W9-ABQ-938

THE NEW HANDBOOK OF TEXAS

The NEW HANDBOOK *of* TEXAS

IN SIX VOLUMES

Volume 1

AUSTIN
THE TEXAS STATE HISTORICAL ASSOCIATION
1996

Published by the Texas State Historical Association
in cooperation with the Center for Studies in Texas History
at the University of Texas at Austin.

This publication has been supported by a grant from the National Endowment for the Humanities, an independent federal agency, and is made possible in part by a grant from the Texas Committee for the Humanities, a state program of the National Endowment for the Humanities.

Printed in the United States of America.

ISBN 0-87611-151-7

10 9 8 7 6 5 4 3 2 1 96 97 98 99 00 01 02 03 04 05

Library of Congress Cataloging-in-Publication Data

The new handbook of Texas / Ron Tyler, editor in chief ; Douglas E. Barnett, managing editor ; Roy R. Barkley, editor ; Penelope C. Anderson, Mark F. Odintz, associate editors.

p. cm.

Includes bibliographical references (p.).

ISBN 0-87611-151-7 (cloth : alk. paper)

1. Texas—Encyclopedias. I. Tyler, Ronnie C., 1941– . II. Barnett, Douglas E., 1954– . III. Barkley, Roy R., 1941– . IV. Texas State Historical Association.

F384.N48 1996

976.4'003—dc20 96-12861

CIP

Designed by David Timmons

The paper used in this book meets the minimum requirements of the
American National Standard for Permanence of Paper for Printed Library Materials, Z39.48—1984.

This volume of the *New Handbook of Texas* is dedicated to

EDWARD A. CLARK, J. CONRAD DUNAGAN, FRED H. MOORE, and A. FRANK SMITH, JR.,

in recognition of their unwavering support of the

Texas State Historical Association and the study of Texas history.

STAFF

Editors in Chief
L. Tuffly Ellis
James W. Pohl
Ron Tyler

Managing Editors
Douglas E. Barnett
Thomas W. Cutrer

Editor
Roy R. Barkley

Senior Editors
Lawrence L. Graves
Harwood Hinton
J. Milton Nance
Anders S. Saustrup

Associate Editors
Penelope C. Anderson
Paul F. Cecil
Nancy Baker Jones
Mark F. Odintz

Assistant Editors
Cecil Harper, Jr.
Rachel A. O. Jenkins
Linda Newland
Jerrell Dean Palmer
Mary Jo Powell
Vivian Elizabeth Smyrl
Mary M. Standifer
Sherlyn R. Wiggs

Illustrations Editor
Kendall Curlee

Visiting Scholars
Randolph B. Campbell
James C. Maroney
Robert Wooster

Staff Writers
Donald R. Abbe
Teresa Palomo Acosta
Julius A. Amin
H. Allen Anderson
Priscilla Myers Benham
Megan Biesele
Sherilyn Brandenstein
Jeff Carroll
Carole E. Christian
Debbie Mauldin Cottrell
María-Cristina García
Alicia A. Garza
Aníbal A. González
John S. Gray III
Rebecca H. Green
James L. Hailey
Stephen L. Hardin
Peggy Hardman
Brian Hart
William R. Hunt
Charles Christopher Jackson
Glenn Justice
Diana J. Kleiner
Martin Donell Kohout
John Leffler
Christopher Long
Paul M. Lucko
James T. Matthews
Lisa C. Maxwell
Judith N. McArthur
Vista K. McCroskey
Angela Shelf Medearis
David Minor
John Minton
Kharen Monsho
Matthew Hayes Nall
Ruben E. Ochoa
Mary H. Ogilvie
Cynthia E. Orozco
Joan Jenkins Perez
Craig H. Roell
Megan Seaholm
Julia Cauble Smith
Nolan Thompson
Cindy Wilke

Senior Research Assistants
Caroline Castillo Crimm
J. Kaaz Doyle
Patricia L. Duncan
Ann Graham Gaines
Brian C. Hosmer
Laurie E. Jasinski

Research Assistants
Richard Bruhn
Richard Allen Burns
Manuel Callahan
Francine Carraro
Helen Peeler Clements
Chris Cravens
Shannon Davies
Charles G. Davis
Timothy Davis
Kathy Edwards
David L. Fisher
Tracé Etienne-Gray
Susan Friesell
Federico Garza
Anthony Gaxiola
Daniel P. Greene
Linda M. Greenwood
James B. Heckert-Greene
Rebecca J. Herring
John G. Johnson
Jack Lala
Jeanne F. Lively
Paula Mitchell Marks
Richard B. McCaslin
Victoria S. Murphy
Erika Murr
Linda Peterson
Geoffrey Pivateau
Alice J. Rhoades
Marvin E. Schultz
Deborah Schwartz
Susan Shaw
Jim Steely
Joan E. Supplee
Robert E. Veselka
Karen Yancy
Nancy Beck Young

Administrative Staff
Marianne Braine
Peggy Caffrey
Dyana Hernández Chahda
Eliza Esquivel
Anne Francis
Kathleen McCarthy
Mary-Lou Pilkinton
Savita Rao
Kim Stark

Volunteers
Caroline Bass
Sally Reese Goach
Arthur K. Leatherwood
Jennifer Watson

EDITORIAL ADVISORY BOARD

PUBLISHER'S PREFACE

With this new edition, the Texas State Historical Association fulfills the first part of its goal of remaking the *Handbook of Texas* into a reference work that will provide concise and accurate information about Texas history for generations to come. Our objective in compiling the *New Handbook of Texas* has not changed from that described in 1952 by Walter Prescott Webb and H. Bailey Carroll, the editors of the original *Handbook*: "to assemble into one usable, practical, ready-reference work the most significant information about the widest possible range of Texas topics." We have cast a much larger loop than those historical pioneers and have had far more help in rounding up our material, but their brilliant accomplishment constantly illuminated our path, its shadow a daily reminder of the high level of professionalism and scholarship to which we would be held.

This new edition, prepared with the assistance of more than 3,000 volunteer authors and a cumulative *Handbook* staff of 130 individuals over a fourteen-year period, incorporates all the information that you have come to expect of the *Handbook*—biographies of notable individuals, histories of important events, counties, cities, and towns, descriptions of physical features, thematic histories—into a new format with essay-length articles on historical periods, regions, and topics and carefully selected illustrations that enhance the appearance of the book as well as our understanding of the past. We have also told the story of the events that have occurred during the more than four decades since the original *Handbook* was published. Significant changes occurred during those years, changes that frequently are at odds with the traditional image of the state, especially the development of "Texas chic" in the last two decades. The Texas Medical Center in Houston, for example, is now recognized as the largest and one of the most sophisticated medical complexes in the world. The Lyndon B. Johnson Space Center near Houston seemed almost out of place when it was built (1961–63), but now appears to lag behind the rest of the high-tech industry that motivates much of the state's economy. And Texans, used to thinking of themselves as rural in origin, now must adjust to the notion that Houston, Dallas, and San Antonio are among the ten most populous cities in the nation, that there are twenty-five other metropolitan centers among the state's population of 18.4 million, and that the sets of twin cities along the border with Mexico—El Paso–Ciudad Juárez, Del Rio–Ciudad Acuña, Eagle Pass–Piedras Negras, McAllen–Reynosa, and Brownsville–Matamoros—all have developed into significant urban centers.

Texans have also continued to recognize the significant role that women and minorities have played in the state's history, a recognition evident in the *Handbook Supplement* of 1976 and strongly reflected in the *New Handbook* by essay-length articles, biographies, topical entries, and illustrations. We have benefited from four symposia that we organized and a virtual explosion of historical studies on women and on Mexican Americans, African Americans, and other ethnic groups. Nevertheless, much of the material found here is based on original research that the *Handbook* staff carried out because no other sources were available. In this, we are reminded again of Webb's goal that the *Handbook* contain "pertinent facts on a multitude of subjects, many of which, prior to this publication, could be found only in definitive works, great libraries, rare or unique books and documents, [or] highly specialized collections" in archives around the world.

Although accuracy has been uppermost in our minds, we know that this book contains errors and omissions, just as the original one did. We can only hope that we got it right as often as they did.

That the Texas State Historical Association should publish a comprehensive history of the state, an idea almost as old as the organization itself, dates from one of its early meetings in 1897. The suggestion surfaced again as various commemorative anniversaries, such as the state's centennial in 1936, came and went. Not until July 1939 did Walter Prescott Webb, the new director of the association, embrace the idea and define it more clearly. Webb named the project the *Handbook of Texas* and said that it would be patterned after Frederick W. Hodge's remarkable *Handbook of American Indians*, which had won universal plaudits. "Such a work" on the Lone Star State "would be indispensable to every editor, reporter, library, scholar, and teacher in Texas," Webb believed. "It would set the standard for spelling...and furnish the starting point for every investigation of things pertaining to Texas history." In time, Webb turned the *Handbook* project over to H. Bailey Carroll, and the first two volumes appeared under their joint editorship in 1952.

Eldon Stephen Branda updated and revised the *Handbook* in the supplementary volume that appeared in 1976. Carroll had recognized errors in some of the 15,896 entries in the first two volumes and knew that other articles were rapidly becoming outdated. He consequently directed his staff to begin a file for corrections and additions. But Branda carried the changes further. "There was an article on Poetry, Texas, but none on poetry in Texas," he noted in explaining that the *Supplement* contained not only an article on the Poetry Society of Texas but a much longer survey of Literature in Texas. Branda also added articles on many of the ethnic groups of Texas, art and music, women, and many other subjects. By 1982, however, the *Handbook* had celebrated its thirtieth anniversary, and it was apparent that it needed further revision and updating to maintain its usefulness. Branda remarked that a complete revision was in order. Association director L. Tuffly Ellis, supported primarily by Ambassador Edward A. Clark, Fred H. Moore, J. Conrad Dunagan, and A. Frank Smith, all presidents or honorary presidents of the association and members of its Executive Council, initiated the revision project and began the fund-raising necessary to finance the effort. The University of Texas at Austin has provided constant assistance through the Center for Studies in Texas History, and Ellis organized a consortium of academic and educational organizations (see Acknowledgments) to assist in the work. Fourteen years later, the *New Handbook of Texas* is the result of that effort.

We have been chided frequently during the intervening years about how such a large work could be called a "handbook," which, as Branda observed, "sounded like something you could roll up and stuff in your pocket." We realize that we have compounded the problem by expanding the work to six volumes. We even thought of changing the name—perhaps to something noble-sounding such as *The Historical Encyclopedia and Biographical Dictionary of Texas*—but reconsidered when we reflected that "the *Handbook*" is a shorthand term that lovers of Texas history instantly recognize. Upon its publication, the original work quickly won a reputation as the place to look for historical information about the state, as the reference librarian in any local history section would tell you. A symposium on state and local history, convened at Yale University in the latter 1960s, underscored the *Handbook*'s contribution by considering how other states might duplicate the Texas accomplishment, and Walter Muir Whitehill, the formidable director of the Boston Athenæum, writing in the *Times Literary Supplement* (November 13, 1970), called it "the best systematic work of reference on any of the fifty United States." As Branda concluded, "you just don't give up a name with that kind of integrity." We were therefore greatly relieved when our indefatigable editor, Roy Barkley, pointed out that in Germany a *Handbuch* can be a compendium of information of almost any size, published serially or all at once; as the *New Handbook* went to press, the *Handbuch der Physik* (*Handbook of Physics*), for instance, was at fifty-four volumes and counting.

We are also mindful of another of Branda's admonitions, that "everything changes," a truth that directly affects the implementation of the second part of our goal: keeping the *Handbook* up to date and available. We frequently wonder how Webb and Carroll and their assistants and students ever managed to compile and publish such a comprehensive and complex work as the *Handbook* without the use of computers. Nor did Branda employ a computer in the compilation of the *Supplement* (which the University of Texas Printing Division set in Linotype). Now computers are commonly used in every phase of historical research and writing, and the *New Handbook* would have been even more labor-intensive without them. The computer also makes change easier. When we began the revision project in 1982, we surveyed Texas librarians and historians and book collectors as to what the format of the *New Handbook* should be. They replied overwhelmingly that it should be published as a book. No other format—microfilm, microfiche, CD-ROM, on-line electronic version—attracted as much as one percent of our total response. We repeated the survey in 1987 with the same result, although by then computers had become so widely used that people had started to inquire about an electronic version. Recognizing the potential of the computer, the Executive Council of the association agreed, in undertaking this revision, that the *Handbook of Texas* project is now a permanent part of the Texas State Historical Association program. The *New Handbook* will be continually updated and improved on disk so that massive revision will not be required in the future. The format of subsequent editions will depend upon the needs of our members and users.

RON TYLER
March 1996

ACKNOWLEDGMENTS

The Texas State Historical Association is the originator and chief sponsor of the *New Handbook of Texas.* We have, however, enjoyed substantial support from individuals and institutions all along the way. When former director L. Tuffly Ellis began the project, he envisioned a network of cosponsors through which the intellectual and financial resources of academic institutions around the state could be brought to bear on the task at hand. Twenty-eight colleges, universities, research centers, and historical associations agreed to participate in the project as cosponsors; they are mentioned individually on the cosponsors' page elsewhere in the front matter of this volume. These institutions have assisted with revision of the *Handbook* by contributing financial support, assigning staff members to work on the project, facilitating access to scholarly collections, and providing office space and logistical support.

The University of Texas at Austin led the way in this effort through its support of the Center for Studies in Texas History, a component of the College of Liberal Arts. Deans Robert T. King, Standish Meacham, and, now, Sheldon Ekland-Olson have provided continued encouragement and, through the Center, paid the salaries of two senior editors, as well as providing office space and assisting with logistical support. Nowhere has the collaborative nature of this relationship been more clearly demonstrated than through the assistance provided by the state's leading Texas history collection, the Center for American History at UT Austin. Director Don E. Carleton and Associate Director Katherine J. Adams recognized the tremendous importance of the center's collections for research on the *New Handbook* and committed the CAH to supporting that work. *Handbook* staff were treated as members of the CAH staff and given unparalleled access to research materials. We want to mention particularly the assistance of Trudy B. Croes, Ralph L. Elder, William H. Richter, and Stefanie A. Wittenbach in using the CAH collections, John R. Wheat for assistance with materials on music history, Stephen C. Stappenbeck for information on the newspaper collections, and John H. Slate and Donna J. Coates for assistance in locating illustrations. Librarians and staff members at most of UT Austin's other libraries assisted at one time or another. Particularly helpful was the access provided by Stephen W. Littrell and the staff of the Map Room of the Perry-Castañeda Library. Thousands of USGS topographical maps loaned to our research staff were invaluable in preparing community and geographical feature articles.

The accuracy and completeness of articles relating to North and Northeast Texas stem in large part from support provided by the University of North Texas. For many years Randolph B. Campbell supervised first one and then two research assistants annually, graduate students in the UNT history department, who researched, wrote, and checked thousands of articles. Articles related to the High Plains and the Panhandle owe a similar debt to Texas Tech University and to senior editor Lawrence L. Graves, who supervised as many as three research assistants annually. For several years Texas A&M University funded the salaries of two research assistants who researched and wrote articles related to Central Texas under the supervision of faculty members Robert A. Calvert and Larry D. Hill. Professor emeritus J. Milton Nance also served as a senior editor during early years of the project. For ten years the history department at Southwest Texas State University funded the salaries of SWTSU graduate students who worked as research assistants in the TSHA offices. The Foundation for Women's Resources and Texas Woman's University helped fund for several years a research assistant working specifically in women's history, and the Texas Catholic Conference underwrote a similar effort on Catholic history.

Libraries and research centers around the state provided additional institutional support. The Texas State Library and Archives gave frequent advice to our research staff on archival holdings.

The Texas Historical Commission staff were helpful in many ways; special thanks need to be extended to Cynthia Beeman and other staff members associated with the Historical Marker program, who made their extensive files available to our research staff and welcomed our frequent visits and questions over the years. The Sam Houston Regional Library and Research Center, in Liberty, provided substantial assistance with the preparation of articles related to the Atascosito region of Southeast Texas and for several years provided office space and access to materials for a *Handbook* staff member working in the region.

The making of the *New Handbook of Texas* depended upon a multitude of informed decisions about topics and authors. We have relied heavily on the advice of advisory editors in making these evaluations. Our board of advisory editors is composed of a wide range of individuals who possess substantial expertise on one or more aspects of Texas history. Collectively, the advisory editors worked with the editorial staff to define the scope of subject areas covered in the *New Handbook* and determine the most important topics; to identify and help recruit the most appropriate authors; to review, evaluate, and sometimes edit the submitted entries; and, in many cases, to research and write on topics in their area of expertise. Advisory editors served without remuneration from the TSHA. As a group, they contributed thousands of hours to the project.

A complete list of advisory editors appears above. Although limits on space prohibit mentioning the important contributions of each individual, several merit comment for extraordinary participation. Randolph B. Campbell, of the University of North Texas, provided sage advice from the beginning of the project, rendered scholarly judgments on an enormous range of questions, guided research assistants and students through massive lists of writing assignments, and, not least, read and critiqued all of the 254 county entries. Arnoldo De León of Angelo State University developed the list of topics pertaining to Tejanos and Mexican Americans in Texas. Through patient and persistent efforts over the life of the project he solicited scores of articles from leading scholars in the area, reviewed the resulting articles, and wrote many himself. Chester R. Burns of the University of Texas Medical Branch at Galveston coordinated a collaborative effort among health science centers to document the medical history of Texas. Over the course of more than ten years, he built a systematic list of topics chronicling the people, institutions, events, and trends of medical practice throughout Texas history. In the process, he and the other authors have brought attention to a major aspect of Texas history and produced a significant new body of literature. An area of Texas history more frequently chronicled—the Spanish Colonial period—benefited tremendously from the untiring efforts of two advisory editors, Robert S. Weddle and Donald E. Chipman. Each read hundreds of new manuscripts and entries from the first *Handbook*, painstakingly ensuring that they reflected the best current knowledge about this vital era.

Primary credit for the content of the *New Handbook* goes, of course, to the more than 3,000 authors and readers who researched, wrote, and critiqued the entries. Walter Webb, in describing his vision for the original *Handbook*, called it the "product of the collective literary genius of the people of Texas." We have remained true to that vision and reached beyond it. *Handbook* authors, who hail from all walks of life, reside not only throughout the state of Texas but also in every other state of the United States and in several other countries. We acknowledge them individually in bylines. Here again, however, the outstanding contributions of a few compel special mention. George C. Werner devoted a great deal of time to the 320 railroad articles; he wrote many of them and read and evaluated the others. Howard N. Martin drew on his vast knowledge of the Alabama-Coushatta Indians in advising us and wrote forty articles related to them. Natalie Ornish enriched our coverage of Jewish history in Texas through her suggestions and by writing more than fifty articles. Bill Groneman contributed articles on 186 of the Alamo defenders as well as an article on the noncombatants. W. H. Timmons provided us with invaluable assistance on topics related to the El Paso area, as did Dick D. Heller, Jr., for Starr County. Frank Wagner contributed numerous articles on the Corpus Christi area. Throughout the project we benefited from the participation of members of county historical commissions who reviewed potential topic lists, critiqued submitted manuscripts, and wrote entries. Several commissions were particularly helpful. Merle R. Hudgins reviewed and wrote many entries about Wharton County, as did Norman W. Black for Gregg County. Jane G. McMeans of Fort Bend County and Audrey D. Kariel of Harrison County were most helpful in coordinating article reviews by members of their county historical commissions. Ann Washington coordinated the efforts of a local group, the Rio Grande Valley *Handbook of Texas* Volunteers, in writing and reading entries related to that region. Charles D. Spurlin and the Victoria County Historical Commission, Patricia B. Hensley and the Trinity County Historical Commission, and John R. Ross and the Cherokee County Historical Commission also assisted in the coverage of their counties.

Professors at several Texas colleges and universities organized classes and seminars to contribute to the *New Handbook*. For several years Randolph B. Campbell had students in his undergraduate Texas history classes at the University of North Texas write *Handbook* articles, as did Paul D. Lack and Jodella Kite Dyreson at McMurry University, Archie P. McDonald at Stephen F. Austin State University, and Martha M. Allen at Southwestern University. The *New Handbook* also benefits from articles written by students of Floyd S. Brandt and Patrick L. Brockett at the UT Austin College of Business Administration and by students of Glen McClish in the communications department at Southwestern University. Under the direction of Jerry Thompson, students at Texas A&M International University prepared a number of entries on Webb County. In addition, Martha M. Allen and Jan C. Dawson at Southwestern University have referred Southwestern history students to us for internships.

The charitable foundations and people of Texas have been exceptionally generous in providing financial resources to sustain the *Handbook* revision, especially the six foundations that collectively contributed $1,250,000 toward the project: The Brown Foundation, Inc., The Cullen Foundation, The Fondren Foundation, Houston Endowment Inc., The Summerfield G. Roberts Foundation, and The Summerlee Foundation. Major financial support also came from the National Endowment for the Humanities and the Texas Committee for the Humanities, a state program of the NEH. The major financial contributors are recognized individually in the following pages. We want to thank everyone who contributed to the fund-raising efforts in any way, for each contribution, regardless of size, was helpful; the *New Handbook* could not have been done without them. Four members of our development committee warrant special mention for their vision, guidance, and enthusiasm: Edward A. Clark, J. Conrad Dunagan, Fred H. Moore, and A. Frank Smith, Jr.

David Timmons, whose graphic design skills will be familiar to many readers of TSHA publications, designed the *New Handbook*. G&S Typesetters of Austin converted the data files into electronic pages, and Digital Press and Imaging of San Antonio prepared the color separations. Edwards Brothers of Ann Arbor, Michigan, printed and bound the volumes. Special thanks go to Brian Slavin for his advice and support on a challenging printing job.

We conclude with a short note about our staff. In the end, it is they who have lived with this project day in and day out for the past fourteen years. Due to its size the *New Handbook* was managed as a separate project with its own staff for core functions such as research and writing, editing, and data entry. The entire TSHA staff, however, provided logistical and administrative support as well as moral encouragement throughout the project. At times, it must surely have seemed as though the *Handbook* had become the tail that wags the dog. Colleen T. Kain, the association's executive assistant throughout the project, patiently counseled, advised, and assisted the *Handbook* staff in coping with myriad administrative matters. She also contributed her outstanding skills as a meeting coordinator to the several *Handbook* conferences. George B. Ward, assistant director and coordinator of TSHA's publication program, provided cheerful and friendly advice on editorial and production matters. David C. De Boe, director of educational programs for TSHA, advised the editorial staff on educators' needs and graciously served as liaison between the *Handbook* project and Texas teachers. Evelyn G. Stehling responded to countless requests for administrative assistance with good cheer and consistently superior work. Ann Russell, the association's bookkeeper for most of the project, worked gamely through the avalanche of financial paperwork generated by the project. To them, and all the other TSHA staff members from 1982 through 1996, we extend our sincere appreciation for not only putting up with it all but for helping immeasurably.

More than 100 people served in one capacity or another on the *Handbook* staff between 1982 and 1996. They have been a magnificent and dedicated group of individuals and a joy to work with. It is by now a truism to say that people do not work in the field of academic scholarship and publishing solely for the monetary reward. The work itself, and its value to society, provided much of our motivation. Time and time again, *Handbook* staff members held to that mission and completed their objectives, regardless of the difficulty. We note especially the contributions of Arthur K. Leatherwood, a volunteer who has worked on the *New Handbook* almost every Monday for fourteen years. A complete list of the staff appears earlier in the front matter of this volume. We extend to all of them our appreciation for a job well done.

COSPONSORS

Cosponsors of the *New Handbook of Texas* have contributed financial and/or staff support to the *New Handbook.*

Abilene Christian University
Lamar University
Permian Historical Society
Prairie View A&M University
Sam Houston Regional Library and Research Center
Sam Houston State University
San Jacinto College
Southern Methodist University
Southwestern University
Southwest Texas State University
Stephen F. Austin State University
Sul Ross State University
Texas A&M University
Texas A&M University at Corpus Christi
Texas Tech University
Texas Woman's University
The University of Houston
The University of North Texas
The University of Texas at Austin
The University of Texas Health Science Center at Houston
The University of Texas Health Science Center at San Antonio
The University of Texas Medical Branch at Galveston
The University of Texas of the Permian Basin
The University of Texas at San Antonio Institute of Texan Cultures
The University of Texas Southwestern Medical Center at Dallas
The University of Texas System Cancer Center
West Texas A&M University
West Texas Historical Association

The Alamo Council

Members of the Alamo Council have contributed $50,000 or more to the *New Handbook of Texas.*

Abell-Hanger Foundation
The Brown Foundation, Inc.
Amon G. Carter Foundation
The Cullen Foundation
The Dunagan Foundation
The Fondren Foundation
The Don and Sybil Harrington Foundation
Hoblitzelle Foundation
Houston Endowment Inc.
Robert J. Kleberg, Jr., and Helen C. Kleberg Foundation
Meadows Foundation
Mrs. Fred H. Moore
National Endowment for the Humanities
The Summerfield G. Roberts Foundation
Rockwell Fund, Inc.
Erwin E. Smith Foundation Trust
Nelda C. and H. J. Lutcher Stark Foundation
The Summerlee Foundation
T. L. L. Temple Foundation
Texas Committee for the Humanities

The San Jacinto Council

Members of the San Jacinto Council have contributed from $25,000 to $50,000 to the *New Handbook of Texas.*

Mrs. Clara Elisabeth Bates-Nisbet
The R. W. Fair Foundation
Dr. Angie Stiles Hamilton
The Moody Foundation
Scurlock Foundation
Texas Commerce Bank
An anonymous foundation

The Ranger Council

Members of the Ranger Council have contributed from $10,000 to $25,000 to the *New Handbook of Texas.*

The Armstrong Foundation
J. Clifton Caldwell
Communities Foundation of Texas, Inc.
Jean and Price Daniel Foundation, Inc.
Davidson Family Charitable Foundation
Foundation for Women's Resources
George and Mary Josephine Hamman Foundation
Harwood P. and Ann B. Hinton
King Ranch Family Trust
The King Ranch, Inc.
Al and Darlyne Lowman
The Priddy Foundation
A. Frank Smith, Jr.
Texas Catholic Conference
Texas College of Osteopathic Medicine
Trull Foundation
Margaret D. Wells
An anonymous foundation

Republic of Texas Council

Members of the Republic of Texas Council have contributed from $1,000 to $10,000 to the *New Handbook of Texas.*

John G. Adams
Mr. and Mrs. Ward Noble Adkins
Pierce M. Allman
Mary and Ben M. Anderson
Richard S. Anderson
Thomas D. Anderson
Austin Community Foundation for Capitol Area
Thomas D. Barrow
Carlton Beal
Lloyd M. Bentsen
Alfred and Annette Cheek Bishop
Eliza H. Bishop
H. L. Brinson
George W. Brown, Jr.
Mr. and Mrs. Maurice R. Bullock
John P. and Alva D. Butler
The CH Foundation

COSPONSORS

Mr. and Mrs. John C. Carey
Margaret Farrar Carmichael
John B. Carter, Jr.
Edward A. Clark
C. W. Conn, Jr.
Conn Appliance Charitable Foundation
Denton A. Cooley Foundation
Joseph H. Coreth
John L. Cox
Mr. and Mrs. Earle M. Craig, Jr.
Donna Galloway Crow
Roy H. Cullen
Ellen V. Daniel
H. W. Davidson
Davidson Foundation
Mr. and Mrs. Ronald K. Deford
Franklin W. Denius
R. R. Donnelley and Sons Company
The James R. Dougherty, Jr., Foundation
J. Conrad Dunagan
R. Sylvan Dunn
Fredda and Lynn D. Durham
Eugene Edge
Billie J. Ellis
El Paso National Bank
Exxon Company, U.S.A.
Murray Fasken
Joe J. Fisher
James C. Fourmy, Sr.
L. R. French, Jr.
Mr. and Mrs. N. C. Galloway
Nathan C. Galloway III
Jenkins Garrett
Mr. and Mrs. L. P. Gilvin
H-E-B Grocery Company
Mr. and Mrs. Dow Hamm, Jr.
Mr. and Mrs. Newt Hasson
Lloyd Hayes
Harriet and Harvey Heard
Hillcrest Foundation
William P. Hobby
Hobby Foundation
Mr. and Mrs. Thomas W. Houghton
Mr. and Mrs. Sherwood Inkley
B. R. Inman
Robert Isham
Mr. and Mrs. Belton K. Johnson
Belton Kleberg Johnson Foundation, Inc.
Mrs. Lyndon B. Johnson
J. E. Jonsson
Mrs. Jean W. Kaspar
Harris and Eliza Kempner Fund
Carl B. and Florence E. King Foundation
Mrs. B. Koontz
Lamar University Foundation
Mr. and Mrs. John H. Lindsey
Sara Scott Bransford Lint
Gilbert I. Low
Mr. and Mrs. Argyle A. McAllen
Eugene McDermott Foundation
Margaret McDonald
Malcolm and Margaret McLean
Mr. and Mrs. Wales Madden, Jr.
Elizabeth H. Maddux
Alex Massad
Wilbur L. Matthews
Bill Milburn, Inc.
Mr. and Mrs. Menton J. Murray
C. Schreiner Nelson
Nelson Puett Foundation
Louise S. O'Connor
B. D. Orgain
Natalie Ornish
Patrick J. Parma
Martha Sue Parr
J. R. Parten
Joe and Lois Perkins Foundation
Perkins-Prothro Foundation
Mr. and Mrs. O. Scott Petty
B. J. Pevehouse
T. Boone Pickens, Jr.
Mrs. Dow Puckett
RGK Foundation
Mr. and Mrs. D. E. Ramsey
John J. Redfern, Jr.
John and Rosalind Redford
Robert A. Rieder
Louis Rochester
Ben Rogers
John N. Rowe III
Earl C. Sams Foundation, Inc.
San Jacinto Museum of History Foundation
William Scanlan, Jr.
Tom and Mary V. Sealy
Shell Oil Company Foundation
C. B. Smith, Sr.
Gregory Soechting
Dr. and Mrs. Vernie A. Stembridge
Mrs. Joe Sullivan
Texas Jewish Historical Society
Dr. and Mrs. Sellers J. Thomas
Mrs. Emory B. Thompson
Libbie Moody Thompson
John G. Tower
Tracor, Inc.
Vinson & Elkins
Cyril Wagner, Jr.
A. W. Walker, Jr.
Mamie McFaddin Ward Heritage Foundation
Mr. and Mrs. Patrick H. Welder
Peter Wells
John R. Willis
Mr. and Mrs. Will E. Wilson
R. D. Woods
Herman Wright
Katherine K. Yarborough
W. B. Yarborough
An anonymous foundation

INTRODUCTION

The *New Handbook of Texas* is a multidisciplinary encyclopedia of Texas history, geography, and culture. It comprises more than 23,000 articles on people, places, events, historical themes, institutions, and a host of other topic categories. The scope is broad and inclusive, designed to provide readers with concise, authoritative, and accessible articles that provide factual, nonpartisan accounts on virtually every aspect of Texas history and culture.

A natural question in making such an encyclopedia is Where to start? What subjects to include and who to write them? The starting point for the editors of the *New Handbook* was clear. The two-volume *Handbook of Texas*, published in 1952, and the *Supplement*, published in 1976, provided a wealth of information and a solid conceptual base from which to develop this new edition. Consequently, almost every topic that received an entry in those three volumes has been retained in the *New Handbook*. The primary exception to that rule involves subjects which, upon further examination, proved not to have an adequate connection with Texas history. In many cases, particularly with biographical subjects, it was possible to reprint the original entry with only minor changes and to include new bibliographical material. For some articles, significant corrections and revisions were needed. And in other instances it was necessary to prepare completely new entries in order to represent the current state of historical knowledge. To the *Handbook* base of approximately 16,000 articles the editors have added another 7,500 entries that dramatically expand both the scope of topical coverage and the level of detail. All in all, the *New Handbook* includes an almost fourfold increase in material.

Its articles represent the efforts of more than 3,000 authors from many walks of life. They include professional scholars, amateur historians and genealogists, college and university students, and numerous other individuals with special knowledge and a willingness to write about it. Given the diverse nature of our authorship and the special enthusiasm they have brought to the *New Handbook*, the editors have made special efforts to give credit where credit is due. Most entries carry a byline designating their author or authors. The primary exceptions are unsigned entries from the original *Handbook* for which authorship could not be determined and the large number of staff-written entries on minor geographic features, where bylines were omitted in order to conserve space. Reprinted entries from the original *Handbook* bear the names of the original authors where they were known; in the event of substantial corrections or revisions the name of the reviser is also generally given.

Editorial Notes

THE SUBJECT PYRAMID. Articles in the *New Handbook of Texas* are arranged alphabetically with each article heading in boldface type. The entry titles for biographical articles and battles are inverted. In addition, our approach to broad subjects suggested a three-tiered pyramid. At the top, a general essay on a major topic such as HEALTH AND MEDICINE provides an overview of the subject and refers the reader to more specific, related articles such as EPIDEMIC DISEASES, MEDICAL EDUCATION, and MEDICAL RESEARCH. In the next tier, the "mid-level" entry on medical education, for example, provides increased detail on the historical development of medical schools in Texas and leads the reader to third-level entries on specific schools, hospitals, doctors, organizations, and events. This pyramidal structure works in reverse fashion as well; internal cross-references lead readers from individual entries to related articles at a more general level.

CROSS-REFERENCES. The text of the *New Handbook of Texas* employs two types of cross-reference, the symbol [qv] and the *see* or *see also* reference. (1) The symbol [qv] denotes Latin *quod vide*, "which see." The plural of [qv] is written [qqv]. A [qv] is printed beside a noun phrase that is the subject of an article in the *New Handbook*; [qqv] means that each item in the preceding series is represented by an article. Occasionally the noun phrase so marked is not the exact equivalent of the title, though the [qv] should lead the reader unambiguously to the intended article. Several categories of article are not regularly cross-referenced—counties and rivers, for instance. When the [qv] appears with such a topic, it signifies that important information about the subject at hand may be found in the referenced article, not merely that the article exists. The editors have not tried to insert all possible cross-references, since to do so would have added clutter to an already packed book. Nevertheless, they have employed the [qv] somewhat more broadly than did the editors of the earlier *Handbook* and the *Supplement*. In particular, whereas the earlier edition did not cross-reference major topics such as Stephen F. Austin and the battle of San Jacinto, the editors of the *New Handbook* have thought it wise to do so. Texas has grown much less insular during the last twenty (not to say forty) years than it once was, and many more residents come from other states or foreign countries. What would have been an obvious topic to the born Texan of twenty years ago might not be such to some newer residents. Further, in order that the *New Handbook* can be the best possible reference tool for young students as well as more seasoned readers, the editors have taken less for granted and adopted more explicit cross-referencing.

Be that as it may, article titles in certain categories are not regularly followed by [qv]. This is especially the case for categories in which all available topics are the subjects of articles: as the *New Handbook* contains an article on every Texas county, for instance, no [qv] is needed after a county name. Rivers and missions, for other examples, are rarely cross-referenced, since every Texas river or mission is treated in a separate article. (San Juan Bautista is a notable separate case, however, since this frequently mentioned mission was in Mexico, not Texas.) Following is a list of topic categories that generally get no [qv]:

- counties
- towns and cities
- rivers and streams (see inclusion criteria for creeks below)
- minor physical features
- railroads
- government positions
- fields of endeavor
- institutions of higher learning
- Indian group or tribal names
- forts
- missions
- presidios

Usually, [qv] is inserted at the first mention of a subject. Sometimes, however, it is employed at a subsequent mention. The word *buffalo*, for instance, is not cross-referenced at its first occurrence in the article on Lee County, where it is a mere item in a list of county wildlife species. The cross-reference occurs at its next mention, where reference to the article BUFFALO (and from there to other related articles) can illuminate the hunting activities of the Tonkawa Indians. Though the editors have tried to eliminate ambiguity in [qv] references, sometimes it has been unavoidable. Congress of the Republic of Texas,[qv] for instance, is ambiguous since both the Congress and the Republic of Texas are the subjects of articles.

SPELLING. For its spelling authority the *New Handbook of Texas* has generally used *Webster's Ninth New Collegiate Dictionary* (1983) and its successor, *Merriam Webster's Collegiate Dictionary* (Tenth Edition, 1993). American spellings are used where possible, though the occurrence of British spellings in proper nouns often requires an exception; theatre is probably the most common British spelling in the *New Handbook*.

Misspellings that occur in quotations are not marked by *sic*. The editors have attempted to quote accurately and to avoid sprinkling editorial exculpations around.

The numerous variant spellings of names of Indian groups result in general from the wide variation in how Europeans heard the names. Frenchmen heard and spelled group designations differently from Spaniards, and Anglo-Americans heard and spelled something else again. Moreover, individual Spaniards, for instance, multiplied spellings from person to person. One Franciscan heard and wrote one thing, and the next heard and wrote differently. To compound the difficulty, authors of secondary works sometimes introduced new terms or took as group designations words that denoted something else. The occasional consequence is a dazzling array of different spellings of the same word, or, occasionally, a group name that denotes no group. The editors have followed the lead of the first edition of the *Handbook* and its *Supplement* in the entry forms of Indian group names. This does not, however, imply that these are the "right" spellings; they are merely convenient. Variant spellings are listed in parentheses.

FOREIGN WORDS, NATURALIZED WORDS, AND DIACRITICS. The editors of the *New Handbook* have cast a large net for naturalized words by choosing as an authority the latest (and perhaps last) "unabridged" dictionary, *Webster's Third New International* (1961). Though that decision means that some unusual words, such as *alferez* and *ejido*, are treated as naturalized, it also greatly reduces the use of italics. The naturalization process seems to have accelerated in recent years, as speakers of foreign languages move in increasing numbers to English-speaking nations and as the globe shrinks through electronic communication.

In accord with standard practice, foreign words that are parts of proper names are not italicized unless they are being discussed as words. The editors have generally capitalized foreign adjectives derived from proper nouns (*Tejano*, for instance), regardless of foreign editorial practice. In general, the editors have employed English in article titles, though exceptions occur when they are warranted. *La Mujer Moderna*, for instance, being a newspaper title, could hardly have been translated.

When a word occurs in a Spanish-language context, it is written with its native diacritics. The word *Béxar* in *San Fernando de Béxar* is an example. When such a word has become a standard Texas place name written without diacritics, however, and when it occurs in the absence of a Spanish-language context, it is written without accent: *Bexar County*. Some words lose their diacritics through morphological alteration. *Querétero*, for instance, is occasionally made into an English adjective, *Quereteran*, which, because it is not a Spanish form, has no accent. Others lose their accents during the same process in the Spanish language: *México* and *Mexicano*, for instance. Contrary to general Spanish or French editorial practice, in the interest of informing readers how to pronounce such foreign names as Álvar Núñez Cabeza de Vaca, the editors have printed accents on capital letters.

BIOGRAPHIES. In the article titles, the editors have tried in most cases to enter biographies under names given at birth or, in the case of a married woman, under her married name. Religious names, stage names, screen names, pen names, changed names, and nicknames are generally given as biographical information within the article. Consequently, for instance, Billy the Kid is entered under what was evidently his birth name, Henry McCarty, and Joan Crawford is entered under the name Lucille Fay LeSeur. Some exceptions to the rule occur. Gustav Elley, for instance, was born Gustavus von Elterlein, but because he was always known in Texas under the shorter name, it is the entry form for his biography. Nicknames are usually given in parentheses at the beginning of the articles: "William (Alfalfa Bill) Murray, a famous political figure...."; "Timothy Isaiah (Longhair Jim) Courtright, two-gun marshal of Fort Worth...." Maiden names of the mothers and, in some contexts, the wives, of biographical subjects are given in parentheses, in the belief that this practice will aid the reader to make genealogical connections within the *New Handbook* and outside of it. Also given in parentheses are variant spellings of names. The names of many historical figures are spelled in more ways than one in both primary and secondary sources. Often it is difficult to choose the "right" spelling. In spite of much research and vacillation, the editors were unable to be certain how, for instance, Philip Dimmitt spelled his surname—or if he always spelled it the same way.

In most cases, the editors have entered biographies of people with Spanish names under their proper surnames. This means, for instance, that Manuel de Mier y Terán is listed under Mier, not Terán. When Spanish names occur in a pre-twentieth-century context, the editors have generally written them with diacritics.

ARTICLES INVOLVING PHYSICAL GEOGRAPHICAL DESCRIPTIONS. In articles about physical features—mountains, canyons, streams, bodies of water, and so forth—and in other articles, such as those about counties, that include physical description, the editors and writers have used as much precision as practical. Nevertheless, the directions, acreages, elevations, distances, coordinates, and other parameters of physical geographical description in the *New Handbook*, including verbal designations of location, are only approximations. Analogously, descriptions of soils, florae, and faunae include only salient elements and are not intended to be exhaustive.

NEWSPAPERS. In newspaper names the editors, following the practice of the first edition of the *Handbook*, have treated city names as adjectives denoting the point of origin, not as part of the title. The result is that the title strictly speaking is italicized and the city name is not: Houston *Post*, Brownwood *Bulletin*. In the first edition, if a newspaper had a name without a city in its masthead, it was listed with the city in parentheses: *Redlander* (San Augustine). But there is no essential difference between this entry form and the form Dallas *Morning News*, since both declare some independence from the masthead. For the sake of bibliographical simplification, the editors of the *New Handbook* have tried to be uniform in their practice. When a newspaper was published at several locations, however, the name is given without a city; the *Telegraph and Texas Register* is a case in point.

Research Notes

GUIDELINES. In the planning stage of the project, the editors studied the features of various subjects that were to be widely represented in the *New Handbook* and prepared guidelines for authors. These listed salient features that should, if possible, appear in every article of a given genre—the spouse's name or the subject's death date in a biography, for instance, or the date of founding in a community history. The genres varied widely, from county and community histories to organizations and institutions to newspapers and miscellaneous historical events. The reader who explores the *New Handbook* will soon know what the guidelines required in most article types. If guideline information does not appear in an article, that fact means that it was unavailable, not that it was not sought. The guidelines in general required, for instance, that books, plays, movies, paintings, and other works be dated by year in the text. But occasionally it is impossible to discover when a book was published or when a painting was done. Despite the best efforts of authors and staff members, the birth or death date or parents' names of a biographical subject sometimes eluded the editors' grasp, and an unmentioned omission resulted.

PHYSICAL FEATURES, COMMUNITIES, AND COUNTIES. Three of the major categories of articles in the *New Handbook of Texas* are physical features, communities, and counties. The 4,200 physical features, 7,200 communities, and 254 counties make up almost half of the articles in the book, but, because of the brevity of many of these articles, considerably less than half its pages. Although many excellent community and county articles were written by volunteers during the course of the project, it became clear fairly early that the great bulk of the towns, counties, and physical features would have to be done by staff members or by student volunteers working under supervision. In order to research and write the large number of short articles on creeks and rural communities before the projected publication date, while ensuring the accuracy of the articles and the most efficient use of the sources available, our advisory editor for local history and the project staff developed what became known internally as the "county writing system." A staff writer, given a list of all topics pertaining to a given county, went to a series of standard sources, supplemented by county and community histories, and revised the list of communities and physical features for the county before writing the articles. The system worked particularly well for towns; the editors identified thousands of small school, church, and store communities missed in the first edition of the *Handbook*.

Most of the physical features described by articles in the original *Handbook* are included in the present volumes. For the most part, coverage of summits, physical regions, and miscellaneous features is derived from the first edition. In order to ensure comprehensive and systematic coverage of watercourses, however, the editors chose to supplement previous coverage with articles on streams and reservoirs listed on the 1:500,000 United States Geological Survey maps. Physical feature articles locate features by their coordinates and by their distance from communities readily identifiable on county highway maps. The source of the feature's name and evidence of historical usage of the site is included when available. Guideline information includes the length and direction of flow of all watercourses, as well as the topography and vegetation of the terrain through which they flow. The length of all streams was measured on topographical maps from the United States Department of the Interior Geological Survey. For mountains the *New Handbook* provides elevation, often in comparison to the surrounding terrain. Articles about lakes include the purpose of the reservoir and a description of the dam, as well as its construction history.

Because communities are central to the historical development of Texas the *New Handbook* includes an article on every community in the state's history about which the editors and researchers were able to find significant information. The defining criterion was the presence of two focuses of community life, such as a church, school, store, cemetery, or post office. The editors attempted, however, to be as inclusive as possible, adding any community that was identified as such in local-history sources, regardless of the focus. Community articles generally locate the town in its county by distance from the county seat or another readily identifiable community, and in relation to roads, railroads, and prominent physical features. The rest of the article is a chronological historical narrative, often beginning with site usage prior to the establishment of the community, and ending with either the community's demise or the most recent population figures. Most articles focus on the development of town institutions and businesses, the growth and decline of population, the impact of transportation developments on a community's fortunes, the role of the town in the surrounding rural area, and dramatic events in the history of the community. Population figures, taken from the *Texas Almanac*, were based when possible upon census data. Recent developments have underscored the fact that no population count is completely accurate.

In county articles, the name of the county is followed by a locator code, such as (C-8), which corresponds to the county's place on the 1988 *Official Highway Travel Map of Texas*. The physical descriptions of counties are based on standard cartographic sources, not on, for instance, historical narratives. County history, for the most part, is heavily weighted toward economic and demographic developments, since such emphasis seemed to be the most efficient way to discuss the inhabitants and what they were doing most of the time without producing hopelessly lengthy articles. Because of the variations in coverage, accuracy, and availability of published county histories, the *New Handbook of Texas* depends fairly heavily on the United States population, agricultural, and manufacturing censuses in county articles. As a result, most county articles will take the reader through the flow of immigration into the county, the racial makeup of its population at different times, and the relative importance of cotton, wheat, sharecropping, ranching, cattle, sheep, oil, and the other main features of county economy and society. The county articles also supplement the book's coverage of ethnic minority topics by discussing demographics and the impact of race on economics, education, and politics at the county level.

BIOGRAPHIES. The *New Handbook of Texas* includes more than 7,200 biographies of significant Texans.

1. *Inclusion criteria and methodology.* Only deceased people are the subjects of biographical articles. Beyond that clear criterion, selection has been more difficult. The editors have taken a fairly broad approach to defining who is a Texan and who is not. In general the subjects are individuals who had some impact on society and were either born in Texas, as were Audie Murphy and Janis Joplin; lived in Texas for a considerable period of time, as did William Sydney Porter (O. Henry) and Sam Houston; or were out-of-staters who had a hand in shaping Texas society, as did Jefferson Davis and Antonio López de Santa Anna. Individuals who made a difference in almost any field of human endeavor, including such negative fields as crime, are represented by articles. Further, subjects were required to have regional or greater significance. Due to space limitations, the *New Handbook* could not, with a few exceptions, include individuals who were important to the development of a single community or county. Individuals were proposed as topics by advisory editors, volunteers, and staff, and selected for inclusion by the editors in consultation with advisory editors. The majority of our biographical articles were written by volunteers—local historians, academics, descendants of subjects, or students. A substantial body of biographical work, particularly in the fields of art, African-American history, Mexican-American history, the history of women, business history, and military history, was produced by staff writers. Although the research sources and methods varied according to the subject of the article, in the biographies, as in all other articles in the book, an attempt was made to ensure uniform coverage through the use of guidelines. Guideline information for all biographies included the birth date, place of birth, parentage, education, religious and organizational affiliations, marriage date, name of spouse, number of children, professional honors, date and place of death, and location of grave. This information is missing only when the editors failed to find it.

2. *Special biographical categories*

(a) Following the lead of the old *Handbook*, the editors included an article on all of Stephen F. Austin's Old Three Hundred colonists. Also included are articles on individuals who arrived in Texas before 1836, though the prerevolutionary population is not systematically covered.

(b) The editors generally included "firsts": the first settlers in a county, the first members of a profession in the state, the first members of a minority group to achieve membership in a profession or hold a certain level of office. This category allowed the editors to include some pioneers in locales and in fields of endeavor.

(c) As a partial guide to the elite of Texas in the immediate antebellum period, the editors have included articles on almost all the figures identified as owning 100 slaves or more in the census of 1860.

(d) Certain categorical inclusion criteria were used for military figures in addition to prominence. All known Alamo defenders are included. All Texans who have received the Medal of Honor are the subjects of articles, as are Medal of Honor winners who entered the military in Texas. Several articles are about soldiers from elsewhere who won the Medal of Honor for actions against Indians in Texas.

Other categories. The "other" articles in the *New Handbook* are about a host of subjects, including ranches, religious bodies, organizations, museums, historical events, archeological sites, and numerous smaller categories. Several of the "other" categories are:

1. *Educational institutions.* All degree-granting institutions of higher education are represented by articles. Extant institutions are entered under their 1995 names, and successive name changes are given in the articles. Most of the discussion of education at the local level is in the relevant town and county articles and in articles on the educational efforts of religious groups. A number of nineteenth-century and early twentieth-century private academies, as well as a number of private religious schools, are the subjects of their own articles.

2. *Railroads.* Every railroad chartered and constructed in Texas is represented by an article. Railroad articles cover the date of chartering, a list of the initial board of directors, an account of additions and deletions to the line, and a discussion of successive mergers and consolidations.

3. *Oilfields.* The oilfields covered in the *New Handbook of Texas* include only the largest and the most historically significant.

4. *Businesses.* Business coverage in the *New Handbook of Texas* is drawn from the three categories of largest, earliest, and representative. Many of the largest business enterprises that have been active in the state (wherever they might actually be chartered) are covered, including most airlines and most of the important oil companies. A number of early businesses, including many of the largest and most historically significant plantations and ranches, are included, as are many of the great mercantile establishments. The *New Handbook* also includes representative articles on insurance companies, supermarket chains, manufacturers, and businesses that extract and process minerals besides oil and gas.

5. *Newspapers.* Most of the major newspapers in the state, most of the earliest, and many of the longest in continual operation are included. Many county seat and small town newspapers not represented by articles of their own are mentioned in the relevant town and county articles.

6. *Government.* The state government of Texas is covered by a general article on government. Additionally, every major state agency is treated in a separate article, as are state and county offices such as attorney general and sheriff. Many minor state agencies fall under the category of examining boards.

7. *Sites.* The *New Handbook of Texas* includes an article on each of the Texas state parks, state historic sites, and state wildlife-management areas. Every national park, national historic site, national forest, national grassland, and national wildlife refuge is the subject of an article. Many sites, whether under state or federal jurisdiction, are centered on missions, presidios, or forts, all of which are represented by articles. Parks are continually being added to the state system, and the reader should consult the *Texas Almanac* for a current list.

Source Material and Bibliographies

In the course of researching and editing articles on communities and physical features, the staff of the *New Handbook of Texas* found that many of the same sources were used in virtually every article of a given type. In order to save space, we list the works that form the "standard bibliography" for a given genre here rather than at the end of each article.

Articles on geographic features, including water features, reference the following sources: Bureau of Economic Geology, University of Texas at Austin, *Vegetation Types of Texas* map; General Land Office, land grant maps; State Department of Highways and Public Transportation, general highway maps; *Water for Texas: A Comprehensive Plan for the Future* (Austin: Texas Department of Water Resources, 1984); C. L. Dowell and R. G. Petty, *Engineering Data on Dams and Reservoirs in Texas* (Texas Water Development Board Report 126 [3 pts., Austin, 1971–74]); United States Department of Agriculture Soil Conservation Service and Texas Agricultural Experiment Station, general soil maps; United States Department of the Interior Geological Survey, topographical maps and *State of Texas 1:500,000 Map.*

Articles on towns, counties, and railroads reference the following sources, as applicable: all relevant maps listed for geographic features; John Clements, *Flying the Colors: Texas, a Comprehensive Look at Texas Today, County by County* (Dallas: Clements Research, 1984); Charles Deaton, *Texas Postal History Handbook* (Houston, 1980; 2d ed. 1981); John J. Germann and Myron Janzen, *Texas Post Offices by County* (1986–); Marker Files, Texas Historical Commission, Austin; Fred I. Massengill, *Texas Towns: Origin of Name and Location of Each of the 2,148 Post Offices in Texas* (Terrell, Texas, 1936); S. G. Reed, *A History of the Texas Railroads and of Transportation Conditions under Spain and Mexico and the Republic and the State* (Houston: St. Clair, 1941; rpt., New York: Arno Press, 1981); Fred Tarpley, *1001 Texas Place Names* (Austin: University of Texas Press, 1980); *Texas Almanac*; *Texas State Gazetteer and Business Directory* (Chicago: R. L. Polk, 1884, 1890, 1892, 1896, 1914); Texas State Library, Archives Division: School Superintendent Reports; Texas State Department Railroad Charters; Texas State Library, Genealogy Division: County Tax Rolls; United States Bureau of the Census: *United States Census of Agriculture, United States Census of Population, United States Census of Manufacturing*; United States Postal Route Maps for the State of Texas; Charles P. Zlatkovich, *Texas Railroads: A Record of Construction and Abandonment* (Austin: University of Texas Bureau of Business Research, 1981).

During the course of the project, the bibliographies at the ends of articles in the *New Handbook* came to amount to more than 13,000 items. Ideally, each bibliography gives some guidance to sources, suggests further secondary reading, and leads the reader to primary sources. In most cases, no attempt has been made to give all the available references. The goal, rather, has been to list works through which a more complete bibliography can be reached. In many cases, however, the paucity of available materials is reflected in a lean bibliography that may in fact include all of the published sources on a given topic. The editors in general have not listed localized primary sources, even when they were used. To include, for instance, such items as deed records of a given county would have enlarged the bibliography needlessly with items not available to most readers. On the other hand, the *New Handbook* frequently cites primary collections of papers or manuscripts when they are accessible in archives.

Many articles lack bibliographies. Most do so because they are based only on the "standard" sources listed above for communities, physical features, and railroads. A substantial number do so because no published, extant, "bibliographable" material is available. Articles about publications often lack bibliographies because the bibliography is intrinsic to the subject; an article on a scholarly journal, for instance, may be based on nothing but the journal itself. In general, articles about institutions that publish regular reports on themselves—college catalogs, for example—do not cite those reports, though the reader may assume they were consulted. When a work is cited in the text of an article, the editors as a rule do not cite it again at the end. In biographies, works of the subjects are not listed in the bibliographies unless they are autobiographical.

Inevitably, in a large project one encounters apparently reliable but dateless and authorless sources—informational leaflets, local reports in the form of manuscripts or mimeographs, unpublished correspondence in private hands, even records in family Bibles. To list such sources in a published bibliography would constitute a purposeless waste of space. Every entry in the *New Handbook*, however, is represented by a file in the offices of the Texas State Historical Association, where the whole bibliographical story behind the article is available.

Illustrations

Almost 700 illustrations accompany the text of the *New Handbook of Texas,* acquired from a number of sources. In most cases the source of an image is fully noted in the accompanying legend. A few institutions have been particularly helpful in providing numerous illustrations and, in these cases, the institutional name is abbreviated in order to save space. The following abbreviations are used in the legends:

CAH	The Center for American History, The University of Texas at Austin
ITC	Institute of Texan Cultures, San Antonio, Texas
HRHRC	Harry Ransom Humanities Research Center, The University of Texas at Austin
TSL	Texas State Library, Archives Division

THE NEW HANDBOOK OF TEXAS

A Portfolio of Texas History

SPANISH AND MEXICAN ERA

La relacion y comentarios del gouerna dor Aluar nuñez cabeça de vaca, de lo acaescido en las dos jornadas que hizo a las Indias.

Con priuilegio.

Esta tassada por los señores del consejo en Ochenta y cinco mrs.

PLATE 1: *Title page of* La relacion y comentarios del gouernador Aluar nuñez cabeça de vaca, de lo acaescido en las dos jornadas que hizo a las Indias..., *by Álvar Núñez Cabeza de Vaca (Valladolid, 1555). Hand-colored woodcut. 7⅛" × 5¼". Courtesy CAH; CT 0058. The written history of Texas began in 1542, when Cabeza de Vaca published his memoirs of his shipwreck on Galveston Island in 1528 and his time among the Texas natives. Valladolid printer Francisco Fernández de Córdova designed this handsome title page for the second edition of his book, published in 1555.*

PLATE 2: Father Antonio Margil de Jesús, *by Noriega, date unknown. Oil on canvas. 82" × 52". Courtesy San Jacinto Museum of History, Houston. Franciscan missionary Antonio Margil de Jesús founded four of the approximately forty missions in Texas between 1632 and 1793, including missions in Nacogdoches (1716) and San Antonio (1719). This work of hagiography was produced to honor Margil's missionary works and, perhaps, as a part of the effort to have him canonized.*

PLATE 3: Destruction of Mission San Sabá in the Province of Texas and the Martyrdom of the Fathers Alonso Giraldo de Terreros, Joseph Santiesteban, *by José de Páez (attrib.), ca. 1763. Oil on canvas. 83" × 115". Courtesy Instituto Nacional de Antropología e Historia, Mexico City. When the wealthy mining magnate Don Pedro de Terreros learned that his cousin had been killed in an attack by Comanche, Bidai, Tejas, and Tonkawa Indians at Santa Cruz de San Sabá Mission in 1758, he commissioned this painting to commemorate the martyrdom of Fathers Alonso Giraldo de Terreros (left) and José Santiesteban (right). This is the earliest extant easel painting depicting a historic event in Texas and predates by several years Benjamin West's* The Death of General Wolfe *(National Gallery of Canada, 1770), generally considered the earliest history painting to depict the characters in modern garb.*

PLATE 4: Soldado de cuera, *by Ramundo de Murillo, ca. 1803. Watercolor. Courtesy Archivo General de Indias, Seville. After serving on the Texas frontier, Sergeant Ramundo de Murrillo included this depiction of a Spanish soldier in a report recommending that the regular thigh-length leather jacket, which was part of the soldier's armor, be cut to jacket size, as shown.*

PLATE 5: Comanches, *by Lino Sánchez y Tapía after Jean Louis Berlandier, ca. 1830. Watercolor. 12¼" × 8½". Courtesy Gilcrease Museum, Tulsa; acc. no. 4016.336, plate II. Naturalist Berlandier was present when General Manuel de Mier y Terán's Comisión de Límites entered Texas in 1828 to determine the eastern boundary between the United States and Mexico and collect data on the geography, natural resources, and plant and animal life of the region. This painting of Comanche warriors is one of dozens of watercolors that Berlandier and Lieutenant José María Sánchez y Tapía did to document the many cultures of the state.*

PLATE 6: Ranchero de Texas, *by Lino Sánchez y Tapía, ca. 1830. Watercolor. 12" × 8½". Courtesy Gilcrease Museum, Tulsa; acc. no. 4016.336, plate XXXV. Mier y Terán noted that the Anglos occupied the eastern half of Texas, but he encountered numerous Spanish ranchos in South Texas. Sánchez y Tapía probably drew this characteristic portrait of a rancher from field notes after the expedition had returned to Mexico.*

PLATE 7: Stephen F. Austin, *by William Howard, 1833. Watercolor. 5¼" × 4⅝". Courtesy CAH; CT 0008. While Austin was in Mexico City in 1833, British artist William Howard painted two miniature portraits of the empresario. This one shows him as the pioneering frontiersman who opened up Texas to Anglo-American settlement.*

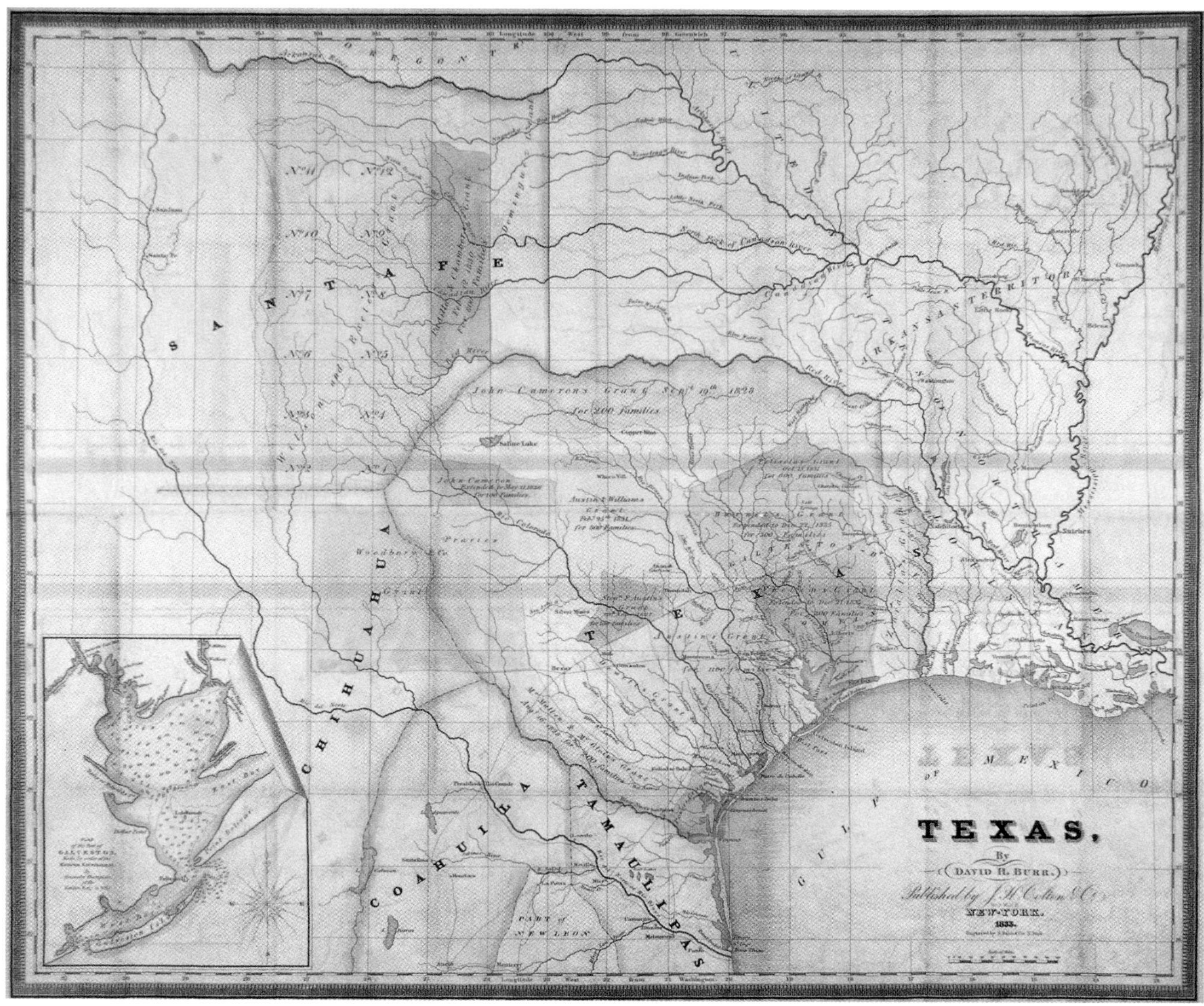

PLATE 8: Texas, *by David H. Burr, 1833. Hand-colored engraving. 17" × 21⅓". Courtesy Paul G. Bell, Houston. Juan N. Almonte included Burr's map as a part of his secret report on Texas in 1834. Thought to be the most accurate and up-to-date map at that time, it shows the Nueces River as the boundary between Texas and Coahuila.*

PLATE 9: The Backwoodsman, Portrait of Col. David Crockett, *by John Gadsby Chapman, date unknown. Oil on canvas. 24½" × 16½". Courtesy HRHRC. In 1834, two years before he arrived in Texas, Crockett participated in the making of this stereotypical frontiersman image by commenting that if artist Chapman could only "catch" him "on a bear hunt in a harricane," then he might produce a portrait "better worth looking at." Crockett scoured Washington to come up with appropriate props: the soiled and used shirt, knife, hatchet, and rifle. The state of Texas acquired the larger version of this painting to hang in the Capitol, but it was destroyed in the 1881 fire.*

PLATE 10: George Childress, *by unknown artist, ca. 1830. Watercolor on ivory. Courtesy CAH; CN 01094. An attorney and former newspaper editor from Tennessee, Childress arrived in Texas in January 1836 and was immediately elected to represent Robertson's colony at the convention at Washington-on-the-Brazos. Childress served as chairman of the committee to draft the Texas Declaration of Independence and read it to the assembled convention on March 2. He is generally considered its author.*

PLATE 11: Juan N. Seguín, *by Thomas Jefferson Wright, 1838. Oil on canvas. 26½" × 24¼". Courtesy TSL. Following the example of several artists who painted the portraits of American Revolutionary heroes, Wright established himself in a Houston hotel in 1837 and invited Texas Revolutionary heroes to have their portraits made for his "Gallery of National Portraits." He probably painted Seguín's portrait in Nacogdoches the following year. Unlike other heroes, however, Seguín found life in an increasingly Anglo-dominated state untenable and emigrated to Mexico in 1842.*

PLATE 12: Whooping Crane, *by John James Audubon, 1834. Engraving with aquatint (hand-colored). 38⅛" × 25¼". Courtesy Stark Museum of Art, Orange, Texas. Audubon was an international celebrity by the time he arrived in Texas in April 1837 in search of additional species for his great book,* The Birds of America *(1827–38). He visited Galveston and Houston, collected skulls of Mexican soldiers from the San Jacinto battlefield, and concluded that more than two-thirds of the birds of America, including the lumbering whooping crane, were native to the republic.*

PLATE 13: Collared Peccary, *by John James Audubon, 1844. Lithograph (hand-colored). 21⅝" × 27¼". Courtesy Stark Museum of Art, Orange, Texas. Audubon's son, John Woodhouse, gathered information on this South Texas javelina in 1845, while in the republic to find additional specimens for his father's second great book,* Viviparous Quadrupeds of North America *(1845–46).*

PLATE 14: Tehuacana Creek Indian Council, *by John Mix Stanley, 1849. Oil on canvas. 17" × 24". Courtesy Susan and Pierce Butler, Nashville, Tennessee. This Indian council, held near Torrey's Trading Post in the future McLennan County in 1843, was one of several inspired by President Sam Houston, who espoused a peaceful policy toward the Indians, as opposed to President Mirabeau Lamar's bellicosity. Stanley, the artist, was on hand to depict this council because he had accompanied American commissioner Pierce M. Butler to the conference.*

PLATE 15: George Allen's Residence, *by Friedrich Jacob Rothaas, 1845. Watercolor. 20" × 24". Courtesy Texas Memorial Museum, Austin. Comforts came quickly for the founding families of Houston. This sketch, by artist, surveyor, and architect Rothaas, a German immigrant, shows Allen's two-story, frame plantation house near Houston. Black slaves attend the children in their kite-flying.*

PLATE 16: General Wool Crossing the Military Plaza, San Antonio, *by Samuel Chamberlain, ca. 1867. Watercolor. 7" × 12⅛". Courtesy San Jacinto Museum of History, Houston. Chamberlain, en route to Mexico as a member of Wool's force, noted the diverse audience that witnessed this 1846 scene: "wild looking Texans, Mexicans in their everlasting blankets, Negro Slaves, with a sprinkling of Lipan Indians, in full dress of paint and feathers, White women, Squaws and Senoretas [sic]."*

PLATE 17: Mission San José, *by Seth Eastman, ca. 1848. Oil on canvas mounted on panel. 15½" × 22". Courtesy Witte Museum, San Antonio, Texas. As a member of the U.S. Army that occupied Texas after statehood, Eastman traveled from Indianola to San Antonio and on to the Hill Country, where he served at Fort Martin Scott. Along with other visitors to the state, he was struck by the almost century-old mission structures.*

PLATE 18: Fort Martin Scott, *by Richard Petri, 1857. Oil on canvas. 16½" × 23". Courtesy Texas Memorial Museum, Austin. German artist Petri's unfinished painting is a fascinating document of multiculturalism on the Texas frontier. James Longstreet, the commander of the post (shown in the background), has an Indian woman on his arm, while Germans, Mexicans, and Indians of various tribes look on. Petri was probably working on the painting at the time of his death.*

PLATE 19: Canyon, Fort Davis–1, *by Capt. Arthur T. Lee, Eighth U.S. Infantry, ca. 1855. Watercolor. 4¾" × 7⅝". Department of Rare Books and Special Collections, University of Rochester Library. The federal military presence in Texas was increased when Fort Davis was established in the Davis Mountains of West Texas in 1854. Captain Lee, one of the founding officers, documented his service there with a number of watercolors.*

PLATE 20: West Side Main Plaza, San Antonio, Texas, *by W. G. M. Samuel, 1849. Oil on canvas mounted on panel. 22" × 36". Courtesy Witte Museum, San Antonio, Texas. As a veteran of Indian fights and the war with Mexico, Samuels was "one of the best known characters" in San Antonio and "a dead shot." He also applied his naïve artistic abilities to a series of paintings of the city's Main Plaza. This view of the west side, with San Fernando Cathedral in the background, suggests some of the activity that routinely went on: water and wood vendors, an arriving stage coach, cowboys (including one trying to rope a runaway steer), and two men watching a dog fight.*

PLATE 21: View on the Guadalupe—Seguin-Texas, *by Sarah Ann Lily Bumstead Hardinge Daniels, 1853. Watercolor, gouache, and graphite on paper. 6" × 9⅜". Courtesy Amon Carter Museum, Fort Worth; gift of Mrs. Natalie K. Shastid, 1984.3.14. Like many of her contemporaries, Hardinge sketched and painted for her and her family's pleasure. Thus, we have this appealing scene of Morrison's ferry on the Guadalupe, near where the Hardinges lived for a short time.*

PLATE 22: Courthouse in Houston, *by Thomas Flintoff, March 24, 1852. Watercolor. 10" × 14". Courtesy Houston Metropolitan Research Center, Houston Public Library. An itinerant English limner who was in Texas for about a year, Flintoff produced a series of small watercolors along the Texas coast for his own enjoyment. Pictured here is the first courthouse in Houston, a brick building designed by Friedrich Jacob Rothaas, which was dedicated in October 1851. The barrenness of the landscape and the wagon tracks in the mud suggest the newness of the site.*

PLATE 23: Corrida de la sandía *(Watermelon Race), by Theodore Gentilz, 1890[?] copy of 1848 painting? Oil on canvas. 9" × 12". Courtesy Daughters of the Republic of Texas Library; gift of the Yanaguana Society. Gentilz came to Texas in 1844 as the surveyor for the Castro colony, but moved to San Antonio in 1846 and soon became the visual historian of the Tejano community. Here he depicts the watermelon race, in which the object of the game was to cross the finish line with the melon. The other team could use almost any means necessary to prevent their opponents from winning.*

PLATE 24: Julius Meyenberg's Farm, *by Louis Hoppe, 1864. Watercolor on paper. 8¼" × 11¾". Courtesy Witte Museum, San Antonio, Texas. In what may be a typical scene, farmer Meyenberg, who built his house on a high bluff in Fayette County, is shown in his garden with his wife and six of his eight children and numerous farm animals. Little is known of Hoppe, who was obviously self-taught and might have been an itinerant laborer.*

PLATE 25: Sugar Harvest in Louisiana and Texas, *by Franz Hölzlhuber, ca. 1860. Watercolor on paper. 6" × 8¾". Courtesy Glenbow Museum, Calgary, Alberta, Canada. Hölzlhuber, a young Austrian traveler who spent four years in the U.S., took one of the well-known "floating palaces" down the Mississippi River to visit Louisiana and Texas, where he documented the sugar harvest by slaves. This scene is one of the few contemporary records of slavery in what may be Texas.*

PLATE 26: Guadalupe River Landscape, *by Hermann Lungkwitz, 1862. Oil on canvas. 18¼" × 24⅛". Courtesy Museum of Fine Arts, Houston; Bayou Bend Collection, gift of Miss Ima Hogg. Trained in Dresden, German immigrant Lungkwitz saw the Texas Hill Country in the same Romantic terms that dominated the vision of European and American landscapists of the day. The two boaters peering into the distant cave evoke the mystery of Romanticism, while the handsome painting itself draws attention to the natural beauty of the land.*

PLATE 27: Plains Indian Warrior in Blue, *by Richard Petri, date unknown. Pencil and watercolor, 6½" × 4⅝". Courtesy Texas Memorial Museum, Austin. The Indians of the Hill Country fascinated Petri, who was Hermann Lungkwitz's brother-in-law and who had been trained in the same Romantic tradition. Petri thought that the Indians he saw were the remnants of a noble people who had been defeated by Anglo-European expansion and would soon be extinct as a people, but who, nevertheless, maintained their dignity and nobility.*

PLATE 28: Plains Woman in Red-and-Blue Dress, *by Richard Petri, ca. 1852. Watercolor and pencil. 8¼" × 6¾". Courtesy Mrs. Hunter P. Harris. Here Petri demonstrates his painterly ability as well as his observational skills by portraying this Lipan Apache woman in some detail: a red and blue dress made from trader's cloth, with a beaded awl case, narrow bracelets, a large abalone-shell pendant, and carefully groomed hair tied up with a strip of orange-red fabric, which apparently reaches to the floor.*

PLATE 29: Guadalupe Mountains, *by John Russell Bartlett, ca. 1751. Pencil and sepia wash. 9½" × 13". Courtesy John Carter Brown Library at Brown University. Bartlett was the commissioner of the U.S. Boundary Survey, ordered to mark the boundary between the United States and Mexico in cooperation with the Mexican survey after the war with Mexico. The artists, naturalists, and surveyors who made up his command produced an unprecedented record of the southwestern border in William H. Emory's* The U.S. and Mexican Boundary Survey. *Bartlett used his own paintings in his* Personal Narrative of Explorations and Incidents in Texas, New Mexico, California, Sonora, and Chihuahua... *(1854).*

PLATE 30: Plaza and Church of El Paso, *by Augustus de Vaudricourt, 1857. Chromolithograph by Sarony Major and Knapp, New York. 6" × 8⁵⁄₁₆". Prints and Photographs Collection, El Paso file 2, CAH; CT 0059. When the final boundary between the United States and Mexico was drawn, the Hispanic community of El Paso (now Ciudad Juárez) remained a part of Mexico, and the American village of Franklin became the new El Paso. El Paso looked exotic to Americans who were unfamiliar with the newly acquired Southwest.*

PLATE 31: Vista de la Cierra de los Chisos, *by Enrique Barchesky, 1851. Watercolor. 8½" × 13". Courtesy Yale Collection of Western Americana, Beinecke Rare Book and Manuscript Library, Yale University. As a member of Colonel Emilio Langberg's Mexican Boundary Commission team, Barchesky painted the first view of the Chisos Mountains, now a part of Big Bend National Park, from across the Rio Grande.*

PLATE 32: Sam Houston, *by Martin Johnson Heade, ca. 1846. Oil. 29½" × 24½". Courtesy TSL. Sam Houston was the dominant political personality in Texas until he was deposed as governor for his Unionist sentiment by the Secession Convention in 1861. He served as first president of the republic and one of the first U.S. senators when Texas entered the Union. He probably posed for this portrait, which now hangs in the Governor's Mansion, shortly after he arrived in Washington in 1846. It was exhibited at the Pennsylvania Academy of the Fine Arts in 1847.*

PLATE 33: The Terry Rangers, *by Carl G. von Iwonski, ca. 1862. Oil on canvas. 11½" × 15". Courtesy Witte Museum, San Antonio, Texas. Iwonski, a German immigrant and Unionist, painted this portrait of the young Sam Maverick of San Antonio (in red shirt), who served the Confederacy throughout the Civil War, first in Benjamin Franklin Terry's famous Terry's Texas Rangers (Eighth Texas Cavalry), then in an independent bushwhacking company.*

GILDED AGE

PLATE 34: Antelope Hunters, *by Chester Loomis, Texas 1887. Oil on canvas. 23" × 37". Photograph by James O. Milmoe. Courtesy the Anschutz Collection, Denver. Trained in Paris and London, Loomis and his brother purchased a ranch near San Angelo in 1886, and he and his family spent many summers there. Here Loomis has pictured himself standing by his horse while his brother skins a recently slain antelope.*

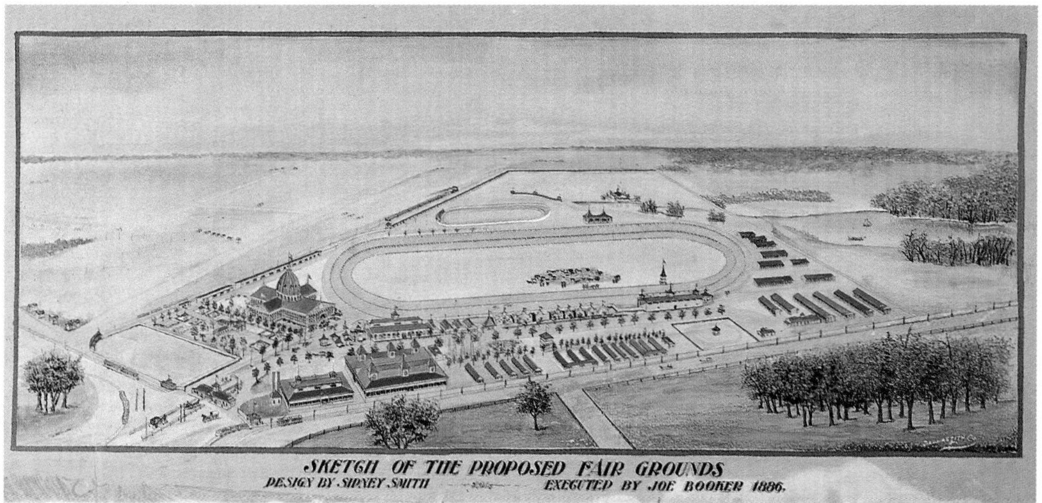

PLATE 35: Sketch of the Proposed Fair Grounds, *by Joe Booker, 1886. Pen and ink and watercolor. 21" × 45". From the collections of the Dallas Historical Society. The first recorded State Fair of Texas was held in Dallas in 1859. It continued sporadically until it was formally chartered in 1886, when the directors voted to expand the fair with the acquisition of additional property. The State Fair of Texas is now held at Fair Park in Dallas, which encompasses this area.*

PLATE 36: San Antonio River at St. Mary's Street Bridge, *by Ida Weisselberg Hadra, ca. 1883. Oil on canvas. 24" × 30". Courtesy Witte Museum, San Antonio, Texas. The winding San Antonio River has given the Alamo City an alternative nickname, "City of Bridges." The river has also proved irresistible to artists, and Castroville-born Hadra was no exception. She completed this painting shortly after moving to San Antonio.*

PLATE 37: Surrender of Santa Anna, *by William A. Huddle, 1886. Oil on canvas. 71¼" × 113¾". Courtesy State Preservation Board, Austin. Mexican general Antonio López de Santa Anna stands before the wounded Houston in this commemorative painting. His aide, Colonel Juan N. Almonte, is shown at Houston's right. Erastus (Deaf) Smith occupies a place of honor at Houston's left, while Thomas J. Rusk and Mirabeau B. Lamar stand behind Almonte. This painting has become the accepted visual account of the surrender scene, despite the facts that Santa Anna is pictured in an enlisted man's jacket rather than the civilian clothing that he actually wore, and that the surrender might have taken place in Houston's tent rather than under this large oak tree.*

PLATE 38: Dawn at the Alamo, *by Henry McArdle, 1905. Oil on canvas. 84¼" × 144". Courtesy State Preservation Board, Austin. The Texas legislature's 1888 acquisition of Huddle's* Surrender of Santa Anna *for the new Capitol probably prompted McArdle to begin work on his version of the heroic battle of the Alamo, which he depicted as a visual morality play. He moved the cannon platform to the center of the picture, intending that it serve as the metaphorical altar upon which the Texans sacrificed their lives for independence. The sun rises behind the altar, signifying the dawn of a new republic. The painting now hangs in the Texas Senate chamber.*

PLATE 39: The Mier Expedition: The Drawing of the Black Bean, *by Frederic Remington, 1896. Oil on canvas. 20⅛" × 40". Courtesy Museum of Fine Arts, Houston; Hogg Brothers Collection, gift of Miss Ima Hogg. Author and artist Remington drew upon a famous event from Texas history when he painted the men of the Mier expedition as heroic but doomed (if they drew a black bean), a metaphor for his view of the Old West, which he felt stood in sharp contrast to a United States that had succumbed to continued immigration, industrialization, and modernization. An engraving of this painting accompanied the article in* Harper's Monthly *(December 1896).*

PLATE 40: Gen. Sam Houston, *by Stephen Seymour Thomas, 1893. Oil on canvas. 144" × 108". Courtesy San Jacinto Museum of History, Houston. Thomas, born in San Augustine, was only twenty-four years old when he began work on this portrait of Houston for the Texas Building at the Chicago World's Fair in 1893. He chose to depict the general at the decisive moment in which he tells his motley band of rebels to charge the Mexican lines at San Jacinto. Both of Thomas's grandfathers were involved in the decisive battle, and among the research items that he compiled for the picture was a portrait of Houston that his aunt had painted during one of the general's visits to her father's home.*

PLATE 41: Galveston Wharf Scene, *by Julius Stockfleth, 1885. Oil on canvas. 21½" × 31". Courtesy Rosenberg Library, Galveston, Texas. Galveston was the leading port and most sophisticated city in Texas when Stockfleth depicted the wharf, the source of its wealth, from the east side of Twenty-first Street looking west. The railroad, the link with the mainland, is shown running along the wharf, with sailboats at dock while a large steamer enters the port. At the peak, approximately 4,000 immigrants entered the United States through Galveston each month.*

PLATE 42: Ellis County Courthouse, Waxahachie, Texas, *by James Riely Gordon, ca. 1895. Watercolor on paper. 34½" × 29". Architectural Drawings Collection, Architecture and Planning Library, University of Texas at Austin General Libraries. A number of Texas counties exhibited their local pride at the turn of the century by building elegant courthouses, and Romanesque-inspired Gordon of San Antonio was the architect of choice. His masterpiece may be the Ellis County Courthouse in Waxahachie, which employed cut red sandstone, pink granite, and terra cotta to achieve the polychrome look so popular at the time.*

PLATE 43: Market Plaza, *by Thomas Allen, 1878–79. Oil on canvas mounted on panel. 26" × 39 ½". Courtesy Witte Museum, San Antonio, Texas. Although Tejanos were a minority in San Antonio by 1876, their culture continued to make the city one of the most colorful in the country. Allen, an American artist trained in the United States, Paris, and Germany, was much impressed with the Hispanic culture during his 1878–79 visit. The Hispanic habit of dining al fresco continued until the public plazas were turned into parks early in the twentieth century.*

PROGRESSIVE ERA, WORLD WAR I, AND THE TWENTIES

PLATE 44: Still Life With Books, *by Robert Onderdonk, date unknown. Oil on canvas. 12" × 18". Courtesy Witte Museum, San Antonio, Texas. Onderdonk's deft still life, a purely aesthetic depiction probably made for his own pleasure, is representative of the impact that he had on the arts in Texas. He painted and taught in San Antonio and Dallas, helped found the first formal art organizations in the state, attracted numerous patrons, and ultimately became known as the "Dean of Texas Artists."*

PLATE 45: Bluebonnet Field, *by Julian Onderdonk, 1912. Oil on canvas. 16" × 20". Courtesy Witte Museum, San Antonio, Texas; gift of Mrs. Grace Irvin Golsing. Raised in an artistic family, Onderdonk was the first Texas artist to apply the impressionism that he had learned at the Art Students' League in New York to the Texas landscape. He painted Texas wildflowers from his return to the state in 1909 until his death in 1922 and was the first of many Texas artists to paint fields of bluebonnets, the state flower.*

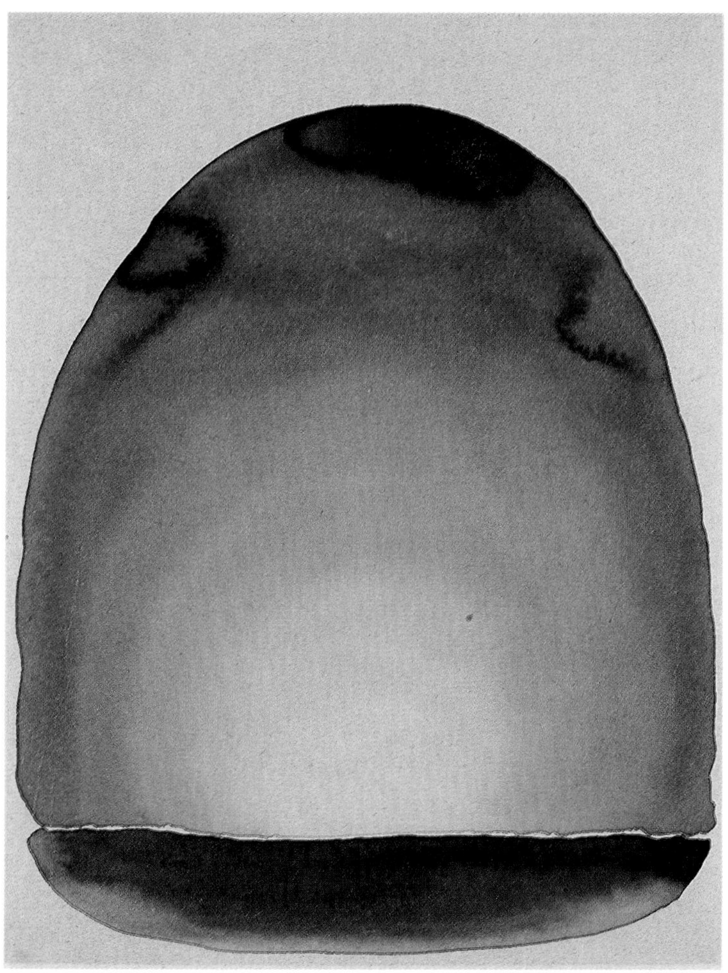

PLATE 46: Light Coming on the Plains II, *by Georgia O'Keeffe, 1917. Watercolor on paper. 11⅞" × 8⅞". Courtesy Amon Carter Museum, Fort Worth; 1966.32. While impressionism ruled in the academies, West Texas Normal College professor Georgia O'Keeffe created avant-garde watercolors of the Panhandle landscape that won her an exhibition at Alfred Stieglitz's 291 Gallery in New York City. O'Keeffe said that the inspiration for this painting, one of a series, was the headlight of a train coming over the night horizon.*

PLATE 47: Cactus Flowers, *by Dawson Dawson-Watson, 1929. Oil on canvas. 26" × 21". Courtesy Witte Museum, San Antonio, Texas. Dawson-Watson was to cacti what Julian Onderdonk was to bluebonnets. He was attracted to Texas by the Texas Wildflower Competition that oilman Edgar B. Davis sponsored, and he continued to paint different versions of cacti thereafter. One of Dawson-Watson's cactus paintings won the 1927 contest.*

PLATE 48: Fort Worth, *by Murray P. Bewley, ca. 1920s. Oil on canvas. 15½" × 12". Courtesy Gretchen B. Denny, Fort Worth. The son of a Fort Worth flour-milling family, Bewley studied art in New York and Paris and returned to his hometown only to visit his mother and to paint portraits of family friends. He was primarily a portraitist and figure painter, but also took time to produce this shimmering view of downtown Fort Worth, similar in style to American artist Childe Hassam's depictions of New York City.*

PLATE 49: Street Scene in San Antonio, *by Boyer Gonzales, Jr., 1938. Oil on canvas. 16" × 20". Courtesy Witte Museum, San Antonio, Texas. Like Stephen S. Thomas and Murray Bewley, Gonzales was born into a prominent Texas family. His father had continued the family cotton brokerage in Galveston until selling it and turning his full attention to painting. After study in Virginia and New York, Boyer, Jr., returned to Texas, where he joined the new art department at the University of Texas.* Street Scene *won the San Antonio artists' exhibition in 1938 because of its well-organized pattern of shapes and colors.*

PLATE 50: Le Taureau au Rodeo, *by Mary Bonner, 1926. Etching. 10" × $42\frac{11}{16}$". Courtesy Walter N. Mathis, San Antonio. After study in Switzerland, New York, and Paris, and international acclaim as a printmaker, Bonner returned to her memories of growing up on a ranch in Uvalde County to produce a vigorous series of art deco cowboys during the 1920s. Her understanding of animals and feel for action may be seen in these rodeo scenes.*

PLATE 51: *Design for fashion by Gordon Conway: cover of* Eve: The Lady's Pictorial, *vol. 34, no. 439, August 8, 1928. Theatre Art Collection, Gordon Conway Costume Design Collection, HRHRC. Cleburn-born Conway excelled as a graphic designer and illustrator for dozens of publications and clients during the golden age of American illustration. She captured the essence of the quintessential New Woman, tall, elegant, and sophisticated—like Conway herself—and popularized it through her numerous magazine covers and stage and film designs.*

PLATE 52: Long Distance Aero Immer, *by C. A. A. Dellschau, 1910. Watercolor. 15¾" × 19¼". Courtesy Witte Museum, San Antonio, Texas. Among the German immigrants to Texas, at least two, Jacob Brodbeck and Dellschau, gave serious thought to aviation. Brodbeck tried (perhaps successfully) to fly an airplane of his own design in 1865, while Dellschau drew exotic but imaginary aircraft designed during the 1850s by the members of the Sonora, California, Aero Club.*

PLATE 53: Neighbors, *by Merritt Mauzey, 1938. Oil on masonite. $23\frac{7}{8}$" × $29\frac{7}{8}$". Courtesy Dallas Museum of Art; Arthur Kramer and Fred Florence Purchase Prize, Ninth Annual Dallas Allied Arts Exhibition, 1938. Contrasting the old with the new, Mauzey, who grew up on a farm in Nolan County, shows that modernization had come to many Texas farms despite the hardships of the Great Depression.*

PLATE 54: Cotton Boll, *by Otis Dozier, 1936. Oil on masonite. 20" × 16". Courtesy Dallas Museum of Art; gift of Eleanor and Tom May. For decades, Texas had a rural, agriculturally based economy dominated by cotton. Dallas artist Dozier, who was raised on a cotton farm near Forney, illustrates this with an enticingly beautiful, almost surreal portrait of the cotton plant in all its permutations: new spring foliage at the top, the sensuous blossom, the mature boll, and, finally, the red stalks of autumn, all set against the endless rows in the background.*

PLATE 55: Boomtown, *by Thomas Hart Benton, 1927–28. Oil on canvas. 46⅛" × 54½". Courtesy Memorial Art Gallery of the University of Rochester, Marion Stratton Gould Fund. The discovery of oil changed Texas dramatically, and artist Benton suggests the impact that new oil had in the fast-growing and raucous Panhandle community of Borger.*

PLATE 56: Oil Field Girls, *by Jerry Bywaters, 1940. Oil on board. 30" × 25". Photograph by George Holmes. Courtesy Archer M. Huntington Art Gallery, University of Texas at Austin, Michener Collection Acquisition Fund, 1984. The discovery of oil radically changed the face, economy, and culture of Texas, as Bywaters, a leading proponent of Regionalism, demonstrates here. By focusing on the improbably tall and overdressed women, and depicting a desolate landscape broken by an oilfield fire, discarded tires, garish signs, and a unkempt building, Bywaters subtly compares the excesses of profit and pollution in the oilfield to prostitution.*

PLATE 57: Winding Road, *by Charles T. Bowling, 1942. Watercolor/arches paper. 26" × 34". Courtesy Dallas Museum of Art. Much aware of the changes being wrought throughout Texas by improved highways, Bowling often used the road as a metaphor for change—old v. new, rural v. urban, tradition v. change.*

PLATE 58: Ellis County Landscape, *by Florence McClung, 1936. Oil on canvas. 24" × 30". Courtesy Panhandle-Plains Historical Museum, Canyon, Texas; gift of the artist. As head of the art department at Trinity University at Waxahachie, McClung had the opportunity to paint nearby landscapes, which are strongly reminiscent of contemporary American artist Grant Wood's strong, regional works.*

PLATE 59: Dallas Broadway, *by George Grosz. Watercolor on paper. 19½" × 15½". Gift of Leon Harris, Jr., University Art Collection, Southern Methodist University, Dallas, Texas. As the oil economy boomed, the state's two largest cities, Dallas and Houston, developed in eastern Texas. Their cultural lives have usually lagged behind their economies, but German artist Grosz captures in his passionate and characteristic cubism some of the post–World War II excitement of the Dallas entertainment scene.*

PLATE 60: Cowboy Dance, *by Jenne Magafan, 1941. Mural. Photographed by Wyatt McSpadden. Courtesy Texas Historical Commission, Austin. With people out of work all over the country, President Franklin D. Roosevelt established government programs to provide employment. The Public Works of Art Project and subsequent programs offered artists employment to paint murals and other pictures for public buildings. The only restriction was that their work interpret the American scene. Magafan's work in the Anson post office is characteristic of the many Texas murals.*

THE COLD WAR

PLATE 61: Hog Killing Time, *by H. O. Kelly, ca. 1950. Oil on canvas-covered board. 14" × 20". Courtesy Dallas Museum of Art; Dallas Art Association Purchase. As Texas became increasingly urban, several artists remembered how good life had been and often painted nostalgic events from their childhood. "Cowboy" Kelly, from Blanket, remarked that "These folks are getting right along. Scalding, cutting up and trimming off fat. Cats and Dogs are pilfering and feasting.... These boys are... mak[ing] pig bladder balloons. Coffee is coming for the ladies. The men will have a snort of 'oh be joyful.' They earn it."*

PLATE 62: Building of the Railroad, *by Clara McDonald Williamson, 1949–50. Oil on panel. 27" × 29½". Courtesy A. H. Belo Corporation, Dallas. "Aunt Clara," as Williamson was called, did not begin painting her "memory pictures" until late in life. Here she portrays the excitement that the community of Iredell felt when the railroad arrived in 1880. "I'm not afraid of that big iron thing," she recalled telling her mother just before the whistle blew and the steam hissed. "I was, oh, so scared, and I grabbed Mama's skirt, and, oh, just hid!" Clara is the little girl in the blue dress.*

PLATE 63: How High is Aunt Fanny's Porch, *by Velox Ward, 1970. Oil on board. 24" × 36". Courtesy Barbara Elizabeth Gary, Aspen, Colorado. Ward, a lay preacher who grew up in rural Texas communities, portrays the perception of a child that the world is much larger than it really is.*

PLATE 64: Tamalada *(Making Tamales), by Carmen Lomas Garza, © 1987. Gouache. 20" × 27". Photograph by Wolfgang Dietze. Collection of Leonila Ramirez, Don Ramon's Restaurant, San Francisco. Many Mexican-American families still get together to make tamales for the holidays.*

PLATE 65: Ranger Escort West of the Pecos, *by Tom Lea, 1965. Oil on canvas. 36¼" × 52". Courtesy State Preservation Board, Austin. El Paso artist and author Tom Lea captures the Romanticism surrounding the historic image of the Texas Rangers in this canvas. Lea recalled that the sergeant on the dun horse wrote many years ago, "How happy I am now in my old age that I am a native Texan and saw the grand frontier before it was marred by the hand of man." This picture on the cover of Walter Prescott Webb's* The Texas Rangers *helped make it a best-seller.*

PLATE 66: East Texas Spring, *by E. M. (Buck) Schiwetz, 1957. Watercolor. 7½" × 10¾". Courtesy HRHRC. For decades, Buck Schiwetz traveled all over Texas to portray the state for millions of Texans in* The Humble Way *and in three different collections of his work. "In April, there is a sedative-like beauty in East Texas," he recalled of this picture. "I found all the ingredients in one spot.... the deep green of the pine groves provides an appropriate backdrop for the clean white of the dogwood blossoms and... the sandhill cranes, egrets, and white herons were everywhere."*

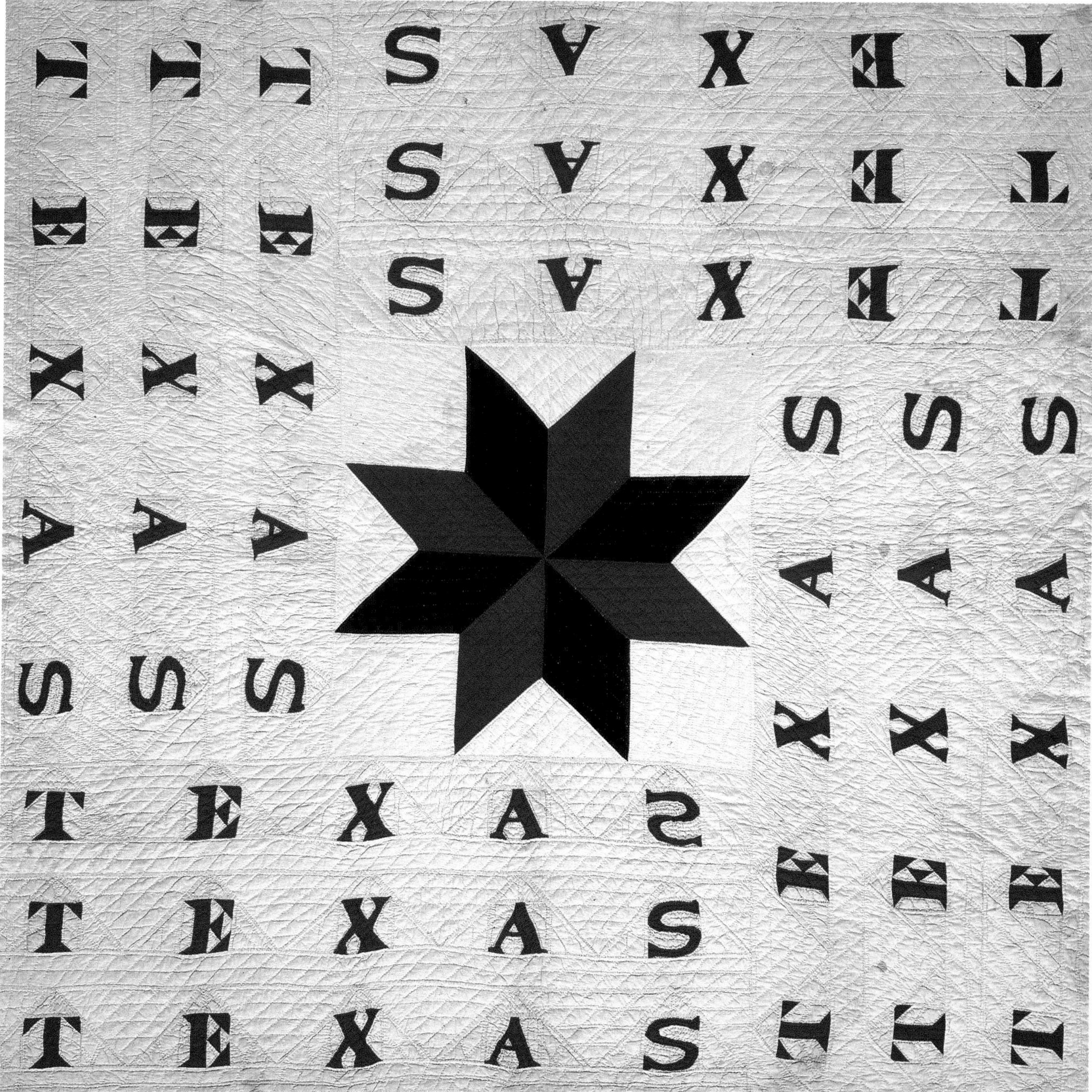

PLATE 67: Texas Quilt, *by Nancy Rebecca Dickson Callan, ca. 1886. From* Lone Stars: A Legacy of Texas Quilts, 1836–1936, *by Karoline Patterson Bresenhan and Nancy O'Bryant Puentes, © 1986. Courtesy the authors and the University of Texas Press. The history of Anglo-American Texas can be traced in quilts, from the colonial period to the present day. In addition, it is frequently said that the anonymous quilt (few of them are signed) is a historical document that provides us a cultural continuity with the past. This "word" quilt honors the fiftieth anniversary of Texas independence and, perhaps, quiltmaker Callan's daughter, Texanna.*

PLATE 68: Drouth Stricken Area, *by Alexandre Hogue, 1934. Oil on canvas. 30" × 42¼". Courtesy Dallas Museum of Art; Dallas Art Association Purchase. Embracing a new aesthetic, and repelled by the devastation of the Dust Bowl, Hogue, who grew up in Denton, denounced the "mediocre paintings of Texas wildflowers" and produced a series of fierce landscapes "because I was there before, during and after the holocaust and could see the awesome, terrifying beauty of it with my own dust-filled eyes."*

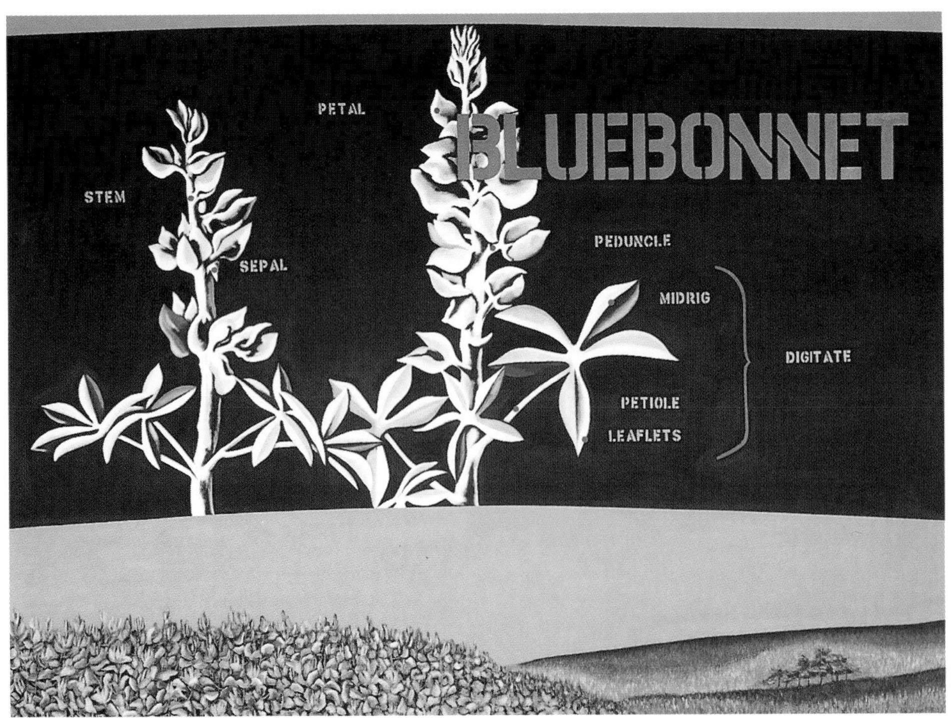

PLATE 69: Humanscape #57, *by Mel Casas, 1969. Acrylic on canvas. 73" × 76¾". Courtesy San Antonio Museum of Art, San Antonio, Texas. Perhaps sharing Hogue's disdain for the clichéd wildflower painting, Casas has employed humor (and a bit of Texas chic) to celebrate the Texas icon in the ultimate bluebonnet painting.*

PLATE 70: Standard Station, Amarillo, Texas, *by Edward Joseph Ruscha, 1963. Oil on canvas. 65" × 121⅝". Courtesy Hood Museum of Art, Dartmouth College, Hanover, New Hampshire; gift of James J. Meeker, Class of 1958, in memory of Lee English. A century ago, nature molded our world in much the same way that man-made culture does today. Ruscha's stereotypical image from U.S. Route 66 is, therefore, familiar to all Americans, not just Texans.*

PLATE 71: Amarillo Boot, *by Jack Boynton, 1976. Color lithograph with collage. 29½" × 22". Courtesy Amarillo Museum of Art. The boot, by Fort Worth artist Boynton, is a complex piece of Texas chic masquerading as Texas kitsch in honor of the American Bicentennial. It synthesizes various familiar images from modern Texas: the boot, the Yellow Rose, Texan James Surls's sculpture juxtaposed with Barnett Newman's* Broken Obelisk *(installed at the Rothko Chapel at the University of St. Thomas in Houston), a rainbow with the University of Texas tower in the background. And, at the top, a play on the landscape and climate of Amarillo, where art (suggested by pencil shadow above the I) nevertheless flourishes.*

PLATE 72: Grand Opening of the Armadillo World Headquarters, *by Jim Franklin, 1970. Poster.* $11\frac{3}{16}" \times 16\frac{13}{16}"$*. Texas Poster Art Collection, CAH; CT 0057. Sam Lewis of San Angelo made the familiar nine-banded armadillo into a "folk critter" and emblem of Texas with his armadillo races during the 1960s, but Austin artist Franklin turned this mammal into the symbol of the Austin underground with his cartoons. When Franklin became the artist for Armadillo World Headquarters, which was to Austin's music scene as the Grand Ole Opry is to Nashville's, he made this poster for the opening and turned the former National Guard Armory into what one reporter called the "Sistine Chapel of armadillo art."*

PLATE 73: The Orange Show, *by Jeff McKissack. Completed in 1979. Photograph by Hickey-Robertson, Houston. Courtesy Orange Show Foundation, Houston. Over a period of years, McKissack, a former worm farmer, welder, shipbuilder, and postman, built his vision, now recognized as an authentic folk creation, on one-tenth of an acre at 2401 Munger Street in Houston. It was not a tribute to the University of Texas orange and white, but to the fruit that grows abundantly throughout the Rio Grande valley. Why? Because, as he explained to one visitor, he could never find the perfect juicer.*

PLATE 74: Vaquero *by Luis A. Jimenez, modeled 1980, cast 1990. Acrylic urethane, fiberglass, steel armature. 199" × 114" × 67". Courtesy Luis A. Jimenez, © 1980. Jimenez's sculpture draws power from several traditional symbols of the Southwest—the vaquero with a pistol in his hand, the horse, and the prickly pear cactus. In other works he has employed Indians and buffalo, skulls, coyotes, rabbits, and other critters.*

PLATE 75: Howdy Arts! *by Tomi Ungerer, 1965. Watercolor. 13" × 11" (sheet size). From* The Poster Art of Tomi Ungerer. *Copyright © 1971 by Diogenes Verlag AG Zurich. Ungerer, a well-known cartoonist and magazine illustrator, produced this caricature of President Johnson on the occasion of the White House Festival of the Arts, which resulted in the establishment of the National Endowment for the Arts. Ungerer deftly contrasts Johnson's western heritage with the cultural sophistication that he was trying to encourage.*

PLATE 76: Shotguns, Fourth Ward, *by John Biggers, 1987. Acrylic and oil on board. 41¾" × 32". Courtesy Hampton University Museum, Hampton, Virginia. Biggers combines images of shotgun houses in the Fourth Ward of Houston with elements of traditional African-American yard art—vessels by the door represent certain practical domestic acts, for example—to produce an intense painting.*

A. C. SAUNDERS SITE. The A. C. Saunders Site, in extreme northeastern Anderson County, is a site of the late prehistoric Frankston Phase. This phase is directly ancestral to the Caddoan-speaking Hasinai tribes encountered by the Spaniards and French in the late seventeenth and early eighteenth centuries. The site consists of an ash mound and a midden beneath which was a circular house pattern. A. T. Jackson of the University of Texas anthropology department did tests there in 1931 and excavated in 1935; he called it a perpetual fire site. E. B. Sayles of Gila Pueblo, Arizona, did tests in the midden in 1933, and copies of his notes are housed in the Texas Archeological Research Laboratory.

Jackson's excavations consisted of two trenches dug into the ash mound and complete excavation of the midden. During the later work was found a circular pattern of postholes that represent a former structure about forty-six feet in diameter. The entrance may have been one of several gaps in the posthole pattern. Evidence of a hearth and several support posts was found on the interior. Additional postholes and hearths were found on the exterior of the large house and may represent the position of a lean-to. The ash mound, which contained few artifacts, was 152 feet from north to south and 123 feet from east to west. The maximum height was about 7 feet. The ash had been placed on a natural knoll of red sand. Covering the ash was an ash-free deposit of sandy loam about 1.5 feet thick.

Spaniards who visited East Texas told of a large, round, thatched house set aside for the maintenance of a perpetual fire and associated ceremonies; they stated that ashes accumulated on the outside. Jackson believed that the A. C. Saunders Site was such a site. In 1982 Ulrich Kleinschmidt tentatively supported Jackson's hypothesis but noted that there is no information to support the contemporaneity of the ash accumulation and the large structure. Yet, as Kleinschmidt points out, in the nearby six-county area, where 668 sites are known, only one other site, Pace MacDonald in Anderson County, has an ash accumulation. But it is smaller and appears to be earlier than that at the A. C. Saunders Site. The Saunders Site is therefore unique in the eastern Texas area.

Several different pottery types were found in the midden. Effigy bowls with mammals and birds and ceramic elbow pipes were also found, as well as projectile points, mainly Perdiz. Stone and bone tools were also recovered, as well as altered mussel shells that were probably used as tools. Food remains consisted principally of deer, wild turkey, and fish bones. Jackson's notes and artifacts from the site are stored at the Texas Archeological Research Laboratory, Austin.

BIBLIOGRAPHY: A. T. Jackson, "A 'Perpetual Fire' Site," *Bulletin of the Texas Archeological and Paleontological Society* 8 (1936). Ulrich Karl Wilhelm Kleinschmidt, Review and Analysis of the A. C. Saunders Site, 41AN19, Anderson County, Texas (M.A. thesis, University of Texas at Austin, 1982). Dee Ann Suhm et al., "An Introductory Handbook of Texas Archeology," *Bulletin of the Texas Archeological Society* 25 (1954).

Kathleen Kirk Gilmore

A. H. BELO CORPORATION. A. H. Belo Corporation, publisher of the Dallas *Morning News* and the *Texas Almanac,*[qqv] is a media corporation encompassing both newspaper publishing and television broadcasting across the country. It is the oldest continuously operated business institution in Texas, having been founded on April 11, 1842, with the first edition of the *Daily News* in Galveston. Founder Samuel Bangs[qv] sold the business within a year to Wilbur F. Cherry and Michael Cronican,[qqv] and Cherry soon acquired sole ownership. Willard Richardson[qv] became editor of the paper a few years later and in 1857 founded the *Texas Almanac.* Alfred Horatio Belo,[qv] a former Confederate colonel from North Carolina, joined the firm as a bookkeeper after the Civil War[qv] and became Richardson's partner in 1866. In 1870 the firm was renamed Richardson, Belo, and Company. In 1876 Belo became sole owner, following Richardson's death the previous year, and renamed the firm A. H. Belo and Company. In 1885 Belo sent George Bannerman Dealey,[qv] who had joined the Galveston *News*[qv] as an office boy nine years earlier, to Dallas to establish a sister paper. The Dallas *Morning News* began publication on October 1, 1885. The Dallas and Galveston papers, linked across 315 miles by telegraph and a network of correspondents that divided the state north and south, heralded the start of "chain journalism." Belo died in 1901, and his son, who succeeded him as head of the company, died in 1906. Dealey continued to head the company on behalf of the Belo heirs, and in 1923 the company sold the Galveston paper, in order to focus its resources on the more thriving newspaper in Dallas. In July 1926, with a few others, G. B. Dealey acquired the company and renamed it A. H. Belo Corporation.

Part of the company's focus in Dallas was radio station WFAA, a "Radio Service of the Dallas *Morning News,*" which began broadcasting on June 26, 1922; WFAA was the first network radio station in Texas. The company sold the last of its radio properties in 1987. In 1963 Belo purchased seven suburban newspapers, the Arlington *Daily News,* the Garland *Daily News,* the Grand Prairie *Daily News,* the Irving *Daily News,* the Mid-Cities *Daily News,* the Richardson *Daily News,* and the *Suburban News,* since renamed *Metrocrest News,* which together form the wholly owned subsidiary DFW Suburban Newspapers, Incorporated. Belo entered the television broadcasting business in 1950 with the acquisition of its principal station WFAA-TV, Channel 8, the ABC affiliate in Dallas. The station had begun broadcasting five months earlier as KBTS-TV. In 1984 Belo purchased four television stations from Dun and Bradstreet: KHOU in Houston; KXTV in Sacramento, California; KOTV in Tulsa, Oklahoma; and WVEC in Hampton-Norfolk, Virginia. In 1994 it purchased WWL in New Orleans, Louisiana. In December 1981 A. H. Belo Corporation became a publicly held entity, with its common stock traded on the New York Stock Exchange. In May 1987 the company reincorporated in the State of Delaware, although its headquarters and operations did not move. In December 1991 Belo acquired the assets of the Dallas *Times Herald*[qv] when that paper ceased publication.

G. B. Dealey remained at the helm of the company until his death in 1946, at which time he was succeeded by his widow, Olivia Allen Dealey, who died in 1960. Subsequent chairmen of the board of directors have been E. M. (Ted) Dealey,[qv] the fourth of Dealey's five children (1960–64); James M. Moroney, husband of the Dealeys' daughter Maidie (1964–68); H. Ben Decherd, grandson of the Dealeys

(1968–72); Joe M. Dealey, another grandson of the Dealeys (1980–84); James M. Moroney, Jr., grandson of the Dealeys (1984–86); and, beginning in 1987, Robert W. Decherd, great-grandson of G. B. Dealey. The position of board chairman was vacant from 1972 to 1980.

BIBLIOGRAPHY: Sam Hanna Acheson, *35,000 Days in Texas: A History of the Dallas "News" and Its Forbears* (New York: Macmillan, 1938). *A. H. Belo Corporation: Commemorating 150 Years, 1842–1992* (Dallas, 1992). Ernest Sharpe, *G. B. Dealey of the Dallas News* (New York: Holt, 1955). *Texas Almanac*, 1994–95. Vertical Files, Barker Texas History Center, University of Texas at Austin.

Judith M. Garrett and Michael V. Hazel

AMR CORPORATION. AMR Corporation, headquartered in Fort Worth, was established in 1982 when American Airlines stockholders, interested in increased flexibility for financing and investment, voted to approve a reorganization plan and establish a holding company. The new firm serves as the parent company of American Airlines (its principal component) and a number of other subsidiaries: AMR Eagle owns American Eagle carriers; American Airlines Decision Technologies provides decision-support systems for industry worldwide; AMR Information Services offers information-management services; AMR Investment Services provides investment management; AMR Services Corporation provided aircraft handling services, cargo handling, warehousing, and distribution services; and the AMR Training and Consulting Group offers consulting services in airline-related businesses. American Airlines divisions include AA Cargo, which provides freight and mail service; SABRE (Semi-Automated Business Research Environment) Travel Information Network and SABRE Computer Services, which provides travel information services from the world's largest privately owned real-time computer network; and SABRE Development Services, which offers information and computer services, including risk assessment. An additional unit, American Airlines Television or AATV, provides video-production services at the airline's television facilities.

American Airlines was founded as a domestic airline after the Aviation Corporation, a New York City–based holding company, was organized in 1929 and began to acquire young aviation firms along with bus lines, radio stations, and airport construction companies. Among the firm's initial acquisitions were some eighty-five small airlines, including Colonial Airways, the Embry-Riddle Company, Interstate Air Lines, Southern Air Transport, Universal Air Lines System, and one of Universal's holdings, Robertson Aircraft of Missouri, for which Charles A. Lindbergh had once served as chief pilot. The consolidation gave the new company a system of partially interconnected routes, a fleet of various types of airplanes, and a variety of local managements. In 1930 routes were redrawn, managements reorganized, and the pieces incorporated to form American Airways. Three years later the company introduced flight attendants and Curtiss Condor airplanes. A further reorganization followed the reapportioning of airmail contracts by the government, and in 1934 American Airways became American Airlines. Credited with the firm's early success was Cyrus Rowlett Smith,[qv] a former Texas Air Transport and Southern Air Transport executive, who served as president of American Airlines from 1934 until 1968, when he was named secretary of commerce by President Lyndon B. Johnson.[qv]

The first innovation of the new company was an air-traffic-control system administered by the government and later adopted by all airlines. Between 1936 and 1942 the airline inaugurated flights between Chicago and New York, became the nation's major domestic carrier in revenue passenger miles (a revenue passenger mile equals one passenger flown one mile), and established service to Mexico. Domestic freight service began in 1944, and in 1945 European service began with a trans-Atlantic division called American Overseas Airlines. All services declined during World War II,[qv] however, after the company turned over almost half its fleet to the Air Transport Command. After the war, the company pioneered nonstop transcontinental and cargo service, and in 1959 began its first jet service with the use of Boeing 707 aircraft. American's computerized reservation system, known as SABRE, was established in 1959, and by the 1990s it served 25,000 travel agencies.

By the 1960s fears of airline deregulation had scared off investors, and conditions worsened as airlines faced rising labor costs and fuel prices, declining profits, and a growing recession. George Spater, who headed the firm in 1967, was forced to resign in 1973 after confessing to illegal contribution of corporate funds to the Committee to Re-Elect the President in the 1972 national presidential campaign. Another executive was convicted on embezzlement charges, leaving the company with a leadership vacuum that Smith in 1973 returned temporarily to fill as chairman and chief executive officer. Boston resident Albert V. Casey, former president of the Times Mirror Company, became president and chief executive officer in 1974 and served until 1985. By the end of the 1970s, American Airlines had moved its headquarters from the New York metropolitan area to Dallas–Fort Worth, where it also established training facilities and a southern reservations office.

Robert L. Crandall became president and chief operating officer in 1980, and chairman and chief executive officer in 1985. He had worked at Eastman Kodak, Hallmark Cards, Trans World Airlines, and Bloomingdale's before moving to American, and was known for his use of computers and advanced technology to achieve efficiency and cost control. Crandall, who assumed the management of American Airlines after passage of the Airline Deregulation Act of 1978, which removed government control of airline routes and prices, opened markets, and encouraged the formation of new airlines, began to invent new strategies for adapting the airline to a new economic environment. Among the innovations that he helped develop were Super-Saver fares, frequent-flyer programs, loyalty fares, participatory employee-relations policies, and the establishment of a system of hubs in Dallas–Fort Worth, Chicago, Miami, Nashville, Raleigh-Durham, and San Juan. This system began with the opening of the Dallas–Fort Worth hub in 1981. The hub system enabled the airline to increase its daily flights from 100 to 300 and, despite the strike of air-traffic controllers, to report profits for that year of $47 million.

In the 1980s American Airlines reduced its labor costs but faced Federal Aviation Administration violations and ongoing deregulation. In 1984 Crandall started the American Eagle system, a network of regional airlines that linked hubs to smaller communities as a fully integrated part of the American Airlines domestic route system. The American Eagle system was originally a network of independent airlines; later eight carriers were reduced to four to become AMR Eagle, Incorporated, a wholly owned subsidiary of AMR Corporation. In 1987 the airline completed underground facilities to house its computer equipment and software in Tulsa, Oklahoma, and merged with a West Coast airline known as Air Cal. In 1988 the airline earned $477 million in net profits and $806 million in operating profit and had developed its first profit-sharing plan. A buyout attempt by Donald Trump failed in 1989, and that year American established its first route from San Francisco to Japan. By 1992, however, though American had revenues of more than $14 billion, it showed a net loss of $935 million, as conditions for the nation's airlines continued to present significant challenges. By the early 1990s the airline employed over 96,000 workers, with more than 58,000 represented by three labor unions: the Allied Pilots Association, the Association of Professional Flight Attendants, and the Transport Workers Union. In the early 1990s groundbreaking ceremonies were held for a major expansion of American facilities at Dallas–Fort Worth International Airport,[qv] a western reservations office opened in Tucson, and the American Airlines C. R. Smith Museum opened. By 1994 the company was operating a fleet of 681 aircraft, which flew a daily average of more than 269,000,000 revenue passenger miles and provided air service to 201 cities worldwide. The company served 361 cities through its American Eagle domestic service.

BIBLIOGRAPHY: Dan Reed, *American Eagle* (New York: St. Martin's Press, 1993).

Diana J. Kleiner

A. S. GAGE RANCHES. The A. S. Gage Ranches in Brewster and Presidio counties form one of the largest cattle ranching operations in the state. It began in 1883, when Edward L. Gage, a native of Vermont and the partner of E. M. Powell in a Dallas land firm, organized the Presidio Live Stock Company in what was then Presidio County. Powell and Gage had already begun ranching on their holdings on Maravillas Creek in the area of present Brewster County. In November 1882 they bought 2,000 cattle and the Running W Bar brand from George J. Reiger of Mitchell County. Powell remained in Dallas, while Gage moved to the Big Bend area to supervise the ranch. By March 1883 they had decided to dissolve their partnership, as Gage planned to devote himself wholeheartedly to the cattle business. He organized the Presidio Live Stock Company with a group of New England investors; he was president and his younger half-brother, Alfred S. Gage,[qv] was superintendent or manager. In May 1883 the company leased 68,000 acres of rangeland from Edward Gage and in November purchased his personal herd of 700 cattle and his Running W Bar brand. Shortly thereafter the company purchased an additional 5,000 head from Milton Faver[qv] and 9,000 more from ranchers in Goliad and Uvalde and from the Reed brothers in the Chisos Mountains.

The mid-1880s was a rough period for ranchers. Two years of severe drought followed the harsh winter of 1885, while the price of cattle dropped from thirty dollars a head in 1882–83 to five dollars a head in 1887. While many Presidio County ranchers were ruined financially, Presidio Live Stock hung on grimly. Seeking to improve the efficiency of its operation, the company put up fifty-four miles of drift fencing and constructed a concrete dam (which was shortly washed away in a flood) on Dugout Creek. To cut costs, the company returned six sections of leased land to Edward Gage because they were outside the fenced area. In an effort to find additional sources of revenue, the company also bought a mercantile store in Alpine, installing another of Edward's half-brothers, Seth Gage, as manager; contracted to supply Camp Peña Colorado[qv] with 500 cords of wood; and attempted an ill-fated farming project near Peña Colorado Creek. Despite these steps, however, the company's financial problems mounted.

In 1886 Edward Gage had organized another ranching concern, the Santiago Cattle Company. This company had leased 52,500 acres and was also experiencing difficulties. In 1891 Gage merged the two companies under a new charter for the Roscillo Land and Cattle Company in Colorado. He deeded 124,800 acres in Texas to the new firm, hoping that the Presidio and Santiago stockholders would exchange their shares in the older companies for shares in the new firm, but they proved reluctant to do so. In desperation, Gage decided to go north, hoping to sell some of the Roscillo stock. On April 21, 1892, apparently distraught over his inability to get his new venture off the ground, he killed himself in the washroom of a Chicago railroad station. Gage's death apparently brought home to Presidio and Santiago officials the serious nature of their problems. They determined to merge the two companies as Gage had intended and in the winter of 1892 bought the cattle and brand of the Presidio Live Stock Company. In 1893 they purchased 50,400 acres from Gage's widow, and in January 1897 they formally chartered the Alpine Cattle Company, with Alfred S. Hall as president and A. S. Gage as secretary and superintendent. With the exception of Gage, who owned seven shares, and director Louis Hess, all the stockholders were from the Northeast or Midwest.

Under A. S. Gage's management, the Alpine Cattle Company enjoyed great success. In 1900 the company contracted to purchase an additional 76,000 acres and also bought the personal herds of Gage and his mother, bringing its total holdings to 14,000 cattle and 130,000 acres of rangeland. Meanwhile, Gage himself bought two ranches to the east of the Alpine Cattle Company range and the remains of the old Dubois-Wentworth holdings in the Toronto Mountain area. By 1910 his personal operation was larger than that of the Alpine Cattle Company.

Three years later he had accumulated 35 percent of the stock in the company and determined to buy the rest. He paid off all debt within three years, thanks to the high cattle prices during World War I,[qv] and in July 1917 Gage dissolved the company, after selling the firm's holdings to himself for ten dollars. He dropped the Running W Bar brand in favor of his personal brand, called Lightning. At that time one could ride horseback from southeast of Marathon almost to Fort Davis on lands owned or leased by Gage, with only one railroad right-of-way and several roads, all of which had livestock crossings, intervening.

Before his death in 1928 Gage built up a total operation of 10,000 cattle on 503,000 acres; he owned 700 sections of land himself and leased an additional 100. His estate was divided between his two daughters, Dorothy Gage Holland Forker and Roxana Gage Negley Catto. The former continued to use the Lightning brand, and the latter resumed use of the Running W Bar. By 1936 the estate consisted of slightly more than 400,000 acres, usually running between 4,000 and 6,000 cattle. In the late 1940s the estate owned 500,000 acres extending along the Southern Pacific Railroad tracks from Marathon almost to Marfa, with a total acreage of 368,026 within Brewster County and additional land in Uvalde and Kinney counties. In the mid-1950s the Gage ranches were the sixth-largest in Texas, with a total acreage of 398,314 acres in Brewster and Presidio counties. The ranch east of Alpine, 370,000 acres, was the fourth-largest in Texas made up of a single block of land.

In 1965 family members formed A. S. Gage Ranches, Inc., which was liquidated in 1986 and replaced by the A. S. Gage Partnership Ltd. In 1992 the partnership held 174,029 acres in Brewster County and 17,439 acres in Presidio County. The land was leased to the Paisano Cattle Company, also controlled by family members, which grazed 200 cattle on it.

BIBLIOGRAPHY: Walter Roberts, Early Developments Leading to the Establishment of the A. S. Gage Ranches of the Big Bend–Davis Mountain Area of Texas, 1883–1917 (Senior thesis, Trinity University, 1957).

Martin Donell Kohout

ABA INDIANS. In 1683–84 Juan Domínguez de Mendoza[qv] led an exploratory expedition from El Paso as far eastward as the junction of the Concho and Colorado rivers east of the site of present San Angelo. In his itinerary he listed the names of thirty-seven Indian groups, including the Abas, from whom he expected to receive delegations on the Colorado River. Nothing further is known about the Abas, who seem to have been one of many Indian groups of north central Texas that were swept away by the southward thrust of the Lipan Apache and Comanche Indians in the eighteenth century. However, it is possible that the Abas were the same people as the Hapes, a Coahuiltecan band of the same period that ranged from northeastern Coahuila across the Rio Grande into the southwestern part of the Edwards Plateau[qv] in Texas, though this identification has yet to be demonstrated.

BIBLIOGRAPHY: Herbert Eugene Bolton, ed., *Spanish Exploration in the Southwest, 1542–1706* (New York: Scribner, 1908; rpt., New York: Barnes and Noble, 1959). Charles W. Hackett, ed., *Pichardo's Treatise on the Limits of Louisiana and Texas* (4 vols., Austin: University of Texas Press, 1931–46).

Thomas N. Campbell

ABAMILLO, JUAN (?–1836). Juan Abamillo, Alamo defender, was born in Texas. He was one of twenty-four native Texans who enlisted for six months' service during the Texas Revolution[qv] under the command of Juan N. Seguín.[qv] Abamillo took part in the siege of Bexar.[qv] He returned to San Antonio in January 1836 with part of Seguín's company. On February 23, 1836, he entered the Alamo with the rest of the Texan garrison at the approach of the Mexican army. Abamillo died in the battle of the Alamo[qv] on March 6, 1836.

BIBLIOGRAPHY: Daughters of the American Revolution, *The Alamo Heroes and Their Revolutionary Ancestors* (San Antonio, 1976). Bill Groneman, *Alamo Defenders* (Austin: Eakin, 1990). Thomas L. Miller, "Mexican-Texans at the Alamo," *Journal of Mexican-American History* 2 (Fall 1971). Phil Rosenthal and Bill Groneman, *Roll Call at the Alamo* (Fort Collins, Colorado: Old Army, 1985). Amelia W. Williams, A Critical Study of the Siege of the Alamo and of the Personnel of Its Defenders (Ph.D. dissertation, University of Texas, 1931; rpt., *Southwestern Historical Quarterly* 36-37 [April 1933-April 1934]).

Bill Groneman

ABAU INDIANS. The similarity in the names Abau and Aba suggests that they may be variants of the same Indian group name, but this is contradicted by the fact that both Abau and Aba appear on the same list of Indian groups recorded by Juan Domínguez de Mendoza[qv] in 1683–84, when he was in the western part of the Edwards Plateau.[qv] If Mendoza's Abas were the same as the Hapes, then it is also likely that the Abaus were the same as the Xiabus, who in other Spanish sources of the same time are identified with the Rio Grande just downstream from the site of modern Eagle Pass, Texas. In both cases it is possible to argue for Coahuiltecan affiliation and conclude that the ethnic identities were lost early in the eighteenth century.

BIBLIOGRAPHY: Herbert Eugene Bolton, ed., *Spanish Exploration in the Southwest, 1542–1706* (New York: Scribner, 1908; rpt., New York: Barnes and Noble, 1959). Charles W. Hackett, ed., *Pichardo's Treatise on the Limits of Louisiana and Texas* (4 vols., Austin: University of Texas Press, 1931–46). *Thomas N. Campbell*

ABBIE'S PEAK. Abbie's Peak is a small hill four miles northeast of Dickens in central Dickens County. It was named by an early surveyor names Hayes after his fiancée. At various times the hill has also been called Saddleback for its peculiar shape. Abbie's Peak was part of the Jack Gipson ranch in the 1970s.

BIBLIOGRAPHY: Fred Arrington, *A History of Dickens County: Ranches and Rolling Plains* (Quanah, Texas: Nortex, 1971).

ABBOTT, JOSEPH (1840–1908). Joseph (Jo) Abbott, lawyer, judge, and congressman, one of twelve children of William and Mary (McMillan) Abbott, was born near Decatur, Alabama, on January 15, 1840. At the age of thirteen he moved with his family to Freestone County, Texas. After attending private school, Abbott left home to study law with Franklin L. Yoakum[qv] in 1859. The Civil War,[qv] however, interrupted his studies, and he joined Company B, Twelfth Texas Cavalry. As a first lieutenant, he fought in a half dozen battles before being wounded. After several months of medical treatment and rest, he rejoined his unit and remained in active duty until 1865.

After the war he moved to Limestone County and resumed legal studies with Lochlin J. Farrar[qv] at Springfield. He also studied with D. M. Pendergast. In 1866 he was admitted to the bar and began his legal career as Farrar's partner. Because of the political and legal uncertainties facing a former Confederate officer in Reconstruction[qv] Texas, Abbott abandoned his law practice and moved to Hill County in 1867. He taught school near Hillsboro for five months. In 1868, however, he resumed his law career. In December of that year he married Rowena Sturgis. The couple had five children. Abbott was elected to the Texas House of Representatives in 1869 and served one term in the Eleventh Legislature.

His lifelong interest in politics and loyalty to the Democratic party[qv] resulted in his selection as head of the Democratic Executive Committee of Hill County. His legal skills and work for the party were rewarded in February 1879, when Governor Oran M. Roberts[qv] appointed Abbott judge of the Twenty-eighth Judicial District (Hill, Johnson, and Bosque counties). In November 1880 voters elected Abbott to this position for a term of four years. In 1886 there was an effort to place Abbott's name in nomination for a vacancy on the Texas Supreme Court. This effort failed, but a few months later Abbott was elected to the United States Congress. The Texas lawyer represented District Twenty (Ellis, Hill, Kaufman, and Navarro counties) from 1887 to 1897. He retired from political life in 1898 and returned to Hillsboro, where he continued his legal career. He died at his home on February 11, 1908, and was buried at the old cemetery at Hillsboro.

BIBLIOGRAPHY: Lewis E. Daniell, *Personnel of the Texas State Government, with Sketches of Representative Men of Texas* (Austin: City Printing, 1887; 3d ed., San Antonio: Maverick, 1892). Hill County Historical Commission, *A History of Hill County, Texas, 1853–1980* (Waco: Texian, 1980). *Anne W. Hooker*

ABBOTT, TEXAS. Abbott is a half mile west of Interstate Highway 35 and ten miles south of Hillsboro in south central Hill County. It was founded as a railroad town on the Missouri, Kansas and Texas line in 1881 and named for Jo Abbott.[qv] An Abbott post office was established in 1882 and served the town until 1928. The United Methodist church was organized in 1883 by Rev. G. W. Swofford, pastor of the Hillsboro Circuit. A sanctuary was built in 1884 and a parsonage in 1885 on land that W. W. Treadwell donated. In the 1890s cotton was a major crop in the area around Abbott. During that decade two cotton gins, a gristmill, and more than fifteen other businesses were in operation in the community. Early establishments included general stores, doctors' offices, a drugstore, barbershops, two hotels, two blacksmith shops, a photographer's studio, a newspaper, and a bank. The town had three churches.

Abbott suffered disastrous fires in 1897, 1903, and 1904 and was rebuilt after each. Electricity came in 1913 with the building of an interurban railway by the Southern Traction Company (*see* ELECTRIC INTERURBAN RAILWAYS). The Katy and the interurban transported passengers as well as goods and products. The community was incorporated in 1916 with C. W. Thompson as mayor and A. R. Crocker and W. R. Hammonds as commissioners. In 1920 the highway was built through the middle of town parallel to the Katy and the interurban. Abbott declined as a result of the Great Depression,[qv] however, and by 1932 the train stopped only when flagged. Czech farmers came and bought much of the rich black farmland of the area. The first Czechs[qv] had come as early as 1870 and have maintained a Catholic parish in the town.

The local school system began in 1885 or 1886 with an enrollment of over 140 pupils. In 1927–28 the school was accredited through the eleventh grade, and the 1930 enrollment was 240. As smaller schools were consolidated with Abbott, local enrollment increased to over 500 in the late 1930s and early 1940s. L. C. McKamie served twenty nonconsecutive years as superintendent between 1926 and 1948.

The population of Abbott was 156 in 1890 and grew to a high point of 713 by 1914. It had declined to 264 by 1941. In 1989 the town had 364 residents, a post office, a cotton gin, three churches, and a school with 192 students. A local cave, Hooker Cave, on nearby Old Carr Ranch, is explored by many avid spelunkers and is the subject of numerous local legends. More than 2,000 people attended a day-long celebration of the centennial of Abbott in 1981. Country music star Willie Nelson is from Abbott. In 1990 the population was 314.

BIBLIOGRAPHY: Abbott Centennial Planning Committee, *Abbott, Texas, 1881–1981: A History* (Belton, Texas: Centex, 1981). Ellis Bailey, *A History of Hill County, Texas, 1838–1965* (Waco: Texian Press, 1966). Hill County Historical Commission, *A History of Hill County, Texas, 1853–1980* (Waco: Texian, 1980). *A Memorial and Biographical History of Johnson and Hill Counties* (Chicago: Lewis, 1892).

Virginia Sullins

ABE, TEXAS. Abe was a rural community five miles southwest of Lovelady in southwestern Houston County. The site was settled in the mid-1880s. A post office operated there in 1887 and 1888. At that time Abe had a store, a mill and gin, and a number of houses. By the mid-1930s the community no longer appeared on highway maps.

Christopher Long

ABELL-HANGER FOUNDATION. The Abell-Hanger Foundation was incorporated by George Thomas Abell and his wife, Gladys Hanger Abell, in 1954. George Abell, a native of Kansas, moved to Midland in 1927 to work in the West Texas oilfields. A graduate of Colorado A&M University with degrees in civil and mechanical engineering, Abell was a self-taught geologist who made a fortune as an independent oil producer. He was a charter member of the Permian Basin Petroleum Pioneers Association as well as a cofounder of the Permian Basin Petroleum Museum, Library and Hall of Fame. A major supporter of the city of Midland, Abell served as president of the board of the Midland Independent School District and as director of the Midland Chamber of Commerce. He was a dedicated and successful fund-raiser for a variety of charities, including the Midland Memorial Hospital and the Boy Scouts of America. The latter honored him with the Silver Beaver Award in recognition of his leadership in the fund drive that secured the scouts a 6,000-acre camp in the Davis Mountains.[qv] Gladys Hanger Abell, born and raised in Fort Worth, was an alumna of Texas Christian University and the University of Texas. She served on the board of governors of the Midland Memorial Hospital and on the board of trustees of the Midland Presbyterian Homes. Along with her husband, she was an active board member of the Permian Basin Petroleum Museum, Library and Hall of Fame. The couple's commitment to community was a driving force in their lives and in the work of their foundation. As George Abell explained, "Business success provides the opportunity to do some of the things most of us dream about doing for our community and its various institutions, organizations and agencies." The purpose of the Abell-Hanger Foundation is to support higher education, youth activities, cultural programs, health services, and social-welfare agencies. In 1995 the foundation had assets of $107 million and an annual income of $6,785,000. In the 1994–95 fiscal year it gave $4,817,681 in 137 grants; cumulative giving from 1954 through that fiscal year totaled $65,783,452.

ABERCROMBIE, JAMES SMITHER (1891–1975). James (Jim or Mr. Jim) Smither Abercrombie, oilman, Houston civic leader, and philanthropist, was born in Huntsville, Texas, on July 7, 1891, the fourth of thirteen children of James Buford and Evelina (Wood) Abercrombie, Jr. He spent his childhood in Huntsville, where he attended grammar school. In 1900 his family was forced to move because of harsh winters and boll weevil[qv] infestations of the local cotton crops. They moved to Esperanza and then to Richmond, where J. B. Abercrombie worked on the Harlem Prison Farm (*see* JESTER STATE PRISON FARM), a branch of the state prison system.[qv] Jim enrolled in school and got a job jerking sodas at Cranston's Drug Store. After he had attended three years of school and held many odd jobs to help make money for his family, they moved to the outskirts of Houston and started a dairy farm around the time of his fifteenth birthday. They then moved into the Fourth Ward, Houston.[qv] Abercrombie worked for the family's dairy business until he was over seventeen. He and a brother went to look for work in the Houston oil business, where they would make enough money to hire extra manpower to work at the dairy. In 1909 Jim's cousin, Charles Abercrombie, hired him to work as a roustabout—an unskilled deckhand on a drilling rig—for the Goose Creek Production Company. By 1910 Jim had become a driller for Goose Creek. When he was in his early twenties, Crown Petroleum hired him as the field superintendent for some of its wells, and while working for Crown he was the first to use salt water to put out a derrick fire, a discovery he made because there was no fresh water available. In 1918 he used his savings and a loan to buy a used drilling rig to drill on his own in the Burkburnett oilfield,[qv] north of Wichita Falls. At the same time, he continued as a superintendent at Crown. He had several wells at Burkburnett by 1920, and soon left Crown Petroleum to work on his own in South Texas and in the Gulf Coast oilfields. He helped his brother, Bolling, finance the Houston Carbonate Company, which sold carbonic gas to soda fountains, creameries, and bottlers. On July 9, 1920, he bought, with Harry Cameron, the Cameron-Davant Company (*see* CAMERON IRON WORKS, HOUSTON), a business that sold oil-drilling supplies and parts for rigs and wells. Jim Abercrombie became the unsalaried president of Cameron Iron Works, and before his thirtieth birthday he was the president of the expanding James S. Abercrombie Company, an independent drilling operation with five rigs.

In late 1921 the Monarch Oil and Refining Company gave Cameron Iron Works a contract to find a way to control the increasing gas pressure in deep wells. Repeated attempts to solve this growing problem, found in many oil wells around the world, failed. But through Abercrombie's persistence, he and Harry Cameron developed the Type MO blowout preventer, which, after additional refinements by Cameron, led to a patent for its solution to the high gas pressure. After this invention, sales by Cameron Iron Works rose to $67,000 in 1925 and subsequently to six-figure levels. The company grew increasingly successful as additional patented inventions, such as a casing-cutter and various joints and clamps, followed. Also, in 1924 the J. S. Abercrombie Company drilled several wells at Lake Charles, Louisiana—where Abercrombie met his future wife, Lillie Frank—for Socony-Vacuum, an early venture of John D. Rockefeller. Abercrombie and Lillie Frank were married on May 6, 1925; the couple had one daughter.

Between 1924 and 1929 Abercrombie traveled internationally to solve oilfield problems. In 1929, with Dan Harrison, he formed Harrison and Abercrombie, which invested and drilled in many oilfields in Texas and Louisiana, especially the Old Ocean field in Brazoria County. The Great Depression[qv] hit Cameron Iron Works hard: sales dropped from $479,000 in 1930 to $87,000 in 1932. In 1939, however, Cameron Iron Works developed a list of wartime products that it could produce for the United States military to use in World War II.[qv] The military eventually moved Cameron Iron Works up from subcontractor status to direct supplier. By 1941 the company had a contract to build K-guns and arbor bombs; this led to a 1942 contract to build .50-caliber gun barrels. Improved techniques developed by Cameron engineers drastically cut production time for rifling and machining the barrels. Cameron Iron Works also built the Tiny Tim rockets that were used in beach invasions by the navy. In 1942 President Franklin D. Roosevelt asked Harrison and Abercrombie to build an aviation gas refinery at the Old Ocean oilfield; the refinery was completed by 1943. Around this time Harrison sold his share in Harrison and Abercrombie to the Magnolia Petroleum Company,[qv] which had Abercrombie administer its newly purchased share. Abercrombie sold the James S. Abercrombie Company and his part of Old Ocean to Stanolind of Indiana for $54 million on May 23, 1946. By November of that year, however, he had formed J. S. Abercrombie Interests, Incorporated.

Also in 1946 Abercrombie, always a man interested in cattle and ranches, bought a ranch on the Guadalupe River just a few miles east of Gonzales. Its fertile lowlands were a perfect place to invest money in agriculture and animal husbandry. This ranching operation built a feed factory for ranch animals. In 1959 Abercrombie Interests was reorganized into the J. S. Abercrombie Mineral Company, which drilled wells in Texas, Louisiana, and the neutral zone between Kuwait and Saudi Arabia. Also, Cameron Iron Works continued to prosper, and by 1960 had some 2,000 employees and sales topping $40 million.

On March 10, 1950, Abercrombie and several other prominent Houston citizens chartered the Texas Children's Hospital[qv] in Houston to treat sick and critically ill children. Abercrombie, the first to donate money to this project, gave $1 million of the $2.5 million donated to cover construction costs. He requested that absolutely no restrictions be made on which sick children could be admitted. He also donated all proceeds from the Pin Oak Horse Show to the hospital. Then in 1968 the James S. Abercrombie Foundation was established as a trust to hold gifts and grants primarily for the Texas Children's Hospital and for the Texas Heart Institute of St. Luke's Episcopal Hospital. While living in Houston, Abercrombie joined many clubs and organizations, among them the Masons, the Old Colony Club, the Houston Yacht Club, the River Oaks Country Club, and the Houston Club. He died in Houston on January 7, 1975, and was buried at Glenwood Cemetery there.

BIBLIOGRAPHY: Marcellus E. Foster and Alfred Jones, eds., *South and Southeast Texas* (n.p.: Jas. O. Jones, 1928). Patrick J. Nicholson, *Mr. Jim: The Biography of James Smither Abercrombie* (Houston: Gulf, 1983). Vertical Files, Barker Texas History Center, University of Texas at Austin. Clarence R. Wharton, ed., *Texas under Many Flags* (5 vols., Chicago: American Historical Society, 1930). *David Littlefield*

ABERCROMBIE, LEONARD ANDERSON (1832–1891). Leonard Anderson Abercrombie, lawyer, Confederate Army officer, and legislator, was born in Macon County, Alabama, on December 1, 1832, the son of Milo B. and Sarah (Anderson) Abercrombie. He was educated in Alexandria, Virginia, and read law in Tuskegee, Alabama. He was admitted to the bar in 1854 but later that same year moved to Madison County, Texas, then to Huntsville. In 1860 he was elected prosecuting attorney for Galveston, Grimes, Harris, Montgomery, and Walker counties. On January 1, 1860, he married Lavinia Chilton in Tuskegee, Alabama; the couple eventually had seven children. From January 28 until February 4, 1861, Abercrombie represented Walker County as a delegate to the state Secession Convention.[qv] During the Civil War[qv] he served as lieutenant colonel of Col. Henry M. Elmore's Twentieth Texas Infantry. This regiment, organized in the spring of 1862, was composed primarily of middle-aged men, many of whom were prominent citizens. It was assigned to guard duty on the Texas Gulf coast from Galveston to the Sabine River and did not see duty outside of the state. It did, however, play an important role in the Confederate recapture of Galveston in January 1863 (*see* GALVESTON, BATTLE OF). After the war Abercrombie returned to his legal practice at Huntsville and was elected to represent the Ninth District as a state senator in the Twentieth Legislature. He was reelected to a seat in the Twenty-first Legislature. He died at Philadelphia, Pennsylvania, on December 23, 1891, and his body was returned to Huntsville for burial.

BIBLIOGRAPHY: Norman Kittrell, *Governors Who Have Been and Other Public Men of Texas* (Houston: Dealy-Adey-Elgin, 1921). Marcus J. Wright, comp., and Harold B. Simpson, ed., *Texas in the War, 1861–1865* (Hillsboro, Texas: Hill Junior College Press, 1965).

Thomas W. Cutrer

ABERDEEN, TEXAS (Collingsworth County). Aberdeen, in northeastern Collingsworth County, was a division headquarters of the Rocking Chair Ranch.[qv] The town was named for the earl of Aberdeen, one of the British owners, and planned in 1889 to be the nucleus of this ranching enterprise. A post office was granted in December of that year with Henry J. Nesper, a ranch foreman, as postmaster. M. M. French, an agent for the Rocking Chair, purchased the tract and formed the Aberdeen Townsite Company in January 1890. A hotel and a blacksmith shop were constructed on the site, and by 1891 Judge Edward H. Small was operating a supply store for the cowboys. Small also served as the local physician and banker, and later as postmaster.

When Collingsworth County was organized in 1890 Aberdeen was one of several contenders for the role of county seat, after the initial election between Pearl and Wellington was declared void by the state Supreme Court. With the support of the Rocking Chair's London management, Archibald J. Marjoribanks, the ranch bookkeeper and brother of the baron of Tweedmouth, eagerly promoted the townsite's advantages. A grocery store was established, several lots were sold, and money was donated for a school. The state legislature confirmed Wellington as the county seat, however, thus dashing local hopes and prompting French to deed the townsite back to the Rocking Chair company in June 1891. By 1900 financial failure of the ranch had put the land on the market. Settlement was slow because of inadequate transportation. Nevertheless, Aberdeen managed to survive as a community with a general store, a school, a church, and a population of twenty-five from 1930 to 1960. The post office was discontinued in 1942, and by 1963 the town had fallen into oblivion.

BIBLIOGRAPHY: Clyde Chestnut Brown, A Survey History of Collingsworth County, Texas (M.A. thesis, University of Colorado, 1934). Arthur Hecht, comp., *Postal History in the Texas Panhandle* (Canyon, Texas: Panhandle-Plains Historical Society, 1960). Estelle D. Tinkler, ed., *Archibald John Writes the Rocking Chair Ranche Letters* (Burnet, Texas: Eakin Press, 1979). Estelle D. Tinkler, "Nobility's Ranche: A History of the Rocking Chair Ranche," *Panhandle-Plains Historical Review* 15 (1942). *H. Allen Anderson*

ABERDEEN, TEXAS (Medina County). Aberdeen was twelve miles northwest of Castroville on Quihi Creek in north central Medina County. Around 1858 J. C. Reid, a traveler who left a journal called "Reid's Tramp," noted two grocery stores and three residents in Aberdeen. The grocery stores, which also served liquor, were used by the community members as places to socialize. Reid recalled in his journal that the surrounding fields appeared to yield good corn. The exact location of Aberdeen and its development beyond that described in Reid's journal are unknown.

BIBLIOGRAPHY: Castro Colonies Heritage Association, *The History of Medina County, Texas* (Dallas: National Share Graphics, 1983).

Ruben E. Ochoa

ABERDEEN-ANGUS CATTLE. Aberdeen-Angus cattle originated from the polled (hornless) black cattle in Scotland that were recorded there as early as 1523. Two types of polled black cattle—from the counties of Aberdeen and Angus in southeastern Scotland—were crossbred, and over the years the Aberdeen-Angus breed was developed. Hugh Watson of Keillor, Scotland, has been credited with the movement to upgrade and promote the breed, which was prized for being able to range well on grass and withstand the dramatic weather changes of the Scottish climate. The breed is characterized by its short black hair and large size—up to 2,000 pounds or more. The cattle are hornless, and in crossbreeding tend to produce polled offspring a majority of the time. Aberdeen-Angus cattle do well under range conditions and are generally hardy and disease-resistant. They are noted for producing choice beef, and the beef industry has touted Angus beef for its high quality and flavor. The first Angus cattle imported to the United States arrived in 1873; Scotsman George Grant brought in four bulls to his ranch in Victoria, Kansas. He showed two of them at the Kansas City Fair, and this generated much interest among ranchers, who wanted Aberdeen-Angus cattle for crossbreeding. Soon Aberdeen-Angus cattle had been introduced into Texas. About 1885 rancher John V. Farwell[qv] may have purchased, from the cattle firm of Findlay and Anderson in Illinois, the first Angus bull to arrive in Texas. He pastured it at Buffalo Springs and crossbred it with longhorn cattle.[qv] Beginning in the 1880s the XIT Ranch[qv] brought many Angus bulls to Dallam County to crossbreed with their longhorns. Hundreds of Angus cattle were shipped to Texas in the last decade of the 1800s, and Texas breeders were among the first to use the cattle for crossbreeding, as the calves produced were generally thicker and heavier at weaning time. Around 1900 there were very few purebred Aberdeen-Angus herds in Texas, but interest in the breed continued to increase. San Angelo rancher Sam H. Hill owned one of the largest early herds of purebred animals in the state, and Koss Berry of Meridian also had a large herd. In the twentieth century Aberdeen-Angus were favorites at stock shows, winning numerous grand championships. This breed has also done well in crossbreeding programs. During the first half of the twentieth century the Brangus breed, consisting of five-eighths Angus and three-eighths Brahman cattle,[qv] was developed, and in the early 1990s Texas was home to 36 percent of all registered Brangus. In 1938 the Texas Aberdeen-Angus Breeders' Association was organized, and by 1941 more than 250 breeders were in the association, with a listing of over 60,000 head of cattle. In the latter half of the twentieth century the breed continued to grow in popularity. In 1995 more than 1,200 members and registered breeders in Texas were affiliated with the American Angus Association. Its Texas office, the Texas Angus Association, was located in Fort Worth.

BIBLIOGRAPHY: *Cattleman,* October 1941, June 1959. James Cox, *Historical and Biographical Record of the Cattle Industry* (2 vols., St. Louis: Woodward and Tiernan Printing, 1894, 1895; rpt., with an introduction by J. Frank Dobie, New York: Antiquarian, 1959).

Laurie E. Jasinski

ABERFOYLE, TEXAS. Aberfoyle is on Farm Road 512 fifteen miles northeast of Greenville in northeastern Hunt County. The settlement was begun soon after the Civil War[qv] and received a post office in 1884. By 1900 it had 100 residents, a cotton gin, and a general store. The post office ceased operation in 1904, and the mail was routed through Wolfe City. Aberfoyle's population was 100 in 1933, fell to twenty-five in 1945, and was reported as twenty-five from 1976 to 1989. Businesses declined from four in 1933 to none in the 1980s. In 1990 the population was thirty-five. *Brian Hart*

ABERNATHY, MOLLIE WYLIE (1866–1960). Mollie D. Wylie Jarrott Abernathy, rancher and businesswoman, was born on April 27, 1866, in Hood County, Texas, the daughter of John N. M. and Elizabeth (Robertson) Wylie, both members of prominent ranch families. She grew up at Thorp Spring and was a member of the first class at Add-Ran College (forerunner of Texas Christian University). She spent the summers on her father's ranches in Erath and Runnels counties, where she acquired knowledge of the cattle industry. On September 26, 1886, she married James William Jarrott, who served that year in the Texas legislature. The next year the couple moved to a ranch near Phoenix, Arizona, where their first child was born. In 1889 the family returned to Thorp Spring and in 1890 moved to Stephenville. There Jarrott became county attorney for Erath County. The couple had three more children in Stephenville.

In 1901 the Jarrotts filed for themselves and twenty-three other families under the Four-Section Act[qv] on a mile-wide strip of vacant land extending from the western boundary of Lubbock County to New Mexico. The tent that they pitched on their claim was the only human habitation within a thirty-mile radius; by 1902 they had settled all of the other families on the land. The influx of small landowners living in tents and dugouts aroused the hostility of the area ranchers, and on August 28, 1902, Jarrott was shot and killed. Mollie was in a hotel in town convalescing from an illness at the time of the murder, but she returned to the claim and operated the Swastika Ranch alone. She expanded it from four to sixteen sections and developed a prime herd of registered Hereford cattle. In 1905 she married Monroe G. Abernathy, a real estate developer, for whom the South Plains towns of Monroe (later New Deal) and Abernathy were named. Together they successfully promoted the construction of the Santa Fe Railroad into Lubbock. The ranch properties were sold in 1920, after the extension of the railroad caused a demand for farmland.

During the same period, Mollie Abernathy was investing in business property in the fledgling city of Lubbock, and in 1916 she financed the construction of the J. C. Penney building, one of the largest downtown commercial structures. On the eastern and northeastern borders of town she and her husband acquired more than a thousand acres of undeveloped land. Portions of the properties were later developed into Mackenzie State Recreation Area[qv] and a residential addition overlooking it. Her astute management of her ranch and business holdings led to Mrs. Abernathy's reputation as Lubbock's first businesswoman. She was a charter member of the Business and Professional Women's Club and served as president of both the League of Women Voters and the Woman's Christian Temperance Union[qqv] in Lubbock. She chaired the first Woman's Democratic League in Texas and actively promoted full citizenship responsibility for women. She was a member of the First Christian Church. She died in Lubbock on June 4, 1960, and was buried in the city cemetery.

BIBLIOGRAPHY: Seymour V. Connor, ed., *Builders of the Southwest* (Lubbock: Southwest Collection, Texas Technological College, 1959). Lubbock *Avalanche-Journal,* June 5, 1960. J. W. Turner, "A Woman's Ranch and Its Products," *Farm and Ranch,* September 4, 1915. *Who's Who of the Womanhood of Texas,* Vol. 1 (Fort Worth: Texas Federation of Women's Clubs, 1923–24). *Seymour V. Connor*

ABERNATHY, TEXAS. Abernathy, on Interstate Highway 27 and U.S. Highway 87 eighteen miles north of Lubbock in Hale County, was founded in 1909 when the Santa Fe Railroad built from Plainview to Lubbock. It was apparently named for M. G. Abernathy, who along with J. C. Roberds and Marvin C. Overton[qv] formed the South Plains Investment Company to establish and promote the town. Many of the buildings from Bartonsite, a small community seven miles to the northwest, were moved to Abernathy, which gained a post office in 1910. By 1914 the town had a population estimated at 300, four churches, several stores, and a bank.

The community was incorporated in 1924 and by 1926, when it had forty-five businesses and about 1,500 people, was known as a cotton and grain center. The businesses included a flour mill, which opened during the early 1920s and operated until its destruction by fire in 1934 or 1935. In 1929 a cheese factory began operation. It survived until 1951 and at its height produced 1,800 pounds of cheese daily. The community acquired electricity in 1929–30, a public water system in 1934, and a sewer system in 1949. Population figures fell to around 850 in 1930 and remained relatively stable for the next two decades. The number of businesses ranged between thirty and forty from 1933 to 1946. The discovery of oil near Abernathy in 1946 and 1947 caused a boom, resulting in a rise in both the number of businesses (sixty-five) and the population (1,962) by the early 1950s.

With a variety of businesses offering goods and services, the town has remained an agribusiness and trading center since that time. However, after a high of 114 businesses in 1967, the number steadily declined to a low of forty-five in 1985. The population was 2,491 in 1960, 2,625 in 1970, and 2,904 in 1980, when 699 of the town's residents lived in Lubbock County. In 1990 the population was 2,720.

BIBLIOGRAPHY: Vera D. Wofford, ed., *Hale County Facts and Folklore* (Lubbock, 1978). *Patricia L. Duncan*

ABERT, JAMES WILLIAM (1820–1897). James William Abert, army officer and explorer, was born on November 18, 1820, in Mount Holly, New Jersey, the son of Maj. John James Abert, an officer in the Corps of Topographical Engineers. In his teens he attended Princeton University, where he graduated, probably from its academy, in 1838; he entered the United States Military Academy at West Point in September of that year. In 1842 he was assigned to the Fifth United States Infantry. After an uneventful year of garrison duty in Detroit, Abert was transferred to the Corps of Topographical Engineers in May 1843. His first assignment in the corps was that of assistant topographical engineer in an extensive survey of the northern lakes, 1843–44. During that time he married Jane Stone, and they had a son.

In the summer of 1845 Abert was attached to the third expedition of John Charles Frémont, whose assignment was "to make reconnaissance southward and eastward along the Canadian River through the country of Kiowa and Comanche." Frémont, however, chose to take his main party on to California, and gave command of the Canadian River mission to Abert, with an assistant, Lt. William G. Peck. The legendary mountain man Thomas Fitzpatrick was employed as a guide, and Bent employees John L. Hatcher[qv] and Caleb Greenwood were hired temporarily as hunters. Except for the two young officers, the entire party of thirty-three was composed of civilians.

The expedition struck the headwaters of the Canadian and followed it through the breaks in eastern New Mexico and into the Texas Panhandle. Continuing along the north bank of the Canadian, Abert noted many Panhandle[qv] landmarks, including Atascosa Creek and the Alibates Flint Quarries (see ALIBATES FLINT QUARRIES NATIONAL MONUMENT), which he labeled Agate Bluffs. The expedition arrived at Bent's trading house in what is now Hutchinson County on September 14, rested there for a day, and exchanged gifts with a party of Kiowas and Comancheros.[qv] Three Kiowas had briefly joined the expedition to help keep the peace. On September 16, after Hatcher and Greenwood had left to return to Bent's Fort, the remainder of Abert's party crossed the Canadian and turned toward the southeast. Near the site of present Laketon, in Gray County, the party struck the North Fork of the Red River, which they mistook for the Washita and followed for a while, then turned back northeast toward the Canadian. They crossed the present Oklahoma boundary before reaching the Canadian, which they followed to its confluence with the Arkansas. At Fort Gibson, in eastern Indian Territory, the expedition was disbanded, and Abert and Peck went on to St. Louis.

In his report Abert described in detail the geology, flora, and fauna of the Canadian valley. His maps of the region were the most accurate of the time, and later explorers found them quite useful, especially for finding campsites and watering places. The abundance of wild game in the valley had kept the expedition well supplied with food. Abert's description of the habits and customs of the Kiowa and Comanche Indians proved valuable to the federal government later. Along with his maps and written accounts, Abert made several sketches and watercolors of activities at Bent's Fort, native animals, and outstanding Indian personalities, including the Kiowa chief Dohäsan,[qv] whose village the expedition had visited on September 17.

In the summer of 1846 Abert and Peck accompanied Gen. Stephen W. Kearny's Army of the West to New Mexico. Abert came down with a fever in July and had to remain behind at Bent's Fort to recuperate. While he was sick he continued his studies in natural science and ethnology and compiled a tribal dictionary. Afterward he joined Peck in Santa Fe, and the two lieutenants conducted a thorough survey of New Mexico as far south as Socorro. They visited each of the Rio Grande pueblos and, as before, took note of the geology and wildlife of the new American territory, as well as of the habits and customs of its native residents. Abert then went to Washington to submit his report to Congress.

From 1848 to 1850 he served on the faculty at West Point, where he taught drawing. He was promoted to first lieutenant in 1853 and to captain in 1856. After the death of his first wife he married Lucy Taylor, with whom he had several children. In 1860, after serving two years in Florida, he traveled in Europe to study military affairs and visit various forts and arsenals. When the Civil War[qv] broke out Abert served in the Shenandoah valley from June 1861 to September 1862. On March 3, 1863, he was promoted to major and assigned to the United States Army Corps of Engineers. He was later severely injured by a fall from his horse, and in 1864 he resigned from the army. He had been brevetted lieutenant colonel for his "faithful and meritorious service." During the next five years, Abert and his family engaged in the mercantile business in Cincinnati, Ohio. From 1869 to 1871 he served as examiner of patents in Washington. He taught English literature at the University of Missouri from 1877 to 1879 and afterward was president of the Examining Board of Teachers of Public Schools in Kentucky. Abert was reappointed a major in the United States Army on January 14, 1895, and retired almost immediately. He died at his home in Newport, Kentucky, on August 10, 1897.

Despite the value of Abert's western frontier journals, they lay almost forgotten in government files until 1941, when H. Bailey Carroll[qv] first published the 1845 report in the Panhandle-Plains Historical Review.[qv] William A. Keleher published Abert's New Mexico report in 1962. In 1967 and 1970 special publications of the Abert journals were edited under the title *Through the Country of the Comanche Indians in the Fall of the Year 1845* by John Galvin, a California historian. They featured illustrations of Abert's watercolors, many of which were obtained from his descendants. A species of finch that Abert discovered was named Pipilo aberti in his honor.

BIBLIOGRAPHY: W. H. Goetzmann, *Army Exploration in the American West, 1803–1863* (New Haven: Yale University Press, 1959; 2d ed., Lincoln: University of Nebraska Press, 1979; rpt., Austin: Texas State Historical Association, 1991). Frederick W. Rathjen, *The Texas Panhandle Frontier* (Austin: University of Texas Press, 1973).

H. Allen Anderson

ABILENE, TEXAS. Abilene is in the northeast corner of Taylor County. It is situated 1,708 feet above sea level on generally flat terrain. The city is connected east–west by Interstate Highway 20, U.S. Highway 80, and State Highway 36 and north–south by U.S. highways 83, 84, and 277. Reflecting its beginning as a railroad townsite, Abilene is bisected by the Texas and Pacific tracks, which run east–west.

Abilene owes its genesis to the Texas and Pacific and a group of ranchers and land speculators. Before the coming of the railroad, the Abilene area had been sporadically inhabited by nomadic Indians and United States military personnel and later by buffalo hunters and ranchers. By the 1870s the Indians had been driven out, and cattlemen began to graze their herds in the area. Taylor County was organized in 1878, and Buffalo Gap was designated the county seat. When the Texas and Pacific Railway began to push westward in 1880, several ranchers and businessmen—Claiborne W. Merchant,[qv] John Merchant, John N. Simpson,[qv] John T. Berry, and S. L. Chalk—met with H. C. Whithers, the Texas and Pacific track and townsite locator, and arranged to have the railroad bypass Buffalo Gap. They agreed that the route would traverse the northern part of the county and consequently their own land, and that a new town would be established between Cedar and Big Elm creeks east of Catclaw Creek. C. W. Merchant apparently suggested the name Abilene, after the Kansas cattle town.

After the Texas and Pacific arrived at the site in January 1881 the railroad promoted Abilene as the "Future Great City of West Texas." J. Stoddard Johnston and other railroad officials platted the townsite. Several hundred people arrived in Abilene before the sale of town lots and began to establish businesses and a church. The lots were auctioned on March 15, 1881; in two days buyers purchased more than 300 lots, and Abilene was officially established. On January 2, 1883, the residents voted to incorporate, and in an election held on October 23, 1883, Abilene became the county seat. By 1890 the city had a population of 3,194; twenty years later the number of residents was 9,204.

In slightly more than 100 years Abilene developed from an almost entirely agricultural economy to a diversified economy based on oil, agriculture, commerce, light manufacturing, and service. World War II[qv] was the watershed for the city's growth and economic development. The initial and most obvious drawback to Abilene's economic development was a lack of water, since the normal annual rainfall is only 23.59 inches. The city excavated Lytle Lake (1897), Lake Abilene (1919), Lake Kirby (1927), and Lake Fort Phantom Hill (1937) to assure a municipal water supply. Local farmers were urged to diversify their crops in order to protect both themselves and processors in Abilene from losses due to weather, pests, price fluctuations, and other causes outside their control. The city began holding fairs in 1884 to promote the region's agricultural products. Severe droughts in 1909–10 and 1917–18 and the decline of farm prices in the 1920s and 1930s retarded economic growth.

Since prosperity depended also on adequate transportation, civic leaders vigorously sought additional railroad connections and succeeded when the Abilene and Northern and the Abilene and Southern railroads provided north–south connections in the early twentieth century. Efforts to attract the Santa Fe Railroad to Abilene failed. Internal transportation improved with the establishment of the Abilene Street Railway (called the Abilene Traction Company after 1919), which ran streetcar lines from 1908 to 1931. Abilene Electric Light and Power began operation in 1891; a private telephone service began in 1895. City water and electricity were combined in one firm, Abilene Light and Water Company, in 1905. West Texas Utilities was organized in 1923; the gas operations were acquired by Lone Star Gas.

The modern era began for Abilene, as for the rest of Texas, with World War II.[qv] The acquisition of Camp Barkeley,[qv] a United States Army post, in 1940 changed the demographic composition, urban landscape, leadership, and outlook of the town. One and one-half million soldiers who spent some time at Barkeley and at the air base at Tye (established in 1943) infused millions of dollars into the local economy. After World War II civic leaders aggressively sought an air force base to maintain the flow of federal dollars, and Congress approved the establishment of Dyess Air Force Base[qv] in 1952. In the early 1960s Nike and Atlas missile installations and launching sites were built near the city, but they were phased out within three years.

The oil industry, including the development of exploration, drilling, refining, and oilfield service industries, expanded significantly after World War II. Manufacturing plants increased from 111 in 1979 to 145 in 1982. Parallel expansion occurred in banking, construction, and retail and wholesale business. Service employment expanded dramatically, as it did statewide. Per capita income remained well below the state average until 1950, when figures reflected an 89 percent increase; afterward it approximated the state figure.

In 1986 Abilene had seven commercial radio stations and one public one, three television stations, and two newspapers, including the Abilene *Reporter News*,[qv] the oldest continuously operated business in the city. Abilene improved its municipal airport in the 1960s and has been served by major carriers and commuter lines.

The population rose from 10,274 to 23,175 between 1920 and 1930. Between 1940 and 1950 it increased from 26,612 to 45,570, and then doubled in the following decade to 90,638. In 1988 the population was 108,157; in 1990 it was 106,654. As in most of West Texas, Anglo-Saxon Protestants predominate in Abilene. Since the first census in 1890, the percentage of whites, including Hispanics, has been 93 percent or above. The 1980 census revealed 6.7 percent black and 12.6 percent Hispanic population.

Although Abilene began its existence as a rowdy frontier town and shipping point, the citizens quickly founded schools and churches. The first class graduated from Abilene High School in 1888. Black children attended a separate school, founded by their parents in 1890, until they were incorporated into the Abilene school district. The Woodson elementary and high schools were built for black students in 1953 but were closed in 1969 in the general movement to integrate schools. A second high school, Cooper High, opened in 1960. In 1986 Abilene had two high schools, five middle schools, and seventeen elementary schools. Early in the twentieth century private schools were established; the longest-lived of these was St. Joseph's Academy, founded by the Sisters of Divine Providence[qv] in 1916. St. Joseph's (later called Central Catholic) educated hundreds of students before it closed in the 1960s. The Episcopal Church opened St. John's School in 1950. Abilene sought and acquired a Baptist college, Simmons College (now Hardin-Simmons University), in 1891. Abilene Christian College (now Abilene Christian University) first opened as Childers Classical Institute in 1906. McMurry College, a Methodist school, opened in 1923. Cisco Junior College began offering courses in Abilene in the 1970s.

The dominant religious groups in Abilene have been Baptist, Church of Christ, and Methodist; Presbyterians, Lutherans, Episcopalians, Disciples of Christ, and Catholics have been present in smaller numbers. From the beginning, there was an attempt to tame the frontier and make Abilene a town congenial for rearing families. The initial efforts to abolish saloons were successful in 1903; the city was legally dry until 1978, when a fiercely contested election to legalize the sale of alcoholic beverages barely succeeded. Abilene had already been bracketed by two wet communities—Impact and Buffalo Gap—since the 1960s. Until the 1930s virtually all local charity was conducted by the churches; they sponsored and funded day-care centers and nurseries and programs for elderly citizens, civic improvement, disadvantaged youth, and disaster relief. For decades churches provided the principal arena for women's community involvement. This religious environment has been reinforced by the presence of the three church-related colleges. In 1986 there were over 100 churches in the city.

Cultural interests are reflected in the profusion of dramatic clubs, Chautauqua circles, community bands, and literary guilds. The first social and cultural organization for women was founded in 1883; the City Federation of Women's Clubs dates from 1898. The women's clubs were successful in establishing the Carnegie Library, which opened in 1909. The original building served the city until the 1950s, when it was razed to make way for a new library building. In the 1960s citizens approved bonds for the construction of the Abilene Civic Center and the Taylor County Coliseum. The Abilene Philharmonic Orchestra gave its first concert in 1950. Active little-theater groups, ballet companies, a civic chorus, an art museum, a community band, and an opera association support the fine arts.

In the 1930s Abilenians enjoyed polo and horse and auto racing at Fair Park. In the 1950s the Abilene Blue Sox competed in semipro baseball. In 1981 the LaJet Classic at Fairway Oaks Golf and Racquet Club was added to the PGA tour. Popular recreation areas near Abilene are Fort Phantom Hill Reservoir and Abilene State Park.[qqv] Abilene has public swimming pools, a zoo, and numerous city parks. The West Texas Fair attracts large crowds to the city annually.

At its incorporation Abilene adopted a mayoral form of government and elected Dan B. Corley first mayor. In 1911 the city changed to a home-rule charter that provided for a mayor, four commissioners, and several city offices. Since 1947 it has had a city-manager form of government. For the last several decades Abilenians have generally favored Republican candidates in national elections.

In 1959 Abilene made extensive improvements to the downtown area. But major population movement in the 1970s and 1980s, spurred by the location of Cooper High School, the Mall of Abilene, and Fairway Oaks, was south toward Buffalo Gap. Most commercial establishments left downtown Abilene. The ruins of Fort Phantom Hill,[qv] north of Abilene, and Buffalo Gap Historic Village, south of the city, are the major historic sites nearby.

BIBLIOGRAPHY: Fane Downs, ed., *The Future Great City of West Texas: Abilene, 1881–1981* (Abilene: Richardson, 1981). Katharyn Duff, *Abilene . . . On Catclaw Creek: A Profile of a West Texas Town* (Abilene, Texas: Reporter Publishing, 1969). Katharyn Duff and Betty Kay Seibt, *Catclaw Country: An Informal History of Abilene in West Texas* (Burnet, Texas: Eakin Press, 1980). Paul D. Lack et al., *The History of Abilene* (Abilene, Texas: McMurry College, 1981). Juanita Daniel Zachry, *Abilene* (Northridge, California: Windsor, 1986).

Fane Downs

ABILENE CHRISTIAN UNIVERSITY. Abilene Christian University opened on September 11, 1906, with twenty-five students. The school was founded by A. B. Barrett and named Childers Classical Institute, after J. W. Childers, who sold the board five acres and a large house at a reduced rate for a campus. During the first six years the college had four presidents: Allen Booker Barret (1906–08), H. C. Darden (1908–09), R. L. Whiteside (1909–22), and Alonzo B. Cox[qv] (1911–12). In 1912 Jesse Parker Sewell, an energetic young preacher who had originally come from Tennessee to West Texas because of tuberculosis, accepted the presidency. He served from 1912 to 1924 and solidified the school. Batsell B. Baxter was the next president, from 1924 to 1932. During his administration the college grew steadily. The institution was officially renamed Abilene Christian College on April 16, 1920, though from the beginning it had been known as the Christian College or the Abilene Christian College. In February 1976 the name of the institution was again officially changed, this time to Abilene Christian University.

The college was originally beside the railroad tracks in what was then the west part of Abilene. The 5½-acre campus became 6½ acres, and several good buildings were erected. By the 1920s the board of trustees saw that the growing institution would have to have additional land. They bought 680 acres of open ranchland on the northeast edge of Abilene and received some additional acreage by donation. They set aside a tract of land for a campus and subdivided the remainder of the property into residential and commercial lots. In 1928 and 1929 eight new buildings were erected, and in the fall of 1929 the twenty-fourth session opened on the new campus. To finance the move the trustees voted bonds totalling $500,000. The crash of 1929 impeded sales of the bonds, and lots that had been sold were turned back to the college by buyers who were no longer able to pay for them. Abilene Christian College was faced with possible foreclosure. But in 1934 John G. Hardin[qv] and his wife, benefactors from Burkburnett, gave the college good securities that retired the entire debt. This one act put the institution on a sound footing.

Since its founding, Abilene Christian University has been governed by a board of trustees composed of members of the Church of Christ.[qv] Its principal support and the majority of its students have always come from that church. Many of its benefactors, however, have not been affiliated with the Church of Christ; the ACU student body includes members of many faiths.

In its earlier years the college was referred to as an ungraded educational institution; that is, classes were offered at all levels from elementary through junior college level. A student could enroll in one course at the high school level and another at the college level and receive credit for both. In 1912 the institution officially became a junior college. Senior college status was attained in 1919, and the graduate school was added in 1953.

In 1940 Donald H. Morris was elected president. He was the first alumnus of the school to assume that post. During his tenure of twenty-nine years a trio of long-time administrators headed the institution. Walter H. Adams was dean for thirty-seven years, and Lawrence L. Smith was business manager for forty-one years. Great growth came to the college after World War II.[qv] Within a short time enrollment jumped from about 500 to 3,000. Great efforts had to be made to acquire a faculty and physical plant adequate to the students' needs.

For the first forty-five years the institution was unaccredited. Its graduates were admitted to outstanding graduate and professional schools, but frequently their admission was conditional. In 1951 full accreditation was granted by the Southern Association of Colleges and Schools.

The university has from its beginning been primarily a liberal arts institution with a strong emphasis on biblical studies. At the same time, it has been noted for its offerings in education and teacher training and for its programs in the sciences and preprofessional studies. In 1944 ACC became the first church-related college in the Southwest to open an agriculture department, which included a 225-acre experimental farm. In 1988, in addition to the graduate school, ACU comprised five colleges: liberal and fine arts, natural and applied sciences, professional studies, business administration, and biblical studies. Nursing education was provided through a dual degree program offered in conjunction with the Abilene School of Nursing.

By the mid-1980s the campus in northeast Abilene consisted of approximately 350 acres. The physical plant included forty-one buildings with 1,400,000 square feet of floor space in 1988. Endowment assets were approximately $50 million. The annual budget of the institution for 1988–89 was $30 million. Enrollment in fall 1990 was 4,053. Students came from every state of the United States and about twenty-five other nations.

In addition to membership in the Southern Association of Colleges and Schools, ACU is accredited by the National Council for Accreditation of Teacher Education, the American Chemical Society, the American Industrial Arts Association, the National Association of Schools of Music, the Council on Social Work Education, the Texas State Board of Nurse Examiners, and the National League for Nursing. William J. Teague, the ninth president of the university, began his administration in the fall of 1981. In 1988 H. Lynn Packer of Dallas, chairman of the board of Wyatt's Cafeterias, was chairman of the board of trustees.

BIBLIOGRAPHY: Guy A. Scruggs, "Abilene Christian College," West Texas Historical Association *Year Book* 21 (1945). *John C. Stevens*

ABILENE AND NORTHERN RAILWAY. The Abilene and Northern Railway Company was fostered by Edward S. Hughes[qv] and his associate D. T. Bomar, who had been one of the promoters of the Wichita Valley Railway. On February 5, 1906, they obtained a charter to build from Hamlin southeastward to Brady, with a branch from a point near Anson to Stamford, the terminus of the Wichita Valley line. The construction contract was given to the Fidelity Construction Company of Wichita Falls, which in 1907 built the thirty-nine miles from Stamford via Anson to Abilene. The Abilene and Northern was open for service on January 1, 1907. The capital was $200,000, and the business office was at Abilene. Members of the first board of directors included C. H. Steel of Anson, R. L. Penick of Stamford, Bomar of Fort Worth, and Hughes, William G. Swenson,[qv] Henry James, H. O. Wooten, A. Holt, and George L. Paxton, all of Abilene.

By February 1908 the company had sold its securities to the Colorado and Southern Railway, another backer of the project. Though the road received no state funds, financial backing from people in Abilene, Anson, and Stamford and landowners along the line amounted to $86,805.85. No more track was built, and the Abilene and Northern was leased for operation to another Colorado and Southern subsidiary, the Wichita Valley Railway Company. The Abilene and Northern formed the south end of a through route between Wichita Falls and Abilene. The company was merged into the Fort Worth and Denver in June 1952. *H. Allen Anderson*

ABILENE *REPORTER-NEWS*. The Abilene *Reporter-News* began as a weekly newspaper called the Abilene *Reporter* on June 17, 1881. The paper was founded by Charles Edwin Gilbert from Navasota, Texas, and printed at the Abilene Steam Printing House. A daily edition appeared by 1885. The paper was operated by Dr. Alfred H. H. Tolar from March 1886 to the fall of 1887 and by John Hoeny, Jr., and F. S. Brittain between July 1888 and February 1895. It subsequently went into financial receivership. In 1896 George S. Anderson and several investors formed a partnership known as the Abilene Publishing Company to purchase the paper and publish it as the Abilene *Daily Reporter*. The paper continued with intermittent weekly or semi-weekly supplements thereafter as the Abilene *Reporter*, *Morning Reporter*, *Morning Reporter News*, and *Weekly Reporter*.

In 1906, when the paper was incorporated, Bernard Hanks became its general manager and one of several stockholders. Hanks, who had joined the firm in 1897, retained independent ownership even after 1921, when he entered the partnership with Houston Harte[qv] that later became Harte-Hanks Communications.[qv] In 1923 the paper divided into separate printing and publishing companies, and in 1930 Hanks was named president of the publishing company. A morning edition, the Abilene *Morning News*, appeared from 1926 until about 1934. In 1937 the paper merged the Abilene *Morning News* and the *Reporter* to form the daily Abilene *Reporter News*, which was published in morning, evening, and Sunday editions in the 1950s. After Hanks's death in 1948, the paper was run by his wife until her death in 1967. Hanks's daughter, Mrs. Andrew B. Shelton, served subsequently as chairman of the board. In the 1990s the paper had a circulation of 43,437, and was published by Andrew B. Shelton.

The *Reporter-News* was the first newspaper in West Texas to fight the open range, to advocate crop diversification and stock farming, and to join the Associated Press. It claims to have been the first daily in Texas to ban whiskey advertisements and to be among the first in American journalism to use special columns for classified advertising.

BIBLIOGRAPHY: Naomi Hatton Kincaid, The Abilene *Reporter-News* and Its Contribution to the Development of Abilene (M.A. thesis, Hardin-Simmons University, 1945). *Texas Newspaper Directory* (Austin: Texas Press Service, 1991). *Naomi Hatton Kincaid*

ABILENE AND SOUTHERN RAILWAY. The Abilene and Southern Railway Company was chartered on January 13, 1909, to build from Abilene south to Sonora, about 160 miles. A branch was also proposed from Ballinger northwest to San Angelo, about forty miles. The initial capital for the road was $200,000, and the business office was located in Abilene. Members of the first board of directors included Morgan Jones, Edward S. Hughes,[qqv] and J. M. Radford, of Abilene; D. T. Bomar, John W. Broad, and E. H. Holcomb, of Fort Worth; C. A. Doose and C. S. Miller, of Ballinger; and Grenville M. Dodge of Council Bluffs, Iowa.

By 1909 fifty-four miles of track had been laid from Abilene to Ballinger, and in 1911 eighteen miles was built from Anson to Hamlin. The company operated over the Abilene and Northern Railway between Abilene and Anson. In 1916 thc company owned seven locomotives, sixty-nine freight cars, seven passenger cars, and three company cars; earnings included $55,838 in passenger revenue, $165,187 in freight revenue, and $2,550 in other revenue.

The road became part of the Texas and Pacific system in 1926. In 1931, when it had four locomotives, fifteen freight cars, and two passenger cars, it earned $1,125 in passenger revenue, $148,385 in freight revenue, and $5,843 in other revenue. The line to Hamlin was abandoned in 1937, and in 1972 the sixteen miles between Winters and Ballinger was abandoned. In 1972 the company rented all of its equipment; its net income was $347,816. The Abilene and Southern was merged into the Missouri Pacific Railroad Company on November 1, 1978. *Chris Cravens*

ABILENE STATE PARK. Abilene State Park is off Farm Road 89 nineteen miles southeast of Abilene in Taylor County. Elm Creek, which flows through the 621.4-acre park, was for many years a popular camping ground for the Tonkawas and Comanches, who hunted buffalo[qv] during their annual migrations through Buffalo Gap, five miles to the northeast. In 1921 the city of Abilene built a dam across the creek to impound water for municipal use. In 1933 the city donated the land below the dam to the State Parks Board. During the mid-1930s the Civilian Conservation Corps[qv] built a number of structures, including a swimming pool and a concession building with an adjoining dance terrace. Shelters and campgrounds were added in the 1960s and 1970s. The heavily wooded park is home to a wide variety of wildlife, ranging from deer and raccoons to armadillos and coyotes. A portion of the official Texas longhorn herd is also kept in the park. Lake Abilene, a popular fishing and recreation spot, is adjacent to the park, and Buffalo Gap, one of the early frontier settlements of the region, is nearby. Facilities include a hiking trail, a dining hall, and playgrounds.

BIBLIOGRAPHY: Ray Miller, *Texas Parks* (Houston: Cordovan, 1984). *Christopher Long*

ABILENE STATE SCHOOL. Abilene State School is located on seventy-five acres just outside the southeast city limit of Abilene. The school is charged with the responsibility of caring for the mentally retarded citizens of 115 Texas counties. It was originally an epileptic colony authorized by the Twenty-sixth Texas Legislature in 1899, though it was actually established by the Twenty-seventh Legislature in 1901 with an appropriation of $50,000. Subsequent appropriations increased that figure to $250,000 for the construction of the colony.

The colony was built on a 640-acre tract of land donated by the city of Abilene. Brick buildings constructed on forty acres constituted the colony proper. Of the remaining 600 acres, 400 were under cultivation and 200 were in pasture. Dr. John Preston, the colony's first superintendent, admitted its first patients on March 26, 1904. Treatment was a combination of proper diet and hygiene, regular habits, and exercise. The state provided free treatment for indigent patients; others paid five dollars a week.

In 1919 the Texas legislature abolished the colony's original board of managers and replaced it with the state Board of Control.[qv] In 1925 Abilene State Hospital became the institution's new name, although the hospital continued to treat epileptics exclusively. In 1949 responsibility for the hospital was transferred to the Board for Texas State Hospitals and Special Schools. At that time the complex consisted of thirty wards and numerous associated buildings. That same year the legislature allowed the hospital to admit black patients, but none was actually admitted until the completion of two black wards in 1952. In 1957 the institution was renamed Abilene State School. The name change signified the new functions of the institution as a residential center for the mentally retarded citizens of Texas.

In 1963 the Abilene State School discontinued livestock operations. By 1964 fifteen single-story units had replaced the original structures. In 1965 the Texas legislature passed the Texas Mental Health and Mental Retardation Act. Subsequent legislation directed the school to intensify its efforts in caring for the mentally retarded. Also in 1965 the Board for Texas State Hospitals and Special Schools was abolished and replaced by the Texas Department of Mental Health and Mental Retardation.[qv] The new policy also deemphasized residential care in favor of a variety of outpatient and community-oriented services.

Because education and training of the mentally retarded are the focus of Abilene State School, the institution provides workshops for those clients with the capability to use them. Academic instruction for the clients takes place in two buildings under the supervision of the school's education department. In 1985, 325 clients received instruction in socialization, communication, and basic motor skills from eleven teachers. Employees give therapy and instruction in basic living skills continuously in the dormitories.

In 1993 Abilene State School had 720 clients and more than 1,700 workers with an annual payroll of $27 million. The completion of a new administration building, six cottage-type dormitories, and a chapel brought the number of buildings to about seventy-five, with a value of $17,671,000.

BIBLIOGRAPHY: Board for Texas State Hospitals and Special Schools, *Report* (Austin, 1949–65). Margery Taylor, "The Establishment and Early History of the Abilene State School," West Texas Historical Association *Year Book* 37 (1961). *Jennifer Hopkins*

***AB INITIO* QUESTION.** The *ab initio* question arose in the Constitutional Convention of 1866[qv] over the legal status of secession.[qv] Radical Republicans led by Morgan C. Hamilton[qv] maintained that secession was null and void *ab initio* ("from the beginning") and that all laws and transactions based on laws passed since secession in 1861 were null and void. Moderates led by Andrew J. Hamilton[qv] contended that secession was null and void as a result of the war but preferred to validate all laws not in conflict with the laws and constitution of the United States. Moderates opposed *ab initio* because of possible economic and political consequences. Had the radicals won, no government act in Texas between 1861 and 1866 would have been valid. The *ab initio* theory was rejected by Elisha M. Pease,[qv] by the military, by the constitutional conventions, and by the Republican state committee.

BIBLIOGRAPHY: James A. Baggett, "Birth of the Texas Republican Party," *Southwestern Historical Quarterly* 78 (July 1974). Dale A. Somers, "James P. Newcomb: The Making of a Radical," *Southwestern Historical Quarterly* 72 (April 1969). *Seymour V. Connor*

ABLE, MARY NEES (1927–1988). Mary Nees Able, pilot and founder of Able Aviation, the daughter of Gordon S. and Corinne (Gary) Nees, was born on August 23, 1927, in Bremond, Texas. She attended Stephens College in Columbia, Missouri, Texas Tech in Lubbock, and the University of Houston. On October 15, 1945, she married Conover Harris Able; the couple had two children. Mrs. Able first began flying as an activity to share with her husband. She later became the chief flight instructor and senior pilot of a local flight school, and subsequently founded her own flight school. She also became an examiner and safety counselor for the Federal Aviation Administration. She founded M. Able Aviation Company at Andrau Airpark and was later involved in charter operations and aircraft sales. She received numerous aviation achievement awards and was a participant in Powder Puff derbies, an Angel derby, and numerous rallies. She was also the fifth woman in the world to hold a Lear-jet flight rating. Mary Able held a number of offices—including vice governor, international secretary, and member of the board of directors (two terms)—in the Ninety-Nines, Incorporated, an organization of woman pilots. She also belonged to the Women's Airline Transport Pilots Association. She served on the Women's Committee on Aviation in Washington, D.C., and later on the Citizens' Committee on Aviation (also in Washington). Her flying career ended when she became ill in July 1981; she eventually had open-heart surgery at the Texas Heart Institute to replace a faulty mitral valve. She later had open-heart surgery again. She died on August 18, 1988.

BIBLIOGRAPHY: Houston *Post*, August 20, 1988. *Who Houston* (Houston: Who Houston, Inc., 1980). *Diana J. Kleiner*

ABLES, TEXAS. Ables, in northeastern Hudspeth County, was named for pioneer settler W. S. Ables. The settlement was established before 1909, when a post office was established there with James W. Hammack as postmaster. In 1914 the area had eight livestock breeders, including W. S., Oscar, and Sid Ables and James Hammack, as well as one real estate broker. By the mid-1930s, however, only one business was still operating in Ables. When the post office was moved to Salt Flat in 1941, the estimated population of Ables was twenty-five. That estimate remained constant until the late 1940s, when the settlement ceased to appear on maps. *Martin Donell Kohout*

ABLES SPRINGS, TEXAS. Ables Springs is on Farm Road 429 ten miles northeast of Terrell in northeastern Kaufman County. It was for many years a center for local religious and school activities. In 1853 James and Eliza Godfrey Ables settled there on land that had been granted in 1848 by the state of Texas to James's father, Ezekiel. In 1878 Mr. and Mrs. Ables deeded to the Methodist Episcopal Church, South, 8.75 acres "to be used as a campground or for any other purposes they might desire." On this land were built a tabernacle, a church, and a school, and a portion was set aside for the cemetery. Camping facilities were available. In 1915 a writer made note of the community's "old-fashioned religious camp meetings." Few people actually settled on the spot. In the mid-1980s a Baptist church met where the Methodist church once flourished; a Church of Christ met nearby. The freshwater spring that once flowed is dry today. The school, which many alumni still remember, is now part of the Terrell school system.

BIBLIOGRAPHY: *Daily Comet* (State Fair of Texas), October 29, 1915. *Jack Stoltz*

ABNER, DAVID, SR. (1826–1902). David Abner, black legislator, was born in Selma, Alabama, in 1826 and brought to Texas in 1843 by the daughter of his master, who, with her husband, settled in Upshur County. Abner remained there until after the Civil War.[qv] In 1866 he moved to Marshall. There he came in contact with Mrs. Fannie Richardson, the sister of his first owner in Alabama. Mrs. Richardson rented a mule, some farm equipment, and forty acres of land known as the Nathan Smith Plantation to Abner on credit. After settling in Harrison County the former slave became a prosperous farmer, and after a few years of hard labor and frugal living he managed to buy the farm. By 1876 he was signing notes, bonds, and securities for thousands of dollars for whites as well as blacks. According to oral sources, Abner was a natural politician. After settling in Marshall, he was appointed to the State Executive Committee of the Colored Men's Convention of 1873 and was later elected Harrison county treasurer. In 1874 he was elected to the Texas legislature. The next year he was also elected a member of the Constitutional Convention of 1875,[qv] and in 1876 he was a member and a vice president of the Republican state convention.

Abner participated in many civic activities in Harrison County. He helped to organize Bethesda Baptist Church and became one of its first deacons. He also helped to establish the first elementary school for blacks in Harrison County. After leaving the legislature he continued his interest in education. He was at the forefront of the movement to establish Bishop College and served as one of the two original black trustees.

The 1880 census listed him as a farmer. He and his wife, Mollie, reported eight children in their household. Seven were Abner's children from a previous marriage, including David Abner, Jr.,[qv] and two stepchildren; one child, Lucy, was Mollie's daughter from a previous marriage. When Abner retired from the legislature he went into the ice business in order to enhance an already sizable estate, which included over 300 acres of land in East Texas. He died in 1902 and was buried in a family plot in the Old Powder Mill Cemetery, Marshall.

BIBLIOGRAPHY: J. Mason Brewer, *Negro Legislators of Texas and Their Descendants* (Dallas: Mathis, 1935; 2d ed., Austin: Jenkins, 1970). Randolph B. Campbell, *A Southern Community in Crisis: Harrison County, Texas, 1850–1880* (Austin: Texas State Historical Association, 1983). Alwyn Barr, *Black Texans: A History of Negroes in Texas, 1528–1971* (Austin: Jenkins, 1973). *Merline Pitre*

ABNER, DAVID, JR. (1860–1928). David Abner, Jr., the first black professor of Bishop College, minister, and president of Guadalupe College, the son of David Abner, Sr.,[qv] was born in Upshur County, Texas, on November 25, 1860. After attending public schools and studying classics at Straight University in New Orleans, Louisiana, he went to Fisk University in Nashville, Tennessee, in 1877. While he was at the university, one of his compositions in Greek was placed on display at the Nashville exposition. Abner became the first black person to graduate from a Texas institution of higher learning when he received his degree from Bishop College in 1881. After graduation, he became a professor for the Baptist Home Mission Society of New York. In 1883 he was chosen as a delegate to the National Convention of Black Men in Louisville, Kentucky. He served as a Baptist minister, as corresponding secretary for the Baptist State Convention of Texas, and as editor of the *Baptist Journal* and two other newspapers. Abner was president of Guadalupe College from its founding until 1905, when he became president of Conroe College. He lectured, wrote, and traveled until 1917, when he left the college to head the National Baptist Convention Theological Seminary at Nashville. He was among the founders of the Odd Fellows Lodge in Texas, and a District Grand Master of the organization in Texas, New Mexico, and Arizona. Abner married Ella Wheeler, with whom he had two children. He died on July 21, 1928.

bibliography: J. Mason Brewer, *Negro Legislators of Texas and Their Descendants* (Dallas: Mathis, 1935; 2d ed., Austin: Jenkins, 1970). Andrew Webster Jackson, *A Sure Foundation and a Sketch of Negro Life in Texas* (Houston, 1940). Merline Pitre, *Through Many Dangers, Toils and Snares: The Black Leadership of Texas, 1868–1900* (Austin: Eakin, 1985). Martin Rywell, ed., *Afro-American Encyclopedia* (10 vols., North Miami, Florida: Educational Book Publishers, 1974).

Diana J. Kleiner

ABNER, TEXAS. Abner is in east central Kaufman County on Farm Road 2727, seven miles northeast of Kaufman. The site, which bordered the College Mound community on the north, was first known as Johnson's Point. It was settled in the late 1840s by Abner Johnson, who had piloted a keelboat up the Trinity River two years before. A Johnson's Point post office was opened in 1871 but closed two years later, when service was moved to Terrell. The post office was reopened in 1885 under the name Abner. The Johnson's Point school district was established by the Kaufman County Commissioners Court in 1885. In 1890 Abner had one barber, two doctors, one general store, and a population of twenty-five. In 1896 the population was estimated at thirty-five. The Abner post office was closed in 1903, and mail was routed through Kaufman. The community finally settled down to become a quiet neighborhood of rural homes when the school district was annexed to the Kaufman school system in 1949.

Jack Stoltz

ABOLITION. Abolition sentiment was never significant in Texas, although antebellum Texans often expressed fear concerning its presence. There were Unionists in Texas, but few, if any, were abolitionists, though many had strayed away from solid Southern sentiment enough to wonder whether slavery[qv] did not operate to retard Southern progress. At times, particularly in 1860, during the so-called Texas Troubles,[qv] public excitement reached an advanced stage of hysteria in contemplating the presence of abolitionists. Fires of unknown origin destroyed large parts of Dallas, Denton, Kaufman, Waxahachie, and other North Texas towns. Rumors spread that the fires were started by abolitionists to demoralize the people in preparation for a slave uprising. Gruesome stories of slave insurrections[qv] were circulated, always exaggerated or wholly without foundation, as were tales of wholesale poisonings, which seem to have been the product almost entirely of fertile imaginations. The Texas press in particular played an important role in promoting the fears of an abolitionist-led uprising. Charles Pryor, editor of the Dallas *Herald*, in a letter printed by the *Texas State Gazette* in July of 1860 declared: "It was determined by certain abolitionist preachers, who were expelled from the country last year, to devastate, with fire and assassination, the whole of Northern Texas, and when it was reduced to a helpless condition, a general revolt of slaves, aided by the white men of the North in our midst, was to come off on the day of election in August." Such stories were picked up and carried by papers around the state and throughout the South. Several scholars have argued that at least some of the events related to the Texas Troubles were the result of an organized though ineffective plot, but conclusive evidence is lacking.

To offset these dangers, whether real or imaginary, vigilance committees were organized to ferret out offenders and administer proper punishment. The result was that justice through regular channels disappeared at times and was replaced by mob action. Three blacks were hanged in Dallas in the interest of public safety. A white man in Fort Worth accused of tampering with slaves was also put to death. The most definitive charge against any one of them, as reported to the press, was that "he had prowled about the country." Texans often dealt harshly with Mexicans as well, fearing that they encouraged unrest among slaves. In 1856 the editor of the San Antonio *Zeitung* was threatened with a coat of tar and feathers for printing criticisms of slavery. Three years later, Northern Methodists in conference at Bonham made derogatory remarks about slavery and slaveowners and were immediately threatened by intolerant inhabitants. Hostility towards Northern Methodists reached a peak in August 1860 with the lynching of Rev. Anthony Bewley,[qv] an ordained missionary suspected of being an abolitionist and slave agitator. A few people in antebellum Texas[qv] criticized slavery, but there were few outright abolitionists.

bibliography: Walter L. Buenger, *Secession and the Union in Texas* (Austin: University of Texas Press, 1984). Randolph B. Campbell, *An Empire for Slavery: The Peculiar Institution in Texas, 1821–1865* (Baton Rouge: Louisiana State University Press, 1989). Wesley Norton, "The Methodist Episcopal Church and the Civil Disturbances in North Texas in 1859 and 1860," *Southwestern Historical Quarterly* 68 (January 1965). Frank H. Smyrl, Unionism, Abolitionism, and Vigilantism in Texas, 1856–1865 (M.A. thesis, University of Texas, 1961). William W. White, "The Texas Slave Insurrection of 1860," *Southwestern Historical Quarterly* 52 (January 1949).

Claude Elliott

ABRA, TEXAS. Abra, at the junction of Farm roads 1547 and 3143 in northwestern Collingsworth County, was one of thirty-nine school districts established in the county during the early 1900s. An Abra post office was established in July 1908 and remained in operation until May 1917, when the community was included in the Shamrock mail route. In 1934 the Abra school district was consolidated with that of Samnorwood. The community listed a population of ten in 1940 and was afterward eclipsed by Dozier, three miles to the east.

bibliography: Arthur Hecht, comp., *Postal History in the Texas Panhandle* (Canyon, Texas: Panhandle-Plains Historical Society, 1960). *A History of Collingsworth County and Other Stories* (Wellington, Texas: Leader Printing, 1925).

H. Allen Anderson

ABRAHAM, NAHIM (1885–1965). Nahim Abraham, community builder, was born on February 15, 1885, in Kafracab, Lebanon. He left his homeland in 1901 on the first of three trips he made to America before deciding to immigrate permanently. On his second return to Lebanon he was married to Alia Abdullah Bulos Malouf, the daughter of a doctor. After returning to America the third time in 1912, Abraham worked as a traveling salesman. He settled briefly in Utah, then in Amarillo, Texas, before moving to Canadian in the summer of 1913. Later that year he brought Alia and his two sons to join him; the couple had two more sons in Canadian. Abraham established a mercantile business called the Fair Store, which he managed until his retirement in 1955; the store was noted throughout the Panhandle[qv] for its quality merchandise. Abraham was an elder in the First Presbyterian Church of Canadian. He and his wife visited Lebanon over the years, the last time in the summer of 1939. In June 1950 Abraham purchased the old Moody Hotel, which dated from 1903. After his son Edward died in 1961, Abraham gave a gift to build the Edward Abraham Memorial Home, a nursing facility. Abraham died of a heart attack on January 10, 1965. His surviving sons became prominent local businessmen; Malouf (Oofie) served as mayor of Canadian and was a state legislator.

bibliography: Amarillo *Daily News*, January 11, 1965. Sallie B. Harris, *Cowmen and Ladies: A History of Hemphill County* (Canyon, Texas: Staked Plains, 1977). F. Stanley [Stanley F. L. Crocchiola], *The Canadian, Texas, Story* (Nazareth, Texas, 1975).

H. Allen Anderson

ABRAM, TEXAS. Abram is on Farm Road 1427 a mile north of the Rio Grande and five miles southwest of Mission in southwest Hidalgo County. The site was near the route of the original military highway from Brownsville to Fort Ringgold and was on part of the common grazing grounds of old Reynosa, Tamaulipas. Later the Ojo de Agua ("Watering Hole") Ranch was established on the site. The community was named for Abram Dillard, Texas Ranger and prominent citizen of the area of Ojo de Agua Creek. An Abram post office was established in 1901. The railroad was built in 1904 a few miles to the north to avoid river flooding. In 1914 the settlement had fifty residents and three businesses. On September 3, 1915, Abram was the site of a skirmish between United States Cavalry troops and bandits. Through the 1930s and 1940s the population was seventy-five. In the 1950s it dropped to twenty-five, where it remained in the 1960s. A colonia (*see* COLONIAS) developed beside Abram over two or three decades; in 1990 its 927 residents lived in 206 dwellings and received water from the La Joya Water District. In 1990 Abram and the colonia had an estimated total population of 3,999. The colonia is variously called Abram, Ojo de Agua, or Chapa Joseph.

BIBLIOGRAPHY: *Colonias in the Lower Rio Grande Valley of South Texas: A Summary Report* (Policy Research Project Report No. 18, Lyndon B. Johnson School of Public Affairs, University of Texas at Austin, 1977). Winnie Maddox, History of the Donna Community (M.A. thesis, Texas College of Arts and Industries, 1955). J. Lee and Lillian J. Stambaugh, *The Lower Rio Grande Valley of Texas* (San Antonio: Naylor, 1954). *Robert E. Norton*

ABRAMS, LUCIEN (1870–1941). Lucien Abrams, painter, the son of Maj. William Henry and Ella Murray (Harris) Abrams, was born in Lawrence, Kansas, on June 10, 1870. He probably moved to Marshall, Texas, with his parents in 1874; in 1883 the family moved to Dallas. Abrams graduated with a degree in art and architecture from Princeton in 1892 and began his career as an artist. He studied at the Art Students League, New York, from 1892 to 1894, then at the Académie Julien in Paris under Benjamin Constant and Jean Paul Laurens. He also studied with James A. McNeil Whistler in Paris. From 1894 to 1905 Abrams lived in Paris or at the family villa on the Mediterranean. He also painted in Belgium, Provence, Brittany, Italy, and Spain. He produced a number of works during a six-month stay in Algeria (1905–06). The following year he worked in Rockport, Massachusetts, and New York City. He returned to France in 1908 for a six-year stay; there he worked chiefly in Provence. Although strongly influenced by Whistler, during his years of travel Abrams developed his own style, in which are merged elements of Impressionism, Post-Impressionism, and Fauvism.

Abrams exhibited at the New Salon of the Société National des Beaux Arts from 1899 to 1901; from 1902 to 1914 he exhibited annually at the Salon d'Automne and the Société des Independents in Paris. He also exhibited at the Pennsylvania Academy of Fine Arts in 1903 and 1911, at the National Academy of Design in New York City in 1907, and with the Society of Independent Artists in 1917 and 1919; his works were shown at the Art Institute of Chicago, the Dallas Art Association, the Dallas Women's Forum, the Fort Worth Museum of Art (*see* MODERN ART MUSEUM OF FORT WORTH), and the Witte Memorial Museum,[qv] San Antonio. He was represented at the 1925 Texas State Fair Art Exhibition by a group of flower pieces and landscapes. One-man shows of his work were held at the Dallas Woman's Club, the Pabst Galleries in San Antonio, and the Durand-Ruel Galleries in New York City.

On March 11, 1915, Abrams married Charlotte Gina Onillon, a native of Paris and graduate of the Sorbonne; they had one daughter. They returned to the United States and purchased a residence in Old Lyme, Connecticut, where Abrams became an active member of the Lyme Art Association. He was also a member of the Dallas Art Association, the San Antonio Art Association, the American Federation of Arts, and the Society of Independent Artists. Although Old Lyme was the artist's principal residence, he maintained a studio at his father's home in Dallas and another house in San Antonio. Abrams died in New Haven, Connecticut, on April 14, 1941. Several of his works are in the permanent collection of the Dallas Museum of Art.[qv]

BIBLIOGRAPHY: Diana Church, *Guide to Dallas Artists, 1890–1917* (Plano, Texas, 1987). Gallery Files, Marion Koogler McNay Art Museum, San Antonio. *Diana Church*

ABRAMS, WILLIAM H. (1843–1926). William H. Abrams, railroad official and oilman, the son of Isaac and Ellen (Rittenhouse) Abrams, was born on January 10, 1843, in Peru, Illinois. He studied at Beloit College in Wisconsin and Monmouth College in Illinois, served in the Union Army in 1864–65, and graduated with a bachelor's degree from Monmouth in 1866. From October of that year until 1873 he was employed by the land department of the Kansas Pacific Railroad, later part of the Union Pacific system. On June 16, 1869, Abrams married Ella (Fanny) Murray Harris, with whom he had three sons. He lived in Marshall, Texas, from 1873 to 1875, after which he was employed by the Texas and Pacific Railway as land commissioner, succeeding James W. Throckmorton.[qv] In 1883 Abrams moved to Dallas, where he represented the land interests of the Missouri, Kansas and Texas Railroad and auxiliary lines, beginning in 1884. As the company extended the railroad from Fort Worth to El Paso and from Marshall to New Orleans, Abrams aided in establishing new towns along the line. As general agent for the Texas Pacific Land Trust he sold and administered up to four million acres of land and later leased thousands of acres for oil and gas development.

He also bought land and made another fortune from oil. The Abrams No. 1 oil well, drilled by the Texas Company (later Texaco[qv]), blew in on July 2, 1920, on Abrams's 1,650-acre tract in Brazoria County and established the West Columbia oilfield as a major field that produced up to 30,000 barrels of crude oil daily. Oil discovered on Abrams's land in Mitchell County that same year initiated some of the first petroleum production in the Permian Basin.[qv] Abrams was an Episcopalian and one of the founders of the Dallas Club. He died in Dallas on April 16, 1926, and was buried in that city.

BIBLIOGRAPHY: *Memorial and Biographical History of Dallas County* (Chicago: Lewis, 1892; rpt., Dallas: Walsworth, 1976). Marker Files, Texas Historical Commission, Austin. *Diana J. Kleiner*

ABRIACHE INDIANS. The Abriache (Abriade) Indians, who are generally considered to be Jumanos, lived in the vicinity of present Presidio during the late sixteenth century. Their settlements seem to have been along the south bank of the Rio Grande, but they must have crossed to the north bank on occasion. The Abriaches disappeared during the seventeenth century.

BIBLIOGRAPHY: J. Charles Kelley, "The Historic Indian Pueblos of La Junta de Los Rios," *New Mexico Historical Review* 27, 28 (October 1952, January 1953). William W. Newcomb, *The Indians of Texas* (Austin: University of Texas Press, 1961). Carl Sauer, *The Distribution of Aboriginal Tribes and Languages in Northwestern Mexico* (Berkeley: University of California Press, 1934). *Thomas N. Campbell*

ACADEMY OF THE SACRED HEART. On September 23, 1873, Mother Emelie, American provincial of the Sisters of St. Mary of Namur,[qv] Lockport, New York, accompanied by Sister Mary Angela and Sister Stanislaus, arrived in Waco at the urging of Bishop Claude Marie Dubuis,[qv] the second bishop of Galveston, for the purpose of opening a Catholic school. On October 1, 1873, in a residence on the southwest corner of Sixth and Washington the school opened, and one pupil, Thomas Bloomer, a Catholic, enrolled. The third day, six more students, faith undisclosed, enrolled. Subsequent to that, the enrollment grew steadily.

On June 12, 1874, Sister Angela bought a lot on the northwest corner of Eighth and Washington, later the site of the M Bank Building. The date of purchase was the feast of the Sacred Heart, so the school was named Academy of the Sacred Heart. The first brick was laid on July 15, 1874. The academy, in its red-brick Victorian buildings surrounded by magnolia trees, was enclosed by a typical period-style iron-post fence. In November 1873 Mother Emelie returned to New York, and Sister Angela remained as superior of the academy for many years. She is said to have fought carpetbaggers, ignorance, and anti-Catholicism to bring the school to popularity and academic excellence. The school eventually came to be accredited by both the Catholic University of America and the University of Texas.

From 1873 to 1946 the boarding and day school provided grades one through twelve to boys and girls. Boys attended through grammar school only, and none were boarding students. The first graduating class (1881) was four girls. The academy was a popular boarding school for girls whose families lived on surrounding farms. Growth in enrollment and plans to build a new school encouraged the sisters to purchase two tracts of land in northwest Waco. Plans to relocate and enlarge never materialized, however. In 1946 the nuns, probably because of declining student enrollment, a decline in religious vocations from the students, and an emerging interest in parochial rather than private schools in Waco, closed the Academy of the Sacred Heart. The sisters donated twenty-three acres they had purchased for expansion to the Diocese of Galveston in 1941. St. Louis School and Reicher High School were later opened at that site.

BIBLIOGRAPHY: Waco *News-Tribune*, May 24, 1946.

Mary Catherine Henry

ACADEMY OF SCIENCE OF TEXAS. The Academy of Science of Texas was founded on October 27, 1880, in Austin, Travis County, by Samuel Botsford Buckley, Franklin L. Yoakum,[qqv] and Quintius Cincinnatus Smith. At the first meeting the members selected a name for the organization, elected Governor Oran M. Roberts[qv] as president, and voted other top government officials to membership, hoping for state sponsorship and cooperation. Evidently the politicians did not cooperate, and the founders shortly moved the academy to Palestine, where they reorganized it with Buckley as president and Yoakum as secretary. Membership grew from about thirty to 100. Scientific publications were planned, although there is no evidence that anything was published. However, Yoakum and another member, Thomas Volney Munson,[qv] regularly contributed articles on horticulture and the affairs of the academy to Texas Farm and Ranch, a bimonthly newspaper published in Dallas during the late 1800s. Their primary interest seems to have been a museum of natural history, the nucleus of which was Yoakum's private collection of rocks, shells, and botanical specimens. Buckley died in 1883, and in 1886 Yoakum moved the museum to Tyler. In 1886 it was exhibited at the State Fair of Texas[qv] in Dallas. In an article about the academy in Texas Farm and Ranch in 1886, the objectives of the organization were listed as the "mutual improvement of its members," the collection of specimens, the promotion of a scientific interest among the people, "fortifying our people against the false analysis of mineral waters," and facilitating the identification of specimens within Texas without having to make "humiliating" inquiries beyond the state. Yoakum died in 1891, and Smith died in 1911. The last known published mention of the academy was in 1889, when Texas Farm and Ranch published an article by Yoakum on "The Academy of Science of Tyler." There is no record of what happened to the museum, although part of it may have ended up at Southern Methodist University.

BIBLIOGRAPHY: S. W. Geiser, "Fifty Years of Texas Biology," *Proceedings and Transactions of the Texas Academy of Science* 30 (1946). S. W. Geiser, "The First Texas Academy of Science," *Field and Laboratory* 13 (January 1945). *Texas Farm and Ranch*, December 1, 1886. Ethel Ward-McLemore, "The Academies of Science of Texas, 1880–1987," *Texas Journal of Science* 41 (August 1989, suppl.).

Ethel Ward-McLemore

ACADIA. The *Acadia* was a River Clyde–type steamship built at Sorel, Quebec, in May and July of 1864. She was expressly constructed to be a blockade runner and was larger and faster than the norm. She was a 738 tonner, whereas the usual range of vessels in this occupation was from 400 to 600 tons. The *Acadia* was 211 feet long and had a beam of thirty-one feet and a hold twelve feet deep. She was a sidewheeler with one 900-horsepower engine. Under the command of Capt. Thomas Leach, the *Acadia* was on her first voyage as a blockade runner when she was run aground and abandoned by her crew on February 6, 1865. As soon as the morning fog lifted she was spotted in fifteen feet of water ten miles northeast of the mouth of the Brazos, her intended destination, by the USS *Virginia,* the Union navy ship on patrol in the area. The *Acadia* was destroyed by gunfire, although much of her cargo was salvaged by shore parties. The wreck site was examined by Wendell E. Pierce during the late 1960s and early 1970s under permit from the Texas Antiquities Committee[qv] and under the supervision of Frank Hole, an archeologist at Rice University. Artifacts from the site are housed at the Houston Museum of Natural Science.[qv] The wreck of the *Acadia* is a designated state archeological landmark protected under the Texas Antiquities Code.

BIBLIOGRAPHY: Frank Hole, *The Acadia: A Civil War Blockade Runner* (Houston: Rice University Department of Anthropology, 1974). Marker Files, Texas Historical Commission, Austin.

J. Barto Arnold III

ACALA, TEXAS. Acala is on the Rio Grande and State Highway 20, thirty-four miles northwest of Sierra Blanca near the Southern Pacific tracks in southwestern Hudspeth County. It was founded before 1925, when a post office was established with Mrs. Julia A. Vaughn as postmistress. In 1927 Acala had a population of fifty; two years later that figure had doubled. By the mid-1930s, however, the population had fallen to an estimated ten. It increased gradually over the next three decades, from an estimated seventy-five in the late 1930s to ninety in the late 1940s and 100 in the late 1950s. Subsequently, however, it fell again; in the late 1960s it was estimated at fifty and in the early 1970s at twenty-five, where it remained in 1990. Acala was named for the long-staple cotton of Mexican origin grown in the area; it is the site of numerous canals and wells dug for irrigation.

Martin Donell Kohout

ACE, TEXAS. Ace is on Farm Road 2610 seventy-five miles northeast of Houston in south central Polk County. In 1830 Samuel G. Hirams established a community called Smithfield about a mile south of the present site of Ace. The settlement, a stopping point on the Liberty–Nacogdoches road, was originally known as Smith's Field, after an early settler named Robert Smith. A group of Coushatta Indians lived nearby. The town was moved nearer its present location in 1840 and became a steamboat landing on the Trinity River. Several sawmills were established, and the post office existed by 1840. Yet the community remained small, as other riverports captured the steamboat trade. In 1871 the post office was discontinued. However, a new post office was opened in 1915, named Ace after its postmaster, Ace Emanuel. Oil was found in the area in 1952, and more substantial returns were made from discoveries in 1969. The population, estimated to be twenty-five in the mid-1940s, grew to forty by the early 1970s and remained at that level in 1990.

BIBLIOGRAPHY: *History of Polk County* (2 vols., Livingston, Texas: Keen Printing, 1968). *A Pictorial History of Polk County, Texas, 1846–1910* (Livingston, Texas: Polk County Bicentennial Commission, 1976; rev. ed. 1978).

Robert Wooster

ACEBUCHE DRAW. Acebuche Draw originates in southwestern Pecos County near Panther Mesa (at 30°25′ N, 103°10′ W) and runs northeast for forty-five miles before emptying into Lake Leon near Interstate Highway 10, eight miles west of Fort Stockton (at 30°53′ N, 103°01′ W). The draw runs through an area of steep to gentle slopes surfaced with clayey and sandy loams. In the local vegetation creosote bush, tarbush, mesquite shrubs, and juniper shrubs predominate.

ACEQUIAS. The building of acequias, or irrigation canals, was an important element in Spanish efforts to colonize Texas. Much of the region occupied by the Spanish in Texas was semiarid, and irrigation was vitally necessary for the success of agriculture. Acequias had been widely used throughout Spain since the time of the Moorish conquest, and the early Spanish colonists brought with them sophisticated knowledge of how to construct large-scale irrigation systems. The earliest acequias were dug near Ysleta, below El Paso, after 1680 by Pueblo Indians under the supervision of Spanish friars. These first acequias eventually became part of a large irrigation network, portions of which were still in use in the early 1990s.

In the mid-1700s acequias were also planned or constructed at Nuestra Señora del Rosario Mission, near the site of present Goliad, at Nuestra Señora de la Candelaria Mission, near the site of present Montel, and at a number of other sites. Later, particularly after Mexican independence from Spain, numerous private acequias were built by the owners of ranchos or small farms.

The most extensive network of acequias, however, was found in San Antonio and the surrounding area. The oldest acequia there was the Concepción, or Pajalache, built in 1729, which followed a route running along what is now Garden and Roosevelt streets to Nuestra Señora de la Purísima Concepción de Acuña Mission, and from there to its lands further south. The Concepción acequia was the largest of the irrigation canals in the region and, according to tradition, was of ample size to allow the Franciscans[qv] to employ small boats to transport themselves to and from the mission and to repair the canal. It was in continual use until 1869, when it was abandoned.

Other acequias in the San Antonio area included the Acequia Madre de Valero, dug between 1718 and 1744, which ran from San Pedro Springs[qv] through the town to the farmlands below; the Upper Labor acequia in the northern portion of the city, begun in 1776; the San José y San Miguel de Aguayo Mission acequia, built around 1730; the San Juan Capistrano Mission acequia, constructed in 1731; and the San Francisco de la Espada Mission acequia, constructed between 1731 and 1745. The last included the stone Espada aqueduct, which spanned an arroyo; it is claimed to be the only Spanish structure of its type still in working use in the United States.

In addition to the irrigation canals built by the missions, several public acequias and ancillary ditches were built in the San Antonio area to serve the presidio and the lands of the Canary Islanders[qv] at the Villa de San Fernando. The construction and maintenance of the acequias required considerable amounts of labor, and some of the larger canals took more than two decades to complete. Because of their high cost, the amount of irrigated land was limited, and competition for such land was strong. Much of the better land went to the Canary Islanders, who constituted the local political and socioeconomic elite. Water rights were strictly controlled and were sometimes sold or bought separately from the land. Landowners were expected to help dig new irrigation ditches and to defray the expense of upkeep. Those who failed to comply with regulations to keep the canals in working order were subject to fines.

After the missions were secularized in the early 1790s, the city authorities undertook to oversee the distribution of water. City control was discontinued in the later half of the nineteenth century, and the remaining acequias were operated for a time as informal community enterprises or, in the case of the San Juan acequia, by an incorporated mutual company. With the expansion of San Antonio in the twentieth century most of the canals were abandoned, though traces of most of them are still evident. *See also* IRRIGATION.

BIBLIOGRAPHY: Edwin P. Arneson, "Early Irrigation in Texas," *Southwestern Historical Quarterly* 25 (October 1921). Herbert Eugene Bolton, *Texas in the Middle Eighteenth Century: Studies in Spanish Colonial History and Administration* (Berkeley: University of California Press, 1915; rpt., Austin: University of Texas Press, 1970). Carlos E. Castañeda, *Our Catholic Heritage in Texas* (7 vols., Austin: Von Boeckmann–Jones, 1936–58; rpt., New York: Arno, 1976). Jesús Francisco de la Teja, Land and Society in 18th Century San Antonio de Béxar: A Community on New Spain's Northern Frontier (Ph.D. dissertation, University of Texas at Austin, 1988). Thomas F. Glick, *The Old World Background of the Irrigation System of San Antonio* (El Paso: Texas Western Press, 1972). William H. Holmes, The Acequias of San Antonio (M.A. thesis, St. Mary's University, 1962). Wells A. Hutchins, "The Community Acequia: Its Origins and Development," *Southwestern Historical Quarterly* 31 (January 1928). Marker Files, Texas Historical Commission, Austin. Michael C. Meyer, *Water in the Hispanic Southwest: A Social and Legal History, 1550–1850* (Tucson: University of Arizona Press, 1983). Gerald E. Poyo and Gilberto M. Hinojosa, eds., *Tejano Origins in Eighteenth-Century San Antonio* (San Antonio: Institute of Texan Cultures, 1991).

Christopher Long

ACHESON, ALEXANDER W. (1842–1934). Alexander W. Acheson, soldier, mayor, and physician, was born to Judge Alexander Wilson and Jane (Wishart) Acheson on October 12, 1842, at Washington, Pennsylvania. In 1861 he entered the Civil War[qv] as a private in the Thirteenth Pennsylvania Regiment. He was transferred to the 140th Pennsylvania Regiment during the following year and with this unit rose to the rank of sergeant in 1862 and captain in 1863. As a captain he served as aide-de-camp to Gen. Nelson A. Miles.[qv] Acheson was the first United States Army officer to mount captured breastworks at the center of the Confederate lines at the battle of Spotsylvania, Virginia, in May 1864. He was shot in the face during the course of this five-day battle but survived the injury.

At the end of the war Acheson returned to his hometown, where the local university, Washington and Jefferson College, awarded him an honorary A.B. degree. He received the M.D. degree from the University of Pennsylvania the following year. He established a practice in Philadelphia in 1872 but abandoned it the same year and moved to Denison, Texas. Apparently aware of the benefits that the Grayson County town derived from the presence of the Missouri, Kansas and Texas Railroad, which extended its tracks into Denison from Oklahoma in 1872, Acheson secured an interview with railroad magnate Jay Gould.[qv] During this meeting he argued successfully for the building of the tracks of Gould's Texas and Pacific Railway through Denison. Acheson served four terms as mayor of Denison. He ran unsuccessfully as the Republican nominee for governor in 1906, for the United States Senate in 1916, and for the United States House of Representatives in 1920. He served as city physician of Denison from 1923 through 1929 and sat on the boards of directors of the local State National Bank and the Denison and Suburban Railway.

As a staunch advocate of efforts to make the Red River navigable and to control its flooding, Acheson was an honorary lifetime vice president of the Red River Flood Control and Navigation Association. He also served as the Texas director of the Mississippi Valley Association and as a delegate to conventions on rivers at New Orleans, Washington, and Chicago.

He married Sarah M. Cooke on June 20, 1864; they had a daughter. Acheson was a Presbyterian and a member of the Benevolent and Protective Order of Elks, the Knights of Pythias, and various state and national medical associations. He was also the only honorary member of the Veterans of Foreign Wars[qv] in North Texas. He died at his home in Denison on September 7, 1934.

BIBLIOGRAPHY: Dallas *Morning News*, September 8, 1934. *Who Was Who in America*, Vol. 1.

Brian Hart

ACHESON, SAM HANNA (1900–1972). Sam Acheson, journalist and historian, was born to Alexander Mahon and Alice (Hanna) Acheson on August 21, 1900, in Dallas, Texas. He attended Dallas public schools, Austin College, and then, from 1917 to 1921, the University of Texas, where he received a bachelor's degree in English in 1921. In 1918 he was selected as an officer candidate by the United States Marine Corps, but he was still in training at Camp Mabry when World War I[qv] ended.

For two years in the early 1920s Acheson worked as a reporter for the Dallas *Times Herald*, then moved to the Dallas *Morning News*[qqv] in 1925. There he worked as a reporter, an editor, and an editorial writer until his retirement in 1966. During World War II[qv] he was appointed to the Enemy Alien Hearing Board for the Northern District of Texas but quit to join the army as a captain. He served in Europe, received the Bronze Star, and attained the rank of major. He later retired from the reserves as a lieutenant colonel.

Acheson's works include *Joe Bailey: The Last Democrat* (1932), nominated for the Pulitzer Prize; *35,000 Days in Dallas* (1938), a history of the Dallas *Morning News* and its parent news agencies hailed as "one of the first socioeconomic histories of the state"; and a historical play dramatizing the fall of the Alamo, *We Are Besieged* (1941). Acheson was a contributor to *American Mercury,* the *Dictionary of American Biography,* and the *Dictionary of American History.* He was a compiler of *Texian Who's Who* (1937) and an editor of *George Washington Diamond's Account of the Great Hanging at Gainesville, 1862,* published in 1963 by the Texas State Historical Association,[qv] of which he was a fellow. Acheson was considered the leading authority on Dallas during his lifetime; after he retired he continued to write a weekly series, "Dallas Yesterday," for the *News.* This column was assembled into a book and published posthumously in 1977.

Acheson served as secretary of the Dallas Historical Society[qv] from 1935 until his death and was instrumental in persuading the city of Dallas to lease the Hall of State[qv] from the state and invite the historical society to maintain the library and museum there. He was secretary of the Philosophical Society of Texas[qv] from 1940 to 1972, a director of the Dallas Civic Federation and Community Chest Foundation, and a member of the American Legion,[qv] the Military Order of the World Wars, the Texas Institute of Letters,[qv] the University Club, and the Beta Theta Pi fraternity. At the time of his death he was serving as consultant to the executive vice president of the Southwestern Legal Foundation.

Acheson was a Presbyterian and a Democrat; he never married. On March 7, 1972, he died at his home in Dallas. He was buried in Denison.

BIBLIOGRAPHY: Dallas *Morning News,* March 8, 1972. Herbert Gambrell, "Sam Hanna Acheson," *Proceedings of the Philosophical Society of Texas* 35 (1971). *Who's Who in the South and Southwest,* 12th ed.

Joan Jenkins Perez

ACHESON, SARAH C. (1844–1899). Sarah Acheson, suffragist and temperance reformer, was born on February 20, 1844, in Washington, Pennsylvania, and was married there in 1863. She had four children, two of whom survived to adulthood. In 1872 she and her husband moved to Texas and settled in Denison. After serving as president of the Denison chapter of the state Woman's Christian Temperance Union,[qv] Mrs. Acheson was elected president of the state organization and held office from 1888 to 1891. She declined reelection because of ill health and afterward served as state vice president.

When the prohibition[qv] amendment failed at the polls in 1887, an equal-franchise department was added to the WCTU program in the conviction that enfranchised women would vote for prohibition. Mrs. Acheson helped organize and served as first president of the Denison Equal Rights Association, the first suffrage club in the state. She signed the call for a statewide suffrage convention that resulted in the formation of the Texas Equal Rights Association[qv] in 1893. She was elected fourth vice president at the organizing meeting and represented TERA at the National American Woman Suffrage Association conventions in 1894 and 1895. She became superintendent of educational opportunities for women and children in 1894 and served on the business committee in 1895. Sarah Acheson died on January 16, 1899, in Denison and was buried in Fairview Cemetery. *See also* WOMAN SUFFRAGE.

BIBLIOGRAPHY: May Baines, *A Story of Texas White Ribboners* (1935?). Elizabeth Brooks, *Prominent Women of Texas* (Akron, Ohio: Werner, 1896). Denison *Sunday Gazetteer,* January 22, 1899. Grayson County Frontier Village, *History of Grayson County, Texas* (2 vols., Winston-Salem, North Carolina: Hunter, 1979, 1981). H. A. Ivy, *Rum on the Run in Texas: A Brief History of Prohibition in the Lone Star State* (Dallas, 1910). Texas Equal Suffrage Association Scrapbook, Austin History Center.

Judith N. McArthur

ACHUBALE INDIANS. The Achubale Indians were one of twenty groups that joined Juan Domínguez de Mendoza[qv] on his journey from El Paso to the vicinity of present San Angelo in 1683–84. Since Domínguez did not indicate at what point the Achubales joined his party, it is impossible to determine their range or affiliations. Indians between the Pecos River and the San Angelo area were being hard pressed by Apache Indians at that time, and it seems likely that the Achubales ranged between these two localities.

BIBLIOGRAPHY: Herbert Eugene Bolton, ed., *Spanish Exploration in the Southwest, 1542–1706* (New York: Scribner, 1908; rpt., New York: Barnes and Noble, 1959).

Thomas N. Campbell

ACKERLY, TEXAS. Ackerly is on U.S. Highway 87 and at the junction of Farm roads 2002 and 2212, partly in the southeastern corner of Dawson County and partly in Martin County. It was established in 1923 with the breakup of the Slaughter Ranch into farming tracts. The town was named for its founder, Paul Ackerly, who was from Georgia. W. A. Wilson served as the first postmaster when the post office opened in 1924. A school district composed of portions of Dawson, Borden, Martin, and Howard counties was organized the following year, and a school was built and later expanded. Ackerly was the center for the local agricultural area and was incorporated in the early 1960s. In 1948 it had a population of 500, four gins, and thirty businesses. By 1980 the population had declined to 317. In 1990 the population was 243.

BIBLIOGRAPHY: Matthew Clay Lindsey, *The Trail of Years in Dawson County* (Fort Worth: Wallace, 1958?).

William R. Hunt

ACME, TEXAS. Acme, on U.S. Highway 287 four miles west of Quanah in central Hardeman County, developed around cement and plaster industries established there in the 1890s. In 1890 James Sickler, who operated a gypsum-processing plant in Kansas, discovered a large gypsum bed on Grosbeck Creek and reestablished his milling plant at the Texas site. He and his partners formed the Lone Star Cement Plaster Company, and later other Kansas manufacturers established another gypsum mill about a mile downstream from the first plant. The town's post office was established in 1898, and the Fort Worth and Denver City and Quanah, Acme, and Pacific railroads provided service. The Acme Tap Railroad Company was formed in 1909 when one of the gypsum plants refused to give its rival rail access. By the early 1900s the town had a hotel, a railway depot, a general store, and a school. Over the years a number of historic objects were discovered as a result of the open-pit gypsum excavations, including the remains of some prehistoric mastodons, which were said to have been sent to museums in St. Louis.

In 1945 the population of Acme was estimated at 400. The gypsum industry remained important to the town through the middle twentieth century, when Acme served as the home of the CertainTeed Products Corporation, once among the country's largest gypsum plants. The plant and mine closed during the 1960s, however, causing the community to decline. The population was estimated at fourteen in 1975. By the mid-1980s the old gypsum plant was owned and operated by the Georgia Pacific Corporation, which produced gypsum wallboard for the construction industry. Though little remained of the town except for scattered dwellings and the ruins of old buildings, Acme still reported a population of fourteen in 1990.

BIBLIOGRAPHY: T. Lindsay Baker, *Ghost Towns of Texas* (Norman: University of Oklahoma Press, 1986). Bill Neal, *The Last Frontier: The Story of Hardeman County* (Quanah, Texas: Quanah *Tribune-Chief,* 1966).

Alice J. Rhoades

ACME TAP RAILROAD. The Acme Tap Railroad, only 1.51 miles long, was one of the shortest common-carrier railroads in Texas. It began and ended in Acme, Hardeman County, where for several years there were two plaster plants, one operated by the Acme Cement Plaster Company, the other by the Salina Cement Plaster Company. One plant had a private side track, but the other could be reached only by crossing land belonging to the rival plant, which refused to grant an easement to the Fort Worth and Denver City for an industrial spur. Thus the Salina Company, on January 7, 1899, took out a charter for the Acme Tap Railroad Company as a common carrier to be built under contract by the FW&DC. Except for the period between April 1903 and January 1914, when it was leased by the Acme, Red River and Northern and its successor, the Quanah, Acme and Pacific, the Acme Tap was operated under lease by the FW&DC from the date of completion until the company was abandoned. The Acme Tap was never recognized by the Railroad Commission[qv] as a separate carrier. In 1931 the operation of the Salina Company plant ceased, and application was made to the Interstate Commerce Commission for authority to abandon the track, which was granted in January 1938.
H. Allen Anderson

ACOL, TEXAS. Acol was a boxcar post office of the Angelina County Lumber Company;[qv] the name of the office is an acronym of the company name. The Acol post office is associated with a site on the Southern Pacific Railway in northern Tyler County four miles northeast of Colmesneil. It served the lumber company's logging camps in Angelina, Tyler, and Polk counties during the 1930s and 1940s. When the office needed to be moved, it was hooked to a locomotive and rolled to its new location. *Megan Biesele*

A Chicano, *by Manuel G. Acosta, ca. 1971. Courtesy Baker Gallery of Fine Art, Lubbock, Texas.*

ACOSTA, MANUEL GREGORIO (1921–1989). Manuel Acosta, painter, sculptor, and illustrator, was born on May 9, 1921, in Aldama, Chihuahua, Mexico, the son of Ramón P. and Concepción Sánchez Acosta. The family moved in 1924 to El Paso, where a daughter and five more sons were born. Acosta grew up in various barrios of southern El Paso and graduated from Bowie High School in 1941. As a child he copied illustrations in newspaper advertisements and later sketched pin-up girls. He continued to sketch and paint while serving in the United States Air Force during World War II[qv] and decided to become an artist after seeing the work of Francisco de Goya and other masters while on tour in Europe.

After his discharge Acosta became an American citizen. In the fall of 1946 he attended the College of Mines and Metallurgy (now the University of Texas at El Paso), where he studied drawing and sculpture under sculptor Urbici Soler.[qv] He then studied for a year at the Chouinard Art Institute in Los Angeles and six months at the University of California, Santa Barbara, before returning to El Paso, where he established a home and studio and resumed his studies at Texas Western (1951–52). During this period Soler introduced Acosta to Peter Hurd,[qv] whom Acosta assisted in painting murals for the Prudential Insurance Company in Houston and the pioneer murals at the Museum of Texas Tech University[qv] in Lubbock. Hurd encouraged Acosta to use his Mexican-American heritage in his work, and the people and scenes in El Paso's barrios subsequently became Acosta's primary subject matter.

Acosta's talents began to be recognized in the mid-1950s, when he was commissioned to paint murals at the Casa Blanca Motel in Logan, New Mexico; the First National Bank in Las Cruces, New Mexico; and the Bank of Texas in Houston. He began exhibiting his work by participating in the Art U.S.A. exhibition in Missouri (1958), the Texas Watercolor Society exhibition (1960), the American Watercolor Society exhibition in New York City (1965), and the Hurd-Wyeth Family Group show in Roswell, New Mexico (1965). His first solo exhibition was mounted by the Chase Gallery, New York City, in 1962. His work was also exhibited at the Dallas Museum of Art,[qv] the Diamond M Foundation Museum in Snyder, the Chihuahua Art Museum in Mexico, and museums and galleries in Santa Fe, New Mexico, Lubbock, Texas, Scottsdale, Arizona, Santa Barbara, California, Tucson, Arizona, and Juárez, Chihuahua. The El Paso Museum of Art[qv] mounted a solo exhibition of his work in 1974, and in 1984 his work was included in a touring exhibition of watercolors sponsored by the Burlington Foundation. Acosta served as an advisor to the Texas Commission on the Arts[qv] and Humanities during the 1970s.

He painted the people and scenes of El Paso's barrios in a realistic style enlivened by lush colors and, in some works, a dramatic chiaroscuro effect. He worked primarily in oils, though he was fluent in such other media as watercolor, charcoal, casein, and tempera. He also sculpted some works in bronze. Acosta painted series of bullfighters, children, floral arrangements, and allegorical works based on popular songs of the Mexican Revolution.[qv] Perhaps his most successful works were his self-portraits and portraits of elderly Mexican-American women. In his painting of Doña Maria Caldera, for example, he conveyed the subject's dignity, humble character, and a life of hard work by focusing not only on her face, but also on her hands, which he described as the "question mark, the exclamation point to the person."

Acosta's paintings of El Paso's Mexican Americans won new appreciation and recognition during the Chicano[qv] movement of the mid-1960s and early 1970s. He painted a portrait of César Chávez for a 1969 *Time* magazine cover, and in 1971 illustrated *Canto y Grito Mi Liberación,* a book of poems and prose by Chicano activist Ricardo Sánchez. Acosta's painting *A Chicano-Portrait of Gonzalo Gómez,* which graces the cover of Sánchez's book, provides another example of his skill as a portraitist. The book also depicted people being beaten, Brown Berets, children playing in tenement hallways, and the humble dwellings in El Paso's barrios.

In the early 1970s Acosta was forced to move from his studio home to make way for a new highway. With the help of his family and friends he built a large stucco and adobe[qv] studio at his new home at 366 Buena Vista, which became the site for theatrical and musical performances as well as art activities. Although not an activist, Acosta supported the Chicano movement with his art and by making his studio available for political rallies and fund-raisers. He was murdered in his home on October 25, 1989, by Cesar Nájera Flores, a Mexican national. His work is represented in a number of public and private collections throughout the United States, including the National Portrait Gallery, Washington; the El Paso Museum of Art; the Museum of Texas Tech University, Lubbock; the Museum of New Mexico, Santa Fe; Harmsen's Western Collection, Colorado; and the Time, Incorporated, collection, New York City.

BIBLIOGRAPHY: "Acosta, A Man and His Art," *Nosotros* (El Paso, Texas), September 1972. Manuel Acosta, Interview by John H. McNeely, 1973, Institute of Oral History, University of Texas at El Paso. Dallas *Morning News*, October 27, 1989. El Paso *Times*, October 31, 1989. Dorothy Harmsen, *Harmsen's Western Americana: A Collection of One Hundred Western Paintings with Biographical Profiles of the Artists* (Flagstaff, Arizona: Northland Press, 1971). Salvador Valdez, "The Roots of Awareness," *Nosotros*, February 1, 1971.

Kendall Curlee

ACREE, ROBERT FRED (1878–1945). Fred Acree, businessman and collector of rare books and Texas memorabilia, was born to George Wren and Elizabeth Virginia (Grimes) Acree on March 26, 1878, at Cross Roads, Navarro County, Texas. He attended McGregor High School, Toby's Business College, and the University of Texas. He worked in a dry-goods store at Moody, then later formed a partnership, under the name Johnson and Acree, with another mercantile owner there. He also at one time owned a grocery store in Chilton with Clay Gilmore. Acree was mayor of Moody for several terms and also served as president of the local school board. He married Anna Byrd McLeod on September 19, 1906; they had three children. Acree moved his family to Waco on January 1, 1927, and established a real estate business there.

In 1892, at age fourteen, he had begun his book collecting when he purchased a pine bookcase filled with rare books. He preferred Texas, religious, and poetry books, and by the early 1940s his collection comprised some 5,000 volumes. He was also noted for about fifty drawings that he had done from photographs of famous people. Acree was a Baptist, a Mason, an Elk, and a member of the Democratic party,[qv] which he served for many years as the Moody precinct chairman. He was also a supporter of prohibition.[qv] Acree had memberships in various historical and literary organizations, including the McLennan County Historical Society, the Texas Poetical Society, and the Sons of the Republic of Texas.[qv] He died on August 29, 1945, and was buried at McGregor. After his death, much of his book collection was given to Baylor University, while many of his papers went to the University of Texas at Austin.

BIBLIOGRAPHY: Fred Acree Papers, Barker Texas History Center, University of Texas at Austin. Dayton Kelley, ed., *The Handbook of Waco and McLennan County, Texas* (Waco: Texian, 1972). Vertical Files, Barker Texas History Center, University of Texas at Austin.

Melanie Watkins

ACRES HOMES, TEXAS. Acres Homes, once considered the South's largest unincorporated black community, is south of Aldine and ten miles northwest of downtown Houston in Harris County. It developed around the time of World War I,[qv] when landholders began selling off homesites in plots big enough to allow small gardens and maintain chickens or farm animals. The town derived its name from the fact that land was sold by the acre and not by the lot. The first settlers came from rural areas, attracted by the community's inexpensive land, low taxes, and the absence of city building standards. Residents dug wells and built sanitary facilities, but conditions in the settlement subsequently declined. When the city of Houston approved a plan to annex the area and install water and sewer lines, Acres Homes was a 12½-square-mile, heavily wooded, dispersed slum settlement without transportation or educational facilities. Though 90 percent of the residents were homeowners, most housing was substandard.

In the 1960s congressman and future president George H. W. Bush sponsored a girls' softball team, the Bush All Stars, which played at Carver Park in the community. Acres Homes resident George F. Sampson was involved in a case that charged the Aldine Independent School District with racial discrimination against Sampson's sons. Though Sampson won his case in 1964, the district was not integrated until 1965. In 1970 a group of ministers persuaded the United States Department of Housing and Urban Development to build Lincoln Park, a 264-unit low-income housing project, at Acres Homes. Six years later the development, having fallen into disrepair, was repossessed by HUD. Rehabilitation began in the 1980s, but by then the project was troubled by crime and drug abuse. Lincoln Park reopened in 1986 after a $4.2 million federal investment brought central heat, a day-care center, and other major improvements. The community itself had become a sprawling working-class neighborhood of well-kept brick and frame homes interspersed with abandoned and dilapidated shacks. After November 1987 the War on Drugs Committee organized antidrug parades through the park, sponsored drug-prevention workshops, and encouraged reporting of illegal drug use. In 1989 President Bush and William Bennett returned to participate in events relating to the War on Drugs campaign in an effort to rid the park, renamed Winzer Park, of drug dealers. In 1988 a Citizens Chamber of Commerce was formed to help revive the community and handle growing conflict between local residents and Asian owners, primarily Vietnamese,[qv] of the twenty-six businesses that had moved into the community after 1975.

BIBLIOGRAPHY: Houston Metropolitan Research Center Files, Houston Public Library. Erika Sampson, "George Franklin Sampson: The Effect of One Man," *Texas Historian*, March 1990.

Diana J. Kleiner

ACRES HOMES TRANSIT COMPANY. The Acres Homes Transit Company, a small suburban transportation organization established in 1959, operated in response to the need for public commuter services in the predominantly African-American community of Acres Homes, nine miles northwest of downtown Houston. Acres Homes was outside of the city limits until the late 1960s, when it was annexed to Houston. Prior to 1959 local bus service in the community had been provided by the Yale Street Bus Line, which was owned by the Pioneer Bus Company, the largest of the suburban, privately owned transit companies in Houston. The Yale Street Bus Line ceased commuter services in Acres Homes in the fall of 1958. Left with no adequate system of public transportation, many of the area residents used "jitneys," or small, used-car taxis driven by independent operators. In Acres Homes these operators were usually residents of the community and went about their daily routine in open violation of municipal transportation codes. By July 1959 several residents from the area, including teachers, ministers, businessmen, and civic leaders, petitioned city hall for a permit to operate a suburban bus franchise from Acres Homes. The AHTC received a charter from the state of Texas and, on July 1, 1959, the city council granted a temporary permit to the company. Four buses made forty-three round trips a day between downtown Houston and Acres Homes. The AHTC became the first bus franchise in the South owned and operated by African Americans.[qv] The buses were driven by local drivers hired especially for the task. Acres Homes was annexed to Houston in 1967. The AHTC board members sold the company to the Houston Rapid

Transit Lines, the largest privately owned transit company in the city, in June of 1968 for $5,000.

BIBLIOGRAPHY: Inez Elmore, *Times to Remember: A Dynamic Autobiography* (Hicksville, New York: Exposition Press, 1979). Houston Metropolitan Research Center Files, Houston Public Library (City of Houston Public Service/Public Transportation).

Roger Townsend Ward

ACTON, TEXAS. Acton is on State Highway 4 five miles east of Granbury in Hood County. The site was cleared in 1866, when the area was in Johnson County. Acton is the oldest known settlement in Hood County. As early as 1845 there were reports of surveyors working in the area. Among the first white settlers was Charles Barnard,[qv] who built a trading post on the Brazos River in order to trade with the nearby Indians. It was reported that the friendly Caddo Indians in the area assisted in the defense of the settlers against the fierce Comanches. In 1856 the settlement received a post office with the orthographically strange name Camanche Peak.

In 1855 a church building was built for use by Baptists, Methodists, Presbyterians, and "Reformed Christians"; each group used the structure once a month. That year Aaron Farris erected a water mill at nearby Walnut Creek. The mill became a natural gathering place for the townspeople, so Farris established a type of "exchange store" in his home. The first permanent store was built by Clarence Hollis. The building served the community as a general store, post office, saloon, and blacksmith shop. Soon, teacher William Wright began to conduct the first school in the area. The first local physicians, J. C. Cornelius and S. R. McPherson, arrived in 1855 and 1858, respectively. Construction on the Masonic Hall commenced, and upon its completion in 1868 many new families chose to settle permanently in Acton.

Around 1861 the townspeople were commissioned to select a new name for the area. Several suggestions were offered, but the permanent choice was Acton. There are several explanations for the new name. The most common is that Hollis proposed the name in honor of his sweetheart, Miss Acton. It was also suggested that the name was derived from Oak Town, due to the large number of oak trees growing in the area. The Acton post office was officially established in 1861 and operated until 1906. By 1903 it was on a daily delivery route out of Granbury.

During the mid-1850s Elizabeth Crockett, the second wife of David Crockett,[qv] and two of her sons settled on the David Crockett survey, 320 acres granted to the widow by the state of Texas. Upon her death she was buried in the Acton Cemetery. In 1911 the state placed a statue of her in the cemetery. The Crockett plot, called the Acton State Historic Site,[qv] consists of .006 acres of land and now holds the distinction of being the smallest registered state park in Texas.

By 1887 the population of Acton was estimated to be 200. It was 164 in 1927, 142 in 1933, and 75 from 1949 through the early 1960s. The 1970 tally, however, reached 210. The population increased because of the construction from the mid-1960s to 1970 of the De Cordova Bend[qv] Dam nearby. Upon completion of Lake Granbury the population leveled off once again at 130. Another surge in the population occurred by 1988, when it was 450; at this time the Comanche Peak Steam Electric Station was being constructed in nearby Somervell County. Acton is surrounded by farm and ranch land and has several residential subdivisions, in which new residents are employed by the nuclear plant. Three neighboring communities, Pecan Plantation, De Cordova Bend Estates, and Port Ridglea, are highly populated. In 1990 the population of Acton was still 450.

BIBLIOGRAPHY: Thomas T. Ewell, *History of Hood County* (Granbury, Texas: Gaston, 1895; rpt., Granbury Junior Woman's Club, 1956). C. L. Hightower, ed., *Hood County in Picture and Story* (Fort Worth: Historical Publishers, 1970; rpt. 1978). Vertical Files, Barker Texas History Center, University of Texas at Austin. *Kristi Strickland*

ACTON STATE HISTORIC SITE. Acton State Historic Site, the smallest park in the state park system, is on Farm Road 1190 just outside of Acton in northeast Hood County. The .006-acre site comprises only the Crockett family plot in the old Acton Cemetery. The significant grave at the site is that of David Crockett's[qv] second wife, Elizabeth. The state does not own the site, but the Texas Parks and Wildlife Department[qv] maintains the plot.

BIBLIOGRAPHY: Ray Miller, *Texas Parks* (Houston: Cordovan, 1984).

Christopher Long

ACUFF, TEXAS. Acuff is on Farm roads 40 and 789 ten miles east of Lubbock in east central Lubbock County. The town is said to have been named for Michael S. Acuff, who reportedly arrived in the area in February 1891. Other early settlers were the Thomas Acuff, L. O. Burford, and Jim Brown families. Acuff's first school was constructed in 1902. It was a wooden structure built from lumber hauled in from as far away as Amarillo or Big Spring. A six-room brick schoolhouse was built in 1924, and in 1925 Acuff was designated an independent school district. However, by 1942 the community's children were attending the Roosevelt school, and by 1947 Acuff was a part of the Roosevelt district. Acuff had a post office from 1903 to 1912. During the 1940s one church building was used for both Baptist and Methodist church services, and in 1989 the Church of Christ was the only church in the community. Acuff recorded a steady population of approximately twenty-five during the 1930s and early 1940s. The population rose to fifty during the 1950s and 1960s and fell by 1990 to thirty. The Lubbock International Dragway is located near Acuff.

BIBLIOGRAPHY: Lawrence L. Graves, ed., *A History of Lubbock* (Lubbock: West Texas Museum Association, 1962). Mary Louise McDonald, The History of Lubbock County (M.A. thesis, University of Texas, 1942). *June Melby Benowitz*

ACWORTH, TEXAS. Acworth is thirteen miles northeast of Clarksville in northern Red River County. The town was named by J. H. Cox, an early settler, for his former home, Acworth, Georgia. Frank H. Clark became postmaster when a post office was established there in 1902. The population was fifty in 1910; in 1940 the settlement had the post office, a church, a school, a store, and a population of twenty. By 1956 the post office had been closed. From 1940 through 1986 the estimated population was consistently reported as twenty. In 1990 it was fifty-two. *Claudia Hazlewood*

ADA, TEXAS (Lampasas County). Ada, six miles southeast of Lometa on School Creek in central Lampasas County, was settled in 1875. A post office was established there in 1878, and the town was named for the daughter of William Malony, who became postmaster in 1880. Cotton was the chief product of this agricultural community. A Methodist church, a district school, a general store, and a population of twenty-five made up the settlement in 1885. The post office was discontinued in 1886, and no community center was reported in 1948. There have been no population listings for Ada since 1904.

Claudia Hazlewood

ADA, TEXAS (Nolan County). Ada was on Farm Road 1809 east of the Atchison, Topeka and Santa Fe Railway and north of Lake Trammell; the site is eight miles southwest of Sweetwater in central Nolan County. In 1897 Irving Wheatcroft, a railroad promoter, persuaded the citizens of Sweetwater to finance the construction of the Kansas City, Mexico and Orient Railway to link up Sweetwater with other lines to the south. The railroad was soon built to a point eight miles southwest of Sweetwater, and the new community laid out at that site was called Ada, after Wheatcroft's stenographer, Ada Cooper. The building of the railroad was delayed by financial difficulties, and the community developed slowly. In 1900 the owners of the railroad removed the rails and used them for another project, and when the

railroad was eventually built later in the decade it was laid out to the west of Ada. Ada Common School was built in 1899, and by 1904 it had one teacher and twenty-two pupils. In 1914 Lake Trammell was built to south of the community. By 1940, when the site was identified on maps as both Ada School and, a little to the west, Lake Trammell, it had the school and scattered dwellings. The school was consolidated with the Sweetwater schools in 1941, and the site was deserted by the 1980s.

BIBLIOGRAPHY: E. L. Yeats and Hooper Shelton, *History of Nolan County* (Sweetwater, Texas: Shelton, 1975).

Monica Smith and Rachel Piñeda

ADAES INDIANS. The Adaes (Atais, Atayos) were a Caddoan tribe inhabiting the Red River area north of the site of present Natchitoches, Louisiana. In 1699 Pierre le Moyne d'Iberville called them Natao. San Miguel de Linares de los Adaes Mission was established for them in 1716, destroyed in 1719, and restored in 1721. The Adaes were also found at San Francisco de los Tejas Mission. John R. Swanton said the Adaes spoke a divergent dialect and seemed to have had a more primitive culture than the other Caddoan tribes of the area.

BIBLIOGRAPHY: Frederick Webb Hodge, ed., *Handbook of American Indians North of Mexico* (2 vols., Washington: GPO, 1907, 1910; rpt., New York: Pageant, 1959).

Margery H. Krieger

ADAIR, ANTHONY GARLAND (1889–1966). Anthony Garland Adair, historian and curator of the Texas Memorial Museum,[qv] son of J. B. and Mattie (Palmer) Adair, was born in Queen City, Texas, on March 28, 1889. His father was a Methodist minister. Adair attended Wesley College in Terrell, Texas, and the University of Texas, where he was president of the Students' Assembly and Council and a member of the Cofer Law Society. After leaving the university and before World War I,[qv] Adair was editor of the Marshall *Messenger.* He entered the army in 1917; on September 1, 1918, he was commissioned a second lieutenant. On September 22 of that year he married Gladys Marie Ingram, a schoolteacher, of Texarkana. They became the parents of two daughters and one son.

After the war Adair edited and published newspapers at Hico, Mexia, Breckenridge, and McCamey. He was twice named a delegate to national Democratic conventions, from Hico in 1920 and from Mexia in 1924. He became active in the American Legion[qv] and was made commander of the Fifth Division in 1930. In 1932 he moved his family to Austin and assumed the duties of department historian for the legion. In 1935 he was named chairman of the Centennial Committee of the American Legion of Texas, which sponsored legislation to authorize the organization of a state museum. Adair conceived the idea of selling souvenir coins to raise money for the project, and fifty-cent silver coins commemorating the Texas Centennial[qv] were minted by the federal government. Sales raised some $92,000. Adair was named curator of patriotic exhibits when the Texas Memorial Museum opened in 1939; he later became curator of history, a position he held until his retirement in 1959.

He was coauthor of several books, among them *Texas, Its History,* with Ellen B. Coats (1954), and *Austin and Commodore Perry,* with E. H. Perry, Sr. (1956). He edited a series of Texas history periodicals during the 1940s and 1950s, including the *Texas Pictorial Handbook* and *Under Texas Skies.* He compiled a book of political cartoons depicting John Nance Garner[qv] (1958).

The Forty-seventh Texas Legislature named Adair commissioner for the 1945–46 observance of the Texas Centennial of Statehood.[qv] He was an honorary life member of the Sons of the Republic of Texas,[qv] a life member of the Texas State Historical Association,[qv] a fellow of the Texas Academy of Science,[qv] a member of the Texas Press Association and the Knights of the Order of San Jacinto,[qqv] an executive director of the Texas Heritage Foundation, and a Methodist. He died in Temple on December 14, 1966, and was buried in the State Cemetery[qv] at Austin.

BIBLIOGRAPHY: Austin *American,* March 28, 1964, December 15, 16, 1966. Vertical Files, Barker Texas History Center, University of Texas at Austin.

Willena C. Adams

ADAIR, CHRISTIA V. DANIELS (1893–1989). Christia Adair, black civil-rights activist and suffragist, was born on October 22, 1893, in Victoria, Texas, one of four children of Hardy and Ada (Crosby) Daniels. She attended a small school in Edna, then went to Austin with her brother in 1910 to attend high school at Samuel Huston College (now Huston-Tillotson College). She later went to Prairie View State Normal and Industrial College (now Prairie View A&M University), then taught at Edna and later at Vanderbilt, Texas. In 1918 she married Elbert H. Adair, a brakeman for the Missouri Pacific Railroad. The couple moved to Kingsville, where Christia Adair started a Sunday school and joined a biracial group of women opposed to gambling. She also became one of the few black suffragists in the state. When she attempted to vote after passage of the Nineteenth Amendment, however, she learned that state law concerning primary elections prevented her.

Hurt that she could still be denied the vote, she began shifting her focus to racial issues. When presidential candidate Warren G. Harding appeared in Kingsville in 1920, she had carefully situated several black children close to Harding, but when he finished speaking he reached over them to shake the hands of white listeners behind them. "I was offended and insulted and I made up my mind I wouldn't be a Republican ever," she later recalled. The Adairs moved in 1925 to Houston, where Mrs. Adair became an early member of the local branch of the National Association for the Advancement of Colored People.[qv]

Elbert Adair died in 1943, and for the next sixteen years Christia Adair remained active in the NAACP, which she served as executive secretary for twelve years. The Houston branch brought suit against a local election judge in *Smith v. Allwright* for denying the vote to a local black dentist, Dr. Lonnie Smith.[qv] The case, argued by NAACP special counsel Thurgood Marshall, was decided in favor of Smith by the United States Supreme Court in 1944. *Smith* was important in the history of civil rights law because it ended the use of race as a barrier to voting in Texas Democratic primaries (*see* WHITE PRIMARY). This and similar NAACP activities made the chapter a target for its opponents. Bomb threats were not uncommon. Although Christia Adair was sometimes frightened and told people she kept a gun in her home, she was remembered by others as unafraid. In 1957 Houston police attempted for three weeks to locate the chapter's membership list. While the official charge was barratry—the illegal solicitation of clients by attorneys—Adair believed the real purpose was to destroy the organization and its advocacy of civil rights. She testified for five hours in a three-week trial over the attempted seizure of NAACP records. Two years later, on appeal to the Supreme Court, Thurgood Marshall again won a decision for the organization. Adair never admitted having membership lists or having member's names. In 1959 the chapter disbanded and she resigned as executive secretary, though she later helped rebuild the group's rolls to 10,000 members.

She also helped desegregate the Houston Public Library,[qv] airport, veterans' hospital, and city buses. Partly as a result of her work, blacks became able to serve on juries, and the city's newspapers began referring to blacks with the same titles they used for whites; blacks became able to be hired for county government jobs. Christia Adair successfully desegregated a department store's dressing rooms when she insisted on using a room reserved for white women only. With Frankie Randolph,[qv] she founded the Harris County Democrats, an integrated alternative to the county's segregated Democratic organization. She was precinct judge of the third ward, one of the first blacks in Houston to serve as a judge. In 1960 a Harris County grand jury investi-

Christia Adair (far left) and friends at Samuel Huston College, Austin, ca. 1910–13. Courtesy Houston Metropolitan Research Center, Houston Public Library. In 1905, about the time Christia Adair would have begun to dream of going to college, Texas ranked sixth among the states in terms of African-American college graduates, but only a very few black Texans went to college.

gated the records of an election in her ward, and the process embittered her. In 1966 she was one of the first two blacks elected to the state Democratic committee. In response, the state party refused to seat the Harris County delegation, then agreed to seat only its two black members. She refused the offer.

Christia Adair was active in the Methodist Episcopal Church and was the first black woman elected to its general board. She was chairman of the Christian Social Concern program at Boynton United Methodist Church and served on its national board of missions. She was also active in the Texas Club, part of the National Association of Colored Women's and Girls' Club. She was one of fifty black women interviewed for an oral history of black women conducted by the Radcliffe College Schlesinger Library of History of Women in America, and in 1974 the Houston chapter of the National Organization for Women honored her for suffrage activism. She worked as a county clerk of absentee voting when she was well into her eighties. On her eighty-fourth birthday a county park in Houston was dedicated in her name. Christia Adair died on December 31, 1989.

BIBLIOGRAPHY: Doris T. Asbury, Negro Participation in the Primary and General Elections in Texas (M.A. thesis, Boston University, 1951). Alecia Davis, "Christia V. Adair: Servant of Humanity," *Texas Historian*, September 1977. Michael L. Gillette, The NAACP in Texas, 1937–1957 (Ph.D. dissertation, University of Texas at Austin, 1984). Houston *Chronicle*, October 23, 1977, March 10, 1980. Houston *Post*, February 25, 1972. Houston *Informer and Texas Freeman*, April 8, 1944. Mary Beth Rogers et al., *We Can Fly: Stories of Katherine Stinson and Other Gutsy Texas Women* (Austin: Texas Foundation for Women's Resources, 1983). Vertical Files, Barker Texas History Center, University of Texas at Austin. *Nancy Baker Jones*

ADAIR, CORNELIA WADSWORTH (1837–1921). Cornelia Wadsworth Adair, diarist and rancher, the second of the six children of Gen. James Samuel and Mary Craig (Wharton) Wadsworth, was born on April 6, 1837, in Philadelphia. She spent her early years at Hartford House, her father's country estate near Geneseo, New York. In 1855 the family left for a two-year sojourn in France and England. Soon after their return in 1857 Cornelia married Montgomery Ritchie, a grandson of Harrison Otis of Boston. Two sons were born to them. Her father and her husband died in 1864. The widowed Cornelia took her two small sons to Paris, where the older son died a few years later.

In 1867, while attending a ball in New York City given in honor of Congressman J. C. Hughes, Cornelia Ritchie met broker John G. Adair[qv] of Ireland. They were married in 1869 and afterward divided their time between America and their estates in England and Ireland. In the fall of 1874 they left Ireland to see the American West and to experience a buffalo hunt along the South Platte River in Nebraska and northeastern Colorado. Her brother had served as an aide to Philip H. Sheridan,[qv] and Cornelia Adair probably used the general's influence to obtain a military escort under Col. Richard Irving Dodge to accompany the party, which departed from Sydney Barracks in Nebraska Territory. She kept a detailed diary of the two-month journey, which included attending a council of cavalry officers and Oglala Sioux, near the South Platte. In 1918 she had it published.

In the summer of 1877, when her husband and Charles Goodnight[qv] formed a partnership to found the JA Ranch,[qv] Cornelia accompanied the party from Pueblo, Colorado, to the new ranch headquarters Goodnight had established in Armstrong County, Texas. Because the Adairs lived at the ranch only sporadically, Goodnight became its manager and, under orders from Cornelia Adair, paid high salaries for experienced, law-abiding ranchhands. After Adair died in 1885, Cornelia became Goodnight's partner. In 1887 she traded a second ranch for his one-third interest in the JA, a share that comprised 336,000 acres, 48,000 cattle, assorted mules, horses, and equipment, and rights to the JA brand. Although she was a naturalized British subject and spent most of her time in Ireland, Cornelia Adair also maintained a home in Clarendon and contributed generously to various civic projects in the vicinity of the JA Ranch, which by 1917 covered half a million acres. She provided funds to build the Adair Hospital and the first YMCA building in Clarendon and strongly supported that community's Episcopal church. She also vigorously promoted the Boy Scout movement since she knew Lord Baden-Powell and many other of its British organizers. She died on September 22, 1921, and was buried next to her husband in Ireland. In 1984 the Adairs' Glenveagh Castle, which sheltered Belgian refugees during World War I,[qv] became an Irish national park.

BIBLIOGRAPHY: Cornelia Adair, *My Diary: August 30 to November 5, 1874* (Austin: University of Texas Press, 1965). Armstrong County Historical Association, *A Collection of Memories: A History of Armstrong County, 1876–1965* (Hereford, Texas: Pioneer, 1965). Virginia Browder, *Donley County: Land O' Promise* (Wichita Falls, Texas: Nortex, 1975). Harley True Burton, *A History of the JA Ranch* (Austin: Von Boeckmann–Jones, 1928; rpt., New York: Argonaut, 1966). J. Evetts Haley, *Charles Goodnight* (Norman: University of Oklahoma Press, 1949). *Nancy Baker Jones*

ADAIR, JOHN GEORGE (?–1885). John George Adair, Panhandle[qv] cattleman, was an English aristocrat of Scots-Irish descent who owned vast estates in England and Ireland. He was educated and trained for the diplomatic service but entered the world of finance instead. In 1866 he made his first visit to the United States and established a brokerage firm in New York City for the purpose of placing British loans in America at higher interest rates than those in Britain. The following year, at a ball given in honor of Congressman J. C. Hughes, he met Mrs. Cornelia Wadsworth Ritchie, whom he married in 1869 (*see* ADAIR, CORNELIA W.).

Over the next several years the couple divided their time between Ireland and America. In the fall of 1874 they went on a buffalo hunt along the South Platte River in Nebraska and northeastern Colorado, accompanied by a military escort from Sydney Barracks under Col. Richard Irving Dodge. Adair killed no buffalo but accidentally shot his horse and almost killed himself. Nevertheless, he liked the opportunities the West had to offer and in 1875 moved his brokerage business to Denver, Colorado. The firm made a loan to Charles Goodnight[qv] in March 1876, and Adair sought him out when he decided to enter the cattle business. They entered into a partnership on June 18, 1877, in which Adair furnished the money and Goodnight the herd for the JA Ranch[qv] in Palo Duro Canyon.[qv] The Adairs accompanied the Goodnight party from Pueblo, Colorado, to the ranch headquarters in Armstrong County and stayed just long enough to inspect the range, help tally the cattle, and hunt game before departing for their estate near Rathdair. Adair's conventional, and sometimes arrogant, British mannerisms were received poorly by the cowboys; even Goodnight later admitted that his partner's overbearing attitude was irritating. However, when the original agreement expired in 1882, the ranch showed a profit of $512,000, and the owners renewed the partnership for five more years.

In the spring of 1885 Adair made his third and final trip to the JA, accompanied by his personal valet. He died on his return trip at St. Louis, on May 14, 1885. His body was shipped to Rathdair for burial on his estate. His wife maintained the partnership with Goodnight until it expired in 1887.

BIBLIOGRAPHY: Cornelia Adair, *My Diary: August 30 to November 5, 1874* (Austin: University of Texas Press, 1965). Harley True Burton, *A History of the JA Ranch* (Austin: Von Boeckmann–Jones, 1928; rpt., New York: Argonaut, 1966). Willie Newbury Lewis, *Between Sun and Sod* (Clarendon, Texas: Clarendon Press, 1938; rev. ed., College Station: Texas A&M University Press, 1976). *H. Allen Anderson*

ADAIR NORMAL SCHOOL. Adair Normal School was a private school in Whitesboro, west central Grayson County. In 1894 C. L. and Noah Adair leased the building that previously was the home of the Shilow Baptist Institute. The two-story facility, constructed in 1889 at the corner of Main and College streets, housed the Adair Normal School for two years. During that time the Adairs attempted to establish a college-level academic institution. Enrollment and financial problems, however, led to the closing of the school in 1896.

BIBLIOGRAPHY: Grayson County Frontier Village, *History of Grayson County, Texas* (2 vols., Winston-Salem, North Carolina: Hunter, 1979, 1981). Graham Landrum and Allen Smith, *Grayson County* (Fort Worth, 1960; 2d ed., Fort Worth: Historical Publishers, 1967).
David Minor

ADALIA, TEXAS. Adalia was twelve miles northeast of Lockhart in northeast Caldwell County. The settlement, named by early settler Walton Rife for his daughter, Ada, began in the 1870s as a center for cattle raising. By the turn of the century its economy had shifted to crops, primarily cotton, corn, and cane. A post office was established at Walton Rife's Blue Store in 1901 and discontinued in 1904. The Adalia school was consolidated with the Lytton Springs school in the 1930s. Adalia had ceased to exist by the 1970s.

BIBLIOGRAPHY: Carl C. Wright, "Prairie Scenes and Moods," *Southwestern Historical Quarterly* 72 (January 1969). *Carl C. Wright*

ADAMS, ANDY (1859–1935). Andy Adams, author, was born on May 3, 1859, in Whitley County, Indiana, to Andrew and Elizabeth (Elliott) Adams, who belonged to a cultured pioneer Scots-Irish family. He became one of the few writers of the West who had a knowledge based on experience that enabled him to record cowboy life authentically. From early youth he helped his two brothers with cattle and horses on their father's farm. After attending a rural elementary school for a few years, he left home and worked for a year at a lumbermill in Arkansas. Adams traveled to Texas in the early 1880s and remained there for ten years, eight of which he spent in traildriving. He had become a foreman before he left the trail in 1890. After that he remained in Texas two more years, during which he was a partner in an unsuccessful mercantile venture in Rockport. In 1892 he drifted to gold-mining camps in Colorado and Nevada and in 1894 moved to Colorado Springs, where he lived until his death, with the exception of one year in Nevada (1908–09) and two years in Kentucky (1920–22). Adams was forty-three when he began writing. After his first book was published in 1903, he ran unsuccessfully for sheriff of El Paso County, Colorado. He ran two more times but was never elected.

Texas was Adams's literary domain. He waited a score of years for the belated recognition that finally came when he was an old man, but he never relinquished a vital interest in the state as a literary source. His available published works comprise seven books and one article. Also, the copyright for a play, "Corporal Segundo, A Pastoral in Three Parts," was issued in 1898, but no copy has been found. While he lived in Colorado, Adams wrote dozens of manuscripts—novels, dramas, short stories, and lectures—that were never published. Because he knew the real West, he was able to write with a remarkable verisimilitude—a quality he maintained without compromise, though it led to many rejected manuscripts, since publishers seemed to demand "Wild West" stories. In spite of his admitted limitations of style, he was an honest interpreter of western culture. In later years he took great interest in sponsoring authentic western fiction among younger writers. *The Log of a Cowboy,* Adams's best work, was published in 1903. It tells of a five-month drive of over 3,000 cattle from Brownsville to Montana in 1882 and has been called the best chronicle written of the great days in the cattle country. Other books followed: *A Texas Matchmaker* (1904), *The Outlet* (1905), *Cattle Brands* (1906), *Reed Anthony, Cowman* (1907), *Wells Brothers* (1911), and *The Ranch on the Beaver* (1927). Five of the books were sold in England by London publishers. The books and an article, "Western Interpreters," in the *Southwest Review*[qv] (October 1924), make up the available works published over Andy Adams's name.

Adams, a large man of strong physique, enjoyed good health until his last year. He was bachelor by choice who lived quietly and simply and was reticent about himself. He died on September 26, 1935, and was buried in Colorado Springs, Colorado.

BIBLIOGRAPHY: J. Frank Dobie, *Andy Adams, Cowboy Chronicler* (Dallas: Southern Methodist University Press, 1926). Jean Shelley Henry, Andy Adams (M.A. thesis, Texas Christian University, 1938). Wilson Mathis Hudson, *Andy Adams: His Life and Writings* (Dallas: Southern Methodist University Press, 1964). Wilson Mathis Hudson, *Andy Adams: Storyteller and Novelist of the Great Plains* (Austin: Steck–Vaughn, 1967). A. L. Schafer, "Andy Adams, Author," *True West*, December 1964. Vertical Files, Barker Texas History Center, University of Texas at Austin. *Jean Shelley Henry*

ADAMS, CARLETON W. (1885–1964). Carleton W. Adams, architect, was born in Alma, Nebraska, on November 26, 1885, the son of Jay E. Adams, a prominent real estate developer. In 1890 the elder Adams moved his family to San Antonio, Texas, where he was involved in developing the north-side area now in the Monte Vista Historic District.qv Adams attended Main Avenue High School in San Antonio and subsequently studied architecture at Columbia University, where he graduated with a bachelor of architecture degree in 1909. He returned to San Antonio and together with his uncle Carl C. Adams founded the architecture firm of Adams and Adams. After Carl Adams died in 1918, Max C. Friedrich, a senior employee, became an associate member of the firm.

Among Adams's early works was the Mediterranean-style Santa Gertrudis ranchhouse at the King Ranch,qv completed in 1917. Although he continued to design houses for many of San Antonio's elite, Adams specialized in large commercial and public structures. During the late teens and 1920s he and his associates produced a number of multistory buildings in the Beaux-Arts style then reigning, including the San Antonio Drug Company Building (1919), the San Antonio National Bank of Commerce, the Great American Life Insurance Building in San Antonio (1925), the Kerr County Courthouse in Kerrville, the Sames-Moore Building in Laredo, and the Nixon Office Building in Corpus Christi. Like most architects at the time, however, Adams produced works in a variety of styles and types. Among the best known of these is the Spanish Colonial–revival Jefferson High School in San Antonio (1930–32), which received national attention. In the early 1930s Adams also began to experiment with Art Deco style; he produced several of the state's best examples in the Texas State Highway Building in Austin (1931), the Alamo Cenotaphqv in San Antonio (1936, with sculptures by Pompeo Coppiniqv), and the Hall of Stateqv (1936) at the State Fair of Texasqv in Dallas. Among Adams's other important works were the Student Union Building at Texas A&M in College Station (1950) and the State Archives and Library Building in Austin (1962).

Adams married Marcia Booth in 1909. The couple had three children. Adams was a member of the American Institute of Architects and the Presbyterian Church. He was also active in the San Antonio Rotary Club and served for a time as its president. He died of a heart attack while on a hunting trip on his ranch in Devine on November 20, 1964, and was buried in Mission Burial Park, San Antonio.

BIBLIOGRAPHY: Ellis A. Davis and Edwin H. Grobe, comps., *The New Encyclopedia of Texas* (2 vols., Dallas: Texas Development Bureau, 1925?). Christopher Long, "Adams and Adams," *Texas Architect*, November–December 1989. San Antonio *Express News*, November 21, 1964. *Christopher Long*

ADAMS, JED COBB (1876–1935). Jed Cobb Adams, lawyer and politician, the son of Z. T. and Elizabeth (Ratliff) Adams, was born on January 14, 1876, in Kaufman, Texas. He attended Southwestern University in Georgetown from 1889 to 1891 and Bingham School in Asheville, North Carolina, in 1892–93. He was admitted to the State Bar of Texasqv in 1895. On December 1, 1897, he married Allie Nash, also from Kaufman. The couple had two children.

Although Adams was active politically throughout his life, he held comparatively few public offices. From 1898 to 1902 he was state's attorney in Kaufman County. He was a major in the judge advocate general's department of the United States Army in Governors Island, New York, from October 1918 to April 1919. Afterward he received a commission as a lieutenant colonel in the reserve corps. From October 1919 until his resignation in January 1920, he was United States attorney for the Northern District of Texas. He was a member of the United States Board of Tax Appeals from May 1933 until his death.

For most of his adult life Adams maintained a successful private law practice, first at Kaufman and then in Dallas, to where he moved in 1909. He was a lifelong Democrat and was active in the party at the state and national level. He was a delegate to the 1904 Democratic national convention, a member of the Democratic state executive committee in 1906, and a Democratic presidential elector in 1908. From 1924 to 1934 he was a member of the national Democratic executive committee. Although he had long opposed James and Miriam Ferguson,qqv Adams supported Miriam for governor in 1924 because her principal opponent was backed by the Ku Klux Klan;qv Adams spoke at several of Ma Ferguson's anti-Klan rallies during the campaign. In 1928 he gained nationwide attention for his opposition to the Texas Democrats who supported Herbert Hoover for president. Claiming that continued national Republican rule would endanger the South's Jim Crow laws and lead to integrated public schools, Adams called for the ouster of any Texas Democratic party leader who refused to support Al Smith.

Adams was a member of the Texas Bar Association, the American Bar Association, the American Legion,qv and the Methodist Church. In 1931 he received an honorary LL.D. degree from the Jefferson School of Law. After a brief illness he died in Washington, D.C., on January 29, 1935. He was buried in Kaufman, Texas.

BIBLIOGRAPHY: Norman D. Brown, *Hood, Bonnet, and Little Brown Jug: Texas Politics, 1921–1928* (College Station: Texas A&M University Press, 1984). Dallas *Morning News*, January 31, 1935.

Cecil Harper, Jr.

ADAMS, NATHAN (1869–1966). Nathan Adams, banker and civic leader, was born on November 26, 1869, near Pulaski, Tennessee, the youngest of seven children of Nathan and Susan (Pankey) Adams. His father, a major in the Confederate Army and a lawyer, died when Adams was five years old, and afterward Mrs. Adams taught at Giles College to support her family. Adams attended public schools in Pulaski, but a foot injury caused him to quit Giles College after a year, and the financial needs of his family prevented his return. He began his business career as cash boy in a general store and later became a runner for the People's National Bank of Pulaski, manager of a bookstore, and bookkeeper for both the Giles National Bank and a grocery store.

When Adams adeptly prepared a statement for a family friend, who was also treasurer of the Texas and Pacific Railway, the friend invited him to come to Dallas. In December 1887 Adams borrowed seventy-five dollars to make the trip and soon thereafter began work as an agent in the auditing department of the railroad. By the next year, however, he had returned to banking as a utility and relief man at the National Exchange Bank. During a series of mergers he rose swiftly through the ranks. He became the president of the First National Bank of Dallas, the largest bank in the South, in 1929. In 1944 he became chairman of the board. He retired in 1950 at the age of eighty as honorary board chairman.

Adams was sometimes called the "dean of Texas bankers." He is credited with developing programs that averted disasters for the Texas cotton industry in 1907 and for the Texas wool industry in 1931. He also helped build the independent oil and gas industry in the state by accepting proved underground oil reserves as collateral for the financing of large-scale production. He secured the location of the Federal Reserve Bank of Dallas[qv] as well as the Texas Centennial[qv] Central Exposition, the board of which he chaired. Accordingly, he has been credited with the regional financial preeminence of Dallas. Adams was president of the Texas Bankers Association[qv] (1913–14), a member of the executive council of the American Bankers Association, a Hoover appointee to the Federal Home Loan Bank Board, and a director of the United States Chamber of Commerce (1931–32).

During World War I[qv] he managed the sale of treasury certificates worth $75 million. During World War II[qv] he headed a Texas sales campaign that totaled over $4.5 billion worth of government securities. He was instrumental in the founding of the Texas Scottish Rite Hospital for Crippled Children, served on its board for over twenty-five years, and collected more than $1 million in contributions. He was a Shriner and Scottish Rite Mason.

Adams married Elizabeth Kirtley Ardinger on November 4, 1891; they had one daughter. He was a member of the Episcopal Church. Although a conservative Democrat, he opposed prohibition.[qv] He lived at the Scottish Rite Hospital in failing health for the last four years of his life and died there on June 17, 1966.

BIBLIOGRAPHY: Dallas *Morning News*, April 20, 1939, June 18, 1966. Dallas *Times Herald*, April 23, 1930, June 19, 1966. *Joan J. Perez*

ADAMS, RAMON FREDERICK (1889–1976). Ramon Adams, writer and bibliographer of the American West, son of Cooke M. and Charlie (Colby) Adams, was born at Moscow, Texas, on October 3, 1889. When he was thirteen the family moved to Sherman, where his father operated a jewelry business for twenty years. Adams enrolled in the Sherman Private School, run by John H. LeTellier, in 1903 and entered Austin College as a subfreshman in 1905. He was literary editor of the students' monthly magazine, *Reveille*, in 1907 but dropped out in 1909; he subsequently returned, however, and graduated in 1912. He also studied violin under Carl Venth[qv] at Kidd-Key College in Sherman.

In 1912 he joined the music department at the University of Arkansas, where he taught violin until 1914. While there he married Allie Jarman before moving to Chicago for further training and teaching. After a few years he returned to Texas to head the violin department at Wichita Falls College of Music and lead the orchestra at the Majestic Theater. Later he moved to the Dallas–Fort Worth area, where he continued to play in theater orchestras. His musical career ended when he broke his wrist cranking a Model T Ford. In 1929 Adams and his wife opened a retail candy business in Dallas. It became so successful that they expanded it into a wholesale operation, which lasted until 1955.

Adams had long been interested in Western lore, especially that pertaining to cattle. He privately printed his first book, *Poems of the Canadian West*, in 1919. He sold his first story to *Western Story Magazine* in 1923 and published *Cowboy Lingo* in 1936. A flood of publications followed these. One of his major contributions was capturing the language and habits of the men who rode the range. *Cowboy Lingo* was followed by *Western Words, A Dictionary of the Range* (1944); *The Old-Time Cowhand* (1961), narrated entirely in the language of a cowpuncher; and *The Cowman Says It Salty* (1971). With these and other works, such as *Come an' Get It: The Story of the Old Cowboy Cook* (1952), Adams added significantly to the literature of range life. With Homer Britzman he also wrote *Charles M. Russell, the Cowboy Artist: A Biography* (1948).

With grants from several foundations, Adams ranged far and wide to gather his material, interviewing old-timers, examining private and public collections, and amassing his own sizable library. He became an expert bibliographer and developed a passion for separating the myth from the reality of the West, especially as it related to gunmen. He produced five bibliographical gems: *Six-Guns and Saddle Leather* (1954), *The Rampaging Herd* (1959), *Burrs under the Saddle* (1964), *The Adams One-Fifty* (1976), and *More Burrs Under the Saddle* (1979).

Adams was a Presbyterian and a member of the Texas Institute of Letters.[qv] He was honored by Austin College in 1968 with a Litt.D. degree and remained active into his eighties. He died in Dallas on April 29, 1976.

BIBLIOGRAPHY: Ramon F. Adams, "The Cowman's Philosophy," *American West*, Fall 1965. Dallas *Morning News*, May 1, 1976. W. David Laird, "A Dedication to the Memory of Ramon F. Adams, 1889–1976," *Arizona and the West* 28 (Winter 1986). Howard R. Lamar, ed., *The Reader's Encyclopedia of the American West* (New York: Crowell, 1977). *Southwestern Historical Quarterly*, Clippings, January 1977. Vertical Files, Barker Texas History Center, University of Texas at Austin.
Edward Hake Phillips

ADAMS, REBECCA ANN PATILLO BASS (1826–1867). Rebecca Ann Patillo Bass Adams, pioneer, daughter of Hamblin Bass[qv] and Elizabeth (Saunders) Harris Bass, was born on December 11, 1826, in Hancock County, Georgia. Hamblin Bass owned a plantation near the Oconee River. Rebecca attended Eatonton Female Seminary in Eatonton, Georgia. According to her correspondence at the time, she probably studied a variety of subjects including history, chemistry, geography, and Greek literature. She was also an accomplished pianist. On January 15, 1845, she married Robert Adams, the son of a planter who lived nearby. After the couple's first child was born in 1846, Robert left Rebecca and their son with her parents and went to Philadelphia to begin studying to become a physician; in 1848 he completed his education at South Carolina Medical College, Charleston. After living in Eatonton for about ten years, the Adams family decided to move to Texas to join Hamblin Bass, who had bought the famous Waldeck Plantation[qv] near the site of present East Columbia. Leaving behind a plantation, a medical practice, and a real estate business, in December 1859 the Adamses packed up their six children, fifty slaves, and seven hounds and started the long journey to Texas. They were delayed in Mobile, Alabama, when Rebecca had her seventh child. Hamblin Bass traveled by boat to Mobile, picked up the couple's two sons, the slaves, and the wagons, and took them overland to Texas. When Rebecca recovered, she and the other members of the family traveled by ship from Mobile to Galveston and then overland to Waldeck. She and her family lived there with Hamblin Bass for about a year until they bought the Huckaby Plantation, in Freestone County near Fairfield. In December 1860 they moved into their first log house. During the Civil War,[qv] Dr. Adams and his eldest son, Robert, served in the Confederate Army. The two men were stationed in various camps in Texas and were able to make frequent trips home. The task of running the plantation, however, fell to Rebecca, and she endured great hardship as she managed the extensive property, bore another child, cared for fifty slaves, and nursed the slaves as well as her children through many bouts with life-threatening illness, including smallpox.

After the war ended, the Adams family moved to Houston. Rebecca became ill, and she and the children moved to Waldeck for a short time. Her health deteriorated rapidly, and the family moved back to Freestone County. On October 5, 1867, Rebecca died of tuberculosis. She was buried in Fairfield, Texas. She had borne eleven children. During her life she had saved hundreds of family letters, many of which were edited and published by her granddaughter, Gary Doyle Woods, in a book entitled *The Hicks-Adams-Bass-Floyd-Patillo and Collateral Lines, Together with Family Letters, 1840–1868*. This book is a valuable resource for information on plantation life in Texas. Rebecca Adams meticulously saved records of plantation parties, social programs, and inventories of goods. Her letters after her family arrived in Texas revealed the economics of the area as well as the daily happenings of life. They give insight into that era's expectations of husbands for their wives regarding motherhood. Robert Adams, for example, expected a large family, and in one letter to Rebecca after the birth of another child, her sister-in-law offered to "sympathize with and congratulate" her on the new birth.

BIBLIOGRAPHY: Jo Ella Powell Exley, ed., *Texas Tears and Texas Sunshine: Voices of Frontier Women* (College Station: Texas A&M University Press, 1985). Freestone County Historical Commission, *History of Freestone County, Texas* (Fairfield, Texas, 1978). Elizabeth Silverthorne, *Plantation Life in Texas* (College Station: Texas A&M University Press, 1986). Abner J. Strobel, *The Old Plantations and Their Owners of Brazoria County* (Houston, 1926; rev. ed., Houston: Bowman and Ross, 1930; rpt., Austin: Shelby, 1980).

Jo Ella Powell Exley

ADAMS, ROBERT (1847–1944). Robert Adams, rancher and pioneer, was born in Norfolk, England, on March 9, 1847, the son of Robert and Sarah (Anderson) Adams. The family moved to Corpus Christi, Texas, in 1852. During the Civil War[qv] Adams and his brother William Adams[qv] hauled cotton to Brownsville to be shipped through Mexico to Europe. In 1867 the two brothers formed a partnership and began to raise sheep in the area that was then northwest Nueces County and later became Jim Wells County. In 1869 they preempted 320 acres on Tecolote Creek, fourteen miles north of Alice, the beginning of the Tecolote Ranch. In 1878 they fenced their land and began to breed and raise cattle; they were among the first to bring Durham bulls to Texas. In 1888 they purchased the Farías grant, two leagues adjoining their property. In 1893 the brothers divided their property, and Robert kept the Tecolote Ranch. Both brothers were involved in the establishment of Jim Wells County in 1912. Robert Adams married Lorena McWhorter on August 8, 1867. They had eight children. He died on August 26, 1944, and was buried on the ranch.

BIBLIOGRAPHY: *Cattleman*, June 1930, October 1944. James Cox, *Historical and Biographical Record of the Cattle Industry* (2 vols., St. Louis: Woodward and Tiernan Printing, 1894, 1895; rpt., with an introduction by J. Frank Dobie, New York: Antiquarian, 1959). Ellis A. Davis and Edwin H. Grobe, comps., *The New Encyclopedia of Texas*, 1929. *Frontier Times*, May 1929.

John G. Johnson

ADAMS, WALTER R. (1897–1971). Walter R. Adams, poet, was born at Purmela, Texas, on January 25, 1897, one of fourteen children of James and Emma Adams. He attended Ireland High School and Baylor Normal College, served in the United States armed forces during World War I,[qv] and then taught school at Hay Valley, Purmela, and Ireland. He spent the rest of his life farming and writing. Three collections of his verse, *The Dead Lie Down* (1934), *Bachelor's Poppy* (1940), and *High to the Fruits* (1949), were published by the Kaleidograph Press of Dallas (see KALEIDOGRAPH). His poetry was published in many periodicals and anthologies, and he received numerous honors and literary awards. He was a charter member of the Texas Institute of Letters[qv] and the Fort Belknap Archives Association. At the time of his death at Gatesville, on June 27, 1971, he was honorary vice president of the Poetry Society of Texas.[qv] A collection of his works is on display at the restored Fort Belknap Museum near Graham. Adams never married.

BIBLIOGRAPHY: Vaida Stewart Montgomery, *A Century with Texas Poets and Poetry* (Dallas: Kaleidograph, 1934). Vertical Files, Barker Texas History Center, University of Texas at Austin.

William E. Bard

ADAMS, WAYMAN (1883–1959). Wayman Adams, portrait artist, son of Nelson Perry and Mary Elizabeth (Justice) Adams, was born in Muncie, Indiana, on September 23, 1883. His father, a farmer and amateur painter, died when Adams was young, and the youth received no formal education beyond the sixth grade. His artistic ability was recognized early. At twelve he won first prize at the Indiana State Fair, and at sixteen he received his first portrait commission, to paint a picture of a prize heifer for five dollars. He first studied painting at the John Herron Institute in Indianapolis under William Forsythe. At the urging of Booth Tarkington he went to New York and studied at the Grand Central Art School. He also studied under Robert Henri in Spain and William Merritt Chase in Italy. In 1914 he won his first major award, the Thomas R. Proctor Prize of the National Academy of Design in New York. On October 1, 1918, Adams married Margaret Graham Burroughs, another student of Chase in Italy; they had one son.

Adams was considered one of America's leading portrait painters long before he established permanent residence in Austin, Texas, in 1948. He had exhibited at the National Academy of Design (1914, 1926, 1932), the Art Institute of Chicago (1918), the American Watercolor Society (1930), the Salmagundi Club (1931, 1940), the Pennsylvania Academy of Fine Arts (1929, 1933), the Carnegie Institute (1943), the Hoosier Salon (1925–26, 1929, 1931, 1935), and many other institutions. He maintained a studio in New York City for most of the years of his career.

His first sizable commission was a portrait of Booth Tarkington. He subsequently painted such notables as presidents Warren G. Harding, Calvin Coolidge, and Herbert Hoover, Vice President Henry Wallace, generals Jonathan Mayhew Wainwright[qv] and Walter Krueger,[qv] industrialist B. F. Goodrich, Col. Edward M. House,[qv] Clara Driscoll,[qv] golfer Bobby Jones, Texas governors Beauford Jester[qv] and Allan Shivers,[qv] and J. Frank Dobie.[qv] One of his best-known works, a portrait of the Russian cellist Gregor Piatigorsky, won a $1,000 prize when it was exhibited in the 1943 Painting in the United States exhibition held at the Carnegie Institute in Pittsburgh. Adams worked in a fluid style heavily influenced by the bravura technique of his teacher William Merritt Chase. He finished portraits in one or two days, depending on their size. He preferred oil paints, but occasionally worked in watercolors.

He taught at the Grand Central Art Galleries in New York, the John Herron Art Institute in Indianapolis, and a school and art colony in Elizabethtown, New York, that he and his wife established. In 1935 and 1936 he conducted an art school in Taxco, Guerrero, Mexico. He received an honorary doctor of arts degree at Syracuse University in 1943. He was a member of the National Academy of Design, the National Institute of Arts and Letters, the New York Society of Painters, the National Association of Portrait Painters, the American Water Color Society, the Allied Artists of America, the Salmagundi Club, and the Texas Fine Arts Association.[qv] Adams and his wife lived from 1948 to 1959 in Austin, where their home became a magnet for artists and authors. Adams died of a heart attack on April 7, 1959. His work is represented in the Indianapolis Museum of Art, the Art Institute of Chicago, the Yale University Art Gallery, the San Antonio Museum Association,[qv] the Texas State Library,[qv] and other institutions.

BIBLIOGRAPHY: Austin *American-Statesman*, March 3, 1950, April 8, 1959. Peter Haskins Falk, ed., *Who Was Who in American Art* (Madison, Connecticut: Sound View, 1985). F. N. Levy, ed., *American Art Annual* (37 vols., Washington: American Federation of Arts, 1898–1948). Vertical Files, Barker Texas History Center, University of Texas at Austin. *Who's Who in American Art.*

Joseph E. Blanton and Kendall Curlee

ADAMS, WILLIAM (1846–1939). William Adams, sheep rancher and public servant, son of Robert and Sarah (Anderson) Adams, was born in Norfolk, England, on January 3, 1846. With his brother, Robert Adams,[qv] and his parents he moved to Corpus Christi, Texas, in 1852. He began sheep ranching in partnership with Robert in 1867. The partnership operated in the Nueces River valley until 1893, when Adams moved to a large ranch near Alice that he had bought in 1891. He later moved into Alice. For sixteen years he was county commissioner of Nueces County. He became president of the Alice Cotton

Oil Company and vice president of the South Texas Cattle Loan Company and the Alice Broom Corn Drying Company. He helped organize Jim Wells County in 1912 and served as ex officio county judge for a while. He married Sarah Dodson in January 1867, and after her death in 1894 he married Nina O. Young. He was the father of seven children. He died on January 12, 1939, at his home in Alice and was survived by two daughters and three sons.

BIBLIOGRAPHY: James Cox, *Historical and Biographical Record of the Cattle Industry* (2 vols., St. Louis: Woodward and Tiernan Printing, 1894, 1895; rpt., with an introduction by J. Frank Dobie, New York: Antiquarian, 1959). *Frontier Times*, May 1929.

Richard Allen Burns

ADAMS, WILLIAM WIRT (1819–1888). William Wirt Adams, son of Judge George and Anna (Weissiger) Adams, was born at Frankfort, Kentucky, on March 22, 1819. Returning from college in Bardstown, Kentucky, in 1839, he enlisted as a private in Col. Edward Burleson's[qv] command for service in the Republic of Texas.[qv] Adams was soon made adjutant of the regiment and was in the campaign against the Indians in northeast Texas. In autumn of 1839 he returned to Mississippi. Throughout the 1840s and 1850s Adams made a living in banking and agriculture. He married Sallie Huger Magrant in 1850. They had no children. In 1858 he served in the Mississippi legislature, and in 1861 he worked as a Confederate commissioner in Louisiana attempting to convince the state to secede. After the formation of the Confederate States of America, Adams declined Jefferson Davis's offer to serve as postmaster general. He subsequently raised a regiment, the First Mississippi Cavalry to fight in the Civil War.[qv] In September 1863 Adams was commissioned a brigadier general. Following the war he lived in Vicksburg and Jackson, where he served as postmaster in 1885. In 1888 Adams died in Jackson in a street fight with a local newspaper editor who had written a critical editorial of the statesman.

BIBLIOGRAPHY: *Dictionary of American Biography.*

ADAMS, TEXAS (Lamar County). Adams is 2½ miles northeast of Paris on Farm Road 195 in central Lamar County. The settlement had been established by 1896, when Adams Common School reported one female teacher and twenty-four students. The community was unidentified on maps for 1936, but at the site were the school, a church and cemetery, a business, and a cluster of dwellings. In 1964 the Paris Country Club and a few scattered dwellings were located at Adams. Local students attended school in the Powderly Independent School District. Adams still appeared on maps in 1983 and was listed, without statistics, in later editions of the *Texas Almanac.*[qv]

BIBLIOGRAPHY: Thomas S. Justiss, An Administrative Survey of the Schools of Lamar County with a Plan for Their Reorganization (M.A. thesis, University of Texas, 1937). *Vista K. McCroskey*

ADAMS, TEXAS (Schleicher County). Adams is twenty miles northeast of Eldorado and four miles east of Farm Road 2084 in eastern Schleicher County. By 1903 the settlement was the focus of a common school district; in 1947 it was made part of the Schleicher County rural high school district. A few scattered houses marked the community on county highway maps in the late 1940s, and in the 1980s maps showed a community center in the area.

BIBLIOGRAPHY: Schleicher County Historical Society, *A History of Schleicher County* (San Angelo: Anchor, 1979).

Vivian Elizabeth Smyrl

ADAMS BAYOU. Adams Bayou rises 1½ miles east of the hamlet of Robertson, Jasper County, in southwestern Newton County (at 30°18′ N, 93°53′ W) and flows southeast across Newton and Orange counties before entering the Sabine River southeast of West Orange (at 30°03′ N, 93°44′ W). The stream is intermittent near its point of origin. It flows through woodlands and marshland and is briefly paralleled by a levee just south of the Newton county line. Adams Bayou has been used to provide water for irrigation and power for sawmills. It is crossed by several highways and railroads, including Interstate Highway 10, U.S. Highway 90, the Missouri Pacific Railroad, and the Sabine River and Northern Railroad. The towns of Orange, West Orange, and Pinehurst are all bordered by Adams Bayou.

Catherine P. Eggers

ADAMS BRANCH. Adams Branch rises six miles northwest of Brownwood in central Brown County (at 31°47′ N, 98°59′ W) and runs southeast for seven miles through Brownwood to its mouth on Pecan Bayou (at 31°42′ N, 98°57′ W) just east of the city. It traverses flat terrain with local shallow depressions surfaced by clay and sandy loams that support water-tolerant hardwoods, conifers, and grasses. The creek is named for Ichabod Adams, who settled on the stream prior to the Civil War.

ADAMS CREEK. Adams Creek, an intermittent stream, rises seven miles west of Electra in northeastern Wilbarger County (at 34°06′ N, 99°06′ W) and runs northeast for fourteen miles to its mouth on the Red River, on the Texas-Oklahoma border in Wichita County (at 34°09′ N, 98°54′ W). The stream crosses flat to rolling plains surfaced by sand and sandy loam that support bunch grasses. It was probably named for a cattleman who camped on it when driving a herd to Dodge City, Kansas.

BIBLIOGRAPHY: Glenn A. Gray, *Gazetteer of Streams of Texas* (Washington: GPO, 1919).

ADAMS GARDENS, TEXAS. Adams Gardens, a mobile park, is located on the Missouri Pacific Railroad off U.S. Highway 83 one mile northeast of La Feria in western Cameron County. It was incorporated in 1972. It is serviced by the Harlingen water district and receives its mail from Harlingen. In 1978 and 1992 Adams Gardens had an estimated population of 200. It can accommodate up to 230 dwellings. The community is governed by an elected board of directors made up of nine members and a president who is elected yearly. Children who live in Adams Gardens attend school in the La Feria school district. *Alicia A. Garza*

ADAMS HILL, BATTLE OF. The so-called battle of Adams Hill occurred on May 9, 1861, between federal forces under Lt. Col. Isaac Van Duzer Reeve and Texas Confederate troops under Col. Earl Van Dorn.[qv] The confrontation took place on the military road between San Antonio and El Paso, about fifteen miles west of downtown San Antonio. Under the terms of the surrender of the Department of Texas, Reeve proceeded from Fort Bliss to the Texas coast to join other federal troops in the evacuation of Texas. His force consisted of companies B, E, F, H, I, and K and a detachment of Company G, Eighth United States Infantry,[qv] which represented the garrisons of Fort Bliss, Fort Quitman, and Fort Davis. Reeve reported the total strength of his command at 320 men, including two hospital stewards, twelve musicians, and ten officers. Col. James V. Bomford of the Sixth United States Infantry also accompanied the column.

Upon arriving at Fort Clark, Reeve became aware of the Confederate internment of paroled federal troops in Texas and of concern by Confederate officials in San Antonio that Reeve's force was, in fact, hostile. He nevertheless resolved to continue his march to the coast to evacuate his command in compliance with former Department of Texas commander David Twiggs's[qv] terms of surrender. On May 8 Reeve camped his command on the east side of the Medina River opposite Castroville. At midnight, having received further word of Van Dorn's advance from San Antonio with the purpose of confronting the column, Reeve resolved again to push forward to San Antonio.

Upon the advice of Lt. Zenas Randall Bliss,qv Reeve halted his column on a high hill a few hundred yards from San Lucas Springs. There was a small collection of buildings and corrals, which Reeve supplemented with his wagons for defense purposes. At around nine that morning, two officers representing Colonel Van Dorn arrived under a white flag with the Confederates' demand that Reeve surrender unconditionally. With no actual hostile force in sight and his position a strong one, Reeve declined.

Van Dorn, on the march, soon arrived in full force. His command, which consisted of six companies of Col. Henry E. McCulloch'sqv cavalry regiment, a squadron of Col. John S. Ford'sqv State Troops (under the command of Lt. Col. John Robert Baylor,qv) Capt. William Edgar's battery of light artillery, and a battalion of infantry under Lt. Col. James Duff,qv comprised nearly 1,370 men and six pieces of artillery. Van Dorn's representative now offered Reeve an opportunity to inspect the Confederate force. Lieutenant Bliss was sent forward and examined it, then quickly reported the strength of the force to Reeve. Inasmuch as the federals' effective strength had been reduced to 270 by sickness, desertion, and stragglers, Reeve resolved that resistance would be futile and surrendered his command to Van Dorn. The Confederates, satisfied with this turn of events, retired, allowing Reeve to continue his march, under arms, at his own leisure. The federals arrived at San Antonio on May 10, and the next day a Confederate officer was sent to recover all arms and public property.

Period accounts of the confrontation refer to the event as having taken place at San Lucas Springs. Later accounts say Adams Hill. There were no shots fired; it appears that both sides were eager to avoid bloodshed.

BIBLIOGRAPHY: San Antonio *Daily Ledger and Texan,* May 9, 13, 1861. John Titcomb Sprague, *Treachery in Texas: The Secession of Texas and the Arrest of the United States Officers and Soldiers Serving in Texas* (New York: Press of the Rebellion Record, 1862). *The War of the Rebellion: A Compilation of the Official Records of the Union and Confederate Armies* (Washington: GPO, 1880–1901). *Kevin R. Young*

ADAMS-ONÍS TREATY. The Adams-Onís (or Florida) Treaty, signed on February 22, 1819, by John Quincy Adams for the United States and by Louis de Onís for Spain, renounced the United States claim to Texas. It fixed the western boundary of the Louisiana Purchase as beginning at the mouth of the Sabine River and running along its south and west bank to the thirty-second parallel and thence directly north to the Río Roxo, or Red River, "then following the course of the Río Roxo westward to the degree of longitude 100 west from London and 23 from Washington; then, crossing the said Red River, and running thence, by a line due north, to the river Arkansas; thence, following the course of the southern bank of the Arkansas to its source, in latitude 42° north; and thence by that parallel of latitude to the South Sea. The whole being as laid down in Melish's map of the United States" (*see* MELISH MAP).

BIBLIOGRAPHY: William M. Malloy, comp., *Treaties, Conventions, International Acts, Protocols and Agreements between the United States of America and Other Powers, 1776–1909* (2 vols., Washington: GPO, 1910). *Evelyn Turk*

ADAMS STORE, TEXAS. Adams Store, a rural community off U.S. Highway 79 seventeen miles northeast of Carthage in northeastern Panola County, was named for the proprietor of a store that operated on Waterman's logging tram in the early 1900s. In 1940 the community had a store and a number of houses; the reported population was twenty-five. After World War IIqv the settlement reported two businesses, but by the mid-1960s only a few scattered houses remained in the area; the estimated population in 1965 was fifty. In the early 1990s Adams Store was a dispersed rural community for which no recent population estimates were available.

BIBLIOGRAPHY: John Barnette Sanders, *Index to the Cemeteries of Panola County* (Center, Texas, 1964). *Christopher Long*

ADAMSVILLE, TEXAS. Adamsville is at the junction of U.S. Highway 281 and Farm Road 581, on the Lampasas River 16½ miles north of Lampasas in northern Lampasas County. It was founded around 1856. Early ranchers in the area included Joseph Leland Straley, who built one of the first houses in the area, and the brothers Jasper and Perry Townsen. During the 1870s a number of small cattle drives were organized in the community, in which cattle were driven short distances to join the larger cattle trails to the north. In 1872 Jasper Townsen built a mill on Mill Branch, near the spot where the creek joins the Lampasas River, two miles southeast of the current town. This mill was originally established to saw lumber from the Round Rock area; eventually a mill for wheat and corn was added, and the mills served communities throughout the entire county.

One of the earliest stores was operated by McCall Smith, a Presbyterian minister, and John Adams. A second general store was located near the mills; when a post office was established in this store in 1876, with Perry Townsen as the first postmaster, the community took the name Townsen Mills. Some of the first public surveying in Lampasas County was carried out on nearby Simms Creek in the late 1870s, and the surveyors suffered several Indian attacks while carrying out their work. Adamsville's first church, the Cumberland Presbyterian, was established in 1881. In 1885 the first local school, called Straley's School, was built north of town; this building also doubled as a church for the Baptists and the Presbyterians.

On January 1, 1891, Perry Townsen, who helped his brother run the mills, was killed in an accident. Jasper Townsen then asked that the post office be moved, and it was transferred to the second store in town and renamed Adamsville after John Adams, who was by that time the store's sole proprietor. Townsen eventually sold the mill, and the entire building was moved to Hamilton County. By that time, however, Adamsville had several other mills in operation.

In 1918 a new school building was erected; it burned on March 27, 1942. Due to the wartime shortage of building materials, the town obtained an existing school building from Mount View and moved it to Adamsville. As of 1974 the town had two churches, several stores, a cafe, and a locker plant. The population remained fairly stable at seventy-five to 100 from the mid-1880s to the early 1930s. In 1933 an estimate of ten was reported in the *Texas Almanac.*qv By 1941 the population had risen again. It continued at 150 to 200 until 1961, at which time it began to decline slowly. It was reported as twenty-eight in 1972 and 1990.

BIBLIOGRAPHY: Jonnie Ross Elzner, *Relighting Lamplights of Lampasas County, Texas* (Lampasas: Hill Country, 1974). Kathleen E. and Clifton R. St. Clair, eds., *Little Towns of Texas* (Jacksonville, Texas: Jayroe Graphic Arts, 1982). *Alice J. Rhoades*

ADDICKS, TEXAS. Addicks, known at various times as Letitia, Bear Hill, and Bear Creek, is just north of Interstate Highway 10 on the outskirts of Houston in western Harris County. It was the railroad stop for the Bear Creek community, which was established around 1850 by German immigrants who homesteaded along Bear, Lanham, and South Mayde creeks. The town was named after its first postmaster, Henry Addicks, in 1884. In 1891, when the Missouri, Kansas and Texas Railroad was built, the town became a commercial center for local farmers and ranchers. Both the Bear Creek community and the town of Addicks were destroyed in the Galveston hurricane of 1900.qv The community rebuilt and listed a population of forty in 1925. The Bear Creek German Methodist Church, founded in 1879, continued in 1989 as the Addicks United Methodist Church, although it quit conducting services in German during World War I.qv Addicks Bear Creek Cemetery, located at the intersection of State

Highway 6 and Patterson Road, contains the graves of the descendants of many of the original German settlers. Addicks had a population of 200 when the site was covered with water in the mid-1940s by the Addicks Dam Reservoir, built to protect nearby Houston from floods. By 1947 forty homes and buildings had been moved or destroyed, and the residents had been required to resettle under the auspices of the Federal Flood Control Project. The relocated town, a suburb of Houston, had a population of 150 in 1988.

BIBLIOGRAPHY: Margaret Ann Howard and Martha Doty Freeman, *Inventory and Assessment of Cultural Resources at Bear Creek Park, Addicks Reservoir* (Austin: Prewitt and Associates, 1983).

Margaret Hopkins Edwards

ADDICKS RESERVOIR. Addicks Reservoir is on South Mayde Creek a mile east of Addicks in western Harris County (at 29°47′ N, 95°37′ W). The filled rolled-earth dam is 61,166 feet long, and the drainage area above the dam covers 129 square miles. The elevation of the dam is 121 feet at the top, and the crest of the spillway reaches seventy-one feet. The United States Army Corps of Engineers completed the dam in 1948 in an effort to provide flood control in Buffalo Bayou and the San Jacinto River basin. The dam helps protect the city of Houston from floodwaters. Water is stored only for flood control and is released when flooding is no longer a danger. The total storage capacity of Addicks Reservoir and the adjacent Barker Reservoir is 411,500 acre-feet.

BIBLIOGRAPHY: *Water for Texas,* Vol. 1: *A Comprehensive Plan for the Future;* Vol. 2: *Technical Appendix* (Austin: Texas Department of Water Resources, 1984).

ADDIELOU, TEXAS. Addielou, eleven miles northeast of Detroit in northwestern Red River County, was founded about 1910. Sam H. Patterson operated a post office in his general store there from 1916 to 1925, when rural delivery from Manchester replaced the office. The population was fifteen in 1920 and 100 in 1930; in 1940 one store and fifty persons were reported. In 1986 and in 1990 the community had a population of thirty-one. *Claudia Hazlewood*

ADDISON, OSCAR MURRAY, SR. (1820–1898). Oscar Murray Addison, Methodist minister, was born in Baltimore, Maryland, on November 20, 1820, the son of Isaac Simmonds and Sarah (Murray) Addison. The family moved to Texas in 1835 and settled in Burleson County. Oscar was converted to Methodism in 1844 and licensed to preach in 1846. He was admitted to the East Texas Conference of Methodists that year but immediately transferred to the Texas Conference. Bishop James O. Andrew ordained him a deacon in 1849 and an elder in 1850. His first charge was the New Washington Mission, at which his chief activity was going from one cotton plantation on the Brazos to another and preaching to the slaves. As a circuit rider he covered an area from Huntsville to Brownsville and also served the Victoria and Springfield districts. Another transfer in 1866 made him a charter member of the Northwest Texas Conference. Addison married Mary F. Hines in 1866. She died six years later, and in 1879 he married T. H. Smith of Johnson County. He retired in 1889 and settled on a farm near Eulogy in Somervell County, where he assembled a large collection of historical material concerning Texas Methodists.

Sometime before the Civil War[qv] Addison wrote and published *Yankee Slave Trader,* intended as an answer to offset *Uncle Tom's Cabin* (1852), but the book did not receive wide distribution. During the Civil War he served as chaplain in Colonel Bates's regiment at Velasco and kept a journal of his war experiences. He later wrote his memories of the Runaway Scrape[qv] and the experience of his family during the Texas Revolution.[qv] In retirement he wrote works on sanctification and the liquor question. Addison died at his farm on October 11, 1898, and was buried at Eulogy. His papers are at the Barker Texas History Center[qv] at the University of Texas at Austin.

BIBLIOGRAPHY: Methodist Episcopal Church, South, *Journal of the Northwest Texas Conference,* 1898. Macum Phelan, *History of Early Methodism in Texas, 1817–1866* (Nashville: Cokesbury, 1924); *A History of the Expansion of Methodism in Texas, 1867–1902* (Dallas: Mathis, Van Nort, 1937). *Karen Yancy*

ADDISON, TEXAS. Addison is on Belt Line Road, the St. Louis Southwestern Railway, and Dallas North Tollway thirteen miles north of downtown Dallas in northern Dallas County and southern Collin County. The area was first settled by Peters colony[qv] residents in the 1840s. The first prominent settlers in the area were Preston and Pleasant Witt, who settled on White Rock Creek and built an ox-powered gristmill by 1849. In 1888 W. W. Julian, W. E. Horten, and S. S. Noell donated right-of-way to the St. Louis, Arkansas and Texas Railway in exchange for a coaling station, later known as Noell Junction. After the railroad arrived, several buildings were moved from nearby Frankford to the railway station.

In 1902 Noell Junction became the site of a depot on the St. Louis Southwestern, which built a spur to Dallas in 1903. Residents of the area rode into Dallas from 1903 to 1917 on the "Plug," a small Cottonbelt train consisting of an engine, a coal tender, and a passenger car. In 1904 a post office opened at the junction, but since a community named Noell already existed in Leon County, the office was named after Addison Robertson, the first postmaster. W. W. Julian platted the six blocks of the community that year.

By 1914 Addison had a population of seventy-five, three grocers, a dry-goods store, and the Addison State Bank. In 1926 the population was forty and the bank had failed. Addison was incorporated in 1953 in an effort to avoid annexation by Dallas. In the mid-1950s it had a population of 600 and eight businesses. In 1956 the Addison *Times Chronicle* was founded and Addison Airport was built.

In 1970 Addison had a population of 595 and eighty businesses; by 1980 it had 5,553 residents and 263 businesses. The town took a number of measures to promote industrial development and lose its small-town image. Residents voted to legalize alcoholic beverages in 1976, unlike the majority of the communities in Dallas County, to attract restaurants and hotels. In addition, Addison attracted businesses by a property-tax rate that was only one-sixth that of Dallas. The major industries in Addison were the airport and manufacturers and suppliers of aviation equipment. Addison's 189 businesses in 1974 included manufacturers of plastics, rubber and metal products, and pharmaceutical products. In 1990 the town had a population of 8,783 and 251 businesses. Area office buildings and restaurants served a daily population of 50,000. From 1986 to 1991 the number of restaurants grew from forty-nine to 118 and the number of hotels from five to nine. In 1991 Addison supported three banks, three malls, one daily and one weekly newspaper, and a Baptist church. The town had a council-mayor form of government, fifty policemen and fifty-four firemen, and received water from the city of Dallas.

BIBLIOGRAPHY: Dallas *Morning News,* June 20, 1983. Kathleen E. and Clifton R. St. Clair, eds., *Little Towns of Texas* (Jacksonville, Texas: Jayroe Graphic Arts, 1982). *Lisa C. Maxwell*

ADDRAN, TEXAS. Addran (Add Ran) is near State highways 19 and 154 ten miles north of Sulphur Springs in north central Hopkins County. The area was first settled in the late 1850s. The community was later named by a minister who had attended Add-Ran College. A post office opened there in 1890 but closed in 1906. A local Baptist church, organized in 1915, continued to hold services until 1948. In the mid-1930s the community had a school, two churches, one business, and a number of scattered dwellings. The population reached a peak of thirty-one in 1933. Thereafter it was consistently reported at twenty-five until the mid-1970s. The school was consolidated with North Hopkins High School, and the churches and business closed. In the late 1980s a few scattered farmhouses remained.

J. E. Jennings

ADELL, TEXAS. Adell is near Farm Road 1885 twelve miles northwest of Weatherford in northwest Parker County. Settlement of the site began in the late 1880s. The first business was a grocery store built and operated by J. R. Fondren in 1889. In 1890 Denton County resident B. B. Barton moved into the area and petitioned for a post office for the community. He reportedly received the suggestion for a name from Alexander Sanger,[qv] owner of the Sanger Mercantile Company in Dallas, who wanted the town named in honor of the prettiest girl in Dallas, his daughter Adell. Postal service to Adell began in 1890. At one time the town had three churches, a public school, a cotton gin, a gristmill, and a corn crusher. The population of Adell never exceeded 100. Postal service ended in 1904.

BIBLIOGRAPHY: Gustavus Adolphus Holland, *History of Parker County and the Double Log Cabin* (Weatherford, Texas: Herald, 1931; rpt. 1937).

David Minor

ADELSVEREIN. The Adelsverein, also known as the Mainzer Verein, the Texas-Verein, and the German Emigration Company, was officially named the Verein zum Schutze deutscher Einwanderer in Texas (Society for the Protection of German Immigrants in Texas). Provisionally organized on April 20, 1842, by twenty-one German noblemen at Biebrich on the Rhine, near Mainz, the society represents a significant effort to establish a new Germany on Texas soil by means of an organized mass emigration. Such German publications as Charles Sealsfield's *Das Kajütenbuch, oder Schilderungen aus dem Leben in Texas* (1841), Detlef Dunt's *Reise nach Texas nebst Nachrichten von diesem Lande* (1834), and G. A. Scherpf's *Entstehungsgeschichte und gegenwärtiger Zustand des neuen, unabhängigen Staates Texas* (1841), which depicted in glowing terms the great personal liberty and the plentiful and productive land to be found in Texas, had served to direct the nobles' attention to the Republic of Texas as the best destination for an increasing German emigration. Accordingly, in May 1842 the association sent two of its members, counts Joseph of Boos-Waldeck and Victor August of Leiningen-Westerburg-Alt-Leiningen[qqv] to Texas to investigate the country firsthand and purchase a tract of land for the settlement of immigrants. Once in Texas, the two agents discussed colonizing a land grant with President Sam Houston,[qv] who, under the provisions of a law passed on February 5, 1842, was authorized to grant entire tracts of land to contractors who would colonize them. Boos-Waldeck and Alt-Leiningen declined Houston's offer of a grant, however, when they learned that it would be in frontier territory west of Austin and still inhabited by hostile Indians. In January 1843 Boos-Waldeck purchased a league of land (4,428 acres) in what is now Fayette County, near Industry, as the base for future colonization, and named it Nassau Farm,[qv] in honor of Duke Adolf of Nassau, the patron of the society. Boos-Waldeck remained in Texas a year developing the farm, and in May 1843 Alt-Leiningen returned to Mainz. Though Boos-Waldeck recommended against an immediate large-scale colonization effort, Alt-Leiningen supported such a venture. Accordingly, on June 18, 1843, the association was reorganized as a joint-stock company with a capital stock of 200,000 gulden ($80,000) for the acquisition of more land in Texas. In September the association was approached by Alexander Bourgeois d'Orvanne,[qv] a speculator, who with Armand Ducos[qv] held a colonization contract for a tract of land west of San Antonio. On March 25, 1844, the association was formally constituted as the Society for the Protection of German Immigrants in Texas with Prince Carl Emich III of Leiningen[qv] as president and Count Carl of Castell-Castell[qv] as business manager.

The society's goals were both philanthropic and commercial. They included the economic relief of the German proletariat by the direction of emigration to Texas and the establishment of German settlements in Texas, which would supply markets abroad for German industry and promote the development of German maritime commerce. In April 1844, when the society purchased from Bourgeois the colonization rights to his grant, the contract had already expired. Nevertheless, later that month the society dispatched Prince Carl of Solms-Braunfels[qv] as general commissioner and Bourgeois as colonial director to Texas to seek renewal of the grant and to prepare for the arrival of colonists. Upon his arrival in Texas in July, Solms learned that Bourgeois could not renew his contract and that the society had acquired from him neither land nor colonization rights in Texas. In the meantime the society had already severed its ties with Bourgeois and, on June 26, 1844, had purchased colonization rights from another

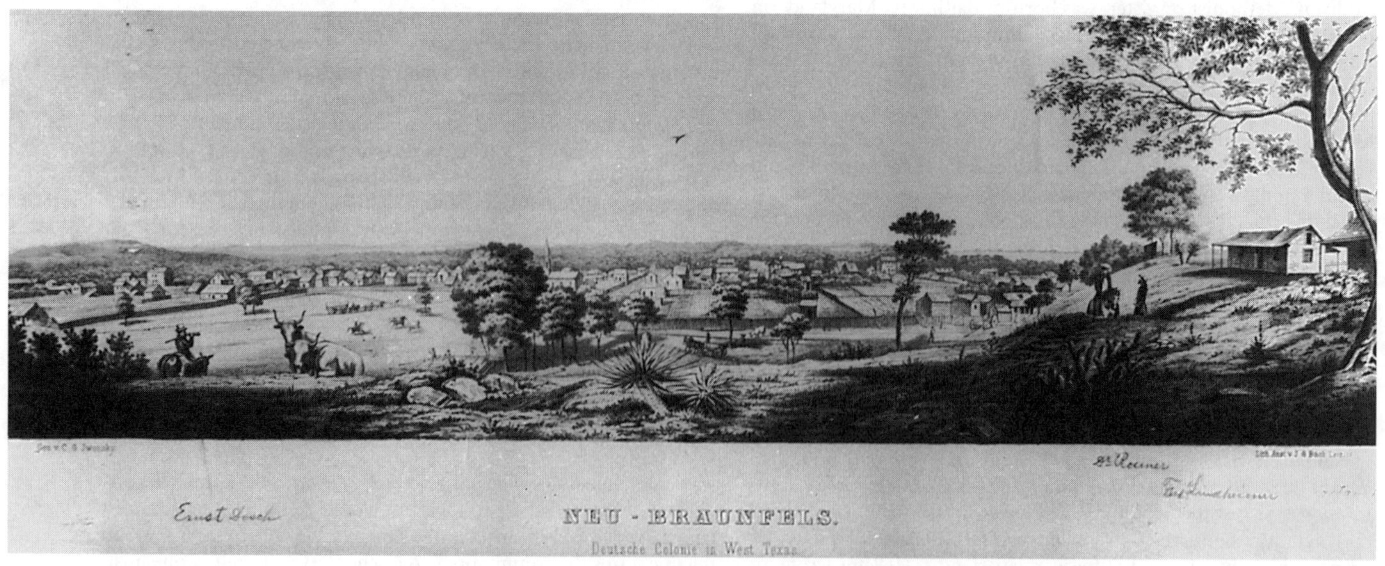

Neu-Braunfels, Deutsche Colonie in West Texas, *by Carl G. von Iwonski, 1857. Toned lithograph. 7¼″ × 13⅜″. Courtesy Witte Museum, San Antonio, Texas. This panoramic view of New Braunfels, which Duke Paul of Württemberg took back to Germany to be lithographed, shows at least fifty wooden buildings, some two-story, and a steepled church.*

speculator, Henry Francis Fisher,[qv] who with Burchard Miller[qv] held a colonization contract for a tract of land between the Llano and Colorado rivers. The first immigrants disembarked in Texas in December 1844, near Carlshafen (later Indianola), the society's port of entry established by Prince Solms. Since no preparations had been made for settlement on the Fisher-Miller land grant,[qv] the immigrants were settled on two leagues of land at Comal Springs that Solms purchased on March 15, 1845, and named New Braunfels after his estate in Germany. On May 8, 1845, John O. Meusebach,[qv] Solms's successor as general commissioner in Texas, arrived at Carlshafen; in November he began making preparations for the arrival of 4,000 new immigrants. Fredericksburg, the society's second colony, was established by Meusebach in 1846 near the Pedernales River, where the year before he had bought over 11,000 acres of headright land.

Under Meusebach's administration, from May 1845 to July 20, 1847, when he resigned as general commissioner, the major part of the society's work in Texas was accomplished. Between October 1845 and April 1846 a total of 5,257 German emigrants were brought to Texas. In 1847 five settlements—Bettina, Castell, Leiningen, Meerholz, and Schoenburg—were established in the Fisher-Miller grant on the banks of the Llano River. Under Meusebach's successor, Hermann Spiess,[qv] no new settlements were founded.

By the end of 1847 the society was facing bankruptcy. Neither the appointment of Gustav Dresel[qv] as special business agent nor the attempt in 1848 to sell the society's holdings to another company was able to save the Adelsverein. Fisher attempted to revive the society under a new name, German Emigration Company. Spiess and Louis Bene, who succeeded Spiess in 1852 as general commissioner, carried on the society's business in Texas under that name until September 1853, when the company assigned all its properties and colonization rights to its creditors. Besides bringing over 7,000 German emigrants to Texas, the chief contribution of the society was to establish Texas as a major goal of subsequent emigration from Germany.

During its brief existence and long after its demise, the Adelsverein was beset by controversy. Though most of its critics acknowledged the philanthropic motives of the society's aristocratic founders—the desire to ease economic pressures on the German proletariat by providing in Texas a refuge for surplus German labor—they were also aware of the society's commercial objectives—assured markets for German industry, a reliable source of raw materials for her factories, and dividends and profits for the society's shareholders. Contemporary criticism of the society came chiefly from two sources: victims of the society's inept planning and mismanagement, who published in Germany letters to friends and book-length exposés of the hardships that they suffered in Texas; and German travelers to Texas who had visited the society's settlements there. The reports of the latter group, which included such writers as Viktor Bracht, Friedrich Kapp, and Ferdinand Roemer,[qqv] were generally much more balanced than the former in their view of the society's motives and its achievements. Some later accounts, written often by journalists, emphasized the more sensational and anecdotal features of the society's history. Chief among the popular chroniclers was August Siemering,[qv] a journalist and Forty-eighter, who even alleged that the Adelsverein had been founded at the instigation of Great Britain as a measure to halt the spread of slavery[qv] in Texas and to prevent the annexation[qv] of Texas by the United States. Recent historical research supports, however, a mixed view of the society's motives and achievements. As an effort to establish a new Germany in Texas, the venture was a fiasco. The chief causes of its failure were not greed or the mean-spirited parsimony of its members, however, but their lack of business sense, the intrigues of land speculators and some members of the society, the naïveté of the nobles involved, and a lack of trust even in their own officers in Texas.

BIBLIOGRAPHY: Adelsverein Archives, Beinecke Rare Book and Manuscript Library, Yale University. Rudolph L. Biesele, *The History of the German Settlements in Texas, 1831-1861* (Austin: Von Boeckmann–Jones, 1930; rpt. 1964). Don Hampton Biggers, *German Pioneers in Texas* (Fredericksburg, Texas: Fredericksburg Publishing, 1925). Chester William and Ethel Hander Geue, eds., *A New Land Beckoned: German Immigration to Texas, 1844-1847* (Waco: Texian Press, 1966; enlarged ed. 1972). Irene M. King, *John O. Meusebach, German Colonizer in Texas* (Austin: University of Texas Press, 1967). Ferdinand Roemer, *Texas* (Bonn: Marcus, 1849; trans., San Antonio: Standard, 1935; rpt., Waco: Texian Press, 1976). William von Rosenberg, "*Kritik*: A History of the Society for the Protection of German Immigrants to Texas," trans. Louis E. Brister, *Southwestern Historical Quarterly* 85 (October 1981, January, April 1982). Solms-Braunfels Archives (transcripts, Sophienburg Museum, New Braunfels, Texas; Barker Texas History Center, University of Texas at Austin). Moritz Tiling, *History of the German Element in Texas* (Houston: Rein and Sons, 1913).

Louis E. Brister

AD HALL, TEXAS. Ad Hall is on Farm Road 466 six miles west of Cameron in western Milam County. The post office, named for early settler Adam J. Hall, was opened in 1874, and the community became a voting precinct in 1880. The Gulf, Colorado and Santa Fe Railway passed within a half mile of Ad Hall when its track was built through the area in 1881. The community enjoyed a brief period of prosperity in the 1880s, when it had a cotton gin, a gristmill, three churches, a district school, and 200 residents. In the 1890s, however, the population fell to thirty-five. The post office was discontinued in 1912, and by the 1930s only fifteen residents were reported. A school, a business, and several scattered houses marked the community on county highway maps in 1948. The school closed in 1958, and the students were sent to Cameron. A church and two cemeteries were all that appeared on county maps in 1988.

BIBLIOGRAPHY: Lelia M. Batte, *History of Milam County, Texas* (San Antonio: Naylor, 1956). Milam County Heritage Preservation Society, *Matchless Milam: History of Milam County* (Dallas: Taylor, 1984).

Vivian Elizabeth Smyrl

ADINA, TEXAS. Adina is a rural community four miles north of Farm Road 696 and four miles west of Farm Road 122 in northwestern Lee County. The area was first settled after the Civil War.[qv] R. L. Cain, an early settler, donated five acres for a school and cemetery, and for a time the community was known as Cain School House. In 1895 the town received a post office, and the name was changed to Adina, after a character in a novel Cain was reading at the time. In 1896 the population was estimated at forty, and just after the turn of the century the town had a school, a store, a blacksmith shop, and a cotton gin. After 1905 many residents began to move to larger towns, and in 1908 the post office was closed. In the mid-1930s the school, a cemetery, and a number of scattered dwellings marked the site. The school continued to operate until 1945, when it was consolidated with the Lexington school district. The school district later deeded the land and the old school building to the Adina Christian Church. In 1982 only the church and a nearby cemetery remained at Adina.

BIBLIOGRAPHY: Lee County Historical Survey Committee, *A History of Lee County* (Quanah, Texas: Nortex, 1974). *Christopher Long*

ADINOSA CREEK. Adinosa Creek, an intermittent stream, rises just south of U. S. Highway 67 in east central Presidio County (at 30°02′ N, 104°12′ W) and runs southeast for sixteen miles to its mouth on Alamito Creek, where the latter stream is crossed by Farm Road 169, just north of Plata (at 29°53′ N, 104°01′ W). The surrounding desert mountain terrain, volcanic-rock canyons, and wash deposits of sand and gravel support sparse grasses, desert shrubs, and cacti.

AD INTERIM GOVERNMENT. The ad interim government of Texas operated from March 16 to October 22, 1836. The Convention of 1836[qv] declared independence and framed the Constitution of the

Republic of Texas,[qv] but the advance of the Mexican army made immediate ratification and establishment of constitutional government impossible. The last act of the convention was the selection of an ad interim government with David G. Burnet, president; Lorenzo de Zavala, vice president; Samuel P. Carson, secretary of state; Bailey Hardeman, secretary of treasury; Thomas J. Rusk, secretary of war; Robert Potter, secretary of the navy; and David Thomas,[qqv] attorney general. This temporary government, without any legislative or judicial departments, fled with the people in the Runaway Scrape[qv] and was located successively at Washington-on-the-Brazos, Harrisburg, Galveston Island, Velasco, and Columbia; nevertheless, it continued to function until regular elections could be held and the constitution ratified. One of its major concerns was controlling the revolutionary army[qv] and dealing with low supplies and morale. It was also in place when the two treaties of Velasco[qv] were signed. The ad interim government ended with the inauguration of Sam Houston[qv] as president on October 22, 1836.

BIBLIOGRAPHY: Rupert N. Richardson, *Texas: The Lone Star State* (New York: Prentice-Hall, 1943; 4th ed., with Ernest Wallace and Adrian N. Anderson, Englewood Cliffs, New Jersey: Prentice-Hall, 1981).

ADJUTANT GENERAL. The present state office of adjutant general was established by the Texas legislature in 1905. A similar office existed under the Republic of Texas[qv] but was abolished in 1840. It was reestablished as a state office in 1846, but activities were limited to the verification of veterans' land claims. The office operated intermittently from 1846 until 1905. The adjutant general, appointed by the governor for a two-year term, heads the Adjutant General's Department. He is assisted by two assistant adjutants general, who are appointed by the governor upon his recommendation. All three officials must have previous military service and at least ten years' experience as commissioned officers in an active unit of the Texas National Guard.[qv] The adjutant general serves as the governor's aide in supervising the military department of the state. Responsibilities include providing military aid to state civil authorities and furnishing trained military personnel from the state's military forces—the Texas State Guard, the Texas Army National Guard, and the Texas Air National Guard—in case of national emergency or war. The Adjutant General's Department is located at Camp Mabry[qv] in Austin. In the early 1990s annual working budgets totaled over $14 million.

BIBLIOGRAPHY: Seymour V. Connor, "A Preliminary Guide to the Archives of Texas, " *Southwestern Historical Quarterly* 59 (January 1956).
Dick Smith and Laurie E. Jasinski

ADKINS, WALTER SCOTT (1890–1956). Walter Scott Adkins, geologist, was born on December 24, 1890. He was an only child and was orphaned at the age of twelve and raised by an uncle. He graduated from the University of Tennessee with a B.S. in 1910, having achieved one of the highest scholastic averages ever made at the university at that time, and did subsequent graduate work in entomology. Adkins went on to Columbia, where he specialized in the study of *Drosophila* under Thomas H. Morgan and belonged to a group called the "*Drosophila* gang." He was well on the way to a doctorate in genetics when he started teaching. He taught as professor of geology at Texas Christian University from 1913 to 1915, instructor in anatomy at the Illinois Medical School from 1916 to 1918, and assistant professor of anatomy at Baylor Medical School in Dallas during the 1918–19 term. He was with the Texas Bureau of Economic Geology from 1919 to 1921. From 1921 to 1925 he worked for the Mexican petroleum company El Águila. At the Sorbonne in the 1925–26 term he studied under Emil Haug and Leon Perviquiere. In 1926 he returned to the Bureau of Economic Geology, where he spent several fruitful years before joining Shell Development Company in 1934. In 1931 he became the first paleontologist to hold a John Guggenheim Memorial Fellowship. During this period he studied with L. F. Spath at the British Museum. He served Shell Development as chief stratigrapher and head of the special-problems research group until his retirement in 1950, after which he served as a consultant until his death.

Adkins was vice president of the Society of Economic Paleontologists and Mineralogists in 1931 and served as the first chairman of the society's research committee in 1929 and 1930. He is perhaps best remembered for his *Handbook of Texas Cretaceous Fossils* (1928) and his *Mesozoic Systems in Texas* (1933). With Will McClain Winton he coauthored *Paleontological Correlation of the Fredericksburg and Washita Formations in North Texas* (1920), the first detailed biostratigraphical study to come out of Texas. His *Stratigraphy of the Woodbine and Eagle Ford, Waco Area, Texas* (1951), written in collaboration with Frank E. Lozo, is another outstanding work about solving geologic problems through biostratigraphy. Among Adkins's reports to the Shell company, his works on the distribution of shoestring and barrier sands in the subsurface of the Miocene (1935) and the "Time of Origin and Migration of Oil" (abstracted at the International Geological Congress, Mexico, 1956) were particularly important.

Adkins was married early and was divorced in the 1920s. One child, Jack, who died in combat in World War II,[qv] resulted from this union. Adkins later married Mary Grace Muse, a former student of his, who taught English for many years at the University of Texas. Colleagues and students at the university called Adkins Si ("scientist") and, though he never earned a doctorate, Doc.

In the early 1920s Adkins collected linguistic works in Mexico, and a close associate, R. Wright Barker, collected ethnological works. When the Adkins library was obtained by the University of Texas, the geological part went to what became the Joseph C. and Elizabeth C. Walters Geology Library, and the linguistic part went to the Nettie Lee Benson Latin American Collection[qv] at the University of Texas. When Wright Barker learned of this, he made his ethnological collections available to the university; they too are housed in the Latin American Collection. The university also obtained Adkins's extensive paleontological collections, amounting to about 14,000 catalogued items. These are now housed with the other paleontological collections of the university under the care of the Texas Memorial Museum.[qv] Adkins died of a heart ailment on September 22, 1956, shortly after his return from the International Geological Congress meeting in Mexico City, and was buried in Austin Memorial Park.

BIBLIOGRAPHY: John T. Lonsdale, "Walter Scott Adkins (1890–1956)," *Geological Society of America Proceedings for 1956*, 1957. Frank E. Lozo, "Walter Scott Adkins (1890–1956)," *Bulletin of the American Association of Petroleum Geologists* 41 (1957). Keith Young, "The Adkins Collections of Mesozioc Fossils," *Texas Quarterly* 3 (1960).
Keith Young

ADKINS, TEXAS. Adkins, on Loop 1604 fourteen miles east of downtown San Antonio in eastern Bexar County, became a flag station on the Galveston, Harrisburg and San Antonio Railway in the 1880s. The settlement was named for William Adkins Jones, who gave land for the depot and switchyard. An Adkins post office was established in 1896. In 1910 the community had two churches, a school, and a population of 100. In 1940 four businesses and a population of 150 were reported. With the expansion of nearby San Antonio and the construction of Loop 1604 the community grew, and in 1990 it had thirty-two businesses and a population of 241.

Claudia Hazlewood

ADMIRAL, TEXAS. Admiral is eleven miles southwest of Baird in central Callahan County. The community, established in the late 1890s, was granted a post office in 1897; Henry L. Buchin, an early settler, became the first postmaster. During the first quarter of the twentieth century Admiral developed into a thriving farming town. In 1900 the settlement had two churches, a gin, and a population of 100.

By 1914 residents were also supporting two general stores and a blacksmith. After the post office was discontinued in 1929 the community quickly declined. In 1950 Admiral had one business and a population of twenty-five. By 1980 the population had declined to eighteen. In 1989 all that was left of the town was the cemetery and a church building with no congregation.

BIBLIOGRAPHY: Callahan County Historical Commission, *I Remember Callahan: History of Callahan County, Texas* (Dallas: Taylor, 1986).

Julius A. Amin

ADMIRAL NIMITZ STATE HISTORICAL PARK. Admiral Nimitz State Historical Park in Fredericksburg includes the restored Nimitz Hotel,[qv] which now houses the Nimitz Museum of the Pacific War and the Nimitz Art Gallery, the Pacific War History Walk, and the Japanese Garden of Peace. The state park grew out of the Fleet Admiral Chester W. Nimitz[qv] Memorial Naval Museum, which opened on February 24, 1967, the anniversary of the birth of Chester Nimitz, and featured artifacts of old Fredericksburg and of Admiral Nimitz's career. The museum was dedicated at Nimitz's request to the two million men and women who served with him in the Pacific during World War II.[qv] It officially became a state agency, with an appointed commission administration, in June 1970. On September 1, 1981, the Texas legislature placed the museum under the jurisdiction of the Texas Parks and Wildlife Department,[qv] although the local Admiral Nimitz Foundation continued fund-raising activities. The Japanese Garden of Peace behind the hotel was donated by the Japanese government; it was designed by Taketora Saita of Tokyo and built by Japanese craftsmen who came to the United States on funds raised by popular subscription in Japan. The garden includes a replica of the study of Admiral Heihachiro Togo, a leader whom Nimitz greatly admired; it displays a number of Japanese-style, American-grown plants, such as dwarf maples, apricots, magnolias, Japanese pines, and several crape myrtles that were a gift from the people of Fredericksburg. The garden was dedicated on May 8, 1976, the 130th anniversary of the founding of Fredericksburg.

The Pacific War History Walk, located two blocks northeast of the hotel, features a number of relics of the Pacific Theater of Operations, including dive bombers, tanks, guns, mines, and a "Fat Man" atomic bomb case made to house a bomb like that dropped on Nagasaki. The park's location in downtown Fredericksburg makes it a convenient stop for the many tourists who visit the Hill Country[qv] every year. The Lyndon B. Johnson State and National Historical parks[qqv] are eleven miles east of Admiral Nimitz Park, and the Enchanted Rock State Natural Area[qv] is eighteen miles to the north.

BIBLIOGRAPHY: Vertical Files, Barker Texas History Center, University of Texas at Austin.

Martin Donell Kohout

ADOBE. Although usually associated with the architecture of New Mexico and Arizona, adobe construction—building with a sun-dried mixture of earth, grass, and water—is also common throughout parts of West and South Texas and the Panhandle.[qv] The use of sun-dried mud is among the oldest building technologies. Recent archeological evidence suggests that adobe first appeared in the ancient Middle East, but various forms of earth construction are common in dry regions around the world. Indians of the American Southwest were familiar with this technology and used it to build the impressive pueblos in Taos and Acoma Pueblo, New Mexico. The Spanish, who first arrived in the Southwest in the sixteenth century, brought with them their own tradition of adobe construction. In early Spanish Texas[qv] adobe bricks, fashioned by Spanish and Indian workers, were used to build a variety of structures, including missions, fortifications, and dwellings. Among the examples of early adobe construction in Texas are portions of San Antonio de Valero Mission (the Alamo) and Nuestra Señora de la Purísima Concepción de Acuña Mission in San Antonio, and the ruins of San Lorenzo de la Santa Cruz Mission in Real County.

Adobe bricks are formed in wooden molds. They are then left in the sun to dry, typically for about two weeks. Because they are not fired they are a low-strength material and can bear only small weight loads; as a result, adobe structures are rarely taller than two stories. To prevent collapse, the walls of large structures are usually tapered at the top or braced with large buttresses, as in the famous church at Ranchos de Taos, New Mexico. The thick walls of adobe structures provide excellent insulation and thus are particularly desirable in the desert Southwest with its extreme temperatures. The rooms of adobe structures are usually quite narrow. Their length depends on the length of their *vigas*, wooden beams that support the weight of the roof. In traditional adobe construction, smaller wooden poles, known as *latillas*, extend between the *vigas* and support layers of twigs covered with packed adobe mud. The roofs are generally flat with shallow parapets; water drains off through wooden or tile *canales*.

Mexican Americans[qv] used the adobe technology introduced by the Pueblo Indians in New Mexico and the Jumano and Apache Indians in Texas, as well as their Spanish and Mexican forebears, to construct family dwellings. They often built modest, flat-topped adobe structures of one or several rooms, with neither connecting doors nor parapets. However, during the late nineteenth century many second-generation Mexican Americans in Alpine and Marfa altered the interior of their dwellings, adding doors to connect the rooms and expensive gabled roofs. Adobe structures remained typical of Texas Hispanic domiciles up to 1900.

Because of a shortage of wood during the eighteenth century, residents of San Antonio de Béxar erected both adobe homes and business shops, which they washed with blue or yellow. They also added Moorish-style radiating stone or lattice work to some of the buildings. Among the Pueblo people of New Mexico, women were the architects and builders in adobe. They dominated all aspects of plaster mixing and wall building, using only their hands and the simplest of tools to design their dwellings. Indian and Mexican women throughout the Southwest have maintained a significant role in adobe construction, with skills passed down through the generations. Some have specialized in such aspects of interior finishing as fogón (fireplace) building. Mexican-American women in West Texas have continued to build adobe structures.

With the arrival of the railroads in the 1880s, adobe buildings began to sport such nontraditional materials as sheet metal, shingles, tile, and sawed lumber; hip roofs also began to appear. In early adobe structures the floors were usually constructed of fired adobe brick, brick, tile, wood, or flagstone; concrete, sometimes covered with linoleum, later came into use. Several West Texas cities, notably El Paso and Fort Stockton, have passed ordinances curtailing or limiting the use of adobe, but it continues to be used through much of West Texas. In the 1980s adobe construction grew in popularity, and numerous new adobe structures were built in Lajitas and the Terlingua area.

BIBLIOGRAPHY: Francis Edward Abernethy, *Built in Texas*, Publications of the Texas Folklore Society 42 (Waco: E-Heart Press, 1979). *Building with Adobe: A West Texas Legacy* (Austin: Texas Historical Commission, 1984). Arnoldo De León, *The Tejano Community, 1836–1900* (Albuquerque: University of New Mexico Press, 1982). Joe Graham, "Folk Housing in South and West Texas: Some Comparisons," in *An Exploration of a Common Legacy: A Conference on Border Architecture* (Austin: Texas Historical Commission, 1978). Ramón A. Gutiérrez, *When Jesus Came, the Corn Mothers Went Away: Marriage, Sexuality, and Power in New Mexico, 1500–1846* (Stanford: Stanford University Press, 1991). Terry McKay, "Carmen Velarde: La Fogonera, The Art of the Fireplace Builder," *Traditions Southwest: The Adobe Quarterly*, Fall 1990. Del Scott, The Significance of Adobe to the Spanish Colonization of the Southwest (M.A. thesis, Abilene Christian College, 1962). Myrtle and Wilfred Stedman, *Adobe Architecture*

(Santa Fe: Sunstone Press, 1978). Vertical Files, Barker Texas History Center, University of Texas at Austin.

Teresa Palomo Acosta and Christopher Long

ADOBE CREEK. Adobe Creek rises in its northern branch in northeastern Hutchinson County (at 36°01′ N, 101°11′ W) and flows southeast for eight miles to its mouth on the Canadian River, twelve miles northeast of Plemons (at 35°53′ N, 101°08′ W). The creek crosses an area of flat to rolling plains surfaced with mesquite and various grasses. The stream received its name from the sandy and clayey soils along its banks, which were used to make adobe bricks. Bent, St. Vrain and Company used these soils to construct their adobe trading house in 1843. The Adobe Walls trading post of 1874 was also located near the creek (*see* ADOBE WALLS, TEXAS).

BIBLIOGRAPHY: Pauline D. and R. L. Robertson, *Cowman's Country: Fifty Frontier Ranches in the Texas Panhandle, 1876–1887* (Amarillo: Paramount, 1981).

ADOBE DRAW. Adobe Draw rises two miles northwest of Mount Livermore and four miles south of Farm Road 166 in north central Jeff Davis County (at 30°40′ N, 104°11′ W) and runs northeast for forty miles to its mouth on San Martine Draw, four miles southwest of San Martine Peak in southeastern Culberson County (at 31°08′ N, 104°06′ W). The last 3½ miles of the draw, below Levinson Reservoir, are dry. The streambed traverses an area of steep to gentle slopes surfaced by variable soils that support scrub brush and sparse grasses.

ADOBES, TEXAS. Adobes is located on Farm Road 170 and the Rio Grande near Arroyo Borracho, six miles southeast of Chinati in southwestern Presidio County. It developed as a farming community in the 1870s. Antonio Madrid was an eleven-year-old boy when he came to Adobes from Mexico to herd sheep in 1882. He grew to adulthood there and married Panfilia Estrade de Anda from the Borracho community. The Madrids raised eight children at Adobes. By 1914 irrigation and cotton growing had revolutionized the community's agricultural methods. Adobes had 750 acres of irrigated cottonfields in 1930. The community operated a school in 1939 as part of the Presidio school district. In the late 1980s Adobes remained a small farming community.

BIBLIOGRAPHY: John Ernest Gregg, History of Presidio County (M.A. thesis, University of Texas, 1933). Cecilia Thompson, *History of Marfa and Presidio County, 1535–1946* (2 vols., Austin: Nortex, 1985).

Julia Cauble Smith

ADOBE WALLS, FIRST BATTLE OF. The first battle of Adobe Walls occurred on November 26, 1864, in the vicinity of Adobe Walls, the remains of William Bent's abandoned adobe fort near the Canadian River in what is now Hutchinson County. The battle was one of the largest engagements between whites and Indians on the Great Plains. It resulted from the determination of Gen. James H. Carleton,[qv] commander of the military units in New Mexico, to halt Comanche and Kiowa attacks on Santa Fe wagontrains; the Indians saw the wagoners as trespassers who killed their game.

Col. Christopher (Kit) Carson,[qv] commanding the First Cavalry, New Mexico Volunteers, was ordered to lead an expedition against the winter campgrounds of the Comanches and Kiowas, believed to be somewhere on the south side of the Canadian. On November 10 he arrived at Fort Bascom with fourteen officers, 321 enlisted men, and seventy-five Ute and Jicarilla Apache scouts and fighters he had recruited from Lucien Maxwell's ranch near Cimarron, New Mexico. Two days later the column, supplied with two mountain howitzers under the command of Lt. George H. Pettis, twenty-seven wagons, an ambulance, and forty-five days' rations, marched down the Canadian into the Panhandle[qv] of Texas. Carson's destination was Adobe Walls, where he had been employed by Bent nearly twenty years earlier. After a delay caused by snowstorms the column set up camp for the night of November 25 at Mule Springs, in what is now Moore County, thirty miles west of Adobe Walls. Two of Carson's scouts reported the presence of a large group of Indians, who had recently moved into and around Adobe Walls with many horses and cattle. Carson immediately ordered all cavalry units and the two howitzers to move forward, leaving the infantry under Lt. Col. Francisco P. Abreau to follow later with the supply train. After covering fifteen miles Carson halted to await the dawn. No loud talking or fires were permitted, and a late-night frost added to the men's discomfort.

At about 8:30 A.M. Carson's cavalry attacked Dohäsan's[qv] Kiowa village of 150 lodges, routing the old chief and most of the other inhabitants, who spread the alarm to several Comanche groups. Pushing on to Adobe Walls, Carson forted up about 10 A.M., using one corner of the ruins for a hospital. One of the several Indian encampments in the vicinity, a Comanche village of 500 lodges, was within a mile of Adobe Walls. The Indians numbered between 3,000 and 7,000, far greater opposition than Carson had anticipated. Sporadic attacks and counterattacks continued during the day, but the Indians were disconcerted by the howitzers, which had been strategically positioned atop a small rise. Dohäsan led many charges, ably assisted by Stumbling Bear and Satanta;[qv] indeed, Satanta was said to have sounded bugle calls back to Carson's bugler.

With supplies and ammunition running low by late afternoon, Carson ordered his troops to withdraw to protect his rear and keep the way open to his supply train. Seeing this, the Indians tried to block his retreat by torching the tall bottomland grass near the river, but Carson set his own fires and withdrew to higher ground, where the battery continued to hold off the attacking warriors. At dusk Carson ordered a force to burn the Kiowa and Kiowa-Apache lodges, which the soldiers had attacked that morning. The Kiowa-Apache chief, Iron Shirt, was killed when he refused to leave his tepee.

Concerned with protecting the supply wagons and Abreau's infantry column moving up from Mule Springs, Carson decided to retreat. The reunited forces encamped for the night, and on the morning of November 17 Carson ordered a general withdrawal from the area. In all, Carson's troops and Indian scouts lost three killed and twenty-five wounded, three of whom later died. Indian casualties were estimated at 100 to 150. In addition 176 lodges, along with numerous buffalo robes and winter provisions, as well as Dohäsan's army ambulance wagon, had been destroyed. One Comanche scalp was reported taken by a young Mexican volunteer in Carson's expedition, which disbanded after returning to Fort Bascom without further incident.

General Carleton lauded Carson's retreat in the face of overwhelming odds as an outstanding military accomplishment; though the former mountain man was unable to strike a killing blow, he is generally credited with a decisive victory. Carson afterward contended that if Adobe Walls was to be reoccupied, at least 1,000 fully equipped troops would be required. The first eyewitness account of the battle other than Carson's military correspondence was published in 1877 by George Pettis, who had served as the expedition's artillery officer.

BIBLIOGRAPHY: M. Morgan Estergreen, *Kit Carson: A Portrait in Courage* (Norman: University of Oklahoma Press, 1962). C. Boone McClure, ed., "The Battle of Adobe Walls, 1864," *Panhandle-Plains Historical Review* 21 (1948). George Henry Pettis, *Kit Carson's Fight with the Comanche and Kiowa Indians at the Adobe Walls* (Providence: Rider, 1878; rpt., Santa Fe, 1908).

H. Allen Anderson

ADOBE WALLS, SECOND BATTLE OF. The second battle of Adobe Walls occurred on June 27, 1874, when a buffalo[qv] hunters' camp, built in the spring of that year in what is now Hutchinson County, about a mile from the adobe ruins known as Adobe Walls was attacked by a party of about 700 Plains Indians, mostly Cheyennes, Comanches, and Kiowas, under the leadership of Quanah Parker and Isa-tai.[qqv] Most of the hunters at the camp were awake repairing a broken ridgepole when the Indians charged at dawn. The defenders, twenty-eight men and one woman, gathered in (Jim) Hanrahan's Saloon, (Charlie) Myers and Leonard's Store, and (Charles) Rath and Wright's Store and repelled the initial charge with a loss of only two men. One more man was lost in later charges, which continued until about noon, and a fourth man was accidentally killed by the discharge of his own gun. The Indians, who had been urged into the fight by a medicine man, Isa-tai, conducted a desultory siege for about four or five days but made no other attacks. On the second day a group of fifteen or twenty of the Cheyennes appeared on a high mesa overlooking the post. Their appearance led to the famous gunshot of William (Billy) Dixon,[qv] when Dixon, inside the stockade, shot an Indian off his horse seven-eighths of a mile away. Hunters in the vicinity were notified of the attack on Adobe Walls, and by the end of the fifth day there were more than 100 men at Adobe Walls. A rescue party arrived after the Indians had given up the fight and retired. The significance of this fight is that it led to the Red River War[qv] of 1874–75, which resulted in the final relocation of the Southern Plains Indians to reservations in what is now Oklahoma. A monument was erected in 1924 on the site of Adobe Walls by the Panhandle-Plains Historical Society.[qv]

BIBLIOGRAPHY: T. Lindsay Baker and Billy R. Harrison, *Adobe Walls: The History and Archaeology of the 1874 Trading Post* (College Station: Texas A&M University Press, 1986). Olive K. Dixon, *Life of "Billy" Dixon* (1914; rev. ed., Dallas: Turner, 1927; facsimile, Austin: State House, 1987). Evetts Haley, Jr., "Adobe Walls," *Junior Historian*, January 1948. Mildred P. Mayhall, *Indian Wars of Texas* (Waco: Texian Press, 1965). Rupert N. Richardson, "The Comanche Indians at the Adobe Walls Fight," *Panhandle-Plains Historical Review* 4 (1931). G. Derek West, "The Battle of Adobe Walls," *Panhandle-Plains Historical Review* 36 (1963).

ADOBE WALLS, TEXAS. Adobe Walls was the name given several trading posts and later a ranching community located seventeen miles northeast of Stinnett and just north of the Canadian River in what is now northeastern Hutchinson County. The first trading post in the area seems to have been established in early 1843 by representatives of the trading firm of Bent, St. Vrain and Company, which hoped to trade with the Comanches and Kiowas. These Indians avoided Bent's Fort, the company's main headquarters on the upper Arkansas River near La Junta, Colorado, because enemies, the Cheyennes and Arapahoes, lived in the area. The new satellite post was situated on a stream that became known as Bent's (now Bent) Creek. Company traders worked originally from tepees and later from log structures. Probably no real fort was built on the site before 1846. Sometime after September 1845 William Bent and Ceran St. Vrain, chief partners in the firm, arrived with Mexican adobe makers to replace the log establishment with Fort Adobe, a structure eighty feet square, with nine-foot walls and only one entrance.

Occupation of Fort Adobe was sporadic, and by 1848 Indian hostility had resulted in its closure. That fall a momentary peace was effected, and Bent sought to reopen the post by sending Christopher (Kit) Carson,[qv] Lucien Maxwell, and five other employees to the Canadian. Resistance from the Jicarilla Apaches, however, forced Carson's group to cache the trade goods and buffalo robes they had acquired and return to Bent's Fort. Soon after, several Comanches persuaded Bent to make another try at resuming trade at Fort Adobe. A thirteen-man party, led by R. W. (Dick) Wootton, encountered restive Comanches at the fort and finally conducted trade through a window cut in the wall. In the spring of 1849, in a last concerted effort to revive the post, Bent accompanied several ox-drawn wagons to the Canadian. After part of his stock was killed by Indians, he blew up the fort's interior with gunpowder and abandoned the Panhandle[qv] trade to the Comancheros.[qv]

The adobe ruins thus became a familiar landmark to both Indians and Comancheros and to any white man who dared to venture into the heart of Comanchería. In November 1864 Carson, now a colonel of volunteers, used the walls of Fort Adobe to rest his 300 men and their horses after sacking a Kiowa village during a campaign against the tribes of the southern Plains. The group withstood several Indian attacks at the fort before withdrawing (see ADOBE WALLS, FIRST BATTLE OF).

In March 1874 merchants from Dodge City, Kansas, following the buffalo[qv] hunters south into the Texas Panhandle, established a large complex, called the Myers and Leonard Store, about a mile north of the Fort Adobe ruins. This business, which included a corral and restaurant, was joined in April 1874 by a second store operated by Charles Rath[qv] and Company. Shortly afterward James N. Hanrahan and Rath opened a saloon, and Tom O'Keefe started a blacksmith shop. By the end of spring, 200 to 300 buffalo hunters roamed the area, and trade at Adobe Walls boomed. After an Indian uprising called the second battle of Adobe Walls (June 1874) both merchants and hunters abandoned the site.

In the early 1880s James M. Coburn[qv] established his Turkey Track Ranch[qv] headquarters near the old battle site and persuaded William (Billy) Dixon,[qv] a scout and survivor of the 1874 battle, to homestead several sections nearby. Dixon built his house at the ruins of Fort Adobe. In August 1887 a post office was established at the Dixon homestead, where Dixon and S. G. Carter also operated a ranch-supply store. Dixon served as postmaster until 1901, when he was elected the county's first sheriff. He resigned shortly afterward and about 1902 moved to Plemons. A school was also established; after the first building burned in 1920, school was conducted on the second floor of Dixon's old home until a new structure could be built. Although the Dodge City Times advertised Adobe Walls as "a fine settlement with some twenty families," there never was a real community in the area except for the ranchers and their employees and families. The post office remained in operation until October 1921. From 1940 until 1970 Adobe Walls was listed in the Texas Almanac[qv] as having a population of fifteen. In 1987 a few scattered ranch dwellings marked the area.

During the 1920s several local and state projects were launched to mark the battle site at Adobe Walls and make it more accessible. In 1923 the Panhandle-Plains Historical Society[qv] acquired a six-acre tract that contained the remains of the 1874 trading post. The society conducted major archeological excavations at this site in the 1970s. In 1978 the complex was added to the National Register of Historic Places and recognized as a Texas state archeological landmark.

BIBLIOGRAPHY: T. Lindsay Baker and Billy R. Harrison, *Adobe Walls: The History and Archaeology of the 1874 Trading Post* (College Station: Texas A&M University Press, 1986). T. Lindsay Baker, *Ghost Towns of Texas* (Norman: University of Oklahoma Press, 1986). George Bird Grinnell, "Bent's Old Fort and Its Builders," *Collections of the Kansas State Historical Society, 1919–1922* 15 (1923). Arthur Hecht, comp., *Postal History in the Texas Panhandle* (Canyon, Texas: Panhandle-Plains Historical Society, 1960). Hutchinson County Historical Commission, *History of Hutchinson County, Texas* (Dallas: Taylor, 1980). David Lavender, *Bent's Fort* (Garden City, New York: Doubleday, 1954). Mildred P. Mayhall, *The Kiowas* (Norman: University of Oklahoma Press, 1962; 2d ed. 1971). John L. McCarty, *Adobe Walls Bride* (San Antonio: Naylor, 1955). Frederick W. Rathjen, *The Texas Panhandle Frontier* (Austin: University of Texas Press, 1973).

H. Allen Anderson

ADOBE WALLS MOUNTAIN. Adobe Walls Mountain is located twelve miles north of Study Butte, Texas, and two miles east of State Highway 118 in southwestern Brewster County (at 29°29′ N, 103°30′ W). It rises on its northern side in a long slope from the desert floor and falls off in sheer cliffs of bare rock some 500 feet high on its southern face. The elevation of its highest point is 4,510 feet above sea level. Vegetation in the area consists primarily of Chihuahuan Desert scrub, characterized by various shrubs and semisucculents that have partially replaced grassland as a result of overgrazing. Adobe Walls Mountain marks the northern edge of the historic Terlingua quicksilver district (*see* MERCURY MINING). The mountain is named for the incomplete adobe walls that once surrounded the main ranchhouse of the G4 Ranch.[qv]

BIBLIOGRAPHY: Clifford B. Casey, *Soldiers, Ranchers and Miners in the Big Bend* (Washington: Office of Archeology and Historic Preservation, U.S. Department of the Interior, 1969). Virginia Madison and Hallie Stillwell, *How Come It's Called That? Place Names in the Big Bend Country* (Albuquerque: University of New Mexico Press, 1958). Kenneth B. Ragsdale, *Quicksilver: Terlingua and the Chisos Mining Company* (College Station: Texas A&M University Press, 1976). Ronnie C. Tyler, *The Big Bend* (Washington: National Park Service, 1975).

ADOBE WALLS TRAIL. The Adobe Walls Trail, perhaps a subroute of the Jones and Plummer Trail,[qv] ran from Dodge City, Kansas, to the vicinity of Adobe Walls, Texas. The success of the buffalo[qv] hunters encouraged a group of Dodge City merchants in March 1874 to establish Adobe Walls as a trading center on the Canadian River in Hutchinson County. Their stores and stockade were located four miles east of Bent's Fort, the original Adobe Walls trading post. A. C. Meyers, who hired Ed "Dirty Face" Jones to organize a caravan of thirty wagons, and Charles Rath,[qv] who used his own teams, freighted in more than $70,000 worth of goods. The route established by the merchants and other buffalo hunters, such as J. Wright and John Mooar,[qqv] was heavily used by hunters and hide freighters even after Quanah Parker's[qv] raid. But after the buffalo hunting ended, the Adobe Walls Trail became primarily a cattle trail, while the Jones and Plummer, the Tascosa–Dodge City,[qv] and the Fort Supply trails were preferred by freighters and stage operators.

The Adobe Walls Trail ran due south out of Dodge City and crossed Mulberry Creek some twelve miles out, near the common crossing for all trails leading south from Dodge. It then veered southwest, gradually away from the more popular Jones and Plummer, and skirted Crooked Creek, which it crossed near the Meade-Ford county line. The trail caught a corner of Seward County as it angled south toward the Cimarron crossing near the Price and Davies Ranch headquarters in Indian Territory. It traveled west of the Beaver River and entered Texas just east of Palo Duro Creek, then continued to Adobe Walls on a nearly straight line south through Hansford County east of Horse Creek. It entered the breaks of the Canadian River west of Adobe Creek and followed that bank to Adobe Walls, where it extended south a few more miles to connect with the east-west Tascosa Trail.

The trail varied as travelers picked it up at different points or branched off to travel other routes. The Adobe Walls Trail remained generally on the high, dry flats, which provided grass but limited access to water. Ranches were few, and landmarks were scarce. Though the trail was a somewhat quicker route to Dodge from the western Panhandle[qv] than the others, by the late 1880s it had been abandoned.

BIBLIOGRAPHY: T. Lindsay Baker and Billy R. Harrison, *Adobe Walls: The History and Archaeology of the 1874 Trading Post* (College Station: Texas A&M University Press, 1986). Harry E. Chrisman, *Lost Trails of the Cimarron* (Denver: Sage, 1961). Frederick W. Rathjen, *The Texas Panhandle Frontier* (Austin: University of Texas Press, 1973).

C. Robert Haywood

ADOUE, JEAN BAPTISTE, SR. (1846–1924). Jean Baptiste Adoue, Sr., banker, was born in Aurignac, France, on October 24, 1846, the son of Jean Marie and Paule (Dorleac) Adoue. In 1861 he arrived in New Orleans with his younger brother. The trip from France to the United States took six months and was planned by the boys' older brother, who was already in the United States. The next year Adoue moved to Bryan, Texas. He subsequently operated a grocery store in Waco for a year before moving to Bremond, where he established a general store and private bank. In 1879 or 1880 he moved to Dallas and with several partners established a bank, Flippen, Adoue, and Lobit. Five years later he married Mittie Simpson, and the couple eventually had four children, including Jean Baptiste Adoue, Jr.[qv] Adoue became the president of his bank when it became the National Bank of Commerce in 1892. He continued as president until his death. In addition to his banking endeavors he was a partner in an investment firm and the director of two insurance companies. He was director and treasurer of the Old Dallas Club, a member of the City Club, a Mason, and a Shriner. He was the treasurer of the State Fair of Texas[qv] from 1899 until his death. He was appointed a French consular agent to settle the affairs of the La Réunion[qv] colony, a task he had just completed at the time of his death. He was a trustee of the Oak Cliff College for Young Ladies. On June 20, 1924, Adoue committed suicide in his Dallas home.

BIBLIOGRAPHY: Dallas *Morning News*, June 21, 1924. Ellis A. Davis and Edwin H. Grobe, comps., *The Encyclopedia of Texas* (2 vols., 1922?). Vertical Files, Barker Texas History Center, University of Texas at Austin.

Wayne Gard

ADOUE, JEAN BAPTISTE, JR. (1884–1956). Jean Baptiste Adoue, Jr., Dallas banker and mayor, was born on November 4, 1884, to Jean Baptiste and Mary or Mittie Neosha (Simpson) Adoue. He attended Dallas public schools and took his law degree from the University of Texas in 1906. He returned to Dallas, practiced law for a year, and then worked with his father at the National Bank of Commerce, of which he became president upon his father's death in 1924. He served as director and chairman of the board of numerous other businesses ranging from hotels to insurance and construction companies.

Adoue served two terms as president of the Dallas Chamber of Commerce (in 1939–40). His two terms as head of the Dallas Community Chest, during which he overhauled and strengthened its financial base, and his conduct of the War Chest 1943 Fund Drive earned him the Linz Award for outstanding community service in 1943. He was elected national vice president of the Community Chest and Councils in 1946 and 1947. He also served as vice president of the National War Fund.

In 1942 he was appointed to fill a vacancy on the city council, to which the voters returned him in 1943 and 1945. On the council he acquired a reputation as the champion of the common man and the underdog. His election to the council in 1949 resulted in a dispute that changed the city charter. His supporters successfully petitioned for a referendum election on the direct election of the mayor when Adoue did not win that office but had received the most votes of all those elected to the council. In 1951 Dallas voters made Adoue the first mayor elected by direct popular vote in more than twenty years. His term in office saw passage of one of the city's largest public-works programs, including an expansion of the Love Field.[qv] His administration, however, was one of the city's most turbulent, and he was often at odds with the Citizens' Charter Association. Although urged by supporters to run again for mayor in 1953, Adoue declined because of bad health.

He also held Texas, Southwest, and Southern tennis titles for a number of years and was ranked in the nation's top ten tennis players. He was a member of the board of directors of the United States Lawn Tennis Association for thirty years and in 1938 acted as the nonplaying captain of the United States Davis Cup team. He married Hester Ann Allen on October 12, 1909; they had two sons. After his first wife died he married Mary J. Wilson, on May 12, 1937. Adoue was a political conservative and an Episcopalian. On November 17, 1956, while at his desk at the bank, he died of a heart attack.

BIBLIOGRAPHY: Dallas *Morning News*, November 18, 1956. *Who Was Who in America*, 1960.

Joan J. Perez

ADRIAN, TEXAS. Adrian, on Interstate Highway 40 and U.S. Highway 66 in south central Oldham County, originated in 1900 when the Rock Island survey west of Amarillo picked the site as a station.

The first settler in the vicinity was Calvin G. Aten,[qv] a former Texas Ranger, who built a dugout for his family west of the site. The town was named for Adrian Cullen, an early farmer in the area, and officially began in the summer of 1909, when the Chicago, Rock Island and Gulf Railway was completed through that portion of the county. Promotion by the Iowa-based American-Canadian Land and Townsite Company quickly attracted prospective farmers and businessmen. J. P. Collier, who owned several lots, set up a printing press and provided a city water well and a few two-inch water mains. By 1910 Adrian had a post office, a pool hall, a school, a general store, a lumberyard, a bank, a blacksmith shop, a brick factory, and a newspaper, the Adrian *Eagle*. In 1915 the town had two churches, a drugstore, telephone service, and a population of fifty. The reason for this slow growth was a lengthy drought, coupled with the difficulty of maintaining a sufficient water supply. Nevertheless, Adrian survived famines and black dusters to become a stopping place for travelers on Route 66 and a shipping point for area wheat growers. The town's first grain elevator was built in 1929. During the 1940s Adrian organized a volunteer fire department, and in 1953 the citizens voted to incorporate with a mayor-council government. By 1984 the population had grown to 222. In 1990 the population was 220.

bibliography: Oldham County Historical Commission, *Oldham County* (Dallas: Taylor, 1981). Kathleen E. and Clifton R. St. Clair, eds., *Little Towns of Texas* (Jacksonville, Texas: Jayroe Graphic Arts, 1982). *H. Allen Anderson*

ADRIANCE, JOHN (1818–1903). John Adriance, early Texas merchant and legislator, son of George C. and Gertrude Adriance, was born at Troy, New York, on November 10, 1818. He was educated at Troy and Truxton, New York. After the death of his parents, he lived with an uncle, John Miller, a physician and United States congressman. He received his early training in merchandising in the stores of Truxton and Berlin, New York, and was eventually employed by the New York City firm of John Haggerty Sons, an auction house. For reasons of health he left New York, on October 8, 1835, and settled at Bell's Landing, Texas, later called Columbia. During the Texas Revolution,[qv] under Capt. Jacob Eberty, he helped protect the escaping residents of Marion during the Runaway Scrape;[qv] he later guarded Gen. Antonio López de Santa Anna[qv] and his officers on their way to imprisonment at Velasco.

Adriance was a partner with C. Beardslee in a mercantile business at West Columbia from 1836 to 1839, when he formed a partnership with Morgan L. Smith[qv] in Columbia. The firm marketed cotton in New York, New Orleans, and England. The partners purchased Waldeck Plantation[qv] as a place to send animals and implements taken as payment for debts. The merchant partnership was dissolved in 1844 and the plantation partnership in 1847. Adriance continued in the mercantile business until the end of the Civil War.[qv] He owned slaves, favored secession,[qv] and was named a member of the Brazoria County Committee of Correspondence on November 17, 1860. During the war Adriance acted as a deputy for the commissary department of the Confederacy at Columbia. He was wealthy in 1860 but suffered heavy losses during the war.

After the war he and his son operated a real estate firm. Adriance contributed to the Houston Tap and Brazoria Railroad and its extension to Wharton. For three years he headed the Immigration Department of the International–Great Northern Railway in Palestine. While serving as a member of the Thirteenth Texas Legislature, he influenced the founding of the Agricultural and Mechanical College of Texas (now Texas A&M University), Prairie View College (now Prairie View A&M University), and the University of Texas. He served as a director and finance-committee member of Texas A&M. He was a Mason and Episcopalian.

Adriance married Lydia Ann Cooke on September 24, 1846. They had three daughters and one son. Lydia died in 1871. After her death Adriance married his sister-in-law, Catherine Nash. He died at Columbia on December 7, 1903.

bibliography: John Adriance Papers, Barker Texas History Center, University of Texas at Austin. James A. Creighton, *A Narrative History of Brazoria County* (Angleton, Texas: Brazoria County Historical Commission, 1975). Llerena B. Friend, "Additional Items for the Winkler Check List of Texas Imprints, 1846–1860," *Southwestern Historical Quarterly* 65 (July 1961). Abigail Curlee Holbrook, "Cotton Marketing in Antebellum Texas," *Southwestern Historical Quarterly* 73 (April 1970). Louis Wiltz Kemp, "The Capitol at Columbia," *Southwestern Historical Quarterly* 48 (July 1944). *Memorial and Genealogical Record of Southwest Texas* (Chicago: Goodspeed, 1894; rpt., Easley, South Carolina: Southern Historical Press, 1978). *Southwestern Historical Quarterly*, Texas Collection, July 1960. Ralph A. Wooster, "Wealthy Texans, 1870," *Southwestern Historical Quarterly* 74 (July 1970). Ralph A. Wooster, "Wealthy Texans, 1860," *Southwestern Historical Quarterly* 71 (October 1967). *Ruth Munson Smith*

ADSUL, TEXAS. Adsul is west of the main unit of E. O. Siecke State Forest,[qv] one-half mile north of Farm Road 82 and about forty-three miles north of Beaumont, in west central Newton County. B. F. Yoakum[qv] extended the Orange and Northwestern Railway north of Buna shortly after he acquired the line in 1905. As lumbermen entered the heavily forested area, a number of small towns formed around the new sawmills. Among these was Adsul, named for the Adams-Sullivan Lumber Company sawmill. A post office was established there in 1907 with James K. Sullivan as postmaster. Population at the lumber town peaked at 500. As local timber was cut out, however, the mill at Adsul was shut down, and the post office was discontinued in 1911. One 1920 estimate set the population as high as 250. Only a few scattered buildings remained in 1984.

bibliography: S. G. Reed, *A History of the Texas Railroads* (Houston: St. Clair, 1941; rpt., New York: Arno, 1981). *Robert Wooster*

ADVANCE, TEXAS. Advance is a dispersed rural community near Farm Road 1885 sixteen miles northwest of Weatherford in northwest Parker County. In 1890 B. B. Barton, of Denton County, moved to Adell in Parker County. Four years later he opened a general store four miles northwest of Adell and encouraged Adell residents to move to his new community, which he named Advance. Postal service began in 1894. A cotton gin was erected, and by the late 1890s the new community had twenty residents. Postal service was discontinued in 1906.

bibliography: Gustavus Adolphus Holland, *History of Parker County and the Double Log Cabin* (Weatherford, Texas: Herald, 1931; rpt. 1937). *David Minor*

ADVENTIST CHURCHES. The Adventist movement, which developed from a schism in the religious following of William Miller and broke into several different groups, apparently reached Texas in the late 1880s. The town of Keene in Johnson County was established by a group of Seventh-Day Adventists in 1893. In 1894 the church members organized Keene Industrial Academy, which became Southwestern Assemblies of God College. Tenets of the Adventist creed include biblical literalism, the personal and imminent second advent of Christ on earth, and the celebration of Saturday as the Sabbath. The church stresses promotion through education, evangelism, and publication.

The religious census of 1906 reported a total membership of 1,825 in all the Adventist bodies in Texas. In 1926 the Advent Christian Church had ten churches with 623 members, the Seventh-Day Adventists had fifty-two churches with 3,011 members, the Church of God (Adventist) had two churches with 100 members, and the Church of God in Christ Jesus had four churches with 117 members.

In 1936 the Advent Christian Church had four organizations with 370 members, the Seventh-Day Adventists had sixty-seven churches with 4,102 members, the Church of God (Adventist) had two branches of three churches each and a total of 244 members. By 1936 the Church of God in Christ Jesus had separated from the Adventist groups and had 128 churches with a membership of 5,052. Seventh-Day Adventist membership in Texas increased from 6,259 on January 1, 1950, to 9,495 on June 30, 1966. During the same period the number of churches increased from 79 to 118. Thirty-eight new churches were constructed between 1959 and 1966, in such key cities as Dallas, Fort Worth, Houston, San Antonio, Austin, and Amarillo. In 1962 a camp-meeting pavilion with seating capacity for 5,000 was constructed in Keene.

In 1995 the Texas Conference employed 120 pastoral and church workers. In addition, the conference operated forty-five elementary schools, four secondary schools, and Southwestern Adventist College (*see* adventist schools). The conference operated five medical institutions—Huguley Memorial Medical Center, Fort Worth; Willow Creek Psychiatric, Arlington; Metroplex Hospital, Killeen; Rollins Brook Community Hospital, Lampasas; and Central Texas Medical Center, San Marcos. It also operated an ambulance service in San Antonio. More than 100 physicians and dentists operated self-supporting clinics as officials of the Seventh-Day Adventist Medical and Dental Association. Church headquarters for the Texas Conference of Seventh-Day Adventists is in Alvarado, near Fort Worth. In 1990 the Adventist Christian Church had five churches and 221 members. The Seventh-Day Adventists had grown to 258 churches and 41,470 members.

bibliography: *Dictionary of American History* (New York: Scribner, 1940).

ADVENTIST SCHOOLS. The early development of the Seventh-Day Adventist educational system dates back to 1874. The first schools in Texas were established in the 1890s. In 1995 the Texas Conference of Seventh-Day Adventists operated 45 elementary schools; 110 teachers were employed for an annual enrollment of approximately 1,800 students. In addition, the denomination maintained four secondary schools in Texas—Jefferson Adventist Academy, Jefferson; Valley Grande Academy, Weslaco; Chisholm Trail Academy, Keene; and Burton Adventist Academy, Arlington. The schools accommodated both boarding and community students. The enrollment of the four academies was 465 students, with 50 teachers. The conference also runs Southwestern Adventist College in Keene, which has approximately 900 students. These schools, which are all coeducational, are operated on the philosophy that education should be threefold: equal development of mental, physical, and spiritual faculties is stressed. To accomplish this purpose, the schools adhere closely to educational standards established by the state, adding courses in Bible and allotting time for worship or inspirational studies. Health principles are taught, and opportunity is given for students to work. Academy students assist with office work, janitorial services, laundry, cafeteria, grounds, broom making, cabinet making, and other work. *I. V. Stonebrook*

ADY, TEXAS. Ady, on Farm Road 1061, is in a farming and ranching area south of the Canadian River in northwestern Potter County. The first settler in this vicinity was Agapito Sandoval, one of Casimero Romero's[qv] *pastores,* who located his family and sheep on Corsino Creek near the north bank of the Canadian. Ady, on the opposite bank, began as a switch on the Fort Worth and Denver City Railway in 1887. The Texas Sand and Gravel Pit was started here in 1941. In 1984 there was a cemetery at Ady but no community center or listed population.

bibliography: Della Tyler Key, *In the Cattle Country: History of Potter County, 1887–1966* (Amarillo: Tyler-Berkley, 1961; 2d ed., Wichita Falls: Nortex, 1972). José Ynocencio Romero and Ernest R. Archambeau, "Spanish Sheepmen on the Canadian at Old Tascosa," *Panhandle-Plains Historical Review* 19 (1946). *H. Allen Anderson*

AERONAUTICS AND AEROSPACE INDUSTRY. In Texas all types of aircraft, from small one-man planes to vehicles capable of landing on the moon, have been manufactured, and several major commercial airlines have originated in the state. Many years before the space age dawned with the orbiting of the first artificial earth satellite in 1957, Texas played an important part in the development of American military aviation and aircraft technology. Before World War II[qv] a complex of army airfields (later air force bases) surrounded San Antonio, and Randolph Field (*see* randolph air force base) was known as the "West Point of the Air." During the war other military installations were built in the state. The United States Air Force School of Aviation Medicine at San Antonio grew into the nation's outstanding aeromedical center and became a center for the new field of space medical research and applications.

Aircraft manufacture did not begin in Texas until 1940, although since World War I[qv] repair shops had operated in the state and had been successfully rebuilding airplanes. In May 1939 the Southern Aircraft Corporation was formed in Houston, and in July 1940 this plant completed its first plane, a biplane designed for use as an army trainer. In that month also the Hall-Aluminum Aircraft Corporation announced plans for a $5 million plant to be constructed near Dallas. In August 1940 the Bennet Aircraft Company opened a plant near Fort Worth, and the Worth Garment Company bought and moved to a plant near Fort Worth the equipment of the Roos Aircraft Company of Kansas City. On September 28, 1940, ground was broken at Hensley Field, Dallas, for the $7 million North American Aviation factory. The original unit consisted, when finished, of six buildings on a 180-acre site. The large main building of the plant was completely windowless, air-conditioned, and artificially lighted. In December 1940 Southern Aircraft began excavation for a plant near Garland and in February 1941 moved from Houston and began production of military primary-training planes.

In January 1941 the Consolidated Aircraft Corporation announced plans for the construction of a $10 million plant near Fort Worth to construct four-motor bombers, under United States Army auspices. It was estimated that the erection of this plant, one of the largest factories of any kind in the world, more than doubled the number of industrial wage earners in the Fort Worth area. Ground was broken in May and included a housing project and a community center called Avion Village. The main building of the factory, completed in December, was fourteen city blocks long and more than a block wide; it covered thirty acres.

By the close of 1941 six companies supplied parts and equipment for aircraft factories in the Dallas–Fort Worth area. Several oilfield-equipment factories were converted to wartime production, and the Hughes Tool Company (*see* baker hughes) at Houston manufactured bomber parts for nationwide distribution. Workers at these plants came from all over the nation. Industrial-training schools emphasizing aircraft techniques were operated at Texas colleges and universities as well as at factories themselves.

Some decline in Texas aircraft manufacture occurred in the immediate postwar years, as most aircraft factories and supplemental equipment companies were converted to peacetime production on a smaller scale of operation. Equipment designed for working aluminum was newly employed in prefabricated houses, household furnishings, and industrial supplies. Chance-Vought, one of the four divisions of United Aircraft, Incorporated, took over the North American plant in May 1949 to produce and experiment with jet aircraft. The Texas Engineering and Manufacturing Company was organized to utilize the facilities of what by then had become one of the world's largest centers of aircraft production, and in 1950 Lawrence Bell established in a Hurst-Euless cow pasture the world's first plant specifically designed to manufacture helicopters.

By the 1960s aircraft manufacture was located chiefly in North

Texas, particularly in the area of Grand Prairie, Richardson, Hurst, Euless, Arlington, and Fort Worth, an area that ranked second only to the entire state of California in aircraft production. Other aircraft-manufacturing enterprises or their subsidiaries could be found in Bexar, Cameron, Harris, Harrison, Hunt, Kerr, McLennan, Medina, Stephens, and Young counties. After the North American facility (later Ling-Temco-Vought), the Fort Worth General Dynamics or "Convair" plant was completed in 1941. This firm, noted for bomber production and its controversial TFX contract, ranked first in the nation in the export of defense weapons in 1965.

In 1944 the United States Army established an Air Defense Center for guided missiles at Fort Bliss,[qv] near El Paso. The missile center and its test range were subsequently used to test German rockets, principally V-2 missiles, captured at the end of the war. In the 1950s, as national security needs dictated an expensive ballistic-missile program involving all three military services, millions of federal dollars found their way to Texas in development and fabrication contracts to such firms with large Texas plants as the General Dynamics Corporation, the Boeing Company, and Texas Instruments.[qv] During this decade the space industry came to Texas in the form of manufacture for military rocket projects, ballistics research, and testing at the United States Navy's Daingerfield Ordnance Test Facility and research into the psychophysiological conditions of space flight at San Antonio. Aircraft manufacture and its later concomitant, the electronics industry, added significantly to the Texas economy. With the advent of electronics, companies such as Texas Instruments and Collins Radio developed in Dallas County and branched out elsewhere in Texas.

The decision of the National Aeronautics and Space Administration in September 1961 to locate its Manned Spacecraft Center (*see* LYNDON B. JOHNSON SPACE CENTER) in Houston, planned as the command post for the national effort to send men to the moon, marked the culmination of the growing identification of Texas with the development of atmospheric and extra-atmospheric transport. In the 1990s NASA cooperated with other agencies to explore outer space, firms like Space Services Incorporated in Houston developed privately funded rocket launchers and other innovations, and area universities developed programs relating to needs of the industry. Among these were the Rice University Department of Space Physics and Astronomy and the University of Houston Space Vacuum Epitaxy Center and Institute for Space Architecture, working to support the space-shuttle mission and establish the nation's first permanent space station.

Aircraft manufacture in the 1960s ranked sixth in the state in number of employees, sixth in payroll accounts, and eighth in value added by manufacturing. (These figures did not include data from the National Aeronautics and Space Administration complex, certain government contractors in North Texas, or satellite plants.) In 1967 sixty aircraft-manufacturing establishments operated in the state, employing 58,000 workers; 50,900 workers were employed in aircraft manufacturing in 1986.

BIBLIOGRAPHY: E. C. Barksdale, *The Genesis of the Aviation Industry in North Texas* (Austin: University of Texas Bureau of Business Research, 1958). Roger Bilstein and Jay Miller, *Aviation in Texas* (Austin: Texas Monthly Press, 1985). Lloyd L. Turner, "The South's Biggest War Baby," *Editor and Publisher*, October 31, 1953.

Charles C. Alexander and E. C. Barksdale

AEROSPACE MEDICINE, AIR FORCE. Aerospace medicine is a medical specialty that deals with ways to adapt to the stresses experienced by those who fly far from the earth, including sustained acceleration, weightlessness, decompression sickness, temperature extremes, noise, vibration, confinement, and radiation. After the Wright brothers pioneered airplane flights in 1903, the Signal Corps established an Aeronautical Division (1907) to supervise all matters pertaining to "air machines." In 1917 Theodore Charles Lyster became the first chief surgeon, Aviation Section, Signal Corps, United States Army. Lyster guided the development of aviation medicine during World War I,[qv] including the foundation of the Air Service Medical Research Laboratory at Hazelhurst, New York (1918). This laboratory evolved into a training academy for flight surgeons and was renamed the School of Aviation Medicine in the same year that Brooks Field (later Brooks Air Force Base[qv]) in San Antonio became a center for primary flight training in the army (1922). In 1926 the army transferred the School of Aviation Medicine to Brooks, where it remained for five years. The SAM was then moved to Randolph Field (later Randolph Air Force Base[qv]), then back to Brooks in 1959. Harry G. Armstrong, another pioneer in aviation medicine, commanded SAM between 1946 and 1949. Armstrong had participated in the establishment of the Aeromedical Laboratory in Dayton, Ohio, in 1935. He studied physiological problems of flight and developed ways to prevent them. He and others developed partial-pressure and full-pressure suits, keys to the beginnings of aerospace medicine. When Charles Yeager became the first man to break the sound barrier in October 1947, he wore a T-1 partial-pressure suit developed by the Aeromedical Laboratory.

When the United States Air Force became an independent agency in 1947, a separate Medical Service was established. Maj. Gen. Malcolm C. Grow and Maj. Gen. Harry Armstrong became the first and second USAF surgeons general. Armstrong believed that a medical center must embrace all fields of science related to human biology and medicine, and that it should have close association with other civilian and military scientific, engineering, and medical-research centers. A new Aerospace Medical Center opened at Brooks AFB in 1959. The center brought together the School of Aviation Medicine (transferred from Randolph AFB), the Lackland Hospital and the Air Force Epidemiology Laboratory (both from Lackland Air Force Base[qv] in San Antonio), and the Medical Service School from Gunter AFB, Alabama. The center completed some research projects for NASA before it was incorporated into a newly established Aerospace Medical Division at Brooks in 1961. Many experiments were conducted before the Mercury series—the first United States manned space flights. Many of the human subjects were USAF basic trainees who volunteered for pressure-chamber, isolation, and weightlessness studies. One of the first was Airman Donald R. Farrell, a finance specialist stationed at Randolph AFB, Texas. In 1958 he volunteered to test the "space cabin simulator" that the SAM had received in 1954. Much was learned from his seven-day stay in a tiny cabin, and Farrell was honored by the presence of Lyndon B. Johnson,[qv] then the Senate majority leader, when he emerged on February 16, 1958.

Officials wanted the new Aerospace Medical Center to expand its traditional role in flight medicine. For four decades, doctors and scientists had addressed the medical needs of pilots and astronauts. Now they hoped that the center would become the single agency for studies in the life sciences and aerospace medicine. Under the direction of Lt. Gen. Bernard A. Schriever, the USAF School of Aerospace Medicine (the renamed School of Aviation Medicine), much of the former Aerospace Medical Center, and several other laboratories became the Aerospace Medical Division in 1961. AMD commanded virtually all of the USAF facilities for aerospace medical-research development and testing; postgraduate training of medical officers, nurses, and technicians in aerospace medicine and related specialties; and clinical services for flyers afflicted with aerospace disorders. In August 1962 the Department of Defense and NASA agreed that NASA would assume responsibility for all of the United States space bioscience programs, including animal flights. NASA would continue to need support from the air force, since the military supplied launch vehicles, experiments, and research animals. Since NASA managed the only operational programs for the support of man in space, control of nearly all research in manned space flight and aerospace medicine was lifted from the USAF. Nevertheless, AMD continued to work with NASA in several ways. AMD's hospital facilities were used by the astronauts and their families. Contracts were given to AMD to test pure-oxygen atmospheres and the Gemini-Apollo pressure suit.

One program of the USAF School of Aerospace Medicine graduated thirty-nine veterinarians who specialized in the care of animals used in aerospace research. USAFSAM began courses in Aerospace Nursing at Cape Kennedy, Florida, in July 1965. In 1963, AMD began several studies associated with the Manned Orbiting Laboratory, the first United States space-laboratory program assigned to the USAF. Because of a need to reduce defense spending, the Manned Orbiting Laboratory program was canceled in 1969, but AMD continued with several aerospace-research projects.

Studies were conducted on nuclear survivability, decompression, sustained accelerative forces, and cardiographic parameters for NASA's space-shuttle system. Other studies involved the effects of ionizing radiation and the effects of protons on nonhuman primates. Some of the first experiments in the space-shuttle launches of the early 1980s involved tests in visual functions, since astronauts had commented on both increased and decreased ability to see in space. A short-arm centrifuge was studied as a way to prevent the physiological deconditioning caused by weightlessness in space. The current protective measures employed in the shuttle operations evolved directly from twenty years of joint studies by NASA and USAFSAM on altitude-decompression sickness. Beginning in 1991 all astronauts were trained for G exposure at USAFSAM and a crew reentry anti-G suit was developed at the school. *See also* AEROSPACE MEDICINE, LYNDON B. JOHNSON SPACE CENTER.

BIBLIOGRAPHY: *Aerospace Medicine* (Baltimore: Williams and Wilkins, 1961; 2d. ed., 1971). Edward B. Alcott and Robert C. Williford, *Aerospace Medical Division: Twenty-Five Years of Excellence, 1961–1986* (San Antonio: Aerospace Medical Division, Brooks Air Force Base, 1986). Harry G. Armstrong, *Principles and Practice of Aviation Medicine* (Baltimore: Williams and Wilkins, 1939). Charles A. Berry, "The Beginnings of Space Medicine," *Aviation Space and Environmental Medicine* 57 (October 1986). *Edward B. Alcott*

AEROSPACE MEDICINE, LYNDON B. JOHNSON SPACE CENTER. As the center of the national space program, the Lyndon B. Johnson Space Center[qv] has become the focus of research in aerospace medicine.

NASA and aerospace medicine. The successful launch of Earth's first artificial satellite by the Soviet Union on October 4, 1957, was the initial step in a series of events that made the state of Texas the home of the United States manned space-exploration program. *Sputnik I* provided the impetus for President Dwight D. Eisenhower[qv] to propose and Congress to approve the National Aeronautics and Space Act, which was signed into law on July 29, 1958. To implement the act, Eisenhower selected the National Advisory Committee for Aeronautics. The NACA was soon renamed the National Aeronautics and Space Administration, and T. Keith Glennan and Hugh Dryden were named administrator and deputy administrator, respectively. Although plans for manned space flight were well under way before the establishment of NASA, one of NASA's highest priorities was to consolidate the work done by the NACA laboratories and the military services and focus on the goal of launching a person into orbital flight and returning that person safely to Earth. To accomplish this goal, Glennan established a Space Task Group on November 5, 1958, at Langley Research Center under the direction of Robert R. Gilruth, who had been at Langley since graduating from the University of Minnesota in 1936. During the years before NASA, Glennan assembled an extremely competent and vigorous group of engineers. Included in it were many who later became highly influential, both in technical and management roles, in all NASA's manned space flight programs. Among these were Maxime A. Faget, Christopher C. Kraft, Jr., Paul E. Purser, Charles W. Mathews, Robert O. Piland, and Charles J. Donlan. The technology for manned space flight came from this dedicated and ingenious cadre of engineers, but the aerospace medical expertise resided in the military service and in universities supported by the military. The United States Air Force, in particular, held the required expertise in the physiological aspects of space flight.

After World War II,[qv] 130 German scientists and engineers, led by Werner von Braun, were brought to the United States and stationed at Fort Bliss in El Paso, Texas, to continue their work on rockets. The United States Air Force also enlisted the service of a number of German physicians, physiologists, and psychologists who had been the nucleus of the Luftwaffe medical-research program in support of high-altitude and high-speed airplane flight. Six of these were assigned as research physicians to the Air Force School of Aviation Medicine at Randolph Air Force Base in San Antonio. Although they concentrated primarily on aviation medicine, the natural extension of their high-altitude research programs drew their interests to space.

In 1948, nine years before *Sputnik I,* Col. Harry G. Armstrong, commandant of the school, convened a panel to discuss "Aeromedical Problems of Space Travel." The panel discussion included presentations by Hubertus Strughold and Heinz Haber, two of the German physicians, and commentary from six noted university and military scientists. At this panel, Strughold coined the term "space medicine." Later, through the excellence of his work, he was nicknamed "the father of space medicine." The foundation of aerospace medicine in support of manned space flight had been established. As research continued, concern grew throughout this medical community that weightless flight would gravely affect the physiological systems of those who flew. German physicians Heinz Haber and Otto Gauer, who supported the air force aviation-medicine program, noted that weightlessness could seriously affect the "autonomic nervous functions and ultimately produce a very severe sensation of succumbence associated with an absolute incapacity to act." This concern for physiological and psychological dangers associated with space flight resulted in the establishment of an operational aerospace medical group within the Space Task Group to address the problem. The first members of the medical group were two air force physicians, Lt. Col. Stanley C. White and Maj. William S. Augerson, and one navy psychologist, Lt. Robert Voas; their primary interest was flight-crew selection and training. To provide contact between the Space Task Group medical group, NASA Headquarters, and external medical and life-sciences groups, the Life Sciences Advisory Committee was established, with W. Randolph Lovelace II as chairman. The committee played a role in the selection of the Mercury astronauts.

The Manned Spacecraft Center and Project Mercury. The accomplishments of the Space Task Group over the next three years were phenomenal. The Redstone and Atlas rockets were selected and, after extensive testing, man-rated for suborbital and orbital missions, respectively. The Mercury capsule was designed, tested, and flown. Life-support systems were developed to provide a breathable atmosphere at regulated pressure with temperature and humidity control. Food and water systems were developed. A couch was designed to protect the astronaut from the forces of high acceleration launch and landing.

Astronaut-selection planning began seriously in 1958. On April 9, 1959, at a Washington news conference, Glennan introduced the seven military test pilots selected for space flight. They were selected from thirty-two candidates who had passed the initial screening and evaluation process, had been through a rigorous physical examination at the Lovelace Clinic in New Mexico, and had been through extensive mental and physical environmental tests at the Wright Air Development Center in Dayton, Ohio. America's first astronauts were Lt. Cdr. Alan B. Shepard, Lt. Cdr. Walter M. Schirra, Jr., and Lt. M. Scott Carpenter from the navy; Capt. Donald K. Slayton, Capt. L. Gordon Cooper, and Capt. Virgil I. Grissom from the air force; and Lt. Col. John H. Glenn from the marines. Doctors Stanley White and Robert Voas were members of the first astronaut-selection committee, which was chaired by Charles Donlan, assistant project manager of the Space Task Group. Two years later, on May 5, 1961, Alan Shepard became the first American in space when the Redstone rocket boosted his Mercury space capsule into suborbital flight for five minutes and sixteen seconds of weightlessness. Shortly after Shepard's flight, President John F. Kennedy, in a special message presented to Congress on May 25, 1961, made a statement that profoundly affected America's space program. He said, "I believe this nation should commit itself to achieving the goal, before this decade is out, of landing a man on the Moon and returning him safely to the Earth. No single space project in this period will be more impressive to mankind, or more important for the long-range exploration of space; and none will be so difficult or expensive to accomplish."

President Kennedy's statement gave the Space Task Group both a future and a challenge. The STG had grown from thirty-three persons at its inception to 794 by mid-1961. A new facility dedicated to manned space flight was necessary to accomplish the challenge. Kennedy approved the new facility in principle as an adjunct to his emphasis on an enlarged space program. Congress, sensing the interest of the American people in responding to the earlier successes of the Soviet Union, approved the budget, and a site-survey team was established in August 1961. On September 19, 1961, James E. Webb, the new NASA administrator, announced that a new NASA center named the Manned Spacecraft Center would be built near Houston, Texas, on 1,000 acres of land transferred to the government by Rice University and an adjacent plot that the government purchased. The site was in Harris County near Clear Lake and was connected through Galveston Bay to the Gulf of Mexico. There was criticism that Vice President Lyndon B. Johnson and Houstonian Albert Thomas,[qqv] chairman of the Independent Offices Subcommittee of the House Appropriations Committee, had exercised undue political influence in the selection of Houston as the site of MSC. The charges were denied by NASA. Gilruth, now officially director of MSC, moved quickly to lease facilities in the nearby Houston area, while plans were completed for the construction of fourteen buildings at an estimated cost of $60 million to accommodate more than 3,000 persons. During the next year, as construction began on a permanent facility, NASA successfully launched three orbital missions. On May 15, 1963, Gordon Cooper completed twenty-two orbits of Earth in the final Mercury mission.

Aerospace medicine and manned space flight. Project Mercury provided confidence in the ability of the astronaut to perform satisfactorily in the weightless environment and in the capability of the spacecraft environmental-control system to support life in space. In addition, many worries about psychological and physiological dangers that could be associated with space and the weightless environment were dispelled. Several physiological problems did, however, emerge from the Mercury project. Dehydration was observed in every crew member, accompanied by decreased water consumption and increased urine output. Some degradation of performance capability was evident and was thought to be related to fatigue associated with sleep disturbances. Two astronauts experienced orthostatic hypotension after flight; soon after leaving the spacecraft their pulse rate increased and their blood pressure decreased as their cardiovascular systems were challenged by Earth's gravitational forces following their exposure to weightlessness. Postflight clinical evaluations indicated blood and urine electrolyte imbalances and bone demineralization, as evidenced by the increased levels of calcium and phosphorus in body-fluid samples collected and analyzed after the flight. The medical implications of these physiological changes in the Mercury astronauts heightened the awareness of management officials at MSC of the need for a more aggressive medical program in support of the planned longer-duration Gemini and Apollo projects.

In 1963, at the height of Project Mercury, MSC had grown to 2,500 civil-service employees, but only about 500 supported Project Mercury. The rest of the employees were involved in preparing for the Gemini and Apollo projects. Gemini was planned to demonstrate that spacecraft rendezvous was possible, that an astronaut could exit the spacecraft in space and function safely in a pressurized space suit, and that he could endure and perform satisfactorily during extended periods of time in the weightless environment. Capt. Charles A. Berry, an air force physician, had been assigned from the School of Aerospace Medicine in San Antonio to participate in medical examinations for the Mercury astronauts. He was reassigned to MSC to provide medical care and medical-operations support for Project Mercury. Dr. Lawrence F. Dietlein, a physician from the United States Public Health Service, was assigned to MSC to develop a medical-research program to investigate the physiological changes observed on Mercury flights and evaluate these changes for the longer missions. These two physicians, plus Dr. Stan White's life-systems group, which was transferred from Langley to MSC, formed the major elements of biomedical support for Gemini and Apollo.

Project Gemini included twelve manned space flights. The Gemini spacecraft, launched by a modified Titan missile, carried two astronauts. The two longer flights, Gemini V (eight days) and Gemini VII (almost fourteen days), included nine medical experiments designed to investigate the problems identified during the Mercury missions. These experiments provided an opportunity for the medical community outside NASA to participate in the space-flight experiment program: Dr. Pauline Mack of Texas Woman's University and doctors Harry Lipscomb and Peter Kelloway of Baylor College of Medicine were selected as principal investigators for two of the nine Gemini experiments. The results of the medical experiments, the performance of the Gemini astronauts, and the information obtained from the extensive medical examinations conducted before and after each mission gave MSC medical officials increased confidence as the challenge of Apollo—to land on the moon and return safely to Earth—approached. As Dr. Berry stated in a technical paper presented at the Gemini Summary Conference held at MSC in February 1967, "Although much remains to be learned, it appears that if man is properly supported, his limitations will not be a barrier to the exploration of the universe."

Preparations to take the first step in exploring the universe continued unabated as the Mercury and Gemini projects provided the information necessary to send men to the moon and return them to Earth. As the manned Gemini launches proceeded, the three unmanned launches testing Apollo's powerful Saturn boosters and the three-man spacecraft were completed. The first Apollo manned launch, an orbital flight of Earth, was scheduled for February 21, 1967, less than four months after the final Gemini mission. This mission did not take place as scheduled, for, on January 27, 1967, during a final manned checkout of the complete vehicle, a fire in the spacecraft resulted in the death of Virgil I. Grissom, Edward H. White II, and Roger B. Chaffee, who were trapped inside. A twenty-month delay followed as NASA strove furiously to investigate the cause of the fire and correct every factor involved. The Apollo fire had a profound effect on the aerospace medical program at MSC. The complexity, diversity, and growth of the medical elements at the center during Gemini resulted in combining these elements into one organization—the Medical Research and Operations Directorate, with Dr. Berry as director. Although ensuring the health and safety of the flight crew had always been the primary objective of the medical program, the emphasis of the in–flight program was now almost entirely on medical support and safety. A planned series of in-flight experiments to investigate cardiovascular function, the musculoskeletal system, and metabolic function in space was eliminated. The medical-research program concentrated on preflight and postflight examinations, clinical analyses of collected body-fluid samples, and preflight and postflight physiological investigations. One potentially serious medical problem emerged during the Apollo missions. Space motion sickness, thought to be associated with disturbances of the vestibular system's ability to function normally in the weightless environment, had been reported by Russian cosmonauts but had not been evident in either the Mercury or Gemini astronauts. However, of the thirty-three Apollo astronauts, eleven reported motion-sickness symptoms ranging from slight stomach awareness to severe vomiting and degraded performance capability.

The biomedical results of Apollo were impressive. The number of flights and the number of astronauts provided the medical investigators with extensive information to examine the physiological changes observed in previous flights and to plan and design the detailed medical experiments to be flown on the longer missions of the world's first space station, Skylab. The legacy of Apollo, however, was pride in meeting a challenge. President Kennedy's challenge was answered on July 20, 1969, when Neil A. Armstrong, from the lunar lander sitting on the surface of the moon, reported, "Houston, Tranquility Base here—the Eagle has landed." People throughout the world shared in the pride of accomplishing the first step in the manned exploration of the universe.

The Skylab missions, which occurred between May 1973 and February 1974, differed significantly from all previous manned missions. From its inception, Skylab was intended to be a science program. The space laboratory, a modified Saturn IV-B stage, provided a large area (294 cubic meters) for science investigations and living in space. Skylab was launched unmanned; and during its time in orbit, it was occupied by three crews of three astronauts per crew for 171 days. The first manned mission lasted twenty-eight days; the second, fifty-nine days; and the final, eighty-four days. These long-duration missions, which included twelve primary medical experiments, were the answer to the medical scientists' dreams. The investigators had an opportunity to study in flight, over a much longer period of time, the physiological changes observed on earlier missions. The twelve in-flight medical experiments included investigators from areas throughout the United States. Six of the experiments included principal investigators from the Lyndon B. Johnson Space Center (as the Manned Spacecraft Center was now called) and two from Baylor College of Medicine. These experiments and fourteen other special in-flight medically related tests, which were added to the second and third manned Skylab missions, provided a wealth of biomedical information. This information answered many of the questions raised concerning physiological changes observed in earlier missions and established that man can adapt to the weightless environment, perform effectively over an extended time, and successfully readapt to the gravity of Earth. The medical data indicated that some physiological changes observed in earlier, shorter flights were apparently self-limiting. These changes related to blood volume, body-fluid output, and body-fluid biochemistry. Other changes, such as bone demineralization and muscle degeneration, continued throughout the longer missions. Though the cardiovascular system appeared to stabilize after four to six weeks in space, problems of orthostatic intolerance continued to appear postflight. Many biomedical questions were answered by the Skylab missions, and the data were useful in designing measures, such as regimented exercise programs, to counteract some of the physiological changes. However, there were still many unanswered questions that only long-term flights and an increased number of flight crew members could address.

The final flight of an Apollo spacecraft took place on July 15, 1975. The Apollo-Soyuz Test Project was a nine-day international mission that featured the rendezvous and docking of the Apollo spacecraft with a Russian Soyuz spacecraft. While some in-flight biomedical data were obtained, the inadvertent exposure of the crew to nitrogen tetroxide fumes during reentry and their subsequent development of chemical pneumonitis negated most postflight medical-experiment data collection. The Apollo-Soyuz mission was the final opportunity for medical scientists to conduct in-flight experiments or tests in an American spacecraft for more than six years.

The Medical Research and Operations Directorate was renamed the Life Sciences Directorate on September 5, 1972. On October 17, 1977, the Life Sciences Directorate was combined with the Science and Applications Directorate and became the Space and Life Sciences Directorate. This organizational change increased the functional responsibilities of the directorate by adding lunar and planetary science, Earth observations, and space science, and by retaining responsibility for life sciences, medical research, medical operations, experiment development, and payload management. Although no in-flight experiments were conducted, the next six years were busy ones for the Space and Life Sciences Directorate. The ground-based medical-research program, which supported the development of flight experiments and devised and tested countermeasures to the physiological problems identified in previous missions, was expanded and accelerated in anticipation of more frequent space missions when flights were resumed. In-flight experiments were designed to address the primary concerns of weightless flight—space motion sickness, cardiovascular deconditioning, fluid and electrolyte imbalance, bone demineralization, and muscle atrophy. Medical and environmental requirements were defined for the next generation of United States spacecraft. The spacecraft design chosen was the Space Shuttle. Launched into orbit with the aid of two reusable solid rocket boosters, the shuttle would reenter the Earth's atmosphere, land, and after refurbishment be available for another mission. The shuttle was to be capable of carrying satellites and other free-flying scientific payloads into orbit and launching them into space. Additionally, the cargo bay of the shuttle could carry an attached laboratory, called Spacelab, in which science programs could be conducted in orbit. Though the shuttle could not provide the extended-duration missions of Skylab, the frequency of the seven to fourteen day shuttle missions and the ability to carry larger crews to serve as subjects and operators of medical experiments provided a valuable test venue to assess the progress made during six years of ground-based studies. The first shuttle orbital flight was launched on April 12, 1981. Commanded by John W. Young with pilot Robert L. Crippen, this mission was a flight test of the Space Shuttle *Columbia.* The shuttle program was an outstanding success. Its performance was even better than anticipated until January 27, 1986, when the Shuttle *Challenger* exploded shortly after liftoff. One of the solid rocket boosters malfunctioned, and the resulting explosion killed the seven crew members. This catastrophe resulted in a twenty-month period of investigation and reengineering of the shuttle and its launch systems to provide the highest possible assurance that such an accident could not happen again.

In addition to the Spacelab, the Shuttle middeck offers an area in which approved operationally oriented medical tests and investigations can be conducted. These tests, called Detailed Supplementary Objectives, are approved with the provision that they will not interfere with the mission's primary objectives. The third shuttle flight, launched on March 22, 1982, carried the first medical DSO. The DSOs flown on shuttle missions have contributed significantly to understanding the important mechanisms of physiological change in weightlessness, testing of medical equipment, and developing operational medical procedures. By late 1994 Spacelab had flown eight times, and each mission included biomedical investigations. Two missions, moreover, were dedicated life-sciences missions and were the most intensive biomedical-research missions ever conducted by NASA. The second of these life-sciences missions was concluded on November 1, 1993, and, at fourteen days, was the fourth-longest mission ever flown by NASA. Sixteen medical experiments were conducted.

The Space Station currently being built is intended to provide a sophisticated orbital laboratory to investigate human responses to space travel. With the help of principal scientists from Texas colleges, universities, medical institutions, and industries, the Space Station missions may provide the information necessary to establish a permanent human presence in space, so that we will have the knowledge to establish lunar bases, to explore Mars, and—someday—to explore the universe. *See also* AEROSPACE MEDICINE, AIR FORCE.

bibliography: R. E. Bilstein, *Stages to Saturn: A Technological History of the Apollo/Saturn Launch Vehicles* (NASA SP-4206, Washington, 1980). W. D. Compton and C. D. Benson, *Living and Working in Space: A History of Skylab* (NASA SP-4208, Washington, 1983). R. S. Johnston and L. F. Dietlein, *Biomedical Results from Skylab* (NASA SP-377, Washington, 1977). R. S. Johnston, L. F. Dietlein, and C. A. Berry, eds., *Biomedical Results of Apollo* (NASA SP-368, Washington, 1975). M. M. Link, *Space Medicine in Project Mercury* (NASA SP-4003, Washington, 1965). NASA, Marshall Space Flight Center, *Science in Orbit: The Shuttle and Spacelab Experience, 1981–1986* (NASA NP-119, Washington, 1988). H. E. Newell, *Beyond the Atmosphere: Early Years of Space Sciences* (NASA SP-4211, Washington, 1980). A. E. Nicogossian, C. L. Huntoon, and S. L. Pool, *Space Physiology and Medicine* (2d ed., Philadelphia and London: Lea and Febiger, 1989). J. A. Pitts, *The Human Factor: Biomedicine in the Manned Space Program to 1980* (NASA SP-4213, Washington, 1985). L. S. Swenson, Jr., J. A. Grimwood, and C. C. Alexander, *This New Ocean: A History of Project Mercury* (NASA SP-4201, Washington, 1966).

Carolyn Leach Huntoon

AFFLECK, ISAAC DUNBAR (1844–1919). Isaac Dunbar Affleck, Texas Ranger and entomologist, son of Anna (Dunbar) and Thomas Affleck,[qv] was born on October 24, 1844, in Washington, Mississippi. He came to Texas with his parents in 1858 and spent most of his life at Glenblythe Plantation,[qv] near Brenham. He attended Bastrop Military Institute (*see* texas military institute, austin) from 1859 to 1861. During the Civil War[qv] he served in Terry's Texas Rangers (the Eighth Texas Cavalry[qv]). On December 26, 1876, he married Mary Foster Hunt of Kentucky (see affleck, mary hunt). Affleck was a student of politics, science, and Texas history and contributed frequently to the press. He made intensive study of ants. Part of his findings on the Texas agricultural ant and the cutting ant are contained in H. M. McCook's *The Natural History of the Agricultural Ant of Texas* (1880). Affleck edited August Santleben's[qv] *A Texas Pioneer* in 1910. He died in Austin on April 18, 1919, and was buried at Brenham. Much of his Civil War correspondence has been edited and published.

bibliography: S. W. Geiser, "Notes on Some Workers in Texas Entomology, 1839–1880," *Southwestern Historical Quarterly* 49 (April 1946). San Antonio *Light and Gazette*, January 2, 1910. *A Twentieth Century History of Southwest Texas* (2 vols., Chicago: Lewis, 1907).

AFFLECK, MARY HUNT (1847–1932). Mary Hunt Affleck, poet, daughter of J. A. and Anna (Adair) Hunt, was born in Danville, Kentucky, on January 20, 1847. She was educated at Harrodsburg Female College, Harrodsburg, Kentucky, moved to Texas in 1874, and settled in Burleson County. In Texas she won wide recognition as a nature poet; her works, generally published in newspapers, were widely read. She was also a member of the Daughters of the American Revolution, the United Daughters of the Confederacy,[qqv] the Daughters of 1812, and the Texas Editorial Association. She was married to Isaac Dunbar Affleck[qv] on December 26, 1876; they were parents of three children. Mrs. Affleck died in Galveston on November 28, 1932.

bibliography: Sam Houston Dixon, *The Poets and Poetry of Texas* (Austin: Dixon, 1885). San Antonio *Express*, November 29, 1932.

AFFLECK, THOMAS (1812–1868). Thomas Affleck, planter, son of Thomas and Mary (Hannay) Affleck, was born on July 13, 1812, in Dumfries, Scotland. He studied agriculture at the University of Edinburgh before coming to the United States, where he arrived on May 4, 1832. On April 19, 1842, he married Anna Dunbar Smith, the niece of Jane Wilkinson Long,[qv] at Washington, Mississippi, where he established one of the earliest nurseries in the South and operated several plantations. In 1858 he moved to Texas and established Glenblythe Plantation[qv] and the Central Nurseries near Brenham. His *Cotton Plantation Record and Account Book* and *Sugar Plantation Record and Account Book*, prepared as a record of Glenblythe, became models for other planters in the area.

Through experimentation and publication of books and articles, Affleck contributed to the progress of agriculture in Texas and the South. From 1840 to 1842 he was junior editor and editor of the *Western Farmer and Gardener* at Cincinnati, Ohio. He published *Bee-Breeding in the West* in 1841 and in 1848 edited *Norman's Southern Agricultural Almanac. Affleck's Southern Rural Almanac and Plantation and Garden Calendar* had a wide annual circulation from 1851 to 1861. *Hedging and Hedging Plants in the Southern States* (1869) and "Report on Agricultural Grasses," which appeared as a Senate executive document in 1879, were published after his death. He made several trips to Europe to encourage English and Scottish immigration to Texas and promoted European interests in the establishment of beef-packing houses with direct shipping lines from Texas to Europe. He died at Glenblythe on December 30, 1868.

bibliography: Fred C. Cole, The Texas Career of Thomas Affleck (Ph.D. dissertation, Louisiana State University, 1942). Abigail Curlee, A Study of Texas Slave Plantations, 1822–1865 (Ph.D. dissertation, University of Texas, 1932). *Dictionary of American Biography.* S. W. Geiser, *Horticulture and Horticulturists in Early Texas* (Dallas: University Press, 1945).

AFRICA, TEXAS. Africa is three miles southeast of Center in central Shelby County. This predominantly black community was settled in the last quarter of the nineteenth century by former slaves who cleared the heavily wooded area for farming. The focus of the community was originally a one-room building that served as a school and as a meetingplace for the congregation of St. John's Baptist Church. Later a building was constructed for the church. Residents also built a two-story town hall, which served as a school building and community center where lodge meetings and other social affairs were held. Although periodic attempts were made to establish other churches in the community, none of them was successful. The school had forty-seven students in 1899, twenty in 1903, and seventy-six in 1938. At one time Africa also had a gristmill, a syrup mill, and three stores. During the 1940s and 1950s the population of the area declined, and improved transportation led to the consolidation of the school district with the Center school district. By 1983 only St. John's Baptist Church, a cemetery, and a few houses remained.

bibliography: Charles E. Tatum, *Shelby County: In the East Texas Hills* (Austin: Eakin, 1984).

Cecil Harper, Jr.

AFRICAN-AMERICAN CHURCHES. African Americans[qv] who entered Texas from the 1820s through the Civil War[qv] years generally did so as slaves. In this country they developed a faith born from the union of African traditions and Christian evangelism. Through the eighteenth century slave traders delivered cargoes of men and women either recently enslaved in Africa or transported from plantation islands in the Caribbean. The former usually had had little contact with Christianity, though the Catholic Church[qv] had long maintained missions in sub-Saharan Africa. The latter had nurtured the concepts, rituals, and customs of Africa in the diaspora. The Europeans with whom slaves had contact on the plantations of Barbados and elsewhere in the Caribbean basin exerted scant influence on slave religion. By the time owners and traders began transporting slaves to Texas, however, distinctively African-American patterns of worship had evolved. Most slaves had some form of contact with organized Christian churches and merged the ideas they learned there with what they remembered individually or collectively from Africa.

Many slaves congregated in churches that whites provided for them. Some masters felt responsible for offering spiritual guidance to their chattels, especially their personal servants. Albert C. Horton,[qv] a

Baptist deacon who was heavily invested in slave property, built a church for the benefit of his people. Other masters, in light of the Christian-based, militant abolitionist movement, sought pragmatically to supervise the slaves' religious instruction in order to filter the subversive messages from the Christian Gospel. They wanted slaves to hear that God expected them to obey their masters and not steal from them. Frequently on larger plantations slaves attended services in the same churches that whites used, usually gathering in the afternoon when their masters had returned home. In some churches whites and blacks actually worshipped together. The Methodist Church[qv] reported approximately 7,500 black congregants in 1860, the largest number of recorded black members in any communion. The Baptist Church[qv] listed at least 1,087 African-American members. And both the Presbyterian and Protestant Episcopal churches[qv] acknowledged blacks as full members of their congregations. Biracial churches, however, were not really the slaves' churches. Whites controlled them, ordinarily assigned blacks to separate pews, and rarely permitted black preachers to ascend to the pulpit. How slaves responded to this type of worship varied from one individual to the next, but in most cases they preferred churches of their own and preachers who also were slaves. They tired of hearing whites preach about obedience and honesty with, as Wes Brady later recalled, "nary a word about having a soul to save." They preferred contemplating the uplifting Christian messages of freedom and equality, and they enjoyed the rhythmic elements of music and dancing, derived from Africa, that suffused their worship services.

Just how formally the slaves' churches were organized depended largely on whether owners sanctioned them or not. Slaves on many plantations gathered surreptitiously because their masters would not allow churches on their places. Sarah Ashley, who lived near Coldspring, testified that her master whipped slaves whom he caught at prayer meetings; however, she stated that she and others "run off at night and go to . . . camp meetings." Where whites did permit them, black churches occasionally functioned as regular congregations. In 1840 the First Baptist Church of Galveston allowed five slave members to worship by themselves; within a few years they had a building of their own named the First Africa Church. Slaves in La Grange, Fayette County, constructed and organized the Ebenezer Baptist Church in 1860. In 1854 the Colorado Baptist Association recognized a separate slave congregation as a member of the organization, and just before the beginning of the Civil War the Methodist Church reported thirty-seven slave missions. However, the Union Baptist Association expressed the prevailing view among whites when it stated that for slaves to have separate congregations was "inconsistent with their condition as servants, and with the interests of their masters."

The buildings that independent slave congregations occupied ran the gamut from brush arbors, which were mere clearings in the woods with log benches sheltered by tree branches, to plank buildings. The most substantial ones were those that the slaves' masters allowed them to build. Not infrequently, white congregations passed older buildings on to slaves when whites moved into new buildings. When Federal military authorities read the Emancipation Proclamation to slaves in 1865 (*see* JUNETEENTH), all slaves in Texas became free. Even the small group of blacks who had not been slaves before the Civil War felt a sudden liberation from oppression. An overwhelming urge to try on their new "freedom clothes" took hold of most black people. Freed slaves walked away from their plantations, sought out long-separated loved ones, and celebrated their redemption with parades, picnics, and general revelry. A more lasting gesture of their new status, however, was their withdrawal from white-controlled congregations and the formation of churches of their own. At first, whites hoped to maintain some measure of control or direct influence over the former slaves, but gradually they came to the conclusion that separation was best all the way around since in a white church, as the officers of one white Baptist association put it, they "never will be . . . permitted to exercise equal rights . . . with the white members of the church."

After slavery,[qv] when they gained a free choice in church membership, most black Texas churchgoers became Baptists. In organizing new churches blacks usually found Northern missionaries, white and black, ready to assist them. Israel S. Campbell,[qv] a black missionary from the Midwest, moved to Galveston in 1865 and organized a church there. Baptist theology, worship, and ecclesial structure appealed strongly to the freed people. The Baptists' egalitarian ideas about redemption and baptism by total immersion were particularly attractive. Baptists believed that salvation was available to all who repented of their sins, a thought that at least partially compensated for worldly hardship and injustice. Baptism in creeks or rivers dramatized the sinner's spiritual death and rebirth as a Christian. Congregations enjoyed the social aspect of baptisms, converting them into occasions for picnics and fellowship. But beyond that, Christian baptisms resonated with ancient West African water rites that were embedded in African-American culture. As when they were slaves, the freed people enjoyed the informality of the Baptist worship service, one that accommodated singing, shouting, and vocal interaction with their preachers. They also appreciated the fact that Baptist organization was congregational. They had had enough of control during slavery; they craved freedom to join with other churches in associations if they so desired or to break away and form new organizations.

Although essentially congregational, Baptist organization united local churches into district associations and state conventions. Black Texans formed their first district association in 1868 and made plans in 1874 for a statewide convention that convened the following year. These organizations allowed churchgoers to recognize each other's hard work in Christian activity as well as to bring together resources in support of schools, old-age pensions, indigent care, and other social causes.

Before emancipation, black Methodists were affiliated with the Methodist Episcopal Church, South. But missionaries representing three Northern-based denominations accompanied Union military forces into Texas at the end of the Civil War. Some were chaplains who ministered to the spiritual needs of black troops and civilians. Michael M. Clark, who arrived late in 1865, was the first regular African Methodist Episcopal Church[qv] missionary to work in the state. Houston Reedy, another AME missionary, organized a church in Galveston at about the same time. By 1868 the church claimed 3,000 members. In 1875, though originally attached to an episcopal district that included Mississippi and Louisiana, the African Methodists of Texas received their own bishop, who presided over the Texas Annual Conference. The African Methodist Episcopal Zion Church[qv] was smaller than the AME Church and sponsored fewer missionaries, but it had enough members by 1881 to warrant the formation of an annual conference. Northern whites controlled the Methodist Episcopal Church; however, it aggressively and successfully pursued black members. Claiming to be a biracial organization without segregation, ME missionaries appealed to African Americans who envisioned a racially integrated society. For the most part, though, ME churches in Texas and elsewhere in the South were predominantly white. Only slowly did blacks gain entry into the Methodist Episcopal ministry, and not until the twentieth century did they rise in the organizational hierarchy. Through its relationship with the Freedmen's Bureau, however, the ME Church was able to secure ownership of church buildings, a valuable asset in the Methodist competition for black adherents who owned little property. Methodist Episcopal leaders met at Trinity Church in Houston in 1867 and organized the Texas Conference, which by 1871 claimed 7,934 black members and fifty-one ministers. The Methodist Episcopal Church, South, attempted to retain its black membership in segregated churches by transferring title to church property to congregations that remained affiliated with it. The desire to be free of their former masters exceeded the lure of real estate, however, and in 1870, in the wake of sharply declining black membership, denominational leaders established a separate organization called the Colored Methodist Episcopal Church (later the Christian Methodist Episcopal Church[qv]).

The Episcopal and Presbyterian churches also admitted black members. African Americans in Crockett organized the first black Presbyterian church in the state in 1874, and in 1888 seven black Presbyterian churches formed the Negro Presbytery of Texas. The Cumberland Presbyterian Church, Colored, listed approximately 1,700 members in 1890, worshipping in thirty congregations across Texas. Black Episcopalians and Presbyterians tended to be comparatively well-to-do business and professional people. George T. Ruby[qv] was among the prominent black Presbyterians. Despite their presence in those denominations, however, the vast majority of African-American churches in Texas after the Civil War were either Baptist or Methodist.

In many ways their churches aided the former slaves' social progress. During years immediately after emancipation, black Texans sought to satisfy their hunger for education. Officials in Washington recognized that appetite, and many education-minded private citizens in the North insisted that schooling was essential to the freedmen's progress and social order. Accordingly, the Freedmen's Bureau joined hands with such groups as the American Missionary Association and negotiated with church officials for the use of their buildings as schools. Many churches conducted their own schools, both Sunday schools and secular day schools, for the benefit of children and adults. The Constitution of 1869[qv] acknowledged the state's responsibility for providing public primary and secondary education, and afterward the churches concentrated on higher education and vocational training. The AME Church established Paul Quinn College in 1872. The campus was initially located in Austin but moved to Waco in 1881 and to Dallas in 1990. In 1873 the all-black Methodist Episcopal conference founded Wiley College in Marshall, the first postsecondary school for African Americans west of the Mississippi River. Baptists established several preparatory and collegiate institutions after Reconstruction.[qv] Bishop College, founded in Marshall in 1881, had the support of the American Baptist Home Mission Society of New York. Texas Baptists also operated Guadalupe College in Seguin (which they purchased from the Catholic Church in 1884), Houston College, Conroe College, and Hearne Academy.[qv] During Reconstruction and after, the churches provided black Texans with political leadership. Many preachers were active in Republican party[qv] politics. They held public office and discussed political issues with their congregations. Church buildings were often the sites of political rallies. At a time when business opportunities for African Americans were still limited, the churches also taught their members how to raise and sometimes how to manage money. In areas of finance, the women of the churches usually asserted themselves. They often were in charge of raising funds to finance church activities, including building projects. Occasionally they even kept the account books. They actually made many of the decisions that affected the regular operation of churches.

African-American churches in Texas grew steadily through the late nineteenth and early twentieth centuries. When the census bureau counted church members in 1890, the Baptist state convention tallied 111,138. The African Methodist Episcopal Church showed 23,392 members and the African Methodist Episcopal Zion Church 6,927. The Colored Methodist Episcopal Church, with 14,895 adherents in 1890, was the third largest black church in the state. The Methodist Episcopal Church enrolled 23,392 congregants in two conferences, Texas and West Texas, but because it was a biracial church it is impossible to know exactly how many of them were black. By 1900 the African-American determination to realize the full promise of freedom had resulted in many remarkable individual and collective achievements. Unfortunately, progress often came over stubborn white resistance. Even benevolent whites often exhibited a stifling paternalism that raised the hackles of many blacks. At Bishop College in Marshall, a white administration and the controlling influence of the white Home Mission Society drew complaints from many black Baptists. When, in 1891, the Home Mission Society proposed to downgrade black-run Guadalupe College to a secondary school feeding Bishop, the simmering resentment of such blacks as David Abner, Jr.,[qv] Texas Baptist State Convention leader Lee L. Campbell,[qv] and Richard H. Boyd,[qv] who a short time later organized the Publishing Board of the National Baptist Convention, suddenly boiled over. Meeting in San Antonio in 1893, convention delegates debated the Home Mission Society's plan. Allen R. Griggs[qv] from Dallas, agent of the Home Mission Society and brother of novelist and churchman Sutton A. Griggs,[qv] backed the proposal. Many of the delegates agreed that continued cooperation with supportive whites was essential to race progress, while critics of the Home Mission Society and its allies, "who have deprived the Negro Baptists of this State from owning and controlling Institutions of Higher Learning," refused to accept the plan. This bitter debate led to a division of African-American Baptists into two state conventions, the General Missionary Baptist State Convention and the Baptist Missionary and Education Convention. Subsequent attempts to heal the Baptist breech failed. Baptists were no more able to reconcile their differences than national leaders such as William E. B. Du Bois and Booker T. Washington were able to agree in their prescriptions for race advancement. As a matter of fact, disputes and theological differences continued to divide the state's Baptists and bring about the formation of additional organizations. Ultimately, four statewide conventions came into being. The American Baptist Free Mission General State and Educational Convention of Texas grew out of the antebellum American Free Mission Baptist Society of Boston. It became the American Baptist Free Mission Association of Texas in 1930 and has been known as the American Baptist Convention of Texas since 1940. A split in the Missionary Baptist General Convention in 1981 led to the formation of the Central Missionary Baptist General Convention of Texas.

From the 1890s through the early decades of the twentieth century, increasing numbers of blacks abandoned farm tenancy[qv] for jobs and new lives in the city. Many left for the "promised land"—Chicago—while others crowded into Dallas, San Antonio, Galveston, and Houston. Though the once-small black urban population of the state had been diverse in class terms, in many ways a relatively well-to-do elite and an expanding middle class had dominated it. Members of these groups sometimes worshipped in Presbyterian and Episcopal congregations; however, more commonly, upper and middle class churchgoers attended Baptist and Methodist churches. Eschewing the style of the old slave preachers, the pastors of these urban churches usually were college or seminary trained. The men and women of the congregations dressed well and behaved in a restrained way. For black folk arriving from the country and small towns, the urban churches lacked the excitement that made going to church a thrilling spiritual experience. Moreover, they felt uncomfortable sitting next to people they believed—often rightly—to be snobs. This may account, at least in part, for a decline in black church membership from slightly over 396,000 in 1916 to approximately 351,000 in 1926. However, a more important phenomenon than this temporary slip in church membership was the steady drift of largely working-class, urban blacks into so-called "holiness" churches. These included the Church of the Living God, General Assembly, organized in 1902 with headquarters in Waco, the Christian Workers for Fellowship, the Pillar and the Ground of Truth, and the Apostolic Church. Pentecostalism seeded itself in the same discontent with mainline Protestant churches. William Joseph Seymour, a black man and one of the founders of Pentecostalism, settled for a while in Houston early in the century. By the 1930s the "holiness" churches ranked second to Baptists among adherents in such cities as Houston, where one black congregation in five was a "holiness" church, and evangelists like J. Gordon McPherson and J. L. "Sin Killer" Griffin[qv] stirred the passions of rapt audiences.

In 1939 the Methodist Episcopal Church completed a long- sought merger with the Methodist Episcopal Church, South. At issue between the two groups had been the status of African Americans. Bowing to Southerners' demands for a segregated church, the Methodist Church organized a separate black organization called the Central Jurisdiction. All of the denomination's black conferences from every part of the country, including the Texas Conference and the West Texas Conference, were included in the Central Jurisdiction. For the first time, blacks elected their own bishops, but they reported to the Central Jurisdiction rather than an integrated general conference. Some blacks registered displeasure with this segregation by withdrawing from the church. Others remained but voiced their resentment. All in all the church lost much of its influence among black Texans as a consequence of the merger. Then in 1968, amid the civil-rights movement,[qv] the church abandoned the detested Central Jurisdiction. Meeting in Dallas, it joined with two other Methodist organizations to form the United Methodist Church and did away with its policy of racial segregation. Moreover, the church responded to demands from blacks for hymnals and instructional materials that included black contributions and that related directly to African-American history and culture.

From the 1960s to the 1990s, black churches have maintained the tradition of active involvement in the social lives of their congregants. During the campaigns for voting and other civil rights, ministers and members were major participants, sometimes leading marches and voter-registration drives and at other times seeking accommodation with conservative white leaders, as the Baptist minister Sylvester M. Wright of Dallas did. The churches have generally espoused conservative social values; thus, even though women have been powerful figures in church affairs, they have remained mostly outside of the ministry and church leaders have condescendingly referred to female organizations as "auxiliaries." The churches have sought to counter social threats to blacks by opposing liquor, gambling, drugs, and gangs. Furthermore, they have encouraged young people to remain in school, organized activities that keep youth busy in productive pursuits, and rewarded them for positive achievements. Just as much of the effort in race relations over the past 150 years has been toward integrating American society, in Texas many black congregations are affiliated with and feel welcome in predominantly white churches. In 1994, for instance, approximately 400 black churches belonged to the white Baptist state convention. Yet church integration has not worked in reverse. No predominantly white congregation belonged, for instance, to the black Missionary Baptist General Convention. Many voices have asserted that eleven o'clock Sunday morning remains the most segregated time of the week. *See also* BLACK CATHOLICS, EDUCATION FOR AFRICAN AMERICANS, *and* BLACK COLLEGES.

BIBLIOGRAPHY: Alwyn Barr, *Black Texans: A History of Negroes in Texas, 1528–1971* (Austin: Jenkins, 1973). Randolph B. Campbell, *An Empire for Slavery: The Peculiar Institution in Texas, 1821–1865* (Baton Rouge: Louisiana State University Press, 1989). Marvin C. Griffin, *Texas African-American Baptists: The Story of the Baptist General Convention of Texas* (Austin: Publisher's Marketing House, 1994). William E. Montgomery, *Under Their Own Vine and Fig Tree: The African-American Church in the South, 1865–1970* (Baton Rouge: Louisiana State University Press, 1993).

William E. Montgomery

AFRICAN AMERICANS. People of African descent are some of the oldest residents of Texas. Beginning with the arrival of Estevanico[qv] in 1528, African Texans have had a long heritage in the state and have worked alongside Americans of Mexican, European, and indigenous descent to make the state what it is today. The African-American history of Texas has also been paradoxical. On the one hand, blacks have worked with others to build the state's unique cultural heritage. But on the other hand, African Americans have been subjected to slavery,[qv] racial prejudice, and exclusion from the mainstream of state institutions. Their contributions to the state's development and growth in spite of these obstacles have been truly remarkable.

From the beginning of European settlement in Texas, people of African descent were present. In 1528 Estevanico, a Moor, accompanied Spanish explorer Álvar Núñez Cabeza de Vaca[qv] across the territory known today as Texas. Estevanico was an important member of Cabeza de Vaca's mission because he could interpret the languages of many of the Indians that the expedition encountered. Along with the other members of the expedition he was captured by Indians and enslaved for five years. After escaping, Estevanico and the surviving members of the expedition made their way to Mexico. In 1539 he accompanied a second expedition into the Southwest. This time he was murdered by the Zuñi Indians and the mission failed. Other pioneer Africans accompanied the Spanish into the Southwest, and some settled with them in the region known today as Texas. By 1792 Spanish Texas[qv] numbered thirty-four blacks and 414 mulattoes. Some of them were free men and women.

Unlike Estevanico and some of the Africans who inhabited the province prior to settlement by Anglo-Americans, most African Americans entered the area as slaves. The first Anglo-Americans who settled in Texas came from the southern United States and were accustomed to using African slaves as an important source of labor. During the first fifteen years of white settlement in Texas, from 1821 to the Texas Revolution[qv] of 1836, slavery grew very slowly. On the eve of the Revolution only about 5,000 blacks were enslaved in Texas. With independence from Mexico, however, whites made African slavery an integral part of the state's economic development, and the institution of slavery grew rapidly. By 1840, 11,000 African Americans were enslaved in Texas. By 1850, 58,000 were enslaved, and by 1860,

[Official.]

HEADQUARTERS DISTRICT OF TEXAS,
GALVESTON TEXAS, June 19, 1865.

General Orders, No. 3.

The people are informed that, in accordance with a proclamation from the Executive of the United States, all slaves are free. This involves an absolute equality of personal rights and rights of property, between former masters and slaves, and the connection heretofore existing between them, becomes that between employer and hired labor.—The Freedmen are advised to remain at their present homes, and work for wages. They are informed that they will not be allowed to collect at military posts; and that they will not be supported in idleness either there or elsewhere. By order of
Major-General GRANGER.
(Signed,) F. W. EMERY, Maj. & A. A. G.

"All slaves are free." Notice printed in the Galveston Tri-weekly News, *June 21, 1865. Texas Newspaper Collection, CAH; CN 06520. On June 19, 1865, Union major general Gordon Granger landed in Galveston and declared the state subject to federal authority. The same day he also issued an order, in the name of President Andrew Johnson, declaring all slaves free. Newspapers across the state printed Granger's order. Texas African Americans have celebrated "Juneteenth," or emancipation day, ever since.*

Hal and Jane Mason. Photograph by Samuel B. Hill. Austin, ca. 1895–1900. Andrew W. George Papers, CAH; CN 02926. Hal and Jane Mason began their lives as slaves. By the mid-1880s Hal Mason was assistant jailer at the Travis County Jail.

182,000—30 percent of the Texas population. According to historian Randolph Campbell, slavery in Texas was similar to that in other parts of the American South. The records gathered by Campbell as well as the testimony of African Americans enslaved in Texas attest to the fact that black slaves in Texas had as harsh and as easy a lot as slaves in other parts of the South. Two cases illustrate this fact. In 1861 a Canadian newspaper published the story of Lavinia Bell, a black woman who had been kidnapped at an early age and sold into slavery in Texas. She escaped from bondage and told of being forced to work naked in the cottonfields near Galveston. She also told about how after her first escape attempt, she was physically mutilated and beaten severely by her owner. Other African Americans who were enslaved in Texas told similar stories of violence and cruelty by their owners. Hundreds sought escape, especially to Mexico. But there were also cases such as that of Joshua Houston,[qv] one of the slaves of Sam Houston.[qv] Joshua, owned initially by Houston's second wife, became an important member of Houston's family. He was treated well, taught to read and write, and prepared well for his eventual emancipation by the Houston family. After the Civil War[qv] Joshua became a politician in Huntsville, and, as if to underscore his loyalty to his former owners, on one occasion he offered to lend money to Sam Houston's widow when she faced financial difficulties.

While the treatment of African Americans enslaved in Texas may have varied on the basis of the disposition of individual slaveowners, it was clear that white Texans in general accepted and defended slavery. Moreover, slavery in Texas had all of the characteristics that had made it successful in other parts of the South. For instance, slaveholders dominated the state's economic and political life. The government of the Republic of Texas[qv] and, after 1845, the state legislature passed a series of slave codes to regulate the behavior of slaves and restrict the rights of free blacks. The census counted about 400 free blacks in 1850, although there may have been close to 1,000. White Texans also restricted the civil liberties of white opponents of slavery in order to suppress dissent about the institution. When rumors of a slave insurrection circulated in the state in 1860, Texans virtually suspended civil liberties and due process in the state. Suspected abolitionists were expelled from the state, and one was even hanged. A vigilante group in Dallas lynched three African-American slaves who were suspected of starting a fire that burnt most of the downtown area. Other slaves in the county were whipped.

The Texas vote for secession[qv] in February 1861 hastened the end of slavery and set in motion the eventual liberation of the state's African-American population. For blacks in Texas, freedom did not come until Juneteenth,[qv] June 19, 1865. In contrast to other parts of the South, where the approach of the Union Army encouraged thousands of enslaved blacks to free themselves and run away, Texas blacks remained enslaved until the end of the Civil War. Few were able to run away and enlist in the Union Army, as black men did in other parts of the South.

The Reconstruction[qv] era presented black Texans another challenge. Many had to rebuild their lives, locate lost family members, and begin to live their lives as self-sufficient, free men and women. The establishment of the Freedmen's Bureau[qv] in the state aided this transition from slavery to freedom. But given the continuing racial animosity that separated blacks and whites after the war, this was not an easy task. The state legislature and several Texas cities passed Black Codes[qv] to restrict the rights of blacks, to prevent them from having free access to public facilities, and to force them back to the rural areas as agricultural laborers. The use of the political and legal system to regulate black behavior was accompanied by a literal reign of terror in the state. From 1865 to 1868 white Texans committed over 1,500 acts of violence against blacks; more than 350 blacks were murdered by whites. These were attempts to reestablish white supremacy and to force blacks back into their "place." Only the intervention of Congress and the imposition of military rule in the state after 1867 eliminated the Black Codes and brought a modicum of safety to African Americans. The arrival of military and Congressional efforts to protect black rights ushered in the second phase of Reconstruction in the state. In this period African Americans made a substantial contribution to the transition of Texas from a slave-labor state to one based on free labor. Ten African-American delegates at the Constitutional Convention of 1868–69[qv] helped to write a constitution that protected civil rights, established the state's first public education system, and extended the franchise to all men. Between 1868 and 1900, forty-three African Americans served in the state legislature, and they helped to move the state toward democracy. Such black Reconstruction leaders as George T. Ruby and Norris Wright Cuney[qqv] became important members of the Republican party[qv] and, along with other blacks, dominated state Republican politics through the turn of the twentieth century. During the course of the Reconstruction period, many African Americans moved from the state's rural areas to cities such as Dallas, Austin, Houston, and San Antonio. On the outskirts of these cities they established "freedmantowns," which became the distinct black neighborhoods that still exist today. Black labor also contributed substantially to the economic development of these cities and helped the state to begin the transition from its near-total depen-

Republican county convention, Fayette County, 1904. Courtesy Fayette Heritage Museum/Archives, La Grange; 81.83.58. About 200 African-American delegates attended the 1904 Fayette County Republican convention. This photograph shows convention chairman Charles Gates seated in the judge's chair and convention secretary Charles Toney speaking from the judge's stand. By 1906 white Democrats and Republicans had virtually eliminated black participation in the two major parties.

dence on agriculture to industrialization. In 1879 a few thousand black Texans moved to Kansas seeking greater opportunities. Other black Texans participated in the postwar cattle boom (*see* BLACK COWBOYS), while the presence on the frontier of black soldiers, called Buffalo Soldiers[qv] by their Indian foes, exemplified the desire of many blacks to enter into the military responsibilities of citizenship.

As in other parts of the South, Reconstruction lasted only a short time in Texas. Democrats regained control of the state in 1873 and proceeded to reverse many of the democratic reforms instituted by black and white Republicans. Between 1874 and 1900 the gains that African Americans had made in the political arena were virtually lost. In the 1890s, for example, more than 100,000 blacks voted in Texas elections. But after the imposition of a poll tax in 1902 and the passage of the white primary[qv] law in 1903, fewer than 5,000 blacks voted in the state in 1906. In addition, segregation was established in all facets of public and private life in Texas for African Americans. In Dallas, Houston, and San Antonio, public transportation and accommodations, schools, and, eventually, neighborhoods were segregated by law. Blacks in Houston and San Antonio challenged segregation on public transportation by forming their own bus and jitney companies. Dallas blacks won a case in 1916 that overturned a residential segregation ordinance. But nothing succeeded in stemming the tide of segregation that restricted the rights of black Texans by the early twentieth century. The victims of lynching,[qv] which did not end until the 1940s, were predominantly black. Riots[qv] destroyed black neighborhoods. African Americans became disfranchised, second-class citizens, denied the basic human rights other citizens in the state took for granted. As a result, several thousand black Texans moved out of the state to the North and West in the twentieth century. Although the percentage of blacks in Texas fell to 20 percent of the population by 1900 and declined further in the twentieth century, their numbers grew to more than 600,000 in 1900 and 900,000 in 1940.

Despite their second-class status, African Americans still built viable and progressive communities throughout the state. Almost immediately after Civil War, they established churches, schools, and other social organizations to serve their own needs. They established newspapers (the Dallas *Express,* Houston *Informer* and *Texas Freeman,* and San Antonio *Register*[qqv]), grocery stores, funeral homes, and other business establishments that served a predominant African-American clientele. In the late nineteenth century black farmers formed a cooperative to encourage black land ownership and to raise crop prices. From 1900 to 1940 a majority of black Texans remained in farming, with about 20 percent owning their land while most rented farms as tenants. The Great Depression[qv] of the 1930s hastened a trend toward urbanization. In the same period blacks in Dallas organized a cotton-processing mill, but it failed in less than five years. These self-help and economic development efforts by black Texans indicate that they did not allow the oppression of white racism to deter them from striving to build successful communities. After the Civil War, African Americans also developed their first educational institutions. Black colleges[qv] such as Bishop, Paul Quinn, and Wiley were founded by several religious denominations, primarily Baptist and Methodist organizations. African-American churches[qv] such as Boll Street African Methodist Episcopal in Dallas also started the first schools in that city for black children. The city of Houston provided schools for its black citizens beginning in 1871. By 1888 the city government in Dallas followed suit.

African Americans also contributed to the state's social and cultural heritage in the late nineteenth and twentieth centuries. Musicians such as Blind Lemon Jefferson, Huddie (Leadbelly) Ledbetter, Eddie Durham, Scott Joplin,[qqv] Bobbi Humphrey, and many others became innovators in blues, jazz,[qqv] and ragtime. Singers such as Julius L. C. Bledsoe[qv] and Osceola Mays sang songs from the African-American folk tradition as well as their own contemporary compositions. Such writers as Maude Cuney-Hare, J. Mason Brewer, and Sutton Griggs[qqv] wrote biographies and novels and recorded the folklore of black Texans. Artist John Biggers of Houston became one of the nation's most important mural painters and an internationally recognized artist. In sports, such black Texans as Charlie Taylor, Ernie Banks, Jack Johnson,[qv] and George Foreman earned national fame in football, baseball, and boxing. After the integration of the state's universities, black Texas athletes such as Earl Campbell of the University of Texas at Austin, Elvin Hayes of the University of Houston, and Jerry Levias of Southern Methodist University had outstanding college athletic careers.

One of the most significant achievements of blacks in the state was their participation in the Texas Centennial[qv] of 1936. This event was important because it allowed African Americans to highlight the contributions that they had made to the state's and the nation's development. Through the efforts of A. Maceo Smith[qv] of the Dallas Negro Chamber of Commerce and Samuel W. Houston[qv] of Huntsville, the Hall of Negro Life[qv] was built at Fair Park[qv] in Dallas to bring to the state the works of Harlem Renaissance painter Aaron Douglass as well as to exhibit the paintings of Texas artists Samuel A. Countee of Houston and Frank Sheinall of Galveston. More importantly, the Negro Day event held in Dallas as the black celebration of the Texas Centennial proved to be an important opportunity for black Texans to meet and plan strategy to end the segregation and discrimination that they faced. Three organizations emerged from the Negro Day celebration of 1936: the Texas State Conference of Branches of the National Association for the Advancement of Colored People, the Texas State Negro Chamber of Commerce, and the Texas Negro Peace Officers Association (now the Texas Peace Officers Association[qv]). All three organizations had as their objective to improve the lot of blacks in Texas.

The Texas Centennial was indeed a watershed event for African Americans. After it they launched a campaign to win the citizenship rights that the state's segregation laws and racist tradition denied them. Texas blacks won two of the nation's most significant civil-rights cases. They renewed challenges to the state's white primary system four times, and, eventually, they won a Supreme Court decision in *Smith v. Allwright* (1944), which declared the white primary unconstitutional. This landmark case won by black Texans opened primaries for blacks throughout the South. In 1950, black Texans also won one of the major legal cases that eliminated segregation in the South's graduate and professional schools. The *Sweatt v. Painter*[qv] case, filed by Thurgood Marshall, legal counsel of the NAACP, and local NAACP attorney William J. Durham of Dallas, forced the University of Texas Law School to admit black students. Although the *Sweatt* case was one of several cases that the NAACP filed to gain entry for black students into graduate and professional schools, it also became one of the cases that laid the groundwork for the NAACP's challenge to segregation in pubic schools in the famous *Brown v. Board of Education*, Topeka, Kansas case.

Despite the notion among some historians that Texas did not need a civil-rights movement[qv] to end its legacy of racial discrimination, African Americans had to use both the courts and direct action in the 1950s and 1960s to win access to public services throughout the state.

Sharecroppers picking cotton in the Dallas area, ca. 1907. Stereograph. Prints and Photographs Collection, Cotton file, CAH; CN 01281. At the turn of the century relatively few who farmed, whether black or white, owned the land they worked. In counties where many black people vied for jobs in cotton, some planters still employed whip-cracking overseers. A few strikes were held, but wages for fieldhands remained low.

Using a variety of methods, black citizens won the right to sit on juries, equal pay for equal work for black teachers, the elimination of residential segregation in the state's major cities, jobs on the police forces of Dallas and Fort Worth, and open seating on public transportation throughout the state. They also used sit-ins in Houston and Marshall to end segregation in public accommodations. By the mid-1960s, only one area of citizenship rights continued to elude black Texans: serving in elective office. In 1958, Houstonian Hattie White became the first African American to win an elective office in the state since Reconstruction by winning a seat on the school board. But many citizens thought that she was white and voted for her in error. She served ten turbulent years on the Houston school board, fighting constantly to force other members of the board to implement court-ordered desegregation of the school system. After Mrs. White's election black Texans did not win another elective office until 1966, when several black candidates throughout the state won political races. Among the pioneers were Joe Lockridge of Dallas, who won a seat in the state house of representatives, and Barbara Jordan of Houston, who won a seat in the Texas Senate. In 1971, Judson Robinson became Houston's first black city councilman since Reconstruction. A year later Barbara Jordan was elected to the United States House of Representatives, thus becoming the first African American in Texas history to represent the state in Congress.

Her election symbolized the progress that blacks had made in the state after over 100 years of racial segregation and exclusion. Despite the lingering effects of the old racist and segregationist legacy, African Americans continued to achieve in both the private and public spheres in the state. They won elective office on the city, county, and statewide levels. In 1992, for example, Morris Overstreet of Amarillo became the first African American to win a statewide office when he was elected a judge on the Texas Court of Criminal Appeals.[qv] Employment opportunities also increased significantly for black Texans, especially in the larger urban areas such as Dallas and Houston. In 1983, for instance, Dallas was named "one of the ten best cities for blacks" because of the social, political, and economic opportunities available there for African Americans. In addition, African Americans continued to participate in the state's social and cultural life and to add their creative talents to the state's as well as the nation's artistic development. Two of many examples are the works added to American literature by Houston playwright and author Ntozake Shange and short story writer J. California Cooper of East Texas. Shange's work "for colored girls who have considered suicide when the rainbow is enuf" played on Broadway and toured the country for several years. Her novels *Sassafras, Cypress, and Indigo* (1982) and *Betsey Brown* (1985) were national best-sellers. Cooper's short stories in *A Piece of Mine* (1984) and *Family* (1991) also earned her national acclaim.

These achievements were the result of black Texans' ongoing struggle for equal opportunity and human dignity. African Americans have lived in the area known as Texas as long as any other ethnic group except American Indians. Throughout their history in the state, they have contributed their blood, sweat, and hard labor to

The Bronze Peacock nightclub, Houston, ca. 1950. Courtesy Galen Gart/Big Nickel Publications, Milford, New Hampshire. The Bronze Peacock, a highly successful dinner and dance club in the business district of the Fifth Ward, Houston, opened in 1945. Its founder, Don Deadric Robey, promoted the careers of many important black artists through his record companies and talent-booking agency.

State and national leaders of the National Association for the Advancement of Colored People (top row, left to right: John J. Jones, M. T. Blanton, Thurgood Marshall; bottom row, left to right: unidentified, Juanita Craft, Walter White, Peyton Medlock), Dallas, 1948. Juanita Jewel Shanks Craft Collection, CAH; CN 00674. Juanita Craft, a field worker with the National Association for the Advancement of Colored People, helped organize 182 branches in Texas.

make Texas what it is in the 1990s. Although the 2,000,000 black Texans in 1990 formed only 12 percent of the state's population, blacks had made major contributions to Texas history and culture. The previous thirty years of African-American history in Texas had been quite eventful. During that period black citizens had taken major steps toward reversing the negative aspects of the previous 100 years. Yet, they had only begun to reap the benefits of their labor and persistence.

See also CIVIL RIGHTS, ANTEBELLUM TEXAS, TEXAS TROUBLES, SLAVE INSURRECTIONS, ABOLITION, NATIONAL ASSOCIATION FOR THE ADVANCEMENT OF COLORED PEOPLE, ELECTION LAWS, BLACK EXTENSION SERVICE, COLORED FARMERS3 ALLIANCE, FARM TENANCY, *and* DALLAS BLACK CHAMBER OF COMMERCE.

BIBLIOGRAPHY: Alwyn Barr, *Black Texans: A History of Negroes in Texas, 1528–1971* (Austin: Jenkins, 1973). Howard Beeth and Cary D. Wintz, eds., *Black Dixie: Afro-Texan History and Culture in Houston* (College Station: Texas A&M University Press, 1992). Randolph B. Campbell, *An Empire for Slavery: The Peculiar Institution in Texas, 1821–1865* (Baton Rouge: Louisiana State University Press, 1989). Barry A. Crouch, *The Freedmen's Bureau and Black Texans* (Austin: University of Texas Press, 1992). Chandler Davidson, *Biracial Politics: Conflict and Coalition in the Metropolitan South* (Baton Rouge: Louisiana State University Press, 1972). W. Marvin Dulaney and Kathleen Underwood, eds., *Essays on the American Civil Rights Movement* (College Station: Texas A&M University Press, 1993). Darlene Clark Hine, *Black Victory: The Rise and Fall of the White Primary in Texas* (Millwood, New York: KTO Press, 1979). Merline Pitre, *Through Many Dangers, Toils and Snares: The Black Leadership of Texas, 1868–1900* (Austin: Eakin, 1985). Lawrence D. Rice, *The Negro in Texas, 1874–1900* (Baton Rouge: Louisiana State University Press, 1971). James Smallwood, *Time of Hope, Time of Despair: Black Texans during Reconstruction* (London: Kennikat, 1981). Ruthe Winegarten, *Black Texas Women: 150 Years of Trial and Triumph* (Austin: University of Texas Press, 1995).

W. Marvin Dulaney

AFRICAN AMERICANS AND POLITICS. Racial conflict is a basic feature of Texas history. From 1865 onward its primary political manifestation has been the struggle of African Americans[qv] to vote, have their ballots fairly counted, elect their preferred candidates, develop effective coalitions with other groups, and thereby achieve equality of opportunity in a white-dominated society that, from its beginning, relegated people of color to the status of an inferior caste.

Congresswoman Barbara Jordan and Democratic party national chairman Robert Strauss at the Democratic national convention, Madison Square Garden, New York, July 1976. Courtesy AP/Wide World Photos, New York. Barbara Jordan became nationally known for a speech she delivered while serving on the House Judiciary Committee during impeachment hearings on President Richard Nixon in 1974. Here she prepares to deliver the keynote address at the Democratic national convention in 1976.

In 1860, on the eve of the Civil War,[qv] blacks made up 30 percent of the state's population. Most were slaves, and even the few who were free could not vote. Emancipation was announced in Texas on June 19, 1865 (Juneteenth[qv]), but the newly formed government withheld black political rights. An all-white constitutional convention in 1866 refused to grant suffrage even to literate blacks. The all-white legislature then refused to ratify the Fourteenth Amendment forbidding states from depriving citizens of equal protection of the laws. Seeking to restore plantation discipline, it passed Black Codes[qv] that severely restricted freedmen's economic options. And it prohibited voting, officeholding, jury service, and racial intermarriage by freedmen.

These actions by white lawmakers, similar to those in other Southern states, prompted the Republican-dominated Congress to respond with a series of statutes applicable to the former Confederacy, including one to enfranchise black males. The implementation of these statutes was known as Congressional Reconstruction. In Texas the Republican reformers, called radicals, entered into an uneasy alliance with the great majority of freedmen. Another Republican faction, the conservatives, sometimes joined with Democrats, who generally opposed most civil rights for blacks.

In July 1867 twenty whites and 150 blacks attended a Republican convention in Houston, where they endorsed free common schools and free homesteads from public lands for blacks and whites alike. Thus began a decades-long tradition of black Republicanism in the state. Despite widespread violence and intimidation by the Ku Klux Klan[qv] and Democrats, many black men registered for the first election in which they could participate—the 1868 referendum on whether to hold another constitutional convention and elect delegates. More blacks than whites cast ballots, and, with their white allies, they overcame the opposition of the majority of white voters and voted to hold another convention. The Convention of 1868–69,[qv] dominated by Republicans, included ten African-American delegates out of ninety. Among them was George T. Ruby[qv] of Galveston, a Northern journalist and teacher who had moved to Texas to work in freedmen's schools; he became a well-known Republican leader. All ten were active on committees and presented important resolutions. Though frustrated in attempts to secure certain constitutional safeguards for their people, they contributed to the accomplishments of the convention, which paved the way for the readmission of Texas to the Union in March 1870.

The election of Edmund J. Davis,[qv] a white radical, as governor in 1869 gave blacks additional influence, as did the election of two black state senators—G. T. Ruby and Matthew Gaines,[qv] a minister and former slave—and twelve representatives to the Twelfth Legislature. Dominated by reform-minded Republicans, this body ratified the Fourteenth and Fifteenth amendments and passed several important though controversial laws, including ones establishing a militia and the Texas State Police,[qv] open to blacks, to control lawlessness and violence in the state. The legislature also passed a homestead act, a measure protecting homesteads from forced sale, and a law establishing public schools.

Reconstruction ended in 1873 with the defeat of Davis, an event hailed by a former governor as "the restoration of white supremacy and Democratic rule." The number of blacks in the legislature dropped, and white Democrats began reestablishing control of Texas politics. This was accomplished primarily by the Constitutional Convention of 1875,[qv] which was accompanied by continuing violence and intimidation aimed at blacks. In a state now controlled by white Democrats, African Americans experimented with three options: involvement in the Republican party,[qv] alliance with factions of Democrats, and collaboration with third parties. None of these proved satisfactory, however, given blacks' worsening legal status and shrinking share of the state's population. (Black Texans declined from 31 to 20 percent of the population between 1870 and 1900.) African-American activity in the Republican party focused on preventing the conservative faction from gaining control and driving out blacks, who in the 1880s formed 90 percent of the party's membership. By attracting like-minded whites, conservative Republicans hoped to compete effectively with the Democrats. Norris Wright Cuney[qv] of Galveston, an early protégé of Senator Ruby, was the astute leader of the black Republicans from the death of E. J. Davis in 1883 to his own death in 1897. Black influence in the party of Lincoln was sharply curtailed at the turn of the century, when a combination of factors—mainly the struggle among black leaders over the inheritance of the late Cuney's mantle and the success of the conservatives' efforts to obtain control of federal patronage—led to the lily white movement.[qv] The conservative Republicans, who now called themselves "lily whites," gained ascendancy over the Black and Tans, the Negro faction of the party.

Alliances with Democrats also offered limited prospects. Their party, after all, was the home of most white supremacists. For tactical reasons, however, blacks sometimes "fused" with a Democratic faction. Though he was a Republican national committeeman in 1892, Cuney, for example, urged blacks to support George Clark,[qv] the conservative Democratic candidate, against the economically progressive governor, James S. Hogg,[qv] in hopes of dividing the Democrats and increasing Cuney's influence. Only about half the black vote went to Clark, however, and Hogg was reelected.

Alliances with third parties proved alluring but were also unsuccessful. The Greenback party,[qv] addressing farmers' economic troubles, attracted black support in 1878, shortly before it collapsed. The People's party[qv] also garnered black support in statewide races—roughly 20, 35, and 50 percent of the black vote in 1892, 1894, and 1896, respectively. This upsurge came from the educational efforts of the Colored Farmers' Alliance,[qv] the organizing work and oratorical skills of such black Populists as John B. Rayner,[qv] a schoolteacher from Calvert, and the Populists' inclusion of platform planks addressing blacks' concerns and election of blacks to party-leadership posts. Ironically, these actions probably contributed to the defeat of Populism and black disfranchisement soon thereafter.

Disfranchisement, however, had been under way since the end of Reconstruction. Intimidation, harassment of black leaders, violence (including the lynching[qv] of 300 to 500 blacks late in the century), the growth of Jim Crow institutions, repeated efforts by conservative legislators to pass a poll-tax law from 1875 onward, and Democrats' fear of the third parties' biracial appeal culminated in the effective removal of blacks from the electorate. The last of forty-two black Reconstruction-era legislators, Robert L. Smith[qv] of Colorado County, attended his final sessions in 1897, offering an impassioned resolution on May 4 against lynching. Gerrymandering had cut the numbers of black legislators sharply. Violence had taken a toll on black voter turnout even before the constitution was amended in 1902 to impose the poll tax. But the tax, which fell hardest on those least able to pay, had an independent effect, as did restrictive registration laws mandated in 1903 and 1905, and county Democratic leaders' widespread adoption of the white primary.[qv] As nomination by the Democratic party[qv] was tantamount to election, the white primary denied most blacks the ballot in state contests. By 1906 African Americans were no longer a significant force in most elections.

Black Texans nonetheless continued to pursue their rights through such institutions as the National Association for the Advancement of Colored People,[qv] established in 1910; black civic, political, religious, business, and professional groups; a few interracial groups; the urban black press, a source of information and an instrument of social protest; and the courts, a somewhat more promising avenue for progress than the other branches of government. The NAACP was especially important. Until 1923 the white primary operated at the discretion of county executive committees, and blacks in some areas could still vote in Democratic contests. That year, however, the legislature passed a law preventing blacks from participating in any Democratic primary election. Lawrence A. Nixon,[qv] a black El Paso physician, challenged the law with the help of NAACP legal assistance and funding. The United States Supreme Court, in *Nixon v. Herndon* (1927), invalidated the statute as violating the equal-protection clause. The state legislature then shifted authority to prohibit black participation in political parties' state executive committees. The Democratic committee limited primary participation to "white Democrats . . . and none other." Dr. Nixon sued and won again in the Supreme Court, which held in *Nixon v. Condon* (1932) that the new law was just an extension of the earlier one. The Democratic committee, the court reasoned, lacked authority to act for the party and was acting for the state. But the party's state convention had such authority, the court said. Predictably, the state convention adopted a rule excluding blacks from its primaries. Houstonian Richard Randolph Grovey,[qv] against the advice of the national NAACP, attacked this rule in *Grovey v. Townsend* (1935), arguing that the Democratic party was an instrument of the state, not a voluntary association. This time the Court, quoting a Texas Supreme Court opinion holding that political parties were voluntary associations, let the law stand.

A major upswing in black Texans' involvement in the NAACP occurred in the 1930s. At the initiative of Antonio Maceo Smith,[qv] a black Dallas businessman, the State Conference of NAACP Branches was formed in 1937. Mobilizing civic leaders and lawyers in black communities, the conference revived the five state branches and before long had more than 170 local chapters. It cooperated with the national office to finance and execute successful legal attacks on the Texas white primary and racial segregation at the University of Texas law school and to file legal actions throughout the state attacking segregated municipal facilities, juries, and schools. Leaders in the state conference during this period, in addition to Smith, were Juanita Craft[qv] of Dallas, William J. Durham[qv] of Sherman, and Carter Wesley, Lulu White, and Christia Adair[qqv] of Houston. White and Craft were effective fieldworkers who helped revive dormant local chapters, raise money, and develop strategy. Conference activity declined sharply after 1956 when the state, in reaction to the conference's many achievements, temporarily enjoined the NAACP from doing business in Texas and charged it with violating the state's barratry statutes.

But in the 1940s the state NAACP was boldly advancing. Lonnie Smith,[qv] a Houston dentist, was prevented from voting in the Democratic primary. Represented by local and national attorneys, including Texan W. J. Durham and Thurgood Marshall, general counsel of the newly formed NAACP Legal Defense Fund, Smith filed suit in 1942. In *Smith v. Allwright* (1944) the Supreme Court overrode its prior reasoning in *Grovey*, holding that the Democratic primary, because regulated by Texas law, was an agency of the state and violated the Fifteenth Amendment's protection against racial discrimination in voting. The white primary, by then the major Texas disfranchising barrier, was dead. By 1946 75,000–100,000 blacks—at a maximum, 20 percent of those eligible—voted in the primary, compared to 33 percent of whites.

In earlier years, while still locked out of the Democratic organization, blacks had also been marginalized in the Republican party by the dominant lily whites. In 1932, Texas black precincts began to vote for the national Democratic ticket, a trend encouraged by the New Deal's popularity. After *Smith* was decided, blacks quickly joined the emerging liberal wing of the Texas Democrats, who were locked in conflict with party conservatives, and they supported liberal Ralph Yarborough in his campaigns for governor and United States senator from 1952 to 1972. They also supported other liberal white and Hispanic candidates in Democratic primaries and joined the liberals in party conventions. Several black Texans ran for office after Smith, but two of the first to succeed were Garlington J. Sutton,[qv] who won a post in 1948 on the governing board of a San Antonio junior-college district, and Hattie Mae White, who in 1958 won a Houston school-board post with a plurality of the votes but less than a majority. By 1965, the year Congress passed the Voting Rights Act and more than two decades after the end of the white primary, at most only a half-dozen black Texans held office.

As a result of legislative reapportionment in 1966—mandated by the Supreme Court's recent one-person, one-vote decisions—blacks were nominated for posts above the level of precinct chairmen in the Texas Democratic primary for the first time, at least, in this century. Barbara Jordan, a young Houston attorney, won election that year from a newly drawn single-member senatorial district in which blacks and Mexican Americans[qv] made up about half the population, after twice having unsuccessfully run at large in Harris County—which had a 20 percent black population—for a seat in the legislature. She was elected to Congress in 1972 from a district less than half white. In 1973 she was one of the first two Southern blacks to serve in Congress since 1901; she went on to a distinguished political career, achieving national recognition on the House Judiciary Committee during the Watergate hearings after the 1972 presidential election. Two blacks won seats in the Texas House in 1966—Curtis Graves of Houston and Joe Lockridge of Dallas. Each succeeding legislature also had black members. In 1993 two black senators and fourteen black representatives composed 9 percent of the legislature, while about 11 percent of the Texas voting-age population was black. All black members were Democrats that year, and all were elected from districts in which blacks, or blacks and Hispanics, were a majority.

Across the state African-American elected officials increased from fewer than seven in 1964 to 472 in 1993. These included Morris Overstreet, a justice on the Texas Court of Criminal Appeals[qv] and the first black elected statewide in Texas history, who in 1990 had defeated a single opponent, a black appointed by the Republican governor to fill an unexpired term. Among the other officials were 2 members of Congress, 13 mayors, 128 city-council members, 85 school-board members, and 17 county commissioners. The three black members of Congress elected since Jordan—Mickey Leland[qv] and Craig Washington of Houston and Eddie Bernice Johnson of Dallas—had served first in the legislature; all were elected from districts in which whites were a minority.

The increase in black officeholding would have been much smaller without extensive revision of discriminatory election laws, beginning in the 1960s. The Twenty-fourth Amendment abolished the poll tax in federal elections in 1964, and the Supreme Court overturned its use in state and local elections in *Harper v. Virginia State Board of Elections* (1966). The onerous annual voter registration system that a conservative-dominated legislature had substituted when the poll tax was invalidated was ruled unconstitutional in *Beare v. Smith* (1971). The Supreme Court in *Bullock v. Carter* (1972) struck down the state's candidate filing fees, which the Court said weighed "more heavily on the less affluent segment of the community." Another form of discrimination was attacked in a series of vote-dilution cases. In white-majority jurisdictions where whites voted as a bloc against candidates preferred by most black or Mexican-American voters, the whites could systematically deny election to the minorities' candidates, who often belonged to minorities themselves. This occurred when certain election structures or practices existed. These were mostly of two kinds: at-large systems with a majority-runoff requirement; or, where elections were by district, gerrymandering. In either case, white bloc voting often defeated candidates of minority voters and weakened their political strength. The Supreme Court first found minority vote dilution unconstitutional in *White v. Regester* (1973), which held that the round of legislative redistricting in Texas during the 1970s violated the equal-protection clause. As a remedy, district boundaries were redrawn in San Antonio and Dallas. Further litigation soon attacked other districts and produced a sharp increase in black and Hispanic legislators in the 1970s. In 1975 Congress extended to Texas coverage of Section 5 of the Voting Rights Act, requiring all proposed changes in voting procedure, including redistricting, to be precleared by the United States attorney general. Justice Department oversight diminished gerrymandering against minorities by the legislature and other entities such as cities and counties. In addition, minority plaintiffs invoked the Constitution and the Voting Rights Act to sue numerous cities, school districts, county commissioners' courts, and other entities, alleging minority vote dilution and demanding changes from at-large to district elections or the establishment of more fairly drawn districts. From the early 1970s on, these suits enabled many blacks and Hispanics to win office. In addition, the Justice Department from 1975 on refused to preclear numerous proposed election changes in Texas that would have undercut minority voting strength.

Most of these measures securing black and Hispanic voting rights were fashioned during the so-called Second Reconstruction, the period beginning with *Brown v. Board of Education* (1954), when several federal statutes and judicial decisions were formulated to destroy the Jim Crow system, discourage racial discrimination, and enable Southern blacks to participate equally in politics. The new laws were largely a response to the black-led civil-rights movement,[qv] in which Texans, both black and white, participated. The Second Reconstruction also led to a party realignment in Texas. As Senate majority leader, Lyndon B. Johnson[qv] guided the 1957 Civil Rights Act through the upper house; and as president he played a crucial role in the enactment of the 1964 Civil Rights Act, which abolished the Jim Crow system of segregated public accommodations, and the 1965 Voting Rights Act. Ralph Yarborough, the only Democratic United States senator from Texas from 1961 to 1971, was the only Southern senator to support the 1964 bill and only one of three Southern senators to support the Voting Rights Act. Backing epochal civil-rights policies in the late 1950s and 1960s, these two Texas Democrats, dependent on a solid black vote, were among the leaders of the national party's mainstream. At the same time, virtually no Texas Republican leader supported civil-rights legislation of the era. Senator John Tower[qv] opposed both the 1964 and 1965 bills. George H. W. Bush, opposing Yarborough for the Senate in 1964, attacked him for supporting the Civil Rights Act. That year Bush and Tower backed Barry Goldwater, who opposed the Civil Rights Act as a violation of states' rights and who was the first modern Republican presidential candidate to employ a "Southern strategy" in a campaign appealing to conservative whites while largely ignoring black voters. The polarized positions of party leaders on civil-rights issues resulted in a gradual exodus of white voters from the Democratic party, the strengthening of black and Hispanic ties to it, and a remarkable growth in Republican voting and officeholding. The Texas Democratic party became disproportionately black, Hispanic, and liberal, while the Republicans remained overwhelmingly white and conservative.

If a survey of the history, status, and prospects of black Texans had been conducted as the 1990s began, it would have revealed that many hard-fought battles for political equality had been won, even as challenging problems remained and others loomed on the horizon. The right of blacks to vote was obtained during Reconstruction, lost at the turn of the century, and won again long decades later. The same was true for their ability to hold office and participate in government. As a racial minority that had made striking social and economic progress since the 1940s even while struggling with serious social problems—including discrimination, poverty, unemployment, crime, family breakdown, infant mortality, and drug abuse—black Texans attempted to shore up and expand their own community institutions while looking to politics and government for additional support. Yet even when they coalesced at the polls and in governmental bodies with white and Mexican-American Democrats—who were their most reliable allies from the 1950s onward—the coalition's size was often insufficient to achieve such goals as equal school funding, a more progressive tax base, adequate protection from discrimination, fair provision of municipal services, and similar items on black Texans' long-term egalitarian agenda. Moreover, the rapid growth of the Mexican-American population in Texas in the latter part of the century, partly from illegal immigration, encouraged the perception that scarce jobs were being taken by newcomers from Mexico. This, along with clashes of culture between the two groups in inner-city neighborhoods and struggles over political turf, created tensions that threatened to weaken the liberal Democratic coalition. It was thus not only with pride in past achievements against great odds but also with a wariness of what the political future held in store that thoughtful African Americans anticipated the new century. *See also* RECONSTRUCTION, ELECTION LAWS.

BIBLIOGRAPHY: Melvin J. Banks, The Pursuit of Equality: The Movement for First Class Citizenship among Negroes in Texas, 1920–1950 (Ph.D. dissertation, Syracuse University, 1962). Alwyn Barr, *Black Texans: A History of Negroes in Texas, 1528–1971* (Austin: Jenkins, 1973). Alwyn Barr, *Reconstruction to Reform: Texas Politics, 1876–1906* (Austin: University of Texas Press, 1971). William Joseph Brophy, The Black Texan, 1900–1950: A Quantitative History (Ph.D. dissertation, Vanderbilt University, 1974). Barry A. Crouch, *The Freedmen's Bureau and Black Texans* (Austin: University of Texas Press, 1992). Chandler Davidson, *Race and Class in Texas Politics* (Princeton University Press, 1990). Michael L. Gillette, The NAACP in Texas, 1937–1957 (Ph.D. dissertation, University of Texas at Austin, 1984). Bruce Alden Glasrud, Black Texans, 1900–1930: A History (Ph.D. dissertation, Texas Tech College, 1969). Darlene Clark Hine, *Black Victory: The Rise and Fall of the White Primary in Texas* (Millwood, New York: KTO Press, 1979). Barbara Jordan and Shelby Hearon, *Barbara Jordan: A Self-Portrait* (Garden City, New Jersey: Doubleday, 1979). J. Morgan Kousser, *The Shaping of Southern Politics: Suffrage Restrictions and the Establishment of the One-Party South, 1880–1910* (New Haven: Yale University Press, 1974). Merline Pitre, *Through Many Dangers, Toils and Snares: The Black Leadership of Texas, 1868–1900* (Austin: Eakin, 1985). Lawrence D. Rice, *The Negro in Texas, 1874–1900* (Baton Rouge: Louisiana State University Press, 1971). James Smallwood, *Time of Hope, Time of Despair: Black Texans during Reconstruction* (London: Kennikat, 1981). James R. Soukup, Clifton McCleskey, and Harry Holloway, *Party and Factional Division in Texas* (Austin: University of Texas Press, 1964).

Chandler Davidson

AFRICAN METHODIST EPISCOPAL CHURCH. The African Methodist Episcopal Church grew out of a protest by Richard Allen against racial discrimination in St. George's Methodist Episcopal Church, Philadelphia, in 1787. Rather than suffer indignities in that white-controlled church, Allen formed a separate black congregation. In 1816 he organized several black Methodist congregations into a new denomination called the African Methodist Episcopal Church. In the tense times leading to the Civil War,[qv] the AME Church was not permitted to operate in Texas, or in most other parts of the slaveholding South.

The first African Methodist Episcopal Church missionary in Texas, M. M. Clark, arrived in Galveston in 1866, after the surrender of the Confederacy and the end of slavery.[qv] Like African Methodist missionaries elsewhere in the former slave states, Clark wanted to organize black Methodists. Although Texas had had no AME congregations previously, many black Methodists had worshipped in the Methodist churches of their masters. Clark intended to bring them into the AME Church and to recruit others to Methodism. The congregations that he and other missionaries organized were originally supervised by Bishop Jabez P. Campbell from New Orleans.

A meeting to organize an annual conference in Texas took place in Galveston, probably in 1867. (Administrative and doctrinal matters for the church as a whole are attended to in general conferences held every four years. Annual conferences handle church affairs within states.) On October 22, 1868, the first Texas conference met in Galveston, presided over by Bishop James A. Shorter. Among those present were the early leaders of African Methodism in Texas, Houston Reedy (*see* REEDY CHAPEL AME CHURCH), Steven Patton, Emmanuel Hammitt, and Johnson Reed.[qv] The conference claimed 3,000 members and probationers that year, and membership grew steadily though not spectacularly afterward. By 1890 membership in Texas had reached 23,000, and by 1926 it had reached 34,000, ranking second to Baptists among black churchgoers.

In the early years of the Texas Conference most member churches were located within a triangle formed by Galveston, Bryan, and San Antonio. Eventually, however, the number of AME members in Texas increased and spread across the state. The West Texas Conference was organized in 1875 and the Central Texas Conference in 1883. The church had four conferences by 1890 and nine by 1926.

The Texas Conference founded Paul Quinn College in the Metropolitan AME Church in Austin in 1872. The school was later moved to Waco. In addition to its religious functions, the African Methodist Church has helped blacks maintain a sense of community and provided them with a place to express their demands for civil rights.

BIBLIOGRAPHY: Hightower T. Kealing, *History of African Methodism in Texas* (Waco, 1885). Daniel Alexander Payne, *History of the African Methodist Episcopal Church* (Nashville: A.M.E. Sunday School Union, 1891; rpt., New York: Arno, 1969). Charles Spencer Smith, *A History of the African Methodist Episcopal Church* (Philadelphia: A.M.E. Church Book Concern, 1922; rpt., New York: Johnson Reprint, 1968). Richard R. Wright, Jr., ed., *Centennial Encyclopaedia of the African Methodist Episcopal Church* (Philadelphia: Book Concern of the A.M.E. Church, 1916). *William E. Montgomery*

AFRICAN METHODIST EPISCOPAL ZION CHURCH. The Texas Conference of the African Methodist Episcopal Zion Church, an offshoot of the African Methodist Episcopal Church,[qv] was organized in 1883. Zion missionaries had entered the South with the Union army and had been slower than the parent AME Church to move into Texas. The first conference meeting, in Stoneham, produced plans to organize the Zion congregations in the state and promote discipline among them. Bishop Thomas H. Lomax presided. The Zion AME Church numbered 6,927 after organization in 1890. However, in 1936 the census showed only 614 members in the state. In 1986–87 there were seven active churches, 1,752 confirmed members, and 2,095 total adherents in Texas. Evangelical theology, spiritual and material support for its members, and worship services that are also social occasions characterize the church. Through journals such as the Star of Zion, members have been kept informed.

BIBLIOGRAPHY: Alwyn Barr, *Black Texans: A History of Negroes in Texas, 1528–1971* (Austin: Jenkins, 1973). Olin W. Nail, ed., *History of Texas Methodism, 1900–1960* (Austin, 1961). Lawrence D. Rice, *The Negro in Texas, 1874–1900* (Baton Rouge: Louisiana State University Press, 1971). Carter G. Woodson, *The History of the Negro Church* (Washington: Associated Publishers, 1921; 2d ed. 1945).

William E. Montgomery

AFTON, TEXAS (Dickens County). Afton is on Farm Road 193 seventy miles east of Lubbock in north central Dickens County. Before 1891 a hunter named Patton camped near springs in the area that became known as Patton Springs. Soon after, a settlement developed south of the springs. The community's first post office, which opened in 1891, was named Beckton after the first postmaster, Francis E. Beck. In 1895 it closed, but by 1900 a new post office had opened. Although the town had by this time become known as Cottonwood, the postal authorities rejected this name since another Texas town was already using it. At this time Myra Kelly, applying the sentiments of the song "Flow Gently, Sweet Afton" to a local stream, named the settlement Afton. In 1900 Afton had a population of only ten, and the tent grocery store operated by R. L. Sitton was its only business. Ed Chambers evidently built the first gin in 1904, and Uncle Wash Robertson started a blacksmith shop in 1906. During the late teens and early twenties Afton thrived and was referred to as "Little Fort Worth." The town had an estimated population of 100 in 1970 and 1990. It still maintained a post office, a Baptist church, and a consolidated school in 1980, but the only businesses remaining were a gin and a grocery store.

BIBLIOGRAPHY: Fred Arrington, *A History of Dickens County: Ranches and Rolling Plains* (Quanah, Texas: Nortex, 1971). Kathleen E. and Clifton R. St. Clair, eds., *Little Towns of Texas* (Jacksonville, Texas: Jayroe Graphic Arts, 1982). *Edloe A. Jenkins*

AFTON, TEXAS (Fisher County). Afton is on Farm Road 92 five miles west of Hamlin in northeastern Fisher County. The area was settled by the Afton family in the late nineteenth century. About 1889 a school was built at the site of the Afton cemetery. Church services were held in the school for a time, and a church building was erected nearby some years later. In 1892 Afton was granted a post office, which closed the following year. The school was consolidated with that of nearby Hitson a few years later. In 1940 Afton had a church, a cemetery, and scattered dwellings, and by 1965 all that remained was the cemetery.

BIBLIOGRAPHY: Fisher County Historical Commission, *History of Fisher County, Texas* (Rotan, Texas: Shelton, 1983). *Daniel L. Ruth*

AGISTHA, TEXAS. Agistha was on the northwestern edge of the site of present Longview in north central Gregg County. The settlement was probably established in the 1890s. A post office opened there in 1899 and closed in 1901. Around 1900 the community had a general store and a number of houses. By the early 1920s it no longer appeared on maps. *Christopher Long*

AGNES, TEXAS. Agnes is on State Highway 199 eighteen miles north of Weatherford in north central Parker County. Settlement began there in the late 1870s, when B. B. Barnard opened a general store. The community petitioned for postal service in 1879 under the name Agnes, in honor of Agnes Mull, the daughter of a pioneer physician in North Texas. By the mid-1880s two churches, a public school, a blacksmith shop, and Barnard's General Store served the seventy-five residents. Area farmers brought their crops to Agnes to be processed at the cotton gin and gristmill. Cotton, corn, and oats were shipped on the Texas and Pacific Railway. Postal service was discontinued in 1907, though Agnes continued as a dispersed rural community throughout the twentieth century. Its population has never exceeded 100.

BIBLIOGRAPHY: John Clements, *Flying the Colors: Texas, a Comprehensive Look at Texas Today, County by County* (Dallas: Clements Research, 1984). Gustavus Adolphus Holland, *History of Parker County and the Double Log Cabin* (Weatherford, Texas: Herald, 1931; rpt. 1937). Kathleen E. and Clifton R. St. Clair, eds., *Little Towns of Texas* (Jacksonville, Texas: Jayroe Graphic Arts, 1982). *David Minor*

AGREDA, MARÍA DE JESÚS DE (1602–1665). María de Jesús de Agreda (the Lady in Blue) was born in the Spanish village of Agreda near the border of Aragon and Navarre in April of 1602, the eldest daughter of Francisco Coronel and Catalina of Arana. In her youth María, baptized María Coronel, demonstrated unusual piety and remarkable memory. At the age of sixteen, she convinced her father that he should convert the family castle into a convent for Franciscan nuns. She took religious vows on February 2, 1620, and the name María de Jesús. The new order soon expanded beyond the confines of the castle and moved to the convent of the Immaculate Conception in Agreda. The nuns' habit was colored Franciscan brown (*pardo*) with an outer cloak of coarse blue cloth.

Throughout the 1620s María de Jesús would repeatedly lapse into deep trances. On these occasions she experienced dreams in which she was transported to a distant and unknown land, where she taught the Gospel to a pagan people. Her alleged miraculous bilocations took her to eastern New Mexico and western Texas, where she contacted several Indian cultures, including the Jumanos. Sister María related her mystical experiences to her confessor, Fray Sebastián Marcilla of Agreda. His superiors contacted the archbishop of Mexico, Francisco Manso y Zúñiga. The archbishop, in turn, wrote the religious superior of New Mexico in May of 1628, requesting information regarding a young nun's alleged transportations and teachings in northern New Spain. That communication arrived in New Mexico shortly before a delegation of some fifty Jumano Indians appeared at the Franciscan convent of old Isleta, south of present Albuquerque, in July 1629. The Jumanos had come to request religious teachers for themselves and their neighbors. They demonstrated rudimentary knowledge of Christianity, and when asked who had instructed them replied, "the Woman in Blue."

An expedition headed by Fray Juan de Salas,[qv] organized in New Mexico, set out for the land of the Jumanos. Guided by the chief of the Jumano delegations, it reached a locale in Southwest Texas where it was met by a large band of Indians. The Indians claimed that they had been advised by the Woman in Blue of approaching Christian missionaries. Subsequently, some 2,000 natives presented themselves for baptism and further religious instruction. Two years later, Fray Alonso de Benavides,[qv] a former religious superior in New Mexico, traveled to Spain, where he sought more information about the mysterious nun. He interviewed María de Jesús at Agreda. Sister María admitted that she had experienced some 500 bilocations to New Spain and acknowledged that she was indeed the Lady in Blue.

During the last twenty-two years of her life, María de Jesús was an active correspondent with the Spanish king, Philip IV. She died at Agreda on May 24, 1665. Her story was published in Spain several years after her death. Although the abbess said her last visitation to the New World was in 1631, the mysterious Lady in Blue was not quickly forgotten in Texas. In 1690 a missionary working with the Tejas Indians heard the legend. In the 1840s a mysterious woman in blue reportedly traveled the Sabine River valley aiding malaria victims, and in the twentieth century her apparition was reported as recently as World War II.[qv]

BIBLIOGRAPHY: *The Age of Mary: An Exclusively Marian Magazine*, January–February 1958. Carlos E. Castañeda, *Our Catholic Heritage in Texas* (7 vols., Austin: Von Boeckmann–Jones, 1936–58; rpt., New York: Arno, 1976). Aníbal A. González, "The Lady in Blue," *Sayersville Historical Association Bulletin*, Summer 1982. Vertical Files, Barker Texas History Center, University of Texas at Austin.

Donald E. Chipman

AGRICULTURAL ADJUSTMENT ADMINISTRATION. The Agricultural Adjustment Act of 1933, which provided for the Agricultural Adjustment Administration to adjust production of dairy products, wheat, corn, cotton, hogs, and rice, was declared unconstitutional by the United States Supreme Court in January 1936. Prior to the Supreme Court ruling, 237 out of 254 Texas counties had complied with AAA production quotas. The 1936 Soil Conservation and Domestic Allotment Act was supplemented in 1938 by a new Agricultural Adjustment Act providing compensation to producers who adjust the acreage of their soil-depleting crops, parity of price adjustments to those who do not overplant, federal crop insurance, and other benefits. The two programs combined provided Texas farmers with $292,821,000 in direct payments. In 1948 the only payments being made were those to assist farmers in carrying out soil-conservation practices; the Texas allocation for that purpose was $11,130,000. Between 1936 and 1946 Texas farmers engaged in thirty types of conservation, including terracing, construction of dams, contouring, pasture sodding, and tree planting. In 1938 county offices were set up, and the farmers in each community elected a committee of three to administer the program and a delegate to the county convention. The county convention chose a committee of three to direct the county program. The secretary of agriculture appointed a state director and a state committee of five farmers. The Agriculture Stabilization and Conservation Service[qv] replaced the Agricultural Adjustment Administration in 1945 when the AAA was absorbed by the Production and Marketing Administration of the United States Department of Agriculture.

BIBLIOGRAPHY: Nancy Blanpied, ed., *Farm Policy: The Politics of Soil Surpluses and Subsidies* (Washington: Congressional Quarterly, Inc., 1984). Donald Blaisdell, *Government and Agriculture: The Growth of Federal Farm Aid* (New York: Farrar and Rinehart, 1940). Robert A. Calvert and Arnoldo De León, *The History of Texas* (Arlington Heights, Illinois: Harlan Davidson, 1990). Van L. Perkins, *Crisis in Agriculture: The Agricultural Adjustment Administration and the New Deal* (Berkeley: University of California Press, 1969).

AGRICULTURAL EDUCATION. Agricultural education in Texas has been conducted on the high school and college levels and, through the Texas Agricultural Extension Service,[qv] among farmers. Vocational agricultural education was introduced into twenty-eight white and four black high schools in 1917 under provisions of the federal Smith-Hughes Bill. In 1947 there were vocational agriculture departments in 631 high schools; more than 25,000 boys received daily instruction, and approximately 2,130 received part-time instruction, while 17,650 adults took evening courses. The Future Farmers of America, a national organization of students, had chapters wherever vocational agriculture was offered as a course. An agricultural education specialist program was established in 1958, which provided part-time instruction for 6,750 adults in all phases of agriculture. The Vocational Education Act of 1963 provided for the expansion of vocational agricultural education to include production agriculture training and off-farm occupation training for persons of all ages. In 1965 there were vocational agriculture departments in 1,022 high schools, representing a substantial increase over the 631 extant in 1947. Some 48,895 high school students received daily instruction in 1965, as compared to the 1947 figure of 25,000. Adult agricultural education more than tripled from 1947, with 67,653 persons enrolled in 1965. In addition to regular courses in classrooms, laboratories, and research centers, vocational agriculture teachers provided individual instruction to 41,895 young and adult farmers in 1965. In 1994–95 Texas had 1,462 agricultural science and technology teachers providing instruction to 1,011 departments in Texas high schools. More than 92,000 students received daily instruction in those departments, compared to 48,895 in 1965 and 25,000 in 1947. During the 1994–95 school year twenty-nine courses were offered. Agricultural science and technology teachers were trained at nine universities in the state: Texas A&M University, Southwest Texas State University, Texas Tech University, Sam Houston State University, Stephen F. Austin State University, Texas A&M University at Kingsville, Prairie View A&M University, Tarleton State University, and East Texas State University. By the mid-1990s, those institutions were graduating between 150 and 200 teachers a year. Agricultural science and technology teachers also taught 3,356 adults in various agriculture and agribusiness education courses in 1995. *See also* AGRICULTURE.

AGRICULTURAL RESEARCH. Agricultural research has generally had a regional focus, and Texas research has been no exception. However, the state's research also has had lasting national and international implications since its formal organization in the late 1800s. In its second century, Texas research has continued to increase its global focus and impact and to aid economic growth. Vast amounts of land, variable fertility, and short water supplies helped define Texas research, as did the national research model that gave a central role to the land-grant college and the state agricultural experiment stations. These stations were based on practices already developed before the mid-1800s in Europe, where systematic, scientific methods were used to improve the process of agricultural observation and selection. Those practices led to improved yields and less labor devoted to food production—developments that had long marked the progress of various cultures from subsistence economies to more stable and varied social systems. Such progress marked the period in which the United States established its agricultural research system. The Industrial Revolution was expanding and requiring more labor; the American West was being settled, cities were growing, and trade, especially for manufactured goods, was increasing. In 1887, hoping to improve agricultural efficiency, the Congress approved the Hatch Act, which established federally supported experiment stations as components of state land-grant colleges (themselves established by the Morrill Act of 1862). The colleges often possessed the farmlands, laboratories, and faculty needed by the stations, and students would benefit from the close working relationship between state colleges and experiment stations. The structure of these stations is fairly uniform throughout the United States. As in Texas, they usually conduct a three-pronged effort involving education, research, and extension carried out by a land-grant college or college system, a state experiment station (often with several research sites), and a state extension service. Most state experiment station scientists traditionally spend some time teaching in the colleges.

The Texas Agricultural Experiment Station[qv] was established on April 2, 1887, when Governor Lawrence Sullivan Ross[qv] signed legislation establishing the station and designating Texas A&M as administrator of its program. This was during the midst of a depression in American agriculture, when rapid plowing of the Great Plains, increased farm productivity, and steady appreciation of the dollar brought low prices for farm commodities. An advisory body of Texas farmers and ranchers went to College Station to confer with the station on agricultural research. Together they decided to focus initial research on seven projects with a practical bent: improving feeding methods for beef and dairy cattle, finding the best-adapted fruit varieties for Texas, studying the adaptability and feeding value of various grasses and forage plants, comparing the usefulness of barnyard manure and commercial fertilizers, determining the value of tile drainage for gardens and farms, controlling cotton blight (or root rot), and protecting cattle from Texas fever.[qv] Within a few years of its establishment, the station had successfully met major research goals in six of the seven projects. Texas fever, once a nationwide problem, had been effectively wiped out, largely through TAES efforts in cooperation with others. Root rot, however, remained a major problem, even though its effects can be somewhat controlled through various cultural practices. The remaining five initial projects became successful bases for later work in the areas of irrigation,[qv] fertilization, livestock feeding, new or improved crops, and range management. Early field trials were conducted at the TAES College Station headquarters, but researchers suspected that many findings were dependent on local conditions. By 1880 several state prison farms also were used for trials, as were fields at Prairie View Normal College. Occasionally, private farms and ranches cooperated with TAES by providing funding, livestock and their own facilities for research. The King Ranch[qv] in South Texas, for example, was a partner in the successful effort to eradicate Texas fever. This beef-cattle disease caused many northern states to ban imports of Texas cattle from the 1870s to the 1890s. After TAES scientists confirmed it was carried by ticks, joint development of a method of dipping cattle into vats of sheep dip and other fatty solutions to kill the ticks helped defeat the disease. By 1900, growing demands for agricultural products in a rapidly increasing urban population led to higher commodity prices, and agricultural research and education had also improved and grown dramatically across the United States. TAES had begun expanding its efforts and throughout the next century it was able to improve productivity of all the state's major crops and livestock.

For cotton, since the 1800s the top cash crop in Texas, TAES worked extensively to breed plants that fruited early and more rapidly as a method of defeating the boll weevil.[qv] One of the first of quick-growing varieties was jointly bred by TAES and USDA in the first years of the 1900s. TAES also introduced TAMCOT, some of the first varieties suited to harsh conditions on the High Plains, and has introduced many new varieties with superior fiber strength. The station did extensive work with mechanical strippers during the first decades of the 1900s, and in 1971 developed a cotton module system that compresses cotton directly to compact field-storage units of ten to fifteen bales, making it easier for farmers to store and transport their cotton. The project was carried out cooperatively with cotton farmers and supported financially by the trade association, Cotton, Incorporated, through producer check-off funds collected on each harvested bale. Wheat, sorghum, corn, and rice are also among the biggest cash crops in Texas, and new lines of each have been developed by the station. The first successful semi-dwarf hard red winter wheat varieties led to higher yields and insect resistance and ability to produce crops late in the year; by 1990 improved varieties were grown on about half of the state's wheat acreage and almost a quarter of all wheat acreage in Texas, Oklahoma, Nebraska, Colorado, and Kansas. The station developed sorghum hybrids in the 1940s and 1950s that more than tripled sorghum yields by the 1980s and also produced more effective corn hybrids. An example of successful state and federal cooperation resulted from requests in the 1970s by rice producers, who helped fund an aggressive research agenda from TAES and USDA that began in 1982. By 1986, the Texas Econo-Rice initiative had boosted production by some 2,000 pounds per acre, to a state average of about 6,300 pounds, and cut costs to $8.20 per hundredweight from some $13 per hundredweight—far exceeding program goals. In addition, new semi-dwarf varieties enabled producers to grow two crops each year. Similar successes have been achieved with smaller Texas crops. In the 1980s an investment of $10 million from both state and industry sources in onion research yielded the Texas Grano 1015Y onion, a larger, sweeter variety with such a vast market appeal that by 1991 it was worth some $150 million annually to the state's economy, including $42 million in wholesale income alone. TAES had a number of other notable achievements in both beef and dairy cattle research. Among these were the use of electrical stimulation of carcasses to improve tenderness and extensive crossbreeding and feeding studies to improve the productivity of the Texas cattle industry. Because of the high cost of irrigation in drier areas of Texas, particularly the High Plains, water conservation has always been a major area of concern for both state and federal agencies. The effects of different types of plowing, forms of rows for crops, mulches, and irrigation systems were key projects. A major TAES accomplishment was the Low Energy Precision Application irrigation system, the first mobile drip system of field size. Developed in 1976, LEPA achieved irrigation efficiencies that are expected to lighten demands on the Ogallala Aquifer in the Panhandle.[qv] TAES research is now carried on at substations throughout the state. The first permanent TAES substation was established on 151 acres near Beeville in 1894, and it was still carrying on research on forage and reproduction of beef cattle into the 1990s. Substations opened and closed over the next seven decades, and beginning in the 1960s, several units were converted to regional research and extension centers. This was partly an effort to improve communication among scientists, extension specialists, and farmers and also to bring together larger groups of researchers for more complex, interdisciplinary projects. There are now fourteen such regional research and extension centers, shared by TAES and the Texas Agricultural Extension Service[qv] (both agencies of the Texas A&M University System). Additional TAES research facilities with more limited functions are located in ten other communities across Texas.

TAES substations in Weslaco, Amarillo, Beaumont, and Temple share facilities with the Agricultural Research Service of the United States Department of Agriculture, which supervises federal agricultural research and allocates research funds to state experiment stations. The oldest of the ARS centers still in use is at Big Spring, where experiments in dry-land crop rotation and tillage began in 1915. It pioneered techniques for using layers of cotton-gin trash to decrease erosion on sandy soils and developed field equipment now used worldwide to measure wind erosion. An ARS facility with similar purposes was established in 1936 at Bushland, near Amarillo, and it has developed improvements in stubble-mulch tillage, water conservation, wind-erosion control, wheat improvement, grass reseeding, and livestock management, including reduction of losses to bovine respiratory disease. In 1931 the ARS established its cooperative relationship with the TAES center at Beaumont to work on rice breeding. The resulting program serves the entire United States with research on cooking and processing qualities of various lines and improved disease and insect resistance, among other projects. Similarly, the USDA in 1932 established a pecan-breeding facility in Brownwood that is the only one of its kind in the world, and added a second worksite near College Station in 1987. The pecan program has introduced nineteen improved cultivars used throughout the country. Three-fourths of the cultivars recommended for planting in Texas were introduced through these facilities. The ARS established the United States Livestock Insects Laboratory in 1946 in Kerrville to conduct research on biology and control of parasitic insects affecting livestock and human beings. Its most notable achievement was development of the process for sterilizing male screwworms, which when released into the environment overwhelmed populations of the flies. Because they breed only once, the screwworms were unable to produce their flesh-eating larvae. TAES, which had studied the problem since at least 1890, played a cooperative role in the eradication, as did producers and several other state and federal agencies. In 1982 the last case of screwworms was reported in Texas. Other accomplishments included development of a cattle-grub vaccine, ear tags that decrease environmental contamination by 98 percent, and microencapsulation techniques used for long-term pest control in livestock. The Food Animal Protection Research Laboratory in College Station, which focuses on solving problems related to food safety in livestock and poultry, has increased understanding of how natural and synthetic poisons affect livestock and poultry and improved methods for eliminating chemical and microbial hazards associated with meat products. Other ARS units in College Station include the Southern Crops Research Laboratory and the Veterinary Toxicology and Entomology Laboratory. The Grassland, Soil and Water Research Laboratory of the ARS, in Temple, has been a leader in controlling undesirable plants that compete with grasses on rangelands, developing new strains of pasture and range grasses, and pioneering efforts to develop computer simulation of agricultural processes. By the 1990s many of its projects focused on computer models and databases used for soil and water testing, geographic-information systems, and other projects based on large sets of data on soils, water, and other natural resources throughout Texas and the world. The Subtropical Agricultural Research Laboratory in Weslaco focuses on national and international agricultural needs, many centered on preventing the spread of exotic pests such as the boll weevil or the Africanized honey bee, which invaded the United States through the Rio Grande valley. The facility's research dramatically improved cotton-production efficiency in South Texas through development of short-season, early-maturing crops planted in narrower rows. Use of high-altitude infrared photography to detect citrus-blackfly infestations and discovery of methods to control tracheal mites, which harm honey bees, are also among its accomplishments.

TAES and ARS also cooperate with other educational institutions and with numerous private foundations and commodity groups. Several universities have extensive agricultural education programs and have carried out successful, smaller-scale research programs, including Texas A&M University at Kingsville (wildlife), Tarleton State University (soil and water), and Prairie View A&M University. Prairie View's Cooperative Agricultural Research Center has specialized facilities for small-animal research and meat research; in addition to poultry and swine complexes and a computerized feed mill, it has greenhouses and other facilities for small-animal research on various crops. Each of these universities is part of the Texas A&M system, and agricultural research at each is supported by TAES funding. Texas Tech University, established in 1925, is not a landgrant university and therefore initially lacked the resources of Texas A&M and TAES. Its plans for agricultural research were hindered through the 1930s by funding shortages, although it cooperated with TAES on several projects. Among the earliest and most important was the work both did in livestock feeding with crops available from High Plains farms. That and other research led to development of the area's extensive feedlot industry. The university organized a farm and ranch research facility in the late 1940s under a lease agreement with TAES and the USDA. Experiments on livestock feeding and additives, digestibility of feedstuffs, and crossbreeding were of primary importance to the area, as was research involving forage sorghum varieties, fertilizers, the use of sewage effluent for irrigation, soils, herbicide tests, seeding of rangeland grasses, the effects of fire on High Plains rangeland vegetation, and the control of greenbugs and aphids. Texas Tech's research in agriculture of arid regions has drawn international attention. A private foundation that significantly added to the state's research effort was the Texas Research Foundation,[qv] which began at Southern Methodist University in 1944 as the Institute of Technology and Plant Industry. The institute was founded to solve regional problems that Dallas-area businessmen and others felt received too little attention from existing state and federal institutions. By 1945, fund-raising and demand for research projects had risen enough that the institute was separated from SMU and set up as a private foundation. Originally called the Texas State Research Foundation, it was moved from SMU to 107 acres of land at Renner, which the university deeded to the foundation in 1946. Operating independently, the foundation focused on soil and soil fertility, with an emphasis on using forage grasses and then grains to restore organic matter to the soil in cropping systems. In 1972 the foundation went out of business and turned over its research facilities and a portion of its land to TAES, which closed its Denton substation and moved into the former foundation buildings. This Dallas TAES substation became a center for urban agricultural research, including work related to the multibillion-dollar turf, landscaping, and nursery industries; biological control of insects; and management of fertilizer and other chemicals, both in agricultural production and maintenance of lawns and urban landscaping. A similar effort, the High Plains Research Foundation, was organized near Halfway by area businessmen and farmers with the help of the Texas Research Foundation in the late 1950s and turned over to TAES in 1973. The foundation's initial research laid a foundation for continuing work in soil and water research and equine and crop breeding programs. Businesses have also improved Texas agricultural production through their own research and with financing of public projects. Among the more successful research efforts is that by the Texas seed-sorghum industry, whose High Plains–based firms lead the world in providing hybrid seed. Much of their output results directly from USDA-TAES efforts to collect sorghum varieties from all over the world, which are then interbred for improved disease and insect resistance, yield, and nutritional quality. Seed producers in corn, cotton, and other crops are also among the state's leading exporters of agricultural products.

By the 1980s private firms and commodity groups began playing an increasing part in funding agricultural research and in cooperative public-private efforts. This coincided with a changing role of United States experiment stations, which increasingly began emphasizing research on issues of environmental and consumer concern. By that time, the American public enjoyed the benefits of food that was both abundant and relatively cheap by world standards. However, criticism of the agricultural system increased because of problems of groundwater pollution, soil erosion, declines in rural communities as farming and ranching became more concentrated in larger operations, and other issues. By the 1990s, TAES, ARS and other public and private groups faced these issues and others, including the concerns of animal-rights groups, increasing pressure from regulatory agencies, and increased research costs. The research agendas of these groups reflect those concerns, with efforts focusing on systems to take into account the complexities of modern agriculture. Integrated pest-management systems, for instance, focus on combinations of the best-known methods of chemical and biological control, with decreasing emphasis on chemicals, that would allow high output with low production and environmental costs. Interdisciplinary research, biotechnological methods, sophisticated electronics, and other techniques have become standard approaches in the research effort. Still, agricultural research in Texas has, in some ways, changed little. Though root rot still affects cotton and many other plants throughout Texas, interdisciplinary efforts to understand the fungus causing the disease may lead to more effective methods of controlling it. Research into genetic material that increases yields, resistance to disease, or tolerance of drought in various crops could produce new genetically engineered crops of all types; similar research for livestock may produce cattle that provide leaner, healthier beef that still has the flavor and texture consumers previously associated only with beef containing more fat. Scientists in Texas and throughout the United States are continuing to seek new ways to produce, process, package, and distribute foods that are lighter, fresher, faster to prepare and more healthful. Computer-based information and decision systems are becoming more important in such operations as pest management and irrigation. Computerized tractors and harvesting equipment may soon plant, prune, selectively harvest, and even cool and pack many crops automatically. Two research centers opened in the 1990s and affiliated with TAES and Texas A&M illustrate the use of the new approaches. The Institute of Biosciences and Technology in Houston's world-renowned medical center focuses on links between agriculture, human medicine, and veterinary medicine. Among its initial research projects were basic studies in genetic structure with applications in both human medicine and agricultural production. The Crop Biotechnology Center, located on the Texas A&M campus, was organized to bring together researchers and new technology in genetic identification, molecular biology, and applied plant breeding. Key goals in each of the new centers were to encourage further diversification and provide a competitive edge to the Texas economy. Agricultural research has helped lead to production efficiencies that gave Texas agriculture $14 billion in gross sales in 1991, when one-fifth of all Texans worked in jobs related to the production, processing, or marketing of agricultural products. New technology-intensive approaches were expected to help future Texas researchers continue to find better answers to the age-old questions about how best to feed people and livestock, but with increased emphasis on caring for the environment that supports both. *See also* AGRICULTURE.

BIBLIOGRAPHY: Henry C. Dethloff, *A Centennial History of Texas A&M University, 1876–1976* (2 vols., College Station: Texas A&M University Press, 1975). Donald E. Green, *Fifty Years of Service to West Texas Agriculture: A History of Texas Tech University's College of*

Agricultural Sciences, 1925–1975 (Lubbock: Texas Tech University Press, 1977). Don F. Hadwiger, *The Politics of Agricultural Research* (Lincoln: University of Nebraska Press, 1982). Robert L. Haney, *Milestones: Marking Ten Decades of Research* (College Station: Texas Agricultural Experiment Station, 1989). Cyrus L. Lundell, *Agricultural Research at Renner* (Renner, Texas: Texas Research Foundation, 1967). Clarence Ousley, *History of the Agricultural and Mechanical College of Texas* (College Station: A&M College of Texas, 1935).

Dudley T. Smith and Steve Hill

AGRICULTURAL STABILIZATION AND CONSERVATION SERVICE. During the 1940s the Agricultural Stabilization and Conservation Service replaced the Agricultural Adjustment Administration[qv] in the administration of federal laws related to agriculture. The ASCS has regional, state, and county offices. As was the case under the AAA, each county has a farmers' committee working in cooperation with federal employees. The mission of the ASCS is to promote conservation and price stability. Virtually every county in Texas has its own county ASCS office. Services include distribution of price-support payments and cost-share programs for various conservation projects. Each office also stores aerial photographic maps of its county. The maps are used for road planning and other development projects.

BIBLIOGRAPHY: Nancy Blanpied, ed., *Farm Policy: The Politics of Soil Surpluses and Subsidies* (Washington: Congressional Quarterly, Inc., 1984). Bruce L. Gardner, *The Governing of Agriculture* (Lawrence: Regents Press of Kansas, 1981). Allen Matusow, *Farm Policies and Politics in the Truman Years* (Cambridge: Harvard University Press, 1967). Luther Tweeten, *Foundations of Farm Policy* (Lincoln: University of Nebraska Press, 1970).

Tracé Etienne-Gray

Jaranames *(Aranamas), by Lino Sánchez y Tapia, after a sketch by Jean Louis Berlandier. Near Goliad, ca. 1830. Watercolor. Courtesy Gilcrease Museum, Tulsa, Oklahoma; accession no. 4016.336, plate XI. Some Indians, such as the Caddos, farmed in Texas before the arrival of Europeans. The Aranamas, however, probably took up agriculture as mission Indians. By 1843 the Aranamas were extinct.*

AGRICULTURE. Modern Texas agriculture evolved from the agriculture of prehistoric Texans and agricultural practices transferred from Europe, Asia, and Africa. Crops native to North America included the food staples corn, beans, and squash, and such diverse vegetables as tomatoes, "Irish" potatoes, chili peppers, yams, peanuts, and pumpkins. Spanish colonists introduced wheat, oats, barley, onions, peas, watermelons, and domestic animals, including cattle, horses, and hogs.

Prior to European settlement, most of Texas was occupied by nomadic hunting and gathering groups for whom agriculture was peripheral. When Europeans first arrived, however, advanced agriculture existed among the Caddo Indians in the east and in the pueblo cultures concentrated in New Mexico. The Caddos lived in permanent villages and depended for food primarily on the cultivation of corn, beans, and squash, with hunting and gathering to supplement the crops. They prepared fields for planting by burning and girdling, and cultivated with wooden hoes, stones, and sharpened sticks. In extreme west Texas, pueblo cultures also depended heavily on corn, beans, and squash, raised cotton for fiber, and practiced irrigation.[qv]

Livestock industries, predominantly for cattle, sheep, goat, and hog production, developed in Spanish Texas.[qv] Farming was largely limited to small garden plots adjacent to missions and settlements—San Antonio, El Paso (Ysleta), and Nacogdoches, for instance. By 1727 a 2½-mile irrigation ditch was watering fields and gardens in San Antonio. Ranching and farming expanded only slightly in Texas over the next 100 years, since Comanches, Apaches, and other nomadic and warring tribes dominated the land.

After its independence from Spain in 1821, Mexico encouraged settlement in its vast provinces north of the Rio Grande. Moses Austin[qv] secured the first empresario[qv] or colonial grants from Spain. His son, Stephen F. Austin,[qv] initially led 300 families from the United States into an area extending from the Gulf Coast into Central Texas. Settlers received a sitio[qv] or square league of land (about 4,338 acres) for grazing, and a labor (177 acres) of farming land. The American settlers quickly introduced the slave-based cotton-plantation system, expanded commercial livestock production, and developed concentrations of small, nonslaveholding family farms. The large influx of Anglo-American settlers led to the Texas revolt, the independence of Texas, and the subsequent war between the United States and Mexico, followed by the admission of Texas into the Union.

As time passed the essentially pastoral character of Texas agriculture became more heavily a plow and commercial system. The plantation system, small family farming, and the range cattle industry expanded rapidly between 1836 and the Civil War.[qv] Annual cattle drives were being made from points in south central Texas south and east along the Opelousas Trail to New Orleans, and on the Old Government Road to Little Rock and Fort Smith, Arkansas; and on other trails or extensions to Alexandria and Shreveport, Louisiana, or Natchez and Vicksburg, Mississippi. In 1846 Edward Piper drove a herd of

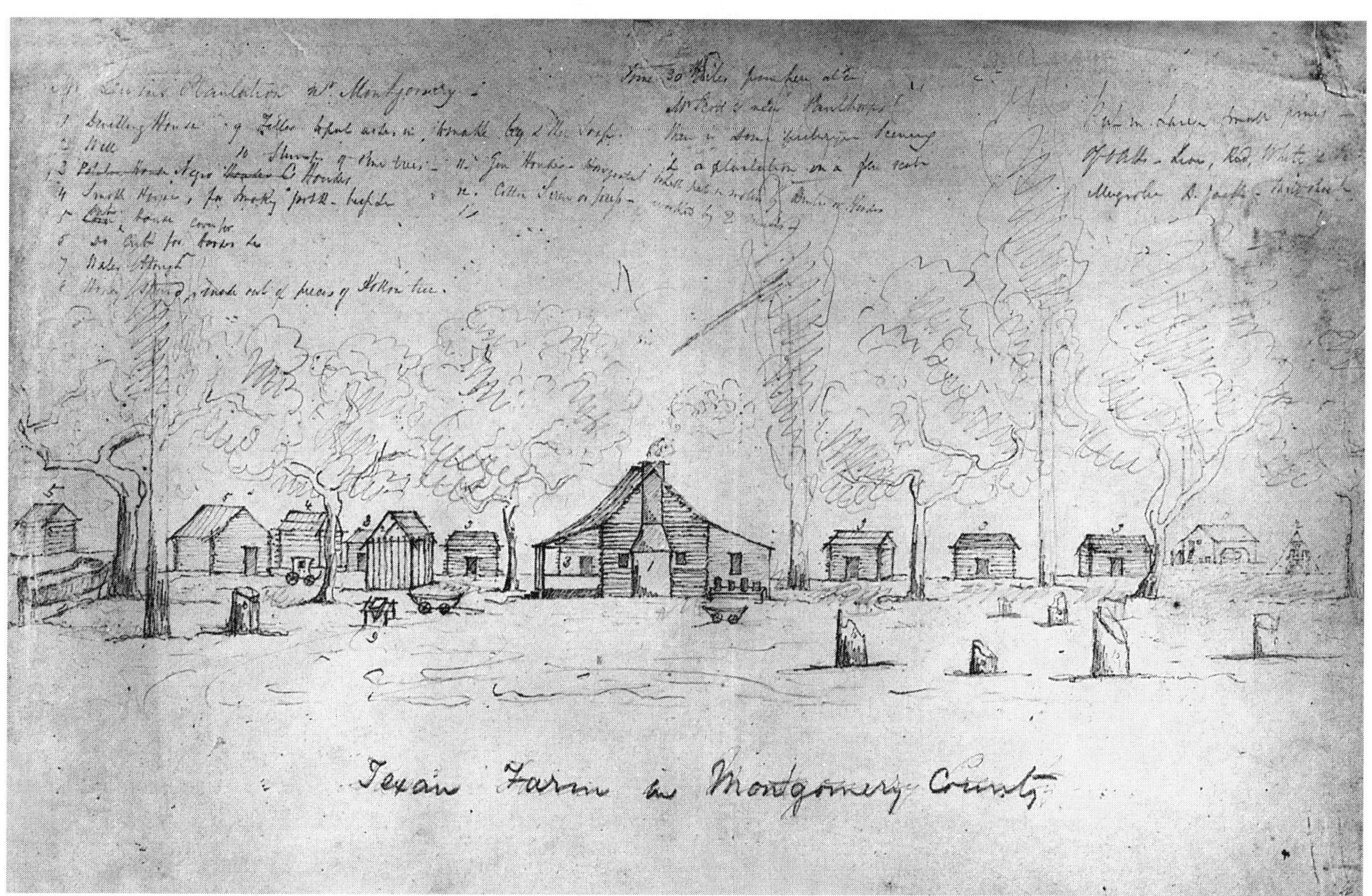

Texan Farm in Montgomery County, *by William Bollaert, ca. 1841–44. Sketch. Edward E. Ayer Collection, Newberry Library, Chicago. This sketch shows a prosperous farm, with its main house, a cotton press or mill (at the far right), a smokehouse, and six slave cabins that have neither windows nor chimneys. Numerous trees have been felled to clear land for animals or planting.*

Texas cattle to Ohio. In the 1850s Texas herds were being driven to Chicago and Illinois markets, to California, and to railheads in Iowa. The value of livestock on Texas farms rose from about $10.5 million to $43 million between 1850 and 1860.

The cotton-plantation system, concentrated in south central Texas on the lower Colorado, Brazos, and Trinity rivers, generated much of the state's agricultural production before the Civil War. Cotton production rose massively from 58,000 bales in 1850 to over 431,000 bales in 1860. Numbers of slaves grew from 58,161 to 182,566 in the same period, while the total population approximately tripled, from 212,592 to 604,215. The primary export was cotton; cattle were second.

Most agriculture before the Civil War involved small, subsistence family farms. The great majority of people were nonslaveholders. Germans[qv] established small farms and communities such as New Braunfels, Brenham, and Boerne. Czechs[qv] settled heavily in Fayette and Brazos counties. Other settlers streamed in from the South and Midwest and spread across the Blackland Prairies and Cross Timbers of north central Texas by 1860.

Agricultural practices on the small farm, which typically ranged in size from 120 to 160 acres, varied from purely pastoral to a combination of pastoral, crop, and garden farming. Hunting and gathering provided an important supplement to family food provisions. In Washington County a farmer with 120 acres might be expected to use 100 acres for unfenced cattle and hog raising, firewood gathering, and hunting. Of the remaining twenty acres, ten to twelve would ordinarily be devoted to corn, a staple for both human beings and farm animals. An acre or less might be used variously for sweet sorghum or sugarcane, a fruit orchard, home garden and herb plot, and tobacco. Cash income, always minimal, came from the cultivation and harvest of two or three acres of cotton.

Farms and plantations primarily utilized teams of oxen for plowing, and occasionally horses or mules. Mules became much more prevalent after the Civil War. Plows were fabricated locally, or, when cash was available, farmers might import farm equipment such as the Eagle plow through New Orleans and Galveston. Commerce generally depended on wagons to and from the port of Galveston; some produce was floated down the rivers. Although steamboat transportation and railroad construction began in Texas before the Civil War, river steamer and rail transportation were generally postwar developments.

After the war the traditional cotton plantation system continued, but with tenant farmers in place of slaves. Tenants were both black and white, but the latter far outnumbered the former by 1880. As the economy became more of a money-based system, small farmers increasingly slipped into tenancy or left farming. Generally, in tenant farming the landlord or planter contracted with the tenant for the cultivation of a small plot of land (usually in the range of 16–20 acres) on which the tenant was expected to raise as much cotton as possible. The planter ordinarily received one-third of the income from the crop for supplying the land, and one-third for provisioning the farmer with tools and housing, while the tenant received one-third for the labor. Credit was extremely expensive and scarce for the planter and disabling for the tenant, who commonly ended a year more deeply in debt than before.

African-American man plowing on a farm. Photograph by Henry Stark. Cherokee County, ca. 1895–96. From the collections of the Dallas Historical Society. At the turn of the century almost two-thirds of employed blacks worked in agriculture. Most were sharecroppers and tenant farmers; only 31 percent owned the land they worked.

Despite the difficulties, the number of farms in Texas rose from about 61,000 in 1870 to 174,000 in 1880 and 350,000 by 1900. Stimulated largely by the extension of railroads[qv] throughout Texas between 1870 and 1900, farm and ranching enterprises expanded rapidly as emphasis on commercial production and marketing grew. Subsistence farming and small farm operations declined. Cattle and cotton production dominated farming operations through the remainder of the nineteenth century, but wheat, rice, sorghum, hay, and dairying became important.

Under the terms of the Morrill Land-Grant College Act, approved on July 2, 1862, Texas established the Agricultural and Mechanical College of Texas (later Texas A&M University), which began operation near Bryan in 1876. A&M College established the Texas Agricultural Experiment Station[qv] in January 1886 and sponsored instructional farmers' institutes throughout Texas beginning in 1889. Dr. Mark Francis,[qv] the veterinarian for the experiment station, initiated research that helped lead to the eradication of Texas fever[qv] in cattle and greatly improved livestock production everywhere. He also headed efforts to establish a school of veterinary medicine, which opened under the auspices of A&M College with Francis as dean in September 1916.

A&M sponsored the organization of a Texas Farmers' Congress, which met annually on the campus between 1898 and 1915. The congress, in turn, sponsored a Farm Boys' and Girls' Progressive League (1903), which became the predecessor of the 4-H Club. In cooperation with Seaman A. Knapp, a special agent of the United States Department of Agriculture Bureau of Plant Industry, Texas A&M established a demonstration farm program at Greenville and Terrell in September 1903. In 1905 the college assumed responsibility for the greatly expanded demonstration farm program and appointed special agents to direct demonstration farm work. This activity became the impetus for the development of formal cooperative extension farm programs, entered into by agreements between the college and the United States Department of Agriculture. Cooperative extension work became a national farm program under the terms of the Smith-Lever Act of 1914, which established the Agricultural Extension Service.

Advanced cultivation practices, improved plant varieties, the mechanization of agriculture, and the greater availability of capital contributed to both higher yields and increased acreage in cultivation. Bonanza farming and large-scale cattle operations, often funded by foreign investors, developed in Texas in the 1880s. Many of these ventures failed in the depression of the 1890s. New corporate operations developed intermittently after 1900.

After the Civil War falling prices, high credit and transportation costs, and after 1893 a national depression, precipitated farm organization and revolt. Although some farmers in the state joined the

Grange[qv] (the National Grange of the Patrons of Husbandry), first established in 1867 in the Midwest, Texas participation in that group was weak. The Grange sought to impose state regulation on railroad freight rates and grain-elevator charges, to lower credit costs and put more money in circulation, and to reduce tariffs on nonfarm products. Texas farmers began to seek these measures through their own association, the Farmers' Alliance,[qv] which originated in Lampasas County in 1872. Under the leadership of Charles W. Macune,[qv] the Texas Farmers' Alliance embraced the Grange objectives and stressed the development of farm cooperatives.

The merger of the Texas Farmers' Alliance and the Louisiana Farmers' Union in January 1887 resulted in the creation of the National Farmers' Alliance and Industrial Union of America (better known as the Southern Alliance). This organization grew rapidly throughout the South and into the Midwest. The independent Colored Farmers' Alliance[qv] and Cooperative Union was organized in Houston in 1886. These organizations, like the Northern Farmers' Alliance, advocated paper money as legal tender, the unlimited coinage of silver, government control or ownership of railroads and telegraph systems, lower tariffs, a graduated income tax, the Australian or secret ballot, and the direct election of United States senators, as well as expanded public education. The Alliance movement, in turn, led to the organization of a national farmers' political party called the People's party[qv] of America or Populist party. Although the party generally failed to achieve its objectives, by the time of its demise after 1896 Populism had began to influence the programs of the major political parties.

Prosperity returned to Texas farmers in the first two decades of the twentieth century. As both rapid urbanization in the United States and the advent of World War I[qv] increased the demand for agricultural commodities, their prices rose more rapidly than those of nonfarm goods and services. Because of the resulting favorable economic position for farmers, between 1900 and 1920 the number of cultivated acres on Texas farms grew from fifteen to twenty-five million. Cotton production expanded from 3.4 to 4.3 million bales, and corn stabilized at approximately 100 million bushels, though it declined afterwards. The value of livestock more than doubled, from $240 to $590 million. Rice farming, which had been introduced in the 1880s on the Coastal Plains, produced nine million bushels annually by 1910. Wheat, introduced to Texas near Sherman in 1833, had emerged as a major export by 1900; production and milling centered in the north central area, around Fort Worth, Dallas, and Sherman.

Such favorable conditions brought further expansion to the state's agricultural system. In South Texas land promoters launched campaigns to attract investors to the lower Rio Grande valley and the Winter Garden Region.[qv] With mild winters and available irrigation water from the Rio Grande, the area became one of the state's most prolific farm sections. By first planting sour orange rootstocks in 1908, Charles Volz and others such as John H. Shary[qv] launched the citrus fruit industry in Cameron, Hidalgo, and Willacy counties, where, by 1929, 85 percent of the five million trees were grapefruit. Furthermore, those same counties, with the Winter Garden area to the north, became a major site for commercial truck farming of such vegetables as onions, cabbage, lettuce, carrots, beets, and spinach.

During the same period the High Plains also emerged as a major area for crop production. As cattlemen placed their large ranches on the market, cheap land prices in an area without the boll weevil[qv] made the region particularly attractive to cotton farmers. With the development of cotton types adapted to the plains environment by scientists at the Texas Agricultural Experiment Station at Lubbock, the planting of hard red winter wheat varieties, and the widespread adoption of the tractor, the one-way disk plow, and the combine, the High Plains became one of the state's premier areas for both cotton and wheat production by the end of the 1920s.

By that time the basic structure of the state's modern farming system appeared to be in place. While livestock producers focused upon raising cattle, sheep, and goats on the grazing areas that covered approximately 70 percent of the state's acreage, farmers grew crops on 17.5 percent of the land. Cotton, planted on 60 percent of the state's cultivated acreage, outdistanced all other commodities as a cash crop. Though it was grown in most areas of the state, the heaviest concentration was on the Blackland Prairies, the Coastal Plains around Corpus Christi, and the Southern High Plains. Acreage devoted to corn was usually second to cotton in the eastern half of the state, while sorghum was the leading livestock feed in the western half. Wheat, which was produced most extensively on the Northern High Plains and in the counties along the Red River, led the small grains and ranked second to cotton in cash-crop receipts. Besides the citrus and vegetable industries in South Texas, such truck-farming goods as tomatoes, watermelons, and peas were marketed in northeastern Texas. On the Coastal Prairie rice was raised, and timber was important in the Piney Woods of East Texas. In most areas of the state cropland was interspersed with pastureland; stock farming was therefore more common than other farming.

Kiyoaki Saibara (fourth from left) standing with workers in rice field owned by his father, Seito Saibara. Webster, Texas, 1904. Courtesy ITC. Seito Saibara brought about seventy Japanese families to the area around Webster in Harris County beginning in 1902. Around the turn of the century, the first attempt to cultivate rice using irrigation was made. Many of the Japanese who came to Texas at the beginning of the century became rice farmers.

Texas farmers like those throughout the nation experienced hard times during the 1920s. The decade began with the agricultural crisis of 1920–21, when postwar commodity surpluses caused a sharp decline in the prices farmers received for their crops. Instead of making efforts to curb production, farmers turned to various panaceas to remedy their plight. Some joined marketing cooperatives such as the Texas Wheat Growers Association or the Texas Farm Bureau Cotton Association, in which producers pooled their harvests with the hope of forcing processors to negotiate prices. Others sought to cut costs by replacing draft animals with tractors and increasing their crop acreage.

Yet the imbalance in the marketplace continued on to the end of the decade, thus contributing to the economic catastrophe of the Great Depression.[qv] The number of farms in Texas increased from 436,038 in 1920 to 495,489 ten years later, while cropland harvested grew by 3.5 million acres. Despite the surpluses, the acreage planted in wheat virtually doubled, from 2.4 million to 4.7 million, and cotton acreage increased from 12.9 million to 16.6 million. As wheat prices plunged from $2.04 to thirty-three cents per bushel, income declined from $41 million in 1920 to $9.4 million in 1932; cotton sales receipts dropped from $376 million to $140 million between 1920 and

Threshing wheat on the Halff Farms, east Midland County, 1916. Courtesy Midland County Historical Society, Midland. It took seven men to keep up with this mechanical combine, which separated chaff from straw, in 1916. Earlier machines were pulled more slowly by animals, and farmers plowed and planted less.

1932, as the price fell from seventeen cents to less than six cents a pound. The farmers' plight grew even worse when a drought accompanied by high winds brought about the Dust Bowl,qv which was particularly severe on the High Plains, where crop production virtually halted. With these developments rural poverty spread across Texas.

The implementation of Franklin D. Roosevelt's New Deal farm programs had both an immediate and long-range impact upon the Texas agricultural system. The Agricultural Adjustment Act of 1933 launched a series of programs designed to control surpluses and to maintain a minimum level of income. For such basic commodities as cotton, corn, wheat, rice, hogs, and milk, farmers accepted acreage allotments and marketing quotas and engaged in soil conservation practices, in exchange for receiving payments or guarantees of parity prices through nonrecourse loans. In addition, the availability of both long and short term credit through agencies of the Farm Credit Administration made money more accessible. Furthermore, the Soil Conservation Service was established to awaken farmers to the need of protecting their land through such techniques as terracing, contour listing, strip cropping, and the maintenance of vegetative cover.

The combination of the government programs and the nation's involvement in World War IIqv laid the basis for a major shift in the structure of Texas agriculture. First, farm tenancy declined from 60 percent of the state's farm operators in 1930 to 37.6 percent fifteen years later, as some landowners took advantage of government checks and cheap credit to replace tenants with machines. Furthermore, the rapid growth of good industrial jobs in urban areas during the war years contributed to a decrease in farm population from 2.16 million to 1.52 million and a loss of approximately 115,000 farm units in the ten years following 1935, when farms had numbered a half million. Yet farm income grew from approximately $500 million to $1.1 billion as wartime demand forced prices higher. The improved economic situation for Texas farmers, along with a guarantee of 90 percent of parity prices for at least two years after the war, set the stage for the modernization of the Texas agricultural system.

A major step towards the transformation of Texas farm life occurred with increased mechanization. The foremost factor in this change was the emergence of the tractor. Though steam tractors had been introduced at the turn of the century and gasoline tractors had appeared before World War I,qv mules and horses remained a common source of power until the 1940s. However, both the growth in farm income and the enhanced versatility of the all-purpose tractor contributed to the virtual elimination of draft animals from Texas farms. The increase in tractor horsepower in subsequent years from forty to as much as 200 or more permitted the use of larger auxiliary equipment. The one and two row implements of the World War II era were replaced with breaking plows, listers, tandem disks, rotary hoes, grain drills, and other tools that could cover up to sixteen rows, thus allowing a farmer to till or seed as much as 200 acres in a day.

In addition, major innovations in harvesting equipment further transformed Texas farming. By the 1920s the general acceptance of the combine, capable of doing the work of a binder or header and a thresher, spurred the expansion of wheat production in the state. Whether owned by individual farmers or itinerant custom cutters, the combine underwent a series of technical improvements after World War II that ranged from the replacement of the tractor-drawn models with self-propelled machines to the enlargement of the header size from six feet to thirty feet and the development of attachments that allowed for cutting grain sorghum, corn, and similar commodities, all of which increased the farmers' efficiency and versatility. In addition, machines for harvesting hay, spinach, potatoes, beans, sugar beets, pecans, peanuts, and other commodities reduced much of the labor requirements for producers.

The marketing of mechanical cotton harvesters in the 1940s represented a major breakthrough in production. Almost immediately the use of spindle-type pickers and roll or finger strippers reduced the labor requirements for producing and gathering an acre of cotton from an average of 150 to 6.5 man hours. Once engineers had refined some of the technical problems with harvesting and gin equipment and scientists had developed cotton varieties that could be gathered more easily, as well as herbicides and defoliants that eliminated much of the weed and leaf trash prior to ginning, farmers acquired enough machines that by the late 1960s cotton production was almost fully mechanized. Furthermore, as a reduction in the number of gins delayed processing, during the 1970s inventors developed the module, which by compacting the crop in the field postponed the ginning without causing damage. By the 1990s most Texas cotton was machine harvested and processed, with approximately one-fourth gathered by spindle pickers, three-fourths collected by strippers, and 70 percent ginned from modules.

While advances in mechanization allowed farm operators to handle more land with less labor, the expansion of irrigation after World War II greatly enhanced the state's agricultural productivity. Although approximately 900,000 acres was being watered in 1939, primarily from surface sources in the lower Rio Grande valley, the Winter Garden, the Coastal Prairie, and the Trans-Pecos regions, the major thrust for crop irrigation developed when farmers of the High Plains who had suffered through the Dust Bowl began tapping the Ogallala Aquifer extensively. The availability of financial resources and equipment technology initially spurred the drilling of wells and the installation of furrow systems utilizing drainage ditches and plastic, rubber, or aluminum siphon tubes in the shallow-water belt south of the Canadian River. However, after operators north of the river observed how irrigation enhanced yields by 50 or 60 percent, permitted greater crop diversification, and provided production stability even in the drought years of the 1950s, they too drilled wells and installed ditches or center-pivot sprinkler systems. In 1979, when the state's irrigated acreage reached a high of 7.8 million—a third of all of the Texas land in production—87 percent of the watered land was located on the High Plains, where farmers received approximately 40 percent of the state's cash crop receipts.

In conjunction with such capital investments, Texas farmers who recognized that profitability depended upon achieving higher crop yields at reduced labor costs readily incorporated the application of chemicals as part of their agricultural programs. The use of fertilizers, particularly ammonia-based and nitrogen products, generally enhanced commodity returns. Furthermore, the introduction of herbicides at the preplanting, preemergence, or postemergence of the crops usually reduced weed growth and cut labor expenses. In addition, insecticides applied by tractor-mounted equipment or by aircraft helped lessen damages inflicted by insects and diseases.

As farming became more complex after World War II, the role of research scientists and advisors from the state and federal agricultural experiment stations, the colleges of agriculture, and the cooperative extension services expanded. Besides supplying operators with information about effective methods or discoveries, the researchers' success in developing higher-yielding crop varieties had an immense influence upon the state's production. By the 1980s their efforts contributed to the rise of average wheat yields from ten bushels to thirty bushels an acre; irrigated semidwarf winter varieties exceeded 100 bushels per acre, corn production grew from 15 to 120 bushels per acre, rice from 2,000 pounds to 4,600 pounds per acre, and cotton from approximately 200 pounds to 400 pounds per acre on dry land and 500 pounds on watered acreage.

A prime example of the impact of agricultural research was demonstrated with the emergence of grain sorghum as a major Texas commercial crop. Sorghum varieties such as hegari and kafir, originally planted in the state's more arid western areas due to their drought-resistant qualities, were grown for livestock forage; hand-cut milo maize was fed as a grain. Marketing sorghum as a feed grain began in the late 1940s, when breeders succeeded in reducing the plant's height so as to permit harvesting with a combine and farmers with irrigation discovered the prolific nature of the crop when watered. Yet this was only a beginning, for after several years of experimentation researchers introduced hybrid grain sorghum, which was first distributed for planting in 1957. Immediately, average yields of 1,200 pounds an acre doubled, and as improved varieties were bred farmers of irrigated milo maize frequently harvested as much as 5,000 pounds per acre. Though production centered on the High Plains initially, the lower Rio Grande valley, the Coastal Bend, the Blackland Prairies, and the Rolling Plains also became regions where the crop achieved importance.

Grain sorghum hybridization supplied the impetus for the rise of the cattle-feeding industry on the High Plains. In the area where cattle raising thrived and the locally produced feed grain supply was greater than the demand by the 1960s, entrepreneurs and promoters conceived the idea of combining the two resources to prepare beef animals for slaughter. By the end of the decade large feedlots capable of handling several thousand animals had been erected and expanded to the extent that in the early 1970s more than three million head were being marketed annually. With 70 percent of the cattle being fattened on the High Plains, Texas became the leader of fed-cattle production in the nation.

The cattle-feeding industry stimulated the resurrection of corn as an important commodity in Texas. Though corn was a major household-food and livestock-feed crop from the time of initial settlement of the state, acreage devoted to its production declined after World War II as reliance upon animal power dwindled. However, when skyrocketing sorghum prices threatened the profitability of the cattle-feeding industry after a trading agreement with the Soviet Union in 1973, High Plains irrigation farmers turned to corn hybrids. With normal yields in excess of 100 bushels of grain per acre plus the silage, growers found that they could achieve a good return on their investment and meet the requirements of the feeders. Besides serving as a cattle feed, corn was valuable as a sweetener, starch, and fuel. The lower Rio Grande valley, the Coastal Plains, and the Blackland Prairies also became centers for corn production.

Just as scientific and technological achievements had influenced corn raising, they gave farmers a greater flexibility in crop selection. Along with the introduction of commercial vegetable and sunflower production on the High Plains, sugar beets emerged as a valuable crop there during the 1960s, following the erection of the Holly Sugar Company plant at Hereford, Deaf Smith County. Soybeans, which normally were grown in the humid region of the Upper Coastal Plain, fared well in Hale County on the High Plains as well as in Northeast Texas. In addition to the vegetable and citrus industries in the Valley, sugarcane reemerged as a crop in the late 1970s. The Spanish and, after 1973, the Florunner varieties of peanuts, the production of which had been centered in such north central Texas counties as Comanche and Eastland for decades, flourished in sandy soils on the High Plains, while commercial orchards in thirty counties of Central

Sugarcane harvesting, Rio Grande valley, ca. 1986. Courtesy Texas Department of Transportation/Bill Reaves. The sugarcane being harvested in this picture was crushed at a mill in Santa Rosa (Cameron County), one of the most modern in the country. The truck shown here on the right accommodated ten tons of cane, which could be unloaded at the mill in two minutes.

and West Texas propelled the state to second place in the production of pecans. By the 1980s wineries had appeared in West Texas as vineyards added an additional commercial crop.

The move towards crop diversification often occurred in reaction to restraints imposed by federal governmental policies. Continuing the goals established in the 1930s of attempting to prevent the accumulation of price-depressing surpluses and to provide stable incomes, such instruments as acreage allotments and marketing quotas remained in use, while such other approaches as set-aside or diversion programs were tried as a means of maintaining control over the production of the basic commodities grown in Texas—wheat, feed grains, cotton, rice, and peanuts. Further long-term limitation efforts included the Soil Bank program of 1956, the 1965 Cropland Adjustment Program, and the Conservation Reserve Program in 1985, by which cropland was removed from production and replaced with grasses or hay. The rewards for participating in such programs came in the form of income or price-support policies that varied from benefit payments for idling acreage to nonrecourse loans for commodities placed in storage. In the 1970s those who cooperated became eligible to receive disaster payments when emergency situations caused crop losses or deficiency payments for those farmers whose average cash receipts for cotton, wheat, corn, sorghum, and oats were less than the target price that political authorities deemed acceptable. After 1940 annual federal governmental payments to Texas farmers ranged from a low of $25 million in the 1950s to a high of $1.4 billion in 1987.

Though the governmental restriction programs applied primarily to crop production, the livestock industry maintained a significant role in Texas agriculture, for cash receipts from livestock and livestock products exceeded crop sales continuously after 1970. In a state where two-thirds of the space was pastureland, beef-cattle enterprises, which normally furnished more income than any other agricultural endeavor, operated in every Texas county. On farms and ranches the basic cow-calf operations, including the breeding of registered animals, prevailed. Though a portion of the calves were maintained on the pastureland, others were either sent to graze on winter wheat from late fall to late winter or went directly or indirectly to feedlots for fattening before slaughter. Another aspect of cattle production, dairying, grew as urbanization spread in the state. With 95 percent of the milk produced east of a line from Wichita Falls to Corpus Christi, large dairy farms often consisted of herds in excess of 100 cows, which gave an average of 15,000 pounds of milk per animal annually. Sheep and goat ranching, with its wool and mohair harvest, continued to be centered on the Edwards Plateau. Along with raising hogs for pork, poultry operations provided income through the sale of eggs and broilers; Angelina and Camp counties in East Texas and Gonzales County in south central Texas were the leading producers.

With the convergence of technological, scientific, economic, and political factors after World War II, large commercial farms and ranches became dominant in the Texas agricultural system. As their operators acquired sophisticated machines that allowed them to handle more acreage with less labor, began to use chemicals and improved seed varieties that enhanced their crop productivity, and introduced livestock and poultry breeding techniques to develop more marketable goods, large numbers of poorly capitalized marginal farmers found the costs beyond their capability and left the profession. Consequently, between 1945 and 1990 the farm population fell from 1.52 million to about 245,000, or 1.1 percent of the state total, and the number of farms declined from 385,000 to 185,000. Yet the average value of farm assets, including land and buildings, rose from approximately $9,000 to $475,000, and the cash receipts from crop and livestock marketings jumped from $1.1 billion to $11.8 billion as the average farm size grew from 367 acres to 700 acres. Though approximately three-fourths of the farms in the state were smaller than 500 acres by 1990, 80 percent of the commodity sales came from 8.7 percent of the farm units, an indication of the impact of the large commercial operations upon agricultural production.

Four areas—the High Plains, the lower Rio Grande valley, the upper Coastal Prairie, and the Blackland Prairies—had become the primary centers for large commercial units by the 1980s. With the exception of the Blackland Prairies, where diversified dry-land stock farms were prevalent, the other regions included heavily capitalized operations with extensive irrigated acreage. In the upper coastal region of Southeast Texas, rice and soybeans generated the most income. The mild winters of the lower Rio Grande valley allowed for a great variety of produce, ranging from citrus fruits and vegetables to cotton, grain sorghum, and corn. On the northern High Plains, where large farms averaged more than 2,000 acres, wheat, grain sorghum, and corn were raised in fields adjacent to mammoth cattle feedlots. A more intensive cropping system in the southern High Plains counties made the area the state's leader in cotton production.

In most of the remaining farm areas of the state, stock farming, which usually combined cattle raising and dry-land raising of wheat, sorghum, or cotton, continued, with variations dependent upon the land and climate. However, major changes did occur in some regions such as East Texas, where the expense of modernization and federal controls upon production caused a shift from small cotton farms to an emphasis upon cattle raising, with hay as the primary crop.

Yet, whether they produced livestock, raised crops, or operated stock farms, Texas agriculturalists found themselves a part of an infrastructure that influenced their actions and decisions. Increasingly, loan officers at such lending institutions as commercial banks, federal land banks, production credit associations, and insurance companies offered advice on planning. Oftentimes, the ability of an array of

Estate surrounded by citrus trees. Young trees surround the landscaped grounds—two miles north of Weslaco. *Photograph by Russell Lee, 1948. Standard Oil (New Jersey) Company Collection, Photographic Archives, University of Louisville; neg. no. SONJ 57267. This photograph was taken in one of the peak years in Texas citrus production. Freezes over the next two years killed seven million of the Rio Grande Valley's nine million grapefruit and orange trees.*

agribusinessmen from private enterprises or cooperatives to supply such goods and services as implements, seeds, fertilizers, chemicals, fuel, repair facilities, and other necessities affected their decision making. In addition, representatives from federal agencies supervised their compliance with production programs or counseled them on conserving their land. Information gathered by researchers at federal and state agricultural experiment stations, universities, or private firms became available through county agents, farm magazines, radio and television broadcasters, and other sources. Whether farmers raised rice, corn, wheat, cotton, grain sorghum, fruits, livestock, or other commodities, they usually belonged to a general organization such as the American Farm Bureau Federation, the National Farmers Union, or the American Agriculture Movement, and perhaps to more than one commodity association; both the general organizations and the commodity associations became the farmers' instruments for promoting their interests in political arenas or in marketing their produce.

Marketing also underwent change. Instead of sending their crops and livestock to distant terminal points on railroads, farmers and ranchers profited from the introduction of motor vehicles, particularly trucks, in the 1920s and the subsequent improvement in the roadways, which gave growers more options for delivering their produce directly to nearby gins, elevators, packing sheds, or livestock auctions for sale through cooperatives or to private buyers. Some producers engaged in futures trading through commercial brokers as a hedge against possible price declines. Though much of the produce went to fresh fruit and vegetable markets or cottonseed mills, flour mills, textile mills, meat-packing plants, canneries, or other processors both within the state and outside, the Texas Gulf ports as well as those on the Atlantic and Pacific coasts became the debarkation points for Texas crops sent to all areas of the world. With rice, cotton, cottonseed oil, peanuts, and livestock products as the leading export goods, the annual $2.5 billion international sales of Texas commodities by the 1990s represented approximately 20 percent of the state's cash receipts from crop and livestock marketings.

Lifestyles for Texas farm families changed significantly after World War II. As electricity became available through rural cooperatives, farmers began enjoying the same household conveniences as those who lived in the city. In addition, the construction of farm roads and improved roadways made areas beyond the immediate community more accessible. Besides virtually eliminating the small country stores, the roads made shopping at supermarkets in nearby towns easy; milk cows and laying hens disappeared from many farmsteads. As consolidation programs led to the closing of rural schools, children were bused to larger educational facilities, which usually offered access to more programs than such groups as 4-H Clubs or Future

Women packing broccoli in the Vahlsing shed, Elsa, 1947. *Photograph by Russell Lee. Standard Oil (New Jersey) Company Collection, Photographic Archives, University of Louisville; neg. no. SONJ 57121. Hidalgo County produces many winter vegetables, including broccoli.*

Farmers of America. From the towns young men and women increasingly went to colleges and universities, either to pursue careers in urban areas or to return to their home communities trained in agricultural practices. Though some farmers chose to live in nearby towns and commute to their farms, by the 1980s a majority of Texans residing on farms earned their principal income elsewhere. Along with the advent of radio and television, which both entertained and kept farmers aware of world events and the latest crop and livestock market quotations, such devices as two-way radios and computers became helpful management tools, particularly at large commercial operations.

Even as changes came in the Texas agricultural system, several challenges existed with which farmers and livestock producers had to deal. Regardless of where farming and ranching occurred, environmental or climatic problems had always arisen. In some years there was little rain and in others too much. Sometimes crops suffered when diseases and insects struck. Though the application of scientific and technological practices could ameliorate some of these difficulties, plains farmers felt a sense of hopelessness when their crops were destroyed by hail, for instance; citrus growers in the lower Rio Grande valley saw their orange and grapefruit orchards frozen on four occasions between 1950 and 1990. In addition, the fear of being caught on the wrong side of the cost-price squeeze was ever present. As commercial operators became dependent upon agribusiness suppliers, any variations in costs or slippage in prices oftentimes placed them in jeopardy. For example, the rapid rise in natural gas prices during the 1970s forced both Upland and Pima irrigated cotton producers in Pecos and Reeves counties to reduce their acreage by two-thirds. Besides the costs, irrigation farmers on the High Plains faced the threatened depletion of the Ogallala Aquifer, which had made the region one of the most prolific in the state. Despite such remedial efforts as the organization of water-conservation districts, the return of substantial watered acreage to dry land, the institution of minimum tillage techniques, and the installation of more efficient equipment such as the center pivot sprinkler or the low-energy pressure-application systems, the concern remained. Furthermore, though farmers and ranchers recognized that both national and international incidents could influence their livelihood, an element of insecurity existed when political leaders assumed the authority to render decisions affecting agriculture.

Yet even with these and other issues, Texas agriculture remained a vital industry both in the state and the nation at the end of the twentieth century. By the 1990s crop and livestock cash receipts continued to grow. Agricultural receipts of approximately $12 billion combined with agribusinesses to add about $40 billion to the state's economy, thus making Texas one of the leading farm states.

See also CITRUS FRUIT CULTURE, FRUITS OTHER THAN CITRUS, GRAPE CULTURE, PECAN INDUSTRY, PEANUT CULTURE, PEPPERS, SWEET POTATO CULTURE, ONION CULTURE, SPINACH CULTURE, SUGAR PRODUCTION, CORN CULTURE, WHEAT CULTURE, RICE CULTURE, SORGHUM CULTURE, HAY CULTURE, COTTON CULTURE, COTTON COMPRESS INDUSTRY, COTTONSEED INDUSTRY, LUMBER INDUSTRY, PLANT DISEASES, BEE INDUSTRY, HORSE AND MULE INDUSTRY, CATTLE FEEDING, MEAT PACKING, DAIRY INDUSTRY, DAIRY CATTLE, DAIRY PRODUCTS, SHEEP RANCHING, GOAT RANCHING, WOOL AND MOHAIR INDUSTRY, SWINE RAISING, POULTRY PRODUCTION, AGRICULTURAL ADJUSTMENT ADMINISTRATION, ENVIRONMENTAL HISTORY, HIGHWAY DEVELOPMENT, RURAL ELECTRIFICATION, WATER LAW *and related articles under* WATER, *and* WEATHER.

BIBLIOGRAPHY: Irvin Milburn Atkins, *A History of Small Grain Crops in Texas: Wheat, Oats, Barley, Rice, 1582–1976* (Bulletin 1301, College Station: Texas Agricultural Experiment Station, 1980). Donna A. Barnes, *Farmers in Rebellion: The Rise and Fall of the Southern Farmers Alliance and People's Party in Texas* (Austin: University of Texas Press, 1984). Jan Blodgett, *Land of Bright Promise: Advertising the Texas Panhandle and South Plains, 1870–1917* (Austin: University of Texas Press, 1988). Paul H. Carlson, *Texas Woolybacks: The Range Sheep and Goat Industry* (College Station: Texas A&M University Press, 1982). Henry C. Dethloff, *A History of the American Rice Industry, 1685–1985* (College Station: Texas A&M University Press, 1988). Henry C. Dethloff and Irvin M. May, Jr., eds., *Southwestern Agriculture: Pre-Columbian to Modern* (College Station: Texas A&M University Press, 1982). Donald E. Green, *Land of the Underground Rain: Irrigation on the Texas High Plains, 1910–1970* (Austin: University of Texas Press, 1973). R. Douglas Hurt, *The Dust Bowl: An Agricultural and Social History* (Chicago: Nelson-Hall, 1981). Richard G. Lowe and Randolph B. Campbell, *Planters and Plain Folk: Agriculture in Antebellum Texas* (Dallas: Southern Methodist University Press, 1987). Janet M. Neugebauer, ed., *Plains Farmer: The Diary of William G. DeLoach, 1914–1964* (College Station: Texas A&M University Press, 1991). William N. Stokes, Jr., *Oil Mill on the Texas Plains* (College Station: Texas A&M University Press, 1979).

Henry C. Dethloff and Garry L. Nall

AGUA AZUL CREEK. Agua Azul Creek rises four miles southwest of Mirando City in southeastern Webb County (at 27°22′ N, 98°59′ W) and runs southwest for eighteen miles to its mouth on Cerrito Creek, eleven miles southwest of Aguilares (at 27°21′ N, 99°13′ W). The area's low-rolling and flat terrain is surfaced by clay and sandy loams that support grasses, mesquite, chaparral, and water-tolerant hardwoods.

AGUA CABALLO CREEK. Agua Caballo (or Horse) Creek, an intermittent stream, rises in the extreme northwestern corner of Oldham County (at 35°37′ N, 103°02′ W) and flows southeast for thirteen miles through Sidle Canyon to its mouth on the Canadian River, fifteen miles northwest of Adrian (at 35°29′ N, 102°54′ W). It travels over terrain characterized by somewhat steep to rolling slopes, with locally high relief and shallow to moderately deep silt and clay loams that support mesquite, juniper, cacti, and grasses. The area has been part of the LE Ranch,[qv] the Ojo Bravo Division of the XIT Ranch,[qv] and John M. Shelton's[qv] Bravo Ranch.

BIBLIOGRAPHY: Oldham County Historical Commission, *Oldham County* (Dallas: Taylor, 1981).

AGUA DULCE, TEXAS. Agua Dulce is located on the Texas Mexican Railway at the intersection of Farm Road 70 and State Highway 44 in west central Nueces County. The name, Spanish for "sweet water," refers to a nearby creek. The settlement existed by the 1900s. In August 1908 the post office was established with James l. Petray as postmaster. In 1910 the Agua Dulce Independent School District was founded; Sophinia Thompson was the first teacher. The school system was consolidated with that of Bentonville in 1932. Agua Dulce profited from an oil boom in the 1930s. The first seismographic survey done in Nueces County was done in Agua Dulce by E. E. Rosaire. Several gas wells are located there, as well as the Agua Dulce oilfield, which was opened in 1928. In 1914 the population of Agua Dulce was 100, and the town had a general store, a lumber mill, a cotton gin, a blacksmith, a confectioner, and a grocer. Between 1940 and 1945 the population increased from 200 to 750. In 1961 thirty businesses were in operation. In 1990 the population was 996, and Aqua Dulce had nine businesses.

BIBLIOGRAPHY: Nueces County Historical Society, *History of Nueces County* (Austin: Jenkins, 1972). Vertical Files, Barker Texas History Center, University of Texas at Austin. *Robin Dush*

AGUA DULCE CREEK. Agua Dulce Creek, intermittent for all but the last two miles of its roughly forty-five mile length, rises in northwestern Jim Wells County (at 27°59′ N, 98°12′ W) and runs southeast until it joins Banquete Creek to form Petronila Creek one mile east of

Banquete in western Nueces County (at 27°48′ N, 97°47′ W). Its name is from the land grant given by the Spanish government to Rafael García. The surrounding flat to rolling terrain is surfaced by clay and sandy loams and dark clays that support water-tolerant hardwoods, conifers, grasses, scrub brush, mesquite, and some cacti.

AGUA DULCE CREEK, BATTLE OF. The battle of Agua Dulce Creek, an engagement of the Texas Revolution[qv] and an aftermath of the controversial Matamoros expedition of 1835–36,[qv] occurred twenty-six miles below San Patricio on March 2, 1836. Dr. James Grant[qv] and his party of twenty-three Americans and three Mexicans were surprised and defeated by a Mexican force under José de Urrea.[qv] Six of the volunteers escaped, five of whom joined James W. Fannin, Jr.,[qv] at Goliad and were killed in the Goliad Massacre[qv] on March 27; six were captured and taken to Matamoros as prisoners; all others were killed in the engagement.

BIBLIOGRAPHY: Harbert Davenport, "Men of Goliad," *Southwestern Historical Quarterly* 43 (July 1939). Cyrus Baird Tilloson, "The Battle of the Agua Dulce," *Frontier Times*, December 1947. Vertical Files, Barker Texas History Center, University of Texas at Austin. Henderson K. Yoakum, *History of Texas from Its First Settlement in 1685 to Its Annexation to the United States in 1846* (2 vols., New York: Redfield, 1855).

Curtis Bishop

AGUA FRIA MOUNTAIN. Agua Fria Mountain is a large mesa eighteen miles north of Terlingua in southwestern Brewster County (at 29°31′ N, 103°39′ W). Its steep, deeply cut and eroded sides rise some 1,500 feet above the surrounding Chihuahua Desert floor. Near its southeastern edge the mesa reaches an elevation of 4,828 feet above sea level. Its name, Spanish for "cold water," refers to a large spring at the base of a cliff several hundred feet high on the western side of the mountain. The spring is surrounded by willows and large boulders and harbors an abundant growth of watercress. The cliff forms a large protective overhang, beneath which are deep accumulations of ashes and burned rock, as well as numerous flakes of flint, obsidian, jasper, and chalcedony. Colorful pictographs cover the lower reaches of the cliff face and many of the nearby boulders. One modern historian of the region cites evidence of a rather extensive irrigation system built by Indians to the north and northeast of Agua Fria Mountain. A camel train under the command of Lt. William Echols camped in 1859 at Agua Fria Mountain (*see* CAMELS). In the 1880s, Agua Fria Mountain was the northern extent of the G4 Ranch,[qv] one of the earliest and largest ranches in the Big Bend. The ranch maintained a line camp near the spring at the foot of the mountain. Agua Fria Mountain is clearly visible from State Highway 118, seven miles to the east.

BIBLIOGRAPHY: Clifford B. Casey, *Mirages, Mysteries and Reality: Brewster County, Texas, the Big Bend of the Rio Grande* (Hereford, Texas: Pioneer, 1972). Clifford B. Casey, *Soldiers, Ranchers and Miners in the Big Bend* (Washington: Office of Archeology and Historic Preservation, U.S. Department of the Interior, 1969). Forrest Kirkland and W. W. Newcomb, Jr., *The Rock Art of Texas Indians* (Austin: University of Texas Press, 1967).

AGUAJUANI INDIANS. The Aguajuani Indians are known from a Spanish document of 1754, which placed them an unspecified distance north or northwest of Nacogdoches. They were evidently not the Yojuanes, whose name (Jujuane) also appears in the same document. Aguajuani resembles Ahehouen, the name of an Indian group recorded in documents of the La Salle expedition.[qv] These French documents indicate that in the late seventeenth century the Ahehouens lived inland somewhere north of Matagorda Bay, probably near the Colorado River. No relationship between the Aguajuanis and the Ahehouens has thus far been established, and the linguistic and cultural affiliations of both groups remain unknown.

BIBLIOGRAPHY: Isaac Joslin Cox, ed., *The Journeys of René Robert Cavelier, Sieur de La Salle* (2 vols., New York: Barnes, 1905; 2d ed., New York: Allerton, 1922). Frederick Webb Hodge, ed., *Handbook of American Indians North of Mexico* (2 vols., Washington: GPO, 1907, 1910; rpt., New York: Pageant, 1959). Henri Joutel, *Joutel's Journal of La Salle's Last Voyage* (London: Lintot, 1714; rpt., New York: Franklin, 1968).

Thomas N. Campbell

AGUA NEGRA CREEK. Agua Negra Creek rises sixteen miles south of Lytle in northern Atascosa County (at 29°09′ N, 98°39′ W) and runs southeast for eight miles to its mouth on Palo Alto Creek, three miles northwest of Poteet (at 29°03′ N, 98°37′ W). The terrain at the source is flat to rolling and exhibits local escarpments; there deep, fine sandy loam supports brush and grasses. Towards the mouth, locally active blowout areas replace the escarpments, and clay and sandy loam supports bunch grasses. The land is predominantly forested. The creek was named for a spring that fed it with water darkened by iron sediment or oil. The spring has been dry since 1915.

BIBLIOGRAPHY: Margaret G. Clover, The Place Names of Atascosa County (M.A. thesis, University of Texas, 1952).

AGUA NUEVA, TEXAS. The site of Agua Nueva, thirty-five miles south of Hebbronville on Farm Road 1017 in southeastern Jim Hogg County, was first settled before 1900. It was probably named for the Spanish land grant Agua Nueva de Abajo, which went to Juan Manuel Ramírez, but some sources suggest that it was named for a local spring. Sixto García opened a store there in 1903 and a post office in 1910. In 1915 the estimated population was 200. By 1936 the community had two businesses, a row of dwellings, a school, and a population estimated at ten. Between the mid-1940s and mid-1960s the number of residents fluctuated between forty and fifty; in 1968 and 1990 it was twenty. In 1988 Agua Nueva had three businesses and a cemetery.

BIBLIOGRAPHY: Hebbronville Chamber of Commerce, *Fiftieth Anniversary, Jim Hogg County* (Hebbronville, Texas, 1963).

Alicia A. Garza

AGUAPALAM INDIANS. The Aguapalam Indians appear to have been first recorded in 1670, under the distorted name Gamplam, as one of thirty-four small Indian groups said to have been involved in raiding Spanish settlements north of Monterrey and Saltillo. They were reported living under native conditions only in 1691, at which time they were on lower Hondo Creek southwest of San Antonio, apparently near the boundary between the future Frio and Medina counties. The Aguapalams shared that area with twelve other Indian groups, probably because their combined manpower gave them better protection from attacks by Apaches of the Edwards Plateau[qv] to the north. No population figures were recorded for any of these groups. After 1691 the Aguapalams may have moved farther to the east. They evidently declined in numbers, but a few of them managed to maintain their ethnic identity until 1741, when three adults and four children were recorded at San Antonio de Valero Mission of San Antonio. Between 1741 and 1768 they and their descendants were recorded by missionaries under such name variants as Ajuiap, Aujuiap, and Ujuiap. Scholars have failed to note that Aguapalam, minus the suffix *-alam*, is Aguap, which in Spanish phonetics is virtually the same as the Valero recordings. H. E. Bolton[qv] saw no similarities in these names and, through faulty analysis of the Valero registers, concluded that Ujuiap was the name of a separate Indian group of Tonkawan affiliation. No evidence of this Tonkawa linkage has been found in European documents. The Ujuiaps of Valero were almost certainly the Aguapalams of 1691, who were associated with Indian groups southwest of San Antonio and who, according to the observations of Damián Massanet,[qv] spoke the language now known as Coahuilteco. Jean Jarry,[qv] the Frenchman who deserted the La Salle expedition[qv] and became a leader of Indians in the area east of Eagle Pass, seems to have known the Aguapalams/Ujuiaps by the name Huiapico. No documents have been found that contain descriptive details of Aguapalam culture, but circumstantial evidence indicates that they lived by hunting and gathering.

BIBLIOGRAPHY: Lino Gómez Canedo, ed., *Primeras exploraciones y poblamiento de Texas, 1686–1694* (Monterrey: Publicaciones del Instituto Technológico y de Estudios Superiores de Monterrey, 1968). William B. Griffen, *Culture Change and Shifting Populations in Central Northern Mexico* (Tucson: University of Arizona Press, 1969). Mattie Alice Hatcher, trans., *The Expedition of Don Domingo Terán de los Ríos into Texas,* ed. Paul J. Foik (Preliminary Studies of the Texas Catholic Historical Society 2.1 [1932]). Frederick Webb Hodge, ed., *Handbook of American Indians North of Mexico* (2 vols., Washington: GPO, 1907, 1910; rpt., New York: Pageant, 1959). Alonso de León et al., *Historia de Nuevo León* (Monterrey: Centro de Estudios Humanísticos de la Universidad de Nuevo León, 1961). San Antonio de Valero Mission, Baptismal and Burial Registers, San Antonio.

Thomas N. Campbell

AGUA DE PIEDRA CREEK. Agua de Piedra Creek, an intermittent stream, rises five miles southeast of Adrian in southwestern Oldham County (at 35°16′ N, 102°46′ W) and flows northwest for thirteen miles to its mouth on Trujillo Creek (at 35°26′ N, 102°53′ W). The streambed runs across flat terrain with some moderately steep slopes. The soils, shallow to moderately deep silt loams and loose sand, support brush, mesquite, and grasses. The Spanish name means "stony water." The stream is in the heart of a vast ranching area, successively part of the LE, XIT, and Matador ranches.[qqv]

BIBLIOGRAPHY: Oldham County Historical Commission, *Oldham County* (Dallas: Taylor, 1981).

AGUA POQUITA CREEK. Agua Poquita Creek rises twenty miles west of Benavides in southwestern Duval County (at 27°36′ N, 98°43′ W) and runs southeast for twenty-four miles, then joins Concepcion Creek to form Los Olmos Creek eight miles south of Benavides (at 27°30′ N, 98°27′ W). Its Spanish name, appropriately enough, means "little water." The surrounding terrain is flat and marked with shallow depressions. The land surface is clay and sandy loams that support water-tolerant hardwoods, conifers, and grasses.

AGUASTAYA INDIANS. Although there is evidence indicating that the Aguastaya Indians ranged an area somewhere south of San Antonio, no pre-mission document records a Spanish encounter with them. Aguastaya families seem to have entered only one of the San Antonio missions, San José y San Miguel de Aguayo. Because the registers of this mission are lost, there is no way to determine the number of Aguastaya individuals in residence. A few documents say that some of the Aguastayas entered San José when it was founded in 1720, but others mention that they came at a later date. It is certain that they entered this mission by 1734, because a document in the Bexar Archives[qv] refers to two Aguastaya males from Mission San José giving legal testimony in that year. Some writers have stated that the Aguastayas spoke a dialect of the Coahuilteco language, but there is not enough evidence to demonstrate this linguistic affiliation. Contrary to what has long been assumed, languages other than Coahuilteco were spoken in the inland area south of San Antonio. The name Aguastaya is phonetically similar to two additional Indian group names recorded for southern Texas: the Yguaz, known to Álvar Núñez Cabeza de Vaca[qv] in 1533–34, and the Oaz, listed by Isidro Félix de Espinosa[qv] in 1708. Name similarities and linkage with the same region suggest that Aguastaya, Oaz, and Yguaz refer to the same Indian population, but this cannot be proved because of scanty documentation for the 200-year period involved.

BIBLIOGRAPHY: Thomas N. Campbell, *The Payaya Indians of Southern Texas* (San Antonio: Southern Texas Archeological Association, 1975). Peter P. Forrestal, trans., *The Solís Diary of 1767,* ed. Paul J. Foik (Preliminary Studies of the Texas Catholic Historical Society 1.6 [March 1931]). J. Villasana Haggard, "Spain's Indian Policy in Texas: Translations from the Bexar Archives, No. 9," *Southwestern Historical Quarterly* 46 (July 1942). Juan Agustín Morfi, *History of Texas, 1673–1779,* trans. Carlos E. Castañeda (2 vols., Albuquerque: Quivira Society, 1935; rpt., New York: Arno Press, 1967). Pedro de Rivera y Villalón, *Diario y derrotero de lo caminado, visto y obcervado en el discurso de la visita general de precidios situados en las provincias ynternas de Nueva España* (Mexico City: Porrúa, 1945).

Thomas N. Campbell

AGUA SUCIA INDIANS. The Agua Sucia ("dirty water") Indians are known from a single Spanish document of 1683 that does not clearly identify their area. They seem to have lived somewhere in west central Texas. Their affiliations remain unknown.

BIBLIOGRAPHY: Charles W. Hackett, ed., *Pichardo's Treatise on the Limits of Louisiana and Texas* (4 vols., Austin: University of Texas Press, 1931–46). *Thomas N. Campbell*

AGUAYO, MARQUÉS DE SAN MIGUEL DE (?–1734). José de Azlor y Virto de Vera, soldier and governor, the son of Artal de Azlor, was born in Spain, a member of a family long distinguished in the service of the Spanish crown. He married Ignacia Xaviera, daughter and heiress of Agustín de Echevers, first Marqués de San Miguel de Aguayo. Through this marriage José de Azlor became the second Marqués de Aguayo.

In 1712 he and his wife went to Mexico to live on one of their haciendas, Patos, which included almost half of Coahuila. In 1719, after offering to drive the French out of the area claimed by Spain, Aguayo was appointed governor and captain general of the provinces of Coahuila and Texas, an office he assumed on October 21. In 1720 he received a commission from the viceroy of New Spain to reoccupy the East Texas missions and presidios that had been abandoned during the French invasion in 1719. Aguayo offered to finance the expedition himself, but the viceroy declined that proposal. The Aguayo expedition[qv] so solidified the Spanish claim to Texas that it was never again challenged by the French. When Aguayo entered Texas the province had only one presidio and two missions, one of which, San José y San Miguel de Aguayo, had been established only a few months earlier under the patronage of the Marqués. When he left, Texas had four presidios and ten missions. Aguayo was also responsible for the beginnings of colonization in Texas. He recommended that steps be taken to settle 400 families between San Antonio and the East Texas missions, one-half of the settlers to be recruited from Galicia, the Canary Islands, and Havana and the other half to be composed of loyal Tlaxcalán Indians.

On June 13, 1722, Aguayo resigned the governorship of Coahuila and Texas because of ill health resulting from the hardships of the expedition. In 1724 he was rewarded for his efforts with promotion to field marshal by the Spanish king. He died on March 7, 1734, and was buried in the chapel of Santa María de las Parras.

BIBLIOGRAPHY: Eleanor Claire Buckley, "The Aguayo Expedition in Texas and Louisiana, 1719–1722," *Quarterly of the Texas State Historical Association* 15 (July 1911). Charles W. Hackett, "The Marquis of San Miguel de Aguayo and His Recovery of Texas from the French, 1719–1723," *Southwestern Historical Quarterly* 49 (October 1945).

Lewis W. Newton

AGUAYO EXPEDITION. The Aguayo expedition, a project of the Marqués de Aguayo,[qv] resulted from the French invasion of 1719, which caused the Spanish to retreat from East Texas. In response to Aguayo's offer, the viceroy commissioned him to reoccupy the area.

Aguayo gathered together a force of about 500 men, organized as a mounted infantry, which he called the Battalion of San Miguel de Aragón. Four thousand horses and other livestock provided transportation and provisions. Juan Rodríguez[qv] acted as guide.

After numerous delays the expedition crossed the Rio Grande, on March 20, 1721, and reached San Antonio on April 4. A detachment under Domingo Ramón[qv] occupied La Bahía del Espíritu Santo on the same day Aguayo reached San Antonio. Accompanied by the friars who had been in San Antonio since the French invasion, the main body of the expedition went on to East Texas. The party proceeded by way of the sites of present New Braunfels and San Marcos to a crossing of the Colorado River a few miles below the site of present Austin, crossed Little River at the Griffin Crossing east of the site of Belton and the Brazos near the site of Waco, marched southeast to the Old San Antonio Road[qv] above the site of Navasota and followed the road to the former Spanish settlements between the Trinity and Red River. Detours necessitated by heavy rains caused the Aguayo trail to skirt the Apache country and run in sight of the Balcones Escarpment.[qv]

The Indians east of the Trinity welcomed the Spanish, as did Louis Juchereau de St. Denis,[qv] who, as commander of the French forces in the area, agreed to withdraw to Natchitoches. While in East Texas Aguayo reestablished six missions: San Francisco de los Tejas (renamed San Francisco de los Neches), San José de los Nazonis, Nuestra Señora de la Purísima Concepción de los Hainai, Nuestra Señora de Guadalupe de los Nacogdoches, Nuestra Señora de los Dolores de los Ais, and San Miguel de Linares de los Adaes. He also reestablished the presidio of Nuestra Señora de los Dolores de los Tejas[qv] and built and garrisoned the presidio of Nuestra Señora del Pilar de los Adaes[qv] for the protection of the missions against hostile Indians or possible French encroachment.

In the fall of 1721 the members of the expedition not stationed in East Texas returned to San Antonio, which Aguayo strengthened by the establishment of a third mission there, San Francisco Xavier de Náxara,[qv] and by the rebuilding of San Antonio de Béxar Presidio.[qv] On a side trip to La Bahía he established the presidio of Nuestra Señora de Loreto[qv] and the mission of Nuestra Señora del Espíritu Santo de Zúñiga.[qv] He also initiated a direct sea route from La Bahía to Veracruz as a course of supply for the Texas mission establishments.

Leaving 219 of his men at various presidios in Texas, Aguayo returned to Coahuila, where the force was disbanded on May 31, 1722. The expedition resulted in the increase in the number of missions in Texas from two to ten, the increase in the number of presidios from one to four, the strengthening of the military force from fifty to 269 soldiers, and the establishment of so definite a Spanish claim to Texas that it was never again disputed by France or by the French in Louisiana. *See also* SPANISH TEXAS, SPANISH MISSIONS.

BIBLIOGRAPHY: Eleanor Claire Buckley, "The Aguayo Expedition in Texas and Louisiana, 1719–1722," *Quarterly of the Texas State Historical Association* 15 (July 1911). Carlos E. Castañeda, *Our Catholic Heritage in Texas* (7 vols., Austin: Von Boeckmann–Jones, 1936–58; rpt., New York: Arno, 1976). Charles W. Hackett, "The Marquis of San Miguel de Aguayo and His Recovery of Texas from the French, 1719–1723," *Southwestern Historical Quarterly* 49 (October 1945).

Charles W. Hackett

AGUIDA INDIANS. In 1683–84 Juan Domínguez de Mendoza[qv] led an exploratory expedition from El Paso as far eastward as the junction of the Concho and Colorado rivers east of the site of present San Angelo. In his itinerary he listed the names of thirty-seven Indian groups, including the Aguidas, from whom he expected to receive delegations. Nothing further is known about the Aguidas, who seem to have been one of the many Indian groups of north central Texas that were swept into oblivion by the southward thrust of the Lipan Apache and Comanche Indians in the eighteenth century.

BIBLIOGRAPHY: Herbert Eugene Bolton, ed., *Spanish Exploration in the Southwest, 1542–1706* (New York: Scribner, 1908; rpt., New York: Barnes and Noble, 1959). Charles W. Hackett, ed., *Pichardo's Treatise on the Limits of Louisiana and Texas* (4 vols., Austin: University of Texas Press, 1931–46).

Thomas N. Campbell

AGUILARES, TEXAS. Aguilares is on State Highway 359 and the Texas-Mexican Railway twenty-four miles east of Laredo in southeastern Webb County. It is named for Locario, José, Francisco, Próspero, and Librado Aguilar, who settled in the area in the 1870s. The town started as a ranching community. In 1881 it became a water and wood stop on the railroad. It received a post office in 1890. Some oil has been produced in the area. In 1907 the town had two schools with eighty-nine pupils and two teachers, and in 1910 it reportedly had a population of 1,500. By 1914 the population had decreased to 300; two businesses, the larger being the Aguilares Mercantile Company, served the community. The post office was closed after 1930, and in 1939 the population was ten. In 1945 the population was twenty-five, and one of the two stores had closed. In 1990 only ten people were reported, and most of the houses were in disuse.

BIBLIOGRAPHY: Michael F. Black, ed., *Mirando City: A New Town in a New Oil Field* (Laredo: Laredo Publishing, 1972).

Alfredo B. Barrera III

AGUIRRE, PEDRO DE (1678–?) Pedro de Aguirre, soldier, was born in Aranaz, Navarra, Spain, on April 24, 1678, the son of Pedro and María (Sagardia) de Aguirre; the family line can be traced back to the year 1200. Aguirre, a captain in the Spanish army and commander of Presidio del Río Grande del Norte, was ordered by a special council held August 7, 1708, to escort fathers Antonio de San Buenaventura y Olivares and Isidro Félix de Espinosa[qqv] to what is now the Colorado River to meet the Tejas Indians and their allies. The Spanish, who believed that the French were illegally trading in Texas (*see* SPANISH TEXAS), planned to use the Indians to keep watch on the French. The expedition left San Juan Bautista[qv] on April 5, 1709, and reached the Colorado on May 19. Upon reaching their destination, they learned that they were still three days' travel from the land of the Tejas Indians, whereupon they returned to the Rio Grande, since Aguirre did not have orders to proceed farther. During the trip they arrived at the site of what is now San Antonio, on April 13, 1709, and named the nearby springs San Pedro Springs,[qv] and the river San Antonio de Padua.

BIBLIOGRAPHY: Yjinio Aguirre, *Echoes of the Conquistadores: History of a Pioneer Family in the Southwest* (1983). Carlos E. Castañeda, *Our Catholic Heritage in Texas* (7 vols., Austin: Von Boeckmann–Jones, 1936–58; rpt., New York: Arno, 1976).

John G. Johnson

AGUJA PEAK. Aguja Peak is 6½ miles south-southwest of Terlingua in southwestern Brewster County (at 29°13′ N, 103°38′ W). *Aguja*, meaning "needle" or "spire" in Spanish, is descriptive of the peak, which rises in the northwest part of a short, rugged uplift called the Sierra Aguja. The Sierra Aguja is some 2½ miles long by one mile wide and runs northwest-southeast astride the boundary of Big Bend National Park.[qv] Vegetation in the area consists predominantly of juniper, oak, grasses, chaparral, and cacti. With an elevation at its summit of approximately 3,280 feet above sea level, Aguja Peak is the highest point in the Sierra Aguja. Among residents of the region the mountain is more commonly known as Needle Peak.

AGULA CREEK. Agula Creek rises near the intersection of Farm roads 444 and 1686 in eastern Victoria County (at 28°47′ N, 96°49′ W) and flows intermittently southeast for eleven miles to its mouth on Placedo Creek, two miles west of Lavaca Bay (at 28°43′ N, 96°41′ W). It traverses flat to rolling prairie surfaced by clay and loam that support mesquite and grasses.

AHEHOUEN INDIANS. The Ahehouen (Ahehoen, Ahekouen) Indians are known only from records of the La Salle expedition.[qv] In

1687 they lived somewhere north of Matagorda Bay, probably near the Colorado River. In 1754 Indians with a similar name, Aguajuani, lived an unspecified distance north or northwest of Nacogdoches. The Aguajuanis are not to be confused with the Yojuanes, whose name (Jujuane) also appears in the same document. No relationship between the Ahehouens and the Aguajuanis has yet been established, and the linguistic and cultural affiliations of both groups remain unknown.

BIBLIOGRAPHY: Isaac Joslin Cox, ed., *The Journeys of René Robert Cavelier, Sieur de La Salle* (2 vols., New York: Barnes, 1905; 2d ed., New York: Allerton, 1922). Frederick Webb Hodge, ed., *Handbook of American Indians North of Mexico* (2 vols., Washington: GPO, 1907, 1910; rpt., New York: Pageant, 1959). Henri Joutel, *Joutel's Journal of La Salle's Last Voyage* (London: Lintot, 1714; rpt., New York: Franklin, 1968). *Thomas N. Campbell*

AHOUERHOPIHEIM INDIANS. In the latter part of the seventeenth century, according to records of the La Salle expedition,[qv] the Ahouerhopiheim (Abonerhopiheim, Ahonerhopiheim) Indians occupied an inland area somewhere north of Matagorda Bay, probably near the Colorado River or between the Colorado and Brazos rivers. Although this name has passed into American Indian literature, there is some question about its accuracy. There is some evidence that on Henri Joutel's[qv] original manuscript two names appeared, Ahouergomahe and Kemahopiheim, and that a printer, through error, manufactured a hybrid name, using the first and last parts of these names respectively. The linguistic and cultural affiliations of the Indians bearing these names remain unknown.

BIBLIOGRAPHY: Isaac Joslin Cox, ed., *The Journeys of René Robert Cavelier, Sieur de La Salle* (2 vols., New York: Barnes, 1905; 2d ed., New York: Allerton, 1922). Frederick Webb Hodge, ed., *Handbook of American Indians North of Mexico* (2 vols., Washington: GPO, 1907, 1910; rpt., New York: Pageant, 1959). Henri Joutel, *Joutel's Journal of La Salle's Last Voyage* (London: Lintot, 1714; rpt., New York: Franklin, 1968). *Thomas N. Campbell*

AIELI INDIANS. In 1683–84 Juan Domínguez de Mendoza[qv] led an exploratory expedition from El Paso as far eastward as the junction of the Concho and Colorado rivers east of the site of present San Angelo. In his itinerary he listed the names of thirty-seven Indian groups, including the Aielis (Ayeles), from whom he expected to receive delegations. Nothing further is known about the Aielis, who seem to have been one of the many Indian groups of north central Texas that were swept into oblivion by the southward thrust of the Lipan Apache and Comanche Indians in the eighteenth century.

BIBLIOGRAPHY: Herbert Eugene Bolton, ed., *Spanish Exploration in the Southwest, 1542–1706* (New York: Scribner, 1908; rpt., New York: Barnes and Noble, 1959). Charles W. Hackett, ed., *Pichardo's Treatise on the Limits of Louisiana and Texas* (4 vols., Austin: University of Texas Press, 1931–46). *Thomas N. Campbell*

AIKEN, HERMAN (1809–1860). Herman Aiken, soldier, surveyor, and pioneer, was born in 1809 in Deering, New Hampshire, reared in Illinois, and left home at age fourteen to support himself. He arrived in Texas in 1833 and in 1835 was captain of a vessel carrying men and supplies for the revolutionary army[qv] from New Orleans to Galveston. After Texas won its independence, he established a general store at Old Nashville and later another at Caldwell. Aiken undertook several exploratory trips to the future area of Bell County in the mid-1840s, and from 1846 to 1848 he served as captain in the Mexican War.[qv] In 1851 he moved to his home, Casa Blanca, in Bell County; he moved to Troy in 1857 and to Salado in 1859. When Coryell County was established in 1854, Aiken was hired to survey the new county. In the same year he helped build the Cumberland Baptist Church in Belton. During the 1850s he assisted in the promotion of two Bell County communities—Aiken, which flourished briefly during the 1850s and 1860s, and the more permanent community of Salado. Herman Aiken was a member of the founding board of trustees of Salado College in 1859. He married a German emigrant named Margaret in the 1830s and had at least four children. He died on November 27, 1860, and was the first person buried in the old cemetery at Salado.

BIBLIOGRAPHY: Temple *Telegram*, December 16, 1934. George Tyler, *History of Bell County* (San Antonio: Naylor, 1936). *L. W. Kemp*

AIKEN, TEXAS (Bell County). Aiken was a mill and farming community on the Leon River twelve miles northeast of Belton in northwest Bell County. A steam saw and flour mill was constructed on the site by Abner Kuykendall[qv] in 1857, and a settlement grew up around it, on land owned by Herman Aiken.[qv] By 1860 Aiken was a thriving community with an estimated 200 inhabitants. During the Civil War[qv] the population of 600 produced a number of goods formerly imported; the town supported a cabinet shop, a tanyard, a shoe and saddle shop, a hat factory, a Confederate distillery, and wood and blacksmith shops for the manufacture and repair of wagons. Aiken had a post office from 1868 to 1872. The town seems to have declined in the later nineteenth century; it was not shown on the state highway map of 1948. The townsite was inundated by Belton Lake in the 1950s.

BIBLIOGRAPHY: Bell County Historical Commission, *Story of Bell County, Texas* (2 vols., Austin: Eakin Press, 1988). Temple Junior Chamber of Commerce, *Bell County History* (Fort Worth, 1958). George Tyler, *History of Bell County* (San Antonio: Naylor, 1936).
Mark Odintz

AIKEN, TEXAS (Floyd County). Aiken is on U.S. Highway 70 and the Santa Fe Railroad four miles northwest of Lockney in northwest Floyd County. The settlement was named for Frank Aiken, who owned the townsite and secured a post office in August 1922. In 1923 the new Aiken school district replaced an earlier school named Meteor. Aiken had four businesses, a school, and 110 residents by 1947. During the mid-1950s it had two grocery stores, two cafes, two service stations, and a Methodist church. Early residents included the Elam, Marshall, Young, Lucas, Roach, Langfeldt, and Owens families. Most of the services have closed, partly because of changes in agricultural production and farming. Paymaster Seeds, a division of Cargill, Incorporated, once operated a plant at Aiken that shipped an annual average of 300,000 to 400,000 fifty-pound bags of seed worldwide. Cargill also had a research facility three miles north of the community. A Southwestern Grain elevator was located there. North of the town was a community Baptist church. Although some Aiken residents believed the number to be too high, the 1980 census reported a population of 140. In 1990 the population was sixty.

BIBLIOGRAPHY: Floyd County Historical Museum, *History of Floyd County, 1876–1979* (Dallas: Taylor, 1979). *Charles G. Davis*

AIKEN, TEXAS (Shelby County). Aiken is twelve miles from Center on State Highway 7 in southwestern Shelby County. The community was purportedly named after Herman Aiken.[qv] A post office that opened there in 1889 was described in 1890 as a "country post office." By 1892, however, the community had a sawmill, a blacksmith's shop, and a school. In 1896 the population was estimated at seventy-five, and two churches, a cotton gin, and a general store had been added to the earlier institutions. The post office was closed in 1909, but Aiken remained a church and school community for farmers in the area. By 1955 the school district had been consolidated with other districts. In 1990 Aiken had a population of seventy-five and no rated businesses.

BIBLIOGRAPHY: John Clements, *Flying the Colors: Texas, a Comprehensive Look at Texas Today, County by County* (Dallas: Clements Research, 1984). *Cecil Harper, Jr.*

AIKEN CREEK. Aiken Creek, sometimes called Harber Creek, rises at the northeastern edge of the Lone Star Army Ammunition Plant,[qv] about a mile south of Leary in eastern Bowie County (at 33°27′ N, 94°12′ W). The stream is intermittent in its upper reaches. It flows southeast for 14½ miles to its mouth on Elliott Creek, 9½ miles south of Nash (at 33°18′ N, 94°08′ W). The soils that flank the streambed are loamy in the upper and middle reaches and clayey around the mouth. The area is heavily wooded, with pines and various hardwoods predominating. The stream may have been named for James Akin, an original grantee of land through which it flows.

AIKIN, A. M., JR. (1905–1981). A. M. Aikin, Jr., legislator, son of A. M. and Mattie (Stephens) Aikin, was born at Aikin Grove in Red River County, Texas, on October 9, 1905. His parents moved to Lamar County in 1907 to operate a country store. Aikin attended a three-teacher school in Milton, then rode horseback four miles to Deport each day until he graduated from high school. He credited his lifetime interest in education to the early personal difficulties he encountered in acquiring his own education. He milked cows to earn room and board at Paris Junior College and worked in a department store in Paris from 1925 to 1931 to earn enough money to attend Cumberland University in Lebanon, Tennessee, where he graduated with a bachelor of laws degree in 1932. In 1929 Aikin married Welma Morphew, a lifelong advocate of landscape beautification, whose career included serving as a regent of Paris Junior College. The Aikins had one son.

Aikin, a Democrat, began his political career in 1932, when he was elected to the Texas House of Representatives. He completed two terms before going to the Senate in 1937. He served forty-six years in the state's two legislative chambers and missed only 2½ legislative days in his career. From his first year in elective office, he supported every major educational bill passed by the legislature. He was an advocate of all-weather farm-road legislation on the grounds that schools were of little value to students if they were inaccessible.

Aikin, "the father of modern Texas education," is best remembered as the cosponsor with Representative Claud Gilmer of Rocksprings of the Gilmer-Aikin Laws.[qv] These measures, passed in 1949, established a centralized state education system and the Minimum Foundation school program, which provided state-financed minimum teachers' salaries and set guaranteed public school funding levels for other related expenditures. In addition Aikin authored legislation to increase state aid to public schools, including colleges, and sponsored a bill in 1933 to establish the Teacher Retirement System, which became a constitutional amendment in 1937. In 1956 he sponsored an amendment to establish a minimum retirement compensation of $100 a month to attract capable teachers to the profession.

Aikin served on the Senate Finance Committee beginning in 1937, when he became a senator, and chaired that committee from 1967 until he retired in 1979. In 1943 he was president pro tem of the Senate and acting governor for fourteen days in the absence of Governor Coke Stevenson.[qv] Aikin became dean of the Senate in 1963 and dean emeritus upon his retirement.

The A. M. and Welma Aikin Regional Archives, a part of the Mike Rheudasil Learning Center at Paris Junior College, was established to honor Aikin in 1978 and houses his papers, a replica of his Senate office, and a gallery of memorabilia related to his career. The archives also houses local-history manuscript collections from Delta, Fannin, Lamar, and Red River counties and is a regional depository for the local records division of the Texas State Library.[qv] The Aikin Monolith, a Texas red granite monument, towers outside the entrance to the Aikin Archives, a gift of the Texas Association of Public Junior Colleges.

Aikin died in Paris on October 24, 1981. In 1985 the A. M. Aikin Regents Chair in Junior and Community College Education and the A. M. Aikin Regents Chair in Education Leadership were established at the University of Texas, with a total endowment of $1 million. Former Paris Junior College president Louis B. Williams led the fund-raising effort. The total gift of $500,000 was matched from the Permanent University Fund[qv] to establish the memorial.

BIBLIOGRAPHY: Frances T. Davis, The Role of Senator A. M. Aikin, Jr., in the Development of Education in Texas, 1932–1974 (Ph.D. dissertation, East Texas State University, 1975). *Focus on Paris Junior College*, January 1982. Vertical Files, Barker Texas History Center, University of Texas at Austin. *Daisy Harvill*

AILEY, ALVIN (1931–1989). Alvin Ailey, black dancer, choreographer, and founder of the Alvin Ailey American Dance Theater, was born in Rogers, Bell County, Texas, on January 5, 1931. His mother, Lula, was seventeen when he was born; six months later, her husband abandoned them. By all accounts, Ailey and his mother were very close. They earned a living by picking cotton and doing laundry and domestic work after they moved to Navasota and then Los Angeles, California. Later in his career, in honor of his mother's birthday, Ailey choreographed a solo work, *Cry*, that was performed by his leading dancer and the artistic director of his company, Judith Jamison. The piece was dedicated to "black women everywhere." As a child, Ailey spent time drawing and attending the True Vine Baptist Church. He was introduced to performance dance on a junior high class trip to see the Ballet Russe de Monte Carlo. Later, he saw performances by Katherine Dunham and took dance lessons from a member of her company.

Ailey was profoundly influenced by the work of Lester Horton, a choreographer and teacher in Los Angeles. Horton's company is believed to be the first racially integrated dance company in the United States. He drew inspiration from American Indian dance and Japanese theater, and those inclusions greatly impressed Ailey. In 1949, Ailey gave up studying romance languages at UCLA and began to study with Horton. He made his debut as a dancer in 1953 and took over the company when Horton died that year. In 1954 he made his Broadway debut as a featured dancer in Truman Capote's *House of Flowers*. The play ran only four months, after which Ailey decided to stay in New York to study ballet, acting, and modern dance with Martha Graham and others. From 1954 to 1958 he appeared in a number of musicals both on and off Broadway. He performed in *The Carefree Tree* (1955), played opposite Mary Hinkson in Harry Belafonte's *Sing, Man, Sing* (1956), and was the leading dancer in *Jamaica* (1957), starring Lena Horne. Ailey also appeared in the film *Carmen Jones* (1954), directed the revue *African Holiday* (1960), and co-directed Langston Hughes's off-Broadway song-play *Jericho Jim Crow* (1964). He acted in *Call Me by My Rightful Name* (1961) and the Broadway production of *Tiger Tiger, Burning Bright* (1962). He choreographed both Samuel Barber's opera *Antony and Cleopatra,* the first production at the new Metropolitan Opera at Lincoln Theater, and Leonard Bernstein's Mass for the debut performance of the Kennedy Center for the Performing Arts in Washington. On one evening in March 1958, at the 92d Street Y in New York, Ailey and six other dancers performed three works, including his first choreographic success, *Blues Suite.* That performance led a New York *Times* dance critic to name Ailey one of the six outstanding artists that season. The performance was also the genesis of his dance company, which subsequently performed for more than fifteen million people around the world. Beginning in 1962, the State Department sent the company to Southeast Asia and Australia on the first of several successful foreign tours.

Ailey retired from dance in 1965 but continued to devote himself to choreography and his company. The Ailey Troupe became a resident company at the Brooklyn Academy of Music in 1969 and remained there for three seasons. In 1970 it became the first American modern-dance company to tour the Soviet Union since Isadora Duncan in the 1920s. The Ailey company received a twenty-three-minute ovation in Leningrad. In 1972, the Alvin Ailey American Dance Center became the company's official school and home of the Alvin Ailey Repertory Ensemble, the company's junior troupe.

Before 1963 the company was composed exclusively of black dancers; when Ailey integrated, he was criticized by some black Americans. In a 1973 interview with Ellen Cohn in the *New York Times Magazine* Ailey explained that he had "met some incredible dancers of other colors who could cut the work," and that he had run "into reverse racism." To maintain an all-black company would be "like saying only French people should do Racine or Molière." Critics also accused Ailey of being too overtly theatrical, but he explained in the same interview that his performances were based on the concept of total dance theater. He wanted to put "something on stage that will have a very wide appeal without being condescending; that will reach an audience and make it part of the dance; that will get everybody in the theater."

Though most of Ailey's choreography is rooted in African-American history and culture, including jazz, blues, Gospel music, and folk heroes, many of his works are developed from pure movement, abstract and plotless. Moira Hodgson refers to Ailey's choreography as lyrical and theatrical. Theatrical works such as *Blues Suite* and *Revelations,* his best-known work, combine drama and dance, while abstract pieces such as *The Lark Ascending* and *Streams* are stylistically classic. Ailey received the Kennedy Center Honors from President Ronald Reagan in 1988 and the New York City Handel Medallion for achievement in the arts. His dance honors also include the 1987 Samuel H. Scripps American Dance Festival Award, the 1979 Capezio Award, and the 1975 *Dance Magazine Award.* He received honorary doctorates from Princeton University, Bard College, and Adelphi University, and in 1976 he was awarded the Spingarn Medal of the National Association for the Advancement of Colored People. Ailey died in New York on December 1, 1989, of blood dyscrasia.

BIBLIOGRAPHY: Peter A. Bailey, "Alvin Ailey at the Met," *Ebony,* October 1984. Susan Cook and Joseph H. Mazo, *The Alvin Ailey American Dance Theater* (New York: Morrow, 1978). Lynne Fauley Emery, *Black Dance from 1619 to Today* (2d ed., Princeton, New Jersey: Princeton Book Company, 1988). Moira Hodgson, *Quintet: Five American Dance Companies* (New York: Morrow, 1976). Richard G. Kraus, *History of the Dance in Art and Education* (Englewood Cliffs, New Jersey: Prentice-Hall, 1969). New York *Times,* December 2, 1989. Vertical Files, Barker Texas History Center, University of Texas at Austin.

Kharen Monsho

AIMABLE. The *Aimable,* one of the vessels that carried the La Salle expedition[qv] to the Matagorda Bay area, was variously described as a flyboat, flute, pink, or hooker, of 250 to 300 tons burden. She was lost when the expedition was making its initial entry into the bay at the seaward end of Cavallo Pass[qv] in February 1685. Most of the supplies brought along to assist in the founding of the French colony, originally intended to be at the mouth of the Mississippi River, were lost with the ship.

BIBLIOGRAPHY: Kathleen Gilmore, *The Keeran Site: The Probable Site of La Salle's Fort St. Louis in Texas* (Austin: Texas Historical Commission, 1973). Henri Joutel, *Joutel's Journal of La Salle's Last Voyage* (London: Lintot, 1719; rpt., New York: Franklin, 1968).

J. Barto Arnold III

AIR-CONDITIONING. The earliest home air cooling in Texas was practiced by the Mexican and Spanish population. At an early date Spanish Americans constructed adobe[qv] houses with thick masonry walls with a door or a closable opening in each of the four walls. At night the opened doors and openings permitted an all-night flow of air through the rooms. This lowered the temperature of the entire adobe wall. All openings were closed from sunup until sundown. The owner thus captured a mass of cool air in his home that lasted until siesta time, after the midday meal. During the day, the semitropical sun would heat up the outer walls by direct radiation. For the night sleeping hours, while the house was cooling for the next day, the adobe inhabitant and his family sometimes slept out-of-doors, where they could obtain the benefit of natural night cooling. The Spanish-speaking people learned this practice from African and Asiatic Arabs who had learned to employ the existing forces of nature to keep cool. From Spain this practice entered Mexico and then Texas. The early white settlers in the state also built their homes so that they could be cooled by this system of cross-ventilation.

Well water was also introduced as an air-cooling medium at an early date. The water was pumped from the well to fan radiators installed in the space to be cooled. Unless the water was pumped for other uses subsequent to its application as a coolant, this was not an economical procedure in Texas since the well water was usually 62° to 72° F and thus had little cooling potential.

In the dairy regions of Central Texas, nineteenth-century German farmers adopted evaporative cooling. This system, which was practiced extensively in Central and West Texas, was originated for milk cooling. The evening milk was placed in metal cans; fans blew air through wetted blankets covering the cans. This air took on "wet bulb" temperatures and cooled the milk to 70° or 75° F. This system was easily modified for home cooling, as is evident today in the wide range of evaporative coolers ranging from the desert variety to the sophisticated designs used in large homes, commercial structures, and government buildings. During this same period the cities in low elevations in eastern North Texas experimented with every type of fan, with ice and dry ice, and with evaporative and sky-cooling devices to combat the summer heat waves.

Manufacturing of cooling devices began in Texas cities as early as 1870 and provided the beginning of a new type of industry. Air cooling with commercial ice dates back to approximately 1910, when ice could be purchased for as little as four dollars a ton. At first the 300-pound blocks of ice were placed in a vault through which a fan blew air into an outlet duct and thence to the space to be cooled. By 1920 the ice had been placed in an enclosed pool and the ice water circulated to fan radiators in order to cool rooms, auditoriums, and restaurants. The First Baptist churches of Dallas and Austin and the Highland Park Methodist Church were ice-water cooled for many years. The first refrigerated air-cooled building in the Houston area was the Rice Hotel cafeteria, air-conditioned in 1922. The Milam building in San Antonio, which opened in 1928, was the first air-conditioned high-rise office building in the country.

By 1940 Texas had become a national manufacturing center for air-cooling machines and inventions, which ranged from lowly desert coolers to the most sophisticated forms of evaporative coolers and reversed cycle refrigerators, as well as heaters for winter heating and summer refrigerated air cooling. The latter system was designed into one machine, usually called the "heat pump." Also in the 1940s the air-conditioning industry began to include units for automobiles. By the 1950s Dallas had become a major center for the manufacture of car air conditioners. In the early 1960s Don Dixon of San Antonio broadened the potential market for the industry by inventing a unit to fit Volkswagens (cars previously considered "uncoolable"). By the 1960s air-conditioning was a multi-million-dollar industry, with manufacturing and retail establishments accounting for more than 240 businesses in the state. By the 1990s the Texas Air Conditioning Contractors Association had licensed about 8,000 contractors.

Environmental questions arose in the 1980s concerning the hypothetical deleterious effect of the chlorofluorocarbons used in air-conditioning systems. Passage of the Clean Air Act by the United States Congress in 1992 gave the Environmental Protection Agency the power to require that refrigerants be recovered and recycled. The cost of such procedures prompted the air-conditioning industry to make plans to phase out freon-based units and replace them with supposedly less harmful systems. *See also* REFRIGERATION.

bibliography: Vertical Files, Barker Texas History Center, University of Texas at Austin. *Willis R. Woolrich*

AIR LINE RAIL ROAD. The Air Line Rail Road was chartered on January 30, 1860, to construct a railroad from Brenham to Austin. Incorporators were George W. Glasscock, John B. Banks, John W. Brown, and W. S. Oldham of Travis County; L. D. Moore and J. B. McGinnis of Bastrop County; and J. D. Giddings of Washington County, James Shaw of Burleson County, and Thomas Oates of Williamson County. The Air Line graded about five miles before the Civil War,[qv] but no other work was done by the company. Its charter gave the Air Line the right to consolidate with the Washington County Rail Road Company. This consolidation was effected, but the date of the merger is not known. In 1869 the Washington County was acquired by the Houston and Texas Central Railway Company, which used the rights granted by the Air Line charter to build its Western Division between Brenham and Austin in 1870 and 1871.

S. G. Reed

AIRVILLE, TEXAS. Airville is at the intersection of Farm roads 2904 and 437, eleven miles east of Temple in northeast Bell County. The community had three businesses in 1931, but by 1944 it had only a single business, a school, and several houses. By 1964 Airville had only ten inhabitants living in scattered dwellings. The population was still ten in 1990. *Mark Odintz*

AIS INDIANS. The Ais (Ayis, Ays, Eyeish, Ayish) Indians, an East Texas group associated with the Hasinais, spoke a language different from the Caddos of the region. For this reason, it has been suggested by some authorities that the Ais represented a culture older than the confederacy known to the French and Spanish. Their early home was on Ayish Bayou between the Sabine and Neches rivers. In 1717 Nuestra Señora de los Dolores de los Ais Mission was founded for them in the vicinity of present San Augustine. According to historical accounts the Ais were distrusted alike by the Caddo and by French and Spanish authorities. In the later part of the eighteenth century they were placed under the jurisdiction of the officials residing at Nacogdoches. They were later placed on the Wichita reservation in Oklahoma.

bibliography: Frederick Webb Hodge, ed., *Handbook of American Indians North of Mexico* (2 vols., Washington: GPO, 1907, 1910; rpt., New York: Pageant, 1959). *Margery H. Krieger*

AJAX, TEXAS. Ajax was a post office community five miles southwest of Deberry and just east of the Sabine River in north central Panola County. It was established in the late 1890s. A post office opened there in 1900 with Chapple W. Rogers as postmaster. At its height the small settlement had a general store, a cotton gin and mill, and a number of houses. The post office closed in 1907, and the mail was routed through Tacoma. By the mid-1930s Ajax no longer appeared on highway maps.

bibliography: John Barnette Sanders, *Postoffices and Post Masters of Panola County, Texas, 1845–1930* (Center, Texas, 1964).

Christopher Long

AKASQUY INDIANS. The Akasquy Indians, an otherwise unidentified group, possibly Caddoan, were visited by René Robert Cavelier, Sieur de La Salle,[qv] in 1687, when they were living near the Palaquesson Indians on the lower Brazos River.

bibliography: Frederick Webb Hodge, ed., *Handbook of American Indians North of Mexico* (2 vols., Washington: GPO, 1907, 1910; rpt., New York: Pageant, 1959). *Margery H. Krieger*

AKOKISA INDIANS. The Akokisa (Arkokisa, Orcoquiza) Indians were Atakapan-speaking Indians who lived in extreme southeastern Texas between the Trinity and Sabine rivers. They were most commonly encountered around Galveston Bay. It seems likely that the Han and Coaque Indians encountered by Álvar Núñez Cabeza de Vaca[qv] in the early sixteenth century were Akokisas, as well as the Caux, who held Simars de Bellisle[qv] captive in the early eighteenth century. Most of what is known about the Akokisas comes from mission records. In 1748–49 some of them entered San Ildefonso Mission on the San Gabriel River near the site of present Rockdale, but they left this area when the mission was abandoned in 1755. Nuestra Señora de la Luz Mission was built near the mouth of the Trinity River for the Akokisas and the Bidais in 1756–57 and lasted until 1772. Thereafter little is reported about the Akokisas, although in 1805 they seem to have lived in two settlements, one on the lower Colorado River and the other near the coast between the Neches and Sabine rivers. It seems likely that the Akokisa survivors joined their relatives, the Atákapas, in southwestern Louisiana shortly before the Texas Revolution.[qv]

bibliography: Herbert Eugene Bolton, ed. and trans., *Athanase de Mézières and the Louisiana-Texas Frontier, 1768–1780* (2 vols., Cleveland: Arthur H. Clark, 1914). Herbert E. Bolton, "The Founding of the Missions on the San Gabriel River, 1745–1749," *Southwestern Historical Quarterly* 17 (April 1914). Herbert Eugene Bolton, *Texas in the Middle Eighteenth Century* (Berkeley: University of California Press, 1915; rpt., Austin: University of Texas Press, 1970). Melvin Chandler Burch, "The Indigenous Indians of the Lower Trinity Area of Texas," *Southwestern Historical Quarterly* 60 (July 1956). Joseph O. Dyer, *The Lake Charles Atakapas (Cannibals) Period of 1817 to 1820* (Galveston, 1917). Albert S. Gatschet and J. R. Swanton, *A Dictionary of the Atakapa Language* (Smithsonian Institution Bureau of American Ethnology Bulletin 108, Washington: GPO, 1932). William W. Newcomb, *The Indians of Texas* (Austin: University of Texas Press, 1961). John R. Swanton, *Indian Tribes of the Lower Mississippi Valley and Adjacent Coast of the Gulf of Mexico* (Washington: GPO, 1911). John R. Swanton, *The Indian Tribes of North America* (Gross Pointe, Michigan: Scholarly Press, 1968). John R. Swanton, *The Indians of the Southeastern United States* (Washington: GPO, 1946).

Thomas N. Campbell

AKRON, TEXAS. Akron, also known as Lavender and Holly, was on Ray's Creek five miles north of Tyler in central Smith County. It was established in 1877 as a station on the Tyler Tap Railroad. In 1936 it consisted only of a station and two dwellings north of Pleasant Grove School on a graded and drained dirt road. The community no longer appeared on government survey maps by the 1960s.

bibliography: "Post Offices and Postmasters of Smith County, Texas: 1847–1929," *Chronicles of Smith County*, Spring 1966. Smith County Historical Society, *Historical Atlas of Smith County* (Tyler, Texas: Tyler Print Shop, 1965). Albert Woldert, *A History of Tyler and Smith County* (San Antonio: Naylor, 1948). *Vista K. McCroskey*

ALABAMA, TEXAS (Houston County). Alabama was a post office community and steamer stop on the Trinity River ten miles southwest of Crockett in western Houston County. It was established in the 1830s. In 1841 the Texas Congress chartered Trinity College, which operated in the community before the Civil War.[qv] An Alabama post office opened in 1846 with A. T. Monroe as postmaster. The community prospered for many years as a shipping point for plantations in western Houston County but began to decline in the 1870s, when the railroad supplanted the Trinity steamboats. The post office was closed in 1878, and by the 1880s many of the businesses and residents had moved away. A school was still operating at Alabama in 1897, but by the mid-1930s only a few scattered houses remained. Alabama appeared as a place name on maps as late as 1946.

bibliography: Armistead Albert Aldrich, *The History of Houston County, Texas* (San Antonio: Naylor, 1943). Viktor F. Bracht, *Texas im*

Jahre 1848 (Iserlohn, Westphalia: J. Bädeker, 1849; trans. C. F. Schmidt, San Antonio: Naylor, 1931). Houston County Historical Commission, *History of Houston County, Texas, 1687–1979* (Tulsa, Oklahoma: Heritage, 1979).
Cyrus Tilloson

ALABAMA, TEXAS (Trinity County). Alabama, a rural community also known as Alabama Creek, is sixteen miles northeast of Groveton on Farm Road 357 and Alabama Creek in eastern Trinity County. The site was settled around 1865 and named for the Alabama Indians, who had moved to the area from Mississippi in the 1820s. Around 1900 the community had a store, a cotton gin, and a sawmill. A school operated there until the 1930s, when it was consolidated with the Centerville district. By the mid-1950s only scattered houses remained. The estimated population in 1990 was twenty.

BIBLIOGRAPHY: Patricia B. and Joseph W. Hensley, eds., *Trinity County Beginnings* (Groveton, Texas: Trinity County Book Committee, 1986).
Christopher Long

ALABAMA-COUSHATTA INDIANS. The Alabama-Coushatta Indian Tribe of Texas, Incorporated, occupies a 4,593.7-acre reservation on U.S. Highway 190, seventeen miles east of Livingston in Polk County. In 1993 the names of 893 Alabama-Coushattas were recorded on the tribal roll, of whom approximately 500 lived on the reservation. Although recognized as two separate tribes, the Alabamas and Coushattas have been closely associated throughout their history. Both are of Muskhogean language stock. Both lived in adjacent areas in what is now Alabama, followed similar migration routes westward after 1763, and settled in the same area of the Big Thicket[qv] in Southeast Texas. Culturally, these two tribes have always been one people, in spite of minor differences. Their languages are mutually understandable, although some differences occur in individual words. Their closest tie has been that of blood, as intermarriage between the tribes has been practiced since earliest times. An early interpretation of *Alabama* indicated that the name meant "Here we rest." This explanation was generally accepted until T. M. Owen, director of the Alabama State Department of Archives and History, pointed out in 1921 that the name is derived from a combination of words meaning "vegetation gatherers." *Coushatta* is a popular form of "Koasati," which probably contains the words for "cane," "reed," or "white cane."

The first written references to the Alabamas, dated 1541, relate the contacts of the explorer Hernando De Soto with these Indians, probably in the future state of Mississippi. After De Soto, the Alabamas were lost to view until the appearance of the French in the region bordering the Gulf of Mexico.[qv] The Alabamas, who had migrated eastward during the intervening century and a half, then lived near the junction of the Coosa and Tallapoosa Rivers, the two main tributaries of the Alabama River. The Coushattas also moved to this area and established villages among those of the Alabamas. Beginning north of the site of present Montgomery, Alabama, the villages of the Alabamas and Coushattas extended southward for forty miles on both sides of the Alabama River. Both tribes were members of the Upper Creek Confederacy—the name given to a loose organization built around a group of dominant tribes called Creek or Muskogee in what is now Alabama. One of the principal objectives of the Creek Confederacy seems to have been to achieve a defensive alliance against certain enemies—including the Choctaw and Chickasaw Indians in what is now Mississippi and western Alabama and the Cherokee Indians in Tennessee.

While the French were establishing themselves at Mobile, they became involved in skirmishes with the Alabama and Mobile tribes. Peace was soon established, however, and thereafter the Alabamas remained loyal to French interests. This friendship was cemented in 1714 by the establishment of Fort Toulouse in the heart of the Alabama-Coushatta homeland. When it was built in 1714, the fort became a cause of great anxiety to the English in the region. It was also a depot for exchange of French articles for skins and other products, brought by the Indians from their hunting grounds and then floated down the Alabama River to the sea at Mobile. Papers of French governor Sieur de Bienville provide information relating to the French-Alabama friendship and the rivalry between the English and French for the loyalty of the Alabamas, Coushattas, and other Indians in the vicinity. Bienville wrote that "the Alabamas have the reputation among all nations of being people of intelligence and of good counsel . . . of all the Indians . . . most attached to the interests of the French." The Alabama River and the state of Alabama were named for the Alabama Indians.

In 1763 Alabamas and Coushattas began migrating from the Fort Toulouse area for several possible reasons. The development of a "deerskin economy" among North American Indians, brought about by trade with Europeans, had led to shortage of animals and conflict over hunting territories, resulting in a constant search for improved hunting conditions. In the short run, trade with Europeans helped the Indians obtain supplies and equipment. But they became dependent upon traders to furnish many items they needed, and their increased skin-hunting brought a disastrous shortage of game comparable to the disappearance of the buffalo[qv] on the plains. Moreover, settlers were pressing inland along the Atlantic coast. In 1763 the struggle between England and France for supremacy in America ended, and control of formerly French territory—including the Alabama-Coushatta homeland—passed to the English. When English administrative officials and settlers began arriving in the Fort Toulouse area, substantial numbers of Indians in this region began moving westward. In this movement they followed their French friends to Louisiana, where they expected better treatment from the Spanish. According to Charles Martin Thompson,[qv] chief of the Alabama-Coushattas from 1928 to 1935, it is unlikely that the Indians moved in a mass exodus; rather, they probably traveled in family or clan groups and left Alabama sporadically after 1763. Thompson also stated that they most likely traveled down the Alabama River to avoid the country of the Choctaws, their bitter enemies in western Alabama, Mississippi, and eastern Louisiana. One small group attempted to detour by the Tombigbee River but was driven back by the Choctaws. After descending the Alabama River to Mobile, the Alabamas and Coushattas probably used a well-known protected route along the coasts of Alabama and Mississippi, across lakes Pontchartrain and Maurepas, up the Amite River, and finally through the Iberville or Bayou Manchac to a spot on the Mississippi River about fourteen miles below Baton Rouge. After entering Louisiana about 1766 the mainstream of Alabama and Coushatta movement was westward across the southern part of the future state of Louisiana. However, small groups of both tribes established villages along the Red River and in other sections of Louisiana. In the early nineteenth century Governor William C. C. Claiborne reported that in 1766 a small group of Alabamas had settled near Opelousas but that a larger number had established homes on the Sabine River.

The Coushattas settled first on Bayou Chicot. In the 1780s some of them moved across the Sabine River and settled on the Trinity River in Texas. Others moved to a site on the Sabine River eighty miles southwest of Natchitoches, Louisiana. A small group of Coushattas settled on the Red River north of Natchitoches. The Pakana branch of the Muskogee or Creek Indian tribe had lived among the Alabamas and Coushattas in the Fort Toulouse area and migrated westward after 1763. In 1797 the Pakana Muskogees were located on the Calcasieu River about fifty miles southeast of the Coushatta village on the Sabine River.

In the 1780s Alabamas and Coushattas began moving across the Sabine River into Spanish Texas.[qv] There they found a welcome, since the Spanish considered Texas the outer cordon standing guard against first the French and then, after 1803, the Americans. In 1800 Napoleon attempted to reestablish the French empire in America. Three years later he sold Louisiana to the United States. Immediately after the Louisiana Purchase, the United States began to pursue a policy of friendly relations with the Indians in the new territory. On February 4, 1804, Edward Turner was given a commission for the District of Natchitoches. A few months later he informed Governor Claiborne that certain Indians in the vicinity had visited him and said the Spaniards had given them presents. They now wished the same from the Americans. Turner recommended the establishment of American factories at Natchitoches to lure the Indians' allegiance away from Spain. From the Spanish point of view, maintenance of the Texas defense line depended substantially upon the loyal service of friendly Indian tribes between the Trinity and Sabine rivers. Only about thirty cavalrymen, operating from Nacogdoches, were usually available to patrol the long border between Texas and Louisiana as well as the Old San Antonio Road and the Atascosito Road[qqv] into the Texas interior. Indians were needed to assist the Spanish regulars. Accordingly, Spain appropriated large sums of money to buy clothing, medals, guns, axes, knives, and other items for the Indians. These gifts were presented to Indians who visited Nacogdoches, the Spanish headquarters in East Texas.

In 1805 Dr. John Sibley[qv] was asked to serve as United States agent to keep the Indians in the vicinity of Natchitoches friendly toward the American government. He advocated alliances with the Indians and, like Turner, the establishment of an Indian factory at Natchitoches to divert Indian trade from the Spanish factory at Nacogdoches. Sibley made advantageous trade arrangements for the Indians and also distributed various types of gifts among them. His trading post was a popular gathering point for Indians in the area. There the Alabamas and Coushattas expressed loyalty to the Americans and received gifts. Then, at the first opportunity, they would travel to Nacogdoches for Spanish gifts and friendship. Both tribes probably understood that the Spanish and the Americans were engaged in a tug-of-war for their loyalty, and they capitalized on the opportunities intrinsic to this conflict. Soon, however, strained relations developed between the Indians and the white population of Louisiana. Each group accused the other of murdering members of its community. Representatives of the white population asked for the assistance of the militia, but Louisiana governor Claiborne refused this request. Instead, he called for a calm approach and took steps to avoid war.

Meanwhile, Alabamas and Coushattas had been moving into the Big Thicket region of Spanish Texas since the 1780s. There they found an awesome junglelike wilderness that, early observers said, covered most of the area between the Sabine and Brazos rivers. Travel through much of this region was so difficult that the Spanish skirted the northern edge of the Big Thicket when they laid out the road from Nacogdoches to San Antonio. The Atascosito Road provided an alternate route into Texas along the southern boundary of this wilderness. For the incoming Alabamas and Coushattas, this unique natural region was an excellent hunting and gathering area with an abundant food supply that supported many kinds of animals, birds, and fish. It was a barrier to prospective settlers. The Indian newcomers developed a material culture adapted to the characteristics of the Big Thicket, where they could be relatively free from Spanish or other interference.

The earliest Alabama hunting camps, *rancherías,* and villages were located along Attoyac Bayou, the Angelina River, and the Neches River. In 1830 the Alabamas lived in three communities in what is now northwestern Tyler County. The largest and most prominent of these was Peach Tree Village,[qv] located about two miles north of the site of present Chester. The Alabama Trace and the Coushatta Trace[qqv] passed through this village, and it was the northern terminus of the Long King Trace.[qv] Fenced-In Village[qv] ranked second in importance among the Alabama tribal settlements in the Big Thicket. It was located on the Liberty–Nacogdoches Road about five miles southeast of Peach Tree Village in northwestern Tyler County. Another Alabama community, Cane Island Village,[qv] was between Peach Tree Village and Fort Terán on the Neches River, about twenty-two miles northwest of the site of present Woodville. In 1830 about 600 Coushattas lived in three communities on or near the Trinity River. The Upper Coushatta Village (Battise Village[qv]) was located where the Coushatta Trace crossed the Trinity in what is now San Jacinto County, on the opposite side of the River from the future site of Onalaska, Polk County. The site is now under Lake Livingston.[qv] Long King's Village,[qv] the Middle Coushatta Village, was located at the confluence of Tempe Creek and Long King Creek, approximately two miles north of the site of Lake Livingston dam on the Trinity River. In the Lower Coushatta Village lived Colita,[qv] one of the best-known Indian leaders in East Texas, who succeeded Long King[qv] as principal chief of the Coushattas. Colita's Village[qv] was located on the Logan league in a great bend of the Trinity River—the "Shirt-tail Bend," as the steamboat sailors named it—now in San Jacinto County. Typically, an Alabama-Coushatta village was actually a community in which cabins were located in a succession of neighborhoods scattered for miles through the woods and along streams and connected by a network of trails. Cabins were usually grouped in family or clan units, with adequate land around each cabin for cultivating vegetables and growing fruit trees. Near the center of each community was a square used for a variety of governmental, social, entertainment, and religious activities. Alabamas and Coushattas relied primarily upon hunting, gathering, fishing, and vegetable cultivation for subsistence. The search for food was continuous, and members of these tribes used their trails and water routes extensively to obtain food. Both tribes prospered. In 1809 the combined population of Alabamas and Coushattas within seventy miles of Nacogdoches totaled approximately 1,650.

To facilitate land travel through their wilderness territory, the Alabamas and Coushattas developed a remarkable network of trails. These traces were usually laid as straight as practical between villages or other terminals. In many instances, they followed ridges between the drainage basins of streams, thus avoiding major water crossings. The proximity to streams made fresh water available. The density of most of the Big Thicket underscored the importance of this network: travel through the region was impractical except along the Alabama and Coushatta trails. It is ironic that these trails expedited the penetration of white settlers into this region and thus contributed to the later deterioration of the Alabama-Coushatta culture. Moreover, fieldnotes of the earliest land grants now in Polk County and several adjoining counties show that most of the original white settlers in the area selected homesites along the Indian trails.

During the early decades of the nineteenth century, Antone[qv] served as principal chief of the Alabamas, and Long King served in the same capacity for the Coushattas. Before the Alabama-Coushatta tribal council was organized in the 1930s, most governmental affairs were in the hands of the principal chief. His duties included serving as tribal spokesman, representing the tribe at meetings and functions, serving as moral leader, settling disputes, keeping tribal records including deeds to land, leading religious and educational activities, assigning land to individuals, directing hunts, calling meetings, throwing out balls to begin ballgames, and directing dances.

Both tribes preferred to remain at peace with their neighbors, but proved to be effective warriors when forced to fight. For many years the Alabamas and Coushattas defended their territory in Alabama, especially against the Choctaws, and their record indicates that they readily fought any enemy when necessary. John Sibley mentioned that Alabamas and Coushattas had participated in raids against the Osages, had taken Osage scalps, and had returned horses the Osages had stolen from the Caddos. Jean Louis Berlandier[qv] wrote in 1830 that hunting and farming were principal occupations of the Alabamas, but that they "can be just as warlike as their neighbors." Coushattas participated in the Mexican war of independence[qv] in 1812–13; their bravery and skill were mentioned by several chroniclers of the fighting around San Antonio in this rebellion against Spain. Stephen F. Austin,[qv] in the administration of his Texas colony, was aware of the Alabamas' and Coushattas' military capabilities, and his plans for campaigns against the Karankawa Indians and the Nacogdoches-area Fredonians usually included use of these two tribes. Gen. Sam Houston[qv] also planned to utilize the fighting ability of the Alabamas and Coushattas in the Texas Revolution.[qv] Early in 1836 Houston's army was retreating eastward across Texas, pursued by the Mexican army under Santa Anna. Many Texas settlers fled toward the Sabine River in this "Runaway Scrape."[qv] As the revolutionary army[qv] marched toward San Jacinto, Houston sent a delegation to ask the Alabamas and Coushattas for assistance. The tribes could provide about 250 warriors, and this group was the only noncommitted fighting force with any chance to arrive at San Jacinto in time to participate in the impending battle. The delegation dispatched by General Houston to negotiate for the services of the Alabamas and Coushattas arrived at Long King's Village several days before the battle of San Jacinto.[qv] The delegation brought a message from Houston and tried to persuade the Indians to join the army. While the discussions were proceeding, the battle of San Jacinto was fought, and the services of the Indians were no longer needed by the Texas army. Although the Alabamas and Coushattas did not participate militarily in the war, they were generous in their efforts to feed and care for settlers who passed through their villages in the Runaway Scrape. The Coushattas, however, did not entirely escape the turbulence of the 1836–39 period. In 1839 a Comanche raiding party approached the Long King Village from the north. Coushattas met the Comanches in the valley of Long King Creek and, in a fiercely fought battle, defeated the invaders, who were forced to retreat.

After Texas won independence in 1836, the government of the republic confronted a multitude of problems, including formulating an Indian policy. President Houston's plans for the Indian population provided for peace, friendship, trade, and frontier protection. Mirabeau B. Lamar,[qv] who succeeded Houston as president, adopted a program that included exterminating the hostile tribes and removing friendly tribes from the republic or moving them to reservations in Texas. It is remarkable that Lamar's harsh policy was not applied to the Alabamas and Coushattas. While all other East Texas tribes were removed, Lamar expressed friendship toward these two tribes, requested white settlers in the Trinity River area to respect their rights, and appointed an agent to assist them in their relations with their neighbors. Furthermore, in 1840—during Lamar's administration—the Republic of Texas Congress granted each of these two tribes two leagues of land. When surveyors came to survey the land, the Alabamas, thinking the grant was for white settlers, departed for other homesites, leaving their hogs, cattle, and 200 acres of fenced land suitable for cultivation. The Coushattas fared no better. One league of their land included Colita's Village, and the other included the Battise Village. The two leagues were surveyed and the fieldnotes were filed, but the grants never became effective; white settlers had already claimed the land.

After leaving Fenced-In Village, the Alabamas drifted southward and formed a settlement near the junction of Big and Little Cypress creeks. Next, they lived briefly at a site on Woods Creek called Rock Village.[qv] On October 29, 1853, Chief Antone, the tribal subchiefs, and prominent citizens of Polk County presented a petition to the Texas legislature requesting land for a reservation. It was approved, and the state of Texas purchased 1,110.7 acres of land for the Alabama Indian reservation. About 500 tribe members settled on this land during the winter of 1854–55. In 1855 the Texas legislature appropriated funds to purchase 640 acres for the Coushattas. Because suitable open land was no longer available in Polk County, however, this grant remained only a scrap of paper. With the permission of the Alabamas, most of the Coushattas settled on the Alabamas' reservation in 1859. When the state attempted to move the Polk County Indians to the Lower Brazos Reserve in 1858, Indian Agent James Barclay[qv] rode across Texas on horseback with a delegation of Alabamas and Coushattas to inspect the new reservation. The Lower Brazos Reserve was a barren, dreary land compared to the forested hills of their Polk County reservation. The Indian leaders told Barclay that they did not want to move from East Texas.

The Polk County Indians played only a minor role in the Civil War.[qv] John Scott,[qv] later chief of the Alabama-Coushattas, and nineteen members of his tribe were sworn into Confederate service on April 11, 1862. After serving briefly in Company G, Twenty-fourth Texas Cavalry, at Arkansas Post, they returned home and were organized by Capt. William H. Beazley[qv] into a cavalry company unattached to any regiment. In December 1864 this company listed 132 men on its roster and was part of the Sixth Brigade, Second Texas Infantry.[qv] The primary job of this new organization was to construct and operate flat-bottom boats for transporting farm produce to the Confederate forces along the Gulf Coast. Beazley's cavalrymen built most of their scows at Magnolia, a Trinity River port in Anderson County. Each boat, manned by an Indian crew, moved slowly downriver, stopping at plantation landings to pick up produce and other supplies requisitioned by Confederate authorities. At Liberty the boatmen delivered the boats and supplies to Confederate officials. To return upriver after each trip, the Indian cavalrymen-sailors rode horses driven to Liberty by their sons. Through no fault of their own, the Polk County Indians did not fight as a group in any battles of the war. In helping to move key military supplies, however, they contributed to the success of Confederate forces along the Texas Gulf Coast. Texas governors Francis R. Lubbock and Pendleton Murrah[qqv] commented favorably on the service of the Polk County Indians, and the state legislature provided funds to pay the salary of an agent for them from 1861 to 1865.

After 1865, however, the Indians had a home but little else. Few could speak English effectively, and few could find jobs. The state government was busy with other matters, primarily with problems of Reconstruction.[qv] A great tide of settlers sweeping west brought bitter fighting between whites and such warlike tribes as the Apaches, Comanches, and Sioux. One result was the development of a negative attitude among the settlers toward most Indians, and it was difficult to arouse public sympathy for the Polk County Indians. In 1866 Texas governor James W. Throckmorton[qv] proposed in vain that the United States government assume guardianship of the Indians in Polk County. During the administration of Edmund J. Davis,[qv] another effort was made to give the Indians federal protection, and in 1870 they were placed under military jurisdiction. Capt. Samuel M. Whitside, commander of the federal Military Post of Livingston, reported that the Polk County Indians needed an agent for their protection and volunteered to serve in the role until other arrangements could be made. The 1870s brought rapid deterioration in the Alabama-Coushatta culture. The influx of white settlers, the clearing of forests, and the plowing of farmland nearly destroyed the hunting, fishing, and gathering practices of the Indians, who were forced either to rely primarily on farming their limited, worn-out reservation lands or to seek employment outside the reservation. In February 1873 a bill was introduced in the United States House of Representatives to remove the Alabama, Coushatta, and Pakana Muskogee Indians from Texas to the Creek Nation in Oklahoma. The bill required that the proposed removal be approved by the Polk County Indians. There is no record that the proposal was approved by them, however, and the secretary of the interior recommended against passage of the bill. In 1876 the Alabamas discovered that they did not have title to 263 acres they had been occupying as part of their reservation. This tract had been surveyed for them in 1854, but the surveyor failed to file the necessary fieldnotes with the General Land Office.[qv] The tract was included subsequently in a grant of land to the International–Great Northern Railroad, although the Alabamas continued to occupy the area. The Polk County Indians' fortunes continued to decline, and neither the national government nor the state of Texas seemed willing to help. In the fourth quarter of the nineteenth century the indifference of the United States toward the Indians was so complete that the Bureau of Indian Affairs did not bother even to make a count of the Indian residents in Polk County. For many years the bureau simply reported the same total number of Indians—290—in the county. The state government made no move to help. The Alabamas and Coushattas reached the lowest point of their history in 1879, when the state abolished the post of agent for them.

After 1880 the picture began to brighten. This period was marked by three factors that had a vast influence on the Alabamas, Coushattas, and Pakana Muskogees. The first was construction of a Houston–Shreveport railroad that passed through Polk County. The Houston, East and West Texas Railroad reached Polk County in 1881 and opened the gate for development of the lumber industry.[qv] Many of the Indians soon became expert in lumbering jobs. As sawmills spread through the Big Thicket, so did opportunities for employment; many Indian families had steady cash incomes for the first time in their history. Job opportunities in the timber industry became increasingly important in subsequent years. Even more important was the coming of Christianity and education. The first Presbyterian mission was established on the Alabama-Coushatta reservation in Polk County in 1881, and since that time the church has played a major role in the lives of these Indians. Early missionaries were ministers, teachers, doctors, nurses, and friends, and their total impact is beyond measure.

The third prominent influence at this turning point was the work of J. C. Feagin, an attorney from Livingston who demonstrated his interest in the local Indians by maintaining a constant barrage of letters, reports, demands, and appeals on their behalf to public officials on every level of state and national government until his death in 1927. Feagin convinced Congressman Samuel Bronson Cooper[qv] that assistance should be provided for the Polk County Indians. Cooper introduced a bill in January 1896 and again in March 1897 to grant 25,000 acres to the Alabama-Coushattas. The commissioner of Indian affairs reported unfavorably on the bill both times, and it failed both times. In an act of April 1910 the Sixty-first Congress directed the Department of the Interior to investigate the status of the Alabama Indians in Texas. William Loker was appointed commissioner. In his report, Loker opined that the principal needs of these Indians were more land and a school with manual training. He added that if they had about 5,000 acres, they would be able to compete successfully with their white neighbors in farming and stock raising, and could become self-sufficient. Congress did nothing for the Polk County Indians in 1910, but Feagin had succeeded in bringing the Indians to the attention of the national government. His efforts constituted a successful opening phase of a campaign that involved, in subsequent years, the work of many other interested persons to improve dramatically the lot of the Alabama-Coushattas.

In the years after Loker's report, several requests for federal assistance for the Alabama-Coushatta Indians were submitted, a number of them by Feagin. Chief Clerk Hauke wrote the commissioner of Indian affairs suggesting the purchase of land, farm equipment, a school, a hospital, and a demonstration farm. In the next year Congress appropriated $8,000 for education and for investigation about whether to purchase land for the Alabama-Coushattas. In a report to Secretary of the Interior Franklin K. Lane of September 1918, Inspector James McLaughlin recommended an appropriation of $100,000 for the purchase of lands for the Alabama-Coushattas. In 1928 Clem Fain, Jr., of Livingston was appointed Texas agent for the Alabama-Coushattas, and he continued the campaign to focus public attention on them. Early in 1928 he accompanied principal chief Charles Martin Thompson and second chief McConnico Battise to Washington to appeal for assistance. This campaign was successful: in June 1928 Congress appropriated $40,000 for the Alabama-Coushattas. Of this amount, $29,000 was used for the purchase of 3,071 acres of land adjoining the original reservation, and the remainder was spent primarily for horses, cattle, hogs, and livestock feed. The deed for this additional land was issued to the Alabama and Coushatta tribes, and the name "Alabama-Coushatta" has been used since 1928 as the official title of the enlarged reservation. In 1929 the state of Texas appropriated $47,000 for the construction of a gymnasium, a hospital, a home for the reservation administrator, and twenty-five cottages.

In a report to the commissioner of Indian affairs in 1931, special commissioner Roy Nash recommended that Alabama-Coushatta affairs be left to the state of Texas. The state Board of Control[qv] served as the supervising board until September 1, 1950, when the Board for Texas State Hospitals and Special Schools[qv] was given the administration of all state institutions and agencies classed as eleemosynary. From 1929 to July 1, 1955, trusteeship of the Alabama-Coushatta reservation was in the hands of the federal government. In June 1934 Congress passed what has been termed the Indian Reorganization Act, which authorized Indian tribes to organize for their welfare, as individual tribes or with other tribes living on the same reservation. Specifically, the act gave the tribes the right to incorporate under a federal charter, which was to become effective when ratified by a majority vote of the adult Indians living on a reservation. The Alabama and Coushatta Indians were organized under the act as a single tribe with both a constitution and charter. The constitution and by-laws for the corporation were approved on August 19, 1938, and the charter was ratified by the Alabama-Coushattas on October 17, 1939. By means of a quitclaim deed effective July 1, 1955, the federal government relinquished the trusteeship of the Alabama-Coushatta land and other assets, and the state of Texas assumed full responsibility. The state's trusteeship of the Alabama-Coushattas continued until August 1987, when the state withdrew as trustee and the federal government assumed full responsibility for the Polk County Indians.

The governing body under the Alabama-Coushatta constitution and by-laws is the Tribal Council, composed of seven members elected by tribe members. The chief of the Alabama-Coushatta Tribe is an advisory member and votes only to break a tie. The officers of the Tribal Council are chairman, vice chairman, secretary, and treasurer. All are selected by the Tribal Council from its own membership at the first meeting of the newly elected council.

The Alabama-Coushattas passed other milestones in 1924, when American Indians became citizens; in 1934, when the Polk County Indians formed a school district; in World War II,[qv] when forty-seven tribe members served in the armed forces (Indians had not been allowed to serve in World War I[qv]); in 1948, when the Texas attorney general confirmed the voting rights of the Alabama-Coushattas; in 1963, when the state allocated $40,000 to finance a museum, a restaurant, and an arts and crafts shop on the reservation; in 1970, when construction began on new brick homes as a Mutual Help Housing Project administered by the Department of Housing and Urban Development; in 1975, when a Multipurpose Community Center was built to house the tribal kindergarten program, adult education, library, youth activities, counseling, vocational training, and recreational activities; in 1988, when the Tribal Council contracted for health care from the Indian Health Service of the Department of Health and Human Services and the Bureau of Indian Affairs began providing social and economic programs on the reservation, especially adult vocational training and scholarships; in 1989, when the Chief Kina (Robert Fulton Battise[qv]) Medical Center was dedicated; and in 1994, when ground was broken for the large, multipurpose Alabama-Coushatta Cultural Center.

BIBLIOGRAPHY: Frederick Webb Hodge, ed., *Handbook of American Indians North of Mexico* (2 vols., Washington: GPO, 1907, 1910; rpt., New York: Pageant, 1959). Howard N. Martin, "Texas Redskins in Confederate Gray," *Southwestern Historical Quarterly* 70 (April 1967). Anna Muckleroy, "The Indian Policy of the Republic of Texas," *Southwestern Historical Quarterly* 25–26 (April 1922–January 1923). William W. Newcomb, *The Indians of Texas* (Austin: University of Texas Press, 1961). Alvin W. Roseler, The Indian Policy of Sam Houston (M.A. thesis, St. Mary's University, 1949). Harriet Smither, "The Alabama Indians of Texas," *Southwestern Historical Quarterly* 36 (October 1932). John R. Swanton, *Indian Tribes of the Lower Mississippi Valley and Adjacent Coast of the Gulf of Mexico* (Washington: GPO, 1911). Mary Donaldson Wade, *The Alabama Indians of East Texas* (Livingston, Texas: *Polk County Enterprise*, 1931; rev. ed. 1936). Dorman H. Winfrey and James M. Day, eds., *Texas Indian Papers* (4 vols., Austin: Texas State Library, 1959–61; rpt., 5 vols., Austin: Pemberton Press, 1966). Dudley Goodall Wooten, ed., *A Comprehensive History of Texas* (2 vols., Dallas: Scarff, 1898; rpt., Austin: Texas State Historical Association, 1986). *Howard N. Martin*

ALABAMA CREEK. Alabama Creek rises two miles south of Centerville in east central Trinity County (at 31°10′ N, 95°02′ W) and flows southeast for twelve miles to its mouth on the Neches River, two miles northeast of Alabama (at 31°09′ N, 94°51′ W). The stream is intermittent in its upper reaches. The surrounding terrain is flat to rolling and surfaced by clay and sandy loam that supports conifers, water-tolerant hardwoods, and grasses.

ALABAMA TRACE. The Alabama Trace was an Indian trail that extended from a point on the Old San Antonio Road[qv] about three miles west of what is now San Augustine, Texas, to the Lower Coushatta Village (Colita's Village[qv]) on the Trinity River in what is now San Jacinto County. The route of this trail is shown on Stephen F. Austin's[qv] memorandum for a map of Texas in 1827. Surveyors' passing calls in field notes for original land surveys in selected East Texas counties confirm the location of this trail, which passed through four Alabama Indian village sites in the Texas counties of Angelina, Tyler, and Polk. From the Old San Antonio Road this trail went southwest through an Alabama village on the Angelina River near the junction of this river and Attoyac Bayou, and then crossed the Neches River at the Spanish-designated "pass to the south," where Fort Terán was constructed in 1831. The next important locations on the Alabama Trace were the Cane Island Village[qv] and the Peachtree Village[qv] of the Alabamas in northwestern Tyler County, after which the trail crossed into eastern Polk County and went south along the east side of Bear Creek, passed through an abandoned Alabama village on what is now the Alabama-Coushatta Indian Reservation, went through a prominent Indian campground at the junction of Big Sandy Creek and Bear Creek, and from this point went on south to terminate at the Colita Village of the Coushatta Indians on the Trinity River. The Alabama Trace was used extensively not only by Indians but also by illegal immigrants and contraband traders who entered Spanish Texas[qv] from Louisiana on the Old San Antonio Road. They found that they could avoid Spanish military patrols operating from Nacogdoches by using out-of-the-way trails such as the Alabama Trace to bypass Nacogdoches. During the Republic of Texas[qv] period, Samuel T. Belt began operating a ferry across the Neches River at the Fort Terán site. Stagecoaches traveling from Houston to San Augustine went via Montgomery, Swartwout, Livingston, and the Fort Terán site, and then used a segment of the Alabama Trace for the remainder of the trip to San Augustine.

BIBLIOGRAPHY: Ellen Marshall, Some Phases of the Establishment and Development of Roads in Texas, 1718–1845 (M.A. thesis, University of Texas, 1934). Howard N. Martin, "Polk County Indians: Alabamas, Coushattas, Pakana Muskogees," *East Texas Historical Journal* 17 (1979). Stephen F. Austin's Memorandum for a Map of Texas, 1827 (S. F. Austin Collection, Barker Texas History Center, University of Texas at Austin). *Howard N. Martin*

ALACHOME INDIANS. In the late seventeenth and early eighteenth centuries the Alachome Indians, apparently Coahuiltecans, ranged from northeastern Coahuila northward across the Rio Grande into the adjoining part of Texas south of the Edwards Plateau. The Alachomes are not to be confused with the Chomes; both names appear in the same document.

BIBLIOGRAPHY: Mattie Alice Hatcher, trans., *The Expedition of Don Domingo Terán de los Ríos into Texas*, ed. Paul J. Foik (Preliminary Studies of the Texas Catholic Historical Society 2.1 [1932]). Frederick Webb Hodge, ed., *Handbook of American Indians North of Mexico* (2 vols., Washington: GPO, 1907, 1910; rpt., New York: Pageant, 1959). *Thomas N. Campbell*

ALAMÁN Y ESCALADA, LUCAS (1792–1853). Lucas Alamán y Escalada, politician and historian, son of Juan Vicente Alamán and María Ignacia Escalada, was born in Guanajuato, Mexico, in 1792. He obtained his primary education in his hometown, the wealthiest mining site of the colonial period. When still a young man, he narrowly escaped the Alhondiga de Granaditas massacre during the Mexican war of independence[qv] against Spain in 1810. It was an experience he never forgot, and he condemned the "tumultuous" character of that early movement. He went to Mexico City and attended the Real Seminario de Minería; later he studied at Freyburg, Göttingen, and Paris. When the Constitution of 1812 was reestablished in Spain, he was elected as representative from Mexico to the Cours (parliament) in the metropolis. There, he participated in an attempt to divide the empire into three kingdoms, each one headed by a Spanish prince. Witnessing, however, the lack of interest of the peninsular politicians, he became convinced of the need for independence; therefore, he went back to Mexico and served in some of the newly established administrations. Alamán was minister of foreign affairs in the provisional government established after the failure of Agustín de Iturbide's[qv] empire, and then with the first Republican president, Guadalupe Victoria. He resigned, however, a few months later over political differences within the cabinet. In the following years he occupied himself as agent of the British-financed Compañía Unida de Minas.

In 1830 Alamán returned to politics, once again as minister of foreign affairs. Through tight control this administration straightened out the finances of the federal government. In order to promote the development of the textile industry through government loans, Alamán established the Banco de Avío. In combination with these efforts he reacted towards Manuel de Mier y Terán's[qv] warnings about foreigners in Texas by trying to direct the Texas cotton crop to Mexican factories. He established a trade network with Galveston and other Texas ports. Other sections of this law, commonly known as the Law of April 6, 1830,[qv] prohibited any further immigration from the United States into Texas. The bill favored colonization by other nationalities and proved controversial among the colonists. Finally, this restriction was derogated once Alamán was out of office in 1833. In the administration of 1830–32 he signed a treaty of limits with the United States, which ratified the borders established in the Adams-Onís Treaty[qv] in 1819. Although it is probable that Alamán was involved in the centralization of Mexico in 1835–36, no evidence as yet proves it. In 1840, as member of the Council of Government, and clearly reacting to British advice, he recommended the recognition of Texas independence in order to have a stable border and to avoid any further conflict.

Five years later, as the annexation[qv] of Texas was completed, Alamán participated in a monarchist conspiracy that could have brought European support to Mexico, both to fight American expansionism and to stop the internal political turmoil. Though he and the Spanish minister, Salvador Bermúdez de Castro, preferred a pacific solution to the Texas question, the military leader that they chose opted for a bellicose demonstration against the United States. Indeed, Mariano Paredes y Arrillaga accused President José Joaquín de Herrera of being a traitor for trying to avoid a "glorious and necessary war." Thus, their plot became intrinsically connected to an open confrontation with the northern neighbor, as their newspaper *El Tiempo* expressed it. As it turned out, once the military defeats of the Mexican army began, Bermúdez decided to conclude the monarchist project; as a result of this Mexico fought—and lost—the war with the United States alone. With a strong mood of defeat, between 1849 and 1852,

Alamán published his famous five-volume *Historia de México,* which condemned the early movement for independence of Miguel Hidalgo y Costilla[qv] and José María Morelos y Pavón. It was also a petition for help from European powers to ensure Mexico's survival.

Alamán was a strong advocate of the Spanish inheritance of Mexican society, as he argued extensively in his *Disertaciones* (1844). With José Fernando Ramírez, he profusely annotated William Prescott's *Conquest of Mexico* and became a member of various academic institutions, among them the Sociedad Mexicana de Geografía y Estadística and the Massachusetts Historical Society. He also reorganized the Archivo General de la Nación in Mexico. His complex thought clearly exemplifies the serious contradictions of Mexican monarchists. Even though they favored the economic development of the country through industrialization, they opposed the redistribution of church property. Thus, they specifically called for a prince who would maintain the social and economic privileges of the Catholic Church.[qv] As Maximilian's adventure proved, these expectations were misleading and unreal, since no European ruler was willing to grant such privileged status to the clergy. Alamán died on June 2, 1853.

BIBLIOGRAPHY: Jaime Delgado, *La monarquía en México, 1845–1847* (Mexico City: Porrúa, 1990). Charles A. Hale, *Mexican Liberalism in the Age of Mora, 1821–1853* (New Haven: Yale University Press, 1968). Miguel Soto, *La conspiración monárquica en México, 1845–1846* (Tepepan, Xochimilco: Eosa, 1988). José C. Valades, *Alamán: Estadista e Historiador* (Mexico City: Universidad Nacional Autónoma de México, 1977).

Miguel Soto

ALAMEDA, TEXAS. Alameda was a rural community six miles northwest of Desdemona in eastern Eastland County. The settlement was started by William A. Mansker in 1859 and called Mansker's Lake. Other early settlers were James P. and Ike Schmick, J. S. Stuart, and M. T. Duvall. Mail came from Stephenville. There was a mill at the nearby Allen Ranch, just east of Mansker's Lake. The first school in the settlement was built in 1874; a post office named Alameda operated from 1876 until 1882. A general store, a blacksmith shop, and a Woodmen's hall were built near the lake. It is not likely that the community ever reached the population of ninety-nine claimed in 1860. A map of 1936 shows only four houses near the cemetery and a school on State Highway 571. Later maps indicate only a community center and the cemetery, but on still later maps the settlement is not shown.

John G. Johnson

ALAMITA, TEXAS. Alamita, a small Mexican settlement at the crossing of the La Bahía Road and Alamita Creek in Karnes County, was the predecessor of old Helena, which was established in 1852. The name Alamita, meaning "little cottonwood," was also applied to nearby Alamita Crossing on the San Antonio River and to Alamita Lodge No. 200, A. F. and A. M., which was originally chartered in Helena in 1857 and moved to Karnes City in 1925 (*see* HELENA, TEXAS).

BIBLIOGRAPHY: Thomas H. Puckett, *Alamita Lodge No. 200, A.F. & A.M.* (Karnes City, 1957). Robert H. Thonhoff, History of Karnes County (M.A. thesis, Southwest Texas State College, 1963).

Robert H. Thonhoff

ALAMITO, TEXAS. Alamito is on Farm Road 169 at Alamito Creek, three miles north of Plata in eastern Presidio County. The community was established in 1870, when John Davis settled there with several Hispanic families in his employ. For protection against Indian attack Davis built a large adobe[qv] house with a corral for horses and mules attached to the back and a chapel for religious services when a priest was available. He raised horses and cattle on the open range, cultivated a large peach orchard, and made peach brandy. His employees' families raised corn, wheat, beans, and other vegetables, which Davis freighted to Fort Stockton for sale. With a good supply of food and peach brandy and with plenty of water and shade from the creek, the settlement was a favorite stop for travelers. Alamito had a post office from 1884 until 1892. The community operated a school as early as 1908, when Selena Hord was the teacher. In the 1911 Presidio County scholastic census Alamito's Precinct No. 2 reported fifty-seven students from a total population of 392.

BIBLIOGRAPHY: John Ernest Gregg, History of Presidio County (M.A. thesis, University of Texas, 1933). Carlysle Graham Raht, *The Romance of the Davis Mountains and Big Bend Country* (Odessa, Texas: Rahtbooks, 1963).

Julia Cauble Smith

ALAMITO CREEK (Presidio County). Alamito Creek, an intermittent stream, rises at the confluence of two forks three miles north of Marfa in northern Presidio County (at 30°22′ N, 104°02′ W) and runs southwest for eighty-two miles to its mouth on the Rio Grande, five miles southeast of Presidio (at 29°31′ N, 104°17′ W). The North Fork of Alamito Creek rises on the southeastern flank of Paradise Mountain three miles north of Bloys Camp Meeting in southern Jeff Davis County (at 30°36′ N, 104°08′ W) and runs southeast for nineteen miles. The South Fork rises a mile southeast of Bloys Camp Meeting in southern Jeff Davis County (at 30°32′ N, 104°08′ W) and runs southeast for fifteen miles. The surrounding flat terrain with local shallow depressions is surfaced by clay and sandy loams that support water-tolerant hardwoods, conifers, scrub brush, and grasses. The expedition of Antonio de Espejo[qv] is thought to have camped beside the stream in 1583.

____ (Webb County). Alamito Creek, an intermittent stream, rises in a tank fifteen miles north of Oilton in southeastern Webb County (at 27°43′ N, 99°02′ W) and runs nine miles north to its mouth on Salado Creek, twenty-three miles east of Callaghan (at 27°52′ N, 99°02′ W). The surrounding low-rolling and flat terrain has local shallow depressions and a surface of clay and sandy loams; grasses, mesquite, chaparral, and water-tolerant hardwoods predominate in nearby vegetation.

ALAMO. San Antonio de Valero Mission[qv] (originally referred to as San Antonio de Padua) was authorized by the viceroy of Mexico in 1716. Fray Antonio de Olivares,[qv] who brought with him Indian converts and the records from San Francisco Solano Mission near San Juan Bautista[qv] on the Rio Grande, established the mission at the site of present San Antonio in 1718 and named it San Antonio de Valero in honor of Saint Anthony de Padua and the Duke of Valero, the Spanish viceroy. The present site was selected in 1724; the cornerstone of the chapel was laid on May 8, 1744. Founded for the purpose of Christianizing and educating the Indians, the mission later became a fortress and was the scene of many conflicts prior to the siege of 1836. Its activity as a mission began to wane after 1765, and it was abandoned in 1793, the archives being removed to nearby San Fernando Church.

In 1803 the Second Flying Company of San Carlos de Parras,[qv] a company of Spanish soldiers from Álamo de Parras, Coahuila, Mexico, occupied the abandoned mission, using its buildings as barracks for a number of years. From this association probably originated the name Alamo. According to some historians, the name was derived from a grove of cottonwood trees growing on the banks of the acequia, *álamo* being the Spanish word for "cottonwood." The Alamo was occupied by Mexican forces almost continuously from 1803 to December 1835, when the fortress under Gen. Martín Perfecto de Cos[qv] was surrendered to Texan forces.

On February 23, 1836, Col. William B. Travis[qv] entered the Alamo with a force that later totaled approximately 187 men. Mexican forces under the command of Gen. Antonio López de Santa Anna[qv] totaled approximately 5,000 men. The siege of the Alamo lasted thirteen days and was climaxed on March 6 with a complete loss of all the combatant Texans (*see* ALAMO, BATTLE OF THE).

After the fall of the Alamo, the building was practically in ruins, but no attempt was made at that time to restore it. The Republic of Texas,[qv] on January 13, 1841, passed an act returning the church of

Ruins of the Church of the Alamo, San Antonio de Bexar, *by Edward Everett, 1847. Pen and ink, watercolor, and gouache on paper. 6″ × 9⅜″. Courtesy Amon Carter Museum, Fort Worth, Texas; gift of Mrs. Anne Burnett Tandy in memory of her father, Thomas Loyd Burnett, 1870–1938. Edward Everett, noted for his ability as a scientific draftsman, made several views of the Alamo, both from the inside and outside, which were later lithographed and distributed widely in a congressional publication.*

the Alamo to the Catholic Church.qv After Texas was annexed to the United States, it was declared that the Alamo was property of the United States, and in 1848 the United States government took over the building and grounds and until the Civil Warqv used them for quartermaster purposes. For some time the Alamo was claimed by the city of San Antonio, the Catholic Church, and the United States government. The United States government finally leased the property from the Catholic Church and made some improvements. During the Civil War the Confederates used the building, but after the close of the war the United States government again took over and used it until 1876.

Under an act of April 23, 1883, Texas purchased from the church the Alamo property and placed the Alamo in the custody of the city of San Antonio on condition that the city should care for the building and pay a custodian for that purpose. This system continued until January 25, 1905, when the Texas legislature passed a resolution ordering the governor to purchase that part of the old Alamo fortress occupied by a business concern. It was further ordered that the governor should deliver the property thus acquired, with the property then owned by the state (the chapel of the Alamo), to the Daughters of the Republic of Texas.qv

A controversy over custody of the Alamo developed between the Daughters of the Republic of Texas and the De Zavala chapter of that organization at San Antonio, and for a time there was a controversy between the Daughters of the Republic of Texas and Governor O. B. Colquittqv concerning restoration. Several appropriations for funds to improve the Alamo have been made, the largest being in connection with the celebration of the Texas Centennial.qv In the 1990s the Alamo was in custody of the Daughters of the Republic of Texas and remained the center of disputes over the custody, presentation, and boundaries of the site.

BIBLIOGRAPHY: Frederick Charles Chabot, *The Alamo: Mission, Fortress and Shrine* (San Antonio: Lenke, 1935). Anne A. Fox, *Archaeological Observations at Alamo Plaza* (Center for Archaeological Research, University of Texas at San Antonio, 1977). Anna B. Story, The Alamo from Its Founding to 1937 (M.A. thesis, University of Texas, 1938). Henry Ryder Taylor, *History of the Alamo and of Local Franciscan Missions* (San Antonio: N. Tengg, 1908).

Amelia W. Williams

ALAMO, BATTLE OF THE. The siege and the final assault on the Alamoqv in 1836 constitute the most celebrated military engagement in Texas history. The battle was conspicuous for the large number of illustrious personalities among its combatants. These included Tennessee congressman David Crockett,qv entrepreneur-adventurer James Bowie,qv and Mexican president Antonio López de Santa Anna.qv Although not nationally famous at the time, William Barret Travisqv achieved lasting distinction as commander at the Alamo. For many Americans and most Texans, the battle has become a symbol of patriotic sacrifice. Traditional popular depictions, including novels, stage plays, and motion pictures, emphasize legendary aspects that often obscure the historical event.

To understand the real battle, one must appreciate its strategic context in the Texas Revolution.qv In December 1835 a Federalist army of Texan (or Texian,[qv] as they were called) immigrants, American volunteers, and their Tejano[qv] allies had captured the town from a Centralist force during the siege of Bexar.[qv] With that victory, a majority of the Texan volunteers of the "Army of the People" left service and returned to their families. Nevertheless, many officials of the provisional government[qv] feared the Centralists would mount a spring offensive. Two main roads led into Texas from the Mexican interior. The first was the Atascosito Road,[qv] which stretched from Matamoros on the Rio Grande northward through San Patricio, Goliad, Victoria, and finally into the heart of Austin's colony. The second was the Old San Antonio Road,[qv] a *camino real* that crossed the Rio Grande at Paso de Francia (the San Antonio Crossing[qv]) and wound northeastward through San Antonio de Béxar, Bastrop, Nacogdoches, San Augustine, and across the Sabine River into Louisiana. Two forts blocked these approaches into Texas: Presidio La Bahía (Nuestra Señora de Loreto Presidio) at Goliad and the Alamo at San Antonio. Each installation functioned as a frontier picket guard, ready to alert the Texas settlements of an enemy advance. James Clinton Neill[qv] received command of the Bexar garrison. Some ninety miles to the southeast, James Walker Fannin, Jr.,[qv] subsequently took command at Goliad. Most Texan settlers had returned to the comforts of home and hearth. Consequently, newly arrived American volunteers—some of whom counted their time in Texas by the week—constituted a majority of the troops at Goliad and Bexar. Both Neill and Fannin determined to stall the Centralists on the frontier. Still, they labored under no delusions. Without speedy reinforcements, neither the Alamo nor Presidio La Bahía could long withstand a siege.

At Bexar were some twenty-one artillery pieces of various caliber. Because of his artillery experience and his regular army commission, Neill was a logical choice to command. Throughout January he did his best to fortify the mission fort on the outskirts of town. Maj. Green B. Jameson,[qv] chief engineer at the Alamo, installed most of the cannons on the walls. Jameson boasted to Gen. Sam Houston[qv] that if the Centralists stormed the Alamo, the defenders could "whip 10 to 1 with our artillery." Such predictions proved excessively optimistic. Far from the bulk of Texas settlements, the Bexar garrison suffered from a lack of even basic provender. On January 14 Neill wrote Houston that his people were in a "torpid, defenseless condition." That day he dispatched a grim message to the provisional government: "Unless we are reinforced and victualled, we must become an easy prey to the enemy, in case of an attack."

By January 17, Houston had begun to question the wisdom of maintaining Neill' s garrison at Bexar. On that date he informed Governor Henry Smith[qv] that Col. James Bowie and a company of volunteers had left for San Antonio. Many have cited this letter as proof that Houston ordered the Alamo abandoned. Yet, Houston's words reveal the truth of the matter:

> I have ordered the fortifications in the town of Bexar to be demolished, and, *if you should think well of it, I will remove all the cannon and other munitions of war to Gonzales and Copano, blow up the Alamo and abandon the place, as it will be impossible to keep up the Station with volunteers, the sooner I can be authorized the better it will be for the country* [italics added].

Houston may have wanted to raze the Alamo, but he was clearly requesting Smith's consent. Ultimately, Smith did not "think well of it" and refused to authorize Houston' s proposal.

On January 19, Bowie rode into the Alamo compound, and what he saw impressed him. As a result of much hard work, the mission had begun to look like a fort. Neill, who well knew the consequences of leaving the *camino real* unguarded, convinced Bowie that the Alamo was the only post between the enemy and Anglo settlements. Neill's arguments and his leadership electrified Bowie. "I cannot eulogize the conduct & character of Col. Neill too highly," he wrote Smith; "no other man in the army could have kept men at this post, under the neglect they have experienced." On February 2 Bowie wrote Smith that he and Neill had resolved to "die in these ditches" before they would surrender the post. The letter confirmed Smith's understanding of controlling factors. He had concluded that Bexar must not go undefended. Rejecting Houston's advice, Smith prepared to funnel additional troops and provisions to San Antonio. In brief, Houston had asked for permission to abandon the post. Smith considered his request. The answer was no.

Colonel Neill had complained that "for want of horses," he could not even "send out a small spy company." If the Alamo were to function as an early-warning station, Neill had to have outriders. Now fully committed to bolstering the Bexar garrison, Smith directed Lt. Col. William B. Travis to take his "Legion of Cavalry" and report to Neill. Only thirty horsemen responded to the summons. Travis pleaded with Governor Smith to reconsider: "I am unwilling to risk my reputation (which is ever dear to a soldier) by going off into the enemy' s country with such little means, and with them so badly equipped." Travis threatened to resign his commission, but Smith ignored these histrionics. At length, Travis obeyed orders and dutifully made his way toward Bexar with his thirty troopers. Reinforcements began to trickle into Bexar. On February 3, Travis and his cavalry contingent reached the Alamo. The twenty-six-year-old cavalry officer had traveled to his new duty station under duress. Yet, like Bowie, he soon became committed to Neill and the fort, which he began to describe as the "key to Texas." About February 8, David Crockett arrived with a group of American volunteers.

On February 14 Neill departed on furlough. He learned that illness had struck his family and that they desperately needed him back in Bastrop. While on leave, Neill labored to raise funds for his Bexar garrison. He promised that he would resume command when circumstances permitted, certainly within twenty days, and left Travis in charge as acting post commander. Neill had not intended to slight the older and more experienced Bowie, but Travis, like Neill, held a regular army commission. For all of his notoriety, Bowie was still just a volunteer colonel. The Alamo's volunteers, accustomed to electing their officers, resented having this regular officer foisted upon them. Neill had been in command since January; his maturity, judgment, and proven ability had won the respect of both regulars and volunteers. Travis, however, was unknown. The volunteers insisted on an election, and their acting commander complied with their wishes. The garrison cast its votes along party lines: the regulars voted for Travis, the volunteers for Bowie. In a letter to Smith, Travis claimed that the election and Bowie's subsequent conduct had placed him in an "awkward situation." The night following the balloting, Bowie dismayed Bexar residents with his besotted carousal. He tore through the town, confiscating private property and releasing convicted felons from jail. Appalled by this disorderly exhibition, Travis assured the governor that he refused to assume responsibility "for the drunken irregularities of any man"—not even the redoubtable Jim Bowie. Fortunately, this affront to Travis's sense of propriety did not produce a lasting breach between the two commanders. They struck a compromise: Bowie would command the volunteers, Travis the regulars. Both would co-sign all orders and correspondence until Neill's return. There was no more time for personality differences. They had learned that Santa Anna's Centralist army had reached the Rio Grande. Though Travis did not believe that Santa Anna could reach Bexar until March 15, his arrival on February 23 convinced him otherwise. As Texans gathered in the Alamo, Travis dispatched a hastily scribbled missive to Gonzales: "The enemy in large force is in sight. We want men and provisions. Send them to us. We have 150 men and are determined to defend the garrison to the last." Travis and Bowie understood that the Alamo could not hold without additional forces. Their fate now rested with the General Council[qv] in San Felipe, Fannin at Goliad, and other Texan volunteers who might rush to assist the beleaguered Bexar garrison.

Santa Anna sent a courier to demand that the Alamo surrender. Travis replied with a cannonball. There could be no mistaking such a concise response. Centralist artillerymen set about knocking down the walls. Once the heavy pounding reduced the walls, the garrison would have to surrender in the face of overwhelming odds. Bottled up inside the fort, the Texans had only one hope—that reinforcements would break the siege.

On February 24 Travis assumed full command when Bowie fell victim to a mysterious malady variously described as "hasty consumption" or "typhoid pneumonia." As commander, Travis wrote his letter addressed to the "people of Texas & all Americans in the world," in which he recounted that the fort had "sustained a continual Bombardment and cannonade for 24 hours." He pledged that he would "never surrender or retreat" and swore "Victory or Death." The predominant message, however, was an entreaty for help: "I call on you in the name of Liberty, of patriotism & everything dear to the American character, to come to our aid, with all dispatch." On March 1, thirty-two troops attached to Lt. George C. Kimbell's[qv] Gonzales ranging company made their way through the enemy cordon and into the Alamo. Travis was grateful for any reinforcements, but knew he needed more. On March 3 he reported to the convention at Washington-on-the-Brazos that he had lost faith in Colonel Fannin. "I look to the colonies alone for aid; unless it arrives soon, I shall have to fight the enemy on his own terms." He grew increasingly bitter that his fellow Texans seemed deaf to his appeals. In a letter to a friend, Travis revealed his frustration: "If my countrymen do not rally to my relief, I am determined to perish in the defense of this place, and my bones shall reproach my country for her neglect."

On March 5, day twelve of the siege, Santa Anna announced an assault for the following day. This sudden declaration stunned his officers. The enemy's walls were crumbling. No Texan relief column had appeared. When the provisions ran out, surrender would remain the rebels' only option. There was simply no valid military justification for the costly attack on a stronghold bristling with cannons. But ignoring these reasonable objections, Santa Anna stubbornly insisted on storming the Alamo. Around 5:00 A.M. on Sunday, March 6, he hurled his columns at the battered walls from four directions.

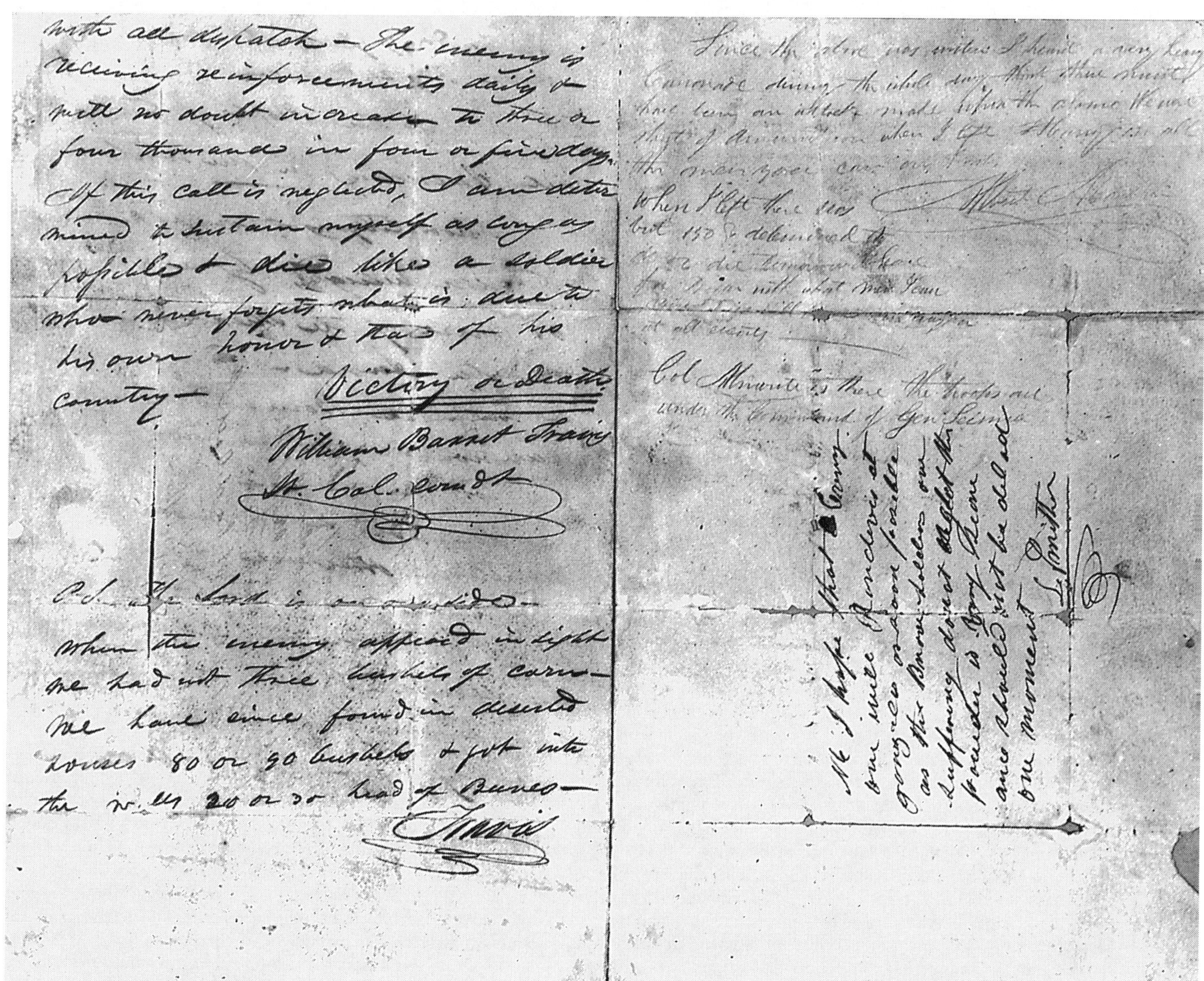

with all dispatch — The enemy is receiving reinforcements daily & will no doubt increase to three or four thousand in four or five days. If this call is neglected, I am determined to sustain myself as long as possible & die like a soldier who never forgets what is due to his own honor & that of his country —

Victory or Death.

William Barret Travis
Lt. Col. comdt

P.S. The Lord is on our side — When the enemy appeared in sight we had not three bushels of corn — We have since found in deserted houses 80 or 90 bushels & got into the walls 20 or 30 head of Beeves —

Travis

Since the above was written I heard a very heavy Cannonade during the whole day [illegible] there must have been an attack made upon the alamo We were short of Ammunition when I left [illegible] all the men you can [illegible]

Albert Martin

When I left there was but 150 determined to [illegible] die tomorrow [illegible] for Bejar with what men I can [illegible] at all events.

Col Almonte is there the troops are under the Command of Gen Seisma

N.B. I hope that Every one will Randeves at gonzales as soon poseble as the Brave Soldiers are suffering do not neglect the powder is very Scarce and should not be delad one moment

L. Smither

"To the People of Texas & All Americans in the World . . ." Letter written by William Barret Travis, February 24, 1836. Original in TSL. Photograph courtesy HRHRC. Captain Albert Martin saddled up and carried the message to the town of Gonzales, the only town that sent reinforcements to the Alamo. At Gonzales the message went into the hands of another courier, who carried it to San Felipe. From there it went on to Galveston and eventually New Orleans and the eastern seaboard. On the right page, one can still read another postscript the second courier, Launcelot Smithers, scribbled on it: "I hope that Every one will Randeves at Gonzales as soon as poseble, as the Brave Soldiers are suffering. do not neglect the powder. is very scarce and should not be delad one moment."

Battle of Bexar—Heroism of Col. Crockett.

Battle of Bexar—Heroism of Col. Crockett, *anonymous, 1837. Wood engraving. From* Davy Crockett's Almanack of Wild Sports in the West, Life in the Backwoods, and Sketches of Texas, *Vol. 1, No. 3 (Nashville: Published by the heirs of Col. Crockett, [1836?]). Courtesy Huntington Library, San Marino, California.*

This woodcut appeared in one of the popular "Crockett almanacs," essentially the equivalent of modern comic books with lunar charts attached. According to the text, Crockett fought with four pistols, a dagger, and a rifle in his final standoff at the Alamo and killed seventeen men in his final moments.

Texan gunners stood by their artillery. As about 1,800 assault troops advanced into range, canister ripped through their ranks. Staggered by the concentrated cannon and rifle fire, the Mexican soldiers halted, reformed, and drove forward. Soon they were past the defensive perimeter. Travis, among the first to die, fell on the north bastion. Abandoning the walls, defenders withdrew to the dim rooms of the Long Barracks. There some of the bloodiest hand-to-hand fighting occurred. Bowie, too ravaged by illness to rise from his bed, found no pity. The chapel fell last. By dawn the Centralists had carried the works. The assault had lasted no more than ninety minutes. As many as seven defenders survived the battle, but Santa Anna ordered their summary execution. Many historians count Crockett as a member of that hapless contingent, an assertion that still provokes debate in some circles. By eight o'clock every Alamo fighting man lay dead. Currently, 189 defenders appear on the official list, but ongoing research may increase the final tally to as many as 257.

Though Santa Anna had his victory, the common soldiers paid the price as his officers had anticipated. Accounts vary, but best estimates place the number of Mexicans killed and wounded at about 600. Mexican officers led several noncombatant women, children, and slaves from the smoldering compound (*see* ALAMO NONCOMBATANTS). Santa Anna treated enemy women and children with admirable gallantry. He pledged safe passage through his lines and provided each with a blanket and two dollars. The most famous of these survivors were Susanna W. Dickinson, widow of Capt. Almaron Dickinson, and their infant daughter, Angelina Dickinson.[qqv] After the battle, Mrs. Dickinson traveled to Gonzales. There, she reported the fall of the post to General Houston. The sad intelligence precipitated a wild exodus of Texan settlers called the Runaway Scrape.[qv]

What of real military value did the defenders' heroic stand accomplish? Some movies and other works of fiction pretend that Houston used the time to raise an army. During most of the siege, however, he was at the Convention of 1836[qv] at Washington-on-the-Brazos and not with the army. The delay did, on the other hand, allow promulgation of independence, formation of a revolutionary government, and the drafting of a constitution. If Santa Anna had struck the Texan settlements immediately, he might have disrupted the proceedings and driven all insurgents across the Sabine River. The men of the Alamo were valiant soldiers, but no evidence supports the notion—advanced in the more perfervid versions—that they "joined together in an immortal pact to give their lives that the spark of freedom might blaze into a roaring flame." Governor Smith and the General Council ordered Neill, Bowie, and Travis to hold the fort until support arrived. Despite all the "victory or death" hyperbole, they were not suicidal. Throughout the thirteen-day siege, Travis never stopped calling on the government for the promised support. The defenders of the Alamo willingly placed themselves in harm's way to protect their country. Death was a risk they accepted, but it was never their aim. Torn by internal discord, the provisional government could not deliver on its promise to provide relief, and Travis and his command paid the cost of that dereliction. As Travis predicted, his bones did reproach the factious politicos and the parade ground patriots for their neglect. Even stripped of chauvinistic exaggeration, however, the battle of the Alamo remains an inspiring moment in Texas history.

The sacrifice of Travis and his command animated the rest of Texas and kindled a righteous wrath that swept the Mexicans off the field at San Jacinto. Since 1836, Americans on battlefields over the globe have responded to the exhortation, "Remember the Alamo!" *See also* REVOLUTIONARY ARMY.

BIBLIOGRAPHY: Stephen L. Hardin, *Texian Iliad: A Military History of the Texas Revolution* (Austin: University of Texas Press, 1994). John H. Jenkins, ed., *The Papers of the Texas Revolution, 1835–1836* (10 vols., Austin: Presidial Press, 1973). Walter Lord, *A Time to Stand* (New York: Harper, 1961; 2d ed., Lincoln: University of Nebraska Press, 1978).

Stephen L. Hardin

ALAMO, TEXAS. Alamo is on U.S. Highway 83 nine miles southeast of McAllen in southern Hidalgo County. Between 1902 and 1909 Peter Ebenezer Blalock and George T. Hawkins accumulated 32,000 acres of land surrounding the townsite and extending fifteen miles north of the Rio Grande. By 1908 they had laid out the town, built shipping pens, and named the railroad depot Ebenezer. The site became known as Camp Ebenezer when a community of prospective buyers housed in temporary dwellings developed. In 1909 the land was sold to the organizers of the Alamo Land and Sugar Company, which moved the town from Camp Ebenezer to higher, better-drained ground. The Alamo Townsite Company was formed by C. H. Swallow and Rentfro B. Creager,[qv] who promoted the site to prospective settlers. In 1909 a post office was established. The town was reportedly first called Forum and later Swallow. It may have been subsequently named for the mission in San Antonio. In 1919 the Alamo Progressive Club was formed; it later became the chamber of commerce. The First State Bank of Alamo opened in 1920. After incorporation in 1924 the town grew steadily, and its population was reported at 200 in 1925. In 1936 Alamo had 1,018 residents and fifty businesses. During the 1940s and 1950s the town served mainly as a shipping point for vegetables and citrus fruits. The population was 1,944 in 1940 and 3,017 in 1950. In 1990 it was 8,210.

BIBLIOGRAPHY: T. R. Fehrenbach, Mario Lorenzo Sanchez, and Aura Nell Ranzau, *A Shared Experience: The History, Architecture, and Historical Designations of the Lower Rio Grande Heritage Corridor* (Austin: Los Caminos del Rio Heritage Project and the Texas Historical Commission, 1991). Winnie Maddox, History of the Donna Community (M.A. thesis, Texas College of Arts and Industries, 1955). Marker Files, Texas Historical Commission, Austin.

Alicia A. Garza

ALAMO ALTO, TEXAS. Alamo Alto is on State Highway 20 some 4½ miles southeast of Tornillo and thirty-five miles southeast of El Paso in southeastern El Paso County. The settlement was founded before 1931, when three businesses were reported there. Its estimated population grew from ten in the mid-1930s to twenty-five in the mid-1940s. The community consisted of a few scattered dwellings on maps in the early 1970s. In 1990 the population was twenty-five.

Martin Donell Kohout

ALAMO ARROYO. Alamo Arroyo, through which an intermittent stream flows, begins fifteen miles northeast of Fort Hancock in southwestern Hudspeth County (at 31°28′ N, 105°42′ W) and runs southwest for twenty miles to disembogue into the Rio Grande 1½ miles southeast of Acala (at 31°19′ N, 105°54′ W). Three dams have been constructed along the arroyo to trap water for irrigation. The surrounding flat to rolling terrain is surfaced by sandy and clay loams that support scrub brush, cacti, and grasses.

ALAMO BEACH, TEXAS. Alamo Beach, a community two miles southeast of Port Lavaca and just north of the junction of Farm roads 2717 and 2760 in Calhoun County, is bound on the east by Lavaca Bay. The settlement was established during the first decade of the twentieth century and had a post office from 1907 to 1915. About 1915 residents erected a seaside pavilion to attract tourists. That year the community had a telephone connection, a dairy, a real estate and life insurance business, and an estimated population of fifty-five. Although an Alamo Beach school district existed, there is no evidence that a school building was ever built at the site. By the school year 1935–36 the nine students of the district were attending schools in neighboring communities. In the 1970s the site was marked by a few scattered dwellings. In 1990 the community was listed in the *Texas Almanac*,[qv] but without population figures.

BIBLIOGRAPHY: Calhoun County Historical Commission, *Shifting Sands of Calhoun County, Texas* (Port Lavaca, Texas, ca. 1980).

Stephen L. Hardin

ALAMO CEMENT COMPANY. The Alamo Cement Company was chartered in 1880 after Englishman William Loyd discovered what he believed to be a natural cement rock near San Antonio. With the help of chemist George H. Kalteyer, who confirmed that the rock's lime and clay could produce Portland cement, Loyd organized a group of investors to form the Alamo Portland and Roman Cement Company, the first Portland cement plant west of the Mississippi and one of the earliest in the United States. The original plant was powered by steam engine and ground ten barrels of cement daily.

The company diversified its enterprise with lime burning and the sale of building stone and entered the sidewalk construction business to help it survive. It obtained the patent rights for the process by which sidewalk blocks were cut into sections to accommodate expansion and contraction in changing temperatures from the original inventor. In 1881 the company changed its name to Alamo Cement Company. Its principal product was known by the brand name Alamo. Construction of the Texas state Capitol[qv] and the Driskill Hotel,[qv] as well as many other buildings in the state, used cement from this plant, and Kalteyer later organized the Buckeye Portland Cement Company in Ohio to produce what was known as "artificial stone" before use of the term "concrete." After Kalteyer's death in 1897, Charles Baumberger became company president and led the firm's further expansion. In 1908 the company was reorganized under the name San Antonio Portland Cement Company and, after material at its original site was exhausted, the plant was moved to a place that came to be known as Cementville. The area became Baumberger Plaza in 1944, and in 1990 the smokestack and kilns of the original plant remained on the site. The quarry became the Japanese sunken gardens at Brackenridge Park, in San Antonio.

Baumberger was succeeded by his son, C. Baumberger, Jr., who served until 1968. In 1979 Robert Koch of Vigier Cement a Swiss firm, and Sandro Buzzi of Presa, Limited, in Italy purchased the firm and changed its name back to Alamo Cement Company. In 1977 the original plant site was placed on the National Register of Historic Places, and in 1980 the new owners constructed a modernized plant with updated equipment. In keeping with Charles Baumberger's will, assets of his estate, including the proceeds from the sale of the company (1979), were used to set up a trust fund to provide college scholarships to San Antonio high school students. Between 1979 and 1993 the estate generated over $20 million and sent 1,802 students to college.

BIBLIOGRAPHY: *Grinstead's Graphic*, October 1922. Sid Levine, "One Hundred Years with Alamo Cement," *Pit and Quarry*, December 1982. San Antonio *Express*, June 20, 1973. *Men of Affairs of San Antonio* (San Antonio Newspaper Artists' Association, 1912).

Diana J. Kleiner

ALAMO CENOTAPH. The Alamo Cenotaph, on Alamo Plaza in front of the Alamo[qv] in San Antonio, was erected in 1939 by the Texas Centennial[qv] Commission. The memorial stone of gray Georgia marble rests upon a slab base of pink Texas granite. The shaft rises sixty feet from its base and is forty feet long and twelve feet wide. The theme of the monument is the Spirit of Sacrifice, represented on the main (south) face of the shaft by an idealistic figure rising twenty-three feet from the long sloping capstone emblematic of the tomb. This monolithic slab twenty feet long bears appropriate ornamental tracery. The east and west ledges are decorated with background panels of eight figures in low relief depicting the men who died in the Alamo. Before the east panel stand the portrait statues of James Bowie and James B. Bonham;[qqv] before the west panel, the portrait statues of William B. Travis and David Crockett.[qqv] On the north side appears a feminine figure symbolizing the state of Texas, holding the shields of Texas and the United States. Pompeo Coppini[qv] conceived and executed the sculptural parts of the monument, which was designed by Adams and Adams, architects, with Frank T. Drought as consulting engineer. Dr. Amelia W. Williams[qv] compiled for the inscription the list of men who died in the battle of the Alamo.[qv]

BIBLIOGRAPHY: Harold Schoen, comp., *Monuments Erected by the State of Texas to Commemorate the Centenary of Texas Independence* (Austin: Commission of Control for Texas Centennial Celebrations, 1938).

ALAMO DE CESARIO CREEK. Alamo de Cesario Creek rises just south of Bandera Mesa in eastern Presidio County (at 29°33′ N, 103°50′ W) and runs east for fourteen miles to its mouth on Terlingua Creek, north of Agua Fria Mountain in western Brewster County (at 29°34′ N, 103°46′ W). The surrounding desert mountain terrain, canyonland of volcanic rock, and moderate to high slopes of clay and limestone are surfaced by generally light reddish-brown to brown sand, clay loam, and rough stony soils that support sparse grasses, cacti, scrubby desert conifers, and oaks. The creek's name comes from a legend about a Mexican girl named Cesaria, who was captured by Mescalero Apaches and taken to their camp at Agua Fria. There they tied her to an *alamo*, or cottonwood, tree. Friends and relatives of Cesaria followed the trail of her captors and rescued her, but the tree and the area became known as Alamo de Cesaria, or Cesaria's Cottonwood.

BIBLIOGRAPHY: Virginia Madison and Hallie Stillwell, *How Come It's Called That? Place Names in the Big Bend Country* (Albuquerque: University of New Mexico Press, 1958).

ALAMOCITOS CREEK. Alamocitos (or Alamocita) Creek rises in three prongs thirteen miles northeast of Adrian in Oldham County (at 35°26′ N, 102°36′ W) and flows north sixteen miles to its mouth on the Canadian River (at 35°32′ N, 102°35′ W). It runs over flat to rolling terrain with local escarpments and mostly deep, fine, sandy loam that supports brush, grasses, and some hardwoods. The Spanish name means "little cottonwoods," a name perhaps conferred by *pastores* in the 1870s. The creek occupies a prominent place in Panhandle[qv] ranching history. In the fall of 1878 the British owners of the New Zealand Sheep Company[qv] established their initial headquarters on Alamocitos Creek a few miles south of the Canadian River. The site later became the location of the second headquarters of the LS Ranch[qv] after W. M. D. Lee[qv] bought it in 1882. In 1885 it became the nucleus of the Alamocitos Division of the XIT Ranch,[qv] in 1902 part of the Matador Land and Cattle Company,[qv] and subsequently the Alamocitos Cattle Corporation, owned and operated by Clarence Sharbauer, Jr., after 1952.

BIBLIOGRAPHY: Oldham County Historical Commission, *Oldham County* (Dallas: Taylor, 1981). Pauline D. and R. L. Robertson, *Cowman's Country: Fifty Frontier Ranches in the Texas Panhandle, 1876–1887* (Amarillo: Paramount, 1981).

ALAMO CREEK. Alamo Creek, also known as Willow Creek, rises five miles northeast of the Maverick Ranger Station and just south of the park road between the ranger station and Panther Junction in Big Bend National Park,[qv] southwestern Brewster County (at 29°19′ N, 103°25′ W), and runs southwest for nineteen miles to its mouth on the Rio Grande, two miles northwest of Castolon (at 29°09′ N, 103°33′ W). It flows beneath steep to gentle slopes surfaced by variable soils that support scrub brush and grasses.

ALAMO HEIGHTS, TEXAS. Alamo Heights, off U.S. Highway 281 five miles northeast of the center of San Antonio in north central Bexar County, has always been economically and socially a part of San Antonio. The area below the headwaters of the San Antonio River in Brackenridge Park in Alamo Heights was an Indian campground and haven for many explorers, travelers, and troops; visitors included álvar Núñez Cabeza de Vaca, Domingo Terán de los Ríos, and Fray Damián Massanet.[qqv] Massanet celebrated Mass at the spot in 1691 and changed the name from Yanaguana to San Antonio de Padua. In 1718, with the founding of San Antonio de Béxar, the use of the headwaters was guaranteed to the missionaries and early settlers under the rules of the Recapitulation of the Indies. In 1731 the Canary Islanders[qv] were granted similar rights to the use of the river.

In 1836 the land known as Alamo Heights was included as public land in the original survey of the city of San Antonio, but in December 1837 a city ordinance provided for sale of public lands at auction to provide funds for city improvements. Despite controversy over the proposed sale, the site of Alamo Heights was purchased by James R. Sweet.[qv] After several sales the property was bought by Mrs. Isabel Brackenridge in 1869. In 1897 her son, George W. Brackenridge,[qv] sold the family estate, Fernridge, and 200 acres of land containing the springs of the San Antonio River to the Sisters of Charity of the Incarnate Word.[qv] Incarnate Word College is on the boundary line between San Antonio and Alamo Heights, and Fernridge is preserved by the sisters as a museum building.

Alamo Heights was also the location of the "Arsenal Lot," donated by San Antonio to the federal government as an arsenal site in 1852 and returned to the donor in 1859. Charles Anderson[qv] bought the site in 1860, established a ranch, and built a home that subsequently became the Argyle Hotel.[qv] William McLane bought the property in 1861. In 1893 his son, Hiram H. McLane,[qv] sold the area to the Alamo Heights Land and Improvement Company. Progress was slow until 1909, when Clifton George took over the company and began a program of expansion that included an adequate school building for the growing community.

With the completion of the Olmos Dam, which furnishes water for San Antonio, and subsequent impetus to home building, San Antonio developed annexation schemes to bring Alamo Heights into the city government; but, following two mass meetings, in 1922 Alamo Heights was voted an independent municipality. Voters also approved an independent school system.

Located in Alamo Heights are Texas Military Institute,[qv] a public swimming pool, a post office, and a shopping center; the McNay Art Institute[qv] adjoins the municipality on the north. Adjacent to the Argyle Hotel is Cathedral House, headquarters of the Episcopal Diocese of West Texas, with conference center and chapel housed in the Spanish-style former Harry Halff residence and offices in a contemporary stone building. On Cathedral House grounds are the headwaters of the San Antonio River, described in diaries of Mary Adams Maverick[qv] in 1839 and a visiting Englishman, James Freemantle, in 1863. Newspapers that have been published in Alamo Heights include the Alamo Heights *Herald* in the 1920s and the Alamo Heights *News*, from 1939 to the early 1960s. The population in 1950 was 7,950, 7,552 in 1960, and 6,933 in 1970. In 1990 Alamo Heights had a reported 6,502 residents. *Minnie B. Cameron*

ALAMO MONUMENTS. Two Alamo monuments and the Alamo Cenotaph[qv] have been dedicated to the defenders of the Alamo. The first monument, the work of an Englishman named William B. Nangle, was made in 1841 from stones of the Alamo at the suggestion of Col. Reuben M. Potter.[qv] It was ten feet high and consisted of a pyramid that rested upon a square pedestal ornamented with carved work and inscriptions. On two sides of the pedestal were escutcheons bearing the names of the men at the Alamo. For a number of years the monument was on display at various Texas cities and in New Orleans. On February 6, 1858, the Texas legislature passed an act providing for the purchase of this monument, which was placed in the vestibule of the old Capitol. After the Capitol fire in 1881, the ruins of the monument were acquired by the Daughters of the Republic of Texas[qv] and in 1950 were on display in the Old Land Office Building.[qv] In 1881 the Twenty-first Legislature appropriated funds for an Alamo monument to be erected on the grounds of the new Capitol.[qv] The monument, made from Texas granite, was built in 1891 by James S. Clark and Company of Louisville, Kentucky, and placed at the right of the main entrance of the Capitol. The foundation forms a floor nineteen feet square, which rises about two feet above the level of the ground. At each corner of this foundation is a three-foot-square marginal base. These bases support four massive polished pillars, seven feet high by two feet three inches square. These pillars in turn support arches that unite in a dome, upon which stands a typical soldier of early Texas. The whole structure is thirty-five feet six inches high. On the four columns are engraved the names of the heroes of the Alamo. Some forty names on this monument are inaccurate.

BIBLIOGRAPHY: C. W. Raines, "The Alamo Monument," *Quarterly of the Texas State Historical Association* 6 (April 1903). Vertical Files, Barker Texas History Center, University of Texas at Austin.

Amelia H. Williams

ALAMO NONCOMBATANTS. When the Mexican army appeared at San Antonio de Béxar on February 23, 1836, a number of civilian noncombatants retired to the dubious safety of the Alamo, along with the Texan forces of Lt. Col. William B. Travis.[qv] Some of these civilians remained in the Alamo during the entire siege. Most, but not all, survived the battle of March 6.

Some of the survivors are well known: Susanna and Angelina Dickinson, wife and daughter of Capt. Almaron Dickinson;[qqv] Ana Salazar Esparza and Enrique Esparza,[qv] wife and eldest son of Pvt. José María Esparza;[qv] Juana Navarro Alsbury, wife of Dr. Horace Alsbury,[qqv] who was away from the Alamo on a scouting mission; and Joe,[qv] Travis's slave, who fought in the battle but survived.

There were, however, a number of lesser known occupants of the Alamo during the siege and battle. Gertrudis Navarro (November 26, 1816–April 1895) was the sister of Juana Alsbury and the daughter of the second José Ángel Navarro[qv] and Concepción Cervantes. She and her sister were raised by the Veramendi family of San Antonio de Béxar and probably entered the Alamo under the protection of James Bowie,[qv] the Veramendis' son-in-law. Gertrudis survived the Alamo battle and married José Miguel Felipe Cantú on July 26, 1841. They had eight children. She lived the remainder of her life in San Antonio.

Alejo Pérez, Jr. (March 23, 1835–October 19, 1918), was the son of Juana Alsbury and her first husband, Alejo Pérez, Sr. He was brought into the Alamo by his mother and was seventeen days short of his first birthday at the time of the Alamo battle. He survived the battle and grew up in San Antonio, where he was later a policeman. On December 27, 1853, he married Antonia Rodríguez; they had four children. Alejo was still living in San Antonio in 1900. Some evidence indicates that he was married again, to Florenzia Valdez, at the age of eighty-one, on March 1, 1916. He died on October 19, 1918, probably the last survivor of the Alamo.

Manuel Esparza (October 19, 1830–1886) and Francisco Esparza (1833–July 1887) were the younger sons of Gregorio and Ana Salazar Esparza and were present during the entire siege and battle. On September 7, 1853, Manuel married Melchora Leal (January 4, 1834–February 13, 1922); they had eleven children. In the 1850s Manuel moved with his brothers Enrique and Francisco to Atascosa County, where they farmed and ranched. They also built the church of San Agustine. Manuel was described as being much like his brother Enrique. Both liked history and were Democrats. Francisco Esparza married Petra Zamora (1827–1924). They had five children. At the outbreak of the Civil War[qv] he left Atascosa County to serve in the Confederate Army. After the war he did not return to his family but settled in Tucson, Arizona. He remarried and had two children with his second wife.

María de Jesús Castro Esparza (January 11, 1826–1849) was the daughter of Ana Salazar Esparza and her first husband, Victor de Castro. She accompanied her mother and stepfather into the Alamo and survived the siege and battle. Some confusion has always surrounded this Alamo survivor. At least one newspaper reported that Ana Salazar Esparza brought an infant daughter into the Alamo, but there is no evidence that she and Gregorio ever had a daughter. There is further confusion since Enrique Esparza gave several newspaper interviews in his old age, in which he stated that three brothers, one an infant, entered the Alamo with his parents and half-sister. San Fernando de Béxar Cathedral[qv] records, however, indicate that the Esparza family had four children, one of whom was María de Jesús Esparza.

The family of Alamo defender José Toribio Losoya[qv] actually lived for a time within the Alamo compound. Toribio Losoya's mother, Concepción, his younger brother Juan, and his sister, Juana Francisca Melton, were present in the fort and survived the siege and battle. Juana Francisca Melton was the wife of the Alamo garrison's quartermaster, merchant Eliel Melton.[qv] Enrique Esparza later remembered that when he entered the Alamo, one of the first things he saw was Mrs. Melton drawing circles on the ground with an umbrella. The image remained vivid in his mind since he had seen very few umbrellas. He also remembered that after the Alamo battle and before the survivors were brought before Santa Anna, Mrs. Melton, through her brother Juan, asked Ana Esparza not to reveal to Santa Anna that she was married to an American. Mrs. Esparza told her not to be afraid.

A Victoriana de Salinas and her three small daughters survived the battle. Little is known of them, but Enrique Esparza remained acquainted with two of the girls in later life. Petra Gonzales, an old woman known as "Doña Petra" to Enrique Esparza, also survived the battle. She may have been an elderly relative of Ana Esparza, since both her paternal grandmother and her maternal grandfather were named Gonzales. Trinidad Saucedo, a twenty-seven-year-old former servant of the Veramendi family, was present during the siege, but left the fort before the final battle. Besides the identified survivors, there were also a number of unidentified slaves who lived through the battle. A number of the Alamo's defenders were slaveholders, and Joe, Travis's slave, reported that several blacks were in the fort.

The Alamo's noncombatants suffered casualties among their small number. Joe remembered a black woman killed attempting to cross the Alamo during the battle. Her body was found lying between two cannons. Enrique Esparza stated that a young American boy, no older than he (eight to nine years) was shot down and killed right beside him, while the boy was drawing a blanket around his shoulders. Susanna Dickinson remembered that the two young sons of artilleryman Anthony Wolf,[qv] ages eleven and twelve, were bayonetted, along with their father, before her eyes.

BIBLIOGRAPHY: Files, Daughters of the Republic of Texas Library, San Antonio.

Bill Groneman

ALAMO RANCH RAID. Alamo Ranch was located between Alamito and Black Hills creeks, 5½ miles southeast of the Cienega Mountains in southern Presidio County. It was established by Victoriano Hernández, who settled preemption land on the so-called Chihuahua Trail (*see* CHIHUAHUA EXPEDITION) in 1874. Hernández built an adobe[qv] house of eight large rooms with thick walls, wooden floors, and heavy doors. He planted a large orchard and garden to feed his family, workers, and guests. Many celebrations and fiestas were held at Alamo Ranch over the years. The ranch was a hospitable stop on the route of traders and travelers. In February 1891 bandits attacked the ranch, wounded Hernández, and killed his grandson Oscar. The family buried Oscar at Alamo Ranch and erected a small chapel with a four-foot crucifix by the side of the grave. Presidio County provided funds for the prosecution of the bandits, but the names of the defendants and any verdict the court reached remained secret.

BIBLIOGRAPHY: Virginia Madison and Hallie Stillwell, *How Come It's Called That? Place Names in the Big Bend Country* (Albuquerque: University of New Mexico Press, 1958). Cecilia Thompson, *History of Marfa and Presidio County, 1535–1946* (2 vols., Austin: Nortex, 1985).
Julia Cauble Smith

ALAMOSA CREEK (Motley County). Alamosa Creek, once known as Alamo Creek, rises just north of Farm Road 97 and twenty miles northwest of Matador in northwestern Motley County (at 34°14′ N, 101°01′ W) and runs northeast for eight miles to its mouth on Quitaque Creek, six miles northeast of Flomot (at 34°15′ N, 100°53′ W). It crosses flat to gently sloping terrain surfaced by quartz sand and silt that support scrub brush and grasses.

____ (Oldham County). Alamosa Creek is made up of three intermittent branches that all rise in east central Oldham County north and east of Vega. West Alamosa Creek flows from its source fifteen miles northeast of Vega (at 35°25′ N, 102°30′ W) to its junction with Middle Alamosa Creek (at 35°29′ N, 102°25′ W). Middle Alamosa Creek rises four miles south of the head of West Alamosa Creek (at 35°15′ N, 102°30′ W) and flows twenty miles northeast to the point where the two streams join, four miles south of the Canadian River. East Alamosa Creek, the shortest of the streams, rises near Middle Alamosa Creek (at 30°24′ N, 102°23′ W) and parallels the latter for its last six or seven miles, then joins the main stream (at 35°30′ N, 102°21′ W) halfway between the junction of West and Middle Alamosa creeks and the mouth (at 35°31′ N, 102°21′ W) of the main creek on the Canadian River. The streams traverse an area of low hills and moderately steep slopes with densely dissected gullies. The soils are chiefly mud and sand that support mesquite, grasses, and some oaks. The third headquarters of the LS Ranch[qv] was located on the Alamosa in 1886; in 1905 this property was purchased and operated by the Landergin brothers.[qv] It later became the nucleus of the Mansfield Cattle Company.

ALAMO AND SAN JACINTO MONTHLY. The *Alamo and San Jacinto Monthly* was a literary magazine published in Georgetown and edited by students of Southwestern University. Two rival male literary and debating clubs, the Alamo and the San Jacinto, originated and sponsored the magazine in the later nineteenth century. The journal contained student musings on a variety of literary, historical, cultural, and political topics. It was edited by Jonathan L. Brooks in 1893.

BIBLIOGRAPHY: Clara Stearns Scarbrough, *Land of Good Water: A Williamson County History* (Georgetown, Texas: Williamson County Sun Publishers, 1973).
Mark Odintz

ALAMO VILLAGE. Alamo Village is six miles north of Brackettville on the Shahan Angus Ranch in Kinney County. This replica of an old Texas town was first a set for a Western movie on the battle of the Alamo,[qv] but it remains a tourist attraction. The idea for the complex was developed by James Tullis (Happy) Shahan after he was elected mayor of Brackettville in 1950. The town's economy had been ailing since the army deactivated Fort Clark in 1946. Shahan persuaded Paramount Studios to film *Arrowhead* at Brackettville in 1951. Two other movies followed before John Wayne filmed *The Alamo* on Shahan's ranch near Brackettville. From December 1957 to September 1959, when the filming of *The Alamo* was begun, the Batjac Company preproduction crew supervised a $12 million building program that involved up to 400 workmen at one time. Artisans from Mexico made adobe[qv] bricks as they were made three centuries ago. More than a million bricks were used to construct 200,000 square feet of permanent buildings. The Alamo replica was based on careful research that included obtaining plans sent to Spain by the Catholic priests who built the mission. There were no "false front" streets. Electrical and telephone wiring was concealed in more than ten miles of underground casing.

After production of *The Alamo* Shahan acquired the set, which houses a cantina and restaurant, a trading post, an Indian store, a church, a jail, a blacksmith shop, museums of western artifacts, and a gallery of celebrities who have performed on the dusty streets of this little village. Alamo Village is filled with antique tools and vehicles. A herd of longhorn cattle[qv] contributes to the Old West atmosphere. Although several movies, television shows, documentaries, and commercials have been made on the set since *The Alamo* was filmed, Alamo Village today operates primarily as a tourist attraction. From Memorial Day to Labor Day live entertainers are hired to perform country and western music, western melodramas, and stage shootouts. Horseback and stagecoach rides are available. The activity of the summer months culminates in the Labor Day Horse Races, which draw the largest annual crowds to Alamo Village. All of the buildings and facilities are open to the public year-round.

BIBLIOGRAPHY: Mike Blakely, "Alamo Village," *Texas Highways*, May 1985. New York *Times*, October 4, 1959. Vertical Files, Barker Texas History Center, University of Texas at Austin (Brackettville).
D. Shaw

ALANREED, TEXAS. Alanreed is on Interstate Highway 40 and U.S. Highway 66 in southern Gray County. In the early 1880s a group of farmers clearing timber from the basin of McClellan Creek selected the site, which was on the stage line from Mobeetie to Clarendon. By 1884 the Clarendon Land and Cattle Company began selling townsite lots. F. R. McCraken and R. P. Reeves were among the first settlers. In 1886 a post office called Eldridge was established six miles north of the present site of Alanreed. At various times the town was also called Springtown or Spring Tank, for a large spring-fed tank; Prairie Dog Town, for one located nearby; and Gouge Eye, for a saloon fight. The present townsite was laid out in 1900 by a surveyor for the Choctaw, Oklahoma and Texas Railroad. The town's present name was reputedly derived from the name of the contracting firm, Alan and Reed.

In 1901 the first school was built. In 1902 the post office was moved from Eldridge and renamed Alanreed. After the Rock Island line was completed in 1903 the town became a shipping point for cattle. G. E. Castleberry's land company sold parcels at $2.25 an acre. By 1904 Alanreed was the largest town in Gray County. In 1907 it had a bank, a hotel, a depot, Baptist and Methodist churches, a saloon, two grocery stores, a hardware store, a livery stable, and a blacksmith shop. Watermelons became a major crop; the town shipped an average of 500 cars annually. In 1912 a two-story school was built. By 1917 the town had telephone service and an estimated population of 250.

Like its neighbor McLean, Alanreed made several unsuccessful bids to be the county seat. The oil boom of the 1920s led to a temporary increase in population, but it also shifted development to other towns in the area. Although the population was estimated at 500 in 1927, by 1929 both the hotel and the bank had closed. In 1930 the Alanreed school was consolidated with three other area schools. In 1933 the number of residents was estimated at 150. By 1939 the population had grown to 200, and fifteen businesses were reported. In 1947 Alanreed reported eleven businesses and a population of 300. In the early 1960s the Alanreed school district merged with that of McLean, and a new school was built in 1964. The town reported a population of 200 and five businesses in 1967, but over the next decade both continued to decline. In 1977 the population was estimated at sixty, and no businesses were reported. In 1990 the population was still reported as sixty.

BIBLIOGRAPHY: *Gray County 50th Anniversary, 1902–1952: Souvenir Program* (Pampa, Texas: Pampa *Daily News,* 1952). Gray County History Book Committee, *Gray County Heritage* (Dallas: Taylor, 1985).
H. Allen Anderson

ALARCÓN, MARTÍN DE (?–?). Martín de Alarcón was a knight of the Order of Santiago, governor of Coahuila, governor of Texas, and founder of San Antonio, Texas. Before arriving in the Indies he had served in Oran (North Africa) and as a sailor in the royal navy. On May 31, 1691, Viceroy Conde de Galve appointed Alarcón *sargento mayor* of a company of militia in Guadalajara, and he later selected Don Martín as *alcalde mayor* and *capitán a guerra* of Jacona and Zamora, both now in Michoacán. On September 11, 1696, Viceroy Juan de Ortega y Montañez appointed Alarcón as *capitán a guerra* and protector of Indians in the locale of Mazapil. Subsequent viceroys continued to employ his services as an agent of pacification on the northern frontier of New Spain, especially in the environs of Saltillo. On December 9, 1716, Viceroy Marqués de Valero appointed Alarcón in Mexico City as commander of Presidio San Francisco de Coahuila and as governor of the province of Texas. As chief executive, Alarcón was to resupply Spaniards who had gone to Texas earlier in 1716 under the command of Domingo Ramón.[qv] In June 1717 Alarcón arrived at Saltillo, where he was delayed for several months while investigating the trading activities of Louis Juchereau de St. Denis.[qv] In April 1718 Alarcón crossed the Rio Grande with an entrada numbering ten families and seventy-two persons. On May 1, 1718, he assisted Father Antonio San Buenaventura y Olivares[qv] in the founding of San Antonio de Valero Mission. Four days later Alarcón founded San Antonio de Béxar Presidio. The families clustered around the presidio and mission formed the beginnings of Villa de Béxar, destined to become the most important town in Spanish Texas.[qv] Alarcón visited the six missions that had been set up in East Texas previously (in 1716 and 1717), completing his assignment on November 21, 1718. While in East Texas he confiscated a variety of illegal merchandise, all of French origin. Alarcón returned to San Antonio in January 1719 and from there on May 28 wrote Jean Baptiste Bénard de La Harpe,[qv] advising him to withdraw from Spanish territory. In the fall of 1719, Alarcón was relieved of his duties as governor of Texas. His record of merits and services to the Spanish crown was filed in Mexico City on January 18, 1721.

BIBLIOGRAPHY: Fray Francisco Céliz, *Diary of the Alarcón Expedition into Texas, 1718–1719,* trans. F. L. Hoffman (Los Angeles: Quivira Society, 1935; rpt., New York: Arno Press, 1967). Donald E. Chipman, *Spanish Texas, 1519–1821* (Austin: University of Texas Press, 1992). Fritz L. Hoffman, ed. and trans., "Mezquía Diary of the Alarcón Expedition into Texas, 1718," *Southwestern Historical Quarterly* 41 (April 1938). Robert S. Weddle, "San Juan Bautista: Mother of Texas Missions," *Southwestern Historical Quarterly* 71 (April 1968).
Donald E. Chipman

ALARM CREEK. Alarm Creek rises five miles southwest of Stephenville in central Erath County (at 32°12′ N, 98°18′ W) and runs southeast for thirteen miles to its mouth on the North Bosque River, four miles northeast of Alexander (at 32°05′ N, 98°09′ W). It crosses an area of steep slopes and benches, with an elevation of 1,200 to 1,300 feet and with a land surface of shallow clay loams that support juniper, live oak, mesquite, and grasses. The creek reportedly got its name when Maj. George B. Erath[qv] and a group of surveyors camped on it and promised to give an alarm to the settlers in case of an Indian raid.

ALAVEZ, FRANCITA (?–?). Francita Alavez, the "Angel of Goliad," accompanied Capt. Telesforo Alavez to Texas in March 1836. Her first name is variously given as Francita, Francisca, Panchita, or Pancheta, and her surname as Alavez, Alvárez, or Alevesco. Her real surname and place of birth are not known. Some writers claim that she was with Gen. José de Urrea's[qv] army at San Patricio, but this is highly unlikely since Captain Alavez came by ship from Matamoros to Copano Bay. Because Francita was with Captain Alavez in Texas, it was long assumed that she was his wife. However, research carried out in 1935 by Marjorie Rogers revealed that the army officer's legitimate wife was María Augustina de Pozo, who was abandoned by Alavez in 1834.

Francita was at Copano Bay when Maj. William P. Miller's[qv] Natchez volunteers were held prisoner there by General Urrea's troops. She noticed that the men were tightly bound with cords that restricted the circulation of blood in their arms. Taking pity on the men, she persuaded the Mexican soldiers to loosen their bonds and to give them food.

From Copano Bay she went with Alavez to Goliad and was there at the time of the Goliad Massacre.[qv] She is credited with persuading the officer in charge of the fortress not to execute Miller's men, who had been brought from Copano to Goliad. In addition, it is believed that Francita entered the fort the evening before the massacre and brought out several men and hid them, thereby saving their lives. Francita and Captain Alavez proceeded to Victoria, where she continued to aid the Texans held prisoner at Goliad by sending them messages and provisions. When the Mexicans retreated from Texas after Santa Anna's defeat at San Jacinto, Francita followed Captain Alavez to Matamoros, where she aided the Texans held prisoner there. From that town she was taken by Alavez to Mexico City and there abandoned. She returned to Matamoros penniless, but was befriended by Texans who had heard of her humanitarian acts on behalf of Texans captured by the Mexican army.

Dr. Joseph Barnard and Dr. John Shackelford,[qqv] two of the Goliad prisoners spared by the Mexicans, later testified to Francita's saintly behavior, thus causing her deeds to be more widely known. She came to be called the Angel of Goliad and gained recognition as a heroine of the Texas Revolution.[qv]

BIBLIOGRAPHY: Samuel Erson Asbury Papers, Barker Texas History Center, University of Texas at Austin. Joseph H. Barnard, *Dr. J. H. Barnard's Journal: A Composite of Known Versions,* ed. Hobart Huson (Refugio?, Texas, 1949). Harbert Davenport, "Men of Goliad," *Southwestern Historical Quarterly* 43 (July 1939). Henry Stuart Foote, *Texas and the Texans* (2 vols., Philadelphia: Cowperthwait, 1841; rpt., Austin: Steck, 1935). Kathryn Stoner O'Connor, *The Presidio La Bahía del Espíritu Santo de Zúñiga, 1721 to 1846* (Austin: Von Boeckmann-Jones, 1966).
George O. Coalson

ALAZAN, TEXAS. Alazan is at the junction of Farm roads 225 and 2782, seven miles west of Nacogdoches in western Nacogdoches County. The site was settled before 1900 and named for nearby Alazan Creek. A post office operated there from 1901 to 1911, and a school opened before 1904. During the 1930s the settlement comprised the school, a church, and a number of houses. The school was closed during the 1940s, and by the early 1990s only a church, a cemetery, and a few scattered houses remained. *Christopher Long*

ALAZAN-APACHE COURTS. The Alazan-Apache Courts is a public housing project built between 1939 and 1942 on San Antonio's predominantly Mexican-American West Side. It was still operating in the early 1990s. During the 1930s more than 100,000 Mexican Americans[qv] lived in San Antonio, many of them in little more than shacks with tin roofs, dirt floors, and scrap-material walls. These dwellings had no indoor plumbing, and sanitation was primitive. In 1937, during the Great Depression,[qv] the United States Housing Authority was established. San Antonio began its own San Antonio Housing Authority on June 17, 1937. Among the five SAHA commissioners the one most responsible for promoting the Alazan-Apache project was the Italian-born Father Carmelo Tranchese,[qv] pastor of the Our Lady of Guadalupe Church. In September 1937 the USHA agreed to fund the San Antonio housing program. Five projects were scheduled: Alazan and Apache Courts for Mexican Americans, Lincoln Heights and Wheatley Courts for blacks, and Victoria Courts for whites. Many of the nearly 500 landlords who had to be bought out, however, demanded compensation beyond that allocated. Angered, the USHA administrator ordered the projects stopped in early March 1939. Eleanor Roosevelt intervened, and work began on the Alazan project in July with the demolition of the 929 substandard structures that occupied the site.

Alazan opened some of its units in August 1940 and the rest by early 1941. The project cost nearly $4 million. In less than a year the smaller, adjacent Apache Courts was scheduled for completion at a cost of $1,116,000. The USHA requirement that union labor be used for construction prevented local Mexican Americans from working on the project and added to its cost. The total cost of the five housing projects was over $10 million. The federal government loaned 90 percent of the necessary funding, while the required 10-percent local contribution was raised through a bond drive. All debts were repaid though rents. By the end of 1942 the 2,554 single-family units in all five projects were open for nearly 10,000 tenants, including 4,994 tenants in the 1,180 single-family dwellings in the Alazan-Apache projects. The carefully constructed buildings contained multiple single-family dwellings, which ranged from three to 6½ rooms each, including private bathrooms and kitchens. All were equipped with modern appliances. On-site services included library facilities, health clinics, and social, recreational, and educational programs. The cost of the utilities and services was included in the tenants' rent, which ranged from $8.75 to $14.00 a month. Eligibility for the housing was determined by minimum and maximum annual salary limits, which varied depending on family size. United States citizenship was required by the SAHA as one way of reducing the number of applicants, who far outnumbered the units available. The occupants of the Alazan-Apache Courts formed a tenants' association to maintain the project, and their courts were judged by some observers to be "the best maintained housing project in the United States." The success of the projects led to demands for more. Tranchese headed the cause. Lack of funding, however, and the developing World War II[qv] made the effort unproductive, and public housing development in San Antonio ceased until the 1950s.

bibliography: Lyndon Gayle Knippa, San Antonio, Texas, during the Depression, 1933–1936 (M.A. thesis, University of Texas at Austin, 1971). Robert Garland Landolt, *The Mexican American Workers of San Antonio, Texas* (New York: Arno Press, 1976). Selden Menefee and Orin C. Cassmore, *The Pecan Shellers of San Antonio* (Washington: GPO, 1940). Carmelo A. Tranchese Papers, Microfilm Collection, St. Mary's University Library. Donald L. Zelman, "Alazan-Apache Courts," *Southwestern Historical Quarterly* 87 (October 1983).

Donald L. Zelman

ALAZAN BAY. The center of Alazan Bay, a small bay opening onto Baffin Bay,[qv] is at 27°20′ north latitude and 97°31′ west longitude. The whole bay, at the mouth of Petronila Creek in the southeast corner of Kleberg County, is surrounded by the Laureles Division of the King Ranch. It takes its name from El Alazán, the Spanish grant of Vicente de Ynojosa, which borders the bay on the northwest. The Spanish name means "sorrel-colored" and may have referred to wild horses, cattle, or the soil.

bibliography: Tom Lea, *The King Ranch* (2 vols., Boston: Little, Brown, 1957).

ALAZAN BAYOU. Alazan Bayou, also known as Bayou Alazan, rises one mile south of Grayback in western Nacogdoches County (at 31°37′ N, 94°46′ W) and flows southeast for twelve miles to its mouth on the Angelina River, 1½ miles west of Procella (at 31°29′ N, 94°45′ W). The stream is intermittent in its upper reaches. It crosses an area of flat terrain with local shallow depressions, surfaced by clay and sandy loam. Water-tolerant hardwoods, conifers, and grasses predominate in the local flora.

ALBA, TEXAS. Alba, also known as Simpkins Prairie and Albia, is at the intersection of U.S. Highway 69 and Farm Road 17, south of Lake Fork Reservoir and ten miles west of Quitman on the western border of Wood County. Probably the first to settle in the area was gunsmith Joseph Simpkins, who arrived with his family from Missouri around 1843. Next came W. W. Dale, who settled on Dale's (now Dale) Creek near the site of Alba. In 1881 the Missouri, Kansas and Texas Railroad came through Alba. One of the earliest shipments to the community was a telegraph office, and among the first telegraphs received was one telling of the assassination of President James Garfield (d. September 19, 1881). Late in 1881 Alba received a post office, which closed briefly early in 1882, then reopened later that year. For a time the railroad station and school may have been known as Albia. According to one story the town got its name because it was intended for white settlers only; another says it was named for the son of a railroad official. By 1882 the townsite had been laid out and several stores were opened to serve the influx of railroad-tie cutters. By 1884 the population of fifty was served by a church and a school. The population reached 300 by 1896, when the community had at least fifteen businesses, as well as Methodist, Baptist, and Christian churches and a school with 134 students.

Around 1900 lignite coal was discovered in the vicinity, and in 1902–03 the Texas Short Line Railway was built to ship coal from Alba and Hoyt to Grand Saline. By 1908 the Alba weekly *News* had been established, and the community had expanded its school and acquired a large farmers'-union warehouse. By 1911 five area mines were producing 40,000 tons of coal a month, and Alba had two banks and a population of around 1,500. In 1914 the community also had a waterworks, a telephone company, and a hotel. By the mid-1920s Alba was incorporated. The population ranged from 1,600 to 2,000 in the late 1920s, then fell to 662 in the early 1930s, by which time the banks had closed. At that time the community newspaper was the *Herald;* it was probably followed by the *Reporter.* Although the Alba oilfield was discovered by F. R. Jackson just south of the community in 1948, by 1952 the population had fallen to 545. That year the town had twenty-two businesses. Alba had 408 residents in the late 1960s, 676 residents and ten businesses in 1980, and 594 residents and fifteen businesses in 1988. In 1990 the community had extended into Rains County and had a population of 489. *See also* coal and lignite mining.

bibliography: Adele W. Vickery, *A Transcript of Centennial Edition, 1850–1950, Wood County Democrat* (Mineola, Texas, 1974). *Wood County, 1850–1900* (Quitman, Texas: Wood County Historical Society, 1976).

Rachel Jenkins

ALBA CLUB. The Alba Club was started in the fall of 1946 at the University of Texas at Austin by a group of Mexican-American students—many of them World War II[qv] veterans—to promote cultural and social interests and to confront the discrimination faced by Spanish-speaking people in the state. Membership, open to all faculty and students at the university, initially numbered about forty-five, grew by 1952 to a little more than seventy, then leveled off to forty-four by 1958. The club's sponsors were education professor George I. Sánchez and history professor Carlos E. Castañeda.[qqv] The assembly took the name Alba, which means "dawn" in Spanish, to represent the new era the founders envisioned for themselves and their people.

This new age, according to Alba's first president, university student Charley Gonzales Kidder, then twenty-one, had been ushered in by his generation who, through their service in the war, had been exposed to the larger world outside the segregated towns in which they had grown up. The Alba Club was thus intended to provide these "G.I. activists," the majority of the group, with the opportunity to assist the Mexican-American community while also providing members with a network for socializing. The Alba Club also collaborated with other student groups at the University of Texas, such as the Laredo Club and the Disabled American Veterans.qv Though in the club's early years its female members served mainly as secretaries to the group, at least one woman was known to have been elected president of the organization.

While Alba members opposed such discrimination against Mexican Americans qv as exclusion from restaurants or barbershops, the club tackled a situation it considered more severe—public school segregation. The club soon joined with the League of United Latin American Citizens qv and the newly organized American G.I. Forum qv to challenge public school discrimination in the 1948 case *Delgado* v. *Bastrop Independent School District.*qv Alba Club members interviewed parents of children in the Bastrop schools and gathered other significant information, helping bring to twenty the total number of plaintiffs involved in the case. The group took part in another school-equity case the next year, when on January 7, 1949, Cristóbal Aldrete qv of the Alba Club filed on behalf of the organization a racial discrimination complaint with the Texas Department of Education against the Del Rio public schools. Officials responded to the charge by withdrawing the school district's accreditation; the state legislature, however, soon passed a bill that removed jurisdiction for accreditation decisions from the state superintendent of education to a new appointed position—commissioner of education. The Alba Club probably ceased functioning in the late 1950s. It was significant because of its probable role as one of the earliest Mexican-American student organizations at the University of Texas. Alba's involvement in the problems facing Mexican Americans foreshadowed the Chicano qv activism, as exemplified by the Mexican American Youth Organization,qv during the 1960s and 1970s. The Alba Club also had a significant impact on desegregation of education.

BIBLIOGRAPHY: George I. Sánchez Papers, Benson Latin American Collection, University of Texas at Austin. *Teresa Palomo Acosta*

ALBANY, TEXAS. Albany, the county seat of Shackelford County, is at the intersection of State Highway 6 and U.S. Highway 283, in the central part of the county. The townsite was donated by Henry C. Jacobs, the first sheriff. William Cruger named the town for his former home, Albany, Georgia. One of the town's Bicentennial projects was a rock fountain dedicated to the memory of the Georgia volunteers killed in the Goliad Massacre qv during the Texas Revolution.qv

The site was selected for a county seat to supersede Fort Griffin on November 8, 1874. The public sale of town lots took place on August 2, 1875; within a few months T. E. Jackson built a general store. Cattle drivers going up the Western Trail qv to Dodge City soon began to use the town as a supply point. The arrival of the Texas Central Railroad in December 1881 made Albany a shipping point for cattle. An election on July 20, 1883, authorized Albany's first public school system, which covered eight square miles; by 1986 the Albany system covered 560 square miles. In 1883 the Albany *News* superseded the Albany *Star.* The Shackelford County Courthouse was built that same year.

Cattle and sheep raising dominated the local economy until the emergence of the oil industry in the twentieth century. Discovery of the Cook oilfield in 1926, and later discoveries have made Albany an oil drilling, producing, and supply center. Ranching continues to be an important part of the town's economic life; since 1920 the town slogan has been "Albany, the Home of the Hereford."

The Old Jail Foundation, chartered in 1978, restored the 1878 stone building, the first permanent jail in the county seat. The Old Jail Foundation Art Research Center opened in 1980; the museum houses a collection of Chinese tomb figures dating from the third century B.C., and nineteenth and twentieth century painting and sculpture, including works by Henry Moore, Aristide Maillol, Pablo Picasso, Amadeo Modigliani, Giacomo Manzu, John Marin, and others. The Fort Griffin Fandangle,qv an outdoor theater production of local history that originated in 1938, is presented during the last two weekends in June. In 1982 the population of the immediate area was 2,450. In 1990 the population of Albany was 1,962.

BIBLIOGRAPHY: Don Hampton Biggers, *Shackelford County Sketches* (Albany, Texas: Albany *News* Office, 1908; rpt., ed. Joan Farmer, Albany and Fort Griffin, Texas: Clear Fork Press, 1974). Fort Worth *Star-Telegram,* April 11, 1954, December 13, 1981. San Angelo *Standard Times,* February 18, 1979. *Shackelford County* (Albany, Texas: Shackelford County Historical Survey Committee, 1974).

Marilynne Howsley Jacobs

ALBERCA DE ARRIBA RANCH. A scenic South Texas ranch, the Alberca de Arriba Ranch is located along the Bordas Escarpment ten miles south of Mirando City. The Alberca spring, one of the few flowing springs in Webb County, is located near the old ranch headquarters. The ranch was founded in 1830 by Valentín de las Fuentes and his wife Tomasa de la Peña on a bluff overlooking the Alberca spring. Fuentes died in 1833, but the following year, the Mexican government granted his widow title to the land she and her husband had settled, a grant comprising 22,142 acres. In 1836 Indians, probably fighting for their seasonal camping site by the spring, forced the widow, her workers and tenants to flee. Tomasa soon returned and reestablished the ranch operation. Indian raids continued; often many of the ranch structures were burned, but Tomasa tenaciously had them rebuilt. Notwithstanding the Indian attacks and the constant threat posed by the stern surroundings, the ranch became a self-sustaining community. The Alberca spring provided the basis for existence in this harsh, remote environment. Cattle and horses were raised and by 1857 large fields were placed under cultivation. The ranch became a crossroads of wagon trails going from Laredo to the lower Gulf coast and from the Rio Grande valley to points north. In a renowned Spanish encyclopedia published in 1907 the settlement is described as a "locality and sweet water well situated southeast of Laredo on the road . . . from that city to Santo Domingo." By 1859 there were some forty stone structures at the ranch. Tomasa de la Peña, a remarkable Hispanic frontier woman who spent her life developing and defending her ranching enterprise in one of the most desolate sections of South Texas, died around 1860.

The village was again abandoned during the Civil War qv when Confederate irregulars forced the inhabitants to flee. Tomasa's son and grandson, Sabas and Valentín, promptly volunteered in Edmund Jackson Davis's qv First Texas Cavalry, U.S.A.,qv organized near Matamoros, Tamaulipas. At the end of the war, the family returned to the ranch but had to pursue almost half a century of litigation against the state of Texas to establish clear title. During this period, William von Rosenberg qv unsuccessfully tried to gain possession of the ranch by locating thirteen Confederate land scrips on the ranch. In 1907 the state Supreme Court finally established that the heirs of Valentín de las Fuentes and Tomasa de la Peña held a valid title to the ranch. In 1918 Antonio M. Bruni qv paid $82,198.11 for 12,749 acres of the original grant, including the old settlement, which he converted into his ranch headquarters. The ranch was the site of a famous gunfight between Texas Rangers qv and liquor smugglers from Guerrero, Tamaulipas, that occurred during Prohibition.qv Three *tequileros* were ambushed and shot dead by the rangers and buried on the spot. A *corrido, Los Tequileros,* which depicted the smugglers as tragic heroes, soon became popular along both sides of the Texas-Mexican border (*see* CORRIDOS). The southern section of the historic Aviator's oilfield, discovered in Webb County in 1922, is located at the ranch.

Of some forty houses that originally existed in the nineteenth century settlement, only three remain—a schoolhouse, a chapel that doubled as a commissary, and the large main house, all made from hand-hewed caliche block. The extant structures are fine examples of nineteenth-century South Texas ranch architecture. The main ranch-house shows the transition from the fortress-like, windowless structure with narrow *troneras* (gunports) that was necessary for defense to the more refined, spacious style that could be built once the region became pacified. Ruins of the workers' quarters indicate they were built of stone, as contrasted with the mesquite jacal that was the typical housing provided in most other ranches of South Texas at the time.

BIBLIOGRAPHY: Gunnar Brune, *Springs of Texas, Vol. 1* (Fort Worth: Branch-Smith, 1981). *Enciclopedia Universal Illustrada Europeo-Americana*. T. R. Fehrenbach, Mario Lorenzo Sanchez, and Aura Nell Ranzau, *A Shared Experience: The History, Architecture, and Historical Designations of the Lower Rio Grande Heritage Corridor* (Austin: Los Caminos del Rio Heritage Project and the Texas Historical Commission, 1991). William E. Galloway et al., *Atlas of Major Texas Oil Reservoirs* (Austin: University of Texas Bureau of Economic Geology, 1983). Joe S. Graham, *El Rancho in South Texas: Continuity and Change from 1750* (Denton: University of North Texas Press, 1994). *Guide to Spanish and Mexican Land Grants in South Texas* (Austin: Texas General Land Office, 1988). Américo Paredes, *A Texas-Mexican Cancionero: Folksongs of the Lower Border* (Urbana: University of Illinois Press, 1976).

Manuel Guerra

ALBERS BRANCH. Albers Branch rises about a mile south of Waldeck Church in north central Fayette County (at 30°03′ N, 96°48′ W) and flows northeast intermittently for two miles before disemboguing into Hellers Branch about one mile east of Waldeck (at 30°04′ N, 96°46′ W). The first half of the streambed runs through gently sloping hills surfaced by shallow, highly erodible, loamy topsoil over a dense clay subsoil containing volcanic materials. The lower half of the branch flows over deep deposits of sand and gravel mixed with clay. These soils are marginal for agriculture and are used primarily for pasture and wildlife habitat. The vegetation combines native and introduced grasses with post oak forests, hackberry, and yaupon. The stream is named for Gerhard Albers, a German immigrant who, with other Germans, settled in the Waldeck area before the Civil War.[qv] During that war Captain Albers commanded the Long Prairie German Company, which was formed in June 1861.

ALBERT, TEXAS. Albert is on Williams Creek sixteen miles southeast of Fredericksburg and one mile west of the Blanco county line in southeastern Gillespie County. The earliest known settlers in the area were George Cauley, Ben White, Sr., and a man named Jacobs. The town dates from 1877, when Fritz Wilke, George Maenius, and John Petri moved from Fredericksburg seeking new grazing lands for their cattle. Wilke, a blacksmith, bought his land from a man named Elmeier, who was murdered in a robbery several years later. The town was originally called Martinsburg after an early settler and was a stop on the Fredericksburg-Blanco stage route. The Martinsburg post office operated from 1877 to 1886, when mail was routed through nearby Hye in Blanco County. In 1892, however, Martinsburg got a new post office and a new name, thanks to Albert Luckenbach, who sold his store in Luckenbach, moved to Martinsburg, and opened a new post office, which he registered as Albert. The first local school was established in 1891, and in 1897 postmaster Otto Schumann opened the town's first store. The Albert Echo, a singing society, was founded the following year. In 1900 a new school building was erected; there the young Lyndon Baines Johnson[qv] was enrolled for a year. A local Lutheran mission was established in 1902 and eventually grew into what was often called the Lutheran Church of Stonewall, which Johnson attended. Albert had fifty residents in 1925, four in 1964, and twenty-five in 1972. By 1985 the store had been torn down, the school was a community club, and the town's dance hall was partitioned and used for storage; Albert still had twenty-five residents and two businesses. The reported population in 1990 was twenty-five.

BIBLIOGRAPHY: Kathleen Bauer, "Settlement and Progress of the Albert Community," *Junior Historian*, September 1968.

Martin Donell Kohout

ALBION, TEXAS. Albion is at the junction of State Highway 37 and Farm roads 195 and 1159, sixteen miles north of Clarksville in northern Red River County. The site was first settled during the antebellum period, but a community did not begin to grow up until after the Civil War.[qv] A local post office operated from 1886 until 1904 and from 1912 until 1929. During the 1930s the community had a store, a church, and a few houses; the population in 1940 was twenty. After World War II[qv] several new stores opened, and in 1991 the community had four or five businesses, a church, a cemetery, and a population of fifty. *Christopher Long*

ALBRIGHT, ALEX (1861–1937). Alex Albright, merchant and sheep breeder, son of German immigrants, was born on September 11, 1861. His father's trade was shoemaking, but Alex developed a love for livestock, quit college, and bought shorthorn cattle. In 1890 he moved to Dundee, Texas, and opened a mercantile business. Albright bought his first 320 acres for $3.24 an acre. He married in 1892. After his wife died in 1900, Albright read an ad in the Fort Worth *Star-Telegram* of a lady tutor. He went to see her, fell in love, and returned with a mother for his three children. She was French.

Albright named his place Elm Lodge Ranch. Through the influence of Mrs. Albright he started breeding Lincoln sheep. After three years of experimentation he had animals that produced wool of thirty-two inches length, which sold for a dollar a pound. In 1912 he became interested in Karakul sheep imported by his neighbor, Dr. C. C. Young. Albright soon bought the unusual-looking animals and began breeding them. To expand his breeding stock, he enlisted the aid of President Theodore Roosevelt to import Karakuls from Russia and in 1929 went to Germany to buy an experimental flock from the university at Halle. The ewes gave birth at least once a year. A photograph and carefully taken data were kept on each lamb; the best lambs were reserved for breeding, but the majority were slaughtered for their hide at birth or in the next four days. The tanned pelts were sold to furriers in New York for coats and hats for the royalty of Europe. A single pelt, which sold for eight to forty dollars, could make a coat costing as much as $2,000. With over 1,000 head, Albright had a thriving business, even during the Great Depression.[qv] His lands increased to 1,800 acres and his herd to 1,500. Some furriers declared his furs to be the finest in the world. His mercantile business thrived also; at times he was called Mr. Dundee. Albright died on April 3, 1937, and was buried at Dundee.

BIBLIOGRAPHY: Jack Loftin, *Trails Through Archer* (Burnet, Texas: Nortex, 1979). *Southwestern Sheep and Goat Raiser*, May 15, 1937.

Jack O. Loftin

ALBUQUERQUE, TEXAS. Albuquerque was on the Clear Fork of Sandies Creek two miles south of the junction of Gonzales, Wilson, and Guadalupe counties in Gonzales County. The site was believed to be in Wilson County until a 1914 survey showed it inside the Gonzales county line. Probably the settlement was named by South Texans who had fought in New Mexico under Henry H. Sibley.[qv] The town's official life spanned the years 1870 through 1883. A United States post office, with William W. Davis as postmaster, operated from 1870 to

1877; later that year it was reestablished by Mrs. Martha H. McCracken and operated until 1883. Henry S. Hastings and Samuel McCracken—Mississippian brothers-in-law—were the earliest settlers. At one time the town had a cotton gin, a blacksmith shop, a mercantile store, a saloon, a post office, a school, and several dwellings. On May 17, 1873, John Wesley Hardin killed Jack Helm[qqv] in Albuquerque, one of a series of violent acts of the Sutton-Taylor feud.[qv] Albuquerque quickly declined after business activities shifted to a new village, Union (sometimes referred to as Union Valley), two miles south of the Albuquerque site. By 1912 only deserted structures remained at the town site.

BIBLIOGRAPHY: Roy Sylvan Dunn, "Life and Times in Albuquerque, Texas," *Southwestern Historical Quarterly* 55 (July 1951).

Roy Sylvan Dunn

ALCALDE. The alcalde, the most important official in the Spanish municipality, acted not only as the chief executive in a Spanish town, but also functioned as a judge of minor cases and as the head of the ayuntamiento,[qv] or town council. His responsibilities combined components of the executive, legislative, and judicial branches of government. One of his primary duties was to act as a judge. Though his judicial authority was limited to lesser civil and criminal issues, in practice he handled most judicial matters occurring within the limits of his jurisdiction. The major exceptions to this were those cases involving military or ecclesiastical courts. Most alcaldes lacked any formal training in the law and generally relied on unwritten Spanish tradition to resolve disputes. The decisions reached by the alcalde were not final and could be appealed to the ayuntamiento, the *justicia mayor,* who served as chief assistant to the governor, or to the governor himself.

The alcalde served as the chief officer of the ayuntamiento. Although he held an equal vote, his authority extended beyond that of the other regidors, or councilmen (*see* REGIDOR). The alcalde not only officially issued laws for a municipality but also held the authority to arrest and punish those who violated city ordinances. In addition, he served as a link between the governor and city officials. He sent reports and requests to colonial administrators and acted on instructions from higher authorities. In a paternalistic manner, he took whatever measures he deemed best for the city. He served many different functions, such as supervising local records and helping to determine the use of municipal lands. Though the alcalde was generally chosen by the regidors, he could be appointed by the governor or directly elected by the people. Larger cities often provided for the election of two alcaldes, with the one receiving the most votes regarded as higher in rank.

The term *alcalde* generally referred to the *alcalde ordinario,* or municipal administrator, but other officers also received the title. The *alcalde mayor,* also known as the *justicia mayor,* assisted the governor in the administration of a district. He was responsible for Indian relations, the regulation of public travel, and a variety of other duties.

Neither the independence of Mexico nor the increasing number of American immigrants in Texas changed the alcalde's position. Despite cultural difficulties, immigrants adapted easily to the Spanish system of local government. American alcaldes functioned in the same manner as their Mexican counterparts until the Texas Revolution.[qv] *See also* SPANISH TEXAS.

BIBLIOGRAPHY: Eugene C. Barker, "The Government of Austin's Colony, 1821–1831," *Southwestern Historical Quarterly* 21 (January 1918). Gilbert Cruz, ed., "The City Ordinances of San Antonio of Bejar, 1829," *Texana* 7 (Summer 1969). Charles Gibson, *Spain in America* (New York: Harper and Row, 1966). Mattie Alice Austin, "The Municipal Government of San Fernando de Bexar," *Quarterly of the Texas State Historical Association* 8 (April 1905). John Preston Moore, *The Cabildo in Peru under the Bourbons* (Durham: Duke University Press, 1966). John Preston Moore, *The Cabildo in Peru under the Hapsburgs* (Durham: Duke University Press, 1954). David J. Weber, *The Mexican Frontier, 1821–1846* (Albuquerque: University of New Mexico Press, 1982).

Geoffrey Pivateau

ALCANTRA, BATTLE OF. The battle of Alcantra was fought on October 3 and 4, 1839. The opposing forces were both Mexican, as Mexico struggled with civil war sometimes known as the Federalist Wars. The Federalist forces were commanded by Gen. Antonio Canales and included 231 Texans. The Texans were a company of Frontier Guards authorized by the Texas government and commanded by Reuben Ross.[qv] Colonel Ross, claiming to have discretionary powers, chose to pursue frontier security from the Mexican side of the Rio Grande and joined with the Federalist forces; for a time he even operated under the Texas Lone Star flag. The Centralist troops were under the command of Col. Francisco González Pavón and had occupied the Mexican Rio Grande border town of Mier. On the morning of October 3, 1839, Pavón left Mier with 500 regulars and four pieces of artillery and retreated to the Alamo River twelve miles southwest of the town. Pursued by Canales, Pavón took up positions on high ground and attacked the Texan positions with artillery fire followed by infantry attack but failed to dislodge them. A second charge was also repulsed by the Texans. After a third attack, which resulted in a fierce counterattack by the combined Texan and Federalist force, both armies withdrew for the night. The following morning Pavón and the Centralist forces, who were without water, tried to move towards a source of water but were cut off by the Texans and a battalion of Canales's cavalry. After a brief skirmish, Pavón surrendered. Two Texans were killed during the battle, five more died later from their wounds. The Centralists lost 150, with 350 taken captive. Pavón and his officers were paroled; Pavón was later court-martialed by his government. The Federalist forces returned to Mier to rest and regroup.

BIBLIOGRAPHY: Joseph Milton Nance, *After San Jacinto: The Texas-Mexican Frontier, 1836–1841* (Austin: University of Texas Press, 1963).

Art Leatherwood

ALCEDO, TEXAS. Alcedo was a stop on the Texas South-Eastern Railroad a mile east of the Neches River in southwestern Angelina County. It was originally on the river, but when the Southern Lumber Company of Diboll opened a logging camp, it was moved to higher ground. An Alcedo post office opened in 1916 and operated with a brief hiatus in 1919 until in 1924, when the logging camp was closed. The community was still shown on maps as late as the mid-1930s, but most of the residents evidently left the area by the mid-1920s.

BIBLIOGRAPHY: Angelina County Historical Survey Committee, *Land of the Little Angel: A History of Angelina County, Texas,* ed. Bob Bowman (Lufkin, Texas: Lufkin Printing, 1976).

Christopher Long

ALCINO, TEXAS. Alcino was two miles northwest of the site of the present community of Cedar Hill in northeast Floyd County. The settlement was named either for a town in New Mexico or for postmaster John Dillard's wife, Alcinie. An Alcino post office existed from March 10, 1917, until August 31, 1923, when services were moved to Lockney. Businesses included Dillard's store and post office and a blacksmith's shop. By the 1940s only the school district of Cedar Hill remained in the area. The Cedar Hill school was consolidated with the Floydada schools in 1950.

BIBLIOGRAPHY: Floyd County Historical Museum, *History of Floyd County, 1876–1979* (Dallas: Taylor, 1979).

Charles G. Davis

ALCO, TEXAS. Alco was on the Angelina and Neches River Railroad ten miles northeast of Lufkin in northeastern Angelina County. The settlement became a flag station around 1911 after the railroad was built from Keltys through the area. By the 1930s Alco had a sawmill, a school, and a number of houses. Around the time of World War II[qv] the sawmill closed, and the site was abandoned. In the early 1990s only a few scattered houses remained in the area.

Christopher Long

ALCOA LAKE. Alcoa Lake is on Sandy Creek in the Brazos River basin, seven miles southwest of Rockdale in Milam County (its midpoint is at 30°35′ N, 97°03′ W). Sandy Creek is a tributary of Yegua Creek, which in turn empties into the Brazos River. The lake is owned and operated by the Aluminum Company of America for industrial and recreational purposes. Construction was started on February 17, 1952, and the dam and spillway were completed in October 1952; the gates were not installed until January 31, 1953. Impoundment of water began in early 1952. The 12½-mile pipeline from the Little River pumping plant to the lake was placed in operation on January 13, 1953. In 1966 the lake had a capacity of 10,500 acre-feet and a surface area of 703 acres at the top of the spillway gates. The lake was maintained at near-spillway level by pumping from Little River when necessary, and the water was used for condenser-cooling purposes at a steam-electric generating station. The drainage area was only six square miles, but this was an off-channel storage. Most of the water was pumped from Little River.

BIBLIOGRAPHY: C. L. Dowell, *Dams and Reservoirs in Texas: History and Descriptive Information* (Texas Water Commission Bulletin 6408 [Austin, 1964]).

Seth D. Breeding

ALCORN, ELIJAH (ca. 1769–1844). Elijah Alcorn (Allcorn), early settler, was born about 1769 in the area of present York County, South Carolina. He may have been the son of James and Catherine Alcorn. Early in life he moved to Georgia, and between 1793 and 1800 he served in the Georgia State Militia as an infantryman under Capt. John Hodge. Sometime in the 1790s he married Nancy (Hodge?); they had six children. Alcorn resided in Georgia as late as 1816 and was listed in the Illinois state census in 1818. He took his family to Texas in December 1821 as one of Stephen F. Austin's[qv] Old Three Hundred.[qv] On January 1, 1822, Alcorn was with the group that camped on a stream they named New Year's Creek, in an area between the sites of present Independence and Brenham. Alcorn received title to 1½ sitios and a labor of land now in Fort Bend, Washington, and Waller counties on July 10, 1824. He brought in freight for the settlers at San Felipe de Austin, participated in local elections, served on a jury in 1825, and acted as road supervisor. The census of Austin's colony in March 1826 indicated that he was a farmer and stock raiser aged over fifty, with a household including his wife, four sons, a daughter, and two servants. In 1835 he signed a petition requesting the organization of Washington Municipality. In May 1840 he filed a mortgage-foreclosure suit in Harris County. Alcorn died on March 21, 1844, in Washington County.

BIBLIOGRAPHY: Eugene C. Barker, ed., *The Austin Papers* (3 vols., Washington: GPO, 1924–28). Eugene C. Barker, ed., "Minutes of the Ayuntamiento of San Felipe de Austin, 1828–1832," 12 parts, *Southwestern Historical Quarterly* 21–24 (January 1918–October 1920). Lester G. Bugbee, "The Old Three Hundred: A List of Settlers in Austin's First Colony," *Quarterly of the Texas State Historical Association* 1 (October 1897). *Telegraph and Texas Register*, January 6, 1841.

ALDERBRANCH, TEXAS. Alderbranch (Alder Branch) is on Farm Road 323 and the Alder Branch of Squirrel Creek eleven miles southeast of Palestine in southeastern Anderson County. The Alder Branch post office operated from 1863 to 1913. B. F. Chambers established a sawmill on the branch in the early 1880s, and by 1884 the community had water-powered sawmills, two churches, two general stores, cotton gins, a district school, and forty inhabitants. Alder Branch reached an estimated peak population of sixty around 1890, but by 1896 the district school was gone. The population was only thirty, though the community still had Methodist and Baptist churches, two sawmills, two cotton gins, a flour mill and gin, and one general store. In the 1930s the community was called Alderbranch and had an estimated twenty-five inhabitants and one business; a sawmill was located less than a mile east. In 1982 the community consisted of several scattered dwellings, and it was still listed on state highway maps in 1985.

Mark Odintz

ALDERSON, EUGENE WEBSTER (1854–1939). Eugene Webster Alderson, Methodist preacher, was born on October 15, 1854, in Hart County, Kentucky, the son of Rev. and Mrs. A. L. Alderson of the Louisville Conference. He was licensed to preach at nineteen and went to Texas in 1875. There he taught for a few years and founded North Trinity College at Gainesville. He was ordained a deacon in 1878, and in 1879 he joined the North Texas Conference and became a popular leader. He debated vigorously in defense of Methodist theology and polity. He was a delegate to four general conferences of the church. At the 1910 general conference he was chairman of the Committee on Revisals (of the Methodist ritual). He died on March 9, 1939, and was buried at Bonham.

BIBLIOGRAPHY: Methodist Episcopal Church, South, *Journal of the Northwest Texas Conference*, 1939. Macum Phelan, *History of Early Methodism in Texas, 1817–1866* (Nashville: Cokesbury, 1924); *A History of the Expansion of Methodism in Texas, 1867–1902* (Dallas: Mathis, Van Nort, 1937).

Walter N. Vernon

ALDINE, TEXAS (Harris County). Aldine is on Farm Road 525, the Missouri Pacific Railroad, and the Hardy Toll Road, on the northern outskirts of Houston in central Harris County. It was originally built on the International–Great Northern Railroad and named for a local farm family. The community had a post office from 1896 until 1935, when mail was delivered from Houston. By 1914 Aldine had two general stores, a fig preserver, and several poultry breeders and dairymen. The population briefly reached 100 in 1925 but fell in the 1930s and 1940s to between thirty and forty. The Aldine schools were integrated by federal order in 1965. The community began growing again in the late 1970s. It had a population of 12,623 in 1986 and 11,133 in 1990.

BIBLIOGRAPHY: Durward Harvey Blackmon, An Educational Survey of a Portion of North Harris County, Texas (M. Ed. thesis, University of Texas, 1939).

Diana J. Kleiner

ALDINE, TEXAS (Uvalde County). Aldine is on Farm Road 1051 and the Dry Frio River two miles north of the junction of U.S. Highway 83 and Farm Road 1051 in north central Uvalde County. A post office operated there from 1885 to 1891. Some of the original settlers around 1880 were the Mousers, the Blakneys, and Josh and Billy Cox. The land used for the Aldine school and cemetery was donated by Cox. In 1900 the school had twelve students and one teacher. The school and a scattering of dwellings were at the site in 1946. By 1971 the school had been abandoned, and all that remained of Aldine by 1988 was the cemetery.

BIBLIOGRAPHY: *A Proud Heritage: A History of Uvalde County* (Uvalde, Texas: El Progreso Club, 1975).

Ruben E. Ochoa

ALDREDGE, GEORGE N. (1846–1908). George N. Aldredge, attorney and judge, was born on April 14, 1846, in Dougherty County, Georgia, to Dr. J. F. and Mary (Oglesby) Aldredge. In 1856 the family moved from Marietta, Georgia, to Pittsburg, Texas. At the age of sixteen Aldredge enlisted as a private in the Confederate Army. He served two years in Company F, Clark's Texas Infantry Regiment, and transferred in January 1864 to Company F, Chisholm's Cavalry Regiment, Thomas Green's[qv] Brigade, in the Army of the Trans-Mississippi.

About two years after the war Aldredge graduated from McKenzie College, then studied law under Oran M. Roberts[qv] at Gilmer. In 1869 he was admitted to the bar in Tyler by the state Supreme Court. After practicing law for a year in Gilmer, then for two years in Waxahachie, Aldredge arrived in Dallas in 1873. Without opposition he was elected county attorney of Dallas County in 1875 and served until 1878, when he was elected judge of the Eleventh Judicial District, which was reorganized in 1883 as the Fourteenth District. Aldredge was judge until 1888, the year he retired and returned to private practice with A. T. Watts and J. J. Eckford. He was a director of the National Exchange Bank of Dallas. He ran for Congress as a Democrat but withdrew in protest against the party's support of free silver. A speech he gave to the American Bankers' Association in 1895 in Atlanta, Georgia, was widely quoted and read into the Congressional Record. In 1897 he gave the eulogy for Robert E. Lee[qv] at the unveiling of the Lee monument in Dallas.

Aldredge was a master Mason and a Knight of Pythias. From 1875 to 1877 he served as chairman of the Democratic committee of the Third Congressional District. In January 1881 he married Bettie Hearne, and they had five children, two of whom died very young. A son, Sawnie Robertson Aldredge, was mayor of Dallas from 1921 to 1923. Aldredge practiced law until ill health forced his retirement. He became ill when an old kidney ailment flared up on a train trip home from Colorado Springs and died at his home in Dallas on September 5, 1908.

BIBLIOGRAPHY: Berry B. Cobb, *A History of Dallas Lawyers, 1840 to 1890* (Bar Association of Dallas, 1934). Dallas *Morning News*, September 6, 1908. Dallas *Daily Times Herald*, September 5, 1908. William S. Speer and John H. Brown, eds., *Encyclopedia of the New West* (Marshall, Texas: United States Biographical Publishing, 1881; rpt., Easley, South Carolina: Southern Historical Press, 1978).

Joan Jenkins Perez

ALDRETE, CRISTÓBAL (1924–1991). Cristóbal (Cris) Aldrete, civil rights lawyer, was born in Del Rio, Texas, on January 16, 1924, the son of Felipe and Dolores (Pool) Aldrete. He was reared in Del Rio and worked throughout his adolescence in the family's grocery store, picking cotton, or with the local English and Spanish language dailies. He was the seventh of eleven children but the first in his family to graduate from high school. He joined the United States Army and studied Japanese at the University of Denver but later transferred to the University of Texas to complete a degree in government. In 1951 he received a law degree from the South Texas College of Law in Houston. He married Oralia Vera of Brownsville in August of 1954; they had five children.

After completing law school, Aldrete returned to Del Rio to practice law. He was a member of the city council from 1952 to 1958 and was elected city attorney in 1959. Between 1961 and 1965 he was Val Verde county attorney. He resigned during his second term to accept employment with the federal government. His pursuit of civil rights in the courts began when his father became a plaintiff in *Del Rio Independent School District v. Salvatierra*[qv] (1930), in which the court opposed the segregation of Mexican Americans[qv] on grounds of national origin but allowed segregation on an educational basis in elementary schools. In 1946 Aldrete founded the Alba Club at the University of Texas to provide Hispanic students the opportunity to focus attention on social problems faced by their people. In 1947, as a student, he participated in the American Veterans Committee at the University of Texas and protested the segregation of Mexican Americans in Texas schools. In 1949 he lodged a complaint with the state department of education against the segregated Del Rio school system on behalf of Alba. Within a few weeks of his charge, T. M. Trimble, the assistant state superintendent of public instruction, made an inspection tour of the Del Rio schools and reported that Aldrete's complaint was warranted. Consequently, the state withdrew its accreditation of the Del Rio Schools on February 12, 1949, a decision that the new commissioner of education overruled once he was installed. Ultimately the state required that public schools in Texas end segregation on the basis of national origin by September of 1949. The Delgado decree in the case of *Delgado v. Bastrop Independent School District*,[qv] however, permitted separate classes for first graders on pedagogical grounds if all students were subjected to "scientific and standardized tests." After his return to Del Rio to practice law, Aldrete, a member of the American G.I. Forum,[qv] became involved in a campaign to make the organization national in scope. In August 1952 he and Hector P. García,[qv] the founder of the forum, traveled throughout the Southwest promoting the organization. In *Hernández v. State of Texas*, the United States Supreme Court overturned the conviction of Pete Hernández, a farm worker who had been found guilty of the murder of Joe Espinosa in Edna, because the jury that convicted him had no Mexican panelists. In fact, no Texas Mexican had served on a jury in the county for the preceding twenty-five years. Aldrete was one of five attorneys representing Hernández on behalf of the American G.I. Forum and the League of United Latin American Citizens[qv] when the case was argued before the Supreme Court on January 11, 1954. In a unanimous decision, Chief Justice Earl Warren found in favor of Hernández and ordered the state to reverse his conviction.

Aldrete was elected state chairman of the forum in 1953. In 1965 he became a regional administrator for the Community Action Programs of the Office of Economic Opportunity. Two years later he was named special assistant to the chairman of the Democratic National Committee to assist in the effort among Hispanic voters to reelect Lyndon Johnson.[qv] He was an assistant to Representative Abraham Kazen, Jr. (D-Texas), in 1969; he worked for Senator Lloyd Bentsen, Jr. (D-Texas), as a legislative and executive assistant in the 1970s. In 1977 President Jimmy Carter appointed Aldrete to serve as cochairman of the Southwest Border Regional Commission to organize a $10 million economic development plan for the region.

Aldrete spent his later years in Austin. He served as executive director of the Texas Senate Hispanic Caucus from 1987 to 1989. On occasion he participated in public forums, such as the 1990 Martín De León[qv] Symposium on the Chicano[qv] movement in Texas from 1940 to 1960. Aldrete died on September 17, 1991, of cancer, at Methodist Hospital of Houston.[qv] A memorial Mass was offered for him at St. John Neumann Catholic Church in Westlake Hills, outside of Austin. He was buried in Del Rio after another service at Sacred Heart Catholic Church in that city.

BIBLIOGRAPHY: Austin *American-Statesman*, September 23, 1991. Veronica Salazar, *Dedication Rewarded: Prominent Mexican Americans* (2 vols., San Antonio: Mexican American Culture Center, 1976, 1981). Guadalupe San Miguel, Jr., *"Let All of Them Take Heed": Mexican Americans and the Campaign for Educational Equality in Texas* (Austin: University of Texas Press, 1987). *Teresa Palomo Acosta*

ALDRETE, JOSÉ MIGUEL (?–?). José Miguel Aldrete, Mexican official and early Texas patriot, son of José de Jesús Aldrete, was born in Texas, probably at La Bahía. At an early age he married Candelaria De León, daughter of Martín De Leon.[qv] For a number of years he served in the ayuntamiento[qv] at Goliad and was alcalde in 1823–24 and from 1830 to 1833. For several years he was collector at the port of El Cópano. He maintained residences both at Goliad and Refugio and on occasion lived at Nuestra Señora del Refugio Mission, near his ranch. In 1830 he represented the Mexican government in the secularization of the mission.

Aldrete, probably the largest landowner in the Refugio area at the time, was land commissioner of the state of Coahuila and Texas[qv] in 1835 and was functioning as such when Antonio López de Santa Anna[qv] dissolved the state government. He immediately espoused the Federalist cause and was a member of Ira Westover's[qv] Lipantitlán expedition,[qv] after which he went to San Antonio de Béxar[qv] where, according to some accounts, he was a member of the Texan army during the siege of Bexar.[qv] He was a member of Philip Dimmitt's[qv] garrison at Goliad and a signer of the Goliad Declaration of Independence.[qv] Aldrete furnished many animals and supplies to the Texas army during the Texas Revolution[qv] and was one of the few Mexicans who enjoyed the confidence and friendship of Dimmitt.

About 1840, after living in Goliad and Victoria, Aldrete moved back to Refugio County. He, like many other family members, was a warm abettor of the Mexican Federalists. From 1841 to 1844 he was a justice of Refugio County. Upon him was conferred one of the orders of the papal nobility. In addition to their holdings in Refugio County, the Aldretes owned large ranches in the Nueces River region. Aldrete lived in Corpus Christi in 1854. About the time of the fall of Maximilian's empire, he moved to Chihuahua, Coahuila, where he died sometime before 1873.

BIBLIOGRAPHY: Hobart Huson, *Refugio: A Comprehensive History of Refugio County from Aboriginal Times to 1953* (2 vols., Woodsboro, Texas: Rooke Foundation, 1953, 1955).

Hobart Huson

ALDRICH, ARMISTEAD ALBERT (1858–1945). Armistead Albert Aldrich, judge and historian, was born in Crockett, Texas, to Oliver Cromwell and Eliza Jane (Masters) Aldrich on April 10, 1858, the day his father was elected Houston county clerk. He was educated privately and sent on horseback to attend the University of Virginia in 1877. In 1883 he was admitted to the Texas bar. In Crockett he served as a school board member from 1890 to 1892, county judge from 1892 to 1896, member of the 1918 District Exemption Board and the 1936 Texas Centennial[qv] Advisory Committee, and chairman of the Democratic Executive Committee from 1926 to 1936. Aldrich was also a representative to the Twenty-seventh Texas Legislature. Austin College in Sherman, where he was a trustee from 1900 to 1930, awarded him an honorary LL.D. on May 31, 1937. He was a Presbyterian elder and Sunday school superintendent. He was a popular orator and served as master of ceremonies when a crowd of 5,000 attended the dedication of San Francisco de los Tejas Mission Park on July 4, 1935. He wrote a weekly history column in the Crockett *Courier* and wrote a *History of Houston County* (1943). He was a member of the Knights of Pythias, president of a chapter of the Sons of the Republic of Texas,[qv] president of the David Crockett Memorial Association, president of the Houston County bar, and organizer of the David Crockett Building and Loan Association and the Aldrich Abstract Company.

In 1881 Aldrich married Willie Arledge. They had seven children. Two Aldrich family homes are now museums in Crockett: the Greek Revival Monroe-Crook (1854), where four generations of Aldriches lived; and the Eastlake-style Downes-Aldrich House (1893), where Aldrich died on August 25, 1945. Aldrich's papers are in the Barker Texas History Center,[qv] University of Texas at Austin.

BIBLIOGRAPHY: Armistead Albert Aldrich, *The History of Houston County, Texas* (San Antonio: Naylor, 1943). A. A. Aldrich Papers, Barker Texas History Center, University of Texas at Austin. Clarence R. Wharton, ed., *Texas under Many Flags* (5 vols., Chicago: American Historical Society, 1930). Suzanne Winckler, "Home Sweet Home," *Houston Home and Garden*, April 1986.

Mary Ann Edwards

ALDRICH, COLLIN (1801–1842). Collin Aldrich, first chief justice of Houston County, son of George and Polly (Bowen) Aldrich, Jr., was born on May 2, 1801, in Mendon, Massachusetts. His brother George came to Texas before the Texas Revolution,[qv] formed a partnership with Robert Anderson Irion[qv] of Nacogdoches in land trade, and later became first county surveyor of Houston County. Aldrich arrived in Red River County in 1829 and settled near Clarksville. In 1835 he obtained land on the Trinity River now in Houston County. He served as first postmaster at Aldrich (later Mustang Prairie) and helped organize the county government. He fought in the battle of San Jacinto[qv] and was appointed chief justice of Houston County by Sam Houston[qv] in 1837. His suitability for office was questioned by D. H. Campbell, a political adversary, who charged him with corruption and malpractice. Aldrich appealed to president-elect Mirabeau B. Lamar,[qv] and in 1838 his appointment was confirmed. Aldrich and his wife, Elizabeth (Lawrence Crownover), had at least four children. Aldrich died in June 1842 in Houston County.

BIBLIOGRAPHY: Armistead Albert Aldrich, *The History of Houston County, Texas* (San Antonio: Naylor, 1943). Robert Bruce Blake Research Collection, Steen Library, Stephen F. Austin State University; Barker Texas History Center, University of Texas at Austin; Texas State Archives, Austin; Houston Public Library, Houston. Joe E. Ericson, *Judges of the Republic of Texas (1836–1846): A Biographical Directory* (Dallas: Taylor, 1980).

Pamela Lynn Palmer

ALDRICH, ROY WILKINSON (1869–1955). Roy Wilkinson Aldrich, of the Texas Rangers,[qv] was born in Quincy, Illinois, on September 17, 1869. He spent his early childhood in Golden City, Missouri, and as a youth lived in Arizona, Idaho, and Oklahoma Territory. When the Spanish-American War began he was commissioned a second lieutenant in the Second Missouri Volunteer Regiment; he saw service on the island of Mindanao during the Philippine Insurrection. He served with the British army's remount service in South Africa during the Boer War. From 1903 to 1907 he was sheriff of Kiowa County, Oklahoma Territory, and from 1907 to 1915 he was in the real estate business in Corpus Christi and San Antonio.

In 1915 he enlisted in Company A, Texas Rangers. He was promoted to captain and quartermaster in 1918 and retired from that post in 1947; his term of service at the time of his retirement was longer than that of any other ranger. During his years on the force Aldrich became known in Texas academic circles for his interest in history and natural history. He aided Walter Prescott Webb[qv] while Webb was doing research in South Texas for his book *The Texas Rangers* (1935); Aldrich's collections of flora and Indian artifacts provided specimens for botanists and anthropologists at the University of Texas. The woods and pond of his home near Austin were the source of an important collection of fruit flies used by the university's Genetics Foundation. Aldrich never married. He died on January 29, 1955, and was buried in Oakwood Cemetery, Austin. In 1958 Sul Ross State College (now Sul Ross State University) acquired his 10,000-volume library.

BIBLIOGRAPHY: Austin *American*, August 15, 1952. Austin *American-Statesman*, January 30, 1955. Dallas *News*, January 16, 1927. Houston *Chronicle*, January 17, 1960.

Morris G. Cook

ALDRIDGE, TEXAS (Angelina County). Aldridge was on the Neches River near Boykin Springs in southern Angelina County. The settlement was founded in 1903 by Rockland lumberman Hal Aldridge, who built a sawmill at the site. A local post office operated briefly in 1906. The sawmill closed in 1920 after most of the surrounding forest had been cut, and within a short time the town died.

BIBLIOGRAPHY: Angelina County Historical Survey Committee, *Land of the Little Angel: A History of Angelina County, Texas*, ed. Bob Bowman (Lufkin, Texas: Lufkin Printing, 1976).

Christopher Long

ALDRIDGE, TEXAS (Jasper County). Aldridge was on the Burr's Ferry, Browndell and Chester Railroad, about seventy miles north of Beaumont in extreme northwestern Jasper County. The area's rich forests attracted outside lumber interests by the late nineteenth century, and the Aldridge Lumber Company, with W. H. and F. W. Aldridge as president and vice president, respectively, had begun operations in Jasper County by 1898. In 1905 the firm increased its property holdings in Jasper and Angelina counties substantially with a large purchase from the Vaughan Lumber Company. The Aldridge mill gained a railroad outlet in 1907 via the BFB&C.

On August 26, 1911, fire destroyed the Aldridge sawmill, and company owners went heavily into debt in the process of rebuilding. Although some assistance from the giant Kirby Lumber Company was forthcoming, shipments from Aldridge remained "a disappointment" in 1915. The mill burned again that year, and the post office, opened in 1907, discontinued operations at Aldridge in 1916. With heavy investments in nearby forests, John Henry Kirby[qv] remained interested in the Aldridge operations. Indeed, the efforts of the Texas and New Orleans Railroad to extend the old BFB&C line across the Angelina River seemed to spark new life in the region. The Aldridge post office was reopened from 1920 to 1923.

However, because loggers had depleted the locally available timber, the railroad spur from Rockland to Turpentine, which passed through Aldridge, was abandoned in 1927, thus destroying all hopes for another recovery at Aldridge. The area has been most noted by subsequent generations for the recreational opportunities at Blue Hole, formed when a stone quarry collapsed during the town's heyday.

BIBLIOGRAPHY: Kirby Lumber Corporation Papers, Steen Library, Stephen F. Austin State University. S. G. Reed, *A History of the Texas Railroads* (Houston: St. Clair, 1941; rpt., New York: Arno, 1981).

Robert Wooster

ALEDO, TEXAS. Aledo is on Farm Road 2376 fifteen miles west of Fort Worth in east central Parker County. The first settlers in the area were from Georgia. They called the place Parker's Station. The name, however, caused confusion for postal authorities, and after the tracks of the Texas and Pacific Railway were laid nearby and businesses were built close to the rail line, a Texas and Pacific official suggested that the new site be named after his hometown, Aledo, Illinois. An Aledo post office was opened in 1882. By the mid-1880s the settlement had an estimated 150 residents and had become a shipping point for area farmers. The town's steam cotton gin, corn mill, bank, and twenty-one businesses established Aledo as a retail center for eastern Parker County by 1915. The population grew to 400 by the early 1920s. In 1963 the community was incorporated. Beginning in the mid-1970s the town grew rapidly as a result of the growth of nearby Fort Worth. In 1980 it had an estimated 1,027 residents and twenty-three businesses. In 1990 the population was 1,169.

BIBLIOGRAPHY: Gustavus Adolphus Holland, *History of Parker County and the Double Log Cabin* (Weatherford, Texas: Herald, 1931; rpt. 1937). Kathleen E. and Clifton R. St. Clair, eds., *Little Towns of Texas* (Jacksonville, Texas: Jayroe Graphic Arts, 1982).

David Minor

ALEMAN, TEXAS. Aleman, at the junction of Farm roads 932 and 3340 eight miles southeast of Hamilton in central Hamilton County, was settled by German immigrants from Washington County. In 1886 Rev. Thomas Kohn held the first church services there, and St. Paul's Lutheran Church subsequently became the center of a community. Originally the settlement was called Pleasant Point, but in 1907, when it was moved a mile to the railroad line, it was renamed Piggtown, after promoter Mack Pigg. The name was later changed to Aleman, Spanish for "German," used by Mexican railroad workers. For some years a cotton gin, blacksmith shop, and cafe operated there. In 1954 Aleman had the church, an elementary school, and a store. An Aleman post office operated from 1914 until 1943. In 1980 and 1990 the population was sixty.

BIBLIOGRAPHY: Hamilton County Historical Commission, *A History of Hamilton County, Texas* (Dallas: Taylor, 1979). Oran J. Pool, A History of Hamilton County (M.A. thesis, University of Texas, 1954).

William R. Hunt

ALESSANDRO, VICTOR NICHOLAS (1915–1976). Victor Alessandro, Jr., orchestra conductor, was born in Waco, Texas, on November 27, 1915, son of a prominent music teacher and conductor. The Alessandros moved to Houston in 1919. Victor was introduced to music at an early age and studied horn with his father. He is said to have made his conducting debut at age four, when he led a children's band in a performance of Victor Herbert's "March of the Toys." In 1932 he entered the Eastman School of Music in Rochester, New York, where he studied composition with Howard Hanson. He afterward studied at the Salzburg Mozarteum and the St. Cecilia Academy in Rome, where he studied with Ildebrando Pizzetti. In 1938 he became conductor of the Oklahoma City Symphony Orchestra, an organization that he led from a WPA project to an accomplished ensemble with broad civic support. When Max Reiter,[qv] conductor of the San Antonio Symphony Orchestra,[qv] died in December 1950, Alessandro took over much of the remaining season; he signed a contract as permanent conductor in April 1951. The next year he also assumed leadership of the San Antonio Symphony Society's Grand Opera Festival. In 1955 he married flutist Ruth Drisko; they had two children.

Alessandro was at his best in works by Peter I. Tchaikovsky and Richard Strauss. He was a sympathetic interpreter of Johannes Brahms and the odd-numbered symphonies of Ludwig van Beethoven. He introduced works by Anton Bruckner, Gustav Mahler, and Alban Berg to San Antonio audiences before they became fashionable elsewhere. He conducted memorable performances of *Elektra, Salome, Nabucco, Boris Godunov, Susannah, Die Meistersinger,* and the standard operas of Giuseppe Verdi and Giacomo Puccini. In building the San Antonio orchestra he was an exacting, often irascible taskmaster of high musical standards. But he was capable of less formidable moments as well; in February 1962, for instance, he dedicated a performance of *Ein Heldenleben* to the memory of Bruno Walter.

Alessandro received honorary doctorates from the Eastman School and Southern Methodist University and the Alice M. Ditson Award for service to American music. Recordings of his work include Claude Debussy's *Martyrdom of St. Sebastian* (1950), light accompaniments (ca. 1953), Antonio Vivaldi and Rodrigo guitar concertos and works by Richard Strauss and John Corigliano (1967–68). With his health declining, Alessandro retired in 1976. He died in San Antonio on November 27, 1976, his sixty-first birthday.

BIBLIOGRAPHY: Theodore Albrecht, "101 Years of Symphonic Music in San Antonio," *Southwestern Musician/Texas Music Educator,* March, November 1975. *Baker's Biographical Dictionary of Musicians,* 1978. Hope Stoddard, *Symphony Conductors of the U.S.A.* (New York: Crowell, 1957).

Theodore Albrecht

ALEXANDER, ALMERINE M. (ca. 1821–1865). Almerine Alexander, merchant and Confederate officer, was born in Kentucky about 1821. He came to Texas with his brothers, C. C. and L. C. Alexander, in the 1840s. All of the brothers were merchants, and at various times they owned large stores in Paris, Clarkesville, Bonham, Dallas, and Sherman. A. M. Alexander first appears on county tax rolls in 1847 in Lamar County, where he and his brother L. C. were apparently partners in a store at Paris. In 1848 the Alexanders moved to Dallas and opened a store, A. M. Alexander and Brothers. It became the largest retail firm in Dallas before closing in 1853. In the spring of 1849 Alexander married Josephine B. King of Burkesville, Kentucky, in Nashville, Tennessee. The couple had three children. In late 1850 Alexander left the Dallas store to be run by a manager and moved to Sherman, where he opened a firm in his own name. He closed that store a year later and moved to Bonham, where he and his brothers had a store. In late 1854 he moved back to Sherman and opened a store in partnership with S. B. Allen. Alexander continued to live in Sherman until he left for service in the Confederate Army; the firm of Alexander and Allen remained in operation until Alexander's death.

In the winter of 1861–62 Alexander raised the Thirty-fourth Texas Cavalry regiment, also known as the Second Texas Partisans, in Sherman. This regiment was one of three Texas cavalry regiments brigaded for the first time in July 1862. They were charged with defending the Trans-Mississippi Department and for the next three years were marginally successful in doing so. After engaging federal troops at Spring River and Newtonia, Missouri, in the fall of 1862, the Thirty-fourth, weakened by sickness, poor morale, and frequent desertions, was reduced to an infantry unit. On December 7, 1862, the newly designated Thirty-fourth Texas Dismounted Cavalry engaged Union forces at Prairie Grove, Arkansas. Although the regiment was successful in fending off a series of charges, dwindling ammunition forced them to retreat.

Following Prairie Creek, the Thirty-fourth was merged with the Fifteenth Texas Infantry. In February 1863 Alexander was made acting commander of Lt. Col. Joseph Warren Speight's[qv] brigade, a position he held until May of that year, when poor health forced him to resign. He died in New Orleans in the summer of 1865.

BIBLIOGRAPHY: Alwyn Barr, *Polignac's Texas Brigade*, Texas Gulf Coast Historical Association Publication Series 8.1 (November 1964).

Cecil Harper, Jr.

ALEXANDER, BIRDIE (1870–1960). Birdie Alexander, music teacher, was born in Lincoln County, Tennessee, on March 24, 1870, the daughter of George Washington and Mary Jane (Shores) Alexander. The family moved to Texas, where she was educated in Forney and at Mary Nash College in Sherman. She then attended Ward Seminary in Nashville, Tennessee, where she majored in piano and voice, and graduated with honors in 1891. After her family moved to Dallas she began teaching in the public schools, where she became supervisor of music in 1900. In Dallas she is credited with having laid the foundation for the system of music education in the public schools. She established the teaching of singing in all grades and was the first to form citywide choral groups for public performance. Under her direction the first operetta was performed at Turner Hall on May 24 and 25, 1901, to raise funds for the children's department of the Dallas Public Library. She produced and directed the music festival in May 1912 at the coliseum and the first cantatas given by the schools. In 1910 she organized the Dallas High School orchestra, which continued to function with annual concerts. In the same year she inaugurated music appreciation lessons in the schools with the purchase of the first record player and recordings with funds subscribed by interested citizens. She instituted folk-dancing classes to teach rhythm in the lower grades.

Miss Alexander was a charter member of the first board of directors of the Music Supervisors' National Conference, and as chairman of the MSNC was responsible for the formation of the music department of the Texas State Teachers Association.[qv] In the summers of 1908, 1909, and 1910 she organized and taught courses in music education at the University of Texas. She also taught on the summer faculty at Northwestern University in Evanston, Illinois. In 1912 she edited *Songs We Like to Sing*. Because of her health she moved to El Paso in 1913, and there until her death she taught piano and was a leader in musical activities. In 1941 the Texas Music Teachers' Association[qv] made her a life member "in recognition of her distinguished contribution to American music." She died in El Paso on August 2, 1960.

BIBLIOGRAPHY: Dallas *Morning News*, May 16, 1966.

Lelle Swann

ALEXANDER, ISAAC (1832–1919). Isaac Alexander, Methodist minister, youngest of fourteen children of David B. and Margaret (Gilmore) Alexander, was born on July 24, 1832, in Russell County, Virginia. His father was born in Ireland and came to America with his parents at age two. When Isaac was a year old, his family moved to Tennessee. At sixteen years of age he became a Methodist. He grew up at Cumberland Gap and Strawberry Plains, where he later graduated from high school. From there he went to Emory and Henry College, where he received an M.A. at the age of nineteen.

Upon graduation from college, Alexander moved to Henderson, Texas, to teach at Fowler Institute.[qv] In 1855 he was ordained an elder in the East Texas Conference of the Methodist Episcopal Church, South, and promptly persuaded the conference to authorize him to open a female academy in Tyler. After two years there, he taught for a year at the Chappell Hill Female College,[qv] after which he returned to East Texas to marry Miss Hall, the daughter of the Methodist preacher in Jamestown, Smith County, and open a school in his wife's home. The couple had two daughters. In 1859 the family moved to Gilmer, where Alexander taught school and preached. In 1860 he was hired as principal of the four-year-old New Danville Masonic Female Academy. He kept this school open though the war and the yellow fever epidemic that carried off his wife and many of his students in 1864. In 1873 Alexander, the academy, and most of the population of New Danville moved to the new railroad town of Kilgore, where the academy reopened as a coeducation facility named Alexander Institute under the sponsorship of the local Methodist congregation. Alexander remained as principal when the school, which later became Lon Morris College, was turned over to the East Texas Conference in 1875. In 1888 his home burned. In 1890 he resigned as president of the institute (though he remained a member of its board until his death) and moved once more to Henderson. There he married Mrs. Margaret Lockens. Two children were born to them. At Henderson, Alexander taught for four years before entering the full-time pastorate. In 1908 he became a superannuate preacher and associate editor of the *Rusk County News*. In 1911 he became chaplain of the Agricultural and Mechanical College of Texas, where he also taught history. He died on June 5, 1919.

BIBLIOGRAPHY: Glendell A. Jones, Jr., *Mid the Pine Hills of East Texas* (Jacksonville, Texas: Progress, 1973). *Connie Snodgrass*

ALEXANDER, JAMES MINOR (1867–1954). James Minor Alexander, builder and physician, was born on September 18, 1867, in Spring Hill, Tennessee, to James Franklin and Elizabeth (Minor) Alexander. He attended the Kentucky School of Medicine and graduated with honors in 1889 from Louisville Medical College. Later he did postgraduate work in New York, at Johns Hopkins in Baltimore, at the Mayo Clinic in Rochester, and in 1913 in hospitals in London, Paris, Rome, Naples, and Berlin. In 1889 he moved to Victoria, Texas, then to Abilene, where he started a practice.

He opened Alexander Sanitarium, a hospital with eighteen beds, on June 1, 1904, in a two-story frame building. In 1918 he converted the structure into a school for nurses and moved his hospital into an adjacent three-story brick building with forty beds. He was joined in his Abilene practice by his brother, Dr. Sydney McLemore Alexander. Jim Alexander was credited with many medical firsts in West Texas, including the first Caesarean operation and the first two complete hysterectomies. He installed Abilene's first X-ray equipment. He closed his sanitarium in 1934 to join the staff of Hendrick Medical Center,[qv] where he later became chief of staff. He was a member of the Taylor-Jones County Medical Society, the Texas Medical Association,[qv] the Southern Medical Association, and the American Medical Association.

In 1925 he constructed the Alexander Building, then the tallest building in Abilene. That same year he established the Alexander Trust Estate, which placed most of his holdings in the names of his children. After his medical career was established, he acquired ranchland in Jones, Stonewall, King, Knox, and Shackelford counties. His ranching operations continued through his grandchildren and great-grandchildren. He was married twice, first to Madge Quarles, then to Anna Lee Burnes. He retired from medical practice in 1949 and died on November 10, 1954. He was buried in Cedar Hill Cemetery, Abilene.

BIBLIOGRAPHY: Abilene *Reporter-News*, November 27, 1950, November 11, 1954, April 8, 1956. Hugh E. Cosby, *The History of Abilene* (Abilene, Texas, 1955). Katharyn Duff and Betty Kay Seibt, *Catclaw Country: An Informal History of Abilene in West Texas* (Burnet, Texas: Eakin Press, 1980). *Katharyn Duff*

ALEXANDER, JAMES PATTERSON (1883–1948). James Patterson Alexander, chief justice of the Texas Supreme Court, was born in Moody, McLennan County, Texas, on April 21, 1883, the son of John Newton and Mary (Patterson) Alexander. He attended Baylor University in 1901 and received a law degree from the University of Texas in 1908. After a summer of postgraduate work at the University of Chicago in 1908, he began a law practice in McGregor. He moved his practice to Waco in 1911 and was elected county judge of McLennan County in 1916. He married Elizabeth Akin of Waco on August 2, 1916, and they had two daughters. From 1920 to 1924 Alexander served as judge for the Nineteenth District Court. He retired to private practice in 1924 but in 1930 became an associate justice of the Tenth Court of Civil Appeals at Waco. From 1920 to 1940 he was a member of the Baylor law faculty. While there, he taught civil trial procedure and instituted a series of student practice trials. In 1940 he was elected chief justice of the Texas Supreme Court, in which he served until his death. One of his primary concerns was to revise the code of civil procedure so that cases would move through the judicial process more efficiently.

Alexander was a Baptist, a Mason, and a member of the Philosophical Society of Texas.[qv] He also served as director of the State Bar of Texas[qv] and as president of the National Council of Judicial Councils. He farmed and raised bees as a hobby. He died in Austin on January 1, 1948, and was buried in the State Cemetery.[qv]

BIBLIOGRAPHY: *National Cyclopaedia of American Biography*, Vol. 51. Vertical Files, Barker Texas History Center, University of Texas at Austin.

A. L. Weinberger

ALEXANDER, JEROME B. (?–1842). Jerome B. Alexander, soldier of the Republic of Texas,[qv] moved to Texas in January 1832. During the Texas Revolution[qv] he served as a private in Capt. John York's[qv] volunteer company at the siege of Bexar[qv] and as a private in Capt. Moseley Baker's[qv] Company D of Col. Edward Burleson's[qv] First Regiment, Texas Volunteers, at the battle of San Jacinto.[qv] He was elected clerk of the Third Judicial District court in January 1838 and was reelected in January 1842. During this period he was a resident of Fayette County with title to 200 acres of land and an additional 611 acres under survey. He also owned two town lots in La Grange, four horses, fifty cattle, and a silver watch. He had an additional 1,476 acres under survey in Gonzales County.

When Adrián Woll[qv] raided San Antonio in 1842, Alexander was elected lieutenant in the volunteer company of Capt. Nicholas M. Dawson.[qv] He was killed in action in the infamous Dawson Massacre[qv] on September 18, 1842. He was buried with his companions at Monument Hill[qv] near La Grange, Fayette County.

BIBLIOGRAPHY: *Compiled Index to Elected and Appointed Officials of the Republic of Texas, 1835–1846* (Austin: State Archives, Texas State Library, 1981). Daughters of the Republic of Texas, *Muster Rolls of the Texas Revolution* (Austin, 1986). Sam Houston Dixon and Louis Wiltz Kemp, *The Heroes of San Jacinto* (Houston: Anson Jones, 1932). Joseph Milton Nance, *Attack and Counterattack: The Texas-Mexican Frontier, 1842* (Austin: University of Texas Press, 1964). *Southwestern Historical Quarterly*, Notes and Fragments, July 1903.

Thomas W. Cutrer

ALEXANDER, ROBERT (1811–1882). Robert Alexander, Methodist minister and missionary to Texas, the ninth child of Daniel and Rachael (Moffat) Alexander, was born in Smith County, Tennessee, on August 7, 1811. He joined the Methodist Episcopal Church about 1826. He was admitted into the Tennessee Conference in 1830 and ordained a deacon in 1832 and an elder in 1834. He transferred to the Mississippi Conference in 1835 and in April 1837 was appointed missionary to Texas with Martin Ruter and Littleton Fowler.[qqv] Alexander, the first of the three to enter the new republic, crossed the Sabine on August 19 and preached his way westward, thus beginning a ministry of forty-five years in Texas. During a camp meeting at the McMahan settlement, he held a "quarterly conference" and formed the San Augustine circuit on September 16. In mid-October he formed the first Methodist missionary society in Texas during a camp meeting held at Caney Creek, southwest of Washington-on-the-Brazos.

When Ruter died in May 1838, Alexander took up Ruter's plans for a college and organized a board of proprietors for Rutersville College. Under Alexander's chairmanship the board raised funds, purchased a site, elected Chauncey Richardson[qv] president, obtained a charter and a generous grant of land from the Texas Congress, and opened the school in 1840.

In the meantime, the mission had been organized into the Texas Conference, and Alexander was appointed first presiding elder of the Rutersville District. In the following years he also served as presiding elder of the Galveston, Huntsville, and Chappell Hill districts. His pastoral appointments included Belton, Chappell Hill, Galveston, and Waco. From 1855 to 1858 he was agent for the American Bible Society in Texas.

When the Methodists split over slavery[qv] in 1844, Alexander's colleagues elected him delegate to the Louisville Convention that organized the Methodist Episcopal Church, South, in 1845. They subsequently elected him to nine succeeding General Conferences. In 1848 he was instrumental in establishing the *Texas Wesleyan Banner*, which later became the *Texas Christian Advocate* (now the *United Methodist Reporter*[qv]), published in Cincinnati, Nashville, New Orleans, New York, and Galveston. After the failure of Rutersville College, Alexander played a prominent role in the effort to establish a central university for Texas Methodism. He was a member of the board of commissioners that located Soule University at Chappell Hill in 1856 and was a trustee there. From 1870 to 1873 he was president of the educational commission that founded Texas University (later Southwestern University) at Georgetown.

Alexander married Eliza Ayres on January 25, 1838. They had a daughter. His wife died on August 30, 1878, and on November 11, 1879, he married Mrs. Patience N. Wilson of Bryan. Alexander died on April 25, 1882, in Chappell Hill, where he is buried.

BIBLIOGRAPHY: Ralph W. Jones, *Southwestern University, 1840–1861* (Austin: Jenkins, 1973). Ann Ayers Lide, *Robert Alexander and the Early Methodist Church in Texas* (La Grange, Texas: Press of La Grange *Journal*, 1935). Walter N. Vernon et al., *The Methodist Excitement in Texas* (Dallas: Texas United Methodist Historical Society, 1984).

Norman W. Spellmann

ALEXANDER, WILLIAM (1814–1872). William Alexander, lawyer and judge, was born in Glasgow, Scotland, on September 10, 1814. His family immigrated to Jackson County, New York, in 1822, when Alexander was eight. He graduated from Yale Law School and moved to Tuskegee, Alabama, where he practiced in the supreme court of that state after receiving his license on January 11, 1850. Alexander moved to Galveston, Texas, in 1850. In 1851 John Byler Mallard[qv] persuaded him to move to Palestine, Anderson County, to form a law partnership with Mallard and John H. Reagan,[qv] and on February 1, 1851, Alexander received his license to practice before the Supreme Court of Texas. He married Mallard's widow, Susan Scott Mallard, on March 8, 1857; they had two children. He served as a trustee for Palestine Female Academy[qv] in 1858 and was chief justice of Anderson County from 1860 to 1865. He was a Mason and a Presbyterian. Alexander died in Palestine on January 11, 1872.

BIBLIOGRAPHY: C. K. Chamberlain, "East Texas," *East Texas Historical Journal* 4 (October 1966). Marker Files, Texas Historical Commission, Austin (William Alexander, Mallard-Alexander House).

Mark Odintz

ALEXANDER, WILLIAM (1819–1882). William Alexander was born in 1819 in Woodford County, Kentucky, to a prominent family of farmers and stock raisers. He graduated from Centre College, Kentucky, and Yale University. He later studied law at Frankfort, Kentucky, and began his practice after moving to Galveston, Texas, in May 1846. In 1857 he moved to Austin. He opposed secession[qv] and left Texas during the Civil War[qv] to travel in Mexico and study Spanish and Mexican law. After the war he served as attorney general of Texas under provisional governor Andrew J. Hamilton[qv] in 1865–66. In September 1867 he again was appointed attorney general of Texas by Gen. Charles Griffin,[qv] commander of the Fifth Military District.[qv] He resigned in October, however, after a difference of opinion with Governor E. M. Pease[qv] over the validity of the state Constitution of 1866.[qv] Alexander was appointed attorney general of Texas for the third time in 1870 by Governor Edmund J. Davis[qv] and served until 1874. Thereafter he continued practicing law in Austin, where he died on February 16, 1882.

BIBLIOGRAPHY: Austin *Daily Statesman*, February 19, 1882. Charles W. Ramsdell, *Reconstruction in Texas* (New York: Columbia University Press, 1910; rpt., Austin: Texas State Historical Association, 1970).

Alwyn Barr

ALEXANDER, TEXAS. Alexander, at the junction of State Highway 6 and Farm Road 914 in southern Erath County, was named Harper's Mill when a post office was established there in 1876. John D. St. Clair was the first postmaster and was still serving in 1881, when the name was changed to Alexander, possibly after an official of the Texas Central Railroad Company. The railroad laid out the townsite after buying land from W. C. Keith in 1880. Alexander expanded after the railroad came in 1881, but growth was checked after the railroad reached Stephenville in 1889. Alexander had a population of 381 and twenty-one businesses in 1890. In 1900 the population was the same, but the number of businesses had declined. By 1940 the town had 200 people, a post office, and five businesses. The post office closed before 1970, when the population was forty. In 1990 the population was still reported as forty.

BIBLIOGRAPHY: Vallie Eoff, A History of Erath County, Texas (M.A. thesis, University of Texas, 1937).

ALEXANDER CREEK. Alexander Creek, in central Hamilton County, rises three miles south of Hamilton (at 33°40′ N, 98°05′ W) and runs east for eight miles to its mouth on the Leon River (at 31°42′ N, 97°59′ W). The steep slopes and benches of the area are surfaced by shallow clay loams that support juniper, live oak, mesquite, and grasses.

ALEY, TEXAS. Aley is on Farm Road 85 twenty-seven miles northwest of Athens in far northwestern Henderson County. The settlement was evidently founded soon after the Civil War.[qv] A post office operated there from 1894 to 1907. In the early 1900s J. O. Hall and W. C. Higgins operated a local general store, and by 1910 the settlement had a combination church and school, a store operated by James Burns, and a population of twenty-five. In the mid-1930s it had a population of sixty-five, two churches, a store, and a school. After World War II[qv] the population dropped to fifty and the school closed. In the early 1990s a cemetery and two stores remained.

Christopher Long

ALFORD, GEORGE G. (1793–1847). George G. Alford, merchant, planter, and fighter in the Texas Revolution,[qv] was born near Ithaca, New York, on June 17, 1793, the son of Capt. George G. and Elizabeth (Hulbert) Alford, Sr. During the War of 1812 he served as a lieutenant of artillery on the staff of Gen. Winfield Scott. In 1815 he moved with his family to Detroit, Michigan. About 1819 he settled in New Madrid, Missouri, where he opened a store and served as county court judge from 1822 to 1825 and as treasurer from 1834 to 1836. In the winter of 1835, at the request of Sam Houston,[qv] Alford joined the revolutionary army[qv] as quartermaster general. Shortly after the battle of San Jacinto[qv] in April 1836, he was sent by the provisional government[qv] of the Republic of Texas[qv] to New Orleans to purchase supplies for the army. Alford's group was returning with two vessels loaded with provisions, when it was intercepted by a Mexican fleet commanded by José V. Matios off Galveston. The two vessels and their cargos were seized, and Alford and the other members of the expedition were captured and imprisoned in Matamoros. Alford and his brother, Maj. Johnson H. Alford, were condemned to death but were eventually released through the intervention of President Andrew Jackson.

In April 1837 Alford settled his affairs in New Madrid and moved his family and slaves to Texas. They settled first in Nacogdoches, then in 1840 in newly organized Houston County, where Alford acquired extensive landholdings and established a plantation at what became known as Alford's Bluff, on a small rise overlooking the Trinity River. During the 1840s Alford served as justice of the peace and associate justice for Houston County and was senior warden of the first Masonic lodge in Crockett. He married Christine Lesieur, the daughter of French Canadian settlers, in 1821, while in New Madrid. She died in 1824, leaving him one daughter. About 1829 Alford married Ann Barfield, with whom he had four children. He died in Crockett on April 1, 1847, two months after his wife's death, and was buried in the Glenwood Cemetery. A state historical marker was placed at the gravesite in 1981.

BIBLIOGRAPHY: Armistead Albert Aldrich, *The History of Houston County, Texas* (San Antonio: Naylor, 1943). Carolyn Reeves Ericson, *Nacogdoches, Gateway to Texas: A Biographical Directory* (2 vols., Fort Worth: Arrow-Curtis Printing, 1974, 1987). *History of Southeast Missouri* (Chicago: Goodspeed, 1888). *Memorial and Biographical History of Dallas County* (Chicago: Lewis, 1892; rpt., Dallas: Walsworth, 1976). Marker Files, Texas Historical Commission, Austin. Vertical Files, Barker Texas History Center, University of Texas at Austin.

Christopher Long

ALFORD, NEEDHAM JUDGE (1789–1869). Needham Judge Alford, Methodist preacher, was born July 12, 1789, in North Carolina, the son of Jacob and Elizabeth (Bryant) Alford. He held a two-day meeting near the present site of Milam in the spring of 1832 with Sumner Bacon,[qv] a Cumberland Presbyterian. The meeting was a test of their determination to preach in the area against the opposition of James Gaines[qv] and others. When a man named Johnson threatened to horsewhip the first preacher who entered the stand, Alford, a strong man, said, "I am as able to take a whipping as any man on this ground," and Johnson, taking notice of the muscular preacher, quietly retired. Before coming to Texas, Alford had been known in Louisiana as the "bulldog preacher." He was married to Martha Waddell (Waddle) in Franklin County, Mississippi, on February 18, 1815; they had nine children. He died on September 19, 1869, near Horn Hill in Limestone County.

BIBLIOGRAPHY: George L. Crocket, *Two Centuries in East Texas* (Dallas: Southwest, 1932; facsimile reprod., 1962). Homer S. Thrall, *A Brief History of Methodism in Texas* (Nashville: Publishing House of the Methodist Episcopal Church, South, 1889; rpt., Greenwood, South Carolina: Attic, 1977).

Helen Gomer Schluter

ALFORD'S BLUFF. Alford's Bluff was a cotton plantation and landing on the Trinity River a mile upriver from Sebastopol and seven miles southeast of Trinity in southwestern Trinity County. It was described in 1867 as being "just below Whiterock shoals," which was probably near the confluence of White Rock Creek and the Trinity River. The same report also described it as being located "on the site of the ancient Puebla of Trinidad," which was incorrect. The villa of Santísima Trinidad de Salcedo,[qv] on a site later known as Spanish Bluff, was on the east bank of the Trinity River twenty-four miles to the northwest in Houston County.

A plantation owned by George G. Alford[qv] was established at Alford's Bluff by 1841. Although Alford moved shortly thereafter to Crockett, in neighboring Houston County, the property appears to have stayed in the family. In 1859 two of Alford's sons, George Frederick and Hulbert Mallory Alford, moved to Alford's Bluff from Palestine, where they had been involved in the mercantile business. Describing Trinity County in the 1867 *Texas Almanac,* George F. Alford identified Alford's Bluff and Sebastopol as the two shipping points for the county. Cotton, corn, and beeves, he wrote, could be shipped from either place and "landed on the wharf at Galveston in sixty hours." The traveler setting out from either place could reach Galveston in twenty-four hours, Houston in twenty. Alford also observed that Alford's Bluff was noted for its chalybeate springs. With the expansion of railroads in East Texas during the 1870s, river traffic on the Trinity declined, and with it, the importance of Alford's Bluff as a shipping point. Hulbert Alford died in 1864. In 1866, following a disastrous flood on the Trinity, George F. Alford moved his family to Galveston, where he became wealthy as a cotton factor and banker. He died in Dallas in 1910.

BIBLIOGRAPHY: George F. Alford, "Trinity County," *The Texas Almanac for 1867* (Galveston: W. Richardson, 1866?). Clement Anselm Evans, ed., *Confederate Military History* (Atlanta: Confederate, 1899; extended ed., Wilmington, North Carolina: Broadfoot, 1987–89). Louis Wiltz Kemp Papers, Barker Texas History Center, University of Texas at Austin. *Memorial and Biographical History of Dallas County* (Chicago: Lewis, 1892; rpt., Dallas: Walsworth, 1976).

Mary M. Standifer

ALFRED, TEXAS. Alfred is on State Highway 359 twelve miles northeast of Alice in northeastern Jim Wells County. The community was founded in 1888, when the site was in Nueces County, and was originally named Driscoll. A post office was established there in 1890. In 1904, when the St. Louis, Brownsville and Mexico Railway built through the Robert Driscoll[qv] ranch to the east, Driscoll wanted the station to be named after himself. Since there could not be two post offices with the same name, N. T. Wright, the postmaster of old Driscoll, agreed to change the name of his post office to Alfred, in honor of his father, Alfred Wright, the first postmaster of the community. The Texas and New Orleans Railroad built through the area in 1907. In 1912 a school district was formed there, and in 1914 the town had a population of fifty, a general store, and six cattle breeders. The population of Alfred peaked in 1927, when it was estimated at 300. In 1936 Alfred comprised a school, several dwellings, and surrounding farms. During the 1940s and 1950s the community's population continued to decrease, and by 1969 it was estimated at twenty. In 1979 and 1990 Alfred was a dispersed rural community with a population of ten. *Cyrus Tilloson*

ALFRED DISTRICT. The Alfred District was an electoral district for selecting delegates to the Convention of 1832.[qv] Its representatives were William D. Lacey, Samuel Bruff, David Wright, William R. Hensley, and Jesse Burnam.[qqv] Colorado County now includes the area of the colonial district.

BIBLIOGRAPHY: Hans Peter Nielsen Gammel, comp., *Laws of Texas, 1822–1897* (10 vols., Austin: Gammel, 1898).

ALGERITA, TEXAS. Algerita is on U.S. Highway 190 about 7½ miles west of San Saba in central San Saba County. In 1885 Charles Cadwaleder Yarborough opened a general store and post office near Richland Creek four miles north of the present site and called it Algerita after the local algerita (agarita) shrub. The post office was closed in 1890. In 1907 the Gulf, Colorado and Santa Fe Railway constructed a line several miles from town, and the settlement gradually moved to its present location next to the railroad. Walter Thomas established a post office at the new townsite in 1914, but the community declined after the railroad property was removed because ranchers west of town refused to open cattle lanes across their land. The population fell to twenty by 1925 but increased to sixty by 1949, when the community had a church, a school, and a combination filling station and store. The population was twenty-five in 1952 and was estimated at forty-eight in 1990.

BIBLIOGRAPHY: Alma Ward Hamrick, *The Call of the San Saba: A History of San Saba County* (San Antonio: Naylor, 1941; 2d ed., Austin: Jenkins, 1969). *San Saba County History* (San Saba, Texas: San Saba County Historical Commission, 1983). *Karen Yancy*

ALGOA, TEXAS. Algoa, located on State Highway 6 in northern Galveston County, was founded in 1880 on the Gulf, Colorado and Santa Fe Railway, which later formed a junction with the St. Louis, Brownsville and Santa Fe at the townsite. The community was named Hughes and was equipped with telephone service as early as 1893. The Algoa post office opened in 1897. Some sources have claimed that the town was named for a British tanker, the *Algoaian,* which was blown ashore during the Galveston hurricane of 1900,[qv] but the name clearly predates that event. Local farmers grew pears, satsumas, strawberries, and magnolia figs. The Alvin Fruit and Nursery Company, incorporated by R. H. Bushway in 1900, expanded rapidly. The first Algoa school was built near the Brazoria county line and in 1910 employed three teachers. By the 1920s rice and dairy farming had become major parts of the economy. Schools in Algoa became a part of the Santa Fe Consolidated School District in 1928. Algoa grew from a population of fifty in 1920 to 350 in 1940. In 1957 the Milwhite Mud Industry was built to serve the nearby oilfields. The post office closed in 1972, and mail was sent through Alvin or Arcadia. In 1982 Algoa had a drive-in grocery store, a gas station, a restaurant, an auction barn, an antique shop, a roller rink, a horse-race training track, four to five beer parlors, three fig farms, and the mud industry. The 1980 and 1990 the population was reported as 135.

BIBLIOGRAPHY: Galveston *Daily News,* September 6, 1972. Kathleen E. and Clifton R. St. Clair, eds., *Little Towns of Texas* (Jacksonville, Texas: Jayroe Graphic Arts, 1982). Vertical File, Rosenberg Library, Galveston. *Leigh Gard*

ALGUACIL. The alguacil served as the sheriff of a Spanish municipality. He also acted as executive officer of the courts, the equivalent of a modern bailiff, and executed the decisions of the alcalde,[qv] or local judge. The alguacil could gain his office in a number of ways. Though in some towns he was elected, usually an alguacil was appointed to the position, either by the alcalde, the governor, or the ayuntamiento,[qv] the town council. The alguacil was a member of the ayuntamiento and had a vote equal to the other councilmen. He also had numerous duties, most of which consisted of acting upon the orders of the governor, alcalde, and ayuntamiento and serving as chief constable. As the principal police officer, the alguacil and his assistants, or *tenientes,* were allowed to carry arms as they patrolled the town. In addition, the alguacil maintained the security of the prison, if one existed. To avoid possible conflict and interference with his position, the alguacil could not hold another office or have a business. Instead, he received a percentage of the judgments he executed for his duties as administrative officer of the alcalde's court. The exact amount varied and was never standardized. In some areas he was also paid based on his number of arrests. The alguacil did not receive a fee for collecting fines owed to the royal treasury. The Spanish Constitution of 1812 and the subsequent independence of Mexico, which transformed many colonial institutions, did not substantively alter the alguacil's position.

BIBLIOGRAPHY: Eugene C. Barker, "The Government of Austin's Colony, 1821–1831," *Southwestern Historical Quarterly* 21 (January 1918). Frank W. Blackman, *Spanish Institutions of the Southwest*

(Baltimore: Johns Hopkins Press, 1891; rpt., Glorieta, New Mexico: Rio Grande Press, 1976). Mattie Alice Austin, "The Municipal Government of San Fernando de Bexar," *Quarterly of the Texas State Historical Association* 8 (April 1905). O. Garfield Jones, "Local Government in the Spanish Colonies as Provided by the Recopilación de Leyes de los Reynos de las Indias," *Southwestern Historical Quarterly* 19 (July 1915). John Preston Moore, *The Cabildo in Peru under the Bourbons* (Durham: Duke University Press, 1966). John Preston Moore, *The Cabildo in Peru under the Hapsburgs* (Durham: Duke University Press, 1954). Marc Simmons, *Spanish Government in New Mexico* (Albuquerque: University of New Mexico Press, 1968). David J. Weber, *The Mexican Frontier, 1821–1846* (Albuquerque: University of New Mexico Press, 1982). *Geoffrey Pivateau*

ALIANZA HISPANO-AMERICANA. The Alianza Hispano-Americana was founded on January 14, 1894, in Tucson, Arizona, by Carlos I. Velasco, Pedro C. Pellón, and Mariano G. Samaniego, as a fraternal benefit society. It fanned out across the rest of the Southwest over the next sixteen years, spreading to Texas by June 1906. It grew into the biggest and best known of the Mexican-American sociedades mutualistas[qv] in the Southwest. Although AHA was set up to offer life insurance at low rates and provide social activities for Mexican Americans,[qv] one source suggests that it was initially organized in response to hostile attitudes against Mexican Americans in Tucson. Its goals were similar to those of other fraternal aid groups in the United States, which began to multiply in the late nineteenth century among European immigrants. When AHA was established, most United States citizens could not depend on government social security programs, labor unions, or commercial life insurance to provide economic assistance to a family upon the loss of the chief family provider, usually the father. Besides tendering such services, AHA, like other mutual-aid groups, also sought to preserve the culture of its constituents and taught its members democratic traditions, such as free speech, by involving them in organizational activities.

Membership in AHA was limited to Mexican Americans who were committed to altruism toward their fellows, the work ethic, and good moral virtues; it did not offer membership to exconvicts or individuals of African or Asian descent. However it joined forces with the NAACP in 1954 to fight discrimination and offered musician Louis Armstrong an honorary membership in 1957. Women were allowed to join AHA in 1913 as a response to the woman suffrage[qv] movement. Monthly dues subsidized the death-benefits package. An executive board oversaw AHA's activities, and by 1916 the national headquarters in Tucson moved into the Alianza building.

Texas-based AHA lodges were established in major cities, such as San Antonio and El Paso, but there were some affiliates in such small towns as Luling and Lytton. Expansion into Texas and other Southwestern cities in the 1910s improved services to the immense Mexican immigrant population that had been driven across the border by the Mexican Revolution.[qv] After 1929 the establishment of the League of United Latin American Citizens[qv] cut Texas participation in the AHA.

The June 1955 issue of the AHA *Alianza* noted two goals: equal opportunities for citizens of Mexican descent and expansion of AHA's services to those citizens. In Texas, George I. Sánchez[qv] spearheaded AHA's civil rights efforts in the mid-1950s as a consultant to Ralph Estrada, who headed the group's civil-liberties division. AHA's original work in the state sought legal remedies to end the segregation of prisoners. The organization hoped to use a two-pronged approach in attacking segregation—activism by a wide array of civil-rights leaders, and negotiations with Governor Allan Shivers.[qv] The Robert Marshall Civil Liberties Trust assisted AHA through a grant to Sánchez of $5,000.

In 1939 AHA membership climbed to 17,366, a monumental growth from its 1,171 members in 1907. It also organized lodges in Mexico and allied itself with the National Fraternal Congress, the largest organization for mutual-aid societies in the country. Although AHA ended most of its operations in the mid-1960s, a staff of two apparently remained at its Tucson headquarters through the early 1970s to finish its business. Budgetary woes forced AHA into receivership, and its president, James Carlos McCormick, was indicted, tried, and sentenced to a six-to-eight-year prison term for embezzlement. Later, all twenty-one counts against him were dismissed, and his sentence was reduced to five years' probation.

BIBLIOGRAPHY: Kaye Lynn Briegel, Alianza Hispano-Americana, 1894–1965 (Ph.D. dissertation, University of Southern California, 1974). Sylvia Alicia Gonzales, *Hispanic Voluntary Organizations* (Westport, Connecticut: Greenwood Press, 1985). George I. Sanchez Papers, Benson Latin American Collection, University of Texas at Austin.
Teresa Palomo Acosta

ALIBATES FLINT QUARRIES. The Alibates flint quarries are located along the Canadian River in Moore and Potter counties in the central part of the Panhandle.[qv] Alibates flint is an agatized dolomite outcropping in the Alibates dolomite of the Permian Age on both the north and south sides of the Canadian River valley. The flint can be found in an area of about ten square miles. It is characterized by its distinctive coloring and banded patterns. Colors are typically maroon and white, but blue, brown, red, and yellow also occur. The flint was utilized for the manufacture of chipped-stone tools from the time that man first inhabited the Southern High Plains, beginning with the Clovis cultures of about 10,000 years ago, through the Archaic and Neo-Indian stages and into the Historic stage, perhaps until the 1800s. The working of Alibates flint could be characterized as one of the earliest and longest-lived industries in early America. Floyd V. Studer[qv] has been credited with the discovery of the quarries in modern times.

In the areas of the outcrops, the flint was quarried from pits dug into the bedrock. These are shallow, circular depressions located along many of the canyon rims. They frequently are about three meters in diameter and about half a meter in depth. When they were active quarries, they may have ranged in depth from about three to six feet. Over the years they have been partially or completely filled with blown dirt. The flint was also frequently gathered from the gravel located downstream from the outcrops. Around the circumference of each pit is a low mound of quarry debris. Intermixed are occasional large Alibates quarry blanks (quarry bifaces) and quartzite hammers. The smaller hammers were used to shape the quarry bifaces, and the larger ones were probably used to remove the flint from the pits. The larger hammers may have been used with wooden wedges to loosen the flint. No wedges, however, have been found.

None of the quarry pits has ever been scientifically excavated and reported. Little detailed study of the quarrying activities of any of the prehistoric inhabitants of the region has been done. It is believed, however, that the Paleo-Indian hunters, the Archaic hunter-gatherers, and the Woodland–Palo Duro complex hunter-gatherers most often used readily available sources of flint—gravels or actual outcrops—rather than excavating pits into the source. The later sedentary group, the Panhandle Aspect, probably is responsible for excavating most of the quarry pits. Archeological surveys in the nearby Canadian valley have recorded numerous Panhandle Aspect slabhouse villages, occupied during the period from about A.D. 1150 to 1450. A major activity at some of these villages appears to have been the reduction of the quarry bifaces into blades and tool blanks. This suggests that the quarriers' economy depended a great deal on the mining, preparation, and trading of the flint. Testing and excavations have been conducted at several of these sites, including the Alibates Ruins, PT-8, and the Ozier Site, although none of the studies presents detailed discussion or analysis of lithic technology as it relates to the quarrying activities. The Alibates blades and quarry bifaces were used as trade items by the Panhandle Aspect peoples and were traded for Puebloan ceramics from the Rio Grande valley in New Mexico, obsidian from the Jemez Mountains in New Mexico, catlinite from Minnesota, and olivella shell from the Pacific coast. Frequently caches of Alibates blades or quarry blanks are found, but only a few are reported and described in the literature.

Alibates Flint Quarries National Monument was set aside in 1965 to preserve the flint quarries. Located above the Canadian River in Potter County, it consists of 1,079 acres with hundreds of the quarries and several village sites. Guided tours are presented by park rangers during the summer months and at other times by reservation. In 1992, 3,419 people visited the area. Other quarries are located within Lake Meredith National Recreation Area, the Lubbock Lake National Historic and State Archeological Landmark,[qqv] the Miami Site near the town of Miami and the Folsom Bison Kill and Blackwater Draw sites in northern New Mexico. The total number of quarry pits would undoubtedly be in the thousands. At some of the sites the remains of the flint have been found with the bones of the imperial mammoth. Most collections and records from the sites are at the Panhandle-Plains Historical Museum[qv] and the West Texas State University Archeological Research Laboratory, in Canyon, and also at the National Park Service Archeological Laboratory, Lake Meredith Recreation Area, in Fritch. Others are curated at Texas Tech University in Lubbock.

BIBLIOGRAPHY: *Alibates Flint Quarries and the Texas Panhandle Pueblo Culture* (Amarillo: Panhandle Historical Society, 1963). H. Mewhinney, "Alibates Flint Quarry," *Texas Parks and Wildlife,* August 1965.

Meeks Etchieson

ALICE, TEXAS. Alice, the county seat of Jim Wells County, is intersected by U.S. Highway 281 and State highways 44 and 359, forty-four miles west of Corpus Christi. The town originated in the defunct community of Collins, three miles to the east. About 1880 the San Antonio and Aransas Pass Railway attempted to build a line through Collins, which then had 2,000 inhabitants. The townspeople were not amenable to selling their land to the railroad company; consequently, the railroad site was moved three miles west, and in 1883 a depot called Bandana was established at its junction with the Corpus Christi, San Diego and Rio Grande Railway. Bandana soon became a thriving cattle-shipping point, and application for a post office was made under the name Kleberg in honor of Robert Justus Kleberg.[qv] The petition was denied because a town named Kleberg already appeared on the post office list, so residents then chose the name Alice, in honor of Alice Gertrudis King Kleberg, Kleberg's wife and the daughter of Richard King.[qv] The Alice post office opened for business in 1888. Within a few years the remaining residents of Collins moved to Alice, which was by then a thriving community.

The town's first school was established in 1888 on the second floor of the Becham Place, a boardinghouse for men. The private school had nine students. Until 1886 Alice students who chose to continue their education attended Goliad College. The Catholic church at Collins was moved to Alice in 1889. Methodist services were held at Mrs. E. D. Sidbury's lumberyard until 1890, when they were moved to a new school built by George Hobbs. A school board of trustees was elected, and a public school was started. In 1892 the town was served by a hotel, two saloons, two general stores, a weekly newspaper named the Alice *Reporter,* and a cotton gin. The San Antonio and Aransas Pass Railway had completed its line to Alice. By 1894 Alice was the busiest shipping point in South Texas. The Alice Circuit of the Methodist Church was formed in 1895. By 1896 the town had an estimated population of 885, a library, a bank, the Episcopal Church of the Advent, and a second weekly newspaper, *El Eco.* The first telephone exchange in Alice was established by the Beeville, Alice, and Wade City Telephone Company in 1896. The first two telephones in the community were located at Trinidad Salazar's[qv] general store and home. In 1898 Alice flooded, forcing residents to move their houses. In February 1899 a smallpox epidemic hit one of Alice's Mexican subdivisions, then located on the outskirts of the town. Consequently, the area was quarantined, and the two private Mexican schools in Alice were forced to close down. The epidemic became so widespread that the county commissioner ordered all schools closed and fumigated and authorized the county health officer to vaccinate every one in the area free of charge.

By 1900 the town had five churches, three public schools, a kindergarten, and a private Mexican school. The two weekly newspapers serving the town were the *Reporter* and the *Echo.* During that period Alice acquired the nickname the "Windmill Town" for its numerous windmills. In 1903 Eulalio Velázquez[qv] started publication of *El Cosmopolita,* a Spanish-language newspaper. Alice was incorporated on June 2, 1904, at which time it had a population of 887. F. B. Nayer owned the townsite and donated land for early civic buildings. With the completion of the St. Louis, Brownsville and Mexico Railway to Brownsville in 1904, the Alice-to-Brownsville stagecoach was discontinued. The telephone company was sold to the Eureka Telephone Company in 1904, and the Southwestern Telephone and Telegraph Company started providing long-distance service. Trinidad Salazar was instrumental in getting Alice a new elementary school, which was named for original settler F. B. Nayer. In 1909 a fire destroyed half of the Alice business section, but it was rebuilt and the town continued to grow. Alice was chosen county seat of Jim Wells County shortly after the county's organization in 1911. The town also became the headquarters for Texas Rangers[qv] serving in South Texas during the 1912–16 border raids. By 1914 Alice had an estimated population of 3,500, two banks, a cottonseed oil mill, a cotton gin, an ice plant, and two weeklies, the Alice *Echo* and the *News.* The introduction of irrigation[qv] helped to continue Alice's importance as a shipping center, and a shift was made from transporting livestock to transporting fruits and vegetables. During the 1920s, as a result of the oil boom in Jim Wells County, Alice adopted the slogan "Hub City of South Texas." The town served as the distribution point for both supplies and construction to south Texas. Its population was estimated at 4,239 in 1931. In 1935 a public library opened. The town had an oil boom in 1938, when the Alice oilfield was discovered. By 1940 the population was 7,792.

Alice made national headlines during the 1948 primary election for state senator. Lyndon Baines Johnson and Governor Coke Stevenson[qqv] both ran for the Democratic party[qv] nomination. It was alleged that Johnson won the primary because he had stolen the election with the help of George B. Parr,[qv] political boss, who controlled both Duval and Jim Wells counties. Alice became the focal point of a federal investigation when it was alleged that Alice's Precinct 13 ballot box had been stuffed. By 1949 violence erupted in Alice. W. H. (Bill) Mason, a local broadcaster, was shot by deputy sheriff Sam Smithwick after he had alleged on the air that Smithwick was the owner of a dime-a-dance palace.

During the 1940s and 1950s Alice had an economy based on the oil and gas industry, livestock production, and the marketing of cotton, flax, grain, and vegetables. Industries manufactured oil-well chemicals and supplies, fiberglass, products, cottonseed oil products, and foods. Census figures indicated a population of 16,414 in 1950. In September 1951 Alice was struck by a flood. In 1960 the population was 20,861. In 1963 Alice had thirteen churches and seven schools. In 1966 the town reported 429 businesses, nineteen manufacturers, twenty churches, two libraries, two newspapers, three banks, a radio station, and a hospital. Around 1966 Mexican-American youths boycotted Alice High School in protest against discrimination on the part of students, teachers, and administrators. Alice had an estimated population of 25,100 and 462 businesses in 1970. During the 1970s the city continued to be an oil and agricultural center. Agribusiness in Alice contributed nearly $34 million annually to the gross income of Jim Wells County. The Alice trade territory embraced a population of more than 150,000 in a forty-mile radius. In 1982 naphthalene and penanthene were found in Alice's water supply and traced to an oilfield drilling company working in the area. In 1985 there were over 250 oil and mineral industry companies in the area. At the time Alice had eleven public schools and two parochial schools, twenty-nine churches, a museum, a public library, a private hospital, 557 businesses, and ninety-four major employers. In 1990 Alice had a population of 19,788.

Recreational facilities in Alice include city parks, golf courses, and swimming pools. Proximity to Lake Corpus Christi, Padre Island,[qqv] and the Gulf of Mexico makes Alice an attractive haven for winter Texans. The Fiesta Bandana is held annually in May. A historical marker noting Alice's 100th anniversary was unveiled on August 28, 1993.

BIBLIOGRAPHY: Evan Anders, *Boss Rule in South Texas: The Progressive Era* (Austin: University of Texas Press, 1982). Agnes G. Grimm, *Llanos Mesteñas: Mustang Plains* (Waco: Texian Press, 1968). Laredo *Times,* March 11, 1975. David Montejano, *Anglos and Mexicans in the Making of Texas, 1836–1986* (Austin: University of Texas Press, 1987). Neva Virginia Pollard, The History of Jim Wells County (M.A. thesis, Texas A&I University, 1945). Vertical Files, Barker Texas History Center, University of Texas at Austin. *Alicia Salinas*

ALICE SOUTHWEST, TEXAS. Alice Southwest was southwest of Alice off U.S. 281 and State Highway 359 in central Jim Wells County. The settlement had a population of 1,813 in 1961 and 1,950 in 1986. By 1993 it had been annexed by the city of Alice. *Alicia A. Garza*

ALICE TERMINAL RESERVOIR. Alice Terminal Reservoir, also known as Lake Alice, is on Chiltipin Creek in the Nueces–Rio Grande coastal basin three miles north of Alice in Jim Wells County (at 27°49′ N, 98°03′ W). Construction of the reservoir started on September 27, 1963, and was completed in 1965. The project is owned by the Alice Water Authority and is operated as a municipal water supply for the city of Alice. The lake is also used for recreation. Its water is obtained from Chiltipin Creek, supplemented by Nueces River water that is purchased by contract from the city of Corpus Christi. The reservoir has a normal capacity of 2,780 acre-feet and surface area of 700 acres; its maximum capacity is 7,316 acre-feet. An intake structure and a pumping plant were built at Lake Corpus Christi to deliver purchased water through 20.4 miles of pipeline. The drainage area to the reservoir is some 157 square miles.

BIBLIOGRAPHY: C. L. Dowell, *Dams and Reservoirs in Texas: History and Descriptive Information* (Texas Water Commission Bulletin 6408 [Austin, 1964]). *Seth D. Breeding*

ALIEF, TEXAS. Alief, a residential suburb of Houston originally known as Dairy and Dairy Station, is on the Southern Pacific Railroad and Bray's Bayou in western Harris County. The site was first settled in 1861, when Reynolds Reynolds claimed 1,250 acres of land at the bayou headwaters. Jacamiah Seaman Daugherty[qv] purchased Reynolds's land in 1888 and in 1889 granted the San Antonio and Aransas Pass Railway a right-of-way. Daugherty's plans failed, however, and in 1893 Francis I. Meston of Colorado purchased the land. Meston hired W. D. Twitchell (perhaps Willis D. Twichell[qv]) to plat the town in 1895 and retained Daugherty to oversee land sales at his Houston land office. Meston granted a free lot in town for the purchase of every forty acres of farmland and in 1900 donated land for the Alief cemetery. In 1894 county surveyors named the community Dairy, but application for a post office in 1895 resulted in changing the name to Alief in honor of the first postmistress, Alief Ozella Magee. The population was twenty-five in 1896, when the community had a two-room schoolhouse for white children and a one-room schoolhouse for black children.

Alief suffered heavy damage from the flood of 1899 and the Galveston hurricane of 1900,[qv] which destroyed the Methodist Episcopal church and cotton and corn crops ready for harvest. When the International–Great Northern Railroad Company offered free transportation to anyone who wanted to leave, many residents left for Ellis County, where they had previously resided. The town reverted to prairie; only six of its thirty families and the Bassinger General Mercantile Store remained, and wolves were seen during the daytime. In 1900 Daugherty convinced local farmers that rice was particularly suited to Alief's easily flooded land and spent large sums of money to raise the first crops. His effort made rice a prominent cash crop until 1915, when cotton production resumed. Daugherty also acquired and distributed free Egyptian cottonseed.

In 1901 Andrew Jackson Martin became the first of a small group of German immigrants to arrive in the community and purchase land for farming. Many who left after the hurricane returned by 1904. Resettlement brought a new commercial district along the tracks of the San Antonio Aransas Pass, where depots were constructed in 1904. The town's first cotton gin was built in 1905, and an independent school district was established in 1911. In 1908 the city of Houston built the Upper Brays Bayou Wastewater Treatment Plant in Alief, and in 1909 residents formed the first Harris County Flood Control District. Daugherty promoted the Cane Belt Canal, whose irrigation system reached Alief in 1934 and caused a resurgence in rice as a major cash crop (*see* RICE CULTURE). In the 1930s the population of Alief fell from 112 to thirty-five. In 1942 the town had 200 residents and eight businesses. From the end of World War II[qv] through the 1950s it had a population of 150. In 1964 work began on a new school building for the district, which comprised nearly thirty-seven square miles; but between 1964 and 1968 school enrollment declined by more than 50 percent. By the 1970s much of the community had been annexed by Houston, though the town retained its identity. From 1962 until 1990 the population was reported at 1,400. Businesses peaked in 1983 at sixty.

BIBLIOGRAPHY: Houston Metropolitan Research Center Files, Houston Public Library. *Claudia Hazlewood*

ALIEN LAND LAW. An alien land law passed on April 13, 1891, during the administration of James Stephen Hogg,[qv] was designed to prohibit land speculation by foreign-controlled corporations and provided that no alien or alien company might obtain deed to or interest in Texas land except for a limited time. The law was inapplicable to aliens who became citizens within six years after they acquired land; all aliens not exempt by the law were given six years to surrender their land. The law was declared unconstitutional on December 11, 1891, in *Gunter v. Texas Land and Mortgage Company* on the technical ground that the subject was not expressed in the title and that although the law was passed as an amendment, it did not specify what law it was amending. On April 12, 1892, a new alien land law, passed by the called session of the Twenty-second Legislature, did not include a prohibitive measure on alien corporations and altered the time limit from six to ten years. The 1892 law operated until 1921, when a new law again included a prohibitive measure against land ownership by alien corporations and changed the time limit from ten to five years. In 1965 the Fifty-ninth Texas Legislature repealed the laws from the 1921 act on the grounds that they imposed "unreasonable and discriminatory restrictions" on alien ownership and militated against efforts by the state to entice foreign investment and stimulate economic development and industrial growth.

BIBLIOGRAPHY: Mary Louise Wimberley Barksdale, The Gubernatorial Administration of James Stephen Hogg (M.A. thesis, University of Texas, 1932). Hans Peter Nielsen Gammel, comp., *Laws of Texas, 1822–1897* (10 vols., Austin: Gammel, 1898). C. W. Raines, ed., *Speeches and State Papers of James Stephen Hogg* (Austin: State Printing Company, 1905). *Revised Civil Statutes of the State of Texas* (Austin: Baldwin, 1925).

ALKALI CREEK. Alkali Creek rises nine miles west of Roby and three miles southeast of the intersection of U.S. Highway 180 and Farm Road 611 in west central Fisher County (at 32°42′ N, 100°31′ W) and runs sixteen miles northeast to its mouth on the Clear Fork of the Brazos River, two miles north of Roby and just east of State Highway 70 (at 32°47′ N, 100°23′ W). It crosses flat, flood-prone terrain with local shallow depressions, surfaced by clay and sandy loams that support water-tolerant hardwoods, conifers, and grasses.

ALLAMOORE, TEXAS. Allamoore (Allamore, Carrizo), is a ranching community on the Missouri Pacific Railroad just north of Interstate 10 and U.S. Highway 80, twenty-two miles southeast of Sierra Blanca in southeastern Hudspeth County. A post office under the name Acme was established there in 1884 with Robert B. McGrew as postmaster. It closed in 1886, but a new one opened two years later under the name Allamoore, after the postmistress, Mrs. Alla R. Moore. At that time the community consisted of "mining and stock camps." In 1890 the town had 200 inhabitants. Among them were Plato Clifford, a geologist and assayer, and H. C. Clifford, manager of the Hazel Mining Company. The Hazel Mine in nearby Culberson County was for several decades among the most productive silver and copper mines in Texas. The post office closed in 1895, but two years later a third post office, also called Allamoore, was established. By 1914 the population of the settlement had fallen to ten, and two cattle breeders were operating in the town. In the mid-1920s the population was estimated at twenty-five; by the late 1920s it was seventy-five. In the mid-1930s, when seventy pupils from the surrounding ranches attended the Allamoore school, the population was again estimated at twenty-five. A rock-crushing plant owned by Gifford-Hill and Company was operating five miles east of town in 1938. From the mid-1940s to the mid-1960s the population was estimated at seventy-five; it subsequently dropped to fifty. At that time Allamoore comprised scattered dwellings and a church. During the 1960s a local rancher reportedly paid a teacher to sit in the empty one-room schoolhouse, just in case a student happened to walk in. The Pioneer Talc Company opened at Allamoore in 1960 and the Westex Talc Company in 1971, but the latter was gone by the mid-1970s, and the Gifford-Hill rock crusher apparently ceased operation in the early 1980s. By 1988 the Allamoore school had the smallest enrollment of all Texas schools: only eight children from the ten families scattered throughout the district's 2,100 square miles attended. *Martin Donell Kohout*

ALLAN, JOHN T. (1821–1888). John T. Allan, sometimes called the "Father of Industrial Education in Texas," was born in Edinburgh, Scotland, on May 21, 1821, the son of a wheelwright. He attended public schools in Edinburgh and Inverness and was apprenticed to a German cabinetmaker at Inverness. About 1842 he left Scotland. He eventually landed in New Orleans, worked as a bookkeeper for a cotton plantation near Alexandria, Louisiana, then moved to Arkansas and studied law before acquiring title to land in Texas and settling in Nacogdoches, where he worked as a carpenter and wheelwright. He moved to Austin in 1850 and opened a law office two years later. For a number of years beginning in the early 1850s he served as justice of the peace.

In 1863 Allan left for Louisiana and became an officer in the Confederate Army. From 1864 to 1865 he was district attorney for the Fourth Judicial Circuit in Louisiana. After the Civil War[qv] he moved back to Texas. On September 1, 1867, he was appointed state treasurer, and before the close of his term about $7,000 was stolen from the treasury. On February 28, 1870, a board of military officers appointed by the headquarters of the Fifth Military District[qv] heard testimony. Allan appeared before the board and was acquitted. He served as a member of the board of trustees for the Deaf and Dumb Institute (later the Texas School for the Deaf[qv]). He was a Republican and Presbyterian. He died a bachelor on January 22, 1888, and left to the city of Austin an estate valued at about $43,000, with a request that an industrial school be established for the purpose of teaching the practical use of tools and scientific principles. In September 1896 a manual-training department was established at Austin High School as a result of his benefaction, the first department of its kind in the South. John T. Allan High School (later John T. Allan Junior High) was named for him and opened in 1900. Allan was buried in Oakwood Cemetery, and his remains were moved to the State Cemetery[qv] in 1930.

BIBLIOGRAPHY: Austin History Center Files. Frank Brown, Annals of Travis County and the City of Austin (MS, Frank Brown Papers, Barker Texas History Center, University of Texas at Austin). Dallas *Herald*, May 15, 1869. *Evidence of the Case of Mr. John T. Allan, Late State Treasurer* (Austin: Tracy, 1871). *Texas State Gazette*, August 28, 1852, August 27, 1853. Vertical Files, Barker Texas History Center, University of Texas at Austin. *Laurie E. Jasinski*

ALLEE, ALFRED YOUNG (1905–1987). Alfred Young Allee, Texas Ranger, the son of Alonzo W. Allee, was born on September 14, 1905, in La Salle County, Texas. He was a member of the Texas Rangers[qv] for thirty-seven years, following in the footsteps of his father and his grandfather, Alfred Y. Allee I, both of whom also served in the rangers. Allee's first work in law enforcement was as a special game warden on the 7D Ranch in Zavala County in 1926. The next year, he became a Zavala County deputy sheriff. In 1931 he applied to Capt. William W. Sterling[qv] to join the Texas Rangers and was assigned to Capt. Light Townsend's C Company. His early years were spent preventing smuggling and cattle rustling on the Rio Grande border. In 1933, however, Allee, like many of the rangers, resigned following the election of Miriam "Ma" Ferguson[qv] as governor. During this period he served as a deputy sheriff in Beeville. With the election of James Allred[qv] as governor in 1935, most Texas Rangers, including Allee, returned to duty. In 1952 Governor Allan Shivers sent Allee's D Company into San Diego, Texas, to protect the newly founded Freedom party from molestation by the Duval County political machine run by George Parr.[qv] In January 1954 Allee was involved in a scuffle with Parr in the hallway of the Alice City Courthouse when Parr tried to take a ranger's gun after a disagreement. The fight ended with Parr sustaining light injuries and filing attempted murder charges against Allee. Parr later dropped these charges "for the good of the community."

In April 1963 Allee's company was sent to Crystal City to supervise the city elections, for which local Hispanics had organized in an attempt to gain proportional representation in the city government (*see* CRYSTAL CITY REVOLTS). The rangers remained in Crystal City after the election of Los Cinco Candidatos and the subsequent resignation of the majority of city workers, who were predominantly Anglo. Allee soon found himself once again the subject of a lawsuit, this time filed by the new mayor of Crystal City, Juan Cornejo, who accused the ranger of physically and verbally abusing him. The charges were later dropped because of a lack of witnesses, and in fact most of the witnesses Cornejo named stated that Allee did not lay a hand on the mayor. In 1967 Allee and the rangers were again sent into a racially charged situation, this time to prevent violence during the Starr County strike[qv] by melon pickers. Once on the scene, the rangers began to enforce the state's antipicketing laws; more than fifty arrests resulted. Numerous reports began to surface of alleged ranger brutality and use of excessive force. Two of these cases, the arrests of Rev. Edgar Krueger and Magdeleno Dimas, drew heavy attention in the media. In June 1967 and December 1968 congressional subcommittees on civil rights met in Texas and found that the rangers had used excessive force in their handling of the striking farmworkers. In 1974 the United States Supreme Court concurred with the subcommittees and found in favor of the workers in the class-action suit *Allee et al. v. Medrano et al.* Allee, the last of the pre–Department of Public Safety rangers, retired on September 30, 1970. He died of cancer on January 13, 1987, in San Antonio. He had married Pearl Leach in 1928, and their son, Alfred Young Allee, Jr., also joined the Texas Rangers.

BIBLIOGRAPHY: Charles Schreiner III et al., *A Pictorial History of the Texas Rangers* (Mountain Home, Texas: Y-O Press, 1969). John Staples Shockley, *Chicano Revolt in a Texas Town* (Notre Dame, Indiana:

University of Notre Dame Press, 1974). Robert Stephens, *Tribute to a Ranger: Captain Alfred Y. Allee, Company D, Texas Rangers* (1968). Vertical Files, Barker Texas History Center, University of Texas at Austin.

Norman Youngblood

ALLEN, AUGUSTUS CHAPMAN (1806–1864). Augustus Chapman Allen, early settler and founder of Houston, son of Roland and Sarah (Chapman) Allen, was born at Canaseraga, New York, on July 4, 1806. At the age of seventeen he graduated from the Polytechnic Institute at Chittenango, New York, and began to teach mathematics there. In 1827 he resigned his professorship to accept a place as bookkeeper for the H. and H. Canfield Company, New York. Two years later he and his brother John K. Allen[qv] bought an interest in the Canfield business. In the summer of 1832 the Allen brothers withdrew from the firm to move to Texas, where they settled first at San Augustine. By June 1833 they were established in Nacogdoches. There they joined a coterie of land speculators and soon were engaged in a variety of enterprises, chief of which was traffic in land certificates. When the Texas Revolution[qv] broke out, the Allens did not join the Texas army, but they rendered services to the country by fitting out, at their own expense, a vessel to protect the Texas coast and to land troops and supplies for the army.

Late in 1836 the Allen brothers bought the John Austin[qv] half league, which lay along Buffalo Bayou not far from Harrisburg. Upon investigation they found that the bayou contained sufficient water for navigation and that the site was beautiful, so they decided to establish a town and name it for Sam Houston.[qv] Early in 1837 the father, mother, four brothers, and a sister of the Allens arrived in Texas to make their home. All six brothers became prominent figures in the economic and social life of Texas. In developing their town the Allens pursued a policy of donating many town blocks to institutions, municipal and religious, and to various persons whom they wished to honor. Perhaps their cleverest scheme for inducing growth was to have the Texas Congress select Houston as capital of the Republic of Texas.[qv] In October 1836 John Allen promised Congress that the Allens would construct, by their own means, an adequate capitol as a donation to the government. Other buildings to accommodate the officials were to be rented at the nominal sum of seventy-five dollars a month. In the event of the removal of the government from Houston, the capitol and the other buildings were to revert to the builders. Congress accepted the proposal, and early in May 1837 the seat of government was moved from Columbia to Houston.

In 1837 it was difficult for travelers in Texas to find accommodations or food. The Allens opened their own comfortable home, without charge, to all who needed lodging. Their bookkeeper, William R. Barker, testified that although this hospitality cost more than $3,000 a year, the Allens considered it an expense that would bring rich returns in the development of their city. In addition to developing Houston, the Allens had other extensive interests. They were owners of more than a hundred leagues of land, shareholders in the Galveston City Company (*see* GALVESTON, TEXAS), and partners of Thomas F. McKinney and Samuel May Williams[qqv] in the firm of McKinney, Williams and Company.[qv] It is said that the Allens obtained funds from friends in New York and placed their youngest brother, Harvey H., in the business to represent their interests.

On August 15, 1838, John Allen died of congestive fever. He left no will. At a family conference, his brothers waived their rights to share in his estate in favor of their father and mother, but by 1841 both parents were dead, and the four other brothers demanded of Augustus Allen their shares in John K. Allen's estate. Various interests made the business so complex that the only way to settle such an estate was by assignment. Allen began the tedious process of winding up the business in 1843, when a more perplexing problem arose. Much of the money that Augustus C. and John K. Allen had used in their early enterprises was the inheritance of Augustus's wife, Charlotte Allen.[qv] She became dissatisfied with the methods being employed in the settlement of the Allen brothers' business, and this dissatisfaction finally resulted in a separation, without divorce, from her husband in 1850; both husband and wife pledged to keep the details of their troubles secret.

Allen's health failed completely, and he decided to leave Houston. He signed over to his wife the bulk of what remained of his many enterprises and went to Mexico to seek health and a new start in life. During the early years of the 1840s he had engaged in business relations with Benito Juárez; in Mexico the two men became friends. In 1852 Allen was appointed United States consul for the port of Tehuantepec on the Pacific Ocean, and in 1858 he was given the same position for the port of Minotitlán. These offices gave him control of the consular affairs of the United States for the entire Isthmus of Tehuantepec, a commercially important position since a trade route—probably a canal—through that region was contemplated. Allen, in partnership with an Englishman named Welsh, developed an extensive private shipping business. Allen was never able to recover his health, however, and realized in 1864 that he was critically ill; he closed his private business and went to Washington to resign his consulships. Soon after arriving there he contracted pneumonia. He died on June 11, 1864, and was buried in Greenwood Cemetery, Brooklyn, New York.

BIBLIOGRAPHY: O. F. Allen, *The City of Houston from Wilderness to Wonder* (Temple, Texas, 1936). Eugene C. Barker, ed., *The Austin Papers* (3 vols., Washington: GPO, 1924–28). William Campbell Binkley, ed., *Official Correspondence of the Texan Revolution, 1835–1836* (2 vols., New York: Appleton-Century, 1936). John Henry Brown, *Indian Wars and Pioneers of Texas* (Austin: Daniell, 1880; reprod., Easley, South Carolina: Southern Historical Press, 1978). Amelia W. Williams and Eugene C. Barker, eds., *The Writings of Sam Houston, 1813–1863* (8 vols., Austin: University of Texas Press, 1938–43; rpt., Austin and New York: Pemberton Press, 1970). Dudley Goodall Wooten, ed., *A Comprehensive History of Texas* (2 vols., Dallas: Scarff, 1898; rpt., Austin: Texas State Historical Association, 1986).

Amelia W. Williams

ALLEN, CHARLOTTE M. BALDWIN (1805–1895). Charlotte Allen, called "the mother of Houston," was born on July 14, 1805, in Onondaga County, New York, the daughter of James C. Baldwin, a turnpike and canal builder who founded Baldwinsville, New York. On May 3, 1831, she married Augustus Chapman Allen,[qv] a New York businessman. The following year Allen and his brother, John Kirby Allen,[qv] came to Texas and settled at San Augustine, then at Nacogdoches. Charlotte Allen probably arrived in Texas in 1834, and her inheritance helped the brothers to speculate in land.

In August 1836 the Allen brothers purchased a half league of land on Buffalo Bayou for $5,000. Four days later they advertised the establishment of a prosperous new city called Houston, which may have been so named at Charlotte's suggestion. In any event, the name apparently attracted settlement to the area and influenced the decision to make Houston the capital of the Republic of Texas,[qv] a role it held from 1837 to 1839. The Allen brothers built the first statehouse, near Charlotte and A. C. Allen's home at Prairie and Caroline streets. Sam Houston[qv] lived next door to the Allens, and from their home Mary Austin Holley[qv] drew the first sketches of the capitol. When John Allen died in 1838 Charlotte and Augustus disagreed over the estate settlement, and they separated in 1850. Augustus moved on to Mexico and Washington, D.C., where he died in 1864; Charlotte remained in Houston and became one of the city's best-known citizens over the next forty-five years. In 1857 she sold the capitol site, which had become the location of the Capitol Hotel, for $12,000. The following year the hotel was the scene of Anson Jones's[qv] suicide; the land eventually became the site of the Rice Hotel.

After the Civil War[qv] Charlotte Allen's home became the headquarters for the commanding general of federal troops in Houston. She deeded property, eventually called Market Square, to the city for a city hall and markethouse; because the original deed was lost she deeded it a second time, in 1895. In 1890, the day after her eighty-fifth birthday, the Houston *Daily Post* (*see* HOUSTON POST) referred to her as the "connecting link between Houston's past and present history." Charlotte Allen had four children, only one of whom survived to maturity. She died on August 3, 1895, in Houston, at the age of ninety and was buried in Glenwood Cemetery. In 1911 her home was razed to provide a site for the Gulf Building.[qv]

BIBLIOGRAPHY: Elizabeth Brooks, *Prominent Women of Texas* (Akron, Ohio: Werner, 1896). Houston *Post*, August 4, 1895. David G. McComb, *Houston: The Bayou City* (Austin: University of Texas Press, 1969; rev. ed., *Houston: A History*, 1981). Ann Quin Wilson, *Native Houstonian: A Collective Portrait* (Norfolk, Virginia: Donning, 1982). WPA Writers Program, *Houston* (Houston: Anson Jones, 1942).

Nancy Baker Jones

ALLEN, EBENEZER (?–1863). Ebenezer Allen, early state official and railroad promoter, a native of Maine, migrated to Texas in the 1830s. He became attorney general of Texas under Anson Jones[qv] in December 1844, served a while as secretary of state, and assisted Jones in framing the terms of annexation[qv] to the United States. He was attorney general under Governor Peter Hansbrough Bell[qv] from 1849 to 1853. In 1848 Allen was instrumental in securing the charter for the Galveston and Red River Railroad Company, and in the 1850s he was a promoter and manager of the Houston and Texas Central Railway. He supported secession[qv] and entered the Confederate service at the outbreak of the Civil War.[qv] He died in Virginia in 1863.

BIBLIOGRAPHY: S. G. Reed, *A History of the Texas Railroads* (Houston: St. Clair, 1941; rpt., New York: Arno, 1981). Amelia W. Williams and Eugene C. Barker, eds., *The Writings of Sam Houston, 1813–1863* (8 vols., Austin: University of Texas Press, 1938–43; rpt., Austin and New York: Pemberton Press, 1970). *Claudia Hazlewood*

ALLEN, FRANCES DAISY EMERY (1876–1958). Frances Daisy Emery Allen, physician, was born on September 5, 1876, in Kaufman County, Texas, the daughter of James Wallace and Elizabeth Jane (Brown) Emery. When she was a teenager the family moved to Fort Worth, where her father taught school and she attended public school. Her father strongly supported her plan, which she expressed as early as the age of four, to become a doctor; when the Fort Worth Medical School was opened, she talked with physicians she knew, secured an application form, and applied. At first she was refused, but when she pointed out that the entrance requirements did not specifically exclude women, she was admitted to the charter medical class at Fort Worth University in 1894. Three years later she became the first woman to graduate from medical school in Texas, finishing second in a class of seventeen. After graduation she went into private practice, but in 1899 she moved to Washington, D.C., to secure postgraduate training. She returned to Texas in 1901, taught at Dallas Medical College, and had private patients. She married Dr. James Walter Allen, a classmate from medical school, on November 30, 1903. The Allens were partners in a succession of rural practices for the next ten years. They first lived in Vinson, Oklahoma Territory, where James Allen had been residing. They were building a house and an office there when a storm and fire on April 2, 1904, destroyed much of the town. Invited by a resident of Content, Runnels County, Texas, to relocate there, they moved back to Texas and practiced in Content and the surrounding area from 1904 to 1910. When Content was bypassed by the railroad, the Allens moved to nearby Goldsboro, a new town located on the Pecos and Northern Texas Railway. After spending 1910–12 in Goldsboro, they moved to Newark, about twenty miles northwest of Fort Worth. They were making plans to go to China as Methodist missionaries when James died unexpectedly in December 1913. With her two young daughters Dr. Allen returned to Fort Worth, accepted a position as clinical professor of children's diseases at Fort Worth University, and opened a private practice. After the university closed in 1917, she continued her practice, largely with women and children. She was on the staffs of Harris, All Saints, and St. Joseph[qv] hospitals and was a volunteer physician at City-County Hospital and Wesley House Clinic. She was a member of both the Tarrant County Medical Society and the Tarrant County Association for Mental Health. She held a life membership in the Texas Medical Association.[qv] She retired in 1950 at the age of seventy-four. She died on December 7, 1958, and was buried in Greenwood Cemetery, Fort Worth. *See illustration in article* HEALTH AND MEDICINE.

BIBLIOGRAPHY: Daisy Emery Allen, M.D., 1876–1958: Scholarship and Loan Funds (brochure, University of Texas Medical Branch, Office of University Relations). *Judith N. McArthur*

ALLEN, GEORGE R. (1830–?). George R. Allen was born in Connecticut in 1830 and moved, probably in 1849, to Huntsville, Texas, where he advertised as a portrait painter. There he painted portraits of Henderson K. Yoakum[qv] and members of Sam Houston's[qv] family, including Nancy Lea and Margaret Moffette Lea Houston.[qv] The severe style that characterizes his art is reminiscent of eighteenth-century Dutch portraiture. His work is stiff and rather two-dimensional with little modeling to the forms; and with the exception of flesh tones, his palette is almost colorless. After leaving Huntsville, Allen seems to have made Galveston the center of his activities.

BIBLIOGRAPHY: Pauline A. Pinckney, *Painting in Texas: The Nineteenth Century* (Austin: University of Texas Press, 1967).

Pauline A. Pinckney

ALLEN, GLENN HINCKLEY (1860–1943). Glenn Hinckley Allen, architect, was born in Pennsylvania on April 30, 1860, the son of Truman D. and Harriet (Hinckley) Allen. He was evidently in Houston by 1884, when he worked for a time in the office of Eugene T. Heiner.[qv] Around 1898 he practiced in association with another Houston architect, F. S. Glover, and from 1899 to 1902 was in partnership with Houston architect George E. Dickey.[qv] Like most of the architects of the period, Allen had a varied and prolific practice, in which he designed a wide variety of buildings, including residences, schools, churches, hotels, courthouses, libraries, and commercial structures. Among his most important works in Texas are the Highlands Mansion in Marlin (1898–1900), the First National Bank of Marlin (1892), Marlin National Bank (1900), the Madison Alexander Cooper House in Waco (1905–07), the James Archer Dunkum House in Marlin (1900), the Scottish Rite Temple in Dallas (1905), the Artesian Manufacturing and Bottling Company Building (now the Dr Pepper Museum) in Waco in 1906, and the Arlington Hotel (1900); the hotel served as the spring-training home of several baseball teams, including the Chicago White Sox, the Philadelphia Phillies, the Cincinnati Reds, the St. Louis Browns, and the New York Giants. Allen also designed elementary schools in Comanche, Killeen, Mount Calm, Lott, Brandon, Brownwood, and Markham; high schools in Beaumont, Corsicana, Marlin, Gatesville, Angleton, Valley Mills, Whitney, Morgan, Plano, and Sweetwater; and the Mess Hall at Texas A&M, College Station (1898). He was first married to a woman named Laurette and later to Mildred Weiss, with whom he had one son. Allen moved from Texas to San Francisco, California, in 1907. By 1912 he had permanently moved to Stockton, California, where he lived and worked the rest of his life. He died there on November 1, 1943.

Naomi S. Michalsky and Joydelle G. Wolfram

ALLEN, HENRY TUREMAN (1859–1930). Henry Tureman Allen, the commanding general of the Ninetieth (Texas-Oklahoma) National Army Division in World War I,[qv] was born at Sharpsburg, Kentucky, on April 13, 1859, to Ruben Sanford and Susannah (Shumate) Allen. He attended Georgetown College in Kentucky and was commissioned in the cavalry upon his graduation from West Point in

1882. He and his wife, Jennie Dora (Johnston), had three children. Henry, Jr., served as his father's aide in the war.

Between 1882 and 1917 Allen was an aide to Gen. Nelson A. Miles,[qv] taught at West Point, served as attaché to Russia and Germany, fought in the Spanish-American War and the Philippine Insurrection, organized the Philippine Constabulary, served on the general staff, and accompanied John J. Pershing's[qv] expedition into Mexico in 1916. He was promoted to brigadier general in May 1917 and to major general on August 5.

Allen assumed command of Camp Travis, in San Antonio, on August 23, 1917, and supervised the assignment of Texas and Oklahoma draftees to the new Ninetieth Division. Despite several problems, training proceeded at a relatively rapid rate. Allen was absent for about three months, beginning late in November 1917, on an official visit to the western front. Although General Pershing usually favored younger combat commanders, Allen was found acceptable for overseas duty and led the Ninetieth to France. The division underwent additional training at Aignay-le-Duc, entered the line in August 1918, participated in the St. Mihiel operation in September, and was advancing in the Meuse-Argonne on November 11. The Ninetieth was rated by Pershing's headquarters as one of the top six divisions in the American Expeditionary Forces, and its operations were subsequently studied by the AEF General Staff College and the General Service Schools at Fort Leavenworth. While in France Allen conceived the T-O design of the Ninetieth's insignia. Nevertheless, the T-O Division remained to some the Alamo Division, a designation Allen had rejected at Camp Travis.

On November 24, 1918, Allen left the Ninetieth while it was attached to the Seventh Corps, to become commander of the Eighth Corps. From July 1919 until shortly before his retirement in 1923 he commanded the American forces in Germany. During his career he received several decorations and wrote many articles and books, including *My Rhineland Journal* and *The Rhineland Occupation.* He died at Buena Vista Springs, Pennsylvania, on August 30, 1930.

BIBLIOGRAPHY: *Dictionary of American Biography.* George Wythe, *A History of the 90th Division* (New York: 90th Division Association, 1920).

Lonnie J. White

ALLEN, JAMES C. (?–?). James C. Allen, soldier, arrived in Texas on June 29, 1836, as captain of the seventy-five-member Buckeye Rangers.[qv] He was a former editor of the Cincinnati *Republican* and a friend of its owner, Richard Disney, a member of James W. Fannin's[qv] command massacred at Goliad. He was also a relative of Henry S. Stouffer, who participated in the battle of San Jacinto.[qv] The Buckeye Rangers left Cincinnati on June 5, 1836, for New Orleans and Texas. Allen may have been the Captain Allen referred to in a letter from Edward Hall to Bailey Hardeman[qv] dated June 18, 1836, at New Orleans. This Captain Allen was given $4,000 to charter a boat for 100 men. Four or five days later he had not done so, and he refused to take passage on the *Pennsylvania.* The Buckeye Rangers eventually arrived on the *San Jacinto.*[qv] When forces led by Col. Henry W. Millard[qv] went to Velasco to capture Gen. Antonio López de Santa Anna and arrest President David Burnet,[qqv] Captain Allen promised Burnet the protection of the Buckeye Rangers.

In September 1836 Allen was told that his command was attached to the command of Gen. Thomas Jefferson Green.[qv] Ill will arose between Allen and Green's adjutant, Leon Dyer, after which Allen's company was assigned to Colonel Harrison's regiment. By October 9, 1836, Allen had resigned his captaincy and been appointed aide-de-camp to Gen. Thomas J. Rusk.[qv] His company had broken up because of discontent over the election of a new captain and their assignment. A letter to the *Telegraph and Texas Register*[qv] of July 7, 1838, signed "A Buckeye Ranger," defends Allen from criticism printed in another paper over an event in October 1836, when Allen delivered four prisoners to Columbia. An officer there refused to accept them, so Allen left the papers on them with Gen. Sam Houston's[qv] secretary and maintained custody of the prisoners. Two days later Houston returned and sent a message to Allen asking him to come at once. Allen had the messenger take a reply to Houston asking to be excused until the next day. Houston then ordered his arrest, and when Allen was brought to him harsh words were exchanged; Houston told Allen that he would receive a dishonorable discharge. Friends of Houston intervened, and Allen was allowed to retire and close his account with the paymaster. Allen was married and had children. He did not apply for bounty land.

BIBLIOGRAPHY: Mary Whatley Clarke, *Thomas J. Rusk: Soldier, Statesman, Jurist* (Austin: Jenkins, 1971). Daughters of the Republic of Texas, *Muster Rolls of the Texas Revolution* (Austin, 1986). John H. Jenkins, ed., *The Papers of the Texas Revolution, 1835–1836* (10 vols., Austin: Presidial Press, 1973). Louis Wiltz Kemp Papers, Barker Texas History Center, University of Texas at Austin. Marilyn McAdams Sibley, "Letters from the Texas Army, Autumn, 1836: Leon Dyer to Thomas J. Green," *Southwestern Historical Quarterly* 72 (January 1969).

John G. Johnson

ALLEN, JAMES C. (ca. 1810–?). James C. Allen (Allan), soldier and judge, was born in Kentucky and entered Texas as a first lieutenant with a battalion recruited in New York by colonels Edwin H. Stanley and Edwin Morehouse.[qv] This unit left New York on November 21, 1835, but did not reach Velasco until March 8, 1836, because the ship was seized by the United States Navy and held for fifty days. The battalion was assigned the job of escorting fleeing colonists to a safe place. By December 31, 1836, Allen was captain in command of Company B of the First Volunteer Regiment, under Col. Joseph D. Rogers. He received a bounty warrant for 1,280 acres for service from January 1, 1836, to January 16, 1838. He also received a headright grant of one-third league in Victoria County. On June 10, 1837, President Sam Houston[qv] nominated Allen for judge advocate general, but he was not confirmed by the Texas Senate. On November 10, 1837, he was nominated for chief justice of Refugio County; he was confirmed the next day but did not arrive at the post until the middle of 1838. In September 1839 it was reported to Secretary of War Albert Sidney Johnston[qv] that Allen was involved in cattle rustling. Allen served as chief justice in Refugio until March 30, 1840, when he resigned and moved to Victoria. His application there for the post of judge of the Fourth Judicial District was defeated in the Republic of Texas Senate. In 1847 he was mayor of Victoria and in 1848 was chosen an elector for the Whig party.[qv] On May 2, 1839, Allen married Catharine Hay. The census of 1850 indicates that he was forty years old at that time and had four children. Catharine Allen was alive during the Civil War.[qv] In 1878 two Victoria lots belonging to a James Allen were sold for unpaid taxes.

BIBLIOGRAPHY: Daughters of the Republic of Texas, *Muster Rolls of the Texas Revolution* (Austin, 1986). Charles Adams Gulick, Jr., Harriet Smither, et al., eds., *The Papers of Mirabeau Buonaparte Lamar* (6 vols., Austin: Texas State Library, 1920–27; rpt., Austin: Pemberton Press, 1968). Hobart Huson, *Refugio: A Comprehensive History of Refugio County from Aboriginal Times to 1953* (2 vols., Woodsboro, Texas: Rooke Foundation, 1953, 1955). John H. Jenkins, ed., *The Papers of the Texas Revolution, 1835–1836* (10 vols., Austin: Presidial Press, 1973). Louis Wiltz Kemp Papers, Barker Texas History Center, University of Texas at Austin. Thomas L. Miller, *Bounty and Donation Land Grants of Texas, 1835–1888* (Austin: University of Texas Press, 1967). Amelia W. Williams and Eugene C. Barker, eds., *The Writings of Sam Houston, 1813–1863* (8 vols., Austin: University of Texas Press, 1938–43; rpt., Austin and New York: Pemberton Press, 1970). E. W. Winkler, ed., *Secret Journals of the Senate, Republic of Texas* (Austin, 1911).

John G. Johnson

ALLEN, JAMES L. (1815–1901). James L. Allen, the last messenger from the Alamo,[qv] son of Samuel and Mary (Lamme) Allen, was born in Kentucky on January 2, 1815, the eldest of seven children. His father, a veteran of the Indian wars, had served under Gen. William Henry Harrison. Allen was a student at Marion College, Missouri, when he joined other students to volunteer for military service in Texas. He left the Alamo on courier duty on March 5, 1836, the night before the battle of the Alamo[qv] took place. He served at San Jacinto as a scout under Erastus (Deaf) Smith[qv] and helped burn bridges behind Mexican lines to cut off their retreat. After the victory at San Jacinto, he returned to the United States, where he stayed for two years. He then settled in Texas, became a Texas Ranger, and served in the companies of Captain Ward and later Capt. Peter H. Bell.[qv] In July 1844 Allen took part in an Indian battle at Corpus Christi. In 1849 he settled in Indianola, where he dealt in the stock business and also served for a time as mayor and justice of the peace. In 1849 he married Federica M. Manchan; they raised seven children. At the outbreak of the Civil War,[qv] Allen was serving as tax assessor-collector of Calhoun County. He refused to take the oath of allegiance when Union soldiers took Indianola and was placed under guard on Saluria Island, from which he escaped by swimming to the mainland and going to Port Lavaca. In 1865 he moved to Hochheim, where he owned a farm of 260 acres. He was a Baptist and Mason. He died at his home, five miles west of Yoakum, on April 25, 1901.

There was a James B. Allen at the siege of Bexar,[qv] and in June 1836 a James C. Allen[qv] of Kentucky arrived in Texas as captain and commanding officer of the Buckeye Rangers. Another James C. Allen,[qv] also born in Kentucky, came to Texas from New York and participated in the Texas Revolution.[qv] Historians have confused James L. Allen with the James C. Allens and perhaps also with James B. Allen.

BIBLIOGRAPHY: Daughters of the Republic of Texas, *Muster Rolls of the Texas Revolution* (Austin, 1986). Bill Groneman, *Alamo Defenders* (Austin: Eakin, 1990). Louis Wiltz Kemp, *The Honor Roll of the Battle: The Complete List of Participants and Personnel on Detached Service* (San Jacinto, Texas: San Jacinto Museum of History Association, 1965). Walter Lord, *A Time to Stand* (New York: Harper, 1961; 2d ed., Lincoln: University of Nebraska Press, 1978). *Memorial and Genealogical Record of Southwest Texas* (Chicago: Goodspeed, 1894; rpt., Easley, South Carolina: Southern Historical Press, 1978). Vertical Files, Barker Texas History Center, University of Texas at Austin. Amelia W. Williams, A Critical Study of the Siege of the Alamo and of the Personnel of Its Defenders (Ph.D. dissertation, University of Texas, 1931; rpt., *Southwestern Historical Quarterly* 36 (April 1933), 37 (July, October 1933, January, April 1934).

Bill Groneman

ALLEN, JOHN KIRBY (1819–1838). John Kirby Allen, founder of Houston, legislator, and backer of the Texas Revolution,[qv] fourth son of Roland and Sarah (Chapman) Allen, was born at Orrville, near Syracuse, New York, in 1819. He took his first job—that of callboy in a hotel at Orrville—when he was seven. Three years later he became a clerk in a store. At sixteen he went into partnership with a young friend named Kittredge in a hat store at Chittenango, New York, where his brother, Augustus C. Allen,[qv] was professor of mathematics until 1827. John Allen sold his interest in the hat store and followed his brother to New York City, where they were stockholders in H. and H. Canfield Company until 1832, when they moved to Texas.

At the beginning of the Texas Revolution the Allen brothers did not join the armed forces but rendered more valuable, and equally dangerous, service in other ways. At their own expense they fitted out the *Brutus*[qv] for the purpose of protecting the Texas coast and for assisting troops and supplies from the United States to land safely in Texas. When some of the members of the Texas provisional government objected to the activities of privateers under letters of marque, the Allens, in January 1836, sold the *Brutus* to the Texas Navy[qv] at cost. The brothers also served on committees to raise loans on Texas lands and became receivers and dispensers of supplies and funds without charge to the republic. In spite of these services there was considerable gossip and censure concerning the Allens because they were not in the armed services.

In September 1836 John Allen was elected a representative from Nacogdoches to the Texas Congress. While he was serving, he and his brother decided to found the city of Houston.[qv] John Allen served as congressman from Nacogdoches and on the president's staff with the rank of major. In partnership with James Pinckney Henderson[qv] he operated a shipping business. Allen was never married. He died of congestive fever on August 15, 1838, and was buried in Founders Cemetery, Houston.

BIBLIOGRAPHY: William Campbell Binkley, ed., *Official Correspondence of the Texan Revolution, 1835–1836* (2 vols., New York: Appleton-Century, 1936). James E. Buchanan, comp. and ed., *Houston: A Chronological and Documentary History, 1519–1970* (Dobbs Ferry, New York: Oceana, 1975). *Diplomatic Correspondence of the Republic of Texas*, ed. George Pierce Garrison (3 parts, Washington: GPO, 1908–11). Clarence Pekham Dunbar, *Houston, 1836–1936: Chronology and Review* (Houston: Business Research and Publications Source, 1936). Jim Hutton, *Houston: A History of A Giant* (Tulsa, Oklahoma: Continental Heritage, 1976). Marie Phelps McAshan, *A Houston Legacy: On the Corner of Main and Texas* (Houston: Gulf, 1985). Texas House of Representatives, *Biographical Directory of the Texan Conventions and Congresses, 1832–1845* (Austin: Book Exchange, 1941).

Amelia W. Williams

ALLEN, JOHN M. (?–1847). John M. Allen (Tampico Allen), soldier and first mayor of Galveston, was a native of Kentucky. He joined the United States Navy in the aid of the Greek revolution against Turkey and was with Lord Byron at Missolonghi when Byron died (1824). Allen came to Texas in 1830 and joined the Tampico expedition[qv] in 1835 but escaped imprisonment. He returned to Texas in December, enlisted in the revolutionary army,[qv] was appointed captain of infantry, and served as acting major at the battle of San Jacinto.[qv] He commanded the *Terrible* in the summer of 1836 but did not see action; he was sent to the United States on recruiting service and enrolled about 230 men for the army. He was discharged on December 2, 1836, and received a headright for a league and labor of land on June 7, 1838. Later he moved to Galveston, where he was elected mayor in March 1839. In 1840 Samuel May Williams,[qv] seeking to rid the threat Allen posed to the Galveston City Company,[qv] called for a new election with a change in the franchise. Allen, refusing to give up his office since his term was not over, removed the city archives to his home and the protection of two cannons. Thomas F. McKinney[qv] and a posse removed the archives after the district court ruled on the matter, and so ended the "charter war." Allen was reelected annually until 1846. After annexation[qv] he was appointed United States marshal for the Eastern District of Texas, an office he held until his death on February 12, 1847. Allen was a Mason. He was buried in an unmarked grave in Galveston.

BIBLIOGRAPHY: Daughters of the Republic of Texas, *Muster Rolls of the Texas Revolution* (Austin, 1986). Sam Houston Dixon and Louis Wiltz Kemp, *The Heroes of San Jacinto* (Houston: Anson Jones, 1932). Earl Wesley Fornell, *The Galveston Era: The Texas Crescent on the Eve of Secession* (Austin: University of Texas Press, 1961). David G. McComb, *Galveston: A History* (Austin: University of Texas Press, 1986). Homer S. Thrall, *A Pictorial History of Texas* (St. Louis: Thompson, 1879).

Wesley N. Laing

ALLEN, MARTIN (1780–1837). Martin Allen, early settler and a member of Stephen F. Austin's[qv] Old Three Hundred,[qv] was born in Kentucky in what is now Newport on November 28, 1780, son of Benjamin Allen. He married Elizabeth Vice in Campbell County, Kentucky, on September 24, 1804; the couple had ten children. By 1810 he, his wife, and three children were living in Old Attakapas District, Louisiana, and in 1811 he was appointed justice of the peace in

Opelousas Parish, Louisiana. In 1812 Allen, his father, a brother Hiram, and a nephew joined the Gutiérrez-Magee expedition[qv] in an unsuccessful effort to wrest Texas from Spain. Allen's father, brother, and nephew were killed at the battle of Medina[qv] the following year, but Allen, who was in Louisiana on a recruiting mission, survived. By 1817 he and his family were living in Arkansas Territory. A year or two later he settled at Flat Lick in northwest Louisiana. He was living in Allen's Settlement, Natchitoches Parish, Louisiana, in 1821, when be joined Stephen F. Austin. By December 22, 1821, Allen was building a cabin and planting a garden on the Colorado River. When he returned to the United States for his wife and eight children, he found his wife too ill to move. He wrote Austin in March 1822 indicating his intention to return to Texas and asking approval of his land title. He was given title to a sitio[qv] of land now in Wharton County in July 1824. When his wife's illness continued, Allen sent his two oldest sons to Texas by November 1824 to plant a crop. Sometime after May 12, 1825, and before the census of March 1826, Allen arrived in Texas with his wife and seven children. In April and May 1826 he was in a volunteer company fighting the Tonkawa Indians. He was living in Mina Municipality in January 1827, when he signed resolutions of loyalty to Mexico and opposition to the Fredonian Rebellion.[qv] The ayuntamiento[qv] of San Felipe de Austin made Allen a road supervisor in February 1830 and in April 1830 granted him the right to operate a ferry across Buffalo Bayou opposite Harrisburg. Allen was fifth regidor[qv] and a member of the ayuntamiento in February 1832; in June 1832 he signed the call for the Convention of 1832.[qv] In December 1837 the Congress elected him associate land commissioner for Austin County. He died at his home, Eight Mile Point, on December 20, 1837, and was buried in the Allen-Johnston family cemetery. James B. and Elizabeth Allen, his administrators, were ordered by the probate court of Austin County to sell his residence and perishable goods. In 1993 a Texas historical marker in Allen's memory was erected in Austin County.

BIBLIOGRAPHY: Eugene C. Barker, ed., *The Austin Papers* (3 vols., Washington: GPO, 1924–28). Eugene C. Barker, ed., "Minutes of the Ayuntamiento of San Felipe de Austin, 1828–1832," 12 parts, *Southwestern Historical Quarterly* 21–24 (January 1918–October 1920). Lester G. Bugbee, "The Old Three Hundred: A List of Settlers in Austin's First Colony," *Quarterly of the Texas State Historical Association* 1 (October 1897). *Telegraph and Texas Register*, December 16, 1837, July 21, 1838, July 8, 1840. *Texas Gazette*, September 25, 1830. Marker Files, Texas Historical Commission, Austin.

ALLEN, MILES N. (1805–1834). Miles N. Allen, early settler and member of Stephen F. Austin's[qv] second colony, was born on September 7, 1805, in Campbell County, Kentucky, the oldest son of Elizabeth (Vice) and Martin Allen.[qv] He was sent to Texas with a brother, James Bud Allen, in 1824 to plant a crop and live on the property granted to his father, now in Wharton County. He married Mary P. Dobson and had two children: James W. Allen, who married Penelope Johnston, and Elizabeth Miles Allen. Allen received a quarter league of land now in southern Austin County on May 21, 1827. It was called Eight Mile Point because of the distance from San Felipe de Austin and was on Allen's Creek, named in his honor. On November 29, 1832, Allen was issued title to ¾ league of land in central Austin County. He died on May 6, 1834, at his home and is buried in the Allen Johnston Cemetery on this property.

BIBLIOGRAPHY: Eugene C. Barker, ed., *The Austin Papers* (3 vols., Washington: GPO, 1924–28). Marker Files, Texas Historical Commission, Austin. Vertical Files, Barker Texas History Center, University of Texas at Austin (Martin Allen). *Katherine Allen Harrison*

ALLEN, MOSES (1808–1865). Moses Allen, soldier and settler, was born on December 14, 1808, in St. Helena Parish, Louisiana, the son of William and Hannah (Pride) Allen. He moved to Texas in 1826 and in 1838 was granted a headright certificate for a league and a labor of land by the Board of Land Commissioners of Jefferson County as a first-class grantee under the Constitution of the Republic of Texas.[qv] The 1840 tax roll listed Allen as living in Jefferson County and owning thirty-eight cattle and one wooden clock. The tax list for 1846 lists Moses Allen with property in Jefferson County. He was an original landowner in Bell County, which was established by an act of the Texas legislature in 1850.

He and six of his brothers participated in the Texas Revolution.[qv] Moses was in B. J. Harper's Company for three months in 1836, for which he was issued a bounty certificate for 320 acres of land. For his participation in the siege of Bexar[qv] he received a donation certificate for 640 acres of land that he located in Bell County. He is on the muster roll of volunteers in Captain Chesshire's Company in 1835 and received 320 acres of land for this service. His name is on a list of volunteers who marched from the Natchez River on November 16, 1835, under the command of Martin B. Lewis.[qv]

Allen married Nancy A. Williams, the daughter of Hezekiah and Nancy (Reams) Williams, who also came to Texas from Louisiana before 1830. In the 1850 census Moses and Nancy were living in the Milam and Williamson district with their three children; also living with them was Marvin Williams, age twenty, born in Louisiana, and probably a relative of Nancy's. By 1860 Allen had moved to Belton in Bell County, where he resided until his death on October 1, 1865.

BIBLIOGRAPHY: Bell County Historical Commission, *Story of Bell County, Texas* (2 vols., Austin: Eakin Press, 1988). Daughters of the Republic of Texas, *Muster Rolls of the Texas Revolution* (Austin, 1986). Madeleine Martin, *More Early Southeast Texas Families* (Quanah, Texas: Nortex, 1978). Worth Stickley Ray, *Austin Colony Pioneers* (Austin: Jenkins, 1949; 2d ed., Austin: Pemberton, 1970). Gifford E. White, *1830 Citizens of Texas* (Austin: Eakin, 1983).

Patricia Gilleland Young

ALLEN, RICHARD (1830–1909). Richard Allen, political and civic leader, was born a slave in Richmond, Virginia, on June 10, 1830. He was brought to Texas in 1837 and ultimately to Harris County, where he was owned by J. J. Cain until emancipation in 1865. While a slave he earned a reputation as a skilled carpenter; he is credited with designing and building the mansion of Houston mayor Joseph R. Morris.[qv] After emancipation Allen became a contractor and bridge builder and at times a commission agent and saloon owner. The first bridge built across Buffalo Bayou is his work. Although he was without a formal education, he became literate by 1870. Allen entered politics as a federal voter registrar in 1867. In 1868 he served as an agent of the Freedmen's Bureau[qv] and as the supervisor of voter registration for the Fourteenth District of Texas. He also participated in the organization of the Republican party[qv] in Harris County. After assuming an active role in the Radical Republican meeting that nominated Edmund J. Davis[qv] for governor in 1869, Allen was elected to the Twelfth Legislature that November and became one of the first and most active black legislators. As a representative of the Fourteenth District, which included Harris and Montgomery counties, he advocated general measures for education, law enforcement, and civil rights. In 1870 he unsuccessfully sought the Republican nomination for United States Congress. In 1871 the Union League,[qv] which supported the Republican party, made him one of its vice presidents. Allen apparently was reelected to the legislature in 1873, but the House seated his Democratic opponent, who contested the election. Allen remained a leader of the Republican party in Houston, at state conventions, and as a delegate to national conventions through 1896. He was elected street commissioner in Houston as an independent candidate in January 1878 and served for one term. Later that year the conservative wing of the Republican party nominated him for lieutenant governor, thereby making him the first black to seek statewide office in Texas. Allen served as quartermaster for the black regiment of Texas militia in 1881–82, and from 1882 to 1885 he acted as storekeeper and then inspector and deputy collector of United States customs at Houston.

As a political leader Allen occasionally took unpopular positions.

In 1879 he broke with most other black leaders in Texas and became a spokesman for the short-lived Exodus Movement, which told blacks that they would never enjoy educational or economic opportunity in Texas and therefore should move to Kansas. As customs collector Allen became involved in the labor dispute that occurred at the port of Houston in 1890. He defied white labor leaders but urged black workers to remain peaceful during the protests. In 1872 and 1879 he served as a delegate to the National Colored Men's Convention. He acted as a vice president in 1873 and as chairman in 1879 of black state conventions[qv] that voiced African Americans'[qv] concerns about civil rights, education, and economic issues. When the Prince Hall Masons organized in Texas, Allen presided over the meeting at Brenham in 1875. Two years later he became the state's grand master. In Houston he led emancipation celebrations, promoted a park, and served as the superintendent of the Sunday school at Antioch Baptist Church. He also sat on the board of directors of Gregory Institute, Houston's first black secondary school. He married a woman named Nancy soon after emancipation. They had one son and four daughters. Allen died on May 16, 1909, in Houston and was buried in the city cemetery.

BIBLIOGRAPHY: J. Mason Brewer, *Negro Legislators of Texas and Their Descendants* (Dallas: Mathis, 1935; 2d ed., Austin: Jenkins, 1970). Merline Pitre, *Through Many Dangers, Toils and Snares: The Black Leadership of Texas, 1868–1900* (Austin: Eakin, 1985).

Alwyn Barr and Cary D. Wintz

ALLEN, ROBERT (?-1836). Robert Allen, Alamo defender, was born in Virginia. He was a member of Capt. John H. Forsyth's[qv] cavalry company, which accompanied Lt. Col. William B. Travis[qv] to the Alamo in January 1836. He died in the battle of the Alamo[qv] on March 6 of that year.

BIBLIOGRAPHY: Bill Groneman, *Alamo Defenders* (Austin: Eakin, 1990). Amelia W. Williams, A Critical Study of the Siege of the Alamo and of the Personnel of Its Defenders (Ph.D. dissertation, University of Texas, 1931; rpt., *Southwestern Historical Quarterly* 36-37 [April 1933-April 1934]).

Bill Groneman

ALLEN, ROBERT THOMAS PRITCHARD (1813–1888). Robert Allen, military instructor, was born in Maryland in 1813 and graduated fifth in his class at West Point in 1834. After brief service in the Seminole War, he resigned his commission to become, in turn, a civil engineer; a Methodist minister; and a professor successively at Allegheny College in Pennsylvania, at Transylvania University in Kentucky, and at Kentucky Military Institute. He moved to the Far West in 1849 and worked as a special agent for the United States Post Office Department in California and Oregon. He later owned and published the San Francisco *Pacific News* before moving in 1857 to Texas, where he established Bastrop Military Institute (*see* TEXAS MILITARY INSTITUTE, AUSTIN). There the cadets reportedly "loved and honored him."

With the outbreak of the Civil War[qv] Allen was placed in charge of Camp Clark,[qv] a camp of instruction on the San Marcos River near Martindale. He briefly commanded the Fourth Texas Infantry regiment of what was to become the famed Hood's Texas Brigade,[qv] but "although a man of thorough military education," according to the regiment's chaplain, Nicholas A. Davis,[qv] Allen "was not acceptable to either men or officers." In fact, the high-spirited Texans literally drove him from their camp because of the reputation as a "Rarin', Tearin', Pitchin'" martinet that he had attained while supervising their training at Camp Clark.

Allen returned to Bastrop and on February 26, 1862, recruited the Seventeenth Texas Infantry Regiment of John G. Walker's[qv] Texas Division, which he commanded until November 1863, when he was given charge of Camp Ford, a prisoner of war camp near Tyler. After the war Allen returned to his old position as superintendent of Kentucky Military Institute, where he continued to serve until 1874. On July 9, 1888, he drowned while swimming in the Kissimmee River in Florida.

BIBLIOGRAPHY: Norman D. Brown, ed., *Journey to Pleasant Hill: The Civil War Letters of Captain Elijah P. Petty* (San Antonio: University of Texas Institute of Texan Cultures, 1982). Ezra J. Warner, *Generals in Gray* (Baton Rouge: Louisiana State University Press, 1959).

Thomas W. Cutrer

ALLEN, RODERICK RODMAN (1894–1970). Roderick Rodman Allen, an army officer who served in three wars, the son of Jefferson Buffington and Emma (Albers) Allen, was born on January 29, 1894, in Marshall, Texas, and spent his youth in Palestine, Texas. He graduated from Texas A&M in 1915 with a bachelor of science degree in agriculture. In 1946 A&M granted him an honorary LL.D. degree. On April 25, 1917, he married Maydelle Campbell; the couple reared Nancy Campbell Allen and Gail Random Allen. Allen was commissioned a second lieutenant, Sixteenth Cavalry, Regular Army, on November 29, 1916, and subsequently a first lieutenant. He was stationed at Mercedes, Texas, on the Mexican border. He was transferred to the Third Cavalry in June 1917, was promoted to captain on October 17, and served with the regiment in France in the American Expeditionary Force. His troop and squadron were on remount duty at six locations. From November 1917 to January 1918 Allen was an aerial observer, First Observation Squadron, Aviation Section, Signal Corps, in World War I.[qv] During the spring of 1919 he attended the University of Toulouse in France. In July 1919 he returned with the Third Cavalry to Fort Ethan Allen, Vermont. In 1919–21 and 1923 he rode 300-mile endurance tests in the United States Mounted Service. In 1920 Allen was an instructor, Texas National Guard,[qv] Dallas. In February 1921 he transferred to the Sixteenth Cavalry, Fort Sam Houston, San Antonio, and in October he moved to the Fourth United States Cavalry.[qv] He was a member of the Cavalry Engineer Rifle Team from 1921 to 1923. Beginning in the 1920s Allen graduated from several advanced military schools. He attended the Cavalry School and was assigned (1923) to command Company A, Seventh Cavalry, Fort Bliss, and served as regimental adjutant. He graduated from the Command and General Staff School (1928), was promoted to major on June 20, and was ordered to the Personnel Section (of which he became chief in 1930), Office of Chief of Cavalry, in Washington, D.C. In 1929 he was captain of the Cavalry Rifle and Pistol Team. He was an instructor at the Command and General Staff School (1932–34). He graduated from the Chemical Warfare School (1934), the Army War College (1935), and the Naval War College (1936). Allen was a staff officer, Plans and Training Division, War Department, from 1936 to 1940. He was promoted to lieutenant colonel on August 1, 1938.

During World War II[qv] he commanded various armored units. In July 1940 he was operations officer, First Armored Regiment, Fort Knox, Kentucky. In April he was transferred to the Third Armored Division, Camp Beauregard, Louisiana. He was promoted to colonel, Army of the United States, on October 14, 1941, and took command of the Thirty-second Armored Regiment. Allen became chief of staff, Sixth Armored Division, in January 1942 and was promoted to brigadier general, Army of the United States, on May 23. He commanded Combat Command A, Fourth Armored, and participated in maneuvers in Tennessee (1942) and California (1942–43). From October 1943 to September 1944 he commanded the Twentieth Armored Division at Camp Campbell, Kentucky. He was promoted to major general, Army of the United States, on February 23, 1944. He commanded the Twelfth Armored Division in Europe from September 1944 to August 1945. The division was attached to the United States Seventh Army (in France), detached to the First French Army, then to the Third Army to spearhead the Twentieth Corps drive from Trier to the Rhine. His division accompanied the Twenty-first Corps into Austria. From August 1945 to February 1946 he commanded the First Armored in Germany, then was director of operations, plans, and training at European Theater headquarters. He was promoted to colonel, regular army, on November 1, 1945, and to brigadier general on January 24, 1948.

In the United States he served from October 1947 to April 1948 as director of intelligence, Army Ground Forces, Fort Monroe, Virginia.

He was promoted to major general on May 27, 1949. He commanded the Third Armored, Fort Knox, from 1948 to 1950. In July 1950, at the outbreak of the Korean War, he reported to Douglas MacArthur's headquarters, Far East Command, Tokyo, Japan. He was designated deputy chief of staff, Far East Command, deputy chief of staff, United Nations Command, and chief of staff, Korean Operations. From April 1951 to February 1952 Allen commanded the Sixteenth Corps, headquartered at Sendai, Japan. After being reassigned to the states, he commanded the Ninth Infantry Division, Fort Dix, from February to July 1952. At Dix, Allen briefly made national news when a House subcommittee on appropriations criticized his expenditures for kennels and dog runs for his fancy dogs (Samoyeds). His last assignment was as commanding general, New England Sub-area, Boston Army Base, Fort Devens, Massachusetts. He retired from the army on May 31, 1954, and resided in Washington, D.C., until his death, on February 1, 1970. He is buried in Arlington National Cemetery. Allen received the Distinguished Service Medal, Silver Star Medal, Legion of Merit, Bronze Star Medal, Army Command Ribbon, Distinguished Marksman award, Officer Legion of Honor award, Croix de Guerre with Palm (French), Order of the White Lion and Victory, and War Cross (Czechoslovakia).

BIBLIOGRAPHY: Vertical Files, Sterling C. Evans Library, Texas A&M University. *Who Was Who in American History: The Military* (Chicago: Marquis Who's Who, 1975). *Harwood P. Hinton*

ALLEN, RUTH ALICE (1889–1979). Ruth Alice Allen, university professor, was born on July 28, 1889, in Cameron, Texas, to Thomas Franklin and Jennie (Adams) Allen. She grew up and attended public schools in Milam and Falls counties, where her father was a teacher and later county school superintendent. After graduation from high school she passed the teacher certification examination and then taught school for several years. She attended summer school at Baylor University and at Southwest Texas State Teachers College (now Southwest Texas State University) and earned her diploma or permanent teaching certificate in 1914. She entered the University of Texas in 1918 and received a B.A. in 1921 and an M.S. in economics in 1923 with a thesis on the minimum wage. At a time when few women earned doctorates and even fewer studied economics, Allen was awarded a Ph.D. in the subject at the University of Chicago in 1933. Her dissertation, The Labor of Women in the Production of Cotton, was based on one of the first on-site investigations into the living and working conditions of women in Texas, and because the workers reflected an ethnic variety, also of the condition of African and Mexican Americans in Texas.

From 1923 until 1959 Allen taught economics at the University of Texas, where she achieved the rank of professor in 1941. For several years she was department chairman and graduate advisor. In the early 1940s, when the politically outspoken members of the economics department attracted the hostile attention of the board of regents and the state legislature, she joined her faculty colleagues in speaking out to defend academic freedom. She served on a series of faculty committees, among them the Committee of Eleven, which fought the dismissal of University of Texas president Homer Rainey[qv] by the regents in 1944.

Allen was the first economist to focus sustained scholarly attention upon the history of the Texas working people and their unions, and she was among the first to document such early labor struggles as the Cowboy Strike of 1883.[qv] She was also the first to perceive the urgent need to preserve the written documents of organized labor and to attempt to establish a labor archives for the state. Her publications, especially *Chapters in the History of Organized Labor in Texas* (1941) and *The Great Southwest Strike* (1942), influenced much later research and lay interest in the area.

In 1934–35 Allen served as supervisor for the southwestern region of the Cost of Living Division of the Bureau of Labor Statistics, and during World War II[qv] she was a member of Division Eight of the War Labor Board and a member of the War Manpower Commission's Women's Policy Committee. She was a board member of the Social Science Research Council and, from 1942 to 1947, editor of the *Southwestern Social Science Quarterly* (now *Social Science Quarterly*[qv]). She was a member of numerous professional organizations, among them the American Economic Association, the Economic History Association, the Texas Association of College Teachers,[qv] and the American Association of University Professors. She was a Presbyterian.

Allen taught courses well in advance of their time, such as one on the economic status of women. She taught on a university faculty whose female members were around 10 percent in the late 1920s and concentrated primarily in such "female professions" as home economics. Allen never married. She was a member of an early suffrage organization. She was an outspoken advocate of organizing and collective bargaining for working people and the "discoverer" of their history. After her retirement from the University of Texas in 1959, she taught economics at Huston-Tillotson College for several years. She died in Austin on October 7, 1979, at the age of ninety.

BIBLIOGRAPHY: Ruth Alice Allen Papers, Barker Texas History Center, University of Texas at Austin. Labor Movement in Texas Papers, Barker Texas History Center, University of Texas at Austin. Austin *American*, January 8, 1950. Austin *American-Statesman*, April 2, 1972. Vertical Files, Barker Texas History Center, University of Texas at Austin. *Barbara K. Byrd*

ALLEN, SAMUEL EZEKIEL (1848–1913). Samuel Ezekiel Allen, rancher, was born in Harris County, Texas, on June 8, 1848, the son of Rebecca Jane (Thomas) and Samuel W. Allen.[qv] He attended Harrisburg public schools and Bastrop Military Academy. He was a rancher like his father, whose property he inherited and consolidated with some of his mother's land originally granted to her father, Ezekiel Thomas,[qv] and her great-uncle, Mosis A. Callihan.[qv] At the time of Allen's death in 1913 he owned 10,000 to 20,000 acres along Buffalo Bayou and was one of the largest taxpayers in Harris County. He also maintained a 10,000-acre "winter pasture" on the San Bernard River in Brazoria County and had additional grazing land in Galveston and Fort Bend counties. Earlier his holdings had extended to the Colorado River near Columbus.

For the headquarters of his ranch Allen chose a location near the mouth of Sims Bayou and used Buffalo Bayou for the transportation of cattle. Also he shipped cattle by rail, through his private station, El Buey. Besides his ranching activities he had varied business interests, including banking, shipping, and manufacturing. He founded and was one of the principal stockholders in the Oriental Textile Mills, at that time the largest manufacturer of press cloth for the cotton industry in the world, with offices in New York, London, and other major cities. Allen was also among the founders of a bank.

In 1874 he married Rosa Christie Lum. They had six children. Allen died on June 23, 1913. In 1917 Mrs. Allen began the dissolution of the Allen Ranch, which continued until her death in 1931. She was assisted by her grandson, Robert Cummins Stuart, who helped her subdivide Allen Dale, Allen Farms, and Lum Terrace. Through those and other subdivisions many streets in Houston bear names connected with the Allen Ranch. Both Allen and his wife were buried in Glendale Cemetery, Harrisburg.

BIBLIOGRAPHY: Houston *Chronicle*, June 24, 1913. Marguerite Johnston, *Happy Worldly Abode: Christ Church Cathedral, 1839–1964* (Houston: Cathedral Press, 1964). *Francita Stuart Koelsch*

ALLEN, SAMUEL TABOR (1809–1838). Samuel Tabor (Taber) Allen, early Texas public figure, son of Thomas and Eunice (Johnson) Allen, was born in 1809 in Connecticut. He sailed to Texas by way of New Orleans in 1830 and joined his uncle George Allen in Harrisburg. His goal was to seek a fortune and acquire land. Allen was active in prerepublic politics and was arrested and imprisoned with William B. Travis qv and others during the Anahuac Disturbances qv in 1832. He was a delegate from Milam to the Consultation qv of 1835 and was a member of the General Council.qv He also represented Milam in the House of Representatives of the First Congress, 1836–37. He and a group of his neighbors missed fighting at the Alamo by five days, and he missed participation in the battle of San Jacinto qv because he was moving his family to safety at San Augustine during the Runaway Scrape.qv In 1835 he married Matilda (or Hester) Roberts Connell, the daughter of Elisha Roberts,qv who settled in the San Augustine area in 1820. Matilda was a widow with two children, and she and Samuel had two additional children. Allen acquired over 20,000 acres of land and had many business interests. In October 1838 he was a member of a surveying team of some twenty men who were ambushed by a group of Kickapoo Indians near Dawson in Navarro County. Allen was killed; only five escaped. In 1850 Matilda Allen gave 120 acres of land to establish the town of Belton in Bell County. She died in April 1879.

BIBLIOGRAPHY: *A Memorial and Biographical History of McLennan, Falls, Bell, and Coryell Counties* (Chicago: Lewis, 1893; rpt., St. Louis: Ingmire, 1984). Texas House of Representatives, *Biographical Directory of the Texan Conventions and Congresses, 1832–1845* (Austin: Book Exchange, 1941). *Margaret A. Cox*

ALLEN, SAMUEL WILLIAM (1826–1888). Samuel Allen, cattleman, was born in Frankfort, Kentucky, on January 2, 1826. He was married in Harris County, Texas, on May 9, 1844, to Rebecca Jane Thomas, daughter of Ezekiel Thomas.qv Allen was not related to the Allen brothers who founded the city of Houston (*see* ALLEN, AUGUSTUS CHAPMAN). Samuel Allen was a rancher and a partner in the Galveston-based firm of Allen and Poole, the largest shippers of cattle in Southeast Texas, and later was a partner in a cattle enterprise with Abel Head (Shanghai) Pierce.qv He bought Pierce's interest for $110,000 in 1871. The Allen Ranch qv centered around the site of present South Houston and extended from Clear Lake to Harrisburg. When the Galveston, Houston and Henderson Railroad opened in 1860, one stop was at Allen's private station, known as Dumont. The name was retained for the railroad station in South Houston. Allen died on August 8, 1888, and was buried in Glendale Cemetery, Harrisburg.

BIBLIOGRAPHY: Chris Emmett, *Shanghai Pierce: A Fair Likeness* (Norman: University of Oklahoma Press, 1953; rpt. 1974). Frances Richard Lubbock, *Six Decades in Texas* (Austin: Ben C. Jones, 1900; rpt., Austin: Pemberton, 1968). Samuel O. Young, *A Thumb-Nail History of the City of Houston* (Houston: Rein, 1912). Jesse A. Ziegler, *Wave of the Gulf* (San Antonio: Naylor, 1938). *Francita Stuart Koelsch*

ALLEN, THOMAS (1849–1924). Thomas Allen, painter, son of Thomas and Annie G. Allen, was born in St. Louis, Missouri, in 1849. In his second year of business school at Washington University, St. Louis, Allen accompanied his professor, J. W. Paterson, on a sketching expedition to the Rocky Mountains. His notes and sketches from that trip increased his interest in art. In 1871 he went to Paris, then to Düsseldorf, where he studied at the Royal Academy from 1872 to 1876.

In the winter of 1878–79 he traveled to San Antonio, Texas, before returning to France. In San Antonio he painted three notable works: *The Market Place, San Antonio* (exhibited in the Paris Salon in 1882); *Mexican Woman Washing at San Pedro Spring*, and *The Portal of San José Mission*. The colors of his romantic scenes are muted, and his subjects are presented with little detail. Allen's work shows an appreciation of the simple and commonplace.

The first American showing of Allen's work was at the National Academy of Design in New York. He was made a member of the American Society of Artists, and in 1884 he became an associate member of the National Academy. In 1893 he was a member of the International Board of Judges at the World's Columbian Exposition in Chicago, and he was chairman of the jury of paintings at the World's Fair in St. Louis. He was vice president of the Boston Art Club and chairman of the Art Commission of Boston. Before his death in 1924 he became president of the board of trustees of the Boston Museum of Fine Arts. His paintings are in the collections of the San Antonio Public Library, the Witte Memorial Museum,qv the St. Louis Art Museum, the Boston Museum of Fine Arts, the Berkshire Museum in Pittsfield, Massachusetts, and the Joslyn Art Museum in Omaha, Nebraska. Allen died in Worcester, Massachusetts, on August 25, 1924.

BIBLIOGRAPHY: Pauline A. Pinckney, *Painting in Texas: The Nineteenth Century* (Austin: University of Texas Press, 1967). Vertical Files, Barker Texas History Center, University of Texas at Austin.
Pauline A. Pinckney

ALLEN, WILLIAM YOUEL (1805–1885). William Youel Allen, clergyman, the son of Benjamin and Margaret (Youel) Allen, was born in Shelbyville, Kentucky, on May 7, 1805. He began to study law at the age of twenty-one but soon changed his focus to the ministry. He attended Centre College, graduated in 1831, and taught there for 2½ years while studying theology. He later studied at Princeton Theological Seminary. He was licensed to preach in 1836 by the Presbytery of New Brunswick, New Jersey, and spent some time working for a black colonization society in Pennsylvania before traveling to Texas in March 1838. He conducted Sunday school and preached in Houston on his first Sunday there. He served as chaplain of the Texas Senate in 1838 and, perhaps, of the House of Representatives in 1839, although the latter is disputed. Allen organized a church in Houston in March 1839, one in Austin in October, and one in Columbia the following year. He also participated in the organization of the Presbytery of the Brazos in April 1840.

While in Houston he served as a member of the school board and organized, with the support of President Sam Houston,qv the first temperance meeting in Texas. He helped organize the first Texas temperance society as well as the Texas National Bible Society. He drafted the first Texas congressional legislative enactment for education. While serving in Texas Allen made several trips to the United States. On his first trip (1838) he was ordained an evangelist, and on the fourth trip (1841) he was ordained a minister in the Presbyterian Church and married Sarah Stonestreet. After her death in April 1848, he married Margaret Maxwell. He left Texas on February 18, 1842, but visited the state in 1857.

After his return to Kentucky, Allen was elected president of Centre College, Danville, on September 2, 1845. Later he served as pastor at Bethany, Kentucky, and spent fourteen years at Rockville, Indiana, where he died on February 13, 1885.

BIBLIOGRAPHY: Frederick Eby, *Education in Texas: Source Materials* (Austin: University of Texas, 1918). Marguerite Johnston, *Houston, The Unknown City, 1836–1946* (College Station: Texas A&M University Press, 1991). *Presbyterian Expansion in the Synod of Texas of the Presbyterian Church, U.S.* (n.p: Texas Synod, 1927). S. C. Red, *A Brief History of the First Presbyterian Church, Houston, Texas, 1839–1939* (Houston: Wilson, 1939). William S. Red, ed., "Allen's Reminiscences of Texas, 1838–1842," *Southwestern Historical Quarterly* 18 (January 1915). William S. Red, ed., "Extracts from the Diary of W. Y. Allen, 1838–1839," *Southwestern Historical Quarterly* 17 (July 1913).

ALLEN, WINNIE (1895–1985). Winnie Allen, archivist and historian, was born on April 13, 1895, in Henrietta, Texas, to W. T. and Ethel (Youree) Allen. She graduated from Henrietta High School and taught school from 1917 to 1923 in Henrietta, San Antonio, El Paso, and Dallas. In 1920 she received her A.B. degree from the University of Texas. From 1923 to 1925 she was acting archivist at the Texas State Library qv in Austin. She collaborated with Charles Adams Gulick, Jr., to edit Volume IV of the *Lamar Papers* (1924, 1925). In 1925 she received her M.A. in history from the University of Texas and became assistant archivist at the University of Texas archives, under Mattie Austin Hatcher. When Hatcher retired in 1936, Allen replaced her as archivist, a position in which she served for thirty-five years.

Her major focus was to collect new materials for the University archives, and she drove all over Texas to obtain documents. When she began the job the archives contained only the Austin papers and about twenty other manuscript collections; by the time of her retirement in 1960 the archives comprised between 3,500 and 4,000 collections. Winnie Allen also supervised the transcription of a number of important collections during her tenure, including the Bexar Archives,qv *The Writings of Sam Houston, 1813–1863*, the Robert Bruce Blake Collection, and the papers of James Stephen Hoggqv and his son William Clifford Hogg.qv As a strong believer in the use of tape recordings as an archival tool, Allen began in 1952 to organize and supervise a project to preserve the oral history of Texas oil pioneers.

She wrote or contributed to a number of articles and books on Texas history. She coauthored *Pioneers in Texas: True Stories of the Early Days* with Carrie Walker Allen (1935); this book became the state-adopted reader for the sixth grade. In 1936 she collaborated with Eugene C. Barkerqv and Marius Perron in compiling the *Texas Centennial Roster* and served on the advisory board for the Texas Centennialqv Historical Exhibits in Dallas. She also wrote a number of historical feature articles for the Dallas *News* and reviews and research articles for the *Southwestern Historical Quarterly*qv throughout her career.

In 1952 Allen proposed a nonpartisan state board to coordinate all efforts directed toward the location, documentation, preservation, and publication of materials related to Texas history and the development of a state-backed foundation to fund approved historical projects. This idea led to the establishment of the first Historical Survey Commission in 1952. This organization, chartered as the Texas Historical Foundation in 1954, eventually became the Texas Historical Commission.qv Winnie Allen was also a founding member of the Society of American Archivists. She helped organize the first Institute of Archival Management in the Southwest in the 1960s. The Daughters of the Republic of Texasqv appointed her to the Committee on Awards for their Texas History Scholarship Fund in 1943 and also made her an honorary member. She was president of the Austin Library Club in 1945–46, served on the board of directors of the Heritage Society of Austin, and was a member of the Texas Library Associationqv and the Texas State Historical Association.qv

After her retirement in August 1960 she moved to Hutchins, to be near friends. Eventually, failing health caused her to move to the Texas Health Center, a nursing home in Lancaster where she died on August 1, 1985.

BIBLIOGRAPHY: Don E. Carleton and Katherine J. Adams, "'Work Peculiarly Our Own': Origins of the Barker Texas History Center," *Southwestern Historical Quarterly* 86 (October 1982). Malcolm D. McLean, comp. and ed., *Papers Concerning Robertson's Colony in Texas* (13 vols., Fort Worth: Texas Christian University Press, 1974–76; Arlington: University of Texas at Arlington Press, 1977–87). *Proceedings of the Philosophical Society of Texas*, 1985. Vertical Files, Barker Texas History Center, University of Texas at Austin.

Alice J. Rhoades

ALLEN, TEXAS. Allen is on Farm Road 2478 eight miles southwest of McKinney in southwestern Collin County. The town was established in 1870 by a purchasing agent for the Houston and Texas Central Railway and named in 1872 for Ebenezer Allen,qv former attorney general of Texas and a promoter of the railroad. In 1876 a post office opened there. Four years later Denton outlaw Sam Bassqv supposedly committed the first train robbery in the state at Allen. By 1884 Allen had a population estimated at 350, three churches, a school, a chair factory, and a flour mill. In 1908 the Texas Traction Company built an electric railway through the town. The population had increased to 550 by 1915. In the mid-1940s the number of residents declined to 400, and in 1948 train service was discontinued. Beginning in the late 1960s, however, Allen's population grew rapidly. Between 1970 and 1980 the number of residents jumped from 1,940 to 8,314. This increase was influenced by the economic growth of Dallas and nearby Plano and the construction of Dallas–Fort Worth International Airport.qv In 1990 Allen had a population of 18,309 and was the third largest town in Collin County.

BIBLIOGRAPHY: Roy Franklin Hall and Helen Gibbard Hall, *Collin County: Pioneering in North Texas* (Quanah, Texas: Nortex, 1975). J. Lee and Lillian J. Stambaugh, *A History of Collin County* (Austin: Texas State Historical Association, 1958).

David Minor

ALLEN ACADEMY. Allen Academy, a private school in Bryan, traces its beginnings to 1886, when John Hodges Allen became the principal of Madison Academy, at Madisonville. After nine years of successful operation of Madison Academy, Allen requested and received a charter from the state to establish Madison College, a secondary school. Rivers O. Allen, Allen's younger brother, moved from Tennessee to become coprincipal at Madison College. In 1896 the name of the school was changed to Allen Academy.

In 1899 the Allens decided to reorganize Allen Academy as a private boarding school for boys. They moved it to Bryan that summer. During the early years the Allens were the only teachers in the school, but the academy prospered and overcame many obstacles similar to those that forced other private schools to close. In 1899 the Allens purchased five acres and a two-room building; in 1968 the school had 470 acres and thirty-eight buildings. From an initial enrollment of twenty-seven students in six grades, the number of students reached an average of 600 students enrolled in eight grades. In 1916 military training was introduced into the academy, and three years later an ROTC was organized there. The military program made rapid progress, and in 1927 Allen Academy was selected as an honor military school, the highest rating given to a military school in the United States. The academy continued to retain this rating throughout the years that it maintained its ROTC program.

Under the supervision of the Agricultural and Mechanical College of Texas (now Texas A&M University), the first year of junior college was added to the Allen curriculum in 1927. The courses were instituted primarily to accommodate students who lacked a few high school credits to satisfy the entrance requirements for college. Therefore, a student was able to complete his high school work and at the same time receive some college credit. In 1947 the second year of college work was added to the curriculum, thus completing the requirements of the junior college division of the school. The academy continued to offer a junior college curriculum until 1968, when Blinn College in Brenham assumed the responsibility and began to teach the courses at the Allen Academy location.

The changing economic climate persuaded the Allen family to relinquish private ownership of the academy, and in June 1953 Allen Academy was transferred to the Allen Academy Foundation, a nonprofit educational trust. During the 1970s and 1980s the administration modified the school to meet educational demands. The military program was discontinued in 1982, and the next year the school had 250 students. In the summer of 1988 the school property was sold to the federal government for a minimum-security unit of the federal prison system. Allen Academy was moved to a modern facility located between Bryan and College Station. In 1994 the school was coeducational and offered instruction to students from preschool through high school. The enrollment was 305.

BIBLIOGRAPHY: Glenna Fourman Brundidge, *Brazos County History: Rich Past—Bright Future* (Bryan, Texas: Family History Foundation, 1986). Barbara LeUnes, A History of Allen Academy, 1886–1968 (M.A. thesis, Texas A&M University, 1970). Vertical Files, Barker Texas History Center, University of Texas at Austin.

Barbara LeUnes Pearson

ALLEN CHAPEL, TEXAS. Allen Chapel, a mile south of Ratcliff off State Highway 7 in eastern Houston County, was established in the 1870s by the emancipated slaves of area landowners. An African Methodist Episcopal church was organized there around 1900 and built a building in 1903 on land purchased from Nat Allen, after whom the community was named. A one-room schoolhouse was built in 1910. In the mid-1930s the community comprised the church, the school, and a number of houses. The school building was moved to Kennard in 1968 but returned in 1985. In the early 1990s Allen Chapel was a dispersed farming community with a church, a community center, and a number of houses. Descendents of many original settlers still lived in the area.

BIBLIOGRAPHY: Houston County Historical Commission, *History of Houston County, Texas, 1687–1979* (Tulsa, Oklahoma: Heritage, 1979). *Houston County Cemeteries* (Crockett, Texas: Houston County Historical Commission, 1977; 3d ed. 1987). Marker Files, Texas Historical Commission, Austin. *Christopher Long*

ALLEN CREEK (Cherokee County). Allen Creek rises two miles northeast of Alto in southern Cherokee County (at 31°41′ N, 95°02′ W) and runs southeast for six miles to its mouth on the Angelina River, three miles east of Linwood (at 31°40′ N, 94°57′ W). The stream is intermittent in its upper reaches. It traverses flat to gently rolling terrain surfaced by clay and sandy loam that supports mixed hardwoods and pines.

____ (Fayette County). Allen Creek rises in Fayetteville in eastern Fayette County (at 29°54′ N, 96°41′ W) and flows east intermittently for four miles to its mouth on Pool Branch, one mile southeast of the community of Rek Hill (at 29°55′ N, 96°38′ W). Throughout its length the stream generally parallels the route of the Missouri, Kansas and Texas Railroad. The area soils vary from deep sand and gravel to sandy loam topsoil with firm clay subsoil. The surrounding land is used primarily as pasture. Area vegetation consists primarily of mesquite and grasses. The stream flows through an area of low-rolling hills and prairies.

____ (Lee County). Allen Creek, also known as Allens Creek, rises six miles northwest of Lexington in extreme northern Lee County (at 30°30′ N, 97°04′ W) and flows northeast for thirteen miles through southern Milam County and northern Lee County before emptying into East Yegua Creek on the Lee-Burleson county line 4½ miles west of Hicks (at 30°32′ N, 96°55′ W). The stream is intermittent in its upper reaches. It flows through generally flat terrain with local shallow depressions and clay loam and sandy loam soils that support water-tolerant hardwoods and grasses.

____ (Van Zandt County). Allen Creek rises just east of State Highway 64 and a mile southeast of Wills Point in northwestern Van Zandt County (at 32° 40′ N, 95° 58′ W) and flows southwest for ten miles to its mouth on Cedar Creek, two miles northeast of Cedarvale in Kaufman County (at 32° 36′ N, 96° 05′ W). The terrain is chiefly flat with local shallow depressions. The soil surface of clay and sandy loams supports water-tolerant hardwoods, conifers, and grasses.

ALLENDALE, TEXAS (San Patricio County). Allendale was centered around the home and store of George Allen, two miles south of the site of present-day Aransas Pass in eastern San Patricio County. A school built there in the early 1870s existed until at least 1910. After it was closed and the city of Aransas Pass expanded, Allendale disappeared.

BIBLIOGRAPHY: Keith Guthrie, *History of San Patricio County* (Austin: Nortex, 1986). *Keith Guthrie*

ALLENDALE, TEXAS (Wichita County). Allendale is on Farm Road 2650 just southwest of Wichita Falls in southeastern Wichita County. The settlement was established in 1889 and named for Elbert Allen and B. Dale Hinkle. These two men, with A. D. Butcher, purchased a plot on the center block of Wichita County land from Denton County and founded Allendale. By 1892 the small farming community had a post office, a general store, and a school. The post office ceased operation in 1895, was reopened in 1903, and closed permanently sometime after 1930. The Allendale school closed sometime during the 1940s. State highway maps of 1936 showed a church and scattered dwellings at the townsite on the Burlington Northern tracks.

BIBLIOGRAPHY: Louise Kelly, *Wichita County Beginnings* (Burnet, Texas: Eakin Press, 1982). *Brian Hart*

ALLENFARM, TEXAS. Allenfarm is on Farm Road 159 and the Atchison, Topeka and Santa Fe Railroad twenty-four miles south of Bryan in southern Brazos County. The area was settled by Stephen F. Austin's[qv] second group of colonists between 1821 and 1831. The original grants were issued to Jarrell and Robert H. Millican.[qv] The community was named for Robert A. Allen, an area plantation owner. His name however, does not appear on the known land deeds. The post office operated from 1885 until after 1940. In 1902 the town had a three-story depot, two gins, a general store, a commissary, three saloons, and a population of 100. In the 1940s it had two stores, two schools, a church, two factories, and a population of seventy-five. By 1964 the population had fallen to fifteen. In 1970 it was forty. Allenfarm had one business in 1986. Will Terrell, the owner, preserved several of the original local buildings and their contents. In 1990 Allenfarm had a population of thirty.

BIBLIOGRAPHY: Glenna Fourman Brundidge, *Brazos County History: Rich Past—Bright Future* (Bryan, Texas: Family History Foundation, 1986). *Molly Kate McCaughey*

ALLENHURST, TEXAS. Allenhurst is on Caney Creek six miles northeast of Bay City in northeast Matagorda County. It was named after Allentown, Pennsylvania, the birthplace of Jeff N. Miller, an official of the St. Louis, Brownsville and Mexico Railway, which was built through the area in 1905. Allenhurst was a stop for passenger trains from Brownsville to Houston. By the mid-1930s it was part of the Van Vleck common school district and had a church and cemetery, a number of dwellings, and a one-room frame elementary school building. By 1952 the school was gone. County highway maps for 1989 showed one business in the community, though no population count was available for the 1990 census.

BIBLIOGRAPHY: Frank J. Balusek, Survey and Proposed Reorganization of the Schools of Matagorda County, Texas (M.Ed. thesis, University of Texas, 1939). Matagorda County Historical Commission, *Historic Matagorda County* (3 vols., Houston: Armstrong, 1986).
Rachel Jenkins

ALLEN RANCH. The Allen Ranch, with headquarters in Harris County, was established in the early 1840s and operated for more than 100 years. It became the largest ranch in the region. Its operations ranged from the Trinity to the Lavaca rivers and extended into four counties.

Samuel William Allen[qv] started ranching on the south side of Buffalo Bayou, now the Houston Ship Channel,[qv] about eight miles east of Houston. His wife, Rebecca Thomas, daughter of Ezekiel Thomas,[qv] inherited 350 acres from her uncle, M. A. Callihan,[qv] that became part of the Allen Ranch. Like his neighbors and friends Andrew Briscoe and Francis R. Lubbock,[qqv] Allen started his ranch by rounding up the prolific longhorn cattle[qv] that had run wild since Spanish times along the Gulf Coast. By the 1860s Allen had acquired exclusive cattle-shipping rights from the Morgan Lines[qv] and had a virtual monopoly on the trade to New Orleans and Cuba. He formed cattle partnerships with other ranchers, including Abel H. (Shanghai) Pierce.[qv] Pierce once estimated that he and Allen owned over 100,000 cattle. In 1871, as a personal favor, Allen bought out Pierce's interest. He also helped out former governor Lubbock by buying his ranch and then hiring Lubbock to represent Allen's Galveston-based firm, Allen, Poole, and Company. The Galveston, Houston and Henderson Railroad was built through the Allen Ranch in 1859. Allen shipped cattle by steamer from Galveston, Palacios, and his dock on Buffalo Bayou. He also operated tallow and hide-rendering plants on Buffalo Bayou and in Galveston.

As a result of internal financial misdealings, Allen, Poole, and Company went into bankruptcy in 1874, but S. W. Allen's ranch continued and prospered under the management of his son, Sam Ezekiel Allen.[qv] In 1876 the Morgan Lines moved operations from Galveston to a new wharf opposite the Allen Ranch's docks. The Gulf, Colorado and Santa Fe Railway was built through the ranch in 1883, as was the La Porte, Houston and Northern Railroad in 1893. In 1900 the Allen Ranch extended over 17,000 acres in Harris County and had pastures in Galveston, Fort Bend, and Brazoria counties. S. E. Allen concentrated on upgrading the quality of the herd and shipped trainloads of feeder cattle to the finishing ranches of the West Texas plains.

After Allen died in 1913 his grandson, Robert C. Stuart, began liquidating the ranch holdings. Many streets and subdivisions of southeastern Harris County bear the names of the Allen family because they were once part of the ranch. S. E. Allen's son, Sam Milton Allen, continued to ranch on 386 acres in Harris County and 10,000 acres in Brazoria County. S. M. Allen's ranch was liquidated in 1947, after his death. Afterward, other descendents still maintained small ranching operations on land inherited from the original ranch.

BIBLIOGRAPHY: Chris Emmett, *Shanghai Pierce: A Fair Likeness* (Norman: University of Oklahoma Press, 1953; rpt. 1974). Houston *Chronicle*, June 24, 1917. Frances Richard Lubbock, *Six Decades in Texas* (Austin: Ben C. Jones, 1900; rpt., Austin: Pemberton, 1968). C. David Pomeroy, Jr., *Pasadena: The Early Years* (Pasadena, Texas: Pomerosa Press, 1994). Jesse A. Ziegler, *Wave of the Gulf* (San Antonio: Naylor, 1938). *C. David Pomeroy, Jr.*

ALLEN'S CHAPEL, TEXAS. Allen's Chapel, on Farm Road 1396 thirteen miles northeast of Bonham in eastern Fannin County, is an offshoot of nearby Allen's Point. It served area farmers as a school and church community. In the 1950s the school district was consolidated with that of Honey Grove. The population in Allen's Chapel was forty-one in 1990.

BIBLIOGRAPHY: *Fannin County Folks and Facts* (Dallas: Taylor, 1977). Floy Crandall Hodge, *A History of Fannin County* (Hereford, Texas: Pioneer, 1966). *David Minor*

ALLEN'S (ALLENS) CREEK (Austin County). Allen's (Allens) Creek, also known as Eight Mile Creek, rises near Sealy in southeastern Austin County (at 29°47′ N, 96°10′ W) and flows southeast through mostly open country for fifteen miles to its mouth on the Brazos River, two miles north of Wallis (at 29°40′ N, 96°03′ W). The area is gently sloping to nearly level and surfaced with loam and clay that support elm, hackberry, post oak, black hickory, and blackjack oak. Settlement along the stream began in the 1820s. The creek heads in the four-league tract that Stephen F. Austin[qv] donated to his colony as a site for its capital, San Felipe de Austin. The stream is named for Miles N. Allen, who patented a quarter league of land on the creek in 1827. It was formerly known as Eight Mile Creek because it was thought to head eight miles below San Felipe de Austin. During the late 1870s Sealy was established near the headwaters by the Gulf, Colorado and Santa Fe Railway on a three-acre tract purchased from the San Felipe de Austin town corporation.

____ (Fannin County). Allen's Creek rises a mile northwest of Gober in south central Fannin County (at 33°29′ N, 96°07′ W) and flows generally southeast for five miles before joining the waters of the North Sulphur River about 1½ miles southeast of Gober (at 33°27′ N, 96°04′ W). It flows over rolling prairie surfaced with shallow to deep clays and clay loams. Mesquite, juniper, oak, and cacti border the banks of the stream. For most of the county's history the Allen's Creek area has been used as crop and range land.

ALLEN'S LANDING, TEXAS. Allen's Landing is located at the site of the original city of Houston on the south bank of Buffalo Bayou and a fork of White Oak Bayou in central Harris County. The landing, at a natural turning basin, originally served as a boat dock for Houston real estate development at the "head of navigation" on Buffalo Bayou. Oceangoing ships, steamers, and sailing vessels loaded from its wharves, and the steamer *Laura*[qv] first docked there on January 26, 1837. The city of Houston officially established the port in June 1841, and in 1910 the federal government approved funding for the dredging of a ship channel from the Gulf to the present turning basin four miles to the east of Allen's Landing. A historical marker was placed at the nearly two-acre parksite when it was dedicated as Allen's Landing Memorial Park in 1967. The park serves as a memorial to Houston founders John K. and Augustus Chapman Allen.[qqv] The Southern Pacific Railroad also donated 4,000 square feet of land to the park, which was developed by the Houston Chamber of Commerce, the City of Houston, and the Harris County Navigation District. In 1990 the landing was a dock for the *Laura*.

BIBLIOGRAPHY: Houston Metropolitan Research Center Files, Houston Public Library. Marie Phelps McAshan, *A Houston Legacy: On the Corner of Main and Texas* (Houston: Gulf, 1985). David G. McComb, *Houston: The Bayou City* (Austin: University of Texas Press, 1969; rev. ed., *Houston: A History*, 1981). Ray Miller, *Ray Miller's Houston* (Houston: Cordovan Press, 1982). *Diana J. Kleiner*

ALLEN'S POINT, TEXAS. Allen's Point is on Farm Road 100 fifteen miles northeast of Bonham in eastern Fannin County. The settlement began in 1836, when its founder, Tennessean Wilson B. Allen, established a homestead near Honey Grove Creek and a crossing called Allen's Point. The success of Allen's sugarcane farm attracted other farmers to the area. Soon thereafter, the settlers organized what are believed to be the first Methodist and Baptist churches in the county. The Methodist church was built about five miles west of Allen's Point and called Allen's Chapel. Gradually a separate community developed around the Methodist church. Throughout its history, Allen's Point has served area farmers as a school and church community. Nearby Meade Springs became a tourist attraction, but its development as a health resort failed. From 1899 to 1903 a post office called Yew, probably in honor of H. C. Yew, an early settler, lodge owner, and bricklayer, operated in the community. After the closing of the post office, the town reverted to its original name. At one time a reported seven cotton gins operated nearby. The community's population, however, never exceeded 100. Though passed by the railroads and overshadowed by nearby Honey Grove, Allen's Point remained a community center for area farmers. In 1964 the Texas Agricultural Extension Service[qv] awarded Allen's Point the first place in its Rural Community contest. In 1990 the population was seventy-six.

BIBLIOGRAPHY: *Fannin County Folks and Facts* (Dallas: Taylor, 1977). Floy Crandall Hodge, *A History of Fannin County* (Hereford, Texas: Pioneer, 1966). *David Minor*

ALLENTOWN, TEXAS. Allentown is on Farm Road 843 eight miles north of Lufkin in northwestern Angelina County. In the 1930s the settlement had a store, a church, and a number of houses. After World War II[qv] many residents left the area, but in the early 1990s the church and a store still remained. *Christopher Long*

ALLEY, ABRAHAM (1803–1862). Abraham (sometimes Abram) Alley, early settler, son of Thomas and Catherine (Baker) Alley, was born on October 22, 1803, in Missouri. He traveled to Texas in the spring of 1822, accompanied by two of his brothers, John C. and

Thomas V. Alley.[qqv] He landed on Galveston Island and journeyed on foot to the Fort Bend settlement on the Brazos River but later settled on the Colorado River, where another brother, Rawson Alley,[qv] had located in 1821. The Alley family, of French Huguenot descent, had been friends of the family of Stephen F. Austin[qv] in Missouri. A fourth brother to Abraham, William Alley,[qv] immigrated to Texas in 1824. That year Abraham Alley took part in a campaign against the Waco and Tawakoni Indians. In 1825 he was reported as a farmer in Stephen F. Austin's colony. He was a member of an 1829 expedition against the Indians in the San Saba area. On April 26, 1835, Abraham Alley married Nancy Millar, daughter of Texas pioneers John and Elizabeth (Payne) Millar. The Alleys had five children. On June 17, 1835, Alley and his wife applied for land on the Atascosito Road[qv] north of the Colorado River. During the Texas Revolution[qv] he enlisted as a volunteer guard under Capt. William Walker. He was assigned to escort women and children to the Trinity River and did not participate in any battles. For his service, February 20 to May 20, 1836, he was awarded several hundred acres of land in Leon County. In December 1837 he was appointed president of the Colorado County committee on the state land bill. In 1840, he declared for tax purposes that he had title to 3,800 acres of land, with 4,444 acres under survey, and that he also had four slaves, seventy-five cattle, and one horse. In 1850 he owned seven slaves and in 1860, fourteen. Alley died May 16, 1862, and was buried in the family cemetery. His wife died on October 28, 1893.

BIBLIOGRAPHY: John Henry Brown, *Indian Wars and Pioneers of Texas* (Austin: Daniell, 1880; reprod., Easley, South Carolina: Southern Historical Press, 1978). Evelyn M. Carrington, ed., *Women in Early Texas* (Austin: Pemberton Press, 1975). Daughters of the Republic of Texas, *Founders and Patriots of the Republic of Texas* (Austin, 1963–). Daughters of the Republic of Texas, *Muster Rolls of the Texas Revolution* (Austin, 1986). J. H. Kuykendall, "Reminiscences of Early Texans," *Quarterly of the Texas State Historical Association* 6–7 (January, April, July 1903). Thomas L. Miller, *Bounty and Donation Land Grants of Texas, 1835–1888* (Austin: University of Texas Press, 1967). Annie Doom Pickrell, *Pioneer Women in Texas* (Austin: Steck, 1929). *Telegraph and Texas Register*, December 16, 1837. Vertical Files, Barker Texas History Center, University of Texas at Austin.

John Q. Anderson

ALLEY, JOHN (?–?). John Alley, early colonist, soldier, and politician, was among Stephen F. Austin's[qv] Old Three Hundred.[qv] He immigrated to Texas as early as 1826, when a Mexican census listed him as a farmer and stock raiser between twenty-five and forty years of age. The census indicated that he was married at the time and had two small sons. In 1827 Mexican officials granted him title to a league of land now in Jackson and Lavaca counties. On July 17, 1835, Alley was present at William Millican's[qv] gin, where delegates adopted resolutions condemning Mexican policies on American colonists. On October 3, 1835, the day after the battle of Gonzales,[qv] Austin wrote Alley to inform him of the outbreak of hostilities and request intelligence regarding the approach of Mexican general Martín Perfecto de Cos.[qv] By November Alley had been appointed captain in the Texan "Army of the People," in which capacity he served on General Austin's headquarters staff. On December 6, 1835, he was elected commissioner to organize the militia for Jackson Municipality. In February he served as judge at the election of delegates to the Convention of 1836.[qv] Alley left Texas on April 18, 1838, and named Darwin M. Stapp[qv] his agent during his absence from the republic.

BIBLIOGRAPHY: Eugene C. Barker, ed., *The Austin Papers* (3 vols., Washington: GPO, 1924–28). Lester G. Bugbee, "The Old Three Hundred: A List of Settlers in Austin's First Colony," *Quarterly of the Texas State Historical Association* 1 (October 1897). *Telegraph and Texas Register*, January 16, 1836, April 18, 1838. Louis Wiltz Kemp, *The Signers of the Texas Declaration of Independence* (Salado, Texas: Anson Jones, 1944; rpt. 1959).

Stephen L. Hardin

ALLEY, JOHN C. (?–ca. 1822). John C. Alley, one of the Old Three Hundred,[qv] was the son of Catherine (Baker) and Thomas Alley. He immigrated to Texas from Missouri in the spring of 1822 with his brothers Abraham and Thomas V. Alley.[qqv] A fourth brother, Rawson Alley,[qv] had moved to the Austin colony the year before, and a fifth, William A. Alley, Jr.,[qv] joined them in the winter of 1824. The three brothers sailed from New Orleans on the schooner *James Lawrence* and landed on the west end of Galveston Island. They proceeded on foot up the Brazos River to the Fort Bend settlement and from there to the Atascosito Crossing[qv] of the Colorado, where they settled on the east side of the river. During the fall of 1822 or the winter of 1822–23, while canoeing up the Colorado, Alley, John C. Clark,[qv] and another man were attacked by a band of Karankawa Indians near the mouth of Skull Creek, and Alley and the third man were killed. The party of Indians also attacked and severely wounded Robert Brotherton.[qv] A group of Austin colonists tracked and defeated the Indian party near the scene of Alley's death. On May 16, 1827, Alley's estate was awarded a sitio[qv] of land now in Fayette County.

BIBLIOGRAPHY: Lester G. Bugbee, "The Old Three Hundred: A List of Settlers in Austin's First Colony," *Quarterly of the Texas State Historical Association* 1 (October 1897). J. H. Kuykendall, "Reminiscences of Early Texans," *Quarterly of the Texas State Historical Association* 6–7 (January, April, July 1903).

Thomas W. Cutrer

ALLEY, RAWSON (ca. 1796–ca. 1833). Rawson Alley, pioneer settler and public official, the oldest son of Thomas Alley and his first wife, was born about 1796. He migrated in 1821 from Missouri to Texas, where, over the next three years, he was joined by his half-brothers John C., Abraham, Thomas V., and William Alley.[qqv] In 1823 he joined a party, including Stephen F. Austin, the Baron de Bastrop,[qqv] and several slaves, in surveying 170 acres on the Colorado River intended as the site of the headquarters of the Austin colony and capital of Colorado Municipality. Although the capital was instead established at San Felipe de Austin, settlement begun on the original site soon grew into the town of Columbus. As one of the Austin colony's Old Three Hundred[qv] Alley received title to a league and a half of land on both banks of the Colorado River, five miles below Columbus in what is now Colorado County. The 1823 census of the Colorado District describes him as a carpenter and joiner, and census reports of 1825 and 1826 list him as a surveyor and a single man twenty-five to forty years of age. An election of militia officials was held at his home in March 1825, and in 1826 he was a captain of militia in command of an attack against Waco and Tawakoni Indians. He was a member of the first electoral assembly held at San Felipe de Austin in 1828 and that year was elected *síndico procurador*.[qv] In August 1830 he was appointed to collect subscriptions for a fund to supply an army to be organized against a possible invasion, and in November of that year he announced as a candidate for sheriff. He was again *síndico* in February 1832, and in June, as a member of the ayuntamiento,[qv] he signed the call for the Convention of 1832.[qv] He died before October 7, 1833, when William B. Travis[qv] examined his will and wrote the petition for the admission of his heirs, Abraham and William Alley and Cynthia Alley Daniels.

BIBLIOGRAPHY: Eugene C. Barker, ed., *The Austin Papers* (3 vols., Washington: GPO, 1924–28). Colorado County Historical Commission, *Colorado County Chronicles from the Beginning to 1923* (2 vols., Austin: Nortex, 1986). William Barret Travis, *Diary*, ed. Robert E. Davis (Waco: Texian Press, 1966).

ALLEY, THOMAS V. (?–1826). Thomas V. Alley, one of Stephen F. Austin's[qv] Old Three Hundred[qv] colonists, was the son of Catherine (Baker) and Thomas Alley. He left Missouri in the spring of 1822 with his brothers, Abraham and John C. Alley.[qqv] Carrying letters and supplies for Austin, he and his brothers arrived at Galveston by way of New Orleans on the schooner *James Lawrence* and traveled to the Atascosito Crossing[qv] of the Colorado River, where other members of the Alley family settled. Alley posted bond as constable of the Colorado District in January 1824; he and his brother William A. Alley, Jr.,[qv] received title to a league of land now in Brazoria County on July 29, 1824. The Austin colony census of 1826 listed Thomas Alley as a farmer, single and aged between twenty-five and forty. During the spring of 1826, while on a campaign against the Waco and Tonkawa Indians, Alley was crossing the Colorado River when he fell from his horse and drowned.

BIBLIOGRAPHY: Eugene C. Barker, ed., *The Austin Papers* (3 vols., Washington: GPO, 1924–28). Lester G. Bugbee, "The Old Three Hundred: A List of Settlers in Austin's First Colony," *Quarterly of the Texas State Historical Association* 1 (October 1897). J. H. Kuykendall, "Reminiscences of Early Texans," *Quarterly of the Texas State Historical Association* 6–7 (January, April, July 1903).

ALLEY, WILLIAM A. (ca. 1800–1869). William A. Alley, one of Stephen F. Austin's[qv] Old Three Hundred[qv] colonists, the son of Catherine (Baker) and Thomas Alley, was born in Missouri in either 1799 or 1800. He moved to Texas in 1824 to join his brothers John C., Thomas V., Rawson, and Abraham Alley,[qqv] who lived near the Colorado River. With his brother Thomas, he received title to a league of land now in Brazoria County in July 1824. The 1825 census for the Colorado District listed Alley as a farmer and stockman. He was probably the same William Alley who received bounty lands for service in the Texas army from about April 11 to July 11, 1836, and from June 26 to September 26, 1836. He was one of a nine-member committee of Colorado County citizens who nominated James Pinckney Henderson[qv] for governor in 1845. Alley, who never married, died at his home in Alleyton on August 15, 1869.

BIBLIOGRAPHY: Eugene C. Barker, ed., *The Austin Papers* (3 vols., Washington: GPO, 1924–28). Lester G. Bugbee, "The Old Three Hundred: A List of Settlers in Austin's First Colony," *Quarterly of the Texas State Historical Association* 1 (October 1897). Dallas *Herald*, September 4, 1869. Thomas L. Miller, *Bounty and Donation Land Grants of Texas, 1835–1888* (Austin: University of Texas Press, 1967). Annie Doom Pickrell, *Pioneer Women in Texas* (Austin: Steck, 1929). *Telegraph and Texas Register*, June 7, 1843. *Texas National Register*, November 15, 1845.

ALLEY CREEK. Alley Creek rises on the fringes of a strip mine four miles south of Hughes Springs in southwestern Cass County (at 32°56′ N, 94°39′ W) and flows southeast for nine miles to its mouth on Lake O' the Pines in northwestern Marion County (at 32°48′ N, 94°35′ W). The soils along the creekbed are loamy, and the gently rolling to hilly land is heavily wooded, with pines and various hardwoods predominating. In 1847 Jefferson Nash constructed what is presumed to be the first iron furnace in Texas beside a small unnamed tributary of Alley Creek, on land now in Marion County (*see* NASH'S IRON FOUNDRY). Alley Creek was named for an early settler who constructed a sawmill on its banks.

BIBLIOGRAPHY: Robert L. Jones, "The First Iron Furnace in Texas," *Southwestern Historical Quarterly* 63 (October 1959).

ALLEY THEATRE. The Alley Theatre in Houston is a nonprofit professional residential theater company that offers new plays, classic works, and music theater, as well as providing a home for artists from around the world to develop their work. Alley productions have been seen throughout the United States and abroad. In the 1990s the resident company had twenty actors, and its associate artists included Robert Wilson, Edward Albee, Jose Quintero, and Frank Wildhorn. The artistic director in 1993 was Gregory Boyd and the executive director, Stephen J. Albert. The theater produced its first play in 1947, under the direction of Nina Vance.[qv] Vance, a drama teacher at San Jacinto High School at the time, initiated the project by sending postcards to 150 persons whom she knew to be interested in the theater. As a result, 100 people met to discuss forming a local theater group. Vance was business manager, producer, and director. The group became professional in 1954 and existed without patronage until 1963, when other personnel were first employed to allow Vance to concentrate on the role of director.

The first location for the group was in a former dance studio with an opening on Main Street. A brick corridor led from Main to the back of the studio, hence the name Alley Theatre. The theater seated eighty-seven. After a season and a half at this location, the group moved to a building on Berry Street that seated 215. Here the theater remained for 18½ years before moving to the new $3.5 million structure in Houston's cultural complex, which included the Jesse H. Jones Hall for the Performing Arts[qv] and the Albert Thomas[qv] Convention Center.

Impetus for the new building came in 1962, when Houston Endowment, Incorporated, a charitable organization established by Mr. and Mrs. Jesse H. Jones, donated a downtown site at 615 Texas Avenue. The Ford Foundation pledged $1 million for construction, contingent on Houston residents' raising $900,000. The local money was raised in 1963, and the Ford Foundation then boosted its pledge to $2 million, the largest grant ever given a resident professional theater. The foundation also pledged for operating expenses for ten years. Architect Ulrich Franzen designed the building to include two separate theaters, one seating 800 and another seating 300. The larger theater was designed with a modified thrust stage and allows for unusual exits and entrances. Lighting takes the place of curtains. The smaller theater is a replica of the playhouse's original small square arena under a hooded light grid. The exterior of the structure is concrete, sandblasted to give the look of aged stone. Nine towers are both decorative and utilitarian, housing elevators and air-conditioning equipment. A tunnel entrance gives credit to the original alley entryway. Polished concrete, curved wood, and rich colors decorate the interior. The new theater opened officially in November 1968, with a special performance of Bertolt Brecht's *Galileo*. Tony Van Bridge, a Canadian, played the lead. By opening night more than 20,000 subscriptions had been paid. After Nina Vance died in 1980, the theater was known as the Nina Vance Alley Theatre. *See also* THEATER.

BIBLIOGRAPHY: William Beeson, ed., *Thresholds: The Story of Nina Vance's Alley Theatre* (Houston: Alley Theatre, 1968). Ray Miller, *Ray Miller's Houston* (Houston: Cordovan Press, 1982).

ALLEYTON, TEXAS. Alleyton is on the east bank of the Colorado River and Farm Road 102 between Interstate Highway 10 and the main line of the Southern Pacific Railroad, three miles east of Columbus in central Colorado County. The area, once the site of a prehistoric Indian encampment, was settled in 1821 by Rawson Alley,[qv] who was joined by his brothers Abraham, John C., Thomas V., and William A. Alley, Jr.,[qqv] in 1822. In 1859 William arranged for the extension of the Buffalo Bayou, Brazos and Colorado Railway to his property and donated land for the right-of-way and for the building of shops, a roundhouse, a depot, and loading facilities. The town was surveyed, and all city lots, with the exception of one reserved for William Alley's home, were auctioned to the public. The proceeds of the sale were divided equally between William Alley and the railroad.

Completion of the railroad to Alleyton in 1860 made the town the terminus for the southernmost railroad in the state. Alleyton became the largest and most active town in Colorado County. A post office was established there in 1860. During the Civil War[qv] Alleyton was the beginning of the "cotton road," which carried cotton, brought by rail, to Mexico by wagon train, in order to bypass the Union blockade of Texas ports. Returning wagon trains brought military and domestic supplies, which were then shipped by rail to the rest of the Confederacy. After the war the Colorado River was bridged, and the railroad extended to Columbus, the county seat, and points west. Alleyton declined in importance as a rail terminus but remained important as the supply center for a heavily populated agricultural area. In 1890 the town reported a population of 200 and two churches, a school, five general stores, a drugstore, and a saloon. In 1896 the population was estimated at 320, but by 1914 the number had fallen. It remained at 200 well into the 1940s.

Cotton was the primary agricultural product of Alleyton during the first half of the twentieth century, with some emphasis on rice, corn, and pecans. The removal of gravel in large strip-mining operations near the river resulted in the destruction of some rich farming and grazing land and the formation of many lakes, which are locally popular for fishing. The rise of the use of synthetics during the post–World War II period and increasing government regulation of cotton production eliminated cotton as a viable crop during the 1950s, by which time Alleyton's population had declined to about 125. In 1986 the community had a population of sixty-five and six businesses, including several places of entertainment, a welding and well-drilling service, and an auto-salvage yard. In 1990 the population was 165.

BIBLIOGRAPHY: *Colorado County Sesquicentennial Commemorative Book* (La Grange, Texas: Hengst Printing, 1986). *Jeff Carroll*

ALLHANDS, JAMES L. (1879–1978). James L. Allhands, contractor and writer, was born on September 23, 1879, in Iroquois County, Illinois, the son of Erastus J. and Elizabeth (Wilkins) Allhands. The family moved to Wichita, Kansas, in 1890. Although his public education ended in the fifth grade, Allhands took a stenographic course at a Wichita business college and completed a privately taught telegraphy course. In 1897 he became a railroad clerk and worked for railroads in Missouri, Kansas, Illinois, and the Indian Territory.

He went to work for the Johnston Brothers Construction Company of St. Elmo, Illinois, in 1900. As a troubleshooter for the company he made his first trip to Texas in 1903 to determine the best route for a projected railroad from Houston to Brownsville. In 1907 he joined P. M. Johnston to establish the P. M. Johnston, Son and Allhands Company, also in St. Elmo. Their business built a number of railroads in Texas, including the Stamford and Northwestern and the Port O'Connor branch of the St. Louis, Brownsville and Mexico line. After the termination of the company in 1911 Allhands did construction work for various railroad companies. Later he became associated with J. H. Hedges and J. H. Jarrett in forming the Allhands-Hedges Construction Company in Springfield, Missouri. As president of the company Allhands joined with other contractors to found the Associated General Contractors of America, an organization that promoted legislation favorable to the construction industry.

When the Allhands-Hedges Construction Company was dissolved in 1919 Allhands formed a partnership with R. E. Davis. Their company engaged in all types of construction throughout Texas and several other states; they built railroads and highways, dug irrigation canals, and erected dams. The partnership ended in 1939, and Allhands joined Jesse J. Briley to found Allhands and Briley, a construction company that built highways and railroads in the state until 1967. He acquired considerable real estate in Dallas and invested in oil exploration with moderate success. In Dallas he served on the board of the Richmond Freeman Memorial Clinic and helped establish the Children's Medical Center as well as the Presbyterian Hospital. He was a member of the Dallas Citizens Council, the Texas Geographic Society,[qv] and the Advisory Board of the Salvation Army.

Allhands was a prolific writer whose first book, *Gringo Builders,* was published in 1931. He followed it with *Boll Weevil* (1946), *Uriah Lott* (1949), *Tools of the Earth Movers* (1951), *Railroads to the Rio* (1960), and an autobiography, *Looking Back over 98 Years* (1978), the best source of information about his life.

He married Reba E. Warren in 1933. The marriage ended with her death in 1951, and in 1953 he married Margareth C. Welton. Allhands died on January 6, 1978, and was buried in Dallas.

George O. Coalson

ALLIANCE HALL, TEXAS. Alliance Hall was a rural community on Farm Road 667 two miles north of Navarro Mills in western Navarro County. It grew up around a meetinghouse built before 1900. A local school had an enrollment of sixty in 1906. In the mid-1930s the community had a church, a school, a cemetery, and a number of houses. The school was later consolidated with the Blooming Grove school, and by the mid-1960s only a cemetery and a few widely scattered houses remained. *Christopher Long*

ALLIED HEALTH SCIENCES. As new diagnostic and therapeutic methods enlarged the scope of health care after the 1920s, physicians, dentists, hospital administrators, and other health professionals employed many different kinds of assistants. Technical and "on-the-job" training for assistants evolved into certificate, diploma, or degree programs in such fields as dental hygiene, dietetics, respiratory therapy, speech pathology, physical therapy, and occupational therapy. In 1966 Mary Switzer, director of the Division of Rehabilitation in the United States Department of Health, Education, and Welfare, labeled these new groups "allied health." Congress adopted landmark legislation, the Allied Health Professions Training Act of 1966, to provide federal money for increasing the number of allied health schools in the United States. Today there are more than 200 health occupations classified as allied health.

The first recognized school of the allied health professions in Texas was chartered on April 8, 1968, as the School of Allied Health Sciences at the University of Texas Medical Branch in Galveston. This school was the first of its kind in Texas and the Southwestern United States. More than 4,500 students graduated from it during its first twenty-five years; 85 percent of the graduates practiced in Texas. In 1993 the school enrolled more than 500 students seeking degrees or certificates in a dozen fields. Schools of allied health sciences are affiliated with the University of Texas Health Science centers in Dallas, Houston, and San Antonio, with the Texas Tech University Health Science Center, with Baylor College of Medicine, and with the United States Army Academy of the Health Sciences at Fort Sam Houston. Additionally, numerous colleges and hospitals offer training programs in specific allied health fields.

Five training fields are commonly found in four-year colleges or academic health science centers: health information management, medical technology, occupational therapy, physical therapy, and physician assistant studies. Many vocational, technical, and associate degree programs are offered in junior colleges and technical institutes. Academic credentials therefore vary considerably, from certificates given by technical institutes and hospitals, to associate and baccalaureate degrees awarded by colleges, to graduate degrees offered by university health science centers.

Even with the large number of programs, there is still a severe shortage of allied health professionals. This problem has resulted in delays in opening rehabilitation facilities, in increased costs, and in intense competition among employers seeking allied health personnel. A survey by the Association of Schools of the Allied Health Professions in 1992 indicated that 95 percent of allied health students are employed upon graduation. With more emphasis on primary health care in the future, the demand for allied health professionals will be robust because they work in many settings—hospitals, health maintenance organizations, community clinics, school systems, and long-term care facilities. Trends toward more outpatient care, home care, long-term care and community-based care are fueling the demand for many more types of allied health workers. This will have a profound impact on state laws that govern licensure of these practitioners. In 1994 the state regulated fourteen allied health occupations through licensing, certification, or registration: audiologists, dental hygienists, dental laboratory technologists, dietitians, emergency care attendants, emergency care technicians, massage therapists, nursing-home administrators, occupational therapists, occupational therapy assistants, physical therapy assistants, speech and language pathologists, radiologic technologists, and respiratory therapists. The Texas Society of Allied Health Professions is the professional organization in the state.

BIBLIOGRAPHY: Gloria C. Gupta, "Student Attrition: A Challenge for Allied Health Education Programs," *JAMA: Journal of American Medicine,* August 21, 1991. Institute of Medicine, *Allied Health Services: Avoiding Crises* (Washington: National Academy Press, 1989). J. W. Perry, "The Next Decade: Issues and Challenges," *Journal of Allied Health* 7 (Winter 1978). Barbara Weithaus, "Committee on Allied Health Education and Accreditation: Assessing Educational Outcomes and Assuring Quality," *JAMA: Journal of American Medicine,* August 21, 1991. *Billy U. Philips, Jr.*

ALLIGATOR BAYOU. Alligator Bayou originally rose three miles northwest of Port Arthur in eastern Jefferson County (at 29°58′ N, 93°57′ W) and flowed nine miles south to its mouth on Taylor's Bayou, two miles southwest of Port Arthur, at a point crossed by the Texas and New Orleans Railroad (at 29°52′ N, 93°58′ W). With the growth of the community, however, the creek is now part of an urban area and has been channeled and dammed in its upper and middle reaches.

ALLIGATOR CREEK (Falls County). Alligator Creek rises six miles southeast of Reagan in southeastern Falls County (31°11′ N, 96°42′ W) and runs southwest for ten miles to its mouth on the Little Brazos River, seven miles southwest of Bremond in Robertson County (at 31°06′ N, 96°46′ W). The streambed traverses flat to rolling prairie surfaced by clay and sandy loams that support oak, juniper, mesquite, and grasses.

—— (Freestone County). Alligator Creek rises four miles west of Oakwood in extreme southern Freestone County (at 31°33′ N, 95°58′ W) and flows south for eight miles to its mouth on Buffalo Creek, in northeastern Leon County (at 31°29′ N, 95°55′ W). The stream traverses steeply sloping to nearly level terrain surfaced by sandy loam that supports pecan, elm, water oak, hackberry, post oak, and black hickory. Settlement in the vicinity of the stream began in the mid-nineteenth century. In 1872 the International–Great Northern Railroad constructed a line through the area and established Oakland as a rail station east of the creek. Keechi is located on the west bank of the creek.

—— (Hill County). Alligator Creek rises a mile northwest of Abbott in south central Hill County (at 31°54′ N, 97°05′ W) and runs southwest for ten miles to its mouth on Aguilla Creek (at 31°50′ N, 97°11′ W). The streambed traverses flat to rolling terrain surfaced by shallow, stony clay loams and clay to sandy loams that support juniper, oak, cacti, scrub brush, and grasses. For most of the county's history, the Alligator Creek area has been used as range and crop land.

—— (Leon County). Alligator Creek rises a mile northwest of Jewett in northwestern Leon County (at 31°22′ N, 96°10′ W) and flows northeast for eleven miles to its mouth on Buffalo Creek, just west of Interstate Highway 45 in extreme southern Freestone County (at 31°29′ N, 96°06′ W). The stream traverses gently sloping to nearly level terrain surfaced by sandy to loamy soils. Pecan, elm, water oak, hackberry, post oak, and black hickory trees grow beside the creek. Settlement near the stream began in the mid-nineteenth century. In 1872 the International–Great Northern Railroad constructed a line through the area; Jewett, near the headwaters of the creek, and Buffalo, south of the mouth, were established as rail stations. The Cedar Creek community is located on the south bank.

—— (Navarro County). Alligator Creek rises near Long Prairie in southeastern Navarro County (at 32° 04′ N, 96° 13′ W) and flows southeast for twelve miles to its mouth on Richland Creek, near the junction of U. S. Highway 287 and Farm Road 488 in northeastern Freestone County (at 31° 57′ N, 96° 05′ W). The stream, which is intermittent in its upper reaches, flows through flat to rolling terrain surfaced with clayey and sandy loams that support water-tolerant hardwoods and grasses.

—— (Van Zandt County). Alligator Creek, also known as the West Fork of Kickapoo Creek, rises a mile north of Tundra in southwestern Van Zandt County (at 32°29′ N, 95°53′ W) and runs ten miles to its mouth on Kickapoo Creek, three miles southwest of Martin's Mill (at 32°24′ N, 95°50′ W). The stream traverses rolling prairie surfaced by clay loam that supports mesquite, grasses, and mixed hardwood and pine forests; toward the mouth the terrain becomes flatter, and water-tolerant hardwoods, conifers, and grasses predominate.

—— (Williamson County). Alligator Creek rises three miles east of Bartlett in northeastern Williamson County (at 30°46′ N, 97°07′ W) and runs southeast for 21½ miles, through Bell and Milam counties, to its mouth on the San Gabriel River, five miles east of San Gabriel in Milam County (at 30°42′ N, 97°07′ W). Alligators lived in the region in the nineteenth century. The creek flows through flat or gently rolling terrain characterized by clayey soils used predominantly for agriculture.

ALLIGATOR LAKE. Alligator Lake is a small intermittent natural lake on the west bank of the Trinity River 1½ miles above the mouth of Upper Keechi Creek, one-half mile east of Clear Lake in far eastern Leon County (at 31°24′ N, 95°42′ W). The oval-shaped body, scarcely a tenth of a mile in length, is fed by runoff in the Trinity bottoms. The surrounding level terrain is surfaced by clay that supports various hardwoods.

BIBLIOGRAPHY: James Young Gates and H. B. Fox, *A History of Leon County* (Centerville, Texas: Leon County *News,* 1936; rpt. 1977). Frances Jane Leathers, *Through the Years: A Historical Sketch of Leon County and the Town of Oakwood* (Oakwood, Texas, 1946). *Leon County Historical Collections,* Vol. 1 (Centerville, Texas: Leon County Genealogical Society, 1981).

ALLIGATOR POINT. Alligator Point, a narrow promontory at the western end of the small island formed by the Gulf Intracoastal Waterway[qv] across from Galveston Island (at 29°10′ N, 95°07′ W), is eighteen miles southeast of Angleton in extreme east central Brazoria County. The point consists of grass-covered sand dunes.

ALLIGATOR SCHOOL HOUSE, TEXAS. Alligator School House was a rural community on State Highway 309 two miles north of Round Prairie in southeastern Navarro County. It grew up around a school of that name built after 1900. In the mid-1930s the community had a church, a school, a cemetery, and a number of houses. The school was later consolidated with the Kerens school. In the mid-1960s a church and a cemetery were at the site, but the community no longer appeared on highway maps. *Christopher Long*

ALLISON, ALVIN RAY (1907–1987). Alvin Ray Allison, attorney and state representative, was born on September 16, 1907, at Kopperl, Texas, one of seven children of L. H. and Lillie (Henderson) Allison. When his father moved the family to West Texas in 1925, Alvin stayed behind to complete his high school education. In 1926 he was admitted to Texas Tech, where he helped organize the first Pre-Law

Club and in 1928 was the business manager of the school paper, the *Toreador*. Allison received a bachelor's degree in government from Texas Tech in 1930. The Great Depression[qv] interrupted his law studies at the University of Texas in 1934, but he was admitted to the bar by examination and was licensed to practice in Texas on September 12. That year he was elected Hockley county judge; he held the office from 1935 to 1938. In 1937 he was elected president of the West Texas Judges Association.

After completing his second term as county judge, Allison decided to seek the office of state representative for the 119th District, a substantially populated district. Allison defeated five candidates without a run-off. He served as a Democrat in the legislature during the term of Governor W. Lee O'Daniel.[qv] Allison's most controversial contribution was a law that made it a felony to write a hot check. He did not run for a second term but returned to his general law practice in Levelland. On December 17, 1941, he received a license to practice law before the United States Supreme Court.

Allison was first appointed to the Texas Tech board of directors in 1961 by Governor Price Daniel[qv] and was reappointed to an additional six-year term in 1967 by Governor John Connally. He promoted establishment of a law school at Texas Tech, which became a reality in 1964. He served as president of the Texas Tech Law School Foundation for several years beginning in 1968. He established two scholarships and a loan fund for law students. He was also on the board of regents that worked to establish the Texas Tech Health Sciences Center. His portrait hangs in the Law School building, where a courtroom bears his name. He received many other honors at Tech, including an honorary doctorate in 1981.

Allison was a member of the American Judicature Society. He was a Mason and a Baptist. He married Aletha Faye Atchison on December 2, 1933, and the couple had two children. When Allison died on June 28, 1987, he was survived by his wife, two daughters, and four grandchildren. He was buried in the Levelland Cemetery.

BIBLIOGRAPHY: Anton *News*, June 5, 1942. Lillian Brasher, *Hockley County* (2 vols., Canyon, Texas: Staked Plains, 1976). Hockley County Historical Commission, *From the Heart of Hockley County: Recollections* (Dallas: Taylor, 1986). Levelland *Herald*, March 17, 1965. Lubbock *Avalanche-Journal*, June 29, 1989. Vertical Files, Barker Texas History Center, University of Texas at Austin (Texas Tech University).
Jeanne F. Lively

ALLISON, IRL, SR. (1896–1979). Irl Allison, Sr., pianist, music educator, and founder of the National Guild of Piano Teachers,[qv] was born on April 8, 1896, in Warren, Texas, the son of John Van and Mary (Richardson) Allison. He attended Bryan Military Academy and in 1915 received an A.B. from Baylor University. After studying at Chicago Music College and Columbia University he returned to Baylor, where he received an A.M. in 1922. He was awarded an honorary doctorate in music by Southwestern Conservatory, Dallas, in 1947 and by the Houston Conservatory of Music in 1955. He also received an honorary law degree from Hardin-Simmons University. As a young man Allison was a silent-film pianist in a Waco theater. He later studied piano with Rudolph Hoffman, Joseph Evans, Percy Grainger, Ernest Hutcheson, Harold von Mickwitz, and Walter Gilewicz. He married Jessie Johnson on July 3, 1918, and they had four children. A son, Irl, Jr., succeeded his father as president of the National Guild of Piano Teachers.

Although Allison was best known to hundreds of thousands of music teachers and their pupils by his signature on certificates awarded by the National Guild for participation in the Annual National Piano Playing Auditions, he was also a renowned music teacher. He served as dean of music at Rusk College in 1918–19, was a piano instructor at Baylor College for Women from 1921 to 1923, and was dean of fine arts at Montezuma College from 1923 to 1927. He was dean of music at Hardin-Simmons University from 1927 to 1934, where he organized the National Guild and began the National Guild Auditions in 1929. He was also the founder and president of the guild-sponsored American College of Musicians and of the National Fraternity of Student Musicians. Allison edited the guild yearbook from 1936 to 1945 and *Piano Guild Notes* from 1951 to 1963. He contributed to several musical publications and newspapers and wrote *Through the Years* (1925). He also founded the Golden Rule Peace Movement and began the World Peace Programs for radio in 1948. Under the auspices of the guild, Allison compiled and edited the Irl Allison Library of Music in thirty-three volumes; he also initiated and promoted into an international event the Van Cliburn International Piano Competition. In Austin, where the Allisons made their home after 1943, he was largely responsible for developing the Azalea Trail, and presented to Lady Bird Johnson azaleas for the Lyndon B. Johnson Library.[qv] Allison died on September 6, 1979.

BIBLIOGRAPHY: Austin *American-Statesman*, June 12, 1949, October 14, 1962. *The Guild Syllabus*, 1986–87. *Who's Who in America*, 1980–81.
Craig H. Roell

ALLISON, JOHN (1791–1871). Judge John Allison, son of Sarah Ogilvie and Robert Allison, Jr., was born in Granville County, North Carolina, in March 1791. He and his wife, Naomi (Gillespie), moved with his parents to Bedford County, Tennessee, in 1815, and then to Pulaskie, Mississippi, in 1836, to become cotton planters. Due to financial reverses from the 1837 depression, Allison moved on to Montgomery County, Texas, by 1840. Health problems encouraged another move in 1842, to what is now Horton, Panola County.

When Panola County was organized in 1846, Allison became the first chief justice (county judge) of the county. Pulaski, on the east bank of the Sabine River, became the temporary county seat. Since Allison had come from Panola County, Mississippi, he asked that the new county be called Panola, an Indian word meaning "cotton." Though he is said to have named Pulaski also, a Sabine ferry was called that before he arrived in the area. When his term as county judge ended in 1848 Allison bought John Williams's[qv] headright on the western side of the county and established his family on the "Old Grand Bluff-to-Douglas Road." There he put his slaves to work on the farm and opened a store and wagonyard camp for travelers. The community known today as Fairplay developed at the site. Allison lived there until his death, in 1871. The Allisons had five children. They and two generations of their descendants are buried at the Old Williams Cemetery, near Fairplay.

BIBLIOGRAPHY: S. T. Allison, *The History of Fairplay, Panola County, Texas* (Henderson, Texas: Park Print, 1948?). *History of Panola County*. (Carthage, Texas: Carthage Circulating Book Club, 1935?). Leila B. LaGrone, ed., *History of Panola County* (Carthage, Texas: Panola County Historical Commission, 1979). Lawrence R. Sharp, History of Panola County, Texas, to 1860 (M.A. thesis, University of Texas, 1940).
Leila B. LaGrone

ALLISON, JOHN C. (?–?). John C. Allison, soldier, enlisted in Kentucky for service in the Texas army on December 18, 1835. He arrived in Texas in Sidney Sherman's[qv] company in January 1836, swore allegiance to the Texas government at Nacogdoches on January 14, was promoted to second sergeant on March 15, and fought at the battle of San Jacinto[qv] under William Wood. He was discharged from the army in December 1837. He probably left Texas in 1837 and did not return. He did not apply for the headright or the donation land due him for his military services.

BIBLIOGRAPHY: Sam Houston Dixon and Louis Wiltz Kemp, *The Heroes of San Jacinto* (Houston: Anson Jones, 1932).
L. W. Kemp

ALLISON, ROBERT CLAY (1840–1887). Clay Allison, gunfighter, the fourth of nine children of John and Nancy (Lemmond) Allison, was born on a farm near Waynesboro, Tennessee, on September 2, 1840. His father, a Presbyterian minister who was also engaged in the cattle and sheep business, died when Clay was five. When the Civil War[qv] broke out, Allison joined the Confederate Army. In January 1862 he was discharged for emotional instability resulting from a head injury as a child, but in September he reenlisted and finished the war as a scout for Gen. Nathan Bedford Forrest. He was a prisoner of war from May 4 to 10, 1865, in Alabama.

After the war Allison moved to the Brazos River country in Texas. At a Red River crossing near Denison he severely pummeled ferryman Zachary Colbert in a fist fight. This incident reportedly started a feud between Allison and the Colbert family that led to the killing of the ferryman's desperado nephew, "Chunk" Colbert, by Allison in New Mexico on January 7, 1874.

Allison soon signed on as a cowhand with Oliver Loving and Charles Goodnight[qqv] and was probably among the eighteen herders on the 1866 drive that blazed the Goodnight-Loving Trail.[qv] In 1867–69 Allison rode for M. L. Dalton and was trail boss for a partnership between his brother-in-law L. G. Coleman and Irvin W. Lacy. During this time he befriended the John H. Matthews family in Raton and accidentally shot himself in the right foot while he and some companions stampeded a herd of army mules as a prank. In 1870 Coleman and Lacy moved to a spread in Colfax County, New Mexico. Allison drove their herd to the new ranch for a payment of 300 cattle, with which he started his own ranch near Cimarron. Eventually he built it into a lucrative operation.

He is alleged to have had a knife duel with a man named Johnson in a freshly dug grave in 1870. On October 7 of that year he led a mob that broke into the jail in Elizabethtown, near Cimarron, and lynched an accused murderer named Charles Kennedy. Allison was a heavy drinker and became involved in several brawls and shooting sprees. On October 30, 1875, he led a mob that seized and lynched Cruz Vega, who was suspected of murdering a Methodist circuit rider. Two days later Allison killed gunman Pancho Griego, a friend of Vega, in a confrontation at the St. James Hotel in Cimarron. In January 1876 a drunken Allison wrecked the office of the Cimarron *News & Press* because of a scathing editorial. He allegedly later returned to the newspaper office and paid $200 for damages. In December of that year Clay and his brother John were involved in a dance-hall gunfight at Las Animas, Colorado, in which a deputy sheriff was killed. For this Allison was arrested and charged with manslaughter, but the charges were later dismissed on grounds of self-defense. Allison was arrested as an accessory to the murder of three black soldiers the following spring, but evidence was sketchy and he was soon acquitted. In 1878 he sold his New Mexico ranch and established himself in Hays City, Kansas, as a cattle broker.

In September 1878 Allison and his men supposedly terrorized Dodge City and made Bartholomew (Bat) Masterson[qv] and other lawmen flee in fear. Later, Wyatt Earp was said to have pressured Allison into leaving. Though Dodge City peace officers may have questioned him about the shooting of a cowboy named George Hoy, there is no evidence of any serious altercation.

By 1880 Clay and John Allison had settled on Gageby Creek, near its junction with the Washita River, in Hemphill County, Texas, next door to their in-laws, the L. G. Colemans. Clay registered an ACE brand for his cattle. On March 28, 1881, he married Dora McCullough. The couple had two daughters. Though Allison served as a juror in Mobeetie, and though age and marriage had slowed him down some, his reputation as the "Wolf of the Washita" was kept alive by reports of his unusual antics. Once he was said to have ridden nude through the streets of Mobeetie. In the summer of 1886 a dentist from Cheyenne, Wyoming, drilled the wrong one of Allison's teeth, and Allison got even by pulling out one of the dentist's teeth.

In December 1886 he bought a ranch near Pecos and became involved in area politics. On July 3, 1887, while hauling supplies to his ranch from Pecos he was thrown from his heavily loaded wagon and fatally injured when run over by its rear wheel. He was buried in the Pecos Cemetery the next day. On August 28, 1975, in a special ceremony, his remains were reinterred in Pecos Park, just west of the Pecos Museum.

BIBLIOGRAPHY: Carl W. Bretham, *Great Gunfighters of the West* (San Antonio: Naylor, 1962). Norman Cleaveland, *Colfax County's Chronic Murder Mystery* (Santa Fe: Rydal, 1977). J. Frank Dobie, "Clay Allison of the Washita," *Frontier Times*, February 1943. Chuck Parsons, *Clay Allison: Portrait of a Shootist* (Seagraves, Texas: Pioneer, 1983). Richard C. Sandoval, "Clay Allison's Cimarron," *New Mexico Magazine*, March–April 1974. F. Stanley [Stanley F. L. Crocchiola], *Clay Allison* (Denver: World, 1953).
C. L. Sonnichsen

ALLISON, WILMER LAWSON (1904–1977). Wilmer Lawson (Lee) Allison, tennis player, was born in San Antonio, Texas, on December 8, 1904, one of two children of Dr. and Mrs. Wilmer L. Allison. His family moved to Fort Worth in his youth, and he graduated from Fort Worth Central High School, where he was an outstanding amateur baseball player. He enrolled at the University of Texas in 1925 after his father refused to permit him to sign a professional baseball contract with the Beaumont team of the Texas League.[qv] At UT he began an internationally acclaimed career as a tennis player. Under the tutelage of Daniel A. Penick[qv] he won the Southwest Conference[qv] and National Collegiate Athletic Association championships in 1927.

Allison won the Wimbledon doubles title in 1929 and 1930 with partner John Van Ryn. They are considered by many tennis historians to be the best doubles combination of the period. Perhaps Allison's finest moment as a singles player came on June 30, 1930, when he upset the legendary Henri Cochet of France in the quarter-final round of the 1930 Wimbledon tournament. However, he lost the championship in the finals to fellow American Bill Tilden in straight sets.

Allison achieved the number-one ranking in the United States in 1934 and again in 1935 and won the United States National Open Championship in 1935 by defeating Fred Perry in the semifinals and then Sydney Wood for the title at Forest Hills, New York. Along with partner Van Ryn he claimed National Doubles in 1931 and 1935 and finished second in 1930, 1932, 1934, and 1936. Allison competed on behalf of the United States in Davis Cup competition from 1928 until 1937. He retired from full-time competition in 1937 after a serious injury to his lower abdomen. Upon retirement, he served as an assistant to Penick at the University of Texas from 1938 to 1941, when he left to join the army air corps; he achieved the rank of colonel. After his discharge he returned to the university in 1947 and served as Penick's assistant until 1957. That year he became the head tennis coach at the university, where he served until his retirement in 1972. He instituted a policy restricting athletic scholarships for tennis to players from Texas. His teams won four Southwest Conference team championships, three singles titles, and one doubles title. He was elected to the Texas Sports Hall of Fame[qv] in 1957 and is a member of the Longhorn Hall of Honor. In 1963 he was enshrined in both the national and international tennis halls of fame.

Allison died on April 20, 1977, of a heart attack, only four days after the dedication of the new University of Texas tennis facility in his and Penick's honor. He is buried at Oakwood cemetery in Austin. He was survived by his wife, Ann (Caswell). The couple had no children.

BIBLIOGRAPHY: Nancy Gilbert, *Wimbledon* (Minneapolis: Creative Education, 1990). *International Who's Who in Tennis* (Dallas: World Championship Tennis, 1983). New York *Times Book Review*, April 21, 1977. Arthur Voss, *Tilden and Tennis in the Twenties* (Troy, New York: Whitson, 1985).
Jack Lala

ALLISON, TEXAS (Wheeler County). Allison is at the junction of Farm roads 1046 and 277 in northeastern Wheeler County. The settlement became a station on the Panhandle and Santa Fe Railway in 1929 and was named for R. H. Allison, general manager of the railroad. A local post office was opened in October of that year, and by 1930 the settlement had a general store, two lumberyards, and three gins. Allison was laid out by the Lone Star Townsite Company and soon had electricity and gas. In 1932 the Allison Consumers' Water Club obtained a franchise for a public water system, and the town absorbed nearby Zybach. Uproarious by reputation, Allison was said to have had as many as twenty-five bootleggers operating stills during the prohibition[qv] era. Considerable excitement occurred in 1934 when two men robbed the bank and escaped in the cashier's car. By 1940 Allison had five stores, a filling station, and three churches. In 1965 a new telephone system was installed. In 1984 Allison had four businesses, a gin, a grain elevator, four churches, and a school. The population was estimated at 200 in 1941 and 135 in 1974 and 1990.

BIBLIOGRAPHY: Sallie B. Harris, comp., *Hide Town in the Texas Panhandle: 100 Years in Wheeler County and Panhandle of Texas* (Hereford, Texas: Pioneer, 1968). William Coy Perkins, A History of Wheeler County (M.A. thesis, University of Texas, 1938). Millie Jones Porter, *Memory Cups of Panhandle Pioneers* (Clarendon, Texas: Clarendon Press, 1945).
H. Allen Anderson

ALLISON, TEXAS (Williamson County). Allison was a farming community on Willis Creek near Granger in northeast Williamson County. The community, also called Old Friendship, was founded by Elihu Crosswell Allison in 1847. In 1878–80 the Conel post office was located in the community, and an Allison post office existed there from 1892 to 1894. A community school built around 1873 was enlarged in 1902 and served sixty-three pupils in 1903. The Woodmen of the World helped enlarge the building and used it for lodge meetings. In the late nineteenth century a store, a gin, and a church were located in the community, but all three were moved closer to the neighboring farm community of Friendship in the early twentieth century. Allison's decline was hastened by a flood in 1921 that destroyed the school and encouraged resettlement on the higher ground of Friendship. In 1948 Allison no longer appeared on county maps. In the 1950s, with the construction of Laneport Dam and the impoundment of Granger Lake,[qv] the site of the former community was inundated, and the Allison cemetery was removed to Granger.

BIBLIOGRAPHY: Clara Stearns Scarbrough, *Land of Good Water: A Williamson County History* (Georgetown, Texas: Williamson County Sun Publishers, 1973).
Mark Odintz

ALLISON, TEXAS (Wise County). Allison is a farm community on a spur of U.S. Highway 380 two miles west of the Denton county line in eastern Wise County. The site was originally owned by cattleman Daniel Waggoner and his son William Thomas Waggoner.[qqv] In the 1870s outlaws Jesse and Frank James and Texas bandit Sam Bass[qv] hid from the law near the site. In 1909, five years after the death of his father, W. T. Waggoner divided half of the family's ranch among his three children. In 1910 Electra Waggoner, W. T.'s daughter, sold her interest to J. L. Gamman and a syndicate of businessmen from Waxahachie and Dallas for $250,000. On the supposition that the land would be located along the route of a promised rail line between Decatur and Denton, Gamman and the syndicate laid out forty-six lots and constructed buildings, including a school. The lots sold quickly, and in 1911 the new community chose the name Allison in honor of E. M. Allison, Wise county judge from 1911 to 1915. A general store, a blacksmith shop, and a church made Allison a community center for the corn and cotton farmers in the area. When the promised rail line did not materialize, however, the town failed. In 1990 the church building and several houses were at the site.

BIBLIOGRAPHY: Rosalie Gregg, ed., *Wise County History* (Vol. 1, n.p: Nortex, 1975; Vol. 2, Austin: Eakin, 1982).
David Minor

ALLISON SPRING. Allison Spring is 100 yards east of the Pecos River in northwestern Loving County (at 31°55′ N, 103°54′ W). Since Red Bluff Reservoir was built in 1936 the spring has usually been covered by its waters. The area is surrounded by deposits of gravel, sand, and silt. The surrounding desert terrain is flat to rolling with locally steep slopes and active sand dunes. Soils are dark chocolate-red clay and fine sandy loam. Area vegetation consists of desert shrubs, mesquite, sage, salt cedar, and sparse grasses. Allison Spring offered fresh water to prehistoric Indians, who left behind projectile points, manos, and metates. In 1583 the entrada of Lt. Antonio de Espejo[qv] traveled along the Pecos near the spring. Capt. John Pope[qv] and his surveying expedition came to the area in 1854 and reported a spring of fine water located 100 yards from the east bank of the Pecos. Pope made his camp at the spring and drilled unsuccessfully for artesian wells. After he left the area, the Butterfield Overland Mail[qv] operated a way station at the spring. In the mid-1880s Clay Allison[qv] established the headquarters of his ranch at the spring and gave it his name.

BIBLIOGRAPHY: Gunnar Brune, *Springs of Texas*, Vol. 1 (Fort Worth: Branch-Smith, 1981). Robert W. Dunn, The History of Loving County, Texas (M.A. thesis, University of Texas, 1948; condensed in West Texas Historical Association *Year Book*, 1948).

ALLMON, TEXAS. Allmon is located at the intersection of Farm roads 54 and 378, seventeen miles southwest of Floydada in extreme southwestern Floyd County. The community was named for the Charles L. Allmon family and evolved around a rural school that had been established by 1909 or 1910. Classes continued until about 1935, when the school was consolidated with the one in Petersburg. A cotton gin was established at Allmon around 1950 or 1951, and a grain storage and elevator was built later in the decade. A general store operated intermittently. In the late 1980s the community consisted of a scattered farm population and a grain elevator, a branch of Barwise Elevator and Fertilizer, with its office located in the old Allmon school building. *Charles G. Davis*

ALLRED, JAMES BURR V (1899–1959). James V Allred, Texas jurist and governor, was born in Bowie, Texas, on March 29, 1899, son of Renne and Mary (Henson) Allred, Sr. (V was a name, not an initial.) After completing Bowie High School in 1917, he enrolled at Rice Institute (now Rice University) but withdrew for financial reasons. He served with the United States Immigration Service until his enlistment in the United States Navy during World War I.[qv] After the war Allred began the study of law as a clerk in a Wichita Falls law office. In 1921 he received an LL.B. from Cumberland University, Lebanon, Tennessee, and began practice in Wichita Falls.

In 1923 he was named by Governor Pat M. Neff[qv] to an unexpired term as district attorney for the Thirtieth Texas District, which included Wichita, Archer, and Young counties. In that office Allred earned a reputation as "the fighting district attorney" for his forthright opposition to the Ku Klux Klan.[qv] He was a candidate for the office of state attorney general in 1926 but was defeated by Claude Pollard[qv] in a close second-primary vote. In 1930 Allred made a successful race for the same position by defeating the incumbent, Robert Lee Bobbitt. As attorney general, Allred won popular approval through a continuing campaign against monopolies and large businesses and against the efforts of corporations to influence state taxation and fiscal policies.

His activities as attorney general, aided by the depression-born distrust of large corporations, made him a logical candidate for the governorship in 1934. He entered the campaign on a platform proposing a state commission for regulating public utility rates and practices, the imposition of a graduated tax on chain stores to neutralize the competitive power of chain enterprises, a system for regulating the activities of lobbyists, and opposition to a state sales tax as a revenue-increasing device because of the economic burden the tax

Governor James Allred presents Alabama-Coushatta chief Ti-ca-i-che with a Texas flag at the centennial celebration of the signing of the Texas Declaration of Independence. Washington-on-the-Brazos, 1936. Courtesy Star of the Republic Museum, Washington, Texas.

would place on low-income groups. Other planks were his proposal to submit to the people the problem of state repeal of prohibition[qv] (in spite of his personal opposition to repeal), and his desire to see the basic pardoning power, used so freely by governors James Edward Ferguson and Miriam Amanda Ferguson,[qqv] transferred to a board of pardons and paroles. Allred believed that sufficient state revenue should be raised by a more equitable system of property valuation and a more efficient use of existing revenues, rather than by increased general taxation.

His principal Democratic opponents in 1934, both from Wichita Falls, were Tom F. Hunter, regarded as more liberal than the attorney general, and Charles C. McDonald, regarded as the candidate of the Ferguson faction. Allred gained a plurality in the first primary and won over Hunter by 40,000 votes in the runoff. In addition to attempting to legislate his campaign proposals, the governor devoted this term to cooperating with federal programs designed to combat the Great Depression.[qv] To this end he used the Texas Planning Board.[qv] Although several programs were approved in regular and special sessions, the legislature refused to provide the revenues necessary for financing them. As a result, measures providing increased financial support to education, expanded highway construction, the establishment of the Texas Department of Public Safety,[qv] and the framework for old-age pensions and expanded state welfare services remained on insecure foundations. During his first term Allred also engineered the Interstate Oil Compact Commission, which forestalled federal control of petroleum production.

Several significant factors worked to Governor Allred's credit in the election of 1936. He had been commended highly by President Franklin D. Roosevelt for the state's cooperation and performance in the national recovery program, and that recognition had been a factor in causing the national Junior Chamber of Commerce to name Allred "Outstanding Young Man in America in 1935." Moreover, he had secured the enactment of many of his 1934 pledges to the voters of the state. As a result, he polled a majority of 52 percent in the first primary in a field of five candidates and won by a landslide in the general election of 1936. Allred's second administration brought passage of a teacher retirement system, broadened social security and welfare provisions, additional funds for education, expansion of the services of most existing state agencies, and increased compensation for state officials. Nevertheless, the legislature again failed notably to provide the additional revenues for the services.

Late in Allred's second term as governor, his nomination by President Roosevelt to a federal district judgeship was confirmed, and upon the completion of his gubernatorial term, he assumed his position on the bench. He resigned from the judgeship in 1942 to seek the Democratic nomination for the United States Senate, and after his defeat in that race by former governor W. Lee O'Daniel[qv] he returned for a time to private law practice in Houston. Senator O'Daniel opposed Allred's appointment to the Fifth Circuit Court of Appeals in 1943. In 1949 President Harry S. Truman returned Allred to the federal bench, where he remained until his death.

Allred married Joe Betsy Miller of Wichita Falls on June 20, 1927; they had three sons. He died on September 24, 1959, and was buried in Riverside Cemetery, Wichita Falls. Mrs. Allred died in 1993.

BIBLIOGRAPHY: James V Allred Papers, Special Collections, University of Houston. James V Allred Papers, Texas State Archives, Austin. James V Allred Scrapbook, Barker Texas History Center, University of Texas at Austin. William Eugene Atkinson, James V Allred: A Political Biography, 1899–1935 (Ph.D. dissertation, Texas Christian University, 1978; rpt., Ann Arbor: University Microfilms, 1982). Dallas *Morning News*, June 19, 1993. Houston *Post*, September 25, 1959. George N. Manning, Public Services of James V Allred (M.A. thesis, Texas Technological College, 1950). Vertical Files, Barker Texas History Center, University of Texas at Austin. *Who's Who in America*, 1948.

Floyd F. Ewing

ALLRED, RENNE, JR. (1901–1977). Renne Allred, Jr., attorney, the son of Renne and Mary (Henson) Allred, was born on June 6, 1901, in Bowie, Texas. From the age of twelve to fourteen he attended Bowie Commercial College, or, as it was commonly referred to, "the Knowledge Box," where he learned typing and shorthand. At the age of fifteen he moved to Carthage and worked as a stenographer in the office of the superintendent of the Fort Worth and Denver Railway. Before becoming a court reporter in 1920 he worked in various cities. As a court reporter he read law under his brother, James Allred.[qv] He passed the Texas bar in 1925 and received his license to practice in 1926. From 1927 to 1928 he was prosecuting attorney of Montague County. He then moved to Henderson County to set up practice during the oilfield boom. He served as district judge of Rusk and Gregg counties from 1932 to 1934 and later practiced law in Dallas and Tyler.

From 1940 to 1954 Allred reached the height of his career with his appointment as attorney for the receiver of Texas Insolvent Insurance Company. His investigation of the first Texas insurance scandals led to closer regulation of insurance companies. After his tenure as a receiver he worked as a member of the law firm Allred and London in Bowie until 1961. He was a receiver for US Trust ICT Insurance Company from 1957 to 1960.

In addition to his duties as a lawyer he was active in his church. In 1959 he was elected the president of District 18 Christian Churches (Disciples of Christ). He was already serving the First Christian Church of Bowie as an elder and chairman of the board. Allred died on July 18, 1977, in Bowie, Texas, and was buried in Elmwood Cemetery. He was survived by his wife, Velma (Bunch), and their only son.

BIBLIOGRAPHY: Renne Allred, Jr., Oral History Number 23, University of North Texas Archives. Renne Allred, Jr., Papers, University of North Texas Archives. James Allred Scrapbook, Barker Texas History Center, University of Texas at Austin. *Texas Observer*, December 28, 1955, January 25, 1956, February 26, December 13, 1957, December 5, 1958.

Lisa C. Maxwell

ALLRED, TEXAS. Allred is just north of State Highway 83 and seventy miles southwest of Lubbock in southern Yoakum County. At the site was once the largest undeveloped oilfield in Texas. The town was conceived by Walter E. Young and M. A. Shields in 1937, soon after the first oil discoveries, and probably named for Governor James

Allred;[qv] actual building started in January 1938. The Allred water well was dug in January. The first lot of the original forty-acre townsite was sold to Alva Willis on February 12, 1938, and the town's post office opened in May. Later, three additions of forty acres each were added so that the town could handle a population of 3,000. The Graves Grocery, operated by Harold W. Graves, the first business establishment of Allred, opened in March 1938. Young sold his interest in the townsite to Pat Malone in January 1939; Malone enlarged the light plant and provided the town with an adequate telephone system. In 1939 the town's population of 1,200 made it the largest in Yoakum County, and new people were moving in daily. On May 25, 1939, Roy Royal published the first and only issue of the Allred *Times*. That same year a new school was built on the north side of town. The population declined to 750 by 1940 and to 150 by 1947.

In 1956 the Allred school district and the Sligo school district were consolidated. The Allred school building was abandoned and later used as a community building. In 1957 the Yoakum County Gas Company, which had served Allred since 1939, found it unprofitable to serve the five remaining families and discontinued service to the town. Later that year the church, the post office, and the grocery store closed. The last recorded population of Allred was fifty in 1964, though a few people still lived there in the 1980s.

BIBLIOGRAPHY: Denver City *Press*, August 23, 1956, March 7, 1957.

Leoti A. Bennett

ALLRIGHT CORPORATION. Allright Corporation, originally known as Allright Auto Parks, headquartered in Houston, provides diversified parking services for airports, banks, hospitals, municipalities, hotels, office buildings, and stores, often organized in partnership with government authorities or private developers. The company, which claims to be North America's largest parking company, also designs and engineers computerized parking facilities, conducts site-planning and economic feasibility studies, and develops industry-related innovations such as watchdog systems and ticketing systems.

The parking industry traces its beginnings to Detroit, Michigan, where an all-day parking lot opened in 1917. Allright, among the first companies of its kind in the nation, began in 1926 when Rice University law student Durell M. Carothers began working for his uncle W. W. Towell's Billie's Auto Parks in Houston. By 1930 the firm owned seven Houston locations. Carothers took over the firm in 1932, and Towell died in 1933. By 1962 the company had expanded to major cities across the country, and Carothers was involved in forty-seven corporations and twenty-two partnerships that had come to be known as the "Allright organization." The firm eventually operated through a network of subsidiaries, usually one incorporated subsidiary in each city. In this system, the city manager served as chief operating officer, and a regional manager coordinated local operations with the company as a whole.

Allright Auto Parks, Incorporated, was formed in 1962 and made its first public stock offering in 1963. The company developed a standard parking-lot lease and diversified into demolition, property leasing, and the design and construction of parking facilities. Acquisition of properties, largely through outright fee ownership, enabled the company to invest in rising property values in major urban locations. A system of regional managers was devised in 1974.

In 1982 Hong Kong investors engaged in real estate development acquired the firm through a cash merger valued at about $120 million. In 1993 the chairman of the board was A. J. Layden, a native of Forney, Texas, and the president was Bernard M. Meyer, who had previously headed Allright's Eastern Division. By then Allright operated over 2,000 parking facilities in ninety cities in the United States and Canada and owned eight subsidiaries in Texas; its Allright Planning Division provided garage-design capability to a wide clientele. At one time the company parked forty-three million cars a year and owned prime downtown real estate totalling more than eight million square feet in central business districts or adjacent to major airports. In 1993 the firm employed 3,000 workers.

Diana J. Kleiner

ALL-WOMAN SUPREME COURT. The only All-Woman Supreme Court in Texas was appointed by Gov. Pat M. Neff[qv] in 1925 to hear the case *W. T. Johnson et al. v. J. M. Darr et al.* The case focused on whether trustees of the fraternal organization Woodmen of the World (Darr et al.) were entitled to two tracts of land in El Paso. After a trial court granted the trustees only one tract, the El Paso Court of Civil Appeals overruled and awarded them full title to both tracts. The case then was submitted on appeal to the state Supreme Court. *Johnson v. Darr* presented a problem to the three-member, all-male Supreme Court. The Woodmen of the World was a powerful political organization in Texas, and its membership included numerous elected officials. In 1924, when the Darr case made its way to the Supreme Court, all three of its justices were Woodmen members and were, by state law, disqualified from hearing the case. State law also provided that in cases where the elected judges were disqualified, the governor was to act immediately to appoint special justices. Governor Neff, however, found it difficult to name suitable replacements quickly. Beginning in March 1924, when the court disqualified itself, he made numerous attempts to find justices for the special court, but discovered, with increasing frustration, that each prominent male attorney he approached was also a member of the Woodmen. Ultimately, Neff decided that he would appoint women attorneys to the special court, as the Woodmen was a male-only organization and females would be safe from disqualification. Neff had named women to serve on numerous state boards and was also the first Texas governor to appoint a woman as his private secretary. Still, the use of female justices was not common, and Neff resorted to it only after determining that he simply would not be able to appoint qualified men to the court.

On January 1, 1925, shortly before his term as governor ended, Neff officially named three women to serve on the special court: Nellie Robertson of Granbury, Edith Wilmans[qv] of Dallas, and Hortense Ward[qv] of Houston. Robertson was named special chief justice, with the other two women to serve as special associate justices, and Neff specified that the first hearing in the case would occur one week later. Apparently, however, Neff had not verified that each of his appointees had seven years of legal experience, a requirement stipulated by the state constitution for any Supreme Court justice. After several resignations and reappointments, the special court was finally set with Ward as chief justice and Ruth V. Brazzil (*see* ROOME, RUTH BRAZZIL) of Galveston and Hattie L. Henenberg[qv] of Dallas as associate justices. These were all well-established lawyers. The appointments were finalized one day before the first hearing in the case.

The All-Woman Supreme Court met in the state Capitol[qv] on January 8, 1925, to hear court procedure reviewed by Chief Justice C. M. Cureton[qv] and to determine if a writ of error would be granted in the case. The women agreed to review the decision of the El Paso Court of Appeals, and they set January 30 as the date for oral argument before the court by the opposing attorneys, both from El Paso. The special court announced its ruling on May 23, 1925, upholding the El Paso appeals court and allowing the Woodmen of the World full title to the two tracts. Ward, as chief justice, wrote the majority opinion in the case, with the two associate justices submitting concurring opinions. The decision was based primarily on upholding the state law on registration of deeds and trust agreements, specifically the provision that recognized the validity of verbal secret trusts in land without ownership being recorded with a county clerk. Soon after the All-Woman Supreme Court began its work, the state's first woman governor, Miriam A. Ferguson,[qv] took office. The novelty of an all-woman court, believed to have been the only such court to exist in the country, and the election of a woman to the state's highest office, gave some distinction to the role of women in Texas politics. It was some thirty years later, however, before Texas women were allowed to serve on juries. And it was not until 1982 that a woman was named to serve full-time on the state Supreme Court, when Gov. William Clements appointed a woman to fill an unexpired term on the court.

BIBLIOGRAPHY: Hattie L. Henenberg, "Women of the Supreme Court of Texas," *Women Lawyers' Journal* 19 (August 1932). Houston *Post, Texas Star Magazine*, February 11, 1973. Leila Clark Wynn, "History of the Civil Courts in Texas," *Southwestern Historical Quarterly* 60 (July 1956). *Debbie Mauldin Cottrell*

ALMA, TEXAS. Alma is on U.S. Highway 75 four miles south of Ennis in southeastern Ellis County. The first settlers in the area arrived in the early 1840s. Among them was Thomas Smith, who bought a thousand acres of land beside a lake named Willow Pond. The Willow Pond site served as a stagecoach station between Waxahachie and Marshall. By 1872 the Houston and Texas Central Railway had come through. Around 1881 the settlement received a post office, named Alma, possibly after the daughter of a local banker. In 1900 Alma had a school, a church, 150 residents, and six businesses. A local school built in 1912 operated until the district was consolidated with the Ennis school district. By 1915 the town had a bank. The number of residents reached a high of 250 by the mid-1920s, dipped briefly to about 100 by the end of World War II,[qv] then climbed to 200, where it remained through the early 1960s. By 1964 Alma had lost its post office and had a population of thirty and three or four businesses. In the late 1970s the population had increased to 117, and the town incorporated. In 1990 the population was 205.

BIBLIOGRAPHY: John Clements, *Flying the Colors: Texas, a Comprehensive Look at Texas Today, County by County* (Dallas: Clements Research, 1984). Edna Davis Hawkins et al., *History of Ellis County, Texas* (Waco: Texian, 1972). *Memorial and Biographical History of Ellis County* (Chicago: Lewis, 1892; rpt., as *Ellis County History*, Fort Worth: Historical Publishers, 1972).
Rachel Jenkins and David Minor

ALMA INSTITUTE. Alma Male and Female Institute, in Hallettsville, the county seat of Lavaca County, was founded in 1852 by builder L. W. Layton and constructed on land donated by Mrs. Margaret Hallett.[qv] The wooden building near the town square contained classrooms, a dormitory, and a music room, all of which cost $5,000 to erect. The institute's first session ran from May 1853 to October 1853 and was conducted by C. L. Spencer, a Methodist minister. A joint-stock company was formed in 1854, and a board of trustees was established out of the primary stockholders, A. W. Hicks, Amasa Turner,[qv] J. C. Finney, L. W. Layton, Collatinus Ballard, A. G. Andrews, M. B. Bennett, and Silas Bennett. Although the school was usually run by ministers, its charter disallowed control of the institute by any Christian denomination and prohibited religious screening of prospective administrators or teachers; students could not be dismissed or punished for their political or religious views. The board of trustees generally controlled administrative and scholastic duties.

The institute flourished after it was incorporated, attaining a student enrollment of eighty-five by 1854. It was run by a succession of principals, the most famous being John Van Epps Covey,[qv] who later founded Concrete College in Concrete, Texas. He was a Baptist minister sent to the institute in 1857 by the mission board of the Southern Baptist Convention. The Baptists were very important in the growth of the school, which drew many of its students from the Colorado Baptist Association. The institute continued to provide a liberal education for its students at a tuition of five dollars a month for weekly students attending Monday through Friday and seven dollars a month for full-time students, until it closed during the Civil War.[qv] The war was a difficult time for schools in Texas, but the Alma Institute was also hurt by the management of J. E. Murray, the principal. By 1861 he had rented the building out as a private home. Although the school closed permanently, the building was still used as a hotel until it was dismantled in 1888.

BIBLIOGRAPHY: Paul C. Boethel, *The Free State of Lavaca* (Austin: Weddle, 1977). Paul C. Boethel, *The History of Lavaca County* (San Antonio: Naylor, 1936; rev. ed., Austin: Von Boeckmann–Jones, 1959).
Mary Ramsey

ALMEDA, TEXAS. Almeda, on State Highway 288 and the Missouri Pacific tracks eleven miles south of Houston in southwestern Harris County, was named for Almeda King, daughter of Dr. Willis King, who promoted the townsite in the early 1880s. The town was built on the International–Great Northern Railroad and served as a trading center for an agricultural and lumbering community. It had a post office from 1893, when the population was fifty, to 1959. In 1905 the local school had thirty-one students and a single teacher. The population reached 200 by 1914, when the town supported two general stores and a lumber company. It was eighty in 1925, 125 in 1948, and 1,200 in 1962. State highway maps in 1936 showed two schools within a mile of the community and several buildings. Businesses increased from four in the 1930s to twenty in the 1950s and forty by the 1960s. As late as 1960, however, local residents remained without public water service or a fire department. Sewers were first built in 1963. In the 1980s a school, three churches, an abandoned railroad station, and scattered dwellings remained at the townsite.

BIBLIOGRAPHY: Houston Metropolitan Research Center Files, Houston Public Library. *Claudia Hazlewood*

ALMIRA, TEXAS. Almira is located at the junction of Farm roads 995 and 1399, eight miles northwest of Linden in northwestern Cass County. The area was settled before the Civil War.[qv] A post office was established there in 1886 with Elijah J. Hanes as postmaster and was discontinued in 1905. During the 1890s the settlement comprised a store and blacksmith shop and a population of twenty-five. In 1904 the community had 102 residents, but no population figures have been recorded since then. In 1936 Almira had a school, a business, and scattered houses. By 1983 the school had been closed, and one small business was in operation at the site. *Cecil Harper, Jr.*

ALMONT, TEXAS. Almont, twelve miles north of DeKalb in northwestern Bowie County, was named for Almont Hill, where the first houses were built. A post office was opened there in 1893 with Edwin Thompson as postmaster. In 1896 the settlement had a population of twenty-five. The post office was closed in 1904. In 1984 Almont consisted of a church, a business, and a few scattered houses.

BIBLIOGRAPHY: J. J. Scheffelin, *Bowie County Basic Background Book*. *Cecil Harper, Jr.*

ALMONTE, JUAN NEPOMUCENO (1803–1869). Juan Nepomuceno Almonte, Mexican official and diplomat, was born in Necupétaro, Michoacán, on May 15, 1803. He was reputed to be a son of an illustrious priest, José María Morelos, by an Indian woman named Brigida Almonte, but conclusive evidence is lacking. In 1815 Almonte was sent to be educated in the United States, where he acquired both social and political principles that influenced a considerable portion of his public life and career. A resolute enemy of Spain, he joined Vicente Ramón Guerrero's[qv] supporters upon his return to Mexico. Almonte was on the staff of José Félix Trespalacios[qv] in Texas in 1822 and in 1824 was sent as a part of the Mexican legation to London, where he was instrumental in negotiating a commercial treaty with England in 1825—Mexico's first treaty with one of the major powers. In 1830, while serving in the national Congress, Almonte became an object of government persecution and was forced to hide. About this time he, as editor of *El Atleta*, accused President Anastasio Bustamante[qv] of permitting foreign intervention in Mexican affairs. The paper succumbed under heavy fines imposed by the government. In 1834 Almonte made an inspection tour of Texas and wrote a detailed and comprehensive report on what he found (*see* almonte's report on texas). He accompanied Antonio López de Santa Anna[qv] to Texas in 1836 and was taken prisoner at San Jacinto. He was subsequently sent with Santa Anna to the United States and returned to Mexico with him in February 1837. He continued in diplomatic and military service and rose to the rank of general of a division. In 1839 he headed the Mexican legation in Belgium but in 1840 returned to the War Department. Almonte was accredited minister plenipotentiary to Washington in 1841 and held the position until 1845, when he returned to Mexico upon the annexation[qv] of Texas. He was appointed minister to France, but on his arrival in Havana he joined Santa Anna and returned to Mexico. During the Mexican War[qv] Almonte served for a time as secretary of war. He went to Europe in 1856 as minister plenipotentiary to London, but neglected his duties somewhat and devoted himself to the promotion of foreign intervention and monarchical schemes that culminated in the French intervention in Mexico. He returned to Mexico with the French troops. In March 1862 he landed at Veracruz to aid in establishing the monarchy. He was declared supreme chief of the nation by the French and was president of the regency that brought Maximilian to the throne. After Maximilian appointed him envoy to France, Almonte died in Paris on March 21, 1869.

bibliography: Juan Nepomuceno Almonte Papers, Barker Texas History Center, University of Texas at Austin. Juan Nepomuceno Almonte, "The Private Journal of Juan Nepomuceno Almonte, February 1–April 16, 1836," *Southwestern Historical Quarterly* 48 (July 1944). Juan N. Almonte, "Statistical Report of Texas," *Southwestern Historical Quarterly* 28 (January 1925). Vicente Filisola, *Memorias para la historia de la guerra de Tejas* (Mexico City, 1848, etc.; abridged trans. by Wallace Woolsey, *Memoirs for the History of the War in Texas*, Austin: Eakin Press, 1985). Celia Gutiérrez Ibarra, *Como México perdió Texas: Análisis y transcripción del informe secreto 1834 de Juan Nepomuceno Almonte* (Mexico City: Instituto Nacional de Antropología e Historia, 1987). Helen W. Harris, The Public Life of Juan Nepomuceno Almonte (Ph.D. dissertation, University of Texas, 1935).

Winifred W. Vigness

ALMONTE'S REPORT ON TEXAS. In January of 1834, when Mexican authorities feared that Texas was about to secede or revolt, Col. Juan Nepomuceno Almonte[qv] was dispatched to Texas to make an accurate inspection and to promise reforms to gain time. He entered Texas by way of Nacogdoches, where he spent May, June, and half of July. He traveled through the various departments, studying the situation in each, as well as searching for any evidence that might point to an impending revolution. The result of his inspection was his Statistical Report on Texas, an analytical account of Texas as a whole and of the departments in particular. The report is extremely detailed; each department is discussed under some twenty-five divisions. Several tables were set up in the appendix to clarify the text. The report gives an overall description and evaluation of Texas and describes conditions in each of the departments. Such inaccuracies as exist are usually the result of faulty estimation of distances and quantity. No other inspection was made in Texas during this period; it is to Almonte's report that the historian must go to find an account of the state at that time.

bibliography: Juan N. Almonte, "Statistical Report of Texas," *Southwestern Historical Quarterly* 28 (January 1925). Celia Gutiérrez Ibarra, *Como México perdió Texas: Análisis y transcripción del informe secreto 1834 de Juan Nepomuceno Almonte* (Mexico City: Instituto Nacional de Antropología e Historia, 1987).

ALOE, TEXAS. Aloe is on U.S. Highway 59 five miles southwest of Victoria in central Victoria County. The site became a stop on the Gulf, Western Texas and Pacific route, completed from Victoria to Beeville in 1889, and soon had a hotel, a Wells Fargo office, and a rural common school. The community was named for the yucca plants in the vicinity. The station was the site of Aloe Army Air Field[qv] from 1943 to 1945 and Victoria County Airport from 1949 to 1960. In 1986 the school, which joined the Victoria Independent School District as Aloe Elementary in 1951, still served the Yucca Heights residential development.

bibliography: Roy Grimes, ed., *300 Years in Victoria County* (Victoria, Texas: Victoria *Advocate*, 1968; rpt., Austin: Nortex, 1985). Victoria *Advocate*, Historical Edition, May 12, 1968. *Craig H. Roell*

ALOE ARMY AIR FIELD. Aloe Army Air Field, an advanced single-engine training field for fighter pilots, was opened in January 1943 on a 1,820-acre tract five miles southwest of Victoria. The field, named for a nearby railway station, became the new home of the Lake Charles Army Flying School from Lake Charles, Louisiana; Lt. Col. Charles B. Harvin was director. Using the North American AT-6 "Texas" and Curtis P-40 trainers, cadets were schooled in flying and in ground and aerial gunnery. The first class of pilots graduated on February 16, 1943. Soon after V-J Day the government made plans to reassign the field as a subpost of Foster Army Air Field,[qv] but both Aloe and Foster were closed on October 31, 1945. Aloe Field, with its 304 buildings, was transferred to Victoria County by the War Assets Administration in 1948, after which the site became Victoria County Airport. In 1960 the airport was moved to Foster Field, and Aloe returned to private ownership.

bibliography: Roy Grimes, ed., *300 Years in Victoria County* (Victoria, Texas: Victoria *Advocate*, 1968; rpt., Austin: Nortex, 1985). *Life*, June 29, 1941. Robert W. Shook and Charles D. Spurlin, *Victoria: A Pictorial History* (Norfolk, Virginia: Donning, 1985). Victoria *Advocate*, Historical Edition, May 12, 1968. *Craig H. Roell*

ALPHA, TEXAS. Alpha was on Preston Road (now State Highway 289) and Alpha Road four miles west of Richardson at a site now inside Dallas, in northern Dallas County. It was originally a freedmen's community that developed out of Farmers Branch and was on the principal route of transportation between Farmers Branch and Garland. A post office operated in Alpha from 1893 until 1904. E. C. Bramlett opened the first general store in 1895, and by 1933 the community had two businesses. The population was 111 in 1904 but decreased to fifty in 1933, where it remained in 1987, the last year it was listed as a community.

bibliography: Daniel Hardy, *Dallas County Historic Resources Survey* (Dallas: Dallas Historical Commission, 1982). David S. Switzer, *It's Our Dallas County* (Dallas: Switzer, 1954). *Matthew Hayes Nall*

ALPINE, TEXAS. (Brewster County). Alpine is located in a wide valley in the foothills of the Davis Mountains in northwest Brewster County. Cattlemen lived in tents near their herds in the area between 1878 and 1882. The town began in the spring of 1882, when a few railroad workers and their families pitched their tents along a small spring-fed creek at the foot of what is now known as "A" Mountain. The railroad section was given the name of Osborne, and for a brief period the name Osborne was applied to the small community of settlers. The best of the springs was on a section belonging to Daniel and Thomas Murphy. The railroad needed control of the spring as a source of water for its steam engines, so it entered into an agreement with the Murphys to change the name of the section and settlement to Murphyville in exchange for a contract to use the spring. In November of 1883 the Murphys registered a plat for the town of Murphyville with the county clerk of Presidio County.

As the town grew the residents petitioned for its name to be changed to Alpine, and on February 3, 1888, the name of the local post office was officially changed. In 1888 a description of the town mentioned a dozen houses, three saloons, a hotel and rooming house, a livery stable, a butcher shop, and a drugstore, which also housed the post office.

Alpine grew very slowly until 1921. Then came the opening of Sul Ross State Normal College (now Sul Ross State University) and the construction of the first paved roads into the area. The college, along with ranching and the transcontinental railroad, made Alpine the center of activities in the Big Bend area of Texas. At this time city utilities, including water, sewerage, and electricity, came to the community. In the early 1940s, with the establishment of Big Bend National Park,[qv] Alpine came to be looked upon as the entrance to the park. Since the early 1960s the rapid influx of affluent retired people into the area has been an important factor in the town's continued growth.

Alpine is listed as one of the fifty safest and most economical places for retirement in the United States. It is often spoken of as the "heart of the Big Bend," the "Alps of Texas," "out where the West begins," and the "economic, cultural, and recreational center for Trans-Pecos Texas." Alpine was incorporated by 1929. The town is served by the Southern Pacific and South Orient railroads, Amtrak, and several bus lines and is crossed by U.S. highways 90 and 67 and State Highway 118. The Big Bend Telephone Company has its headquarters in Alpine and serves customers who are not served by Southwestern Bell. In addition to the facilities of three major petroleum companies Alpine has a number of financial institutions and small businesses. The medical needs of the area are met by Big Bend Regional Medical Center. The town has three public schools and more than eighteen churches. Recreational facilities include public parks, swimming pools, a golf course, tennis courts, and an outdoor theater. Alpine also has a TV cable system, two radio stations, and the campus communications program at Sul Ross.

The population was estimated at 396 in 1904. By 1927 it had risen to 3,000. The 1950 census reported Alpine's population at 5,256, but the 1960 census reported only 4,740 residents. A high of approximately 6,200 was reached by 1976. In 1980 residents numbered 5,465 and businesses 108. In 1990 the population was 5,637.

BIBLIOGRAPHY: Valerie Bluthardt, "Urban West Texas: Alpine," *Fort Concho Report* 18 (Winter 1986–87). P. C. Burney, "Alpine, the Roof Garden of Texas," *Texas Magazine*, March 1911. Clifford B. Casey, *The Trans Pecos in Texas History* (West Texas Historical and Scientific Society Publication 5, 1933).

Clifford B. Casey

ALPINE, TEXAS (Gregg County). Alpine, a rural community formerly on Alpine Road and now in north Longview in northeastern Gregg County, grew up around the Alpine Presbyterian Church, which was established before 1900. In the mid-1960s the community had a church, a store, a cemetery, and a number of houses. In the early 1990s only a church, a cemetery, and a few scattered dwellings remained. *Christopher Long*

ALPINE CREEK. Alpine Creek rises three-quarters of a mile south of Ranger Peak near Alpine (at 30°17′ N, 103°43′ W) in northwestern Brewster County and flows northeast for twenty-three miles to its mouth on Musquiz Creek, a half mile below the crossing of the Santa Fe tracks over the latter stream (at 30°31′ N, 103°34′ W). Alpine Creek runs through Alpine and across a broad, open valley surrounded by rugged mountains and mesas. Its last six miles, beginning about six miles northeast of Alpine, was formerly known as Paisano Creek. The area has attracted human habitation for thousands of years, as artifacts attest. In historical times various trails into Mexico all crossed the area. Explorers in the valley were singularly impressed by the deep grasses, abundant wildlife, and flowing water. As early as 1682, Juan Domínguez de Mendoza[qv] described the valley as "for miles . . . covered with grass that looked like a field of waving grain." When Maj. W. H. Emory[qv] entered the valley through Paisano Pass in 1852, he found it "watered by a limpid stream from crystalline rocks, clothed with luxuriant grass, sufficient to feed a million of cattle." By the late 1870s stockmen had begun moving into the area, and in 1882 the Southern Pacific was built across Alpine Creek. The town grew around the crossing. Heavy grazing eliminated most of the deep grasses described in earlier accounts, and Alpine Creek became a dry wash. In some areas along the course of the creek, the former grassland has been invaded by desert scrub. For the most part, however, the area still supports grasses typical of semiarid climates, such as various gramas and tobosa grass, though much less abundant than was once the case.

BIBLIOGRAPHY: Clifford B. Casey, *Alpine, Texas, Then and Now* (Seagraves, Texas: Pioneer, 1981).

ALSA, TEXAS. Alsa, a farming community twenty-two miles north of Canton in northwest Van Zandt County, had a post office from 1894 to 1907. According to one source the town was established by Bill Starnes, a Confederate veteran who opened a store shortly after the Civil War[qv] and named the settlement for his boyhood sweetheart. The population reached a high of fifty in 1896, when the community had a combined cotton gin and gristmill, Baptist and Methodist churches, and a general store. The school, established sometime after 1890, had an enrollment of seventy-five in 1904 and was consolidated with the Wills Point school by the early 1950s. Two businesses, a church, Center School, and Howell Cemetery were located in or near the town in 1936. By 1964 the businesses were gone, and the population was estimated at fifteen. Diversified farming and stock raising were the principal industries of the community: cotton, fruits, and vegetables were the chief crops; dairy and beef cattle, hogs, and poultry were grown commercially. By 1979 only scattered dwellings marked the site. *Diana J. Kleiner*

ALSBURY, CHARLES GRUNDISON (?–?). Charles Grundison Alsbury, one of Stephen F. Austin's[qv] Old Three Hundred[qv] colonists, was in Texas in company with Addison Harrison in August 1822, when some of the immigrants who came on the *Lively*[qv] found them on the Brazos River. Alsbury took part in a colony election in April 1824 and became a partner of his brothers James Harvey and Horace A. Alsbury.[qqv] They received title to 1½ sitios (*see* SITIO) of land now in Brazoria County on August 3, 1824. Charles Alsbury took part in the alcalde[qv] election at San Felipe in December 1824 and in early Indian campaigns. The census of 1826 listed him as a single man aged between twenty-five and forty. In 1839 the Alsbury family planned a town to be named Monticello at the mouth of Cow Creek and advertised the site as healthful, with plenty of timber to build a city.

BIBLIOGRAPHY: Eugene C. Barker, ed., *The Austin Papers* (3 vols., Washington: GPO, 1924–28). Lester G. Bugbee, "The Old Three Hundred: A List of Settlers in Austin's First Colony," *Quarterly of the Texas State Historical Association* 1 (October 1897). W. S. Lewis, "Adventures of the 'Lively' Immigrants," *Quarterly of the Texas State Historical Association* 3 (July 1899). Daniel Shipman, *Frontier Life: 58 Years in Texas* (1879). Clarence Wharton, *Wharton's History of Fort Bend County* (San Antonio: Naylor, 1939).

ALSBURY, HORACE ARLINGTON (1805–1847). Horace (Horatio, Horacio) Arlington (Alex, Alexander) Alsbury (Alsberry, Allsbury; variant spellings occur in the surname of related Alsburys), possibly a native of Hopkinsville, Kentucky, came to Texas as one of Stephen F. Austin's[qv] Old Three Hundred.[qv] With two of his brothers, James Harvey and Charles Grundison Alsbury,[qqv] he received title to a league and a half of land now in Brazoria County on August 3, 1824. Although he called himself a doctor, it is not known where he studied medicine. He rode horseback across the Rio Grande between Mexico and Texas numerous times. He wrote voluminously to important persons in the Texas government and volunteered for numerous military activities. In January 1834 Stephen F. Austin[qv] wrote from Monterrey that he was sending by "Mr. Allsbury," probably Horace Alsbury, two portrait miniatures of himself to his Texas kin. In late August 1835, after perhaps being at the legislature of Coahuila and Texas[qv] in Monclova, Alsbury published a handbill in Columbia, "To The People Of Texas," warning of Antonio López de Santa Anna's[qv] plans to drive Anglo-Americans from Texas. In the siege of Bexar[qv] (November–December 1835) he was a member of Capt. John York's[qv] Company. In early 1836 Alsbury married Mrs. Juana Navarro Pérez, daughter of José Ángel Navarro,[qv] a Santa Anna loyalist of Bexar. She remained in the Alamo during the siege and final assault by Mexican forces (*see* ALSBURY, JUANA NAVARRO). Alsbury rode from the Alamo as one of the messengers on February 23, during the first hours after Santa Anna captured Bexar. On March 1 he possibly accompanied the thirty-two Gonzales volunteers on their way to the Alamo, and on March 3 he was in Gonzales with other Texas volunteers after failing to contact James W. Fannin's[qv] division expected to reinforce the Alamo.

Alsbury was a member of Henry W. Karnes's[qv] company at San Jacinto and was one of the 154 Masons to take part in the fighting. After the battle he joined in the surveillance of Mexican troops retreating from San Jacinto toward La Bahía and Mexico. He returned to Bexar in May 1836 and took his wife and her young son away from the devastated town to Calavero Ranch, on the Goliad road.

He received a military donation and bounties for his service at San Jacinto. The Congress of the Republic of Texas[qv] allowed him payment for service as major of the infantry and as interpreter for the post of Bexar, 1835 and 1836. He secured a land grant south of San Antonio near the site of present Von Ormy. In 1837 he successfully bid for office of tax assessor for Bexar County, which he may have held for some time before John W. Smith[qv] assumed the position. In early 1838 Alsbury and Joseph Baker, as Indian agents of the republic, led a group of men from Bexar and met with the Comanches on a peace mission on the Pedernales. They barely escaped with their lives.

In late 1838 Alsbury wrote from San Antonio regarding the favorable business in South Texas with self-proclaimed Federalist traders from Mexico. In late 1839 and early 1840 Alsbury served as commander of Federalist leader Antonio Canales's bodyguard along the Rio Grande during the running battles of Mexican general Mariano Arista's[qv] forces against Canales and Samuel W. Jordan's[qv] movement to establish the Republic of the Rio Grande.[qv] During desperate fighting, Alsbury and his command, fleeing for their lives, escaped into Texas.

In 1839 Alsbury joined other San Antonio citizens to ask for government protection of their lives and those of their families against Indian and Mexican incursions. In early September 1842 he was among the Texans captured by Mexican general Adrián Woll[qv] and marched to Mexico's Perote Prison, where he remained until his release on March 24, 1844. According to Juana Alsbury her husband accompanied the American army across the Rio Grande in 1846 during the Mexican War[qv] and was killed somewhere between Camargo and Saltillo in June 1847.

BIBLIOGRAPHY: Eugene C. Barker, ed., *The Austin Papers* (3 vols., Washington: GPO, 1924–28). Sam Houston Dixon and Louis Wiltz Kemp, *The Heroes of San Jacinto* (Houston: Anson Jones, 1932). Rena Maverick Green, ed., *Samuel Maverick, Texan* (San Antonio, 1952). Vertical Files, Barker Texas History Center, University of Texas at Austin.

Crystal Sasse Ragsdale

ALSBURY, JAMES HARVEY (?–?). James Harvey Alsbury was a partner of his brothers Horace A. and Charles Grundison Alsbury[qqv] as one of Stephen F. Austin's[qv] Old Three Hundred[qv] colonists. On August 3, 1824, they received title to a sitio[qv] and a half of land that later became part of Brazoria County.

James Harvey has been confused with Hanson Alsbury, his brother, who was born in Virginia on October 18, 1801, came to Texas in 1824, lived temporarily at San Felipe, and later moved to the Trinity River area, where he spent some months in surveying and became a father in 1825. In 1826 his wife, Harriet Raymond (Plummer), became ill, and the family returned to Mississippi, where they remained until 1840; then they returned to Brazoria County. They moved to Galveston in 1842 and later to San Antonio.

BIBLIOGRAPHY: Eugene C. Barker, ed., *The Austin Papers* (3 vols., Washington: GPO, 1924–28). Lester G. Bugbee, "The Old Three Hundred: A List of Settlers in Austin's First Colony," *Quarterly of the Texas State Historical Association* 1 (October 1897).

ALSBURY, JUANA GERTRUDIS NAVARRO (1812–1888). Juana Navarro Alsbury, among the survivors of the battle of the Alamo,[qv] one of three daughters of José Ángel Navarro[qv] and Concepción Cervantes, was born in San Antonio de Béxar in 1812 and baptized on December 28 of that year. Her father was a long-time government official of San Antonio de Béxar and a Mexican loyalist during the Texas Revolution.[qv] Her uncle José Antonio Navarro,[qv] a loyal Tejano, signed the Texas Declaration of Independence.[qv]

After her mother's death Juana was reared by her godmother and aunt, Josefa Navarro Veramendi, and her husband Juan Martín de Veramendi[qv] in the Veramendi Palace near Main Plaza in San Antonio. As a young woman she met prominent Texans who came there. Her cousin and adopted sister Ursula Veramendi was married to James Bowie,[qv] who is thought to have brought Juana, her baby son Alejo Pérez, and her younger sister Gertrudis to the Alamo (*see* ALAMO NONCOMBATANTS) when Antonio López de Santa Anna[qv] captured San Antonio on February 23, 1836. Dr. Horace Alexander Alsbury,[qv] Juana's husband, left the Alamo that same day, probably with messenger Dr. John Sutherland.[qv] He may have been looking for a safe home for his family. Juana helped nurse Bowie during his illness in the Alamo. Months later Susanna Dickinson[qv] accused Juana of being the legendary Mexican woman who carried Travis's parley message to Santa Anna on March 4 from the Alamo, as well as saying Juana left the Alamo with her father before the siege on March 6. Other sources refute these stories. According to Juana's personal account, she remained at the Alamo throughout the siege. On the final day she was protected by two men who were killed by Mexican soldiers who broke into a trunk and took valuables of Juana and her family. After the battle of the Alamo[qv] Juana, her son, and her sister stayed at her father's home.

Juana was first married in 1832 to Alejo Pérez Ramigio, with whom she had a son, Alejo. Some sources say that she also had a daughter who died in infancy. Perez died in 1834, possibly in the cholera epidemic. Juana married Horace Alexander Alsbury, by some accounts, in early January 1836. During their eleven-year marriage Alsbury was often away from San Antonio involved in revolutionary activities in Mexico, along the Rio Grande, and in South Texas. He did not survive his Mexican War[qv] military service and died, presumably in Mexico sometime in 1847. Alejo Pérez, Juana's son, was a long-time local San Antonio city official whose descendants still live in San Antonio.

When Alsbury was marched to Mexico with other San Antonio captives of Adrián Woll's[qv] invasion in September 1842, Juana followed the Texan prisoners as far as Candela, Coahuila, where she waited for Alsbury's return. He came there for her after his release from Perote prison in 1844, and the couple again made their home in San Antonio. After Alsbury's death Juana married Juan Pérez, her first husband's cousin.

Although she probably wrote few letters, her signature appears on numerous Bexar County land documents and in the state archives on legal petitions to the Texas legislature. She petitioned the legislature in 1857 and received a pension for the belongings she lost at the Alamo and for her services there. She probably died on July 23, 1888, at her son's Rancho de la Laguna on Salado Creek in east Bexar County. She is said to have been buried there, although other information gives her burial place as a Catholic cemetery in San Antonio.

BIBLIOGRAPHY: John S. Ford, Mrs. Alsbury's Recollections of the Alamo (MS, John Salmon Ford Papers, Barker Texas History Center, University of Texas at Austin). John Ogden Leal, San Fernando Church Baptismals, 1812–1825 (MS, DRT Library at the Alamo, San Antonio). San Antonio *Daily Express*, July 26, 1888, May 12, 19, 1907. Glenn Scott, "Juana Navarro de Alsbury," in *Women in Early Texas*, ed. Evelyn M. Carrington (Austin: Jenkins, 1975).

Crystal Sasse Ragsdale

ALSBURY, THOMAS (1773–?). Thomas Alsbury, Jr., one of Stephen F. Austin's[qv] Old Three Hundred,[qv] was born in West Virginia in 1773. He married Leah Jane Catlett on August 7, 1796; they had ten children. Alsbury fought in the War of 1812. The family came to Austin from Kentucky between May and July 1824. On July 8, 1824, Alsbury received title to two leagues and 1½ labores of land that later became part of Fort Bend, Brazoria, and Waller counties. The census of 1826 listed him as a farmer and stock raiser, aged over fifty. He was accompanied to Texas by his wife, sons Charles, J. Harvey, and Horace Alsbury,[qqv] and two daughters.

BIBLIOGRAPHY: Eugene C. Barker, ed., *The Austin Papers* (3 vols., Washington: GPO, 1924–28). Lester G. Bugbee, "The Old Three Hundred: A List of Settlers in Austin's First Colony," *Quarterly of the Texas State Historical Association* 1 (October 1897).

Katherine P. Miller

ALSDORF, TEXAS. Alsdorf was on a spur off State Highway 34 five miles northeast of Ennis in east central Ellis County. The catalyst for settlement was the arrival of the Texas and New Orleans Railroad in the 1880s. The town was named Faulkner after Alsdorf Faulkner, general passenger agent for the railroad. Faulkner's home was an early social center. The name Alsdorf was adopted in 1895 when the settlement received a post office. By 1900 Alsdorf had a general store and a frame church and school building. In addition, two cotton gins and the tracks of the Texas and New Orleans Railroad combined to make the town a shipping point for local cotton. Alsdorf's population never exceeded 100. In 1920 the post office closed. In 1933 the community had an estimated seventy-five residents and two businesses. By 1949, the last year for which figures are available, the population had declined to fifty.

BIBLIOGRAPHY: Edna Davis Hawkins, et al., *History of Ellis County, Texas* (Waco: Texian, 1972).

David Minor

ALSUP, NELSON FISHER (1877–1952). Nelson Fisher Alsup, politician, was born on July 20, 1877, in Wilson County, Tennessee, the son of Joseph Franklin and Rachel Baskin Alsup. He was educated at home, at the Belton Male Academy (Wedemeyer's Academy), and at Sam Houston Normal (now Sam Houston State University) in Huntsville. He taught school at Durango, Paige, and other small Central Texas communities. Alsup married Laura Kate Johnson of Day's Lake near Waco on August 23, 1905. They had six children.

In 1906 Alsup ran unsuccessfully against Thomas T. Connally[qv] for justice of the peace in Falls County. When the anti-Ferguson faction of the Democratic party[qv] joined with the Ku Klux Klan[qv] to control state offices, Alsup ran for superintendent of public instruction on the American (Know-Nothing) party[qv] ticket. Pat M. Neff,[qv] a leader of the anti-Ferguson faction, had not registered under the conscription act of 1917, claiming he was overage. Alsup obtained photographs of the Neff family Bible showing an erasure in the name of Patty M. Neff, born in 1871. There was no entry for Pat Morris Neff. The Neff family burial ground showed tombstones for each of the Neff children except Patty M. Neff, though there was some disturbance of the gravestones. Alsup published this information in the *Ferguson Forum*. After Neff's election as governor, an indictment for criminal libel was issued in McLennan County, and about two the next morning Alsup was taken from his home on Little River in Bell County by persons claiming to be Texas Rangers.[qv] He remained hidden for some time. Attempts to serve a writ of habeas corpus at several jails in Central Texas were unsuccessful because he was being held in a camp in secluded cedarbrakes west of Waco. Once the camp was discovered, Alsup was placed under arrest, brought to trial in Waco, and quickly convicted. The Court of Criminal Appeals confirmed the conviction, saying "The evil design, which is an essential element of criminal libel, requires no specific proof..." and "the truth of a statement charging acts which were disgraceful but not penal is no defense to a prosecution for publishing such statement." Another hearing was denied by the court on March 8, 1922. Neff's second term as governor expired, and Governor Miriam A. Ferguson[qv] pardoned Alsup and fully restored his civil rights. Alsup never again swayed from his support of the Democratic party.

Under patronage of George W. West,[qv] he became editor of a Live Oak County newspaper. During this time he wrote a novel, *The Lost Crucifix of Our Lady of Guadalupe* (1977), a thinly veiled fictional account of the life and some adventures of George West. Alsup lobbied the Texas legislature during the 1930s and 1940s for the Texas Sheep and Goat Raisers, the Texas Soil Conservation Association, and others. Some of his most earnest lobbying was for the State Soil Conservation Act, which was passed in 1939. He led an unsuccessful write-in campaign against Commissioner of Agriculture McDonald. The largest write-in vote ever recorded in Texas was levied against McDonald. Alsup died on February 29, 1952 at Temple.

BIBLIOGRAPHY: Temple *Daily Telegram*, March 1, 1952.

Frank Wagner

ALTAIR, TEXAS. Altair is on State Highway 90A in south central Colorado County. The community dates from the late 1880s. A post office was established there in 1888. The town was originally named Stafford's Ranch in honor of a leading local rancher. Because a Stafford, Texas, already had a post office, the name Altair, for the star, was approved by the residents in 1890. That same year Altair obtained service from a branch of the Texas and New Orleans Railroad. Stafford's Ranch has sometimes been mistakenly called Spafford's Ranch. During the 1960s Altair had a population of 200. From 1974 until 1986 its population was estimated at eighty. In 1986 the community supported a few stores and rice-drying facilities. In 1990 the population was thirty.

BIBLIOGRAPHY: *Colorado County Sesquicentennial Commemorative Book* (La Grange, Texas: Hengst Printing, 1986). Fred Tarpley, *1001 Texas Place Names* (Austin: University of Texas Press, 1980).

Ken Hendrickson

ALTA LOMA, TEXAS. Alta Loma, on State Highway 6 in southwestern Galveston County, was settled by Asa Brigham,[qv] who received a grant on Hall's Bayou from the Mexican government in 1830. This area had previously been occupied by roaming Karankawa Indians. In 1878 the Gulf, Colorado and Santa Fe Railway was built through the settlement, and in 1883, after booms in pears, figs, and oranges, the Alta Loma Improvement and Investment Company established the townsite and sponsored the building of a school, a depot, a store, churches, and houses. James W. Skirvin led the first settlers to Alta Loma in 1894, and that year the Alta Loma post office was established. In 1895 the first artesian well was brought in in the settlement. By 1897 there were thirty such wells that provided nearby Galveston with 6,000,000 gallons of fresh drinking water daily. At that time Alta Loma had a population of 200 and more than a dozen businesses, including a fruit cannery. Throughout the early 1900s the community's economy was based on fruit, dairy farming, and beef cattle. The Hoyland and Johnson Creamery was built in 1912. In 1907 the local school had sixty-eight pupils and two teachers. Alta Loma's population was 500 in 1915. By 1948 the community had eleven local businesses, which served the nearby oilfields. The population grew from 540 in 1920 to 1,350 in 1940. The Alta Loma Business Association was founded in 1966. At that time Steelco, which produced galvanized boat trailers, was built at the community, and the Alta Loma post office was among the largest in the county. By 1970 Alta Loma had a population of 1,536 and some thirty businesses, including six gas stations, several beauty shops, three cafes, two drive-ins, two drugstores, a clinic, and a concrete business. On January 21, 1978, nearby Santa Fe incorporated Alta Loma into its city limits and in 1982 changed the post office name to Santa Fe. During the 1980s recreational facilities in the area included Hall's Bayou for boating and fishing, the Knights of Columbus[qv] hall, the Veterans of Foreign Wars[qv] hall, and two private parks.

BIBLIOGRAPHY: Galveston *Daily News*, January 19, 31, 1966, February 22, 1970. *Leigh Gard*

ALTAVISTA, TEXAS. Altavista is off Farm Road 1017 twenty-two miles south of Hebbronville in east central Jim Hogg County. The site was first settled in 1890, when the Jones family purchased the Jones–Alta Vista Ranch. A post office called Altavista and a store were in operation by 1906. One business and a population estimated at twenty-five were recorded for the year 1936. In the mid-1940s Altavista had a business, a school, and row of dwellings. In the early 1990s Altavista was a dispersed community.

BIBLIOGRAPHY: Hebbronville Chamber of Commerce, *Fiftieth Anniversary, Jim Hogg County* (Hebbronville, Texas, 1963). *Jim Hogg County Enterprise*, March 9, 1939. *Alicia A. Garza*

ALTGELT, EMMA FRANZISKA MURCK (1833–1922). Emma Franziska Murck Altgelt, pioneer, teacher, and author, daughter of Friedrich D. E. and Ambrosine (Reinbach) Murck, was born at Barmen (now in Wuppertal), Prussia, on December 4, 1833. Her father, a former army officer serving as the city's police commissioner, died of typhoid at age thirty-three, when she was only 3½. Her only sibling soon followed him. Before Emma was five, her maternal grandmother and aunt assumed her upbringing in Heinzberg, near the Dutch border. A precocious pupil and the lone girl in a supplementary evening class with forty boys, she studied algebra, history, literature, and French twelve hours weekly. Before Emma left for Liège to prepare herself as a teacher of German and English, her family moved to the Cologne area.

Charmed by stories her kinsmen the Brachts told of Texas, she sailed from Bremen on the *Franziska* in October 1854 and landed in Galveston just days before her twenty-first birthday. Her mother settled in Texas also. Emma's determination never to marry did not survive Ernst Hermann Altgelt's[qv] wooing. After their marriage (July 23, 1855), their home for some twelve years was Comfort, which Altgelt had founded. For 2½ years, starting when the eldest Altgelt child was barely seven, Mrs. Altgelt conducted the Comfort school in their home. During the Civil War[qv] in 1863, Altgelt, ardently Confederate in a town of strong Union sentiments, left for Germany at his wife's urging to preserve his fragile health and visit his aging father. After his return in 1865, the family could not rejoin him until a cholera epidemic had subsided in San Antonio, where he soon became the law partner of D. Y. Portis. For a brief time their residence in the city was the neglected Spanish Governor's Palace,[qv] which Altgelt had purchased and attempted to renovate. When he acquired a tract on which he laid out what he named King William Street (*see* KING WILLIAM HISTORIC DISTRICT), the family moved into a home constructed for them there. Hoping Altgelt's health would benefit, they next lived on their farm, Wassenberg, near Boerne. Almost immediately (1869) an infant son died of a childhood illness. In 1878 another small son's fatal fall hastened the father's death. Soon daughter Antonia's husband Adolph Benner was murdered and the Benners' infant died. For forty-four years a widow, Emma Altgelt had to sell properties disadvantageously. Nevertheless she helped her six remaining children to become educated.

Two visits to her homeland during the 1880s revived her wish to become a writer. She visited California and also studied Spanish intensively. At age seventy she was visiting close friends and grandchildren in the interior of Mexico. She lived briefly in New Braunfels, then returned to San Antonio, home of most of her children. Late in life her devoted companion was a longtime family servant, Virginia, a former slave. When Emma Altgelt died on July 19, 1922, twelve of her twenty surviving grandchildren were men named Altgelt. Some of her reminiscences, observations, and sentimental descriptive verses have been published, occasionally in translation (her recollections of the early years in Texas are especially prized). Her published works include a collection entitled *Beobachtungen und Erinnerungen* ("Observations and Memories"), published in 1930 by the *Neu-Braunfelser Zeitung* (*see* NEW BRAUNFELS *HERALD-ZEITUNG*), and "Schilderungen aus texanischem Leben" ("Descriptions from Texas Life"), translated by Guido Ransleben and published in the Comfort *News* weekly from May 22, 1969, through August 5, 1970.

BIBLIOGRAPHY: Henry B. Dielmann, trans., "Emma Altgelt's Sketches of Life in Texas," *Southwestern Historical Quarterly* 63 (January 1960). Ethel Hander Geue, *New Homes in a New Land: German Immigration to Texas, 1847–1861* (Waco: Texian Press, 1970). Crystal Sasse Ragsdale, ed., *The Golden Free Land: The Reminiscences and Letters of Women on an American Frontier* (Austin: Landmark, 1976). Guido E. Ransleben, *A Hundred Years of Comfort in Texas* (San Antonio: Naylor, 1954; rev. ed. 1974). San Antonio *Express*, June 29, 1977. *Minetta Altgelt Goyne*

ALTGELT, ERNST HERMANN (1832–1878). Hermann Altgelt was born on July 17, 1832, at Düsseldorf on the Rhine, the son of a privy counselor of that city. Upon completing military service, he immigrated at age twenty to New Orleans and worked briefly for the cotton firm of John Vles. In 1854 he led a surveying party into the Hill Country[qv] of Texas and laid out the town of Comfort on property owned by Vles. Soon, German freethinkers from New Braunfels began to settle in the area and to develop the communal life that they wanted. The Comfort area, in spite of floods and drought, offered lands for both farming and ranching, as well as an abundance of timber and water. Altgelt began lumber and grist mills, but neither was successful. He married another immigrant from the Rhineland, Emma Murck (*see* ALTGELT, EMMA MURCK), in July 1855 and thereafter took up the practice of law. Though he was never a fire-eating supporter of secession,[qv] during the Civil War[qv] Altgelt aligned himself with the Southern cause. He traveled to Germany, allegedly as a result of strained relations with his fellow countrymen. After this trip he joined the Confederate Army in time to participate in the battle of Palmito Ranch[qv] after Lee's surrender.

He moved to San Antonio in 1866, continued his practice of law, and increased his real estate investments. According to some sources, he built the first house on King William Street (see KING WILLIAM DISTRICT, SAN ANTONIO) in 1867 and was thus accorded the privilege of naming the street, allegedly after Wilhelm I of Prussia. His neighborhood rapidly attracted successful families of German and other nationalities. Altgelt built a more elaborate second home in 1877–78 at 226 King William Street. He died on March 28, 1878, at the family ranch, Wassenberg, twenty-five miles from San Antonio. Altgelt had nine children, seven of whom grew to maturity.

BIBLIOGRAPHY: Frederick Charles Chabot, *With the Makers of San Antonio* (Yanaguana Society Publications 4, San Antonio, 1937). Henry B. Dielmann, trans., "Emma Altgelt's Sketches of Life in Texas," *Southwestern Historical Quarterly*, January 1960. Glen E. Lich,

The German Texans (San Antonio: University of Texas Institute of Texan Cultures, 1981). San Antonio *Daily Herald*, March 29, 30, 1878.
Donald E. Everett

ALTHAUS, CHRISTIAN (1821–1915). Christian Althaus, pioneer doctor, was born in Westphalia on February 11, 1821. He received his medical training in the Prussian army and, with other Germans who emigrated in the 1840s, traveled to Texas. He sailed from Antwerp on August 14, 1846, and arrived at Galveston in October. He was settled in Fredericksburg when town lots were distributed in 1847. On October 5, 1847, he married Anna Maria Elisabetha Behrens, also a German immigrant, whose mother brought her and her brother to Fredericksburg with the first colonists after her father died on the boat.

In the spring of 1847 Althaus signed the Meusebach-Comanche Treaty,[qv] which brought some stability to the Hill Country[qv] frontier. He gave the Indians medical treatment and followed the advice of his friend Chief John Carnor to "be friendly and never pull a gun." Althaus spoke several Indian dialects and worked for a time at nearby Fort Martin Scott distributing food to the Indians as an agent of the United States government. He also made and sold saddles and other supplies to the Forty-niners on their way to California. In 1857 he moved his family sixteen miles to Cave Creek to start ranching. He built his otherwise conventional dwelling over a spring to provide water inside the house and a cool place to store his medicine. Althaus opposed slavery and secession,[qqv] but he organized the home guard during the Civil War[qv] and was a Gillespie county commissioner from 1861 to 1864 and again in 1866.

He served as a community doctor until the 1880s, and his practice of medicine was carried on under many difficulties. Medical instruments were scarce; before Althaus amputated a crushed arm, he had to have the operating instrument (now at Pioneer Museum, Fredericksburg) made by a local blacksmith. He used locally grown herbs, roots, and bark to make his own medicines. When the government sent him to Bandera to treat diphtheria patients, he used medicine he made from honey, almond juice, and the bark of the blackjack tree. Thirty-four out of thirty-five people survived. Elizabeth Althaus not only raised seven children but also ran a makeshift hospital, orphanage, and shelter for wayfarers in their home. In addition she tended the farm during her husband's trips, which sometimes lasted for weeks. Althaus died on August 10, 1915, at the age of ninety-four. He was buried at Cave Creek beside St. Paul Lutheran Church, which he had helped found in 1883.

BIBLIOGRAPHY: Fannie Althaus, "Reminiscences of a Pioneer Doctor," *Junior Historian*, May 1948. Gillespie County Historical Society, *Pioneers in God's Hills* (2 vols., Austin: Von Boeckmann–Jones, 1960, 1974). *Barbara Donalson Althaus*

ALTHEA, TEXAS. Althea was on Farm Road 487 in the southeastern corner of Bell County. The town was headquarters for farm and ranch operations of the Thompson F. Fowler family; the Fowler General Store and gin operated there. Althea had a store, a gin, a blacksmith shop, and a school in the early twentieth century and a post office between 1900 and 1904. It comprised one business and a population of forty in 1933, and its school, which had been part of the Williamson County School District, was consolidated with the Bartlett district in 1948. In 1964 the population had fallen to ten, and the community was no longer shown on government topographical maps.

BIBLIOGRAPHY: Bell County Historical Commission, *Story of Bell County, Texas* (2 vols., Austin: Eakin Press, 1988). Clara Stearns Scarbrough, *Land of Good Water: A Williamson County History* (Georgetown, Texas: Williamson County Sun Publishers, 1973).
Mark Odintz

ALTITA CREEK. Altita Creek rises five miles northeast of Cotulla in west central La Salle County (at 28°27′ N, 99°08′ W) and runs south for seven miles to its mouth on the Nueces River, seven miles southwest of Cotulla (at 28°21′ N, 99°09′ W). Its course lies over low-rolling to flat terrain with locally shallow depressions, surfaced by clay and sandy loams that support grasses, mesquite, and chaparral. Downstream, water-tolerant hardwoods and grasses predominate.

ALTO, TEXAS. Alto, also known as Branchtown, is an incorporated community at the junction of U.S. Highway 69, State highways 21 and 249, and Farm roads 752 and 1911, eleven miles south of Rusk in southern Cherokee County. The settlement was founded around 1849 by Robert F. Mitchell on land acquired in a lawsuit with John Durst.[qv] The site was once a part of an extensive grant to Nacogdoches merchants William Barr and Samuel Davenport.[qqv] A local post office opened in 1850 under the name Branchtown. In 1852 the town was renamed Alto ("high"), reportedly at the suggestion of Henry Berryman,[qv] because of its location at the highest point between the Angelina and Neches rivers. Because it was situated on the Old San Antonio Road,[qv] the settlement quickly developed into a commercial center and stopping point for travelers. Mitchell opened a store in 1851, and by the eve of the Civil War[qv] Alto had several stores, a blacksmith and livery shop, a saloon, a cotton gin, and a school for girls. After the construction of the Kansas and Gulf Short Line Railroad through the town in the mid-1880s, Alto drew residents and businesses from many nearby communities. By 1885 the town had four gristmill–cotton gin combinations, a sawmill, a church, a district school, a saloon, several general stores, and a population of 600. A newspaper, the Alto *News*, was begun in 1893; under the name Alto *Herald* it continued to be published in the early 1990s. A bank was established in Alto in 1903, and in 1909 the town was incorporated.

Alto continued to prosper. In 1929 it reported a peak population of 1,600. With the onset of the Great Depression[qv] in the early 1930s, however, the population fell, and in 1936 the community reported 1,053 residents and eighty businesses. The population was 1,500 in the mid-1960s. In 1990 the town had 1,252 residents and twenty-seven businesses. Cattle ranching, oil and gas, and lumber are its chief industries.

BIBLIOGRAPHY: *Cherokee County History* (Jacksonville, Texas: Cherokee County Historical Commission, 1986). Hattie Joplin Roach, *A History of Cherokee County* (Dallas: Southwest, 1934).
Christopher Long

ALTOGA, TEXAS. Altoga is on Farm Road 1827 ten miles northeast of McKinney in northeastern Collin County. It was named by Dock Owensby, who wanted the town to have a motto and suggested "all together." By 1910 the community had seven stores, a public school, two cotton gins, and a popular brass band. A local post office operated from 1889 until 1900 and reopened in 1915. Early contradictory estimates give Altoga a population of fifty or 133 residents in 1915. By 1929 the town had grown to 250, but it declined to 150 by 1941. Mail was discontinued in 1937, when the number of businesses was four. By 1970 Altoga had only fifty residents. However, the population, benefitting from the growth of nearby McKinney, was 358 in 1980. In 1990 it was 367.

BIBLIOGRAPHY: Roy Franklin Hall and Helen Gibbard Hall, *Collin County: Pioneering in North Texas* (Quanah, Texas: Nortex, 1975). J. Lee and Lillian J. Stambaugh, *A History of Collin County* (Austin: Texas State Historical Association, 1958). *David Minor*

ALTON, TEXAS (Denton County). Alton, established by the state legislature on February 24, 1848, to replace Pinckneyville as county seat of Denton County, was less than a mile from the site of present-day Corinth in the east central part of the county. For three years the residence of W. C. Baines, the only person living in Alton, served as the legal center of the county. On November 26, 1850, because of a lack of water at the original site, the state legislature chose a new site for the county seat, five miles south of the site of present-day Denton near Hickory Creek. This new site kept the name Alton. By 1855 at least two stores, a hotel, and a post office had been constructed there. In 1856, however, residents of the county demanded a new county seat. They argued that Alton was not in the center of the county, that the water from the standing pools in Hickory Creek had made a number of families ill, and that the development of the town had been unsatisfactory. As a result of these complaints, in an election held in November 1856, Denton County voters accepted an offer from Hiram Cisco, William Loving, and William Woodruff to provide 100 acres of their property for a new county seat. This new site, near the center of the county, was named Denton. Soon after the establishment of the new county seat Alton disappeared.

BIBLIOGRAPHY: Edward Franklin Bates, *History and Reminiscences of Denton County* (Denton, Texas: McNitzky Printing, 1918; rpt., Denton: Terrill Wheeler Printing, 1976). C. A. Bridges, *History of Denton, Texas, from Its Beginning to 1960* (Waco: Texian Press, 1978). E. Dale Odom and Bullitt Lowry, *A Brief History of Denton County* (Denton, Texas, 1975).
David Minor

ALTON, TEXAS (Hidalgo County). Alton is four miles north of Mission on State Highway 107 in Hidalgo County. It originated as a stop on the San Benito and Rio Grande Valley (Spiderweb) Railway in 1911, when the population was fifty. A post office operated there from 1913 to 1916. In the late 1920s the Alton Independent School District was formed. The small, six-grade Alton school was later consolidated with the Sharyland Independent School District. A grade school was in operation in the community in 1990, when Alton was a rural bedroom community for McAllen; the population of 3,069 was 80 percent Spanish-speaking and included many migrant workers. Beginning in the late 1980s the community had a contract sub-post office. San Martín de Porres Catholic Church, originally a mission, was constructed in 1967 and declared a parish in 1969, when a large parish hall and other improvements were added for the 1,000 families it served. Water District No. 7 was formed in the 1930s to serve Alton; in 1990 it was called the United Water District. A sewage disposal plant, volunteer fire station, city hall, and community center were among the public buildings. The community voted to incorporate on April 10, 1978. At 7:30 a.m. on September 21, 1989, a Dr. Pepper truck hit a Mission school bus, knocking it into the caliche pit at the corner of Five-Mile Road and Bryan Road. Twenty children from the Alton area were drowned, and sixty were injured. This was the worst school bus accident to date in Texas history.

BIBLIOGRAPHY: Austin *American-Statesman*, September 22, 1989. Valley By-Liners, *Roots by the River: A Story of Texas Tropical Borderland* (Mission, Texas: Border Kingdom Press, 1978).
Dick D. Heller, Jr.

ALTONIA, TEXAS. Altonia was thirteen miles southwest of San Augustine in southwestern San Augustine County. The community was granted a post office named Ransom in 1886, and in 1895 the name was changed to Altonia, supposedly for the site's location on an elevated sandy ridge. By 1914 Altonia had a general store, and in 1933 it comprised a business and twenty-five inhabitants. By the 1940s the community was no longer shown on county highway maps.
Mark Odintz

ALTO SPRINGS, TEXAS. Alto Springs is on Farm Road 2745 thirteen miles east of Marlin in eastern Falls County. The settlement began as a relay point for an early Central Texas stage route and a supply station for area settlers. Local tradition has it that Sam Houston[qv] gave an address at the Alto Springs station in 1842 in an effort to increase the Texas army. Cynthia Ann Parker[qv] is also said to have stayed there after she had been recovered from the Indians. A post office was established at the stage stop in 1846. Alto Springs had a church, a school, and a brush arbor that was used as a community center; it served for several years as a gathering place for political rallies and stump speeches. Alto Springs was considered a possible county seat when residents of Falls County were deciding on a location in 1851. The possibility faded, however, when it became clear that the Houston and Texas Central Railway would bypass the town by about three miles. The Alto Springs post office was discontinued in 1868, and when the railroad was completed two years later, the community lost its function as a supply station. Shortly after the turn of the century Alto Springs had a one-teacher school for forty-nine white students and two one-teacher schools for 140 black students. The community had at least one school, a church, and several residences in the 1940s. The Alto Springs schools were consolidated with the Marlin Independent School District in 1949. By the 1980s only a church marked the community on county highway maps.

BIBLIOGRAPHY: Walter W. Brawn, The History of Falls County (M.A. thesis, Baylor University, 1938). Marlin *Daily Democrat*, July 16, 1936.
Vivian Elizabeth Smyrl

ALTSHELER, JOSEPH ALEXANDER (1862–1919). Joseph Alexander Altsheler, reporter and western writer, son of Joseph and Louise (Snoddy) Altsheler, was born at Three Springs, Kentucky, on April 29, 1862. He attended Liberty College in Glasgow, Kentucky, and Vanderbilt University. In 1885 he worked as a reporter and in various editorial positions at the Louisville *Courier-Journal*. In 1892 he worked for the New York *World* and in 1898 served as that paper's correspondent in Honolulu. Working as a reporter, feature writer, and editor, he became a storywriter almost by chance when he was unable to secure a desirable serial for boys and decided to write one himself. This began a long list of juvenile stories, grouped in six main series: the French and Indian War, Great West, Young Trailers, Civil War, World War, and Texas. Altsheler was interested in American history and took care to ensure authentic historical facts in his books. On May 30, 1888, he married Sarah Boles; they had one son, Sidney. The Altshelers were caught in Germany when World War I[qv] broke out in 1914, and the hardships they endured in returning to America broke Altsheler's health. He was a semi-invalid until his death, in New York on June 5, 1919. His principal works on Texas were *The Border Watch* (1912), *The Texan Star* (1912), *Apache Gold* (1913), *The Texan Triumph* (1913), and *The Texan Scouts* (1913).

BIBLIOGRAPHY: *Dictionary of American Biography*. Stanley Kunitz, ed., *Twentieth Century Authors* (New York: Wilson, 1942; Supplement, 1955).
Ida Jo Marshall

ALUM, TEXAS. Alum was just off State Highway 123 sixteen miles northeast of Floresville in northeastern Wilson County. The community was settled before 1900. In 1910 it reported a population of twenty-five. G. A. Burris operated a general store until about 1920. Maps of 1936 showed a rural school. In the early 1990s only a church and a few scattered houses remained.
Christopher Long

ALUM CREEK. Alum Creek rises three miles south of McDade in northeastern Bastrop County (at 30°14′ N, 97°13′ W) and flows southward for eighteen miles to its mouth on the Colorado River (at 30°03′ N, 97°12′ W). Before entering the Colorado River floodplain, the stream travels through gently to strongly sloping uplands characterized by post oak woods and sandy soil, then enters the Lost Pines[qv] area. The water flows over and through aluminum sulfate deposits and so has a high alum content. In 1856 Fred and Jacob Steussy were advertising their "steam mill pinery" on the creek below Bastrop.

BIBLIOGRAPHY: William Henry Korges, Bastrop County, Texas: Historical and Educational Development (M.A. thesis, University of Texas, 1933). Bill Moore, *Bastrop County, 1691-1900* (Wichita Falls: Nortex, 1977).

ALUM CREEK, TEXAS. Alum Creek is located where Highway 71 crosses Alum Creek about four miles southeast of Bastrop in central

Bastrop County. It is one of the oldest communities in Bastrop County, having been settled about 1829 by seven families from Stephen F. Austin's[qv] lower colonies. The Cottles, Highsmiths, Crafts, Parkers, Grimeses, Ridgeways, and Whites built a fort for protection against Indians near the mouth of the creek and located their cabins and farms nearby. By 1835 a private school had been established in the community, and in 1846 a five-acre plot was deeded by James Craft for an Alum Creek campground and meetinghouse. An Alum Creek post office was established in 1851, and by 1853 a local Methodist Episcopal church had been formed. In 1884 the community had a population of 200 that supported three mills, two general stores, a blacksmith shop, and a saloon. By 1896 the population had dipped to forty, and two years later the post office was discontinued. Though an Alum Creek school continued until at least 1932, the community failed to maintain enough people to be included in twentieth-century population estimates. During the 1930s Alum Creek was the site of a community club. By the mid-1980s the community consisted of a few houses and a cluster of country antique shops.

BIBLIOGRAPHY: Bastrop *Advertiser*, Historical Edition, August 29, 1935. Bastrop Historical Society, *In the Shadow of the Lost Pines: A History of Bastrop County and Its People* (Bastrop, Texas: Bastrop *Advertiser*, 1955). William Henry Korges, Bastrop County, Texas: Historical and Educational Development (M.A. thesis, University of Texas, 1933). Bill Moore, *Bastrop County, 1691-1900* (Wichita Falls: Nortex, 1977).

Paula Mitchell Marks

ALVARADO, HERNANDO DE (?–?). Hernando de Alvarado, captain of artillery on the Coronado expedition,[qv] saved the life of his commander during the storming of Hawiku pueblo. On August 29, 1540, he commanded a side expedition commissioned to explore the region to the east and the north for eighty days and to investigate the reports of cows or buffalo.[qv] Alvarado's command passed the Acoma pueblo, the land of the Tiguex Indians, and at the Pecos pueblo acquired El Turco[qv] as a guide to the cow herds. El Turco's tales of gold and silver caused the group to lose interest in cows, but the Spaniards continued until buffalo herds had been sighted, thus becoming the first known Europeans to visit the High Plains.

After rejoining Coronado at Tiguex, where he had moved for the winter at Coronado's suggestion, Alvarado went back to Pecos to demand some gold bracelets that El Turco reported had been taken from him at the time of his capture. No bracelets were found, and, feeling he had been deceived by the Indians of Pecos, Alvarado seized the Indian governor and his aide and put them in chains. This seizure of the Indian chief in violation of Spanish assurances of friendship caused the Indians to cease cooperation.

BIBLIOGRAPHY: Hubert Howe Bancroft, *History of Arizona and New Mexico, 1530–1888* (San Francisco: History Company, 1889; facsimile ed., Albuquerque: Horn and Wallace, 1962). Carlos E. Castañeda, *Our Catholic Heritage in Texas* (7 vols., Austin: Von Boeckmann–Jones, 1936-1958; rpt., New York: Arno, 1976). Frederick Webb Hodge and Theodore H. Lewis, eds., *Spanish Explorers in the Southern United States, 1528-1543* (New York: Scribner, 1907; rpt., Austin: Texas State Historical Association, 1984).

ALVARADO, TEXAS. Alvarado, the oldest town in Johnson County, is at the junction of U.S. highways 67 and 81 and Interstate Highway 35W, fifteen miles east of Cleburne in eastern Johnson County. In the winter of 1849 William Balch staked out a claim near an old Indian trail. His family did not last until spring but returned in 1851. Two years later Balch and a fellow settler, G. H. Sigler, laid out half-acre town lots. The community's first sheriff, A. H. Onstoott, is credited with naming Alvarado for Alvaredo, Vera Cruz, Mexico, where he fought in a battle during the Mexican War.[qv] By the summer of 1854 Alvarado had an estimated 100 families and postal service. The focus of the town was a two-story building, where the Masonic lodge held its meetings and an elementary school conducted classes. There was also an Alvarado College, operated by John C. Collier.[qv] The town had four churches, more than a dozen businesses, and 350 residents. In 1881 the tracks of the Gulf, Colorado and Santa Fe and the Missouri, Kansas and Texas railroads arrived. Within a few years the population surpassed 1,000. Residents voted to incorporate in June 1885. By that time the community had a bank chartered in 1880, a newspaper named the Alvarado *Bulletin*, two schools, a number of gins, a hotel, and an opera house. By 1890 a second bank opened and the reported population exceeded 2,000. By the mid-1920s Alvarado had an estimated 1,200 residents and more than fifty businesses. Unlike many of its sister communities, Alvarado did not decline during the Great Depression and World War II,[qqv] when the town actually managed to grow. The population reached 1,324 in 1943 and 4,129 in 1988, when sixty local businesses were in operation. Proximity to Cleburne and the Dallas–Fort Worth area contributed to the growth. In 1990 the population was 2,918.

BIBLIOGRAPHY: Frances Dickson Abernathy, The Building of Johnson County and the Settlement of the Communities of the Eastern Portion of the County (M.A. thesis, University of Texas, 1936). Viola Block, *History of Johnson County and Surrounding Areas* (Waco: Texian Press, 1970). Johnson County History Book Committee, *History of Johnson County, Texas* (Dallas: Curtis Media, 1985).

David Minor

ALVARADO PARK LAKE. Alvarado Park Lake is formed by a dam on Turkey Creek, a tributary of Chambers Creek and the Trinity River, two miles southwest of Alvarado in central Johnson County (at 32°22′ N, 97°13′ W). The county-owned reservoir was built in 1966 by Jack P. McKinney for floodwater retention, municipal water storage, and recreation. The lake's drainage area is thirty-one square miles, and its capacity is 4,700 acre-feet. The dam is 3,500 feet long and forty-nine feet high and has a crest width of fourteen feet. The top of the dam has an elevation of 704.1 feet, and the normal water level is 691.8 feet.

ÁLVAREZ BARREIRO, FRANCISCO (16?–17?). Francisco Álvarez Barreiro traveled from Spain to New Spain in the company of Viceroy Marqués de Valero (1716–22). Shortly after his arrival in the New World, Álvarez Barreiro was appointed military engineer for the expedition of Governor Martín de Alarcón,[qv] charged with founding religious, military, and civilian settlements on the San Antonio River and the resupply of missions in East Texas. According to his own testimony he assisted in the construction of the chapel for San Antonio de Valero Mission.

In 1720 Álvarez Barreiro was apparently obliged to return to Spain under a general order, which stated that Spaniards with wives in Spain should return there. However, by 1724 he was back in Mexico. In that year he began his most important work as surveyor, map maker, and experienced engineer for a massive inspection of northern New Spain (1724–28), carried out by Brigadier General Pedro de Rivera y Villalón.[qv]

Álvarez Barreiro left the capital on November 21, 1724, on a trek that eventually covered nearly 7,000 miles. The inspection began at Zacatecas and progressed to all presidios in northern New Spain. Prolonged stopovers were often necessary in order for him to complete his surveys and maps. Rivera completed his tour of inspection in Texas in the latter months of 1728. In all, Álvarez drafted six maps, five of which are located in the Archivo General de Indias. From presidio La Bahía, he spent thirty-five days exploring the coast and land that lay between it and the Neches River. His efforts represented "the most comprehensive reconnaissance of the upper Texas coast yet achieved." The resulting map, entitled *Plano, corographico é hidrographico*, is preserved in the British Museum. While it repeats a few errors, such as the misconception that the Guadalupe River flows into Matagorda Bay, its accuracy in other respects is surprising. Contained within it are the configuration of the coast, some rivercourses, and Indian villages and Spanish settlements.

In Álvarez Barreiro's final landmark survey, he recorded logging 363 leagues, or about 944 miles. He rejoined the Rivera inspection caravan at San Juan Bautista[qv] on December 23, 1728. There he received a new assignment, after which he disappears from known historical records.

BIBLIOGRAPHY: Thomas H. Naylor and Charles W. Polzer, comps. and eds., *Pedro de Rivera and the Military Regulations for Northern New Spain, 1724–1729* (Tucson: University of Arizona Press, 1988). Henry R. Wagner, *The Spanish Southwest, 1542–1794* (2 vols., Albuquerque: Quivira Society, 1937; rpt., New York: Arno Press, 1967). Robert S. Weddle, *The French Thorn: Rival Explorers in the Spanish Sea, 1682–1762* (College Station: Texas A&M University Press, 1991).

Donald E. Chipman

ÁLVAREZ DE PINEDA, ALONSO (?–1520). Alonso Álvarez de Pineda commanded a Spanish expedition that sailed along the Gulf of Mexico coastline from Florida to Cabo Rojo, Mexico, in 1519. He and his men were the first Europeans to explore and map the Gulf littoral between the areas previously explored by Juan Ponce De León[qv] and Diego Velázquez. Álvarez de Pineda's voyage of "more than 300 leagues" ended when he encountered Hernán Cortés, who perceived him as a rival and arrested the messengers he sent ashore near Cortés's base at Villa Rica de la Vera Cruz on the Bay of Campeche. Álvarez de Pineda then withdrew back up the Mexican coast to the Río Pánuco, where he established a settlement of his own near the site of the future city of Tampico. Despite his pioneering exploration, however, Álvarez remains a shadowy figure. The only original source connecting his name with the reconnaissance ordered in 1519 by Francisco de Garay,[qv] Spanish governor of Jamaica, is Bernal Díaz del Castillo, historian of the Mexican conquest. Díaz was present when Cortés confronted Garay's four ships in late July or early August 1519 and relates that Álvarez de Pineda was in command of the vessels. Both Díaz and Cortés, who fails to mention the captain's name, reveal that Álvarez de Pineda already had been in contact with the natives on the Pánuco, and Díaz says that he was settling there.

No account of the voyage itself, by either Álvarez or Garay, has come to light. Garay's report to the Spanish crown, however, is summarized in a 1521 royal *cédula* granting him the territory, called Amichel, that Álvarez de Pineda had explored in his name. Although the document identifies neither Álvarez nor other participants in the voyage, it comprises the only extant description of the exploration. The four ships, carrying 270 men, sailed from Jamaica by late March 1519—about six weeks after Cortés had sailed from Cuba on the expedition that led to the conquest of Mexico. The stated purpose of Álvarez de Pineda's voyage was to explore the coast between the discoveries of De León on the Florida peninsula and those made on behalf of Velázquez along the southern Gulf, in hope of finding a strait to the Pacific Ocean. After clearing the Yucatán Channel, which separates Cuba and the mainland, the ships continued north until the Florida panhandle was sighted, then turned east, expecting to find the passage that was supposed to separate the "island of Florida" from the mainland. The ships probably neared the end of the Florida peninsula before contrary wind and strong current forced them to turn about, then sailed west and south along the coast until they found Cortés's nascent settlement of Villa Rica, the first European settlement on the North American mainland.

Álvarez de Pineda thus proved that Florida was not an island, as De León had reported it to be in 1513. On or about the feast day of Espíritu Santo (Pentecost), which fell on June 2 in 1519 by the Julian calendar, Álvarez registered the discharge of a mighty river and named it, for the religious occasion, Río del Espíritu Santo. This was the Mississippi, although various writers have attempted to show that it was some other.

Garay's royal *cédula* describes the coast viewed by Álvarez de Pineda only in the most general terms. Although he undoubtedly examined the Texas coast and was, as is so often proclaimed, the first European to do so, there is no precise description that can be definitely linked to his trip.

After their encounter with Cortés, the *cédula* relates, the voyagers sailed six leagues up a "very large and fluent river," the banks of which were populated with forty native villages, and there spent forty days cleaning and repairing the ships. This river has been variously taken for the Rio Grande or the Mississippi. Yet Díaz del Castillo's identification of it as the Pánuco is unequivocal.

When the ships departed for Jamaica—to reach the home port in the late fall of 1519—it seems likely that Álvarez de Pineda and a sizable company remained as settlers. In early January 1520 a ship commanded by Diego de Camargo[qv] set sail from Jamaica with supplies for the Pánuco colony. Upon arrival, Camargo found the settlement besieged by Huastec Indians. Except for sixty colonists evacuated to Villa Rica by Camargo, Álvarez de Pineda and "all the horses and soldiers" were slain.

When the ships of the 1519 voyage returned to Jamaica, the pilots presented Garay with a map sketch of the entire Gulf coast in more or less accurate proportions. This first known map of the Gulf presumably is the one found in Spanish archives by the noted compiler Martín Fernández de Navarrete, attached to a copy of Garay's royal *cédula*. It is housed today in the Archivo General de Indias, Seville.

The Río de las Palmas has often been associated with Álvarez de Pineda and the erroneous conclusion drawn that this was the Rio Grande. Actually, the Río de las Palmas was discovered by Garay in 1523, when he sailed for the Pánuco to renew Álvarez's settlement and was carried off course by contrary wind and current. Numerous maps and documents spanning the colonial period show that the river called Las Palmas in colonial times was the Soto la Marina, in Mexico. Nothing but supposition connects either Álvarez de Pineda or the Río de las Palmas to the Rio Grande.

BIBLIOGRAPHY: Donald E. Chipman, *Nuño de Guzmán and the Province of Pánuco in New Spain, 1518–1533* (Glendale, California: Clark, 1967). Robert S. Weddle, *Spanish Sea: The Gulf of Mexico in North American Discovery, 1500–1685* (College Station: Texas A&M University Press, 1985).

Robert S. Weddle

ÁLVAREZ TRAVIESO, VICENTE (1705–1779). Vicente Álvarez Travieso, a leader of the Canary Islanders,[qv] was born in 1705 on the island of Tenerife, the son of Juan and Catarina (Cayetano) Álvarez Travieso. He joined the Canary Islander migration en route to Texas and married Mariana Curbelo at Cuatitlán, Mexico. After arrival at their new home, San Antonio de Béxar, the *isleños* organized a municipal government, and Álvarez Travieso was elected *alguacil*[qv] *mayor* (chief constable) for life. He soon became a leading spokesman for the colonists and something of a problem for the colonial administration.

When the islanders were refused permission to travel to Saltillo for medical attention, Álvarez Travieso launched a series of lawsuits on behalf of his disgruntled companions. One in 1740 was directed toward securing the labor of mission Indians on the settlers' farms and the right to sell produce to the presidio. The missionaries appealed to the viceroy, however, and managed to retain their privileges. Another celebrated case in 1756 was aimed against the missions' virtual monopoly on lands and water rights around the villa. When Don Vicente's claim to a ranch on the banks of Cibolo Creek was contested by the Quereteran friars at Nuestra Señora de la Purísima Concepción de Acuña Mission, he sued again in 1771. Although the ruling obtained in Mexico City was favorable to the private stockmen of Bexar, it was not implemented, and Álvarez's title to Rancho de las Mulas remained clouded.

This technicality did not keep the Álvarez Travieso clan from vigorously pursuing the stray cattle of the area, many of which were unbranded and had wandered away from neighboring mission pastures.

To stop such "excesses" Governor Vicencio de Ripperdá qv conducted two rustling trials against the ranchers of the San Antonio River valley. Álvarez Travieso died just after these proceedings, on January 25, 1779, and the controversy was left to the younger generation. He and Mariana had eleven children. After her death in 1785, Las Mulas became the property of their son Tomás, who was executor of his father's estate, but other heirs challenged Tomás's rights. Nonetheless, the ranch was deeded to Vicente, son of Tomás, in 1809 and remained in his hands after Mexican independence despite the prominent role that Vicente had played in the revolutionary years against Royalist authority.

BIBLIOGRAPHY: Frederick Charles Chabot, *With the Makers of San Antonio* (Yanaguana Society Publications 4, San Antonio, 1937). Jack Jackson, *Los Mesteños: Spanish Ranching in Texas, 1721–1821* (College Station: Texas A&M University Press, 1986). *Jack Jackson*

ALVIN, TEXAS. Alvin is twelve miles southeast of Houston in northeast Brazoria County, on land originally granted to the Houston Tap and Brazoria Railroad. In the 1860s the Santa Fe Railroad established a flag station near the head of Mustang Slough on its Galveston-to-Richmond branch line. Santa Fe hired Alvin Morgan in 1872 to supervise the loading and shipping of cattle at the stock pens. Morgan built the first house in the area in 1879 and persuaded many travelers to settle there. In 1881 the settlement acquired a post office, and the residents named the community Morgan but renamed it Alvin upon learning of another Morgan, Texas. City folklore recalls Morgan's inseparable companions—a dog, a goose, and a white buzzard. Alvin was incorporated in 1891 and again in 1893.

By the mid-1890s Alvin had experienced a population explosion, with the number of residents increasing from 100 in 1890 to an estimated 2,000 by 1896. Businesses in the community included an ice factory, a pickle works, a cotton gin, a bank, an opera house, six hotels, four churches, and two weekly newspapers. Alvin's economy was based primarily on farming and fruit growing. Methodists organized the first church in Alvin in 1881, and other denominations soon followed: Baptist in 1886, Presbyterian in 1892, Episcopal in 1896, Nazarene in 1934, and Lutheran in 1938. Alvin's first public school classes met in the Methodist church building, but by the 1890s the school had facilities of its own. In 1910 the community raised funds for a two-story brick schoolhouse. Alvin became an independent school district in 1925. A community college opened at the high school in 1949 but moved to a separate campus in 1963.

Alvin had a population reported at 3,087 in 1940 and 3,701 by the mid-1950s. The community's economic growth was based on livestock, poultry, dairying, agriculture, jasmine, oil, natural gas, and petrochemicals. During World War II qv businessmen persuaded the United States government to place an internment camp in Alvin. About 500 Germans from the camp worked in the local canning factory and rice fields for two years.

Between 1960 and 1970 Alvin grew 89 percent, from 5,643 to 10,671. In addition to the public schools and community college, it had several private schools and more than 100 civic organizations. Alvin had 100 acres set aside for parks and recreational facilities in 1980. In 1988 the population stood at 18,484; in 1990 it was 19,220. Annually, from July through November, the city braces for floods, hurricanes, qv and tornadoes. qv The Galveston hurricane of 1900 qv destroyed or damaged most Alvin businesses and homes. In 1979 hurricane Claudette dumped forty-three inches of rain near Alvin within twenty-four hours, a state record. Four years later Alicia, generally called the most expensive storm in American history, battered the Alvin area (*see also* WEATHER).

At least two Alvinites have achieved widespread recognition. Dr. F. R. Winn, an Alvin resident, was nationally praised for his 1898 Cuban Report to Theodore Roosevelt and his eyewitness newspaper report of the battle of Santiago. His distinguished record as medical corpsman in World War I qv brought international recognition and requests for assistance from foreign governments. Alvin's baseball superstar Nolan Ryan pitched for New York and Los Angeles before signing with the Houston Astros; qv he finished his career with the Texas Rangers qv in 1993, having set many major-league records.

BIBLIOGRAPHY: Ida M. Blanchette, *Babe on the Bayou* (Waco: Texian Press, 1979). *Ida M. Blanchette*

ALVIN COMMUNITY COLLEGE. Alvin Community College was established in 1948 as Alvin Junior College. The college and the Alvin Independent School District had the same boundaries. The system's 6-4-4 plan, which provided six grades in elementary school, four grades in junior high, and four grades in high school and college, was the first such plan in Texas. The registrar was elected president of the Texas Junior College Teachers Association in 1950, and in 1951 AJC was chosen to participate in a Kellogg Foundation cooperative program. In 1959 the Southern Association of Colleges and Secondary Schools granted AJC full membership. Two years before court-ordered integration, the college provided adult education for blacks.

With the implementation of additional programs in 1965, expansion was necessary. In 1966 the college moved to its new million-dollar plant on its sixty-acre campus, and the first Texas prison extension program began at the Ramsey Unit in Rosharon with AJC faculty teaching sixty inmates on Saturdays. By 1983 the college's inmate enrollment was more than 1,000.

During the 1970s two new programs brought distinction to the college. The Texas legislature provided a special appropriation to establish a court-reporting program in 1975. Within a decade it became the largest department of the college and was attracting students nationwide. In 1978 Alvin Junior College, in cooperation with the University of Texas at Austin, became the first community college in the United States involved in geothermal exploration.

In 1971 AJC became a separate administration and tax district. An elected board of trustees assumed the management, control, and operation of the district and in 1975 approved an $8 million bond issue for major expansion. The college was renamed Alvin Community College in 1976. ACC continues to expand its programs and to increase its enrollment. The college is respected for its University Parallel and Occupational-Technical programs, which prepare students for universities and for skilled job markets. It is also involved in community services. ACC facilities are available for community use, even as a disaster shelter. In January 1994 the college had an on-campus enrollment of 3,466 and an additional 801 students enrolled through programs with the Texas Department of Criminal Justice (*see* PRISON SYSTEM).

BIBLIOGRAPHY: Ida M. Blanchette, *Babe on the Bayou* (Waco: Texian Press, 1979). *Ida M. Blanchette*

ALVORD, TEXAS. Alvord is on U.S. Highway 287/81 ten miles northeast of Decatur in northeast Wise County. Settlement began there in the early 1880s. The community, originally called Nina, adopted its present name in 1882 in honor of the president of the Forth Worth and Denver Railway Company. A post office was established there in 1882. By the time the town was incorporated eight years later, it had become a prosperous retail center for area farmers. In 1925 Alvord had 1,376 residents, a high school, an elementary school, four churches, and a weekly newspaper; the Burlington-Northern Railroad stopped there. The town was also the site of a Magnolia Petroleum Company qv pumping station. The population of Alvord declined as the Great Depression qv reduced the number of nearby watermelon farms and livestock ranches. In 1940 the residents numbered 821 and the businesses thirty-five. Twenty years later the population was 720, and the businesses had declined to nineteen. In 1990 Alvord had 1,112 residents and sixteen businesses.

BIBLIOGRAPHY: Rosalie Gregg, ed., *Wise County History* (Vol. 1, n.p: Nortex, 1975; Vol. 2, Austin: Eakin, 1982). *David Minor*

AMALADEROS CREEK. Amaladeros Creek, also known as Arroyo Amaladeros, rises a mile southeast of Mount Gillion Church in southeastern Nacogdoches County (at 31°36′ N, 94°26′ W) and flows southeast for eleven miles to its mouth on Attoyac Bayou, one mile east of Chireno (at 31°29′ N, 94°19′ W). The stream is intermittent in its upper reaches. It traverses flat terrain with local shallow depressions, surfaced by clay and sandy loam that supports water-tolerant hardwoods, conifers, and grasses. Amaladeros is believed to be a misspelling of the Spanish word *amoladero*, "grindstone," and the creek may have been named for the stones along its banks.

AMANDA, TEXAS. Amanda, also known as Olds, was on the Texas and New Orleans Railroad sixteen miles northwest of Brackettville in far west central Kinney County. The community was established in the 1880s as a rail supply point for Mexican sheep ranchers and named for Amanda Dignowity, wife of a prominent local landowner. A post office operated between 1888 and 1890; G. N. Farrar served as postmaster and railway agent. In 1890 Amanda had an estimated population of twenty-five and two general stores. The community appears to have been abandoned by 1909. *Ruben E. Ochoa*

AMANGUAL, FRANCISCO (c. 1739–1812). Francisco Amangual, soldier, was born on Majorca about 1739. He entered the Spanish army in 1762 and served two years in the Batavian Regiment of Dragoons and fourteen years in the Spanish Regiment of Dragoons. After distinguishing himself in a cavalry company in the Sonora expedition of 1767–71, he was stationed at San Antonio de Béxar Presidio, Texas, where he became paymaster in 1784. In 1797 he commanded an unsuccessful pursuit of Comanche Indians who had raided the cattle ranch at Nuestra Señora del Refugio Mission. Later he was elected alferez of his company at La Bahía.[qv] He was ordered to guard the coast against invasion at the time of the Philip Nolan[qv] expedition of 1800 and escorted Nolan's captured companions to Saltillo. In 1804–05 Amangual captained the Company of San Carlos de Parras at La Bahía. He had charge of the finances of the military hospital in Bexar for a brief period before his resignation in March 1808. Between March 30 and December 23, 1808, he led an expedition of 200 men from San Antonio to Santa Fe, through the Comanche country, and back by way of El Paso. After his return he retired with the rank of captain. He was married three times. He died on May 19, 1812.

BIBLIOGRAPHY: Bexar Archives, Barker Texas History Center, University of Texas at Austin. Carlos E. Castañeda, *Our Catholic Heritage in Texas* (7 vols., Austin: Von Boeckmann–Jones, 1936–58; rpt., New York: Arno, 1976). *A. P. Nasatir*

AMARGOSA, TEXAS. Amargosa (Armagosa) is a mile off U.S. Highway 281 and eight miles northwest of Alice in northwestern Jim Wells County. It was originally a ranch settlement on Amargosa Creek, owned by Manuel Barrera of Mier, Tamaulipas, Mexico, who received title to the Tinaja de Lara grant on September 28, 1836. By 1849 Amargosa was a prominent South Texas ranch, well-stocked with sheep, goats, and horses, and dealing in wool and hides. During the early 1850s, however, repeated Indian raids forced the occupants to leave. In 1852 Hamilton P. Bee[qv] and associates took over the ranch, but in 1854 Barrera's heirs won back the land in a suit. Amargosa had grown into a settlement of 100 residents by 1877, when a school was established to serve forty children. When the San Antonio and Aransas Pass Railway bypassed Amargosa in 1898, the town lost its importance as a trade center. Its school stayed in operation and became the Amargosa common school district, but the name was changed to El Carro in 1926. In 1935 another school was built four miles north of the original and was named Armagosa. In 1965 two fort-shaped houses from the old Amargosa were still in the area. Amargosa was shown on a 1989 map of the area with its original spelling. In 1993 it was a dispersed rural community with a cemetery and a quarry. *Amargosa* is Spanish for "bitter." *Agnes G. Grimm*

AMARGOSA CREEK. Amargosa Creek rises two miles south of Mendita in northeastern Duval County (at 27°57′ N, 98°15′ W) and runs southeast for eleven miles to its mouth on Chiltipin Creek, eleven miles northeast of San Diego in northwestern Jim Wells County (at 27°54′ N, 98°08′ W). The stream is dammed four miles above its mouth. *Amargosa* means "bitter" in Spanish. The creek crosses flat to gently rolling terrain with local shallow depressions, surfaced by clay and sandy loams that support scrub brush and grasses.

AMARILLA MOUNTAIN. Amarilla Mountain is four miles northeast of Lajitas in southwestern Brewster County (at 29°19′ N, 103°45′ W). The summit rises to 3,013 feet above sea level. The name, which means "yellow" in Spanish, probably refers to the yellowish color of the mountain, which results from the mixture of iron oxides and clay minerals in the soils. Amarilla Mountain lies deep within the Chihuahuan Desert. The surrounding vegetation, characteristic of Chihuahuan Desert scrub, includes various shrub species and semisucculents such as lechuguilla, sotol, yucca, ocotillo, and the ubiquitous creosote bush.

AMARILLAS, AGUSTÍN AHUMADA Y VILLALÓN, MARQUÉS DE LAS (?–1760). Agustín Ahumada y Villalón, Marqués de las Amarillas, the forty-second viceroy (1755–1760) of New Spain, was born in Spain, probably in the last years of the seventeenth century. Before his arrival in New Spain, he had been governor of Barcelona and lieutenant colonel of the Regiment of Royal Guards. Military experience in Italian campaigns had also earned him a measure of fame. He arrived in Mexico City at a critical juncture for Spanish Texas.[qv] Attempts to expand missionary enterprises beyond San Antonio had collapsed on the San Gabriel River, and the Franciscans[qv] had already redirected their missionary efforts toward the Lipan Apaches on the San Saba River. The new viceroy saw no reason to depart from that course. On April 29, 1756, Amarillas summoned Father Alonso Giraldo de Terreros,[qv] a veteran missionary, to a conference in Mexico City. When the two men met on May 9, the viceroy informed Terreros that his cousin, Pedro Romero de Terreros,[qv] was considering sponsorship of missions for the Apaches. The two priests worked out details, which were formalized by the viceroy. Subsequently a new presidio, San Luis de las Amarillas, was founded on the San Saba River in 1757 and named for the viceroy.

Amarillas also directed Spanish settlement of the lower Trinity River basin. In response to French penetration of this region, he called for the establishment of a garrison of thirty soldiers and a supporting mission manned by two friars from the Franciscan missionary college at Zacatecas. The viceroy also deemed it advisable to found a villa populated by fifty families, but that proviso was never realized. Near what is now Anahuac in Chambers County, another presidio named for the Marqués, San Agustín de Ahumada, took shape in 1756. The Marqués de las Amarillas likewise directed the founding of Santa Cruz de San Sabá Mission, which was established in 1757. One year later, Comanches and their northern allies attacked the mission and totally destroyed it. Under express orders of the viceroy, a punitive campaign of 1759, led by Col. Diego Ortiz Parrilla,[qv] sought vengeance against the offending Indians. News of Parrilla's defeat on the Red River came near the end of Amarilla's tenure. He died at Cuernavaca in 1760; his interment was at the Santuario de la Piedad. He had profited so little from government service that he left his widow, the Marquesa de las Amarillas, without means of subsistence, forcing her to return to Spain where she was provided for by the generosity of Archbishop Rubio y Salinas. The military garrisons in Texas that had been named in honor of Amarillas were both abandoned in 1770.

BIBLIOGRAPHY: Donald E. Chipman, *Spanish Texas, 1519–1821* (Austin: University of Texas Press, 1992). *Diccionario Porrúa de historia, biografía y geografía de México* (3d ed., 2 vols., Mexico City: Editorial Porrúa, 1970, 1971). Robert S. Weddle, *San Juan Bautista: Gateway to Spanish Texas* (Austin: University of Texas Press, 1968).

Robert S. Weddle, *The San Sabá Mission* (Austin: University of Texas Press, 1964). *Donald E. Chipman*

AMARILLO, CATHOLIC DIOCESE OF. The Catholic Diocese of Amarillo comprises twenty-six counties in the Panhandle;[qv] the southern boundary of the diocese is the line that forms the southern boundary of Childress, Hall, Briscoe, Swisher, Castro, and Parmer counties. In 1993 the Catholics of the area numbered 36,795, about 10 percent of the total population.

White settlers entered the Panhandle after the Indians were removed to Indian Territory in 1875. Priests from New Mexico and Kansas served the few Catholics until the Fort Worth and Denver Railway crossed the Panhandle in 1887, and priests came up from Gainesville, Texas. The first Catholic church in the Panhandle, St. Mary's at Clarendon, was built in 1892 for a congregation of predominantly Irish and German railroad employees. The Sisters of Charity of the Incarnate Word,[qv] the first nuns to work in the Panhandle, established a school, St. Mary's Academy, in Clarendon in 1899 and St. Anthony's Sanitarium in Amarillo in 1901. Father David Henry Dunn moved church headquarters from Clarendon to Amarillo, the railroad crossroads, in 1902. At the breakup of the big ranches, Catholic farming parishes were established, largely by settlers of German descent. First among these was that at Nazareth, founded in 1903, and by 1913 there were thirteen such rural Catholic parishes around Amarillo. After irrigation with underground water developed in West Texas, Catholic Hispanic migrant laborers moved to the area. When the gas and oil industry grew in the Panhandle and the Permian Basin,[qv] Catholic parishes were formed in the oil towns of Borger and Pampa.

In 1926 the church responded to the influx of people by establishing the Diocese of Amarillo, which included the Panhandle and the area as far south as Kimble, Sutton, and Crockett counties, for a total of 70½ counties. The first bishop, Rudolph A. Gerken[qv] (1927–33), built churches and schools and founded Price Memorial College, now Alamo Catholic High School. The diocesan Catholic Charities opened in 1932. Bishop Robert E. Lucey[qv] (1934–41) established the diocesan newspaper in 1936. A mission to black Catholics was opened in 1940. A diocesan Council of Catholic Women was organized. When Lucey was made archbishop of San Antonio in 1941, Bishop Laurence J. FitzSimon[qv] replaced him in Amarillo. After World War II[qv] West Texas experienced a surge in economic growth, which the church shared. Facilities expanded. Hispanic families coming to work in cotton and vegetable fields settled down in towns. Between 1945 and 1965, forty predominantly Hispanic parishes were established in the Lubbock area alone. FitzSimon established a Catholic Children's Home in the town of Panhandle. When FitzSimon died in 1958, John L. Morkovsky,[qv] auxiliary bishop since 1955, was made bishop of Amarillo. During his tenure (1958–63) St. Ann's Nursing Home was built in Panhandle. New demographics, however, reduced the size of the diocese. Growth led to the establishment of the Diocese of San Angelo[qv] in 1961, when the 21½ southernmost counties of the Diocese of Amarillo were transferred to the new diocese.

Morkovsky, transferred to the Diocese of Galveston-Houston,[qv] was followed in 1963 in Amarillo by Bishop Lawrence M. DeFalco,[qv] who introduced reforms issuing from the Second Vatican Council. A Diocesan Pastoral Council, a Priests' Senate, and a Sisters' Council were formed. By authority of Vatican II the permanent diaconate, which had fallen into disuse in the church centuries earlier, was reestablished. During the same period a program for refugees was developed, and St. Joseph's Home for retired priests was built in Panhandle. After the death of Bishop DeFalco in 1979, Leroy T. Matthiesen became bishop of Amarillo in 1980. He built the Bishop DeFalco Retreat Center, brought contemplative Franciscan nuns to Amarillo, and established the seminary of Missionaries of Christ the Priest. He also had the Museum-Archives Building constructed.

In 1983 the twenty-three southern counties of the diocese were transferred to the new Diocese of Lubbock.[qv] In 1993 the Diocese of Amarillo included forty-two parishes and missions and seventeen chapels, served by sixty-eight priests and thirty permanent deacons. One religious brother and 154 religious sisters worked in the diocese. The diocese had one Catholic high school and eight elementary schools.

BIBLIOGRAPHY: Archives of the Catholic Diocese of Amarillo. John Michael Harter, *The Creation and Foundation of the Roman Catholic Diocese of Amarillo, 1917–1934* (Amarillo: Catholic Historical Society of the Diocese of Amarillo, 1975). Sister M. Nellie Rooney, A History of the Catholic Church in the Panhandle-Plains Area of Texas from 1875 to 1916 (M.A. thesis, Catholic University of America, 1954).

Sister Nellie Rooney, O.S.F.

AMARILLO, TEXAS. Amarillo, commercial center of the Texas Panhandle, is in southern Potter County and extends into Randall County. When the Fort Worth and Denver City Railway began building across the Panhandle[qv] in 1887, a group of Colorado City merchants chose the site to establish stores. In April 1887 J. T. Berry arrived from Abilene to plat the new town. He chose a well-watered section of school land, located along the FW&DC right-of-way in Potter County, which contained a large playa known as Amarillo, or Wild Horse, Lake.[qv]

Berry and the Colorado City merchants sought to make their new townsite the Potter county seat and the region's main trade center. Since most of the qualified voters were LX Ranch[qv] employees, Berry enlisted the ranchers' support by promising each cowhand a business lot and residence lot in the new town if it should be chosen county seat. On August 30, 1887, Berry's townsite was elected for that honor. The settlement was originally called Oneida but was by majority consent renamed Amarillo after the nearby lake and creek. These natural features had been named by New Mexican traders and *pastores*,[qv] probably for the yellow soil along the creek banks or the yellow wildflowers that were abundant during the spring and summer. Charles F. Rudolph,[qv] editor of the Tascosa *Pioneer*, blamed the FW&DC employees for ignoring the word's Spanish pronunciation; in 1888 he prophetically stated, "Never again will it be Ah-mah-ree-yoh." Most of the town's first houses were painted yellow in commemoration of the name change.

The railroad arrived shortly after the county election, and by October 1887 freight service was made available. Amarillo boomed as a cattle-marketing center. Holding grounds, complete with pens, were built near the tracks to corral the numerous herds that came from ranches in the Panhandle, South Plains, and eastern New Mexico for shipment. A post office was established in 1887 with Robert M. Moore as postmaster. George S. Berry soon replaced Moore, and the office was moved to Berry's real estate office nearby. By the spring of 1888 the patent to Berry's townsite had been obtained. Eight other men, including William Buford Plemons,[qv] John Hollicott, and Warren W. Wetzel, held equal interest in it. After the passenger station and freight depot were built near the FW&DC tracks, people from nearby townsites began moving to Amarillo. H. T. (Tuck) Cornelius, formerly of Jacksboro, operated the town's first livery stable. His father, Dr. J. C. Cornelius, was the first physician in Amarillo, and on June 18, 1888, Tuck's daughter Mayvi became the first child born in Amarillo. Meanwhile a lumberyard and a twenty-five-room hotel were established, and H. H. Brookes began publication of the town's first weekly newspaper, the Amarillo *Champion*, on May 17, 1888. Bonds were voted for a two-story brick courthouse to replace the small frame building and for Amarillo's first school. On May 29 town lots were sold to the public by auction. People were brought in by excursion trains. Most of the lots sold for $50 to $100 each.

Although Berry's cowtown seemed to be well established, Henry B. Sanborn,[qv] part owner of the Frying Pan Ranch,[qv] argued that Berry's site was on low ground that would flood during rainstorms. Sanborn and his partner, Joseph F. Glidden, began buying land to the east to move Amarillo out of its "mudhole." On June 19, 1888, they purchased four sections and offered to trade lots in the new location for those in the original site and contribute to the expense of moving buildings. Sanborn's enticements gradually won over people like Tuck Cornelius and H. H. Brookes, who moved their businesses to Polk Street in the new commercial district. Sanborn erected the elegant, forty-room Amarillo Hotel, which became the town's social center and the unofficial headquarters of area cattle buyers. He also donated a half-block for Amarillo's first union church. In the spring of 1889, when heavy rains almost flooded "Old Town," the railroad embankment prevented effective drainage and prompted more people to move to Sanborn's higher location. Despite a successful lawsuit filed against Sanborn by the Murphy-Thomason-Wisner interests over ownership of block 88, even the county and city officials eventually joined the cattlemen's project; by 1890 the town's nucleus was one mile east at the city's Glidden and Sanborn addition. That year the First National Bank opened for business, and the three Wolfin brothers from Gainesville established a mercantile store. In 1891 Phillip H. Seewald moved from Tascosa and opened a jewelry store. The depot and courthouse remained at the old site, since the law decreed that they could not be moved until five years after the 1887 election. In 1893 another county-seat election officially transferred the title to Sanborn's town, and the records were housed in a newer building there. In the meantime the FW&DC had installed a second depot at the Polk Street crossing for the convenience of passengers. By 1894 Amarillo had three newspapers: H. H. Brookes's *Livestock Champion*, Frank Cates and A. R. Rankin's Amarillo *Northwest*, and J. L. Caldwell's Amarillo *Weekly News*. Ellwood Park, the first of Amarillo's many city parks, was established in the 1890s. Three churches were constructed during the decade, and other denominations organized local congregations. From 1897 to 1899 Willis Day Twichell[qv] operated Amarillo College in a building donated by the Sanborn family; the public school met at the former old-town courthouse until late in 1900, when a three-story red-brick school opened. On February 18, 1899, the citizens of Amarillo voted to incorporate and elected Warren W. Wetzel mayor. However, the inauguration of city government was restrained by injunctions, and municipal administration was carried on by county officials and Texas Rangers[qv] for a while. The first annual Tri-State Fair was held in Amarillo in the fall of 1899.

By 1890 Amarillo had emerged as one of the world's busiest cattle-shipping points. The population grew from 482 in 1890 to 1,442 by 1900. Construction of the Southern Kansas, the Pecos and Northern Texas, and the Chicago, Rock Island and Gulf railroads by 1903 added to the shipping facilities and helped to increase the population to 9,957 by 1910. The sudden influx of people with the railroads resulted in the rise of Amarillo's Bowery district, notorious for its saloons, brothels, and desperadoes; crime there was commonplace, but after prohibition[qv] was imposed in 1911 the Bowery faded away. In 1902 the two-story St. Anthony's Hospital, the first hospital in the Panhandle, was erected; it served the entire area. Electrical service also came that year with the establishment of the Amarillo Light and Water Company, precursor to Southwestern Public Service. The Amarillo Independent School District was formed in 1905, and by the following year a new stone courthouse and jail were completed, after a bitter court battle over ownership of the courthouse square. The Amarillo Street Railway Company began operating its electric streetcar lines in January 1908. Amarillo Academy operated from 1904 to 1907, the first Amarillo College closed in 1910, and the Amarillo Public Library was founded by the Just Us Girls (JUG) Club. The Grand Opera House opened in 1909. In 1913 a second hospital, Northwest Texas, was added. St. Mary's Academy, Amarillo's first Catholic school, opened in 1914, the same year the Board of City Development was formed. Increasing production of wheat and small grains made Amarillo an elevator, milling, and feed-manufacturing center during the early 1900s. Prior to the railroad's extension into the South Plains area, cotton farmers often brought their produce to Amarillo for shipment.

Industry and culture developed in Amarillo after World War I.[qv] Gas was discovered in 1918 and oil three years later. The Panhandle added a zinc smelter, oil refineries, and oil-shipping facilities. In 1928 the discovery of the Cliffside gas field, with its high helium content, led to the establishment of the United States Helium Plant by the Federal Bureau of Mines four miles west of town (*see* HELIUM GAS PRODUCTION). Two United States Army Signal Corps biplanes commanded by Lt. Robert H. Gray arrived at Amarillo on April 27, 1918. Lee Bivins,[qv] W. E. Fuqua, and others promoted the aviation[qv] industry, and in 1929 the Panhandle Air Service and Transportation Company was established; at one time Amarillo had five airfields, including the Municipal Airport. By 1924 automobiles and buses had made Amarillo's streetcar system obsolete. In 1926 Eugene A. Howe and Wilbur Clayton Hawk[qqv] bought the Nunn family's Amarillo *News* and merged it with the *Globe* to form the Amarillo *Globe-News*.[qv] J. Lawrence Martin started Amarillo's first radio station, WDAG, in 1922; a municipal auditorium was completed in 1923; a twelve-piece Philharmonic Orchestra was formed in 1925; and the Amarillo Little Theater was organized in 1927. The Bivins addition became the first suburban extension in southwest Amarillo. In 1928 Rudolph Aloysius Gerken,[qv] the first bishop of the Catholic Diocese of Amarillo,[qv] opened Alamo Catholic High School, and the following year Amarillo Junior College began at the Municipal Auditorium with 350 students.

The 1930s brought drought and black dusters to Amarillo (*see* DUST BOWL). However, the city was a regional center for numerous federal relief programs, especially the Work Projects Administration,[qv] whose funds helped improve Amarillo streets, water, and sewerage facilities. The popularity of Art Deco architecture was reflected in several new public buildings, including the Santa Fe Building, headquarters of the Panhandle and Santa Fe Railway, and the new Potter County Courthouse. Howe made news with his "Tactless Texan" column and merged the competing WDAG and KGRS radio stations as KGNC. The arrest and suicide of attorney Alfred D. Payne made national headlines in the summer of 1930, while Ernest Othmer Thompson[qv] was mayor. Payne had pleaded insanity in the murder of his wife in an auto explosion, partly because of financial problems and an extramarital affair. In 1934 Cal Farley[qv] founded the Maverick Club for underprivileged boys; from that program later grew Kid, Incorporated. Amarillo College moved to its present campus on Washington Street in 1938. Between 1930 and 1940 the Amarillo High School football team won several district titles and four state championships. Four U.S. highways—60, 87, 287, and the fabled Route 66—merged at Amarillo, making it a major tourist stop with numerous motels, restaurants, and curio shops. Although many local oil companies folded during the Great Depression,[qv] the firm of Hagy, Harrington, and Marsh was formed in 1933 with offices in Amarillo.

By 1940 Amarillo's population numbered 51,686. A United States veterans' hospital was built west of the city. During World War II[qv] Amarillo Army Air Field[qv] was a school for basic pilot training, and the nearby Pantex Ordnance Plant (*see* PANTEX, TEXAS) produced bombs and ammunition. The influx of servicemen and their families and the new jobs ended the city's depression and boosted its chamber of commerce. On May 15, 1949, a tornado killed seven people and caused damage estimated at $2.5 million (*see* TORNADOES). Between 1950 and 1960 Amarillo grew 85 percent, from 74,443 to 137,969. In 1951 the city's first television station began broadcasting. S. B. Whittenburg published the Amarillo *Times*, which he merged with the *Globe-News* when he and his associates bought the company in 1955. During the late 1960s a municipal building, a civic center, a branch library, a corporation court building, High Plains Baptist Hospital, and a multimillion-dollar medical center were built. The closing of Amarillo Air Force Base on December 31, 1968, contributed to a decrease in population to 127,010 by 1970. In September 1970 the Texas State Technical Institute opened a campus on the former base grounds.

The 1970s saw the opening of the Amarillo Art Center[qv] on the AC campus, the establishment of the Amarillo Copper Refinery of ASARCO, Incorporated, and the opening of the Donald D. Harrington Discovery Center, which contains the first computer-controlled planetarium in the nation. Iowa Beef Processors and Owens-Corning Fiberglass also built plants at Amarillo. By 1980 Amarillo had a population of 149,230 and encompassed in its city limits more than sixty square miles in Potter and Randall counties. At that time it had 164 churches, forty-seven schools, five hospitals, nine radio stations, and four television stations. Between 1969 and 1986 new oil companies were formed, and as oil prices dropped, seven mergers occurred; Mesa Petroleum Company, headed by T. Boone Pickens, Jr., became one of the nation's largest oil firms.

Gas, petroleum, agriculture, and cattle are Amarillo's principal sources of income. In 1982 the 2,708 local businesses included petrochemicals, grain storage, processing, meat packing, clothing, feed, leather goods, and cement manufacture. The Helium Monument, located near the Harrington Discovery Center and containing time capsules, designates Amarillo the "Helium Capital of the World." In the 1980s the Santa Fe and Burlington National railroads provided freight service, and Amarillo International Airport served five major airlines. New housing developments and shopping centers in south and west Amarillo followed the completion of Interstate Highway 40, and during the 1980s Interstate 27 was constructed from Lubbock to Amarillo. In 1988 Amarillo was the home of the world's largest feeder-cattle auction and headquarters of the American Quarter Horse Association, which publishes a monthly magazine, the *Quarter Horse Journal* (*see* QUARTER HORSE). Accent West, Incorporated, headed by Don Cantrell, published its monthly *Accent West* magazine. Amarillo was home for such celebrities as country music pioneer Alexander C. (Eck) Robertson and Thomas A. Preston, Jr., better known among card players as Amarillo Slim. Actresses Carolyn Jones[qv] and Cyd Charisse and humorist Grady Nutt[qv] spent their early years in Amarillo, which was celebrated in song by George Strait's "Amarillo by Morning." In 1990 the population of Amarillo was 157,615.

BIBLIOGRAPHY: Lana Payne Barnett and Elizabeth Brooks Buhrkuhl, eds., *Presenting the Texas Panhandle* (Canyon, Texas: Lan-Bea, 1979). J. R. Hollingsworth, "Trail and Travail of an Editor, or 'I'll Do Anything for Block'," *Panhandle-Plains Historical Review* 48 (1975). Della Tyler Key, *In the Cattle Country: History of Potter County, 1887–1966* (Amarillo: Tyler-Berkley, 1961; 2d ed., Wichita Falls: Nortex, 1972). David L. Nail, *One Short Sleep Past: A Profile of Amarillo in the Thirties* (Canyon, Texas: Staked Plains, 1973). Thomas Thompson, *North of Palo Duro* (Canyon, Texas: Staked Plains, 1984).

H. Allen Anderson

AMARILLO AIR FORCE BASE. Amarillo Air Force Base, originally Amarillo Army Air Field, was activated in April 1942 and formally named an army air field in May. It was eleven miles east of Amarillo on a 1,523-acre tract of land adjacent to English Field, a commercial airfield serving the Panhandle.[qv] Col. Edward C. Black, the first commanding officer, arrived in April 1942 with the first cadre of troops. Construction was only half completed when the first classes were begun in September 1942. The field, one of the largest installations in the Western Technical Training Command, was established for training of air crew and ground mechanics to service B-17 aircraft. From 1943 to 1945 basic training and special courses of instruction were conducted, and the school was later designated to train technicians for B-29 aircraft in addition to the B-17 technical training. Flying operations were also inaugurated. The field was closed on September 15, 1946, and its buildings were converted to peacetime uses or destroyed.

The base was reactivated as Amarillo Air Force Base in March 1951 and became the first air force all-jet mechanic-training base. In December 1951 the first trainees from foreign countries arrived. By 1952 the program reached a planned maximum of 3,500 students. Mechanic training continued throughout 1953 and 1954 and included a course on the B-47 jet bomber. The base was declared a permanent installation in 1954. Four new courses were added a year later, and the number of students climbed to about 5,000. When the two-phase system of basic training began in 1956, Amarillo Air Force Base was selected as one of the bases to administer the technical second phase. The base continued to grow in the late 1950s. In 1957 a missile-training department was established, and facilities were expanded to accommodate an air wing of the Strategic Air Command. In July 1958 a supply and administration school previously stationed in Wyoming was moved to the Amarillo base. The base was redesignated Amarillo Technical Training Center in 1959, when the 4128th Strategic Air Wing concluded a joint-tenancy agreement with Air Training Command.

By May 1960 the jet-mechanic school had graduated 100,000 students. At that time Amarillo was the site of all Air Training Command resident training in administrative, procurement, and supply fields; it continued to train thousands of jet aircraft mechanics, jet engine mechanics, and air-frame repairmen. The center changed in February 1966 with the formation of the 3330th Basic Military School. A personnel-processing squadron was added the same month to support the school. In 1967 the center's facilities covered 5,273 acres and had about 16,300 assigned personnel.

By 1964 the United States Department of Defense had decided to close the base. The last class was graduated on December 11, 1968, and the base was deactivated on December 31, 1968. The closing damaged the economy of Amarillo. On September 2, 1970, the Amarillo branch of Texas State Technical Institute[qv] was opened on the former base grounds. Another part of the base was used for the Amarillo Air Terminal, which opened on May 17, 1971.

BIBLIOGRAPHY: B. Byron Price and Frederick W. Rathjen, *The Golden Spread: An Illustrated History of Amarillo and the Texas Panhandle* (Northridge, California: Windsor, 1986).

Ross Phares and Paul O. Cormier

AMARILLO AREA FOUNDATION. The Amarillo Area Foundation, based in Amarillo, is a nonprofit charitable organization dedicated to improving life in the Panhandle.[qv] During the early 1990s the area served included twenty-six counties. In 1988 Mrs. Sybil Harrington changed the status of her family's private foundation, the Don and Sybil Harrington Foundation,[qv] to public and turned over its control to the Amarillo Area Foundation. This gave the latter, which had assets of about $25 million, control over a much larger supporting foundation, with assets of about $73 million. These combined assets make the foundation one of the largest community foundations in the country. During the early 1990s all grant proposals were reviewed by the Amarillo Area Foundation's twenty-five-member board of directors. Proposals not funded were then passed on with recommendations to be reviewed by the seven-member Harrington Foundation board; four of those seven board members were also members of the Amarillo Area Foundation board. The Harrington and Amarillo Area foundations share these four board members and also share the position of president and executive director; in all other regards the two foundations function separately. In 1994 the Amarillo Area Foundation emphases included public education, child care, youth development, and the elderly. In the 1990s the Foundation initiated Achievement through Commitment to Education, a community-supported scholarship program guaranteeing every qualified student from Palo Duro High School access to a college education. ACE included the formation of informal supportive coalitions of diverse ethnicities and social and civic institutions as a base for neighborhood self-help action. ACE was intended to benefit the student who had never considered a college education a possibility. In 1994 the Amarillo Area Foundation offices were at First National Place I in Amarillo, and the foundation's director was Jim Allison.

BIBLIOGRAPHY: Vertical Files, Barker Texas History Center, University of Texas at Austin (Don Harrington).

AMARILLO ART CENTER. The Amarillo Art Center, located on the campus of Amarillo College, opened in 1972 under the sponsorship of the Amarillo Art Center Association, which was founded in 1966. The first chairman of the board of trustees was Betty Bivens Childers. This board cooperated with regents and the administration of Amarillo College to build a $2.2 million arts complex designed by Edward Durell Stone that consisted of three buildings. One of these buildings houses the Amarillo Art Center; it contains five exhibition galleries placed around an atrium, labs for ceramics and sculpture, an art reference library, and service areas and offices in a total usable space of over 32,000 square feet.

Amarillo College owns the building and provides the salary of the director. All acquisition programs, exhibitions, seminars, and classes are the responsibility of the board of trustees. Operating funds are raised by the board and the staff. Two volunteer organizations, the Amarillo Art Alliance and the Docent Council, assist the paid staff in raising funds and operating the center. Additional support for the center has been provided by the Texas Commission on the Arts[qv] and other government grants and an endowment fund initiated by Betty Bivins Childers. The Amarillo Art Center has been fully accredited by the American Association of Museums since 1979 and is also a member of the Texas Association of Museums.[qv]

The exhibition program sponsors traveling and original exhibits in all media and styles. Among the exhibits that have been displayed since 1972 are Legendary Costumes of the Metropolitan Opera (1984), Archeological Treasures of Ancient Egypt (1982), Early French Moderns (1982), Eight Modern Masters (1985), and Georgia O'Keeffe[qv] and her Contemporaries (1985). Each year at least twenty changing exhibits are presented. The center encourages emerging artists by offering exhibits to selected individuals each year. Some artists who had their first single exhibitions at the Amarillo Art Center include Melissa Miller and Jesús Batista Moroles.

The permanent collection has been assembled from gifts by collectors and artists and focuses on twentieth-century American art. In 1986 the collection numbered just under 500 pieces. In the collection are works by Georgia O'Keeffe, Franz Kline, Fritz Scholder, Elaine de Kooning, Larry Bell, Jack Boynton, Larry Calcagnyo, Martin Schrieber, Warren Davis, Arthur Rothstein, Dorothea Lange, Edward Steichen, Walker Evans, Alfred Stieglitz, Russell Lee,[qv] Luis Jiménez, Ellio Porter, Jeanne Reynal, and others.

Each year the center mounts seminars relating to exhibitions that attract scholars and artists from around the nation. In recent years Clement Meadmore, Walter Horn, Karl Kilinski, John Canaday, Philip Perlstein, and Marilyn Swezey have presented lectures. An education program offers preschool through adult classes in painting, drawing, weaving, ceramics, papermaking, caligraphy, and sculpture. The center sponsors an annual Jubilee of the Arts festival at which regional artists and craftsmen exhibit and sell their work and a Very Special Arts Festival for disabled children.

BIBLIOGRAPHY: Amarillo *Sunday News-Globe*, January 18, 1976, August 22, 1982. Dallas *Morning News*, September 10, 1972. Clara Thornhill Hammond, comp., *Amarillo* (Amarillo: Autry, 1971; 2d ed., Austin: Best Printing, 1974). Vertical Files, Barker Texas History Center, University of Texas at Austin. *Al Kochka*

AMARILLO COLLEGE. The original Amarillo College grew out of several college-level classes conducted in Amarillo by Willis D. Twichell.[qv] In 1897 Twichell and James D. Hamlin[qv] purchased two store buildings and moved them to a four-block tract. The buildings were made into an assembly hall and four classrooms, and simple equipment was installed. Four directors of the new institution chose Hamlin as the president, and when the school opened in September he, Twichell, Maud Tannehill, and Mrs. James Bolton composed the first faculty. At the beginning of the second semester Twichell retired, and Hamlin induced four former classmates from the University of Kentucky to join the faculty; one of them, Russell Briney, combined his teaching duties with his pastorate of the local Disciples of Christ church. Although none of the faculty received stated salaries, all shared the school's revenue, which was derived wholly from the tuition fee of five dollars a month per pupil. The ambitious curriculum included natural sciences, history, Latin, Greek, English, an introductory course in law, and classes in physiology and hygiene. Mrs. Bolton headed the music department.

Hamlin resigned the presidency in 1909, and Briney continued the institution for one more year. In 1910 Hamlin sold the buildings to S. S. Lightburne, who moved them near the old Potter County Courthouse and converted them to offices. The four-block campus was reconveyed to Henry B. Sanborn[qv] for a consideration of $600. The site, now occupied by the post office and Federal Building, is in the heart of the city of Amarillo, although at the time of its operation the college was a mile from town.

BIBLIOGRAPHY: James D. Hamlin, *The Flamboyant Judge: As Told to J. Evetts Haley and William Curry Holden* (Canyon, Texas: Palo Duro, 1972). *James D. Hamlin*

AMARILLO COLLEGE. The later Amarillo College was established in 1929 as Amarillo Junior College. Amarillo had failed in earlier efforts to get a state college and in 1929 was the largest city in Texas without a public college. Amarilloans, led by George Ordway and James O. Guleke,[qv] introduced a house bill that established junior college districts; Amarillo Junior College was the first college established under this act. Governor Daniel J. Moody[qv] signed the bill on April 2, 1929, and Amarillo began its campaign on April 3, 1929. The college started in September 1929 with B. E. Masters as president and was accredited rapidly, in April 1930 by the Association of Texas Colleges and Universities[qv] and in 1933 by the Southern Association of Colleges and Secondary Schools.

Vocational courses were offered in the 1930s, when a specific demand developed, but the college had no continuing programs. In 1939, in line with Southern Association recommendations that the junior colleges begin to stress vocational courses, a flying school was established to train pilots under the authority of the Civil Aeronautics Administration, and in 1941 a National Defense Vocational Training School was started to supply personnel to defense industries during World War II.[qv] After the war all programs expanded steadily. A technical school was established in 1960 and a biomedical school in 1967.

In 1951 Amarillo College became the first publicly supported college in Texas to admit blacks to undergraduate classes. It began courses in radio in 1949 and in television in 1956 in its own studios. In 1962 it became the first junior college in the state to offer courses in data processing, and for many years it was the only college in the state offering a major in photographic technology. It was among the first to have Bible chairs established adjacent to the campus. In 1965 AC was the only junior college in the eleven southern states accorded a commendation of excellence by the Southern Association. In 1984, after twelve years of work by Richard Howard and the biology department, Amarillo College opened the largest natural history museum of any two-year college in the country, with a public collection valued at over $1 million and a research division that includes over 26,000 identified insects, plus hundreds of spiders, plants, mammals, birds, fish, reptiles, and other specimens.

On campus is the Amarillo Art Center,[qv] a three-building complex (art museum, museum building, and concert hall) designed by Edward Durrell Stone Associates. The center, opened in 1972, provides a major focus for the arts. The library has a large southwestern collection and is a member—along with West Texas A&M University, the Texas Tech medical school branch in Amarillo (*see* TEXAS TECH UNIVERSITY HEALTH SCIENCE CENTER), and the public libraries of Amarillo and Canyon—of the Harrington Library Consortium. The Amarillo College Foundation, established in 1962, had grown to $1 million by August 1985.

From seven faculty members and eighty-six students the first year, Amarillo College grew by 1984 to 220 full-time and 471 part-time faculty members. Full-time enrollment in fall 1990 was 5,952; the college enrolled many additional students in trade-related short courses and community-service classes. Classes were first held in a wing of the municipal auditorium. In 1937 the college moved to its own campus. In 1985 there were three campuses in Amarillo, satellite campuses in Hereford and Dumas, and classes in Tulia, Dimmitt, and Canyon. The college had a teacher-exchange program with West Texas A&M and maintained cooperative programs with Clarendon College, Frank Phillips College, West Texas A&M, and the Texas Tech medical branch in Amarillo. West Texas A&M and Amarillo College cooperate in a photographic technology program.

BIBLIOGRAPHY: Joe F. Taylor, *The AC Story: Journal of a College* (Canyon, Texas: Staked Plains, 1979). *Joe F. Taylor*

AMARILLO *DAILY NEWS.* The Amarillo *Daily News* was an outgrowth of the Amarillo *News,* first published as a weekly in 1894, the Amarillo *Weekly News,* which appeared in 1898, and the Amarillo *Evening News,* which began as a daily in 1899. In 1909 Delbert Davenport and W.A. Allen moved to Amarillo from Kansas and started the *Evening American.* William Beck of Indiana bought an interest in the paper, and a plant was established at Fifth and Tyler streets. A new Amarillo corporation seeking to promote prohibition[qv] acquired the paper, and it was subsequently published, beginning on November 4, 1909, as the Amarillo *Daily News.* This paper, which absorbed the Amarillo *Daily Tribune* and the *Daily Panhandle,* was produced by the Amarillo Publishing Company, claimed to be independent, and called itself the "morning newspaper of the golden spread." Among the incorporators of the Amarillo Publishing Company were Dr. J. E. Nunn, president; W. A. Askew, secretary; and J. W. McGammon, editor. Other owners included R. E. Underwood and J. W. Crudgington. Financial troubles forced a foreclosure sale of the publication in 1912, after which it was purchased by J. W. Williams and Willis D. Twichell.[qv] At a second foreclosure in 1916, the paper was returned to one of its original owners, J. E. Nunn, whose son, J. Lindsay Nunn,[qv] became publisher and general manager in the fall of 1920. In January 1926 Eugene A. Howe[qv] and his associates, then publishers of the Amarillo *Globe,* acquired the paper; they soon combined the two as companion morning and afternoon newspapers and named the operation the Globe-News Publishing Company. In 1955 S. B. Whittenburg and associates purchased the company, which by 1966 published the *Daily News* each morning, along with the evening Amarillo *News and Globe-Times*[qv] and the Amarillo Sunday *News-Globe.* In 1967 the Amarillo *Daily News* (the morning paper), the *Globe-Times* (the evening paper), and the Sunday *News-Globe* were sold to the Southwestern Newspapers Corporation. By the 1990s the paper had merged with the Amarillo *Globe-Times* to form the Amarillo *News and Globe-Times,* which had a circulation of about 65,000.

BIBLIOGRAPHY: *Texas Newspaper Directory* (Austin: Texas Press Service, 1991). *Robert W. Wylie*

AMARILLO LAKE. Amarillo Lake, a playa also known as Wildhorse Lake, is within the city limits of Amarillo in southern Potter County (at 35°13′ N, 101°15′ W). Since it was once a relatively dependable source of water, mustangs, buffalo,[qqv] and other game formerly frequented it. It was a landmark for Indians, Comancheros,[qv] Spanish explorers, and trailblazers; Josiah Gregg's[qv] party camped beside it on March 14, 1840. Later, free-range cattle raisers often watered their stock there. These considerations, plus the location of the Fort Worth and Denver City right-of-way, prompted J. T. Berry to plat the original townsite of Amarillo, initially called Oneida, on the section of school land that encompassed the lake. Amarillo Lake, now located between North Hughes and McMasters streets south of Amarillo Boulevard, no longer holds much water because the town's sewage system has diverted most of the surface drainage. The lakebed itself is now marked by shallow depressions and sparse grassy areas in the variable soil. The area surrounding it is flat to gently sloping, with a loose sandy soil that supports scrub brush and grasses.

AMARILLO *NEWS AND GLOBE-TIMES.* The Amarillo *News and Globe-Times* was formed in the 1990s by the combination of the Amarillo *Daily News* and the Amarillo *Globe-Times.* The *Globe,* first published on February 20, 1924, was established by Eugene A. Howe[qv] and associates. On January 12, 1926, the firm acquired the Amarillo *Daily News.* Howe combined the *News* and *Globe* as companion morning and afternoon newspapers, and published them in a newly acquired plant at Sixth and Fillmore. The Globe-News Publishing Company became associated with the Lubbock *Avalanche-Journal* and later with radio and television stations. In November 1951 the afternoon *Globe* merged with another afternoon daily, the Amarillo *Times,* the Amarillo *Globe-Times* resulted. The *Times* had been published since 1937 and was widely known as the only tabloid in Texas. At the time of the merger it became a full-sized newspaper. The morning and afternoon papers had separate staffs, and the editorial policies of the two were independent. S. B. Whittenburg was publisher and editor of the *Globe-Times,* for which T. E. Johnson served as managing editor, and Wesley S. Izzard[qv] was editor of the *Daily News.* In 1955 S. B. Whittenburg and associates, owners of the earlier Amarillo *Times,* purchased the stock of the Globe-News Publishing Company. In 1961 the Amarillo *Globe-Times* received the Pulitzer Gold Award for Community Service for its work under the leadership of editor Thomas Thompson in uncovering corruption in the governments of Potter and Randall counties. In 1966 its circulation reached 91,500, and in 1967 the newspapers moved to new quarters. In that year the papers, including the Amarillo *Daily News* (the morning paper), the *Globe-Times* (the evening paper), and the Sunday *News-Globe,* were sold to the Southwestern Newspapers Corporation. Among the papers' outstanding editors was W. L. (Putt) Powell, a sportswriter, editor, and columnist who began at the paper in 1931 and was later inducted into the Texas High School Sports Hall of Fame. Circulation of the Amarillo *News and Globe-Times* in 1993 was almost 65,000.

BIBLIOGRAPHY: *Texas Newspaper Directory* (Austin: Texas Press Service, 1991). *Diana J. Kleiner*

AMATEIS, LOUIS (1855–1913). Louis Amateis, sculptor, was born in Turin, Italy, on December 13, 1855, the son of Gen. Paolo and Carolina Amateis. He studied architecture at the Institute of Technology and sculpture at the Royal Academy of Fine Arts, both in Turin, and received a gold medal from the Royal Academy for outstanding work. In 1880 he received a silver medal at the National Exposition in Turin. He also studied art in Paris and Milan before immigrating to the United States in 1883. Amateis settled first in New York City, where he did some architectural sculpture, primarily for the firm of McKim, Mead, and White. He married Dora Ballin in New York City on February 24, 1889; they had four sons. After his marriage Amateis moved to Washington, D.C., to found the School of Architecture and Fine Arts at Columbian University (later George Washington University), where he served as chairman of the Department of Fine Arts from 1892 to 1902. Among some of his best known works are the bronze doors (1909) intended for the west main entrance to the United States Capitol, a monument to the heroes of the Texas Revolution[qv] (1900) in Galveston, and busts of such prominent men as President Chester A. Arthur, Gen. Winfield Scott Hancock,[qv] and philanthropist Andrew Carnegie.

Amateis executed a number of monumental works in Texas. Four of his sculptures are in Galveston: the monument to the heroes of the Texas Revolution commissioned by Henry Rosenberg,[qv] a statue of Rosenberg himself (1906), a monument erected over the grave of Maj. Gen. John Bankhead Magruder[qv] (n.d.), and a bronze monument to the Confederate soldiers of the Civil War[qv] located in City

Park (1894–1912). His other works in Texas include Spirit of the Confederacy (1907) in Houston and Call to Arms (1907–08) in Corsicana. The seventy-four-foot-high monument to the heroes of the Texas Revolution in Galveston, with its combination of classical allegory, historical friezes, and portraits of Texas heroes, typifies Amateis's style.

Amateis was represented at the Pan-American Exposition in Buffalo, New York (1901), and the Louisiana Purchase Exposition in St. Louis (1904). He also exhibited his work at the National Academy of Design in New York City and at the Art Society in Philadelphia. He was a member of the Society of Washington Artists, the National Sculpture Society, and the National Art Society. He died on March 16, 1913, in West Falls Church, Virginia, where he maintained a studio. His son, Edmond Romulus Amateis, became a prominent sculptor during the first half of the twentieth century.

BIBLIOGRAPHY: *Dictionary of American Biography.* Peter Haskins Falk, ed., *Who Was Who in American Art* (Madison, Connecticut: Sound View, 1985). Esse Forrester-O'Brien, *Art and Artists of Texas* (Dallas: Tardy, 1935). James M. Goode, *The Outdoor Sculpture of Washington, D.C.* (Washington: Smithsonian Institution, 1974). Patricia D. Hendricks and Becky D. Reese, *A Century of Sculpture in Texas, 1889–1989* (Huntington Art Gallery, University of Texas at Austin, 1989). *Rebecca H. Green and Kendall Curlee*

AMBER UNIVERSITY. Amber University is at the intersection of Interstate Highway 635 and Northwest Highway, in Garland, Texas. It began in 1971 as a branch of Abilene Christian College called ACC Metrocenter. Before it opened its own campus in 1974, most of its classes were held on the campus of the defunct Christian College of the Southwest in Mesquite or at the former campus of Fort Worth Christian College. In its early years the school primarily offered criminal-justice degrees to police officers. This program was phased out by 1978.

When ACC Metrocenter received its own campus in 1974 its name was changed to Abilene Christian College at Dallas. The campus was a two-story, 60,000-square-foot office building with two-thirds of its space leased to other businesses, including a trucking school. In 1976, in order to stay in line with its main campus, which changed its name from Abilene Christian College to Abilene Christian University, ACC Metrocenter was renamed Abilene Christian University at Dallas. On June 1, 1981, ACU Dallas became a separate institution, after its four-year search for its own accreditation. The name Amber University was chosen by a group of students and staff members because they liked the sound of the name.

The university was devoted to the mature student. It described itself as an "independent, non-denominational institution committed to Christian values." As a nonprofit, private institution, it directed all funds from tuition to education rather than athletics or research. No social clubs or athletics were available. No one under the age of twenty-one was allowed to enroll, and the average student age was thirty-seven. Bachelor's and master's degrees were offered in business, management, human behavior, and professional development. Classes primarily met in the evenings and on weekends, and the year was divided into four sessions of ten weeks each. Amber University restricted its enrollment to 1,000 students in order to give them individual attention, and the enrollment stayed near that figure. Enrollment in 1990 was 1,498.

BIBLIOGRAPHY: Dallas *Morning News,* December 18, 1983, August 2, 1987. Donald W. Whisenhunt, *The Encyclopedia of Texas Colleges and Universities* (Austin: Eakin, 1986). *Lisa C. Maxwell*

AMBIA, TEXAS. Ambia, on the Atchison, Topeka and Santa Fe Railroad, Farm Road 1506, and Mallory Creek five miles southwest of Paris in southern Lamar County, was established in 1886 as a stop on the Gulf, Colorado and Santa Fe tracks. A justice of the peace from nearby Roxton named the site Amber because of the streams of tobacco juice spat by chewers at the local store. The post office opened in 1886. In 1890 postmaster John K. Boyd reported a population of twenty-three. His general store was the sole business. By 1892, however, Western Union had opened a local telegraph office, the population was thirty-nine, and two cotton gins, a grocery, and two saloons were open. Postal service was discontinued in 1905. In 1933 Ambia had a population of twenty and two businesses. A common school district had been established by 1936, and maps for that year also identified a church. The number of residents in Ambia peaked at fifty immediately after World War II.[qv] By 1957 the school had been absorbed into the Roxton Independent School District. In 1964 the population was forty-five. From 1974 until 1990 it was reported as twenty. Maps for 1983 showed a community hall.

BIBLIOGRAPHY: Thomas S. Justiss, An Administrative Survey of the Schools of Lamar County with a Plan for Their Reorganization (M.A. thesis, University of Texas, 1937). Fred Tarpley, *1001 Texas Place Names* (Austin: University of Texas Press, 1980).

Vista K. McCroskey

AMBROSE, TEXAS. Ambrose is on Highway 69 six miles southeast of Denison in the far northeastern corner of Grayson County. It is near the site of Old Warren, which is just across the Fannin county line. Ambrose was named after Ambrose Bible, who came to Texas from eastern Tennessee in 1883. He bought land from S. E. Elliott out of the Daniel Montague[qv] survey dated February 20, 1845, and settled in the old Fannin County, out of which Grayson County was formed in 1846. The Denison, Bonham and New Orleans Railway Company bought right-of-way from J. P. N. Haun and Ambrose Bible on March 3, 1887, to run a spur from the Missouri, Kansas and Texas Railroad in Denison. The company's first attempt failed.

On January 10, 1902, land was surveyed, laid out, and mapped for Ambrose, and in September a post office opened with James B. Moore as postmaster. On July 28, 1903, Bible deeded the land for the right-of-way and the station grounds to the original railway company. He donated an entire block for the school, which was built in 1907. The town had three churches—Methodist, Church of Christ, and Baptist. Dr. Frank Miller was the first doctor. Oscar Sanford owned the hardware store, C. D. Jordan the drugstore, and Calmy Brown the bank. The town had a restaurant, a general store, and a blacksmith shop. The farmers shipped cotton, watermelons, sand, and gravel. In 1917 a new school building was erected. In 1919 the town reached its zenith. The population never rose above sixty because the majority of people lived on farms. By 1927 the DB&NO railroad had failed. The post office was moved to Bells in 1930 and served Ambrose on a rural route. In 1940 the school was consolidated with that of Bells. The census in 1980 reported a population of forty-one and no businesses in Ambrose. The school building was being used as a community center. The population was still forty-one in 1990.

BIBLIOGRAPHY: Grayson County Frontier Village, *History of Grayson County, Texas* (2 vols., Winston-Salem, North Carolina: Hunter, 1979, 1981). *Leslie Keith*

AMEDICHE INDIANS. The Amediche (Nabiti, Naviti, Namidish) Indians were a Hasinai group of Caddos who lived near the Anadarkos in East Texas. According to Bénard de La Harpe[qv] the Spanish established a temporary settlement among them, and they were at war with the Natchitoch Indians from 1714 to 1716.

BIBLIOGRAPHY: Frederick Webb Hodge, ed., *Handbook of American Indians North of Mexico* (2 vols., Washington: GPO, 1907, 1910; rpt., New York: Pageant, 1959). *Margery H. Krieger*

AMELIA, TEXAS. Amelia, formerly a separate community, is at the junction of Farm Road 364 and U.S. Highway 90 in western

Beaumont, northern Jefferson County. The Amelia post office was established in 1885 on the Texas and New Orleans Railroad. A section house built by the Southern Pacific system was located at Amelia. Soon after the construction of the Beaumont, Sour Lake and Western Railway in 1903, a depot in Amelia was named Elizabeth, in honor of Elizabeth McClain, daughter of a nearby resident.

The Amelia oilfield, established in 1936, had 114 producing wells by 1939. The Sun Oil Company established a geophysical lab at Amelia in 1948, and moderate amounts of crude oil continued to be recovered there through the mid-1980s. The Amelia schools were consolidated with Beaumont's South Park Independent School District in 1949. Amelia voters incorporated their town in August 1955 by a vote of 146 to 108. Less than three months later, however, they voted 129 to 79 to abolish the corporation. The city of Beaumont annexed Amelia in 1957. In the mid-1980s the Amelia area, once known as Corn Street, was a center for rice growers; a rice warehouse was located there, as was an agricultural extension station operated by Texas A&M University since 1911.

BIBLIOGRAPHY: WPA Federal Writers' Project, *Beaumont* (Houston: Anson Jones, 1939).

Robert Wooster

AMERICAN ASSOCIATION OF UNIVERSITY WOMEN. The Texas branch of the American Association of University Women, a network of women and men who have a bachelor's or higher degree, was formed in Dallas in October 1926. The national organization of AAUW was organized in Boston, Massachusetts, in 1881 to open graduate education to women. Ten local community groups had formed before the state organized in 1926 with Jessie Daniel Ames[qv] as its first president. Assisted by national committees and a national headquarters staff of professionally trained educators, committees of the Texas division worked with local branches in the state in a program for practical educational work. Early goals included improvement of rural schools and extension of the Sheppard-Towns Act. The founders believed that education was the key to achieving equity for women of all ages, races, creeds, and nationalities.

In 1994 Texas had 5,000 members in seventy branches. AAUW has examined the fundamental issues of the times—educational, social, economic, and political—and has taken action, often far ahead of popular opinion. The association spoke out early for racial integration and against McCarthyism, supported Margaret Sanger and *Roe v. Wade*,[qv] and lobbied to remedy injustices from child labor to modern pay inequities. Its vision is equity and education for women and girls. In 1991, AAUW launched the *Initiative for Educational Equity*, a long-term, comprehensive effort to eliminate systematic gender bias in American schools and set the stage for concrete solutions; and *Hostile Hallways: The AAUW Survey on Sexual Harassment in America's Schools*, the first scientific national survey on sexual harassment in American public schools.

AAUW turns credible research into grassroots action to make tomorrow's classrooms more equitable by organizing community meetings, mentoring girls, conducting math-science institutes, and working with educators to develop new approaches. The philanthropic arm of AAUW is its Educational Foundation, which was formed in 1886. AAUW members raise millions of dollars each year to support the foundation. In 1993, $2.75 million was awarded to women through national and international fellowships, grants, and awards. The foundation has helped more than 6,000 women reach their personal and professional goals. Named endowments for Texans include those for Ida Green, Jessie Daniel Ames, and Charlotte Wyatt. AAUW's Legal Advocacy Fund was formed in 1981 to provide funding and a support system for women seeking judicial redress for sex discrimination in higher education. LAF helps students, faculty, and administrators challenge discriminatory practices involving sexual harassment, denial of tenure or promotion, and aid for women's athletics programs. The AAUW's international connection is the International Federation of University Women, which provides a worldwide forum where university women from fifty-nine nations interact on international issues. The federation is committed to improve the status of women and girls.

BIBLIOGRAPHY: *AAUW Journal*, January 1911. *AAUW Outlook*, January–February 1989. American Association of University Women, *Bulletin of the Texas Division*, May 1930, September 1936.

Betty Anderson

AMERICAN COUNCIL OF SPANISH SPEAKING PEOPLE. The American Council of Spanish Speaking People was a national Mexican-American civil-rights organization founded in 1951, based in Austin, and funded by the Robert C. Marshall Trust Fund of New York. It provided grants-in-aid, legal assistance, and research to Mexican-American civil rights groups across the nation. In 1943 the Marshall Trust had funded the Texas Civil Rights Fund, a group concerned with policies affecting Mexican Americans. Its members included George P. Sánchez,[qv] and attorney M. C. Gonzales[qv] collaborated with the group. By the 1950s Sánchez reported that Mexicans and Indians were "orphans" to foundations and were ignored by the NAACP, the National Council on Naturalization and Citizenship, and the National Council of Agricultural Life and Labor. In 1952 the chairman of the American Civil Liberties Union, Roger Baldwin, who had ties to the Marshall Fund, contacted and funded Lyle Saunders of New Mexico to help establish a Spanish-American association that would be self-sustaining. Saunders contacted Sánchez, who assembled organizers in El Paso on May 18 and 19, 1951. Those attending elected Sánchez executive director. The name American Council of Spanish Speaking Persons reflected the Marshall Fund's hope to promote unity among the "Spanish-American" community, in which it included Puerto Ricans and Cubans. The foundation believed that the Latino community needed visibility. The first board of directors included New Mexico lieutenant governor Tibo Chávez; Arturo Fuentes, the national president of the Alianza, which was especially strong in Arizona; Los Angeles publisher Ignacio López; Anthony Ríos of the Community Service Organization; and Bernard Valdez, Director for Community Councils in Colorado. Representing Texas were attorney Gustavo C. García[qv] and Sánchez. Valdez was initially elected secretary but became treasurer for the organization's duration.

The Marshall Trust Fund granted $53,000 over four years. Associate, regular, and contributing patrons contributed less than $1,000. The fund expected ACSSP to become self-supporting, but Sánchez noted that the indigenous organizations were "still too poor." The ACSSP opened its office in downtown Austin at the Nalle Building and moved to the Driskill Hotel[qv] in 1953; when funds were short in 1954 it moved to the Littlefield Building at the University of Texas. Paid staff included Sánchez, director; Ed Idar, Jr., assistant director and state chairman of the Forum; Abraham Ramírez; and Luisa Solís, secretary. García served as legal consultant.

Despite the Marshall Trust's wishes, ACSSP directed its money and efforts to the area it believed deserved attention: litigation, especially test cases to challenge discriminatory practices. ACSPP gave grants-in-aid to fund specific cases, including a segregation case in Glendale, Arizona; *Hernández v. State of Texas* (1954); the Anthony Ríos police brutality case in Los Angeles (1954); the Robert Galvan alleged Communist alien deportation case in California (1954); and the Winslow, Arizona, swimming pool desegregation case (1954). In Texas ACSSP helped desegregate Austin and Houston public housing and Zavala and Nixon schools (1951). It also funded school desegregation cases in Carrizo Springs (1955), Mathis (1956), and Driscoll (1957) and worked on the Federico Gutiérrez case in Beeville, for which it covered traveling expenses for lawyers and consultants. Lawyers who collaborated with ACCSP included Gonzales, John J. Herrera,[qv] Chris Alderete, Albert Peña, Jr., James De Anda, Carlos Cadena, Ricard M. Casillas,

Carlos Castillon, and, outside of Texas, A. L. Wirin of the ACLU in Los Angeles.

ACSSP funded and assisted *Raza* organizations. In its attempt to empower other organizations and strengthen the national cause, ACSSP's strategy was to give credit to local and state organizations for its work. This was especially true for the Forum and the Alianza. ACSSP made grants-in-aid to the CSO, the Colorado Latin-American Conference, and the Alianza. In 1954–55 the Alianza received $5,000. ACSSP also worked with the Mexican-American Council of Chicago. ACSPP can be credited with providing leadership, legal advice, and research for litigation involving desegregation and racial discrimination. Sánchez, Idar, and García volunteered much of their time. ACSPP maintained a newsletter in 1953. The ACSPP offices closed in 1956, and in 1958, when funding ceased, the council also ceased operations.

BIBLIOGRAPHY: George I. Sánchez Papers, Benson Latin American Collection, University of Texas at Austin. *Cynthia E. Orozco*

AMERICAN DAM. American Dam is located on the Rio Grande at El Paso, 140 feet north of where the Mexican border leaves the river and goes overland toward the Pacific Ocean. On May 21, 1906, the United States and Mexico signed a treaty for "an equitable distribution of the waters of the Rio Grande." To carry out the treaty, the United States Bureau of Reclamation built Elephant Butte Dam on the Rio Grande at Truth or Consequences, New Mexico, 125 miles north of El Paso. Impounding the water at the dam guaranteed Mexico a maximum of 60,000 acre-feet of Rio Grande irrigation water a year, available on demand, to be delivered at the main irrigation canal in Ciudad Juárez, Chihuahua, known as the Acequia Madre. The canal's mouth is two miles downstream from the international border. The remainder of the water would be used by American farmers in the ninety-mile-long El Paso valley. In times of drought both Mexican and American shares would be reduced on a percentage basis.

The system did not provide a way for the United States to allot Mexico its rightful portion and keep the rest. As a result, Mexico took its share first and channeled the remainder into the Franklin Canal for the farms in the El Paso valley. According to some American estimates this permitted Mexico to siphon off up to three times its portion of irrigation water. Responding in 1935, Congress authorized two diversionary projects, the American Dam and the American Canal. The dam caught the water in New Mexico short of the international border, measured Mexico's share and allowed it to continue to the Acequia Madre, and diverted everything else into the American Canal, a two-mile feeder leading to the Franklin Canal. The project has proved a successful solution to the problem of dividing the waters.

BIBLIOGRAPHY: J. C. Day, "Urban Water Management of an International River: The Case of El Paso–Juarez," *Natural Resources Journal* 15 (July 1975). *Leon C. Metz*

AMERICAN ENTERPRISE FORUM. The American Enterprise Forum, a nonprofit organization promoting free enterprise and economic education, began as the Hill Country Project, a cooperative educational effort organized in 1948 for school superintendents in Travis, Burnet, Lampasas, and San Saba counties. Its organizers, who included J. E. Edgar, then Austin superintendent of schools and later Texas Commissioner of Education, thought that "progressive education" did not adequately stress traditional values. Teachers in the cooperating schools prepared and exchanged lesson plans emphasizing freedom, patriotism, the Judeo-Christian ethic, and the importance of the individual. The organization was incorporated as the Texas Bureau for Economic Understanding, a nonprofit educational corporation, on June 10, 1954. R. H. Lawrence served as executive director of the corporation until his death in September 1969. He was succeeded by Leon Blair. The bureau operated through regional American Heritage programs, supervised by local school officials, which encouraged the development of students' academic and leadership skills. In 1973 the legislature required public schools to teach economics with an emphasis on free enterprise. In February 1974 the bureau organized a symposium in Austin to define the parameters of the free-enterprise system and inaugurate an instructional program for teachers. At one time some twenty Texas universities used the bureau's instructional program. The bureau showed an increased interest in fostering historical awareness and heritage programs in the 1970s and 1980s. In 1983 the bureau had a budget of $388,150 and sponsored a variety of educational programs, including an economic awareness conference, regional history conferences for secondary school students, and teacher workshops. It also provided financial support for a number of publications, including the *Texas Historian,* the journal of the Junior Historians of Texas[qv] and *Touchstone,* the journal of the Walter Prescott Webb Historical Society.[qv] In 1987 Blair retired, Sheridan Grace Nichols took over as executive director, and the name of the organization was changed to the American Enterprise Forum. The group continued to promote the study of economics at the secondary-school level. Between 1987 and 1994 the forum provided more than $2 million in scholarships for teachers to return to school for further education in the social sciences. Among its board members at different times were Richard Armey, Texas congressman and speaker of the house, members of the Dealey family of Dallas, and Congressman Jim Collins. The American Enterprise Forum ceased operations in 1994.

Leon B. Blair

AMERICAN ENVIRONMENTAL HEALTH FOUNDATION. The American Environmental Health Foundation, in Dallas, was founded in 1975 by William J. Rea of the Environmental Health Center to promote environmental medicine, a branch of medical science dedicated to the study and treatment of adverse environmental effects. It was first named the Human Ecology Research Foundation of the Southwest. The foundation is funded by private donations and endowments and an international medical conference, the International Symposium on Man and His Environment in Health and Disease. It had an office staff of four in 1992. Services have included publications on environmentally triggered diseases, products designed for sensitive individuals, and referral and information services. The foundation also funds research projects to help physicians diagnose and treat environmentally induced illness and publishes semiannual and quarterly newsletters. *Kim L. Rice*

AMERICAN G.I. FORUM OF TEXAS. On March 26, 1948, 700 Mexican-American veterans, led by Hector P. Garcia, met in Corpus Christi and organized the American G.I. Forum, a civil-rights organization devoted to securing equal rights for Hispanic Americans. The first issue the forum dealt with was the failure of the Veterans Administration to deliver earned benefits through the G.I. Bill of Rights of 1944. After securing those benefits, the forum addressed other veterans' concerns, such as hospital care and Mexican-American representation on draft boards. In 1949 the director of the Rice Funeral Home in Three Rivers refused the use of his chapel for the funeral of Private Felix Longoria (*see* FELIX LONGORIA AFFAIR). Garcia and the Corpus Christi forum organized a widespread protest that gained national attention. Eventually, through the intervention of Lyndon B. Johnson,[qv] Longoria was buried in Arlington National Cemetery. The incident in Three Rivers established the forum as an effective civil-rights advocate for Hispanics and expanded the scope and nature of its activities.

The organizational structure promoted this goal. The local chapter was the basic unit; the membership of each local chapter had to be 75 percent veterans. Beyond the local chapter were the district, state, and (after 1958) national governing bodies. In some areas, auxiliary (female) and junior G.I. forums developed. The charter of each unit emphasized loyalty and patriotism. The forum also prohibited official endorsement of a political party or candidate. This sanction blunted possible charges of bloc voting. Skills and experience developed in the forum were, however, applied by members in political campaigns.

In 1954 forum lawyers, in conjunction with attorneys for the League of United Latin American Citizens,[qv] successfully argued before the Supreme Court in *Hernández v. State of Texas*[qv] that Mexican Americans,[qv] although technically classified as Caucasian, suffered discrimination as a class and were entitled to the protection of the Fourteenth Amendment. In 1957 the Texas forum ended a ten-year struggle when a federal court agreed that school segregation of Mexican-American children in Texas schools was unjustified. In the same decade the forum helped thousands of Mexican Americans in the Rio Grande valley to register to vote, and incidents of police brutality were confronted in forum efforts. Health care and veterans' needs remained important concerns, as did scholarship donations, back-to-school drives, and the problems of migrant workers.

In 1958 the American G.I. Forum became a national organization, and its members led Mexican Americans into national politics. In the 1960 presidential campaign Viva Kennedy–Viva Johnson clubs,[qv] administered by forum and LULAC leaders, helped to win Texas and New Mexico for John F. Kennedy. Robert Kennedy stated that the Spanish-speaking vote won the election for his brother. Although the Kennedy administration did not reciprocate with much federal aid, the Johnson administration did. The G.I. Forum played a significant role in the application of Great Society programs in the barrios, and for the first time Latin Americans were appointed to influential positions and agencies. When Johnson established the first cabinet-level office for Hispanic issues, he selected a former national chairman of the G.I. Forum, Vicente Ximenes, for the position. The American G.I. Forum continued its work through the 1970s with such efforts as the first application of the due-process clause of the Fourteenth Amendment to de facto Mexican-American school segregation in Corpus Christi. In 1983 Garcia received an award for distinguished accomplishment from President Ronald Reagan.

BIBLIOGRAPHY: Carl Allsup, *The American G.I. Forum: Origins and Evolution* (University of Texas Center for Mexican American Studies Monograph 6, Austin, 1982). Carl Allsup, "Education Is Our Freedom: The American G.I. Forum and Mexican American School Segregation in Texas, 1948–1957," *Aztlán* 8 (Spring–Summer–Fall 1977). Robert Cuellar, *A Social and Political History of the Mexican American Population of Texas, 1929–1963* (San Francisco: R and E Research Associates, 1974). Chris F. Garcia and Rodolfo O. de la Garza, *Chicano Political Experience: Three Perspectives* (North Scituate, Massachusetts: Duxbury, 1977).

V. Carl Allsup

AMERICAN G.I. FORUM WOMEN'S AUXILIARY. The American G.I. Forum of Texas[qv] established its Women's Auxiliary at the first national conference of the Forum in 1956. A group of female members led the movement to formalize the supportive roles that women already played in the organization. Women's involvement in the Forum's activities had always been considered natural because the organization stressed the Mexican-American family, in which women were central, as a major source of its strength. In the earlier years of the Forum, women had helped raise funds by such activities as *tamaladas* (tamale sales), dances, and "queen" contests. When the organization expanded its role beyond Mexican-American veterans' matters to larger civil-rights issues, women led some of its membership and voter-registration drives and became lobbyists for equal-opportunity legislation. In Texas Dr. Clotilde García, a physician and teacher and the sister of Dr. Hector P. García, founder of the Forum, became an example for other women in leading Forum activities.

With the establishment of the auxiliary, women were able to become leaders and help define the Forum's mission. In 1957 the auxiliary organized a women's leadership conference, an unusual move at the time. By running their own caucus, women gained political skills and contributed to the Forum's success in rallying Mexican-American support for its struggle against prejudice. The auxiliary members set up scholarships for Mexican-American students and developed community or women's education. In most cases, the women were interested in equalizing opportunities for all Mexican Americans[qv] rather than advancing a feminist agenda.

The auxiliary continued to involve its members in public issues through conferences on the state legislative process. In addition, it used the Forum's newsletter, *The Forumeer Today*, to bring members' attention to both the needs of the developing female Hispanic labor force and the great increase in the numbers of Hispanic female immigrants. The Women's Auxiliary predated Mexican-American women's involvement in the Democratic and Republican parties and foreshadowed their contributions to the Chicano[qv] Movement.

BIBLIOGRAPHY: Henry A. J. Ramos, *A People Forgotten, A Dream Pursued: The History of the American G.I. Forum, 1948–1972* (N.p.: American G.I. Forum, 1983).

Teresa Palomo Acosta

AMERICAN GENERAL CORPORATION. American General Corporation, headquartered in Houston and parent of the American General Life Insurance Company, is one of the nation's largest insurance and financial-services organizations. It incorporated in Houston in 1926 as the American General Insurance Company, a fire and casualty insurance business, with Gus Sessions Wortham as president and John W. Link[qv] as chairman of the board. Wortham, a Houston native, learned the business at the John L. Wortham and Son Agency, founded in 1915 by his father. When his father died, Wortham responded to a new ruling by the Commission of Appeals of Texas that enabled him to organize one of the nation's first multiple-line insurance companies, or firms permitted to underwrite both fire and casualty insurance. Initially the agency managed the new company, absorbed its costs of expansion, and directed business to it.

American General paid a dividend in 1929 and every year thereafter. The company grew in the 1930s despite the Great Depression[qv] and by 1936 had capital and surplus exceeding a million dollars. Diversification began in 1939, when the company established its first subsidiary, the American General Investment Corporation, to finance real estate, automobiles, and other purchases. By that time the company was licensed to operate in nine states and had assets of over $2 million. Further diversification in 1945 resulted in the acquisition of Seaboard Life Insurance Company, a Houston-based life and health insurance company that did business solely in Texas. Burke Baker[qv] served as president and R. H. Baker,[qv] formerly of Equitable Life Insurance Company of New York, as chairman.

Benjamin N. Woodson, a former managing director of the National Association of Life Underwriters and later American General president, joined the firm in 1953. Before his retirement as chairman and chief executive officer in 1978, Woodson expanded the company into national markets. Between 1954 and 1964 American General acquired a fire and casualty company in Marshall, Texas, and life insurance companies in Hawaii, Nebraska, Oklahoma, and Pennsylvania, and in the 1960s it diversified into financial services other than insurance, including the distribution of mutual funds, mortgage banking with real estate subsidiaries, the sale of variable annuities and title insurance, equipment leasing and financing, and investment counseling. In 1964 it acquired the Commercial and Industrial Life Insurance Company of Houston and the Maryland Casualty Company of Baltimore, a property and liability company founded in 1898. The acquisition made American General a major property and casualty insurer and expanded its reach to every state and Canada. Company headquarters on Buffalo Bayou in Houston were completed in 1965.

American General acquired the Patriot Life Insurance Company of New York in 1966 and between 1975 and 1982 made thirteen divestitures and twelve acquisitions, among the latter the Variable Annuity Life Insurance Company, an innovator in sales of tax-deferred annuities to the employees of nonprofit organizations. In 1968 it acquired the Life and Casualty Insurance Company of Nashville, a regional insurer with $1 billion in assets, and a majority interest in California–Western States Life Insurance Company, whose leader, Harold Swanson Hook, joined the firm in 1975. By 1974 American General, with $674 million of capital and surplus, was the largest financial organization in Texas. As the company's third president, Hook embarked on a new growth program that brought twenty new firms into the company and nearly tripled its size.

In 1980 American General Insurance Company became a general-business holding corporation to simplify its regulatory environment and reflect its evolving structure. The American General Corporation, as this parent company was named, coordinated the operation of company subsidiaries throughout the decade as it developed a reputation for buying other insurance companies and profitably assimilating them. In 1982 Hook completed a merger with NLT, the parent company of the National Life and Accident Insurance Company of Nashville, Tennessee, and entered the consumer-credit business by acquiring Credithrift Financial of Indiana. He also acquired the General Finance Corporation and Gulf United Corporation's insurance properties. By this time the company employed 13,205 workers and had assets of over $32 billion dollars. American General moved to new corporate headquarters in 1985. In 1988 the company doubled its consumer-finance operations by acquiring the consumer-finance division of Manufacturers Hanover, but in 1989 sold its property-liability segment to a Swiss-based insurer and group life and health insurance operations to Associated Insurance Companies.

In 1991 American General merged California–Western States Life Insurance Company into a subsidiary, the American General Life Insurance Company of Delaware. American General Corporation is the parent company of a number of subsidiaries. In the 1990s, with $23 billion in assets, American General offered home-service insurance, special-markets insurance, and the services of a finance and real estate division. It continued to obtain more than half its earnings from door-to-door insurance sales and employed 16,000 workers and 48,000 agents and salesmen.

bibliography: *American General Corporation: History, 1926–1986* (Houston: American General Corporation, 1986). Benjamin N. Woodson, *Financial Services Supermarket: The American General Story* (New York: Newcomen Society in North America, 1974).

Jason M. Olson

AMERICAN HISTORY CLUB. On December 1, 1893, eight women met in the Austin home of Mrs. Thomas F. Taylor to form a club for the study of American history and literature. Mrs. Taylor had been a newspaper correspondent and drama critic in Washington, D.C., who on her return to Austin in 1883 foresaw the good influence women could exert in a community. At the first meeting a temporary organization was set up, membership was limited to fifteen, and a bylaws committee and program committee were appointed. At the second meeting Mrs. Taylor was elected president, and the constitution was adopted. Meetings were held every other week, a practice that lasted until World War II.[qv] Members presented papers and answered roll call with information on the topic of study.

In 1897 the club printed a yearbook that listed programs presented during the organization's first five years. In that same year the club became a charter member of the newly established Texas Federation of Women's Literary Clubs. On March 5, 1897, the treasurer purchased a trunk for $1.50. All papers were to be placed in the trunk, and any member who failed to deposit her paper would be fined one dollar. The trunk was kept by members until it was placed in the Austin Travis County Collection, now the Austin History Center.[qv]

Membership limits had increased to twenty-five by 1914 and were eventually set at thirty. Interests of the club broadened to include the arts and civic, educational, and philanthropic concerns, as well as history. The club's contributions were important in establishing the Texas Federation of Women's Clubs[qv] headquarters in Austin, in increasing the number and quality of recitals and art lectures at the University of Texas, in establishing Big Bend National Park,[qv] and in endowing the Austin Public Library. The club lobbied for increased school taxes in 1902 and for improved dairy sanitation in 1915. Between 1925 and 1929 the club worked with a women's-club organization that acquired the Ira H. Evans[qv] home for the Austin Woman's Club. With the advent of World War II, the club's lecture topics began to reflect an interest in international affairs; papers were presented on Germany, China, Japan, and the Soviet Union. This trend continued into the 1950s and early 1960s, when lecture topics included United States relations with Latin America and Canada, the Middle East, Africa, the Caribbean, and Southeast Asia, and the exploration of space. By the mid-1960s, however, the club returned to more traditional themes drawn from early American history, biography, and culture. Afterward, club fare reflected an interest in science, medicine, technology, and social issues.

bibliography: American History Club Papers, Austin History Center.

Helen B. Frantz

AMERICAN INDEMNITY. The American Indemnity Company, headquartered in Galveston, offers insurance in Texas and twenty-seven states, primarily in the South. It was incorporated in 1913, the first stock-casualty company incorporated under Texas statutes, by Joseph F. Seinsheimer, who had founded the Seinsheimer Insurance Agency in 1901. The first president of American Indemnity was Sealy Hutchings, and Seinsheimer served as general manager until 1920. Seinsheimer became president after Hutchings resigned in 1931 and was succeeded by his son, J. F. Seinsheimer, Jr., in 1951. In 1931 American Indemnity became a "multiple line insurer," able to write all lines of insurance except life. The company expanded into departments: American Fire and Indemnity Company, founded in 1936; Texas General Indemnity Company, which grew from a company founded in 1919; American Computing Company, founded in 1973; and American Indemnity Lloyds, organized in 1983. In 1973 the firm organized a holding company, American Indemnity Financial Corporation, to assume financial control, but in the 1990s remained under the direction of the Seinsheimer family with J. F. Seinsheimer III as president and chief executive officer. At that time, the company wrote 80 percent of its direct premiums in Texas, was represented by 500 agents nationwide, and employed 300 people.

bibliography: *History of American Indemnity Company* (Galveston: American Indemnity Company, 1993). Hugh Williamson, ed., *The Story of Insurance in Texas* (Dallas: John Moranz Associates, 1954).

Lisa A. Parker

AMERICAN LEGION. The Texas Department of the American Legion is a nonpolitical and nonpartisan organization. Its principal aim is to secure legislation for the benefit of veterans in Texas, including adequate hospitalization, physical and vocational rehabilitation, and preference in public jobs. The organization also supports legislation for assistance to underprivileged children. The legion was founded by service veterans from World War I[qv] at a meeting held in San Antonio on San Jacinto Day, April 21, 1919. Col. Claude V. Birkhead[qv] was elected first chairman. The organization was originally known as the Texas Division of World War Veterans, but the name was changed a short time later to Texas Department, American Legion, to conform to the constitution adopted by the national organization in December 1919.

Among the most important concerns of the early members was the need to secure adequate hospital facilities for sick and injured former servicemen. Donations were collected from posts and individuals throughout the state, and within a short time more than $500,000 was raised. In 1921–22 the department built the American Legion

Memorial Hospital at Legion, Texas, with funds raised through legion activities, supplemented by state aid. The hospital was sold to the United States in 1925 and became a Veterans Administration facility.

While rehabilitation for veterans remained the number-one goal of the legion through the early 1920s, the agenda was soon expanded to include employment, legislation, and the care of needy families, widows, and orphans of veterans. In 1920 the American Legion Auxiliary, composed of the wives and widows of veterans, was formed, with the purpose of augmenting and supporting the organization's activities. During the early 1920s, the Legion also turned its attention toward fighting what it perceived as a growing tide of anti-Americanism. The Americanism committee at the 1923 convention called for "vigilance against teaching in public or private schools in Texas false or 'doctored' history, or subversive doctrine" and "against textbooks tainted with foreign or special propaganda and careful study of textbooks used in schools." It also endorsed a measure adopted at the national convention calling for the "total cessation of immigration until assimilation shall catch up with immigration." The legion also sponsored a variety of civic projects. Some posts erected community Christmas trees or made donations to the needy; others sponsored parks and playgrounds, built swimming pools, and equipped lighted baseball parks. After 1923 most of the posts in the state also sponsored local Boy Scout troops and took part in scouting activities. During the 1920s and early 1930s legion posts throughout Texas also began to sponsor baseball teams and oratorical contests. Beginning in 1938 the Americanism program organized the annual Boys State convention (*see* LONE STAR BOYS' STATE and BLUEBONNET GIRLS' STATE), held each summer in Austin, to promote citizen education for young men.

Between 1919 and 1942 membership in the legion ranged from 10,540 to 37,709. In 1942 veterans of World War II[qv] were made eligible, and after the war large numbers of returning soldiers joined the organization. Black Texas veterans were made eligible in 1945, though at first they were confined to a separate district-at-large, with the posts sponsored and guided by existing white posts. In the period just after World War II, when the demand for veterans' services exploded, the legion lobbied for additional hospitals, rehabilitation facilities, and other benefits. Korean War veterans began joining the organization in large number in the mid-1950s, and in 1979 Vietnam veterans were made eligible for membership. By the early 1990s the statewide membership was 90,000. Subsequently, the legion continued its earlier charitable activities and added new ones, including programs for abused children, the mentally retarded, missing children, and drug-abuse prevention. The state organization has been headquartered in Austin since 1927.

BIBLIOGRAPHY: Harold M. Branton, *The American Legion Department of Texas, 1919–1986: An Official History* (Waco: American Legion Department of Texas, 1987). Carrie Wilcox, *The American Legion in Texas, 1919–1949* (Dallas: Banks, Upshaw, 1951).

Carrie Wilcox and Christopher Long

AMERICAN NATIONAL INSURANCE COMPANY. American National Insurance Company, headquartered in Galveston, covers seven million policy owners throughout the United States, Canada, Guam, American Samoa, and Western Europe. It was founded on the Strand[qv] in 1905 by William Lewis Moody, Jr.,[qv] who served as company president until his death in 1954. In 1900 Moody became convinced that he could break into the Eastern-dominated insurance industry. In 1904 he became associated with the American National Insurance and Trust Company of Houston, which he moved to Galveston and incorporated in 1905 as the American National Insurance Company. The firm received its charter and made its first stock offering in 1905, using its initial profits to finance growth. The first dividends were paid in 1911. Insurance in force reached over $22 million by 1910, and by 1912 the firm employed seventy workers in its home office and 700 representatives in the field. By 1920 the firm was known as the "Giant of the South." Moody went on to purchase the Galveston *News*[qv] and *Tribune* and to become active in the hotel industry and ranching.

By 1928 the company employed 500 persons in its home office and had absorbed twenty-seven other insurance companies. Company assets increased by over 100 percent during the 1930s, and insurance in force declined only minimally. In the 1930s the firm was widely known for its sponsorship of award-winning girls' basketball teams made up of company employees. By 1945 insurance in force passed the billion-dollar mark, and in 1950 the firm acquired the Commonwealth Life and Accident Insurance Company of St. Louis and entered the fields of health, hospitalization, and credit life insurance through the purchase of companies in St. Louis and Dallas.

At his death in 1954 Moody willed the majority of the company stock to the Moody Foundation,[qv] which subsequently controlled both ANICO and the banks, newspapers, hotels, and ranches he had accumulated. He was succeeded as president of the company by his daughter, Mary Moody Northen.[qv] By 1963 American National was one of the top ten stock life and health insurance companies, i.e., firms that sold shares of stock in their enterprise by 1961 and had assets of over $1 billion, in the nation. In 1968 the company acquired the Trans World Life Insurance Company of New York, expanded its operations across the entire United States, Canada, and Western Europe, and acquired a mutual fund management company called Citadel, Incorporated, which it renamed the American National Growth Fund; in 1970 it started the American National Income Fund. In the 1970s American National headquarters moved to the twenty-story American National Tower, designed by Neuhaus and Taylor of Houston, on Moody Plaza in Galveston, which housed the Mary Moody Northen Auditorium and the corporation's art collection of American painters, sculptors, weavers, and watercolorists. At the time the firm had branch offices in 400 cities in forty-nine states. By 1983 the company was the second largest employer in Galveston.

Total life insurance in force reached almost $29 billion by 1991, by which time the company had assets of over $4 billion. In the 1990s the American National "family of companies" included Standard Life and Accident Insurance Company of Oklahoma City; Garden State Life Insurance Company of League City, Texas; American National Property and Casualty Company, American National Insurance Service Company, and American National General Insurance Company of Springfield, Missouri; the American National Life Insurance Company of Texas and American National Insurance Company; ANREM Corporation; and Securities Management and Research of Galveston. Presidents of the firm have included W. L. Vogler, Phil B. Noah, Glendon E. Johnson, and Orson C. Clay.

BIBLIOGRAPHY: David G. McComb, *Galveston: A History* (Austin: University of Texas Press, 1986). Hugh Williamson, ed., *The Story of Insurance in Texas* (Dallas: John Moranz Associates, 1954).

Sandia Sullivan and Philip Boydston

AMERICAN PARTY. The antiforeign, anti-Catholic secret society called the American Order, more popularly known as the Know-Nothing movement, reached Texas by the mid-1850s. Many Texans joined the movement and especially its political manifestation, the American party. Some feared "foreign ideas," especially the anti-slavery views often attributed to persons of Mexican and German origin in the state. Others believed that the state Democratic party[qv] was drifting dangerously toward a secessionist position and hoped that the new party might save the Union. Still others were Whigs who, realizing that their party was dying, did not want to join the Democrats. Some Texans were attracted by the secret character of the movement. Texas Know-Nothings, like their counterparts elsewhere in the nation, pledged to vote only for native-born Protestants for public office and to work to increase the residence requirement in the federal naturalization law from five to twenty-one years.

The party's first success in Texas came in December 1854, when Know-Nothing candidates swept the San Antonio municipal election. Then, in March 1855, Galvestonians elected a mayor who belonged to the secret order. In both towns native-born white voters seemed to be reacting to the growing number of foreign-born residents.

Early in the summer of 1855 Texas Know-Nothing leaders launched a plan to gain political control of the state by subverting the Democratic party. By that time they had secretly won over several Democratic leaders, including John S. Ford,[qv] chairman of the state Democratic committee, and Lieutenant Governor David C. Dickson.[qv] On June 11, under cover of a river-improvements convention at Washington-on-the-Brazos, the Know-Nothings nominated a slate of candidates to run for state offices and for Congress in the August election. Dickson headed the ticket in opposition to Democratic governor Elisha M. Pease's[qv] reelection bid. Though the true purpose and actions of the convention were public knowledge within twenty-four hours of its adjournment, the participants and candidates steadfastly denied—then and throughout the ensuing campaign—that they were members of the American Order.

A spirited campaign followed. On June 16 the Texas Democrats held a convention in Austin, at which they passed resolutions condemning secret political factions and the imposition of tests for voting or officeholding. On July 24 United States senator Sam Houston[qv] issued a public letter criticizing the sectionalism of the John C. Calhoun wing of the Democratic party and endorsing the principles of the American Order. Throughout the campaign Dickson and his supporters criticized Governor Pease's unpopular proposal to pay for a railway system for Texas with state funds, while the Democratic leadership hammered away at Dickson's defection to the American party.

On August 6 Pease defeated Dickson by a vote of 26,336 to 17,968. Most of the Know-Nothing vote was concentrated in the western part of East Texas and in a group of western counties in the vicinity of Travis County. The American party succeeded in electing Lemuel D. Evans[qv] to Congress from the eastern district, Stephen Crosby[qv] as land commissioner, and about a dozen members of the legislature. The party faithful celebrated their limited victories in November at a rally in Austin at which Senator Houston spoke.

On January 21, 1856, the American party of Texas, abandoning secrecy, met in open convention in Austin. Participants elected delegates to the national convention, nominated candidates for several state offices, and adopted resolutions endorsing the party's nativism and calling for the preservation and perpetuation of the federal Union, a strict construction of the United States Constitution, the preservation of states' rights, and the denial of the right of Congress to legislate on the issue of slavery[qv] in the states.

In February two Texans, Lemuel D. Evans and Benjamin H. Epperson,[qv] attended the party's national convention in Philadelphia, which nominated Millard Fillmore for president. The failure of the party to include any statement in its platform about protecting the institution of slavery disappointed many Texas Know-Nothings and may have discouraged them from active participation in the campaign. At any rate, the American party candidates suffered local and national defeats in the general election. The movement then declined as it split nationally over slavery. In Texas the opposition of the Democrats was very effective. By 1857 the American party had virtually disappeared in Texas, though many of its former members supported Houston's unsuccessful bid for the governorship that year.

In its short life, the American party made its mark on the Texas political scene by forcing the Democratic party to organize effectively throughout the state and by focusing on Unionist, nationalist, and nativist issues that perdured long after the movement's demise.

BIBLIOGRAPHY: Litha Crews, The Know Nothing Party in Texas (M.A. thesis, University of Texas, 1925). Waymon L. McClellan, "1855: The Know Nothing Challenge in East Texas," *East Texas Historical Journal* 12 (1974). Ralph A. Wooster, "An Analysis of the Texas Know Nothings," *Southwestern Historical Quarterly* 70 (January 1967).

Roger A. Griffin

AMERICAN RIO GRANDE LAND AND IRRIGATION COMPANY. In 1900 Benjamin Franklin Yoakum,[qv] manager of the Frisco railroad system, developed a plan to extend the St. Louis, Brownsville and Mexico Railway from Houston to Brownsville. He recognized the agricultural potential of the area and soon collected a group of St. Louis capitalists to form the American Rio Grande Land and Irrigation Company with a capital stock of $1.25 million. A charter for the corporation was granted by the state of Texas on September 30, 1905. The main accomplishment of the American Company was integrating the development of irrigation, the coming of the railroad, the sale of farmland, and the establishment of the town of Mercedes. The developers were fully aware that irrigation would be unprofitable if there was no way to get the produce to distant markets; hence the railroad. Production required producers; hence the intensive recruitment of land buyers from the Midwest. Coordination of the operation required central facilities; hence the town.

The land was purchased from the heirs of the original grantees, Juan José Hinojosa and Rosa Hinojosa de Ballí,[qv] in the Llano Grande and La Feria grants. The first office of the company was a boxcar on a railroad siding; the second was a two-story building in Mercedes. W. F. Shaw served as chief engineer, vice president, and general manager from 1907 to 1930. He planned and developed the irrigation and drainage system for the project. A settling basin, a pumping plant on the river, a canal, and an electrical plant were built in Mercedes in 1906–07. The canals and river pump station began operation in 1908. By 1920 the system consisted of three large canals, five pumping plants, reservoirs and settling basins, and extensive drainage works.

On January 27, 1922, controlling stock in the company was bought by Harry L. Seay and Charles Linz of Dallas. In 1927 Hidalgo and Cameron Counties Water and Control District No. 9 was formed by the farmers who owned land in the district, and in 1929 they purchased the irrigation portion of the company.

BIBLIOGRAPHY: James Lewellyn Allhands, *Gringo Builders* (Joplin, Missouri, Dallas, Texas, 1931). James Lewellyn Allhands, *Railroads to the Rio* (Salado, Texas: Anson Jones Press, 1960). William Kenneth Matthews, A History of Irrigation in the Lower Rio Grande Valley (M.A. thesis, University of Texas, 1938). Vertical Files, Barker Texas History Center, University of Texas at Austin (Mercedes, Texas).

Mrs. Goldsby Goza

AMERICAN WELL AND PROSPECTING COMPANY. In Kansas in 1890 Charles Rittersbacher and Horace Greeley Johnston organized a water-well-drilling business that they named the American Well and Prospecting Company. In 1894 they contracted with the Corsicana Water Development Company for three water wells in Corsicana, Texas. Work began on the first well in June at a site on South Twelfth Street, a few blocks from the business district. At a depth of 1,035 feet they struck oil and thus opened the state's first commercial oilfield. By 1900 the Corsicana oilfield[qv] was producing more than 800,000 barrels of crude annually and had the first refinery west of the Mississippi River.

Although they continued drilling some wells, Rittersbacher and Johnston soon concentrated primarily on repairing drilling rigs and other equipment. They had opened a small shop in Corsicana to repair their own equipment, but meeting demands for repairs from other drillers became a full-time endeavor. About 1900 Rittersbacher and Johnston purchased patent rights for hydraulic rotary drilling equipment from M. C. and C. E. Baker, brothers who had pioneered in that field. From that time the American Well and Prospecting Company began manufacturing and distributing oilfield equipment under the trade name Gumbo Buster. A rig manufactured by American Well and Prospecting and operated by the Hamill brothers of Corsicana was used to drill the A. F. Lucas[qv] well at Spindletop in 1901, thus ushering in the petroleum industry on the Texas Gulf Coast (*see* SPINDLETOP OILFIELD). Eventually Gumbo Buster equipment was used in every major oilfield in the world.

With the outbreak of World War II,[qv] American Well and Prospecting, like many other industries, converted its operations to the production of war-related materials. Among the items manufactured by the company were 1,000-pound semi-armor-piercing bombs and 240-millimeter shells. The plant operated around the clock and employed 1,000 people during peak wartime production.

American Well and Prospecting was a family-controlled operation for the first several decades of its existence. Johnston served as president until his death in 1930. Rittersbacher died in 1919, but his sons, Elmer and Edgar, held management positions in the company, as did Eliot Johnston and Lowell Estes, son and son-in-law of Johnston. On June 30, 1944, Bethlehem Steel of Pennsylvania purchased all the outstanding stock and assets of American Well and Prospecting Company. At the conclusion of the war Bethlehem resumed production of oilfield equipment at the Corsicana plant. Increased competition in the business of manufacturing oilfield equipment and hard times in the petroleum industry forced Bethlehem to close the plant in 1959.

BIBLIOGRAPHY: Walter Rundell, Jr., *Early Texas Oil: A Photographic History, 1866-1936* (College Station: Texas A&M University Press, 1977). Tommy Stringer, "American Well and Prospecting Company," *East Texas Historical Journal* 22 (1984). *Tommy W. Stringer*

AMERICA'S FAVORITE CHICKEN. America's Favorite Chicken, headquartered in Atlanta, Georgia, is the parent company of Popeye's Fried Chicken and Biscuits and Church's Fried Chicken, headquartered in San Antonio, Texas; these fast-food chains specialize in Southern-style fried chicken. George W. Church, Sr., of San Antonio, Texas, founded Church's in 1952, at a time when only hot dogs and ice cream were being marketed as fast food. Church, a retired incubator salesman in his sixties, drew on his knowledge of the poultry industry in conceiving the idea of marketing low-cost, freshly fried chicken as a convenience food. The first Church's Fried Chicken To Go, in downtown San Antonio across the street from the Alamo, sold only fried chicken. French fries and jalapeño peppers were added to the menu by 1955, and at the time of Church's death in 1956, four stores were in operation.

In 1962, when the chain operated at eight San Antonio locations, George W. "Bill" Church, Jr., took over the family business. He and his brother Richard are credited with concocting the unique marinade used on Church's chicken. George initiated the firm's rapid expansion and started the company's first units outside the state in 1967. Church's did not initially franchise its business as did other convenience food chains.

By 1968, when the company reported revenues of $2.7 million, it was operating seventeen stores in five Texas cities. That year Church's reorganized to allow the original family firm to expand into a chain, and in 1969 Church's Fried Chicken, Incorporated, became a publicly held company with new company headquarters in northwest San Antonio. By the end of 1975 the company had 554 stores in twenty-two states, primarily in Texas, the South, and the Midwest, and had begun to diversify into speciality hamburger shops under the name "G.W. Jrs." Franchising began in 1976, and international expansion started with the opening of the first Church's in Japan in 1979. Sixty-two Texas hamburger shops were in operation by 1982, but the hamburger business was discontinued in 1985.

Church's restaurants displayed a distinctive architecture, designed and engineered to stress productivity by Shikatani Lacroix Design, a Toronto-based firm noted for establishing corporate identity. Each restaurant was a modular building, constructed for adaptability to any part of the country. Sufficient cash flow enabled the company to purchase its real estate rather than lease it. Church's established a San Antonio plant to manufacture its own equipment with the help of computer-aided design machinery and robotics.

In the 1980s, growing competition prompted Church's to close 112 outlets, and the Bass family of Texas to trim its stake in the company. A hostile takeover attempt by Alvin Copeland of Popeye's Famous Fried Chicken and Biscuits, headquartered in New Orleans, Louisiana, succeeded in a 1989 leveraged buyout, resulting in the ousting of company president Ernest E. Renaud and in significant layoffs. By 1991, Popeye's faced bankruptcy. A new company called America's Favorite Chicken, incorporated in Minnesota with offices in Atlanta, replaced Al Copeland Enterprises as Church's parent company in 1992, after federal bankruptcy-court action confirmed a plan for reorganization. Church's was the nation's second-largest fried chicken chain that year (behind Kentucky Fried Chicken), with sales exceeding $510 million. Chairman and chief executive officer of AFC in 1993 was Frank J. Belatti. In 1993, the company entered a purchasing cooperative with its franchisees to provide reduced freight charges and manufacturing prices, eliminate broker fees, and reduce distribution costs to restaurants. It continued to manufacture its own spices at a San Antonio plant, and to acquire its raw materials by contracting with such vendors as Pilgrim's Pride, Tyson's, and Coca-Cola. In 1994, AFC owned 605 Church's and 111 Popeye's restaurants and had 335 domestic Church's franchises and 655 Popeye's franchises, along with 143 international Church's and fifty Popeye's. Church's restaurants could be found in Mexico, Puerto Rico, Canada, Indonesia, Saudi Arabia, the Philippines, and Korea. In the 1990s, the firm was ripe for takeover attempts because of its large real estate holdings.

Church's philanthropic activities have included a major donation in 1992 to the United Negro College Fund and the 1993 founding of an annual Kids Fair in conjunction with KABB, an independent children's television station in San Antonio. Its Operation Kid Print promotes child safety. AFC subsequently announced its plan to become a major corporate sponsor for Habitat for Humanity, a program dedicated to rebuilding inner cities and providing low-income housing.

BIBLIOGRAPHY: *Forbes*, May 28, 1990. Burt Hochberg, ed., *San Antonio '72* (New York: Chess, 1973). *Institutional Investor*, May 26, 1992. New York *Times*, March 15, December 13, 1988. *Rajni Madan*

AMES, HARRIET A. MOORE PAGE POTTER (?–?). Harriet Ames, subject of a an early Texas community-property case, the daughter of Francis Moore, left her home and small retail business in New Orleans and accompanied her improvident husband, Solomon C. Page, to Texas before the revolution of 1836. Not long after their arrival Page joined the army, abandoning Harriet and their two small children without provisions in an isolated house on the prairie surrounding Austin Bayou. They survived by gathering wild plants until they were finally rescued and brought to Brazoria, where Harriet sold some store goods she had brought from New Orleans and learned farming from her brother's wife. During the Runaway Scrape[qv] Robert Potter,[qv] secretary of the Texas Navy,[qv] took her and her children to Galveston under his protection and gave them refuge on a navy vessel until after the battle of San Jacinto.[qv] Refusing Solomon Page's plea for reconciliation, she journeyed to New Orleans with the intention of setting out for Kentucky to live with her grandmother. Potter, who was with her, offered to arrange the journey; but instead, he executed a series of deceptive maneuvers that ultimately took them back to Texas and his property on the Sabine River in Shelby (now Harrison) County.

Harriet refused Potter's proposals of marriage until he convinced her that her marriage to Page was invalid in Texas because it had not been solemnized by a priest, and in September 1836 they were married by bond. They lived for a year on the Sabine while they built a home at Potter's Point on Ferry (Caddo) Lake in Red River (now

Marion) County. They had two children, and Robert Potter served in the Fifth and Sixth Texas congresses; he assured Harriet that he had introduced a law in Congress validating marriages like theirs. Potter became involved in the Regulator-Moderator War,[qv] and on March 2, 1842, he was murdered by William P. Rose[qv] and a contingent of Regulators. When his will, made in Austin less than a month before his death, was probated, it revealed that he had left the land on which the homestead stood to a Sophia Mayfield of Austin, and another part of his headright and some horses, slaves, and all of the household furnishings and farming stock to Harriet, named in the will as Mrs. Harriet A. Page.

Harriet remarried in August or September 1842, and with her new husband, Charles Ames, continued to reside on the Potter homestead. Sophia Mayfield died in 1852 without ever attempting to take possession of Potter's bequest, and it was sold by the administrator of her estate. In July 1857 the purchasers filed suit to try title against Harriet and Charles Ames. After years of amended pleadings the case of Lewis *v.* Ames was tried in Marion County District Court in April 1872 and judgment was rendered in Harriet's favor (Ames had died in 1866). The case was reversed and remanded by the Texas Supreme Court in 1875. The controlling issue was whether Harriet had been Potter's legal wife and was therefore entitled to assert a community interest in the property. Chief Justice O. M. Roberts[qv] held that the remedial statutes passed by the Texas legislature to validate irregular marriages contracted under Mexican sovereignty did not affect Harriet Ames's alleged bond marriage: Potter's failure to mention a wife or children among the enumerated beneficiaries and his reference to Harriet as Mrs. Page indicated that he did not regard their living arrangement as a marriage. Harriet was dispossessed from the property at Potter's Point and lived for the remainder of her life in New Orleans with the children of her third marriage. At the age of eighty-three she wrote her reminiscences, which are now in the Barker Texas History Center,[qv] University of Texas at Austin.

BIBLIOGRAPHY: Louis Wiltz Kemp, *The Signers of the Texas Declaration of Independence* (Salado, Texas: Anson Jones, 1944; rpt. 1959). James Norvell, "Ames Case Revisited," *Southwestern Historical Quarterly* 63 (July 1959). Texas Supreme Court, *Texas Reports: Cases Adjudged in the Supreme Court*, Vol. 44. *Judith N. McArthur*

AMES, JESSIE HARRIET DANIEL (1883–1972). Jessie Ames, suffragist and antilynching reformer, daughter of James Malcolm and Laura Maria (Leonard) Daniel, was born in Palestine, Texas, on November 2, 1883. In 1893 the family moved to Georgetown, where Jessie entered the Ladies Annex of Southwestern University at the age of thirteen. She graduated with a B.A. degree in 1902 and moved with her family to Laredo. There in June 1905 she married Roger Post Ames, an army surgeon and friend of her father. They had a son and two daughters, the last born in 1914, the year Roger Ames died in Guatemala of blackwater fever.

Because her marriage was an unhappy one, she and her husband lived apart; he was a doctor in Central America, while she and the children lived with her parents and older sister. After the death of her father in 1911, Jessie Ames helped her mother run their Georgetown telephone company. In 1916 she organized and became the first president of the Georgetown Equal Suffrage League and began to write a weekly "Woman Suffrage Notes" column for the *Williamson County Sun*. As the protégée of Minnie Fisher Cunningham,[qv] president of the Texas Equal Suffrage Association,[qv] Jessie Ames was elected treasurer of the state association in 1918; from this position she helped to make Texas the first southern state to ratify the Nineteenth Amendment.

In 1919 she became the founder and first president of the state League of Women Voters;[qv] she represented the national League of Women Voters at the Pan American Congress in 1923. She served as a delegate-at-large to the national Democratic party[qv] conventions of

Jessie Daniel Ames. Courtesy Austin History Center, Austin Public Library; photo no. E.4 D (20).

1920 and 1924 and as an alternate delegate in 1928. She also was president of the Texas branch of the American Association of University Women and an officer of the Women's Joint Legislative Council,[qv] the Board of Education (Women's Division) of the Methodist Church, the Texas Committee on Prisons and Prison Labor, and the Texas Federation of Women's Clubs.[qv] In 1924 she became director of the Texas Council of the Commission on Interracial Cooperation, based in Atlanta. In 1929 she moved to Atlanta to become the national director of the CIC Woman's Committee; a year later, financed primarily by the CIC, she founded the Association of Southern Women for the Prevention of Lynching,[qv] a group of white women organized to fight racial violence and vigilante executions. By February 1937 eighty-one state, regional, and national organizations or groups had endorsed the antilynching platform. Jessie Ames directed the Association of Southern Women until 1942, when the CIC was replaced by the Southern Regional Council. She retired to Tryon, North Carolina, then returned in October 1968 to Texas to live with her younger daughter. The next year she presented the family library of some 1,200 books to the Cody Memorial Library[qv] of Southwestern University. She died in Austin of pneumonia on February 21, 1972, and is buried in the family plot in the I.O.O.F. Cemetery in Georgetown. In 1985 the Jessie Daniel Ames Lecture Series was inaugurated at Southwestern University, and Jessie Ames's life and work were the subject of both the university's 1985 Freshman Symposium and its 1986 Brown Symposium.

BIBLIOGRAPHY: Jessie Daniel Ames Papers, Dallas Historical Society, Hall of State, Dallas; Southern History Collection, University of North Carolina at Chapel Hill; Texas State Library, Austin. Jacquelyn Dowd Hall, "Jessie Daniel Ames," in *American Reformers*, ed. Alden Whitman (New York: Wilson, 1985). Jacquelyn Dowd Hall, *Revolt Against Chivalry: Jessie Daniel Ames and the Women's Campaign Against Lynching* (New York: Columbia University Press, 1979). *Notable American Women: A Biographical Dictionary* (4 vols., Cambridge, Massachusetts: Harvard University Press, 1971–80). Jon D. Swartz and Joanna Fountain-Schroeder, eds., *Jessie Daniel Ames: An Exhibition at Southwestern University* (Georgetown, Texas: Cody Memorial Library, Southwestern University, 1986). *Jon D. Swartz*

AMES, TEXAS (Coryell County). Ames is on State Highway 36 eight miles northwest of Gainesville in north central Coryell County. It was originally located on the Leon River two miles to the south, but moved closer to the highway. The community was probably named for William Ames, an early settler. In 1889 the Methodist church, which had been located next to the cemetery, was rebuilt near the center of the settlement. It was originally called Union Grove and later known as the Ames Methodist Church. The Ames post office opened in 1893 and was housed in the community store, whose successive proprietors served as postmaster. The church, store, and a school named Enterprise were all located together and stood on land belonging to the Liljeblad family.

Ames acquired telephone service in 1905. At one time it had two switchboards, one of which was used especially to call across the Leon River to Ater and Levita. The community also had a gin and a shop. Electricity reached Ames in 1941. The school, which had been served by two teachers, closed in the early 1940s, and the children were bused to Gatesville. The post office was discontinued in 1957, the same year that the church disbanded. Most members transferred to a church in Jonesboro. The Ames school and the church were torn down, and the store seems to have closed by the early 1960s. Weaver's Chapel Cemetery, the second cemetery established for the community, was still accessible off Highway 36 in the late 1980s. Ames reported a population of ten in 1896 and twenty-five from 1925 through 1967, the last year for which statistics are available. Still living on or near their ancestors' original land holdings in the late 1980s were descendants of the Liljeblad, Wilson, Wilhelm, Quicksall, Coward, Bell, Yows, and Byrom families.

BIBLIOGRAPHY: Coryell County Genealogical Society, *Coryell County, Texas, Families, 1854–1985* (Dallas: Taylor, 1986).
Doris A. Coward

AMES, TEXAS (Liberty County). Ames is at the junction of Farm Road 1909 and U.S. Highway 90, forty-two miles west of Beaumont in south central Liberty County. Once known as Rachal Station after pioneer Darius Ciriaque Rachal,[qv] Ames was renamed for a section foreman on the Texas and New Orleans Railroad. The community had a flag station during the Civil War[qv] and a full station by 1890. A local Catholic rectory was built in 1915. Ames had a population of twenty-five in 1930. The county set up a new voting box there in 1945. In 1972 Ames voters incorporated their town by a margin of 69 to 8. During the mid-1970s the town's population was estimated at 350, and by 1980 Ames had 1,155 residents and an array of businesses. In 1990 the population was 989.

BIBLIOGRAPHY: Miriam Partlow, *Liberty, Liberty County, and the Atascosito District* (Austin: Pemberton, 1974). *Robert Wooster*

AMHERST, TEXAS (Lamar County). Amherst is three miles northeast of Paris in central Lamar County. A post office operated there in 1904–05, and maps for 1936 showed a school and a cluster of dwellings at the site. In 1964 Amherst students attended school in Powderly. By 1970 Amherst was part of the North Lamar Independent School District. The community still appeared on maps in 1983 and was listed, without statistics, in later publications.

BIBLIOGRAPHY: Thomas S. Justiss, An Administrative Survey of the Schools of Lamar County with a Plan for Their Reorganization (M.A. thesis, University of Texas, 1937). *Vista K. McCroskey*

AMHERST, TEXAS (Lamb County). Amherst, on U.S. Highway 84 and the Santa Fe tracks in west central Lamb County, began in 1913 as a Pecos and Northern Texas Railway station for William E. Halsell's[qv] Mashed O Ranch.[qv] A townsite was platted a mile from the Santa Fe depot in 1923 and named for Amherst College by a railroad official. The post office opened in 1924. By 1930 thirty-five businesses and 964 people constituted a lively trade center, and amenities included a newspaper, the Amherst *Argus*. For many years the Amherst Hotel, the town's first permanent building, was the most popular stopping place between Clovis and Lubbock. The population in Amherst was 749 in 1940, when the first co-op hospital in Texas was built there. Incorporation came in 1970, when the population was 825. In 1980 the population was 971, and businesses included five cotton gins and two grain elevators. Sod House Spring Monument, commemorating the first cow camp in the area, is located six miles northwest of Amherst, and Plant X, one of Southwestern Public Service's largest generating plants, is nine miles north. The population of Amherst in 1990 was 742.

BIBLIOGRAPHY: Vincent Matthew Peterman, *Pioneer Days: A Half-Century of Life in Lamb County and Adjacent Communities* (Lubbock: Texas Tech Press, 1979). Evalyn Parrott Scott, *A History of Lamb County* (Sudan, Texas: Lamb County Historical Commission, 1968).
William R. Hunt

AMICHEL. When Alonzo Álvarez de Pineda[qv] explored the Gulf Coast from peninsular Florida to Veracruz in 1519, the territory was named Amichel. The name is known from only two sources: the royal patent granted Francisco de Garay[qv] (Álvarez's sponsor) to settle the region and a map known as the Cortés map, published in 1524. Although Garay's report of the Álvarez voyage was sent to Spain before the end of 1519, it was not acted upon until 1521. On June 4 that year the royal *cédula* was issued at Burgos. Royal officials acting for King Charles II (Emperor Charles V of the Holy Roman Empire) exulted that through the efforts of Garay, Diego Velázquez, and Juan Ponce De León,[qv] the entire Gulf Coast had been discovered and proved to be contiguous mainland. According to this document, the entire coast was pleasant and fruitful, inhabited by pacific natives of affectionate nature who gave every indication of being suitable subjects for conversion to the Catholic faith. In places the people were as much as seven feet tall; in others they were midgets of no more than 3½ to four feet. Some of the natives, it is said, wore gold jewelry in their nostrils and earlobes, and there was wide distribution of the precious metal in the territory.

The voyage made for Garay having shown the new lands "suitable for settlement," the crown granted him permission to send a colonizing expedition at his own expense with the title of Adelantado. The land recently discovered, it was noted, "is called the province of Amichel and is so named."

Garay launched two efforts to establish a colony in Amichel. An error in the historical literature has placed these attempts at the mouth of the Rio Grande. Actually, they were on the Río Pánuco. Both ended in abject failure. Not having been disposed to await the ponderous turning of official wheels, Garay sent Álvarez de Pineda back to the Pánuco in late 1519 or early 1520. The colony he sought to establish there was destroyed shortly afterward in a Huastec uprising that cost Álvarez his life.

Garay himself led the second attempt. He sailed from Jamaica on June 14, 1523, unaware that his authority had been revoked in favor of Hernán Cortés and his province of Amichel attached to New Spain. On reaching the Pánuco, Garay found Cortés's minions firmly in control. Seeing his own troops defecting to Cortés while his ships rotted in the harbor, Garay went to Mexico to treat with Cortés personally and died there the following December of pneumonia.

The name Amichel does not appear on the map sketch attributed to Álvarez de Pineda, the first to show the Gulf of Mexico and the Texas coast in reasonably accurate proportions. It does appear on the "Cortés map," published with the August 1524 Nuremberg edition of Cortés's second letter to the crown. Authorship of the map, however, is not known. Use of Amichel, which originated with his rivals, in preference to names of his own origin, suggests that the author definitely was not Cortés.

BIBLIOGRAPHY: Martín Fernández de Navarrete, *Colección de los viages y descubrimientos que hicieron por mar los españoles desde fines del siglo XV* (5 vols., Buenos Aires: Guarania, 1945–46). Robert S. Weddle, *Spanish Sea: The Gulf of Mexico in North American Discovery, 1500–1685* (College Station: Texas A&M University Press, 1985).

Robert S. Weddle

AMIGO, TEXAS. Amigo was a railroad community seven miles northeast of Tyler and just south of Winona on the St. Louis Southwestern Railway in eastern Smith County. In 1910 one store and a population of twenty-five were reported there; in 1940 two businesses and a population of forty were reported. Maps of 1947 indicated only a service station. The community was no longer listed on government survey maps by the 1960s.

BIBLIOGRAPHY: Smith County Historical Society, *Historical Atlas of Smith County* (Tyler, Texas: Tyler Print Shop, 1965).

Vista K. McCroskey

AMIGOS DEL VALLE. Amigos del Valle functions as a consortium of county and city governments to implement and administer comprehensive human services to the eligible elderly of the lower Rio Grande valley. It was established as part of the Lower Rio Grande Development Council-Area Agency on Aging, organized under the federally funded Title VII Nutrition Project as authorized by the Older Americans Act of 1965. It began service to the aged in Cameron, Hidalgo, and Willacy counties in 1975, under a four-month Title VII grant from the Governor's Committee on Aging. It started with an operating cost of $357,000, and by February 1976 the agency's budget had increased to $1.9 million. In 1979 an Outreach Services program was initiated to provide individual, family, and group counseling on health care, transportation needs, and financial problems for the elderly.

In 1990 the ADV had an annual budget of over $4 million, employed 102 persons, and operated seventeen multipurpose senior service centers and fifteen satellite nutrition sites, from which 3,000 older Texans were provided nutritionally balanced hot meals daily, as well as educational, recreational, and social services. The ADV operated a fleet of fourteen buses and twelve vans that daily transported 400 senior participants from their homes on field trips and to shopping sites and medical facilities. The ADV also provided supportive services during natural disasters. Through the United States Department of Housing and Urban Development the ADV provided housing projects for Valley elderly. By 1990 the agency owned and managed elderly housing units in Brownsville (100 units), McAllen (72), Harlingen (55), Pharr (40), Raymondville (38), and Weslaco (71). It was estimated that 50,000 Senior Citizens in the three-county area had been served by 1990. Amigos del Valle also provided home health care and home delivered meals for those individuals who were homebound. ADV also published a monthly newspaper available at all the centers or delivered to homebound individuals. Aside from the paid staff ADV depended on volunteers to carry out its objectives. In 1980 1,200 volunteers worked an estimated 240,000 hours a year at the senior service centers. ADV holds a Volunteer Appreciation Banquet annually in May.

BIBLIOGRAPHY: *Amigos del Valle, Inc.: Programs for Older Americans* (McAllen, Texas, 198?).

Alicia A. Garza

AMISTAD RESERVOIR. Amistad Reservoir is located in the Rio Grande basin in southern Val Verde County, Texas, and Coahuila, Mexico, twelve miles northwest of Del Rio (at 29°27′ N, 101°03′ W). The lake is surrounded by massive limestone and wash deposits on flat terrain surfaced by dark, calcareous, stony clays and clay loams that support grasses and water-tolerant hardwoods and conifers.

Many limestone caves and rockshelters along the banks of the Rio Grande and Devils River, which feed into the lake, were inhabited by prehistoric Indians, who left their art on the walls of the caves. When Amistad Lake was filled after the fall of 1969, the paintings were inundated. In the fall of 1848 the expedition of Col. John Coffee Hays[qv] passed over the lower San Pedro River, where part of the lake is now located. Hays and his explorers renamed the stream the Devils River. In 1853 Julius Froebel[qv] came through the area of the lake and wrote of its beauty.

Construction on Amistad Dam and Reservoir began in December 1964 and was completed in November 1969. The dam is an earthfill and concrete structure. The lake and dam are owned by the United States and Mexico and operated by the International Boundary and Water Commission.[qv] The lake surface covers 89,000 acres, and its capacity is 5,658,600 acre-feet. Amistad Lake was built for flood control, conservation, irrigation, power, and recreation. In honor of the cooperation and goodwill exhibited by both counties in the project, the dam and reservoir were named the Spanish word meaning "friendship."

BIBLIOGRAPHY: C. L. Dowell, *Dams and Reservoirs in Texas: History and Descriptive Information* (Texas Water Commission Bulletin 6408 [Austin, 1964]). C. L. Dowell and R. G. Petty, *Engineering Data on Dams and Reservoirs in Texas* (Texas Water Development Board Report 126 [3 pts., Austin, 1971–74]). Roy L. Swift and Leavitt Corning, Jr., *Three Roads to Chihuahua* (Austin: Eakin Press, 1988).

AMISTAD NATIONAL RECREATION AREA. Amistad National Recreation Area is on the shores of Amistad Reservoir off U.S. highways 90 and 277, northwest of Del Rio in Val Verde County. The reservoir was formed on the Rio Grande through a cooperative effort by the United States and Mexico. The recreation area follows the twisting contour of the reservoir on the United States side of the border, extending twenty-five miles into Devil's Canyon, fourteen miles up the Pecos River, and seventy-four miles up the Rio Grande. The vegetation growing in the area's dry rocky terrain is mainly blackbrush acacia, guajillo, sotol, and yucca. The locale provides habitat for a variety of wildlife, including javelinas, white-tailed deer, rattlesnakes, and lizards. Indian artifacts, some dating back 12,000 years, have been found in the vicinity. The recreation area has camping and picnicking facilities, several marinas, and nature trails.

BIBLIOGRAPHY: George Oxford Miller, *Texas Parks and Campgrounds: Central, South, and West Texas* (Austin: Texas Monthly Press, 1984).

Christopher Long

AMITY, TEXAS. Amity is on a country road off State Highway 36 two miles from the Brown county line and eighteen miles northwest of Comanche in the northwestern corner of Comanche County. It was settled in the 1870s; the oldest grave in Amity cemetery dates from 1877. According to one source the community chose its name because of the amicable relations of the early settlers. It had a school from 1902 to 1906. In 1940 the community had a church, a cemetery, and scattered dwellings. Little was altered by 1966, and in 1992 the church was still standing and the community was still listed on county maps.

BIBLIOGRAPHY: Comanche County Bicentennial Committee, *Patchwork of Memories: Historical Sketches of Comanche County, Texas* (Brownwood, Texas: Banner Printing, 1976). *Mark Odintz*

AMMANSVILLE, TEXAS. Ammansville, on Farm Road 1383 nine miles southeast of La Grange in southeastern Fayette County, was settled during the 1870s by German and Czech immigrant farmers on lands originally allotted to the Fayette County schools. The first settler in the community was Andrew Ammann, who arrived on March 12, 1870. He was a noted architect as well as a farmer. Other early family names included Kossa, Sobolik, Heller, Stefek, Fietsam, Munke, Bartos, Holster, Lidiak, Ohnheiser, and Zoesper. In 1876 the first business opened, and by 1879 the town had a post office and a public school. A Catholic church and school opened in 1890 with Father Jules Vrana as priest. The church was destroyed by a storm in 1909 and rebuilt and dedicated on November 24, 1910. Shortly thereafter it was destroyed by fire and again rebuilt. In 1900 Ammansville had three stores and saloons, two blacksmith shops, one drugstore, one physician, and two gins. The post office was discontinued in 1906; mail was delivered from Weimar until the 1920s and subsequently from Schulenburg. The public school closed in 1909. The First State Bank of Ammansville was chartered in 1914, when the population of the extended community was estimated at 800, with 100 living in town. In the 1980s fewer than fifty people lived in Ammansville. The Catholic church, surrounded by a few remnant businesses, remained the focal point of community life. In 1990 the population was forty-two.

BIBLIOGRAPHY: Mary Hinton, *Weimar, Texas: First 100 Years, 1873-1973* (Austin: Von Boeckmann-Jones, 1973). Frank Lotto, *Fayette County: Her History and Her People* (Schulenburg, Texas: Sticker Steam Press, 1902; rpt., Austin: University of Texas Press, 1981). *Jeff Carroll*

AMON CARTER MUSEUM. The Amon Carter Museum, in Fort Worth, was founded in 1961 under the terms of the will of the late Amon G. Carter,[qv] founder and publisher of the Fort Worth *Star-Telegram*[qv] and for many years prominent in the development of Fort Worth and West Texas. Carter asked that the museum be an "artistic enterprise" that would be free and open to the public, particularly stimulating the "artistic imagination of young people." In addition to his large and distinguished collection of pictures and sculpture by Frederic Remington and Charles M. Russell, the two best-known western American artists of the late nineteenth and early twentieth centuries, the museum houses the state's preeminent collection of American art, which has grown from the original 400 paintings, watercolors, prints, and sculpture to more than 6,400 works of arts (not including the large photographic collection).

The founding director, Mitchell A. Wilder, established a program of exhibitions, publications, and public programs based on the concept of "westering America," a phrase borrowed from historian Bernard DeVoto that referred to the great nineteenth-century movement of the people westward across the continent. As a result, the museum became the leading research organization in the field, developing pioneering exhibitions and publications on many western artists and topics.

One of the first institutions devoted to showing western art, the museum was originally called the Amon Carter Museum of Western Art, but in 1967 Wilder announced that the board of trustees had broadened its collecting policy to include American art of the nineteenth and early twentieth centuries, thereby placing the works associated with the American West in the larger context of American art. This was an innovative departure from the practice of many museums of western art, which chose to view that genre apart from American and European cultures. Subsequently, the museum added many fine examples of both American and western American paintings, sculpture, prints, and photographs, to its collection. Jan Keene Muhlert became the museum's second director in 1980. A reference library specializing in American and western American art and history is housed in the museum and may be visited by appointment during regular hours. The library also contains a significant collection of newspapers on microfilm.

The museum began to develop an important collection of photographs in its second decade and now houses more than one-half million photographs and photographic negatives, including the photographic estates of Erwin E. Smith,[qv] Laura Gilpin, Eliot Porter, Clara Sipprell, and Carlotta Corpron.[qv] A catalogue of the photographic collection was published in 1993.

Situated on a hill in west Fort Worth, the museum faces east and opens onto a large plaza containing Texas shrubs and trees and three large bronze sculptures, *Upright Motives Nos. 1, 2, and 7*, by the English sculptor Henry Moore. The building, designed by Philip Johnson of New York, is constructed of buff-colored Texas shellstone. An office annex was added in 1964, and a major addition that more than doubled the size of the building was completed in 1977. It included library, office, storage, and work space. The museum is governed by a board of trustees chaired by Carter's daughter, Ruth Carter Stevenson. It receives most of its funding from the Amon G. Carter Foundation of Fort Worth, which the senior Carter established in 1945. The museum is part of the Fort Worth cultural district that includes the Kimbell Art Museum, the Modern Art Museum of Fort Worth, the Fort Worth Museum of Science and History,[qqv] Casa Mañana Theater, and the Will Rogers Coliseum, where the annual Southwestern Exposition and Livestock Show[qv] and Rodeo are held.

BIBLIOGRAPHY: Linda Ayres et al., *American Paintings: Selections from the Amon Carter Museum* (Birmingham: Oxmoor House, 1986). Paula and Ron Tyler, *Texas Museums: A Guidebook* (Austin: University of Texas Press, 1983). *Ron Tyler*

AMON G. CARTER FOUNDATION. Amon G. Carter[qv] and his wife, Nenetta Burton Carter, of Fort Worth incorporated the Amon G. Carter Foundation in 1945 and funded it in 1947 with $8,511,712 from the sale of their Wasson Field oil interests, 60 percent coming from Carter and 40 percent from his wife. The foundation received a substantial portion of Carter's estate after his death in 1955. In his will, Carter requested that the foundation establish a museum of Western American art to house his significant collection of paintings and bronzes by Frederic Remington and Charles M. Russell. The Amon Carter Museum[qv] of Western Art opened its doors in 1961 in what is now the cultural district of Fort Worth. The foundation continues to support the museum by dedicating one-half of its annual grant budget to it, along with funding various building improvements and additions to the permanent collection. The foundation also supports many other good works, primarily in Fort Worth and Tarrant County. In the early 1970s it participated in a clean-up and revitalization of downtown Fort Worth by facilitating the city's purchase of several blocks adjacent to a proposed convention center. The foundation commissioned New York architect Philip Johnson to design the Fort Worth Water Gardens and funded its construction as a gift to the city. In 1974, Carter Publications, the holding company for the Fort Worth *Star-Telegram*,[qv] WBAP Radio, and WBAP-TV, sold its media interests. Because the foundation owned a portion of the stock of Carter Publications, the market value of the foundation almost doubled to slightly more than $82 million. By that time the foundation had made cumulative grants of more than $34 million. The Carter Foundation has played a significant role in most major projects in Fort Worth. It funds grants supporting the visual and performing arts, education, health care, social and human services, programs benefiting youth and the elderly, and civic and community endeavors. Among the major beneficiaries are Texas Christian University and the University of Texas, as well as many other organizations. As of December 31, 1993, the foundation had market value of $235,065,097 and had made charitable gifts totalling $177,020,939. *Ron Tyler*

AMORY, NATHANIEL C. (1809–1864). Nathaniel C. Amory, Mexican land agent, member of the Republic of Texas[qv] State Department, and partner of James Harper Starr,[qv] was born in Massachusetts in 1809. He traveled to Texas in 1835 as a private agent of United States citizens who believed they held land in Texas. Upon discovering that the land scrip they held was fraudulent, Amory became translator for Mexican land commissioner George A. Nixon.[qv] He received a quarter-league grant from the Mexican government on October 5, 1835. After the Texas Revolution[qv] he was employed by the Republic of Texas State Department and served as chief clerk in 1838 and 1839. He was secretary of the Texas legation at Washington, D.C., from 1839 to 1842 under Bernard E. Bee and James Reily.[qqv] He was acting chargé d'affaires in Washington from January to March 1842, and with the assistance of the United States he secured the release of the Texan prisoners captured when the Texan Santa Fe expedition[qv] failed to conquer New Mexico for the Republic of Texas. Amory became the Texas consul at Boston, Massachusetts, on December 14, 1842, but returned to Nacogdoches in 1844 and formed a land and banking agency with James Harper Starr.

In 1854 Amory was elected a member of the Democratic party[qv] state central committee. He left the partnership with Starr on April 1, 1858, and returned to Boston, Massachusetts. Amory and Starr remained business associates and corresponded regularly until Amory's death on December 27, 1864, in Boston. Amory left two thousand dollars to Starr and the rest of his estate to his family in Massachusetts.

BIBLIOGRAPHY: Alma Howell Brown, "The Consular Service of the Republic of Texas," *Southwestern Historical Quarterly* 33 (January, April 1930). Carolyn Reeves Ericson, *Nacogdoches, Gateway to Texas: A Biographical Directory* (2 vols., Fort Worth: Arrow-Curtis Printing, 1974, 1987). Thomas Maitland Marshall, "Diplomatic Relations of Texas and the United States, 1839–1843," *Southwestern Historical Quarterly* 15 (April 1912). Pauline Shirley Murrie, *Early Records of Nacogdoches County* (Waco, 1965). William S. Speer and John H. Brown, eds., *Encyclopedia of the New West* (Marshall, Texas: United States Biographical Publishing, 1881; rpt., Easley, South Carolina: Southern Historical Press, 1978). Virginia H. Taylor, *The Spanish Archives of the General Land Office of Texas* (Austin: Lone Star, 1955).
Linda Sybert Hudson

AMOS CREEK. Amos Creek rises in north central Concho County three miles southwest of Paint Rock (at 31°29′ N, 99°53′ W) and flows eight miles northeast to its mouth on the Concho River, seven miles east of Paint Rock (at 31°31′ N, 99°48′ W). It traverses an area of steep slopes and benches surfaced by shallow clay loams that support grasses, live oaks, junipers, and mesquite.

AMPHION, TEXAS. Amphion is nine miles northwest of Pleasanton in west central Atascosa County, just east of Ranch Road 2146. The majority of settlers came to the site in the late 1880s. Some have claimed that Amphion was the first county seat. A Masonic lodge and a summer normal school were established in the town before 1900, and Amphion had a post office from 1881 to 1916. The origin of the name is not known. By 1887 Amphion had a general store and two cotton gins. The population was listed as 100 in 1896, when a hotel, church, and school had been added. In 1904 the Amphion school had seventy-two students and two teachers. The town declined in importance when the Artesian Belt Railroad bypassed it in favor of Jourdanton in 1909. The population remained at 100 in 1914, but the number of students in the school had declined to fifty-four, and the general store was the only business. In the 1940s Amphion had a school, a cemetery, and scattered dwellings. No population figures have been listed for Amphion since 1914, and by 1956 it was said to be a ghost town. In the late 1960s only the cemetery and a few structures remained at the site, which was designated a community on county maps in the 1980s.

BIBLIOGRAPHY: *Atascosa County Centennial, 1856-1956* (Jourdanton, Texas: Atascosa County Centennial Association, n.d). *Atascosa County History* (Pleasanton, Texas: Atascosa History Committee, 1984). Margaret G. Clover, The Place Names of Atascosa County (M.A. thesis, University of Texas, 1952). Janie Foster, History of Education in Atascosa County (M.A. thesis, University of Texas, 1936).
Linda Peterson

AMPUDIA, PEDRO DE (1803–1868). Pedro de Ampudia, Mexican general, was born in Cuba in 1803. As an artillery officer in the Mexican army, he participated in the capture of the Alamo and, after the Mexican defeat at San Jacinto, retreated with José de Urrea's[qv] army. Ampudia was commander of the units of the Mexican army stationed at Matamoros at the time of the Mier expedition,[qv] defeated the Texans at Mier in December 1842, and in January 1843 marched them as prisoners to Matamoros. He was appointed general in chief of the Mexican Army of the North just before the outbreak of the Mexican War[qv] and arrived at Matamoros on April 11, 1846, where he demanded that Gen. Zachary Taylor[qv] retreat to the Nueces River. After being succeeded in command by Mariano Arista,[qv] who arrived at Matamoros on April 24, 1846, Ampudia fought in the battles of Palo Alto and Resaca de la Palma,[qqv] regained command of the army, and was the commanding officer at the siege and fall of Monterrey. He surrendered the city to Taylor on September 23, 1846. In February 1847 he took part in the battle of Buena Vista. In 1864 Ampudia commanded the eastern liberal army. He died on August 7, 1868, and was buried in the Panteón de San Fernando.

BIBLIOGRAPHY: Vito Alessio Robles, *Coahuila y Texas en la época colonial* (Mexico City: Editorial Cultura, 1938; 2d ed., Mexico City: Editorial Porrúa, 1978). Miguel ángel Peral, ed., *Diccionario Biográfico Mexicano* (Mexico City: Editorial P.A.C., 1944).
David M. Vigness

AMSTERDAM, TEXAS. Amsterdam is on Chocolate Bayou ten miles west of Angleton in east central Brazoria County. A post office operated there from 1897 until 1905, when mail was routed through Liverpool. The town shipped cotton to Galveston from area plantations and depended on water traffic in the 1890s. At its height around 1900, Amsterdam had a hotel and school. However, the Galveston hurricane of 1900[qv] did considerable damage, and afterward the town failed to grow. State highway maps of 1936 showed only scattered dwellings at the townsite. By the 1970s construction of a nearby chemical plant had increased the number of local residences, and 1988 state highway maps showed several buildings.

BIBLIOGRAPHY: James A. Creighton, *A Narrative History of Brazoria County* (Angleton, Texas: Brazoria County Historical Commission, 1975).
Diana J. Kleiner

AMY, TEXAS. Amy was on the East Fork of Big Creek three miles north of Cooper in central Delta County. The site, located on the A. Askey survey, was settled early in the 1800s. The Amy school opened sometime around 1890; Jim Smith was one of the first instructors. In 1894 Robert Andrew Nicholson began a postal service, and the settlement was officially named Amy, but only after the postal department rejected the name Hobbs. The school was the center of the community. Records for 1904 listed seventy-six students and one teacher. The following year the post office was closed, and the area began to decline. In 1929 the school merged with Mulberry to form Clark School. By 1936 Amy was no longer identified on maps, but in 1939 it reported one business and twenty-five residents. In 1952 the store had closed, but twenty-five residents remained in the area. In 1964 a few scattered dwellings marked the old community site.

BIBLIOGRAPHY: Paul Garland Hervey, A History of Education in Delta County, Texas (M.A. thesis, University of Texas, 1951).

Vista K. McCroskey

ANACACHO, TEXAS. Anacacho was a ranching community eleven miles southeast of Brackettville on the Galveston, Harrisburg and San Antonio Railway, west of the Anacacho Mountains in southeastern Kinney County. A railroad depot named Leonhard is shown at the site on county maps in 1884. The community was established around the depot, chiefly by railroad employees. By 1909 the name had been changed to Anacacho. There is evidence that a game preserve was maintained near the community. By 1946 the community appears to have been abandoned. *Ruben E. Ochoa*

ANACACHO MOUNTAIN. Anacacho Mountain, the northwesternmost elevation in the Anacacho range, is located a mile southeast of Farm Road 1572 and the Southern Pacific Railroad in southeastern Kinney County (at 29°11′ N, 100°12′ W). With an elevation of 1,383 feet above sea level, its summit rises 400 feet above Farm Road 1572. The mountain is sometimes said to have been named for Ana Cacho, the wife of an early Spanish rancher in the area. According to other accounts the name was derived from a ceremonial rite honoring an Indian god, but the Indian name for the mountain was Decate. Early Spaniards, including Fernando del Bosque and Diego Ramón,[qqv] called the range Sierra Dacate y Yacasole.

ANACHOREMA INDIANS. In the latter part of the seventeenth century the Anachorema Indians lived north of Matagorda Bay on or near one of the major streams now in Jackson County, apparently the Lavaca River. Their village, which was visited by La Salle[qv] in 1687, was one of many Indian settlements along this river. Of these various settlements, only the Anachorema and Quara villages are identified in the records of the La Salle expedition.[qv] The Anachoremas are not referred to by this name in later times, and their ethnic affiliation remains unknown. Since they lived in an area dominated by Karankawan groups, it is possible that they too, were Karankawan. However, it is also possible that Anachorema is a French rendition of Aranama, the name of an Indian group that lived nearby at about the same time.

BIBLIOGRAPHY: Charles W. Hackett, ed., *Pichardo's Treatise on the Limits of Louisiana and Texas* (4 vols., Austin: University of Texas Press, 1931–46). John Gilmary Shea, *Discovery and Exploration of the Mississippi Valley* (New York: Redfield, 1852). *Thomas N. Campbell*

ANACHOREMA VILLAGE. The Anachorema Indian village was visited by René Robert Cavelier, Sieur de La Salle,[qv] in 1687 and was located northeast of Fort St. Louis, possibly on the Colorado River.

BIBLIOGRAPHY: Frederick Webb Hodge, ed., *Handbook of American Indians North of Mexico* (2 vols., Washington: GPO, 1907, 1910; rpt., New York: Pageant, 1959).

ANADARKO CREEK. Anadarko Creek rises in south central Rusk County four miles southeast of Laneville (at 31°54′ N, 94°47′ W) and flows west for eight miles to its juncture with the East Fork of the Angelina River, four miles southeast of New Salem (at 31°56′ N, 94°53′ W). The stream flows over flat to rolling prairie surfaced by dark calcareous clays that support pine forest.

ANADARKO INDIANS. The Anadarko (Anadaca, Anduico, Nadaco, Nandacao) Indians, a tribe of the southwestern or Hasinai division of the Caddo Indians, lived near the future boundary between Nacogdoches and Rusk counties during the late seventeenth and early eighteenth centuries. Anadarko Creek in Rusk County received its name from these Indians. H. E. Bolton[qv] has suggested that Nabiri may have been an early name for the Anadarko, but this has yet to be demonstrated. In the late eighteenth century, after their numbers had been greatly reduced by disease and warfare, some of the Anadarkos moved northward and lived along the Sabine River in the area that became Panola County. After the Texas Revolution[qv] they migrated westward and, at various times, had settlements along the Brazos River and between the Brazos and Trinity rivers north and northwest of present Waco. In 1854 they were placed on the Brazos Indian Reservation[qv] in future Young County and in 1859 were removed to Indian Territory, now Oklahoma. Today their descendants live near the town of Anadarko (named for these Indians) in Caddo County, Oklahoma.

BIBLIOGRAPHY: Herbert E. Bolton, "The Native Tribes about the East Texas Missions," *Quarterly of the Texas State Historical Association 11* (April 1908). Jesse Clifton Burt, *Indians of the Southeast: Then and Now* (Nashville: Abingdon Press, 1973). John R. Swanton, *Source Material on the History and Ethnology of the Caddo Indians* (Smithsonian Institution, Bureau of American Ethnology Bulletin 132, Washington: GPO, 1942). Dorman H. Winfrey and James M. Day, eds., *Texas Indian Papers* (4 vols., Austin: Texas State Library, 1959–61; rpt., 5 vols., Austin: Pemberton Press, 1966). *Thomas N. Campbell*

ANAGADO INDIANS. The Anagados, an otherwise unidentified Indian group, was reported by Álvar Núñez Cabeza de Vaca[qv] as living in southern Texas near the Yguaces Indians between 1528 and 1534. *Margery H. Krieger*

ANAHUAC, TEXAS. Anahuac, the county seat of Chambers County, is on the northeast bank of Trinity Bay on the Texas Gulf Coast. The earliest inhabitants of the Anahuac area were Atakapan Indians. In 1721 French explorer Jean Baptiste de La Harpe[qv] visited a village of some 200 Atakapans located between the future site of Anahuac and Round Point. The site was originally known by Anglos as Perry's point, a name attributed to Col. Henry Perry,[qv] a noted filibuster, who established a camp there in 1816. Col. John Davis Bradburn,[qv] the newly appointed Mexican commander, arrived there in October 1830 with three officers and forty men to begin construction of a fort. Gen. Manuel de Mier y Terán,[qv] commanding officer of the Mexican states of Coahuila and Texas,[qv] officially named the town Anahuac in January 1831, after the ancient capital of the Aztecs.

Fort Anahuac was the scene of incidents in 1832 and 1835 that preceded the Texas Revolution[qv] (*see also* ANAHUAC DISTURBANCES). Although the town flourished briefly prior to the 1832 battle, the population declined dramatically afterward. A long-running civil dispute between Gen. Thomas Jefferson Chambers and Charles Willcox[qqv] over ownership of the townsite began in 1838 and was not fully resolved until after the assassination of Chambers in 1865. This dispute obviously hindered the development of the town. General Chambers briefly called the town Chambersea in his own honor, but the town did not follow suit. A small Confederate outpost was established here in 1862 and was called Fort Chambers.

The first significant commercial development came with the establishment of a large sawmill in 1894 by Jesse and Charles R. Cummings. The mill was moved to Wallisville in 1898. The construction of the Lone Star Canal Company began in 1902 under the direction of Berriman Richard Garland and A. L. Williams. The Anahuac Townsite Company, under the direction of William Duncan Willcox, George R. Fahring, and Francis M. Hamilton, began real estate development of the town in the early 1900s. Business leaders were successful in an April 11, 1907, election to make Anahuac the county seat instead of Wallisville. Legal efforts to reverse the election failed, and the First Court of Civil Appeals ordered county records transferred to Anahuac in 1908.

The Anahuac Independent School District was established in 1917 and in 1990 covered the middle portion of Chambers County, including the communities of Double Bayou, Eminence, Hankamer, Oak Island, Smith Point, and Wallisville. All school facilities are located in Anahuac. The 1935 discoveries of the Anahuac and Turtle Bay oilfields brought another period of economic development for Anahuac. Voters approved the incorporation of the city of Anahuac on October 30, 1948, and elected attorney Everett Cain mayor on January 8, 1949. The Anahuac National Wildlife Refuge[qv] was established in 1963 by the United States Fish and Wildlife Service. The refuge is located sixteen miles southeast of Anahuac. The Anahuac Area Chamber of Commerce organized the first annual Gatorfest in September 1989, an event that drew 14,000 people to Fort Anahuac Park. In 1990 the population of Anahuac was 1,993.

BIBLIOGRAPHY: Anahuac *Progress*, May 19, 1939. Bexar Archives, Barker Texas History Center, University of Texas at Austin. John V. Clay, *Spain, Mexico and the Lower Trinity: An Early History of the Texas Gulf Coast* (Baltimore: Gateway Press, 1987). Jewel Horace Harry, A History of Chambers County (M.A. thesis, University of Texas, 1940; rpt., Dallas: Taylor, 1981). Margaret S. Henson, *Anahuac in 1832: The Cradle of the Texas Revolution* (Anahuac, Texas: Fort Anahuac Committee of the Chambers County Historical Commission, 1982). Margaret S. Henson, *Juan Davis Bradburn: A Reappraisal of the Mexican Commander of Anahuac* (College Station: Texas A&M University Press, 1982). Margaret S. Henson and Kevin Ladd, *Chambers County: A Pictorial History* (Norfolk, Virginia: Donning, 1988). Sally Hill, Lone Star Canal: Application for Official Texas Historical Marker (MS, Chambers County Historical Commission, Anahuac, Texas, 1978). William Kennedy, *Texas: The Rise, Progress, and Prospects of the Republic of Texas* (London: Hastings, 1841; rpt., Fort Worth: Molyneaux Craftsmen, 1925). *Official Records of the Union and Confederate Navies* (Washington: Department of the Navy, 1894–1927).

Kevin Ladd

ANAHUAC DISTURBANCES. Two major events at Anahuac, in 1832 and 1835, upset those who wanted to maintain the status quo with Mexican authorities and thus helped to precipitate the Texas Revolution.[qv] Both difficulties centered around the collection of customs by the national government of Mexico.

Col. Juan Davis Bradburn[qv] and approximately forty officers and men landed at the bluff overlooking the mouth of the Trinity, called Perry's Point, on October 26, 1830, with orders to establish a garrison and a town. The garrison was originally chosen as a protected, strategic point from which to prevent smuggling on the Trinity and San Jacinto rivers; accordingly, it also aided the collector of customs, George Fisher,[qv] after he arrived in November 1831, to collect national tariffs and prevent smuggling. Bradburn was also charged with preventing the entrance of immigrants from the United States in accord with the recently passed Law of April 6, 1830,[qv] which was designed to encourage Mexican and European settlement of Texas and to restrict Anglo-American settlement.

The first trouble for Bradburn came in January 1831, when a state-appointed land commissioner, José Francisco Madero,[qv] arrived to issue titles to those residents of the lower Trinity who had settled prior to 1828. Although both the state and national governments had previously approved granting titles, Bradburn believed that the Law of April 6, 1830, had annulled the earlier grants. The matter was complicated by politics because Bradburn represented the Centralist administration, which believed in a strong central government and weak states, and Madero stood for the opposition, the states'-rights-minded Federalists of northern Mexico. Bradburn arrested Madero, but he was soon released by the state authorities, who appealed to Bradburn's superiors, and the land commissioner quickly issued more than fifty titles to local residents before he returned to his home near the Rio Grande. Madero also organized an ayuntamiento[qv] at the Atascosito Crossing of the Trinity (*see* ATASCOSITO ROAD) and named it Villa de la Santísima Trinidad de la Libertad, shortened to Liberty by Anglo settlers (*see* LIBERTY, TEXAS [Liberty County]). Although this was an act within his powers, it roused the ire of Bradburn and the Centralists, who saw it as a challenge to the national government's control of the area.

Another crisis followed the visit of Gen. Manuel de Mier y Terán,[qv] the commandant of the eastern interior provinces, in November 1831. He did not want the ayuntamiento at Liberty and ordered it moved to Anahuac. Because he did not approve of Anglo-American lawyers practicing before the court without certification from Mexican authorities, he ordered Bradburn to inspect their licenses. The general also ordered an inspection of land titles. But his greatest offense, as far as the colonists were concerned, was ordering George Fisher to begin collecting duties from all ships already in the Brazos River and Galveston Bay. The ship captains complained about retroactive laws. Moreover, the assistant collector for the Brazos had not yet arrived, and all vessels would have to clear their papers at Anahuac for the time being. This arbitrary decision was inconvenient for Brazos captains. Several left the river without stopping for clearance at the mouth, where a small number of soldiers were garrisoned, and shots were exchanged between the ships and the troops.

Further trouble stemmed from Anglo-American animosity against Bradburn and his troops, some of whom were former convicts sent to the frontier to do heavy construction work in order to earn their freedom. At peak strength, Bradburn had fewer than 300 men under his command both at Anahuac and at Fort Velasco on the Brazos, and of these probably fewer than twenty were convicts. But Anglo neighbors attributed petty thievery and an attack against a woman to the presence of prisoners among the military. Bradburn had also incorporated two or three runaway slaves from Louisiana into his garrison. Mexico allowed no slavery[qv] but had permitted Austin's colonists to bring blacks in as indentured servants; thus Bradburn acted correctly when the fugitives applied for asylum. A slave catcher arrived but was unsuccessful in his efforts to recover the Louisiana runaways, and he hired William B. Travis[qv] to attempt to recover the escaped slaves. Travis and his law partner, Patrick C. Jack,[qv] had already antagonized Bradburn by starting a civil militia, contrary to Mexican law, to fight the "Indians," a euphemism for Mexican soldiers. Bradburn briefly incarcerated Jack for parading this militia. Later Travis decided to trick Bradburn into releasing the runaway slaves. A man, perhaps Travis, wrapped in a concealing cloak, delivered a note purportedly from an acquaintance of the commander warning that a force of Louisianans was on the march to recover the fugitives he was harboring. When he realized that he had been given false information, Bradburn arrested Jack and Travis; because the jail was not adequately secure he placed them in an empty brick kiln. Brazos valley hotheads organized a rescue force of perhaps 200 men, who reached Turtle Bayou, six miles north of Anahuac, on June 9, 1832. On their way, they captured Bradburn's entire cavalry force of nineteen men and held them hostage, planning to exchange them for Travis and Jack and a couple of others Bradburn had arrested. After a day of skirmishing, an exchange was arranged by the rebels, most of whom withdrew to Turtle Bayou, where they released the captured cavalrymen. When Bradburn discovered that not all the insurgents had evacuated as they had promised, he refused to release his prisoners and instead announced that he would fire on the town. After a skirmish between Bradburn's men and the remaining Anglos, the latter also fell back to Turtle Bayou to await the arrival of artillery. A large party bringing the ordnance up from the Brazos settlements met Mexican troops in a major engagement at the battle of Velasco.[qv] Meanwhile, the party on Turtle Bayou composed and signed the Turtle Bayou Resolutions,[qv] which explained their rebellion against Bradburn as part of the reform movement of Federalist general Antonio López de Santa Anna,[qv] who had recently won a victory over administration forces at Tampico.

The matter was resolved when Col. José de las Piedras,[qv] Bradburn's immediate superior, arrived from Nacogdoches and, thinking he was outnumbered, bowed to the wishes of the insurgents. He removed Bradburn, reinstalled the ayuntamiento at Liberty, and turned over the Anglo-American prisoners to this body. The prisoners were soon released, and after Piedras left, Travis, Jack, and the others returned to Anahuac, where they incited the garrison to rebel against its Centralist officers. A Federalist officer, Colonel Subarán, assumed command of the troops and, within a month, boarded the garrison on ships and moved to the Rio Grande.

Merchants returned to Anahuac, and business continued without national tariffs until 1835, when the government sent collectors and support troops back to Texas. The national government depended entirely upon customs duties for revenue, and Texas had to pay its share. Andrew Briscoe,[qv] a local merchant, complained that the duties were not collected uniformly in all the ports and refused to cooperate at Anahuac. He intentionally tricked the new commander, Capt. Antonio Tenorio,[qv] by loading his boat in such a manner as to excite curiosity, while stowing bricks, not smuggled goods, in the hull. Tenorio, much aggravated, arrested Briscoe and his associate, DeWitt Clinton Harris,[qv] on June 12, but Tenorio's force of some forty troops was no match for the Anglo response. When Travis learned of Briscoe's arrest, he raised volunteers who marched to Harrisburg from the Brazos and commandeered a vessel to sail for Anahuac. Tenorio surrendered on June 20 to twenty-five Anglo insurgents, who disarmed the government troops and returned with them to Harrisburg. But Travis had acted without real community support. He felt the necessity to make a public apology for his rash actions in order to keep from endangering Stephen F. Austin,[qv] who was in Mexico City.

BIBLIOGRAPHY: Margaret S. Henson, *Anahuac in 1832: The Cradle of the Texas Revolution* (Anahuac, Texas: Fort Anahuac Committee of the Chambers County Historical Commission, 1982). Margaret S. Henson, *Juan Davis Bradburn: A Reappraisal of the Mexican Commander of Anahuac* (College Station: Texas A&M University Press, 1982). Adele B. Looscan, "Harris County, 1822–1845," *Southwestern Historical Quarterly* 18–19 (October 1914–July 1915).

Margaret Swett Henson

ANAHUAC FIELD. Anahuac field is an oval-shaped oil and gas field near Turtle Bay in central Chambers County, on the coast of Southeast Texas. Its discovery and development were scientifically guided by its primary operators, Humble Oil and Refining Company, Sun Oil Company, and Gulf Oil Corporation. The field draws oil and gas from a faulted domal uplift in massive sands of the Marginulina and upper Frio formations. The source of its primary recovery was a strong water-drive and gas-cap expansion, but since April 1957 the reservoir has been maintained by reinjection into the Frio formation of all the nonassociated and most of the casinghead gas produced in the field. Between its discovery on March 6, 1935, and January 1, 1993, the field produced more than 277 million barrels of oil, and between 1974 and 1993 the field yielded more than 43.3 billion cubic feet of gas. The field is significant because the small number of operators in it followed a systematic drilling program that spaced wells for optimal oil recovery and economic return. Anahuac field was named for the county seat, situated five east of it.

In 1925 and again in 1927 and 1929 Humble Oil and Refining Company conducted early forms of geophysical measures and tests in the area of the future Anahuac field, looking for evidence of an oil-bearing structure. When geophysics offered no encouragement, Humble management allowed the company leases to expire. However, the management did not lose exploratory interest in the area. Late in 1932 Humble made a trade for the right to explore a block of 21,000 acres for thirty-five cents an acre. In the trade Humble gained the right to select any part of the acreage for drilling at five dollars an acre. In May 1933 the company used a reflection seismograph, the latest in geophysical equipment, on the block and found evidence of a structure. With these encouraging results, Humble leased three-fourths of the original block. On December 8, 1934, Humble spudded the No. 1 A. D. Middleton in Section 58, Houston and Texas Central Railway Company survey, in central Chambers County. The well had a show of high-gravity oil at the section between 7,024 and 7,050 feet in the Frio sand in February 1935. On March 6, 1935, the well reached a depth of 7,052 feet with an initial daily production of 120 barrels of oil and a gas-to-oil ratio of 12,500 cubic feet per barrel. The No. 1 Middleton was deepened to 7,088 feet on March 16, 1935, in an attempt to reduce the gas-oil ratio. From the lower depth, the well yielded 547 barrels of oil a day with an improved gas-oil ratio of 435 cubic feet to one barrel of oil.

After the success of the No. 1 Middleton, four more wells were completed in the field by early May. On May 8, 1935, the Railroad Commission[qv] of Texas set well spacing at one well to every twenty acres. At the same time the commission based production allowable 50 percent on acreage and 50 percent on well potential. On July 21 an independent partnership, Glenn H. McCarthy[qv] and R. A. Mason, brought in the No. 1 White in the James McGahey survey, with initial production of 588 barrels of oil a day, and extended the field about three miles to the north. Although nine wells were completed in the field by the end of July, it was the No. 1 White that proved the substantial size of the field and influenced leasing to the north and east. Although intense leasing drove prices as high as $1,000 an acre, the drilling of wells was cheap and quick in the new field. The average cost of drilling and completing a well to 7,100 feet was $23,000. The average time needed to drill a well through the soft sand and shale of the subsurface was twenty-one days. Even with cheap drilling costs and short drilling time, operators completed only thirty-eight wells by the end of 1935, when annual production for the field was 342,239 barrels of oil. The few operators in the field faced no competition or time constraints in field development. They chose safe locations by staking direct offsets to producing wells because they wanted an orderly development of the field and because they knew little about the producing structure.

Until the summer of 1935, when leasing excitement gripped the town of Anahuac, the county seat consisted of 200 families and few accommodations for newcomers. To meet the demand, new hotels and cafes sprouted as quickly as mushrooms after rain. Although the town had no railroad, a bus company scheduled service through Anahuac. In the field, Humble constructed a camp of twenty-five houses for employees, three warehouses, and a one-unit high-pressure pump station to carry oil through a six-inch line to its carrier in Barbers Hill oilfield[qv] and on to its Baytown refinery. In September 1935 Sun Oil Company built a four-inch pipeline in the field that eventually reached its refinery, and Gulf Production Company completed a six-inch line to run to the Hankamer field. Humble built a modern road through the field to replace an earlier wooden one. A canal was dug to supply water for the field from the Trinity River. With these new constructions, operators were set to continue field development.

During 1936, development of the field progressed with the drilling of 106 additional wells. By the end of the year only three operators were working the field, and it was estimated that 50 percent of the field was developed. Production for 1936 was 2,603,280 barrels of oil, almost 2,000 barrels below the set allowable. Although 1937 production almost doubled the 1936 figure, yields were held to just over 2.5 million barrels a year through 1940. By February 1941 Anahuac field covered 7,300 acres and Humble owned 75 percent of it. Four other companies held the remaining 25 percent. At the end of 1941, when the field reached full development, annual production was 4,649,833 barrels of oil from 356 wells and 378,438,000 cubic feet of gas from three producing wells. Annual oil production climbed during the early 1940s until peak production was reported at the end of 1944, when 11,916,137 barrels of oil were brought to the surface. Production was maintained above five million barrels of oil a year through 1975, the fortieth anniversary of the discovery of the field. By 1985, after fifty years of operation, the field gave up over 1.3 million barrels of oil annually. At the end of 1992 Anahuac field reported cumulative production of 277,086,782 barrels of oil, proving the effectiveness of the optimal oil-recovery program set in place by Humble, Sun, and Gulf fifty-seven years earlier.

BIBLIOGRAPHY: William E. Galloway et al., *Atlas of Major Texas Oil Reservoirs* (Austin: University of Texas Bureau of Economic Geology, 1983). Frank J. Gardner, *Texas Gulf Coast Oil* (Dallas: Rinehart Oil New Company, 1948). Edgar Wesley Owen, *Trek of the Oil Finders: A History of Exploration for Petroleum* (Tulsa: American Association for Petroleum Geologists, 1975). Railroad Commission of Texas, *Annual Report of the Oil and Gas Division,* 1943.
Julia Cauble Smith

ANAHUAC NATIONAL WILDLIFE REFUGE. Anahuac National Wildlife Refuge was established in 1963 by the United States Fish and Wildlife Service on 12,000 acres at the juncture of Oyster Bay and East Bay in Chambers County. The refuge had doubled in size by 1982, when the Nature Conservancy, a nonprofit organization based at Arlington, Virginia, purchased an additional 12,670 acres from Ralph J. Barrow's ranch in 1981. The refuge provides a safe habitat for wintering ducks, geese, and other waterfowl, shelters alligators and other species, and provides a year-round home for mottled ducks.

BIBLIOGRAPHY: Margaret S. Henson and Kevin Ladd, *Chambers County: A Pictorial History* (Norfolk, Virginia: Donning, 1988).
Diana J. Kleiner

ANAMIS VILLAGE. Anamis was an Indian village found by René Robert Cavelier, Sieur de La Salle,[qv] in 1686 on his way from Matagorda Bay toward the Mississippi. It was possibly associated with the Caddoans. The actual site has not been identified.

BIBLIOGRAPHY: Frederick Webb Hodge, ed., *Handbook of American Indians North of Mexico* (2 vols., Washington: GPO, 1907, 1910; rpt., New York: Pageant, 1959).
Margery H. Krieger

ANAO INDIANS. In a Spanish missionary report of 1691, the Anao Indians were listed among the enemies of the Hasinais of eastern Texas. Twelve names occur on this list, and it is said that two or three of the groups named lived southeast of the Hasinais; the others lived to the west. The identity of the Anaos remains undetermined. It is evident that they were not the same as the Annahos, listed in documents of the La Salle expedition[qv] (1687) as allies of the Kadohadachos on the Red River. The Annahos were Osage Indians, whose base area at that time was western Missouri, and there is no record of their having lived as far south as eastern Texas or western Louisiana.

BIBLIOGRAPHY: Pierre Margry, ed., *Découvertes et établissements des Français dans l'ouest et dans le sud de l'Amérique septentrionale, 1614–1754* (6 vols., Paris: Jouast, 1876–86). Ralph A. Smith, trans., "Account of the Journey of Bénard de La Harpe," *Southwestern Historical Quarterly* 62 (July, October 1958, January, April 1959). John R. Swanton, *Source Material on the History and Ethnology of the Caddo Indians* (Smithsonian Institution, Bureau of American Ethnology Bulletin 132, Washington: GPO, 1942).
Thomas N. Campbell

ANAQUA, TEXAS. Anaqua, possibly the first site in Texas to receive a name, is on the San Antonio River twenty miles south of Victoria in Victoria County. It is described by Álvar Núñez Cabeza de Vaca,[qv] as the habitat of the "Iguaces" Indians, whom authorities believe to have been the Anaquas, a Tonkawa group. The locale was named for the anaqua trees (Ehretria *elliptica*) common in the area. Carlos de la Garza[qv] built a chapel there as early as 1820, and Anglo settlers came after 1836. These early homesteaders used the wood from the "knock-away" or anaqua trees for posts, wheel spokes, axles, yokes, and tool handles. Anaqua became a trading post at which a ferry operated for many years. A post office, which at first was simply a box nailed to a big anaqua tree, was established in 1852, and the community also erected a rural school. The population grew from fifteen in 1884 to twenty-five in 1890. In 1906, however, the settlement's focus was drawn five miles east when the St. Louis, Brownsville and Mexico Railway established a station at McFaddin. The Anaqua post office had been closed by 1919, and the school had become part of Kemper City Common School by 1963. The Anaqua area is the site of the Anaqua oilfield. (*See also* CARLOS RANCHO, TEXAS.)

BIBLIOGRAPHY: Hobart Huson, *Refugio: A Comprehensive History of Refugio County from Aboriginal Times to 1953* (2 vols., Woodsboro, Texas: Rooke Foundation, 1953, 1955). Victoria *Advocate,* Progress Edition, March 10, 1963. *The Victoria Sesquicentennial "Scrapbook"* (Victoria, Texas: Victoria *Advocate,* 1974).
Kathryn Stoner O'Connor

ANARENE, TEXAS. Anarene, in south central Archer County, was named for Annie Lawrence Graham, daughter of pioneer settler J. M. Keen, who, after serving in the Confederate Army, began ranching in the area and built up his herd to 15,000 head. He used a terrapin emblem for a brand because he found a rock painting of a terrapin at Terrapin Springs, three miles northwest of Olney. His daughter Annie married Charlie Graham, whose family came to Archer County to raise sheep. Joy Graham, their son, claimed that "the only reason he was born was due to the invention of barbed wire,[qv] which kept peace, leading to a marriage between the sheepman and cattleman."

Anarene was founded on the Wichita Falls and Southern Railroad in 1908. Its primary economic activity was hauling coal from the recently opened Newcastle Mine, some twenty miles south. Charlie Graham built a two-story hotel, opened a post office, and laid out the town with the help of J. H. Kemp and Frank Kell,[qv] officials of the Wichita Falls and Southern Railroad Company. Most businesses were on First Street; the school was to the west of Graham Street and south of Dallas Avenue. The railroad buildings, old store, dipping vat, cotton gin tank, loading ramps, cattle pens, and baseball field were across the tracks to the east.

From the Anarene pens thousands of cattle were shipped to market. Early in World War I[qv] Sam Cowan sent a shipment of several hundred four-year-old steers weighing 1,800 pounds each from Anarene to St. Louis and received eighteen cents a pound, the record high price at the time. In 1929 Anarene had a store, a schoolhouse, a post office, a blacksmith shop, a filling station, and a two-story hotel. Graham owned a stock farm of several thousand acres nearby and took part in school and church affairs in Anarene. The *Texas Almanac*[qv] reported a population of 100 for 1929, but by 1933 the number had declined to only twenty. The railroad station closed in 1951 and the post office in 1955.

BIBLIOGRAPHY: Jack Loftin, *Trails Through Archer* (Burnet, Texas: Nortex, 1979).
Jack O. Loftin

ANATHAGUA INDIANS. The Anathagua (Anatagu) Indians are known from a Spanish document of 1748 that lists twenty-five Indian groups of east central and southeastern Texas who had asked for missions in that general area. About half the names on this list, including Anathagua, cannot be identified. It is possible but not demonstrable that the Anathaguas were the same as the Quanataguos reported at San Antonio de Valero Mission at San Antonio in the 1720s. J. R. Swanton included the Quanataguos in his list of Coahuiltecan groups, apparently because one Quanataguo woman was said to have married a Coahuiltecan. The list of twenty-five groups that includes Anathagua contains no names that can be identified as Coahuiltecan; the identifiable names indicate only Caddoans (including Wichita), Tonkawans, Atakapans, and Karankawans. Both Anathagua and Quanataguo bear some resemblance to Quiutcanuaha, the name of a group identified in 1691 as living an unspecified distance southwest of the Hasinai

Indians of eastern Texas, but no identities can be established. The affiliations of all three groups remain undetermined.

BIBLIOGRAPHY: Herbert Eugene Bolton, *Texas in the Middle Eighteenth Century* (Berkeley: University of California Press, 1915; rpt., Austin: University of Texas Press, 1970). Charles W. Hackett, ed., *Pichardo's Treatise on the Limits of Louisiana and Texas* (4 vols., Austin: University of Texas Press, 1931–46). Frederick Webb Hodge, ed., *Handbook of American Indians North of Mexico* (2 vols., Washington: GPO, 1907, 1910; rpt., New York: Pageant, 1959). J. R. Swanton, *Linguistic Material from the Tribes of Southern Texas and Northeastern Mexico* (Washington: Smithsonian Institution, 1940). John R. Swanton, *Source Material on the History and Ethnology of the Caddo Indians* (Smithsonian Institution, Bureau of American Ethnology Bulletin 132, Washington: GPO, 1942).
Thomas N. Campbell

ANCHIMO INDIANS. In 1683–84 Juan Domínguez de Mendoza[qv] led an exploratory expedition from El Paso as far eastward as the junction of the Concho and Colorado rivers, east of the site of present San Angelo. In his itinerary he listed the names of thirty-seven Indian groups, including the Anchimos, from whom he expected to receive delegations. Nothing further is known about the Anchimos, who seem to have been one of the many Indian groups of north central Texas that were swept into oblivion by the southward thrust of the Lipan Apache and Comanche Indians in the eighteenth century.

BIBLIOGRAPHY: Herbert Eugene Bolton, ed., *Spanish Exploration in the Southwest, 1542–1706* (New York: Scribner, 1908; rpt., New York: Barnes and Noble, 1959). Charles W. Hackett, ed., *Pichardo's Treatise on the Limits of Louisiana and Texas* (4 vols., Austin: University of Texas Press, 1931–46).
Thomas N. Campbell

ANCHOR, TEXAS. Anchor is at the intersection of Farm roads 521 and 44 four miles northwest of Angleton in central Brazoria County. A two-story residence that was once the Whistler Hotel is all that remained in the 1980s to mark a once thriving town that stood at the junction of three railroads. The Columbia Tap, from Houston to East Columbia, was built through the area about 1852. The Houston and Brazos Valley crossed the original line in 1893, at a point first called Chenango Junction. In 1908 a third line was built through to Sugar Land. Four passenger trains ran through Anchor each day until World War I;[qv] afterward the passenger and freight traffic increased. A depot built in the 1890s handled all railroad business from West Columbia and Brazoria, and many "special trains" took people to the circus in Houston, to tours of a ship in port at Galveston, to a baseball game at Velasco, or elsewhere.

The town was established near the site of an earlier settlement known as Fruitland, at the junction of the International–Great Northern and the Velasco Terminal railroads. Jacob Whistler moved his family to this junction in 1895 and changed its name to Anchor, in honor of his former hometown in Illinois. Lots were sold at the site, but the development failed, and Fruitland lots later became an extension of the Anchor townsite. The Whistlers built a hotel and restaurant to accommodate passengers who switched trains there. A post office was established in 1897 with George W. Richey as postmaster. Eventually Anchor had two general stores, two sawmills, a cotton gin, a blacksmith shop, a cafe, a plant for processing frog legs, day and night Western Union service, two churches, and its own school, where Miss Minnie McMillan (later Mrs. Holland) taught from about 1914 to 1917.

Anchor was a trading center for the many farms in the area. Cotton and corn were the main crops, but onions, cabbage, tomatoes, and other crops were also marketed. Most families raised cattle for milk, butter, and meat, as well as hogs and chickens. A canning factory, mainly for tomatoes, was operated by a man named Burchard. By the time good roads and affordable automobiles became available, the area had had several storms and floods. The post office was discontinued on June 15, 1920, and mail was subsequently distributed from Angleton. In 1933 the community had two businesses and a population of fifty, but war rationing brought a further store closing in the 1940s. When State Highway 288 was constructed, it bypassed the town to the east. Development of the Angleton-Anchor oilfield caused little local growth, and by 1950 the town no longer appeared in the census.

BIBLIOGRAPHY: James Lewellyn Allhands, *Gringo Builders* (Joplin, Missouri, Dallas, Texas, 1931). Angleton *Times*, September 14, 1900, May 11, July 20, 27, August 3, 1986. Brazoria County Federation of Women's Clubs, *History of Brazoria County* (1940). James A. Creighton, *A Narrative History of Brazoria County* (Angleton, Texas: Brazoria County Historical Commission, 1975). Houston *Chronicle*, December 20, 1959.
Marie Beth Jones

ANCHORAGE, TEXAS. Anchorage is just east of Ranch Road 2504 and fourteen miles northwest of Pleasanton in west central Atascosa County. In 1889 Scottish seaman Thomas Whittet bought 200 acres of land there from Francisco de la Garza and was granted a post office, which he called Anchorage because he had "anchored" there. In 1890 the town had a general store. By 1896 the population was recorded as fifteen, and the town had two general stores and one gin. The population increased to 120 by 1914 and included a physician, Mrs. M. J. Whittet. Anchorage was listed as having one business in 1933. The post office was closed in 1935. In the 1940s the town had a cemetery, a church, a factory, and a few scattered dwellings. The factory no longer appeared on maps in the 1960s. In 1990 the site of Anchorage was marked on state highway maps, but without further information.

BIBLIOGRAPHY: *Atascosa County History* (Pleasanton, Texas: Atascosa History Committee, 1984). Margaret G. Clover, The Place Names of Atascosa County (M.A. thesis, University of Texas, 1952). Fred Tarpley, *1001 Texas Place Names* (Austin: University of Texas Press, 1980).
Linda Peterson

ANCHOSE INDIANS. The Anchose (Anchosa) Indians are known from a Spanish document of 1748 that lists the names of twenty-five Indian groups of east central and southeastern Texas who had asked for missions in that general area. About half the names on this list, including Anchose, cannot be identified. The identifiable groups include Caddoans, Tonkawans, Atakapans, and Karankawans.

BIBLIOGRAPHY: Herbert Eugene Bolton, *Texas in the Middle Eighteenth Century: Studies in Spanish Colonial History and Administration* (Berkeley: University of California Press, 1915; rpt., Austin: University of Texas Press, 1970). Charles W. Hackett, ed., *Pichardo's Treatise on the Limits of Louisiana and Texas* (4 vols., Austin: University of Texas Press, 1931–46). Juan Agustín Morfi, *History of Texas, 1673–1779* (2 vols., Albuquerque: Quivira Society, 1935; rpt., New York: Arno, 1967).
Thomas N. Campbell

ANDACAMINO INDIANS. A few individuals are identified by this name (Spanish for "wanderer") in the records of San José y San Miguel de Aguayo Mission at San Antonio. It seems likely that this was a convenient term used by mission personnel to refer to displaced Indians of unidentifiable band or tribal origins. No such name appears in other eighteenth-century documents. J. R. Swanton listed Andacamino as a Coahuiltecan band, but he presented no evidence in support of this linguistic identification.

BIBLIOGRAPHY: Frederick Webb Hodge, ed., *Handbook of American Indians North of Mexico* (2 vols., Washington: GPO, 1907, 1910; rpt., New York: Pageant, 1959). John R. Swanton, *The Indian Tribes of North America* (Gross Pointe, Michigan: Scholarly Press, 1968).
Thomas N. Campbell

ANDER, TEXAS. Ander, on Farm Road 1961 in northern Goliad County, was settled during the pre–Civil War German immigrations by families from Prussia, Saxony, Alsace, and Lorraine. The community was originally named Hanover after the German city and duchy. The settlers earned their livelihood from farming and raising hogs, sheep, poultry, and some cattle. Since the town was never on a railroad, freight had to be hauled by wagon from Cuero and Yorktown; turkeys were herded to market in Cuero several times a year. A general store, one of the community's most important institutions, operated under various owners from the 1860s to 1972. In time Ander had a horse-powered cotton gin, which was later converted to steam; a blacksmith shop, which became a garage and filling station in a later era; and a hospital, which operated from 1896 to 1920. A mission Lutheran church, administered by the pastor of Meyersville, was conducted in various homes until 1876, when St. Peter's Lutheran Church was established and became the first church in Goliad County and the focus of the community's life. The present structure was built in 1966.

Mail was picked up weekly at Meyersville until a post office was established in 1881 at Weser, two miles away, allowing mail delivery twice a week. In 1900 the citizens of Hanover applied for their own post office, only to discover that another Hanover already existed in Texas. They then chose the name Ander, in honor of Theodore N. Ander, pastor of the Lutheran church. The Ander post office operated until 1920, when mail was again delivered from Weser until the rural route was established in 1927.

The Ander school was conducted through the Lutheran church until 1944, when bus service to Goliad closed rural schools. The last schoolhouse now serves as the Ander Community Club. In 1914 Ander recorded a population of fifty, which decreased to about twenty by the 1930s but climbed again to about fifty in the late 1940s. In 1986 Ander had thirty residents. In 1990 it had thirty-five.

BIBLIOGRAPHY: Goliad County Historical Commission, *The History and Heritage of Goliad County*, ed. Jakie L. Pruett and Everett B. Cole (Austin: Eakin Press, 1983). *Craig H. Roell*

ANDERS CREEK. Anders Creek, also known as Andys Creek, rises five miles southeast of Mount Vernon in southeastern Franklin County (at 33°07′ N, 95°11′ W) and runs southeast for six miles to its mouth (at 33°03′ N, 95°08′ W) on Lake Bob Sandlin in southwestern Titus County, three miles southwest of Monticello. The area is gently undulating, loamy, and heavily wooded, with pines and various hardwoods predominating.

BIBLIOGRAPHY: John Clements, *Flying the Colors: Texas, a Comprehensive Look at Texas Today, County by County* (Dallas: Clements Research, 1984).

ANDERSON, BAILEY, SR. (1753–1840). Bailey Anderson, Sr., Revolutionary War veteran and Texas pioneer, the son of John and Sarah (Carney) Anderson, was born on November 13, 1753, in Stafford County, Virginia. He married a woman believed to be named Mary Wyatt about 1770. The family moved to South Carolina, and Anderson, his father, and two brothers were in the Revolutionary War. His father and two brothers were killed. In 1795 Anderson moved to Kentucky, where he represented Warren County in the state legislature in 1800–02. In 1805 he moved to Indiana. Anderson Township in Warrick County, Indiana, was named in his honor.

The family started for Texas in 1816. Mary Anderson died and was buried on the shore of the Mississippi River in a hollowed-out cottonwood log. The family settled in Arkansas Territory (now Oklahoma), where they remained for two years. On August 4, 1817, Anderson signed a petition complaining about an Osage Indian attack on family members at Clear Creek. The family arrived in Texas by January 1819. Anderson had two great-grandsons born in Texas that year. During the Long expedition[qv] troubles, the family went back to Arkansas Territory but subsequently returned to the Ayish Bayou District of Texas in 1821. Anderson had a total of nine children. He is listed on the Texas Roll of Patriots as one of the forty-six Revolutionary War heroes buried in Texas. He died in Harrison County, Texas, on August 1, 1840, and is buried at Elysian Fields. A historical marker was dedicated to him on June 1, 1975.

BIBLIOGRAPHY: George L. Crocket, *Two Centuries in East Texas* (Dallas: Southwest, 1932; facsimile reprod., 1962). Max S. Lale, "Bailey Anderson: Revolutionary War Veteran," *East Texas Historical Journal* 14 (Fall 1976). Rex W. Strickland, "Miller County, Arkansas Territory," *Chronicles of Oklahoma* 18 (March 1940). *Dixie Engle*

ANDERSON, BAILEY, JR. (1788–1865). Bailey Anderson, Jr., soldier and pioneer, the son of Mary (Wyatt?) and Bailey Anderson,[qv] was born on February 25, 1788, in South Carolina. He received a common-school education. In 1795 he and his family moved to Warren County, Kentucky. Anderson enlisted in the War of 1812 on September 11, 1812, at Vincennes, Indiana, as a private in Capt. Thomas Spencer's Fourth Regiment, Indiana Militia. He married Winneford Bozeman of Warren County on January 10, 1814, but she died sometime after the birth of their son. Anderson married Elizabeth McFadden, also of Warren County, on June 4, 1817; they had eight children. The family moved to Arkansas Territory (now Oklahoma) in 1817. By 1821 they had settled in San Augustine County, Texas. Anderson was alcalde[qv] of the Ayish Bayou District in the late 1820s. He commanded a company of San Augustine volunteers at the battle of Nacogdoches[qv] in 1832 and offered the terms of surrender to Col. José de las Piedras.[qv] His most heroic service was at the siege of Béxar[qv] in December 1835. With thirty picked men noted for bravery, he captured Colonel Navarro's house in the heart of San Antonio. He moved to Harrison County in 1837 and was appointed a trustee of Marshall University in 1842. Anderson moved to McLennan County in 1853. He died on July 14, 1865.

BIBLIOGRAPHY: Nugent E. Brown, comp., *The Book of Nacogdoches County, Texas* (Nacogdoches, 1927). George L. Crocket, *Two Centuries in East Texas* (Dallas: Southwest, 1932; facsimile reprod., 1962). John H. Jenkins, ed., *The Papers of the Texas Revolution, 1835–1836* (10 vols., Austin: Presidial Press, 1973). *Memorial and Biographical History of Navarro, Henderson, Anderson, Limestone, Freestone, and Leon Counties* (Chicago: Lewis, 1893). Helen G. S. Thomas and Dolly R. G. Barmann, *Gilmore-Carter and Allied Families* (Bowling Green?, Kentucky, 1962). *Marjorie Rouse Willard*

ANDERSON, CHARLES (1814–1895). Charles Anderson, attorney and rancher, son of Richard Clough and Sarah (Marshall) Anderson, was born on June 1, 1814, in Louisville, Kentucky. He graduated from Miami University, Ohio, in 1833. He then became minister to Turkey at Constantinople. He was admitted to the bar in 1835 and in 1844 was elected to the Ohio Senate. He visited Texas in 1858 and in 1859 returned with his family. At San Antonio he bought a ranch, where he bred horses that he expected to sell to the United States Cavalry. He built what became the Argyle Hotel[qv] in San Antonio as his ranch headquarters. Because of his Union sympathies, Anderson was arrested and imprisoned by Col. Henry E. McCulloch[qv] in September 1861. He escaped a month later, however, and made his way back to Ohio, where he became colonel of the Ninety-third Ohio Volunteer Infantry. After being wounded in the battle of Stone River, he resigned his commission, on February 21, 1863. He was elected lieutenant governor of Ohio later the same year and, after the death of Governor John Brough in August 1865, served as governor until January 1866. He later returned to Kentucky and was elected governor there. Anderson was the author of various pamphlets and speeches, including *On the State of the Country* (1860), *The Cause of the War* (1863), and *Texas, Before and on the Eve of the Rebellion* (1884). He died on September 2, 1895, at Paducah, Kentucky.

BIBLIOGRAPHY: M. L. Crimmins, "Colonel Charles Anderson Opposed Secession in San Antonio," West Texas Historical Association *Year Book* 29 (1953). San Antonio *Weekly Herald*, October 5, 26, 1861. *Twentieth Century Biographical Directory of Notable Americans*

(10 vols., Boston: Biographical Society, 1904). Vertical Files, Barker Texas History Center, University of Texas at Austin.

Clinton P. Hartmann

ANDERSON, CHARLES EDWIN (1852–1924). Charles Edwin Anderson, rancher, the son of Winifred P. and James M. Anderson,[qv] was born on September 28, 1852, at Rusk, Texas. He attended the Waco public schools, Baylor University, and Eastman Business College in New York. After returning to Texas he was associated with the Day Land and Cattle Company[qv] and worked in the General Land Office.[qv] Later he went into the cattle business, established the Matagorda Land and Cattle Company, and became president of the Cattle Raisers Association (now the Texas and Southwestern Cattle Raisers Association[qv]). He was an organizer of the Heywood Oil Company, of which he was vice president. Anderson married Myrtle Rogers Looney at Bastrop, and they had three children. He was a founder of the Austin Country Club and served on the Austin City Council. He died on February 27, 1924, in Austin.

BIBLIOGRAPHY: Ellis A. Davis, and Edwin H. Grobe, comps., *The New Encyclopedia of Texas*, 4 vol. ed.

ANDERSON, DILLON (1906–1974). Dillon Anderson, statesman and writer, son of Joseph Addison and Besnie (Dillon) Anderson, was born in McKinney, Texas, on July 14, 1906. He enrolled at Texas Christian University before transferring to the University of Oklahoma, where he received a B.S. degree in 1927. He graduated from the Yale law school in 1929; that same year he was admitted to the Texas bar and began practicing with the Houston firm of Baker, Botts, Andrews, and Shepherd (*see* BAKER AND BOTTS). He was made a partner of the firm in 1940.

Anderson served as a colonel in the United States Army from 1942 to 1945. He won the Army Commendation Ribbon and the Legion of Merit. He was appointed consultant to the National Security Council in 1953, and President Dwight D. Eisenhower[qv] chose Anderson to be his special assistant for national security in 1955. In that capacity, Anderson presided over the National Security Council and accompanied Eisenhower to the summit conference in Geneva in 1955. He resigned in 1956.

In 1948 Anderson met Edward Weeks, editor of *Atlantic*, who complained that J. Frank Dobie, Tom Lea, and John Lomax[qqv] were the only Texans who ever sent contributions to his magazine. When Weeks asked Anderson if he knew of other Texas writers, Anderson volunteered to contribute, even though none of his fiction had been published. Anderson's first submission was "The Revival," a story that Weeks returned several times for revision. It was finally published in 1949 and won the Doubleday company's O. Henry prize for short fiction. Anderson then began publishing other stories in *Atlantic, Saturday Evening Post,* and *Collier's.*

In 1951 Little, Brown, and Company brought out *I and Claudie*, which won the Texas Institute of Letters[qv] award that year. Little, Brown also published Anderson's second book, *Claudie's Kinfolks*, in 1954. Both books are accounts of the picaresque adventures of two fun-loving rogues who philosophize in homespun, practical fashion about life and the world. Though published as novels, both *I and Claudie* and *Claudie's Kinfolks* had been written as series of short stories. The same was true of *The Billingsley Papers* (1961), published by Simon and Schuster, although Anderson did develop a logical sequence for the stories. The "papers" make up a report in which attorney Gaylord Boswell Peterkin reveals the true character of fellow attorney Richard K. Billingsley to the university faculty committee conferring an honorary doctorate of laws degree on Billingsley. Despite their loose structure, all three books won praise for their picture of life among the folk and the exuberant, if not always tasteful, pursuits of the Texan.

Anderson was a director of Westinghouse Electric Corporation, a trustee of the Carnegie Endowment for International Peace, and a member of the Texas Institute of Letters. He married Lena Carter Carroll on May 30, 1931. The Andersons and their three daughters made their permanent home in Houston. Dillon Anderson died in Houston in 1974 and is buried there.

BIBLIOGRAPHY: Austin *American-Statesman*, March 16, 1955. Dallas *News*, November 7, 1954. Vertical Files, Barker Texas History Center, University of Texas at Austin. *Who's Who in the South and Southwest*, Vol. 2.

Joyce Glover Lea

ANDERSON, E. H. (1850–1885). E. H. Anderson, black college president, was born on September 2, 1850, in Memphis, Tennessee. He was a graduate of Fisk University and was trained for the Methodist ministry. He moved to Texas to head Prairie View Normal School, established in 1879 as a school to train black teachers (*see* PRAIRIE VIEW A&M UNIVERSITY). During his tenure Prairie View experienced severe financial hardships as the Sixteenth and Seventeenth legislatures debated over the constitutionality and the funding of the school. The school, with fifty students, was overcrowded and did not have a fixed course of study, but toward the end of Anderson's tenure he was optimistic at the support of the black communities around the state. Anderson died at Prairie View on October 29, 1885. He was succeeded by his brother, Laurine Cecil Anderson,[qv] who had served as his first assistant.

BIBLIOGRAPHY: George Ruble Woolfolk, *Prairie View* (New York: Pageant, 1962).

Kharen Monsho

ANDERSON, EDWARD EWELL (1905–1969). Edward Ewell (Eddie) Anderson, novelist, the son of Edward Houston and Ellen Sara (Sexton) Anderson, was born on June 19, 1905, at Weatherford. His father, a country printer, worked in a number of small towns before settling in Ardmore, Oklahoma, where Eddie went through high school before he ran off with the mayor's son to a wheat harvest, fought one professional boxing match, played trombone a season in a carnival band, and, eventually, learned the reporter's trade at the *Daily Ardmorite.*

Anderson worked on newspapers in Oklahoma, Arkansas, El Paso, Fort Worth, and Tyler, before settling for a time in Abilene in the late 1920s. While working for Max Bentley on the newly established Abilene *Morning News*, he covered the trial of Marshall Ratliff, ringleader in the Santa Claus Bank Robbery (*see* CISCO, TEXAS). In 1930 Anderson worked his passage on a freighter to Europe and back. He returned to Abilene, where his parents and three sisters had settled, to try seriously to write fiction. A year later he began collecting material for hobo fiction by riding freight cars across the nation. He returned to write a picaresque novel about an out-of-work musician hoboing aimlessly around the United States. He also wrote short stories about hoboes, and *Story* magazine accepted two of them.

Anderson married Polly Anne Bates in Abilene in 1934. They went to New Orleans, where he sold pieces to detective magazines and worked on a New Orleans newspaper. His hobo novel, *Hungry Men*, was published by Doubleday, Doran, and Company in 1935. It won the Doubleday-*Story* Prize that year and was a Literary Guild selection. Anderson returned to Texas and lived in Kerrville, where he began work on a second novel about two desperadoes who resembled Bonnie Parker and Clyde Barrow.[qqv]

By the time this second novel, *Thieves Like Us* (1937), was published, Anderson was working for the *Rocky Mountain News* in Denver, where he also wrote a successful radio series. After good reviews of *Thieves Like Us* Anderson went to Hollywood, where he worked for B. P. Schulberg at Paramount and for Warner Brothers. When his screenwriting faltered, he worked for the Los Angeles *Examiner* and the Sacramento *Bee*. By then the Andersons had three children. Anderson returned to Texas after World War II[qv] and worked for the Associated Press and the Fort Worth *Star Telegram*,[qv] among other papers. His marriage ended in divorce in 1950.

For a time he took to the road again and drifted almost as much as he had during the early 1930s. He wrote for an underground newspaper in New York at one time. He then drifted back to Texas and lived principally at Brownsville, where he eventually married a Mexican national named Lupe. They had a son and a daughter. Anderson's later fiction projects did not reach print. After two years of retirement from newspaper work, he died of heart disease on September 5, 1969, in Brownsville. *Thieves Like Us* has been made into motion pictures twice, as *They Live by Night* in 1948 and as *Thieves Like Us* in 1974. In 1985 *Hungry Men* was reissued.

BIBLIOGRAPHY: Patrick Bennett, *Rough and Ready Ways: The Life and Hard Times of Edward Anderson* (College Station: Texas A&M University Press, 1988). Susan Mernit, "The Second Time Around," *Saturday Review*, May–June 1985. Vertical Files, Barker Texas History Center, University of Texas at Austin. *Patrick Bennett*

ANDERSON, HATTIE MABEL (1887–1965). Hattie Mabel Anderson, college professor, writer and cofounder of the Panhandle-Plains Historical Society,[qv] one of six children of Swedish immigrant parents, was born on a farm near Norborne, Missouri, on February 9, 1887. Her father served for several years as a justice of the peace. She began teaching at the age of sixteen in a one-room country school. For the next few years she taught in the winters and attended school during the summers. She attended Central Missouri State Teachers' College, where she received a bachelor of pedagogy degree, and then transferred to the University of Missouri. There she worked as a teaching assistant and earned her B.A., A.M., and Ph.D degrees in history. For a time she taught at Synodical College in Fulton, Missouri, and at Missouri Wesleyan College.

In 1920, after pursuing studies for a year at the University of Chicago, Anderson accepted a position with the history faculty at West Texas State Teachers' College (now West Texas A&M University). Her interest in the Panhandle's[qv] pioneer heritage was quickly fueled by her realization that the region had only recently emerged from its frontier phase and that many pioneers were living. Recognizing a unique opportunity for professional historians to know and work with the pioneer generation, Anderson sought ways to turn this opportunity to account. With the backing of the college president, Joseph A. Hill,[qv] she organized the Panhandle-Plains Historical Society[qv] in February 1921. She chaired the committee that drew up the constitution and bylaws and cosigned the state charter. She was also instrumental in allying the society with the Panhandle Old Settlers Association and was a leader in the establishment of the Panhandle-Plains Historical Museum[qv] in 1932.

As a college professor Hattie Anderson took charge of the history department's teaching methods and supervised the training of history teachers after the student teaching program was developed at WTSC. She helped organize the Pi chapter of the Delta Kappa Gamma Society[qv] in Amarillo and founded Amarillo and Canyon branches of the American Association of University Women.[qv] She served as president of both organizations and was a state board member of AAUW. In addition she joined the Business and Professional Women's organization in Canyon and for several years taught Sunday school classes at the First Baptist Church in Canyon. She published numerous articles in historical journals, and in 1943 she and Hill collaborated on the American history text *My Country and Yours* (1944), which was adopted by schools in five states and subsequently came out in two revisions.

Anderson retired in 1957 but continued writing and volunteered her services at the Panhandle-Plains Museum, often as a guide for groups. She died on March 25, 1965, and was buried in Dreamland Cemetery at Canyon. Her papers are housed in the Museum Research Center.

BIBLIOGRAPHY: Canyon *News*, April 1, 1965. Joseph A. Hill, *More Than Brick and Mortar* (Amarillo: Russell Stationery, 1959). Joseph A. Hill, *The Panhandle-Plains Historical Society and Its Museum* (Canyon, Texas: West Texas State College Press, 1955). Ruth Lowes and W. Mitchell Jones, *We'll Remember Thee: An Informal History of West Texas State University* (Canyon: WTSU Alumni Association, 1984). B. Byron Price and Frederick W. Rathjen, *The Golden Spread: An Illustrated History of Amarillo and the Texas Panhandle* (Northridge, California: Windsor, 1986). *H. Allen Anderson*

ANDERSON, JAMES MONROE (1824–1889). James Monroe Anderson, legislator and Confederate soldier, was born in Lawrence County, Alabama, on July 30, 1824, the son of Edmond P. and Adaline A. (Derchard) Anderson. The family moved to Winchester, Tennessee, in 1827, and at the age of twelve Anderson became a clerk. He graduated from Cumberland University in Lebanon, Tennessee, in 1848 and for two years thereafter taught school at Winchester Academy. During his spare time he read law in the office of Judge Nathan Green, chief justice of Tennessee and father of Gen. Thomas Green.[qv] Anderson was admitted to the bar at Winchester in 1849. He moved to Rusk, Texas, in 1850 and established a partnership with Judge Stockton P. Donley.[qv] At age thirty-five Anderson was elected to represent Cherokee County in the Secession Convention,[qv] January 28 through February 4, 1861. On September 29, 1861, he enlisted as a private in Capt. John F. F. Dottery's Company H of Col. James Reily's[qv] Fourth Texas Mounted Volunteers but was discharged the following month. Later in the Civil War[qv] he served briefly as a Confederate private during the Red River campaign.[qv]

In 1866 Anderson moved to Waco and there reestablished his practice in partnership with Richard Coke.[qv] In 1873 he was elected to the Thirteenth Legislature as a Democrat. He was twice married, first on September 18, 1849, to Jane Buchanan, who died in March 1850, and then on November 26, 1851, to Winifred Polk of Rusk. He was a Baptist. He died at his home in Waco on June 3, 1889.

BIBLIOGRAPHY: *Biographical Encyclopedia of Texas.* Martin Hardwick Hall, *The Confederate Army of New Mexico* (Austin: Presidial Press, 1978). James D. Lynch, *The Bench and Bar of Texas* (St. Louis, 1885). Marcus J. Wright, comp., and Harold B. Simpson, ed., *Texas in the War, 1861–1865* (Hillsboro, Texas: Hill Junior College Press, 1965). *Thomas W. Cutrer*

ANDERSON, JOHN D. (1819–1849). John D. Anderson, early settler, soldier, and politician, the son of Dr. Thomas Anderson, was born in Pittsylvania County, Virginia, on June 21, 1819. He arrived with his father and brother, Washington Anderson,[qv] at Port Lavaca, Texas, in February 1835 and afterward settled in Benjamin R. Milam's[qv] colony. He was a member of Jesse Billingsley's[qv] company but missed seeing action at the battle of San Jacinto[qv] because he had been assigned to the detail left at Harrisburg to guard the baggage. Anderson studied law at Webber's Prairie in the office of Barrie Gillespie, and on February 5, 1844, President Sam Houston[qv] appointed him district attorney for the Fourth Judicial District, an act that automatically rendered Anderson a member of the Supreme Court of the Republic of Texas.[qv] He served as a Gonzales delegate to the Convention of 1845[qv] and fought in the Mexican War[qv] in 1846. In 1847 he was a member of the Second Legislature from Gonzales County. Anderson was twice married. Little is known about the first Mrs. Anderson. The second, Ellen P. Erskine, was the daughter of Michael H. Erskine.[qv] Anderson apparently died in Guadalupe County on April 10, 1849, and was buried in the Erskine family cemetery near Capote Ranch, a few miles from Seguin.

BIBLIOGRAPHY: Texas House of Representatives, *Biographical Directory of the Texan Conventions and Congresses, 1832–1845* (Austin: Book Exchange, 1941). *William L. Mann*

ANDERSON, JOHN QUINCY (1916–1975). John Quincy Anderson, Texas folklorist, author, and professor, was born on May 30,

1916, in Wheeler, Texas, to Albert Slayton and Emily (Grant) Anderson. He attended Oklahoma State University, where he received his B.A. degree in 1939. He was in the United States Army from 1940 until 1946 and was decorated with the French Médaille de la Reconnaissance. He earned a master's degree from Louisiana State University in 1948 and completed his Ph.D. in 1952 at the University of North Carolina. Anderson began teaching at McNeese State College as an assistant professor in 1952. He then taught in the English department at Texas A&M University from 1953 to 1966. He chaired the department from 1962 to 1966. He taught in the University of Houston American literature department from 1966 until his death, when he was professor emeritus.

Anderson was a member of the Modern Language Association and the South Central Modern Language Association. From 1963 to 1964 he was president, and from 1964 to 1967 he was on the executive council of the American Studies Association. He was an editor of the *Southwestern Historical Quarterly*[qv] in the 1970s. He was also a member of the Western American Literature Association and in 1955–56 the American Literature Association of Texas. He was also active in the Texas Folklore Society.[qv]

He wrote many books, including *Brokenburn: The Journal of Kate Stone* (1955), *A Texas Surgeon in the C.S.A.* (1957), *Louisiana Swamp Doctor: The Life and Writings of Henry Clay Lewis* (1962), *Tales of Frontier Texas* (1966), *Campaigning with Parsons' Texas Cavalry Brigade, C.S.A.* (1967), *John C. Duval: First Texas Man of Letters* (1967), *Texas Folk Medicine* (1970), and *The Liberating Gods: Emerson on Poets and Poetry* (1971). Anderson married Marie Loraine Epps; they had no children. He died on February 19, 1975, in Houston.

BIBLIOGRAPHY: Vertical Files, Barker Texas History Center, University of Texas at Austin. *Who's Who in the South and Southwest,* Vol. 14.

Melanie Watkins

ANDERSON, JONATHAN (1798–ca. 1889). Jonathan Anderson, early settler, the son of Wyatt and Mary (McFadden) Anderson, was born in Warren County, Kentucky, on February 11, 1798. When he was five, his father moved to Indiana; in 1816 the family moved to Indian Territory. In the summer of 1817 he was living in the Clear Creek Settlement of the Red River valley. He and his first wife, Nancy (Whetstone), arrived in Texas on his twenty-first birthday (1819) and settled in the Ayish Bayou area (now San Augustine). Nancy died not long thereafter, and Anderson was married in 1826 to Hannah English Payne (1797–1862), a widow who was the sister of William English.[qv] They had six children. In 1824 Anderson and his family moved to the Teneha area (now Shelby County) and settled near a town called Patroon. Anderson participated in the Fredonian Rebellion.[qv] He consistently voted for Democratic candidates in elections after Texas became a state. He moved in 1849 to Panola County, where he was a pioneer settler and where he remained the rest of his life. Anderson married Sarah A. Biggers on February 10, 1864. He died about 1889.

BIBLIOGRAPHY: George L. Crocket, *Two Centuries in East Texas* (Dallas: Southwest, 1932; facsimile reprod. 1962). Gifford E. White, *Character Certificates in the General Land Office of Texas* (1985). Gifford E. White, *1830 Citizens of Texas* (Austin: Eakin, 1983).

Richard D. English

ANDERSON, KENNETH LEWIS (1805–1845). Kenneth Lewis Anderson, lawyer and vice president of the republic, son of Kennith and Nancy (Thompson) Anderson, was born on September 11, 1805, in Hillsborough, North Carolina. There he attended William Bingham's school. He worked as a shoemaker at an early age. By 1824 he was living in Bedford County, Tennessee, where he became deputy sheriff in 1826 and sheriff in 1830; he was a colonel in the militia by 1832. About 1825 Anderson married Patience Burditt; the couple had three children. Two sons, Theophiles and Malcolm, and a grandson, William, became judges in San Antonio.

In 1837 the family moved to San Augustine, Texas, where Mrs. Anderson's brother-in-law Joseph Rowe[qv] had lived for five years. In 1838 Anderson served successively as deputy sheriff and sheriff. It was probably after he arrived in Texas that he studied to become a lawyer. President Mirabeau B. Lamar[qv] appointed him collector of customs for the district of San Augustine, and he was confirmed on November 21, 1839. He served until he became a candidate from San Augustine County for the House of Representatives of the Sixth Congress in 1841; he won with the largest majority in the county's history at that time. As a partisan of Sam Houston,[qv] Anderson was elected speaker of the House on November 1, 1841. He immediately led an unsuccessful attempt to impeach Lamar and Vice President David G. Burnet.[qv] Anderson had for a time been considered for secretary of the treasury, a post that went to William Henry Daingerfield.[qv] In 1842 he helped convince Houston to veto the popular but dangerous war bill, which sought to force an invasion of Mexico.

After one term, and despite President Houston's pleas, Anderson retired in 1842 to practice law in San Augustine with Royal T. Wheeler;[qv] he eventually formed a partnership with J. Pinckney Henderson and Thomas J. Rusk.[qqv] In December 1842 Anderson became district attorney of the Fifth Judicial District. In 1844 Anderson was frequently mentioned as a candidate for president, but eventually he became the Houston party candidate for vice president, on a ticket headed by Anson Jones.[qv] Anderson's opponent, Patrick Jack,[qv] died before the election, and Anderson won nearly unanimously. He presided over the Senate at Washington-on-the-Brazos in June 1845, when the Texas Congress approved annexation.[qv] After adjournment he immediately left for home despite being sick. After only twenty miles, at the Fanthorp Inn,[qv] his fever flared. There he died on July 3, 1845, and was buried in the Fanthorp cemetery. The vice president had been considered the leading candidate to become the first governor of the state. His law partner, Pinckney Henderson, was instead elected governor in December. Anderson was a Mason. Fanthorp was renamed for him in 1846, and on March 24, 1846, Anderson County was established and named in his honor.

BIBLIOGRAPHY: James T. DeShields, *They Sat in High Places: The Presidents and Governors of Texas* (San Antonio: Naylor, 1940). John S. Ford, *Rip Ford's Texas*, ed. Stephen B. Oates (Austin: University of Texas Press, 1963). Thomas Clarence Richardson, *East Texas: Its History and Its Makers* (4 vols., New York: Lewis Historical Publishing, 1940). Leslie H. Southwick, "Kenneth L. Anderson, Last Vice President, Almost First Governor of Texas," *East Texas Historical Journal* 30 (Fall 1992).

Leslie H. Southwick

ANDERSON, LAURINE CECIL (1853–1938). Laurine Cecil (L. C.) Anderson, black teacher and school administrator, was born in Memphis, Tennessee, in 1853 and received his B.A. from Fisk University. He trained for the Methodist ministry and taught at Tuskegee, Alabama, with Booker T. Washington before moving to Texas in 1879 to assist his brother E. H. Anderson,[qv] who was a minister and teacher at Prairie View Normal Institute (now Prairie View A&M University). In 1882 L. C. Anderson lobbied for university status for the school. Upon his brother's death on October 9, 1885, Anderson succeeded him as principal of Prairie View. During his tenure there Anderson helped form and was elected the first president of the Colored Teachers State Association (*see* TEACHERS STATE ASSOCIATION OF TEXAS). He served as president of the college from 1885 to 1889 and worked to unify African-American leaders in business, politics, and religious and fraternal organizations, as well as for to improve conditions for black Texans through education. After heading Prairie View for seventeen years, Anderson moved to Austin to serve as principal of the school for blacks that later became Anderson High School, named in his honor. He was principal for thirty-two years and taught Latin until he was forced to resign in 1928 because of ill health. Anderson died in Austin on January 8, 1938, and was buried at Oakwood Cemetery.

BIBLIOGRAPHY: Austin *American-Statesman*, August 25, 1953. Vernon McDaniel, *History of the Teachers State Association of Texas* (Washington: National Education Association, 1977). George Ruble Woolfolk, *Prairie View* (New York: Pageant, 1962). *Kharen Monsho*

ANDERSON, MONROE DUNAWAY (1873–1939). M. D. Anderson, philanthropist, was born on June 29, 1873, in Jackson, Tennessee, the sixth of eight children of James Wisdom and Ellen (Dunaway) Anderson. James Anderson was first president of the First National Bank of Jackson. As a young man M. D. Anderson was a banker in Jackson, Tennessee. In 1904 he joined his brother, Frank Ervin Anderson, and the latter's brother-in-law, William Lockhart Clayton,[qv] in establishing Anderson, Clayton and Company,[qv] a partnership that eventually grew into the world's largest cotton merchandiser. Anderson moved to Houston, Texas, about 1907 to take advantage of the city's proximity to the port of Galveston and its superior banking resources. Houston became the company's headquarters in 1916, and Anderson served as its treasurer until illness forced his retirement in 1938. The University of Texas M. D. Anderson Cancer Center[qv] in Houston, initially funded by a substantial gift from the M. D. Anderson Foundation[qv] to the University of Texas, is Anderson's best-known philanthropy. The foundation, established before Anderson's death, received the bulk of his large estate. Anderson was a member of the Cumberland Presbyterian Church and the Democratic party,[qv] but was not active in church or in politics. He never married. He lived for thirty years in a succession of downtown Houston hotels. He died in that city on August 6, 1939, after a year-long illness and was buried in Jackson, Tennessee.

BIBLIOGRAPHY: William B. Bates, "Monroe D. Anderson: His Life and Legacy," *Texas Gulf Coast Historical Association Publications* 1.1 (February 1957). Houston *Post*, August 7, 1939. *Thomas D. Anderson*

ANDERSON, RALPH ALEXANDER, SR. (1890–1956). Ralph A. (Andy) Anderson, Sr., sportswriter and humanitarian, son of John and Anna Anderson, was born on May 14, 1890, in Pittsburgh, Pennsylvania. After two years at Carnegie Institute of Technology, he enlisted in the United States Army in 1917 at Fort Logan, Colorado, and served in the mounted engineers. After the armistice he was city editor and sports editor of the Houston *Post*[qv] from 1919 to 1923. In 1920 he married Ruby Rose Ellison. They had one son, Ralph A. Anderson, Jr.[qv]

While with the *Post*, Anderson was honored for his efforts in helping to establish sandlot baseball in Houston and the Houston Amateur Baseball Federation. In 1923 he went into the business of constructing and operating golf courses in several small towns around Houston. In 1923 he became sports editor of the Houston *Press*,[qv] with which he was affiliated the rest of his life. He wrote a column on hunting and fishing along the Texas Gulf Coast and conducted a radio program on outdoor sports for several years.

During World War II[qv] Anderson promoted the sale of war bonds and subsequently began rehabilitation work with returning disabled war veterans. This work included developing special social and recreational activities, with emphasis on the outdoors. He invented attachments for sports equipment to permit persons of various disabilities to participate. Under his direction annual wild-game dinners were instituted in several veterans' hospitals in South Texas; in addition to those hospitals, Anderson visited 172 other Veterans Administration hospitals over the United States as volunteer-at-large to entertain and instruct the veterans in recreational pursuits. Through his efforts a park for handicapped veterans was established on the east shore of Lake Houston. Later the park was named for him. Anderson's office at the Houston *Press* became a one-man bureau for helping the poor, the troubled, and parolees. Through his column he served as an intermediary between those in need and those in a position to help, and he received national recognition for his work. In 1953 he was also chosen National Fisherman of the Year and was elected to the Fishing Hall of Fame of the Sportsman's Club of America. An elementary school in southwest Houston was named for him in 1961. He died on January 24, 1956, at his home in Houston.

L. C. Anderson. Courtesy Austin History Center, Austin Public Library; photo no. PICB 04553.

BIBLIOGRAPHY: Mary Grimm Frazer, "Andy Anderson Brings Great Outdoors to Aid Disabled Veterans of World War II," *Texas Press Messenger*, October 1945. D. M. Frost, "A Heart as Big as Texas," *Coronet*, June 1952. *Time*, July 5, 1954. *Ruby E. Anderson*

ANDERSON, RALPH ALEXANDER, JR. (1923–1990). Ralph Alexander Anderson, Jr., Houston architect, the son of Ruby (Ellison) and Ralph Alexander Anderson, Sr.,[qv] was born in Houston on January 1, 1923. He received a B.A. in architecture from Rice Institute (now Rice University) in 1943 and a B.S. in 1947. From 1943 to 1945 Anderson served in the United States Infantry in the European Theater of Operations. After graduation he worked for the firm of Wilson, Morris, and Crain, in which he became a partner in 1952; by 1978 the firm was known as Crain and Anderson. Among Anderson's notable Houston works, executed in the late stripped-down modernist style, are the World Trade Center (1962), the Kelsey-Seybold Clinic (1963), the Astrodome[qv] (1965), the West National Bank (1967), and the Houston *Post*[qv] Building (1969). He also designed the Austin *American-Statesman*[qv] building in Austin; KHOU-TV, Houston; WISH-TV in Indianapolis, Indiana; event centers at the University of Texas at Austin and El Paso, Baylor University, and several out-of-state universities; and award-winning homes in Texas and Louisiana. Architecture critic Stephen Fox described Anderson's *Post* building as one of the first examples of "freeway architecture," a rectangular box with concrete silos attached, projecting an image that could be apprehended from a speeding car. Anderson served as president of the Contemporary Art Museum, Houston,[qv] in 1957, the Houston Botanical Society in 1967, and the Houston chapter of the American Institute of Architects in 1966. He was a member of Phi Beta Kappa and a fellow of the American Institute of Architects. Anderson died in Houston on February 5, 1990.

BIBLIOGRAPHY: Austin *American-Statesman*, February 6, 1990. Stephen Fox, *Houston Architectural Guide* (Houston: American Institute of Architects, Houston Chapter, 1990). *Who's Who in America*, 1974–75.
Diana J. Kleiner

ANDERSON, REUBEN (1793–1861). Reuben (Ruben) Anderson, plantation owner, was born in Twiggs County, Georgia, on December 22, 1793. He moved to Montgomery County, Alabama, where he raised two sons and one daughter. In January 1839 he made a gift of fifty slaves to his sons. The entire family moved to Robertson County, Texas, in 1852. They established plantations in the Brazos Bottom near the Port Sullivan community. Reuben Anderson is listed as a wealthy Texan in 1860, where he owned 100 slaves, personal property valued at over $93,000, and real estate worth over $80,000. He was a Freemason. He died on May 2, 1861, and is buried in the Port Sullivan Cemetery.

BIBLIOGRAPHY: J. W. Baker, *History of Robertson County, Texas* (Franklin, Texas: Robertson County Historical Survey Committee, 1970). Randolph B. Campbell, *An Empire for Slavery: The Peculiar Institution in Texas, 1821–1865* (Baton Rouge: Louisiana State University Press, 1989). Mrs. John T. Martin and Mrs. Louis C. Hill, *Milam County, Texas, Records* (2 vols., Waco, 1965, 1968). Richard Denny Parker, *Historical Recollections of Robertson County, Texas* (Salado, Texas: Anson Jones, 1955). Ralph A. Wooster, "Wealthy Texans, 1860," *Southwestern Historical Quarterly* 71 (October 1967).
James L. Hailey

ANDERSON, RICHARD ALLEN (1948–1969). Richard Allen Anderson, Medal of Honor recipient, was born at Washington, D.C., on April 16, 1948. He entered the military service in Houston, Texas. On August 24, 1969, Lance Corporal Richard Anderson, United States Marine Corps, Company E, Third Reconnaissance Battalion, Third Marine Division, was serving as assistant team leader against an armed enemy in Quang Tri Province, South Vietnam. While conducting a reconnaissance patrol his team came under heavy automatic-weapon fire that severely wounded Anderson. He continued firing in an attempt to repulse the enemy and was wounded a second time. While a companion attended his wounds he continued relentless fire. When a grenade landed between him and the other marine, Anderson rolled over and covered the grenade to absorb the detonation. By his courage and self sacrifice he saved several Marines from injury and possible death. Anderson is buried in Forest Park Cemetery, Houston, Texas.

BIBLIOGRAPHY: Committee on Veterans' Affairs, United States Senate, *Medal of Honor Recipients, 1863–1973* (Washington: GPO, 1973).
Art Leatherwood

ANDERSON, SIMEON ASA (?–?). Simeon Asa Anderson, one of Stephen F. Austin's[qv] Old Three Hundred,[qv] received title on August 10, 1824, to a league of land now in Fayette County. The census of Austin's colony of March 1826 listed him as a farmer and stock raiser aged between twenty-five and forty; his household consisted of his wife, a son, two daughters, and a slave. Anderson wrote Austin in May 1826 that he had had no opportunity to see him but was making arrangements to pay for his land.

BIBLIOGRAPHY: Eugene C. Barker, ed., *The Austin Papers* (3 vols., Washington: GPO, 1924–28). Lester G. Bugbee, "The Old Three Hundred: A List of Settlers in Austin's First Colony," *Quarterly of the Texas State Historical Association* 1 (October 1897).

ANDERSON, THOMAS (1789–1857). Thomas Anderson, physician and soldier, son of Maj. Richard and Frances Anderson, was born in Buckingham County, Virginia, on June 16, 1789. His father was a major of the Virginia line in the Revolutionary War. On December 21, 1815, Thomas married Chloe Glascock, daughter of William and Elizabeth Sanford Glascock. Two sons, John D. and Washington Anderson,[qqv] were born to this couple before Chloe died on September 5, 1819. When Anderson's second wife, Sarah (Tunstell), died, he and his two young sons headed for Texas. They debarked at what is now Port Lavaca in February 1835 and stayed for a few days with Mrs. Martha Suttles. Then they went to Washington County, and when Thomas received title to a league of land in Benjamin R. Milam's[qv] colony, the trio settled there.

Anderson joined the revolutionary army[qv] near Gonzales and served until after the victory at San Jacinto. When Capt. Jesse Billingsley's[qv] company (later Company C of the First Regiment) joined them, Anderson found his two sons among Billingsley's men. He claimed he had left them at Mina (Bastrop) to protect the women from the Mexicans and Indians.

During the battle of San Jacinto[qv] Anderson remained as a volunteer physician at Harrisburg in Captain Splane's company, which had been left at the upper encampment under the command of Maj. Robert McNutt[qv] to care for the ill and wounded. When Gen. Edward Burleson[qv] and others offered to obtain Thomas a compensation from the Texas government, he refused to receive any reward for his services. On May 22, 1838, he was, however, given a certificate for 640 acres for his services at Harrisburg. The land was located at Webber's Prairie (Webberville), where Anderson continued to practice medicine. He treated Josiah Wilbarger,[qv] who had been scalped by Indians and left to die. Because of Anderson's skill Josiah's injury was reduced to the permanent inconvenience of wearing a skull cap. On December 6, 1837, Anderson was appointed medical censor, the physician elected in every senatorial district of the republic to grant either temporary or permanent licenses to those who practiced medicine, for Mina and Gonzales. He further served the republic as surgeon on the flagship *Austin*[qv] in December 1842. His salary of $100 a month was the second highest salary paid an officer under the command of Capt. Edwin W. Moore.[qv] By 1850 Anderson was living and boarding in Austin. He died in Round Rock, probably at the home of his son Washington, on April 26, 1857.

BIBLIOGRAPHY: Jane H. DiGesualdo and Karen R. Thompson, *Historical Round Rock, Texas* (Austin: Eakin Press, 1985). William L. Mann, comp., *The Andersons: A Father and Two Sons with General Sam Houston's Army* (Corpus Christi: U.S. Naval Hospital, 1941; rev. ed., Georgetown, Texas, 1946). Noah Smithwick, *The Evolution of a State, or Recollections of Old Texas Days* (Austin: Gammel, 1900; rpt., Austin: University of Texas Press, 1983).
Mrs. Harmon Watts

ANDERSON, THOMAS SCOTT (1830?–1868). T. Scott Anderson, attorney and Texas secretary of state, was born in Tennessee between 1827 and 1830 and moved to Texas in 1852. He began a law career in Austin, where he advertised his services in the local newspaper. In 1852 he served on the Provisional Railroad Association of Travis County. He was at one time a law partner of Horace Cone[qv] in Houston. Anderson served as secretary of state under Governor Hardin R. Runnels,[qv] beginning on December 22, 1857. In the gubernatorial election of 1859 Runnels lost to Sam Houston,[qv] and Anderson resigned his position on December 27 of that year. While Anderson was secretary of state, he married Mary McNeill Harper, on January 30, 1858. Shortly after their marriage the couple moved to

Dallas, where they lived until 1860, when they moved to Columbus. Anderson served as a Colorado County delegate to the Secession Convention[qv] in Austin in 1861. On August 21 of that year Captain Anderson, now in the Texas State Militia, was mustered into the Confederate Army in Colorado County, with a rank of colonel. Anderson's Second Texas Regiment, a division of the Third Texas Cavalry, saw action in the Arkansas valley as well as in Tennessee, before Anderson assumed command of the Confederate Military Prison, Camp Ford, near Tyler. Once the war ended he moved back to Colorado County, to Eagle Lake, a town easily accessible to Galveston by train. He made frequent trips to the seaside city, at that time a thriving cultural and business center. Anderson died on September 25, 1868, at his home in Eagle Lake and was buried near the graves of Confederate soldiers who had died while encamped there.

BIBLIOGRAPHY: C. L. Greenwood Collection, Barker Texas History Center, University of Texas at Austin. *Journal of the Secession Convention of Texas, 1861* (Austin: Texas Library and Historical Commission and Texas State Library, 1912). C. W. Raines, *Year Book for Texas* (2 vols., Austin: Gammel-Statesman, 1902, 1903). *The War of the Rebellion: A Compilation of the Official Records of the Union and Confederate Armies* (Washington: GPO, 1880–1901). Ralph A. Wooster, "An Analysis of the Membership of the Texas Secession Convention," *Southwestern Historical Quarterly* 62 (January 1959).

Mary Jayne Walsh

ANDERSON, WASHINGTON (1817–1894). Washington (Wash) Anderson, hero of the battle of San Jacinto,[qv] was born in Pittsylvania County, Virginia, where his grandfather, Richard Anderson, had been a captain in the Revolutionary War. He arrived at Port Lavaca, Texas, in February 1835 with his father, Dr. Thomas Anderson, and brother John D. Anderson.[qqv] His mother was Chloe Glascock Anderson, who died when Wash was three years old.

Anderson served in Capt. Jesse Billingsley's[qv] company in the battle of San Jacinto,[qv] where he was wounded in the ankle. Several years later John Osburn Nash was quoted in the Houston Chronicle: "The old pioneer Wash Anderson was the true hero of San Jacinto, although history gives him no praise. Wash was never known to shout 'go on' in battle, but was always known to say 'come on' instead. He had more to do with turning the tide of the battle than Sam Houston[qv] did." Anderson is pictured in William H. Huddle's[qv] painting *The Surrender of Santa Anna*, which hangs in the Capitol[qv] in Austin. He also fought in the battle of Brushy Creek[qv] in 1839. The Andersons received several land grants for service.

On March 25, 1838, Anderson married his cousin Mary Ann Glascock. They had one daughter. Anderson, a devout Baptist, a Democrat, and a successful businessman, circulated and signed the petition to form Williamson County in 1848. He was one of the first county commissioners there. He built the county's first sawmill and gristmill and was one of the most prominent settlers of Round Rock, where he sold land to have the town platted. He also sold the land for the first college in the county, Greenwood Institute. After living in several log houses, the Andersons built a large rock house with separate slave quarters in 1859. The home is still standing on Brushy Creek in Round Rock; it received a Texas historical medallion in 1962. The Andersons were active in state affairs, especially the Texas Veterans Association.[qv] Wash Anderson died in 1894 and was buried in Oakwood Cemetery, Austin.

BIBLIOGRAPHY: Sam Houston Dixon and Louis Wiltz Kemp, *The Heroes of San Jacinto* (Houston: Anson Jones, 1932). Bill Moore, *Bastrop County, 1691–1900* (Wichita Falls: Nortex, 1977). Clara Stearns Scarbrough, *Land of Good Water: A Williamson County History* (Georgetown, Texas: Williamson County Sun Publishers, 1973). Vertical Files, Barker Texas History Center, University of Texas at Austin.

Karen R. Thompson

ANDERSON, WILLIAM L. (?–1864). William "Bloody Bill" Anderson, Confederate guerilla and outlaw, was born in Missouri and in 1861 was a resident of Council Groves, Kansas, where he and his father and brothers achieved a reputation as horse thieves and murderers. At the outbreak of the Civil War[qv] he was forced by his Unionist neighbors to flee to Clay County, Missouri, where he became a guerilla leader notorious for leading raids along the Kansas-Missouri border and infamous for scalping his victims. Especially heinous was his raid against the German settlers of Lafayette County, Missouri, in July 1863. When in August 1863 two of his sisters were killed and a third crippled for life in the collapse of a makeshift jail in which they were being held by Union authorities, the already ferocious Anderson redoubled his frenzy of killing. Prominent in his band were Archie Clement, Frank James, and later Jesse James. On August 21, 1863, Anderson and his gang of about thirty joined William C. Quantrill[qv] in the celebrated Lawrence, Kansas, raid, in which Anderson was reputed to have been the most bloodthirsty of all of the 450 raiders. "I am here for revenge," he declared, "and I have got it!"

In the winter of 1863 Quantrill led his band into Texas, where the men fell under the command of Gen. Henry E. McCulloch.[qv] In the reorganization that followed their muster into the Confederate Army, Anderson was elected first lieutenant, but he soon broke with Quantrill and deserted the army to rejoin his mistress, one Bush Smith, at Sherman. From there Quantrill chased Anderson to Bonham, where Anderson informed McCulloch that Quantrill was robbing civilians. Thereupon McCulloch ordered Quantrill to report to him at his headquarters and arrested him. When Quantrill made good his escape, McCulloch ordered his return, dead or alive, and Anderson and his gang joined in the pursuit. After some skirmishing between the two bands of bushwhackers, Quantrill escaped across the Red River.

In 1864 Anderson returned to raiding in Kansas and Missouri, and between July and October of that year was said to have made more raids, ridden more miles, and killed more men than any other bushwhacker of the war. On August 9, 1864, his band received a serious setback when it attempted unsuccessfully to sack Fayette, Missouri, but it continued to scourge the state. On August 27 Anderson and his men perpetrated the Centralia Massacre, which involved some of the most vicious atrocities of the Civil War. In conjunction with the Confederate invasion of Missouri by Gen. Sterling Price, Anderson's gang sacked Danville, Florence, and High Hill in October, but failed to do serious harm to the federal communications net in Missouri or to render Price any practical assistance.

On the morning of October 26, 1864, Anderson was brought to bay by a force of 150 Union militia near the Ray County community of Albany. In the pitched battle that resulted, Anderson rode through the Union line only to be shot twice in the back of the head. His men made a vigorous effort to recover his body but failed; at least one man and, according to one account, as many as ten, died in the attempt. The body was decapitated and dragged through the streets of Richmond, Missouri, by the victorious Unionists. The head was hoisted onto a spiked telegraph pole. Finally, Anderson's corpse was buried in an unmarked grave in the Richmond cemetery. According to unsubstantiated rumor, however, Anderson survived the Albany fight, and the mutilated body was that of another man. The real Anderson, according to the story, took advantage of his supposed death to move to Brown County, Texas, where he married and lived a settled and respectable life. The Brown County Anderson died at his home on Salt Creek on November 2, 1927.

BIBLIOGRAPHY: Carl W. Breihan, *Quantrill and His Civil War Guerrillas* (Denver: Sage, 1959). John P. Burch, *Charles W. Quantrell* (Vega, Texas, 1923). Albert Castel, *William Clarke Quantrill: His Life and Times* (New York: Fell, 1962). William Elsey Connelley, *Quantrill and the Border Wars* (New York: Pageant, 1909; rpt. 1956). W. C. Stewart, "Bill Anderson, Guerrilla," *Texas Monthly*, April 1929.

Thomas W. Cutrer

ANDERSON, WILLIAM MADISON (1889–1935). William Madison Anderson, clergyman, son of William M. and Sarah Knott (Latta) Anderson, was born on September 29, 1889, at Rock Hill, South Carolina. He attended Vanderbilt University from 1907 to 1910, then moved to Texas and attended Austin College, where he received his A.B. degree in 1911. In 1914 he graduated from Austin Presbyterian Theological Seminary, was ordained to the Presbyterian ministry, and was named pastor of East Dallas Presbyterian Church. In 1915 he served as secretary of schools and colleges of the Presbyterian Church[qv] in Texas. On October 23, 1916, he married Nancy Lee Gossett; they had two daughters. Anderson became associated with his father as assistant pastor of the First Presbyterian Church of Dallas and on his father's death in 1924 assumed the pastorate. In 1924 Austin College conferred on him an honorary doctorate. Anderson was a member of Phi Delta Theta fraternity, a thirty-second-degree Mason, and a Shriner. He organized the Evangelical Theological College of Dallas and founded a Presbyterian charity clinic for babies in Dallas. He died on November 11, 1935.

BIBLIOGRAPHY: Dallas *Morning News*, November 12, 1935. *Who Was Who in America*, 1943. Vertical Files, Barker Texas History Center, University of Texas at Austin.

Wesley N. Laing

ANDERSON, WILLIAM T. (1859–1934). William T. Anderson, clergyman and physician, was born a slave in Seguin, Texas, on August 20, 1859. During the Civil War[qv] he and his mother moved to Galveston, where he joined the African Methodist Episcopal Church.[qv] The congregation sponsored him at Wilberforce University in Ohio for three years, and he received a theology certificate from Howard University in 1886. In 1888 he graduated from the Homeopathic Medical College of Cleveland. He then pastored AME congregations in Toledo, Urbana, Lima, and Cleveland, Ohio. In 1897 President William McKinley appointed Anderson chaplain of the Tenth United States Cavalry,[qv] with the rank of captain. In April 1898 the regiment departed for the Chickamauga area from its headquarters at Fort Assinniboine, Montana. Anderson remained behind and is believed to be one of the first black officers to command an American military post. On July 24, 1898, he joined the Tenth near Santiago, Cuba, where he treated the sick for fever and dysentery. After the war he coedited *Under Fire with the Tenth Cavalry* (1899, 1969), a book about the heroism of black soldiers in the war based on eyewitness accounts.

From mid-1899 to 1902 the regiment occupied Manzanillo, Cuba. In Cuba and later in Nebraska, Anderson helped enlisted men organize a regimental YMCA as a means to engage in self-help, address issues of concern, and discuss racial matters. In April 1907 he and the regiment were sent to Fort William McKinley, near Manila, Philippines. Anderson was promoted to major in August 1907 and commanded the United States Morgue.

On January 10, 1910, he retired because of a disability caused by a fever contracted in Cuba in 1898. He returned to Wilberforce and worked as an accountant and secretary to the bishop in the Third Episcopal District. Anderson died in Cleveland on August 21, 1934. He was survived by his wife Sada J. Anderson, who was also active in the AME church. An American Legion[qv] post was named for him in the Cleveland area.

BIBLIOGRAPHY: Rayford W. Logan and Michael R. Winston, eds., *Dictionary of American Negro Biography* (New York: Norton, 1982).

Kharen Monsho

ANDERSON, TEXAS. Anderson is on State Highway 90 and Farm roads 149 and 1774 ten miles northeast of Navasota in central Grimes County. Bidai, Coushatta, and Kickapoo Indians roamed this area before the arrival of Stephen F. Austin's[qv] first settlers. Francis Holland,[qv] one of the first settlers in the area, received his deed to a league of land from Austin on August 10, 1824. In 1833 Henry Fanthorp[qv] purchased the east quarter of Holland's league for twenty-five cents an acre and built a corn-storage building that served also as a dwelling and grain market. In 1834 he built a larger, dog-run house to live in. In order to take advantage of the stage lines, he enlarged this dwelling into a tavern known as the Fanthorp Inn.[qv] Mail was delivered here weekly, starting in 1835; the inn was thus the first post office in what was to be Grimes County.

In 1846 Grimes County was organized, and Fanthorp offered land for the county seat. In the following election a site between Alto Mira and Randolph was chosen. It was named Anderson, in honor of Kenneth L. Anderson,[qv] last vice president of the Republic of Texas,[qv] who had recently died at the Fanthorp Inn. In time the community encompassed Alto Mira, Randolph, and the inn.

Good soil, good crops, good water supply, and numerous stagecoach routes across Grimes County contributed to Anderson's growth. Lawyers, teachers, preachers, physicians, and political leaders from the southern United States, along with skilled farmers of German and Polish descent, came together in Anderson. The Masons opened Masonic Collegiate Institute, also known as Patrick Academy, in 1846; other schools followed: St. Paul's Episcopal College (1852), a Lutheran school (1882), a Catholic school (1890), and the school of Anderson Independent Free District (1893). Numerous churches provided worship services. The town boomed from 1846 to 1885; it had two steam sawmills, six cotton gins, five hotels, a drugstore, a mercantile house, a hardware store, a tailor, a blacksmith, a pistol factory that provided handguns for the Confederacy (*see* DANCE BROTHERS), and a population of 3,000. At least six different Anderson newspapers were published between 1854 and 1900.

For all of its promise in the stagecoach days, no major development in road or rail line construction passed through Anderson. Local landowners refused to give right-of-way to the Houston and Texas Central in 1857. In 1903 they agreed to construction of the Madisonville Branch of the Missouri Pacific, from Navasota to Madisonville. This line was discontinued in 1944, leaving Anderson without a public carrier. The first highway to pass through Anderson was not begun until 1930. Growth was also retarded by the lack of city government. Although the town was incorporated, records show elected officials only for the years 1867 and 1875. In 1983 a movement to revive city government was defeated at the polls.

Although Anderson is the county seat and was once the fourth largest town in Texas, its population in 1990 was only 320, composed of the residents within a half-mile radius of the historic county courthouse. The town has a number of historic homes. Special events that attract tourists are Texas Trek in April, a County Fair and Juneteenth[qv] celebration in June, and Texan Days in September, as well as church festivals and activities of fraternal organizations. By 1990 a dozen or more commercial business and offices, a post office, the bank, the school, law enforcement offices, and the county jail were within a three-block radius of the courthouse. Livestock, dairy farming, hay, and honeybees were the means of livelihood for the surrounding community. Many residents worked out of town.

BIBLIOGRAPHY: Irene Taylor Allen, *Saga of Anderson—The Proud Story of a Historic Texas Community* (New York: Greenwich, 1957). E. L. Blair, *Early History of Grimes County* (Austin, 1930). Grimes County Historical Commission, *History of Grimes County, Land of Heritage and Progress* (Dallas: Taylor, 1982). Vertical Files, Barker Texas History Center, University of Texas at Austin.

Jan M. Hennigar

ANDERSON, CLAYTON AND COMPANY. Anderson, Clayton and Company, cotton merchants, was founded by brothers-in-law Frank E. Anderson and William Lockhart Clayton,[qv] cotton merchants, and Monroe D. Anderson,[qv] a banker. The partnership was established in Oklahoma City on August 1, 1904. In 1905 Benjamin Clayton, Will's younger brother and an expert in rail and steamship transportation, joined the firm. Company headquarters moved to Houston in 1916 to be nearer the deep-water port facilities of the Houston Ship Channel.[qv]

World War I[qv] demands for cotton enhanced the company's fortunes. As its buying and distributing organization expanded, the firm acquired storage and compressors for American cotton handling and improved its finance and insurance arrangements. As United States exports and banking accommodations grew, Anderson, Clayton set up overseas distributing agents. By the mid-1920s company trading firms were operating in Europe, Egypt, India, and China.

In the Great Depression,[qv] Farm Board price-support legislation and the Smoot-Hawley Tariff Act necessitated geographical diversification to protect the firm's interests from the uncertainties of government policy. Development of an organization for accumulating, handling, selling, and distributing cotton abroad allowed Anderson, Clayton ultimately to sell any nation's cotton to any nation's spinners. New South American subsidiaries were set up, and, as cotton growing in other countries spread, the firm followed, offerings its services. At home, cottonseed-oil refineries produced salad oils, shortenings, and cattle feed under a variety of trademarks. By 1940 Anderson, Clayton could provide American cotton growers with service and supervision at all stages of cotton production, ginning, by-products merchandising, and finance. Before World War II[qv] the company purchased Gulf Atlantic Warehousing to improve its access to cotton resources and built a lab for the development of disease-resistant cottonseed.

From 1928 to 1930 and again in 1936 Anderson, Clayton and Company was investigated by the United States Senate on charges of manipulating the market. William L. Clayton, later assistant United States secretary of state, responded to the charges, and no action was taken. Clayton's successful negotiations with northern investors for "Southern delivery" to non–New York ports on cotton futures contracts altered a long-standing tradition and aided the firm.

After initial war-related setbacks Anderson, Clayton continued to sell cotton in Europe in the 1940s, avoiding conflict by quick turnover of its supplies. To aid in the war effort, the company used its line of barges and tugs to transport fuels, and the Long Reach Machine Works, built in 1942 to manufacture cotton-handling machinery, was converted to army ordnance production.

The company was incorporated in 1929 and remained private until 1945. At that time it went public and was listed on the New York Stock Exchange. The move allowed the M. D. Anderson Foundation[qv] to purchase land for the Texas Medical Center[qv] through sale of company stock. By 1945, with 223 gins, 33 cottonseed oil plants, and 123 warehouses worldwide, Anderson, Clayton and Company was called the largest buyer, seller, storer, and shipper of raw cotton in the world by *Fortune Magazine.* Its subsidiaries included a marine insurance company, the barge line, bagging and cotton-blanket mills, a Mexican loan bank, and the machine works. After 1950 sales in the international market reached 3½ percent of all the world's production, and the multimillion-dollar corporation came to be known as ACCO, or the Big Store.

When rayon threatened the cotton market after the war, ACCO further diversified, reducing its cotton interests by half and adding industrials, government warehousing services, and other interests. A Foods Division was organized after the purchase of Mrs. Tucker's Foods of Sherman, Texas, in 1952 and by 1954 ACCO sold Chiffon margarine and Seven Seas dressing and owned some of the first consumer-product franchises in Mexico. By 1965 the company handled approximately 15 percent of Brazilian coffee exports and a substantial quantity from other countries, as well as cocoa exports and soybean processing.

By 1977 Anderson, Clayton and Company maintained firms or exclusive agents for cotton in over forty nations; had expanded its Ranger trademark insurance ventures, founded in 1923, with acquisition of Pan Am Insurance in 1968 and American Founders Life in 1977; and had acquired Igloo Corporation, a producer of thermoplastic beverage containers and ice chests. The company climaxed its shipping investments as cooperator of the first nuclear-powered merchant ship, the *Savannah.*

Pruning of operations began in the 1960s, and by 1973 the firm had withdrawn from cotton merchandising everywhere except in Brazil and Mexico and considered itself chiefly a producer of food products. In the fiscal year 1982 gross sales reached $1.9 billion and net income $55.4 million. The company employed 15,000 persons worldwide. Anderson, Clayton and Company became a wholly owned subsidiary of the Quaker Oats Company in 1986, when Quaker Oats purchased the Anderson Clayton stock. Some food products, notably Gaines dog food, continued to be marketed under the name Anderson Clayton, but the company's Houston headquarters was closed and the stock was delisted.

BIBLIOGRAPHY: Houston *Chronicle*, December 2, 1979.

Thomas D. Anderson

ANDERSON COUNTY. Anderson County (G-20) is located in East Texas between the Trinity and the Neches rivers. Palestine, the county's largest town and its county seat, is 108 miles southeast of Dallas and 153 miles north of Houston. U.S. highways 287, 79, and 84 provide the major transportation routes through the county. The county's center lies at 95°36′ west longitude and 31°47′ north latitude. Anderson County has a total area of 1,077 square miles or 689,280 acres. The county is partly in the Texas Claypan area and partly in the East Texas Timberlands of the Southern Coastal Plains. Almost half of the soil is Fuquay-Kirvin-Darco, deep, sandy, and loamy. The terrain is nearly level to moderately steep in the uplands. The 66,000 acres in the western Claypan area are used mainly for pasture. The Timberlands are used mostly for pasture and woodland. Cattle are grazed on 200,000 acres of open land and about 127,000 acres of forest land; commercial timber grows on 200,000 acres; cultivated land comprises 86,000 acres, of which 23,000 is in row crops and the rest is either fallow or in close-grown crops or hay; and urban development covers 28,000 acres. Anderson County ranks twenty-second in production of commercial timber of the forty-three counties in the East Texas pine-hardwood region known as the Piney Woods. Many varieties of timber grow abundantly, including red oak, post oak, white oak, pecan, walnut, hickory, elm, ash, and pine (*see* LUMBER INDUSTRY). The soil also supports a wide variety of fruits, vegetables, and nuts.

The terrain is hilly and slopes to the Trinity and Neches rivers, with an elevation of between 198 and 624 feet above sea level. The entire eastern area of the county is bordered by the Neches and is drained by Hurricane Creek, Lone Creek, and Brushy Creek. The western area is bordered by the Trinity River and is drained by Massey Lake, Mansion Creek, and Keechie Creek. Mineral resources include oil and gas and iron ore. Temperatures range from an average minimum of 37° F in January to an average maximum of 94° in July. Rainfall averages about 40.5 inches annually, and the growing season averages 264 days.

The territory that became Anderson County was home to the Comanche, Waco, Tawakonis, Kickapoo, and Kichai Indians. These and others, originally on the southern flanks of the Wichita peoples, were in the vanguard of the southern migration. By 1772 they had settled on the Brazos at Waco and on the Trinity upstream from the site of present Palestine.

In 1826 empresario[qv] David G. Burnet[qv] received a grant from the Mexican government for colonization of the area that is now Anderson County. In 1833 members of the Pilgrim Predestinarian Regular Baptist Church settled at the site of Parker's Fort in Limestone County, and others settled near the site of present Elkhart, where they established "Old Pilgrim," reputedly the oldest Protestant church in Texas. On June 10, 1835, Willison Ewing and Joseph Jordan bought a tract of land, which is now the John H. Reagan[qv] homesite, about two miles southeast of the present city of Palestine, and erected Fort Sam Houston as protection from the Indians. In 1836 a settlement known as Fort Houston grew at this site. During the incursion of Antonio López de Santa Anna[qv] in the spring of 1836 most of the settlements west of the Trinity were destroyed. Settlers fled to Fort Houston, but many of them returned to Parker's Fort after Santa Anna's defeat. On May 19, 1836, Parker's Fort was attacked by Indians, and most of the families there were killed. Those who survived made their way to Fort Houston. Some residents of Anderson County are related to Cynthia Ann Parker,[qv] who was captured in this raid. In October 1838, while Gen. Thomas J. Rusk[qv] marched with two hundred men on his way to Fort Houston in pursuit of Mexicans and Indians, he learned that hostile Indians were at a site called Kickapoo, near Frankston, in what is now northeastern Anderson County. His successful raid ended the engagements with the Indians in eastern Texas for that year.

After the removal of the Indians in the 1840s, settlement proceeded rapidly until the area had sufficient inhabitants to form a new county. In response to a petition presented by settlers at and around Fort Houston, the First Legislature of the state of Texas formed Anderson County from Houston County on March 24, 1846. A suggestion was made that the new county be called Burnet in honor of David G. Burnet. The county was named Anderson, however, after Kenneth Lewis Anderson,[qv] a prominent member of Congress and the last vice president of the Republic of Texas.[qv] Fort Houston was two miles from the center of the county, so a committee, composed of Dan Lumpkin, William Turner Sadler,[qv] and John Parker was appointed to lay out the site for and name a new county seat. They chose a 100-acre tract in the center of the county. The Parkers had come from Palestine, Crawford County, Illinois, and upon their suggestion, the new county seat was named Palestine.

On July 30, 1846, the first session of the Anderson County court was called. Road building was of foremost importance, and a road from Palestine to the Neches River was ordered. Other roads from Palestine to Fort Houston, Parker's Bluff, Cannon's Ferry, and Kingsboro in Henderson County followed. Authorization for construction of a courtroom and jail with an underground dungeon was given. In August 1846 a county tax was levied, and Thomas Hanks was appointed county treasurer. In October election precincts were arranged. District court was held on November 9, 1846, with Judge William B. Ochiltree,[qv] of the sixth judicial district of Texas, presiding. The first cases were civil cases involving title to land and slaves.

In 1851 the Palestine Masonic Institute was established, with both male and female departments. In 1856 it became Franklin College. When the male department failed, the Palestine Female College was formed and stayed in operation until 1881, when a vote was taken to establish public schools. A school established in 1852 at Mound Prairie was one of the most famous in antebellum Texas.[qv]

Most of the settlers in the county came from the southern states and from Missouri. In 1850 the county population was 2,884, of which 600 were slaves, but by 1860 the population had increased to 10,398, of which 3,668 were slaves. During the same time, cotton production had grown from 784 bales to 7,517 bales. Anderson County showed steady growth in population and agricultural production during the antebellum period.

When the Civil War[qv] broke out, Anderson County almost unanimously supported secession[qv] and sent her ablest men to fight. Judge John H. Reagan served in the cabinet of the Confederate government as postmaster general. Even after the defeat of the South, Anderson County resisted federal rule. During Reconstruction,[qv] one loyalist called District Judge Reuben A. Reeves,[qv] a resident of Palestine, "the greatest curse of the latter part of the nineteenth-century so far as this District is concerned" because of his refusal to allow blacks to participate as jurors in the judicial process. When the Democratic party[qv] gained control statewide, Anderson County voted Democratic in all national elections until 1924 and 1928, when it voted Republican for Calvin Coolidge and Herbert Hoover. In 1932 Anderson County again supported the Democrats. In 1952 and 1956 the county voted for Republican Dwight D. Eisenhower,[qv] and in 1960, Richard Nixon. The county voted for Republican candidates in 1980, 1984, and 1992.

By 1870 the population of Anderson County had declined to 9,229, 52 percent white and 48 percent black. In 1875, under the leadership of Judge Reagan, the citizens of Palestine and the county joined in voting a bond issue of $150,000 to be given as a bonus to the International–Great Northern Railroad for locating its machine and repair shops and general offices in Palestine. The company employed over 300 men. As a direct result, by 1880, Palestine doubled in size to more than 4,000 people, and the county population nearly doubled in size to 17,395. The county was traversed north to south by the railroad, which branched at Palestine, one set of tracks running to Houston and Galveston and the other to Laredo. The I–GN, currently the Missouri Pacific, still serves Palestine. Palestine is also a hub for the Texas State Railroad. The county population grew steadily upward to 37,092 in 1940, and the white majority increased to 68 percent. Between 1940 and 1970, however, the county declined in population by 25 percent, from 31,875 to 27,162. The white majority increased to 75 percent of the total. Between 1970 and 1980 the population increased to 38,381; whites numbered 29,399, or 77 percent.

Between 1880 and 1940 Anderson County was predominantly agricultural. Corn, cotton, sweet potatoes, hay, and, by the 1920s, peanuts were the most important crops. The timber industry gained importance in the 1930s. Between 1940 and 1982 the number of farms dropped by 70 percent, from 4,422 to 1,356. Crops that remained important in the 1980s included peanuts, sweet potatoes, hay, and fruits and nuts.

In 1881 traces of oil were found. The first rotary rig was shipped to the county in 1902. Good showings of oil caused more local citizens to drill, but no commercial wells were made at that time. In 1916 the Texas Company proved the existence of the Keechi Salt Dome, and in 1926 the Boggy Creek Dome was discovered. In January 1928 the first successful oil producer in Anderson County, known as the Humble–Lizzie Smith No. 1, was brought in. The discovery brought prosperity, and this may account for the county's voting Republican in the 1924 and 1928 elections. The oil discoveries also meant that the Great Depression[qv] had a less severe impact than elsewhere.

Manufacture of diverse products, including glass containers, garments, automotive parts, metal and wood products, aluminum, and furniture played an important role in the economy of the county. Manufacturing-related and retail employment rose from 2,006 in 1965 to 3,663 in 1980, accounting for over 55 percent of total employment. Oil and natural gas discoveries, valuable timber regions, rich ranchlands for grazing cattle, iron ore deposits, and the conversion to peanut production kept the price of farm and ranch land steadily increasing. Three units of the Texas Department of Corrections (*see* PRISON SYSTEM) were located at Tennessee Colony in the southwestern part of the county. Education levels advanced. In 1950 only 24 percent of those aged twenty-five or older had at least a high school education. By 1980, however, 51 percent met this standard.

Anderson County experienced growth in oil and gas production, transportation, retail and wholesale trade, finance, and the service industries throughout the 1970s and 1980s, while the population increased 60 percent, from 27,789 to 46,400. Population in 1990 was 48,024. The county attracts numerous visitors, who come to enjoy the beautiful Dogwood Trails in the spring, balloon launchings at the United States government's Scientific Balloon Base, picturesque train rides to Rusk on the Texas State Railroad, the Engeling Wildlife Management Area,[qv] the 900-acre Palestine Community Forest, and other historic sites and museums. Educational opportunities increased with the opening in 1980 of Trinity Valley Community College.

BIBLIOGRAPHY: Pauline Buck Hohes, *A Centennial History of Anderson County, Texas* (San Antonio: Naylor, 1936). Anderson County

Genealogical Society, Pioneer Families of Anderson County Prior to 1900 (Palestine, Texas, 1984). *Georgia Kemp Caraway*

ANDERSON CREEK. Anderson Creek rises in central Angelina County about six miles east of Lufkin (at 31°21′ N, 94°37′ W) and runs northeast for 7½ miles to its mouth on Sam Rayburn Reservoir (at 31°23′ N, 94°32′ W). The surrounding East Texas piney woods are characterized by flat to moderately rolling terrain surfaced by red sandy clays and loams.

ANDERSON MILL, TEXAS. Anderson Mill, sometimes called Anderson's Mill or Anderson's Mills, was located on Cypress Creek in northwestern Travis County, about sixteen miles northwest of Austin. It was named for Thomas Anderson, who came to Texas from Virginia in the late 1850s. In the early 1860s he built a mill to make gunpowder for the Confederacy; when the war was over he converted the operation to a gristmill. Farmers came from miles away to have their corn ground, sometimes having to camp near the mill for several days to wait their turn. In the early 1870s Anderson added a cotton gin to his operation. A post office opened at Anderson Mill in 1876 with Anderson as postmaster. In 1884 the community had a population of thirty. When the post office was discontinued later that year, mail for area residents was sent to Duval. The development of steam-powered mills and gins gradually forced Anderson out of business. After his death in 1894 his family sold the equipment and moved to Austin. A historical marker was placed near the mill site in 1936.

BIBLIOGRAPHY: John J. Germann and Myron Janzen, *Texas Post Offices by County* (1986). Ellen Seals, ed., *A Legend Collection: Fact and Fantasy* (Austin, 1981). *Vivian Elizabeth Smyrl*

ANDICE, TEXAS. Andice, also called Berry's Creek and Stapp, is at the intersection of Farm Roads 2338 and 970, five miles southwest of Florence in northwest Williamson County. The site was first settled by Joshua Stapp, who built a log structure to serve as a school and church in 1857. In 1876 Andrew Jackson, the proprietor of a small store on Berry Creek near the site of the future town, was appointed postmaster of the Berry's Creek post office, which continued in operation until 1879. When a local resident, Rev. William Isaac Newton, applied for a new post office in 1899 and suggested it be named after his son, Audice, postal officials misread the name as Andice and granted a post office under that name. White House School was built south of Andice before 1877 and had three teachers and 119 pupils in 1903. It was replaced by Andice School about 1925, and the latter was consolidated with the Florence school in 1967. Andice had 150 inhabitants in 1929. Its population peaked at 200 in 1931, when the town had ten businesses, then fell to fifty in 1933. In 1941 it was 190, and from 1970 until 1990 it remained stable at twenty-five. In 1973 Andice had two stores and two churches.

BIBLIOGRAPHY: Clara Stearns Scarbrough, *Land of Good Water: A Williamson County History* (Georgetown, Texas: Williamson County Sun Publishers, 1973). *Mark Odintz*

ANDRADE, JUAN JOSÉ (?–?). Juan José Andrade, commander of a cavalry brigade under Antonio López de Santa Anna[qv] during the Texas Revolution,[qv] was left in charge of Bexar after the battle of the Alamo[qv] on March 6, 1836. On April 1, he was ordered to prepare to leave for San Luis Potosí, since Santa Anna thought the Texan forces were routed. Andrade and his command were still in Bexar, however, on May 24, 1836, when Vicente Filisola[qv] ordered him to demolish the fortifications of the Alamo and march down the left bank of the San Antonio River to Goliad. Filisola met Andrade at Goliad, and the combined force continued to retreat. When the troops were nearing Matamoros on June 8, José de Urrea,[qv] who, unknown to Filisola, had replaced him as commander of the Mexican forces, sent orders for Andrade to return to Goliad. The retreat was continued, however, and on June 12 Filisola was notified that Urrea had replaced him. Since Urrea was not with the force, Filisola resigned his command to Andrade. Although the order for Andrade to return to Goliad was repeated on June 12, Andrade thought that the safety of the troops depended on their reaching Matamoros. He therefore defied his orders and took his command into Matamoros on June 18, 1836, thus ending the campaign.

BIBLIOGRAPHY: Hubert Howe Bancroft, *History of the North Mexican States and Texas* (2 vols., San Francisco: History Company, 1886, 1889). Antonio López de Santa Anna et al., *The Mexican Side of the Texan Revolution*, trans. Carlos E. Castañeda (Dallas: Turner, 1928; 2d ed., Austin: Graphic Ideas, 1970). Dudley Goodall Wooten, ed., *A Comprehensive History of Texas* (2 vols., Dallas: Scarff, 1898; rpt., Austin: Texas State Historical Association, 1986). *Winifred W. Vigness*

ANDREWARTHA, JOHN (1839–1916). John Andrewartha, architect and civil engineer, was born on August 25, 1839, in Falmouth, Cornwall, England, the son of William Guy and Mary Elizabeth Andrewartha. After attending primary school he trained as an engineer in the Royal Navy. On June 11, 1860, he married Jemima Louisa Whillier; the couple had twelve children, seven of whom survived to adulthood. In 1865, with his wife and other members of his family, Andrewartha moved to Louisville, Kentucky, where he worked as an architect and engineer. He moved to Austin, Texas, in 1881 in the hope that he would be chosen to design the new Capitol.[qv] Although he failed to secure the commission, he elected to settle in Austin and set up practice as an architect and civil engineer. In 1883 he was commissioned to design a building for the *Daily Statesman* (*see* AUSTIN AMERICAN-STATESMAN), but the project fell through because of financial problems at the paper. In 1884 he designed the new Austin City-County Hospital (razed 1929). The imposing Queen Anne style structure, located at 1405 Sabine Street, was the first public hospital in Texas. Andrewartha's residential work included a number of large houses, among them the Henry Hirschfeld house (1885; now listed in the National Register of Historic Places), and the Louis N. Grissom house (1898; razed). He was also responsible for the design of the Montopolis bridge across the Colorado River (destroyed by flooding in 1935) and St. John's Home for Negro Orphans (1911, burned 1956). Andrewartha died in Austin on November 7, 1916, and was buried there in Oakwood Cemetery.

BIBLIOGRAPHY: Vertical Files, Austin History Center. Roxanne Williamson, *Austin, Texas: An American Architectural History* (San Antonio: Trinity University Press, 1973). *Christopher Long*

ANDREW FEMALE COLLEGE. Andrew Female College, at Huntsville, was founded in 1852 and chartered on February 7, 1853, by the Texas Conference of Methodist Churches. The institution was named for Bishop James Osgood Andrew, and the first president was James M. Follansbee. Among the original trustees were Charles G. Keenan, Henderson Yoakum, and Daniel Baker;[qqv] Tom H. Ball[qv] was an early president of the school. The college was erected on the site of present Huntsville High School. Andrew Female College provided young women a classical education and classes in music, art, and embroidery. The college closed in 1879, and the building was moved to house a school for black children.

BIBLIOGRAPHY: D'Anne McAdams Crews, ed., *Huntsville and Walker County, Texas: A Bicentennial History* (Huntsville, Texas: Sam Houston State University, 1976). Hans Peter Nielsen Gammel, comp., *Laws of Texas, 1822–1897* (10 vols., Austin: Gammel, 1898).

ANDREWS, FRANK (1864–1936). Frank Andrews, railroad attorney and state assistant attorney general, son of Rev. Green Lee and Martha Ann (Sellers) Andrews, was born in Fayetteville, Texas, on June 15, 1864. He graduated from Southwestern University in 1885, was admitted to the Texas bar in 1887, and from 1888 to 1891 served as city attorney at Belton. He was assistant attorney general of Texas from 1891 to 1895. On December 22, 1891, he married Rosalee Smith, with whom he had two children.

In 1895 he moved to Houston, where he organized the law firm of Andrews, Kelley, Kurth, and Campbell and became interested in railroad building. As attorney for the Houston and Texas Central Railway Company, he represented the company before the Railroad Commission.[qv] With E. M. House and Robert Holmes Baker,[qqv] he chartered the Trinity and Brazos Valley Railway in 1902 and later the Yoakum Lines, which became part of the Missouri Pacific. In 1913, when the Frisco System in Texas went into receivership, Andrews served as receiver of Texas properties, and in 1916 he became chairman of the board for a newly chartered New Orleans, Texas and Mexican Railway.

He declined three appointments to Texas judgeships, including a nomination to the state Supreme Court in 1918. With others he established the Union Bank and Trust Company and developed the Montrose addition in Houston. He was a member of the cotton exchange and chamber of commerce and was a developer of the Houston Ship Channel.[qv] He was a member of the American, state, and county bar associations and a Mason. Andrews died at his home in Houston on December 7, 1936.

BIBLIOGRAPHY: Houston *Post*, December 9, 1936. *National Cyclopædia of American Biography*, Vol. 27. S. G. Reed, *A History of the Texas Railroads* (Houston: St. Clair, 1941; rpt., New York: Arno, 1981). *Who Was Who in America*, Vol 2.

Erma Baker

ANDREWS, HENRY BARCLAY (1828–1895). Henry Barclay Andrews, soldier, statesman, and railroad builder, son of English citizens named Barclay, was born on the island of St. Thomas, West Indies, on September 21, 1828. His father died in 1829, and in 1830 his mother moved to Columbia, Texas, where she married Judge Edmund Andrews, who adopted her three children and gave them his name. Henry was sent to Yale University but was recalled before graduation because of the death of his adopted father. In 1844 he entered the mercantile business at Galveston, where he married Martha Wynne in 1845. After reading law with Elisha M. Pease[qv] and being admitted to the bar, Andrews became attorney of the Galveston district court in 1846. He served as postmaster at Galveston from 1857 until 1861, when he organized and commanded a company of cavalry coast rangers for Texas defense during the Civil War.[qv] In 1863 he was made chief of the Texas Labor Bureau, and in 1864 he was elected to the Texas legislature. Andrews began his career as a railroad man in 1868, when he became general freight and passenger agent for the Galveston, Houston and Henderson Railroad. Later he was vice president and general manager of the Galveston, Harrisburg and San Antonio. He moved to San Antonio in 1877. He was appointed one of three commissioners to represent Texas at the World's Fair Exposition at Paris by Governor Richard B. Hubbard.[qv] Andrews was the father of ten children, nine born to his first wife and one to his second wife, Mrs. Frank Smith, formerly Mollie Houston of Alabama. Andrews was a Democrat, a Mason, an Odd Fellow, and an Elk. He died in San Antonio on April 14, 1895, and was buried there.

BIBLIOGRAPHY: Vinton Lee James, *Frontier and Pioneer Recollections of Early Days in San Antonio and West Texas* (San Antonio, 1938).

Claudia Hazlewood

ANDREWS, JESSE (1874–1961). Jesse Andrews, lawyer and public servant, was born on April 9, 1874, in Waterproof, Louisiana, the son of Mark and Helen (McFerran) Andrews. He attended Jefferson College in Mississippi from 1887 to 1889 and then embarked on a career in the hardware business. He enrolled in the University of Texas in 1891 and received his B.Litt. in 1895 and LL.B. in 1896, after which he passed the bar examination. In 1899 Andrews entered the law firm of Baker, Botts, and Lovett (now Baker and Botts[qv]), with which he remained throughout his career. He became a partner in 1906, and in 1933 his name was added to the firm's name. One of Andrews's major accomplishments was his stewardship of the Long-Bell Lumber Company, the world's largest lumber company in the 1920s. After leading the company through legal channels during the Great Depression,[qv] he became the chairman of its board of directors. Andrews was a trustee of the University of Kansas and maintained residences in both Houston and Kansas City. He was a member of the first zoning committee of the city of Houston and served as chairman of the Houston City Planning Commission for sixteen years. He also was a member of the Philosophical Society of Texas[qv] and served as both president and director of that organization. He married Emilia Celeste Bujac on November 8, 1900, and they had one son. At the time of his death in Houston on December 29, 1961, Andrews was an active Democrat, director and vice chairman of the executive committee of the Bank of the Southwest, director of the American General Life Insurance Company, and a trustee of the Robert A. Welch[qv] Foundation.

BIBLIOGRAPHY: Sam Hanna Acheson, Herbert P. Gambrell, Mary Carter Toomey, and Alex M. Acheson, Jr., *Texian Who's Who*, Vol. 1 (Dallas: Texian, 1937). *Proceedings of the Philosophical Society of Texas*, 1961.

ANDREWS, JESSIE (1867–1919). Jessie Andrews, the first woman teacher at the University of Texas, one of five children of Jesse and Margaret L. (Miller) Andrews, was born in Washington, Mississippi, on February 17, 1867. She moved to Texas with her mother about 1874; her father, who had come earlier for his health, died less than a year later, and Margaret Andrews opened a boarding house near the Capitol[qv] to support the family. Jessie graduated from Austin High School, where she won the Peabody Award as the outstanding honor graduate. She became the first female to complete the entrance examinations and enter the new University of Texas in 1883. She majored in German. In 1886 she received a B.Litt. degree and thus became the first woman to graduate at UT. At the commencement ceremony she was presented a special award as the first female graduate and member of the Alumni Association. When a chapter of Phi Beta Kappa was established at the university in 1904, she was elected to membership.

After teaching for a year in Mrs. Hood's Seminary for Young Ladies in Austin, Jessie Andrews taught German and French at the University of Texas, beginning in 1888. She thus became the first woman teacher at UT. In 1918, after becoming disillusioned with Germany because of World War I,[qv] she resigned and joined her sister in operating a store. She was a Presbyterian and an active member of the YWCA. She was chosen poet laureate[qv] by the Texas Woman's Press Association. A book of her poems was published in 1910 under the title *Rough Rider Rhymes*, and her verse also appeared in several magazines. She earned a master of philosophy degree from the University of Chicago in 1906, after studying there for nine summers. She died of pneumonia on December 23, 1919. Jessie Andrews Dormitory, built on the University of Texas campus in 1936, is named for her.

BIBLIOGRAPHY: *Alcalde* (magazine of the Ex-Students' Association of the University of Texas), May 1920. Austin *American-Statesman*, May 5, 1989. Vertical Files, Barker Texas History Center, University of Texas at Austin.

Margaret C. Berry

ANDREWS, JOHN (?–?). John Andrews, one of Stephen F. Austin's[qv] Old Three Hundred,[qv] was living in Texas as early as March 1824; he probably came from Mississippi, where his son, John Jr., was born. He received title to a league and a labor of land now in Waller, Fayette, and Colorado counties in July 1824. The 1826 census of Austin's colony listed Andrews as a farmer and stock raiser aged over fifty. His household included his wife, a son, a daughter, and a servant. Andrews gave testimony in a lawsuit in the Colorado District in 1827 and in February 1828 was one of the secretaries of the colonial assembly held at San Felipe de Austin. In 1830 his home on the Navidad River was the site of a precinct meeting to choose a representative to a district meeting to be held in San Felipe.

BIBLIOGRAPHY: Eugene C. Barker, ed., *The Austin Papers* (3 vols., Washington: GPO, 1924–28). Lester G. Bugbee, "The Old Three Hundred: A List of Settlers in Austin's First Colony," *Quarterly of the Texas State Historical Association* 1 (October 1897). *Telegraph and Texas Register*, December 16, 1837, August 17, 1842. *Texas Gazette*, October 16, 1830. *Texas Sentinel*, February 5, 1840. Vertical Files, Barker Texas History Center, University of Texas at Austin.

ANDREWS, JOHN DAY (1795–1882). John Day Andrews, mayor of Houston, planter, and businessman, was born in Spotsylvania County, Virginia, on August 30, 1795. He managed a hotel, probably in Hanover County, Virginia, and married a widow, Mrs. Eugenia Price Tighlman, of Rocketts, Virginia, in 1830. She was granddaughter of Mary Randolph Price of the Randolph family of Virginia. With his wife, her two children, whom he adopted, and their small daughter, he moved to Houston in 1837. Their second daughter was born in 1840. By 1840 Andrews owned twenty-two slaves and a small farm in Harris County, as well as seventeen town lots. He built Houston's first multiple-dwelling unit, which housed his family and, for a brief time, that of Thomas M. League. From 1838 to 1840 League and Andrews were partners in a general merchandise and produce business. By 1850 Andrews was worth $25,000, and in spite of the Civil War[qv] he reported his wealth at $100,000 in the 1870 census, a fortune amassed from his plantations and real estate transactions throughout Texas.

He and his wife were devout Episcopalians and helped organize Christ Church in 1838. As a businessman, Andrews recognized the necessity of civic as well religious improvements. During the administration of Mayor Francis Moore, Jr.[qv] (1839), the firm of League, Andrews, and Company was on the list of $100 contributors for the purchase of an engine house for the volunteer fire company. Andrews served as president of the board of health, also established in 1840. Since the progress of Houston depended in large measure upon the city's being reached by steamboat, Andrews helped organize and became president of the Buffalo Bayou Company, which took responsibility for removal of obstructions on Buffalo Bayou in the five-mile section between Harrisburg and Houston. His work on behalf of the town's commercial welfare contributed to his being elected mayor in 1841 and 1842. Under his direction the city government established a Port of Houston Authority, which regulated all wharves, slips, and roads adjacent to Buffalo and White Oak bayous and used wharfage fees to pay for keeping the waterway navigable. Andrews was also responsible for building Houston's first city hall, which was completed early in 1842.

While Houston was the capital of the Republic of Texas,[qv] President Sam Houston[qv] lived on property owned by Andrews and was a frequent dinner guest in his home. In one of the largest homes in Houston, Andrews often entertained visiting dignitaries such as French chargé d'affaires Dubois de Saligny,[qv] and he was a friend of Texans Anson Jones, Ashbel Smith, and Lorenzo de Zavala.[qqv] In 1842 Houston asked Andrews to become secretary of the treasury, but he declined.

After his terms as mayor, Andrews sought to improve educational opportunities by becoming the first president of the first school board of Houston City School. He remained interested in the activities of the Houston Chamber of Commerce and expanded his real estate investments. He was blind for the last four years of his life and was cared for by his daughter and son-in-law, Eugenia and Robert Turner Flewellen.[qv] He died on August 30, 1882, and was buried in Glenwood Cemetery in Houston.

BIBLIOGRAPHY: Pearl Hendricks, "Houston—One Hundred Years of Progress," *Houston*, April 1940. Houston *Post*, October 3, 1937.

Priscilla Myers Benham

ANDREWS, MATTHEW THOMAS (1866–1939). Matthew Thomas (M. T.) Andrews, Baptist preacher, son of Thomas J. and Margaret (Rollins) Andrews, was born on a plantation near McComb City, Mississippi, on April 13, 1866 or 1869. He received his early education at Gillsburg Collegiate Institute and subsequently earned his A.B. degree in 1894 at Clinton College (now Mississippi College) in Clinton, Mississippi. He was awarded an honorary doctorate by Howard Payne College, Brownwood, Texas, in 1919. Andrews was ordained a Baptist minister by the East Fork Baptist Church in 1895. He served as pastor in many places: Amite City, Louisiana, 1891–94; Hammond, Louisiana, 1894–96; Clinton, Louisiana, 1896–98; First Baptist Church, Marshall, 1898; First Baptist Church, Marlin, 1899–1909; First Baptist Church, Denton, 1909–12; First Baptist Church, Hillsboro, 1912–18; First Baptist Church, Temple, 1919–23; and First Baptist Church, Texarkana, 1924–38. He also served on the board of trustees of Southwestern Baptist Theological Seminary, the executive board of the Baptist General Convention of Texas, and the home mission board of the Southern Baptist Convention. He was a delegate to the Baptist World Alliance in Stockholm, 1923; in Toronto, 1928; and in Berlin, 1934. He made many speaking tours, including trips to Europe and China. After his retirement from the Texarkana First Baptist Church in 1938, Andrews assisted in the fund-raising campaign for the Tidwell Bible Building at Baylor University. He wrote many articles for Southern Baptist periodicals as well as several books, including *Growing a Soul* (1926), *Comrades of the Road* (1939), and *Adults and the Art of Learning* (1936).

Andrews was married to Theodocia Ernest Cook of Liberty, Mississippi, on December 22, 1891. They had seven children—six daughters and one son. Mrs. Andrews died on September 30, 1936, in Texarkana, while her husband was in China. In April 1938 Andrews married Gertrude Wright of Chattanooga, Tennessee. Soon after their marriage they traveled to Africa to review Baptist missions there. After returning from the Baptist World Congress in Atlanta, Andrews died of a heart attack in Chattanooga, on July 31, 1939. His funeral was held at the First Baptist Church of Texarkana, and he was buried in a family lot in Hillsboro.

BIBLIOGRAPHY: *Baptist Standard*, September 21, 1939. L. R. Elliott, ed., *Centennial Story of Texas Baptists* (Dallas: Baptist General Convention of Texas, 1936). George William Lasher, ed., *The Ministerial Directory of the Baptist Churches in the United States of America* (Oxford, Ohio: Ministerial Directory Company, 1899). John S. Ramond, ed., *Among Southern Baptists* (Shreveport, Louisiana, 1936).

Alan J. Lefever

ANDREWS, REDDIN, JR. (1848–1923). Reddin Andrews, Jr., Baptist preacher, college president, writer, and politician, was born in La Grange, Fayette County, Texas, on January 18, 1848, to Reddin and Mary Jane (Talbert) Andrews. His mother died in 1852, and he grew up in the home of his brother-in-law, J. L. Gay. In 1863 Andrews joined the Confederate infantry as a scout and courier. After the war he returned to Fayette County, attended school, and joined the Shiloh Baptist Church. In 1871 he graduated from Baylor University as valedictorian, was ordained, and left for a two-year course of study at Greenville Seminary in South Carolina. He returned to Texas in 1873 to a pastorate in Navasota. During his ministry he worked with churches in Millican, Hempstead, Calvert, Tyler, Lampasas, Bastrop, Goodman, Webberville, Hillsboro, Woodbury, Rockwall, and Lovelady. In August 1874 he married Elizabeth Eddins. They had nine children and were survived by seven.

In 1871–72 Andrews joined the faculty of Baylor University, where he taught primary classes in exchange for tuition. In 1886 he was professor of Greek and English literature. He resigned in 1878 for financial reasons and became principal of the Masonic Institute at Round Rock. In 1881 he accepted a pulpit in Tyler and became contributing editor to John B. Link's[qv] *Texas Baptist Herald.*[qv] Andrews had a filial relationship with Baylor president William C. Crane,[qv] and when Crane died Andrews became Baylor's first Texas-born president. Because of financial pressures he agreed to move the institution to Waco in 1885. Waco University president Rufus C. Burleson[qv] served as president, and Andrews became vice president of the consolidated institution. Andrews also served on the unification committee that merged the Baptist State Convention and Baptist General Association into the Baptist General Convention of Texas in 1886.

In 1889 Andrews moved to Atlanta, Georgia, to edit W. T. Martin's *Gospel Standard and Expositor,* a publication that challenged the Southern Baptist Convention. In 1890 he returned to Lampasas, Texas. Although his association with Martin produced tensions within the denomination, he was considered an expert on the problems of rural congregations. In 1892 Andrews moved to Belton to teach and worked as an organizer for the People's (Populist) party.[qv] Populists mentioned him for state office, but he did not receive a formal nomination. He continued to fill pulpits in Hill County on a periodic basis from 1902 to 1905 and remained active in radical politics because he thought the ethics of Christianity and socialism were identical. In 1907 Andrews was editor of the *Sword and Shield* at Tyler. As a socialist gubernatorial candidate he received 11,538 votes in 1910 and outpolled all but the Democratic nominee in 1912 with 25,258 votes. In 1911 he collected various original poems composed for sermons and special occasions and published them in a volume entitled *Poems.* In 1916 he moved to Lawton, Oklahoma, where he died on August 16, 1923.

BIBLIOGRAPHY: Reddin Andrews, "The Baylor I Knew," *Baylor Bulletin,* December 1915. Robert A. Baker, *The Blossoming Desert—A Concise History of Texas Baptists* (Waco: Word, 1970). *Baptist Standard,* Centennial Issue, June 11, 1936. James Milton Carroll, *A History of Texas Baptists* (Dallas: Baptist Standard, 1923). J. C. Daniel, *A History of the Baptists of Hill County, Texas* (Waco: Hill-Kellner-Frost, 1907). *Minutes of the Ministers Conference of the Baptist General Convention,* October 7, 1891. Lois Smith Murray, *Baylor at Independence* (Waco: Baylor University Press, 1972). Thomas E. Turner, *The Presidents of Baylor* (Waco: Baylor University, 1981). Vertical File, Texas Collection, Baylor University. Mamie Yeary, *Reminiscences of the Boys in Gray* (McGregor, Texas, 1912; rpt., Dayton, Ohio: Morningside, 1986). *Keith L. King*

ANDREWS, RICHARD (?–1835). Richard Andrews, early settler and soldier in the revolutionary army,[qv] son of William Andrews,[qv] traveled to Texas with his father and family to settle in the Fort Bend area on the Brazos River at the site that became Richmond. He and his brother Micah became Indian fighters, and both joined the army at the beginning of the Texas Revolution.[qv] Richard Andrews, called Big Dick because of his immense stature and strength, was wounded in the battle of Gonzales[qv] on October 2, 1835. He was with James Bowie and James W. Fannin, Jr.,[qqv] on October 28, 1835, at the battle of Concepción,[qv] in which he was killed. Andrews County was named in his honor in 1876.

BIBLIOGRAPHY: Zachary T. Fulmore, *History and Geography of Texas As Told in County Names* (Austin: Steck, 1915; facsimile 1935). Clarence Wharton, *Wharton's History of Fort Bend County* (San Antonio: Naylor, 1939). *Claudia Hazlewood*

ANDREWS, ROBERT (?–?). Robert Andrews, doctor, was a member of the Arkansas territorial legislature about 1820. Both he and Stephen F. Austin[qv] had been interested in land certificates in the Little Rock area. On November 3, 1821, Andrews wrote from Arkansas to Austin in New Orleans that he would do surveying in Texas requested by Austin and that he would leave with James Clark[qv] for San Antonio about November 17. By January 29, 1822, he was on his surveying expedition. He left San Antonio on March 21, 1822, to accompany Austin to Mexico City to secure the authorization of the Austin colonization contract. Dr. Andrews stopped either in Laredo or Monterrey and by July 8, 1822, was practicing medicine in Saltillo. Immediately after March 4, 1823, he left Saltillo for Parras, where he wrote Austin on May 9, 1823, that he had applied through Ramos Arispe for the office of surveyor in Texas to replace the Baron de Bastrop.[qv] On June 13, 1824, Andrews was in Durango, but by August 23 he had returned to Parras, where he wrote on October 4 that he intended to petition the Mexican government for title to the entire Red River country including Pecan Point and to request a right of citizenship and appointment to the position of surveyor of Texas. Austin was asked to use his influence in securing the surveying position.

BIBLIOGRAPHY: Eugene C. Barker, ed., *The Austin Papers* (3 vols., Washington: GPO, 1924–28). Eugene C. Barker, *The Life of Stephen F. Austin* (Nashville: Cokesbury Press, 1925; rpts., Austin: Texas State Historical Association, 1949; New York: AMS Press, 1970). Pat Ireland Nixon, *The Medical Story of Early Texas, 1528–1853* (Lancaster, Pennsylvania: Lupe Memorial Fund, 1946). *Marie Giles*

ANDREWS, STEPHEN PEARL (1812–1886). Stephen Pearl Andrews, lawyer, abolitionist, and education innovator, the son of Elisha and Ann (Lathrop) Andrews, was born on March 22, 1812, at Templeton, Massachusetts, the youngest of eight children in a Baptist family. In 1828 he enrolled in the Classical Department of Amherst College. Two years later he accompanied an older brother and sister to Louisiana, where he was an instructor at Jackson Female Seminary. There he met Mary Ann Gordon, whom he married in 1835; the couple had four sons. Andrews began to study law and was admitted to the state bar in 1833. Shortly thereafter, he moved to New Orleans, where he established a successful law practice and became acquainted with abolitionist Lewis Tappan. The panic of 1837 and yellow fever epidemics resulted in Andrews's departure for Texas. In 1834 he settled with his family in Houston, where he achieved some prominence as a lawyer and became involved in real estate. During this time he devised a plan to abolish slavery in the republic through the purchase of slaves. Though he gained some support for his efforts, many people blamed him for stirring up trouble among the slaves. Because of his abolitionist efforts his home was mobbed in 1843, and he and his family were forced to leave Texas. The summer of that year he accompanied Tappan to England, where he endeavored to raise money for the purchase of slaves in the form of a loan from Great Britain to Texas. He influenced many British leaders, but the project was dropped when he was repudiated by Ashbel Smith,[qv] Texas chargé d'affaires.

While in England, Andrews became interested in the shorthand system of Isaac Pitman and, when he returned to the United States, opened a school of phonography in Boston. He added spelling reform to the list of his interests, moved to New York in 1847, and edited two magazines printed in phonetic type, the *Anglo-Saxon* and the *Propagandist.* In collaboration with Augustus F. Boyle, he compiled and published *The Comprehensive Phonographic Class-Book* (1845) and *The Phonographic Reader* (1845). In 1856 Andrews married his second wife, Esther Hussey Bartlett Jones. They did not have children. Andrews was reputed to have a good knowledge of thirty-two languages. He presented a deductive science of the universe, "universology," in his *Basic Outline of Universology* (1871). He was also involved in the woman suffrage[qv] movement and studied the works of Karl Marx. Andrews died on May 21, 1886.

BIBLIOGRAPHY: *Appleton's Cyclopaedia of American Biography* (7 vols., New York: Appleton, 1888–91). *Dictionary of American Biography. National Cyclopaedia of American Biography,* Vol. 6. Madeleine B. Stern, *The Pantarch: A Biography of Stephen Pearl Andrews* (Austin:

University of Texas Press, 1968). *Who Was Who in American History: The Military,* Historical volume, 1607–1896. *David L. Fisher*

ANDREWS, WILLIAM (?–ca. 1840). William Andrews, one of Stephen F. Austin's[qv] Old Three Hundred[qv] colonists, married Susan Clark on August 20, 1805, in St. Landry Parish, Louisiana. He moved to Texas before December 1821 and received title to a league and a labor of land in what is now Fort Bend County on July 15, 1824. His daughter Martha (Polly), aged fourteen, married Randal Jones[qv] on October 12, 1824. Twin daughters were born to the Andrews family on January 7, 1825, but one of them must have died before the census was taken in 1826, for at that time Andrews had with him his wife, four sons, one daughter, and two slaves. He was classified as a farmer and stock raiser aged between forty and fifty. Sometime before the Texas Revolution[qv] Andrews sold his league in Fort Bend County and moved to the San Bernard area, where he operated a trading post. A son, Walter, who spelled his name Andrus, was still living in Fort Bend County in 1850. Andrews died before January 10, 1840.

BIBLIOGRAPHY: Eugene C. Barker, ed., *The Austin Papers* (3 vols., Washington: GPO, 1924–28). Lester G. Bugbee, "The Old Three Hundred: A List of Settlers in Austin's First Colony," *Quarterly of the Texas State Historical Association* 1 (October 1897). William Barret Travis, *Diary,* ed. Robert E. Davis (Waco: Texian, 1966). Clarence Wharton, *Wharton's History of Fort Bend County* (San Antonio: Naylor, 1939).

ANDREWS, WILLIE ANN HUDSON (1848–1895). Willie Ann Hudson Andrews, school founder and teacher, was born in Virginia on May 26, 1848. In 1867, after her marriage to Whit W. Andrews, she moved to the Harris Chapel community in Gonzales County, Texas, where she established the first of several innovative coeducational schools in south central Texas. Mrs. Andrews conducted schools at the Josey community (now Luling), at Prairie Lea in Caldwell County, and at Mountain City in Hays County, before she opened Science Hall Institute between Buda and Dupre (now Kyle) in 1876. The curriculum at Science Hall, which covered mathematics, science, business, art, and music, was considered a model course of study and drew students from across the state. School officials built a dormitory after the available boarding spaces with local families were taken up. The school boarded both male and female students, an unusual arrangement at the time. Willie Andrews traveled as far as West Texas during the summers distributing the school's catalogue and recruiting students.

After Science Hall was destroyed by fire in the early 1880s, Mrs. Andrews accepted an offer to consolidate her operations with Kyle Baptist Seminary, a coeducational boarding school. After an unsatisfactory year at the seminary, she opened Science Hall Home Institute,[qv] a private boarding school, in 1884. In 1888, at the request of a group of Austin citizens who donated a school site, she left Hays County and established the Austin Home Institute, which operated until 1895. This school attained such standing as a preparatory institution that its graduates could enter the University of Texas without entrance examinations.

Willie Andrews died on September 10, 1895, of injuries sustained in a carriage accident, and was buried in Oakwood Cemetery in Austin. In 1929 a group of her former students, including her three children, formed the Ex-Students of the Willie Andrews Pioneer Schools of Texas to commemorate her pioneer promotion of coeducational and public schools in the state. The former students held an annual reunion and memorial service until 1960.

BIBLIOGRAPHY: Austin *American,* November 3, 1957. Willie Andrews Pioneer School Records, Barker Texas History Center, University of Texas at Austin. Walter Edward Willis, The History of Education in Hays County (M.A. thesis, University of Texas, 1937).

Chester V. Kielman

ANDREWS, TEXAS (Andrews County). Andrews, the seat of Andrews County and the only incorporated town in the county, is on U.S. Highway 385 thirty-four miles north of Odessa. The town, like the county, was named for Richard Andrews,[qv] the first man to die in the war for Texas independence in 1835. The town began around 1908 with a general store and a schoolhouse. There were only eighty-seven people living in the county, most of them ranchers. A post office was established in 1909, and Andrews became the county seat in 1910 after a spirited contest against Shafter Lake; in 1911 residents built their first courthouse. In 1903 the Means Memorial Methodist Church became the first Andrews church to organize officially. It was joined in 1910 by the Andrews Baptist Church.

Development in Andrews proceeded slowly until 1929, when the Deep Rock Oil Company made the first major strike in the county. As a result of the national economic depression and the slow flow of the oil, Deep Rock eventually sold its holdings to J. W. Tripplehorn, for $7,500. Tripplehorn brought in the wells J. S. Means No. 1 and R. M. Means No. 1 in 1934, and the pace of development quickened. In 1937 Andrews was incorporated. The town's population, 611 by 1940, did not reflect the increasing importance of the region, for most of the oilmen and their families lived outside of town in company camps. The same year that Tripplehorn's first wells came in, the *Andrews County News* began publication. A library, established in one room in the county courthouse in 1947, was moved to its own new building in 1967.

Oil may have had its greatest local impact on the public school system. A one-room schoolhouse had opened in Andrews in 1907; by 1909 it had twenty-five students. A year later six county school districts were established. In the 1930s the original districts were consolidated into one, based in Andrews. A new high school was built in 1945 and a new middle school in 1954. In 1962 another new high school was built, and 1973 saw the construction of a new middle school, complete with planetarium. The modern and well-equipped schools reflected the system's reputation as one of the best and the wealthiest in the state.

After the opening of new oilfields in 1942, 1943, and 1944, the industry slumped, and by the 1960s most of the oil companies had closed their camps. Left with the choice of diversification or evacuation, many residents stayed on and developed a broader economic base for the town. The population fluctuated during these years, changing from 3,294 in 1950 to 11,135 in 1960, and back to 8,655 in 1970. In 1980 Andrews had a population of 11,061 and 258 businesses, was served by a bus line, two motor freight lines, and a small airport, and had hospitals, a mental health center, and a rest home. Recreational sites included an eighteen-hole golf course and six public parks. The population in 1990 was 10,678.

BIBLIOGRAPHY: *Andrews County History, 1876–1978* (Andrews, Texas: Andrews County Heritage Committee, 1978). Wilson Bond, Ruth Kindiger, and James Roberts, "Andrews' First Fifty Years," *Texas Permian Historical Annual* 2 (1962). *Tracey L. Compton*

ANDREWS, TEXAS (Wood County). Andrews was 6½ miles east of Quitman in northeastern Wood County. The settlement received a post office in 1885 and the following year reported a population of six. By 1892 the community had grown to 100, had two Methodist ministers, and supported a carpenter, a distiller, and two combination gristmill-gins. The population declined to fifteen by 1896, and by 1906 the post office had closed. *Rachel Jenkins*

ANDREWS COUNTY. Andrews County (E-8), in the southern High Plains, is bounded on the west by New Mexico, on the north by Gaines County, on the east by Martin County, and on the south by Winkler and Ector counties. The center of the county is at 32°18′ north latitude and 102°50′ west longitude, 110 miles southwest of Lubbock. Andrews County encompasses 1,504 square miles of level, rolling prairieland typical of the southern High Plains. Sandy soils predominate except in the east, where red clay loam is found. The elevation varies from 3,000 feet in the south to 3,400 feet in the north. The average annual rainfall is 14.37 inches, and temperatures range from a January average minimum of 30°F to a July average maximum of 96°F. The growing season is 213 days. Livestock production accounts for roughly two-thirds of the $11 million average agricultural income. Crops of cotton, sorghums, grains, corn, and hay account for the rest. About 8,000 acres of land is irrigated. Oil and gas production and related services produce most of the county's income. With an income of $146,055,000 and oil production valued at $1,213,228,209 in 1982, Andrews ranks among the leading counties of the state in median annual income and in annual oil production. The oil industry is a major source of employment; by the end of 1982 the county had produced over two billion barrels of oil. Some 293,000 acres of valuable county land have been owned by the state university since 1883.

Angostura type arrowheads discovered by archeologists indicate the possibility of an aboriginal population as early as 6,000–4,000 B.C., but pottery sherds and other evidence establish occupation by the Anasazi people from around A.D. 900. In more recent times the Apaches and Comanches occupied the region, until the United States Army campaigns of 1874–75 cleared the way for white settlement.

The county was formed from Bexar County on August 21, 1876, a year after the first detailed explorations made by Col. William R. Shafter[qv] from his military base at Fort Concho. The county was named for Richard Andrews,[qv] a hero of the Texas Revolution[qv] who was killed at the battle of Concepción in 1835. Subsequent boundary alterations occurred in 1902, 1931, and 1932. For administrative purposes the area was placed within the jurisdiction of Shackelford County in 1876, within the Howard Land District from 1882 to 1887, and within the Martin Land District from 1887 to 1891. The area was placed within the jurisdiction of Martin County from 1891 until 1910, when Andrews County was formally organized with Andrews as its county seat.

In 1886 O. B. Holt first filed on county lands, although the huge Chicago Ranch, founded by Nelson Morris, a Chicago meat packer, purchased 228,000 acres in the southeastern corner in 1884. The county's aridity and its lack of surface streams encouraged novel rainmaking experiments in 1891 by the United States Department of Agriculture. Sixty mortars charged with blasting powder and thirty kites suspending dynamite loosed their destructive forces at clouds while a number of ten-foot balloons, each holding a thousand cubic feet of oxygen and hydrogen gas were simultaneously discharged. Despite these notable bombardments no rain fell locally, although a copious precipitation to the east and south was, perhaps, a result of the experiment. After the draughts of 1886 and 1887, Nelson Morris introduced windmills to draw ground water until he had seventy-nine of the wind machines spaced on his ranch. Morris also introduced barbed wire[qv] drift fences to contain cattle.

In 1894 the Scharbauers purchased the Wells Ranch, which with Morris's C-Ranch occupied most of the eastern part of the county. A year later the Texas legislature passed the four-section law, which helped to end open-range ranching in Texas by encouraging the breakup up of great ranches for the benefit of homesteaders and small tract purchasers.

In the early 1880s the building of the Texas and Pacific Railway through Midland, Midland County, the supply point of Andrews County, gave promise of future growth. The railroad promoted immigration and had millions of acres to offer settlers. But since there was plenty of land in West Texas with better access to transportation than Andrews County, the population grew slowly; the census showed only twenty-four residents in 1890, and as late as 1900 only eighty-seven people lived in Andrews County

By 1910, however, the population was 975, principally farmers and ranchers. Though only 70 acres of farmland had been classified as improved in the 1900 census, by 1910 the census counted 1,105 improved acres; and by 1920 the area was more than 6,000 acres. Almost 2,700 acres was planted in corn, at that time the county's most important crop. Still, actual cropland accounted for relatively little of the county's economic activity; ranching, while declining somewhat between 1910 and 1920, continued to dominate the local economy. The 2,700 acres devoted to corn production in 1920, for example, was only a small fraction of the 366,755 total productive acres in the county that year. The county had more than 53,000 cattle in 1900, and more than 54,000 in 1910.

The terrible drought of 1917–18, World War I,[qv] the great influenza epidemic of 1917–18, blizzards, and a drop in cattle prices reduced county population to 350 in 1920. It was clear by this time that much county land was not suitable for farming. Cattle ranchers bought the abandoned lands of disappointed farmers to extend their ranges. Land owned by the University of Texas, some fourteen blocks scattered around the county, accounted for 29 percent of the total acreage, and much of this was leased for grazing purposes. Nevertheless, agricultural activity did rebound during the 1920s; seventy-five farms and ranches were counted in Andrews in 1930, nearly a 32 percent increase over the figure for 1920. During this same decade cotton came to be the single largest crop raised by the farmers of the county. While the number of acres devoted to corn production fell more than 50 percent between 1920 and 1930, by 1930 almost 1,900 acres was planted with cotton. By the 1940s, sorghum had become another leading crop.

The 1920s also saw the beginning of oil production in Andrews County. On December 5, 1929, the gusher drilled in the Deep Rock Ogden No. 1 came in. The oil had been tapped at 4,345 feet and flowed in prodigious quantities. While the excitement was general in oil-industry circles and among county residents, who braced for a great boom, prosperity did not come at once. The timing of the new field could not have been worse. East Texas fields were in full production, and the 1929 crash had devastated the market. By 1931 oil was selling for as little as ten cents a barrel. Even at that price the Andrews County oil, of low gravity and heavy in sulfur, would not have sold. Investors declined to build a pipeline into the county until 1934, when J. W. Tripplehorn bought up leases, began drilling, and encouraged Humble Oil Company (later Exxon Company, U.S.A.[qv]) to lease other lands and to build a pipeline.

Though five new oilfields drilled during the 1930s continued local petroleum development, the industry did not really boom in Andrews County until the 1940s, when twenty-six new fields were discovered. Extravagant drilling efforts during this time added an entirely new dimension to life in the county, as thousands of people traveled to the area seeking jobs in the oilfields and service industries. The population of Andrews County rose from 1,277 in 1940 to more than 5,000 in 1950, and with the growth came housing problems and overcrowded conditions in Andrews, which, like the rest of the county, experienced unprecedented growth and prosperity thanks to the oil boom.

Petroleum production continued to rise in Andrews County during the 1950s, when ninety new fields were discovered. Oil income from royalties and tax dollars provided residents with many of modern services and conveniences that could not be afforded earlier, but oil production fell off in the 1960s, when only fifty-three new fields were found, and particularly in the early 1970s, when only thirteen new fields were discovered. Unemployment mounted, and county leaders called for some diversification of industry.

Water flooding of old fields and the Arab oil embargo of 1973–74 stimulated oil production again in the 1970s, and prosperity became general through the decade. The population was 10,352 in 1970 and was estimated at 15,000 in 1982, before declining slightly to 14,338 in 1992. Most people in the county live in the town of Andrews, the county seat, which had a population of more than 11,000 in 1982 and 10,678 in 1990. In the early 1990s cattle ranching continued to be the most important agricultural activity in the county, while sorghum, cotton, and corn were the most significant crops (*see* corn culture, cotton culture, sorghum culture).

The county's road network includes Highway 385 (north-south), Highway 176 (west-east), and Highway 115, which bisects the other roads at Andrews. Communities include Andrews, Frankel City (pop. 1,344), and Florey (25). Prairie Dog Town and the Oil Museum are two of the county's most popular tourist attractions.

bibliography: *Andrews County History, 1876–1978* (Andrews, Texas: Andrews County Heritage Committee, 1978). *William R. Hunt*

ANDROSS, MILES DEFOREST (1809–1836). Miles DeForest Andross, Alamo defender, was born in Vermont in 1809. He moved to Texas and settled in San Patricio. He took part in the siege of Bexar,[qv] became ill afterwards, and remained in Bexar as part of Lt. Col. James Clinton Neill's[qv] command. Andross served in the Alamo garrison as part of Capt. William Blazeby's[qv] infantry company. He died in the battle of the Alamo[qv] on March 6, 1836.

bibliography: Daughters of the American Revolution, *The Alamo Heroes and Their Revolutionary Ancestors* (San Antonio, 1976). Daughters of the Republic of Texas, *Muster Rolls of the Texas Revolution* (Austin, 1986). Bill Groneman, *Alamo Defenders* (Austin: Eakin, 1990). Phil Rosenthal and Bill Groneman, *Roll Call at the Alamo* (Fort Collins, Colorado: Old Army, 1985). *Bill Groneman*

ANDRY, LUIS ANTONIO (?–1778?). Luis Antonio Andry, a French engineer, was chosen by Louisiana governor Bernardo de Gálvez[qv] to map the Gulf of Mexico coast from the Mississippi River to Matagorda Bay. Andry sailed from New Orleans on December 13, 1777, on the schooner *Señor de la Yedra* with a crew of thirteen, including his young son, a cadet. The expedition represents an early manifestation of Gálvez's interest in exploration and mapping of the Louisiana-Texas coast that later brought forth the coastal survey voyage of José Antonio de Evia.[qv] Andry's survey ship reached Matagorda Bay by early March 1778, its work essentially complete. Shortly thereafter, it fell victim to the trickery of apostate Karankawas from the Texas missions.

Andry's qualifications came to the attention of General Alejandro O'Reilly after O'Reilly took possession of Louisiana from rebellious French colonists in 1769. The Irish-expatriate general named him to a three-man commission to inspect the installation called La Balisa on an island at the mouth of the Mississippi. Andry continued to serve Spain thereafter. In 1776 Governor Luis de Unzaga y Amezaga recommended the engineer, a "brevet captain and second adjutant" of the Spanish post at New Orleans, for appointment as commandant of the Acadian Coast. Besides experience in the service of both France and Spain, said Unzaga, Andry had "personal merits, talents, and a knowledge of mathematics . . ., which he employs to the benefit of the service."

The mapping expedition had not been heard from by October 1778. Apprehension that the ship had been lost mounted in New Orleans, where the loss was to be felt severely. By the following January a report came through Natchitoches that the charred remains of a schooner fitting *Yedra's* description had been found on the Texas coast near Nuestra Señora de Loreto Presidio, also known as La Bahía.[qv] Verification came in March 1779, when a lone survivor of the massacre was released from Karankawa captivity. Tomás de la Cruz, a Mayan sailor from Campeche, related how Andry, in need of provisions, had been victimized by the apostates Joseph María and Mateo who, feigning friendship, claimed to be soldiers from La Bahía. After first disposing of two parties sent ashore to obtain provisions, the renegade brothers brought their companions on board the ship, seized the crew's unguarded weapons, and murdered the rest of the crew. Cruz was spared by Joseph María, who wanted him as his slave. The natives, Cruz related, at La Bahía stripped their victims' bodies and threw them into the bay. After removing the guns and other useful gear from the ship, they burned the vessel and with it perhaps the most detailed Spanish map of the Texas-Louisiana coast to that time.

The Andry expedition came between that of the trespassing survey crew of the British Admiralty cartographer George Gauld in the summer of 1777 and the two expeditions of José de Evia, which approached the Texas coast from different directions in 1785 and 1786. The Evia survey has most often been considered as having resulted from Bernardo de Gálvez's encounter with imprecise coastal maps while campaigning against the English on the Gulf Coast during the American Revolution. It now may be seen as a renewal of Andry's failed effort, postponed by Spain's entry into the war with England.

bibliography: Lawrence Kinnaird, *Spain in the Mississippi Valley, 1765–1794* (3 vols., Washington: GPO, 1949). *Robert S. Weddle*

ANGEL CITY, TEXAS. Angel City, on State Highway 239 ten miles west of Goliad in western Goliad County, is an agricultural community that was originally owned and operated by the C. C. Ramsey Enterprises to serve its tenant farmers. The settlement was named Angel City, according to one version, because of the violent fights that often accompanied regular Sunday night dances. Another story tells that two local young women, dressed in white and watching a crew drill the town water well, reminded a worker of a couple of angels. The community, established by 1931, once had a general store, a grocery, a blacksmith shop, a dairy, a cotton gin, a dance hall, and two schools, one for Hispanic children and one for Caucasians. A population of twenty was listed from 1933 to 1948. With the decline of cotton the tenant farmers moved, the gin and store closed, and the town disappeared, although maps of the 1980s continued to mark the site as a community.

bibliography: Goliad County Historical Commission, *The History and Heritage of Goliad County*, ed. Jakie L. Pruett and Everett B. Cole (Austin: Eakin Press, 1983). *Craig H. Roell*

ANGELINA (?–?). Angelina is a name supposedly given by Spanish founders of missions in eastern Texas in 1690 to an Indian woman who served as guide and interpreter. In 1712 André Pénicaut,[qv] who was accompanying Louis Juchereau de St. Denis,[qv] mentioned a "woman named Angélique, who has been baptizéd by Spanish priests . . . . She spoke Spanish, and as M. de St. Denis too spoke that language fairly well, he made use of her to tell the Assinais chiefs to let us have some guides for hire." Angelina is believed to be the same woman who rescued French officer François Simars de Bellisle[qv] from the Hasinais and sent him back to the French. She is mentioned by Father Isidro Félix de Espinosa[qv] as interpreter for the Domingo Ramón[qv] expedition of 1716, by Francisco de Céliz during the Martín de Alarcón[qv] expedition of 1718–19, and by Juan Antonio de la Peña during the Aguayo expedition[qv] of 1721, being described variously as "learned" and "sagacious." Her name was given to the Angelina River as early as 1768, in Gaspar José de Solís's[qv] diary. Espinosa, Peña, and, much later, Juan Agustín Morfi[qv] (1774–75) state that she had learned Spanish in the missions along the Rio Grande, perhaps at San Juan Bautista.[qv]

Ethnographers indicate a high degree of mobility among Indians generally in Texas. Angelina might have accompanied her family to Coahuila, been traded from the area as a slave, and returned; or she may come from elsewhere, and her appearance in East Texas might be due to chance. Espinosa says of her that "she had been reared in Coahuila, since her parents had been there a long time when the Spaniards left Texas in 1693." She has been the object of much romanticizing, including a painting by Texas artist Ancel Nunn.

bibliography: Eleanor Claire Buckley, "The Aguayo Expedition in Texas and Louisiana, 1719–1722," *Quarterly of the Texas State Historical Association* 15 (July 1911). Fray Francisco Céliz, *Diary of the Alarcón*

Expedition into Texas, 1718–1719, trans. F. L. Hoffman (Los Angeles: Quivira Society, 1935; rpt., New York: Arno Press, 1967). Henri Folmer, "De Bellisle on the Texas Coast," *Southwestern Historical Quarterly* 44 (October 1940). Juan Agustín Morfi, *History of Texas, 1673–1779* (2 vols., Albuquerque: Quivira Society, 1935; rpt., New York: Arno, 1967). Gabriel Tous, trans., *Ramón Expedition: Espinosa's Diary of 1716*, Preliminary Studies of the Texas Catholic Historical Society 1.4 (April 1930). *Diane Lu Hughes*

ANGELINA, TEXAS. Angelina was located on the Houston, East and West Texas Railway eight miles north of Lufkin in northern Angelina County. The area was settled prior to the Civil War.[qv] A post office opened there in 1855 under the name Angelina and operated with several interruptions until 1893, when the name was changed to Durst. In 1896 the settlement had several sawmills, a church, and a population of 150. In 1898 the name of the post office was changed back to Angelina, and in 1902 service was suspended. After logging in the region ended around 1900 most of the residents moved away. As late as the 1930s a sawmill and church were still in the vicinity, but by the early 1990s only a few scattered houses remained.

BIBLIOGRAPHY: Angelina County Historical Survey Committee, *Land of the Little Angel: A History of Angelina County, Texas*, ed. Bob Bowman (Lufkin, Texas: Lufkin Printing, 1976). *Christopher Long*

ANGELINA COLLEGE. Angelina College, a two-year institution in south Lufkin, Angelina County, opened in the fall of 1968. It is a vocational and academic college under both state and local jurisdiction that began as a project of the Angelina County Chamber of Commerce. In the early 1960s the chamber appointed a steering committee whose purpose was to gain support from area individuals, business, and industry for the construction of a two-year public community college. The efforts of this committee resulted in the Angelina County Junior College District, the sale of bonds for building purposes, a maintenance tax, and a seven-member board of trustees. In its first semester the college enrolled 660 students in both credit and noncredit programs.

Fifty-five percent of Angelina College students come from the school's tax district. The remainder list permanent residences in many Texas counties and many states. As the student population has increased, the percentage of students living within the college tax district has declined; the demand for Angelina College's educational programs has expanded beyond the boundaries of the district. Jack W. Hudgins, original president of the college, was still president in 1990. On October 26, 1969, the gymnasium was dedicated. At that time, the president of the board of trustees was Oscar Brookshire, a prominent East Texas grocer (*see* BROOKSHIRE GROCERY COMPANY).

Angelina College operates six satellite campuses in nearby communities: Crockett, Groveton, Jasper, Livingston, San Augustine, and Woodville. The college offers thirty-four degree programs through its four academic instructional divisions and twenty technical, vocational, and occupational training programs through the two occupational divisions. Students pursue associate degrees in arts, science, and applied science, as well as one-year certificates in a number of technical programs.

Angelina College is located on a 140-acre wooded campus. By the mid-1980s it had up-to-date computer labs, a computer-aided design laboratory, and a learning resource center with more than 40,000 bound volumes and subscriptions to 300 periodicals and twenty-five newspapers. The college is a member of the National Junior College Athletic Association and competes in both basketball and baseball. It is approved by the Texas Higher Education Coordinating Board[qv] and accredited by the Southern Association of Colleges and Schools. It is also a member of the Association of Texas Colleges and Universities[qv] and the American Association of Community and Junior Colleges. In the fall of 1990 Angelina College had a student enrollment of 3,145. *Megan Biesele*

ANGELINA COUNTY. Angelina County (G-22) is on U.S. Highways 59 and 68 northeast of Houston in the East Texas Timberlands region of northeast Texas. Lufkin, the county seat and largest town, is ninety-six miles northwest of Beaumont and 120 miles northeast of Houston, at 31°20′ north latitude and 94°43′ west longitude. The county is bounded on the north by the Angelina River and on the south by the Neches River. It comprises 807 square miles of gently rolling terrain and is densely forested with pine and a great variety of hardwoods. Altitudes range from 200 to 380 feet above sea level. The Angelina River drains the northern and eastern parts of the county, and the Neches drains the southern and western parts. The largest body of water in the county is Sam Rayburn Reservoir,[qv] on the Angelina River; the lake, which extends into Jasper, Sabine, Nacogdoches, and San Augustine counties, covers 114,500 acres and affords county residents good boating, fishing, and swimming, as well as water storage for municipal, agricultural, and industrial needs and for flood control and electric power. Most of the county is surfaced by sand and mud containing lignite and bentonite. This soil underlies rangeland and cropland and is exploited for mineral production. The northernmost edge of the county (generally, the area north of Lufkin) is covered by thin to moderately thick clayey sands over steep slopes and rolling hills. In the piney woods area, longleaf, shortleaf, loblolly, and slash pines provide excellent timber. Hardwoods in Angelina County include several types of gum, magnolia, elm, hickory, and oak. Between 21 and 30 percent of the land is considered good for farming. Mineral resources include natural gas and oil. Temperatures range from an average high of 94° F in June to an average low of 39° in January. Rainfall averages 42.99 inches per year. The growing season extends for 244 days.

The area that is now Angelina County was originally occupied by agricultural Indians of Caddoan and Atakapan-related stock. The county was named for a Hainai Indian girl who, according to Spanish legend, helped early Spanish missionaries of the area around 1690. Settlers who came to the county in the early nineteenth century found Indians of the Hasinai branch of the Caddo confederacies. The Hasinai, to which the Indian girl's group belonged, had an abundant food supply, a relatively dense population, and a complex social organization.

The settlement by whites in the future Angelina County began before the Texas Revolution[qv] of 1836. The first deed on record, dated May 10, 1801, conveyed 5½ leagues of land to Vincente Micheli from Surdo, chief of the Bedias Indians, in exchange for a white shirt, eight brass bracelets, a handful of vermilion, a fathom of ribbon, a gun, and fifty charges of powder and ball. The first Anglo settlers in the district were the Burris family, who in 1820 settled in the northern part of what is now Lufkin at a place then called Burris Prairie. Within a few years other families came from Alto and Nacogdoches, and from other states, to settle along the rivers. Mexican authorities made land grants in the area in 1834–35.

Settlement was still thin when Texas won its independence. Angelina County was organized on April 22, 1846, when Nacogdoches County was divided. The first permanent settler after the county was formed is thought to have been George W. Collins. The population increased quickly thereafter due to the good farming land and to the rivers, which made steamboat transportation possible. The population reached 1,165, 196 of whom were slaves, in 1850. The first county seat was Marion; successively, Jonesville became county seat in 1854, Homer in 1858, and Lufkin in 1892. Lufkin was favored by the route of the Houston, East and West Texas Railway (now the Southern Pacific), which had been built in 1882 from Houston to Shreveport.

Angelina County was settled predominantly by natives of the southern United States, some of them slaveowners who established plantations in their new Texas home. Large plantations were owned by the Stearns, Oates, Kalty, Stovall, and Ewing families. However, many Angelina County farmers were relatively poor men who owned no slaves. In 1847 slaves numbered 154, out of a total population of 834. In 1859 the number of slaves had grown to 427, valued at $269,550, and the total population was 4,271. Cotton culture,[qv] however, occupied only 2,048 acres of county land in 1858, a relatively small area for East Texas. Between 1850 and 1860 improved land in the county increased from about 3,000 to about 16,000 acres.

In 1861 Angelina County was the only county in East Texas, and one of only a handful of other Texas counties, to reject secession.[qv] This election result was startling when compared with that of Angelina County's neighbor to the immediate south, Tyler County, which supported secession by a 99 percent vote. Angelina County had also given the Constitutional Union party[qv] candidate, John Bell, a strong minority vote in the 1860 election. Two companies of county men were organized to fight in the Civil War,[qv] but they saw only limited action; only nineteen Angelina County men lost their lives in the war, and no Union soldiers entered the county before 1866.

Before the war, a principal source of wealth in Angelina County was the raising of livestock, since most of the early settlers were not slaveholding planters able to concentrate on agriculture. After the war, livestock was largely supplanted by the lumber industry,[qv] and therefore the numbers of cattle did not increase proportionately with the population. Residents declined by 1870 to 3,985, but in 1880 they numbered 5,239. In 1890 the population was 6,306; in 1900, 13,481; and in 1910, 17,705, 2,435 of whom were black.

Economically Angelina County improved greatly in the 1880s because of the arrival of the railroads. Exploitation of the county's pine and hardwood timber became possible, and lumber began quickly to return a bonanza. The construction in 1882 of the Houston, East and West Texas Railway was followed in a few years by the Kansas and Gulf Short Line, which later became the Cotton Belt. Other railroads of the county included the St. Louis and Southwestern, the Texas Southeastern, the Shreveport, Houston and Gulf, the Groveton, Lufkin and Northern, and the Texas and New Orleans, as well as many small tram lines for lumbering. Lufkin is the hub at which most of these rail lines met.

In 1880 county farmers cultivated only about 25,000 acres; landowners were waiting for the railroads so that they could develop their timber. The county had 10,000 cattle and twice as many hogs at this time. It was estimated that the county had 1.3 billion board feet of longleaf and a billion board feet of loblolly pine. After the railroads arrived, the foundation was laid for a way of life and an economy in Angelina County built upon timber and forest products. By 1900 there were at least seventeen sawmills operating in the county, and the population, which had increased only from 4,271 to 5,239 in the period 1860–80, more than doubled in the period 1880–1900, when it reached 13,481. It doubled again by 1930, when it was 27,803.

The World's Fair of 1893 gave a boost to the popularity of southern pine as a building material, and thus to the new economic base of Angelina County. The Angelina County Lumber Company, founded by Joseph H. Kurth, Sr.,[qv] and others in 1887 at Keltys, along with the Southern Pine Lumber Company, founded at Diboll in 1893 by T. L. L. Temple,[qv] became giant industries as southern pine became the chief commercial wood used in America. In addition to the two large mills, about fifteen other lumber companies were begun around the turn of the century in Angelina County. From a modest beginning in 1855, when Dr. W. W. Manning operated the first Angelina County sawmill and employed twelve men, to today, when the annual payroll of a single sawmill may be in the millions of dollars, Angelina County has built steadily on its timber resources. Property increased in value from $401,000 in 1870 to $732,282 in 1881, to $4,372,655 in 1903, and to $10,078,407 in 1913. The county also profited greatly from the development of a method for turning southern pine wood into paper. The Southland Paper Mill, established in 1939 near Lufkin, was the pioneer in the manufacture of newsprint from southern pine.

Lumber and other industries such as foundry and the manufacture of oilfield equipment made Lufkin the fifth largest industrial area in Texas by the mid-1980s. Such smaller towns in the county as Diboll, Huntington, Fuller Springs, Hudson, Zavalla, and Burke were maintained chiefly by the lumber industry. Still other towns, now defunct or severely depopulated, flourished around early sawmills until the timber was cut out: these included Homer, Baker, Clawson, Emporia, Hamlet, Lay, Popher, Yuno, Baber, Davisville, Renova, and Retrieve. Despite the many ghost towns, lumbering continued to form the economic backbone of Angelina County through the early part of the present century. However, after the lumber industry's 1913 peak in the area, Angelina County's potential as an agricultural center was much discussed. Of 601,600 total acres in the county, 158,646 was in cultivation in 1916, when the county had 1,569 farms, as compared with 1,403 in 1900. In 1916 the agricultural census counted 18,877 cattle, 3,300 horses and mules, 32,266 hogs, 4,500 sheep and goats, and 50,000 chickens and turkeys. As timber production began to fall off due to wasteful harvesting practices, conservation and sustained maintenance of forest resources led to more stable town and population growth as well. By 1950, lumber-related industries were still the major employer for the county, providing work for many.

The Great Depression[qv] hit Angelina County quite hard. By 1933 more than 2,500 residents were on relief rolls—about 10 percent of the county population. This was mainly because the timber industry in Texas was particularly vulnerable to the depression. The boom in housing and other businesses that depended on lumber ceased abruptly with the failure of banks and lending institutions and with unemployment. Many Angelina County lumber companies were forced to close or to decrease their activities sharply. County inhabitants turned back to small farming and stock raising to feed themselves; the 1935 census numbered more than 18,000 cattle and 17,000 hogs. The Civilian Conservation Corps[qv] for East Texas was headquartered in Lufkin during the depression. It served twenty-six counties and seventeen camps in efforts to bring about financial recovery.

Angelina County had a respectable total of both state highways (103.22 miles) and county roads (871.56 miles) by 1937, towards the end of the depression. It also had more farms (2,802) and more cattle (18,659) than five of the eight counties that bound it. By 1944, Angelina County had forty-four firms employing 400 persons, and the value of manufactured goods in 1945 was $25 million. Principal industries at that time were foundries, a creosoting plant, sawmills, and a $10 million newsprint mill, Southland Paper Mills. In 1954 and 1958 wholesale trade in Angelina County amounted to $37,114,000; the county topped a list of ten East Texas counties. Angelina County was also at or near the top of these ten counties in the 1950s and 1960s for retail trade, retail trade increases, service industries receipts, bank deposits, poll taxes, auto registrations (16,518), and chamber of commerce budgets.

The population of Angelina County was 36,032 in 1950, 39,814 in 1960, and 67,600 in 1986. Between 1970 and 1980 the rural population increased by 34 percent, while urban areas had a slightly lower growth rate. The largest ethnic group in the county is English (24 percent), with Irish (20 percent) and African Americans[qqv] (15 percent) next. In 1984 the county had 36,081 persons aged twenty-five and over; 22 percent had only an elementary education, 29 percent high school, and 8 percent college. In 1979 about 10 percent of Angelina County residents[qv] income was below the poverty level. The county is a major producer of timber products. It ranked only twenty-first in the state for agricultural receipts in 1982, 82 percent of which were from livestock. County farmers also raise hay, rye, potatoes, sweet potatoes, tomatoes, watermelons, peaches, and pecans.

Between 1970 and 1980 the number of housing units increased by 42 percent. Current production of minerals includes bentonite, clay, fire clay, and drilling mud. In 1982 tourism generated 939 jobs and $7,529,000 in payrolls. Angelina County has generally been staunchly Democratic, although Republican presidential candidates won a majority of votes in the 1972, 1984, and 1988 elections, and Democrat Bill Clinton managed to win only by a narrow margin in the 1992 election. Republican senatorial candidates also fared well during this time. Nevertheless, as in most Texas counties, Democratic officials continued to maintain control of most county offices.

Alcoholic beverages are not sold legally in Angelina County. The county's 117 churches have about 38,000 members. The county supports one daily newspaper, the Lufkin *Daily News*, and two weeklies, the Diboll *Free Press* and the Zavalla *Herald*. Recreational institutions include the Texas Forestry Museum, the Lufkin Historical and Creative Arts Center, and the Ellen Trout Zoo, all at Lufkin. The population of Angelina County in 1990 was 69,884.

BIBLIOGRAPHY: Effie Mattox Boon, The History of Angelina County (M.A. thesis, University of Texas, 1937). *Megan Biesele*

ANGELINA COUNTY LUMBER COMPANY. The Angelina County Lumber Company was founded in 1890 by Joseph H. Kurth, Sr.,[qv] Simon W. Henderson, Sr., and Sam Wiener. In 1888 Kurth, a German immigrant, purchased a sawmill on the outskirts of Lufkin from Charles L. Kelty. Needing additional capital to expand the operation, he formed a partnership with Corrigan merchant Simon W. Henderson, and in 1890 the two organized a corporation with Wiener under the name Angelina County Lumber Company. Kurth served as president. Eli Wiener, Sam's brother, later became a partner. The company had grown into a million-dollar corporation with several thousand acres of timberland by 1912. It was centered at Keltys. In addition to a large sawmill and mill pond, the factory complex included a company-run commissary, a community doctor and dentist, a power plant, employee housing, recreational facilities, and garden plots. To transport the timber to the mill the company built a tram railroad. In 1900 Kurth and his partners chartered the railroad as a common carrier under the name Angelina and Neches River Railroad and extended the line to Chireno in Nacogdoches County.

During the early 1900s the company had some 1,200 employees, including some of the first occupational foresters in East Texas. In 1916 Kurth, Henderson, and the Wieners organized a new corporation, the San Augustine Lumber Company, and purchased the mill. The original Angelina County Lumber Company was dissolved in 1923, and the San Augustine Lumber Company charter was changed to assume the name of the former. The company continued to operate until 1966, when the plant and remaining timber reserves were sold to Owens-Illinois, Incorporated. Owens-Illinois closed the sawmill and replaced it with a plywood plant constructed jointly by Angelina and Southland Paper Mills, Incorporated.

BIBLIOGRAPHY: Angelina County Historical Survey Committee, *Land of the Little Angel: A History of Angelina County, Texas*, ed. Bob Bowman (Lufkin, Texas: Lufkin Printing, 1976). Angelina County Lumber Company Papers, Forest History Collections, Stephen F. Austin State University Library. Robert S. Maxwell and Robert D. Baker, *Sawdust Empire: The Texas Lumber Industry, 1830–1940* (College Station: Texas A&M University Press, 1983). *Christopher Long*

ANGELINA NATIONAL FOREST. Angelina National Forest surrounds Sam Rayburn Reservoir off U.S. Highway 69 east of Lufkin. The preserve, which is administered by the United States Department of Agriculture Forest Service, with local headquarters in Lufkin, has a total of 153,176 acres, with 58,535 acres in Angelina County, 21,011 acres in Jasper County, 9,238 acres in Nacogdoches County, and 64,392 acres in San Augustine County. The national forests in Texas were established by an act of the Texas legislature in 1933, authorizing the purchase of lands for the National Forest system. President Franklin D. Roosevelt proclaimed these purchases on October 15, 1936. Angelina National Forest has five parks with campgrounds: Bouton Lake, Boykin Springs, Caney Creek, Harvey Creek, and Sandy Creek. The area consists of pine and hardwood woodlands growing on flat to gently rolling terrain. Facilities include boat ramps, hiking trails, and camping and picnicking areas.

BIBLIOGRAPHY: George Oxford Miller, *Texas Parks and Campgrounds: Central, South, and West Texas* (Austin: Texas Monthly Press, 1984). *Christopher Long*

ANGELINA AND NECHES RIVER AUTHORITY. The Angelina and Neches River Authority was originally established in 1949 as the Neches River Conservation District. Before that time it had been part of the Sabine-Neches River Conservation District, established by the Texas legislature in 1935. The Neches River Conservation District was inactive until 1971, when Governor Preston Smith appointed nine members to the board of directors. In 1977 the district's name was changed to Angelina and Neches River Authority. It held jurisdiction over parts of sixteen East Texas counties and included the upper Neches River basin.

Throughout the 1970s the agency implemented various plans and projects to promote water-resource development, water-quality management, and water conservation. It managed water-quality studies of the upper Neches basin, assisted wastewater treatment plants, and conducted field analysis, sample collection, and industrial-waste analysis for the cities of Jacksonville and Lufkin. Additionally, the organization also provided analyses for the forest service and petroleum service industries, cities, water-supply corporations, and private citizens to test for drinking water contamination. The Texas legislature authorized the Angelina and Neches River Authority Industrial Development Corporation in the late 1970s. It is a nonprofit corporation established to furnish certain kinds of bond financing for private industry.

In the 1980s the Texas Department of Water Resources contracted the ANRA to conduct studies on various aspects of sewage treatment. These included the evaluation of the operation and maintenance of seven municipal sewage-treatment plants in East Texas in 1982 and a study of sludge-disposal methods for all municipal sewage-treatment plants in the upper Neches basin in 1985. Also in 1985 the Texas Water Commission approved the construction of Lake Eastex, a proposed reservoir in Cherokee County.

In 1990 the authority conducted the Nacogdoches County Water Study to determine the need for an increased water supply over the next fifty years. It concluded that water consumption should move toward greater use of surface water such as Lake Nacogdoches for the city of Nacogdoches and Lake Naconiche, a proposed United States Soil Service lake, for a number of county water-supply entities. During the early 1990s the Angelina and Neches River Authority continued to proceed with the necessary permits and acquisitions for Lake Eastex. It conducted analyses for treatment plants, monitored wastewater discharge into the Angelina River, and examined water quality of twelve stream locations for the United States Forest Service. It regulated a septic-tank licensing program around the Sam Rayburn Reservoir.[qv] The agency operated nine wastewater plants and one water-treatment plant and performed wastewater analyses and coliform testing of drinking water for cities, school districts, water corporations, industrial groups, and other clients. In 1992 it submitted its first report on the water quality of the upper Neches basin in accord with the rules of the 1991 Clean Rivers Act. The Angelina and Neches River Authority does not have any taxing authority. It receives income through customer payments for agency services. Agency headquarters are located in Lufkin. *Laurie E. Jasinski*

ANGELINA AND NECHES RIVER RAILROAD. The Angelina and Neches River Railroad Company was chartered on August 23, 1900, to connect Keltys in Angelina County with Manton, twelve miles to the east. The railroad had a capital stock of $75,000. The principal place of business was Keltys. The members of the first board of directors were Joseph H. Kurth,[qv] S. W. Henderson, Eli Wiener, and E. T. Clark, all of Keltys; E. J. Mantooth and W. M. Glenn, both of Lufkin; and Sam Wiener, Jr., of Shreveport, Louisiana.

The line originated as a narrow-gauge tram road constructed by the Angelina County Lumber Company[qv] in 1895. The Angelina and Neches River acquired ten miles of track running eastward from Keltys in August 1900, and in August 1906 purchased an additional ten miles to Alco from the lumber company. At this time the railroad was converted to standard gauge. Additional track was acquired from Angelina County Lumber Company: Alco to Naclina in June 1910 and Naclina to Chireno in June 1912. The Angelina and Neches was one of the roads involved in the Tap Line Case before the Interstate Commerce Commission in 1910. The Railroad Commission[qv] did not recognize this line as a common carrier until 1911. In 1916 the A&NR owned one locomotive and five cars and reported passenger earnings of $6,000 and freight earnings of $40,000. In 1944 Southland Paper Mills was established on the railroad. In 1963 the line removed twenty-one miles of track between Dunagan and Chireno. It reported a total net income of $290,000 in 1972, when it owned two locomotives and eleven cars; it rented some of its rolling stock. The Angelina and Neches River acquired terminal tracks at Lufkin from the St. Louis Southwestern in the 1980s, when that company abandoned its line from Jacksonville to Lufkin, and about a mile of track from the Southern Pacific from Dunagan to Buck Creek.

Nancy Beck Young

ANGELINA RIVER. The Angelina River is formed by the junction of Barnhardt and Shawnee creeks three miles northwest of Laneville in southwest central Rusk County (at 32°01′ N, 94°50′ W). The river flows southeast for 110 miles, forming the boundaries between Cherokee and Nacogdoches, Angelina and Nacogdoches, and Angelina and San Augustine counties. It empties into the Neches River twelve miles north of Jasper in northwestern Jasper County (at 31°54′ N, 94°12′ W). Sam Rayburn Reservoir[qv] is on the southern part of the stream. The river traverses flat to rolling terrain surfaced by sandy and clay loams that support water-tolerant hardwoods, conifers, and grasses.

The stream was named for a Hasinai Indian girl whom Spanish missionaries called Angelina.[qv] It was well known to Spanish and French explorers and to missionaries in East Texas. Spanish land grants along the stream date back to the later eighteenth century, and there was considerable settlement in the area during the Mexican period. The river was navigable from Ayish Bayou nearly to Nacogdoches in the 1840s and furnished a significant means of transportation to settlers. The earliest attempts at commercial navigation of the Angelina began in 1844 when Moses and Robert Patton, using a barge-like craft known as the *Thomas J. Rusk,* transported 192 bales of cotton from Pattonia Landing (located on the Angelina twelve miles southeast of Nacogdoches) by way of the Neches to Sabine Pass. The Patton brothers continued to operate their barge service for three years, hauling cotton and other produce downriver and returning with provisions and merchandise from Galveston and New Orleans. In 1847 they purchased a steamship, the *Angelina,* capable of hauling 350 to 400 bales of cotton and making the round trip to Sabine Pass in fifteen to twenty days. Several other steamboats plied the Angelina during the heyday of river traffic around the time of the Civil War.[qv] The largest of these was the 115-foot *Laura,*[qv] built in Evansville, Indiana, powered by a forty-horsepower engine; the *Laura* was capable of carrying 525 bales of cotton or 1,700 barrels of other goods. River traffic on the Angelina began to die in the 1880s with the arrival of the railroads. By 1900 the stream was no longer navigable. Farming and clear-cutting by the growing lumber industry[qv] in the river's watershed caused the river to silt up, and numerous sandbars formed along its course.

Bibliography: Angelina County Historical Survey Committee, *Land of the Little Angel: A History of Angelina County, Texas,* ed. Bob Bowman (Lufkin, Texas: Lufkin Printing, 1976). *Carolyn Hyman*

ANGELITA, TEXAS. Angelita was located on the St. Louis, Brownsville and Mexico Railway two miles south of Odem in central San Patricio County. The community originated as a shipment point for local ranchers and farmers, and John J. Welder's[qv] ranch built cattle-shipping pens there shortly after the coming of the railroad in 1904. A packing shed was soon constructed to accommodate large shipments of watermelons from nearby farms to eastern and northern markets. W. M. Spessard laid out the townsite, and a depot was built on the site of the old Nelson home. A one-room school also served as a community center and church. On April 30, 1907, Kotiet Miller was appointed the first postmaster; he was shortly succeeded by Spessard, who operated the office in his general store. Norman Smith operated the community's other store, and a cotton gin processed the crops of local farmers. Angelita's population never exceeded fifty, and as the nearby city of Odem grew, Angelita faded. The post office was discontinued and moved to Odem in June 1916. The school was in existence until 1914. The Spessards moved to Taft, Smith moved his store to Odem, the gin was moved, and the community ceased to exist.

Bibliography: Keith Guthrie, *History of San Patricio County* (Austin: Nortex, 1986). *Keith Guthrie*

ANGELO STATE UNIVERSITY. Angelo State University, in San Angelo, was founded in 1928 as San Angelo College; it offered a junior college program within the San Angelo Independent School District. Originally, the college was located downtown. In 1945 a county junior college district was established, and the first board of trustees was elected. In 1947 the first building was built on the new campus. The official name was changed to Angelo State College in 1963 by a legislative act that made the college a four-year institution. The effective date of the change was September 1, 1965. Raymond M. Cavness, president starting in 1954, remained as president during the transition, and the first baccalaureate degrees were awarded in May 1967. In September of that year Lloyd Drexell Vincent became president of the college. In May 1969 the official name was changed to Angelo State University. In 1975 Angelo State became a member of the Texas State University System and has since been governed by the system's board of regents. A graduate school was authorized in May 1970 and approved in October by the Coordinating Board, Texas College and University System (now the Texas Higher Education Coordinating Board[qv]). The graduate school was officially initiated in the fall of 1971.

Expansion of the university at the 268-acre campus has been significant. In the fall of 1967 the Porter Henderson Library was completed. The Raymond M. Cavness Science Building was completed in the spring of 1968. In September 1968 a ten-story women's dormitory was opened, and a similar residence for men was completed the following year. In the summer of 1972 a physical-education complex was opened. The Robert and Nona Carr Education–Fine Arts Building, with one of the few comprehensive modular theaters in the United States, was completed in the spring of 1976. Between 1979 and 1985, a multipurpose sports facility, two new residence halls, a computer science building, and a nursing and physical science complex opened.

The university's Management, Instruction, and Research Center is located at O. C. Fisher Lake on 4,645 acres leased from the United States Army Corps of Engineers. The center supports instructional programs in animal science and biology; management and research programs in sheep, goat, and cattle production; range management and improvement; and wildlife management and ecology. A $1.25 million supporting complex was completed in August 1975.

In 1976 the Roy E. Moon Distinguished Lectureship in Science was established by local physicians in honor of the late Dr. Moon, who practiced obstetrics and gynecology for twenty-eight years in San Angelo. The lectureship brings a nationally prominent scientist to Angelo State each year. The university offers a large scholarship program through the Robert G. Carr[qv] and Nona K. Carr Scholarship Foundation. The foundation awards full and partial scholarships in all departments. Over 900 scholarships totaling more than $1.6 million are awarded annually. In addition to the Carr academic scholarship program, a $1 million endowment fund also established by Mr. and Mrs. Carr provides Air Force ROTC scholarships totaling approximately $130,000 annually. The university awards about 750 other scholarships of varying amounts each year.

The Angelo State University curriculum provides for studies leading to baccalaureate degrees in thirty-three major fields. Teacher certification is available at all levels. Graduate programs are offered in seventeen disciplines leading to seven graduate degrees. The university's nursing programs are accredited by the National League for Nursing and offer clinical experience through internships with area hospitals and community facilities. The medical technology program has affiliations with hospitals in San Angelo, Midland, and Abilene. The university offers programs in the arts, sciences, teacher education, nursing education, and business administration, as well as courses designed to meet entrance requirements for dentistry, engineering, law, and medicine. In the fall of 1990, 6,298 students representing every region of Texas and the United States and many foreign countries were enrolled. *Sangeeta Singg*

ANGIER, SAMUEL TUBBS (1792–1867). Samuel Tubbs Angier, physician and Old Three Hundred[qv] pioneer, was born in Pembroke, Plymouth County, Massachusetts, on August 26, 1792, the son of Samuel and Mary Tubbs. On February 29, 1812, he changed his name to Samuel Tubbs Angier, taking as his surname the maiden name of his paternal grandmother, Katurah (Angier) Tubbs. He received his A.B. degree in 1818 and his M.D. degree in 1823 from Brown University, Providence, Rhode Island. Angier had married and had a daughter before his second marriage on January 18, 1821, in Easton, Massachusetts, to Rowena Hayward. They also had a daughter.

Angier was a partner of Thomas W. Bradley and George B. Hall[qqv] as one of Stephen F. Austin's[qv] Old Three Hundred colonists. The three men received title to a sitio[qv] of land on the west bank of Chocolate Bayou three leagues above its mouth on August 16, 1824; the land is now in Brazoria County. Additionally, Angier was granted a labor of land on the east bank of the Brazos four miles above its mouth on August 24, 1824. In a quiet ceremony at the home of James Briton (Brit) Bailey[qv] on April 30, 1829, he married Old Three Hundred colonist Mrs. Permelia Pickett, in a ceremony conducted by Alexander Hodge,[qv] *comisario*[qv] of the precinct of Victoria. Consequent to his marriage, Angier requested, and on December 10, 1830, received, two-thirds of a league of land "on the right margin of Chocolate Bayou within the littoral Belt, above and adjacent to the league conceded to the petitioner together with Bradley and Hall."

Angier was one of the four established physicians of Brazoria Municipality who early in the 1830s were appointed by the ayuntamiento[qv] as a standing committee to examine the qualifications of persons wishing to practice surgery and medicine in the municipality. David G. Burnet,[qv] one of the delegates from Liberty, stopped at the Chocolate Bayou home of Dr. Angier after becoming ill on his way to the Consultation.[qv] On February 1, 1836, Angier served as an election judge for Brazoria Municipality when delegates were chosen for the Constitutional Convention of 1836,[qv] to convene at Washington-on-the-Brazos.

On September 5, 1837, Permelia Angier died. In April of 1838 Angier, who gave his place of residence as Liverpool, was one of several signatories from across Texas of a memorial to the Congress of the Republic of Texas[qv] requesting the establishment of a system of public education. Angier married Mary Ann Augusta Kendall, the daughter of Horace and Mary (Cogswell) Kendall, in Monroe County, Alabama, on June 28, 1842. He was a Methodist and she a Presbyterian. Angier's return to Texas from New Orleans aboard the *Neptune* was reported in the March 20, 1844, in the Houston *Telegraph and Texas Register.*[qv] *The* Columbia *Planter*[qv] of September 12, 1845, carried an advertisement for the Columbia Female Seminary,[qv] which was to open on the twenty-ninth, with Mrs. Angier as headmistress. Samuel and Mary Angier had a son in 1846. Mary died near West Columbia in 1854, and Angier married Mrs. Mary O'Brien Millard on May 25, 1857, in the Methodist Episcopal Church, South, in Galveston. Dr. Angier died in West Columbia on April 17, 1867. He is buried in the Columbia Cemetery in West Columbia.

Angier was one of the twenty Old Three Hundred settlers known to have been Freemasons. He was a charter member of St. John's Lodge Number 49 (later to become St. John's Lodge Number 5), organized in Columbia in 1848, and was selected grand master of the lodge on June 1, 1848. He served as lodge treasurer in 1849 and 1850 and was junior steward in 1858 and junior warden in 1861.

BIBLIOGRAPHY: Lester G. Bugbee, "The Old Three Hundred: A List of Settlers in Austin's First Colony," *Quarterly of the Texas State Historical Association* 1 (October 1897). Virginia H. Taylor, *The Spanish Archives of the General Land Office of Texas* (Austin: Lone Star, 1955). *Telegraph and Texas Register,* October 4, 1837, August 11, 1838, March 20, 1844. *Ronald Howard Livingston*

ANGLETON, TEXAS. Angleton, on State highways 288, 35/227, and the Union Pacific Railroad, was founded in 1890 by Lewis R. Bryan, Sr., and Faustino Kiber[qqv] near the center of Brazoria County and named for the wife of the general manager of the Velasco Terminal Railway. The founders deeded one-half interest in the original townsite to that railroad in 1892 for $1,000, with the stipulation that the rail line be routed through the town and a depot be built on Front Street, between Mulberry and Myrtle streets. An Angleton post office was established in 1892.

In 1896 Angleton was chosen the new county seat of Brazoria County. The move followed a political battle so bitter that county records were said to have been moved to Angleton at night by citizens who feared they would be destroyed. The controversy resurfaced in 1913, when another election was called to make Brazoria the county seat again. The proposal failed, 1,348 to 1,058. The courthouse built in Angleton in 1897 has been restored for use as a museum. A five-story courthouse was completed in 1940 and a five-story annex added in 1976. In 1989 several smaller buildings were also being used to house county offices.

The Angleton schools began operation in 1897 as a county district, and in 1899 citizens voted to incorporate as a school district only. A two-story brick school was built but was destroyed in the Galveston hurricane of 1900.[qv] A second two-story brick school went down in the hurricane of 1909 and was rebuilt. The third school, which stood for many years, was named in honor of one of the county's most famous former residents, Albert Sidney Johnston.[qv] A college, the University of South Texas, operated briefly at Angleton, but closed after its buildings were demolished in the 1900 storm. In 1989 Angleton Independent School District employed a staff of 359 and enrolled 6,000 students.

On November 12, 1912, Angleton residents voted to incorporate as a city and elected the first city officials, headed by F. M. Harvin as mayor. Soon afterward electrical service was made available. Angleton's founders donated block 25 of their town to the Methodists, and soon afterward the first church in the new town was built. It was used by all denominations until others built their own. Early social life of the community included amateur theatricals, ice cream suppers to help raise money for the churches, and a "reading and rest room" provided by women of the community to give area farmers' wives and children a place to wait while the men transacted business in town. A volunteer fire department was organized and was still in operation in 1989. A community baseball team was so popular that special trains took citizens to out-of-town games. Several clubs were organized, one of which, the Angleton Embroidery Club, was begun in 1923 and was still active in 1989. W. F. Reed, editor of the local newspaper, organized a community band in 1907 and taught the twenty or so members to play their instruments. Attired in snappy white uniforms, the band marched in parades throughout the Houston-Galveston area and played for local citizens downtown each week. What is believed to be the last legal hanging in Texas occurred in Angleton on August 31, 1923. The largest county fair in the state, the Brazoria County Fair, is headquartered on a 120-acre, county-owned site just south of the city. During World War II[qv] the fairgrounds were turned over to the federal government for use first as a prisoner of war camp and later as a base for a United States Signal Corps radar unit.

Angleton was originally a trade center for agriculture, devoted primarily to cotton, corn, truck farming, and cattle, and later to rice and soybeans. It still derives considerable income from agriculture but has followed the general industrial trend of Brazoria County, which began in 1940 with the location of Dow Chemical Company at Freeport and continued with the introduction of a number of other petrochemical manufacturing companies. In 1989 Angleton was a banking and distribution center for a large oil, chemical, and agricultural area. The 1980 federal census showed a population of 13,929; it was 80 percent white, 8.6 percent black, 13.6 percent Hispanic, and 6.1 percent other. The population in 1990 was 17,140.

Angleton is served by one local newspaper, the Angleton *Times*, which was established in Velasco in 1892 and about 1894 moved to Angleton, where it grew from a weekly to a five-day daily. The Brazoria County Historical Commission and Brazoria County Historical Museum conduct historical-preservation programs. Restoration of the 1897 courthouse, which is leased to the museum association, was recognized by a state marker dedicated in 1983. In 1989 the city had five parks, in one of which was a swimming pool. A flagpole and marker were placed on the courthouse grounds to commemorate the Texas Sesquicentennial.

BIBLIOGRAPHY: Brazoria County Federation of Women's Clubs, *History of Brazoria County* (1940). James A. Creighton, *A Narrative History of Brazoria County* (Angleton, Texas: Brazoria County Historical Commission, 1975). Vertical Files, Barker Texas History Center, University of Texas at Austin. *Marie Beth Jones*

ANGLO-AMERICAN COLONIZATION. Anglo-American colonization in Mexican Texas[qv] took place between 1821 and 1835. Spain had first opened Texas to Anglo-Americans in 1820, less than one year before Mexico achieved its independence. Its traditional policy forbade foreigners in its territory, but Spain was unable to persuade its own citizens to move to remote and sparsely populated Texas. There were only three settlements in the province of Texas in 1820: Nacogdoches, San Antonio de Béxar, and La Bahía del Espíritu Santo (later Goliad), small towns with outlying ranches. The missions near the latter two, once expected to be nucleus communities, had been or were being secularized (i.e., transferred to diocesan from Franciscan administration), while those near Nacogdoches had been closed since the 1770s. Recruiting foreigners to develop the Spanish frontier was not new. As early as the 1790s, Spain invited Anglo-Americans to settle in Upper Louisiana (Missouri) for the same reason. The foreigners were to be Catholic, industrious, and willing to become Spanish citizens in return for generous land grants. Spain expected the new settlers to increase economic development and help deter the aggressive and mobile Plains Indians such as the Comanches and Kiowas. Mexico continued the Spanish colonization plan after its independence in 1821 by granting contracts to empresarios who would settle and supervise selected, qualified immigrants.

Anglo-Americans were attracted to Hispanic Texas because of inexpensive land. Undeveloped land in the United States land offices cost $1.25 an acre for a minimum of 80 acres ($100) payable in specie at the time of purchase. In Texas each head of a family, male or female, could claim a headright of 4,605 acres (one league—4,428 acres of grazing land and one labor[qv]—177 acres of irrigable farm land) at a cost about four cents an acre ($184) payable in six years, a sum later reduced by state authorities.

Beginning in 1824 when the Mexican Republic adopted its constitution, each immigrant took an oath of loyalty to the new nation and professed to be a Christian. Because the Catholic Church[qv] was the established religion, the oath implied that all would become Catholic, although the national and state colonization laws were silent on the matter. Religion was not a critical issue, however, because the church waited until 1831 to send a resident priest, Michael Muldoon,[qv] into the Anglo-Texan communities. This was inconvenient for those wishing to marry because there was no provision for civil ceremonies, and only priests had authority to perform nuptial rites. Anglo-Texans unwilling or unable to seek a priest in Catholic communities received permission from the authorities to sign a marriage bond, a practice common in the non-Anglican foothills of Virginia and the Carolinas before 1776, promising to formalize their union when a priest arrived.

Two other reasons brought Anglo-American settlers to Texas. Through the 1820s, most believed that the United States would buy eastern Texas from Mexico. Many thought that that portion of Texas had been part of the Louisiana Purchase and that the United States had "given" it away to Spain in exchange for Florida in the 1819 Adams-Onís Treaty,[qv] which established the Sabine River boundary. The Texas pioneers expected annexation would stimulate immigration and provide buyers for their land. A second attraction was that Mexico and the United States had no reciprocal agreements enabling creditors to collect debts or to return fugitives. Therefore, Texas was a safe haven for the many Mississippi valley farmers who defaulted on their loans when agricultural prices declined at the end of the War of 1812 and bankers demanded immediate payment. Faced with seizure of their property and even debtors' prison in many states, men loaded their families and belongings into wagons and headed for the Sabine River, where creditors could not follow and there was opportunity to start over.

Against this background, Moses Austin[qv] traveled from Missouri to Spanish San Antonio in 1820 to apply for an empresario[qv] grant to bring Anglo-American families to Texas. Like so many others, he had suffered losses in banking failures and hoped to restore his family's fortunes by charging small fees—12½ cents an acre—for land within his assigned area. He had become a Spanish citizen in 1798, when he moved from Virginia to the St. Louis area where he acquired an empresario grant to develop a lead mine and import workers. The Spanish governor at San Antonio gave tentative approval to Austin's plan, subject to review by his superiors, to bring 300 moral, hardworking, Catholic families from the former Spanish territory of Louisiana. Although the authorities wanted him to settle close to San Antonio, Austin opted for a still-to-be-defined area along the lower Colorado River, where he hoped to establish a port. On his return to Missouri he became ill and died at home in June 1821, leaving the plan with his eldest son, Stephen Fuller Austin.[qv]

Austin's advertisements for colonists coincided with Mexican independence and the presumption that a republic would be organized. Stimulated by these events, some families began moving immediately to the Red River near future Texarkana and across the Sabine along the old Spanish road leading to Nacogdoches. There they remained as squatters, some with intentions of joining the Austin colony, but others engaged in trading with the Indians and Mexicans.

The younger Austin visited San Antonio in mid-1821 as his father's heir and received permission to explore the lower Colorado for a site for the colony. His roaming convinced him that the Brazos watershed should be added to his grant. Upon returning to Texas in early 1822, Austin discovered he must go to Mexico City to confirm the contract with the national government, even though his first settlers were on their way with only vague instructions about where to settle. Soon after he reached the capital, a coup established an empire, and the resulting turmoil delayed Austin for a year. In April 1823 he finally received a contract under the Imperial Colonization Law, which had been passed in January. Because the empire collapsed in April and the republic was reestablished, Austin's empresario contract was the only one issued under this law. The reinstated republican Congress immediately approved the imperial contract, and Austin rushed back to Texas to organize his colony.

The Imperial Colonization Law specified that colonists must be Catholic, so Austin's first 300 families were affected. The 1824 National Colonization Law and the 1825 Coahuila and Texas[qv] State Colonization Law said only that foreigners must be Christian and abide by the laws of the nation, thereby implying they would be members of the established church. Protestant preachers occasionally visited Texas, but they seldom held public services. In 1834 the state decreed that no person should be molested for political or religious beliefs as long as he did not disturb public order. This was as close as Texans came to freedom of religion and speech before 1836.

Slavery[qv] was also an issue. Mexicans abhorred slavery as allowed in the United States, but pragmatic politicians shut their eyes to the system in their eagerness to have the Anglos produce cotton in Texas. National and state laws banned the *African* slave trade, but allowed Anglo-Americans to bring their family slaves with them to Texas and buy and sell them there until 1840. Grandchildren of those slaves would be freed gradually upon reaching certain ages. The state inferred in 1827 that it might emancipate slaves earlier, and the immigrants took the precaution of signing indenture contracts with their illiterate servants binding them for ninety-nine years to work off their purchase price, upkeep, and transportation to Texas. Mexican officials recognized the subterfuge as debt peonage, and black slaves continued to arrive in Texas. The most serious threat to Anglo slaveholders occurred when President Vicente Ramón Guerrero[qv] emancipated all slaves on September 15, 1829, in commemoration of independence. Austin's Mexican friends quickly secured an exemption from the law for Texas.

Austin, the most successful Texas empresario, made four six-year contracts between 1823 and 1828 for a potential 1,200 families. They were to be settled between the watersheds of the Brazos and Colorado rivers and as far as the Lavaca River below the Old San Antonio Road,[qv] as well as eastward to the San Jacinto River (but not including Galveston Island) and a small area around the site of present-day Austin. A fifth contract issued in 1831 for 800 families to be settled along the Brazos above the old Spanish Road was challenged by Sterling Clack Robertson,[qv] who had an expired prior claim. The ensuing conflict made accurate tallies difficult.

Empresarios did not own the land within their grants, nor could they issue titles; the state appointed a land commissioner to give deeds only after 100 families had been settled. Surveyors laid off leagues and labores along the watercourses and roads, after which colonists could choose vacant tracts. The settlers paid fees to the state, the surveyor, the land commissioner, and the clerk, who wrote the deeds on stamped paper and recorded the payments. Austin's plan to restore his family's well-being by selling land was denied because empresarios could not receive fees. The state gave them a bonus of 23,000 acres for each 100 families settled. By 1834, at the virtual end of the empresario system, Austin had settled about 966 families and earned 197,000 acres of bonus land that he could locate where he chose. He could sell the land, but only to those willing to live in Texas.

Austin, as the pioneer empresario in Texas, was burdened with more duties than later contractors. With no published compendium of the Mexican laws, administrative and judicial authority rested with Austin, and the result was a mix of Mexican decrees with pragmatic Anglo-American implementation. Local settlements within his colony elected alcaldes, similar to justices of the peace, and constables. Austin sat as superior judge until 1828, when sufficient population permitted the installation of an ayuntamiento[qv] at San Felipe, the capital of the colony. This council, with elected representatives from the settlements, had authority over the entire Austin colony and acted like a county government. As population grew, other settlements within the colony qualified for ayuntamientos. These councils settled lawsuits, regulated the health and welfare of the residents by supervising doctors, lawyers, taverns, and ferries, surveyed roads, and sold town lots. Capital cases were referred to authorities in Monterrey and later Saltillo. The remoteness of the court disturbed Anglo-Texans, who wanted accessible courts.

Austin also commanded the local militia to defend the colony against Indians and to keep the peace. His contract area had only a few small Indian villages belonging to such sedentary groups as the Bidais and Coushattas, who wanted only to trade. Less friendly were the seasonally migrant remnant coastal tribes of Karankawas or the inland Tonkawas, who foraged for game and targeted the settlers' livestock. Pioneers along the Colorado River suffered most. Austin led several punitive expeditions between 1823 and 1826; he also negotiated moderately successful treaties with these declining tribes. North and west of the Austin colony Indians continued to resist the flow of immigrants well beyond the colonial period.

Other men besides Austin wanted empresario contracts in Texas, and a few were in Mexico City in 1822. Because of the changing political scene and the slow passage of the colonization laws, they had to wait until 1825, after the passage of national and state colonization laws passed in August 1824 and March 1825. The national law prohibited foreigners from settling within twenty-six miles of the Gulf of Mexico[qv] or within fifty-two miles of the Sabine River[qv] border without special executive permission. To encourage immigration, settlers were free from national taxes for four years. Land ownership was limited to eleven leagues. Owners had to be residents of Mexico. Preference was given to native Mexicans in the selection, and the national government could use any portion of land needed for the defence and security of the nation.

The state colonization law detailed how to apply for land, how much would be given to heads of families, including females or single persons, and the fees to be paid. The law granted freedom from tithes and the *alcabala*, an internal excise tax, for ten years. Within three weeks four contracts were signed: Haden Edwards[qv] could settle 800 families in the Nacogdoches area, Robert Leftwich[qv] 800 along the Brazos valley above the Old San Antonio Road, Green DeWitt[qv] 400 on the Guadalupe River, and Frost Thorn[qv] 400 north of Nacogdoches. DeWitt, who developed the area around Gonzales, was the second most successful empresario in Texas. He settled 189 families before his contract expired in 1831. His colony suffered Indian attacks and also controversy with his neighbor, Mexican native empresario Martín De León.[qv]

De León, a native of a small town 100 miles southwest of the site of present Matamoros, moved his family north across the Nueces River and into the province of Texas in the early 1800s. He lived by catching mustangs[qv] and wild cattle and raising mules, then selling the animals in San Antonio or even trailing them to Louisiana. In April 1824, before the passage of the national colonization law, he received permission from the provincial deputation in San Antonio to establish a town for forty-one families about twenty miles northeast of La Bahía on the banks of the Guadalupe River. No boundaries were mentioned. By October, De León and twelve families had arrived at a cypress grove, the site of the town of Guadalupe Victoria (now Victoria, Texas), named for the first president of Mexico, who took office that year.

Unaware of the colonization grant to De León in San Antonio, the state assigned the same area of the Guadalupe valley with specific boundaries to DeWitt in April 1825. When DeWitt's settlers arrived, trouble was inevitable. Because the colonization laws gave preference to native Mexicans, De León petitioned the state for redress, and the authorities told DeWitt in October 1825 to respect De León's prior claims but failed to establish boundaries. The state named land commissioners for both De León's and DeWitt's colonies. The commissioners issued titles in 1831, the year DeWitt's six-year contract expired permanently. The boundaries remained unresolved. Eventually sixteen non-Hispanic families, some of whom were Anglo-Americans with Irish roots, received headrights in De León's otherwise Hispanic community.

De León also quarreled with neighboring empresarios James Power

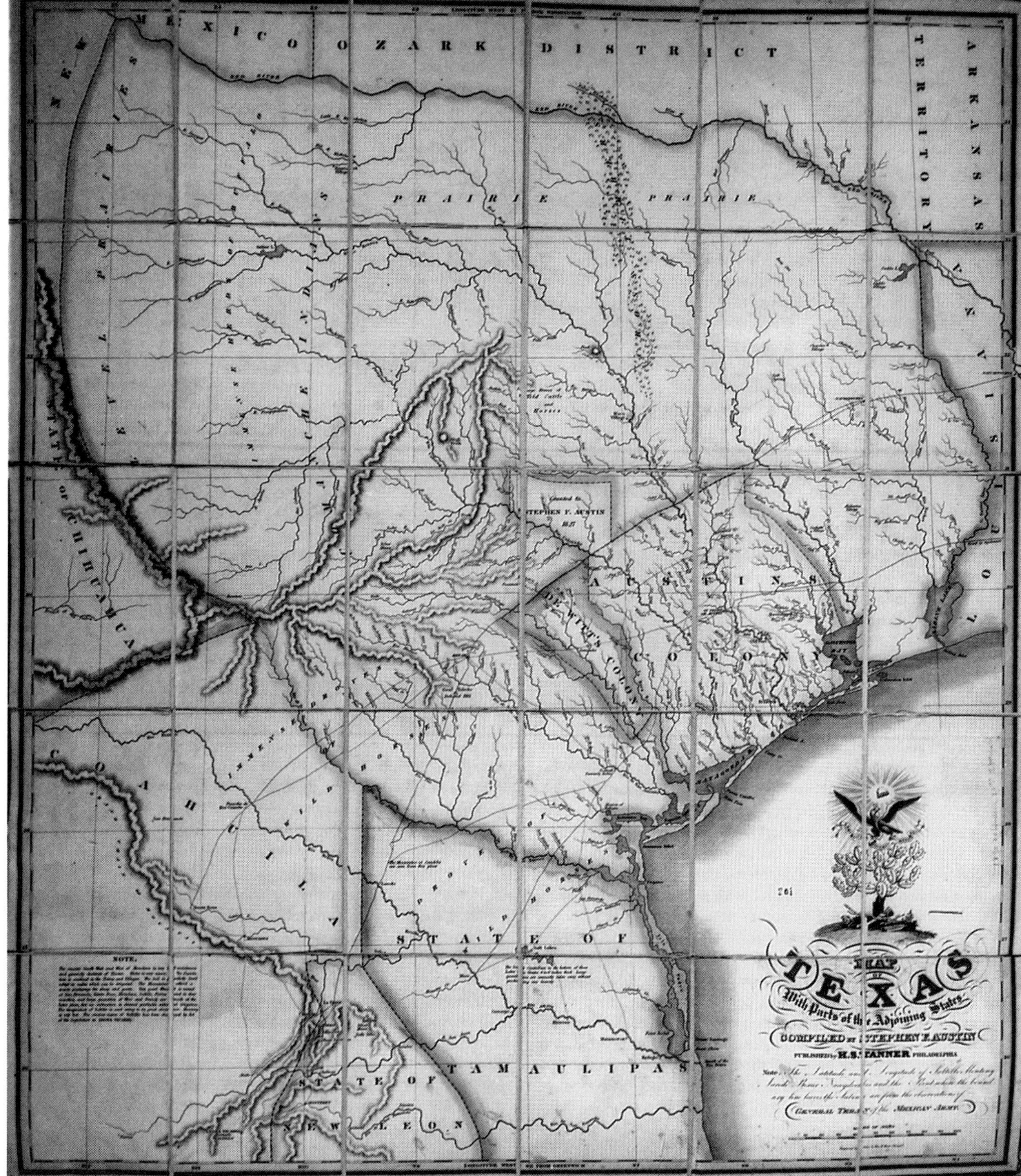

Map of Texas, with Parts of the Adjoining States, *compiled by Stephen F. Austin. Published by H. S. Tanner, Philadelphia, 1830. Map Collection, CAH; CN 04810. This map, intended by Austin to encourage immigration from the United States, was the first separately published map of Texas to provide generally accurate information. It was issued six times by Tanner during the 1830s and served as a pattern for the maps of other publishers.*

and James Hewetson,[qqv] natives of Ireland and residents of the United States and Mexico. They received a state contract in June 1828 to settle 200 families—half Mexican and half Irish—in the twenty-six-mile coastal reserve between the mouth of the Guadalupe and the mouth of the Lavaca River, an area that received approval from the president. In 1829 their boundary was extended south to the Nueces River. Two hundred titles were issued to Europeans, but because many were single men the colonial contract was left incomplete, since the law specified families. Nearby, two other Irish natives, residents of Matamoros, secured a contract in 1828 to bring 200 European families to the Nueces above the Power-Hewetson grant. John McMullen and James McGloin's[qqv] colony was known as the Irish Colony; most of its residents clustered around San Patricio, where the land commissioner issued eighty-four titles.

Of more importance to the development of Anglo-Texan communities were the large grants made in 1825 to Edwards and Leftwich that were adjacent to the Austin colony on the east and north. Edwards's contract specified land for up to 800 Anglo-American families in a large area of East Texas from northwest of Nacogdoches, including the forks of the Trinity, west to the Navasota River, thence southeast along the Trinity River valley to upper Galveston Bay. The tract did not include Galveston Island or the twenty-six-mile-wide coastal reserve forbidden to foreigners. The eastern boundary was the fifty-two-mile-wide border reserve along the Sabine River running north from the Gulf of Mexico to the thirty-second parallel. The state instructed Edwards to respect the property of long-time residents in the Nacogdoches area, some of whom had been there since the 1780s. Edwards, insensitive to Hispanic culture, reached Nacogdoches in October 1825 and threatened to dispossess those who had no proof of ownership unless they paid him for the land. The Spanish process to acquire land on the remote frontier was lengthy and expensive, and almost nobody had deeds. But besides Hispanics, there were a number of Anglo-American hunters and traders who had moved there in the 1790s, as well as new squatters who had arrived since 1821. Although local alcaldes were authorized for the scattered settlements, there was no ayuntamiento until 1828, so all official business had to be conducted in San Antonio. In general, Hispanics and old-time Anglos opposed Edwards and complained to the political chief in San Antonio; some newcomers supported the empresario, while others remained aloof. Tensions mounted during 1826, and in response to complaints against Edwards the state abrogated his contract in October and banished him from Texas. Anglo-Texans, even those not involved in the controversy, were disturbed that a contract, almost sacred in Anglo culture, could be canceled. Did that mean that the provisions of the colonization laws might change regarding slavery? Were other empresario contracts vulnerable?

At the time of the cancellation, Haden Edwards was recruiting colonists in Mississippi, but his brother, Benjamin W. Edwards,[qv] rallied supporters to protest the order. In November they seized the alcalde (an Anglo old-timer) and tried others at a drumhead court; after a few days all were released. The following month the insurgents declared independence from Mexico by decreeing the Republic of Fredonia. Benjamin Edwards forged an alliance with some disaffected Cherokee leaders who were unable to secure titles to their villages northwest of Nacogdoches, and Edwards promised to divide Texas between the red men and the whites. The Indians reconsidered, however, and failed to support Edwards, who fled towards Louisiana in January 1827, when soldiers from San Antonio accompanied by Austin's militia approached Nacogdoches. Thus ended the quixotic Fredonia Rebellion,[qv] which aroused fears of widespread Anglo-Texan revolt among Mexican leaders. The state banished the ringleaders, promised to send a land commissioner to issue titles to families who had settled the area in good faith, and established a permanent garrison at Nacogdoches to guard against ruffians and filibusters from the United States.

Almost as troublesome was the Leftwich contract, which, unknown to the authorities, was intended as a profit-making undertaking for the benefit of stockholders. This empresario grant eventually was known as Robertson's colony.[qv] Leftwich, who was in Mexico City when Austin was there, represented seventy Tennessee investors called the Texas Association. The land assigned was in the upper Brazos valley just north of Austin's grant and touching that of Edwards on the east. When Leftwich returned to Nashville in 1825 with the empresario contract in his name instead of the company's, the investors had to buy out his interest. They sent several agents to Coahuila-Texas to get the contract in their name, but the suspicions raised by the Fredonia Rebellion deterred their efforts. With Austin's help, the Nashville Association (as it was now called) was finally recognized as successor to Leftwich in October 1827. But the stockholders failed to send settlers until October 1830, only six months before the end of their contract. Shareholder Sterling C. Robertson and six others reached the garrison at Fort Tenoxtitlán, one of the new military posts established in 1830; Tenoxtitlán guarded the old Spanish road crossing on the Brazos River. Nine families trailed Robertson, and when they reached Nacogdoches the commandant detained them. The newly passed Law of April 6, 1830,[qv] prohibited the entrance of Anglo-Americans into Texas unless they had a passport to Austin's or DeWitt's colony. Austin had quickly secured an exemption from the restriction for his and DeWitt's colonies when he discovered an ambiguous phrase seeming to allow immigration to "established" colonies. This he interpreted as those with more than 100 families in residence. The authorities acquiesced. The Law of April 6 also forbade the immigration of slaves, but even the authorities admitted that this restriction was impossible to enforce.

Passage of the restrictive law was the result of heightened suspicions that the United States intended to seize Texas. Between 1825 and 1829, the United States minister to Mexico, Joel R. Poinsett,[qv] unsuccessfully pressured the new nation to sell eastern Texas, and his successor, Anthony Butler,[qv] had similar instructions. Mexican leaders feared a rebellion of Anglos and annexation[qv] to the United States, just as Spain had lost Baton Rouge and Mobile in the early 1800s. Thus the Fredonian Rebellion inspired an official inspection tour in 1828 from San Antonio to Nacogdoches which revealed that Anglo-Americans greatly outnumbered native Mexicans in Texas. Although there was no obvious subversive activity, the Anglos continued to speak only English and conducted legal matters primarily in Anglo tradition. The authorities concluded that Mexico might lose Texas if more Anglo-Americans were allowed to enter and that native Mexicans must be encouraged to settle in the frontier state to "Mexicanize" it. The government dispatched troops to strategic entrances to Texas in late 1830 to enforce the law and also to aid the newly installed customs collectors in levying national import duties. The special exemption from the tariff for Texas pioneer settlers had expired. It was hoped that the new garrisons would produce native Mexican communities and that the tariff would pay for the troops needed to preserve Texas. However, this understandable response to save Mexican hegemony inflamed Anglo-Texans, who inherited their grandfathers' distaste for standing armies and troops billeted in residential communities, and who had come to believe that their exemption from tariffs was permanent.

Robertson's colonists surreptitiously passed Nacogdoches and reached the Brazos in November. Amid a flurry of letters to officials, Austin offered the unlucky settlers sanctuary, a step approved officially in September 1831. Meanwhile Robertson asked Austin, who was leaving to take his seat in the state legislature at Saltillo, to intercede for an extension of the six-year contract. Austin agreed, although he believed the case dead—the six years was up, the Law of April 6, 1830, prevented Anglo settlement, and a French immigration company had already applied for the old Leftwich grant. In early February, however, Austin asked the state for a contract in his name and that of his associate, Samuel May Williams,[qv] to settle 800 European and Mexican families on the former Nashville grant, plus some additional land north and west. The application was approved on February 25, 1832.

This action caused trouble with Robertson, who felt betrayed. Austin defended his action by saying that Robertson's cause was hopeless. Austin wanted, he stated, a more dependable frontier neighbor than a French company on his northern frontier, which was still exposed to Indian raiders. Robertson appealed to the ayuntamiento in San Felipe for relief in November 1833 by offering testimony from various persons that the Nashville company had sent 100 families before the expiration of the contract in 1831. The council, influenced by anti-Austin sentiment, agreed that Robertson should be reinstated, and he left for Saltillo, where he presented his documents on April 2, 1834. In

May the governor returned the contract to Robertson despite arguments by Austin and Williams's attorney; Robertson's land commissioner began granting titles immediately. Sam Williams attended the 1835 session of the state legislature and won back the colony in May. Austin and Williams's new land commissioner began issuing deeds, while Robertson's commissioner continued to act until the end of the year. The resulting overlapping claims kept lawyers employed past midcentury.

The most controversial of all of the empresario grants, however, were those of David G. Burnet, Joseph Vehlein, and Lorenzo de Zavala,[qqv] who sold their respective contracts to New York and Boston speculators. This action was contrary to the intent of the national and state colonization laws. The sale was not only illegal, but also deleterious to the purchasers. As a result of it, small and large investors and innocent colonists lost their promised land and sometimes their lives. Burnet, a native of New Jersey and resident of Ohio, had traded with the Indians in Spanish Texas about 1818 but soon returned to Ohio. In December 1826 he received a contract to settle 300 families in the northwestern area of the former Edwards grant near Nacogdoches. At the same time, Vehlein, a Mexico City merchant, contracted through agents to settle 300 families in the southern portion of the canceled Edwards grant. Neither man visited the land and neither sent a single colonist. Burnet, a younger son of a prominent family, tried to recruit antislavery settlers in Ohio, but lacked the financial means to succeed. In 1829, with time running out, he unsuccessfully offered half of his future bonus land to wealthy and powerful individuals if they would send 300 families to his grant. Finally, in October 1830, he negotiated the sale of his grant to the Galveston Bay and Texas Land Company,[qv] as did Vehlein's agent. Joining in the sale was Lorenzo de Zavala,[qv] a native of Yucatán, a prominent politician and currently a political refugee in New York City. He had acquired the long fifty-two-mile-wide border reserve on the Sabine River as his empresario grant in 1828, when he agreed to settle 500 European or Mexican families. He, too, never saw his Texas land nor sent a colonist.

The Galveston Bay company issued stock entitling investors to scrip in denominations of leagues and labores. Some investors, such as James Prentiss,[qv] used their scrip to create separate ventures such as the Union Land Company and the Trinity Land Company.[qqv] Those companies dispatched two schooners to Galveston Bay in January 1831 with a few European settlers recruited in New York City. Though the Law of April 6, 1830, prohibited sending Anglo-Americans, some American workmen accompanied the settlers. John Davis Bradburn,[qv] the commandant at Anahuac, allowed the unfortunate immigrants to land briefly. A few stayed and farmed, but most returned to the United States as best they could.

The entire undertaking was extortionate. Upon landing, each immigrant was to apply for a headright, of which he would receive 177 acres after three years of labor. The remaining 4,428 acres was signed over to the company. The company employed agents in Mexico to lobby for revocation of the restrictive law of 1830, a step that succeeded in 1834. Moreover, those squatters who had lived in East Texas since 1821 without titles discovered they were now colonists of the three empresarios. Although the state had approved naming a land commissioner in 1828, politics delayed implementation. Finally, in 1834, land commissioners arrived to give deeds to those long-time squatters and also the newcomers. One called himself the agent of the empresario and tried to collect fees until complaints to the state ended the illegal practice.

There were a number of lesser empresarios, including Benjamin R. Milam, Arthur G. Wavell, John Cameron, Stephen Julian Wilson, John Charles Beales, and Richard Exeter,[qqv] as well as a few native Mexicans. All failed to complete their contracts within the allotted time. Most of their grants were located on the southwestern and northern perimeters of Texas.

Settlers continued to arrive in the established colonies and the area claimed by the Galveston Bay Company until the land offices were closed by the General Council[qv] on October 27, 1835, and confirmed by the Consultation[qv] the next month. By this time most residents, except in Robertson's colony on the northern frontier, no longer thought of themselves as colonists dependent on an empresario. De León was dead, DeWitt died in 1835, Austin was a sort of elder statesman, and few people in the Burnet, Vehlein, or Zavala grants were acquainted with the phantom empresarios. By 1834 Texas was divided into three departments: Bexar, the Brazos, and Nacogdoches, each with its own political chief reporting directly to the governor and each having more than one town with an ayuntamiento. This gave the residents a feeling of self-government. Their main goal was achieving separate statehood from Coahuila. The old Austin colony continued to attract newcomers, including some of those unable to secure titles in other colonies. Its stability, its guaranteed deeds, and its easy accessibility by water from New Orleans through Galveston Bay and the Brazos river were drawing cards.

The Anglo-American settlers imported their culture to Texas and resisted Mexicanizing even after 1830, when purchase by the United States was increasingly unlikely. Rich or poor, Anglo immigrants were independent-minded, self-sufficient republicans suspicious of the traditional deferential society of Hispanic culture, even though Mexican reformers were struggling to build a republic. The spirit of Jacksonian democracy pervaded even those not admiring President Andrew Jackson. Moreover, collecting national tariff duties in Texas in 1830 coincided with the growing anti-tariff movement in South Carolina, which resulted in the Nullification Crisis. Texans, like other agrarians, manufactured nothing and disliked import duties on necessities. It was not surprising, then, that American ship captains, supported by Anglo-Texan merchants, refused to pay the new duties and exchanged fire with the fort at the mouth of the Brazos River in December 1831. At this same time, Colonel Bradburn, charged with enforcing Mexican laws regarding immigration and the tariff at Anahuac, arrested civilians and held some without bail for trial before the commandant general at Matamoros. Anglo-Texans believed Bradburn was acting arbitrarily. They did not understand that his actions were required under Mexican law, which lacked anything like a Bill of Rights. Angry men from the Brazos marched to confront Bradburn at Anahuac, while others loaded illegal cannons on a ship to join them. At the mouth of the river, the Anglo-Texans forced the surrender of the fort. The first of the Anahuac Disturbances[qv] and the battle of Velasco[qv] took place in June 1832, just as the Federalist party's army defeated that of the conservative administration, thus ending a four-year-old civil war. The Texans claimed to be helping the Federalists, who were led by Antonio López de Santa Anna,[qv] and convinced authorities sent to investigate that they were not revolutionaries against Mexico. Their action resulted in the departure of all Centralist troops and customs collectors from Texas.

Wanting to capitalize on their support of Santa Anna, who was to be the new president, the Anglo-Texans drafted petitions for separate statehood, a better judicial system, and similar reform measures. In April 1833 Austin took the requests to Mexico City, where most were approved except for separate statehood. In a moment of despondency, Austin wrote an incriminating letter urging the leaders at San Antonio to act unilaterally on separation. For this act of sedition he was arrested in January 1834 and incarcerated in Mexico City until July 1835.

Texans remained relatively quiet during Austin's absence fearing for his life. After Santa Anna's installation as president in 1833, he left governing to his Federalist-reformer vice president. By 1835, however, Santa Anna reversed himself, became a Centralist dictator, and sent the army to punish his political enemies. Garrisons and customs collectors returned to Texas in January 1835 and the Anglo-Texan response was predictable. A second attack recaptured Anahuac in June, and when Austin reached Texas in September he surprised many by endorsing the resistance movement against the oppressive administration. Though at first supporting reform of the Mexican government, public opinion moved quickly to favoring a separate Texas nation.

There are no accurate figures detailing the number of Anglo-Americans who settled in Texas between 1821 and 1835. Although Mexican law required an annual census of all residents, the Anglo-Texans resisted such bureaucratic demands. Existing tallies reveal that in 1826 Austin had 1,800 people, including 443 slaves; DeWitt counted 159 whites and 29 slaves; and the lower Trinity River, then outside of any empresario grant, was populated by 407 settlers with 76 slaves. Subsequent extant records show Austin's colony with 2,201 people in 1828, 4,248 in 1830, and 5,565 in 1831, while DeWitt had only 82 persons, including 7 slaves, in 1828. In 1834 the English-speaking Col. Juan N. Almonte[qv] made an official inspection of Texas and estimated that 4,000 people lived in the Department of Bexar, 2,100 in the Department of the Brazos (Austin's colony), and 1,600 in the Department of Nacogdoches. The 3,000 decrease in Austin's colony suggests that Almonte's figures were wrong. A few lists of residents in the Nacogdoches area in 1834–35 and scattered other records are extant, but such incomplete records only hint at the Texas population. Anglo-American colonization in Texas was obviously a success, although not what Mexican leaders envisioned. Neither side worked to understand, appreciate, nor resolve the cultural differences intrinsic to the union proposed by Mexico and accepted by Anglo-American immigrants.

See also SPANISH TEXAS, MEXICAN TEXAS, TEXAS REVOLUTION, MEXICAN COLONIZATION LAWS, BOUNDARIES, *and* LAND GRANTS.

BIBLIOGRAPHY: Eugene C. Barker, *The Life of Stephen F. Austin* (Nashville: Cokesbury Press, 1925; rpt., Austin: Texas State Historical Association, 1949; New York: AMS Press, 1970). A. B. J. Hammett, *The Empresario Don Martín de León* (Waco: Texian Press, 1973). Mary Virginia Henderson, "Minor Empresario Contracts for the Colonization of Texas, 1825–1834," *Southwestern Historical Quarterly* 31, 32 (April, July 1928). Margaret Swett Henson, *The Cartwrights of San Augustine* (Austin: Texas State Historical Association, 1993). Margaret S. Henson, *Juan Davis Bradburn: A Reappraisal of the Mexican Commander of Anahuac* (College Station: Texas A&M University Press, 1982). Margaret S. Henson, *Samuel May Williams: Early Texas Entrepreneur* (College Station: Texas A&M University Press, 1976). Edward Albert Lukes, *De Witt Colony of Texas* (Austin: Jenkins, 1976). Malcolm D. McLean, comp. and ed., *Papers Concerning Robertson's Colony in Texas* (19 vols., Arlington: University of Texas at Arlington Press, 1974–93). Ernest Wallace and David M. Vigness, eds., *Documents of Texas History* (Austin: Steck, 1963). David J. Weber, *The Mexican Frontier, 1821–1846* (Albuquerque: University of New Mexico Press, 1982).

Margaret Swett Henson

ANGLO-TEXAN CONVENTION OF 1840. The Anglo-Texan Convention of November 14, 1840, resulted from a proffer of British mediation to secure Mexican recognition of the independence of the Republic of Texas.[qv] Texas and England attended the convention, but Mexico refused and countered the invitation with the expedition of Adrián Woll[qv] in September 1842.

BIBLIOGRAPHY: Annie Laura Middleton, Studies Relating to the Annexation of Texas by the United States (Ph.D. dissertation, University of Texas, 1938). Henderson K. Yoakum, *History of Texas from Its First Settlement in 1685 to Its Annexation to the United States in 1846* (2 vols., New York: Redfield, 1855).

Claudia Hazlewood

ANGLO-TEXAN SOCIETY. The Anglo-Texan Society was founded in London in December 1953. Author Graham Greene, its founding president, suggested that friendly relations between the two realms could best be promoted by sponsoring cultural exchanges and generally looking after any Texan who finds his way to London. The idea for such an organization first came to Greene and actor-producer John Sutro when they heard some visiting Texans complain about British reserve. Membership was open "to persons of either sex who have some definite connections with both Texas and Great Britain." In addition to Britons-who-love-Texas, Texans in England in the 1950s were numerous by virtue of military service or business interests, especially petroleum. The oil crisis caused by the end of the British occupation of the Suez Canal zone stimulated a demand for Texas oil in Great Britain. The first Texas Instruments[qv] plant in England was begun in 1957, when TI architect O'Neil Ford[qv] became an enthusiastic member of the society.

The Anglo-Texan Society's first function, a barbecue on March 6, 1954, in observance of Texas Independence Day, was attended by 1,500 guests. The menu for the affair, held at Denham Film Studios, featured 2,800 pounds of beef donated by the Houston Fat Stock Show. Greene's interest in the organization quickly waned when the cultural directions he charted were supplanted by a more convivial agenda. Early on, leadership responsibilities were assumed by Sir Alfred Bossom,[qv] member of Parliament (1931–59), whose ties with Texas were extensive. In the course of his architectural practice in the United States (1903–26) he designed landmarks in several Texas cities. Under the genial Sir Alfred, the organization's only purpose was pure fun, with no demands made on anyone. The society met four times a year. Memorable luncheons with Mexican food imported from Texas were often held at Bossom's Regency house at 5 Carlton Gardens. Distinguished Texans might also be invited to address the organization. Clarence T. McLaughlin[qv] of Snyder, rancher and oilman extraordinaire, flew to London to be the featured speaker for the society's 1960 annual dinner in the dining room of the House of Commons.

In his capacity as president of the Anglo-Texan Society, Sir Alfred made several trips back to Texas. During a 1958 visit to Dallas, he was feted by society members, including Dallas mayor Robert L. Thornton;[qv] William Burrow, head of the society's Texas branch; and Lawrence and Edward Marcus of Neiman-Marcus.[qv] The press now spoke of the "world-wide Anglo-Texan Society." With so many eager to celebrate the bonds between Texas and Britain, Bossom invited London attorney Michael Bryceson to assume administrative responsibilities as the society's chairman. During World War II[qv] as a Royal Navy cadet, Bryceson completed his flight training at Corpus Christi Naval Air Station.

In 1963, on the initiative of Alfred Bossom, the Anglo-Texan Society erected a brass plaque at the corner of No. 3 St. James's Place to mark the location of the Texas Legation in Great Britain during the final years of the Republic of Texas,[qv] 1842–45. The plaque, unveiled by Texas governor Price Daniel, Sr.,[qv] is now the only monument to the existence of the Anglo-Texan Society.

With Bossom's death in 1965, the glory years of the society were over. The organization survived but in a more sedate mood. Men of great distinction who succeeded to the presidency included Lord Caccia of Abernant, who was followed by Sir Patrick Dean. Both men had previously served as British Ambassador to Washington. The more serious tone was a portent that the ties that had long united Great Britain and the United States were unraveling. At the 1972 annual meeting, Sir Patrick Dean commented on the imminent entry of Britain into the Common Market, observing that "the natural emphasis placed on this new and historic development...has turned the eyes of many away from our special relationship with the U.S.A." In these more strident times, an organization that made no demands other than that a civilized good time be had by all may have seemed frivolous. At a special meeting in May 1979, the Anglo-Texan Society voted to disband.

Mary Carolyn Hollers George

ANGUS, TEXAS. Angus is on the Burlington Northern Railroad and Interstate Highway 45, six miles south of Corsicana in Navarro County. It was established in 1871 by A. Angus and had the first hay press in that part of Texas. It was also known for its cattle industry, oil refineries, and vast amounts of fertile soil good for corn and wheat production. The first church was built in 1872 and the first school in 1874. An Angus post office opened in 1877 but was later discontinued. A money-order office was established in 1911, when the population of

Angus was twenty. In 1945 the population had increased to twenty-five. In 1987 it was 244, and in 1990 it was 363.

BIBLIOGRAPHY: Annie Carpenter Love, *History of Navarro County* (Dallas: Southwestern, 1933). *David Allen*

ANHALT, TEXAS. Anhalt, twenty-eight miles west of New Braunfels in western Comal County, was settled by German pioneers in 1859 and known as Krause Settlement. The settlers united in early years for protection against Indians and reorganized in 1876 as the Germania Farmers Verein to safeguard and improve their livestock. The society grew in succeeding decades to include mutual insurance and social activities. In 1887 the verein leased land from George Krause and built a meeting hall, which they enlarged in 1896. As late as the mid-1970s, hundreds of people still gathered at the Farmers Hall for annual spring and harvest festivals. Two explanations have been offered for the name Anhalt: one, that it derives from the German word for "stopping place" and was suggested by an early settler when a post office opened in 1879 in the Krause Store; the other, that it refers to a region of the same name in Germany. The post office closed in 1907. In the 1970s the population along Anhalt Road between Farm Road 475 and the Farmers Hall was estimated at ten. The site is now called Farmers Hall.

BIBLIOGRAPHY: *Atlas of the World* (Washington: National Geographic Society, 1963; 5th ed. 1981). New Braunfels *Zeitung*, August 21, 1952. *Oscar Haas*

ANIGSTEIN, LUDWIK (1891–1975). Ludwik Anigstein, medical scientist, was born in Warsaw, Poland, on February 2, 1891, to Isidore and Helen (Steinkalk) Anigstein. His father sent him to the University of Heidelberg, where he graduated magna cum laude with a Ph.D. in natural sciences in 1913. His studies included a year's study of marine zoology in France. He enrolled at the University of Dorpat, Estonia, in 1914 and earned an M.D. diploma in 1915. He then went to the University of Poznan in Poland for a second medical degree, which was granted in 1923. That same year he attended the London School of Tropical Medicine and Hygiene and received a postgraduate certificate. Between 1915 and 1939 Anigstein served the Thai and Liberian governments and the League of Nations as an expert in tropical medicine, attended international congresses, and worked with the Soviet Red Cross.

He specialized in parasitology and tropical medicine. He worked as a parasitologist with the State Institute of Hygiene in Warsaw, Poland, from 1919 until 1940, when he immigrated to the United States as a refugee from the Nazis. The Jewish Emigré Committee in New York and the Hooper Foundation found him a temporary position with the University of California; that same year he accepted a permanent position as a research associate at the University of Texas Medical Branch at Galveston, where he later became an assistant, then associate, professor. He became a United States citizen in 1945. After the death of his wife, Luba Esther (Heller), a pediatrician, he married Dorothy Whitney, a laboratory scientist with whom he coauthored numerous research papers. He was the father of a son and daughter by his first marriage.

Anigstein wrote or shared in the writing of nearly 2,000 articles and papers for scientific journals. He also coauthored a textbook. His first great contribution came during studies of rickettsial diseases borne by ticks. He discovered that one of the rickettsiae caused a disease that infected hundreds of soldiers during World War II.[qv] Anigstein also did pioneering work in antibiotics. His discovery of a blood-derived antibiotic made news on two continents and provided material for the first official report on the use of blood as a source of antibiotics (antibiotics had previously been extracted only from molds or bacteria). He served as director of the UTMB Rickettsial Laboratory from 1941 to 1962 and of the UTMB Tissue Immunity Laboratory from 1962 to 1970.

Even though he was older than fifty when the United States entered World War II, Anigstein joined the Texas State Guard[qv] in 1943 and became a major in the infantry and an executive officer of the Forty-ninth Battalion. At the end of the war he returned to Poland to teach on communicable diseases with the United Nations Medical Teaching Mission. In 1950 he acted as a consultant for the Medical Division of the United States Atomic Energy Commission at the Oak Ridge Institute for Nuclear Studies.

In 1955 Anigstein received the James W. McLaughlin Faculty Fellowship to study tropical diseases in Peru and Brazil. In 1956 the Royal Society of Health in London elected him to membership. In 1961 he served as the Gabriel Kempner Visiting Professor to the University of Hamburg. He died in 1975 in Galveston.

BIBLIOGRAPHY: *Who's Who in World Jewry*. Vertical Files, Barker Texas History Center, University of Texas at Austin.

Natalie Ornish

ANIMAL DISEASE INVESTIGATIONS LABORATORY. The Animal Disease Investigations Laboratory, at Marfa, was a field laboratory of the Texas Agricultural Experiment Station System[qv] of the Agricultural and Mechanical College of Texas (now Texas A&M University). The plant was established near Alpine in 1930, when it was called the Loco Weed Laboratory. The station initially received funds from the Texas legislature and, until 1949, from the United States Department of Agriculture Bureau of Animal Industry. The laboratory's veterinarian and an assistant researched effects of poisonous plants and infectious diseases on cattle. Investigations showed that the loco weed and thirty-one other plants were responsible for livestock losses in the Trans-Pecos area. The laboratory was renamed and moved in 1946 to a 400-acre tract at an abandoned air force base three miles from Marfa. It ceased operation in 1962.

BIBLIOGRAPHY: Frank P. Mathews, *Locoism in Domestic Animals* (Texas Agricultural Experiment Station Bulletin 456 [College Station, September 1932]). Texas Agricultural Experiment Station, *Annual Report*, 1930.

ANNA, TEXAS. Anna is on State Highway 5, Farm Road 455, and the Southern Pacific Railroad eleven miles northeast of McKinney in north central Collin County. Although Collin McKinney[qv] settled within a few miles of the future townsite in 1846, John L. Greer, who arrived in 1867, is credited with building the first home and store there. The Houston and Texas Central Railway, at that time building between Dallas and Denison, passed through the area in 1873. By the time Anna was platted in 1883, it had a population of twenty, two stores, a steam gristmill, and a Baptist church. A post office also opened in that year. By 1890 the town had a population of 100 to 200. It incorporated in 1913, with Greer as first mayor. Two years later the Greenville and Whitewright Northern Traction Company built the Greenville and Northwestern Railway between Anna and Blue Ridge via Westminster. The line proved unsuccessful, however, and was abandoned in 1920. Anna's first bank, the Continental Bank, was organized in 1902, and the Collin County State Bank was organized in 1913 with R. C. Moore as president. The population of Anna was 538 in 1929 and 467 in 1931. Some sources suggest that the community was named after Greer's daughter. Others report that the town was named in honor of Anna Quinlan, daughter of George A. Quinlan, former superintendent of the Houston and Texas Central. Still another story suggests that Anna Quinlan was the wife of George Quinlan and the daughter of J. L. Greer. Finally, another story attributes the name to Anna Huntington, daughter of C. P. Huntington, who built the Dallas-Denison railroad line. In the mid-1980s Anna had 855 residents and several businesses. The population was 904 in 1990.

BIBLIOGRAPHY: Roy Franklin Hall and Helen Gibbard Hall, *Collin County: Pioneering in North Texas* (Quanah, Texas: Nortex, 1975).

Chester A. Howell, *A Town Named Anna* (Waco, 1993). Kathleen E. and Clifton R. St. Clair, eds., *Little Towns of Texas* (Jacksonville, Texas: Jayroe Graphic Arts, 1982). J. Lee and Lillian J. Stambaugh, *A History of Collin County* (Austin: Texas State Historical Association, 1958). *David Minor*

ANNAHO INDIANS. The Annaho Indians were mentioned in documents (1687) of the La Salle expedition[qv] as enemies of the Kadohadacho Indians on the Red River. Annaho was an early name used by the French for the Osage Indians, whose base area at that time was in western Missouri. The Annahos are not to be confused with the Anaos, who were mentioned in a Spanish missionary report of 1691 as living near the Hasinai tribes of eastern Texas.

BIBLIOGRAPHY: Pierre Margry, ed., *Découvertes et établissements des Français dans l'ouest et dans le sud de l'Amérique septentrionale, 1614–1754* (6 vols., Paris: Jouast, 1876–86). Ralph A. Smith, trans., "Account of the Journey of Bénard de La Harpe," *Southwestern Historical Quarterly* 62 (July, October 1958, January, April 1959). John R. Swanton, *Source Material on the History and Ethnology of the Caddo Indians* (Smithsonian Institution, Bureau of American Ethnology Bulletin 132, Washington: GPO, 1942). *Thomas N. Campbell*

ANNA JUDSON FEMALE INSTITUTE. Anna Judson Female Institute opened at Starrville in northern Smith County in 1860. The school, founded by the Bethel Baptist Church, had forty-three students that year. Levi Wilcoxen served as principal of the literary department, and Sallie A. McGilvary, his cousin, assisted him. J. B. Norman was principal of the music department. The school failed during the Civil War,[qv] but perhaps not before 1864.

BIBLIOGRAPHY: Vicki Betts, *Smith County, Texas, in the Civil War* (Tyler, Texas: Smith County Historical Society, 1978). Donald W. Whisenhunt, comp., *Chronological History of Smith County* (Tyler, Texas: Smith County Historical Society, 1983).
Vista K. McCroskey

ANNA ROSE, TEXAS. Anna Rose (Annarose), on Farm Road 624 eighteen miles south of George West in south central Live Oak County, is noted for raising cattle and sheep. The settlement is associated with nearby Clegg and Ramirena. An Anna Rose post office was established in 1915 but closed sometime after 1930. State highway maps of 1936 showed a business, a school, and scattered dwellings at the townsite, and the local population rose from ten in 1933 to eighty in 1945. Black and white schools in the community were combined by 1944 and annexed to the George West Independent School District in 1948. A dance hall owned by the daughter of Tom Weston, an early settler, drew area residents from 1926 until the 1950s, but after 1947, when three businesses remained, the population declined.

BIBLIOGRAPHY: Live Oak County Centennial Association, *Live Oak County Centennial* (George West, Texas, 1956). Ervin L. Sparkman, *The People's History of Live Oak County* (Mesquite, Texas, 1981).
Brian Michael Todd Kryszewski

ANNAS, HARRY FORREST (1897–1980). Harry Forrest Annas, photographer, son of Frederic Druf and Viola Mae (McGee) Annas, was born on February 27, 1897, in Washington, Iowa. He married Marjorie Mae Iliff on June 22, 1933; they had four children. After World War I[qv] service in the Rainbow Division in France, Annas enrolled in Dad Lively's Southern School of Photography at McMinnville, Tennessee. In 1926, shortly after he graduated, he opened a studio in Columbus, Ohio; he subsequently moved his business to Webster, Iowa. In search of prosperity during the Great Depression,[qv] he and his wife moved to Lockhart, Texas, in 1933. Annas's photography achieved national recognition when his photographs were included in Barbara Norfleet's *The Champion Pig* (1979). Norfleet described his photographs as "the best in the country" and acquired a number of them for the Carpenter Center for the Visual Arts at Harvard University. Annas claimed to specialize in "all kinds of photography"; his work, like that of other small-town studio photographers, filled many needs in the community. He worked at his studio on the south side of the courthouse square in Lockhart until his retirement in 1970. He died on November 19, 1980.

BIBLIOGRAPHY: Walter Barnes, "Salute to Harry Annas," *Texas Professional Photographer*, October–November 1979. Lockhart *Post-Register*, November 27, 1980. *Richard Pearce-Moses*

ANNAS INDIANS. This name, reported by Pedro de Rivera[qv] in 1736, refers to a small band of Indians who lived somewhere in the southern part of Texas. It seems likely that the Annas are the same as the Teanames, a Coahuiltecan group of northeastern Coahuila and adjoining parts of Texas, who in missions were also known as Peana and Teana.

BIBLIOGRAPHY: Vito Alessio Robles, *Coahuila y Texas en la época colonial* (Mexico City: Editorial Cultura, 1938; 2d ed., Mexico City: Editorial Porrúa, 1978). Frederick Webb Hodge, ed., *Handbook of American Indians North of Mexico* (2 vols., Washington: GPO, 1907, 1910; rpt., New York: Pageant, 1959). *Thomas N. Campbell*

ANNAVILLE, TEXAS. Annaville was on Highway 9 at Violet Road just west of Calallen in northern Nueces County. It was established in 1940 by Leo and Anna Stewart of Corpus Christi, who divided up their land into lots, opened a store, and named the site Annaville. An elementary school was opened; it later became part of the Calallen Independent School District. In 1952 the community had a reported population of 240 and twelve businesses. During the mid-1960s the area was annexed by Corpus Christi.

BIBLIOGRAPHY: Nueces County Historical Society, *History of Nueces County* (Austin: Jenkins, 1972). *Christopher Long*

ANNETTA, TEXAS. Annetta is on Farm Road 1187 six miles southeast of Weatherford in southeastern Parker County. Settlement began there in the late 1870s, when a Mr. Fraser established a station for the convenience of freighters who traveled east to Dallas and on to Jefferson. Fraser named his station Annetta after his daughter. In the early 1880s, after the tracks of the Texas and Pacific Railway passed near his station, Fraser built a general store on the rail line, and gradually a community developed at the site. An Annetta post office operated from 1876 until 1907. By the mid-1890s Annetta had a population of twenty-five, three churches, a public school, and a general store; it was a shipping point for cotton and local crops. For most of the twentieth century Annetta served area farmers as a school and church community. The number of residents remained well below fifty until the late 1970s. At that time the community grew suddenly, probably as a result of the dramatic growth of nearby Fort Worth. By the 1980s the northern and southern sections had split off from central Annetta. Annetta North incorporated in the mid-1980s and reported 281 residents. Annetta South also incorporated during the 1980s and claimed a population of 115. In 1990 Annetta had a population of 678; Annetta North had 265, and Annetta South had 413.

BIBLIOGRAPHY: John Clements, *Flying the Colors: Texas, a Comprehensive Look at Texas Today, County by County* (Dallas: Clements Research, 1984). Gustavus Adolphus Holland, *History of Parker County and the Double Log Cabin* (Weatherford, Texas: Herald, 1931; rpt. 1937). Kathleen E. and Clifton R. St. Clair, eds., *Little Towns of Texas* (Jacksonville, Texas: Jayroe Graphic Arts, 1982). *David Minor*

ANNEXATION. The annexation of Texas to the United States became a topic of political and diplomatic discussion after the Louisiana Purchase in 1803 and became a matter of international concern between 1836 and 1845, when Texas was a republic. In September 1836 Texas voted overwhelmingly in favor of annexation, but when the Texas minister at Washington, D.C., proposed annexation to the Martin Van Buren administration in August 1837, he was told that the proposition could not be entertained. Constitutional scruples and fear of war with Mexico were the reasons given for the rejection, but antislavery sentiment in the United States undoubtedly influenced Van Buren and continued to be the chief obstacle to annexation. Texas withdrew the annexation offer in 1838; President Mirabeau B. Lamar[qv] (1838–41) opposed annexation and did not reopen the question. Sam Houston,[qv] early in his second term (1841–44), tried without success to awaken the interest of the United States.

In 1843 the United States became alarmed over the policy of Great Britain toward Texas. The British were opposed to annexation and even contemplated the use of force to prevent it. They did not wish to add Texas to the British Empire, but they did want to prevent the westward expansion of the United States, to reap commercial advantages from Texas trade, and to tamper with the American tariff system and the institution of slavery.

President John Tyler, concluding that Texas must not become a satellite of Great Britain, proposed annexation. After some sparring, Houston consented to the negotiation of a treaty of annexation, which was rejected by the United States Senate in June 1844. Annexation then became an issue in the presidential election of 1844; James K. Polk, who favored annexation, was elected. Tyler, feeling the need of haste if British designs were to be circumvented, suggested that annexation be accomplished by a joint resolution offering Texas statehood on certain conditions, the acceptance of which by Texas would complete the merger. The United States Congress passed the annexation resolution on February 28, 1845, and Andrew Jackson Donelson[qv] proceeded to Texas to urge acceptance of the offer.

The British still hoped to prevent annexation by having Texas decline the American offer. On British advice, the government of Mexico agreed to acknowledge the independence of Texas on condition that she not annex herself to any country. Public opinion in Texas, fanned by special agents from the United States, demanded acceptance of the American offer. President Anson Jones[qv] called the Texas Congress to meet on June 16, 1845, and a convention of elected delegates was assembled on July 4. He placed before both bodies the choice of annexation or independence recognized by Mexico. Both Congress and the convention voted for annexation. A state constitution, drawn up by the convention, was ratified by popular vote in October 1845 and accepted by the United States Congress on December 29, 1845, the date of Texas's legal entry into the Union. The formal transfer of authority from the republic to the state was not made until a ceremony held on February 19, 1846. President Anson Jones[qv] handed over the reins of state government to Governor James Pinckney Henderson[qv] having declared "The final act in this great drama is now performed; the Republic of Texas is no more."

BIBLIOGRAPHY: E. D. Adams, *British Diplomatic Correspondence Concerning the Republic of Texas, 1836–1846* (Austin: Texas State Historical Association, 1918?). Eugene C. Barker, "The Annexation of Texas," *Southwestern Historical Quarterly* 50 (July 1946). *Diplomatic Correspondence of the Republic of Texas*, ed. George Pierce Garrison (3 parts, Washington: GPO, 1908–11). Joseph William Schmitz, *Texan Statecraft, 1836–1845* (San Antonio: Naylor, 1941). Justin Harvey Smith, *The Annexation of Texas* (New York: Baker and Taylor, 1911; 2d ed., New York: Macmillan, 1919; 3d ed., New York: Barnes and Noble, 1941; 4th ed., New York: AMS Press, 1971).

C. T. Neu

ANNONA, TEXAS. Annona is on the Missouri Pacific Railroad and U.S. Highway 82 eight miles southeast of Clarksville in eastern Red River County. It was established in the early 1870s on the proposed route of the railroad. When the post office was moved from nearby Savannah in 1874 the new town was called Walker Station, in honor of G. W. Walker, founder of the town and first postmaster. In 1884, at Walker's suggestion, the name was changed to Annona, the name of an Indian girl. After the completion of the railroad in 1876 the town grew rapidly. In 1881 a correspondent of the Clarksville *Standard* called Annona "the most important trading point in the county outside of Clarksville." In 1890 the community had three churches, a school, two gins, two mills, a machine shop, and a population of 250. By 1914 the population had grown to 600, and the town had added two small banks and a newspaper, the Annona *News*, published by C. R. Floyd. The population of Annona had fallen to around 500 by 1926, but in the late 1920s the town began to grow again. By 1929 the population was estimated at 800. Annona was incorporated around this time. In 1931 the population was 426, and it remained fairly stable after that. The number of businesses in Annona fell from twenty in 1931 to six in 1986. In 1984 Annona's businesses included two feed stores, a packaging and processing plant, and a cattle company. The population in 1990 was 329. *Cecil Harper, Jr.*

ANSON, TEXAS. Anson, the county seat of Jones County, is at the intersection of U.S. highways 83/277 and 180 at the center of the county. The town was established at Fort Phantom Hill but was moved to its present location when an enterprising speculator, John Merchant, anticipated that the Texas and Pacific Railway would go through the new site. Merchant's offer of land induced McD. Bowyer and P. S. Tipton to open a general store and a hotel. Though the railroad never materialized, the founding of Anson, then known as Jones City, had occurred. On July 17, 1881, Jones City was declared county seat. By 1882 the town had been renamed Anson, again in honor of Anson Jones,[qv] last president of the Republic of Texas.[qv] By 1883 Dick Davis had established the *Texas Western*, Anson's first newspaper. In 1909 county commissioners engaged Elmer Withers to design a new courthouse, which was completed in 1910 at a cost of $100,000.

In 1926 the Phillips Petroleum Company struck oil southwest of Anson, a discovery that led to exploration throughout Jones County. The Bullard oilfield opened one mile southwest of Anson in 1950. In addition to serving as a supply center for the county's agricultural and oil industries, in 1980 Anson produced concrete, magnetic signs, and polished rock. The population of 2,831 was served by a bank, a savings and loan, 100 businesses, and a newspaper, the *Western Observer*. Despite its modern economic activities, the town has not forgotten its western heritage. The Cowboys' Christmas Ball, initiated in December 1885 by M. G. Rhoads at his Star Hotel, continues to be a traditional event (*see* CHITTENDEN, WILLIAM LAWRENCE). In 1990 the population was 2,644.

BIBLIOGRAPHY: Hooper Shelton and Homer Hutto, *The First 100 Years of Jones County* (Stamford, Texas: Shelton, 1978). Anson *Western-Enterprise*, August 24, 1933.

Connie Ricci

ANSON JONES PRESS. The Anson Jones Press was founded in Houston in 1929 by Herbert Herrick Fletcher,[qv] a New Yorker by birth who was head of the rare-book department at Wanamaker's in Philadelphia before opening his own bookstore in Akron, Ohio. With World War I[qv] and the inevitability of the draft before him, he sold out, joined the army, and eventually landed in San Antonio as a medical librarian for Fort Sam Houston. There he met his future wife, Thelma Rawls, employee of Moose's Old Book Store on Broadway. She was the daughter of the Presidio County rancher and legendary lawman John Fletcher Rawls. The couple moved to Houston in 1927 and opened Fletcher's Books on the corner of Rusk and San Jacinto. In the spring of 1929 the Williams family of Galveston offered the Fletchers 585 copies of Anson Jones's[qv] *Memoranda and Official Correspondence Relating to the Republic of Texas*. They were the original printing published by Appleton and Sons in 1861 and were refused by Jones's widow. The books had remained in storage in Galveston in the Williams family warehouses since then. Fletcher formed a small company and purchased the books for $500. Profits from selling them enabled him to enter the publishing world. The press was appropriately named after Anson Jones and was headquartered in Fletcher's bookstore. Fletcher's first publication was a little book of verse titled *Ourselves* and compiled by the Owen Wister Literary Society of Rice Institute in 1930. In 1932 the press published *The Heroes of San Jacinto* by Sam Houston Dixon and Louis Wiltz Kemp;[qqv] in 1936, *Texas 1844–1845,* translated from the German, by Prince Carl of Solms-Braunfels;[qv] also in 1936, *Interwoven, A Pioneer Chronicle,* by Sallie Reynolds Matthews;[qv] and in 1950 *Texas and Its Revolution,* by Frederic LeClerc.[qv] In 1954 the Fletchers moved to Salado, where they continued the Anson Jones Press and opened another bookstore. In 1961 they published *The French in Mexico and Texas* by Louis Eugène Maissin.[qv] In all, the Anson Jones Press has published more than 100 books and pamphlets relating to Texas history. In 1995 it was co-located with Fletcher's Books in Salado.

BIBLIOGRAPHY: Vertical Files, Barker Texas History Center, University of Texas at Austin (Herbert Herrick Fletcher).

Tyler Herrick Fletcher

ANTEBELLUM TEXAS. In the drama of Texas history the period of early statehood, from 1846 to 1861, appears largely as an interlude between two great adventures—the Republic of Texas and the Civil War.[qqv] These fifteen years did indeed lack the excitement and romance of the experiment in nationhood and the "Lost Cause" of the Confederacy. Events and developments during the period, however, were critical in shaping the Lone Star State as part of the antebellum South. By 1861 Texas was so like the other Southern states economically, socially, and politically that it joined them in secession[qv] and war. Antebellum Texans cast their lot with the Old South and in the process gave their state an indelibly Southern heritage.

When President Anson Jones[qv] lowered the flag of the republic for the last time in February 1846, the framework for the development of Texas over the next fifteen years was already constructed. The great majority of the new state's approximately 100,000 white inhabitants were natives of the South, who, as they settled in the eastern timberlands and south central plains, had built a life as similar as possible to that experienced in their home states. Their economy, dependent on agriculture, was concentrated first on subsistence farming and herding and then on production of cotton as a cash crop. This meant the introduction of what southerners called their "Peculiar Institution"—slavery.[qv] In 1846 Texas had more than 30,000 black slaves and produced an even larger number of bales of cotton (*see* COTTON CULTURE). Political institutions were also characteristically Southern. The Constitution of 1845,[qv] written by a convention in which natives of Tennessee, Virginia, and Georgia alone constituted a majority, depended heavily on Louisiana's fundamental law as well as on the existing Constitution of the Republic of Texas.[qv] As befitted an agricultural state led by Jacksonians, the constitution prohibited banking and required a two-thirds vote of the legislature to charter any private corporation. Article VIII guaranteed the institution of slavery.

With the foundations of their society in place and the turbulence of the republic behind them, Texans in 1846 anticipated years of expansion and prosperity. Instead, however, they found themselves and their state's interests heavily involved in the war between Mexico and the United States that broke out within a few months of annexation[qv] (see *also* MEXICAN WAR). Differences between the two nations arose from a variety of issues, but disagreement over the southwestern boundary of Texas provided the spark for war. Mexico contended that Texas reached only to the Nueces River, whereas after 1836 the republic had claimed the Rio Grande as the border. President James K. Polk, a Jacksonian Democrat from Tennessee, backed the Texans' claims, and in January 1846, after unsuccessful attempts to make the Rio Grande the boundary and settle other differences by diplomacy, he ordered Gen. Zachary Taylor[qv] to occupy the disputed area. In March Taylor moved to the Rio Grande across from Matamoros. Battles between his troops and Mexican soldiers occurred north of the river in May, and Congress, at Polk's request, declared war. Approximately 5,000 Texans served with United States forces in the conflict that followed, fighting for both General Taylor in northern Mexico and Gen. Winfield Scott on his campaign to capture Mexico City. In the Treaty of Guadalupe Hidalgo,[qv] which ended the war in February 1848, Mexico recognized Texas as a part of the United States and confirmed the Rio Grande as its border.

Victory in the Mexican War soon led to a dispute concerning the boundary between Texas and the newly acquired Mexican Cession. This conflict arose from the Lone Star State's determination to make the most of the Rio Grande as its western boundary by claiming an area reaching to Santa Fe and encompassing the eastern half of what is now New Mexico. In March 1848 the Texas legislature decreed the existence of Santa Fe County, and Governor George T. Wood[qv] sent Spruce M. Baird[qv] to organize the local government and serve as its first judge. The people of Santa Fe, however, proved unwilling to accept Texas authority, and United States troops in the area supported them. In July 1849, after failing to organize the county, Baird left. At the same time a bitter controversy was developing in Congress between representatives of the North and the South concerning the expansion of slavery into the territory taken from Mexico. The Texans' western boundary claims became involved in this larger dispute, and the Lone Star State was drawn into the crisis of 1850 on the side of the South.

President Zachary Taylor, who took office in March 1849, proposed to handle the Mexican Cession by omitting the territorial stage and admitting California and New Mexico directly into the Union. His policy angered southerners in general and Texans in particular. First, both California and New Mexico were expected to prohibit slavery, a development that would give the free states numerical superiority in the Union. Second, Taylor's approach in effect pitted the federal government against Texas claims to the Santa Fe area and promised to stop the expansion of slavery at the Lone Star State's western boundary. Southern extremists resolved to break up the Union before accepting the president's proposals. They urged Texas to stand firm on the boundary issue, and the Mississippi state legislature called for a convention in Nashville during June 1850 "to devise and adopt some means of resistance" to Northern aggression. Ultra-Southern spokesmen in Texas took up the cry, demanding that their state send delegates to Nashville and take all steps necessary to prove that it was not "submissionist."

In December 1849 the Texas legislature responded to the crisis with an act designating new boundaries for Santa Fe County, and Robert S. Neighbors[qv] was sent to organize the government there. The legislature also provided for the election in March 1850 of eight delegates to attend the Nashville convention for "consultation and mutual action on the subject of slavery and Southern Rights." By June, when Neighbors reported that the people of Santa Fe did not want to be part of Texas, the state appeared ready to take aggressive action. Moderation prevailed, however, in Washington, Nashville, and Texas. By September 1850 Congress had worked out a compromise to settle the crisis. After much wrangling, Senator James A. Pearce of Maryland proposed that the boundary between Texas and New Mexico be a line drawn east from the Rio Grande along the 32d parallel to the 103d meridian, then north to 36°30′, and finally east again to the 100th meridian. In return for its New Mexican claims, Texas would receive $10 million in United States bonds, half of which would be held to satisfy the state's public debt. Some Texans bitterly opposed the "Infamous Texas Bribery Bill," but extremism was on the wane across the state and the South as a whole. In Texas the crisis had aroused the Unionism of Sam Houston,[qv] the state's most popular

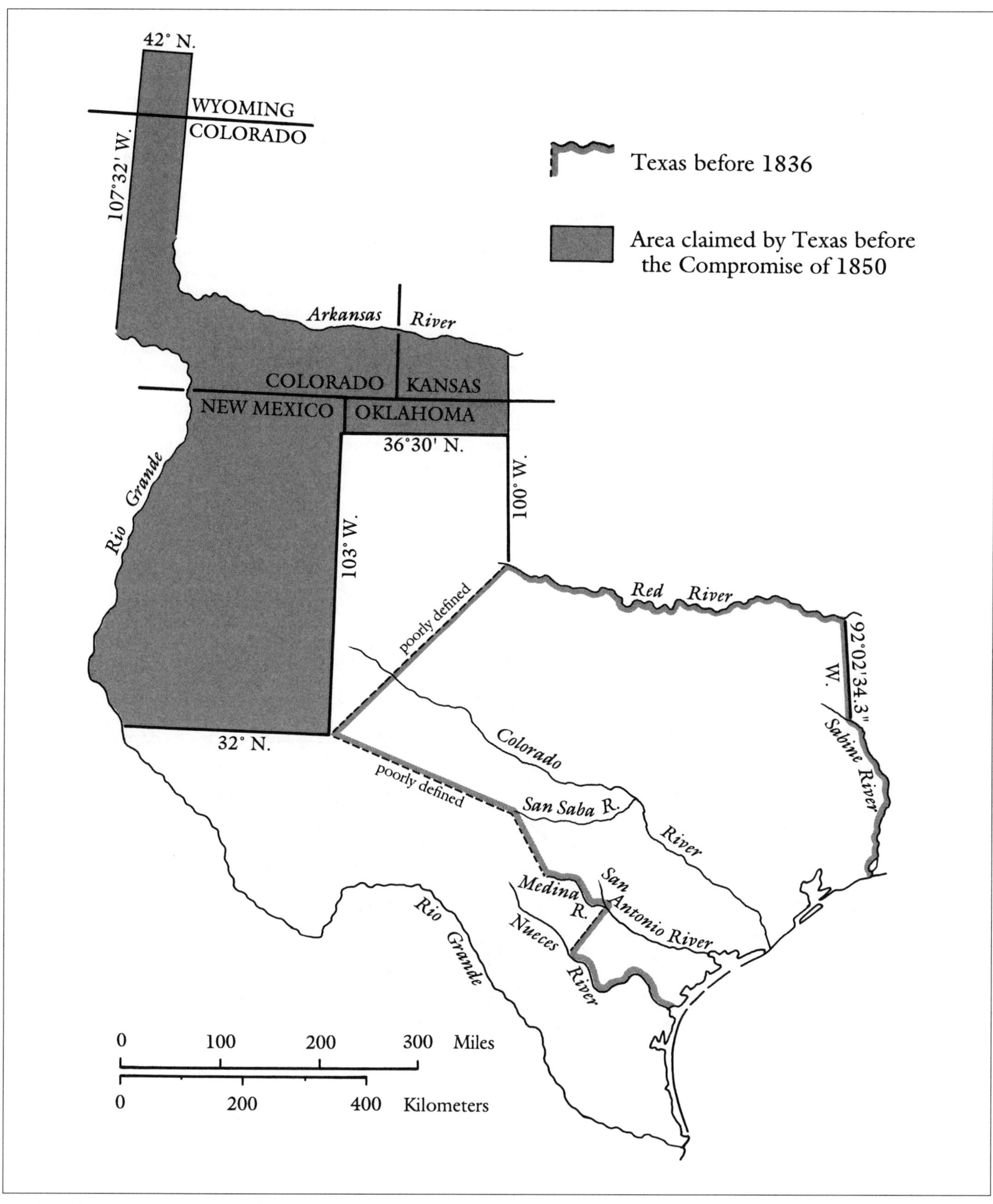

Boundary settlements of 1848 and 1850. Drawn by John Cotter. As both republic and young state, Texas declared its south and west boundary to be the Rio Grande from its source to its mouth. The Treaty of Guadalupe Hidalgo of 1848 declared the Rio Grande to El Paso to be the boundary between Texas and Mexico. As part of the Compromise of 1850, Texas relinquished its claim to territory in the present-day states of New Mexico, Colorado, Wyoming, Kansas, and Oklahoma in exchange for $10 million.

politician. He made fun of the election to choose delegates to the Nashville convention. The vote had been called too late to allow effective campaigning anyhow, and of those elected only former governor J. Pinckney Henderson[qv] actually attended the meeting in Tennessee. (Incidentally, in this same election Texans approved the permanent choice of Austin as state capital.) The Nashville convention, although it urged Texas to stand by its claim to New Mexico, generally adopted a moderate tone. In November 1850 Texans voted by a two-to-one margin to accept the Pearce Bill (*see* COMPROMISE OF 1850).

The crisis of 1850 demonstrated the existence of strong Unionist sentiment in Texas, but it also revealed that the Lone Star State, in spite of its location on the southwestern frontier, was identified with the Old South. Charles C. Mills of Harrison County summarized this circumstance perfectly in a letter to Governor Peter H. Bell[qv] during the crisis: "Texas having so recently come into the Union, should not be foremost to dissolve it, but I trust she will not waver, when the crisis shall come."

As the boundaries of antebellum Texas were being settled and its identity shaped during the first years of statehood, new settlers poured in. A state census in 1847 reported the population at 142,009. Three years later a far more complete United States census (the first taken in Texas) enumerated 212,592 people, excluding Indians,[qv] in the state. Immigrants arriving in North Texas came primarily from the upper South and states of the old Northwest such as Illinois. Settlers entering through the Marshall-Jefferson area and Nacogdoches were largely from the lower South. On the Gulf Coast, Galveston and Indianola served as entry points for many lower southerners. Numerous foreign-born immigrants, especially Germans, also entered through these ports during the late 1840s.

The Texas to which these migrants came was a frontier state in the classic sense. That is, it had a line of settlement advancing westward as pioneers populated and cultivated new land. Also, as in most American frontiers, settlers faced problems with Indians. By the late 1840s Texas frontiersmen had reached the country of the fierce Comanches and were no doubt relieved that, since annexation, the task of defending the frontier rested with the United States Army. In 1848–49 the army built a line of eight military posts from Fort Worth to Fort Duncan, at Eagle Pass on the Rio Grande. Within two years, under the pressure to open additional lands and do a better job of protecting existing settlements, federal forces built seven new forts approximately 100 miles to the west of the existing posts. This new line of defense, when completed in 1852, ran from Fort Belknap, on the Brazos River, to Fort Clark, at the site of present-day Brackettville. Conflict with the Comanches continued for the remainder of the decade as federal troops, joined at times by companies of Texas Rangers,[qv] sought to protect the frontier. They were never entirely successful, however, and Indian warfare continued after the Civil War. With the

Creek Nation,
October 26th 1851.

I, Sarah McClish, of the Chickasaw Nation, do relinquish my right, title, and all claim whatsoever, to seventeen negroes (17), in Texas, viz— six boys, 5 women, and 6 female children, named as follows: Bean, woman aged 38; Lorene, woman aged 17; Anna, aged 16; Nero, aged 14; Sambo, aged 12; Morris, aged 10; Philis, aged 8; Polly, aged 6; Sandy, aged 4; Samuel aged 1; Amanda, 5 month old; Dicy, aged 40; Lady, aged 20; Hannah, aged 8; Peggy, aged 6; Manuel, aged 4; Henry, aged 2; to Mrs Rebecca Hagerty, of Texas, for the sum of $800.00;

her
Sarah McClish
mark

In Witness
R. Lewis
W. F. Buckner

Record of slave sale, Creek Nation, October 26, 1851. Rebecca McIntosh Hawkins Hagerty Papers, CAH; CN 08001. Sarah McClish made her mark on this document recording her sale of seventeen slaves, including five women, six boys, and six girls, to Rebecca Hagerty "of Texas" for a total of $800. The oldest person Hagerty bought was Dicy, aged forty, and the youngest was Amanda, five months.

Mr. Polley's Plantation, Harrie's birthplace, *by Sarah Ann Lillie Bumstead Hardinge Daniels, ca. 1856. Watercolor, gouache, and graphite on paper. Courtesy Amon Carter Museum, Fort Worth, Texas; gift of Mrs. Lucinda Shastid. Many Texans aspired to the planter class in the antebellum years, yearning for a life of leisure. This primitive watercolor shows Joseph H. Polley's two-story house and slave cabins surrounded by snake fences. Three female members of his family lounge on porches. About fifteen slaves appear in the yard, some with baskets or pitchers on their heads. Cattle can be seen in the field to the left.*

Comanches and the lack of water and wood on the western plains both hampering its advance, the Texas frontier did not move during the 1850s beyond the seven forts completed at the onset of the decade. Areas immediately to the east of the military posts continued to fill, but the rush westward slowed. In 1860 the line of settlement ran irregularly from north to south through Clay, Young, Erath, Brown, Llano, Kerr, and Uvalde counties.

Important as it was to antebellum Texas, this western frontier was home to only a small fraction of the state's population. The great majority lived well to the east in areas where moving onto unclaimed land and fighting Indians were largely things of the past by 1846. These Texans, not frontiersmen in the traditional sense, were yet part of an extremely significant frontier—the southwesterly march of slaveholding, cotton-producing farmers and planters. "King Cotton" ruled the Old South's agricultural economy, and he came to rule antebellum Texas as well. Anglo-American settlers had sought from the beginning to build a plantation society in the region stretching from the Red River through the East Texas timberlands to the fertile soils along the Trinity, Brazos, Colorado, and lesser rivers that emptied into the Gulf of Mexico. During the 1850s this cotton frontier developed rapidly.

At the census of 1850, 95 percent of the 212,592 Texans lived in the eastern two-fifths of the state, an area the size of Alabama and Mississippi combined. Ten years later, although the state's population had grown to 604,215, the overwhelming majority still lived in the same region. The population had far greater ethnic diversity than was common elsewhere in the South. There were large numbers of Germans[qv] in the south central counties, many Mexican Americans from San Antonio southward, and smaller groups of Poles, Czechs,[qqv] and other foreign-born immigrants scattered through the interior. Nevertheless, natives of the lower South constituted the largest group of immigrants to Texas during the 1850s, and southerners headed three of every four households there in 1860. Like immigrants from the Deep South, slaves also constituted an increasingly large part of the Lone Star State's population (27 percent in 1850 and 30 percent in 1860). Their numbers rose from 58,161 to 182,566, a growth of 214 percent, during the decade.

The expansion of slavery correlated closely with soaring cotton production, which rose from fewer than 60,000 bales in 1850 to more than 400,000 in 1860. In 1850 of the nineteen counties having 1,000 or more slaves—ten in northeastern Texas and nine stretching inland along the Brazos and Colorado rivers—fifteen produced 1,000 or more bales of cotton. The census of 1860 reported sixty-four counties having 1,000 or more slaves, and all except eight produced 1,000 or more bales. These included, with the exception of an area in extreme Southeast Texas, virtually every county east of a line running from Fannin County, on the Red River, southwestward through McLennan County to Comal County and then along the San Antonio River to the Gulf. Only six counties in this area managed to grow at least 1,000 bales of cotton without a matching number of slaves.

Slavery and cotton thus marched hand-in-hand across antebellum Texas, increasingly dominating the state's agricultural economy. Plantations in Brazoria and Matagorda counties produced significant sugar crops, but elsewhere farmers and planters concentrated on cotton as a source of cash income. By 1860 King Cotton had the eastern two-fifths of Texas, excepting only the north central prairie area around Dallas and the plains south of the San Antonio River, firmly within his grasp.

Perhaps, as Charles W. Ramsdell[qv] suggested, the cotton frontier was approaching its natural limits in Texas during the 1850s. The soil and climate of western Texas precluded successful plantation agriculture, and proximity to Mexico, with its offer of freedom for runaways, reinforced these geographical limitations. In reality, however, regardless of these apparent natural boundaries, slavery and cotton had great potential for continued expansion in Texas after 1860. Growth had not ended anywhere in the state at that time, and the north central prairie area had not even been opened for development. The fertile soils of the Blackland Prairie and Grand Prairie counties would produce hundreds of thousands of bales of cotton once adequate transportation reached that far inland, and railroads would soon have met that need. The two prairie regions combined were more than three-fourths as large as the state of South Carolina but had only 6 percent as many slaves in 1860. The cotton frontier of antebellum Texas constituted a virtual empire for slavery, and such editors as John F. Marshall[qv] of the Austin *State Gazette* wrote confidently of the day when the state would have two million bondsmen or even more.

Only a minority of antebellum Texans, however, actually owned slaves and participated directly in the cash-crop economy. Only one family in four held so much as a single slave, and more than half of those had fewer than five bondsmen. Small and large planters, defined respectively as those owning ten to nineteen and twenty or more slaves, held well over half of the state's slaves in both 1850 and 1860. This planter class profited from investments in land, labor, and cotton and, although a decided minority even among slaveholders, provided the driving force behind the state's economy.

Agriculture developed rapidly in antebellum Texas, as evidenced by a steady expansion in the number of farms, the amount of improved acreage, the value of livestock, and the size of crops produced. Slave labor contributed heavily to that growth. On the other hand, during the 1850s Texas developed very slowly in terms of industry, commerce, and urban growth. In both 1850 and 1860 only about 1 percent of Texas family heads had manufacturing occupations. Texas industries in 1860 produced goods valued at $6.5 million, while, by contrast, Wisconsin, another frontier state that had entered the Union in 1846, reported nearly $28 million worth of manufactures. Commercial activity, retarded no doubt by inadequate transportation and the constitutional prohibition on banking (*see* BANKS AND BANKING), also occupied only a small minority (less than 5 percent) of Texans. With industry and commerce so limited, no urban area in the state reached a population of 10,000 during the antebellum years. In 1860 San Antonio (8,200), Galveston (7,307), Houston (4,800), and Austin (3,500) were the state's only "cities." By contrast, Milwaukee, Wisconsin, reported a population of 20,000 as early as 1850.

Antebellum Texans failed to diversify their economy for several reasons. Part of the explanation was geographical: climate and soil gave Texas an advantage over most regions of the United States, certainly those outside the South, in plantation agriculture and thus helped produce an overwhelmingly agricultural economy. Slavery appears also to have retarded the rise of industry and commerce. Slave labor made the plantation productive and profitable and reduced the need for the invention and manufacture of farm machinery. Planters concentrated on self-sufficiency and on the cultivation of cotton, a crop that quickly passed out of Texas for processing elsewhere with a minimum involvement of local merchants along the way. Opportunities for industry and commerce were thus reduced by the success of the plantation. Moreover, the planters, who were, after all, the richest and most enterprising men in Texas and who would have had to lead any move to diversify the economy, benefited enough financially and socially from combining land and slave labor that they generally saw no need to risk investments in industry or commerce.

Planters did have an interest in improving transportation in their state. From the 1820s onward Texans had utilized the major rivers from the Red River to the Rio Grande to move themselves and their goods and crops, but periodic low water, sand bars, and rafts of logs and brush made transportation by water highly unreliable. Moving supplies and cotton on Texas roads, which became quagmires in wet weather, was simply too slow and expensive. Thus, as the cotton frontier advanced inland, the movement of crops and supplies, never an easy matter, became increasingly difficult. Railroads[qv] offered a solution, albeit not without more financial difficulties than promoters could imagine. The state legislature chartered the state's first railroad, the Buffalo Bayou, Brazos and Colorado, in February 1850. Intended to run from Harrisburg, near Houston, westward to Alleyton, on the Colorado River, and tap the commerce on both the Brazos and Colorado, this road became operational to Stafford's Point in 1853 and reached its destination by 1860. Dozens of other railroads received charters after 1850, but for every one that actually operated six came to nothing.

Railroad promoters, faced with a difficult task and armed with arguments about the obvious importance of improved transportation in Texas, insisted that the state should subsidize construction. Their efforts to gain public aid for railroad corporations focused on obtaining land grants and using the United States bonds acquired in the settlement of the New Mexico boundary as a basis for loans. Some Texans, however, led by Lorenzo Sherwood, a New York–born lawyer who lived in Galveston, opposed the whole concept of state subsidies for private corporations. Sherwood developed a State Plan calling for the government in Austin to construct and own a thousand-mile network of railroads. Those who favored private promoters managed early in 1854 to obtain a law authorizing the granting of sixteen sections of land for each mile of road built to all railroads chartered after that date. However, the struggle between those who favored loans and supporters of the State Plan continued into 1856, as Sherwood won election to the legislature and continued to fight effectively for his ideas. His opponents finally seized upon statements Sherwood made against reopening the African slave trade, accused him of opposing slavery, and forced him under the threat of violence to resign from the legislature. Within less than a month, in July 1856, the legislature passed a bill authorizing loans of $6,000 to railroad companies for every mile of road built.

Antebellum Texans thus decided that private corporations encouraged by state aid would built their railroads. Progress was limited, however. By 1860 the state had approximately 400 miles of operating railroad, but almost all of it radiated from Houston. Major lines included the Buffalo Bayou, Brazos and Colorado, from Harrisburg to Alleyton through Houston; the Galveston, Houston and Henderson, from Galveston to Houston; and the Texas and New Orleans, from Houston to Orange through Beaumont. Only the San Antonio and Mexican Gulf Railway, which ran from Port Lavaca to Victoria, and the Southern Pacific Railroad (not to be confused with the future system of that name) in Harrison County did not connect in some fashion with Houston. Railroad building progressed slowly because antebellum Texas did not have the native capital to finance it, the industrial base to produce building materials, or the population and diversified economy to provide traffic the year around. At least the stage had been set, however, for building an adequate network of rail transportation after 1865.

Thus, as the cotton frontier of Texas developed during the 1850s, the state's economy increasingly mirrored that of the Deep South. A majority of Texans lived as small, nonslaveholding farmers, but plantation agriculture and slave labor produced the state's wealth and provided its economic leaders. At the same time, there was little development in terms of industry, commerce, urban growth, and transportation. With an economy of this nature and a Southern-born population predominant in most areas, antebellum Texas naturally developed social practices and institutions that also were Southern to the core.

Market Place and Gaol, Houston, Texas, March 20th, 1852, *by Thomas Flintoff, 1852. Watercolor. Courtesy Houston Metropolitan Research Center, Houston Public Library. The earliest images of Houston known to have been made at the scene by a professional artist are those by Thomas Flintoff. This view shows the market building, with lattice-covered openings for ventilation, and the two-story city hall, surmounted by a cupola. The buildings were built in 1840–41 on Market Place.*

Women in antebellum Texas found their role in society shaped by traditions that, while by no means unique to the South, were strongly entrenched in that region. The ideal female was a homemaker and mother, pious and pure, strong and hardworking, and yet docile and submissive. She was placed on a pedestal and admired, but she had no political rights and suffered serious disabilities before the law. Women could not, for example, serve on juries, act as lawyers, or witness a will. Texas women, however, did enjoy significant property rights. Married women retained title to property such as land and slaves owned before they wed, had community rights to all property acquired during a marriage, and had full title to property that came into their hands after divorce or the death of a husband. These rights allowed Texas women to head families, own plantations, and manage estates in ways that were anything but passive and submissive.

Antebellum Texans favored churches in the evangelical tradition of the Old South. Methodists far outnumbered other denominations. By 1860 the Methodist Episcopal Church, South, as it was called after the North-South split of 1844, had 30,661 members. Baptists constituted the second largest denomination, followed by the Presbyterian, Christian, Cumberland Presbyterian, Catholic, Lutheran, and Episcopal churches. These institutions provided spiritual and moral guidance and offered educational instruction as well. Moreover, religious activities brought people together in settings that encouraged friendly social interchange and relieved the isolation of rural life.

Education in antebellum Texas was largely a matter of private enterprise, both secular and church affiliated. At the most basic level, would-be teachers simply established common schools and offered primary and elementary instruction to children whose parents could pay tuition. More formal education took place in state-chartered institutions, which often bore names promising far more than they could deliver. Between 1846 and 1861 the Texas legislature chartered 117 schools, including forty academies, thirty colleges, and seven universities. Most of these institutions lasted only a few years, had relatively few students, and, regardless of their titles, offered little beyond secondary education. The University of San Augustine and Marshall University, for example, both chartered in 1842, had primary departments teaching reading, writing, and arithmetic. The quality of education at all levels in Texas schools suffered from a variety of problems, including the fact that teachers who were dependent for their pay on the good will of parents could not afford to be very demanding. Schools often covered their shortcomings and bolstered their academic reputations by holding public oral examinations that the whole community could attend. Parents and most observers greatly appreciated these events and overlooked the fact that generally they were watching rehearsed performances rather than true examinations.

Regardless of its doubtful quality, private school education lay beyond the means of most antebellum Texas families. In general only the well-to-do could afford to buy schooling for their children, a situation that conflicted with democratic ideals and growing American faith in education. Texans expressed considerable interest during the 1850s in establishing a free public school system. Action came, however, only after the legislature devised a scheme to establish a fund

Main building of Rutersville College, Rutersville, Texas. Completed 1842. Courtesy Mood-Heritage Museum, Southwestern University, Georgetown, Texas. Higher education flourished before the Civil War as churches established small colleges and academies. Rutersville College, a Methodist coeducational school, opened in 1840. The main building, pictured here, had a bell tower atop its second floor. The school granted thirty-six degrees between 1840 and 1856. By the latter year it had merged with the Texas Monumental and Military Institute.

that could be used for loans to promote railroad building, with the interest going to support public schools. In January 1854 the legislature set aside $2 million of the bonds received from the boundary settlement in 1850 (*see* BOUNDARIES OF TEXAS and COMPROMISE OF 1850) as a "Special School Fund." Two years later another act provided for loans from this fund to railroad corporations. Interest from the school fund was to go to the counties on a per-student basis to pay the salaries of public school teachers, but counties had to provide all the necessary buildings and equipment. Knowing that this would be expensive and doubtless feeling pressure from private school interests, the legislature permitted local authorities to hire teachers in existing educational institutions. It quickly became apparent that the interest from the school fund would be totally inadequate to do more than subsidize the schooling of children from indigent families. The private schools benefited, and public education remained only a dream. (*See also* HIGHER EDUCATION.)

Educational opportunities notwithstanding, literacy, at least as measured by census enumerators, was high in antebellum Texas. The state's many newspapers (three dailies, three triweeklies, and sixty-five weeklies by 1860) constituted the most widely available reading matter. Among the most influential publications were the *Telegraph and Texas Register*, the Clarksville *Northern Standard*, the Marshall *Texas Republican*, the Nacogdoches *Texas Chronicle*, the Austin *State Gazette*,[qqv] the Dallas *Weekly Herald* (*see* DALLAS *TIMES-HERALD*), and the Galveston *Daily News* (*see* GALVESTON *NEWS*). What the papers lacked in news-gathering facilities they made up for with colorful editors and political partisanship. Virtually anyone who cared to could find both information on current events and entertainment in an antebellum newspaper.

Texans had a notable variety of amusements. Amateur theater groups, debating societies, and music recitals, for example, provided cultural opportunities. Many other amusements were notably less genteel. Horse racing, gambling, and drinking were popular, the last to such a degree that the temperance crusade against liquor was by far the most important reform movement of the era. Cruder amusements often sparked violence, although antebellum Texans needed very little provocation. The constitution had outlawed duels, the Old South's traditional method of settling affairs of honor, but violence in Texas was generally more spontaneous and less stylized, anyhow. In June 1860, for example, a man named Johnson spotted on the street in Hempstead one McNair, with whom he had a long-standing quarrel. Firing three times from his second-floor hotel room window, he hit McNair in the neck, side, and thigh. As Johnson prepared to ride away, a crowd gathered around the dying McNair. "By God, a good shot that," one said.

Politics in antebellum Texas reflected the state's preeminently Southern economic and social structure. Institutionally, political arrangements were highly democratic by the standards of that era. The Constitution of 1845 permitted all adult white males, without regard to taxpaying or property-holding status, to vote and hold any state or local office. In practice, however, wealthy slaveholders dominated officeholding at all levels and provided the state's political leadership. Their control was democratic in that they were freely elected, and they governed without having to coerce nonslaveholders into supporting their policies. Nevertheless, leadership by a minority class whose status depended on the ownership of slaves introduced an element of aristocracy and gave a pro-Southern cast to antebellum Texas politics.

Virtually all of the men who governed Texas from 1846 to 1861 were identified with the Democratic party.[qv] "We are all Democrats," Guy M. Bryan[qv] wrote in 1845, "since the glorious victory of that party, who fearlessly espoused our cause and nailed the 'Lone Star' to the topmast of their noble ship." When the Whig party[qv] displayed a lack of enthusiasm for the Mexican War and supported President Zachary Taylor in denying Texas claims to New Mexico territory in 1849–50, Bryan's statement became even more accurate. The Democrats won every presidential and gubernatorial election between 1845 and 1861. Indeed, so complete was their domination that the closest contests during these years came as a result of intraparty divisions, usually with the towering figure of Sam Houston occupying center stage.

J. Pinckney Henderson easily won the first race for state governor in December 1845 and took office in February 1846. He presided over the transition from republic to state and spent the latter part of 1846 commanding Texas troops in Mexico. Worn out from the war and in failing health, Henderson declined in 1847 to run for reelection. He was succeeded by George T. Wood,[qv] a Trinity River planter who had the support of Sam Houston. Wood served from 1847 to 1849, as the dispute over the New Mexico boundary built to crisis proportions. During his term Texans participated in their first presidential election and gave Democrat Lewis Cass 69 percent of the vote in his contest with the Whig Zachary Taylor. Wood lost the governorship to Peter Hansborough Bell[qv] in 1849, probably because of lukewarm support from Houston and Bell's promise of a more aggressive policy on the boundary question. The Compromise of 1850, although considered a shameful surrender by some extremists, did not seriously injure Bell's pro-Southern reputation. He defeated four opponents in 1851, including the Whig Benjamin H. Epperson,[qv] and served a second term before resigning in 1853 to take a seat in Congress. In the meantime the Democratic presidential candidate, Franklin Pierce, carried Texas overwhelmingly in the election of 1852. The Whigs made their most serious bid for the governorship in 1853 with the candidacy of William B. Ochiltree.[qv] Democrats met this challenge by agreeing to support one man, Elisha M. Pease,[qv] rather than their usual multiplicity of candidates. Pease's first term was significant for efforts to start a public school system and encourage railroad building. It also marked the appearance of a new political party that offered the most serious threat to Democratic domination of state politics during the 1850s. The American (Know-Nothing) party,[qv] an antiforeign, anti-Catholic organization that had originated in the Northeast, appeared in Texas during 1855 and attracted many Whigs, whose party had disintegrated as a result of the Kansas-Nebraska Act in 1854. The Know-Nothings supported Lieutenant Governor David C. Dickson[qv] for governor in 1855 and forced the Democrats to call a hurried state convention and

Theatre at the Old Casino Club in San Antonio, *by Carl G. von Iwonski, ca. 1860. Oil on canvas. 9½″ × 14″. Courtesy Witte Museum, San Antonio. The Casino Club, founded in 1854, served as the social and cultural center of the German community in San Antonio.*

unify in support of Governor Pease. The new party had considerable success in legislative and local elections, but Pease defeated Dickson with relative ease. The Know-Nothings lost badly in their support of Millard Fillmore during the presidential race of 1856 and rapidly withered into insignificance thereafter.

During Pease's second term (1855–57), Texas politics came to focus on pro- and anti-Houston issues as they had not since the end of the republic. Senator Houston's consistent Unionism in the crisis of 1850 and in voting against the Kansas-Nebraska Act greatly irritated ultra-Southern Democrats in Texas. A flirtation with the Know-Nothings had the same effect. Believing that he would not be reelected to the Senate when his term ended in 1859, Houston decided to run for governor in 1857 as an independent. The regular Democrats nominated Hardin R. Runnels,[qv] a native Mississippian with strong states'-rights beliefs, and a bitter campaign followed. Houston presented himself as a champion of the Union and his opponents as disunionists, while regular Democrats said that Old Sam was a Free-Soil traitor to Texas. Runnels won by a vote of 32,552 to 23,628, handing Houston the only defeat he ever suffered in a major political campaign. As governor, Runnels pursued an aggressive policy toward Indians in Northwest Texas, and there was more bloodshed on the frontier in 1858–59 than at any other time since 1836. The Comanches, although pushed back, mounted destructive raids on exposed settlements in 1859, creating considerable dissatisfaction with the Runnels administration. Also, during Runnels's term sectional tensions increased as the governor endorsed an extreme version of states' rights, and leading Democrats, including John Marshall,[qv] state party chairman and editor of the Austin *State Gazette,* advocated ultra-Southern policies such as reopening the African slave trade.

These developments under Runnels set the stage for another bitter and exciting gubernatorial contest in 1859. The regular Democrats renominated Runnels and Lieutenant Governor Francis R. Lubbock[qv] on an ultra-Southern platform, while Houston and Edward Clark[qv] opposed them by running as Independent or Union Democrats. This time, in his last electoral contest, Houston defeated Runnels, 36,227 to 27,500. The victory may have resulted in part from a lack of pro-Southern extremism among Texas voters, but Houston's personal popularity and the failure of Runnels's frontier policy played key roles, too. In any case, the state legislature's choice of Louis T. Wigfall[qv] as United States senator only two months after the gubernatorial election demonstrated that Unionism by no means had control in Texas. Wigfall, a native of South Carolina, was a fire-eating secessionist and one of Houston's bitterest enemies in Texas.

Houston's inaugural address, which he delivered publicly rather than to the hostile legislature, concluded with a plea for moderation. "When Texas united her destiny with that of the United States," he said, "she entered not into the North, nor South. Her connection was not sectional, but national." The governor was at least partly correct about the attitude at the time of annexation, but by 1860 Texas had become so much a part of the Old South that not even Sam Houston

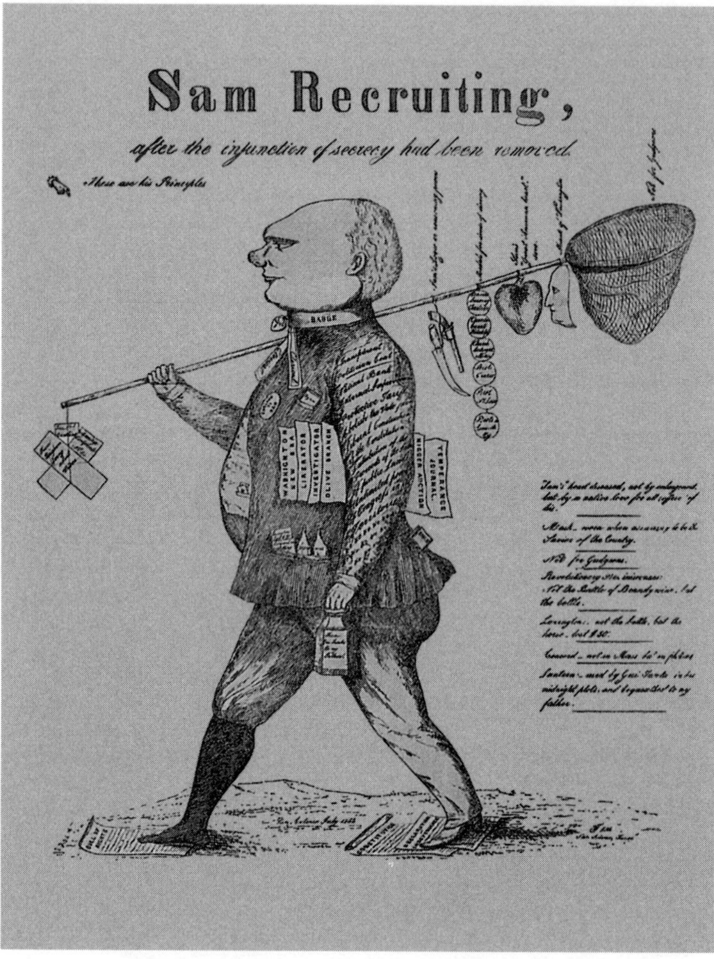

Sam Recruiting, after the injunction of secrecy had been removed, *1855. Lithograph by Wilhelm C. A. Thielepape. Broadsides Collection, CAH; CN 00694. In 1854 the American (Know-Nothing) party became active in Texas, and Houston adopted some of its tenets. The reference to secrecy in this cartoon alludes to Houston's connection with the party, which was in many ways a secret society.*

could restrain the state's rush toward secession. Ultrasoutherners controlled the Democratic state convention in 1860 and sent a delegation headed by Runnels and Lubbock to the national convention in Charleston, South Carolina. Rather than accept a platform favoring Stephen A. Douglas, the northern Democrat who called for popular sovereignty to decide the matter of slavery in the territories, the Texans joined other Deep South delegations in walking out of the convention. This step opened a split in the Democratic party that soon resulted in the nominations of Douglas by the Northern wing and John C. Breckinridge by the Southern. In the meantime the Republican party[qv] nominated Abraham Lincoln on a platform opposing the spread of slavery, and conservatives from the upper South formed a Constitutional Union party[qv] aimed at uniting those who wished to avoid disunion. Sam Houston received serious consideration for the presidential nomination of the new party but lost to John Bell of Tennessee.

Regular Democrats in Texas supported Breckinridge and threatened immediate secession if the "Black Republican" Abraham Lincoln won. The Opposition, as those who opposed the Democrats were now called, turned to Bell and the Constitutional Unionists in the hope of preventing disunion. This group, which generally sought to carry on the traditional unionism of the Whigs, Know-Nothings, and Houston Independent Democrats, did not oppose slavery or Southern interests. They simply argued that secession amounted to revolution and would probably hasten the destruction of slavery rather than protect it. A minority from the outset, the Opposition saw their cause weakened further during the late summer of 1860 by an outbreak of public hysteria known as the Texas Troubles.[qv] The panic began with a series of ruinous fires in North Texas. Spontaneous ignition of phosphorous matches due to extremely hot weather may have caused the fires. Several masters, however, forced their slaves to confess to arson, and Texans decided that a massive abolitionist-inspired plot threatened to destroy slavery and devastate the countryside. Slave and white suspects alike fell victim to vigilante action before the panic subsided in September. "It is better," said one citizen of Fort Worth, "for us to hang ninety-nine innocent (suspicious) men than to let one guilty one pass." (See also SLAVE INSURRECTIONS.)

In November 1860 Breckinridge defeated Bell in Texas by a vote of 47,458 to 15,463, carrying every county in the state except three—Bandera, Gillespie, and Starr. Abraham Lincoln received no votes in Texas, but free-state votes made him the president-elect, scheduled to take office in March 1861. His victory signaled the beginning of a spontaneous popular movement that soon swept the Lone Star State out of the Union. True to its antebellum heritage as a growing part of the cotton frontier, Texas stood ready in 1860 to join the other Southern states in secession and war.

BIBLIOGRAPHY: Walter L. Buenger, *Secession and the Union in Texas* (Austin: University of Texas Press, 1984). Randolph B. Campbell and Richard G. Lowe, *Wealth and Power in Antebellum Texas* (College Station: Texas A&M University Press, 1977). Abigail Curlee, A Study of Texas Slave Plantations, 1822–1865 (Ph.D. dissertation, University of Texas, 1932). Earl Wesley Fornell, *The Galveston Era: The Texas Crescent on the Eve of Secession* (Austin: University of Texas Press, 1961). Llerena B. Friend, "The Texan of 1860," *Southwestern Historical Quarterly* 62 (July 1958). Robert Kingsley Peters, Texas: Annexation to Secession (Ph.D. dissertation, University of Texas at Austin, 1977). Charles W. Ramsdell, "The Natural Limits of Slavery Expansion," *Mississippi Valley Historical Review* 16 (September 1929). Ernest Wallace, *Texas in Turmoil: The Saga of Texas, 1849–1875* (Austin: Steck-Vaughn, 1965).

Randolph B. Campbell

ANTELOPE. The American antelope that appear in Texas (*Antilocapra americana* and *A. mexicana*) are only two of the five subspecies of the pronghorn antelope that occur in North America. A mature buck of the Texas pronghorn stands about three feet tall at the shoulder and rarely exceeds 110 pounds. Adult females average about eighty-four pounds. The animals are generally tan. The bucks have a black patch at the corner of the jaw. All pronghorns have a white rump patch that is highly visible from a substantial distance. Both sexes have horns that they shed annually. They are the only hollow-horned ruminant in North America that sheds its horns every year. Before the European settlement of West Texas, antelope ranged over all of Texas west of the ninety-seventh meridian. At the beginning of the twentieth century they occurred as far north as the Wichita Falls area and as far east as Alice. They shared the same range as the buffalo,[qv] and numbers were estimated in the millions in the Trans-Pecos and Panhandle.[qqv] Later, hunted for food and starved as the result of cattle overgrazing, populations were in danger of extinction. The first comprehensive survey of pronghorns, made in 1924, showed a population of only 2,407, with 692 occurring in the Trans-Pecos. At that time the hunting season was closed. The population subsequently improved, and controlled hunting was established in 1944. From 1977 to 1991, under managed conditions, the population averaged 18,500, 70 percent in the Trans-Pecos, 20 percent in the Panhandle, and 10 percent in the Lower Plains. With the dissemination of research findings regarding life history, range use, ecology, behavior, restocking, and proper harvest, the Texas pronghorn is thriving.

BIBLIOGRAPHY: Danny A. Swepston and Tommy L. Hailey, *Texas Pronghorns* (Austin: Texas Parks and Wildlife Department, 1991).

Art Leatherwood

ANTELOPE, TEXAS (Coryell County). Antelope was six miles north of Copperas Cove in southwestern Coryell County. Settlers arrived in the area as early as the 1850s. The school at Antelope grew as the Refuge, Table Rock, Salem, Eliga, Ross, and House Creek schools were consolidated with it. In 1920 the Antelope school had three rooms and ten grades. Residents of Antelope had to leave their homes in the early 1940s in order to make room for the Fort Hood military reservation.

BIBLIOGRAPHY: Coryell County Genealogical Society, *Coryell County, Texas, Families, 1854–1985* (Dallas: Taylor, 1986). Anice Thompson Vance et al., comps., *Antelope Community, Coryell County, Texas* (Temple, Texas, 1992). *Vivian Elizabeth Smyrl*

ANTELOPE, TEXAS (Jack County). Antelope is near the intersection of Loop 187, U.S. Highway 281, and Farm Road 175, twenty miles northwest of Jacksboro in northwestern Jack County. In 1858 Antelope received a post office, and in 1859 B. F. Spear was postmaster. The community was in a ranching area near the West Fork of the Trinity River and became an overnight stop and supply point on the cattle trails. In 1875 Walter S. Jones platted and surveyed the six blocks around the town square, but the papers were not filed until 1889. By 1890 Antelope had a population of 300, a hotel, several general stores, Methodist and Baptist churches, a school, and daily stages to Henrietta and Graham for a two-dollar fare. A saw and grist mill operated in the community until 1900, when a cotton mill replaced the gristmill. The area was a popular overnight stop for drummers. By 1914 the population was 200. The community still had several general stores, a physician, and a blacksmith but no hotel or mill. The population was 166 in the 1940s. The Mullins Brothers general store, which had opened in 1883, was still in business, and the community had a garage and filling station, the Methodist and Baptist churches, and a school. The community's economy was supported by stock raising and nearby oilfields. In the 1980s the population fell to sixty-five, where it remained in 1990. Two businesses remained in the community.

BIBLIOGRAPHY: Ida Lasater Huckabay, *Ninety-Four Years in Jack County* (Austin: Steck, 1949; centennial ed., Waco: Texian Press, 1974). Kathleen E. and Clifton R. St. Clair, eds., *Little Towns of Texas* (Jacksonville, Texas: Jayroe Graphic Arts, 1982). *Lisa C. Maxwell*

ANTELOPE CREEK (Archer County). Antelope Creek rises just west of Holliday in north central Archer County (at 33°49′ N, 98°44′ W) and runs north eight miles to its mouth on the Wichita River, three miles south of Iowa Park in Wichita County (at 33°54′ N, 98°42′ W). The stream, which is intermittent in its upper reaches, traverses an area of rolling hills surfaced by clay and sandy loams that support scrub brush, mesquite, cedar, and grasses. For most of the county's history the area has been used as rangeland and for farming.

____ (Briscoe County). Antelope Creek rises east of Silverton in east central Briscoe County (at 34°32′ N, 100°59′ W) and flows northeast for seven miles to its mouth on the Prairie Dog Town Fork of the Red River in Hall County (at 34°38′ N, 100°56′ W). The surrounding area, once a part of the Shoe Bar Ranch,[qv] is now the site of Antelope Flat, a sparse ranching community. The creek crosses an area of flat to gently sloping terrain and shallow to moderately deep soils over limy earth. The vegetation consists mainly of mesquite and grasses.

____ (Carson County). Antelope Creek starts where its east and west forks join, northwest of Panhandle in northwestern Carson County (at 35°35′ N, 101°32′ W), and flows north through a ranching and oil area for twelve miles to its mouth on the Canadian River, east of Sanford in southwestern Hutchinson County (at 35°44′ N, 101°29′ W). The stream was once a part of the LX Ranch.[qv] It gave its name to the Antelope Creek Focus, the common term used by archeologists for sites of pre-Columbian Indian slab-house ruins in the general area. The stream crosses an area of rolling to steeply sloping terrain and loamy and clayey soils. The vegetation includes juniper, cacti, and sparse grasses.

____ (Lampasas County). Antelope Creek rises four miles west of Lometa in northwest Lampasas County (at 31°18′ N, 98°27′ W) and runs southwest for ten miles to its mouth on the Colorado River, five miles west of Lometa (at 31°12′ N, 98°32′ W). North Antelope Creek rises one mile east of Scallorn in southeast Mills County (at 31°18′ N, 98°30′ W) and runs southeast six miles. The two creeks join near the county line in Lampasas County (at 31°16′ N, 98°30′ W). Antelope Creek is intermittent in its upper reaches. It crosses an area of steep slopes and benches and flat to rolling terrain surfaced by sandy and clay loams that support juniper, oak, live oak, mesquite, elm, and grasses.

____ (Nolan County). Antelope Creek rises twenty miles northwest of Blackwell in southwest Nolan County (at 32°07′ N, 100°30′ W) and flows southeast for fourteen miles before emptying into Oak Creek 1½ miles southwest of Blackwell in northeast Coke County (at 32°04′ N, 100°20′ W). The vegetation along the creek's course includes water-tolerant hardwoods, conifers, and various grasses. The creek flows through flat terrain with locally shallow depressions; soil beds consist of expansive clays.

____ (San Saba County). Antelope Creek rises nine miles northwest of Richland Springs in northwestern San Saba County (at 31°22′ N, 99°04′ W) and flows northeast for 12½ miles to its mouth on the Colorado River, which forms the Mills county line (at 31°28′ N, 99°00′ W). The creekbed crosses an area of moderately to steeply sloping hills with live oak, Ashe juniper, mesquite, and grasses growing in clayey and sandy loam soils.

____ (Shackelford County). Antelope Creek rises southwest of Antelope Hills in northwest Shackelford County (at 32°55′ N, 99°23′ W) and runs northwest for seven miles to its mouth on the Clear Fork of the Brazos River east of the Whistler oilfield (at 32°56′ N, 99°28′ W). It traverses an area of steep slopes and benches surfaced by clay loam that supports juniper, live oak, mesquite, and grasses.

____ (Throckmorton County). Antelope Creek rises nine miles northwest of Throckmorton in northwest Throckmorton County (at 33°20′ N, 99°16′ W) and runs northwest for eight miles to its mouth on Millers Creek Reservoir, in southeast Baylor County (at 32°25′ N, 99°22′ W). It crosses an area of steep slopes and benches surfaced by shallow clay loams that support juniper, live oak, mesquite, and grasses.

ANTELOPE CREEK PHASE. Antelope Creek phase is the cultural designation assigned to a series of prehistoric sites in the upper Texas and Oklahoma panhandles utilized by semisedentary, bison-hunting, and horticultural groups during a period of aridity between A.D. 1200 and 1500. General similarities in architecture, subsistence, and artifact assemblages indicate that the Antelope Creek people participated in the Plains Village horizon, which included many bison-hunting and horticultural village societies with similar adaptations resident in the mixed-grass prairies extending from north central Texas to North Dakota. The Antelope Creek phase and adjacent Buried City complex (found along Wolf Creek in the northeastern Texas Panhandle) are the two southwesternmost societies of the Plains Village horizon and the only two to reside in contiguous-room, pueblo-like villages and to employ stone masonry routinely in the foundations and walls of their structures. Village sites attributed to these two societies are generally riverine and extend from Tule Creek below Palo Duro Canyon[qv] north to the North Canadian River valley in the Oklahoma panhandle and across the width of the Texas Panhandle.

The first excavation, conducted in 1907 by T. L. Eyerly at the "Buried City" south of Perryton, drew widespread attention to village ruins on the Plains. Other early fieldwork consisted mainly of reconnaissance surveys by Warren Moorehead of Phillips Academy, Andover, Massachusetts, Ronald Olson of the American Museum of Natural History, J. Alden Mason of the Pennsylvania Museum, and Floyd V. Studer[qv] of the Panhandle-Plains Historical Museum.[qv] Most of these studies attempted to examine cultural influences on areas between the Southwestern Puebloan and the Mississippian mound builders. The diligent work of William C. Holden,qv of Texas Tech, during the 1930s at Tarbox Ruin, Antelope Creek 22 Ruin, and Saddleback Ruin in the Canadian River valley demonstrated the Plains orientation of the phase. Considerable information on the artifact assemblage and village structure was gained from the Work Projects Administrationqv excavations (1938–41) at eight sites in Texas (including the type sites of Antelope Creek 22 and Alibates Ruin 28, north of Amarillo), and the 1964 salvage work at sites within Lake Meredithqv along the Canadian River. Other important excavations in the Canadian River valley of Texas were conducted at the Sanford, Roper, Pickett, Cottonwood Ruins, and Jack Allen sites, sponsored by the Panhandle-Plains Historical Museum;qv excavations in three ruins along Big Blue Creek and the Buried City by the Texas Archeological Society;qv work at Landergin Mesa, north of Vega, by the Texas Historical Commission;qv and surveys around Lake Meredith by the Bureau of Reclamation. In the Oklahoma panhandle, excavations have focused on the Stamper Site, McGrath Site, and Two Sisters Site, in the vicinity of Guymon.

The first major interpretive synthesis of the Antelope Creek phase was developed by Alex Krieger (1946), who systematically described the cultural remains, employed the Midwest Taxonomic System (which defines cultures on the basis of artifact similarities) to coin the term "Antelope Creek focus" for sites in Texas, and grouped them with similar materials in adjacent regions into a poorly defined "Panhandle aspect." Subsequently, Lintz (1986) focused on examining intracultural variability for twenty-eight excavated sites in a fifty-mile segment of the Canadian River valley centered on Lake Meredith.

The age of the Antelope Creek phase is established from more than eighty radiocarbon dates, five archeomagnetic dates, and five obsidian-hydration dates. In addition, eighteen Puebloan ceramic types linked to tree-ring dates in their source areas permit the cross-dating of additional site contexts. The phase abruptly started by about A.D. 1200 and terminated by A.D. 1500. Sites immediately predating the Antelope Creek phase have not been identified; however, general cultural similarities in cord-marked ceramics suggest that Antelope Creek may have developed from an indigenous "Woodland Period" manifestation present in the Panhandleqv by A.D. 400. The extensive collection of dates has allowed the delineation of some trends in culture change through time for the Antelope Creek–phase components in the Canadian River valley.

The excavation emphasis on architectural sites has produced a distorted image of Antelope Creek settlement patterns, since activities at nonarchitectural sites are poorly understood. Three classes of architectural sites have been delineated: multiple family hamlets with twenty or more "residential rooms," single-family "homesteads," and subhomesteads or field-hut sites that lack residential rooms. Each of these site types may also be associated with a series of smaller architectural features. The structures at any of these site types may consist of one or more free-standing buildings, or small-to-large contiguous-room blocks made of multiple, repetitious residential rooms and other associated room types. Contiguous-room structures tend to be earlier than single-room buildings.

Typically, an Antelope Creek residential room is a large (135 to 650 square-foot) rectangular building, oriented roughly in cardinal directions with a low, eastward-extended entryway. The walls often have unshaped, vertically placed, stone-slab foundations either aligned with the wall axis or, in the Buried City area, set perpendicular to the wall. Upper walls may be of horizontal masonry or adobe.qv The roof configuration is uncertain but might have been flat or hipped with grass thatch. Four interior roof-support posts often occur around a central hearth. The floor level of residential structures is a foot or more below the ground surface, with the distinctive presence of slightly elevated plastered activity areas or benches flanking a depressed work-area "channel" extending east–west through the central third of the room. Pit features or bins may be present on the benches. Many residential rooms contain a dais, or platform-altar, located within the channel against the west wall or recessed into the west wall. The intact extended entryways with polished stones flanking the low tunnels at Alibates Ruin 28 indicate that access was gained by crawling or stooping.

Other auxiliary rooms include small (75 to 430 square-foot) circular to rectangular areas. These are rarely semisubterranean, but construction methods are similar to those used in the wall and foundations of residential rooms, except that they lack the distinctive central channel and roof-support posts. Some of these rooms may contain interior hearths or storage pits, but most do not. The entrance was gained through ground-level or upper-wall openings. In addition, extramural slab-lined cists, hearths, and storage pits are relatively common.

Burials occur either inside rooms, in exterior midden areas, or in defined cemeteries located 150 to 300 feet from structures. Burials are often flexed single interments beneath slabs. The occurrence of burials above floor levels within a six-foot-tall mound covering a contiguous room structure at Alibates Ruin 28 suggests that wall remnants in abandoned buildings served as mnemonic markers for burials. Few burials display evidence of violence; although at the Footprint Site (Lake Meredith) several disarticulated individuals occurred on the house floor, and a cluster of ten skulls was intrusive to the burned structure. Three ossuary pits inside the same room contained seven to ten individuals interred with Antelope Creek–phase artifacts. The cranial pile may comprise trophy skulls obtained in retaliation for hostile raids. Grave goods are rare, but when present reflect gender-related utilitarian tool kits. No significant status differentiation is evident from the grave goods.

The economy is based on a hunting-gathering-horticulture pattern. Bison was the preferred game, followed by deer and antelope; however, a broad exploitation pattern may be inferred from a wide range of small mammals, amphibians, reptiles, fish, clams, and waterfowl. Most bones are extensively smashed, indicating the extraction of marrow and bone grease. A wide range of charred wild and domestic plant remains has been found in small quantities. These include hackberry, mesquite, plums, cattail stems, persimmons, prickly pear, purslane, goosefoot, grass seeds, sunflower seeds, corn, squash, and beans. Local foods may have been supplemented by products obtained from trading blanks and nodules of the local chert resources. The occurrence of extensive quarry pits at the Alibates Flint Quarries,qv northeast of Amarillo, and caches of large, thin bifaces at the Alibates Ruin document the intensive prehistoric mining and manufacturing occurring during the Antelope Creek phase.

The artifacts from Antelope Creek–phase sites reflect specialized tool kits for mundane activities. The hunting and animal-processing kits consist of an abundance of small side-notched and unnotched arrow points; alternately beveled, diamond-shaped, and oval knives; end and side scrapers; guitar-pick–shaped scrapers or preforms; gravers; bone awls, pins, and spatulate tools; bone wrenches; freshwater clamshell scrapers; hammerstones and anvil stones; globular, cord-marked (or fabric-impressed) pots; and perhaps scored-rib rasps. Horticultural and construction implements are best represented by an abundance of socketed hoes, "squash knives," and digging-stick tips made from bison scapulae and leg bones. Domesticated and wild seeds were ground on basin-shaped stone slabs and one-handed manos. Woodworking implements are suggested by drills, scrapers, gravers, expedient flake knives and rarely hafted axes. Stone and bone or wood tool manufacturing is represented by the presence of hammerstones, antler billets, pressure flakers, shaft straighteners, awl sharpeners, abrading stones, biface caches, and abundant chipping debris. Evidence of weaving and basketry is represented by a few charred, coiled baskets, bone needles, awls, and sherd spindle whorls. Little is known about Antelope Creek–phase arts or religion. Elbow and tubular pipes are relatively common. Pecked rock art at hamlet sites depicts human footprints, quadrupeds, stick figures, and bas-relief turtles. Occasional building stones and thin bifacial knives are smeared with red hematite.

Quantities of trade materials are present on many Antelope Creek–phase sites. Sites postdating A.D. 1350 on the average show a 4,600 percent increase in the occurrence of trade goods over the earlier sites. Most materials are from the Southwestern Pueblos, where exotic painted ceramics and lithic resources occur; foreign objects from the Plains may be more difficult to identify and are underreported. Trade goods from the west include eighteen types of Southwestern ceramics, turquoise beads and pendants, obsidian nodules and tools, marine-shell beads (both disc and whole *Olivella* shells), conch-shell gorgets, conus-shell tinklers, and tubular pipes. Trade goods from the Central Plains may be represented by some collared-rim ceramic vessels and Niobrara jasper, whereas East Texas influences are represented by rare Caddoan ceramics. The trade goods seldom occur in special settings (as grave goods or in platform-altar contexts), and they are mostly redundant with indigenous tool forms and functions. For example, more than 4,100 Southwestern obsidian flakes were recovered from Alibates Ruin 28, located less than a half mile from the Alibates chert quarries. The redundancy in trade and the marked increase in frequency suggest that the goods may represent gifts used to solidify reciprocal relations that may have extended to trade in tobacco and staple foods that reduced local risks of economic failure.

The Antelope Creek phase was able to flower on the High Plains during drought because of fossil springwater reserves that continued to flow from the Ogallala Aquifer. The people were able to capitalize on local conditions and develop a mode of living similar to that of groups to the north and east. The change in architecture from contiguous room structures to one-room buildings may reflect greater periods of seasonal mobility and shorter duration of village occupation. Shifts in settlement toward springs, the intensification of trade in redundant goods and perhaps foods, and intercultural raiding are all regarded as attempts by Antelope Creek people to maintain a stable village life while coping with deteriorating climatic conditions. Worse droughts, coupled with the arrivals of Apachean groups around A.D. 1500, ended this adaptation. Cultural continuity with modern Indian groups is tenuous; presumably the Antelope Creek people moved northeastward and merged with similar Plains Caddoan peoples, such as the Pawnees or Wichitas.

Large collections of artifacts and records from all of the WPA excavations and many other projects are on file at the Panhandle-Plains Historical Museum, Canyon. Artifacts from W. C. Holden's early studies and F. E. Green's excavations at sites within Lake Meredith are at Texas Tech University, Lubbock. Artifacts from other excavated sites within Lake Meredith are at the Texas Archeological Research Laboratory, University of Texas at Austin. Most materials from the Oklahoma panhandle sites are at the Stovall Museum, University of Oklahoma, Norman. Small collections and notes from other surveys are on file at the National Park Service, Fritch, Texas; the American Museum of Natural History, New York; the Arizona State Museum, Tucson; the University of Pennsylvania Museum, Pittsburgh, and the No Man's Land Museum, Goodwell, Oklahoma.

BIBLIOGRAPHY: Alex D. Krieger, *Culture Complexes and Chronology in Northern Texas, with Extension of Puebloan Datings to the Mississippi Valley* (University of Texas Publication 4640 [Austin, 1946]). Christopher Lintz, *Architecture and Community Variability within the Antelope Creek Phase of the Texas Panhandle* (Norman: Oklahoma Archaeological Survey, 1986).

Christopher Lintz

ANTELOPE DRAW (Brewster County). Antelope Draw begins about twelve miles east of Alpine in northern Brewster County (at 30°22′ N, 103°34′ W) and runs northeast for eighteen miles to its mouth on Coyanosa Draw (at 30°39′ N, 103°20′ W) in western Pecos County. The desert grassland vegetation along the draw includes blue grama and other gramas, tobosa grass, bluestems, and scattered clumps of sacahuiste. Desert scrub has invaded the heavily grazed area, however; plants such as lechuguilla, allthorn, creosote bush, and mesquite are very much in evidence. Antelope Draw is among a number of land features in this region named for the pronghorn antelope, which were at one time extremely abundant here. Although pronghorns were hunted almost out of existence in the late 1800s, their numbers have recovered somewhat, so that they may again be seen grazing along the course of Antelope Draw.

____ (Hudspeth County). Antelope Draw begins 1½ miles east of Tepee Butte in west central Hudspeth County (at 31°40′ N, 105°42′ W) and runs northeast for thirty-two miles to its mouth on Eightmile Draw, four miles east of Hueco Station (at 31°43′ N, 105°15′ W). The stream that flows through the draw is intermittent in its upper reaches. It traverses an area of steep to gentle slopes surfaced by variable soil that supports scrub brush and grasses.

ANTELOPE GAP. Antelope Gap is a notch between two summits 5½ miles northwest of Lometa and one-half mile east of U.S. Highway 183 in northern Lampasas County (at 31°17′ N, 98°27′ W). The area is characterized by steeply to moderately sloping hills and thin, stony, sandy and clay loams that support grasses and open stands of live oak, mesquite, and Ashe juniper.

ANTELOPE GAP, TEXAS. Antelope Gap was located on North Antelope Creek in southern Mills County, thirteen miles southeast of Goldthwaite on U.S. Highway 183. It was named after a nearby pass in Lampasas County through which the main branch of Antelope Creek runs. Some sources claim that antelope herds were abundant in the area until around 1900. The community was settled around 1884 in what was then Lampasas County. A flag stop and siding on the Gulf, Colorado and Santa Fe Railway was built for the surrounding ranching section and named Antelope Gap. When Mills County was established in 1887, Antelope Gap fell within the boundaries of the new county. A post office was established there in 1892. By 1896 the community, which was chiefly engaged in livestock raising, had an estimated population of seventy-five, a district school, a union church, a cotton gin, and a gristmill; and a rock mill was in operation on the Colorado River some eight miles distant. The post office was discontinued in 1914, and the railroad stop was abandoned sometime after 1920. As of 1952 Antelope Gap was described as an active community. Its population has not been listed in the *Texas Almanac* since 1904.

Alice J. Rhoades

ANTELOPE HILLS. The Antelope Hills are located five miles west of Fort Griffin State Historical Park[qv] in northern Shackelford County (at 32°56′ N, 99 °23′ W) and may take their name from nearby Antelope Creek. With an elevation of 1,748 feet they rise ninety-eight feet above the surrounding terrain. The area is marked by steep slopes and benches surfaced by shallow clay loam that supports juniper, live oak, mesquite, and grasses.

ANTELOPE MESA. Antelope Mesa is a half mile west of Gemelo Mesa in east central Presidio County (at 29°58′ N, 103°55′ W). With an elevation of 4,826 feet above sea level, its summit rises 594 feet over Paradise Valley, which runs along its southeastern edge. The mesa is formed of sandstone, tuff, and conglomerate. Loose rubble covers its surface. It stands in an area of desert mountain terrain cut by numerous canyons. Area vegetation consists primarily of sparse grasses, cacti, and desert scrub of conifers and oaks.

ANTELOPE MOUND. Antelope Mound, also known as Antelope Hill, is six miles north of Copperas Cove in southern Coryell County (at 31°12′ N, 97°53′ W). It rises 1,040 feet above sea level, forty feet above the surrounding countryside. It has been part of Fort Hood since 1942.

BIBLIOGRAPHY: Coryell County Genealogical Society, *Coryell County, Texas, Families, 1854-1985* (Dallas: Taylor, 1986).

ANTELOPE MOUNTAIN. Antelope Mountain, with an elevation of 1,375 feet, is located eight miles west of Palo Pinto in west central Palo Pinto County (at 32°45′ N, 98°26′ W). The area is surfaced by thin, stony soil that supports scrub brush, mesquite, cactus, and grasses.

ANTELOPE SPRING CREEK. Antelope Spring Creek rises twenty miles southwest of Hartley in south central Hartley County (at 35°41′ N, 102°39′ W) and flows seven miles south to its mouth on Pederosa Creek, just across the northern border of Oldham County (at 35°35′ N, 102°38′ W). The stream crosses flat to rolling terrain with clayey and loamy soils that primarily support mesquite and grasses. Antelope Spring Creek is in the heart of a vast ranching area, once part of the XIT Ranch's[qv] Rito Blanco Division.

ANTELOPE SPRINGS. Antelope Springs (Ojos del Berrendo) was located 1½ miles south of the Atchison, Topeka and Santa Fe tracks in northeastern Presidio County (at 30°12′ N, 103°55′ W). The springs, which once flowed from caliche rock, are now dry. The gentle slopes of the surrounding terrain are covered with alluvial deposits of sand and gravel. The land surface in the area is generally light reddish-brown to brown sand, clay loam, and stone. Vegetation consists of range grasses and a grove of large cottonwoods that circles the site. Antelope Springs provided water to early Indians, Spanish explorers, and Chihuahua Trail traders. In 1684 the expedition of Capt. Juan Domínguez de Mendoza[qv] passed by Antelope Springs and planted a cross at the site. In the 1880s cattlemen began using the surrounding range. Cattle overgrazed and trampled the native grasses, which had held the rainwater until it filtered into the subsurface. With the loss of the grass and the installation of a windmill well, Antelope Springs went dry.

BIBLIOGRAPHY: Gunnar Brune, *Springs of Texas*, Vol. 1 (Fort Worth: Branch-Smith, 1981). Cecilia Thompson, *History of Marfa and Presidio County, 1535-1946* (2 vols., Austin: Nortex, 1985).

ANTHONY, DANIEL W. (?–1833). Daniel W. Anthony, early Texas newspaperman, book publisher, and attorney, was possibly born in Kentucky. He arrived at the mouth of the Brazos River as a passenger aboard the schooner *Sabine* in late May or early June 1832, after a two-week voyage from New Orleans. On June 20, 1832, he joined the military organization then forming at Brazoria for the purpose of attacking Fort Velasco. He fought in the battle of Velasco[qv] aboard the schooner *Brazoria*[qv] as fourth sergeant.

Later that month he purchased from Godwin Brown Cotten[qv] the press on which Cotten had printed the *Texas Gazette and Brazoria Commercial Advertiser.*[qv] Anthony's initial publication was an extra edition of the paper, dated July 23, 1832, in which he reported the arrival on June 16 of a Mexican fleet at the mouth of the Brazos River carrying Col. José Antonio Mexía and Stephen F. Austin[qqv] and described the subsequent festivities and speeches. "Documents and Publications, explanatory of the late commotions" at Anahuac and Velasco were carried in the extra (*see* ANAHUAC DISTURBANCES), as well as the announcement by Anthony that "The Press of the 'Gazette,' having been transferred to the subscriber, will hereafter be conducted under the style of *The Constitutional Advocate and Brazoria Advertiser.*"[qv] Possibly reflecting a business decision to bring his paper wider acceptance, he actually published it as the *Constitutional Advocate and Texas Public Advertiser.* Anthony used his press to print the *Proceedings of the General Convention of Delegates Representing the Citizens and Inhabitants of Texas* in December 1832. It was the second book published in Texas. (Cotten had published the first in 1829–30.)

In November 1832 Anthony received title to a quarter league of land on the San Bernard River in what is now Fort Bend County. In December he wrote Stephen F. Austin to request more land for himself and to remind Austin that Anthony's brothers Henry and Jacob also wanted land. He wrote the empresario[qv] again in 1833 on behalf of his brothers. Shortly before his death Anthony advertised himself in his paper as a lawyer. Alcalde Henry Smith[qv] hired him in July 1833 as curator for William Parks,[qv] who was accused of taking property from the home of John McCroskey.[qv]

Anthony died of cholera at the tavern of Henry Brown in Brazoria on August 10, 1833. Very likely his brothers died at the same establishment from the same illness. Letters of administration of Anthony's estate were granted to Dr. Thomas F. L. Parrott[qv] on August 16, 1833. A claim against the estate was made by the Browns, who sought payment for board and lodging for all three Anthony brothers. Administering the estate, including Anthony's press, took quite a while and involved a conflict between citizens of Brazoria and citizens of San Felipe. In San Felipe was filed, on September 11, 1833, a petition on behalf of Luke Lesassier, Francis W. Johnson, Samuel May Williams, Oliver Jones,[qqv] and Stephen F. Austin to stay the sale of the press, type, and fixtures belonging to the estate. The same month in Brazoria Robert M. Williamson,[qv] acting for the San Felipeans, obtained an injunction against Parrott to keep him from selling the press and other property belonging to the estate. The press was eventually placed into operation by John A. Wharton[qv] and Oliver H. Allen, who began publishing the Brazoria *Advocate of the People's Rights*[qv] in November 1833. In the February 22, 1834, issue of this paper Wharton noted that there had been five claimants for Anthony's press. Cotten, who had worked for Anthony for several months, brought suit on February 19, 1834, to recover wages from the Anthony estate.

The name D. W. Anthony appears on a document drawn up at Harrisburg on June 4, 1835, which states that the signatories agree to meet again in Harrisburg on June 6 to elect officers and to proceed to Anahuac to attack the Mexican garrison commanded by Capt. Antonio Tenorio.[qv] Obviously this was not the D. W. Anthony who had published the newspaper in Brazoria.

BIBLIOGRAPHY: Eugene C. Barker, ed., *The Austin Papers* (3 vols., Washington: GPO, 1924–28). Eugene C. Barker, "Notes on Early Texas Newspapers," *Southwestern Historical Quarterly* 21 (October 1917). Mary D. Boddie, *Thunder on the Brazos: The Outbreak of the Texas Revolution at Fort Velasco, June 26, 1832* (Angleton, Texas: Brazoria County Historical Museum, 1978). James A. Creighton, *A Narrative History of Brazoria County* (Angleton, Texas: Brazoria County Historical Commission, 1975). James M. Day, comp., *Texas Almanac, 1857–1873: A Compendium of Texas History* (Waco: Texian Press, 1967). Charles Adams Gulick, Jr., Harriet Smither, et al., eds., *The Papers of Mirabeau Buonaparte Lamar* (6 vols., Austin: Texas State Library, 1920–27; rpt., Austin: Pemberton Press, 1968). *An Inventory of the Colonial Archives of Texas: No. 3, the Municipality of Brazoria, 1832–1837* (San Antonio: Historical Records Survey, 1937). Marilyn M. Sibley, *Lone Stars and State Gazettes: Texas Newspapers before the Civil War* (College Station: Texas A&M University Press, 1983). Villamae Williams, *Stephen F. Austin's Register of Families* (Nacogdoches, Texas: Ericson, 1984). *Ronald Howard Livingston*

ANTHONY, TEXAS (Bexar County). Anthony was on the Missouri, Kansas and Texas Railroad in the city limits of San Antonio, Bexar County; the site was six miles north of downtown, near the site of the Alamo Portland Cement Company. Anthony was established by the cement company after 1900 as a community for its employees. St. Anthony's Shrine was erected there by Peter M. Baque in 1931. The church for the settlement was called St. Peter, Prince of Apostles, and had a parish school. *Claudia Hazlewood*

ANTHONY, TEXAS (El Paso County). Anthony is on the Atchison, Topeka and Santa Fe Railway and State Highway 20 sixteen miles northwest of downtown El Paso on the Texas–New Mexico border in El Paso County. It was reportedly named by a Mexican-American woman who built a chapel to St. Anthony of Padua sometime before 1884. A post office was established on the El Paso County side in March of that year but was never in operation. The Texas community later became known as La Tuna, after the Federal Correctional Institution[qv] located there, at which a post office was open from 1932 to 1965. In the early 1940s the population was estimated at only twenty, but ten years later, after the community incorporated as Anthony, the population estimate had grown to 1,200. It declined to 1,082 in the early 1960s, then grew to 2,154 in the early 1970s, 2,640 in the early 1980s, and 3,328 in 1990. A post office was established in Anthony in 1981. In 1988 the Anthony Chamber of Commerce named the town the Leap Year Capital of the World, and the Worldwide Leap Year Birthday Club, open to anyone born on February 29, had more than 100 members by 1992.

Martin Donell Kohout

ANTHONY, TEXAS (Fannin County). Anthony is on Farm Road 1753 twelve miles northwest of Bonham in the northwest corner of Fannin County. In the 1880s the Anthony family established a homestead in this area near the Red River. Between 1894 and 1907 a post office branch served the community. The population, which never exceeded fifty, was ten in 1988 and 1990.

BIBLIOGRAPHY: *Fannin County Folks and Facts* (Dallas: Taylor, 1977). *David Minor*

ANTHONY'S NOSE. Anthony's Nose is a peak two miles northwest of Fort Bliss and three miles west of Farm Road 3255 in the Franklin Mountains State Park[qv] in northwestern El Paso County (at 31°58′ N, 106°30′ W). Its summit, at an elevation of 6,927 feet above sea level, rises 2,810 feet above Farm Road 3255. The area's shallow, stony soils support scrub brush and grasses.

Martin Donell Kohout

ANTIMONY SMELTER. The largest antimony smelter in the world in 1945 was just north of Laredo in Webb County. Initially it had been at San Luis Potosí, Mexico, operated by a British firm owned by the Cookson family and founded in 1704. The duty placed on foreign antimony in the 1920s had encouraged domestic production to free the United States from dependence on Chinese antimony supplies. At that time, the smelter company moved north along the railroads to remain as near as possible to the source of Mexican ore, which was produced chiefly at San Luis Potosí and Oaxaca, and reestablished the smelter at Laredo. Known for a time as Lead Industries, this firm by 1930 had become the Texas Mining and Smelting Company. H. P. Henderson, the first president of this company, was succeeded by V. L. Kegler in 1939. At its Laredo location the smelter burned natural gas and Alabama coke. During World War II,[qv] when the British government exchanged its assets in America for weapons and supplies, Texas Mining and Smelting became an American firm known as National Lead, which operated the smelter until it ceased production in 1976. In 1977 the original British firm, then known as the Cookson Group, once again acquired the Laredo operation. At that time Cookson (under the name Anzon, Limited) produced antimony and zircon in Europe. The Laredo operation became Anzon American and later Anzon, Incorporated. Among the company's products is an antimony oxide known as TMS (from Texas Mining and Smelting Company). *J. H. McNeely and Diana J. Kleiner*

ANTIOCH, TEXAS (Cass County). Antioch is on Farm Road 96 seven miles northwest of Atlanta in northeastern Cass County. The settlement, originally called Anti, grew up around a church organized in 1856. It received a post office in 1888, which was discontinued about a year later, reestablished in 1901, and discontinued permanently in 1904. In 1936 Antioch had a church, a cemetery, a school, and several houses. In 1983 it had an estimated population of twenty-nine, a church, a cemetery, and two small businesses. In 1990 the population was still reported as twenty-nine. *Cecil Harper, Jr.*

ANTIOCH, TEXAS (Delta County). Antioch is on Farm Road 64 six miles west of Cooper in western Delta County. The site, originally part of the Moses Williams land grant, was settled by 1849, when four trustees obtained title to land for the Antioch Cemetery. Cotton was an important local crop in the early years, but honey became the major product after Charles H. "Honey" Smith began the industry in 1850. An Antioch school opened in 1879; classes met in the local church. In 1889 the Antioch Baptist Church held membership in the Delta County Baptist Association. The town was established the following year. In 1905 the school had ninety-five students and two teachers. In 1936 the site was not identified on maps, but one business, the school, and a cluster of dwellings were shown. The school was merged with the Pecan Gap and Cooper school districts in 1950. In 1964 the church and a few scattered dwellings were at the site. Antioch reported a population of twenty-five in 1970 and appeared on maps for 1984. In 1990 the reported population was still twenty-five.

BIBLIOGRAPHY: Paul Garland Hervey, A History of Education in Delta County, Texas (M.A. thesis, University of Texas, 1951). Wilma Ross and Billie Phillips, *Photos and Tales of Delta County* (1976).

Vista K. McCroskey

ANTIOCH, TEXAS (Freestone County). Antioch is on Farm Road 1364 six miles southeast of Fairfield in east central Freestone County. The Antioch Baptist Church was organized in 1873, and the church building was also used for a school known as East Antioch School. The school had thirteen pupils enrolled in 1893 and thirty-two in 1899. It was moved to Turlington in 1908. In 1936 the community had a church, a school, and a few scattered dwellings. By the 1960s only the church, the cemetery, and one dwelling remained.

BIBLIOGRAPHY: Freestone County Historical Commission, *History of Freestone County, Texas* (Fairfield, Texas, 1978). *Chris Cravens*

ANTIOCH, TEXAS (Houston County). Antioch, a rural community four miles southwest of Lovelady on Farm Road 230 in southern Houston County, was probably established in the late 1880s. A post office began operating there in 1890, and by 1892 the community had two general stores, a school, two physicians, and a combination gristmill and gin. The estimated population in 1896 was thirty. In the mid-1930s only a school, a cemetery, and a few widely scattered houses remained. In the early 1990s only a church and cemetery marked the site. *Christopher Long*

ANTIOCH, TEXAS (Lee County). Antioch is eleven miles east of Giddings on Farm Road 141 in southeastern Lee County. The community was settled during Reconstruction[qv] when the offer of inexpensive land brought blacks from Washington, Burleson, and Fayette counties. Antioch quickly became the largest black community in Lee County. Some of the settlers supplemented their income, which presumably came from farming, by working periodically at neighborhood plantations such as Black's Quarter. The post office, general store, and cotton gin at nearby Nunnsville served residents of Antioch. The Antioch Juneteenth[qv] celebration was held at the Mays Road Park with all-day festivities. In 1898 the Antioch school had 156 students. Church services were also held in the one-room schoolhouse until the congregation built the Antioch Missionary Baptist Church. In 1953 the Antioch school was consolidated with that of Post Oak. The Antioch Missionary Baptist Church continued to serve afterward as the center of the community.

BIBLIOGRAPHY: Lee County Historical Survey Committee, *A History of Lee County* (Quanah, Texas: Nortex, 1974). *Nolan Thompson*

ANTIOCH, TEXAS (Panola County). Antioch, six miles southeast of Carthage in central Panola County, was established before 1900. A school began operating there around 1900, and in 1906 it had an enrollment of sixty-one. In the mid-1930s the community had a school, a church, a cemetery, and a number of houses. During the 1940s the school was consolidated with the Carthage school, and by the mid-1960s only a cemetery and a few scattered houses remained in the area.

BIBLIOGRAPHY: Leila B. LaGrone, ed., *History of Panola County* (Carthage, Texas: Panola County Historical Commission, 1979).

Christopher Long

ANTIOCH, TEXAS (Smith County). Antioch i?s a small church community three miles northeast of Bullard in southern Smith County. By 1903 the settlement reported a one-teacher school for fifty-two white students and another for twenty-nine black students. In 1936 Antioch had a few houses, a church, the Antioch and Crow cemeteries, and a one-teacher elementary school attended by twenty black pupils. By 1952 the Antioch school district had been consolidated with the Whitehouse Independent School District. In 1973 the church, the cemeteries, a scattered collection of dwellings, and a water tank remained at the site. The community was still designated on maps in 1985.

BIBLIOGRAPHY: Edward Clayton Curry, An Administrative Survey of the Schools of Smith County, Texas (M.Ed. thesis, University of Texas, 1938). "School Sights," *Chronicles of Smith County*, Fall 1969.

Vista K. McCroskey

ANTIOCH, TEXAS (Stonewall County). Antioch was about two miles west of the site of present Peacock, near the Salt Fork of the Brazos River in west central Stonewall County. The settlement was established around 1889 and grew to include two stores and a gin during the 1890s and early 1900s. The Antioch Baptist Church, established in 1895 at the Bilberry settlement near Oriana, lasted until 1918; in 1905 its membership was 135. A local school started in 1897 served also as a community center, church, and Woodmen of the World lodge. When the Stamford and Northwestern Railway laid track south of the community in 1909, citizens and merchants of Antioch moved their town to the nearby settlement of Oriana.

BIBLIOGRAPHY: *A History of Stonewall County* (Aspermont, Texas: Stonewall County Historical Commission, 1979). Jerome R. Whitmire, The History of Stonewall County (M.A. thesis, Texas Technological College, 1936).

Charles G. Davis

ANTIOCH, TEXAS (Trinity County). Antioch, a rural community on Farm Road 233 twelve miles northeast of Groveton in northeastern Trinity County, was founded after the Civil War.[qv] A school for black children was established there in 1884, and a Church of Christ around 1900. The school was closed before World War II,[qv] and in the early 1990s only the church, a cemetery, and a few scattered houses remained.

BIBLIOGRAPHY: Patricia B. and Joseph W. Hensley, eds., *Trinity County Beginnings* (Groveton, Texas: Trinity County Book Committee, 1986).

Christopher Long

ANTIOCH, TEXAS (Van Zandt County). Antioch was ten miles northeast of Canton in northeast Van Zandt County. By 1890 it had a school that reached an enrollment of sixty-two in 1905 and was consolidated with the Grand Saline Independent School District by the 1950s. In 1936 a school and church remained at the site, but by 1965 the community had disappeared.

BIBLIOGRAPHY: Mary E. Valandingham, *Early Scholastic Records for Van Zandt County* (Center, Texas, 1968).

Diana J. Kleiner

ANTIOCH CHURCH, TEXAS. Antioch Church is on Hayes Branch one mile east of Luna in southwest Freestone County. The community had a cemetery, founded in the late 1860s; the earliest death date marked on a grave is 1880. In the 1960s the church and cemetery were still at the site.

BIBLIOGRAPHY: Freestone County Historical Commission, *Freestone County Cemeteries*, Vol. 1 (1976).

Chris Cravens

ANTI-SALOON LEAGUE OF TEXAS. After an abortive attempt in 1902, the Texas Anti-Saloon League was formed in 1907. It was headquartered in Dallas; Benjamin Franklin Riley, a Baptist clergyman, was superintendent. The national league had been formed in 1895; it was modeled on the Ohio Anti-Saloon League, which was founded in 1893 to fight for laws prohibiting the manufacture, transportation, and sale of all alcoholic beverages. The Ohio organization focused on the single issue of prohibition,[qv] was nonpartisan, and attempted to apply big-business professionalism and bureaucracy to its intended reform. The spread of the league to southern states was slowed by the national officers' objections to segregation. Prohibition organizations, including the Woman's Christian Temperance Union,[qv] were already active in Texas, although none adhered to the league's principles of continual expert attention on the single issue.

The Texas Anti-Saloon League quickly embroiled itself in the state's prohibition politics by taking credit in 1907–08 for winning local-option elections to ban the liquor trade in twelve counties. However, it remained an informal organization with only loose ties to the national office, and it was unable to command the state's prohibition forces. Joel H. Gambrell[qv] led the league after 1910. Quarrels among Texas drys hurt the cause at the polling booth, and in 1915 the national office reorganized the Texas league and installed new officers.

Under the leadership of Arthur James Barton the Texas league aggressively raised funds and pursued the prohibition cause. The national league assumed the debt of *Home and State* and turned the paper into the league's voice in Texas. In 1916 the league campaign to initiate state prohibition succeeded with a majority of voters, only to meet defeat in the legislature. The league took credit for adding twelve more counties to the dry column in 1917.

Once national prohibition was won, the Anti-Saloon League in Texas and elsewhere withered, in spite of leaders' pleas to supporters to maintain vigilance. Nationally the league was divided over the question of emphasizing enforcement or education in a dry America. Barton, who had resigned as Texas superintendent in 1918 to be replaced by Atticus Webb, advocated education, and, in fact, in 1927 the state saw an intensive educational campaign begin. In 1928 the Texas league, like its southern counterparts elsewhere, opposed the presidential candidacy of Alfred Smith, an outspoken wet. Although prohibition reduced alcohol consumption and remained widely popular through the 1920s, after the onset of the Great Depression[qv] it quickly lost favor. By 1933 the Anti-Saloon League in Texas and elsewhere stood hopelessly by as the repeal movement succeeded. In 1991 the direct descendant of the Texas League was Drug Prevention Resources, Incorporated, based in Dallas.

BIBLIOGRAPHY: Ernest H. Cherrington, ed., *Standard Encyclopedia of the Alcohol Problem* (6 vols., Westerville, Ohio: American Issue, 1925–30). Lewis L. Gould, *Progressives and Prohibitionists: Texas Democrats in the Wilson Era* (Austin: University of Texas Press, 1973; rpt., Austin: Texas State Historical Association, 1992). K. Austin Kerr, *Organized for Prohibition: A New History of the Anti-Saloon League* (New Haven: Yale University Press, 1985).

K. Austin Kerr

ANTON, TEXAS. Anton, on U.S. Highway 84, Farm roads 168 and 597, and the Atchison, Topeka and Santa Fe Railroad twenty-four miles northwest of Lubbock in northeast Hockley County, was founded in the center of what had been the Spade Ranch's[qv] north pasture. Around 1924 ranch owner W. L. Ellwood sold off more than 200 farms from his ranch and contracted with the Anton Townsite Company to plat a town at the site of Danforth Switch, a spur of the Pecos and Northern Texas Railway. The site was named Anton in honor of J. F. Anton, a Santa Fe railroad executive. On December 3, 1924, the Anton Townsite Company sponsored a "Grand Opening Jubilee" for the town; despite a bad sandstorm, they sold over 200 town lots the first day. Early businesses included a depot, four lumber companies, a gin, a hotel, and a newspaper, the Anton *News* (later the *Four County News*, which ended publication in 1959). The first mayor was Paul Whitfield, and when the post office opened in 1925 the first postmaster was J. C. Arnett. The Anton Independent School District was established in 1925; classes were held in two small frame buildings, though by the end of the year the district had obtained a $40,000 building. By 1926 several churches had been established; by 1929 the town had a bank. In the late 1930s Anton, which then had a population of 400 and twenty businesses, was incorporated. Grain, cotton, and later oil were central to the economy. The town also had for a time a large rabbit-processing plant, though by 1982 it had closed down. Anton had a population of 1,368 and fifty businesses in the 1960s. By the early 1980s the town again had a newspaper, the Anton *Star*. In 1988 Anton's population of 1,198 was served by fourteen businesses. In 1990 the population was 1,212.

BIBLIOGRAPHY: Lillian Brasher, *Hockley County* (2 vols., Canyon, Texas: Staked Plains, 1976). Kathleen E. and Clifton R. St. Clair, eds., *Little Towns of Texas* (Jacksonville, Texas: Jayroe Graphic Arts, 1982). Orville R. Watkins, "Hockley County: From Cattle Ranches to Farms," West Texas Historical Association *Year Book* 17 (1941).

Rachel Jenkins

ANTONE (ca. 1780–ca. 1870). Antone, first chief of the Alabama Indians in Texas, was born near Lafourche, Louisiana, about 1780. He was elected chief about 1806. In September 1839 Gustav Dresel,[qv] the first German consul in Texas, visited Fenced-In Village and referred to Antone as absolute monarch of all the Alabamas. He wrote that Antone had two cabins—a regular log cabin and a summer house with cane walls to admit cooling breezes. From 1800 to 1855 the Alabama Indians moved from one village site to another, seeking permanent homes in western Tyler County and eastern Polk County. As principal chief, Antone directed tribal members in these movements.

The highlight of Antone's service as principal chief was his successful request for a grant of land from the state of Texas for a permanent reservation. While the Alabamas were living at Rock Village in eastern Polk County, a petition for land signed by Antone, the tribal subchiefs, and prominent citizens of Polk County was presented to the Texas legislature, on October 29, 1853. This petition was approved, and the state purchased 1,110.7 acres of land for the Alabama Indian reservation.

After the Alabamas moved onto their reservation, during the winter of 1854–55, they expressed the need for an agent or reservation administrator to assist in tribal business matters, in contacts with government officials, and in relations with their white neighbors. On November 24, 1855, Antone and the subchiefs of the tribe signed a request for an agent, addressed to the Texas Senate and House of Representatives. The state of Texas attempted to move the Polk County Indians to the Lower Brazos Reserve in 1858, and Indian agent James Barclay[qv] rode across Texas on horseback in October of that year with Antone and a delegation of other Alabamas and Coushattas to inspect the new reservation. From the Indians' viewpoint, the Lower Brazos Reserve was a barren, dreary land compared to the forested hills of their Polk County reservation. The Indian leaders told Barclay they did not want to move from East Texas.

In 1862 nineteen members of the Alabama and Coushatta Indians were recruited and sworn into service with Company G, Twenty-fourth Texas Cavalry Regiment (Second Lancers), C.S.A. Antone expressed a desire to enter service with this group, but there is no record that he was accepted. He died about 1870 and was buried in the Coushatta cemetery near the village of Coushatta chief Colita[qv] on the Logan League in San Jacinto County, Texas. *See also* ALABAMA-COUSHATTA INDIANS.

BIBLIOGRAPHY: Anna K. Fain, *The Story of Indian Village* (Livingston, Texas, 1948). Vivian Fox, *The Winding Trail: The Alabama-Coushatta Indians of Texas* (Austin: Eakin Press, 1983). Aline T. Rothe, *Kalita's People* (Waco: Texian Press, 1963). Harriet Smither, "The Alabama Indians of Texas," *Southwestern Historical Quarterly* 36 (October 1932). U.S. House of Representatives, *Alabama Indians in Texas* (document 1232, 61st Cong., 3d Sess., 1911). U.S. House of Representatives, *Alabama Indians of Texas* (document 866, 62d Cong., 2d Sess., 1912).

Howard N. Martin

ANTON WULFF HOUSE. The Anton Wulff House, located at 107 King William Street in the King William Historic District[qv] a half mile from downtown San Antonio, is an Italianate house with a square tower, paired arch windows, and a circular bas-relief in the gable featuring a sculptured bust of Wulff's daughter Carolina, done by his son Henry. Wulff built this house around 1869 or 1870. The land was originally part of the grant made to Pedro Huizar[qv] in 1793 from the large area farmed by Indians who lived at San Antonio de Valero Mission. Until the San Antonio River was diverted about 1926, it bordered the Wulff property, where a boathouse and bathhouse were situated. Part of the property on the Washington Street side was sold before Wulff died in 1894. His family lived in the house until 1902, when Mrs. Wulff sold it to Arthur and Elise Guenther for $7,000. In 1950 Elise Guenther's heirs sold the house to F. G. and Kathryn Antonio for $20,000. Mrs. Antonio made it into apartments. In 1964 a thin layer of pink stucco was applied to the house, and it was remodeled for use by the United Brotherhood of Carpenters and Joiners. It proved unsuitable for their needs, however. It was exempted from historic zoning when the King William Historic District was established in May 1968.

In 1974 the San Antonio Conservation Society[qv] undertook a campaign, headed by Walter Nold Mathis, to raise a fund of $100,000 to match a grant from the Sheerin Foundation to purchase the Wulff property. The cost of restoration ($250,000) was mostly paid for by a grant from the United States Economic Development Agency. In the fall of 1975 the Wulff house became the headquarters of the San Antonio Conservation Society, and that year the house was included in the King William Historic District. A Texas historic landmark medallion was placed on the house in 1976.

BIBLIOGRAPHY: Chris Carson and William B. McDonald, eds., *A Guide to San Antonio Architecture* (San Antonio Chapter, American Institute of Architects, 1986). Carlos E. Castañeda, *Our Catholic Heritage in Texas* (7 vols., Austin: Von Boeckmann–Jones, 1936–58; rpt., New York: Arno, 1976). Frederick Charles Chabot, *With the Makers of San Antonio* (Yanaguana Society Publications 4, San Antonio, 1937). Glen E. Lich, *The German Texans* (San Antonio: University of Texas Institute of Texan Cultures, 1981). San Antonio *Express*, October 3, 1965. San Antonio *Light*, March 23, 1986.

Mary V. Burkholder

ANTONY, EDWIN LEROY (1852–1913). Edwin LeRoy Antony, attorney and legislator, son of Dr. Milton and Margaret Frances (Davis) Antony, Jr., was born in Waynesboro, Georgia, on January 5, 1852. He moved to Texas with his parents in 1859 and settled in Columbia. He graduated from the University of Georgia with honors in 1873, became a member of the state bar the following year, and set up a law practice in Cameron. Antony served as prosecuting attorney for Milam County from 1876 to 1878 and was appointed special judge in 1886 during an illness of the regular district judge. He was an alderman in Cameron from 1890 to 1892 and was elected as a Democrat to the United States House of Representatives in 1892, when Roger Q. Mills[qv] resigned to take a seat in the Senate. Antony lost his bid for renomination later that year and returned to Cameron to resume his law practice.

He married Augusta Houghton on September 20, 1876; the couple had two daughters. Antony died at his brother-in-law's home in Dallas on January 16, 1913, and was buried in Oakland Cemetery.

BIBLIOGRAPHY: *Biographical Directory of the American Congress. History of Texas, Together with a Biographical History of Milam, Wil-*

liamson, Bastrop, Travis, Lee and Burleson Counties (Chicago: Lewis, 1893). Dallas *Morning News,* January 17, 1913. *Anne W. Hooker*

AOY, OLIVES VILLANUEVA (1823–1895). Olives Villanueva Aoy (born Jaime Aoy Olives Vila), school founder, was born in Mahon, Menorca, Spain, on March 24, 1823, the son of Jaime Vila and Margarete Olives. He journeyed from Spain to Havana and for a time lived among the Mayas in Mexico. In Arizona or Utah he was converted to the Church of Jesus Christ of Latter-day Saints and became a valuable assistant in translating the *Book of Mormon* into Spanish. At the Mormon temple in Logan, Utah, probably in November 1884, sacred ordinances were performed for him under the name Jaime Aoy Olives Vila. He left Utah and traveled to Silver City, New Mexico, where he edited a newspaper. Around 1887 he arrived in El Paso. The first public school there had opened in 1883, and surviving rolls from that time do not show a single child with a Spanish surname. A school census from that time, however, listed more than 100 Mexican children of school age. The El Paso school board had not made provisions to teach non–English speakers. Aoy, supported by concerned parents and using funds he had saved from his translation project, in 1887 founded an *escuelita* and began teaching Mexican children in English and Spanish. He also supplied them with food and clothing and cared for their health. In 1888 the school board incorporated Aoy's school on a segregated basis, and it eventually became known as the Mexican Preparatory School. A vacant customhouse building was made available to Aoy in 1891, and with two assistants he taught English to nearly 100 first and second grade students. When he died in El Paso on April 27, 1895, he was virtually penniless, having spent most of his income and savings on supplies for his students. Administrators of his estate used money owed him by the school board to provide a granite headstone for his grave in Evergreen Cemetery. After Aoy's death, the school board fulfilled its commitment to the school and appointed W. H. T. Lopez as principal. By 1897 the small school had grown to an enrollment of 200 students with a staff of three teachers. The board in 1899 built a six-room schoolhouse, named Aoy School, which could accommodate 300 students. In 1900 Aoy School was holding double sessions and reported an enrollment of 500—the largest enrollment of any El Paso school at that time.

BIBLIOGRAPHY: Conrey Bryson, "A Man Named Aoy," *Password* 35 (Summer 1990). Mario T. García, *Desert Immigrants: The Mexicans of El Paso, 1880–1920* (New Haven: Yale University Press, 1981).
Conrey Bryson

APACHE CANYON. Apache Canyon begins seven miles west of Apache Peak in east central Hudspeth County (at 31°28′ N, 105°02′ W) and extends northeast for eight miles to its terminus, one mile north of Apache Peak on the Culberson-Hudspeth county line (at 31°30′ N, 104°55′ W). Through the canyon flows an intermittent stream, Apache Spring Creek. The surrounding steep slopes with local deep and dense dissection are surfaced by shallow, stony soil that supports Mexican buckeye, walnut, persimmon, desert willow, oak, juniper, mesquite, scrub brush, and grasses. The canyon was named for the Mescalero Apaches, who dominated the area until the late nineteenth century.

APACHE INDIANS. The Apache Indians belong to the southern branch of the Athabascan group, whose languages constitute a large family, with speakers in Alaska, western Canada, and the American Southwest. The several branches of Apache tribes occupied an area extending from the Arkansas River to Northern Mexico and from Central Texas to Central Arizona. Generally, the Apaches are divided into Eastern and Western, with the Rio Grande serving as the dividing line. Two groups, the Lipans and the Mescaleros, lived partially or entirely within the confines of Texas. The Apaches went by numerous names. Because of their nomadic nature, it seems probable that several names were used to identify the same band or tribe. Some names of Apache bands in Texas were Limita, Conejero, and Trementina[qqv] (perhaps the same as Limita). But only the names Lipan and Mescalero survived into the nineteenth century. The name Apache most probably came from the Zuñi word *apachu,* meaning "enemy," or possibly Awa'tehe, the Ute name for Apaches. The Apaches referred to themselves as Inde or Diné, meaning "the people." The Apaches arrived in the Southwest between A.D. 1000 and 1400. After somehow being separated from their northern kinsmen, they carved out a home in the Southwest—apparently migrating south along the eastern side of the Rocky Mountains, then spreading westward into New Mexico and Arizona. In time, pressure from the Comanches and other tribes pushed the Apaches farther south and west.

The social unit of the Lipan and Mescalero Apaches was the extended family. Several extended families generally stayed together and were led by their most prominent member, who acted as chief advisor and director of group affairs. A number of the groups lived in close proximity and could unite for defensive or offensive purposes, or for social or ceremonial occasions. The leader of the combined groups was the band leader. The Lipans had no formal organization larger than the band. This loose organization caused problems in relations with the Spanish, and later with the Mexicans, Texans, and Americans. One Apache band, for instance, might make peace with its enemies, while another would remain at war. Likewise, when the Apaches made peace with one enemy Indian settlement, it did not mean that they made peace with other affiliated settlements. Band leaders were always males, but females held a central place within the tribe. Upon marriage, the groom moved in with his wife's family and had to hunt and work with his in-laws. If the wife should die, the husband was required to stay with her family, who would usually supply him with a new bride. The wife had little obligation to the husband's family, but if he died, his family could provide a cousin or brother for her to marry. Men were allowed to marry more than one woman, but few besides wealthy or prestigious leaders did so. On those rare occasions, they were required to marry sisters or cousins of their wives.

The Apaches were nomadic and lived almost completely off the buffalo.[qv] They dressed in buffalo skins and lived in tents made of tanned and greased hides, which they loaded onto dogs when they moved with the herds. They were among the first Indians, after the Pueblos, to learn to ride horses. Learning from runaway or captured Pueblos, the Apaches quickly adapted to their use of horses. Formerly peaceful trade relationships with the Pueblos deteriorated, however, as the Spanish discouraged trade with the Apaches and forced the Pueblos to work their farms. When the Pueblos became unwilling or unable to trade with the Apaches, the nomadic Indians turned their new equestrian skills to raiding for horses and supplies. The Spanish first contacted the Apaches in 1541, when Francisco Vázquez de Coronado[qv] and his men encountered a band of "Querechos" on the journey to Quivira.[qv] From 1656 to 1675, the Spanish settlers and Pueblo Indians of New Mexico suffered heavily from almost continuous Apache raids. These raids, in conjunction with drought, harsh Spanish rule, and missionary activities, led the Pueblo Indians to revolt and to drive the Spaniards out of New Mexico in 1680 (the "Pueblo Revolt"). When the Spaniards reconquered New Mexico in 1692, the Apaches were a powerful nation of mounted Indians who raided with impunity wherever they desired. But the Apaches' dominance was short-lived. Their aggressive behavior turned their neighbors into enemies, and a new, potentially powerful tribe, the Comanches, began pressuring the Apaches from the north. By 1700 the Apaches began migrating southwest as the Comanche, Wichita, and Tejas Indians, better armed through trade with the French, began to occupy the dominant position on the South Plains. In addition, the Apaches had never adapted completely to a Plains culture. They continued to establish *rancherías,* where they built huts and tended fields of maize, beans, pumpkins, and watermelons. This attempt to improve their source of food was a major cause of their defeat by the Comanches. Twice a year, during planting and again during harvesting, the Apaches were tied to their fields. As a result, the Comanches knew where to find their enemies and could launch devastating raids upon the Apache settlements. With each successful raid the Comanches grew stronger and the Apaches weaker.

As the Apaches fled before the Comanche onslaught, many groups moved westward into New Mexico and Arizona. Others, mainly the Lipans and Mescaleros, fled southward into Central Texas as well as into northern Mexico. There, they collided with the Spanish, who were advancing northward. The Spanish had earlier aided the Tejas Indians of East Texas in their raids against the Apaches. When the Spanish founded San Antonio in 1718, the Apaches discovered a convenient, accessible location at which to stage raids against their European enemies. The Spanish at San Antonio attempted to make peace with the Apaches but had little success. After a series of clashes, the viceroy ordered the governor of Texas, Fernando Pérez de Almazán,[qv] to secure peace with the Apaches through gentle means. Noting that the Jicarilla Apaches had made peace with the Spanish in New Mexico, the viceroy saw hope for similar conciliation with the Texas Apaches. The viceroy therefore forbade any further campaigns against the Apaches in 1725, and his decision appeared to be justified by a substantial drop in Apache raiding over the next six years. During this lull in activity, Pedro de Rivera y Villalón[qv] made a general inspection of the entire Spanish frontier and recommended, among other things, a reduction in the size of the garrison at San Antonio. Influenced no doubt by the relative quiet around San Antonio, Rivera suggested that the garrison be reduced. This action raised a storm of protest from the missionaries and settlers at Bexar. They feared renewed raids once the Apaches learned of the smaller force at San Antonio. The Regulation of 1729, based largely on Rivera's recommendations, forbade governors and commanders from waging war on friendly or indifferent Indians, discouraged campaigns against hostile Indians by friendly tribes, and encouraged granting peace to any enemy tribes who sought it. During the 1730s and 1740s, the Apaches and Spaniards continued to wage war on each other. In 1743 Fray Benito Fernández de Santa Ana[qv] urged the establishment of missions for the Apaches in their own lands, arguing that this was the best solution to the most serious Indian problems in Texas. On August 19, 1749, four Apache chiefs with numerous followers buried a hatchet along with other instruments of war in a peace ceremony at San Antonio. For the first time both sides appeared genuinely to desire peace, and the Apaches, decimated by Comanche raids, appeared willing to accept Christian conversion in exchange for protection by the Spaniards.

The missionaries at San Antonio proposed several plans to set up missions for the Apaches, but competition among proposals delayed their implementation. The first formal mission for the Texas Apaches was established not at San Antonio but in the jurisdiction of San Juan Bautista[qv] on the Rio Grande. Late in 1754, Alonso Giraldo de Terreros[qv] established the mission of San Lorenzo, situated in Mexico eighteen leagues west of the presidio at San Juan Bautista. San Lorenzo had a degree of success until Father Terreros retired from the management of that mission to promote a larger project intended for the San Saba River in Texas. Less than a year after San Lorenzo was established, its neophytes became discontented, revolted, burned the mission buildings, and deserted. The missionaries blamed the failure of that first Apache mission on the natural inconstancy of the tribe, as well as on their reluctance to live away from their homelands. The latter reason helped bolster the argument for placing a mission closer to Apache territory. Revived prospects for mining in the region of San Saba, which was located in the heart of Apachería, also boosted the argument for that location. In addition, Terreros's cousin offered generous monetary support for the mission. The plan for a mission-presidio-colony project was soon under way. When Terreros, the presidio commander Col. Diego Ortiz Parrilla,[qv] and their entourage arrived at the San Saba River in April 1757, they found no Indians to greet them. Still, despite Ortiz's objections, the missionaries demanded that construction begin, and Ortiz yielded to their entreaties. In June 1757 the first Indians began to arrive at the site, and within days 3,000 Apaches encamped around the mission. The missionaries were extremely pleased until they learned that the Indians were not willing to enter the mission. Instead, they had gathered for their annual buffalo hunt and for a campaign against their enemies, the northern tribes. The Indians soon departed, promising to return to settle at the missions upon completion of their quest. During the autumn and winter of 1757, small groups of Apaches would appear at the mission; but after partaking of the priests' kindness, they continued their migration to the south. On March 16, 1758, a party of 2,000 Comanche, Tejas, Bidai, Tonkawa, and other Indians swooped down upon Santa Cruz de San Sabá Mission, killed eight of the inhabitants, pillaged the supplies, and burned the buildings.

Despite the disaster at San Saba and the apparent untrustworthiness of the Apaches, the Spanish continued in their efforts to keep the peace. The Apaches for their part did just enough to keep the Spanish interested. They even joined Colonel Ortiz on his campaign in 1759 to punish the northern tribes. Although some of the Lipans retreated before the final battle, most of them apparently served Ortiz well during the campaign. The Lipans continued to ask for a mission but refused to settle in the region of San Saba after the massacre that had occurred there. They desired a location more remote from their Comanche and northern enemies. In January 1762 the new Apache mission, San Lorenzo de la Santa Cruz, was established on the upper Nueces River halfway between San Saba and the Rio Grande. Once the mission was established, several Apache bands visited it, but only one band of more than 300 actually settled at the mission. Within a month, however, an Apache chief requested the establishment of a second mission at a site several miles downstream from San Lorenzo. In February 1762 Nuestra Señora de la Candelaria Mission was established. Life at the missions progressed relatively smoothly until a smallpox epidemic hit the neophytes in 1764. In addition, the missions were too poor to feed the Indians regularly, and the missionaries demanded too much labor from them. Slowly, the Lipans became discouraged with mission life. In 1766 they abandoned Candelaria; and when the Comanches and other northern tribes began raiding San Lorenzo, the Apaches deserted in droves. By the summer of 1767, both missions were devoid of Lipan Apaches.

At approximately this time, the Marqués de Rubí[qv] completed his inspection of the frontier, and upon his return to Mexico set forth his recommendations. He believed that the Comanches and other northern tribes attacked the Spanish only because of the latter's connection with the Lipan Apaches. Rubí felt sure that friendship could be cultivated with the northern tribes and that with their help the Apaches could be exterminated, or at least sufficiently reduced. By the 1790s the Apaches had become relatively quiet, although they continued to raid sporadically. The Spanish made peace treaties with them in 1790 and again in 1793. When the Mexican War of Independence[qv] began in 1811, the decreased attention that the Spanish paid to Indians caused them to become bolder, and they again staged raids. These attacks continued until the end of Spanish rule in Texas and Mexico. Antonio María Martínez,[qv] the last Spanish governor of Texas, reported raids by Lipan and Comanche Indians, even on the capital of Texas, San Antonio (*see* CAPITALS).

The Mexican government quickly signed two treaties with the Lipans. In each, the Mexicans promised to supply the Apaches with annual gifts of gunpowder and corn in exchange for peace. As Anglo-Americans began moving into Central Texas, the Apaches cultivated a friendship with them, each side hoping that the other would help defend them against hostile tribes in the area. The Lipans often raided into Mexico and sold their stolen horses and goods to the Anglos. The Mexican government generally overlooked these depredations, because of the usefulness of the Apaches against the formidable Comanches.

When Texas gained its independence, the relatively cordial relations between whites and Apaches continued. The Texans drew up their own treaty with the Lipans in 1838. The alliance broke down in 1842, and 250 of approximately 400 Lipans left Texas for Mexico, where they joined the Mescaleros on destructive raids across the border for several decades. In 1865–67 alone, Uvalde County reported the theft of more than $30,000 worth of livestock and the deaths of eighteen people. The Mexican government was reluctant to act, because several Mexican border towns profited handsomely from the purchase of plundered goods from the Apaches. Finally, in 1873, Col. Ranald S. Mackenzie[qv] led a force of 400 soldiers into Mexico to destroy the Lipan villages. His army killed or captured virtually all of the surviving Lipans, and they were deported to the Mescalero Reservation in the Sacramento Mountains of New Mexico, which had been assigned to the Mescaleros in 1855 but not officially established until 1873. In 1905 the remainder of the Lipans in Mexico drifted onto the Mescalero Reservation. In 1970 about 1,660 Indians were enrolled there—not only Mescaleros, but Chiricahuas, Lipans, Kiowas, and a few Comanches as well. Thirty-five Lipans were living in Oklahoma in 1940 but were not officially listed among the tribes of the state.

BIBLIOGRAPHY: John Francis Bannon, *The Spanish Borderlands Frontier, 1513–1821* (New York: Holt, Rinehart, and Winston, 1970). Carlos E. Castañeda, *Our Catholic Heritage in Texas* (7 vols., Austin: Von Boeckmann–Jones, 1936–58; rpt., New York: Arno, 1976). William E. Dunn, "The Apache Mission on the San Saba River: Its Founding and Failure," *Southwestern Historical Quarterly* 17 (April 1914). William E. Dunn, "Apache Relations in Texas, 1718–1750," *Quarterly of the Texas State Historical Association* 14 (January 1911). Odie B. Faulk, *The Last Years of Spanish Texas, 1778–1821* (The Hague: Mouton, 1964). George E. Hyde, *Indians of the High Plains: From the Prehistoric Period to the Coming of Europeans* (Norman: University of Oklahoma Press, 1959). Elizabeth A. H. John, *Storms Brewed in Other Men's Worlds: The Confrontation of Indians, Spanish, and French in the Southwest, 1540–1795* (College Station: Texas A&M University Press, 1975). Thomas E. Mails, *The People Called Apache* (Englewood Cliffs, New Jersey: Prentice-Hall, 1974). Paul D. Nathan, trans., and Lesley Byrd Simpson, ed., *The San Sabá Papers* (San Francisco: Howell, 1959). Thomas H. Naylor and Charles W. Polzer, comps. and eds., *Pedro de Rivera and the Military Regulations for Northern New Spain, 1724–1729* (Tucson: University of Arizona Press, 1988). William W. Newcomb, *The Indians of Texas* (Austin: University of Texas Press, 1961). Frank D. Reeve, "The Apache Indians in Texas," *Southwestern Historical Quarterly* 50 (October 1946). Thomas F. Schilz, *Lipan Apaches in Texas* (El Paso: Texas Western Press, 1987). Virginia H. Taylor, trans. and ed., *The Letters of Antonio Martínez, Last Spanish Governor of Texas, 1817–1822* (Austin: Texas State Library, 1957). John Upton Terrell, *The Plains Apache* (New York: Crowell, 1975). Ernest Wallace and David M. Vigness, eds., *Documents of Texas History* (Austin: Steck, 1963). Robert S. Weddle, *The San Sabá Mission* (Austin: University of Texas Press, 1964).

Jeffrey D. Carlisle

APACHE MOUNTAINS. The Apache Mountains stretch from south central to southeastern Culberson County a mile northeast of Kent (their center point is 31°11′ N, 104°21′ W). The highest elevation within the Apaches is 5,650 feet above sea level. The mountains, presumably named for the Mescalero Apaches who roamed the area until the late nineteenth century, are one of three exposed portions of the largest fossil reef in the world (the others are the Guadalupe Mountains in northwestern Culberson County and the Glass Mountains in Brewster County). The reef was formed during Permian times, some 250 million years ago, when the area was submerged in the Delaware basin. Lime-secreting algae were the main reef-builders, with some sponges, bryozoans, and brachiopods; their remains and the lime they secreted formed the reef. The Apaches are steep and rocky with local deep and dense dissection. The shallow, stony soil surface supports oak, live oak, juniper, mesquite, piñon, and grasses. During the 1960s barite was mined from open pits in the Seven Heart Gap area of the Apaches, and some production of zinc was reported from the Buck Prospect.

BIBLIOGRAPHY: Don Kurtz and William D. Goran, *Trails of the Guadalupes: A Hiker's Guide to the Trails of Guadalupe Mountains National Park* (Champaign, Illinois: Environmental Associates, 1978).

APACHE PEAK. Apache Peak is thirty-two miles northeast of Sierra Blanca in central eastern Hudspeth County (at 31°29′ N, 104°55′ W). It straddles the Culberson-Hudspeth county line, although the summit is in Hudspeth County. With an elevation of 5,690 feet above sea level, it rises 2,000 feet above State Highway 54, four miles to the east.

APACHE RANCH, TEXAS. Apache Ranch, formerly known as Los Apaches, is on the Rio Grande forty-six miles northwest of Laredo in western Webb County. The settlement is primarily a ranching community. An Apache Ranch school and a business appeared on county maps during the 1960s and the 1980s. *Eduardo Pupo*

APACHERÍA. The term Apachería is used to designate the area inhabited by the Apache Indians. Since there has been a written record, this has been in a region extending from north of the Arkansas River into the northern states of Mexico and from Central Texas to Central Arizona.

BIBLIOGRAPHY: Frank D. Reeve, "The Apache Indians in Texas," *Southwestern Historical Quarterly* 50 (October 1946).

APAPAX INDIANS. This name is known from a document of 1748 that lists twenty-five Indian groups of east central and southeastern Texas that had asked for missions in that general area. About half of the names on this list, including Apapax, cannot be further identified. The remainder denote groups identifiable as Caddoans (including Wichita), Tonkawans, Atakapans, and Karankawans. The name Apapax bears some resemblance to Atakapa, but this may be fortuitous.

BIBLIOGRAPHY: Herbert Eugene Bolton, *Texas in the Middle Eighteenth Century* (Berkeley: University of California Press, 1915; rpt., Austin: University of Texas Press, 1970). Charles W. Hackett, ed., *Pichardo's Treatise on the Limits of Louisiana and Texas* (4 vols., Austin: University of Texas Press, 1931–46). *Thomas N. Campbell*

APARICIO, FRANCISCO (?–?). Francisco Aparicio was one of six Franciscans[qv] assigned to unsuccessful missions founded on the San Gabriel River in the late 1740s. After the murders of Father Juan José Ganzabal[qv] and Juan José Ceballos (1752), relations between the remaining clergy and the presidio commander, Felipe de Rábago y Terán,[qv] continued to worsen. A second priest at San Gabriel had already died of natural causes; a third determinedly remained at his mission. But Father Aparicio fled to San Antonio with two other clerics, and they did not return to their missions until after the panic had subsided.

In July 1755 Aparicio joined soldiers of the presidio in requesting permission to move the failed settlements to the San Marcos River. By August 16 the two remaining missions and a presidio had been relocated without formal approval of the viceroy. On August 23, 1755, Father Aparicio and two fellow priests petitioned the new military commander, Pedro de Rábago y Terán,[qv] for reassignment among Lipan Apaches on the San Saba River. That request was denied.

Aparicio then participated in the temporary transfer of San Francisco Xavier de Horcasitas Mission to the Guadalupe River. Immediately after the deaths of fathers Alonso Giraldo de Terreros[qv] and José de Santiesteban at Santa Cruz de San Sabá Mission (March 16, 1758), Aparicio was sent there by Mariano de los Dolores y Viana.[qv] Three weeks after the destruction of the mission Aparicio asked that the site be abandoned and that further efforts be directed to the San Marcos or Guadalupe rivers. Widely experienced among diverse enemies of the Apaches, such as the Mayeyes, Yojuanes, Bidais, Orcoquizas, and Cocos, the padre raised serious doubts about further attempts to missionize the Lipans.

By October 1758 Father Aparicio had returned to San Antonio, and he was present during the interrogation of Apache chief Tacu, which centered on the advisability of founding new nations for his people. As plans progressed in San Antonio for a punitive expedition against the northern nations that had destroyed Santa Cruz de San Sabá, Francisco Aparicio supplied ten Indian auxiliaries from Nuestra Señora de la Purísima Concepción Mission.

BIBLIOGRAPHY: Carlos E. Castañeda, *Our Catholic Heritage in Texas* (7 vols., Austin: Von Boeckmann–Jones, 1936–58; rpt., New York: Arno, 1976). Gary B. Starnes, *The San Gabriel Missions, 1746–1756* (Madrid: Ministry of Foreign Affairs, 1969). Robert S. Weddle, *The San Sabá Mission* (Austin: University of Texas Press, 1964).

Donald E. Chipman

APATIN INDIANS. The Apatin Indians were one of five bands of Coahuiltecans encountered near the site of present Corpus Christi by a Spanish expedition in the middle eighteenth century. They are not mentioned in later documents.

BIBLIOGRAPHY: Herbert Eugene Bolton, *Texas in the Middle Eighteenth Century* (Berkeley: University of California Press, 1915; rpt., Austin: University of Texas Press, 1970). Gabriel Saldivar, *Archivo de la historia de Tamaulipas, México* (1946). *Thomas N. Campbell*

APAYSI INDIANS. In 1691 Damián Massanet[qv] listed Apaysi as one of thirteen Indian groups seen by him on lower Hondo Creek southwest of San Antonio, apparently near the boundary line between modern Frio and Medina counties. No recognizable variant of this name has been found in other primary documents. Massanet indicated that the Apaysis and their associates all spoke the same language, the one now known as Coahuilteco. The Apaysis were not the same people as the Apayxams, who were seen by Massanet on the Guadalupe River some 125 miles farther to the east. Unlike the Apaysis, the Apayxams were associated with Indian groups who, according to Massanet, spoke languages other than Coahuilteco. The Apaysis were probably few in number when seen by Massanet, and shortly thereafter they may have lost their identity by merging with one or more of the larger groups. This supposition is suggested by the fact that no Apaysi individuals were ever recorded as having entered Spanish missions. As some of the Hondo Creek groups are known to have hunted animals and collected wild plant products in an area that extended from Hondo Creek southwestward into northeastern Coahuila, it seems likely that the Apaysis originally ranged over some part of the same area.

BIBLIOGRAPHY: Lino Gómez Canedo, ed., *Primeras exploraciones y poblamiento de Texas, 1686–1694* (Monterrey: Publicaciones del Instituto Technológico y de Estudios Superiores de Monterrey, 1968). Mattie Alice Hatcher, trans., *The Expedition of Don Domingo Terán de los Ríos into Texas*, ed. Paul J. Foik (Preliminary Studies of the Texas Catholic Historical Society 2.1 [1932]). *Thomas N. Campbell*

APEX, TEXAS. Apex was at the head of Cold Creek, eight miles southwest of Cherokee in southwestern San Saba County. The community was founded by Warren Potter, justice of the peace, as a trade center for local ranchers. For several years it had a voting box. A post office was maintained in the Potter home in 1880–81, then replaced by the post office at Algerita. The recorded population of Apex in 1884 was twenty. *Alice Gray Upchurch*

APION INDIANS. The Apion Indians, known only from records of San Antonio de Valero Mission in San Antonio, cannot be linked with any known group of Indians. The sounds suggest that the name may be a variant of Hape, but the Hapes are believed to have become extinct by 1689. An early place name near Laredo, La Cañada de los Abiones, suggests residence in Coahuiltecan Indian territory. The records of Mission Valero also contain a reference to Capellone Indians, who may be the same, but nothing is known about the Capellones either.

BIBLIOGRAPHY: Bexar Archives, Barker Texas History Center, University of Texas at Austin. Herbert Eugene Bolton, *Texas in the Middle Eighteenth Century* (Berkeley: University of California Press, 1915; rpt., Austin: University of Texas Press, 1970). *Thomas N. Campbell*

APOLONIA, TEXAS. Apolonia, three miles east of Anderson in south central Grimes County, was founded as a lumbering center about 1835, although settlement had begun in the area in the early 1830s. The Pine Grove Baptist Church was built in the early 1840s, and later a school was established in the vicinity. A black Methodist church, known as Yarborough's Chapel, was constructed after the Civil War.[qv] The settlement was invigorated in the 1880s and 1890s by an influx of Polish immigrants. A local post office established in 1889 was named by Polish Catholic residents in honor of Saint Appolonia. At the turn of the century the community had three general stores and two sawmills. In 1907, however, the post office was discontinued, and mail was redirected through Anderson. In 1910 Apolonia reported a population of thirty. In 1920 two businesses were operating in the town. In 1948, the last year for which figures are available, an estimated twenty-five residents and one accredited business remained.

BIBLIOGRAPHY: Grimes County Historical Commission, *History of Grimes County, Land of Heritage and Progress* (Dallas: Taylor, 1982). Fred Tarpley, *1001 Texas Place Names* (Austin: University of Texas Press, 1980). *Charles Christopher Jackson*

APPLEBY, TEXAS. Appleby is on U.S. Highway 59 and Farm roads 941 and 2609 seven miles northeast of Nacogdoches in central Nacogdoches County. The site was originally a Caddo Indian village. White settlers began arriving in the area in the 1820s but did not develop a community until the early 1880s, when the Houston, East and West Texas Railway was built through the area. The railroad platted a new town and named it for James Appleby, former auditor of the HEWT. In 1885 the community had a reported population of 100, a general store, and two cotton gins; a post office began operating in 1889. At its height during World War I[qv] the town had a population of nearly 1,000, four churches, two gins, four sawmills, two hotels, and several drugstores. The Appleby school, founded before 1900, became the first independent school district in the county. By the mid-1920s the population had fallen to 500; many residents moved to Nacogdoches. Several tornados[qv] damaged the town, especially one in 1942. By the early 1950s the population had dwindled to 250. During the late 1950s and early 1960s most of the remaining businesses closed. The post office was discontinued in 1958, and by 1964 the last store had closed. The town incorporated around 1970, even as the population decline continued. In the early 1980s Appleby began to revive as retirees and others from nearby Nacogdoches began building homes in the area. In 1990 the population was 449.

BIBLIOGRAPHY: Nacogdoches County Genealogical Society, *Nacogdoches County Families* (Dallas: Curtis, 1985). *Christopher Long*

APPLEGATE, TEXAS. Applegate was on the Gulf, Beaumont and Great Northern Railway between Roganville and Jasper in east central Jasper County, about sixty-eight miles north of Beaumont. The railroad was extended north from Roganville into northern Jasper County in 1901–02, thus opening large expanses of timberland to major lumbering operations. As part of this expansion the Jasper Lumber Company, of which H. D. Applegate was an officer, began to acquire large amounts of land in Jasper County. The stop named after Applegate was established sometime after 1905. The Jasper Lumber Company was reorganized as the Texas and Ohio Lumber Company and had extensive property rights in the area as well as 2½ miles of tram lines. The mill at Applegate, however, did not succeed as well as many others in the county. The company went into receivership, and the Applegate post office was discontinued in 1909. The mill at Applegate, which once had a population of about 300, was removed in 1912. Highway and geological survey maps of the 1980s did not designate the site.

BIBLIOGRAPHY: Ed Ellsworth Bartholomew, *800 Texas Ghost Towns* (Fort Davis, Texas: Frontier, 1971). *Robert Wooster*

APPLE SPRINGS, TEXAS. Apple Springs, also known as May Apple Springs, is at the junction of State Highway 94 and Farm roads 357 and 2501, fifteen miles northeast of Groveton in northeastern Trinity County. The community was established after the Civil War[qv] and was originally known as May Apple Springs for the abundant may apples that grew on the banks of a nearby spring-fed creek. When a post office opened in 1884 the name was shortened to Apple Springs. A school began operating around the same time; in 1896 it had an enrollment of twenty-eight. When the Groveton, Lufkin and Northern Railway was built between Groveton and Vair, the town was moved a short distance to the railroad. By the time of World War I[qv] the community had three general stores, a gin, a bank, a cafe, and a population of seventy-five. When the railroad was abandoned in 1931, the town was moved to State Highway 94, which had been constructed two years before. During the mid-1930s Apple Springs had twelve rated businesses and 150 residents. The population continued to grow during the 1950s and 1960s, reaching a high of 285 in 1965. In the early 1990s the town had a reported population of 130 and nine businesses.

BIBLIOGRAPHY: Patricia B. and Joseph W. Hensley, eds., *Trinity County Beginnings* (Groveton, Texas: Trinity County Book Committee, 1986). *Christopher Long*

APPURCEON CREEK. Appurceon Creek rises eight miles southeast of Asherton in south central Dimmit County (at 28°21′ N, 99°46′ W) and runs northeast for nineteen miles to its mouth on the Nueces River, twelve miles east of Asherton (at 28°29′ N, 99°33′ W). It traverses an area of rolling hills surfaced by clay and sandy loam that supports scrub brush, mesquite, cacti, and grasses; in the creek's lower reaches the terrain becomes flat with locally shallow depressions, and the vegetation changes to water-tolerant hardwoods and grasses.

AQUARENA SPRINGS. Aquarena Springs, at San Marcos Springs just off U.S. Highway 81 in San Marcos, Texas, is a resort and amusement park that attracts tourists and visitors year-round. The springs, a cluster of 200 in all, originate in the Edwards Plateau[qv] sixteen miles north and flow from the Edwards Aquifer at the rate of 200 million gallons daily to form the headwaters of the San Marcos River. The area is also distinguished by the eroded Balcones Escarpment,[qv] which rises above the plateau where the park is located. The complex ecosystem of the springs comprises more than fifty varieties of fish and 125 species of plants, as well as the endangered San Marcos dwarf salamander.

To Tonkawa Indians in the area the springs were known as Canocanayesatetlo, meaning "warm water." The expedition of Isidro Félix de Espinosa, Antonio de San Buenaventura Olivares, and Pedro de Aguirre[qqv] in 1709 likely discovered the springs, but the springs were named by Franciscans[qv] exploring the Guadalupe River valley for a place to which to move the San Xavier Missions[qv] and presidio in 1755. Fourteen years after the area became a Mexican land grant in 1831, settlers began to arrive and two ranches were established nearby. In Spanish Texas[qv] the springs were an important stop on the Old San Antonio Road,[qv] which ran between northern Mexico and Nacogdoches, and from 1867 to 1895 they served as a stopping place on the Chisholm Trail.[qv]

A. B. Rogers, owner of a San Marcos funeral home and furniture store, purchased the property in 1926. His son Paul developed it by building the Springlake Hotel in 1928 and introducing glass-bottom boats on Spring Lake. The hotel failed to survive the Great Depression,[qv] but was restored in 1961 as the Aquarena Springs Hotel. In the 1950s, construction of a submarine theater and large spillway at one end of the lake to produce a swimming pool led to the opening of an amusement park at the site in 1951.

The Aquarena Springs Resort, which attracts 250,000 visitors annually, is built around Spring Lake on an archeological site that has yielded Clovis artifacts, including spear points, believed to be 12,000 years old. Among other features the resort offers a Franciscan mission, a 100-year old gristmill, Texana Village, and an underwater show originally designed by Don and Margaret Russell, who developed similar shows in Florida. The current show also features a swimming pig named Ralph. In 1977 the park employed 225 persons, including students from nearby Southwest Texas State University.

In 1993 Southwest Texas State University acquired the property from the Aquarena Springs Corporation with the help of its nonprofit support foundation and revenue bonds authorized by the state legislature; previous owners retained an interest. Plans were to preserve the ecosystem and use the resort for conferences and other educational purposes.

BIBLIOGRAPHY: Gunnar Brune, *Springs of Texas*, Vol. 1 (Fort Worth: Branch-Smith, 1981). *Diana J. Kleiner*

AQUILLA, TEXAS. Aquilla is on Farm Road 933 twelve miles southwest of Hillsboro in southwestern Hill County. Settlers, attracted to the site because it was the nearest point to Hillsboro, where timber could be found, began moving into the area in the 1840s. Aquilla Creek is nearby. The original settlement, near the site of present Aquilla, was called Mudtown. Aquilla received a post office in 1859. Twenty years later the tracks of the Texas Central Railroad crossed southwestern Hill County, passing within a few miles of the timber settlement. Shortly thereafter, businesses and residents moved a few miles south to the rail line. The community's population was 175 in 1886 and 100 in 1892. A series of illnesses resulted from drinking creek water, so a well was dug in 1897 to provide fresh water. One of the state's first chartered banks opened at Aquilla in 1905, when the town also had a health spa. In 1910 the population surpassed 200. By 1914 it had a population of over 500 and thirteen retail stores, three hotels, four churches, a school, a newspaper, a bank, and a thriving lumber company. By the late 1950s there were 250 residents and ten businesses in Aquilla. In 1990 the population was 136.

BIBLIOGRAPHY: Hill County Historical Commission, *A History of Hill County, Texas, 1853-1980* (Waco: Texian Press, 1980).
David Minor

AQUILLA CREEK. Aquilla Creek rises near Parker in extreme southern Johnson County (at 32°14′ N, 97°17 W) and flows south for fifty miles to its mouth on the Brazos River, ten miles northwest of Waco (at 31°40′ N, 97°10′ W). In its upper reaches the creek is dammed to form Aquilla Lake, three miles from Aquilla. Below the lake the stream flows into McLennan County six miles south of Aquilla. The surrounding low-rolling to flat land is surfaced with sandy and clay loams that support brush, cacti, and grass. The area has been used for range and crop land.

ARAGO, JEAN (1788–1836). Dominque François Jean Arago, soldier, was born at Estagel, Pyrénées-Orientales, France, in 1788. In 1815 he was unjustly indicted for official misconduct in the French treasury and fled to the United States, where he joined Francisco Xavier Mina[qv] in an attempt to liberate Mexico. He sailed on the *Calypso* on October 10, 1817, and landed in Galveston, where he joined Louis Michel Aury.[qv] Mina made him military commander of Guanajuato.

After the departure of the Spanish, Arago supported the Plan de Iguala, proclaimed by Anastasio Bustamante.[qv] He participated in the successful Plan de Casamata in 1823 and was put in command of the militia division of Puebla in 1828. His ardent adherence to the York Rite Masons made him a leading liberal influence in the Mexican army. Vicente Guerrero[qv] put Arago in command of the Brigade of Zapadores (Sappers) in 1832. He was named director general of the Corps of Engineers in 1833 and was awarded "Ciudadano Benemérito" by the states of Mexico, Veracruz, Guanajuato, and Tamaulipas. He was pardoned after the overthrow of Guerrero under the Plan de Jalapa and named commanding general in the Army of Mexico. He was a general in command of a division of engineers encamped at Las Chimineas on Nueces Bay, about four miles from Corpus Christi, during the Texas Revolution.[qv] Owing to a severe illness, possibly malaria, that he contracted in May 1836, Arago went for medical treatment to New Orleans, where he died. He was highly esteemed in Mexico as a French supporter of Mexican liberty. *See also* MEXICAN WAR OF INDEPENDENCE.

BIBLIOGRAPHY: Dominique François Jean Arago, *The History of My Youth: An Autobiography of Francis Arago*, trans. Rev. Baden-Powell (London: Longmans, Green, and Longmans, 1862). Hobart Huson, *Captain Philip Dimmitt's Commandancy of Goliad, 1835–1836* (Austin: Von Boeckmann–Jones, 1974). *Frank Wagner*

ARAH, TEXAS. Arah was ten miles west of Snyder in western Scurry County. The settlement developed to serve the needs of surrounding ranches and was named for Arah Gray, daughter of E. W. Gray, a rancher in the area in the early 1890s. C. R. Fellmy may have opened a general store in Arah in 1907. About the same time E. F. Sears laid the foundation for a gin that was never completed. In 1912 Ruth Davis arrived in Arah with her family and recorded the presence of a gin, blacksmith shop, general store, and combined school and church building. The population of Arah was estimated at thirty-five in 1914. The settlement acquired a post office in 1907 with Eugene Gray as postmaster; the office was closed in March 1949, and thereafter the mail was brought from Snyder on a rural route. During the 1930s the Arah school was the center of local activity, according to Mary Ellen Chapman, who served as postmistress from 1930 to 1949. It was consolidated with the Fluvanna school eventually. During the 1930s the population was estimated at thirty, and the community had one business. In 1962 Arah had no businesses, and the population remained at thirty. By 1969 the town had disappeared from maps and listings. Oil leasing increased in the area after the discovery of the Canyon Reef oilfield in 1950. But the highest density of oil activity was mostly to the south and southeast; C. T. McLaughlin's Diamond-M ranch, with its rich wells, was located southeast of Arah, which declined as Snyder became the center of the oil trade.

BIBLIOGRAPHY: Kathryn Cotten, *Saga of Scurry* (San Antonio: Naylor, 1957). *Jeanne F. Lively*

ARAÑA CREEK. Araña (Anranta) Creek rises six miles northwest of Riviera in western Kleberg County (at 27°21′ N, 97°54′ W) and runs east for twenty-one miles to its mouth on Cayo del Grullo, one mile south of Loyola Beach (27°19′ N, 97°41′ W). *Araña* is Spanish for "spider." The surrounding terrain is flat to gently sloping and surfaced by loose sand that supports scrub brush and grasses.

ARANAMA COLLEGE. Aranama College, at Goliad, was established in 1852 under the auspices of the Presbyterian Church as an "educational clinic" for Mexicans. This men's college, named for the eighteenth-century Indian converts of Nuestra Señora del Espíritu Santo de Zúñiga Mission, resulted from the efforts of the Western Presbytery of Texas, which was organized in 1851, and particularly Rev. William C. Blair,[qv] to start a Presbyterian college within the boundaries of the presbytery. A committee, organized by the presbytery in April 1851 and chaired by Rev. Joel T. Case,[qv] who helped establish Victoria Female Academy,[qv] reported in the spring of 1852 in favor of establishing a college. Among the towns vying for the college were Lockhart, Victoria, and Goliad. The last offered as inducement the old Aranama mission and its grounds, amounting to twenty acres, plus a league of the unsold lands of the town tract and an additional $1,000 cash and 20,000 acres from the citizens of the town. Goliad was chosen because of its importance to what was called western Texas, the increased immigration of Mexicans and the proximity of Mexico, and the promise of patronage by influential local Mexican families.

The nine members of the first board of trustees were elected on March 27, 1852, and included Joel Case and J. F. Hillyer,[qv] founder of Hillyer Female College,[qv] a Baptist institution at Goliad. Aranama College, established on the Aranama mission site on the San Antonio River, opened in September 1852 with Blair as president. The Western Presbytery designated $10,000, largely the profit from the sale of the donated lands, to be used over the next five years to erect buildings and a library and to purchase "school apparatus." The school, by its state charter granted on January 25, 1854, was to be "purely literary and scientific." It was open to students of all denominations, whose "moral and religious improvements" were also a goal.

The preparatory department was the first department to function. In 1857 it offered English grammar, orthography, composition, elocution, geography, bookkeeping, elementary and higher mathematics, surveying, Latin, and Greek. Tuition ranged from three to four dollars a month. The college also sponsored the literary contests of the Adelphian Literary Society, which debated in 1859 over the question, "Should the United States re-open the African Slave Trade?"

The college was reorganized in 1860 with the hiring of new faculty members. Its three departments were the four-year college proper, whose graduates received the A.B. degree; the scientific department, designed to prepare students for business; and the preparatory department, maintained to prepare students for college. Tuition was fixed at fifty dollars a term for the college and scientific department, and twenty-five dollars for the preparatory department. Board with respectable families was also available. By 1860 about 100 students were enrolled.

Although financial problems burdened the college throughout most of its existence, it remained open until the Civil War,[qv] when the entire student body enlisted in the Confederate Army. The school building, a three-story stone structure with thirty rooms, was used by both Southern and Northern armies as a headquarters during the war. After the war the Western Presbytery was unable to keep the college in operation. Because the school's lands were given conditionally, the presbytery, following a request from local citizens, donated the land and college to the state in February 1871 on the condition that a penitentiary be located at Goliad. In August the presbytery attempted to lease the college to the state for use as a free school. The attempt apparently failed, since by April 1872 the Western Presbytery no longer laid claim to Aranama College, and the trustees had lost a suit to recover the property during the administration of Governor Edmund J. Davis.[qv] The college building was destroyed in the great storm of 1886 (*see* HURRICANES).

BIBLIOGRAPHY: Goliad County Historical Commission, *The History and Heritage of Goliad County*, ed. Jakie L. Pruett and Everett B. Cole (Austin: Eakin Press, 1983). Eugene Allen Perrin, The History of Education in Goliad County (M.A. thesis, University of Texas, 1933). William Stuart Red, *A History of the Presbyterian Church in Texas* (Austin: Steck, 1936). *Craig H. Roell*

ARANAMA INDIANS. The Aranama (Aname, Arrenamus, Auranean, Hazaname, Jaraname, Xaraname) Indians lived along the lower Guadalupe and San Antonio rivers near the coast. Although the evidence is scant, most writers today classify the Aranamas as Coahuiltecan speakers. Attempts to link them with groups named in the narrative of Álvar Núñez Cabeza de Vaca[qv] (Muruame) and in records of the La Salle expedition[qv] (Anachorema, Erigoana, Quara) have not been very convincing; the affiliations must be considered only as probabilities. Most of what is known about the Aranamas comes from Spanish mission records. Espíritu Santo de Zuñiga Mission was moved in 1722 from Matagorda Bay to the lower Guadalupe River in order to serve the Aranamas and Tamiques. In 1749 this mission was moved to the vicinity of present Goliad, and many Aranamas followed it to the new location. At various times in the late eighteenth century the Aranama deserted this mission and went north to live with other groups, particularly the Tawakonis. Each time the Spaniards induced them to return. A few Aranamas were present at other missions—San Antonio de Valero at San Antonio and Nuestra Señora del Refugio near present Refugio. During the late eighteenth and early nineteenth centuries the Aranamas slowly declined in numbers and finally disappeared about 1843. The last survivors were probably absorbed by Spanish-speaking people near the coastal missions. Some writers have implied that the Aranamas were agricultural Indians in the pre-mission period, but acceptable evidence for this has never been presented.

BIBLIOGRAPHY: Herbert Eugene Bolton, ed. and trans., *Athanase de Mézières and the Louisiana-Texas Frontier, 1768–1780* (2 vols., Cleveland: Arthur H. Clark, 1914). Herbert Eugene Bolton, *Texas in the Middle Eighteenth Century* (Berkeley: University of California Press, 1915; rpt., Austin: University of Texas Press, 1970). Thomas R. Hester, *Ethnology of the Texas Indians* (New York: Garland, 1991). Juan Agustín Morfi, *History of Texas, 1673–1779*, trans. Carlos E. Castañeda (2 vols., Albuquerque: Quivira Society, 1935; rpt., New York: Arno Press, 1967). William W. Newcomb, *The Indians of Texas* (Austin: University of Texas Press, 1961). John R. Swanton, *The Indian Tribes of North America* (Gross Pointe, Michigan: Scholarly Press, 1968). J. R. Swanton, *Linguistic Material from the Tribes of Southern Texas and Northeastern Mexico* (Washington: Smithsonian Institution, 1940). Texas Indian Commission, *The Texas Indian Commission and American Indians in Texas: A Short History with Definitions and Demographics* (Austin, 1986).

Thomas N. Campbell

ARANDA, MIGUEL DE (?–?). Miguel de Aranda, a member of the College of Santa Cruz de Querétaro,[qv] was assigned to Nuestra Señora de la Purísima Concepción Mission in San Antonio. In June 1753 he accompanied an expedition led by Lt. Juan Galván,[qv] of San Antonio de Béxar Presidio,[qv] charged with exploring lands in Apachería to the northwest of San Antonio. The expedition initially reconnoitered lands along the Pedernales and Llano rivers, without finding a suitable site for Spanish settlement. It then pushed on to the San Saba River, where more favorable conditions included abundant water and arable lands. There Father Aranda offered Mass for Apaches of the region. A favorable and optimistic report, signed by Galván but probably authored by Aranda, extoled the land as potentially rich in mineral deposits and the Apaches as prime objects of religious conversion. The account also suggested that missionizing the Apaches would obviate the need for soldiers at Bexar, who could be reassigned to a new presidio situated on the San Saba River. A subsequent entrada (1754) paralleled the findings of Galván and Aranda and served as further impetus for founding a new mission for the Lipan Apaches at the site of present Menard, Texas. After the collapse of missions of the San Gabriel River and their subsequent relocation, first on the San Marcos River and subsequently on the Guadalupe, Miguel de Aranda endorsed the Guadalupe site and later served with Francisco Aparicio[qv] at San Francisco Xavier de Horcasitas Mission[qv] until its closure in March 1758. *See also* FRANCISCANS, SAN XAVIER MISSIONS.

BIBLIOGRAPHY: Carlos E. Castañeda, *Our Catholic Heritage in Texas* (7 vols., Austin: Von Boeckmann–Jones, 1936–58; rpt., New York: Arno, 1976). Robert S. Weddle, *The San Sabá Mission* (Austin: University of Texas Press, 1964).

Donald E. Chipman

ARANSAS, TEXAS. Aransas, on the southwestern end of St. Joseph Island in what became Aransas County, was established about 1845. It was originally called St. Josephs and later named for Aransas Bay. The town was laid out by Ebenezer Allen and William G. Hale.[qqv] A stage line and ferry connected it with the mainland. Most of the inhabitants were seafarers or stockmen; the early settlers included John Baker, William Bryan, William Little, and Peter Johnson. Aransas was a port of call for vessels of the Morgan Lines[qv] and had a post office before 1860. It prospered until the Civil War,[qv] when the federal blockade ruined the shipping industry. Early in the war a Confederate post, Camp Semmes, was located at Aransas and manned by artillery under Benjamin F. Neal[qv] and William H. Maltby. Federal marines who captured the town in February 1863 were driven out by Confederate mounted riflemen under Daniel D. Shea, but the federals recaptured the town in the summer of 1862 and destroyed every building. After the war the island failed to recover its prosperity, and Aransas failed to reappear. In 1871 the site was transferred from Refugio County to Aransas County.

BIBLIOGRAPHY: Aransas County–Rockport Centennial, *A Glimpse at Our Past . . . on the Occasion of the One Hundredth Anniversary of the Incorporation of Rockport, 1870, and the Establishment of Aransas County, 1871* (Corpus Christi: Coastal Printing, 1971).

Claudia Hazlewood

ARANSAS BAY. Aransas Bay (at (28°03′ N, 96°59′ W) connects Corpus Christi Bay on the south, Mesquite Bay on the north, and Copano Bay on the west. It is protected from the Gulf of Mexico by St. Joseph Island. Entry to the bay is through the Gulf Intracoastal Waterway[qv] or through Aransas Pass between Mustang and St. Joseph islands. Aransas Bay and other waterways protected by the barrier islands played a significant role in the movement of freight during the Civil War,[qv] when federal gunboats patrolled the open Gulf waters.

BIBLIOGRAPHY: Brownson Malsch, *Indianola—The Mother of Western Texas* (Austin: Shoal Creek, 1977).

Art Leatherwood

ARANSAS CITY, TEXAS. Aransas City, now a ghost town, was founded about 1837 by James Power[qv] on Live Oak Point in what was Refugio County but is now Aransas County. Before the Texas Revolution[qv] Power built his home at the point; after the war he constructed a commissary and planned the townsite in an area once occupied by a Spanish-Mexican fort called Aránzazu, which guarded the entrance to Copano Bay. Aransas City, with several stores and an estimated population of 500, was the actual seat of government of Refugio County until April 1840, and it was often used as a refugee county seat between 1840 and 1846. The town, incorporated on January 28, 1839, was the location of a Republic of Texas[qv] customhouse. Until Corpus Christi was founded, Aransas City was the westernmost port in Texas. It reached its commercial zenith when the Mexican Federalist army had its rendezvous at Fort Lipantitlán[qv] in 1838 and much contraband traffic in munitions centered in the port. Aransas City was raided on several occasions by Comanche and Karankawa Indians and was sacked by Mexican irregulars in 1838, 1839, and 1841. The choice of Refugio as county seat, the rivalry of Corpus Christi and Lamar as ports, and the loss of the customhouse after annexation[qv] contributed to the decline of the town. It had ceased to exist by 1847.

BIBLIOGRAPHY: Aransas County–Rockport Centennial, *A Glimpse at Our Past . . . on the Occasion of the One Hundredth Anniversary of the Incorporation of Rockport, 1870, and the Establishment of Aransas County, 1871* (Corpus Christi: Coastal Printing, 1971).

Hobart Huson

ARANSAS COUNTY. Aransas County (P-18) is on the Gulf Coast northeast of Corpus Christi. The county, divided into three parts by

Copano, St. Charles, and Aransas bays, is bounded on the north and northwest by Refugio County, on the south by San Patricio and Nueces counties, and on the east by the Gulf of Mexico. The county seat and largest city is Rockport. Several highways cross the county, including State highways 35 and 361, and Farm roads 136, 881, 1781, 2040, 2165, 2725, and 3036. The county is also served by the Gulf Intracoastal Waterway.[qv]

Aransas County has an area of 276 square miles. The altitude ranges from sea level to fifty feet. The level land, part of the Coastal Prairie, is generally poorly drained. Dark, saline, loamy soils cover much of the inland terrain. Along the coastal areas are sandy beaches. In the northwest are loamy, acidic soils, with cracking, clayey subsoils. The Gulf marshes support cordgrasses, sedges, rushes, seashore saltgrass, march millet, and maiden cane. Further inland the native flora includes the tall grasses of the Gulf prairie and some hardwoods such as elms and oaks, which are found particularly along streambeds. Much of the northern portion of the county is in the Aransas National Wildlife Refuge.[qv] Between 11 and 20 percent of the land in the county is considered prime farmland.

The subtropical-humid climate features mild winters and warm summers. Temperatures range in January from an average low of 46° F to an average high of 63°, and in July from 76° to 91°. The average annual rainfall is 36 inches; the average relative humidity is 95 percent at 6 A.M. and 76 percent at 6 P.M. The growing season averages 305 days a year, with the last freeze in early February and the first freeze in mid-December.

The Aransas County area has been the site of human habitation for several thousand years. Archeological artifacts recovered in the region suggest that the earliest human inhabitants arrived around 6,000 to 8,000 years ago. Subsequent inhabitants belonged to a culture known as Aransas. Aransas campsites, some dating back approximately 4,000 years, have been found from Copano Bay in Aransas County to Baffin Bay north of Kenedy County. The Aransas Indians, a nomadic, hunter-gatherer people, appear to have left the Gulf Coast around A.D. 1200 to 1300. The region apparently afterward remained uninhabited for 100 years until the ancestors of the Karankawas moved there around A.D. 1400. During historic times, the Coastal Bend area was occupied by several groups of Indians, including the Karankawas and Coahuiltecans. These nomadic hunter-gatherers never formed a large alliance or organization. After the arrival of the Europeans most fled, succumbed to disease, or were absorbed by other Indian groups in Mexico; by the mid-1800s virtually all trace of them had disappeared.

The earliest European to see the area of the future county may have been Alonzo Álvarez de Pineda,[qv] who sailed along the Texas coast in the early summer of 1519 and may have explored Aransas Bay during his journey. Nine years later Álvar Núñez Cabeza de Vaca[qv] and his crew were shipwrecked on the Texas coast. Although their exact route is unknown, historians believe that he or members of his party may have crossed the area. The Spanish, however, largely ignored the region until the French under René Robert Cavelier, Sieur de La Salle,[qv] established a colony in Texas in 1685. Spanish authorities dispatched an expedition to the area in 1689 under Alonso De León,[qv] but no permanent settlement was founded in the area. In 1766 Diego Ortiz Parrilla[qv] conducted an exploration of the Gulf Coast and gave the names Santo Domingo to Copano Bay and Culebra Island to what is now St. Joseph Island.

By the late colonial period, the Spanish had established a small fort on Live Oak Point that they named Aránzazu, reportedly after a palace in Spain. Several attempts were made to establish settlements in the lower Nueces River valley to the south, but because of the threat of Indian attacks and the distance from other Spanish enclaves the plans came to nothing.

Across Copano Bay in what is now Refugio County, Governor Bernardo de Gálvez[qv] established a port of entry and customhouse in the 1780s, which became known as El Cópano. During the late Spanish and Mexican periods, the port, which served Goliad, Refugio, and San Antonio de Béxar, was considered the best in what was called western Texas, and hundreds of colonists landed there. Most of the colonists, however, moved inland, and only few settled in the coastal region.

The area of Aransas County lay within the border leagues closed to colonization, but the general government of Mexico, on June 11, 1828, gave an empresario[qv] grant embracing the region to James Power and James Hewetson,[qqv] who were to bring in Irish and Mexican settlers. A few Irish[qv] arrived between 1829 and 1833, among them Thomas O'Connor,[qv] Edward St. John, Edward McDonough, Peter Teal, and the Fagan and Lambert families, but the region was only sparsely settled on the eve of the Texas Revolution.[qv]

After Texas independence, the area became part of the newly formed Refugio County. Around 1832 James Power founded Aransas City on Live Oak Point near the site of the Aránzazu fort. A customhouse, a post office, and several stores were established at the settlement, which by April 1840 served as the de facto seat of government for Refugio County. Until the establishment of Corpus Christi, Aransas City was the westernmost port in Texas; its estimated population was several hundred. The town was raided by Comanche and Karankawa Indians on several occasions, and at least three times by Mexican bandits, in 1838, 1839, and 1841.

At about the same time three local figures, Capt. James W. Byrne, George R. Hull, and George Armstrong, were developing another townsite, Lamar, across the pass on Lookout Point. After Mirabeau B. Lamar[qv] became president of Texas, he ordered the customhouse moved to the new town. In 1840 Refugio became the county seat, and as a result Aransas City began to decline; by 1846 it had ceased to exist. After the revolution cattlemen and sailors founded another community, Aransas, on the southern end of St. Joseph's Island, which was a prosperous port in antebellum Texas.[qv]

Despite these developments along the coast, however, the interior of the county was still largely undeveloped. During the 1830s Power and Hewetson had purchased an additional twenty-two leagues of land, which, along with their original grant from the Mexican government, made them the largest landowners east of the Nueces. But in 1839 their title was challenged by Joseph F. Smith and several others, including Stuart Perry, Cyrus W. Egery, James W. Byrne, G. R. Hull, George Armstrong, and Joseph E. Plummer, who claimed that the Mexican grants in the county were void. The case dragged through the courts until 1845, when Smith and his fellow plaintiffs succeeded in having the original grants overturned. Litigation continued to the late 1850s, but in the end Power and Hewetson lost all of their titles, and Smith became the major landholder in the area.

During the Mexican War[qv] the Live Oak Peninsula was the site of Zachary Taylor's[qv] main encampment before he moved his army south. A short time later James W. Byrne and his associates founded the settlement of St. Joseph on the western end of St. Joseph's Island. The community proved to be short-lived, however. Byrne became associated with Pryor Lea[qv] in a plan to develop a railroad from Lamar to Goliad. In 1847 the railroad was incorporated by the legislature, and Byrne induced a number of settlers to move to Lamar, which he hoped to turn into an important port city. The Aransas Railroad Company, as Lea and Byrne called their project, changed its name to Central Transit Company a few years later. The company graded a roadbed across Live Oak Peninsula in 1858, but the threat of the Civil War[qv] terminated their plans.

In the meantime, Joseph F. Smith had begun to develop another port town, St. Mary's of Aransas, on Copano Bay, two miles up the bay from Black Point. The settlement soon became the largest lumber and building-materials center in western Texas. Regular wagon trains hauled goods inland to Refugio, Goliad, Beeville, and San Antonio, and on the eve of the Civil War St. Mary's was an important shipping point for hides, tallow, cattle, and cotton. By 1860 Lamar had two stores and a post office, but St. Mary's had become the more important port.

During the Civil War the area that was to become Aransas County was the site of several engagements between Union and Confederate forces. In February 1862 marines from the USS *Afton* went ashore on St. Joseph's Island and destroyed Aransas. By the summer, civilians had deserted the islands. Vessels of the United States Navy under J. W. Kittredge blockaded the coast, using St. Joseph's Island as a depot to store captured cotton. On May 3, 1863, Capt. Edwin E. Hobby's[qv] Confederate company attacked the Union garrison there and killed twenty, but in November 1863 federal troops under T. C. G. Robinson succeeded in regaining control of the island. St. Mary's, which had been a prime focus for blockade runners, was attacked, and its wharves and warehouses were destroyed. Many of the town's leading citizens moved elsewhere, including Joseph F. Smith, who moved to Tuxpan, Vera Cruz, where he purchased a plantation and lived until his death.

Despite the destruction and economic disruption caused by the war, the future Aransas County area quickly recovered. Aransas, which had been destroyed during the war, became a ghost town, and Lamar, which had burned during the war, declined, but several new towns were founded, including Fulton in 1866 and Rockport in 1867. During the years of the great cattle boom, the new port towns became important shipping and processing points. The first packery in the county was built by W. S. Hall in Fulton just after the war, and over the course of the next eight years the plant slaughtered 400,000 cattle. In nearby Rockport, J. M. Mathis and Dan Doughty built large wharf pens and persuaded the Morgan Lines[qv] to ship the cattle to New Orleans. Numerous other packeries sprang up, most of them located in the Rockport-Fulton area, including the Carruthers and Fulton Company, Lyman Meat Packing and Canning Company, American Meat Company, American Beef Packery, Boston Packing Company, Texas Beef Packery, and Marion Packing Company.

During the early years of the cattle boom, most of the animals were slaughtered for their hides and tallow; the lack of adequate refrigeration or preservation technology dictated that much of the meat was fed raw to pigs or thrown into the bay. Near one of the packeries was a dump for meat and carcasses that covered nearly five acres. The smell of rotting meat reportedly pervaded the area for years. In 1871 Daniel L. Holden installed the first ice machine in a packing house, thus revolutionizing the industry by enabling the packery to process most of the meat instead of disposing of it. The meat-packing industry in the area began to decline after a decade, in large part due to the rising price of cattle and competition from beef-packing plants in Chicago and Kansas City. But as late as 1880 a single factory in the Rockport-Fulton area handled 93 percent of the $500,000 worth of beef slaughtered by Texas factories in 1880.

In March 1871, because the great cattle boom had established it as the most important town in the area, Rockport became county seat of Refugio County. On September 18 of the same year, the legislature voted to divide the county and designated much of the coastal area as a new county named Aransas. Rockport was made the county seat, and on March 26, 1872, the county commissioners' court met for the first time in a rented frame house.

In 1888 the San Antonio and Aransas Pass Railroad (later the Texas and New Orleans) reached Rockport, thus ensuring the town's continued importance as a shipping center. The rise of Rockport, however, marked the beginning of the decline for St. Mary's. Successive storms in 1886 and 1887 destroyed the town's wharves, and by the early 1890s St. Mary's had dwindled to a small village.

Despite the growth of Rockport and Fulton, the county's population remained small; in 1880 it was 996. In 1888, however, all of the unsold land in the Smith and Wood subdivision was acquired by the Aransas Pass Land Company, which instituted a comprehensive plan to develop Rockport and the surrounding region. Lured by the promise of a bright future, numerous immigrants from the Old South and Europe were drawn to the county, and by 1890 the population had grown to 1,824.

A new county courthouse, designed by J. Riely Gordon,[qv] was built in 1889. By 1900 the county had seven post offices and six public schools. Between 1890 and 1900 the number of farms grew from six to forty-seven, and tourism for the first time began to play a significant role in the area's economy.

Local leaders, however, recognized that the county's continued prosperity was dependent on developing Rockport into a deepwater harbor. Several attempts had been made by the end of the nineteenth century to open a deep channel, but the lack of adequate jetties, dredging equipment, and finances had doomed the efforts. Another large construction project was undertaken after the turn of the century under the direction of a Philadelphia engineering firm, but it proved to be a fiasco that made matters worse. Vessels that had previously navigated the channel without difficulty could pass only during high tide. Several other plans failed in execution. Finally, in the 1920s, Aransas Pass became a deepwater port, but by that time the Port of Corpus Christi had been opened to oceangoing vessels, and the Aransas County ports declined in importance.

In 1919 the area was hit by a powerful hurricane (see HURRICANES), and much of Rockport and the surrounding area was destroyed. The combination of the storm and the loss of shipping to Corpus Christi dealt a serious blow to the county's economy, and for much of the next four decades it showed only modest growth. The population, which reached 2,106 in 1910, declined slightly by 1920 to 2,064, and only topped the 3,000 mark in 1940 (3,469).

During the first half of the twentieth century two new industries emerged, fishing and shipbuilding. By the early 1890s commercial fishing was flourishing in the Rockport area, and over the course of the next several decades it continued to expand, eventually outstripping agriculture in net receipts. The shrimping industry[qv] also began to develop in the 1930s, and by 1950 it produced fifty-one million pounds of shrimp.

The area's small shipbuilding industry, which had begun to develop at the end of the nineteenth century, took off during World War I[qv] and continued to prosper during the 1920s and 1930s. During World War II[qv] the United States Navy took over the Rockport Yacht and Supply Company to repair and maintain vessels in the 100-foot class, and another shipyard, owned by Rob Roy Rice, built wooden submarine chasers.

Oil was discovered in the county in 1936, and thirteen wells were in production in 1946, but it was not until the 1950s that oil was produced in large quantities. In 1990 498,703 barrels was produced; total production between 1936 and 1990 was over 77,000,000 barrels. Much of the drilling has been done offshore, and the county benefited greatly from the settlement in 1953 of the Tidelands controversy,[qv] which gave it an additional 208 square miles of submerged land area.

The first school in the county was Lamar Academy, founded around 1850. The first school in Rockport opened in 1881, and in 1884 the first public school opened there. Between 1893 and 1949 seven common school districts operated in the county, but in June 1946 they were consolidated in the Aransas County Independent School District. In the early 1980s Aransas County had three elementary, one middle, and one high school. Private schools enrolled fifty-three elementary students. Fifty-seven percent of the 139 high school graduates planned to attend college. In 1983, 62 percent of the graduates were white, 31 percent Hispanic, 3 percent black, and 5 percent Asian.

From the time of annexation[qv] until the 1950s, Aransas County was staunchly in the Democratic camp. Republican presidential candidate Herbert Hoover received a narrow majority of the county's votes in the 1928 election, but Democrats prevailed in every other election until Dwight Eisenhower's first campaign in 1952. From 1952 through 1992, Republicans won the majority of the elections; the Democrat victors were John F. Kennedy in 1960, Lyndon Baines

Johnson[qv] in 1964, Hubert Humphrey in 1968, and Jimmy Carter in 1976.

The total number of businesses in the county in the early 1990s was about 450. Leading industries included agribusiness, tourism, oil and gas extraction, and fish packing. Gross sales in 1990 totaled $193,138,955. In 1990, approximately 33 percent of the land in the county was in farms and ranches, and 14 percent of the farmland was under cultivation. Aransas County ranked 253d in the state in agricultural receipts, with 69 percent coming from crops. Principal crops included sorghum, fruits, and nuts; the primary livestock products were from cattle.

The county population was 3,469 in 1940, 4,240 in 1950, 7,006 in 1960, and 8,902 in 1970. Subsequently the county grew more rapidly: in 1980 the number of inhabitants was 14,260, and in 1990 it reached 17,892. In 1990, 85.4 percent of the population was white, 1.8 percent black, 3.3 percent Asian, and 0.6 percent American Indian. The largest cities were Rockport, Aransas Pass (part of which is in Nueces and San Patricio counties), and Fulton.

The Gulf Intracoastal Waterway, which runs the length of Aransas Bay, handles a large volume of shipping through the area and is an important element in the economy. In the late twentieth century tourist trade was also a major source of income. Local attractions include Goose Island State Park,[qv] Copano Bay State Fishing Pier, the Rockport Beach, and the Texas Maritime Museum. Special celebrations include Seafair in October, Fiesta en la Plaza in September, and the Fourth of July Fireworks and Art Festival; Oyster Fest occurs in March and the Children's Christmas Tree in November.

BIBLIOGRAPHY: Aransas County–Rockport Centennial, *A Glimpse at Our Past . . . on the Occasion of the One Hundredth Anniversary of the Incorporation of Rockport, 1870, and the Establishment of Aransas County, 1871* (Corpus Christi: Coastal Printing, 1971). Agnes Cummins, The Physical and Cultural Geography of Parts of San Patricio and Aransas Counties, Texas (M.A. thesis, University of Texas, 1953). William H. Oberste, *Texas Irish Empresarios and Their Colonies* (Austin: Von Boeckmann–Jones, 1953; 2d ed. 1973). Vertical Files, Barker Texas History Center, University of Texas at Austin.

Christopher Long

ARANSAS CREEK. Aransas Creek, also known as West Aransas Creek, rises just north of the Singleton oilfield in west central Bee County (at 28°25′ N, 97°54′ W) and runs southeast for eighteen miles to its mouth on the Aransas River, two miles north of Skidmore (at 28°17′ N, 97°40′ W). The creek traverses flat to rolling terrain surfaced by clay and sandy loam that supports water-tolerant hardwoods and grasses.

ARANSAS HARBOR TERMINAL RAILWAY. The Aransas Harbor Terminal Railway was chartered on June 13, 1892, to begin on Aransas Harbor in Aransas County and run east across the north end of Harbor Island, then turn south to Turtle Cove, and then east across Turtle Cove to the north end of Mustang Island, for a total distance of ten miles. The capital was $250,000, and the principal place of business was Aransas Harbor. The members of the first board of directors were J. P. Nelson and Edgar Foster of San Antonio, John W. Maddox of Austin, D. M. Picton of Rockport, T. P. McCampbell of Goliad, Fred S. Løvenskjold of Nueces County, and J. Reiley of Refugio County.

The charter was later amended to provide for the construction of a harbor at Aransas. The Baltimore syndicate managed by Alexander Brown and Company controlled this operation. After several private and government attempts failed to get a deepwater pass between Mustang and St. Joseph islands, the United States Army Corps of Engineers took over the project in 1907 and built Aransas Pass.

The D. M. Picton firm of Rockport was contracted to do the jetty work. Picton and J. P. Nelson began by constructing a railroad to carry granite blocks to be used on the jetties into the Gulf of Mexico. The railroad was built on a series of man-made islands connected by trestles ending at Morris and Cummins Cut, a distance of 3½ miles. Rock for the jetties was brought into Aransas Pass by the San Antonio and Aransas Pass Railway and then onto the Terminal Railway. At the end of the line the rock was loaded onto barges for the trip to the jetty site. Later the barges were equipped with tracks so that the entire car could be transferred to the building site. Old-timers referred to this line as the Old Terminal Railway to distinguish it from one later completed all the way to Harbor Island by a different route. The Old Terminal was abandoned in 1917.

In June 1909 the Aransas Pass Channel and Dock Company filed for a charter with the announced intention of building a channel 8½ feet deep and 100 feet wide from deep water at Harbor Island to Aransas Pass on the mainland. The dredge from this channel was thrown up on one side, and this fill became the roadbed for the new Terminal Railway. The deepwater port and railroad were completed in 1912, and for the next six years the 9½-mile railroad served the booming oil port at Harbor Island. The hurricane of 1916 damaged the line, but it was put back in operation within a short time. The hurricane of 1919 did major damage to the line, and it was 1922 before service was resumed (*see* HURRICANES).

In 1916 the Aransas Harbor Terminal Railway reported passenger earnings of $320 and freight earnings of $58,000 and owned two locomotives and thirty-seven cars. In 1931 it reported total earnings of $11,000 and owned two locomotives and fourteen cars. When Corpus Christi was opened as a deepwater port in 1926, business on the Terminal Railway diminished. During World War I[qv] a Model-T Ford truck was converted to an engine, and a very popular passenger service was opened between Harbor Island and the mainland. Later the little railroad began hauling automobiles on flatcars to Harbor Island, from where they went to Mustang Island by ferry. Still later, planks were put in between the rails, and a road was made for motorists to drive to Harbor Island. A toll road was opened in 1931. After the railroad closed in 1947, auto traffic continued until 1960, when the state constructed a new road to Harbor Island. All that remained in 1990 was a few pilings that offered grandstand seats for sea birds to watch the traffic roar by.

BIBLIOGRAPHY: Aransas Pass *Progress*, November 19, 1909, February 24, 1911, April 21, 1921, September 29, 1922. Keith Guthrie, *History of San Patricio County* (Austin: Nortex, 1986). *Keith Guthrie*

ARANSAS NATIONAL WILDLIFE REFUGE. Aransas National Wildlife Refuge, originally known as Aransas Migratory Waterfowl Refuge, is located on Blackjack Peninsula, eight miles southeast of Austwell and midway between Rockport and Port Lavaca, on the Gulf Coast. The refuge comprises 54,829 acres of scattered blackjack oak woodlands, fresh and saltwater marshes, ponds, and coastal grasslands on the mainland, as well as 56,668 acres on Matagorda Island. Karankawa, Lipan, Tonkawa, and Comanche Indians once occupied the area. The refuge occupies land on which it is believed pirate Jean Laffite[qv] buried treasure. In 1937 surface rights to what was by then the St. Charles Ranch of San Antonio oilman Leroy G. Denman[qv] were purchased by the government with funds raised from the sale of migratory bird stamps, and the refuge was established on December 31, 1937, with 47,261 acres on the Blackjack Peninsula. Continental Oil Company won the right to extract oil and gas within the refuge. In 1967 the refuge acquired an additional 7,568 acres along St. Charles Bay; it also purchased 19,000 acres on Matagorda Island in 1982 and another 11,502 acres in 1986. Another 2,940 acres of the island was added to the refuge in 1993.

The refuge forms a unit in the Central Flyway, which extends from Alaska and Arctic Canada southward. It provides wintering grounds for the rare whooping crane,[qv] 320 species of other birds including wild turkeys and Canadian geese, and thirty-seven species of mammals. Among the inhabitants are deer, armadillos, javelinas, and alligators. Facilities at the refuge include an observation tower, a picnic area, a car tour route, walking trails, and an environmental study area. Hunting for deer and feral hogs is permitted in season. The refuge on the mainland is administered by the United States Fish and Wildlife Service, Department of the Interior; Matagorda Island State Park[qv] is managed by the Texas Parks and Wildlife Department[qv] as a unit of the National Wildlife Refuge System. In the late 1980s the refuge was losing about twenty-five acres of shoreline each year as a result of erosion. By 1991 volunteer projects had succeeded in stabilizing 4,785 feet of shoreline, but the problem was still not solved.

BIBLIOGRAPHY: Wayne H. and Martha K. McAlister, *Guidebook to the Aransas National Wildlife Refuge* (Victoria, Texas: Mince Country Press, 1987). U.S. Fish and Wildlife Service, *National Wildlife Refuges and Fish Hatcheries: Region Two* (GPO, 1988). Vertical Files, Barker Texas History Center, University of Texas at Austin (Aransas National Wildlife Refuge, Whooping Cranes, Matagorda Island).

Diana J. Kleiner

ARANSAS PASS. Aransas Pass is the water passage between Mustang and St. Joseph islands, located at 27°50′ north latitude and 97°03′ west longitude. A deepwater entrance has been dredged into channels leading to Corpus Christi, Aransas, and Red Fish bays. This natural pass over a sandy bar was known to exist as early as 1528, when it was clearly indicated on the Bratton map. It was called Aránzazu by Governor Prudencio de Orobio y Basterra[qv] on his map of 1739; the name was altered to Aransas on the map of a Captain Monroe of the ship *Amos Wright* (1833). Powers and Hewetson colonists came into Copano Bay across the Aransas bar in 1830–34, when the water depth was variously reported to be seven to eighteen feet.

The commercial need for a deepwater entrance and port south of Galveston focused serious attention on the Aransas bar as early as 1853, when considerable material was being lightered to the mainland for trade with settlers and Mexico. By 1854 the Texas legislature had authorized a seven-mile channel from Corpus Christi to the bar. In 1855 a lighthouse was erected on Harbor Island in Red Fish Bay adjacent to the pass (*see* ARANSAS PASS LIGHT STATION), but the lighthouse was soon more than a mile away, since the pass migrated toward the south. In the years following, the construction of dikes, revetments, sand fences, jetties, brush and stone mattresses, and tree plantings all failed to stop the erosion or to deepen the channel across the bar significantly.

By 1885 jetties, a breakwater, and a mattress revetment along the channel face of Mustang Island had greatly retarded the erosion. A south jetty, known as the Mansfield Jetty, was also constructed of brush mattresses and stone. By 1889 an eighteen-inch-thick riprap cover, which effectively curtailed the erosion, had been installed. A government decision to develop Galveston as the Texas deepwater port temporarily prevented appropriations for further major changes.

In 1890 the Aransas Pass and Harbor Company, under government contract, began a major effort to deepen the channel through the pass. The company was to construct two jetties. The south or Nelson jetty was constructed of cylindrical wooden caissons that extended 1,800 feet eastward along the face of the Mustang Island channel. The north, or Haupt, jetty was constructed of stone. It was detached from the shore of St. Joseph Island and curved; it was intended to be 6,200 feet long but was completed only to about three-fourths of its planned length. These jetties failed to increase the channel depth. A subsequent attempt, by a contractor of the company, to blast a channel with thousands of pounds of dynamite was also unsuccessful.

The Rivers and Harbors Act of 1899 provided for the removal of the old Mansfield jetty. After two serious attempts and much difficulty the work was considered complete by 1911. Authorization was given to construct a new south jetty and to join the detached Haupt jetty to St. Joseph Island in 1907. By 1919 the south jetty had been completed to 7,385 feet and the Haupt jetty to 9,241 feet, and the channel began to deepen. With the assurance of deep water across the bar, channels were opened to Aransas Pass, Rockport, and Corpus Christi. The great hurricanes[qv] of 1916 and 1919, with related economic alterations, caused the United States Army Corps of Engineers to declare Corpus Christi the South Texas deepwater port after access to the city was made available through Aransas Pass. The port of Corpus Christi opened in 1926 and has continued to grow and to accommodate larger and deeper-draft vessels.

BIBLIOGRAPHY: Lynn M. Alperin, *Custodians of the Coast: History of the United States Army Engineers at Galveston* (Galveston: U.S. Army Corps of Engineers, 1977). Cyril Matthew Kuehne, S.M., *Hurricane Junction: A History of Port Aransas* (San Antonio: St. Mary's University, 1973). Frank Wagner, ed., and William M. Carroll, trans., *Béranger's Discovery of Aransas Pass* (Friends of the Corpus Christi Museum, 1983).

Art Leatherwood

ARANSAS PASS, TEXAS. Aransas Pass, across Redfish Bay from Port Aransas in Aransas, San Patricio, and Nueces counties, is named for the pass between Mustang and St. Joseph's islands. The town's early developers wanted to found a great deepwater port city on the Gulf of Mexico. The first attempts to develop the area were made by Pryor Lea,[qv] who founded the Aransas Road Company to link the coast with San Antonio by means of both a railroad and a turnpike. The enterprise, however, was a failure. Lea succeeded in building only a short distance of road, and the railroad never advanced beyond the planning stage. In the late 1850s the Central Transit Company, backed by English investors, sought to turn Lea's dream into reality by financing construction of a harbor and the railroad. But with the outbreak of the Civil War[qv] the work was interrupted and funding dried up.

Efforts at making the port also began before the Civil War. The United States Army Corps of Engineers studied the possibility of a deepwater port at Aransas Pass harbor in 1853. But it was not until 1879, when a group from Rockport raised $10,000 for the project, that work began in earnest. Congress passed a resolution in 1879 authorizing the deepening of Aransas Pass. Samuel M. Mansfield worked unsuccessfully on this project from May of 1880 to 1885.

The Texas Homestead and Farmers Association (renamed Aransas Pass Land Company in 1888) took out a charter in 1882 with the intention of purchasing and subdividing land. In 1890 the Aransas Pass Harbor Company and the Aransas Harbor City and Improvement Company were chartered by largely the same people. The harbor company planned to dig a channel from the Gulf to the site where the Harbor City Company proposed to develop Harbor City. Russell B. Harrison, son of the late president William Henry Harrison, and Thomas Benton Wheeler,[qv] former lieutenant governor of Texas, were two of the key organizers.

Nationwide publicity generated interest from all over the United States. The three-story Hoyt Hotel (later renamed Bay View) was opened in 1893 to accommodate and impress the flood of prospects who flocked in by rail and sea to inspect the new port city. The so-called Terminal Railroad that would link Aransas Pass to the mainland began in 1891. Rock for the planned jetty was shipped in on the San Antonio and Aransas Pass Railway, transferred to the Terminal Railroad, and then off-loaded to barges to be taken to the pass.

A double-barreled blow ended the dream. The panic of 1893 dried up funds, and the channel-deepening project turned out to be a failure. People who had flocked into Aransas Pass now vanished just as fast. The promoters eventually offered to turn their $401,554 channel-deeping project over to the federal government at no charge, and in 1899 the United States Corps of Engineers was authorized to tackle the project. By 1907 a second jetty had been installed, and a deepwater channel had been extended to Harbor Island. Deep water had finally arrived after a fifty-year struggle.

Wheeler, who had remained faithfully committed to Aransas Pass, now interested real estate developers in the site. The developers negotiated a deal with Mary McCampbell for 12,000 acres of land, and the stage was set for one of the biggest land sales ever held in South Texas. Six thousand land-lottery tickets were sold for $100 each to people in the Midwest. Each ticket guaranteed the holder one city lot and a chance at three giant prizes. The sale was a huge success, despite the fact that postal inspectors stepped in and forced competitive bidding rather than the agreed-on price of $100.

While the dredging was underway on the pass and Harbor Island, the developers dug a channel 100 feet wide and 8½ feet deep from the mainland to Harbor Island. The dredged material was thrown to one side, forming a roadbed for the Terminal Railroad, which was extended from Harbor Island to the mainland to join the Southern Pacific main line. Oceangoing vessels began to call regularly, and on September 7, 1912, a week-long celebration was staged with the ocean liner *Brinkburn* as the centerpiece. Records show that in the two weeks ending on September 13, 1912, 47,093 bales of cotton were shipped.

W. H. Vernor was elected mayor in April 1910, when the city was incorporated; commission government was approved in 1952. Harbor City and Aransas Pass were just settling into routine shipping when the hurricane of 1916 struck. Damage was heavy, but repairs were completed within two months, and business was back to normal. In September 1919 a second hurricane did tremendous damage to the town of Aransas Pass and the shipping facilities. Visions that Aransas Pass had for becoming the deepwater port for the lower Gulf coast were smashed on June 5, 1920, when the Corps of Engineers announced that Corpus Christi had been chosen over Aransas Pass and Rockport. Aransas Pass sought funds to dig its own channel through a countywide bond issue, but the measure failed. Harbor Island continued as an oil terminal, but for all practical purposes no further cargo shipments were made in and out of Harbor Island after the port of Corpus Christi opened for business in 1926. Eventually the channel dredged by the Aransas Pass Channel and Dock Company in 1909–10 was taken over by the Corps of Engineers.

Although development of Aransas Pass has been primarily centered around the harbor, the town grew on all fronts. The school system originated in 1892 when local Methodists erected a combination church and school building. In 1911 a two-story brick building was constructed, and in 1988 it was still used as the central office for the school district. The first post office was opened in 1892 with Charles T. Black as the postmaster.

After the hurricane of 1919 a seawall was built, and steady growth of the shrimping and fishing fleet brought business into Aransas Pass. Shrimp canneries opened, and later, when quick freezing techniques were developed, packing plants were built on the harbor. With the improvements to Conn Brown Harbor after World War II,[qv] the shrimping fleet grew to be the largest on the Gulf coast. Allied industries have grown up on the port and in the city. In the 1980s Aransas Pass had an estimated population of over 7,000. In 1990 the population was 7,180.

BIBLIOGRAPHY: Lynn M. Alperin, *Custodians of the Coast: History of the United States Army Engineers at Galveston* (Galveston: U.S. Army Corps of Engineers, 1977). Keith Guthrie, *History of San Patricio County* (Austin: Nortex, 1986). Hobart Huson, *Refugio: A Comprehensive History of Refugio County from Aboriginal Times to 1953* (2 vols., Woodsboro, Texas: Rooke Foundation, 1953, 1955).

Keith Guthrie

ARANSAS PASS LIGHT STATION. Aransas Pass Light Station, on Harbor Island in Aransas County, was built in 1855 by the United States government to facilitate navigation on Aransas Bay. The station has a tapered octagonal brick tower, three wooden auxiliary dwellings, and a radio shack. It is the second oldest lighthouse on the Texas coast and the oldest surviving structure in the Aransas Pass–Corpus Christi area. A state historical marker was placed at the site in 1973, and in 1977 the station was added to the National Register of Historic Places.

BIBLIOGRAPHY: Marker Files, Texas Historical Commission, Austin.

Christopher Long

ARANSAS RIVER. The Aransas River rises at the confluence of Olmos, Aransas, and Poesta creeks, two miles north of Skidmore in south central Bee County (at 28°17′ N, 97°40′ W). It flows southeast for forty miles, forming the boundary between San Patricio and Refugio counties and continuing into Aransas County, where it empties into Copano Bay ten miles northeast of Rockport (at 28°05′ N, 97°13′ W). The river, named for an Indian group, traverses flat to rolling terrain with clay loam and sandy loam soils that support water-tolerant hardwoods and grasses. While Texas was attempting to secure separate statehood from Coahuila (*see* COAHUILA AND TEXAS), Juan N. Almonte[qv] wrote that the Aransas formed the southwestern boundary of Texas: "Notwithstanding that up to the present it has been believed that the river Nueces is the dividing line between Coahuila and Texas, for so it appears on maps, I am informed by the government of the State, that in this an error has been committed by geographers, and that the true boundary ought to commence at the mouth of the Aransas and continue up to its source."

ARBADAO INDIANS. The Arbadao Indians were an otherwise unidentified group met by Álvar Núñez Cabeza de Vaca[qv] between 1528 and 1534 at prickly-pear grounds in southern Texas.

BIBLIOGRAPHY: Frederick Webb Hodge, ed., *Handbook of American Indians North of Mexico* (2 vols., Washington: GPO, 1907, 1910; rpt., New York: Pageant, 1959).

Margery H. Krieger

ARBALA, TEXAS. Arbala is on Farm roads 1567 and 2081 eleven miles south of Sulphur Springs in south central Hopkins County. The area was first settled in 1857 by F. L. and Daniel Clinton and called Clinton's Prairie. C. C. Harper built a mill and gin there in 1881 and became postmaster when a post office named Arbala was established in 1899. A local school was opened before 1905, when it had 113 students. By 1914 the community had four general stores and a population of fifty. The post office was closed in 1923. In 1925 the town reported 100 inhabitants. In the mid-1930s Arbala had a church, a cemetery, one business, and a number of scattered dwellings. After World War II[qv] the population began to decline, and in 1952 the community reported only twenty inhabitants. In 1990 Arbala had a population of forty-one, a church, a community center, and a cemetery.

J. E. Jennings

ARBOR GROVE, TEXAS. Arbor Grove, ten miles east of Crockett on Farm Road 232 in southeastern Houston County, was established before 1900. A post office operated there under the name Arbor between 1901 and 1906. In the mid-1930s the community comprised a church and a number of houses. After World War II[qv] many of the residents moved away, and by the early 1990s only the church and a few houses remained.

Christopher Long

ARBUCKLE, MACLYN (1866–1931). Maclyn (Jedge) Arbuckle, character actor, was born at San Antonio on July 9, 1866. His mother was a Virginian and his father a Scot. Arbuckle's father sent him to Glasgow and Boston to prepare for Harvard and the Episcopal clergy, but Arbuckle rebelled and returned home to Galveston in 1883. Next the senior Arbuckle put his son in a drugstore to make a doctor out of him; but Maclyn broke so much glassware that after two months he was put in a hardware store. A succession of jobs followed—in a cotton office, on his father's stock farm near Dallas, and in the legal profession. He was admitted to the bar at Texarkana a few months before his twenty-first birthday, but was not financially successful as a lawyer. He could not afford a room, so he slept on a table in his office. His uncle sent him a measure of cloth to have made into a suit, but since Arbuckle could not afford the expense of a tailor, he used the cloth as a mattress and a volume of philosophy as a pillow. During these difficult financial times he became interested in the study of the classics and philosophy and, as he put it, "gradually worked down the centuries until I landed on Shakespeare, and there I stuck." He spent long hours memorizing Shakespeare's plays and recited passages to his friends whenever they would allow it. He also found an outlet for his interest in theater while campaigning to become justice of the peace in Bowie County. Riding a yellow horse and a mule on alternate days, he frequented all the barbecues and barrooms reciting the dream scene from *Richard III* before gamblers, saloonmen, rangers, cowpunchers, and river-hands. He lost the election but still acquired the nickname "Jedge." Ultimately, Arbuckle decided to leave "the quiet and deliberate starvation of the law and try the stage."

He made his first professional stage appearance at Shreveport, Louisiana, on December 25, 1888, in *The Emigrant,* with Peter Baker. He spent three seasons in the classical atmosphere of the R. D. MacLean company; in 1892–94 he played with Charles Frohman's company in *Men and Women* and *The Girl I Left Behind Me;* in 1895–96 he was with the Frawley Stock Company in San Francisco, most notably in *Brother John* and *The Senator.* According to Arbuckle, playing the role of the senator gave him the "idea of becoming identified with the big, typical, everyday American character as [his] special line of work." In 1898 he made his first London appearance, at the Strand Theatre, as John Smith in *Why Smith Left Home.* Arbuckle portrayed Jim Hackler in *The County Chairman,* a part he played four consecutive seasons, from 1903 to 1907. Another success followed with the role of Slim Hoover in *The Round Up* in 1907. He appeared from 1915 to 1917 as Rev. Murray Hilton in a rewritten revival of *The Henrietta;* he played John Tarleton in William Faversham's production of George Bernard Shaw's *Misalliance* in 1917. He played in *Lord and Lady Algy* and *Home Again* in 1918 and in *The Better 'Ole* in 1920. During his life he performed in more than thirty stage productions; many of these engagements lasted for more than one season, and some ran from two to four seasons.

During the successful run of *The Better 'Ole* on Broadway, William C. Hogg[qv] of Houston and some people from San Antonio approached Arbuckle with the idea of starting a motion picture company. Arbuckle resigned from *The Better 'Ole* and moved to San Antonio, where he formed the San Antonio Pictures Corporation in March 1918. As president and star, he produced Maclyn Arbuckle Photo Plays, one of which was *The Prodigal Judge.* During the 1920s he appeared in light films, primarily as a supporting player: *The Prodigal Judge, Welcome to Our City, Mr. Potter of Texas, Mr. Bingle, The Young Diana* (1922), *Broadway Broke* (1923), *Janice Meredith* (1924), *That Old Gang of Mine* (1925), and *The Gilded Highway* (1926). He also worked in two New York stage plays, *Daddy Dumplins* in 1921 and *Wild Oats Lane* in 1923.

He married Elizabeth Sheldon Carlisle. They had no children. Arbuckle died at Waddington, New York, on March 31, 1931, after a long illness. *See also* FILM INDUSTRY.

BIBLIOGRAPHY: Maclyn Arbuckle, "Some Texas Experiences," *Green Book Album,* April 1909. Johnson Briscoe, *Actor's Birthday Book* (New York: Moffat, Yard, 1908). Larry Langman, *Encyclopedia of American Film Comedy* (New York: Garland, 1987). New York *Times,* April 1, 1931. San Antonio *Express,* March 16, 1919. *Texas Magazine,* November 1910. *Who Was Who in the Theatre* (4 vols., Detroit: Gale Research, 1978).

Donna P. Parker

ARCADIA, TEXAS (Galveston County). Arcadia, on State Highway 6 in northwest Galveston County, was established around 1889 near Hall's Bayou on the Gulf, Colorado and Santa Fe Railway and named for Arcadia, Louisiana. The townsite was laid out by Henry Runge[qv] in 1890 and originally named Hall's Station. It included land for a school and a public park. Early families included the Halls, the Owenses, the Perrys, and the Dauras. The post office was founded in 1891. Several churches were organized in the 1890s, and in 1892 the White Horse Inn was built to impress prospective land buyers. The site of Arcadia was on Stephen F. Austin's[qv] fourth land grant. The area had been occupied by the Coco Indians and explored by Álvar Núñez Cabeza de Vaca.[qv] By 1900 Arcadia had a population of 168, and in 1907 its school had eighty-nine pupils and two teachers. The town grew to 300 by 1920. Dairying became the largest industry. During the 1920s the Arcadia Creamery was founded, and the Farmer's Cooperative Feed and Grocery Store opened. In 1947 Arcadia had a post office, ten businesses, and a population of 275. By the 1980s Arcadia was within the boundaries of Santa Fe, an incorporated town. Arcadia hosted the annual county fair at Runge Park.

BIBLIOGRAPHY: Galveston *Daily News,* January 31, 1966, February 22, 1970. Kathleen E. and Clifton R. St. Clair, eds., *Little Towns of Texas* (Jacksonville, Texas: Jayroe Graphic Arts, 1982).

Leigh Gard

ARCADIA, TEXAS (Shelby County). Arcadia is at the junction of Farm roads 138 and 1645, ten miles southwest of Center in western Shelby County. In 1903 it had two schools, one for white children that had sixty-eight pupils, and one for black children that had sixteen pupils. By 1938 the school district had been consolidated with a nearby common school district. In 1946 the community had a church, two stores, a gin, and a population estimated at twenty-five. From 1972 through 1990 the population was reported as twenty.

BIBLIOGRAPHY: John Clements, *Flying the Colors: Texas, a Comprehensive Look at Texas Today, County by County* (Dallas: Clements Research, 1984).

Cecil Harper, Jr.

ARCAHOMO INDIANS. The Arcahomo (Axcahomo) Indians appear to have been related to the Tacames, a Coahuiltecan group that lived near the Gulf Coast between the San Antonio and Nueces rivers in the eighteenth century. Arcahomo may be a synonym for Tacame, or it may refer to a subdivision of the Tacames. It is also possible that the Arcahomos represent remnants of some former coastal group that became attached to the Tacames. The name Arcahomo appears only in records that pertain to San Francisco de la Espada Mission in San Antonio, chiefly in connection with an episode of 1737, when all Indians deserted this mission.

BIBLIOGRAPHY: Frederick Webb Hodge, ed., *Handbook of American Indians North of Mexico* (2 vols., Washington: GPO, 1907, 1910; rpt., New York: Pageant, 1959).

Thomas N. Campbell

ARCHAMBEAU, ERNEST R. (1891–1987). Ernest R. Archambeau, amateur historian, was born on December 25, 1891, in Perry, Missouri. He arrived in the Texas Panhandle in 1914 as a student at West Texas State Normal College (now West Texas State University), where he received his bachelor's degree in economics. During World War I[qv] he served in France for fifteen months. He also attended Westminster College in Fulton, Missouri, and the University of Montpellier in France. He married Zerah McReynolds in 1920, and they had one son. In 1926 Archambeau moved permanently to Amarillo, where he pursued a long career in the insurance business.

His interest in Panhandle[qv] history began when he interviewed José (Chencho) Romero, the adopted son of Tascosa pioneer Casimero Romero.[qv] Historical research remained his chief hobby, and over the years he made many noteworthy contributions to the field. He traced Josiah Gregg's[qv] Fort Smith–Santa Fe Trail through the Panhandle, including the area where Amarillo was later founded; his location of the wagon ruts on the property of the new Palo Duro High School led to the placement of a granite monument there and the founding of the school's annual Pioneer Day. Archambeau also became an authority on the region's railroad lines. Many of his findings were published in the *Panhandle-Plains Historical Review* and other history journals. He often spoke at meetings and once was invited to address the British Historical Society in London.

Archambeau was an active member of Polk Street United Methodist Church in Amarillo, where he taught Sunday school for fifty years. He was a member of the American Legion,[qv] the American Red Cross, Friends of the Library, the Westerners Club, and the Potter County Historical Society. He was on the Cerebral Palsy board and United Way board. He was a president and district governor of the American Business Club and president of the Knife and Fork Club. He was president of the Panhandle-Plains Historical Society[qv] in 1959–60 and served on its publications committee for several years. Throughout his life Archambeau spent much time and energy promoting Amarillo and the Panhandle. Just before his death he was involved in the "Faces of Amarillo" television spots for the city's centennial. He died on March 3, 1987, and was buried in Llano Cemetery.

BIBLIOGRAPHY: Amarillo *Daily News*, March 4, 5, 1987. Amarillo *Globe-Times*, March 3, 1987. Ernest R. Archambeau Papers, Research Center, Panhandle-Plains Historical Museum, Canyon, Texas.

H. Allen Anderson

ARCHER. The *Archer*, a brig of war in the Texas Navy,[qv] also sailed under the names *Galveston* and *Brazos*. The ship, named in honor of Texas diplomat Branch Tanner Archer,[qv] was 110 feet long and twenty-eight feet across the beam and had a draft of eleven feet. She displaced 400 tons of water and carried a complement of seventeen officers and 123 sailors and marines. Her armament consisted of fourteen eighteen-pound cannons. As the sister ship of the *Wharton*,[qv] she was the last ship of the navy to be delivered under a contract with the shipbuilding firm Schott and Whitney. She was constructed in Baltimore and delivered on April 25, 1840, but not commissioned until 1842, and only then as a response to the raids of Mexican generals Rafael Vásquez and Adrián Woll.[qqv] In April of that year she was sent to New Orleans for refitting and re-arming, most of her guns having been transferred to the *Austin*[qv] and the *Wharton*. The *Archer* was never sent to sea on a major cruise. She was commanded in 1840 and 1841 by John C. Clark[qv] and, on May 11, 1846, was transferred to the United States Navy. She was found "unfit for service" and sold, on November 30, 1846, for $450.

BIBLIOGRAPHY: Alex Dienst, "The Navy of the Republic of Texas," *Quarterly of the Texas State Historical Association* 12–13 (January–October 1909; rpt., Fort Collins, Colorado: Old Army Press, 1987). C. L. Douglas, *Thunder on the Gulf: The Story of the Texas Navy* (Dallas: Turner, 1936; rpt., Fort Collins, Colorado: Old Army Press, 1973). Jim Dan Hill, *Texas Navy in Forgotten Battles and Shirtsleeve Diplomacy* (Chicago: University of Chicago Press, 1937; rpt., Austin: State House, 1987). Tom Henderson Wells, *Commodore Moore and the Texas Navy* (Austin: University of Texas Press, 1960).

Thomas W. Cutrer

ARCHER, BRANCH TANNER (1790–1856). Branch Tanner Archer, legislator and secretary of war of the Republic of Texas,[qv] son of Maj. Peter Field and Francis (Tanner) Archer, was born in Fauquier County, Virginia, on December 13, 1790. Peter Archer was a Revolutionary War officer. Branch Archer attended William and Mary College at Williamsburg in 1804, and in 1808 he received his M.D. degree from the medical school at the University of Pennsylvania. After returning to Virginia he practiced medicine, served one or two terms in the House of Burgesses (1819–20), and was a presidential elector in 1820. Some sources suggest he left Virginia after participating in a duel in which his cousin was killed.

Archer arrived in Texas in 1831 and quickly joined a group in Brazoria agitating for independence from Mexico. He represented Brazoria at the Convention of 1833[qv] and participated in the battle of Gonzales[qv] in October 1835. In November 1835 he traveled to San Felipe as representative of Brazoria and there was elected chairman of the Consultation.[qv] He urged the members to disregard previous factional divisions and concentrate on what was the best course for Texas. Although he favored independence, he voted with the majority, who favored a return to the Constitution of 1824.[qv]

The Consultation then selected Archer to join Stephen F. Austin and William H. Wharton[qqv] as commissioners to the United States to lobby for financial assistance, collect supplies, and recruit men for the Texas cause. The three arrived in New Orleans in January 1836 and negotiated a series of loans that totaled $250,000. Then they proceeded up the Mississippi River, making numerous speeches before turning east for Washington, D.C. During their trip Texas declared its independence, on March 2, 1836. The three commissioners were unable to persuade Congress to support their cause and returned home.

After arriving in Texas Archer worked for the election of Austin as president of the young republic. He also served in the First Congress of Texas and as speaker of the House during its second session. In Congress he and James Collinsworth[qv] sponsored a law establishing the Texas Railroad, Navigation, and Banking Company.[qv] Subsequently, Archer served as President Mirabeau B. Lamar's[qv] secretary of war until 1842.

Archer married Eloisa Clarke on January 20, 1813. They had six children. He was a Mason and helped organize a Masonic lodge in Brazoria. He was grand master of the Grand Lodge of the Republic of Texas in 1838–39. Archer continued to be an active political force until his death. He died on September 22, 1856, at Brazoria and was buried at Eagle Island Plantation[qv] on Oyster Creek in Brazoria County. Archer County was named in his honor.

BIBLIOGRAPHY: *Dictionary of American Biography*. Rebecca Smith Lee, "The Publication of Austin's Louisville Address," *Southwestern Historical Quarterly* 70 (January 1967). Vertical Files, Barker Texas History Center, University of Texas at Austin.

David Minor

ARCHER CITY, TEXAS. Archer City is twenty-five miles southwest of Wichita Falls in the center of Archer County, of which it is the seat. It was named for Branch Tanner Archer,[qv] a leading figure in the Texas Revolution and Republic of Texas.[qqv] The county was established and Archer City designated county seat by the state legislature in 1858, but the county was not organized until after the removal of the Kiowas and Comanches from the area. The townsite was originally surveyed in 1876 and was intended to lie on the projected paths of three railroad lines—the Fort Worth and Denver, the Houston and Texas Central, and the Red River and Rio Grande. A local post office opened in 1878, and in about 1879 C. B. Hutto settled nearby and platted the town; he donated land for a town square, a lot for a county jail, and lots for the construction of Protestant churches. He also donated a "frameless wooden building" to be used as a county courthouse.

Archer County's first church, the First Baptist Church, was organized in the town in 1880 with eight members meeting in a building intended as a saloon. The town soon after voted to ban the sale of alcoholic beverages, so the building continued to serve as a church; from 1881 to 1886 it was the first school building. In 1884 the estimated population of Archer City was 150, and the principal business was county administration. Cotton was the most important shipped product, although the railroad had not arrived yet.

By 1890 the population was an estimated 250, and a weekly newspaper was being published. The town now had daily mail and a daily stage to Wichita Falls. In 1892 the post office name, Archer, was changed to match the town's name. An ornate stone courthouse had been built, two more churches had been organized, and a brickyard and a hotel had opened. By 1900 the town had a bank and three livestock dealers, although cotton remained the staple of outside trade.

The first oil well in the county, twelve miles from town, began producing in March 1912. Although it never produced great amounts it continued in operation at least into the late 1970s. By 1914 Archer City had two railroads, the Wichita Falls and Southern and the Southwestern, and the population was estimated at 825. Archer City was incorporated in 1925 and continued to grow as more oil wells were opened nearby. By late 1926 there were seventeen fields with 411 wells within thirteen miles of Archer City. The largest field by far was Oldham, with 103 wells. Archer City was also a milling and market point for wheat and other grains and had about seventy businesses, including three banks.

By 1930 the town's population was 1,512, and the county hospital had been built there. The county's fiftieth-anniversary celebration had been held in Archer City the year before, a year early in honor of the opening of the county's first highway, State Highway 79. By the 1930s researchers from Harvard University were collecting fossils in Archer County. Two of the best fossil pits are near Archer City, and from one of these came a fossil that was named Archeria in honor of the county.

Archer City continued growing slowly despite the loss of some businesses during World War II.[qv] The population peaked at 2,025 in 1970; the number of businesses had begun falling off in the 1960s. In Larry McMurtry's novel *The Last Picture Show* (1966), which derives its setting from Archer City, the closing of the Royal Theater is a major symbol. McMurtry is a native of Archer County. In 1986 the town had a post office, forty-nine businesses including a bank, and a population of 1,862.

BIBLIOGRAPHY: Jack Loftin, *Trails Through Archer* (Burnet, Texas: Nortex, 1979). Winnie D. Nance, A History of Archer County (M.A. thesis, University of Texas, 1927). *Monte Lewis*

ARCHER COUNTY. Archer County (F-14) is located in north central Texas, bounded on the North by Wichita County, on the west by Baylor County, on the south by Young County, and on the east by Clay and Jack counties. Archer County's center is at 98°30′ west longitude and 35°30′ north latitude, twenty-five miles south-southwest of Wichita Falls. The county comprises 900 square miles of the Central Rolling Red Plains, Central Rolling Red Prairies, and Western Cross Timbers. Soils range from sandy loams and clays to stony soil on the plains and prairies and sand or loams in the timbers. Major deposits of oil and gas, copper deposits, and beds of sand and gravel make up the natural resources of this generally agricultural county. The Big Wichita, the Little Wichita, the West Fork of the Trinity, and the Brazos rivers drain Archer County. The Big Wichita River touches the county's northwestern corner, and the diversion dam of the Wichita Valley irrigation system is located at this point. Lakes Wichita, Kickapoo, and Arrowhead furnish soft water for county towns as well as Wichita Falls. The altitude ranges from 900 to 1,400 feet, the yearly rainfall averages 25.26 inches, the temperature averages range from 28° to 98° F, and the growing season lasts 220 days.

Before white settlement, Apaches, Wichitas, Tawakonis, Kichais, Caddoes, Comanches, and later Kiowas camped and hunted in the area now known as Archer County. Spaniards and Anglos crossed through the area at various times, and in the eighteenth century French traders operated a post close to the two small mesas in the west central area later called Little Arizona. Kichais defeated the Texas Rangers[qv] in the battle of Stone Houses[qv] in southeastern Archer County in 1837, and Kiowas led by Kicking Bird[qv] defeated United States cavalrymen led by Capt. Curwen B. McClellan in the battle of the Little Wichita River[qv] in the northwestern part of the county in 1870. On January 22, 1858, the Texas legislature marked off Archer County from Clay County and named it in honor of Republic of Texas commissioner Branch Tanner Archer.[qv] No settlers had yet arrived. By 1875, however, the United States Army had driven all the Indians from North Texas and the area was open to settlement.

In 1874 the first American settler, Dr. R. O. Prideaux, originally from England, settled on the West Fork of the Trinity River in southeastern Archer County. He had observed that the buffalo[qv] he had shot there were fat. Soon other cattlemen and farmers moved in, and scattered herds of longhorn cattle[qv] were introduced to different parts of the county's grasslands. Along with buffalo hunters, the pioneer cattlemen led the way for other American settlers by eliminating great herds of buffalo and antelope. Imaginary lines were drawn and agreed upon between herd owners. Cowboys rode these lines daily to drive stray animals back to their respective territories. Barbed wire[qv] was introduced in the fall of 1880, and great pastures were fenced. Herd owners divided the county into three portions. The T Fork and 99 pastures controlled the north section, the OX Ranch[qv] and Circle Ranch (*see* PIERCE, ABEL HEAD) pastures formed the central part, and the LM, TIP, JJ, CLA Bar, Mule Shoe, GAR, Figure 3, Lazy H, and other smaller ranches occupied the southern portion.

Meanwhile, farmers were also moving into the area. Colonists located vacant or unpatented lands throughout the county and built dugout[qv] or log, board, or stone houses. By 1880, 596 people lived on fifty-three ranches and farms in Archer County. Over 56,000 cattle were counted by the United States agricultural census in the county that year, along with 1,423 sheep. Over 400 acres was planted in corn in the county in 1880, and smaller areas were planted with oats and wheat. Cotton, grown on about 100 acres, produced forty-three bales.

In November 1879 farmers combined with the small ranchers in Archer County and presented a petition to the commissioners' court of Clay County calling for the political organization of Archer County. Larger cattle interests, bitterly opposed to organization, protested and delayed the process, but in the spring of 1880 the court ordered an election. Archer County was organized on July 27 of that year.

When election results designated Archer City the county seat, Dr. C. B. Hutto, a dentist from South Carolina and founder of the town, gave the county a one-story box house with four small rooms and one large room to be used as a courthouse.The large room served as a courtroom and office space for the county attorney. The county clerk, sheriff, tax collector, surveyor, and treasurer each used a smaller room. Many of the early county officials were Republicans, since numerous early settlers had migrated from old Union states, particularly Illinois, Indiana, and Ohio; but many county Democrats voted for them, anyway, on the basis of ability. Settlers active in county politics included W. B. Hutcheson, T. M. Coulson, William Hutton, and A. J. Ikard.

The Great Plains environment tested Archer County's new settlers early with a blizzard-drought-blizzard series in 1885–87. The bitter winter of 1885–86 killed thousands of cattle in the county; the Circle Ranch was bankrupted because of its losses. Then, in the summer of 1886, hot west winds dried up vegetation and water sources, and a severe drought followed. Cattle drifted down dry creeks to the West Fork of the Trinity River. Some of these animals were scattered as far as Fort Worth, and many were lost permanently. Another severe winter then followed the drought. A state census revealed that the county's population declined from 596 in 1880 to 521 in 1887.

Growth resumed almost immediately, however, as farmers continued to move into the area. By 1890, 2,101 people were counted in Archer County, living on 278 ranches and farms; by 1900, 356 farms had been established in the county, and the population had increased to 2,508.

Railroads played an important role in attracting settlers to the county during the late nineteenth and early twentieth centuries. In 1890 the Wichita Valley Railway crossed northern Archer County, giving rise to the towns of Holliday, Mankins, and Dundee. In 1908 the Wichita Falls and Southern Railway pushed south through Archer City on its way to the coal supply of Newcastle in neighboring Young County. In 1909 the Henrietta and Southwestern began to serve Scotland and Archer City, and the next year the Gulf, Texas and Western built through Megargel on its way to Seymour. This railroad construction helped to tie the county to the national marketplace, and encouraged immigration into the area. By 1910, 6,525 people lived in Archer County and 792 farms had been established. Ranching declined somewhat during this period, but continued to be a crucial mainstay of the local economy. In 1890 more than 75,000 cattle were counted in Archer County; in 1900, 65,627 were counted; in 1910, there were just over 41,000 cattle in the county, and about the same number in 1920.

Meanwhile, farmlands expanded dramatically, and crop production helped to balance the economy. Between 1890 and 1920 farmers in Archer County opened tens of thousands of acres to the production of forage crops as well as such cereal crops as corn, wheat, and oats; by 1920, wheat culture[qv] occupied more than 37,000 acres; wheat was the county's most important crop at that time. Cotton culture[qv] also expanded significantly. In 1890 cotton acreage totaled 221 acres, and in 1900, 2,150. Cotton was one of the county's most important crops by 1910, however, when more than 18,000 acres was given to its production. After dropping significantly between 1910 and 1920, cotton experienced another brief boom after 1920; in 1930, more than 20,000 acres of Archer county land was planted in cotton.

In spite of significant increases in wheat production between 1910 and 1920, however, general farming activity in Archer County had already begun to decline by 1920. The number of farms in the county dropped from 792 in 1910 to 760 in 1920, and in spite of the 1920s cotton boom their number dropped to 692 in 1930. The hard times of the Great Depression[qv] in the 1930s shook out many farmers and cut seriously into the county's crop production. By 1940 only 501 farms remained in Archer County; only 4,391 acres was planted in cotton. Dairy products,[qv] marketed in Wichita Falls, had already become an important part of the economy, along with poultry production.[qv] The county's population dropped from its all-time high of 9,684 in 1930 to only 7,599 in 1940.

But before and after the onset of the depression, agricultural fluctuations were offset by petroleum production. Oil was discovered in Archer County in 1911, and by 1930 the county was a major shallow producer. The production in 1940 was 4,124,500 barrels, and World War II[qv] helped to stimulate oil activity further; in 1944 more than 8,162,000 barrels was produced, and almost 12,000,000 barrels in 1950. Production in the county gradually declined, however; in 1979 it was 3,760,086 barrels and in 1990, 2,814,915. By 1991, more than 467,949,000 barrels of oil had been taken out of Archer County lands since 1911.

The population of Archer County steadily declined after 1930 until the 1970s, when it again began to rise. It was 7,599 in 1940, 6,816 in 1950, 6,110 in 1960, and 5,759 in 1970. By 1980, however, 7,266 people resided in Archer County, and by 1990 the population had increased to 7,973. Postwar dairy production increased, though grazing remained strong. The county's population centers, Archer City, Holliday, Windthorst, Megargel, Lakeside, Scotland, Mankins, Dundee, and part of Wichita Falls, are connected by U.S. highways 281, 277, and 82, and by Texas highways and roads. An annual rodeo, a livestock show, and a rattlesnake roundup provide entertainment. Archer County has produced two fiction writers of national stature, Benjamin Capps and Larry McMurtry.

BIBLIOGRAPHY: Joseph Andrew Blackman, "The Ikard Family and the North Texas Frontier," *Cross Timbers Review* 1 (May 1984). Jack Loftin, *Trails Through Archer* (Burnet, Texas: Nortex, 1979). Winnie D. Nance, A History of Archer County (M.A. thesis, University of Texas, 1927).

Monte Lewis

ARCHER M. HUNTINGTON ART GALLERY. The Archer M. Huntington Art Gallery, a scholarly teaching and research unit of the College of Fine Arts at the University of Texas at Austin, is a major resource for the cultural education of students at the university. The gallery is mandated to contribute to and support the teaching and research responsibilities of the university through close collaboration with the academic departments and to participate in the training of students for professional museum careers. By the early 1990s there were more than 10,000 works of art in the Huntington's permanent collection, which provides the backbone for visual-arts education at the university and serves as a resource for teaching in architecture, history, foreign languages, Latin-American studies, classical studies, design, and other fields.

The gallery began when Archer M. Huntington, who once commented "wherever I put my foot down, a museum springs up," decided to put his foot on the University of Texas campus in October 1927. Huntington, the son of one of the four founders of the Central Pacific Railroad, chose not to follow his father into industry, but instead to devote his life to learning, fellowship, and philanthropic activity. He first became aware of the university's need for art when *Diana of the Chase*, a bronze sculpture by his wife, Anna Hyatt, was donated to the university by a family friend. Huntington offered the University of Texas about 4,200 acres along Galveston Bay "to be dedicated to the support of an art museum." The sale of a portion of this land and income from oil and gas leases generated the endowment fund that now supports public programs, catalogs, exhibitions, and acquisitions at the museum.

In the early 1990s the permanent collection of the Huntington Art Gallery was housed in the Harry Ransom Humanities Research Center[qv] on the main campus. The Huntington's encyclopedic collections range from ancient to medieval, European Renaissance to Baroque, western to contemporary American, and Latin American. The Huntington's gallery space, in the campus art building nearby, serves as home to the museum's print and drawing collection and also shows a variety of temporary and traveling exhibitions. The Huntington's conservation laboratory is also at this site. The gallery was accredited by the American Association of Museums in 1984.

In the 1990s the gallery's American collection included one of the most comprehensive bodies of twentieth-century art on a United States college campus. The American collection as a whole spans more than two centuries, encompasses a variety of styles and media, and includes definitive examples of nineteenth and twentieth century American art. The collection began as a gift from the Longfellow Foundation of New York, in recognition of the opening of the gallery's exhibition spaces in 1963. The museum then received the cornerstone of its American collection, the Mari and James Michener Collection of Twentieth-Century American Painting. The Micheners' original gift of more than 300 works, together with their continued commitment through the years, enabled the museum to obtain a total of 375 paintings by American artists. Cyrus Rowlett (C. R) Smith's[qv] donation of some 100 Western American paintings and sculptures complements the Michener Collection.

The museum's involvement with Latin-American art began in the late 1960s with a major gift from the New York–based collector Barbara Duncan. The collection subsequently grew to include more than 1,500 works in diverse media by 250 artists from Central and South America and the Caribbean. The museum's print and drawing collection of more than 8,500 works provides an in-depth view of Western art since the Renaissance, with significant holdings of Old Master prints, twentieth-century American prints, and Latin-American drawings. Artists represented in this substantial cross section include Dürer, Ribera, the Carracci brothers, Rembrandt, Goya, Géricault, Degas, Rivera, Rauschenberg, and Johns. The museum's collection of ancient art features noted examples of Corinthian, Greek black-figure and red-figure vases, and South Italian vases, as well as Roman portrait sculpture and Urartian metalwork. The William J. Battle[qv] Cast Collection consists of more than sixty restored plaster replicas of important antique sculptures. The collection of ancient art is supplemented by the medieval collection, which spans more than nine centuries and includes thirty objects on long-term loan from the Metropolitan Museum of Art in New York. These collections provide a significant view of the beginnings of Western art.

The European collection of thirty-four paintings completes the diverse range of art at the Huntington. A small but impressive group of works, this collection contains original examples of Renaissance, Mannerist, and Baroque paintings, including works by Luca Giordano, Il Guercino (Giovanni Francesco Barbieri), and Francesco Fontebasso. Eight works from Italy and the Netherlands are a further highlight of the collection, and fourteen additional paintings were bequeathed to the gallery in 1991 by Jack Taylor of Austin. These more recent acquisitions include paintings by Thomas Gainsborough, Jan Brueghel, and Nicolaes Maes.

BIBLIOGRAPHY: Austin *American-Statesman*, July 19, 1989.

Jessie Otto Hite

ARCHITECTURE. Texas architecture reflects a remarkable variety of cultural influences, physiographical conditions, and technological advancements. Over a long period of colonization and settlement, people of different nationalities with ingrained customs and taste erected a variety of buildings in forms recalling their social backgrounds. These were situated in regions with diverse character ranging from arid West Texas, largely treeless, to semitropical East Texas, heavily forested. In the beginning, materials of construction naturally came from the locale of buildings, although eventually technology and taste produced certain similarities of design throughout the state. For analysis, historic Texas architecture can be organized into six periods: Indian or precolonial (to 1682), Spanish colonial–Mexican (1682–1835), Republic–antebellum (1835–61), Victorian (1861–1900), Early twentieth century (1900–1941), and Modern (1941–90).

Indian or precolonial. The earliest residents of what is now Texas were nomadic peoples. They erected no permanent structures, but made use instead of such natural shelters as caves and rock overhangs, or lived in temporary structures made of animal hides, wood, or grasses. Anthropological findings of later Indian peoples reveal that before the Europeans arrived at least four basic cultural groups had evolved in the future Texas, each reflecting its particular geographic and environmental setting. The Coahuiltecan and Karankawan peoples, who inhabited the coast of southern Texas and the Trans-Nueces, lacked formal political organization and, like their more ancient ancestors, did not erect permanent structures. By contrast, in the Trans-Pecos[qv] the Jumanos and Patarabueyes inhabited villages consisting of houses with mud-plastered pickets and roofs of adobe,[qv] probably placed over saplings, grasses, and bark. Farther north in the Panhandle[qv] a pueblo culture, similar to those in Arizona and New Mexico, flourished between A.D. 1200 and 1500. These peoples constructed one-story pueblos with walls of horizontal masonry and double rows of stone slabs set on edge, oriented to the cardinal points of the compass. Dramatically different were the peoples of the Plains region, the Comanches, Lipan Apaches, Kiowas, and Tonkawas. Their culture, based on buffalo hunting,[qv] required them to wander throughout the vast expanses of Central and Northwest Texas in search of the great herds. They relied for shelter on hide-covered tepees that could be readily disassembled and transported. In Northeast Texas, Indians of the Mississippi valley culture flourished, among them the various Caddo groups. A sedentary, agricultural people, they constructed large, round, thatched shelters, some up to fifty feet in diameter. They also built large earthen mounds typical of the Mississippi culture.

Jacal, ca. 1875. Stereograph by H. A. Doerr. Courtesy Lawrence T. Jones III Collection, Austin. South Texas jacals had steeply pitched roofs to shed occasional heavy rains.

Spanish colonial–Mexican. From the end of the seventeenth century through the eighteenth century, Spanish missionaries and soldiers brought to Texas building types and construction techniques they had known at home. On a remote and sometimes dangerous frontier, they established missions with chapels, convents, apartments, and various service structures; presidios[qv] with fortifications, chapels, barracks, and storerooms; ranches with dwellings and, in some instances, defensive works; and towns with plazas, commons, churches, and dwellings—all according to Spanish traditions and laws. Spanish colonists employed familiar methods in the construction of shelters and buildings. In heavily forested East Texas, palisado walls of wooden pickets, well known for centuries in Spain and throughout Europe, enclosed rooms roofed with thatch in both missions and presidios. Chapels, apartments, and other spaces of San Francisco de los Tejas Mission, for instance, had walls of posts planted vertically in the ground. Meanwhile, in West Texas, the jacal, a type indigenous to Mexico, sheltered countless families. Walls were formed with brush or branches contained between pairs of posts spaced several feet apart and plastered with mud. Roofs were either thatched or covered with hides. Particularly in arid and semiarid regions, adobe construction also was common. Walls were made of sun-baked mud bricks laid up in thick beds of mud with openings spanned by wooden lintels. Roofs were either gabled and thatched, or were flat and covered with earth or lime concrete carried upon beams, sometimes hewn. These types of construction, indigenous to the land, remained in use well into the twentieth century, when shingles and other types of roofing replaced thatch and earth. When stone was available, masonry walls enclosed numerous cubical houses, roofed with either thatch or earth. Often, slightly inclined, earthen roofs were surrounded with parapets and drained through *canales,* projecting channeled troughs. In several instances, on locations exposed to attack, loopholes were included and windows were omitted. Commonly, houses were one-room structures, although on occasion, two or more rooms were situated end-to-end. In some instances, as in Spain, rooms and walls were situated to enclose a court. A beehive-shaped *horno,* or oven, made of mud and grass and located outdoors, was employed for cooking.

Numerous mission chapels were hastily thrown up with a variety of building techniques. Jacals, palisados, or small adobe rooms containing altars were among the first shelters set up at any mission. Although missionaries certainly intended to replace these with more durable works, in many instances the mission was abandoned before large permanent structures could be built. Near El Paso and San Antonio, durable chapels were constructed. The chapel of Nuestra Señora de la Concepción de Socorro Mission, adjacent to the Rio Grande, was executed with thick adobe walls. Both the nave and transepts, which were added much later, were spanned with vigas bearing upon corbel blocks. At San Antonio each of the five missions eventually built a stone chapel with a design based upon customs in Mexico.

The most famous of these, San Antonio de Valero Mission, the Alamo,[qv] established in 1718, has an incomplete chapel executed between 1744 and 1756, with a Baroque portal similar to a number of Mexican examples. The Chapel of Nuestra Señora de la Purísima Concepción de Acuña Mission (established in 1731), the best preserved of the Texas missions, has a portal with Plateresque details. A beautiful Ultra-Baroque portal with niche pilasters was completed at San José y San Miguel de Aguayo Mission (established in 1720), commonly regarded as the "Queen of the Missions." At both San Juan Capistrano (1731), and San Francisco de la Espada (1731), durable chapels were built, but with little ornamentation.

During the Mexican period (1821–35), relatively little architectural progress was made beyond the construction of dwellings and some military work, although several new towns were established, including Bastrop (laid out in 1830), Liberty (founded in 1831), and Gonzales (founded in 1832). A poor economy, along with religious and political turmoil, precluded noteworthy undertakings and, for that matter, even maintenance upon existing buildings.

Republic–antebellum period. During the Republic of Texas[qv] and the years that followed until the Civil War,[qv] other cultural traditions were brought to Texas by Anglo-Americans and European immigrants, both seeking land and opportunities. New towns were populated, farms developed, and military posts established, all reflecting the traditions and previous customs of the builders. In regions where trees were available, log cabins were common to Anglo-American settlements as well as those of some European immigrants. They required few tools for construction and were used for virtually every type of building, including dwellings, churches, courthouses, schools, jails, barns, and forts. Both single-crib and double-crib houses were common. In the latter, known as dog-trot or dog-run houses,[qv] the rooms were separated by a breezeway. Ordinarily, log cabins had only a single story, but occasionally attics were included. In any instance, porches ordinarily extended along the south side of dwellings; porch roofs shaded the walls and provided a protected space. A fireplace was usually placed at a gable end of dwellings. Regardless of type, cabins were assembled with horizontal logs, sometimes hewn or partially hewn. Logs were notched together at corners utilizing several types of joints. Spaces between them were filled with wooden chinks, rocks, or moss and mud. Roofs were finished with boards, shakes, or shingles. Though no type of log construction can be specifically attributed to any particular ethnic group, *Fachwerk* structures were peculiar to German settlements. *Fachwerk* consisted of hewn frameworks joined with mortise and tenon joints, secured with treenails (wooden pegs). Panels formed by the framework were infilled with either brick or stone

Log Cabin, New Braunfels, *by Carl G. von Iwonski, ca. 1843–67? Oil on canvas. 8½″ × 11½″. Courtesy Daughters of the Republic of Texas Library, San Antonio. This modest, single-crib log cabin, said to be the Iwonski family's first home in New Braunfels, was typical of early homes built in Texas by Anglo-Americans and Europeans.*

nogging, but some openings were framed for doors and windows. Porches were the adaptation of European custom to the hot Texas climate.

As the country and economy developed in antebellum Texas,[qv] neat wooden, brick, and stone buildings also appeared in various communities and on numerous farms. Texans, like people in other regions of America, yearned for order and cultural refinement reflected in tidy houses and public buildings. Both were considered important to the development of communities as desirable places to live and raise families. Sophisticated architecture, critics believed, refined public taste and positively influenced people's attitudes. Numerous frame and masonry buildings were plain, but others were distinguished by historic styles, including the Greek Revival style, which dominated Texas architecture from 1840 to 1870. Though often referred to as Southern Colonial, the Greek Revival Style is neither southern nor colonial, since it first appeared in the East in the early nineteenth century. It was introduced into Texas by both experienced builders and authoritative publications. It featured geometric order, formal balance, and decorative details. Its principal feature was derived from the classic temple form of ancient Greece, the temple portico or porch with a roof supported by a row of columns. These columns were of three types or orders: Doric, Ionic, and Corinthian. The Greek Revival style is formal in character, the building being arranged symmetrically about a central axis, the hall, which is flanked by rooms of the same width that give the desired balance. The doorway is flanked by an equal number of windows on each side, and centered on the front of the house is a porch that features columns of one of the classical orders. The Greek Revival style marked numerous houses, school buildings, some courthouses and churches, and even an occasional commercial building. Nationally, its simplicity and dignity seemed to make it appropriate for a country with limited means but with needs for refined architecture. Symmetrical porticoes commonly distinguished houses and some churches and courthouses. Dignifying the exteriors of these, pilasters, columns, and entablatures, ordinarily fashioned from wood, were based upon examples found in pattern books, although builders freely innovated upon these. A number of noteworthy plantation houses, as well as city houses, represented these developments. The simple frame house of the Anglo-American settler, however, continued to be the principal type of house built in Texas until the Civil War. But even frame houses were often given a few classic details, such as a cornice, capped posts on the porches, and multipaned double-hung sash windows, all of which gave them a resemblance to the larger Greek Revival houses. As the farthest extension of the Old South, Texas possesses some of the most recently built Greek Revival homes, which can be seen in San Antonio, Austin, Waco, Jefferson, and Marshall. The Governor's Mansion[qv] (1854–56), in Austin, built by Abner Cook,[qv] is one of the most representative examples of the Greek Revival style in Texas. Greek Revival forms and details also marked many other important public buildings. The old Capitol (1852–54; burned 1881) was a monumental work with an Ionic portico. The Galveston Post Office and Custom House (1858–61), designed by the Treasury architect, Ammi B. Young, displays both Doric and Ionic orders. On a smaller scale, the Methodist Episcopal Church, South (1860), in Marshall is a temple-type edifice with square columns and a simplified Doric order.

While the Greek Revival, along with straightforward designs, was common in evangelical churches, Gothic Revival styles marked a number of Catholic and Episcopal churches. Pointed arches, steeply pitched roofs, and buttresses were basic, but a number of variations of Gothic appeared, in some instances reflecting the backgrounds of the builders. Several Catholic Churches, including St. Mary's Cathedral, Galveston[qv] (1847), were designed by French emigré architects. Builders in Fredericksburg, a German community, recalled in St. Mary's Church (1861–63) the Gothic of their homeland. Episcopal houses of worship featured characteristics ultimately derived from rural English churches and disseminated in America through publications and the work of English immigrants.

Adjacent to the public square of Anglo-American communities, a typical spatial form brought west, commercial buildings were executed with masonry fronts, either one or two stories high. Ordinarily, street-level openings were spanned by semicircular arches with French doors and fanlight transoms; when a second story was included, it often had segmental arches and double-hung windows. Ornamentation of parapets with a wide variety of brick or stone patterns is a distinguishing feature—characteristics that continued to mark many commercial buildings during the Victorian period.

Victorian. Following the Civil War, from 1870 to 1900, Texas caught up with the mainstream of American architectural fashion, which was the Victorian, so called in the absence of a better name to encompass the multitude of stylistic expressions of that complex period. The exuberance of the Victorian style reflects a period of rapid expansion and new fortunes. In Texas, as elsewhere in America, the Victorian period was marked by revolutionary changes. Numerous new towns were founded, railroads were rapidly extended, and the westerly regions were progressively opened to farming and ranching. At the same time, in large cities outside investment was solicited and new industries were established, contributing to the prosperity essential to opulent architecture. Meanwhile, such buildings as libraries, opera houses, schools, hospitals, and public markets all improved the life of communities. Evolving technology favored the development of cities and architecture within them. During the last two decades of the nineteenth century, waterworks, sewerage systems, electric-light companies, gas works, ice plants, telephone systems, and rail transportation all improved sanitation and afforded numerous conveniences in many towns. Meanwhile, organized fire departments reduced the amount of damage caused by fires in various cities, virtually every one of which had over time been devastated by one or more incendiaries. Building construction and comfort were facilitated by mass production of building components, both wooden and metal. For interior comfort, ventilation devices were introduced, steam heat was developed, and electrical lighting was installed in many buildings. Economical railroad transportation made building materials and products manufactured elsewhere readily available in Texas, although many were still produced at home.

In the wake of Reconstruction,[qv] turreted mansions began to spring up in cities and towns all over the state. In contrast to the restrained classicism of the Greek Revival style, the Victorian style was rich in detail, exceedingly ornate, and designed to achieve a romantic and picturesque effect. The buildings were seldom symmetrical, but were characterized by the off-center tower and projecting bay. The whole was intended to be a balanced composition. Many materials were now available to the builder; these were often combined to achieve greater richness. Sawmills had become widespread, and frame houses were given elaborate gingerbread trim, made possible by the jigsaw. Architectural motifs from many historic styles were combined in an eclectic fashion, with the Medieval Romanesque and Gothic vying with the Renaissance for popularity. New views on architecture influenced building aesthetics. Appreciation of beauty of proportion and details—characteristic of the antebellum period—was replaced by admiration of character and opulence. In part achieved with historic forms and styles, character denoted the particular purpose of a building combined with a distinctive image. Associations with the historical development of particular styles made function evident—for instance, general knowledge of medieval European cathedrals and churches readily associated the Gothic Revival with churches. Opulence along with picturesqueness was achieved by the use of a variety of materials, and historic styles were characteristic and much admired. The features of various styles sometimes were mixed into eclectic, original compositions, albeit sometimes without unity. Polychromy and patterns achieved through combinations and treatments of materials were char-

The Governor's Mansion, Austin, 1854–56. Abner Cook, master builder. Photograph by William J. Oliphant, ca. 1866. Courtesy Austin History Center, Austin Public Library; photo no. PICA 08592. Abner Cook, the leading designer of Greek Revival buildings in antebellum Texas, incorporated his trademark X-and-stick balustrade (or gallery railing) into the second story of this structure.

acteristic. These attributes were evident in countless houses in picturesque styles, with fanciful towers, porches, chimneys, bay windows, dormers, spindlework, punch work, shingle patterns, and decorative glass. At the beginning of the Victorian period, these were simply applied to traditional plans, but eventually asymmetrical, picturesque forms prevailed. Numerous historic and novel styles appeared in Texas Victorian houses. The Queen Anne, characterized by turrets and picturesque massing, distinguished numerous large dwellings throughout the state. The Eastlake style, with its spindlework and gingerbread, enriched numerous other houses on various scales. The so-called Stick Style, identified by the articulation of exterior wall surfaces of frame buildings into panels, added further variety. Distinguished by Italian Renaissance details, the Italianate style also dignified numerous large dwellings. The Mansard-roofed Second Empire Style and the Roman-arched Romanesque Revival mode lent imposing images to yet others.

Many Texas cities and towns preserve a rich legacy of Victorian architecture. Among the impressive surviving monuments of the era are the Driskill Hotel[qv] (1880), Austin, by Frederick E. Ruffini,[qv] the Turn-Verein Building (1892), San Antonio, by James Wahrenberger,[qv] and the Albert Maverick Building, San Antonio (1881), by Alfred Giles.[qv] Of all the cities in Texas, Galveston was undoubtedly the richest in its collection of Victorian architecture. One of the state's first professional architects, Nicholas J. Clayton,[qv] practiced there and added many fine buildings, including the Gresham house, now known as the Bishop's Palace.[qv] During the Victorian era civic and commercial architecture became important, and many handsome courthouses, banks, opera houses, and hotels were constructed. The most significant building to be built during this period was the Capitol,[qv] completed in 1888. This impressive red-granite structure was designed by Elijah E. Myers[qv] of Detroit, Michigan, in the Renaissance Revival style and inspired by the national Capitol in Washington. The building was originally intended to be of limestone. However, there was not a sufficient supply of the quality required to be found in Texas, so granite was used. The ruggedness of the granite gives the building a unique character, and the tall cast-iron dome has become symbolic of the state's most important building. Many towns took pride in their public buildings, which were collectively viewed as signs of progress. Situated prominently on public squares, county courthouses[qv] were commonly the most imposing buildings of a county, reflecting their importance as both a social and governmental center. Designed in a variety of styles and laid out to facilitate cross-ventilation, they are announced by central clock towers and have four similar fronts. Often they had such technological improvements as iron and wrought-iron structural systems. Among the numerous noteworthy examples are the Hill County Courthouse, Hillsboro (1889), a large edifice in eclectic style with a lofty tower designed by W. Clarke Dodson, and the Renaissance Revival–style Ellis County Courthouse (1894–1896), designed by James Riely Gordon.[qv] Usually standing nearby on the public square was the county jail. Architects and clients occasionally favored the medieval castellated style, which gave the impression of strength, although other styles also were used. Surrounding the courthouses and lining main streets leading to the public square were various types of commercial buildings, also considered as signs of progress. Large plate-glass windows, cast-iron supports, and sheet-metal cornices and window hoods—the products of technology—superseded the all-masonry fronts of antebellum days, although brick and stone were still extensively employed for visual interest. In such large cities as Dallas, Fort Worth, and Houston, commercial buildings of three to six stories incorporating technological advances became sources of considerable pride. Among the best examples of these is the Cotton Exchange in Houston (1888), designed by Eugene T. Heiner,[qv] which, like other buildings, employed a variety of styles and mixture of details and materials to produce an individuality and opulence appealing to the public. Ordinarily standing at the corners of street intersections and reflecting prosperity, banks and opera houses were particularly prominent, a situation well represented by the Sealy Bank Building (1895–97) and Tremont Opera House (1870), both in Galveston. Houses of worship, prominently situated in neighborhoods adjacent to commercial districts, accented the skylines of most communities. Many churches were built during the last two decades of the nineteenth century, with the Medieval styles, Romanesque and Gothic, being favored by the liturgical religions such as Catholic and Episcopal. For example, St. Mark's Episcopal Church, San Antonio (1875), designed by Richard Upjohn, the architect of Trinity Church in New York and the leading Gothic Revival architect in America, was inspired by the Perpendicular Gothic of England; the old San Fernando de Béxar Cathedral[qv] in San Antonio, extensively remodeled by François P. Giraud[qv] between 1868 and 1878, was based on French medieval models; and St. Mary's Cathedral, Austin (1870), designed by Nicholas Clayton, was executed in the High Victorian Gothic style. In numerous instances, evangelical churches were distinguished from liturgical edifices by broad auditoriums and corner entrances, evident in the First Baptist Church, Dallas[qv] (1890), designed by Albert Ullrich. Moorish styles, on the other hand, projecting associations with Near Eastern architecture, characterized a number of nineteenth-century synagogues. Among the other noteworthy Victorian buildings were the railroad depots, which formed gateways to towns. Scaled according to the size of communities, these were linear structures, with both passenger and freight facilities, stretched along the tracks. Various stylistic and decorative devices emphasized their importance, a tendency evident in the Union Depot, Fort Worth (1899). Such service structures as roundhouses—other products of technology—were also numerous, although most are now gone, along with numerous depots.

Early twentieth century. The years following the turn of the century witnessed continuing immigration and growth of towns and cities throughout the state. Cotton, lumber, cattle, and oil aided a growing economy that fostered cultural development. Meanwhile, new industries and trade pumped up the economies of metropolitan areas, facilitating the building of pretentious edifices, both public and private. During this period, architecture throughout the United States embodied new aesthetic ideals aimed at achieving noble images reflecting cultural advancement. Influenced by the École des Beaux Arts in Paris, design principles called for formal compositions and classical vocabularies. The impressive effects attainable with unified classical design based upon monumental Renaissance architecture were well demonstrated by the overall plan and official buildings of the 1893 World's Columbian Exposition in Chicago. This impressive achievement profoundly influenced taste throughout the entire country. The architecture of the first half of the twentieth century reflects the growing unity of architectural expression throughout the United States. Regional characteristics rapidly disappeared as a result of the spread of popular taste and the uniformity of architectural fashion. During the first thirty years of the twentieth century eclecticism was the accepted form of architectural expression. While subscribing to formal principles, numerous critics and architects advocated architecture that reflected some characteristics of its locale. One approach to regional design called for historic styles associated with particular ethnic groups that had settled in an area. Another viewpoint advocated styles that had evolved abroad in certain countries or terrains as types for buildings in regions of Texas with comparable physiographical conditions. A Spanish-inspired mode, the Neo-Plateresque style, of the first buildings of Texas Technological College, for instance, was intended to recall the Hispanic heritage of Texas. The Bhutanese style of the Texas School of Mines and Metallurgy (now the University of Texas at El Paso), located at the foot of the Franklin Mountains,[qv] was inspired by a Tibetan monastery in the Himalayan Mountains. These motifs, along with a variety of others, are displayed in Texas houses. At the turn of the century, some of the picturesqueness of the Victorian period still prevailed, but compositions of forms were bilaterally balanced, and classical details soon replaced Eastlake and other features. Eventually, large houses projected stately images through a variety of Classical styles in formal compositions. Monumental pedimented porticoes and extensive balustraded porches contributed to their stately yet residential character. Small houses featured a variety of styles, including Tudor, Spanish Colonial, Colonial, Georgian, and Italian Renaissance, as well as Mission Revival and Pueblo Revival. By the early years of the twentieth century another influence was being felt in Texas, an attempt to break free of historical precedents, and to forge a new, wholly modern style. The most important of these influences was what became known as the Prairie style. It originated with Frank Lloyd Wright and a group of creative Chicago architects, and rapidly spread through the new suburbs of Texas. Pure examples of the Prairie style, such as the Trost residence (1909), El Paso, by Wright protégé Henry C. Trost,[qv] are rare, but vernacular examples, spread widely by pattern books and popular magazines, appeared throughout the state between 1905 and 1915. Even more influential was the Craftsman or Bungaloid style, inspired primarily by the work of Charles S. and Henry M. Greene in California. Like the vernacular examples of the contemporaneous Prairie style, the Bungaloid style was spread through pattern books and popular magazines. The one-story Craftsman house or bungalow became one of the most popular designs for small houses, and numerous examples were constructed in the state between 1905 and the late 1920s.

While regional or early modern designs appeared in many residential edifices after the turn of the century, civic buildings generally were either Beaux-Arts Classical, a massive, heavy, monumental style, or Neo-Classical Revival, a graceful, dignified mode. The Harris County Courthouse, Houston (1911), a massive work, crowned with a dome designed by the firm of Lang and Witchell, exemplifies the former, while the Museum of Fine Arts, Houston (1924),[qv] a handsome work with an Ionic colonnade designed by William Ward Watkin,[qv] represents the latter. In small towns, commercial buildings largely conformed to Victorian standards, but in the cities office buildings formed new skylines. Houston, Dallas, Fort Worth, San Antonio, and Waco all built noteworthy skyscrapers rising boldly above their surroundings. Such achievements were made possible by technology that had been developed in such cities as Chicago and New York, including methods of structural framing and fire protection of beams and columns. These developments were well represented by the Southwestern Life Insurance Company[qv] Building, Dallas (1911–13), a sixteen-story work with a clearly expressed skeletal structure consistent in design with Chicago School work. Like other types of buildings, both

Lutcher Memorial Church Building (First Presbyterian Church), Orange, 1911. James Oliver Hogg, designer and contractor. Courtesy Texas Historical Commission, Austin. With its copperplate central dome and Ionic columns, this church building exemplifies the Beaux Arts style. The three art-glass windows on the second story of the building won prizes at the 1893 Chicago World's Fair.

churches and schools echo a variety of motifs. Indicating associations with an important chapter in the history of Christianity, a number of Catholic edifices were built in the Italian Renaissance Revival style, which recalls Renaissance Rome, while others were either in Gothic or a Mexican Colonial style, the latter echoing cultural roots in Texas. Reflecting origins in the Church of England, Episcopal churches were mostly in some variation of the English Gothic, consistent with earlier buildings. Classical styles, Gothic modes, and regional variations all marked Protestant churches, although Presbyterians showed a predilection toward the Romanesque Revival. The Palladian Revival, based upon ecclesiastical work of Italian Renaissance architect Andrea Palladio, distinguished yet others, particularly a number of Baptist churches. Similarly, a variety of stylistic features characterizes schools, both public and private. Catholic and Episcopal schools usually reflected their affiliations through Gothic styles. College, university, and high school buildings, often on a large scale, all appeared in a variety of modes, including Neoclassical Revival and Georgian Revival. Among the important developments during this period was the evolution throughout the state of the public high school into a dominant building type. Housing classrooms, auditorium, gymnasium, shops, offices, and other facilities, the high school became a complex entity that accommodated large numbers of students. Spaces were organized into formal yet functional compositions contained within forms juxtaposed to facilitate efficient cross-ventilation and admit high levels of light. On the exteriors, patterns of openings and solids suggested function, while various decorative features, both geometric and stylistic, enriched the buildings, reflecting importance and projecting character. Among the best examples of such educational facilities is El Paso High School (1914–16), designed by Trost and Trost.

The period between 1920 and 1940 also witnessed the emergence of the Art Deco or Moderne style. As its name suggests, Art Deco was inspired by the 1925 Paris Exposition des Art Décoratifs et Industriels Modernes. Much like the Prairie style that flourished a decade earlier, it represented an attempt to come to terms with the dramatic changes brought on by industrialization and modernization, and sought to break free of historical precedents and to forge a modern expression. Early Art Deco buildings, such as the Gulf Building, Houston[qv] (1927–29), designed by Alfred C. Finn,[qv] and the State Highway Building (1932), Austin, designed by Carleton W. Adams,[qv] made use of ornate geometric motifs. After 1930 a more stripped-down variant of the style, sometimes called Moderne, or Streamlined Moderne, became popular. Numerous Moderne shops, gas stations, movie houses, and

The Amicable Building (later the ALICO Building), Waco, 1911. Designed by Sanguinet and Staats of Fort Worth. Photograph by Fred A. Gildersleeve. Courtesy Texas Collection, Baylor University, Waco, Texas. This twenty-two-story skyscraper was the tallest building west of the Mississippi for many years after it was built for the Amicable Life Insurance Company. It remained the central landmark of Waco in 1994.

Tower Conoco Station and U-Drop Inn, Shamrock, ca. 1936. Designed by John Nunn and J. M. Tindall. Courtesy Norbert Schlegel, Shamrock. The Tower Station and cafe, at the intersection of U.S. highways 66 and 83, remained open to highway travelers twenty-four hours a day. The building, which was clad in beige and brown tile, combined Art Deco ornamentation with a Streamlined Moderne style.

roadside diners featuring characteristic smooth surfaces, glass blocks, and curved corners were constructed before World War II.[qv] Hybrid versions of the two styles, such as the remarkable Conoco station on Route 66 in Shamrock (circa 1936), were also common. Unfortunately, these developments were hindered by the Great Depression.[qv] After the crash of 1929, building activity slowed within the state. Although numerous public-works projects were undertaken during the 1930s under the aegis of such federal as the Public Works Administration and the Work Projects Administration,[qv] private building was considerably retarded until after World War II. Numerous public works during the 1930s displayed features of the Art Deco, among them the Texas Centennial[qv] Park, Dallas (1936), planned by George L. Dahl,[qv] the San Jacinto Monument (1936), Houston, designed by Alfred C. Finn, and the Houston City Hall (1939), designed by Joseph Finger.[qv]

Modern. Though World War II brought an upturn in the economy that eventually stimulated the construction industry, much of the new activity initially served the war effort. Upon conclusion of hostilities, construction of houses and public buildings resumed; inflation, however, reduced the return on expenditures. During the postwar years, many clients demanded economical buildings with functional designs based upon historic traditions. The beauty and associations resident in the Georgian Revival and the Gothic Revival still made these styles attractive for numerous types of building, including houses and churches. A number of other institutions, among them colleges and universities, also built conservatively. Southern Methodist University, for example, continued to construct buildings in the Georgian Revival style, maintaining the theme of the institution's earlier buildings. Numerous church buildings were still designed in both the Georgian and Gothic Revival styles. After 1945, however, the so-called International Style increasingly influenced design throughout the state. Calling for the elimination of applied decoration and the rejection of historical styles, architects of the postwar era advocated straightforward, functional planning, machine-produced building components, and asymmetrical composition. Incorporating these characteristics, the International Style featured skeletal structural systems with curtain walls treated as skins "stretched" over them, emphasizing geometrical patterns. Buildings were viewed as compositions of volumes, rather than masses. Plain boxes with large areas of transparency became hallmarks of modernity. Particularly notable examples of this trend include the Tenneco Building, Houston (1963), and One Shell Plaza, Houston (1971), both designed by Skidmore, Owings, and Merrill. In a number of instances, modern appearances were achieved by simplifying traditional forms and the application of new technology. Churches, for instance, still were planned according to traditional spatial requirements, but were designed with laminated wood, steel, and concrete structural systems free of historic stylistic decoration. In numerous instances, the demand for progressive, modern images resulted in the remodeling of old structures, particularly commercial buildings and public edifices. Typically, historical details were either removed or covered, and aluminum, glass, and plastic components were added, all echoing new technology. During the Modern period, developing technology had a phenomenal impact upon architecture. Innovative steel and concrete structural systems made possible unprecedented spans of space, as well as new means of architectonic expression. The Astrodome,[qv] Houston (1965), and Texas Stadium, Irving (1971), are impressive technological achievements. Another important trend in the post–World War II era has been the growth of massive suburban developments on the periphery of the state's larger cites. Tract housing, frequently designed by contractors rather than trained architects and repeated serially, has come to dominate residential building throughout the state, and entire communities, such as Richardson, Plano, and Clear Lake, have grown up as a result.

At midcentury, several leading modern architects from outside the state executed important works in Texas that were certainly inspirational if not influential. In 1958, Ludwig Mies van der Rohe completed a major addition to the Museum of Art, Houston, a steel and glass work with a clearly articulated structure illustrating his idea that "less is more." Shortly thereafter, Philip Johnson, who earlier had executed a number of works in International Style, designed the Amon Carter Museum qv of Western Art, Fort Worth (1960), a clearly ordered work with the stateliness of a Greek temple. At about the same time (1959), Frank Lloyd Wright oversaw the completion of the Kalita Humphreys Theatre, Dallas, a monolithic concrete work exemplifying his concept of organic architecture. And Louis I. Kahn conceived the design for the Kimbell Art Museum qv (1972), Fort Worth, a sublime work with post-tensioned concrete cycloidal vaults, symbolizing a perception of permanence. Such Texas architects as David R. Williams,qv who developed the Texas ranch-style house; O'Neil Ford,qv who designed the Trinity University campus, San Antonio, and the Texas Instruments qv Semi-Conductor Building, Dallas (1958); Caudill, Rowlett, and Scott, who designed the Jesse H. Jones Hall for the Performing Arts,qv Houston; and Howard R. Meyer qv and Max Sandfield, who associated with W. W. Wurster of California to design the Temple Emanu-El, Dallas qv (1953–59), are among those who have achieved national recognition. Noteworthy technological advances in all phases of life brought increasing large and complex building functions. Massive shopping malls, large medical complexes, new college campuses, and expansive airports all were complex products of growth and technological advances, requiring a teamwork approach to design and construction. Representative is Dallas–Fort Worth International Airport qv (1973), an entity architecturally determined by the need to handle complex traffic patterns.

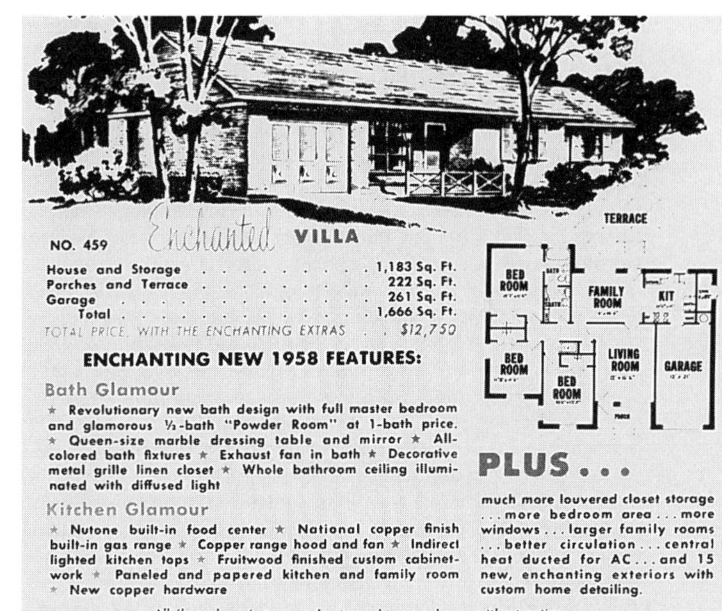

Enchanted Villa, *Dallas, 1958. Courtesy Robert K. and Carole Curlee, Lubbock. This three-bedroom ranch-style house, advertised to cost $12,750 in 1958, is typical of the suburban homes many Texans bought in the postwar era.*

Houston skyline, ca. 1990. Courtesy Texas Department of Commerce/Richard Reynolds. Innovative buildings designed by masters such as Philip Johnson and I. M. Pei distinguish Houston's skyline, here photographed looking east from the hike and bike trail along Buffalo Bayou.

Eventually, the simplicity and lack of poetic content of Modern architecture attracted considerable criticism. Modernity had failed to satisfy the need for decoration and meaning. Consequently, Texas architects, like those elsewhere, searched for new types of expression that included both current technology and references to the past. In the design of Herring Hall (1986) for Rice University, Houston, for instance, East Coast–based architect Cesar Pelli drew upon features of the first campus buildings, yet through technology and spatial organization produced a noteworthy work indicative of its time. Houston-based Taft Architects created a colorful, jazzy postmodern idiom that brought the firm wide recognition. After the disastrous destruction of numerous buildings in central business districts under "urban renewal" programs during the 1950s and 1960s, the preservation movement became a significant force in Texas architecture. As a result of the leadership of such agencies as the San Antonio Conservation Society and the Texas Historical Commission,[qqv] protective legislation was passed and various programs were implemented to assist the preservation and restoration of historic buildings. Among the most significant restoration projects undertaken is the restoration of the Capitol (late 1980s to middle 1990s). Throughout the latter half of the century, much architecture was noted for originality of design. Unique forms and patterns were employed to produce distinctive images, particularly in commercial work. Particularly noteworthy are the skyscrapers of such cities as Dallas, Houston, and San Antonio. At the same time, a revival of interest in regional design character occurred. Such attributes as climate, local traditions, and local materials were viewed as significant informants of design, tying buildings to their locale. Our Lady of Guadalupe Catholic Church, Helotes (1991), a work recalling traditional forms and materials of the Hill Country[qv] by Clovis Heimsath Architects, well represents modern regionalism. Such contrasts between high-tech and vernacular design illustrate the rich diversity of Texas architecture. Variety contributes to the cultural richness of cities, towns, and rural areas, reflecting particular attributes of the people and the land to which they belong.

See also SPANISH TEXAS, MEXICAN TEXAS, SPANISH MISSIONS, GERMAN VERNACULAR ARCHITECTURE, HOUSTON COTTON EXCHANGE AND BOARD OF TRADE, SAN JACINTO MONUMENT AND MUSEUM.

BIBLIOGRAPHY: Drury Blakeley Alexander and (photographs) Todd Webb, *Texas Homes of the Nineteenth Century* (Austin: University of Texas Press, 1966). Joel Warren Barna, *The See-Through Years: Creation and Destruction in Texas Architecture, 1981–1991* (Houston: Rice University Press, 1992). Dorothy Kendall Bracken and Maurine Whorton Redway, *Early Texas Homes* (Dallas: Southern Methodist University, 1956). David G. De Long, *Historic American Buildings, Texas* (2 vols., New York: Garland, 1979). Jay C. Henry, *Architecture in Texas, 1895–1945* (Austin: University of Texas Press, 1993). Historic American Buildings Survey, *Texas Catalog*, comp. Paul Goeldner (San Antonio: Trinity University Press, 1974?). Terry G. Jordan, *Texas Log Buildings: A Folk Architecture* (Austin: University of Texas Press, 1978). Willard B. Robinson, *Gone from Texas: Our Lost Architectural Heritage* (College Station: Texas A&M University Press, 1981). Willard B. Robinson, *The People's Architecture: Texas Courthouses, Jails, and Municipal Buildings* (Austin: Texas State Historical Association, 1983). Willard B. Robinson and Todd Webb, *Texas Public Buildings of the Nineteenth Century* (Austin: University of Texas Press, 1974). Elizabeth Skidmore Sasser, *Dugout to Deco: Building in West Texas, 1880–1930* (Lubbock: Texas Tech University Press, 1993). James Wright Steely, comp., *A Catalog of Texas Properties in the National Register of Historic Places* (Austin: Texas Historical Commission, 1984).

Willard B. Robinson

ARCHIVES OF THE BIG BEND. The Archives of the Big Bend was established in 1976 and is located in the Bryan Wildenthal Memorial Library on the campus of Sul Ross State University in Alpine. The archives is an outgrowth of the collecting efforts of the West Texas Historic and Scientific society, formed in 1926. The WTHSS collected some 200,000 leaves of manuscript material before it ceased operation in 1965. In 1968 all WTHSS collections were turned over to Sul Ross State University. Manuscript materials were placed in the rare book room of the library. This body of papers represents the organic collection of the Archives of the Big Bend. In September 1975 a professional museum director, Kenneth D. Perry, was employed by the university to modernized the museum operation and establish the archives. Archival operations began in earnest in 1976 with the processing of the first manuscript collection, organization of "type" collections, and acquiring a departmental budget within the library. Concomitant with this beginning was selecting a name, Archives of the Big Bend, and developing an Archives Record Manual for processing collections. Today the archives houses broadsides and posters, ephemera, manuscripts, maps, microforms, motion pictures and videotapes, newspapers, oral history, periodicals, photography, artistic pictures, documentary pictures, reference materials, scrapbooks, sheet music, sound recordings, and the Sul Ross State University archives. Since its inception in 1976 the archives has collected more than 1.6 million leaves of manuscript material, along with numerous photographs, oral histories, maps, and other materials. The archives is used extensively for research in the history and culture of the Big Bend region.

Kenneth D. Perry

ARCHIVE WAR. In March 1842 a division of the Mexican army under Gen. Rafael Vásquez[qv] appeared at San Antonio demanding the surrender of the town; the Texans were not prepared to resist and withdrew. On March 10 President Sam Houston[qv] called an emergency session of the Texas Congress. Fearing that the Mexicans would move on Austin, he named Houston as the meetingplace. The citizens of Austin, fearful that the president wished to make Houston the capital, formed a vigilante committee of residents and warned department heads that any attempt to move state papers would be met with armed resistance. President Houston called the Seventh Congress into session at Washington-on-the-Brazos and at the end of December 1842 sent a company of rangers under Col. Thomas I. Smith and Capt. Eli Chandler[qqv] to Austin with orders to remove the archives but not to resort to bloodshed. The Austin vigilantes were unprepared for the raid, and the rangers loaded the archives in wagons and drove away, but not before Mrs. Angelina Eberly[qv] fired a cannon at them. On January 1, 1843 the vigilance committee, under Capt. Mark B. Lewis,[qv] seized a cannon from the arsenal and overtook the wagons at Kenney's Fort on Brushy Creek. Only a few shots were fired before the rangers gave up the papers in order to avoid bloodshed. The archives were returned to Austin and remained there unmolested until Austin became the capital again in 1844.

BIBLIOGRAPHY: Mike Fowler and Jack Maguire, *The Capitol Story, Statehouse of Texas* (Austin: Eakin Press, 1988). Louis Wiltz Kemp, "Mrs. Angelina B. Eberly," *Southwestern Historical Quarterly* 36 (January 1933). Homer S. Thrall, *A Pictorial History of Texas* (St. Louis: Thompson, 1879).

Claudia Hazlewood

ARCINIEGA, JOSÉ MIGUEL DE (?–?). José Miguel de Arciniega, legislator, military explorer, and alcalde[qv] of San Antonio de Béxar, was the son of Gregorio and Josefa (Flores) Arciniega. His father was a soldier from San Carlos de Parras Presidio (*see* SECOND FLYING COMPANY OF SAN CARLOS). In 1816 Arciniega was authorized to go to the United States border to check on possible illegal entry of Americans. In 1818 he and Vicente Gortari gave information secured at Nacogdoches, Texas, and Natchitoches, Louisiana, on foreigners at Galveston and on the Trinity River. Arciniega was a member of the provincial deputation of Texas, which in October 1823 gave consent for abandoned mission lands to be distributed to settlers without property. In 1826, when he was sent to learn the intentions of the Cherokee Indians, he met Richard Fields[qv] and leaders of the Comanche, Tahuallace, Tejas, and Caddo Indians at Laguna de Gallinas, near Nacogdoches. Arciniega was arrested in October 1826 by alcalde Juan José Zambrano[qv] for signing a document for María Josefa Seguín but was evidently exonerated, as in December he was appointed captain of the civil militia. By April of 1827 he and Ángel Navarro[qv] were elected commissioners, and the following month he and José Antonio Navarro[qv] were elected deputies to the state congress at Saltillo, where they managed to pass a law allowing slavery[qv] in Texas. In 1832 Arciniega returned from the United States border to advise Ramón Músquiz[qv] of the cholera epidemic in New Orleans. On February 27, 1833, he was reelected alcalde of Bexar, and in June he assumed the post of political chief because Músquiz was ill.

Arciniega had been appointed land commissioner for Stephen F. Austin's[qv] colonies in November 1830. In this position he signed a four-league grant for the town of Bastrop and with Samuel May Williams[qv] laid out the town in 1832. On September 22, 1835, Arciniega received a Spanish grant of 48,708 acres now in Hunt, Grayson, and Harrison counties. He was chosen interpreter for Gen. Martín Perfecto de Cos[qv] in negotiations for the surrender of Bexar in December 1835. It is unclear whether he supported the Texas Revolution,[qv] as he was appointed Bexar delegate to the Convention of 1836[qv] but did not attend. He had been appointed second judge of Bexar in 1835, and it was probably in that position that he corresponded with Thomas Jefferson Rusk[qv] in August 1836 concerning a cholera epidemic in Brazoria, treatment of Bexar residents, and the theft of cattle. In the cattle case he was ordered to assist the cavalry sent by Rusk to prevent the thefts and to protect anyone who had not opposed the Texans in the war.

Arciniega married Alejandra Losoya, and they had five children. After 1836 his name appears only twice in the records. In 1840 he reported for tax purposes twenty town lots in San Antonio and three slaves. In 1850 Juan N. Seguín[qv] testified that Miguel Arciniega, Jr., was a member of an 1839 campaign against Indian tribes.

BIBLIOGRAPHY: Eugene C. Barker, ed., *The Austin Papers* (3 vols., Washington: GPO, 1924–28). Adán Benavides, Jr., comp. and ed., *The Béxar Archives, 1717–1836: A Name Guide* (Austin: University of Texas Press, 1989). John Henry Brown, *History of Texas from 1685 to 1892* (2 vols., St. Louis: Daniell, 1893). Frederick Charles Chabot, *With the Makers of San Antonio* (Yanaguana Society Publications 4, San Antonio, 1937). Hans Peter Nielsen Gammel, comp., *Laws of Texas, 1822–1897* (10 vols., Austin: Gammel, 1898). William Fairfax Gray, *From Virginia to Texas, 1835* (Houston: Fletcher Young, 1909, 1965). John H. Jenkins, ed., *The Papers of the Texas Revolution, 1835–1836* (10 vols., Austin: Presidial Press, 1973). Kenneth Kesselus, *History of Bastrop County, Texas, Before Statehood* (Austin: Jenkins, 1986). Virginia H. Taylor, *The Spanish Archives of the General Land Office of Texas* (Austin: Lone Star, 1955). Gifford E. White, ed., *The 1840 Census of the Republic of Texas* (Austin: Pemberton, 1966; 2d ed., Vol. 2 of *1840 Citizens of Texas*, Austin, 1984).

John G. Johnson

ARCOLA, TEXAS. Arcola is at the junction of Farm Road 521 and State Highway 6 and the intersection of the Atchison, Topeka and Santa Fe and the Missouri Pacific railroads, twenty miles east of Richmond in southeastern Fort Bend County. The site is on part of the league granted in 1822 to David Fitzgerald,[qv] one of the Old Three Hundred.[qv] A large portion of the grant was sold to Jonathan Dawson Waters[qv] in the middle 1840s. By acquiring the whole league in 1850, Waters became the owner of one of the largest cotton and sugar plantations in Texas, which he called Arcola. The Houston Tap Railroad was built through the area of the plantation in 1858. After Waters' death the plantation lands were purchased by Col. T. W. House[qv] of Houston. The Arcola community was formed predominantly by freed slaves. A post office was established in 1869 and served off and on until 1920. Arcola became a railroad junction in 1878 when the Gulf, Colorado and Santa Fe was built through the county. By 1884 the community had a sugar mill, two steam gristmill–cotton gins, two general stores, a Baptist church, and a school. In 1903 the Arcola school district had two schools serving forty-two white pupils and four schools serving 176 black pupils. In 1914 the community had an estimated fifty inhabitants and one general store. In 1940 Arcola had a church, a school, the Riceton-Arcola cemetery, and four businesses. Arcola's population slowly grew to 120 in 1949, 299 in 1968, and 661 in 1986, when the community incorporated. Some of its growth may be attributed to its proximity to Houston. Arcola had two churches, a school, and a number of scattered dwellings in 1980 and a population of 666 in 1990.

Mark Odintz

ARCOS BUENOS, ARCOS PORDIDOS, AND ARCOS TIRADOS INDIANS. These three groups of Indians are known only from a Spanish document of 1693 that lists them among fifty "nations" that lived north of the Rio Grande and "between Texas and New Mexico." This may be interpreted to mean the southern part of western Texas, since the document also mentions that the Apaches were at war with the groups named. Nothing further is known about these Indians, whose names all refer to the condition of their bows ("good," "rotten," and "long," respectively).

BIBLIOGRAPHY: Charles W. Hackett, ed., *Historical Documents Relating to New Mexico, Nueva Vizcaya, and Approaches Thereto, to 1773* (3 vols., Washington: Carnegie Institution, 1923–37).

Thomas N. Campbell

ARCOS TUERTOS INDIANS. The Arcos Tuertos (Spanish for "twisted bows") Indians were one of twenty Indian groups that joined Juan Domínguez de Mendoza[qv] on his journey from El Paso to the vicinity of present San Angelo in 1683–1684. The meeting occurred east of the Pecos River, possibly in what is now Reagan and Irion counties, and the Arcos Tuertos accompanied Mendoza to the Colorado River beyond San Angelo. They seem to have been one of the numerous bands of unknown affiliation that ranged the transition zone between the southern High Plains and the Edwards Plateau[qv] prior to Apache dominance in the early eighteenth century.

BIBLIOGRAPHY: Herbert Eugene Bolton, ed., *Spanish Exploration in the Southwest, 1542–1706* (New York: Scribner, 1908; rpt., New York: Barnes and Noble, 1959).

Thomas N. Campbell

ARDEN, TEXAS. Arden, on Rocky Creek in northeastern Irion County, was named for John and Katie Arden, who settled a claim at the site by 1885. The community acquired a post office in 1890 with W. P. Moore as postmaster. A local public school was established in 1892. Two short-lived schools had operated before this in the Arden district, one on Rocky Creek and the other at Sawyer. In 1915 Arden had a post office, a school, a church, and a population of fourteen. In 1947, when the community had one business and thirty residents, the Arden school was consolidated with that of Mertzon. All of the businesses had been abandoned as of 1966, except for a polling place used to preserve precinct lines. The passing of the school, low cotton prices, drought, and better opportunities in nearby larger towns were the primary causes for the decline of Arden. Since 1952 an Arden reunion has been held each Labor Day on Rocky Creek.

BIBLIOGRAPHY: Irion County Historical Society, *A History of Irion County, Texas* (San Angelo: Anchor, 1978).

Tracey L. Compton

ARENOSA CREEK (Kinney County). Arenosa Creek rises immediately north of Turkey Mountain and four miles southeast of the intersection of Farm roads 3199 and 334 in east central Kinney County (at 29°24′ N, 100°12′ W) and runs southwest for eighteen miles to its mouth on the East Fork of Elm Creek, at Farm Road 1572 twelve miles southeast of Brackettville (at 29°13′ N, 100°15′ W). It traverses flat terrain with locally deep and dense dissection and locally shallow depressions, surfaced by clays that support oak, juniper, mesquite, and grasses. Downstream, water-tolerant hardwoods, conifers, and grasses predominate. *Arenosa* is Spanish for "sandy."

____ (Victoria County). Arenosa Creek rises three miles southwest of Fordtran in extreme northern Victoria County (at 29°01′ N, 97°01′ W) and flows east and southeast for thirty-five miles to its mouth on Garcitas Creek, eight miles southeast of Inez (at 28°50′ N, 96°43′ W). The stream is intermittent in its upper reaches and is a major drainage tributary of the area. It runs through level to gently sloping terrain surfaced primarily with clay and sandy loams that support a rich rangeland and cropland. Arenosa Creek formed part of the boundaries of the original land grants issued in the early 1830s to Martín De León and his son Fernando,[qqv] colonizers of present Victoria County. After annexation[qv] the state legislature made the creek part of the Victoria-Jackson county line, on March 31, 1846. The community of Arenosa is named after the creek.

BIBLIOGRAPHY: Roy Grimes, ed., *300 Years in Victoria County* (Victoria, Texas: Victoria *Advocate*, 1968; rpt., Austin: Nortex, 1985).

ARENOSA SHELTER. Arenosa Shelter is a limestone overhang in the north wall of the lower Pecos River canyon near the confluence of the Pecos and the Rio Grande. The shelter, now beneath the waters of Amistad Reservoir,[qv] was investigated as part of salvage archeological work in anticipation of the impoundment of that lake in 1969. The shelter was first recorded in 1958, and excavations were conducted during several seasons from September 1965 until July 1968 under the auspices of the Texas Archeological Salvage Project of the University of Texas at Austin and directed by David S. Dibble. The limestone roof of the shelter was about twenty-one meters above the level of the Pecos River and extended out more than eight meters from the back wall. At the time of its discovery in 1958, the shelter was completely filled with stratified, alternating alluvial and cultural deposits. Excavations exposed a series of deposits 12.8 meters thick. Of the forty-nine strata documented, twenty-four contained cultural remains and twenty-five were devoid of cultural debris (these were numbered from the top down, 1 through 49). This remarkable sequence reflects repeated periods of prehistoric human occupation between 9,600 and 1,500 years ago, each followed by flooding. The floods were at times caused by the Pecos River, at other times by backwater from the Rio Grande, and at still other times by both rivers. The most recent (1954) and biggest buried such twentieth-century artifacts as tobacco cans and fishing tackle in the shelter under nearly half a meter of silt.

A series of thirty-two radiocarbon dates of charcoal aided in developing a chronology of the site. The Paleo-Indian period is represented by bison bones and a few nondiagnostic stone artifacts (175 flakes and four unifacial tools) in stratum 38 near the base of the sequence. A single, uncorrected, uncalibrated radiocarbon date of 9550 ± 190 years ago derives from charcoal in stratum 38. From stratum 36 upward into stratum 4 were recovered artifacts resulting from a long sequence of Archaic occupations. These are well-dated with thirty radiocarbon determinations ranging from more than 5,500 to around 1,900 years ago. Cross-dating of diagnostic artifacts in this sequence expands it from ca. 9,000 to ca. 1,300 years ago. Strata 2 and 3 derive primarily from Late Prehistoric occupations, datable from ca. 1,300 to ca. 500 years ago; a single radiocarbon age on charcoal from stratum 2 was determined to be 1,380 ± 60 uncorrected, uncalibrated years old.

Numerous archeological features and important assemblages of artifacts from well-dated, brief intervals of occupation were documented at Arenosa. The site provides the best single-site chronological record in the Trans-Pecos[qv] and one of the best in North America. The flood deposits at the site have also afforded evidence for the history of flooding of the Pecos River. Larger floods occurred during drier climatic intervals over the last 8,000 years, a finding dramatically evident in the catastrophic flood of 1954 during the droughty mid-1950s. There has been no comprehensive analysis and reporting of the data from Arenosa Shelter. The collections and records are housed at the Texas Archeological Research Laboratory at the University of Texas at Austin and have often been referred to by students and scholars researching the prehistory of the lower Pecos region. In this way, the site has contributed significantly to understanding of the area, though its full potential has not been tapped.

BIBLIOGRAPHY: Michael B. Collins, *Test Excavations at Amistad International Reservoir, Fall 1967* (Texas Archeological Salvage Project, Misc. Papers No. 16, University of Texas at Austin, 1969). David S. Dibble, Excavations at Arenosa Shelter, 1965–1966 (MS, Texas Archeological Salvage Project, University of Texas at Austin, 1967). Peter C. Patton and David S. Dibble, "Archeologic and Geomorphic Evidence for the Paleohydrologic Record of the Pecos River in West Texas," *American Journal of Science* 282 (February 1982). Solveig A. Turpin, ed., *Papers on Lower Pecos Prehistory* (Texas Archeological Research Laboratory, University of Texas at Austin, 1991).

Michael B. Collins

ARGENTA, TEXAS. Argenta is a rural community on Farm Road 88 nineteen miles southeast of George West in the southeastern corner of Live Oak County. Richard Bethel Bomar moved to the area from Oklahoma in 1903, cleared land, and sold it to friends from Oklahoma. In 1907 the community was granted a post office with the name of Ego; citizens built a church in 1909 under Bomar's leadership, and in 1910 the settlement was renamed Argenta. Between 1910 and 1926 Argenta grew to include a general store, a gristmill, and a blacksmith shop. In 1917 a schoolhouse was built, and by 1925 the town had an estimated population of fifty. A cotton gin brought from Oklahoma was never put into operation, however, and about 1925 the community began to decline. It lost its post office in 1926, in 1927 the general store closed, and by 1940 only the schoolhouse, the church, and scattered dwellings remained at the site. In 1945 the school was consolidated with the Mathis school district. In 1981 the church was still used by a small Church of Christ congregation; the old schoolhouse was a community center. In the early 1980s new homes were being built in the area.

BIBLIOGRAPHY: Ervin L. Sparkman, *The People's History of Live Oak County* (Mesquite, Texas, 1981). *John Leffler*

ARGO, TEXAS. Argo is on Farm Road 1001 eight miles northeast of Mount Pleasant in northeastern Titus County. The town grew up in the 1880s around the businesses of James S. Rountree, Millard C. Wilhite, and John Arnold. The post office was established in Rountree's general store in 1885 with Rountree as postmaster. By 1890 Argo had become a major trading center for farmers who lived north of Mount Pleasant; it had a population of 150, three churches, a mill, a gin, a tannery, and several stores. Although the population was only sixty-five in 1896, it had increased to 131 by 1900. The post office was closed in 1907, but the town remained fairly stable until the 1940s. By 1954 the population had fallen to thirty, and in 1986 and 1990 it was reported as twenty-six.

BIBLIOGRAPHY: C. L. Embrey, Our Good Old Days (Laird Hill, Texas, 1970). Quasqui Centennial Committee, *Titus County Celebrates 125 Years* (Mount Pleasant, Texas, 1971). Traylor Russell, *History of Titus County* (2 vols., Waco: Morrison, 1965, 1966; rpt. 1975).

Cecil Harper, Jr.

ARGYLE, TEXAS. Argyle is on U.S. Highway 377 and the Missouri Pacific Railroad six miles southwest of Denton in southwestern Denton County. Between 1850 and 1867 fourteen families settled in the area under the auspices of the Peters colony,[qv] and in the 1850s twenty-nine families settled on vacant or unclaimed land in the area. At that time the place was known as Pilot Knob or Waintown. Early settlers raised cattle on the open ranges nearby. The first post office in the area was near Pilot Knob, where Emily Wilson was appointed postmistress in 1878. She had the post office in her log cabin, two miles east of the site of future Argyle, where a stagecoach delivered the mail. The first school in the area was in Graham, one-half mile to the north, in 1875. In 1876, the Graham Baptist Church, the first formal church in the area, was organized in the school. Previously, a ten-day revival had been held every fall at John Wells Campground, two miles west of Argyle.

The Texas and Pacific built its track through the area in 1881. Argyle was founded on November 7, 1881, when James Morrill was given the authority to build and maintain a depot, switches, and side tracks there. The community was named Argyle by a railroad surveyor, after a garden in France. In 1881 the post office was moved from Pilot Knob to Argyle. Mail was delivered by the railroad four times daily. By the late 1880s Argyle had two rural mail routes, each thirty miles long, which took a full day to ride. New cash crops, such as wheat and oats, were grown to ship on the railroad, and hogs and sheep were raised. In 1888 the Argyle State Bank was established. By 1890 Argyle had a population of 148 and several businesses, including two steam gristmills, a cotton gin, two general stores, a hotel, and a hardware store. In 1895 a fire started in a dry goods store and destroyed the entire business section, but it was rebuilt by the early twentieth century.

Denton County was divided into seventy-three school districts in 1884, and Argyle received its own district. It had nine grades; any student wishing more education had to attend school in Denton. In 1885 Argyle built a two-story brick school, and by 1891 the Argyle district was the fifth largest in the county, with 107 students. The town reached a population of 238 and five businesses in 1930. By the mid-1930s Argyle had electric service, and telephones were available from 8:00 a.m. to 5:00 p.m. Monday through Friday through a switchboard operator. The cotton gin burned in 1930 and was never rebuilt, and area farmers started growing peanuts instead of cotton.

After the population peaked in the 1930s, the community began to decline. It reached a low of ninety in 1950. Local soils were depleted. As opportunities to work in Dallas–Fort Worth industries and war factories increased during World War II,[qv] young farmers moved from the country to the city. By the 1960s the population rose slightly, to 125. Argyle voted to incorporate on September 19, 1960, and did so in 1962. M. H. Wilson was elected the first mayor. The next year the Argyle Volunteer Fire Department was founded. Argyle's newspaper, the *Quad Town News*, was published that decade. In the 1970s more businesses were located in Argyle, including two grocery stores, several service stations and garages, beauty shops, a leather and shoe-repair shop, and a cafe and bakery. The railroad depot was moved in the 1970s, when the old section house was being used for Sunday school classes, but the railroad was still shipping agricultural products and manufactured goods. In the next two decades Argyle grew considerably as big-city residents moved to a country atmosphere. In 1990 it had a population of 1,575. That year Argyle's one manufacturing establishment made wooden cabinets.

BIBLIOGRAPHY: Yvonne Allen Jenkins, *History of the Argyle Community in Southwest Denton County* (Argyle, Texas, Bicentennial Committee, 1976). *Lisa C. Maxwell*

ARGYLE HOTEL. The Argyle Hotel, for many years one of San Antonio's finest hotels and restaurants, was built in 1859 by Charles Anderson[qv] as a plantation house for his ranch, which covered most of what is now Alamo Heights. Anderson, a Union sympathizer, was briefly imprisoned in 1861, but escaped and left the state. Confederate authorities discussed the possibility of constructing an arsenal on his property, but the plans never materialized, and the house stood unoccupied for several years. After the war Hiram W. McLane[qv] purchased the house and ranch and started raising horses there. In 1890 the ranch was sold to a Denver investment company, which developed the land into what is now Alamo Heights. The house itself was purchased by two Scots named Patterson, after whom the street in front of the house is named. They converted the house into an inn, the Argyle Hotel. A third story and a southwest wing were added after 1890; the second and third story front porches were modified, and the lower front porch was converted into a garden loggia.

Robert Emmit O'Grady and his sister Alice O'Grady[qqv] purchased the hotel and opened it on St. Patrick's Day, 1893. European furnishings and decoration were added to the twenty-one guest rooms and various public spaces, and antique silver and fine china became part of the daily table service. Alice O'Grady, with George Bannister, the Argyle chef for thirty-five years, served a fine cuisine. Having collected and experimented with recipes from the time she helped her mother in the Kendall House (the O'Grady home and inn in Boerne), Alice brought to the Argyle a creative interest in cooking that made it outstanding in the South for fine food. Her tiered wedding cakes, shipped in sheet-draped Pullman berths, were a must for brides of many South Texas families. Her brother Robert assisted in the operation of the Argyle. Through the years O'Grady sisters Kate, Lizzie, and Mary assisted Alice and Robert in the hotel's management. Guests of national reputation came for meals, and several lived there for years. Alice retired in 1941, and the hotel remained in private hands until it was bought in the 1950s by the Southwest Foundation for Research and Education[qv] of San Antonio and converted into an exclusive club whose members make an annual contribution in support of the medical research underway at the foundation. Restoration and additions to the famous old Argyle Hotel have continued, and it was still in operation as a private club in 1990.

BIBLIOGRAPHY: Ella K. Daggett, "Famous Contemporaries: The Argyle and the Menger," *Southern Home and Garden*, September 1941. Lillie May Hagner, *Alluring San Antonio* (San Antonio: Naylor, 1940). *Christopher Long*

ARHAU. The term Arhau denoted an Indian group or village, possibly Karankawan, described by Henri Joutel[qv] as being between Matagorda Bay and the Colorado River in 1687.

BIBLIOGRAPHY: Frederick Webb Hodge, ed., *Handbook of American Indians North of Mexico* (2 vols., Washington: GPO, 1907, 1910; rpt., New York: Pageant, 1959). *Margery H. Krieger*

ARIEL. The *Ariel,* the first steamboat used in Texas waters, was the property of Henry Austin,[qv] who brought the vessel to the mouth of the Rio Grande in June 1829 to experiment with steam navigation on the river. In October the *Texas Gazette*[qv] reported that the *Ariel* had ascended 300 miles up the river to Revilla and was making regular runs between Matamoros and Camargo. After a year Austin gave up the project and arranged to visit Stephen F. Austin's[qv] colony in Texas. In August 1830 he reached the mouth of the Brazos and ascended to Brazoria. After exploring Brazos waters, he decided that a boat business could not be made profitable and decided to sail for New Orleans. The *Ariel* was almost wrecked attempting to cross the Brazos bar and put out to sea in a damaged condition; it was forced to return. After three attempts to reach the United States, the ship put back into Galveston Bay and was laid up to rot in the San Jacinto River.

BIBLIOGRAPHY: William R. Hogan, Life and Letters of Henry Austin (M.A. thesis, University of Texas, 1932). William Ransom Hogan, "Life of Henry Austin," *Southwestern Historical Quarterly* 37 (January 1934). Bernice Lockhart, Navigating Texas Rivers, 1821–1900 (M.A. thesis, St. Mary's University, 1949). *Wesley N. Laing*

ARIHUMAN INDIANS. The Arihuman Indians are known only from a Spanish document of 1683 that does not clearly identify their area, but it seems to have been east of the Pecos River in west central Texas. Their affiliations remain unknown.

BIBLIOGRAPHY: Charles W. Hackett, ed., *Pichardo's Treatise on the Limits of Louisiana and Texas* (4 vols., Austin: University of Texas Press, 1931–46). *Thomas N. Campbell*

ARIOLA, TEXAS. Ariola is fourteen miles north of Beaumont in southern Hardin County. A small community called Sharon sprang up around a flag stop on the Texas and New Orleans Railroad at a site once called Buzzard Roost. Seeking to utilize the area's forest resources, George W. Hooks built a sawmill there soon after the railroad was completed. The post office, established in 1888, was named Hooks Switch, although the railroad stop continued to be known as Sharon as late as 1905. The depression of the 1890s forced Hooks to transfer his mill, which had a daily capacity of 75,000 board feet, to the J. F. Keith[qv] Lumber Company of Beaumont. The community's name was then changed to Ariola, after the Eduardo and Francisco Ariola leagues, on which the town was built. The post office took the new name in 1901. John Henry Kirby[qv] acquired the Ariola mill in 1902. In 1904 the community, still occasionally referred to as Hooks Switch, had a population of 108. The Kirby Lumber Company dismantled the mill in 1907, and the post office discontinued operations shortly thereafter. Ariola, however, remained a flag stop for several years. In 1932 the first of three oil wells in the Ariola field was brought in. Local residents call the community Chance, in honor of a pioneer family of that name. The population is combined with that of Loeb and Lumberton, a growing suburb of Beaumont. Two of the Ariola oil wells were still producing in 1984.

BIBLIOGRAPHY: Aline House, *Big Thicket: Its Heritage* (San Antonio: Naylor, 1967). Mary Lou Proctor, A History of Hardin County (M.A. thesis, University of Texas, 1950). *Robert Wooster*

ARISPE, TEXAS. Arispe, also known as La Valley, was five miles southeast of Sierra Blanca on the Missouri Pacific Railroad in an area that is now crossed by Interstate 10 and U.S. Highway 80 in south central Hudspeth County. The community was founded in 1885 as a railroad section house. A post office called La Valley operated from 1909 until 1911 with Mrs. Alice Auten as postmistress. The community had fifty-seven inhabitants. By the mid-1940s the estimated population numbered fewer than twenty-five. *Martin Donell Kohout*

ARISTA, MARIANO (1802–1855). Mariano Arista, Mexican general, was born at the city of San Luis Potosí, Mexico, on July 26, 1802. He entered the army as a cadet in the Puebla regiment about 1819 and rose to the rank of brigadier general. After an unsuccessful *pronunciamento* in favor of Centralism in 1833, he went in exile to the United States until he was repatriated and reinstated in the army in 1836. He served on the Supreme Tribunal of War and in the Supreme Military Court and in 1839 was made commandant general of Tamaulipas and general of the Mexican Army of the North. In that capacity he defeated the movement to establish the Republic of the Rio Grande[qv] in northern Tamaulipas in 1840. After a period in private life, he was recalled to active duty just before the outbreak of the Mexican War,[qv] was ordered to command the Army of the North, and was in command of Mexican troops in the battles of Palo Alto and Resaca de la Palma[qqv] on May 8 and 9, 1846. After suffering defeat in both engagements and being criticized by subordinates, he relinquished his command to Francisco Mexía, requested trial by a court-martial, and was absolved of guilt. He became Mexican secretary of war in June 1848. In January 1851 he was declared by the Mexican Congress the constitutional president of Mexico. He resigned in January 1853, was forced into exile, and died near Lisbon, Portugal, on August 7, 1855.

BIBLIOGRAPHY: Hubert Howe Bancroft, *History of the North Mexican States and Texas* (2 vols., San Francisco: History Company, 1886, 1889). *Diccionario Enciclopédico Hispano-Americano de Literatura, Ciencias y Artes* (25 vols., Barcelona: Montaner y Simón, 1887–98). Miguel Ángel Peral, ed., *Diccionario Biográfico Mexicano* (Mexico City: Editorial P.A.C., 1944). Herbert Ingram Priestley, *The Mexican Nation: A History* (New York: Macmillan, 1923). *David M. Vigness*

ARKANSAS CITY, TEXAS. Arkansas City, four miles south of San Isidro on Farm Road 2294 in northeastern Starr County, was a supply point and shipping center for the surrounding ranch area in the days of horse-drawn wagons; by 1936 it had a factory, a business, and two dwellings. In 1940 it had a store and a population of ten. During the 1950s and 1960s the community population increased to forty. In 1991 there were three rural homes in the area but no markers indicating a community. *Dick D. Heller, Jr.*

ARLEDGE FIELD. Arledge Field, at Stamford, was a contract primary flight school operated by the Lou Foote Flying Service to give primary flight training to army aviation cadets. It was established on March 15, 1941, and named for Roy Arledge, a member of the committee that selected and purchased the site. Commanding officers during the base's brief period of activity were Capt. Bob Arnold and majors James B. Knopf and John H. Enders. Cadets from the training school were entertained in homes, and the youth center at the Stamford library was converted into a cadet club. The base was deactivated on September 30, 1944.

BIBLIOGRAPHY: Hooper Shelton and Homer Hutto, *The First 100 Years of Jones County* (Stamford, Texas: Shelton, 1978).

ARLESTON, TEXAS. Arleston was a post office community six miles northwest of Deberry in northeastern Panola County. It was probably established in the late 1870s. Its post office operated from 1881 until 1906, and in the early 1890s the settlement had two general stores, a cotton gin and mill, and an estimated population of thirty. By the mid-1930s Arleston no longer appeared on highway maps.

BIBLIOGRAPHY: John Barnette Sanders, *Postoffices and Post Masters of Panola County, Texas, 1845-1930* (Center, Texas, 1964).

Christopher Long

ARLIE, TEXAS. Arlie is on Farm Road 1034 and Sand Creek in northeastern Childress County. The town was established in 1888 and named for Arlie Griffith Weddington, an early resident. The Arlie post office was granted in June 1888. The community became a trade center for a prosperous farming area and for years had a church, a general store, and a cotton gin. Beginning in 1901 it was part of the Buck Creek (later Loco) school district. In 1930 the Arlie post office changed its name to Loco; it remained in operation until December 1964. In 1946 eight families were reported as permanent residents in Arlie, but improved local transportation led to the community's demise, as local businesses closed; this was also the case with neighboring Loco. In the 1980s only farms and the Arlie community cemetery remained in the vicinity. *Ida Howard Taylor*

ARLINGTON, TEXAS. Arlington is halfway between Dallas and Fort Worth in east Tarrant County. It was founded in 1876 on the Texas and Pacific Railway as a market town for the surrounding farms. From the 1840s the area had attracted farmers because of the fertile blackland in the eastern part of the region and the sandy loam, good for growing fruits and vegetables, in the western part. The place was also well watered by the Trinity River and its tributaries. Early settlements included Bird's Fort, Watson, and Johnson Station, founded by Middleton Tate Johnson.[qv]

The area was not without liabilities for settlers, however. The Village Creek area near the site of present Lake Arlington was one of the largest gathering places of Indians in the region. In a battle of May 24, 1841, Gen. Edward H. Tarrant[qv] attacked and defeated the Indians of the Village Creek encampment, thus opening the Arlington area for white settlement. According to the terms of the Indian Peace Council in 1843, a trading post was set up at Marrow Bone Spring (in present

Arlington), near Johnson Station. A few stores had been set up in Johnson Station before 1876. When the Texas and Pacific planned to lay tracks through the county, a more direct route between Fort Worth and Dallas was chosen, north of Johnson Station. A Presbyterian minister, Andrew S. Hayter, was asked by the railway company to survey the area that became Arlington and the land on either side of the tracks. He is credited with laying out the first town plat. The stores and many of the settlers made the move north to the new location from Johnson Station at that time. Johnson Station had a post office from 1851 to 1905. When citizens of the new settlement applied for a post office under the name Johnson they were turned down because of the proximity to Johnson Station. The post office was established under the name Hayter in 1875 and in 1877 was renamed Arlington, after Robert E. Lee's[qv] hometown in Virginia.

Arlington had as many as five gins at one time to process cotton, the major source of agricultural revenue. Area farmers also raised hay, oats, corn, peanuts, potatoes, sorghum, and other crops, as well as dairy cattle and other livestock. Arlington became the site of large produce sales and a distribution center for shipment to other towns. Another early source of revenue was the mineral well in the center of town. Though it was dug as a public water well, it yielded mineral water, from which medicinal crystals were produced and sold. The water was also bottled for sale, and a sanitarium was built for using it to treat illnesses.

By 1884 the community had an estimated population of 800 and Baptist, Methodist, and Presbyterian churches. In 1890 Arlington reported eighteen businesses, including several stores. By 1910 the citizens had an electric plant, a water system, natural gas lines, telephones, and a public school system. In 1925 the number of residents was estimated at 3,031. Arlington Downs,[qv] a racetrack built in 1933, drew thousands of visitors, including many dignitaries, until pari-mutuel betting was declared illegal in Texas in 1937.

Before World War II[qv] the population of Arlington had grown to 4,240. A General Motors assembly plant was built there in 1951, and the Great Southwest Industrial District was formed in 1956. In 1961 the population was estimated at 44,775, and 122,200 residents were reported in 1978. Arlington has a council-manager government. Tom Vandergriff served as mayor through the period of rapid growth, from 1951 until 1977.

In 1990 the city had two institutions of higher learning, the University of Texas at Arlington and Arlington Baptist College. Recreational, social, and cultural facilities included many public parks, several public swimming pools, public and private golf courses, tennis courts, auditoriums, libraries, theaters, youth centers, seniors' facilities, and a community center. For recreation and water needs Lake Arlington was developed in the southwest section of the city in 1957. The large amusement park Six Flags Over Texas[qv] opened in 1961. It continued to draw thousands to the North Texas area, and Arlington in particular, every year. Restaurants, hotels, motels, and many retail businesses benefited from this tourist attraction. In 1972 Arlington became the home of the Texas Rangers[qv] baseball team, which plays at the Arlington Stadium. In 1988 Arlington had an estimated 213,832 residents and 4,105 businesses. The population in 1990 was 261,721.

BIBLIOGRAPHY: Arista Joyner, comp., *Arlington, Texas: Birthplace of the Metroplex* (Waco: Arlington Bicentennial-Centennial Celebration Committee, 1976). Leonard Sanders, *How Fort Worth Became the Texasmost City* (Fort Worth: Amon Carter Museum, 1973). Janet L. Schmelzer, *Where the West Begins: Fort Worth and Tarrant County* (Northridge, California: Windsor, 1985). Vertical Files, Barker Texas History Center, University of Texas at Austin.

Gayla Weems Shannon

ARLINGTON BAPTIST COLLEGE. Arlington Baptist College, a four-year, private, coeducational institution of higher education, was established in Fort Worth in 1939 as the Fundamental Baptist Bible Institute by Louis Entzminger, an associate of Baptist minister J. Frank Norris.[qv] The school was organized to train ministers and missionaries who would teach the literal inerrancy of the Bible—an objective that has remained central to the institution to the present. Entzminger served as the college's only faculty member during its initial year, when the enrollment was sixteen. The first classes met in an upstairs room of the First Baptist Church of Fort Worth, and its first graduates became pastors or missionaries working through the World Fundamental Baptist Fellowship.

Though it grew some, the school largely maintained its humble origins during its first twenty years of existence. It was apparently moved a number of times to various leased properties in Fort Worth. In 1945 its name was changed to Bible Baptist Seminary. Norris served as president in 1950–51. In 1952 the school moved to Arlington and took on the name Arlington Baptist College. At the same time, it discontinued its high school curriculum and became a four-year, undergraduate institution. In 1956 the school, which had maintained itself through a combination of tuition and fees, gifts, and contributions from churches and individuals, purchased the tract of land on which it is now located. By the 1962–63 school year enrollment had grown to 225.

The college curriculum emphasizes intense study of the Bible and the deepening of the student's faith. Its philosophy holds that "thorough preparation in the Word of God best equips an individual for a useful career and responsible citizenship." The school offers bachelor of science degrees in a number of fields, including pastoral ministries, missions, and music education. A bachelor of arts degree is offered in biblical languages. The school is supported by the World Baptist Fellowship and is an accredited member of the American Association of Bible Colleges. In 1990 the campus had ten buildings, including a library, an administration building, a religious education building, an auditorium, and two dormitories. In 1990 the enrollment was 171.

Brian Hart

ARLINGTON DOWNS RACETRACK. Arlington Downs, a 1¼-mile track with a 6,000-seat grandstand, opened on November 1, 1929, under the guidance of oil and cattle magnate William T. Waggoner.[qv] The track was located on his "Three D" stock farm half-way between Dallas and Fort Worth near Arlington, and the construction cost was nearly $3 million. All of this endeavor was a gamble for the millionaire since pari-mutuel betting, the largest income-producing aspect of horse racing, was illegal at the time of the track's opening. By use of his facility for prize races and for local civic events, Waggoner endeared himself and his track to the local citizenry. Simultaneously, the racing entrepreneur was spending thousands lobbying Austin for legalization of pari-mutuel wagering.

Although lawmakers were unsuccessful in their attempts to pass legislation in support of Waggoner's gamble, a test case arose when two racegoers, O. O. Franklin and J. B. Coulter, were arrested at Arlington Downs in the fall of 1931 for openly betting on the races. The resulting publicity and court case allowed racing proponents to make their case public. In 1933 the Texas legislature legalized pari-mutuel; it issued the first permit to a hastily expanded and remodeled Arlington Downs.

The income generated by pari-mutuel betting breathed new life into the racetrack, and thoroughbred owners from across the country sent their horses by rail to compete at Arlington Downs. During its first year of full operation under the new laws, 650 horses ran on the track, profits averaged $113,731 a day, and the average daily attendance was 6,734. As Arlington Downs increased its financial health, Waggoner's physical health broke. On December 9, 1934, he died of a stroke, thus depriving the racing industry of one of its most vocal and successful boosters. In Austin support was growing for a repeal of pari-mutuel as pro-racing lobbyists scrambled to buy time. By careful maneuvering, a decision on the issue was avoided during the 1936–37 seasons, and the popularity and prestige of Arlington Downs grew throughout the country. In 1937 the Texas Derby was heralded as the "tryouts" for the more famous Kentucky Derby.

At the end of the 1937 regular session the state legislature repealed the pari-mutuel laws. Arlington Downs was sold to commercial developers. The racetrack was used for rodeos and other events until 1958, when the buildings were razed. In 1978 a Texas historical landmark was placed on the site.

BIBLIOGRAPHY: Arlington *Citizen-Journal*, July 4, 1985. Chris Taylor, "Reign of the Tricolors," *Texas Historian*, March 1972.

Donald S. Frazier

ARMADA DE BARLOVENTO. At the urging of Juan de Palafox, influential member of the Consejo de Indias, the Armada de las Islas de Barlovento y Seno Mexicano was authorized by the Spanish Crown about 1635. The name was abbreviated to Armada de Barlovento, or Windward Fleet. Its purpose was to police the sea lanes in the Gulf of Mexico and the Caribbean Sea to protect Spanish shipping and coastal settlements from foreign raiders. The armada's principal activities relating to Texas centered around the La Salle expedition,qv especially the search for La Salle's colony, and support of Domingo Terán de los Ríos qv in his entrada of 1691–92.

Since the 1560s sea commanders of the Armada de la Carrera de las Indias, the Spanish Indies fleet, had requested a separate battle squadron permanently based in the West Indies. It took the Thirty Years' War, which occasioned heavy losses of Spanish shipping and occupation of Spanish islands in the Caribbean by French, English, and Dutch forces, to bring it about. The *alcabala*, a local sales tax of New Spain, was doubled to finance the new fleet, which began operation in 1641 with a few embargoed vessels of various sizes while others were being built.

The armada, first stationed at Veracruz, was alternately ported at Havana, Santo Domingo, and San Juan, Puerto Rico. Under command of Adm. Antonio de la Plaza Eguiluz, it achieved a notable victory on its first voyage. Plaza's force seized three English or Dutch ships in the act of destroying two galleons being built for the armada in the Río de Alvarado, south of Veracruz. Farther down the coast it overhauled three other vessels, killed their captain and inflicted heavy casualties otherwise. The captured vessels expanded the Armada de Barlovento.

The broader picture, however, was not so bright. The plethora of European enemies made it impossible for Spain to guard such extensive possessions. A perpetual manpower shortage afflicted the armada, at times so severely that the ships were unable to sail. From time to time its vessels were assigned to escort the silver fleet to Spain, then were kept there under various pretexts. Intrigues in the Spanish court further inhibited the accomplishments of the fleet.

After a long period in limbo, the Armada de Barlovento was reinstituted in 1664 with four ships purchased in Amsterdam. These vessels, outfitted and manned at Cádiz, were unable to sail for the Indies until July 1667, when they were sent to escort the *azogues* (ships carrying quicksilver for the mines). After reaching Veracruz they served their intended purpose for a time, patrolling the pirate-infested Campeche coast and the Windward Islands. Then the *capitana* again was sent to escort the treasure ships to Spain, leaving Adm. Alonso de Campos and three ships to deal with Henry Morgan's rampage in the southern Caribbean.

Morgan, after sacking Portobelo and Cartagena in the summer of 1668, turned his rapacity on Maracaibo early the following year. Campos interrupted his own reconnaissance of the Antilles to set course for the Venezuela port. Entering boldly into the Gulf of Venezuela, he engaged on April 27 a vastly superior force that destroyed his fleet. His loss included three ships and more than 130 men. It was the Armada's most disastrous encounter to that time.

In 1672 a new Armada de Barlovento was organized by the viceroy of New Spain. The old problems of financing and manning the ships persisted; the fleet was spread too thin, with too wide an area to cover. Its numerous enemies, including a growing band of multinational pirates, always seemed to know where the armada was and to time their raids accordingly. Such was the case in May 1683, when a buccaneer force of eight ships and 1,000 men led by Michel de Grammont and Laurens de Graff (Lorencillo)—the professionals—carried out the rape of Veracruz.

The Armada de Barlovento had better luck a year later against a bunch of amateurs who sought to do the same for Tampico. Headed by Captain-General Andrés Ochoa de Zárate, the fleet caught the freebooters red-handed and captured 104 men, predominantly English and Dutch. Testimony given by the prisoners—fourteen of whom were garroted—indicated that they had recently visited the Texas coast in hope of salvaging a wrecked vessel. Among those spared was a pilot who later revealed expert knowledge of the Matagorda Bay area while serving as a guide on a voyage seeking La Salle's colony.

The first definite news of La Salle's intrusion came from pirates captured by General Ochoa and his armada in a different encounter. On July 6, 1685, Graff and Grammont stormed ashore at Campeche with 750 buccaneers to begin a two-month spree of rape and pillage. Ironically, the armada during that time was in the Caribbean, seeking the pirates' hideaway on the Honduras island of Roatán. Returning in early September from the fruitless voyage, minus three ships lost in a tropical storm, the remaining ships stumbled onto Graff's fleet off Cabo Catoche, retreating from the Campeche raid. The armada succeeded in destroying one pirate ship and capturing another. In pursuit of Graff's flagship, already crippled by the Spaniards' fire, a cannon exploded on one of the armada vessels, killing three men. In the ensuing confusion, Lorencillo was able to right his vessel and escape. Several armada officers held responsible for abandoning the chase were brought to trial and suspended from duty. The several tragic occurrences of this voyage culminated two days later, when Ochoa, stricken by a sudden illness, died at sea. Yet the armada had 120 prisoners, among whom were defectors from La Salle's company willing to disclose—for a chance at escaping the garrote—the Frenchman's plan for planting a settlement on a river called "Michipipi."

Armed with depositions from the captured French pirates, the Spaniards mounted a three-year search for La Salle's colony. The Armada de Barlovento dispatched five voyages seeking the intruders, bringing to the fore names of such officers as Juan Enríquez Barroto, Francisco López de Gamarra, Andrés de Pez y Malzárraga, and Martín de Rivas.qqv The search constituted a rebirth of exploration of the Gulf of Mexico and its coasts. Thus, the Armada de Barlovento figured prominently in the Spanish mapping of Texas qv and the Gulf Coast, providing place names and other data that found their way onto maps of several European nations.

Even after Alonso De León,qv on a 1689 overland march from Coahuila, found La Salle's Fort St. Louis near the head of Lavaca Bay (at a site now in Victoria County), the Armada de Barlovento continued its involvement in matters pertaining to Texas. In 1690 Capt. Francisco de Llanos qv sailed to Matagorda Bay on a multipurpose mission that included mapping the bay area. With him went Capt. Gregorio de Salinas Varona,qv in charge of land operations, and Manuel José de Cárdenas y Magaña qv as mapmaker. In 1691–92 Enríquez Barroto, who lately had mapped the Gulf Coast while piloting the Rivas-Iriarte expedition, ferried men and supplies for the Terán expedition to Matagorda Bay. While his two ships waited offshore for Terán to complete his mission, six of his men drowned in a boating accident.

Spain, meanwhile, was involved in King William's War. The manpower shortage that generally afflicted the fleet became more critical. At a tender age three of the Talon children,qv late of La Salle's colony, were enlisted as soldiers in the Armada de Barlovento of Captain-General Andrés de Pez to serve on *Santo Cristo de Maracaibo*, flagship of Adm. Guillermo Morfi. They thus became witnesses to one of the most shameful episodes in the armada's history. *Santo Cristo*, cut off from the fleet, struck her colors and surrendered to a French squadron off Hispaniola on January 7, 1697. The Talons were repatriated to France, to return to Louisiana and Texas a few years later, and both Pez and Morfi were court-martialed. With the blame assigned to Morfi, Pez was exonerated. The exploration of Pensacola Bay and a portion of the Mississippi Delta by Pez and Carlos de Sigüenza y Góngora in 1693 was followed in 1695 by a coastal reconnaissance from Tampico to Pensacola Bay. The voyage was conducted by Andrés de Arriola, who later became the reluctant founder of Pensacola and, still later, captain-general of the armada.

In 1700 the armada still faced a plethora of problems: the nest of pirates and poachers infesting the Laguna de Términos and the Campeche coast, the Scots invading Darién, and pressure from European enemies across the length and breadth of the Caribbean. Going into the War of the Spanish Succession, the ships were in bad repair or poorly manned, with the exception of the *capitana*, which still served for escort duty to Spain. The fleet dribbled away until, in 1712, a new naval construction program was implemented at Havana. At the end of the war plans for naval reorganization were put forth in Madrid, a move toward centralization that ultimately spelled the end of the Armada de Barlovento as an independent unit. The armada enjoyed a brief resurgence in 1719, but within the next decade its crews were being appropriated for the new navy. Its manpower was depleted further in the years that followed. On January 31, 1748, the crown decreed dissolution of the Armada de Barlovento.

BIBLIOGRAPHY: William Edward Dunn, *Spanish and French Rivalry in the Gulf Region of the United States, 1678–1702: The Beginnings of Texas and Pensacola* (Austin: University of Texas, 1917). Bibiano Torres Ramírez, *La Armada de Barlovento* (Seville: Escuela de Estudios Hispano-Americanos, 1981). Robert S. Weddle, *The French Thorn: Rival Explorers in the Spanish Sea, 1682–1762* (College Station: Texas A&M University Press, 1991). Robert S. Weddle, *Spanish Sea: The Gulf of Mexico in North American Discovery, 1500–1685* (College Station: Texas A&M University Press, 1985). Robert S. Weddle, *Wilderness Manhunt: The Spanish Search for La Salle* (Austin: University of Texas Press, 1973).

Robert S. Weddle

ARMADILLO. The nine-banded armadillo (*Dasypus novemcinctus*), a relatively recent addition to the Texas fauna, is the only species of armadillo that occurs in North America, the other twenty or so species of Dasypodidae being restricted to South and Central America. The Texas armadillo is about the size of a large cat; its overall length is about 2½ feet, and adults weigh from twelve to seventeen pounds. Mature females mate in late summer and autumn and give birth to identical quadruplets the following spring. The armadillo's diet consists chiefly of insects, grubs, and spiders, though it also eats such foods as earthworms, small amphibians, and reptiles.

Before the mid-1850s the armadillo was known only along the lower Rio Grande valley. By 1880 it had extended its range across South Texas, and it reached the Hill Country[qv] and Austin before the turn of the century. Continuing its movement northward and eastward, the armadillo spread throughout most of Texas and into Louisiana and Oklahoma during the 1920s and 1930s.

Armadillos are adaptable animals. They have few natural enemies; hunters, dogs, coyotes, and automobiles are among the chief agents of mortality. Armadillos are able to survive and reproduce in a variety of habitats. They are, however, susceptible to prolonged drought and extended periods of subfreezing weather so that, except for isolated individuals, armadillos are not permanent residents west or north of the Panhandle and Trans-Pecos[qqv] regions. Currently, the range of the armadillo extends into northern Oklahoma and Arkansas and east to Georgia and Florida. Individual animals have been reported in New Mexico, Kansas, Missouri, Tennessee, and South Carolina; a single specimen has been seen in Colorado.

Human beings have contributed significantly to the spread of armadillos. Some have been captured or purchased as curious pets and later escaped or been intentionally released. In these ways breeding populations were initially established in Mississippi, Alabama, and Florida. Some people may have carried armadillos into new territory for human consumption. The animals have long been considered a legitimate game animal in Mexico, and the practice of eating armadillos was adopted by residents of South Texas when the animal migrated there. During the Great Depression,[qv] East Texans stocked their larders with armadillos, which they called "Hoover hogs" because of the animal's supposed pork-like flavor (some say chicken-like) and because they considered President Herbert Hoover responsible for the depression. Currently, barbecued armadillo and armadillo chili are popular foods at various festivals in parts of Texas, Arkansas, and the southeastern United States.

Recent medical research suggests that people who regularly handle armadillos may be increasing their exposure to Hansen's disease (leprosy). Armadillos have very limited natural immunity to leprosy, and they are shipped from Texas and other states to research facilities worldwide for study relating to the diagnosis and treatment of this disease.

Armadillos have been promoted as a Texas souvenir since the 1890s. Charles Apelt, inventor of the armadillo-shell basket, first displayed his wares at the New York World's Fair in 1902. His family operated the Apelt Armadillo Company near Comfort until 1971. In addition to baskets, Apelt's catalog listed lamps, wall hangings, and other curios fashioned from the armadillo's shell. His farm was also a principal supplier of live armadillos to zoos, research institutions, and individuals.

Armadillo racing became a popular amusement in Texas during the 1970s. Several organizations, notably from San Angelo, began promoting races throughout the United States, in Canada, and even in Europe. As a result, the animal is strongly associated with Texas. The Armadillo World Headquarters[qv] in Austin, a rock and country music establishment decorated by the "Michelangelo of armadillo art," Jim Franklin, was from 1970 to 1980 a monument to the association between Texans and the armadillo. In the late 1970s the Texas legislature voted down attempts to make the armadillo the official state mammal, but in 1981 it was declared the official state mascot by executive decree.

BIBLIOGRAPHY: Larry L. Smith and Robin W. Doughty, *The Amazing Armadillo* (Austin: University of Texas Press, 1984).

Larry L. Smith

ARMADILLO WORLD HEADQUARTERS. During the 1970s the Armadillo World Headquarters, a concert hall in Austin, became the focus of a musical renaissance that made the city a nationally recognized music capital. Launched in a converted national guard armory by a group of local music entrepreneurs, the "Armadillo" provided a large and increasingly sophisticated alternative venue to the municipal auditorium across the street. This venture, which capped several years of searching by young musicians and artists to find a place of their own, reflected the emergence nationwide of a counterculture of alternative forms of music, art, and modes of living. The name Armadillo World Headquarters evoked both a cosmic consciousness and the image of a peaceable native critter, the armadillo,[qv] often seen on Texas highways as the victim of high-speed technology.

The Armadillo opened its doors in August 1970, and quickly became the focus for much of the city's musical life. With an eventual capacity of 1,500, the hall featured a varied fare of blues, rock, jazz, folk, and country music in an informal, open atmosphere. By being able to host such top touring acts as Frank Zappa, the Pointer Sisters, Bruce Springsteen, and the Grateful Dead, the Armadillo brought to Austin a variety of musical groups that smaller clubs or other local entities might never have booked. Since outstanding local or regional artists often opened these shows, the Armadillo also gave vital exposure to such future stars as Joe Ely, Marcia Ball, and Stevie Ray Vaughan.[qv] The Armadillo's eclectic concert calendar brought together different, sometimes disparate, sectors of the community. The most dramatic fusion mixed traditional country-music culture with that of urban blues and rock to produce a Texas hybrid character known as the "cosmic cowboy" and a hybrid music called "progressive country" (sometimes referred to as "redneck rock"). The acknowledged godfather of this movement was singer-songwriter Willie Nelson, who made his Armadillo debut in 1972.

To promote its concerts, the Armadillo maintained a staff of poster and mural artists, including Jim Franklin, Micael Priest, Guy Juke, and Danny Garrett. Given free reign for their creative impulses, these and other artists explored many new images and techniques in poster making. The hundreds of Armadillo concert posters they made during the 1970s contributed to the flowering of poster art in Austin. The Armadillo operated on a shoestring budget and much volunteer labor, on a month-to-month basis in an atmosphere of perpetual financial crisis. By 1980 the demands of downtown real estate signalled the end of an era. As its lease expired, the Armadillo World Headquarters held one final New Year's Eve blowout (December 31, 1980), then closed its doors to await demolition. Though the building is gone, the Armadillo's legacy as a vital center of musical and artistic creativity lives on in Texas music history.

BIBLIOGRAPHY: Armadillo World Headquarters Archives, Barker Texas History Center, University of Texas at Austin. David L. Menconi, Music, Media, and the Metropolis: The Case of Austin's Armadillo World Headquarters (M.A. thesis, University of Texas at Austin, 1985). Jan Reid, *The Improbable Rise of Redneck Rock* (New York: Da Capo Press, 1974). Vertical Files, Barker Texas History Center, University of Texas at Austin.
John Wheat

ARMAND BAYOU. Armand Bayou, also known as Middle Bayou, rises in central Pasadena twenty miles south of Houston in southeastern Harris County (at 29°40′ N, 95°09′ W) and runs ten miles southeast along the eastern edge of the Clear Lake oilfield to its mouth on Mud Lake, just west of Taylor Lake Village on the eastern edge of the Lyndon B. Johnson Space Center[qv] (at 29°34′ N, 95°04′ W). The creek flows through urban Pasadena into a flat grassy prairie surfaced by clay and sandy loams that support wild hickory, holly, oak, elm, and ash. The area was the site of an early Cajun settlement. The 1,600-acre Armand Bayou nature preserve surrounding the bayou protects the interlocking ecologies of prairie, marsh, and forest, the indigenous habitat of the area, and was one of the state's first urban wilderness preserves. The preserve was established after a 1970 campaign to rename the bayou for Armand Yramatagui, a leader of the 1960s environmental crusade who was murdered in January 1970, and is operated by the Committee to Preserve Armand Bayou, a nonprofit corporation formed in 1974. The reserve remains outside the state park system.

ARMISTEAD, WILLIAM THOMAS (1848–1920). William Thomas Armistead, politician, lawyer, and soldier, was born in Georgia on October 25, 1848. He enlisted as a private in the Confederate Army during the Civil War,[qv] rose to the rank of captain, was wounded, and was taken prisoner. After the war he attended the University of Georgia, where he graduated in 1871. He moved immediately to Cass County, Texas, where he taught school for a year before settling in Jefferson and becoming the law partner of David B. Culberson.[qv] Armistead was a delegate to every state Democratic convention from 1874 through 1889, a member of the House of Representatives in the Eighteenth and Nineteenth legislatures, a senator in the Twentieth and Twenty-first legislatures, and a representative in the Twenty-fourth Legislature. He was best known as the author of the Texas antitrust law. In 1878 he was one of several defence attorneys in the notorious Rothschild murder trial in Jefferson (*see* JEFFERSON, TEXAS [MARION COUNTY]). After leaving political office in 1889 he opened a law firm in Jefferson in partnership with his brother James. He joined the State Bar of Texas[qv] in 1894. After his final term in the legislature he served on the Committee on Platform and Resolutions at the Democratic state convention in 1896. In 1915 he formed yet another law partnership with J. H. Benefield. Armistead was a bachelor, a Baptist, and a prominent Mason and Knight Templar. He died on September 1, 1920, at Jefferson and was buried in the Jefferson Cemetery.

BIBLIOGRAPHY: John Henry Brown, *Indian Wars and Pioneers of Texas* (Austin: Daniell, 1880; reprod., Easley, South Carolina: Southern Historical Press, 1978). Lewis E. Daniell, *Personnel of the Texas State Government, with Sketches of Representative Men of Texas* (Austin: City Printing, 1887; 3d ed., San Antonio: Maverick, 1892). *Members of the Legislature of the State of Texas from 1846 to 1939* (Austin: Texas Legislature, 1939). George P. Rawick, ed., *The American Slave: A Composite Autobiography*, Supplement, Series 2 (Westport, Connecticut: Greenwood Press, 1979).
Carolyn Hyman

ARMOUR, TEXAS. Armour, also known as Sandy Creek, was on State Highway 171 twelve miles northwest of Mexia in northern Limestone County. The site was laid out in 1882 by James Armour, and when the post office was established in 1883, it was named in his honor. In 1884 the community had two churches, a district school, two steam gristmills, and sixty residents. Population estimates rose to 100 in 1890, but fell to fifty by 1896. In 1903 the Trinity and Brazos Valley Railway Company began laying track between Hillsboro and Mexia, but missed Armour by about a mile. The railroad established a new town called Coolidge. The Armour post office closed later that year, and residents moved their homes and businesses from Armour to the new town.

BIBLIOGRAPHY: John J. Germann and Myron Janzen, *Texas Post Offices by County* (1986).
Vivian Elizabeth Smyrl

ARMSTRONG, A. JOSEPH (1873–1954). A. Joseph Armstrong, Baylor University English professor and founder of the Armstrong Browning Library,[qv] was born in Louisville, Kentucky, on March 29, 1873, the sixth son of Andrew Jackson and Lotta (Forman) Armstrong. He received his B.A. degree from Wabash College, Indiana, in 1902 and his M.A. in 1904. He taught briefly at East Texas Baptist Institute in Rusk, Texas, to earn money for graduate school but returned to Kentucky when the Rusk school was unable to pay him. From 1904 to 1907 he taught at Wesleyan University in Illinois, where he developed a keen interest in the poetry of Robert and Elizabeth Barrett Browning. In 1908 Armstrong received his Ph.D. from the University of Pennsylvania and accepted a one-year appointment in the English department at Baylor University. He returned again to Kentucky the next year and taught English at Georgetown College for three years. On January 24, 1911, he married Mary Maxwell of Waco, whom he had met while both were teaching in Rusk. In September 1912 Armstrong moved to Waco as head of the Baylor English department, a position he held for more than forty years. He soon began collecting items for a Browning library at Baylor and turned over his own Browning collection to the school in 1918. He spent the rest of his life developing the collection into what is widely considered the largest accumulation of Browning materials in the world. He raised funds for the project by bringing poets, scholars, musicians, and lecturers to Baylor, including Robert Frost, Vachel Lindsay, Amy Lowell, Carl Sandburg, and Rabindranath Tagore.

In 1943 Baylor president Pat M. Neff[qv] promised Armstrong a matching grant of $100,000 for a Browning library on the Baylor campus. The professor redoubled his fund-raising efforts, and the Armstrong-Browning Library opened in 1951 with Armstrong as director. Armstrong's other activities included his work as editor of the Baylor Browning Series and the Browning pilgrimages he and his wife led to Europe. The popular professor died on March 31, 1954, and is buried in Oakwood Cemetery, Waco. He and his wife had one son.

BIBLIOGRAPHY: Lois Smith Douglas, *Through Heaven's Back Door* (Waco: Baylor University Press, 1951). Vertical Files, Barker Texas History Center, University of Texas at Austin.
Margaret Royalty Edwards

ARMSTRONG, CAVITT (1808–?). Cavitt Armstrong, planter, was born in Tennessee in 1808 and arrived in Texas in September 1837. He settled near the site of present Mumford in Robertson County and operated one of the first plantations in the area. He served as justice of the peace for the county and was elected associate justice of Robertson County on April 22, 1845. He represented the county in the Convention of 1845.[qv] He subsequently held the office of notary public, first appointed in 1848 and reappointed in 1854. Armstrong owned twenty slaves and ran 600 cattle in 1854.

BIBLIOGRAPHY: J. W. Baker, *History of Robertson County, Texas* (Franklin, Texas: Robertson County Historical Survey Committee, 1970). Lewis E. Daniell, *Personnel of the Texas State Government, with Sketches of Representative Men of Texas* (Austin: City Printing, 1887; 3d ed., San Antonio: Maverick, 1892). Texas House of Representatives, *Biographical Directory of the Texan Conventions and Congresses, 1832–1845* (Austin: Book Exchange, 1941). *James L. Hailey*

ARMSTRONG, FRANK B. (1863–1915). Frank B. Armstrong, ornithologist and taxidermist, son of Richard Sands Armstrong, was born on May 10, 1863, at St. Johns, New Brunswick, Canada. After the death of his father, an amateur naturalist, he moved with the family to Medford, Massachusetts, and then to Boston. There Armstrong attended school, and after graduation he studied taxidermy for two years with Professor C. J. Maynard. At home in Boston, Armstrong wrote his first essays on ornithology, mammalogy, and oology. In his early twenties he began a tour of the sparsely settled Southwest and subsequently spent several years doing field work in Mexico with Laredo, Texas, as a base. During that time he collected Mexican birds and animals. In March 1890, when Armstrong traveled to Brownsville, he was so pleased with wildlife in the area that he moved his collection and taxidermy studio there. He studied subtropical bird life, and his later reputation was based chiefly on his work in tropical ornithology. The Armstrong collection of mounted birds, fishes, and animals attracted many visitors. He had assembled more than 800 different specimens from the vicinity. He also contributed thousands of specimens to museums in Europe and the United States, including the Field Museum in Chicago and the Smithsonian Institution. At one time Southern Methodist University and Southwest Texas State University had specimens of Armstrong's work. He married Marie Isabel Schodts of Brownsville on April 2, 1891. They had three daughters and four sons. Armstrong died on August 20, 1915, and was buried in the Old City Cemetery in Brownsville.

BIBLIOGRAPHY: John Henry Brown, *Indian Wars and Pioneers of Texas* (Austin: Daniell, 1880; reprod., Easley, South Carolina: Southern Historical Press, 1978). Brownsville *Herald*, August 21, 1915. W. H. Chatfield, *The Twin Cities of the Border and the Country of the Lower Rio Grande* (New Orleans: Brandao, 1893; rpt., Brownsville: Brownsville Historical Association, 1959). *Ruby Armstrong Wooldridge*

ARMSTRONG, GEORGE WASHINGTON (1866–1954). George Washington Armstrong, attorney, oilman, industrialist, farmer and rancher, and author, the son of Ramsey Clarke and Matilda Moseley (Smyth) Armstrong, was born on January 26, 1866, in Jasper County, Texas. His father was a minister, principally in the Fort Worth and Waco districts of the Methodist Episcopal Church, South, and was founding trustee and later vice president of Polytechnic College (now Texas Wesleyan University) in Fort Worth. His mother was a daughter of George W. Smyth,[qv] signer of the Texas Declaration of Independence.[qv] Armstrong was the eldest of six children. He was educated at Marvin College and the University of Texas, where he received his bachelor of laws degree in 1886. After practicing two years at Ennis he moved to Fort Worth, where he founded several law partnerships and was elected alderman in 1890. In November 1894 he was elected county judge of Tarrant County; he served two terms before being defeated for renomination in 1898. He was called "Judge" thereafter.

In 1903 Armstrong abandoned his law practice and went into the oil and banking business in South Texas. As an oil producer he was active in the development of the Batson field in Hardin County (1903–05), the Petrolia field in Clay County (1905–07), and several major producing fields in Adams County, Mississippi (1943–54). His banking ventures included significant investments in the First National Bank of Sour Lake, Texas (1903), the Stockyards National Bank (1905), and two privately owned banks organized as George W. Armstrong and Company. He was president and principal stockholder of the Denison Mill and Elevator Company, president and principal stockholder of Hubbell, Slack and Company, a gin and cotton-exporting concern, and founder of the Texas Steel Company, the Texasteel Manufacturing Company, and the Liberty Manufacturing Company. He developed the Horseshoe Ranch at Hickory, Oklahoma, into a 25,000-acre showpiece. He sold it in 1917 and transferred his livestock to newly purchased holdings (ultimately 40,000 acres) in Adams County, Mississippi. These farming and ranching operations were not profitable, but timber and oil income reversed his farming losses. "Farming is my hobby if I have one, and it is an expensive one," Armstrong wrote.

He was the founding president of the Texas Chamber of Commerce and an early advocate of cooperation between Dallas and Fort Worth in civic development. He was a Methodist, a Democrat with a keen interest in politics, and an unsuccessful candidate for Congress in 1902 and for the Democratic nomination for governor in 1932. He wrote numerous tracts over a period of thirty-five years. These publications expressed his frequently controversial views, which included opposition to the Federal Reserve System, advocacy for the repeal of the Fourteenth and Fifteenth amendments, anti-Zionism, anti-Communism, and strong support for segregation and the doctrine of white supremacy. He established the Judge Armstrong Foundation, and in 1949 he organized the Texas Educational Association. Both organizations were dedicated to promoting his views on racial, political, and financial matters. Armstrong attracted national attention in 1949 when he offered to provide Jefferson Military College of Washington, Mississippi, with a large endowment on the condition that the school exclude blacks, Jews, and Asians.

Armstrong was twice married: in 1887 to Jennie May Allen, who died in 1930, and in 1933 to Mary Cozby. Three children were born of his first marriage. Armstrong died on October 1, 1954, in Natchez, Mississippi, after a stroke.

BIBLIOGRAPHY: George Washington Armstrong, *Memoirs of George W. Armstrong* (Austin: Steck, 1958). *Leon B. Blair*

ARMSTRONG, JAMES (ca. 1811–1879). James Armstrong, politician, was born in Kentucky about 1811. He came to Texas shortly before the Texas Revolution[qv] and joined Capt. James Chessher's company of Jasper Volunteers on March 3, 1836. He was discharged on July 26 of that year. Armstrong was elected to represent Jasper County at the Fourth Congress of the Republic of Texas[qv] in 1839–40. He subsequently was district attorney for Jasper in 1840–41 and served as president of the board of land commissioners of Jasper County before moving to Beaumont. Jefferson County voters elected him to serve in the House during the Ninth Congress (1844–45) and in the Convention of 1845.[qv] After annexation[qv] he was elected to the House of the Second Legislature from Jefferson County. Armstrong moved in 1848 to Williamson County, where he became an attorney and a rancher. He subsequently returned to public life and served in the Fourth, Fifth, and Sixth Texas legislatures as the senator from his home district, which included Williamson County. By 1860 he owned three slaves and had a total estate of some $6,000. He had at least five children. He returned to Beaumont about 1868. He served as a member of the Constitutional Convention of 1868–69,[qv] where he was one of the leaders of the conservative faction, and represented the First District, including much of Southeast Texas, in the Thirteenth Legislature. Armstrong was listed as an attorney in the census of 1870, when his estate was valued at $13,000. He was a Mason. He died of pneumonia on December 21, 1879.

BIBLIOGRAPHY: Texas House of Representatives, *Biographical Directory of the Texan Conventions and Congresses, 1832–1845* (Austin: Book Exchange, 1941). W. T. Block, A History of Jefferson County, Texas, from Wilderness to Reconstruction (M.A. thesis, Lamar University, 1974; Nederland, Texas: Nederland Publishing, 1976). Galveston *Daily News*, December 23, 1879. *Members of the Texas Legislature, 1846–1962* (Austin, 1962). *Robert Wooster*

ARMSTRONG, JOHN BARCLAY (1850–1913). John Barclay Armstrong, a Texas Ranger known as "McNelly's Bulldog," was born in January 1850 in McMinnville, Tennessee, the son of Dr. John B. Armstrong. After living for a time in Missouri and Arkansas he moved to Texas, in January 1871. He settled in Austin and married Mollie Durst; they had seven children. In the early 1870s Armstrong was a member of the Travis Rifles, and on May 20, 1875, he joined Capt. Leander McNelly's[qv] company of Texas Rangers.[qv]

Described as well built, with a "full face marked by heavy brows and made distinguished by a finely modeled nose and deep-set languid eyes," Armstrong wore a full beard and was something of a dandy in dress. In 1875 he accompanied McNelly to the Rio Grande and was promoted to the rank of sergeant. He took part in the fighting at Palo Alto Prairie in the so-called Las Cuevas War, and in the fall of 1876 he was involved in the killing or capture of a number of suspected criminals in the area between Eagle Pass and Laredo. In February 1877 he was active in the pursuit of hide thieves on the border, and in December of that year he and a ranger named Deggs killed accused murderer John Mayfield in Wilson County.

When McNelly retired from ranger service, Armstrong was named second lieutenant of the Special Force of Texas Rangers under 1st Lt. Leigh Hall,[qv] on January 26, 1877. Several of the company were outspoken in their belief that Armstrong should have been promoted to captain. He was assigned to the Eagle Pass area, where he operated on both sides of the border, assisted in the breakup of several bands of outlaws, and helped arrest John King Fisher[qv] in April 1877. While recovering from an accidental self-inflicted gunshot wound suffered at Goliad, Armstrong asked to be allowed to arrest the notorious gunman John Wesley Hardin.[qv] The ranger pursued Hardin first to Alabama, then to Florida, then confronted him and four of his gang on a train in Pensacola. In the affray that followed, Armstrong killed one of Hardin's men, rendered Hardin unconscious with a blow from his handgun, and arrested the remaining gang members. After considerable delay in the execution of extradition papers, Armstrong returned Hardin to Texas, where he was tried and sentenced to twenty-five years in prison in September 1877. In July 1878 Armstrong was involved in the killing of outlaw Sam Bass[qv] at Round Rock. Thereafter he was stationed for a time at Cuero.

After retiring from ranger service he was appointed a United States marshal. In 1882 he established the 50,000-acre Armstrong Ranch in Willacy County. The old ranger, known in retirement as "Major" Armstrong, died on May 1, 1913.

BIBLIOGRAPHY: George Durham, *Taming the Nueces Strip: The Story of McNelly's Rangers* (Austin: University of Texas Press, 1962). James B. Gillett, *Six Years with the Texas Rangers, 1875 to 1881* (Austin: Von Boeckmann–Jones, 1921; rpt., Lincoln: University of Nebraska Press, 1976). Frank W. Johnson, *A History of Texas and Texans* (5 vols., ed. E. C. Barker and E. W. Winkler [Chicago and New York: American Historical Society, 1914; rpt. 1916]). Dora Neill Raymond, *Captain Lee Hall of Texas* (Norman: University of Oklahoma Press, 1940). Walter Prescott Webb, *The Texas Rangers* (Boston: Houghton Mifflin, 1935; rpt., Austin: University of Texas Press, 1982). *Thomas W. Cutrer*

ARMSTRONG, MARY MAXWELL (1882–1971). Mary M. Armstrong, cofounder of the Armstrong Browning Library[qv] at Baylor University, was born in Buena Vista, Texas, on September 21, 1882, the tenth child of Baptist minister Wilder Richard Maxwell. She received her bachelor of arts degree from Baylor University and did additional work at the University of Chicago. She taught English at East Texas Baptist Institute[qv] in Rusk, where her brother was president, and there met A. Joseph Armstrong,[qv] a Browning scholar who later became chairman of the English department at Baylor. The couple married in Waco on January 24, 1911, and had one son.

The Armstrongs turned a shared dream into reality by amassing the world's largest collection of Robert Browning and Elizabeth Barrett Browning letters, manuscripts, likenesses, and mementos and raising funds to construct the building that houses them. Together they made twenty-nine trips to Europe to search for Browning materials. During the months of planning and construction of the Armstrong Browning Library, Mrs. Armstrong consulted with architects, builders, designers, and stained-glass experts. Her supervision and expertise are particularly reflected in the library's Elizabeth Barrett Browning Salon. The building was dedicated on December 3, 1951.

Upon her husband's death in 1954, Mary Armstrong assumed the directorship of the library, a post she held until 1959. Thereafter she served as director of the Guardian Angels, a patron group established many years before by her husband. She maintained an office in the library until her retirement in 1966. She was also an active member of the Baylor Round Table and the Domestic Science Club of Waco, as well as a Daughter of the American Revolution and an honorary member of the Waco Woman's Club and the Thursday Club. In 1966 she moved to West Chester, Pennsylvania, to live with her son and his family. She died there on September 1, 1971, and was buried in Oakwood Cemetery, Waco.

BIBLIOGRAPHY: Armstrong Correspondence, Armstrong Browning Library Archives, Baylor University. Helen Pool Baldwin, "Mrs. A. J. Armstrong Moves to Pennsylvania," *Baylor Line*, November–December 1966. Clipping File, Armstrong Browning Library Archives, Baylor University (J. A. Armstrong; Mary Maxwell Armstrong), Lois Smith Douglas, *Through Heaven's Back Door* (Waco: Baylor University Press, 1951). Waco *Tribune-Herald*, September 25, 1966. *Betty A. Coley*

ARMSTRONG, MOLLIE WRIGHT (1875–1964). Mollie Wright Armstrong, optometrist, was born on January 23, 1875, in Bell County, Texas, the daughter of Thomas C. and Elizabeth (Neal) Wright. After attending Baylor Female College, she studied at optometry schools in Georgia, Illinois, and Missouri. When she began her practice in Brownwood in 1899, she was the first woman optometrist in the state and only the second in the United States. She was active in the passage of the first optometry law in Texas, became a member of the Texas Board of Examiners in Optometry, and served as vice president and president of the board, to which she belonged for twenty-four years. She was president of the Texas Optometric Association from 1923 to 1925 and at another time served as the association's director of publicity. When the *Texas Optometrist* was first published, she was its editor. It was largely through her efforts that the first optometric professional liability policy was made available to optometrists nationwide, and she became a trustee of the American Optometric Association. In 1927 Dr. Armstrong was instrumental in organizing the Texas Woman's Auxiliary to the American Optometric Association. That same year she was appointed a regional director of the American Optometric Association Auxiliary. In Brownwood she was the organizer and first president of the American Legion Auxiliary, the Brownwood Business and Professional Women's Club, and the Brownwood Civic League. She served as director of the Brownwood Chamber of Commerce and represented her district as a member of the State Democratic Executive Committee. She was married to Brownwood jeweler Walter D. Armstrong, who died in 1948. She retired from practice in 1962 and died in Fort Worth on May 23, 1964. She was buried in Greenleaf Cemetery, Brownwood. *See also* OPTOMETRY.

BIBLIOGRAPHY: Dallas *Morning News*, May 25, 1964. Fort Worth *Star-Telegram*, May 25, 1964. *Journal of the Texas Optometric Association*, August 1964. Weston A. Pettey, *Optometry in Texas, 1900–1984* (Austin: Nortex, 1985). *Gertrude Chambers*

ARMSTRONG, ROBERT WRIGHT (1892–1966). Robert Wright Armstrong, railroad executive, soldier, and musician, son of Walter David and Mary Elizabeth (Wright) Armstrong, was born in Brownwood, Texas, on December 18, 1892. He received his education in the Brownwood public schools, at Kemper Military Academy in Boonville, Missouri, and at the Missouri Military Academy in Mexico, Missouri. He played in the school bands at Brownwood and at the Missouri Military Academy, where he also directed the band and orchestra. After graduation he performed with the Kryl Concert Band, the Honey Boy Evans Minstrels, and the Al G. Fields Minstrels. When he was tired of performing he moved to the Neil O'Brien Minstrels to become first the assistant manager and then the manager. Later, while working as manager of the Brownwood Chamber of Commerce (1919–24), he organized the Old Gray Mare Band, which became the official band of the West Texas Chamber of Commerce.[qv]

Although he joined the Brownwood Chamber of Commerce after World War I,[qv] Armstrong did not remain there for long. In 1924, at the request of John A. Hulen,[qv] whom he had met during military training at Camp Bowie in Fort Worth, he worked for the Trinity and Brazos Valley Railway as general agent, with assignments in Fort Worth (1924–28), Houston (1928–32), and New Orleans, Louisiana (1932–36). Afterwards he was general freight agent for the Chicago, Burlington and Quincy in Denver, Colorado (1936–38), and in St. Louis, Missouri (1938–43). After active duty in World War II,[qv] Armstrong served as executive assistant from 1945 to 1948 with the Burlington lines. Finally, he served as vice president of the Fort Worth and Denver Railway Company (1948–62). He retired in December 1962. In addition to his connection with the Fort Worth and Denver, Armstrong also was a director of the Houston Belt and Terminal Company of Dallas, and a member of the Board of Control of the Port Terminal Railroad Association of Houston.

The former military school cadet was active in both world wars. He served overseas with the 142nd Infantry, Thirty-sixth Division,[qv] of the United States Army during World War I and achieved the rank of lieutenant. During World War II he was commissioned a major in the Transportation Corps and then assigned to the Twenty-sixth Regulating Station as rail officer. He was awarded the Bronze Star for meritorious service overseas. He was also active in the National Guard.

Armstrong was a member of civic clubs in Fort Worth and Houston and the Western Railway Club of Chicago. He was active in the Fort Worth Chamber of Commerce and was president of the West Texas Chamber of Commerce from 1952 to 1954. In addition, he belonged to the Sons of the American Revolution and the Thirty-sixth Division Association (of which he was president in 1947–48). He also served from 1961 to 1966 on the board of directors of Texas Technological College (now Texas Tech University) and was chairman of that board from 1964 to 1966.

Armstrong was a Methodist. He married Nannie Pauline Lusher on April 23, 1918, and they had three children. He died on September 15, 1966, in Fort Worth and was buried there in Greenwood Cemetery.

BIBLIOGRAPHY: Seymour V. Connor, ed., *Builders of the Southwest* (Lubbock: Southwest Collection, Texas Technological College, 1959). Fort Worth *Star-Telegram*, August 7, 1949. Lubbock *Avalanche-Journal*, September 16, 1966. Vertical Files, Barker Texas History Center, University of Texas at Austin. *Michael Q. Hooks*

ARMSTRONG, TEXAS. Armstrong, a rural community on U.S. Highway 77 twenty miles south of Sarita in west central Kenedy County, is on the Missouri Pacific Railroad, originally constructed here as the St. Louis, Brownsville and Mexico Railway in 1904. The community was named for Capt. James B. Armstrong,[qv] who around 1893 founded the Armstrong Ranch two miles northeast of the site. The railroad stop served the ranch as a shipping point. In 1913 a local post office opened under the name Katherine; it was renamed in 1915. The population of Armstrong peaked in 1929 at an estimated twenty-five. In 1948 the settlement had a railroad station, and in 1956 several dwellings were at the site. From 1931 to 1950 the settlement had one business. In the early 1990s Armstrong was a dispersed community with a post office, an estimated population of twenty, various dwellings, and the railroad station.

BIBLIOGRAPHY: Frank Cushman Pierce, *Texas' Last Frontier: A Brief History of the Lower Rio Grande Valley* (Menasha, Wisconsin: Banta, 1917; rpt., Brownsville: Rio Grande Valley Historical Society, 1962). Marker Files, Texas Historical Commission, Austin.

Alicia A. Garza

ARMSTRONG BROWNING LIBRARY. The Armstrong Browning Library building was dedicated on December 3, 1951, having cost $2 million. Andrew Joseph Armstrong,[qv] chairman of the English Department at Baylor University, presented to the university, soon after joining its faculty, his personal collection of Browning materials. This was the beginning of the Armstrong Browning Library, which for many years was maintained in the Browning Room of the Carroll Library. Armstrong continued to purchase, and frequently received as gifts, many additions to the collection—books, paintings, furniture, and other mementoes of Robert and Elizabeth Barrett Browning. The library has 2,000 original letters and other manuscripts written by and to the Brownings. The collection includes all of the first editions of both poets and most of the books, periodical articles, pamphlets, and other publications that deal with them. Primary and secondary materials for the use of scholars are constantly being added to the collection.

The library has become known as a source of information about the Brownings and researches and acknowledges hundreds of questions each year. It publishes *Studies in Browning and His Circle* and the *Baylor Browning Interests Series.* The library building has two floors. The main floor is divided into the Martin Entrance Foyer, the Leddy-Jones Research Hall, the Hankamer Treasure Room, and the McLean Foyer of meditation. The upper floor includes the Austin Moore–Elizabeth Barrett Browning Salon, the Mary Armstrong Seminar Room, the Charles G. Smith Graduate Research Complex, the International Room, the Browning Classroom, and offices for the director and librarian, workrooms for the library staff, and study carrels for visiting scholars.

A statue of Pippa (modeled from *Pippa Passes*) is in front of the building, and bronze-paneled entrance doors depict themes from ten of Browning's poems. Fifty-four stained-glass windows are designed to illustrate poems and themes by Robert or Elizabeth Barrett Browning. The Cloister of the Clasped Hands in the McLean Foyer of Meditation contains Harriet Hosmer's cast of the clasped hands of the two poets; the Sturdivant Alcove in the Leddy-Jones Research Hall contains the Pied Piper window; letters and manuscripts are displayed in the Hankamer Treasure Room. The Browning Corridor has more than twenty-five different likenesses of Robert Browning. A balcony overlooks the McLean Foyer of Meditation; the entire library shows outstanding workmanship in the walnut paneling, marble, hand-painted ceilings, and parquet floors.

BIBLIOGRAPHY: Vertical Files, Barker Texas History Center, University of Texas at Austin. *Jack W. Herring*

ARMSTRONG COUNTY. Armstrong County (D-9), in the central Panhandle[qv] on the eastern edge of the Texas High Plains, is bounded on the east by Donley County, on the north by Carson County, on the West by Randall County, and on the south by Swisher and Briscoe counties. It is named for one of several pioneer Texas families named Armstrong, though the sources are unclear about which one. The center of the county lies approximately at 34°58′ north latitude and 101°20′ west longitude. Claude, the county seat, is in the north central part of the county thirty miles east of Amarillo. Armstrong County occupies 907 square miles of level plains and canyons. The northern half is generally level, as is the far southwest corner. The rest of the southern half of the county is covered by the great Palo Duro Canyon.[qv] The eastern end of Palo Duro Canyon State Scenic Park[qv] is in Armstrong County. The soil surface of rich deep gray and chocolate loams supports abundant native grasses as well as wheat and grain sorghums in some areas. The county is crossed by three streams, the Prairie Dog Town Fork of the Red River in Palo Duro Canyon, the Salt Fork of the Red River, and Mulberry Creek, all of which run year-round to some degree. Elevation ranges from 2,400 to 3,500 feet, and the average rainfall is 19.98 inches per year. The average minimum temperature is 19°F in January, and the average maximum is 92° in July. The growing season averages 213 days per year.

The Panhandle was occupied by Paleo-Indians perhaps as early as 10,000 B.C. The Apaches were supplanted by the Comanches around A.D. 1700, when the area became a part of the Comanche homelands; Palo Duro Canyon was a favorite haunt of the Comanches. After the Comanche incursion, some Kiowa and Cheyenne Indians also moved into the area. Anglo-Americans have been resident here only since the 1870s. The Red River War[qv] of 1874 led to the final removal of the Comanches to Indian Territory. The campaign culminated in the battle of Palo Duro Canyon, fought on both sides of the present Randall-Armstrong county line. With the Indian threat removed, ranchers soon arrived.

Ranching came to Armstrong County and the Panhandle with Charles Goodnight and John Adair.[qqv] In 1876 Goodnight brought a herd of 1,600 cattle into the Palo Duro Canyon. A short time later, in 1877, he formed a partnership with John G. Adair from Ireland. Their ranch, the JA,[qv] grew to encompass over 1,335,000 acres by the early 1880s. This included most of Armstrong County and parts of five surrounding counties. Although the partnership ended and the assets were divided in 1886, the two ranches continued to dominate the area well into the twentieth century. During 1887 the Fort Worth and Denver City Railway built across the county as it extended its line from Fort Worth across North Texas to New Mexico and Colorado. This provided the local ranchers with improved access to markets and eventually encouraged settlers to enter the area. Homesteaders, intending to raise stock and crops, began to trickle into the county in the late 1880s. They initially settled near the townsites laid out by the railroad: Washburn, Claude, and Goodnight.

Still, the county remained almost totally devoted to ranching throughout the rest of the century. While the area's population rose from 31 in 1880 to 944 in 1890 and 1,205 in 1900, the bulk of this population engaged in ranching or stock farming, or worked for the railroad. The 1890 census, for example, counted 104 ranches and farms in the area encompassing more than 413,000 acres of land, but less than 100 acres was devoted to growing staple cereals such as corn, oats, and wheat. In 1900, only 933 acres was devoted to corn, oats, wheat, and cotton combined. Meanwhile, the number of cattle grew. About 15,000 cattle were counted in Armstrong in 1880, while about 54,000 cattle were counted in both 1890 and 1900.

Although the county was marked off from Bexar County in 1876, it remained unorganized until 1890, when the growing population felt the need for a local government. Accordingly, the county was organized in March of that year, with Claude as the county seat.

In the early years of the twentieth century, the great ranches began to be broken up and land was sold to newly arriving farmers. Between 1900 and 1910, the number of farms in Armstrong County grew from 172 to 384. Many newcomers planted cotton; by 1910, cotton was grown on more than 18,000 acres in the county. Cotton culture[qv] dropped precipitously between 1910 and 1920, however, and a number of farmers went broke. Between and 1920 and 1930, however, the number of farms increased again from 373 to 472, as more than 40,000 acres was turned to wheat production. Meanwhile, the large ranches, though reduced in size, continued to dominate the local economy. The number of cattle in the county declined to fewer than 35,000 in 1910 and about 23,000 in 1920, but rose again to almost 46,000 in 1929.

The county's population statistics during these years mirrored its agricultural developments. The number of people in the county rose from 1,205 in 1900 to 2,682 in 1910 and to 2,816 by 1920. Then the demand for wheat led to another spurt in population so that by 1930 the number had reached 3,329.

During the Great Depression[qv] of the 1930s, the agriculturally based economy suffered; only 408 farms remained in Armstrong County by 1940, and the county required many years to recover. County population dropped from 3,329 in 1930 to 2,495 in 1940 and 2,215 in 1950. This drop in population, first caused by the depression and subsequently spurred on by advances in agricultural mechanization and technology, continued into the 1970s, when the number of people in the county began to rise again. In 1960 only 1,966 people lived in Armstrong County, and the 1970 total was 1,895. The population increased to 1,994 in 1980, however, and to 2,021 in 1990.

The towns in the county have now seen more than a century of growth and decline. Goodnight, laid out in 1887, flourished in the 1890s and early 1900s, even maintaining a college, Goodnight College, from 1898 to 1917. By 1980 only twenty-five people lived in the hamlet. Likewise, Washburn prospered in the 1890s and early decades of the twentieth century. It was established in 1887 and included a railroad section house on the Fort Worth and Denver City line, a depot, stock pens, and a coal chute. By 1888, the Panhandle line from Washburn to Panhandle had been finished. Still, this active community of the 1890s had only seventy residents in 1980. Wayside, a farming community in the southwest corner of the county, has grown but little since the 1920s, and had only forty people in 1980. Like Washburn, Claude, the county seat, was also laid out in 1887. It grew into the leading town in the county, yet only numbered 1,112 people in 1980 and 1,199 in 1990.

The transportation system of the county reflects the nature of the local ranching-farming economy. U.S. Highway 287, originally 370, follows the Fort Worth and Denver City Railway from Fort Worth to Colorado. It was built in the early 1920s and remains the county's only major highway. State roads and farm-to-market roads built between the 1930s and 1950s converge on Claude. State Highway 207, which runs north from Post to Perryton, passes through Claude, and local farm roads link Claude to other communities in the county.

The economic structure of Armstrong County reflects its evolution and its ranching-dominated economy. The JA Ranch, owned by John Adair's descendants Monte Ritchie and his daughter Cornelia, together with seven or eight lesser operations, occupies approximately 70 percent of the land and accounts for 70 percent of the county's agricultural products. Wheat, grain sorghum, and cotton grown on the other 30 percent of the land account for the remaining production. Cultivated land comprises 165,000 acres of the county, while ranching occupies 415,000. No meaningful amounts of oil and gas are produced in Armstrong County. Recreation and tourist attractions include Palo Duro State Park, the pioneer Goodnight Ranch Home, and the Caprock Roundup, which is held each year in July.

BIBLIOGRAPHY: Armstrong County Historical Association, *A Collection of Memories: A History of Armstrong County, 1876–1965* (Hereford, Texas: Pioneer, 1965). Harley True Burton, *A History of the JA Ranch* (Austin: Von Boeckmann–Jones, 1928; rpt., New York: Argonaut, 1966). Duane F. Guy, ed., *The Story of Palo Duro Canyon* (Canyon, Texas: Panhandle-Plains Historical Society, 1979). *Highways of Texas, 1927* (Houston: Gulf Oil and Refining, 1927).

Donald R. Abbe

ARMSTRONG CREEK (Cass County). Armstrong Creek rises 5½ miles east of Douglassville in northeastern Cass County (at 33°12′ N,

94°15′ W) and runs northwest for two miles to its mouth on Wright Patman Lake (at 33°13′ N, 94°16′ W). The soils over which it flows are sandy and loamy, and the gently rolling to hilly area around the creek is heavily wooded, with pines and various hardwoods predominating.

____ (Erath County). Armstrong Creek rises in western Erath County in three branches. The East Fork rises three miles northwest of Mount Zion (at 32°21′ N, 98°26′ W), and the West Fork rises three miles northeast of School Hill Church (at 32°21′ N, 98°29′ W). The two branches run southward roughly parallel for eight miles before merging (at 32°15′ N, 98°27′ W) to form Armstrong Creek two miles east of Lowell. The third branch, the Dry Fork, begins two miles northwest of Lowell (at 32°17′ N, 98°29′ W) and runs southeast for 4½ miles to its mouth on Armstrong Creek, 2½ miles south of the confluence of the East and West forks (at 32°13′ N, 98°27′ W). The consolidated stream runs southwest for twelve miles to its mouth on Proctor Reservoir, three miles east of DeLeon (at 32°05′ N, 98°30′ W). Upstream, the terrain features steep slopes; downstream, the land is generally flat and locally indented. The land surface of shallow sandy soil supports juniper, scattered oaks, and grasses.

ARMY OF THE REPUBLIC OF TEXAS. The army was of immense importance in the life of the Republic of Texas.[qv] Such lawmakers as Mirabeau B. Lamar,[qv] who favored a strong defense establishment, were a powerful element in the Texas government, and the great expense of the army was perhaps the major factor in the republic's chronic financial difficulties. The army's drain on the treasury, however, was at least equalled by its demands on the nation's manpower. Although the land claims of the new republic were vast, including all of present-day Texas and parts of New Mexico, Oklahoma, Kansas, Colorado, and Wyoming, its Anglo-American population probably did not exceed 30,000. Texas Mexicans, Indians, and blacks—almost all of whom were either hostile or of doubtful loyalty—numbered approximately 22,000. As late as 1848 the number of Anglo-Texans had risen to only a little more than 100,000. Yet during the revolution Texas maintained an army that at one time constituted nearly one-tenth of its Anglo population, and in every year of its existence the republic recruited thousands of volunteers to fight Indians or Mexicans. President Lamar's most moderate plan for staffing the regular army required a force of 840 men, an astonishing one soldier for every fifty civilians.

The Army of the Republic of Texas was the direct lineal descendant of the revolutionary army[qv] improvised during the war for independence from Mexico. Though the urgency of military necessity during the revolution never allowed the formation of a regular Texas army, the provisional government was able to keep the "Volunteer Army of the People"—spontaneously organized during the first stages of the revolution—in the field and to make efforts to augment and improve its efficiency. These included the formation, at least on paper, of a regular army. The Consultation[qv] of November 1835 urged the formation of a force of regulars with an organizational and command structure patterned after that of the United States Army, and less than two weeks later the provisional government[qv] authorized the formation of a permanent regular army. Under the terms of this law the army was to consist of one brigade, numbering 1,120 men. The brigade was to consist of one regiment of infantry and one of artillery, each commanded by a colonel. Each regiment was composed of two battalions divided into five fifty-six-man companies. A lieutenant colonel commanded one battalion and a major the other. The infantry companies were commanded by a captain, with a first lieutenant, a second lieutenant, four sergeants, and four corporals as subalterns. The artillery companies were identically structured except that each was allowed a third lieutenant as well. Although no cavalry force was provided for in the law of November 1835, the following month a "Legion of Cavalry" was authorized. Smaller than regimental size, the legion was composed of 384 officers and men commanded by a lieutenant colonel and seconded by a major. The legion, divided into two squadrons of three companies of sixty privates each, was otherwise identical in organization to the infantry.

This regular force was to be supplemented by a corps of "auxiliary volunteers," an "army of reserve" that it hoped to raise in the United States, and a militia force, patterned after the state militias of the United States. Finally, it undertook the formation of a number of irregular ranging companies for duty on the Indian frontier. These four basic military organizations formed during the revolution—the regular army, the volunteer army, the militia, and the ranger corps—evolved into the Army of the Republic of Texas. Financial problems and the almost constant threat of Mexican invasion and Indian depredation beset the republic's ten years of independence. Experimentation and improvisation therefore characterized the Texas government's approach to military problems until the annexation[qv] of Texas to the United States in 1845.

No sooner had the guns of San Jacinto fallen silent than Texas leaders undertook to replace the sometimes unruly and always inefficient volunteers who had won the nation's independence. Although the Texas revolutionary army never came close to recruiting its paper strength and never had more than one hundred regulars in its ranks, David G. Burnet's[qv] ad interim government,[qv] during the six months during which it managed the affairs of Texas, maintained the army laws passed by the Consultation. Sam Houston,[qv] the first constitutional president of the republic, largely reorganized the military forces, however, increasing the regular army to slightly more than 3,600 men in December 1836. This new army was to be commanded by a major general and two brigadier generals. The artillery and cavalry organizations and strengths remained much as they had been under Burnet, but the infantry arm was reinforced from one to four regiments. Also, for the first time, division, brigade, and regimental staffs were authorized. Although a large number of staff positions had been established by the general military ordinances adopted in November and December 1835, this largely improvised administrative corps evolved as need became apparent. No plan for a general staff had been formulated. As a consequence, haphazard and shoddy staff work became a major problem in the army. With Houston's reorganization of December 1836, these deficiencies were partially rectified, and administrative officers were authorized for several departments. During Lamar's administration—the high-water mark of the Republic of Texas army, West Point–trained Hugh McLeod[qv] served as adjutant general, keeping the army's records and dealing with general administrative matters. Paymaster general Jacob Snively[qv] directed the financial bureau. Quartermaster general William Gordon Cooke, commissary general of subsistence William L. Cazneau,[qqv] and a commissary of purchase managed the services of supply. William R. Smith[qv] headed the medical department as surgeon general, while inspection duties fell to Peter Hansbrough Bell[qv] as inspector general. An engineer and an ordnance bureau were also created and were commanded by colonels. Each brigade was also authorized to have a provost martial and chief of staff to oversee the regimental staff officers. At regimental level the staff consisted of an adjutant, an assistant quartermaster, an assistant commissary of subsistence, and a surgeon. Curiously, no judge advocate general was authorized by the December 1836 law. This basic staff structure remained in effect until 1840, when the poverty of the republic compelled a reduction in the number of staff officers and departments.

The Texas army had emerged from the revolution scattered around the new republic in a state of almost total inactivity. After San Jacinto, Sam Houston left the army to seek treatment in New Orleans for a wounded ankle, leaving Thomas Jefferson Rusk[qv] in command. Rusk continued in this capacity until Houston's inauguration as first president of the republic, but then reluctantly accepted the post of secretary of war in Houston's cabinet. Command of the 2,000-man army then devolved upon Felix Huston,[qv] a Mississippi planter of volatile temper and decidedly aggressive intentions toward Mexico. Huston's headquarters and the bulk of the army were located at Camp Johnson[qv] on the Lavaca River, and a small mounted detachment under

Lt. Col. Juan N. Seguín[qv] reoccupied San Antonio. Galveston and Velasco also quartered small garrisons, and a line of crude forts on the Indian frontier was manned by small groups of mounted volunteers. Additionally, a small detachment under Capt. Andrew Neill[qv] guarded the crossing of the Colorado River between army headquarters and the capital at Columbia in order to intercept deserters. The veterans of San Jacinto and fresh volunteers from the United States were disappointed that no campaign against Mexico was forthcoming, while other soldiers were dissatisfied with short rations and meager clothing. Beans, flour, coffee, and sugar were in chronically short supply, and only beef cattle, driven up from the Nueces, seemed to offer an alternative to starvation. The adverse effect on morale and discipline was severe, and not surprisingly the army went into a serious decline as men were mustered out of service while others deserted.

In December 1836 a new senior brigadier general, Albert Sidney Johnston,[qv] was named to succeed Huston in command of the army. This appointment resulted in a near fatal duel when Huston's honor compelled him to call out the new commander and shoot him through the right hip (*see* DUELING IN THE REPUBLIC OF TEXAS). Once recovered from his wound, Johnston attempted to apply the lessons that he had learned as a West Point graduate and a professional soldier of the United States Army to the Army of the Republic of Texas. Under Huston, the camps of the army had become the resting place for idlers and brawlers, and Johnston sought to curtail the sale of whiskey in the army and to impose military routine. Within two months, however, stricter discipline and a worsening supply situation produced serious discipline problems. In late March 1837 the garrison at Velasco under Capt. Martin K. Snell[qv] became unruly and disobedient. A Lieutenant Sprowl sided with the mutineers and left the post without permission. When Snell and a squad of soldiers followed him to a billiard room to apprehend him, he resisted arrest, and the two officers traded blows. Sprowl reached for his sword but Snell drew his pistol first and killed the renegade. Although this incident seems to have quieted the situation at Velasco, the mutinous spirit reached the main army at Camp Preston soon thereafter. Johnston's unpopularity grew with each day of military routine and monotonous rations, and on the night of April 3 six soldiers and a civilian were arrested smuggling whiskey into camp. The soldiers were placed under guard and the civilian was placed in irons. When one of the soldiers was later put in irons for refusing to work, the camp was outraged, and about fifty men rushed the guardhouse that night and released the prisoners. Rioting continued until midnight. Order was at last restored by the camp guard, and the prisoners were rearrested the following day. General Johnston relaxed his pressure on the men and ordered suspension of all drills until regular supply issues could be made.

Although the compromise at Camp Preston seems to have eased the tensions there, a more serious mutiny broke out at one of the detached camps shortly afterward when dissatisfied soldiers placed an artillery shell beneath Capt. Adam Clendennin's bunk. When the shell failed to explode, the mutineers aimed a loaded cannon at the captain's quarters and fired their muskets at him. Clendennin eventually brought the malcontents under control by surrounding their barracks with artillery, but when a court-martial found them guilty their only punishment was dishonorable discharge and the loss of pay and bounty land. Rampant insubordination, combined with his unhealed wound and political difficulties with President Houston, conspired to motivate Johnston to request that he be relieved on April 22, and on May 7 Col. Joseph H. D. Rogers, the senior officer at headquarters, took command of the army. Within a week, however, a soldier who held a grudge against Col. Henry Teal[qv] shot him in his sleep. This incident proved too much for even Sam Houston, who ordered secretary of war William S. Fisher[qv] to go to Camp Bowie (in the future Jackson County), the army headquarters, and to furlough two-thirds of the army. The remaining 500 to 600 men were retained only to garrison the most essential posts. Because of its smaller size, the army could then be more adequately maintained by the government while the remaining units were held in almost total inactivity and allowed to dwindle away by expiration of enlistments. By the end of the year only small garrisons at San Antonio and Galveston remained.

After the inauguration of Mirabeau B. Lamar to the presidency on December 10, 1839, however, the fortunes of the army took a dizzying swing for the better. The Lamar administration pursued an aggressive policy against both the Indians and Mexico as well as a program of territorial expansion. In order to fulfill his mandate Lamar clearly required a powerful military establishment, and the new president began immediately to revitalize the army. First, he named the regular army's most forceful advocate, Albert Sidney Johnston, as secretary of war and then discharged all of the residue of Houston's army so as to have a free hand in the organization of a new fighting force. The principal element of new Texas army, recommended by Johnston and authorized by the Third Congress, was its regular component, designated the Frontier Regiment but more commonly referred to as the First Regiment of Infantry. This fifteen-company regiment, with an authorized strength of 840 men, was to be stationed at forts along the frontier connected by a Military Road[qv] running from the Red River to the Nueces. This line of defense was to be established some distance beyond the inhabited area at most points, and settlement near the forts was encouraged. Since the total military strength of the republic was only that of a regiment in most of the armies of the time, its command devolved upon a colonel. Remarkably, each of the companies could be designated either as infantry or cavalry at the discretion of the colonel commanding.

Edward Burleson,[qv] described by a contemporary as "a remarkable, plain, kind-hearted, benevolent, honest and unambitious man" and "a great Indian fighter," was made colonel and commander of the First Regiment of Infantry. Former secretary of war Fisher was appointed lieutenant colonel and Peyton S. Wyatt[qv] major. Col. Lysander Wells[qv] was given command of the cavalry. Although none of these officers had taken any formal military training, each was popular and experienced in warfare with the Indians and the Mexicans. Lamar's Frontier Regiment was recruited under the overall supervision of a lieutenant colonel, and recruiting stations were established at various towns in Texas. Stations at Galveston and Houston were staffed by a captain and a sergeant each. In New Orleans a recruiting officer was on duty from 1839 through 1841. Troops enlisted there were forwarded to Galveston at the expense of the Texas government. Texas soldiers came from widely varied social and economic backgrounds as well as diverse geographic origins. Rural areas of Texas or the United States supplied many units, while others were composed entirely of men recruited in New Orleans or other large cities. The better class of American or Texan was often led to volunteer by a sense of patriotism or by a taste for adventure. Volunteers from the poorer classes were often attracted to Texas by the promise of generous land bounties, and, according to Noah Smithwick,[qv] a class of men joined the Texas army who were "actuated by no higher principle than prospective plundering." All too often, this type was dominant, if not in fact, at least in the popular image of the Texas army. Although the recruiting of regular soldiers proceeded very slowly because few Texans were willing to submit to army discipline and boredom in exchange for uncertain pay and rations, most soldiers were decent men, even if they were often poor and illiterate.

Immediately upon entering the service, all recruits became the responsibility of the Texas government for clothing and feeding. Procuring and distributing adequate food and clothing for the troops was the responsibility of the quartermaster, subsistence, and purchasing departments, but the strained financial situation of the republic often made their jobs all but impossible. Rations prescribed for the regular army were identical to those issued to the army of the United States. Regulations stipulated a daily ration of three-quarters of a pound of salt pork or bacon or a pound and a quarter of fresh or salted beef; one and a half pounds of bread, hardtack, flour, or cornmeal; some peas or beans; and rice, coffee, vinegar, salt, and sugar.

The issue of small quantities of soap and candles was also authorized. Shortages often compelled commissary officers to make alterations in the standard ration, however, and when sufficient bread was not available, the issue of beef was customarily increased. As much as three pounds of beef a day was sometimes supplied. During such periods, the commissary department made every effort to provide adequate coffee and sugar in order to minimize discontent among the troops. Although perhaps less urgent than feeding them, the problem of clothing and equipping the troops was nevertheless a major challenge to the maintenance of the regular army. Regulations called for abundant supplies of clothing and equipment, with each recruit to receive two pairs of woolen trousers and three of cotton, a woolen and a cotton jacket, a coat appropriate to his branch, two cotton and two flannel shirts, three pairs of boots, three pairs of stockings, two sets of underwear, a greatcoat, a dress coat, a blanket, and a leather stock. In addition to this initial issue, new uniform items were to be supplied at intervals established by regulations.

Although regulations were quite precise regarding uniformity, the army's appearance varied greatly with time and circumstances. Texas army uniforms were meant to be identical to those used by the United States Army during the same period. Dark-blue nondress uniforms with standing collars and long skirts trimmed with white were prescribed for infantry. The cavalry wore an identical uniform with yellow trim and a yellow stripe on each trouser leg. White cotton trousers were prescribed as summer wear for both services. Gray fatigue uniforms for the field completed the soldiers' ensemble. However, although quantities of clothing began to reach the army in summer of 1836, the Texas agent obviously had purchased the garments with little regard to uniformity. As well as some regulation United States Army clothing, cotton duck and red flannel shirts and brown linen and blue twill trousers were forwarded from New Orleans. Prior to 1839, only official Texas army buttons—which had the Lone Stare in the center, T-E-X-A-S above in a semicircle, and T.A. below—could have been regarded as uniform, and they had to be purchased by the soldiers themselves. As most of the troops could not afford even to buy buttons, before 1839 the Texas army never achieved any of the uniformity prescribed by regulation. After 1839 the army was, at least for a time, adequately supported by the Congress, and available evidence indicates that between 1839 and 1841 the Texas army actually dressed according to regulations.

In addition to clothing, the troops were to be provided with a variety of miscellaneous equipment. Tents, ranging in size from the luxurious marquee and wall tents prescribed for generals to the spartan, wedge-shaped tents for each six enlisted men, were part of the regulation issue. Enlisted tent-mates formed a mess, each of which was provided with a hatchet, a camp kettle, and two mess pans. Each company was likewise issued six axes and four spades, and all officers, including the generals, were issued axes and hatchets.

Disciplining officers and men alike proved perhaps the most vexing problem of administration in the Texas army. Regulars, because of their better discipline, were more easily managed than volunteers, and, so long as they were properly fed and clothed, were willing to endure long periods of the monotony of garrison duty or inactivity in the field. Regulars, however, were inclined to mutiny and desertion when food and clothing were in short supply or of poor quality. Courts-martial were specified for numerous breaches of army regulations, and such serious infractions as violence against a superior officer, mutiny, desertion, sleeping on post while acting as a sentinel, the raising of false alarms in camp, and cowardice in battle, were punishable by death. Such judicial proceedings were not infrequent in the regular army, and the death penalty was prescribed on a number of occasions. In almost all such cases, however, clemency was granted to the offender, and no one seems to have been executed for a strictly military crime. Of the 674 enlisted in the First Regiment of Infantry, no fewer than 169 deserted, 61 of whom were apprehended and returned to the custody of the army. No deserter, however, seems ever to have been executed, although desertion was clearly one of the most serious problems in the army of the republic. In fact, between 1839 and 1841 only seven soldiers were dishonorably discharged and three executed. Mutiny, a most serious military crime, was never severely punished in the Texas army, perhaps because authorities who were too weak to prevent mutinies were usually too weak to chastise mutineers. At worst, mutineers were given dishonorable discharges or cashiered. Among the very few executions that did take place in the army was that of a soldier who had stabbed an officer. This felon was tried, convicted, and sentenced within five days of his crime. His sentence was appealed and upheld the same day as the trial, and he was executed less than two weeks later.

Assemblies, drill, and duty constituted the standard daily routine in the Army of the Republic of Texas. A drum or bugle sounded reveille at daybreak, and breakfast call was sounded at seven. Sick call followed at 7:30, and then came assembly for drill, inspection, and assignment of duties at eight. Call to dinner was beaten at one and retreat at sunset. When tattoo was sounded at nine in the evening, all men were required to be in their quarters. Officers, however, were not nearly so fully regulated, and garrison life for them was usually uneventful but often pleasant. According to the diary of Capt. Andrew Neill, commandant of the post on Galveston Island during the summer of 1838, daily activities included the oversight of guard mount, the formation of the troops, and the preparation of administrative reports. The rest of his days he spent in reading, swimming in Galveston Bay, watching the boats passing by, and conversing with visitors to the island. Enlisted men as well had considerable time off duty, which they passed in such simple diversions as hunting, writing letters and occasionally keeping journals, gambling, and drinking illicit whiskey.

Lamar's Frontier Regiment never achieved more than half of its authorized size. It reached a maximum strength of only ten full companies, totaling 560 men. Nevertheless, thanks largely to liberal congressional army appropriations for 1840, this force was superior in organization, discipline, and efficiency to any previous Texas army, as well as better fed, clothed, and equipped. Recruiting in Texas, however, was almost nonexistent, and officers transferred their efforts to New Orleans, where recruits were more plentiful. Even so, the army never reached its authorized strength, and after Albert Sidney Johnston's resignation in March 1840 the army slowly declined, from approximately 540 at the end of September 1840 to only 465 by the end of the year. Failure in recruiting was paralleled by the War Department's inability to establish the line of forts and the Military Road that President Lamar had proposed at the beginning of his term. By December 1839 the army still had no more than five companies along the Texas frontier, a number far too small to open the new posts called for by the law. So small an army was hardly effective as a deterrent either to Indians or to Mexicans, and only in the Cherokee War (1839) and the Council House Fight[qqv] (1840) did the regular army play even a supporting role in actual combat.

The Fifth Congress of the republic, sitting between November 2, 1840, and February 5, 1841, was completely dominated by the Houston faction. Although Lamar argued forcefully for the retention of the regular army, his dream of a powerful military establishment was doomed. Lamar correctly pointed out that certain essential military services such as enduring extended garrison duty or building roads and forts would never be willingly performed by "citizen soldiers." Further, he maintained, the very fact that the army had not participated in many actions during 1839 and 1840 was an indication of its worth, since "It was not its actual fighting, but its existence in the field that was serviceable." Although Lamar's patronage prevented the passage of legislation for disbanding the regular army, his victory was a hollow one. Congress adjourned before making any appropriation for the army's support, thus effectively destroying the Frontier Regiment. Sadly, Lamar was compelled to issue orders to disband the army. The First Regiment of Infantry, the last serious effort by the Republic of Texas to maintain a regular army, thus passed from the scene, a victim of partisanship and the country's financial difficulties.

In addition to the regular army, the Republic of Texas was protected by a militia, by companies of minutemen, and by the paramilitary Texas Rangers.[qv] On December 6, 1836, during Sam Houston's first presidential term, Congress passed legislation establishing the essential militia structure. "Every free able bodied male citizen of this republic, resident therein, who is or shall be . . . seventeen . . . and under the age of fifty years shall . . . be enrolled in the militia." Congress envisioned two divisions, each commanded by a major general and divided into two brigades commanded by brigadier generals. Each brigade would contain two regiments of two battalions each, and each of these battalions would contain five companies. According to the legislation, companies and battalions would muster twice annually for drill, and regiments would gather each year for three days of drill. The organization, on paper, was formidable. The Texas Congress, however, refused to appropriate necessary funds, causing a furious Sam Houston to write the House of Representatives that the "proper organization would have been consummated under the last law, had Congress made any appropriation adequate to the completion of its organization. Not one dollar was placed at the disposal of the Executive." Late in 1837 the Second Congress made another attempt to reorganize the militia. The militia act of 1837 reduced the militia to one division, under the command of a major general, which contained four brigades, each commanded by a brigadier general. Congress selected the initial general officers: Thomas J. Rusk as major general and Edward Burleson, Moseley Baker,[qv] Kelsey H. Douglass,[qv] and John Dyer as commanders of the first to forth brigades, respectively. In 1839 Felix Huston replaced Rusk as major general, but four years later Rusk returned; he held the office for less than a year before being replaced by Sidney Sherman,[qv] who remained in the office until annexation.

Because of the ineffectiveness of the militia and the scarcity of regular army troops, the Texas Congress authorized twenty frontier counties to organize "minutemen companies" under the jurisdiction of the county judge, but, as Texas Ranger James Buckner (Buck) Barry[qv] pointed out, "every settler was a minuteman. In fact, every man in Texas was a soldier." As their title implied, these volunteers anticipated dropping their work in an emergency and rushing to the scene of action with little time wasted on musters and rules and regulations. Each man equipped himself with "a good substantial horse, bridle, and saddle . . . together with a good gun, and one hundred rounds of ammunition." Congress expected these "minute companies" to be mustered only in times of extreme emergency, and the men were paid only for the days spent on actual service, with a maximum limit of four months duty per year. Each squad of rangers daily patrolled its section of the frontier to assure that no Indians took the settlements by surprise. Barry wrote that if the rangers discovered Indians, "it was our business to beat them there and notify the minutemen of their coming." According to him, the minutemen "were really the army of Texas," for John Coffee (Jack) Hays's[qv] ranger battalion was composed only of "spy companies" that watched for the enemy and reported to the minutemen. No more than three rangers from a camp were ever out on patrol at the same time, and these men were to report to a prearranged rendezvous with the patrols from the camps above or below at the terminus of their areas of responsibility. Failure to show usually meant that marauding Indians had "sent them under." The rangers were ordered, therefore, to avoid confrontation with the raiders, for, as Hays said, "no dead man could make a report to the minutemen."

BIBLIOGRAPHY: Eugene C. Barker, "Texan Revolutionary Army," *Quarterly of the Texas State Historical Association* 9 (April 1906). William Campbell Binkley, *The Expansionist Movement in Texas, 1836–1850* (Berkeley: University of California Press, 1925). Daughters of the Republic of Texas, *Defenders of the Republic of Texas* (Austin: Laurel House, 1989). Hans Peter Nielsen Gammel, comp., *Laws of Texas, 1822–1897* (10 vols., Austin: Gammel, 1898). Frances Terry Ingmire, *Texas Frontiersman, 1839–1860: Minute Men, Militia, Home Guard, Indian Fighter* (St. Louis: Fort Ingmire, 1982). John H. Jenkins, ed., *The Papers of the Texas Revolution, 1835–1836* (10 vols., Austin: Presidial Press, 1973). Joseph Milton Nance, *After San Jacinto: The Texas-Mexican Frontier, 1836–1841* (Austin: University of Texas Press, 1963). Gerald S. Pierce, The Army of the Texas Republic, 1836–1845 (M.A. thesis, University of Mississippi, 1963). *Thomas W. Cutrer*

ARNECKEVILLE, TEXAS. Arneckeville is a German community on Farm Road 236 and a branch of Coleto Creek eight miles south of Cuero in south central DeWitt County. Although the community dates from 1859, it had no name until 1872, when the post office opened and was named for Adam Christoph Henry and U. Barbara Arnecke, the first settlers. Their log house stood from 1859 to 1947. Zion Lutheran Church was constructed of logs in 1865 and served as a school until a separate school building was built in 1890 on land Arnecke donated. Arnecke also had the community's first store and kept the post office from 1872 to 1903. Dr. C. A. H. Arnecke, son of the founder, built the first drugstore and opened a hospital. By 1885 Arneckeville had the church, a steam gristmill and cotton gin, and daily stages to Meyersville and Goliad. The population of 130 rose to a reported 250 residents by 1896. By 1925 it had declined to seventy-five. It remained steady until the late 1940s, when about 100 residents and four businesses were reported. The post office was closed in the mid-1950s. In 1961 Arneckeville, Westhoff, and Meyersville were the only consolidated rural school districts left in DeWitt County. The population fell to seventy-five in the late 1960s and to fifty in the mid-1980s. It was still reported as fifty in 1990.

BIBLIOGRAPHY: Nellie Murphree, *A History of DeWitt County* (Victoria, Texas, 1962). *Craig H. Roell*

ARNETT, CULLEN CURLEE (1812–1854). Cullen Arnett, Republic of Texas[qv] congressman, son of Davis and Rhoda (Curlee) Arnett, was born in Alabama on March 27, 1812. He moved to Madison County, Mississippi, in 1828, and four years later to Leake County, where he was elected sheriff. He married Elizabeth Norrid on August 12, 1834, and had at least six children. In 1838, after the death of Cullen's mother, the Arnett family moved to Texas. Arnett secured a land grant in Liberty County on December 5, 1839. He represented Liberty County in the Fifth Congress of the Republic of Texas, from November 2, 1840, to February 5, 1841. By 1845 he had moved to Wolf Creek in Tyler County, and he was appointed notary public there on May 22, 1846. He and his family were living in Milam County by 1850; that year's census reported his real estate to be worth $500. He was elected county commissioner in February 1851. Arnett died at Seguin on July 24, 1854.

BIBLIOGRAPHY: Texas House of Representatives, *Biographical Directory of the Texan Conventions and Congresses, 1832–1845* (Austin: Book Exchange, 1941). *Robert Wooster*

ARNETT, SAM CULLEN, JR. (1908–1985). Sam Cullen Arnett, Jr., South Plains physician, son of Sam Cullen and Alice Ford (Helpman) Arnett, was born at the Arnett ranch headquarters, presently the site of Meadow, Texas, on August 26, 1908. The elder Arnett was a scion of a prominent pioneer ranching family. Young Arnett attended Texas Technological College (now Texas Tech University) the first two years the school was open (1925–27), transferred to the University of Texas for one year (1927–28), then entered Baylor School of Medicine and received his M.D. degree in 1932. After a two-year internship (1932–34) in Kings County Hospital, Brooklyn, New York, he spent six months in the pathology department of the Mayo Clinic. He earned his board certification in internal medicine in 1945.

During his term at Kings County Hospital, Arnett was sent to Boston to study under Dr. E. P. Joslin, one of the leading pioneers in treating diabetes, to learn the clinical use of insulin in the treatment of that disease. After his tenure with Joslin, Arnett returned to Kings County Hospital and set up a diabetes clinic. There he gained expertise in insulin therapy, which he brought to Lubbock. He also introduced the electrocardiograph to Lubbock—the only such instrument within hundreds of miles.

Arnett returned to Lubbock in 1935 and contributed greatly to Lubbock's development as a medical center for the South Plains. In the 1930s Lubbock was not the easiest place to establish a practice. Both hospitals in the city had closed staffs; physicians had either to buy a share of a hospital or to be salaried employees. As part of their refusal to do either, Arnett and doctors Olan Key and Frank B. Malone built their own hospital. The group purchased an acre of land near the Texas Tech campus from W. L. (Bill) Ellwood, of the ranching family for which Arnett's grandfather had worked, and built the most modern hospital in West Texas, using the Ellwoods' old swimming pool as the basement for their twelve-bed facility. The hospital, named Plains Hospital, was opened in 1937. It had modern equipment and was one of the first air-conditioned buildings in Lubbock and reportedly the first completely air-conditioned hospital in Texas. In 1939 the partners sold the hospital to the Sisters of St. Joseph, of Orange, California, who renamed it St. Mary of the Plains Hospital. Arnett continued his active participation in the institution. St. Mary's continued to grow and was moved to its present site bordering Maxey Park in 1970.

Arnett donated twenty acres of land for the campus of Lubbock Christian College and gave the college the "old Arnett home," which was used at varying times for classrooms, as a dormitory, and as the college's administration building. He was also a leader in the move to found a medical school in Lubbock. After Texas Tech University School of Medicine was established, St. Mary's was the major teaching facility in Lubbock for several years. Arnett endowed a chair in the Department of Medicine at Texas Tech University Health Science Center.[qv]

He married Olga Wirchniansky in New York on October 31, 1934. They had two children. Arnett died on February 13, 1985, in the hospital he had started in 1935.

BIBLIOGRAPHY: William Rush Dunnagan, "A Survey of Lubbock's Growth As a Medical Center, 1909–1954," *Museum Journal* 19 (1980). Lawrence L. Graves, ed., *A History of Lubbock* (Lubbock: West Texas Museum Association, 1962). *Robert L. McCartor*

ARNETT, WILLIAM WASHINGTON (1823–1892). William Washington (Fuzzy Buck, Judge) Arnett was born three miles from Tuscumbia in Franklin County, Alabama, on January 5, 1823, the son of David and Rhoda (Curlee) Arnett. The family moved to Mississippi in 1828 and settled first in Madison County, then in Hinds County, and finally near the site of present Carthage in Leake County. In 1837 Arnett's mother died, and the boy contracted "inflammatory rheumatism," from which he never fully recovered. After living with a brother in Tipton County, Tennessee, for a while, Arnett returned to Mississippi in 1839, and on March 1, 1843, became tax assessor of Leake County. He held this position until 1845, when, his proposal of marriage having been rejected by a local heiress, he departed for Texas.

In Texas Arnett resided with his older brother in the Tyler County communities of Town Bluff and Wolf Creek, where he taught school. There he married Emiline Barnell; they eventually had seven children. The couple resided briefly in Milam County. During the Mexican War[qv] Arnett served as a private in Capt. John A. Veatch's[qv] company of Col. Peter H. Bell's[qv] regiment of Texas Mounted Volunteers. This company was recruited primarily in Tyler County, mustered into federal service on October 23, 1847, and left federal service on September 20, 1848. On February 10, 1852, the Arnetts moved to the present site of Uvalde, then a wilderness. There Arnett built a shanty on the banks of the Leona River and delivered hay to Fort Inge under a contract to the army. For years after the family settled in Uvalde County they had no close neighbors and were in constant peril from Indians, wolves, and mountain lions. From January 1 until December 31, 1856, Arnett served as a private in Capt. Reading Wood Black's[qv] company of minutemen.

Mrs. Arnett died in 1871, and Arnett married Mrs. Mary Herrington Copeland at Salado on July 27, 1874. She was a teacher and the daughter of H. H. Herrington, a founder of Marshall, Texas. She and Arnett had five children. Arnett was elected treasurer of Kinney County in 1876, a position he held until his death. In 1885 he began writing a delightful memoir, now on deposit at the Barker Texas History Center,[qv] University of Texas at Austin.

Arnett died in Brackettville on December 23, 1892, and was buried there. He was a Mason, a member of the Disciples of Christ, and a frequent contributor of editorial and historical materials to the Castroville *Quill* and the Uvalde *Hesperian.* His widow died at Uvalde on January 11, 1925.

BIBLIOGRAPHY: W. W. Arnett Papers, Barker Texas History Center, University of Texas at Austin. Frances Terry Ingmire, comp., *Texas Ranger Service Records, 1847–1900* (St. Louis, 1982). Charles D. Spurlin, comp., *Texas Veterans in the Mexican War: Muster Rolls of Texas Military Units* (Victoria, Texas, 1984). *Thomas W. Cutrer*

ARNETT, TEXAS (Coryell County). Arnett is on U.S. Highway 84 in west central Coryell County, nine miles west of Gatesville. The site was settled in the 1880s, and Arnett was supposedly named by a man named Johnson for a friend of his who lived in the vicinity. An Arnett post office, with John T. Taylor as postmaster, was in operation from 1903 until 1906, when mail was rerouted to Gatesville. In 1940 local businesses dealt mainly in farm implements and general merchandise and served an estimated population of 100. By the mid-1950s the number of residents had dwindled to fifty, and the Arnett school district had been consolidated with that of Gatesville. By the 1980s Arnett residents were largely dependent on Gatesville for schools, churches, and stores.

BIBLIOGRAPHY: Coryell County Genealogical Society, *Coryell County, Texas, Families, 1854-1985* (Dallas: Taylor, 1986).

Zelma Scott

ARNETT, TEXAS (Hockley County). Arnett is on Farm Road 1585 eight miles southeast of Levelland in south central Hockley County. It developed around the south headquarters of the Spade Ranch[qv] and was named in 1926 for ranch foreman Tom Arnett. J. C. Arnett was the first postmaster. A store, a filling station, and a gin served the community, which reached its peak in 1946 with about 100 residents. By 1950 the population had declined to fifty and by 1970 to twenty-six, where it remained in 1990. *William R. Hunt*

ARNEY, TEXAS. Arney is twenty-two miles from Dimmitt in the northeast corner of Castro County. The community was named for the Arney family, who settled there in 1901. A post office was established in 1902 at the home of William D. Robinson, who acted as postmaster. Another settler, C. H. Cox, donated five acres of land for a school, which opened in the fall of that year. A Baptist church was organized in 1905. By 1912 the post office had been discontinued. The church disbanded during the early 1930s, and in 1945 the school district was consolidated with that of Dimmitt. Subsequently the school building was turned into a meeting place for the Community Club, which was still active in the 1980s. Arney was still listed as a community in 1990.

BIBLIOGRAPHY: Castro County Historical Commission, *Castro County, 1891-1981* (Dallas: Taylor, 1981). Arthur Hecht, comp., *Postal History in the Texas Panhandle* (Canyon, Texas: Panhandle-Plains Historical Society, 1960). *H. Allen Anderson*

ARNO, TEXAS. Arno is one mile west of the Pecos River on State Highway 302 and the Atchison, Topeka and Santa Fe Railway in northeastern Reeves County. The settlement began as one of many promotional townsites in the county early in the twentieth century. An Arno post office was operated from 1907 until 1915; Ola Solman was postmistress. The community had a population of ten and one business in the 1930s. From 1945 until 1949 the population was reported as twenty. By 1950 no population was reported.

BIBLIOGRAPHY: Alton Hughes, *Pecos: A History of the Pioneer West* (Seagraves, Texas: Pioneer, 1978). *Romantic Old Odessa* (Odessa: Permian Historical Society, 1962). *Julia Cauble Smith*

ARNOLD, HAYDEN S. (1805–1839). Hayden S. Arnold, army officer in the Texas Revolution[qv] and legislator in the Republic of Texas,[qv] was born in Tennessee in 1805 and moved to Texas late in December 1835. At Nacogdoches on January 14, 1836, he took the oath of allegiance to the Mexican government and enrolled for six months' service in the Volunteer Auxiliary Corps. On March 6 he was elected captain of his company, which became the First Company of Col. Sidney Sherman's[qv] Second Regiment, Texas Volunteers. Arnold led the Nacogdoches troops at the battle of San Jacinto,[qv] where his new London Yager rifle was shot from his hands and broken through at the breech. After the company disbanded on June 6, 1836, he was elected to represent Nacogdoches in the House of Representatives of the First Congress of the Republic of Texas. He served from October 3, 1836, to June 13, 1837. In 1836 Sam Houston[qv] appointed him to serve as secretary of a commission to treat with the Indians. He later served as district clerk pro tem of the Nacogdoches District, until at least December 20, 1838. Arnold died on July 3, 1839, at his home in Nacogdoches and was buried in Oak Grove Cemetery there. His widow, Selina, was appointed administrator of his estate. In 1936 the state of Texas erected a monument over his grave. On November 17, 1851, Adolphus Sterne[qv] introduced a bill for the relief of Arnold's heirs before the Senate of the State of Texas.

BIBLIOGRAPHY: Daughters of the Republic of Texas, *Muster Rolls of the Texas Revolution* (Austin, 1986). Sam Houston Dixon and Louis Wiltz Kemp, *The Heroes of San Jacinto* (Houston: Anson Jones, 1932). Archie P. McDonald, ed., *Hurrah for Texas: The Diary of Adolphus Sterne* (Waco: Texian Press, 1969; rpt., Austin: Eakin Press, 1986). Texas House of Representatives, *Biographical Directory of the Texan Conventions and Congresses, 1832–1845* (Austin: Book Exchange, 1941). *Thomas W. Cutrer*

ARNOLD, HENDRICK (?–1849). Hendrick Arnold, guide and spy during the Texas Revolution,[qv] emigrated from Mississippi with his parents, Daniel Arnold, apparently a white man, and Rachel Arnold, who was apparently black, in the winter of 1826. The family settled in Stephen F. Austin's[qv] colony on the Brazos river. Hendrick is referred to as a Negro, although his brother Holly was regarded as white; both were apparently considered free, although there is no evidence that they were ever formally freed by their father. In July or August of 1827 Hendrick and an Arnold slave named Dolly had a daughter, Harriet. Hendrick held Harriet as a slave.

By the fall of 1835 Arnold had settled in San Antonio and married a woman named Martina (María), a stepdaughter of Erastus (Deaf) Smith.[qv] Arnold had a second daughter, Juanita, who may have been Martina's child. While Arnold and Smith were hunting buffalo in the Little River country north of the site of present Austin, Mexican forces under Gen. Martín Perfecto de Cos[qv] occupied San Antonio. On their trip home Arnold and Smith came upon Stephen F. Austin's[qv] encampment at Salado Creek. Arnold, and soon thereafter Smith, who considered remaining neutral because of his Mexican wife, offered their services as guides to the Texans. In October Arnold took part in the battle of Concepción.[qv]

When Edward Burleson,[qv] who had replaced Austin as commander, called a council of officers on December 3, 1835, the council decided to postpone an attack on San Antonio, explaining that Arnold was absent and that the officers of one of the divisions refused to march without him. Arnold's whereabouts during his absence are now unknown. When he returned, Benjamin R. Milam[qv] called for an attack, which was subsequently called the siege of Bexar.[qv] Arnold served as the guide for Milam's division. Francis W. Johnson,[qv] leader of the other division, wrote the official report of the battle for himself and Milam, who was killed during the siege. Johnson acknowledged the bravery of all the Texan forces and cited Arnold specifically for his "important service."

On January 3, 1836, Arnold arrived in San Felipe de Austin with his family and that of Erastus Smith. On January 4 he successfully petitioned the General Council[qv] of the provisional government[qv] of Texas for relief for their families and noted Smith's service for Texas and his wounds suffered in battle. Arnold continued to support the revolution and served in Smith's spy company in the battle of San Jacinto.[qv]

After the revolution Arnold was compensated for his service with land a few miles northwest of the site of present Bandera, a relatively unexplored area that many white men would not accept for grants. Arnold secured adjacent land for his grandmother Catherine Arnold, his father Daniel, and his brother Holly. Holly appears to have been the only family member to settle on the land. Hendrick Arnold lived on the Medina River and operated a gristmill in San Antonio. A portion of the mill was still standing in 1990 near Mission San Juan.

In 1846 Arnold arranged an indentured-servant contract between his daughter Harriet and James Newcomb.[qv] Newcomb agreed to pay $750 for her services and then free her after five years. Both Arnold and Newcomb died of cholera before the expiration of the contract. Newcomb's administrator, George M. Martin, petitioned the Texas House of Representatives to permit Harriet to remain in the state as a free woman of color on December 29, 1849. The resolution passed the House; however, Arnold's family made several attempts to regain Harriet from Martin. Martina Arnold took the matter to court, sued Martin for $2,000 plus the $750 due on the indentured-servant contract, and requested that Harriet be returned to her. The final outcome of the case was cloudy; however, it appears that Harriet was allowed to remain in the state as a free woman. Hendrick Arnold died in the cholera epidemic in Bexar County in 1849 and was buried on the banks of the Medina River.

BIBLIOGRAPHY: *The Afro-American Texans* (San Antonio: University of Texas Institute of Texan Cultures, 1975). John H. Jenkins, ed., *The Papers of the Texas Revolution, 1835–1836* (10 vols., Austin: Presidial Press, 1973). Harold Schoen, "The Free Negro in the Republic of Texas," *Southwestern Historical Quarterly* 39–41 (April 1936–July 1937). *Nolan Thompson*

ARNOLD, JUNE FAIRFAX DAVIS (1926–1982). June Arnold, author and publisher, was born on October 27, 1926, in Greenville, South Carolina, the daughter of Robert Cowan and Cad (Wortham) Davis. She attended Kinkaid School[qv] in Houston and Shipley in Bryn Mawr, Pennsylvania, and made her debut at the Allegro Club ball in 1947. She attended Vassar College in 1943–44 but returned to Houston and completed her B.A. at Rice Institute (now Rice University) in 1948. She earned a master's degree in literature at Rice in 1958.

By 1953 she had married Gilbert Harrington Arnold, a classmate at Rice. The couple had four children before they were divorced. After her marriage ended, June Arnold took her children and moved to New York City to pursue a writing career. She studied writing at the New School for Social Research. Although she reportedly considered her writing career as secondary, she completed four novels, the last two of which drew high praise. In 1967 her first novel, *Applesauce*, was published by McGraw-Hill. The book reflected the author's personal experiences, including her life in Houston and the Rice University area, but it also examined changes in personalities that occur when people marry. Following *Applesauce* Arnold moved to rural

Vermont and founded a press, Daughters, Incorporated, with Parke Bowman. Daughters focused on publishing works that chronicled lesbian experiences, including two by Arnold: *The Cook and the Carpenter,* which appeared in 1973 under the pseudonym Carpenter, and *Sister Gin,* which came out in 1975. Arnold contributed to a number of periodicals, including the *Village Voice,* Houston *Post,*[qv] *Quest, Plexus, Amazon Quarterly,* and *Sister Courage.* She was a member of the National Organization for Women and the Texas Institute of Letters.[qv]

She was one of the organizers of the first Women in Print conference, which met in Omaha in August 1976. Drawing together women from publishing houses, magazines, newspapers, bookstores, printing companies, and distribution services, the conference has been credited with significantly advancing the development of media branches within the women's movement. In the early 1980s she returned to Houston to write a novel recreating her mother's life and time. Her efforts resulted in both a compelling story of a mother-daughter relationship and a richly detailed picture of Houston as a small southern city in the first half of the twentieth-century. Arnold died of cancer in Houston on March 11, 1982. Her manuscript was published posthumously as *Baby Houston* in 1987.

bibliography: June Arnold, "Feminist Presses and Feminist Politics," *Quest* 3 (Summer 1976). *Contemporary Authors* (Detroit: Gale Research, 1962–). Houston *Chronicle,* February 26, 1967. Houston *Post,* March 13, 1982. Janis Kelly, "June Arnold," *Off Our Backs,* April 1982. Beverly Lowry, "June," in June Arnold, *Baby Houston* (Austin: Texas Monthly Press, 1987). Jane Marcus, "Afterword," in June Arnold, *Sister Gin* (New York: Feminist Press, 1989). Jane Marcus, "Bringing Up Baby," *Women's Review of Books* 5 (October 1987). Ellen Morgan, "The Feminist Novels of Androgynous Fantasy," *Frontiers: A Journal of Women Studies* 2 (Fall 1977). *New Directions for Women,* May–June 1982. *New York Times Book Review,* July 26, 1987.

Debbie Mauldin Cottrell

ARNOLD, RIPLEY ALLEN (1817–1853). Ripley Allen Arnold, United States Army officer, the son of Willis Arnold, was born at Pearlington, near Bay St. Louis, in Hancock County, Mississippi, on January 17, 1817, and was appointed to the United States Military Academy at West Point in 1834. He was said to have been a talented song writer whose compositions were popular at the academy. He reportedly fought a duel at an infamous drinking establishment, Benny Haven's, while still a cadet. He graduated thirty-third in his class and was assigned to duty as a second lieutenant of the First Dragoons in Florida on July 1, 1838. On February 1, 1839, he was promoted to first lieutenant. He and Catherine Bryant eloped on her fourteenth birthday (August 26, 1839) and were married in Pass Christian, Mississippi. They had five children.

Arnold was brevetted captain on April 19, 1842, for gallant conduct in the Seminole War and major on May 9, 1846, for his role in the battles of Palo Alto and Resaca de la Palma.[qqv] He served under Gen. William J. Worth[qv] through the battle of Monterrey. He was then transferred to the army of Gen. Winfield Scott and took part in the battle of Molino del Rey and the capture of Mexico City in 1847. Arnold was promoted to captain on May 11, 1846, and served as assistant quartermaster until March 10, 1847.

He was given command of Company F of the Second Dragoons after the Mexican War[qv] and ordered to northern Texas to establish a military post "at or near the confluence of the West Fork and the Clear Fork of the Trinity River." In the latter part of May 1849, after locating a suitable site for the new camp, he left Fort Graham with forty-two dragoons and proceeded to the Trinity, where, on June 6, 1849, he established Camp Worth, which he named after his former commander, who had recently died of cholera in San Antonio. With a portable, horse-powered sawmill his company constructed a barracks, a mess hall, a commissary, an infirmary, stables, and a smithy. Camp Worth, later named Fort Worth, was completed by mid-winter of 1849, and in 1850 Arnold's wife and five children joined him from Washington, D.C. Two of the couple's daughters died shortly after their arrival and were buried near the fort.

Arnold and his company returned to Fort Graham on June 17, 1851. He was detached to duty in Washington in 1852 but returned to command of Fort Graham in 1853. During this period his company launched a preemptive strike against a war party led by Comanche chief Jim Ned.[qv] They pursued the raiding parties of Jim Ned and Feathertail into what is now Palo Pinto County, where they defeated the Indians. Jim Ned was killed in the fighting, and Comanche raiders never ventured as far east as Tarrant County again.

Arnold was known as a strict disciplinarian. When a soldier stole a hog from a nearby farm, Arnold ordered that he remain tied for several hours in front of the officers' quarters in the July sun with the remains of the slaughtered animal hung around his neck.

Arnold was killed at Fort Graham on September 6, 1853, by Josephus Murray Steiner,[qv] in an exchange of shots. Civil and military authorities disputed jurisdiction in the case, and Steiner was ultimately acquitted by both court-martial and a civil jury. He was represented by future governor Richard Coke and future Confederate general William H. Parsons,[qqv] who established that Arnold had been procuring United States government horses under questionable circumstances and selling them for his own profit. Steiner's attorneys claimed that their client had known of this practice and planned to expose it. One witness swore that Arnold had threatened, "I will put him out of the way; he shall not give evidence against me." Arnold was first buried at Fort Graham, then disinterred and removed to Fort Worth, where he was buried in the Pioneer's Rest Cemetery, within a mile of old Fort Worth and near the graves of his two infant daughters. He was said to have received the first Masonic rites ever performed in Fort Worth. His diary and personal papers were destroyed by fire at the Fort Worth home of one of his granddaughters.

bibliography: George W. Cullum, *Biographical Register of the Officers and Graduates of the U.S. Military Academy at West Point, New York* (8 vols., New York [etc.]: D. Van Nostrand [etc.], 1868–1940). Fort Worth *Star-Telegram,* October 30, 1949. Jill Gunter, "The Major and His Fort," *Texas Historian,* January 1978. Francis B. Heitman, *Historical Register and Dictionary of the United States Army* (2 vols., Washington: GPO, 1903; rpt., Urbana: University of Illinois Press, 1965). James V. Reese, "Murder of Major Ripley J. Arnold," West Texas Historical Association *Year Book* 41 (1965). Thomas Thompson, "Ripley Arnold, Frontier Major," *Junior Historian,* May 1949.

Thomas W. Cutrer

ARNOTTVILLE, TEXAS. Arnottville was on State Highway 171 three miles north of Hillsboro in central Hill County. The community was probably named for Albert M. Arnott (Arnot), who owned 2,000 acres in the area on which he ran cattle. Arnott donated half an acre to build a school and church. The church was used as a circuit-rider stop and usually held Church of Christ services. Because of its proximity to cattle trails the area was a popular resting place for cowboys. In 1905 the Arnott school had sixty-nine pupils. In the 1980s the only remnant of the community was the church, which was no longer in use.

bibliography: Hill County Historical Commission, *A History of Hill County, Texas, 1853-1980* (Waco: Texian, 1980). *Lisa C. Maxwell*

AROCHA, SIMÓN DE (1731–1796). Simón de Arocha was the eldest of fifteen children of Francisco and Juana (Curbelo) de Arocha, both Canary Islanders[qv] in Texas. He was born in San Antonio de Béxar seven months after the *isleños* arrived there. In 1752 he married María Ignacia de Urrutia; their union produced eight children. Like his father, who had served as city clerk and public notary, Simón held important administrative posts. He was a judge over distribution of public lands and later an alcalde.[qv] He also served as commander of the provincial militia, in which he was a lieutenant general. In this capacity he escorted the uprooted Adaesaños (*see* LOS ADAES) to the new Trinity River site of Bucareli[qv] in 1774. When Teodoro de Croix[qv] visited Texas in 1778, Arocha prepared a census report of the province for the new commandant general and his historian, Fray Juan Agustín Morfi.[qv]

Simón and his brother Juan obtained title to eight leagues of land north of the site of present Floresville in 1782. With this ranch, called San Rafael de Pataguilla, they and their kinsmen soon became leading cattlemen of the province. Simón was instrumental in forging a roundup agreement with the missions in 1787. Three years later he and other family members virtually controlled the local governing body, the cabildo.[qv] When they attempted to use their influence to obtain another ranch at the junction of the Guadalupe and San Marcos rivers, other stockmen lodged a vigorous protest and were supported by Governor Rafael Martínez Pacheco.[qv] The ensuing feud cost the governor his job. Don Simón died on July 29, 1796; his wife, on April 27, 1812.

During the revolutionary disturbances of the early nineteenth century, in which the Arochas were dedicated insurgents, most of their property was confiscated. With the coming of Mexican independence, however, Arocha's grandson José Ignacio managed to confirm title to the original Arocha grant.

BIBLIOGRAPHY: Bexar Archives, Barker Texas History Center, University of Texas at Austin. Jack Jackson, *Los Mesteños: Spanish Ranching in Texas, 1721–1821* (College Station: Texas A&M University Press, 1986). Nacogdoches Archives, Steen Library, Stephen F. Austin State University; Barker Texas History Center, University of Texas at Austin; Texas State Archives, Austin. Virginia H. Taylor, *The Spanish Archives of the General Land Office of Texas* (Austin: Lone Star, 1955).

Jack Jackson

ARONSFELD, GERSON HENRY (1885–1947). Gerson Henry Aronsfeld, optometrist, writer, and lecturer, was born on May 5, 1885, in Samotschin, Prussia, and immigrated to Newark, New Jersey, with his family in 1891. When he was twelve he moved with his family to Austin, Texas, where he was apprenticed to a local jewelry firm at the age of fourteen. In 1903 he was briefly employed by E. Hertzberg Jewelry in San Antonio. Aronsfeld graduated from Northern Illinois College of Ophthalmology and Otology in 1903. He returned to Texas and was in charge of the optical department of Noble and Roempke in Galveston before beginning medical studies at the University of Texas Medical Branch. After two years he chose to resume optometric practice and organized the Galveston Optical Company with an associate. At this time Texas had no licensing examination for optometrists, but a license from another state was considered prestigious. In 1917 Aronsfeld passed the New Jersey Board of Optometry Examiners requirements for licensing at the head of the candidate class and returned to Galveston and private practice as sole proprietor of the Galveston Optical Company. In 1927 he moved his family and his practice to Houston.

Aronsfeld, who was elected president of the Texas Optometric Association in 1911 and 1919, led the TOA campaign for an optometric statute for Texas. He was appointed to the newly developed Texas State Board of Examiners in Optometry in 1921 and served until 1937. During all but two of those years he was president of the examining board. He was also an intellectual leader in the optometric profession. He began publishing in scientific and technical journals in 1917 and was a regular contributing editor of the *Optical Journal and Review of Optometry* of New York, *The Refractionist* of London, and the *Optische Rundschau* of Berlin. He lectured at the University of California at Berkeley and Ohio State University as well as before optometric societies. He received an honorary doctorate from Northern Illinois College of Optometry in Chicago.

Aronsfeld married Rose Fridner in Galveston on October 25, 1908; they had one daughter. Aronsfeld waged a bitter, unsuccessful battle against the infiltration of the Optometric Extension Program into the Texas Optometric Association. This fight and ill health led to despondency. Aronsfeld died of self-inflicted gunshot wounds in his Houston office on July 24, 1947, and was buried in Galveston. *See also* OPTOMETRY.

BIBLIOGRAPHY: Weston A. Pettey, *Optometry in Texas, 1900–1984* (Austin: Nortex, 1985).

Weston A. Pettey

ARP, TEXAS. Arp is on the Missouri Pacific Railroad and State Highway 135 eighteen miles southeast of Tyler in southeastern Smith County. Kickapoo Creek flows to the south. The area was occupied as early as 1868, when John G. and Eliza Sartain bought six acres from Henry Moore. In 1872 the International–Great Northern Railroad was built, and the community became Jarvis Switch, a stop on the line. Commercial development began in 1897 when truck and fruit farmer J. W. Melton moved there from Troup. He was the first local citizen to ship tomatoes to northern markets. The post office was established in 1898 as Strawberry with Charles P. Orr as postmaster. The following year the town was renamed after William Arp, a popular newspaper editor.

In 1902 the community had a six-month public school, five general stores, one drugstore, one doctor, and Methodist, Baptist, and Presbyterian congregations. The population consisted mostly of small farmers owning ten to 100 acres each, and Arp was a shipping point for fruit and vegetables. Local commercial nurseries specialized in the "Arp Beauty," a peach they had developed. School records for 1903–04 showed both a white and a black school. The Omen post office was transferred to Arp in 1906.

The town continued to grow, and in 1911 Arp Guaranty State Bank opened. In 1912 the town had two businesses, and by 1914 it had 400 inhabitants, a bank, a restaurant, general stores, and a cotton gin and gristmill. Canton Masonic Lodge No. 94 transferred there from Omen in 1923, and an imposing two-story white-brick school dominated the community.

In 1931 Guy V. Lewis drilled the first successful well in the county near Arp. The McMurry Refining Company soon located in Arp, and in 1936 the population peaked at 2,500. That year a white school had twenty-six teachers for grades one through eleven, and a black school had six teachers for one through ten. With the coming of World War II,[qv] the town population declined to approximately 1,000, but seventy businesses remained. By 1952 the Arp Independent School District had been established. During the 1960s the population was still 1,000, and the number of businesses fell to thirty-seven. In 1973 Arp had a population of 816, four churches, and a downtown business district, and Mason Church and Ebenezer Cemetery were in the vicinity. In 1989 there were nineteen businesses and 1,045 citizens. In 1990 the population was 812.

BIBLIOGRAPHY: Edward Clayton Curry, An Administrative Survey of the Schools of Smith County, Texas (M.Ed. thesis, University of Texas, 1938). "School Sights," *Chronicles of Smith County*, Fall 1969. Smith County Historical Society, *Historical Atlas of Smith County* (Tyler, Texas: Tyler Print Shop, 1965). Frank and Carolyn M. Smyrl, *Index to the Chronicles of Smith County, Vols. 1–10* (Tyler, Texas: Smith County Historical Society, 1972). Donald W. Whisenhunt, comp., *Chronological History of Smith County* (Tyler, Texas: Smith County Historical Society, 1983). Albert Woldert, *A History of Tyler and Smith County* (San Antonio: Naylor, 1948).

Vista K. McCroskey

ARPA, JOSÉ (1868–1952). José Arpa y Perea, painter, son of Antonio and María de García Perea Arpa, was born in Carmoria, Spain, on February 19, 1868. He studied in the School of Fine Arts in Seville, where he received special instruction from the historical painter Eduardo Cano de la Peña. While in school he received the Rome Prize three successive times; the award gave him six years of study in

Rome. He was already well known in Europe when the Spanish government sent four of his paintings to the World's Fair at Chicago in 1893. Because of the recognition given his work in Spain and in the United States, the Mexican government invited him to become the director of the Academy of Fine Arts in Mexico City; they sent a man-of-war to Spain to escort the artist to Mexico. Arpa declined the position, but he did stay in Mexico to paint.

Later he traveled to San Antonio, where his painting *A Mexican Funeral*, exhibited at the International Fair, brought him to the attention of Texans. Arpa remained in that city for many years of painting and teaching. His assistant and one of his students was Xavier Gonzales;[qv] he also taught painting to Octavio Medellín[qv] in 1921 and influenced the work of Porfirio Salinas.[qv] Arpa was a brilliant colorist, and his skill in handling sunlight earned him the nickname "Sunshine Man." His style was realistic; his loose, fluid brushwork evoked a sense of atmosphere.

His work was exhibited in the principal galleries of the United States. The San Antonio Museum Association[qv] has ten of his paintings in its collection. Arpa participated in the Texas Wildflower Oil Painting contests held by the San Antonio Art League,[qv] and in 1927 he won the state prize of $1,000 for *Verbena*, which is now owned by the league. In 1952 murals by Arpa were hung in the lobby of the Express Publishing Company of San Antonio. Arpa died in Seville, Spain, in October 1952, at the age of ninety-four.

BIBLIOGRAPHY: Mantle Fielding, *Dictionary of American Painters, Sculptors and Engravers* (New York: Struck, 1945; rev. ed., ed. Glenn B. Opitz, Poughkeepsie: Apollo, 1983). Frances Battaile Fisk, *A History of Texas Artists and Sculptors* (Abilene, Texas, 1928; facsimile rpt., Austin: Morrison, 1986). Ruth Goddard, *Porfirio Salinas* (Austin: Rock House, 1975). Jacinto Quirarte, *Mexican American Artists* (Austin: University of Texas Press, 1973). Cecilia Steinfeldt, The Texas Collection: Regional Art in the San Antonio Museum Association (MS, Barker Texas History Center, University of Texas at Austin). Vertical Files, Barker Texas History Center, University of Texas at Austin.

Caroline Remy

ARREDONDO, JOAQUÍN DE (1768–?). Joaquín de Arredondo, military commandant, son of Nicolás de Arredondo y Palegrí and Josefa Roso de Mioño, was born in Barcelona, Spain, in 1768. His father became a governor of Cuba and a viceroy of Buenos Aires. He entered the Royal Spanish Guards as a cadet in 1787, was commissioned probably by the end of the eighteenth century for service in New Spain, and in 1810 was promoted to colonel and given the command of the infantry regiment of Veracruz. After being made military commandant of the Huasteca and governor of Nuevo Santander in 1811, he was instrumental in suppressing Miguel Hidalgo y Costilla's[qv] revolt and criollo[qv]-related revolts in that province in 1812 and 1813, and was rewarded by being appointed as commandant of the eastern division of the Provincias Internas[qv] in 1813. Reinforced with new troops, he left for San Antonio and on August 18, 1813, defeated the rebels under José Álvarez de Toledo y Dubois[qv] in the battle of Medina.[qv] Arredondo quickly cleared the province of insurgents and appointed Cristóbal Domínguez[qv] ad interim governor of Texas. After completing his assignment in Texas, he returned to Monterrey. He subsequently crushed the filibustering expedition of Francisco Xavier Mina[qv] by overrunning his defenses at the village of Soto la Marina in October 1817. On January 17, 1821, near the end of his tenure as commandant, Arredondo approved the petition of Moses Austin[qv] to bring settlers to Texas. At Monterrey on July 3, 1821, he endorsed the Plan of Iguala and swore allegiance to the new Mexican nation. Shortly after the Mexican War of Independence,[qv] Arredondo surrendered his command and retired to Havana, where he died in 1837.

BIBLIOGRAPHY: Vito Alessio Robles, *Coahuila y Texas en la época colonial* (Mexico City: Editorial Cultura, 1938; 2d ed., Mexico City: Editorial Porrúa, 1978). Hubert Howe Bancroft, *History of the North Mexican States and Texas* (2 vols., San Francisco: History Company, 1886, 1889). Donald E. Chipman, *Spanish Texas, 1519–1821* (Austin: University of Texas Press, 1992). *Enciclopedia de México* (special ed., 14 vols., Mexico City: Secretaría de Educación Pública, 1987–88). David B. Gracy II, *Moses Austin: His Life* (San Antonio: Trinity University Press, 1987). José María Miguel i Vergés, *Diccionario de Insurgentes* (Mexico City: Editorial Porrúa, 1969). Ted Schwarz and Robert H. Thonhoff, *Forgotten Battlefield of the First Texas Revolution: The Battle of Medina* (Austin: Eakin Press, 1985). Henderson K. Yoakum, *History of Texas from Its First Settlement in 1685 to Its Annexation to the United States in 1846* (2 vols., New York: Redfield, 1855).

Robert H. Thonhoff

ARRINGTON, ALFRED W. (1810–1867). Alfred W. Arrington, author and judge, was born in Iredell County, North Carolina, on September 17, 1810. In 1819 he moved to Arkansas, where he was a preacher from 1828 to 1834. He was admitted to the bar in Missouri in 1835, when he returned to Arkansas and was elected to the state legislature; he served until 1845 and moved to Texas. He visited Boston and New York in 1847 and there published *Desperadoes of the South and Southwest* (1849) under the pen name Charles Summerfield. He also contributed "Sketches of the South and Southwest" to various newspapers. After returning to Texas, Arrington was elected judge of the Twelfth (Rio Grande) Judicial District in 1850. He retired in 1856 because of ill health, returned to New York, and, again under a pen name, published *The Rangers and Regulators of the Tanaha, or Life Among the Lawless: A Tale of the Republic of Texas* (1857). He went to Chicago to practice law in 1857 and died there on December 31, 1867, leaving three children. His poems were published posthumously under the title *Poems of Alfred W. Arrington* (1869).

BIBLIOGRAPHY: *Dictionary of American Biography*. Sam Houston Dixon, *The Poets and Poetry of Texas* (Austin: Dixon, 1885). Pat Ireland Nixon, "Judge Alfred W. Arrington, Judge William H. Rhodes, and the Case of Summerfield," *Southwestern Historical Quarterly* 55 (January 1952). Leonidas Warren Payne, *Survey of Texas Literature* (New York: Rand McNally 1928). *Marie Giles*

ARRINGTON, GEORGE WASHINGTON (1844–1923). George Washington (Cap) Arrington, lawman and rancher, was born John C. Orrick, Jr., in Greensboro, Alabama, on December 23, 1844, the son of John and Mariah (Arrington) Orrick. After his father's death in 1848, his mother married William Larkin Williams, who was later killed in the Civil War.[qv] In 1861, at the age of sixteen, he enlisted in the Confederate Army and rode with John S. Mosby's guerrillas, often doing undercover work as a spy. After the war's end, Orrick went to Mexico, but arrived too late to join Emperor Maximilian as a mercenary. After murdering a black businessman at his hometown in June 1867, he made a brief trip to Central America before moving to Texas in 1870. At that time he adopted the name George Washington Arrington to break with his troubled past. He worked for the Houston and Texas Central Railway in Houston and later took a job at a commission house in Galveston. In 1874 he farmed briefly in Collin County; he was subsequently hired to help trail a cattle herd to Brown County.

Arrington was in Brown County in 1875 when he enlisted in Company E of the newly organized Frontier Battalion[qv] of Texas Rangers.[qv] During his first two years of service he distinguished himself in the Rio Grande valley by tracking down fugitives and outlaws. Maj. John B. Jones[qv] recommended his promotion from sergeant to first lieutenant in 1877 because of his successful accomplishment of difficult missions. The following year Arrington was made captain of Company C and stationed at Coleman. In July 1878 he was ordered to Fort Griffin to restore peace in the wake of vigilante activities. In the summer of 1879 his company was moved to the Panhandle[qv] to investigate depredations at area ranches. His opposition to federal

Indian policy soon brought him into sharp conflict with Lt. Col. J. W. Davidson[qv] at Fort Elliott. In September Arrington established Camp Roberts, the first ranger camp in the Panhandle, east of the site of present Crosbyton. From there in January and February 1880 he led his men on a successful forty-day search for the Lost Lakes in eastern New Mexico; the troop also charted the area from Yellow House Canyon to Ranger Lake, in eastern New Mexico, and located watering places and Indian hideouts. In 1880–81 Arrington and his men covered much of the Panhandle and were stationed briefly at both Mobeetie and Tascosa. Because of his rank he received the nickname "Cap."

Arrington resigned from the rangers in the summer of 1882 to take advantage of Panhandle ranching opportunities. After helping area ranchers break up a major rustling ring, he was elected sheriff of Wheeler County and the fourteen counties attached to it. About that time he met Sarah (Sallie) Burnette, who had come to visit her sister Jane (Mrs. Henry L.) Eubank at the Connell-Eubank ranch. They were married at her hometown, Westboro, Missouri, on October 18, 1882. They became the parents of three sons and six daughters; the first son died in infancy. During Arrington's years as sheriff, the family resided at the county jail in Mobeetie. His reputation as the "iron-handed man of the Panhandle" increased with his fatal shooting in November 1886 of John Leverton, who was suspected of cattle rustling. Although murder charges were filed against Arrington by Leverton's widow, he was acquitted on grounds of self-defense.

Arrington served as county sheriff until 1890. During his service he filed on choice ranchland on the Washita River in Hemphill County. After first living in a dugout he erected two cabins as his home and headquarters and in 1885 registered his CAP brand. In 1893 he was appointed manager of the Rocking Chair Ranch[qv] by its British owners. In that position Arrington made considerable improvements by shipping cattle, paying off accounts due, and interviewing prospective buyers. He remained manager until December 1896, when the Continental Land and Cattle Company[qv] bought the Rocking Chair lands.

Arrington resumed management of his own ranch after 1896. As a Mason and Shriner he became involved in the civic affairs of Canadian, where the family lived for seven years in the former home of Cape Willingham[qv] so the older children could attend school. In 1897 Arrington escorted George Isaacs, convicted killer of Hemphill county sheriff Thomas McGee, to the Texas State Penitentiary at Huntsville.[qv] Later the Arringtons built a new house at the ranch and helped establish a rural school in the vicinity. To the end of his life, Cap was cautious about visitors because of enemies he had made as a peace officer and was seldom seen in public without a gun. In his last years he suffered from arthritis and made frequent train trips to Mineral Wells for the hot baths. On one of these trips in 1923 he was stricken with a heart attack. He was taken to his home in Canadian, where he died on March 31. He was buried in the cemetery at Mobeetie. Sallie Arrington remained active in the Canadian WCTU and First Baptist Church, of which she was a charter member, until her death on June 1, 1945. In 1986 the Arrington Ranch, on which oil was later discovered, was owned and operated by the heirs of Cap's younger son, French; Arrington's older son, John, established a ranch near Miami, in Roberts County. Arrington's papers are in the Research Center of the Panhandle-Plains Historical Museum.[qv]

BIBLIOGRAPHY: Millie Jones Porter, *Memory Cups of Panhandle Pioneers* (Clarendon, Texas: Clarendon Press, 1945). Jerry Sinise, *George Washington Arrington* (Burnet, Texas: Eakin Press, 1979). Estelle D. Tinkler, "Nobility's Ranche: A History of the Rocking Chair Ranche," *Panhandle-Plains Historical Review* 15 (1942). *H. Allen Anderson*

ARRINGTON, JOSEPH, JR. (1935–1982). Joseph Arrington [pseud. Joe Tex, Yusef Hazziez], African-American soul singer, son of Joseph Arrington, Sr., and Cherie (Jackson), was born at Rogers, Texas, on August 8, 1935. He moved to Baytown at age five with his mother after her divorce from his father and attended school there. While in Baytown, Arrington performed song and dance routines to enhance his business as a young shoeshine and paper boy. He also sang in the G. W. Carver school choir and the McGowen Temple church choir. During his junior year of high school Arrington entered a talent search at a Houston nightclub. He took first prize over such performers as Johnny Nash, Hubert Laws, and Ben E. King–imitator Acquilla Cartwright. He performed a skit called "It's In the Book" and won $300 and a week's stay at the Hotel Teresa in Harlem. There, Arrington performed at the Apollo Theater. During a four-week period he won the Amateur Night competition four times. After graduating from high school in 1955, he returned to New York City to pursue a music career. While working odd jobs, including caretaking at a Jewish cemetery, he met talent scout Arthur Prysock, who paved the way for him to meet record-company executive Henry Glover and get his first record contract with King Records.

Arrington, now known as Joe Tex, introduced a style of music that has been copied by Isaac Hayes, Barry White, and others. In songs and ballads, in particular, he slowed the tempo slightly and started "rapping," that is, speaking verse that told the story in the middle of the song, before repeating the refrain and ending the song. The biggest hits of Joe Tex included "Hold On To What You Got," "Papa Was Too," "Skinny Legs and All," and "South Country," an album of Country and Western songs; his biggest seller was "I Gotcha," which went platinum (made 1,000,000 sales) in 1971.

In 1972 Arrington gave up show business and began a three-year speaking ministry for the Nation of Islam, which he joined in 1968. He became known as Yusef Hazziez or Minister Joseph X. Arrington. He said he was through with singing, and he would follow Allah and the Honorable Elijah Muhammad. But after Muhammad's death in 1975, and with the approval and blessing of the Nation of Islam, Arrington returned to show business in order to deliver the Nation of Islam's message to his fans. He enjoyed moderate success, with no hit singles, until the 1977 smash hit "I Ain't Gonna Bump No More (With No Big Fat Woman)" put him back on the top of the charts. After that single, he left the music scene and performed at local clubs and benefits. Arrington died on August 12, 1982, of heart failure at his home in Navasota. He was survived by his wife Belilah and six children.

BIBLIOGRAPHY: H. Wiley Hitchcock and Stanley Sadie, eds., *The New Grove Dictionary of American Music* (4 vols., New York: Macmillan, 1986). Vertical Files, Barker Texas History Center, University of Texas at Austin. "Westward," Dallas *Times Herald*, December 13, 1981.
Kirven Tillis

ARRINGTON, WILLIAM W. (?–?). William W. Arrington, early settler and political leader during the Texas Revolution,[qv] arrived in Texas on February 15, 1831, when he settled as a bachelor in Green DeWitt's[qv] colony. He was one of the "Immortal Eighteen" citizens of Gonzales who, in the battle of Gonzales,[qv] refused Gen. Martín Perfecto de Cos's[qv] demand that the Anglo colonists surrender their diminutive piece of artillery and defied his soldiers to "Come and Take It!" Arrington was elected to represent Gonzales in the Consultation of 1835[qv] and on November 7 signed the declaration of war against Gen. Antonio López de Santa Anna[qv] and the Centralist Mexican government. That same day Arrington was appointed one of twelve members of a committee to draw up plans for a provisional government[qv] for Texas. In 1839 he was appointed associate land commissioner of Washington County. Soon thereafter he moved to Grimes County, where, on August 7, 1848, he was elected a county commissioner. The census of 1850 listed him as a Grimes County farmer and stockman.

BIBLIOGRAPHY: *Compiled Index to Elected and Appointed Officials of the Republic of Texas, 1835–1846* (Austin: State Archives, Texas State Library, 1981). John H. Jenkins, ed., *The Papers of the Texas Revolution, 1835–1836* (10 vols., Austin: Presidial Press, 1973). Texas House of Representatives, *Biographical Directory of the Texan Conventions and Congresses, 1832–1845* (Austin: Book Exchange, 1941). Gifford E. White, *1830 Citizens of Texas* (Austin: Eakin, 1983).

Thomas W. Cutrer

ARROWOOD, CHARLES FLINN (1887–1951). Charles Flinn Arrowood, professor and author, son of Robert Sylvanus and Mary Louise (Dickson) Arrowood, was born in Cabarrus County, North Carolina, on November 9, 1887. He received a B.A. degree from Davidson College, North Carolina, in 1909, a B.D. degree from Union Theological Seminary, Virginia, in 1915, a second B.A. degree and an M.A. degree from Rice Institute (now Rice University) in 1918 and 1921, and a Ph.D with honors from the University of Chicago in 1924. Arrowood taught high school at Hemp, North Carolina, in 1909 and was principal of St. Paul's School in North Carolina from 1911 to 1912. He was ordained a Presbyterian minister in 1915 and served until 1920 as pastor of churches in El Campo, Wharton, Pierce, and Houston, Texas.

From 1920 to 1923 he was professor of philosophy and psychology at Southwestern Presbyterian University in Tennessee. He served as assistant professor in philosophy at the University of Chicago in 1923–24. From 1924 to 1928 he worked as an instructor and then assistant professor at Rice Institute. In 1928 he became professor of the history and philosophy of education at the University of Texas. He was a frequent guest professor at several American universities and was appointed by the United States Department of State as a delegate to the Fourth International Conference on Education at Geneva, Switzerland, in 1935. In 1936 he served as chairman of the National Society of College Teachers of Education. Arrowood wrote numerous articles on education, as well as *Thomas Jefferson and Education in a Republic* (1930) and *Theory of Education in the Political Philosophy of Adam Smith* (1945). He coauthored two prominent textbooks with Frederick Eby[qv]—*Development of Modern Education* (1934) and *The History and Philosophy of Education, Ancient and Medieval* (1940). He also edited and translated George Buchanan's *The Powers of the Crown in Scotland* (1949).

Arrowood was a member of the National Society of College Teachers of Education, the Texas State Teachers Association,[qv] the Texas State Historical Association,[qv] Phi Beta Kappa, Phi Delta Kappa, Phi Kappa Sigma, and the National Education Association. He received an honorary D.Litt. degree from Davidson College in 1941. He was a Mason and Democrat. He married Flora Kathleen Register on September 2, 1914. He died in Austin on February 6, 1951, and was buried in Clinton, North Carolina.

BIBLIOGRAPHY: *Daily Texan*, February 7, 1951. *National Cyclopaedia of American Biography*, Vol. 40. Vertical Files, Barker Texas History Center, University of Texas at Austin. *Who's Who in America*, 1946–47.

ARROYO DE LOS ANGELES. Arroyo de los Angeles rises six miles northeast of Oilton in southeastern Webb County (at 27°30′ N, 98°53′ W) and runs southeast for eleven miles to its mouth on Mesquite Creek, six miles northwest of Hebbronville in northern Jim Hogg County (at 27°24′ N, 98°44′ W). The stream was named for Las Cabercas de los Angeles, José Cuellar's original Spanish land grant, which included the area where the stream originates. The stream traverses flat to gently rolling terrain with local depressions, surfaced by shallow clay loams that support grasses and scrub brush.

ARROYO BALLUCO. Arroyo Balluco, a canyon with an intermittent stream in its upper reaches, begins 2½ miles northeast of the Mile High Golf Course and ten miles north of Sierra Blanca in central Hudspeth County (at 31°18′ N, 105°23′ W) and runs southwest for twenty-seven miles to its mouth on the Rio Grande, four miles southeast of Esperanza (at 31°07′ N, 105°40′ W). It runs through steep to gently sloping terrain surfaced by stony clay loams and sandy loams that support scrub brush, grasses, juniper, oak, chaparral, and cacti.

ARROYO BALUARTE. Arroyo Baluarte, also known as Baluarte Creek and San Antonio Creek, rises eight miles southwest of Thompsonville in north central Jim Hogg County (at 27°12′ N, 98°49′ W) and runs southeast for forty-one miles to its mouth on Laguna Salada, four miles south of Falfurrias in northeastern Brooks County (at 27°10′ N, 98°07′ W). In its lower reaches it is dammed to form Laguna Madre, not to be confused with the coastal lagoon of that name. The Arroyo Baluarte traverses flat to gently sloping terrain surfaced by shallow clay and sandy loams and loose sand that support scattered scrub brush and grasses. It is named after a land grant, San Antonio de Baluarte, originally granted to José Luis Salinas.

ARROYO BLANCO. Arroyo Blanco begins four miles southeast of Farm Road 3169 in west central Zapata County (at 27°06′ N, 99°13′ W) and runs southwest for three miles to its mouth on Cavasara Creek, three miles southeast of FM 3169 and nine miles northeast of Ramireño in west Zapata County (at 27°05′ N, 99°16′ W). The arroyo extends through low-rolling hills and prairies surfaced by sandy loams and clay loams that support scrub brush, grasses, and chaparral. The stream is dammed at its middle course.

A second Arroyo Blanco rises five miles southeast of Farm Road 3169 in central Zapata County (at 27°06′ N, 99°12′ W) and runs southeast for eight miles to its mouth on Salomoneño Creek, a mile northeast of State Highway 16 and two miles southwest of Bustamante (at 26°59′ N, 99°09′ W). The area's low-rolling hills and prairies are surfaced by sandy and clay loams that support water-tolerant hardwoods, mesquite, grasses, and chaparral.

ARROYO BURRO. Arroyo Burro rises five miles northeast of Ramireño in western Zapata County (at 27°03′ N, 99°16′ W) and runs southwest for eight miles to its mouth on the Rio Grande, a mile east of Ramireño (at 27°00′ N, 99°22′ W). It crosses low-rolling to flat terrain with locally active dune blowout areas, surfaced by sand and shallow to deep sandy and clay loams in which grow scrub brush, grasses, scattered oak mottes, mesquite, and chaparral.

ARROYO CALERO. Arroyo Calero begins a quarter mile north of Interstate Highway 10 and two miles south of the Malone Mountains in southwestern Hudspeth County (at 31°12′ N, 105°35′ W) and runs southwest for seven miles to its mouth on Fort Quitman Lake, four miles southeast of Esperanza and one mile north of the Rio Grande (at 31°08′ N, 105°39′ W). It traverses steeply to gently sloping terrain surfaced by variable soils that support scrub brush and sparse grasses. *Calero*, Spanish for "calcareous," presumably refers to the limestone found in the area.

ARROYO CITY, TEXAS. Arroyo City, also known as Arroyo, is located on Farm Road 2925 a mile east of Farm Road 1847 and ten miles northeast of Rio Hondo in northeastern Cameron County. The area was settled by Mexican herders in the early 1860s and named for its location on the Arroyo Colorado. In 1904 the community had a school with one teacher and twenty-four students. A post office operated in Arroyo City from 1887 to 1907. In 1910 the settlement had two stores and a population estimated at ten. During the 1930s a few scattered houses remained in the area. In 1970 the community had various dwellings and businesses, and in 1990 Arroyo City was still marked on state highway maps.

Alicia A. Garza

ARROYO CLAREÑO. Arroyo Clareño rises a mile northwest of U.S. Highway 83 in southwest Zapata County (at 26°50′ N, 99°09′ W) and runs north and then southwest for a total of five miles to its mouth on the International Falcon Reservoir, nine miles southeast of Zapata (at 26°48′ N, 99°12′ W). The stream traverses low-rolling to flat terrain with local dunes. Much of the land surface is shallow to deep sandy and clay loams and sand that support scrub brush, grasses, and scattered oak mottes.

ARROYO COLORADO. The Arroyo Colorado, a stream in the Rio Grande delta, originates at Lake Llano Grande in Hidalgo County (at 26°08′ N, 97°56′ W) and flows northeast for fifty-two miles through Cameron and southeastern Willacy counties to its mouth opposite Padre Island on Laguna Madre (at 26°25′ N, 97°22′ W). It is navigable to barges through parts of its dredged channel from the Gulf Intracoastal Waterway[qv] to the port of Harlingen. From that point to near its headwaters it is navigable only to small boats. The arroyo is a former outlet of the Rio Grande and in time of flood still carries excess water from the Rio Grande to Laguna Madre. Its upper drainage area includes rich farm and citrus land and the cities of Harlingen and Rio Hondo. The lower arroyo course runs through an area of farms, ranches, and coastal playas. Typical bankside vegetation consists of reeds overhung by huisache, mesquite, and Texas ebony. The final reaches of Arroyo Colorado pass through Laguna Atascosa National Wildlife Refuge,[qv] where its banks and adjoining thorn forests and marshes shelter ocelots, jaguarundis, indigo snakes, and other rare and endangered animals. The estuary protects roseate spoonbills, brown pelicans, and many other bird species. The first skirmish of the Mexican War[qv] occurred at the Paso Real crossing on the banks of the Arroyo Colorado, on March 20, 1846.

BIBLIOGRAPHY: Raymond J. Fleetwood, *Plants of Laguna Atascosa National Wildlife Refuge* (Albuquerque: U.S. Fish and Wildlife Service, 1973). Florence J. Scott, *Old Rough and Ready on the Rio Grande* (San Antonio: Naylor, 1935). *William MacWhorter*

ARROYO DIABLO. Arroyo Diablo, a canyon through which an intermittent stream runs, begins seven miles northwest of Small in southwestern Hudspeth County (at 31°22′ N, 105°36′ W) and runs southwest for twenty-five miles to its mouth on the Rio Grande, two miles southwest of McNary (at 31°14′ N, 105°49′ W). The stream has been dammed to form Diablo Reservoirs 1 and 2 for irrigation. It crosses flat to rolling terrain surfaced by sand and some clay loams that support scattered oak mottes, scrub brush, cacti, and grasses.

ARROYO LEÓN. Arroyo León, an intermittent stream, rises at U.S. Highway 83 four miles southeast of Zapata in southwest Zapata County (at 26°51′ N, 99°13′ W) and runs south for two miles to its mouth on the International Falcon Reservoir, six miles southeast of Zapata (at 26°50′ N, 99°13′ W). The surrounding low-rolling to flat terrain is surfaced by sandy and clay loams that support scrub brush, grasses, and cacti.

ARROYO MIGUEL. Arroyo Miguel rises twelve miles southeast of Zapata in south central Zapata County (at 26°52′ N, 99°05′ W) and runs southwest for ten miles to its mouth on the International Falcon Reservoir, a half mile east of U.S. Highway 83 (at 26°44 N, 99°06 W). It crosses low-rolling to flat terrain surfaced by shallow to deep sandy and clay loams that support scrub brush, grasses, and cacti.

ARROYO LOS MORENOS. Arroyo los Morenos begins four miles above Roma–Los Saenz in Starr County (at 26°29′ N, 99°01′ W) and runs southeast for five miles before it runs dry a mile northeast of Escobares (at 26°24′ N, 98°57′ W). The name is Spanish for "Gully of the Swarthy Ones." The upper stream crosses flat to rolling terrain with steep margins, surfaced by clay and sandy loams that support pecan, willow, and grasses. Downstream, water-tolerant hardwoods, conifers, and grasses predominate. *Dick D. Heller, Jr.*

ARROYO NEGRO. Arroyo Negro rises near Farm Road 1867 two miles northwest of Loma Vista in southeast Zavala County (at 28°47′ N, 99°37′ W) and runs southeast twenty-four miles to its mouth on the Nueces River, five miles southwest of Big Wells in northeast Dimmit County (at 28°30′ N, 99°35′ W). According to local tradition the last Indian fight in Zavala County took place on Arroyo Negro. The streambed begins in an area of variable terrain surfaced by muddy sand and alluvial material. Scrub brush, cacti, and grasses grow there. Downstream, the land is flat with locally shallow depressions and a clay surface that supports water-tolerant hardwoods, conifers, and grasses.

BIBLIOGRAPHY: Zavala County Historical Commission, *Now and Then in Zavala County* (Crystal City, Texas, 1985).

ARROYO PALO ALTO. Arroyo Palo Alto rises a mile southeast of Victoria in central Victoria County (at 28°47′ N, 96°55′ W) and runs southeast for ten miles to its mouth on Placedo Creek (at 28°44′ N, 96°46′ W). The flat to rolling prairie of the area is surfaced by clay loam that supports mesquite and various grasses.

ARROYO PRIMERO. Arroyo Primero rises in southeastern Presidio County one mile east of Panther Spring (at 29°23′ N, 103°56′ W) and runs six miles southeast to its mouth on Fresno Creek, two miles southwest of Chimney Rock (at 29°22′ N, 103°51′ W). The surrounding desert mountain terrain of volcanic rock is surfaced by sands, clay loam, and rough stone. Sparse grasses, cacti, and desert shrubs grow there.

ARROYO QUEMADO. Arroyo Quemado (Arroyo del Quemada) rises five miles east of Falcon Heights in western Starr County (at 26°34′ N, 99°01′ W) and runs five miles southwest to its mouth on Arroyo La Minita (Casas Blancas Creek) (at 26°31′ N, 99°04′ W). The name means "scorched gully." The creek crosses flat to rolling terrain with steep margins surfaced by sandy loams that support pecan, willow, and grasses. *Dick D. Heller, Jr.*

ARROYO QUIOTE. Arroyo Quiote rises six miles north of Rosita in south central Starr County (at 26°31′ N, 98°56′ W) and runs south for eleven miles to its mouth on the Rio Grande, two miles southeast of Rosita (at 26°22′ N, 98°54′ W). The name is believed to be a misspelling of Quijote. The quixotic stream traverses flat terrain, subject to flooding, surfaced by sand, gravel, and mud that support water-tolerant hardwoods, conifers, and grasses. *Dick D. Heller, Jr.*

ARROYO SALADO. Arroyo Salado, also known as Salado Creek, rises eight miles southeast of Nuestra Señora de los Dolores Hacienda[qv] in northwest Zapata County (at 27°11′ N, 99°18′ W) and runs southwest for ten miles to its mouth on the Rio Grande, six miles north of San Ygnacio (at 27°08′ N, 99°26′ W). The stream is dammed at two points near its origin. It traverses flat terrain with local shallow depressions and prairies, surfaced by clay and sandy loams that support water-tolerant hardwoods, mesquite, grasses, and chaparral.

ARROYO SEGUNDA. Arroyo Segunda rises just north of Panther Mountain in southeastern Presidio County (at 29°24′ N, 103°58′ W) and runs east for seven miles to its mouth on Fresno Creek, at the eastern edge of Rincon Mountain (at 29°24′ N, 103°52′ W). The surrounding desert mountain terrain of volcanic rocks is surfaced by sands, clay loam, and rough stone in which sparse grasses, cacti, and desert shrubs grow.

ARROYO DEL TIGRE CHIQUITA. Arroyo del Tigre Chiquita ("Brook of the Small Tiger") rises in southeastern Zapata County half a mile east of the Starr county line (at 26°38′ N, 99°03′ W) and runs northwest for six miles to its mouth on the International Falcon Reservoir, immediately east of U.S. Highway 83 and one mile southeast of Lopeño (at 26°42′ N, 99°06′ W). It crosses low-rolling to flat terrain surfaced by shallow to deep sandy and clay loams in which grow scrub brush, grasses, and cacti.

ARROYO DEL TIGRE GRANDE. Arroyo del Tigre Grande rises two miles west of the Starr county line in southeastern Zapata County (at 26°45′ N, 99°03′ W) and runs west for four miles to its mouth on the International Falcon Reservoir, a mile east of U.S. Highway 83 (at 26°45′ N, 99°07′ W). It crosses low-rolling to flat terrain with shallow to deep sandy and clay loams and loose sand that support scrub brush, grasses, and cacti.

ARROYO VELEÑO. Arroyo Veleño (Valeño) rises at Arroyo Salado four miles southeast of Bustamante in central Zapata County (at 26°59′ N, 99°09′ W) and runs southwest for four miles to its mouth on International Falcon Reservoir, two miles southeast of State Highway 16 (at 26°56′ N, 99°12′ W). The stream crosses low-rolling to flat terrain with shallow to deep sandy and clay loams in which grow scrub brush, grasses, and cacti.

ARROYO VENADO. Arroyo Venado ("Deer Creek") is a rugged canyon cut by an intermittent stream in the Sierra del Caballo Muerto of the eastern reaches of Big Bend National Park[qv] in southeastern Brewster County. From the head of the arroyo (at 29°22′ N, 102°57′ W) the streambed runs south-southeast for seven miles to its mouth (at 29°17′ N, 102°54′ W) on the Rio Grande in Boquillas Canyon, eleven miles below the entrance to that canyon. In places the walls of the canyon reach a height of 500 to 600 feet above the streambed, before the arroyo opens out in a broad mouth upon the green-clad bottom of Boquillas Canyon several hundred yards from the Rio Grande. For most of its length Arroyo Venado, like the rugged desert mountains surrounding it, is covered with sparse arid vegetation characterized by Chihuahuan Desert scrub, including various semisucculents such as lechuguilla and yucca and shrubs such as creosote bush and ocotillo. Desert willow and other desert riparian species grow in sheltered spots along the arroyo, and the streambed crosses a narrow belt of denser riparian vegetation at its juncture with the Rio Grande. Mule deer are native to the region. The only established route of access to Arroyo Venado is an arduous backpacking trail called the Marufo Vega, which leaves the paved park road near the mouth of Boquillas Canyon and follows a winding route over the Sierra del Caballo Muerto to its terminus near the mouth of the arroyo.

BIBLIOGRAPHY: A. Michael Powell, "Vegetation of Trans-Pecos Texas," in *New Mexico Geological Society Guidebook* (Socorro, New Mexico: New Mexico Geological Society, 1980). David J. Schmidly, *The Mammals of Trans-Pecos Texas* (College Station: Texas A&M University Press, 1977).

ART, TEXAS. Art is on State Highway 29 seven miles east of Mason in eastern Mason County. One of the first settlements in the county, it began around 1856 when five German families settled along upper Willow Creek. Later, German settlers from Fredericksburg established themselves on either side of the creek for about ten miles in both directions. The early community, originally called Willow Creek (or Upper Willow Creek) Settlement, suffered from numerous Indian raids, although nearby Fort Mason offered some protection. Provisions were scarce, and many were forced to get supplies from Fredericksburg.

Most of the early settlers were Methodists. The first church, a log building that doubled as a schoolhouse, was built on the east side of Willow Creek in 1858. It was part of a group of churches, known as the Llano Charge, served by the pioneer missionary Rev. Charles A. Grote. This building was replaced by a stone structure in 1875, and a third church was built in 1890 by the Methodist Episcopal Church, South. The first schools were conducted at home or at a neighbor's house. Eventually, early teachers traveled from community to community. Otto von Donop was probably Willow Creek Settlement's first permanent teacher. The log church was used as the schoolhouse until 1890, when the new church was built. Classes were then held in the old stone church until 1945, when all rural schools in the county were consolidated with the Mason schools.

J. A. Hoerster opened a general merchandise store, one of the town's first, in 1883. Otto Plehwe bought him out in 1885, established a post office in the store in 1886, and became the first postmaster. At that time Plehwe renamed the town Plehweville, but the post office department eventually asked that the name be changed, as the difficulty of spelling it was causing mail to be lost. On December 23, 1920, Eli Dechart, who was then store owner and postmaster, named the town Art after the last three letters of his name.

Throughout most of its history, Art has been primarily a ranching community. As of 1947 the town had a combination general store and post office, a feed store, and a filling station. The population remained steady at twenty-five from 1925 to 1967 and rose to forty-six in 1968. From 1974 until the 1980s the *Texas Almanac*[qv] listed the population as thirty. The post office still existed in 1985, and the store–post office building was being used by the Art Community Club. In 1990 the population was eighteen.

BIBLIOGRAPHY: Kathryn Burford Eilers, A History of Mason County, Texas (M.A. thesis, University of Texas, 1939). *Mason County News*, Centennial Edition, June 19, 1958. Stella Gipson Polk, *Mason and Mason County: A History* (Austin: Pemberton Press, 1966; rev. ed., Burnet, Texas: Eakin Press, 1980). *Alice J. Rhoades*

ARTESIAN BELT RAILROAD. The Artesian Belt Railroad, named for the area of Texas it traversed, was chartered on November 17, 1908, in the interest of Charles F. Simmons to develop his landholdings. The road was projected to run between Macdona, a station on the Galveston, Harrisburg and San Antonio Railway in Bexar County, to Simmons City in Live Oak County, a distance of seventy miles. The railroad had a capital stock of $70,000. The principal place of business was San Antonio. The members of the first board of directors were A. M. Bates, of Excelsior Springs, Missouri; E. P. Simmons, Robert Clarke, C. N. Feamster, J. O. Terrell,[qv] and D. O. Terrell, all of San Antonio; and Jourdan Campbell, of Campbellton, Texas. On September 1, 1909, the Artesian Belt opened a forty-two-mile line between Macdona and Christine. The company crossed the International–Great Northern track at Kirk and operated over that line between Kirk and San Antonio. In 1916 it owned three locomotives and five cars and reported total passenger earnings of $7,000 and freight earnings of $22,000. The Artesian Belt entered receivership for the second time on April 25, 1917, and the property was acquired by the San Antonio Southern Railway Company in 1920.

Nancy Beck Young

ARTESIAN CREEK. Artesian Creek rises a mile southeast of the Lake Pasture oilfield in eastern Refugio County (at 28°24′ N, 97°01′ W) and runs southeast eleven miles to its mouth on Willow Creek (at 28°19′ N, 96°56′ W). Artesian Creek is intermittent in its upper reaches. The surrounding variable terrain is surfaced by muddy sand that supports mixed hardwoods and pines, as well as numerous prairie grasses.

ARTESIAN WELLS. Artesian wells tap the confined groundwater trapped below impermeable strata beneath the surface of the earth. Natural pressure forces the water to rise, sometimes above the surface of the earth (*see* UNDERGROUND WATER). Although extensive drilling for artesian wells did not begin until the 1880s, in 1857 and 1858 John Pope[qv] experimented with artesian wells on the plains of West Texas, and in 1858 a bill introduced by Forbes Britton[qv] became a law authorizing the drilling of public artesian wells on the road between San Antonio and Laredo. These early experiments were typical of the many mistakes made, through lack of knowledge, in an effort to secure water in the arid portion of the state. The artesian-well area is largely confined to the Coastal Plain[qv] east of the Balcones Escarpment,[qv] although there have been other isolated artesian areas, most notable of which were located at El Paso, Fort Stockton, and Balmorhea. By 1897 there were 458 flowing and 506 nonflowing wells in the Black and Grand Prairie regions, somewhat fewer on the Coastal Plain,[qv] and none on the High Plains.

Around the turn of the century there were six artesian districts in Texas: Coastal Prairie system, Hallettsville system, Carrizo system, Black and Grand prairies system, Trans-Pecos Basin system, and Stevens County and Jack County systems. At that time the city of Galveston received its water from approximately thirty-three artesian wells, and Houston had about 100. In 1905 the area comprising most of South Texas from twenty miles south of Corpus Christi to the Rio Grande valley was referred to as the Artesian Belt. Farmers were just beginning to realize the agricultural potential of South Texas and relied on irrigation[qv] from artesian wells to provide water to crops. In a 1905 edition of *Farm and Ranch*[qv] magazine one article stated that 200 wells were in operation, ranging in depths from 600 to 800 feet and averaging flows from 200 to 600 gallons per minute. Wells were also touted in promotional brochures, such as the ad for the town of Sarita, Texas, which estimated that an artesian well would irrigate 100 to 200 acres. Costs for digging those wells ranged from $1,000 to $1,500.

Water from artesian wells was included in the general irrigation act of 1913 (*see* WATER LAW), and in May 1931 the legislature passed a law to prevent the waste of artesian water, which had become an important source of water supply for numerous cities and irrigation projects. Throughout the later part of the twentieth century more cities looked to other options for municipal water such as the use of surface reservoirs. Though the use of wells remained the property of the individual owner, increased government regulation such as the issuing of permits and possibilities of restrictions became the focus of debate. According to Texas law a person can drill an artesian well for domestic or stock purposes, but the well should be properly cased. Records of depth, thickness, and the types of strata penetrated should be kept. Reports of new artesian wells are made to the Texas Water Commission.[qv] Those using wells for other than domestic needs must submit an annual report regarding the well level, quantities used, and methods of use.

BIBLIOGRAPHY: Wm Doherty, "Irrigation, The Great Problem," *Farm and Ranch*, April 15, 1905. Robert Thomas Hill, *Geography and Geology of the Black and Grand Prairies* (Washington: GPO, 1901). Robert Thomas Hill, *On the Occurrence of Artesian and Other Underground Waters in Texas, Eastern New Mexico, and Indian Territory, West of the Ninety-Seventh Meridian* (Washington, 1892). George Getz Shumard, *Artesian Water on the Llano Estacado* (Austin: H. Hutchings, 1892). *West's Texas Statutes and Codes*, Vol. 4 (St. Paul, Minnesota: West, 1984). *Seymour V. Connor*

ARTESIA WELLS, TEXAS. Artesia Wells is on Interstate Highway 35 eleven miles south of Cotulla in western La Salle County. It takes its name from the artesian wells that once provided water for the residents of the area. The town, originally a water stop called Bart on the International–Great Northern Railroad, was one of several new settlements in the Winter Garden region when irrigation opened new land to farming in the early 1900s. A legal plat for Artesia Wells was filed in 1907. Farmers moved into the area, and the town grew slowly over the next thirty years. In 1909 a post office opened, and by 1915 the town also had a general store and a restaurant. By 1925 Artesia Wells had a school and by 1929 an estimated population of 100. In 1936 only fifty people lived there. In 1939 Artesia Wells had four businesses and a population of 125. After the end of World War II[qv] the settlement began a decline. In 1950 it reported two businesses and fifty residents. When I-35 was constructed through the town, many of the buildings were torn down or moved back to make room for the highway. By the early 1970s Artesia Wells had lost its school and had only thirty residents and one small store. In 1988 the town reported four businesses. In 1990 the population was thirty.

BIBLIOGRAPHY: Annette Martin Ludeman, *La Salle: La Salle County* (Quanah, Texas: Nortex, 1975). *John Leffler*

ARTHUR. In the Union blockade of Texas seaports during the Civil War[qv] the USS *Arthur* captured five Confederate vessels and was one of three federal boats to attack Corpus Christi in August 1862. The bark was built in Amesburg, Massachusetts, in 1855 and commissioned on December 11, 1861, with acting volunteer lieutenant J. W. Kittredge in command. The *Arthur* set sail from New York in January 1862, joined the Gulf blockading squadron off the Texas coast, and cruised between Aransas Pass and Cavallo Pass until August of that year. On August 18 the *Arthur* joined the *Sachem*[qv] and the *Corypheus* in an attack on Corpus Christi in which three Confederate vessels were burned. On September 14, 1862, while exploring the Laguna Madre at Flour Bluff, Lieutenant Kittredge and seven men were captured by the Confederates. Between October 1863 and August 1865 the *Arthur* served as a guard ship at Pensacola, Florida. It was sold at New York on September 27, 1865.

BIBLIOGRAPHY: *Dictionary of American Naval Fighting Ships*, 1959. *Martin Donell Kohout*

ARTHUR CITY, TEXAS. Arthur City is on the Red River at the intersection of Farm Road 197 and U.S. Highway 271 in extreme north central Lamar County. The town was founded by Capt. J. G. C. Arthur in 1886 as a stop on the St. Louis–San Francisco Railway. Arthur donated the land for the railroad right-of-way and had it platted into twelve blocks. The post office was established that same year. By 1890 Arthur City had 300 residents, three general stores, a Western Union telegraph office, a blacksmith shop, a furniture maker, and an undertaker. J. H. Arthur was postmaster. In 1892 a new hotel, a doctor's office, and a sawmill were established. A common school had been organized by 1896, when it enrolled twenty-five pupils and employed one teacher. The most prosperous years for the town were the early railroad days, when lumber resources were untapped and prices for farm produce were high. By 1904, however, the local timber supply was becoming exhausted, and many residents began to leave the vicinity in search of other jobs, particularly in cities such as nearby Dallas. In 1914 most commercial enterprises in Arthur City had closed, leaving the telegraph office, a grocery, a telephone exchange, and two general stores. Residents numbered 150. Throughout the 1920s and 1930s, the town had five businesses and 200 residents. By 1943 it had a population of 100 and three businesses. The school had closed by 1957, and local students attended school in the Chicota Independent School District. In 1959 the population was sixty. The growth of nearby Paris, the mechanization of farming, and the development of nearby Pat Mayse Lake led to an economic turnaround in the 1960s and 1970s. In 1961 the town had eleven commercial enterprises and a population of 300. By 1970 the population had stabilized between 200 and 250. Children attended the North Lamar schools. In 1983 Arthur City had eight businesses, two churches, a post office, and a community center. In 1989 it had five businesses and 200 residents, most of whom were part-time farmers and worked in nearby Paris.

BIBLIOGRAPHY: Fred I. Massengill, *Texas Towns: Origin of Name and Location of Each of the 2,148 Post Offices in Texas* (Terrell, Texas, 1936). A. W. Neville, *The History of Lamar County, Texas* (Paris, Texas: North Texas, 1937; rpt. 1986). *Vista K. McCroskey*

ARTHUR CREEK. Arthur Creek rises a mile west of the Brewster county line in northeastern Presidio County (at 30°17′ N, 103°50′ W) and runs southwest for twenty miles to its mouth on Alamito Creek, a mile south of San Esteban Dam (at 30°07′ N, 104°02′ W). Its course crosses desert mountain terrain, canyonland of volcanic rock, alluvial sands and gravel, and rough stony ground where scrub brush, sparse grasses, and desert shrubs grow.

ARTILLERO CREEK. Artillero Creek rises twenty-one miles northeast of Laredo in western Webb County (at 27°47′ N, 99°46′ W) and runs south for two miles to its mouth on the Rio Grande, twenty miles northeast of Laredo (at 27°43′ N, 99°46′ W). It traverses an area of rolling hills and flat terrain with locally shallow depressions, surfaced by clays that support scrub brush, mesquite, cacti, grasses, and water-tolerant hardwoods.

ART MUSEUM OF SOUTH TEXAS. The Art Museum of South Texas, located in Corpus Christi, offers a variety of exhibitions and programs. The museum originated in 1944, when an enthusiastic public response to an art sale prompted the Corpus Christi *Caller-Times*[qv] Publishing Company, the Corpus Christi Art Guild, and the South Texas Art League to establish the Centennial Art Museum. From 1944 to 1972 the museum was located in South Bluff Park, in a small building constructed in 1936 to commemorate the Texas Centennial.[qv]

During the 1960s the museum grew rapidly. In 1960 it hired its first professional director, Cathleen Gallander, and formed a support organization, the Art Auxiliary. The following year the museum was chartered by the state of Texas as a tax-exempt, nonprofit, educational organization that was legally identified as the Corpus Christi Art Foundation, Incorporated. The Junior League of Corpus Christi began offering docent tours for schoolchildren, and the museum's educational program subsequently expanded to include films, lectures, and workshops. Concerned that the original facility would limit the museum's growth, museum supporters, led by Edwin and Patsy Singer, conducted a 1967 fund drive that raised a million dollars for a new facility. During the fund-raising campaign the museum was renamed Art Museum of South Texas in order to emphasize its service to the entire region.

New York architects Philip Johnson and John Burgee designed a striking museum building of white cast concrete accentuated with bronze-tinted windows that flood its galleries with natural light and offer spectacular views of the Corpus Christi Bay. The 30,000 square-foot building includes four galleries, an auditorium, a gift shop, a library, classrooms, administrative areas, and two outdoor sculpture courts. After its completion the $1.3 million facility was deeded to the city of Corpus Christi, which assumed all maintenance and security costs. The new museum opened to the public in October 1972 with the exhibition Johns, Stella, Warhol: Works in Series.

In the new building the museum personnel placed an emphasis on exhibitions and educational activities rather than acquisitions. Thus available funds have supported an ambitious exhibition program that presents art from a variety of periods and locales. In an effort to serve the interests of its constituency, which is over 50 percent Hispanic, the museum organized Spain and New Spain: Mexican Colonial Arts in Their European Context (1978) and featured major traveling exhibitions on Fernando Botero (1980), José Luis Cuevas (1984), and Mexican Colonial painting from the Davenport Museum of Art (1992). The museum also presented a series of group exhibitions of contemporary artists, including American Painting of the 1970s (1979), which was curated by leading art critic Barbara Rose; Numerals 1924–1977 (1979), which examined the use of mathematical systems, numbers, and serial progressions in the work of such artists as Carl Andre, Eva Hesse, and Robert Smithson; and Variants: Drawings by Contemporary Sculptors (1981), which included the work of Laurie Anderson, Joseph Beuys, Judy Pfaff, and James Surls.

The museum staff supplements exhibitions with lectures, gallery talks, readings, films, and music and dance performances. Docent tours serving students in the Corpus Christi public schools form the core of the museum's educational program. The museum offers tours by appointment to other groups, and a Mobile Art program consisting of slide lectures, mini-exhibitions, and hands-on projects serves in peripheral school districts, hospitals, and other sites. Classes in painting, printmaking, drawing, and other media are offered to children in the summer, and special classes that complement various exhibitions are offered to adults throughout the year.

Despite its emphasis on exhibition and education, the museum has gradually acquired a small permanent collection of 400 objects. Included in it are a substantial number of works on paper by contemporary such artists as Sol LeWitt, Ed Ruscha, Robert Motherwell, and Andy Warhol. In addition, the museum owns collections of pre-Columbian artifacts, silk carpets from the Near East, School of Paris paintings, American Regionalist paintings and prints, Color Field paintings, and contemporary sculpture. Such leading Texas artists as Terry Allen, Vernon Fisher, Roy Fridge, James Surls, and Michael Tracy are represented in the museum's collection. Items from the permanent collection are exhibited periodically throughout the year, with curators selecting groups of objects to complement the themes of traveling exhibitions.

A 125-member board of trustees oversees museum activities and elects twenty-one of its members to the Board of Governing Trustees, which meets on a monthly basis to make policy decisions and establish budgets. Daily operations are guided by the museum director. Cathleen Gallander left the museum in 1980 and was succeeded as director by Ric Collier (1981–87) and Gus Teller (1988–90). In October 1990 Lillian Murray became director of the museum, which employed a staff of eighteen in 1991. The city of Corpus Christi, the Corpus Christi Independent School District, and various local, state, and federal agencies provide financial support. The museum also depends on membership and admission fees, income from its gift shop and art classes, and fund-raisers to meet its operating budget, which was $800,000 in 1991. The Art Museum of South Texas is a member of the Texas Association of Museums,[qv] the American Association of Museums, the American Federation of Arts, the Corpus Christi Chamber of Commerce, and the Corpus Christi Arts Council.

BIBLIOGRAPHY: *Art in America*, September–October 1972. Charlotte Moser, "Texas Museums: Gambling for Big Change," *ARTnews*, December 1979. Jim Steely, "Serendipity by the Bay," *Texas Highways*, January 1977. *Studio International*, May–June 1975.

Kendall Curlee

ARVANA, TEXAS. Arvana is at the intersection of U.S. Highway 87, Farm Road 2411, and the Atchison, Topeka and Santa Fe Railway, five miles northeast of Lamesa in north central Dawson County. It was established on the Pecos and Northern Texas Railway before 1909. Ten people were living in the community in 1933, and a population of twenty and one business were reported in 1949. In 1980 and 1990 the population was twenty-five. *Charles G. Davis*

ASA, TEXAS. Asa, at the junction of Farm roads 2643 and 434 in McLennan County, was one of a series of communities along the Old River Road from Waco to Marlin. These communities were prosperous "when cotton was king." The town was formerly named Norwood for early settlers, but the Texas and New Orleans Railroad changed the name to Asa, the first name of Asa Woodward Warner, a Waco businessman who owned the cotton gin, the country store, and four farms in the area. Warner operated as the last of the plantation-style landowners in the area. The cotton gin and a seed warehouse were still in operation in 1983, when the population was about 100. In 1990 the population was forty-six.

BIBLIOGRAPHY: Dayton Kelley, ed., *The Handbook of Waco and McLennan County, Texas* (Waco: Texian, 1972). William Robert Poage, *McLennan County Before 1980* (Waco: Texian, 1981).

Jean Warner Epperson

ASARCO. ASARCO, originally known as the American Smelting and Refining Company, traces its origins to 1881, when Robert Safford Towne arrived in El Paso after touring the mines in the Mexican state of Chihuahua. Two years later he organized the Mexican Ore Company, a small plant that sampled and graded ore from the Mexican mines. In 1887 the ambitious Towne went to Argentine, Kansas, where he secured the backing of the Kansas City Consolidated Smelting and Refining Company for the construction of a major smelter in El Paso to process lead and copper ores from mines in Mexico and in the American Southwest. Towne bought 1,156 acres along the Rio Grande for $3,757, and within five months the El Paso Smelter, with a 100-foot high chimney and a workforce of 250, was ready to begin processing the high-grade Mexican ore. The community that grew up around the plant was called Smeltertown.

In 1899 KSARCO and several other corporations merged into the newly organized American Smelting and Refining Company, which became known as ASARCO. In 1901 a fire destroyed about $100,000 worth of the new company's property and equipment, but ASARCO rebuilt and reopened in 1902 with seven new lead furnaces and the first copper smelter in El Paso. The new facility doubled production and expanded the local payroll to nearly 900 workers. During the 1920s ASARCO was the largest mining operator in Mexico, with twenty-four different units. In 1948 slag fuming facilitators were built for the recovery of zinc from the slag produced by the lead furnaces, and in 1951 ASARCO built a 612-foot smokestack to reduce ground-level concentrations of sulfur dioxide. In 1967 the company built an 828-foot stack, designed to help alleviate local air pollution. In 1969, however, El Paso still had a higher concentration of lead in the air than any other city in Texas.

In the spring of 1970, the city of El Paso filed a $1 million suit, later joined by the State of Texas, charging ASARCO with violations of the Texas Clean Air Act. In December 1971 the El Paso City-County Health Department reported that the smelter had emitted 1,012 metric tons of lead between 1969 and 1971 and found that the smelter was the principal source of particulate lead within a radius of a mile. When lead was discovered in the soil of Smeltertown, the company removed the top foot and a half of soil and replaced it with fresh soil. When lead poisoning was suspected in the children living in Smeltertown, the company bought the land in Smeltertown and removed the residents. Following a 1975 injunction requiring ASARCO to spend $120 million on modernization and environmental improvements, the company by 1978 had reduced emissions of sulfur dioxide by nearly two-thirds from pre-1970 levels. Since that time, lead and zinc operations have been closed, and the smelting of copper has become the plant's principal function. The copper, which is shipped to the ASARCO refinery in Amarillo, is 98 to 99 percent pure.

In 1990 an $81 million modernization program began, involving a smelting technology that improves operating efficiency and production while capturing 98 percent or more of the sulfur dioxide emissions. In the early 1990s ASARCO plant in El Paso employed nearly 1,000 people and produced almost a million tons of raw materials per year. In 1990 the El Paso and Amarillo plants had sales totalling more than $50 million each.

BIBLIOGRAPHY: T. Lindsay Baker, *Ghost Towns of Texas* (Norman: University of Oklahoma Press, 1986). El Paso *Times*, March 30, 1972. Leon C. Metz, *City at the Pass: An Illustrated History of El Paso* (Woodland Hills, California: Windsor, 1980). *Martin Donell Kohout*

ASBERRY, ALEXANDER (1861–ca. 1903). Alexander Asberry, a black Republican party[qv] member who served in the Twenty-first Legislature of 1889, was born on November 2, 1861, in Wilderville, Texas, the son of William and Julia Asberry. He attended Hearne Academy in Robertson County and eventually engaged in the grocery business. Although he failed to win election to the state House of Representatives in 1884, Robertson County voters elected him in 1888, the same year he served as a delegate to the national Republican convention. While in the legislature, Asberry, a resident of Calvert, served on the County Government and County Finances and the Mining and Minerals committees. He expressed interest in legislation designed to make railroad companies liable for livestock killed by their trains and opposed racial segregation on railroad passenger cars. He also supported replacing the convict lease system[qv] with state prison farms.

He was defeated in the election of 1890 but again served as a delegate to the Republican national convention in 1892. He lost the election for the state legislature in 1896 by only twenty-one votes. It is rumored that when he attempted to contest the election an unfriendly white judge shot him instead of hearing his case. A committee in the Twenty-fifth Legislature also rejected the challenge, ruling that Asberry had failed to follow proper contesting procedures. Asberry was a deacon in the Baptist Church; he died sometime before February 19, 1903, when a Robertson County court probated his estate.

BIBLIOGRAPHY: J. Mason Brewer, *Negro Legislators of Texas and Their Descendants* (Dallas: Mathis, 1935; 2d ed., Austin: Jenkins, 1970). Lewis E. Daniell, *Personnel of the Texas State Government, with Sketches of Representative Men of Texas* (Austin: City Printing, 1887; 3d ed., San Antonio: Maverick, 1892). Merline Pitre, *Through Many Dangers, Toils and Snares: The Black Leadership of Texas, 1868–1900* (Austin: Eakin, 1985). *Paul M. Lucko*

ASBURY, SAMUEL ERSON (1872–1962). Samuel Erson Asbury, chemist and Texas historian, was born on September 26, 1872, in Charlotte, North Carolina, one of eight children of Sidney Monroe and Felicia Swan (Woodward) Asbury. In the fall of 1889 he enrolled at the North Carolina State College of Agriculture and Engineering at Raleigh, where he worked his way through school as a janitor in the chemistry building. He graduated in 1893 with a B.S. in chemistry and the next year was employed as an instructor in the chemistry department. At the same time he began work toward a master's degree, which he completed in 1896.

Asbury became assistant state chemist in the North Carolina Experiment Station in 1895 and continued in this capacity until July 1897. During the ensuing years he worked as a chemist in a succession of jobs. He then returned to his old job in the North Carolina Experiment Station in 1899 and worked at the station until November 1, 1904, when he accepted the position of assistant state chemist with the Texas Agricultural Experiment Station (*see* AGRICULTURAL EXPERIMENT STATION SYSTEM) on the campus of the Agricultural and Mechanical College of Texas (now Texas A&M University). He held this position until he retired partially in 1940 and completely in 1945. While at A&M he helped put his brothers and sisters through college. He also took a year's leave of absence to do advanced study in physical chemistry at Harvard. As assistant state chemist Asbury tested seed, feed, and fertilizers and experimented with growing roses. By a judicious combination of aluminum sulfate and water, he succeeded in making roses grow to a height of more than forty feet.

Soon after coming to Texas, he became deeply interested in the early history of the state and became a collector of Texana and of stories about early Texas leaders. After 1930 he became more and more absorbed in historical research, and the Texas Revolution[qv] became his chief concern. He planned the production of a musical drama to tell the story of that event. In 1951 he published a pamphlet, entitled *Music as a Means of Historical Research*, in which he discussed music as a medium for the presentation of historical narrative. He proposed to produce an opera to interpret the Texas Revolution through a cycle of music dramas, but it was never completed. At the time of his death he held membership in the Southern Historical Association and was a fellow of the Texas State Historical Association.[qv] He was the author of one article and the editor of another in the *Southwestern Historical Quarterly*.[qv] He was a member of the Bryan–College Station Poetry Society and was a critic of poetry. He attended the First Methodist Church in Bryan. Asbury died in Bryan on January 10, 1962, and was buried in the City Cemetery, College Station.

BIBLIOGRAPHY: Samuel Erson Asbury Papers, Barker Texas History Center, University of Texas at Austin. Samuel Erson Asbury Papers, University Archives, Texas A&M University. Austin *American*, October 17, 1952. *Battalion*, September 20, 1945, October 1, 1952. Bryan *Daily Eagle*, May 26, 1953, December 29, 1957, January 11, 12, 1962. Dallas *Morning News*, December 18, 1937. *Extension Service Farm News*, January 1938. Houston *Post*, January 12, 21, 1962.

Joseph Milton Nance

ASEN ARCOS INDIANS. This is one of twenty Indian groups that joined Juan Domínguez de Mendoza[qv] on his journey from El Paso to the vicinity of present San Angelo in 1683–84. Since Domínguez did not indicate at what point the Asen Arcos joined his party, it is impossible to determine their range or affiliations. Indians between the Pecos River and the San Angelo area were being hard pressed by Apache Indians at that time, and it seems likely that the Asen Arcos ranged somewhere between these two localities. Asen Arcos is a shortening of Mendoza's phrase "Los que asen Arcos," Spanish for "bow makers." This designation is of special interest because it suggests technological specialization by a single band.

BIBLIOGRAPHY: Herbert Eugene Bolton, ed., *Spanish Exploration in the Southwest, 1542–1706* (New York: Scribner, 1908; rpt., New York: Barnes and Noble, 1959). *Thomas N. Campbell*

ASH, TEXAS. Ash, a farming community sixteen miles southwest of Crockett on Farm Road 1280 in southwestern Houston County, was founded in 1870 and named for James B. Ash, a community leader. A post office opened there in 1890, and by 1896 the community had a gristmill-gin and general store. An Ash school that began operating around the same time had an enrollment of fifty-eight in 1897. Although the post office closed in 1909, in the mid-1930s the town still had a church, two stores, and a number of houses; the estimated population in 1936 was ten. After World War II[qv] the stores closed, and by the early 1970s only a church and a number of scattered houses remained. In the early 1990s Ash was a dispersed rural community for which no population recent estimates were available.

Christopher Long

ASHBURN, ISAAC SEABORN (1889–1961). Isaac Seaborn Ashburn, soldier, publisher, and businessman, the son of Isaac and Hannah (Strother) Ashburn, was born at Farmersville, Texas, on December 19, 1889. His father was a Methodist preacher. Ashburn attended Paris and Greenville public schools and Polytechnic College at Fort Worth, then left college to become a reporter for the Fort Worth *Record* (*see* FORT WORTH *STAR-TELEGRAM*). He rose from beat reporter to city editor but left the paper in 1913 to become publicity director and secretary of the board of directors of the Agricultural and Mechanical College of Texas (now Texas A&M University). In 1917, at the age of twenty-nine, he joined the army. He was twice wounded and gassed and received numerous battlefield commendations, including the Distinguished Service Cross, the Legion of Honor, and the Croix de Guerre with Palm. He was also promoted to lieutenant colonel.

After the war Ashburn returned to Texas A&M, where he became commandant of cadets. During the 1920s he moved to Houston to serve as a vice president and general manager of the Houston Chamber of Commerce. In 1936 he cofounded and published *Texas Parade*.[qv] The magazine, sponsored by the Texas Good Roads Association, which Ashburn headed, initially devoted its pages to promoting highway development.[qv] Within a few years *Texas Parade* became a publicity vehicle highlighting Texas history and sports and encouraging tourism.

During World War II,[qv] after being rejected for active duty, Ashburn served as director of civilian defense for Harris County and executive secretary of the Harris County Association for Industrial Peace. He became director of industrial and public relations in 1943 and later senior vice president and comptroller of the Todd Houston Shipbuilding Corporation. In 1949 Governor Beauford H. Jester[qv] promoted him to major general and appointed him deputy commander of the Texas National Guard.[qv]

The six-foot-three, three-hundred-pound publisher and war hero, nicknamed "General Ike," was a popular public speaker. He was also a friend and confidant to a number of political figures. In 1947 He moved from Houston to Austin, where he remained until a series of strokes forced him to remain bedridden at the Veterans Administration Hospital, Temple.[qv] He died in Temple on February 1, 1961, and was survived by his third wife, Bertha (Smith), and a son by his first wife, Beulah (Cook). He was buried at Austin Memorial Park. Ashburn was a lifelong Methodist, a member of the Army and Navy Legion of Valor and the First Officers Training Camp Association, and past president of the Ninetieth Division of the National Guard Association.

BIBLIOGRAPHY: Dallas *Morning News*, February 2, 1961. *Texas Parade*, March 1961. Clarence R. Wharton, ed., *Texas under Many Flags* (5 vols., Chicago: American Historical Society, 1930).

David Minor

ASHBY, HARRISON STERLING PRICE (1848–1923). H. S. P. (Stump) Ashby was born to Benjamin F. and Martina Virginia (Walton) Ashby on May 18, 1848, on their farm in Chariton County, Missouri. He served in Gen. Joseph O. Shelby's command in the last part of the Civil War[qv] (*see also* SHELBY EXPEDITION), immediately after settling in Texas, where in turn he was an actor, cattle driver, farmer, and schoolteacher. He was converted to Methodism at the age of twenty and, after a theological reading course, was licensed as a preacher in 1872. He spent the next fifteen years in rural Texas pastorates in Belton, Lancaster, Weston, Stephenville, Rice, and finally Grapevine, Tarrant County, where in 1888 he was apparently removed from the itinerant ministry for his political activities, his criticism of the church's failure to support reform, and an alleged fondness for the bottle.

In 1871 Ashby married Sara Sophia Wisdom in Cooke County, Texas. Before she died in 1876 they had four children. On January 12, 1879, he married Amanda Elizabeth Ray (Wray) at Belton, Texas. They had five children, two of whom died in infancy. Ben, one of his children, had by the time of Ashby's death achieved county political office in Oklahoma.

Ashby's interest in politics began through his acquaintance with Judge Thomas L. Nugent,[qv] a member of his Stephenville congregation, who twice ran for governor on the Populist ticket. Ashby was one of the first Farmers' Alliance[qv] speakers and organizers in Texas. With Evan Jones,[qv] James M. Perdue of Mineola, R. M. Humphrey (white founder of the Colored Farmers' Alliance[qv]), William R. Lamb,[qv] Harry Tracy,[qv] and a few others, Ashby led the antimonopoly, Greenback wing of the Texas Farmers' Alliance. As an early supporter within the alliance of independent political action, he helped lead an independent political movement in Fort Worth that succeeded, in the midst of the Great Southwest Strike[qv] of 1886, in electing the mayor of the city. In Waco in May 1888 he helped organize a convention of farmers, laborers, and stockraisers, which led directly to a state Union Labor party convention in July, the first statewide independent political effort in which large numbers of Farmers' Alliance men were involved. As one of the Texas alliance's first district lecturers, Ashby helped pioneer the radicals' tactics of using Democratic hostility to the Sub-Treasury plan of 1889 to split the Farmers' Alliance membership from their traditional Democratic loyalty.

Ashby's Populist career began officially when, with Thomas Gaines[qv] of Comanche County and William R. Lamb, he organized the founding state People's party[qv] convention, held August 17, 1891, in Dallas; this convention was coordinated with the state Farmers' Alliance meeting in the same city. As state party chairman in 1892 and 1894, Ashby organized the increasingly successful Populist state campaigns. Here his organizational skills and his ability to work with and for his black colleagues counted as much as his effective speaking ability, for which he gained his nickname, "Stump." Ashby was a delegate to the organizing convention of the national Populist party in St. Louis in 1892. During his Populist career he remained active in the Texas Farmers' Alliance; he was state lecturer from 1892 to 1894. In 1896 he ran unsuccessfully for lieutenant governor on the Populist ticket.

That year ended Ashby's public prominence for a while, but he had returned to public activity as a Populist by 1900, when he campaigned in North Carolina for Marion Butler in the latter's efforts to retain his United States Senate seat. In 1902 Ashby attended the Texas state Populist convention as a delegate from Smithfield for the purpose of blocking a prohibition[qv] plank in the party's platform.

Soon after this he moved to Mannsville, Indian Territory, where he farmed quite successfully and eventually became president of his local farmers' union. He also returned to politics, this time as a supporter of Democrats William H. (Alfalfa Bill) Murray[qv] and Charles N. Haskell. Ashby served in the Oklahoma House of Representatives as a representative of Marshall County to the First Legislature in 1907 and to the Third and Fourth legislatures from Pushmataha County. He died in Octavia, Oklahoma, in May 1923, as well known in Oklahoma as he had been in Texas for his politics and speaking ability.

BIBLIOGRAPHY: Alwyn Barr, *Reconstruction to Reform: Texas Politics, 1876–1906* (Austin: University of Texas Press, 1971). Dallas *Morning News*, September 16, 1894. Lawrence Goodwyn, *Democratic Promise: The Populist Moment in America* (New York: Oxford University Press, 1976). Robert C. McMath, Jr., *Populist Vanguard: A History of the Southern Farmers' Alliance* (Chapel Hill: University of North Carolina Press, 1975). Roscoe C. Martin, *The People's Party in Texas* (Austin: University of Texas, 1933; rpt., University of Texas Press, 1970). Vertical Files, Barker Texas History Center, University of Texas at Austin.

Bruce Palmer

ASHBY, TEXAS (Houston County). Ashby was a post office community twenty-two miles northeast of Crockett near the site of present Weches in northeastern Houston County. It was probably established after the Civil War.[qv] A post office operated there from 1872 until 1877; in the mid-1870s the community had a store and a number of houses. By the mid-1930s it no longer appeared on highway maps.

Christopher Long

ASHBY, TEXAS (Matagorda County). Ashby is off Farm Road 1095 just north of a residential development called Tres Palacios Oaks, nine miles northeast of Palacios in west central Matagorda County. Before settlers arrived, the area had been a campsite of the Karankawa Indians. Though the settlement may have had a church as early as 1869, it did not receive a post office until 1890, when Capt. W. W. Moore opened a general store on the banks of Tres Palacios River. Moore, a Civil War[qv] veteran, named the community after his commanding officer in the Eighth Texas Cavalry.[qv] Boats made regular stops at his general store; at that time the river was navigable to Deming's Bridge (later known as Hawley), about six miles upriver. Moore, who built a twelve-room house called the Oaks at Ashby to accommodate his large family, donated two acres of land for a Methodist church and cemetery. At one time the Ashby church, served by ministers on the Matagorda Circuit, had as many as 100 members; it was destroyed by fire in 1902.

In 1892 Ashby reported a population of 100, a barber, a carpenter, and a physician, and by 1896 the community had a daily stage to El Campo. Initially Ashby's economic mainstays were rice and cotton, which were warehoused on the banks of the Tres Palacios. Later, grain became a major crop. In 1899 Ashby had a school with one teacher and twenty-eight students; by 1904 the number of students had risen to forty. Until the community built a school in 1911, classes were taught in private homes. In 1914 Ashby reported a population of 150, served by two general stores and the Ashby Farms Company, and by 1917 the community reported white and black schools, each with four grades.

By 1919 the post office had closed, and mail was sent to Blessing. In the mid-1930s Ashby had a number of farms linked by a paved road and a two-room elementary school. In 1948 the Ashby school district was consolidated with the Blessing Independent School District, which by 1949 had become part of the Tidehaven Consolidated Independent District. A Baptist church constructed in 1948 was donated to the black Baptist congregation in Markham around 1958. By 1972 the Tres Palacios Oaks development appeared on maps. The development was just across Trespalacios Creek from Ashby, which then consisted of a few scattered dwellings and a cemetery. The community was still listed, though without statistics, in 1990.

BIBLIOGRAPHY: Frank J. Balusek, Survey and Proposed Reorganization of the Schools of Matagorda County, Texas (M.Ed. thesis, University of Texas, 1939). Matagorda County Historical Commission, *Historic Matagorda County* (3 vols., Houston: Armstrong, 1986).

Rachel Jenkins

ASH CREEK (Brewster County). Ash Creek rises one-half mile east of State Highway 118 and three miles northwest of Mount Ord in northwestern Brewster County (at 30°16′ N, 103°34′ W) and runs south for fifteen miles to its mouth on Calamity Creek, five miles northwest of Elephant Mountain (at 30°05′ N, 103°35′ W). The creek is intermittent for the first seven miles. Its upper reaches pass through rugged terrain with numerous box canyons surfaced by shallow, stony soils that support Mexican buckeye, walnut, persimmon, desert willow, scrub brush, and sparse grasses. Terrain in the creek's lower reaches is flat with local shallow depressions and surfaced by clay and sandy loams in which grow water-tolerant hardwoods, conifers, and grasses.

——— (Hill County). Ash Creek rises 2½ miles northwest of Bynum in central Hill County (at 32°00′ N, 97°03′ W) and runs southeast for twenty miles to its mouth on Navarro Mills Reservoir, five miles south of Irene (at 31°57′ N, 96°46′ W). It traverses flat to rolling terrain surfaced by clay and sandy loams. For most of the county's history, the Ash Creek area has been used as range and crop land.

——— (King County). Ash Creek rises eleven miles southeast of Guthrie in central King County (at 33°33′ N, 100°15′ W) and runs north for four miles to its mouth on the South Wichita River (at 33°36′ N, 100°16′ W). It traverses an area of rolling to steep slopes surfaced by shallow clay and sandy loams that support juniper, cacti, and sparse grasses.

——— (Parker County). Ash Creek rises four miles southwest of Sanctuary in northeast Parker County (at 32°52′ N, 97°42′ W) and flows southeast for fourteen miles to its mouth on the West Fork of the Trinity River, three miles southeast of Azle in northwestern Tarrant County (at 32°52′ N, 97°31′ W). It runs across undulating to gently rolling land surfaced by sandy and loamy soils that support grass and hardwoods. For most of the county's history the Ash Creek area has been used as range and crop land.

ASHE, SAMUEL SWANN (1839–1919). Samuel Swann Ashe, Confederate Army officer and civil servant, was born in Brownsville, Tennessee, on June 14, 1839, the son of John B. and Eliza (Hay) Ashe. The elder Ashe was a member of the United States House of Representatives. Samuel Ashe's grandfather, Samuel Ashe, had been a governor of North Carolina and was the man after whom the city of Asheville was named. Samuel S. Ashe moved to Galveston with his family in 1848 but returned to North Carolina to receive his education at what is now the University of North Carolina at Chapel Hill. Upon graduation he went to work on a ranch in Harris County, Texas. With the outbreak of the Civil War Ashe enlisted as a private in Company B of the famed Eighth Texas Cavalry[qv]—popularly known as Terry's Texas Rangers. When Col. Benjamin Franklin Terry[qv] was killed at the battle of Woodsonville, Kentucky, Ashe helped to remove his body from the field. In 1862 he took part in the battles of Shiloh, where his brother William was killed, and Murfreesboro, Tennessee. He was wounded in action in 1863, but after recovery was promoted to lieutenant and transferred to White's Battery of horse artillery. In that capacity he participated in the battles of Chickamauga and Atlanta and in the campaign in the Carolinas. During the Atlanta campaign he was promoted to captain. After the war he moved to Lynchburg and entered the mercantile business in partnership with John B. Snydor. On May 23, 1866, he married Sallie Anderson of Lebanon, Tennessee. They had a son and a daughter. In 1870 Ashe was elected justice of the peace in Harris County; he served until 1873. He was elected sheriff of Harris County on December 17, 1873, and served for four years. He was elected tax collector in 1880 and served until 1883. From 1893 until 1897 he was clerk of the district criminal court. He died on April 29, 1919.

BIBLIOGRAPHY: Clement Anselm Evans, ed., *Confederate Military History* (Atlanta: Confederate Publishing, 1899; extended ed., Wilmington, North Carolina: Broadfoot, 1987–89). Dermont H. Hardy and Ingham S. Roberts, eds., *Historical Review of South-East Texas* (2 vols., Chicago: Lewis, 1910). *History of Texas, Together with a Biographical History of the Cities of Houston and Galveston* (Chicago: Lewis, 1895).

Thomas W. Cutrer

ASHERTON, TEXAS. Asherton is on U.S. Highway 83 eight miles southeast of Carrizo Springs in central Dimmit County. It was one of several settlements founded in the county between 1909 and 1917 and was named for Asher Richardson, the local rancher and entrepreneur who established it. Richardson began planning Asherton as early as 1902, when he acquired the site in a special sale from the state of Texas. Soon afterward he formed the Asherton Land and Irrigation Company and developed his blueprint for an ambitious 48,000-acre development project. He set up telephone and railroad companies in 1905 and soon afterward began to construct shops, workers' housing, a church, and other buildings on the Asherton townsite. By 1909 the town had a post office, and when the Asherton and Gulf Railway began running in 1910, the community became a shipping point for local farmers. By 1915 the settlement comprised 1,000 residents, four churches, and eighteen businesses, including a bank, two hotels, two blacksmith shops, a lumber company, and three general stores. Asherton continued to grow until the late 1920s. In 1925 it was incorporated. By 1927, thanks to the irrigated farms that surrounded it and its rail link, Asherton had become one of the largest shipping points for Bermuda onions in the United States. By 1929 the town's population had grown to 2,000. Many local small farmers experienced hard times during the 1930s, however, and several businesses closed. By 1931 Asherton's population had dropped to 1,858. In 1941 the town had 1,538 residents and thirty-six businesses; by 1943 only seventeen businesses were reported. The town grew briefly in the 1950s; in 1954 it had 2,425 residents and twenty-two businesses. But in 1962 it had 1,890 residents and fifteen businesses. In 1989 Asherton had one business and a population of 1,609.

BIBLIOGRAPHY: Carrizo Springs *Javelin*, October 28, 1980. Paul S. Taylor, "Historical Note on Dimmit County, Texas," *Southwestern Historical Quarterly* 34 (October 1930). Laura Knowlton Tidwell, *Dimmit County Mesquite Roots* (Austin: Wind River, 1984). Vertical Files, Barker Texas History Center, University of Texas at Austin.

John Leffler

ASHERTON AND GULF RAILWAY. The Asherton and Gulf Railway Company was chartered on January 14, 1905, as the Nueces Valley, Rio Grande and Mexico Railway Company; the name was changed on March 9, 1909. The principal office, originally at Carizzo Springs, was later moved to Asherton. Members of the first board of directors were Asher Richardson, J. C. Dennis, W. W. McKinley, W. A. Milles, John Bivens, J. T. Nesbit, W. W. Williams, A. M. McElwee, and M. C. Wells. Work was begun on a railroad grade between Artesia Wells and Carizo Springs in February 1905, but was discontinued in May after about ten miles had been graded. Following a change of control, construction resumed in 1908. The twelve miles between Artesia Wells and Light opened on June 27, 1909, and the remaining twenty miles between Light and Asherton on August 2, 1909. After the construction of the railroad much of the nearby ranchland was converted to vegetable farming. Most of the Asherton and Gulf's earnings came from freight operations, but passenger service was also provided. In 1916 the line reported passenger earnings of $5,000 and total freight earnings of $26,000, and the railroad owned two locomotives and six cars. The Asherton and Gulf became part of the Missouri Pacific lines on January 2, 1926, but continued to operate as a separate company until it was merged into the Missouri Pacific Railroad Company on March 1, 1956. The line was abandoned in 1958.

Nancy Beck Young

ASHLAND, TEXAS. Ashland, on State Highway 154 fourteen miles southeast of Gilmer in extreme southeastern Upshur County, was established around 1845. In antebellum Texas[qv] the settlement served as a shipping and marketing point for plantations along the bend of Cypress Creek. A post office under the name Asbury opened there in 1894. By 1896 the community had a sawmill, a general store, Baptist and Methodist churches, two doctors, and an estimated population of 110. In 1902 the community was renamed Ashland. At its height around 1914 Ashland had a bank, a Masonic lodge, four general stores, a cotton gin, and a population of 250. After World War I,[qv] however, the town began to decline. The post office was closed in 1921, and by 1933 the population had fallen to 175. In the mid-1930s the community had a church, a store, and a number of scattered houses. By 1945 the population had fallen to twenty. In the mid-1960s Ashland had a church, a cemetery, and a few houses. In 1990 the church and cemetery were still at the site, and Ashland was a dispersed rural community with an estimated population of twenty.

BIBLIOGRAPHY: Doyal T. Loyd, *History of Upshur County* (Waco: Texian Press, 1987).

Christopher Long

ASHLOCK, JESSE (1915–1976). Jesse Ashlock was born in 1915. He started playing violin at age nine. In 1930 he began attending the Crystal Springs Club in Fort Worth, where James Robert (Bob) Wills[qv] played with his band, the Bob Wills Fiddle Band. Wills bought Jesse a fiddle, taught him to play, and included him in a few of the band's performances at Crystal Springs. In 1932 Ashlock joined a band named Milton Brown and His Musical Brownies.[qv] Brown was Wills's chief competition in Western Swing. In 1935 Ashlock joined Wills's Original Texas Playboys as a fiddle player. He stayed with Bob Wills throughout the rest of Wills's career and continued playing shows until three days before his death. While playing for Wills he became an integral part of the band. He was known as a practical joker. He once told Bob Wills during a performance that his pants were unzipped, causing Bob to stop playing his chorus and double over trying to cover up the offending opening. During his career with Wills, Ashlock was also involved with the movies that Wills made. Ashlock's playing style had its roots in jazz. His fiddle style was characterized by hot breaks and hot choruses. His idol was jazz violinist Joe Venuti. Ashlock's attempt to play his fiddle like a horn earned him placement in the category of the "hot fiddlers." He died on August 9, 1976, in Austin, where he had moved from Claremore, Oklahoma, the previous year. At sixty-one years, he had performed at the Broken Spoke, a country and western club, three days before his death from cancer.

BIBLIOGRAPHY: Charles R. Townsend, *San Antonio Rose: The Life and Music of Bob Wills* (Urbana: University of Illinois Press, 1976). Vertical Files, Barker Texas History Center, University of Texas at Austin.

Matthew Douglas Moore

ASHMORE, TEXAS. Ashmore is at the junction of Farm roads 83 and 403, sixteen miles east of Seagraves in northeastern Gaines County. It developed as a community after 1913 and was named for the man who purchased J. H. Belcher's store and post office. Coleman L. Henson surveyed the townsite in 1939. A local school was established in 1923, although one had existed at several nearby locations since 1913. It was consolidated with the Loop school in 1937, and the post office closed in 1948. The population in 1980 and 1990 was twenty-five.

BIBLIOGRAPHY: Gaines County Historical Survey Committee, *The Gaines County Story*, ed. Margaret Coward (Seagraves, Texas: Pioneer, 1974). *William R. Hunt*

ASH SWITCH, TEXAS. Ash Switch, also known as Ash, is on Farm Road 1616 four miles northeast of Athens in north central Henderson County. The settlement was named for John Ash, who built a home there in the 1890s. Before 1900 the St. Louis and Southwestern Railway established a flag station nearby named Ash Switch, which locals eventually shortened to Ash. In the mid-1930s the community had a population of five, one business, a church, and a number of houses. After World War II[qv] residents left the area, and by the early 1990s only a cemetery and a few scattered dwellings remained.

Christopher Long

ASHTOLA, TEXAS. Ashtola, on U.S. Highway 287 nine miles northwest of Clarendon in western Donley County, was established in 1906 as a section house on the Fort Worth and Denver City Railway. The townsite was originally named Southard and was granted a post office in March 1906, with Thomas F. Lewallen as postmaster. Two stores and a one-room schoolhouse were added by 1908. In 1916 W. A. Poovey, acting on the request of postal authorities, sought to have the town's name changed to Poovieville, but the name Ashtola was chosen instead. The town served the SJ and other area ranches. By 1930 it had three stores, a brick school building, and a population estimated at twenty-five. About that time the local ladies organized a home demonstration club, which later became the Ashtola Needle Club. After automobiles became popular, Ben Lovell opened a filling station and a gristmill. The mill remained in operation until 1973. The post office was discontinued in 1956. In 1958 the Ashtola school district was consolidated with that of Clarendon, and the school building was subsequently remodeled into a community center. Between 1949 and 1966 Ashtola had an estimated population of fifty. In 1968 the population was estimated at twenty-five. From 1970 to 1990 it was estimated at twenty.

BIBLIOGRAPHY: Virginia Browder, *Donley County: Land O' Promise* (Wichita Falls, Texas: Nortex, 1975). *H. Allen Anderson*

ASHTON, TEXAS. Ashton was on Farm Road 139 seven miles southeast of Joaquin in northeastern Shelby County. It was apparently originally located on the banks of the Sabine River, just to the east of its later site. Small craft often traveled up the river to Ashton. At its height the community had a ferry, a small sawmill, a cotton gin, at least one church, and at least two schools. A local post office operated from 1847 to 1854 and was probably named for the postmaster, Henry C. Ashton, who was also an original grantee of land in the area. When railroads took over the work of the Sabine riverboats in the mid-1880s, the community seems to have declined. People gradually moved to the west, up the hill from the river. Although the focus of the community changed as most of its institutions closed, the churches and schools remained in operation and preserved the town name. In 1903 the Ashton area supported two schools, one with twenty white students and one with eighteen black students. The area also had at least three Protestant churches. By 1938 the two schools had grown to serve sixty-six white and seventy-three black children. Gradually transportation improvements and a decline in the rural population of the county led to a consolidation of the school system and the end of the community. By 1956 the two schools had closed, and by 1983 the only remaining evidence of Ashton was two cemeteries, one for whites on Farm Road 139, and one for blacks a few miles off the road.

BIBLIOGRAPHY: Charles E. Tatum, *Shelby County: In the East Texas Hills* (Austin: Eakin, 1984). *Cecil Harper, Jr.*

ASHTON VILLA. Ashton Villa, one of the first brick structures in Texas, is located on Broadway in Galveston. It was built in 1859 by James Moreau Brown,[qv] who by the late 1850s had developed the largest hardware store west of the Mississippi. Brown purchased four lots at the corner of Broadway Boulevard and Twenty-fourth Street in Galveston on January 7, 1859. He designed the building and used slave labor and skilled European craftsmen. His wife, née Rebecca Ashton Stoddart, named the new family residence Ashton Villa in memory of one of her ancestors, Lt. Isaac Ashton, a Revolutionary War hero.

The imposing three-story home was in the Victorian Italianate style, distinguished by deep eaves with carved supporting brackets. Its long windows and graceful ornate verandas were topped by lintels made of cast iron. To protect the house from the damp, Brown made the brick walls thirteen inches thick, with an air space between the exterior and the interior walls. Ashton Villa's interior design was based on a central hall floor plan.

Brown died in 1895, leaving ownership of Ashton Villa to his wife. The home withstood the devastation of the Galveston hurricane of 1900,[qv] but its basement was filled with sand and silt from the Gulf, and the surrounding grounds were topped with two feet of soil. In 1927 the villa was sold by a granddaughter to El Mina Shrine. The Shriners made minor modifications to the interior of the house to suit their needs and used it for the next forty years as their business offices and for social functions.

In June 1968 El Mina Shrine placed the Ashton Villa property for sale. It was rumored that the house was also threatened with demolition. In a campaign led by the Galveston Historical Foundation,[qv] $125,000 was raised to purchase Ashton Villa. Further funding from both government and private sources helped restore and refurnish the historic home. Much of the original furniture and art was retrieved and is now a part of the collection. Ashton Villa was opened to the public on July 25, 1974, and is administered by the Galveston Historical Foundation. It served as Galveston's official Bicentennial Headquarters. It is listed in the National Register of Historic Places. Programs at the villa include daily public tours, property rentals, continuing restoration, special events, and a volunteer program. In June 1987, after accomplishing Galveston's first urban archeology, Ashton Villa opened an archeology exhibit that includes an interpretation of domestic life as well as the history of the house and its family.

BIBLIOGRAPHY: David G. McComb, *Galveston: A History* (Austin: University of Texas Press, 1986). Vertical Files, Barker Texas History Center, University of Texas at Austin (James Moreau Brown).

Judy D. Schiebel

ASHWOOD, TEXAS. Ashwood is at the junction of Farm roads 1728 and 3156, thirteen miles north of Bay City in northeastern Matagorda County. The railroad reached this town on Caney Creek when a branch of the New York, Texas and Mexican Railway was built from Wharton to Van Vleck in 1899–1900. Large numbers of ash logs were shipped from the town. In 1914 the community had a population of eighty-seven, a general store, and a mill. By 1925 the population was estimated at 200. In the mid-1930s the town had two schools, a church, a business, and a number of scattered dwellings. In 1942 the population had dropped to around 100 and by 1950 to twenty. In 1967 population estimates show a brief rebound to thirty, but after that year the town was no longer listed. A post office was established in Ashwood in 1910 with Mittie D. Hanson as postmistress. Annie M. Smith succeeded her in 1916 and not only operated the post office, but also the express office and the J. Fisher Smith Mercantile Store until her retirement in 1952. In 1952 the post office was discontinued. In 1917 Ashwood had a one-room school with four grades. In 1938 a two-teacher school for black children was there. In the late 1980s Ashwood had a few scattered houses and the Ashwood Depot, which was restored in 1986.

BIBLIOGRAPHY: Matagorda County Historical Commission, *Historic Matagorda County* (3 vols., Houston: Armstrong, 1986).

Will Branch

ASHWORTH, AARON (ca. 1803–?). Aaron Ashworth, free black colonist and landowner, was born in South Carolina about 1803. In 1833 he followed his brother William Ashworth[qv] to Lorenzo de Zavala's[qv] colony in East Texas, leaving his home in what is now Calcasieu Parish, Louisiana. Other relatives named Ashworth also came to the Zavala colony and were affected when the General Council[qv] passed an ordinance forbidding the immigration of free blacks into Texas. The law was not enforced against any of the Ashworths. When the Texas Congress passed an act on February 5, 1840, ordering all free blacks to leave the republic within two years or be sold into slavery, white support for the Ashworths came in the form of three petitions requesting their exemption from the act. This support was instrumental in the passage of the Ashworth Act[qv] of December 12, 1840. This law exempted the Ashworths and all free blacks resident in Texas on the day of the Texas Declaration of Independence,[qv] along with their families, from the act of February 5.

In 1850 the census listed Aaron Ashworth as a farmer with a substantial amount of property, including six slaves. He and his wife, Mary, from Kentucky, had six children and a white schoolmaster in residence to tutor their four school-aged children. In 1860 Ashworth owned four slaves, and his property value had increased. He and many of his relatives were obviously respected in their community as wealthy and autonomous free blacks.

BIBLIOGRAPHY: Hans Peter Nielsen Gammel, comp., *Laws of Texas, 1822–1897* (10 vols., Austin: Gammel, 1898). Andrew Forest Muir, "The Free Negro in Jefferson and Orange Counties, Texas," *Journal of Negro History* 35 (April 1950). Harold Schoen, "The Free Negro in the Republic of Texas," *Southwestern Historical Quarterly* 39–41 (April 1936–July 1937).

Nolan Thompson

ASHWORTH, WILLIAM (ca. 1793–?). William Ashworth, free black colonist and landowner, was born in South Carolina about 1793. In 1831 he moved from what is now Calcasieu Parish, Louisiana, to Lorenzo de Zavala's[qv] colony in East Texas. His father, Moses Ashworth, a white man, also came to Texas before the Texas Revolution[qv] and settled in San Augustine. William and his brother Aaron Ashworth[qv] obtained an order of survey from George Antonio Nixon,[qv] but before they could locate their lands the revolution began and the Texas provisional government closed the land offices. During the revolution Ashworth sent a substitute, Gipson Perkins, to the Texas army. Perkins served from July 7 to September 7, 1836, in Capt. B. J. Harper's Company of Beaumont Volunteers.

Opposition to the immigration of free blacks into the area of present Jefferson and Orange counties appeared as early as 1835. The committee of public safety at Beaumont warned the General Council[qv] against admitting free blacks into Texas, and the council passed an ordinance forbidding their immigration. The law was not enforced against William Ashworth, however, or any of the many Ashworths who followed him to the area.

In 1838 Ashworth obtained a franchise from the Jefferson County board of roads and revenues to operate a ferry across Lake Sabine and up the Neches River to Beaumont. His ferry and landholdings were threatened, however, by an act of the Texas Congress passed on February 5, 1840, which ordered all free blacks to vacate the republic within two years or be sold into slavery.[qv] White neighbors came to the aid of Ashworth and his relatives with three petitions to the Texas Congress requesting their exemption from the act. This support brought about the passage of the Ashworth Act[qv] of December 12, 1840, which exempted the Ashworths and all free blacks residing in Texas on the day of the Texas Declaration of Independence,[qv] along with their families, from the act of February 5.

In 1842 Ashworth and his relatives again faced a threat to their livelihood when a traveling land board charged with detecting fraudulent claims refused to certify the headrights given them by the Jefferson County board of land commissioners. The land board refused certification on the grounds that their jurisdiction did not cover free blacks. The board members nevertheless joined three members of the Jefferson board, along with some seventy other citizens, in petitioning Congress to make a direct issuance of the certification patents. The suggested bill easily passed the Texas Congress and was signed by President Sam Houston.[qv]

In 1850, of the sixty-three free blacks in Jefferson County, thirty-eight were named Ashworth. William Ashworth probably had the longest residence of any Ashworth in the area at that time. He and his wife, Leide or Delaide, a native white Louisianan, had seven children listed in their household in the 1850 census, although they probably had older children who had started their own families. While other Ashworths experienced legal difficulties because of interracial marriages, William and Leide appear to have been left alone. The 1850 census describes Ashworth as a farmer with large property, including two slaves. He and many of his relatives apparently were respected in their community as wealthy and relatively autonomous free blacks.

BIBLIOGRAPHY: Hans Peter Nielsen Gammel, comp., *Laws of Texas, 1822–1897* (10 vols., Austin: Gammel, 1898). Andrew Forest Muir, "The Free Negro in Jefferson and Orange Counties, Texas," *Journal of Negro History* 35 (April 1950). Harold Schoen, "The Free Negro in the Republic of Texas," *Southwestern Historical Quarterly* 39–41 (April 1936–July 1937).

Nolan Thompson

ASHWORTH ACT. The Ashworth Act, passed by the Texas Congress on December 12, 1840, came in response to an act passed on February 5, 1840, which prohibited the immigration of free blacks and ordered all free black residents to vacate the Republic of Texas[qv] within two years or be sold into slavery.[qv] The earlier act was designed to make color the standard mark of servitude in Texas by eliminating the free black population. It repealed all laws contrary to its provisions and nullified the act of June 5, 1837, which permitted the residence of free blacks living in Texas before the Texas Declaration of Independence.[qv]

Immediately after the passage of the February 5 act, influential whites from around the republic began to prepare petitions for the exemption of their newly disenfranchised friends, neighbors, and servants. Three of the petitions submitted were on behalf of several free black families named Ashworth, who resided in Jefferson County. The first of these petitions requested exemptions for early immigrants Abner and William Ashworth,[qv] David and Aaron Ashworth,[qv] and Elisha Thomas, an early resident and the brother-in-law of William and Abner. The petition, signed by sixty citizens, claimed that Aaron and David had been residents for two years, though in fact they had neglected to apply for permission to remain in Texas during that time. The second petition, which accompanied the first, only addressed the plight of William and Abner, apparently because they were early immigrants and had a stronger case. The petition was signed by seventy-one citizens. It claimed that William and Abner had been residents for six years and stated that they had contributed generously to the Texan cause during the revolution. It argued that the law of February 5, 1840, would "operate grievously" if enforced against them. Sixty-one citizens signed the third petition supporting Elisha Thomas, who had served in the army immediately after the battle of San Jacinto.qv In all three cases the petitions were signed by prominent officials in Jefferson County.

On November 5, 1840, three days after the opening of the Fifth Legislature, Joseph Grigsbyqv of Jefferson County presented the three petitions to the Texas Congress. The petitions were referred to a special committee, of which Grigsby was named chairman. The committee reported favorably on them, and a bill for the relief of the Ashworths passed its first reading without recorded contest.

Many congressmen had received one or more petitions from their constituents. House member Timothy Pillsburyqv of Brazoria, in an effort to conserve the time necessary to consider each of the petitions separately, offered a resolution, adopted by the House, instructing the Committee on the State of the Republic to consider legislation allowing the continued residence of free blacks who were in the country when the constitution was adopted. Such legislation had precedence in the joint resolution of June 5, 1837. If passed, it would dispense favorably with most of the petitions for free blacks. Pillsbury had a personal interest in such a bill, for he carried unpresented petitions supporting Samuel H. Hardin and James Richardson.

When the Committee on the State of the Republic ignored Pillsbury's resolution, he presented the Hardin and Richardson petitions to the House. James Richardson was a vendor of oysters in Brazoria County who had served in the garrison at Velasco in the revolution, although he was sixty years of age. Samuel H. Hardin's petition requested relief for him and his wife, reporting their long residence, industriousness, and good conduct. Sixty-five citizens signed the Hardin petition, including William T. Austin, Henry Austin, and Henry Smith.qqv On November 9, 1840, the Hardin and Richardson petitions were referred to the Committee on the State of the Republic. A bill exempting Samuel McCulloch, Jr.,qv and some of his relatives passed its first reading the same day.

On November 10, 1840, the Ashworth bill passed the House, and the McCulloch bill was read a second time. At this reading attempts were made to amend the bill by adding the names of William Goyens,qv who was supported by Thomas J. Rusk,qv and two other parties. The amendments lost, but the original bill passed.

The Ashworth bill came up in the Senate on November 20, 1840. A successful amendment inserted the words "and all free persons of color together with their families, who were residing in Texas the day of the Declaration of Independence" after the names of the original beneficiaries. The bill thereby addressed the case of all free blacks who had immigrated to Texas before the Declaration of Independence and conferred residency on David and Abner Ashworth, who had immigrated afterward. The House accepted the Senate's amendment, and on December 12, 1840, President Mirabeau B. Lamarqv signed the bill. David and Abner Ashworth became the only free blacks to immigrate subsequent to the Declaration of Independence who were given congressional sanction to remain in Texas.

BIBLIOGRAPHY: Hans Peter Nielsen Gammel, comp., *Laws of Texas, 1822–1897* (10 vols., Austin: Gammel, 1898). Harold Schoen, "The Free Negro in the Republic of Texas," *Southwestern Historical Quarterly* 39–41 (April 1936–July 1937). Texas House of Representatives, *Biographical Directory of the Texan Conventions and Congresses, 1832–1845* (Austin: Book Exchange, 1941). *Nolan Thompson*

ASIA, TEXAS. Asia is a farming community north of U.S. Highway 287 in northern Polk County, two miles west of Corrigan and 100 miles north of Houston. It was founded by Mexican Warqv veteran James Standley about 1859 and developed as a rural settlement around Standley's cabinet and blacksmith shops. During the Civil Warqv Asia residents manufactured wagons and cannon carts for use by the Confederacy. Significant change came in the mid-1880s, when the Trinity and Sabine Railway was constructed through northern Polk County. To harvest the rich supply of timber in the area, the Allen Lumber Company of Houston built a sawmill at Asia; it furnished lumber for the railroad and drew scores of new residents to the site. Although the Allen company expanded operations in 1900, the cutting out of local forests, concentration of mills at nearby Corrigan, and general decline of the lumber industryqv between 1900 and 1910 led to Asia's demise. Only a few scattered residences remain.

BIBLIOGRAPHY: Ed Ellsworth Bartholomew, *800 Texas Ghost Towns* (Fort Davis, Texas: Frontier, 1971). *A Pictorial History of Polk County, Texas, 1846–1910* (Livingston, Texas: Polk County Bicentennial Commission, 1976; rev. ed. 1978). *Robert Wooster*

ASKANASE, REUBEN W. (1908–1991). Reuben W. Askanase, businessman, the son of immigrant parents, was born in Fargo, North Dakota, in 1908 and as a boy began his career selling newspapers. Early in life he helped take care of his family by assisting his mother in their chuck wagon. To earn a living, they followed the migrant workers, cooking and serving them meals on their jobs or boarding them in their home.

Askanase, who worked his way through North Dakota State University, later gifted the school with the Askanase Hall and scholarships. He rose from office boy to the vice presidency of the New York department store, Abraham and Strauss, before moving to Houston in 1945. His success in Houston began with the Columbia Dry Goods store and was furthered when he invested in the purchase of the manufacture of Evenflow baby bottles. He and his partners built the company into Dunhill International, which owned Spaulding sporting goods, along with other properties. He served as chairman of the board.

Askanase was active in the Houston Council on Human Relations, the Houston Symphony, and the Alley Theatre.qv He also served as president of the Houston Sports Association and the Jewish Community Center, chairman of the United Jewish Campaign, trustee of the Rothko Chapelqv and North Dakota State University, and board member of Allied Mercantile Bank and Benjamin Franklin Savings Association. He received the Max H. Nathan Award from the American Jewish Committee in 1964. He raised funds for Citizens for Good Schools and the Houston Area Women's Center and was a member and trustee of Congregation Beth Israel.qv

Reuben Askanase married Hilda Graham, and they had a son and a daughter. Askanase died on January 3, 1991. He was survived by his wife, his children and their spouses, a sister, eight grandchildren, and two great-grandchildren.

BIBLIOGRAPHY: Houston *Post*, January 5, 1991. Ruthe Winegarten and Cathy Schechter, *Deep in the Heart: The Lives and Legends of Texas Jews* (Austin: Eakin Press, 1990). *Merilee Weiner*

ASPERMONT, TEXAS. Aspermont is at the junction of U.S. highways 83 and 380 and Farm roads 610, 2211, and 1263, fifty-nine miles north of Abilene in central Stonewall County. It was platted as a townsite in 1889 by A. L. Rhomberg, who provided the land and gave it the Latin name for "rough mountain." A post office was opened the same year. Earlier area residents called the place Sunflower Flat. The population had reached approximately 250 in 1898, when Aspermont replaced Rayner as county seat. Rayner contested the election, and the courthouse relocation was deferred until 1900, when litigation cleared the way for construction. Aspermont was incorporated in 1909 with a population of 700; construction of a lake and water-supply facilities began in 1914. Local businessmen made donations to encourage railroad construction, and the Stamford and Northwestern Railway line was extended from Stamford in 1909 and leased to the Wichita Valley Railway Company. Aspermont had 400 residents by 1900 and 600 by 1910. World War Iqv reduced the population to 436 in 1920, but it rebounded by 1930 to 769; by 1940, thanks to the discovery of oil, it had increased to 1,041. The local economy relies on ranching and oil. In 1970 the town had 1,198 residents and fifty businesses; in 1980 the population reached 1,357. A hospital was built in 1965. County facilities in town include a library, a swimming pool, and a livestock show barn. An annual rodeo is a feature event. The population in 1990 was 1,214.

BIBLIOGRAPHY: *A History of Stonewall County* (Aspermont, Texas: Stonewall County Historical Commission, 1979). Vertical Files, Barker Texas History Center, University of Texas at Austin.

William R. Hunt

ASPHALT BELT RAILWAY. The Asphalt Belt Railway Company was chartered on June 9, 1923. The railroad was planned to run from a point on the San Antonio, Uvalde and Gulf in Zavala County to the mines of the Texas Rock Asphalt Company and of R. L. White in Uvalde County. The capital of the AB was $20,000. The principal place of business was San Antonio. The members of the first board of directors were H. P. McMillan, R. C. Tarbutton, R. H. Schultz, and Mason Williams, all of San Antonio; E. R. Breaker and F. L. Lewis, both of North Pleasanton; and R. C. Hollifield of Uvalde. The Asphalt Belt was constructed during the later part of 1923 by Frank Kell and W. T. Eldridge and opened January 1, 1924. The line ran from Asphalt Belt Junction on the SAU&G, located about a mile south of Pulliam, at Dabney, a distance of about eighteen miles. The company provided intrastate service only until granted authority to engage in interstate commerce by the Interstate Commerce Commission on August 24, 1926. In November of the same year the Asphalt Belt was acquired by the New Orleans, Texas and Mexico, which was acting for the Missouri Pacific. Although the Asphalt Belt kept its corporate identity, it was operated as a part of the Missouri Pacific lines until 1956, when it was merged into the Missouri Pacific. Throughout its life the Asphalt Belt owned no equipment and never offered passenger service. Extensive flood damage in late 1986 destroyed a bridge near Farm Road 481 and led to the dismantling of the former Asphalt Belt in 1987. *Ruben E. Ochoa*

ASPHALT MOUNTAIN. Asphalt Mountain is three miles southeast of Cline in southwestern Uvalde County (at 29°13′ N, 100°03′ W). With an elevation of 1,292 feet above sea level, its summit rises 330 feet above nearby Farm Road 1022. Cline is an asphalt center.

ASSOCIATION FOR THE ADVANCEMENT OF MEXICAN AMERICANS. The Association for the Advancement of Mexican Americans was established in 1970 by Yolanda Navarro, Luis Cano, and other Houston students, businessmen, and young teachers from the city's barrios to address educational and social problems among local Mexican-American youths and prepare them to become leaders. The AAMA, which initially had only fourteen members, was headed by a board of directors. By the end of the 1970s its membership had grown to 1,000, mostly low-income and middle-class Mexican Americans in Houston.

AAMA sought to improve the students' achievement by curbing their school dropout rate and reducing drug abuse. Working out of an old house on Sampson Street, it set out to organize various community-service programs. In 1970 the association established the Jovita I. Day Care Center, a bilingual preschool program, and offered free neighborhood-based recreational activities for Hispanic teenagers. Financial support for these programs was drawn from both local and federal sources.

In January 1973 AAMA closed temporarily due to an inadequate budget, and its state charter was revoked because of its inactivity. To reinvigorate the organization, Navarro and Cano set up a new board of directors, and by the summer of 1973 AAMA received a Model Cities grant to establish an art center for barrio youth. Cano, a self-described activist, insisted, however, that the funds be used for an alternative school for Mexican-American students. With the AAMA board's support the George I. Sánchez[qv] School began under Sánchez's direction in an old muffler warehouse on Polk Street. Fifteen adolescent males made up the first class.

Sánchez was accredited as a private school by the Texas Education Agency in the late 1970s. At the same time AAMA also obtained federal funds to run a talent-search project to encourage local Mexican-American students' enrollment in college. By the early 1990s the school had graduated more than 300 students, and the talent-search program reached 1,200 students a year.

AAMA established an arts center in 1974, which later produced "The Aztecas and Their Medicine, A Chicano Legacy." The film was awarded the Seventh Annual Robert Kennedy Journalism Award in 1975. In 1976 the organization set up a program to prevent drug abuse, and in 1978 it opened Casa de Esperanza (House of Hope), since renamed Casa Phoenix, to treat inhalant, drug, and alcohol abusers. AAMA eventually set up programs in mathematics and science education for families, foster care, cultural awareness, AIDS education, and adult basic education. All these activities have served such Mexican-American neighborhoods as East End, Magnolia Park, Second Ward, Northside, and Denver Harbor.

By 1990 AAMA had purchased the former Houston Office Center on the Gulf Freeway and renamed it AAMA Park Plaza. It houses the organization's administrative offices, the Sánchez School, and other programs. In 1990 AAMA established a statewide magazine, *Texas Hispanic.* The publication, which covers a broad array of issues on Hispanics, became independent from AAMA in 1992. More recently, AAMA set up a housing revitalization program in Magnolia Central Park.

BIBLIOGRAPHY: Sylvia Alicia Gonzales, *Hispanic Voluntary Organizations* (Westport, Connecticut: Greenwood Press, 1985).

Teresa Palomo Acosta

ASSOCIATION OF SOUTHERN WOMEN FOR THE PREVENTION OF LYNCHING. The Association of Southern Women for the Prevention of Lynching was founded in November 1930 in Atlanta, Georgia, by Jessie Daniel Ames,[qv] a Texas-born southern woman active in suffrage and interracial reform movements. She and twelve founding members established the ASWPL as an arm of the Atlanta-based Commission on Interracial Cooperation, an organization working for racial harmony. The ASWPL's founders, all active in Protestant churches and interracial organizations (they were later joined by members of Jewish women's groups), wanted to prevent lynching[qv] by educating southern whites about its causes and prevention. They were convinced that lynchings were sanctioned murder and the result of "false chivalry," the use by white men of white women's virtue as an excuse for racially motivated violence against blacks. The ASWPL sought to convince white women of their responsibility to refuse to play a helpless role in that process.

The association had no constitution, by-laws, charter, dues, or formal membership roster. It did have standards for affiliation, however. Southern, often prominent, white women who were active in existing reform and church organizations were asked to serve as state and local contact points in the association's information network and to use their respective organizations to spread the word against lynching. Although its structure resembled that of many black antilynching organizations, the ASWPL rejected participation by blacks in its activities because its leaders believed that only white women could influence other white women. The association separated itself from the Commission on Interracial Cooperation to avoid connection with concepts of interracialism, but continued to receive its only financial support from the CIC. Ames met in Atlanta once a year with a volunteer central council of ten to twelve women to make policy, and she headed an executive committee of five that handled routine tasks. Eventually, state councils were formed to funnel information from the central council. Working through existing organizations and securing pledges of active support from individuals, the ASWPL grew rapidly. Georgia and Mississippi women formed the first state councils and were followed by councils in eleven more states. By the early 1940s there were 109 associations, and memberships totaled four million. In Texas efforts were headed by Sallie L. Hanna,[qv] a churchwoman in Dallas who had previously served as the national president of the YWCA.

Once its participants pledged to work to end lynching, the central council provided them with results of their investigations into specific incidents, issued press releases, brochures, pamphlets, and other educational pieces for use in the states, instructed supporters about procedures for preventing lynchings, and urged them to secure antilynching pledges from sheriffs, judges, governors, and other political figures. Letter-writing campaigns and confrontations with law officers and mobs were also among their tactics. The ASWPL concentrated its efforts in the five states where lynchings were most frequent—Mississippi, Georgia, Texas, Louisiana, and Florida.

In Texas in 1934 Sallie Hanna secured the pledges of seven gubernatorial candidates to use the power of the governor's office to end lynching. The Texas council sent questionnaires to each candidate, then offered the results for publication. The Dallas *Morning News*[qv] printed the story on page one. Attorney General James Allred,[qv] who subsequently won the governorship, pledged to support state legislation necessary to control mobs, to prevent lynchings, and to catch and punish perpetrators of lynchings.

By 1942 enough reduction in mob violence and lynchings had been accomplished that Jessie Ames believed the purposes of the ASWPL had been achieved and ended the association's work. In addition many of the association's active supporters had begun to fight for a federal antilynching bill, which she opposed.

BIBLIOGRAPHY: Henry E. Barber, "The Association of Southern Women for the Prevention of Lynching," *Phylon* 34 (December 1973). Jacquelyn Dowd Hall, "Jessie Daniel Ames," in *American Reformers*, ed. Alden Whitman (New York: Wilson, 1985). Jacquelyn Dowd Hall, *Revolt Against Chivalry: Jessie Daniel Ames and the Women's Campaign Against Lynching* (New York: Columbia University Press, 1979). Lewis Nordyke, "The Ladies and the Lynchers," *Reader's Digest*, November 1939. *Notable American Women: A Biographical Dictionary* (4 vols., Cambridge, Massachusetts: Harvard University Press, 1971–80).

Nancy Baker Jones

ASSOCIATION OF TEXAS COLLEGES AND UNIVERSITIES. In November 1916 the former college section of the Texas State Teachers Association[qv] was reorganized as the Association of Texas Colleges in order to provide for duly accredited representation of participating members. C. A. Nichols, of Southwestern University, was the first president. In the 1960s the organization changed its name to Association of Texas Colleges and Universities and relinquished its power to accredit colleges. One of the major goals of the association is the promotion of the needs and benefits of higher education to the general public. The group also serves as a forum for communication among college presidents. The charter prohibits the group from engaging in political lobbying. To join, a school must be fully accredited by the Commission of Colleges of the Southern Association of Colleges and Schools. Affiliate memberships are available to schools classified by the Southern Association as candidates for accreditation. In 1994 the Association of Texas Colleges and Universities had 121 members, representing independent, public senior, community, and public technical colleges. Members meet annually. The association elects a president, a vice president, and a board of directors. The board has six members elected at large for three-year terms and representatives from the Independent Colleges and Universities of Texas, the Texas Association of Community Colleges, and the Council of Public University Presidents and Chancellors. Funds are obtained through membership dues, which are calculated by a school's enrollment.

BIBLIOGRAPHY: Thomas Ferguson, *The Association of Texas Colleges* (Durham, North Carolina, 1945). *Proceedings of the Association of Texas Colleges and Universities Annual Meeting*, 1983.

Tracé Etienne-Gray

ASSUMPTION SEMINARY. Bishop John Shaw[qv] established St. John's Seminary in 1915. Early attempts at a seminary had occurred at St. Mary's Parish in San Antonio (1876–78), Guadalupe College in Seguin (1878–80), and St. Joseph in Victoria (1880–1902). St. John's opened first in the chancery building and was moved next to Nuestra Señora de la Purísima Concepción de Acuña Mission in 1920. It was a high school and college from the beginning. A graduate theology department was added in 1928, two years after San Antonio was named an archdiocese. It is believed that St. John's was the only Catholic seminary in the United States where all twelve years were offered at the same site.

Robert E. Lucey[qv] was installed as archbishop of San Antonio on March 27, 1941. One of his first major decisions was to invite the Vincentian fathers[qv] to administer and teach at St. John's. The old Trinity University campus in the west end of town was purchased. The college and graduate theology students were transferred there in the fall of 1952. The new campus was named Assumption Seminary; St. John's remained as a high school.

The undergraduate students began taking their academic classes at nearby St. Mary's University in 1964. Diocesan priests took over responsibility of administration and pastoral formation in 1967. That same year the graduate theology students began taking their academic classes at St. Mary's University. The theology students transferred to Oblate School of Theology for academic formation in 1970. The undergraduate program began to be phased out in 1975.

In 1990 Assumption Seminary was a house of residence and pastoral formation for students for the Catholic priesthood in a bicultural ministry. All students must make a commitment to Hispanic culture and language. Assumption is the only diocesan seminary in the United States that is connected with a religious house in a collaborative model of education and formation.

Pope John Paul II visited San Antonio on September 13, 1987, and stayed at Assumption that evening. He had lunch there with the Texas bishops and met that evening with about 1,500 Polish people from Panna Maria. Assumption–St. John's concluded seventy-five years of service in 1990. It has produced one martyr, ten bishops, and about 650 priests from its staff and alumni.

BIBLIOGRAPHY: Catholic Archives of Texas, Files, Austin.

James F. Vanderholt

ASTRODOME. The Astrodome, the first fully air-conditioned, enclosed, domed, multipurpose sports stadium in the world, is officially named Harris County Domed Stadium. More than four million persons have visited the Astrodome each year since the stadium was opened in April 1965. It has been used for major-league baseball, major-league soccer, professional and collegiate football, championship boxing, Portuguese-style bullfighting, rodeos, polo, collegiate basketball, special concerts, conventions, and religious meetings. The Astrodome is the prototype of numerous sports structures.

The first tangible efforts toward building the innovative stadium were made when the Harris County Park Commission was established by the Fifty-fifth Texas Legislature. The bill enabled Harris County to submit a revenue-bond issue to property owners for a Houston sports center. Voters approved the issue by a vote of more than three to one on July 26, 1958. Later, the idea of having an all-purpose covered stadium was developed through the leadership of Roy M. Hofheinz,[qv] and it was determined that a new bond issue should be held to authorize general-obligation bonds. On January 31, 1961, the voters of Harris County approved a general obligation bond issue of $22 million. Ground was broken on January 3, 1962. After excavation work was completed it was found that more money was needed to complete the structure. On December 22, 1962, another bond issue of $9 million was approved by Harris County property owners. Although there were two lawsuits and other delays, construction on the stadium itself started on March 18, 1963, and was completed two years later. The stadium structure itself cost $20 million but the overall cost was more than $40 million of which $31.6 million came from two county bond issues and $3.75 million from the state highway department and the city of Houston for off-site improvements, including paved streets, bridges, and storm sewers. The Houston Sports Association, which leased the stadium from the county for forty years, added $6 million for expensive apartments, restaurants, cushioned seats, and a $2 million scoreboard.

The first event in the Astrodome was held on April 9, 1965, when the Houston Astros[qv] played the New York Yankees in exhibition baseball. The Astros play all their home games in the Astrodome. Professional football established itself in the Astrodome when the Houston Oilers[qv] began playing all of their home games there in a preseason exhibition game with the Washington Redskins on August 1, 1968. Seating capacity of the Astrodome for baseball is 52,000, for football about 62,000, and for some events, 66,000. Temperature is a constant 73°F, with humidity at 50 percent. There are five restaurants. The stadium has a clear span of 642 feet, an inside height of 208 feet, a lighting maximum of 300 footcandles, an air-filtering system of activated charcoal, and a man-made field cover called Astroturf. Hofheinz ordered the plastic roof painted because outfielders had trouble tracking fly balls during daylight in the bright glare and crisscross network of girders overhead. The lack of sunlight kills the grass, but Chemstrand, then experimenting with an outdoor artificial carpet, produced what came to be called Astroturf. Hofheinz, starting in 1966, used this instead of natural grass. Questions have been raised about injuries suffered from the harder surface, although numerous other stadiums have it.

In 1987 the dome underwent a $100 million renovation. Seating was expanded by 10,000, and seventy-two luxury boxes were built. As well as being the home for both the Houston Astros and Houston Oilers, the stadium has also hosted the United States Football League Houston Gamblers, World Football League Houston Texans, and the University of Houston Cougars. In 1992 the Republican party[qv] held its national convention at the dome.

bibliography: Vertical Files, Barker Texas History Center, University of Texas at Austin. *Wayne Chandler*

ASTRONOMY AND ASTRONOMERS. Apart from the work of a number of isolated amateurs, early astronomy in Texas mainly consisted of surveys of the state and professionals visiting for special events. From 1686 to 1690, during his five expeditions through Texas, Alonso De León[qv] carried astronomical tables and made latitude observations with an astrolabe. In 1772 Athanase de Mézières[qv] wrote probably the first report of an iron meteorite in Texas, the Texas Iron,[qv] based on accounts he heard from Indians living near the Brazos River. During the Red River expedition[qv] in 1806 Thomas Freeman and Lt. Enoch Humphreys used sextants and a telescope to determine latitudes and longitudes. Two years later Anthony Glass[qv] visited and described the Red River iron meteorite. A United States Army survey included the Panhandle[qv] in 1820 and a Pacific railroad survey in 1855; in 1850–51 the United States–Texas border was surveyed. Tables compiled by the United States Coast Survey include stations marked as early as 1848 at Dollar Point (near Galveston) and 1853 on Galveston Island. A few academic lectures were given, for example by Oscar H. Leland at Baylor and Waco universities, in the 1850s and 1860s.

On May 6, 1878, a transit of Mercury across the solar disk was observed by William Harkness and Lt. George E. Ide, of the United States Naval Observatory, from the grounds of the General Land Office[qv] in Austin. On July 29, 1878, a total eclipse of the sun was observed from Fort Worth by a party directed by Leonard Waldo, then at Harvard College Observatory. Many observers were recruited both locally and from out-of-state academic institutions. The program included drawings and photography of the solar corona, measurements of polarization, and spectroscopic observations of the changing light from the solar chromosphere. From the latter W. H. Pulsifer of Washington University in St. Louis deduced a height of the chromosphere of at least 524 miles. David Todd of the Naval Observatory observed from Dallas and produced sketches of the solar corona.

On December 6, 1882, a transit of Venus across the solar disk occurred. Such transits are very rare events that offer an opportunity of determining the distance of the earth from the sun by mounting expeditions to widely scattered sites over the earth, from which different tracks of the planet across the sun can be observed. On previous occasions the exact moments when the disk of Venus was just fully on the edge of the solar disk were unknown because of a distortion of the planet's image known as the "black drop effect." For the 1882 event many nations sent expeditions to a variety of sites. San Antonio was considered the best observing station in North America, and the city hosted two expeditions, one from the United States Naval Observatory and one from the Belgian Royal Observatory. The Belgian expedition was directed by Jean Charles Houzeau de Lehaie, who had an adventurous career in Belgium, Texas, Mexico, Louisiana, and Jamaica before returning to direct the Belgian Royal Observatory. He occupied a house near Fort Sam Houston and made meticulous observations, some by a novel technique, with a variety of instruments. Many drawings of the black drop effect were produced, both at San Antonio and at the companion station in Chile, but these led again to an uncertain estimate of the earth–sun distance. The American expedition under Asaph Hall was installed in army tents 500 yards to the east of the Belgians. The United States results were equally disappointing, not least because the funds allocated by Congress were cut off.

H. S. Moore, an amateur astronomer from McKinney, Texas, was a codiscoverer of the supernova in the Andromeda nebula in 1885. At the 1910 apparition of Halley's comet almost the only scientific observations in Texas were made at Holy Trinity College in Dallas by Father John Joseph Lesage, who had been giving scientific classes, including astronomy, over a period of eleven years. Again there was wide public interest and alarm.

When the American Association of Variable Star Observers was founded in 1911, a number of Texas amateurs began to contribute observations, notably S. H. Huntington of Kerrville; Oscar Monnig (a renowned meteorite expert) of Fort Worth, who with friends established a small observatory outside the city; Graham Kendall of Houston; and B. F. Grandstaff of Dallas. In 1932 the University of Texas joined with the University of Chicago to found the McDonald Observatory at Mount Locke (*see* university of texas mcdonald observatory). In 1961 plans were announced for the establishment of the Manned Space Center (*see* lyndon b. johnson space center) at Clear Lake in Harris County. From the 1960s into the 1990s the facility continued to function as the control center for the United States space program under NASA. In the 1990s universities with separate astronomy departments were the University of Texas at Austin and Rice University. See also meteorites.

bibliography: David S. Evans and Donald W. Olson, "Early Astronomy in Texas," *Southwestern Historical Quarterly* 93 (April 1990). S. W. Geiser, "Men of Science in Texas, 1820–1880," *Field and Laboratory* 26–27 (July–October 1958, October 1959). Leo J. Klosterman, Loyd S. Swenson and Sylvia Rose, *100 Years of Science and Technology in Texas: A Sigma Xi Centennial Volume* (Houston: Rice University Press, 1986). *David S. Evans*

ATAJAL INDIANS. In 1690 Damián Massanet[qv] reported an encounter with the Atajals and five other Indian groups in the Frio River valley southwest of San Antonio, apparently in what is now Frio County. Massanet's observations on Indian languages spoken in southern Texas seem to indicate that the Atajals and their associates spoke the language now known as Coahuilteco. The Atajals of Massanet were evidently the same people as the Etayax Indians, who are recorded as one of the groups known to Jean Jarry[qv] in 1688. The Atajals appear to have originally lived somewhere along the southern margin of the Edwards Plateau[qv] west of San Antonio. The southward thrust of Apaches must have displaced them from their homeland. In 1708 they were last recorded, under the name Atacal, as living farther south in Texas. After being reduced in numbers, they probably merged with a remnant of some larger group. Although there is some similarity in the names, it is not possible to prove by documentary evidence that the Atajals of Massanet were the same people as the Atayos of Álvar Núñez Cabeza de Vaca.[qv] The Atayos were known to Cabeza de Vaca in the years 1533–34 and appear to have lived in an area 140 miles east of the Atajals. This was more than 150 years before the Atajals were first recorded. The similarity in names is probably fortuitous.

BIBLIOGRAPHY: Thomas N. Campbell and T. J. Campbell, *Historic Indian Groups of the Choke Canyon Reservoir and Surrounding Area, Southern Texas* (San Antonio: Center for Archaeological Research, University of Texas at San Antonio, 1981). Lino Gómez Canedo, ed., *Primeras exploraciones y poblamiento de Texas, 1686–1694* (Monterrey: Publicaciones del Instituto Technológico y de Estudios Superiores de Monterrey, 1968). Alonso de León et al., *Historia de Nuevo León* (Monterrey: Centro de Estudios Humanísticos de la Universidad de Nuevo León, 1961). P. Otto Maas, ed., *Viajes de Misioneros Franciscanos a la conquista del Nuevo México* (Seville: Imprenta de San Antonio, 1915).

Thomas N. Campbell

ATAKAPA INDIANS. The Atakapa (Attakapa, Attacapa) Indians, including such subgroups as the Akokisas and Deadoses, occupied the coastal and bayou areas of southwestern Louisiana and southeastern Texas until the early 1800s. Such groups as the Akokisas and Deadoses lived west of the lower Neches River, while the Atakapas proper occupied the territory east of the lower Neches extending into Louisiana. Archeological studies of this area suggest that settlements have been present since before American Indians learned to make pottery, about the time of the birth of Christ. *Atakapa* means "eaters of men" in Choctaw, but the question has been raised whether the Atakapas' cannibalism was for subsistence or ritual. Village chiefs in the mid-1700s included Canoe, El Gordo, Mateo, and Calzones Colorados.[qv] Atakapan society consisted of loose bands that moved from place to place within a set area or territory gathering, hunting, and fishing. The alligator was important to them, for it provided meat, oil, and hides. The oil of the alligator was used as insect repellent. The Atakapan language has fascinated linguists and is among the better-recorded Indian languages. In 1721 Jean Béranger[qv] recorded and analyzed the language of nine Akokisas, members of a group closely associated with the Atakapas proper. Studies done in the 1920s by John R. Swanton and Albert Gatschet led to the Smithsonian publication *A Dictionary of the Atakapa Language* in 1932. Swanton and Gatschet associated the Atakapas with the Tunican Indians of the lower Mississippi River. Some later linguists have abandoned this linkage and classified Atakapan as an isolated language.

The bands of the Atakapas, including the Akokisas, were reported to have engaged in some type of trade not only with other Indians but also with the French and Spanish. Evidence indicates that the Hans people, whom Álvar Núñez Cabeza de Vaca[qv] encountered in 1528, may have been part of the Atakapan group. French contact was established after François Simars de Bellisle[qv] found himself stranded among the Akokisas in 1719. French exploration and trade of Atakapan territory continued throughout the early 1700s. The Spanish responded to the French presence on the Texas coast by establishing a series of missions along the San Gabriel River. The mission of San Ildefonso was briefly home to a number of Atakapas from the Deadose, which as a whole the Spanish had little success in converting. The San Xavier missions[qv] were abandoned in 1755.

Much of what is known about the Atakapas' appearance and culture comes from eighteenth and nineteenth century European descriptions and drawings. They were said to have been short, dark, and stout. Their clothing included breechclouts and buffalo hides. They did not practice polygamy or incest. Their customs included the use of wet bark for baby carriers and Spanish moss for diapers. Customarily, a father would rename himself at the birth of his first son or if the son became famous. In the Atakapan creation myth, man was said to have been cast up from the sea in an oyster shell. The Atakapas also believed that men who died from snakebite and those who had been eaten by other men were denied life after death, a creed that may give support to the idea that they practiced ritual cannibalism. With the coming of the Europeans, the ranks of the Atakapas thinned rapidly. According to Swanton, there were 3,500 in 1698 and only 175 in Louisiana in 1805. By 1908 there were only nine known descendants. Their demise was primarily caused by the invasion of European diseases rather than through direct confrontations with European settlers.

BIBLIOGRAPHY: Lawrence E. Aten, *Indians of the Upper Texas Coast* (New York: Academic Press, 1983). Lyle Campbell and Marianne Mithune, eds., *The Languages of Native America: Historical and Comparative Assessment* (Austin: University of Texas Press, 1979). Joseph O. Dyer, *The Lake Charles Atakapas (Cannibals) Period of 1817 to 1820* (Galveston, 1917). Henri Folmer, "De Bellisle on the Texas Coast," *Southwestern Historical Quarterly* 44 (October 1940). William W. Newcomb, *The Indians of Texas* (Austin: University of Texas Press, 1961).

Dorothy Couser

ATANAGUAYPACAM INDIANS. The Atanaguaypacam Indians (Atanaguipacane), who were apparently Coahuiltecan in speech, lived on the Gulf Coast near the mouth of the Rio Grande. In the middle eighteenth century their settlements were reported to be along the shores of the numerous small bays and islands near the mouth of the Rio Grande.

BIBLIOGRAPHY: Gabriel Saldivar, *Los Indios de Tamaulipas* (Mexico City: Pan American Institute of Geography and History, 1943).

Thomas N. Campbell

ATASACNEU INDIANS. The Atasacneu (Atasacnau) Indians are known from a Spanish document of 1748 that lists twenty-five Indian groups of east central and southeastern Texas who had asked for missions in that general area. About half the names on the list, including Atasacneu, cannot be identified. The identifiable groups consist of Caddoans (including Wichita), Tonkawans, Atakapans, and Karankawans.

BIBLIOGRAPHY: Herbert Eugene Bolton, *Texas in the Middle Eighteenth Century* (Berkeley: University of California Press, 1915; rpt., Austin: University of Texas Press, 1970). Charles W. Hackett, ed., *Pichardo's Treatise on the Limits of Louisiana and Texas* (4 vols., Austin: University of Texas Press, 1931–46). Juan Agustín Morfi, *History of Texas, 1673–1779* (2 vols., Albuquerque: Quivira Society, 1935; rpt., New York: Arno, 1967).

Thomas N. Campbell

ATASCOSA, TEXAS. Atascosa is off Interstate Highway 35 fourteen miles southwest of downtown San Antonio in southwestern Bexar County. The community, whose name in Spanish means "boggy," was settled just after the Civil War.[qv] A post office opened in 1872, and by 1885 the community had a Baptist church, a district school, a general store, a saloon, two blacksmiths, and a population of 180. A pottery and coal mine operated there around 1900. In the mid-1930s Atascosa had a school, a church, a lodge, several stores, and a population of 300. The population has remained steady since that time, and in the early 1990s the town still reported four businesses.

Minnie B. Cameron

ATASCOSA COUNTY. Atascosa County (P-14) is south of San Antonio on Interstate Highway 37 in the Rio Grande Plain region of south central Texas. Jourdanton, the county seat, is located on Interstate Highway 37 in central Atascosa County thirty-three miles south of San Antonio and 100 miles northwest of Corpus Christi. The geographic center point of the county is 28°50′ N, 98°30′ W. The county covers 1,218 square miles of level to rolling land. Elevation ranges from 350 to 700 feet, and the soils are generally deep with loamy surface layers and clayey subsoils. Along the southern borders the light-colored soils have limestone near the surface. In some areas the soils are gray to black, cracking and clayey, and expand and shrink considerably. In the South Texas Plains vegetation area, the subtropical dryland vegetation consists primarily of cactus, weeds, grasses, thorny shrubs and trees such as mesquite,[qv] and live oak and post oak. Many of the open grasslands have been seeded with buffalo grass. Between 41 and 50 percent of the county is considered prime farmland. Wildlife in Atascosa County includes white-tailed deer, javelina, turkey, fox squirrel, jackrabbits, foxes, ring-tailed cats, skunks, and opossum. The main predators are bobcats and coyotes. Ducks, cranes, and geese migrate across the county. Tanks are stocked with catfish, bass, and sunfish. Mineral resources include clay, uranium, sand and gravel, and oil and gas. Other minerals and products include caliche and clay, lignite coal, construction and industrial sand, sulfur, and uranium.

The climate is subtropical-subhumid; winters are mild and summers are hot. The average annual temperature is 70°F. Temperatures range in January from an average low of 40° F to an average high of 65° and in July from 74° to 97°. The average annual precipitation is twenty-seven inches, with an average relative humidity of 84 percent at six A.M. and 51 percent at six P.M. There is no significant snowfall. The growing season averages 282 days a year, with the last freeze in late February and the first freeze in early December. The sun shines an average 65 percent of the daylight hours.

Archeological evidence suggests that Indians of the Coahuiltecan language group occupied this region for several thousand years before the arrival of Spanish explorers in the sixteenth century. They survived by hunting and gathering until they were taught agriculture by the Spaniards, who also trained them in pottery, masonry, and carpentry skills. After the arrival of Europeans, most of these early residents succumbed to disease, intermarried, or were annihilated by Comanche and Apache invasions. Indians in Atascosa County after Anglo settlement began were primarily Lipan Apaches and Comanches, although by the late nineteenth century these, too, were virtually extinct.

Families from northern Mexico established ranches in the area by the middle of the eighteenth century. The name Atascosa, "boggy" in Spanish, was used to describe the area as early as 1788. The Lower Presidio Road, one of the branches of the Old San Antonio Road,[qv] passed through the area. After the Texas Revolution,[qv] most of the Mexican ranches were broken up, but the first Anglo settlers did not arrive until the late 1840s, when the state began to grant land there to veterans. The most important of these grants, and the one that marked the beginning of extensive colonization in the area, was that of four leagues on the Atascosa River (formerly known as Atascosa Creek) to José Antonio Navarro,[qv] originally deeded to him by the Mexican government in 1825 and acknowledged by the state of Texas in 1853.

The area was sparsely settled by the mid-1850s, and in 1856 the county was marked off from Bexar County. The first county seat, Navatasco, was established in 1857 on land donated by Navarro. Among the county's early settlers were Peter Tumlinson,[qv] who organized one of the first Ranger companies in the state in 1836, Indian fighter Thomas Rodriguez, George F. Hindes, Marshall Burney, and Eli Johnson. In 1858 Pleasanton, a newly founded community, became county seat, and a new courthouse was constructed. Settlers continued to trickle in, but the threat of Indian attack, poor roads, and the area's general isolation kept the population low.

On the eve of the Civil War[qv] subsistence farming and cattle ranching were the dominant occupations. The first census taken in Atascosa County in 1860 recorded a population of 1,578, including eighty-four black slaves. Tax rolls show that there thirty-three slaveholders, with most of them owning only one or two slaves. The number of improved acres was small, only 3,397, spread out among 102 farms.

Because of its isolation Atascosa County was little touched by the Civil War. Some Atascosa County residents fought for the Confederacy, most notably four of José Antonio Navarro's sons, but the way of life for most residents changed little during the war years. Due to the county residents' relatively small investment in slaves, the war and the depression that followed it had little effect on the economy. In marked contrast to most other counties of the state, which saw a dramatic decline in property values, the total taxable assets of Atascosa County actually rose, from $478,408 in 1860 to $497,940 in 1865.

After the war, cattle ranching took center stage, and during the late 1860s the number of livestock increased sharply. In 1860 there were 29,020 cattle in the county; by 1870, during the peak period of the great cattle drives, the figure had risen to 92,047, and livestock, mostly cattle, accounted for 75 percent of the agricultural receipts.

The population also increased rapidly during the postbellum years, to 2,915 by 1870 and to 4,217 in 1880 and 6,459 in 1890. Many of the new settlers were recent immigrants, including a sizable number of English and Germans.[qqv] After 1880 the number of immigrants from Mexico also grew steadily, and by the turn of the century Mexicans made up the largest number of foreign-born residents.

Many of the new residents arrived by railroad. In 1881 an extension of the Great Northern Railway was built through the extreme northern corner of Atascosa County, and the first railroad station in the county was located at Lytle. The influx of new settlers in turn brought a rapid increase in the number of farms and helped boost the agricultural economy. In 1870 there were 400 farms in the county with some 4,800 improved acres; by 1890 there were 886 farms and 50,534 improved acres. During the 1870s and 1880s corn was the principal cash crop, but during the late 1870s cotton was introduced, and by 1900 it had become the leading farm shipment. In 1890 Atascosa County farmers planted 10,553 acres in cotton; by 1910 that figure had increased to 32,125. Production of cotton also grew, from only 465 bales in 1880 to 4,799 in 1910.

The early years of the twentieth century brought other changes as well. In 1908 the Artesian Belt Railroad Company was incorporated and a year later began service between MacDona and Christine. And in 1912 the San Antonio, Uvalde and Gulf Railway was built through Atascosa County, fostering the growth of the towns of Leming, North Pleasanton, McCoy, Charlotte, and Hindes. In 1910 the residents of the county voted to make Jourdanton the county seat, and in 1912 a new mission-style courthouse was constructed, which is still in use.

Irrigation,[qv] first used effectively by Henry Mumme in Poteet in 1911, opened the way for such cash crops as strawberries, peas, and watermelons. But during the first three decades of the twentieth century cotton and cattle continued to be the county's leading products. Cotton production peaked in the mid-1920s, with over 81,000 acres under cultivation in 1924. Falling prices, droughts, and boll weevil[qv] infestations, however, combined to drive down cotton production in the 1930s. Although the amount of land planted in cotton continued to be quite high—as much as 20,000 acres in the late 1920s—both yields and profits dropped significantly, especially after 1932. In 1930

Atascosa County farmers produced only 6,176 bales, less than half of the 1926 figure (16,634).

Partly because of the rapidly growing population, land prices showed a marked increase between 1910 and 1929, and many new farmers found it impossible to buy land. The number of tenants and sharecroppers grew rapidly, particularly in the 1920s, and by 1930 more than half of the farmers—1,087 of 1,809—were working someone else's land. In contrast to many other areas of the state, the overwhelming majority of the tenants were white, but the problem nonetheless had serious results during the Great Depression[qv] of the 1930s. As a result of the poor yields and the reluctance of banks to extend credit to financially strapped farmers, many of those who made a living from the land, particularly tenants, found themselves in a precarious position. Numerous farmers were forced to give up their livelihoods and seek work elsewhere. Between 1930 and 1950 the number of tenants dropped from 1,087 to 532. Oil was discovered in 1917, and oil revenues helped some cash-strapped farmers and ranchers to survive the depression years, but the farming economy did not fully recover until after World War II.[qv]

During the 1950s cotton production continued to decline, and its place was taken by new crops such as sorghum and peanuts. Commercial strawberry raising also grew in importance after World War II, and by 1960 Atascosa County was the third-largest strawberry grower among Texas counties. Poteet strawberries were famous. In the early 1990s beef and dairy cattle, peanuts, hay, corn, grain sorghums, pecans, and strawberries were the leading crops. Approximately 40,000 acres was under irrigation.

After World War II the county population grew slightly, to 20,048 in 1950, but fell during the late 1950s and 1960s, and by 1970 the number of residents stood at 18,696. Subsequently, the population increased steadily; in 1990 it was 30,533. Much of the growth is attributable to the increase in the number of Mexican Americans.[qv] In 1980 Atascosa County was ranked fortieth among all United States counties in percentage of Hispanics, with 48 percent, and by 1990 that number had grown to 55 percent. Other leading ancestry groups included German (15 percent) and English (14 percent).

Total wages paid to employees of nonfarming enterprises increased to approximately $200 million in the 1980s. The percentage of the labor force employed in retailing, wholesaling, and manufacturing was 25; 16 percent were in professional or related service, 21 percent in agriculture, forestry, fisheries, and mining, and 12 percent self-employed. The remainder worked outside the county. Among the leading occupations were general construction and agribusiness.

Oil and gas extraction continued to be a leading industry. Humble Pipe Line Company established operations in Atascosa County in 1927, but the oil industry did not begin in earnest until the opening of Imagine and West Imagine fields in the 1940s, as well as those at Charlotte and Jourdanton. Diverse Humble operations in the Jourdanton area in the 1950s included gasoline, propane, butane, natural gasoline, and natural gas, all of which continued to be productive in the mid-1990s. In 1990 Atascosa County wells produced 1,236,387 barrels of oil; between 1917 and 1990 the total production was 138,595,610 barrels.

The mining of lignite coal, first begun in 1888, also became a major industry as the price of fuel oil and natural gas rose. The first lignite in Atascosa County was burned as fuel in 1981 after a ten-year period of research and development by the Brazos Electric Power Cooperative of Waco and the South Texas Electric Cooperative of Victoria. Another main mineral resource of Atascosa County is silica, used in building and glass-making. Local sand has also been processed for playground use, as blasting and frac sand for the oil industry, and as building material.

Politically, Atascosa County has usually been staunchly Democratic, although in the late twentieth century Republicans made strong inroads, particularly in presidential elections. Republican candidates outpolled Democrats in every election from 1972 to 1992, except for 1976, when Jimmy Carter won. Democrats, however, have continued to dominate local offices. In the 1982 primary 98 percent of the county's residents voted Democratic, and only 2 percent Republican, with 4,923 votes cast.

As of 1980, Atascosa County had forty-five churches with a total estimated membership of over 18,000. The largest denominations were Catholic, Southern Baptist, and United Methodist.

The earliest schools were organized around the time of the Civil War. By 1914 there were thirty-seven schools in the county, including three schools for black students. By the 1940s the school districts had begun to consolidate. The total number of persons over the age of twenty-five who had completed four years of high school rose from 1,300 in 1950 to 2,083 in 1960. In addition, 395 in 1950 and 473 in 1960 had some college education and 415 in 1950 and 358 in 1960 had received undergraduate degrees. In 1982, 384 students graduated from high school in Atascosa County's five consolidated school districts, and 34 percent of these indicated their intention to go on to college. The total number of adults with four years of high school had increased dramatically to over 12,000, almost half the total number of residents, and the number of college graduates over twenty-five was 2,322, or almost 9 percent.

Numerous hunters are attracted to the county, particularly during the fall and winter deer seasons. Other leading attractions include the Poteet Strawberry Festival, Jourdanton Days Celebration, and the Cowboy Homecoming and Rodeo in Pleasanton.

BIBLIOGRAPHY: *Atascosa County History* (Pleasanton, Texas: Atascosa History Committee, 1984). C. L. Patterson, *Atascosa County* (Pleasanton, Texas: Pleasanton *Express*, 1938). Vertical Files, Barker Texas History Center, University of Texas at Austin.

Linda Peterson

ATASCOSA RIVER. The Atascosa River heads in two branches known as the North and West Prongs. The North Prong rises four miles west of Atascosa in far southwestern Bexar County (at 29°16′ N, 98°47′ W) and runs south for six miles. The West Prong rises a mile west of Lytle in eastern Medina County (at 29°15′ N, 98°49′ W) and runs southeast for four miles. The two prongs flow together two miles southeast of Lytle in northwestern Atascosa County (at 29°12′ N, 98°46′ W) to form the Atascosa River proper. From that point the river runs ninety-two miles southeast through Atascosa County and into Live Oak County, where it drains into the Frio River two miles northwest of Three Rivers (at 28°29′ N, 98°12′ W). The river is probably the one called Arroyo de Vino by Alonso De León[qv] in 1689. It traverses flat to gently rolling terrain surfaced by clay and sandy loam that supports water-tolerant hardwoods, mesquite, cacti, and grasses.

ATASCOSITO CROSSING. The most well-known Atascosito Crossing is a historical point (29°40′ N, 96°27′ W) where the Atascosito Road[qv] crossed the Colorado River nine miles downstream from Columbus. Land on both sides of the river at the crossing was granted to Rawson Alley,[qv] one of Stephen F. Austin's[qv] Old Three Hundred[qv] settlers, on August 3, 1824. On Alley Hill, on the east bank of the river, Alley built his home, which became a focal point for early colonial activity. During the Civil War[qv] Alleyton was the western terminus of the Buffalo Bayou, Brazos, and Colorado Railway. From there a steady stream of wagon trains carrying cotton joined the Atascosito Road at the crossing and made their way to Mexico. Herders of cattle from South Texas also used the crossing on their way to Louisiana and Mississippi before and during the Civil War.[qv] Other cattlemen from the Gulf Coast crossed here during the 1870s and 1880s on their way to join the main trails north to the Kansas railheads.

ATASCOSITO ROAD. The Atascosito or Atascosita Road, established by the Spanish before 1757 as a military highway to East Texas (*see* SPANISH TEXAS), took its name from Atascosito, a Spanish settlement and military outpost on the Trinity River near the site of what is now Liberty, Texas. The road extended from Refugio and Goliad to the Atascosito Crossing on the Colorado River, on to the Brazos near San Felipe de Austin, and across the area of what is now northern Harris County to the Trinity. The eastward extension of the trail was known as the Opelousas or La Bahía Road.[qv] After the development of the cattle industry in Texas, the old Atascosito Road was followed by cattle drivers from South Texas to New Orleans. *L. W. Kemp*

ATASTAGONIE INDIANS. The Atastagonies, an otherwise unidentified group reported by Pedro de Rivera[qv] as living in South Texas in 1736, were probably the same as the Taztasagonie Indians.

BIBLIOGRAPHY: Frederick Webb Hodge, ed., *Handbook of American Indians North of Mexico* (2 vols., Washington: GPO, 1907, 1910; rpt., New York: Pageant, 1959).

ATAYO INDIANS. The Atayo (Atoyo, Tayo) Indians were encountered by Álvar Núñez Cabeza de Vaca[qv] near or along the Texas coast, apparently about 1528. Their location cannot be determined, but it seems to have been in the central section of the coast. Attempts to identify the Atayos with groups known to Europeans over 150 years later are largely speculations based on phonetic similarities in names. The Atayos have been linked with the Adais, a Caddoan group of western Louisiana, but this is no longer taken seriously. They have also been linked with the Tohos (or Tojos) and Tohahas, both of which did live inland near the coastal area possibly occupied by the Atayos.

BIBLIOGRAPHY: Adolph F. Bandelier, ed., *The Journey of Álvar Núñez Cabeza de Vaca and His Companions from Florida to the Pacific, 1528–1536* (New York: Barnes, 1905). Frederick Webb Hodge, ed., *Handbook of American Indians North of Mexico* (2 vols., Washington: GPO, 1907, 1910; rpt., New York: Pageant, 1959). John R. Swanton, *Source Material on the History and Ethnology of the Caddo Indians* (Smithsonian Institution, Bureau of American Ethnology Bulletin 132, Washington: GPO, 1942). Texas Indian Commission, *The Texas Indian Commission and American Indians in Texas: A Short History with Definitions and Demographics* (Austin, 1986). *Thomas N. Campbell*

ATCHISON, DANIEL D. (1820–1867). Daniel D. Atchison, lawyer, son of John and Elizabeth Atchison, was born in Fayette County, Kentucky, on April 7, 1820. He attended Centre College, graduated from Harvard Law School in 1844, and opened a law office at Louisville, Kentucky. In May 1846 he settled in Galveston, Texas, where he was in law firms with William Alexander and George W. Brown.[qqv] On January 20, 1847, Atchison married Frances Alexander, who died in July 1847. In 1863 he married Lucy Holt of Augusta, Georgia. He was prominent in Presbyterian church work, contributed to Atchison Free School at Navasota, and took a part in the establishment of Austin College. For twelve years he was clerk of the Texas Supreme Court. As an admirer of Sam Houston,[qv] he supported the governor during the controversy over secession.[qv] Atchison died on October 21, 1867.

BIBLIOGRAPHY: *History of Texas, Together with a Biographical History of the Cities of Houston and Galveston* (Chicago: Lewis, 1895). Amelia W. Williams and Eugene C. Barker, eds., *The Writings of Sam Houston, 1813–1863* (8 vols., Austin: University of Texas Press, 1938–43; rpt., Austin and New York: Pemberton Press, 1970).

ATCHISON, TOPEKA AND SANTA FE RAILWAY SYSTEM. Founded in Kansas in 1859 by Cyrus K. Holliday as the Atchison and Topeka Railroad, the Atchison, Topeka and Santa Fe Railway system became one of the largest and most profitable railroads in the Southwest. Holliday envisioned a line that would link Kansas with the Pacific Ocean in California, with Mexico City, and with the Gulf of Mexico, as well as with Santa Fe. By 1887 the Santa Fe, as it is popularly called, extended to Los Angeles from Kansas City; it completed a line from Kansas City to Chicago the next year. Boston and European investors provided most of the capital to build this rapidly growing system, and, led by William Barstow Strong, the management sought to tap markets in Texas. The Santa Fe reached Texas in 1881 with the completion of its line from Albuquerque to El Paso. By 1888 the Santa Fe had also entered the Panhandle of Texas with a line from southern Kansas to Panhandle City with service later extended to Amarillo. The company's builders sought an outlet on the Gulf of Mexico as a market for Kansas wheat and an entry into the burgeoning cattle and cotton production of Central Texas. In 1886 the Santa Fe arranged to acquire the Gulf, Colorado and Santa Fe Railway to obtain a connection to the Gulf of Mexico.

The GC&SF had been formed in 1873 by leading citizens of Galveston to build a line around Houston toward the northern and northwestern portions of the state. Aided by a grant of state lands, the company slowly constructed lines from Galveston to Lampasas, Fort Worth, and Dallas, with branches to Houston and Conroe. The leaders of the GC&SF and the Santa Fe agreed to construct a line across Indian Territory to link the two companies. The GC&SF built north from Fort Worth to Purcell, Indian Territory, where it joined the Santa Fe's new line from Kansas. After completion of this project in 1887, the Santa Fe began to build additional lines in Texas.

In order to meet the terms of Texas law that required all Texas railroads to be headquartered in the state, the GC&SF was operated as a subsidiary from its offices in Galveston. The track was extended east and north to Beaumont and Longview and northwest to Brownwood. Additional lines were constructed in the Panhandle, and in 1914 the Coleman Cutoff from Brownwood through Lubbock to Texico provided a new, shorter route from Houston to California. The Santa Fe incorporated another subsidiary, the Panhandle and Santa Fe Railway, headquartered in Amarillo, to consolidate its trackage in West Texas and to build new branches to Lamesa, San Angelo, and Stratford. The P&SF line through Pampa, Amarillo, and Hereford became part of the Santa Fe's major freight route from Chicago to California. Though many corporations were formed to construct these lines, the GC&SF and P&SF were the major subsidiaries of the Santa Fe in Texas.

Another significant acquisition, the Kansas City, Mexico and Orient Railway, purchased in 1928, gave the Santa Fe a line south from Wichita, Kansas, through Sweetwater and San Angelo to Presidio. Even in the 1920s and 1930s the Santa Fe continued to build or purchase track in the Panhandle and on the Edwards Plateau. The last major construction of a new branch into Dallas from the mainline at Sanger through Denton occurred in 1955.

In 1972 the Santa Fe operated 1,771 locomotives and 74,008 freight cars; net income for that year was $80,866,000. By 1980 the Santa Fe operated a system 12,209 miles in length, of which 3,508 miles were in Texas. A change in Texas statutes allowed for the merger of the GC&SF and P&SF into the Santa Fe system in 1965.

The Santa Fe acquired diverse business interests in Texas. In the 1930s the railway purchased the Kirby Lumber Company, a major timber operator in East Texas founded by John Henry Kirby.[qv] The railway owned truck lines in the state as well as extensive holdings in oil and natural gas. In 1968 Santa Fe Industries was formed in recognition of the many nonrail functions of the company in Texas and elsewhere. This new holding company reorganized the rail, petroleum, real estate, and pipeline operations into new divisions. Santa Fe Industries acquired Robert E. McKee, Incorporated, of El Paso in 1972, adding a construction company and real estate developer to its already extensive urban real estate holdings in Texas.

In 1983 Santa Fe Industries merged with the Southern Pacific Company to form Santa Fe Southern Pacific Corporation, but the Interstate Commerce Commission rejected the proposed merger of the Atchison, Topeka and Santa Fe Railway with the Southern Pacific Transportation Company.[qv] After defeating a hostile takeover attempt, the firm sold the Southern Pacific Transportation Company (1988),

Kirby Forest Industries (1986), and Robert E. McKee (1987). Several of the pipeline and energy subsidiaries were sold or their securities were distributed to stockholders. The company became Santa Fe Pacific Corporation in 1989.

BIBLIOGRAPHY: Keith L. Bryant, Jr., *History of the Atchison, Topeka and Santa Fe Railway* (New York: Macmillan, 1974). Ira G. Clark, *Then Came the Railroads: The Century from Steam to Diesel in the Southwest* (Norman: University of Oklahoma Press, 1958). E. D. Worley, *Iron Horses of the Santa Fe Trail* (Dallas: Southwest Railroad Historical Society, 1965).

Keith L. Bryant, Jr.

ATEN, CALVIN GRANT (1868–1939). Calvin Grant Aten, Texas Ranger and Panhandle[qv] lawman, the third of four sons of Austin C. and Kate (Dunlap) Aten, was born on December 7, 1868, in Abingdon, Illinois. He was a younger brother of Ira Aten,[qv] in whose steps he followed as a lawman. Cal remained on the family farm until April 1, 1888, when he enlisted in the Frontier Battalion[qv] and was assigned to his brother's Company D, then commanded by Capt. Frank Jones. He later recalled how conspicuous he felt as he walked into the ranger camp near Realitos, in Duval County, without weapons. Ira handed him a gunbelt with a six-shooter and instructions to put it on. Aten served with distinction throughout the Rio Grande border country. His most noted escapade occurred on Christmas Day 1889, when he accompanied John R. Hughes[qv] and two others on a manhunt to Bull Head Mountain, in Edwards County. There they killed Alvin and Will Odle when the two wanted rustlers resisted arrest. Pressing family responsibilities caused Aten to resign from the battalion on August 31, 1890. He returned to Round Rock, where he served for several years as a constable and sheriff and, on May 2, 1894, married Mattie Jo Kennedy. The couple later moved to the Panhandle, where Ira was section foreman for the Escarbadas Division of the XIT Ranch[qv] and head of the ranch's police force. Cal Aten remained in the XIT's employ from 1898 to 1904 and afterward established his own farm and ranch near Lelia Lake, in Donley County, where he spent his remaining years. He died there on April 1, 1939, and was buried in the Citizens Cemetery in Clarendon.

BIBLIOGRAPHY: Jack Martin, *Border Boss* (San Antonio: Naylor, 1942). Robert W. Stephens, *Texas Ranger Sketches* (Dallas, 1972).

H. Allen Anderson

ATEN, EDWIN DUNLAP (1870–1953). Edwin Dunlap Aten, Texas Ranger, the youngest son of Austin C. and Kate (Dunlap) Aten, was born on September 5, 1870, in Abingdon, Illinois. Despite his upbringing, Aten soon developed a rowdy streak and became dissatisfied with farm life. His concerned parents in 1890 sent him to the Panhandle,[qv] where he could be under the watchful eye of his former ranger brother Ira Aten,[qv] foreman of the Escarbada Division of the XIT Ranch.[qv] Although he worked diligently as a cowhand for the XIT Ranch, Ed Aten came to love poker and was involved in various incidents in saloons, climaxed by his shooting of a man in a quarrel over a card game. Ira immediately wrote his former commander, Frank Jones, with the intention of having Ed enlist in Company D of the Frontier Battalion[qv] as soon as a vacancy occurred. Although not enthusiastic at first about the prospect, Edwin joined the Texas Rangers[qv] on September 16, 1892, and began service with his brother's old company, then stationed at Alpine.

He soon became a dedicated member of the ranger company. In June 1893 he was part of the four-man posse that accompanied Captain Jones in pursuit of outlaws near San Elizario. In the resultant gunfight at Pirates' Island on June 30 Jones was killed. Afterward Aten continued his service under Capt. John R. Hughes,[qv] who succeeded Jones as commander of Company D. Aten married Elena Benavídez, who was from a prominent Ysleta family. The marriage ended in divorce after their daughter died.

During his tenure as a ranger, Aten saw duty at several frontier towns, including Marathon, Pecos, and Alpine. He helped settle the railroad strike at Temple in 1894 and for two years did guard service on the Southern Pacific line between El Paso and Del Rio because of the numerous train robberies reported. By the time he submitted his resignation on July 6, 1898, due to an illness, he had risen to the rank of sergeant. Thereafter he returned to the rangers periodically to do undercover work in Texas and Mexico.

Following his ranger service, Aten briefly ran a saloon and gambling hall in El Paso. He then moved to Shafter, where he dealt faro and tended the bar in Ike Herrin's saloon, which he later purchased. In 1906, however, he returned to El Paso and became a special officer for the Southern Pacific Railroad. On February 20, 1915, he married Gertrude Bacus Aiello, a widow from Las Cruces, New Mexico. Both Ed and Ira, along with John Hughes and Ed Bryant, were present for the unveiling of a monument to Frank Jones on May 12, 1938. Ed Aten retained his position with the railroad until his retirement in 1947. Like his brother Ira, he had a legendary reputation as a lawman. He died on January 31, 1953, and was buried in Rest Lawn Cemetery, El Paso.

BIBLIOGRAPHY: Harold Preece, *Lone Star Man* (New York: Hastings House, 1960). Robert W. Stephens, *Texas Ranger Sketches* (Dallas, 1972). Walter Prescott Webb, *The Texas Rangers* (Boston: Houghton Mifflin, 1935; rpt., Austin: University of Texas Press, 1982).

H. Allen Anderson

ATEN, IRA (1862–1953). Ira Aten, Texas Ranger and Panhandle[qv] lawman, the second of four sons of Austin C. and Kate (Dunlap) Aten, was born on September 3, 1862, in Cairo, Illinois. In 1876 the family moved to Texas, where Ira's father, a Methodist minister, rode circuit for his church. They settled on a farm near Round Rock. On July 20, 1878, Ira witnessed the death of Sam Bass[qv] and was inspired to become a lawman. He enlisted in the Texas Rangers[qv] and was assigned to Company D under Capt. Lamar P. Sieker, headquartered at Camp King, near Uvalde. Aten served in McCulloch, Brown, and Navarro counties before 1888. In the summer of 1887 he and John R. Hughes[qv] trailed and killed Judd Roberts, an associate of Butch Cassidy's Hole-in-the-Wall gang. Aten served more than six years with the frontier battalion, during which time he attained the rank of sergeant. In August 1889 Governor Lawrence S. Ross[qv] sent him in charge of a ranger squad to quell the Jaybird-Woodpecker War[qv] in Fort Bend County.

Aten and Imogen Boyce, a cousin of Albert G. Boyce,[qv] were married at the Central Christian Church in Austin on February 3, 1892, and afterward set up housekeeping at Aten's dugout ranchhouse near Dimmitt. They had three sons and two daughters. Citizens of Castro County, led by County Judge Lycius Gough,[qv] drafted Ira as sheriff in 1893. Imogen became the county jailer. By 1895 Aten had organized a ranch police force of some twenty cowboys armed with Winchester rifles. He stayed on for a time as division foreman and helped organize the first bank at Hereford, the new Deaf Smith county seat. In 1904, when the XIT Ranch[qv] began to break up, Aten moved his family to California, where they developed an irrigated farm and ranch. In 1923 Aten was elected to the Imperial Valley District board, which was concerned mainly with bringing water and electricity to the area by such means as Hoover Dam and the All-American Canal. During his later years Aten compiled the memoirs of his Wild West days, which were published in J. Marvin Hunter's[qv] *Frontier Times*[qv] magazine in 1945. At age ninety Aten still could ride and shoot straight. He was called the "last of the old Texas Rangers" when he died of pneumonia, on August 5, 1953, and was buried in the Evergreen Cemetery at El Centro.

BIBLIOGRAPHY: Ira Aten, *Six and One-Half Years in Ranger Service* (Bandera, Texas: *Frontier Times*, 1945). *Deaf Smith County: The Land and Its People* (Hereford, Texas: Deaf Smith County Historical Society, 1982). J. Evetts Haley, *The XIT Ranch of Texas and the Early Days of the Llano Estacado* (Chicago: Lakeside, 1929; rpts., Norman: University of Oklahoma Press, 1953, 1967). Jack Martin, *Border Boss* (San Antonio: Naylor, 1942). Harold Preece, *Lone Star Man* (New York:

Hastings House, 1960). Robert W. Stephens, *Texas Ranger Sketches* (Dallas, 1972). Walter Prescott Webb, *The Texas Rangers* (Boston: Houghton Mifflin, 1935; rpt., Austin: University of Texas Press, 1982).

H. Allen Anderson

ATER, TEXAS. Ater is on the south bank of the Leon River nine miles northwest of Gatesville and one mile north of Farm Road 2412 in northwestern Coryell County. The site was settled in the early 1870s by families from Pontotoc County, Mississippi. The community, first named Sardis after a church at the settlers' former home, was renamed for Joe Ater, owner of the general store and postmaster from 1899 until 1907; in the latter year the office was discontinued and the mail rerouted through Jonesboro. The Stephenville North and South Texas Railway built through the area within a mile of Ater in 1911, but the company went bankrupt in the mid-1930s. The school at Ater was consolidated with the Jonesboro district in 1939. In the mid-1940s Ater was marked on county highway maps as having a church, a business, and a few scattered houses, and the population was reported as twenty-five.

BIBLIOGRAPHY: Coryell County Genealogical Society, *Coryell County, Texas, Families, 1854–1985* (Dallas: Taylor, 1986).

Zelma Scott

ATHENS, TEXAS. Athens, the "Black-Eyed Pea Capital of the World," is located thirty-five miles west of Tyler on State highways 19 and 31 and U.S. Highway 175 at the center of Henderson County. The county seat of Henderson County was first Buffalo (1846), then Centerville by election (1848), and finally Athens (1850); neither of the first two county seats was within the new county boundaries delineated in 1850. The earliest settlers, E. J. Thompson and Joab McManus, arrived early in 1850. Matthew Cartwright[qv] donated 160 acres for a county seat, and the commissioners had Samuel Huffer survey the streets, the city square, and 112 lots. The district court first met in October 1850 under an oak in the square, with Oran Milo Roberts[qv] presiding. The first courthouse, a sixty-five-dollar log building, was ready the next month. A jail of hewn logs was built in 1856 on the same site and cost $500. Dulcina A. Holland suggested the name Athens, hoping that the town would become a cultural center.

By 1855 a Presbyterian congregation was organized, Joab McManus ran a hotel, E. A. Carroll had a store, and the Masonic lodge had been built. Athens was first incorporated in 1856, and a mayor and city marshall were elected in 1874; but the town, in one historian's words, "never moved a peg" until 1900. There were no improved streets or sidewalks, weeds covered the square, and the few houses were unpainted. The early years witnessed a pottery (Levi S. Cogburn, 1857), a brick plant (H. M. Morrison, 1882), a cotton gin, a cottonseed oil mill, a compress, a newspaper (1873), the arrival of the Cotton Belt (1880) and Texas and New Orleans (1900) railroads, a bank (1887), and a telephone company (1901). In 1901 Athens was reincorporated, and newly elected city officials began building roads. From 177 people in 1859, Athens grew to 1,500 in 1890 and 4,765 in 1940.

Cotton was the major agricultural crop until the 1930s. During the Great Depression[qv] farmers shifted to livestock and vegetable production. Oil and gas exploration in the region began in 1928, and some production occurred in the 1940s. In the 1950s Athens had a furniture plant, an electronics manufacturer, an apparel manufacturer, and a cannery. In the 1980s the town businesses included three banks, two savings and loans, oil, gas, and clay production, and manufacturers of televisions, clothing, bricks, steel buildings, mobile homes, medical supplies, boats, and bridge bearing pads. Corn, cotton, tomatoes, and black-eyed peas were once raised in the area, but agricultural revenue in the 1980s came principally from livestock, hay, and nurseries. The town had forty-two churches, a radio station (KBUD), a newspaper (the Athens *Review*, since 1885), and a library. Athens had grown to 10,967 people in 1990. The Old Fiddlers Reunion in May and the Black-Eyed Pea Jamboree in July attracted crowds of visitors. In the fall 1990 semester Trinity Valley Community College, which was founded in Athens in 1946, enrolled more than 4,460 students. For recreation the town offers parks, a YMCA, swimming, golf, tennis, a theater, and Lake Athens.

BIBLIOGRAPHY: "Athens," *The Southland*, February 1903; rpt. in Athens *Review* for the Henderson County Historical Survey Committee, 1975. Athens *Review*, August 2, 1901. Mrs. Claude Corder, comp., *1850–1860 Census of Henderson County, Texas, Including Slave Schedule and 1846 Tax List* (Chicago: Adams, 1984). J. J. Faulk, *History of Henderson County* (Athens, Texas: Athens Review Printing, 1926). Henderson County Historical Commission, *Family Histories of Henderson County, Texas, 1846–1981* (Dallas: Taylor, 1981). Robert H. Ryan, *Athens, Texas: Economy in Transition* (Austin: Bureau of Business Research, University of Texas, 1961).

William R. Enger

ATHENS *REVIEW*. The Athens *Review* is among the oldest newspapers in Henderson County and the longest in continuing operation. It was founded as a weekly newspaper on December 24, 1885, by J. B. Bishop and George M. Johnston, owners and editors. The earliest newspaper in Henderson County, the Athens *Bulletin*, was established in 1873 by J. H. Cox and Professor J. E. Thomas. After it closed, the printing press was used to print the *Athenian*, which lasted from 1883 through early 1885. In late 1885 Bishop and Johnston acquired the press that they used to print the first edition of the *Review*, a six-column, four-page publication with a subscription price of $1.50 a year. In 1886 a nineteen-year-old-printer from Waco, William Dixon Bell, bought the paper, which he operated until 1888, when he sold it to J. H. Walford. Col. R. E. Yantis of Van Zandt County purchased it in 1900 and in 1901 began publication of a second paper, the Athens *Daily Review*. In the early 1990s both papers were still in operation.

BIBLIOGRAPHY: Wanda Forester Alderman, A History of the *Athens Review* (M.A. thesis, East Texas State University, 1967). Marker Files, Texas Historical Commission, Austin.

Christopher Long

ATHENS TILE AND POTTERY COMPANY. Athens Tile and Pottery Company of Athens, Texas, a pottery and clay products manufacturer, was founded in February 1885 by McKendree Miller, who was born in Illinois and had worked for a Louisiana, Missouri, pottery before moving to Texas in 1884. Miller arrived by train in Dallas and walked the tracks to Athens, where he established the Athens Pottery. By locating at Athens, where substantial amounts of clay were available for manufacturing, the business could provide its own raw materials, interrupted only when rain filled the clay pits. The company sold its products through local distributors in cities and towns throughout the Southwest, distributing by railroad until 1930, when it acquired its own trucks. Later it operated a retail store at Athens and diversified into the manufacture of syrup jugs, churns, jars, vases, cups, and mugs. The firm incorporated before World War I[qv] and eventually owned seven potteries in Texas, including facilities at Dallas, Fort Worth, Groesbeck, San Antonio, and near Austin. The pottery sold $3 million worth of products annually by 1925 and at one time employed up to 200 workers, 75 percent of the town population. Miller was succeeded at the head of the firm by his sons, Elmer and Pearl Eli Miller, grandson M. K. Miller II, and great grandson M. K. Miller, Jr. The business failed during the Great Depression,[qv] but M. K. Miller II bought the Athens plant, reorganized it, and renamed it Athens Tile and Pottery in 1934. When plastic replaced clay pots, the firm's business changed to the production of industrial materials as well as domestic wares. In 1961 Athens Tile and Pottery manufactured 10,000,000 flower pots annually. In 1968 the company, including its plants at De Leon, Texas, and Mooringsport, Louisiana, was acquired by Texas Industries.[qv]

BIBLIOGRAPHY: Athens *Review*, November 18, 1909, Special Ed., August 1962. Henderson County Historical Commission, *Family Histo-*

ries of Henderson County, Texas, 1846–1981 (Dallas: Taylor, 1981). Robert H. Ryan, *Athens, Texas: Economy in Transition* (Austin: Bureau of Business Research, University of Texas, 1961).

Diana J. Kleiner

ATIA AND ATIASNOGUE INDIANS. These names occur in a Spanish document of 1748 that lists twenty-five Indian groups of east central and southeastern Texas who had asked for missions in that general area. About half the names on this list, including Atia (Atai) and Atiasnogue, cannot be identified. The others are identifiable as Caddoans (including Wichita), Tonkawans, Atakapans, and Karankawans.

BIBLIOGRAPHY: Herbert Eugene Bolton, *Texas in the Middle Eighteenth Century: Studies in Spanish Colonial History and Administration* (Berkeley: University of California Press, 1915; rpt., Austin: University of Texas Press, 1970). Charles W. Hackett, ed., *Pichardo's Treatise on the Limits of Louisiana and Texas* (4 vols., Austin: University of Texas Press, 1931–46). Juan Agustín Morfi, *History of Texas, 1673–1779* (2 vols., Albuquerque: Quivira Society, 1935; rpt., New York: Arno, 1967).

Thomas N. Campbell

ATKINS CREEK. Atkins Creek rises near Highway 149 in west central Montgomery County (at 30°25′ N, 95°42′ W) and runs southeast for four miles to its mouth on Lake Conroe, three miles northeast of Montgomery (at 30°24′ N, 95°40′ W). It was named for William Atkins, who received a grant of land near its headwaters in 1831. The creek crosses flat terrain with local shallow depressions surfaced by clay and sandy loam that supports water-tolerant hardwoods, conifers, and grasses.

ATKINSON, DONALD TAYLOR (1874–1959). Donald T. Atkinson, ophthalmologist and author, was born on May 31, 1874, in Little Shemogue, New Brunswick, one of five sons of Joseph Silliker and Elizabeth A. (Grant) Atkinson. In 1883 his family moved to the United States, and he was left behind to help care for his grandmother. In 1886 Atkinson left home to go to work in the coal mines of Nova Scotia. After being injured in the mines, he went to sea, but retired from the sailing life in Boston at the age of fourteen. Thereafter, he worked as a stable boy, coachman, and freighter and took night classes at Tufts College. In 1899 he graduated as a psychiatric nurse from McLean Hospital, part of the Harvard medical complex. Shortly after graduation he was hired to accompany a patient on a trip through the Dakotas, only to find himself stranded when the patient tried to commit suicide in a Pierre hotel. He resumed his education at Pierre University, later Huron College. The dean, impressed with his abilities, gave Atkinson a letter of reference to the Hospital College of Medicine in Louisville, Kentucky, where he obtained his M.D. degree in 1902.

He subsequently traveled west with two classmates to practice general medicine in the Oklahoma Territory and in Bonanza and Del Rio, Texas. After further study at the Manhattan Eye and Ear Hospital, he opened a practice in Hillsboro, Texas, where he specialized in eye, ear, nose, and throat surgery. He took further training in Vienna and London, returned to Hillsboro for three years, and then moved to Dallas. He gradually limited his practice to ophthalmology. In 1911 he became ill with tuberculosis. After a stay in the Kerrville Sanatorium, he set up practice in San Antonio, where he stayed for the rest of his life. He became a United States citizen in 1916.

In San Antonio Atkinson was on the staff of both Santa Rosa and Nix hospitals. Except for a period in the 1920s when he became interested in the treatment of throat cancer, he concentrated upon diseases and surgery of the eye. He designed innovative instruments and operative methods in eye surgery. He received a fellowship in the National Surgical Society of Italy and a bronze medal from the University of Florence for his research in glaucoma. He was awarded an honorary doctor of science degree by Center College in Danville, Kentucky, in 1944 and an honorary doctor of law degree by Huron College in 1945.

Atkinson was ophthalmology editor for the *Texas Medical News* from 1913 to 1916 and associate editor of the *Chicago Eye, Ear, Nose, and Throat Journal* for many years. He wrote and illustrated a textbook on the interior of the eye and was the author of eight other books, including *Magic, Myth and Medicine* (1955) and an autobiography, *Texas Surgeon* (1958), which won an award from a national professional journalism fraternity for women in 1958. He was a fellow of the International College of Surgeons in Geneva and of the Royal Academy of Medicine in Dublin and a member of the American Medical Association, the Texas Medical Association,[qv] the Bexar County Medical Society, the American College of Surgeons, the American Academy of Ophthalmology and Otolaryngology, the Southern Medical Association, the National Tuberculosis Association, the American Genetic Association, the American Social Hygiene Association, the National Society of Arts and Letters, the National Association of Authors and Journalists, and the San Antonio River Art Group.

In 1935 Atkinson married silent film star Wanda Wiley, who had returned to Texas with the advent of talking pictures. They had no children. He died on March 20, 1959, in San Antonio, of coronary occlusion.

BIBLIOGRAPHY: *Texas State Journal of Medicine* 55 (May 1959).

Patricia L. Jakobi

ATKINSON ISLAND. Atkinson Island is a long, narrow island in extreme northwest Galveston Bay, southwestern Chambers County (at 29°40′ N, 94°58′ W). The island, south of Hog Island, runs north and south and is about three miles long and less than a half mile wide.

ATLANTA, TEXAS (Caldwell County). Atlanta was a small farming community near the site of present Luling in southern Caldwell County. Settlers may have been in the area as early as the 1850s. After the Galveston, Harrisburg and San Antonio Railway laid its track from Columbus to the new town of Luling in 1874, residents of Atlanta gradually began to associate themselves with Luling, and Atlanta soon faded. The Atlanta school continued to function until the county established new districts in 1887. No population estimates for Atlanta are available, and the community did not appear on county highway maps. A copy of the Atlanta townsite plat was reproduced in the *Plum Creek Almanac* in 1986.

BIBLIOGRAPHY: Mark Withers Trail Drive Museum, *Historical Caldwell County* (Dallas: Taylor, 1984). Carroll L. Mullins, History of the Schools of Caldwell County to 1900 (M.A. thesis, University of Texas, 1929).

Vivian Elizabeth Smyrl

ATLANTA, TEXAS (Cass County). Atlanta, at the junction of U.S. Highway 59, State highways 43 and 77, and Farm roads 96, 249, 251, 995, 1159, 1841, 2327, and 2791, ten miles west of the Texas-Arkansas line, is the largest town and most important economic center in Cass County. The town was established in 1871 with the building of the Texas and Pacific Railway and named for Atlanta, Georgia, former home of many early settlers. A post office opened in 1871, and by 1885 the community had 1,500 residents, three white and two black churches, two schools, a bank, several sawmills, a number of general stores, and a weekly newspaper, the *Citizens' Journal.* Lumbering was the chief industry. The lumber boom reached its peak around 1890, when the population was 1,764. The community was incorporated in 1929, when it had 1,900 residents and 105 businesses. The onset of the Great Depression[qv] forced many businesses to close, and in 1936 Atlanta had only eighty-five rated businesses. The opening of the Rodessa oilfield[qv] in 1935, however, helped mitigate the worst effects of the depression, and by 1940 the town had modern canneries, lumber mills, wholesale houses, a brick plant, a hospital, and a population of 2,453. Subsequently, Atlanta grew steadily, topping the 4,000 mark for the first time in the early 1960s. In 1990 the population was 6,118. Principal industries include farming, forestry, oil, and tourism.

Claudia Hazlewood

ATLANTA STATE RECREATION AREA. The Atlanta State Recreation Area is on the shores of Lake Wright Patman off Farm Road 1154, eight miles northwest of Atlanta in Cass County. The 1,475-acre park was acquired in 1954 by a license from the Department of the Army. The landscape features pine and oak forest with exposed red-clay bluffs. Park facilities include camp and picnic sites, a 3½-mile hiking trail, a boat ramp, an amphitheater, a playground, and a beach.

BIBLIOGRAPHY: Vertical Files, Barker Texas History Center, University of Texas at Austin.

Christopher Long

ATLANTIC AND PACIFIC RAILROAD. The Atlantic and Pacific Railroad Company was chartered in New York State in 1852 for the purpose of constructing a transcontinental railroad. The initial capitalization was $100,000,000. Anson Jones[qv] became a stockholder and director and was made commissioner to Texas. Richard J. Walker, former United States Secretary of the Treasury under President James T. Polk, and former Georgia Congressman T. Butler King were the primary promoters of the project. The company wanted to secure the sole franchise for a transcontinental railroad and acquired the charter of the Texas Western for $600,000 in stock and an option to purchase the other transcontinental projects chartered by the state. As a result, the Atlantic and Pacific was the only company to submit a bid that met the provisions of the Mississippi and Pacific act of 1853. However, the securities the company offered as bond were rejected by Governor Elisha M. Pease[qv] and the contract was canceled. At a meeting held in Montgomery, Alabama, on December 16, 1854, the promoters reorganized under the Texas Western charter, as all hopes of building a transcontinental railroad by the Atlantic and Pacific had ended.

BIBLIOGRAPHY: Alexander Deussen, "The Beginning of the Texas Railroad System," *Transactions of the Texas Academy of Science for 1906* (1907). Marshall *Republican,* January 13, 1855.

George C. Werner

ATLAS, TEXAS. Atlas is at the intersection of Farm roads 2036 and 137, five miles northeast of Roxton and five miles southwest of Paris in south central Lamar County. It was founded in 1884 when the Texas-Midland Railroad began to use a local rock quarry to obtain ballast. Railroad owner Edward H. R. Green[qv] is credited with naming the quarry and the post office Atlas, for the character in Greek mythology who supported the world. The first postal facility opened in 1884. By 1890 Atlas had twenty residents, two cotton gins, and a general store. I. H. Hughes had established a law practice. A triweekly stagecoach ran to Paris and Cooper; the fare was twenty-five and fifty cents respectively. The stage also delivered the mail. By 1896 a local common school district enrolled seventy students and employed one teacher. In 1914 the population was fifty, and the town had a new cotton gin and a telephone exchange. In 1929 Atlas had a population of seventy-six. Maps for 1936 showed a cotton gin, two stores, the school, and a church. The postal service was discontinued in 1943. In 1947 the population peaked at 120, and four businesses were in operation. In 1949 Atlas had fifty people and two businesses. By 1957 no businesses were left, and schoolchildren attended the Roxton schools. The population of Atlas remained at fifty throughout the 1960s, decreased to forty by 1970, and was reported as twenty in 1974. Maps for 1984 showed a church and a few scattered dwellings. The town had twenty inhabitants in 1990.

BIBLIOGRAPHY: Thomas S. Justiss, An Administrative Survey of the Schools of Lamar County with a Plan for Their Reorganization (M.A. thesis, University of Texas, 1937). Fred Tarpley, *1001 Texas Place Names* (Austin: University of Texas Press, 1980).

Vista K. McCroskey

ATLEE, EDWIN A., JR. (1878–1938). Edwin A. Atlee, Jr., lawyer, was born in Corpus Christi, Texas, on March 8, 1878, the son of Betty (Foster) and Edwin Augustus Atlee.[qv] He spent his boyhood with his family in Laredo and acted as page in the House and in the Senate of the Texas legislature while his father was representative and senator from Webb County. He was educated in Austin and Laredo and took his law degree from the University of Texas in 1896. He enlisted in 1898 to fight in the Spanish American War and served as sergeant in Troop K, First Texas Cavalry. He was admitted to the bar in 1902 and practiced law in partnership with his father at Laredo until 1910. Later he formed the law firm of Atlee and Smith at Laredo. He died on October 8, 1938, and was buried in the Elks Cemetery at Laredo.

BIBLIOGRAPHY: Frank W. Johnson, *A History of Texas and Texans* (5 vols., ed. E. C. Barker and E. W. Winkler [Chicago and New York: American Historical Society, 1914; rpt. 1916]).

Jeannette H. Flachmeier

ATLEE, EDWIN AUGUSTUS (1846–1910). Edwin Augustus Atlee, lawyer and state legislator, was born in Athens, Tennessee, in 1846. He received a classical education and taught Latin and Greek in Athens until January 1873, when he moved to Corpus Christi, Texas, where he taught, studied law, and was admitted to the bar in 1874. He was county attorney for Nueces County from 1874 to 1879. In 1874 he married Bettie Foster at Corpus Christi. In 1879 he moved to Laredo. From 1880 to 1896 he practiced in partnership with A. L. McLane. Atlee was mayor of Laredo for about seven years. He represented Webb County in the House of Representatives of the Nineteenth and Twentieth legislatures and in the Senate of the Twenty-first and Twenty-second. In the Senate he was chairman of the committee on frontier protection. In his law practice he had many cases dealing with land titles, one of which was the title to the Borrego grant; this case involved the site of the city of Laredo. Atlee was active in breaking up business combinations harmful to cattle raisers of the Western states. In 1889 he promoted the establishment of a deepwater port for South Texas. He practiced law in partnership with his son, Edwin A. Atlee,[qv] from 1902 to 1910. He died at Rochester, Minnesota, on January 5, 1910, and was buried at Chattanooga, Tennessee.

BIBLIOGRAPHY: Lewis E. Daniell, *Types of Successful Men in Texas* (Austin: Von Boeckmann, 1890). Frank W. Johnson, *A History of Texas and Texans* (5 vols., ed. E. C. Barker and E. W. Winkler [Chicago and New York: American Historical Society, 1914; rpt. 1916]).

Jeanette Flachmeier

ATLEE, TEXAS. Atlee was six miles north of Encinal on the International–Great Northern Railroad in southwestern La Salle County. It was founded some time after 1880 as a stop on the I–GN and in the 1930s comprised a railroad depot and a collection of houses. Atlee appeared on some maps of La Salle County as late as 1980.

John Leffler

ATONEMENT FRIARS AND SISTERS. The Union-That-Nothing-Be-Lost collected alms and dispensed many thousands of dollars to missions, some of them in Texas. It was started as a vehicle for mission work by Fr. Paul James Francis Wattson (born Lewis Thomas Wattson) and Sr. Lurana White, Episcopalians who had founded the Society of the Atonement, a Franciscan order. The friars published a monthly magazine, the *Lamp,* and the sisters published the *Candle.* As a move toward Christian unity the leaders of the Friars and the Sisters of the Atonement joined the Catholic Church[qv] in 1909, along with a group of lay associates. The first mission house for both the friars and the sisters was St. Anthony's Church in Hereford,

Texas, where the pastor, Fr. J. A. Campbell, was struggling to maintain a parish and school. The Atonement nuns conducted St. Anthony's School from 1917 to 1938, then left to devote themselves more exclusively to social services. The friars served as pastors of St. Anthony's Church and its missions from 1920 to 1988. During their tenure they helped develop three other parishes. In addition, St. Ann's in Bovina, founded by Campbell, came under the friars' jurisdiction in 1920. St. Teresa's in Friona was founded through the efforts of Fr. Raymond Gillis, an Atonement friar. Gillis moved to Hereford in 1948 and worked among the migrant laborers in the vegetable fields of the area. His flock lived in the barracks of a former prisoner of war camp. In this setting, dubbed the "Labor Camp," Gillis built a church, school, convent, and clinic. He thus also provided the first Catholic church for nearby Friona. As former migrant families settled down in Hereford, they built a new St. Joseph's Church in the city, and many of the services at the Labor Camp were discontinued. By 1980 St. Joseph's in Hereford was the largest parish in the Catholic Diocese of Amarillo.[qv]

While at Hereford, Campbell had founded the first Catholic periodical in the Panhandle.[qv] In answer to the *Menace*, an anti-Catholic paper, the priest began a monthly, the *Antidote*. He ran the press himself. When the Atonement friars came to Hereford, Father Paul transferred the printing of the *Antidote* to Graymoor, New York, where it was published alongside the *Lamp* until 1931. Gillis served as pastor of Sacred Heart parish in Memphis, Texas, from 1977 to 1981, and built an educational and meeting building there.

The Franciscan Sisters of the Atonement opened a house for religious and social services in Sour Lake in 1925. They transferred their center to Dickinson in 1929 in order to serve more people. They closed their mission in Texas in 1946. In 1990 the Friars of the Atonement operated in North and South America, Europe, Jamaica, and Japan. In 1991 one friar, located in Bovina (Diocese of Amarillo), represented the order in Texas.

BIBLIOGRAPHY: Sister Nellie Rooney, O.S.F., and Mrs. Edna Reinart, *The Society of the Atonement in West Texas, 1917–1988* (Amarillo: Diocese of Amarillo, 1988). *St. Anthony's Fiftieth Anniversary, 1922–1972* (Hereford, Texas, 1972).

Sister Nellie Rooney, O.S.F.

ATOY, TEXAS. Atoy is a rural community on Farm Road 343 and near Atoy Creek eight miles east of Rusk in eastern Cherokee County. The area was first settled in the 1840s, but a community did not develop there until after the Civil War.[qv] An Atoy post office operated in 1870–71, and a school was in operation by the mid-1890s. During the mid-1930s Atoy had a school, a church, a store, and a number of houses. After World War II[qv] the school was consolidated with the Rusk schools, but in the early 1990s Atoy still had a church, a store, a community center, and several houses.

BIBLIOGRAPHY: *Cherokee County History* (Jacksonville, Texas: Cherokee County Historical Commission, 1986).

Christopher Long

ATTORNEY GENERAL. With roots in the British common law and Spanish civil law, the office of Texas attorney general was first established by executive ordinance in 1836. The attorneys general of the Republic of Texas[qv] and the first four attorneys general under the first state constitution (1845) were appointed by the governor; all subsequent attorneys general were directly elected. In the Constitution of 1876[qv] the attorney general is one of seven officers constituting the executive department of Texas state government.

As the chief legal officer of the state of Texas, the attorney general protects state interests through judicial proceedings and legal advice. His constitutional authority is broad but briefly stated, and the Texas legislature and the courts may augment his official powers. Whenever the interests of Texas state government are involved in civil law, the attorney general must represent and defend those interests. The state of Texas is represented by the attorney general in the courts of Texas and of the United States. The office influences all Texas government agencies through its advisory-opinion function, whereby the attorney general provides specified officials with guidance on how to perform their duties legally.

The attorney general works with governmental agencies in a variety of functions, such as assisting the secretary of state and the governor in extradition proceedings, approving the form of official papers, appearing before grand juries in an informational capacity, initiating inquiries into suspected illegal activities, examining the legality of bond issues for state and local governments, and preparing legal instruments for state agencies. The attorney general has regulatory or punitive civil powers over corporations and must protect charitable trusts through court action. Taxation and property are two functional areas significant to the work of the attorney general; the attorney general sues for recovery of taxes owed the state of Texas and protects the public interest with respect to abandoned property that escheats to the state. The attorney general acts against persons or corporations violating the environmental-protection laws of Texas or illegally extracting natural resources. The office also enforces the state's antitrust laws and prosecutes persons who mishandle state funds.

The attorney general broadly reflects a combination of law and politics in his regular duties, uniquely combining administration with regulation and law enforcement, acting as both enforcer and protector. Legal decisions are judged by political standards, and political skills may be technically useful in the position. The attorney general must be a mixture of a good politician, a good administrator, and a skillful lawyer.

The attorney general's actions are by nature collegial. Although daily work is in the hands of assistants, operations are shaped by the priorities and the personality of the attorney general. His formal authority is plenary, whether in litigation or giving legal advice. The incumbent attorney general controls the form and substance of state civil cases and the final form of legal opinions.

During the attorney generalship of Price Daniel, Sr.[qv] (1947–53), for example, one of the most significant projects of the attorney general's office was the Tidelands case (see TIDELANDS CONTROVERSY). This litigation grew out of the federal government's decision to wrest ownership of submerged offshore oil lands from the coastal states, including Texas, and thus to deprive them of the oil revenues from these lands. The state lost its case before the federal courts but ultimately won in Congress. Attorney General Daniels emerged from this case as a leading spokesman for the rights of states in the face of federal efforts to restrict state prerogatives.

Attorney General John Ben Shepperd's[qv] (1953–57) most distinctive enterprise was an investigative campaign and resulting civil suits against the political machine of George B. Parr[qv] in Duval County. This case is an example of how certain projects initiated by the attorney general's office can have political content as well as legal substance. Attorney General Will Wilson (1957–63) probably utilized the civil authority of the office against illegal activities more than any other person in the office. An example is his well-publicized investigations against organized-gambling interests in Galveston.

The attorney general functions from a point of central significance in Texas government—a perspective not precisely duplicated by any other state office. This strategic influence results from formal authority, strict constitutional limits on the powers of other state officials, fluctuating constitutional limits on the powers of other state officials, the fluctuating character of a part-time legislature, the rarity of judicial reversal of the attorney general's actions, and his control over state civil litigation.

The expanded role of the attorney general has accompanied the evolving roles of state and local governments. The general growth of governmental activity was precipitated by political pressures on governments to police, to regulate, and to change. The office has evolved through political, economic, and social turmoil and the imprint of modern technology, as well as the political efforts of racial, ethnic, regional, and special-interest groups to bring about changes through

ATTORNEYS GENERAL

(Articles about bold-faced subjects appear in the *New Handbook of Texas*)

Republic of Texas:

David Thomas	1836
Peter W. Grayson	1836, 1837
J. Pinckney Henderson, John Birdsall	1836–38
John Charles Watrous	1838–40
Joseph Webb, **Francis A. Morris**	1840–41
George W. Terrell, Ebenezer Allen	1841–44
Ebenezer Allen	1844–46

State of Texas:

Name	Years	Name	Years	Name	Years
Volney E. Howard	1846	**George Clark**	1874–76	**Daniel J. Moody, Jr.**	1925–27
John W. Harris	1846–49	**Hannibal H. Boone**	1876–78	**Claude Pollard**	1927–29
Henry P. Brewster	1849–50	**George McCormick**	1878–80	R. L. Bobbitt	1929–31
Andrew J. Hamilton	1850	**James H. McLeary**	1880–82	**James Allred**	1931–35
Ebenezer Allen	1849–53	**John D. Templeton**	1882–86	William McCraw	1935–39
Thomas J. Jennings	1852–56	**James S. Hogg**	1886–90	Gerald C. Mann	1939–44
James Willie	1856–58	**Charles A. Culberson**	1890–94	Grover Sellers	1944–47
Malcolm D. Graham	1858–60	**Martin M. Crane**	1894–98	**M. Price Daniel, Sr.**	1947–53
George M. Flournoy	1860–62	**Thomas S. Smith**	1898–1901	**John Ben Shepperd**	1953–57
Nathan G. Shelley	1862–64	**Charles K. Bell**	1901–04	Will Wilson	1957–63
Benjamin E. Tarver	1864–65	**Robert V. Davidson**	1904–09	Waggoner Carr	1963–67
William Alexander	1865–66	**Jewel P. Lightfoot**	1910–12	**Crawford C. Martin**	1967–72
William M. Walton	1866–67	**James D. Walthall**	1912–13	John Hill	1973–79
William Alexander	1867	B. F. Looney	1913–19	Mark White	1979–83
Ezekiel B. Turner	1867–70	**Calvin M. Cureton**	1919–21	Jim Mattox	1983–91
William Alexander	1870–74	W. A. Keeling	1921–25	Dan Morales	1991–

the courts. The modern office is the result of an intricate combination of rules, traditions, and circumstances. Many of the leading political figures in Texas history have served as attorney general, several of them using the office as a jumping-off place to other offices in state and national government. Attorneys general James S. Hogg (1886–90), Charles A. Culberson (1890–94), Daniel J. Moody, Jr. (1925–27), James Allred (1931–35), Price Daniel, Sr. (1947–53),[qqv] and Mark White (1979–83) were elected governor; Culberson and Daniel were also elected to the United States Senate.

The attorney general acts as an instrument for achieving administrative flexibility in the state's legal system, thus enabling government to adjust to changing policy demands through flexible interpretations of statutory and constitutional law. Wherever the political system and the legal systems converge or conflict, the attorney general is essential to state government. The office effects innovative but incremental change that fosters administrative and political viability and stability. The importance of the office to Texas government results from both the historical character of the office in the United States and the distincitve adaptation in Texas of Anglo-American legal and political traditions.

BIBLIOGRAPHY: James G. Dickson, Jr., *Law and Politics: The Office of Attorney General in Texas* (Manchaca, Texas: Sterling Swift, 1976). Beryl Pettus, "Functions of the Opinions of the Texas Attorney General in the State Legislative Process," in *Practicing Texas Politics*, ed. Eugene Jones et al. (Boston: Houghton Mifflin, 1971; 2d ed. 1974). Leo M. Sabota and J. David Martin, "The Texas Attorney General—An Alternate State Supreme Court," in *Understanding Texas Politics*, ed. Richard H. Kraemer et al. (St. Paul: West, 1975).

James G. Dickson, Jr.

ATTOYAC, TEXAS. Attoyac, seven miles east of Nacogdoches on Farm Road 95 in eastern Nacogdoches County, was laid out in 1836 by John Allen Veatch and Almanzon Huston[qqv] and named for nearby Attoyac Bayou. Over the years the town has sometimes been known as Black Jack, but when a post office was established in 1897 the name Attoyac was used. At its height just prior to World War I[qv] the settlement had three general stores, a school, a physician, and an estimated population of 100. During the 1920s, however, residents began to leave, and by 1925 the population fell to sixty-five. Between the end of World War II[qv] and the 1970s the population was consistently reported at seventy-five. In the same period, however, the post office, the school, and most of the remaining businesses closed. In the early 1990s Attoyac was a dispersed community with a few scattered houses.

BIBLIOGRAPHY: Nacogdoches County Genealogical Society, *Nacogdoches County Families* (Dallas: Curtis, 1985).

Christopher Long

ATTOYAC BAYOU. Attoyac Bayou rises one mile south of Minden School in southeastern Rusk County (at 31°57′ N, 94°39′ W) and flows southeast for sixty miles to its mouth on the Angelina River, at the southeastern corner of Nacogdoches County (at 31°29′ N, 94°19′ W). The stream at various points forms the boundary between Rusk and Shelby, Nacogdoches and Shelby, and Nacogdoches and San Augustine counties. It crosses flat to rolling terrain surfaced by sandy and clay loam that supports water-tolerant hardwoods, conifers, and grasses.

ATTWATER, HENRY PHILEMON (1854–1931). Henry Attwater, naturalist and conservationist, the son of Thomas G. and Rose Ellen (Woolbit) Attwater, was born in Brighton, England, on April 28, 1854. He was educated at St. Nicholas Episcopal College at Shoreham, Sussex, and in 1873 immigrated to Ontario, Canada, where he engaged in farming and beekeeping. Attwater soon became interested in natural history, and during 1883 he and John A. Morden prepared and exhibited natural history specimens. During 1884 the two men collected specimens in Bexar County, Texas, where Attwater made the acquaintance of Gustave Toudouze,[qv] a naturalist and taxidermist from Losoya. During the latter part of 1884 and early 1885 Attwater and Toudouze were employed to prepare and exhibit natural history specimens in the Texas pavilion at the New Orleans World's Fair.

Attwater was married on December 31, 1885, in Chatham, Ontario, to Lucy Mary Watts, a widow with two children. No children were born to Henry and Lucy Attwater. In 1886 the Attwater family moved to London, Ontario, where he opened a small museum at the Mechanics' Institute. This enterprise did not prove successful, and the museum was closed in the summer of 1887.

In 1889 the family moved to Sherman, Texas, where Attwater briefly engaged in the bee industry[qv] before moving to San Antonio. During the 1890s he collected throughout the state as well as lecturing and writing on natural history and agricultural subjects. He was also employed at various times to prepare exhibits of Texas natural products and wildlife at fairs and expositions. In 1900 Attwater moved from San Antonio to Houston to become the agricultural and industrial agent for the Southern Pacific Railroad. In this position he continued to expand his collections and to promote the agricultural and business interests of the state, in addition to assisting the work of commercial clubs, fairs, and farmers' organizations.

Attwater's major contributions to natural history were in the areas of ornithology and conservation. His three ornithological papers deal with the nesting habits of fifty species of birds in Bexar County, Texas, the occurrence of 242 species of birds in the vicinity of San Antonio, and the deaths of thousands of warblers during a blue norther[qv] in March 1892. Attwater also contributed specimens to the Smithsonian Institution, collected birds for George B. Sennett,[qv] and provided notes for W. W. Cooke's *Bird Migration in the Mississippi Valley* (1888) and the mammal section of Vernon Bailey's *Biological Survey of Texas* (1905).

Attwater was elected a director of the National Audubon Society about 1900 and was reelected for a five-year term in 1905. Through his influence with farmers, the Texas Audubon Society had by 1910 gained affiliation with the Texas Farmers' Congress, the Texas Cotton Growers' Association, and the Texas Corn Growers' Association. In April 1910 Attwater and Mervyn Bathurst Davis,[qv] secretary of the Texas Audubon Society, secured the endorsement of the Conservation Congress, which met in Fort Worth.

Attwater worked diligently for passage of the 1903 Model Game Law and, following its passage, arranged for warning notices from the National Audubon Society to be distributed in railroad facilities throughout the state. In 1907 he served on the game-law committee that recommended not only that the 1903 Model Law be reenacted, but also that a license be required for both resident and nonresident hunters and that revenue from licenses and fines be used solely for game protection and propagation. Attwater was also active in the promotion of legislation to protect the mourning dove, which was rapidly declining during the early 1900s. His most important conservation works include *Boll Weevils and Birds* (1903), *Use and Value of Wild Birds to Texas Farmers and Stockmen and Fruit and Truck Growers* (1914), and *The Disappearance of Wild Life* (1917).

In 1913 Attwater retired as industrial agent with the Southern Pacific to devote his entire time to the study of natural history. During the 1920s he sold his collection to the Witte Museum[qv] in San Antonio, and after his death his papers were deposited in the Houston Public Library. Attwater's greater prairie chicken (*Tympanuchus cupido attwateri*), Attwater's white-footed mouse (*Peromyscus attwateri*), Attwater's wood rat (*Neotoma floridana attwateri*), Attwater's pocket gopher (*Geomys bursarius attwateri*), and Attwater's swamp rabbit (*Lepus aquaticus attwateri*) are named in his honor, in recognition of his major contributions as a scientist and conservationist.

H. P. Attwater joined the American Ornithologists' Union as an associate in 1891 and became a member in 1901. He was also a member of the Texas State Horticultural Society, the Scientific Society of San Antonio, the Order of the Eastern Star, and Holland Lodge, A.F. and A.M. He died on September 25, 1931, and is buried in Hollywood Cemetery, Houston.

BIBLIOGRAPHY: Houston *Post-Dispatch*, September 26, 1931. T. S. Palmer, *Biographies of Members of the American Ornithologists' Union* (Washington, 1954). Bess Carroll Woolford and Ellen Schulz Quillin, *The Story of the Witte Museum* (San Antonio Museum Association, 1966).

Stanley D. Casto

ATTWATER PRAIRIE CHICKEN NATIONAL WILDLIFE REFUGE. The Attwater Prairie Chicken National Wildlife Refuge is seven miles northeast of Eagle Lake in eastern Colorado County. Attwater's prairie chicken, a subspecies of the heath hen named for Henry P. Attwater,[qv] was once one of the most abundant prairie residents of Texas and Louisiana. It inhabited eight million acres from the Coastal Plains to the Mississippi River. The bird's natural range now covers only 46,000 acres, and populations are scattered. The chicken was a popular game bird in the late nineteenth and early twentieth centuries, and hunting parties occasionally killed 200 to 300 birds per trip. The prairie chicken became extinct in Louisiana in 1919, and its population in Texas dwindled badly. The state of Texas banned hunting of the bird in 1937, at which time its population was counted at 8,618; in 1967 the number of Attwater prairie chickens had fallen to 1,070, and the bird became an official endangered species. In the mid-1960s the Nature Conservancy of Texas and the World Wildlife Fund purchased 3,500 acres in Colorado County as a preserve for the bird. At that time, the prairie chicken population at the refuge was twenty-five; by the mid-1980s it had risen to more than 200.

The United States government acquired the property in 1972 and made it a national wildlife refuge. Through additional land acquisition, the refuge grew to include 8,000 acres by 1990. The entire Attwater's prairie chicken population of Texas was reported at 900 in 1986 and at 456 in 1992. Additional measures to save the prairie chicken from extinction have included a captive breeding program initiated in 1992 by researchers at Texas A&M University, plans to lease thousands of additional acres of suitable land in Austin and Victoria counties, and efforts to encourage area farmers and ranchers to manage their land in ways that will encourage the chicken's survival.

The Attwater Prairie Chicken Refuge is one of the few preserves managed specifically for an endangered species; controlled grazing and burning, strip row cropping, mowing, pest plant control, and predator control are among the management techniques used to improve the habitat. Visitors are permitted to observe the grounds from an automobile tour route and designated walking paths, but no picnicking facilities are provided, and no hunting, fishing, canoeing, or camping is allowed. Access to some areas is tightly controlled during the birds' mating season.

Although the refuge is dedicated to the preservation of the Attwater's prairie chicken, many other birds and animals take advantage of the area. Birds common to the refuge include the white-tailed hawk, the roseate spoonbill, the white ibis, the tricolored heron, and the fulvous whistling duck. Other animals include white-tailed deer, armadillos, coyotes, the endangered Houston toad,[qv] water moccasins, and king snakes. More than 250 different flowering plants have also been identified within the refuge. *See also* PRAIRIE CHICKENS.

BIBLIOGRAPHY: Dallas *Morning News*, February 14, 1993.

Vivian Elizabeth Smyrl

ATTWELL, JAMES (ca. 1815–?). James Attwell (Atwell), printer, newspaper publisher, and editor, was born in New York and apparently moved to Texas soon after the Texas Revolution.[qv] He was publisher and printer of the Matagorda *Colorado Gazette and Advertiser*,[qv] the first issue of which appeared on May 16, 1839, with W. Donaldson as editor. By December 25, 1839, Attwell had sold the paper to William Douglas Wallach,[qv] but he continued to work on the *Gazette* as a printer. Whenever Wallach was away, Attwell served as his "authorized Agent" and had "entire control" of the paper. The *Gazette* apparently ceased publication in 1843. Attwell later became editor and proprietor of the Matagorda *Weekly Despatch*[qv] (1843–46). He was apparently assisted in the editorial work by Richard Drake Sebring, who died in August 1844. By 1850 Attwell had moved to Lavaca (now Port Lavaca). In early 1854 he published the first number of the Lavaca *Register* with Edward B. Mantor as editor. The *Register* continued to be published for about a year. In 1857 Attwell bought the Lavaca *Herald* (1855–59) from James C. Rowan and became publisher and editor. He issued the paper until late 1859, when it was bought out and became the *Gulf Key.* Attwell likely worked as a printer on other papers in Matagorda and Lavaca during the 1840s and 1850s. In 1844 in Matagorda he printed a four-page prospectus for James Wilmer Dallam's[qv] *Digest of the Laws of Texas.* On March 27, 1841, Attwell was elected justice of the peace for beat two in Matagorda County, and in 1847 he was listed as a contributor to a library fund in Matagorda. In the 1860 census for Lavaca, Attwell claimed $500 each in real and personal property.

BIBLIOGRAPHY: *Compiled Index to Elected and Appointed Officials of the Republic of Texas, 1835–1846* (Austin: State Archives, Texas State Library, 1981). Joe B. Frantz, Newspapers of the Republic of Texas (M.A. thesis, University of Texas, 1940). Matagorda County Historical Commission, *Historic Matagorda County* (3 vols., Houston: Armstrong, 1986). Marilyn M. Sibley, *Lone Stars and State Gazettes: Texas Newspapers before the Civil War* (College Station: Texas A&M University Press, 1983). Thomas W. Streeter, *Bibliography of Texas, 1795–1845* (5 vols., Cambridge, Massachusetts: Harvard University Press, 1955–60).
Mary M. Standifer

ATWELL, WILLIAM HAWLEY (1869–1961). William Hawley Atwell, Republican politician and federal judge, son of Capt. Benjamin and De Emma (Green) Atwell, was born at Sparta, Wisconsin, on June 9, 1869, and moved to rural Dallas County, Texas, with his parents in the 1870s. He attended public school at Hutchins until he entered Southwestern University at Georgetown in 1885; after graduating in 1889 he studied law in the office of Williams and Turney in Dallas and was admitted to the bar in 1890. He entered the University of Texas law school in fall 1890 and received a degree the following spring.

After establishing a practice at Dallas in 1891 Atwell was married to Susie Snyder, on December 7, 1892. Two sons were born to them. Atwell's father, a Union veteran of the Civil War,[qv] led him into Republican politics, and President William McKinley appointed him United States district attorney. He served until 1913 and returned to practice law in Dallas during the years of Democratic ascendancy under Woodrow Wilson. In 1922, while vacationing in Europe, Atwell was nominated to run against Governor Pat M. Neff[qv] by the state Republican convention in Fort Worth. During a time of agitation over the Ku Klux Klan[qv] in Texas politics, Atwell told reporters that the Klan was an outgrowth of failure to enforce the law. Whether his condemnation of the Klan helped or harmed him, he received but 73,329 votes, against his Democratic opponent's 334,199.

A month after Atwell's defeat, President Warren G. Harding appointed him United States district judge for the Northern District of Texas, which comprised 102 counties. He assumed the judgeship in January 1923, and, though he retired in 1958, he remained a judge in special cases until his death. He became well known for his rigorous style, which countenanced no dilatory tactics on the part of the bar, and for his strict adherence to duty and constitutional precepts. In his later years he was sharply critical of the United States Supreme Court because of its civil rights rulings. In 1956 he said from the bench that the 1954 decision concerning desegregation of public schools had been "based on sociological opinion rather than law." He told reporters in 1957 that he considered segregation "neither immoral nor unconstitutional."

Atwell was long active in Dallas civic affairs and served as city zoo commissioner under Mayor William H. Holland. During 1925–26 he was national grand exalted ruler of Elks. He also wrote several books: *A Treatise on Federal Criminal Law Procedure* (1911), *Salmagundi* (1929), *Charges to Juries* (1929), an *Autobiography* (1935), *Some Provocative Decisions and Other Fundamentals* (1945), and *Wandering and Wondering* (1946). Atwell died in Dallas on December 22, 1961. His family dedicated the William Hawley Atwell Chair of Constitutional Law at Southern Methodist University School of Law to his memory.

BIBLIOGRAPHY: Paul D. Casdorph, *A History of the Republican Party in Texas, 1865–1965* (Austin: Pemberton Press, 1965). Dallas *Morning News*, December 23, 1961.
Paul D. Casdorph

ATWELL, TEXAS. Atwell, in eastern Callahan County, was established in the 1870s. Pioneer settlers in the community included Tobie Bell, Uncle Johnny Surles, J. T. Purvis, J. P. Hutchins, and Frank Abbott. Several families moved to the community in 1885 and 1886. Around 1886, residents established a school first named Bell Branch and later Flag Springs. In 1899 a post office was established in the settlement and named for William H. Atwell, district attorney of the Federal District Court of Northern Texas. By 1905 the community had several stores, three churches, a blacksmith shop, and a gin. But the population declined rapidly after 1915, and on June 29, 1929, the post office was discontinued. Atwell's population was listed as sixty-five from 1925 to 1948, after which no further estimates are available.

BIBLIOGRAPHY: Callahan County Historical Commission, *I Remember Callahan: History of Callahan County, Texas* (Dallas: Taylor, 1986). Brutus Clay Chrisman, *Early Days in Callahan County* (Abilene, Texas: Abilene Printing and Stationery, 1966).
Julius A. Amin

ATZ, JOHN JACOB (1879–1945). John Jacob (Jake) Atz, baseball player and manager, was born on July 1, 1879, in Washington, D.C. He is generally considered the greatest baseball manager in Texas League[qv] history. He began his major league playing career in 1902 with Washington of the American League and played for the Chicago White Sox in 1907–09. Here his major league career was ended when he was hit by a pitch thrown by Walter Johnson. Atz signed as a playing manager of the Fort Worth Cats of the Texas League in 1914. After an argument he quit in 1916 but returned in 1917. He led Fort Worth to seven consecutive championships during 1919–25 and remained there until 1929. Thereafter he managed clubs in Dallas, Shreveport, New Orleans, Tulsa, and Galveston. He held the following records: twenty-two years as a player and manager; eighteen years as manager of one club (Fort Worth); longest continuous service at one club (fourteen seasons with Fort Worth); and seven successive first-place finishes. Atz's real name was Zimmerman, but, according to legend, he changed it because he had played on a succession of clubs that went bankrupt, and paying their players alphabetically, the clubs frequently would run out of money before reaching the end of the alphabet. The name change was typical of his flamboyant personality, which has caused many people to call him "the grandest Texas League figure of all time." Atz died on May 22, 1945, in New Orleans, Louisiana.

BIBLIOGRAPHY: Vertical Files, Barker Texas History Center, University of Texas at Austin.
Joe B. Frantz

AUBREY, WILLIAM (1853–1941). William Aubrey, lawyer, the son of William and Rosa Matilda (Forsyth) Aubrey, was born in Mobile, Alabama, on July 29, 1853. He attended Dews School at Columbus, Georgia, and Loyola College and Richard Malcolm Johnston School at Baltimore, Maryland. He was admitted to the State Bar of Texas[qv] in 1874 and began practice at Marshall, where he served as mayor. He moved to San Antonio in 1882 and on February 14, 1883, married Mrs. Sallie E. Weir. They had one son. He married Eugenia Deering Speer on August 25, 1892, and they had three children. Aubrey was dean of San Antonio Law School in 1928 and a director of the *Texas Law Review*.qv He served as president of the San Antonio Bar Association, as well as of the State Bar of Texas and of the Yanaguana Society.qv He died in San Antonio on January 29, 1941.

BIBLIOGRAPHY: San Antonio *Express*, January 30, 1941. *Who Was Who in America*, Vol. 2.

AUBREY, TEXAS. Aubrey is in the Cross Timbersqv region twelve miles northeast of Denton and forty miles north of Dallas in northeastern Denton County. The site was originally named Onega (Ornega, Ornego) when the Texas and Pacific Railway built a section house there in 1881. The same year the name Aubrey was drawn from a hat to replace the name Onega, which was not popular, and a charter for a post office, to be operated in the railroad depot, was granted. Although the Key Schoolhouse settlement, established in 1858 by Dr. George Key, was only about a mile from what became the downtown part of Aubrey, Lemual Noah Edwards, a Civil Warqv veteran from Alabama, is given credit for founding the town. He built the town's second house, a large, imposing, two-story structure, of lumber hauled from Jefferson in 1867. After the first businesses, east of the railroad tracks, burned in 1887, the town was rebuilt west of the tracks, partially on land donated by Edwards. He also helped the town grow by giving each of his ten children land on which to build a home as a wedding present. By 1920 Aubrey had more than thirty businesses and a population of 700. The automobile, the boll weevil,qv and the Great Depressionqv contributed to the decline of the population over the next several years. By the 1980s peanuts had replaced cotton as the number-one crop; an annual average of 3,000 tons is processed in the local drying plant. The sandy, fertile land and the moderate climate have attracted many horse ranchers to the area, which, according to some, is becoming the "horse capital" of Texas. Other farm products include cattle, hay, fruits, and vegetables. A number of cabinet shops are also located in the area. In 1980 Aubrey had a population of 948. In 1986 Ray Roberts Dam was completed nearby on the Elm Fork of the Trinity River. In 1990 Aubrey had a population of 1,138.

BIBLIOGRAPHY: Edward Franklin Bates, *History and Reminiscences of Denton County* (Denton, Texas: McNitzky Printing, 1918; rpt., Denton: Terrill Wheeler Printing, 1976). Mary Jo Cowling, *Geography of Denton County* (Dallas: Banks, Upshaw, 1936).

Jackie Balthrop Fuller

AUBRY, FRANÇOIS XAVIER (1824–1854). François Xavier Aubry (Aubrey), explorer and merchant, was born near Maskinongé, Quebec, on December 3, 1824, to Joseph and Magdeleine (Lupien) Aubry. In his teens he went to St. Louis as a merchant clerk. At the outbreak of the Mexican Warqv he borrowed money, purchased wagons, and entered the Santa Fe trade. He became very successful and was noted for his efficiency and reliability. His solo return trips from Santa Fe to St. Louis were accomplished so quickly and accompanied by such dangers that he received much publicity in the nation's press. He kept journals of most of his trips, and these were printed in papers from St. Louis to New York.

By 1849 Aubry was one of the leading frontier merchants. He believed that Chihuahua and Texas showed promise as trading venues. In February, with merchant Charles White, Aubry traveled via Socorro and El Paso to Chihuahua. He wholesaled his goods, returned by the same route, and was in St. Louis by late August. But the profit was slight because the war was over; Mexican ports were open to European and American vessels, so Chihuahua had less need of the St. Louis–Santa Fe connection.

Still thinking of new ventures, Aubry concluded that the Texas-Chihuahua market might be rewarding if the excessive charges on the Missouri goods could be avoided. On December 1, 1849, he left Santa Fe with twenty empty wagons, turned east at El Paso, followed the Neighbors-Ford route, and traveled beyond San Antonio to Victoria. He filled his wagons at Victoria and on February 15, 1850, headed west; he reached El Paso on April 27, delivered his goods to Chihuahua, and was back in Santa Fe in early June.

The trip was profitable but not easy. Beyond the Pecos Aubry ran into a severe snowstorm and lost forty mules in one night. Indians made the frontier especially dangerous, but Aubry had sixty armed men with him. Near the Davis Mountains he had an encounter with Marco's Apaches. Marco and Aubry discussed travel and friendship, and Marco pledged harmony. However, his pledge did not extend to Mexicans: "We have had for a long time no other food than the meat of Mexican cattle and mules, and we must make use of it still, or perish."

Aubry made one more Texas-Chihuahua trip. He left Santa Fe in mid-August of 1850, arrived in San Antonio in late November and purchased goods, and then went to Chihuahua via El Paso; but he was no longer enthusiastic about this route. He wrote to the *Daily Missouri Republican* from San Antonio, admitting that Indian problems in Texas were so severe and distances so great that San Antonio–El Paso could not replace the St. Louis–Santa Fe route. The *Republican* specified other problems, including the Chihuahua market glut, the shortage of grass and water, and "the class of whites known as gamblers, horse thieves and cut throats."

Aubry made a few more St. Louis–Santa Fe trips and found an important shortcut on the Santa Fe Trail,qv known as the Aubry Cut-Off (northwest of the Cimarron route). Still desiring more adventure, excitement, and profit, he made two Santa Fe–California trips in 1853–54, moving thousands of sheep over inhospitable lands to San Francisco. On his return trips he located an important wagon (later railroad) route along the thirty-fifth parallel. This wagon route led to a dispute with Maj. Richard H. Weightman, a prominent New Mexico figure. On August 18, 1854, the day of his return from California, Aubry met Weightman in a Santa Fe cantina. After a heated argument over the merits of the wagon route, Weightman threw a glass of liquor in Aubry's face, Aubry pulled a pistol, and Weightman fatally stabbed him with a Bowie knife.

BIBLIOGRAPHY: Donald Chaput, *François X. Aubry: Trader, Trailmaker and Voyageur in the Southwest, 1846–1854* (Glendale, California: Clark, 1975). *Donald Chaput*

AUBURN, TEXAS. Auburn was sixteen miles southwest of Waxahachie in western Ellis County. Some of its first settlers were from a caravan of 105 covered wagons that originated in Arkansas in 1852. They were attracted by the water supply from the nearby North Fork of Chambers Creek, the flat and tillable land suitable for crops and livestock, and the climate. Jerry Files opened a general store at Auburn. By 1890 the community had a population of 290; by 1900 it had two cotton gins, a corn mill, a blacksmith shop, and two grocery stores. Four church congregations met regularly—Methodist, Baptist, Presbyterian, and Disciples of Christ. A two-story building, McCarver Chapel, housed a grade school on the first floor and a Masonic lodge on the second floor. An Auburn post office opened in 1877 and operated until 1906, when the mail was rerouted through Maypearl. In 1865 Rezia (or Rezi) Jarvis Banks deeded land to the trustees of the Methodist church, to be used as the site for a church, school, and cemetery. The community name appears first on that deed. Martin P. Nation bought Eureka, a retired world's champion short horse, and brought him to Auburn for breeding. At one time a racetrack was located a half mile from the general store. In 1904 the community reported a population of 136. By the 1940s Auburn consisted of one business, a school, a church, and a few widely scattered dwellings. The 1968 population was reported at twelve. On April 11, 1978, a state historical marker for the cemetery was dedicated as a result of research and documentation done by Cloyd F. Stiles, a great-grandson of Rezia Banks.

BIBLIOGRAPHY: *Ellis County, Texas, Cemetery Records*, Vol. 1 (Waxahachie, Texas: Ellis County Genealogical Society, 1981). Edna Davis Hawkins et al., *History of Ellis County, Texas* (Waco: Texian, 1972). Marker Files, Texas Historical Commission, Austin. *Ubah Stiles*

AUDELIA, TEXAS. Audelia was at the intersection of Forest Lane and Audelia Road, three miles south of present Richardson within the present Dallas city limits in northeastern Dallas County. The first settlers in the Audelia area were the family members of James E. Jackson of Tennessee; his family received a land grant in the Peters colony[qv] in 1842. The area around their homestead became known as Ardelia, after Jackson's daughter, but the name was later changed to Audelia. Although the area was settled in the 1840s, it was not recognized as a community until the 1870s. In October 1899 Audelia received a post office, which opened in a general store at the intersection of Audelia Road and Forest Lane. Its first postmaster was the store's merchant, Junius T. Rhoton. In addition to the post office, Audelia had a cotton gin and a school in 1900. The post office remained in Audelia until January 1904, when it was moved to Richardson. By 1915 Audelia had a population of twenty and by 1940 a population of thirty-five, a store, and a church. In 1981 Audelia was in Dallas.

BIBLIOGRAPHY: Margaret Johnston, "Audelia," *Elm Fork Echoes*, November 1984. David S. Switzer, *It's Our Dallas County* (Dallas: Switzer, 1954). *Lisa C. Maxwell*

AUDIE L. MURPHY MEMORIAL VETERANS HOSPITAL. The Audie L. Murphy[qv] Memorial Veterans Hospital, San Antonio, is a department of Veterans Affairs Medical Center and was officially dedicated on November 17, 1973. It is a 615-bed acute care facility, providing primary, secondary, and tertiary health care in medicine, surgery, neuropsychiatry, and rehabilitation medicine. It also supports a 120-bed nursing home and a thirty-bed Spinal Cord Injury Center. An active ambulatory care program provides primary services to eligible veterans throughout South Texas. This program is carried on at the hospital and in satellite outpatient clinics in San Antonio, Victoria, Laredo, Corpus Christi, and McAllen.

The hospital, built in 1973 as a component of the South Texas Medical Center, serves forty-one counties and a veteran population of 300,000. In 1993 the facility employed 2,000 persons and had an operating budget of $135 million. The Audie Murphy Hospital is affiliated with all five schools that constitute the University of Texas Health Science Center at San Antonio,[qv] and with forty-one other academic institutions.

The Audie Murphy Research Services, among the top ten research and development services in the Department of Veterans Affairs, dedicates 28,000 square feet to medical investigations. In 1992 more than 150 investigators pursued 500 separate studies in such diverse areas as aging, fungal infection, hypertension, and cardiovascular disease. The service is the only Veterans Affairs unit included in a nationwide Interleukin-2 cancer study. The Biomedical Research Foundation of South Texas was established in 1989 to support the research mission of the Audie L. Murphy Memorial Veterans Hospital.

Due to the dedication of its clinical and administrative staff, the hospital is home to many unique and outstanding programs. Dental-implant procedures were pioneered by the facility for the entire federal government. In 1988 the hospital was selected as a Geriatric Research Evaluation and Clinical Center site. The hospital's sharing agreements with the Department of Defense and the private sector result in savings to the federal government and a wide range of services to veterans. Some significant programs established through sharing agreements include lung transplants, liver transplants, heart transplants, bone-marrow transplants, magnetic resonance imaging, linear accelerator treatment, and positron emission tomography. Because the hospital is named for Audie Leon Murphy, the most highly decorated soldier of World War II,[qv] it houses the Audie L. Murphy Memorial Room, which showcases the most complete collection of Audie Murphy memorabilia in the United States.

José R. Coronado

AUDRA, TEXAS. Audra was on Farm Road 1086 1½ miles west of Highway 83 in south central Taylor County. Around the turn of the century a general store was opened there by C. Meno Hunt, Fred Robinson, and Frank Sheppard; Sheppard named the town after his daughter. A school had been established in 1894 one mile southwest of Audra and called South Bluff Creek School and then Red Lake School. A community existed by June 24, 1900, when a post office began operation. It was joined in 1905 by a store operated by Meno Hunt. In that year Audra had a population of about seventy-five with two stores, the post office, a school, and a church in which both Baptists and Methodists worshipped. In response to the coming of the railroad the residents of Audra moved eastward in 1909 to found the new town of Bradshaw. Audra lives on as the name of a general store in Bradshaw, operated by a descendant of its founder.

BIBLIOGRAPHY: Ed Ellsworth Bartholomew, *The Encyclopedia of Texas Ghost Towns* (Fort Davis, Texas, 1982). Juanita Daniel Zachry, *A History of Rural Taylor County* (Burnet, Texas: Nortex, 1980).

Eugene Perry

AUDS CREEK. Auds Creek, also known as Odd's Creek, rises two miles east of Brookston and just south of the Missouri Pacific track in central Lamar County (33°37′ N, 95°40′ W) and runs south for thirteen miles to its mouth on the North Sulphur River at the Delta county line, two miles southeast of Gadston and just west of Slabtown (at 33°28′ N, 95°33′ W). It traverses an area of low-lying floodplains surfaced by sand and gravel that support water-tolerant hardwoods, conifers, and grasses; the area floods several times a year.

AUDUBON, JOHN JAMES (1785–1851). John James Audubon, naturalist and painter of American wildlife, was born on April 26, 1785, in Les Cayes, Santo Domingo (Haiti), the illegitimate son of Jean Audubon and Jeanne Rabin(e), a servant who died soon after his birth. His father, a successful French ship captain, merchant, planter, and slave dealer, took him to Nantes, France, where he was adopted and raised by Jean Audubon's wife, Anne (Moynet). Young Audubon, called variously Fougère, Jean Rabin, Jean Jacques Fougere Audubon, or La Forest, showed an early interest in drawing wildlife. From 1796 until 1800 he attended a naval training academy at Rochefort-sur-Mer. He later claimed to have studied under the renowned French painter Jacques Louis David.

In 1803 he traveled to Pennsylvania to manage an estate that his father had purchased in 1789. After a brief return to France between 1805 and 1806, he returned to the United States and married Lucy Bakewell at her home in Pennsylvania in 1808. They moved west to Kentucky, where he attempted several unsuccessful business ventures. After he was temporarily jailed for debt in 1819, he went to Cincinnati, Ohio, where he worked as a taxidermist, portraitist, and art teacher.

With the idea of documenting American birds and animals by publishing engraved copies of his wildlife drawings, Audubon traveled along the Mississippi and Ohio rivers and the Great Lakes from 1820 to 1824, collecting wildlife specimens while his wife supported their family by running a school. In 1826, after failing to find an American publisher for his project, *The Birds of America*, he went to England. He supported himself by selling oil copies of his watercolor drawings while he canvassed for subscribers to his project among the wealthy and influential in Liverpool, Manchester, Edinburgh, London, and Paris. To engrave his works, Audubon employed William Lizars of Edinburgh and, later, Robert Havell, Jr., of London. In 1829 he briefly returned to America to exhibit his drawings and collect support for his project before heading back to Europe with his wife. His fame grew as the elephant-folio-size plates of *Birds of America* began to appear, and when he returned to the United States in 1831 he exhibited them in the Library of Congress and the Boston Athenaeum. For the next several years he traveled up and down the Atlantic coast from Florida to Labrador in search of birds and subscribers. In Charleston, South Carolina, he met Rev. John Bachmann, a Lutheran minister and amateur naturalist. Audubon's sons, Victor Gifford and John Woodhouse Audubon,[qv] later both married into the Bachmann family, and increasingly the two families assisted Audubon on his various projects. In 1834 and 1835 Audubon was again in Edinburgh, Scotland, to oversee the preparation of *The Birds of America* and its accompanying text, the *Ornithological Biography.* By September 1836 he was back in the eastern United States, where he purchased specimens collected in California.

In April 1837 Audubon and his son John left New Orleans aboard the United States revenue cutter *Campbell* on an expedition along the Gulf Coast to the new Republic of Texas.[qv] They arrived at Galveston Bay toward the end of the month and were officially greeted there by the secretary of the Texas Navy,[qv] Samuel Rhoads Fisher.[qv] They next visited the capitol at Houston, where they met with President Sam Houston[qv] in his dog-trot cabin. While in Texas they observed a large number of previously known birds including blue-winged teals, black-necked stilts, least terns, roseate spoonbills, skimmers, ivory-billed woodpeckers, black-throated buntings, and varieties of sandpipers, ducks, and herons. Later in 1837, after stops in New Orleans and Charleston, Audubon returned to England and Scotland, where for the next couple of years he oversaw the completion of *The Birds of America* and the *Ornithological Biography.* Afterwards he returned to America and worked on the miniature or octavo edition, lithographed by John T. Bowen, which immediately became a best seller. With the money made from its sales, he bought land on the Hudson River and built a home.

During the 1840s Audubon worked on a second great project, *The Viviparous Quadrupeds of North America.* He collected specimens sent to him, toured Canada to canvass for subscriptions in 1842, and made a final expedition up the Missouri River in 1843 to collect specimens and notes. The *Quadrupeds* was issued as lithographs in both large portfolio in 1845–48 and a smaller, multivolume edition in 1854. About half of the original drawings for the work were by Audubon; the rest were by his son John. Audubon died on January 27, 1851, at his home on the Hudson, before his friend, the Reverend Bachmann, had completed the text. He is buried in Trinity Cemetery.

Quadrupeds contains more plates drawn from Texas specimens than does the *Birds of America.* In fact, apparently only one plate from the octavo *Birds of America*, the *Texas Turtle Dove*, fits this category. Among the Texas *Quadrupeds* drawn by John James Audubon are the *Orange-bellied Squirrel*, the *Cotton Rat*, the *Collared Peccary*, and the *Black-Tailed Hare.* Many of the *Quadruped* specimens were obtained by John W. Audubon on his second trip to Texas in 1845–46. Although important parts of John James Audubon's journal, including information on his 1837 Texas trip, were lost, Samuel Wood Geiser[qv] attempted a reconstruction of the Texas trip from the *Birds* in "Naturalists of the Frontier" in the *Southwest Review*[qv] for 1930.

BIBLIOGRAPHY: Alice E. Ford, *Audubon's Animals: The Quadrupeds of North America* (New York: Studio Publications, 1951). Alice Ford, *John James Audubon* (New York: Abbeville, 1988). *Dictionary of American Biography* (New York: Scribner, 1928–81). S. W. Geiser, "Naturalists of the Frontier: Audubon in Texas," *Southwest Review* 16 (Fall 1930). Francis Hobart Herrick, *Audubon the Naturalist: A History of His Life and Times* (2 vols., New York: Appleton, 1917). John H. Jenkins, *Audubon and Texas* (Austin: Pemberton Press, 1965).

Ben W. Huseman

AUDUBON, JOHN WOODHOUSE (1812–1862). John W. Audubon, wildlife and portrait painter, was born on November 30, 1812, at Meadow Brook farm, near Henderson, Kentucky, the second son of Lucy (Bakewell) and John James Audubon.[qv] He spent his youth in Kentucky, Ohio, and Louisiana, where he attended a school taught by his mother. He and his older brother, Victor Gifford Audubon, learned to draw from their father and assisted him in collecting wildlife specimens. Audubon traveled with his father to Labrador in 1833, and from 1834 until 1836 he resided with the family in England. He worked as a portrait painter and helped his father on the publication of *The Birds of America* (1827–38). In 1837 he accompanied his father on a trip to the Republic of Texas,[qv] where they visited Galveston and what was then the capital, Houston. In Charleston, South Carolina, Audubon married Maria Rebecca Bachman in May 1837; they had two daughters. After her death in 1840, he married Caroline Hall, on October 2, 1841; this second marriage produced seven children.

After 1839 Audubon resided in New York City, where he assisted his father by using the camera lucida to make one-half of the 500 small drawings required for the octavo edition of *The Birds of America.* (The senior Audubon made the others.) He also exhibited at the Apollo Association, the American Art-Union, and the National Academy. In 1845–46 he again traveled to Texas to collect specimens, notes, and sketches for one of his father's projects, *The Viviparous Quadrupeds of North America* (1845–51). On this second Texas trip he talked again with Sam Houston[qv] and met Texas Ranger captain John Coffee Hays.[qv] Audubon eventually furnished original drawings for half of the plates in *Quadrupeds*, some of which were credited to his father; he again used a camera lucida to reduce the images for the octavo edition.

After a business trip to England for his father in 1846–47, Audubon joined Col. Henry Webb's California Company expedition as commissary, in 1849. From New Orleans the expedition sailed to the mouth of the Rio Grande; it headed west overland through northern Mexico and over the Gila Trail in Arizona to San Diego, California. Cholera and outlaws caused nearly half of the men to turn back, including the leader. Audubon assumed command of the remainder, which pressed on to California, although he was forced to abandon his paints and canvases in the desert. Upon returning to New York in 1850 he completed *Quadrupeds* and, together with his brother, continued publishing editions of their father's works after his death in January 1851, including a full-sized, chromolithograph edition of *The Birds of America*, which he began with Julius Bien of New York in 1858. Audubon died at his home outside New York City on February 18 or 21, 1862.

BIBLIOGRAPHY: Alice Ford, *John James Audubon* (Norman: University of Oklahoma Press, 1964). George C. Groce and David H. Wallace, *The New York Historical Society's Dictionary of Artists in America, 1564–1860* (New Haven: Yale University Press, 1957). Peggy and Harold Samuels, *The Illustrated Biographical Encyclopedia of Artists of the American West* (Garden City, New York: Doubleday, 1976); Ron Tyler, *Audubon's Great National Work: The Royal Octavo Edition of The Birds of America* (Austin: University of Texas Press, 1993).

Ben W. Huseman

AUGUR, CHRISTOPHER COLUMBUS (1821–1898). Christopher Columbus Augur, United States soldier, son of Ammon and Annis (Wellman) Augur, was born at Kendall, New York, on July 10, 1821. After moving with his widowed mother to Michigan, he was appointed to the United States Military Academy in 1839 and graduated four years later, sixteenth in a class of thirty-nine. He married Jane E. Arnold of Ogdensburg, New York, in 1844. Augur served in the Mexican War[qv] at the battles of Palo Alto and Resaca de la Palma.[qqv] From 1852 to 1856 he participated in fighting against the Yakima and Rogue River Indians in the Oregon and Washington territories. By 1861 Major Augur was serving as commandant of cadets at West Point.

He established a solid but unspectacular Civil War[qv] record in the

Canis Lupus, Linn, Var Rufus. Red Texan Wolf. Male. *After John Woodhouse Audubon. Lithography firm of John T. Bowen, lithograph (hand colored), 1845. Courtesy Amon Carter Museum, Fort Worth. The red wolf once ranged widely in Central and East Texas. In the mid-1990s it was extinct in the wild in Texas and listed by the federal government as an endangered species.*

Union Army. He was promoted to major general of volunteers for his conduct in action in August 1862 at Cedar Mountain, Virginia, where he received serious wounds. He served in the New Orleans campaign and the siege of Port Hudson before receiving command of the Twenty-second Army Corps and the Department of Washington in October 1863, a command that he maintained until the end of the war. In 1865 Congress brevetted Augur major general for his services. The next year he was transferred from command of the volunteer service and made colonel of the Twelfth Infantry. He was made brigadier general, regular army, in 1869.

After the Civil War he commanded the departments of the Platte (1867–71), Texas (1872–75, 1881–83), the Gulf (1875–78), the South (1878–80), and the Missouri (1883–85). He gained a reputation for quiet competence in command rarely equaled during the period. While in Texas he believed that Indians guilty of depredations should be punished severely, and he cooperated fully with Ranald S. Mackenzie's[qv] raid into Mexico, during which Mackenzie burned several Indian villages, as well as with the Red River campaigns of 1874–75 (see RED RIVER WAR). Augur also tried to cooperate with Mexican officials in hope that their combined efforts would crush Indian resistance along the Rio Grande. Yet Indian reformers joined Gen. William T. Sherman[qv] in classifying Augur as a fair man. General Augur was a strong advocate of western railroads, for he recognized that they changed "very materially the conditions of the problem of protection and defense" along the frontier. Augur retired from military service on July 10, 1885, and died at Georgetown, D.C., on January 16, 1898.

BIBLIOGRAPHY: *Dictionary of American Biography.* Francis B. Heitman, *Historical Register and Dictionary of the United States Army* (2 vols., Washington: GPO, 1903; rpt., Urbana: University of Illinois Press, 1965). Raphael P. Thian, comp., *Notes Illustrating the Military Geography of the United States, 1813–1880* (Washington: GPO, 1881; rpt., with addenda ed. John M. Carroll, Austin: University of Texas Press, 1979). *The War of the Rebellion: A Compilation of the Official Records of the Union and Confederate Armies* (Washington: GPO, 1880–1901).

Robert Wooster

AUGUSTA, TEXAS. Augusta is on Farm Road 227 sixteen miles northeast of Crockett in northeastern Houston County. The town was reportedly named for Augusta Smith, daughter of a pioneer settler. Daniel McLean, a member of the Gutiérrez-Magee expedition,[qv] established what is thought to be the first home there in 1821. Other early settlers included the Kyle and Aldrich families, Col. W. W. Davis, and G. W. Wilson, on whose headright the townsite was located. Before the Civil War[qv] Augusta was a trading point for plantations in the area. W. M. Waddell taught at Augusta Male and Female Academy in 1860. An Augusta post office was established in 1882, and by 1885 the town had a Union church, a district school, steam cotton gins, grist and corn mills, three general stores, and a population of 200. The post office was later discontinued, but the community continued to prosper until the 1940s. As late as 1936 Augusta reported 250 residents and three businesses. In the 1940s, however, the population fell to 120, and by 1952 it had dwindled to twenty. It was still reported as twenty in 1990, when a community center and cemetery remained.

Claudia Hazlewood

AUGUSTINE, HENRY WILLIAM (1806–1874). Henry William Augustine, pioneer, soldier, and public official, was born in South Carolina in 1806. He moved to Texas from Autauga County, Alabama, in 1827 and settled in the Ayish Bayou District with his wife, Cynthia. In 1832 he was appointed to a committee of fifteen to select the townsite of San Augustine, which was founded in 1834. At the battle of Nacogdoches[qv] on August 2, 1832, Augustine was battalion commander of the San Augustine regiment. On October 17, 1835, he raised a company in San Augustine to join the Texas volunteer army to march against the Mexican forces at San Antonio de Béxar; meanwhile, he became a delegate to the Consultation[qv] in San Felipe, after which George English[qv] succeeded him as company captain in the siege of Bexar,[qv] December 5–10.

In the First and Second congresses of the Republic of Texas,[qv] Augustine served as senator from San Augustine. He resigned his post on November 24, 1837. During the Córdova Rebellion[qv] in August 1838, Gen. Thomas J. Rusk[qv] dispatched Major Augustine with 150 men to help quell the trouble. While commanding a company in the Cherokee War[qv] in 1838, Augustine received an arrow wound that resulted in the amputation of his leg at the knee. By a special act of the Congress of the republic he was given a wooden leg. He represented San Augustine in the House of the Fifth Congress, 1840–41, and was appointed to the Board of Trustees, San Augustine University, on February 16, 1843. After the death of his wife, Augustine filed for guardianship of their children, on April 30, 1849. About 1855 he moved from San Augustine County to Polk County, where he died in 1874. A state plaque marks his gravesite in Magnolia Cemetery, Segno.

BIBLIOGRAPHY: John Henry Brown, *Indian Wars and Pioneers of Texas* (Austin: Daniell, 1880; reprod., Easley, South Carolina: Southern Historical Press, 1978). George L. Crocket, *Two Centuries in East Texas* (Dallas: Southwest, 1932; facsimile reprod., 1962). Texas House of Representatives, *Biographical Directory of the Texan Conventions and Congresses, 1832–1845* (Austin: Book Exchange, 1941). Gifford E. White, *Character Certificates in the General Land Office of Texas* (1985).

McXie Whitton Martin

AULICK. The USS *Aulick*, the first combatant ship constructed in the state of Texas, was launched on March 2, 1942, at Orange, after patriotic ceremonies marking the celebration of Texas Independence Day and the 106th anniversary of the founding of Orange. The ship was named after nineteenth-century naval commander John H. Aulick. A crowd of 6,000 people watched the launching of this $8.2 million war ship. The ship was commissioned on October 27, 1942, with Lt. O. P. Thomas as the first commander. The *Aulick* was 376 feet long and had a displacement of 2,050 tons. It carried 329 men, had a capacity of 35.2 knots, and was armed with five five-inch cannons and ten twenty-one-inch torpedo tubes.

Following shakedown and training, the *Aulick* joined the Pacific Fleet and Task Force 64 in the Coral Sea for support of the American landing on the Russell Islands. On March 9 she struck a coral reef off the southern tip of New Caledonia while making twenty knots and suffered extensive damage to her hull, propellers, and engines. After being repaired she served from January until May 1944 as a training vessel with the Fleet Operational Training Command. On June 22 she departed for the western Pacific, where she served as a screening vessel during the recapture of Guam, on August 4, 1944, and the seizure of the Palaus, in the southern Philippine Sea (September 6–October 14).

During the Leyte landings the *Aulick* was assigned to the northern fire-support group for shore bombardment, night harassing, and close fire support. From October 29 till November 25 she was assigned escort work and then returned to Leyte to join Task Group 77.2, Leyte Defense Force. On November 29, while on antisubmarine patrol in the east entrance of the Leyte Gulf, the *Aulick* was attacked by six kamikaze Japanese planes. One peeled off and dived toward the destroyer, dropped a bomb, then exploded on hitting the water twenty yards off the ship's bow. Another aircraft approached, struck the starboard side of the bridge with its wing tip, and exploded near the bow just above the main deck. The explosion set the number two gun and handling room on fire. Metal fragments killed several men on the bridge and flying bridge. Casualties were thirty-one men killed, sixty or more wounded, and one missing.

The *Aulick* spent January and February 1945 undergoing repairs. On April 10 she returned to the Philippines and served as an escort during the Mindanao landings. From May 3 until the end of the war she operated off Okinawa, where she served as a radar picket, fighter-director vessel, and air-sea rescue ship. On August 28 she joined the *John D. Henley* in rescuing twelve men from a disabled army bomber.

On September 10, 1945, the *Aulick* left Okinawa for New York. She participated in the presidential review in the Hudson River on October 27 and then steamed to Charleston Navy Yard, where she was placed out of commission in reserve on April 18, 1946. The *Aulick* was transferred on loan to the government of Greece on August 21, 1959. She was later returned to the United States, and her name was struck from the navy list on September 1, 1975. In April 1977 she was sold to the Greek navy, in which she was renamed the *Sphendoni*; she was still serving in 1990. For her action in the Pacific, the *Aulick* received five battle stars.

BIBLIOGRAPHY: Orange *Leader*, March 2, 1942.

Howard C. Williams

AULTMAN, OTIS A. (1874–1943). Otis A. Aultman, photographer, was born on August 27, 1874, in Holden, Missouri. His family moved to Trinidad, Colorado, in 1888. As a young man he learned photography from his older brother, Oliver, many of whose photographs of the Trinidad area are now in the collections of the Colorado State Historical Society. Aultman married and had two children, but the marriage ended in permanent separation in 1908, after which he moved to El Paso. There he first worked for Scott Photo Company, was later in partnership with Robert Dorman, and eventually owned his own studio.

By 1911 El Paso was a gathering place for many of the main personalities of the Mexican Revolution[qv]—Francisco Madero, Francisco (Pancho) Villa, Pascual Orozco[qqv]—and after the shooting began, many American newsmen also flocked to El Paso to cover the event. Aultman was a man in the right place at the right time. He photographed the battle of Casas Grandes, the first battle of Juárez in May 1911, and the Orozco rebellion in 1912. He was a favorite of Pancho Villa, who called Aultman "Banty Rooster" because he was only 5′4″ tall. Aultman worked for the International News Service and Pathé News and experimented with cinematography. In 1916 he was one of the first photographers to arrive at Columbus, New Mexico, after the famous raid on that town by the Villistas.

During the early years of the revolution Aultman's studio on San Francisco Street was a gathering place for both local and out-of-town reporters and photographers, as well as soldiers of fortune. A group called the Adventurer's Club, of which Aultman was a founding member, was formed during this period and continued to meet sporadically for many years, reportedly whenever two or more members were in town.

After the military part of the revolution was over, Aultman settled down to a conventional career as a commercial photographer. He took an interest in photographs depicting early El Paso history and collected many from the 1880s and 1890s. Another of his interests was archaeology; early photographs of archeological sites in the El Paso area are an important part of his work, and he was a founding member of the El Paso Archaeology Society.

Aultman died from a fall in his studio in 1943. Subsequently, the El Paso Chamber of Commerce purchased his negatives from the estate. Over the next twenty years the negatives were moved from one storage place to another, and undoubtedly some disappeared. In the 1960s, due largely to the interest of historian C. L. Sonnichsen,[qv] the remaining 6,000 negatives were purchased, prints were made, and both negatives and prints were placed in the El Paso Public Library. A second set of prints is in the Library of the University of Texas at El Paso. Aultman's photographs are a priceless contribution to the recorded history of El Paso, southern New Mexico, and Ciudad Juárez. Equally important are his photos of the early stages of the Mexican revolution.

BIBLIOGRAPHY: Larry A. Harris, *Pancho Villa and the Columbus Raid* (El Paso: McMath, 1949). Mary A. Sarber, *Photographs from the Border: The Otis A. Aultman Collection* (El Paso Public Library Association, 1977). *Mary A. Sarber*

AUNSPAUGH, VIVIAN LOUISE (1869–1960). Vivian Louise Aunspaugh, painter and art teacher, the daughter of John Henry and Virginia Fields (Yancy) Aunspaugh, was born on August 14, 1869, in Bedford City, Virginia. Her father was a cotton buyer. The family moved from Virginia to Alabama, South Carolina, and Georgia during Vivian's childhood. In Rome, Georgia, she graduated from Shorter College and was awarded the Excelsior Art Medal. In 1885 she taught at the Woman's College of Union Springs, Alabama. Between 1886 and 1890 she studied with John Henry Twachtman in New York and with Cecil Payne and Alphonse Mucha in Paris. She painted landscapes, flowers, figures, portraits, and miniatures. She specialized in watercolors and pastels.

In 1890 she returned from Europe. For the next two years she taught art at McKinney College in McKinney, Texas, then served for a year as art supervisor for the Greenville Public Schools. From 1893 to 1894 she taught at the Masonic Female College in Bonham. Miss Aunspaugh was head of the art department at Patton Female Seminary, Dallas, from 1894 to 1896 and an instructor in decorative arts at St. Mary's College from 1896 to 1900. She exhibited at the Expo Universelle, Paris, France, in 1900 and received a gold medal.

In 1898 she and sculptress Clyde Chandler[qv] established joint studio classes in Dallas. Their studio, designed as a four-year preparatory course for college or public school teaching, became the Aunspaugh Art School in 1902. It was the first art school in the Southwest to offer classes in fine and commercial art, including the use of live models, nude and draped. Clyde Chandler left for Chicago in 1903, but Vivian Aunspaugh continued teaching for the next fifty-seven years. In addition to providing art instruction to the young ladies of Dallas, she was active in the Dallas Woman's Forum and responsible for its annual exhibition of Texas artists between 1912 and 1932. Through these efforts she introduced Texas artists to Dallas collectors, thereby establishing a foundation for the widespread acceptance of local artists in the 1930s.

For many years Vivian Aunspaugh was director of the Gamma Omicron Chapter of Beta Sigma Phi, the young businesswomen's sorority. She was a member of the Episcopalian Church of the Incarnation. She died in Dallas on March 9, 1960.

BIBLIOGRAPHY: Diana Church, *Guide to Dallas Artists, 1890–1917* (Plano, Texas, 1987). Frances Battaile Fisk, *A History of Texas Artists and Sculptors* (Abilene, Texas, 1928; facsimile rpt., Austin: Morrison, 1986). Chris Petteys, *Dictionary of Women Artists* (Boston: Hall, 1985).
Diana Church

AURORA, TEXAS (Jefferson County). Aurora was located near the mouth of Taylor Bayou on Sabine Lake, at the site of present-day Port Arthur. The town was conceived as early as 1837, and by 1840 promoters led by Almanzon Huston[qv] were advertising town lots. Although some lots were sold, Houston's project failed to materialize. The area came to be known as Sparks after John Sparks and his family moved to the shores of Sabine Lake near the Aurora townsite. The Eastern Texas Railroad, completed between Sabine Pass and Beaumont just before the outbreak of the Civil War,[qv] passed about four miles west of Sparks. The railroad passing track at this point was named Aurora after the Houston project. The rails were removed during the Civil War. A few scattered settlers remained until 1886, when a destructive hurricane led residents to dismantle their homes and move to Beaumont. By 1895 Aurora was a ghost town. The abandoned community, however, soon became the site of Arthur E. Stilwell's[qv] new city, Port Arthur.[qv]

BIBLIOGRAPHY: S. G. Reed, *A History of the Texas Railroads* (Houston: St. Clair, 1941; rpt., New York: Arno, 1981). WPA Federal Writers' Project, *Port Arthur* (Houston: Anson Jones Press, 1939).
Robert Wooster

AURORA, TEXAS (Wise County). Aurora is on State Highway 114 ten miles southeast of Decatur in southeastern Wise County. The site is on a gentle rise and is surrounded by mesquite and live oak trees. Settlement began there in the late 1850s. Impressed by the beauty of the place, William O. Stanfield suggested Aurora for the name of the community. For the first twenty years the population grew rapidly, and the town became a trading center for county farmers. A post office was opened in 1873, and the town was incorporated on August 21, 1882. By the mid-1880s Aurora had two schools, two cotton gins, two hotels, fifteen businesses, and a population variously estimated at between 750 and 3,000. An outbreak of spotted fever began during the latter part of 1888, and by 1889 fear of the epidemic had caused a mass exodus from the town. Two years later, when the Burlington-Northern Railroad Company abandoned its plan to lay tracks through Aurora, most of the few remaining inhabitants moved to Rhome, two miles to the southeast, the new site of a railroad stop. Ironically, as its decline continued, the town became the focus of the state's attention. On April 18, 1897, S. E. Hayden, an Aurora cotton buyer, wrote a story describing the crash of a mysterious airship just outside of town. Hayden's fictional article was apparently an attempt to bring attention to the community, but it caused a sensation because stories were already current of unidentified flying objects near Fort Worth. Hayden's tale, however, failed to revive Aurora. In 1901 postal service was discontinued. The construction of State Highway 114 through Aurora in 1939 probably saved the community from extinction. In the early 1970s Aurora underwent a rebirth as the town became a bedroom community of Fort Worth. In 1986 it had an estimated 376 residents. In 1990 the population was 623.

BIBLIOGRAPHY: Rosalie Gregg, ed., *Wise County History* (Vol. 1, n.p: Nortex, 1975; Vol. 2, Austin: Eakin, 1982). *Wise County Messenger*, Centennial Edition, October 4, 1956. *David Minor*

AURY, LOUIS MICHEL (ca. 1788–1821). Louis Michel Aury, pirate, was born in Paris about 1788. He served in the French navy and on

French privateers from 1802 or 1803 until 1810, when accumulation of prize money enabled him to become master of his own vessels. He sailed from a North Carolina port with a Venezuelan commission in April 1813 and reached Cartagena in May. In August 1813 he was given command over the Granadine Republic's privateer schooners, a service that ended in January 1816, when he reached Aux Cayes, Haiti, after successfully running the Spanish blockade of Cartagena.

At Aux Cayes Aury quarreled with Simón Bolívar and transferred his services to a group of New Orleans associates who were planning a Mexican rebel port on the Texas coast, an invasion of the Provincias Internas,[qv] and attacks on Mexican Royalist ports, all part of the Mexican revolt against Spain. Aury left Aux Cayes on June 4 and captured several vessels en route to the Belize, where he arrived on July 17. Then he went on to Galveston. Most of the prize vessels and cargo were lost or damaged in efforts to sail into the harbor. Haitian sailors mutinied on the night of September 7, wounded Aury, and sailed to Haiti with considerable booty. Aid from New Orleans arrived within two or three days. José Manuel de Herrera, Mexican rebel envoy, proclaimed Galveston a port of the Mexican republic, made Aury resident commissioner, and raised the rebel flag on September 13, 1816.

Aury's privateers cruised the Gulf looking for prizes. Of the many that came to Galveston, one carried a cargo of specie and indigo worth about $778,000. Cargoes condemned at Galveston went through New Orleans customs in unlabeled bales or were smuggled into Louisiana.

Aury's settlement of shacks on the Galveston sand was far from peaceful. Henry Perry,[qv] who commanded troops sent by the New Orleans associates for the invasion of Texas, refused obedience to Aury. Another disturbing incident was the arrival, on November 22, 1816, of Francisco Xavier Mina[qv] with his filibustering expedition. Aury, disconcerted by Mina's appearance, at first refused to cooperate, but Perry and others forced him to change his attitude. Then Mina quarreled with his New Orleans associates, who severed connections with him and with Aury; the latter's services were no longer needed after the plans to invade New Spain were dropped. Aury then decided to convoy the Mina expedition to the Santander River. The fleet left Galveston on April 7, 1817, providing Jean Laffite[qv] with an opportunity to undermine the skeleton "government" left on the island. Aury returned from his trip and tried to establish himself at Matagorda Bay. After failing in this effort he went back to Galveston, where he remained until July 21. In preceding weeks, the Laffite brothers, Jean and Pierre, had gained a strong hold on the nondescript inhabitants of Galveston. Aury resigned his commission to rule Galveston Island on July 31, 1817. He then sailed to the Florida coast, where he joined Gregor McGregor, authorized agent of the rebel colonies of Venezuela, New Grenada (Colombia), Mexico, and La Plata (Argentina), in attacking Spanish Florida from Amelia Island. After numerous disappointments, he captured Old Providence Island on July 4, 1818. From that headquarters he participated in several unsuccessful attempts to aid the republican cause. He probably died at Old Providence on August 30, 1821, though some sources state that he was living in Havana in 1845.

BIBLIOGRAPHY: Lancaster E. Dabney, "Louis Aury: The First Governor of Texas under the Mexican Republic," *Southwestern Historical Quarterly* 42 (October 1938). Harry Van Demark, "Pirates of the Gulf," *Texas Magazine,* May 1910. Harris Gaylord Warren, *The Sword Was Their Passport: A History of American Filibustering in the Mexican Revolution* (Baton Rouge: Louisiana State University Press, 1943).

Harris Gaylord Warren

AUSTIN. The *Austin,* a sloop-of-war and flagship of the Texas Navy[qv] first known as the *Texas,* was commissioned into the navy on January 5, 1840. The ship, constructed in Baltimore by the firm of Shott and Whitney, was 125 feet in length and thirty-one feet across the beam, with a displacement of 600 tons and a draft of 12½ feet. She carried a crew of twenty-three officers and warrant officers and 151 sailors and marines and was armed with sixteen medium twenty-four-pound cannons, two eighteen-pound medium cannons, and two eighteen-pound long cannons.

The *Austin* was the flagship of the navy from April 1840 through July 1843 and was commanded, except for the period that she lay in ordinary from July through December 1841, by Edwin Ward Moore,[qv] senior officer of the navy. While in ordinary she was commanded by Lt. Alfred G. Gray.[qv] On July 26, 1840, the *Austin* sailed for the Yucatán port of Sisal to assist the Federalist rebels against Mexico's Centralist government. The ship arrived on July 31, cruised the Bay of Campeche as far as Veracruz by August 23, and blockaded Tampico through October. In November she took part in the capture of the capital of Yucatán, San Juan Bautista; the navy earned for Texas $25,000 in ransom from the city.

After a return to her home port of Galveston for repairs, the *Austin* once again sailed for Yucatán on December 13, 1841, and arrived at Sisal on January 6, 1842. From there she again cruised the Mexican coast in search of prizes. In company with the *San Bernard,*[qv] the *Austin* took the *Progresso* off Veracruz on February 6 and, running northward as far as Tuxpan, took the *Dolorita* and the *Dos Amigos,* out of Matamoros, Tamaulipas. During this cruise Yucatán was paying $8,000 monthly toward the maintenance of the Texas navy.

On April 24 the *Austin* returned to New Orleans for refitting. From there, despite the fact that Commodore Moore, his ship, and his crew had been declared pirates by Sam Houston,[qv] she sailed for the Yucatán on April 15, 1843, hoping to engage the powerful new Mexican steam warship *Moctezuma* and to break up a rumored amphibious assault on Galveston Island. The *Austin,* accompanied by the brig *Wharton,*[qv] intercepted the *Moctezuma,* the steam frigate *Guadaloupe,* and two brigs and two schooners on April 30, and sprang to the attack. Although overwhelmingly the stronger, the Mexican fleet withdrew, and a running fight ensued for about two hours. The *Austin* was struck once in the fighting and lost some of her mizzen rigging. The commander of the *Moctezuma* and twenty of his crew were killed, the Mexican fleet was driven from Yucatán waters, and the siege of Campeche was raised as a result of the action. On May 16 the *Austin* and the *Wharton* pursued the *Moctezuma* and the *Guadaloupe* fourteen miles, during which the *Austin* sustained seventeen hits to hull and rigging. By 3:00 p.m. she could no longer keep up the chase and withdrew to Campeche. This battle became the subject of the engraving on the cylinder of the famed Colt Navy revolver.

A bolt of lightning further damaged the *Austin*'s rigging on June 25, and on June 29 Moore set a course for Galveston, there to answer Houston's piracy charge. The arrival of the *Austin* and the *Wharton* at their home port on July 14, 1843, effectively ended all operations of the Texas Navy. When annexation[qv] occurred, the *Austin* was transferred to the United States Navy, on May 11, 1846. She was thereupon towed to Pensacola, where she served for a while as a receiving ship, the only vessel of the Texas Navy to be commissioned into United States service. The ship leaked so badly, however, that after two years she was run aground and broken up, being, according to the commandant of the Pensacola Navy Yard, "unworthy of repairs."

BIBLIOGRAPHY: Alex Dienst, "The Navy of the Republic of Texas," *Quarterly of the Texas State Historical Association* 12–13 (January–October 1909; rpt., Fort Collins, Colorado: Old Army Press, 1987). C. L. Douglas, *Thunder on the Gulf: The Story of the Texas Navy* (Dallas: Turner, 1936; rpt., Fort Collins, Colorado: Old Army Press, 1973). Jim Dan Hill, *The Texas Navy* (New York: Barnes, 1962). Tom Henderson Wells, *Commodore Moore and the Texas Navy* (Austin: University of Texas Press, 1960). *Thomas W. Cutrer*

AUSTIN, GENE (1900–1972). Gene Austin, singer and composer, was born Eugene Lucas on June 24, 1900, in Gainesville, Texas, the son of Serena Belle (Harrell) Lucas. He later took the surname of his stepfather, Jim Austin. He grew up in small towns in Louisiana, joined the United States Army when he was fifteen, participated in the expedition sent to capture Francisco (Pancho) Villa[qv] in 1916, and served in France during World War I.[qv] He studied both dentistry and law in Baltimore, but decided on a singing career. Though he composed more than 100 songs, Austin never learned to read music. He was one of the original crooners, and his tenor voice was well known in the early days of radio and on the hand-cranked phonographs of the 1920s and 1930s. His RCA Victor recordings sold a total of more than eighty-six million copies; one of the recordings, "My Blue Heaven" (1927), sold over twelve million records. He started his recording career in 1923, and the next year Jimmy McHugh produced his first hit song, "When My Sugar Walks Down the Street," with lyrics by Austin and Irving Mills. Other hit songs Austin introduced were "My Melancholy Baby," "Girl of My Dreams," "Ramona," "Carolina Moon," and "Sleepy Time Gal." His compositions included "When My Sugar Walks Down the Street," "How Come You Do Me Like You Do?" and "Lonesome Road." Austin debuted in the movies in 1932 and ultimately made three: *Sadie McKee, Gift of Gab,* and *Melody Cruise.* Over the years he was also featured on numerous radio programs. In 1939 he began working with Billy Wehle in a tented musical-comedy show that spent the winter in Gainesville and that opened in 1940 during the Circus Roundup of the Gainesville Community Circus.[qv] He was a nightclub entertainer in the 1930s, but then his career waned. After his life was dramatized in a television special in the late 1950s, he resumed nightclub appearances. He continued to write songs until the last ten months of his life, when he developed lung cancer. Austin spent most of his adult life in Las Vegas, Nevada, and in 1962 he ran for governor there, but lost badly to the incumbent, Grant Sawyer. He was married five times. Austin died on January 24, 1972, in Palm Springs, California, and was survived by his wife, Gigi, and two daughters from a previous marriage.

BIBLIOGRAPHY: Austin *American-Statesman,* January 25, 1972. Dallas *Morning News,* August 6, 1956. New York *Times,* January 24, 1972. *Newsweek,* May 6, 1957. *Saturday Evening Post,* August 31, 1957.

AUSTIN, HENRY (1782–1852). Henry Austin, promoter, lawyer, and land dealer, the son of Elijah and Esther (Phelps) Austin, was born in New Haven, Connecticut, on January 31, 1782. At the age of twelve he sailed to China as a cabin boy and, on returning, found that his father's death had left him partly responsible for the family. He had quit the sea by 1805 and was engaged in business in New York and New Haven until 1825. Concerning the period from 1808 to 1812 he wrote, "Scarce a dollar that has gone out of my hands has returned to me." In 1814 he married Mary Tailer of Boston. By 1824 he was in a receptive mood to letters from his cousin, Stephen F. Austin,[qv] urging him to come to Texas, primarily in the interest of his growing family. He first tried unsuccessfully to set up a gin and commission business in Mexico. Then he bought the *Ariel*[qv] to navigate the Rio Grande. Unable to adjust to the temperament of the Mexicans, he sailed up the Brazos to Brazoria in 1830, visited his cousin, and made application to Mexico for a ten-league grant of land. The *Ariel,* being unable to make the trip to New Orleans, where Henry Austin went to visit his sister, Mary Austin Holley,[qv] and to make plans for joining the colony, was abandoned in the San Jacinto River. Henry received news of the approval of his application for land on April 2, 1831, and in May sailed for Texas as a prospective settler. He selected a site on the Brazos for his plantation, named it Bolivar, and employed five men to erect buildings. He welcomed Mary Holley there in October and his wife and five children in December of the same year. Stephen F. Austin spent a week with the family before he went to Saltillo as the representative of Coahuila and Texas.[qv]

Henry Austin's wife died in 1832, and he sent his daughters home with Mary Holley to Lexington, Kentucky; there they spent several years in school before returning to Bolivar, "where Emily kept house while Henrietta waited on her father." Henry spent his life in Texas in the vain effort to make his land pay, but he only succeeded, as did most of the other settlers, in being "land poor" and having to sacrifice much of his holdings for the education of his children. His public contribution to the state was in his relation to Stephen F. Austin, whose firm friend and staunch supporter he remained until his death. The extensive report he drew up for the administration of his cousin's estate proved to be invaluable. He was a promoter, a lawyer, a land dealer, and a politician and in spite of difficulties added significantly to his landholdings for the benefit of his children. His death on January 23, 1852, in the words of his will, ended "a long life of incessant enterprise, toil, privation, and suffering."

BIBLIOGRAPHY: Eugene C. Barker, ed., *The Austin Papers* (3 vols., Washington: GPO, 1924–28). Eugene C. Barker, *The Life of Stephen F. Austin* (Nashville: Cokesbury Press, 1925; rpt., Austin: Texas State Historical Association, 1949; New York: AMS Press, 1970). William Ransom Hogan, "Life of Henry Austin," *Southwestern Historical Quarterly* 37 (January 1934). Mary Austin Holley Papers, Barker Texas History Center, University of Texas at Austin. *Winnie Allen*

AUSTIN, JAMES ELIJAH BROWN (1803–1829). James Austin, brother of Stephen F. Austin[qv] and one of the Old Three Hundred,[qv] son of Moses and Maria (Brown) Austin,[qqv] was born in Missouri on October 3, 1803. From 1811 to 1817 he attended an academy in Washington, Connecticut. He joined his brother Stephen in Texas in December 1821, established residence, and became entitled to land grants from the Mexican government. On August 19, 1824, he received title to three leagues on the west bank of the Brazos River, encompassing Eagle Nest and Manor lakes; a labor in what is now western Brazoria County; and another labor that later became part of Waller County. Austin returned to Missouri in May 1824 to bring his mother and sister Emily (later Emily Austin Perry[qv]) to Texas, but in 1825 he was forced to return to Texas alone.

Shortly after his return he formed a partnership with John Austin[qv] and engaged in the coasting trade and merchandising. In 1826, when the proposed constitution for the state of Coahuila and Texas[qv] threatened to abolish slavery,[qv] Austin lobbied in Saltillo for a continuation of the institution and was instrumental in gaining a modification that recognized those slaves already in Texas. He also brought to Texas 300 Spanish horses from Saltillo in 1826. In 1827 he helped to put down the Fredonian Rebellion.[qv] Austin married Eliza Martha Westall on March 20, 1828; they named their son, born in February 1829, Stephen F. Austin, Jr.[qv] James Austin died of yellow fever in New Orleans on August 14, 1829.

BIBLIOGRAPHY: Lester G. Bugbee, "The Old Three Hundred: A List of Settlers in Austin's First Colony," *Quarterly of the Texas State Historical Association* 1 (October 1897). *Charles A. Bacarisse*

AUSTIN, JOHN (1801–1833). John Austin, participant in the Long expedition,[qv] soldier, alcalde,[qv] and signer of the Turtle Bayou Resolutions, was born in New Haven, Connecticut, on March 17, 1801, the son of Susan (Rogers) and John Punderson Austin.[qv] His middle name was Punderson, but apparently he dropped it before coming to Texas. As a youth he went to sea as a common sailor and joined the Long expedition,[qv] in New Orleans in 1819. He was taken with other members of the expedition as a prisoner to Mexico, where after his release he contacted Stephen F. Austin,[qv] who had just received his grant from the Mexican authorities. Apparently the two men were only distantly related, if at all, but they formed a close personal friendship, and John Austin, after a brief trip to the United States in 1822, joined Stephen Austin at San Felipe and aided him in settling his original colonists.

On January 26, 1824, he made his bond as constable of the district of San Felipe de Austin. With financing mainly from Stephen Austin, he bought a cotton gin on Buffalo Bayou in July 1825, and a few months later he formed a partnership with J. E. B. Austin,[qv] younger brother of the empresario.[qv] The partnership was expanded to include a mercantile store in Brazoria, where both men continued to live until J. E. B. Austin's death in 1829.

John Austin's business interests grew to include cattle and shipping enterprises as well as the gin and store. He became port officer in 1831, alcalde of Brazoria Municipality in 1832, and delegate to the Convention of 1832.[qv] He also participated in the Anahuac Disturbances,[qv] was one of the group that returned to Brazoria for the cannon that occasioned the battle of Velasco,[qv] commanded at the battle of Velasco and received Gen. Domingo de Ugartechea's[qv] surrender, and later signed the Turtle Bayou Resolutions. Austin was subsequently elected brigadier general of the militia. He died at Gulf Prairie on August 11, in the same cholera epidemic in which his two children died. His wife, Elizabeth, survived and married Thomas F. L. Parrott[qv] in 1834. She turned over the upper league of John Austin's 1824 two-league grant to his father. On August 26, 1836, she and her husband sold for $5,000 the lower half of the John Austin league on Buffalo Bayou to Augustus C. and John K. Allen[qqv] for the proposed township of Houston.

BIBLIOGRAPHY: Eugene C. Barker, ed., *The Austin Papers* (3 vols., Washington: GPO, 1924–28). John Henry Brown, *Indian Wars and Pioneers of Texas* (Austin: Daniell, 1880; reprod., Easley, South Carolina: Southern Historical Press, 1978). James A. Creighton, *A Narrative History of Brazoria County* (Angleton, Texas: Brazoria County Historical Commission, 1975). Lois A. Garver, "Benjamin Rush Milam," *Southwestern Historical Quarterly* 38 (October 1934, January 1935). David G. McComb, *Houston: The Bayou City* (Austin: University of Texas Press, 1969; rev. ed., *Houston: A History*, 1981). Edna Rowe, "The Disturbances at Anahuac in 1832," *Quarterly of the Texas State Historical Association* 6 (April 1903). *Southwestern Historical Quarterly*, Texas Collection, July 1962. Texas House of Representatives, *Biographical Directory of the Texan Conventions and Congresses, 1832–1845* (Austin: Book Exchange, 1941).

AUSTIN, JOHN PUNDERSON (1774–1834). John Punderson Austin, son of David and Mary (Mix) Austin, was born in New Haven, Connecticut, on June 28, 1774. After his graduation from Yale in 1794, he went into business in New Haven, where he married Susan Rogers on September 11, 1797. They later lived in Bridgeport and in Norwich, Connecticut, and had thirteen children, two of whom, John Austin and William Tennant Austin,[qqv] came to Texas. After John Austin's death in the cholera epidemic of 1833, John Punderson Austin came to Texas to take over his son's estate, but he too died of cholera, probably in July 1834. His remains were returned to New Haven, Connecticut, for burial.

Another John P. Austin, who is sometimes confused with John Punderson Austin and with John Austin, was a cousin of Stephen F. Austin and the brother of Henry Austin and Mary Austin Holley.[qqv] This John P. Austin was a native of New York. He considered coming to Texas in 1825 but instead became a commission merchant in New York. He maintained his interest in Texas, however, and corresponded frequently with Stephen F. Austin, giving him news of importance to Texas from the United States. He also handled business matters for the Texas colonizer.

BIBLIOGRAPHY: Eugene C. Barker, ed., *The Austin Papers* (3 vols., Washington: GPO, 1924–28). Franklin Bowditch Dexter, *Biographical Sketches of the Graduates of Yale College: With Annals of the College History* (vols. 1–5, New York: Holt, 1885–1912; vol. 6, New Haven: Yale University Press, 1912). Vertical Files, Barker Texas History Center, University of Texas at Austin.

AUSTIN, MARY BROWN (1768–1824). Mary (Maria) Brown Austin, wife of Moses Austin and mother of Stephen F. Austin and Emily Margaret Austin Bryan Perry,[qqv] daughter of Abia and Margaret (Sharp) Brown, was born at Sharpsborough Furnace, New Jersey, on New Year's Day, 1768, one of eight and the oldest living child. Her father had served as a deputy in the provincial congresses of 1775 and 1776 and amassed holdings in real estate in connection with iron mining and smelting. After Mary's mother died in 1780, her father asked the wealthy Philadelphia merchant Benjamin Fuller, connected by marriage to the Sharp family, to board Mary and one of her sisters. After a courtship of no more than two years, Mary married Moses Austin in 1785 and moved to Richmond, Virginia, where Moses established and prospered in a branch of a mercantile partnership he shared with his brother. In Richmond Mary managed a household of up to half a dozen slaves in the most imposing residential structure there. She gave birth to Anna Maria (1787) and Eliza Fuller (1790), each of whom died within months of birth. Mary moved with Moses in 1792 to the frontier at the Lead Mines, soon renamed Austinville, in modern Wythe County, Virginia, where she gave birth to Stephen Fuller (1793), later known as the "Father of Texas," and Emily Margaret (1795). When Austin's business in Virginia began to fail, he moved his family in 1798 to Ste. Genevieve, then to Potosi, the first Anglo-American settlement west of and back from the Mississippi River, in Spanish Upper Louisiana (modern Missouri). Moses built a mansion in the Southern style, over which Mary presided, and where in 1803 she bore their fifth child, James Elijah Brown Austin.[qv]

Maria, as her family came to call her, was a steady, capable woman in whom her husband confided concerning his business affairs. During his extended business trips, she managed both the household and her husband's business affairs at home. Always frugal, she demonstrated a strong capability for handling money and managing finances. Life on the Missouri frontier was hard on her physically. She lost weight and by 1811 endured nearly constant pain. A change of climate, she and her husband decided, might do her good. Moreover, a trip to the East would give her the joy of renewing acquaintances with kin, none of whom, save one sister, she had seen since before she left Virginia thirteen years earlier. Moses and Maria agreed, too, that she should take their two youngest children, seven-year-old Brown so that he could meet his relatives, and sixteen-year-old Emily so that she could enter a good Eastern school to finish her education. Maria and the children were escorted by a brother-in-law of her husband, whose business shortcomings aggravated her, but whose unannounced abandonment of them on the East Coast left her free to manage her own affairs. Maria was happy in the East; she begged her husband to abandon Missouri and establish a business there. Upon declaration of the War of 1812 she curtailed her social life to conserve on the cost of living, but sorrow and loneliness made her life miserable. She returned to Missouri in the summer of 1813, in time for Emily's marriage to James Bryan. The next year Emily bore a son, but fell so ill that Maria had to care for him. When the baby died a month later, Maria was devastated. Thereafter, her health deteriorated steadily. By 1817 rheumatism had destroyed her ability to write. By 1817 financial troubles had bereft Maria and Moses of their home of eighteen years in Potosi. They moved to Herculaneum, a town Moses had founded ten years earlier on the Mississippi. In 1820 Maria's anxiety increased, both on account of the death of close friends, who, without having forewarned her, left their son to Maria's care, and on account of Austin's deteriorated financial condition, which led him to declare bankruptcy in March. In May 1820, against Maria's wishes, Moses left home for Arkansas. He subsequently sought permission to establish an Anglo-American colony in Spanish Texas.[qv] When she saw Moses again ten months later in March 1821, Maria found him terribly debilitated and begged him to rest. He refused. On June 8, 1821, two days before Moses died, Maria, hoping desperately for her husband's recovery, wrote one of the most widely known letters in Texas history in which she told their son, Stephen Fuller, of Moses' wish for him to pursue the Texas colonization venture.

With more liabilities than assets in her husband's estate, the widowed Maria at fifty-three had to support herself, which she did in part by making bonnets for sale. She and Emily, whose husband died in 1822, hoped to recover the home Moses had built in Potosi, but it was not to be. Living with Emily in her last years, Maria focused on religion and her grandchildren. She died at Emily's home on Hazel Run, twenty miles east-southeast of Potosi, on January 8, 1824. Maria was buried beside her husband in the private graveyard on the Bryan property. She had wanted Austin's body moved to a public cemetery. Before Emily and her second husband moved to Texas in 1831, they had the remains of both Maria and Moses reinterred in a public cemetery in Potosi on land once owned by them.

BIBLIOGRAPHY: Eugene C. Barker, ed., *The Austin Papers* (3 vols., Washington: GPO, 1924–28). David B. Gracy II, *Moses Austin: His Life* (San Antonio: Trinity University Press, 1987).

David B. Gracy II

AUSTIN, MOSES (1761–1821). Moses Austin, founder of the American lead industry and the first man to obtain permission to bring Anglo-American settlers into Spanish Texas,[qv] son of Elias and Eunice (Phelps) Austin, was born in Durham, Connecticut, on October 4, 1761. He was in the fifth generation of his line of Austins in America. Abandoning his father's occupations of tailor, farmer, and tavern keeper, Moses at age twenty-one entered the dry-goods business in Middletown, Connecticut, then moved to Philadelphia, Pennsylvania, in 1783 to join his brother, Stephen, in a similar undertaking. In Philadelphia he met and in 1785 married Mary Brown (*see* AUSTIN, MARY BROWN), by whom he had five children, three of whom lived to maturity: Stephen Fuller Austin,[qv] who accepted and successfully carried out Moses' deathbed request to prosecute "the Texas Venture," Emily Margaret Austin (*see* PERRY, EMILY MARGARET AUSTIN), and James Elijah Brown Austin.[qv] Moses extended his business to Richmond, Virginia, where he established Moses Austin and Company. In 1789 he secured a contract to roof the new Virginia capitol in lead, and, since the state promised to pay 5 percent above market price if the contractor used Virginia lead, Moses, again in partnership with Stephen, gained control of Virginia's richest lead deposit. He brought experienced miners and smelterers from England to improve the efficiency of his operation, and the resulting expertise and industry he introduced into the lead business established the American lead industry. Austin founded Austinville (Wythe County) at the lead mines in 1792 after he moved to the mines. When he encountered problems in roofing the capitol and in financing his enterprise, he looked for relief to the rumored lead deposits in Spanish Upper Louisiana. After visiting the mines during the winter of 1796–97, he sought and obtained a grant to part of Mine a Breton (at modern Potosi, Missouri), where in 1798 he established the first Anglo-American settlement west of and back from the Mississippi River. Imbued with the New England Calvinist belief that to those most able to manage assets should go the lion's share of them, Austin sought aggressively to expand his holdings. Using the efficient reverberatory furnace, the design of which he had learned from the English smelterers, he gained control of virtually all smelting in the region and amassed a wealth of $190,000. The second period in the history of the American lead industry is known as the "Moses Austin Period." Austin's contributions influenced the lead industry until heavy machinery revolutionized mining and smelting after the Civil War.[qv]

In his frontier settlement Austin built, in the style of a southern mansion, an imposing home that he called Durham Hall. From this seat he fought for nearly a decade with John Smith for supremacy of the mines. With few exceptions, he made it his business to win the friendship of men in prominent positions. Governor William Henry Harrison appointed him a justice on the Court of Common Pleas and Quarter Sessions for the Ste. Genevieve District. With sales lost because of Aaron Burr's[qv] conspiracy, the War of 1812, and subsequent depressed conditions, Austin joined others seeking to increase the money supply in circulation by founding the Bank of St. Louis, the first bank west of the Mississippi River. When the bank failed in 1819, the repercussions on Austin's finances were severe. Already in 1816 he had relinquished the Potosi mine to his son Stephen, moved to Herculaneum, Missouri, a town he established in 1808 as a river shipping point for his lead, and returned to merchandising.

Unsuccessful in escaping debt through traditional business pursuits, Austin developed a plan in 1819 for settling an American colony in Spanish Texas. Characteristically, he took an aggressive tack in times when holding the line seemed best. After the Adams-Onís Treaty[qv] clarified Spanish title to Texas, he traveled to San Antonio, where he arrived on December 23, 1820, seeking permission to bring his colonists. Spurned by Governor Antonio María Martínez,[qv] he chanced to meet the Baron de Bastrop[qv] in one of the most famous turns of history in Texas. Austin and Bastrop had chanced to meet nineteen years earlier when in New Orleans on unrelated trips and had had no contact during the interim. Nevertheless, the two recognized each other. After Bastrop, a resident of San Antonio, heard the enthusiasm with which Moses spoke of his colonization plan, the baron returned with him to the governor's office to request permission to establish the colony. On December 26, 1820, Governor Martínez endorsed and forwarded the plan to higher authority.

On the trip out of Texas, Moses contracted pneumonia from four weeks of wet and cold weather; he subsisted for the last week on roots and berries. Shortly after he reached home, he learned that permission for the colony had been granted, after which he neglected his health and devoted all of his energies to the "Texas Venture." Austin lived barely two months more. Two days before he died, he called his wife to his bed. "After a considerable exertion to speak," she wrote in one of the most famous letters in Texas history, "he drew me down to him and with much distress an difficulty of speech, told me it was two late, that he was going . . . he beged me to tell you to take his place tell dear Stephen that it is his dieing fathers last request to prosecute the enterprise he had Commenced." Moses Austin died on June 10, 1821, at the home of his daughter, Emily Bryan, and was buried in the Bryan family cemetery. In 1831 the remains of both Moses and his wife were removed to a public cemetery in Potosi on land they once owned. In 1938 the state of Texas tried unsuccessfully to remove the remains to the State Cemetery[qv] in Austin.

BIBLIOGRAPHY: Eugene C. Barker, ed., *The Austin Papers* (3 vols., Washington: GPO, 1924–28). David B. Gracy II, *Moses Austin: His Life* (San Antonio: Trinity University Press, 1987).

David B. Gracy II

AUSTIN, OSCAR P. (1949–1969). Oscar P. Austin, black Medal of Honor recipient, was born at Nacogdoches on January 15, 1949, the son of Frank and Mildred Austin. He graduated from Phoenix High School in 1967 and was inducted into the United States Marine Corps at Phoenix, Arizona, on April 22, 1968. Private First Class Oscar P. Austin was an assistant machine gunner with Company E, Second Battalion, Seventh Marines, First Marine Division, six miles west of Da Nang, South Vietnam, on February 23, 1969. His company was in action during the early morning hours against a large North Vietnamese force. After his post was attacked, he noticed a wounded comrade unconscious in an exposed position. Austin unhesitatingly went to his aid. When a grenade landed near the injured man he leaped between it and the wounded marine and absorbed the effects of the explosion. Badly wounded, he turned to render aid to his fallen comrade and saw an enemy soldier aiming a weapon at the wounded man. Once again he resolutely threw himself between the wounded marine and the enemy soldier and in so doing was mortally wounded. The Medal of Honor was presented to his parents by Vice President Spiro Agnew on April 20, 1970, at the White House.

BIBLIOGRAPHY: Committee on Veterans' Affairs, United States Senate, *Medal of Honor Recipients, 1863–1973* (Washington: GPO, 1973).

Art Leatherwood

AUSTIN, PRESTON ROSE (1872–1929). Preston Rose Austin, cotton grower and land promoter, was born near Marshall, Texas, on November 11, 1872, the son of Hiram G. and Ann Elizabeth (Rose) Austin. His maternal grandfather was Preston Robinson Rose, and his maternal great-grandfather was William Pinckney Rose.[qqv] His family moved in 1875 to Victoria, where he was raised. He attended college in Virginia but returned to Victoria to engage in the cattle business. Ruined by the "Big Freeze" of February 12, 1899, an infamous norther that killed 40,000 cattle overnight, Austin borrowed money from a friend and started afresh.

Over the next few years Austin accumulated extensive farm and ranch interests. With business partner Jesse McDowell he owned some 20,000 acres, primarily in Refugio and Calhoun counties. After considerable experimentation with rice and alfalfa, which proved susceptible to the area's salt water, Austin successfully produced cotton on his plantations. He and McDowell platted the townsite of Tivoli in 1907 and that of Austwell in 1912. Austin built hotels, lumberyards, mercantile companies, and cotton gins, in which he maintained strong financial interests. He donated school and church facilities to communities and in 1912 granted the right-of-way as well as station grounds in Austwell and $20,000 in bonus money to induce the Frisco system to extend its lines from Tivoli and Austwell to Victoria. As president of the Black Land and Improvement Company and as a principal stockholder in the Refugio Land and Irrigation Company, he sold improved farms to buyers in the Tivoli and Austwell areas. He was largely responsible for the development of the cotton industry on the lower Guadalupe River. In 1910 he became a founding director of the Levi Bank and Trust Company, later the Victoria Bank and Trust Company; he directed the bank until his death.

Austin married Mary Jane Traylor Morris on January 12, 1905. They had two daughters. Austin's death has been characterized as "the most baffling mystery in Victoria's history." On his annual vacation in Hot Springs, Arkansas, on September 27, 1929, he was strangled to death in his hotel room—apparently by three men and a woman seen leaving his floor at the approximate time of his death. A nationwide search and the offer of a $6,000 reward failed to turn up the killer or killers. Austin is buried beneath an imposing granite marker in Evergreen Cemetery, Victoria.

BIBLIOGRAPHY: Sid Feder, *Longhorns and Short Tales of Old Victoria and the Gulf Coast* (Victoria, Texas: Victoria *Advocate,* 1958). Lawrence S. Johnson, *Century of Service: The Concise History of Victoria Bank and Trust Company* (Victoria, Texas: Victoria Bank and Trust, 1979). Booth Mooney, *75 Years in Victoria* (Victoria, Texas: Victoria Bank and Trust, 1950). Victor Marion Rose, *History of Victoria* (Laredo, 1883; rpt., Victoria, Texas: Book Mart, 1961).

Thomas W. Cutrer

AUSTIN, STEPHEN FULLER (1793–1836). Stephen Fuller Austin, founder of Anglo-American Texas, son of Moses and Maria (Brown) Austin,[qqv] was born at the lead mines in southwestern Virginia on November 3, 1793. In 1798 Moses Austin moved his family to other lead mines in southeastern Missouri and established the town of Potosi in what is now Washington County. There Stephen grew to the age of ten, when his father sent him to a school in Connecticut, from which he returned westward and spent two years at Transylvania University in Lexington, Kentucky. At Potosi, Moses Austin was engaged in the mining, smelting, and manufacturing of lead and, in addition, conducted a general store. After his return from Transylvania in the spring of 1810, Stephen Austin was employed in the store and subsequently took over the management of most of the lead business. He served the public as adjutant of a militia battalion and for several years was a member of the Missouri territorial legislature, in which he was influential in obtaining the charter for the Bank of St. Louis. After failure of the Austin business in Missouri, he investigated opportunities for a new start in Arkansas and engaged in land speculation and mercantile activities. While he was there the territorial governor appointed him circuit judge of the first judicial district of Arkansas. He took the oath of office and qualified in July 1820, but he only briefly held court, for at the end of August he was in Natchitoches, Louisiana, and in December in New Orleans, where he had made arrangements to live in the home of Joseph H. Hawkins[qv] and study law. At this time Moses Austin was on his way to San Antonio to apply for a grant of land and permission to settle 300 families in Texas.

Though not enthusiastic about the Texas venture, Austin decided to cooperate with his father. He arranged to obtain a loan from his friend Hawkins to float the enterprise and was at Natchitoches expecting to accompany his father to San Antonio when he learned of Moses Austin's death. He proceeded to San Antonio, where he arrived in August 1821. Authorized by Governor Antonio María Martínez[qv] to carry on the colonization enterprise under his father's grant, Austin came to an understanding about certain administrative procedures and was permitted by the governor to explore the coastal plain between the San Antonio and Brazos rivers for the purpose of selecting a site for the proposed colony. Among other details, he arranged with Martínez to offer land to settlers in quantities of 640 acres to the head of a family, 320 acres for his wife, 320 acres for each child, and 80 acres for each slave. For such quantity as a colonist desired, Austin might collect 12½ cents an acre in compensation for his services. Martínez warned Austin that the government was unprepared to extend administration over the colonists and that Austin must be responsible for their good conduct.

Austin returned to New Orleans, published these terms, and invited colonists, saying that settlements would be located on the Brazos and Colorado rivers. The long depression, followed by the panic of 1819 and changes in the land system of the United States, made settlers eager to take advantage of the offer, and the first colonists began to arrive in Texas by land and sea in December 1821. To his great disappointment, Austin was informed by Governor Martínez that the provisional government set up after Mexican independence refused to approve the Spanish grant to Moses Austin, preferring to regulate colonization by a general immigration law. Austin hastened to Mexico City and, by unremitting attention, succeeded in getting Agustín de Iturbide's[qv] rump congress, the *junta instituyente,* to complete a law that the emperor signed on January 3, 1823. It offered heads of families a league and a labor of land (4,605 acres) and other inducements and provided for the employment of agents, called empresarios, to promote immigration. For his services, an empresario[qv] was to receive some 67,000 acres of land for each 200 families he introduced. Immigrants were not required to pay fees to the government, a fact that shortly led some of them to deny Austin's right to charge them for services performed at the rate of 12½ cents an acre. The law was annulled when Iturbide abdicated, but in April 1823 Austin induced congress to grant him a contract to introduce 300 families in accordance with its terms. In August 1824 a new congress passed an immigration law that vested the administration of public land in the states, with certain restrictions, and authorized them to make laws for settlement. In March 1825 the legislature of Coahuila and Texas[qv] passed a law conforming in general to the previous act approved by Iturbide. It continued the empresario system contemplated by that law and offered to each married man a league of land (4,428 acres), for which he was obligated to pay the state thirty dollars within six years. In the meantime, Austin had substantially fulfilled his contract to settle the first 300 families. Under this state law, he obtained three contracts (in 1825, 1827, and 1828) to settle a total of 900 additional families in the area of his first colony, besides a contract in partnership with his secretary, Samuel M. Williams,[qv] for the settlement of 800 families in western Texas. Unfortunately, this partnership contract led to a disagreeable controversy with Sterling C. Robertson.[qv]

Austin had complete civil and military authority over his colonists until 1828, subject to rather nominal supervision by the officials at San Antonio and Monterrey. He wisely allowed them to elect militia officers and local alcaldes, corresponding to justices of the peace in the United States; and, to assure uniformity of court procedure, he drew up forms and a simple civil and criminal code. As lieutenant colonel of militia, he planned and sometimes led campaigns against Indians. When population increased and appeals from decisions of individual alcaldes promised to become a burden, he instituted an appellate court composed of all the alcaldes—ultimately seven in number. The Constitution of Coahuila and Texas[qv] went into effect in November 1827, and Austin seized the opportunity to relieve himself of responsibility for the details of local government by hastening the organization of the ayuntamiento,[qv] over which by virtue of experience he continued to exercise strong influence in relations with the superior government of the state. Aside from the primary business of inducing immigrants to come to his colonies, Austin's most absorbing labor was devoted to the establishment and maintenance of the land system. This involved surveying and allocating land to applicants, with care to avoid overlapping and to keep conflicts at a minimum. The Mexican practice of issuing titles on loose sheets without a permanent record invited confusion, and Austin asked and obtained permission to record titles in a bound volume having the validity of the original. Both copies and originals had to be attested by the land commissioner, who represented the government, but Austin and his secretary had to prepare them.

The labor of directing surveyors, checking their field notes, allocating grants, preparing titles and records, entertaining prospective colonists, corresponding with state and federal officials, punishing hostile Indians, and finding food and presents for friendly visitors to keep them from marauding was heavy and expensive. To meet current costs, Austin's only resource was to assess fees against the colonists. Though his original plan to collect 12½ cents an acre for services rendered was originally welcomed by the first settlers, some of them refused to pay after the imperial colonization law proposed to compensate empresarios by grants of land. Ignoring the facts that the empresario could not claim the grant until he had settled at least 200 families and that he could hardly sell land when every married man could obtain 4,600 acres free, the settlers appealed to the political chief at San Antonio for an opinion, and he ruled that Austin could not collect. At the same time, however, he proclaimed a fee bill, which among other details allowed the land commissioner (the Baron de Bastrop[qv] in the first colony) to charge $127 a league for signing titles, and Austin made a private arrangement with Bastrop to split this fee. A rather veiled provision of the state law of 1825 allowed empresarios to reimburse themselves for costs and services, and under this law Austin required colonists to pay, or promise to pay, first sixty dollars and later fifty dollars a league. Nearly all such collections as he was able to make were consumed in necessary public expenses, which fell upon him because nobody else would pay them. This statement applies, in fact, to all his colonizing experience. Though his personal circumstances became somewhat easier with the growth of the colonies, he wrote shortly before his death that his wealth was prospective, consisting of the uncertain value of land acquired as compensation for his services as empresario.

Besides bringing the colonists to Texas, Austin strove to produce and maintain conditions conducive to their prosperous development. This aim coincided, in general, with that of the government. For example, by an act of September 1823, the federal government relieved the colonists of the payment of tariff duties for seven years; and the state legislature was nearly always reasonably cooperative. Mexican sentiment sometimes clashed, however, with practical needs of the colonists, and Austin had to evolve or accept a compromise. The status of slavery[qv] was always a difficult problem, and Austin's attitude from time to time seems inconsistent. With almost no free labor to be hired and expecting most of the colonists to come from the slave states, Austin prevailed on the *junta instituyente* to legalize slavery in the imperial colonization law, under which the first colony was established. Contrary to his strenuous efforts, the Constitution of Coahuila and Texas prohibited further introduction of slaves by immigration, but the legislature passed a law at his suggestion that evaded the intent of the constitution by legalizing labor contracts with nominally emancipated slaves. He appeared to concur, however, when congress prohibited immigration in 1830, and tried to convince the colonists that the long-time interest of Texas would be served by the prohibition. He vividly pictured the potential evils of slavery and was apparently sincere, but he failed to reconcile the colonists to the law and after 1833 declared consistently that Texas must be a slave state. Whatever his private convictions may have been, it is evident that they yielded to what may have seemed to be the current need of Texas. It is inferable, moreover, that his acceptance of federal and state regulations against the extension of slavery contemplated continuation of the evasive state labor law.

Stephen F. Austin, *by William Howard, 1833. Watercolor on ivory. 5¼″ × 4⅝″. James Perry Bryan Papers, CAH; CN 01436. This portrait, the larger of two miniatures of Austin painted by British artist William Howard in Mexico City in 1833, shows Austin, a slender man with an unruly mop of hair, gazing pensively. Austin himself recorded that one of the miniatures was made in October, "when things were very unfavorable for Texas and I was not in a pleasant humour." The background supposedly shows a spot on the Brazos River just above its mouth. Soon after these portraits were completed, Austin was arrested on his way back to Texas. He then arranged to have both, which had been in his luggage, sent to his sister, Emily Austin Perry, and brother-in-law.*

Another subject in which the interests of the colonists were deeply involved was their protection from efforts of creditors to collect debts incurred by debtors before they moved to Texas. In view of conditions in the United States during the 1820s, it was inevitable that many should have left debts and unpaid judgments behind them. Working through the local ayuntamiento, the political chief at San Antonio, and representatives in the congress, or legislature, Austin secured a state law that closed the courts for twelve years to plaintiffs seeking collection of such debts and permanently exempted land, tools, and implements of industry from execution if a suit was finally won. The law provided further that unsuccessful defendants could not be required to pay produce or money in a way to "affect their attention to their families, to their husbandry, or art they profess." In effect, it was a sweeping homestead exemption law. For a while, in 1832, Austin toyed with the idea of abolishing collateral security for loans and basing "the credit system upon moral character alone . . . avoiding unjust retroactive effects."

Aware of the importance of external trade, Austin consistently urged the establishment of ports and the temporary legalization of coasting trade in foreign ships. In lengthy arguments to various officials, he declared that the coasting trade would establish ties of mutual interest between the colonists and Mexico and enable Mexico to balance imports from England by exporting Texas cotton. Congress legalized the port of Galveston after a survey of the pass by Austin in 1825, and the government winked at the use of the Brazos and other landing places, but the coasting trade in foreign vessels was not established. As a result, external trade was confined to the United States. As early as 1829 and as late as 1835 Austin was giving thought to diversion of the Missouri–Santa Fe trade to Texas, but this was another far-sighted plan that could not be realized.

Harmony with state and federal authorities was indispensable to the success of the colonies. Austin clearly realized this fact and never allowed the settlers to forget the solid benefits that they received through the liberal colonization policy or their obligation to obey the laws and become loyal Mexican citizens. He anticipated and disarmed criticism of inconvenient laws and clumsy administration and then used the patience of the colonists as evidence of good faith in begging the government for concessions. He thwarted the efforts of Haden Edwards[qv] to drag his colonists into the Fredonian Rebellion[qv] and led the militia from the Brazos and Colorado to assist Mexican troops in putting it down. His settled policy before 1832 was to take no part in Mexican party convulsions. "Play the turtle," he urged, "head and feet within our own shells." Two factors finally defeated the policy of aloofness. By 1832 Austin's various colonies comprised 8,000 persons, and other empresarios, though less successful, had brought in a great many more. Naturally, it became more and more difficult for Austin to reconcile them to his cautious leadership. On the other hand, the rapid growth of the colonies, in addition to persistent efforts of the United States to buy Texas, increased the anxiety of Mexican leaders. Their consequent attempt to safeguard the territory by stopping immigration—with other irritations—caused an insurrection, and continued friction led to revolution and independence.

The Law of April 6, 1830,[qv] embodied the Mexican policy of stopping the further colonization of Texas by settlers from the United States. The law proposed to annul general empresario contracts uncompleted or not begun and prohibited settlement of immigrants in territory adjacent to their native countries. In effect, it applied only to Texas and the United States. By ingenious and somewhat tortuous interpretation, Austin secured the exemption of his own colonies and the colony of Green DeWitt[qv] from the prohibition. He thereby gained a loophole for continued immigration from the United States and then turned industriously to the task of getting the law repealed. He succeeded in this in December 1833.

In the meantime, however, military measures to enforce the Law of April 6, 1830, and imprudent administration of the tariff laws, to which the Texans became subject in September 1830, produced the Anahuac Disturbances.[qv] Austin had been away from Texas for several months at Saltillo attending a session of the legislature, of which he was a member. It is probable that he could have averted the uprising, had he been at home. In fact the local authorities, including Ramón Músquiz,[qv] the political chief, had quieted and repudiated it, when irresistible circumstances compelled Austin to abandon his well-tried policy of aloofness from national political struggles and adopt the cause of Antonio López de Santa Anna[qv] against the incumbent administration of President Anastasio Bustamante.[qv] Texas could no longer stand aside. Fortuitously Santa Anna won, and the colonists could not be diverted from claiming the reward of their valorous support.

The Convention of 1832[qv] met in October of that year to inform the government of the needs of the Texans. They wanted repeal of the prohibition against immigration from the United States, extension of tariff exemption, separation from Coahuila, and authority to establish state government in Texas. For reasons not entirely clear these petitions were not presented to the government. Though Austin was president of the convention, he doubted the expediency of the meeting, fearing that it would stimulate suspicion of the loyalty of the colonists—all the more because the old Mexican inhabitants of San Antonio had sent no delegates to the convention. It is easy to conclude that Austin held out hope that he might persuade these local Mexicans to take the lead in asking for reforms in a later convention; at any rate, he was in San Antonio engaged on this mission when the ground was cut from under his feet by publication of a call for a second convention to meet at San Felipe on April 1, 1833. Again Austin acquiesced and served in the convention, hoping in some measure to moderate its action. This Convention of 1833[qv] repeated the more important petitions of the previous meeting and went further in framing a constitution to accompany the request for state government. Though it was well known that Austin thought the movement ill-timed, the convention elected him to deliver the petitions and argue for their approval. Even men who distrusted him acknowledged his great influence with state and federal authorities. He left San Felipe in April, arrived in Mexico City in July, and, after unavoidable delays, persuaded the government to repeal the Law of April 6, 1830, and to promise important reforms in Texas local government. He started home in December, reasonably satisfied with his work and convinced at least that he had left nothing undone; President Santa Anna simply would not approve state government for Texas. Austin was arrested at Saltillo in January, under suspicion of trying to incite insurrection in Texas, and taken back to Mexico City. No charges were made against him, no court would accept jurisdiction of his case, and he remained a prisoner, shifting from prison to prison, until December 1834, when he was released on bond and limited to the area of the Federal District. He was freed by a general amnesty law in July 1835 and at the end of August returned to Texas by way of New Orleans.

Austin was thus absent from Texas for twenty-eight months. Upon his return, he learned that an unofficial call had been issued for a convention, or consultation, to meet in October. Probably he could have quashed this call, but in a notable speech at Brazoria on September 8 he gave it his sanction, and election of delegates proceeded. The Consultation[qv] organized on November 3. In the meantime, during September and early October, Austin had been in effect civil head of Anglo-American Texas, as chairman of a central committee at San Felipe. War began at Gonzales on October 1. Austin was elected to command the volunteers gathered there and led them against the Mexican army at San Antonio. In November the provisional government[qv] elected him to serve, with William H. Wharton and Branch T. Archer,[qqv] as commissioner to the United States. He arrived in New Orleans in January 1836 and returned again to Texas in June. The business of the commissioners was to solicit loans and volunteers, arrange credits for munitions and equipment, fit out warships, and do whatever they could to commit the government of the United States to recognition and eventual annexation[qv] if Texas should declare independence. They were fairly successful in accomplishing this program, except in the effort to obtain assurances from President Andrew Jackson and Congress. Austin was convinced, however, that Congress would have voted for recognition in May, after the battle of San Jacinto,[qv] if the acting president, David G. Burnet,[qv] had cooperated with the commissioners by sending them official reports of conditions in Texas. Somewhat hesitantly, Austin consented to offer himself for the presidency after his return to Texas. He was defeated in the election of September 1836, but accepted the office of secretary of state from the successful candidate. He died in service on December 27, 1836, at the untimely age of forty-three.

Judged by historical standards, Austin did a great work. He began the Anglo-American colonization[qv] of Texas under conditions more difficult in some respects than those that confronted founders of the English colonies on the Atlantic coast. He saw the wilderness transformed into a relatively advanced and populous state, and fundamentally it was his unremitting labor, perseverance, foresight, and tactful management that brought that miracle to pass. Contemporaries who disagreed with his cautious policy of conciliating Mexican officials accused him of weakness and instability, but criticism did not cause him to abandon it. Casually discussing this subject in a letter of April 9, 1832, to his secretary, he wrote, "Some men in the world hold the doctrine that it is degrading and corrupt to use policy in anything. . . . There is no degradation in prudence and a well tempered and well timed moderation." Until the passage of the Law of April 6, 1830, attempting to shut out emigrants from the United States, he believed that Texas could develop into a free and prosperous Mexican state, a goal that he sincerely desired. Passage of that law and continued political turmoil in Mexico certainly shook his confidence, but prudence forbade abandonment of the policy of outward patience and conciliation before Texas seemed strong enough to demand reforms and back the demand by force. Premature action might be fatal, or so he thought. He would have prevented the conventions of 1832 and 1833 if he could have had his way, but, since he could not, he went along and tried to moderate their demands. The same considerations caused him to oppose the Texas Declaration of Independence[qv] by the provisional government[qv] in 1835, while there was hope of winning the support of the liberal party in Mexico. In short, his methods varied with circumstances, but from the abiding aim to promote and safeguard the welfare of Texas he never wavered. As he wrote in July 1836, "The prosperity of Texas has been the object of my labors, the idol of my existence—it has assumed the character of a *religion,* for the guidance of my thoughts and actions, for fifteen years." Consciousness of heavy responsibility dictated his policy of caution and moderation and compelled him to shape his methods to shifting circumstances. *See also* OLD THREE HUNDRED, MEXICAN COLONIZATION LAWS.

BIBLIOGRAPHY: Eugene C. Barker, ed., *The Austin Papers* (3 vols., Washington: GPO, 1924–28). Eugene C. Barker, *The Life of Stephen F. Austin* (Nashville: Cokesbury Press, 1925; rpt., Austin: Texas State Historical Association, 1949; New York: AMS Press, 1970). Rupert N. Richardson, *Texas: The Lone Star State* (New York: Prentice-Hall, 1943; 4th ed., with Ernest Wallace and Adrian N. Anderson, Englewood Cliffs, New Jersey: Prentice-Hall, 1981). *Eugene C. Barker*

AUSTIN, STEPHEN F., JR. (1828–1837). Stephen F. Austin, Jr., son of Eliza Martha (Westall) and James E. Brown Austin,[qv] was born in 1828. After his father's death in August 1829, the child was taken into the home of his aunt, Mrs. Emily Austin Bryan Perry.[qv] His uncle, Stephen F. Austin,[qv] wrote the Perrys from Mexico concerning the child's schooling, and James F. Perry[qv] wrote in May 1835 that the boy was under the instruction of Thomas J. Pilgrim[qv] at Peach Point Plantation.[qv] On December 17, 1835, Stephen F. Austin wrote that he wanted to adopt the nephew who was named for him, but evidently he never actually did so. He wanted the child to learn Spanish and French in preparation for becoming a lawyer. The boy's mother balked at the idea of the adoption, and later she was involved in land disputes with the family. Stephen Austin's will directed that the major portion of his property be divided into two parts, one to Emily Perry and the other to his nephew. If the nephew died without issue, his portion would pass to Emily. Stephen F. Austin, Jr., died at the home of Col. W. G. Hill on February 2, 1837.

BIBLIOGRAPHY: Eugene C. Barker, ed., *The Austin Papers* (3 vols., Washington: GPO, 1924–28). Marie Beth Jones, *Peach Point Plantation: The First 150 Years* (Waco: Texian Press, 1982). *Telegraph and Texas Register,* February 3, 1837. Alice Mitchell Wright, An Abstract of Biographical Data in the Texas Supreme Court Reports, 1857–1874 (M.A. thesis, University of Texas, 1937).

AUSTIN, WILLIAM G. (?–?). William G. Austin, Medal of Honor recipient, was born at Galveston and entered military service at New York, New York. He was a sergeant in Company E, Seventh United States Cavalry, at Wounded Knee Creek, South Dakota, on December 29, 1890. He was commended for assisting "men on the skirmish line, directing their fire, etc., and using every effort to dislodge the enemy," Indians fighting from a ravine.

BIBLIOGRAPHY: Committee on Veterans' Affairs, United States Senate, *Medal of Honor Recipients, 1863–1973* (Washington: GPO, 1973).
Art Leatherwood

AUSTIN, WILLIAM TENNANT (1809–1874). William Tennant Austin, soldier and civil servant of the Republic of Texas,[qv] was born on January 30, 1809, in Bridgeport, Connecticut, the son of Susan (Rogers) and John Punderson Austin.[qv] He began working at the age of eleven and by seventeen was established as a merchant. In 1826 he married Joana Thomas. He was the brother of John Austin[qv] of Brazoria. In October 1830, at the age of twenty-two, he arrived at that town on the schooner *Nelson* with his wife and daughter. His wife was, according to Archibald Austin, "a very pretty little woman" and "a very agreeable acquisition to the Society of Texas." On December 12 Stephen F. Austin[qv] had located land on Buffalo Bayou for William, who had established a mercantile trade before the end of the month. In 1832 William was wounded in the battle of Velasco,[qv] and in 1833 his wife, child, and brother all died in a cholera epidemic. Later that year the Brazos River flooded and washed away his store.

At Harrisburg on June 4, 1835, William Austin, along with William B. Travis,[qv] signed a document protesting the Mexican enforcement of customs duties and other restrictions at Anahuac and pledged himself to overthrow Mexican authority there (*see* ANAHUAC DISTURBANCES). As an early member of the so-called war party, he joined William H. Wharton[qv] and several other citizens of the Columbia District on July 25, 1835, in calling for a general convention of all Texans. On August 15 he was appointed secretary of a meeting at Columbia, at the mouth of the Brazos, which established a committee of safety for the district and on August 20 called for a General Consultation.[qv] When Mexican general Martín Perfecto de Cos[qv] and 400 soldiers landed at Copano to suppress resistance to Antonio López de Santa Anna's[qv] Centralist government, Austin and Branch T. Archer[qv] called for volunteers to resist him with force. On October 2, 1835, Austin and nine other volunteers, including James W. Fannin, Jr., George Sutherland,[qqv] and Archer, left Columbia to reinforce the Texan insurrectionists at Gonzales, thus becoming part of the nucleus of the army with which Gen. Stephen F. Austin and Col. Edward Burleson[qv] besieged Bexar that fall and winter. On October 12 General Austin commissioned William Austin a colonel and appointed him as one of his two aides-de-camp, the other being Peter W. Grayson.[qv] When Stephen Austin left the army to become the spokesman for the Texan cause in Washington, D.C., William Austin continued his duties as aide to the new commander, Edward Burleson. In their official reports on the storming of Bexar (*see* BEXAR, SIEGE OF), both Burleson and adjutant general Francis W. Johnson[qv] commended Austin; Burleson observed to Governor Henry Smith[qv] that Austin's "conduct on this and every other occasion, merits my warmest praise." On March 14, 1836, Sam Houston[qv] appointed Austin his aide-de-camp with the rank of major and ordered him to Columbia to requisition artillery and horses for the army.

After the war Austin, who had married Elizabeth Bertrand on January 25, 1836, returned to his Brazoria County plantation. There in 1837 he was elected clerk of the Brazoria county court and, on January 21, 1838, was appointed collector of revenue for the port of Velasco. In 1840 he was a resident of Brazoria County, but by 1848 he had moved to Washington-on-the-Brazos, where he was once again a merchant. In 1854 he was in Galveston as a commission merchant and cotton factor. During the Civil War[qv] Austin served as Confederate marshal for East Texas and was appointed a brigadier general of state troops. He was a Democrat, a Mason, and an Episcopalian. He died at Galveston on February 25, 1874.

bibliography: *Compiled Index to Elected and Appointed Officials of the Republic of Texas, 1835–1846* (Austin: State Archives, Texas State Library, 1981). Daughters of the Republic of Texas, *Muster Rolls of the Texas Revolution* (Austin, 1986). John H. Jenkins, ed., *The Papers of the Texas Revolution, 1835–1836* (10 vols., Austin: Presidial Press, 1973). Gifford E. White, *1830 Citizens of Texas* (Austin: Eakin, 1983).

Thomas W. Cutrer

AUSTIN, CATHOLIC DIOCESE OF. The presence of the Catholic Church[qv] in what is now the Diocese of Austin dates from the seventeenth century. The Spaniards had established missions in East Texas as early as 1690, largely through the agency of Franciscans[qv] from the colleges of Santa Cruz de Querétaro and Nuestra Señora de Guadalupe de Zacatecas.[qqv] In 1721 three East Texas missions were staffed by Queretarans and three by Zacatecans. By July 27, 1730, the Queretaran missions had been combined and reestablished as one mission on the south side of the Colorado River near the site of present-day Zilker Park in Austin. This mission, the only Spanish mission within the territory of the present diocese, remained in the area for only about seven months, then was moved to San Antonio de Béxar and split into three. After the secularization of the missions in the early eighteenth century, the church maintained its presence in Texas through Mexican dioceses (*see* catholic diocesan church in spanish and mexican texas). As immigration from the United States increased during the later Spanish and Mexican periods, a scattering of Catholics came with the new residents. Mexican law required the rest of the colonists to adopt the Catholic religion. After Texas independence from Mexico, however, the majority of the populace reverted to its Southern Protestant origins. The Catholics who remained were in need of care.

In 1840 the Republic of Texas[qv] was made a prefecture apostolic, and Fr. John Timon[qv] was named prefect apostolic. Timon appointed Jean Marie Odin,[qv] another Vincentian, as his vice prefect. The two Vincentian fathers[qv] arrived in Austin in November and negotiated successfully with the state legislature for the return of mission lands to the Catholic Church. After annexation[qv] the whole of Texas was made a diocese, the Diocese of Galveston, in 1847. Odin was bishop.

The Diocese of Galveston was subsequently split into other dioceses. The Diocese of Austin, the seventh of these, was formed in 1947 by a decree of Pope Pius XII, from territory that had formerly been in the Archdiocese of San Antonio, the Diocese of Galveston, and the Diocese of Dallas. Louis J. Reicher[qv] was made bishop, and St. Mary's Church in Austin became St. Mary's Cathedral.[qv] The new diocese comprised thirty-one counties that cover 25,000 square miles; the Catholic population was counted at 75,495. The original diocese had fifty parishes and forty-three missions served by 132 priests, 196 sisters, and 24 brothers. The Catholic population comprised immigrants from many origins; among them were Germans, Czechs, Poles, Italians, Irish, and French.[qv] Mexican Americans[qv] had long maintained the Catholic faith on Texas soil. Black Catholics[qv] had an established community in Washington-on-the-Brazos as early as 1849; Holy Cross Church, founded in Austin in 1936, operated the first black Catholic hospital in the state, Holy Cross Hospital.

Bishop Reicher lived at the Stephen F. Austin Hotel for a while, then at St. Edward's University. He used two rooms at Newman Hall, near the University of Texas, for a chancery. In 1958 a new chancery, designed by Walter Koch, Jr., of Waco, was opened at Congress Avenue and Sixteenth Street, on property purchased from Southern Methodist University. The diocese began publishing a newspaper, the *Lone Star Catholic*, in 1957; *Catholic Spirit* was the diocesan newspaper in the early 1990s. Reicher conducted a synod in 1960; a second Synod of Austin was begun in 1988 and completed in 1992. In 1959 the Catholic Archives of Texas[qv] were transferred from Amarillo to the chancery building in Austin.

Upon the formation of the Catholic Diocese of San Angelo[qv] in 1961, four northwest counties—Coleman, McCulloch, Brown, and Callahan—were transferred from the Austin see to the new jurisdiction. The Diocese of Austin thus assumed the boundaries it had in the 1990s, reaching from Sealy and Bryan in the east to Mason in the west, and from West in the north and San Saba in the northwest to Luling in the south.

Bishop Reicher established many new parishes and built more than 200 buildings. Upon his retirement in 1971 the diocese had grown to 85 parishes and 31 missions served by 147 priests, 152 nuns, and 37 brothers. Reicher resigned because of ill health in 1971, and Vincent M. Harris,[qv] who succeeded him, presided over continued growth and handled some difficult fiscal problems. Harris had a stroke in November 1984 and resigned the next year. Auxiliary bishop John McCarthy of Houston was named to succeed him and was installed as ordinary on February 26, 1986.

The diocese has long engaged in a wide variety of ministries, especially education, health care, and social service, many of which began while the Austin region was still a part of the Diocese of Galveston. St. Edward's University, founded in 1885, had an enrollment of 3,086 in fall 1990–91. Catholic student centers were located at the campuses of the University of Texas, Texas A&M, Baylor, Southwest Texas State University, Blinn College, and Temple Junior College. Catholic elementary and secondary schools enrolled some 3,500 students annually. Six Catholic hospitals operated within the diocese: Seton Medical Center, Austin; St. Jude, Brenham; St. Joseph, Bryan; St. Edward, Cameron; and Providence, Waco. Holy Cross Hospital closed in 1989, after serving East Austin for nearly fifty years. The St. Vincent de Paul Society and Caritas were two of many social-service organizations operating within the diocese. In the 1990s the Diocese of Austin had grown to eighty-eight parishes and a Catholic population of nearly 250,000. Serving the church were 195 priests, 142 religious women, more than 70 permanent deacons, and 43 religious men.

bibliography: Catholic Archives of Texas, Files, Austin. "History of the Diocese of Austin," in *Diocese of Austin Directory, 1986–87* (Austin: Futura Press, 1986).

Steven P. Ryan, S.J.

AUSTIN, TEXAS (Matagorda County). Though Moses Austin[qv] died before fulfilling his plans for a community called Austina on the mouth of the Colorado River, Austin was the name given as early as 1836 to a site just south of Oliver Point (formerly known as Point Plesant or Pleasant), four miles across Tres Palacios Bay from what is now Palacios, in southwestern Matagorda County. The settlement, also known as Port Austin, was platted to be a town of at least 166 blocks, with blocks reserved for a college, a church, and public buildings, as well as an area labeled Hyde Park. The development was a project of Capt. Thomas Bridges, a Massachusetts shipmaster who had run supplies from New Orleans through the Mexican blockade during the Texas Revolution.[qv] He originally bought land near Oyster Lake but later moved the townsite north toward Oliver Point. In 1838 Bridges traveled to New York and sold several town lots. Around that time he took on two partners, Silas Dinsmore[qv] and William Boyd. Though Austin apparently never developed substantially, in 1840 several parishioners of Christ Episcopal Church in Matagorda recorded their residence as the city of Austin, and the county land-grant map shows a Port Austin at the site. Bridges, his wife, Hannah, and their daughter Alice apparently lived at the site, and Alice Bridges eventually learned the language of the local Karankawa Indians. Bridges died in 1848. The townsite land, the ownership of which had been open to question, eventually became the property of Jonathan Edwards Pierce[qv] and later the LeTulle family.

bibliography: Matagorda County Historical Commission, *Historic Matagorda County* (3 vols., Houston: Armstrong, 1986).

Rachel Jenkins

AUSTIN, TEXAS (Travis County). Austin, the capital of Texas, county seat of Travis County, and home of the University of Texas at Austin, is located in central Travis County on the Colorado River and Interstate Highway 35. Situated at 30°16′ north latitude and 97°45′ west longitude, it is at the eastern edge of the Hill Country and the Edwards Plateau.[qqv] The city was established by the three-year-old Republic of Texas[qv] in 1839 to serve as its permanent capital, and named in honor of the founder of Anglo-American Texas, Stephen F. Austin.[qv] A site-selection commission appointed by the Texas Congress in January 1839 chose a site on the western frontier, after viewing it at the instruction of President Mirabeau B. Lamar,[qv] a proponent of westward expansion who had visited the sparsely settled area in 1838. Impressed by its beauty, healthfulness, abundant natural resources, promise as an economic hub, and central location in Texas territory, the commission purchased 7,735 acres along the Colorado River comprising the hamlet of Waterloo and adjacent lands. Because the area's remoteness from population centers and its vulnerability to attacks by Mexican troops and Indians displeased many Texans, Sam Houston[qv] among them, political opposition made Austin's early years precarious ones.

Surveyors L. J. Pilie and Charles Schoolfield laid out the new town, working under the direction of Edwin Waller,[qv] who was appointed by Lamar to plan and construct Austin. Out of the 7,735 acres they chose a 640-acre site fronting on the Colorado River and nestled between Waller Creek on the east and Shoal Creek on the west. The plan was a grid, fourteen blocks square, bisected by Congress Avenue, and extending northward from the Colorado River to "Capitol Square." Determined to have Austin ready by the time the Texas Congress convened in November 1839, Waller opted for temporary government buildings at temporary locations. The one-story frame capitol was set back from Congress Avenue on a hill at what is now the corner of Colorado and Eighth streets. The first auction of city lots took place on August 1. During October President Lamar arrived, government offices opened for business, Presbyterians organized the first church, and the Austin *City Gazette,*[qv] the city's first newspaper, made its appearance. Congress convened in November, Austin was incorporated on December 27, and on January 13, 1840, Waller was elected the town's first mayor. By 1840 Austin had 856 inhabitants, including 145 slaves as well as diplomatic representatives from France, England, and the United States.

Austin flourished initially but in 1842 entered the darkest period in its history. Lamar's successor as president, Sam Houston, ordered the national archives transferred to Houston for safekeeping after Mexican troops captured San Antonio on March 5, 1842. Convinced that removal of the republic's diplomatic, financial, land, and military-service records was tantamount to choosing a new capital, Austinites refused to relinquish the archives. Houston moved the government anyway, first to Houston and then to Washington-on-the-Brazos, which remained the seat of government until 1845. The archives stayed in Austin. When Houston sent a contingent of armed men to seize the General Land Office[qv] records in December 1842, they were foiled by the citizens of Austin and Travis County in an incident known as the Archive War.[qv] Deprived of its political function, Austin languished. Between 1842 and 1845 its population dropped below 200 and its buildings deteriorated. But during the summer of 1845 a constitutional convention meeting in Austin approved the annexation[qv] of Texas to the United States and named Austin the state capital until 1850, at which time the voters of Texas were to express their preference in a general election. After resuming its role as the seat of government in 1845, Austin officially became the state capital on February 19, 1846, the date of the formal transfer of authority from the republic to the state.

Austin recovered gradually, its population reaching 854 by 1850, 225 of whom were slaves and one a free black. Forty-eight percent of Austin's family heads owned slaves. The city entered a period of accelerated growth following its decisive triumph in the 1850 election to determine the site of the state capital for the next twenty years. For the first time the government constructed permanent buildings, among them a new capitol at the head of Congress Avenue, completed in 1853, and the Governor's Mansion,[qv] completed in 1856. State-run asylums for deaf, blind, and mentally ill Texans were erected on the fringes of town. Congregations of Baptists, Episcopalians, Methodists, Presbyterians, and Catholics erected permanent church buildings, and the town's elite built elegant Greek Revival mansions. By 1860 the population had climbed to 3,546, including 1,019 slaves and twelve free blacks. That year thirty-five percent of Austin's family heads owned slaves.

From 1861 to 1865 the Civil War dominated life in Austin. In February 1861 Austin and Travis County residents voted against the secession[qv] ordinance 704 to 450, but Unionist sentiment waned once the war began. By April 1862 about 600 Austin and Travis County men had joined some twelve volunteer companies serving the Confederacy. The Austin-based Tom Green Rifles served with Hood's Texas Brigade[qv] in Virginia. Austinites followed with particular concern news of the successive Union thrusts toward Texas, but the town was never directly threatened. Like other communities, Austin experienced severe shortages of goods, spiraling inflation, and the decimation of its fighting men. The end of the war brought Union occupation troops to the city and a period of explosive growth of the African-American population, which increased by 57 percent during the 1860s. During the late 1860s and early 1870s the city's newly emancipated blacks established the residential communities of Masontown, Wheatville, Pleasant Hill, and Clarksville, organized such churches as First Baptist Church (Colored), started businesses, and patronized schools. By 1870 Austin's 1,615 black residents composed 36 percent of the 4,428 inhabitants.

On December 25, 1871, a new era opened with the coming of the Houston and Texas Central Railway, Austin's first railroad connection. By becoming the westernmost railroad terminus in Texas and the only railroad town for scores of miles in most directions, Austin was transformed into a trading center for a vast area. Construction boomed and the population more than doubled in five years to 10,363. The many foreign-born newcomers gave Austin's citizenry a more heterogeneous character. By 1875 there were 757 inhabitants from Germany, 297 from Mexico, 215 from Ireland, and 138 from Sweden. For the first time a Mexican-American community took root in Austin, in a neighborhood near the mouth of Shoal Creek. Accompanying these dramatic changes were civic improvements, among them gas street lamps in 1874, the first streetcar line in 1875, and the first elevated bridge across the Colorado River about 1876. Although a second railroad, the International and Great Northern, reached Austin in 1876, the town's fortunes turned downward after 1875 as new railroads traversed Austin's trading region and diverted much of its trade to other towns. From 1875 to 1880 the city's population increased by only 650 inhabitants to 11,013. Austin's expectations of rivaling other Texas cities for economic leadership faded.

Austin solidified its position as a political center during the 1870s and 1880s and gained a new role as an educational center. In 1872 the city prevailed in a statewide election to choose once and for all the state capital, turning back challenges from Houston and Waco. Three years later Texas took the first steps toward constructing a new Capitol[qv] that culminated in 1888 in the dedication of a magnificent granite building towering over the town. In 1881 Austin emerged as a seat of education. In a hotly contested statewide election, the city was chosen as the site for the new University of Texas, which began instruction two years later. Tillotson Collegiate and Normal Institute, founded by the American Missionary Association to provide educational opportunities for African Americans,[qv] opened its doors in 1881. The Austin public school system was started the same year. Four years later St. Edward's School, founded several years earlier by the Holy Cross Fathers and Brothers,[qv] was chartered as St. Edwards College.

In 1888 civic leader Alexander P. Wooldridge[qv] proposed that Austin construct a dam across the Colorado River and use water power to attract manufacturing. The town had reached its limits as a seat of politics and education, Wooldridge contended, yet its economy could not sustain its present size. Proponents of the dam won political control of Austin in 1889. Empowered by a new city charter in 1891 that more than tripled Austin's corporate area from 4½ to 16½ square miles, the city fathers implemented a plan to build a municipal water and electric system, construct a dam for power, and lease most of the waterpower to manufacturers. By 1893 the sixty-foot-high Austin Dam was completed, impounding Lake McDonald behind it. In 1895 dam-generated electricity began powering the four-year-old electric streetcar line and the city's new water and light systems. Thirty-one new 150-foot-high "moonlight towers"[qv] illuminated Austin at night. Civic pride ran strong during those years, which also saw the city blessed with the talents of sculptor Elisabet Ney and writer William Sydney Porter[qqv] (O. Henry). But it turned out that the dam produced far less power than anticipated, manufacturers never came, periodic power shortfalls disrupted city services, Lake McDonald silted up, and, on April 7, 1900, the dam collapsed.

Between 1880 and 1920 Austin's population grew threefold to 34,876, but the city slipped from fourth largest in the state to tenth largest. The state's surging industrial development, propelled by the booming oil business, passed Austin by. The capital city began boosting itself as a residential city, but the heavy municipal indebtedness incurred in building the dam resulted in the neglect of city services. In 1905 Austin had few sanitary sewers, virtually no public parks or playgrounds, and only one paved street. Three years later Austin voters overturned the aldermanic form of government, by which the city had been governed since 1839, and replaced it with commission government. A. P. Wooldridge headed the reform group voted into office in 1909 and served a decade as mayor, during which the city made steady if modest progress toward improving residential life. In 1918 the city acquired Barton Springs,[qv] a spring-fed pool that became the symbol of the residential city. Upon Wooldridge's retirement in 1919 the flaws of commission government, hidden by his leadership, became apparent as city services again deteriorated. At the urging of the Chamber of Commerce, Austinites voted in 1924 to adopt council-manager government, which went into effect in 1926 and remained in the 1990s. Progressive ideas like city planning and beautification became official city policy. A 1928 city plan, the first since 1839, called upon Austin to develop its strengths as a residential, cultural, and educational center. A $4,250,000 bond issue, Austin's largest to date, provided funds for streets, sewers, parks, the city hospital, the first permanent public library building, and the first municipal airport, which opened in 1930. A recreation department was established, and within a decade it offered Austinites a profusion of recreational programs, parks, and pools.

By 1900 segregation of blacks and whites characterized many aspects of city life, and the lines of separation hardened in the early twentieth century. Despite a two-month streetcar boycott organized by blacks, the city implemented an ordinance in 1906 requiring separate compartments on streetcars. While residences of blacks had been widely scattered all across the city in 1880, by 1930 they were heavily concentrated on the east side of town, a process encouraged by the 1928 city plan, which recommended that East Austin be designated a "Negro district." Municipal services like schools, sewers, and parks were made available to blacks in East Austin only. At mid-century Austin was still segregated in most respects—housing, restaurants, hotels, parks, hospitals, schools, public transportation—but African Americans had long fostered their own institutions, which included by the late 1940s some 150 small businesses, more than thirty churches, and two colleges, Tillotson College and Samuel Huston College. Between 1880 and 1940 the number of black residents grew from 3,587 to 14,861, but their proportion of the overall population declined from 33 percent to 17 percent. Austin's Hispanic residents, who in 1900 numbered about 335 and composed just 1.5 percent of the population, rose to 11 percent by 1940, when they numbered 9,693. By the 1940s most Mexican Americans[qv] lived in the rapidly expanding East Austin barrio south of East Eleventh Street, where increasing numbers owned homes. Hispanic-owned business were dominated by a thriving food industry. Though Mexican Americans encountered widespread discrimination—in employment, housing, education, city services, and other areas—it was by no means practiced as rigidly as it was toward African Americans.

During the early and mid-1930s Austin experienced the harsh effects of the Great Depression.[qv] Nevertheless, the town fared comparatively well, sustained by its twin foundations of government and education and by the political skills of Mayor Tom (Robert Thomas) Miller,[qv] who took office in 1933, and United States Congressman Lyndon Baines Johnson,[qv] who won election in 1937. Its population grew at a faster pace during the 1930s than in any other decade during the twentieth century, increasing 66 percent from 53,120 to 87,930. By 1936 the Public Works Administration had provided Austin with more funding for municipal construction projects than any other Texas city during the same period. The University of Texas nearly doubled its enrollment during the decade and undertook a massive construction program. Johnson procured federal funds for public housing and dams on the Colorado River. The old Austin Dam, partially rebuilt under Mayor Wooldridge but never finished due to damage from flooding in 1915, was finally completed in 1940 and renamed Tom Miller Dam. Lake Austin[qv] stretched twenty-one miles behind it. Just upriver the much larger Mansfield Dam was completed in 1941 to impound Lake Travis.[qv] The two dams, in conjunction with other dams in the Lower Colorado River Authority[qv] system, brought great benefits to Austin: cheap hydroelectric power, the end of flooding that in 1935 and on earlier occasions had ravaged the town, a plentiful supply of water without which the city's later growth would have been unlikely, and recreation on the Highland Lakes that enhanced Austin's appeal as a place to live. In 1942 Austin gained the economic benefit of Del Valle Army Air Base, later Bergstrom Air Force Base,[qv] which remained in operation until 1993.

Between the 1950s and 1980s ethnic relations in Austin were transformed. First came a sustained attacked on segregation. Local black leaders and political-action groups waged campaigns to desegregate city schools and services. In 1956 the University of Texas became the first major university in the South to admit blacks as undergraduates. In the early 1960s students staged demonstrations against segregated lunch counters, restaurants, and movie theaters. Gradually the barriers receded, a process accelerated when the United States Civil Rights Act of 1964 outlawed racial discrimination in public accommodations. Nevertheless, discrimination persisted in areas like employment and housing. Shut out of the town's political leadership since the 1880s, when two blacks had served on the city council, African Americans regained a foothold by winning a school-board seat in 1968 and a city-council seat in 1971. This political breakthrough was matched by Hispanics, whose numbers had reached 39,399 by 1970—16 percent of the population. Mexican Americans won their first seats on the Austin school board in 1972 and the city council in 1975.

From 1940 to 1990 Austin's population grew at an average rate of 40 percent per decade, from 87,930 to 465,622. The city's corporate area, which between 1891 and 1940 had about doubled to 30.85 square miles, grew more than sevenfold to 225.40 square miles by 1990. During the 1950s and 1960s much of Austin's growth reflected the rapid expansion of its traditional strengths—education and government. During the 1960s alone the number of students attending the University of Texas at Austin doubled, reaching 39,000 by 1970. Government employees in Travis County tripled between 1950 and 1970 to 47,300. University of Texas buildings multiplied, with the Lyndon Baines Johnson Library[qv] opening in 1971. A complex of state office buildings was constructed north of the Capitol. Propelling Austin's growth by the 1970s was its emergence as a center for high technology. This development, fostered by the Chamber of Commerce since the 1950s as a way to expand the city's narrow economic base and fueled by proliferating research programs at the University of Texas, accelerated when IBM located in Austin in 1967, followed by Texas Instruments[qv] in 1969 and Motorola in 1974. Two major research consortiums of high-technology companies followed during the 1980s, Microelectronics and Computer Technology Corporation and Sematech.[qv] By the early 1990s, the Austin Metropolitan Statistical Area had about 400 high-technology manufacturers. While high-technology industries located on Austin's periphery, its central area sprouted multistoried office buildings and hotels during the 1970s and 1980s, venues for the burgeoning music industry, and, in 1992, a new convention center.

Austin's rapid growth generated strong resistance by the 1970s. Angered by proliferating apartment complexes and retarded traffic flow, neighborhood groups mobilized to protect the integrity of their residential areas. By 1983 there were more than 150 such groups. Environmentalists organized a powerful movement to protect streams, lakes, watersheds, and wooded hills from environmental degradation, resulting in the passage of a series of environmental-protection ordinances during the 1970s and 1980s. A program was inaugurated in 1971 to beautify the shores of Town Lake,[qv] a downtown lake impounded in 1960 behind Longhorn Crossing Dam. Historic preservationists fought the destruction of Austin's architectural heritage by rescuing and restoring historic buildings. City election campaigns during the 1970s and 1980s frequently featured struggles over the management of growth, with neighborhood groups and environmentalists on one side and business and development interests on the other. In the early 1990s Austin was still seeking to balance the economic development it had long sought with the kind of life it had long treasured.

BIBLIOGRAPHY: Austin Human Relations Commission, *Housing Patterns Study: Segregation and Discrimination in Austin, Texas* (Austin, 1979). Kenneth Hafertepe, *Abner Cook: Master Builder on the Texas Frontier* (Austin: Texas State Historical Association, 1992). David C. Humphrey, *Austin: An Illustrated History* (Northridge, California: Windsor, 1985). David C. Humphrey, "A 'Muddy and Conflicting' View: The Civil War as Seen from Austin, Texas," *Southwestern Historical Quarterly* 94 (January 1991). Paul D. Lack, "Slavery and Vigilantism in Austin, Texas, 1840–1860," *Southwestern Historical Quarterly* 85 (July 1981). Stuart MacCorkle, *Austin's Three Forms of Government* (San Antonio: Naylor, 1973). Anthony M. Orum, *Power, Money and the People: The Making of Modern Austin* (Austin: Texas Monthly Press, 1987). *Texas Cities and the Great Depression* (Austin: Texas Memorial Museum, 1973).

David C. Humphrey

AUSTIN *AMERICAN-STATESMAN.* The Austin *American-Statesman*, in 1994 the only daily newspaper in Austin, Travis County, traces its origins back to the *Democratic Statesman*, which began publication every three weeks beginning in July 1871. The paper began as a semiofficial organ of the state executive committee of the Democratic party[qv] and was the only major Democratic newspaper in Texas at that time. It advocated "straight out Jacksonian Democracy" during the Reconstruction[qv] period of Republican control of the state. The paper was prominent in the election campaign of 1873, which resulted in the defeat of the Republican regime in Texas. In 1873 the paper began daily morning publication, and from 1880 to 1889 the publishers were John Cardwell[qv] and a Mr. Morris. In 1914 the *Democratic Statesman* took over the Austin *Tribune* (founded 1889), a competitor that in 1904 had absorbed a smaller local newspaper called the Austin *Daily News.* The newly consolidated paper began to publish each afternoon as the Austin *Statesman and Tribune.* In 1916 this paper changed its name to the *Evening Statesman* to reflect a new time of publication.

The first issue of the Austin *American*, published daily including Sunday, was issued on May 31, 1914, under the direction of Henry Hulme Sevier.[qv] In 1919 Charles E. Marsh and E. S. Fentress bought the *American*, and in December 1924, the Austin *Evening Statesman*, by then one of the oldest dailies in Texas. At this juncture the two papers were merged into one company, but were published as independent newspapers. The *American* remained the morning paper and the *Statesman* an afternoon paper, but the Sunday morning issue of the *American* was renamed the *Sunday American-Statesman.* Early in 1948 all of the Marsh-Fentress newspapers became a part of Newspapers Incorporated. The *American* joined the Associated Press, subscribed to the daily wire services of the United Press International News Service, and acquired comics and other news features on an independent basis from NEA, the Chicago *Tribune*, and other syndicates.

In November 1973 the Austin *American* and the Austin *Statesman* combined to become an all-day newspaper issued in four daily editions as the Austin *American-Statesman.* In 1976 Cox Enterprises purchased the Austin *American-Statesman*, and in April 1987, the paper switched from all-day publication to morning editions only. Its circulation reached 180,345 by 1991, by which time the paper was being published by Roger Kintzel.

BIBLIOGRAPHY: Austin *American-Statesman*, Anniversary Edition, March 26, 1939. *Texas Newspaper Directory* (Austin: Texas Press Service, 1991).

Curtis Bishop and R. L. Schroeter

AUSTIN *ANTI-QUAKER.* The Austin *Anti-Quaker*, a newspaper that may have been published only once, on March 12, 1842, appears to be a successor to the San Antonio *Alarm Bell of the West.* The date of publication and title of the papers seem to indicate that they were established to advocate opposition to a peaceful policy in Mexican relations.

BIBLIOGRAPHY: Marilyn M. Sibley, *Lone Stars and State Gazettes: Texas Newspapers before the Civil War* (College Station: Texas A&M University Press, 1983).

AUSTIN *ARGOS.* The Austin *Argos* was founded in 1962 by a group of black Austin business and professional people. The chairman of the board of the corporation that owned the *Argos* was Everett Givens, an Austin physician. The corporation disbanded, and Mason Smith, a newspaper publisher from Detroit, bought out the other investors and became the sole proprietor. In 1971 Arthur Sims and his wife began helping Smith with the paper, and later that year Smith talked Sims into taking over as publisher. Sims and his wife published and edited the *Argos* until Mrs. Sims died in 1985. A year later Sims sold the paper to Charles Miles. The Austin *Argos* began as a tabloid-size weekly community newspaper. In 1978 Sims began publishing it as a broadsheet. It printed stories of general interest to the black community in Austin and Central Texas, featuring society news, church affairs, sports reports, political issues, and editorial comment. Through the 1970s the *Argos* carried facts and opinion on such subjects as the activities of the Ku Klux Klan,[qv] local black preachers, high prices for food in black neighborhoods, and the education of black students. At its peak the *Argos* published 5,600 copies of the newspaper that were distributed directly to subscribers through the mail and through local stores. The *Argos* eventually became the longest continuously published newspaper of its type produced by blacks in Texas.

William E. Montgomery

AUSTIN BAYOU. Austin Bayou rises 1½ miles east of Rosharon in northwest Brazoria County (at 29°22′ N, 95°26′ W) and runs twenty-eight miles southeast to its mouth on Bastrop Bayou, eight miles southeast of Angleton (at 29°06′ N, 95°18′ W). The creek has been altered at various points to form Peltier Garrett Lakes, McCullough Lake, and other reservoirs. Austin Bayou is named for Henry Austin,[qv] who received a title for land along the stream in 1831. The surrounding flat to rolling terrain is surfaced by clay and clay and sandy loam that supports mesquite, grasses, cacti, water-tolerant hardwoods, and conifers.

BIBLIOGRAPHY: James A. Creighton, *A Narrative History of Brazoria County* (Angleton, Texas: Brazoria County Historical Commission, 1975).

AUSTIN CAVERNS. Austin Caverns, a series of caves on Meredith Street in northwest Austin (at 30°18′ N, 97°47′ W) has been known since the mid-1800s. The caves were exploited commercially for a brief period in 1932 but were judged too dangerous to be open to the public. The entrance was blasted shut. Rainwater and quarrying periodically reopened the cave, requiring further blasting and filling to keep it closed. Part of the cave served as a storm-sewer drain.

BIBLIOGRAPHY: Vertical Files, Barker Texas History Center, University of Texas at Austin (Caves). *A. Richard Smith*

AUSTIN *CITY GAZETTE*. The Austin *City Gazette,* the first newspaper published in Austin, made its initial appearance on October 30, 1839, under the direction of Samuel Whiting,[qv] with Joel Miner[qv] heading the typographical department. The four-page paper appeared each Wednesday, at a subscription price of five dollars a year. It supported the development of agriculture in Texas. In January 1840 George K. Teulon became the editor; Whiting, however, continued as owner and publisher. From January 1840 until March 1842 the paper was publisher to the Texas Congress; 50 percent of its space was occupied with the proceedings of Congress, laws, presidential decrees, and other governmental matters. The paper also carried local news, national news, foreign (including United States) news, one or two columns of editorials, letters to the editor, and, usually, a page or a page and a half of advertising. Fiction, poetry, and essays, usually reprinted from other journals, sometimes appeared. At first the *Gazette* was for Mirabeau B. Lamar[qv] in its editorial policy, but about the time Teulon assumed the editorship, it became anti-Lamar and supported the policies of Sam Houston.[qv] It suspended publication in March 1842 because of the threatened Mexican invasion of Austin, but scattered issues appeared until August 17, 1842. The paper was later continued by the Austin *Western Advocate.*[qv] The Texas State Library[qv] holds a run from October 30, 1839, to March 2, 1842.

BIBLIOGRAPHY: Joe B. Frantz, Newspapers of the Republic of Texas (M.A. thesis, University of Texas, 1940). Mary Glasscock Frazier, Texas Newspapers during the Republic (March 2, 1836-February 19, 1846) (M. Journ. thesis, University of Texas, 1931). Marilyn M. Sibley, *Lone Stars and State Gazettes: Texas Newspapers before the Civil War* (College Station: Texas A&M University Press, 1983).

"AUSTIN CITY LIMITS." "Austin City Limits," a television program of concert performances featuring uniquely American styles of music, was founded in 1974 by Public Broadcasting Service affiliate KLRN-TV (later KLRU-TV) in Austin, Texas, and was carried by 280 stations nationwide in 1990. The program, which usually produces thirteen live weekly shows a season, has showcased performers such as Jimmy Buffett, Rosanne Cash, Ray Charles, Leonard Cohen, B. B. King, Lyle Lovett, Willie Nelson, Roy Orbison,[qv] Bonnie Raitt, George Strait, and Tanya Tucker. The show's success was credited with contributing to the rise of several major country performers and coincided with the growing popularity of country music. The program, known particularly for its "redneck rock" or "progressive country" music, resulted in the mid-1970s from the desire of Bill Arhos, then program director at KLRN, to develop locally produced programming that could attract national attention. With producer Paul Bosner and director Bruce Scafe, Arhos approached PBS's Station Program Cooperative (a program fostered by the network to help individual system stations produce national programming) for funding for a pilot program. Despite resistance from KLRN upper management, the SPC granted support in 1974. The initial show starred Willie Nelson and was an immediate success. Arhos and Bosner sold the show to PBS by convincing station executives, accustomed to shows like *Masterpiece Theater* and *Sesame Street,* that the program was not too far outside the mainstream. In 1975 Arhos convinced Greg Harney, program acquisition head for the PBS's annual national membership drive, to show the pilot at the Station Independence Project meeting, a forum for planning the next year's national pledge drive. Thirty-four stations aired the show; subsequently, PBS and Arhos agreed that if five stations would support it, the program could remain in the market for at least a year. With the help of KQED-TV in San Francisco, Arhos got the five stations only minutes before the network deadline. Videotaping began in September 1975 with a reunion of (Bob) Wills's Original Texas Playboys. Despite technical glitches and limited audiences, the 1976 season defined the show's unique "progressive country" style, a combination of traditional country music with folk and rock influences that flourished in Austin at that time. The show drew on this growing Austin music scene, challenged the dominance of Nashville, and later competed with Music Television (MTV), The Nashville Network (TNN), and Country Music Television (CMT). Although "progressive country" and mainstream country have been staples of the program, it has also featured an eclectic mix of American music: jazz, blues, and folk.

Program highlights have included the premiere of the "Austin City Limits" theme song (Gary P. Nunn's "London Homesick Blues") and the return of Willie Nelson's album *Red-Headed Stranger* to the *Billboard* charts for forty-eight weeks after his performance on the show (both in 1977); appearances by Ray Charles and Chet Atkins (1979); the adoption of the Austin-skyline backdrop (1981); and the three-hour special "Down Home Country Music," which won Best Network Music Program in the New York International Film and Television Festival (1982). Other high points have been the tenth-anniversary show taping, featuring the Texas Playboys, before an open-air crowd of more than 5,000 in Austin (1984); the first all-female "Songwriters Special" (with Emmylou Harris, Rosanne Cash, and others) and the first show appearance by Fats Domino (both in 1986); appearances by Johnny Cash and by Reba McEntire (both in 1987); Garth Brooks's first appearance on the show (1990); the featuring of Nanci Griffith, the Indigo Girls, Mary Chapin Carpenter, and Julie Gold in another "Songwriters Special" (1992); and appearances by humorist Garrison Keillor and the Hopeful Gospel Quartet (1993). After losing Budweiser as an underwriter in 1990, "Austin City Limits" faced a declining PBS budget and network demands that the series raise more than a quarter of its own funding. Performers on the show have always been paid on a union scale. By its nineteenth network season (1993), "Austin City Limits" was focusing less on mainstream country music and more on songwriters and the "new folk movement," and had introduced a variety of new formats to supplement its traditional stage-show settings. *See also* FOLK AND POPULAR MUSIC.

BIBLIOGRAPHY: Austin *American-Statesman,* January 14, 1993. Clifford Endres, *Austin City Limits* (Austin: University of Texas Press, 1987). Houston *Chronicle,* January 14, 1990. *Damon Arhos*

AUSTIN COLLEGE. Austin College, an independent liberal arts college in Sherman, was established by the Brazos Presbytery of the Old School Presbyterian Church as a men's college and theological school. It was founded at Huntsville by Daniel Baker, James Weston Miller, and William Cochran Blair,[qqv] who were appointed by the presbytery in June 1849 to select a college site somewhere between the Brazos and Trinity rivers. Huntsville citizens provided $10,000 and five acres of land to secure the location. When the college was incorporated on November 22, 1849, it was granted a charter, still in use today, modeled after the charters of Harvard, Yale, and Princeton universities. The college was named in honor of Stephen F. Austin[qv] despite suggestions by the Huntsville Presbyterian Church that it be named San Jacinto College and by others that it be named after Daniel Baker. Baker, known as "the father of Austin College," steadfastly objected to the idea of naming the college for him. Sam Houston and Anson Jones[qqv]—both presidents of the Republic of Texas[qv]—were charter members of the board of trustees of Austin College. The board, which included Abner Smith Lipscomb and Henderson King Yoakum[qqv] in its membership, was appointed in 1849, met for the first time on April 5, 1850, and selected Samuel McKinney[qv] as president and Baker as agent. Baker traveled over the settled districts of Texas and over much of the United States raising funds for the college. The school began operating in the fall of 1850, and the Masonic lodge at Huntsville laid the cornerstone of Austin Hall on June 24, 1851. Baker served as president from 1853 until his death in 1857. For a year after his death the college did not have a leader, and even closed for the fall semester of 1858. In general, however, Austin College was prosperous and well patronized until the Civil War and Reconstruction[qqv] periods, when it lost enrollment and suffered financially. In 1876 the Texas Synod of the Presbyterian Church, United States, decided to move the college to Sherman, where the first college building was completed and fifty-three students were enrolled in 1878.

After 1878 Austin College grew slowly but steadily until a fire set by a homesick prep-school student destroyed the main building in 1913. The college recovered when citizens of Sherman contributed $50,000 for a new library and auditorium. The school became coeducational in 1918. After 1930 it was strengthened by its consolidation with Texas Presbyterian College at Milford and financial assistance from Sherman citizens. Austin College has had its most dynamic period of growth in students, endowment, and campus facilities since 1950. The presidents of Austin College succeeding McKinney and Baker were Rufus W. Bailey, Samuel M. Luckett,[qqv] K. B. Boude, E. P. Palmer, Donald MacGregor, Thornton R. Sampson,[qv] Thomas Stone Clyde, E. B. Tucker, W. B. Guerrant, John D. Moseley, and Harry E. Smith.

Students at Austin College reside and attend courses on a beautifully landscaped sixty-acre campus with a mixture of old and new facilities. During the 1983–84 academic year, the college employed 265 persons, 107 of whom were faculty members. In addition to liberal arts studies in twenty-seven areas, Austin College offers preprofessional programs in engineering, business, health sciences, law, theology and church vocations, and teaching. The Austin Teacher Program is a five-year plan that leads to a bachelor's degree in an undergraduate field and a master's in teacher education. Unusual educational opportunities include January Term, which involves students in projects and experiences outside their field of concentration; Field Studies, which allows participation in off-campus projects; Washington Semester, in which students spend a semester in Washington, D.C.; Study Abroad, which allows students to spend either a semester or a year attending college in a foreign nation; and the Social Science Laboratory, which involves fieldwork in the local community. In 1984, $5 million was raised for a new library after a $1 million challenge grant. The new building, completed in October 1986, has space for 240,000 printed volumes. Included in the library are a rare book room and a circulating Texana collection. After a twenty-year delay the Carruth Administration building received a $1.3 million renovation, completed in October 1987. A stained glass window of Stephen F. Austin that survived a fire in 1913 was installed in the new library. Austin College had eighty-five faculty members and 1,174 students in the 1992–93 regular term, when Harry E. Smith was president.

BIBLIOGRAPHY: Dan Ferguson, "The Antecedents of Austin College," *Southwestern Historical Quarterly* 53 (January 1950). George L. Landolt, *Search for the Summit: Austin College through XII Decades* (Austin: Von Boeckmann–Jones, 1970). Percy Everett Wallace, The History of Austin College (M.A. thesis, University of Texas, 1924).

J. D. Fuller

AUSTIN COMMUNITY COLLEGE. Austin Community College, a two-year institution of higher education, was established in Austin late in 1972 to serve the capital area of Texas. Students of all ages, ethnic groups, and educational backgrounds were enrolled; classes opened in September 1973 in several locations in the city with 2,200 students. Administrative offices were on the Ridgeview campus, the old Anderson High School building in East Austin. Thomas M. Hatfield was named president by the school board of the Austin Independent School District, the governing body of the college. The fall 1974 enrollment was 7,061. The college holds membership in the Association of Texas Colleges and Universities,[qv] the American Association of Community and Junior Colleges, the Texas Public Community/Junior College Association, the Southern Association of Colleges and Schools, and the Texas Higher Education Coordinating Board.[qv]

Austin Community College offers college parallel freshman and sophomore courses, occupational programs, and adult education in 147 areas of study. The college confers associate degrees and certificates of completion. In 1994 the school had three main campuses: Northridge, Rio Grande, and Riverside. It also had several satellite campuses, including Cypress Creek, Eastridge, Southwest, and Pinnacle, and various evening and offsite facilities located throughout Travis, Williamson, Bastrop, and Hays counties. Nontraditional instruction was offered via television. Combined, the ACC libraries house over 100,000 volumes of print, audiovisual, and computer software material. In 1991 Dan Angel was president, and the enrollment was 32,000.

AUSTIN COUNTY. Austin County (L-19), in southeastern Texas thirty-five miles west of Houston, is bordered on the north by Washington County, on the east by Waller and Fort Bend counties, on the south by Wharton County, and on the West by Colorado and Fayette counties. Bellville, the county seat and second largest town, is fifty miles west-northwest of Houston. The county's center point is 29°55′ north latitude, 96°18′ west longitude. State Highway 36 is the major north–south thoroughfare, while State Highway 159, U.S. Highway 90, and Interstate 10 span the county east and west. The county is also served by three major railways: the Southern Pacific, the Missouri, Kansas and Texas, and the Atchison, Topeka and Santa Fe.

Austin County covers 656 square miles on the boundary between the Post Oak Savannah and the Coastal Prairie regions of Texas. The terrain varies from rolling hills in the northern, western, and central sections to a nearly level coastal prairie in the south. Elevations range from 460 feet above sea level in the northwest to 120 feet in the southeast. Most of the area lies within the drainage basin of the Brazos River, which forms the eastern border of the county. The margins of the western and southern sections of the county are drained by the San Bernard River, which forms much of the county's western border. The northwestern portion of the county lies in a zone of blackland prairie surfaced by dark clays and grayish-brown sandy and clay loams. The heavily wooded central section of the county is covered by light-colored sandy loams and sands not suited to agriculture, while the southern prairies are surfaced by dark clay loams and lighter colored sandy loams. Stream bottoms consist of very fertile dark reddish brown alluvium. From southwest to northeast across the sandy soils of the county's midsection stretches a five-mile-wide band of oak-hickory forest. North of this timber belt, on the rolling blackland that covers almost half the county's surface, is a "mosaic" zone of interspersed forest and prairie. In the south the coastal prairie exhibits wide expanses of open grassland fringed by stands of oak and elm. Although the timber and grassland were almost equal in extent during the nineteenth century, the woodland has been reduced in the twentieth century by advancing urbanization; yet between one-fourth and one-third of the county remains heavily wooded. In addition to the predominant post oaks, the county's hardwood forests include such species as hickory, live oak, blackjack oak, elm, hackberry, black walnut, sycamore, and mesquite. A number of creeks, the largest of which include Mill, Piney, and Allens, flow southeastward athwart the timber belt to the Brazos; the bottoms of many of these streams are mantled by thick stands of water oak, pecan, and cottonwood. Mill Creek, with its picturesque, broad, wooded valley, was called palmetto by the Spanish, in commemoration of a species of dwarf palm that once grew on its lower course (*see* TEXAS PALM). North of the timber belt the most abundant types of prairie grass include Indian grass, tall bunchgrass, and buffalo grass, while on the coastal prairie the dominant species are marsh and salt grasses, bluestems, and coarse grasses.

Between 11 and 20 percent of the land in the county is regarded as prime farmland. Substantial reserves of petroleum and natural gas are by far the most significant of the county's limited mineral resources. Although the bears, alligators, and buffalo[qv] that once roamed the area disappeared in the nineteenth century, the county still has many wild animal species, including white-tailed deer, coyote, skunk, raccoon, and opossum, and such wild birds as the mourning dove and bobwhite quail. In winter migratory ducks and geese feed on grain in the southern reaches of the county. Recreation areas include the 667-acre Stephen F. Austin State Historical Park[qv] at San Felipe, which attracts thousands of visitors annually. Temperatures range from an average high of 96° F in July to an average low of 41° in January. Rainfall averages forty-two inches annually. The growing season averages 283 days per year.

The scanty archeological evidence available suggests that human habitation in the area began as early as 7400 B.C. during the Paleo-Indian Period. The county lies in what appears to have been during late prehistory a zone of cultural transition between inland and coastal aboriginal peoples. During the early historic era the principal inhabitants were the Tonkawas, a nomadic, flint-working, hunting and gathering people, living in widely scattered bands, who traveled hundreds of miles in pursuit of buffalo and practiced little if any agriculture. Their numbers were greatly reduced by European diseases over the course of the eighteenth century. They were regarded as friendly by the white settlers who moved in during the early nineteenth century, but their petty thievery was a continual source of annoyance to the newcomers. Similarly, the Bedias and other distant groups migrated periodically through this area begging and stealing. To the south and west of what is now Austin County, on the coastal lowlands and littoral, dwelt the more bellicose Karankawas, much feared by the settlers. The Wacos, a southern Wichita people, also launched raids into the area down the Brazos River from their villages near the site of present Waco.

Early settlers were somewhat shielded from the depredations of fierce plains tribes such as the Comanches and Apaches by the settlements on the Colorado River to the west and the buffering presence of the Tonkawas to the north. As early as 1823 Stephen F. Austin[qv] began organizing a militia with which to defend the frontiers of his colony, and the Austin County area contributed many volunteers for the Indian campaigns. Punitive expeditions were mounted against the Tonkawas in 1823, the Karankawas in 1823 and 1824, and the Wacos in 1829. To at least one such campaign in the early 1820s Jared E. Groce,[qv] a wealthy planter, contributed thirty of his own armed and mounted slaves. The success of these operations seems to have sharply curtailed Indian depredations in the Austin County vicinity, and by 1836 they had virtually ceased; until after the Texas Revolution,[qv] however, inhabitants of more exposed settlements to the west continued to abandon their homes periodically and take refuge at San Felipe. The theft of a few horses from homesteads along Mill Creek in 1839 marked the last Indian raid within the bounds of present Austin County. The Indians drifted westward and northward, and by 1850 the federal census found none residing within the county.

During the seventeenth and eighteenth centuries the territory that is now Austin County was part of a vast arena of imperial competition between the Spanish and French. It is likely that the first European to set foot within the boundaries of the present county was René Robert Cavelier, Sieur de La Salle,[qv] who may have traversed the area in the spring of 1686 and crossed the San Bernard near present Orange Hill, while traveling northeastward from his base at Fort St. Louis, above Matagorda Bay, in a desperate attempt to reach the Mississippi River. Some authorities believe that La Salle again crossed the vicinity early in 1687 on his last fatal trek toward the Mississippi. The first Spaniard to reach the area seems to have been Alonzo De León,[qv] governor of Coahuila, who may have ventured through in the spring of 1689 while searching for traces of La Salle's expedition. De León returned to the vicinity in the spring of 1690 in the company of the Franciscan priest Damián Massanet[qv] on a mission to the Tejas Indians, traveling from Garcitas Creek on Lavaca Bay northeastward to the headwaters of the Neches River. His general route, which followed a crude Indian trace through southeastern Texas and is believed to have passed along the northern border of what is now Austin County, later became known as the La Bahía Road[qv] and served as a major thoroughfare between the presidios at Goliad and San Francisco de los Tejas, near the site of present Crockett. In 1718 Texas governor Martín de Alarcón,[qv] having founded the Villa de Béxar and San Antonio de Valero Mission, crossed the territory of the future county on an expedition from Matagorda Bay to the missions of East Texas. Pedro de Rivera y Villalón[qv] traversed the area on an inspection tour of the presidios[qv] of Texas in 1727. Forty years later the Marqués de Rubí[qv] also passed through the vicinity on an official inspection of the Spanish frontier. The Atascosito Road,[qv] a military road linking Refugio and Goliad with Atascosito, a fortified settlement on the lower Trinity River near the site of present Liberty, was constructed by Spanish authorities during the mid-eighteenth century; a section of the road extended through the southern reaches of the future Austin County.

American settlement in the area began in the early 1820s with the founding of Stephen F. Austin's first colony. By November 1821, just ten months after the Spanish government's acceptance of Moses Austin's[qv] colonization application, four families had encamped on the west bank of the lower Brazos. The next month saw the arrival of several additional parties of colonists, and settlement proceeded rapidly. In the fall of 1823 Stephen F. Austin and the Baron de Bastrop[qv] chose a spot on the west bank of the Brazos at the Atascosito Crossing,[qv] now in southeastern Austin County, to be the site of the unofficial capital of the colony, San Felipe de Austin. The settlement quickly became the political, economic, and social center of the colony. By the end of 1824, thirty-seven of the Old Three Hundred[qv] colonists had received grants of land. These early settlers were attracted to the well-timbered, rich, alluvial bottomlands of the Brazos and other major streams; the especially prized tracts combined woodland with prairie. Most of the immigrants came from Southern states, and many brought slaves. By the late 1820s these more prosperous settlers had begun to establish cotton plantations, emulating the example of Jared Groce, who settled with some ninety slaves on the east bank of the Brazos above the site of San Felipe and in 1822 raised what was probably the first cotton crop in Texas. In 1834 more than one-third of the 1,000 inhabitants of the future county were African Americans.[qv]

Industry began here in the mid-1820s, when the Cummins family constructed a water-powered saw and grist mill near the mouth of Mill Creek, probably the first mill of its kind in Texas; not long thereafter the first cotton gins were established. Soon San Felipe, the first true urban community to develop within the Austin colony, ranked second in Texas only to San Antonio as a commercial center. By 1830 small herds of cattle were being driven from San Felipe to market at Nacogdoches. Cotton, however, the chief article of commerce, was carried overland by ox-wagon to the coastal entrepôts of Velasco, Indianola, Anahuac, and Harrisburg. Unreliable water levels and turbulence during the spring rains discouraged steamboat traffic on the Brazos as high as San Felipe, and the stream's meanders rendered the water route to the coast far longer than land routes. After 1830, however, steamboats gradually began to appear on the lower Brazos, and by 1836 as many as three steamboats were plying the water between landings in Austin County and the coast. During the 1840s a steamboat line on the Brazos provided regular service between Velasco and Washington.

The area played an important role in the events of the Texas Revolution. The conventions of 1832 and 1833[qqv] were held at San Felipe and, as the site of the Consultation[qv] of November 3, 1835, the town became the capital of the provisional government[qv] and retained the role until the Convention of 1836[qv] met the following March at Washington-on-the-Brazos. After the fall of the Alamo,[qv] Gen. Sam Houston's[qv] army retreated through Austin County, pausing briefly at San Felipe before continuing northward up the Brazos to Groce's plantation. On March 30, 1836, the small garrison under Moseley Baker[qv] that remained at San Felipe to defend the crossing ordered the town evacuated and then burned to keep it from falling into the hands of the advancing Mexican army. Residents fled eastward during the incident known as the Runaway Scrape.qv After a brief skirmish with Baker's detachment at San Felipe in early April, Antonio López de Santa Anna qv marched his army southward for Harrisburg, but not before his troops had looted the eastern part of the county. In May 1836, as news of the Texans' victory at San Jacinto spread, residents began returning to what remained of their homes and possessions.

Although the state of Coahuila and Texas qv designated San Felipe the capital of its Department of the Brazos in 1834, the first machinery of democratic government in Austin's colony appeared in 1828 with the establishment of the ayuntamiento qv of San Felipe; the municipality over which it exercised authority extended from the Lavaca to the San Jacinto rivers and from the Old San Antonio Road qv to the coast. The jurisdiction was progressively narrowed by the formation from it of fifteen additional municipalities; by 1836 the Municipality of San Felipe had acquired boundaries approximating those of modern Austin County, with the addition of a large region in the south that was broken off to form Fort Bend County in 1837, and a wide strip of territory on the east bank of the Brazos, which remained in the county until the end of Reconstruction.qv The Constitution of the Republic of Texas qv (1836) made counties of the former Mexican municipalities, and by 1837 Austin County, named in honor of Stephen Austin, had been officially organized. Although the burning of San Felipe left the town unavailable to serve as the capital of the republic, the partially rebuilt town became the county seat of Austin County. After a referendum of December 1846, however, Bellville became the county seat; this new community was near the geographical center of the county. The transfer of administrative functions was completed in January 1848.

In 1831 J. Friedrich Ernst,qv a native of Lower Saxony, was granted a league of land on the banks of Mill Creek in what is now northwestern Austin County. Ernst described his new home in glowing terms in a letter to a friend in Germany, and his descriptions were reprinted in newspapers and travel journals in his homeland. Within a few years a steady stream of Germans qv began settling in Austin, Fayette, and Colorado counties. In 1838 Ernst surveyed a townsite on his property on which the community of Industry arose. Between 1838 and 1842 alone, several hundred Germans moved near the town; those not establishing permanent residence soon began rural communities throughout northern and western Austin County. In some instances, as at Industry, Cat Spring, and Rockhouse, the immigrants founded all-German towns; more commonly, however, they formed German enclaves within areas previously settled by Anglo-Americans and often became numerically and culturally dominant.

Most of the early German immigrants were from provinces of northwestern and north central Germany; among them, however, were increasing numbers of Austrians, Swiss, Wends,qqv and Prussians. Most soon acquired land and began cultivating cotton and corn like their Anglo-American neighbors, although many followed the example of prosperous early settlers Friedrich Ernst and Robert J. Kleberg qv and raised tobacco. The crop was either fashioned into cigars locally to be marketed in San Felipe and Houston—the activity that inspired the name Industry—or, during the 1840s, was sold to the German cigar factory at Columbus in Colorado County. In the 1850s a cigar factory was established at New Ulm in Austin County. By the mid-1840s Austin County's growing reputation as a haven for German settlers began attracting immigrants brought to Texas by the Adelsverein.qv The failure of revolution in Germany in 1848 triggered a new wave of immigration to Austin County in the late 1840s and 1850s consisting largely of political dissidents, many well educated.

The newcomers were quick to establish not only educational and religious institutions but a wide array of voluntary associations devoted to such pursuits as literature, singing, marksmanship, agriculture, and gymnastics, as well as mutual aid. A striking indication of the Germans' emphasis upon education was the campaign launched in 1844 to establish a university on the German model at Cat Spring. Among the community's cultural achievements was the founding of an influential German-language newspaper, *Das Wochenblatt*, originally published at Bellville by W. A. Trenckmann qv in 1891; the paper was later moved to Austin. Not until the Civil War qv did German migration into the county subside. By 1850 the county population included 750 German-born residents, 33 percent of the white population; American-born farmers outnumbered their German-born counterparts by the same two-to-one ratio. By 1860, however, German-born farmers outnumbered the American-born.

Bolstered by the area's generous natural endowments and high rates of immigration from both Germany and the southern United States, Austin County quickly recovered from the destruction of the Texas Revolution. In 1836 the county's population stood at an estimated 1,500. During the ensuing quarter-century of agricultural prosperity the population grew rapidly. The upper South—particularly the states of Tennessee, Kentucky, Virginia, and North Carolina—remained the most important source of settlers in the county until after the Civil War. By 1847 the county's population had risen to 2,687; it climbed to 3,841 by 1850 and to 10,139 by 1860.

The steady stream of southerners arriving with slave property pushed the county's slave population steadily upward. From 447 in 1840 it climbed to 1,093 in 1845 and to 1,274 in 1847; at that time slaves constituted more than 47 percent of the total population. Slaves numbered 1,549 by 1850 and 3,914 (39 percent of the population) by 1860. During the 1840s more than thirty Austin County residents were planters, that is, owners of twenty or more slaves or other considerable property; by 1860, 46 residents held twenty or more slaves. With 324 slaveholders in 1860, Austin County was one of only seventeen counties in the state in which the average number of slaves per owner was greater than ten. In 1860 twelve Austin County residents ranked among the wealthiest individuals in the state, i.e., as holders of at least $100,000 in property. Six residents held more than 100 slaves.

Amid the rising tide of servile labor the smallest and undoubtedly most incongruous of the county's minorities was its free black inhabitants. The census found seven free blacks in the county in 1847 and six in 1850. These may have been members of the Allen family, longtime residents of the area, two of whom, George and Sam Allen, had helped evacuate and burn San Felipe in 1836. By 1860, however, no free blacks remained in the county.

From 1824 to 1837 San Felipe was the only town in Austin County. By the early 1850s, however, Industry, Travis, Cat Spring, Sempronius, Millheim, and New Ulm had appeared. Many communities were simply open clusters of farmsteads with a post office and general store in the center of the settlement. Despite a modest increase in steamboat traffic on the Brazos, the chief mode of commercial transportation continued to be the ox wagon, as a brisk trade developed between Austin County and the burgeoning town of Houston. Finally, in the late 1850s, the first railroad arrived in the area, as the Houston and Texas Central extended its main line northward through Hockley to reach the new town of Hempstead, in the eastern district of the county east of the Brazos, in June 1858. Cotton transported to the rail line by wagon from western Austin County crossed the Brazos at a number of ferries between San Felipe and the mouth of Caney Creek.

Austin County agriculture grew remarkably in antebellum Texas.qv The county's 381 acres of improved land in 1850 expanded to 58,869 acres by 1860, and the number of farms multiplied from 230 to 790. Cotton and corn continued to be the most significant crops. In 1850 cotton production was 3,205 bales. By 1860 it had grown almost 500 percent, to an astonishing 19,020 bales. Corn production was 149,230 bushels in 1850 and 400,800 bushels in 1860. Irish potatoes increased from 3,530 bushels in 1850 to 9,809 in 1860. In the same period oat cultivation rose from 1,469 bushels to 2,418. Only sweet potatoes and tobacco fell off, the former from 37,322 bushels in 1850 to 32,273 in 1860, and the latter from 9,663 pounds to 5,175 in the same interval. Stock raising retained its early status as a pillar of the local economy throughout the antebellum period, as herds multiplied rapidly on the open range of the lush coastal prairies south of Bernard Creek. In 1850, 20,791 cattle were raised in the county; just ten years later the figure had increased 242 percent to 71,271. Sheep production registered a 250 percent increase, from 2,104 animals in 1850 to 7,407 in 1860. The number of horses raised in the county more than doubled, from 2,386 in 1850 to 5,497 in 1860. In the same period hog production rose from 12,871 animals to 21,177.

The average German farm was barely half the size of that of the average slaveless Anglo-American in the late antebellum period. Most German immigrants arrived in Texas too late to receive free land, the distribution of which ceased in the early 1840s. Furthermore, most had been compelled to expend so much of their money on the way that they had relatively little to buy land and livestock. In 1856 Germans near Cat Spring formed one of the earliest agricultural societies in Texas, the Cat Spring Landwirthschaftlicher Verein, which continues to the present. Germans also owned few slaves. Yet, except in the case of a relatively small group of Forty-Eighter intellectuals, this circumstance was due far less to philosophical opposition to slavery[qv]—as many Anglo-Americans suspected—than to the fact that most German immigrants lacked the money to buy slaves. The few Germans who did own slaves were generally those who had immigrated during the 1830s and 1840s and had thus accumulated the requisite wealth. By 1860 only about a dozen of Austin County's German residents were listed as slaveholders in the federal census reports; most owned fewer than five slaves, while the largest German slaveholder, Charles Fordtran,[qv] owned twenty-one. Many German farmers raised tobacco, the local production of which they soon dominated, in the belief that the crop required the sort of intensive care that slaves could not provide. German yeomen, moreover, utilized far more hired labor than did their neighbors, drawn from new immigrants, who continued to arrive. German farmhands, who usually preferred to work for Germans, could be hired more cheaply than slaves.

Secession[qv] brought turbulence. In early 1859 mounting fear of slave insurrections[qv] inspired the formation of the county's first patrol system. As early as February 1860 a mass meeting at Bellville advocated secession if the "aggressions of the North upon the South" continued. Six months later the tension had increased; another public meeting at Bellville called upon the county's ministers to cease preaching to blacks in public places. Unionist sentiment, however, was also in evidence during the crisis. "Frequent, enthusiastic, and well-attended" Unionist meetings in which Germans were prominent were reportedly held in Austin, Washington, Fayette, Lavaca, and Colorado counties throughout 1860. When Austin County elected representatives to the Secession Convention[qv] in late 1860, one of the delegates refused to attend the gathering on ground that although a majority of those casting ballots favored a convention, they did not constitute a majority of the county's eligible voters. However, in the referendum of February 23, 1861, Austin County approved secession 825 to 212. Several heavily German precincts had voted decisively against the secession ordinance.

With the coming of the war hundreds of Austin County residents, including many prewar Unionists, enlisted in Confederate or state military units. State formations to which companies organized in the county were attached included the Second, Eighth,[qv] Twenty-first, Twenty-fourth, and Twenty-fifth Texas Cavalry regiments, the First and Twentieth Texas Infantry, and Waul's Legion.[qv] However, much of the rush to enroll in state and county militia companies, so-called "home-guard" units, had less to do with motives of patriotism than with the desire to avoid combat. Many German residents had immigrated to the United States to avoid military service in Austria, Prussia, or other European states; many Germans were reluctant to risk their lives in defense of the "peculiar institution" of slavery. The Confederate government's adoption of conscription in early 1862 deepened the difficulty of the many county residents, both foreign-born and native, who were desperately trying to remain neutral in the conflict. Besides rushing to enlist in home-guard units, many draft-age males gained exemption from conscription as wagoners or teamsters. But as the war dragged on and exemptions became more difficult to obtain, men subject to the draft resorted to increasingly drastic measures. Some county residents fled the state for Mexico. Others, who could not abandon their families entirely, hid in the woods. Some of these returned to their homes at night to plow their fields by moonlight. Some county residents serving with Confederate units deserted upon returning to their homes on furlough. The names of forty such men, most of them German, were published in the Bellville *Countryman* in December 1862. By late 1862 county enrolling officers were claiming that 150 Germans subject to conscription had refused to present themselves for induction. Confederate officials were thoroughly aroused by the situation developing in the county. It was reported that forcible opposition to conscription was being organized in the German settlements of Austin and surrounding counties. Gatherings of from 500 to 600 individuals, conducted in German to foil possible Anglophone spies, were said to have been held at Shelby, Millheim, and Industry in December 1862 and early January 1863. Unionist militias complete with cavalry formations had reportedly begun drilling. One Unionist group published a petition to the governor detailing the grievances of the draft resisters. The petitioners claimed that they could not abandon their suffering families just as spring planting was set to begin, inasmuch as the county had made no provision for the relief of the needy; local merchants, moreover, refused to accept the very currency with which Confederate troops were paid.

The crisis came to a head on January 8, 1863, when martial law was declared in Austin, Colorado, and Fayette counties. Several companies of the First Regiment of Gen. H. H. Sibley's[qv] Arizona Brigade were rushed from New Mexico to suppress the uprising. A detachment of twenty-five soldiers under Lt. R. H. Stone was sent to Bellville to arrest the ringleaders of the Austin County resistance. The detainees were turned over to local authorities; most of those arrested were German, but some of the principal conspirators were not. By January 21 the rebellion had been officially quelled and all who had been conscripted were coming forward for enrollment. However, the arrests left bitterness. The homes of several German farmers had been ransacked, prisoners had been beaten, and their families had been abused. This deepened the contempt of the Germans for the Confederate enrollment officers. Nor did the events of January end the search for subversives in Austin County. In October 1863 Dr. Richard R. Peebles,[qv] a founder of Hempstead and respected local physician, and four coconspirators were arrested on charges of treason for having circulated a pamphlet that urged an end to the war. After brief stints in the jails of San Antonio and Austin Peebles and the other prisoners were exiled to Mexico.

Scores of German county residents loyally served in the Confederate Army. Hempstead, because of its strategic location on the Houston and Texas Central Railway, became an important assembly point for troops from throughout Central Texas. A Confederate military hospital was constructed at Hempstead, and three Confederate military posts were established in the vicinity; one of these, Camp Groce,[qv] was one of only three prisoner of war camps in Texas. At least five smaller military camps were scattered through the county west of the Brazos River. When the Union navy tightened its blockade of the Texas coast, local planters shipped cotton to Matamoros in long caravans of ox wagons to be exchanged for salt, flour, cloth, and other commodities. Even so, expanded domestic manufacturing had to be relied upon to fill most needs. Several county businesses produced munitions: a gunsmith shop in Bellville reconditioned rifles and muskets for the Confederate Army; foundries in Bellville and Hempstead produced canteens, skillets, and camp kettles under contract with the state of Texas; the Hempstead Manufacturing Company made woolen blankets, cotton cloth, spinning jennies, looms, and spinning wheels. Nobody starved in Austin County during the war, but suffering was widespread, especially among families with soldiers in the field.

Unfortunately, the end of the fighting in the spring of 1865 did not bring the expected end to strife; Reconstruction in Austin County, as in much of the rest of Texas, was violent and chaotic. The war years had brought another expansion of the county's black population, as planter refugees from the lower South flocked into the area seeking protection for their slave property. Between 1860 and 1864, according to county tax rolls (which probably understate the matter), slave population increased by 47 percent to 4,702. Though some blacks entering the county returned after the war to the communities from which they had recently been uprooted, many others remained. The war had scarcely ended before the federal government moved to garrison Austin County. From August 26 to October 30, 1865, Hempstead was occupied by elements of the Second Wisconsin Cavalry and several other units under the command of Maj. Gen. George A. Custer.[qv] After Custer went to Austin, Hempstead was garrisoned for a time by a small detachment of the Thirty-sixth Colored Infantry. Two white companies of the Seventeenth United States Infantry were posted in Hempstead from 1867 to 1870. The garrison was controlled by the subassistant commissioner of the thirteenth subdistrict of the Freedmen's Bureau,[qv] which embraced all of Austin County and had headquarters at Hempstead. Charged with protecting the lives, property, and civil rights of all citizens, including freedmen, the troops helped ensure equal access to polling places and the court system, but their numbers were too few and their resources too limited to permit them to enforce the laws everywhere within the county.

Capt. George Lancaster, head of the local Freedmen's Bureau office in 1867, declared that racial animosities in the area were so intense that only a spark was needed to set off an explosion. Violent confrontations between federal soldiers and local residents were common throughout the Union occupation. The numerous reports in the bureau records of violent crimes committed against blacks by whites portray a campaign of intimidation conducted against the freedmen; with Republicans and Democrats struggling for control of the county's black vote, most if not all of these crimes were politically motivated. The appearance of the Republican-sponsored Union League[qv] in the county in early 1867 outraged white Democrats, who responded by forming a Klan-like organization. The violence was most intense in the eastern district of the county, where the black population was concentrated; there the whipping, shooting, and even lynching[qv] of blacks became almost routine; few culprits were ever brought to justice. But blacks were not the only targets of white wrath. In March 1867 two soldiers were shot to death for what subassistant commissioner Lancaster termed the "crime" of wearing the federal uniform, "in the eyes of these white desperadoes a sufficient cause for murder." In the spring of 1869 a white Republican newspaper editor from Houston, visiting Hempstead to address a black audience, was accosted by a mob and run out of town. Interracial altercations characterized as riots broke out on at least two occasions in the eastern district near Hempstead in 1868. Yet with federal troops on hand to safeguard freedmen's rights, a number of blacks in Austin County were elected to positions in local government during Reconstruction. In the gubernatorial election of 1869 black voters helped provide victory in the county for Radical Republican Edmund J. Davis.[qv] By 1873, however, as previously disfranchised Confederate sympathizers recovered their political rights, the Democrats had regained control of the county's electoral machinery; thoroughly intimidated, few blacks risked casting a ballot. The smashing Democratic victory that resulted signaled the end of Reconstruction and the permanent eclipse of Republican power in the county.

Amid all the turmoil, the county's black residents set about constructing new lives for themselves. By 1870 Austin County's population had climbed almost 40 percent above its level of a decade before, to 15,087. Black population had increased about 68 percent, to 6,574, and now amounted to some 44 percent of the county's population. As blacks began to construct their own free institutions, the first black churches in the county appeared; by 1869 the Freedmen's Bureau had established one of the first black schools in the county's history, in a period when schools of any sort were rare. Plantations in the bottoms of the Brazos and other streams were broken into small farms operated by black sharecroppers. Once the initial restlessness had ended, the diligence of free black labor surprised many white observers. However, some of the county's white residents—including A. Thomas Oliver,[qv] who had owned more than 100 slaves—decided not to wait for results from the economic and political experimentation and exiled themselves from the United States in the first years after the war. Oliver and many other of these emigrants settled in Brazil, where they established colonies and raised cotton with slave labor.

Regardless of the freedmen's diligence, as a landless class they soon proved vulnerable to exploitation by white landlords, who often withheld wages from black laborers. However, not all whites were unsympathetic to the blacks' plight. Austin County resident Adalbert Regenbrecht recalled that during Reconstruction he became "probably the first justice of the peace in Texas in whose court a freedman recovered wages for his labor from his former master." Perceiving the exploitation of blacks under the developing crop-lien system, and fearful that immigrants from their homeland would also become trapped in this sort of peonage, German residents of the county wrote to prominent newspapers in Germany in 1866 to warn prospective immigrants not to sign labor or tenant contracts with former slaveowners before arriving in Texas. Driven by such fears, German rates of land ownership in Austin County were not only far higher than those of blacks but higher than those of Anglos as well.

Reconstruction politics was largely responsible for a crucial alteration of the county boundaries. As early as 1853 the residents of the eastern part of the county had begun petitioning the legislature for a separate county east of the Brazos, citing the expense and inconvenience of crossing the river to transact routine business in Bellville. When the petition was revived in 1873, the beleaguered Davis administration, fighting for its existence, decided to grant the request by carving a new county out of eastern Austin and southern Grimes counties. The Republicans expected to dominate the new county, with its large black population, and hoped that by grafting onto it a large section of northwestern Harris County, where hundreds of Democratic voters lived, they could pull Harris County into the Republican column. Waller County, established on May 19, 1873, removed from Austin County not only a fertile agricultural district but also the thriving commercial center of Hempstead, with its cotton mill, iron foundry, and rail facilities. The effects of the loss were mitigated, however, by a postbellum revival of both foreign and domestic immigration. Nevertheless, in 1880 Austin County's population of 14,429 was almost 5 percent below the 1870 figure. Black population, in particular, declined some 67 percent between 1870 and 1880, to 3,939, or 27 percent of the overall population. Renewal of domestic immigration, primarily from Gulf South states—especially Alabama—offset some of the losses. Even more significant was the revival of foreign immigration. Germans continued to settle in Austin County until the end of the nineteenth century, albeit in smaller numbers than during the antebellum period. By the 1980s fully 49 percent of the population was of German ancestry. However, the principal source of postbellum immigration was Czechoslovakia. The first Czechs[qv] had settled as early as 1847 in the vicinity of Cat Spring, where they formed what became the first Czech community in Texas. Throughout the 1850s Czechs continued to arrive in small numbers, taking up farming among the German population on the blackland prairie soils of northern and western Austin County and spilling into adjoining counties. After the Civil War the pace of Czech immigration increased; in the decade after 1870 alone more than 800 Czechs settled in Austin County, and smaller numbers continued to move into the area until after the turn of the century. The Czechs, who usually resided in German localities, only slowly established cultural institutions of their own; yet eventually they created a distinctive Czech-Texan identity. By the end of the nineteenth century at least ten communities in the county had appreciable numbers of Czech residents, and Sealy, Wallis, and Bellville had large Czech populations. Austin County had 1,205 foreign-born residents in 1860; by 1870 that figure had increased 150 percent to 3,010, or 20 percent of the population; the number grew by another 25 percent in the following decade, to 3,752—26 percent of the population. Subsequently the proportion of foreign-born residents declined steadily, to 16 percent by 1900, 13 percent by 1910, and 4 percent by 1940. The black population grew between 1880 and 1890 by 32 percent and then increased another 19 percent the following decade, to crest at 30 percent in 1900. Railroad construction in the county in the late nineteenth century provided employment for hundreds of black workers, many of whom took up residence in segregated sections of such rail towns as Sealy, Wallis, and Bellville. After the turn of the century, however, the county's black population began to decline, both absolutely and as a proportion of the population, a trend that continued into the late twentieth century. Disastrous farming conditions after the 1890s drove many farmers, including blacks, off the land in the early years of the twentieth century, just as railroad employment in the county was also disappearing. In the ten years after 1900 the county's black population fell by 23 percent. After remaining virtually unchanged in the succeeding decade, it decreased again by 14 percent during the lean years from 1920 to 1940. From 1940 to 1950 it fell almost 46 percent, to 3,016—or 21 percent of the population—as farm tenancy[qv] began to disappear and defense-related industrial jobs opened to blacks in urban areas of Texas and the North and West. Over the next thirty years the decline continued at a rate of more than 5 percent a decade; by 1980 the county's black population stood at 2,580, less than 15 percent of the whole. A bare 1 percent increase in absolute numbers between 1980 and 1990 failed to check the relative slide, so that by 1990 blacks constituted just 13 percent of the county population.

Austin County's economy recovered slowly from the havoc of the Civil War. By 1870 county farms had fallen to scarcely 45 percent of their 1860 value. No county resident in 1870 owned property worth so much as $100,000. By the end of the nineteenth century, however, the revival of cotton farming and stock raising had restored much former prosperity. The number of cattle fell by almost 16,700 between 1860 and 1870, and similar declines were registered in each of the two succeeding decades; by 1890 the county's production had fallen to 33,847 animals, or 47 percent of the 1860 figure. In part the decline was attributable to the loss of the territory east of the Brazos. However, with improvements in breeding and production techniques, each animal became more valuable than ever before. From 1890 to 1900 cattle production rebounded more than 20 percent, to 40,771, and in the latter year the value of the county's livestock herds finally surpassed that of 1860. Although the number of cattle grew only modestly over the next four decades, to 44,477 in 1940, their dollar value increased dramatically. Swine raising,[qv] similarly, never regained its antebellum levels in terms of numbers of animals, but remained significant nonetheless. From 1860 to 1890 the county's swine herds declined by more than 30 percent, to 14,492 animals. Over the next ten years, however, the swine count increased almost 29 percent, to a postbellum peak of 18,642. In the four decades after 1900, however, production fell almost 45 percent, to 10,270 in 1940. Sheep ranching[qv] actually exceeded antebellum levels as early as 1870, when 7,554 animals were counted. However, the county's flocks declined by more than 60 percent between 1870 and 1880, to a rather insignificant 2,930, and remained almost unchanged until the mid-twentieth century. The county's impressive poultry production[qv] and dairy products[qv] industry, although mainly devoted to home consumption until after the Civil War, gained substantial commercial importance after the late nineteenth century, when poultry, eggs, and butter began to be shipped by rail to markets in neighboring counties.

As in the antebellum period, cotton culture[qv] remained the most important economic activity in the county. Inasmuch as virtually every farmer raised the valuable staple, the postbellum increase in farms and cultivated acreage inevitably meant increased cotton production. The number of farms in the county increased by an average of almost 570 each decade in the forty years after 1860, to a postbellum peak of 3,064 in 1900. In the same time, acres of improved farmland rose 126 percent, to 133,077. Although cotton production fell by 37 percent between 1860 and 1870 (to 11,976 bales), the chaos of the immediate postwar years was soon overcome and output began to climb. In the thirty years after 1870 cotton production expanded 117 percent, to stand at a historic crest of 26,087 bales in 1900; acres planted in cotton peaked the same year at 53,925. With the move to diversify agriculture in the early twentieth century, cotton production declined again in the four decades after 1900, yet it was still a respectable 14,260 bales in 1940. Cotton acreage remained almost unchanged until 1930, but declined sharply thereafter.

Tobacco continued to be an important crop among the county's German farmers until after 1880, when, with the coming of the railroad, tobacco growers became convinced that cotton offered higher profits. The 3,682 pounds of sotweed raised in 1870 had dwindled to only 596 pounds by 1890; small quantities continued to be produced well into the next century, but local cigar manufacturing ended in the late nineteenth century.

Corn culture[qv] in postbellum Austin County recovered quickly from the effects of the war; production exceeded peak antebellum levels as early as 1870, when more than 445,000 bushels was raised. By the end of the next decade almost 27,000 acres of farmland was planted in corn. Both output and acreage expanded steadily for the next sixty years, until in 1940 a record 805,600 bushels was produced on a record 40,500 acres. Local farmers, especially Germans, experimented with small grains throughout the nineteenth century. Problems of climate and disease, however, hampered rye and wheat crops in Austin County during the nineteenth century. With the advent of the railroad and expansion of cotton culture, most efforts at producing small grains were abandoned until the mid-twentieth century, although oats continued to be raised on a significant scale at times.

Gardening and the cultivation of orchard fruits for home consumption have been important in the county almost from the beginning. However, the commercial production of fruits and vegetables began only with the improvement of rail facilities in the late nineteenth century. Thereafter, truck gardening, especially for the Houston market, grew rapidly. In 1903 the Bellville Truck Growing Association was formed, and other commodity associations, such as the Cat Spring Pickling Cucumber Association, were soon organized. Watermelons were grown commercially as early as 1903; by 1924, 1,450 train cars of melons were shipped from the county annually, and production continued to expand afterward. Dairying, limited to home consumption throughout the early history of the county, became significant commercially with the advent of improved transportation facilities; by the early twentieth century several creameries were in operation. Viticulture has been little practiced in the county; in the 1880s some members of the Cat Spring Agricultural Society reportedly raised Herbemont grapes, and almost 5,000 pounds of grapes were grown in 1900. Wine making has not been significant commercially; in 1870, for example, only 770 gallons of wine was manufactured, while 5,205 was produced in 1900.

Boosted by the postwar revival of immigration, by the end of the nineteenth century Austin County had overcome the loss of its populous eastern district. After falling almost 5 percent between 1870 and 1880, the county's population grew by an average of almost 22 percent a decade over the next twenty years to reach a peak of 20,676 in 1900. Many of the county's postbellum immigrants, like most of its black population, became tenant farmers, as the rapid spread of cotton cultivation produced a rapid expansion of the crop-lien system and agricultural tenancy. As early as 1880 almost 47 percent of the county's farmers were tenants. That proportion remained virtually unchanged until the mid-twentieth century, when the Great Depression[qv] and changes in federal farm policy reduced cotton cultivation and tenancy rates began to decline.

The postbellum economic revival was stimulated by improvements in the county's transportation system. The county received its first rail service in the late 1870s when the Gulf, Colorado and Santa Fe Railway extended its Galveston–Brenham main line through Wallis, Sealy, and Bellville. During the 1880s the GC&SF constructed a branch line from Sealy to Eagle Lake through southwestern Austin County, and by the early years of that decade the Texas Western Narrow Gauge Railway operated a line between Sealy and Houston. In the mid-1890s the Missouri, Kansas and Texas Railroad built its Houston–La Grange spur through Sealy and New Ulm. In 1901 the Cane Belt Railroad constructed a line between Sealy and Eagle Lake, while almost simultaneously the Texas and New Orleans Railroad extended its Houston–Eagle Lake spur through Wallis. The railroads made thriving communities of Sealy, Bellville, Wallis, New Ulm, and Cat Spring, and relegated to insignificance towns deprived of their service, such as San Felipe. With the development of the automobile in the early twentieth century, trucks increasingly assumed the business of transporting produce to market, yet the county's roads remained primitive until after World War I.[qv] Although as early as 1912 some communities had issued bonds for road improvement, during the 1920s a Good Roads movement began in earnest and construction began on a network of paved farm roads, a project that continued through World War II.[qv] State Highway 36 was extended through the county in 1936 and U.S. Highway 90 was built in 1937. With the completion of Interstate 10 in 1965 the county was equipped with an imminently functional road system.

Transportation improvements stimulated industry as well as agriculture. Industrial activity in the early history of the county had been confined to the processing of agricultural and forest products. Gristmills, sawmills, and cotton gins abounded in the county during the antebellum period. By the 1850s the German settlers of New Ulm had established a brewery and a cigar factory, and at least two cigar factories continued in operation in the county in the 1880s. The county's first iron foundries and cottonseed oil mills were also built before the Civil War. By 1860, during the era of small-scale craft production, Austin County led the state in construction of carriages, carts, and wagons; but this ranking slipped after the war, as craft methods were swamped by the competition of market-oriented production. In the late nineteenth century, however, broom and mattress factories were built at Sealy, where the new rail lines provided access to a national market. Bottling works, pickling plants, canneries, and cider distilleries were also established in the county around the turn of the century. The Santa Fe Railroad constructed a roundhouse and machine shop in Sealy, which remained a division headquarters until 1900, when the facilities were moved to Bellville. In 1870, 105 manufacturing establishments in Austin County employed 217 workers; by 1900, 133 establishments had 272 employees. Yet this modest level of industrial development did not alter the overwhelmingly agricultural character of the county's economy. As agriculture slumped in the early twentieth century, so did the county's industries that relied upon it. By 1940 only six manufacturing plants and thirty-eight industrial workers remained in the county.

As black population declined during the era of the First World War, the county's chronic shortages of agricultural labor became acute. To alleviate the condition, increasing numbers of Mexican migrant workers were brought into the county. Many eventually took up residence, so that Mexicans became the largest foreign immigrant group to settle in Austin County during the twentieth century. In 1900 there were 46 Mexican-born residents; by 1920 the figure had increased to 145, and it rose another 60 percent over the next decade, to 242. Although Mexican immigration was sharply curtailed in the early 1940s, the county's Hispanic population has continued to grow and by 1992 constituted 10.5 percent of the total population.

A reconfiguration of the county's agriculture began in the thirties as cotton acreage began to decline under the combined impact of continuing low commodity prices, diminishing soil fertility, the increasing relative inefficiency of small farms, and New Deal acreage-reduction programs. Acres devoted to cotton cultivation in 1930 (52,793) fell by more than 40 percent by 1940. The decline continued over the next half century, so that by 1982 cotton was grown on only 1,633 acres in Austin County. Although the yield remained as high as 10,957 bales in 1960, by 1987 that figure had been reduced to only 1,408. Likewise, the production of corn, an important feature of the county's economy throughout its history, contracted after the Second World War, with yields falling from 805,599 bushels in 1940 to 220,498 in 1987 and acres planted in corn plummeting over the same period from 40,462 to 3,024. King Cotton's demise drove hundreds of tenant farmers off the land. In 1930 more than 47 percent of county farmers were tenants, but two decades later the figure was 26 percent; by 1980 fewer than 7 percent of the county's farmers were tenants. Meanwhile, the cultivation of hay, rice, peanuts, and truck crops—principally pecans, peaches, and watermelons—was expanded. A boom in stock raising stimulated a boom in the cultivation of such feed grains as sorghum; after 1930 sorghum culture[qv] increased enormously, to reach 279,163 bushels in 1987.

Irrigation,[qv] which began on an experimental basis in the county after the turn of the century, became more extensive after World War II; in 1982, 10 percent of the county's cropland was irrigated, with much of the acreage devoted to rice culture.[qv] Most of the former cotton land, however, was converted to livestock production, which after World War II became the county's chief industry. Between 1930 and 1987 harvested cropland was reduced 54 percent from 104,199 acres to 47,928. By 1982 more than 60 percent of the county's cropland was devoted to pasturage. The number of cattle raised in the county more than doubled in the three decades after 1940, then declined slightly in the seventies and early eighties to stand at 84,599 in 1987. Dairying, a lucrative pursuit since the late nineteenth century, declined after World War II, and by 1987 only five dairy farms were in operation. Between 1940 and 1982 swine production fell by 80 percent; yet a respectable 2,724 hogs were fed in 1987. Sheep raising has continued at modest levels since the Civil War, although a decline reduced production in 1987 to 403 animals. Poultry products have remained a significant source of agricultural revenue in the county since the late nineteenth century; more than 101,000 chickens were raised in 1987. By 1982 fully 83 percent of Austin County's agricultural revenues came from livestock and livestock products. In that year the county ranked 100th in the state in agricultural income.

Residents of Austin County participated enthusiastically in this century's two world wars and contributed their sons unreservedly to both. During World War I, an Austin County Council of Defense was organized, on November 23, 1917. The council vigorously promoted conservation and directed the rationing of flour, sugar, and other commodities. The county exceeded its subscription quota in the four Liberty Loan and Victory Loan bond sales. An Austin County chapter of the American Red Cross with branches in ten communities and a membership of more than 2,800 was formed on November 13, 1917, and worked to provide medical and social services to military personnel and their families and relief to poor people. Black residents of the county were enrolled in segregated Red Cross chapters in a number of towns, including Bellville and Bleiblerville. As hostility toward Germany mounted, the county's large German population fell under suspicion of disloyalty. The use of the German language was prohibited in public schools and non-English-speaking citizens of all ethnic backgrounds were pressured to use English exclusively in schools, churches, social organizations, and other venues. More than 860 county residents, including 275 blacks, served in the armed forces; thirty-one servicemen died during the war. Hundreds of Austin County's German-American residents, eager to demonstrate their loyalty to the United States, served in 311 branches of the military. There was virtually no resistance to conscription in the county and only two cases of desertion. The county's response to the call during World War II was at least as enthusiastic. But on the home front, Austin County was less directly affected by this conflict than were many other areas of the state. Undoubtedly the most profound impact of the Second World War upon the county was economic. Even as defense-related jobs in the nearby metropolis of Houston siphoned population from the county, the growth of that city created new markets for Austin County agricultural products and thus laid the foundation for postwar prosperity. Industry was also stimulated by proximity to Houston. The number of factories in the county increased from six in 1940 to thirty-one in 1982, and the number of employees in manufacturing rose from thirty-eight to 1,400. Much of the development occurred after 1970 as a result of the migration of heavy industry out of Houston into neighboring towns. By 1980 the Austin County industries with the largest employment, other than agribusiness, were general and heavy construction and steel.

Petroleum was discovered in Austin County in 1915, but the first significant production began only in 1927 with the opening of the Raccoon Bend oilfield northeast of Bellville. Soon other finds were made near Bellville, New Ulm, and Orange Hill. From the end of World War II until 1980 the county's annual production of crude oil seldom fell below a million barrels and occasionally approached three million. Although output finally declined during the eighties, by 1990 more than half a million barrels of oil and several million cubic feet of natural gas were still being produced in the county annually. In 1980, 15 percent of the county's workers were employed in manufacturing, 13 percent in agriculture, 23 percent in trade, and 14 percent in the professions; 15 percent were self-employed, and 33 percent were employed in other counties. The last figure reflects the county's accelerating suburbanization after the 1970s, as increasing numbers of white collar workers moved in from Houston.

Under the impact of agricultural depression in the first years of the twentieth century, the county's population fell more than 14 percent between 1900 and 1910, to 17,699. Although it managed to grow almost 7 percent during the brief agricultural revival in the decade of the First World War, the population declined over the next forty years to 13,777 in 1960. After remaining virtually unchanged in the succeeding decade it climbed 28 percent between 1970 and 1980, before rising another 12 percent in the next decade, to stand at 19,832 in 1990. By the early years of the twentieth century Sealy had surpassed Bellville to become the county's largest town, a position it maintained throughout the rest of the century.

Politically, Austin County has demonstrated a certain independence. Although the Democratic party[qv] has been dominant since the end of Reconstruction, the Republicans have managed an occasional surprise. In the presidential election of 1880 Republican James Garfield triumphed in the county over former Union general Winfield Scott Hancock, an accomplishment repeated by James S. Blaine in 1884 and William McKinley in 1896. Although familiar third-party movements such as those of the Greenbackers and Populists made little headway in Austin County—the latter especially tainted by suspicions of nativism—in 1920 German-American voters threw the county decisively to the little-known American party[qv] of James E. Ferguson.[qv] With the sole exception of the election of 1964, Austin County voted Republican from 1948 through 1988. The overwhelming majority of voters, nevertheless, remain registered Democrats, and few non-Democrats have won state or local elections in the county. Exceptions to this generalization include victories by Republican senatorial candidate John Tower[qv] in 1966, 1972, and 1978, and Republican gubernatorial candidate William Clements in 1978 and 1986.

BIBLIOGRAPHY: Julia Lange Dinkins, *The Early History of Austin County* (M.A. thesis, Southwest Texas State University, 1940). Noel Grisham, *Crossroads at San Felipe* (Burnet, Texas: Eakin Press, 1980). Corrie Pattison Haskew, *Historical Records of Austin and Waller Counties* (Houston: Premier Printing and Letter Service, 1969). Terry G. Jordan, *German Seed in Texas Soil: Immigrant Farmers in Nineteenth-Century Texas* (Austin: University of Texas Press, 1966). Ruby Grote Ratliff, *A History of Austin County, Texas, in the World War* (M.A. thesis, University of Texas, 1931). *Charles Christopher Jackson*

AUSTIN *DAILY BULLETIN*. The *Daily Bulletin*, published at Austin between November 27, 1841, and January 18, 1842, was a small, two-column, four-page paper that appeared daily except Sunday at a subscription rate of $1.50 a month. The *Bulletin*, printed at the office of the Austin *City Gazette*[qv] and edited by Samuel Whiting[qv] and briefly in 1841 by Charles DeMorse,[qv] contained notes on proceedings of the House of Representatives, editorial comments, and a few local-interest items. A paper also called the Austin *Daily Bulletin* was published daily except Sundays in 1936 by the United Publications of Texas and on Sundays as the Austin *Sunday Review*.

BIBLIOGRAPHY: Joe B. Frantz, Newspapers of the Republic of Texas (M.A. thesis, University of Texas, 1940). Mary Glasscock Frazier, Texas Newspapers during the Republic (March 2, 1836–February 19, 1846) (M. Journ. thesis, University of Texas, 1931). Marilyn M. Sibley, *Lone Stars and State Gazettes: Texas Newspapers before the Civil War* (College Station: Texas A&M University Press, 1983).

AUSTIN *DAILY TEXIAN*. The *Daily Texian* began publication in Austin on November 13, 1841. The paper continued the Austin *Texas Sentinel*,[qv] which began in 1840. Greenberry H. Harrison[qv] established the *Texian* as a journal of Senate activities but gave space to the affairs of both houses of Congress. The *Daily Texian* had four double-column pages, measuring 6½ by 11½ inches. It ran forty-seven issues before stopping publication on February 2, 1842. The paper was also published in a weekly edition.

BIBLIOGRAPHY: Joe B. Frantz, Newspapers of the Republic of Texas (M.A. thesis, University of Texas, 1940). Mary Glasscock Frazier, Texas Newspapers during the Republic (March 2, 1836–February 19, 1846) (M. Journ. thesis, University of Texas, 1931). Douglas C. McMurtrie, "Pioneer Printing in Texas," *Southwestern Historical Quarterly* 35 (January 1932).

AUSTIN DAM AND SUBURBAN RAILWAY. What later became the Austin Dam and Suburban Railway was originally built by the city of Austin in 1891 and ran from the city to the site of Austin Dam, a distance of 4.75 miles. The Austin Dam and Suburban was chartered on July 16, 1895, and purchased the line from the city of Austin for $43,500. The railroad was electrified and operated as a streetcar line through Austin to a pleasure park near the dam. In the spring of 1899 an additional 1.5 miles of track was constructed. After the destruction of Austin Dam by a flood in April 1900, the railroad ceased operations until May 1904. The company was sold at foreclosure on June 7, 1902, and acquired by George J. Gould three days later. Under the provisions of an ordinance approved June 10, 1903, the company abandoned and removed its tracks from certain streets and acquired the right to operate what remained as a steam railroad. Service over the Austin Dam and Suburban was provided by the International and Great Northern Railroad Company, whose successor acquired the line in 1923. On March 1, 1956, the company, along with its parent, was merged into the Missouri Pacific Railroad Company. *George C. Werner*

AUSTIN FEMALE ACADEMY. G. C. Baggerly, pastor of the First Baptist Church, opened the Austin Female Academy in Austin on October 21, 1850. In 1851 the school occupied a new building on Pecan Street (later Sixth Street) and added a "thorough collegiate course." Baggerly asked the Baptist State Convention to send visitors to conduct annual examinations, but his request was declined. Although the Cherokee Baptist Association recommended the school,

Baggerly gave up his project and moved to Tyler in 1853, when he could not convert the school into a Baptist institution.

BIBLIOGRAPHY: Aloise Walker Hardy, A History of Travis County, 1832–1865 (M.A. thesis, University of Texas, 1938). Willie Madora Long, Education in Austin Before the Public Schools (M.Ed. thesis, University of Texas, 1952). Carl Bassett Wilson, History of Baptist Educational Efforts in Texas, 1829–1900 (Ph.D. dissertation, University of Texas, 1934). *Lura N. Rouse*

AUSTIN FEMALE COLLEGIATE INSTITUTE. Austin Female Collegiate Institute, established by Rev. B. J. Smith, was opened in Austin in 1852. Classes met in the Presbyterian church until 1855, when the school moved to a building previously used by the Austin Female Academy[qv] at the corner of Pecan (later Sixth) and Guadalupe streets. By 1856 the school employed seven teachers and had boarding students as well as day students; 125 students enrolled in 1857. The school had chiefly Presbyterian patronage but received state funds from 1858 through 1862. The institute continued to operate throughout the Civil War and Reconstruction,[qqv] although enrollment fell and the faculty declined from seven to five between 1860 and 1869. The school probably closed in the early 1870s.

BIBLIOGRAPHY: Frederick Eby, *The Development of Education in Texas* (New York: Macmillan, 1925). Aloise Walker Hardy, A History of Travis County, 1832–1865 (M.A. thesis, University of Texas, 1938). Willie Madora Long, Education in Austin Before the Public Schools (M.Ed. thesis, University of Texas, 1952). *Louise Kelly*

AUSTIN *FREEMAN'S PRESS*. The Austin *Freeman's Press* was published in 1868, first as the *Freedman's Press* and then briefly as the *Freeman's Press*. An issue appeared simultaneously in Austin and in Galveston on October 24 of that year. *Diana J. Kleiner*

AUSTIN *GOLD DOLLAR*. The Austin *Gold Dollar* was one of the first black newspapers west of the Mississippi and one of forty-eight commercial black newspapers published in Texas between 1870 and 1900. It was founded in August 1876 in the Wheatsville area of Austin by Jacob Fontaine.[qv] Copies are extremely scarce, and records on circulation are scanty, but the *Gold Dollar* certainly existed in 1878 and maybe as late as 1880. The newspaper emphasized needs of freed slaves—family ties, education, frugality, moral and religious instruction, the discipline of youth, and racial justice. It struggled with black illiteracy and poverty, and supported the political and social causes of its founder, a leader in the Republican and Greenback parties[qqv] in Travis County. Fontaine named his paper for a gold dollar given him by his sister Nelly Miller in 1872, when they were reunited in Mississippi after a separation caused by slavery[qv] twenty years before. Fontaine earned sixty dollars to start the newspaper in his home, a structure set afire by arsonists in August 1879 but designated an Austin landmark in August 1977. The *Gold Dollar* was revived shortly in 1979–80 with federal funds, in order to help renew and preserve a nearby black neighborhood, Clarksville, where Fontaine founded the Sweet Home Missionary Church in 1877.

BIBLIOGRAPHY: Jacob Fontaine III and Gene Burd, *Jacob Fontaine* (Austin: Eakin Press, 1983). Charles William Grose, Black Newspapers in Texas, 1868–1970 (Ph.D. dissertation, University of Texas at Austin, 1972). *Gene A. Burd*

AUSTIN HISTORY CENTER. The Austin History Center, the local history and information division of the Austin Public Library, is an extensive research collection of both primary source materials and published materials that document Austin and Travis County. It is located in the former central library building at 810 Guadalupe Street, a 1933 limestone structure designed by Hugo Kuehne in the Italian Renaissance style. The building, which occupies a half-block site overlooking Wooldridge Park, was remodeled in 1959 and renovated in 1983. It is a Texas historic landmark and is listed on the National Register of Historic Places. The collection was begun in 1955 as part of the reference section of the library, became a separate division known as the Austin–Travis County Collection in 1961, and became known as the Austin History Center in 1983. The collection grew to include (in 1995) more than 12,000 books, 2,500 linear feet of manuscripts, 700,000 photographs, 22,000 clipping files, 900 periodical titles, 1,000 maps, 26,000 architectural drawings, and 4,000 video, audio, and electronic recordings. Significant collections of primary source materials include the papers of Texas governor Elisha M. Pease[qv] and his family, suffragist Jane Y. McCallum,[qv] and civic leader Walter E. Long,[qv] as well as the Trueman O'Quinn O. Henry Collection and the Chalberg Photography Collection. The center serves as the depository for historical Travis County records under the Texas State Library's Regional Historical Resource Depository program and as the official archives for city of Austin records. Since 1991 it has also overseen the Records Management Program for the city of Austin. One of the earliest and now one of the largest local history collections in Texas, the Austin History Center was directed by Katherine Drake Hart until 1975, by Audray Bateman Randle from 1975 to 1989, and subsequently by Biruta Celmins Kearl. The center is funded by tax money through the city of Austin; in 1995 the operating budget was $449,388 and the staff numbered fourteen full-time-equivalent positions. The center provides assistance to researchers in person, over the telephone, and by mail. It mounts two or three exhibits each year from materials in its collection and contributes regular articles to the Austin *American-Statesman*.[qv] With the assistance of its citizen support group, the Austin History Center Association, some of the center's collections have been published in its own imprint, the Waterloo Press. Among these have been *An Epitome of My Life, Civil War Reminiscences; Lucadia Pease and the Governor; Letters: 1850–1857;* and *Austin and Travis County; a Pictorial History, 1839–1939*. The association also publishes a biannual newsletter, *Austin Archives*.

Biruta Celmins Kearl

AUSTIN LYCEUM. The Austin Lyceum was planned in October 1839 and organized in February 1840, when President E. L. Stickney presided over its first formal meeting. A charter, the first of its kind granted by the Republic of Texas,[qv] was secured on February 5, 1841; it stated that the purpose of the Lyceum was the cultivation of the minds of the young men of Austin. Membership fees and dues were to fund a library and museum. According to the minutes, eighteen members attended the first meeting; by the end of April 1840 the membership had risen to forty-two. A total of fifty names appear in the extant minutes; the members included lawyers, merchants, doctors, printers, and newspapermen. Meetings featured either a debate on a political or literary topic or a lecture or essay delivered by a member. The organization was dissolved on April 15, 1841. It surrendered its charter to the Texas secretary of state, provided that the money in the treasury should go to the family of county judge J. W. Smith, who had been killed by Indians; the Lyceum sold its other property at auction. The Austin Lyceum was the forerunner of other such groups chartered at Galveston in 1845, at Houston in 1848, and at Brownsville in 1849. Attempts in 1849 and in 1850 to reorganize the Austin group were unsuccessful.

BIBLIOGRAPHY: Louise Jarrell, The Austin Lyceum, 1839–1841 (M.A. thesis, University of Texas, 1941). *Julia L. Vivian*

AUSTIN *NEW ERA*. The *New Era*, a weekly newspaper, was published irregularly by Jacob Cruger and Joel Miner[qqv] from July 23, 1845, until August 28, 1845. It was primarily a journal of the Convention of 1845,[qv] fifteen of the sixteen columns of one issue being devoted to convention proceedings.

Another *New Era*, also at Austin, was announced as early as October 20, 1845, but did not appear until January 1846. John G. Chalmers,[qv] its publisher, described the *New Era* as a successor to the

Austin *City Gazette.*[qv] The name indicated the new era of statehood after annexation.[qv] The paper probably lasted until December 1846.

BIBLIOGRAPHY: Joe B. Frantz, Newspapers of the Republic of Texas (M.A. thesis, University of Texas, 1940). Mary Glasscock Frazier, Texas Newspapers during the Republic (March 2, 1836–February 19, 1846) (M. Journ. thesis, University of Texas, 1931). Marilyn M. Sibley, *Lone Stars and State Gazettes: Texas Newspapers before the Civil War* (College Station: Texas A&M University Press, 1983).

AUSTIN AND NORTHWESTERN RAILROAD. On April 29, 1881, the Austin and North Western Rail Road Company was incorporated to build a line from Austin to a connection with the Texas and Pacific at Abilene, along with branch lines including one to a point on the Rio Grande. The capital was $3 million, and the general office was at Austin. Members of the first board of directors were J. A. Rhomberg, J. K. Graves, and F. T. Walker, all of Dubuque, Iowa; A. H. W. McNeal of Asealoosa, Iowa; and Dr. M. A. Taylor, Rudolph Bertram, Leander Brown, Francis B. Forster, and W. H. Westfall, all of Austin.

The company was able to construct only 106 miles of track. The initial sixty miles of narrow-gauge track between Austin and Burnet opened in May 1882. However, the line did not prove profitable and was placed in receivership in October 1883, with Rhomberg serving as receiver. It was acquired by W. B. Isham, acting for the bondholders, in 1885, and in 1888 it was reorganized under the original charter as the Austin and Northwestern Railroad Company. The railroad carried all of the granite from Granite Mountain,[qv] nearly 16,000 carloads, used to build the state Capitol.[qv] Several cars derailed near Brush Creek in Travis County, and granite blocks can still be found in the streambed. The company extended its line to Marble Falls by using the charter of the Granite Mountain and Marble Falls City Railroad to build the 2.35 miles from Granite Mountain.

The railroad was sold to C. W. Holloway in 1890, and came under the control of the Houston and Texas Central (Southern Pacific) the following year. The line was converted to standard gauge during the summer of 1891, and an extension from Fairland in Burnet County to Llano, in Llano County, was completed in June 1892.

The Austin and Northwestern was profitable throughout the latter half of the 1880s and the 1890s; most of its income was generated by the transport of mineral resources. In 1891 the road showed a profit of $26,862. Three years later, in 1894, it grossed $252,002, of which $102,698 was profit. In 1893 a two-mile spur was built to the Bessemer-Oliver Iron Mine. The market failed to develop, however, and the railroad's profits declined; in 1898 the Austin and Northwestern grossed only $151,820, and operating expenses totaled $136,629. The Bessemer-Oliver Iron Mine spur was abandoned in 1902.

In 1901 the state legislature approved the merger of the Austin and Northwestern into the Houston and Texas Central, which occurred on August 22 of that year. As a condition of the merger, a new passenger terminal was constructed at Austin, and the line was extended from Burnet to Lampasas in 1903. The Lampasas line was abandoned in 1951. In 1986 the Southern Pacific, as successor to the Houston and Texas Central, sold the former Austin and Northwestern as well as trackage between Giddings and Austin to the city of Austin and Capitol Metro. Freight service over the line was leased to RailTex, Incorporated, a short-line railroad company based in San Antonio. Operation of the new Austin and Northwestern Railroad began on August 15, 1986. The capital was initially $1,000, but in 1989 it was raised to $100,000. The principal place of business is Austin. The members of the board of directors were Bruce M. Flohr and Robert R. Lende, both of San Antonio; Fred E. Hamlin of Junction City, Oregon; William P. Ludwig, Jr., of Austin; and Ramsey Clinton of Burnet. In 1990 the line reported revenues of less than $5 million; it hauled nonmetal materials, building materials, scrap paper, and beverages.

George C. Werner

AUSTIN AND OATMANVILLE RAILWAY. The Austin and Oatmanville Railway Company was chartered by the Capitol Syndicate (*see* XIT RANCH) on November 5, 1883, to connect Kouns, a station on the International and Great Northern Railroad five miles south of Austin, with Oatmanville (now the Austin suburb of Oak Hill). The road was built to haul limestone for use in the building of the Capitol.[qv] Although the limestone was unsuitable for the exterior of the building, stone from the quarry was used for the foundation and basement walls, cross walls, and backing for the exterior walls as well as elsewhere in the structure. The capital stock was $100,000. Members of the first board of directors were Abner Taylor and Charles B. Farwell, of Cook County, Illinois; Amos C. Babcock, of Fulton County, Illinois; and John T. Brackenridge, Gustav Wilke,[qqv] A. P. Wooldridge, and W. D. Williams, all of Austin. In 1884 the railroad built six miles of track between Kouns and the quarry at Oatmanville at a cost to the building contractor of $35,000 for grading and bridging, while the International and Great Northern spent $24,100 for rails and cross-ties. Before the end of 1884 nearly 280,000 cubic feet of limestone had been delivered from the Oatmanville quarry. The line was abandoned and the rails removed in 1888.

Nancy Beck Young

AUSTIN PRESBYTERIAN THEOLOGICAL SEMINARY. Austin Presbyterian Theological Seminary, in Austin, opened its doors on October 1, 1902, at Ninth and Navasota streets. The Synod of Texas of the Presbyterian Church[qv] in the United States had appointed a board of trustees that in 1900 appointed Thornton Rogers Sampson[qv] the first president. He had to raise his own salary plus $100,000 as an endowment, put the property (formerly the Stuart Seminary[qv] for young ladies) in readiness, engage a faculty, and encourage candidates for the ministry to matriculate. The initial collection for a library was derived from the books of the Austin School of Theology.[qv] The enabling gift of $75,000 to the endowment was made by Sarah C. (Mrs. George) Ball of Galveston. Later the synods of Arkansas, Oklahoma, and Louisiana of the Presbyterian Church, U.S., joined in the ownership and control of the seminary.

Sampson, on the advice of his physician, resigned from the office of president in December 1904 but continued his duties as professor. By May of 1906 he was taking the lead in arranging for the seminary to move to its present location at 100 East 27th Street, nearer the campus of the University of Texas. The initial 5¼-acre plot at the new site was bought for $5,029 in 1906. In March 1908 the premises were occupied. The first buildings included a refectory, the bequest of the late Governor Francis R. Lubbock,[qv] and a 3½-story dormitory–classroom–administration building later to be known as Sampson Hall.

Robert Ernest Vinson[qv] was president from 1909 to 1916. When Vinson became president of the University of Texas, the choice of the board for president of the seminary was Neal Larkin Anderson, but when Anderson found the seminary's finances nearly exhausted he returned to the Southeast. The chairman of the faculty, Thomas White Currie,[qv] who was also secretary of the University YMCA, was put in charge of the seminary properties while the rest of the faculty and student body became absorbed in the war effort.

A faculty was assembled and students registered again by September 29, 1921. The buildings that had been rented were gradually reoccupied. In 1922 Currie became president of the seminary, a post he held until his death in 1943. The chapel was completed in the spring of 1942.

The fourth president, who came to the post in 1945, was David Leander Stitt. In addition to the original 5½ acres, the campus had been enlarged by property east of Speedway Street. During Stitt's tenure more property was added, Sampson Hall was razed, and the property east of Speedway was sold. New apartments for single and married students were built and administration and classroom accommodations provided by the construction of the Trull and McMillan buildings. Also a handsome library was provided and later named for David L. Stitt and his wife Jane.

After Stitt's resignation in 1971, Prescott Harrison Williams, Jr., became the fifth president. He served until 1976 and was succeeded by Jack Martin Maxwell. During Maxwell's administration the seminary received a bequest of more than $11 million from the estate of Miss Jean Brown of Hot Springs, Arkansas. Maxwell ended his service at the seminary in 1984 and was succeeded in 1985 by Jack L. Stotts, a native of Dallas, who had come from the presidency of McCormick Seminary in Chicago.

By 1985 the campus had been enlarged to about ten acres. The land and the improvements were worth $10 million, the endowments $34 million. Scholarships and grants-in-aid were available. Foreign students were encouraged by scholarships offered through the World Council of Churches, the World Alliance of Reformed Churches, and other such bodies. Austin Seminary maintained reciprocal relations with the Episcopal Theological Seminary of the Southwest[qv] in Austin and with Wartburg Seminary of the American Lutheran Church in Dubuque, Iowa. Austin Seminary is accredited by the Southern Association of Colleges and Schools and by the Association of Theological Schools in the United States and Canada. Since 1983 it has been owned and controlled by the Synod of the Sun of the Presbyterian Church (U.S.A.). During the middle 1980s the student body averaged about 200. The resident teaching faculty numbered about fifteen. The seminary offered master of divinity, master of theology, and doctor of ministry degrees. Proximity to the campus of the University of Texas at Austin afforded opportunities for allied academic and cultural pursuits.

Among graduates of the seminary who became missionaries abroad was John Walker Vinson (class of 1906), who was killed by bandits in China in November 1931. Alumni who became presidents of Presbyterian theological seminaries include Thomas W. Currie, David L. Stitt, James I. McCord (Princeton), and C. Ellis Nelson (Louisville). Rachel Henderlite, the first woman to become an ordained minister of the Presbyterian Church in the United States, joined the faculty in 1965. Most alumni became pastors in Presbyterian congregations in the Southwest. A historical marker was placed at the seminary on February 17, 1989, to commemorate the life of Rebecca Kilgore Stuart Red.[qv] Mrs. Red owned and taught the Stuart Female Seminary at the old Ninth Street location, which eventually became today's seminary. Austin Presbyterian School of Theology had 22 faculty and 300 students for the 1992–93 regular term plus 80 for the 1992 summer session with 110 extension or continuing-education students.

BIBLIOGRAPHY: Thomas White Currie, Jr., *Austin Presbyterian Theological Seminary: A Seventy-fifth Anniversary History* (San Antonio: Trinity University Press, 1978).

Thomas W. Currie, Jr.

AUSTIN *RAMBLER*. The Austin *Rambler*, a weekly newspaper published in Austin by George W. Morris,[qv] first appeared in March 1841. After only four or five issues the paper was discontinued, but it was revived and appeared again on September 28, 1858, with William Carleton[qv] as editor and publisher. According to family records, Carleton moved the paper to Lockhart in 1859 and continued it there for a year before ill health forced him to discontinue publication.

BIBLIOGRAPHY: Joe B. Frantz, Newspapers of the Republic of Texas (M.A. thesis, University of Texas, 1940). Mary Glasscock Frazier, Texas Newspapers during the Republic (March 2, 1836–February 19, 1846) (M. Journ. thesis, University of Texas, 1931). Marilyn M. Sibley, *Lone Stars and State Gazettes: Texas Newspapers before the Civil War* (College Station: Texas A&M University Press, 1983).

AUSTIN SCHOOL OF THEOLOGY. The Austin School of Theology, an institution in Austin for training Presbyterian ministers, was founded by Richmond Kelly Smoot, pastor of the Southern Presbyterian Church in Austin, and Robert L. Dabney.[qv] Smoot began using his study as a classroom for one student in 1882. In 1884 Dabney joined him in teaching, and they used the basement of the Presbyterian church for classes until a small building was constructed to house the college. When the institution ceased operation in 1895 it had trained forty-four ministers. The school's assets were turned over to the Synod of Texas and subsequently utilized by the Austin Presbyterian Theological Seminary.[qv]

BIBLIOGRAPHY: William Angus McLeod, *Story of the First Southern Presbyterian Church, Austin, Texas* (Austin, 1939?). William Stuart Red, *A History of the Presbyterian Church in Texas* (Austin: Steck, 1936).

William A. McLeod

AUSTIN *SIX-POUNDER*. The *Six-Pounder* is listed in a checklist of Texas newspapers as being published in Austin in June 1840. Since the only reference to the paper is a mention in the Austin *City Gazette*[qv] for June 10, 1840, it is possible that the title was the *Gazette's* nickname for another newspaper.

BIBLIOGRAPHY: Joe B. Frantz, Newspapers of the Republic of Texas (M.A. thesis, University of Texas, 1940). Mary Glasscock Frazier, Texas Newspapers During The Republic (March 2, 1836–February 19, 1846) (M. Journ. Thesis, University Of Texas, 1931).

AUSTIN *SOUTHERN INTELLIGENCER*. The first issue of the Austin *Southern Intelligencer* appeared on August 19, 1856. The publishers were William Baker and Irving Root, and the editor was George W. Paschal.[qv] The *Southern Intelligencer* was published every Wednesday under the masthead motto, "Nothing extenuate, nor set down aught in malice." A prospectus published November 19, 1856, states that the paper's "uniform object will be to give the earliest local and general interesting intelligence to every class of its readers whether their tastes and pursuits be agricultural, mechanical, professional or literary." Anthony B. Norton[qv] assumed editorial control of the paper in 1860, and a break in its publication occurred when he moved to Ohio during the Civil War.[qv] The final issue under his editorship was February 22, 1862. Both of the early editors of the *Southern Intelligencer* were antisecessionist supporters of Sam Houston[qv] and the Union. The *Southern Intelligencer* was revived in July 1865 by Frank Brown[qv] and James A. Foster and was printed for about sixteen months. The plant was then sold to Alfred E. Longley and Morgan C. Hamilton,[qv] who began publishing the Austin *Republican*.

BIBLIOGRAPHY: Mary Starr Barkley, *History of Travis County and Austin, 1839–1899* (Waco: Texian Press, 1963). Frank Brown, Annals of Travis County and the City of Austin (MS, Frank Brown Papers, Barker Texas History Center, University of Texas at Austin).

Karen Warren

AUSTIN *SPY*. The Austin *Spy* is listed in a checklist of Texas newspapers as being published in Austin in June 1840. The *Spy* was associated with the humor of Dr. Richard F. Brenham,[qv] who came to Texas from Kentucky in 1836, fought in the Texas Revolution,[qv] and later practiced medicine. Since the only reference to the paper is a mention in the Austin *City Gazette* for June 10, 1840, however, it is possible that the title was the *Gazette's* nickname for another newspaper.

BIBLIOGRAPHY: Joe B. Frantz, Newspapers of the Republic of Texas (M.A. thesis, University of Texas, 1940). Marilyn M. Sibley, *Lone Stars and State Gazettes: Texas Newspapers before the Civil War* (College Station: Texas A&M University Press, 1983).

Diana J. Kleiner

AUSTIN *STATE GAZETTE*. The *State Gazette* was one of the most influential newspapers in Texas from the pre–Civil War era (*see* ANTEBELLUM TEXAS) until Reconstruction.[qv] The paper was founded as the *Tri-Weekly State Gazette* and first published in Austin by William H. Cushney[qv] on August 25, 1849. Its publication schedule varied, from triweekly to semiweekly, weekly, and daily. Its various titles also included *Texas State Gazette* and *Weekly State Gazette.* The paper was known for its strong states'-rights positions and as a voice of the state Democratic party,[qv] a reputation it established during political battles with Sam Houston[qv] in the turbulent times before secession.[qv]

The *Gazette*'s editorial policies were to "oppose a high protective tariff, internal improvements at government expense and a banking system." The paper also proclaimed itself to be "thoroughly democratic" politically. It followed the standard procedure in gathering most of its news by exchanging information with the twenty-nine other newspapers in Texas at that time. Editorially it promoted states' rights, called for the reopening of the slave trade in Africa, opposed the Compromise of 1850,[qv] and blamed the North for the slave problem because of northern reaction to the fugitive-slave laws.

John F. Marshall[qv] purchased the *Gazette* in 1854 and became its best-known editor. He devoted most of his editorials to politics, sectionalism, and support of slavery.[qv] Marshall aimed his most candid remarks against Sam Houston, and his crusade against Houston probably influenced the outcome of the gubernatorial election of 1857. Houston suffered the only election loss of his life in his defeat by Democratic nominee Hardin R. Runnels.[qv] Marshall attributed Houston's 1859 comeback to a conspiracy among postmasters who, he claimed, withheld copies of the *Gazette* until after the 1859 election. But Marshall's strident advocacy of reopening the slave trade probably gave Houston the victory by splintering the Democratic party.

The *Gazette* also fought other battles with competing newspapers over politics and government printing contracts. A principal competitor during the 1850s was the *Texas State Times,* one of whose publishers was John S. (Rip) Ford.[qv] The *Times* supported Houston and other Unionist candidates when the American party[qv] (Know-Nothings) were active. But Ford had a change of heart and left the *Times* once he could no longer tolerate Houston's lack of support for "Southern institutions." Ford then served as editor pro tem of the *Gazette* in 1858 during one of Marshall's lengthy absences.

After Abraham Lincoln was elected president in 1860, the *Gazette* was one of the first papers to demand that Governor Houston call the legislature into session and secede before Lincoln took office. In the November 24, 1860, issue, the editorial declared, "It is clear that nine-tenths of our people are determined to sever their political connection with the Northern States, and that Texas will secede from the Union." On December 8 a *Gazette* editorial called for an election of delegates to meet in special session on January 28 to pass articles of secession. Most of the other newspapers in the state joined the call.

After the Secession Convention[qv] and Houston's refusal to take the oath of office for the Confederacy, the *Gazette* continued its political attacks on the former governor. Marshall was killed in his first battle, that of Gaines' Mill, Virginia (June 27, 1862), and the *Gazette* continued publishing a smaller version throughout most of the Civil War.[qv] It served as an official spokesman for the Southern cause and state government. The Gazette continued supporting the Democratic party through Reconstruction and the restoration of the party in power in the 1870s. It ceased publication by 1879.

BIBLIOGRAPHY: Larry Jay Gage, Editors and Editorial Policies of the *Texas State Gazette,* 1849–1879 (M.A. thesis, University of Texas, 1959). Larry Jay Gage, "The Texas Road to Secession and War: John Marshall and the Texas State Gazette, 1860–1861," *Southwestern Historical Quarterly* 62 (October 1958). Robert A. Nesbitt, Texas Confederate Newspapers, 1861–1865 (M.A. thesis, University of Texas, 1936). W. S. Oldham, "Colonel John Marshall," *Southwestern Historical Quarterly* 20 (October 1916). Marilyn M. Sibley, *Lone Stars and State Gazettes: Texas Newspapers before the Civil War* (College Station: Texas A&M University Press, 1983).

Patrick Cox

AUSTIN STATE HOSPITAL. The Austin State Hospital was established as the State Lunatic Asylum by act of the Sixth Legislature in 1856 and began operation in May 1861 with twelve patients. It is the oldest hospital in Texas for the care and treatment of the mentally ill. Initially, asylums in Texas were operated under individual boards of five members, appointed by the governor, with each board developing its own standards. In 1913 the legislature placed its mental hospitals under individual boards of managers. In January 1920 state hospitals were placed under the Board of Control.[qv] The name of the Austin asylum was changed to Austin State Hospital in 1925. In 1949 control of the hospital was transferred to the Board for Texas State Hospitals and Special Schools.[qv] In 1993 it was operated by the Texas Department of Mental Health and Mental Retardation.[qv]

In 1942 a state dairy and hog farm was established on 308 acres owned by the state, seventeen miles from Austin, to provide milk and meat for Texas mental institutions. An additional 1,140 acres was leased. The Austin State Hospital had from twenty-five to thirty patients stationed at the farm in 1945. That year the hospital had 2,810 beds, 2,774 patients, and 360 nonmedical staff employees, and the medical staff consisted of the superintendent, assistant superintendent, nine assistant physicians, and one dentist. In 1940 the hospital was designated an independent school district and began providing education for school-age psychiatric patients. By 1961 it had a rated capacity of 2,608 patients, and service had been expanded by outreach clinics and follow-up services for furloughed and discharged patients. In 1964 it expanded, within its own grounds, to incorporate patients from the Texas Confederate Home.[qv]

The Austin State Hospital had an average daily population in 1968 of 3,313, and 900 elderly patients were maintained on furlough in private facilities. The institution provided surgical services for residents and for persons from the Austin State School, the Travis State School,[qqv] and the Texas Confederate Home (before it was closed in 1967). An adult out-patient clinic was operated by the hospital, with referrals to the Travis County Mental Health and Mental Retardation Clinic and to various county community health centers around the state. Admissions of younger patients, alcoholic patients, and drug abusers increased in 1970, and the average daily census was 1,994. By 1986–87, with changes in the philosophy of treatment, there was an average of only 711 inmates, while the Austin MHMR center served 7,100. By 1992–93 inmates had decreased to 450, and the MHMR center served 9,000. In 1990 the hospital served thirty-four counties in Central Texas with an annual admittance of 3,500 patients but a daily average of only 518. In 1990 renovation was begun on the original administration building, the third oldest state building in Texas. It was expected to take from four to six years and to cost $4 million.

BIBLIOGRAPHY: Mikel Jean Fisher Brightman, An Historical Survey of the State of Texas' Efforts to Aid the Mentally Ill and the Mentally Retarded (M.A. thesis, University of Texas at Austin, 1971).

John G. Johnson

AUSTIN STATE SCHOOL. The Austin State School, in Austin, Texas, is a ninety-five-acre residential and training facility for adults with developmental disabilities. It is administered by the Texas Department of Mental Health and Mental Retardation.[qv] In 1991 the school had a staff of 1,505, more than two-thirds women, which served about 460 individuals at the west Austin campus and 615 in a fourteen-county region extending south and west of Travis County; about 315 of the off-campus population were under age three. Most campus residents had severe or profound retardation or multiple disabilities.

In 1915 the Texas legislature passed a bill to establish the state's first facility for the retarded, some of whom had been housed at the Austin State Lunatic Asylum until then. Two years later the State Colony for the Feebleminded opened on Austin's outskirts with an initial admission of sixty-five females, ages six to forty-nine. In 1925 it was renamed Austin State School. Dr. John Bradfield, superintendent from 1917 to 1936, faced severe shortages in dormitory space and in personnel trained to teach persons with developmental disabilities, but he worked to build a residential training program. By 1927 a school building, for academic and vocational training on-site, had been added to the facilities. More capable residents were assigned by sex to domestic or farming chores. Beginning in 1930, adult clients also manufactured mattresses and brooms at the campus and assisted in the butcher shop, which provided meat for all state institutions in the area. In 1934 many male residents of Austin State School were moved to the school's new farm on the eastern edge of Travis County, to work in dairy, poultry, and truck farming. This farm, originally called Austin State School Farm Colony, was separated from the Austin school and renamed Travis State School[qv] in 1957. With the farm serving only men and boys until 1973, Austin State School continued to house mostly women and children. Because Bradfield, like most people of his time, thought that persons with mild or moderate retardation easily gravitated toward promiscuity and criminal behavior, he believed that closed, sex-segregated institutions were the most appropriate permanent homes for them. Therefore, during the 1930s and early 1940s, the "colonies" were managed restrictively. Buildings generally were kept locked, employees lived on-site, and residents' families had minimal access during visits.

The post–World War II period witnessed changing treatment philosophies for an expanding population of individuals with developmental disabilities. Texas public schools began offering special-education classes, allowing some youths with disabilities to remain in their home communities. As the National Association for Retarded Citizens urged a shift from custodial care in isolated settings to social, occupational, and life-skills training for community integration, Austin State School administrators worked to improve facilities and programs for residents during the 1950s and 1960s. Yet overcrowding and understaffing limited the number of residents receiving such training. Despite the establishment of four more Texas training schools between 1946 and 1963 and acquisition of a seventy-five-acre annex campus for the Austin State School in 1960, contemporary reports indicate that in 1958 only 400 employees provided twenty-four-hour service for 1,900 individuals at the school. By 1965, 765 employees supervised 2,500 residents, and hundreds still awaited admission. Meanwhile, in 1963 the school implemented racial integration in its hiring and admission policies. The Texas Mental Health and Mental Retardation Act in 1965 authorized county-based training centers for persons with mild or moderate developmental disabilities (*see* MENTAL HEALTH), so Austin State School increasingly served those with more severe retardation or multiple disabilities. To assist the school's residents preparing to move into the community, teachers from the Texas Commission for the Blind[qv] established training for blind children and the Texas Rehabilitation Commission[qv] helped to form specialized vocational workshops at the campus in 1967.

In the 1970s federal requirements for intermediate-care facilities mandated higher state allocations for the school, to provide residents with better housing, staffing ratios, and residential and vocational skills training. In 1972 the ASPEN residential unit began offering specialized training for residents with aggressive or self-destructive behavior. By 1974 the entire facility had 1,400 residents and 1,100 staff members. During the 1970s crowding was eased by construction of several new state schools and by completion of sixteen new one-story homes and a large residence for persons with mobility impairments at the Austin State School. Meanwhile, interdisciplinary staff teams developed individual program plans for residents' development. The school also added more trainers overall and initiated special services for the hearing impaired at the annex campus. Vocational training services were extended to include 450 residents, the largest increase ever. By 1977 the school's Community Services division had set up developmental training centers in Kerrville, San Marcos, Seguin, and New Braunfels and had launched its first community-based center for infant training. Such programs enabled people with developmental disabilities to stay in their home communities and increased the normalcy of their lives compared to that of those still in large residential training facilities. In 1983 residents and future residents of Austin State School were included in the *Lelsz v. Kavanaugh* resolution and settlement, which resulted from a 1974 class-action suit seeking an improved life and treatment for state school residents. To comply with the settlement, the school implemented many changes during the next decade, to help those served achieve as normal a life as possible within their abilities. By 1986 about 700 individuals resided in and received training at the school, while 540 were served in off-campus communities in Central Texas. As more persons with mild or moderate retardation moved to community placements, school administrators reorganized and retrained most residential staff to educate and care for those residents who required more intensive supervision. When the *Lelsz v. Kavanaugh* implementation settlement was signed in 1987, giving the defendants more specific guidelines, it called for Austin State School to increase its staff-to-client ratio within three years and to comply with standards of the Accreditation Council on Services for Persons with Developmental Disabilities.

During the early 1990s, the school consistently achieved ACDD accreditation; it was only the second Texas state intermediate-care facility to comply with the council's 600 standards. By 1988, 1,450 staff members were serving about 550 residents at the facility and several hundred more in Central Texas communities. The Community Services division added eighteen employees to the total 1991 Austin State School workforce of 1,505 to initiate services for about seventy disabled residents of nursing homes in the school's catchment area. With the 1992 final resolution of the *Lelsz v. Kavanaugh* suit, Austin State School increased its emphases on community placement and respite programs, rather than routine institutionalization. The school obtained more commercial work contracts, allowing it to change most prevocational training programs to vocational operations, thereby paying more residents wages for performing even simple jobs. By 1993 the vocational services staff had moved the school's sheltered workshops from the annex campus to a local commercial site. All of these measures contributed to the gradual normalizing of residents' lives to resemble those of the general populace. Meanwhile, Austin State School began routinely admitting individuals transferred from Travis State School in preparation for the latter school's closing.

BIBLIOGRAPHY: Austin *American-Statesman*, November 1, 1990. *Campus Echo*, November 15, 1976, March 1980. *Mental Illness and Mental Retardation: The History of State Care in Texas* (Austin: Texas Department of Mental Health and Mental Retardation, 1975).

Sherilyn Brandenstein

AUSTIN *TEXAS DEMOCRAT*. The Austin *Texas Democrat* was established when John Salmon Ford and Michael Cronican[qqv] purchased the *Texas National Register*[qv] in 1845 and moved it to Austin. The paper was published both as a weekly and a semiweekly beginning January 21, 1846. The semiweekly appeared during sessions of the legislature, and the weekly the remainder of the year through the third volume. Ford and Cronican dissolved their partnership when Ford left to fight in the Mexican War,[qv] and Joel Miner[qv] and Samuel Cummings replaced him on December 15, 1847. In 1848 Cronican took his printing press and equipment to San Antonio, leaving Miner and Cummings as proprietors of the *Democrat*. The weekly continued publication until sometime in 1863, when the two owners sold it to William Cushney,[qv] who changed its name to the *Texas State Gazette*.[qv]

Another Austin *Texas Democrat* was published by Charles G. Norton from February 26, 1937, until April 30, 1937, and continued by the Austin *Times and Texas Democrat*.

BIBLIOGRAPHY: Mary Glasscock Frazier, Texas Newspapers during the Republic (March 2, 1836–February 19, 1846) (M. Journ. thesis, University of Texas, 1931). Marilyn M. Sibley, *Lone Stars and State Gazettes: Texas Newspapers before the Civil War* (College Station: Texas A&M University Press, 1983). *Diana J. Kleiner*

AUSTIN *TEXAS SENTINEL.* Two Austin newspapers were called the *Texas Sentinel.* The first, nominally a weekly, began publication on January 15, 1840. Jacob W. Cruger and George W. Bonnell[qqv] were its publishers until Cruger withdrew from the firm on July 28, 1840. Bonnell continued alone until December 1840, when Cruger and Martin Carroll Wing[qv] became owners. The paper changed the spelling of its name to *Texas Centinel* on April 22, 1841. The paper was bitterly opposed to Sam Houston[qv] in policy and published slander on his personal conduct. During sessions of Congress the paper was a semiweekly, and extra editions were published, such as that of July 1841 on the "Texian Loan." The *Sentinel* appeared at least through November 11, 1841, after which Greenberry H. Harrison[qv] acquired the paper and split it into the *Daily Texian*[qv] and *Weekly Texian* (*see* NATIONAL VINDICATOR).

BIBLIOGRAPHY: Joe B. Frantz, Newspapers of the Republic of Texas (M.A. thesis, University of Texas, 1940). Mary Glasscock Frazier, Texas Newspapers during the Republic (March 2, 1836–February 19, 1846) (M. Journ. thesis, University of Texas, 1931). Marilyn M. Sibley, *Lone Stars and State Gazettes: Texas Newspapers before the Civil War* (College Station: Texas A&M University Press, 1983).

AUSTIN *TEXAS SENTINEL.* The second *Texas Sentinel* was published weekly in Austin beginning in June 1857, after William G. O'Brien and Company purchased it from John S. Ford.[qv] The paper described itself as "an independent, anti-Caucus, anti-Austin clique Democratic journal" and succeeded the *Texas State Times.* Fenton M. Gibson[qv] served as editor. P. W. Humphreys, A. G. Compton, and Xavier B. DeBray[qv] succeeded O'Brien before the paper was discontinued in July 1858.

BIBLIOGRAPHY: Joe B. Frantz, Newspapers of the Republic of Texas (M.A. thesis, University of Texas, 1940). Mary Glasscock Frazier, Texas Newspapers during the Republic (March 2, 1836–February 19, 1846) (M. Journ. thesis, University of Texas, 1931). Marilyn M. Sibley, *Lone Stars and State Gazettes: Texas Newspapers before the Civil War* (College Station: Texas A&M University Press, 1983).

AUSTINIA, TEXAS. Austinia was a settlement on the shores of Moses Lake, on the west bank of Galveston Bay in Galveston County. The exact date of its establishment is unknown. The Congress of the Republic of Texas,[qv] in the first Texas railroad charter, chartered the Brazos and Galveston Railroad Company on May 24, 1838, to make turnpikes, crossings, and a railroad from Austinia on Galveston Bay to Bolivar on the Brazos River. The site was located on Dollar Point in the Stephen F. Austin[qv] league, now within the bounds of Texas City. Austinia was to be the headquarters for the company. After Austin's death in 1836 his sister, Emily Austin Perry,[qv] became sole owner of the Dollar Point league and platted the townsite. She deeded to her son, William J. Bryan, and George L. Hammeken[qqv] part of the townsite to aid in financing the construction of the railroad. James F. Perry[qv] and Hammeken were commissioned to sell subscriptions to the 1,500 Austinia shares. On February 1, 1839, Bryan and Hammeken bought the rest of Austinia and the Dollar Point peninsula. The board of directors elected Hammeken president and Perry treasurer.

Although the location appeared excellent for both a town and a railroad, little improvement occurred. Changes in the route and charter caused the company to direct its efforts to building a canal instead. The developers abandoned Austinia, and the railroad was never built. Part of the property remained in the hands of the family. Guy M. Bryan,[qv] a nephew of Stephen F. Austin, developed there the 1,200-acre Bay Lake Ranch, where he lived from 1865 to 1871. His heirs sold the property to fig growers in the 1920s.

BIBLIOGRAPHY: Galveston *Daily News,* February 24, 1980. Andrew Forest Muir, "Railroad Enterprise in Texas, 1836–1841," *Southwestern Historical Quarterly* 47 (April 1944). *Priscilla Myers Benham*

AUSTONIA, TEXAS. Austonia (Astonia, Astoria) is on Farm Road 984 fifteen miles southeast of Waxahachie in southern Ellis County. Thomas Alston built the first house in the community in 1876 and became the first postmaster when Astonia received a post office in 1879 in his general store. Baptist, Methodist, and Christian groups shared a union church there, and forty students attended school in the church building. In 1890 Astonia had a population of ten, several businesses, three churches, and a school. In 1900 the post office was moved to Rankin, a mile to the west. In the 1980s the community appeared on maps as Austonia, but only the Austonia church and cemetery remained in the area.

BIBLIOGRAPHY: Edna Davis Hawkins et al., *History of Ellis County, Texas* (Waco: Texian, 1972). *Lisa C. Maxwell*

AUSTONIO, TEXAS. Austonio, on State Highway 21 fourteen miles southwest of Crockett in western Houston County, was established before 1900 and named Pearville. In 1930 the community sponsored a contest to choose a new name. The winning entry came from Ruth Tucker, who suggested the name Austonio, a combination of Austin and San Antonio. A consolidated school serving Austonio, Ash, Mapleton, and Creek opened in 1931, and a post office was established the following year. The community prospered in the years just before World War II,[qv] and in 1940 it reached a peak at a population of 150 and four stores. After 1945, however, the town began to decline. The school was consolidated with the Lovelady school in 1964, and the post office was discontinued in 1971. Most of the businesses had closed by the late 1980s. In 1990 Austonio had a population of thirty-seven.

BIBLIOGRAPHY: Armistead Albert Aldrich, *The History of Houston County, Texas* (San Antonio: Naylor, 1943). Houston County Historical Commission, *History of Houston County, Texas, 1687–1979* (Tulsa, Oklahoma: Heritage, 1979). *Eliza H. Bishop*

AUSTRIANS. Although there are no Austrian settlements in Texas, the state has attracted numerous emigrants from the Hapsburg empire and, later, from the Republic of Austria. The history of Austrian nationality has long been problematic and confusing. During the nineteenth century, "Austrian" usually referred to the German-speaking residents of the western portion of the Hapsburg empire, generally those living in the traditional hereditary lands of the Hapsburg dynasty, now roughly the area within the borders of the present Republic of Austria. However, the term has been used both as a geographic and ethnic description. Thus, the German-speaking residents of Bohemia, Moravia, and Galicia were sometimes referred to as Austrian, and the designation "Austrian" was even occasionally used—incorrectly—to refer to anyone living within the Hapsburg empire, regardless of nationality. Moreover, German-speaking Austrians have frequently been referred to or identified themselves simply as Germans. United States census forms in the nineteenth century, which listed national origin, did little to clear up the confusion, since those who came from the region were alternately listed as Germans, Bohemians or "other." Because of this it is impossible to known precisely the number of Austrian immigrants to America, although it was certainly much smaller than that of other Central European groups.

Numerous residents of the multinational Hapsburg empire immigrated to Texas during the nineteenth and early twentieth centuries, including sizable numbers of ethnic Czechs, Poles, and Italians.[qqv] After 1845, small numbers of German-speakers from the region began moving to the state and often settling in predominantly German towns and areas. The 1860 census for Comal County, for example, shows that some two dozen Austrians (including German-speakers from Bohemia) were living there, among them four farmers, a stockman, a wagoner, and three laborers. Other Austrian immigrants to Texas included Jan Reymershoffen, a former legislator in his homeland, who operated an import-export business in Galveston, and Moritz O. Kopperl,[qv] who served as a legislator and president of the Texas National

Bank. Perhaps the most prominent immigrant from Austria in antebellum Texas[qv] was Vienna-born George Bernard Erath,[qv] who fought in the Texas Revolution[qv] and later, as a legislator, played an important role in promoting the annexation[qv] of Texas by the United States. After the Civil War,[qv] the flow of immigration from the Hapsburg empire (after 1867 officially known as Austria-Hungary), increased. Among the most prominent emigrants from the region were Rudolf Gunner, who had served for a time as a naval officer in Mexico under Maximilian, settled in Dallas, and in 1895 established a thriving bookstore; Michael Perl, a former assistant army surgeon from Vienna who lived for a time in Mexico City and Matamoros before settling in Houston, where he practiced medicine and carried out horticultural experiments; and George Dullnig, who founded the Alamo National Bank and helped establish the San Antonio and Gulf Railroad. Anthony Francis Lucas[qv] (born in Hvar, Dalmatia), mining engineer and erstwhile Austrian naval officer, discovered fabled Spindletop.

In 1916 a small group of immigrants from Austria-Hungary in San Antonio, led by Ernst Raba, formed the Österreichisch-Ungarischer Verein, or the Austro-Hungarian Association. The group sent clothes, groceries, and even cattle fodder back to their former homeland, held periodic picnics and dinners, and occasionally put on stage shows; it continued to exist until the 1950s. More recent immigrants from Austria include Theodore W. Alexander, producer of annual German plays at Texas Tech from 1947 to his retirement in 1984, George W. Hoffman, cofounder of the department of geography at the University of Texas at Austin, and Paul Weiss, a researcher and pioneer in nerve regeneration. In 1990 some 2,500 Austrians lived in Texas. San Antonio and Houston both had Austrian clubs. So well assimilated are most contemporary Austrian Texans that many profess no awareness of compatriots, past or present, in the state.

BIBLIOGRAPHY: Rudolph L. Biesele, *The History of the German Settlements in Texas, 1831–1861* (Austin: Von Boeckmann–Jones, 1930; rpt. 1964). *The Czech Texans* (San Antonio: University of Texas Institute of Texan Cultures, 1972). Minetta Altgelt Goyne, *Lone Star and Double Eagle: Civil War Letters of a German-Texas Family* (Fort Worth: Texas Christian University Press, 1982). Glen E. Lich, *The German Texans* (San Antonio: University of Texas Institute of Texan Cultures, 1981).

Minetta Altgelt Goyne

AUSTWELL, TEXAS. Austwell is on Farm Road 774 near Hynes Bay in northeastern Refugio County. It was founded by Preston R. Austin[qv] in 1911; the community name combines the first syllable of Austin's name and the last syllable of that of his partner, Jesse C. McDowell. The farsighted Austin installed a water system with large cypress mains in every street and a fire plug on almost every corner. The community served as the terminus of the Austwell branch of the St. Louis, Brownsville and Mexico Railway. In 1912 Austwell acquired its own post office and erected a small wharf, but the bay was too shallow for any except lighter navigation. Austwell was incorporated by an election held on September 10, 1914. Around that time a town newspaper, the Austwell *Dispatch*, was established. On December 7, 1914, local Masons chartered the Lieuen M. Rogers[qv] lodge. The town was badly damaged by a storm in 1919 and almost destroyed by another on August 31, 1942. The population had dwindled to 300 in 1944. In 1988 Austwell listed a population of 280. In 1990 the population was 189.

BIBLIOGRAPHY: Hobart Huson, *Refugio: A Comprehensive History of Refugio County from Aboriginal Times to 1953* (2 vols., Woodsboro, Texas: Rooke Foundation, 1953, 1955).

Hobart Huson

AUTHON, TEXAS. Authon is near Farm Road 113 twelve miles northwest of Weatherford in northwest Parker County. Settlement began at the site in the late 1870s. The community applied for a post office in 1882 under the name Arthur, but postal authorities substituted Authon. By 1890 the estimated seventy-five residents were served by three churches, a public school, a blacksmith shop, and a general store. Area farmers processed their cotton at the town's steam gin. Other products included grain, livestock, and hides. Postal service was discontinued in 1904. In 1990 the population was five.

BIBLIOGRAPHY: John Clements, *Flying the Colors: Texas, a Comprehensive Look at Texas Today, County by County* (Dallas: Clements Research, 1984). Gustavus Adolphus Holland, *History of Parker County and the Double Log Cabin* (Weatherford, Texas: Herald, 1931; rpt. 1937).

David Minor

AUTRY, MICAJAH (1794?–1836). Micajah Autry, Alamo defender, son of Theophilus and Elizabeth (Greer) Autry, was born in Sampson County, North Carolina, in 1794 or 1795. During the War of 1812 he volunteered for service against the British at age eighteen. He marched to Wilmington, North Carolina, as a member of a volunteer company and later joined the United States Army at Charleston, South Carolina. He served until 1815. Afterward, when his bad health compelled him to quit farming, he became a teacher. Autry moved to Hayesboro, Tennessee, in 1823 and took up the study of law. In 1824 he married a widow, Martha Wyche Putny Wilkinson. They raised two children of their own and Martha's daughter by her first marriage. In 1828 or 1829 Autry was admitted to the bar at Nashville. He practiced law in Jackson, Tennessee, from 1831 to 1835 in partnership with Andrew L. Martin. In Tennessee Autry started an unsuccessful mercantile business with his law partner.

During business trips to New York and Philadelphia, he heard of opportunities in Texas. In 1835 he left his family and slaves in the care of Samuel Smith, his stepdaughter's husband, and set out for Texas by steamboat from Nashville, Tennessee. By January 14, 1836, he was in Nacogdoches, where he enlisted in the Volunteer Auxiliary Corps of Texas. His correspondence indicates that he set out for Washington-on-the-Brazos with David Crockett[qv] and others under the command of Capt. William B. Harrison.[qv] He arrived in Bexar with his company on or about February 9, 1836, and entered the Alamo with the garrison under the command of Lt. Col. William B. Travis[qv] on February 23. He died in the battle of the Alamo[qv] on March 6, 1836. Autry was an amateur poet, writer, artist, and musician. A letter to his wife, dated February 11, 1834, is on display at the Alamo.

BIBLIOGRAPHY: Adele B. Looscan, "Micajah Autry, A Soldier of the Alamo," *Southwestern Historical Quarterly* 14 (April 1911). Phil Rosenthal and Bill Groneman, *Roll Call at the Alamo* (Fort Collins, Colorado: Old Army, 1985). Amelia W. Williams, A Critical Study of the Siege of the Alamo and of the Personnel of Its Defenders (Ph.D. dissertation, University of Texas, 1931; rpt., *Southwestern Historical Quarterly* 36–37 [April 1933–April 1934]).

Bill Groneman

AVAILABLE SCHOOL FUND. The Available School Fund is made up of the money set aside by the state from current or annual revenues for the support of the public school system. As early as 1883 a maximum twenty-cent state ad valorem school tax was adopted to maintain such a fund. There are two major revenue sources for the fund: earnings from the Permanent School Fund[qv] and 25 percent of fuel tax receipts. The fund does not receive annual appropriations by the legislature from the general revenue fund. It is prorated to school districts according to scholastic population. In 1968 a constitutional amendment passed that called for the elimination of the state ad valorem tax over a period of several years; by 1975 this had been accomplished. In 1950–51 the Available School Fund contained $95,225,919. Since then the income of the state fund has increased significantly with a resultant increase in the rate per student distributed to public schools. In the 1969–70 fiscal year the Available School Fund disbursed $288,059,478.32; this amounted to a payment rate per student of $117.65. In 1994 the Legislative Budget Board estimated that the fund amounted to $1.3 billion. It was projected that the fund would distribute $350 per pupil during the 1994–95 school year. The fund also devotes annual revenue to textbook purchases. *See also* FOUNDATION SCHOOL PROGRAM FUND, LAND APPROPRIATIONS FOR EDUCATION.

BIBLIOGRAPHY: Henry H. Goodman, *The Appropriation and Distribution of School Funds in Texas* (Austin, 1922). Roswell W. Rogers, *The Texas School Funds* (Chicago, 1911). *Texas Almanac*, 1994–95.

AVALON, TEXAS. Avalon was a school community west of the site of Roby on Alkali Creek in central Fisher County. It was established in the late 1880s. The school seems to have been initially known as Alkali, although two separate districts, Avalon and Alkali, were reported in 1890. At any rate, the school was known as Avalon after absorbing the nearby Fairview district around 1890. Sometime later Avalon was moved north and reestablished on land given by W. Eaton on the Clear Fork of the Brazos River. While in this second location, the settlement was occasionally referred to as Chickenfoot. The school was used as a church and meetinghouse by area settlers. The attempt to merge the Avalon school with the Roby school in 1924 was defeated in an election. The Avalon district was then divided by Roby and Rotan in 1925.

BIBLIOGRAPHY: Lora Blount, A Short History of Fisher County (M.A. thesis, Hardin-Simmons University, 1947). E. L. Yeats and E. H. Shelton, *History of Fisher County*, (n.p.: Feather, 1971).

Charles G. Davis

AVANT PRAIRIE, TEXAS. Avant Prairie is off State Highway 179 four miles southeast of Teague in southwestern Freestone County. By 1848 a few settlers, including Charles Kilgore, had moved to the area. In 1852 more families from Alabama, including the Comptons, Highs, and Blains, settled there. The community was first called Durham; later the name was changed to Avant or Avant Prairie. It was probably named after Durham Avant, who owned the grant for the land in the area. A post office was established for the community in January 1853, with James W. Brewer as postmaster, but it closed by November of that year. The Sunshine Church was organized in 1854, and a general store was established by D. K. Compton in 1870. The post office was reestablished in 1884 but closed again in 1885, when mail was sent to Luna. In 1903 Avant Prairie's white school had an enrollment of eight pupils, and the black school had fifty-seven. In the 1930s the community had a school, two churches, two cemeteries, and a large number of scattered dwellings. By 1965 it had a church, a school, a cemetery, and three dwellings. In the late 1980s the church and cemetery remained at the site.

BIBLIOGRAPHY: Phillip Dale Browne, The Early History of Freestone County to 1865 (M.A. thesis, University of Texas, 1925). Freestone County Historical Commission, *History of Freestone County, Texas* (Fairfield, Texas, 1978). *Chris Cravens*

AVATON, TEXAS. Avaton was on Little Cypress Bayou nine miles from Longview and twenty miles west of Marshall in western Harrison County. It had a post office from 1884 to 1902. In 1896 the community had a cotton gin and gristmill, a district school, and Methodist and Baptist congregations. Avaton was gone by the 1940s.

Mark Odintz

AVAVARE INDIANS. The Avavare Indians were an otherwise unidentified group for which Álvar Núñez Cabeza de Vaca[qv] became medicine man in South Texas in 1528. They lived west of the Mariames and Yguaces, with whom they traded although they spoke a different language.

BIBLIOGRAPHY: Frederick Webb Hodge, ed., *Handbook of American Indians North of Mexico* (2 vols., Washington: GPO, 1907, 1910; rpt., New York: Pageant, 1959). *Margery H. Krieger*

AVENUE L BAPTIST CHURCH. The Avenue L Baptist Church, one of the oldest black churches in Texas, grew from the slave membership of the First Baptist Church of Galveston. The slaves were organized under the name Colored Baptist Church in 1840 by the Rev. James Huckins.[qv] By the early 1850s they had left First Baptist to worship in a separate building, known as the Africa Baptist Church. In 1855 First Baptist trustees Gail Borden, Jr., John S. Sydnor,[qqv] and Huckins purchased land from the Galveston City Company for use by the congregation. After the Civil War[qv] the property was formally deeded to the members, who were reorganized under Rev. Israel S. Campbell[qv] as the First Regular Missionary Baptist Church in 1867. The present name was adopted during the pastorate of Rev. P. A. Shelton around 1903. Other prominent pastors have included Rev. H. M. Williams (1904–33), who served as moderator of the Lincoln District Baptist Association and had the task of rebuilding the church after the Galveston hurricane of 1900;[qv] Rev. G. L. Prince (1934–56), who later served as president of the National Baptist Convention of America and Mary Allen College in Crockett, Texas; and Rev. R. E. McKeen (1957–78), who also served as moderator of the Lincoln District Association. Construction of the present brick church began in 1916 and was completed at a cost of $18,000. In 1973 the church began renovations that included the installation of air-conditioning and heating and the refurbishing of the stained-glass windows. A historical marker was placed at the church site in 1981. Rev. Andrew W. Berry was elected pastor in 1984. In 1993 the church had more than 200 members.

BIBLIOGRAPHY: Truett Latimer, Avenue L Missionary Baptist Church (MS, Marker Files, Texas Historical Commission, Austin).

AVERITT, TEXAS. Averitt was on Lipan Creek adjacent to Hess, south of Mereta in east central Tom Greene County. In 1931 the school had two teachers and offered nine grades. In 1936 the school was called Hess-Averitt School on state highway maps, and in 1939 the average attendance was ten. By the 1980s the community had disappeared.

BIBLIOGRAPHY: Julia Grace Bitner, The History of Tom Green County, Texas (M.A. thesis, University of Texas, 1931).

Diana J. Kleiner

AVERY, TEXAS. Avery is on the Missouri Pacific Railroad and U.S. Highway 82 sixteen miles southeast of Clarksville in eastern Red River County. When the Texas and Pacific was being constructed through the county in the 1870s, the managers of the railroad planned a station at the site and named it Douglass. Settlement in the community was slow because the surrounding area was so sparsely populated. When a correspondent of the Clarksville *Standard*[qv] visited Douglass in early 1881 he found a collection of families living in tents. Later that year, when Isaac Bradford and his partner opened their general store, a post office was established there, and the name of the town was changed to Isaca. In 1902 the name was changed to Avery, in honor of Ed Avery, the first railway station agent. In 1884 the population was estimated at thirty, and by 1896 it had increased to forty-eight. By 1900 Avery had three churches, a school, and a population of 176. During the first decade of the twentieth century cotton ginning was an important local industry. By 1914 the town had two banks; a weekly newspaper, the *Avery News*, published by H. H. Morgan; and a population estimated at 500. The population reached its highest point in the late 1920s with a reported 800 residents, before falling sharply to a low of 300 in the early 1930s. Avery was incorporated before the 1940 census, when it reported 477 residents. The population subsequently remained relatively stable. The 1980 census recorded 520 residents, and in 1986 nine businesses were reported. In 1990 the population was 430.

BIBLIOGRAPHY: Clarksville *Standard*, April 15, 1881. Fred I. Massengill, *Texas Towns: Origin of Name and Location of Each of the 2,148 Post Offices in Texas* (Terrell, Texas, 1936). *Red River County, Texas* (Marshall, Texas: Texas and Pacific Railway Land Department Office, ca. 1872). *Cecil Harper, Jr.*

AVERY CANYON. Avery Canyon is the bed of an intermittent stream through rugged Chihuahuan Desert terrain to the northeast of the Chisos Mountains in Big Bend National Park.[qv] The head of the canyon, two miles southwest of the park headquarters at Panther Junction (at 29°20′ N, 103°14 W), lies on alluvial fans against the high Chisos Mountains. Following a generally northeasterly course, the canyon then crosses Cretaceous clay and sandstone and becomes a deep defile with walls up to 250 feet high between Hannold Hill to the southeast and the Grapevine Hills to the northwest. At the end of a winding 16½-mile course the canyon empties into Tornillo Creek about one-quarter mile upstream from the U.S. Highway 385 bridge (at 29°25′ N, 103°09′ W). The area's biology is characteristic of the deep Chihuahuan Desert. For the most part, the land is sparsely vegetated; the most common plants include such shrubs as creosote bush and ocotillo and such semisucculents as lechuguilla and yuccas. There are also scattered grasses in the area, including gramas and fluffgrass. The desert scrub in turn shelters and supports the rich variety of animal and bird life typical of the Chihuahuan Desert. The name of the canyon derives from J. C. Avery, who was a rancher in this area of the low Big Bend country from 1901 to 1909.

BIBLIOGRAPHY: A. Michael Powell, "Vegetation of Trans-Pecos Texas," in *New Mexico Geological Society Guidebook* (Socorro, New Mexico: New Mexico Geological Society, 1980). David J. Schmidly, *The Mammals of Trans-Pecos Texas* (College Station: Texas A&M University Press, 1977).

AVES, CHARLES MARION (1881–1944). Charles Marion Aves, neurosurgeon and pioneer in industrial medicine, was born in Cleveland, Ohio, on November 14, 1881, the son of the Rev. Charles S. and Jesse (Hughes) Aves and the brother of Etheldreda Aves.[qv] His father was an Episcopal minister. The family moved to Texas in 1900, when Charles Aves was offered the position of rector at Trinity Episcopal Church in Galveston. Aves received his early schooling in Norwalk, Ohio, and Kenyon Military Academy. He attended Kenyon College and the University of Texas before entering the University of Texas Medical Branch, where he obtained an M.D. in 1907.

After an internship at John Sealy Hospital[qv] in Galveston, Aves completed a residency in neurosurgery at the Episcopal Hospital in Philadelphia. In 1911 he settled in Houston, where he practiced medicine and surgery until World War I.[qv] He accepted a commission as first lieutenant in the United States Army Medical Reserve Corps in 1916 and entered active service in June 1917 as a captain. After receiving special military training at Washington University and the Mayo Clinic, Aves was sent overseas as chief surgeon at an evacuation hospital in France. While in France he was promoted to lieutenant colonel and became commanding officer of the hospital. He returned to Houston in 1919.

Aves was one of the founders of Hermann Hospital[qv] in Houston and served as chief of staff there for many years. He was the founder of the medical department and chief surgeon for Humble Oil and Refining Company from 1919 (now Exxon Company, U.S.A.[qv]) until his death. He also served as neurological surgeon at Jefferson Davis Hospital, chief surgeon of Baytown Hospital, and surgical staff member at St. Joseph's Infirmary.

He was chairman of the Committee on Industrial Safety for the State Medical Association of Texas (*see* TEXAS MEDICAL ASSOCIATION) and a member of the Texas Surgical Society and the Harris County Medical Society. He was a member of the board of directors of the National Safety Council and a fellow of the American Medical Association and the American College of Surgeons. He was an Episcopalian and a Mason. Aves married Mrs. Ruby Lynn Arnim of Houston on May 15, 1915. They had two sons. He died of a cerebral hemorrhage at his home in Houston on April 25, 1944, and was buried in Forest Park Cemetery in that city.

BIBLIOGRAPHY: Galveston *Daily News*, April 26, 1944. *Texas State Journal of Medicine*, June 1944. *Patricia L. Jakobi*

AVES, ETHELDREDA BELLE (189?–1942). Etheldreda (Dreda) Aves, operatic soprano, was born in the 1890s in Norwalk, Ohio, the daughter of Rev. Charles S. and Jessie Olivia (Hughes) Aves. She was taken as a child to Galveston, where her father was rector of Trinity Episcopal Church. She first studied singing with H. T. Huffmeister, director of the Galveston Choral Club and organist at her father's church. Her father reportedly had "vigorous moral objections" to Dreda's singing in public, with the result that she sang only at church services until she left Texas. She attended the University of Texas in 1913–14, during which time Madame Ernestine Schumann-Heink, a renowned contralto, encouraged her to study in the East. Aves attended Columbia University in 1916 and studied for two years at the Damrosch Institute of Musical Art in New York.

She debuted with the De Foe Carlin Opera Company in the title role of *Carmen* in Baltimore in 1922. She sang for a season with the Havana Opera Company, toured with the San Carlo Opera Company in 1924 and 1925, and was a guest artist with the Philadelphia Civic Opera in 1927 and the Dresden Opera in 1928. Although she began her career as a contralto, with the advice and help of Vilonat, her last teacher, she became a dramatic soprano. Aves joined the Metropolitan Opera in 1927 and made her debut in Aïda in 1928. She remained with the Metropolitan through the end of the 1931–32 season and later sang with the San Carlo Opera, an American touring company. During her career she also appeared with the Friends of Music (New York), the Detroit Symphony Orchestra, the Cleveland Symphony Orchestra, and other groups. She moved from New York City to Buckeye Lake in Ohio in 1940 or 1941. She died on April 17, 1942, in the nearby town of Newark, after an illness of several months. Aves was survived by three brothers and a sister.

BIBLIOGRAPHY: *Alcalde* (magazine of the Ex-Students' Association of the University of Texas), April 1928. *Musical America*, April 25, 1942. New York *Times*, April 18, 1942. *Who Was Who in America*, Vol. 2.
Mary M. Standifer

AVES, HENRY DAMEREL (1853–1936). Henry Damerel Aves, Episcopal bishop, son of Frederick William and Frances Elizabeth (Damerel) Aves, was born on July 10, 1853, in Huron County, Ohio. He received a bachelor of philosophy degree from Kenyon College in 1878 and studied law at Cincinnati Law School from 1879 to 1880. In preparation for the ministry, he completed his B.D. degree at Bexley Hall in 1883 and his D.D. degree at Kenyon College in 1905. He married Mary Gertrude Smith on September 11, 1883; they had five children. Aves became a deacon in 1883 and a priest in 1884. He was rector of St. John's Church, Cleveland, Ohio, from 1884 to 1892 and of Christ Church, Houston, Texas, from 1892 to 1904. He was consecrated bishop of Mexico on December 14, 1904. Upon his retirement from the bishopric in 1923, he made his home in Seabrook, Texas, where he died on September 20, 1936.

BIBLIOGRAPHY: *Who Was Who in America*, Vol. 1.

AVIATION. The first people in Texas to fly, in the 1860s, were air-show balloonists and their passengers, although several inventors were also busy with plans for winged flying machines. The alleged flight of Jacob F. Brodbeck[qv] in 1865 has become a Texas legend. After the Wright brothers' controlled airplane flights in 1903, aeronautical progress generally was slow until 1909–10, when European aviation made rapid strides and the United States government acquired its first aircraft. Aerial demonstrations proliferated at sites across America, including Houston, where a Frenchman, Louis Paulhan, made the first airplane flight in the state on February 18, 1910. Flights in other Texas cities soon followed, and some Texans began building their own airplanes. Records of many of these projects are often imprecise, but one of the earliest Texans to fly appears to have been L. L. Walker, of Houston. He apparently flew his aircraft, a Bleriot monoplane, during October and November 1910. Several airplanes and fliers were active around the state before World War I,[qv] and at least two women, Marjorie and Katherine Stinson,[qqv] of San Antonio, became well-known pilots.

Military aviation had already begun to develop in Texas. Lt. Benjamin Foulois, a colorful pioneer pilot, arrived at Fort Sam Houston in February 1910, assembled the army's recently purchased Wright biplane, and took to the air on March 2, 1910. Three years later the newly established First Aero Squadron, with nine airplanes, was assigned to Texas City. After serving in other states, the First Aero returned to Texas in 1916 to support Gen. John J. Pershing[qv] in his pursuit of Francisco (Pancho) Villa[qv] into Mexico. In 1917 American entry into World War I brought the first of many military flight schools to Texas, where students appreciated the level terrain and year-round flying weather. In addition to Kelly and Brooks fields in San Antonio, facilities throughout the state trained thousands of fliers, mechanics, and other aviation personnel and established a legacy of military aviation. Texans such as Wiley Post, Howard Hughes,[qqv] and Douglas "Wrong Way" Corrigan posted records and made headlines during the 1930s. These events dramatized the role of aircraft in reducing time and distance and made Texans more inclined to utilize airplanes in a state where distances were vast and centers of population were far removed from each other and from other urban areas of the United States.

The first commercial line to serve Texas was National Air Transport, one of the private companies incorporated to take advantage of the Air Mail Act of 1925. On May 12, 1926, a National plane left Love Field[qv] in Dallas and headed for Chicago with the first air mail; passenger service was added in the fall of 1927. Braniff Airways, a regional carrier started by Thomas Elmer Braniff,[qv] made Love Field its principal operations and maintenance base in 1934 and eventually moved its home office from Oklahoma to Love Field, in 1942. Under the guidance of Cyrus R. Smith,[qv] of Austin, American Airlines routes through Dallas not only bolstered the area's reputation but also offered Texans rapid transportation to commercial centers on both coasts. Pan American offered international service from Brownsville to Latin America.

As a major agricultural state, Texas became a lively area of activity for crop dusters. Many operations like rice farming used aerial seeding, fertilizing, and dusting against insects. The rapid growth of surveying for oil leases in the booming Texas oilfields propelled Tobin Aerial Surveys of San Antonio into early prominence in the new industry of aerial photogrammetry. Around the "oil patch," with widely scattered operations and a lack of convenient all-weather roads, planes became standard tools of the trade for both corporations and wildcatters in a business noted for its aggressiveness.

During World War II[qv] geography and climate again made Texas a center for aeronautical training. The base at Corpus Christi became the world's largest naval air-training station; Randolph Field was the army air force's "West Point of the Air." At Avenger Field in Sweetwater, the Air Force carried out training for WASPS, the Women's Airforce Service Pilots,[qv] who flew thousands of warplanes from factories to airfields, towed aerial targets, and performed other functions. Some forty military fields in Texas turned out 45,000 pilots, 25,000 bombardiers, and 12,700 navigators. Moreover, the state became a major aircraft manufacturer; new plants employed thousands of workers. During the war years, two companies in Dallas and Fort Worth alone employed some 70,000 men and women who built 50,000 aircraft. Refineries in Texas were principal suppliers for high-octane gasoline used by Allied aircraft in every combat theater of the world.

In the postwar years, the general aviation sector (agricultural, business, and personal flying) rapidly developed throughout the state. As Texas industry grew, many businesses saw the need for rapid air travel to distant business centers from coast to coast. Scheduled air transport did not always offer convenient and timely schedules; for these reasons, business and corporate flying rapidly increased. In agriculture the long growing season and broad fields favored the development of such specialized agricultural aircraft as the trend-setting AG-1 at Texas A&M University, and Texas became a world leader in the design and production of such airplanes. Along the Gulf Coast, dozens of helicopters made their runs to offshore oil rigs, carrying relief crews, mail, groceries, repair parts, and myriad other cargos. In sprawling cities, especially in rush hours when accidents frequently occurred, the versatility of helicopters as ambulances was invaluable.

However, it was the growth of scheduled air travel that necessitated new urban airports. Houston Intercontinental opened in 1969; Dallas–Fort Worth Regional Airport opened in 1974. The convenience of air travel attracted much new business to the state. The airlines serving Dallas–Fort Worth, Houston, and other major cities reflected the revolution in aeronautics since 1945. Piston-engined transports gave way to jets in the 1960s, including long-range jumbo jets capable of nonstop flights to Europe from both DFW and Houston. In times past, when a European visit required at least two or three weeks of sailing on ocean liners, only the very wealthy could afford such luxuries of time and expense. The jets, with rapid travel and lower fares, brought a democratization of foreign and domestic travel.

In the mid-1980s Texas listed some 60,000 licensed pilots and 25,000 registered aircraft. There were 250 airline aircraft based in Texas, and fifty-five different airline companies served the state. But these numbers represented only a small part of the aerospace industry in Texas. Numerous military air bases annually pumped billions of dollars into the state's economy. The United States Air Force Air Training Command, headquartered at Randolph Air Force Base[qv] in San Antonio, trained more Air Force pilots than any other facility. The Naval Air Station at Corpus Christi was the second largest naval aviation center in the free world. After 1945 the Dallas–Fort Worth area, a major military complex, turned out bombers, fighters, and helicopters, as well as missile components and advanced electronics. Because these products played such a significant role in world affairs, such as the multinational production and sales agreements for the General Dynamics F-16 fighter, the aerospace industry helped keep Texans attuned to international economics and politics.

BIBLIOGRAPHY: E. C. Barksdale, *The Genesis of the Aviation Industry in North Texas* (Austin: University of Texas Bureau of Business Research, 1958). Roger Bilstein and Jay Miller, *Aviation in Texas* (Austin: Texas Monthly Press, 1985). *Roger Bilstein*

AVINGER, TEXAS. Avinger is on the Louisiana and Arkansas railway at the junction of State highways 49 and 155, eight miles southeast of Hughes Springs in southwestern Cass County. Hickory Hill, a settlement that began in the early 1840s, was located a mile south of the site of Avinger. A post office was established there in 1848 with Thomas M. Kimball as postmaster, and at its height it had a school house, two or three churches, a store, a gravelyard, a tannery, and several residences. In 1876 the East Line and Red River Railroad was built through the area, and a station was located at the current site of Avinger. Gradually the businesses began to relocate, and when the post office was moved in 1877 it was renamed Avinger in honor of Dr. H. J. Avinger, who operated the first store at the new location. The town became a shipping point for lumbermen and area farmers and by 1884 had two churches, a school, saw and grist mills, a gin, and a population of fifty. By 1892 the population had increased to 100, and by 1914 the town supported numerous businesses including a small bank and had an estimated population of 500.

The population of the town remained stable until the late 1920s; it rose from an estimated 505 in 1925 to an estimated 700 in 1929. By 1931, in the trough of the Great Depression,[qv] the population had dropped to an estimated 450. The town was incorporated in the 1930s. During World War II[qv] the United States Defense Corporation built the Lone Star Steel Plant[qv] a few miles west of Avinger. In 1949 the town began extensive renovations, in the hopes that the large nearby industry would encourage growth. Bonds were voted that built a new high school, water system, and sewer system. The town's antiquated crank telephone system was replaced by a dial system, and many of streets were paved. The population reached its height of 750 in 1960. In 1980 Avinger had a population of 671 and twenty-one rated businesses; by 1990 the number of residents had fallen to 478.

BIBLIOGRAPHY: Avinger *Citizen*, June 18, 1954. Vertical Files, Barker Texas History Center, University of Texas at Austin.

Cecil Harper, Jr.

AVOCA, TEXAS. Avoca is on State Highway 6 at the intersection of Farm roads 600 and 1636, eight miles southeast of Stamford in northeast Jones County. It was first called Spring Creek when it was founded in the early 1880s. The post office was established in 1893 and named Avo. With the construction of the Texas Central Railroad in 1900, J. L. Crostwaite moved his general store three miles to the track at Avo and changed the name of the new post office to Avoca. The population of the town reached a peak of 500 in 1908. Drought, depression, changing transportation patterns, and the appeal of neighboring towns later reduced Avoca's population. The town survived as a shipping point for livestock and cotton, but the population fell to 150 in 1940 and 121 in 1980. Tent show entertainer Harley Sadler[qv] was born in Avoca. The population in 1990 was still 121.

BIBLIOGRAPHY: Hooper Shelton and Homer Hutto, *The First 100 Years of Jones County* (Stamford, Texas: Shelton, 1978). Kathleen E. and Clifton R. St. Clair, eds., *Little Towns of Texas* (Jacksonville, Texas: Jayroe Graphic Arts, 1982). Fred Tarpley, *1001 Texas Place Names* (Austin: University of Texas Press, 1980).

Connie Ricci

AVONDALE, TEXAS. Avondale is sixteen miles northwest of Fort Worth at the intersection of U.S. Highway 287 and Farm Road 718 in northwestern Tarrant County. Its founding was associated with the extension of the tracks of the Fort Worth and Denver City Railway through the area in 1882. Rail officials surveyed and platted the townsite, which they named for its attractive location, and a village soon developed there. A post office opened in 1890. By 1910 it had a population of eighteen, and its school registered forty-six students and employed one teacher. In 1920 State Highway 81 bypassed the settlement, and the post office and the last store closed. The railroad depot closed in 1924. A 1936 map shows scattered dwellings and one business, and a 1976 highway map shows Avondale as a sparsely populated rural community.

BIBLIOGRAPHY: *Historic Resources Survey: Selected Tarrant County Communities* (Fort Worth: Historic Preservation Council for Tarrant County, 1990).

Brian Hart

AWALT, TEXAS. Awalt, among the earliest settlements in Gregg County, was probably founded in the late 1840s. It was located two miles south of Pine Tree Church near the site of the present western edge of Longview. The community was named for Solomon Awalt, the first minister of the Pine Tree Cumberland Presbyterian Church. A ferry known as Awalt's Ferry operated nearby on the Sabine River during the Civil War[qv] era. When the Texas and Pacific Railway was built through Gregg County in 1873 it bypassed the town, and most of the residents apparently moved to the new community of Willow Springs, on the railroad. Awalt had disappeared by 1900.

BIBLIOGRAPHY: Eugene W. McWhorter, *Traditions of the Land: The History of Gregg County* (Longview, Texas: Gregg County Historical Foundation, 1989).

Christopher Long

AXIS DEER. The axis deer, or chital (*Cervus axis* Erxleben), is native to the Indian subcontinent. It is considered to be the most beautiful of deer, with a bright reddish coat marked with rows of white spots that persist throughout life. Antlers of males are large but simple, usually with only three points. Adult males weigh up to 200 pounds and females 35 percent less. The axis deer was first introduced into Texas in the 1930s and now occurs in at least forty-five counties. Largest numbers occur on the Edwards Plateau,[qv] where the semiopen, dry scrub forest vegetation resembles that of its native habitat in India. Essential habitat components include water, woody vegetation for cover, and open areas for feeding. This deer is primarily a grazer, but its food habits are very general, and it can exist quite easily on forbs and woody browse. In contrast to the white-tailed deer, which typically eats only a few foods, the axis deer eats small quantities of a large variety of plant species. This broad-spectrum diet gives it an advantage in competition with other deer.

The reproductive activity of the axis occurs year-round, but most breeding occurs in June and July. Single fawns are born the following spring after a 7½-month gestation period. During the breeding period males bellow loudly and wander in search of receptive females. Females mature sexually and first breed at fourteen to seventeen months of age. Males are probably capable of breeding as yearlings but must achieve adult size to compete for females.

The basic social unit is a family group that consists of an older female and her offspring. A herd consists of two or more family groups. Other social groupings consist of loosely structured male herds and, between February and April, nursery herds composed of females with fawns. Vocalizations are important in axis deer society and one of the most noticeable characteristics of this animal.

Axis deer are more active by day than by night, with greatest activity occurring for two to three hours after dawn and again before dark. The size of the home range varies with habitat and averages 2½ square miles in the coastal live oak region. Axis deer do not seem to be territorial, but males fight, often with serious consequences, for possession of females.

In Texas the major predators of the axis are coyotes and bobcats, but predation does not seem to be serious. Axis deer are also remarkably resistant to disease, a fact that may help explain their success as introduced animals.

With few exceptions, axis deer are not regulated by game laws. They are landowners' property and may be bought, sold, or hunted at any time. Therefore, they are important in sports hunting and offer hunting opportunities at times when native species are not available. Ranchers stock them for this purpose, and this practice explains their wide distribution in the state. As a sporting animal, the axis deer provides a fine trophy. The meat is of excellent quality and lacks the strong game flavor sometimes associated with venison.

BIBLIOGRAPHY: Ernest D. Ables, ed., *The Axis Deer in Texas* (College Station, Texas: Texas A&M Agricultural Experimental Station, 1977). Al Jackson, "Texotics," *Texas Game and Fish*, April 1964. C. W. Ramsey, *Texotics* (Austin: Texas Parks and Wildlife Department, 1969).

Ernest D. Ables

AXSON, STOCKTON (1867–1935). Stockton Axson, university professor, the son of Samuel Edward and Margaret (Hoyt) Axson, was born in Rome, Georgia, on June 6, 1867. He attended Wesleyan University (Connecticut), where he received a B.A. (1890), an M.A. (1892), and an LHD (1914). He also attended Johns Hopkins University and Knox College before becoming a teacher of English at the University of Vermont in 1892. He was staff lecturer for the American Society for University Extension from 1894 to 1896, taught at Adelphi College in Brooklyn from 1896 to 1899, and from 1899 to 1914 was professor of English at Princeton University. Axson moved to Texas to teach at Rice Institute (now Rice University) in 1913. During his career he published numerous lectures and reviews. He also took an interest in government affairs through the influence of his brother-in-law President Woodrow Wilson. From 1917 to 1919 he was national secretary of the American Red Cross. He returned to Rice at the end of World War I[qv] and continued to teach there until his death, on February 26, 1935.

BIBLIOGRAPHY: Houston *Post*, February 27, 1935. Alan Dugald McKillop, "Stockton Axson," *Rice Institute Pamphlet* 24 (January 1937). *Who Was Who in America*, Vol. 1.

AXTELL, TEXAS. Axtell is on Farm Road 1330 between U.S. Highway 84 and State Highway 31, eight miles northeast of Bellmead in eastern McLennan County. It was established in 1881, when the Texas and St. Louis Railway laid track from Corsicana to Waco. A post office, called Axtell in honor of a railroad official, opened in 1882 with Edward P. Rino as postmaster. By the early 1890s Axtell had a population of 200, a gristmill and gin, two general stores, and a hotel. In 1896 Axtell schools had two teachers for eighty-five white students and one teacher for seventy-nine black students. The population had risen to 250. The Axtell State Bank opened in 1912 and provided an economic boost for local businesses by attracting customers from outlying areas. Population estimates for Axtell reached a peak of 400 in 1914. Severe storms and floods in the fall of that year damaged or destroyed crops and property throughout the region, making it impossible for many area farmers to meet their loan payments. The bank at Axtell was forced to close in 1914. In spite of this setback and the Great Depression[qv] a few years later, Axtell managed to hold its own as a small railroad town. The community became the focus of a rural high school district in 1915. The district grew to include the Billington and Watt common school districts of Limestone County and the Elk common school district of McLennan County. Population estimates for the Axtell community remained at 220 from the 1920s through the 1960s; a population of 105 was reported from 1970 through 1990. Axtell had three churches, a post office, and several businesses in the mid-1980s.

BIBLIOGRAPHY: Charles Leroy Hinkle, A History and Analysis of Rural Banking in McLennan County (M.S. thesis, Baylor University, 1959). Dayton Kelley, ed., *The Handbook of Waco and McLennan County, Texas* (Waco: Texian, 1972). William Robert Poage, *McLennan County Before 1980* (Waco: Texian, 1981). Vertical File, Texas Collection, Baylor University. *Vivian Elizabeth Smyrl*

AYALA SITE. The Ayala Site is located 1½ miles south of McAllen, on a fifteen-foot bluff on the north side of the Sardinas Resaca, an old channel of the Rio Grande. It is one of several cemeteries known from the Rio Grande valley. Almost all of these date to the Brownsville Complex and constitute a distinctive mortuary pattern with similar kinds of burials and grave offerings. The site was first discovered in 1948 during construction of a sewer trench on N. E. Ayala's farm. Several human burials were exposed. In July 1948 a University of Texas student, Jack Frizzell, visited the Ayala farm. He helped to uncover a total of eleven prehistoric burial sites. Except for one group burial, the remainder had been individual inhumations. There are two distinct silt (alluvial) layers at the site; the upper ("light silt") goes from the surface to about six feet below ground level, with the lower ("dark silt") beneath. All of the burials came from the light silt alluvium.

A number of ornaments were associated with the burials exposed in 1948. Burial 8, for example, had a necklace of ninety-four shell and bone beads. The group burial, comprising two adults and three children, included more bone and shell beads. Frizzell's excavations also recovered a number of stone tools and animal-bone remains, an indication that the Ayala site burials had been placed in midden deposits.

In 1952 another University of Texas student, Frederick Reucking, Jr., returned to the site. Rather than the hurried salvage work done by Frizzell, Reucking was able to lay out a grid and to excavate several units. His fieldwork was hampered, however, by haphazard digging by local people looking for a "treasure cave" believed to exist on the Ayala farm. This looting turned up additional archeological materials that Ruecking had to document. He apparently excavated seven burials, and he recorded numerous others uncovered by the looting. A plan of the site drawn by Ruecking shows the locations of a total of forty-four burials, including those reported by both Ruecking and Frizzell and those opened by the looters.

The artifacts found in the 1952 fieldwork, both by Ruecking and in the uncontrolled digging, were more varied then the assemblage found by Frizzell. These included a number of olive shell (*Oliva sayana*) beads and "tinklers" (shell bells). There were also numerous disk-shaped beads fashioned of conch shell. A dozen coyote canine teeth were found, all of which had been perforated for use either as pendants or as clappers to hang inside the olive shell tinklers. Other mortuary offerings included a large triangular conch-shell gorget and five rectangular bone pendants, two of which have engraved designs. A fragment of a large white-tailed deer antler was found with one burial, and a turtle shell was with another. The latter probably represents a rattle-type musical instrument.

Data from Frizzell and Ruecking suggest that the burial pits at Ayala were circular in outline and four to five feet deep. Most contained one individual, in a flexed position, with the forearms crossed or the hands adjacent to the face. Some of the burials may represent secondary ("bundle") burials. Red ochre, or hematite, had been placed with Burial 1, excavated by Frizzell. He also noted evidence of violent death for Burial 8 (a strong blow to the right side of the skull) and for Burial 10, with an embedded projectile-point fragment in one of the lumbar vertebrae.

The kinds of artifacts found with the Ayala Site burials are largely typical of the Brownsville Complex (from ca. A.D. 1400 to the time of Spanish contact). However, some of the burials may date to earlier, Archaic occupations of the area. Indeed, Ruecking observed that the lower levels of the midden appeared to him to be related to the Archaic period. The large number of burials may indicate the use of a preferred cemetery location by generations of hunters and gatherers, spanning the time from the Archaic into the Late Prehistoric (Brownsville Complex).

Other burial areas are known near the Ayala Farm. One of these is only a half mile upstream from the Ayala Site. A burial from that site, found at a depth of six feet, was accompanied by many of the same types of artifacts found at the Ayala Site. These included disk-shaped beads, tubular bone beads (including some made from sections of human long bones), olive-shell beads and tinklers, and a large conch-shell pendant.

A number of the burials and many of the artifacts from the Ayala Site are curated at the Texas Archeological Research Laboratory, on the J. J. Pickle Research Campus of the University of Texas at Austin. However, Frizzell and Ruecking both recorded numerous skeletal remains and artifacts that remained the property of the landowner or other individuals in the McAllen area.

BIBLIOGRAPHY: T. N. Campbell and Jack Q. Frizzell, "Notes on the Ayala Site, Lower Rio Grande Valley of Texas," *Bulletin of the Texas Archeological and Paleontological Society* 20 (1949). Michael B. Collins, Thomas R. Hester, and Frank A. Weir, "The Floyd Morris Site (41CF2), a Prehistoric Cemetery Site in Cameron County, Texas," *Bulletin of the Texas Archeological Society* 40 (1969). Thomas R. Hester, *Digging into South Texas Prehistory* (San Antonio: Corona, 1980). Thomas R. Hester and Frederick Ruecking, Jr., "Additional Materials from the Ayala Site, a Prehistoric Cemetery Site in Hidalgo County, Texas," *Bulletin of the Texas Archeological Society* 40 (1969).

Thomas R. Hester

AYCOX, NANIE JENKINS (?–1974). Nanie Belle Jenkins Aycox, teacher and college president, was born in Crockett, Texas, the daughter of Alonza R. and Hattie M. Jenkins, both of whom were East Texas teachers. She attended elementary and secondary school in Crockett,

Livingston, Houston, and Trinity. After receiving a teaching certificate from Prairie View State Normal and Industrial College (now Prairie View A&M University) in 1921, she earned a bachelor's degree from Hampton Normal and Agricultural Institute in Hampton, Virginia (1928); a B.S. in education from the University of Illinois, Urbana (1933); and an M.A. in education at the University of California at Berkeley (1936), where she did further graduate work in the summer of 1952. She also did research at Tuskegee Institute in Tuskegee, Alabama.

Mrs. Aycox taught at Alcorn College in Mississippi (1923–35) and directed the teacher-training program there. After leaving Alcorn she taught at Prairie View State College (1936) and Samuel Huston College (*see* HUSTON-TILLOTSON COLLEGE). She also taught in the public schools of Texas and Louisiana. As a Jeanes Fund supervisor in Travis and Harrison counties she visited rural black schools to introduce training in home economics, promote sanitation and hygiene, organize contests in athletics and industrial work, help improve school facilities, and establish Mothers' Clubs and Parent-Teacher associations. In 1938 she was president of the state organization of Jeanes teachers. She also taught at Tillotson, Wiley, and Bishop colleges. From 1946 to 1951 she served as president of Paul Quinn College in Waco. In September 1951 she joined Texas Southern University as an assistant professor of elementary education, a position she held until July 1958.

In 1950, 1951, and 1954 Mrs. Aycox served as a state officer in the Colored Teachers State Association of Texas, and in 1955 she served as president of the successor organization, the Teachers State Association of Texas.[qv] In the mid-1950s she served on the board of the Texas Commission on Race Relations. The commission operated under the auspices of the Southern Regional Council to help communities make a peaceful transition to desegregated schooling. During Mrs. Aycox's term as president of the Teachers State Association of Texas, the TSAT undertook a cooperative study with the commission to examine ways of improving integration and race relations. She also served as secretary of the Houston Commission on Race Relations.

Nanie Aycox was a member of AKA sorority and of St. Luke Independent Methodist Church in Huntsville, where she was director of publications and her husband was pastor. She died at her home in Houston on December 11, 1974. The funeral service was held at St. Luke, and burial was in the Trinity Cemetery in Trinity, Titus County. Mrs. Aycox was survived by her husband, a stepdaughter, a brother, and two sisters.

BIBLIOGRAPHY: Dallas *Morning News*, March 9, 1948. Houston *Post*, December 14, 1974. Vernon McDaniel, *History of the Teachers State Association of Texas* (Washington: National Education Association, 1977). Vertical Files, Barker Texas History Center, University of Texas at Austin (Paul Quinn College). *Texas Standard*, January–February 1954, May–June 1955. Trinity County Historical Commission, *Trinity County Cemeteries* (Burnet, Texas: Nortex, 1980).

Mary M. Standifer

AYERS, LEWIS T. (1798–1866). Lewis T. Ayers, pioneer settler and soldier, son of Silas and Mary (Bryan) Ayers, was born at Morris Plains, New Jersey, on October 6, 1798. In 1834 he and his brother, who went by the name David Ayres,[qv] set out with their families for Texas. Lewis Ayers became a member of the McMullen-McGloin colony,[qv] where he received his grant on July 25, 1835. He married Rebecca Osborn in 1824. They had seven children. Ayers openly espoused the Texan side of the conflict with Antonio López de Santa Anna.[qv] He was elected to represent San Patricio in the Consultation[qv] but arrived in San Felipe after it had adjourned. On December 1 he was elected to the General Council,[qv] in which he assisted Col. James Power[qv] and others in preparing an address to the Mexican people. He resigned on December 12 to become collector of customs at Lavaca.

On March 9, 1836, Ayers accepted appointment as assistant quartermaster of James W. Fannin, Jr.'s,[qv] regiment. He went with Col. William Ward[qv] and the Georgia Battalion[qv] to extricate Amon B. King[qv] from Refugio, accompanied King in his foray against the ranchos below the mission on March 14, and was in King's fight with the Mexican rear guard. Ayers was captured on March 15 and was one of thirty-three prisoners led out to be shot. He was saved by the intervention of Col. J. J. Holsinger,[qv] who halted the execution so that German prisoners might be reprieved. Ayers was set free supposedly because he gave a Masonic sign that was recognized by the Mexican general. Ayers himself claimed his wife aided in his release. He obtained a passport from Juan Davis Bradburn[qv] and went to New Orleans by way of Matamoros. In 1837 he moved to Mobile, Alabama, where he died on October 11, 1866. *See also* GOLIAD CAMPAIGN OF 1836.

BIBLIOGRAPHY: Charles H. Ayers, "Lewis Ayers," *Quarterly of the Texas State Historical Association* 9 (April 1906). William H. Oberste, *Texas Irish Empresarios and Their Colonies* (Austin: Von Boeckmann–Jones, 1953; 2d ed. 1973).

Hobart Huson

AYERS BAY. Ayers Bay, in northeast Aransas County (at 28°11′ N, 96°50′ W), is a small bay at the south end of Espíritu Santo Bay, between Matagorda Island and the Aransas National Wildlife Refuge.[qqv]

AYETA, FRANCISCO DE (1640–169?). Francisco de Ayeta, missionary, was born in Pamplona, Spain, in 1640. He entered the Franciscan order at the age of nineteen, was ordained a priest the next year, and was assigned to the province of New Mexico. He provided vital assistance to refugees at El Paso del Norte when they arrived after the Pueblo Revolt of 1680. The exiles numbered nearly 2,000, including soldiers and other men, women, servants, children, and Indian allies. Among the last were Tiguas from Isleta pueblo.

Ayeta, a remarkable missionary, had only recently arrived in El Paso with a large train of supplies from New Spain. He agreed to provide rations for the displaced families, especially if Governor Antonio de Otermín[qv] should decide to undertake an immediate reconquest of Pueblo lands. When Otermín chose to delay military initiatives, the refugees were moved to camps near Nuestra Señora de Guadalupe Mission, west of the Rio Grande. Otermín then requested authorization to build a presidio, regarded as essential to the safety of the displaced persons. To lend support to the proposed garrison of fifty men and obtain additional provisions, Father Ayeta traveled to Mexico City.

During the winter months of 1681–82, Otermín attempted an unsuccessful reconquest of New Mexico. This failed campaign determined that Spanish recovery of Pueblo country would be a long and difficult process, and that realization lent a reluctant sense of permanence to the El Paso communities. The desire to resettle the Tigua Indians—including the original refugees and additional ones who returned with Otermín in 1682—away from Spanish settlers prompted Ayeta to assist in the founding of the mission and pueblo of Corpus Christi de la Isleta. The first mission within the borders of present Texas, thanks to a shifting river channel in 1829, was located a few miles east of El Paso near the site of modern Ysleta, Texas.

Father Ayeta, in ill health and physically impaired, left the frontier and returned to Spain in 1683. There he took up his pen in defense of the missionary (regular) clergy, who were increasingly challenged by bishops and the secular clergy. Ayeta died in Spain during the decade of the 1690s. He has been called one of New Mexico's greatest men.

BIBLIOGRAPHY: Carlos E. Castañeda, *Our Catholic Heritage in Texas* (7 vols., Austin: Von Boeckmann–Jones, 1936–58; rpt., New York: Arno, 1976). C. L. Sonnichsen, *Pass of the North: Four Centuries on the Rio Grande* (2 vols., El Paso: Texas Western Press, 1968, 1980). W. H. Timmons, *El Paso: A Borderlands History* (El Paso: Texas Western Press, 1990).

Donald E. Chipman

AYISH BAYOU. Ayish Bayou rises about seven miles north of San Augustine in northern San Augustine County, near the Shelby county line (at 31°37′ N, 94°06′ W). Before the development of Sam Rayburn Reservoir,[qv] the stream ran southeast for forty-seven miles through central San Augustine County before disemboguing into the Angelina River in northern Jasper County (at 31°04′ N, 94°05′ W). With the impoundment of the reservoir, the lower reaches of the creek were inundated. The banks of the stream are heavily wooded in places with pine and hardwood trees; the terrain is nearly level to moderately steep and surfaced by loamy and clayey soils that support farming and lumbering. The stream's name is probably a variant of that of the Ais Indians, who lived in the area. About 1820 the bayou became the site of the earliest settlements in what later became San Augustine County.

BIBLIOGRAPHY: George L. Crocket, *Two Centuries in East Texas* (Dallas: Southwest, 1932; facsimile reprod., 1962).

AYNESWORTH, KENNETH HAZEN (1873–1944). Kenneth Hazen Aynesworth, surgeon and regent of the University of Texas, son of George Levin and Ellen (Hickman) Aynesworth, was born at Florence, Texas, on February 9, 1873. He attended Baylor University (1892–94) and graduated from the University of Texas Medical Department in 1899. As a medical student, Aynesworth was a member of Alpha Mu Pi Omega medical fraternity and Alpha Omega Alpha honorary medical fraternity. He interned in 1899–1900 and served as house surgeon, 1900–01, at John Sealy Hospital,[qv] Galveston. In 1901 he also served as demonstrator in anatomy at the University of Texas Medical Department. Aynesworth took postgraduate courses at Friedrich Wilhelm University in Berlin (1902) and at Johns Hopkins University in Baltimore, Maryland (1909). In 1903 he began medical practice in Waco. He became consulting surgeon for the Missouri, Kansas and Texas Railroad (1906) and the Texas Electric Railroad (1910). He served on several city boards and commissions, including the Waco school board (1907–17) and board of health (1903–13). Aynesworth was a member of the McLennan County Medical Society (president, 1939), Texas State Medical Association, American Medical Association, American Board of Surgery, West Texas Archaeological and Paleontological Society, Texas Academy of Science,[qv] Texas State Historical Association,[qv] and a founder of the Philosophical Society of Texas.[qv] He was a charter member of the Texas Surgical Society (president, 1927) and was elected a fellow of both the Southern Surgical Association and the American College of Surgeons. He was a Baptist and Mason.

In 1933 Aynesworth received an honorary LL.D. from Baylor University and was appointed to the board of regents of the University of Texas. As a regent from 1933 to 1944 he served on the complaints and grievances committee, the medical branch committee, the library committee, the College of Mines (now the University of Texas at El Paso) committee, and the board of lease of university lands. He was instrumental in the acquisition of important new collections for the University of Texas Library on the subjects of Latin America and Texas History. As an avocation he collected Texana and American Indian artifacts. He donated both collections to Baylor University. On December 31, 1902, Aynesworth married Maud Bryan of St. Maurice, Louisiana; they had four children. He died on October 30, 1944, in Waco of a cerebral hemorrhage and was buried in Oakwood Cemetery, Waco.

BIBLIOGRAPHY: Kenneth Hazen Aynesworth Papers, Moody Medical Library, University of Texas Medical Branch at Galveston. *Texas State Journal of Medicine*, February 1945. Vertical Files, Barker Texas History Center, University of Texas at Austin. *Larry J. Wygant*

AYR, TEXAS. Ayr, in Deaf Smith County, was established in January 1890 when the Fort Worth and Denver City Railway sent a party of fifteen surveyors under Robert E. Montgomery and H. H. Granger to survey a projected spur from Washburn southwest through the center of the county. The purpose of the spur was to transport to northern markets the cattle of the ranching region between Roswell, New Mexico, and Big Spring. Since the railroad hoped to take away cattle shipments from the rival Southern Kansas (Santa Fe) line, details of the expedition were kept as secret as possible. On January 26 the surveyors had chosen a place five miles from the center of the county and laid out a townsite, which they named for the city of Ayr in Scotland (although Montgomery reportedly called it "Air" because of the wind). The surveying crew wintered at the site, and by early spring settlers began to come in and file on sections of land for three dollars an acre at 5 percent interest. A few houses were built, and the town grew rapidly as several families settled in the vicinity. By May, W. D. Dulaney had established a general store, and a post office had been granted with James M. Campbell, an elderly Scotsman, as postmaster. The XIT Ranch,[qv] however, had developed a rival town called Grenada (later La Plata), which vied with Ayr to be county seat. During the heated controversy that ensued, Texas Rangers[qv] were stationed at Ayr to prevent trouble. On October 3, 1890, La Plata won the election by ninety-seven to seven votes. Despite rumors that certain XIT cowboys had voted twice, the election was declared valid. Consequently, the projected railroad was never built. By 1895 the post office was discontinued and the townsite of Ayr was abandoned.

BIBLIOGRAPHY: Amarillo *Sunday News-Globe*, August 14, 1938. *Deaf Smith County: The Land and Its People* (Hereford, Texas: Deaf Smith County Historical Society, 1982). Bessie Patterson, *A History of Deaf Smith County* (Hereford, Texas: Pioneer, 1964).

H. Allen Anderson

AYRES, ATLEE BERNARD (1873–1969). Atlee Bernard Ayres, architect, was born in Hillsboro, Ohio, on July 12, 1873, the son of Nathan Tandy and Mary Parsons (Atlee) Ayres. The family moved to Texas, lived first in Houston, and then moved in 1888 to San Antonio, where Nathan Ayres for many years managed the Alamo Flats, a luxury apartment hotel. In 1890 Ayres went to New York to study at the Metropolitan School of Architecture, a subsidiary of Columbia University. There he won first prize in the school's annual design competition. His teachers included William Ware, a student of Richard Morris Hunt. Ayres took drawing lessons at the Art Students League at night and studied painting under Frank Vincent Dumont on Sundays. Upon his graduation from the school of architecture in 1894 he returned to San Antonio and worked for various architects. He subsequently moved to Mexico, where he practiced until 1900. That year he moved back to San Antonio and began a partnership with Charles A. Coughlin that lasted until Coughlin's death in 1905. Ayres designed the Halff house (1908) and a villa for Col. George W. Brackenridge[qv] (date unknown) that was later was torn down.

In 1924 Ayres formed a partnership with his son, Robert M. Ayres.[qv] During the 1920s and 1930s Atlee B. and Robert M. Ayres, as the firm was called, designed numerous residences in the Spanish Colonial Revival style, among them the Hogg house (1924), the Mannen house (1926), the Newton house (1927), and the Atkinson house (1928, now the Marion Koogler McNay Art Museum[qv]). The firm was also adept in using other revival modes, including the Colonial Revival of the H. Lutcher Brown residence (1936) and the English Tudor of the Jesse Oppenheimer residence (1924).

In 1915 Ayres was state architect of Texas, a position that allowed him to design the Blind Institute (now the Texas School for the Blind[qv]), the Texas State Office Building, and other important public buildings. On the University of Texas campus he designed Carothers Dormitory and the original Pharmacy Building. He drew plans for courthouses in Kingsville, Alice, Refugio, Del Rio, and Brownsville. In San Antonio his firm helped design the exterior of the Municipal Auditorium (1923) and the Administration Building at Randolph Air Force Base (1931), known as the "Taj Mahal," with a tower that conceals a 500,000-gallon water tank. It also designed the thirty-story Smith-Young Tower (1929), the Plaza Hotel (1927), and the Federal

Reserve Bank Building (1928) and remodeled the Menger Hotel (1949–53).

Ayres was the author of *Mexican Architecture* (1926). He was a charter member of the Texas Society of Architects[qv] and was one of three architects instrumental in securing passage of state legislation in 1937 for the licensing of architects to practice. He received license number 3. He married Olive Moss Cox in San Antonio in 1896, and the couple had two sons. After Mrs. Ayres's death in 1937 he married Katherine Cox, his second cousin, in 1940. Ayres was still practicing architecture when he died at the age of ninety-six on November 6, 1969, in San Antonio. He was buried in Mission Burial Park.

BIBLIOGRAPHY: Ayres and Ayres Collection, Architectural Drawings Collection (Architecture and Planning Library, University of Texas at Austin). Chris Carson and William B. McDonald, eds., *A Guide to San Antonio Architecture* (San Antonio Chapter, American Institute of Architects, 1986). Stephanie Hetos Cocke, "Atlee B. and Robert M. Ayres," *Texas Architect*, November–December 1989. Vertical Files, Barker Texas History Center, University of Texas at Austin.

AYRES, CLARENCE EDWIN (1891–1972). Clarence Edwin Ayres, economist, philosopher, social critic, and university professor, son of William S. and Emma (Young) Ayres, was born at Lowell, Massachusetts, on May 6, 1891. The family's emphasis on learning and personal and social morality influenced Ayres throughout his life. In 1912 he received a B.A. in philosophy with honors as best scholar from Brown University. He attended Harvard for a year and then returned to Brown to receive a M.A. in economics in 1914. From there he went to the University of Chicago, where he received a doctorate in philosophy and stayed on as an assistant instructor until 1920. He then became an associate professor of economics at Amherst. In 1923 he, along with a large part of the faculty, resigned to protest the dismissal of Amherst president Alexander Meiklejohn. Ayres taught at Reed College in 1923 and 1924 and afterward worked as associate editor of the *New Republic* from 1924 to 1927. In 1927 he and his second wife moved to a ranch in New Mexico, where they remained until 1930. That year he accepted a professorship in economics at the University of Texas, where he remained until his retirement in 1968. Ayres was married twice, in 1915 to Anna Bryan, with whom he had three children, and to Gwendolyn Jane in 1924.

Ayres's consistent interest throughout his career was the integration of philosophy and economics. He had gone to the University of Chicago to study the philosophical instrumentalism developed there by John Dewey and the economic theory of institutionalism that Thorstein Veblen and his followers had developed at the same institution. Ayres's dissertation, The Nature of the Relationship Between Ethics and Economics, first attempted to establish a philosophical base for institutionalism, and he explored this theme in his teaching and popular writings throughout the 1920s. In his first book, *Science: The False Messiah* (1927), he dismissed the utility of pure science and described it as an invention of the technological perspective. In its companion work, *Holier Than Thou: The Way of the Righteous* (1929), Ayres analyzed traditional mores, which he called "ceremonialism," as opposition to technology and therefore inhibiting to human progress. After his Texas appointment he devoted himself to definitions of ethical values for his institutional theory; this activity culminated in his two most important works, *The Theory of Economic Progress* (1944) and *The Industrial Economy* (1952). Veblen and many pragmatists had accepted a cultural and moral relativism, which Ayres countered with the use of Dewey's idea of a continuum of means and ends. Ayres strove to identify universal moral values derived from a "technological continuum," defined as "the sum of human skills and tools." His system denounced mere statistical analyses, savings accumulation, and full employment as moral measures and recommended that governmental policy rather focus on "full production" or technological advance. Ayres's criticism of capitalism led to conflicts with University of Texas administrators and Texas legislators. He was one of four economics professors whom the regents unsuccessfully ordered Homer P. Rainey[qv] to fire in 1940. Ayres continued his outspoken ways and before a 1949 Texas Senate hearing called a proposed loyalty oath for University of Texas employees an insult. In 1951 the Texas House, by a vote of 130 to 1, passed a resolution demanding his dismissal and threatened to block funds for the entire economics department otherwise. Powerful friends and colleagues intervened, and the unrepentant Ayres continued to teach until the mandatory retirement age of seventy-five.

Toward the end of his life he was a member of the Committee on the Southwest Economy for the President's Council of Economic Advisors under president Harry Truman and a director of the San Antonio branch of the Dallas Federal Reserve Bank (1954–59). In the 1960s Ayres was a governor of the Federal Reserve Board, received the University of Texas Students' Association award for teaching excellence, and helped found the Association for Evolutionary Economics in 1966. He was a twenty-year national committeeman of the American Civil Liberties Union and served as president of the Southwestern Social Science Association.[qv] In 1962 his *Toward a Reasonable Society: The Values of Industrial Civilization* was published. He died in Alamogordo, New Mexico, on July 24, 1972.

BIBLIOGRAPHY: Ronnie Dugger, *Our Invaded Universities: Form, Reform, and New Starts* (New York: Norton, 1974). Vertical Files, Barker Texas History Center, University of Texas at Austin.

Mark C. Smith

AYRES, CLAUDIA (1882–1968). Claudia (Mother Mary Angelique) Ayres, teacher and cofounder of Our Lady of the Lake University in San Antonio, the daughter of Eli Snow and Nan Elizabeth (Lowry) Ayres, was born on April 12, 1882, in Kosciusko, Mississippi. Eli Ayres, who was employed building bridges for the International–Great Northern Railroad, moved his family to Palestine, Texas, in 1883 and in 1884 to Troup, where his in-laws had settled. Although the family was not Catholic, Claudia was enrolled in St. Mary's Academy[qv] in Austin in 1896. At the end of her second year there she received Catholic baptism with her father's approval. He objected, however, when soon afterward she expressed a desire to become a member of a religious order, and he did not allow her to return to St. Mary's for her senior year. In the summer of 1899 the family moved to New Braunfels, where two younger Ayres children were enrolled in the parochial school, which was staffed by members of the Sisters of Divine Providence.[qv] Eli Ayres's contact with these women, and with a sister who helped nurse his young son during a fatal bout of typhoid fever, softened his opposition to Claudia's vocation. In 1900 she became a postulant with the Sisters of Divine Providence in San Antonio. In July 1902, at the beginning of her second novitiate year, she took the name Mary Angelique, and in August 1904 she made her first vows.

Claudia finished her senior year of high school at Our Lady of the Lake Academy, which was staffed by her congregation, and in 1901 began teaching at the academy. From 1901 to 1910 she attended summer schools for teachers; she received her first-class teaching certificate in 1906 and her permanent certificate in 1909. She also took correspondence courses from the University of Texas and in 1911 and 1912 attended summer school at Catholic University of America. After examining her record of coursework, a Catholic University professor instructed Our Lady of the Lake College to award her a B.A. degree in 1912. Sister Angelique remained at Catholic University during the 1912–13 academic year, at the end of which she received an M.A. in English. Although her duties at the college prevented her from completing the Ph.D., she did doctoral work at Columbia University during the summers of 1925, 1926, 1927, and 1930. In 1911 she and Mother Philothea Thiry established Our Lady of the Lake College, a junior college devoted mainly to teacher training. Sister Angelique taught

English and math at the school in 1911–12 and English from 1914 to 1943. In 1913 she became the school's first registrar, an office that included the duties of dean. She assumed the office of academic dean in 1923, when that position was officially established, and served in that capacity until her retirement in 1960. She was convinced that accreditation by secular education agencies would strengthen the college and continually sought to raise standards and secure certification. Our Lady of the Lake received state accreditation as a junior college in 1918 and as a senior college in 1919. In 1920 the school became a member of the Association of Texas Colleges (later the Association of Texas Colleges and Universities[qv]), in 1923 of the Association of Colleges and Secondary Schools for the Southern States, in 1924 of the American Council on Education, and in 1925 of the Association of American Colleges. It was placed on the approved list of colleges by the Association of American Universities in 1927. Under Sister Angelique's leadership Our Lady of the Lake developed a strong program in education, the first school of social work in Texas, and the first speech and hearing center in the state to combine professional training with clinical service. The school also offered early programs in librarianship, medical technology, and dietetics. During this time the school's enrollment grew to 1,500 and the number of buildings on its campus increased to seventeen.

Sister Angelique Ayres was elected superior of her congregation in 1925 and served in that office until 1937. In 1943 she became the first American-born woman to serve as superior general of the Sisters of Divine Providence, a position in which she held two consecutive six-year terms. She was a frequent contributor to educational journals and also collaborated with Sister M. Generosa Callahan on *The History of the Sisters of Divine Providence in Texas* (1955). She held offices in various professional associations, including the Southern Conference of College Deans and the Southern Association of Colleges for Women. She was a member of the National Association of Modern Language Teachers and the American Poetry Association; a member and officer of the American Association of University Women[qv] and the National Education Association; an honorary member of Delta Kappa Gamma,[qv] an honor society for education professionals; and a cofounder and member-at-large of Delta Epsilon Sigma, a nationwide Catholic honor society. Mother Angelique died on September 13, 1968, and was buried in Providence Cemetery in San Antonio. Ayres Hall, a women's residence hall at Our Lady of the Lake University, was named in her honor.

BIBLIOGRAPHY: Sister Mary Generosa Callahan, C.D.P., *Mother Angelique Ayres, Dreamer and Builder of Our Lady of the Lake University* (Austin: Jenkins, 1981). Vertical Files, Barker Texas History Center, University of Texas at Austin.

Mary M. Standifer

AYRES, DAVID (1793–1881). David Ayres, pioneer merchant and a founder of the first Methodist missionary society in Texas, son of Silas and Mary (Byram) Ayers, was born in Morristown, New Jersey, on August 10, 1793. He and his wife, Ann, were married in 1815 in the John Street Methodist Church in New York City. From 1817 to 1832 Ayres, who changed the spelling of his name from that of his parents, was a merchant in Ithaca, New York, where he played a significant role in establishing Methodism and building its first church there. In 1832 he came to Texas to buy property and build a home. He landed at the mouth of the Brazos in early 1833 and proceeded up the river to Washington County, where he bought a tract of land thirty miles west of Washington-on-the-Brazos. After clearing part of the land and building a stone house called Montville, he returned to the East.

In May 1834 he, his brother, and their families returned. Ayres brought with him what he believed to be the first box of Bibles ever shipped to Texas and a supply of books from the New York Sunday School Union. The family settled on the Nueces at San Patricio. In November Ayres moved his family and remaining possessions to Montville, Washington County. He distributed Bibles to all who would receive them. In addition to running his mercantile business, he began a school in his home, taught by his wife and Lydia Ann McHenry.[qv] William B. Travis[qv] left his son, Charles Edward Travis,[qv] with the Ayreses to attend that school. Charles stayed there for two years after the battle of the Alamo.[qv]

While attending a camp meeting in Austin County in September 1835, Ayres assisted in the formation of an unofficial Methodist quarterly conference. As secretary, he wrote to the Methodist Missionary Society in New York requesting that missionaries be sent to Texas.

When war with Mexico broke out he furnished supplies for the army. Deafness prevented his participation in active service, but Sam Houston[qv] assigned him to protect the families fleeing in the Runaway Scrape.[qv] Upon returning to Montville after the victory at the battle of San Jacinto,[qv] Ayres found his property in ruins and moved to Washington-on-the-Brazos. By 1837 he had sufficiently recovered financially to purchase land at Center Hill, near Bellville, in Austin County. He organized a Sunday school, led worship services every Sunday, and held thrice-weekly prayer meetings in his home.

In November 1837 he met Martin Ruter[qv] in New Albany, Indiana, and served as companion and guide to the newly appointed superintendent of Methodist missionary work in Texas. During a camp meeting held on Caney Creek, twenty-five miles southwest of Washington-on-the-Brazos, the first Methodist Missionary Society in Texas was formed, and Ayres was elected secretary. He headed the list of subscribers with a $100 contribution. He was also a major contributor to the funding of Rutersville College in 1840.

In 1847 Ayres moved his family to Galveston, where he opened a mercantile business and served for a time as a United States deputy marshall. In 1857–58 he was publisher of the *Texas Christian Advocate* (*see* UNITED METHODIST REPORTER) and wrote some of the earliest accounts of Methodism in Texas. He was a major contributor to the building of St. James Methodist Church in Galveston. Ayres died on October 25, 1881, and is buried in Galveston. *See also* METHODIST CHURCH.

BIBLIOGRAPHY: Charles H. Ayers, "Lewis Ayers," *Quarterly of the Texas State Historical Association* 9 (April 1906). William Campbell Binkley, ed., *Official Correspondence of the Texan Revolution, 1835–1836* (2 vols., New York: Appleton-Century, 1936). May Williams Pennington Papers, Barker Texas History Center, University of Texas at Austin.

Norman W. Spellmann

AYRES, ROBERT MOSS (1898–1977). Robert Moss Ayres, architect, one of two sons of Olive Moss and Atlee Bernard Ayres,[qv] was born on August 19, 1898, in San Antonio. He studied at San Antonio Academy,[qv] boarded at Haverford School, outside Philadelphia, and from 1918 until 1920 attended the School of Architecture at the University of Pennsylvania. There he received training in the theory and method of the école des Beaux-Arts under dean Paul Philippe Cret. After leaving the University of Pennsylvania in 1920, he worked in New York City for a year for the firm of Murchison, Lamb, and French. He returned to San Antonio in 1922 to begin working for his father. Two years later the firm become known as Atlee B. and Robert M. Ayres, Architects.

Ayres married Florence Collet, a native of Kansas City, Missouri, on December 2, 1925, and they had four children. His wife's numerous community activities included the presidency of the Junior League of San Antonio and Timely Topics, a lecture group. She also was a founding board member of the Miss Porter's School Alumni Association of Texas and a member of the Battle of Flowers Association (*see* FIESTA SAN ANTONIO).

Ayres was responsible for many significant public buildings and residences in South Texas and beyond. The publication of fourteen building designs by the firm in *Pacific Coast Architect* in 1925 launched his firm's reputation beyond Texas and the central Southwest. His first major public commission was the thirty-story Smith-Young

Tower (1929), a neo-Gothic skyscraper that still defines the San Antonio skyline. His residence for Mr. and Mrs. Lutcher Brown (1936) in the San Antonio suburb of Terrell Hills is an outstanding suburban Neoclassical home from that era. Other projects include the Administration Building at Randolph Air Force Base, known as the "Taj Mahal" (1931), and five buildings for the University of Texas, all designed with his father.

Among Ayres's architecture-related activities was a position as consulting architect to *Good Housekeeping* magazine in 1936. He was president of the West Texas (now San Antonio) chapter of the American Institute of Architects. His firm was the recipient of numerous awards, including a gold medal from the AIA in 1929 for the design of the San Antonio Municipal Auditorium, done in collaboration with George R. Willis[qv] and Emmett T. Jackson. Ayres served in the cavalry in World War I.[qv] He was a member of Christ Episcopal Church and belonged to several social clubs, including the German Club and the Order of the Alamo, which he served as president. His firm remained small and ceased operation after his death on August 7, 1977.

BIBLIOGRAPHY: *American Architects Directory*. Chris Carson and William B. McDonald, eds., *A Guide to San Antonio Architecture* (San Antonio Chapter, American Institute of Architects, 1986). Files, Architectural Drawings Collection, Architecture and Planning Library, University of Texas at Austin. Anne Henderson, Revival Modes and Regionalism in the Early Twentieth Century: Atlee B. Ayres's Residential Designs for Suburban San Antonio (M.A. thesis, University of Texas at Austin, 1986). *Stephanie Hetos Cocke*

AYRES, TEXAS. Ayres (Ayers) was an early commercial town in Stephen F. Austin's[qv] colony and the Republic of Texas.[qv] Around 1835 David Ayres,[qv] a prominent early settler, founded the settlement, which he named for himself, two or three miles south of the present site of Long Point. The town was located in what is now northwest Washington County in a well-watered area near Sheppard and East Fork Mill creeks. It flourished briefly but disappeared with the growth of other population centers.

BIBLIOGRAPHY: D. Theo Ayers, History of the Ayers Family (MS, Barker Texas History Center, University of Texas at Austin). Ed Ellsworth Bartholomew, *The Encyclopedia of Texas Ghost Towns* (Fort Davis, Texas, 1982). Galveston *Daily News*, August 17, 1902. Mrs. R. E. Pennington, *History of Brenham and Washington County* (Houston, 1915). Macum Phelan, "David Ayers and Robert Alexander," in *Texas Methodist Centennial Yearbook*, ed. Olin W. Nail (Elgin, Texas, 1934). Worth Stickley Ray, *Austin Colony Pioneers* (Austin: Jenkins, 1949; 2d ed., Austin: Pemberton, 1970). Charles F. Schmidt, *History of Washington County* (San Antonio: Naylor, 1949). *Carole E. Christian*

AYTES BRANCH. Aytes Branch rises just north of Westover in southeast Baylor County (at 33°31′ N, 99°03′ W) and runs southwest for eight miles to its mouth on the Brazos River, two miles north of the Baylor-Throckmorton county line and west of Farm Road 2374 (at 33°25′ N, 99°05′ W). It passes through Round Timber shortly before its confluence with the Brazos. The surrounding flat to rolling terrain is surfaced by sand that supports oak mottes with freshwater marsh during the rainy season. Springs named Round Timber Springs, which are found in several large holes, are sources for the creek. The springs were camping sites for hunters and trappers in earlier times but by the 1980s were mostly dry.

BIBLIOGRAPHY: Gunnar Brune, *Springs of Texas*, Vol. 1 (Fort Worth: Branch-Smith, 1981).

AYUNTAMIENTO. The ayuntamiento was the principal governing body of Spanish municipalities. It functioned as the town council and had a wide range of administrative duties. Its size varied and was generally based on the population of the town. The council members consisted of the alcalde,[qv] who served as president, a varying number of regidors (see REGIDOR) or councilmen, and a *síndico procurador*,[qv] the equivalent of a city attorney. Other local administrators—police chiefs and fine collectors, for instance—sometimes held positions in the council, though often these additional members were not allowed to vote. The ayuntamiento was in most cases not a democratic institution. Often it received little voluntary support from the people it represented. Many offices were inherited, and others were sold by the crown or their current holders. Although elected officials did exist, by the late colonial period many ayuntamientos had to resort to forced service, for often few men of consequence volunteered to serve. Spanish colonists in America commonly referred to the ayuntamiento as the cabildo,[qv] though this term first meant the building in which the council met.

The ayuntamiento managed police and security matters, hospitals, health measures such as the inspection of food markets and the removal of stagnant ponds, public roads, weights and measures, taxation, and agriculture. Though the powers of the ayuntamiento seemed wide, the body operated within the limits imposed by a higher authority, whether viceroy or governor. One of its primary functions, in fact, was to relay the orders of officials in Spain or Mexico to the local populace. In turn, the ayuntamiento often represented the interests of town citizens to the royal authority. Thus the ayuntamiento served as a mediating institution between local and central authorities.

The 1812 Constitution of Cádiz called for popular election to the ayuntamientos and thus ended lifetime appointments to the bodies. The new document also officially made the colonies of Spain part of the empire and thus entitled them to representation in the Spanish congress, the Cortes. The writers of the constitution relied on municipal governments to appoint deputies to the congress, and municipalities throughout New Spain restructured their councils as a result. In 1820 San Antonio altered its ayuntamiento to conform, as did Goliad.

Mexican independence did not fundamentally change local government. The number of ayuntamientos increased in Mexican Texas[qv] as the number of colonists grew. Spanish law had allowed any settlement of more than ten married men the right to a local council, and this right continued under Mexico. The constitution that unified Coahuila and Texas[qv] as a state merely formalized office-holding requirements by setting standards for age, residency, and literacy. By incorporating these minor changes, the ayuntamiento continued to function as a viable institution until the Texas Revolution.[qv]

BIBLIOGRAPHY: Eugene C. Barker, "The Government of Austin's Colony, 1821–1831," *Southwestern Historical Quarterly* 21 (January 1918). Frank W. Blackman, *Spanish Institutions of the Southwest* (Baltimore: Johns Hopkins Press, 1891; rpt., Glorieta, New Mexico: Rio Grande Press, 1976). Charles Gibson, *Spain in America* (New York: Harper and Row, 1966). Clarence H. Haring, *The Spanish Empire in America* (New York: Oxford University Press, 1947; 2d ed., New York: Harcourt, 1963). Mattie Alice Austin, "The Municipal Government of San Fernando de Bexar," *Quarterly of the Texas State Historical Association* 8 (April 1905). O. Garfield Jones, "Local Government in the Spanish Colonies as Provided by the Recopilación de Leyes de los Reynos de las Indias," *Southwestern Historical Quarterly* 19 (July 1915). John Preston Moore, *The Cabildo in Peru under the Bourbons* (Durham: Duke University Press, 1966). John Preston Moore, *The Cabildo in Peru under the Hapsburgs* (Durham: Duke University Press, 1954). Marc Simmons, *Spanish Government in New Mexico* (Albuquerque: University of New Mexico Press, 1968). David J. Weber, *The Mexican Frontier, 1821–1846* (Albuquerque: University of New Mexico Press, 1982). *Geoffrey Pivateau*

AZCUÉ, FERNANDO DE (?–?). Fernando de Azcué, *alcalde mayor* of Saltillo, is credited with the first definite crossing of the Rio Grande by a European. In 1665, in response to continuing Indian attacks, Azcué recruited a company of 103 men from Saltillo and Monterrey. His force, bolstered by 300 Indian allies, forded the Rio Grande near the site of present Eagle Pass and penetrated twenty-four leagues beyond it, where it fought an all-day battle with Cacaxtle Indians. At the conclusion of hostilities, more than 100 natives had been killed and an additional seventy had been captured.

BIBLIOGRAPHY: Carlos E. Castañeda, *Our Catholic Heritage in Texas* (7 vols., Austin: Von Boeckmann–Jones, 1936–58; rpt., New York: Arno, 1976). *Donald E. Chipman*

AZLE, TEXAS. Azle is on State Highway 199 sixteen miles northwest of downtown Fort Worth in the northwest corner of Tarrant County; the town extends partly into Parker County. The first recorded settlement at the site occurred in 1846, when a young doctor named James Azle Steward moved into a cabin built by a Dutchman named Rumsfeldt. Other settlers came and established themselves near the local streams, Ash Creek, Silver Creek, and Walnut Creek. The first post office opened in 1881, and the town took the name O'Bar in honor of the man who obtained the postal service. Soon, however, the name was changed at the request of Steward, who donated the land for a townsite in order to have the town named Azle. The community's economy was based on agriculture. Several crops were grown, including wheat, corn, peanuts, sorghum, and cotton. Watermelons, cantaloupes, peaches, plums, and pears were also produced. Dairy farming became important in the early decades of the twentieth century, when local milk products were sold to creameries in Fort Worth. The population of Azle grew steadily, and by 1920 the census recorded 150 residents. By 1933 State Highway 34 (later State Highway 199) had reached Azle from Fort Worth, greatly improving transportation capabilities between the town and the city. Also, Eagle Mountain Lake was formed by a dam on the Trinity River east of Azle. In the late 1930s electricity was supplied to Azle and the surrounding countryside. The population grew between 1940 and 1960 from 800 to 2,696. It was 5,822 by 1980. After the 1930s agriculture gradually declined; fields were converted from wheat and corn production to housing developments. Manufacturing increased, and in 1984 Azle had twenty-six businesses. In 1985 the population was estimated at more than 7,000. The town's proximity to Fort Worth and its position as the "Gateway to Eagle Mountain Lake" have made Azle a popular place to live. In 1990 the population was 8,868.

BIBLIOGRAPHY: Ruby Schmidt, ed., *Fort Worth and Tarrant County* (Fort Worth: Texas Christian University Press, 1984). Kathleen E. and Clifton R. St. Clair, eds., *Little Towns of Texas* (Jacksonville, Texas: Jayroe Graphic Arts, 1982). *W. Kellon Hightower*

AZTLÁN. Aztlán, the name of the legendary homeland of the Aztecs that covered the area of Mexico and the southwestern United States, was used as a name of political power, cultural renewal, and nationalism during the 1970s Chicano[qv] movement. Although there is no clear evidence for the existence of Aztlán in either Mexico or the Southwest, "El Plan Espiritual de Aztlán," a manifesto written in 1969 by Alurista, a poet, called on Hispanic Americans to unite and rescue their homeland from domination by Anglos. In Texas the idea was promoted by the Raza Unida party,[qv] which was established in Crystal City in 1970. The plan advocated that Mexican Texans control their education, economy, politics, and culture. In El Paso in September 1972 delegates to the first national convention of Raza Unida established El Congreso de Aztlán, a national assembly charged with organizing a political agenda.

The Centro Aztlán of Laredo, a volunteer community services agency, provided assistance with immigration or welfare problems, offered cultural awareness classes, and kept books on Mexican-American history in its library. During the 1970s *Tejidos* and *Caracol*, two literary vehicles of the Chicano Literary Renaissance[qv] in Texas, published literary works inspired by Aztlán, and Tejano writers promoted statewide activities. Several movement newspapers added the word Aztlán to their titles. *El éxito* and *La Verdad*, published in Beeville and Crystal City, respectively, used it on their mastheads. In 1989 *Aztlán, Essays on the Chicano Homeland*, edited by Rudolfo Anaya and Francisco Lomelí, brought together the various interpretations of the term.

BIBLIOGRAPHY: José Ángel Gutiérrez Papers, Benson Latin American Collection, University of Texas at Austin.

Teresa Palomo Acosta

BABBITT, EDWIN BURR (1803–1881). Edwin Burr Babbitt, a major in the United States Army Quartermaster Corps who was responsible for the repair of the Alamo[qv] chapel and barracks, was born in Connecticut in 1803. He graduated from the United States Military Academy in 1826 and was posted to the Third United States Infantry at Jefferson Barracks, Missouri. He was a member of the Pawnee expedition in 1829 and was promoted to first lieutenant in 1834. Babbitt was stationed at Fort Jesup, Louisiana, and Fort Towson, Indian Territory, before being made an assistant quartermaster in 1836. His service record until 1846 was quite full and included service in the Seminole War.

In 1846 he was assigned to Gen. Winfield Scott's army in Mexico and established the quartermaster's depot at Tampico. He was brevetted major in May 1848 for meritorious conduct in Mexico. In March of 1849 he was made assistant quartermaster of the post of San Antonio, a position previously held by Capt. Morris Miller. Babbitt completed agreements with the Catholic bishop of Texas, Jean Marie Odin,[qv] for the rental of the Alamo[qv] buildings. In June 1849 he recommended to Gen. Thomas S. Jesup that the existing buildings be demolished and permanent quarters for the army be constructed. Jesup vetoed this suggestion, and during the spring of 1850 Babbitt began to repair the battle-damaged Alamo. He supplied a wooden roof, a second floor, and the now famous parapet over the chapel façade; architect John M. Fries[qv] probably helped design the parapet. In 1854 Babbitt was reassigned to duties in Baltimore, Maryland.

Babbitt's military career continued until 1868 and included service in the Utah expedition and assignment as chief quartermaster of the Division of the Pacific Station at San Francisco. In 1861 he was promoted to lieutenant colonel, in 1866 to colonel. He retired at the rank of brigadier general. He died at his home at Fortress Monroe, Virginia, on December 10, 1881, and was buried at his own request at Jefferson Barracks National Cemetery, outside of St. Louis, Missouri. His son, Lawrence Sprague Babbitt, later commanded the United States Arsenal at San Antonio and was chief ordnance officer for the Department of Texas from 1887 to 1890.

BIBLIOGRAPHY: George W. Cullum, *Biographical Register of the Officers and Graduates of the U.S. Military Academy at West Point, New York.* Jim Steely, "Remembering the Alamo," *Texas Highways,* March 1985. *Kevin R. Young*

BABER, TEXAS. Baber was a sawmill town four miles south of Huntington in east central Angelina County. It was established by S. F. Carter about 1906 on the Texas and New Orleans Railroad and was at first the site of a small mill. Later, J. P. Carter, who had been associated with a mill at Emporia, constructed a larger plant at Baber with a daily capacity of 25,000 to 50,000 board feet. The second Carter owned substantial timberland between Huntington and Zavala, and this acreage sustained the mill at Baber for quite a few years. Baber, named for a lumberman, had its first postmaster, James Burns, in 1907. By 1915 the town had a population of 100 and at least three businesses. But the timber had been exhausted, and the mill was liquidated. In 1915 local mail delivery was transferred to Huntington.

BIBLIOGRAPHY: Angelina County Historical Survey Committee, *Land of the Little Angel: A History of Angelina County, Texas,* ed. Bob Bowman (Lufkin, Texas: Lufkin Printing, 1976). Archie Birdsong Mathews, The Economic Development of Angelina County (M.A. thesis, University of Texas, 1952). *Megan Biesele*

BABY HEAD, TEXAS. Baby Head is on State Highway 16 near Babyhead Mountain, ten miles north of Llano in north central Llano County. A post office was established there in 1879 with Shelby Walling as postmaster; the post office was closed in 1918. Baby Head was at one time the site of an election and justice court precinct and supported several small businesses and a school. By 1968 it was a rural community of twenty people marked only by a cemetery. In 1990 the population was still twenty.

BIBLIOGRAPHY: Wilburn Oatman, *Llano, Gem of the Hill Country: A History of Llano County* (Hereford, Texas: Pioneer, 1970).

James B. Heckert-Greene

BABYHEAD CREEK. Babyhead Creek rises near Babyhead Mountain, eleven miles north of Llano in north central Llano County (at 30°55′ N, 98°40′ W), and runs southwest for eight miles to its mouth on Pecan Creek, seven miles northwest of Llano (at 30°51′ N, 98°43′ W). It traverses an area of the Llano basin characterized by flat to rolling terrain surfaced chiefly with fine sandy loams. Local vegetation consists mostly of open stands of live oak and mesquite.

BABYHEAD MOUNTAIN. Babyhead Mountain is ten miles north of Llano in northern Llano County (at 30°54′ N, 98°40′ W). A baby's skull was reportedly found there. The summit, with an elevation of 1,627 feet, rises 200 feet above State Highway 16 to the northeast. The surrounding terrain is flat to rolling, with local dissection, and surfaced by sandy and clay loams that support open stands of live oak and mesquite.

BIBLIOGRAPHY: Wilburn Oatman, *Llano, Gem of the Hill Country: A History of Llano County* (Hereford, Texas: Pioneer, 1970).

BABYLON, TEXAS. Babylon was midway between Dawson and Purdon, seventeen miles southwest of Corsicana in western Navarro County. It was founded by former slaves who around 1895 established a church that they named for the ancient city of Babylon because of its biblical associations; a school was in operation there by 1900. Residents traded in nearby Dawson, Purdon, or Spring Hill. The school and church were later closed, and after World War II[qv] most of the remaining residents left the area. In the early 1990s only a few scattered houses remained at the site.

BIBLIOGRAPHY: *Navarro County Scroll,* 1966. *Christopher Long*

BACHE, ALEXANDER DALLAS (1806–1867). Alexander Dallas Bache was born in Philadelphia, Pennsylvania, on July 19, 1806, the eldest child of Sophia (Dallas) and Richard Bache.qv He was a great-grandson of Benjamin Franklin and a member of a family distinguished by its physicists and scientists. Bache graduated from the Military Academy at West Point in 1825 and served in the Corps of Engineers. He taught at the University of Pennsylvania and was associated with the Franklin Institute until 1835, when he was appointed the first president of Girard College at Philadelphia. From 1843 to 1861 Bache served as superintendent of the United States Coast Survey, and much of the coast of Texas was surveyed by teams working under his direction. Although Commodore Edwin Moore,qv Capt. George Simpton, and Capt. Perry W. Humphrey of the Texas Navyqv had made surveys and maps of the Texas coast, and engineers attached to Gen. Zachary Taylor'sqv army had surveyed the section of the coast between Corpus Christi and Caballo Pass in 1845–46, the Coast Survey's charting of the Gulf Coast from Point Isabel (later Port Isabel) to Florida appears to have been the first scientific cartography of the coast of Texas. The numerous maps and charts made under Bache's supervision during his tenure are in the National Archives. He wrote many reports of his surveys of the Gulf coast, which appeared in the annual reports of his department. He served as adviser to the United States Navy during the Civil War.qv He made notable contributions to science during his long career. Bache married Nancy Clarke Fowler in 1828. He died on February 17, 1867.

BIBLIOGRAPHY: *Dictionary of American Biography.*

Hobart Huson and Mark Odintz

BACHE, RICHARD (1784–1848). Richard Bache, Galveston County official and state legislator, the son of Richard and Sarah (Franklin) Bache and grandson of Benjamin Franklin, was born in Philadelphia on March 11, 1784. He married Sophia Burrell Dallas, daughter of the United States secretary of the treasury and sister of United States vice president George M. Dallas, on April 4, 1805. The couple had nine children. Bache served as captain of the Franklin Flying Artillery of the Philadelphia Volunteers in the War of 1812. He also served in the United States Navy and as Philadelphia postmaster. In 1836 he abandoned his family, possibly for financial reasons, and traveled to Texas, where he served on the *Zavala*qv in the Texas Navy.qv On May 1, 1836, he was mustered into the Louisiana Independent Volunteers, commanded by J. J. Robinson, and while in service he briefly guarded Antonio López de Santa Anna.qv In 1838–39 he served as chief clerk in the Navy Department at Houston and was enrolling clerk of the House of Representatives in the Third Congress of the republic. In 1842 he moved to Galveston, where he became commissioner of the navy yard and was made justice of the peace for Galveston County. As a member of the Convention of 1845,qv he cast the only vote against the annexationqv of Texas; nevertheless, he helped draw up the Constitution of 1845.qv He was subsequently import inspector at Galveston and represented Galveston in the Senate of the Second Texas Legislature. He was a Mason. Bache died in Austin on March 17, 1848, and was buried there.

BIBLIOGRAPHY: Texas House of Representatives, *Biographical Directory of the Texan Conventions and Congresses, 1832–1845* (Austin: Book Exchange, 1941).

Lura N. Rouse

BACHELOR PEAK. Bachelor Peak (Bachelor's Peak) is on U.S. Highway 183 fourteen miles northwest of Briggs in northern Burnet County (at 31°00′ N, 98°06′ W). It rises 1,391 feet above sea level, nearly 200 feet above the surrounding countryside. Early settler Alexander Brown and six other bachelors once had a picnic on its summit, and the hill was named for them.

BIBLIOGRAPHY: Darrell Debo, *Burnet County History* (2 vols., Burnet, Texas: Eakin, 1979).

BACHELOR PRONG OF HORDS CREEK. The Bachelor Prong of Hords Creek rises four miles south of Novice and six miles west of U.S. Highway 84 in northwestern Coleman County (at 31°56′ N, 99°36′ W) and runs eleven miles southeast to its mouth on Hords Creek, two miles west of Coleman (at 31°51′ N, 99°28′ W). It crosses an area of steep slopes and benches surfaced by shallow clay loams that support juniper, live oak, mesquite, and grasses; the lower reaches of the creek traverse a flat, flood-prone area with local shallow depressions, surfaced by clay and sandy loams that support water-tolerant hardwoods, conifers, and grasses.

BACHMAN, TEXAS. Bachman was on Bachman Branch at a site now adjacent to Bachman Lake on Loop 12, U.S. Interstate 35, and State Highway 354, at the northern edge of Love Fieldqv in central Dallas County. It was located at the intersections of the original land grants of Miles Bennett and Dickerson Parker. The area was settled and named for the John B. and William F. Bachman families, who settled in 1845 on Brownings Branch, a tributary of the Trinity River. The creek was later renamed Bachman Branch in their honor. According to some sources the first camp meeting held in Dallas County in 1845 was near the Missouri, Kansas and Texas crossing of the stream. The area is now the site of Bachman Lake, dammed in 1903, and Bachman Park, a family recreation facility.

BIBLIOGRAPHY: Sam Hanna Acheson, *Dallas Yesterday*, ed. Lee Milazzo (Dallas: Southern Methodist University Press, 1977). William L. McDonald, *Dallas Rediscovered: A Photographic Chronicle of Urban Expansion, 1870–1925* (Dallas: Dallas County Historical Society, 1978). Fred Tarpley, *Place Names of Northeast Texas* (Commerce: East Texas State University, 1969).

Matthew Hayes Nall

BACHMAN BRANCH. Bachman Branch rises at Forest Lane a mile south of Interstate Highway 635 and a half mile west of Dallas North Tollway in northern Dallas County (at 32°55′ N, 96°49′ W) and runs for ten miles south and then west through Bachman Lake to its mouth on the Elm Fork of the Trinity River (at 32°50′ N, 96°53′ W). It crosses variable terrain surfaced by clay loam that supports oaks, junipers, and grasses. Bachman Branch was called Brownings Branch in the 1840s but was renamed after John B. and William F. Bachman, who settled where the stream crosses Lemmon Avenue in Dallas.

BIBLIOGRAPHY: Fred Tarpley, *Place Names of Northeast Texas* (Commerce: East Texas State University, 1969).

BACK, TEXAS. Back, originally Pumpkin Ridge, is a rural community at the junction of State Highway 273 and Farm Road 1321, in eastern Gray County. The area was first settled by farmers in the late 1890s. In October 1899 a post office was opened there and named Northfork because of its proximity to the North Fork of the Red River. John J. Simpkins was the first postmaster. Many of the Pumpkin Ridge farmers built their homes out of lumber procured from the abandoned Fort Elliott near Mobeetie. A one-room school, opened in 1899, was originally taught by Miss Fannie Womble and later by T. M. Wolf, future Gray county judge. The community received its present name after John David Back arrived in the fall of 1904 with his wife and ten children from near Van Alstyne, in Collin County. Back, who became a pillar in the community, gave land for a new school building after the first one was mysteriously plundered for its lumber. The Back school, which served as a church building on Sundays, quickly became a local gathering place. For recreation, area residents enjoyed hunting in the breaks of the North Fork, and in 1905 a local baseball club was organized.

Oil and natural gas discoveries in the area during the 1920s led real estate men to begin platting lots for a proposed Back City in 1927, and roads were graded to the local oil wells, some of which reportedly produced as much as 6,000 barrels a day. A new brick schoolhouse was completed in 1928. The proposed town failed to materialize, however, after the Phillips Petroleum Company constructed a plant on the North Fork and the Fort Worth and Denver Northern Railway completed its line from Childress to Pampa in 1932. The Northfork post office, which had closed in 1928, was reestablished at the oil camp of Denworth in September 1932. Most people found it cheaper to live in either McLean, to the south of Back, or in Denworth, to the north. The Back community school remained in operation until 1950, when its district merged with that of McLean. Afterward the building was used as a community center. The area still produces oil and gas.

bibliography: Arthur Hecht, comp., *Postal History in the Texas Panhandle* (Canyon, Texas: Panhandle-Plains Historical Society, 1960). S. G. Reed, *A History of the Texas Railroads* (Houston: St. Clair, 1941; rpt., New York: Arno, 1981). F. Stanley [Stanley F. L. Crocchiola], *Story of the Texas Panhandle Railroads* (Borger, Texas: Hess, 1976). L. M. Watson, Jr., Back Community (MS, Interview files, Panhandle-Plains Historical Museum, Canyon, Texas). *H. Allen Anderson*

BACKBONE CREEK. Backbone Creek rises at Backbone Ridge, six miles southwest of Burnet in southwestern Burnet County (30°42′ N, 98°18′ W), and runs south for thirteen miles, through the town of Marble Falls, to its mouth on Lake Marble Falls, two miles above Max Starke Dam (at 30°34′ N, 98°17′ W). The terrain is generally flat with local deep dissections and is surfaced by shallow, stony soil that supports oak, juniper, and mesquite.

BACKBONE RIDGE. Backbone Ridge is a small chain of hills between Burnet and Marble Falls in southwestern Burnet County. It extends from a point overlooking Lake Lyndon B. Johnson, a mile south of the intersection of Farm roads 2342 and 1431 (30°39′ N, 98°25′ W), to a point three miles north of State Park Road 4 (30°43′ N, 98°20′ W). The elevation of the range is 1,100 to 1,500 feet, 200 to 400 feet higher than the surrounding countryside. Among its peaks are Backbone Mountain and Bald Knob.

bibliography: Darrell Debo, *Burnet County History* (2 vols., Burnet, Texas: Eakin, 1979).

BACLIFF, TEXAS. Bacliff is on Farm Road 646 and Galveston Bay sixteen miles northwest of Galveston in north central Galveston County. Originally a summer weekend resort, the community was known as Clifton-by-the-Sea until the late 1940s or early 1950s. In 1933 Clifton had a population of fifty and two businesses, and from 1940 to 1949 it had 100 residents and four businesses. Both names, Bacliff and Clifton-by-the-Sea, were used to refer to the community for a time after the Bacliff post office was established in 1961. That year the town registered 1,707 residents and twenty-five businesses. It grew to a population of 1,782 and seventeen businesses by 1966. By 1986 Bacliff had become a residential community for workers who commuted to jobs throughout the area; it had a population of 4,851 and nineteen businesses. In 1990 the community had six churches, a school, twenty-seven businesses, and a population of 5,549.

Diana J. Kleiner

BACON, SUMNER (1790–1844). Sumner Bacon, pioneer Cumberland Presbyterian missionary, was born in Auburn, Massachusetts, on January 22, 1790, to Jonathan and Mollie Bacon. His parents planned a career in law for him, but due to his father's death he left home sometime after 1810 and never returned. For a time he served as a private in the United States Army. His travels took him down the Ohio River valley and eventually, as a member of a surveying party, to Arkansas, where in the mid-1820s he was converted at a Cumberland revival meeting and decided to become a minister.

Because Bacon lacked even a basic grasp of grammar and spelling the Cumberland Presbytery of Arkansas asked him to spend two years improving his education before applying for a license to preach. Unwilling to study, he made little progress. After being refused by the Arkansas Presbytery, he went to Texas as a freelance itinerant evangelist in the fall of 1829. Since Catholicism was the legally required religion of the territory, Bacon did his preaching surreptitiously, moving from place to place when government pressure became too strong. In 1830 he wrote to Stephen F. Austin[qv] unsuccessfully seeking an appointment as chaplain in Austin's colony. His application to the Arkansas Presbytery was again refused in 1832. The following year Bacon met Rev. Benjamin Chase,[qv] a Presbyterian minister and agent for the American Bible Society. On the basis of Chase's recommendation the society commissioned Bacon in 1833 as its first regular agent in Texas. In two years of colportage work for the society, Bacon distributed more than 2,000 Bibles and New Testaments in both English and Spanish. In March of 1835 he presented himself to the newly formed Cumberland Presbytery of Louisiana. With Chase's help and his own persuasive speaking, Bacon was licensed and ordained a minister, although clearly as an exception to normal practices.

The outbreak of the Texas Revolution[qv] in the fall of 1835 temporarily halted Bacon's itinerant ministry. After marrying Elizabeth McCarroll (McKerall) on January 28, 1836, he participated in the hostilities by serving as a chaplain and courier for Gen. Sam Houston.[qv] As a courier he carried dispatches to the Alamo, Goliad, and Victoria and traveled to New Orleans for gunpowder and, secretly, to General Dunlap of Tennessee to seek aid against an expected Mexican invasion.

After the battle of San Jacinto[qv] Bacon resumed his missionary activities. In the summer of 1836 he organized the first Cumberland Presbyterian Church in Texas near San Augustine. The following year he and Cumberland clergymen Amos Roark and Mitchell Smith began the Texas Presbytery at a meeting held at Bacon's home on November 27. Afterwards Bacon's leadership in church activities diminished. Plagued with poor health, he could not maintain an itinerant ministry and was able to preach no more than once a month, although he did serve as the first moderator of the Cumberland Synod of Texas in 1843. He died on January 24, 1844. Although Bacon was not the first Protestant to preach in Texas, evidence indicates that he was the first resident Protestant evangelist to maintain a continuous ministry in the new territory.

bibliography: Robert Douglas Brackenridge, *Voice in the Wilderness: A History of the Cumberland Presbyterian Church in Texas* (San Antonio: Trinity University Press, 1968).

R. Douglas Brackenridge

BADER SETTLEMENT, TEXAS. Bader Settlement was five miles west of Castroville on the Old San Antonio Road[qv] in central Medina County. Joe Bader built and operated a hotel by a spring-fed watering hole there around 1860. He sold the land to August Hutzler and moved the hotel to another location around 1880 after the spring went dry. Bader settlers built a one-room schoolhouse in the late 1800s on property owned by Sterley Jagge. School records indicate an enrollment of fifteen and one teacher in 1897. By 1915 children from the community attended school in Dunlay. In 1935 the original spring at the hotel site resurfaced and continued to flow on land owned fifty years later by Stanley Haby, the grandson of August Hutzler.

bibliography: Castro Colonies Heritage Association, *The History of Medina County, Texas* (Dallas: National Share Graphics, 1983).

Ruben E. Ochoa

BADGER, TEXAS. Badger was located on the Missouri Pacific Railroad northeast of the present Judkins switch in south central Ector County. The station was established on the Texas and Pacific Railway in 1926, and the settlement profited from an oil boom in the late 1920s. Its population reached 200 before falling off to forty by 1940. A permanent community never developed, and only a depot and one supply house were built. In 1980 county maps showed no evidence of the former station.

BIBLIOGRAPHY: Finas Wade Horton, A History of Ector County, Texas (M.A. thesis, University of Texas, 1950). *Charles G. Davis*

BADGETT, JESSE B. (ca. 1807–?). Jesse B. Badgett, signer of the Texas Declaration of Independence,[qv] was born in North Carolina about 1807. With his brother William he enrolled in the Texas army on November 15, 1835. The brothers came from Louisiana to Texas early in December, and Jesse B. Badgett joined the command of William B. Travis[qv] at the Alamo[qv] by February 1, 1836. The soldiers at the Alamo elected him a delegate to the Convention of 1836,[qv] where he was seated on March 1. After signing the Declaration of Independence, he left the convention and evidently returned to his home in Arkansas.

BIBLIOGRAPHY: Louis Wiltz Kemp, *The Signers of the Texas Declaration of Independence* (Salado, Texas: Anson Jones, 1944; rpt. 1959). Texas House of Representatives, *Biographical Directory of the Texan Conventions and Congresses, 1832–1845* (Austin: Book Exchange, 1941). *L. W. Kemp*

BADGETT, TEXAS. Badgett, located on Farm Road 1212 in south central Martin County, was named for the R. A. Badgett family, who moved to the area from Mitchell County. Reported dates for the founding of the school district range from 1916 to 1926. The original school, which had two rooms and two teachers, was consolidated with the Courtney school in the late 1940s. Badgett no longer exists as a community.

BIBLIOGRAPHY: Vernen Liles, Pioneering on the Plains: The History of Martin County, Texas (M.A. thesis, University of Texas, 1953). Martin County Historical Commission, *Martin County, Texas* (Dallas: Taylor, 1979). *Noel Wiggins*

BADILLO, JUAN ANTONIO (?–1836). Juan Antonio Badillo, Alamo defender, was born in Texas. He was one of a number of native Texans who enlisted for six months' service and fought in the siege of Bexar[qv] under Capt. Juan N. Seguín.[qv] After the battle, Badillo accompanied Seguín back to Bexar and the Alamo in February 1836. He remained in the Alamo after Seguin was sent out to rally reinforcements and died in the battle of the Alamo[qv] on March 6, 1836.

BIBLIOGRAPHY: Daughters of the American Revolution, *The Alamo Heroes and Their Revolutionary Ancestors* (San Antonio, 1976). Bill Groneman, *Alamo Defenders* (Austin: Eakin, 1990). *Bill Groneman*

BAFFIN BAY. Baffin Bay, also known as Lago de la Santísima Trinidad and Salt Lagoon, projects inland from Laguna Madre.[qv] Its center point is about 27°15′ north and 97°31′ west. The bay forms part of the eastern boundary between Kenedy and Kleberg counties. The west side of Baffin Bay connects with the mouth of Los Olmos Creek, which flows from the Laguna Salada, Cayo del Grulla, and Alazan Bay. Baffin Bay provided Confederate blockade runners with protected overland access, through the shallow Laguna Madre, to the cotton markets of Mexico. The entire south shore of Baffin Bay forms the northern boundary of the vast Kenedy Ranch (*see* KENEDY, MIFFLIN).

BIBLIOGRAPHY: Tom Lea, *The King Ranch* (2 vols., Boston: Little, Brown, 1957). Marilyn M. Sibley, "Charles Stillman," *Southwestern Historical Quarterly* 77 (October 1973).

BAGBY, ARTHUR PENDLETON (1833–1921). Arthur Pendleton Bagby, lawyer, editor, and Confederate general, was born in Claiborne, Monroe County, Alabama, on May 17, 1833, the son of Arthur Pendleton Bagby. The elder Bagby served in the Alabama state Senate and House of Representatives, where he was the youngest member ever elected speaker. He was also twice elected governor of Alabama, served in the United States Senate, where he supported the annexation[qv] of Texas, and was appointed United States ambassador to Russia by President James K. Polk.

The younger Bagby attended school in Washington, D.C., and the United States Military Academy at West Point. At age nineteen he became the youngest graduate to be commissioned a second lieutenant of infantry. He was stationed at Fort Columbus, New York, in 1852–53 and saw frontier duty at Fort Chadbourne, Texas, in 1853 with the Eighth Infantry, Eighth Military Department. He resigned to study law, was admitted to the bar in Alabama in 1855, and practiced in Mobile until 1858, when he moved to Gonzales, Texas. There he married Frances Taylor in June 1860.

Upon the eruption of the Civil War[qv] he joined the Confederate Army and raised the first company of men from the Victoria area for the cause. He served as a major, Seventh Regiment of Texas Mounted Volunteers, in Gen. Henry H. Sibley's[qv] Army of New Mexico. He was promoted to lieutenant colonel in April 1862 and later to colonel. On January 1, 1863, he led his regiment in the battle of Galveston,[qv] in which his "Horse Marines"[qv] assisted in the capture of the federal ship *Harriet Lane*.[qv] In this encounter Bagby won, according to Gen. John B. Magruder,[qv] "imperishable renown." Bagby later served under generals Richard Taylor and Thomas Green[qv] in western Louisiana, where he was wounded in fighting along Bayou Teche on April 13, 1863. For his service in Louisiana he was promoted for gallantry in action to brigadier general in early 1864 by E. Kirby Smith,[qv] although the rank was not approved in Richmond.

Nevertheless, Bagby's cavalry brigade, formerly Sibley's Brigade,[qv] in which Bagby served during the invasion of New Mexico in 1862, was one of the best mounted commands in the Trans-Mississippi Department. It consisted of the Fourth, Fifth, and Seventh Texas Cavalry and Waller's Thirteenth Texas Cavalry Battalion. In the Red River campaign[qv] at Mansfield and Pleasant Hill in 1864, Bagby also assumed command of Augustus C. Buchel's[qv] cavalry brigade, which consisted of the First and Thirty-fifth Texas Cavalry and Terrell's Texas Cavalry. Bagby commanded a brigade under Hamilton P. Bee[qv] in late April and early May 1864, before replacing Bee in command of the cavalry division in mid-May to harass the Union retreat. Following the surrenders of Lee and Johnston, Bagby was assigned to duty as major general on May 16, 1865, by E. Kirby Smith. He was placed in command of all cavalry forces in Louisiana and held that post until the surrender of the Trans-Mississippi Department. Bagby's latest promotion, however, was not approved in Richmond either. Thus Bagby was a general only as a result of a temporary appointment by Smith's headquarters.

After the war he settled in Victoria, Texas, resumed his law practice, and worked in 1870–71 as assistant editor of the Victoria *Advocate*.[qv] He later moved to Hallettsville, where he continued his law practice. He died there on February 21, 1921. Among his children, W. T. Bagby, also a lawyer, represented Lavaca County in the state legislature, where he earned the nickname "Lion of Lavaca" as an antiprohibition leader. He also figured prominently in the gubernatorial campaigns of Oscar B. Colquitt and James E. Ferguson.[qqv] Another son, A. P. (Penn) Bagby, Jr., served as deputy tax collector and tax clerk of Lavaca County, chief clerk in the Texas secretary of state's office, and tax commissioner of the state of Texas under Governor James Ferguson.

BIBLIOGRAPHY: *Dictionary of American Biography*. Lester Fitzhugh, "Texas Forces in the Red River Campaign, March–May, 1864," *Texas Military History* 3 (Spring 1963). Victoria *Advocate*, 88th Anniversary Number, September 28, 1934. Marcus J. Wright, comp., and Harold B. Simpson, ed., *Texas in the War, 1861–1865* (Hillsboro, Texas: Hill Junior College Press, 1965). *Craig H. Roell*

BAGBY, BALLARD C. (1809–1862). Ballard C. Bagby, planter, merchant, and politician, the son of Daniel and Lucy (Allen) Bagby, was born in Virginia in 1809. He moved to Texas in 1839, and in 1841 he served as a major under Edward H. Tarrant[qv] in the Indian campaigns on the frontier. He was a delegate from Red River County to the Convention of 1845[qv] and represented Red River and Bowie counties in the Senate of the First Congress of the republic. In the late 1840s he moved to Fannin County and settled on a plantation near Honey Grove, where he opened a store. Although he never again served in the legislature, Bagby remained active in the Democratic party[qv] at the local and state levels. The exact date of his death is not known, but his will was filed for probate in Fannin County on December 15, 1862. He left an estate consisting of thirteen slaves and other property, valued at $57,000.

BIBLIOGRAPHY: Texas House of Representatives, *Biographical Directory of the Texan Conventions and Congresses, 1832–1845* (Austin: Book Exchange, 1941).
Cecil Harper, Jr.

BAGBY, GEORGE H. (ca. 1805–1863). George H. Bagby, soldier and legislator, was born in Virginia about 1805 to Daniel and Lucy Bagby. In 1833 he and his wife, Margaret (Latimer), came to Texas, settled in Clarksville, and became charter members of Clarksville's old Presbyterian church. Bagby enlisted in the Texas army as a private in Capt. William Becknell's[qv] company on July 16, 1836, and was discharged on October 16. He served as Red River county clerk from 1854 to 1856 and represented the county at the Secession Convention[qv] in 1861. Though he only participated in the Adjourned Session, he signed the Ordinance of Secession. He was later a member of the House in the Ninth State Legislature (1861–62). Bagby enlisted in the Confederate Army but was discharged from active duty because of his old age. He later served as paymaster and traveled in 1863 Arkansas to pay the Texas troops. On the return trip through Indian Territory he was attacked and killed by Indians.

BIBLIOGRAPHY: Audited Military Claims, Republic of Texas, Texas State Archives, Austin. *Biographical Souvenir of the State of Texas* (Chicago: Battey, 1889; rpt., Easley, South Carolina: Southern Historical Press, 1978). John Henry Brown, *Indian Wars and Pioneers of Texas* (Austin: Daniell, 1880; reprod., Easley, South Carolina: Southern Historical Press, 1978).
J. L. Bryan

BAGBY, THOMAS M. (1814–1868). Thomas M. Bagby, businessman and civic leader, the son of Daniel and Lucy Bagby, was born in Virginia on May 18, 1814. In 1822 the family moved to Montgomery County, Tennessee, where Bagby was reared and became a merchant. He arrived in Texas in 1837, worked for a time as a commission merchant, and by the 1840s was a prosperous cotton factor. In 1847 he was involved in an effort to emancipate a black woman, but his petition to the legislature was denied. On February 23, 1848, he married Marianna Baker, with whom he had six children. He was one of nine original members of the Houston Public Library,[qv] chartered in 1848, which stands on the site of the former Bagby home. He was a Mason and a Presbyterian and served as an alderman of the Fourth Ward, Houston.[qv] He founded and was president of the third national bank established in Texas. In 1850 he was one of the incorporators of the Houston Plank Road Company, and in 1866 he helped found the Houston Direct Navigation Company[qv] to promote barge transport of cotton and improve bayou navigation. A steamboat, the *T. M. Bagby*, was named in his honor. Bagby died in Houston on May 12, 1868.

BIBLIOGRAPHY: *History of Texas, Together with a Biographical History of the Cities of Houston and Galveston* (Chicago: Lewis, 1895). David G. McComb, *Houston: The Bayou City* (Austin: University of Texas Press, 1969; rev. ed., *Houston: A History*, 1981). Andrew Forest Muir, "The Free Negro in Harris County, Texas," *Southwestern Historical Quarterly* 46 (January 1943). Ellen Robbins Red, *Early Days on the Bayou, 1838–1890: The Life and Letters of Horace Dickinson Taylor* (Waco: Texian Press, 1986). Amelia W. Williams and Eugene C. Barker, eds., *The Writings of Sam Houston, 1813–1863* (8 vols., Austin: University of Texas Press, 1938–43; rpt., Austin and New York: Pemberton Press, 1970). WPA Writers Program, *Houston* (Houston: Anson Jones, 1942).
Lura N. Rouse

BAGBY, WILLIAM BUCK (1855–1939). William Buck Bagby, a pioneer Baptist missionary to Brazil, was the son of James and Mary Franklin (Willson) Bagby of Kentucky, who moved to Texas in 1852. He was born in Coryell County on November 5, 1855. The family moved to Waco when he was eight, and he attended the preparatory school for Waco University. He studied theology under Benajah H. Carroll[qv] and graduated in 1875. He farmed for a year and then taught school. In 1880 Bagby married Anne Luther, daughter of John Luther, president of Baylor University at Independence. Several factors influenced Bagby's decision to go to Brazil. Mrs. Bagby had already determined to become a missionary. Bagby's friend and later coworker, Z. C. Taylor, encouraged him to consider Brazil. Finally, A. T. Hawthorne urged the Bagbys to go to Brazil. Hawthorne had led groups of Southerners to Brazil after the Civil War.[qv] The Bagbys arrived in Rio de Janeiro in 1880 and founded an American community in nearby Santa Barbara. They learned Portuguese from Alfonso Teixeria and in 1882 were joined by missionaries Z. C. and Kate Taylor. These five moved to Bahia (Salvador) and established the first Baptist church in Brazil on October 15, 1882. By the time of its centennial the denomination had grown to over one-half million. In 1884 Bagby established a church in Rio de Janeiro. In 1889 Brazil declared itself a republic, and the new government's policy of separation of church and state facilitated Protestant activity in Brazil. Bagby's strategy was to establish churches in major cities. He traveled extensively from Rio for this purpose. He aided new churches in acquiring property, in training ministers, and in erecting buildings. In 1901 the Bagbys moved to São Paulo. Anne organized and operated a school; Bagby continued to organize churches and to help Brazilians organize associations and conventions. He also engaged in preaching missions to Chile and other South American countries. His reports prompted Southern Baptists to send missionaries to other parts of South America. The Bagbys' fourth home in Brazil was Pôrto Alegre in the state of Rio Grande do Sul. They spent the last decade of their lives there. Bagby died on August 5, 1939, of bronchial pneumonia, and was buried there. The Bagbys had nine children; five of these lived to maturity, and all five became missionaries in South America.

BIBLIOGRAPHY: A. R. Crabtree, *Baptists in Brazil* (Rio de Janeiro: Baptist Publishing House of Brazil, 1953). Helen Bagby Harrison, *The Bagbys of Brazil* (Nashville: Broadman, 1954). William L. Pitts, "Baptist Beginnings in Brazil," *Baptist History and Heritage* 17 (October 1982).
William L. Pitts

BAGBY, TEXAS. Bagby is on Farm Road 1550 fifteen miles southeast of Bonham in the southeastern corner of Fannin County. In 1895 the Gulf, Colorado and Santa Fe Railway established the community as a railroad stop. That same year the Bagby post office opened. By 1900 the settlement had a church, a school, a drugstore, two gins, a general store, and a sawmill. In 1904, however, the post office closed. In 1944 the railroad discontinued service to the town. Since the end of World War II,[qv] Bagby has served as a church and school community for area farmers.

BIBLIOGRAPHY: *Fannin County Folks and Facts* (Dallas: Taylor, 1977).
David Minor

BAGDAD, TEXAS. Bagdad was a rural community on the South Fork of Brushy Creek one mile west of Leander in southwest Williamson County. It was surveyed in 1854 by Charles Babcock, who ran an inn at the site, and named for Bagdad, Tennessee, the hometown of an early settler. The settlement had a post office from 1855 to 1882 and was a mail stop on the early stage line between Austin and Lampasas. Bagdad thrived in the 1860s and 1870s and in 1882 had two blacksmith shops, a hotel, two schools, a Masonic lodge, three churches, and several stores. That year, however, the Austin and Northwestern Railroad reached nearby Leander, and the post office was moved from Bagdad to that town; several businesses moved as well. By the turn of the century Bagdad was virtually a ghost town. The site was included as part of Leander on the county highway map of 1977.

BIBLIOGRAPHY: Clara Stearns Scarbrough, *Land of Good Water: A Williamson County History* (Georgetown, Texas: Williamson County Sun Publishers, 1973).
Mark Odintz

BAGGARLY, HERBERT MILTON, JR. (1915–1985). Herbert M. Baggarly, Jr., journalist, son of Herbert Milton and Flora Henry (Parker) Baggarly, was born at Plainview, Texas, on January 1, 1915. He grew up in Happy, where he completed elementary and secondary school. After earning a B.A. at West Texas State University and an M.A. at the University of Missouri, he taught at Tulia High School, from 1938 to 1943. During World War II[qv] he served as a junior aide to Adm. Chester W. Nimitz[qv] in the Pacific. After the war he returned to Tulia, where he taught school and worked at the newspaper.

From 1950 to 1979 Baggarly was editor and publisher of the Tulia *Herald,* which published his column, "The Country Editor." The *Herald* had a weekly circulation of 4,500, with subscribers in every state as well as several foreign countries. This popularity was due in large part to Baggarly's column, which provided sharp, down-to-earth commentary on political issues. His editorial and column writing won numerous state, regional, and national awards. The first of two awards from the National Editorial Association came in 1957, a first-place ranking granted to the *Herald* for column writing. The second, a 1961 award for editorial writing, named the *Herald* as one of the top three newspapers of all sizes and frequencies of publication in the nation. Additional honors for editorial and column writing came from the Texas Press Association, the West Texas Press Association,[qv] the Panhandle Press Association, and the journalism departments at Texas Tech University and West Texas State University. In 1966 Baggarly received the first Editor of the Year Award granted by the Texas Farmers' Union; the next year he was named Tulia's outstanding citizen of the year. In 1968 he declined a personal invitation from Lyndon B. Johnson[qv] to join the president's Washington staff as advisor and speechwriter.

Selected columns from "The Country Editor" were published as *The Texas Country Editor* in 1966 and *The Texas Country Democrat* in 1970. After selling the *Herald* in 1979 Baggarly continued to write a weekly column until his death. He never married. He died at Tulia on September 7, 1985, and was buried in Rose Hill Cemetery.

BIBLIOGRAPHY: Eugene W. Jones, ed., *The Texas Country Democrat: H. M. Baggarly Surveys Two Decades of Texas Politics* (San Angelo: Anchor, 1970). Eugene W. Jones, ed., *The Texas Country Editor: H. M. Baggarly Takes a Grassroots Look at National Politics* (Cleveland: World, 1966). Vertical Files, Barker Texas History Center, University of Texas at Austin.
Eugene W. Jones

BAGGETT CREEK. Baggett Creek rises six miles southeast of Proctor in northeastern Comanche County (at 31°55′ N, 98°24′ W) and flows southwest for four miles to its mouth on the Leon River, three miles north of Gustine (at 31°54′ N, 98°25′ W). The stream was named for John Baggett, an early settler in the region. Although a Baggett community once existed on the creek, only a church building remains in the area. The creek travels through an area of steep slopes surfaced by shallow, stony soils that support cacti and sparse grasses.

BIBLIOGRAPHY: Comanche County Bicentennial Committee, *Patchwork of Memories: Historical Sketches of Comanche County, Texas* (Brownwood, Texas: Banner Printing, 1976).

BAGUAM INDIANS. In 1675 the Baguam Indians were identified in a Coahuila document as a hunting and gathering people who lived in the Sierra de Dacate some seventy-five miles north of the Eagle Pass section of the Rio Grande. The sierra referred to must have been a part of the eroded southern margin of the Edwards Plateau. This would place the Baguam in or near the site of modern Kinney County. The name of these Indians is sometimes given as Bagnam, a misreading of Baguam. The Baguams are evidently the Indians recorded as Pagaiam by Juan Domínguez de Mendoza[qv] in 1684, when he was encamped for six weeks in the western part of the Edwards Plateau. Some writers have speculated that the Baguam language was either Coahuilteco or Tonkawa, but this assumes that no other languages were spoken in their area. The primary documents do not contain enough information to permit linguistic classification. Since the Baguams are not mentioned in documents written after 1684, their ethnic identity was probably lost before 1700.

BIBLIOGRAPHY: Vito Alessio Robles, *Coahuila y Texas en la época colonial* (Mexico City: Editorial Cultura, 1938; 2d ed., Mexico City: Editorial Porrúa, 1978). Herbert Eugene Bolton, ed., *Spanish Exploration in the Southwest, 1542–1706* (New York: Scribner, 1908; rpt., New York: Barnes and Noble, 1959).
Thomas N. Campbell

BAGWELL, TEXAS. Bagwell is at the intersection of Ranch roads 2120 and 2573, seven miles northwest of Clarksville and six miles east of Detroit in western Red River County. It was named for Milas (Miles) Bagwell, who operated a tannery and blacksmith shop in the area, and was built on the Texas and Pacific Railway when it was constructed through the county in 1875–76. The post office in Robbinsville, a small community 2½ miles to the south, seems to have been moved to the new town of Bagwell in 1876. By 1884 Bagwell had cotton gins, a sawmill, a gristmill, a church, a district school, and a population of 200. The town was a railroad shipping point for lumber and shingles produced in town and cotton and cottonseed produced by area farmers. By 1914 the population had reached 300, and two small banks were in operation. The population was 400 in the late 1920s, 250 in the late 1930s and 350 in 1947. By 1961 U.S. Highway 82 had bypassed Bagwell, and the population of the town had begun to decline sharply. It was 195 in 1964, 95 in 1970, and 108 in 1980. In 1986 the town had four businesses. In 1990 the population was 150.
Cecil Harper, Jr.

BAILEY, JAMES BRITON (1779–1832). James Brit(t)on (Brit) Bailey, one of Stephen F. Austin's[qv] Old Three Hundred[qv] colonists, was born in North Carolina on August 1, 1779. He married Edith Smith, and the couple had six children; after her death around 1815, Bailey married her sister, Nancy, also known as Dorothy or Dot Smith, and they had five children. Bailey apparently lived in Kentucky for a number of years and reportedly served in the legislature of that state; however he acquired a controversial reputation and may have been prosecuted for the crime of forgery before he left the state. He also resided in Tennessee for a number of years and fought in the War of 1812. He, his family, and six adult slaves moved to Texas around 1818 and settled near the Brazos River, where Bailey allegedly bought land from the Spanish government. After Mexico gained independence from Spain in 1821 he continued to claim title to his land, although the Mexican government did not recognize his title. Possibly due either to Bailey's reputation in Kentucky or his questionable land claim, Stephen F. Austin[qv] ordered him to leave the Austin colony. However, on July 7, 1824, Austin recognized Bailey's squatter's claim to a league and a labor of land on the east bank of the Brazos River near what is now Bailey's Prairie.

Although Bailey and Austin reportedly disliked one another, Austin convened settlers from the lower Brazos region to Bailey's home to take an oath of fidelity to the Constitution of 1824.[qv] At that meeting Bailey became lieutenant of a company of militia. In 1829 Governor José María Viesca[qv] granted him a commission as captain. Bailey fought in the battles of Jones Creek and Velasco,[qqv] respectively in 1824 and 1832.

He became known for his eccentric behavior and frequently engaged in brawls. He died on December 6, 1832, probably from cholera. He was buried in the family graveyard on Bailey's Prairie. His will, still extant, required that he be buried standing up and facing the West" legend has added "with my rifle at my side and a jug of whiskey at my feet." His ghost is said to wander the area as a white round ball of light, known as Bailey's Light, searching for more whiskey. The Texas Historical Commission[qv] placed a marker near Bailey's Prairie in 1970 to commemorate his life.

BIBLIOGRAPHY: James Briton Bailey Papers, Barker Texas History Center, University of Texas at Austin. Eugene C. Barker, ed., *The Austin Papers* (3 vols., Washington: GPO, 1924–28). James A. Creighton, *A Narrative History of Brazoria County* (Angleton, Texas: Brazoria County Historical Commission, 1975). Edward M. Golson, "Baileys and Polleys among Earliest Texans," *Frontier Times,* February 1936. Josephine Polley Golson, *Bailey's Light: Saga of Brit Bailey and Other Hardy Pioneers* (San Antonio: Naylor, 1950). Noah Smithwick, *The Evolution of a State, or Recollections of Old Texas Days* (Austin: Gammel, 1900; rpt., Austin: University of Texas Press, 1983). Vertical Files, Barker Texas History Center, University of Texas at Austin.

Merle Weir

BAILEY, JAMES ROBINSON (1868–1941). James Robinson Bailey, chemist and professor, son of Frank H. and Mary Ella (Perkins) Bailey, was born in Houston, Texas, on December 11, 1868. He attended Dean Academy in Massachusetts and Phillips Exeter Academy in New Hampshire before entering the University of Texas, where he took his B.A. degree in 1891. He received his Ph.D. at the University of Munich in 1897 and did postgraduate work in Leipzig and London. In 1897 he became instructor of chemistry at the University of Texas. He became professor in 1911 and was research lecturer in 1932–33. He was associate editor of the *Journal of the American Chemical Society* from 1930 to 1941, a member of the American Chemical Society and the American Petroleum Institute, and a fellow in the Texas Academy of Science.[qv]

He wrote more than fifty scientific articles, secured many patents dealing with nitrogen compounds in petroleum and cottonseed meal, and discovered more than twenty drugs. On leave of absence from the university during World War I[qv] he worked with Alcan Hirsch in New York and "cracked" the German formulas for novocaine and synthetic adrenalin. Among his discoveries were adaline, salaphene, novasperin, and a number of analine dyes. His work in developing compounds for pharmaceuticals helped eliminate America's need for foreign medicines. In 1940 he announced the discovery of two new benzoquinolines (white crystals similar to sugar) in petroleum. His laboratory pioneered in research on petroleum bases and derived thirty-two nitrogen compounds from the by-products of petroleum. The laboratory received a grant from the American Petroleum Institute (1926) and a fellowship from the Union Oil Company of California (1931).

On December 18, 1907, Bailey married Mrs. Rosine Mailliot Meyer, who died in 1915. They had one daughter. On January 1, 1924, he married Mrs. Ann Throckmorton Shirley. He died in Austin on March 25, 1941.

BIBLIOGRAPHY: *Alcalde* (magazine of the Ex-Students' Association of the University of Texas), December 1920, May 1941. *Daily Texan,* January 20, 1939. Dallas *Morning News,* March 26, 1941. Vertical Files, Barker Texas History Center, University of Texas at Austin.

BAILEY, JOSEPH WELDON (1863–1929). Joseph Weldon Bailey, United States congressman and senator, was born Joseph Edgar Bailey in Crystal Springs, Mississippi, on October 6, 1863, the son of Joseph and Harriet (Dee) Bailey. He attended five different colleges and universities before completing his law studies in Lebanon, Tennessee, in 1883. During his studies he replaced his middle name with the family name Weldon. He returned to Mississippi in 1883 and, after being admitted to the bar in Copiah County, began practicing law in Hazelhurst, Mississippi. As an avid Democrat who opposed the Republican tariff, he soon became embroiled in local politics. In January 1884 he was called to testify before a United States Senate committee investigating the violent tactics used by Mississippi Democrats in the local elections of 1883. When he was accused of being one of the leaders of the Democratic faction that initiated the violence, Bailey did not appear because he refused to perjure himself. No action was taken against him.

In 1885 he moved to Gainesville, Texas, and began practicing law. He quickly became politically active. He supported the unsuccessful prohibition[qv] amendment to the state constitution in 1887. In 1888 he refused attempts to nominate him as a congressional candidate because he was not old enough. Two years later he successfully ran for Congress, and in 1887 he was elected leader of the Democratic minority. During his terms in the House, he favored free silver and opposed expansionism. He also acquired a reputation as a parliamentary tactician and an orator. Despite political enemies, he was always a popular speaker in his home district; he remained a lifetime friend and hero to the young Samuel T. Rayburn.[qv] Bailey became a United States senator in 1901. In the Senate he advocated regulation of railroad rates and service and the 1909 tax on corporations. During his senatorial term charges were made that he had illegally represented the Waters-Pierce Oil Company, which was expelled from Texas for violating the antitrust laws because of its connections with the Standard Oil trust (*see* WATERS-PIERCE CASE).

Bailey damaged his early promise as a potential leader of the Democratic party[qv] in 1902 when, after a heated debate, he physically assaulted Senator Albert Beveridge. In 1906 *Cosmopolitan* magazine charged that Bailey was one of the senators who controlled the Senate to protect private interests at the expense of the public. He was, nevertheless, reelected and was eventually exculpated by the Texas House and Senate investigations. Nevertheless, these investigations revealed that as a corporate attorney he had received large fees for his work. An additional and perhaps even more damaging event was the revelation that Waters-Pierce had never broken its ties to Standard Oil, contrary to claims that it had severed relations in 1900. Bailey's public career was over; he was never elected to public office again. Facing a stern challenge in 1912 and disillusioned by the progressive movement within the Democratic party, he resigned from the Senate in September 1911 and established a lucrative law practice in Washington. He returned to Texas in 1920 and ran for governor. After his defeat, he established a law office in Dallas.

In 1885 Bailey married Ellen Murray of Oxford, Mississippi. They had two sons, one of whom, Joseph Weldon Bailey, Jr.,[qv] had a long political career. Ellen died in 1926, and Bailey married Mrs. Prudence Rosengren in 1927. He died on April 13, 1929, during a trial in Sherman and was buried in Gainesville.

BIBLIOGRAPHY: Sam Hanna Acheson, *Joe Bailey: The Last Democrat* (New York: Macmillan, 1932; rpt., Freeport, New York: Book for Libraries Press, 1970). Alwyn Barr, *Reconstruction to Reform: Texas Politics, 1876–1906* (Austin: University of Texas Press, 1971). Lewis L. Gould, *Progressives and Prohibitionists: Texas Democrats in the Wilson Era* (Austin: University of Texas Press, 1973; rpt., Austin: Texas State Historical Association, 1992). Bob Charles Holcomb, Senator Joe Bailey: Two Decades of Controversy (Ph.D. dissertation, Texas Tech University, 1969).

Bob C. Holcomb

BAILEY, JOSEPH WELDON, JR. (1892–1943). Joseph Weldon (Little Joe) Bailey, Jr., United States representative-at-large and Dallas attorney, son of Ellen (Murray) and Joseph Weldon Bailey,[qv] was born in Gainesville, Texas, on December 15, 1892. He attended public schools in Gainesville and Washington, D. C., while his father served in the House of Representatives and the Senate. As a young boy accompanying his father on a visit to the White House, he replied to President William McKinley's request that he sit on the president's knee, "Mr. President, I like you, but I can't sit on your knee because you're a Republican."

Bailey graduated from Princeton University in 1915 and received a bachelor of laws degree from the University of Virginia in 1919. In the interim he acquired the rank of first lieutenant in the 314th Regiment of Field Artillery during his military service, from August 15, 1917, to March 24, 1919. In 1920 he was admitted to the state bar and began the practice of law with his father's law firm, Bailey and Shaeffer, located in the Kirby Building in Dallas. He was a delegate to the state Democratic conventions from 1922 to 1934.

In 1932 "Little Joe" threw his hat into the ring to run for one of three new congressman-at-large seats. He campaigned as a states'-rights Democrat in opposition to national government extravagance. He called the Eighteenth Amendment "a mistake" and favored its repeal, while opposing the "open saloon" (*see* PROHIBITION). He eventually received the endorsement of the Texas Federation of Antiprohibition Clubs, headed by John H. Kirby.[qv] Out of a field of eleven in the Democratic primary Bailey received a plurality of the votes, but he was forced into a runoff primary against the second-place finisher, J. H. "Cyclone" Davis,[qv] whom he had led 199,131 to 122,905 in the first primary. Bailey defeated Davis in the runoff by a vote of 519,393 to 361,485. In the November general election he overwhelmed token Republican opposition. As a freshman Congressman he was assigned to committees on Education, Elections, and Expenditures in the Executive Departments.

Despite his personal admiration of President Franklin D. Roosevelt, Bailey's political philosophy put him at odds with some of FDR's New Deal programs. Bailey voted against unemployment relief, the refinancing of home mortgages, and the National Industrial Recovery Act, and he opposed the federal regulation of the oil industry. During the second session of the Seventy-third Congress he was a member of the temporary Committee on World War Veterans Legislation. He was a consistent supporter of veterans' benefits and voted to override the president's veto of the Independent Offices Appropriation bill, which contained generous benefits for veterans of both the Spanish American War and World War I.[qv]

When his Congressman-at-large seat was abolished Bailey chose to challenge U.S. Senator Thomas T. Connally[qv] in his first bid for reelection in 1934. Bailey emphasized his support of veterans and his opposition to prohibition, despite its repeal. As the decided underdog he gambled by accepting the public endorsement of Earle Mayfield,[qv] who had been backed by the Ku Klux Klan,[qv] at a campaign appearance in Tyler. Bailey lost to Connally in a landslide, 567,139 to 355,963, but reemerged politically in 1940 to head the Texas-for-Willkie clubs, groups of conservative Democrats opposed to a third term for Roosevelt. Bailey was an aggressive campaigner in a losing cause. With the aid of his old adversary Senator Connally, he received a commission as a marine captain on May 13, 1942.

He was driving home to Dallas from his military post at Norman, Oklahoma, when he received fatal head injuries in a car wreck north of Gainesville. He died in the Camp Howze army hospital near Gainesville on July 17, 1943. He was survived by his wife, the former Roberta Lewis of St. Louis, Missouri, and one son, Joseph Weldon Bailey III. Bailey was buried in Fairview Cemetery in Gainesville and in 1958 was reinterred at Hillcrest Memorial Park in Dallas, at the request of his widow. He was a Presbyterian.

BIBLIOGRAPHY: *America's Young Men: The Official Who's Who among the Young Men of the Nation* (Los Angeles: Richard Blank, 1937). *Biographical Directory of the American Congress* (Washington, D.C.: GPO, 1859–). Vertical Files, Barker Texas History Center, University of Texas at Austin.

Ronald W. Melugin

BAILEY, LIGHT D'ALBERGO (1908–1972). Light D'Albergo Bailey, teacher, translator, and historical preservationist, was born on January 24, 1908, in New York City, the daughter of Rev. and Mrs. Arturo D'Albergo. She spent her early childhood in Sicily, where she received her first education, and after the family's return to the United States she attended schools in New Jersey and New York. She studied at Birmingham Southern College in Alabama and earned a B.A. from the University of Texas in 1930. After marrying Clay Bailey, a teacher, on July 27, 1930, she taught school for a year in Alabama. From 1931 to 1933 Mrs. Bailey taught high school Spanish, Latin, and Italian in Galveston, and from 1934 to 1942 and again from 1944 to 1951 she was an instructor of Spanish at Southern Methodist University, where she also initiated the first regular coursework in Italian. In 1951 the Baileys and their daughter moved permanently to Houston; there Light Bailey joined the faculty of the University of Houston and introduced Italian to the curriculum. With her husband, she established the Clay and Light Bailey Collection on Italian Culture at the University of Houston in 1966.

Mrs. Bailey published an English translation of Annibale Ranuzzi's *Il Texas*, first published in Bologna in 1842. She reviewed books for the Dallas *Morning News*[qv] and classical records for the Dallas *Times Herald*.[qv] She also lectured frequently on Italian culture to civic, church, and school organizations. The Italian Ministry of Foreign Affairs awarded her its Cultural Medal in 1961, and Unico, the Italian service organization, honored her in 1969 for her contribution to the understanding and preservation of the Italian heritage and history in the United States. Light Bailey died in Houston on January 24, 1972. In recognition of her career in teaching and disseminating Italian language and culture, she was posthumously awarded a decoration by the president of Italy. *See also* ITALIANS.

BIBLIOGRAPHY: Biographical File, University of Texas Institute of Texan Cultures, San Antonio. *The Italian Texans* (San Antonio: University of Texas Institute of Texan Cultures, 1973).

Judith N. McArthur

BAILEY, MOLLIE ARLINE KIRKLAND (1844?–1918). Mollie Bailey, "Circus Queen of the Southwest," the daughter of William and Mary Arline Kirkland, is believed to have been born on November 2, 1844, on a plantation near Mobile, Alabama. As a young woman she eloped with James A. (Gus) Bailey, who played the cornet in his father's circus band, and was married on March 21, 1858. With Mollie's sister Fanny and Gus's brother Alfred, the young couple formed the Bailey Family Troupe, which traveled through Alabama, Mississippi, and Arkansas acting, dancing, and singing. In the Civil War[qv] Gus served as bandmaster for a company of Hood's Texas Brigade.[qv] Leaving their child Dixie, the first of nine children, with friends in Richmond, Virginia, Mollie traveled with the brigade as a nurse and, according to some sources, a spy for Gen. John Bell Hood[qv] and Jubal A. Early. Mrs. Bailey disguised herself as an elderly woman, passed through federal camps pretending to be a cookie seller, and claimed to have taken quinine through enemy lines by hiding packets of it in her hair. She joined her husband and brother-in-law in Hood's Minstrels and on April 5, 1864, performed a "musical and dancing program" with them near Zillicoffer. During this period Gus wrote the words for "The Old Gray Mare," based on a horse who almost died after eating green corn but revived when given medicine. A friend set it to music, and it was played as a regimental marching song. It was later used as the official song of the Democratic national convention of 1928.[qv] After the war the couple traveled throughout the South and then toured by riverboat with the Bailey Concert Company.

Spectators at Mollie Bailey's Circus watch a performer walk a tight-rope stretched from the main tent top. Photograph by Cecil Bouldin James. Hamilton, ca. 1913. Courtesy Maxine Havens, Hamilton.

Their career in Texas began in 1879 when the troupe traded the showboat for a small circus that enjoyed immediate success as the Bailey Circus, "A Texas Show for Texas People." The show became the Mollie A. Bailey Show after Gus's health forced him to retire to winter quarters in Blum, Texas. Mollie came to be known as "Aunt Mollie." Her circus was distinguished by the United States, Lone Star, and Confederate flags that flew over the bigtop and Mollie's practice of giving war veterans, Union or Confederate, free tickets. At its height, the one-ring tent circus had thirty-one wagons and about 200 animals; it added elephant and camel acts in 1902. After her husband's death in 1896, Mollie Bailey continued in the business, buying lots in many places where the circus performed to eliminate the high "occupation" taxes levied on shows by most towns. When the circus moved on, she allowed these lots to be used for ball games and camp meetings and later let many of them revert to the towns. She is also credited for her generosity to various churches and for allowing poor children to attend the circus free. In 1906, when the circus began traveling by railroad, Bailey entertained such distinguished guests as governors James Stephen Hogg and Oscar Branch Colquitt[qqv] and senators Joseph Weldon Bailey and Morris Sheppard,[qqv] along with members of Hood's Brigade, in a finely appointed parlor car. She was also said to be a friend of Comanche chief Quanah Parker.[qv] In 1906 she married A. H. (Blackie) Hardesty, a much younger man, who managed the circus gas lights and who was subsequently known as Blackie Bailey. According to some sources, Mollie Bailey showed the first motion pictures in Texas in a separate circus tent, including a one-reel film of the sinking of the USS *Maine*. After her youngest child, Birda, died in 1917, Bailey ran the circus from home, communicating with the road by telegram and letter. She died on October 2, 1918, at Houston, and was buried there in Hollywood Cemetery. She was survived for nineteen years by her husband, who became a jitney driver between Houston and Goose Creek and resided in Baytown.

BIBLIOGRAPHY: Francis Edward Abernethy, ed., *Legendary Ladies of Texas*, Publications of the Texas Folklore Society 43 (Dallas: E-Heart, 1981). Olga Bailey, *Mollie Bailey: The Circus Queen of the Southwest*, ed. Bess Samuel Ayres (Dallas: Harben-Spotts, 1943). Marj Gurasich, *Red Wagons and White Canvas: A Story of the Mollie Bailey Circus* (Austin: Eakin Press, 1988). *Diana J. Kleiner*

BAILEY, PETER JAMES III (1812–1836). Peter James Bailey, Alamo defender, the son of Gabriel and Sabra (Rice) Bailey, was born in Kentucky in 1812. He graduated from Transylvania University with a degree in law in 1834. In January 1836 he came to Texas in company with Daniel W. Cloud[qv] and others from Logan County, Kentucky. They took the oath of allegiance before John Forbes[qv] at Nacogdoches on January 14, 1836, and were enrolled in the Texas army. Bailey and Cloud were members of the Tennessee Mounted Volunteers.

They perished with David Crockett[qv] in the battle of the Alamo[qv] on March 6, 1836. For Bailey's service to Texas, his heirs received land parcels that are now in Archer, Baylor, and Hamilton counties. Bailey County in the Texas Panhandle was named in Peter Bailey's honor.

BIBLIOGRAPHY: Albert Curtis, *Remember the Alamo Heroes* (San Antonio: Clegg, 1961). Bill Groneman, *Alamo Defenders* (Austin: Eakin, 1990). John H. Jenkins, ed., *The Papers of the Texas Revolution, 1835–1836* (10 vols., Austin: Presidial Press, 1973). Amelia W. Williams, A Critical Study of the Siege of the Alamo and of the Personnel of Its Defenders (Ph.D. dissertation, University of Texas, 1931; rpt., *Southwestern Historical Quarterly* 36–37 [April 1933–April 1934]).

Ronald G. Bailey

BAILEY, RUFUS WILLIAM (1793–1863). Rufus William Bailey, the third president of Austin College, the son of Lebbeus and Sarah (Myrick) Bailey, was born in North Yarmouth, Maine, on April 13, 1793. He graduated as a Phi Beta Kappa from Dartmouth in 1813, studied law under Daniel Webster, and returned to Dartmouth to teach. Later he taught in Virginia and helped to establish Mary Baldwin Seminary. In 1854 he moved to Texas and in 1855 accepted the chair of languages at Austin College, Huntsville. On December 15, 1858, Bailey was elected president of Austin College and was ordered to reorganize and reopen the college. He was married twice: in 1820 to Lucy Hatch of Norwich, Vermont, and after her death to Mariette Perry of Waterbury, Connecticut. He was a prolific writer and was best known for his textbooks on spelling and grammar. He resigned from Austin College in 1862 because of ill health and died on April 25, 1863. He was buried at Huntsville.

BIBLIOGRAPHY: *Dictionary of American Biography. Ministerial Directory of the Presbyterian Church, U.S.*

Carolyn Hyman

BAILEY, TEXAS. Bailey is on State highways 11 and 78 eleven miles south of Bonham in south central Fannin County. Settlement began in the late 1850s, when farmers moved into the area to take advantage of the rich blackland. Cotton and corn became the principal agricultural products. As the community developed, two prominent residents competed to have it named after themselves. Doctors Josiah S. Bailey and A. J. Ray owned land that was to become the townsite. The quarrel between the two men ended in 1885, when the St. Louis Southwestern Railway used the land donated by Bailey for its right-of-way. Two years later a post office branch opened. The railroad stimulated twenty years of economic growth. By the early 1900s Bailey had 300 residents, two churches, a school, a bank, a hotel, one of the few picture shows in the county, and a dozen businesses. In the mid-1920s the population peaked at 350. Bailey was incorporated in 1933. During the years of the Great Depression and World War II[qqv] the population declined. By the mid-1950s the number of residents had decreased to 198. Bailey was the first town in the county to establish a "free lunch" program. By the mid-1970s farmers had abandoned cotton and corn in favor of small grains and cattle. In 1988 Bailey had an estimated 220 residents. In 1990 the population was 187.

BIBLIOGRAPHY: *Fannin County Folks and Facts* (Dallas: Taylor, 1977). Floy Crandall Hodge, *A History of Fannin County* (Hereford, Texas: Pioneer, 1966).

David Minor

BAILEYBORO, TEXAS. Baileyboro, on Farm Road 298 in south central Bailey County, was settled around 1900. In 1921 the community built a school. Muleshoe National Wildlife Refuge,[qv] a migratory bird refuge, was established in 1935 southwest of Baileyboro. In 1940 the community had three stores, a school, and a population of 100, which was its peak. In 1980 the population was sixty-one.

BIBLIOGRAPHY: LaVonne McKillip, ed., *Early Bailey County History* (Muleshoe, Texas, 1978).

BAILEY COUNTY. Bailey County (A-8), in the western Panhandle,[qv] is bordered on the west by New Mexico, on the north by Parmer County, on the east by Lamb County, and on the south by Cochran County. The county center lies at 34°04′ north latitude and 102°50′ west longitude, about seventy-five miles northwest of Lubbock. Bailey County is a part of the Southern High Plains and has an altitude of 3,800 to 4,400 feet above mean sea level. Its 835 square miles of plain are surfaced by sandy loam covered with grasses and mesquite brush. The Double Mountain Fork of the Brazos River drains the northern parts of the county; other sections drain to numerous small playas. The most conspicuous topographic feature is a range of sand hills that runs from northeast to southwest a mile south of Muleshoe. The average annual rainfall is 17.29 inches. The average minimum temperature in January is 20° F; the average maximum in July is 92° F. The growing season of 181 days is shorter than the average for West Texas counties because of the higher elevation and cooler weather. U.S. Highway 70/84 crosses the northeast part of the county. State highways 214 and 298 carry traffic north to south and east to west, respectively.

The county was marked off from Bexar County in 1876 and named for Peter J. Bailey,[qv] an Alamo hero. Bailey and twenty-one other counties newly formed at the time were attached to Jack County for judicial purposes. In 1881 jurisdiction of Bailey County was transferred from Jack to Baylor County; then, in 1887, to Hale County; and in 1892 to Castro County. Settlement of Bailey County did not come early, since the XIT Ranch[qv] held most of its land from 1882 until the division and sale of the ranch in 1901.

The XIT had its origin 1879 when the legislature set aside three million acres in Dallam, Hartley, Oldham, Deaf Smith, Parmer, Lamb, Bailey, Cochran, and Hockley counties to fund the building of the Capitol.[qv] In 1892 the XIT Ranch was organized with British backing; its landholdings included northern and southeastern Bailey County. Fencing in the county was done between 1883 and 1886, and the first cattle reached the ranch in 1885. Among the eight major divisions of the XIT, Bailey County land fell within the Spring Lake, Yellow House, and Bovina divisions. Even after the XIT sold lands in 1901, other large ranches (the VVN, the Snyder, the Bovina Cattle Company, the YL, and the Muleshoe) dominated the region. As late as 1900 the United States census counted only four people living in Bailey County.

The county developed rather quickly during the early twentieth century, however, as old ranchland was divided up and sold to farmers by land developers. From 1906 to 1912 the Coldren Land Company and the Vaughn Land Company held promotions in Bailey County. Midwestern farmers took special excursion trains to nearby Farwell, then were taken south and shown Bailey County lands selling at ten to twenty dollars an acre. In 1909 the county's first irrigation well was dug. By 1910, seventy-one farms had been established in the county and the population had increased to 312.

A severe drought in 1910 drove away many of these early settlers, but others moved in to take their places, particularly after the Santa Fe Railroad extended its tracks through the county in 1913. Hoping to establish a taxing authority that could provide schools and roads for the area, residents decided to organize the county. They raised $1,500 to send delegates to Austin to lobby for a revision of the minimum county-voter requirement to seventy-five. Despite the opposition of ranchmen who feared that organization would bring taxation, the delegates succeeded. A county seat election followed in 1919, with Muleshoe carrying seventy-four of the 111 votes cast. By 1920 there were seventy-nine farms and 517 residents in Bailey County.

During the 1920s and 1930s new conditions helped to transform the county's economy from ranching to farming. Ground water was discovered at depths of twenty to forty feet, and large ranches were broken up and sold as farm tracts. Both the Watson Ranch and the Newsome Ranch, for example, were subdivided in 1924 and 1925.

While many of the new farmers grew wheat, corn, and forage crops, a rapid expansion of cotton farming was responsible for much of the development of the county during these years. In 1920 little if any cotton was grown in the area, but by 1929 over 24,000 acres was planted in cotton and it had become the county's leading crop. The first cotton grown in the area was sent to Plainview for ginning; but Bailey County got a gin in 1923. By 1924 there were 302 farms in the county, and by 1929, 758 farms had been established there. The expansion of cotton farming continued in the county even during the years of the Great Depression,[qv] when cotton farming in other parts of the state suffered severe declines. By 1940 cotton production in Bailey County took up almost 45,000 acres, and the number of farms had increased to 820. Because of this growth, the population of the county rose significantly during this period. The population in 1930 was 5,186, and 6,318 people lived there by 1940. Though many West Texas counties declined in the years immediately after World War II,[qv] Bailey County continued to grow in population until the 1960s. In 1950, 7,592 people lived there, and by 1960 residents numbered 9,090. But the population declined thereafter, to 8,487 in 1970, 8,186 in 1980, and 7,064 in 1990.

In the early 1990s the county had 160,000 acres of irrigated lands and was among the leading counties in agricultural income. It has been said that Bailey County "is one of the few areas in the United States that can produce varying crops such as cotton, wheat, corn, grain, sorghums, soybeans, castor beans, hay, peanuts, cabbage, lettuce, peas, and beans." About 40 percent of agricultural receipts derive from livestock. Manufacturing income in 1980 was almost $2 million, from farm tools.

Communities in Bailey County include Baileyboro, Bula, Circle Back, Enochs, Goodland, Maple, Progress, and Needmore. Muleshoe (1990 population 4,571), the largest town in the county, hosts the Mule Days festival each August and the county fair every September. Muleshoe National Wildlife Refuge[qv] is a major recreation site.

BIBLIOGRAPHY: J. Evetts Haley, *The XIT Ranch of Texas and the Early Days of the Llano Estacado* (Chicago: Lakeside, 1929; rpts., Norman: University of Oklahoma Press, 1953, 1967). LaVonne McKillip, ed., *Early Bailey County History* (Muleshoe, Texas, 1978). Thelma Lee Stevens, History of Bailey County (M.A. thesis, Texas Technological College, 1939).

William R. Hunt and John Leffler

BAILEY CREEK. Bailey Creek rises a mile east of Byers in northern Clay County (at 34°03′ N, 98°12′ W) and flows northeast for slightly more than five miles to its mouth on the Red River (at 34°05′ N, 98°07′ W). It runs through gently sloping rangeland surfaced with loams. Post oak and pecan trees grow along the first mile of the upper banks; there are few trees along the lower reaches. *Clark Wheeler*

BAILEY'S PRAIRIE, TEXAS. Bailey's Prairie is on State Highway 35 and Farm Road 521 between Angleton and West Columbia in southwest Brazoria County. The town was named for James Britton Bailey,[qv] a veteran of the War of 1812 who came to the area in 1818 with his wife and six children to occupy 4,587 acres of rich, flat land granted by the Spanish government. Stephen F. Austin[qv] disputed Bailey's right but ultimately recognized his claim, and Bailey took new title to the land on July 7, 1824, thereby becoming one of the Old Three Hundred.[qv] The town grew up around Bailey's plantation and the league of land granted by the Mexican government to M. S. Munson. Settlers established large sugar plantations, and some plantation owners also ran cattle. A local Methodist church was organized in 1839 by Rev. Jesse Hord.[qv] By 1936 the community had a church, a cemetery, scattered dwellings, and Bailey's Prairie oilfield nearby, but most of the surrounding land remained part of several large family ranches. Bailey's Prairie had a population of 228 in 1972, 410 in 1988, and 634 in 1990.

BIBLIOGRAPHY: Brazoria County Federation of Women's Clubs, *History of Brazoria County* (1940). Lester G. Bugbee, "The Old Three Hundred: A List of Settlers in Austin's First Colony," *Quarterly of the Texas State Historical Association* 1 (October 1897). James A. Creighton, *A Narrative History of Brazoria County* (Angleton, Texas: Brazoria County Historical Commission, 1975). Houston *Chronicle*, October 13, 1980. Houston *Post*, September 23, 1962. Worth Stickley Ray, *Austin Colony Pioneers* (Austin: Jenkins, 1949; 2d ed., Austin: Pemberton, 1970). Noah Smithwick, *The Evolution of a State, or Recollections of Old Texas Days* (Austin: Gammel, 1900; rpt., Austin: University of Texas Press, 1983).

Anna Hallstein

BAILEYVILLE, TEXAS. Baileyville is on Farm Road 2027 sixteen miles northeast of Cameron in northern Milam County. Although the community was once known as Smithland or Bailey's Store, the name Baileyville was chosen when the post office was opened in 1874. By 1884 Baileyville had four combination steam gristmill–cotton gins, good schools, a Baptist church, and 500 residents. The community's population fell to 250 in the 1890s, but the school system continued to thrive. In 1903 the Baileyville district had three one-teacher schools for 118 white students and three one-teacher schools for 238 black students. The post office was discontinued in 1924, and Baileyville's population fell sharply in the 1930s. By 1941 the community reported only two businesses and fifty residents. The Baileyville schools were consolidated with the Rosebud Independent School District by the early 1970s. In 1988 county highway maps showed a community hall and scattered businesses and residences. The population in 1990 was forty-five.

BIBLIOGRAPHY: Lelia M. Batte, *History of Milam County, Texas* (San Antonio: Naylor, 1956).

Vivian Elizabeth Smyrl

BAINE, NOEL MOSES (1800–1864). Moses Baine, early colonist, soldier, and planter, was born in 1800 at Hamilton's Bawn, County Armagh, Ireland, the son of George and Sarah Baine. One source, however, lists his parents as Noel M. and Mary Baine. He immigrated to America in 1818, settling at Baltimore, Maryland. In Baltimore, on February 13, 1830, he married Cecilia Inglesby, daughter of William and Alicia MacKernan Inglesby. On March 6, 1830, they sailed for Texas, landing in New Orleans on April 1, and from there proceeded by water to Brazoria, arriving on April 6. They stayed several weeks with the James Lynch[qv] family, then went on to San Felipe de Austin. Moses Baine received a sitio[qv] of land granted him by the Mexican government through empresario[qv] Stephen F. Austin[qv] on April 26, 1831. The land was in what is now Brazos County, on the east side of the Brazos River. According to Moses Baine's family records, they resided nine miles from San Felipe, and according to family tradition, their house was the only one in the colony that had glass panes in its windows. Also according to family records, they had twelve head of cattle, three horses, and plenty of hogs; it was also noted that Moses Baine taught the children of the colony and in addition farmed. During the Texas Revolution,[qv] on March 5, 1836, Moses Baine enlisted in the Texas army. He also participated in the battle of San Jacinto,[qv] and his name is listed on the bronze plaque at the San Jacinto Battleground State Historical Park.[qv] He received a bounty certificate[qv] for 320 acres of land for this service; the bounty warrant was dated March 19, 1839. On October 17, 1842, Moses Baine enlisted in the Army of the Republic of Texas[qv] under Philip Haddox Coe,[qv] Company A, First Regiment, and marched to Bexar, and then to the Rio Grande. For this service in the Somervell expedition,[qv] he received $67.50. Moses and Cecilia Baine made their home near San Felipe de Austin until 1837, when he purchased land in Washington County from Obadiah Hudson; they settled there permanently. The couple had ten children, two of whom died young. Moses Baine was a successful planter in Washington County until his death on May 28, 1864. His wife died on October 16, 1872. Both are buried in marked graves in Prairie Lea Cemetery, Brenham, Texas. The grave of Moses Baine is further marked with a Texas Historical Commission[qv] marker dedicated in the early 1980s.

BIBLIOGRAPHY: Sam Houston Dixon and Louis Wiltz Kemp, *The Heroes of San Jacinto* (Houston: Anson Jones, 1932). Marker Files, Texas Historical Commission, Austin. Thomas L. Miller, *Bounty and Donation Land Grants of Texas, 1835–1888* (Austin: University of Texas Press, 1967).
Mrs. David H. Peterson

BAINER, TEXAS. Bainer, also known as Yellow House Switch, is located seven miles southeast of Littlefield on the Atchison, Topeka and Santa Fe Railway and U.S. Highway 84 in southeastern Lamb County. The site of the community was part of the Yellowhouse Division of the XIT Ranch[qv] in the late nineteenth century, then became the East Camp of the Yellow House Ranch[qv] in 1901. In 1912 George Washington Littlefield[qv] organized the Littlefield Land Company[qv] and began to sell off portions of the ranch to farmers. In 1913 the Pecos and Northern Texas Railway built through the area and put in a switch by the East Camp. The switch was known as Yellow House Switch until the 1920s, when it was redesignated Bainer. Extensive cattle pens were erected at the depot, which became a major shipping point for the Yellow House Ranch and the neighboring Spade Ranch. A number of businesses served the surrounding farming community. A cotton gin was built in the community in the 1920s, and at various times Bainer has had a grocery store, a filling station, a grain elevator and a blacksmith shop. In 1940 the community comprised three businesses and a number of scattered dwellings. It had a single business in 1990.

BIBLIOGRAPHY: Lamb County History Book Committee, *The Heritage of Lamb County* (Dallas: Curtis Media, 1992).
Mark Odintz

BAINES, GEORGE WASHINGTON, SR. (1809–1882). George Washington Baines, Baptist pastor, teacher, and editor, was born near Raleigh, North Carolina, on December 29, 1809, the eldest son of Thomas and Mary (McCoy) Baines. He was third in a line of four generations of Baptist ministers. His parents moved the family to Georgia in 1817 and to a farm near Tuscaloosa, Alabama, in 1818. Despite a limited academic background Baines entered the University of Alabama, where he paid his expenses by cutting and rafting timber. He was forced to withdraw from school during his senior year (1836) because of poor health. When he twenty-five he was baptized at the Salem Baptist Church. He was licensed to preach on July 20, 1834, by the Philadelphia Baptist Church of Tuscaloosa County and ordained on August 7, 1836, by the Grant's Creek Baptist Church. His father was among the signers of both the license to preach and the certificate of ordination. In 1837, in an effort to recover from his recurring dyspepsia, Baines moved to Carroll County, Arkansas. During his seven years in that state he organized three churches and baptized 150 people while serving as a missionary for the Baptist Home Mission Society of New York City. He was also a representative from Carroll County to the Fourth Legislature of Arkansas, from November 7, 1842, to February 4, 1843. Baines moved to Mount Lebanon, Louisiana, in July 1844 to serve churches there and at Minden and Saline. During his six-year residence in Louisiana, he also served as superintendent of schools in Bienville Parish and assisted John Bryce in organizing the First Baptist Church of Marshall.

In 1850 the family moved to Huntsville, Texas, where Baines preached and began a lifelong friendship with Sam Houston.[qv] During his ministry in Texas he was the pastor of churches at Huntsville, Independence, Anderson, Fairfield, Springfield, Butler, Florence, and Salado. From 1855 to 1860 he was the first editor of the first Baptist newspaper in Texas, the *Texas Baptist*.[qv] Baines served as president of Baylor University in 1861–62. In the face of overwhelming financial obstacles during the Civil War,[qv] he kept the struggling school going at great sacrifice to his health. Baylor University conferred on him an honorary M.A. degree on July 27, 1861.

Baines married Melissa Ann Butler on October 20, 1840. When he left Baylor, he moved to a farm near Fairfield, where his wife and youngest son died. On June 13, 1865, he married a widow, Mrs. Cynthia W. Williams. In 1866 he traveled as field agent for the Baptist State Convention and in 1867 moved his family to Salado, where he was pastor of the First Baptist Church. In 1877 he became an agent for the Education Commission of the Baptist State Convention, but in 1881 the First Baptist Church of Salado insisted that he resume the pastorate there. After the death of his second wife in January 1882 Baines lived with his daughter Anna in Belton until he died, of malaria, on December 28, 1882. He was buried at Salado. One of the ten children of Baines and his first wife, Joseph Wilson Baines, was the father of Rebekah Baines Johnson.[qv]

BIBLIOGRAPHY: James Milton Carroll, *A History of Texas Baptists* (Dallas: Baptist Standard, 1923). *Encyclopedia of Southern Baptists* (4 vols., Nashville: Broadman, 1958–82). L. R. Elliott, ed., *Centennial Story of Texas Baptists* (Dallas: Baptist General Convention of Texas, 1936). *Texas Historical and Biographical Magazine* (1891–92).
Travis L. Summerlin

BAINES, JOSEPH WILSON (1846–1906). Joseph Wilson Baines, lawyer, publisher, and Texas secretary of state, was born at Mount Lebanon, Louisiana, on January 24, 1846, the son of Melissa Ann (Butler) and Rev. George W. Baines.[qv] Four years later the family moved to Anderson, Texas, where George Baines published the first Baptist newspaper in the state. Described as a "precocious" child, Joseph received the educational benefits of a private tutor from England hired by his father. Later he attended Baylor University at Independence, where Reverend Baines had been appointed president. Joseph joined Walter L. Mann's Texas Cavalry Regiment in 1863 and served until the end of the Civil War.[qv]

In 1867 Baines moved to McKinney in Collin County, where he taught school and studied law under James W. Throckmorton.[qv] He was admitted to the bar and practiced civil law, invested in real estate, and in 1878 helped establish the McKinney *Advocate*. A year later he bought his partner's share and soon thereafter consolidated the paper with the McKinney *Citizen*. Baines renamed the weekly newspaper the *Black Waxey* and used it to support the campaign of Democratic gubernatorial candidate John Ireland.[qv] After his election Ireland acted on the advice of influential Democratic party[qv] members and newspaper editors and appointed Baines secretary of state. Baines sold the *Black Waxey* in 1883 and moved to Austin. For the next four years he served in the Ireland administration as a close political advisor to the governor and helped to oversee the construction of the Capitol.[qv]

He left Austin in 1887 and moved to Blanco, where he opened a law office and purchased a farm. Through his activities in the Baptist Church,[qv] support of public education, and the legal services he provided regardless of the clients' ability to pay, Baines established a good reputation. This and his past political experience resulted in his nomination and election to the Twenty-seventh Legislature from the Eighty-ninth District in 1903. At the end of his term he was forced to leave the community that had supported his political return to Austin. Financial losses incurred on the farm forced him to sell his land in Blanco and close his law office. He moved to Fredericksburg, where he lived in a modest house and renewed his law practice. He remained politically active and became chairman of the Democratic Executive Committee of Gillespie County.

He was married in 1869 to Ruth Huffman, and they had two daughters, Josefa and Rebekah, and a son, Huffman. Rebekah Baines Johnson[qv] was the mother of Lyndon Baines Johnson.[qv] The former secretary of state joined few organizations, for, he claimed, "I am a

Baptist and a Democrat, that is enough for me." Baines died in Fredericksburg after a three-month illness, on November 18, 1906.

BIBLIOGRAPHY: Robert A. Caro, *The Years of Lyndon Johnson: The Path to Power* (New York: Knopf, 1982). John Moursund, *Blanco County Families for One Hundred Years* (Austin, 1958). San Antonio *Daily Express*, November 20, 1906. *David Minor*

BAINVILLE, TEXAS. Bainville, on State Highway 72 seven miles southwest of Kenedy in southwest Karnes County, was named after J. L. Bain, who built a store and a cotton gin there in the 1920s. The community was populated largely by Swedes[qv] who had moved there from the Del Valle area of Travis County. Elim Lutheran Church and Cadillac School were nearby. From the early 1940s to the early 1960s the settlement had around sixty residents and two businesses. In 1990 only the church, a scattering of farms, and the name remained.

BIBLIOGRAPHY: Robert H. Thonhoff, History of Karnes County (M.A. thesis, Southwest Texas State College, 1963). *Robert H. Thonhoff*

BAIRD, CHARLES (?–?). Charles Baird, early settler and public official, was a member of Stephen F. Austin's[qv] second colony. His wife, née Francis Elizabeth Daniel, came from Autauga County, Alabama, and Baird may have as well. He was in Texas by October 17, 1832, when he received title to a league of land on the east bank of the San Bernard River in what is now western Fort Bend County. At that time he had two white servants and ten slaves. He represented the Fort Bend area at the Convention of 1833.[qv]

BIBLIOGRAPHY: Texas House of Representatives, *Biographical Directory of the Texan Conventions and Congresses, 1832–1845* (Austin: Book Exchange, 1941). *Stephen L. Hardin*

BAIRD, RALEIGH WILLIAM (1870–1941). Raleigh William Baird, physician and educator, the son of William Leroy and Mary Eleanor (Law) Baird, was born in Coushatta, Louisiana, on April 9, 1870. He spent most of his childhood in Cleburne, Texas, and attended Southwestern University in Georgetown, where he received an A.B. degree in 1893. After his graduation he studied medicine at Bellevue Hospital Medical College in New York and received an M.D. degree in 1896. In 1898 he did postgraduate work at St. Bartholomew Hospital in London, England. He returned to Texas in 1900 to practice medicine in Dallas, where he lived for the next forty-one years. In November 1900 Baird married Lavinia Starley Bishop of Waxahachie. They had four children.

As a specialist in internal medicine, Baird was a member of the first staff of St. Paul Hospital and professor of clinical medicine at Baylor University College of Medicine. In 1915 he founded the Dallas Medical and Surgical Clinic, which he served as president until his death. He also helped organize and was president of the North Texas Medical Association; for a while he was president of the Dallas County Medical Society. He was elected director of the Dallas Surgeons Investment Company and was a charter member of the board of stewards of Highland Park Methodist Church, which was organized in his home. Baird was a fellow of the American College of Physicians and a member of the American Medical Association and the Texas Medical Association.[qv] He was chairman of the TMA section on pathology in 1914 and the section on medicine and diseases of children in 1921. After a short illness he died at his home on July 13, 1941, and was buried in Hillcrest Mausoleum.

BIBLIOGRAPHY: Dallas *Morning News*, July 14, 1941. *Texas State Journal of Medicine*, November 1941. *David Minor*

BAIRD, ROLAND WINFORD, SR. (1899–1988). Roland W. Baird, Sr., founder of Mrs. Baird's Bakeries, was born on September 10, 1899, at Ripley, Tennessee, the sixth of eight children of William Jasper and Ninia Lilla (Harrison) Baird. The family moved to Fort Worth, Texas, in 1900. By 1908 Mrs. Baird had begun baking bread for her neighbors, with young Roland standing on a box at the kitchen table to knead the dough. After their father's death in 1912, all four sons helped support the family by selling their mother's bread in the neighborhood. They built a bakery in their back yard. While attending Draughn's Business College in Fort Worth, Roland baked at night and delivered bread in the afternoons. He married Faye Burrell in 1922, and they had a son and three daughters.

In 1920 the Bairds built their first baking plant, in Fort Worth. In 1928 Baird moved his family to Dallas, where he built a modern bakery. In 1938 he built a third plant in Houston, which was followed in 1948 by a fourth bakery in Abilene. By then Mrs. Baird's Bakeries was the largest independent bakery operation in the United States. Baird originated the practice of twisting equal parts of dough to form each loaf of bread, thus improving the loaf. He also originated the company's slogan, "Stays Fresh Longer," and designed the wrapper.

In 1937 he bought a ranch near Marble Falls. When it was inundated by Lake Lyndon B. Johnson[qv] in 1951, he bought another near Johnson City. Commuting from Dallas to his ranch enabled Baird to enjoy his hobby, flying. He was a director of Mercantile National Bank of Dallas for twenty-five years and served on the boards of Dallas radio station WRR, the Dallas Chamber of Commerce, and Rotary International. He helped organize and served as a director of the Middleton Advertising and the Donovan Uniform companies. He established a scholarship for the Methodist Children's Home in Waco.

He retired from business in 1954. He died on January 15, 1988, and was buried at the Baird family ranch in Johnson City. Roland W. Baird, Jr., of Phoenix, Arizona, directed the business after his father's retirement and expanded Mrs. Baird's Bakeries into Phoenix, Las Vegas, and Hawaii.

BIBLIOGRAPHY: Austin *American-Statesman*, January 16, 1988. Dallas *Morning News*, January 19, 1988. Johnson City *Record-Courier*, December 18, 1975. Vertical Files, Barker Texas History Center, University of Texas at Austin. *Dorothy Baird Mattiza*

BAIRD, SPRUCE MCCOY (1814–1872). Spruce McCoy Baird, jurist and Confederate officer, was born at Glasgow, Kentucky, on October 8, 1814. He taught school there before moving to Texas. He lived at Woodville and San Augustine before beginning his law practice at Nacogdoches. On May 27, 1848, Governor George T. Wood[qv] appointed Baird judge of the newly established Santa Fe County, east of the Rio Grande in what is now New Mexico, an area included in the bounds of the Republic of Texas[qv] but unorganized until after the Treaty of Guadalupe-Hidalgo[qv] concluded the Mexican War.[qv] Baird was unsuccessful in his attempts to set up Texas jurisdiction, for the natives of Santa Fe County were Republican in politics and were opposed to Texas control. Furthermore Baird was opposed by Col. John M. Washington, commanding officer at Santa Fe. When Texas sold her claim to the area as a result of the Compromise of 1850,[qv] Baird was left without a job. He stayed in New Mexico, became a member of the bar there, and in 1852 was Indian agent to the Navajos. In 1860 he was appointed attorney general of New Mexico, but in 1861 he was forced to leave the state because of his sympathy with the Confederacy. On March 4, 1862, he was indicted for high treason and his property was confiscated. Baird returned to Texas, where he recruited and commanded the Fourth Regiment, Arizona Brigade, which served throughout Texas, mostly on the northwest frontier. He was paroled in July 1865 and in 1867 moved to Trinidad, Colorado, where he opened a law office. Baird married Emmacetta C. Bowdry of Kentucky in 1848. On June 5, 1872, he died at Cimarron, New Mexico.

BIBLIOGRAPHY: Vertical Files, Barker Texas History Center, University of Texas at Austin. C. R. Wharton, "Spruce McCoy Baird," *New Mexico Historical Review* 27 (October 1952). *Clinton P. Hartmann*

BAIRD, TEXAS. Baird, at the junction of Interstate Highway 20 and U.S. Highway 283 in north central Callahan County, was established when the Texas and Pacific Railway came through in 1880. It was named for railroad surveyor and engineer Matthew Baird. The community was a division point on the railroad, with a depot, roundhouse, and repair shops. It replaced Belle Plain as county seat in 1883 and gained most of the former county seat's population. New arrivals increased the population to 1,200 by the mid-1880s. The post office, established as Vickery in 1881, was renamed Baird in 1883. A fire that started in S. L. Robinson's store, where the cast of Golden's Opera Company was preparing a show for the residents, did not stop the town's progress in 1884, nor did a tornado in 1895. Baird was incorporated in 1889. W. E. Gilliland began publishing the Baird *Star,* a weekly newspaper in 1887. The hanging of Alberto Vargas in 1907 for the murder of Emma Blakley was Baird's only legal execution. Around 1910 a runaway train in the night precipitated a spectacular three-locomotive pile-up at the Baird depot. The population was 1,502 in 1904 and peaked in 1929 at 3,000, then declined to 1,810 by 1941; it was 1,737 in 1988 and 1,658 in 1990. Industries have included gins, an oil refinery, flour mills, and a feed mill. The county hospital is in Baird, and the town is the center for local oilfield supplies and ranching.

BIBLIOGRAPHY: Brutus Clay Chrisman, *Early Days in Callahan County* (Abilene, Texas: Abilene Printing and Stationery, 1966).

William R. Hunt

BAIRD LAKE. Baird Lake is a natural lake four miles west of the Andrews-Martin county line and eight miles north of the Andrews-Ector-Midland county intersection in southeastern Andrews County (at 32°12′ N, 102°17′ W). The lake is the site of Baird Springs, the only remaining active springs in the county. Extensive windmill and oil drilling, combined with large irrigation projects, has depleted sources of surface water in the area. The lake is located in a remote region of oilfields and ranchlands.

BIBLIOGRAPHY: Gunnar Brune, *Springs of Texas,* Vol. 1 (Fort Worth: Branch-Smith, 1981).

BAIRFIELD, WINTFRY (1858–1931). Wintfry (Wint) Bairfield, Panhandle[qv] rancher, was born in Polk County, Alabama, on June 28, 1858, the son of Seth and Sabrina (Anderson) Bairfield. After her husband's death in the Civil War, Sabrina Bairfield returned to her parents' farm in Georgia with her three sons and an infant daughter, who died soon afterward. Wint and his brothers grew up working on the farm and attended school for half a day whenever convenient. At age twelve he took his first full-time job at a combination gristmill and sawmill near Bainbridge, Georgia. After his mother's death his employer, a man named Powell, took Wint into his own large household.

In 1880, having saved fifty dollars from his meager wages, Bairfield went west to St. Jo, Texas, where several of his friends had already moved from Georgia. Three years later he made his first journey by horseback to the Panhandle, where he punched cattle for one summer. He liked the region and perhaps realized the opportunities there; he returned from St. Jo in the spring of 1884 and began working for Bill Koogle, freighting cedar posts for fences out of Palo Duro Canyon.[qv] His long association with the JA Ranch[qv] began in April 1885, when John Grady, a wagon boss for that outfit, hired him as a horse wrangler. Over the next few years Bairfield participated in three trail drives to Dodge City, Kansas, before the arrival of the Fort Worth and Denver City Railway in 1887. In 1890 Bairfield made his first purchase of dissatisfied settlers' claims on school land within the JA range. He was one of the few JA employees allowed to run cattle of his own; he bought milch calves, grazed them through the winter, and sold them in the spring to JA manager Dick Walsh for a profit.

On March 30, 1896, Bairfield married Lena Elizabeth Scoggins. Their first home was the JA line camp near the head of Mulberry Creek, where Bairfield managed one of the two purebred JJ herds maintained by the JA. In December 1899 the Bairfields left the JA and moved to a claim they had purchased from Joe Beaty at the head of Troublesome Canyon, eight miles southwest of Clarendon. Bairfield obtained a small herd from his father-in-law and started his own ranching operation, using a Lazy R brand. Subsequent purchases made from Cornelia Adair[qv] and the JA in 1909, 1913, and 1915 expanded the Lazy R into eight sections, some of which Bairfield had exchanged for his Mulberry Creek claims.

The Bairfields' first child died in infancy in January 1900; they subsequently had three children. Bairfield was a Mason and member of the Methodist Church in Clarendon. He often served on the grand jury and the local school board and for about four years was the Donley County sheriff's bond. He built a one-room schoolhouse on the Beaty claim that served on occasion as a church and area social center. By 1937, the last year the school was in operation, there was only one teacher and one pupil, a fact duly noted in "Ripley's Believe It or Not."

Lena Bairfield died on February 1, 1922. Bairfield died on November 12, 1931, after being stricken with apoplexy. They were both buried in Clarendon. The Lazy R Ranch continued to be operated by the heirs. The Bairfield schoolhouse was given by the family to the Ranching Heritage Center[qv] in Lubbock in 1972 and formally dedicated on April 16, 1973, by Charles E. Bairfield and his wife, Thelma.

BIBLIOGRAPHY: Armstrong County Historical Association, *A Collection of Memories: A History of Armstrong County, 1876–1965* (Hereford, Texas: Pioneer, 1965). Charles E. Bairfield, "Wint and Lena Elizabeth (Scoggins) Bairfield: Pioneers in the Texas Panhandle," in *RHC Donor Books,* ed. Ernest Wallace (Lubbock: Ranching Heritage Center, 1977). Virginia Browder, *Donley County: Land O' Promise* (Wichita Falls, Texas: Nortex, 1975). B. Byron Price, comp., *Ranching Heritage Center Guidebook* (Lubbock: Museum of Texas Tech University, 1977).

H. Allen Anderson

BAJUNERO INDIANS. In 1683–84 Juan Domínguez de Mendoza[qv] led an exploratory expedition from El Paso as far eastward as the junction of the Concho and Colorado rivers east of the site of present San Angelo. In his itinerary he listed the names of thirty-seven Indian groups, including the Bajunero (Baijunero) Indians, from whom he expected to receive delegations. Nothing further is known about the Bajuneros, who seem to have been one of many Indian groups of north central Texas that were swept away by the southward thrust of the Lipan Apache and Comanche Indians in the eighteenth century.

BIBLIOGRAPHY: Herbert Eugene Bolton, ed., *Spanish Exploration in the Southwest, 1542–1706* (New York: Scribner, 1908; rpt., New York: Barnes and Noble, 1959). Charles W. Hackett, ed., *Pichardo's Treatise on the Limits of Louisiana and Texas* (4 vols., Austin: University of Texas Press, 1931–46).

Thomas N. Campbell

BAKER, ANDERSON YANCEY (1874–1930). A. Y. Baker, political boss of Hidalgo County from 1918 to 1930, was born in Uvalde in 1874, the son of Thomas G. and Verda (Bates) Baker. The elder Baker was a Spanish-American War veteran. A. Y. Baker joined the Texas Rangers[qv] in 1896 and went to the Rio Grande valley. As a ranger he made valuable allies and was accused of brutal acts. In one such incident in Cameron County, Ramón de la Cerda, owner of a small ranch abutting the King Ranch,[qv] was killed. The next year, 1903, Baker was brought to trial for the murders of Cerda and his brother. Baker's defense attorney, James B. Wells, Jr.,[qv] argued self-defense and won an acquittal. In 1904 Baker retired from the rangers and started work as a mounted customs inspector, in which capacity he began to build an agriculture and real estate fortune from lands he acquired inexpensively. During this period he also married Lena Sapington.

He left his job with the United States Customs Bureau in 1908, when he was elected treasurer of Hidalgo County. In 1912 he exchanged offices with Sheriff John Closner,[qv] the county boss who wanted to be treasurer. Baker became boss in early 1918 when Closner was charged with misappropriation of county funds and forced to resign his position as treasurer. The foundation of Baker's political control of Hidalgo County was his patriarchal relationship with local Mexican Americans. He provided charitable favors to them and supported the segregated Mexican schools. Enemies disparaged him as "the multimillionaire sheriff of Hidalgo County." Baker, president of the Edinburg State Bank, was indeed a millionaire, who lived in what his wife described as a "palatial mansion." He died of a stroke on November 1, 1930, in Edinburg and was survived by his wife and three children. *See also* BOSS RULE.

BIBLIOGRAPHY: Evan Anders, *Boss Rule in South Texas: The Progressive Era* (Austin: University of Texas Press, 1982). Catherine Baker, "Through a Woman's Eyes," *Junior Historian*, December 1964. San Antonio *Express*, November 3, 1930. E. F. Smith, *A Saga of Texas Law* (San Antonio: Naylor, 1940).
Laura Caldwell

BAKER, ANDREW JACKSON (1842–1912). Andrew Jackson Baker, land commissioner and legislator, was born on September 4, 1842, near Granada, Mississippi. He was a law student at the University of Mississippi when the Civil War[qv] started. He served in the Confederate Army as a member of Company A, Eleventh Mississippi Regiment, Army of Northern Virginia. He was wounded at Antietam and then at Gettysburg, where he was captured; he spent the rest of the war in a Northern prisoner-of-war camp. After the war Baker returned to Mississippi and served in the legislature. In 1868 he married Corinne Jordan Kearney. After she died in 1872 he married Elizabeth Newsom Kearney. He had at least six children in each marriage.

He practiced law in Oxford, Mississippi, until 1884, when he moved to San Angelo, Texas. He represented Tom Green County in the Twenty-second Legislature (1884). In 1894 and 1896 he won the elections for land commissioner and served from January 26, 1895, to January 16, 1899. Baker believed in the efficient management of the General Land Office.[qv] His efforts were frustrated by what he saw as the continual repurchasing of lands and retraining of personnel. The School Land Acts of 1895 and 1897 placed heavy workloads on the office, which had to sell school lands and reprocess an enormous number of forfeitures, which accounted for some five million of the six million acres originally sold. Baker supported a civil-service system of employment for the land office and believed that the state should drop out of the land business.

He later went into banking in San Angelo. He was a Presbyterian and a Mason. At the Democratic Convention of 1912 he was considered a possible candidate for the vice presidency, but he did not seek nomination because of poor health. He died in Los Angeles on June 21, 1912, and was buried in San Angelo.

BIBLIOGRAPHY: Dallas *Morning News*, June 22, 1912. *A History of Greater Dallas and Vicinity*, Vol. 1., by Philip Lindsley; Vol. 2., *Selected Biography and Memoirs*, ed. L. B. Hill (Chicago: Lewis, 1909). James William Madden, *Charles Allen Culberson* (Austin: Gammel's Bookstore, 1929). Garry Mauro, *Land Commissioners of Texas* (Austin: Texas General Land Office, 1986).
William N. Todd IV and Gerald Knape

BAKER, ARMEL KEERAN KOONTZ (1901–1967). Armel Baker, cattle raiser and breeder, the daughter of Texas cattleman Claude A. Keeran,[qv] was born in San Antonio on November 15, 1901. As a child she developed an interest in Brahman cattle on her father's ranch, and after graduating from college she moved back to the ranch and spent her life raising Brahmans. She was widely known as a Brahman breeder and was an outspoken advocate of the hump-backed cattle. She was the first woman in the United States to raise Brahmans and the second woman to sit on a board of a major cattle association. She developed the largest herd of Brahman cattle in the United States at that time and followed her ranch's tradition of never selling females. She was married to Henry Clay Koontz II of the Koontz Ranch[qv] on January 21, 1928. The couple had four children and were divorced after eleven years of marriage. She later married Hugh Baker. She died of a stroke and complications of diabetes on November 19, 1967, in Victoria.

BIBLIOGRAPHY: Thomas S. Chamblin, ed., *The Historical Encyclopedia of Texas* (2 vols., Dallas: Texas Historical Institute, 1982).
Thomas W. Cutrer

BAKER, BENJAMIN M. (1850–1918). Benjamin M. Baker, the seventh of ten children of Benjamin H. and Eliza (Greer) Baker, was born on January 20, 1850, in Russell County, Alabama. His father was a member of the Alabama Secession Convention in 1861 and fought for the Confederacy as a lieutenant colonel of the Sixth Alabama Infantry. Baker received no formal education. He moved to Carthage, Texas, at the age of nineteen and studied law in the office of A. W. Deberry. He was admitted to the bar in 1871 and began his practice at Carthage, where he married Emily Hull in 1872. They had three daughters and a son, who died at the age of six.

Baker represented Rusk, Panola, and Shelby counties in the Fifteenth, Sixteenth, and Seventeenth legislatures at Austin. In the Seventeenth Legislature he chaired the committee on finance and, in the Eighteenth, the committee on penitentiaries. In January 1883, after practicing law for a short time in Decatur, he became secretary of the State Board of Education, which appointed him first state superintendent of education. He was elected to that office in 1884 and served until 1887, when he moved his family to the new rail town of Canadian, in the Panhandle.[qv] There he resumed his private law practice and in 1891, with John Pugh, founded the Canadian *Enterprise*, which under later owners merged with the Canadian *Record*. In 1890 Baker was elected judge of the Thirty-fifth Judicial District, and he served in that position until 1917, when he retired to his private practice. He died at Canadian on May 21, 1918, and is buried there. B. M. Baker School in Canadian is named for him.

BIBLIOGRAPHY: Sallie B. Harris, *Cowmen and Ladies: A History of Hemphill County* (Canyon, Texas: Staked Plains, 1977). Frank W. Johnson, *A History of Texas and Texans* (5 vols., ed. E. C. Barker and E. W. Winkler [Chicago and New York: American Historical Society, 1914; rpt. 1916]). F. Stanley [Stanley F. L. Crocchiola], *Rodeo Town (Canadian, Texas)* (Denver: World, 1953).
H. Allen Anderson

BAKER, BURKE (1887–1964). Burke Baker, businessman and philanthropist, was born in Waco, Texas, on August 9, 1887, the son of Nellie (Faulkner) and Robert Homes Baker.[qv] He attended the University of Texas, where he received a B.A. degree in 1909. The following academic year he studied at Harvard University. He married Bennie Brown of Cleburne on October 11, 1911, and they had two sons and two daughters. After service in Houston with the Texas Trust Company and the Bankers Trust Company in 1915, Baker moved to Philadelphia, where he was named president of American Briquet Company. In 1919 he returned to Houston and became first an independent oil operator and then an insurance executive. In 1925 he founded Seaboard Life Insurance Company. He later became president and chairman of the board of American General Life Insurance Company and was also a director of the United Gas Corporation and the Manchester Terminal Corporation. Baker was general director of the city's first Community Chest campaign, chairman of the Civil Service Commission, and director of the Philosophical Society of Texas.[qv] In December 1961 he contributed $250,000 for the establishment of the Burke Baker Planetarium in the Houston Museum of Natural Science.[qv] Baker died on April 9, 1964, in Houston.

BIBLIOGRAPHY: Houston *Chronicle*, August 30, 1957, April 13, 1964. *Who's Who in the South and Southwest*, Vol. 7. *Clay Bailey*

BAKER, CHARLES LAURENCE (1887–1979). Charles Laurence Baker, structural geologist, was born in Coe Township, Rock Island County, Illinois, on October 10, 1887, the son of Rudolphus James Rodney and Alice (Drennan) Baker. He attended Port Byron Academy, Illinois; received a bachelor's degree from Monmouth College, Illinois, at the age of eighteen; and took a master's degree in 1916 from the University of California, Berkeley, where he had gone to recover from tuberculosis. He later served as an instructor at Oberlin College, Ohio, and did graduate work at the University of Chicago, where he completed all the work for the doctorate except the dissertation. While in school, Baker worked with the United States Geological Survey in Wyoming.

His subsequent career, which was divided between academic positions and mineral and petroleum exploration projects conducted by various agencies, took him to Oklahoma and Kansas, Brazil, and Mexico. As a geologist, he worked for the Southern Pacific Railway, Standard Oil Company of California, Rio Bravo Oil Company, L. E. Hanchett, East Coast Oil Company of America, and Tidewater Oil Company. From 1935 to 1944 he served as chairman of the geology department at the Agricultural and Mechanical College of Texas (now Texas A&M University) and from 1931 to 1935 as a geologist for the Bureau of Economic Geology at the University of Texas and as a lecturer at various universities. From 1945 to 1953 he worked both for the South Dakota State Geological Survey and in teaching.

Baker is remembered for his forays of two to three weeks alone and on foot into the desert, for his extensive explorations in Mexico, and for his search for hydrocarbons in California. In September 1909 in Baylor County, Texas, he discovered the Craddock Ranch "bone bed," an extensive deposit of Permian amphibian and reptilian fossils. He wrote nearly fifty books and papers on the geology of the western United States, Mexico, and the River Plate basin of South America. His works about Texas include *Review of the Geology of Texas* (1916), which he coauthored with Johan A. Udden and Emil Böse,[qqv] *Exploratory Geology of a Part of Southwestern Trans-Pecos Texas* (1927), and "Major Features of Trans-Pecos Texas," which appeared in *The Geology of Texas*, Volume II: *Structural and Economic Geology* (1935).

In 1915 Baker married Minnie Louise Perkins. The couple had three children. Baker retired in 1953 to the farm in Cordova, Illinois, where he had grown up, and died on April 7, 1979, at East Lansing, Michigan. He was a fellow of the Royal Scottish Geological Society of Edinburgh and the Geological Society of America.

BIBLIOGRAPHY: Walter Scott Adkins Papers, Barker Texas History Center, University of Texas at Austin. J. E. Wilson, "Charles Laurence Baker (1887–1979)," *Bulletin of the American Association of Petroleum Geologists* 66 (January 1982). Keith Young, "Memorial to Charles Laurence Baker, 1887–1979," *Geological Society of America Memorials* 15 (1985). *Keith Young*

BAKER, CULLEN MONTGOMERY (1835?–1869). Cullen Montgomery Baker, infamous desperado and guerilla, the son of John and Elizabeth Baker, was born in Weakley County, Tennessee, probably on June 22, 1835. The family moved to Texas in 1839 and eventually settled in Cass County, where John received a land grant of 640 acres from the Texas Congress. Cullen soon became a hard drinker, quarrelsome and mean-spirited. He temporarily ceased his dissipated ways and married Mary Jane Petty on January 11, 1854, but nine months later he killed his first man. In the years before the outbreak of the Civil War[qv] he spent considerable time at the farm of his mother's brother, Thomas Young, in Perry County, Arkansas. After Mary Jane died on July 2, 1860, and Baker had murdered another man, he returned to Texas. By now the war had begun.

Baker joined Company G, Morgan's Regimental Cavalry, on November 4, 1861, at Jefferson. His name is on the muster roll for September–October 1862, and he received pay through August 31, but he is designated a deserter on January 10, 1863. On February 22, 1862, he joined Company I of the Fifteenth Texas Cavalry at Linden. He is listed on the muster roll from February 1862 to February 1863; after "August 1862" beside his name is written, "left sick on the Arkansas River." After his service he was paid $252.80 and discharged due to disability. He married Martha Foster on July 1, 1862. His activities until the war's end are surrounded by numerous legends. Some believe he led a band of Arkansas guerrillas that preyed upon everybody, regardless of wartime sympathies, although there is no evidence for this. When peace returned, Baker and his wife briefly settled in Cass County, where Baker attempted to earn a living in the ferry business. Martha died on March 1, 1866, and, by most accounts, her death deeply depressed Baker; nevertheless, he proposed to her sister, Belle Foster, two months later.

But Belle married Thomas Orr, a schoolteacher and later a prominent community activist and politician, and he and Baker became bitter enemies. Somewhat later, the Union Army and the Freedmen's Bureau[qv] came to the area, and Baker focused his attention upon harassing and killing employees of the bureau and their clients. In December 1867 Baker also wrought havoc upon Howell Smith's family because of their alleged "unorthodox" relations with the black laborers they employed. He was wounded, but the local citizenry and the army failed to capture him. Baker returned to the Reconstruction[qv] scene again in mid-1868 as the leader of various outcasts and killers. He and his group are credited with murdering two Freedmen's Bureau agents, one in Texas and another in Arkansas, and numerous black men and women, all the time eluding the army.

When his gang disbanded in December 1868, Baker returned to his home in Cass County. There a small group of neighbors led by Orr, whom Baker had earlier attempted to hang, killed him and a companion on January 6, 1869. Legend has it that the whiskey Baker drank was laced with strychnine. Orr collected some of the reward offered for Baker. Baker may have had links with the Ku Klux Klan.[qv] Although he began his killing long before that organization appeared, he abetted the Klan's rise to prominence. As an obstacle to federal Reconstruction, he became notorious in the Southwest and even drew the notice of the New York *Tribune*. He received the nickname "Swamp Fox of the Sulphur" because of the area where he grew to manhood. Although he was not the legendary quick-draw artist some have maintained, writers have made much of Baker's prowess with a six-gun, his harassment of the United States Army, and his defense of "Southern honor" during and after the Civil War. Others see him as a mean, spiteful, alcoholic murderer. Louis L'Amour memorialized Baker in his novel *The First Fast Draw*.

BIBLIOGRAPHY: Ed Ellsworth Bartholomew, *Cullen Baker, Premier Texas Gunfighter* (Houston: Frontier Press of Texas, 1954). Al Eason, "Cullen Baker: Purveyor of Death," *Frontier Times*, August–September 1966. Boyd W. Johnson, "Cullen Montgomery Baker: The Arkansas Desperado," *Arkansas Historical Quarterly* 25 (1966). James Allen Marten, Drawing the Line: Dissent and Loyalty in Texas, 1856 to 1874 (Ph.D. dissertation, University of Texas at Austin, 1986). Thomas Orr, ed., *Life and Times of the Notorious Desperado, Cullen Baker* (Little Rock: Price and Barton, 1870). William L. Richter, *The Army in Texas during Reconstruction, 1865–1870* (College Station: Texas A&M University Press, 1987). William L. Richter, *Overreached on All Sides* (College Station: Texas A&M University Press, 1991). T. U. Taylor, Swamp Fox of the Sulphur, or the Life and Times of Cullen Montgomery Baker (MS, Barker Texas History Center, University of Texas at Austin). Yvonne Vestal, *The Borderlands and Cullen Baker* (Atlanta, Texas: Journal Publishers, 1978). *Barry A. Crouch*

BAKER, DANIEL (1791–1857). Daniel Baker, Presbyterian minister, was born on August 17, 1791, at Midway, Liberty County, Georgia, the youngest of seven children of William Baker and his first wife, who died in Daniel's infancy. Later William Baker died, leaving Daniel to be raised by an older brother and an aunt. After clerking in stores in Savannah for several years, Daniel went in 1811 to prepare himself for the ministry at Hampden-Sidney College in Virginia. He joined the Presbyterian Church there on April 19, 1811. Because of disturbances related to the war with Britain he moved to Princeton, where he graduated with honors in 1815.

To further his theological studies he associated himself with Rev. William Hill at Winchester, Virginia. He was married to Elizabeth McRobert by Moses Hoge, president of Hampden-Sidney, on March 28, 1816; the couple had four children. Baker was ordained and installed as pastor of the Presbyterian congregations at Harrisonburg and New Erection in March 1818; he supplemented his income by teaching school. In 1821 or 1822 he became pastor of the Second Presbyterian Church, Washington, D.C., where John Quincy Adams and Andrew Jackson were members. Baker also clerked at the Washington land office during this period. In 1828 he became pastor of the Independent Presbyterian Church, Savannah, Georgia. Following a brief pastorate in Frankfort, Kentucky, he went in 1836 to Tuscaloosa, Alabama. Although he was never a slaveowner, he was also not an abolitionist, and at the division of the Presbyterian Church in 1836 his sympathies and membership remained with the "old school."

In 1839 Baker, influenced by Rev. John Breckinridge, resigned his pastorate and headed for Texas. He hoped to get there in time to claim 640 acres promised any head of a family who settled before January 1, 1840, but demands for him to preach and conduct protracted meetings were so insistent that his arrival at Galveston was delayed until early February 1840. As an evangelist he witnessed the first conversion to Presbyterianism in Galveston and helped to administer the first Protestant baptism and conduct the first Presbyterian communion there. The Presbyterian church at Galveston was organized by Rev. John McCullough[qv] in January 1840, and Baker went to Houston, which he described as "not handsome, and the streets very muddy. It was like treading mortar." The Presbyterian church there had been organized by Rev. William Y. Allen[qv] in 1839. In Chriesman Settlement, near Independence, an independent presbytery was organized in April 1840. Baker was invited to sit as a corresponding member from the Presbytery of Tuscaloosa. It may have been at this meeting on April 6 that the matter of establishing a college was broached. Afterward, Baker returned to the United States, conducted many revivals, and settled as pastor at Holly Springs, Mississippi.

On June 25, 1848, at the urging of Rev. Stephen F. Cocke, Baker arrived back in Texas, at Port Lavaca. Before returning to Holly Springs he preached in Victoria, Cuero, Clinton, Goliad, Gonzales, New Braunfels, and San Antonio. As a result of a brush with danger on the way from San Antonio to Austin the rumor spread as far as Washington, D.C., that he had been murdered. The news of his safety ruined some flowery obituaries. After preaching in Austin, Bastrop, Wharton, Columbia, and other places, he returned to Port Lavaca. He had organized churches in Port Lavaca and La Grange. After a brief return to Holly Springs he accepted the pastorate of the First Presbyterian Church in Galveston in 1848 and brought his family to Texas the following year. As a member of the committee to locate a college, Baker toured East Texas. He organized a church at Palestine. When he preached in Huntsville and mentioned the possibility of a college, the citizens subscribed $8,000 to be paid over a five-year period. They wanted the college named for the preacher, but Baker declined the honor. The school, under the name of Austin College,[qv] was located in Huntsville, its charter was signed by Governor George T. Wood[qv] on November 22, 1849.

Baker preached at Brownsville, Rio Grande City, and other towns before returning to Huntsville, his new home. In 1850 he was appointed general agent to collect funds for Austin College. To this end he toured throughout the East, North, and South that year and each of the next five years, preaching and fund-raising. He became president of Austin College in 1853, when Samuel McKinney[qv] resigned, and held the post until he resigned in 1857. By then he had acquired approximately $100,000 for the college.

He wrote several pamphlets and a volume of sermons. He received an honorary doctor of divinity degree from Lafayette College in 1848. After a life of single-minded service to his church, he died in the home of his son, William, in Austin on December 10, 1857. Daniel Baker College in Brownwood was named in his honor. *See also* PRESBYTERIAN CHURCH.

BIBLIOGRAPHY: William M. Baker, *The Life and Labours of the Rev. Daniel Baker, D.D., Pastor and Evangelist* (Philadelphia: Presbyterian Board of Publication, 1858). George L. Landolt, *Search for the Summit: Austin College through XII Decades* (Austin: Von Boeckmann–Jones, 1970). William Stuart Red, *A History of the Presbyterian Church in Texas* (Austin: Steck, 1936). *Thomas W. Currie, Jr.*

BAKER, DANIEL DAVIS D. (1806–1843). Daniel D. D. Baker, San Jacinto soldier and Texas legislator, was born in Massachusetts in 1806 and moved to Texas in February 1831. In May 1831 he was granted a quarter league in Stephen F. Austin's[qv] second colony in what is now Wharton County. At the outbreak of the Texas Revolution[qv] he was elected a second lieutenant in Capt. T. L. F. Parrott's[qv] artillery company. He took part in the siege of Bexar[qv] but was discharged on November 23 before the city fell. After reenlisting on March 18, 1836, he was elected captain of artillery, but at the battle of San Jacinto[qv] he was attached to Capt. Moseley Baker's[qv] company. After San Jacinto, Gen. Thomas Jefferson Rusk[qv] detached him to fortify and take command of the defenses at Cavallo Pass. Baker was discharged on July 18, 1836, and moved to Matagorda, where he was elected to represent the county in the House of Representatives of the First Congress of the Republic of Texas in October 1836. On January 3, 1837, he married Mary Ann Cayce of Matagorda. In the spring of 1838 he was involved in real estate development in Matagorda County, where he attempted to establish a town called Preston 4½ miles from the Colorado River. Davis died in Matagorda on May 2, 1843.

BIBLIOGRAPHY: Daughters of the Republic of Texas, *Muster Rolls of the Texas Revolution* (Austin, 1986). Sam Houston Dixon and Louis Wiltz Kemp, *The Heroes of San Jacinto* (Houston: Anson Jones, 1932). John H. Jenkins, ed., *The Papers of the Texas Revolution, 1835–1836* (10 vols., Austin: Presidial Press, 1973). Virginia H. Taylor, *The Spanish Archives of the General Land Office of Texas* (Austin: Lone Star, 1955). Texas House of Representatives, *Biographical Directory of the Texan Conventions and Congresses, 1832–1845* (Austin: Book Exchange, 1941). Annie Lee Williams, *A History of Wharton County* (Austin: Von Boeckmann–Jones, 1964). *Thomas W. Cutrer*

BAKER, DEWITT CLINTON (1832–1881). DeWitt Clinton Baker, businessman, was born in Portland, Maine, on November 23, 1832, the son of Symonds William and Mary Ann (Watson) Baker. He was educated at Gorham Academy and Bowdoin College in Maine and was believed to have been an apprentice in the printing business in Portland. He made a trip to Texas from Maine by way of New Orleans in a sailboat, the *Billow*, with a group of surveyors before 1850. About the same time he moved with his family to Austin, where he was in the drug business for twenty-five years. He married Mary Elizabeth Graham on May 28, 1861, and they became the parents of nine children. Baker was appointed to keep official weather records in Texas. He helped establish public schools in Austin and was the inspector of schools from 1872 to 1877; Baker School in the Hyde Park area of Austin was named in his honor. He probably organized the first Bible society and the first public library in Austin and was treasurer of the Austin Library Association in 1875. He was the author of a number of poems; one called "Sketches of Travel in Texas" appeared in the Portland *Transcript.* He published *A Brief History of Texas from Its Earliest*

Settlement (1873) and *A Texas Scrap-Book* (1875). Because of ill health he retired from the drug business and was employed by the Internal Revenue Department. Baker was a member of St. David's Episcopal Church and served as senior warden and superintendent of the Sunday school for several years. He died in Austin on April 17, 1881, and was buried in Oakwood Cemetery. The Baker home, which was built in 1871, was purchased by a University of Texas sorority in 1968; a historical marker was dedicated at the property in 1971.

BIBLIOGRAPHY: Austin *Statesman*, April 19, 1881. Frank Brown, Annals of Travis County and the City of Austin (MS, Frank Brown Papers, Barker Texas History Center, University of Texas at Austin). Vertical Files, Barker Texas History Center, University of Texas at Austin. Vertical Files, Austin History Center.

Jeanette H. Flachmeier

BAKER, FRANCIS C. (1821–?). Francis C. Baker, newspaper editor and railroad promoter, was born in Indiana in 1821. Information about his education is lacking, but he was called Dr. F. C. Baker by the time he became an editor of the Jefferson *Democrat* at Jefferson, Texas, in 1848. In the same year he undertook a scientific exploration of Texas with J. Eppinger and J. D. Baker. In 1851 F. C. Baker and Eppinger compiled a pocket map of Texas. Apparently Baker contributed to *DeBow's Review* a group of unsigned articles describing the climate and geography of Texas as an inducement to settlers. He attended the railroad convention at Monroe, Louisiana, in 1852. In 1853 he wrote to the *Texas State Gazette* (*see* AUSTIN *STATE GAZETTE*) a letter in defense of routing the Pacific railroad through Texas. In it Baker said that on his trip across Texas via El Paso to California in 1848, he kept a journal of natural topography that might have a bearing on the railroad. In 1870 Baker was a bookkeeper with the Jefferson Insurance, Savings, and Exchange Company and was married and had two children. He was still living in 1871.

BIBLIOGRAPHY: Clarksville *Northern Standard*, January 8, April 22, 1848. James M. Day and Ann B. Dunlap, comps., *Map Collection of the Texas State Archives, 1527–1900* (Austin: Texas State Library, 1962). James M. Day and Ann B. Dunlap, comps., "Map Collection of the Texas State Archives, 1888–1900," *Southwestern Historical Quarterly* 66 (October 1962). *Texas State Gazette*, March 22, 1851, November 11, 1853.

Clinton P. Hartmann

BAKER, HINES HOLT, SR. (1893–1982). Hines Holt Baker, Sr., business executive, the tenth child of John B. and Octavia (Weaver) Baker, was born in Big Valley, Texas, on September 22, 1893. He attended public schools at Medina, taught school at Laxson Creek and Saratoga, and graduated from the University of Texas with B.A. and LL.B. degrees in 1917. After military service he practiced law in Beaumont before joining Humble Oil and Refining Company (*see* EXXON COMPANY, U.S.A.) in 1919. From 1919 until 1937 he practice law in the Humble legal department, where he pioneered the development of legal policies regarding oil leases, conservation, and the selling and handling of crude oil. A generalist rather than a specialist, Baker became a director in 1937 and then vice president under his mentor, Harry C. Wiess,[qv] as an expert on conservation and oil-production regulations.

From May 10, 1948, to April 29, 1957, he served as president and CEO of Humble. During his administration Humble became first in Texas gasoline sales and expanded exploration and production of oil, automation in pipelines, and petrochemistry. Baker championed the position of Texas in the Tidelands Controversy.[qv] From May 1957 until his retirement at the end of 1958, he was vice president (finally executive vice president) and director of Standard Oil Company (New Jersey), now Exxon Corporation, in New York.

During World War II[qv] Baker served on several government committees to coordinate oil production and policy for the war effort under the Petroleum Administration for War. He was a member of the National Petroleum Council and a founder of the Texas Research League.[qv] He served as TRL chairman in 1955. He was an organizer and the first chairman of the United Fund board of trustees for Houston and Harris County, a trustee of Methodist Hospital of Houston,[qv] a member of the Board of Visitors of the University of Texas M. D. Anderson Hospital and Tumor Institute (now the University of Texas M. D. Anderson Cancer Center[qv]), a local and district Methodist leader, and an organizer of St. Luke's Methodist Church. Baker was devoted to increasing the quality of teaching and research at the University of Texas. He served as president of the Ex-Students Association and chairman of the University of Texas Development Board. He was on the advisory committee to select the chancellor in 1953 and was a member of the Law School Dean's Council and the University of Texas Centennial commission. He helped organize and was a trustee of the Texas Law School Foundation, and with his wife, Thelma (Kelley), whom he married on April 25, 1920, endowed a professorship.

In 1952 Baker received the good citizenship medal from the Texas Society of the Sons of the American Revolution and an honorary LL.D. degree from Texas Christian University. In 1953 he received the Distinguished Service Award from the Texas Mid-Continent Oil and Gas Association, and later the Brotherhood Award of the Houston chapter of the National Conference of Christians and Jews. He received the outstanding alumnus award from the University of Texas law school, the distinguished award from the Ex-Students Association, and the Santa Rita Award from the regents of the University of Texas. Baker died on July 19, 1982, in Houston. He was survived by his wife and two of his four children.

BIBLIOGRAPHY: Henrietta M. Larson and Kenneth Wiggins Porter, *History of Humble Oil and Refining Company* (New York: Harper, 1959). Irvin M. May, Jr., "Hines Holt Baker, 1893–1982," *Townes Hall Notes*, Winter 1983.

Irvin M. May, Jr.

BAKER, ISAAC G. (1804–1836). Isaac G. Baker, Alamo defender, was born in Arkansas in 1804. He immigrated to Texas in 1830 and settled in Green DeWitt's[qv] colony. On June 14, 1832, he received title to property in Gonzales. Baker joined the relief force from Gonzales and arrived at the besieged Alamo on March 1, 1836. He died in the battle of the Alamo[qv] five days later.

BIBLIOGRAPHY: Daughters of the American Revolution, *The Alamo Heroes and Their Revolutionary Ancestors* (San Antonio, 1976). Bill Groneman, *Alamo Defenders* (Austin: Eakin, 1990). Ethel Zivley Rather, "DeWitt's Colony," *Quarterly of the Texas State Historical Association* 8 (October 1904).

Bill Groneman

BAKER, JAMES ADDISON (1821–1897). James Addison Baker, attorney and judge, was born on March 3, 1821, in Madison County, Alabama, near Huntsville. After leaving the county at the age of eighteen, he taught school for two years. Later he became a clerk of the chancery court and prepared himself for the bar by reading law at night. He was admitted to practice in May 1843. After admission to the bar he entered practice with Samuel W. Probasco, his mentor. In 1845 Probasco died, and Baker fell heir to the firm. Two years later he formed a partnership with Richard W. Walker, a lawyer who later became an associate justice of the Supreme Court of Alabama. In May 1849 Baker married Caroline Hightower, who died in 1852. No children were born of this marriage. In April 1852 Baker moved to Huntsville, Texas, and became active in legal circles, the Masonic lodge, and higher education. On September 24, 1854, he married Rowena Crawford, the principal of the Huntsville Female Brick Academy. They had five children.

Baker first set up a law practice in Huntsville with D. P. Wiley, under the name Wiley and Baker. He later formed a partnership with W. A. Leigh, and his last partner in Huntsville was Judge James M. Maxey. Baker became a Mason as early as 1853 and served three terms as grand master of Forest Lodge No. 19. On January 23, 1857, a lodge was chartered at New Hope, Texas, and named in his honor. He served three stints as trustee of Austin College, Huntsville: 1854–58, 1864–67, and 1873. In 1854 he was appointed to a committee of three to consider adding a law school to Austin College. As a result, the first law school in Texas was established, on March 17, 1855.

In 1861 Baker was elected to the state legislature. A year later, while serving in the Confederate Army, he was elected district judge for what is now the Eleventh District Court in Houston. During Reconstruction[qv] he was removed from his judgeship by Republican governor A. J. Hamilton.[qv] In 1872 he joined Peter W. Gray[qv] and Walter Browne Botts in Houston in the law firm of Gray and Botts; during his partnership the firm was called Gray, Botts, and Baker.

Baker was the father of another James A. Baker[qv] and the great-grandfather of James A. Baker III, presidential cabinet member under Ronald Reagan and George Bush. Baker died on February 24, 1897, and was buried in Huntsville.

BIBLIOGRAPHY: D'Anne McAdams Crews, ed., *Huntsville and Walker County, Texas: A Bicentennial History* (Huntsville, Texas: Sam Houston State University, 1976). George L. Landolt, *Search for the Summit: Austin College through XII Decades* (Austin: Von Boeckmann–Jones, 1970).
J. H. Freeman

BAKER, JAMES ADDISON (1857–1941). James Addison Baker, lawyer, son of Rowena and James Addison Baker[qv] was born in Huntsville, Texas, on January 10, 1857. He graduated from Texas Military Institute[qv] in Austin and was admitted to the bar in 1880. On January 10, 1883, he married Alice Graham; they had five children. Baker practiced law in Houston, where he eventually headed Baker, Botts, Andrews, and Wharton, a 100-year-old law firm (*see* BAKER AND BOTTS). After the Commercial National Bank, which he organized, merged with South Texas National Bank, he became chairman of the board. He was founder and board member of the Houston Gas Company, organizer and first president of the Guardian Trust Company, and one of the organizers of the Galveston, Houston and Henderson Railway and the Southwestern Drug Company. Baker was also president of the Houston Bar Association and a member of the Philosophical Society of Texas[qv] and the Presbyterian Church. He won special renown as the personal attorney of William Marsh Rice[qv] in the litigation concerning Rice's will, which left Rice Institute a trust fund. Baker, as an executor of the will, was instrumental in proving that Rice had been murdered and that a second will, leaving the bulk of Rice's estate to Albert Patrick, was forged. He then became the first chairman of the board of trustees for the institute and served in that capacity until his death. Baker died in Houston on August 2, 1941, and was buried there in Glenwood Cemetery. In his will he left his home, the Oaks, to Rice Institute.

BIBLIOGRAPHY: Houston *Post,* August 3, 1941. Andrew Forest Muir, *William Marsh Rice and His Institute: A Biographical Study,* ed. Sylvia Stallings Morris (Rice University Studies 58.2 [Spring 1972]). Vertical Files, Barker Texas History Center, University of Texas at Austin. *Who Was Who in America,* Vol. 2.

BAKER, JAMES B. (1847–1918). James B. Baker, soldier and civic leader, was born in Louisville, Kentucky, on January 30, 1847, the son of Amanda (Saunders) and John Holland Baker.[qv] He moved to Crawford, Texas, in 1858, when his family established a stock ranch on Tonk Creek in McLennan County. Baker left school in 1860 to become manager of his father's ranch, and when the elder Baker was wounded in Confederate military service, James, at age fifteen, took his place in the ranks of Company H of Col. Nathaniel M. Burford's[qv] Nineteenth Texas Cavalry. He served in the Trans-Mississippi Department, saw action in the Red River campaign,[qv] and by the end of the war had been promoted to regimental sergeant major. After returning to his father's ranch in 1865, he worked as a stockman until

James A. Baker (second from right) with the faculty and board members of Rice Institute, Houston, ca. 1912. Courtesy Woodson Research Center, Rice University Library, Houston. Baker was the personal attorney of William Marsh Rice, who founded Rice Institute (now known as Rice University).

1877, when he moved to Waco to become a contractor and brickmaker. His account book from 1908 through 1914 is in his papers at the Barker Texas History Center,[qv] University of Texas at Austin. Baker was elected alderman and then, in 1904, mayor of Waco, a post he held until 1910. He was also president of Waco Savings Bank. On August 6, 1876, he married Sallie C. Fordtran; the couple had three children. Baker died in Savannah, Missouri, on September 12, 1918, and is buried in Oakwood Cemetery, Waco.

BIBLIOGRAPHY: *A Memorial and Biographical History of McLennan, Falls, Bell, and Coryell Counties* (Chicago: Lewis, 1893; rpt., St. Louis: Ingmire, 1984).
Thomas W. Cutrer

BAKER, JAMES H. (1800–1854). James H. Baker, early settler, was born in Virginia on June 10, 1800. He married Frances Hancock, also of Virginia, and they became the parents of eight children. A James H. Baker received 1,280 acres in San Saba County for seventeen months service in the Texas army, from October 1836 to May 1838; this may or may not have been the same person. Baker brought his family to Texas from Tennessee in 1837, settled temporarily in Washington County, and moved to Bastrop County in 1838. In 1840 he established a farm on Onion Creek, eight miles from Austin. He raised horses and cattle and owned several slaves. Baker died at his home on February 15, 1854. His sons James and George took a herd of 6,000 cattle from Travis County to holdings in San Saba County in 1856.

BIBLIOGRAPHY: Vertical Files, Austin History Center. Vertical Files, Barker Texas History Center, University of Texas at Austin.
Vivian Elizabeth Smyrl

BAKER, JAMES MCCULLOCH (1797–1882). James McCulloch Baker, judge, was born on November 27, 1797, in South Carolina, the son of Joseph and Jane (McCulloch) Baker of Rowan County, North Carolina. He moved to Tennessee while still a youth and in 1834 to Mississippi. After becoming a prosperous planter in Madison County, Mississippi, he moved to the Upper Cuero Creek Settlement in Gonzales County, Texas, in 1840. He established his cotton plantation on the Guadalupe River above the site of present-day Concrete, which is now in DeWitt County. In Maury County, Tennessee, on July 27, 1818, he married Miss Martha Jane Smith. To this union were born thirteen children, all of whom became citizens of the Republic of Texas[qv] except the eldest son, Samuel Smith Baker, who stayed in Mississippi and managed the Baker Plantation in Madison County. In 1841, with his friend James Norman Smith,[qv] Baker established the First Presbyterian Church in what is now DeWitt County; it was also the first Protestant church there. It was originally located on Cuero Creek near Concrete, and later moved to Hochheim as a Cumberland Presbyterian church. In 1844 Baker was elected chief justice (county judge) of Gonzales County. In 1846, at annexation,[qv] he became the first chief justice of Gonzales County, state of Texas, a position in which he helped the county make the transition from the republic to the state. In 1846, DeWitt County was formed by the Texas legislature. In his capacity as chief justice of Gonzales County, Baker swore in the first set of county officers of DeWitt County. He became the first probate judge of the new county, and afterwards served as county judge from 1850 to 1852 and 1865 to 1867. He was also a trustee of Concrete College. Baker, one of the "Founding Fathers" of DeWitt County, died in March 1882 and is buried on his plantation in DeWitt County beside his wife. Their graves are located in the Baker Family Cemetery on a hill overlooking the Guadalupe River valley.

BIBLIOGRAPHY: Nellie Murphree, *A History of DeWitt County* (Victoria, Texas, 1962). *Ross Booth, Jr.*

BAKER, JESS ALEXANDER (1856–1921). Jess Alexander Baker, merchant and state representative, the son of Daniel Marlin and Angeline E. (Chism) Baker, was born near Georgetown, Texas, on October 11, 1856. In 1871 he moved with his father and younger brother to Granbury, where he worked as a tinner, making and repairing tin kitchen utensils. Four years later he opened a store in partnership with his brother Daniel Oscar to sell leather goods, wagons, buggies, and farm implements. By 1895 he was also vice president of the Hood County Milling Company, the Granbury Quarry Company, and the First National Bank of Granbury; he held the latter position until his death.

Baker was elected in 1906 as the Democratic candidate for the Seventy-sixth legislative district (after 1913, the Ninety-seventh district). He sat in the Texas House of Representatives for Hood, Erath, and Somervell counties for five terms (1907, 1909, 1911, 1915, 1917). Throughout his political career he supported progressive measures and became especially noted for his advocacy of compulsory school attendance and woman suffrage.[qv] During his first term in the Thirtieth Legislature (1907) he introduced a suffrage amendment to the Texas constitution and did so again during his third term in the Thirty-second Legislature (1911). In 1917, during the Thirty-fifth Legislature, Baker cosponsored two suffrage bills, one to grant women primary suffrage and another to submit a women's suffrage amendment to the state's voters. Baker married Alice Ballen in 1880; they had a daughter and a son who survived into adulthood and a daughter who died in infancy. Baker died in Granbury on May 18, 1921.

BIBLIOGRAPHY: Willie D. Bowles, History of the Woman Suffrage Movement in Texas (M.A. thesis, University of Texas, 1939). Minnie Fisher Cunningham Papers, Houston Metropolitan Research Center, Houston Public Library. Dallas *Morning News*, May 19, 1921. A. Elizabeth Taylor, *Citizens at Last: The Woman Suffrage Movement in Texas* (Austin: Temple, 1987). Texas Legislature, *House Journal.*
Elizabeth York Enstam

BAKER, JOHN HOLLAND (1822–1891). John Holland Baker, farmer, stockraiser, and soldier, was born in Frankfort, Kentucky, on April 6, 1822, the son of Lucinda (Edwards) Baker. In 1846 he married Amanda Saunders in Kentucky. The couple had six children, among them John W., Waller S., and James B. Baker.[qqv] In 1858 Baker moved to the McLennan County community of Crawford and became a farmer and stockman on Tonk Creek. At the death of his wife in 1860 he considered returning to Kentucky, but when the Civil War[qv] broke out he enlisted in Company H of Col. Nathaniel M. Burford's[qv] Nineteenth Texas Cavalry. After sustaining a disabling wound in a skirmish at Patterson, Missouri, on January 20, 1863, he returned to his ranch and was replaced in service by his son James. In 1862 Baker married Eva Loughridge; they had four children. Baker died on November 9, 1891, at his ranch. He is buried in Oakwood Cemetery, Waco.

BIBLIOGRAPHY: *A Memorial and Biographical History of McLennan, Falls, Bell, and Coryell Counties* (Chicago: Lewis, 1893; rpt., St. Louis: Ingmire, 1984). *Thomas W. Cutrer*

BAKER, JOHN REAGAN (1809–1904). John Reagan Baker, Republic of Texas[qv] soldier, son of Peter and Margaret Laura (Reagan) Baker, was born near Blue Springs, Green County, Tennessee, on August 6, 1809. He made a trip to Texas in 1836. In 1839 he returned to Texas and became a member of the Texan auxiliary corps of the *Federalista* army encamped at Fort Lipantitlán. He followed Ewen Cameron[qv] through the campaign, was in the battle of October 23, 1840, at Ojo de Agua, near Saltillo, and cut his way back to Texas with his comrades. When the corps was disbanded, he went to Refugio County and settled in Aransas City. He was elected sheriff of Refugio County on February 1, 1841, and organized a company of minutemen, of which he was captain, although he retained membership and became a first lieutenant in Cameron's Rangers.

In March 1842 he went with Cameron's company to San Antonio on the occasion of the Rafael Vásquez[qv] raid, served with the company on the Nueces when Antonio Canales[qv] was repulsed on June 6, 1842, and distinguished himself in hand-to-hand fighting at the battle of Salado Creek[qv] on September 18, 1842. As a member of the Somervell and Mier expeditions[qv] he commanded a spy company and was one of the leaders of the break at Salado on February 11, 1843, when he was wounded. Unable to escape, he was put in the hospital, and there avoided the Black Bean Episode,[qv] but he was held in Perote Prison until September 16, 1844.

Baker returned to Refugio County and established a mercantile business at Saluria, on Matagorda Island. At the outbreak of the Civil War,[qv] he organized a home-guard company and was elected its captain. After the war he lived in Goliad County for a while, then moved to Indianola and again entered the mercantile business. In 1876 he moved to Wilson County, to a ranch near Stockdale, where he died on January 19, 1904.

BIBLIOGRAPHY: Thomas J. Green, *Journal of the Texian Expedition Against Mier* (New York: Harper, 1845; rpt., Austin: Steck, 1935). Hobart Huson, *Refugio: A Comprehensive History of Refugio County from Aboriginal Times to 1953* (2 vols., Woodsboro, Texas: Rooke Foundation, 1953, 1955). William P. Stapp, *The Prisoners of Perote: A Journal* (Philadelphia: Zieber, 1845). *Hobart Huson*

BAKER, JOHN W. (1850–1931). John W. Baker, lawyer and county official, was born in Lexington, Kentucky, on November 30, 1850, the son of Amanda (Saunders) and John Holland Baker.[qv] He attended private schools and graduated from Waco University (later Baylor University) and the Jesuit College of St. Louis (later St. Louis University). Baker read law in the offices of Coke, Herring, and Anderson and entered into private practice in Waco. He married Louise Brown in 1875, and they had five children. Baker was named county clerk of McLennan County in 1876 and held that office until 1892. He was county treasurer in 1893–94 and then served as sheriff for ten years. He became a county judge in 1904 but returned to private practice in 1908. He resumed his duties as county clerk in 1912 and continued in that position until his death, on November 23, 1931.

BIBLIOGRAPHY: Betty A. M. McSwain, ed., *The Bench and Bar of Waco and McLennan County* (Waco: Texian Press, 1976). *A Memorial and Biographical History of McLennan, Falls, Bell, and Coryell Counties* (Chicago: Lewis, 1893; rpt., St. Louis: Ingmire, 1984).

Vivian Elizabeth Smyrl

BAKER, JOHN W. (1871–1924). John W. Baker, banker and state treasurer, son of Robert and Mary Nancy (Woods) Baker, was born in Bastrop County, Texas, on May 27, 1871. About 1883 the family moved to Williamson County, where Baker married Lora F. Shaw of Georgetown on November 23, 1893; they had four children. Baker moved to West Texas in 1896, first to Taylor County and subsequently to Lubbock. He was a prominent banker at Lubbock and at Crosbyton before he was elected state treasurer in a special election in 1918. During World War I[qv] he did distinguished work in Liberty Bond drives. Baker was reelected as state treasurer in 1920, but he resigned in July 1921 to become vice president of the Breckenridge State Bank. He was a Baptist, Mason, Woodman, and Odd Fellow. He died at his home in Austin on May 22, 1924, and was buried at the Oakwood Cemetery annex.

bibliography: Austin *American*, May 24, 1924. Buckley B. Paddock, *History of Texas: Fort Worth and the Texas Northwest Edition* (4 vols., Chicago: Lewis, 1922).

Lura N. Rouse

BAKER, JOSEPH (1804–1846). Joseph Baker, newspaperman and public official, son of William and Jane (Gerrish) Baker, was born in Maine in 1804. On December 7, 1831, he arrived at San Felipe de Austin, where he taught school for three years and was secretary of the ayuntamiento[qv] in 1835. On October 5, 1835, he was issued title to one-fourth league of land on the west bank of Fish Pond Creek, a mile north of the site of Hempstead, in what is now Waller County. A ten-league grant made to him in December 1835 was cancelled by the Republic of Texas.[qv] With Gail Borden, Jr., and Thomas H. Borden,[qqv] Baker, or Don José, as he was called, established the *Telegraph and Texas Register*[qv] at San Felipe; the first issue appeared on October 10, 1835. Baker severed his connection with the paper on April 5, 1836, to join the Texas army, in which he served from February 29 to June 1. He was a member of Moseley Baker's[qv] company at the battle of San Jacinto.[qv] In 1836 he was chosen second judge of Austin Municipality and became a charter member of the Texas Philosophical Society.[qv] He was appointed translator to the state on October 23, 1836, and was elected first chief justice of Bexar County on December 16, 1836. In 1837–38 he represented Bexar County in the House of the Second Congress. In 1841–42 he published the Houston *Houstonian*.[qv] He was Spanish translator in the General Land Office[qv] in 1845. Baker died in Austin on July 11, 1846, and was buried there in Oakwood Cemetery. In 1936 the state of Texas placed a monument at his grave.

bibliography: Texas House of Representatives, *Biographical Directory of the Texan Conventions and Congresses, 1832–1845* (Austin: Book Exchange, 1941).

L. W. Kemp

BAKER, KARLE WILSON (1878–1960). Karle Wilson Baker, writer, daughter of William Thomas Murphey and Kate Florence (Montgomery) Wilson, was born on October 13, 1878, in Little Rock, Arkansas. Her first name was originally spelled Karl; the *e* was added later, first appearing in Kate Wilson's diary in 1893. She attended public schools, Little Rock Academy, and Ouachita Baptist College and returned to graduate from Little Rock Academy, a high school, in 1898. She attended the University of Chicago periodically from 1898 to 1901 and later attended Columbia University (1919) and the University of California at Berkeley (1926–27). The only university degree that she held, however, was an honorary doctorate of letters conferred in 1924 by Southern Methodist University.

From 1897 to 1901 Karle Wilson alternately studied at the University of Chicago and taught at Southwest Virginia Institute in Bristol, Virginia. In 1901 she joined her family, which had moved to Nacogdoches, Texas. She went back to Little Rock to teach school for two years but returned to Nacogdoches, and there, on August 8, 1907, she married Thomas E. Baker, a banker. They had a son and daughter. Karle Baker devoted the remainder of her life to maintaining her household, to writing, and to teaching (from 1925 to 1934) at Stephen F. Austin State Teachers College (now Stephen F. Austin State University). She wrote personal and historical essays, novels, nature poetry, and short stories. Her early writing appeared in such journals as *Atlantic Monthly, Century, Harper's, Poetry: A Magazine of Verse, Scribner's, Putnam's,* and the *Yale Review,* under the pen name of Charlotte Wilson. Yale University Press published her first volume of poetry, ninety-two lyrics collected under the name of the title poem, *Blue Smoke* (1919), which received favorable reviews in the United States and England. Yale also published a second collection of her poems, *Burning Bush* (1922), as well as two prose volumes, *The Garden of Plynck* (1920), a children's fantasy novel, and *Old Coins* (1923), twenty-seven short allegorical sketches. Baker was anthologized in *The Best Poems of 1923, English and American,* published in London, and in 1925 she won the Southern Prize of the Poetry Society of South Carolina, a competition open to poets living in the states of the former Confederacy.

In 1931 a third volume of her poems, *Dreamers on Horseback,* was nominated for the Pulitzer Prize for poetry. By that time, however, she had begun to concentrate mainly on prose writing. As early as 1925 she had written *The Texas Flag Primer,* a Texas history for children that was adopted for use in the public schools. In 1930 *The Birds of Tanglewood,* a collection of essays based on her birdwatching, appeared. Tanglewood was the name that she gave to an area around her parents' second home in Nacogdoches. A second reader for children, *Two Little Texans,* was published in 1932. Her most notable prose works were two novels published when she was in her late fifties and early sixties. *Family Style* (1937), a study of human motivation and reaction to sudden wealth, is set against the background of the East Texas oil boom (*see* east texas oilfield). *Star of the Wilderness* (1942) is a historical novel in which Dr. James Grant,[qv] a Texas revolutionary, figures. It later became a selection of the Book-of-the-Month Club.

In 1958 Baker was designated an honorary vice president of the Poetry Society of Texas,[qv] of which she was a charter member. She had served in 1938–39 as president of the Texas Institute of Letters,[qv] of which she was a charter member and the first woman fellow. Still other recognition was given her by the Authors League of America, the Philosophical Society of Texas,[qv] and the Poetry Society of America. She died on November 9, 1960, and is buried in Nacogdoches.

bibliography: Florence Elberta Barns, *Texas Writers of Today* (Dallas: Tardy, 1935). Edwin W. Gaston, Jr., *The Early Novel of the Southwest* (Albuquerque: University of New Mexico Press, 1961). Edwin W. Gaston, Jr., "Karle Wilson Baker: First Woman of Texas Letters," *East Texas Historical Journal* 15 (1977). *Library of Southern Literature* (16 vols., Atlanta: Martin and Hoyt, 1909–13). Mabel Major et al., *Southwest Heritage: A Literary History with Bibliography* (Albuquerque: University of New Mexico Press, 1938; 3d ed. 1972). Pamela Lynn Palmer, "Dorothy Scarborough and Karle Wilson Baker: A Literary Friendship," *Southwestern Historical Quarterly* 91 (July 1987).

Edwin W. Gaston, Jr.

BAKER, MOSELEY (1802–1848). Moseley (Mosley) Baker, pioneer legislator and soldier, was born in Norfolk, Virginia, on September 20, 1802, the son of Horace and Rebecca (Moseley) Baker. His family soon thereafter moved to Montgomery, Alabama, where he studied law and was admitted to the bar. Finding journalism more to his liking, however, Baker founded and edited the Montgomery *Advertiser.* In 1829 he was elected to the state legislature from Montgomery County and served as speaker of the House. According to some accounts, three years later he moved to Texas. These reports have him living in San Felipe as early as 1833. According to a claim by John J.

Linn,[qv] Baker was forced to flee Alabama for the forgery of a $5,000 check. Although he subsequently repaid the bad debt, Baker was then a fugitive from justice. He and his wife, Eliza (Ward), and their daughter certainly moved to Liberty, Texas, in March 1835. On October 9 Baker secured a league and a labor of land in Lorenzo de Zavala's[qv] colony on the east shore of Galveston Bay.

As a leading advocate of Texas independence from Mexico, Baker claimed to have made the first speech in favor of disunion. He was one of nine men whom Col. Domingo de Ugartechea[qv] ordered arrested at San Felipe in July 1835. The following month Baker accompanied Francis W. Johnson[qv] into East Texas to recruit men for the revolutionary army.[qv] As a member of the Consultation[qv] of 1835 Baker delivered a speech calling for the dissolution of that body. This proposal was met by a stern response from Sam Houston[qv] who, "drawing his majestic figure up to his full height," declared "I had rather be a slave, and grovel in the dust all my life, than a convicted felon!"

Baker was one of the military leaders of the Texas Revolution.[qv] He served as a private at the battle of Gonzales, at the Grass Fight, and at engagements connected with the siege of Bexar[qqv] in December 1835. On March 1, 1836, he was elected captain of Company D, First Regiment of Texan Volunteers, the largest company in Sam Houston's army. John P. Borden[qv] served as his first lieutenant. On Houston's retreat into East Texas after the disasters at the Alamo and Goliad, Baker refused to abandon the line of the Brazos River. For several days his company, on detached duty, guarded the ford at San Felipe, where most of his men resided, thus preventing Santa Anna's army from turning Houston's left flank and forcing his retreat toward the San Jacinto River. On March 29, 1836, when Houston abandoned his position at Groce's Retreat,[qv] Baker burned San Felipe to prevent its capture by the enemy. He contended that the destruction of the town was a result of Houston's orders; Houston said otherwise. Baker rejoined the main army on April 14, 1836, and commanded Company D of Col. Edward Burleson's[qv] First Regiment of Texas Volunteers at the battle of San Jacinto,[qv] where he was slightly wounded.

After San Jacinto Baker helped to incorporate the Texas Railroad, Navigation, and Banking Company[qv] and was elected as a representative from Austin County to the First Congress of the Republic of Texas. During his term, which ran from October 3, 1836, to June 13, 1837, he drew up charges of impeachment, stemming from his earlier disagreements with Sam Houston, against the chief executive. Although the proceedings against Houston failed, Baker was elected to the Third Congress from Galveston County, to which he had moved in 1837, and served from November 5, 1838, to January 24, 1839. He then moved to a league of land near Goose Creek in Harris County, where he established a plantation that he called Evergreen. In the election for the Sixth Congress in 1841 Baker was defeated by Archibald Wynns[qv] by a single vote. In 1839 the Congress appointed him a brigadier general in the militia of the republic for a campaign against the Indians on the Brazos. In 1842 he was reappointed brigadier general and raised a company in response to Gen. Adrián Woll's[qv] seizure of San Antonio. He paraded his company on the Harris County courthouse square on September 28, and "made a very eloquent and appropriate reply" to the presentation of his company flag. Taken ill with a fever, however, he was unable to accompany his men on the subsequent Somervell expedition,[qv] and passed the command over to Gardiner Smith.

Still feuding with Houston in 1844, Baker wrote an open letter to the governor, stating his objections to his policies and actions and characterizing Houston as "the greatest curse that Providence in its wrath could have sent upon the country." According to Linn, Baker "afterwards became a religionist, and after the death of his wife took to preaching." As a Methodist, he published a newspaper in Houston called the *True Evangelist*, which expounded somewhat heterodox religious views. Even when the denomination enjoined him to silence he continued publication. On November 4, 1848, Baker died in Houston of yellow fever. He was first buried in what became known as the Jefferson Davis Cemetery in that city, but his body was later removed to the Episcopal Cemetery. On September 17, 1929, his remains and those of his wife were reinterred in the State Cemetery[qv] in Austin.

BIBLIOGRAPHY: Moseley Baker Papers, Barker Texas History Center, University of Texas at Austin. Daughters of the Republic of Texas, *Muster Rolls of the Texas Revolution* (Austin, 1986). John J. Linn, *Reminiscences of Fifty Years in Texas* (New York: Sadlier, 1883; 2d ed., Austin: Steck, 1935; rpt., Austin: State House, 1986). Joseph Milton Nance, *Attack and Counterattack: The Texas-Mexican Frontier, 1842* (Austin: University of Texas Press, 1964). Texas House of Representatives, *Biographical Directory of the Texan Conventions and Congresses, 1832–1845* (Austin: Book Exchange, 1941). Amelia W. Williams and Eugene C. Barker, eds., *The Writings of Sam Houston, 1813–1863* (8 vols., Austin: University of Texas Press, 1938–43; rpt., Austin and New York: Pemberton Press, 1970). *Thomas W. Cutrer*

BAKER, RHODES SEMMES (1874–1940). Rhodes Semmes Baker, attorney, was born to Andrew Jackson and Elizabeth (Newsome) Baker at Duck Hill, Mississippi, on May 30, 1874. The family moved to Texas in 1884 and settled at San Angelo, where the elder Baker operated a hardware store and served as commissioner of the General Land Office[qv] for a short time in 1896. Baker, while working in his father's business, educated himself in hopes of becoming an attorney. Despite the fact that he had no academic coursework, he was accepted at the University of Texas. In Austin he not only pursued legal studies but edited a number of student publications. He graduated at the top of his class in 1896, moved to Dallas, and established a law practice that immediately prospered. Three years later he married Edna Miller Rembert; they had two daughters.

Baker was admitted to practice before the United States Supreme Court in April 1901 and successfully argued a number of cases. In his most famous one, *Hopkins v. Baker*, he convinced the justices of the legality of a state law allowing married couples to file separate tax returns, thereby reducing their tax burden. He was a member of the American Bar Association, as well as the state and local bar associations, and served at one time as president of the University of Texas Ex-Students Association. He was a member of the First Presbyterian Church, where he taught Bible classes for thirty-seven years, and was president, on a number of occasions, of the Young Men's Christian Association.

Baker acquired an impressive selection of paintings, including works by George Inness, Thomas Gainsborough, Joshua Reynolds, and George Romney, and was a member and one-time president of the Dallas Art Association (*see* DALLAS ART INSTITUTE). This largely self-educated man maintained a great interest in higher education, as seen in his participation in the campaign that brought Southern Methodist University to Dallas and in his service on the board of trustees of Austin College, which awarded him an honorary Ph.D. in 1924. At the time of his death he was a partner in the law firm of Thompson, Knight, Baker, and Harris, chairman of the board of the Dallas Building and Loan Association, and a member of the board of directors of Republic National Bank. Baker died in Dallas on February 6, 1940.

BIBLIOGRAPHY: *Alcalde* (magazine of the Ex-Students' Association of the University of Texas), March 1940. Dallas *Morning News*, February 7, 1940. *A History of Greater Dallas and Vicinity*, Vol. 1., by Philip Lindsley; Vol. 2., *Selected Biography and Memoirs*, ed. L. B. Hill (Chicago: Lewis, 1909). *Texan* (Austin, Texas), February 8, 1940. *University of Texas Record*, August 1899. *Brian Hart*

BAKER, ROBERT ANDREW (1910–1992). Robert Andrew Baker, seminary professor, Baptist historian, and author, was born on December 22, 1910, in St. Louis, Missouri, the second of three sons of Benjamin William and Grace (Hartman) Baker. He had two older stepsisters. His father was an English immigrant, and his mother of Pennsylvania Dutch descent. William Baker died when Robert was two years old. Grace Baker moved her children to Kansas City, Kansas, where she went to work to support them. Robert was converted at the age of twelve and baptized at Immanuel Baptist Church, Kansas City, Kansas. Beginning in 1929 he attended night sessions of a business college for two years while working as an attorney's clerical assistant and a court reporter using stenotype by day. From 1932 through 1936 he was an operative in the United States Secret Service Division of the Treasury Department, with the Oklahoma City, Oklahoma, office as his headquarters. Although Baker had for years been convinced that God was leading him into full-time Christian service, he worked at secular jobs until he had put his younger brothers through college. In December 1936 the First Baptist Church of Oklahoma licensed him to preach, and he enrolled in Baylor University. He was ordained to the ministry by Bellmead Baptist Church, Waco, Texas, on March 14, 1938. His degrees included a B.A. from Baylor University, 1939; a Th.M. in 1941 and a Th.D. in 1944 from Southwestern Baptist Theological Seminary, Fort Worth; a Ph.D. from Yale University, New Haven, Connecticut, in 1947; and an honorary doctor of laws degree from Baylor University in 1981. He married Fredona C. McCaulley on June 5, 1939, in Waco. They had a son and a daughter. From 1940 to 1942 Baker studied at Southwestern Baptist Theological Seminary and taught evening classes. He joined the church-history faculty at Southwestern in 1942 and retired in 1981. He was chairman of the Committee on Graduate Studies for twenty-nine years and served for six years on the commission on accreditation of the American Association of Theological Schools. He served as president of the Texas Baptist Historical Society and as chairman of the Southern Baptist Historical Commission. He was the first to receive the Distinguished Service Award from the latter group in 1981. He was awarded the Distinguished Alumnus Award by Southwestern Seminary in 1968. Among the dozen books Baker wrote are *A Summary of Christian History* (1959), *J. B. Tidwell Plus God* (1947), *Relations Between Northern and Southern Baptists* (1948), and *The Blossoming Desert: A Concise History of Texas Baptists* (1970). On November 15, 1992, Baker died at his home in Fort Worth. A memorial service was held at Travis Avenue Baptist Church on November 19, 1992, and burial was at Laurel Land Cemetery, Fort Worth.

BIBLIOGRAPHY: William R. Estep, ed., *The Lord's Free People in a Free Land: Essays in Baptist History in Honor of Robert A. Baker* (Fort Worth: School of Theology, Southwestern Baptist Theological Seminary, 1976). Fort Worth *Star-Telegram*, November 17, 1992.

Samuel B. Hesler

BAKER, ROBERT HOMES (1858–1935). Robert Homes Baker, businessman, prison reformer, and prison administrator, the son of Robert and Annie (Miller) Baker, was born in Memphis, Tennessee, on September 4, 1858. He attended East Tennessee University for two years before moving to Texas, where from 1882 to 1896 he was a merchant at Waco. From 1896 to 1904 he was Texas manager for Equitable Life Assurance Society. He was a business partner of political leader Edward M. House.[qv] Baker was president and general manager of the Trinity and Brazos Valley Railway from 1904 to 1911. In 1912 he bought the Texas Central Railroad and served as president of the line until 1914, when he bought the Wichita Falls Railroad to sell both lines to the Missouri, Kansas and Texas system. Later Baker became president of the Houston Terminal Warehouse and Cold Storage Company and chairman of the board of the Seaboard Life Insurance Company. He was captain of the Waco Light Infantry, Texas National Guard,[qv] from 1886 to 1889 and from 1902 to 1904 was a colonel on the staff of Governor S. W. T. Lanham.[qv]

From 1924 until about 1927 Baker served as chairman of the Texas Committee on Prisons and Prison Labor,[qv] an organization committed to penal reform. Governor Dan Moody[qv] appointed Baker to the reorganized Texas Prison Board, which he served as chairman from June 16, 1927, through March 25, 1929, when he resigned. While leading the administrative agency for the prison system,[qv] Baker worked closely with advisor Elizabeth Speer, whom he and other reformers regarded as an expert in the field of penology. He fired employees who mistreated prisoners, reduced corporal punishments, and supported the publication of an inmates' newspaper, the *Echo.* Baker also advocated the sale of existing prison properties in East Texas and the Gulf Coast region and their replacement with a modern prison to be constructed near Austin. However, he and Moody failed to persuade the Texas legislature to support the proposal.

Baker, who resided in Austin before the final eight years of his life in Houston, was instrumental in perfecting plans for the enlargement of the campus of the University of Texas. He married Nellie Faulkner on October 19, 1886; they had three children, including philanthropist Burke Baker.[qv] Baker was a Democrat and a Baptist. He died in Houston on January 9, 1935, and was buried there.

BIBLIOGRAPHY: Houston *Post*, January 10, 1935. Paul M. Lucko, "A Missed Opportunity: Texas Prison Reform during the Dan Moody Administration, 1927–1931," *Southwestern Historical Quarterly* 96 (July 1992). Paul M. Lucko, "The 'Next Big Job': Women Prison Reformers in Texas, 1918–1930," in *Women and Texas History: Selected Essays*, ed. Fane Downs and Nancy Baker Jones (Austin: Texas State Historical Association, 1993). Rupert N. Richardson, *Colonel Edward M. House: The Texas Years, 1858–1912* (Abilene, Texas: Hardin-Simmons University, 1964). *Who Was Who in America*, Vol 1.

BAKER, WALLER SAUNDERS (1855–1913). Waller Saunders Baker, lawyer, was born in Lexington, Kentucky, on March 30, 1855, the son of Amanda (Saunders) and John Holland Baker.[qv] The family moved to Texas in the late 1850s and settled on a farm near Crawford in McLennan County. Baker graduated from Baylor University in 1875, read law for a year in the office of Thomas Harrison,[qv] was admitted to the bar, and practiced law in Waco the rest of his life. He was attorney for the San Antonio and Aransas Pass Railway and a law partner of Pat M. Neff.[qv] In 1884 he became chairman of the Democratic executive committee for McLennan County and in 1887 served one term in the state Senate. In 1892 he was a delegate to the Democratic convention in Houston and campaign manager for James S. Hogg.[qv] Baker married Mary Mills of Galveston in January 1886. He died on September 9, 1913, while on vacation in San Francisco, and was buried in Oakwood Cemetery, Waco.

BIBLIOGRAPHY: John Henry Brown, *Indian Wars and Pioneers of Texas* (Austin: Daniell, 1880; reprod., Easley, South Carolina: Southern Historical Press, 1978). Frank W. Johnson, *A History of Texas and Texans* (5 vols., ed. E. C. Barker and E. W. Winkler [Chicago and New York: American Historical Society, 1914; rpt. 1916]). Betty A. M. McSwain, ed., *The Bench and Bar of Waco and McLennan County* (Waco: Texian Press, 1976).

Lura N. Rouse

BAKER, WILLIAM CHARLES M. (?–1836). William Baker, Alamo defender, was born in Missouri. He came to Texas as a volunteer from Mississippi during the Texas Revolution.[qv] He joined Capt. Thomas F. L. Parrott's[qv] company at Bexar on November 26, 1835, and took part in the siege of Bexar.[qv] During the subsequent reorganization of the Texan forces he became part of Capt. John Chenoweth's[qv] company. Baker left Bexar but returned with the rank of captain as commander of the volunteers accompanying James Bowie[qv] on January 19, 1836. He died in the battle of the Alamo[qv] on March 6, 1836.

BIBLIOGRAPHY: Daughters of the American Revolution, *The Alamo Heroes and Their Revolutionary Ancestors* (San Antonio, 1976). Daughters of the Republic of Texas, *Muster Rolls of the Texas Revolution* (Austin, 1986). Bill Groneman, *Alamo Defenders* (Austin: Eakin,

1990). John H. Jenkins, ed., *The Papers of the Texas Revolution, 1835–1836* (10 vols., Austin: Presidial Press, 1973). *Bill Groneman*

BAKER, WILLIAM MUMFORD (1825–1883). William Mumford Baker, Presbyterian minister and author, son of Elizabeth and Daniel Baker,[qv] was born in Washington, D.C., on June 6, 1825. He graduated from Princeton College in 1846 and from Princeton Seminary in 1848. He was ordained an evangelist by the Presbytery of Little Rock on April 22, 1849, and for a short time served as minister at the Presbyterian church in Batesville, Arkansas. In 1849 Baker and his mother, sister, and brother joined his father in Galveston. On May 26, 1850, he reorganized the Presbyterian church in Austin with five people. The church met at the old Capitol and at the Baggelley School. A new church building was completed in 1851. When the Presbyterian General Assembly in Philadelphia, of which the Austin church was a member, officially endorsed the Union during the Civil War,[qv] the Austin church withdrew its membership and joined the Southern General Assembly of Presbyterian Churches. Baker himself was a Unionist, a fact that caused several families to break with the church. Baker submitted his resignation in December 1865 to a congregation of seventy-three persons, and in 1866 he asked the Central Texas Presbytery to dissolve his pastoral relations with the Austin church. The presbytery did not comply. In 1866 Baker published *Inside: A Chronicle of Secession* in New York under the alias G. F. Harrington. At the close of the war he and his family moved north. He served churches in Zanesville, Ohio, from 1866 to 1872, Newburyport, Massachusetts, from 1872 to 1874, and Boston, Massachusetts, from 1874 to 1876. From 1877 to 1881 he resided in Boston and concentrated on his writing. He wrote one biography, *The Life and Labours of the Reverend Daniel Baker;* a religious work, *The Ten Theophanies* (1883); and twelve novels, most of them about his Texas experiences. He died on August 20, 1883, after a two-year illness, and his body was transported back to Austin for burial beside his father in Oakwood Cemetery.

BIBLIOGRAPHY: *Library of Southern Literature* (Atlanta: Martin and Hoyt, 1909–13), Vol. 15. William Angus McLeod, *Story of the First Southern Presbyterian Church, Austin, Texas* (Austin, 1939?). William Stuart Red, *A History of the Presbyterian Church in Texas* (Austin: Steck, 1936). *Mary Jane Walsh*

BAKER, WILLIAM ROBINSON (1820–1890). William Robinson Baker, Houston mayor, Texas state legislator, and railroad official, the son of Asa and Hannah (Robinson) Baker, was born in Baldwinsville, New York, on May 21, 1820. He moved to Texas in 1837, worked as a bookkeeper for the Houston Town Company, and in 1841 was elected Harris county clerk, a position he filled for the next sixteen years. Baker made his considerable fortune as a land dealer. He married Hester Eleanor Runnels on December 15, 1845, and the couple had one child. Between 1852 and 1877 Baker served as secretary, vice president, general manager, president, and board member of the Houston and Texas Central Railway. In 1860 he had real property valued at $300,000, personal property worth $75,000, and twenty-three slaves, but by 1870 the value of his assets had declined to real property valued at $218,000 and personal property valued at $8,000. In 1874 he was elected as a Democrat to the state Senate and from 1880 to 1886 served as mayor of Houston. He purchased an interest in the Houston *Post*[qv] in 1883 and was president of the City Bank of Houston. He was a Mason. He died on April 30, 1890.

BIBLIOGRAPHY: *Biographical Encyclopedia of Texas* (New York: Southern, 1880). *History of Texas, Together with a Biographical History of the Cities of Houston and Galveston* (Chicago: Lewis, 1895). William S. Speer and John H. Brown, eds., *Encyclopedia of the New West* (Marshall, Texas: United States Biographical Publishing, 1881; rpt., Easley, South Carolina: Southern Historical Press, 1978). Ralph A. Wooster, "Wealthy Texans, 1860," *Southwestern Historical Quarterly* 71 (October 1967). *Diana J. Kleiner*

BAKER AND BOTTS. The law firm Baker and Botts was officially established in 1866 by Houston lawyer Peter W. Gray[qv] and Walter Browne Botts under the name Gray and Botts. Botts, a member of a distinguished family of lawyers in Virginia, served in the Texas legislature and as a lieutenant colonel in the Confederate Army. The firm became Gray, Botts, and Baker when former Harris County district judge James Addison Baker[qv] joined in 1872. Gray died in 1874, and James A. Baker[qv] joined in 1887, when the firm became Baker, Botts, and Baker.

For the first thirty-four years of the firm's history, its partners were primarily trial lawyers, railroad lawyers, or both. In the late 1800s, as the commercial importance of Houston grew, Baker, Botts, and Baker became general counsel for several railroads—the Missouri Pacific, the Houston and Texas Central, and the Houston, East and West Texas (the latter two later became part of the Southern Pacific system). As railroad work increased, Robert S. Lovett[qv] joined the firm, which by 1892 was known as Baker, Botts, Baker, and Lovett. The firm then served as general attorneys for all the Southern Pacific lines in Texas. Lovett became general counsel for the Union Pacific and Southern Pacific railroads in 1904 and later served as chairman of both systems.

After the turn of the century, not only did the number of attorneys increase, but the firm's areas of practice expanded, and its structure changed to resemble that of modern law firms with a managing partner and strong centralized management. The first managing partner was Edwin B. Parker,[qv] who came in 1894, wrote the firm's first organization plan, and developed its system of hiring and training young lawyers, now called associates. Parker resigned from the firm in 1922. In 1904 the firm changed its name to Baker, Botts, Parker, and Garwood. Hiram M. Garwood,[qv] an outstanding trial lawyer known for his view of the firm as "a permanent institution, just as Harvard or the Bank of England is an institution," became a partner in 1904, and his name was associated with the firm for twenty-seven years. Subsequently, when Jesse Andrews[qv] joined the firm in 1895 and became a partner in 1906, the name changed to Baker, Botts, Andrews, and Wharton. Under Andrews's direction, the firm opened an office in Kansas City, where it represented lumber interests. As general counsel to Long-Bell Lumber Company, Andrews was instrumental during the Great Depression[qv] in saving from creditors what was then the largest lumber company in the world and is now International Paper Company. Both Andrews and Clarence Wharton,[qv] a trial lawyer and historian who represented the public utilities industry, which came to play a prominent role in the firm's future, became partners in 1906.

Ralph B. Feagin served as managing partner in the aggressive style set by Parker. He expanded the firm's public utility work before he left in 1926 to become vice president of Electric Bond and Share Company in New York, then a large-utility holding company. He returned in 1933 and later resumed his position as managing partner. Outside the firm Parker organized and served as first president of the United Gas Corporation and was a board member and officer for Houston Lighting and Power. In 1943 he and others represented the company in the first public offering of its stock. In 1946 the firm became Baker, Botts, Andrews, and Walne. Walter H. Walne, a trial lawyer, joined in 1912. Although he served as managing partner of the firm, his greatest contribution was his aggressive policy of hiring outstanding lawyers from other sections of the state. John Bullington, a Yale graduate who became a partner in 1935, served as firm recruiter and began to recruit young lawyers nationwide. He was also active in the national bar association.

In 1948 the firm became Baker, Botts, Andrews, and Parish. W. A. Parish was employed in 1910 and became a partner in 1922. As a corporate lawyer, he handled financing for the firm's gas and utility clients and for a brief period was co-managing partner with Ralph B. Feagin. He left the firm in 1953 to become president and later chairman of Houston Lighting and Power. In 1954 the firm became Baker, Botts, Andrews, and Shepherd. James L. Shepherd, Jr., who was known nationally as a leader in oil and gas law, mineral law, and water rights law, was employed in 1917 and became a partner in 1929. In 1947, with impetus furnished by trial lawyer Dillon Anderson[qv] and Henry Holland, the firm formed a law partnership in Mexico that grew to more than fifty lawyers under the direction of Fausto Miranda. In 1973 the Mexico office became the independent Mexico City firm of Santamarina y Steta, which remains linked to Baker and Botts by an agreement of association covering the training of lawyers and other reciprocal arrangements. Anderson became managing partner after serving on the National Security Council as President Eisenhower's personal representative. He also served as chairman of the board of Texas National Bank, and on the boards of several national corporations.

Francis G. Coates came to the firm from Fort Worth in 1929, when it first started to add outstanding lawyers from across the state. He specialized in corporate and public utility work and for many years held a position on the board of Tenneco, Incorporated. When the firm adopted the name Baker, Botts, Shepherd, and Coates in 1962, Coates was the last partner to be so honored. The firm reverted to its 1874 name of Baker and Botts in 1971 and subsequently retained that name.

Between 1900 and 1920, after the predominance of railroad and trial lawyers, the firm developed a strong managing-partner form of organization. In 1929 it began seeking lawyers statewide, and in the 1930s it began national recruiting. The firm experienced its most dramatic growth, however, after World War II.[qv] In 1945 it had forty-two lawyers, one location, and no departments; in 1986 it had offices in Houston, Washington, Dallas, and Austin and had 136 partners, 173 associates, and a total staff of 885, under the direction of managing partner E. William Barnett. As the East Coast's team in Southeast Texas, Baker and Botts has represented northern brokerage houses, utilities, lumber companies, and other absentee landlords and railroads. Although it requires that its lawyers give priority attention to clients, the firm encourages lawyers to participate in professional and civic organizations as well. Attorneys for Baker and Botts have been presidents of the Houston and Texas bar associations, the Houston Chamber of Commerce, and many civic and educational organizations.

BIBLIOGRAPHY: Kenneth J. Lipartito and Joseph A. Pratt, *Baker and Botts in the Development of Modern Houston* (Austin: University of Texas Press, 1991). E. F. Smith, *A Saga of Texas Law* (San Antonio: Naylor, 1940). Griffin Smith, Jr., "Empires of Paper," *Texas Monthly*, November 1973. *Texas Bar Journal*, January 1976. *J. H. Freeman*

BAKER CREEK. Baker Creek rises 4½ miles north of Queen City in northeastern Cass County (at 33°13′ N, 94°10′ W) and runs northeast for eight miles to where it joins a small unnamed stream to form Baker Slough near Domino (at 33°16′ N, 94°06′ W). The stream is intermittent in its upper reaches. It flows over sandy and loamy soils that support pines and hardwoods. The creek may have been named for John Baker, original grantee of land near its mouth.

BAKER HUGHES. Baker Hughes, Incorporated, in the mid-1990s the leading producer of rock-drilling bits in the world, was formed by the merger of Hughes Tool and Baker Oil Tools in 1987. Howard Robard Hughes, Sr.,[qv] an early Texas oilman, solved the problem of drilling for oil through rock by developing a drill bit with cone-shaped revolving cutters and steel teeth capable of pulverizing rock. He patented his inventions in 1909, and the Hughes Rock Bit revolutionized the well-drilling process. In 1909 Hughes and Walter B. Sharp[qv] formed the Sharp-Hughes Tool Company and opened a plant in Houston to manufacture the bit. When Sharp died in 1912, Hughes took over management of the company, which he incorporated as Hughes Tool. In 1918 Hughes purchased the remaining company stock, which had been sold by Sharp's widow to Ed Prather. Hughes continued to improve on his bit and maintained a near monopoly in bit technology by patenting every part of the bit and by buying the patents of competitors. He held some seventy-three patents when he died in 1924 and his son, Howard Robard Hughes, Jr.,[qv] took over control of the company. During his dramatic career as film producer, aviation pioneer, and Las Vegas casino entrepreneur, the younger Howard Hughes drew on Hughes Tool as a source of investment income. In the 1930s he pursued his interest in aviation by forming the Hughes Aircraft Company as a division of Hughes Tool. Over the years a number of Hughes Tool executives, including Noah Dietrich, Chester Davis, Raymond Holliday, and Bill Gay, played leading roles in managing Hughes's extensive and varied empire. In 1972 Hughes sold the tool division of Hughes Tool to the public and renamed his holding company Summa Corporation. Hughes Tool continued to prosper through the 1970s and expanded into the field of aboveground oil-production equipment. The company suffered from declining revenues and expansion-related debt by the mid-1980s and in 1987 merged with Baker Oil Tools.

Carl Baker, a drilling contractor, had founded the Baker Casing Shoe Company in California in 1913 to profit from several of his oil-tool inventions. He began to manufacture his own tools in 1918 and expanded into national and international markets in the 1920s. He formed Baker Oil Tools in 1928. The company prospered with the growth of domestic drilling operations from the 1930s through the 1950s. It dramatically increased its foreign sales in the 1960s and purchased a pumping-equipment company, Kobe, in 1963. Baker Oil Tools diversified into mining-equipment production in the late 1960s and early 1970s, and purchased Reed Tool, an oil drill bit manufacturer, in 1975. The company earned more than a billion dollars for the first time in 1979, but fell in the mid-1980s on hard times that led to the merger with Hughes in 1987.

Baker Hughes, with its headquarters in Houston, consolidated and trimmed operations and was able to make a profit by 1988. In 1990 the company purchased Eastman Christensen, a leading manufacturer of directional and horizontal drilling equipment, and in 1992 added Teleco Oilfield Services, another leader in the field. In 1992 Baker Hughes had sales of more than $2.5 billion and almost 20,000 employees. The company was divided into three operating groups: Baker Hughes Drilling Technologies, Baker Hughes Production Tools, and EnviroTech.

BIBLIOGRAPHY: Donald L. Bartlett and James B. Steele, *Empire: The Life, Legend, and Madness of Howard Hughes* (New York: Norton, 1979). *The Texas 500: Hoover's Guide to the Top Texas Companies* (Austin: Reference Press, 1994). *Mark Odintz*

BAKERSFIELD, TEXAS. Bakersfield is at the intersection of Interstate Highway 10 and Farm Road 11, thirty-six miles east of Fort Stockton and nine miles south of the Pecos River in eastern Pecos County. It was named for J. T. Baker, a promoter who hoped to develop the townsite in 1929 after the discovery of oil in the Taylor-Link field. A post office was established at Bakersfield the same year. The community grew rapidly as a grocery store, a cafe, a hotel, a real estate office, a pool hall, and numerous rent houses were hastily built. The population of Bakersfield was estimated to be more than 1,000 in 1930. Declining oil production and prices in 1930 caused Bakersfield to be abandoned, however, as rapidly as it was built. Many of the buildings were moved from the townsite. In 1945 the town had two businesses and an estimated population of fifty. The population declined by 1976 to thirty, where it remained in 1990.

BIBLIOGRAPHY: Pecos County Historical Commission, *Pecos County History* (2 vols., Canyon, Texas: Staked Plains, 1984).

Glenn Justice

BAKER SLOUGH. Baker Slough originates where Baker Creek joins a small unnamed stream near Domino in northeast Cass County (at 33°16′ N, 94°06′ W) and runs east for 3½ miles to its mouth on Long Slough (at 33°16′ N, 94°03′ W). The loamy and clayey soils in this nearly level to gently undulating area are flood-prone, and native vegetation includes water-tolerant hardwoods, conifers, and grasses. Baker Slough is reported to have been named for Cullen Montgomery Baker,[qv] who is said to have camped in the area frequently.

BALCH, TEXAS. Balch was a mile southwest of the Lubbock county line on U.S. Highway 62/82 and the Atchison, Topeka and Santa Fe Railway in southeast Hockley County. The settlement was named for A. P. Balch, a director of the railroad from 1868 to 1871. It served area farmers as a shipping station. Although Balch remained on county maps of the 1980s, a grain elevator and several abandoned buildings are all that remains. *Charles G. Davis*

BALCH SPRINGS, TEXAS. Balch Springs is on Interstate highways 635 and 20 and U.S. Highway 175 ten miles southeast of Dallas in Dallas County. It was founded around 1870, when the family of John Balch settled in the area and found three springs, one of which was never dry. The perennial spring was kept cleaned and bricked up and became a gathering place for families in the area to fill their buckets and talk. In 1900 the area had only a cemetery and scattered farms. Several years later a school was built and named after the springs.

Balch Springs received electricity from Texas Power and Light in 1939. Gas service by Lone Star Gas and telephone service began shortly after World War II.[qv] On June 13, 1953, Balch Springs was incorporated, with a mayor-council form of government, in order to avoid annexation by Dallas. The site encompassed sections of Rylie, Kleberg, Five Points, Zipp City, Jonesville, Balch Springs, and Triangle. By 1956 Balch Springs had a population of 3,500. The population grew rapidly in the next several decades, and by 1976 it was 13,050. In 1958 the community had a modern fire department with three fire trucks, and a post office opened in Balch Springs in September 1964. Children attended school in either the Dallas or Mesquite school districts. In 1965 the town began levying its first taxes, and in 1966 a vote to disincorporate failed.

Because of proximity to Dallas, land values in Balch Springs began to rise in the early 1970s. The town became more important as a residential community when Interstate Highway 635 went through and made commuting to Dallas more rapid. By the late 1970s 95 percent of the residents commuted to work in Dallas or Garland. In 1970 Balch Springs had three manufacturers, two printers, and a foundry; by 1991 the community had seventeen manufacturers, including manufacturers of shipping pallets and machine parts. In 1988 Balch Springs voted to combine with the city of Mesquite, but the vote was ruled invalid and Balch Springs remained an independent community. In 1991 the town had two banks, a weekly newspaper, a library, and a number of churches. The population in 1990 was 17,406.

BIBLIOGRAPHY: Dallas *Morning News*, February 13, 1971. Vertical Files, Texas-Dallas History and Archives Division, Dallas Public Library. *Lisa C. Maxwell*

BALCON CREEK. Balcon Creek rises two miles northwest of the High Lonesome Ranch headquarters in southern Terrell County (at 29°57′ N, 102°02′ W) and runs southeast for five miles to its mouth on Indian Creek, three miles east of Shafter Crossing Road (at 29°53′ N, 102°02′ W). It sharply dissects massive limestone and crosses variable terrain that overlies hard limestone. The surface soil, generally dark, calcareous, stony clays and clay loams, supports oaks, junipers, grasses, and mesquites. Balcon Creek is a small stream in an area of many large canyons, creeks, and arroyos.

BALCONES CREEK. Balcones Creek rises a mile southwest of the junction of the Bandera, Kendall, and Bexar county lines in northeastern Bandera County (at 29°43′ N, 98°48′ W) and runs east for thirteen miles to its mouth on Cibolo Creek, at the junction of Kendall, Bexar, and Comal counties (at 29°45′ N, 98°39′ W). Live oak, mesquite, Ashe juniper, prickly pear, and a variety of grasses grow in the clayey loams that cover the steep slopes and benches of the surrounding terrain. Balcones Creek has served as the boundary between Kendall and Bexar counties since the establishment of Kendall County in 1862.

BALCONES ESCARPMENT. The Balcones Escarpment is a geologic fault zone several miles wide consisting of several faultings, most of which both dip and are downthrown to the east. It extends in a curved line across Texas from Del Rio to the Red River and is visible eastward from Del Rio, where it is about 1,000 feet high, and northeastward from San Antonio to Austin, where it is about 300 feet high. It was observed by zoologist G. W. Marnoch and was described by Robert Thomas Hill[qv] in 1890. The escarpment, which appears from the plains as a range of wooded hills, separates the Edwards Plateau[qv] in the west from the Coastal Plains. The Balcones zone was formed under conditions of strain during the Tertiary era, when a downwarping occurred near the Gulf Coast with a moderate uplift inland. Water-bearing formations passing beneath the plateau to the plains are broken across by the Balcones fault group, and much water is forced to the surface by artesian pressure. Barton Springs, San Marcos Springs, and Comal Springs[qqv] are examples of the resulting artesian wells or springs.

BIBLIOGRAPHY: Patrick Abbott and C. M. Woodruff, eds., *The Balcones Escarpment: Geology, Hydrology, Ecology* (San Antonio: Geological Society of America, 1986). Edward Collins and Stephen Lauback, *Faults and Fractures in the Balcones Fault Zone* (Austin: Austin Geological Society, 1990). Robert T. Hill, "The Geologic Evolution of the Non-Mountainous Topography of the Texas Region: An Introduction to the Study of the Great Plains," *American Geologist* 10 (August 1892). E. H. Sellards, W. S. Adkins, and F. B. Plummer, *The Geology of Texas* (University of Texas Bulletin 3232, 1932).

BALCONES HEIGHTS, TEXAS. Balcones Heights is near the junction of Interstate highways 10 and 410, six miles north of downtown San Antonio in north central Bexar County. It was developed in the late 1940s and had a population of 950 in 1960 and 2,504 in 1970. The community was incorporated in the 1970s, and in 1990 it had 3,022 residents. *Christopher Long*

BALD EAGLE CREEK. Bald Eagle Creek, also known as Dry Creek, rises just above the Tom Green county line in south central Coke County (at 31°43′ N, 100°29′ W) and runs south for twenty miles to its mouth on O. C. Fisher Lake, at the northwest city limits of San Angelo (at 31°32′ N, 100°33′ W). It traverses rolling prairie, mostly rangeland, surfaced by shallow clay loam and stony soils that support sparse vegetation; grasses and occasional clusters of hardwood trees line the creekbed.

BIBLIOGRAPHY: Glenn A. Gray, *Gazetteer of Streams of Texas* (Washington: GPO, 1919).

BALD EAGLE HILL. Bald Eagle Hill is a mile north of State Highway 36 and thirteen miles southwest of Baird in west central Callahan County (at 32°17′ N, 99°35′ W). Its summit rises 2,213 feet above sea level, 150 feet above State Highway 36.

BALD EAGLE MOUNTAIN. Bald Eagle Mountain, so named because a nest of eagles was discovered there, is located near Ovalo in southeastern Taylor County (at 32°10′ N, 99°48′ W). Its elevation is 2,276 feet. The soil in the area is a combination of limestone, claystone, and sandstone, and shrubs are the only noticeable vegetation. A dirt path runs up the peak. A gap on one side suggests a former mine.

BIBLIOGRAPHY: Paul D. Lack et al., *The History of Abilene* (Abilene, Texas: McMurry College, 1981). Juanita Daniel Zachry, *A History of Rural Taylor County* (Burnet, Texas: Nortex, 1980).

Colleen Tedford

BALD HILL, TEXAS (Angelina County). Bald Hill is on Farm Road 326 eight miles southeast of Lufkin in central Angelina County. The area was settled before 1900. By the 1930s the settlement had three churches, several stores, a school, and a number of houses. After World War II[qv] many residents left the area, but in the early 1990s Bald Hill had three churches, a community center, and a few scattered houses. *Christopher Long*

BALD HILL, TEXAS (Limestone County). Bald Hill was located at the junction of Farm roads 27 and 638, 2½ miles north of Tehuacana in northern Limestone County. In 1942 the settlement had three businesses and a population of seventy-five. In 1946 it had a school. In 1948 Bald Hill had one business, a school, and a number of scattered dwellings, but by 1984 it no longer appeared on state highway maps. *Stephanie Panus*

BALD KNOB (Bell County). Bald Knob is four miles south of Killeen in southwestern Bell County (at 31°03′ N, 97°46′ W). With an elevation of 1,080 feet above sea level, its summit rises 140 feet above nearby State Highway 195.

——— (Burnet County). Bald Knob, sometimes called Bald Mountain, is twelve miles southwest of Burnet and a mile north of the Austin and Northwestern Railroad in southwestern Burnet County (at 30°39′ N, 98°23′ W). It is one of several hills in a small range known as Backbone Ridge. Its elevation is 1,326 feet, more than 300 feet higher than that of the surrounding countryside.

——— (Williamson County). Bald Knob is located about two miles northwest of Andice in northwestern Williamson County (at 30°48′ N, 97°53′ W). With its elevation of 1,160 feet above sea level, it rises forty-four feet above nearby U.S. Highway 183.

BALD MOUNTAIN (Stephens County). Bald Mountain is nine miles southeast of Breckenridge in southern Stephens County (at 32°36′ N, 98°50′ W). It has an elevation of 1,488 feet. The surrounding landscape features rugged hills and scarps surfaced by shallow, stony, sandy loams that support post oak, grasses, and chaparral.

——— (Travis County). Bald Mountain is twenty-six miles northwest of Austin and two miles north of Farm Road 1431 in northwestern Travis County (at 30°33′ N, 98°05′ W). It rises 1,262 feet above sea level, more than 250 feet above the surrounding countryside.

BALD PRAIRIE, TEXAS. Bald Prairie is at the intersection of Farm roads 979 and 2096, two miles east of Twin Oak Reservoir in the northeast corner of Robertson County. The community was established in 1865. Early Texas settlers considered the open prairies undesirable for farming and selected sites along the banks of creeks and streams. However, frequent attacks of "creek fever" drove the farmers to higher ground, which they soon discovered provided a healthier climate than the bottoms. The bald prairies proved to be favorable for growing cotton, corn, and livestock. Bald Prairie was a favorite gathering site for camp meetings in the 1860s. In the nineteenth century the community had several stores, churches, gins, and gristmills. A post office was established in 1875 with J. C. Jennings as postmaster. By 1885 Bald Prairie had a population of 100. The coming of the railroad to other sections of the county facilitated the growth of towns along its course, leading to the decline of Bald Prairie. In 1940 the community had one store and a post office. From 1970 to 1990 the estimated population was thirty-one; this estimate includes the surrounding area. The Ross store closed in the 1960s, and in 1990 the community had two churches, a cemetery, and the abandoned store building. There is another cemetery, Wesley Chapel, one mile north of Bald Prairie. Each year a community reunion is held on the first Saturday in June at the Church of Christ.

BIBLIOGRAPHY: Jewel Gibson, *Joshua Beene and God* (New York: Random House, 1946). *James L. Hailey*

BALDRIDGE, TEXAS. Baldridge was a railroad-station community on the Atchison, Topeka and Santa Fe tracks sixteen miles northeast of Fort Stockton in north central Pecos County. It was named for the physical characteristics of its location. The Kansas City, Mexico and Orient Railway completed track to Baldridge in 1913. The community had two rated business establishments and an estimated population of 200 in 1939. By 1945 the estimated population had declined to fifty. The town was abandoned by the 1950s.

BIBLIOGRAPHY: John Leeds Kerr and Frank Donovan, *Destination Topolobampo: The Kansas City, Mexico & Orient Railway* (San Marino, California: Golden West, 1968). Charles P. Zlatkovich, *Texas Railroads* (Austin: University of Texas Bureau of Business Research, 1981). *Glenn Justice*

BALDRIDGE CREEK. Baldridge Creek begins two miles northwest of Waelder in northern Gonzales County (at 29°44′ N, 97°20′ W) and runs southeast for twelve miles to its mouth on Peach Creek (at 29°36′ N, 97°15′ W). It traverses moderately rolling terrain surfaced by acid and sandy clay that supports mixed hardwoods and pines.

BALDWIN, FRANCIS LEONARD DWIGHT (1842–1923). Frank D. Baldwin, United States general, son of Francis L. and Betsy Ann (Richards) Baldwin, was born on June 26, 1842, near Manchester, Michigan. With two half-sisters he was reared and schooled in Constantine, Michigan, then briefly attended Hillsdale Baptist College in that state. On September 5, 1862, during the Civil War,[qv] Baldwin enlisted as a first lieutenant in the Nineteenth Michigan Infantry. He was captured at the battle of Thompson's Station, Tennessee (March 4–5, 1863), confined briefly at Libby Prison in Richmond, and then exchanged. In March 1864 Baldwin, now a captain, joined William T. Sherman's[qv] campaign against Atlanta and the March to the Sea. He earned a Medal of Honor at the battle of Peachtree Creek, Georgia, on July 20, 1864. He entered the postwar regular army as a second lieutenant early in 1866, was promoted to first lieutenant in the Nineteenth United States Infantry, and was then reassigned to the Thirty-seventh United States Infantry, stationed in Kansas. On January 10, 1867, he married Alice Blackwood, who later that year gave birth to a daughter, the Baldwins' only child.

In 1869 Baldwin was assigned to Col. Nelson A. Miles's[qv] Fifth United States Infantry. During the Red River War[qv] in the Panhandle[qv] (1874–75) he served as chief of scouts and fought in the first battle of Palo Duro Canyon,[qv] where he earned a captain's brevet on August 30. After the battle he commanded a group of four who rode to Fort Supply carrying dispatches, a journey known as Baldwin's Ride (September 7–10). On November 8, in leading an attack against a Cheyenne camp on McClellan Creek in Gray County in which he rescued two of the German sisters[qv] from captivity, he earned a second Medal of Honor. After the massacre of George A. Custer[qv] and his troops at the Little Bighorn in 1876, Baldwin was transferred with Miles's regiment to Montana, where they established Fort Keogh, near Miles City. On December 18, 1876, Baldwin commanded a detachment that dispersed Sitting Bull's camp at the head of Redwater Creek. At the battle of the Wolf Mountains on January 8, 1877, Baldwin rallied the troops in an assault against Crazy Horse and earned a brevet to major. He also participated in the Lame Deer expedition and the campaign against Chief Joseph's Nez Percés later that year. In 1879 he was promoted to captain. From 1881 to November 1885 Baldwin served on General Miles's staff as judge advocate of the Department of the Columbia. In 1884 he negotiated a solution to unrest on the Moses and Coleville reservations in Washington Territory. From November 1885 to 1890 he served with his regiment in Montana, North Dakota, Texas, and New Mexico. He joined Miles again in December 1890 and served in the campaign against the Sioux until the spring of 1891. He investigated the Wounded Knee tragedy of December 1890. From 1891 to October 1894 Baldwin was inspector of small arms practice for the Department of the

Missouri, headquartered at Chicago. From October 1894 to May 1898 he served as agent at the Anadarko Agency in Indian Territory. In 1898 he was promoted to major and subsequently to lieutenant colonel of volunteers.

Early in 1900 Baldwin was promoted to lieutenant colonel of the regular army and assigned to the Fourth United States Infantry stationed in the province of Cavite on the Philippine Island of Luzon, where his troops captured hundreds of insurrectos, including Lt. Gen. Mariano Trias. Baldwin was promoted to colonel in the summer of 1901 and received his own regiment, the Twenty-seventh United States Infantry. He sailed to Mindanao, where his troops defeated the Moros at Bayan on May 2, 1902. Baldwin was promoted to brigadier general in June 1902. In February 1903 he was appointed commander of the Department of the Colorado, a post he held until his retirement in 1906. He was promoted to major general (retired) in 1915 but left retirement briefly to serve as Colorado's World War I[qv] adjutant general. Baldwin died of cirrhosis of the liver on April 22, 1923, and was buried at Arlington National Cemetery. In 1929 his wife published her memoirs of his career and of her life as an army officer's wife on the frontier.

BIBLIOGRAPHY: Alice Blackwood Baldwin, *Memoirs of the Late Frank D. Baldwin, Major General, U.S.A.*, ed. W. C. Brown, C. C. Smith, and E. A. Brininstool (Los Angeles: Wetzel, 1929). Nelson A. Miles, *Personal Recollections and Observations* (Chicago: Werner, 1896; rpt., New York: Da Capo Press, 1969). Joe F. Taylor, comp., "The Indian Campaign on the Staked Plains, 1874–1875," *Panhandle-Plains Historical Review* 34 (1961), 35 (1962).

Robert H. Steinbach

BALDWIN, JOSEPH (1827–1899). Joseph Baldwin, teacher and author, son of Joseph and Isabel (Cairns) Baldwin, was born in Newcastle, Pennsylvania, on October 31, 1827. He attended Bartlett Academy in Newcastle and prepared for ministry in the Disciples of Christ (Christian) Church at Bethany College, where he received the B.A. degree in 1852. After his marriage to Ella Sophronia Fluhart of Ohio, he decided to become a teacher and began his career in Platte City, Missouri, in 1852. In 1856 he helped found the Missouri State Teachers Association. He studied in Millersville Normal School and was principal of Lawrence County Normal School. He taught in Indiana for nine years and served a year in the Union Army before he established a private normal at Kirksville, Missouri, in 1867. The school became a state normal in 1870. In 1881, while on a lecture tour in Texas, Baldwin was elected principal of Sam Houston Normal Institute (now Sam Houston State University) at Huntsville. He served there until 1891, when he was selected as the first professor of pedagogy at the University of Texas. While living in Texas he wrote several books on education: *Art of School Management* (1881), *Elementary Psychology and Education* (1887), *Psychology Applied to the Art of Teaching* (1892), and *School Management and School Methods* (1897). He died on January 13, 1899.

BIBLIOGRAPHY: *Dictionary of American Biography.*

BALDWIN, TEXAS (Harrison County). Baldwin is on the Louisiana and Arkansas Railway fourteen miles northeast of Marshall in northeastern Harrison County. The settlement was named for the J. B. Baldwin family of Marshall and had a post office from 1902 to 1915. In 1914 Baldwin had an estimated population of 350 inhabitants and two sawmills, two general stores, one cotton gin, and an apiarist. By 1933 the population had declined to twenty-five, and there was one business in the town. In 1990 Baldwin consisted of a few scattered dwellings. *Mark Odintz*

BALDWIN, TEXAS (Polk County). Baldwin, in southwestern Polk County, was on the Houston, East and West Texas Railway, which was built through the county in 1880 and generated the construction of numerous sawmills along its line. At Baldwin, a switch on the railroad south of Livingston, the M. D. Tackaberry sawmill cut locally available timber during the late nineteenth century. E. M. Ward also operated a mill there. He moved the Lima Lumber Company's mill, formerly at Lamont, to Baldwin in 1903. The site appears on a 1905 railroad map of Texas but is not shown on 1913 or 1918 maps of this type.

BIBLIOGRAPHY: *A Pictorial History of Polk County, Texas, 1846–1910* (Livingston, Texas: Polk County Bicentennial Commission, 1976; rev. ed. 1978).

Robert Wooster

BALERIO, CECILIO (1796?–1868). Cecilio Balerio, rancher and soldier, whose birthdate was recorded both as May 12, 1796, and as May 12, 1800, was born at or near Mier, Tamaulipas, Mexico, the son of Juana María Valero. He operated a small horse and mule trade at Corpus Christi during the 1850s. At the beginning of the Civil War[qv] he and his family chose to remain loyal to the United States. He was engaged by Edmund J. Davis[qv] to attack the Confederate cotton trains between Corpus Christi and the lower Rio Grande valley. His men were supplied with gold coin, munitions, and clothing from United States Navy vessels standing off Padre Island. Balerio's son Juan was captured when he made a visit to Corpus Christi in March 1864. Maj. Mat Nolan coerced the son into leading about eighty men to the Balerio encampment at Los Patricios, a place said to be about fifty miles southwest of Banquete. At the final moment before the ambush was sprung early on the morning of March 13, 1864, while the Balerio company were sleeping, Juan shouted an alarm. The surprised guerrillas grouped themselves, "charged and fought most gallantly, and could only be repulsed after a desperate fight at cost of much blood and property," according to Nolan's account. The bodies of five of Balerio's men were found, along with a document indicating that Col. John L. Haynes was on the march to reinforce the guerrilla band. Balerio may have had another hidden encampment with about forty men at another location. He and Juan returned to Mier after the end of the conflict. For Balerio's services to the United States, Governor E. J. Davis awarded his heirs a quarter section of land in 1870. A corrido recalling the salient features of the skirmish at Los Patricios was still a part of oral tradition in South Texas as late as 1950 (*see* CORRIDOS).

BIBLIOGRAPHY: *The War of the Rebellion: A Compilation of the Official Records of the Union and Confederate Armies* (Washington: GPO, 1880–1901).

Frank Wagner

BALIS, DANIEL E. (?–?). Daniel E. Balis (Bayles, Bayless) was a partner of Isaac Van Dorn[qv] as one of Stephen F. Austin's[qv] Old Three Hundredqv families. In October 1824 Balis was living in the San Jacinto area when he nominated Dr. Johnson C. Hunter[qv] as the surveyor for the vicinity. In March 1826 he worked for Austin as a hand on the boat *Mexican*. His title to a sitio[qv] of land now in Matagorda County was granted on April 14, 1828. Balis lived in Washington County at or near Chapel Hill. He died before 1837, when his estate was settled.

BIBLIOGRAPHY: Eugene C. Barker, ed., *The Austin Papers* (3 vols., Washington: GPO, 1924–28). Lester G. Bugbee, "The Old Three Hundred: A List of Settlers in Austin's First Colony," *Quarterly of the Texas State Historical Association* 1 (October 1897). Worth Stickley Ray, *Austin Colony Pioneers* (Austin: Jenkins, 1949; 2d ed., Austin: Pemberton, 1970).

BALL, GEORGE (1817–1884). George Ball was born in Saratoga, New York, on May 9, 1817. At the age of twelve he moved to Albany, where he was reared and trained for business in the family of his uncle. He arrived in Texas during the cholera epidemic of 1839 and in Galveston opened a dry goods business, which he operated in partnership with his brother Albert. In 1847 he became a director of the

Commercial and Agricultural Bank at Galveston, the first incorporated bank in Texas, and in 1854 he opened the banking house of Ball, Hutchings, and Company. During the Civil War[qv] he moved to Houston and used the facilities of his banking house and mercantile experience to aid the Confederate government by getting goods shipped through Mexico. At the close of the war he reestablished his banking business in Houston and invested in the Mallory Steamship Line. He contributed generous sums to hospitals, asylums, and public schools but always endeavored to keep his charities concealed. On April 19, 1848, he married Sarah Catherine Perry; they were parents of six children. He died in Galveston on March 13, 1884. Ball High School in Galveston is named for him.

BIBLIOGRAPHY: John Henry Brown, *Indian Wars and Pioneers of Texas* (Austin: Daniell, 1880; reprod., Easley, South Carolina: Southern Historical Press, 1978). Galveston *News*, March 13, 1884. S. C. Griffin, *History of Galveston, Texas* (Galveston: Cawston, 1931). *History of Texas, Together with a Biographical History of the Cities of Houston and Galveston* (Chicago: Lewis, 1895). David G. McComb, *Galveston: A History* (Austin: University of Texas Press, 1986). Ruth G. Nichols, "Samuel May Williams," *Southwestern Historical Quarterly* 56 (October 1952).

BALL, THOMAS HENRY (1819–1858). Thomas Henry Ball, Methodist minister and college administrator, was born on October 29, 1819, in Northumberland County, Virginia, the son of Hannah (Gaskins) and David Thomas Ball. He married Susan Perrie, and they had one son and two daughters. His wife died in 1853, and in the fall of 1855 he took his mother and three children to Huntsville, Texas, where he became president of Andrew Female College,[qv] a Methodist school. In 1857 Ball married a widow, Mrs. M. O. (Spivey) Cleveland; they had one son, Thomas Henry Ball.[qv] The senior Ball died of typhoid fever on November 30, 1858, and was buried in Huntsville.

Mrs. Albert Ball

BALL, THOMAS HENRY (1859–1944). Thomas H. Ball, lawyer, prohibitionist politician, and promoter of publicly owned Houston port facilities, son of M. O. (Spivey) Cleveland and Rev. Thomas Henry Ball,[qv] was born on January 14, 1859, in Huntsville, Texas. His father, a Methodist minister, had moved to Huntsville from Virginia in 1856 to become president of Andrew Female College.[qv] Ball's parents died, and he was left at the age of six in the care of his uncle, Lt. Sidney Spivey, a Confederate veteran, who sent him to private schools for his primary and secondary education. After graduating from Austin College[qv] in 1871, Ball worked as a farmhand and clerk and attended lectures at the University of Virginia, where he was elected president of the law class. He returned to Texas, was admitted to the bar in 1888, and was thrice elected mayor of Huntsville, a post he held from 1877 to 1892. He practiced law in Huntsville until 1902, when he moved to Houston.

Ball first became active in Texas politics in 1887 as an advocate of a prohibition[qv] amendment to the state constitution. He held many state Democratic party[qv] posts and was elected to the United States Congress in 1896. He resigned in 1903 to return to a Houston law practice that primarily served railroad and corporate clients. In 1911 he was selected chairman of the Prohibition Statewide Executive Committee, and many prohibitionists encouraged him to run against incumbent governor Oscar Branch Colquitt,[qv] who was up for reelection in 1912. Ball declined, and lent his support to Judge William F. Ramsey,[qv] who was easily defeated by the antiprohibitionists. In 1914 at a pre-primary elimination convention, Ball emerged as the prohibitionist standard-bearer with the slogan "Play Ball." Both wet and dry forces assumed he would win the coming gubernatorial nomination. But political newcomer James Edward Ferguson[qv] won support by focusing on farm tenant reform. Late endorsements of Ball by President Woodrow Wilson and William Jennings Bryan backfired when Ferguson also asserted that national politicians should stay out of Texas politics. Ferguson won the nomination in July. Ball lost because of his refusal to embrace other prohibitionist demands, growing uneasiness about his legal service for large corporations, his friendship with Joseph Weldon Bailey,[qv] his own lackluster campaigning, and Ferguson's skillful demagogy.

In addition to Ball's prohibitionist activities, he was also a lifelong, vigorous promoter of publicly owned port facilities in Texas. As a member of the Rivers and Harbors Committee in the United States House of Representatives, he secured the first federal aid for development of the Houston Ship Channel[qv] in 1899. After leaving Washington he lobbied the state legislature and the United States Congress heavily, determined to facilitate local, state, and federal efforts to upgrade Houston port facilities. Both bodies soon passed measures significantly aiding local navigation districts. Following the development of Buffalo Bayou, Ball served as general counsel to the Port Commission of Houston.

He married Minnie F. Thomason in 1882. They had three children and adopted three more. In 1907 the community of Peck, just northwest of Houston, was renamed Tomball in Ball's honor. Ball died in Houston on May 7, 1944.

BIBLIOGRAPHY: *Biographical Directory of the American Congress* (Washington, D.C.: GPO, 1859–). Lewis L. Gould, *Progressives and Prohibitionists: Texas Democrats in the Wilson Era* (Austin: University of Texas Press, 1973; rpt., Austin: Texas State Historical Association, 1992). George P. Huckaby, Oscar Branch Colquitt: A Political Biography (Ph.D. dissertation, University of Texas, 1946). Frank W. Johnson, *A History of Texas and Texans* (5 vols., ed. E. C. Barker and E. W. Winkler [Chicago and New York: American Historical Society, 1914; rpt. 1916]). Vertical Files, Barker Texas History Center, University of Texas at Austin (Tomball, Texas). Clarence R. Wharton, ed., *Texas under Many Flags* (5 vols., Chicago: American Historical Society, 1930).

Gary Price

BALL, WILLIAM B. (1839–1923). William B. Ball, black soldier, school official, and minister, was born in Danville, Kentucky, on February 5, 1839. He grew up at his parents' farm and then moved to Xenia, Ohio, where he worked his way through Oberlin College. He enlisted in the Union Army in 1860 and served in the cavalry of the Ninety-ninth Division, 149th Regiment. He received an honorable discharge in 1868 and moved to Texas in 1869. He organized a military company at San Antonio, obtained a commission as captain, and served for a time on the frontier. Ball moved to Seguin in 1871, and on March 21, 1872, he married Rachel Cartwright. The couple had ten children. In 1871, with the help of Rev. Leonard Ilsley, Ball organized the first school for blacks in Guadalupe County, the Abraham Lincoln School in Sequin. He was its principal for many years. In 1884 he and an association of black Baptists founded Negro Baptist College at the site of the present Joe F. Saegert Middle School in Seguin. In 1887 it was reorganized as Guadalupe Colored College. Ball later obtained the help of philanthropist George W. Brackenridge,[qv] who funded the expansion of the college's physical plant in 1904 and purchased a new site for the institution in 1905. Ball served as the president of the college for eight years. In 1920, after thirty years of service as pastor of the Second Baptist Church at Seguin, he resigned from his position. He died on January 26, 1923, at Seguin. In 1925 Lincoln High School was renamed Ball High School, and on June 19, 1939, a swimming pool and an auditorium-gymnasium for the school were dedicated and named in his honor. The building was used for an elementary school in the 1980s but still carried Ball's name. A major street in Seguin is also named for W. B. Ball.

BIBLIOGRAPHY: Andrew Webster Jackson, *A Sure Foundation and a Sketch of Negro Life in Texas* (Houston, 1940). Arwerd Max Moellering, A History of Guadalupe County, Texas (M.A. thesis, University of Texas, 1938).

Nolan Thompson

William B. Ball. Courtesy Lawrence T. Jones III Collection, Austin.

BALLARD CREEK. Ballard Creek begins four miles southwest of Matador in southwest Motley County (at 33°59′ N, 100°50′ W) and flows twenty miles northeast, skirting the southern limits of Matador, to enter the Middle Pease River in east central Motley County (at 34°04′ N, 100°38′ W). A main source for the creek is Ballard Springs.[qv] The area around the springs was the first land acquired by the Matador Land and Cattle Company.[qv] Both the creek and the springs were named for a buffalo hunter who camped at the site about 1876. The area terrain is sloping and surfaced by thin silt loams that support mesquite and grasses.

BIBLIOGRAPHY: Gunnar Brune, *Springs of Texas*, Vol. 1 (Fort Worth: Branch-Smith, 1981). Claude V. Hall, *Early History of Floyd County* (Canyon, Texas: Panhandle-Plains Historical Society, 1947).

BALLENGER BEND. Ballenger Bend is on the Brazos River five miles west of Mineral Wells in east central Palo Pinto County (at 32°49′ N, 98°12′ W). The surrounding flat to rolling terrain is surfaced by moderately deep to deep sandy and clay loam that supports hardwoods, conifers, and grasses.

BALLENTINE, JOHN J. (?–1836). John J. Ballentine, Alamo defender, was born in Pennsylvania. He was a single man and lived several years in Bastrop before the Texas Revolution.[qv] He served in the Alamo garrison as a member of Capt. William R. Carey's[qv] artillery company and died in the battle of the Alamo[qv] on March 6, 1836.

BIBLIOGRAPHY: Daughters of the American Revolution, *The Alamo Heroes and Their Revolutionary Ancestors* (San Antonio, 1976). Daughters of the Republic of Texas, *Muster Rolls of the Texas Revolution* (Austin, 1986). Bill Groneman, *Alamo Defenders* (Austin: Eakin, 1990).

Bill Groneman

BALLENTINE, RICHARD W. (1814–1836). Richard W. Ballentine, Alamo defender, was born in Scotland in 1814. He traveled to Texas from Alabama aboard the *Santiago* and disembarked on December 9, 1835. He and the other passengers signed a statement declaring, "we have left every endearment at our respective places of abode in the United States of America, to maintain and defend our brethren, at the peril of our lives, liberties and fortunes." Ballentine died in the battle of the Alamo[qv] on March 6, 1836.

BIBLIOGRAPHY: Daughters of the American Revolution, *The Alamo Heroes and Their Revolutionary Ancestors* (San Antonio, 1976). Bill Groneman, *Alamo Defenders* (Austin: Eakin, 1990). John H. Jenkins, ed., *The Papers of the Texas Revolution, 1835–1836* (10 vols., Austin: Presidial Press, 1973).

Bill Groneman

BALLEW, SYKES (1902–1984). Sykes (Smith) Ballew, singer, actor, and bandleader, son of May and William Y. Ballew, was born in Palestine, Texas, on January 21, 1902. After attending Sherman High School in Sherman, Ballew attended Austin College and the University of Texas from 1920 to 1922. At the University of Texas he organized a jazz combo, Jimmie's Joys, first playing banjo and later becoming the group's vocalist. Leaving the university after the fall 1922 semester, he continued with the combo until forming the Texajazzers in March 1925. By then primarily a vocalist, Ballew accepted work with a number of noted bandleaders, including Ted Weems, Hal Kemp, and Tommy and Jimmy Dorsey. In 1929 Ballew organized the Smith Ballew Orchestra, which highlighted his singing and which included associations with jazzmen such as Glenn Miller and Bunny Berigan. In the same year Ballew signed his first recording contract, with Okeh Records of Chicago. Ballew's recording career as vocalist and bandleader spanned some twenty years, during which he cut records for more than thirty labels, including Okeh, Victor, Brunswick, Columbia, and Decca. From 1936 to 1950 Ballew mixed an acting career with singing. In 1936, after moving his family to Hollywood and landing a contract with Paramount Pictures, Ballew made his acting debut in the motion picture *Palm Springs.* He appeared in twenty-four films, primarily Westerns. Among his pictures were *Western Gold* (1937), *Roll Along Cowboy* (1937), *Under Arizona Skies* (1946), *Panamint's Bad Man* (1938), *Hawaiian Buckeroos* (1938), and *The Red Badge of Courage* (1951). During World War II,[qv] as his singing and film career waned, and until his retirement in 1967, Ballew worked in the aircraft industry, including stints at Northrup and at Convair (which later became part of General Dynamics). In 1952, after living in California and Arizona, Ballew settled in Fort Worth. He was married twice, first in 1924 to Justine Vera, with whom he had a daughter. Justine died in 1960, and that same year Ballew married Mary Ruth Clark, who died in 1972. Ballew died in Longview, Texas, on May 2, 1984, and was buried in Fort Worth.

BIBLIOGRAPHY: Geoffery J. Orr, *Texas Troubador: A Bio-Discography of the Life and Times of Smith Ballew, 1902–1984* (Melbourne: Exact Science Press, 1985).

John H. Slate

BALLÍ, JOSÉ NICOLÁS (ca. 1770–1829). José Nicolás Ballí, a secular Catholic priest, the oldest son of José María and Rosa María Hinojosa de Ballí,[qv] was born in Reynosa, Mexico, about 1770. His parents were both Spaniards. Padre Ballí was an original grantee of the Texas coastal island later named Padre Island[qv] in his honor. He led an active civic and religious life in South Texas and the state of Tamaulipas as a missionary, a rancher, a colonist, and an explorer. His parents, prominent settlers and landowners at Reynosa, Camargo, and Matamoros and in the lower Rio Grande valley, owned over a million acres of land in South Texas. His two brothers, Juan José and José María Ballí, were officers of the Militia of Provincial and Frontier Cavalry. Nicolás spent his childhood in the company of his two younger brothers in Reynosa and received his elementary education there. His parents sent him to the Conciliar Catholic Seminary in Monterrey to complete his secondary and ecclesiastical education. He was probably ordained in 1790 or 1791.

Ballí conducted religious services in all the villas and haciendas in the lower Rio Grande valley. He lived in Matamoros and was a secular priest in Nuestra Señora del Refugio Mission from 1804 to 1829. In 1830 he began the construction of the present Church of Nuestra Señora del Refugio in Matamoros. Ballí became the official collector of building funds for the churches of the villas on the Rio Grande. He was well known in South Texas and officiated in more than 500 baptisms, marriages, and funerals between 1800 and 1829.

The properties that he owned in South Texas were the La Feria grant, the Las Castañas grant, part of the Llano Grande grant, the Guadalupe grant, and the Isla de Santiago grant, known as Padre Island. Padre Island had been granted to his grandfather, Nicolás Ballí, by King Carlos III of Spain in 1759, and Padre Ballí requested a clear title to the property in 1827. He was the first to have the island surveyed and was the first settler on the island who brought in families. He also built the first church on the island for the conversion of the Karankawa Indians and for the benefit of the settlers. Twenty-six miles north of the island's southern tip the priest founded El Rancho Santa Cruz de Buena Vista (later known as Lost City), where he kept cattle, horses, and mules.

Ballí died on April 16, 1829, and was buried near Matamoros. Title to the island was granted to him posthumously on December 15, 1829, issued jointly in the name of the padre and his nephew Juan José Ballí. The priest had requested that half of the island be given to his nephew, who had been helping him there. Juan José lived on the island from 1829 to his death in 1853.

BIBLIOGRAPHY: Vidal Covián Martínez, *Cuatro Estudios Históricos* (Ciudad Victoria: Universidad Autónoma de Tamaulipas, Instituto de Investigaciones Históricas, 1977). Nueces County Historical Society, *History of Nueces County* (Austin: Jenkins, 1972). Florence J. Scott, *Royal Land Grants North of the Rio Grande, 1777–1821* (Waco: Texian Press, 1969).
Clotilde P. García

BALLINGER, BETTY EVE (1854–1936). Betty Eve Ballinger, cofounder of the Daughters of the Republic of Texas,[qv] was born on February 3, 1854, in Galveston, one of four children of Harriett Patrick (Jack) and William Pitt Ballinger.[qv] Her maternal grandfather, William Houston Jack,[qv] fought at the battle of San Jacinto[qv] and later became a lawyer and a statesman for the Republic of Texas.[qv] Her father received the first license to practice law issued by the state of Texas; Ballinger, Texas, is named for him. Betty was raised in the Ballinger home, the Oaks, at Avenue O and Twenty-ninth Street in Galveston. She received her education, along with her sister Lucy (Mrs. Andrew G. Mills), in the French school of Miss Hull in New Orleans and later in the Southern Home School in Baltimore. In the spring of 1891 she and her cousin Hally Ballinger Bryan Perry[qv] decided to form an organization dedicated to the perpetuation of the memory of the heroes of San Jacinto. Their interest in this pursuit was aroused by the recent discovery in an old Galveston cemetery of the neglected graves of two Texas patriots, David G. Burnet,[qv] first president of the Republic of Texas, and Sidney Sherman,[qv] a veteran of the battle of San Jacinto. After reading Henderson K. Yoakum's[qv] *History of Texas* (1855) in the Ballinger library, the cousins planned to solicit support from other women of Texas whose husbands or ancestors had helped the republic achieve and maintain its independence. To this end Hally's father, Guy M. Bryan,[qv] president of the Texas Veterans Association,[qv] introduced the women to Mary Smith (Mrs. Anson) Jones,[qv] widow of the last president of the Republic of Texas, and to Mary Harris Briscoe,[qv] widow of a Texas patriot. The organization was approved, and on November 6, 1891, seventeen women assembled in Houston to form the Daughters of the Lone Star Republic. Ballinger was chosen a member of the Executive Committee that drew up the organization's constitution and by-laws.

The first annual meeting of the Daughters took place on April 20, 1892, in Lampasas; at that time the organization was officially named Daughters of the Republic of Texas. The next year Ballinger delivered the keynote address to the Daughters, in which she explained the purpose of the DRT. The future of Texas, she said, "is in the hands of her sons [who,] dazzled by the splendor of the present . . . have forgotten the heroic deeds and sacrifices of the past. But it is not so with woman. . . . Surrounded by the history of the family life, it is her duty to keep alive the sacred fire of tradition. . . . Daughters of the Republic of Texas, our duty lies plain before us. Let us leave the future of Texas to our brothers, and claim as our province the guarding of her holy past." These were the words of a woman born in the antebellum South, where cultural proscriptions confined "ladies" to the traditions of family, children, domesticity, and church. Ironically, however, such women's organizations as the DRT, whose purpose was to perpetuate domestic values, encouraged women to participate in the future of Texas primarily through emphasis on improvement in education for Texas children and the maintenance of historic sites such as the Alamo[qv] and the San Jacinto battlefield. In the twentieth century, Miss Ballinger (she never married) no longer believed that the future of Texas should be left in the hands of the men alone. Between 1891 and 1912 she fulfilled her duties as a guardian of tradition, but also helped to form new women's organizations, each of which brought women more and more into public life.

After the initial organization of the state DRT, she organized and presided over (1891–93) the Galveston chapter of the DRT, named for Sidney Sherman. The group's first task, not surprisingly, was the removal of the remains of Burnet and Sherman to a new cemetery in Galveston, where in 1894 a twenty-three-foot stone obelisk was formally placed as a memorial. A dedication ceremony attended by 1,600 dignitaries and citizens marked the occasion. Betty Ballinger also served from 1895 to 1899 as DRT chairman of the Stephen F. Austin Statue Fund, the purpose of which was to commission Elisabet Ney[qv] to produce statues of Sam Houston and Stephen F. Austin[qqv] to be placed in Statuary Hall at the Capitol in Washington. The project was completed in 1903.

By 1912 Betty Ballinger had become a staunch supporter of woman suffrage.[qv] Her interest in various women's associations, including other hereditary–patriotic organizations, led her to seek membership in the Daughters of the American Revolution and the Texas Society Colonial Dames.[qqv] She contributed to her church (First Baptist Church of Galveston) by serving as president in 1892 of the Woman's Aid Society, and to the Johanna Runge Free Kindergarten by becoming a charter member in 1898, by serving on the board of directors, and by taking up the duties of corresponding secretary in 1912 and 1921. She was also a member of the board of trustees of the Rosenberg Library.[qv] In the same year that the DRT was established, Betty, her sister Lucy, and Mrs. Maria Cage Kimball founded the Wednesday Club, one of the first women's literary clubs in Texas and an early affiliate of the General Federation of Women's Clubs. Although initially organized for the study of Shakespeare, Balzac, Hugo, and other literary giants, the club had turned by 1912 to "sociological" topics: "Women in Industry," "Modern Educational Movements," and "Woman Suffrage." Miss Ballinger was an active member from the club's inception through 1929. She acted as delegate to the first state general convention of women's clubs in Waco in 1897 and served as president of the Wednesday Club from 1909 to 1911.

Until the Galveston hurricane of 1900[qv] her life interests revolved around those women's organizations that filled the leisure hours of the ladies of "polite society." Although she would have claimed that these groups were of noble purpose, in fact, all but one (the Johanna Runge Free Kindergarten) did little to ameliorate conditions of poverty in the city, nor did they seek to bring about reform either within the city or for women. But a change in the city's fortunes transformed women's private and organizational lives. The storm of 1900 brought the worst kind of social disorder. In its wake, however, emerged the Women's Health Protective Association,[qv] the most effective of all the women's associations. Though it was organized to give decent burial to the victims of the storm who were not cremated, the WHPA remained active from 1901 to 1920 as a progressive reform association. Its members worked to revegetate the island, to enact updated city building ordinances, to institute regular inspection of dairies, bakeries, groceries, and restaurants, to eliminate breeding grounds for flies and mosquitoes, and to establish medical examinations for schoolchildren, hot-lunch programs, public playgrounds, and well–baby and tuberculosis clinics. Betty Ballinger quickly became involved in the WHPA, which she served as corresponding secretary in 1909. This shift to reform activities no doubt influenced her to take an active interest in the suffrage movement. At the age of sixty-eight she and a number of younger women spoke before an audience of 150 people for the right of women to vote. She served as the first vice president of the Galveston Equal Suffrage Association in 1912. Her ability to develop from a Southern lady to a progressive activist helped open the way toward greater public roles for women in the future of Texas. Betty Ballinger died on March 23, 1936, in Galveston.

BIBLIOGRAPHY: Shirley Abbot, *Womenfolks: Growing Up Down South* (New Haven, Connecticut: Ticknor and Fields, 1983). Betty Ballinger Papers, Rosenberg Library, Galveston. Daughters of the Republic of Texas, *Fifty Years of Achievement: History of the Daughters of the Republic of Texas* (Dallas: Banks, Upshaw, 1942). Emma Barrett Reeves, comp., *Three Centuries of Ballingers in America* (Nacogdoches, Texas, 1977). Vertical Files, Barker Texas History Center, University of Texas at Austin. Larry J. Wygant, "A Municipal Broom: The Woman Suffrage Campaign in Galveston," *Houston Review* 6 (1984).

Elizabeth Hayes Turner

BALLINGER, WILLIAM PITT (1825–1888). William Pitt Ballinger, attorney, was born at Barbourville, Kentucky, on September 25, 1825, the son of James Franklin and Olivia (Adams) Ballinger. He attended St. Mary's College in Bardstown, Kentucky, moved to Galveston in 1843, and began the study of law with an uncle, James Love.[qv] He was admitted to the bar in 1847. During the Mexican War[qv] he enlisted as a private and advanced through the ranks to be adjutant of Albert Sidney Johnston's[qv] regiment.

In 1850 Ballinger married Hallie P. Jack of Brazoria County; the couple had three daughters and two sons. Ballinger served as a United States district attorney for Texas from 1850 until 1854, when he became a partner in a Galveston law firm with Thomas McKinney Jack[qv] and M. L. Mott. He successfully represented a group of Galveston wharf owners, who wished to retain possession of their property, against the City of Galveston. The case went to the Texas Supreme Court in 1859. In 1861 Ballinger was appointed Confederate receiver by Judge D. G. Hill of the Confederate District Court.

Gov. Pendleton Murrah and Gen. John Bankhead Magruder,[qqv] commander of the district of Texas, appointed Ballinger and Ashbel Smith[qv] special commissioners at the end of the Civil War[qv] to secure terms of peace for the state. The commissioners arrived in New Orleans on May 29, 1865, and petitioned for a conference with Gen. Edward R. S. Canby,[qv] but he was without authority to treat the subjects broached by the Texans. Ballinger declined appointments to the Texas Supreme Court in 1871 and in 1874. He participated in the Constitutional Convention of 1875[qv] as a member of the Judicial Committee. Texans offered Ballinger the Democratic nomination for governor in July 1878, but he refused.

His daughter Betty, with Hally Bryan Perry,[qv] organized the Daughters of the Republic of Texas.[qv] Ballinger died in Galveston on January 20, 1888. The county seat of Runnels County was named in his honor.

BIBLIOGRAPHY: William Pitt Ballinger Papers, Barker Texas History Center, University of Texas at Austin. William Pitt Ballinger Papers, Rosenberg Library, Galveston, Texas. Louise C. Curtsinger, "The Career of Judge William P. Ballinger," West Texas State Historical Association *Yearbook* 18 (1942). James L. Hill, The Life of Judge William Pitt Ballinger (M.A. thesis, University of Texas, 1936). C. Richard King, "William Pitt Ballinger: Texas Bibliophile," *Texas Libraries* 31 (Winter 1969).

C. Richard King

BALLINGER, TEXAS. Ballinger is at the junction of U.S. highways 67 and 83 and State Highway 158, fifty-two miles northeast of San Angelo in south central Runnels County. The Colorado River and Elm Creek converge there, and the Atchison, Topeka and Santa Fe Railway runs through the town. Ballinger was established when the Gulf, Colorado and Santa Fe Railway built westward out of Brownwood in 1886. Runnels City, the original county seat, campaigned for selection as the new railroad terminal but could not compete with the superior water supply offered at the future site of Ballinger, five miles to the south.

Extensive advertising in the Dallas, Fort Worth, Austin, San Antonio, and Galveston newspapers brought 6,000 people to the sale of town lots in Ballinger on June 29, 1886. As early as June 7 railroad-company ads in the Dallas *Morning News*[qv] promoted the sale, offering half-price excursion trains from Dallas. The 1.7-square-mile area was laid out in large lots, with a courthouse square and public park set aside for future use. Roughly half of the lots sold on the first day. To ensure the success of their new terminal, Santa Fe officials offered free property to anyone who would move a home from Runnels City to Ballinger and to any church that would erect a building.

The town was originally called Gresham and then Hutchings (in honor of Santa Fe stockholders Walter Gresham and John H. Hutchings[qqv]); it was officially named in honor of William Pitt Ballinger,[qv] a Galveston attorney and stockholder of the Gulf, Colorado and Santa Fe. Rapid growth and opportunity brought a boomtown atmosphere, attracting a crowd of drifters, fugitives, gamblers, and ruffians to the town's nine saloons and gambling halls. Stagecoach robberies were not uncommon. By 1888, however, the railroad extended to San Angelo, the overland stage business ended, and new, permanent settlers came to the land.

A post office was established in Ballinger on June 1, 1886, with William A. Procter as postmaster. The town was incorporated in 1892 and began using the commission form of city government. In 1886 I. C. Huege moved his newspaper, the *Runnels County Record*, from Runnels City to Ballinger and changed its name to Ballinger *Eagle.* Two more newspapers quickly appeared on the scene—the Ballinger *Ledger*, published by P. E. Truly, and the *Banner Leader*, published by C. P. Shepherd. In 1911 the *Ledger* and the *Banner Leader* were consolidated as the Ballinger *Daily Ledger*, which published a weekly edition, the *Banner Ledger.*

Under the influence of the advertising of such groups as the Ballinger Business Men's Club and the Pecan, Colorado, and Concho Immigration Society, the population grew from 1,128 in 1900 to 3,536 in 1910. The area had long been regarded as excellent stock land, but the decade from 1900 to 1910 witnessed the ascendance of farming over stock raising in Ballinger and Runnels County. By 1904 the town had four cotton gins, an ice plant, a steam laundry, a steam bakery, a city waterworks, a telephone company, three newspapers, two large furniture stores, three drugstores, a grain and feed store, two hardware stores, four lumber yards, two saddle stores, several dry goods stores, coal yards, blacksmith shops, a wagonyard, cotton yards, a public school building, churches, hotels, and a restaurant.

In 1909 Ballinger received a $12,500 gift from Andrew Carnegie to build a library, which opened in 1911. The open auditorium on the second level was converted during World War II[qv] to an Army-Navy Club to entertain cadets from nearby Harmon Training Center, a primary flight school for United States Army Air Force cadets. In 1975, after many years of neglect, the building was in ruins. The Ballinger Bicentennial Committee organized a renovation effort, and the library was placed on the National Register of Historic Places.

The drought years of 1916–18 brought a major crisis for this largely agricultural area. The population of Ballinger dropped from 3,536 in 1910 to 2,767 in 1920. Subsequently, with improved weather conditions in the 1920s, the town began to grow steadily, reaching a peak of 5,302 in 1950. A pattern of slow decline followed until the population reached 3,975 in 1992.

Ballinger is the main shipping and distribution center for Runnels County. The major sources of employment are light manufacturing, mining, and retail trade. The number of businesses in the town reached a high of 290 in 1940, dropped to 146 immediately after World War II, and climbed back to a postwar high of 210 in 1950. In 1990 the town had ninety businesses. The health care needs of the town are met by two general hospitals with a combined capacity of fifty-five beds. In addition, Ballinger Memorial Hospital supports a vocational nursing school that provides both training and jobs. Ballinger is home to numerous churches, the largest of which are Southern Baptist, Catholic, and United Methodist. The community also maintains paid fire and police departments and supports radio station KRUN-AM, KRUN-FM. Each spring the town is host to two special events, the Rattlesnake Roundup (March) and the Texas State Festival of Ethnic Cultures Arts and Crafts Fair (April). In the fall Ballinger presents the Pinto Bean Cookoff (October) and the Miss Ballinger Pageant and Parade (December).

BIBLIOGRAPHY: Ballinger *Ledger*, 75th Anniversary Edition, June 29, 1961. John Clements, *Flying the Colors: Texas, a Comprehensive Look at Texas Today, County by County* (Dallas: Clements Research, 1984). Keith Elliott, "Ballinger's Carnegie Library," *Texas Highways*, January 1989. Frank D. Jenkins, ed., *Runnels County Pioneers* (Abilene, Texas: R&R Reproduction, 1975). Charlsie Poe, *Runnels Is My County* (San Antonio: Naylor, 1970). Houston Bailey Self, A History of Runnels County (M.A. thesis, Texas Technological College, 1931). A. E. Skinner, *The Rowena Country* (Wichita Falls: Nortex, 1973). Glenn Smith, "Drought in Runnels County: 1915–1918," West Texas Historical Association *Yearbook* 40 (1964). Vertical Files, Barker Texas History Center, University of Texas at Austin. *Kathryn Pinkney*

BALLINGER CITY LAKE. Ballinger City Lake, popularly known as Lake Ballinger, is located on Valley Creek in the lower Colorado-Llano basin, six miles northwest of Ballinger in west central Runnels County (at 31°46′ N, 100°03′ W). The earthfill dam was completed in 1947; it is thirty feet high and 4,400 feet long, has a 400-foot spillway, and impounds up to 8,215 acre-feet. The lake was engineered by Parkhill, Smith, and Cooper and is owned by the city of Ballinger. It is used for debris control and municipal water supply.

BIBLIOGRAPHY: Inventory of Dams, Report No. WR0703, Water Rights and Uses Division, Dam and Flood Plain Safety Section, Texas Water Commission, Austin.

BALLÍ TIJERINA, CARLOS MANUEL (1889–1947). Carlos Ballí, physician, was born on November 23, 1889, in Reynosa, Tamaulipas. He studied in the Colegio civil in Monterrey, Nuevo León. His father was a poor shoemaker in Reynosa. Ballí moved to McAllen, Texas, to practice medicine in 1918; the Mexican Revolution[qv] and a severe epidemic of Spanish influenza were in progress. He had the support of doctors J. G. Harrison and Frank E. Osborn. He rode on horseback through high waters to attend the sick and the needy. After many nights without sleep, constant closing of schools, and interruptions by war, he was able to finish medical school and obtain his M.D. degree on September 2, 1918, in Mexico City. Two months later he took his medical examination in Austin, Texas, and passed with high honors. He settled in 1920 in McAllen, where he established a clinic and pharmacy on the corner of Seventeenth Street and Beaumont Avenue with the help of Victorino Garza Chapa. Ballí was the first Hispanic doctor to practice in McAllen. On April 18, 1921, he married Elenita García Cerón of Actopan, Hidalgo, Mexico. Elenita gave anaesthesia to patients and also took X rays. Ballí died on May 26, 1947, and was buried in the cemetery El Panteón del Roble.

BIBLIOGRAPHY: Octavio García, *Otros Días* (Westford, Massachusetts: Grey Home Press, 1984). *Herminia Ballí de Chavana*

BALMORHEA, TEXAS. Balmorhea is on Toyah Creek, the Pecos Valley Southern Railway, Farm Road 1215, and U.S. Highway 290, one mile southwest of Brogado in southwestern Reeves County. Indian and Mexican settlers farmed around the area from early times, taking advantage of the good supply of water from nearby San Solomon Springs. The town was laid out in 1906 in the center of a 14,000-acre tract watered by the springs. Balmorhea was named for the three land developers who sent their agent, Ira M. Cole, to file the plat for the townsite. Their names were Balcum, Moore, and Rhea. A public school was organized, and a post office opened in 1908. In 1911 the Pecos Valley Southern laid its tracks from Pecos to Toyahvale through Balmorhea, and a hotel was built in the town that same year. In 1925 fifty people were reported living in Balmorhea, and by 1927 that number increased to 500. A bank opened in 1928 and operated until 1933. The population reached 1,220 in the 1930s, and the number of businesses bounced between twenty-five and thirty-three. A gradual decline began after World War II.[qv] Throughout the 1950s and most of the 1960s the population was around 600, and the number of businesses declined to nineteen. In 1961 the town was incorporated. In 1968 Balmorhea had a population of 1,009 and thirty businesses. By 1988 it had four businesses and a population of 528. The 1990 United States census set the population of Balmorhea at 765. Balmorhea State Recreation Area[qv] is located at San Solomon Springs.

BIBLIOGRAPHY: Alton Hughes, *Pecos: A History of the Pioneer West* (Seagraves, Texas: Pioneer, 1978). Pecos County Historical Commission, *Pecos County History* (2 vols., Canyon, Texas: Staked Plains, 1984). *Julia Cauble Smith*

BALMORHEA LAKE. Balmorhea Lake, an irrigation tank also called Lower Parks Reservoir, is located three miles southeast of Balmorhea in southern Reeves County (at 30°58′ N, 103°44′ W). The surrounding steep to gentle slopes are generally surfaced by reddish-brown to brown sands, clay loams, and clays that support scrub brush and sparse grasses. The lake was built near the prolific San Solomon Springs, which had a reported flow of twenty-two million gallons daily. In 1583 the entrada of Antonio de Espejo[qv] stopped at the spring when Jumano Indians guided the Spaniards up the Toyah valley. Dr. John S. Ford[qv] passed through the Toyah valley in 1849 and noted productive land along its banks. Madera Valley, near the reservoir, was farmed by prehistoric Indians and Hispanic settlers. After Fort Davis was reoccupied by the army at the end of the Civil War,[qv] a lucrative market opened for the grains, vegetables, and cattle of these farmers, who irrigated their fields from San Solomon Springs. In 1909 the Toyah Valley Irrigation Company was organized to supervise water use of the area. By 1915 Reeves County Water Improvement District No. 1 had acquired the water rights and built Balmorhea Lake and Dam. Construction began on the earthfill dam in 1916 and was completed in 1917. The lake surface covers 573 acres, and its capacity is 6,350 acre-feet of water. Sandia Creek feeds into the reservoir from the northeast, and Kountz Draw empties into it from the south. Runoff from Toyah Creek comes into Balmorhea Lake from Madera Diversion Dam and its canals. Surplus water from Phantom Lake Canal, which is supplied by several springs, is stored in Balmorhea Lake until it is needed for irrigation.

bibliography: Alton Hughes, *Pecos: A History of the Pioneer West* (Seagraves, Texas: Pioneer, 1978). Roy L. Swift and Leavitt Corning, Jr., *Three Roads to Chihuahua* (Austin: Eakin Press, 1988). Del Weniger, *The Explorers' Texas* (Austin: Eakin Press, 1984).

BALMORHEA STATE RECREATION AREA. Balmorhea State Recreation Area is located at Toyahvale, at the northern entrance to the Davis Mountains on U.S. Highway 290 in southeastern Reeves County. The park, including its large rock-walled swimming pool, was built around San Solomon Springs by the Civilian Conservation Corps[qv] in 1933. The springs, which have been called Mescalero and Head Springs at various times, issue from caverns in the bottom of the swimming pool. The pool covers one and three-quarters acres, is thirty feet deep in places, and has aquatic plants and fish living in its 76-degree water. Before 1933, 950 acres for the park was deeded to the state by private owners and by Reeves County Water Improvement District No. 1. In the 1940s the state legally lost all of the land except the present forty-eight acres.

Prehistoric Indians and Mexican settlers farmed in Madera Valley near the park in early times. In 1583 the entrada of Antonio de Espejo[qv] met Jumanos in the Pecos valley who guided them up the Toyah valley to the springs. In 1849 Dr. John S. Ford[qv] passed through the Toyah Creek area, noting its productive land and the corn farmed by Mescalero Indians near the springs. After Fort Davis was reoccupied by the army at the end of the Civil War,[qv] farmers found a profitable market at the fort for grains, vegetables, and cattle. They irrigated their fields from San Solomon Springs, from which reportedly flowed twenty-two million gallons of water daily. In 1909 the Toyah Valley Irrigation Company was organized to supervise water use. By 1915 Reeves County Water Improvement District No. 1 had built Balmorhea Dam and Lake; later the district donated land for Balmorhea State Recreation Area.

bibliography: Gunnar Brune, *Springs of Texas*, Vol. 1 (Fort Worth: Branch-Smith, 1981). C. L. Dowell, *Dams and Reservoirs in Texas: History and Descriptive Information* (Texas Water Commission Bulletin 6408 [Austin, 1964]). Ray Miller, *Texas Parks* (Houston: Cordovan, 1984). *Julia Cauble Smith*

BALSORA, TEXAS. Balsora is on Farm Road 920 nine miles south of Bridgeport in southwestern Wise County. The area was originally called Wild Horse Prairie because it was frequented by mustangs.[qv] Balsora was established in the late 1880s or early 1890s. Postal service to the community began in 1894, was halted two years later, and began again in 1900. By that time Balsora had a general store, a church, and a school. The population, however, never exceeded fifty, and in 1924 postal service to the community ended. After the 1930s the population hovered between forty and fifty. In 1990 it was fifty.

bibliography: John Clements, *Flying the Colors: Texas, a Comprehensive Look at Texas Today, County by County* (Dallas: Clements Research, 1984). Rosalie Gregg, ed., *Wise County History* (Vol. 1, n.p: Nortex, 1975; Vol. 2, Austin: Eakin, 1982). *David Minor*

BALTIC, TEXAS. Baltic, a short-lived farming and post office community ten miles northeast of Rusk in central Cherokee County, was probably established soon after the Civil War.[qv] A post office opened there in June 1889 but was closed the following November. In the early 1890s Baltic had a mill, a store, and a few scattered farmhouses; the reported population in 1890 was twenty-five. By 1900 the settlement no longer appeared on maps. *Christopher Long*

BAMMEL, TEXAS. Bammel, eighteen miles north of downtown Houston at the intersection of Farm Road 1960 and Kuykendahl Road in north central Harris County, was established after the neighboring towns of Klein, Westfield, and Spring. It was named for Charles Bammel, a German Houstonian who built the Bammel and Kuehnle Merchandise store with his partner in 1915 and moved to the community for health reasons. A Bammel post office, at which Herman Kuehnle was the first postmaster, operated from 1916 until 1929. Bammel's store burned in 1927 but was later rebuilt to serve the new Bammel Forest subdivision. The town's population was reported as roughly fifty from 1929 until oil was discovered in the area in 1938. In 1943 the community reported two stores and a population of 200, but in 1949 its population was estimated at twenty. During the 1980s Bammel's residents were mainly commuters who worked in Houston. The community included two shopping centers, several schools, a hospital, and nearby cemeteries.

bibliography: *The Heritage of North Harris County* (n.p: North Harris County Branch, American Association of University Women, 1977). Houston Metropolitan Research Center Files, Houston Public Library. *Claudia Hazlewood*

BANCO NACIONAL DE TEXAS. The Banco Nacional de Texas, or Texas National Bank, was established as a bank of issue by Governor José Félix Trespalacios[qv] in San Antonio on October 21, 1822. Members of the city council were made officers in the bank, and four soldiers were given the task of hand-producing the notes. Just under 12,000 pesos was issued in two installments on November 1 and December 1, 1822, before the bank was suspended. The short-lived experiment in emergency financing proved costly to most noteholders, who had to wait until 1830 for redemption of the Texas money by the Mexican government.

Upon his arrival in Texas, Trespalacios found the province's troops in such a deplorable state that he hit upon the idea of issuing paper money, to be backed by the specie due from the central government, as wages to the soldiers. Although the currency was declared legal tender for public and private debts, the doubtful money soon led to trouble. Citizens readily paid their taxes to the municipality in the notes, but many individuals had to be forced to accept the paper money. The matter was further complicated by the arrival of Mexican emperor Agustín de Iturbide's[qv] own paper currency and orders that Texas paper be exchanged for imperial.

Holders of the notes refused to accept national paper in return for the Texas notes, arguing that Trespalacios had guaranteed the Bank of Texas money in specie. Negotiations dragged on between 1823 and 1829 before the Mexican Congress passed a law in 1829 ordering that the Texas notes be redeemed with specie. In 1830 the controversial currency was finally exchanged in Saltillo for coin provided by the customhouses of Matamoros and Tampico.

bibliography: Carlos E. Castañeda, "The First Chartered Bank West of the Mississippi: Banco Nacional de Texas," *Bulletin of the Business Historical Society* 25 (December 1951). *Jesús F. de la Teja*

BANCOS OF THE RIO GRANDE. A 1905 treaty between the United States and Mexico called for the elimination of bancos. A banco is a curve in a river channel, a bend oftentimes resembling a horseshoe or oxbow. Some are so large as to be unnoticeable except from the air or by surveys. Bancos usually form where the ground is level, the drop or grade is slight, and the river is sluggish. During floods, since the water encounters resistance in these curves, the channels frequently shift. Where the Rio Grande is the boundary between the United States and Mexico the shifts have had international repercussions. Boundary commissioners described the Rio Grande border as having three divisions. From El Paso to Rio Grande City, the fall was steep and the banks usually solid. From Rio Grande City to the Gulf of Mexico, a straight distance of 108 miles, the river meandered through 241 miles of curves (bancos) to reach the coast. The soil was alluvial, the fall measured in inches. River channels frequently twisted back upon themselves, creating cut-offs and confusions about where the border was. By 1970 American and Mexican boundary commissions had sliced through 241 bancos by straightening the river. Those bancos that protruded into Mexico went to Mexico, the others to Texas. More than 30,000 acres of land changed hands, most of it in the lower Rio Grande valley. The United States got 18,505 acres, and Mexico received 11,662.

BIBLIOGRAPHY: International Boundary and Water Commission, Files, El Paso. Jerry E. Mueller, *Restless River* (El Paso: Texas Western Press, 1975). Charles A. Timm, *The International Boundary Commission* (Austin: University of Texas Press, 1941). Robert M. Utley, *International Boundary: United States and Mexico* (Santa Fe: National Park Service, Southwest Region, 1964).

Leon C. Metz

BANCROFT, HUBERT HOWE (1832–1918). Hubert Howe Bancroft, historian, the son of Ashley and Lucy (Howe) Bancroft, was born at Granville, Ohio, on May 5, 1832. In 1852 he went to California, where in 1856 he opened a book and stationery shop in San Francisco. With publishing, subscription, and music departments added, the shop became the largest west of Chicago. In 1859 Bancroft began collecting Californiana. His interest soon spread to include all the Pacific states from Panama to Alaska and eastward through Texas. Eventually he amassed books, pamphlets, newspapers, and manuscripts to the amount of 60,000 volumes. After it was moved to the University of California in 1905, his library became the chief center of research in western history and, incidentally, the training ground for a number of specialists in Texas history.

Bancroft determined not only to collect historical materials on the West but to try to chronicle that history comprehensively. With hired assistants, who eventually numbered 600, he began to index his holdings, to take notes, and to write. Between 1874 and 1890 he published thirty-nine massive volumes detailing the history of the western half of the continent. Unfortunately, he published the set as his *Works* and did not precisely credit the writings of his assistants. These books, however, are said to be the greatest compendium of information on their vast subject and the best reference on many of its parts. Although the set is California-centered, the six volumes on Mexico are immediate background for Texas history, and the two on the north Mexican states and Texas were acclaimed by Eugene C. Barker[qv] in 1925 as "the most satisfactory comprehensive history of Texas available."

Selling his histories by subscription, Bancroft made them gross more than a million dollars. The *Works* were followed by eight volumes of subsidized biographies, *The Chronicles of the Builders* (1891), and by several volumes of essays. In his later years Bancroft was berated for his methods of collecting, publishing, and selling; but since his death on March 2, 1918, his repute has greatly improved because of the vast amount of research that has been dependent upon his *Works*. He was married to Emily Ketchum in 1859 and to Matilda B. Griffin in 1875.

BIBLIOGRAPHY: John Walton Caughey, *Hubert Howe Bancroft: Historian of the West* (Berkeley: University of California Press, 1946). *Dictionary of American Biography. Who Was Who in America*, Vol. 2. Vertical Files, Barker Texas History Center, University of Texas at Austin.

John Walton Caughey

BANCROFT, TEXAS (Chambers County). Bancroft was on what is now Farm Road 1663 thirty miles southwest of Beaumont in northeastern Chambers County. It was named by pioneer settler F. M. Richmond for his maternal grandmother. The community organized a school in 1898 and secured a post office two years later. Although Bancroft lost its post office in 1907, it had 112 inhabitants in 1909. In the severe hurricane of 1915, which devastated much of Chambers County, saltwater flooding ruined many of the area's citrus and rice crops (*see* HURRICANES). Low prices for rice in the post–World War I years, poor drainage (which contributed to an outbreak of malaria), and the lack of good roads led to the community's further decline. No record has been found of Bancroft after 1928, when it appeared on a United States Army topographic map.

BIBLIOGRAPHY: Jewel Horace Harry, A History of Chambers County (M.A. thesis, University of Texas, 1940; rpt., Dallas: Taylor, 1981).

Robert Wooster

BANCROFT, TEXAS (Orange County). Bancroft is at the crossing of Interstate Highway 10 and the Missouri Pacific Railroad, twenty miles east of Beaumont in east central Orange County. The Bancroft-Roach subdivision plat was filed on September 15, 1903, and the community was named for the Bancroft family, influential in Orange County lumbering since the 1870s. The site was on the Orange and Northwestern Railway and served as a shipping point for lumber and rice. The Bancroft school district stubbornly resisted efforts to consolidate it with the Little Cypress and West Orange districts during the 1950s. Most of the community's residential areas had by 1974 been annexed by Orange, although several industrial and business sites remained outside the Orange city limits. *Robert Wooster*

BANDERA, TEXAS. Bandera is on State Highway 16 fifty miles northwest of San Antonio in east central Bandera County. A townsite plat for the settlement, designated county seat at the formation of Bandera County in 1856, was filed with the first county commissioners' court that year by John James, Charles DeMontel,[qqv] and John Herndon. The site, on a cypress-lined bend of the Medina River, had been occupied by Indians, then by white campers making shingles. The town and county were named for nearby Bandera Pass.[qv] The founders formed a partnership in 1853 to build a town and water-powered lumber mill. They recruited immigrant workers from Upper Silesia by way of the Polish colony in Karnes County (*see* POLES). These workers arrived in 1855, and each family received purchase rights to town lots and farmland.

The presence of the United States Cavalry at Camp Verde[qv] after 1856 encouraged increased activity and settlement. Bandera served the needs of the military and of settlers who took up small holdings in the area. After the Civil War[qv] the town boomed as a staging area for cattle drives up the Western Trail.[qv] Farm boys became cowboys. Ranchers built holding pens and signed on as trail bosses. Storekeepers contracted as outfitters. Cotton was a commercial crop during this period. An ornate courthouse begun in 1890 announced prosperity from the town square. For local stockraisers, sheep and goats proved more profitable on the shallow limestone soil than cattle, but not until 1920 did the Bandera County Ranchers and Farmers Association organize cooperative storage and marketing of wool and mohair (*see* WOOL AND MOHAIR INDUSTRY).

The local economy declined after 1900; a series of floods destroyed sawmills, gins, and businesses, and the cattle drives ceased. Until the San Antonio highway was constructed in 1936 Bandera remained relatively inaccessible. Other roads remained unpaved as late as the 1950s.

In 1920 Cora and Ed Buck began taking summer boarders at their ranch on Julian Creek. Other families soon advertised for guests, and by the 1930s Bandera had become well known as a resort offering riverside camps, restaurants, dance halls, and rodeos to complement surrounding dude ranches.

Bandera was incorporated in 1964. A Medina River flood in 1978 caused heavy loss of life and property and emphasized the necessity for strict control of the floodplain. In 1988 state and city officials joined in proposing that most of the floodplain within the city be made open parkland. Although Bandera County's population almost doubled after 1970, the population of Bandera has varied little; it has remained in the range of 1,000 since 1928. In 1988 the town had a population of 1,012 and seventy rated businesses, including crafts stores, medical and veterinary clinics, a sawmill, a weekly newspaper, the county library, seven churches, and the Frontier Times Museum.[qv] Bandera offers opportunities for tourism, camping, horse racing, and dude ranching. In 1990 the population was 877.

BIBLIOGRAPHY: T. Lindsay Baker, *The First Polish Americans: Silesian Settlements in Texas* (College Station: Texas A&M University Press, 1979). J. Marvin Hunter, *One Hundred Years in Bandera, 1853–1953* (Bandera, Texas: Hunter's Printing, 1953). J. Marvin Hunter, *Pioneer History of Bandera County* (Bandera, Texas: Hunter's Printing, 1922). Frank W. Johnson, *A History of Texas and Texans* (5 vols., ed. E. C. Barker and E. W. Winkler [Chicago and New York: American Historical Society, 1914; rpt. 1916]). *Peggy Tobin*

BANDERA COUNTY. Bandera County (Q-14) is twenty-five miles northwest of San Antonio in the Edwards Plateau[qv] region of southwest Texas. It is bordered by Kerr and Kendall counties on the north, Bexar County on the east, Medina and Uvalde counties on the south, and Real County on the west. The county seat and largest town is Bandera, and the center of the county lies at 29°45′ north latitude and 99°11′ west longitude. The county is crossed by State highways 16, 46, and 173 and Farm roads 187, 337, 470, and 1283.

Bandera County comprises an area of 793 square miles, with elevations that range from 1,200 to 2,300 feet. The western part of the county is drained by the Sabinal River and the eastern part by the Medina River. The alkaline and generally shallow soils overlie limy subsoils. The vegetation consists primarily of grasses such as bluestems, grama, buffalo grass, winter grass, and wild ryes. Along the many streams of the county grow cedar, post oak, Spanish oak, live oak, pecan, and cypress trees. Deer and turkey are plentiful, but there are no large predators. Sheep, goat, cattle, and poultry raising are the chief occupations. Only 11 to 20 percent of the land in the county is considered prime farmland. Crops include corn, oats, hay, pecans, and some grain sorghums.

The climate features dry and mild winters and warm summers. Temperatures range in January from an average low of 36° to an average high of 69° F, and in July from 69° to 95° F. The average annual rainfall is twenty-nine inches; the average relative humidity is 76 percent at 6 A.M. and 45 percent at 6 P.M. There is no significant snowfall. The growing season averages 235 days a year, with the last freeze in late March and the first freeze in mid-November.

The region has been the site of human habitation for several thousand years. Archeological artifacts suggest that the earliest human inhabitants arrived around 6,000 to 10,000 years ago and settled in rockshelters. Lipan Apaches and, later, Comanches subsequently drifted into the area.

The first Europeans to set foot in what is now Bandera County were the Spanish, who probably explored the region in the early eighteenth century. *Bandera* is Spanish for "flag," and there are a number of colorful accounts as to how the county was named. One has it that a Spanish general named Bandera led a punitive expedition in the area against the Apaches after the Indians raided San Antonio de Béxar. Another relates that after pursuing the Indians to Bandera Pass[qv] the Spanish left a flag or flags to warn them against future raids. And a third legend claims that in 1752 (or 1732) a council was held between Spanish and Indian leaders, during which the Spanish pledged never to go north of the pass if the Indians agreed to cease their raids in the south, and a red flag was placed on the pass as a symbol of the treaty.

Though it is not clear if one or any of these accounts is true, the name was in use by 1842, when a group of Texas Rangers[qv] under the command of Col. John Coffee (Jack) Hays[qv] defeated a large party of Comanches at Bandera Pass. In 1852 John James, Charles S. DeMontel,[qqv] and John J. Herndon entered into a partnership to acquire land "in and above the mountains, commencing ten or fifteen miles above Castroville." Their purpose was to establish a town on the Medina River with a sawmill in order to cut the huge cypress trees that grew there for shingles. In 1853, James and DeMontel surveyed and platted the town of Bandera, and in early 1853 A. M. Milstead, Thomas Odem, P. D. Saner, and their families camped along the river and began making cypress shingles. By the fall of the same year the firm of James, Montel and Company built a horse-powered sawmill and opened a commissary store.

In March 1854 a group of Mormons[qv] led by elder Lyman Wight[qv] reached Bandera. The colony, numbering approximately 250, eventually settled a few miles below the town at a site known for many years as "Mormon Camp," which is now covered by Medina Lake. For a time the Mormons manufactured tables, chairs, and other furnishings, which they sold in San Antonio. But Wight died before the colony was fully established, and many of the colony moved on to Utah or settled in San Antonio. A small number, however, stayed, and their descendants still live in the area.

In February 1855 sixteen Polish families arrived in Bandera to work in James and DeMontel's sawmill, and in August of the same year August Klappenbach opened the first store and post office. On January 25, 1856, the legislature marked off Bandera County from portions of Bexar County; the new county was formally organized on March 10, 1856.

Though Bandera County had schools in 1857 and 1858, taught by teachers named P. P. Pool and Koenigheim, the area maintained its frontier character until well after the Civil War.[qv] Indian attacks were frequent. Despite the establishment of Camp Verde just over the line in Kerr County, settlers lived in constant fear of raids. As late as 1860 the population was only 399, the majority of whom were recent immigrants from East Texas or from the states of the Old South. As was typically the case on the western edge of settlement, men outnumbered women (222 to 167), and the county had only twelve slaves. Farming was still at a subsistence level; as late as 1860 improved acres in the county totaled only 1,461, planted in wheat, corn, beans, and a few vegetables.

Because of its distance from the battlefields and the fact that there were so few slaves in the county, Bandera County was spared much of the trauma of the war and Reconstruction.[qv] The population continued to grow slowly, and by 1870 the number of residents in the county was still only 649, most of whom lived in or near the settlement of Bandera. The decade of the 1870s, however, brought signs that Bandera County was slowly losing its frontier character. Indian attacks became less and less frequent, new stores opened, and stone increasingly replaced cedar logs as a building material.

Much of the economy in the early postwar period was dependent on cattle ranching. In 1870 the county had 4,740 cattle, and Bandera County was a staging area for cattle drives up the Western Trail.[qv] Local farm boys became cowboys, ranchers built holding pens and signed on as trail bosses, storekeepers contracted as outfitters, and the town of Bandera briefly boomed. During the late 1870s, however, the era of the great cattle drives was waning, and sheep, which were easier to feed on the sparse vegetation in the county, gradually replaced cattle. By 1880 sheep outnumbered cattle 32,974 to 9,471, and Bandera County became an increasingly important source of wool. In 1880, the county produced 296,578 pounds of wool, which accounted for its most important export product. Angora goats also began to raised in large numbers in this period, and mohair began to be shipped in significant quantities during the late 1880s (*see* SHEEP RANCHING, GOAT RANCHING, WOOL AND MOHAIR INDUSTRY). The lack of good roads, however, kept the county relatively isolated. Because of the county's hilly terrain, the railroads bypassed it to the north or south, and ranchers were forced to use the arduous overland road to ship their products to market in San Antonio.

Despite the relative hardships, numerous new settlers arrived during the 1870s. In 1880 the population had grown to 2,158, and by 1890 the number of residents stood at 3,795. As before, the great majority of new settlers came from the South, though recent immigrants, especially Germans, formed an increasingly larger portion of the county's residents.

During the late 1880s attempts were made to introduce large-scale farming in Bandera County; for a time cotton was grown as a commercial crop. The amount of cropland harvested, however, remained small, and most landowners found it more profitable to raise sheep and goats on the thin limestone soils. Angora goats in particular proved to be well-adapted to the climate and terrain. By 1910 there were 73,853 goats in the county, nearly twice the number of sheep (42,247) and almost five times the number of cattle (15,308). During the ensuing two decades the trend away from farming and cattle continued. In 1930 the county reported 128,950 goats, 89,594 sheep, and only 7,668 cattle; the same year 470,311 pounds of mohair and 588,943 pounds of wool were shipped.

With the cattle drives over and much of the best land worn out from farming and overgrazing, however, the economy declined. The county population peaked in 1900 at 5,332, and then began to fall as more and more residents moved on to seek their fortunes elsewhere. By 1920 the residents numbered 4,001, and by 1930, 3,784. The onset of the Great Depression[qv] brought a marked downturn in prices for wool and mohair, and by the early 1930s many ranchers and residents found themselves economically strapped. Road building and other government-funded projects helped to employ some locals, but the economy did not completely recover until the onset of World War II,[qv] when wool and mohair were in demand for the defense industries.

The county's population grew in the late 1930s and in 1940 reached 4,234, but in the years after World War II it fell again; between 1950 and 1960 it fell from 4,385 to 3,892. During the 1960s, however, the number of inhabitants grew modestly, and in 1970 the population was 4,747. Subsequently the county has seen impressive growth, largely due to the influx of new residents from San Antonio. In 1980 the population reached 7,084, and in 1991 it was 10,562. In 1990, 94.9 percent of the population was white, .2 percent black, .2 percent Asian, and .6 percent American Indian. Of the total population, 1,172 (11.1 percent) were of Hispanic descent. The largest towns were Bandera and Medina.

In the early 1980s Bandera County had two school districts, with two elementary, one middle, and two high schools. The average daily attendance in 1981–82 was 1,192, and expenditures per pupil were $2,381. Forty-seven percent of the 103 high school graduates planned to attend college. In 1983, 88 percent of the school graduates were white, 12 percent Hispanic, .3 percent black, and .2 percent Asian.

Religion has always played an important role in Bandera County. The Mormons organized their church shortly after arriving in 1854, and the following year the Polish immigrants, all of whom were Catholic, built a small log church where Father Leopold Moczygemba[qv] came to offer Mass and administer the sacraments once a month. St. Stanislaus Church is the second oldest Polish parish in the United States. The First Methodist Church was organized just after the Civil War, a Church of Christ began meeting in the 1870s, and the First Baptist Church was organized in 1883. In the mid-1980s Bandera had fifteen churches, with a estimated combined membership of 3,319. The largest denominations were Baptist, Catholic, and Methodist.

In the nineteenth century Bandera County voters generally preferred Democratic candidates in presidential elections. Republican presidential candidates fared well in the 1920s; Calvin Coolidge and Herbert Hoover received a majority of the county's votes in 1924 and 1928, respectively. Democrat Franklin D. Roosevelt received slim majorities in the 1932 and 1936 elections, but subsequently, Republican presidential candidates won virtually every election, an exception being Lyndon Baines Johnson[qv] in 1964. Democrats, on the other hand, have generally dominated local elections. In the 1982 primary 82 percent of county voters voted Democratic and 18 percent Republican, with a total of 1,842 votes cast.

The total number of businesses in the county in the early 1980s was 118. In 1980, 19 percent of workers were self-employed; 22 percent were employed in professional or related services, 7 percent in manufacturing, 19 percent in wholesale and retail trade, and 16 percent in construction; 37 percent worked in other counties; 907 retired workers lived in Bandera County. Leading industries included tourism and the manufacture of leather purses. Nonfarm earnings in 1981 totaled $63,665,000.

In 1982, 82 percent of the land in the county was in farms and ranches, with 4 percent of the farmland under cultivation. Bandera County ranked 238th among Texas counties in agricultural receipts, with 95 percent coming from livestock and livestock products. The primary crops were oats, hay, wheat, and sorghum; pecans were also grown in sizable quantities. During the 1980s Baxter Adams, a former petroleum geologist, introduced commercial apple growing at his Love Creek Ranch, and subsequently the area around Medina became an important apple-growing region, with more than 30,000 bushels picked annually in the late 1980s.

The tourist trade has also become a major source of the county's income. In 1920 Cora and Ed Buck began taking summer boarders at their ranch on Julian Creek. Other families soon advertised for guests, and Bandera, despite its relative isolation, became well known as a resort, with numerous restaurants, dance halls, and dude ranches. Such attractions such as the Frontier Times Museum,[qv] Bandera Pass, and the site of Camp Montel[qv] also bring in thousands of tourists and vacationers annually. Lost Maples State Natural Area,[qv] near Vanderpool in the west end of the county, is a birder's paradise known for its fall foliage display; Hill Country State Natural Area[qv] is a 4,253-acre primitive camping area with trails for hiking and horseback riding. Numerous hunters are also drawn to the county because of its large deer and turkey population. Since 1990 many tourists come to Bandera Downs for pari-mutuel quarter horse[qv] and thoroughbred racing.

BIBLIOGRAPHY: Bandera County History Book Committee, *History of Bandera County, Texas* (Dallas: Curtis, 1986). Douglas E. Barnett, Mohair in Texas: Livestock Experimentation on the Edwards Plateau (M.A. thesis, University of Texas at Austin, 1983). James B. Gibson, "Indian Raids in Bandera County," *Frontier Times*, June 1936. J. Marvin Hunter, *A Brief History of Bandera County* (Bandera, Texas: Frontier Times, 1949). J. Marvin Hunter, *One Hundred Years in Bandera, 1853–1953* (Bandera, Texas: Hunter's Printing, 1953). J. Marvin Hunter, *Pioneer History of Bandera County* (Bandera, Texas: Hunter's Printing, 1922). Mrs. Albert Maverick, "Ranch Life in Bandera County after 1878," *Frontier Times*, April 1928. T. U. Taylor, "Bandera County Pioneer Cattle Brands," *Frontier Times*, June 1937. WPA Texas Historical Records Survey, Inventory of the County Archives of Texas (MS, Barker Texas History Center, University of Texas at Austin).

Christopher Long

BANDERA CREEK. Bandera Creek rises in Bandera Pass, 2½ miles south of Camp Verde in northeastern Bandera County (at 29°51′ N, 99°06′ W), and flows south for thirteen miles to its mouth on the Medina River, a mile east of Bandera (at 29°44′ N, 99°03′ W). The stream traverses flat to steep terrain with slopes, benches, and deep, dense local dissections. The area vegetation consists primarily of juniper, live oak, and grasses that grow in thin, stony clay loams. The creek is named after Bandera Pass.[qv] It was shown on Stephen F. Austin's[qv] 1829 map of Texas as Puerta de la Bandera.

BIBLIOGRAPHY: J. Marvin Hunter, *Pioneer History of Bandera County* (Bandera, Texas: Hunter's Printing, 1922).

BANDERA FALLS, TEXAS. Bandera Falls is on Farm Road 1283 five miles south of Pipe Creek in eastern Bandera County. In 1966 it was a residential community of some ten houses. It was still listed as a community in 1990, though without census figures.

BANDERA MESA. Bandera Mesa straddles the south central part of the Brewster-Presidio county line twenty-six miles north of Lajitas (at 29°37′ N, 103°46′ W). Most of the mesa, which is about seven miles across, lies in Presidio County, but its highest elevation is at its eastern edge in Brewster County. That point, with an elevation of 4,836 feet above sea level, rises some 1,240 feet above Alamo de Cesario Creek, three miles south. The local terrain is rugged, with numerous box canyons, and is surfaced by shallow, stony soils that support Mexican buckeye, walnut, persimmon, desert willow, scrub brush, and sparse grasses.

BANDERA PASS. Bandera Pass is a narrow, V-shaped natural erosion cut in the long limestone ridge separating the Medina and Guadalupe valleys just south of the Bandera-Kerr county line. There a twentieth-century highway follows the route successively traversed for centuries by Indians, Spaniards, United States Army units, Texas Rangers,[qv] and cattle drovers.

Although a number of persistent legends seek to explain the naming of Bandera—"Flag"—Pass, the origin of the name remains a mystery. Some stories tell of a flag being placed to mark a battle between Indians and Spaniards, at a date somewhere about 1732. Others say the Spanish commander was named Ciro or Manuel Bandera. There was indeed a Manuel Bandera who owned property at the confluence of the Arroyo de Alazán and the Arroyo de San Pedro near Nuestra Señora de la Purísima Concepción de Acuña Mission at San Antonio. But various popular accounts crediting Bandera as the Spanish general cannot be corroborated, nor has his name been found on any Bexar muster roll.

Capt. José de Urrutia[qv] discovered the pass in 1739 while campaigning against the Apaches, who had been threatening Spanish settlements at Bexar. Urrutia had proceeded to the region of San Sabá de la Santa Cruz Mission by a direct route through rough country, where he surprised a band of Apaches and took captives. His recommendation for a presidio on the upper Guadalupe, presumably to guard the pass, was ignored. It is probable that once the easy, though risky, pass route became known, it provided faster communication between Bexar and the mission outpost of San Sabá.

Possibly the earliest map showing Bandera as a place name is an anonymous one, dated around 1815 to 1819, that indicates an Apache village just north of "Puerta de la Bandera." The pass is indicated as the terminal point of an Old Comanche Trail from Nacogdoches. Stephen F. Austin,[qv] in preparing his 1829 map for presentation to the Mexican government, designated the creekbed that runs into the Medina River from the vicinity of the pass Puerta de la Bandera. A map of Spanish Texas issued in 1835 by W. A. Ely shows the Old Comanche Trail intersecting the "Trail to Mission San Saba" but does not specifically show the pass. However, maps beginning with that of John Arrowsmith, as compiled by H. S. Tanner of London in 1841, consistently show either Bandera Creek or Bandera Pass.

The 1849 reconnaissance of routes from San Antonio to El Paso made for the United States Army by Lt. Col. Joseph Eggleston Johnston[qv] included the route traversed by the expedition of Lt. W. H. C. Whiting[qv] across Texas. Whiting's trail began at Fort Washita and bore south through Preston, Fort Worth, Fort Graham, Fort Croghan, the German settlement at Fredericksburg, and Fort Martin Scott. Whiting then crossed the Guadalupe, rode down the remote North Prong of the Medina, cut across to Bandera Pass, recrossed the Guadalupe at a lower point, and then returned to Fredericksburg.

The pass had long been a well-worn trail for whites as well as Indians, but it did not come under white control until the Republic of Texas[qv] era. In 1843 there was a battle at the pass between Comanches and a band of Texas Rangers led by John Coffee Hays.[qv] The ambushed rangers defeated the Indians with their new Colt revolvers. The event is commemorated by a Texas Centennial[qv] marker.

In the 1850s Bandera Pass saw a stream of soldiers and new settlers passing between the lumber camp on the Medina named Bandera and the new cavalry post of Camp Verde beyond the pass in the valley of Verde Creek. Probably the strangest procession ever to cross the pass was that on August 26 and 27, 1856, of the herd of camels[qv] on the last leg of their journey from the Middle East to Camp Verde, where they were employed as beasts of burden in the short-lived Camel Corps of the United States Cavalry.

District of Bexar Survey Number 341, made for George Cole by surveyor Gustav Schleicher,[qv] shows Puerta de la Bandera with the trail heading northwest on the edge of the property and going through the pass, labeled "Road from San Antonio to Fort Terrett" (*see* CAMP TERRETT). The survey, dated July 25, 1855, is noted as postdating that made in 1841 by John James[qv] for Bernardino Ruiz. Early records seem to indicate, however, that land containing Bandera Pass was part of Survey Number 562, actually granted to A. C. Hyde in 1847 and transferred the same year to James Randall, whose first name is variously given as James, John, or Jonas. That the tract in question was subject to confusion and speculation, fueled by the location of the cavalry post guarding the growing nearby communities of Bandera and Kerrville, is evidenced by the survey recorded on July 21, 1856, for John Randall, assignee of Hyde, again by Gustav Schleicher.

The state of Texas gave title to the property to James Randall on January 7, 1858. William G. Randall and James W. Randall of Calhoun County thereupon gave John James a location interest in 640 acres for Jonas Randall, assignee of A. C. Hyde, for which John James was to receive 320 acres on the waters of Verde or Green Creek, tributary of the Guadalupe, in Kerr and Bandera counties. The sought-after Hyde Survey, straddling the road and the pass, could possibly have been intended for use in the establishment of a toll gate, as was the case in other sections of the western frontier, notably at Raton Pass on the Santa Fe Trail.[qv] There is no evidence, however, that any such commercial venture was undertaken.

With safety guaranteed by the presence of the cavalry, the pass continued to gain prominence as the gateway between the ranch country of South Texas and the high plains. After the abandonment of Camp Verde by both Union and succeeding Confederate forces, local minutemen and vigilantes stood guard at the pass throughout the Civil War and Reconstruction.[qqv] Their duty was to intercept carriers of contraband and livestock rustlers who were taking advantage of the wartime breakdown of law and order in the remote area.

After the return of normalcy, Bandera Pass again saw streams of heavy traffic, now of cattle being driven north to Kansas on what came to be known as the Western Trail.[qv] During the period of the trail drives from Texas to northern railheads, Bandera became a booming center for trail outfitters and contractors, as did Kerrville, and most young men of the locality found employment as cowboys. The old trail became the road for wagons and later automobiles from Bandera to Kerrville and was first paved about 1940. It was designated Farm Road 689 and later incorporated by the State Department of Highways and Public Transportation into State Highway 173, which originates at Devine and ends at State Highway 16 near the city limit of Kerrville.

BIBLIOGRAPHY: Herbert Eugene Bolton, *Texas in the Middle Eighteenth Century: Studies in Spanish Colonial History and Administration* (Berkeley: University of California Press, 1915; rpt., Austin: University of Texas Press, 1970). *Frontier Times*, April 1944. J. Marvin Hunter, *One Hundred Years in Bandera, 1853–1953* (Bandera, Texas: Hunter's Printing, 1953). San Antonio *Express*, December 25, 1921.

Peggy Tobin

BANE, JOHN P. (ca. 1835–?). John P. Bane, at age twenty-six, formed the Guadalupe (County) Rangers in Seguin and became their first captain. They reported for duty on July 4, 1861, at Camp Clar, a training center on the San Marcos River, and were mustered in on July 27, 1861. After a brief training period they gathered at Houston before going to Virginia, where they became Company D, Fourth Texas Infantry (see HOOD'S TEXAS BRIGADE). Bane was present at the battles of Eltham's Landing, Seven Pines, and Gaines' Mill. He received an arm wound in the last battle and was absent from the unit's next five encounters. He again saw action at Gettysburg, where he took command of the Fourth Texas after Col. John C. G. Key was wounded. Some weeks later Key resumed command, but he apparently never became completely well. Bane again assumed command of the Fourth Texas in the spring of 1864, before the opening of the Wilderness Campaign. Confederate records indicate that he returned to Texas in the summer of 1864 for recruiting purposes and was there when the war ended. He signed a document in San Antonio on August 25, 1865, listing his home as Guadalupe County, Texas.

BIBLIOGRAPHY: Nicholas A. Davis, *Chaplain Davis and Hood's Texas Brigade*, ed. Donald E. Everett (San Antonio: Principia Press of Trinity University, 1962). *Donald E. Everett*

BANGS, SAMUEL (ca. 1798–1854). Samuel Bangs, pioneer printer and publisher, son of Samuel and Hannah (Grice) Bangs, was born about 1798, probably in Boston, Massachusetts. During the five years preceding September 1816, when he sailed from Baltimore as a printer for Francisco Xavier Mina's[qv] expedition, he served as a printer's apprentice in the shop of Thomas G. Bangs, a printer and distant relative. En route to Mexico the expedition stopped on Galveston Island, where, on February 22, 1817, Bangs and John J. McLaren issued a *Manifesto* for Mina, using a portable press brought from England. The proclamation was similar to one Mina had earlier issued in Pennsylvania. On the back of this first documented Texas imprint were the names of the young printers, Juan J. McLaren and S. Bangs. No original copy survives, but a reprint is in Carlos María Bustamante's *Cuadro histórico de la revolución de la America Mexicana* (1843–46). On April 12, 1817, Bangs was at the mouth of the Rio Grande, where the two probably printed another proclamation, which Mina addressed to his *compañero de armas.* If it was printed in the area that later became Texas territorial waters, it is the second documented Texas imprint. No original copy has survived. It too was reprinted in *Cuadro histórico.* Two copies of a contemporary printing by Mina's press at Soto la Marina have survived.

Louis M. Aury[qv] left Mina, his men, and the printing press at Soto la Marina in mid-April. Having established his press on the mainland of Mexico, Bangs published a patriotic song composed by Joaquín Infante, the auditor of the expedition, in honor of the successful debarkation. On April 25, 1817, the Río Bravo proclamation was printed again under the title *Boletín I de la División Austiliar de la República Mexicana.* Two copies of the *Boletín* have survived, one in the National Museum of Mexico and the other in the Thomas W. Streeter[qv] Collection, Yale University.

At Soto la Marina, Mina's force disintegrated and scattered. McLaren vanished forever. Shortly after landing, Bangs printed a broadside entitled *Canción Patriótica—que al desembarcar general Mina y sus tropas en la Barra de Santander compuso Joaquín Infanta auditor de la división.* A copy is in the Streeter Collection. The Royalists captured Bangs and his press and spared his life only because he knew how to operate the press. He printed for the Royalists at Monterrey until the successes of the Mexican War of Independence[qv] freed him and he began printing for the new government.

Bangs soon returned to his home in New England, married Suzanne Payne, and, not finding satisfactory employment in the United States, returned to Mexico and established himself in Tamaulipas as a government printer in Ciudad Victoria. There in the summer of 1827 he collected and printed the *Colección de Leyes y Decretos de la Primera Legislatura Constitucional del Estada Libre de Tamaulipas.* Bangs and Suzanne had two sons. She died at Victoria in the yellow fever epidemic of 1837. In 1838, after the success of the Texas Revolution,[qv] Bangs visited the United States, taking his two sons to be placed in school. He inspected printing presses in Baltimore and New York and worked on others in Cincinnati and Mobile. He then established himself at Galveston, where he acquired a printing press and published a succession of newspapers—the Galveston *News*[qv] and others. The Galveston *Commercial Intelligencer*[qv] was attributed to him but was really published by Moseley Baker.[qv] The successor to the San Luis *Advocate*[qv] appeared from Bangs's press on October 11, 1842, as the Galveston *Texas Times,*[qv] with Ferdinand Pinchard continuing as editor. Bangs rented his press to others to print the Galveston *Independent Chronicle,*[qv] the *Daily Globe and Galveston Commercial Chronicle* (*see* GALVESTON *DAILY GLOBE*), and the *Texas State Paper.*[qv] By 1839 Bangs had married Caroline H. French, sister of Robert H. and George H. French,[qv] who at times were his associates in the printing business.

With the coming of the Mexican War,[qv] Bangs followed Gen. Zachary Taylor's[qv] troops to Corpus Christi in the summer of 1845 and with George W. Fletcher, a local physician, began printing the Corpus Christi *Gazette*[qv] on January 1, 1846. He also did job printing for both the army and civilians. When Taylor moved to the Rio Grande, Fletcher and Bangs dissolved their partnership, and Bangs planned to publish a new paper, the *Rio Grande Herald,* at Matamoros in partnership with Gideon K. Lewis,[qv] but instead, on June 24, 1846, began publication of the *Reveille* in both English and Spanish, the Spanish section being entitled *La Diana de Matamoros.* Lewis and Bangs soon stopped publishing *La Diana* and rented their press to a Mexican who printed *El Liberal,* a Spanish-language newspaper that strongly defended the Mexican side of the war, thus causing General Taylor to order the *Reveille's* office closed and the printers jailed. Lewis departed in haste and left Bangs to explain that he had had no part in the editorial policy of *El Liberal,* but had merely rented his press to its publisher. He convinced the authorities of his innocence and obtained permission to resume publication of the *Reveille,* but never did so. Instead, he joined his competitors in the publication of the *American Flag,* sold his printing materials and press to them, and worked as a printer at their office until February 17, 1847, when for lack of paper the *Flag* was temporarily suspended.

Bangs moved to Point Isabel to operate a hotel and to establish a newspaper. He soon returned to Galveston, liquidated his business, and shipped his household effects and printing office to Point Isabel, but all was lost in a wreck at sea. For a while he and his wife operated a hotel at Point Isabel, and in the summer of 1848 he made his last attempt to establish a paper there, to be entitled the *Texas Ranger.* It never appeared, owing to Indian depredations, the gold rush to California, and controversy over plans to form a new government to be called the Sierra Madre in northern Mexico—a revival of the old Republic of the Rio Grande.[qv] In 1849 Indians captured the stage between Point Isabel and Brownsville and took Bangs, a passenger, prisoner. Bangs and a companion escaped in a state of nudity. Shortly thereafter, Bangs abandoned his venture in Texas and Mexico and moved to Kentucky, where he worked for the Georgetown *Herald.* He died of typhoid fever on May 31, 1854, in Georgetown, Kentucky.

BIBLIOGRAPHY: Douglas C. McMurtrie, "Pioneer Printing in Texas," *Southwestern Historical Quarterly* 35 (January 1932). Ike H. Moore, "The Earliest Printing and First Newspaper in Texas," *Southwestern Historical Quarterly* 39 (October 1935). Marilyn M. Sibley, *Lone Stars and State Gazettes: Texas Newspapers before the Civil War* (College Station: Texas A&M University Press, 1983). Lota M. Spell, "Anglo-Saxon Press in Mexico, 1846–1848," *American Historical Review* 38 (October 1932). Lota M. Spell, *Pioneer Printer: Samuel Bangs in Mexico and Texas* (Austin: University of Texas Press, 1963). Lota M. Spell, "Samuel Bangs: The First Printer in Texas," *Southwestern Historical Quarterly* 35 (April 1932). *Joseph Milton Nance*

BANGS, TEXAS. Bangs is on U.S. highways 67 and 84 and the Santa Fe Railroad six miles west of Brownwood in west central Brown County. The town was named for its location in the Samuel Bangs[qv] survey. In 1886 a post office was established there, and in 1892 Bangs had eight businesses and a population of fifty. A school was begun that year. In 1900 the population was 136, and by 1915 Bangs had 600 residents and twenty-one businesses, including four churches, a bank, and a weekly newspaper. In 1989 Bangs had twenty-five businesses and an estimated population of 1,869. Growth was attributed to the nearness of Brownwood and the influx of hundreds of followers of a religious cult. In 1973 Bangs became home to the New Testament Holiness Church, Incorporated. David Heze Terrell, who also ran World Ministries, Incorporated, of Dallas and was known to his followers as the Prophet, led the group. In 1974 activities of Terrell, such as using an extremely loud public address system well past midnight, caused conflicts with older residents of the community. It was also claimed that he led an extravagant life while many of his followers lived in abject poverty after contributing much of their income to his church.

BIBLIOGRAPHY: Vertical Files, Barker Texas History Center, University of Texas at Austin.

John G. Johnson

BANISTER, EMMA DAUGHERTY (1871–1956). Emma Susan Daugherty Banister, probably the first woman sheriff in the United States, daughter of Bailey and Martha Ann (Taylor) Daugherty, was born in Forney, Texas, on October 20, 1871. Her father, who had come to the area from Alabama before the Civil War,[qv] was murdered in 1878. After her mother remarried, Emma stayed with her family for two or three years, then went to live with the family of her uncle, Lou Daugherty, in Goldthwaite. There she completed her schooling and studied to become a teacher. She taught in Turkey Creek, Mills County, and at Needmore (now Echo), on Jim Ned Creek in Coleman County. There she boarded in the home of the Sam Golson family.

On September 25, 1894, in Goldthwaite, she married John R. Banister,[qv] a former Texas Ranger and special agent of the United States Treasury Department. After several months of travel the couple settled in Santa Anna, where Emma assumed the duties of rearing John's four small children from a previous marriage and bearing five of her own. Having had experience tracking cattle rustlers, Banister began working for the Texas Cattle Raisers' Association and organized its Field Inspection Service, of which he was the first chief. He was elected sheriff of Coleman County in 1914, and the family moved from the farm to the first floor of the Coleman County Jail. Emma served as John's office deputy. She bought supplies, ran her household, and oversaw the preparation of meals for the family and the prisoners.

On August 1, 1918, the sheriff died, and the commissioners of Coleman County appointed his wife to complete his term in office. Newspapers across the country did not fail to notice that a woman, even in the era before woman suffrage,[qv] had been made a sheriff in Texas. Under the heading "Woman a Sheriff!" the New York World classed Emma Banister among "a stock of westerners that does not know fear." She ran the office efficiently by day, answering mail, instructing deputies, replying to inquiries, and managing the prisoners. In the evenings she kept the records up to date, planned meals, and took care of domestic duties. She declined the county commissioners' offer to place her name on the ballot for the November elections for a further term in office. At the completion of the term the family moved back to the farm in Santa Anna.

Mrs. Banister was a member of the United Daughters of the Confederacy[qv] and a Baptist. In later years she took little credit for her service as sheriff of Coleman County. Oil income enabled her to travel and to deal in real estate in Santa Anna and in Elida, New Mexico. She and her husband had collected Indian artifacts and trophies of his forty-four years in law enforcement; most of the collection is now in the museum at Fort Concho National Historic Landmark,[qv] San Angelo. She died in Brownwood Memorial Hospital on June 4, 1956, and was buried in Santa Anna.

BIBLIOGRAPHY: Leona Bruce, *Banister Was There* (Fort Worth: Branch-Smith, 1968). Leona Bruce, *Four Years in the Coleman Jail, Daughter of Two Sheriffs* (Austin: Eakin Press, 1982).

Margaret White Banister

BANISTER, JOHN RILEY (1854–1918). John Riley Banister, law officer, was born in Banister, Missouri, on May 24, 1854, to William Lawrence and Mary (Buchanan) Banister. His father deserted the family after Civil War[qv] service and settled in Texas. John, who had only three months of schooling, moved to Texas in 1867. He became a cowboy on Rufus Winn's ranch near Menardville, then worked for Sam Golson in Coleman and Mason counties in 1873. Banister fought off several Indian raids and joined his first cattle drive to Kansas in 1874. After another drive in 1876 he joined the Texas Rangers[qv] in Austin for Frontier Battalion[qv] service. His company was involved in escorting murderer John Wesley Hardin[qv] from Austin to Comanche for trial, skirmishes with Indians and outlaws, and the capture of outlaw Sam Bass.[qv]

After leaving ranger service in 1881 Banister moved to San Saba and made cattle drives to Kansas from 1881 to 1883. In 1883 he married Mary Ellen Walker and settled on a ranch near Brownwood, then moved to Coleman to run a livery stable. The couple had six children. Mrs. Banister died in 1892, and Banister married Emma Daugherty on September 25, 1894, in Goldthwaite; they had five children. For several years after 1889 he accepted special assignments as a detective for the Santa Fe and other railroads. In 1892 he became a treasury agent assigned to help police the Mexican border against cattle smugglers. After six years he resigned for full-time service as an inspector for the Texas Cattle Raisers Association (now the Texas and Southwestern Cattle Raisers Association[qv]). He originated the field-inspection service for the association and was its first chief. Banister investigated cattle rustling for the association in Texas, New Mexico, Kansas, and Oklahoma until 1914, when he became sheriff of Coleman County.

Banister's career is documented by a collection of his papers in the Southwest Collection of Texas Tech University. Documents detailing his investigations of cattle theft are particularly valuable in detailing the longtime efforts of the cattlemen's association in protecting livestock. Banister died of a stroke on August 1, 1918, in Coleman, and was buried in Santa Anna. His wife then took over his job and in so doing became the first female sheriff in the United States (*see* BANISTER, EMMA DAUGHERTY).

BIBLIOGRAPHY: Leona Bruce, *Banister Was There* (Fort Worth: Branch-Smith, 1968).

William R. Hunt

BANKERSMITH, TEXAS. Bankersmith, thirteen miles north northeast of Comfort in northwestern Kendall County, was established in 1913, when the San Antonio, Fredericksburg and Northern Railroad laid its track between Fredericksburg and Comfort. The community was named for Temple Doswell Smith,[qv] president of the first bank to be established in Fredericksburg and one of the primary donors for the railroad construction. Just south of the community was the only railroad tunnel in the state. A local post office was established in September 1914 with Rudolph Habenicht as postmaster. The office was sometimes listed as being in Gillespie County, depending on where the postmaster lived. At its peak in the 1920s Bankersmith had a store, a dance hall, a lumberyard, and about fifty residents. The population fell to ten by 1930, and the railroad abandoned its track in 1935. A business and a few scattered houses marked the community on county highway maps in the 1940s, but the post office had already been discontinued. A population of twenty was reported from 1949 through 1961. The ruins of the old railroad tunnel were still visible in the 1980s.

BIBLIOGRAPHY: Kendall County Historical Commission, *A History of Kendall County, Texas* (Dallas: Taylor, 1984).

Vivian Elizabeth Smyrl

BANKS, JOHN WILLARD (1912–1988). John Willard Banks, black self-taught artist, the son of Charlie and Cora Lee (McIntyre) Banks, was born on November 7, 1912, near Seguin, Texas. At the age of five his parents took him to San Antonio, where he attended Holy Redeemer School until the age of nine, when his parents were divorced and John returned to his grandparents' farm near Seguin. From childhood Banks's favorite pastime was drawing pictures on his Big Chief tablet. He later recalled, "As a kid I used to lie flat on my stomach, drawing and drawing. . . . My mother had to kick me off the floor to sweep."

While helping out on his grandparents' farm, Banks completed the tenth grade before striking out on his own. His favorite activities during his youth were singing in a gospel quartet and playing baseball. In his adult years he worked in oilfields and cottonfields, drove a truck, and tended a San Antonio service station. During World War II[qv] he joined the army; he held the rank of sergeant and was stationed in the Philippines. After the war he returned to San Antonio, where he worked as a custodian at Kelly Air Force Base, at Fort Sam Houston, and at a local television station. Banks married Edna Mae Mitchell in 1928, and they had five children. The marriage ended in divorce around 1960. In 1963 he married Earlie Smith.

His art career began in 1978 while he was recuperating from an illness for which he had been hospitalized. Banks's wife admired her husband's drawings and secretly took several of them to a San Antonio laundromat. There she hung the drawings on the wall, offering them for sale at the price of fourteen dollars. They were purchased and taken to a gallery for framing. Quite by chance, a San Antonio physician and collector of works of art by black artists, Joseph A. Pierce, Jr., saw one of the drawings in the gallery. He telephoned Banks and arranged for a meeting to see his other work. Pierce and his wife, Aaronetta, became friends with John and Earlie Banks and began to advise them on Banks's art career.

Banks's first solo exhibition was held at Caroline Lee Gallery in San Antonio in 1984, when Banks was seventy-two years old. Subsequently, he had a dual exhibition with fellow Texas artist George White at Objects Gallery in San Antonio; was shown in the Southwest Ethnic Arts Society's inaugural exhibition of black artists in San Antonio, where he won a prize; was included in two traveling exhibitions, Handmade and Heartfelt, organized by Laguna Gloria Art Museum[qv] and Texas Folklife Resources in 1987, and Rambling on My Mind: Black Folk Art of the Southwest, organized by the Museum of African-American Life and Culture in Dallas in 1987. Also in 1987 he was included in a dual exhibition with fellow San Antonio artist John Coleman at the O'Connor Gallery in the McNamara House Museum, Victoria, and in 1989 he was one of six artists included in the traveling exhibition Black History/Black Vision: The Visionary Image in Texas, organized by the University of Texas Archer M. Huntington Art Gallery. Also in 1989 Banks was included in the exhibition Innate Creativity: Five Black Texas Folk Artists, sponsored by the Museum of African-American Life and Culture and held at the Dallas Public Library.

Banks developed a distinct style, outlining figures in pencil or ballpoint pen and shading them in with colored pencil, crayon, and felt-tipped marker. Sometimes his art was influenced by his early, rural memories, including scenes of baptisms, church meetings, hog killings, funerals, and Juneteenth[qv] celebrations. These works serve as excellent documents of black life in early twentieth-century Texas. At other times, Banks's work was the result of an inner vision that led him to such revelations as his *Second Coming of Christ*, in which he drew his view of the activities man might be found engaging in should Christ return today. Whether his subjects were religious or rural, they took place in lush landscapes, often with tree-lined rivers flowing through the composition. He did a series of African scenes drawn from his imagination, in which he depicted idyllic villages where communal activities took place. Often they included references to the bounty of nature and the virtue of working together toward a common goal. In other pictures Banks told more somber stories, of slave auctions and inner-city ghetto scenes. Through the facial expressions and gestures of the figures, Banks revealed their psychological states and personalities. When Banks died in San Antonio on April 14, 1988, he left behind several hundred drawings.

BIBLIOGRAPHY: Francis E. Abernethy, *Folk Art in Texas*, Publications of the Texas Folklore Society 45 (Dallas: Southern Methodist University Press, 1985). Lynne Adele, *Black History/Black Vision: The Visionary Image in Texas* (Austin: University of Texas Press, 1989). San Antonio *Light*, April 29, 1984.

Lynne Adele

BANKS, NATHANIEL PRENTISS (1816–1894). Nathaniel Prentiss Banks, congressman, governor of Massachusetts, and Union general, was born on January 30, 1816, in Waltham, Massachusetts, to Nathaniel P. and Rebecca (Greenwood) Banks. Working in the cotton mill where his father was superintendent later earned him the sobriquet "Bobbin Boy of Massachusetts." He married Mary Theodosia Palmer in 1847 and was a member of the Massachusetts House from 1849 until 1852; he was speaker for two years. Banks was elected as a coalition Democrat to the Thirty-third Congress in 1853 and as a candidate of the American (Know-Nothing) party[qv] to the Thirty-fourth Congress, which he served as speaker. He was elected as a Republican to the Thirty-fifth Congress and served from 1853 until he resigned in 1857 to become governor.

After his service as governor of Massachusetts from 1858 to 1861, Banks was commissioned major general of volunteers, on May 16, 1861. After setbacks against Confederates in Virginia in 1862, he journeyed to New Orleans and succeeded Benjamin F. Butler as commander of the Department of the Gulf. Acting in concert with Ulysses S. Grant's campaign to open the Mississippi River, Banks attempted to storm Confederate defenses at Port Hudson in May and June 1863 and received the surrender of the city on July 9. He received an official "Thanks of Congress" for his Port Hudson campaign, then at the government's direction prepared to move against Texas in an attempt to influence the French presence in Mexico, to secure stores of cotton, and to restore a Unionist government to the state.

Banks planned a quick thrust at the mouth of the Sabine River, then an overland move upon Houston and Galveston. The invasion resulted in a Union disaster at the battle of Sabine Pass.[qv] Six weeks later Banks left New Orleans with twenty-three ships and landed an invasion force at Brazos Santiago, near the mouth of the Rio Grande, on November 2, 1863. Union troops soon occupied nearby Brownsville, Texas, and began to drive northward along the coast and up the Rio Grande to shut off the trade coming through "the Confederacy's back door."

Banks returned to New Orleans just one month after the landing at Brazos Santiago, pressed by his superiors to invade East Texas by way of the Red River. The Red River campaign ended in a Union failure and was Banks's last active command. He was honorably discharged from military service on August 24, 1865, and subsequently entered the House of Representatives. During his last years he served in Congress, as a member of the Massachusetts Senate, and as United States marshal. With his health broken during his last term in Congress, he returned to Waltham, where he died on September 1, 1894, survived by a son and two daughters.

BIBLIOGRAPHY: Nathaniel Prentiss Banks Papers, Barker Texas History Center, University of Texas at Austin. *Dictionary of American Biography.* Fred Harvey Harrington, *Fighting Politician: Major General N. P. Banks* (Philadelphia: University of Pennsylvania Press, 1948). Ludwell H. Johnson, *Red River Campaign: Politics and Cotton in the Civil War* (Baltimore: Johns Hopkins Press, 1958). Robert L. Kerby, *Kirby Smith's Confederacy: The Trans-Mississippi South, 1863–1865* (New York: Columbia University Press, 1972). United States Congress, *Biographical Directory of the United States Congress, 1774–1989* (Washington: GPO, 1989). *The War of the Rebellion: A Compilation of the Official Records of the Union and Confederate Armies* (Washington: GPO, 1880–1901). *David Paul Smith*

BANKS, WILLETTE RUTHERFORD (1881–1969). Willette Rutherford (Scrap) Banks, teacher and university administrator, was born on August 8, 1881, in Hartwell, Georgia, the second of thirteen children of J. M. and Laura Banks. J. M. Banks was a Georgia populist and founder of the Colored Zion Elementary School at Hartwell, which Willette attended as a youth. The younger Banks attended Atlanta University, where he met the two most abiding influences on his life—W. E. B. DuBois, his role model, and Glovina Virginia Perry, his wife and cultural mentor.

When Banks graduated in 1909, President E. T. Ware of Atlanta University recommended him for a teaching position at Fort Valley Normal and Industrial Institute in Georgia, and later, in 1912, for a principalship at Kowiliga Community School in Elmore County, Alabama. Colored Methodist Episcopal Church bishop R. A. Carter offered Banks the presidency of Texas College at Tyler in May 1915. At the end of his tenure in 1926 Banks had recruited the second largest student body in a Texas black college and had gained a reputation as a builder and as a master of the difficult craft of financing church-related education.

As principal at Prairie View A&M College (now Prairie View A&M University, a part of the Texas A&M University System[qv]), Banks was challenged by the opportunity to test his skill at running a minority institution governed by whites. He welcomed the reputed "unsavory" post as a "divine call." As an administrator he used the "North-South pivot," a combination of support from private philanthropy with the assistance of the state Interscholastic League of Colored Schools and the federal extension service, to achieve many of his goals, including the construction of new buildings on the campus. In the spring of 1930 he revived the idea of DuBois's Atlanta Conferences. With the aid of the National Association of Teachers in Colored Schools and the General Education Board, Banks founded an ongoing Texas "Educational Conference."

Willette Rutherford Banks. Courtesy George R. Woolfolk, Prairie View.

In the late 1930s he came under criticism from the leaders of black denominational colleges and white liberals for supporting the establishment of a graduate school at Prairie View. His opponents supported out-of-state aid for black students to attend schools in the North and emphasized the need of state black colleges to strengthen their undergraduate programs before expanding. Texas A&M president Walton, however, concerned that out-of-state aid was too heavily tainted by the desire to keep blacks from applying to white institutions, wanted to set up a "separate but equal" graduate school for blacks in Texas. Walton offered Banks a two-year fund of $9,000 a year to start the school. Banks opened his graduate school in June 1938 with thirty-five students and E. M. Morris as dean. By Banks's rationale, he had settled all doubts at Texas A&M about his public acceptance of segregation. In 1938 the United States Supreme Court outlawed out-of-state aid and regional black schools in *Lloyd Gaines v. University of Missouri.* As a result, the leaders of state-supported black colleges soon began accepting money for graduate programs, as Banks had done.

During World War II[qv] Banks was influenced by wartime race riots, by Gunnar Myrdal's *American Dilemma* (1944) and Rayford Logan's *What the Negro Wants* (1944), by the Supreme Court case *Smith v. Allwright* (1944), and by W. E. B. DuBois's call for black colleges to devise methods to emancipate blacks through cooperative research. Banks successfully used his "North-South pivot" to influence the Forty-ninth Texas Legislature, which authorized the Texas A&M board to establish courses at Prairie View in law, engineering, pharmacy, and journalism. The courses were to be "substantially equivalent" to those offered at the University of Texas. Banks thus defeated the faction led by Joseph J. Rhoads,[qv] president of Bishop College, which favored a new state-supported liberal arts college for blacks. Banks then went over the heads of Texas A&M officials, who failed to back the legislative mandate, with a request to the legislature for funds. He received his money from the legislature, but as he had been warned by a Texas A&M dean, his retirement was announced in the spring of 1946. He then became the vice chairman of the board of regents of Texas Southern University and served on the boards of Atlanta University, Morehouse College, and Paine College. He died on October 16, 1969, in Corsicana, and was buried at Memorial Park in Prairie View.

BIBLIOGRAPHY: Alwyn Barr and Robert A. Calvert, eds., *Black Leaders: Texans for Their Times* (Austin: Texas State Historical Association, 1981). George Ruble Woolfolk, *Prairie View* (New York: Pageant, 1962). *George R. Woolfolk*

BANKS, TEXAS. Banks was on Sheep Creek two miles south of the site of present McGregor in western McLennan County. It was established in 1880 by the Gulf, Colorado and Santa Fe Railway, when that line was laying track between Temple and Fort Worth. A post office, with Thomas H. Baker as postmaster, was established at Banks in April 1882, when the community's population was estimated at 200. Later that year the Texas and St. Louis Railway crossed the GC&SF two miles north of Banks; the railroad company decided that the second site would be a better place for a town, and McGregor was established. Many residents of Banks accepted the railroad's offer to exchange their property for lots in McGregor, and several businesses moved as well. In October 1882 the post office was transferred to McGregor, and Banks faded quickly.

BIBLIOGRAPHY: Dayton Kelley, ed., *The Handbook of Waco and McLennan County, Texas* (Waco: Texian, 1972). William Robert Poage, *McLennan County Before 1980* (Waco: Texian, 1981).

Vivian Elizabeth Smyrl

BANKS AND BANKING. The first institution designated a bank in Texas and authorized to conduct banking activity was the Banco Nacional de Texas,qv established by decree of a Mexican governor of Texas, José F. Trespalacios,qv in 1822, shortly after Mexico won its independence from Spain. Its primary function was to issue banknotes, but in 1823 the Mexican government repudiated the redemption of the notes in specie and ended its life. This institution has been referred to as the "first chartered bank west of the Mississippi." In 1835 the legislature of Coahuila and Texasqv chartered the Banco de Commercia y Agricultura. This, the first commercial bank in Texas, provided a variety of banking services. The principals of the bank, which was based in Galveston, were merchants Samuel May Williams and Thomas F. McKinney.qv This bank helped arrange loans for the Texas Revolutionqv and for funding the republic.

No banks were chartered in the Republic of Texas.qv Several banking projects were authorized, but the promoters were unable to raise funds to begin operations. The Constitution of the Republicqv contained no provisions for banks, but the Texas Congress apparently contemplated the establishment of a banking system. President Mirabeau B. Lamar,qv in his message to Congress on December 31, 1838, urged the organization of a National Bank of Texas, but the proposal was not approved. Private firms carried on banking activities for both businessmen and for government. The most prominent was the mercantile firm of McKinney, Williams and Company,qv based in Galveston, which issued paper money.

The state Constitution of 1845qv prohibited the incorporation of banks and the private issuance of paper money. Merchants increasingly performed limited banking functions, as commission merchants, factors, insurance agents, and bankers. Financial agents flourished first in Galveston, but other agencies opened offices as agricultural development spread to the interior. In time, moneylenders could be found in most towns and many villages; in 1859 they numbered more than 3,000, with loans in excess of $3 million.

The Commerce and Agricultural Bank opened in 1847 in Galveston, and was the only chartered bank in Texas before the Civil War.qv Both the republic and the state of Texas recognized its Mexican charter (1835), but the investors had difficulty raising the $100,000 in specie required to operate. The bank could establish branches, but a branch at Brownsville was the only one opened. The bank issued notes, underwritten by deposit currency, and engaged in various types of lending. It catered to customers in the mercantile business, but also provided exchange and other financial services to the public. After a decade of activity, an adverse state court decision prohibited the bank from issuing circulating notes, and it closed in 1859.

The constitutions of 1861 and 1866qv prohibited state chartered banks. Under the Reconstructionqv government the Constitution of 1869qv omitted this feature, and during the next four years several state banks were established by special acts of the legislature. Ten additional banks were authorized under a general banking law in 1874. The Constitution of 1876qv again prohibited state-chartered banks.

From 1865 to 1900, state banks, national banks, and private banks flourished in Texas. Private banks dominated the financial scene immediately after the war. They were built around cotton exporting and other trade and mercantile businesses, and were unregulated and unsupervised. Between 1869 and 1876, only a few state-chartered banks opened for business. The first nationally chartered bank was the First National Bank of Galveston, established on September 22, 1865. Partly because of the $50,000 capital requirement, only thirteen national banks were organized up to 1880. The number grew to 68 in 1885, 189 in 1890, and 440 in 1905.

Expanding agricultural, commercial, industrial, and mining activities produced a need for additional financial facilities. A movement for a state banking system began in the 1890s, supported by public officials, the private sector, and the Texas Bankers Association.qv In 1904 the state constitution was amended to permit state banks, and under the leadership of Thomas B. Love,qv the system was established in 1905. State banks numbered more than 300 by 1908 and two years later exceeded the number of national banks in the state.

National money and banking panics focused attention on the need for banking reform. The Panic of 1907 saw the establishment of the National Monetary Commission to address money ills. Laws guaranteeing deposits in state-chartered banks were enacted in Texas, Oklahoma, Kansas, Nebraska, Mississippi, South Dakota, North Dakota, and Washington. As many Texas banks restricted cash withdrawals during the panic, agitation grew for a system to protect depositors. In the fall of 1907 the Dallas *Morning News*qv campaigned for a depositors' guaranty-fund law, and the state banking commissioner proposed a guaranty bill in his biennial report. Robert R. Williams and Thomas M. Campbell,qqv both candidates for governor in 1908, endorsed the idea. When the legislature failed in 1909 to pass a guaranty act, Governor Campbell called a special session. William Jennings Bryan addressed the legislators, urging immediate passage of the bill; in a second special session, they voted approval.

The guaranty law took effect in January 1910 and empowered Texas state banks to secure deposits by a guaranty-fund system or by a bond security system. Most bankers chose the guaranty-fund option. By this arrangement banks contributed a percentage of their average daily deposits during the preceding year to the fund. If a bank failed, assessments could be levied on other guaranty banks up to 2 percent of their average daily deposits in any one year. Under the bond security system, banks had to furnish bond, policy of insurance, or other guaranty of indemnity equal to the capital stock of the bank. The amount of the bond could be increased as deposits rose above a specified ratio to capital.

The guaranty fund appeared successful. The number of state banks increased from 515 in 1910 to 1,035 in 1920, while the number of national banks remained at about 500. Paid-in capital of the state banks tripled, while total resources increased sixfold. Guaranty-fund receipts easily covered operating expenses. The depression of 1921 changed the situation. An epidemic of bank failures prompted heavy calls on the fund, and it became de facto insolvent by 1925. An amendment to the banking law in 1925 destroyed its effectiveness, and the guaranty-fund system was abolished two years later. By that time many state banks had become national banks to escape assessments under the fund system.

The Federal Reserve Bank of Dallasqv was established in 1914 and soon began operating branches in El Paso, Houston, and San Antonio. All national banks were required to be, and the large state-chartered banks were encouraged to become, members of the Federal Reserve System and the Federal Deposit Insurance Corporation. State banks responded favorably to the new system. In 1933 Texas embarked on an alternative plan to insure state bank deposits, but it attracted only seventeen banks and was abolished in 1937.

The Texas banking scene preceding World War IIqv was turbulent. Downturns in the business cycle, chartering of too many banks, dishonest and incompetent bank managers, and an ill-conceived state deposit-insurance system all contributed to failures that prompted efforts to strengthen the supervisory and statutory frameworks of bank operation. More responsible bankers emerged to steer their institutions toward better service for business and the general public.

Texas banking operations expanded during the postwar years. Commercial banks, savings and loan institutions (more than 150 by the early 1950s), federal and state credit unions, investment banks that issued and distributed securities of local corporations, and brokerage houses connected with firms in New York and other financial centers all appeared. A variety of federal lending agencies emerged to fill in gaps and improve existing facilities, particularly those for agricultural credit. Lending policies and funding practices changed. As interest rates rose in the mid-1950s, there was an increased emphasis on consumer services. Credit cards came into vogue.

By the early 1970s, multibank holding-company systems had developed in Texas—particularly in metropolitan areas—encouraged by the state prohibition of branch banking. These "group banking systems," about a dozen of which were multibillion-dollar statewide entities, became the dominant organizational form. By the summer of 1985, some 130 such systems controlled almost half of the more than 1,800 separately incorporated banks and held nearly three-quarters of the bank deposits of the state. The remaining banks, principally independent banks, generally were located in the smaller cities and towns; about 500 became one-bank holding companies, mainly for federal income tax reasons. Beginning in the mid 1970s, the largest group banking organizations reduced the reliance of major Texas-based companies on out-of-state capital (especially money centers in New York and Chicago) for financing. In so doing, they facilitated capital formation and hastened economic growth in the state.

Innovations in the Texas banking industry followed. Included were electronic payment systems (such as the South Western Automated Clearing House in Dallas, which serves Texas and adjoining states), automated teller machine networks; and evolving point-of-sale funds transfer facilities in retail establishments. These technological advancements enhanced the integration of Texas industries with national commercial banking and financial services. Politically, and otherwise, the Texas Bankers Association and, to a lesser degree, the Independent Bankers Association of Texas, promoted these ties.

During the late 1980s the Texas banking industry experienced a traumatic downturn. This was caused by an overextension of bank credit and by loose lending to energy and energy-related industries and to the commercial real estate field. These lending policies, principally by major statewide multibank holding companies, coincided with declining world petroleum prices and rising speculation in commercial real estate. Excessive real estate lending caused more damage to the Texas banking system than did lending in the energy and energy-related areas. Commercial and industrial loans to oil and gas producers, unsecured by real estate, followed the pattern of oil-price changes. On the other hand, secured construction and land-development loans of sixty months or less to developers and oil and gas producers did not follow the changes in the real estate or oil-price sphere. Texas banks churned out loans through 1987, despite increasing rates of vacancy in offices and declining crude-oil prices. They soared substantially above the national average from 1978 to 1987. By the mid-1980s commercial real estate markets in the major metropolitan areas in Texas were overbuilt. As commercial real estate returns and values declined, banks were unable to shift financing from completed projects to long-term, nonbank financiers. Nonperforming assets increased from 1.75 percent in 1982 to 6.6 percent in 1987. The Texas banks that failed had a nonperforming-assets ratio of 10.4 percent. As a result the Texas commercial banking industry suffered net losses every quarter from 1986 to 1990.

Seven of the ten largest commercial banks in Texas failed between 1987 and 1990. Only Texas Commerce Bancshares and Allied Bancshares survived. They merged with major out-of-state banks and were recapitalized without governmental assistance. Seven other banks adjudged insolvent were absorbed by out-of-state interests and recapitalized with assistance from the FDIC. These included the First RepublicBank Corporation, the largest commercial banking institution in Texas, founded when RepublicBank Corporation merged with InterFirst Corporation, both in Dallas. First RepublicBank was absorbed by NCNB Texas National Bank with generous federal aid. It became the largest bank in the state, and a subsidiary of NCNB Corporation, headquartered in Charlotte, North Carolina.

Other failed institutions included MCorp, Texas American Bancshares, National Bancshares Corporation of Texas, BancTexas Group, and First City Bancorporation of Texas. The FDIC consolidated 20 MCorp banks into a branch banking system and sold them to Banc One Corporation of Columbus, Ohio. The institution is now Bank One, Texas (National Association), and second in size to NCNB Texas National Bank (renamed NationsBank of Texas, National Association, in January 1992). Texas American Bancshares (Fort Worth) became the Team Bank statewide branch system. In June 1990 the FDIC closed nine of the twelve subsidiary banks of National Bancshares Corporation of Texas and sold them to NCNB Texas National Bank as branches.

First City Bancorporation experienced financial problems by year-end 1986. In April 1988 the FDIC injected about $1 billion in "note capital" into the restructured bank holding company. This facilitated the raising of over $500 million of new equity by an investor group headed by A. Robert Abboud, who became board chairman and chief executive officer. The Abboud administration proved inefficient, and federal and state regulators closed First City and its twenty-bank system in October 1992.

Texas Commerce Bancshares was the first major statewide commercial bank in the late 1980s to seek acquisition by an out-of-state organization. Chief executive officer Ben F. Love earlier had pushed legislative changes in Texas to allow regional banks to operate across state boundaries within the Southwestern–Mountain State area. Because Love and his supporters thought the Texas economy could no longer be tied to the petroleum industry, they sought to remove state legal obstacles to external capital infusions.

Major Texas banks, with state banking-industry support, persuaded the governor to call the Texas legislature into special session in the summer of 1986. The legislature passed an interstate banking law and approved a public referendum in the November election to amend the state's constitution to permit limited branch banking. The interstate banking law took effect on January 1, 1987. Despite the depressed energy industry and collapsed commercial real estate markets in Texas, major out-of-state bank holding companies responded favorably. Texas Commerce Bancshares merged with Chemical New York Corporation (renamed Chemical Banking Corporation), and Allied Bancshares merged with First Interstate Bancorp, of Los Angeles. These combinations occurred before federal aid for distressed banks began. The first massive federal assistance bailed out the First RepublicBank Corporation in late July of 1988 and supported its merger with NCNB Corporation.

In sum, "statewide" banking giants in Texas tried to seek more efficient formats via branching systems authorized in late 1986; to secure intrastate mergers with holding company systems; and to attract external capital without losing control to outside interests.

The banking crisis in Texas in the 1980s was affected by problems in the savings and loan industry, which had grown rapidly and irresponsibly since the 1970s. Both industries suffered from inadequate federal regulation and supervision. Because of widespread fraud and incompetent management the S&L industry collapsed in Texas—and in the nation generally. Congress passed a law entitled the Financial Institutions Reform, Recovery and Enforcement Act of 1989, by which the government established the Resolution Trust Corporation to address S&L failures. Federal deregulation had played a crucial role in S&L operations in the early 1980s, particularly "thrift" institutions or savings associations. The Depository Institutions Deregulation and Monetary Control Act of 1980 was an effort to improve the efficiency of depository institutions by encouraging competition among institutions and pushing the phaseout of time-deposit interest-rate ceilings (completed in 1986). This legislation also increased the service powers of depository institutions, particularly thrift institutions, with relation to commercial banks. Further deregulation followed under the Garn–St. Germain Depository Institutions Act of 1982, which permitted thrifts to make nonresidential real estate loans up to

40 percent of their portfolio assets. Since S&Ls had been mostly residential mortgage lenders, they surprisingly expanded rapidly, substantially, and haphazardly into construction, real estate development, and other real estate lending—credit areas where commercial banks had been prominent since World War II. The thrifts mounted aggressive competition for deposits and exploited their new character and lending activities, thus prompting more competitive behavior within the commercial banking industry as well. The 1980 law produced a disincentive to fund management in federally insured depository institutions by increasing the insurance coverage in a single account from $40,000 to $100,000.

These statutory acts, plus other factors, caused a deterioration of bank-loan-portfolio quality, bank operating losses, and erosion of capital. These results occurred first in Texas and the Southwest, because the region entered a recession earlier than other parts of the nation. The 1980–82 deregulatory legislation occurred when the market environment was shifting from an inflationary to a disinflationary situation, a movement that most banks and financiers failed to perceive. Hence there was an overchartering of new banks in Texas during the first half of the 1980s, a development that compounded banking difficulties. Infrequent, lax, and limited governmental regulatory supervision hastened the excessive growth and unsound behavior in the banking world. Federal examination of bank supervision in Texas and the Southwest was limited. In fact, there were fewer examinations in the state than elsewhere in the nation. The federal lowering of S&L capital requirements in the early 1980s was indiscreet and poorly timed, and exacerbated other problems that brought down the S&L industry and magnified the collateral effects on commercial banking.

In the late 1980s federal bank authorities, spearheaded by the FDIC, made a strong effort to alter the control, management, and behavior of the major Texas banks. The economy began a slow, protracted recovery. Additional large banking consolidations and restructurings began. In late 1992 the Federal Reserve Board approved the merger of Team Bancshares into Banc One Corporation, the parent company of Bank One, Texas.

During the turbulent decade that began in the mid-1980s, the Texas commercial banking industry shrank significantly. The number of banks declined from 1,800 preponderantly small institutions at the end of 1985 to slightly over 1,100 still mainly small entities in 1992. There were approximately 470 failures, some of which led to mergers with sound banking firms. The decline also saw many conversions to branches. Fewer statewide organizations now existed. With the exception of Texas Commerce Banchares and First City–Texas, these organizations are large branch-banking networks owned by major out-of-state multibank holding-company organizations. In 1993 the approximately 2,500 commercial banking offices operating in Texas (1,100 banks plus more than 1,400 branch offices) varied in size, ownership, and control. As bank assets fell from $209 billion at the end of 1985 to around $170 billion at the end of 1991, Texas banks tightened their lending policies. Like their counterparts elsewhere in the nation, they began selling existing loans and other assets in secondary markets.

By the end of 1993 the Texas banking scene was definitely improving. Only ten banks failed during the year, the lowest since six failed in 1984. None of the state's sixty-three S&Ls failed—for the first year since 1985. Of the 433 state-chartered banks, fewer than 17 had problems. This was a far cry from the preceding decade, when more than 470 banks and 200 thrifts were closed in Texas.

BIBLIOGRAPHY: William Hubert Baughn, *Changes in the Structure of Texas Commercial Banking, 1946–1956*, Studies in Banking and Finance No. 2 (Austin: Bureau of Business Research, University of Texas, 1959). Avery Luvere Carlson, *A Monetary and Banking History of Texas* (Dallas: Texas Publication House, 1930). Lawrence L. Crum, *Transition in the Texas Commercial Banking Industry, 1956–1965*, Studies in Banking and Finance No. 9 (Bureau of Business Research, University of Texas at Austin, 1970). T. Harry Gatton, *Texas Bankers Association: First Century, 1885–1985* (Austin: Texas Bankers Association Historical Committee, 1984). Joseph M. Grant and Lawrence L. Crum, *Development of State Chartered Banking in Texas* (Austin: University of Texas Press, 1978). Hobart Key, Jr., and Max S. Lale, *Of Money...and Men* (Marshall, Texas: Port Caddo Press, 1965).

Lawrence L. Crum

BANNISTER, TEXAS. Bannister is at the intersection of a country road and State Highway 147 by Bannister Lake, thirteen miles southwest of San Augustine in southwestern San Augustine County. It grew up as a shipping point on the St. Louis Southwestern Railway in the 1890s and was granted a post office in 1914. In 1925 Bannister had fifty inhabitants, and in 1933 it had a business. The post office closed in 1925, the railroad was abandoned in the early 1930s, and by the 1940s Bannister was deserted, though the site was still marked as a triangulation point on state highway maps. *Mark Odintz*

BANQUETE, TEXAS. Banquete is at the intersection of State Highway 44 and Farm Road 666, nine miles south of San Patricio and seven miles west of Robstown in northwestern Nueces County. It was named for a four-day feast commemorating the completion of a road linking the Nueces River with the Rio Grande and San Patricio, Texas, with Matamoros, Tamaulipas. Banquete was also on the Texas-Mexican Railway. A post office was established there in 1859 with Mary Madray as postmistress. A one-room school was built in the 1870s and used until 1917, when the Maria, Schroeder, and Leona schools were consolidated with the Banquete school. In 1884–85 the population of Banquete was fifteen; it rose to seventy-five by 1936. A 1946 county map indicates a number of businesses, residences, churches, and a school. That year the population was 300. It reached 450 in 1972, and in 1990 it was 449.

BIBLIOGRAPHY: John J. Germann and Myron Janzen, *Texas Post Offices by County* (1986). Nueces County Historical Society, *History of Nueces County* (Austin: Jenkins, 1972). *Karen S. Parrish*

BANTA, WILLIAM (1827–?). William Banta, Indian fighter, Civil War[qv] soldier, and autobiographer, was born in Warrick County, Indiana, on June 23, 1827, the son of Isaac and Abiah Banta. The family immigrated to Texas in 1839 and settled briefly at Clarksville in Red River County. The following year they moved to Lamar County; they finally settled on Bullard Creek, not far from Bonham in Fannin County, where Isaac Banta was the county's first justice of the peace. In 1843 he sold his headright and moved to South Sulphur, where he assisted in organizing Hunt County. William Banta moved to Austin in 1849, then to Burnet, where he married Lucinda Hairston on March 4, 1850. They had fourteen children.

Banta organized and commanded the first company of minutemen in Burnet County and participated in nearly every engagement against Indians in the region throughout the 1850s. He saw service on the Texas frontier during the Civil War as lieutenant, then captain, of Company A of the Frontier Regiment.[qv] In the spring of 1864 he was stationed at Camp Davis in Gillespie County, where he attempted to enforce the law when a series of murders, robberies, and outrages perpetrated by bushwhackers, state troops of the Third Frontier District, and men of the Frontier Regiment, excited the populace of Gillespie and Kendall counties into a frenzy. Banta's participation in the arrest and execution of an outlaw in Gillespie County led to his arrest. He and six other men were incarcerated in Fredericksburg. Maj. James Hunter, commander of state troops of the Third Frontier District, wrote to Governor Pendleton Murrah[qv] and requested that he be allowed to send the men to prison in Austin or San Antonio. Shortly afterward, an armed group of more than 200 men rode into Fredericksburg and overcame the twelve-man guard stationed at the jail. They pushed their way into the stone jail and opened fire upon the prisoners, who were located in two small rooms separated by a hallway. They killed one of the prisoners instantly and critically wounded four others, two of whom died the next day. Banta survived the episode but was badly wounded in both legs. With J. W. Caldwell he wrote an account of his life in Texas, *Twenty-Seven Years on the Texas Frontier*, published in 1893.

BIBLIOGRAPHY: Amelia W. Williams and Eugene C. Barker, eds., *The Writings of Sam Houston, 1813–1863* (8 vols., Austin: University of Texas Press, 1938–43; rpt., Austin and New York: Pemberton Press, 1970). Dorman H. Winfrey and James M. Day, eds., *Texas Indian Papers* (4 vols., Austin: Texas State Library, 1959–61; rpt., 5 vols., Austin: Pemberton Press, 1966). *David Paul Smith*

BANTON, TRAVIS (1894–1958). Travis Banton, Hollywood costume designer known for the "Paramount Look," the son of Rennie B. and Maggie (Jones) Banton, was born at Waco, Texas, on August 18, 1894. When he was two the family moved to New York. Banton's parents later joined him in Hollywood. During his early years in New York his talents developed in art, theater, and custom fashion design. He served in the navy during World War I,[qv] enrolled at Columbia University to please his parents, and studied at the Art Students League and the New York School of Fine and Applied Art. He worked on his own as a dress designer and at the fashion house of Lucile. While he was an apprentice with Madame Francis (or Frances) his designs were selected by Mary Pickford for her wedding to Douglas Fairbanks. After designing for Norma Talmadge in the East Coast film *Poppy* (1917), he soon distinguished himself with costumes for the Ziegfeld Follies and other stage productions, an interest he resumed at the end of his life by dressing Rosalind Russell in the 1956 Broadway production of *Auntie Mame*. At the time of his death, Banton was designing for Dinah Shore's television show.

He won accolades for dressing some of the world's most popular and glamorous actresses during Hollywood's golden era. His best work was executed before the establishment in 1948 of the now-coveted Academy Award for costume design. In 1924 Walter Wanger brought Banton to Hollywood, where he was contracted by Paramount studios as an assistant to Howard Greer. Banton garnered instant acclaim for dressing star Leatrice Joy and mannequins in the style show for *The Dressmaker from Paris* (1925). As Paramount's chief designer between 1929 and 1938, followed by freelance film and TV work as part of his couture business, Banton dressed more than 160 films. He played a major role in creating images for movie greats Marlene Dietrich, Carole Lombard, Claudette Colbert, and Mae West. The essence of film-costume elegance appears in the visual classics of Dietrich vehicles such as *The Scarlet Empress* (1934) and *Angel* (1937). For the latter, Banton's staff labored weeks; one hand-sewn garment was a Fabergé-inspired gown of chiffon lavished with beading and bordered with Russian sable at a reported cost of $8,000.

Banton also designed for Tallulah Bankhead, Clara Bow, Kitty Carlisle, Ruth Chatterton, Kay Francis, Miriam Hopkins, Ida Lupino, Pola Negri (*see* CHALUPEC, BARBARA A.), Merle Oberon, Gail Patrick, Sylvia Sidney, Lilyan Tashman, and Florence A. Vidor.[qv] Of the films he dressed, many are recognized as classics—1927: *Wings;* 1928: *The Wild Party;* 1930: *Morocco;* 1931: *Dishonoured, Dr. Jekyll and Mr. Hyde;* 1932: *Shanghai Express, Blonde Venus, Night After Night, Trouble In Paradise, A Farewell to Arms, No Man of Her Own, The Sign of the Cross, Sinners In the Sun;* 1933: *Design for Living, I'm No Angel, Death Takes A Holiday, Bolero;* 1934: *We're Not Dressing, Rumba, Belle of the Nineties, Ruggles of Red Gap, The Gilded Lily;* 1935: *The Devil is A Woman, The Crusades, Goin' to Town, So Red the Rose, Anything Goes;* 1936: *Desire, My Man Godfrey, The Big Broadcast of 1937, Love Before Breakfast;* 1937: *Maid of Salem, I Met Him in Paris, Nothing Sacred;* 1938: *Made for Each Other, Fools for Scandal;* 1939: *Intermezzo, A Love Story;* 1941: *Charley's Aunt;* 1946: *Sister Kenny;* 1947: *Mourning Becomes Electra;* 1948: *Letters From An Unknown Woman;* and 1950: *Valentino.*

Praising Banton's inspiration, imagination, and intensity, distinguished designers have acknowledged his influence. Edith Head, former Banton assistant at Paramount who went on to win a record number of Oscars, declared: "He was a god there . . . nobody [would] dare oppose him about anything, including the budgets . . . Travis was a marvelous designer. Any talent I might have would have lain undiscovered if he hadn't lighted the way for me. In my opinion, he was the greatest." In explaining his adaptations of two Banton dresses, Norman Norell observed that Banton "has been underrated and that his talent surpassed Adrian's, since Banton's costumes were timeless and established many famous images, as with the Mae West look." Two decades after the designer's death, Cecil Beaton praised the *Angel* creations and judged Banton "one of the most important of the golden years of Hollywood."

Though Banton has been lauded through the years for the originality, fine workmanship, and understated elegance of his costumes, scholars have neglected his genius as an image maker, both on and off screen, for celebrated women such as Marlene Dietrich. Banton's ability paralleled Adrian's acknowledged role as creator of the Greta Garbo and Joan Crawford (Lucille Fay Leseur[qv]) image. Banton helped invent the Dietrich look along with a unique apparel style that included male attire, like the tuxedo in *Morocco* (1930), the leather flight suit in *Dishonored* (1931), and the military uniform in *The Scarlet Empress* (1934). On her arrival in Hollywood, Dietrich's new svelte and chic silhouette was engineered by Banton. This contrasted with her pudgy appearance as star of *The Blue Angel*, a 1930 landmark film produced by UFA in Germany. Often credited, however, for the Dietrich look are director Josef von Sternberg and, to a lesser extent, Marlene Dietrich's lighting director, cinematographer, and stills and portrait photographer. This evaluation has relegated Banton to the pages of glossy coffee-table books. Yet Banton acted like a sculptor of cloth and flesh, influencing Dietrich's regimen of weight loss, massage, and exercise. In addition he advised her on demeanor, attitude, and body presentation. Banton's sketch pad and valued counsel likewise transformed Carole Lombard into a new persona of taste and class, reminiscent of Parisian haute couture, a world that he admired and emulated in private life. For the Mae West image, he produced a shapelier and more sexually explicit silhouette with a touch of parody that has been labeled high camp. Though he preferred sophisticated modern dress, his skill in interpreting historical periods inspired such trend-setting consumer adaptations as Claudette Colbert's garb in *Cleopatra* (1934).

Paramount rewarded these Banton products with salary, publicity, a private domain of artisan workrooms, and a luxury office. Convinced of the commercial value of screen fashion, Adolph Zukor, a former furrier, demanded costume excellence and reveled in the Banton fashion gems. The highly charged position, however, proved bittersweet and gradually took a toll on Banton's life. One studio crisis requiring Zukor's negotiation focused on Claudette Colbert, a longtime Banton admirer, and the costuming for *Cleopatra*. After rejecting two sets of costume sketches, she streaked Banton's third set of beautifully painted drawings with blood deliberately drawn from her finger to emphasize her displeasure. Another conflict involved a fitting with an ungrateful Nancy Carroll, who slowly ripped an exquisitely crafted garment from her body while Banton and his staff stared in dismay. Frustration and wounded pride escalated with each clash of taste with executives and actresses who were prone to costuming that Banton judged tacky, gaudy, and vulgar. During his tenure at Twentieth Century-Fox (from 1939 to 1941), where he worked for Howard Greer, a feud began with Alice Faye, who resented Banton's references to Dietrich's good taste; Faye later acknowledged the successful costuming for *Lillian Russell* (1939). From 1945 to 1948 Banton worked as head stylist for Universal Studios. His erratic behavior involving absenteeism and alcohol shortened his life; in this he was not unlike other talented colleagues with emotional and alcohol-related problems, such as Orry-Kelly, Howard Greer, and Irene, who committed suicide at age sixty-one. Banton once quipped that he should have left movies when Adrian did in 1942. He agreed with fellow film and couture colleague Howard Greer that life amid all that world-famous glamour, luxury, and notoriety was not what it seemed and that he missed the theater, opera, ballet, shops, and cuisine of New York and Paris. Late in life he recalled that in Hollywood he had "*loathed* those endless barbecue things, deadly-dull afternoons spent staring at people wallowing in swimming pools . . . [in a place where] even the French champagne went flat as soon as it was poured." He admitted, however, to a certain ambivalence, for he needed the studio earnings that supplied the art, antiques, and extravagant lifestyle compatible with his tastes.

Throughout his troubled times women who were grateful for their metamorphosis remained loyal. Carole Lombard requested Banton's designs for her costumes at other studios, including her David O. Selznick pictures. Marlene Dietrich performed in the signature white top hat and tails until the end of her career. Merle Oberon summarized the feelings of this loyal following when she insisted that Banton dress her as George Sand in the 1945 film *A Song to Remember*. She explained that Banton "knew what the character ought to look like but also understood what an actress was happiest wearing, which is very rare for a costume designer. I never found it necessary to make a single change on any of his drawings." Banton died on February 2, 1958, in Los Angeles. He was buried on February 4 at the Little Church of the Flowers in Glendale, California. An extensive collection of Banton's drawings is housed in the Brooklyn Museum.

BIBLIOGRAPHY: W. Robert LaVine, *In a Glamorous Fashion: The Fabulous Years of Hollywood Costume Design* (New York: Scribner, 1980). Elizabeth Leese, *Costume Design in the Movies* (Bembridge, Isle of Wight: BCW, 1976). Los Angeles *Times*, February 3, 1958. Edward Maeder, ed., *Hollywood and History: Costume Design in Film* (London: Thames and Hudson, 1987). Vertical Files, Barker Texas History Center, University of Texas at Austin. *Raye Virginia Allen*

BAPACORA INDIANS. This poorly documented Indian group, evidently not the same as the Bacora Indians, was first recorded as living in northern Coahuila more or less due north of modern Monclova and not far from the Rio Grande. In some secondary sources, through clerical error, the names Bapacora and Pinanaca were combined to give the hybrid name, Bapacorapinanaca. The Bapacoras also seem to have ranged northward across the Rio Grande, for in 1693 Joseph Francisco Marn entered their name on a long list of Indian groups said to be living north of the Rio Grande in what is now western Texas. At that time, according to Marn, all of these groups were being threatened by Apaches. The most likely Texas location of the Bapacoras in 1693 would be in the Eagle Pass–Del Rio area. What language they spoke is not known.

BIBLIOGRAPHY: William B. Griffen, *Culture Change and Shifting Populations in Central Northern Mexico* (Tucson: University of Arizona Press, 1969). Charles W. Hackett, ed., *Historical Documents Relating to New Mexico, Nueva Vizcaya, and Approaches Thereto, to 1773* (3 vols., Washington: Carnegie Institution, 1923–37).

Thomas N. Campbell

BAPTIST CHURCH. Although the Catholic Church[qv] was the established religion of Texas until March 1834, by the summer of 1820 Joseph L. Bays,[qv] a North Carolinian Baptist reared in Kentucky and a friend of Moses Austin,[qv] was preaching regularly in Texas. He was arrested in 1823 and escaped en route to San Antonio to stand trial. About that same time Freeman Smalley,[qv] an Ohio Baptist minister, entered Texas and apparently preached at old Pecan Point, near the site of present Clarksville. In 1825 Thomas Hanks, a Tennessee parson, delivered the first Baptist sermon west of the Brazos River, near San Felipe. Thomas J. Pilgrim[qv] traveled from New York in 1828 and established the first Baptist Sunday school in Texas. Mexican officials suppressed the venture, but Pilgrim resumed his efforts and worked to propagate Baptist Sunday schools in Texas until his death in 1877.

The Mexican government gave Texas settlers religious freedom in 1834. The first Baptist church in Texas was organized in Illinois in July 1833 and moved to Texas as a body, called the Pilgrim Church of Predestinarian Regular Baptists, in January 1834. It was led by the antimissionary Daniel Parker.[qv] Providence Church, founded in March 1834 twelve miles south of Bastrop, was the first Baptist congregation actually formed in Texas. Under the leadership of Zachariah N. Morrell,[qv] a major figure among early Texas Baptists, another congregation emerged in November 1837 at Washington-on-the-Brazos. In May 1838 the Union, or Old North, Church was organized four miles north of Nacogdoches, and in 1839 the Plum Grove Church began just south of Bastrop.

A bitter controversy from the divergent views of Parker and Morrell plagued these early congregations. Parker, a "Primitive" or "Hardshell" Baptist, objected to organized mission societies, Sunday schools, Bible societies, and seminaries as both unscriptural and a threat to congregational independence. Morrell, by contrast, applauded the cooperative ventures of locally autonomous congregations. Though intensely aggressive in the 1830s and 1840s, antimissionary Baptists steadily lost ground to Morrell, whose heirs forged the Baptist General Convention of Texas in 1885, the largest Baptist body in Texas.

Texas Baptists have always been intensely evangelistic. Beginning in the 1840s they proselytized in the German communities of Central Texas. J. Frank Kiefer,[qv] a young German immigrant converted under the influence of Rufus C. Burleson,[qv] in turn made significant headway among the Germans in the 1860s.

Baptists educational and eleemosynary institutions have been important since the days of the Republic of Texas.[qv] William Milton Tryon and Robert E. B. Baylor[qqv] convinced the republic to charter Baylor University[qv] at Independence on February 1, 1845. The university was consolidated with Waco University in 1885 and moved to Waco. By 1860 Baptists operated at least a dozen colleges, most of them for women and many of brief duration; by the turn of the twentieth century Baptist colleges were in operation in Waco, Brownwood, Abilene, Jacksboro, Decatur, Rusk, Greenville, Waller, and Belton. Baylor Theological Seminary was begun in Waco in 1905 and moved to Fort Worth in 1910 to become the Southwestern Baptist Theological Seminary.[qv] It has since become the largest seminary in the world.

Robert Cooke Buckner[qv] opened the Buckner Orphans Home (*see* BUCKNER BAPTIST CHILDREN'S HOME) at Dallas with three children in December 1879. A century later the Buckner Baptist Benevolences[qv] operated major facilities in Dallas, Lubbock, Beaumont, Burnet, and San Antonio and provided an array of services, such as adoption, resident child and foster care, assistance for unwed mothers, in-home mother's aid, family counseling, and retirement and nursing care. Along with James B. Cranfill and George W. Truett,[qqv] Buckner also encouraged Baptists to build a hospital in Dallas; it opened in March 1904. Baptists in Houston established another in September 1907. Baptists currently provide medical care in Dallas, Beaumont, San Antonio, Abilene, Amarillo, Waco, and Harlingen.

On such specific social issues as racial discrimination and prohibition,[qv] Baptists have generally mirrored their environment. Texas was a slave state, and most Texas Baptists supported slavery[qv] and justified secession.[qv] After the Civil War,[qv] white churchgoers were divided over whether to allow blacks in their congregations. In 1866, after a heated discussion, the Colorado Association voted to keep black members, convinced they would succumb to error without "the superior intelligence of the whites." While whites debated, however, blacks resolved the matter by withdrawing en masse from white-controlled congregations. The first black Baptist church in Texas was organized at Galveston in 1865 with Israel S. Campbell[qv] as pastor. The next year the state's first black Baptist association was formed. By 1890 black Baptists totaled 111,138 statewide, and in 1916, 72 percent of the state's black churchgoers were Baptists.

Baptists enthusiastically endorsed the Anti-Saloon League[qv] when it came to Texas in 1907. The league's presidents from 1907 to 1918 were prominent Baptist leaders: Benjamin F. Riley, 1907–09; Joel H. Gambrell,[qv] 1910–15; and Arthur J. Barton, 1915–18. Involvement in the prohibition crusade led to broader social awareness. In 1908 the Baptist General Convention of Texas concluded that the saloon was "so interlaced . . . into commerce, politics, society, and the . . . law" that the organization challenged Baptists to become politically active and socially alert. Texas Baptists, contrary to some opinion, took part in the social gospel movement of the late nineteenth and early twentieth centuries. In 1915 the BGCT formed the Social Service Committee, which directed attention to conflicts between labor and capital, disputes between landowners and tenant farmers, and the need of prison and child-welfare reforms. The principal advocate of applied Christianity in these early years was Joseph Martin Dawson,[qv] longtime pastor of the First Baptist Church in Waco.

Though distracted in the 1920s by John Franklyn Norris,[qv] the flamboyant fundamentalist (*see* FUNDAMENTALISM) and pastor of the First Baptist Church in Fort Worth, socially concerned Baptists persevered, and in 1950 the BGCT formed the Christian Life Commission to attend to race relations, economic matters, family life, church and state relations, political involvement, and such public moral issues as alcoholism, gambling, and pornography. In 1961 the Mexican Baptist Convention of Texas and the BGCT were united.

When the Civil War began Baptists were a distant second to the Methodists. By 1906 the Baptist Church had become the largest church in Texas. In 1980 Baptists numbered approximately 4,500,000. The majority were Southern Baptists affiliated with the BGCT, whose membership totalled 2,600,000. The rest were divided among the American Baptist Association, American Baptist Churches of the U.S.A., the Baptist Missionary Association, the North American Baptist Conference, the Seventh Day Baptist General Conference, and various black conventions. In 1994, despite an ongoing intramural struggle between fundamentalists and progressivists, Baptists continued their numerical lead in the state.

BIBLIOGRAPHY: Robert A. Baker, *The Blossoming Desert—A Concise History of Texas Baptists* (Waco: Word, 1970). James Milton Carroll, *A History of Texas Baptists* (Dallas: Baptist Standard, 1923). Zane Allen Mason, *Frontiersmen of Faith: A History of Baptist Pioneer Work in Texas, 1865–1885* (San Antonio: Naylor, 1970). John W. Storey, *Texas Baptist Leadership and Social Christianity, 1900–1980* (College Station: Texas A&M University Press, 1986). *John W. Storey*

BAPTIST MISSIONARY ASSOCIATION THEOLOGICAL SEMINARY. The Baptist Missionary Association Theological Seminary, in Jacksonville, was established as the North American Theological Seminary in 1955 by the education committee of the North American Baptist Association. Ground was broken in 1956 on a seventeen-acre site given by J. M. Travis and William S. Gober. An administrative wing, a reading room, and five classrooms were completed for the opening, which took place on September 8, 1957. A charter class of fifty-seven students enrolled, and the chapel was dedicated in January 1958. Later additions to the campus included a bookstore, a student center, a music hall, a library, and student housing projects. The library contained 7,880 volumes in 1969. The seminary provided specialized training for Baptist pastors, evangelists, missionaries, ministers of education, and ministers of music. Degrees offered in 1966 were bachelor, master, and doctor of theology; bachelor of divinity; and bachelor, master, and doctor of religious education. Admission to degree programs required some college work, although certification and diploma courses in Christian training and music were open to all, regardless of academic background. In the late 1980s the institution's name was changed to Baptist Missionary Association Theological Seminary. During the 1990–91 regular term the school had a faculty of fourteen and an enrollment of seventy-three.

BAPTIST MISSIONARY AND EDUCATIONAL CONVENTION OF TEXAS. Black Baptists formed the Baptist Missionary and Educational Convention of Texas in 1871. As was typical of Baptist state organizations, the BME Convention promoted missionary and educational activity in the state. Because of the poverty of black Texans the BME depended for many years on assistance from the American Baptist Home Mission Society of New York to support its missionaries and conduct institutes to train its preachers. The ABHMS owned and operated Bishop College in Marshall (later Dallas), which it established to train black ministers. The BME Convention supported two schools of its own, Hearne Academy and Guadalupe College.[qqv] By 1890 the convention represented more than 110,000 black Baptists. In the 1890s a plan put forth by the ABHMS to consolidate black Baptist schools divided the BME Convention. The plan called for making Bishop College the flagship school for educating black Baptists in Texas and subordinating Hearne Academy and Guadalupe College to it. The proposal drew strong objections from several ministers, who argued that the plan would lead to the demise of Guadalupe College. They resented the idea that a black-administered college was being sacrificed to the white-operated ABHMS school. The BME Convention accepted the plan in 1892, and in 1893 the dissident ministers organized the General Baptist Convention. Later disputes further divided the BME Convention. In 1929 dissatisfaction over financial affairs led to the founding of the Texas Baptist Convention. In 1946 the Trinity Baptist State Convention was organized, and in 1981 the Central Baptist Convention was established.

BIBLIOGRAPHY: Alwyn Barr, *Black Texans: A History of Negroes in Texas, 1528–1971* (Austin: Jenkins, 1973). William Edward Montgomery, Negro Churches in the South, 1865–1915 (Ph.D. dissertation, University of Texas at Austin, 1975). *William E. Montgomery*

BAPTIST STANDARD. The *Baptist Standard,* a Baptist newspaper, began as the *Baptist News,* first published in Honey Grove, Texas, on December 6, 1888, as an alternative to the *Texas Baptist and Herald.*[qv] Rev. Lewis Holland was the editor and proprietor, and Rev. J. A. Boyet soon became joint editor and proprietor. The *Baptist News* circulated mainly in Fannin and adjoining counties. It was a four-page paper with five columns per page but was enlarged to seven columns in August 1889 and published every Thursday. On October 1, 1889, Holland bought Boyet's interest in the paper and moved it to Elm Street in Dallas. One of the reasons for this move was to increase the circulation to more counties. Another reason was that Dallas was the center of a conflict between Samuel A. Hayden,[qv] the editor of the *Texas Baptist and Herald,* and leading Baptists with whom Holland identified. Hayden was in dispute especially with R. T. Hanks, pastor of the First Baptist Church, Dallas.[qv] The controversy developed into personal attack, although a First Baptist Church committee found Hanks innocent of immorality but guilty of indiscretions. Twenty-four members withdrew from the congregation and formed another church, and Hayden gave aid and council to them. Hanks resigned as pastor in June 1889 and bought from Holland half interest in the *Baptist News* that same year. Holland remained as coeditor. Toward the end of 1889, when the format of the *Baptist News* became eight pages with five columns a page and its name was changed to *Western Baptist,* the newspaper's circulation was 3,000. It was enlarged to six columns a page on January 9, 1890. The subscription rate was $1.50 a year ($1.00 for active ministers). Holland bought back part of the paper in May 1891.

James B. Cranfill,[qv] superintendent of missions for the Baptist General Convention of Texas, wrote a regular column for the *Western Baptist* called " Dr. Cranfill's Paragraph." James M. Carroll and J. Frank Kiefer[qqv] also had articles in the paper. Hanks used his position at the paper to argue his defense in the Hayden-Hanks controversy, as he had in the *Baptist News.* Hayden, meanwhile, alienated his readers and friends, and the *Western Baptist* grew in circulation. Some thought that both papers should be bought to end the strife, but the price of the *Texas Baptist and Herald* was too high. As the problems with Hayden and the *Texas Baptist and Herald* grew steadily worse, Rev. M. V. Smith, pastor of the First Baptist Church in Belton, and Cranfill, then corresponding secretary of the Baptist General Convention of Texas, met and discussed the need for a Baptist paper in Texas that could be published as a "peace paper." With the finances of W. L. Williams, a deacon of the First Baptist Church in Dallas, Smith and Cranfill bought the *Western Baptist* for $3,000 on March 1, 1892. It had 6,000 subscribers. After February 25, 1892, the name of the paper was changed to *Texas Baptist Standard* and later shortened to *Baptist Standard.*

When Smith died in 1893, Cranfill became the sole proprietor of the paper. The *Standard* was published in Waco from 1894 until 1898, when it moved back to Dallas. After a bitter dispute with Hayden, Cranfill sold the *Standard* in 1904 to George W. Carroll,[qv] who in turn sold the paper to T. B. Butler. Joel H. Gambrell[qv] became the editor and served from 1904 until 1907. J. Frank Norris[qv] became the owner in 1907; Joseph M. Dawson[qv] was editor in 1907–08, and Norris was editor in 1908–09. In 1909 a group headed by George W. Truett[qv] of the First Baptist Church in Dallas bought the paper, and James B. Gambrell[qv] was made the editor. Gambrell and Truett transferred ownership of the *Baptist Standard* to the Baptist General Convention of Texas on March 19, 1914. The Baptist Standard Publishing Company, a nonprofit corporation, was organized to publish the paper as a subsidiary of the convention. The purpose of the publishing corporation was "to aid and support the Baptist General Convention of Texas and to interpret events and movements that affect the welfare of the people of God." In 1969 the Baptist Standard Publishing Company published a history of the *Baptist Standard* by Presnall H. Wood and Floyd W. Thatcher, entitled *Prophets With Pens.* Those serving as editor of the *Baptist Standard* from 1914, when the paper came under the ownership of the Baptist General Convention of Texas, were: E. C. Routh (1914–28), F. M. McConnell (1928–44), David M. Gardner (1944–54), E. S. James (1954–66), John J. Hurt (1966–77), and Presnall H. Wood (1977–95). In 1990, as the official weekly publication of the Baptist General Convention of Texas, the *Standard* distributed information, inspiration, and interpretation to 300,000 homes in Texas, other states, and many countries in the world.

BIBLIOGRAPHY: *Baptist Standard,* September 17, 1896, February 9, 1922. James Milton Carroll, *A History of Texas Baptists* (Dallas: Baptist Standard, 1923). Texas Baptist Historical Society, "Contributions of the *Baptist Standard* to Baptist Life, 1888–1988," *Texas Baptist History* 9 (1989). Presnall H. Wood, History of the *Texas Baptist Standard,* 1888–1959 (Ph.D. dissertation, Southwestern Baptist Theological Seminary, 1964).

Samuel B. Hesler and Presnall H. Wood

BARADO, TEXAS. Barado was located eight miles southeast of Huntsville on what is now Farm Road 2296. The village served the region surrounding Kelly's Switch on the Great Northern Railroad. The switch was located a mile north of the present intersection of Farm Road 2296 and U.S. Highway 75 and served the sawmill operated nearby by John F. Kelly, Jr., and Hervey Kelly. Barado was established in 1893 and had a population of fifteen in 1896. At one time the community had a store and a school. The post office was in operation from 1892 until 1912. In later years a boiler explosion at the mill killed John Kelly, and the mill was closed. By the 1930s nothing remained in the area except the ruins of the old mill.

BIBLIOGRAPHY: Walker County Genealogical Society and Walker County Historical Commission, *Walker County* (Dallas, 1986).

James L. Hailey

BARBAROSA, TEXAS. Barbarosa (Barbarossa) is ten miles north of Seguin on Farm Road 758 and Alligator Creek in northwestern Guadalupe County. The area was settled soon after the Civil War[qv] by German immigrants and was probably named in honor of Holy Roman Emperor Frederick Barbarossa. A post office opened at Barbarosa on July 6, 1900, but closed on October 15 of the same year. The population was thirty in 1933 and rose to seventy-five by 1941. During World War II[qv] an auxiliary airfield established in the vicinity was called Barbarosa Air Field. Two businesses and several houses appeared on the 1946 county highway map. In 1990 twenty-five residents were reported. *Willie Mae Weinert*

BARBED WIRE. By the 1870s westward expansion of the agricultural frontier across the Great Plains had been halted by the lack of adequate fencing material to protect crops from cattle. Texas substitutes for the stone and wood fences common in the East included ditches, mud fences, and thorny hedges, the most popular being those of Osage orange or bois d'arc. Bois d'arc is native to Texas and Arkansas, and export of its seed was an early enterprise in Texas. Hedges of it were claimed to be "pig tight, horse high, and bull strong." Experiments with varieties of thorn hedges and smooth wire failed to solve the problems of plains ranchers and farmers, however, and so their features were combined into barbed wire fences.

On November 24, 1874, Joseph F. Glidden of DeKalb, Illinois, was granted a patent for fencing material consisting of barbs wrapped around a single strand of wire and held in place by twisting that strand around another. Known as the "Winner," this was the most commercially successful of the hundreds of eventual barbed wire designs. Another DeKalb inventor, Jacob Haish, who had applied for a patent on a similar "S barb" design earlier in 1874, undertook a protracted legal battle that failed to halt the progress of the Glidden design. In partnership with Isaac L. Ellwood,[qv] Glidden sold his interests, which included other barbed wire patents, to the Massachusetts wire manufacturer Washburn and Moen in May 1876. Ellwood remained an active partner in the new organization as sole agent and distributor for the South and West. Washburn and Moen, eventually absorbed by United States Steel Corporation, had acquired all major barbed wire patents, except that of Haish, by 1876, thus achieving a near-monopoly on this important product.

Henry Bradley Sanborn[qv] traveled to Texas in 1875 as representative of Glidden and Ellwood's Barbed Fence Company. Though he sold the first barbed wire in the state, he failed to exploit the large potential market. In 1878 John Warne (Bet-a-Million) Gates[qv] conducted a famous demonstration on the Military Plaza in San Antonio in which a fence of Glidden's "Winner" wire restrained a herd of longhorn cattle.[qv] Gates reportedly touted his product as "light as air, stronger than whiskey, and cheap as dirt." Sales grew quickly thereafter, and barbed wire permanently changed land uses and land values in Texas.

Charles Goodnight,[qv] a pioneer of the open plains, fenced along the Palo Duro Canyon,[qv] accepting the need for clear title to grazing rights and hence the eventual end of the open range. Enclosure of the open range upon which the early cattle industry had been based resulted in the fence-cutting[qv] conflicts of the early 1880s. More controlled livestock breeding was made possible by the enclosure of herds, thus virtually eliminating the demand for the longhorn cattle, which were most suited to the open range. The wire simultaneously contributed to the end of the long cattle drives and Indian raids. Barbed wire, still an essential tool in the livestock industry, is today a popular collector's item. The official depository of the papers of the Texas Barbed Wire Collectors Association is the Panhandle-Plains Historical Museum[qv] in Canyon.

BIBLIOGRAPHY: Robert T. Clifton, *Barbs, Prongs, Points, Prickers, and Stickers* (Norman: University of Oklahoma Press, 1970). Henry D. and Frances T. McCallum, *The Wire That Fenced the West* (Norman: University of Oklahoma Press, 1965). Walter Prescott Webb, *The Great Plains* (Boston: Ginn, 1931).

Frances T. McCallum and James Mulkey Owens

BARBER, AMOS (1814–1885). Amos Barber, first settler of Mont Bellview (now Mont Belvieu), Texas, the son of Samuel and Elizabeth (Barrow) Barber, was born on November 26, 1814, probably in St. Landry Parish, Louisiana. The family moved to Texas between 1829 and 1831 and settled five miles north of the site of present Mont Belvieu on the banks of the Old River. Amos Barber was a rancher and cattleman who started out as early as 1841 with sixty-five head of cattle and increased his holdings moderately. He had eight slaves working his lands by the time the Civil War[qv] ended. Like most of his contemporaries, he suffered severe financial reverses from the war and never recovered the prosperity he had enjoyed. Barber was married to Susan Ann (Hodges) Fitzgerald, an eighteen-year-old widow, in 1848 on the Old River. They had ten children and also raised Susan's two Fitzgerald children. In 1849 Barber built the first home on "the hill" a double-pen, dog-trot log house. The homesite was purchased by the Mont Belvieu Church of Christ in 1974. Amos and Susan Barber donated four acres of land to the Methodist congregation in 1878. Although Amos never joined the church, his wife was a lifelong Methodist. Barber was also instrumental in establishing a public school at Barbers Hill in 1877. He died on October 1, 1885, at his home and is buried in the Barber Family Cemetery, Mont Belvieu.

BIBLIOGRAPHY: Jewel Horace Harry, A History of Chambers County (M.A. thesis, University of Texas, 1940; rpt., Dallas: Taylor, 1981).

Kevin Ladd

BARBER MOUNTAIN. Barber Mountain is four miles southwest of Mineral Wells in east central Palo Pinto County (at 32°46′ N, 98°12′ W). With its elevation of 1,097 feet above sea level, it rises 226 feet above nearby Farm Road 1195. The surrounding rolling hills are surfaced by clayey and sandy loam that support scrub brush, mesquite, cacti, and grasses. Barber Mountain was named for George Barber, who settled in the area between 1850 and 1857.

BARBERS HILL OILFIELD. The Barbers Hill oilfield is located in northwestern Chambers County at the junction of State Highway 146 and Farm Road 1942, near Mont Belvieu, approximately thirty miles northeast of Houston. The field was discovered in April 1916 and named for Barbers Hill, a salt dome named in turn for an early settler, Amos Barber.[qv] A water well in the Barbers Hill region had shown traces of natural gas as early as 1889, and serious efforts to find oil were made following the discovery of the Spindletop oilfield[qv] in 1901. After some twenty-eight failures, drillers completed a small well at a depth of 1,571 feet in 1916. Although commercial production began two years later, development remained slow until the latter 1920s, when vast quantities of oil were found at greater depths. In 1930 the first well to produce from below the salt dome on the Gulf Coast was brought in at Barbers Hill, at below 5,000 feet.

Peak annual production came in 1931, when 8,085,278 barrels was recovered at Barbers Hill. In 1951 production still stood at more than two million barrels annually, and the cumulative total exceeded ninety-five million barrels. By 1974 oil had been discovered at deeper than 10,000 feet below the surface at Barbers Hill. The total output reached nearly 130 million barrels by the end of 1984. Large quantities of natural gas have also been recovered from the field.

In addition to yielding oil and natural gas, the field has in more recent years served as an underground storage facility. Man-made caverns have been carved from the huge salt dome to store liquid propane gas for the area's numerous refineries. On November 5, 1985, an explosion killed two workers and threatened Mont Belvieu, thus redoubling efforts of local residents to force the petrochemical industries to buy out homes in the immediate vicinity so residents can move elsewhere.

BIBLIOGRAPHY: Jewel Horace Harry, A History of Chambers County (M.A. thesis, University of Texas, 1940; rpt., Dallas: Taylor, 1981).

Robert Wooster

BARBIER, GABRIEL MINIME, SIEUR (?–1689). Gabriel Minime, Sieur Barbier, early explorer, was probably born in Canada. He accompanied René Robert Cavelier, Sieur de La Salle,[qv] on his trip down the Mississippi River in 1682. He was commissioned lieutenant for La Salle's 1684 voyage to the Gulf of Mexico. The party landed in Texas in February 1685 aboard the *Joly*. Barbier accompanied La Salle on his first expedition west of Fort St. Louis[qv] but was lamed on the journey and was unable to take part in later extended trips. He is believed to be the first European married in Texas, being married in June 1686 by Henri Joutel[qv] to a young woman who also had come on the expedition. Joutel had at first opposed the marriage, but relented believing "they might have anticipated upon matrimony." A child born to the couple in 1688 was the first white child known to have been born in Texas. In March 1686 Barbier and others were sent to find the bark *Belle* but were unsuccessful. In January 1687 he was left in charge of Fort St. Louis when La Salle left in an attempt to reach the Mississippi. Barbier was killed when the fort was destroyed by Karankawa Indians in 1689. One report states that his wife and three-month-old child were initially saved from the massacre at Fort St. Louis by Indian women but were later killed by warriors upon return to their village.

BIBLIOGRAPHY: Carlos E. Castañeda, *Our Catholic Heritage in Texas* (7 vols., Austin: Von Boeckmann–Jones, 1936–1958; rpt., New York: Arno, 1976). Charles W. Hackett, ed., *Pichardo's Treatise on the Limits of Louisiana and Texas* (4 vols., Austin: University of Texas Press, 1931–46). Henri Joutel, *Joutel's Journal of La Salle's Last Voyage* (London: Lintot, 1719; rpt., New York: Franklin, 1968). Robert S. Weddle et al., eds., *La Salle, the Mississippi, and the Gulf: Three Primary Documents* (College Station: Texas A&M University Press, 1987).

John G. Johnson

BARBIER INFANT. In the fall of 1688 a child was born to Gabriel Minime, Sieur de Barbier,[qv] and his wife in the Texas colony founded almost four years previously by René Robert Cavelier, Sieur de La Salle.[qv] This infant, of whom neither the given name nor the sex is known, was the first child of record born in Texas of European parents and the offspring of the first recorded European marriage there. Like Virginia Dare of the Roanoke colony, the first English child born in America, the infant Barbier suffered an early and cruel fate. Three months old when Karankawa Indians destroyed the French settlement of Fort Saint-Louis, the infant and its mother, like the Talon children, were spared by the native women and taken to their village. When the Indian men returned from the massacre, however, they first killed Madame Barbier, then her babe, "which one of them dashed against a tree while holding it by a foot."

BIBLIOGRAPHY: Robert S. Weddle, "La Salle's Survivors," *Southwestern Historical Quarterly* 75 (April 1972). Robert S. Weddle et al., eds., *La Salle, the Mississippi, and the Gulf: Three Primary Documents* (College Station: Texas A&M University Press, 1987).

Robert S. Weddle

BARBONE CREEK. Barbone Creek begins nine miles northwest of Sandia in northern Jim Wells County (at 28°03′ N, 98°02′ W) and runs east for nine miles to its mouth on Lake Corpus Christi, six miles northwest of Sandia (28°03′ N, 97°55′ W). It traverses flat terrain with local shallow depressions, surfaced by clayey and sandy loams that support water-tolerant hardwoods, conifers, mesquite, grasses, and some cacti.

BARCLAY, JAMES (1816–1871). James Barclay, legislator, county official, and Indian agent, was born in Tennessee on February 11, 1816, the son of Walter and Elizabeth (McQueen) Barclay. In 1826 he came to Texas with his father and brother, but they all returned to Tennessee the same year. In February 1836 the family settled permanently in Texas. On April 16, 1841, Barclay married Virginia Ann Foster; they eventually had twelve children. Barclay was one of the earliest settlers in what is now Tyler County. In 1852 he bought land in the John Wheat survey that included a village of the Alabama Indians. These Indians had begun moving southward about 1840 from their Fenced-In Village[qv] in northwestern Tyler County to a location on Cypress Creek. The Alabamas referred to this village as Jim Barclay Village[qv] and continued to live there after 1852 with Barclay's permission.

After the organization of Tyler County in 1846, Barclay served in many of the county's elective positions. He was elected the first tax assessor-collector; in 1850 he was elected sheriff; and he was the county's chief justice during terms that began in 1856 and 1858. On February 3, 1854, Barclay and Samuel Rowe were appointed commissioners to purchase a tract of land for an Alabama Indian reservation in Polk County. This land is now a part of the Alabama-Coushatta Indian Reservation. On May 12, 1858, Governor H. R. Runnels[qv] appointed Barclay agent for the Alabama, Coushatta, and Pakana Muskogee Indians. From November 7, 1859, to February 13, 1860, he served as the Tyler County representative in the Texas legislature. He returned to the legislature in December 1863 to represent Tyler and Hardin counties and served on several legislative committees, including Indian Affairs. During the administration of Governor Pendleton Murrah,[qv] Barclay served a second term as agent for the Polk County Indians, from November 9, 1864, until he was replaced on August 29, 1865, by A. J. Harrison, an appointee of provisional governor A. J. Hamilton.[qv]

Barclay continued to operate his large plantation and to participate in civic affairs until his death at his Tyler County home on November 14, 1871. He was buried in the Hart Cemetery, three miles south of Woodville.

BIBLIOGRAPHY: *Members of the Legislature of the State of Texas from 1846 to 1939* (Austin: Texas Legislature, 1939). J. E. and Josiah Wheat, "The Early Days of Tyler County," *Tyler County Dogwood Festival Program*, 1963. James E. and Josiah Wheat, "Tyler County and the Texas Republic," *Tyler County Dogwood Festival Program*, 1967. Dorman H. Winfrey and James M. Day, eds., *Texas Indian Papers* (4 vols., Austin: Texas State Library, 1959–61; rpt., 5 vols., Austin: Pemberton Press, 1966).

Howard N. Martin

BARCLAY, WILLIAM ANDERSON (1849–1927). William Anderson Barclay was born on December 23, 1849, in Woodville, Texas, the son of Jeremiah Todd and Elizabeth Anne (Rigsby) Barclay. After his father's death and his mother's remarriage, he was reared by his uncle, James Barclay.[qv] He left home at the age of sixteen and went to Cameron, where he worked as a store clerk. He married Martha King Ledbetter on February 14, 1871. Shortly afterward he was made a deputy sheriff of Milam County. He continued to work in the store. At night he delivered papers from one county seat to another and was paid fifty dollars a night because of danger from Indians. He also clerked in a Rockdale store before purchasing a mercantile business at Yarrellton in 1873. In 1875 he sold his store and entered the cattle business with his wife's brother-in-law, William Sewell Goodhue Wilson, of Belle Bayou. The Wilson-Barclay cattle were branded with "28" and the Barclay cattle with the brand reversed, "82." Headquarters were established on Little Pond Creek in what is now Falls County. In 1876 Barclay opened a store in Hico, and in 1878 he opened another store near his homestead between Cameron and Waco. His plantation, Crenshaw, eventually comprised 6,000 acres.

Barclay established the first plow factory in Texas and the first cottonseed oil mill in the state; he had invented his own formula for extracting the oil (*see* COTTONSEED INDUSTRY). He also helped to establish railroads, banks, lumberyards, furniture stores, and general stores. He was president of the Mexican-American Smelting and Refining Company and owned private mines in Mexico. He invented a method of rewashing slag that proved to be extremely profitable. His Mexican mining ventures stopped abruptly when Porfirio Díaz was overthrown. He then turned to copper mines in Arizona and an apple orchard in Oregon. As he grew older he gradually converted his holdings into stocks and bonds. Although he had little formal education, Barclay was an inveterate reader, particularly of Texas history. He died on October 24, 1927, and was buried in Temple.

BIBLIOGRAPHY: Lillian S. St. Romain, *Western Falls County, Texas* (Austin: Texas State Historical Association, 1951).

Margaret Barclay Megarity

BARCLAY, TEXAS. Barclay, on State Highway 53 nineteen miles southwest of Marlin in southwestern Falls County, was named for William Anderson Barclay,[qv] a pioneer resident of Central Texas who, in partnership with his brother-in-law, W. S. G. Wilson, established the Barclay Ranch in the adjoining corners of Bell, Falls, and Milam counties. From 1895 to 1898 Barclay cleared and farmed 3,500 acres. The present site of Barclay was the location of a general mercantile store that he established in 1877 or 1878. Barclay also became postmaster of the community's post office when it opened in 1881. The post office was discontinued in 1906, and mail was routed through Rosebud and Lott. In 1881 pioneer Lyddleton Smith of Washington County assigned three acres of land for a Baptist church. The congregation became known as Beulah (later Barclay) Baptist Church. Part of the property was set aside for a burial ground. Confederate veteran Paul Pieper, Sr., who moved his family to Barclay in 1882, donated part of his acreage for a cemetery in 1886 and set aside plots for Pieper family members. Paul Pieper, Jr., deeded his inherited hay land to the cemetery at his death in 1926. The graveyard has been maintained by the Barclay Cemetery Association since 1915. On April 8, 1984, Barclay Cemetery received a Texas historical marker in a special ceremony in Barclay. A Barclay school district was organized in 1882, when Paul and Katherine Wendel Pieper deeded land for the school. School trustees in 1889 were A. J. Murray, J. F. Knox, and H. Ernst. The teachers were J. F. O'Shea and A. M. Kolb; they each received fifty dollars a month for three months' teaching. Fifty-five students were attending classes in 1889. Local population was reported at fifty by 1890 and at 100 by 1896. The community also had a livestock farm and a cotton gin and gristmill.

About 1910 Barclay had a general store, a drugstore, a doctor's office, a Woodman of the World hall, a Baptist church, a school, a public cemetery, a cotton gin, a butcher shop, a blacksmith shop, a corn mill, a molasses mill, and a water system. By 1933 the number of businesses had fallen to three, and the population was reported at sixty-six. A Red Cross Society was organized in 1917 as an auxiliary to the Marlin chapter. During its early years the Barclay community hosted the first Corn Club (later known as the 4-H Club) in Falls County. The Texas Farmers Union posted a chapter in Barclay before 1920.

After the Great Depression[qv] the people of Barclay voted a bond for materials for a new school with four classrooms, a gymnasium, and a duplex for the teachers. The construction provided jobs for thirty to forty people, and the labor cost was furnished by the Work Projects Administration.[qv] After consolidation of the school with the Rosebud-Lott Independent School District, the building became the community center. A citizens' organization elects officers each year and conducts major repairs. Barclay Community Center is the site of numerous reunions, meetings, volleyball games, and domino parties. In spring of 1982, with the help of the Falls County extension agent, Barclay initiated the Barclay Beautification Committee to improve the area. The community received special recognition for two years from the Beautify Texas Council during its annual Governor's Community Achievement Awards contest. Barclay's population was seventy-five in 1945 and 100 in 1949, when it also reported five businesses. The population rose to 151 by 1964. It was 125 by 1970 and seventy-two by 1972. In 1990 the population was still reported at seventy-two.

BIBLIOGRAPHY: Roy Eddins, ed., and Old Settlers and Veterans Association of Falls County, comp., *History of Falls County, Texas* (Marlin, Texas?, 1947). Lillian S. St. Romain, *Western Falls County, Texas* (Austin: Texas State Historical Association, 1951). *Doris Voltin*

BARCUS, JOHN M. (1860–1928). John M. Barcus, Methodist minister, the son of Edward Rosman and Mary Frances (Smith) Barcus, was born in Tulip, Dallas County, Arkansas, on December 23, 1860. In 1874 his father, an itinerant Methodist minister, transferred to the Northwest Texas Conference, and the family settled on a farm ten miles from Waco. Barcus was licensed to preach at the Bruceville Camp Meeting in McLennan County in 1880, and in 1882 he was admitted to the Northwest Texas Conference. In the latter year he received the first M.A. degree granted by Southwestern University. Barcus married Mary T. McCrary in Belton on November 5, 1885, and the couple became the parents of eight children. Barcus held many pastorates in Texas. He was secretary of the Central Texas Conference for twenty-one years and was elected to the General Conference six times. For twelve years he was a member of the General Board of the Epworth League.[qv] He was secretary of the Committee of Appeals for the church from 1910 to 1922, a member of the publications board of the Texas Christian Advocate, and a trustee of Southwestern University for thirty-two years. In 1911–12 he served as president of Alexander Collegiate Institute (now Lon Morris College). In 1893 the Northwest Texas Conference passed a resolution drafted by Barcus and two other ministers denouncing the holiness movement and urging clerics to withhold their support. Barcus wrote on religious subjects and published several articles in the Texas Methodist Historical Quarterly. In 1905 Southwestern University awarded him an honorary doctor of divinity degree. He was a Democrat, a Mason, and a Rotarian. He died of spinal meningitis on June 12, 1928, and was buried in Greenwood Cemetery in Fort Worth. Seven children survived him.

BIBLIOGRAPHY: John M. Barcus, "A Trip through the Panhandle in 1887," *Texas Methodist Historical Quarterly* 1 (April 1909). Dallas *Morning News,* June 13, 1928. Methodist Episcopal Church, South, *Journal of the Central Texas Conference,* 1928. Walter N. Vernon et al., *The Methodist Excitement in Texas* (Dallas: Texas United Methodist Historical Society, 1984). *Who Was Who in America,* Vol. 2.
Mary M. Standifer

BARD, JOHN PETER (1846–1920). John Peter (Pierre, Padre Pedro) Bard, a priest of the San Diego parish and mission churches in the Catholic Diocese of Corpus Christi,[qv] was born on the island of Martinique in 1846. He was educated in France and became the head of a private school for French boys. He had been seriously ill as a baby, and his mother had promised to offer him to the church if God spared his life. In 1866 he and four parents chaperoned a group of his students on a tour of the Caribbean Sea and the Gulf of Mexico. The natural beauty of the port of Corpus Christi so entranced Pierre that he determined to return as a priest, though he had had no desire to become a priest until that time. Upon his return to France, he began study for the priesthood.

Bard returned to Texas in 1876 and remained in Galveston for several months studying English, German, and Spanish, since he spoke only French. He was ordained at the age of thirty by Bishop Dominic Manucy[qv] of Brownsville, then returned to Corpus Christi and was sent to assist Father Claude C. Jaillet[qv] with his visitation. Bard arrived in San Diego, Texas, on April 14, 1877.

The San Diego parish and mission area consisted of 200 ranches and missions spread from the Nueces River southward 100 miles, and from Banquete westward sixty miles. The area included a Spanish-speaking population of 5,000 to 6,000, about a dozen English-speaking families, and several immigrant German families. Bard's English, French, German, and Spanish library books were frequently used. On his visitations he usually rode in a buggy pulled by two horses. Comanche Indians and American and Mexican outlaws were a danger, and parishioners insisted that Father Bard carry a gun in his buggy with his polyglot Bibles. Though he knew how to use a gun, he accidently killed one of his horses in 1883 and thereafter rode unarmed.

Bard built chapels at Concepción in 1879 and at Collins in 1885; he helped build the chapel at Falfurrias in 1903. The chapel at Collins was moved to Alice in 1889. In 1884 Father Jaillet was sent to Corpus Christi, and Bard was the only priest in San Diego until 1911. He served as the master of ceremonies at the dedication of St. Francis de Paula Church in San Diego on April 18, 1909. Soon after the church was dedicated, he built an underground adobe[qv] vault for the safekeeping of church papers, Communion wine, books, and other valuables. Bard died of influenza on March 4, 1920, and was buried in his vault in the churchyard. When St. Francis de Paula Church was enlarged in 1933, his remains were buried under the floor of the vestibule, and an inscription in Spanish was placed over his grave.

BIBLIOGRAPHY: Sister Mary Xavier Holworthy Papers, Chancery, Catholic Diocese of Corpus Christi. *Agnes G. Grimm*

BARDWELL, TEXAS. Bardwell is on Farm Road 984 and State Highway 34 just west of Bardwell Lake and ten miles southeast of Waxahachie in southeastern Ellis County. The community developed in the early 1880s when John W. Bardwell built a cotton gin a mile southwest of the present townsite. Bethany school and cemetery, a mile south of present Bardwell, also served the new community as a place of worship until Bardwell's first school was built in 1892 and a Baptist church was organized the following year. Residents also established a Methodist church and opened a post office branch in 1893. When the Trinity and Brazos Valley Railway was routed through the county in 1907, the gin was moved to the nearest stretch of track. The community followed, and a townsite was surveyed. Due to its location in an outstanding cotton producing area, Bardwell prospered through the 1920s. Besides its three cotton gins, the town had two banks, six grocery stores, four dry goods stores, a gristmill, a lumberyard, and a weekly newspaper, the *Herald.* By 1914 Bardwell had its own telephone system and electric power supplied by new lines from Ennis. Residents built an open-air tabernacle to shelter political meetings, revivals, traveling Chautauquas, and popular summer singing programs. In 1929 the population reached a high of 650, served by more than twenty-five businesses. The Great Depression[qv] and drought drained Bardwell's economy in the 1930s, and when the main road was rerouted to the new State Highway 34 in the early 1940s, most of the businesses either closed or moved to the highway. In 1958 the Bardwell school was consolidated with the Ennis schools. In 1972 Bardwell had 277 residents, two gins, three churches, and a handful of small businesses. The population in 1988 was 348; in 1990 it was 387.

BIBLIOGRAPHY: Edna Davis Hawkins et al., *History of Ellis County, Texas* (Waco: Texian Press, 1972). *David Minor*

BARDWELL RESERVOIR. Bardwell Reservoir, also known as Bardwell Lake, is located in the Trinity River basin between Bardwell and Ennis in south central Ellis County (at 32°15′ N, 96°37′ W), a mile south of U.S. Highway 287. The dam on Waxahachie Creek was authorized by the Flood Control Act of 1960 and constructed between 1963 and 1965 by the United States Army Corps of Engineers, Fort Worth District. The reservoir is owned by the United States government and operated by the Trinity River Authority.[qv] Bardwell Reservoir has a total capacity of 140,000 acre-feet at the top of flood-control storage, including 53,550 acre-feet of conservation storage, 1,320 acre-feet of dead storage, and 85,130 acre-feet allocated to flood control. The top of conservation storage is at an elevation of 421 feet above mean sea level, where the surface area is 3,570 acres. The drainage area above the dam is 176 square miles. Water from Bardwell Reservoir supplies Waxahachie, Ennis, and other surrounding communities.

BIBLIOGRAPHY: C. L. Dowell, *Dams and Reservoirs in Texas: History and Descriptive Information* (Texas Water Commission Bulletin 6408 [Austin, 1964]).

BARE BUTTE. Bare Butte is located in the KMA oilfield, three miles southeast of Iowa Park and just south of the Wichita River in southeastern Wichita County (at 33°53′ N, 98°38′ W). The mesa was probably named by a county settler who arrived in the area in the 1850s. The name has no relation to the topography of the summit, for the hill is covered with a thick growth of grass. The elevation of Bare Butte is 1,070 feet.

BARILLOS CREEK. Barillos Creek rises eleven miles south of Fort Davis in southern Jeff Davis County (at 30°26′ N, 103°51′ W) and runs northeast for ten miles to its mouth on Musquiz Creek, a half mile north of Farm Road 1837 and twelve miles southeast of Fort Davis (at 30°29′ N, 103°45′ W). It traverses rugged terrain surfaced by shallow, stony soils that support Mexican buckeye, walnut, persimmon, desert willow, scrub brush, and sparse grasses. Mitre Peak Girl Scout Camp is on the creek four miles from its mouth. The name of the creek is possibly from *barrillo*, from *barro*, Spanish for "clay."

BARKER, ELLIOTT SPEER (1886–1988). Elliott Speer Barker, conservationist, author, and the "father" of Smokey Bear, was born in Moran, Texas, on December 25, 1886, the son of Squire L. and Priscilla (McGuire) Barker. When he was three years old the family moved to the Sangre de Cristo Mountains in New Mexico for his asthmatic mother's health. When he was thirteen his mother moved to Las Vegas, New Mexico, from the family ranch near Sapello so that he and those of his ten siblings who were of school age could attend school there. He finished high school in three years and graduated in 1905, then took a six-month course at a college of photography in Effingham, Illinois. He worked briefly with his brother-in-law, a photographer, in Texico, New Mexico.

Barker worked as a professional guide and hunter near Las Vegas for two years before passing the United States Forest Service ranger examination in April 1908. He worked as an assistant forest ranger in the Jemez National Forest in Cuba, New Mexico, in 1909. In November of that year he was transferred to the Pecos National Forest in Pecos, New Mexico, and promoted to ranger. In November 1912 he was transferred to the Carson National Forest near Tres Piedras, New Mexico, where he worked under the famous American conservationist Aldo Leopold. In the fall of 1914 Barker was promoted to deputy forest supervisor and moved to Taos, New Mexico. He spent a year as acting supervisor, then transferred to the Coconino National Forest in Arizona as forest supervisor.

During World War I[qv] he was a first lieutenant in the National Guard, a deputy United States marshal, and the chairman of the Taos County Red Cross. He almost died during the flu epidemic in 1917. He resigned in April 1919 and acquired 640 acres, including the old family homestead, near Las Vegas. He ranched from 1919 to 1930 and worked as a guide for deer and cougar hunts. Barker went broke at the onset of the Great Depression[qv] and sold out. In April 1930 he went to work for Harry Chandler, the publisher of the Los Angeles *Times-Mirror,* as wildlife and predator-control manager at Chandler's Vermejo Park Ranch. A year later, however, Barker was appointed state game warden and director of the New Mexico Department of Game and Fish. He held that position until 1953, when he retired to devote himself full-time to writing.

His first book, *When the Dogs Bark "Treed": A Year on the Trail of the Longtails,* was published in 1946. His other books included *Beatty's Cabin: Adventures in the Pecos High Country* (1953), *Ramblings in the Field of Conservation* and *Eighty Years with Rod and Rifle* (both 1976), and *Smokey Bear and the Great Wilderness* (1982). Barker also published two books of poetry, *A Medley of Wilderness and Other Poems* (1962) and *Outdoors, Faith, Fun and Other Poems* (1968). His best-known book was *Western Life and Adventures, 1889–1970,* originally published in 1970 and reprinted in 1974 as *Western Life and Adventures in the Great Southwest.* It won the Golden Spur Award from the Western Writers of America for the best nonfiction book of the year.

The best-remembered monument to Barker's memory, however, had nothing to do with his literary accomplishments. In May 1950 a huge fire broke out on Capitan Mountain, New Mexico. A fireman rescued a small bear cub, badly burned, clinging to a charred tree, and the cub was flown to Santa Fe and nursed back to health. On behalf of the New Mexico Department of Game and Fish, Barker donated Smokey to the Forest Service in Washington, D.C., specifying that the cub should become a symbol of forest-fire prevention and wildlife conservation. Smokey lived for more than twenty-six years at the National Zoo and became the most recognized animal in the world.

Barker married Ethel M. Arnold on May 17, 1911, and they had one son and two daughters. Barker was a member of the International Association of Game, Fish, and Conservation Commissioners, the Western Writers of America, the National Wildlife Federation, and the Western Association of Game and Fish Commissioners. He received a meritorious-service citation from the New Mexico Wildlife Conservation Association in 1953, and the National Wildlife Federation named him conservationist of the year in 1965. In 1966 the United States Game Commission dedicated a 5,000-acre wildlife area to Barker in recognition of the assistance he had given to the regional Girl Scout council. In 1976 he received an honorary doctorate from New Mexico State University. Barker died at the age of 101 on April 3, 1988, in Santa Fe, New Mexico.

BIBLIOGRAPHY: *Contemporary Authors,* Vol 89.

Martin Donell Kohout

BARKER, EUGENE CAMPBELL (1874–1956). Eugene C. Barker, historian, was born near Riverside, Walker County, Texas, on November 10, 1874, the son of Joseph and Fannie (Holland) Barker. Shortly after his father's death in 1888, his mother moved the family to Palestine, where fourteen-year-old Eugene found employment in the Missouri Pacific railroad shops. In the months that followed, he became a fine blacksmith while working during the day and attending evening school in the home of Miss Shirley Green. He entered the University of Texas in September 1895 and thus started an association that continued until his death.

Despite financial handicaps in his job as night mail clerk on the Missouri Pacific Austin-to-Houston run, Barker received the B.A. degree in the spring of 1899 and the M.A. in 1900. He served the university history department as tutor (1899–1901), instructor (1901–08), adjunct professor (1908–11), associate professor (1911–13), professor (1913–51), and professor emeritus (1951–56)—almost six decades altogether.

On August 6, 1903, Barker married Matilda LeGrand Weeden. In 1906 he took a leave of absence to complete his graduate work at the University of Pennsylvania, where, after a brief interval at Harvard, he received his Ph.D. in 1908. On the death of George P. Garrison[qv] in 1910, Barker became chairman of the University of Texas Department of History, a position he held until 1925. When the title of distinguished professor was inaugurated in 1937, Barker was among the first three distinguished professors chosen.

He did the bulk of his scholarly work during the thirty-eight years of his full professorship. His first major research project, inherited from Lester G. Bugbee[qv] and George P. Garrison, was on the life of

Eugene C. Barker, Austin, 1937. Prints and Photographs Collection, Eugene C. Barker file, CAH; CN 02350. When the University of Texas created the title of distinguished professor in 1937, Barker was one of the first three chosen for the honor.

Stephen F. Austin.[qv] Before finishing the classic biography of Austin, Barker collected, edited, and published *The Austin Papers,* a collection of correspondence that covered the years from 1789 to 1837 (published by the American Historical Association, 1924–28, and the University of Texas Press,[qv] 1927). *The Life of Stephen F. Austin* was published in 1925 and republished several times. Barker's other major publications included *Mexico and Texas, 1821–1835* (1928); *Readings in Texas History* (1929); *The Father of Texas* (1935); in collaboration with Amelia W. Williams,[qv] *The Writings of Sam Houston* (1938–43); and a series of public school textbooks for Row and Peterson done in collaboration with William E. Dodd, Henry S. Commager, and Walter Prescott Webb.[qv]

Barker served as managing editor of the *Southwestern Historical Quarterly*[qv] and director of the Texas State Historical Association[qv] from 1910 until 1937. During that time he not only edited the *Quarterly* but contributed numerous articles to the publication, most of them on some aspect of Texas or Mexican history. Through his articles Barker showed the effect that Texas history had on the history of the American West. In this connection he exploded some of the earlier myths that had gained widespread acceptance among American historians. He explored and corrected misconceptions, among them the "conspiracy theory" of the conquest and annexation[qv] of Texas and the war with Mexico; and the idea that the Texas Revolution and Mexican War[qqv] were solely the fault of the Mexicans.

Barker was a lifetime member of the American Historical Association. Also, along with Clarence V. Alvord and others, he helped establish the Mississippi Valley Historical Association (now the Organization of American Historians, publishers of the *Journal of American History*) and served this organization as its president in 1922–23. During his later years he challenged Professor Charles A. Beard's economic interpretation of the Constitution of the United States.

Barker was instrumental in the origin of the Latin American Collection (now the Nettie Lee Benson Latin American Collection[qv]) and the Littlefield collection of source materials on the history of the South, both important components of the University of Texas libraries. Barker's greatest contribution to the university, however, was in building the history department, which, during his career, came to rank with the best in the state universities of the nation. After the Ferguson controversy of 1917–18 (see FERGUSON, JAMES EDWARD) Barker exercised a remarkable influence as one of the leaders of the university faculty. As the years passed he became a legend on the campus; one of the great intangibles of his long and fruitful career was his influence on the thousands of students who sat in his classes. When the University of Texas named the Barker Texas History Center[qv] (dedicated in 1950) for him, it was the first time that such an honor had been accorded a living member of the faculty. Barker died on October 22, 1956, and was buried in Oakwood Cemetery, Austin.

BIBLIOGRAPHY: William C. Pool, *Eugene C. Barker, Historian* (Austin: Texas State Historical Association, 1971).

William C. Pool

BARKER, WILLIAM LOUIS (1852–?). William Louis Barker, son of William O. and Julia (Crane) Barker, was born in Upshur County, Texas, on July 2, 1852. He studied medicine in his father's office and graduated from the medical department of the University of Louisiana in March 1874. He married Mollie (Mary) F. Barnes in October 1874 and, in 1879, moved to Longview, where he practiced medicine and ran a drugstore. He moved to Waco in 1882, was city health officer there in 1885, and became division surgeon for the St. Louis and Southwestern Railway. Dr. Barker was superintendent of the Southwestern Insane Asylum (later the San Antonio State Hospital[qv]) from 1891 to 1895. He was a member of the San Antonio City Council from 1898 to 1904. He was reappointed superintendent of the asylum in 1907 and served until 1909.

BIBLIOGRAPHY: *A Memorial and Biographical History of McLennan, Falls, Bell, and Coryell Counties* (Chicago: Lewis, 1893; rpt., St. Louis: Ingmire, 1984). *Texas State Journal of Medicine,* July 1921. *A Twentieth Century History of Southwest Texas* (2 vols., Chicago: Lewis, 1907).

BARKER, TEXAS. Barker is on Interstate Highway 10 seventeen miles west of downtown Houston in western Harris County. In 1895 the Missouri, Kansas and Texas Railroad had laid tracks and was operating through Barker. The town was named for the track-laying contractor, Ed Barker. George Miller built two houses in early Barker. One was north of the railroad tracks and served as an inn. It was destroyed in the Galveston hurricane of 1900.[qv] The second house, south of the tracks, was a two-story home, store, telephone office, and post office. In 1898 Miller became the first postmaster of Barker. Barker had an inn, a brick factory, a twine mill, a general store, a telephone company, a depot, two churches, a one-room public school, and a saloon. By 1915, when the town's population was eighty, rice farming, dairying, and ranching were the chief occupations. Whole trainloads of cattle were shipped from Barker's shipping pens. The last dairy in the area became a residential subdivision in 1982. In 1985 the Texas Antiquities Committee[qv] awarded a state archeological landmark to the LH7 Ranch[qv] home, owned by the Emil Henry Marks family. In 1974 Park Ten Industrial Park developed a business park just north of the Katy Railroad tracks. Trendmaker now has two multistory office buildings In Barker just south of Interstate 10, where rice once grew and cattle grazed in the 1970s. The population in Barker stood at 100 from 1925 to 1949, when it declined to fifty. From 1972 to 1990 the census reported a population of 160.

BIBLIOGRAPHY: Houston *Chronicle,* February 23, 1938.

Atha Marks Dimon

BARKER RESERVOIR. Barker Reservoir is southwest of the intersection of U.S. Highway 90 and State Highway 6, about one mile south of Addicks in western Harris County (at 29°46′ N, 95°39′ W). The reservoir is formed on Buffalo Bayou by a rolled-earth dam 72,900 feet long and 112.5 feet high. The spillway elevation is 73.2 feet, and the drainage area covers 128 square miles. The storage capacity of the reservoir, 199,000 acre-feet, expands to 209,000 acre-feet at flood stage. The purpose of the reservoir is to provide flood control on the Buffalo Bayou watershed in the San Jacinto River basin for the city of Houston. Water is stored in the reservoir until it can be released to flow downstream without endangering property. The United States

Army Corps of Engineers completed the Barker dam in February 1946, but the reservoir had already been used in 1945 for spring flood control. The total storage capacity of the Barker Reservoir and the adjacent Addicks Reservoir[qv] is 411,500 acre-feet.

BIBLIOGRAPHY: *Water for Texas*, Vol. 1: *A Comprehensive Plan for the Future*; Vol. 2: *Technical Appendix* (Austin: Texas Department of Water Resources, 1984).

BARKER TEXAS HISTORY CENTER. The Eugene C. Barker Texas History Center, today known as the Eugene C. Barker Texas History Collections and since 1991 a division of the Center for American History[qv] at the University of Texas of Austin, opened on April 27, 1950. At the time of its dedication the center brought together for the first time two departments of the University Library: the Archives department and the Texas Collection Library, as well as the offices of the Texas State Historical Association.[qv] The Barker Center was named for Eugene C. Barker,[qv] distinguished professor of history at the university. The center was the first element on the campus to be given the name of a living member of the University of Texas faculty. It originally occupied the Old Library Building (now called Battle Hall), which was designed by Cass Gilbert[qv] and built in 1910. In 1971 the center moved to Sid Richardson Hall Unit 2, located on the eastern edge of the campus adjacent to the Lyndon Baines Johnson Library.[qv] In 1991 the Barker Center became a division of the university's newly organized Center for American History, established to consolidate and make more visible the university's extensive holdings documenting the historical development of the United States. Until 1994 the Center for American History remained a unit of the University of Texas at Austin General Libraries;[qv] in August 1994 it became an independent operating unit on campus. The Barker Collections house more than 130,000 books and periodicals about Texas, published in Texas, or produced by writers strongly associated with Texas; some 3,500 individual collections of personal papers and official records of individuals, families, groups, and businesses significant to the history of Texas; an extensive newspaper collection containing original editions of some of the earliest known newspapers published in Texas, as well as more than 2,500 locally published newspapers from nearly all of the state's 254 counties; approximately 750,000 photographs documenting Texas persons, places, scenes, and events; 30,000 phonographs relating to Texas music and musicians; and more than 30,000 printed and manuscript maps depicting Texas from the era of the European encounter with the New World to the present.

BIBLIOGRAPHY: Don E. Carleton and Katherine J. Adams, "'Work Peculiarly Our Own': Origins of the Barker Texas History Center," *Southwestern Historical Quarterly* 86 (October 1982). Herbert Gambrell, "The Eugene C. Barker Texas History Center," *Southwestern Historical Quarterly* 54 (July 1950). *Katherine J. Adams*

BARKLEY, BENJAMIN FRANKLIN (1822–1882). Benjamin Franklin Barkley, physician and county official, was born in Kentucky on November 14, 1822. His father was from Virginia, and his mother was born in New Jersey. Before moving to Texas he practiced medicine in Mason, Bracken, and Harrison counties, Kentucky. In 1855 he and his wife, Malinda Elizabeth (Duncan), emancipated the slaves on their Kentucky farm and traveled to Texas. They settled in Birdville, the county seat, with only one horse and $100 worth of medicine. Barkley practiced both law and medicine and helped provide supplies and assistance to struggling families. He donated land for the town's first school and in 1856 fought unsuccessfully to keep Fort Worth from becoming county seat.

"Squire" Barkley began to fall out of favor during the movement toward secession.[qv] He continually spoke out against slavery[qv] and secession, but he kept an open house at Birdville to feed the widows and orphans of Confederate soldiers, and when necessary he treated or lodged returning soldiers. After the war he was named to the Tarrant County Registration Board, and in November 1867 he was appointed county judge, a position he held until 1870. He also served as subassistant commissioner of the Freedmen's Bureau[qv] in 1867–68. Barkley reported misconduct and conducted hearings on Ku Klux Klan[qv] activities; he became so unpopular that he was escorted by black soldiers from his home to his office in Fort Worth. During this time he also served as the local postmaster. He received an appointment as county treasurer from Governor Edmund J. Davis[qv] in November 1871 and served until January 1873. Following the return of state and county government to Democratic control, Barkley resumed his practices of medicine and law in Birdville. Additionally, he advertised as a land agent with 7,000 acres for sale in the county. He was named a United States commissioner for his efforts during the crisis.

Barkley died on December 24, 1882, and was buried on land that he had donated for Birdville Cemetery. A historical marker honoring him was placed at the site in 1979.

BIBLIOGRAPHY: Evelyn D'Arcy Cushman, *Cemeteries of Northeast Tarrant County, Texas* (Arlington, Texas, 1981). Ruby Schmidt, ed., *Fort Worth and Tarrant County* (Fort Worth: Texas Christian University Press, 1984). Mack H. Williams, *In Old Fort Worth: The Story of a City and Its People as Published in the News-Tribune in 1976 and 1977* (1977). Amelia W. Williams and Eugene C. Barker, eds., *The Writings of Sam Houston, 1813–1863* (8 vols., Austin: University of Texas Press, 1938–43; rpt., Austin and New York: Pemberton Press, 1970).

Kristi Strickland

BARKLEY, DAVID BENNES (1899?–1918). David Bennes Barkley, Medal of Honor winner, was born, probably in 1899, to Josef and Antonia (Cantú) Barkley in Laredo, Texas. When the United States entered World War I,[qv] Barkley enlisted as a private in the United States Army. Family records indicate he did not want to be known as of Mexican descent, for fear he would not see action at the front. He was assigned to Company A, 356th Infantry, Eighty-ninth Division. In France he was given the mission of swimming the Meuse River near Pouilly, in order to infiltrate German lines and gather information about the strength and deployment of German formations. Despite enemy resistance to any allied crossing of the Meuse, Barkley and another volunteer accomplished the mission. While returning with the information, Barkley developed cramps and drowned, on November 9, 1918, just two days before the armistice went into effect. His sacrifice earned praise from Gen. John J. Pershing,[qv] the commander of the American Expeditionary Force. Barkley was one of three Texans awarded the nation's highest military honor, the Congressional Medal of Honor, for service in World War I. He was also awarded the Croix de Guerre (France) and the Croce Merito (Italy). In 1921 an elementary school in San Antonio was named for him. He lay in state at the Alamo,[qv] the second person to be so honored. He was buried at San Antonio National Cemetery. On January 10, 1941, the War Department named Camp Barkeley[qv] for the Texas hero.

BIBLIOGRAPHY: Abilene *Reporter-News*, January 12, 1941. Austin *American-Statesman*, January 4, 1992. San Antonio *Express-News*, May 21, 1989. Committee on Veterans' Affairs, United States Senate, *Medal of Honor Recipients, 1863–1973* (Washington: GPO, 1973).

James M. Myers

BARKLEY, HOWARD T., SR. (1901–1981). Howard T. Barkley, Sr., thoracic surgeon, was born in Tucson, Arizona, on November 30, 1901. He graduated from the University of Arizona in 1931 and obtained an M.D. degree from Columbia University School of Physicians and Surgeons in 1935. He remained in New York to serve an internship at Lenox Hill Hospital and a surgical residency at Presbyterian Hospital. After further training at the University of Michigan Hospital at Ann Arbor, he moved to Houston, Texas, in 1941.

During World War II[qv] Barkley served as a flight surgeon with the

United States Army Air Corps, in which he attained the rank of lieutenant colonel. He was an associate professor of clinical surgery at Baylor University College of Medicine from 1943 to 1980 and chief of thoracic surgery at M. D. Anderson Hospital from its inception in 1944 to 1968 (*see* UNIVERSITY OF TEXAS SYSTEM CANCER CENTER). Barkley was also on the staff at Hermann Hospital,[qv] Houston, from 1942 to 1972 and served as chief of thoracic surgery there from 1946 to 1968. In 1948 he was appointed chairman of the medical staff at the Houston AntiTubercular Clinic. Among his many professional offices, Barkley was president of the Houston Surgical Society (1952), the Texas Tuberculosis Association (1956–58), the Harris County Medical Society (1967), and the Houston chapter of the American Tuberculosis Association. In 1963–64 he served as vice president of the National Tuberculosis Association. He was a founding member of the American Association for Thoracic Surgery (1948) and the Society of Thoracic Surgeons (1964).

He married Helen Margaret Bugbee. They had one son, H. T. Barkley, Jr., also a Houston physician. The senior Barkley died on January 26, 1981.

BIBLIOGRAPHY: Howard T. Barkley Papers, Houston Academy of Medicine–Texas Medical Center Library, Harris County Medical Archive. *Texas Medicine*, May 1981.

Patricia L. Jakobi

BARKMAN CREEK. Barkman Creek, sometimes called Big Creek, rises 3½ miles northeast of New Boston in northern Bowie County (at 33°29′ N, 94°22′ W) and runs northeast for sixteen miles to its mouth on McKinney Bayou, seven miles northwest of Texarkana (at 33°32′ N, 94°08′ W). The stream is intermittent in its upper reaches. It traverses an area of woods and pasturelands, in which a soil surface of loams and clays supports post oak, blackjack oak, and elms, as well as crops.

BARKSDALE, TEXAS. Barksdale, formerly known as Dixie, is on the Nueces River at the intersection of Farm Road 335 and State Highway 55, twenty-four miles southeast of Rocksprings in southeastern Edwards County. The community is named for Lewis Barksdale, who patented a league and a labor of land in the area in 1847. Settlers moved into the area in the 1860s, and Barksdale moved to the site of the community in 1869. A settlement gradually developed there, and in its early years the community was called Dixie, for nearby Camp Dixie. By 1880 Dixie had a saloon, a hotel, and a small store. When the community applied for a post office in 1882, its residents were told that another community named Dixie had already secured that name, so citizens selected Barksdale as the name. In 1884 the community had a population of twenty, and by 1890 Barksdale had two general stores and a grocery. School was held in a small house until a school building was erected in 1887; the new schoolhouse doubled as a church. Over the next two years a gristmill and a cotton gin were built in the town, and by 1900 Barksdale had 106 residents. The community received telephone service soon thereafter, a Baptist church was built in 1906, and a bank opened in 1907. Barksdale's population was estimated at 200 through the mid-1940s. In 1948 the town had a school, a church, and five businesses, but by 1950 its population had fallen to an estimated 150. A Methodist church was built there in 1950, and a new high school building was built in 1957. By 1973 Barksdale consisted of the high school, two businesses, several dwellings, and a cemetery, and its population had fallen to seventy-one. The town grew dramatically in the late 1980s as a number of housing subdivisions were built there. In 1990 Barksdale had 617 inhabitants and six businesses.

BIBLIOGRAPHY: Rocksprings Woman's Club Historical Committee, *A History of Edwards County* (San Angelo: Anchor, 1984).

Mark Odintz

BARLOW, IMA CHRISTINA (1899–1990). Ima Christina Barlow, teacher, daughter of Walter Anthony and Ida (Jackson) Barlow, was born in Williamson County, Texas, on February 11, 1899. She graduated from Taylor High School and entered the University of Texas. She began teaching in a one-room rural school and alternated teaching and university studies until she graduated. Among other places, she taught in Beaumont, Vernon, San Marcos, and Brownwood while she completed an M.A. in history. While in Brownwood she applied for a position teaching European history at West Texas State Teachers College (now West Texas A&M University). As she later stated, President Joseph A. Hill[qv] said to "come on up and they'd see how I worked out." She remained at the institution for thirty-four years. Barlow completed the Ph.D. degree in 1939 under the directorship of Professor Thad W. Riker[qv] and published her dissertation, a study of the Agadir crisis, the following year.

Although her teaching specialization and research interests centered on modern Europe, Barlow was a well-informed Texas historian, having studied under professors Eugene C. Barker and Walter Prescott Webb.[qqv] She coauthored a junior high school Texas history text, occasionally taught the senior-level course in Texas history, and supervised many master's theses relating to Texas topics. She was an active member of the Panhandle-Plains Historical Society,[qv] contributed to the *Panhandle-Plains Historical Review*, and edited the journal for four years (1949–52). For many years she sponsored a campus honor society designed to encourage and recognize academic achievement of freshman and sophomore students. She was a Methodist and a member of the Texas State Teachers Association.[qv] She retired in 1964 and moved to Austin, where she continued research and pursued other interests. She died in Austin on October 13, 1990, and is buried in Austin Memorial Park Cemetery.

BIBLIOGRAPHY: Austin *American-Statesman*, October 14, 1990.

Frederick W. Rathjen

BARNARD, CHARLES E. (1823–1900). Charles E. (Uncle Charley) Barnard, pioneer Indian trader, son of Henry B. Barnard, was born at Hartford, Connecticut, on August 10, 1823. At the age of twenty-one he joined his brother, George Barnard,[qv] at Tehuacana Trading Post near the site of present-day Waco and subsequently assisted him in operating it and other Indian trading posts along Central Texas rivers. In 1846 at Tehuacana Trading Post George Barnard ransomed a Comanche captive, Juana Cavasos (*see* BARNARD, JUANA CAVASOS), daughter of a prominent Spanish family of Matamoros, Mexico. In 1848 Charles married her. In 1849 they established their home at Comanche Peak Trading House on the Brazos River in Hood County. To them were born fourteen children. In 1860 Barnard's Indian customers moved to reservations. He built a huge stone gristmill on the Paluxy River and, nearby, a family home. The town of Glen Rose grew up around it. In 1870 Charles sold the mill and moved back to the Brazos River location, where he had large landholdings. He was a literate gentleman who had one of the finest libraries on the frontier. He gave generously of himself and his considerable means to better his area of Texas. He is credited with contributing substantial funds and slave labor to the construction of housing for Acton Masonic Institute in Hood County. Barnard died at his home on June 22, 1900, and is buried beside Juana in the family plot near their first homesite.

BIBLIOGRAPHY: Pearl Andrus, *Juana: A Spanish Girl in Central Texas* (Burnet, Texas: Eakin Press, 1982). W. C. Nunn, *Somervell: Story of a Texas County* (Fort Worth: Texas Christian University Press, 1975).

Pearl Andrus

BARNARD, GEORGE (1818–1883). George Barnard, Indian trader and pioneer merchant, was born in Hartford, Connecticut, on September 18, 1818, the son of Henry B. Barnard. He arrived in Galveston, Texas, in 1838 and soon moved to Houston, where he became a clerk in the firm John F. Torrey and Brothers. In June 1841 he joined Thomas S. Torrey[qv] and about 270 others in the Texan Santa Fe expedition.[qv] After capture by the Mexicans, he suffered considerably during his confinement in Perote prison.[qv] He was released by the fall of 1842 and returned to Houston, where he became a member of the Torrey firm. In 1843 Sam Houston[qv] asked the Torreys to establish the Torrey Trading Houses[qv] trading posts to help pacify the Indians of the republic, and Barnard and Thomas Torrey located a site on a small tributary of Tehuacana Creek, which came to be called Trading House Creek, about eight miles south of the location of present Waco. The site was already well known as a place where Indians and representatives of the Republic of Texas[qv] met. Early in 1844 Barnard began trading with Indians. In 1849 he became the sole proprietor of the post, and the next year he and his brother Charles moved the post to the Brazos River near Comanche Peak in what is now Hood County. They were following the Indians, who were withdrawing from growing white settlement in Central Texas. Barnard's other ventures included trade with soldiers and settlers at Fort Graham, near Whitney. He or his brother may have supplied Indians with liquor and firearms and probably did disrupt the efforts of federal agents trying to remove the Indians to reservations, a move that would have limited the Barnards' trade. In the four years immediately before the Indians' removal (1851–55), the Barnards shipped 59,000 pounds of undressed deer skins, as well as other traded goods, to northern merchants. By 1851 Barnard had moved his operation to Waco Village, where he invested heavily in land. In 1857 he sold his business to Fox and Jacobs, the town's first Jewish merchants, and entered semiretirement. He was a charter member of Bosque Masonic Lodge, begun in 1852, and was active in the local company of Texas Rangers.[qv] He married Mary Rebecca Ross, daughter of ranger captain Shapley P. Ross and sister of Lawrence Sullivan Ross,[qqv] in 1850. George and Mary Barnard had twelve children. Barnard died at his home in Waco on March 6, 1883.

BIBLIOGRAPHY: Pearl Andrus, *Juana: A Spanish Girl in Central Texas* (Burnet, Texas: Eakin Press, 1982). Henry C. Armbruster, *The Torreys of Texas* (Buda, Texas: Citizen Press, 1968). George Barnard Papers, Texas Collection, Baylor University. W. C. Nunn, *Somervell: Story of a Texas County* (Fort Worth: Texas Christian University Press, 1975). John K. Strecker, *Chronicles of George Barnard* (Baylor University Bulletin, September 1928; rpt., *Waco Heritage and History,* Fall 1971). John Willingham, "George Barnard: Trader and Merchant on the Texas Frontier," *Texana* 12 (1974). Dorman H. Winfrey and James M. Day, eds., *Texas Indian Papers* (4 vols., Austin: Texas State Library, 1959–61; rpt., 5 vols., Austin: Pemberton Press, 1966).

John Willingham

BARNARD, JOSEPH HENRY (1804–1861). Joseph Henry Barnard, military surgeon and diarist, was born in Deerfield, Massachusetts, on April 21, 1804. He was a sailor for three years before graduating from Williams College in 1829. He practiced medicine in Canada until 1835, when he moved to Chicago. He left for Texas on December 14, 1835, and enlisted in the revolutionary army[qv] as a private with the Red Rovers.[qv] While surgeon to James W. Fannin, Jr.'s,[qv] command, he was captured at Goliad, but his life was spared so that he might treat the wounded Mexicans at Goliad and San Antonio. In San Antonio he lived with José Ángel Navarro.[qv] Barnard's diary is one of the best sources of information covering this period. He served in the army in Galveston from June 10 to October 28, 1836. He moved to Fort Bend County in 1837, was county clerk in 1838–39, and represented the county in the House of the Eighth Congress, 1843–1844. He married Mrs. Nancy M. Danforth on July 30, 1841. Dr. Barnard moved to Goliad and lived there until 1860, when he went on a visit to Canada, where he died in 1861.

BIBLIOGRAPHY: Joseph H. Barnard, *Dr. J. H. Barnard's Journal: A Composite of Known Versions,* ed. Hobart Huson (Refugio?, Texas, 1949). Texas House of Representatives, *Biographical Directory of the Texan Conventions and Congresses, 1832–1845* (Austin: Book Exchange, 1941). Pat Ireland Nixon, *The Medical Story of Early Texas, 1528–1853* (Lancaster, Pennsylvania: Lupe Memorial Fund, 1946).

BARNARD, JUANA JOSEFINA CAVASOS (1822–1906). Juana Cavasos Barnard, Indian captive, slaveowner, and pioneer in the area of present Somervell County, was born in Mexico to María Josefina Cavasos and was reportedly of Spanish and Italian lineage and a descendent of the Canary Islanders.[qv] Her family lived in Matamoros, Tamaulipas. Her grandfather, Narciso Cavasos, had received the largest Spanish land grant in Texas. In 1848 she married Charles E. Barnard[qv] of Connecticut, considered the first permanent non-Indian settler in the area of present Somervell County. They had fourteen children, six of whom survived into adulthood. She had twenty-five grandchildren and thirteen great grandchildren.

On August 15, 1844, Comanche Indians raided South Texas near the Rio Grande and captured Juana, who was then eighteen. One account reports that she was held captive for seven months, while another reports three years, but Juana's own testimony suggests she may have been captive less than a month. The Comanches visited the Tehuacana Creek Trading House operated by George Barnard[qv] in north central Texas. Barnard traded $300 in horses and merchandise for Juana. Shortly afterwards she married George's brother Charles. Charles Barnard has been recognized as having cordial relations with various Indian tribes. Juana noted that she lived in the Somervell County area for many months without seeing a white woman.

The Barnards accumulated some wealth through landholdings, trade, and income from a gristmill. In 1849 Charles and George established a trading post to trade with Indians. Juana may have helped operate the trading post, since she stated that they kept their trading house for the Indians for fifteen or twenty years. Charles bought out George's share in 1859. That year the United States government moved the Indians from the Fort Belknap reservation to Oklahoma, and thus the Barnards' customers decreased.

Using slave labor Barnard had a mill built in 1859–60, the first building at the site of present Glen Rose. Around 1860 he was considered an extensive slave owner. Juana apparently had one or several slaves in her household, since she noted they had "plenty of Negro slaves." In 1860 their real estate was valued at $50,000 and their personal estate at $60,400. In the early 1870s Charles sold the mill for $65,000. Charles and Juana's wealth declined in the 1890s. In their last years they resided in a small log house. When Charles died in 1900, Juana sold 200 acres to her children, but the bill of sale was not to take effect until her death, probably because she would have been homeless otherwise.

Juana and Charles were considered social leaders. Juana acted as a midwife and had some skill with medicinal herbs. She was reportedly an excellent horsewoman, and at the ripe age of seventy-eight she still maintained a garden. She was one of the few Spanish-Mexican women known to be an Indian captive, and she gave oral testimony to her granddaughter Verdie Barnard Alison in 1900, entitled "My Life with the Indians." In it she discussed the day of her capture and described the violent deaths she witnessed. She noted that she was captured for purposes of trade. Juana is the subject of *Juana, A Spanish Girl in Central Texas* by Pearl Andrus, a fictional account based on interviews with descendants and research. Juana Cavasos Barnard died of natural causes on February 1, 1906.

BIBLIOGRAPHY: Raymond Elliott and Mildred Padon, *Of a People and a Creek* (Cleburne, Texas: Bennett Printing, 1979). W. C. Nunn, *Somervell: Story of a Texas County* (Fort Worth: Texas Christian University Press, 1975). S. W. F. Prewett, "The Adventurous Career of Charles Barnard," *Texas Magazine,* December 1910.

Cynthia E. Orozco

BARNARD KNOB. Barnard Knob is 1½ miles northeast of Fort Spunky in extreme southeastern Hood County (at 32°20′ N, 97°38′ W).

It was probably named for George Barnard,[qv] who maintained a trading post on the nearby Brazos River in the mid-nineteenth century. The summit reaches a height of 956 feet above mean sea level.

BARNES, CHARLES MERRITT (1855–1927). Charles Merritt Barnes, journalist, was born on January 6, 1855, in Waterproof, Louisiana. He attended Louisiana State University and the military college at Baton Rouge. He enlisted in the Louisiana State Militia and in 1872 moved with his family to Texas, where he settled in San Marcos and was soon admitted to the bar. After living a short time at Luling, he went to San Antonio in 1874 and practiced law for several years. His interests then turned to journalism, the military, and politics. He enlisted in the Alamo Rifles in 1875 and remained with that group until 1917, when he retired with the rank of major. During this period he saw active duty along the Mexican border. He was color sergeant of Company G, First Texas Infantry (San Antonio Zouaves) in 1898, but he did not accompany his outfit to Cuba in the Spanish-American War.

Barnes became a reporter for the San Antonio *Express*[qv] about 1880. He gained considerable prominence with stories featuring exploits of frontier individuals. His articles appeared regularly in Sunday editions between 1902 and 1910. They were illustrated with line drawings by Leo Colton, a talented *Express* artist. In 1910 Barnes published *Combats and Conquests of Immortal Heroes,* a collection based on nineteenth-century San Antonio families, personalities, and events. He also published and wrote some verse. He retired from the *Express* just before World War I.[qv] Barnes died on April 7, 1927, in San Antonio.

BIBLIOGRAPHY: O. V. Mergele, "Col. Chas. M. Barnes and the Flowers for the Living Club," *Texas Pioneer* 4 (September–October 1923). San Antonio *Express,* April 11, 1886, May 4, 11, 18, 1902, April 8, 1927.

Hobart Huson

BARNES, NED EASTMAN (1866–1950). Ned Eastman Barnes, a black inventor, was born in January 1866 in Waller County, Texas. He attended public schools and then moved to Willis, where he acquired a farm and joined the Farmers' Improvement Society. He then turned to invention and had an office in Houston by 1915. He developed a brace to maintain the distance between train tracks, an electric projector for display of railroad arrival and departure times, and several other items of railway equipment. He was a Mason and Knight of Pythias and became a lay leader in his Baptist congregation. Barnes married Ada Barnes in the 1880s, and they had three sons who reached adulthood, as well as an adopted daughter. He died in Montgomery County on November 14, 1950.

BIBLIOGRAPHY: *The Red Book of Houston* (Houston: Sotex, 1915).

Alwyn Barr

BARNES, WILLIAM WRIGHT (1883–1960). William Wright (W. W.) Barnes, preacher, seminary professor, and Baptist Church[qv] historian, was born on February 28, 1883, in Elm City, North Carolina, the youngest son of six children of Wright and Nettie Ralph (Bridgers) Barnes. His father and brother were physicians, and his mother was class valedictorian at Chowan College. Barnes joined the Elm City Baptist Church on October 12, 1898, and was baptized four days later. He graduated from Wake Forest College with B.A. and M.A. degrees. He was ordained to the ministry on July 31, 1904, at Elm City Baptist Church. In 1904–05 he taught the children of American families in Santiago, Cuba. In 1905 he returned to Wilson, North Carolina, and became both principal and teacher at a public school. Barnes entered Southern Baptist Theological Seminary in Louisville, Kentucky, in 1906 and received a Th.M. degree in 1909. After returning to Havana, Cuba, he served from February 1909 until May 1912 as principal of El Colegio Cubano-Americano.

In 1913 he received a Th.D. degree from Southern Seminary and became professor of church history at Southwestern Baptist Theological Seminary[qv] in Fort Worth, where he stayed until his retirement in 1953. During the frequent absences of Dr. Lee R. Scarborough,[qv] president of Southwestern from 1914 to 1942, Barnes served as acting president and at times as dean and registrar. He ministered as interim pastor at many Baptist churches and as moderator of the Tarrant Baptist Association for 1914, 1922–27, and 1933–35. He also served on committees and commissions in the Baptist General Convention of Texas and the Southern Baptist Convention. In 1936 Barnes served on the Southern Baptist Committee for the Preservation of Baptist History, which established the Southern Baptist Historical Commission on May 13, 1938. He served also as president of the Texas Baptist Historical Society, organized on November 10, 1938. He received honorary doctorates from Wake Forest College in 1934 and Hardin-Simmons University in 1952.

Barnes wrote articles for *Review and Expositor, Southwestern Journal of Theology,* and *Encyclopedia of Southern Baptists.* He also published *The Southern Baptist Convention: A Study in the Development of Ecclesiology* (1923) and *The Southern Baptist Convention, 1845–1953* (1954). Barnes was a Mason. He and Ethel Dalrymple were married on October 20, 1909, in Amory, Mississippi. They had two sons. Barnes died on April 6, 1960, in Fort Worth and was buried there in Greenwood Cemetery.

BIBLIOGRAPHY: Robert A. Barker, "William Wright Barnes," *Baptist History and Heritage* 5 (July 1970). William Wright Barnes Collection (Texas Baptist Historical Collection, A. Webb Roberts Library, Southwestern Baptist Theological Seminary). James F. Carter, *Cowboys, Cowtowns and Crosses: A Centennial History of the Tarrant Baptist Association* (Fort Worth: Tarrant Baptist Association, 1986). *Encyclopedia of Southern Baptists* (4 vols., Nashville: Broadman, 1958–82).

Samuel B. Hesler

BARNES, TEXAS. Barnes is at the junction of Farm roads 942 and 1745, about seventy-five miles northwest of Beaumont in east central Polk County. The first recorded settler in the area was Dan Hamilton, who arrived during the 1850s. The community derived its name from an early black family of the region. General stores operated by John S. Havis and John A. Handley served residents of this largely rural settlement during the nineteenth century. A few scattered dwellings remained in the late 1980s. Barnes was listed as a community in 1990, but without census figures.

BIBLIOGRAPHY: *A Pictorial History of Polk County, Texas, 1846–1910* (Livingston, Texas: Polk County Bicentennial Commission, 1976; rev. ed. 1978).

Robert Wooster

BARNES MOUNTAIN. Barnes Mountain overlooks the Colorado River eighteen miles northwest of Burnet in northwestern Burnet County (at 30°57′ N, 98°25′ W). It rises 1,347 feet above sea level, nearly 250 feet higher than the surrounding countryside. It was probably named after a local family.

BARNES SWITCH, TEXAS. Barnes Switch, also known as Barnes, is at the junction of State Highway 19 and Farm Road 1893, in western Trinity County. The settlement grew up near a switch on the Waco, Beaumont, Trinity and Sabine Railway in the early 1920s and was named for Dr. S. E. Barnes, a prominent physician. In the mid-1930s there were several stores in the area. In the early 1990s a single store remained, and the community reported a population of fifteen.

BIBLIOGRAPHY: Patricia B. and Joseph W. Hensley, eds., *Trinity County Beginnings* (Groveton, Texas: Trinity County Book Committee, 1986).

Christopher Long

BARNESVILLE, TEXAS. Barnesville was twelve miles east of Cleburne in eastern Johnson County. The site was settled in 1853 by Moses, Ben, and Andrew Barnes and Jaud and John Dee, and it grew through the 1880s. Moses Barnes built a cotton gin there in 1868; by 1873 a local post office opened. Three years later a townsite was laid out. By 1879 a school had opened, and the community was a stop on the Waxahachie-Cleburne stagecoach road. The Methodist church served as the focal point of the community. In the mid-1880s Barnesville had a population of 150, a cotton gin, two gristmills, a school, and two churches. In 1897 the local school had seventy-nine pupils and two teachers. The Gulf, Colorado and Santa Fe and the Missouri, Kansas, and Texas railroads bypassed Barnesville in 1881. A single teacher and forty-nine pupils were registered in the local school in 1903, but the community was apparently abandoned thereafter.

BIBLIOGRAPHY: Johnson County History Book Committee, *History of Johnson County, Texas* (Dallas: Curtis Media, 1985).

Brian Hart

BARNETT, GEORGE WASHINGTON (1793–1848). George Washington Barnett, early settler, son of William and Margaret Barnett, was born in Lancaster County, South Carolina, on December 12, 1793. He attended Waxhaw Academy in South Carolina, received medical training, probably under direction of a preceptor, and began practice in Williamson County, Tennessee. In 1823 he went to Mississippi and in 1834 to what later became Burleson County, Texas. Later that year he purchased a farm near the site of present-day Brenham and resumed the practice of medicine. Barnett's name appears on the petition of July 2, 1835, requesting permission from the "political chief" of the Mexican government to form the new Municipality of Washington. On July 20, 1835, he was chosen captain of one of four volunteer companies under Col. John Henry Moore,[qv] organized to attack the Tawakoni Indians. He joined Capt. James G. Swisher's[qv] Washington Company on October 8, was elected second lieutenant on October 27, and was discharged on December 22, 1835, after participating in the siege of Bexar.[qv] He represented Washington in the Convention of 1836,[qv] after which he joined the army but left it to look after his family, which was involved in the Runaway Scrape.[qv] He spent the spring of 1836 at San Augustine transporting supplies for United States troops under Edmund P. Gaines.[qv] Between July 3 and October 3, 1836, he was enrolled in William W. Hill's[qv] company of rangers. On December 18, 1837, Barnett received a bounty certificate for 320 acres of land as payment for his services with Hill. On January 5, 1838, he received a headright of a league and a labor. He was a member of the Senate of six congresses of the Republic of Texas,[qv] from September 25, 1837, to January 16, 1843.

In 1846 Barnett moved to Gonzales County. On October 8, 1848, while hunting deer fifteen miles west of Gonzales, he was killed by marauding Lipan-Apache Indians. He was buried in the old cemetery at Gonzales. The Texas Centennial[qv] Commission set up a monument to his honor in 1936. Barnett was a member of the Cumberland Presbyterian Church. He married Eliza Patton in Tennessee on July 6, 1820, and had six children.

BIBLIOGRAPHY: Louis Wiltz Kemp, *The Signers of the Texas Declaration of Independence* (Salado, Texas: Anson Jones, 1944; rpt. 1959). Worth Stickley Ray, *Austin Colony Pioneers* (Austin: Jenkins, 1949; 2d ed., Austin: Pemberton, 1970). Texas House of Representatives, *Biographical Directory of the Texan Conventions and Congresses, 1832–1845* (Austin: Book Exchange, 1941).

L. W. Kemp

BARNETT, MARGUERITE ROSS (1942–1992). Marguerite Ross Barnett, the first black president of the University of Houston, was born on May 22, 1942, in Charlottesville, Virginia, to Dewey Ross and Mary (Douglass) Barnett. She grew up in Buffalo, New York, and graduated from Bennett High School in 1959. She married Stephen A. Barnett, and they had one daughter. Mrs. Barnett received her A.B. in political science from Antioch College in 1964 and a Ph.D. in political science at the University of Chicago in 1972. She later divorced Stephen and married Walter Eugene King, a former member of the Bermuda Parliament, in 1980.

She began her university teaching career at the University of Chicago in 1969 and joined the Princeton University faculty in 1970. She was the James Madison Bicentennial Preceptor at Princeton from 1974 to 1976. She then took a position at Howard University and chaired the political science department between 1977 and 1980 before leaving to assume a teaching post at Columbia University. In 1983 she accepted a position as vice chancellor for academic affairs at City University of New York. She remained there until she joined the University of Missouri–Saint Louis as chancellor in 1986. In 1990 she was named president of the University of Houston, a position she held for a year and a half.

Barnett arrived at UH intent on transforming the school into the nation's best public urban university. Considered a highly energetic and committed leader, she was well-liked by her UH colleagues, who touted her ability to garner widespread support for the university. Her brief tenure as the eighth president of UH was marked with innovative changes, including the addition of ten new minority faculty members shortly after her arrival and the establishment of the Texas Center for University School Partnership, an effort to promote cooperative ventures among business, education, and community leaders, which thirty-seven of the state's institutions joined. Under President Barnett's leadership, the university also undertook its most rigorous program to raise private funds. The campaign garnered the institution an initial $42 million, which Barnett announced during her UH inaugural address. Soon afterwards, the university received a record $51.4 million from John and Rebecca Moores, UH alumni. Their endowment was considered the largest single gift to a public university in the country's history.

Barnett edited or wrote five books and won an award from the American Political Science Association for the best book on cultural pluralism, *The Politics of Cultural Nationalism in South India* (Princeton University Press, 1976). In 1986 she was again recognized by the American Political Science Association with an award for excellence in scholarship and service to the profession. She was also a member of various boards and commissions, including the Council on Foreign Relations, the Houston Grand Opera, the American Council on Education, and the President's Commission on Environmental Quality.

In November 1991 Barnett took a medical leave of absence to seek treatment for cancer. She died on February 26, 1992, in Wailuku, Hawaii. A memorial service for her was held on the UH campus, and a private family service was conducted in Scottsville, Virginia. A special endowment in her name was set up by university officials to honor her accomplishments and contributions to the institution.

BIBLIOGRAPHY: Jessie Carney Smith, ed., *Notable Black American Women* (Detroit: Gale Research, 1992).

Teresa Palomo Acosta

BARNETT, S. SLADE (ca. 1807–1877). S. Slade Barnett, farmer and legislator, was born about 1807 in Kentucky. He married Talitha Cumi Woods in that state, and they had at least three children. The family moved to Sabine County, Texas, sometime between August 26, 1838, when his daughter Frances was born in Kentucky, and December 21, 1839, when he received a conditional certificate for land in Texas. Barnett represented Sabine County in the House of the Fifth Congress of the Republic of Texas; he took his seat on November 13, 1840, eleven days after the beginning of the session. He later moved to Rusk County, where he was elected a county commissioner in 1848 and a justice of the peace in 1850. On July 15, 1860, Barnett married Mary E. Kilgore in Rusk County. Two years earlier his daughter had married Constantine Buckley Kilgore.[qv] Barnett's estate was filed for probate in Gregg County on August 10, 1877.

BIBLIOGRAPHY: Texas House of Representatives, *Biographical Directory of the Texan Conventions and Congresses, 1832–1845* (Austin: Book Exchange, 1941). Dorman H. Winfrey, *A History of Rusk County* (Waco: Texian, 1961).

Cecil Harper, Jr.

BARNETT, THOMAS (1798–1843). Thomas Barnett, pioneer settler and public official, was born on January 18, 1798, in Logan County, Kentucky. Before 1821 he moved to Livingston County, Kentucky, where he was sheriff for two years. In 1823 he moved to Texas as one of Stephen F. Austin's[qv] Old Three Hundred[qv] and on July 10, 1824, received title to a league of land on the east bank of the Brazos River in what is now southeastern Fort Bend County. The 1826 census of Austin's colony noted that Barnett owned two slaves. About 1825 he married Mrs. Nancy Spencer (*see* GRAY, NANCY). They had six children. On February 10, 1828, Barnett was elected comisario[qv] of the district of Victoria in the ayuntamiento[qv] of San Felipe de Austin. In 1829 he was elected alcalde;[qv] he represented Austin Municipality at the Consultation[qv] and on November 18, 1835, was elected a supernumerary member of the General Council.[qv] He was one of the three delegates from Austin Municipality to the Convention of 1836[qv] at Washington-on-the-Brazos, where he signed the Texas Declaration of Independence.[qv] On December 20, 1836, President Sam Houston[qv] appointed him chief justice of Austin County. Barnett represented Fort Bend County in the House of the Third and Fourth congresses of the republic, 1838–40. He died at his home in Fort Bend County on September 20, 1843, and was buried in the family cemetery, eight miles from Richmond.

BIBLIOGRAPHY: Lester G. Bugbee, "The Old Three Hundred: A List of Settlers in Austin's First Colony," *Quarterly of the Texas State Historical Association* 1 (October 1897). Louis Wiltz Kemp, *The Signers of the Texas Declaration of Independence* (Salado, Texas: Anson Jones, 1944; rpt. 1959). Texas House of Representatives, *Biographical Directory of the Texan Conventions and Congresses, 1832–1845* (Austin: Book Exchange, 1941).

L. W. Kemp

BARNETT BRANCH. Barnett Branch rises three miles northwest of Click in southern Llano County (at 30°36′ N, 98°35′ W) and runs southeast for five miles to its mouth on Sandy Creek, a mile southeast of Click (at 30°33′ N, 98°34′ W). It crosses rolling to steep slopes surfaced by shallow, stony soils that support oak, mesquite, scrub brush, cacti, and grasses. The creek was probably named for James Finley Barnett, who settled in the area in 1857.

BIBLIOGRAPHY: Martha Gilliland Long, ed., *Llano County Family Album: A History* (1989).

BARNETT CREEK. Barnett Creek rises in a pool just east of Ladonia and south of Pleasant Grove in southwest Fannin County (at 33°25′ N, 95°56′ W) and flows southeast for thirteen miles, passing through the northeastern edge of Hunt County, to its mouth on the Middle Sulphur River in southwest Delta County (at 33°17′ N, 95°50′ W). Near the origin it traverses flat to rolling terrain with some local steep scarps, surfaced by sand that supports oak, juniper, and grasses. The low-lying floodplains downstream are surfaced by mud, sand, and gravel that support water-tolerant grasses, conifers, and hardwoods.

BARNHARDT CREEK. Barnhardt Creek rises five miles south of New Prospect in central Rusk County (at 32°08′ N, 94°45′ W) and runs southwest for eleven miles to its mouth on Shawnee Creek above the East Fork of the Angelina River, seven miles south of Henderson (at 32°01′ N, 94°49′ W). It flows through an area of flat to rolling prairie with local escarpments. The soil varies from thick, fine, sandy loams to clay loams. Native vegetation consists primarily of pine and hardwood forests.

BARNHART, TEXAS. Barnhart, off U.S. Highway 67 and State Highway 163 in southwestern Irion County, was established in 1910 at the building of the Kansas City, Mexico and Orient Railway and was named for William F. Barnhart, agent for the railroad. In 1912 a post office was acquired with C. C. Luther as postmaster, and the first school was established with Mrs. Maude Branch as the teacher. The Barnhart Independent School District was established on February 27, 1917; the school operated until 1969. By 1920 the town also had the Barnhart State Bank, which was moved to Rankin in 1927, and a newspaper, the Barnhart *Range,* published by Ed Downing. In the 1920s and 1930s Barnhart became a large-volume shipping point, due to its location between major railroad lines. The population was reported as fifty in 1915. In 1947 Barnhart had 250 residents and six businesses and in 1980 seventy-four residents, a business, and a post office. In 1990 the population was 135.

BIBLIOGRAPHY: Leta Crawford, *A History of Irion County, Texas* (Waco: Texian, 1966). Irion County Historical Society, *A History of Irion County, Texas* (San Angelo: Anchor, 1978).

Tracey L. Compton

BAR 96 RANCH. The Bar 96 Ranch was established on the northeast range of the Shoe Bar Ranch[qv] by the Finch, Lord, and Nelson cattle firm in 1886 to breed thoroughbred bulls. Orville H. Nelson[qv] represented the company in the Panhandle,[qv] and the ranch became the area's major source of Hereford cattle. The bull ranch, which used the Bar 96 brand, covered 43,000 acres in Hall County. It included 30,000 acres in Lesley, north of the Red River, land purchased from the Shoe Bar in 1885 and subsequently fenced. Headquarters was established on twenty additional sections located on the Red River ten miles south of the site of present Memphis. Nelson, who managed the enterprise from 1886 to 1889, began with 1,500 blooded Herefords. These prize animals were soon in great demand, and the Bar 96 supplied bulls for ranches in the Panhandle, New Mexico, and Arizona.

After Nelson's departure from the Bar 96 in 1889, the Finch, Lord, and Nelson firm was reorganized as L. E. Finch and Company. Nelson's share was purchased by Alfred Ogden of Brooklyn, New York, who used an O Bar brand. Ogden soon sold his interest in the firm back to W. H. Lord, but he bought a number of cattle from the ranch and moved to Childress County, where he developed one of the state's largest herds of registered Herefords. J. A. Finch took over active management of the Bar 96 in 1890 and brought his family from Kansas to the headquarters. Fred Lord brought his bride out to the ranch through Wichita Falls. Roundups, dinners, and dances at the ranch became major social events.

Economic recession in 1892–93 resulted in the demise of the Bar 96. Finch and Company was liquidated. J. A. Finch subsequently laid claim to several sections of land in Hall County on which he ran cattle until he sold his claim to his sons about 1904. Alfred Ogden purchased a controlling interest in the rapidly shrinking Bar 96. By that time settlers had crowded in on the east side of the ranch until they left only eight sections for grazing. In 1913 the ranch ownership was transferred to D. A. Neeley and W. B. Quigley; the latter married Finch's daughter, Winnie. The ranch name was changed to Red River Hereford Ranch. Although most of the original 43,000 acres had been parceled out to farmers, a portion of the former Bar 96 Ranch continued to be operated by Neeley and Ogden, who used the O Bar brand.

BIBLIOGRAPHY: Inez Baker, *Yesterday in Hall County* (Memphis, Texas, 1940). Laura V. Hamner, *Short Grass and Longhorns* (Norman: University of Oklahoma Press, 1943). Jo Stewart Randel, ed., *A Time to Purpose: A Chronicle of Carson County* (4 vols., Hereford, Texas: Pioneer, 1966–72). Pauline D. and R. L. Robertson, *Cowman's Country: Fifty Frontier Ranches in the Texas Panhandle, 1876–1887* (Amarillo: Paramount, 1981).

H. Allen Anderson

BARNSTONE, HOWARD (1923–1987). Howard Barnstone, architect, was born on March 27, 1923, in Auburn, Maine, the son of Robert C. and Dora (Lempert) Barnstone. He spent his childhood in Auburn and in New York City, then attended Amherst College (1940–42), Yale College (A.B. 1944), and Yale University (B. Arch. 1948). From 1944 to 1946 he served as a lieutenant, junior grade, in the United States Navy. He moved to Houston in 1948 and remained there for the rest of his life, teaching and practicing architecture.

Barnstone's early work was strongly influenced by the New York architect Philip Johnson and the Chicago architect Ludwig Mies van der Rohe, both of whom executed modernist buildings in Houston in the 1950s. This type of architecture was especially identified in Houston with the collectors Dominique and John de Menil,[qv] whose house had been designed by Johnson and who were patrons of Barnstone's for the duration of his career. While in partnership with Preston M. Bolton (1952–61), Barnstone produced a series of rectilinear, flat-roofed houses in the manner of Johnson and Mies that brought Bolton and Barnstone to national attention. These included the Gordon (1955), Moustier (1955), Farfel (1956), and Owsley (1961) houses in Houston, the Blum house in Beaumont (1954), and the Cook house in Friendswood (1959).

During the 1960s, however, Barnstone moved away from this precisionist approach. His public buildings—Piney Point Elementary School (1962), the *Galveston County News* Building in Galveston (1965), and the Center for the Retarded (1966)—exhibited differentiated massing shapes and emphatic articulation of reinforced concrete structural members. His houses, especially those produced during his partnership with Eugene Aubry (1966–69), tended to be architecturally introverted. Though self-effacing externally, they were opened internally with high ceilings, simple planar walls, and dramatic expanses of glass. The Mermel (1961), Maher (1964), Bell (1969), and Kempner (1969) houses, the Levin house in Galveston (1969), the Vassar Place Apartments (1965), and Guinan Hall at the University of St. Thomas (1971) exhibited these tendencies, as did the Rice Museum (1969, now altered) and Media Center (1970) at Rice University and the Rothko Chapel[qv] (1971).

During the 1970s and 1980s Barnstone's work became even more varied architecturally. Marti's specialty store in Nuevo Laredo, Tamaulipas, Mexico (1972), built for his stepmother, Marti Franco; the Graustark Family Townhouses, Houston (1973); a country house in Carefree, Arizona, for Mr. and Mrs. Jean Riboud (1976); alterations and additions to a group of Long Island colonial houses in East Hampton, New York (1977); the Encinal apartments, Austin (1979); the Schlumberger-Doll Research Center, Ridgefield, Connecticut (1980); the De Saligny apartments, Austin (1983, with Robert T. Jackson); and the Schlumberger Austin Systems Center, Austin (1987, with Robert T. Jackson) were his major projects of this period.

Barnstone married Gertrude Levy of Houston in 1955; they were divorced in 1969. They had three children. Barnstone joined the faculty of the University of Houston in 1948. He became associate professor of architecture in 1952 and professor in 1958. He taught as a visiting instructor at Yale University (1964) and the University of St. Thomas (1965). He wrote two books on Texas architectural subjects, *The Galveston That Was* (1966) and *The Architecture of John F. Staub, Houston and the South* (1979). Barnstone became a member of the American Institute of Architects in 1951 and was elected to fellowship in the institute in 1968. He served at various times on the boards of numerous civic and cultural organizations. He was a member of Congregation Beth Israel in the 1950s and 1960s. In 1985 he was baptized and became a parishioner of Christ Church. Howard Barnstone suffered from manic-depressive psychosis and endured periods of severe depression in 1969 and in 1985–87. As a result of the latter episode, he killed himself, on April 29, 1987, in Houston. He is buried at Forest Park East Cemetery in League City. His papers are deposited at the Houston Metropolitan Research Center of the Houston Public Library.[qqv]

BIBLIOGRAPHY: *American Architects Directory*, 1955, 1962. Stephen Fox, "Howard Barnstone, 1923–1987," *Cite*, Fall 1987. Mark Hewitt, "Neoclassicism and Modern Architecture, Houston Style," *Cite*, Fall 1984. Houston *Post*, May 2, 1987. New York *Times*, May 2, 1987. *Texas Observer*, May 29, 1987. *Who's Who in America*, 1972–73, 1982–83.

Stephen Fox

BARNUM, TEXAS. Barnum is on U.S. Highway 287 seventy-five miles northwest of Beaumont in northeast Polk County. The community was founded in 1881, when W. T. Carter built a sawmill at the site on the Trinity and Sabine Railway. The Carter and Brother operation at Barnum eventually included a sawmill, a planer, storage bins, seven miles of tram roads, and two locomotives. By 1889 Barnum had a hotel, a post office, a general store, a school, a public hall, and about 350 residents. A fire in 1887 consumed the sawmill and planer, causing an estimated $10,000 worth of damage. Another fire in 1897 again destroyed the Carter facilities at Barnum. After the latter blaze, Carter decided to reestablish his Polk County mill at Camden. Although many residents subsequently left Barnum, the settlement continued to be a stop on the railroad, which became part of the Missouri, Kansas and Texas system in 1882. The Barnum post office also remained open. The small rural community still had two businesses in 1984 and twenty-nine residents in 1990.

BIBLIOGRAPHY: W. T. Block, ed., *Emerald of the Neches: The Chronicles of Beaumont from Reconstruction to Spindletop* (Nederland, Texas: Nederland Publishing, 1980).

Robert Wooster

BAROMEO, CHASE (1892–1973). Chase Baromeo, operatic bass-baritone, was born Chase Baromeo Sikes, son of Clarence Stevens and Medora (Rhodes) Sikes, on August 19, 1892, in Augusta, Georgia. He received B.A. (1917) and M.M. (1929) degrees from the University of Michigan. Before going to the University of Texas in 1938 to head the voice faculty in the music department of the new College of Fine Arts, he had a highly successful operatic career. He made his debut in 1923 at the Teatro Carcano in Milan, Italy. From 1923 to 1926 he was a member of La Scala in Milan, where he sang under Arturo Toscanini. Because of the Italians' difficulty in pronouncing his last name, Sikes became known professionally as Chase Baromeo, and he used that name for the rest of his life. He also sang at the Teatro Colón in Buenos Aires, Argentina, in 1924, with the Chicago Civic Opera Company from 1926 to 1931, and with the San Francisco Opera Company in 1935. From 1935 to 1938 he was with the Metropolitan Opera Company in New York. He also performed with many of the leading symphony orchestras in the United States. He was married to Delphie Lindstrom on May 12, 1931; they had three children, one of whom predeceased him. While with the University of Texas, he directed and performed in many university-staged operas. Baromeo left the university in 1954 to join the University of Michigan faculty. He died in Birmingham, Michigan, on August 7, 1973.

BIBLIOGRAPHY: Austin *American-Statesman*, August 8, 1973. Vertical Files, Barker Texas History Center, University of Texas at Austin.

Eldon S. Branda

BARONS CREEK. Barons (Barrons) Creek rises a mile southwest of Cherry Mountain in north central Gillespie County (at 30°23′ N, 98°56′ W). The stream, intermittent in its upper reaches, flows south-southeast for 16½ miles to its mouth on the Pedernales River, southeast of Fredericksburg (at 30°14′ N, 98°50′ W). It rises in limestone hills on the eastern edge of the Edwards Plateau[qv] and traverses flat to rolling terrain with local escarpments and a surface ranging from shallow stony and clayey soil to deeper sandy and clayey loams. Vegetation consists primarily of open stands of live oak and Ashe juniper woods. The stream was named for Baron John O. Meusebach[qv] by the German settlers of Gillespie County.

BIBLIOGRAPHY: Gillespie County Historical Society, *Pioneers in God's Hills* (2 vols., Austin: Von Boeckmann–Jones, 1960, 1974).

BARR, AMELIA EDITH HUDDLESTON (1831–1919). Amelia Barr, writer, daughter of William Henry and Mary (Singleton) Huddleston, was born in Ulverston, Lancashire, England, on March 29, 1831. Her father was a Methodist minister. She was educated in music and literature and taught in a girls' school before she married Robert Barr, an accountant, of Glasgow. After Barr lost his fortune, the couple sailed for America. They lived briefly in Chicago and Memphis and in 1856 settled in Austin, Texas, where Barr found employment as an auditor for the state of Texas. During the ten years in which Austin was their home, Amelia Barr took an active part in the social life of the frontier capital and wrote in her diary vivid pictures of many Texans and local events and scenes. In 1914 much of this material appeared in her autobiography, *All the Days of My Life!* Her accounts included women, Sam Houston,[qv] Indians who visited the capital, and local affairs concerning the Civil War.[qv] Though she did not show it outwardly, Amelia Barr was a mystic and deeply religious. Her life was governed by intuitions and prophetic dreams, many of which she related in striking detail. In 1866 the family moved to Galveston, where Barr had found new employment. In the yellow fever scourge of the next year, Barr and three sons died, leaving Mrs. Barr and three daughters. For a while she operated a boardinghouse on Tremont Street, but when this venture failed she went to New York. She was employed as a governess before turning to writing, a profession in which she found a ready market for scores of articles, poems, and short stories. Her reputation as a novelist was firmly established with the publication in 1885 of *Jan Vedder's Wife. Remember the Alamo,* the novel for which Texans know her best, was published in 1888. From 1885 to 1911 a single firm published forty-two novels by Amelia Barr. Other publishers launched additional books, and countless shorter pieces flowed from her pen. Her literary success brought her comfort, security, and considerable means, as well as fame. Mrs. Barr died in New York on March 10, 1919, and was buried in Sleepy Hollow Cemetery.

BIBLIOGRAPHY: Paul Adams, "Amelia Barr in Texas, 1856–1868," *Southwestern Historical Quarterly* 49 (January 1946). Amelia Edith Barr Papers, Barker Texas History Center, University of Texas at Austin. Hildegarde Hawthorne, "Amelia E. Barr—Some Recollections," *Bookman,* May 1920. M. N. Howard, The Novels of Amelia Barr (M.A. thesis, University of Texas, 1943). Kate Dickinson Sweetser, "Amelia Barr and the Novice," *Bookman,* October 1923.

Paul Adams

BARR, ROBERT (1802–1839). Robert Barr, soldier and first postmaster general of the Republic of Texas,[qv] was born in Ohio in 1802 and arrived in Texas before December 5, 1833. At the battle of San Jacinto[qv] he served as a private in Capt. William H. Patton's[qv] Fourth Company of Col. Sidney Sherman's[qv] Second Regiment, Texas Volunteers. On December 22, 1836, Sam Houston[qv] appointed Barr postmaster general. Mirabeau B. Lamar[qv] reappointed him, but Barr died in Houston on October 11, 1839, soon after the Lamar administration was inaugurated, and was buried with Masonic and Odd Fellows honors. Three of his sons were living in 1878.

BIBLIOGRAPHY: *Compiled Index to Elected and Appointed Officials of the Republic of Texas, 1835–1846* (Austin: State Archives, Texas State Library, 1981). Daughters of the Republic of Texas, *Muster Rolls of the Texas Revolution* (Austin, 1986). Sam Houston Dixon and Louis Wiltz Kemp, *The Heroes of San Jacinto* (Houston: Anson Jones, 1932). Amelia W. Williams and Eugene C. Barker, eds., *The Writings of Sam Houston, 1813–1863* (8 vols., Austin: University of Texas Press, 1938–43; rpt., Austin and New York: Pemberton Press, 1970).

Thomas W. Cutrer

BARR, WILLIAM (ca. 1760–1810). William Barr, early Nacogdoches merchant, was born in Londonderry, Ulster County, Ireland, around 1760, the son of John and Inez (Gibson) Barr. When he was twelve, his parents took him to Pennsylvania, where they lived first in Philadelphia and later in Pittsburgh. After serving three years as a captain in the United States Army, Barr moved to the Spanish province of Louisiana, about 1786. In 1787 he took the oath of allegiance to Spain before Governor Esteban Miró and in 1793 moved to Nacogdoches, Texas. In 1798 Barr associated himself with Luther Smith, Edward Murphy, and Peter Samuel Davenport[qv] in a commercial firm later known as the House of Barr and Davenport. In 1800 the Spanish government gave Barr a commission to supply the Indians in Texas with certain presents and to trade with them for pelts, furs, and livestock. In this capacity he operated until his death, in 1810. His estate in Natchitoches alone was appraised at $156,945. Barr, who never married, left part of his estate to his mother and two sisters and part to Davenport.

BIBLIOGRAPHY: Carolyn Reeves Ericson, comp., *Citizens and Foreigners of the Nacogdoches District, 1809–1836* (2 vols., Nacogdoches, Texas: Ericson, 1981). J. Villasana Haggard, "The House of Barr and Davenport," *Southwestern Historical Quarterly* 45 (July 1945). J. V. Haggard, "The Neutral Ground between Louisiana and Texas, 1806–1821," *Louisiana Historical Quarterly* 28 (October 1945).

John V. Haggard

BARRACETO CREEK. Barraceto (Barrocito) Creek rises eleven miles east of Aguilares in southwestern Webb County (at 27°16′ N, 99°08′ W) and runs northwest for nine miles to its mouth on Agua Azul Creek, sixteen miles south of Laredo (at 27°20′ N, 99°13′ W). It traverses low-rolling and flat terrain with locally shallow depressions, surfaced by clay and sandy loams that support grasses, mesquite, chaparral, and water-tolerant hardwoods.

BARREDA, CELESTINO PARDO (1858–1953). Celestino Pardo Barreda, pioneer merchant and landowner, son of Eugenio Pardo and Fermina de Barreda y Liaño, was born in La Penilla, Santander, Spain, on January 1, 1858. He immigrated to New Orleans in 1871 on the German steamship *Germania* and sailed to Port Isabel, Texas, shortly thereafter. After working a few months with his uncles in Brownsville, he was sent to schools in New Jersey and Massachusetts. In 1874 Barreda returned from the East to work for his uncles, but he soon established a dry goods business for himself. By 1880 he was a United States citizen and was accumulating ranchlands and city properties in Texas and Mexico. He acquired sugar plantations in Cuba and began shipping cattle throughout the southern United States and Cuba. As early as 1908 he was using the Rio Grande for irrigation purposes. By the 1920s he had extensive landholdings in South Texas and was vice president of the First National Bank in Brownsville, organizer of the Texas Bank and Trust Company, and a member of many civic and social organizations. He deeded land for railway and highway development, promoted the county water-improvement district, and served as director of the chamber of commerce. On December 17, 1906, Barreda married María de Guinea in Matamoros, Tamaulipas, and although they had no children of their own, they reared their orphaned niece and nephew. Barreda was a Catholic of Immaculate Conception Parish. He died on February 3, 1953, in Brownsville and was buried in Buena Vista Cemetery there.

BIBLIOGRAPHY: Ellis A. Davis and Edwin H. Grobe, comps., *The New Encyclopedia of Texas* (2 vols., Dallas: Texas Development Bureau, 1925?; 4 vols. 1929?). Vertical Files, Barker Texas History Center, University of Texas at Austin.

C. C. Stewart and Celia S. Santiso

BARREL CANYON. Barrel Canyon, through which runs an intermittent stream, rises a mile east of Bullis Gap in eastern Brewster County (at 29°49′ N, 102°35′ W) and extends northeast for fourteen miles to its mouth on San Francisco Creek, five miles east of the junction of the Brewster-Terrell county line and the Rio Grande (at 29°53′ N, 102°24′ W). The terrain is flat with local shallow depressions and some deep, dense dissection. Soils in the area are clay and sandy loams and shallow, stony soils; they support water-tolerant hardwoods, conifers, and grasses, as well as oak, juniper, and some mesquite.

BARRELL CREEK. Barrell Creek heads in the breaks at the edge of the Llano Estacado[qv] in east central Briscoe County (at 34°29′ N, 101°08′ W) and flows north for about nine miles to its mouth on the

Prairie Dog Town Fork of the Red River (at 34°37′ N, 101°05′ W). Part of the land near the creek's upper waters, ten miles east of Silverton, was once known as Barrel Creek Ranch. The creek crosses terrain surfaced by shallow to moderately deep silt loams. The vegetation consists primarily of mesquite and grasses.

BIBLIOGRAPHY: Briscoe County Historical Survey Committee, *Footprints of Time in Briscoe County* (Dallas: Taylor, 1976). Harley True Burton, *A History of the JA Ranch* (Austin: Von Boeckmann–Jones, 1928; rpt., New York: Argonaut, 1966).

BARREL SPRINGS CREEK. Barrel Springs Creek begins 2½ miles northwest of Montague in central Montague County (at 33°40′ N, 97°45′ W) and runs northwest for twelve miles to its mouth on Salt Creek, a mile east of Belcherville (at 33°48′ N, 97°48′ W). It traverses generally flat terrain surfaced by clayey and sandy loams that support water-tolerant hardwoods, conifers, and grasses. For most of the county's history, the Barrel Springs Creek area has been used as rangeland.

BARRET, LYNE TALIAFERRO (1832–1913). Lyne Taliaferro (Tol) Barret, pioneer oilman also known as Lynis T. Barrett, the youngest of nine children of Charles Lee and Sarah (Taliaferro) Barret, was born at Appomattox, Virginia, on November 7, 1832. After her husband died in 1842 while the family was on its way to Texas, Mrs. Barret moved her children first to San Augustine County and then to the Barret plantation at Melrose, where she employed a tutor when school was not in session. Lyne Barret's writings attest to his excellent training. He began his career as a clerk and by 1862 had become a partner in the mercantile firm Hardeman Brothers and Barret. He first became interested in the oil industry before the Civil War.[qv] He contracted with Lucy W. Skillern to lease 279 acres near Oil Springs on December 15, 1859, but the war stopped his preparations. On July 31, 1862, he received an exemption from military service to oversee his mother's plantation. From about 1863 to 1865 he served as captain of the Quartermaster Corps, Confederate States of America, for the Nacogdoches district.

On December 21, 1865, Barret, Benjamin P. Hollingsworth, Charles A. Hamilton, John T. Flint, and John B. Earle organized the Melrose Petroleum Oil Company. Three drilling contracts had already been made for the benefit of the company, including another one with Skillern heirs on October 9, 1865. Drilling began during the summer of 1866 and resulted in the first producing oil well in the state, which came in at a depth of 106 feet by September 12, 1866. The well, located at Oil Springs, produced about ten barrels a day. Samples were forwarded to the Department of Emigration in New York, which pronounced the oil "superior in all its properties." On the advice of oilmen in Shreveport, Barret went to New York and Pennsylvania to examine equipment before purchase. There he met John F. Carll, a civil engineer, and on March 1, 1867, Barret and others made financial obligations to Carll, who had agreed to run tests and assist in development of the property. According to Barret, Carll's financial backer, Brown Brothers of Titusville, Pennsylvania, wrote on the day of the test that the low price of oil and the political unrest caused by Reconstruction[qv] made the development of the field unfeasible. Impatient investors wanted to sell their interest in the company but turned down Barret's offers of land and demanded cash. Despite encouragement by Carll in 1868, when oil prices went up again, the field was never developed. Barret suffered extensive financial loss and returned to the mercantile business in Melrose. Later he saw the field developed with an oil boom in 1887 at what became known as Oil City.

Barret was the first secretary of Ochiltree Masonic Lodge No. 143 of Melrose when it was founded in 1855, and was later master. He was secretary of the Melrose Methodist Church in October 1865 and served as justice of the peace in Melrose in 1862 and 1899. He married Angelina Martha Thomas on August 26, 1857, and they had eleven children. Barret died in Melrose on March 23, 1913. Though he received little acclaim during his lifetime, in 1966 memorial markers were dedicated at his grave in Melrose Providence Baptist Church Cemetery and at Stephen F. Austin State University to mark the 100th anniversary of the drilling of the first producing oil well in Texas. In 1981 a marker was also placed at Barret's home, off Farm Road 2863 five miles south of Nacogdoches.

BIBLIOGRAPHY: Lyne Taliaferro Barret Papers, Special Collections Department, Ralph W. Steen Library, Stephen F. Austin State University. C. K. Chamberlain, "Lyne Taliaferro Barret, A Pioneer Texas Wildcatter," *East Texas Historical Journal* 6 (March 1968). Linda Ericson, "A History of Oil Springs: Texas' First Oil Field," *Texas Historian,* January 1972. Charles K. Phillips, Builder of Texas Collection to 1942: Honoring Lyne Taliaferro Barret (MS, Steen Library, Stephen F. Austin State University, Nacogdoches).

Linda E. Devereaux

BARRETT, DON CARLOS (1788–1838). Don Carlos Barrett, lawyer and legislator, was born on June 22, 1788, at Norwich, Vermont, the eldest son of Jonathan and Elizabeth (Murdock) Barrett. In 1810 at Natchez, Mississippi, he married Lucy Walton, also of Norwich. The couple had one son. After the death of his first wife Barrett married Eliza De Cressy, sometime in the early 1820s. He had met Mrs. De Cressy in New York City, and they lived for a time in Wilkes-Barre, Pennsylvania; they had four children. In 1820 Barrett was licensed to practice law in Luzerne County, Pennsylvania, and in 1827 he was admitted to practice before the Supreme Court of Western Pennsylvania.

On April 13, 1835, he took the oath of allegiance to Mexico in Mina Municipality, now Bastrop, and became a citizen of Texas. At Mina he formed a law partnership with Elisha M. Pease,[qv] with whom he had come to Texas. With the approach of the Texas Revolution,[qv] Barrett was elected president of the newly formed committee of public safety at Mina, on May 8, 1835, and on July 4 he was appointed to initiate correspondence with similar committees in the Brazos District with a view toward closing the breach between Texas and the Mexican government. Later that month he was named Mina delegate to a meeting at San Felipe that was to draw up assurances of Texan loyalty to the Mexican government. In August 1835 the joint committee sent Barrett and Edward Gritten[qv] as commissioners to meet with Gen. Martín Perfecto de Cos[qv] at Matamoros and explain to him the cause of the settlers' displeasure with the Mexican Centralist government. The two commissioners were intercepted at San Antonio by Col. Domingo de Ugartechea,[qv] however, and told that Cos would not receive them but demanded the surrender of insurrectionary leaders Lorenzo de Zavala, William B. Travis, and Robert M. Williamson[qqv] before the disturbances in Texas could be forgiven. In his absence a portion of Barrett's property was attached to satisfy an old debt, an action that he bitterly resented.

Barrett returned to San Felipe and then to Mina, where he was elected a delegate to the Consultation,[qv] to take place at Washington-on-the-Brazos on October 15. There he initially opposed the declaration of Texas independence for fear that such a move would unite all of Mexico against the Texans. He voted with the majority on the Declaration of November 7, 1835,[qv] a declaration that the Texans were fighting in favor of the Mexican Constitution of 1824.[qv] Barrett was a principal author of this important document. He then was selected chairman of a committee of twelve delegates to draft a plan for a provisional government[qv] for Texas. The work of this committee provided for the establishment of a civil government and military force for Texas.

When the provisional government took power on November 14, Barrett was elected to the General Council[qv] as representative from Mina. As a member of the council he was chairman of the standing Committee on State and Judiciary as well as the chairman or member of more than twenty other committees. In addition, he sponsored a great many of the laws passed by the provisional government and was a close friend of both Stephen F. Austin and Sam Houston.[qqv] On December 11 he was elected judge advocate of the Texas army, but his appointment was vetoed with a vicious attack by Governor Henry Smith.[qv] Smith claimed, among other charges, that Barrett had forged an attorney's license in North Carolina, that he had accepted fees from both prosecution and defense on a case, that he had knowingly passed counterfeit money, and that he had embezzled money appropriated for his and Gritten's mission to Matamoros to petition Cos the previous July. The council denied not only Smith's charges but his right to veto its appointments. Due at least in part to this clash of wills, Smith ordered the council dissolved on January 11, 1836, and the body responded by naming Lieutenant Governor James W. Robinson[qv] governor of Texas. Barrett made no personal response to Smith's charges, but his colleagues on the council testified that he "has been one of the leading members of the Consultation and General Council and has been industrious and useful to the country. We do most sincerely recommend him as a gentleman of high order, talents and learning, a patriot and an honest politician."

On February 15 Barrett resigned from the council due to failing health. Early in April he went to New Orleans and from there to Blue Sulphur Springs in Greenbriar Springs, Virginia, to recover his health. In May 1837 he returned to New Orleans, and by August 26 he was again in Galveston. He died at the home of Col. Warren D. C. Hall[qv] at Brazoria on May 19, 1838, and was buried in the old cemetery there. The Texas Centennial[qv] Commission placed a marker at his grave. His estate, valued at $140,000, included five slaves and a home in Quintana. Barrett's papers are preserved at the Barker Texas History Center,[qv] University of Texas at Austin.

BIBLIOGRAPHY: Eugene C. Barker, ed., *The Austin Papers* (3 vols., Washington: GPO, 1924–28). Eugene C. Barker, "Don Carlos Barrett," *Southwestern Historical Quarterly* 20 (October 1916). Don Carlos Barrett Papers, Barker Texas History Center, University of Texas at Austin. John H. Jenkins, ed., *The Papers of the Texas Revolution, 1835–1836* (10 vols., Austin: Presidial Press, 1973).

Thomas W. Cutrer

BARRETT, JOHN W. (1814–1862). John W. Barrett, Unionist and editor, was born in South Carolina on July 14, 1814. He immigrated with his family to Indiana at an early age, and in 1838 he moved to Texas. At his death he was cited by a rival newspaper publisher as having "participated in the struggle for Texas independence." Barrett bought the *Star State Patriot,* which succeeded the *Soda Lake Herald,* in April 1848 from Josiah Marshall and in June 1856 renamed it the *Harrison Flag.* The *Flag* supported Sam Houston,[qv] the American (Know-Nothing) party,[qv] and the Constitutional Union party[qqv] of 1860. Robert W. Loughery,[qv] owner and editor of the Marshall *Texas Republican* and an ardent secessionist, classed Barrett and the *Flag* as oppositionist and submissionist during the secession[qv] crisis. Barrett insisted that Lincoln was a moderate and that fears that he would assail the institution of slavery[qv] where it already existed were unfounded. Therefore the fact of his election, Barrett argued, was not sufficient cause for resistance on the part of the South. In editorial after editorial during November and December 1860, Barrett opposed secession;[qv] he declared on December 15, 1860, that breaking up the United States would be "the most momentous political decision that has ever demanded the attention of mankind."

The same winter, ill and confined to his room, he suspended publication of the *Flag* with the issue of January 12, 1861. Writing five days afterward, Loughery called off their long political feud to reminisce about the problems they had encountered as publishers and editors: "He has been sick nine months with little chance of improvement. . . . He has a large family depending on him, with children to educate. He needs every dollar coming to him. Those owing him should not be insensible to his condition." Barrett died of tuberculosis on May 12, 1862, at New Salem (Rusk County). His son William (Billy) Barrett revived the *Flag* on November 15, 1865, at the end of hostilities and continued its publication in Marshall until October 22, 1868, when it was renamed the *Weekly Harrison Flag,* which continued publication until 1870.

BIBLIOGRAPHY: Randolph B. Campbell, *A Southern Community in Crisis: Harrison County, Texas, 1850–1880* (Austin: Texas State Historical Association, 1983). Marilyn M. Sibley, *Lone Stars and State Gazettes: Texas Newspapers before the Civil War* (College Station: Texas A&M University Press, 1983).

Max S. Lale

BARRETT, P. MONTGOMERY (1897–1949). P. Montgomery (Monte) Barrett, cartoonist and author, the son of Edward Wesley and Clara May (Prow) Barrett, was born in Mitchell, Indiana, on June 19, 1897. He attended the University of California and DePauw University but left college in his senior year, 1917, to join the navy for service during World War I.[qv] He was foreign correspondent during the Villareal revolution in Mexico. Barrett came to Texas for a short time in 1920 but soon went to Chicago as feature editor of the Chicago *Herald and Examiner.* He returned to Texas in 1922 and worked on newspapers in several Texas cities until his retirement from active newspaper work in May 1928. In 1927 he began the "Jane Arden" comic strip, which was syndicated. Barrett made his home in San Antonio and wrote various magazine articles and historical novels. Three of his books with Texas backgrounds were *Sun in Their Eyes* (1944), *Tempered Blade* (1946), and *Smoke up the Valley* (1949). He died in New York on October 8, 1949, and was buried in San José Cemetery in San Antonio. He was survived by his wife, Mary Helen (Caruth).

BIBLIOGRAPHY: Florence Elberta Barns, *Texas Writers of Today* (Dallas: Tardy, 1935). San Antonio *Express,* October 9, 10, 1949.

Dorman H. Winfrey

BARRETT, THOMAS C. (1809–1892). Thomas C. Barrett, jurist during the Great Hanging at Gainesville,[qv] son of Thomas and Jane (Christian) Barrett, was born in Anson County, North Carolina, on June 21, 1809. He married Martha Alexander in Tennessee in January 1833. They had five children. Barrett became a minister and a self-taught physician during the 1830s. The family moved from Tennessee to Missouri in 1842 and was living there when Mrs. Barrett died, on September 14, 1844. Barrett afterward married Alsay Linley of Kentucky and fathered another seven children.

The Barretts moved to Texas in 1848. They lived first in Hopkins County, then Titus County, and in 1860 settled on a farm three miles east of Gainesville. In October 1862, upon hearing about a supposed plot by the "Union Peace Party" to overthrow the Confederate government and return the North Texas area to the government of the United States, Barrett rode to Gainesville to investigate. He learned that a jury had been chosen to hear the cases and that he had been selected to serve. The jury decided that only a majority vote would be necessary to determine guilt or innocence, but Barrett was in favor of an unanimous or at least a two-thirds vote. After eight men were tried, found guilty, and sentenced to hang, Barrett and another juror stated that they would remove themselves from the jury unless at least a two-thirds vote was required for a guilty verdict. The jury agreed. Barrett later speculated that the citizens of Gainesville and the surrounding area would have been satisfied with the execution of these eight men if James Dickson and Col. William C. Young[qv] had not been murdered from ambush north of Gainesville. These killings caused renewed excitement, and more prosecutions ensued. At the end of the trial forty men had been found guilty and hanged.

After the trial ended, Barrett, fearing reprisals, decided to move his family to a safer place. The Barretts moved to Mount Vernon in the fall of 1863 and remained there until June 1865, when they moved to

Bell County. In Bell County Barrett heard that federal soldiers were arresting people who had committed crimes during the Civil War.[qv] He spent several nights sleeping out of doors and hiding before he decided to leave Texas until proper authorities were again in control. He went to Mount Pleasant, Mississippi, in January 1866 and visited relatives in Tennessee before returning to Gainesville in December 1866. He demanded a jury trial for his part in the hangings and was found not guilty on December 11, 1868. In 1885 Barrett published his memoirs in a book, The Great Hanging at Gainesville. He deprecated the role of emotion in the jury's decisions and argued that his being on the jury had saved large numbers of lives. He spent the remainder of his life as a preacher for the Church of Christ, a doctor, and a farmer in Cooke County, where he died on July 24, 1892.

BIBLIOGRAPHY: Thomas Barrett, The Great Hanging at Gainesville (Gainesville, Texas, 1885; rpt., Austin: Texas State Historical Association, 1961). *Biographical Souvenir of the State of Texas* (Chicago: Battey, 1889; rpt., Easley, South Carolina: Southern Historical Press, 1978). *Robert Wayne McDaniel*

BARRETT, WILLIAM (1800?–1853?). William Barrett (Barret, Barett), early Texas settler, may have been a member of Stephen F. Austin's[qv] Old Three Hundred.[qv] Although he was not listed on Austin's 1826 census, some sources pair him with Abner Harris[qv] as one of the original three hundred families. On his application for land he stated that he was aged twenty-six and single. The document also indicated that he was from Pennsylvania, but it is uncertain if he was born there. It is equally unclear when he came to Texas, but in June 1827 he and Harris were granted title to a sitio[qv] of land now in Fort Bend County. Barrett and Elizabeth Wient (Wiant) were married on July 8, 1829, before Alexander Hodge.[qv] Barrett pledged a dowry of $5,000, and the couple vowed to be married by a priest as soon as possible, a necessary step under Mexican law. Whether they were ever married by a priest is unknown, but they had at least two children who survived into adulthood. Barrett served in the Texas army under William Hester Patton and Edward Burleson[qqv] in 1835–36. He was paid twenty-six dollars and honorably discharged, after which he returned home to Brazoria County. A William Barret was listed as a passenger on the steamer *Sam Houston* from Houston to Galveston in October 1837, and in 1842 a Capt. William Barett was listed as serving under Alexander Somervell[qv] at San Antonio; whether either of these men was the subject of this article is uncertain. The exact date of Barrett's death is also unknown, but he was posted as deceased and his estate was inventoried in March 1853.

BIBLIOGRAPHY: Austin Land Papers, Spanish Collection (Archives and Records Division, Texas General Land Office, Austin). Lester G. Bugbee, "The Old Three Hundred: A List of Settlers in Austin's First Colony," *Quarterly of the Texas State Historical Association* 1 (October 1897). *Telegraph and Texas Register*, October 7, 1837, December 21, 1842. *Deurene Oates Morgan*

BARRETT, WILLIAM MARTIN (1812–1867). William Martin Barrett, builder, was born in Dinwiddie, Virginia, in 1812, and came to Texas in 1841. He was appointed architect and contractor for the first permanent building of Austin College in Huntsville in 1851. When the college was moved to Sherman in 1876, the building was used for public school purposes; in 1879 it became the first building of Sam Houston Normal Institute (now Sam Houston State University). It is still in use by the college and is the oldest building in Texas used continuously for educational purposes. Barrett was a colonel in the Mexican War[qv] and also served as an officer in the Civil War.[qv] He was allegedly a cousin of William Barret Travis[qv] and a friend of Sam Houston,[qv] who was an Austin College trustee. Barrett married Mrs. Nancy Keenan Hamilton in Huntsville on December 5, 1847; they had four children. Barrett died in Huntsville on September 18, 1867, of yellow fever.

BIBLIOGRAPHY: Frank W. Johnson, *A History of Texas and Texans* (5 vols., ed. E. C. Barker and E. W. Winkler [Chicago and New York: American Historical Society, 1914; rpt. 1916]). *Aline Law*

BARRETT, TEXAS. Barrett, just south of U.S. Highway 90 on Farm roads 1942 and 2100 in eastern Harris County, began during Reconstruction[qv] as a black community. The community was named for former slave Harrison Barrett, known as "Uncle Harrison," who had been born in Texas around 1845 to slave parents. After emancipation, Barrett settled his family on part of Reuben White's[qv] league east of the San Jacinto River and, in 1889, purchased the land for fifty cents an acre. It became one of the largest holdings in Harris County to be acquired by a former slave. Barrett named the property Barrett's Settlement. The community began with seven houses, which Barrett helped to build with lumber from his land. He helped members of his family to set up farms, established a sawmill, a gristmill, and a coffee mill and granted others open access to fish and crayfish in the spring and gully near his homestead. Harrison donated land for Shiloh Baptist Church, which also served as a school. In 1947 a high school and a post office branch known as Barrett Station opened. Barrett, who died in 1917, was buried in Journey's End Cemetery in the settlement, and a museum and park were later named in his honor. State highway maps in 1936 showed a school, St. Martin Cemetery, and a camp at the townsite. The population reached 2,364 in 1960. U.S. Highway 90 was built through the area in the 1970s, and by 1990 the population was 3,644. The town celebrates its heritage every Juneteenth.[qv]

Diana J. Kleiner

BARRILLA DRAW. Barrilla Draw begins between Major Peak and the Barrilla Mountains in east central Jeff Davis County (31°00′ N, 103°27′ W) and runs north for fifty miles across the southwestern edge of Pecos County to its mouth on the eastern edge of Toyah Lake in east central Reeves County (at 31°07′ N, 103°25′ W). The surrounding steep to gentle slopes and broken flat terrain of alluvial pebbles, gravel, sand, and mud are surfaced by light reddish-brown to brown sand, clay loam, and rough stony soils that support scrub brush, sparse grasses, creosote bush, and cacti. Barrilla Draw was named for the salt cedars, or barillas, that grow in the Trans-Pecos.

BIBLIOGRAPHY: Fred Tarpley, *1001 Texas Place Names* (Austin: University of Texas Press, 1980).

BARRILLA MOUNTAIN. Barrilla Mountain, a summit in the Barrilla range also known as Flat Top Mountain, is in the southeastern corner of Reeves County (at 30°47′ N, 103°37′ W). With an elevation of 4,672 feet above sea level, Barrilla Mountain is the highest peak in Reeves County and rises 555 feet above the adjacent canyonland. The surrounding flat terrain and rugged canyonland of desert mountain volcanic rock is surfaced by wash deposits of sand, gravel, and mud that support live oak, piñon, juniper, grasses, maple, ponderosa pine, madrone, and water-tolerant hardwoods and conifers. Prehistoric people lived in rock shelters around the edge of the Barrilla Mountains and left behind pictographs. The mountain and the range were named for the salt cedars that grow in the Trans-Pecos region.

BIBLIOGRAPHY: Alton Hughes, *Pecos: A History of the Pioneer West* (Seagraves, Texas: Pioneer, 1978).

BARRILLA MOUNTAINS. The Barrilla Mountains are twenty miles northeast of Fort Davis in northeastern Jeff Davis County (their center is at 30°48′ N, 103°40′ W). They stretch fourteen miles from northwest to southeast, roughly paralleling the county line but crossing into Reeves and Pecos counties. The highest elevation in the Barrillas is 5,180 feet above sea level, 1,400 feet above the intersection of Ranch Road 1832 and State Highway 17, three miles east. The surrounding shallow, stony soils support Mexican buckeye, walnut, persimmon, desert willow, scrub brush, and sparse grasses. The Spanish word *barrilla* can refer either to a form of impure soda or to the saltwort plant, but one source claims that in this case it is actually a version of Varela, the name of an early settler.

BARRINGTON. Barrington, the plantation home of Anson Jones,[qv] served as the last presidential residence of the Republic of Texas.[qv] The site, three miles from Washington-on-the-Brazos in Washington County, was purchased from Moses Austin Bryan[qv] in 1844, and the construction was supervised by a J. Campbell. The home and two log cabins were paid for with 200 acres of land, $200 cash, and $100 in stock. The plantation grew cotton and tobacco. Campbell had two slaves of his own and hired four from neighbors to work in the construction crew. The Texas Centennial[qv] Commission purchased the structure in 1936 and moved it to Washington State Park, where the building has been restored and is open to viewing by the public (*see* WASHINGTON-ON-THE-BRAZOS STATE HISTORICAL PARK).

Jones named the house after his place of birth, Great Barrington, Massachusetts. After annexation[qv] he continued to reside at Barrington until November 23, 1857. When his hope of election to the United States Senate was dashed by the Texas legislature, he sold the house and began moving his family to Galveston, where he planned to resume his medical practice. He was returning to Barrington, where the family waited, when he stopped in Houston to visit some old friends and committed suicide on January 1, 1858.

James P. Flewellen, an 1850 graduate of West Point and a native of Macon, Georgia, purchased the property from Jones. Flewellen moved to Texas with the intention of farming. At the outbreak of the Civil War[qv] he was commissioned a major and served as an artillery officer under Gen. John B. Magruder.[qv] After the war Flewellen returned to Barrington and lived there until shortly before his death in 1909. Jones's widow, Mary Smith Jones,[qv] made an annual pilgrimage to Barrington, where she was received as a guest of the Flewellens. The home was sold to Henry Quebe in 1910. His son sold it to Henry Goeking in 1916. In 1935 it was purchased from Goeking's heirs by William Stegemueller. The property was turned over to the Texas Parks and Wildlife Department[qv] in 1976 for administration and continued restoration.

BIBLIOGRAPHY: W. O. Dietrich, *The Blazing Story of Washington County* (Brenham, Texas: Banner Press, 1950; rev. ed., Wichita Falls: Nortex, 1973). Herbert Gambrell, *Anson Jones: The Last President of Texas* (Garden City, New York: Doubleday, 1948). Vertical Files, Barker Texas History Center, University of Texas at Austin.

James L. Hailey

BARRIO JUNCO Y ESPRIELLA, PEDRO DE (?–?). Pedro de Barrio Junco y Espriella, son of Felipe de Barrio Junco y Espriella and Ana María Noriega Rubín de Celis, was born in Cardozo, Llanes, Asturias. He was the provincial alcalde[qv] of the Santa Hermandad of all New Spain and became governor ad interim of Texas on June 3, 1748. He had been governor of Nuevo León for six years and conducted many Indian campaigns. On the whole he was unsympathetic with the mission interests and opposed without success the location of the San Xavier missions[qv] on the site selected by the friars. His administration was arbitrary, and for a time he imprisoned the first regidor[qv] of San Antonio. After being accused of disregarding the royal *cédula* prohibiting gambling and of engaging in illegal trade with the French, he was removed from office late in 1750, and the charges against him were investigated. His last official appointment appears to have been as captain of Paso del Norte Presidio on March 27, 1765. He was married to María Antonia Rodríguez, and they had two children.

BIBLIOGRAPHY: Hubert Howe Bancroft, *History of the North Mexican States and Texas* (2 vols., San Francisco: History Company, 1886, 1889). Bexar Archives, Barker Texas History Center, University of Texas at Austin. Herbert Eugene Bolton, *Texas in the Middle Eighteenth Century: Studies in Spanish Colonial History and Administration* (Berkeley: University of California Press, 1915; rpt., Austin: University of Texas Press, 1970). Carlos E. Castañeda, *Our Catholic Heritage in Texas* (7 vols., Austin: Von Boeckmann–Jones, 1936–58; rpt., New York: Arno, 1976). Juan Agustín Morfi, *History of Texas, 1673–1779* (2 vols., Albuquerque: Quivira Society, 1935; rpt., New York: Arno, 1967). Elizabeth Howard West, trans., "Bonilla's Brief Compendium of the History of Texas, 1772," *Quarterly of the Texas State Historical Association* 8 (July 1904).

BARRIOS Y JÁUREGUI, JACINTO DE (?–?). Jacinto de Barrios y Jáuregui entered the service of the Spanish king about 1718 and rose from ensign to lieutenant colonel of cavalry in campaigns against the Italians. After appointment as governor and captain-general of Texas in 1751, he arrived in Los Adaes[qv] in June of that year. Events of his administration included the founding of the San Agustín de Ahumada Presidio on the site of Joseph Blancpain's[qv] arrest; the moving of the San Xavier missions[qv] and San Francisco Xavier Presidio to the San Marcos River; the recommending of the Apache expedition of Diego Ortiz Parrilla;[qv] the sending of Bernardo de Miranda[qv] to investigate the rumored silver in the Hill Country[qv] north of San Antonio; and the founding of Santa Cruz de San Sabá Mission[qv] and the San Sabá Presidio (*see* SAN LUIS DE LAS AMARILLAS PRESIDIO).

In the summer of 1756 ángel de Martos y Navarrete[qv] was appointed governor of Texas, and Barrios received the governorship of Coahuila, but the appointments were interchanged to permit Barrios to remain in Texas until 1759 to complete the founding of San Agustín de Ahumada Presidio and a civil settlement nearby. Barrios made a great deal of money by making the fur trade with the Bidais, Orcoquizas, and other Indian groups a strict personal monopoly; he bought goods from the French in Natchitoches and sold them the furs. These actions contributed to his being the governor of Texas most criticized for contraband trade with the French in Louisiana. He served two terms as governor of Coahuila after leaving Texas.

BIBLIOGRAPHY: Herbert Eugene Bolton, *Texas in the Middle Eighteenth Century: Studies in Spanish Colonial History and Administration* (Berkeley: University of California Press, 1915; rpt., Austin: University of Texas Press, 1970). Carlos E. Castañeda, *Our Catholic Heritage in Texas* (7 vols., Austin: Von Boeckmann–Jones, 1936–58; rpt., New York: Arno, 1976). Charles W. Hackett, ed., *Pichardo's Treatise on the Limits of Louisiana and Texas* (4 vols., Austin: University of Texas Press, 1931–46).

BARRON, SAMUEL BENTON (1834–1912). Samuel Benton Barron, lawyer and judge, was born near Gurley, Madison County, Alabama, on November 9, 1834, the third child of Samuel Boulds and Martha (Cotten) Barron. Both parents died when Barron was young. The youth clerked in a store at nearby Huntsville, Alabama, and began reading law in 1858. He moved the following year to Rusk, Texas, where he found employment as a clerk until the summer of 1860, when he began his legal practice. At the outbreak of the Civil War[qv] Barron joined the "Lone Star Defenders," the first company of Confederate volunteers raised in Cherokee County, in May 1861. This unit became Company C of Col. Elkanah B. Greer's[qv] Third Texas Cavalry[qv] when the regiment was organized the following month. Barron entered service as a sergeant and was elected lieutenant in 1863. He served throughout the war in the Third Texas, from its first battle at Wilson's Creek, Missouri, to its final encounter with the enemy at Sugar Creek, Tennessee, on December 26, 1864.

After the war Barron returned to civilian life at Rusk, where he operated a store for about five years before resuming his law practice. From 1880 until his death he was repeatedly elected to the offices of county clerk (1880–91) and justice of the peace (1907–12); he also served as county judge between 1897 and 1899. Barron was a Presbyterian and Mason. His first wife was Eugenia Wiggins, with whom he had three children. After her death, he married Mrs. Olympia Scott Miller, who died in 1893. His third wife was Mrs. Agatha Scott Leftwich. Barron died in Palestine on February 2, 1912.

He is best remembered for his colorful and accurate memoir of his life as a Rebel cavalryman, *The Lone Star Defenders,* published originally in 1908. Without bombast or excessive sentimentality, he recounts his day-to-day experiences in camp and field. It is among the most authentic and reliable accounts of a Texas soldier in the Civil War.

BIBLIOGRAPHY: Sidney S. Johnson, *Texans Who Wore the Gray* (Tyler, Texas, 1907). J. A. Templeton, "Capt. S. B. Barron," *Confederate Veteran* 20 (June 1912).
Douglas Hale

BARRON, THOMAS HUDSON (1796–1874). Thomas Hudson Barron, early settler and Texas Ranger, son of Susan (Mattingly) and John M. Barron, was born on March 8, 1796, probably in Kentucky. The family lived in Hardin County, Kentucky, in the early 1800s. He enlisted in the Kentucky militia at Leitchfield, Kentucky, on November 15, 1814, and participated in the battle of New Orleans on January 8, 1815. He received for his service a bounty grant of 160 acres. By 1817 he was one of the early settlers on the upper Red River in the area of Miller County, Arkansas.[qv] He married Elizabeth Curnell in Arkansas on February 20, 1820. In late 1821 Barron, his wife, and first child passed through Nacogdoches with several of the first of Stephen F. Austin's[qv] Old Three Hundred[qv] colonists. Barron was a member of the Austin colony for a year before returning to Arkansas Territory. He was commissioned magistrate of Jefferson Township, Miller County, on March 8, 1826. He appears on the tax records for Hempstead County, Arkansas, in 1828, 1829, 1830, and in the census for Hempstead County in 1830.

In January 1831 he returned to Texas, according to Austin's Register of Families. In 1832 he received from Austin a grant of one league of land in Brazos County, located east of Edge on the Old San Antonio Road.[qv] During this period Barron contracted to settle at Nashville in Sterling C. Robertson's[qv] colony. He was granted twenty-four labores of land now in McLennan County on March 25, 1835, and one labor near the site of present Viesca on June 10, 1835. Throughout his career Barron was active in defense of the frontier. From before until after the Texas Revolution[qv] he served as captain of Texas Rangers[qv] at Viesca, Nashville, Washington-on-the Brazos, and Tenoxtitlán, where he was commandant. In January 1836 a ranging company was formed at Viesca with Sterling C. Robertson as captain and Barron as sergeant. Soon thereafter, Barron was promoted to captain. As the struggle for Texas independence heightened, Barron, now in middle age, was allowed to return home to assist in moving families and slaves ahead of the advancing Mexican front in the Runaway Scrape.[qv] At the battle of San Jacinto[qv] on April 21, 1836, his company, in his absence, was commanded by Lt. Albert G. Gholson.[qv]

Early in 1837 Barron's company of rangers established Fort Fisher at Waco Village on the Brazos, at a site within the city limits of present Waco. The reconstructed post is now the site of the headquarters of Company F of the Texas Rangers and the Texas Ranger Hall of Fame and Museum.[qv] At Independence, also in 1837, Barron built a house later purchased by Sam Houston.[qv] In 1847 Barron homesteaded 320 acres on the Brazos and built the first white homestead on Waco grounds. His daughter Mozilla was the first white child born in the Waco settlement, on January 7, 1850, although another child was the first white born within the formal city limits. On April 14, 1851, Barron, as clerk, opened the first district court of McLennan County, with Judge Robert E. B. Baylor[qv] presiding. In 1857 or 1858 Barron opened a steam mill on Barron's Branch in Waco, using the bolting system to grind wheat and corn. Machinery for carding wool and cotton was added in 1860. Throughout much of the 1860s Barron served as tax assessor-collector of McLennan County. A street, an elementary school, a creek, and Barron Springs in Waco were named for him.

Barron and his first wife had twelve children, and he and his second wife had ten children. Three of his sons served in the Confederacy during the Civil War.[qv] Late in his life he moved to Falls County, near Blevins. He died on February 2, 1874, at the home of his daughter Mozilla Mixson in Mastersville (now Bruceville-Eddy). His remains were moved in December 1976 to First Street Cemetery, Waco, beside the entrance to old Fort Fisher and the Texas Ranger Hall of Fame.

BIBLIOGRAPHY: Malcolm D. McLean, comp. and ed., *Papers Concerning Robertson's Colony in Texas* (19 vols., Arlington: University of Texas at Arlington Press, 1974–93). William Robert Poage, *McLennan County Before 1980* (Waco: Texian, 1981). Villamae Williams, *Stephen F. Austin's Register of Families* (Nacogdoches, Texas: Ericson, 1984).
Theron Palmer

BARRON FIELD Barron Field, also known as Taliaferro No. 3, was a World War I[qv] pilot-training field a half mile west of Everman in southeastern Tarrant County. Construction began in September 1917. The field was closed about 1921 and reverted to farm land. It was used to train Canadian pilots.

BIBLIOGRAPHY: Robert E. Hays, Jr., Military Aviation Activities in Texas, World Wars I and II (M.A. thesis, University of Texas, 1963).
Art Leatherwood

BARROW, BENJAMIN (1808–1877). Benjamin Barrow, "Ben the Bearhunter," an early settler, rancher, and official of Chambers County, the son of Reuben and Mary Jane (Johnson) Barrow, Sr., was born on April 24, 1808, near Opelousas, Louisiana. Although he may have traveled to Texas with family members as early as 1824, he did not permanently settle there until 1827. In 1838 he received a headright near the site of present Devers in Liberty County, but he does not appear to have lived on the grant. He was married on June 4, 1835, to Permelia Jane White, daughter of cattleman James Taylor White.[qv] Family legend has it that Benjamin was caught in a rainstorm around 1830, stayed at White's home for the night, and resolved to wait until Permelia, then about ten, was old enough to marry. They had nine children. After Permelia died in 1861, Barrow married Mrs. Mary Jane Middleton Bryan. They had no children.

Barrow received a pension for service in the Texas army from May 10 to August 10, 1836. He is also listed as a second lieutenant in a Liberty militia company organized during the Republic of Texas period. He established a cattle ranch on Turtle Bayou five miles northeast of Anahuac and became one of the county's largest ranchers and wealthiest men. He was a substantial slaveholder and raised cattle, blooded horses, swine, and sheep on his ranch. His upside-down-wineglass brand was a familiar sight on the prairies of Southeast Texas.

A number of legends revolve around Barrow's bear-hunting exploits. On one occasion when his dogs surrounded a bear in a briar patch, he is said to have climbed into the briars and killed the bear with a knife in order to save his hounds. Family members recall that he also kept pet bears around his house. Barrow was elected justice of the peace in 1843 and county commissioner in 1854. In April 1868, during Reconstruction,[qv] he was appointed district clerk, a position he held for a year. He died during a smallpox epidemic on February 7, 1877. Mrs. Barrow died of the same disease three days later.

BIBLIOGRAPHY: Jewel Horace Harry, A History of Chambers County (M.A. thesis, University of Texas, 1940; rpt., Dallas: Taylor, 1981). Margaret S. Henson and Kevin Ladd, *Chambers County: A Pictorial History* (Norfolk, Virginia: Donning, 1988).
Kevin Ladd

BARROW, CLYDE CHESNUT (1909–1934). Clyde Chesnut Barrow, outlaw and partner of Bonnie Parker,[qv] was born just outside Telico, Texas, on March 24, 1909, the son of Henry Barrow. The family moved to Dallas in 1922, and in 1926 Barrow was first arrested for stealing an automobile. During the next four years he committed a string of robberies in and around Dallas. In 1930 he met Bonnie Parker, but their relationship was cut short when Barrow was arrested and jailed in Waco on charges of burglary. While awaiting trial he escaped with a handgun slipped to him by Bonnie and fled north, but was captured a week later in Middletown, Ohio. Barrow was found guilty and sentenced to a fourteen-year term at hard labor in the state penitentiary. Unwilling to endure the work at one of the state-operated plantations, he had another convict chop two toes off his right foot with an axe.

Ironically, a short time later in February 1932, Barrow was given a general parole and released. Reunited with Bonnie and joined by bank robber Raymond Hamilton, Barrow began a series of violent holdups in the Southwest and Midwest. He and his accomplices made national headlines after murdering a number of people, including several law officers, and their exploits continued to hold the public's fascination for the next two years.

After Hamilton was captured in Michigan, Bonnie and Clyde were joined by Clyde's brother, Buck, who had been recently released from prison, and his wife, Blanche (Caldwell) Barrow. They rented a small garage apartment in Joplin, Missouri, as a hideout, but suspicious neighbors tipped off the police. On the afternoon of April 13, 1933, law officers raided the hideaway. In the shootout that followed, two lawmen were killed. The gang narrowly escaped, but they left behind a roll of film from which many of the famous photographs of the pair originated. For most of the remainder of the their brief criminal careers, Clyde and Bonnie were constantly on the move, committing one robbery after the next while managing to stay one step ahead of the law. In Platte City, Missouri, the gang once again was ambushed by police officers; Buck Barrow was killed, and Blanche was taken into custody, but Bonnie and Clyde escaped once again. In January 1934 the two made a daring attack on the Eastern State Prison in Texas to free Raymond Hamilton and another prisoner, Henry Methvin, in the process machine-gunning several guards and killing one. With Hamilton and Methvin in tow, Barrow and Parker went on another robbery rampage in Indiana. After a short time, however, Hamilton quarreled with Barrow and struck out on his own, leaving Methvin with the gang.

Officials, led by former Texas Ranger Francis A. (Frank) Hamer[qv] and FBI special agent L. A. Kindell, finally tracked down the Barrow gang at Methvin's father's farm near Arcadia, Louisiana. Hamer arranged a roadside ambush in Gibsland, Louisiana. On May 23, 1934, at 9:15 a.m., Clyde and Bonnie, traveling alone, were killed in a barrage of 167 bullets. The bodies were taken to Arcadia and later put on public display in Dallas before being buried in their respective family burial plots.

In later years Clyde Barrow and Bonnie Parker were sometimes characterized as latter-day Robin Hoods. Their exploits became the basis of more than a half dozen movies, most notably *Bonnie and Clyde* in 1967, starring Warren Beatty and Faye Dunaway as the title characters. The originals were often compared with the other criminal figures of the Great Depression[qv] era, including John Dillinger and Al Capone. Barrow and Parker, however, despite their later glamorous image, were both ruthless killers who displayed very little in the way of a social conscience or remorse. In marked contrast to the legendary gangsters of the era, they were in reality small-time hoods whose largest haul was only $1,500.

BIBLIOGRAPHY: Jan I. Fortune, *Fugitives: The Story of Clyde Barrow and Bonnie Parker as Told by Bonnie's Mother and Clyde's Sister* (Dallas: Ranger Press, 1934). H. Gordon Frost and John H. Jenkins, *"I'm Frank Hamer": The Life of a Texas Peace Officer* (Austin: Pemberton Press, 1968). Ted Hinton, *Ambush: The Real Story of Bonnie and Clyde* (Austin: Shoal Creek, 1979). Vertical Files, Barker Texas History Center, University of Texas at Austin.

Christopher Long

BARROW, LEONIDAS THEODORE (1895–1978). Leonidas Theodore (Slim) Barrow, petroleum geologist, the son of Thomas Heskew and Sarah (Graves) Barrow, was born on June 16, 1895, in Manor, Texas. He was educated in the public schools of Austin and entered the University of Texas in 1917, but in 1918 he left the university to join the Signal Corps of the United States Army. He returned to the university upon his military discharge in 1919 and was awarded the bachelor's degree in geology in 1921. During his undergraduate days he played on the Longhorn football and basketball teams, where he earned his nickname. He received his master's degree in 1923 and served as instructor in geology at the University of Texas from 1921 to 1924. In 1923 he married Laura Thomson, a geology student at the university.

Barrow joined the Humble Oil and Refining Company (*see* exxon company, u.s.a.) as field geologist in San Antonio in 1924. He did surface geologic mapping in Caldwell and Guadalupe counties, where his company discovered the Salt Flat and Darst Creek oilfields. He recognized the igneous origin of the material that makes up the pay section of the Lytton Springs oilfield in Caldwell County. By 1929 he was made chief geologist for Humble in Houston. There he became associated with Wallace E. Pratt,[qv] a member of the board of directors of the company. Pratt and Barrow, working together, established the highest type of business and professional ethics in the petroleum industry. Barrow was promoted to the board of directors of his company in 1937, to vice president in 1938, and to chairman of the board in 1948. He retired in 1955.

Barrow and his wife aided the University of Texas by helping to organize and donating to the Geology Foundation in 1952. The foundation provides loans for needy students, travel funds for teachers, scholarship and fellowship funds, library funds, and endowments establishing named professorships and chairs in geological sciences. Barrow served on the Geology Foundation Council from 1957 to 1963 and was elected a lifetime honorary member in 1964. He was also a member of the American Association of Petroleum Geologists, the Society of Petroleum Engineers, and the Geophysical Union, as well as a fellow of the Geological Society of America. He and his wife were the founders of the Wallace E. Pratt Publication fund of the American Association of Petroleum Geologists. They also made important contributions to many other geological, charitable, and church organizations. Barrow died in Houston on March 4, 1978.

BIBLIOGRAPHY: M. J. Davis, "Memorial to L. T. Barrow," *Bulletin of the American Association of Petroleum Geologists* 62 (October 1978). Samuel P. Ellison, Jr., "Memorial to Leonidas Theodore Barrow," *Geological Society of America Memorials* 10 (1980).

Samuel P. Ellison, Jr.

BARRY, JAMES BUCKNER (1821–1906). James Buckner (Buck) Barry, Texas Ranger, was born in North Carolina on December 16, 1821, the son of Bryant Buckner and Mary (Murill) Barry. He immigrated to Texas in 1841 and received a headright grant of 640 acres of land near Corsicana. There he occupied himself, in his own words, with a "little farming and with a great deal of hunting." Barry soon joined the Texas Rangers,[qv] first as a member of an independent company at San Antonio and then, from September 15 through December 15, 1845, as a member of Capt. Thomas J. Smith's Robertson County Rangers. Barry then saw service with John Coffee Hays's[qv] company. He subsequently went to work surveying headrights in the Robertson district. In 1846 he was elected second sergeant of Capt. Eli Chandler's[qv] Company K of Colonel Hays's First Regiment,

Texas Mounted Riflemen, for service in the Mexican War.[qv] He was wounded at the storming of Monterrey on September 21, 1846, and mustered out of service on October 2, 1846, of that year.

Barry returned to North Carolina, where, on February 24, 1847, he married Sarah Anapolis Matticks. The couple eventually had six children. The family returned to Texas and settled on Bazette Bluff on the Trinity River. For the next ten years Barry was deeply involved in Indian fighting and was especially outspoken as an advocate of the removal of the Comanches and Caddos from their reservations on the upper Brazos River. In 1849 he was elected sheriff of Navarro County and moved to Corsicana. In 1852 he was elected county treasurer and in 1854 was reelected sheriff. In December 1855 he moved his family to Bosque County, where he settled on the East Bosque River east of Meridian. He owned about twenty slaves.

Barry served as a private in Lt. Dixon Walker's Mounted Volunteers in the spring of 1860. In October he raised a company at Meridian that accompanied Lawrence Sullivan Ross[qv] into Indian Territory on the expedition responsible for the recapture of Cynthia Ann Parker.[qv] During the same period he was the sergeant of Allison Nelson's[qv] company of minutemen. On January 10, 1861, Governor Sam Houston[qv] issued Barry a commission as first lieutenant with authority to raise a company at Fort Belknap for frontier defense. After secession[qv] Barry reenrolled his company into Confederate service in Col. Henry E. McCulloch 's[qv] regiment and assisted in the removal of federal garrisons from Texas frontier forts. Barry, from his headquarters at Camp Cooper, continued to range the frontier from the Red River to the Rio Grande throughout the Civil War,[qv] during which he rose to lieutenant colonel. He also participated in the battle of Dove Creek.[qv]

Barry was an active member of the Grange.[qv] He was elected in 1883 to the Twelfth Legislature, where he was presented "the finest gun that could be bought" in appreciation of his service in protection of the frontier. He worked in the interest of stock raisers and unsuccessfully sought legislation to outlaw fence-cutting.[qv] In 1898 he ran for state treasurer on the People's party[qv] ticket but was defeated. He then retired to his ranch near Walnut Springs.

After the death of his first wife in 1862, Barry married Mrs. Martha Anne Peveler Searcy at Fort Belknap, on July 14, 1865. They had three daughters and one son. Barry became blind near the end of his life and died on December 16, 1906.

bibliography: James Buckner Barry Papers, Barker Texas History Center, University of Texas at Austin. James Buckner Barry, *Buck Barry, Texas Ranger and Frontiersman*, ed. James K. Greer (1932; new ed., Waco: Friends of the Moody Texas Ranger Library, 1978; rpt., Lincoln: University of Nebraska Press, 1984). Frances Terry Ingmire, comp., *Texas Ranger Service Records, 1847–1900* (St. Louis, 1982).

Thomas W. Cutrer

BARRY, MAGGIE HILL (1863–1945). Maggie Wilkins Hill Barry, educator and leader in efforts for Texas rural women, was born in Palo Alto, Mississippi, on January 5, 1863, the daughter of Samuel Van Dyke and Jennie (Calvert) Hill. Her father was a physician and surgeon, and her mother came from a large landholding and slaveowning family in eastern Mississippi. Maggie began her formal education in the private schools of Macon, Mississippi, and later studied at Tuscaloosa (Alabama) Female College and Murfreesboro (Tennessee) Institute. After attaining a master's degree at Murfreesboro, she spent several years studying music, theater, and modern languages in Boston, New Orleans, Paris, and Berlin.

Her early career included serving as head of a private school in Ardmore, Oklahoma, and holding faculty positions in modern languages and music at Murfreesboro Institute and Whitworth College in Mississippi. While teaching at Whitworth she worked under principal Lucy Kidd (*see* kidd-key, lucy thornton). When Mrs. Kidd moved to Sherman, Texas, in 1888 to become president of North Texas Female College (later Kidd-Key College), Maggie Barry moved with her to serve as head of the English department. In 1891 she returned to Mississippi and married Frederick George Barry, a lawyer and former United States congressman. The Barrys had one daughter, Jennie Hill, who later taught voice at Texas Presbyterian College.

Barry died in 1909 but his wife had already apparently returned to her position at North Texas Female College. In addition to resuming her teaching and administrative duties in Sherman, Mrs. Barry also organized a Girls Shakespeare Club at the college in 1900, joined the Texas Federation of Women's Clubs[qv] in 1907, and spent several summers in Europe. In 1911 she organized the All Southwestern Social Center Conference, which was held in Dallas. Her particular effort was to reduce the immigration of rural youth to large cities. In 1914 the United States Congress passed the Smith-Lever Act, which encouraged state agricultural colleges to work cooperatively with other groups in providing demonstrations on home economics and agriculture. In Texas this act resulted in the establishment of the Texas Agricultural Extension Service,[qv] which was to work in conjunction with the Agricultural and Mechanical College of Texas (now Texas A&M University) in demonstration efforts. A&M president William Bennett Bizzell[qv] hired Maggie Barry to serve as a liaison between the Texas Agricultural Extension Service and organized women's groups in the state. In 1918 she moved to College Station to begin her work, drawing on her background as an educator and her increasing interest in rural problems.

Her efforts at A&M focused on the home demonstration[qv] movement in Texas, which was largely a rural effort that utilized demonstrations and models to illustrate how to perform domestic tasks more effectively and improve social interaction. Although home demonstration work existed in Texas before Maggie Barry began her work, she is credited with providing the structure it needed to flourish. She emphasized local interest and community ties as a basis for home demonstration success. She taught organizing principles and practices to district agents, who supervised the county agents who actually went into interested communities to work with individuals and groups. Mrs. Barry, who was the first specialist in rural women's work in Texas, utilized her position to organize, educate, and write for rural women until her retirement in 1940. In 1941 a Texas Home Demonstration Association scholarship was named in her honor. She also served as an advocate for rural women through leadership positions in the national General Federation of Women's Clubs. In that federation she organized surveys of social hygiene in schools and equipment in rural and urban homes and was instrumental in having "homemaker" listed as an occupation on United States census rolls in 1930. She was an active member of the Parent-Teachers Association and the Texas State Teachers Association[qv] she was nominated for the presidency of the latter in 1916. She was a lifelong Democrat. Maggie Barry died in College Station on April 30, 1945, and was survived by her daughter.

bibliography: Sam Hanna Acheson, Herbert P. Gambrell, Mary Carter Toomey, and Alex M. Acheson, Jr., *Texian Who's Who*, Vol. 1 (Dallas: Texian, 1937). Maglin Dupree, "The Social Center Movement in Texas," *Texas Magazine*, April 1911. Kate Adele Hill, *Home Demonstration Work in Texas* (San Antonio: Naylor, 1958). *Houston Chronicle Magazine*, May 1, 1945. Texas Agricultural Extension Service Historical Files, 1914–1970, Evans Library, Texas A&M University. *Who's Who of the Womanhood of Texas*, Vol. 1 (Fort Worth: Texas Federation of Women's Clubs, 1923–24).

Debbie Mauldin Cottrell

BARRY, TEXAS. Barry is on State Highway 22 and the St. Louis Southwestern Railway ten miles northwest of Corsicana in northwestern Navarro County. It derived its name from Bryan T. Barry of Corsicana and Dallas, the original owner of at least 300 acres of land sold to early area settlers at the site. In 1886 the town, which had a gin and a newly established post office in Taylor's General Store, was located a mile south of its present site. When the railroad completed a line between Corsicana and Hillsboro in 1888, residents of Barry moved the town to the tracks. The train shipped cotton and delivered the mail. Rural residents of the new site first received mail service on May 16, 1904; E. W. Miller was the first postmaster. The first public school had opened in 1896, and by 1906 it had two teachers and an enrollment of 127 pupils. In 1914 the community had 400 residents and numerous businesses, including two banks, a blacksmith shop, a cafe, a hotel, a gin, general stores, and a newspaper, the weekly *News.* It supported three churches, Methodist, Baptist, and Presbyterian. In 1939 Barry had 350 residents and seven businesses, but forty years later the population had fallen to 143 and only two businesses remained. The Barry school district was consolidated with that of Blooming Grove in 1952. In 1983 state highway maps showed a community or town hall at the townsite; in 1989 Barry recorded a population of 196 and a single business. In 1990 the population was 175.

BIBLIOGRAPHY: Wyvonne Putman, comp., *Navarro County History* (5 vols., Quanah, Texas: Nortex, 1975–84). *Todd Gantt*

BARSOLA, TEXAS. Barsola is eight miles south of Alto on Farm Road 1911 in southern Cherokee County. It was established in June 1835 by Roland W. Box, who purchased one-third league of land in the Stephen Burham grant west of Larrison Creek. Box built a log fort for his father, John M. Box, and brothers, Samuel C., William, James, and John A. The settlement was named for José Barcela, to whom the first land in the area had been granted. Most of the site later reverted to ranchland. The church was torn down, and a pavilion replaced it.

BIBLIOGRAPHY: *Cherokee County History* (Jacksonville, Texas: Cherokee County Historical Commission, 1986). Hattie Joplin Roach, *A History of Cherokee County* (Dallas: Southwest, 1934).

Phyllis Aswell

BARSTOW, GEORGE EAMES (1849–1924). George Eames Barstow, capitalist and irrigation pioneer, was born on November 19, 1849, in Providence, Rhode Island, the son of Amos Chafee and Emeline (Mumford) Eames. He was educated at the public school and at Mowry and Goff's English and Classical School in Providence. The son of a manufacturer and banker, Barstow himself began a business career at the age of seventeen. He eventually founded, financed, or organized five worsted and paper industries in Rhode Island. He became a member of the Providence school board at the age of twenty-one and served for fourteen years. He also served four years on the Providence common council and three terms in the Rhode Island House of Representatives. He married Clara Drew Symonds on October 19, 1871, and they had nine children.

For a number of years Barstow was involved in irrigation projects and in the draining of swamp lands. His attention turned to the Pecos valley in Texas after the state legislature passed an act in March 1889 to encourage the development of irrigation in West Texas. The Pioneer Canal Company, with Barstow as treasurer, was chartered on July 6, 1889. On September 30, 1889, Pioneer took over the Ward County Irrigation Company. Barstow served as president of at least one of the Pioneer Canal Company's later incarnations, the Pecos Valley Land and Irrigation Company. An ad for the latter company, with a picture of Barstow as president, appeared in a 1909 issue of Cosmopolitan.

In 1891 Barstow joined other land developers in a project to promote a town on the Texas and Pacific Railway in western Ward County. The townsite, laid out in 1891, was deeded by Mr. and Mrs. B. K. Brant and O. F. Brant to the Barstow Improvement Company in 1892. Disagreement surfaced early over a name for the town, but by 1895 the community had taken the name of Barstow. Barstow himself moved to Barstow in 1904 from New York City. He also reportedly participated in organizing other irrigation and drainage systems throughout the West. He was president of the National Drainage Congress in 1907–08 and of the Eleventh International Irrigation Congress in 1908–09. He also served as vice president of the Texas Conservation Commission and president of the West Texas Reclamation Association. He was a member of the Conference of Governors in 1908, a delegate to the World Court Congress in Cleveland in 1915, a life director of Euphrates College (Turkey), a fellow of the Royal Society of Arts (London), a member and fellow of the Society of Applied Psychology (San Francisco), a member of the committee on conferences of the American Agricultural Association, and a member of the advisory committee of the University Forum (New York). He was also a member of the American Society of International Law, the National Institute of Social Sciences, the Southern Sociological Congress, the National Child Labor Committee, the National Civic Federation, the American Institute of Civics, the Academy of Political Science, the American Society of Judicial Settlement of International Disputes, the International Peace Forum, the League to Enforce Peace, the International World Conscience Society (Rome), the Navy League, the Rhode Island Historical Society, the Empire State Society of the Sons of the American Revolution, the Pennsylvania Academy of Fine Arts, and the New York Museum of Natural History. He was also a councilor of the World's Purity Congress. In addition, Barstow wrote pamphlets on such varied subjects as immigration, cooperatives, Sino-Japanese relations, and Americanism. He was a Republican and attended the Congregational church in Providence and the Methodist church in Barstow. He died in Barstow on April 30, 1924, and was buried in the Barstow Cemetery.

BIBLIOGRAPHY: Fort Worth *Star-Telegram*, May 2, 1924. *National Cyclopaedia of American Biography*, Vol. 18. Texas Permian Historical Society, *Water, Oil, Sand and Sky: A History of Ward County* (Monahans, Texas, Junior Chamber of Commerce, 1962). Ward County Historical Commission, *Ward County, 1887-1977* (Dallas: Taylor, 1980?). Clarence R. Wharton, ed., *Texas under Many Flags* (5 vols., Chicago: American Historical Society, 1930). *Who Was Who in America*, Vol. 2.

Claudia Hazlewood

BARSTOW, TEXAS. Barstow is at the intersection of U.S. Highway 80 and Farm Road 516, on the Missouri Pacific Railroad, five miles east of Pecos in southwestern Ward County. The town was named for George E. Barstow,[qv] a Rhode Island land promoter who established it. The Texas and Pacific Railway reached Barstow in 1881. Ten years later the townsite was laid out and a post office established. Barstow became the county seat when Ward County was organized in 1892. That same year George E. Barstow formed the Barstow Improvement Company to promote the sale of land irrigated by the Pecos River. He constructed irrigation canals and a dam and brought trainloads of prospective settlers to the town in land promotions. A red sandstone courthouse was constructed in 1893. By 1900 Barstow had a population of 1,103. In 1914 the community had three churches, a bank, a hotel, an opera house, and a weekly newspaper, the *West Texas Journal.* Two years later a power plant was built to generate electricity. The farms around Barstow grew grapes, peaches, pears, and melons. In 1904 the Barstow Irrigation Company won a silver medal for grapes at the World's Fair. The same year an earthen dam on the rain-swollen Pecos River burst, and the resulting floodwaters raised soil salinity levels, thus ruining many of the farms. In 1907 and 1910 serious droughts plagued Barstow farmers. Vineyards and orchards began to decline in 1911, and by 1918 farming ceased. The population fell from 1,219 in 1910 to an estimated 490 in 1925. Barstow had 468 residents in 1930. In June 1938, after the discovery of oil in Winkler County and eastern Ward County, Monahans replaced Barstow as the county seat of Ward County. Barstow had a population of 683 in 1955. Four businesses and an estimated 637 residents remained in 1982. The population in 1990 was 535.

BIBLIOGRAPHY: Texas Permian Historical Society, *Water, Oil, Sand*

and Sky: A History of Ward County (Monahans, Texas, Junior Chamber of Commerce, 1962). Ward County Historical Commission, *Ward County.* (Dallas: Taylor, 1980?). *Glenn Justice*

BARTHELME, DONALD (1931–1989). Donald Barthelme, author of short fiction and novels, was born on April 7, 1931, in Philadelphia, Pennsylvania, the son of Helen (Bechtold) and Donald Barthelme, Sr., a professor at the University of Houston. He attended parochial schools and was raised as a Catholic. While in school he served as editor of a variety of school newspapers. He entered the University of Houston in 1949 and worked on a journalism degree sporadically through 1957. There he edited the college paper, the *Cougar*, worked for a news service, edited the faculty newspaper, *Acta Diurna*, and founded *Forum*, a university literary magazine. He was drafted into the army in 1953 and served in Fort Polk, Louisiana, Japan, and Korea. In 1955–56 he worked for the Houston *Post*[qv] as an entertainment editor and critic.

He served as the director of the Contemporary Arts Museum[qv] in Houston in 1961–62. In 1963 he moved to Manhattan, New York, where he began his writing career as managing editor of *Location.* He published his first story in 1961 in the *New Yorker* and his first novel, *Come Back, Dr. Caligari*, in 1964. In 1966 he received a Guggenheim fellowship and continued to receive honors throughout his years in New York. By the time he returned to Houston in the early 1980s he had published more books, including *Snow White* (1967), *City Life* (1970), *The Dead Father* (1975), *Amateurs* (1976), and several other short story collections.

He began teaching creative writing at the University of Houston in the early 1980s and was an important influence on his students. At his death, on July 23, 1989, in Houston he had written fifteen books; *The King* was published posthumously in 1990. In addition Barthelme had contributed many stories to the *New Yorker.* He won a National Book Award in 1972 for a children's book, *The Slightly Irregular Fire Engine* (1971), and a PEN/Faulkner Award in 1982 for *Sixty Stories* (1981). He was a member of the American Academy of Arts and Letters, the Authors League of America, and PEN.

BIBLIOGRAPHY: *Contemporary Authors*, New Revision Series, Vol. 20 (1987). Lois Gordon, *Donald Barthelme* (Boston: Twayne, 1981). *Lisa C. Maxwell*

BARTHOLF, MARJORIE (1899–1986). Marjorie Bartholf, first dean of the School of Nursing, University of Texas Medical Branch at Galveston, was born in Chicago, Illinois, on January 13, 1899, to Grace (Bullock) and Charles Steven Bartholf. She was one of five children. Her father was a public school official. She graduated from the University of Wisconsin in 1920 with a baccalaureate in economics. She then enrolled and obtained a diploma in nursing from the Evanston (Illinois) Hospital Training School for Nurses in 1925. Before assuming the position of director of the nursing program at the University of Texas, she was head nurse in the Evanston Hospital, public-health nurse, obstetrics supervisor at St. Luke's Hospital in Kansas City, clinical instructor at the Elizabeth McGee Hospital in Pittsburgh, assistant professor at Yale School of Nursing, and assistant director of the Cook County School of Nursing, Chicago. In 1937 she was in the first class to receive master of science degrees in nursing from the University of Chicago.

Bartholf arrived in Galveston in 1942 to become administrator of the nursing program. As dean she quickly opened the program to black nursing student affiliates from Prairie View A&M. The UTMB School of Nursing was one of the first schools to admit black students and males to nursing programs. In 1952, through her work, graduate education in nursing was first offered in Texas; experimentation in the diploma program pioneered in developing a two-year program, a forerunner of the associate degree program; and the curriculum was changed to provide an education in addition to on-the-job training in nursing. Bartholf implemented an accelerated nursing program during World War II[qv] in order to allow graduate nurses to join the war effort. Under her administration, the College of Nursing was approved for membership in the Association of Collegiate Schools of Nursing. The basic professional program was accredited by the National League for Nursing Education, and the name of the school appeared in the first list published by the National Nursing Accrediting Service in the *American Journal of Nursing* in 1949. In the early 1950s the University of Texas established a master's degree program in nursing as a part of the graduate school at Austin. This program's emphasis was to educate teachers, supervisors, and administrators in medical and surgical nursing. Throughout her tenure from 1942 to 1963 Bartholf was a leader in improving the standards of nursing education, not only in her school but in other nursing schools in Texas and nationally. In 1966 she received the first Ella Goldthwaite Award. She died in 1986.

BIBLIOGRAPHY: *The University of Texas Medical Branch at Galveston: A Seventy-five Year History* (Austin: University of Texas Press, 1967). Vertical Files, Barker Texas History Center, University of Texas at Austin. *Billye J. Brown*

BARTHOLOMEW, EUGENE CARLOS (1839–1923). Eugene Carlos Bartholomew, government official and banker, was born in Hanover, Michigan, on January 3, 1839, the son of Orange Adams and Sarah (Wright) Bartholomew. About 1850 the family moved to Jonesville, Michigan, where Bartholomew helped his father operate a stage line. He graduated from Hillsdale College, Michigan, in 1861. He entered the United States Army as a civilian employee in 1864 and became chief clerk in the Quartermaster's Division of the Fourth Army Corps, a unit that was sent to Victoria, Texas, in July 1865. Bartholomew was among a group of federal soldiers sent to help oust Emperor Maximilian from Mexico, but they heard of the emperor's execution by the time they reached Indianola. When the army was disbanded, Bartholomew worked for the Freedmen's Bureau[qv] at Galveston and Austin, his duty being to establish schools. In July 1870 he was appointed superintendent of education and second assistant clerk of the House of Representatives. In 1871 he became chief clerk in the office of superintendent of public instruction and first assistant clerk of the House. In 1873 he began a real estate and loan business in Austin. From 1909 to 1919 he was water and light commissioner in Austin. He was also one of the founders and directors of the Austin National Bank and for many years a United States grand jury commissioner.

Bartholomew married Elizabeth Morley Brown on February 1, 1870, and they had one son. Bartholomew was a Republican, an Episcopalian, and a Mason. He died in Austin on October 27, 1923, and was buried in Oakwood Cemetery.

BIBLIOGRAPHY: Austin *Statesman*, October 29, 1923. Eugene Carlos Bartholomew Papers, Barker Texas History Center, University of Texas at Austin. Vertical Files, Austin History Center. *Jeanette H. Flachmeier*

BARTHOLOMEW, SUSAN EMILY REYNOLDS (1848–1921). Susan Emily Bartholomew, diarist, daughter of Barber Watkins and Anne Maria Reynolds, was born on September 27, 1848, on a cotton farm in Shelby County, Texas. The family, including Susan's brothers George Thomas and William David Reynolds,[qqv] were pioneer West Texans who moved to Palo Pinto in 1859 and then later to Buchanan (now Stephens) County. In 1862 Susan married Samuel P. Newcomb,[qv] and in 1865 the couple "forted up" with neighbors at Fort Davis on the Clear Fork of the Brazos in Stephens County. In 1866, after the Civil War[qv] ended and the threat of Indian raids diminished, the Newcombs moved to Stone Ranch, established by Susan's father. In 1867 the Newcombs moved to a home of their own on Collins Creek, one mile west of Stone Ranch. Newcomb died of measles in 1870.

In 1872 Susan married Nathan L. Bartholomew, a Connecticut

man and former Union soldier. The couple moved that year to a ranch near Merriman in Eastland County, but returned to Stephens County in 1876 to build a stone house near Susan's father's place. Later the Bartholomews moved to a farm near Albany. They adopted Nathan's daughter from his first marriage.

Like her first husband, Mrs. Bartholomew kept a diary of daily events. Diaries from 1865 to 1869, 1871 to 1873, and 1884 to 1896 record her perceptions of aspects of the Texas frontier, including life at Fort Davis during the Civil War, frontier schools, buffalo hunting,[qv] and homemaking. At times she expressed the dismay that must have haunted most pioneer households: "Such a country as this I almost wish I had never seen it, if I had wings to fly I would abandon it forever, it is surely the last place on earth for a woman to live, or anyone else. I don't believe it was ever intended for civilized people, it was made for wild Indians and buffalo." Susan Bartholomew's diaries have been valuable historical resources for scholars and for Texas history enthusiasts. Directors of the Fort Griffin Fandangle,[qv] an annual outdoor pageant held near Albany, have often used Susan Bartholomew's and Samuel Newcomb's diaries in productions about the history of the region. Susan Bartholomew died at Fort Worth on June 5, 1921.

BIBLIOGRAPHY: Anne Watts Baker Collection, Southwest Collection, Texas Tech University. Frances M. Holden, Chronology of the Reynolds and Matthews Families (MS, Southwest Collection, Texas Tech University, 1982). Frances Mayhugh Holden, *Lambshead Before Interwoven: A Texas Range Chronicle, 1848–1878* (College Station: Texas A&M University Press, 1982). Sallie Reynolds Matthews, *Interwoven: A Pioneer Chronicle* (Houston: Anson Jones, 1936; 4th ed., College Station: Texas A&M University Press, 1982).

William R. Hunt

BARTLETT, CHURCHILL JONES (1862–1930). Churchill Jones Bartlett, legislator and Texas secretary of state, was born in Marlin, Texas, on June 6, 1862, the son of Zenas and Sarah Kendrick (Jones) Bartlett, and the grandson of Churchill Jones.[qv] He attended the Agricultural and Mechanical College of Texas (now Texas A&M University) in 1878–79 and became city secretary and treasurer at Marlin about 1885. He served in this capacity until 1895, when he was elected justice of the peace. On November 30, 1892, he married Bodie Christian of Eddy, who died in 1894. Bartlett became postmaster at Marlin about 1896 but retired to go into the insurance business. In 1906 and again in 1908 he was elected from the Sixty-seventh District to the Texas House of Representatives, where he served as chairman of the Committee on Public Lands and Land Office. He was secretary of state under Governor James E. Ferguson.[qv] Bartlett was a Democrat, a Mason, and an Elk. He died in Marlin on September 27, 1930, and was buried in Calvary Cemetery.

BIBLIOGRAPHY: Falls County Historical Commission, *Families of Falls County* (Austin: Eakin Press, 1987). Houston *Press*, September 29, 1930. Buckley B. Paddock, *History of Central and Western Texas* (2 vols., Chicago: Lewis, 1911). Vertical Files, Barker Texas History Center, University of Texas at Austin. *Marie Giles*

BARTLETT, JOHN RUSSELL (1805–1886). John Russell Bartlett, boundary commissioner, was born on October 23, 1805, in Providence, Rhode Island, to Smith and Nancy (Russell) Bartlett. The family moved to Kingston, Ontario; Bartlett was educated in the common schools there and at Lowville Academy in upstate New York. His schooling brought him a knowledge of accounting and a love of history and literature that gave his writings a romantic turn. In addition, he also was an artist of considerable competence.

In 1824 he returned to Providence, where he clerked in a drygoods store and entered banking in 1828. In 1836 he moved to New York City. There he and Charles Welford opened a shop, Bartlett and Welford, to sell literary and scientific publications; the store became a gathering place for literary figures and scientists. Bartlett was a founding father of the American Ethnological Society in 1842 and wrote *The Progress of Ethnology* in 1847. His most famous work was his *Dictionary of Americanisms* (1848), which went through four editions before 1900.

On June 15, 1850, thanks to his standing in the Whig party,[qv] Bartlett was appointed United States boundary commissioner to carry out the provisions of the Treaty of Guadalupe Hidalgo.[qv] Despite his ignorance of the Southwest he accepted this post because he wanted to travel, because he wanted to see Indians, and because he needed the money.

Bartlett left New York with a large party on August 3, 1850, and landed at Indianola, Texas, twenty-seven days later. After traveling overland, he arrived at El Paso del Norte (Juárez) to begin work with the Mexican boundary commissioner, Pedro García Conde. The point where the southern boundary of New Mexico was to begin on the Rio Grande proved difficult to determine because of inaccuracies in Disturnell's 1847 "Map of the United Mexican States," and Bartlett allowed the boundary to be set forty-two miles north of El Paso. When American boundary surveyor Andrew B. Gray[qv] refused to agree to this, Bartlett departed for a tour of northwestern Mexico. He arrived in California, he then traveled east through Arizona and New Mexico to Texas, where he learned that Congress had rejected the Bartlett–García Conde line. Because of Bartlett's error, the United States in 1853 had to negotiate the Gadsden Purchase, which set the boundary of New Mexico at 31°47′ north latitude. The Gadsden Purchase, which transferred mainly desert lands to the United States, was viewed as essential for establishing a southern route for the transcontinental railroad.

Bartlett returned to Rhode Island and wrote a two-volume *Personal Narrative of Explorations and Incidents in Texas, New Mexico, California, Sonora, and Chihuahua, Connected with the United States and Mexican Boundary Commission, during the years 1850, 51, 52, and 53* (1854), which became a standard early source of information about Texas and the Southwest. From 1855 to 1872 he was secretary of state for Rhode Island. He helped put together the collection that is the nucleus of the John Carter Brown Library and published numerous books, including a *Bibliography of Rhode Island* (1864), *Records of the Colony of Rhode Island and Providence Plantation* (10 vols., 1856–65), *The Literature of Rebellion* (1866), *Bibliographic Notices of Rare and Curious Books Relating to America . . . in the Library of the Late John Carter Brown* (4 volumes, 1875–82), *Letters of Roger Williams, 1632–1682* (1874), and *Letters of Roger Williams to Winthrop* (1896), in addition to various monographs and bibliographies of lesser importance.

Bartlett married Eliza Allen Rhodes on May 15, 1831, and they had seven children. She died on November 11, 1853. Bartlett married Ellen Eddy on November 12, 1863. He died on May 28, 1886, in Providence, Rhode Island. *See also* BOUNDARIES, GEOLOGICAL SURVEYS.

BIBLIOGRAPHY: John Russell Bartlett Papers, John Carter Brown Library, Providence, Rhode Island. *Dictionary of American Biography.* Robert V. Hine, *Bartlett's West: Drawing the Mexican Boundary* (New Haven: Yale University Press, 1968). *Odie B. Faulk*

BARTLETT, TEXAS. Bartlett is a station on the Katy Railroad, State Highway 95, and the border between Williamson and Bell counties. Though there were settlers in the area as early as 1851, Bartlett was founded when the Missouri, Kansas and Texas Railway Company began surveying for a right-of-way in 1881. The town is named for John T. Bartlett, who with J. E. Pietzsch donated the land for a townsite. Town lots were offered for sale in 1881, and there were two stores by the time the railroad reached the town in 1882. A post office opened the same year. In 1884 Bartlett had 300 inhabitants, a gin, a hotel, a grocer, a meat market, four churches, and a school; the town shipped wool and cotton. When Bartlett incorporated in 1890, it had a bank, two weekly newspapers (the *Democrat* and the *Tribune*), a Masonic lodge, and a waterworks. In 1909 investors chartered the Bartlett-

Florence Railway Company (eventually renamed the Bartlett Western), which slowly built a new railway west from Bartlett; the town prospered as the eastern terminus and main depot of the line. Bartlett served as a shipping point for cotton, grain, livestock, and produce in 1914, the same year it reached its peak population of some 2,200 inhabitants and had three banks, electric lighting, and three cotton gins. With the decline of the cotton industry in the 1920s and 1930s, the Bartlett Western experienced financial difficulties and eventually closed in 1935. The town was also heavily dependent on cotton and declined somewhat in this period, though in 1931 it was still a substantial community of 1,873 people and ninety-five businesses. Bartlett continued to shrink during the depression; by 1940 its population was estimated at 1,668, and it had seventy-five businesses. The population was 1,622 in 1970 and 1,567 in 1980. In 1988 the town had 1,556 inhabitants and fifteen businesses. In 1990 the population was 1,439.

BIBLIOGRAPHY: Clara Stearns Scarbrough, *Land of Good Water: A Williamson County History* (Georgetown, Texas: Williamson County Sun Publishers, 1973).
Mark Odintz

BARTLETT-FLORENCE RAILWAY. The Bartlett-Florence Railway Company was chartered on September 15, 1909 (one source says September 17, 1905), to build from Bartlett to Florence, a distance of twenty-three miles. The organizers hoped to profit from Williamson County cotton production. The road was initially capitalized at $25,000, and the business office was located at Bartlett. Members of the first board of directors included F. W. Johnston of St. Elmo, Illinois, John C. Collins of Houston, C. C. Bailey of Bartlett, G. W. Hubbard of Teague, John McDaniel and John Brewster of Florence, and W. J. McDaniel, H. W. Peck, G. D. Fairtrace, and John R. Graham, all of Dallas. The road was opened to traffic between Bartlett and Jarrell on February 1, 1910, and graded as far as Florence by early April. However, the Bartlett-Florence encountered financial problems, and was sold under foreclosure on May 29, 1911. A new company, Bartlett Western, was organized and completed the line to Florence in 1912. *Chris Cravens*

BARTLETT–GARCÍA CONDE COMPROMISE. The Bartlett–García Conde Compromise of 1850 was intended to resolve a dispute over the southern boundary of New Mexico resulting from errors in the map used by the negotiators of the Treaty of Guadalupe Hidalgo.[qv] Instead, the compromise became a partisan political issue, and the question of New Mexico's southern boundary was not finally settled until the Gadsden Purchase in 1853. The boundary sketched by the negotiators of the Treaty of Guadalupe Hidalgo on the 1847 "Map of the United Mexican States" by J. Disturnell began on the Rio Grande eight miles north of El Paso and proceeded west three degrees. Unfortunately, Disturnell's map contained two major errors: it drew the Rio Grande two degrees farther west than it really was, and it showed El Paso thirty miles farther north than it really was.

These problems did not become immediately apparent, in part because of the difficulties of the United States in settling on a commissioner. In December 1848 President James K. Polk named Ambrose Sevier as the United States commissioner, but Sevier died before he could be confirmed by the Senate. John B. Weller replaced Sevier and ran the portion of the line from the Pacific Ocean to the junction of the Gila and Colorado rivers but departed sometime after February 15, 1850, the victim of political intrigues and infighting. John C. Frémont was to be Weller's successor, but Frémont resigned upon his election as the first Senator from California.

On June 19, 1850, John Russell Bartlett[qv] was named to replace Frémont. While the United States had gone through four commissioners, Mexico had had only one: Gen. Pedro García Conde, the former Mexican secretary of war and the navy, director of the Mexican Military College at Chapultepec, and deputy from Sonora to the Mexican legislature. After Weller and García earlier that year had agreed to recess until late 1850 and to arrange for the survey of the El Paso area, at the other end of the line, Weller departed. Bartlett arrived in late November, and García Conde shortly thereafter. Bartlett later described García as "an accomplished engineer, and a most amiable and estimable gentleman," while García Conde apparently felt much the same way about Bartlett, although García later refused to budge in the compromise once it was set. This mutual respect came in handy during the dispute over the New Mexico line.

When their surveyors made astronomical observations in the field, they discovered the errors in the Disturnell map, of which García was aware even before any survey work. He argued that the line should be laid down according to the latitude and longitude shown on the map. By this reasoning, the line would have begun at a point on the Rio Grande thirty miles north of El Paso and proceeded west one degree, then north to the first tributary of the Gila, giving Mexico the Mesilla valley and the copper mines of Santa Rita del Cobre. Taken by surprise by such errors, Bartlett was nevertheless prepared to be conciliatory but argued that the negotiators of Guadalupe Hidalgo had obviously intended the southern boundary of New Mexico to extend more than one degree west.

After much discussion the two commissioners agreed on a compromise. García Conde agreed that the boundary should run three degrees west, regardless of the true position of the Rio Grande. Bartlett in turn agreed that the initial point on the Rio Grande should be at 32°22′ north latitude and not eight miles north of El Paso, which was at 31°45′ north. Bartlett, García Conde, and the chief Mexican surveyor, José Salazar Ylarregui, signed the agreement, but it remained unofficial without the signature of the chief United States surveyor, Andrew B. Gray,[qv] who was in Texas recovering from an illness.

On April 24, 1851, a stone marker was placed on the Rio Grande at 32°22′ N. The surveyors established their headquarters at the Santa Rita mines and began working west. On July 19, however, Gray arrived and immediately concluded that Bartlett had been duped. Gray refused to sign the agreement and ordered all surveying work halted until another meeting could be held with García Conde. Gray argued that latitude and longitude should be discounted, and the line should be placed on the earth in the same relation to the town of El Paso that it had on the map, that is, eight miles north of the plaza. He believed that the area between 31°45′ N and 32°22′ N contained the only practicable route for a transcontinental railroad to California. Gray was replaced by Maj. William H. Emory[qv] as chief surveyor a few months later. García Conde died of typhus on December 19, 1851, but his successor, Salazar, proved equally unwilling to renegotiate the New Mexico line, since the Mexican commission had earlier been heavily criticized for giving away too much in California. In the meantime, the Bartlett–García Conde Compromise had become a political issue, with the members of the Texas congressional delegation, including Sam Houston,[qv] and other Democrats accusing the Whigs of having given up too much of New Mexico.

Emory's signature on the agreement would make it official and binding, but the Democrats wanted to leave a loophole for renegotiation. On the other hand, the secretary of state had expressly ordered the chief surveyor to sign the agreement. Emory delicately sidestepped the issue by signing the agreement but insisting that in doing so he was merely witnessing the previous agreement between Bartlett and García Conde.

Under pressure from the Democrats, the Boundary Commission was disbanded on December 22, 1852, and the United States turned its attention to surveying the Rio Grande from Laredo to the Gulf of Mexico. Just over a year later the Gadsden Treaty finally resolved the initial-point controversy by purchasing enough territory for the coveted railroad route. The surveying of the United States–Mexico line was finally completed in October 1855.

BIBLIOGRAPHY: John Russell Bartlett, *Personal Narrative of Explo-*

rations . . . Connected with the United States and Mexican Boundary Commission (New York: Appleton, 1854; rpt., Chicago: Rio Grande Press, 1965). Odie B. Faulk, *Too Far North, Too Far South* (Los Angeles: Westernlore Press, 1967). W. H. Goetzmann, *Army Exploration in the American West, 1803–1863* (New Haven: Yale University Press, 1959; 2d ed., Lincoln: University of Nebraska Press, 1979; rpt., Austin: Texas State Historical Association, 1991). Harry P. Hewitt, "The Mexican Boundary Survey Team: Pedro García Conde in California," *Western Historical Quarterly* 21 (May 1990). Robert V. Hine, *Bartlett's West: Drawing the Mexican Boundary* (New Haven: Yale University Press, 1968).

Martin Donell Kohout

BARTLETT WESTERN RAILWAY. The Bartlett Western Railway was chartered on June 17, 1911, by J. W. Jackson and others as a successor to the Bartlett-Florence Railway Company, which had been sold under foreclosure on May 29, 1911. The line was located in Williamson County. The capital was $25,000, and the business office was at Bartlett. The road was mainly chartered by non–county residents who sought to make a profit from the traffic in cotton. Members of the first board of directors included W. J. McDaniel, H. W. Peck, and John R. Graham, all of Dallas; and G. W. Hubbard of Teague, John C. Collins of Houston, C. C. Bailey of Bartlett, and John McDowell of Florence.

The Bartlett Western acquired eleven miles of railroad operating between Bartlett and Jarrell, and in 1912 completed its line to Florence. Its stations between Bartlett and Florence were named St. Matthew, St. Mark, St. Luke, and St. John. The company was successful for a number of years, during which it primarily hauled cotton; in 1912 it carried 53,750 tons of the fiber. In 1916 the company owned one locomotive, eighteen freight cars, two passenger cars, and eight company cars and earned $3,817 in passenger revenue and $30,327 in freight revenue. In 1926 the road was listed by the Railroad Commission[qv] as a Class II railroad and owned one locomotive, thirty freight cars, two passenger cars, and three company cars. Earnings for that year included $1,611 in passenger receipts and $27,467 in freight revenue.

But cars jumped the tracks so often that the line became known as the "Bullfrog line." In 1926 Texas began to experience a decline in cotton prices. By 1931 the Bartlett Western was listed as a Class III railroad, and its earnings for that year were down to $6,908. The company's last president was Marie Cronin. The Bartlett Western and its twenty-three miles of track were abandoned on October 11, 1935.

BIBLIOGRAPHY: Clara Stearns Scarbrough, *Land of Good Water: A Williamson County History* (Georgetown, Texas: Williamson County Sun Publishers, 1973).

Chris Cravens

BARTON, ALFRED HIGHTOWER. (1848–1921). Alfred Hightower (Al) Barton, Motley County pioneer, cattleman, and founder of Barton Community, was born on December 21, 1848, near Greenville, South Carolina, to Decater (or Decator) and Catherine (Hightower) Barton. Accounts of his life differ. In 1854 the family joined the Barton wagon train headed for Texas. They settled on the frontier near Round Rock, then in Burnet County, where Indian raids were still common. When he was twenty-two, Al hired out to drive 2,500 cattle to California to sell to gold miners there. With the help of twenty cowboys he arrived with the herd, 100 horses, and two wagons intact, having lost none to Indians or stampedes. He delivered the proceeds to his employer, Dudley H. Snyder,[qv] in Denver, and the Snyder brothers hired him to trail a herd to the Texas plains.

In 1878 Barton returned to Burnet County and married Mollie Moreland. Taking a herd of cattle to Cimarron, Kansas, they moved north. A blizzard in the late 1880s wiped out most of the cattle. Mollie died soon afterward, leaving motherless her three small sons. Barton returned to Texas, temporarily leaving the two older boys with his parents and permanently leaving the youngest son with his sister Milda.

He found work on the F Ranch, owned then by Charles Goodnight[qv] and Lysander Moore, on Quitaque Creek in Floyd and Briscoe counties. He sent for his oldest son, Wilburn, who quickly became a ranchhand. Barton continued as manager when Goodnight sold his part to Moore in 1890 and when Moore sold out to the Cresswell Cattle Company in 1898. In 1889 Al married Mollie (or Millie) Sams of Della Plain; they had six children. When Mollie and her eight-month-old daughter died of pneumonia, they were buried together near the ranch headquarters in the Grey Mule Cemetery, overlooking Quitaque Creek. By this time Barton's eldest son had filed on land, built a dugout,[qv] and married, while the next, Sam, had moved to Canada.

While working for the F Ranch, Barton had accumulated sizable acreage on the Middle Pease River. When the F Ranch was dissolved, he bought some of its cattle and moved them a few miles southeast onto his ranch in Motley County. At the age of fifty-five he married Addie Bishop Seay, a widow with a son and daughter. Alfred and Addie Barton had four children. The new Mrs. Barton was very strict about cursing and drinking, but loved to dance and threw parties that often lasted all night. One time a local fiddler from Turkey, Texas, unable to make it to the dance at the Barton place, sent his fifteen-year-old son, a guitar player named James Robert (Bob) Wills,[qv] who was to play many times at the Barton dances in the years to come.

Barton Community grew as Al's many children began their own farms and ranches nearby. School was held in the east bedroom of the ranchhouse; by 1919 the students filled a one-room school built on a knoll northeast of the home. In 1930 this building was replaced with a two-room red brick building, and a teacherage was provided. At one time as many as seventy-two students were enrolled in Barton School. After 1935 students were transported to Matador so that they might graduate from state-accredited schools. Al Barton died in 1921, probably in May or June.

BIBLIOGRAPHY: Harry E. Chrisman, *Lost Trails of the Cimarron* (Denver: Sage, 1961). Darrell Debo, *Burnet County History* (2 vols., Burnet, Texas: Eakin, 1979). Eleanor Traweek, *Of Such as These: A History of Motley County and Its Families* (Quanah, Texas: Nortex, 1973).

Marisue Potts

BARTON, D. WILBORN (1850–1946) D. Wilborn (Doc) Barton, rancher, son of Decator and Catherine (Hightower) Barton, was born in Bertram, Texas, in 1850. The family had moved to Texas from Virginia that year and settled in Burnet County, where they endured occasional Comanche depredations. They had fourteen children, of whom Wilborn was the second. As a young man Barton left home with his older brother, Alfred, and boyhood friends Tom Connell and J. D. Eubank (*see* CONNELL AND EUBANK RANCHES), in search of greener pastures. He may have been one of the first men to bring Texas cattle to the Santa Fe line in Kansas. As early as 1872 he began driving as many as 3,000 cattle from Mason County to the railhead at Dodge City, Kansas, and for a time he and Alfred ranged a herd around nearby Pierceville, just south of the Arkansas River. On one trip Barton took his wife, Belle (Vandover), whom he had married at Mason, with him; he received his nickname Doc after helping her deliver their second child on the range. In 1878 Doc joined Alfred on Wolf Creek, just west of the present Lipscomb-Ochiltree county line, where he had a herd and a dugout home on the creek. Later that year the Bartons turned the dugout over to Connell and Eubank, who had come in with their herds, and moved farther downstream into Lipscomb County. There they occupied the abandoned Jones and Plummer stockade (*see* JONES AND PLUMMER TRAIL), which contained a three-room picket house and cellar. Their black trail cook, Uncle Ed, stayed with them until an unexpected encounter with reservation Indians from Indian Territory who were breaking in to steal food. The scare was mutual, but Uncle Ed returned to Burnet County shortly thereafter. In 1881 the Bartons sold their stockade home and 1,200 cattle to Henry W. Cresswell[qv] for eighteen dollars a head.

Encouraged by Cresswell, Barton invested in more cattle and choice pastureland in Lipscomb County. Over the next several years his younger brothers Alex, Clay, Dick, Will, Henry, and Walter moved to the county, worked for various ranches, including the Box T and Seven K, established farms, and stayed to become influential Panhandle[qv] citizens. Numerous Barton descendents still reside in the Panhandle and neighboring Oklahoma. D. Wilborn Barton died in Dodge City, Kansas, on January 12, 1946, at the age of ninety-five.

BIBLIOGRAPHY: *Cattleman*, February 1946. *A History of Lipscomb County, Texas, 1876–1976* (Lipscomb, Texas: Lipscomb County Historical Survey Committee, 1976). Millie Jones Porter, *Memory Cups of Panhandle Pioneers* (Clarendon, Texas: Clarendon Press, 1945).

H. Allen Anderson

BARTON, DONALD CLINTON (1889–1939). Donald Clinton Barton, geologist, son of George Hunt and Eva May (Beede) Barton, was born in Stow, Massachusetts, on June 29, 1889. He received a B.A. degree from Harvard in 1910, an M.A. in 1912, and a Ph.D. in 1914. Barton taught engineering and geology at Washington University from 1914 to 1916, when he became field geologist for the Empire Gas and Fuel Company. During World War I[qv] he was weather forecaster with the Meteorological Section of the Signal Corps. He was a geologist for the Gulf Coast division of Amerada Petroleum Corporation from 1919 to 1925, chief geologist for Rycade Oil Corporation from 1923 to 1927, and chief of the Torsion Balance and Magnetometer Division, Geophysical Research Corporation, from 1925 to 1927. He wrote many articles on geology and geophysics. He became research and consulting geologist and geophysicist for Humble Oil and Refining Company (now Exxon Company, U.S.A.[qv]) in 1935. He married Margaret Dunbar Foules on June 26, 1923. They had one daughter. Barton died on July 8, 1939.

BIBLIOGRAPHY: *Who Was Who in America*, Vol. 2.

BARTON, JAMES M. (?–1879). James M. Barton, soldier, farmer, and merchant, was born in Pickens District, South Carolina, about 1842, to Benjamin Barton, who was killed in the Regulator-Moderator War[qv] in Harrison County. Barton's mother's maiden name was Baker. Soon after his father's death, he moved to the Rusk County community of Millville, where he was elected sheriff and served for eight or ten years. With the outbreak of the Mexican War[qv] Barton was elected second lieutenant of Capt. Ferguson Ashton's Company G of Col. George T. Wood's[qv] Second Regiment, Texas Mounted Volunteers. This company was recruited primarily in the vicinity of Sand Hill, Texas, and was in federal service from June 25 through October 2, 1846. Under Gen. Zachary Taylor[qv] it saw action in the Monterrey campaign in September 1846. During the Civil War[qv] Barton was elected lieutenant colonel of the Tenth Texas Cavalry. This regiment served in Arkansas, Louisiana, and Texas during the first months of the war, before being transferred to Ector's Brigade[qv] of the Army of Tennessee, where it was consolidated with the Fourteenth Texas Cavalry. Due to ill health, Barton resigned his commission before the close of the war.

Afterward, he was a successful merchant, first at Bellview, later at Hallville, and finally at Longview. When his Longview store burned, however, he retired to his Bellview farm. He was serving as sergeant at arms of the Texas Senate at the time of his death in September 1879, one year after the death of his wife, Emily (Miller). Barton was the father of five children and the father-in-law of James Harvey (Cyclone) Davis.[qv]

BIBLIOGRAPHY: Frank W. Johnson, *A History of Texas and Texans* (5 vols., ed. E. C. Barker and E. W. Winkler [Chicago and New York: American Historical Society, 1914; rpt. 1916]). Charles D. Spurlin, comp., *Texas Veterans in the Mexican War: Muster Rolls of Texas Military Units* (Victoria, Texas, 1984). Marcus J. Wright, comp., and Harold B. Simpson, ed., *Texas in the War, 1861–1865* (Hillsboro, Texas: Hill Junior College Press, 1965).

Thomas W. Cutrer

BARTON, THOMAS DICKSON (1875–1944). Thomas Dickson Barton, soldier, son of George and Ellen Barton, was born at Kilgore, Texas, on January 20, 1875. He was in the newspaper business for about ten years, worked as a drug salesman for a Kansas City firm, and operated a retail drugstore in Amarillo. He became a private in the Sixth Texas Infantry on July 10, 1892, and was commissioned first lieutenant, Company F, in February 1895. During the Spanish-American War, from May 1898 to August 1899, he was first sergeant in the First Montana Infantry, stationed in the Philippine Islands. Barton was captain of Company E, Fourth Texas Infantry, from 1905 to 1917, when he entered the federal service. He commanded Company G, 142nd Infantry, through its training period and in France. In October 1918 he was promoted to major and awarded the Distinguished Service Cross, the Croix de Guerre, and the Italian Croce al Merite de Guerra. He was in charge of the military police of the Thirty-sixth Division[qv] and later served on the military mission for repatriation of Russian prisoners in Berlin. After discharge from the United States Army on October 10, 1919, he was appointed adjutant general of Texas, on January 20, 1921, and served until January 23, 1925. In 1924 he ran for governor as a Democrat on a platform of limiting state government responsibility to police protection, the judiciary, and education. He retired from the army as a major general on July 6, 1938.

Barton married Rowena McCoy on November 5, 1905. After her death he married Mrs. Lillian Leman, who survived him. He died in San Antonio on November 28, 1944, and was buried in Fort Sam Houston National Cemetery, San Antonio.

BIBLIOGRAPHY: Austin *Statesman*, June 26, 1921. Ellis A. Davis, and Edwin H. Grobe, comps., *The New Encyclopedia of Texas*, 4-vol. ed. San Antonio *Express*, November 29, 1944. Vertical Files, Barker Texas History Center, University of Texas at Austin.

Jeanette H. Flachmeier

BARTON, WELBORN (1821–1883). Welborn Barton, physician, the eldest son of Wilson and Mildah (McKinney) Barton, was born on September 25, 1821, in Greenville, South Carolina, of Scotch-Irish ancestry. His mother died at a rather early age, and his father then married a woman named Rebecca. When he was nine he was permanently crippled in an accident. Because of his handicap his stepmother encouraged him to receive an education. In 1844 Barton entered the Medical Department of Transylvania College, Lexington, Kentucky, where, in 1846, he received an M.D. degree with a major in obstetrics. After his graduation in 1847 he moved to Bastrop, Texas, where he practiced medicine for two years. He then returned to South Carolina and prepared to seek his fortune in California, but returned instead to Lexington to take a postgraduate course. At Lexington on December 12, 1850, he married Louisa Adeline Cox, daughter of a wealthy planter. In time they had at least seven children. Barton returned to Greenville, South Carolina, and practiced medicine there until October 1854, when, leading a party of around eighty persons, including his father, his brothers Alexander, Wilson Perry, David, Joel Poinsett, Columbus, and Decatur, he set out from Tigerville, again intending to go to California. On the way through Texas he stopped off in Williamson County, before moving in 1855 to Burnet County, where his father had settled. The latter soon was elected county judge of Burnet County.

Barton established a medical practice in the area. On the frontier of Texas danger from Indians was ever present; he often had to travel for miles to see the sick, and carried a shotgun for protection. He also frequently found it necessary to make his own surgical instruments. During the Civil War[qv] he served briefly as a surgeon in the Confederate forces, but because of his physical handicap he was soon ordered home to look after the sick and injured on the home front. Throughout his career as a doctor he kept up with advances in the medical profession and occasionally went to the East to attend lectures and do research. Two of his sons (Welborn, Jr., and Robert) followed him in the medical profession. In 1864 Barton became a Royal Arch Mason in Mount Horeb Chapter No. 57. After the war he moved to Salado so that his children might take advantage of the educational facilities available there. His home in Salado bears a Texas Centennial[qv] marker. Barton served as a trustee of Salado College for many years. He was a Sunday school teacher in the First Baptist Church of Salado. He died of a stroke at Salado on May 13, 1883, and was buried there.

BIBLIOGRAPHY: Darrell Debo, *Burnet County History* (2 vols., Burnet, Texas: Eakin, 1979). George Plunkett [Mrs. S. C.] Red, *The Medicine Man in Texas* (Houston, 1930). *Hazel Adams Richardson*

BARTON, WILLIAM (1782–1840). William Barton, early settler called the "Daniel Boone of Texas," son of Thomas and Bethire (Williamson) Barton, was born at Greenville, South Carolina, in 1782. About 1807 he and his first wife, née Charlotte Anderson, moved to Kentucky, where several of his brothers lived. Mrs. Barton died there in 1809, after the birth of their daughter, Minerva. Barton then moved to Alabama and during the Indian rebellion of 1816 was listed as living in Marengo County. His father died during that time, and Barton inherited five slaves. In 1828 he came to Texas with two of his brothers, Elisha and Benjamin, as part of Stephen F. Austin's[qv] second colony. Barton received a headright grant from the Mexican government for a league on the west side of the Colorado River, in what became Bastrop County. He was elected local *comisario*[qv] in 1830. He was a loner with an independent nature, and when a neighbor settled within ten miles of his cabin he moved forty-five miles up the Colorado River, to a site near that of present-day Austin. In 1837, with his second wife, Stacy (Pryor), he patented and settled on land near the springs. Barton had six children. He was known as a fearless and skillful Indian fighter and once saved his own life by pretending to signal other white men to come to his rescue. His friends heard gunshots and soon saw him running toward them saying, "It's a good thing it wasn't one of you, you would have been killed shore!" Barton died on April 11, 1840, and was buried near Barton Springs. His body was reportedly reinterred in Williamson County, near Round Rock, in 1862, but no record of reburial has been found.

BIBLIOGRAPHY: Eugene C. Barker, ed., "Minutes of the Ayuntamiento of San Felipe de Austin, 1828–1832," 12 parts, *Southwestern Historical Quarterly* 21–24 (January 1918–October 1920). Sam Houston Dixon and Louis Wiltz Kemp, *The Heroes of San Jacinto* (Houston: Anson Jones, 1932). J. W. Wilbarger, *Indian Depredations in Texas* (Austin: Hutchings, 1889; rpt., Austin: State House, 1985). Villamae Williams, *Stephen F. Austin's Register of Families* (Nacogdoches, Texas: Ericson, 1984). *Mary Jayne Walsh*

BARTON COMMUNITY, TEXAS. Barton Community is located on Farm Road 1585 twelve miles south of Lubbock in southwestern Lubbock County. The settlement was named for an early landowner who donated the site for a school. By 1927 the Barton school was one of twenty-six school districts in the county. The two-room school building, in which grades one through seven were taught, served also as a community center and church. The school at Barton was combined with similar institutions at Slide, Woodrow, New Hope, and Union in the mid-1930s to constitute the Cooper Rural School District. Early residents of Barton included the Thompson, Morton, Mabry, Potts, and Robertson families. Leading citizens included George Hindman, a farmer and gin manager, and Mr. and Mrs. Russell Dennison, early schoolteachers. In the 1980s Barton Community was an unincorporated farming community; the Barton Gin and the Irish Acres Pecan Orchard were the only businesses.

BIBLIOGRAPHY: Mary Louise McDonald, The History of Lubbock County (M.A. thesis, University of Texas, 1942).

Charles G. Davis

BARTON CREEK (Donley County). Barton Creek rises fourteen miles northeast of Howardwick in north central Donley County (at 35°11′ N, 100°51′ W) and runs southeast for eleven miles to its mouth on Saddlers Creek, ten miles northeast of Clarendon (at 35°04′ N, 100°45′ W). The stream was named for S. B. Barton, a former buffalo hunter and surveyor who had a horse ranch on McClellan Creek. One of three line camps on Lewis H. Carhart's[qv] Quarter Circle Heart Ranch was on Barton Creek, as was J. F. Evans's original Spade Ranch[qv] headquarters; this property was later owned successively by the families of Charlie McMurtry and Thomas L. Griffin. The surrounding terrain is flat to rolling to steeply sloped and surfaced with locally stony loams and clays. Native vegetation includes mesquite scrub and grass.

BIBLIOGRAPHY: Virginia Browder, *Donley County: Land O' Promise* (Wichita Falls, Texas: Nortex, 1975). Willie Newbury Lewis, *Between Sun and Sod* (Clarendon, Texas: Clarendon Press, 1938; rev. ed., College Station: Texas A&M University Press, 1976).

—— (Erath County). Barton Creek rises five miles west of Huckabay in northwestern Erath County (at 32°22′ N, 98°25′ W) and runs north eighteen miles to its mouth on Palo Pinto Creek, two miles south of Lake Palo Pinto in Palo Pinto County (at 32°35′ N, 98°21′ W). It traverses flat terrain surfaced by deep loam that supports elms and a variety of short grasses.

—— (Hays County). Barton Creek rises six miles northeast of Dripping Springs in northern Hays County (at 30°13′ N, 98°11′ W) and flows east for forty miles to its mouth on the Colorado River, at Town Lake in southwest Austin (at 30°16′ N, 97°46′ W). It passes between limestone bluffs, sheer cliffs, and heavily wooded hills that characterize the Hill Country[qv] and drops 1,000 feet between its source and its mouth. It falls through the limestone fissures of the Edwards Aquifer recharge zone in southwest Austin and reemerges several hundred yards downstream at Barton Springs.[qv] The shallow clay and sandy loam near the creek supports juniper, oak, cottonwood, pecan, willow, dogwood, and redbud trees, as well as at least seven endangered plant species.

Tonkawa and Comanche Indians camped in the Barton Creek area in the seventeenth and eighteenth centuries, and Spanish explorers in the eighteenth century commented on the site's beauty. William Barton,[qv] for whom the creek is named, built a home near the springs in 1837. The creek subsequently became a popular resort. An Austin newspaper referred to Barton Springs as "Austin's Eden" in the 1880s, and the swimming hole at the springs was built into a more modern pool in the 1930s.

Although sections of the creek carry little water during dry spells, periods of extended rainfall and high runoff can make the stream ideal for canoeing and kayaking. For decades Barton Creek has provided area residents and visitors opportunities for swimming, hiking, biking, rock climbing, and simply enjoying long stretches of unspoiled natural beauty. However, increased development of southwest Austin in the 1970s and 1980s began to threaten both water quality and wildlife, and the creek became the subject of numerous studies and greenbelt proposals and a bone of contention between developers and environmentalists. More and more frequently the pool at the springs was closed after heavy rains because of contamination from runoff and seepage from sewer lines. Public outcry against development near the creek forced the Austin City Council to adopt the Barton Creek Watershed Ordinance in 1980 and the Comprehensive Watersheds Ordinance in 1986. A 1990 proposal to develop 4,000 acres within the creek's watershed prompted unprecedented opposition and resulted in the passage of the Save Our Springs Citizens Initiative of 1992, an ordinance that severely limited the construction of impervious cover within the watershed, limited exemptions, established pollution-prevention standards, and attempted to reduce the risks of accidental contamination.

BIBLIOGRAPHY: Paul Burka, "The Battle for Barton Springs," *Texas Monthly*, August 1990. Vertical Files, Barker Texas History Center, University of Texas at Austin. Dale Weisman, "Austin's Heart of Green," *Texas Highways*, May 1991.

—— (Ochiltree County). Barton Creek rises at the edge of timber brakes in southeastern Ochiltree County (at 36°05′ N, 100°35′ W) and flows south for eight miles to its mouth on the Canadian River, in northeastern Roberts County (at 35°59′ N, 100°34′ W). The stream was formerly part of Henry Cresswell's[qv] Bar CC property and was probably named by him for his neighbors, the Barton brothers. The terrain is flat to rolling with local escarpments. The soil, mostly thick, fine, sandy loam, supports hardwood forest, brush, and grasses.

BIBLIOGRAPHY: *Wheatheart of the Plains: An Early History of Ochiltree County* (Perryton, Texas: Ochiltree County Historical Survey Committee, 1969).

BARTON'S CHAPEL, TEXAS. Barton's Chapel is on Farm Road 2210 twelve miles south of Jacksboro in south central Jack County. The first settlements in the county, Salt Hill and Burns Valley, were in this area. Although a few farmers and ranchers were scattered throughout the Barton's Chapel area by the mid-1850s, it is possible that a series of Indian raids inhibited the development of a permanent community until the mid-1870s, when the Indians were driven from the county. By the early 1880s Oak Glen and Brown each had Methodist schools that served the cotton farmers and cattle ranchers who had begun to make the area their home. During the years 1908–09 the two communities decided to build a new church and schoolhouse at the intersection of the newly completed Jacksboro-to-Palo Pinto and Graham-to-Perrin roads. The buildings were constructed under the leadership of Rev. L. S. Barton. The new school community was called Barton; later residents referred to it as Barton's Chapel. The population of the community was estimated at twenty through the 1930s and 1940s.

BIBLIOGRAPHY: John Clements, *Flying the Colors: Texas, a Comprehensive Look at Texas Today, County by County* (Dallas: Clements Research, 1984). Ida Lasater Huckabay, *Ninety-Four Years in Jack County* (Austin: Steck, 1949; centennial ed., Waco: Texian Press, 1974).

David Minor

BARTONS CREEK (Bastrop County). Bartons Creek rises three miles southeast of Rosanky in southern Bastrop County (at 29°53′ N, 97°15′ W) and flows eastward for 16½ miles to its mouth on the Colorado River, northwest of West Point in Fayette County (at 29°58′ N, 97°04′ W). The stream runs through an area of eroded terraces and uplands with loamy surface soil. Vegetation in the area consists primarily of post oak woods and crops.

—— (Fayette County). Bartons Creek rises in wooded and broken land in northwest Fayette County (29°53′ N, 97°16′ W) and flows 11½ miles, first northerly into Bastrop County, and then northeasterly back into Fayette County, to its mouth on the Colorado River, 2½ miles east of Kirtly (at 29°58′ N, 97°04′ W). Near the Colorado River the soil produces good crops of grain, pecans, and hay. This area has been subject to frequent flooding in the past, and there are at least fifteen flood-control impoundments of varying sizes along the creek and its unnamed tributaries. The upland slopes are dotted with numerous oil and gas wells and with mixed oak and cedar, which provide good wildlife habitat. The creek is named for Wayne Barton, early settler and participant in the battle of San Jacinto,[qv] who lived in the area.

BIBLIOGRAPHY: Leonie Rummel Weyand and Houston Wade, *An Early History of Fayette County* (La Grange, Texas: La Grange *Journal*, 1936).

BARTONSITE, TEXAS. Bartonsite, a ghost town in southwestern Hale County, was platted in 1907 on the expectation of a Santa Fe line from Plainview to Lubbock. The Barton Ranch community reached a population of 250 by 1909, but the rails were not laid through the area. Most buildings were moved to Abernathy, thirteen miles to the southeast. The post office closed in 1921.

BIBLIOGRAPHY: Ed Ellsworth Bartholomew, *800 Texas Ghost Towns* (Fort Davis, Texas: Frontier, 1971).

William R. Hunt

BARTON SPRINGS. Barton Springs, the fourth largest springs in Texas, is located in Zilker Park in southwest Austin. There artesian water issues from the cavernous Edwards and associated limestones in the Balcones fault zone. For thousands of years the springs were a gathering place for Indians. Spanish explorers wrote in 1714 that wild horses were numerous there. The springs were named after William Barton,[qv] an early settler in the area. Saw, flour, and grist mills as well as ice-making machines have used the water power of the springs. The springs have always been popular for swimming and other recreational activities. During the 1980s, however, use of the springs began to be periodically curtailed because of pollution. The average flow from 1895 to 1978 was nearly thirty-seven gallons per second. In 1992 a highly publicized campaign resulted in legislation for higher standards of water control.

BIBLIOGRAPHY: Gunnar Brune, *Springs of Texas,* Vol. 1 (Fort Worth: Branch-Smith, 1981).

Gunnar Brune

BARTON SPRINGS, TEXAS. The name Barton Springs is often given as an early name for Fredonia in Mason County, though the former seems to have been a separate community. Barton Springs was located in northeastern Mason County near the site of Fredonia and was supposedly named for Dick Barton, the owner of nearby springs.

Alice J. Rhoades

BARTONVILLE, TEXAS. Bartonville, eight miles south of Denton in south central Denton County, was originally part of the Chinn's Chapel settlement, established in 1853 by Elisha Chinn. Chinn's Chapel eventually became three small communities: Shiloh, Waketon, and Bartonville. Bartonville was settled in 1878 and named for T. Bent Barton. In 1886 a local post office was established. In 1890 Bartonville had twenty-five residents and a general store, a gristmill, and a cotton gin, all owned by the Barton family. By 1896 Bartonville's population was estimated at 100, and the town had three general stores. The post office was discontinued in 1905. In 1933 Bartonville had an estimated population of 300 and one business. In 1966 the population was 380, and in 1990 it was 849.

BIBLIOGRAPHY: Edward Franklin Bates, *History and Reminiscences of Denton County* (Denton, Texas: McNitzky Printing, 1918; rpt., Denton: Terrill Wheeler Printing, 1976). C. A. Bridges, *History of Denton, Texas, from Its Beginning to 1960* (Waco: Texian Press, 1978).

David Minor

BARWISE, JOSEPH HODSON (1829–1927). Joseph Hodson Barwise, farmer, businessman, and pioneer settler of Wichita Falls, was born to Thomas Henry and Julia (Collins) Barwise in Cincinnati, Ohio, on November 13, 1829. When he was four the family moved to a small community just north of New Trenton, Indiana, where Thomas Barwise farmed 360 acres. They remained in Indiana until April 1846, when the elder Barwise traded his farm for a large, uncleared tract of land near St. Charles, Missouri. J. H. Barwise, accompanied by one of his brothers, moved to this farm and cleared it in preparation for the arrival of the rest of the family in 1847. Moving to Missouri ended Barwise's formal education, the entire eight months of which had taken place in Indiana, largely at the hand of a tutor, Will Taft, the father of William Howard Taft, later president of the United States. In Missouri on October 18, 1852, Barwise married Lucy Hansell, whom he had met in St. Charles after rafting timber cleared from the family farm down the Quiver River; the couple settled on a farm provided by Barwise's father and eventually raised seven children.

Barwise was a staunch Unionist. He organized Company A of the Twenty-seventh Missouri Division and served as captain of this home-defense unit, which saw no action during the Civil War.[qv] When he was advised in the mid-1870s to move to a drier climate, he took his family to Texas and settled at Cedar Springs, near Dallas, in January 1877. He had little success as a wheat-separator salesman there. In December 1879, "after prospecting in various parts of the state," he and his family became the first permanent settlers at the site of Wichita Falls. He purchased the single existing cabin there, as well as a quantity of land, for $105.

Barwise immediately broke ground for a farm and soon afterward established a freight service. He sank the community's first water well. Soon after his arrival he began manufacturing bricks of native clay to supply local construction. He acquired sizable landholdings and prospered. He donated 55 percent of his land to a bonus designed to induce the Wichita Falls and Denver City Railway Company to extend the road through the community. By the second decade of the twentieth century he had acquired a ranch near Dalhart and begun trading in grain in the Panhandle.[qv] Barwise was chosen as one of two original justices of the peace for Wichita County. He held the position of county judge on three separate occasions. He also served as a member of the Wichita Falls school board during the 1880s and 1890s and was elected president in 1890. He was a charter member of the local Elks and Masonic organizations, the Business Men's League, and the First Presbyterian Church, which he served as an elder. He died in Wichita Falls on January 11, 1927, and was buried in Riverside Cemetery there.

BIBLIOGRAPHY: Louise Kelly, *Wichita County Beginnings* (Burnet, Texas: Eakin Press, 1982). Jonnie R. Morgan, *The History of Wichita Falls* (Wichita Falls, 1931; rpt., Wichita Falls: Nortex, 1971).

Brian Hart

BARWISE, TEXAS. Barwise is at the intersection of the Fort Worth and Denver Railway with Farm Road 784, eleven miles west of Floydada in west central Floyd County. The town was laid out in February 1928 after the FW&D had built through the area and was originally named after J. W. Stringer, a local farmer and the owner of the original townsite; the name was changed when it was discovered that another Texas town was named Stringer. Some residents wanted the name Granary, but the final designation became Barwise, after Judge Joseph Hodson Barwise[qv] of Wichita Falls, supposedly the first person off the train to register at the local hotel. Originally the town comprised some seven city blocks with streets named for early settlers. By the 1930s it had a hotel, a general store, a fertilizer dealer, a fueling station, a cotton gin, and two grain elevators. A population of about twenty-five was reported during the 1940s. Farm Road 784 reached Barwise in the 1950s. Although about half the original townsite had reverted to farmland by 1986, two businesses continued to operate in the community: Barwise Elevator and Fertilizer, which provided a grain elevator as well as farm supplies, seed, and fuels, and Henricks Barwise Gin, which began operations around 1948 as the Barwise Gin. Although the 1986–87 *Texas Almanac*[qv] listed a population of thirty, local residents stated that nine persons lived within the town limits during that period. The 1990 population was still reported as thirty.

BIBLIOGRAPHY: *Floyd County Hesperian*, July 15, 1965.

Charles G. Davis

BARZIZA, DECIMUS ET ULTIMUS (1838–1882). Decimus et Ultimus Barziza, lawyer, politician, author, businessman, and officer in the Confederate Army, was born on September 4, 1838, in Virginia, the tenth and last son of Phillip Ignatius and Cecelia Amanda (Bellett) Barziza. He was the great-grandson of eighteenth-century English scholar John Paradise and a direct descendant of the Ludwells, who owned extensive property in colonial Virginia. In 1857, after graduating from William and Mary College, Barziza followed three of his brothers to Texas and studied law at Baylor University. He graduated in 1859, moved to Owensville, Robertson County, and set up his law practice.

At the outbreak of the Civil War[qv] he volunteered for service in the Confederate Army and was soon elected first lieutenant in Company C of the Fourth Texas Infantry, which became part of Gen. John Bell Hood's[qv] famed Texas Brigade in Robert E. Lee's[qv] Army of Northern Virginia. Barziza was promoted to captain and led Company C into the battle of Gettysburg. During the attack on Little Round Top on July 2, 1863, he was wounded and left behind when the Confederate troops were forced to retreat. Although feigning death, he was discovered by Union troops and taken prisoner. After a year in federal hospitals and the prison camp at Johnson's Island, Maryland, he managed to escape by diving through the open window of a train on which he was being transported farther north, near Huntingdon, Pennsylvania.

After his escape he made his way to Canada, where he was one of the first escapees to use a network set up by rebel agents and Canadians to send escaped Confederates back to the South via Nova Scotia and Bermuda. Barziza arrived at Wilmington, North Carolina, in April 1864, and was allowed to return to Texas to recover from the hardships of his escape. In February 1865 he published his war memoirs anonymously in Houston under the title *The Adventures of a Prisoner of War, and Life and Scenes in Federal Prisons: Johnson's Island, Fort Delaware, and Point Lookout, by an Escaped Prisoner of Hood's Texas Brigade.*

Barziza settled in Houston, where he established a well-known law practice. He also became active in politics as a staunch Democratic opponent of Reconstruction.[qv] He joined other prominent Texans in calling for a "conservative state convention," which was held in the Harris County Courthouse on January 20, 1878. In July of that year he served on a statewide committee that organized the state Democratic convention at Bryan. He was instrumental in removing scalawag Governor Edmund J. Davis[qv] from office, and in 1873 Barziza was elected as a representative from Harris County to the Fourteenth Legislature. In 1875 he was reelected but subsequently lost the speakership of the House, by a vote of forty-five to forty-three, to Thomas R. Bonner[qv] of Smith County.

During the Fifteenth Legislature Barziza was part of a minority group that clashed with the House majority over a bill to give the Texas and Pacific Railway Company an extension of time for complying with the requirements for a land grant. The bill passed the Senate but could not get past the House before the session was scheduled to adjourn, at noon on July 31, 1876. Proponents of the bill lobbied for an extension of the session and managed to have the House recess until 3:30 p.m. on July 31. Barziza attempted to prevent the continuance of the session by absenting himself from his seat along with thirty-three other House members. However, the speaker ordered the missing members arrested and returned to their seats. In protest, Barziza, ill and in bed, tendered his resignation from the House, on August 2, 1876. He returned to Houston, where he continued his successful law practice and helped found the state's first trust company, the Houston Land and Trust Company, which he served as chairman of the board.

Barziza married Patricia Nicholas of Buckingham County, Virginia, in March 1869. They had no children, but in July 1872 they adopted Barziza's orphaned nephew Phillip Dorsey Barziza. Decimus et Ultimus Barziza died after a lingering illness in his home at the corner of San Jacinto and Walnut streets in Houston, on January 30, 1882.

BIBLIOGRAPHY: R. Henderson Shuffler, "Decimus et Ultimus Barziza," *Southwestern Historical Quarterly* 66 (April 1963). R. Henderson Shuffler, "A Texas Profile: Decimus et Ultimus Barziza," *Texas Bar Journal*, April 22, 1963. R. Henderson Shuffler, ed., *Decimus et Ultimus Barziza* (Austin: University of Texas Press, 1964).

Jeffrey William Hunt

BARZYNSKI, VINCENT (1838–1899). Vincent Barzynski, priest, son of Joseph and Mary (Sroczynska) Barzynski, was born at Sulislawice, Sandomir, Russian Poland, on September 20, 1838. His early education was private; he entered the diocesan seminary at Lubin and was ordained a Catholic priest on October 28, 1861. After being forced to leave his country for participating in a military uprising in 1863, Father Barzynski traveled for two years until he reached Rome, where he joined the newly formed Congregation of the Resurrection. Bishop Claude Marie Dubuis[qv] of Galveston, Texas, solicitous for the spiritual welfare of the Poles[qv] at such settlements in Texas as Panna Maria, San Antonio, Bandera, St. Hedwig, and Yorktown, invited the Resurrectionist Fathers to Texas. In 1866 Barzynski and two companions arrived. Laboring particularly as pastor in San Antonio and St. Hedwig, Barzynski did illustrious work before he was transferred to Chicago in 1874 to enter upon the great work of his life, the building of St. Stanislaus Church and school. He influenced the entire Catholic Polish population of Chicago and became a commanding figure in the history of his countrymen in America. He died in Chicago on May 2, 1899.

bibliography: Edward J. Dworaczyk, *The Millennium History of Panna Maria, Texas* (1966). James Talmadge Moore, *Through Fire and Flood: The Catholic Church in Frontier Texas, 1836–1900* (College Station: Texas A&M University Press, 1992).

Joseph W. Schmitz

BASCOM, TEXAS. Bascom is at the junction of State Highway 64 and Farm Road 848, a mile east of Tyler in central Smith County. The Texas State Quail Farm is located just to the south. The area was the site of a spring at the crossing of Indian trails and was settled as early as 1846, when William McAdams built one of the first gristmills in the county. John Pinkerton was buried in the Bascom Methodist Church cemetery the following year, when the Chancellor family owned most of the local land. In 1849 workers at the mill helped build the nearby Tyler-Henderson road. In 1856 a Bascom post office opened with Suzannah W. Smith as postmistress; the office closed after six months. The community was apparently named for Bishop Henry Biddleman Bascom of the Methodist Episcopal Church, South. In 1857 Jesse Cook deeded two acres to the community for a Methodist church; Rev. Caleb H. Smith was the first pastor. Bascom also had a doctor, Lazaira W. Smith, and a corn mill owned and operated by Rice Knowles. A Bascom school had opened by 1860, with classes taught by Dr. Smith and George A. Martin. Harmony Baptist Church was also established that year, when William R. Griffen donated seven acres for the church and a cemetery, later called Bascom Cemetery East; Griffen later gave another acre that became Bascom Cemetery West. In 1869 Walter Funderburgh bought the mill and added a cotton gin upstairs. By 1872 the school had a one-room wooden building in which students sat on plank benches. The average enrollment was twelve, and the school was moved at least three times.

In 1894 the third Methodist church building was completed. The following year the mill exploded, killing owner John Speer and ending a vital business in Bascom. The structure was never rebuilt; a few years later the ruins were completely destroyed by fire. A new post office opened in 1899 with James B. Taylor as postmaster, but mail service was moved to Tyler in 1901. In 1900 local voters established Bascom School District No. 32 and built a new white two-story school with tax and bond revenues. The one-teacher school enrolled twenty-six pupils in 1903; in 1907 the Chitwood school district was consolidated with Bascom. School enrollment in 1911 was approximately sixty-three, and the system employed two teachers. In 1921 the Macedonia school district was also consolidated with Bascom.

During the 1920s farming declined in the area, and many of the young people moved to Tyler. Horace Crawford Alfred opened a general store at which customers paid bills in cash or eggs on a monthly basis. The school system continued to succeed. By 1936 one local school had six teachers and 170 white elementary students, and another school had one teacher and twenty-three black elementary students. That same year the community had a church and two cemeteries. In 1941 citizens voted to merge with the Murph (later Sharon) Independent School District, and in 1945 Bascom became part of the Chapel Hill Independent School District.

In the 1970s Bascom had Methodist and Assembly of God churches. Traffic passed through the community on the road to Lake Tyler. Most residents worked at the nearby General Electric plant or in Tyler. Maps showed a church and a collection of farms at the site. In the 1980s Bascom had about fifteen businesses and numerous residences.

bibliography: Edward Clayton Curry, An Administrative Survey of the Schools of Smith County, Texas (M.Ed. thesis, University of Texas, 1938). Andrew Leath, "Bascom, Texas: Typical Texana," *Chronicles of Smith County*, Summer 1974. "Post Offices and Postmasters of Smith County, Texas: 1847–1929," *Chronicles of Smith County*, Spring 1966. "School Sights," *Chronicles of Smith County*, Fall 1969. Smith County Historical Society, *Historical Atlas of Smith County* (Tyler, Texas: Tyler Print Shop, 1965). Donald W. Whisenhunt, comp., *Chronological History of Smith County* (Tyler, Texas: Smith County Historical Society, 1983).

Vista K. McCroskey

BASFORD BAYOU. Basford (Basford's) Bayou rises one mile southwest of Hitchcock in southwest Galveston County (at 29°20′ N, 95°02′ W) and flows seven miles southeast to its mouth on Jones Bay, across from North Deer Island in West Bay (at 29°18′ N, 94°57′ W). The bayou is channeled in its upper reaches. It traverses flat to rolling terrain, surfaced by clay and sandy loam that supports water-tolerant hardwoods, conifers, and grasses; at the mouth, brackish saltwater marsh covers mud and sand that supports rushes and grasses.

BASILIAN FATHERS. Basilian priests moved to Texas from Toronto, Ontario, in 1899. Subsequently, they became the largest men's religious order in the Catholic Diocese of Galveston-Houston.[qv] They have been primarily committed to teaching, although they also maintain parishes and do mission work.

The Congregation of the Priests of St. Basil was founded in France around 1799 by a group of priests who, when they came out of hiding after the French Revolution, moved to Annonay, a small city on the Rhône, and devoted themselves to education. They became a religious community in 1822 and took St. Basil (330–379), bishop of Caesarea, as their patron. Patrick Moloney, the first Basilian to come to North America, arrived in Toronto in 1850 and, by 1852, had convinced his superiors in France of the need for schools and seminaries in the New World. The Basilians opened a minor seminary, St. Michael's College, in Toronto in 1865. From Toronto they spread their work to Owen Sound, some 140 miles northwest, where they staffed the eight Owen Sound Missions; and to Detroit, where they took over St. Anne's parish for French-speaking Catholics, as well as Assumption College and parish.

In 1899 the fathers of St. Basil established a college preparatory school in the district of Waco known as Provident Heights, their first Texas school, and named it St. Basil's College. The founder was Father James Peter Clancy, and presidents included fathers Thomas Hayes, Francis Forster, and Thomas Gignac. The catalog of 1906–07 reveals the study program as an impressive collection of subjects to be mastered by youngsters from rural backgrounds. The school offered a program in commercial subjects as well and had a heated swimming pool. An unexpected drop in enrollment made the institution financially nonviable, and the Basilians withdrew in 1915. In 1900 Basilians had established a similar school in Houston, St. Thomas College.

From 1901 to 1911, at the request of Bishop Nicholas Gallagher,[qv] the Basilians operated St. Mary's Seminary[qv] in La Porte for the Diocese of Galveston. In a former resort hotel Father James T. Player, the rector, began with one other Basilian to teach classes of about a dozen students. The enrollment increased steadily under Basilian guidance, which continued until December 1911, when the seminar was taken over by the diocese. Subsequent Basilian rectors were E. Albert Hurley (1903–07) and Thomas F. Gignac (1907–11).

Basilian operation of parishes began in Houston in 1928 when Bishop Christopher Byrne[qv] asked the order to take charge of the fledgling St. Anne's at Westheimer and Shepherd. The Basilians had long maintained parishes in Canada and France before that; they were thus able to fulfill this role when called upon. Byrne also requested help in seeing to the spiritual needs of Mexican people in his diocese, and so from the mid-1930s Basilians began missionary parishes in Fort Bend and Brazoria counties. In Rosenberg they assumed management of Our Lady of Guadalupe mission, which became the Basilians' center for work among the Spanish-speaking population of the Diocese of Galveston. Later, the priests expanded this work to Angleton, Sugar Land, Missouri City, Manvel, Richmond, Wharton, Bay City, and Freeport. Many of these missions were subsequently turned over to the diocesan clergy.

In 1945 the Basilian fathers accepted Bishop Byrne's invitation to establish a coeducational Catholic university in Houston. Thus began the University of Saint Thomas.[qv] The Basilians have worked for over eighty-five years in education in the Diocese of Galveston-Houston. The congregation is committed to the academic and spiritual instruction of the young and to the performance of their duties as priests.

BIBLIOGRAPHY: Archives of the Western Region of the Basilian Fathers, Houston. Catholic Archives of Texas, Files, Austin. *Texas Catholic Herald*, March 4, 1980.

R. E. Lamb, C.S.B.

BASKIN, TEXAS. Baskin, near Lancaster in southeastern Dallas County, was originally included in the Peters colony[qv] grant and first settled around 1847. In 1854 settlers from Kentucky led by A. A. Bledsoe[qv] established farms along the nearby valley of Ten Mile Creek.

Claudia Hazlewood

BASS, HAMBLIN (1816–?). Hamblin Bass, Brazoria County planter and committee of correspondence member, was born in Georgia in 1816 and lived in Alabama before moving to Texas. In November 1859 he acquired Waldeck,[qv] a sugar plantation three or four miles from the site of present West Columbia, from Morgan L. Smith.[qv] Sources differ about whether Bass owned the plantation or managed it for Count Ludwig von Boos-Waldeck[qv] as an agent of Spofford and Company of New York. In 1859 Waldeck was one of only two Texas plantations devoted solely to the cultivation of sugar (*see* SUGAR PRODUCTION). That year the plantation slaughtered more animals than any other plantation in Texas; their value was $9,700. In the 1860 census Bass reported real property valued at $163,830 and personal property valued at $97,705, including 172 slaves. In 1860 he served as a member of the Brazoria County committee of correspondence.

BIBLIOGRAPHY: Randolph B. Campbell, *An Empire for Slavery: The Peculiar Institution in Texas, 1821–1865* (Baton Rouge: Louisiana State University Press, 1989). James A. Creighton, *A Narrative History of Brazoria County* (Angleton, Texas: Brazoria County Historical Commission, 1975). Abigail Curlee Holbrook, "A Glimpse of Life on Antebellum Slave Plantations in Texas," *Southwestern Historical Quarterly* 76 (April 1973). Ralph A. Wooster, "Notes on Texas' Largest Slaveholders, 1860," *Southwestern Historical Quarterly* 65 (July 1961).

Diana J. Kleiner

BASS, SAM (1851–1878). Sam Bass, outlaw, was born on a farm near Mitchell, Indiana, on July 21, 1851, a son of Daniel and Elizabeth Jane (Sheeks) Bass. He was orphaned before he was thirteen and spent five years at the home of an uncle. He ran away in 1869 and worked most of a year in a sawmill at Rosedale, Mississippi. Bass left Rosedale on horseback for the cattle country in the late summer of 1870 and arrived in Denton, Texas, in early fall. For the winter he worked on Bob Carruth's ranch southwest of town. But, finding cowboy life not up to his boyhood dreams, he went back to Denton and handled horses in the stables of the Lacy House, a hotel. Later he worked for Sheriff William F. Egan, caring for livestock, cutting firewood, building fences, and spending much of his time as a freighter between Denton and the railroad towns of Dallas and Sherman.

Before long Bass became interested in horse racing, and in 1874, after acquiring a fleet mount that became known as the Denton Mare, he left Egan's employ to exploit this horse. He won most of his races in North Texas and later took his mare to the San Antonio area. When his racing played out in 1876, he and Joel Collins gathered a small herd of longhorn cattle[qv] to take up the trail for their several owners. When the drovers reached Dodge City they decided to trail the cattle farther north, where prices were higher. After selling the herd and paying the hands, they had $8,000 in their pockets, but instead of returning to Texas, where they owed for the cattle, they squandered the money in gambling in Ogallala, Nebraska, and in the Black Hills town of Deadwood, South Dakota, which was then enjoying a boom in gold mining.

In 1877 Bass and Collins tried freighting, without success, then recruited several hard characters to rob stagecoaches. On stolen horses they held up seven coaches without recouping their fortunes. Next, in search of bigger loot, a band of six, led by Collins and including Bass, rode south to Big Springs, Nebraska, where, in the evening of September 18, they held up an eastbound Union Pacific passenger train. They took $60,000 in newly minted twenty-dollar gold pieces from the express car and $1,300 plus four gold watches from the passengers. After dividing the loot the bandits decided to go in pairs in different directions. Within a few weeks Collins and two others were killed while resisting arrest. But Bass, disguised as a farmer, made it back to Texas, where he formed a new outlaw band.

He and his brigands held up two stagecoaches and, in the spring of 1878, robbed four trains within twenty-five miles of Dallas. They did not get much money, but the robberies aroused citizens, and the bandits were the object of a spirited chase across North Texas by posses and a special company of Texas Rangers[qv] headed by Junius Peak.[qv] Bass eluded his pursuers until one of his party, Jim Murphy, turned informer. As Bass's band rode south intending to rob a small bank in Round Rock, Murphy wrote to Maj. John B. Jones,[qv] commander of the Frontier Battalion[qv] of Texas—the rangers. In Round Rock on July 19 Bass and his men became engaged in a gun battle, in which he was wounded. The next morning he was found lying helpless in a pasture north of town and was brought back to Round Rock. He died there on July 21, his twenty-seventh birthday. He was buried in Round Rock and soon became the subject of cowboy song and story.

BIBLIOGRAPHY: Wayne Gard, *Sam Bass* (Boston: Houghton Mifflin, 1936).

Wayne Gard

BASS, THOMAS COKE (ca. 1830–1878). Thomas Coke Bass, attorney and Confederate cavalry officer, was born about 1830 in Mississippi. He was admitted to the Mississippi bar about 1858 and moved to Sherman, Texas, where he established a practice specializing in land law. With the election of Abraham Lincoln to the presidency in 1860, Bass became an outspoken advocate of secession.[qv] He is credited with raising the first Confederate flag over the Grayson County Courthouse. With the onset of the Civil War,[qv] he raised a cavalry regiment in Grayson and Cooke counties and in June 1862 was commissioned a colonel in the Twentieth Texas Cavalry. In this position he saw action in Texas and Indian Territory and commanded the force that captured Fort Washita. In addition, his cavalry unit participated in the battle of Prairie Grove, Arkansas, on December 7, 1862. Bass spent the remainder of the war defending Indian Territory. After the war he returned to his law practice in Sherman. In addition to this business, he published a newspaper, the Sherman *Courier,* for a short time in 1866. He married Ada Dalton Hocker on July 10, 1867. The couple had two sons and a daughter.

As a land agent Bass developed a system to verify land claims, which he published as *Best System of Abstract.* He advertised the pamphlet, which explained his system and listed the legally available lands in Grayson, Denton, Collin, Cooke, and Fannin counties, in numerous national publications. This system and his advertisement of it apparently brought him considerable business. He gained local notoriety in 1874 when he purchased the decrepit, twenty-five-year-old Grayson County Courthouse, had it leveled, and sold the bricks for use in chimneys. In 1878 he responded to an appeal from Memphis, Tennessee, for aid in combating a devastating yellow fever epidemic. Bass and a companion, Dr. T. J. Heady, contracted the disease upon their arrival in Memphis, and Bass died there on September 22, 1878.

BIBLIOGRAPHY: Grayson County Frontier Village, *History of Grayson County, Texas* (2 vols., Winston-Salem, North Carolina: Hunter, 1979, 1981).

Brian Hart

BASS, TEXAS. Bass, twenty miles east of Tyler in eastern Smith County, was named for a family of local settlers and granted a post office in 1886. In 1890 and 1892 John B. Bass was both postmaster and owner of a local cotton gin. In 1890 the town, which received mail semiweekly, had a population of four and businesses including a blacksmith, a corn mill, two cotton gins, and a sorghum plant. By 1892 the number of inhabitants had increased to eighteen and a druggist had opened a new business. The post office was discontinued in 1903.

BIBLIOGRAPHY: "Post Offices and Postmasters of Smith County, Texas: 1847–1929," *Chronicles of Smith County,* Spring 1966.

Vista K. McCroskey

BASSET CREEK. Basset Creek, or Bassets Creek, rises just west of Palestine in south central Anderson County (at 31°47′ N, 95°39′ W) and runs southwest for 5½ miles, through southwestern Anderson County, to its mouth on Town Creek, three miles southwest of Palestine (at 31°44′ N, 95°42′ W). The stream is intermittent in its upper reaches. Its banks are heavily wooded in places with post oaks, and the surrounding nearly level to steeply sloping terrain is surfaced by sandy and clayey upland soils used predominantly for agriculture.

BASSETT, HOUSTON A. P. (1857–1920). Houston A. P. Bassett, a black man who represented Grimes County in the Texas House of Representatives during the Twentieth Legislature, was born on March 14, 1857, in Grimes County, the son of poor farmers. He did not attend school until he was ten years old but was able to enroll in Straight University in New Orleans, Louisiana, in 1875. From 1879 to 1882 he attended Fisk University in Nashville, Tennessee. He returned to Grimes County, where he became active in Republican party[qv] politics. In 1886 he won election to the House. J. P. S. Thompson, his opponent, alleged that ineligible voters had aided Bassett's victory, but the House Committee on Privileges and Elections ruled in Bassett's favor because Thompson lacked sufficient proof.

Bassett resided in Anderson during his single term in the legislature. He sat on the Educational Affairs, Stock and Stock Raising, and Military Affairs committees. He also served as chairman of a special committee that investigated the state insane asylum, introduced legislation to permit the chartering of cooperative associations, and attempted to secure a state constitutional amendment that would temporarily exempt capital investments in manufacturing from taxation. Bassett also tried to increase the amount of money that the state received from the lease of convicted felons. He married Cordelia Foster on September 9, 1886, and the couple had four children. Bassett was an active member of a Baptist Church. He died on July 17, 1920, in Grimes County.

BIBLIOGRAPHY: Lewis E. Daniell, *Personnel of the Texas State Government, with Sketches of Representative Men of Texas* (Austin: City Printing, 1887; 3d ed., San Antonio: Maverick, 1892). Merline Pitre, *Through Many Dangers, Toils and Snares: The Black Leadership of Texas, 1868–1900* (Austin: Eakin, 1985).

Paul M. Lucko

BASSETT, JULIAN MARCUS (1874–1947). Julian Marcus Bassett, rancher, land promoter, and principal founder of Crosbyton, Texas, was born in New York City on December 4, 1874, to R. M. and Fannie Louisa Bassett. He was brought to Texas in 1882; the family settled in Crosby County. He left the area to work for the McCormack Harvester Company in Chicago but returned after two years to work as a cowboy on the Three H Ranch.

While delivering cattle to market in Chicago, Bassett contracted with the Coonley Brothers (Avery, John Stuart, Howard, and Prentiss) to invest in a sheep ranch in Crosby County. The successful partnership resulted in the founding of the CB Livestock Company in 1901. The company purchased the Two-Buckle Ranch[qv] property and used the Bar N Bar brand. The company began to sell its ranchlands in 1908, and the town of Crosbyton was founded. Bassett served as the first postmaster. By 1910 he was also working as the general manager of the Crosbyton–South Plains Railroad, vice president of the Crosbyton South Plains Townsite Company, and a copartner in the Crosbyton Company. He was president of the First National Bank of Crosbyton and of the Crosbyton Telephone Company, and he owned the Bassett Land Company. These companies promoted Crosbyton and two additional townsites, Lorenzo and Idalou, located in Crosby and Lubbock counties. Crosbyton, the most successful of the towns, reached a population of 1,200 by 1917.

Bassett married Cora Belle Drake on August 1, 1915; they had four children. The family moved in 1916 to San Antonio, where Bassett purchased the Block Y Ranch and the townsite of Dryden in Terrell County. He was less successful with this promotion and moved to Gila, New Mexico, in 1928. He returned to Dryden in 1930 and operated a store there until the late 1930s. He died on December 9, 1947, and was buried in the Crosbyton Cemetery.

BIBLIOGRAPHY: Julian Marcus Bassett Papers, Southwest Collection, Texas Tech University. Crosby County Pioneer Memorial Museum, *A History of Crosby County, 1876–1977* (Dallas: Taylor, 1978). Ellis A. Davis and Edwin H. Grobe, comps., *The New Encyclopedia of Texas,* 4 vols. (1929?).

Jan Blodgett

BASSETT, OSCAR T. (1850–1898). Oscar T. (O. T.) Bassett, businessman and financier, was born in Vermont in 1850 and orphaned early. With little formal education, he drifted in and out of the army before settling in Clinton, Indiana, where he was a contractor and lumber dealer. He married Myrtle Nebeker and in 1879 moved to Fort Worth, Texas, where he started a lumber business. With Charles R. Morehead,[qv] he traveled by stagecoach to El Paso in 1880 to buy real estate for the Texas and Pacific Railway and to investigate some Arizona mines. On February 15 of that year he wrote in his diary: "Plenty of room here for a big city, which it will be in time after the railroads come." Bassett returned to Indiana in time for the birth of his son. His wife died soon thereafter, and Bassett returned to El Paso. On the way he stopped in St. Louis to arrange financing for El Paso's first bank. The State National Bank was organized with Morehead as president, Joseph Magoffin,[qv] son of El Paso's foremost pioneer James Magoffin,[qv] as vice president, and Bassett a major stockholder. In 1991 the bank, called MBank El Paso, had been in continuous operation for ninety years. Bassett also opened a lumber business, for which he took orders until the first train arrived from the Pacific Coast with a supply of California redwood. His business expanded rapidly from Texas to California; he maintained headquarters in El Paso, where he acquired considerable land. He was named president of the first El Paso school board in December 1882, and the first classrooms were opened on March 5, 1883. Bassett also served as city councilman. He died in his office above a lumberyard on January 3, 1898. His son, who had been left with relatives in Indiana, came to El Paso to carry on his father's business and became an officer of the bank. In 1921 he became the bank's president. A downtown building and a shopping center carry the Bassett name.

BIBLIOGRAPHY: Harriot Howze Jones, comp. and ed., *El Paso: A Centennial Portrait* (El Paso, 1972). Vertical Files, Southwest Collection, El Paso Public Library. Owen P. White, *Out of the Desert: The Historical Romance of El Paso* (El Paso: McMath, 1924).

Arthur H. Leibson

BASSETT, TEXAS. Bassett is on the St. Louis and Southwestern Railway fourteen miles south of DeKalb in southwestern Bowie County. The town was named for John Bassett, on whose land grant the site is located. A post office was opened there in 1882 with G. B. Dalby as postmaster. By 1884 the town had two sawmills and a population of twenty-five and served as a shipping point for local farm products and lumber. In 1890 the population was 100. It was seventy-five in 1914 and fifty-eight in 1925. The post office was closed in 1958. In 1982 the town had a population of forty and no rated businesses. In 1990 the population was 373.

BIBLIOGRAPHY: J. J. Scheffelin, *Bowie County Basic Background Book.*

Cecil Harper, Jr.

BASSETT CREEK. Bassett Creek is formed by the junction of Blythe and Weaver creeks twelve miles south of DeKalb in southwestern Bowie County (33°20′ N, 94°36′ W). It flows southeast for eleven miles to its mouth on the Sulphur River, thirteen miles southwest of New Boston (at 33°17′ N, 94°31′ W). The soils of the area are clayey; flooding is frequent. The land is heavily wooded, with post oak, blackjack oak, and elm predominating. The stream was probably named for John Bassett, an original grantee of land through which it flows.

BASTROP, BARON DE (1759–1827). Felipe Enrique Neri, colonizer, legislator, and self-styled Baron de Bastrop, was born Philip Hendrik Nering Bögel in Paramaribo, Dutch Guiana, on November 23, 1759, the son of Conraed Laurens Nering and Maria Jacoba (Kraayvanger) Bögel. He moved to Holland with his parents in 1764, and in 1779 enlisted in the cavalry of Holland and Upper Issel. Bögel married Georgine Wolffeline Françoise Lijcklama à Nyeholt in Oldeboorn, Holland, on April 28, 1782; they had five children. The family settled in Leeuwarden, where Bögel served as collector general of taxes for the province of Friesland.

His military service, marriage, and appointment as tax collector suggest that he was a staunch supporter of the aristocracy during the late-eighteenth-century revolutionary period. He always gave the French invasion of Holland as his reason for leaving the country, but he actually left for different reasons. In 1793 he was accused of embezzlement of tax funds and fled the country before he could be brought to trial. After the Court of Justice of Leeuwarden offered a reward of 1,000 gold ducats to anyone who brought him back, Bögel adopted the title Baron de Bastrop.

By April 1795 he had arrived in Spanish Louisiana, where he represented himself as a Dutch nobleman. During the next decade he received permission from the Spanish government to establish a colony in the Ouachita valley and engaged in several business ventures in Louisiana and Kentucky. After Louisiana was sold to the United States in 1803, Bastrop moved to Spanish Texas and was permitted to establish a colony between Bexar and the Trinity River. In 1806 he settled in San Antonio, where he had a freighting business and gained influence with the inhabitants and officials. In 1810 he was appointed second alcalde[qv] in the ayuntamiento[qv] at Bexar.

One of his most significant contributions to Texas was his intercession with Governor Antonio María Martínez[qv] on behalf of Moses Austin[qv] in 1820. Because of Bastrop, Martínez reconsidered and approved Austin's project to establish an Anglo-American colony in Texas. After Austin's death, Bastrop served as intermediary with the Mexican government for Stephen F. Austin,[qv] who would have encountered many more obstacles but for Bastrop's assistance and advice. In July 1823 Luciano García[qv] appointed Bastrop commissioner of colonization for the Austin colony with authority to issue land titles. On September 24, 1823, the settlers elected Bastrop to the provincial deputation at Bexar, which in turn chose him as representative to the legislature of the new state of Coahuila and Texas[qv] in May 1824.

During his tenure as representative of Texas at the capital, Saltillo, Bastrop sought legislation favorable to the cause of immigration and to the interests of settlers; he secured passage of the colonization act of 1825 (*see* ANGLO-AMERICAN COLONIZATION); and he was instrumental in the passage of an act establishing a port at Galveston. His salary, according to the Mexican system, was paid by contributions from his constituents. The contributions were not generous; Bastrop did not leave enough money to pay his burial expenses when he died, on February 23, 1827. His fellow legislators donated the funds to reimburse Juan Antonio Padilla[qv] for the expenses of the funeral. Bastrop was buried in Saltillo.

Even in his last will and testament, Bastrop continued to claim noble background, giving his parents' names as Conrado Lorenzo Neri, Baron de Bastrop, and Susana Maria Bray Banguin. Some of his contemporaries believed him to be an American adventurer; historians have thought him to be a French nobleman or a Prussian soldier of fortune. Only within the last half-century have records from the Netherlands been found to shed light on Bastrop's mysterious origins. Although his pretensions to nobility were not universally accepted at face value even in his own lifetime, he earned respect as a diplomat and legislator. Bastrop, Texas, and Bastrop, Louisiana, as well as Bastrop County, Texas, were named in his honor.

BIBLIOGRAPHY: Charles A. Bacarisse, The Baron de Bastrop: Life and Times of Philip Hendrik Nering Bögel (Ph.D. dissertation, University of Texas, 1955). Charles A. Bacarisse, "Baron de Bastrop," *Southwestern Historical Quarterly* 58 (January 1955). Eugene C. Barker, ed., *The Austin Papers* (3 vols., Washington: GPO, 1924–28). Baron de Bastrop Documents, Barker Texas History Center, University of Texas at Austin. Baron de Bastrop Papers, Barker Texas History Center, University of Texas at Austin. Richard Woods Moore, The Role of the Baron de Bastrop in the Anglo-American Settlement of the Spanish Southwest (M.A. thesis, University of Texas, 1932). Vertical Files, Barker Texas History Center, University of Texas at Austin.

Richard W. Moore

BASTROP, TEXAS. Bastrop, county seat of Bastrop County, is located in the center of the county, about thirty miles southeast of downtown Austin. The town is at the junction of State highways 71, 21, and 95, and on the Colorado River and the Missouri, Kansas and Texas Railroad. The site was first occupied in 1804, when a fort was established at the strategic Colorado River crossing of the Old San Antonio Road[qv] and named Puesta del Colorado. The Baron de Bastrop[qv] obtained permission from the Spanish to found a German colony and selected the site in 1823, but subsequently failed to establish a settlement. The town was probably named Bastrop by Stephen F. Austin[qv] in honor of the baron, a longtime friend and coworker. Austin, interested in developing the upper reaches of his original colony, used this name after the German colonization attempt failed and he obtained permission in 1827 to locate a "Little Colony" of 100 families on the site. He had seen the future townsite on his first journey to Texas, and had noted it favorably in his journal. By 1830 such pioneers as Josiah Wilbarger, Reuben Hornsby, James Burleson, Edward Burleson,[qqv] and Jess Barker had located in the Bastrop area. But the Indian depredations that had doomed the German colonization attempt continued to slow settlement. In 1830 a traveler wrote that the population of Bastrop consisted of a bachelor and two families, with John F. Webber[qv] and the Wilbarger family living a short distance to the north.

On June 8, 1832, land commissioner José Miguel de Arciniega[qv] officially platted the town along conventional Mexican lines, with a square in the center and blocks set aside for public buildings. He also officially named the site Bastrop, but two years later the Coahuila and Texas[qv] legislature renamed it Mina (*see* MINA MUNICIPALITY), in honor of Francisco Xavier Mina,[qv] a Mexican martyr and hero.

On January 1, 1835, Juan N. Almonte[qv] reported a population of 1,100 in the area, and at the outbreak of the Texas Revolution[qv] the town's population was approximately 400. Bastrop served as a business, commercial, and political center for an area that stretched far beyond Bastrop County; it was the place where settlers rallied for retaliation and forted up for protection when Indian depredations occurred in the vicinity. Until the railroad reached the county in the early 1870s, Bastrop was the only town in the county. In May 1835, Mina citizens became the first to organize a committee of safety to stockpile arms and keep citizens informed of revolutionary developments. The town suffered in the Runaway Scrape[qv] of 1836, when residents returned to find it completely destroyed by the Mexican army and Indians. Indians, particularly the Comanches, who hunted in the area every fall, continued to provide a major threat until after annexation[qv] to the United States in 1846.

The town was incorporated under the laws of Texas on December 18, 1837, and the name changed back to Bastrop. The community then comprised a courthouse, a hotel, a stockade, a gunsmith shop, a general store, and a number of residences. With farming, the timber industry provided a mainstay for the local economy from 1836 to 1860. The Lost Pine Forest,[qv] the westernmost stand of the eastern pine forest and the only timber available in what was then western Texas, contributed to the economy. In 1839, when Austin became the capital of the republic, Bastrop began supplying the city with lumber. Soon, ox teams were carting Bastrop lumber to San Antonio, along the western frontier, and into Mexico.

Though Protestant services were held in Bastrop as early as 1835, official organization of a Protestant congregation did not occur until three years later, when a Methodist church with fifteen members was begun. The introduction of slaves to the area helped make cotton a major part of the local economy after 1839 and lessened the priority of lumber. A post office was established in 1846, and a one-room log school was in operation the next year. By the 1850s Bastrop was developing rapidly. In 1851 Bastrop Methodists built the county's first church, a weekly newspaper was founded, and the Bastrop Educational Society opened Bastrop Academy.[qv] By the following year, the Bastrop *Advertiser* had begun its long publishing history, the academy had been incorporated as Bastrop Female Academy, and a subscription library had begun. In 1856 Bastrop Military Institute (later Texas Military Institute, Austin[qv]) opened.

Although Bastrop County residents voted against secession[qv] by a narrow margin, the citizens of Bastrop aided the Confederate cause in a number of ways, including raising money to equip companies and providing a supply warehouse. Fire destroyed most of the downtown buildings in 1862, but flood posed an even greater threat. A flood of area creeks in 1869 forced evacuation of the town as waters rose as high as forty-six feet. Periodic inundations continued to plague the area until dams were built in the 1930s. Despite natural disasters, the period during and after the Civil War[qv] saw the rise of varied industry in Bastrop. Through the 1860s and 1870s such businesses as the Bastrop Iron Manufacturing Company, the Bastrop Coal Company, and Lone Star Mills got their start. By 1884 Bastrop had a population of 2,000 and three schools, two cotton gins, several general stores, and a number of other businesses. A wrought-iron bridge erected across the Colorado in 1890 put the ferries out of business.

With the turn of the century, stock raising increased. Bastrop established a public library, and by 1909 had graded schools and two banks. The population in 1910 was 1,707. It hovered around the 2,000 mark through the early twentieth century. In the 1920s the Bastrop area was the scene of oil drilling, and between 1928 and 1935 lumber operations were revived; a Bastrop mill produced thirty million board feet of lumber annually during those years. Although coal was known to exist in large quantities a few miles from Bastrop as early as 1837, and was mined between 1860 and 1870, major lignite extraction began only around 1910 and from then until 1940 was the community's predominant industry.

The population peaked at about 5,000 during World War II,[qv] after the establishment of nearby Camp Swift. When the camp gradually closed after the war, Bastrop shrank to 4,000, then 3,158 in 1950. Industries in 1947 included a pecan-shelling plant, a cedar-chest factory, and a cedar-oil manufacturer. From 1950 through the 1970s Bastrop's population ranged between 2,950 and 4,050. The 1980s brought new challenges for the community as Austin grew eastward, Austin sewage polluted the Colorado, and strip-mining began pressing from the east. In the mid-1980s the town had a population of almost 4,000. In 1990 the population was 4,044. Residents had restored many historic buildings, and commuters from Austin lived in Bastrop. As a consequence of the town's proximity to Austin, land values soared. Bastrop remained a center for agribusiness. Its industries included oil-well supply and furniture manufacturing.

BIBLIOGRAPHY: Bastrop *Advertiser,* Historical Edition, August 29, 1935. Bastrop Historical Society, *In the Shadow of the Lost Pines: A History of Bastrop County and Its People* (Bastrop, Texas: Bastrop *Advertiser,* 1955). Louis Wiltz Kemp, *The Signers of the Texas Declaration of Independence* (Salado, Texas: Anson Jones, 1944; rpt. 1959). William Henry Korges, Bastrop County, Texas: Historical and Educational Development (M.A. thesis, University of Texas, 1933). Bill Moore, *Bastrop County, 1691–1900* (Wichita Falls: Nortex, 1977). Vertical Files, Barker Texas History Center, University of Texas at Austin. WPA Texas Historical Records Survey, Inventory of the County Archives of Texas (MS, Barker Texas History Center, University of Texas at Austin). *Paula Mitchell Marks*

BASTROP ACADEMY. Bastrop Academy, under the jurisdiction of the Methodist Episcopal Church, South, opened at Bastrop in 1851 and was chartered on February 7, 1853. Administrators built a two-story pine building for $15,000; it had separate male and female study halls and a library of 1,000 volumes. The enrollment was 132 for the first session and increased to 194 by 1857. William Hancock, the first principal, was succeeded by John Carmer. On May 25, 1872, the property of the academy became a part of the Bastrop public school system.

BIBLIOGRAPHY: William Henry Korges, Bastrop County, Texas: Historical and Educational Development (M.A. thesis, University of Texas, 1933). Bill Moore, *Bastrop County, 1691–1900* (Wichita Falls: Nortex, 1977).

BASTROP BAY. Bastrop Bay is west of Follets Island and off the west end of West Bay in Brazoria County (its center is at 29°06′ N, 95°11′ W). It can be reached through San Luis Pass and Cold Pass or through Mud Cut.

BASTROP BAYOU. The channel of Bastrop Bayou begins near the Missouri Pacific Railroad two miles southwest of Angleton in central Brazoria County (at 29°09′ N, 95°27′ W) and runs thirty-two miles south and then northeast, through Cox Lake, Lost Lake, the Gulf Intracoastal Canal, and Bastrop Bay[qqv] to its mouth on Christmas Bay,[qv] in east central Brazoria County (at 29°06′ N, 95°12′ W). Austin Bayou,[qv] a major tributary, enters Bastrop Bayou eight miles southeast of Angleton near Demi-John Island (at 29°06′ N, 95°18′ W). Bastrop Bayou is intermittent in its upper reaches. Upstream, it crosses rolling terrain surfaced by sandy loam that supports post oaks and grasses; downstream, it traverses brackish saltwater marshland surfaced by mud and sand that support rushes and grasses.

BASTROP COUNTY. Bastrop County (L-17), located on State highways 71, 95, 21, and 304, on the upper Gulf coastal plains just below the Balcones Escarpment, encompasses 895 square miles of southeast central Texas. Its seat of government, Bastrop, is situated in the center of the county at approximately 30°04′ north latitude and 97°22′west longitude, a location about thirty miles southeast of downtown Austin. The terrain throughout most of the county is characterized by rolling uplands and broken hills with surface layers of primarily sandy, loamy soils, and woods where post oaks predominate but where cedar, hickory, elm, and walnut also occur. In the northwestern corner of the county and along the central southeastern border, the topography changes to blackland prairie with waxy clay soil and tall grass cover. The Colorado River bisects the county from northwest to southeast; along this waterway and its tributaries can be found rich alluvial silts and clays. Near the river, the Lost Pine Forest[qv] extends through an east central section of the county. Elevations range from 400 to 600 feet above sea level. The county's climate has been described as subtropical humid, with a low average January temperature of 40° F, a high average July temperature of 96° F, and an average annual rainfall of 36.82 inches; the growing season is 270 days long. Mineral resources include clay, oil, gas, lignite, sand, gravel, and surface and underground water.

The McCormick site near McDade has produced archeological evidence of human life in the area during the Neo-American period, a thousand years ago. By the beginning of the nineteenth century, Tonkawa Indians inhabited the area, and Comanche Indians came to hunt along the river each autumn. With an early road between Nacogdoches and San Antonio running through the region, in 1804 Spanish governor Manuel Antonio Cordero y Bustamante[qv] established a fort at the Colorado River crossing where the town of Bastrop now stands. The Baron de Bastrop[qv] planned a German community at the site, but it was not until after Stephen F. Austin[qv] obtained a grant for a "Little Colony" from the Mexican government in 1827 that settlement began. Pioneers met with intense Indian resistance, but by 1830 the town of Bastrop, named for the baron, had been founded and settlers from Austin's lower colonies were clearing farms over the southern portion of the county.

In 1831 Austin received a second land grant; the two grants, Mina Municipality,[qv] took in almost all of what is now Bastrop County. The district was presumably named in honor of Spanish general Francisco Xavier Mina.[qv] In 1834 the vast municipality, comprising all or part of sixteen present-day counties, was established by the government of Coahuila and Texas,[qv] and the town of Bastrop also took the name Mina. When Texas became a republic, Mina Municipality assumed its place as one of twenty-three original counties. In 1837 the Congress of the Republic of Texas[qv] changed the county name to Bastrop in honor of the baron and allowed the town to revert to the name as well. Congress also began whittling away at the boundaries of the huge county; in 1840, when Travis County was formed, Bastrop County shrank almost to its present dimensions.

The year 1837 had seen the arrival of slaves and cotton cultivation in the county. Though Bastrop County was never a leader in cotton production, this crop was favored over others for the next fifty years. In 1838 another significant industry began when the Bastrop Steam Mill Company started operation. It initiated Lost Pines lumbering activity that reached a peak in the early 1840s, as Bastrop mills supplied lumber to Austin, San Antonio, Houston, and other settlements. Lumber production continued for decades until available timber declined, but agriculture remained the predominant means of making a living. In 1850 the county had a population of 2,180, including 919 slaves. The county produced about 1,500 bales of cotton that year and harvested, in addition, 148,360 bushels of Indian corn and 18,552 bushels of sweet potatoes.

In 1853 a county courthouse was constructed in Bastrop to replace the rented building that had been serving the purpose. The next year twenty-three common-school districts were reported in the county. Settlement was spreading through the southern two-thirds of the county, with many immigrants arriving from the southern United States. In addition, hundreds of German emigrants were joining the Americans or establishing their own communities, such as Grassyville.

Between 1850 and 1860 the population of Bastrop County more than tripled, reaching 7,006, with 2,248 slaves making up almost a third of the total and foreign-born residents totaling 700. The county had 596 farms in 1860, and livestock raising was growing; the number of cattle increased from about 12,000 in 1850 to over 40,000 in 1860. Six churches were reported in an 1860 survey: two Methodist, two Lutheran, one Christian, and one Baptist.

Despite the fact that the county possessed a large slave population and a growing cotton economy, Bastrop County residents voted 352 to 335 against secession.[qv] But they rallied for the Confederate cause, arming and equipping military companies and providing for soldiers' families. Reconstruction[qv] brought tensions similar to those experienced across the South, with racial confrontations flaring around the community of Cedar Creek.

In 1870 Bastrop County's population topped 11,000, and it had thirty-four manufacturing establishments. The following year brought a further stimulus to growth in the form of the Houston and Texas Central Railway, completed through the northern part of the county to connect Austin and Brenham. Towns soon sprang up along the railroad, the most substantial being Elgin. Now many farmers had a freight outlet for their harvests of corn and cotton.

In 1874 Bastrop County assumed its present size with the establishment of Lee County. Nine years later, the Bastrop County Courthouse burned and a new one, still in use more than 100 years later, was built. Further railroad development occurred in the 1880s and 1890s, when the Taylor, Bastrop and Houston Railway connected the Bastrop County towns of Smithville and Bastrop with Lockhart, Waco, San Antonio, and Houston. In 1894 the Missouri, Kansas and Texas Railroad, which had taken over the Taylor, Bastrop and Houston, selected Smithville as the site of its central shops. This move soon made the community rival Bastrop and Elgin in size.

At the turn of the century Bastrop County had 26,845 residents and was still primarily agricultural, with a peak number of farms (3,509) and peak production of cotton (41,730 bales) reported in the 1900 census. In this year the county also reported its largest number of manufacturing establishments, though the eighty-seven concerns employed only 293 people.

The discovery of oil in the county in 1913 led to years of oil testing and drilling at various sites. The pool found at the Yost farm four miles east of Cedar Creek in 1928 was representative of those discovered—productive but unspectacular. In the 1920s, however, oil was not the only resource being developed. County coal belts were being mined, with the Winfield mines providing lignite to various state institutions. Clay deposits around Elgin were making the town the "Brick Capital of the Southwest," and the lumber industry around Bastrop was reviving.

At the same time, changes were occurring in Bastrop County agriculture. Farmers had continued to raise corn and cotton primarily, and 1920 was a peak year for corn, with almost a million bushels harvested. Although most of the county's cultivated land was still set aside for cotton, the county picked only 14,250 bales that year. A farm depression that began in 1920 forced changes in land use, with greater agricultural diversification and increased cattle production.

The 1920s farm depression was followed by the general economic depression of the 1930s. The number of farms in Bastrop County dropped between 1920 and 1940 from 3,325 to 2,473, and farm value decreased from over $17 million to $7,246,372. Population, too, was sliding. In 1920 the county reported a population of 26,649, with the ratio of white to black about two to one. In 1940 the population was 21,610.

The World War II[qv] years brought an acceleration in cattle production and an economic upsurge for Bastrop, Elgin, and other communities with the foundation of the army training facility Camp Swift in the north central part of the county. But the war also drew residents off farms to work in war plants, and many did not come back. In the late 1940s, Bastrop County faced an economic decline. Camp Swift was phased out, the coal mines were closed, and lumbering had exhausted the remaining commercial timber. Cotton cultivation occupied only one-sixth its 1920 acreage.

However, farmers were diversifying successfully. Sorghum was being produced in large quantities, watermelons were a significant cash crop, and increasing crops of peanuts and pecans were being produced. In 1950 alone, Bastrop County farmers harvested 1,719,200 pounds of peanuts. More significantly, the number of cattle in the county had grown to 41,529 in 1950 as agricultural emphasis shifted from crop production to beef-cattle raising and more land was set aside for pasture.

Only fourteen manufacturing establishments employing 387 workers were reported in the county in 1947; the steadiest industry was probably brick and tile manufacturing at Elgin, where two large plants were operating in the 1940s, to be joined by a third in the 1950s.

Bastrop County population continued to decline, hitting a low of 16,925 in 1960. The number of farms continued to decline as well, reaching a low of 1,029 in 1969. But by then, population was gradually rising. The number of cattle continued to rise, too, with 68,769 reported in that year.

The beef industry remained strong through the 1970s and early 1980s, with 70,066 cattle reported in the 1982 census. But pasturelands were being taken over by suburban development as the growth of nearby Austin produced growth in Elgin, Bastrop, and such smaller communities as Cedar Creek and Red Rock. By 1980 the county population had risen to 24,726 and was soon to surpass the 1900 high of 26,845. The census classified three-fourths of the population as white, among these 3,402 Hispanic; the black population numbered 4,259. The three largest communities remained Elgin, with 4,535 people, Bastrop, with 3,789, and Smithville, with 3,470. The county population in 1990 was 38,263.

In 1982 the county reported 1,507 farms. Over one-third of these were producing hay; ninety-seven were harvesting nuts and fruits, while only twenty-eight were producing vegetables for sale. In the same year, the county had twenty-eight manufacturing establishments employing 700 workers. Wages paid were over $9.5 million, and product value was almost forty million dollars. Industries ranged from two brick plants still operating in Elgin to an oil-well supply in Bastrop. Both towns had furniture plants. Bastrop had a tourist industry stimulated by historical preservation efforts and by the proximity of Lake Bastrop and Bastrop and Buescher State parks.[qqv] In the early 1990s, residents of Bastrop County were coping with the challenges of growth brought on by the suburban development of nearby Austin and were seeking further opportunities for agricultural and industrial diversification.

For most of its history Bastrop County has been staunchly Democratic, although Republicans made inroads in the late twentieth century, particularly in presidential and statewide races. Republican presidential candidates won in the 1972 and 1984 elections, but Democrats Michael Dukakis and Bill Clinton managed to garner a majority of the votes in the 1988 and 1992 elections respectively. Democratic officials have also continued to maintain control of most county offices. In the 1982 primary 97 percent voted Democratic and 3 percent Republican, with a total of 5,578 votes cast.

BIBLIOGRAPHY: Bastrop *Advertiser*, Homecoming and Progress Edition, July 21, 1980. Kenneth Kesselus, *History of Bastrop County, Texas, Before Statehood* (Austin: Jenkins, 1986). William Henry Korges, Bastrop County, Texas: Historical and Educational Development (M.A. thesis, University of Texas, 1933). Bill Moore, *Bastrop County, 1691–1900* (Wichita Falls: Nortex, 1977).

Paula Mitchell Marks

BASTROP STATE PARK. Bastrop State Park is located on State Highway 71 three miles east of Bastrop in central Bastrop County. It was established in 1938, when the city of Bastrop gave the state 2,100 acres. The Civilian Conservation Corps[qv] built the original park facilities. The park featured part of the Lost Pine Forest[qv] and offered swimming, camping, and picnicking facilities, as well as a nine-hole golf course. Park Road 1, which connected Bastrop and Buescher state parks, was a popular route for both cyclists and motorists. The state acquired an additional 1,450 acres for the park in 1979. In 1990 the park attracted nearly half a million visitors.

BIBLIOGRAPHY: Ross A. Maxwell, *Geologic and Historic Guide to the Texas State Parks* (Bureau of Economic Geology, University of Texas at Austin, 1970). A. Gayland Moore, "Woodland Parks," *Texas Parks and Wildlife*, March 1989.

Vivian Elizabeth Smyrl

BATA INDIANS. The Batas are known from a 1691 Spanish missionary report that identifies them as living about eighty leagues southwest of the Hasinai Indians of eastern Texas. Their affiliations remain unknown.

BIBLIOGRAPHY: John R. Swanton, *Source Material on the History and Ethnology of the Caddo Indians* (Smithsonian Institution, Bureau of American Ethnology Bulletin 132, Washington: GPO, 1942).

Thomas N. Campbell

BATAYOGLIGLA INDIANS. Batayogligla (Batayolida) is the name of one band of Chizo Indians, who are considered by some writers to be a branch of the Conchos. In the seventeenth and early eighteenth centuries the Chizos occupied the area now covered by northeastern Chihuahua, northwestern Coahuila, and the lower part of the Big Bend region of the Trans-Pecos.[qv]

BIBLIOGRAPHY: Charles W. Hackett, ed., *Historical Documents Relating to New Mexico, Nueva Vizcaya, and Approaches Thereto, to 1773* (3 vols., Washington: Carnegie Institution, 1923–37). Carl Sauer, *The Distribution of Aboriginal Tribes and Languages in Northwestern Mexico* (Berkeley: University of California Press, 1934).

Thomas N. Campbell

BATEMAN, ISAAC (ca. 1790–1848). Isaac Bateman, pioneer Red River County settler, was born in North Carolina, probably around 1790. Around 1816 he moved to Arkansas Territory with Charles Burkham[qv] and others who settled in the Red River valley. Around 1820 he moved across the river into Texas, where he joined the Burkham Settlement[qv] in northeastern Red River County, thus becoming one of the earliest settlers in the region. He purchased 400 acres from Ahijah Burkham in Bowie County in 1844. He evidently died in the summer of 1848, for his estate was probated in July of that year.

BIBLIOGRAPHY: Pat B. Clark, *The History of Clarksville and Old Red River County* (Dallas: Mathis, Van Nort, 1937). Claude V. Hall, "Early Days in Red River County," *East Texas State Teachers College Bulletin* 14 (June 1931). Blewett Barnes Kerbow, The Early History of Red River County, 1817–1865 (M.A. thesis, University of Texas, 1936). *Red River Recollections* (Clarksville, Texas: Red River County Historical Society, 1986). Rex W. Strickland, Anglo-American Activities in Northeastern Texas, 1803–1845 (Ph.D. dissertation, University of Texas, 1937).

Christopher Long

BATEMAN, TEXAS. Bateman, two miles south of Red Rock in southern Bastrop County, was established in the early 1880s and named for one of the original settlers. With the coming of the railroad a few years later, the community became a shipping point, and in 1900 a post office was established with William S. Friar, Jr., as postmaster. At the end of 1904 the post office closed. In the 1930s Bateman had two businesses, a population of fifty, and a two-room school. The population estimate remained at fifty through 1948. Bateman was still listed as a community in 1990, but without population figures.

BIBLIOGRAPHY: William Henry Korges, Bastrop County, Texas: Historical and Educational Development (M.A. thesis, University of Texas, 1933). *Paula Mitchell Marks*

BATEN, ANDERSON EDITH (1855–1924). Anderson Edith Baten, teacher and minister, son of Thomas James and Katherine Matilda (Lunsford) Baten, was born at Haw Ridge, Alabama, on October 5, 1855. He attended Baylor University, was ordained a Baptist minister in 1881, and served as pastor of several churches in Texas from 1883 to 1905. He was professor of Bible at Howard Payne College from 1907 to 1911 and again in 1914, president of Oklahoma State Baptist College at Blackwell from 1911 to 1913, and acting president of Howard Payne in 1915. Baten was recording secretary of the Baptist General Convention from 1889 to 1910, a charter member of the Texas Baptist Education Board, and a trustee of Southwestern Baptist Theological Seminary in 1910–11. His home was in Brownwood. He died on November 3, 1924, and was buried in Greenleaf Cemetery, Brownwood.

BIBLIOGRAPHY: *Who Was Who in America*, Vol. 2.

BATES, JOSEPH (1805–1888). Joseph Bates, politician and soldier, was born in Mobile, Alabama, on January 19, 1805. Though a businessman rather than a lawyer, he became a prominent Whig politician and served as a representative in the Alabama legislature in 1829, 1836, 1837, and 1840. He was defeated in the election for the state Senate in 1838. He took part in the Seminole War of 1835 and became a major general of the Alabama militia.

He moved to Galveston, Texas, in 1845 and was elected mayor three years later. President Millard Fillmore appointed him United States marshal for the eastern district of Texas from 1850 to 1853, when he was succeeded by Benjamin McCulloch.[qv] In 1854 he moved to a large plantation on the west side of the San Bernard River in Brazoria County, where he engaged in farming and ranching until his death.

At the outbreak of the Civil War[qv] Bates was appointed a colonel in the Confederate Army. He raised a regiment that later became, after several reorganizations, the Thirteenth (Bates's) Texas Infantry. He was placed in command of the coast defenses between Galveston and Matagorda Island and established headquarters at Velasco. From May to September 1863 he and his regiment served in Louisiana under Maj. Gen. Richard Taylor.[qv] For a time Bates was commander of the post at Brashear City.

His moderation and firmness during Reconstruction[qv] went far in bringing about a peaceful adjustment of affairs in Brazoria County. He was noted for his commanding physical appearance and for his abilities as a public speaker. He was a member of the Brazoria Lodge No. 327, A.F. and A.M. He was twice married. By his first wife he had seven children. By his second, Mrs. Mary Love Morris of Galveston, whom he married in 1851, he had five children. Bates died on February 18, 1888, and was buried in the Episcopal Cemetery in Galveston.

BIBLIOGRAPHY: John Henry Brown, *Indian Wars and Pioneers of Texas* (Austin: Daniell, 1880; reprod., Easley, South Carolina: Southern Historical Press, 1978). William Garrett, *Reminiscences of Public Men in Alabama, for Thirty Years* (Atlanta, Georgia: Plantation, 1872). Charles Cooper Nott, *Sketches in Prison Camps* (New York: Randolph, 1865). *The War of the Rebellion: A Compilation of the Official Records of the Union and Confederate Armies* (Washington: GPO, 1880–1901). *Cooper K. Ragan*

BATES, WILLIAM BARTHOLOMEW (ca. 1889–1974). William B. (Colonel) Bates, lawyer, foundation trustee, and banker, was born on August 16, 1889 or 1890, in Nat, Texas, the sixth of thirteen children of James Madison and Mary Frances (Cook) Bates. He attended and later taught in rural schools in Nacogdoches County. He earned an elementary teaching certificate at Sam Houston Normal Institute (now Sam Houston State University) in 1911, graduated from the University of Texas law school in 1915 at the top of his class, practiced law briefly in Bay City, and enlisted in the Leon Springs First Officers Training Camp[qv] when the nation entered World War I.[qv] He was commissioned a second lieutenant in August 1917 and was twice wounded in France; he held the rank of captain when he was discharged in July 1919. Bates returned to Nacogdoches and was elected district attorney in 1920 for the Second Judicial District. Partly because the Ku Klux Klan[qv] strongly opposed him in 1922, he did not win reelection.

On January 1, 1923, he moved to Houston and joined the law firm of Fulbright and Crooker (later Fulbright and Jaworski) as an associate. He soon became a partner and continued as such until he retired in 1971. As a lawyer, Bates was most successful in his firm's business and corporate practice, in which he represented cotton firms, banks, and clients in the oil and gas business. He became chairman of the board of San Jacinto National Bank in 1942 and of the Second National Bank in 1944. He merged the two banks with Guardian Trust in 1945 under the name Second National Bank (later Bank of the Southwest and subsequently MBank). He remained chairman until 1967 and was a member of the board and advisory chairman at the time of his death.

Bates was an original trustee of the M. D. Anderson Foundation[qv] and became its chairman when the founder, Monroe D. Anderson,[qv] died in 1939. The foundation played a key role in building the Texas Medical Center[qv] in Houston. Bates was also vice president of the Benjamin Clayton Foundation for Research and was a trustee of the San Jacinto Museum of History Association. He served as a member of the Houston Board of Education (1927–35), president of that board (1932–35), a regent (1943–71) and president (1934–35) of the University of Houston, and a trustee of Trinity University.

Though he never ran for political office after 1922, Bates retained an active interest in civic matters. In appreciation of his support, Governor Daniel J. Moody[qv] commissioned him an honorary colonel, a title that Bates used for the remainder of his life. On February 21, 1921, Bates married Mary Estill Dorsey of Nacogdoches. They had two daughters. Bates was a Presbyterian. He died in Houston on April 17, 1974.

BIBLIOGRAPHY: N. Don Macon, *South from Flower Mountain: A Conversation with William B. Bates* (Houston: Texas Medical Center, 1975). *Newton Gresham*

BATES, TEXAS. Bates, about twenty miles east of Denton in Denton County, was originally part of the Hawkins settlement. The community was named after Kentuckian William E. Bates, who, along with Harry Hawkins, founded the Hawkins settlement in 1853. Bates was known in the area primarily for its Zion Methodist Church and its camp meetings. Reverend Bates used the village as a base of operations to spread Methodism in North Texas. Like many of the pioneer settlements in Denton County bypassed by the railroads, Bates failed to sustain itself. The post office closed in 1904, and by the 1930s the community no longer existed.

BIBLIOGRAPHY: Edward Franklin Bates, *History and Reminiscences of Denton County* (Denton, Texas: McNitzky Printing, 1918; rpt., Denton: Terrill Wheeler Printing, 1976). C. A. Bridges, *History of Denton, Texas, from Its Beginning to 1960* (Waco: Texian Press, 1978). *David Minor*

BATES CREEK. Bates Creek rises two miles south of Big Head Mountain in northern Comal County (at 29°58′ N, 98°20′ W) and runs southeast for five miles to its mouth on the Guadalupe River (at 29°55′ N, 98°17′ W). With the construction of Canyon Lake in the 1960s, the lower reaches of Bates Creek were inundated. The terrain through which the creek passes is generally flat with local deep dissections surfaced by shallow, stony soil that supports oak, juniper, and mesquite.

BATESVILLE, TEXAS (Red River County). Batesville is 3½ miles east of Clarksville in central Red River County. In 1933 the community had seven residents and one business, and in 1940 the population was fifty. In 1984 Batesville was a small community of scattered houses with no businesses. The population was fourteen in 1990.

Cecil Harper, Jr.

BATESVILLE, TEXAS (Zavala County). Batesville is on the Leona River at the intersection of U.S. Highway 57 and Farm Road 117, fifteen miles east of La Pryor in northeast Zavala County. The first settlers in the area were ranchers Mont Woodward in the mid-1860s and the Bates family around 1869. By 1870 the Bates brothers, Elijah, Felix, and Finis, had developed a large ranch in the area; it spawned the development of a small community known as Bates Ranch.

Elijah Anderson Bates chartered the Comanche Irrigation Company in 1876 in partnership with his two brothers to develop the region's first irrigation project on two sections of land granted to them by the state of Texas. To comply with provisions of the state-subsidized project Bates proceeded to dam the Leona River and channel its water through a canal system to over 500 acres of farmland. The Bates brothers sold the irrigated area in two-acre plots. The farm complex matured as a community and was thereafter known as Bates Ditch. With the organization of Zavala County in 1884, Bates Ditch became the county seat, and its name changed to Batesville. The Zavala county courthouse was built in Batesville in 1884 from bricks made of Leona River soil on land donated by Elijah Bates. It was the county's first rock structure and became the social center for the surrounding area. The same year a post office was established in the community. Throughout the 1880s residents of Batesville joined with those of Loma Vista for camp meetings at the Leona River; these early summer religious meetings were the social event of the year.

By 1892 Batesville had an estimated 500 inhabitants, three churches, a gristmill, and three general stores. In 1897 the community had two schools, three teachers, and a student body of sixty-one; by 1908 Batesville's three schools had an enrollment of 130 and four teachers. In 1914 the community had Baptist, Christian, and Methodist Episcopal (South) churches, telephone connections, and a weekly newspaper, the *Herald.* The Holmes Hotel, built on the southwest side of the courthouse plaza, burned down in 1915. Although Crystal City became the Zavala county seat in 1927, Batesville remained a trading center for the northeastern part of the county. Aggressive water-well drilling into the Leona gravel by a Mr. O'Keefe and the subsequent clearing of over 500 acres for irrigation south of the city ushered in large-scale farming. By 1933 Batesville had an estimated population of 200 and four businesses. In the late 1930s the population was two-thirds Anglo and one-third Hispanic. Immediately after World War II[qv] the community installed electricity and developed an even larger irrigation system. In 1947 it had six businesses and an estimated population of 200. Neglect in maintaining the dam and canal system throughout the 1950s and a period of extreme drought until late in the decade led to the expiration of the Comanche Irrigation District Charter in 1959. In 1963 Batesville had 250 inhabitants and thirty businesses. Over the next decade, though, it lost over one-third of its population and nearly half its businesses. Local tradition indicates that political and racial tensions in Crystal City in the 1960s helped fuel a modest population increase in Batesville (*see* CRYSTAL CITY REVOLTS). By 1988 Batesville had an estimated population of 200 and twelve businesses, three churches, and a school; numerous cafes and service stations were located on the frontage road for U.S. Highway 57 on the north edge of town. The community continued to revolve around its circular town plaza and its adjacent post office in 1990, when the population was 1,313.

BIBLIOGRAPHY: Early History of Batesville, Organization of Zavala County, and Biographical Sketch of Elijah Anderson Bates (MS, Texas State Archives, Austin). Zavala County Historical Commission, *Now and Then in Zavala County* (Crystal City, Texas, 1985). *Zavala County Sentinel*, Centennial edition, July 25, 1958.

Ruben E. Ochoa

BATESVILLE HILL. Batesville Hill is nine miles northwest of Batesville in north central Zavala County (at 29°02′ N, 99°43′ W). With an elevation of 956 feet above sea level, it rises 128 feet above nearby Farm Road 117.

BATH, TEXAS. Bath, originally called Possum Walk, was a community on Farm Road 1374 eight miles west of Interstate Highway 45 in southwestern Walker County. The Union Hill Baptist Church was established there in 1872. The Possum Walk community changed its name to Bath when its post office was established in 1887; James H. Bell served as the first postmaster. Bath reported twenty-five residents in 1892 and forty in 1896. The Union Hill church building served as both a place of worship and a schoolhouse until a separate facility for the school was provided in 1899. Around 1900 two cotton gins, a gristmill, and a sawmill operated at Bath. The post office closed in 1905. In 1911 the community still had its school, which had seven grades, and the church. As late as 1936 Bath persisted as a community of scattered farm dwellings clustered around the school and church. By the early 1990s only the Union Hill Baptist Church and a cemetery remained.

BIBLIOGRAPHY: D'Anne McAdams Crews, ed., *Huntsville and Walker County, Texas: A Bicentennial History* (Huntsville, Texas: Sam Houston State University, 1976).

James L. Hailey

BATISTE CREEK. Batiste (Baciste) Creek rises three-fourths of a mile northeast of Moss Hill in eastern Liberty County (30°16′ N, 94°42′ W) and runs southeast for twenty-three miles, dipping briefly into southwestern Hardin County before reentering Liberty County, to its mouth on Willow Creek, four miles northeast of Devers (at 30°03′ N, 94°31′ W). The stream is intermittent in its upper reaches. It cuts through a region characterized by loamy soils and mixed pine and hardwood forests.

BATSON, TEXAS. Batson is on State Highway 105 and Farm Road 770 in southwestern Hardin County. It had a post office from 1891 to 1898 called Otto, for settler R. Otto Middlebrook. The community was settled before 1840 by the Batson brothers and others, who lived in mud houses. They later built a church that also served as a school. Two schools known as Batson Prairie operated in the area in 1897 with twenty-four and forty-four students, respectively. With the discovery of an oilfield a half mile north of Otto in October 1903, the town and post office were moved to a site just south of the oilfield, and a city of 10,000 sprang up overnight. This new community was named for pioneer Eli Batson. Four hotels, ten saloons, general merchandise stores, a livery, and a blacksmith were soon in operation. By 1906 Batson had three schools, five teachers, and 252 students, and by 1914 it had three churches and a bank. The population declined to 600 by 1927 as oil production decreased, but another oilfield, New Batson, was discovered in March 1935. State highway maps in 1936 showed two churches, two stores, a school, and the post office in the community. The population rose to 1,000 and the number of businesses to fifteen in the 1930s. From 1950 until 1970 Batson declined to a population of 200 and eight businesses. In the 1980s two churches, multiple businesses, and nearby Jordan Cemetery remained. In 1990 the population was 140.

bibliography: L. I. Adams, Jr., *Time and Shadows* (Waco: Davis Brothers, 1971). Hardin County Historical Commission, *The History of Hardin County, Texas* (Dallas: Curtis, 1991). Miriam Partlow, *Liberty, Liberty County, and the Atascosito District* (Austin: Pemberton, 1974).

Diana J. Kleiner

BATSON-OLD OILFIELD. The Batson-Old field is an oil-producing area on Pine Bayou a mile north of Batson in southwestern Hardin County. The field draws oil and negligible amounts of gas from an anhydrite and limestone reservoir in a caprock structure above a piercement salt dome in the Miocene and Oligocene formations at an average depth of 1,100 feet. Along with three other highly prolific piercement-salt-dome fields—Spindletop (1901), Sour Lake (1901), and Humble[qqv] (1905)—Batson (1903) helped to establish the basis of the Texas oil industry when these shallow fields gave up the first Texas Gulf Coast oil. Batson field was still producing in its tenth decade when its cumulative production reached more than 45 million barrels in 1993. The area surrounding Batson field gained the attention of oil prospectors as early as 1900, when gas seeps and paraffin dirt on the surface suggested that oil could be found in the shallow subsurface. In 1901 the Libby Oil Company staked a location three miles south of the future site of Batson field. The test had a small show of oil near the 1,000-foot depth, but no commercial well was made. Two years later, S. W. Pipkin and W. L. Douglas, who had no prior oil-industry experience, organized the Paraffine Oil Company with backing from a number of Beaumont businessmen. In late October 1903 Paraffine staked a location for a test, the No. 1 Fee, on evidence of paraffin dirt that Douglas found on the surface. This was the first known use of paraffin dirt as a prospecting guide. On October 31, after nine days of drilling, the location proved to be near the center of the salt dome when oil was found at a depth of 790 feet in the sandstone above the caprock. Initial production for the No. 1 Fee was 600 barrels a day. In mid-December, six weeks after completion of the No. 1 Fee, Paraffine completed the No. 2 Fee in the same sandstone. It produced more than 4,000 barrels of oil a day from a depth of 1,000 feet. Drilling of the No. 3 Fee quickly followed; it penetrated the caprock below the sandstone and initially produced 10,000 barrels of oil a day. By the end of December 1903, Batson field reported annual production of 4,518 barrels of oil as twenty-eight rigs continued to drill for new pay.

In January 1904 the J. M. Guffey Petroleum Company No. 1 Brooks came in with initial production of 18,000 barrels a day. Drilling excitement seized operators in the field, motivating them to sink densely-spaced wells into the shallow caprock quickly and pull out all the oil they could reach. Because no Texas fields were prorated before 1930, no regulations prevented operators from overproduction of the field. Peak daily production was reached in the field by March 4, 1904, when more than 150,000 barrels of oil was brought to the surface. Full production continued through the end of the year. In 1904 the field reported a dramatic yield of 10,904,737 barrels of oil, the peak yearly production. Flush production in the field may have been driven by gas-cap expansion and gravity drainage, but excessive overproduction in the first year allowed salt-water encroachment and the loss of any gas drive. In the winter of 1904 and 1905 salt water was detected in some deeper wells and drilling was restricted to four new wells on the west side of the field, where encroachment was less evident. However, by mid-March 1905 water invasion had continued westward, engulfing even shallower wells. By this time, the limits of Batson field were defined by dry holes as covering 400 acres. In 1905 production in the field plummeted to 3,790,629 barrels of oil, just over one-third the 1904 production.

Production continued a steady decline for the next twenty years. In 1924, however, a practice was established in the field that kept it producing. Although no secondary or enhanced recovery was attempted over the years, the field production was maintained through additional yields from newly discovered sectors in the flanks of the dome. The 1924 discovery was the result of deeper wells drilled on the northwest flank of the dome to reach oil held by a stratigraphic trap in the Miocene and Frio formations at a depth of 3,600 feet. At the end of 1924 annual yields had increased by almost 150,000 barrels. In 1925 the Kirby Petroleum Company No. 1 Hodges was brought in, boosting annual production for the field by 4,000 barrels. Production and field development again slipped downward by 1931 and continued declining until early November 1934, when new oil was found in the southwest flank of the dome. At that time the John Deering and Batson Oil Company No. 1 Hooks found the productive Yegua sands pinched against the salt mass. In 1935, with the Yegua–Southwest Flank yields, annual production increased markedly to 616,474 barrels of oil. The Yegua–Southwest Flank sector remained a part of Batson field until 1939, when the Railroad Commission[qv] of Texas separated it under the name Batson-New field. At that time, the old field reported 190 wells, nine operators, and a reduced annual production of only 217,277 barrels. Even though drilling continued on the southwest and northwest flanks of the dome, the limits of the areas were defined by 1947. At the end of 1948 the total number of wells drilled in the field was reportedly 1,450. Most oil left the field by the carriers of Sun Pipe Line Company and Gulf Pipe Line Company.

In 1951 another sector, called Yegua–Northwest Flank, was brought into production when Stanolind and Freeport Sulphur Company No. 1 Kirby Lumber Company came in. This sector, like the Yegua–Southwest Flank, produced from accumulations in the Yegua sands that were pinched against the salt mass. In 1953, after fifty years of production, the annual yield was 111,429 barrels. On October 5, 1961, a new sector, called North Flank–North Extension, was added to the field when the Pan American Petroleum Corporation No. 2-C. C. G. Hooks Fee was completed in Basal Frio sands on the north flank of the salt mass. In 1963 the field reported a yield of 169,713 barrels. On December 31, 1973, the seventy-year-old field reported annual production of 86,576 barrels of oil and 1,183,000 cubic feet of casinghead gas. By the field's eightieth anniversary, the annual production rebounded to 108,863 barrels of oil and 1,699,000 cubic feet of casinghead gas. But as the field neared its ninetieth anniversary, production fell to 69,772 barrels of oil and 1,285,000 cubic feet of casinghead gas from 185 producing wells. On January 1, 1993, Batson-Old field reported cumulative production of 45,150,379 barrels of oil.

bibliography: N. M. Fenneman, *Oil Fields of the Texas-Louisiana Gulf Coastal Plain* (U.S. Geological Service Bulletin 282, Washington: GPO, 1906). William E. Galloway et al., *Atlas of Major Texas Oil Reservoirs* (Austin: University of Texas Bureau of Economic Geology, 1983). Edgar Wesley Owen, *Trek of the Oil Finders: A History of Exploration for Petroleum* (Tulsa: American Association for Petroleum Geologists, 1975). David F. Prindle, *Petroleum Politics and the Texas Railroad Commission* (Austin: University of Texas Press, 1981). Railroad Commission of Texas, *Annual Report of the Oil and Gas Division* (Austin, 1953). George Sawtelle, "The Batson Oil Field, Hardin County, Texas," *Bulletin of the American Association of Petroleum Geologists* 9 (December 1925). Fred L. Smith, Jr., and J. T. Goodwyn, Jr., "Batson Field," in *Typical Oil and Gas Fields of Southeast Texas,* ed. R. L. Denham (Houston: Houston Geological Society, 1962).

Julia Cauble Smith

BATTISE, ROBERT FULTON (1909–1994). Fulton (Kina) Battise, principal chief of the Alabama-Coushatta Indians from 1970 to 1994, was born on the reservation in Polk County on March 16, 1909, the son of McConico and Mabel (Sylestine) Battise. His father was a farmer and woodsman on the reservation, and Fulton lived there his entire life. He grew up with five sisters and one brother in a one-room log cabin. Electricity was not available, and the only running water was a spring a half-mile behind their house. He helped his parents draw water from this spring, picked cotton, gathered corn, and tended cows. He went to school at the Presbyterian Mission School on the reservation through the eighth grade. While in school he and his sister Ivy earned money chopping wood for the steam locomotive used by the W. T. Carter Lumber Company on the logging railroad through the reservation. As a boy he helped on his father's farm, but money was scarce, and he tried several other activities to improve family finances. During the Great Depression[qv] years he joined the Civilian Conservation Corps.[qv] Also, while visiting the Indian Exposition in Oklahoma, he wrestled a twelve-foot alligator for forty dollars. Later, he worked for the W. T. Carter and Kirby Lumber companies and became an expert log scaler for the Carter firm.

Fulton was elected second chief (*Mikko Atokla*) of his tribe at the young age of twenty-six and was inaugurated on January 1, 1936. After the death of Principal Chief Bronson Cooper Sylestine in 1969, Fulton was elected principal chief (*Mikko Choba*) and installed on January 1, 1970. He was active in community affairs and served as elder, Sunday school teacher, church secretary, and choir leader for the Indian Presbyterian Church on the reservation. The local Boy Scout and Girl Scout programs were among his other interests. The office of chief involves only ceremonial duties, and the principal chief is the ceremonial head of the tribe. Despite lack of authority, the word of Principal Chief Fulton Battise carried great weight among the Alabama-Coushattas. He was respected, admired, and liked by nearly everyone, members of the tribe as well as nonmembers. He was progressive and helped to stabilize thinking for the benefit of the reservation as a whole. He encouraged the development of such improvements as tourist facilities on the reservation, construction of modern housing through a federally funded housing project, construction of a multipurpose community center, organization of a kindergarten Head Start Program, and the construction of a medical-services clinic.

Chief Battise received many distinguished visitors at the reservation. Also, he was available consistently to meet with special groups that visited the reservation—school groups, scouts, groups from state schools, senior citizens, media personnel, and politicians. Also, he traveled throughout the state and nation as the Alabama-Coushatta representative in dedications, parades, programs, meetings, and presentations. He made numerous appearances before governmental agencies asking for assistance for the Alabama-Coushattas, including appealing to the Texas legislature to help the Indians help themselves. In 1966 he asked the Housing and Urban Development Administration to allow Indian Mutual Help Home Ownership houses to be built on the reservation. He appealed to congressmen and other federal officials in 1971 for assistance in developing a tourist industry to provide jobs for the Alabama-Coushattas and revenue for tribal operations. In 1972 he traveled to Washington, D.C., to testify before the Indian Claims Commission in relation to land that had been taken from the tribe in the early 1800s.

Battise frequently lamented that his formal education had been limited, and he was always interested in the welfare and education of children. Two scholarships were established in his name: the Chief Kina Scholarship at Sam Houston State University and the Chief Kina Scholarship at the Alabama-Coushatta reservation.

A summary of the highlights of Chief Battise's accomplishments and contributions during his fifty-eight years of tribal leadership was inserted into the Congressional Record on February 9, 1994. On March 3, 1934, Fulton and Eva Bullock were married. Their daughter, Zetha, graduated from Southeastern State Teachers College, Durant, Oklahoma, and taught school for twenty-five years in New Mexico. Battise died on February 8, 1994, and was buried three days later in the Alabama–Coushatta tribal cemetery.

BIBLIOGRAPHY: Houston *Post,* June 25, 1970, May 21, 1982.

Howard N. Martin

BATTISE TRACE. The Battise Trace was one of the trails radiating from the village of Long King,[qv] the principal chief of the Coushatta Indians in Texas during the first three decades of the nineteenth century. This trace connected Long King's Village in southern Polk County with Battise Village, near the mouth of Kickapoo Creek on the Trinity River in San Jacinto County. From Long King's Village the Battise Trace extended northwestward on the east side of the Trinity River in Polk County, went across Garner's Prairie south of Blanchard, led through the headwaters of Penwa Slough, and then crossed Caney Creek, Sandy Creek, and Kickapoo Creek. Next, the trail turned southeast near Onalaska, crossed the Trinity River near the mouth of Kickapoo Creek at a point where Duncan's Ferry (later Patrick's Ferry) was established, and proceeded to Battise Village in San Jacinto County. The Coushatta Trace[qv] crossed the Trinity at the same place, and Patrick's Ferry continued to be used until the development of automobiles and a state system of roads and bridges.

The trail between Long King's Village and Battise Village is mentioned six times in surveyors' field notes for land surveys in western Polk County. A typical entry related to the Battise Trace may be found in the field notes for the Thomas Burrus Survey, which refer to "a road leading from the Long King's Village to the Baptiest (Battise) Village."

Howard N. Martin

BATTISE VILLAGE. Battise (Baptiste, Battiste) Village was the upper village of the three principal communities established by the Coushatta Indians on the Trinity River in what is now Polk and San Jacinto counties. In western Polk County, near the site of present Onalaska, the Coushatta Trace[qv] crossed the Trinity River. Battise Village was at this strategic point on the west bank of the Trinity. Specifically, the location was opposite the mouth of Kickapoo Creek, and the site was included at least partly in land granted subsequently to James H. Duncan in the area that became San Jacinto County. This major Coushatta village is mentioned in surveyors' field notes for eleven original land grants in this area, including a survey for Isham T. Patrick, which was described as being immediately above the upper Coushatta village.

Battise Village was a reference point in defining the boundaries of Liberty County, which during the years of the Republic of Texas[qv] included the present counties of Polk and San Jacinto. On April 25, 1837, Daniel P. Coit,[qv] chief justice of Liberty County, wrote a letter to James P. Henderson,[qv] Republic of Texas secretary of state, in which he described the boundaries of Liberty County and said that the northern boundary should extend northward to the "Battiste" village. George T. Wood,[qv] the second governor of the State of Texas, moved to Texas in 1839 and established a plantation on the Trinity River near Battise Village.

In 1840 the Republic of Texas Congress granted two leagues of land to the Coushatta Indians for permanent reservations; one league included Colita's Village and the other league included Battise Village. The land was surveyed and the field notes were filed, but the grants never became effective because white settlers had already claimed the land.

Near the end of the 1830–40 decade ferry service was established at the Coushatta Trace crossing of the Trinity. The ferry was referred to first as Duncan's Ferry, and by 1844 it was known as Patrick's Ferry, which continued in use until the development of automobiles and a state system of roads and bridges.

The pressure of white settlement nearby resulted in a gradual decline of Battise Village population during the 1840s, but John R. Swanton quoted William Bollaert's[qv] estimate that in 1850 there were 500 warriors in Battise Village and Colita's Village. A General Land Office[qv] map of Polk County dated 1856 does not show Battise Village, and it is assumed that the residents had left their homes in the Patrick's Ferry area and joined their Coushatta kinsmen in either Long King's Village or Colita's Village.

BIBLIOGRAPHY: *A Pictorial History of Polk County, Texas, 1846–1910* (Livingston, Texas: Polk County Bicentennial Commission, 1976; rev.

ed. 1978). Harriet Smither, ed., *Journals of the Fourth Congress of the Republic of Texas, 1839–1840, to Which Are Added the Relief Laws* (3 vols., Austin: Von Boeckmann–Jones, n.d.).

Howard N. Martin

BATTLE, MILLS M. (1800–1856). Mills M. Battle, early settler and public official, was born in New Orleans, Louisiana, on February 20, 1800. He was a partner of M. Berry and John Williams, Sr.,[qqv] as one of the families of the Old Three Hundred.[qv] One sitio[qv] of land now in Matagorda County was deeded to them by the Baron de Bastrop[qv] on August 10, 1824. Battle was a carpenter and contractor in business with Berry at San Felipe de Austin, where he voted in alcalde[qv] elections as early as December 1824, and where he himself was alcalde in 1827. The census of March 1826 listed him as a married man with a small daughter. His wife, Mary, died before August 26, 1837. Battle was president of the election at Stafford's Prairie to choose delegates to the Convention of 1836.[qv] He was justice of the peace of Fort Bend County in 1837–38 and in 1839 was deputy clerk of the probate court. He met with other citizens of the county at Richmond in 1839 to appoint delegates to a railroad meeting at Fayetteville. Battle married Mrs. Treasy Springer on December 29, 1842. He was notary public in Fort Bend County in 1843 and county clerk in 1851. He participated in meetings to nominate Sam Houston[qv] for president in 1841 and James B. Miller[qv] for governor in 1847. Battle died at Richmond on January 15, 1856, and is buried in Morton cemetery.

BIBLIOGRAPHY: Eugene C. Barker, ed., *The Austin Papers* (3 vols., Washington: GPO, 1924–28). Eugene C. Barker, ed., "Minutes of the Ayuntamiento of San Felipe de Austin, 1828–1832," 12 parts, *Southwestern Historical Quarterly* 21–24 (January 1918–October 1920). *Telegraph and Texas Register*, August 26, 1837, April 14, 1838. Louis Wiltz Kemp, *The Signers of the Texas Declaration of Independence* (Salado, Texas: Anson Jones, 1944; rpt. 1959). "Reminiscences of Mrs. Dilue Harris," *Quarterly of the Texas State Historical Association* 4, 7 (October 1900, January 1901, January 1904). Andrew Jackson Sowell, *History of Fort Bend County* (Houston: Coyle, 1904; rpt, Richmond, Texas: Fort Bend County Historical Museum, 1974). *Texas Gazette*, October 9, November 6, 1830.

BATTLE, NICHOLAS WILLIAM (1820–1905). Nicholas William Battle, judge and soldier, was born on January 1, 1820, in Warren County, Georgia, the son of Thomas and Mary (Baker) Battle. The elder Battle was a Methodist minister. Nicholas Battle was educated in Monroe County, Georgia, and in 1842 graduated from the College of William and Mary with a degree in law. He returned to Georgia, continued his legal studies, and was admitted to the bar at Macon in 1844. In 1846 he married Mary Ann Cabaniss. He established a practice in Forsythe, but in 1850 moved to Texas and settled in Waco.

In 1854 and 1856 Battle was elected district attorney, and in 1858 he was elected judge of the Third Judicial District. In May 1852 he was a leader in the movement to bring the railroad to Waco. In December 1852 he was appointed chairman of a committee to plan and build the Waco Masonic Institute, a "Female Academy and Male High School." With the outbreak of the Civil War[qv] Battle resigned his seat on the bench to join the army and was soon elected lieutenant colonel of Col. Edward Jeremiah Gurley's[qv] Thirtieth Texas Cavalry, also known as the First Texas Partisan Cavalry. This regiment was organized in late 1862 and served primarily in Indian Territory. In August 1862, soon after the regiment's formation, Battle transferred to the staff of Brig. Gen. Samuel Bell Maxey[qv] and served as his inspector general.

At the end of the war Battle resumed his practice in Waco and in 1874 was appointed district judge by Governor Richard Coke.[qv] One of his decisions on the bench was that no freedman could sell himself into slavery[qv] under the laws of the state of Texas and that any such contract was ab initio null and void. His opinion was upheld by the Texas Supreme Court in the case of *Westbrook vs. the State*. Judge Battle's district was abolished by the Constitution of 1876.[qv]

Battle was a Baptist. In 1888 he moved to Seattle to live with his sons. He died there in December 1905. The community of Battle in southeast McLennan County was named for him.

BIBLIOGRAPHY: *Biographical Encyclopedia of Texas* (New York: Southern, 1880). James D. Lynch, *The Bench and Bar of Texas* (St. Louis, 1885). *A Memorial and Biographical History of McLennan, Falls, Bell, and Coryell Counties* (Chicago: Lewis, 1893; rpt., St. Louis: Ingmire, 1984). *Texas State Gazette*, June 19, December 25, 1852.

Thomas W. Cutrer

BATTLE, WILLIAM JAMES (1870–1955). William James Battle, professor of classics and university administrator, son of Kemp P. Battle, was born in Raleigh, North Carolina, on November 30, 1870. He later moved to Chapel Hill, where his father served as president of the University of North Carolina. He received a B.A. degree from that institution in 1888 and a Ph.D. from Harvard University in 1893. In his first year at Harvard he held a Thayer scholarship, and the last two years a Morgan fellowship.

Battle was a tutor in Latin at the University of Chicago before going to the University of Texas in 1893 as associate professor of Greek. He was promoted to professor in 1898 and was made dean of the College of Arts in 1908. Three years later he was made dean of the faculty, and in 1914 he was elected acting president of the university. His two years as president were unhappy ones because he was severely attacked by Governor James E. Ferguson,[qv] who charged that Battle had deceived the legislature and the governor about the university appropriation bill of 1915 and had used state money for purposes other than the items specified in the bill. Ferguson urged that Battle be dismissed from the faculty, but in October 1916 the board of regents declared that the charges against the professor were unsubstantiated. In October 1915 Battle had asked that he not be considered for a permanent appointment as president. When he stepped down in April 1916 the board of regents elected Robert E. Vinson[qv] president.

As a result of political pressure Battle left the university in 1917 to teach at the University of Cincinnati. He remained there until 1920, when he returned to the University of Texas as professor of classical languages and chairman of the faculty building committee. He served in the latter position until 1948. In addition to his academic work, he designed the seal of the university in 1901, edited the first student directory in 1900, and founded the first ex-students' magazine. He furnished the money in 1898 to establish the University Co-Op and served as its first manager. The publication of a final announcement of courses was his idea, as was the English comprehension requirement. Battle Hall at the University of Texas was named for him.

In 1929 Southwestern University awarded Battle an honorary LL.D. degree, and he was honored with a second LL.D. degree by the University of North Carolina in 1940. He was a devout member of the Episcopal Church and long served as senior warden of All Saints' Chapel, near the University of Texas campus. He was a charter member of the Texas State Historical Association[qv] and served as president of the Texas Fine Arts Association (1920–29), the Philosophical Society of Texas[qv] (1941), the Texas Classical Association, the Classical Association of the Middle West and South (1919–30), Phi Beta Kappa (Texas Alpha chapter), and the Harvard, Town and Gown, and University clubs of Austin. He retired from active duty in 1948 at the age of seventy-eight but continued to maintain an office on campus as professor emeritus. Books and papers published by Battle include *A Sketch of Grace Hall and All Saints' Chapel* (1940); *The Story of All Saints' Chapel, Austin, Texas, 1900–1950* (1951); and *Town and Gown Club, Memories of Past Days* (1952).

Battle returned to Rocky Mount, North Carolina, in April 1955 and died there on October 9, 1955. In his will he left his property in Austin and his 14,000-volume library to the University of Texas. He also provided means for setting up scholarships for the study of classical languages. He is buried at Raleigh, North Carolina.

BIBLIOGRAPHY: Eugene C. Barker, *Two Gentlemen of the University of Texas: An Appreciation of Henry Winston Harper and William James Battle* (Houston: Rein, 1941). *Proceedings of the Philosophical Society of Texas*, 1955. Henry Peyton Steger, *Letters* (Austin: University of Texas Ex-Students Association, 1915). Vertical Files, Barker Texas History Center, University of Texas at Austin. *James C. Martin*

BATTLE, TEXAS. Battle, once known as Battle Institute, is between State Highway 164 and Farm Road 2957 three miles northwest of Mart in eastern McLennan County. The area was settled about 1880 and named for Nicholas William Battle,[qv] who donated land for a school and two churches. A post office called Battle Institute was established in 1886 with James Riggs as postmaster. The name was changed to Battle in 1890, when the community had a general store and a population of eleven; the principal occupation of area residents was stock raising. Battle became the focus of a common school district in 1891. In 1896 the district had two teachers and 139 students, and the community had Baptist and Methodist churches and two general stores to serve its ninety residents. The International–Great Northern Railroad laid track from Marlin through Battle to Waco in 1902. The population rose to 113 by the early 1900s. Improved roads and the new rail service enabled residents to shop in nearby Mart or Waco. This circumstance greatly reduced Battle's reliance on local businesses, with the result that local establishments soon faded. The post office was discontinued in 1906, and mail for the community was sent to Mart. The Battle school district was consolidated with the Mart Independent School District in 1927. By the mid-1940s Battle had a church, a few residences, a cemetery, and a population of fifty. Maps from the 1970s showed several houses and a cemetery, as well as some new development along the shore of a nearby lake. The community was still listed in 1990, but without census figures.

BIBLIOGRAPHY: Martin Luther Bannister, The Historical Development of the Public School System of McLennan County (M.A. thesis, Baylor University, 1945). Dayton Kelley, ed., *The Handbook of Waco and McLennan County, Texas* (Waco: Texian, 1972). William Robert Poage, *McLennan County Before 1980* (Waco: Texian, 1981). Vertical File, Texas Collection, Baylor University.

Vivian Elizabeth Smyrl

BATTLE CREEK (Armstrong County). Battle Creek rises at the breaks of the Llano Estacado[qv] south of Paloduro and the JA Ranch[qv] headquarters in southeastern Armstrong County (at 34°48′ N, 101°12′ W) and flows southeast for twenty miles, across the sloping mesquite plains of northern Briscoe County, before emptying into the Prairie Dog Town Fork of the Red River near the boundary between Briscoe and Hall counties (at 34°38′ N, 100°57′ W). The stream is so named because it was the site of a battle at Palo Duro Canyon on August 30, 1874, when troops under Col. Nelson A. Miles[qv] fought off an attack by about 500 Cheyenne warriors. Most of the action, which lasted five hours, occurred at the head of the creek (*see* PALO DURO CANYON, BATTLE OF, *and* RED RIVER WAR).

—— (Callahan County). Battle Creek rises four miles north of Cottonwood and three miles east of Spring Mesa in southeast Callahan County (at 32°13′ N, 99°10′ W) and winds through eastern Callahan, northwestern Eastland, southeastern Shackelford, and southwestern Stephens counties to its mouth on Big Sandy Creek, ten miles southwest of Breckenridge (at 32°39′ N, 99°01′ W). The mostly intermittent stream passes through numerous oilfields on its fifty-mile course. A Battle Creek Cemetery and the communities of Eureka and Eolian, all in Stephens County, lie near the creek. The upper area of Battle Creek was first settled in the late 1860s. A skirmish near the stream in 1840 between Indians and a frontier militia under the command of James F. Smith gave the stream its name. The creek passes through a flat area with local shallow depressions and a clay and sandy loam surface that supports water-tolerant hardwoods, conifers, and grasses.

BIBLIOGRAPHY: Callahan County Historical Commission, *I Remember Callahan: History of Callahan County, Texas* (Dallas: Taylor, 1986).

—— (Van Zandt County). Battle Creek rises a half mile south of Midway in southeast Van Zandt County (at 32°23′ N, 95°34′ W) and runs nine miles southeast to its mouth at Kickapoo Cove on Lake Palestine in Henderson County (at 32°18′ N, 95°30′ W). The creek takes its name from an event of 1839. President Mirabeau B. Lamar[qv] appointed Gen. Albert Sidney Johnston[qv] to induce Cherokee Indians in East Texas to cede their lands to the Republic of Texas[qv] and vacate the country. Instructions to pay the Indians or remove them by force led to two battles, one at the Indian village at the creek. The surrounding low-rolling to flat terrain is surfaced by sandy and clay loam that supports scrub brush, cacti, mixed hardwoods, and pines.

BIBLIOGRAPHY: Wentworth Manning, *Some History of Van Zandt County* (Des Moines, Iowa: Homestead, 1919; rpt., Winston-Salem, North Carolina: Hunter, 1977).

BATTLE CREEK FIGHT. The Battle Creek Fight, also known as the Surveyors' Fight, a skirmish between a surveying party and an Indian force, took place on October 8, 1838, just east of Battle Creek, near the site of present Dawson in western Navarro County. The Indian force probably numbered around 300 and included a large number of Kickapoos as well as other groups, including Wacos, Tehuacanas, and Caddoes. About twenty-five white surveyors, including William Fenner Henderson, Walter Paye Lane,[qqv] and James Smith, took part in the battle, although historians continue to disagree about the precise number. The surveyors' original mission was to map what is now southern Navarro County for bounty and headright grants for soldiers who had served in the Texas Revolution.[qv] The Indians, resentful of incursions, first asked the surveyors to leave and then attacked en masse. In the ensuing twenty-four-hour battle about thirty Indians and eighteen surveyors were killed. Three of the seven surviving whites managed to reach another Kickapoo camp. There they reported that they had been fighting with different Indians, and the Kickapoos supplied provisions and a guide to Fort Parker. Several of the surveyors, with a group of about fifty men from Old Franklin, returned to the site of the battle several days later to bury the dead. The battlefield site is marked by a state plaque on State Highway 31 a mile west of Dawson.

BIBLIOGRAPHY: Harry McCorry Henderson, "The Surveyors' Fight," *Southwestern Historical Quarterly* 56 (July 1952). Annie Carpenter Love, *History of Navarro County* (Dallas: Southwestern, 1933). Dudley Goodall Wooten, ed., *A Comprehensive History of Texas* (2 vols., Dallas: Scarff, 1898; rpt., Austin: Texas State Historical Association, 1986).

Harry McCorry Henderson

BATTLEGROUND CREEK. Battleground Creek rises three miles southwest of Taylor in southeastern Williamson County (at 30°33′ N, 97°27′ W) and flows southeast for eight miles to its mouth on Brushy Creek, five miles southeast of Taylor (at 30°31′ N, 97°21′ W). The stream may have been named for its proximity to the battle of Brushy Creek.[qv] Battleground Creek flows through gently sloping terrain characterized by clayey soils used predominantly for agricultural purposes, and the banks of the creek are heavily wooded in places with mesquite and hardwood trees.

BIBLIOGRAPHY: Clara Stearns Scarbrough, *Land of Good Water: A Williamson County History* (Georgetown, Texas: Williamson County Sun Publishers, 1973).

BATTLESHIP *TEXAS* STATE HISTORIC SITE. The Battleship

Texas State Historic Site, near the San Jacinto Monument[qv] in east Harris County, is the final resting place of the former United States Navy battleship *Texas.*[qv] The ship was acquired through the efforts of the Battleship *Texas* Commission, established by an act of the Fiftieth State Legislature, which helped Texans raise money to bring the ship back to Texas and initially administered the site. On April 21, 1948, the ship was decommissioned, presented to the state of Texas, and recommissioned as flagship of the Texas Navy (not the Texas Navy[qv] of the republic era). Restorations were begun in 1988, based on plans drawn up by a naval architect in 1984 and funded by the Texas Parks and Wildlife Department,[qv] which acquired the ship in 1983.

BIBLIOGRAPHY: Vertical Files, Barker Texas History Center, University of Texas at Austin. *Diana J. Kleiner*

BATTS, ROBERT LYNN (1864–1935). Robert Lynn Batts, attorney, judge, and University of Texas regent, was born in Bastrop, Texas, on November 1, 1864, the son of Andrew Jackson and Julia Priscilla (Rice) Batts. He studied law at the University of Texas and served as editor of the university's first student publication, a magazine called *The Texas University*; he received his law degree in 1886. Batts married Harriet Fiquet Boak of Austin on November 12, 1889, and they became the parents of three children.

Batts practiced law in Bastrop until 1892, when he became assistant Texas attorney general in the administration of Charles A. Culberson.[qv] His most significant victory in this position was the recovery of 920,000 acres of land for the public school fund in *Galveston, Harrisburg, and San Antonio Railway Company v. Texas.* In 1893 Batts resigned to become professor of law at the University of Texas, but he returned to private practice in Austin in 1901. As a member of the firm Gregory and Batts, he served as Texas counsel in the Waters-Pierce Case.[qv] In 1914 he became special assistant attorney general of the United States. In March 1917 President Woodrow Wilson appointed him judge of the Fifth Circuit Court of Appeals. Batts resigned from the court in 1919 to become general counsel for the Gulf Petroleum Company (*see* GULF OIL CORPORATION). He lived in New York and Pittsburgh until 1923, when he returned to Texas.

Batts was a member of the board of regents of the University of Texas from 1927 to 1933. He served as chairman during the last three years of his appointment; in this role he was largely responsible for the financing and planning of the university's building program. He wrote several legal texts, including *Annotated Revised Civil Statutes of Texas* (1897–99) and *The Law of Corporations in Texas* (1902). He was made an honorary member of the Texas Alpha chapter of Phi Beta Kappa in 1915. Batts died in Austin on May 19, 1935, and was buried in Oakwood Cemetery. Batts Hall at the University of Texas was dedicated to him in April 1953.

BIBLIOGRAPHY: Austin *American*, May 20, 1935. *Dictionary of American Biography.* Vertical Files, Barker Texas History Center, University of Texas at Austin. *Who Was Who in America*, Vol. 1.

BAUDIN, CHARLES (1784–1854). Charles Baudin, French naval officer, was born in Sedan, France, on July 21, 1784, the son of Pierre Charles Louis Baudin. His father was known for his justice and moderation during the French Revolution. Legend says he died of joy at the news that Napoleon Bonaparte was coming to power in 1799. That year Charles Baudin entered the navy at age fifteen and was accepted into service aboard the *Foudroyant* as a novice seaman. By 1808 he had risen to command successively the frigates *Piémontaise* and *Sémillante.* Despite losing his right arm in combat with the English in the Indian Ocean that year, he continued his career and became a captain in 1812. With Gen. Charles Lallemand[qv] (future founder of Champ d'Asile[qv]), William Lee (American consul at Bordeaux), and Gen. Bertrand Clausel, he plotted the escape of Napoleon from France after Waterloo; but the emperor refused, preferring to throw himself upon the mercy of the British. With the second restoration of the Bourbons, Baudin was forced to resign his commission, though he subsequently prospered as a merchant in Le Havre. In this capacity he befriended the penniless Pierre Soulé, who became a well-known lawyer, senator, and diplomat of New Orleans, and later provided for Baudin's voyage to America.

After the July Revolution in 1830, the government of King Louis Philippe restored Baudin's naval command and in 1838 dispatched a blockading squadron to Mexico under his command, accompanied by the king's third son, Prince Joinville. During the siege, known in Mexican history as the "Pastry War," all of the French provisions (including drinking water) were shipped from Havana. President Mirabeau B. Lamar[qv] sent Col. Bernard E. Bee[qv] to Veracruz to obtain Mexican recognition of Texas independence, but the Mexicans refused to see Bee, who consulted with Baudin and Joinville. Through the blockade of Veracruz, by engaging the military and depriving Mexico of import duties, its principal source of revenue, France impeded Mexico's attempts to reconquer its rebellious northeastern province, Texas, and avenge the Mexican defeat at the battle of San Jacinto.[qv] When negotiations failed to satisfy France's complaints, Baudin's squadron leveled the supposedly impregnable citadel of San Juan de Ullóa on November 27, 1838, earning Baudin international fame as the "hero of San Juan de Ullóa." During the bombardment of the citadel, Baudin's forces further disabled the Mexican army by capturing Gen. Mariano Arista[qv] (a future president) and wounding Gen. Antonio López de Santa Anna,[qv] whose leg had to be amputated. The Duke of Wellington proclaimed this victory to be the only known instance in history of a regularly fortified citadel's being taken solely by naval force. Accounts vary regarding the ultimate success of the mission, however, because Mexico expelled the French soon after Baudin's departure for Texas, where he became an honorary Galvestonian in May 1839. Louis Eugène Maissin,[qv] his aide-de-camp and later chief of staff, published a book in Paris at the end of 1839 describing their military experiences with Mexico and their friendly visit to Texas. His report on the commercial and military potential of the Republic of Texas[qv] and the brave and industrious Texans contributed to France's decision to recognize the republic. The role of Baudin in Texas history has been compared to that of the Marquis de Lafayette in the American Revolution, because Baudin and Lafayette personified France's aid to the young republics during their struggles for independence. After a distinguished career Baudin was promoted to admiral by Napoleon III only days before his death, on June 7, 1854.

BIBLIOGRAPHY: Pierre Blanchard and André Dauzats, *San Juan de Ulúa, ou Relation de l'expédition française au Mexique, sous les ordres de M. le contre-amiral Baudin* (Paris: Gide, 1839). Mary Katherine Chase, *Négociations de la République du Texas en Europe, 1837–1845* (Paris: Champion, 1932). Jurien de la Gravière, "Une expédition d'outre-mer en 1838," *Revue des Deux Mondes* 73 (February 1886). Eugène Maissin, *The French in Mexico and Texas, 1838–1839* (Salado, Texas: Anson Jones Press, 1961). *Betje Black Klier*

BAUER, J. H. VON (?–?). J. H. von Bauer, a land surveyor, left Europe in 1844 and traveled to Texas in 1845. He was a charter member of the Naturforschender Verein, organized by early German settlers at New Braunfels to study the natural sciences.

BIBLIOGRAPHY: S. W. Geiser, "A Century of Scientific Exploration in Texas," *Field and Laboratory* 7 (January 1939). Solms-Braunfels Archives (transcripts, Sophienburg Museum, New Braunfels, Texas; Barker Texas History Center, University of Texas at Austin). *Clinton P. Hartmann*

BAUER, PAUL (1855–1934). Paul Bauer, saddlemaker, son of Friederick and Matilda (Ehrenberg) Bauer, was born on October 30, 1855, at Yorktown, Texas, where his father, a German immigrant and master saddler, taught him the saddle and harness business. He moved successively to Helena, San Diego, Pearsall, Oakville, and, in 1895, to Beeville. In 1878 he married Carrie Reagan, and of their six children, two sons continued in the saddle business. For nearly 100 years the Bauers made saddles for cattlemen, Texas Rangers,[qv] sheriffs, and law enforcement officers throughout Texas, other states, Mexico, and South America. J. Frank Dobie[qv] was particularly fond of the Bauer saddle. In 1890 Bauer was justice of the peace in Live Oak County. He was in partnership with a son until his death. He died on October 28, 1934, and was buried in Beeville.

BIBLIOGRAPHY: Grace Bauer (Lillian Grace Schoppe), The History of Bee County, Texas (M.A. thesis, University of Texas, 1939). Beeville *Bee-Picayune*, November 1, 1934. Live Oak County Centennial Association, *Live Oak County Centennial* (George West, Texas, 1956). Live Oak County Historical Commission, *The History of the People of Live Oak County* (George West, Texas, 1982). San Antonio *Express*, December 22, 1960.
Grace Bauer

BAUGH, JOHN J. (1803–1836). John J. Baugh, adjutant of the Alamo garrison, was born in Virginia in 1803. He traveled to Texas in 1835 as a first lieutenant of Thomas H. Breece's[qv] company of New Orleans Greys[qv] and took part in the siege of Bexar.[qv] After the battle he was promoted to captain and served as Lt. Col. James C. Neill's[qv] adjutant with the Texan force left to garrison the town. Baugh entered the Alamo with the garrison under Lt. Col. William Barret Travis[qv] on February 23, 1836, when the Mexican army arrived. He died in the battle of the Alamo[qv] on March 6, 1836.

BIBLIOGRAPHY: Daughters of the American Revolution, *The Alamo Heroes and Their Revolutionary Ancestors* (San Antonio, 1976). Bill Groneman, *Alamo Defenders* (Austin: Eakin, 1990). Amelia W. Williams, A Critical Study of the Siege of the Alamo and of the Personnel of Its Defenders (Ph.D. dissertation, University of Texas, 1931; rpt., *Southwestern Historical Quarterly* 36–37 [April 1933–April 1934]).
Bill Groneman

BAULARD, VICTOR JOSEPH (1828–1889). Victor Joseph Baulard, painter and merchant, son of Jean Antoine Baulard, was born in Besançon, France, in 1828. He immigrated with his father to Texas in 1843 and settled at Galveston, where he apprenticed himself to Joseph W. Rice, a painter and merchant. In 1853 the two men established the firm of Rice and Baulard, dealers in paints, oils, glass, and allied goods. The firm developed a trade extending throughout Texas and western Louisiana. Baulard was active in various civic, social, and benevolent organizations. In 1851 he married Clothilde L. Gillet; they had seven children. He died on October 3, 1889.

BIBLIOGRAPHY: Galveston *News*, October 4, 1889. Andrew Morrison, *The Industries of Galveston* (Galveston?: Metropolitan, 1887).

BAUMANN BRANCH. Baumann Branch rises at the base of Lone Oak Mountain, four miles east of the community of Field Creek in extreme northwestern Llano County (30°54′ N, 98°53′ W), and runs south for six miles to its mouth on San Fernando Creek, four miles southwest of the Valley Spring settlement (at 30°50′ N, 98°53′ W). It traverses an area of the Llano basin characterized by flat to rolling terrain surfaced with fine, sandy loams. The vegetation consists primarily of open stands of live oak and mesquite.

BAXTER, TEXAS. Baxter is on State Highway 804 five miles southeast of Athens in south central Henderson County. The site, like much of Henderson County, was settled during the 1850s. Baxter became a station for the Texas and New Orleans Railroad in 1900, and a Baxter post office operated from 1901 to 1912. In 1945 two businesses and a population of fifty-six were reported. By 1950 the population decreased to twenty; it was still reported as twenty in 1990.
Jack Long

BAY CITY, TEXAS. Bay City, the county seat of Matagorda County, is an incorporated city at the junction of State Highways 35 and 60, in the north central portion of the county ninety miles southwest of Houston. The community is named for its location on Bay Prairie, between the richly productive bottomlands of the Colorado River and Caney Creek. It was established in 1894, when David Swickheimer,[qv] a Colorado mining millionaire and participant in a promotional organization called the Enterprise Land and Colonizing Company, formed the Bay City Town Company in partnership with G. M. Magill, N. M. Vogelsang, and Nicholas King. Planning that Bay City would one day supplant Matagorda as county seat, the men selected two cow pastures on Bay Prairie as the site for a new community. The company bought 320 acres from D. P. Moore and another 320 acres from the Mensing brothers of Galveston. One square mile was given to the townsite, on which the promoters laid out wide, regular streets. Elliott's Ferry (*see* ELLIOTT, TEXAS), two miles away, provided transportation across the Colorado River.

In August 1894, before a single building had been erected, Magill and Vogelsang released the first issue of the Bay City *Breeze* and began to promote the new community. Distributed countywide, the newspaper, coupled with the promoters' promise to build a new courthouse if the county government were moved, succeeded in convincing county residents to support the new town. At the time, the population of the county totaled roughly 3,000 people, of which 75 percent were black. On September 18, 1894, Matagorda County voters elected to make Bay City the new county seat. A week later, when editor Vogelsang announced the victory in the *Breeze*, he also revealed that the town did not yet actually exist: "As soon as it can be surveyed, lots will be put on the market, buildings will go up and Bay City will be a reality." Bay City was a tent city before construction began on its first buildings. The Town Company office, which housed the printing presses of the Bay City *Breeze*, was among the first completed. A small frame house, formerly used as the grand jury room at Matagorda, was moved overland to Bay City to serve as a makeshift courthouse, as was D. P. Moore's dry-goods store, which housed the post office. Education for black and white children began immediately. The town's first telephone was installed in 1900, and the Wharton–Bay City Telephone Company was awarded a franchise in 1903. Bay City Rice Mills completed construction on its rice warehouse in 1901, and the next year it opened the town's first mill. Other businesses at that time included four groceries, three implement stores, three saloons, and two each of butcher shops, barbershops, confectioneries, and drugstores, as well as several dry-goods stores and a bakery, a laundry, a blacksmith shop, a brickmaking plant, a broom factory, a cotton gin, and a lumberyard.

In 1901 the Cane Belt Railroad reached Bay City, the first of several lines to serve the town. By that time the *Breeze* had ceased publication and been replaced by the *Matagorda County Tribune*, edited by J. L. Ladd, and the *Weekly Visitor*, edited by W. E. Green. Methodist, Baptist, Christian, Episcopalian, and Presbyterian congregations held services in the community. An eight-room, two-story frame school building had opened, and residents had the services of one dentist, four physicians, six lawyers, and three teachers. In 1902 the city, with about 2,000 inhabitants, incorporated, but it failed to replace its plank roads with streets until some time later. Also in 1902 the New York, Texas and Mexican Railway came into Bay City. Oil was discovered in the county in 1904, and that year the St. Louis, Brownsville and Mexico Railway arrived. By 1914 Bay City, with 3,156 residents, was a thriving community at the center of the largest rice-producing area in the nation and was served by three railroads: the St. Louis, Brownsville and Mexico, the Galveston, Harrisburg and San Antonio, and the Gulf, Colorado and Santa Fe. In 1914 the town had four cotton gins, three banks, two rice mills, a brick and tile factory, a nursery, a creamery, an ice factory, a municipal waterworks, and a large cooling station for fruits and vegetables. By 1915 residents had built a library, and Bay City Business College offered the community's first higher education.

In 1916, as revolution developed in Mexico, a company of men from the community served on the border. The town grew slowly during World War I[qv] and reached a population of 3,454 by 1920. Bay City was regularly flooded by the Colorado River until levees and dams were built along the river in 1924. The population rose by roughly 600 between 1920 and 1930, and during that period the town reported a maximum of 165 businesses. In the 1930s Bay City had a canning plant, a bottling works, a hollow-tile factory, two rice mills, two gins, three hatcheries, and six dairies. LeTulle Park, named for local rice grower Victor L. LeTulle,[qv] was developed in 1934, despite the Great Depression.[qv] In the 1937–38 school year, the local school district employed thirty-eight teachers to instruct 1,146 white students through the eleventh grade, and ten teachers to instruct 377 black students through the tenth grade. Bay City continued to grow steadily, and its population reached 9,427 by 1940. A United Service Organizations building was constructed in 1941, and World War II[qv] increased the city's building program. A new football stadium and high school were finished by 1949. The 1950s saw the completion of a new public library and a United States Army Reserve building. Between 1960 and 1970 an airport was built, and a barge canal was constructed to link Bay City to the Gulf Intracoastal Waterway.[qv] The manmade port of Bay City was completed, and an inflatable rubber dam, designed to impound water for rice irrigation, improved use of the river. In 1960 the population of Bay City was about 77 percent white, 10 percent Hispanic, and 23 percent black. Over the ensuing decade the population rose by less than 100, and businesses increased from 285 to 330. The town attracted new industry beginning in 1960, when the Celanese Chemical Company built a petrochemical plant that would become the city's largest employer. The population of Bay City grew in the 1970s and early 1980s as Celanese, the South Texas Nuclear Project (later known as the South Texas Project), Occidental Chemical Company, and other employers entered the county. Between 1980 and 1990 the city's population rose from 14,291 to 19,684, and the number of businesses increased from 335 to 391. During this time the city limits were expanded to include more than six square miles. In the early 1990s the town was served by the Union Pacific and the Atchison, Topeka and Santa Fe railways and was a shipping center for the county oil industry.

BIBLIOGRAPHY: Bay City Chamber of Commerce, *Bay City Story* (1957). Matagorda County Historical Commission, *Historic Matagorda County* (3 vols., 1986–88). Junann J. Stieghorst, *Bay City and Matagorda County* (Austin: Pemberton, 1965). *Diana J. Kleiner*

BAYLAND ORPHANS' HOME FOR BOYS. Bayland Orphans' Home for Boys, a county home for dependent and delinquent boys, was chartered as the Confederate Orphans' Home on September 24, 1866, and organized in Houston on January 15, 1867, by Texas Confederate veterans. The institution was first located at Bayland on the west side of Galveston Bay near Morgan's Point, at a place that later became part of the Goose Creek oilfield.[qv] The nonsectarian home, planned to care for and educate up to 250 orphans of deceased Confederate soldiers, opened on August 13, 1867. Henry F. Gillette[qv] was superintendent from 1867 to 1882, and Col. Ashbel Smith[qv] served as staff doctor. Private support for the home came primarily from Galveston and Houston. In the 1870s the home received a share of state public lands, including acreage in Shackelford, Stevens, and Callahan counties. Agents for the institution were kept in the field to gather and accept donations of all kinds, and a small community church at Harmony Grove was moved to the site for use as a school. By 1878 the home owned a 328-acre farm and several buildings and had cash reserves.

In 1887, when Houston-Galveston packet travel ceased and Bayland became inaccessible, a decision was made to move the home to Houston. A charter amendment made on January 29, 1888, designated the new institution Bayland Orphans' Home Association and provided that it could accept any white orphan child from any county in the state. Mrs. Kezia Payne DePelchin,[qv] later connected with the DePelchin Faith Home, was elected matron of the new home on June 4, 1888. Around 1900 the home was moved from its original location on Galveston Bay to a thirty-six-acre tract in the Woodland Heights area three miles from Houston, with space for forty-two children.

Financial difficulties developed in the 1890s. A fire in 1914 destroyed the Bayland Avenue home, and the institution moved again in 1916 to a new tract ten miles south of Houston, near Bellaire, on land donated by Joseph F. Meyer. At this time a decision was reached to accept only boys, and the home was renamed Bayland Orphans' Home for Boys. In 1922 the institution was taken over by the county, which also agreed to erect a new building at Bellaire, to be known as Harris County Bayland Home, for dependent white female juveniles.

In 1936 the school and home were consolidated with the Harris County School for Boys and moved to a 115-acre tract in southeastern Harris County, four miles east of Webster. The institution became partially self-supporting from the diversified agriculture of its own plant. In 1946 the average age of the sixty-six boys at the home was thirteen. After this time the institution ceased to function strictly as the Bayland Orphans' Home. Boys attended public school at Webster, and efforts were made to place children in foster homes. On September 20, 1964, the Harris County Historical Survey Committee unveiled a bronze marker at the original site of the home.

BIBLIOGRAPHY: Houston Metropolitan Research Center Files, Houston Public Library. Albert A. Walls, Study of Administrative Problems at Bayland Orphans' Home for Boys (M.A. thesis, University of Texas, 1947). *Diana J. Kleiner*

BAYLISS, JOSEPH (1808–1836). Joseph Bayliss, Alamo defender, son of John and Patience Bayliss, was born in Tennessee in 1808. He traveled as a single man to Texas in January 1836 and enlisted in the Volunteer Auxiliary Corps of Texas at Nacogdoches. He went to the Alamo as a member of Capt. William B. Harrison's[qv] company, which included David Crockett.[qv] Bayliss died in the battle of the Alamo[qv] on March 6, 1836.

BIBLIOGRAPHY: Daughters of the American Revolution, *The Alamo Heroes and Their Revolutionary Ancestors* (San Antonio, 1976). Daughters of the Republic of Texas, *Muster Rolls of the Texas Revolution* (Austin, 1986). Bill Groneman, *Alamo Defenders* (Austin: Eakin, 1990). Phil Rosenthal and Bill Groneman, *Roll Call at the Alamo* (Fort Collins, Colorado: Old Army, 1985). *Bill Groneman*

BAYLOR, GEORGE WYTHE (1832–1916). George Wythe Baylor, Confederate military officer and Texas Ranger, the son of John Walker Baylor,[qv] was born in Fort Gibson, Cherokee Nation, on August 2, 1832. His father died in January 1834. On June 5, 1860, Baylor, then living in Weatherford with John R. Baylor[qv] and others, ran down a party of Indian raiders on Paint Creek in Parker County and killed and scalped nine of them. Baylor is reputed to have raised the first Confederate flag in Austin. He was commissioned a first lieutenant in Company H of the Second Cavalry, John Robert Baylor's Arizona Brigade, and served as regimental adjutant before resigning to become senior aide-de-camp to Gen. Albert Sidney Johnston[qv] in August or September 1861. After Johnston's death at the battle of Shiloh, Tennessee, on April 6, 1862, Baylor returned to Texas and was elected lieutenant colonel and commander of the Second Battalion of Henry H. Sibley's[qv] army. When the battalion merged with the Second Cavalry regiment of the Arizona Brigade, Baylor was elected its colonel.

He also commanded a regiment of cavalry during the Red River campaign[qv] of 1864 and was commended for gallantry at the battles of Mansfield and Pleasant Hill.

On April 6, 1865, at the headquarters of Gen. John B. Magruder[qv] in the Fannin Hotel in Galveston, Baylor quarreled with and killed fellow staff officer John Austin Wharton.[qv] Their fight was said to have been about "military matters," specifically the reorganization of the Trans-Mississippi Department of the Confederate States. Wharton reportedly slapped Baylor's face and called him a liar, whereupon Baylor drew his revolver and shot the unarmed Wharton. Baylor later said that the incident had a been a "lifelong sorrow" to him.

After the Civil War,[qv] when Lt. John B. Tays, commander of Company C, Frontier Battalion[qv] of Texas Rangers[qv] in El Paso, resigned to enter the customs service, Baylor was commissioned a first lieutenant and appointed to take his place. At this time, according to Walter Prescott Webb,[qv] Baylor "was in his prime, forty-seven years of age, six feet two inches, a fine type of the frontier gentleman. He had a fair education, a flair for writing for newspapers and an inclination to fill his reports with historical allusions." Baylor left San Antonio on August 2, 1879, with his wife, two young daughters, and a sister-in-law, riding in an ambulance and with two wagons full of provisions and household goods, the latter including a piano and a game cock and four hens. The caravan, guarded by Sgt. James B. Gillett[qv] and five other rangers, was forty-two days on the road to Ysleta, where Baylor established his headquarters. From there he opened his campaign against raiding Apaches, whom he often pursued beyond the Rio Grande, in cooperation with Mexican officials. Soon after arriving on the border Baylor "generously extended" to the Mexican government "the privilege of coming over on our side and killing all the Reservation Indians" they could find. Through the rest of 1879 and most of 1880 Baylor's rangers were occupied in the pursuit of the Mescalero Apache chief Victorio[qv] and his band, an endeavor that proved largely ineffective. In September 1880 Baylor was transferred and promoted to captain of Company A. In 1882 he was promoted to major and given command of several ranger companies. During this period he was active in the fence-cutting[qv] conflict in Nolan County.

After resigning from ranger service in 1885 Baylor was elected to the Texas House of Representatives from El Paso and served as clerk of the district and circuit courts for a number of years. He died at San Antonio on March 17, 1916, and was buried in the Confederate Cemetery there. Baylor, according to Wilburn Hill King,[qv] the nineteenth-century historian of the rangers, was "noted for excellence of personal character and conduct, and soldierly courage and zeal," but Webb, more reserved in his judgment, wrote that "though a courageous individual fighter," Baylor "lacked reserve, was a poor disciplinarian, and an indifferent judge of men."

Bibliography: Anne J. Bailey, *Between the Enemy and Texas: Parsons's Texas Cavalry in the Civil War* (Fort Worth: Texas Christian University Press, 1989). Walter Prescott Webb, *The Texas Rangers* (Boston: Houghton Mifflin, 1935; rpt., Austin: University of Texas Press, 1982). Dudley Goodall Wooten, ed., *A Comprehensive History of Texas* (2 vols., Dallas: Scarff, 1898; rpt., Austin: Texas State Historical Association, 1986). Marcus J. Wright, comp., and Harold B. Simpson, ed., *Texas in the War, 1861–1865* (Hillsboro, Texas: Hill Junior College Press, 1965).

Thomas W. Cutrer

BAYLOR, HENRY WEIDNER (1818–1854). Henry Weidner Baylor, physician and soldier, was born in Paris, Kentucky, in 1818, the son of Sophie Marie (Weidner) and John Walker Baylor.[qv] In 1839 he visited his brother John Robert Baylor,[qv] who had moved to Texas in that year, and joined him on Col. John H. Moore's[qv] campaign against the Comanches. He then returned to Kentucky. After taking both literary and medical degrees at Transylvania University he moved to Texas and began his practice in La Grange, Fayette County.

At the outbreak of the Mexican War[qv] he enlisted as a private in Capt. Claibourn C. Hebert's Company E of Col. John Coffee Hays's[qv] First Regiment, Texas Mounted Riflemen, raised at Columbus, Texas. He took part in the storming of Monterrey and, on September 6, was promoted to regimental surgeon. In October, at the end of the regiment's enlistment period, Baylor raised Company E. of Maj. Michael Chevallie's[qv] battalion of Texas mounted volunteers and was elected its captain. Baylor's company was recruited in San Antonio and was in federal service from June 17, 1847, through June 30, 1848, attached to Gen. Zachary Taylor's[qv] headquarters. It spent much of its enlistment period on garrison duty in Monterrey, Nuevo León, but experienced severe fighting with Indians near Las Tablas on August 5, 1847, in which the company lost six men killed and an unknown number wounded. After the war Baylor moved to Independence and there established a medical practice and farm. He died on August 4, 1854. On his gravestone are the words, "Keep My Memory Green." Henry Weidner Baylor was the brother of George Wythe Baylor[qv] as well as John Robert Baylor; he was the nephew of Robert Emmett Bledsoe Baylor.[qv] Baylor County was named in his honor.

Bibliography: Frank W. Johnson, *A History of Texas and Texans* (5 vols., ed. E. C. Barker and E. W. Winkler [Chicago and New York: American Historical Society, 1914; rpt. 1916]). Charles D. Spurlin, comp., *Texas Veterans in the Mexican War: Muster Rolls of Texas Military Units* (Victoria, Texas, 1984). Marcus J. Wright, comp., and Harold B. Simpson, ed., *Texas in the War, 1861–1865* (Hillsboro, Texas: Hill Junior College Press, 1965).

Thomas W. Cutrer

BAYLOR, JOHN ROBERT (1822–1894). John Robert Baylor, Indian fighter, Civil War[qv] officer, and rancher, the son of John Walker and Sophie Marie (Wiedner) Baylor, was born at Paris, Kentucky, on July 27, 1822. When he was a small boy he moved with his family to Fort Gibson, Indian Territory, where his father was an assistant surgeon in the Seventh Infantry. At an early age he was sent to Cincinnati for an education, but after the death of his father he went to live with his uncle at Rocky Creek, south of La Grange in Fayette County, Texas. In 1840 Baylor joined a Texas volunteer army under Col. John H. Moore,[qv] but he arrived too late for the battle of Plum Creek.[qv] Two years later he joined Capt. Nicholas M. Dawson[qv] to avenge the seizure of San Antonio by Mexican general Adrián Woll[qv] but was able to avoid the subsequent Dawson Massacre.[qv] In late 1842 he returned to Fort Gibson to teach school at the Creek agency. One year later he was with his brother-in-law, James Dawson, when Dawson killed an Indian trader named Seaborn Hill. Charged as an accomplice, Baylor fled across the Red River to Texas. He married Emily Hanna at Marshall in 1844. The Baylors eventually became the parents of seven sons and three daughters.

In Texas Baylor took up farming and ranching at Ross Prairie in Fayette County. In 1851 he was elected to the state legislature, and two years later he was admitted to the bar. In September 1855 he was appointed Indian agent to the Comanches on the Clear Fork of the Brazos. He was dismissed in 1857, after accusing certain of the reservation Comanches of aiding their non-reservation-bound fellow tribesmen in raids on the frontier and feuding with his supervisor, Robert S. Neighbors.[qv] In the years that followed he traveled widely in North Texas preaching hatred of the Comanches and other Indians and attempting to have Neighbors replaced with someone more to his own liking. A man of considerable vigor and magnetism, he addressed mass meetings, organized a vigilante force of some 1,000 men, and even edited an anti-Indian newspaper, the *White Man,* published by H. A. Hamner at Jacksboro and later at Weatherford. In June 1860 Baylor led a band of frontiersmen in the defeat of a small party of Comanches in the battle of Paint Creek, to avenge the murder and scalping of a young white boy.

With secession[qv] and the Civil War, Baylor came as lieutenant colonel to command the Second Texas Mounted Rifles, which was ordered to occupy a chain of forts protecting the overland route between Fort Clark and Fort Bliss. Baylor reached Fort Bliss in July 1861 and immediately began preparations to occupy the Mesilla valley. He seized Mesilla without opposition and, on the basis of reports of the arrival of massive reinforcements and artillery, caused a large part of the Seventh Infantry under Maj. Isaac Lynde to evacuate Fort Fillmore. After pursuing the retreating federals east into the Organ Mountains, where they were weakened by lack of water, Baylor secured their surrender at San Augustine Pass on July 27, 1861 (*see* MESILLA, BATTLE OF).

At Mesilla Baylor established the Confederate Territory of Arizona and proclaimed himself military governor in 1861. On December 15 of that year he was promoted to colonel. In response to a series of critical articles in the pro-Confederate Mesilla *Times,* he challenged the editor, Robert P. Kelley, to a fight and injured him so severely that he died a few weeks later. Preoccupied with the hostile Apaches of the region, Baylor led a raid deep into the mountains of Chihuahua and supposedly killed a large number of Apaches, although no official correspondence exists to prove this. In March 1862 he sent a letter ordering the extermination of the hostile Apaches in the area to Capt. Thomas Helm, who was guarding the Pinos Altos mines. When word of Baylor's controversial order reached Richmond, President Jefferson Davis qv removed him from civil and military command. In Texas Baylor fought as a private during the battle of Galveston qv on January 1, 1863, and beat Malcolm D. Graham qv in the election to the Second Confederate Congress. Two weeks before Lee's surrender Baylor was reinstated as colonel, but he did not see action.

After the war he moved to San Antonio, where in 1873 he competed unsuccessfully with Richard Coke qv for the Democratic nomination for governor. He dabbled in Greenback and Populist politics and in 1876, at the age of fifty-four, offered his services to the army during the Sioux War. In 1878 he moved to Montell, on the Nueces River northwest of Uvalde, and acquired a sizable ranch. He continued to be involved in violent confrontations and reputedly killed a man in a feud over livestock in the 1880s. He was not charged with murder, however, or prosecuted in any way. He died at Montell on February 6, 1894, and is buried in Ascension Episcopal Cemetery there.

BIBLIOGRAPHY: Martin Hardwick Hall, "The Baylor-Kelley Fight: A Civil War Incident in Old Mesilla," *Password,* July 1960. Jerry Don Thompson, *Colonel John Robert Baylor* (Hillsboro, Texas: Hill Junior College Press, 1971). *Jerry Thompson*

BAYLOR, JOHN WALKER (ca. 1813–1836). John Walker Baylor was born at Woodlawn, Bourbon County, Kentucky, around December 1813 to John Walker and Sophia Marie (Weidner) Baylor. His father, an army physician, was the son of Capt. Walker Baylor, who commanded George Washington's Life Guard in the Third Continental Division at the battle of Germantown. Baylor briefly attended Bardstown College in Kentucky and was appointed to the United States Military Academy at West Point on July 1, 1832. He had disciplinary problems there and was once reinstated by President Andrew Jackson. He left in 1833 and studied medicine under his father until the elder Baylor's death in 1835.

He registered at Fort Gibson, Arkansas, under the name Walker Baylor, then joined George M. Collinsworth's qv volunteers at Matagorda, Texas, on October 5, 1835. He signed an agreement with other members of Collinsworth's company to protect the citizens of Guadalupe Victoria (now Victoria, Texas). He fought at Goliad on October 9 in the capture of La Bahía from a small Mexican garrison. He was a member of Philip Dimmitt's qv Goliad garrison and fought under James Bowie and James Fannin qqv in the battle of Concepción qv on October 28. (*See also* GOLIAD CAMPAIGN OF 1835.) On November 21, 1835, he was part of a committee at Goliad assigned to prepare a document expressing the volunteers' defiance of an order from Stephen F. Austin qv directing Dimmitt to turn over control of the post to Collinsworth. Baylor was in the five-day siege of Bexar qv on December 5–9, 1835. He signed the Goliad Declaration of Independence qv on December 20. Dimmitt's command was disbanded in 1836, and Baylor went to San Antonio with either Bowie or Dimmitt.

After the attack on the Alamo began, Baylor was one of four or five couriers sent by William B. Travis qv to La Bahía to urge Fannin to come to his aid. At Goliad, Baylor became a member of Capt. John (Jack) Shackelford's qv Red Rovers. qv He joined Capt. Albert C. Horton's qv cavalry on March 14 and participated in several skirmishes against Gen. José de Urrea's qv Mexican cavalry. Horton's troopers were scouting ahead of Fannin's retreating army and so were not captured with the other Texans in the battle of Coleto qv and consequently were not executed in the Goliad Massacre qv (*see also* GOLIAD CAMPAIGN OF 1836). Some of the troops, including Baylor, were bitter that Horton did not come to the aid of the beleaguered encampment. Baylor made his way to Houston's army on the Brazos, where he joined William H. Patton's qv company in Col. Sidney Johnson's qv Second Texas Volunteer Regiment. He was named drillmaster because of his West Point experience. In the battle of San Jacinto qv he received a thigh wound that he considered so slight he did not report it. On May 29 he joined a group of mounted rangers under Maj. Isaac Burton. qv The rangers were sent by Gen. Thomas J. Rusk qv to patrol the coast and watch for a possible Mexican attack from the sea. At Copano these "Horse Marines" qv captured three ships bearing supplies for the Mexican army.

On July 25 Baylor drew sixty-four dollars in back pay and went on furlough to the home of his uncle, Robert Emmett Bledsoe Baylor, qv in Alabama. His wound had become inflamed. He developed a fever and died on September 3, 1836, in Cahaba, Alabama, an unreported casualty of the battle of San Jacinto. He was possibly the only Texan to fight in every major battle of the Texas Revolution. qv His brothers George W., Henry W., and John R. Baylor qqv became prominent as Texas Rangers, qv soldiers, and Indian fighters.

BIBLIOGRAPHY: Sam Houston Dixon and Louis Wiltz Kemp, *The Heroes of San Jacinto* (Houston: Anson Jones, 1932). Bill Groneman, *Alamo Defenders* (Austin: Eakin, 1990). Hobart Huson, *Captain Philip Dimmitt's Commandancy of Goliad, 1835–1836* (Austin: Von Boeckmann–Jones, 1974). Hobart Huson, *El Copano: Ancient Port of Bexar and La Bahia* (Refugio, Texas: Refugio *Timely Remarks,* 1935). Louis Wiltz Kemp Papers, Barker Texas History Center, University of Texas at Austin. Kathryn Stoner O'Connor, *The Presidio La Bahía del Espíritu Santo de Zúñiga, 1721 to 1846* (Austin: Von Boeckmann–Jones, 1966). *Bill Walraven*

BAYLOR, ROBERT EMMETT BLEDSOE (1793–1873). R. E. B. Baylor, lawyer, college founder, and Baptist leader, was born in Lincoln County, Kentucky, on May 10, 1793, the son of Walker and Jane (Bledsoe) Baylor. His father had been a captain in the Continental Army during the American Revolution, in a company of dragoons that often assisted George Washington. Baylor received his formal education at a country school and at academies around Paris, Kentucky. After service in the War of 1812 he studied law in the office of his uncle, Judge Jesse Bledsoe, and was elected in 1819 to the Kentucky legislature. Around 1820 he moved to Tuscaloosa, Alabama, where he practiced law. In 1824–25 he served in the Alabama legislature. He was elected a representative from Alabama to the Twenty-first Congress of the United States in 1829 and was defeated in the election of 1831. In 1833 he moved to Dallas County, Alabama. Baylor raised a few volunteers and served as a lieutenant colonel against the Creek Indians in Alabama in 1836.

He was converted in 1839 during a Baptist revival meeting conducted by his cousin Thomas Chilton at Talladega, Alabama. The same year he was ordained a Baptist minister and, at the age of forty-six, went to Texas. He settled near La Grange in Fayette County and organized a school. He assisted in the organization of the Union Baptist Association in 1840 and the Texas Baptist Education Society around 1841. With two other Baptist ministers, Z. N. Morrell and Thomas W. Cox,[qqv] he served under Edward Burleson[qv] at the battle of Plum Creek[qv] in 1840.

On January 7, 1841, Baylor was elected judge of the Third Judicial District of the Congress of the Republic of Texas and consequently became an associate justice of the Supreme Court, an office he held until the end of the republic. He was a delegate from Fayette County to the Convention of 1845[qv] and served on three committees: Annexation, Judiciary, and General Provisions of the Constitution. He helped to write the first state constitution and favored free public schools, homestead exemptions, annual elections, and the exclusion of clergy from the legislature. He opposed the veto power for the governor. In 1846 the first Texas state governor, J. P. Henderson,[qv] appointed Baylor judge of the state's Third Judicial District. Baylor served in that capacity until 1863.

With William M. Tryon[qv] and J. G. Thomas, Baylor prepared the petition that led to the establishment of Baylor University in 1845. He may have donated the first $1,000 to the university; he served as a member of the board of trustees and taught law intermittently, without pay. While traveling through his judicial districts on horseback to enforce the law, he held court by day and preached in the evenings. He presided at the first district court held in Waco and perhaps delivered the first sermon ever preached in that city, at the hotel owned by Shapley P. Ross.[qv] Baylor became a Mason in 1825; he served as chaplain of the Grand Lodge of Texas Masons in 1843, 1845, and 1847. In 1853 he assisted in the organization of a lodge at Gay Hill in Washington County, his home until his death.

Baylor never married. He died on December 30, 1873, and was buried, as he had requested, on the campus of Baylor University at Independence. His remains were reinterred in 1917 on the campus of Baylor Female College (now the University of Mary Hardin-Baylor).

BIBLIOGRAPHY: R. E. B. Baylor Papers, Texas Collection, Baylor University. James Milton Carroll, *A History of Texas Baptists* (Dallas: Baptist Standard, 1923). *Dictionary of American Biography.* L. R. Elliott, ed., *Centennial Story of Texas Baptists* (Dallas: Baptist General Convention of Texas, 1936). *Encyclopedia of Southern Baptists* (4 vols., Nashville: Broadman, 1958–82).

Travis L. Summerlin

BAYLOR COLLEGE OF DENTISTRY. Ignoring the opposition of Dallas dentists who feared additional competition and favored apprenticeship as a means for dental training, two dentists from St. Louis, David E. Morrow and T. G. Bradford, received a charter from the Texas secretary of state on February 28, 1905, to establish State Dental College, the forerunner of Baylor College of Dentistry. The college's first thirty-week term began on October 3, 1905, on the second floor of the Juanita Building on Commerce Street in Dallas, later the location of the entrance to the Adolphus Hotel. Morrow was elected dean of the first faculty, which also included Bradford, Allen N. Kearby, Charles F. Barham, Henry L. Alder, W. C. Rice, J. A. Pelkey, and J. H. Nicholson. By August 1907 the degree of doctor of dental surgery had been granted to seven students, most of whom had begun their work at other dental schools. T. G. Bradford replaced Morrow as dean in 1907 and supervised the move to a more spacious building on South Ervay Street. By the time of Bradford's resignation in 1912, the college had moved again and the graduation classes had increased in size to about eighteen. Fred C. Kingsley was selected to replace Bradford, who, with C. L. Morey, remained the largest stockholder in the school.

Although both classes and curriculum grew, the college experienced difficulties from its founding until 1916, when its owners agreed to transfer control to an advisory board. J. J. Simmons, president of the newly organized Dallas District Dental Society, also served as president of the advisory board. He was assisted by Bush Jones as vice president and C. L. Morey as secretary-treasurer. This arrangement proved to be effective in increasing the number of students for the next two years. The school remained a proprietary one, however, and in the early years of World War I,[qv] when the War Department considered drafting students of unrecognized professional schools, the advisory board sought a new arrangement that would enhance the school's status—absorption by Baylor University Medical College, which was then located in Dallas. On May 28, 1918, after graduating twenty-six dentists, Bradford and Morey sold their interest to Baylor University, and State Dental College formally became Baylor Dental College, with Bush Jones as dean.

The difficulties faced by institutions throughout the country during the Great Depression and World War II[qqv] years were experienced by Baylor Dental College as well, but were complicated by the move of Baylor College of Medicine to Houston in 1943. The dental school was left to rebuild its basic science curriculum without the help of professors from the medical college and in overcrowded postwar conditions. By 1950, when the enrollment had reached 241, a new clinic building was completed that eased overcrowding and provided the college with its first quarters built specifically for dental education. George Powers guided the postwar growth, and, following his retirement in 1952, Harry B. McCarthy became dean. During the fiftieth anniversary year of the college in 1955, the Caruth School of Dental Hygiene was opened, the result of a gift from Dallas philanthropist Walter W. Caruth and the Caruth Foundation. Patricia A. Clendenin served as first director of the Caruth School, where in May 1957 the first class of dental hygienists ever to graduate in Texas received diplomas. Graduate programs in basic sciences and clinical fields were added to Baylor's curriculum beginning in the early 1950s. By 1960 the freshman class included eighty-five students.

On August 1, 1971, Baylor Dental College became Baylor College of Dentistry, and its association with Baylor University ended. The college became a private, nonprofit, nonsectarian educational corporation. Kenneth V. Randolph, dean following McCarthy's retirement in 1968, was named president, academic dean, and chief executive officer. At the same time, the college entered into an agreement with the coordinating board of the Texas College and University System (*see* TEXAS HIGHER EDUCATION COORDINATING BOARD), whereby Baylor agreed to increase the number of Texas residents in its undergraduate classes so that it would receive state financial support. Between 1974 and 1977 a combined program of new construction and renovation of the existing building more than doubled the classroom, clinic, and laboratory space. When the new facilities were dedicated on October 2, 1977, the address was delivered by L. M. Kennedy, an alumnus of the college, who had served as president of the American Dental Association. Randolph retired in August 1980 and was succeeded by Richard E. Bradley, former dean of the dental school of the University of Nebraska. At that time, undergraduate enrollment had grown to 522, and graduate enrollment stood at forty-eight. In 1992 the undergraduate enrollment was 355 and graduate enrollment was 71. Dominick P. De Paola had been dean since August 1990. In 1995 the college trustees voted to merge Baylor College of Dentistry with Texas A&M University.

BIBLIOGRAPHY: Bush Jones, History of the State Dental College (MS, Baylor College of Dentistry Archives). Walter C. Stout, *The First Hundred Years: A History of Dentistry in Texas* (Dallas: Egan, 1969). Gladys Yates, The History of Baylor College of Dentistry, 1905–1980 (MS, Baylor College of Dentistry Archives, 1980).

James E. Makins

BAYLOR COLLEGE OF MEDICINE. Baylor College of Medicine, the only private medical school in the Southwest and the first institution to locate in the Texas Medical Center[qv] in Houston, occupied the Roy and Lillie Cullen Building there in 1947. The school was founded in Dallas in 1900, when Texas had only two other schools of medicine—the University of Texas School of Medicine, which started in Galveston in 1891, and the Fort Worth School of Medicine, which began in 1894. It was the first of eight medical schools to be organized in Dallas during the first decade of the twentieth century. With three physicians as incorporators and a charter filed with the Texas secretary of state on September 15, 1900, this proprietary school was named the University of Dallas Medical Department, even though the University of Dallas did not exist. Having leased the former Temple Emanu-el[qv] at what is now 1306 Commerce Street, the school enrolled eighty-one students for its opening on November 19, 1900. Some of these students had previously attended medical lectures elsewhere; some had already been practicing medicine without degrees. At the first commencement, held on April 18, 1901, fifteen diplomas were awarded, and in 1902–03 twenty-two more were bestowed.

On June 29, 1903, the University of Dallas Medical Department became Baylor University College of Medicine. Over time, other "Baylor units in Dallas" evolved around the College of Medicine—schools of pharmacy and nursing and a college of dentistry—all associated with Baylor University Hospital (now Baylor University Medical Center[qv]). The Baylor College of Medicine and the University of Texas Medical Branch in Galveston were the only medical schools in Texas to survive Abraham Flexner's stern criticisms of low standards of medical education in his harsh and famous report of 1911. Between 1903 and 1943 Baylor awarded M.D. degrees to 1,670 graduates.

The latter year, 1943, marks a watershed in Baylor's evolution, because a severe conflict arose between civic leaders and physicians in Dallas and Baylor administrators over the denominational character of the College of Medicine. Governance of Baylor derived its authority from the Baptist General Convention of Texas, even though the college had not required sectarian allegiances with respect to faculty appointments and student admissions. Dr. Walter H. Moursund,[qv] its dean from 1923 to 1953, was a Presbyterian, not a Baptist. But Baylor faced unpalatable alternatives: in exchange for fiscal support and new quarters in a proposed new medical center to be erected on Hines Boulevard in Dallas, the medical college was expected to relinquish administrative control and denominational affiliation. Otherwise it would be excluded from the envisioned medical center in favor of a newly founded nonsectarian medical school. Baylor extricated itself by accepting an invitation from the M. D. Anderson Foundation[qv] and other Houston benefactors to move to Houston. The move was completed by July 12, 1943, when the Baylor College of Medicine began its Houston era in a former Sears-Roebuck building on Buffalo Drive. These renovated quarters housed the college until the Cullen Building was ready for occupancy.

The other Baylor units in Dallas continued to operate in that city. Shortly after Baylor moved the medical school to Houston, the newly organized Southwestern Medical College—which in 1949 became the University of Texas Southwestern Medical College—was formed by the physicians and community leaders who were displeased with Baylor's denominational affiliation. The relationship between the Baptist General Convention of Texas and the Baylor College of Medicine was terminated by a mutual agreement in 1969, and the school became a freestanding corporation, nonsectarian and nonprofit, governed by a self-perpetuating board of trustees. With "University" dropped from its name, and with Dr. Michael E. DeBakey occupying its presidency from 1969 to 1979, Baylor College of Medicine was superbly positioned to appeal for support from Houston philanthropy and benefactors elsewhere and to receive federal funds for biomedical research, without hindrances imposed by traditional Baptist antipathy towards breaching the separately perceived realms of church and state.

Despite its status as a private school Baylor, since 1971, has annually received state appropriations from the Texas legislature to subsidize the medical education of Texas residents. This partnership allowed Baylor to double the size of each entering class to 168 registrants, of whom no fewer than 70 percent are Texans, who in turn pay tuition fees no higher than those levied by state medical schools. Three major fund-raising campaigns from 1971 to 1982 raised $114.5 million in gifts. In 1993 Baylor stood first among Texas medical schools and third among the state's universities for receiving federal funds for research and development. Nationally, Baylor ranks among the top medical schools in federal research support.

Since its founding Baylor has trained more than 11,251 physicians and residents. In 1993 almost 4,400 of this number were in practice in Texas, more than 2,000 of them in the Houston area. One of every seven physicians now practicing in Texas was trained at Baylor.

Baylor's graduate school enrolls 237 students in thirteen Ph.D. programs in the biomedical sciences and an M.S. program in nurse anesthesiology. About 835 resident physicians receive training in twenty-two medical specialties offered jointly by Baylor and its eight primary affiliated teaching hospitals. Another 443 students are either postdoctoral fellows or students in allied health programs, where they learn nuclear medicine technology, nurse midwifery, and similar skills and earn certification as physicians' assistants. In 1972 Baylor and the Houston Independent School District started this nation's first high school for health professions, and between 1983 and 1990 the college developed similar programs for high school students in Mercedes and Corpus Christi. Altogether, 4,146 students of varying levels and ages attend Baylor or Baylor-supported schools.

In 1993 the Baylor faculty numbered 3,526 (1,368 full-time, 103 part-time, 2,007 voluntary, and 48 emeritus). Its staff consisted of 3,586 employees (2,964 full-time and 622 part-time). Baylor is fully accredited by the Liaison Committee on Medical Education, administered jointly by the American Medical Association and the Association of American Medical Colleges, and also by the Southern Association of Colleges and Schools.

Since occupying the Roy and Lillie Cullen Building in 1947, Baylor has expanded its physical plant by erecting Jesse H. Jones[qv] Hall (1964), M. D. Anderson[qv] Hall (1964), the Jewish Institute for Medical Research (1964), the Michael E. DeBakey Center for Biomedical Education (1980), the Family Practice Center (1983), the Ben Taub Research Center (1986), and the Vivian and Bob Smith Medical Research Building (1989). Together with Methodist Hospital of Houston[qv] it has administered the Neurosensory Center of Houston since 1977, and with Texas Children's Hospital[qv] and the United States Department of Agriculture it has operated the Children's Nutrition Research Center since 1988. A Woodlands campus, north of Houston, is the site of the Baylor Center for Biotechnology, which is dedicated to marketing commercially viable products from laboratory research done by Baylor scientists.

An ambitious capital gifts campaign, launched in 1988 to expand Baylor's physical plant, endow professorships, and provide student aid, exceeded its goal of $175 million in 1992. In 1993 the college's endowment stood at $253.1 million. Its total research support (including affiliated institutions) was nearly $160 million, and this research capability generated more than $900 million annually for the Texas economy. Baylor research gives special priority to studies of the molecular basis of genetic ailments.

BIBLIOGRAPHY: John S. Chapman, *The University of Texas Southwestern Medical School: Medical Education in Dallas, 1900–1975* (Dallas: Southern Methodist University Press, 1976). Lana Henderson, *Baylor University Medical Center* (Waco: Baylor University Press, 1978). Walter H. Moursund, *A History of Baylor University College of Medicine* (Houston, 1956).

Charles T. Morrissey

BAYLOR COUNTY. Baylor County (B-14), in North Central Texas, is bounded on the south by Throckmorton County, on the east by Archer County, on the north by Wilbarger County, and on the west by Knox and Foard counties. Its center is 30°37′ north latitude and 99°12′ west longitude, fifty miles southwest of Wichita Falls. The county is level to hilly. It comprises 845 square miles with an average elevation of 1,250 feet. The land is drained by the Salt Fork of the Brazos and the Big Wichita rivers. The soils vary from sandy to loam and red, and the ground cover is largely grasses, mesquites, and junipers.

The average annual rainfall is 26.36 inches. Temperatures range from an average high of 98° F in July to an average low of 28° in January. The growing season averages 214 days.

Before it was settled, the area that is now Baylor County lay within the range of the Wanderers, a nomadic Comanche band, who relied upon buffalo[qv] for food, clothing, shelter, tools, and ornaments. In 1848 special Indian agent Robert S. Neighbors[qv] found 250 Comanche, fifty Tonkawa, and ten Wichita lodges on Lewis Creek at the site of present-day Seymour. When the first surveys were made in the area in 1853 the Indians were still using it as a major hunting ground for buffalo, a fact that made settlement nearly impossible. This continued until the final defeat of the Comanches in 1874 by the United States Army and their removal to a reservation in Indian territory (*see* RED RIVER WAR). Baylor County was separated from Fannin County in 1858 and named for Henry W. Baylor,[qv] a surgeon in a regiment of Texas Rangers[qv] during the Mexican War.[qv] The county was attached to Jack County for administrative and judicial purposes.

The first settlement was at Round Timber, nineteen miles southeast of the site of present Seymour. Tradition holds that the first settler was Col. C. C. Mills, who may have been at Round Timber during the Civil War[qv] and was certainly there by 1870. He was driven out by Indian raids, but returned by 1875 to join J. W. Stevens, who had arrived a year earlier.

This was the era of free-grass ranches, a time in which farmers and ranchers sometimes violently contested for land. Settlers from Oregon, led by Col. J. R. McClain, moved to the site of Seymour in 1876, for example, but were driven off when cowboys ran cattle over their corn. In 1879 the Millett brothers—Eugene C., Alonzo, and Hiram—came from Guadalupe County to begin ranching in Baylor County. They ran a tough outfit and used their armed cowhands to intimidate would-be settlers and the citizens of newly founded Seymour. Violence and contention plagued the county during the first years of settlement. Baylor County's first two county attorneys were forced to resign, and in June 1879 county judge E. R. Morris was shot and killed by saloon keeper Will Taylor. Later the Texas Rangers[qv] gradually brought peace.

Baylor County was formally organized in 1879 with Seymour as county seat. That same year both Seymour and Round Timber were assigned the county's first post offices. By 1880, fifty farms and ranches encompassing 13,506 acres had been established in the county, supporting a population of 708 people; more than 13,506 cattle were counted in the county that year. Baylor County's first newspaper was the *Cresset,* which began publishing in 1880 and lasted for several years. It was followed by the Seymour *Scimeter,* which failed in 1886. Early settlers were tested by a drought and severe winters in 1886 and 1887, but these hard times were followed by seasons of bumper wheat crops, which led to a settlement boom. By 1890 there were 169 farms and ranches in the county, and the population had climbed to 2,595.

In 1890 county residents raised $50,000 to insure the completion of the Wichita Valley Railway, which linked Seymour to Wichita Falls, fifty-two miles to the east. By 1892, the Texas *Gazetteer* reported that Seymour was a thriving town, with two newspapers (the *Monitor* and the *News*), the First National Bank, two physicians, and a dentist. The town also had three hotels and was home to a number of lawyers, storekeepers, shoemakers, saddlers, and county officials who served its population of 1,900. In 1895 another newspaper, the *Baylor County Banner,* printed its first edition; it was still being published in the 1990s. By 1900 the county had 327 farms and the population had grown to 3,052. Ranching was still a crucial component of the local economy, and the number of cattle in Baylor County had increased to almost 45,000. But crop farming was quickly rising in importance as more and more farmers moved to the area to grow wheat, oats, corn, and, increasingly, cotton.

Between 1900 and 1910 Baylor County had another boom as old ranchland was divided up into hundreds of new farms. By 1910 there were 1,040 farms in the county (616 of them operated by tenants), and cotton had replaced wheat as the most important crop. Only seventy-seven acres of Baylor County land was planted in cotton in 1880, and only 3,065 in 1900. But by 1910, cotton cultivation had expanded to more than 38,000 acres in the county. During that same period, land devoted to wheat production had dropped from about 9,500 acres to 2,621 acres. Meanwhile, the number of cattle in the county also dropped from almost 45,000 to about 25,000. The cotton boom brought with it a marked increase in the county's population, which rose from 3,052 in 1900 to 8,411 in 1910. That same year the Gulf, Texas and Western Railroad reached Seymour. Droughts and falling prices after World War I[qv] helped to put an end to this boom, however, and the local economy contracted. By 1920 only about 29,600 acres was planted in cotton, and the number of farms had dropped to 811. The population of the county also fell; by 1920, 7,027 people remained in the county. During the 1920s Baylor County had another brief but intense cotton boom. By 1929 more than 66,000 acres was devoted to cotton, and the number of farms in the county had increased again to 867. Meanwhile, the population rose to 7,418 by 1930. The Great Depression[qv] of the 1930s put an end to this expansion, however, and by 1940 only about 27,000 acres was planted in cotton in Baylor County; the number of farms had dropped to 718.

Petroleum production helped diversify the local economy and nurse it through the depression. Oil was discovered in Baylor County in 1924; in 1938 more than 520,000 barrels of crude was pumped from county lands. In 1948, production was 507,268 barrels; in 1958, 1,658,508 barrels; and in 1963, 2,073,000 barrels. By the 1980s production ranged between 300,000 and 400,000 barrels a year; in 1990, 313,912 barrels was produced. By 1991 more than 55,139,000 barrels had been taken from Baylor County lands since discovery in 1924.

Politically Baylor County has been predominantly Democratic. Since the elections of 1952 Republicans have outpolled Democrats in Baylor County in only two presidential races, in 1972 and 1984; and only in 1986 did the Republicans beat the Democrats in a gubernatorial race.

The population of the county dropped steadily after World War II.[qv] From its 1940 population of 7,755, the number of people in Baylor County declined to 6,875 in 1950, to 5,221 in 1970, to 4,919 in 1980, and to 4,385 in 1990. The county remained fundamentally agricultural. The United States agricultural census for 1982 reported that the county harvested 2,423,530 bushels of wheat that year, when Baylor County was one of the leading wheat producers in the state. The census also credited the county with 100,981 bushels of barley, 82,190 bushels of oats, 59,937 bushels of sorghum, and 249,524 pounds of peanuts; cotton production was 4,607 bales; 42,271 cattle and lesser numbers of other livestock were reported, to round out a fairly well diversified agricultural economy. The total agricultural income for the county averaged nearly $20 million in the 1980s. At that time the arable land included 5,000 irrigated acres, The county had two banks with total assets of $59,667,000. Except in Seymour there is little industry in the county, and employment in towns is mainly for local enterprises.

Baylor County is served by the Fort Worth and Denver Railway (Burlington Northern). U.S. Highway 183/283 runs from north to south across the county, and U.S. 82/277 goes from southwest to northeast. These are supplemented by several farm-to-market and local roads. Baylor County communities include Bomarton, Red Springs, Round Timber, Westover, and Seymour. Recreation in the county is mainly outdoor activities. The oldest event is the annual Cowboys' Reunion, which was first held in 1896 and in its early years featured Indians; it has been renamed the Settlers' Reunion. Lake Kemp,[qv] on the Wichita River,[qv] was opened in 1924 behind its new dam and in the 1980s provided recreational as well as irrigation[qv] water for Wichita Falls and other towns.

BIBLIOGRAPHY: Baylor County Historical Society, *Salt Pork to Sirloin,* Vol. 1: *The History of Baylor County, Texas, from 1879 to 1930* (Quanah, Texas: Nortex, 1972); Vol. 2: *The History of Baylor County,*

Texas, from 1878 to Present (1977). Sarah Ann Britton, *The Early History of Baylor County* (Dallas: Story Book Press, 1955). Floyd Benjamin Streeter, "The Millett Cattle Ranch in Baylor County, Texas," *Panhandle-Plains Historical Review* 22 (1949).

Lawrence L. Graves

BAYLOR CREEK (Fayette County). Baylor Creek rises on land granted to William J. Russell in 1831 a mile southeast of Oldenburg in southeastern Fayette County (at 29°58′ N, 96°46′ W) and flows southwest for eight miles to its mouth on the Colorado River, about five miles southeast of La Grange on lands granted to George Duty[qv] in 1824 (at 29°52′ N, 96°48′ W). Throughout much of its course the stream roughly parallels the Wilbarger Trace, which connected early settlements on the Colorado River with the La Bahía Road.[qv] Baylor Creek traverses gently rolling country with deep topsoil that once supported good cotton crops. Since the 1960s the land has been used mainly as pasture for horses and cattle. The vegetation along the stream is a mixture of oaks, cedars, and sycamores, with an understory of yaupon and wild grape.

—— (Hall County). Baylor Creek is formed where North Baylor and South Baylor creeks join in eastern Hall County (at 34°27′ N, 100°29′ W). North Baylor Creek rises in the remote rangeland of southeastern Hall County (at 34°26′ N, 100°31′ W) and runs northeast for seven miles. South Baylor Creek rises just south of the north creek's head (at 34°24′ N, 100°29′ W) and travels northwest for seven miles. The two branches converge to form Baylor Creek just west of the Hall-Childress county line and six miles south of Estelline. Baylor Creek flows through west central Childress County for eight miles to its mouth on the Prairie Dog Town Fork of the Red River, ten miles northwest of Childress (at 34°31′ N, 100°21′ W). The stream was once fed by numerous small springs, although most were dry by the 1980s. Baylor Creek is the main source of Baylor Lake, located seven miles northwest of the county airport. The area has moderately steep slopes, locally high relief, and a shallow to moderately deep silt loam surface. The vegetation consists primarily of mesquite and grasses.

BAYLOR CREEK RESERVOIR. Baylor Creek Reservoir is on Baylor Creek in the Red River basin, ten miles northwest of Childress in western Childress County. The project is owned and operated by the city of Childress for municipal water supply and recreation. Construction of the earthfill dam was started on April 1, 1949, and completed in February 1950. Deliberate impoundment of water was begun in December 1949, and use of the water began in 1954. Lake Childress is adjacent to this reservoir, which has a capacity of 9,220 acre-feet and a surface area of 610 acres at the operating elevation of 2,010 feet above mean sea level. The drainage area above the dam is forty square miles.

BIBLIOGRAPHY: C. L. Dowell, *Dams and Reservoirs in Texas: History and Descriptive Information* (Texas Water Commission Bulletin 6408 [Austin, 1964]).

Seth D. Breeding

BAYLOR MOUNTAINS. The Baylor Mountains begin two miles north of Van Horn and stretch nine miles to the north, terminating south of Salt Lake in western Culberson County (with their center at 31°15′ N, 104°46′ W). The highest elevation in the mountains is 5,564 feet above sea level. The Baylors are part of an uplifted fault block that includes the Sierra Diablo and Beach Mountains and forms the steep west flank of the salt flats. The Baylors are capped by Permian Hueco limestone, some 250 million years old. Ordovician and Silurian rocks, from 400 to 500 million years old, are exposed on their eastern flank; exposed Silurian rocks are relatively rare in the western United States, so the Baylors are of some interest to geologists studying that period. The Baylors are steep and rocky, with local deep and dense dissection. On them a surface of shallow, stony soil supports oaks, live oaks, piñons, mesquites, junipers, and grasses. The mountains are named for Col. George W. Baylor,[qv] who led the Texas Rangers[qv] against the Mescalero Apaches in this region in the late nineteenth century.

BAYLOR UNIVERSITY. Baylor University owes its founding to Robert E. B. Baylor, James Huckins, and William Milton Tryon,[qqv] who in 1841 organized an education society in the Texas Union Baptist Association with the purpose of establishing a Baptist university in Texas. Baylor was chartered by the Republic of Texas[qv] on February 1, 1845, and was opened in 1846 at Independence. Professor Henry F. Gillette[qv] directed the school until the arrival of its first president, Henry Lee Graves,[qv] who received notice of his election on January 12, 1846, arrived in Independence in December 1846, and entered upon his duties on February 4, 1847. That year Graves organized a collegiate department and in 1849 added lectures in law. He resigned in 1851 and was succeeded by Rufus C. Burleson,[qv] who, during his first year as president announced a course of study leading to graduation. The university granted its first degree in 1854. In 1861, as a result of continued disagreement with the board of trustees, Burleson and the entire faculty of the male department resigned. George W. Baines, Sr.,[qv] became president and in 1863 was succeeded by William Carey Crane,[qv] during whose presidency the curriculum was broadened and the female department became a separate institution, Baylor Female College (*see* UNIVERSITY OF MARY HARDIN-BAYLOR). From 1866 to 1886 Baylor University was a male school. After Crane's death in 1885, Reddin Andrews, Jr.,[qv] an alumnus, was made president.

In 1886 the Baptist General Association of Texas and the State Convention, under the control of which Baylor had been operating since 1848, were combined to form the Baptist General Convention, and as a result Baylor University and Waco University, which Burleson had headed since he resigned as president of Baylor at Independence, were consolidated and rechartered as Baylor University in Waco. Under the control of the Baptist General Convention, Baylor was established on the Waco campus by the end of 1887. Burleson was made president emeritus in June 1897. Professor John C. Lattimore,[qv] as chairman of the faculty, directed the school until 1899, when Oscar Henry Cooper[qv] was made president. Cooper secured two new buildings and raised academic standards.

Samuel Palmer Brooks[qv] succeeded Cooper in 1902 and served as president until his death in 1931. Brooks added new departments and organized the schools of education, law, business, and music. In addition, Baylor acquired four professional schools in Dallas: the College of Medicine (1903), the School of Nursing (1909), the School of Pharmacy (established in 1903 and discontinued in 1930), and the College of Dentistry (1918). In 1919 the Texas Baptist Memorial Sanitarium in Dallas became Baylor Memorial Hospital and was a part of the School of Medicine until 1943, when the school was transferred to Houston. Baylor Theological Seminary, established in 1905, became a separate institution, Southwestern Baptist Theological Seminary,[qv] in 1908 and was moved to Fort Worth in 1910. During the Brooks administration the enrollment grew, the campus was enlarged, four new buildings were erected, the summer term was made a regular part of the school year, the endowment was increased, and Baylor was admitted to membership in various college and university associations.

After Brooks's death, W. S. Allen, dean of the college, served as acting president until June 1932, when former governor Pat M. Neff,[qv] alumnus and president of the board of trustees, became president. Under Neff's direction the endowment was increased and salaries were raised; the campus was enlarged and landscaped; the departments of home economics, drama, and radio were added; library and laboratory facilities were improved and extended; four new buildings were built, and the Union Building was begun. In 1945, despite difficulties incident to World War II,[qv] Baylor celebrated her centennial anniversary. During the war the university instructed students for the army and navy. With the influx of veterans the enrollment reached 4,589 in the fall of 1947. Neff resigned on December 31, 1947, and was made president emeritus. W. T. Gooch, dean of the graduate school, was named president ad interim. William Richardson White[qv] was elected president in January 1948 and took office on February 1. Baylor University made unprecedented growth in both capital assets and academic standards during the thirteen-year administration of President White. Between 1948 and 1959 the university departments were affiliated with the highest accreditation agencies. Baylor's plant was increased in value some $10 million by the addition of eleven new buildings, including the Armstrong Browning Library,[qv] dormitories and apartments, a music hall, the School of Law, and a Bible building. Library holdings increased by 93,209 volumes between 1948 and 1965. The nucleus of the library collection was acquired in 1902, when the Erisophian, Philomathesian, Adelphian, Calleopean, and Burleson societies presented their libraries to the university. The F. L. Carroll Library, completed in 1903, was gutted by fire in 1922, but students were credited with saving most of the books. The rebuilt structure housed the main library. Special collections in music, theology, law, Texas studies, and Robert Browning supplemented the general library, which in 1969 consisted of 460,600 books and periodicals housed in fifteen units on the campus.

In June 1959 Judge Abner V. McCall, former dean of the School of Law, was made executive vice president with administrative responsibility, and White assumed public relations duties. In April 1962 McCall was named president of the university. That same year White became Baylor's first chancellor, and in 1963 he was president emeritus. McCall's administration was characterized by an emphasis on scholastic excellence with efforts to upgrade faculty, students, and facilities and to extend the graduate program. The university's College of Arts and Sciences provided special programs in American studies; B.S. degrees could be obtained in dental hygiene and preprofessional work in medical technology, physical therapy, dentistry, medicine, engineering, and forestry. A senior division of the United States Air Force Reserve Officers' Training Corps was located at Baylor. Doctoral programs were offered in English, chemistry, psychology, physics, and education. Graduate programs in many aspects of dentistry, medicine, and allied fields were sponsored in cooperation with the College of Medicine (Houston), the College of Dentistry (Dallas), and the Graduate Research Center (Dallas). The master of hospital administration degree was offered for military personnel in cooperation with the Medical Field Service School at Brooke Army Medical Center,[qv] Fort Sam Houston, and in 1971 a graduate program in physical therapy was added. In 1972 this facility changed its name to the Academy of Health Sciences of the United States Army.

By 1965 Baylor's enrollment at Waco, including 268 students in the School of Law, reached 6,432—considered the maximum figure consistent with available facilities. The administration and teaching staff totaled 364, of whom eighty-eight worked part-time. Approximately one-fourth of the faculty was involved in research, supported by various sources. Between 1845 and 1965 the institution graduated 36,121 students. In 1965, 74 percent of the students were Texans; the remainder represented every state in the Union and twenty-one foreign countries. Although Baptist in affiliation, Baylor had students from over thirty religious denominations.

Between 1960 and 1965 the Waco campus was extended by fifty-five acres; construction of a student health center, school of business, science building, and auxiliary buildings brought the investment in a total of thirty-two buildings to $24 million. A second science building was constructed, and a new library was ready for occupancy by 1968, when investments in Baylor's campuses at Waco, Dallas, and Houston totaled $53 million. The school also had $42 million in endowments and other investments and assets. In 1970 the enrollment was 6,532, and the faculty numbered 398. By 1974 the enrollment had increased to 8,130.

In 1994 Baylor was organized into the College of Arts and Sciences (founded in 1919), the Hankamer School of Business (organized in 1923 and renamed in 1959), the School of Education (organized in 1919), the Graduate School (organized in 1947), the School of Law (organized in 1857, closed in 1883, reopened in 1920), the School of Music (organized in 1919 as the College of Fine Arts and renamed in 1921), the School of Nursing (reorganized in 1950 to offer the B.S.N.), the University School (organized in 1987), and the Allied Graduate Program at Baylor College of Dentistry in Dallas and the United States Army Academy of Health Science in San Antonio. The University School operated the honors program, the university scholars program, and interdisciplinary-study programs in archeology, biblical and related languages, church-state studies, and environmental studies, as well as programs in American studies, Asian studies, Latin-American studies, Slavic studies, museum studies, and university studies.

Baylor holds accreditation and memberships in the Southern Association of Colleges and Schools, Association of American Colleges, American Council on Education, Southern Universities Conference, Texas Council on Church Related Colleges, Southern Association of Baptist Colleges and Schools, American Association of University Women,[qv] and American Society of Allied Health Professions. In addition, the various colleges, schools, and departments at Baylor hold numerous affiliations. The university offers a variety of bachelor degrees, including several in aviation sciences and home economics. The graduate programs include master's degrees in clinical gerontology, environmental science, international journalism, speech pathology and audiology, taxation, international management, and public policy and administration, and a Ph. D. in such fields as education and psychology. The campus library facilities include the Armstrong Browning Library; the Baylor Collections of Political Materials, which houses the manuscript collections of several former members of Congress and the Texas legislature; the Moody Memorial Library, which houses general collections, public services, circulation, government documents, music, periodicals, and reserves; the Jesse H. Jones[qv] Library, which houses the public service departments of the reference services and the science and engineering collections; the Texas Collection Library and Archives; University Libraries Technical Services; Academic Publications; Institute for Oral History; Regional Studies; and the Strecker Museum. A faculty of 611 served 11,810 students in 1991. Herbert Reynolds was president.

BIBLIOGRAPHY: Eugene W. Baker, *To Light the Ways of Time: An Illustrated History of Baylor University, 1845–1986* (Waco: Baylor University Press, 1987). Jefferson Davis Bragg, "Baylor University, 1851–1861," *Southwestern Historical Quarterly* 49 (July 1945). James Milton Carroll, *A History of Texas Baptists* (Dallas: Baptist Standard, 1923). Kent Keeth, *Looking Back at Baylor: A Collection of Historical Vignettes* (Waco: Baylor University, 1985). Zenos N. Morrell, *Flowers and Fruits from the Wilderness* (Boston: Gould and Lincoln, 1872; rpt. of 3d ed., Irving, Texas: Griffin Graphic Arts, 1966). *The Story of Baylor University at Independence, 1845–1886* (Waco: Baylor University, 1986).

Lillie M. Russell and Lois Smith Murray

BAYLOR UNIVERSITY MEDICAL CENTER. Baylor University Medical Center in Dallas began in 1903 as Good Samaritan Hospital, a two-story brick house converted into a private hospital. A year later, after being purchased by the Baptist General Convention of Texas, the hospital became Texas Baptist Memorial Sanitarium. Fifty-five years later, that institution became Baylor University Medical Center. BUMC comprises five connecting patient hospitals and a cancer center; Baylor is the second largest nonprofit private hospital in the United States. The center, licensed for 1,509 beds, treated 408,581 patients in fiscal 1992. As a major referral center, it offers specialized treatment centers for cancer, heart disease, diabetes, digestive diseases, alcohol and drug abuse, psoriasis, asthma, hair loss, breast disease, eating disorders, neonatology, pediatrics, infectious diseases, and weight management.

In 1943 the hospital faced a severe blow when its medical school, Baylor University College of Medicine (now Baylor College of Medicine), moved to Houston. The school's poor financial status, coupled with plans to build a second medical school in Dallas, precipitated its acceptance of an offer by the M. D. Anderson Foundation[qv] in Houston. Although the Dallas medical school officially graduated its last class in June 1943, the tradition of medical education continued at Baylor University Medical Center. Each year medical residents and fellows as well as nursing students complete their education there, and more than 300 individuals are trained in allied health sciences.

In addition to liver transplants, Baylor surgeons perform kidney, heart, lung, and bone marrow transplants. In 1987 Baylor's liver-transplant program, one of the largest adult programs in the United States, had the highest survival rate in the country. That year the National Institutes of Health named Baylor's program one of only five "centers of excellence." Like many major medical centers, Baylor supports medical research. The Baylor Research Institute underwrites much of the funding available for nine major areas targeted for study: digestive diseases, photobiology, transplantation biology, oncology, immunology, biomedical science, metabolic diseases, radiology, and surgical research. In all, Baylor sponsors 327 ongoing research projects.

Baylor University Medical Center is the hub of the Baylor Health Care System, a nonprofit network founded in 1981. The system comprises five North Texas hospitals: Baylor University Medical Center, Baylor Institute for Rehabilitation, and Baylor Medical centers at Ennis, Garland, Grapevine, and Waxahachie.

BIBLIOGRAPHY: Lana Henderson, *Baylor University Medical Center* (Waco: Baylor University Press, 1978). *Susan Hall*

BAYLOR UNIVERSITY SCHOOL OF NURSING. Baylor University School of Nursing was established in Dallas by Mildred Bridges, superintendent of nursing, as the Nurses' Training School of the Texas Baptist Memorial Sanitarium in October 1909. The sanitarium, chartered by the Baptist General Convention of Texas to replace Good Samaritan Hospital as the clinical facility for the Baylor University College of Medicine, reopened at that time in a new building. The first graduation exercises were held at Gaston Avenue Baptist Church during the summer of 1912.

Helen Holliday, a graduate of Johns Hopkins School of Nursing and Columbia University Teacher's College, assumed leadership of the school in 1912. She stabilized the institution, which had had seven superintendents during its first three years. The number of students and staff increased, and facilities were improved. A graded course of instruction lasting three scholastic years of nine months was implemented by the superintendent of nurses; new positions included an assistant to the supervisor, a head nurse of the operating room, and an instructor in dietetics. Lectures were given by the faculty of Baylor College of Medicine. Students were housed in residences in the immediate neighborhood. In 1915 an instructor of nurses, whose entire time was devoted to theoretical work with the students, was added. In 1918 a new building was completed, providing classroom and office space for the school as well as residence for the students and faculty. This building was known as the nurses' home and training-school building until 1945, when it was named Holliday Hall.

In 1921 the Baptist General Convention of Texas consolidated the Texas Baptist Memorial Sanitarium and the professional schools (medical, dental, pharmacy, and nursing). The hospital became Baylor Hospital, and the nursing school became Baylor Hospital School of Nursing. In 1936 the name was changed to Baylor University Hospital and Baylor University School of Nursing. These combined institutions were known as "Baylor-in-Dallas" and were regarded as integral parts of Baylor University. However, the School of Nursing continued to operate as a hospital-controlled nurses' training school. Although there was no national accreditation for schools of nursing at this time, the school was registered by the University of the State of New York through the New York Board of Nurse Examiners and the State Education Department of New York. The school was one of two schools in the Southwest to receive a Class A rating by the New York Board of Nurse Examiners. Holliday resigned when she married Dr. John Lehmann in 1923 but was asked to return as superintendent of nurses in 1930. Changes were made in the curriculum to conform with the standard curriculum published by the National League of Nursing Education.

Zora McAnelly Fiedler became superintendent of nursing and dean of the School of Nursing upon Lehmann's retirement in 1943. She accepted the position with the goal of establishing a baccalaureate school of nursing. The first step was eliminating the dual responsibilities for nursing service and education. A director of nursing service for Baylor Hospital was appointed in 1946. Application was made to the National League of Nursing Education for accreditation. The school ranked in Group I of the 1949 *Interim Classification of Institutions Offering Basic Programs in Nursing.*

A new plan of organization under the governing board of the School of Nursing was instituted in 1949. The School of Nursing would be directly under the control and supervision of an official of Baylor University in Waco. The headquarters of the school moved to Waco. Students in both diploma and degree courses studied their first year in Waco, then took two years of clinical work in Dallas. Those students desiring a degree returned to Waco for an additional year of study. By October 1950 the transfer of the School of Nursing to the Waco campus was complete. The first degree class had been admitted. Hillcrest Hospital in Waco and Arkansas Baptist Hospital in Little Rock, as well as Baylor Hospital in Dallas, provided sites for clinical work. The first baccalaureate degrees in nursing were awarded in 1954. Fiedler retired as dean of the school in 1951, after seeing her goal accomplished.

Temporary accreditation was approved by the National League of Nursing. By 1960 the school was in danger of being closed because of financial deficits. However, the Baylor-in-Dallas board of trustees agreed to supply the needed support so that the school could continue in a time of nursing shortages. The office of the dean was moved back to the Dallas campus, and clinical courses at Hillcrest and Arkansas Baptist Hospital were discontinued. Anne Taylor was appointed dean in 1962. Under her leadership the curriculum was revised, and the first full accreditation was awarded by the National League of Nursing in 1964.

Dr. Geddis McLaughlin, who became dean of the School of Nursing in 1964 after Taylor resigned, instituted the first integrated nursing curriculum in Texas. The school grew to more than 200 students in the nursing portion of the program. Dr. Opal Hipps was appointed dean following the retirement of McLaughlin in 1979. She was responsible for clarifying the relationship of the school to the hospital and to Baylor University. The dean again was responsible to a university official rather than the hospital administrator. Dr. Phyllis Karns became dean in 1987. A graduate program focusing on patient-care management was initiated in 1990.

BIBLIOGRAPHY: Dallas *Morning News*, May 9, 1964. Lana Henderson, *Baylor University Medical Center* (Waco: Baylor University Press, 1978). Powhatan W. James, *Fifty Years of Baylor University Hospital* (Dallas: Baylor University Hospital, 1953). *Linda F. Garner*

BAYOU, TEXAS (Sabine County). Bayou was nine miles southeast of Hemphill in southeastern Sabine County. The settlement received a post office in 1908 and had one rated business and a population estimated at thirty in 1933. The post office was closed in the late 1930s, but there is no evidence that the population had declined. In 1946 Bayou comprised a school, a business, and a population estimated at thirty. By 1955, however, the school district had been consolidated with that of Hemphill. The site of Bayou was inundated by Toledo Bend Reservoir, which became operational in 1968.

BIBLIOGRAPHY: *Water for Texas*, Vol. 1: *A Comprehensive Plan for the Future*; Vol. 2: *Technical Appendix* (Austin: Texas Department of Water Resources, 1984). *Cecil Harper, Jr.*

BAYOU, TEXAS (San Patricio County). Bayou, between San Patricio and Mathis on a bayou that drained an area of fertile San Patricio County land, was settled in the post–Civil War period. Thomas Bernard Magowan settled on a farm on the bayou in 1876, and other families followed until perhaps a dozen lived in the area. The community had its own school, administered by the schools of San Patricio, and the loose community of families considered themselves a settlement apart from San Patricio. The later history of Bayou is unknown; most of its area is now ranchland.

BIBLIOGRAPHY: Keith Guthrie, *History of San Patricio County* (Austin: Nortex, 1986). *Keith Guthrie*

BAYOU BEND. Bayou Bend, the estate of Ima Hogg,[qv] which now contains the Bayou Bend Collection of the Museum of Fine Arts, Houston,[qv] is located at 1 Westcott Street in the Homewoods section of River Oaks in Houston. The fourteen-acre estate slopes to the north from Lazy Lane, the street from which the grounds were entered during Miss Hogg's residence, down to a broad oxbow curve of Buffalo Bayou. The two-story, twenty-four-room house and an adjacent two-story garage and service building were designed and built between 1926 and 1928 for Ima Hogg and her two unmarried brothers, William C. Hogg[qv] and Michael (Mike) Hogg, the developers of River Oaks. John F. Staub[qv] was the architect, Birdsall P. Briscoe[qv] the associate architect, and Christian J. Miller the general contractor. The house cost about $217,000 to build. It is of tile block construction, finished externally with pink stucco, with a raised-seam copper roof. The house is tripartite in composition, with a central block and flanking wings. A double-height tetrastyle Tuscan portico is centered on the north elevation of the house, on an axis with a terraced lawn that steps down toward the Diana Garden and the bayou. The house is modeled stylistically on early-nineteenth-century English precedents, though many of its details were inspired by eighteenth and early-nineteenth-century houses of the American South. The result is an eclectic amalgam that Ima Hogg called "Latin Colonial" and considered especially appropriate to Houston. Houston landscape architect Ruth London designed the East Garden, and the north terrace and Diana Garden were the work of the firm of Fleming and Sheppard, also Houston landscape architects.

After the marriage of Mike Hogg in 1929 and the death of Will Hogg in 1930, Ima Hogg occupied the house alone until 1965. Beginning in 1920 with the purchase of an eighteenth-century American Queen Anne armchair, she gradually acquired an extensive collection and filled the house with seventeenth, eighteenth, and early-nineteenth-century American furniture, paintings, and artifacts. In 1956 she offered the estate and its contents to the Museum of Fine Arts, which accepted the gift in 1958. Conversion of the house into a museum began in the mid-1960s, though the principal rooms in the center of the house retain the character they had during Miss Hogg's residence. The Museum of Fine Arts opened the collection to the public on March 5, 1966. David B. Warren was the first curator of the collection.

The Bayou Bend Collection of American decorative arts and paintings is one of the finest such collections in the United States. It comprises works produced from the 1660s to the 1860s and is displayed in twenty-four settings within the house. Also included is a small collection of decorative arts that pertain to the Mexican War[qv] (1846–48). Located in the former garage and service building are a decorative-arts research library of some 3,000 volumes, a bookstore, and offices. The gardens are maintained under the supervision of the River Oaks Garden Club. The Friends of Bayou Bend, a members' support group, sponsors lectures and symposia. The house and gardens are open to the public by reservation. Bayou Bend was marked with a Texas Historical Commission[qv] marker in 1973 and was listed in the National Register of Historic Places in 1979.

BIBLIOGRAPHY: Howard Barnstone, *The Architecture of John F. Staub: Houston and the South* (Austin: University of Texas Press, 1979). Vertical Files, Barker Texas History Center, University of Texas at Austin (Houston Museum of Fine Arts). David B. Warren, *Bayou Bend: American Furniture, Paintings and Silver from the Bayou Bend Collection* (Boston: New York Graphic Society for the Museum of Fine Arts, Houston, 1975). *Stephen Fox*

BAYOU CARRIZO. Bayou Carrizo, also known as Carrizo Creek, rises a mile south of Appleby in east central Nacogdoches County (at 31°42′ N, 94°36′ W). It formerly flowed southeast for twenty-one miles to empty into the Angelina River near Kingtown. Since the construction of Sam Rayburn Reservoir[qv] in the mid-1960s, the creek has been inundated in its lower reaches and now enters the lake a mile north of Kingtown (at 31°25′ N, 94°31′ W). The stream is intermittent in its upper reaches. It traverses flat terrain with local shallow depressions, surfaced by clay and sandy loam that supports water-tolerant hardwoods, conifers, and grasses along the bank.

BAYOU CITY. The *Bayou City* was a small steamer used on mail, passenger, and freight service between Galveston and Houston before the Civil War.[qv] Although several of her passengers were killed during a boiler explosion in 1859, the *Bayou City* continued to ply the inland waters, and on September 26, 1861, the ship was leased for state service from the Houston Navigation Company by W. W. Hunter, the Confederate commander of the Texas Marine Department. Supplied with men and material from the former revenue schooner *Henry Dodge* and strengthened with bales of cotton and cottonseed against enemy attack, the *Bayou City* was operated by the state until purchased by the Confederate War Department in October 1862. After service as a police boat the *Bayou City,* along with the *Neptune,* led the Confederate assault on the small Union fleet in the battle of Galveston.[qv] Under the command of Capt. Henry S. Lubbock, the *Bayou City* carried one thirty-two-pound gun and some sixty volunteer riflemen commanded by Capt. Leon Smith against the more heavily armed *Harriet Lane.*[qv] The *Bayou City*'s single cannon burst after only a few rounds, and the *Neptune* was sunk in short order. Nonetheless, the *Bayou City* rammed the Union vessel, which her erstwhile marines boarded and captured. Little is known about the *Bayou City*'s fate after the recapture of Galveston. In June 1863 she was reported ready to steam at Harrisburg but had no armament. By March 1864 she had been moved to Galveston, where she mounted two heavy guns and a single brass cannon.

BIBLIOGRAPHY: *Civil War Naval Chronology, 1861–1865* (Washington: Naval History Division, Department of the Navy, 1961–66; rpt. 1971). Charles C. Cumberland, "The Confederate Loss and Recapture of Galveston, 1862–1863," *Southwestern Historical Quarterly* 51 (October 1947). *Official Records of the Union and Confederate Navies,* Vol. 19). *Robert Wooster*

BAYOU CREEK. Bayou Creek, formerly known as Arroyo Nombre de Dios or Creek of the Name of God, rises at the Live Oak–San Patricio–Bee county line (at 28°12′ N, 97°49′ W) and runs south for fifteen miles to its mouth on the Nueces River, four miles south of Mathis at the San Patricio–Jim Wells county line (at 28°02′ N, 97°48′ W). It crosses flat to rolling terrain surfaced by deep, fine sandy loam that supports hardwood forest, brush, and grasses.

BAYOU DIN. Bayou Din rises seven miles north of Fannett in central Jefferson County (30°01′ N, 94°15′ W) and flows southeast for sixteen miles to its mouth on Hillebrandt Bayou, ten miles south of Beaumont (at 29°57′ N, 94°08′ W). The stream is marshy and intermittent in its upper reaches. Much of the surrounding land is used for rice culture.[qv] Two pumping stations on minor tributaries of Bayou Din aid efforts at irrigation and drainage.

BAYOU LA NANA. Bayou La Nana (Lanana) rises three miles north of the Nacogdoches city limits in north central Nacogdoches County (at 31°42′ N, 94°36′ W) and flows southwest, through the center of Nacogdoches, for eighteen miles to its mouth on the Angelina River, one mile southeast of Procella (at 31°28′ N, 94°43′ W). The stream is intermittent in its upper reaches. It traverses flat terrain with local shallow depressions, surfaced by clay and sandy loams that support water-tolerant hardwoods, conifers, and grasses close to the stream.

BAYOU LOCO. Bayou Loco, also known as Loco Creek, rises just south of Caro in north central Nacogdoches County (at 31°44′ N, 94°41′ W) and runs southwest for twenty-two miles to its mouth on the Angelina River, three miles west of Procella (at 31°29′ N, 94°48′ W). The stream has been dammed just north of Farm Road 225 to form Lake Nacogdoches. Bayou Loco is intermittent in its upper reaches. It traverses flat terrain with local shallow depressions, surfaced by clay and sandy loam that supports water-tolerant hardwoods, conifers, and grasses.

BAYOU SIEPE. Bayou Siepe (Siepe Bayou or Sip Bayou) rises eleven miles southeast of Center in southeastern Shelby County (at 31°43′ N, 94°01′ W) and runs east for ten miles to its mouth on Toledo Bend Reservoir (at 31°43′ N, 93°52′ W). The surrounding terrain is nearly level and is surfaced by clay and loam. The streambed is wholly within the boundaries of Sabine National Forest.[qv]

BAYS, JOSEPH L. (1786–1854). Joseph L. Bays, Baptist minister, was born on December 28, 1786, in North Carolina to Isaiah and Abigail (March) Bays. Isaiah Bays, a Scots-Irish nonconformist, died near Boonesboro, Kentucky, when Joseph was seven. Abigail taught her children to memorize and read from the Bible, and Joseph Bays was preaching at the age of sixteen. In Missouri, at the age of eighteen, he married Rosenia (or Roseina) Whicher; they had three children. In 1825 the family came with thirty-two others to Texas. Although Stephen F. Austin[qv] granted Bays a league and a labor of land in June 1825 and Bays preached at Moses Shipman's[qv] home the same year, he left Texas because he was hindered from preaching by the authorities. He therefore settled in Louisiana and crossed the Sabine River to preach in Texas. In 1827 he moved to the area of present San Augustine County, Texas, where he was arrested by Mexican authorities for preaching a religion other than Catholic. Bays again left Texas but again returned and lived in the area of present San Augustine County in 1833–34, then left Texas yet again on the advice of his friends. He fought several battles against Indians before 1836. He returned to Texas in 1839 and lived in Montgomery County. On July 10, 1839, he petitioned the Republic of Texas[qv] Congress for compensation for his land, but the petition was denied. In 1846 missionaries of the Church of Jesus Christ of Latter Day Saints came through Texas, and Bays's wife and son Henry joined the Mormons.[qv] Bays petitioned the Texas legislature on April 9, 1851, for the return of his land, and this time the petition was granted. Bays died at the home of his daughter Susan DeMoss in June 1854 and was buried in Matagorda County, Texas.

BIBLIOGRAPHY: James Milton Carroll, *A History of Texas Baptists* (Dallas: Baptist Standard, 1923). Dan Ferguson, "Forerunners of Baylor," *Southwestern Historical Quarterly* 49 (July 1945). Zenos N. Morrell, *Flowers and Fruits from the Wilderness* (Boston: Gould and Lincoln, 1872; rpt. of 3d ed., Irving, Texas: Griffin Graphic Arts, 1966). Daniel Shipman, *Frontier Life: 58 Years in Texas* (1879).

Samuel B. Hesler

BAYSIDE, TEXAS. Bayside, on Farm Road 136 twenty-five miles north of Corpus Christi in southeastern Refugio County, stretches more than 3½ miles along the southwestern shore of Copano Bay. The town was founded near the site of the former community of Black Point in 1908 by E. O. Burton and A. H. Danforth, who sought to attract fruit and vegetable growers to the area. Burton and Danforth had part of their property divided into 505 five-acre tracts designed for truck farming. The original townsite consisted of nineteen blocks and one hotel block; land along the shore was set aside for use as public parks. The proprietors also built a bathhouse and a wharf for community use. A well was drilled at the edge of town to provide free water to residents. Burton and Davenport were experienced developers and advertised nationwide. A purchaser of a five-acre tract was to receive a town lot. Although many people bought property with the intention of becoming residents, most of the land was purchased by speculators. The demand for land was overwhelming, and to comply with all the orders for property, Burton and Danforth acquired and subdivided what remained of the abandoned townsite of St. Mary's of Aransas,[qv] two miles to the northeast. They annexed this property to Bayside in 1909 and 1910.

A Bayside post office was established in 1909, but residents had to travel by dirt road to Woodsboro, eighteen miles away, or by boat or stage to Rockport, twelve miles across the bay, for shipping and banking transactions. In 1912 Bayside citizens built a wooden schoolhouse. In 1946 the school was consolidated with the Woodsboro Independent School District. The Church of Christ of Bayside built its first church in 1913 with lumber shipped by barge from Rockport. Other groups, including Methodists, Catholics, Baptists, and Presbyterians, also used the building. Bayside acquired electricity in 1926, when Central Power and Light built a highline to the town. In 1919 a hurricane destroyed the local wharves, outbuildings, nearby bridges, and at least three homes. Another hurricane in August 1942 resulted in even greater devastation. (*See* HURRICANES.)

Of the initial purchasers who came with the intention of settling in Bayside, an estimated twenty to twenty-five remained. Many of those who had bought property for speculative purposes let their taxes go unpaid, and in 1938 hundreds of the tracts and town lots were sold at a tax sale. Bayside had estimated populations of 300 in 1914–15 and seventy-five in 1925. The population subsequently climbed slowly to 383 by 1988. In 1990 it was 400. The town was incorporated in 1977. Bayside's economy is largely based on tourism and fishing. Maj. John H. Wood[qv] built a magnificent home in Bayside in 1875; it was still standing in 1989.

BIBLIOGRAPHY: Katharine E. Henkel and Bobbye Warrick, *Sketches of Refugio* (1976). Hobart Huson, *Refugio: A Comprehensive History of Refugio County from Aboriginal Times to 1953* (2 vols., Woodsboro, Texas: Rooke Foundation, 1953, 1955). *History of Refugio County* (Dallas: Curtis, 1985).

June Melby Benowitz

BAYTOWN, TEXAS. Baytown, a highly industrialized city of oil refining, rubber, chemical, and carbon black plants, is on Interstate Highway 10 and State Highway 146, thirty miles east of downtown Houston in southeastern Harris and western Chambers counties. Among its first settlers were Nathaniel Lynch,[qv] who in 1822 set up a ferry crossing at the junction of the San Jacinto River with Buffalo Bayou that is still in operation, and William Scott,[qv] one of Stephen F. Austin's[qv] Old Three Hundred,[qv] who received a land grant in 1824. His two leagues and one labor of land, over 9,000 acres, covered most of the area of present Baytown. Near his home on San Jacinto (Scott's) Bay, a settlement grew to include a small store and a sawmill. It was called Bay Town.

Later area settlers included Ashbel Smith,[qv] who in 1847 purchased a plantation named Evergreen on Tabbs Bay. He lived there for forty-nine years. Also living in the area for a time were Mrs. Anson (Mary Smith McCrory) Jones, David G. Burnet, and Sam Houston.[qqv] At the outbreak of the Civil War[qv] Smith organized a local unit called the Bayland Guards for Confederate service. They later became part of the Second Texas Regiment and saw action at Shiloh and Vicksburg.

A shipyard established at the mouth of Goose Creek in the early

1850s by John and Thomas S. Chubb built one ship, the *Bagdad*, which was launched in 1864 and had to run a Yankee blockade at Galveston to escape. In 1867 Dr. Smith and several associates founded the Bayland Orphans' Home for Children of Confederate soldiers (*see* BAYLAND ORPHANS' HOME FOR BOYS) on the west side of Goose Creek. The orphanage moved into Houston in 1888 and became the DePelchin Faith Home (*see* DEPELCHIN, KEZIA PAYNE).

The area, though, remained largely undeveloped and isolated into the twentieth century. A rough county road ran from Crosby to Cedar Bayou, a small community of stores, shipyards, and brickyards. The only other entry into the area was by boat. Then, in 1908, after two unsuccessful drilling attempts, an oil strike was made beside Tabbs Bay. In 1916 the Goose Creek oilfield[qv] became famous as the first offshore drilling operation in Texas (second in the nation) and the third-largest producing field, after the Humble and Sour Lake oilfields.[qqv]

The towns of Pelly and Goose Creek developed near the oilfield in 1917–18. In 1917 Ross S. Sterling[qv] and his associates decided to build a refinery near the Goose Creek field and founded the Humble Oil and Refining Company (Exxon Company, U.S.A.[qv]). They bought some 2,200 acres in the William Scott survey and called their site Baytown. Construction began in the fall of 1919.

Baytown grew up around the refinery. At first the community was only a collection of army tents, barracks, and small shacks; it became permanent in 1923 when Humble laid out streets, provided utilities, sold lots, and even furnished financing for employees' homes. Humble also furnished housing for its supervisors and skilled employees in a special "company addition" and built a large community building for their recreational needs. A special management-labor Joint Conference was formed to handle work-related problems. Later, this group also discussed municipal problems and became, in effect, the city council for the community. These and other employee-relations programs were initiated to reduce labor problems like those that had occurred in the Texas-Louisiana oilfield strike of 1917. Leading up to that incident, management policies, inflation, and poor working conditions had brought about the organization of a union local in Goose Creek in December 1916. When the oil producers refused to discuss grievances with union representatives in October 1917, 2,000 Goose Creek workers joined approximately 10,000 oilfield workers in seventeen Texas and Louisiana oilfields in a walkout on November 1, 1917. With hired guards and army troops maintaining order, the producers negotiated directly with the Department of Labor in January 1918 and effected a settlement that rejected all significant union demands. This near total victory for the producers undermined union effectiveness for several years. In the late 1930s and early 1940s the Congress of Industrial Organizations made several attempts to represent Humble employees instead of the Joint Conference, and later the Baytown Employees Federation attempted to organize, but each time Humble employees voted for the company union by large margins.

Due to this pervasive paternalism of Humble, the community of Baytown never incorporated, and this enabled Pelly to annex the "contiguous and unincorporated" territory of Baytown in December 1945. But, when Pelly and Goose Creek voted to consolidate in early 1947, the citizens selected the name Baytown for their new combined city. On January 24, 1948, the city of Baytown was established.

Baytown grew in population from 20,958 in 1948 to 67,117 in 1990 and in area from 7½ square miles to more than thirty-two. Its boundaries stretch from near the San Jacinto River eastward into Chambers County and include several former communities such as Cedar Bayou and Wooster.

Exxon, still a major employer, runs one of more than ten major petrochemical plants now in the Baytown area. In 1970 United States Steel opened the Texas Works near Baytown, and during its peak years the plant employed more than 2,000 workers with an annual payroll of $35 million. Due to the nation's economic downturn and the decline of American steel in the early 1980s, the plant closed in July 1986.

In 1992 Baytown had twenty-three public schools, Lee College (a two-year community college), sixty-seven churches, seven banks, two savings and loan associations, three credit unions, three modern hospitals, a daily newspaper, a radio station, cable television, and a large public library. One of the nation's largest single-level shopping malls houses major retailers and employs nearly 2,000. The city is served by two railroads, an interstate highway, and, since September 1953, the Baytown–La Porte Tunnel, which crossed the Houston Ship Channel.[qv] In the mid-1990s an eight-lane, 450-foot, twin-tower suspension bridge replaced the forty-year-old tunnel.

BIBLIOGRAPHY: Anne Rebecca Daniels, Baytown during the Depression, 1929–1933 (M.A. thesis, Lamar University, 1981; Ann Arbor: University Microfilms, 1983). Margaret Swett Henson, *History of Baytown* (Baytown, Texas: Bay Area Heritage Society, 1986). Henrietta M. Larson and Kenneth Wiggins Porter, *History of Humble Oil and Refining Company* (New York: Harper, 1959). Walter Rundell, Jr., *Early Texas Oil: A Photographic History, 1866–1936* (College Station: Texas A&M University Press, 1977). Buck A. Young, "A Remembered Utopia," *East Texas Historical Journal* 20 (1982).

Buck A. Young

BAYVIEW, TEXAS. Bayview was a row of houses and scattered dwellings on Galveston Bay north of present Farm Road 646 and east of State Highway 146, between Kemah and Clifton-by-the-Sea in northwest Galveston County. A post office operated there from 1902 until 1913, when mail was rerouted to Kemah. The community appeared on state highway maps as late as 1937. After 1936 the settlement was taken in by the adjacent communities of Kemah and Bacliff.

Diana J. Kleiner

BAY VIEW COLLEGE. Bay View College, in Portland, San Patricio County, was founded in 1893 by Alice and Thomas M. Clark,[qv] members of the family that established Texas Christian University (then called Add-Ran College) in Thorp Springs. The Clarks took over a vacant twenty-room hotel in Portland, built during a land boom that fizzled. During the first two years of operation students from the public school system in Portland attended the college, a move approved by the local school board to help the college get started. The state granted a charter in 1897 authorizing the school to grant degrees. As the institution grew, additional buildings were built—dormitories for boys and girls, a chapel, a gymnasium, and a number of utility buildings. In 1903 tuition and board were listed at fifteen dollars a month. At its peak the college had 164 boarding students enrolled from twenty-two Texas counties. Over 2,000 students went through the school in its twenty-three years of operation. The chapel was used by the community for church services and as a meeting place for community events. Enrollment declined as public schools in Texas began to fill educational needs. The school was closed after the storm of 1916 seriously damaged the college buildings (*see* HURRICANES).

BIBLIOGRAPHY: Cecil Eugene Evans, *The Story of Texas Schools* (Austin: Steck, 1955). Keith Guthrie, *History of San Patricio County* (Austin: Nortex, 1986). Vertical Files, Barker Texas History Center, University of Texas at Austin.

Keith Guthrie

BAZETTE, TEXAS. Bazette, on Farm Road 636 near the Trinity River in northeast Navarro County, was established around 1845 on the river, but the settlers had to move to higher ground because of floods. A Baptist preacher named Bazette operated a ferry on the Trinity River. Some of the early settlers were the Barnetts, the Ellisons, John Street, and a Baptist parson named Rickman. The post office was established in 1847 by a man named Ellison but was closed in 1851; it was reopened in 1874 and moved in 1906. Bazette had a population of 300 in 1884 and 250 in 1890. Its largest population, 400, was recorded in 1896, when the town had three general stores, a gristmill, three churches, and a school. In 1904 the population was 100. In 1906 Bazette had one school with eighty-seven students. The town's population was listed as 250 from 1933 until 1944, when it was recorded as 150. In 1949 only twenty residents remained, but the community reported a population of thirty in 1964 and 1990.

Bazette was a religious center for Navarro County in the mid-1800s. People from many miles away traveled to congregate in a grove of oak trees and hear sermons of local ministers. A regularly convened camp meeting developed. Most of Bazette's early pioneers are buried near the oak grove in Prairie Point Cemetery. In the 1930s the town had two schools, two churches, and a number of scattered dwellings, as well as a row of homes and businesses. Highway maps of the 1980s showed Bazette as a community with a cemetery and a church. The town still held a yearly picnic and revival meeting at Prairie Point Cemetery.

BIBLIOGRAPHY: Alva Taylor, *History and Photographs of Corsicana and Navarro County* (Corsicana, Texas, 1959; rev. ed., *Navarro County History and Photographs*, Corsicana, 1962). *Molly McKee*

BEACH, HARRISON LEROY (1863–1942). Harrison Leroy Beach, newspaperman, son of Myron H. and Helen Mary (Hoskins) Beach, was born in Dubuque, Iowa, on January 12, 1863. He entered newspaper work in Chicago in 1889 and was with the Associated Press from 1892 to 1911. He was a correspondent at Santiago, Cuba, and other points during the Spanish–American War. For many years he was superintendent of the central division of the Associated Press, with headquarters at Chicago, and represented the organization at national political conventions. He married Jesse M. Bowen on September 5, 1905. With Charles P. Taft, Charles S. Diehl, and others, Beach owned and published the San Antonio *Light* [qv] from 1921 to May 1924. He died in San Antonio on February 18, 1942.

BIBLIOGRAPHY: *Who Was Who in America,* Vol. 1.

BEACH CREEK. Beach Creek rises three miles northwest of Linden in central Cass County (33°03′ N, 94°23′ W) and flows southeast for seven miles to its mouth on Iron Ore Lake, three miles southeast of Linden (at 32°58′ N, 94°20′ W). The stream, intermittent in its upper and middle reaches, traverses gently undulating to rolling terrain surfaced by loamy soils. The downstream area has been the site of extensive strip-mining.

BEACH MOUNTAINS. The Beach Mountains are located two miles northwest of Van Horn in southwestern Culberson County (with their center at 31°08′ N, 104°51′ W). Their highest elevation is 5,827 feet above sea level. The mountains are a domed and faulted block of Ordovician and Cambrian rocks, some 500 million years old; Precambrian rocks more than 570 million years old are found on their western flanks. The Beach Mountains, along with the Baylor and Sierra Diablo Mountains, form an uplifted block along the western edge of a broad valley of salt flats. They are steep and rocky and surfaced by shallow, stony soil that supports live oaks, piñons, junipers, and grasses. The mountains are named for J. H. Beach, a pioneer settler who arrived in Van Horn in 1886.

BEACON LIGHT LAKE. Beacon Light Lake, a playa, is 2½ miles northeast of Wheat oilfield and a half mile west of Rudd Draw in south central Loving County (at 31°47′ N, 103°34′ W). The lake is surrounded by flat to rolling desert terrain of calichefied bedrock, alluvial deposits of sand and gravel, and windblown sand. The soil is fine-grained, brownish-red, loamy sand. Area vegetation consists primarily of small mesquites, yuccas, bear grass, and sparse range grasses. Beacon Light Lake is representative of the many playas in Loving County. Immature streambeds and normally dry draws feed rainwater into these shallow depressions, which vary in size from a few feet to hundreds of rods. The playas become sheets of water after downpours and disappear gradually through evaporation. They may provide some groundwater for livestock, but they are never dependable or long-term sources. Beacon Light Lake was likely named for a nearby signal tower.

BEADLE, TEXAS. Beadle was on the St. Louis, Brownsville and Mexico Railway twelve miles southwest of Bay City in southwestern Matagorda County. The settlement was established in the early 1900s as an irrigated farm project managed by Levi E. Beadle. In 1910 it secured a post office with Beadle as postmaster. That year the Ashby Mill and Warehouse Company operated a store, and the population was fifty. By 1914 the community had a telephone connection, but population estimates remained unchanged. The post office ceased operation in 1918, and by 1920 the Ashby Company had closed its store. By 1936 the community no longer appeared on county highway maps.

BIBLIOGRAPHY: Matagorda County Historical Commission, *Historic Matagorda County* (3 vols., Houston: Armstrong, 1986).

Stephen L. Hardin

BEAD MOUNTAIN. Bead Mountain is located a mile from Valera in the west central part of Coleman County (at 31°45′ N, 99°35′ W). It has an elevation of 2,050 feet and rises from stairstep terrain with steep slopes and benches surfaced by shallow clay loams that support juniper, live oak, mesquite, and glasses.

BEAD MOUNTAIN CREEK. Bead Mountain Creek rises north of Bead Mountain and west of Valera in west central Coleman County (at 31°45′ N, 99°36′ W) and runs southeast for four miles to join Home Creek (at 31°45′ N, 99°33′ W). The stream runs through steep slopes surfaced by shallow clay loams that support juniper, live oak, mesquite, and grasses.

BIBLIOGRAPHY: Glenn A. Gray, *Gazetteer of Streams of Texas* (Washington: GPO, 1919).

BEAL, JOHN T. (1847–1916). John T. Beal, son of John and Mary (Cullins) Beal, was born in Milam County, Texas, on October 24, 1847. He attended school at Salado during the winter of 1866–67 before beginning a freighting business between Cameron and Bryan. He was also in the lumber trade at Belton for a time. He later entered the cattle business with J. W. Powers and drove several herds of cattle to Kansas. He and his son H. D. moved a herd of cattle to Borden County in 1879. In 1880 Beal became general manager and part owner of the Jumbo Cattle Company. When the company failed in 1898, he became foreman of the St. Louis Cattle Company in Crosby County. He moved to Lubbock in 1900 and to Ranger Lake, New Mexico, about 1905. Beal was married to Anna Stoneham and was the father of eight children. He ranched in New Mexico until his death, at Elida, New Mexico, on December 24, 1916.

BIBLIOGRAPHY: James Cox, *Historical and Biographical Record of the Cattle Industry* (2 vols., St. Louis: Woodward and Tiernan Printing, 1894, 1895; rpt., with an introduction by J. Frank Dobie, New York: Antiquarian, 1959).

BEALES, JOHN CHARLES (1804–1878). John Charles Beales, speculator in Texas lands, the son of John Charles and Sarah (Waller) Beales, was born at Alburgh, Norfolk County, England, on March 20, 1804. Upon completion of a six-year course of study at St. George's Hospital, London, in 1826, he accepted appointment as company surgeon at a salary of $3,000 per year with the Tlalpujahua Mining Association, a British-backed venture in the Mexican state of Michoacán. After that company halted its operations in October 1828 Beales entered private practice in Mexico City, and he later served on the hospital staffs of the state of Mexico and of the Federal District. Before 1833 he gave up the practice of medicine to devote his time to promoting the development of several empresario[qv] contracts he acquired in the region north of the Rio Grande. He resumed medical practice in New York City in 1835 in partnership with Dr. William Barrow. For many years thereafter he was a medical examiner for the Eagle and Albion Life Insurance companies. He continued the practice of medicine until the 1870s.

On August 3, 1830, Beales married María Dolores Soto y Saldaña, the widow of Richard Exter,[qv] an English merchant and land speculator, who had left his widow and infant daughter his interests in two empresario contracts of 1826 and 1828 encompassing some 48 million acres in eastern New Mexico, the Texas and Oklahoma panhandles, and southeastern Colorado; Exter had held these contracts jointly with Stephen Julian Wilson.[qv] Beales and his wife had four children. Within weeks of his marriage Beales took over the management of these contracts for his wife and stepdaughter. In New York on April 27, 1831, he transferred their interests to the Arkansas and Texas Land Company.

After this, Beales entered the empresario sweepstakes on a grand scale and for his own account. In an eight-month period in 1832 he persuaded officials of the state of Coahuila and Texas[qv] to grant him and three different sets of partners three empresario contracts for an estimated 55 million acres of land north of the Rio Grande. The first of these, dated March 14, authorized Beales and José Manuel Royuela to settle 200 families on the same tract originally granted Stephen Julian Wilson in 1826. The second, issued on May 1, permitted the so-called Mexican Company (Beales and three Mexican partners) to locate 450 families on some 2 million acres in two parcels lying between the Colorado and Guadalupe rivers that had been granted to Green DeWitt[qv] in 1825 and Benjamin Rush Milam[qv] in 1826. The third, dated October 9, permitted Beales and Dr. James Grant[qv] to settle 800 families on 8 million acres in two separate tracts—one lying between the Rio Grande and the Nueces, the other including that portion of the 1826 grant to John Lucius Woodbury and Joseph Vehlein[qqv] lying east of the 100th meridian.

In addition to his role in securing these empresario contracts, Beales appears to have masterminded the actions of his wife and eight other Mexican citizens, each of whom, on October 16–18, purchased in fee simple an eleven-league tract of "unoccupied land" in the Department of Monclova. In the week after acquiring title, each of the purchasers gave Beales a power of attorney granting him the authority to sell or transfer title to his respective purchase.

Armed with these authorizations and those of his partners in the empresario contracts, Beales again approached New York speculators. Between April 1833 and January 1835 he was intimately involved in the machinations of the directors of three land companies to which he sold his interests in the lands over which he had acquired control in 1832. To the New Arkansas and Texas Land Company, established in 1833, he ceded one-half of his interest in the Beales-Royuela grant; to the Rio Grande and Texas Land Company he deeded a large part of the Beales-Grant contract and the nine eleven-league purchases; and to the Colorado and Red River Land Company he transferred control over approximately one-half of the land in the Mexican Company contract lying between the Colorado and Guadalupe rivers. In addition he concluded agreements with a number of individuals, including John Woodward,[qv] to whom he passed title to some 4 million acres in different grants.

During the same period Beales spent much time and money recruiting colonists for a colonization project located between the Rio Grande and Nueces. In the end he was able to persuade fewer than 100 persons to settle at Dolores, the village named for his wife that he established in the area of present Kinney County on Las Moras Creek, some eighteen miles above its junction with the Rio Grande. Beales's attempt to plant a colony in that dry region came to an end when the colonists abandoned the site after the outbreak of the Texas Revolution.[qv]

From 1836 until his death Beales sporadically fought in the courts and the legislative halls of the United States and Texas to validate his claims to lands in Texas and adjoining states. For the most part, neither judges nor legislators looked favorably on his petitions or his suits. His heirs were able to salvage only a fraction of the millions of acres to which he once had laid claim. After his death their titles to the eleven-league purchases in Southwest Texas were upheld by the courts.

Beales's dreams of gaining great wealth from his land grants were not fulfilled. In the absence of his journals and financial records, it is impossible to estimate how much he received from the transfer of his interests to the land companies. The total must have been considerable, if, as reported, the Rio Grande and Texas Land Company paid him as much as $100,000 for a portion of his interests in several grants.

Beales was admitted to membership in the Royal College of Surgeons of England in 1839. In 1835 he had become a life member of St. George's Society in New York City and later served as its president. In 1847 he became a fellow of the New York Academy of Medicine. Described by a contemporary as one of the most handsome men he had ever seen, Beales, who stood about five feet eleven inches and weighed about 170 pounds, was described as a "tall, well-built specimen of an Englishman, fond of society, a giant in energy, and a Demosthenes in speech." He became a United States citizen on May 29, 1850, and died in New York City on July 25, 1878. His wife had died in 1873.

BIBLIOGRAPHY: Lucy Lee Dickson, Speculation of John Charles Beales in Texas Lands (M.A. thesis, University of Texas, 1941). Raymond Estep, "The First Panhandle Land Grant," *Chronicles of Oklahoma* 36 (Winter 1958–59). Mary Virginia Henderson, "Minor Empresario Contracts for the Colonization of Texas, 1825–1834," *Southwestern Historical Quarterly* 31, 32 (April, July 1928). Carl Coke Rister, *Comanche Bondage: Dr. John Charles Beales's Settlement of La Villa de Dolores on Las Moras Creek in Southern Texas of the 1830s* (Glendale, California: Clark, 1955).
Raymond Estep

BEALES'S RIO GRANDE COLONY. On November 11, 1833, the *Amos Wright* sailed from New York for Texas with fifty-nine men, women, and children aboard, the vanguard of a proposed colony backed by the Rio Grande and Texas Land Company and under command of John Charles Beales.[qv] From 1830 to 1832 Beales and other contractors had received several colonial grants totaling more than fifty million acres and embracing much of western Texas, eastern New Mexico, and the Rio Grande valley. On May 1 and October 9, 1832, Beales and James Grant[qv] had acquired two tracts and obligated themselves to settle 800 families in the region between the Rio Grande and the Nueces; they set up the joint stock company to promote their venture.

The first colonists landed at Copano Bay on December 12, 1833, and journeyed in ox wagons to their destination. The site chosen for the colony was on Las Moras Creek, a short distance down the Rio Grande from Presidio del Rio Grande and a few miles up the creek from its confluence with the river. Here, on March 12, 1834, the emigrants—American, English, German, and Spanish American—planted their settlement and named it Dolores, in honor of Beales's Mexican wife. Although the colony was in an inhospitable country, semiarid, and overgrown with dense thickets of mesquite, chaparral, and prickly pear, the settlers cleared out the flats along the stream, plowed their fields, and experimented with irrigation. They set up a saw and grist mill, built jacals and brush huts and a church, organized a government, and prepared for permanent occupation.

Beales brought at least one other band of colonists to Dolores, and the settlement grew in spite of marauding Indians and drought. But the colony was doomed to failure. Blighted crops and poor prospects caused general disappointment, and the settlers left in ones and twos for the Mexican town of San Fernando or elsewhere. The outbreak of the Texas Revolution[qv] and Antonio López de Santa Anna's[qv] invasion with a large army to drive Americans out of Texas caused a general exodus. One large wagon train was attacked by Comanche Indians on the Matamoros road, and all the settlers were massacred except two women and their small children, who were taken captive.

BIBLIOGRAPHY: Lucy Lee Dickson, Speculation of John Charles Beales in Texas Lands (M.A. thesis, University of Texas, 1941). Carl Coke Rister, *Comanche Bondage: Dr. John Charles Beales's Settlement of La Villa de Dolores on Las Moras Creek in Southern Texas of the 1830s* (Glendale, California: Clark, 1955). Carl Coke Rister, "The Rio Grande Colony," *Southwest Review* 25 (July 1940).

Carl Coke Rister

BEALL, BENJAMIN LOYD (?–1863). Benjamin Loyd Beall, United States Army officer, was born in Washington, D.C. He was admitted to the United States Military Academy at West Point on January 1, 1814, but left on October 15, 1818, without graduating. He was elected captain of the Washington City Volunteers for service in the Seminole War on June 1, 1836, and was commissioned as a captain of the Second Dragoons in the regular United States Army on June 8, 1836. He was brevetted major on March 15, 1837, "for gallantry and successful service" against the Florida Indians. In April 1846 he was stationed in San Antonio, where he was ordered to escort German immigrants to Fredericksburg and the Pedernales. He was promoted to major of the First Dragoons on February 16, 1847, and on March 16, 1847, received a second brevet, to lieutenant colonel, for his part in the battle of Santa Cruz de Rosales. After the Mexican War[qv] he was stationed in New Mexico until February 1848, when he took the First Dragoons into El Paso and established Fort Bliss. He remained at the new post for only a few months, however, and was responsible for no construction. He was promoted to the substantive grade of lieutenant colonel on March 3, 1855. At the beginning of the Civil War,[qv] on May 3, 1861, he was promoted to colonel; he was then assigned to command the First Cavalry, formerly the First Dragoons, on August 3, 1861. Colonel Beal retired from active duty on February 15, 1862, and died in Maryland on August 16, 1863.

BIBLIOGRAPHY:Albert G. Brackett, *History of the United States Cavalry* (New York: Harper, 1865). Francis B. Heitman, *Historical Register and Dictionary of the United States Army* (2 vols., Washington: GPO, 1903; rpt., Urbana: University of Illinois Press, 1965).

Thomas W. Cutrer

BEALL, JACK ANDREW (1866–1929). Jack Andrew Beall, lawyer, congressman, and business executive, the son of Richard and Adelaide (Pierce) Beall, was born at Mountain Peak, Texas, on October 25, 1866. He attended public schools in Ellis County, then attended the University of Texas from 1886 to 1889. He was admitted to the bar in 1890 and returned to Ellis County, where he established a law office in Waxahachie. He served in the Texas House as a Democrat for one term, 1892–94, before entering the State Senate in 1894. He left the legislature in 1898 to return to private practice. Early that year he married Patricia Martin of Waxahachie. The couple had one child. Beall returned to the campaign trail in 1903 and was elected representative of the Fifth District of Texas to the Fifty-eighth Congress. He was reelected until he retired from public office at the end of the Sixty-third Congress, in 1915. After his retirement he moved to Dallas to become a partner in the legal firm of M. B. Templeton and Tony B. Williams. He concentrated on his legal career until June 1921, when he became president of the Texas Electric Railway upon the death of J. F. Strickland. Two years later Templeton died, and Beall became the senior partner in the reorganized law firm, now known as Beall, Watson, Rollins, Burford, and Ryburn. In addition, he was elected president of Dallas Union Trust Company in 1927. He was a Mason and a Methodist. Beall died of a heart attack in Dallas on February 11, 1929.

BIBLIOGRAPHY: *Biographical Directory of the American Congress.* Dallas *Morning News*, February 13, 1929. *Who Was Who in America*, Vol. 2.

David Minor

BEALL, THOMAS J. (1836–1921). Thomas J. Beall, attorney and Confederate officer, son of Dr. Jeremiah and Susan V. (Neal) Beall, was born at Thomaston, Georgia, on May 12, 1836. He received his primary and secondary education in local schools. After moving with his family to Marshall, Texas, in 1850, he attended Tulane College in New Orleans, Louisiana, and subsequently entered the law department of Cumberland University in Lebanon, Tennessee, where he graduated in 1858. He then returned to Marshall and practiced law until the onset of the Civil War.[qv]

Beall joined the Confederate Army as a member of the Marshall Guards, a company organized and commanded by Capt. Khleber Miller Van Zandt.[qv] After serving in the initial battles near Vicksburg, Mississippi, he took part in the first battle of Fort Donelson, Tennessee, where he was wounded and captured on February 16, 1861. He was exchanged for captured Union soldiers in September of that year and participated in the defense of Vicksburg when the city was assaulted by Gen. William T. Sherman.[qv] After Sherman's defeat Beall became a captain. He eventually took part in the Wilderness campaign, in which he was wounded, and the battles at Spottsylvania Court House, Richmond, and Petersburg.

After the war he returned to Texas and established a law practice at Bryan. There he married Laura Wilson in 1866. She bore one daughter before her death in 1867. Beall later married Margaret Ragsdale, and the couple raised four children. In 1866 Beall and Bennett Hillsman Davis formed the law firm of Davis and Beall. By 1876 Wyndham Kemp[qv] had joined the firm, which was renamed Davis, Beall, and Kemp. About 1881 Beall and moved to El Paso, while Kemp stayed behind to close the law firm in Bryan. Eventually the firm Davis, Beall, and Kemp established an office in El Paso and became one of the most successful firms there. Beall accepted a position as attorney for the Santa Fe Railroad in 1884 and moved to Fort Worth, where he made his headquarters until 1887. That year he returned to El Paso, where he practiced law with his firm until his retirement in 1914. He was selected president of the State Bar of Texas[qv] in 1886.

Beall was a Mason and served as grand commander of the Order of the Knights Templar of Texas. He also helped organize the El Paso chapter of the Benevolent and Protective Order of the Elks and was first exalted ruler. He died at El Paso in July 1921.

BIBLIOGRAPHY: J. Morgan Broaddus, *The Legal Heritage of El Paso* (El Paso: Texas Western College Press, 1963). Frank W. Johnson, *A History of Texas and Texans* (5 vols., ed. E. C. Barker and E. W. Winkler [Chicago and New York: American Historical Society, 1914; rpt. 1916]). *Texas Bar Journal*, April 1976.

Brian Hart

BEALS, DAVID THOMAS (1832–1910). David Thomas Beals, merchant, rancher, and banker, was born in North Abington, Massachusetts, on March 8, 1832, the youngest child of Thomas and Ruth (Faxon) Beals. His father was a boot and shoe manufacturer. Beals received a public school education and briefly attended New Hampshire Academy. He entered business at the age of fifteen as a clerk for a Boston merchant but after some months returned to Abington to learn the shoe trade. In 1859 he traveled west and established several boot and shoe businesses, first in Missouri, then in mining districts in Colorado, Montana, Idaho, and Utah. In 1873 he sold his mercantile interests, went east and secured several partners, and started a ranch on the Arkansas River near Granada in southern Colorado. In July 1877 he organized the Beals Cattle Company in Dodge City, Kansas, and sent W. H. "Deacon" Bates into the Texas Panhandle with a small herd to locate a range. Bates selected a pasture for the LX Ranch[qv] that extended along the Canadian River for twenty-five miles, south twenty miles to the site of Amarillo, and from the river north thirty-five miles to the headwaters of Blue Creek. Line camps were placed on the borders. The headquarters were located on Ranch Creek, two miles east of a small trading store, later the Wheeler post office, at the mouth of Pitcher Creek. Within two years Beals had driven his cattle from Colorado to the Canadian and brought down a series of steer herds from Kansas to accumulate a holding of 50,000 head.

Unlike other Texas ranchers seeking free grass, Beals, beginning in 1881, systematically bought land—first from the Houston and Texas Central Railway (23,680 acres) and later from Jot Gunter and William B. Munson[qqv] (100,000 acres); Gunter and Munson had received various tracts as payment for their services as state surveyors. Beals occasionally visited the ranch, but left its operation to a series of managers. When settlers began entering the area he purchased more land, especially tracts with water. However, he was allowed to buy only two sections out of every four—hence the checkerboard pattern of LX lands on contemporary maps.

Beals made a major effort to produce and market improved stock. He imported blooded Durham and Hereford bulls and set up satellite "feeding" ranches in the Cherokee Strip and Caldwell, Kansas, to fatten his cattle for sale. He also sent fine horseflesh to the LX, where trotting and running sires were mated with half-breed mares to produce unusually fast and durable animals.

In the summer of 1884 he and his partners sold the LX Ranch to the American Pastoral Company of London, England, at a price variously listed from $1,200,000 to $1,650,000. The sale included 187,141 acres, 34,000 cattle, and 1,000 horses. Before the sale of the LX, Beals had settled in Kansas City, Missouri. There in 1887 he organized the Union National Bank and amassed large holdings in real estate, including the LX Building. But he maintained his ties with the Texas cattle industry and in 1908 purchased a major interest in the extensive Callaghan Ranch[qv] at Encinal, near San Antonio.

Beals married Ruth Cobb of Maine on April 20, 1851, and they had two children. Ruth died in 1881. On October 14, 1884, Beals married Arista Thurston of Mount Vernon, Ohio, and they had two children. Beals was a Unitarian. He became sick in San Antonio and died in Kansas City on April 21, 1910.

BIBLIOGRAPHY: *History of the Cattlemen of Texas* (Dallas: Johnson, 1914; rpt., Austin: Texas State Historical Association, 1991). Kansas City *Star*, April 21, 1910. Margaret Sheers, "The LX Ranch of Texas," *Panhandle-Plains Historical Review* 6 (1933). Carrie W. Whitney, *Kansas City, Missouri* (3 vols., Chicago: Clarke, 1908).

Anne B. Hinton

BEALS CREEK. Beals Creek rises from a salt lake at the intersection of Mustang Draw and Sulphur Springs Draw, four miles west of Big Spring in Howard County (at 32°12′ N, 101°36′ W). The stream runs through Big Spring and is crossed by Farm roads 821 and 163. It flows sixty-seven miles east to its mouth on the Colorado River, near Pecan Crossing in southern Mitchell County (at 32°11′ N, 100°51′ W). Beals Creek traverses a geologic floodplain surfaced by sand, gravel, and mud substrata with some bedrock areas. Water-tolerant hardwoods, conifers, and grasses grow in the clay and sandy loams along the creek.

BEAN, PETER ELLIS (1783–1846). Peter Ellis Bean (or Ellis P. Bean), filibuster and Mexican revolutionary, was born to Lydia and William Bean, Jr., on June 8, 1783, at Bean Station, Tennessee. In 1800 he joined Philip Nolan's[qv] last filibustering expedition to Texas, lured by promises of wealth from captured mustangs[qv] and by talk of gold and silver. He was captured by the Spaniards, established residences in both Mexico and in Texas, and became a minor, though colorful, figure in the history of both regions.

In Texas Bean found only misfortune. At dawn on March 21, 1801, Spanish troops attacked Nolan's fortified camp, in what became McLennan County or Hill County, killed Nolan, captured Bean and the other survivors, and took them deep into Mexico, where they held them in a succession of towns. Mexican revolutionaries led by a priest, José María Morelos y Pavón, gave Bean his chance for freedom at Acapulco in 1810. He had been released from jail there to fight for the besieged Royalists, but he deserted to Morelos and helped capture the town. He stayed with Morelos and rose in favor.

Fifteen years after leaving his native land Bean returned as a Mexican colonel to seek United States aid for Morelos's cause, but with scant success. During the journey he joined Andrew Jackson's army and fought at the battle of New Orleans. On February 18, 1815, he departed for Mexico on the Águila. Thereafter, as a man of split loyalties, he divided his time between visits to Mexico and the United States. The royalists eventually executed Morelos, and in 1816 Bean barely escaped capture himself by leaving his wife, Magdalena Falfán de los Godos, at Jalapa, Vera Cruz, and fleeing to the United States. In 1818 he married a Tennessean, Candace Midkiff, and they eventually had three children. In 1820 the family moved to Arkansas and in 1823 to East Texas. There Bean served Mexico again as Indian agent. He persuaded the Cherokees to remain neutral during the Fredonian Rebellion.[qv] In 1830 he commanded a small military force at Fort Terán. However, neither Texans nor Mexicans trusted him. After Texas independence he began yearning for Mexico and his other wife and so traveled to Jalapa and there, on October 3, 1846, died in her home.

BIBLIOGRAPHY: Peter Ellis Bean Papers, Barker Texas History Center, University of Texas at Austin. Bennett Lay, *The Lives of Ellis P. Bean* (Austin: University of Texas Press, 1960). John Edward Weems, *Men Without Countries* (Boston: Houghton Mifflin, 1969). Henderson K. Yoakum, *History of Texas from Its First Settlement in 1685 to Its Annexation to the United States in 1846* (2 vols., New York: Redfield, 1855).

John Edward Weems

BEAN, ROY (ca. 1825–1903). Roy Bean, a frontier justice of the peace known as the "Law West of the Pecos," was born in Mason County, Kentucky, the son of Francis and Anna Bean. The only sources of information about his boyhood and youth are stories told by friends in whom he confided and the reminiscences of his older brother Samuel, published in the Las Cruces, New Mexico, *Rio Grande Republican* in 1903. Sam came home after serving in the Mexican War[qv] and took Roy with him down the Santa Fe Trail[qv] to Chihuahua, Mexico, where the brothers set up shop as traders. Roy got into trouble, how-

Roy Bean on a horse thought to be his beloved Old Bayo, in front of his saloon at Langtry. Photograph by N. H. Rose. Courtesy Western History Collections, University of Oklahoma Library.

ever, and had to make a quick exit; he turned up a short time later in San Diego at the home of his oldest brother, Joshua, who was mayor of the town and a major general of the state militia. Roy was jailed for dueling in February 1852 but broke out and moved on to San Gabriel, where Joshua by this time had established himself as owner of the Headquarters Saloon. Roy inherited the property when Joshua was murdered in November 1852, but made another hasty departure after a narrow escape from hanging in 1857 or 1858.

His next stop was Mesilla, New Mexico, where Sam was sheriff of a county that stretched at that time all the way across Arizona. Roy arrived destitute, but Sam took him in as partner in a saloon, and he prospered until the Civil War[qv] reached the Rio Grande valley. Bean may have had some unofficial military experience, but he found it prudent to leave the country and began a new life in San Antonio. In an area on South Flores Street that soon earned the name of Beanville, he became locally famous for circumventing creditors, business rivals, and the law.

On October 28, 1866, he married eighteen-year-old Virginia Chávez, who bore him four children. The couple were not happy together, however. Early in 1882 Roy left home, probably at the suggestion of his friend W. N. Monroe, who was building the "Sunset" railroad toward El Paso and had almost reached the Pecos. Moving with the grading camps, Bean arrived at the site of Vinegarroon, just west of the Pecos, in July. Crime was rife at the end of the track; it was often said, "West of the Pecos there is no law; west of El Paso, there is no God." To cope with the lawless element the Texas Rangers[qv] were called in, and they needed a resident justice of the peace in order to eliminate the 400-mile round trip to deliver prisoners to the county seat at Fort Stockton. The commissioners of Pecos County officially appointed Roy Bean justice on August 2, 1882. He retained the post, with interruptions in 1886 and 1896, when he was voted out, until he retired voluntarily in 1902.

By 1884 Bean was settled at Eagle's Nest Springs, some miles west of Vinegarroon, which acquired a post office and a new name, Langtry, in honor of the English actress Emilie Charlotte (Lillie) Langtry,[qv] whom Bean greatly admired. Bean's fame as an eccentric and original interpreter of the law began in the 1880s. There was, however, a sort of common sense behind his unorthodox rulings. When a track worker killed a Chinese laborer, for example, Bean ruled that his law book did not make it illegal to kill a Chinese. Since the killer's friends were present and ready to riot, he had little choice. And when a man carrying forty dollars and a pistol fell off a bridge, Bean fined the corpse forty dollars for carrying a concealed weapon, thereby providing funeral expenses. He intimidated and cheated people, but he never hanged anybody. He reached the peak of notoriety on February 21, 1896, when he staged the Fitzsimmons-Maher heavyweight championship fight on a sandbar just below Langtry on the Mexican side of the Rio Grande, where Woodford H. Mabry's[qv] rangers, sent to stop it, had no jurisdiction. Fitzsimmons won in less than two minutes.

Bean died in his saloon on March 16, 1903, of lung and heart ailments and was buried in the Del Rio cemetery. His shrewdness, audacity, unscrupulousness, and humor, aided by his knack for self-dramatization, made him an enduring part of American folklore.

BIBLIOGRAPHY: Everett Lloyd, *Law West of the Pecos* (San Antonio: University Press, 1931; rev. ed., San Antonio: Naylor, 1967). C. L. Sonnichsen, *Roy Bean, Law West of the Pecos* (New York: Macmillan, 1943; rpt., Albuquerque: University of New Mexico Press, 1986).

C. L. Sonnichsen

BEAN, WOODROW WILSON, SR. (1917–1985). Woodrow Wilson (Woody) Bean, lawyer, judge, and state representative, was born on a ranch near Esperanza, Texas, on August 28, 1917, the son of Mr. and Mrs. J. B. Bean and the fifth cousin of Judge Roy Bean.[qv] After being orphaned at the age of two, he lived in a Masonic orphanage for the next eleven years. During the late 1930s he attended Texas A&M for a year before transferring to Southern Methodist University for three years, where he majored in government. In 1940, Bean was elected to the Texas House as a representative from El Paso. The next year, he left the legislator to join the marines and fight in World War II.[qv] He left as a private, but came back from the war as a first lieutenant in 1946. He was reelected to the House in 1947 and 1948, before returning to the military in 1950 for service in the Korean War. He then went on to earn his law degree from the University of Texas, and was admitted to the Texas bar in 1953. Bean was elected El Paso County Democratic party chairman in 1954, and was reelected to that position in 1956. In 1958 he was elected El Paso county judge. He was elected chairman of the El Paso Housing Authority in 1972, and in 1974 won election to the State Board of Education. He is known for helping to make the Sun Bowl[qv] and the Trans Mountain Road in El Paso a reality, and for building housing for the poor. He was a liberal Democrat and a Methodist turned Roman Catholic. He married Fay McAdoo, but the couple were divorced in the 1960s. Bean married and was divorced again, and finally married Theresa Lama Webber. He had two children with his first wife. Bean died of lung cancer on July 14, 1985, and is buried at St. Mary's Catholic Church in El Paso.

BIBLIOGRAPHY: Vertical Files, Barker Texas History Center, University of Texas at Austin. *Ryan Britton*

BEAN CREEK. Bean Creek rises just below Reservoir Number 2, 4½ miles west of Lampasas in south central Lampasas County (at 31°04′ N, 98°15′ W). About 1½ miles downstream from its source the creek has been dammed to form Reservoir Number 6. It flows southeast for two miles to a point just below Reservoir Number 6 and three miles southwest of Lampasas, where it joins Pillar Bluff Creek to form Sulphur Creek (at 31°02′ N, 98°13′ W). Its course crosses an area of the Grand Prairies characterized by relatively flat to steeply sloping terrain surfaced by shallow and stony sandy loams. The vegetation consists primarily of grasses and open stands and woods of oak, live oak, mesquite, and juniper.

BEAN HILL, TEXAS. Bean Hill was on Farm Road 3369 nine miles northeast of Temple in northeastern Bell County. The community had one business and forty inhabitants in 1933 and twenty inhabitants in 1946. Its population was reported as ten in 1964, but Bean Hill did not appear on the United States topographical map for 1963.

BIBLIOGRAPHY: Bell County Historical Commission, *Story of Bell County, Texas* (2 vols., Austin: Eakin Press, 1988). *Mark Odintz*

BEAN INDIANS. The Bean Indians (native name; does not refer to a legume) are known from a single Spanish document of 1683, which does not clearly identify their area. Although it cannot be demonstrated, the Beans may have been the same people as the Teanames, also known as Teana and Peana Indians, who at that time lived in northeastern Coahuila and the adjoining part of Texas (the southwestern part of the Edwards Plateau).

BIBLIOGRAPHY: Charles W. Hackett, ed., *Pichardo's Treatise on the Limits of Louisiana and Texas* (4 vols., Austin: University of Texas Press, 1931–46). Frederick Webb Hodge, ed., *Handbook of American Indians North of Mexico* (2 vols., Washington: GPO, 1907, 1910; rpt., New York: Pageant, 1959). Vito Alessio Robles, *Coahuila y Texas en la época colonial* (Mexico City: Editorial Cultura, 1938; 2d ed., Mexico City: Editorial Porrúa, 1978). *Thomas N. Campbell*

BEANS CREEK (Cherokee County). Beans Creek rises two miles east of Alto in southern Cherokee County (at 31°39′ N, 95°01′ W) and runs southeast for six miles to its mouth on the Angelina River, five miles southeast of Linwood (at 31°37′ N, 94°57′ W). The stream is intermittent in its upper reaches. It flows through an area of flat to gently rolling country surfaced by clay and sandy loam that supports grasses and mixed hardwoods and pines. The creek was named for Peter Ellis Bean,[qv] who settled in the area around 1839.

—— (Jack County). Beans Creek rises four miles north of Perrin in southeastern Jack County (at 33°05′ N, 98°03′ W) and flows northeast for 12½ miles through steep to moderately sloping terrain surfaced with clay and sandy loam in which prairie grasses grow. Post oak and mesquite trees shade the banks of the creek. The stream, which is intermittent in its upper reaches, was named for Thomas C. Bean, who owned land along its banks in the mid-1850s. For most of the county's history the area has been used as range and crop land. Until the construction of Lake Bridgeport in 1931 the creek flowed into the West Fork of the Trinity River. Today it empties into the lake just northeast of Wizard Wells (at 33°14′ N, 97°56′ W).

BEANS PLACE, TEXAS. Beans Place, also known as Beans, Cross, and Horger, is on the west bank of the Angelina River just west of State Highway 63 and twelve miles northwest of Jasper in northwestern Jasper County. It was settled by 1904, when Ira S. Bean built a store and established a post office called Horger, named for John Miller Horger, president of the W. H. Ford Male and Female College at Newton. In 1914 the area had a population of twenty. Because of the name's similarity to the names of the other Texas towns of Spurger and Borger, the United States Post Office Department in 1925 opened a new post office named Bean's Place, and the Horger office closed in 1929. The community's population was recorded as twenty-five from 1934 to 1944. The 1936 county highway map showed scattered dwellings and a campsite on State Highway 63, and in 1948 the community was on a rural mail route. The town was still shown on county maps in the 1980s as Beans Community, but by that time no population figures were available. *Diana J. Kleiner*

BEAN'S PRAIRIE, TEXAS. Bean's Prairie, also known as Bean's Creek, was a rural community on Beans Creek west of Alto in southeastern Cherokee County. Peter Ellis Bean[qv] settled there about 1839. At one time Bean's Prairie had a church, a mill, a gin, and a school, but in the early 1990s only a few scattered houses remained in the area.

BIBLIOGRAPHY: *Cherokee County History* (Jacksonville, Texas: Cherokee County Historical Commission, 1986). Hattie Joplin Roach, *A History of Cherokee County* (Dallas: Southwest, 1934).

Christopher Long

BEAR BAYOU. Bear Bayou rises four miles south of Timpson in northwestern Shelby County (at 31°50′ N, 94°21′ W) and flows southwest for seven miles to its mouth on Attoyac Bayou (at 31°47′ N, 94°25′ W). The surrounding terrain, gently sloping to moderately steep, is surfaced with sandy loam. The area is heavily wooded, with pines and various hardwoods predominating.

BEAR BRANCH (Gonzales County). Bear Branch rises in a tank 1½ miles northwest of Moulton in northern Gonzales County (at 29°37′ N, 97°10′ W) and runs west for four miles to its mouth on Obar Creek (at 29°37′ N, 97°14′ W). It traverses moderately rolling terrain surfaced by fine sandy loam or clay that supports mixed hardwoods and pines.

—— (Lampasas County). Bear Branch rises near Franklin Mountain two miles south of Izoro in northern Lampasas County (at 31°16′ N, 98°04′ W). The spring-fed but intermittent stream flows southwest for five miles to its mouth on the Lampasas River, about three miles northwest of Rumley (at 31°13′ N, 98°06′ W). Its course crosses an area of the Grand Prairies characterized by hills, slopes, and limestone benches, which often give a stairstep appearance to the landscape. Soils in the area are generally thin, stony, sandy and clay loams, and vegetation consists primarily of grasses and open stands of live oak, mesquite, and juniper.

—— (Stephens County). Bear Branch begins south of Farm Road 576 in southwest Stephens County (at 32°39′ N, 99°06′ W) and runs east for five miles to its mouth on Battle Creek, two miles south of Eolian (at 32°38′ N, 99°01′ W). Its course extends through rolling hills surfaced by clay and sandy loam that supports scrub brush, mesquite, cacti, and grasses.

BEAR CREEK (Angelina County). Bear Creek rises six miles south of Lufkin in south central Angelina County (at 31°15′ N, 94°43′ W) and flows south for 14½ miles to its mouth on the Neches River (at 31°06′ N, 94°41′ W). Upstream the rolling land is surfaced with sand and mud mixed with lignite and bentonite; there hardwood and pine forests grow. As the creek enters the floodplain of the Neches the terrain becomes flatter, and willow oak, water oak, black gum, and other water-tolerant species predominate.

—— (Brewster County). Bear Creek rises five miles northwest of Pine Mountain in east central Brewster County (at 29°57′ N, 102°58′ W) and runs south for twenty-one miles to its mouth on Maravillas Creek, nine miles northwest of Stillwell Mountain (at 29°40′ N, 102°59′ W). It crosses an area of steep to gentle slopes surfaced by variable soils that support scrub brush and grasses.

—— (Burnet County). Bear Creek rises two miles northwest of Bertram in eastern Burnet County (at 30°45′ N, 98°06′ W) and runs east for thirteen miles to its mouth on the North Fork of the San Gabriel River, five miles north of Liberty Hill in Williamson County (at 30°44′ N, 97°55′ W). The stream is intermittent in its upper reaches. It traverses an area of steep slopes and benches surfaced by shallow clay loams that support juniper, live oak, mesquite, and grasses.

—— (Carson County). Bear Creek rises at the junction of its east and west forks in central Carson County (at 35°31′ N, 101°18′ W) and flows to the north for seventeen miles to its mouth on the Canadian River, northeast of Borger in southern Hutchinson County (at 35°46′ N, 101°19′ W). The stream, in the Dixon Creek Division of the Four Sixes Ranch,[qv] is in the center of the vast Panhandle oilfield,[qv] a harsh, mostly flat area of sandy soils that support brush, grasses, mesquite, and cacti.

—— (Cass County). Bear Creek rises in northwestern Cass County (at 33°11′ N, 94°29′ W) and runs southwest for seven miles to its mouth on Kelley Creek, five miles south of Marietta (at 33°06′ N, 94°33′ W). The stream is intermittent in its upper reaches. It flows through an area of loamy and sandy soils that overlie gently undulating to rolling terrain. The area around the creek is flood-prone, and native vegetation includes water-tolerant hardwoods and conifers.

—— (Cherokee County). Bear Creek rises two miles west of Sycamore Grove Church in northern Cherokee County (at 32°07′ N, 95°17′ W) and runs southeast for eight miles to its mouth on Mud Creek, 1½ miles west of Gould (at 32°04′ N, 95°11′ W). The stream is intermittent in its upper reaches. It crosses flat to gently rolling terrain surfaced by clay and sandy loam that supports grasses and mixed hardwoods and pines.

—— (Collin County). Bear Creek, also known as Bear-Pen Creek, rises just southeast of Nevada in the southeast corner of Collin County (at 33°02′ N, 96°23′ W) and runs southwest for just under seven miles, over flat to rolling land surfaced by dark, calcareous clays that support mesquite and cacti. For most of the county's history the Bear Creek area has been used as range and cropland. The stream joins Camp Creek (at 32°59′ N, 96°28′ W) a mile before the latter empties into Lake Ray Hubbard.

—— (Comal County). Bear Creek rises three miles southeast of Startz Hill in central Comal County (at 29°48′ N, 98°16′ W) and flows east for 7½ miles to its mouth on the Guadalupe River, 10½ miles northwest of New Braunfels. Dry Bear Creek, a tributary of Bear Creek, rises near Startz Hill in central Comal County (at 29°49 N, 98°18′ W) and flows east for 5½ miles to its mouth on Bear Creek, near its crossing of Farm Road 2722 (at 29°49′ N, 98°14′ W). Little Bear Creek, a second tributary, rises in central Comal County near Valley View (at

29°47′ N, 98°15′ W) and flows east for about three miles to its mouth on Bear Creek, near its convergence with Dry Bear Creek (at 29°48′ N, 98°13′ W). Bear Creek and its tributaries cross an area of the Balcones Escarpment[qv] characterized by steep slopes and limestone benches that give the landscape a stairstep appearance. Soil in the area is generally dark, calcareous stony clay and clay loam with rock outcroppings, and vegetation consists primarily of live oak and Ashe juniper woods. In the nineteenth century Bear Creek was the site of a farming and stock-raising community. In 1924 the area was designated a fish and game preserve.

——— (Dallas County). Bear Creek rises just south of De Soto and 1½ miles north of the Ellis county line in southwestern Dallas County (at 32°34′ N, 96°52′ W) and runs southeast for fifteen miles to its mouth on Red Oak Creek in northeastern Ellis County (at 32°29′ N, 96°33′ W). The stream is intermittent in its upper reaches. It traverses flat to rolling prairies surfaced with dark and clayey soils that support heavy woods of oak, juniper, and mesquite. Although settlement began along the upper reaches of the creek as early as 1849, the area remained sparsely settled until after the Civil War.[qv]

BIBLIOGRAPHY: Sam Hanna Acheson, *Dallas Yesterday*, ed. Lee Milazzo (Dallas: Southern Methodist University Press, 1977).

——— (Eastland County). Bear Creek rises four miles east of Ranger in northeastern Eastland County (at 32°26′ N, 98°36′ W) and runs northeast for seven miles to its mouth on Palo Pinto Creek, near the Palo Pinto county line (at 32°30′ N, 98°29′ W). It traverses flat terrain with local deep dissections, surfaced by moderately deep loam that supports mesquite, oak, juniper, grasses, and shrubs.

——— (Erath County). Bear Creek rises three miles southwest of Patilo in northern Erath County (at 32°29′ N, 98°12′ W) and runs north for six miles to its mouth on Big Sunday Creek, in the extreme southern part of Palo Pinto County (at 32°32′ N, 98°15′ W). It runs beneath rolling and moderately to steeply sloping hills surfaced by stones, gravel, and loam that support scrub brush, mesquite, cacti, oaks, and grasses.

——— (Fannin County). Bear Creek rises two miles southeast of Trenton in southwest Fannin County (at 33°25′ N, 96°18′ W) and flows southwest for ten miles, passing under Farm Road 1562 and within a mile of Pike, in Collin County. The streambed extends through gently rolling land surfaced by clayey soils and empties into Indian Creek about two miles from Lavon Lake (at 33°16′ N, 96°21′ W).

——— (Fayette County). Bear Creek rises four miles east of Warda in northwest Fayette County (at 30°01′ N, 96°50′ W) and flows west for 6½ miles to its mouth on Rabbs Creek (at 30°00′ N, 96°55′ W). Throughout its course the stream meanders through low to moderately rolling land with a highly erodible thin sandy loam topsoil and a heavy clay subsoil. The area's open pasturelands alternate with mixed oak forests underlain by yaupon and hackberry. The land is marginal for agriculture and is used primarily for grazing and wildlife habitat.

——— (Hamilton County). Bear Creek begins five miles west of Hamilton in western Hamilton County (at 31°40′ N, 98°12′ W) and extends northeast for eight miles to its mouth on the Leon River (at 31°47′ N, 98°09′ W). It flows beneath steep slopes and benches surfaced by shallow clay loams that support juniper, live oak, mesquite, and grasses.

——— (Harris County). Bear Creek rises in the area of Wolf Hill in northwest Harris County (at 95°49′ N, 29°53′ W) and flows southeast for eighteen miles to its mouth on Buffalo Bayou, near Addicks Reservoir in northwest Harris County (at 95°37′ N, 29°47′ W). The stream runs through flat to rolling terrain with local escarpments and dissections and a surface of sandy or clay loams that support cultivated row or cover crops and occasional grasslands of the type usually associated with crop rotation.

——— (Harrison County). Bear Creek rises just north of Harleton in northwestern Harrison County (at 32°42′ N, 94°31′ W) and runs southeast for 7½ miles through northwestern Harrison County to its mouth on Little Cypress Bayou, three miles northwest of Nesbitt (at 32°39′ N, 94°29′ W). It crosses gently undulating to hilly terrain surfaced by loam and clay that support dense patches of pine and hardwood trees. The cleared land is used predominantly for agriculture.

——— (Hays County). Bear Creek rises eight miles northwest of Hays in northern Hays County (at 30°12′ N, 97°59′ W) and flows southeast for 16½ miles to its mouth on Onion Creek, a mile south of Manchaca in Travis County (at 30°08′ N, 97°49′ W). The stream is intermittent in its upper reaches. It flows over limestone and chalky soils in which Ashe juniper and live oak trees grow. From 1852 to 1872 Bear Creek was the site of Johnson Institute,[qv] perhaps the first Texas secondary school west of the Colorado River. After World War II[qv] the facilities of the old institute were renovated and developed by Walter Prescott Webb[qv] for Friday Mountain Ranch.[qv]

BIBLIOGRAPHY: Tula Townsend Wyatt, *Historical Markers in Hays County* (San Marcos, Texas: Hays County Historical Commission, 1977).

——— (Hill County). Bear Creek rises three miles northeast of Steiner Valley Park in northwestern Hill County (at 32°05′ N, 97°24′ W) and flows south for three miles to its mouth on Lake Whitney, a few miles east of Steiner Valley Park (at 32°00′ N, 97°24′ W). It traverses variable terrain surfaced by shallow, stony clay loams that support juniper, oak, cacti, and grass. The Bear Creek area has been used as range and crop land.

——— (Kerr County). Bear Creek rises nine miles west of Mountain Home in west central Kerr County (at 30°10′ N, 99°32′ W) and flows southeast for 12½ miles to its mouth on the North Fork of the Guadalupe River, five miles west of Hunt (at 30°04′ N, 99°25′ W). The stream, intermittent in its upper reaches, traverses the loamy soils and rocky outcrops of the Edwards Plateau.[qv] Stands of live oak, mesquite, and Ashe juniper grow along the creekbed.

——— (McCulloch County). Bear Creek rises five miles north of the Calf Creek community in southwestern McCulloch County (at 31°04′ N, 99°31′ W) and runs northeast for 11½ miles to its mouth on Brady Reservoir, two miles west of Brady (at 31°08′ N, 99°23′ W). It traverses generally flat terrain with shallow depressions and a surface of clay and sandy loams in which water-tolerant hardwoods, conifers, and grasses grow.

——— (Menard County). Bear Creek rises a mile north of the Kimble county line in south central Menard County (at 30°44′ N, 99°53′ W) and flows south for twenty miles through Kimble County to its mouth on the North Llano River, east-northeast of Junction (at 30°31′ N, 99°50′ W). Bear Creek's only major tributary is West Bear Creek, which rises 1½ miles south of the Menard-Kimble county line in northwestern Kimble County (at 30°41′ N, 100°04′ W) and runs southeast for twenty-seven miles to join Bear Creek a half mile southeast of Cleo. Raleigh Gentry, one of the first settlers in Kimble County, lived five miles above the mouth of Bear Creek in 1859. At that time native pecans and white oaks lined the creek, and turkeys, deer, and wild cattle inhabited the area. Bears were frequently seen at the stream, which at one time was called Viejo Creek.

BIBLIOGRAPHY: Ovie Clark Fisher, *It Occurred in Kimble* (Houston: Anson Jones Press, 1937). Glenn A. Gray, *Gazetteer of Streams of Texas* (Washington: GPO, 1919).

——— (Motley County). Bear Creek rises twelve miles northeast of Matador in east central Motley County (at 34°08′ N, 100°41′ W) and flows southeast for six miles before it joins the Middle Pease River four miles west of Tee Pee City (at 34°04′ N, 100°37′ W). The stream traverses an isolated part of eastern Motley County characterized by sloping terrain surfaced by thin silt loams that support mesquite and grasses.

——— (Parker County). Bear Creek rises three miles northwest of Parsons in southeastern Parker County (at 32°37′ N, 97°44′ W) and runs southeast for fifteen miles, across nearly level to rolling land surfaced by shallow to deep clayey and loamy soils that lie over limestone. For most of the county's history the grassy Bear Creek area has been used as rangeland. One of Parker County's first schools was conducted under a large oak tree near the banks of the creek. Bear Creek flowed into the West Fork of the Trinity River until the early 1950s, when the stream was diverted to its present mouth on Benbrook Lake, ten miles southwest of Fort Worth in Tarrant County (at 32°36′ N, 97°30′ W).

BIBLIOGRAPHY: Gustavus Adolphus Holland, *History of Parker County and the Double Log Cabin* (Weatherford, Texas: Herald, 1931; rpt. 1937).

—— (Polk County). The longest of five Bear creeks that rise in Polk County begins a mile north of Hortense in the eastern part of the county (at 30°50′ N, 94°42′ W) and runs south for 14½ miles to its mouth on Big Sandy Creek, 1½ miles east of Camp Ruby (at 30°42′ N, 94°41′ W). The stream rises in the East Texas timberlands and crosses an area of flat to low-rolling hills and prairies, surfaced with sandy and clayey loams that support open stands and forests of ponderosa pine and Douglas fir, as well as areas of young forest and grass. The creek flows through the Alabama-Coushatta Indian Reservation.

—— (Sabine County). Bear Creek rises a mile southeast of Bronson in west central Sabine County (at 31°20′ N, 94°00′ W) and flows south for twelve miles to its mouth on Sam Rayburn Reservoir (at 31°11′ N, 94°00′ W). Before the impoundment of Sam Rayburn Reservoir in the late 1950s, Bear Creek extended to Ayish Bayou and formed part of the boundary between San Augustine and Jasper counties. The area is gently sloping to moderately steep, surfaced with loams, and heavily wooded, with pine trees predominating.

—— (San Jacinto County). Bear Creek rises in south central San Jacinto County (at 30°28′ N, 95°15′ W) and runs southeast for three miles to its mouth on Winter's Bayou (at 30°27′ N, 95°12′ W), which then joins the East Fort of the San Jacinto River. The stream is in the southwestern part of Sam Houston National Forest.[qv] It traverses generally level country surfaced by sandy soils that support pine and hardwood forest.

—— (Stephens County). Bear Creek rises near the Shackelford county line in southwestern Stephens County (at 32°37′ N, 99°06′ W) and runs east for seven miles to its mouth on Big Sandy Creek, near Hog Mountain (at 32°38′ N, 99°00′ W). For most of its course the creekbed runs at the feet of rolling hills surfaced by clay and sandy loams that support scrub brush, mesquite, cacti, and grasses. At the mouth the terrain flattens somewhat and becomes sandy, and the vegetation includes scattered oak mottes and bunch grasses.

—— (Tarrant County). Bear Creek rises in two branches, Little Bear and Big Bear creeks, which meet a mile northeast of Euless near the Dallas–Fort Worth International Airport[qv] in northeastern Tarrant County (at 32°52′ N, 97°04′ W). Bear Creek runs southeast for ten miles to its mouth on the West Fork of the Trinity River, south of Irving and northeast of Grand Prairie in west central Dallas County (at 32°47′ N, 96°57′ W). The surrounding flat terrain with local shallow depressions is surfaced by clay and sandy loam that supports water-tolerant hardwoods, conifers, and grasses.

BEAR CREEK, TEXAS (Comal County). Bear Creek, a farming and stock-raising community on a creek of the same name eight miles northwest of New Braunfels in the hills of central Comal County, was settled in the 1860s. A spring in the Balcones Fault furnishes water for game and livestock there. Bear Creek Game Reserve was chartered in 1924 for the protection and propagation of fish and game.

Oscar Haas

BEAR CREEK, TEXAS (DeWitt County). Bear Creek was on Bear Creek and Farm Road 682 eleven miles southeast of Yoakum in southeastern DeWitt County. The community center was the Bear Creek school, organized when the Terryville school was moved there in 1887 and consolidated with the Hebron school. The Bear Creek school closed in 1935 when its students were transferred to Yoakum. The Bear Creek community shared the Hebron church and cemetery and one business. By 1962 only the church and cemetery marked the area. No post office existed for the settlement, and population figures are unavailable.

BIBLIOGRAPHY: Nellie Murphree, *A History of DeWitt County* (Victoria, Texas, 1962).

Craig H. Roell

BEAR CREEK, TEXAS (San Jacinto County). Bear Creek was on Farm Road 1725 in southwestern San Jacinto County, fifty-seven miles north of Houston. The area was settled by 1870; included among its early inhabitants were Pete McShan, J. H. Ellis, Dee McIlvan, and William Moody. Many early residents came from Alabama and cleared farms from the dense underbrush and thick woods. A local post office, known as Drury, served residents from 1890 to 1909, when it was discontinued and mail sent to Maynard. Numerous gravel pits now mark the surrounding countryside.

BIBLIOGRAPHY: Ruth Hansbro, History of San Jacinto County (M.A. thesis, Sam Houston State Teachers College, 1940).

Robert Wooster

BEARD, ANDREW JACKSON (1814–1866). Andrew Jackson Beard, son of William and Martha (Harris) Beard, was born in Missouri on May 29, 1814. He moved to Liverpool, Texas, with his parents in 1831, and shortly thereafter to Big Creek, where he later bought land from his uncle, Abner Harris,[qv] an Old Three Hundred[qv] colonist. In the fall of 1835 Beard served the Texas army for several months before receiving an honorable discharge from Stephen F. Austin[qv] at a camp near Bexar. In the early spring of 1836 he entered William H. Patton's[qv] Columbia Company, which was attached to the Second Regiment of the revolutionary army.[qv] With this unit Beard served as a private at the battle of San Jacinto.[qv] Payroll records reveal that A. J. Beard served the Texas Rangers[qv] for several months in 1839. In 1842, during the Vásquez–Woll campaign, Beard and his two younger brothers, William H. and Robert Sidney, assisted the Texas militia in repelling the Mexican invaders from San Antonio. Andrew returned home to Fort Bend County, but Robert and William had the misfortune to wind up in the Mier expedition.[qv] Even though neither drew a black bean in the Black Bean Episode, both died in Mexican prisons before the Mexican government released the group in 1844. In Fort Bend County in 1847 Andrew Beard married Sarah Jane Pentecost, a daughter of Old Three Hundred colonist George S. Pentecost.[qv] In 1850 Andrew and Sarah were living in Seguin, where Beard's father had relocated the family; however, about 1852–53 Andrew returned to Big Creek to farm and raise cattle. He served several terms as overseer of the Big Creek Road District and was the postmaster at Big Creek for several years. He died in office in 1866. Sarah preceded him in death in 1857. Both are buried in the Old Pentecost Graveyard, now known as the Brown–Beard Cemetery, on Cuming's Road near Big Creek. They had six children, and numerous descendants still live in Fort Bend County. Most of Beard's original acreage on what is now Sawmill Road is still in possession of his heirs. In 1974, when the Texas Family Land Heritage program was initiated, the Beard Ranch on Big Creek was included in the first edition of the registry.

BIBLIOGRAPHY: Lester G. Bugbee, "The Old Three Hundred: A List of Settlers in Austin's First Colony," *Quarterly of the Texas State Historical Association* 1 (October 1897).

Esther Beard

BEARD, CHARLES EDMUND (1900–1982). Charles Beard, airline executive, was born in Toledo, Ohio, on November 23, 1900, the son of Hiram Edmund and Mamie (Reiser) Beard. He received his early education at Lake Forest Academy. At the age of sixteen he convinced the United States Navy that he was eighteen and enlisted as a carpenter's mate. He signed up for aerial-gunnery school and graduated third in a class of 400. He then worked as an instructor at the Great Lakes training station as chief gunner's mate. After being discharged he went to Lake Forest College and the University of Toledo, where he studied English, journalism, and history to prepare himself for a career in newspapers. He then moved to Chicago to work as a reporter for the Chicago Daily News. This lasted only a short time because he tried to pursue a stage career in New York on what was at that time called the Subway Circuit. In 1922 he met Rose Ester Wheaton, a native of Kokomo, Indiana. He moved with her to Toledo, Ohio, where he took a job working in a warehouse for eighteen dollars a week. Charles and Rose were married on February 23, 1923. In 1928 Beard left the warehouse, where he had risen to the office of sales manager. In 1929 he took a job as a consolidated ticket manager for the Chicago Air Traffic Association. He was called to New York in 1932 to organize a consolidated ticket office there. He was offered the job of passenger-traffic manager for Northwest Airways in 1933 and remained there until President F. D. Roosevelt restructured the existing airmail contracts and pushed the airline business into a slump. Between 1933 and 1935 Beard worked for Chevrolet at the Chicago Worlds Fair and for Goodyear Rubber.

In October 1935 he accepted a job with Braniff Airways as general traffic manager. By 1937 he had become a vice president and a member of the board of directors and was in charge of all traffic, sales, and advertising. In 1943 he was made a member of a five-man executive committee established by the board. By 1947 he was executive vice president. He was elected president of Braniff in January 1954, following the death of Thomas E. Braniff[qv] in a plane crash. During his time as president Braniff Airways[qv] grew into a top-ten national carrier. Beard initiated flights to Latin America and South America and was decorated for doing so; in May 1957 he was given the Order of Merit (Peru), and in February 1960 he was given the Order of Balboa (Panama) for his contributions to goodwill between the United States and Latin America. He was given an honorary doctorate of commercial science by the University of Toledo in April 1964. He retired from Braniff in April 1965.

Beard was also a director of the First National Bank of Dallas, a member of the executive committee of the Frito-Lay Corporation,[qv] and a director of the Lone Star Cement Company. He was involved in many civic groups, such as the Boy Scouts of America, the Texas Tourist Council, and the Southwestern Legal Foundation. He was director of the Air Transport Association for several years and president of the Air Traffic Conference. He was also a member of the Air Transport Committee of the United States Council of the International Chamber of Commerce. In 1955 he wrote a short profile of Thomas E. Braniff that was published by the Newcomen Society.

He had a son and a daughter, seven grandchildren, and fifteen great-grandchildren. In September of 1963 his wife died, and he shortly thereafter was remarried to a second wife, Barbara. Beard died on July 18, 1982, in Dallas, Texas.

BIBLIOGRAPHY: Vertical Files, Barker Texas History Center, University of Texas at Austin. *Matthew D. Moore*

BEARD, JAMES (1801?–?). James Beard (Baird), one of Stephen F. Austin's[qv] Old Three Hundred[qv] colonists, was a saddler from St. Louis, Missouri, who was later known as "Deaf" Beard. He joined Austin in New Orleans on June 18, 1821, and accompanied him on the *Beaver* to Natchitoches, Louisiana, and then to Texas. On November 22, 1821, he signed an agreement with Austin to come to Texas on the *Lively*[qv] and to work for him until December 1822 at building cabins and a stockade and cultivating five acres of corn. According to the terms of the agreement, Austin was to provide tools, provisions, a section of land, and a town lot. Beard served as a cook and steward aboard the *Lively* and was left in command of the vessel while some of the passengers explored the Brazos River. On August 10, 1824, he received a sitio[qv] of land and settled on the San Bernard River in what later became Fort Bend County. The census of 1826 listed Beard as a single man aged between twenty-five and forty. In 1846 John G. Owings owned the Beard headright.

BIBLIOGRAPHY: Eugene C. Barker, ed., *The Austin Papers* (3 vols., Washington: GPO, 1924–28). Lester G. Bugbee, "The Old Three Hundred: A List of Settlers in Austin's First Colony," *Quarterly of the Texas State Historical Association* 1 (October 1897). W. S. Lewis, "Adventures of the 'Lively' Immigrants," *Quarterly of the Texas State Historical Association* 3 (July 1899). *Telegraph and Texas Register*, March 4, 1846. Clarence Wharton, *Wharton's History of Fort Bend County* (San Antonio: Naylor, 1939). Dudley Goodall Wooten, ed., *A Comprehensive History of Texas* (2 vols., Dallas: Scarff, 1898; rpt., Austin: Texas State Historical Association, 1986).

BEARD, TEXAS. Beard was on Farm Road 3080 and North Chamblee Creek fourteen miles southwest of Canton in extreme southwest Van Zandt County. In 1906 the Beard school had thirty-seven pupils; by the 1950s the school had been consolidated with the Mabank Independent School District. State highway maps showed a church and cemetery at Beard from 1936 to 1981. The site is located near Odom, and its cemetery is frequently called Odom-Beard or Odom-Baird Cemetery. *Diana J. Kleiner*

BEAR GRASS, TEXAS. Bear Grass is near the intersection of Farm roads 1512 and 1146, eight miles northwest of Jewett in the northwest corner of Leon County. The site was settled in the 1850s. The Bear Grass post office was established in Limestone County in 1858 and closed in 1867. On the other side of the county line, in Leon County, Little Flock Cemetery was established about 1860. The center of the community shifted to the south over the years, placing it in Leon County. Little Flock Baptist Church, sometimes called Old Bear Grass Church, was built by 1900, and the Little Flock school met in the church building. In 1906 the Bear Grass Coal Company developed coal mines in the community and built a company store, the Bear Grass Mercantile Company, and a new school building, which had one teacher and thirty-four pupils in 1907. The school later burned. When a new church was built in 1918, it also served as the new schoolhouse. The supply of soft coal was exhausted by 1930, and by 1930 the community had twenty-five inhabitants and two stores. In 1939 the Little Flock school was consolidated with the Jewett school, and in 1940 Bear Grass had two stores, a church, and a number of scattered dwellings. In the late 1940s the population of the town was estimated at fifty. Bear Grass was still indicated on state highway maps in 1990.

BIBLIOGRAPHY: Leon County Historical Book Survey Committee, *History of Leon County* (Dallas: Curtis Media, 1986).

Mark Odintz

BEARHEAD CREEK. Bearhead Creek begins a mile southwest of Sivells Bend in north central Cooke County (at 33°51′ N, 97°15′ W) and flows southeast for 5½ miles to its mouth on Fish Creek (at 33°47′ N, 97°12′ W). It traverses a sparsely settled area of rural Cooke County where, according to a county historian, predatory animals once abounded, including an occasional bear. Bearhead Creek flows through gently undulating to hilly terrain with loamy, clayey, and sandy soils. Indigenous trees found along the creek are elm, oak, ash, pecan, cottonwood, and willow.

BIBLIOGRAPHY: C. N. Jones, *Early Days in Cooke County: 1848–1873* (Gainesville, Texas, 1936; rpt., Gainesville: Cooke County Heritage Society, 1977). *Robert Wayne McDaniel*

BEAR HOLLOW Bear Hollow, a valley through which runs an intermittent creek, begins eleven miles southeast of Seguin in southeastern Guadalupe County (at 29°26′ N, 97°52′ W) and extends south for two miles to its mouth on Sandies Creek, one mile west of Farm Road 1117 (at 29°25′ N, 97°51′ W).

BEAR MOUNTAIN. Bear Mountain is twenty-three miles northwest of Fort Davis in central Jeff Davis County (at 30°41′ N, 104°15′ W). It rises to an elevation of 7,256 feet above sea level, some 1,700 feet above State Highway 166, a mile to the south. The shallow, stony soils on the mountain support scrub brush and grasses.

BEAR PEN CREEK. Bear Pen Creek rises just northeast of Mount Vernon in central Franklin County (at 33°11′ N, 95°12′ W) and runs north for 7½ miles to its mouth on White Oak Creek, about seven miles north of Mount Vernon (at 33°16′ N, 94°13′ W). The stream, intermittent in its middle and upper reaches, crosses nearly level to rolling land surfaced with loams and clayey subsoils. The area is generally heavily wooded, with pines and various hardwoods predominating.

BIBLIOGRAPHY: John Clements, *Flying the Colors: Texas, a Comprehensive Look at Texas Today, County by County* (Dallas: Clements Research, 1984).

BEARS FOOT CREEK. Bears Foot Creek rises a half mile north of U.S. Highway 67 and five miles northeast of Ballinger in central Runnels County (at 31°46′ N, 99°53′ W) and flows southeast for six miles before emptying into the Colorado River three miles southeast of Ballinger in central Runnels County (at 31°43′ N, 99°54′ W). Mesquite and grasses grow on the surrounding flat to gently sloping land.

BEASLEY, TEXAS. Beasley is on the Southern Pacific Railroad and U.S. Highway 59 eleven miles southwest of Richmond in southwestern Fort Bend County. It was laid out on the Galveston, Harrisburg and San Antonio Railway in the mid-1890s by Cecil A. Beasley, a Richmond banker, who called the town Dyer in honor of Miss Isabel Dyer, who later became Mrs. Beasley. When it was found that another community was called Dyer, the town was named Beasley instead; it was granted a post office in 1898. In 1910 the Stern and Stern Land Company of Kansas City began to promote the community and the surrounding prairielands, and Beasley became a supply and shipping point for settlers. By 1914 the town had a population of 325, Baptist and Lutheran churches, a bank, a hotel, a lumber company, two cotton gins, three general stores, and telephone service. By the 1920s the community also had a filling station and a movie house. In 1930 the Beasley schools served 252 white pupils and thirty-two black pupils. The schools were merged with Lamar in 1948. The population remained static at 350 until the 1940s, when Beasley had seven churches. The town's population fell to 300 in 1949 and 175 in 1960 but began to revive in the 1960s to reach 275 in 1968, 447 in 1980, and 485 in 1990. The community incorporated in 1970.

BIBLIOGRAPHY: S. A. McMillan, comp., *The Book of Fort Bend County* (Richmond, Texas, 1926). *Mark Odintz*

BEASON CREEK. Beason Creek, a perennial stream, rises seven miles southeast of Navasota in south central Grimes County (at 30°20′ N, 95°57′ W) and flows southwest for sixteen miles to its mouth on the Brazos River near the Waller county line (at 30°14′ N, 96°05′ W). It traverses gently sloping to nearly level terrain surfaced by clayey loam that supports post oak, blackjack oak, elm, and hackberry trees along the creekbed. Settlement in the vicinity of the lower creek began in the early 1820s, when Jared E. Groce[qv] began farming a large tract of land near the mouth. His second plantation home, Groce's Retreat,[qv] was constructed on Wallace Prairie beside the middle creek in 1833. The present Retreat, two miles upstream, was founded in 1851. The town of White Hall is on the west bank of the upper creek, and downstream is Courtney.

BIBLIOGRAPHY: Grimes County Historical Commission, *History of Grimes County, Land of Heritage and Progress* (Dallas: Taylor, 1982).

BEATTIE, TEXAS. Beattie, on Farm Road 588 in north central Comanche County, was named for pioneer Charles F. Beatty, who settled there in 1892. The community had a grocery store, cotton gin, drugstore, barbershop, and telephone exchange in the early 1900s. A Beattie post office operated from 1902 to 1908. The population was listed as 115 in 1930, when the town had four businesses. By 1945 the residents had declined to fifty and the businesses to two. By the late 1980s the community had no businesses. The population was still fifty in 1990.

BIBLIOGRAPHY: Comanche County Bicentennial Committee, *Patchwork of Memories: Historical Sketches of Comanche County, Texas* (Brownwood, Texas: Banner Printing, 1976). *Julius A. Amin*

BEATY, JOHN OWEN (1890–1961). John Owen Beaty, teacher and author, was born to James Robert and Eula (Simms) Beaty at Crow, West Virginia, on December 22, 1890. He received his B.A. and M.A. degrees from the University of Virginia in 1913 and enlisted in the United States Army in 1917; he remained on active duty through World War I,[qv] then stayed in Europe and took graduate courses at the Université de Montpellier, France, before returning to the United States, where he joined the faculty of Southern Methodist University in Dallas in 1919. He married Josephine Mason Powell in 1920. The couple raised four children. Beaty completed his Ph.D. in 1921 at Columbia University. In 1926–27 he was an American Kahn fellow in Asia and Europe.

In 1922 he was promoted to professor; he was selected chairman of the Department of English in 1927. He retained this position until 1940 and was honorary chairman until his retirement from the university in 1957. From 1926 to 1934 he was visiting professor during the summers at various universities, including the University of Texas. He authored and coauthored a number of articles for popular and professional journals and several books, including *An Introduction to Poetry* (1922), *An Introduction to Drama* (1927), *Texas Poems* (1936), *Swords in the Dawn* (1937), *Image of Life* (1940), and *Crossroads* (1956). In 1951 he published *The Iron Curtain Over America.* This highly controversial and widely criticized book contended that Jews not only were largely responsible for the success of the Bolshevik Revolution but dominated the Democratic party[qv] in the United States.

Beaty was chairman of the Modern Language Association's Old English group, 1938–39; president of the Texas branch of the Conference of College Teachers of English, 1937–38; and a member of the American Academy of Political Science. He also served as pronunciation consultant for the second edition of *Webster's New International Dictionary,* published in 1934. In addition, he was a member of the United States Army Reserve until 1950; he retired with the rank of colonel.

After his retirement from SMU, Beaty and his wife moved to Campbellton Farm, which his father had established, near Barboursville, Virginia. He died on September 9, 1961, while hospitalized at Gordonsville, Virginia. He was a Baptist and a member of the Order of the White Cross, the Masonic order, and the Woodmen of the World.

BIBLIOGRAPHY: Dallas *Morning News,* September 10, 1961. New York *Times,* September 13, 1961. *Who Was Who in America,* Vol. 4.

Brian Hart

BEAUCHAMP, JENNY BLAND (1833–?). Jenny Bland Beauchamp, temperance reformer and writer, was the second president of the Woman's Christian Temperance Union[qv] in Texas and the first to undertake vigorous guidance. She was a resident of Denton and the wife of Rev. S. A. Beauchamp, a Baptist minister. Mrs. Beauchamp had no previous leadership experience when she took over as president of the WCTU in 1883. During the four years that she held office she organized local unions in more than twenty counties, despite the meagerness of funds to defray travel expenses. Her attempt to defend families against the destructive effects of alcohol led her to a parallel concern for child welfare and social conditions affecting children.

Under WCTU auspices she organized a rescue home in Fort Worth for girls; a similar one for bootblacks later became the Tarrant County Orphans Home. Jenny Beauchamp initiated the WCTU tradition of petitioning the state legislature for specific social reforms, and under her administration the organization lobbied successfully for a state orphanage at Corsicana. A year after she visited Rusk Penitentiary[qv] and launched a petition drive to have juvenile inmates separated from adult criminals, the legislature authorized the Gatesville State School for Boys.[qv]

During the final year of her presidency, Mrs. Beauchamp traveled more than 5,000 miles lecturing and organizing for temperance; by the close of her administration Texas had 1,600 WCTU members, organized into about 100 local unions. Jenny Beauchamp was elected to a fifth presidential term in 1888 but declined to serve because of ill health. Like her husband, she was also an active worker in the state prohibition[qv] movement in the 1880s. She was a member of the platform committee at the 1886 state convention and the following year served as a delegate to the national convention in Chicago. She also wrote the first article on woman suffrage[qv] published in Texas. She contributed material on the legal status of women in Texas to *The History of Woman Suffrage* (1887) and published poems and prose. She wrote *Maplehurst; or Campbellism not Christianity* (1867) and *Our Coming King* (1895).

BIBLIOGRAPHY: May Baines, *A Story of Texas White Ribboners* (1935?). Jenny Beauchamp, "The Ballot as Educator," *Texas Journal of Education*, December 1881. Sam Houston Dixon, *The Poets and Poetry of Texas* (Austin: Dixon, 1885). H. A. Ivy, *Rum on the Run in Texas: A Brief History of Prohibition in the Lone Star State* (Dallas, 1910). A. Elizabeth Taylor, "The Woman Suffrage Movement in Texas," *Journal of Southern History* 17 (May 1951; rpt., in *Citizens at Last: The Woman Suffrage Movement in Texas*, ed. Ruthe Winegarten and Judith N. McArthur, Austin, 1987). *Judith N. McArthur*

BEAUCHAMP, THOMAS D. (?–?). Thomas D. Beauchamp, early settler, moved to Texas in 1832 and attended the Convention of 1832[qv] as a delegate from the Snow (Neches) River District, now in Tyler County. He served on a committee to petition the state of Coahuila for a law permitting the use of the English language except in matters directly pertaining to government. In 1838 Beauchamp, a single man, was issued a headright for eight and one-third labores of land in what is now Falls County.

BIBLIOGRAPHY: John Henry Brown, *History of Texas from 1685 to 1892* (2 vols., St. Louis: Daniell, 1893). Texas House of Representatives, *Biographical Directory of the Texan Conventions and Congresses, 1832–1845* (Austin: Book Exchange, 1941). *Melissa G. Wiedenfeld*

BEAUCHAMPS SPRINGS. Beauchamps Springs is a group of springs at the foot of Johnson Street in Houston, Harris County (at 29°47′ N, 95°22′ W). In the early days of Houston the springs were the city's chief water supply. The water feeds a pond covered with water hyacinths. Confederates had a campsite at the spring during the Civil War.[qv] On April 11, 1978, the water flow was only 1.7 gallons per minute. Heavy groundwater pumping in the vicinity has greatly lowered the water table.

BIBLIOGRAPHY: Gunnar Brune, *Springs of Texas*, Vol. 1 (Fort Worth: Branch-Smith, 1981). *Gunnar Brune*

BEAUCHAMPS SPRINGS, TEXAS. Beauchamps Springs, also known as Beauchampville, was on White Oak Bayou near Woodland Park on the north side of Houston. In 1838 efforts by the Houston Water Works Company to pipe water from a shallow artesian well in Beauchamps Springs two miles into Houston failed. According to various sources, the name may have attached to four separate springs, among them Riordan's Spring, which were described in 1838 as providing an "inexhaustible supply" of pure water. Beauchamps is thought to have been named for a man who camped in the forest at one of the springs with a group of Bidais Indians sometime before 1847. He acquired fifty acres at the site and hauled water for sale at seventy-five cents for a thirty-gallon barrel to Houston citizens compelled to use the noxious water of Buffalo Bayou before central water or sewage systems. He also laid out lots and sold properties; "two straight rows of houses were built in the pine forest before yet the timber had been cut from the main street, Beauchamp Street." During the Civil War[qv] a Confederate campsite was located at the springs. Sources suggest that the community of Beauchamps Springs later grew up near the springs. By the 1980s, after nearby highway development, little more than a trickle of water remained of the springs or of Beauchamps Creek, which formerly flowed from the springs.

BIBLIOGRAPHY: Gunnar Brune, *Springs of Texas*, Vol. 1 (Fort Worth: Branch-Smith, 1981). Andrew Forest Muir, "Railroads Come to Houston, 1857–1861," *Southwestern Historical Quarterly* 64 (July 1960). Edward Stiff, *A New History of Texas* (Cincinnati: George Conclin, 1847). *Diana J. Kleiner*

BEAUJEU, TANGUY LE GALLOIS DE (?–?). Tanguy le Gallois de Beaujeu, a captain of the Royal French Navy, was the son of Robert Le Gallois, Sieur de Saint Aubin and *valet de chambre* (manservant) of the queen Marie de Médicis, and of Marie de Saint Aubin, daughter of a court physician of Louis XIII. He was captain of the thirty-six-gun man-of-war *Joly*, which took part in the 1684 La Salle expedition[qv] to the Gulf of Mexico. King Louis XIV also gave him the overall sea command during the voyage, a division of responsibility that gave rise to conflict between the two leaders and seriously affected the course of the enterprise.

Beaujeu, like La Salle, was a Norman. In the royal service, he was accorded the rank of *capitaine de frégate* in 1671 and *capitaine de vaisseau* shortly thereafter. In 1675 his career took an unfortunate turn, as he was imprisoned, for cause that has not been established, in the tower of La Rochelle. He was set free after three months but was temporarily stripped of his rank, which was restored about a year later. In 1682 Beaujeu took part in the bombardment of Algiers, and it is believed to have been on that occasion that he fell into the hands of the Berbers.

His difficulties with La Salle notwithstanding, Beaujeu appears to have been an able and conscientious officer whose greatest failing was his inability to suffer La Salle's abuse with humility. Though never taken into La Salle's confidence, he showed exceptional navigational abilities in crossing the uncharted Gulf of Mexico, of which he had no prior knowledge. Despite La Salle's incivility Beaujeu seems to have done all that he could to aid the expedition leader and to leave him in comfortable circumstances when he set sail to return to France in March 1685. No evidence has surfaced to indicate that his departure stemmed from a sinister motive or that it constituted willful desertion of La Salle, who actually seems to have wanted the naval commander off his hands. Beaujeu, in fact, had ample reason to return to France: his ship lay in an anchorage exposed to both the weather and to the Armada de Barlovento,[qv] a Spanish fleet. It seemed that the best he could do for La Salle was to return to France with a report as soon as possible.

Little is known of Beaujeu after his return to France. It is said that Claude Delisle, gathering data for maps that appeared under the name of his son Guillaume, sought the naval officer's advice on certain aspects of New World geography. When the Sieur d'Iberville began preparations for a new French enterprise in the Gulf of Mexico, advice was sought from several participants in the La Salle fiasco. Beaujeu was not among them. He nevertheless offered his opinion of the undertaking in a letter to the noted geographer Cabart de Villermont—two weeks after Iberville had sailed. The sailing, he said, was three months later in the season than it should have been; he expected that Iberville would be thinking of turning back by the time he reached the Gulf.

BIBLIOGRAPHY: Francis Parkman, *The Discovery of the Great West* (London: Murray, 1869; new ed., *La Salle and the Discovery of the Great West,* New York: New American Library, 1963). Marc de Villiers, *L'expédition de Cavelier de La Salle dans le Golfe du Mexique* (Paris: Adrien-Maisonneuve, 1931). Robert S. Weddle et al., eds., *La Salle, the Mississippi, and the Gulf: Three Primary Documents* (College Station: Texas A&M University Press, 1987). *Robert S. Weddle*

BEAUKISS, TEXAS. Beaukiss is an abandoned townsite on Middle Yegua Creek about one mile from the Lee county line in southeastern Williamson County. The settlement was founded in 1880 by Samuel M. Slaughter, an Indian, who was also appointed its first postmaster that year. Beaukiss was a prosperous rural community by 1884, when it had a church, a school, a gristmill, a cotton gin, and seventy-five inhabitants. The population had climbed to 100 by 1890, and in the early years of the twentieth century the community had a variety of businesses, several doctors, three fraternal organizations, a school, and a string band. The town declined to a population of seventy-five in 1920 and only two businesses in 1931. The oil boom in eastern Williamson County revived Beaukiss briefly in the 1930s, when a well came in at the nearby Abbott oilfield, but the Beaukiss school closed in 1947, and the population of the town had declined to twenty by 1949. In 1977 Beaukiss was the site of a cemetery and a church. Its population in 1990 was twenty, according to the United States census.

BIBLIOGRAPHY: Clara Stearns Scarbrough, *Land of Good Water: A Williamson County History* (Georgetown, Texas: Williamson County Sun Publishers, 1973). *Mark Odintz*

BEAUMIER, WALTER RAYMOND (1906–1965). Walter Raymond (Beau) Beaumier, newspaper publisher and civic leader, was born on October 7, 1906, in Hallettsville, Texas, the son of Walter R. Beaumier, Sr. He went to school in Bartlett, Schwertner, Salado, and Belton. He became a reporter as a young man and was, in succession, a reporter and city editor for the San Antonio *Express* (*see* SAN ANTONIO *EXPRESS-NEWS*), city editor of the Galveston *News,* and city editor of the Beaumont *Enterprise-Journal* (*see* BEAUMONT *ENTERPRISE*). At age nineteen, in Galveston, he became the youngest news editor of a metropolitan newspaper in the United States. Beaumier left the newspaper field in 1938 to work as a chamber of commerce executive in Beaumont. In 1941 he moved to Lufkin to manage the chamber of commerce there. In April 1943 he became vice president and general manager of the Lufkin *News.*

He served as president of the Texas Daily Newspaper Association, the Texas Press Association,[qv] the North and East Texas Press Association, the Texas Gulf Coast Press Association, and the UPI Editors' Association. He also served on the Advisory Council of the University of Texas School of Journalism. He was a director of the Texas Forestry Association[qv] and of FACTS for East Texas, an information group on forestry problems. He was also regional vice president of the Texas Manufacturers Association.[qv] Beaumier worked with numerous civic organizations and belonged to both the Lufkin Rotary Club and the Lufkin Elks Lodge. He was also a longtime member of the First Presbyterian Church. In August 1965 he resigned from the Texas Historical Survey Commission to accept appointment from Governor John Connally[qv] to the Texas Commission for Indian Affairs (*see* TEXAS INDIAN COMMISSION).

For many years Beaumier's daily column, "I Could Be Wrong," appeared on the editorial page of the Lufkin *Daily News.*[qv] Although he was a Republican in fiercely Democratic Angelina County, Beaumier remained a popular editor. During his tenure the *News* won more excellence awards than any paper its size in the South. Twice during a three-year period, Beaumier was awarded the George Washington Honor Medal by the Freedom Foundation. In 1929 he married a woman named Mary, a native of Paducah, Kentucky, in Pearsall, Texas; they had one daughter. Beaumier died on September 1, 1965, and was buried in the Garden of Memories Memorial Park in Lufkin.

BIBLIOGRAPHY: Houston *Chronicle,* April 4, 1954. Lufkin *Daily News,* September 25, 1965. Vertical Files, Barker Texas History Center, University of Texas at Austin. *Megan Biesele*

BEAU MONDE. The *Beau Monde* was a weekly Dallas society magazine founded in November of 1895 and edited by Alice Parsons Fitzgerald[qv] and Kate Scurry Terrell. Two months later Terrell left the *Beau Monde,* and Fitzgerald remained as the paper's sole owner and editor. The magazine was a nine-by-twelve-inch publication of sixteen pages that cost ten cents an issue or three dollars a year. In the *Beau Monde* Mrs. Fitzgerald reported on a wide variety of social events and was known for florid language and the use of French phrases. The magazine not only reported on Dallas society but also that of high society of the eastern United States and Europe. Alice Fitzgerald remained editor of the *Beau Monde* until her death, in December 1910. Production of the magazine continued under C. E. Fitzgerald, then under Mrs. G. D. de Jarnette. The last issue was published in 1912.

BIBLIOGRAPHY: Sam Hanna Acheson, *Dallas Yesterday,* ed. Lee Milazzo (Dallas: Southern Methodist University Press, 1977). John William Rogers, *The Lusty Texans of Dallas* (New York: Dutton, 1951; enlarged ed. 1960; expanded ed., Dallas: Cokesbury Book Store, 1965).
Matthew Hayes Nall

BEAUMONT, EUGENE BEAUHARNAIS (1837–1916). Eugene Beauharnais Beaumont, United States Cavalry officer, the son of Andrew and Julia (Colt) Beaumont, was born in Wilkes-Barre, Luzerne County, Pennsylvania, on August 2, 1837, and appointed to the United States Military Academy at West Point on July 1, 1856. His father had served in the United States Congress from 1832 to 1836 and was descended from a line of *Mayflower* colonists. His classmates included Confederate major general Thomas L. Rosser[qv] of Texas. Beaumont graduated thirty-second in his class and was commissioned a second lieutenant in the First United States Cavalry on May 6, 1861. From then through June he drilled volunteer troops in Washington, D.C., and participated in the battle of First Manassas or Bull Run as a volunteer aide-de-camp to Col. Ambrose E. Burnside in the First Cavalry. After transfer to the Fourth United States Cavalry[qv] on August 3, 1861, he served as acting adjutant general of the regiment. He was promoted to first lieutenant on September 14, 1861, and on February 1, 1862, was assigned as aide-de-camp to Gen. John Sedgwick. In this capacity he took part in guarding the upper Potomac River and was engaged in the Peninsular campaign from March through May of 1862. He was posted as aide-de-camp to Gen. Henry W. Halleck on August 7, 1862, but was promoted to captain in the volunteer army and returned to Sedgwick's staff on May 13, 1863. Beaumont served in the Rappahannock campaign with the Army of the Potomac in the spring of 1863 and in the Gettysburg campaign in July. He was brevetted to captain in the regular army on November 7, 1863, for "gallant and meritorious service" in the battle of Rappahannock Station, Virginia. After fighting in the battles of the Wilderness and Spotsylvania, where General Sedgwick was killed in May 1864, Beaumont was transferred as aide-de-camp to Gen. James H. Wilson. He served in the Petersburg campaign and in the Shenandoah valley in the summer of 1864 before transferring with Wilson on October 1 to the cavalry corps of the Army of the Mississippi, where he served as assistant adjutant general. On October 20 he was promoted to major of volunteers. He subsequently saw action in the battle of Nashville (December 1864) and the battle of Harpeth River, Tennessee (December 17, 1864); for his performance at Harpeth River he was awarded a Medal of Honor on March 30, 1898. Beaumont was brevetted lieutenant colonel of volunteers on March 13, 1865, for "gallant and meritorious service" during the pursuit of John Bell Hood's[qv] army in Tennessee. On April 2, 1865, his attack on the Confederate breastworks at Selma, Alabama, won him a brevet to major in the regular army and to colonel of volunteers for "gallant and distinguished service" as well as a second Medal of Honor. When Confederate president Jefferson Davis[qv] was captured in Georgia, he was placed in Beaumont's charge.

At the end of the war Beaumont was mustered out of the volunteer army, on March 19, 1866. He retained his prewar rank in the regular army and was advanced to captain of the Fourth Cavalry on July 25, 1865. He commanded Troop A, which garrisoned San Antonio from April through October 1866 and served at Camp Sheridan, Texas, in November and December. The following months saw him at Fredericksburg, Fort Mason, Fort Chadbourne, and Fort McKavett. After a brief leave of absence he returned to the regiment in May 1869 as commander of the garrison at Lampasas. After recruiting service in 1871 and 1872, he was stationed at Fort Richardson and Fort Clark in 1873 and 1874. On May 18, 1873, he took part in Col. Ranald S. Mackenzie's[qv] raid on Kickapoo and Lipan villages at Remolino, Mexico. When Beaumont observed that his officers and men would be "justified in refusing to obey your orders, which you now admit as being illegal, and exposing them to such peril," Mackenzie replied that he would have any officer or man shot who refused to follow him across the Rio Grande. From August 18 through December 29, 1874, Beaumont accompanied Mackenzie on his expedition into Indian Territory after the Warren Wagontrain Raid,[qv] and on September 28, 1874, he commanded the advance battalion that attacked Quanah Parker's[qv] Comanche encampment in the battle of Palo Duro Canyon.[qv]

On March 1, 1875, Beaumont was appointed assistant instructor at the United States Military Academy, where he taught cavalry tactics until August 1879. He was promoted to major on November 12, 1879, and subsequently served in Indian Territory, Colorado, New Mexico, Arizona, and Kansas. On December 24, 1888, he was appointed acting inspector general of Texas, a post that he held until 1892, when he was promoted to lieutenant colonel of the Third United States Cavalry. Beaumont retired from active service on May 16, 1892, and settled at Wilkes-Barre, Pennsylvania.

He was married to Margaret Rutter on September 18, 1861. She died on April 22, 1879, and he married Maria Lindsley Orton on December 20, 1883. After the death of his second wife on November 19, 1901, he married her sister, Stella S. Orton Rushing, in 1905. Beaumont was the father of four children. According to Robert Goldthwaite Carter,[qv] an officer in his regiment, Beaumont was "one of the finest types of an 'all around,' efficient" cavalry officer in the army; "with his jet black hair and moustache, soldier's slouch hat, riding pants tucked into his boots, pistols in his belt, and off-hand soldierly way of putting things," Beaumont "favorably impressed" the men of his troop. He died at Harvey's Lake, Pennsylvania, on August 17, 1916.

BIBLIOGRAPHY: Robert G. Carter, *On the Border with Mackenzie, or Winning West Texas from the Comanches* (Washington: Eynon Printing, 1935). Francis B. Heitman, *Historical Register and Dictionary of the United States Army* (2 vols., Washington: GPO, 1903; rpt., Urbana: University of Illinois Press, 1965). *Thomas W. Cutrer*

BEAUMONT, JEFFERSON (1801–1865). Jefferson Beaumont, early settler and public official, was born in Carter County, Kentucky, on March 12, 1801, the son of William Henry and Elizabeth (Cooper) Beaumont. On January 5, 1823, he married Sarah Greenleaf. The couple settled in Natchez, Mississippi, where Beaumont became a leading merchant. In 1845 he moved his family to Texas, accompanied by his brother Franklin and Franklin's family. Beaumont served as chief justice (county judge) of Calhoun County from August 22, 1848, to August 18, 1856. According to at least one source the city of Beaumont may have been named for him. He died at Carancahua, Jackson County, on July 25, 1865, and was buried there.

BIBLIOGRAPHY: Homer S. Thrall, *A Pictorial History of Texas* (St. Louis: Thompson, 1879) *L. W. Kemp*

BEAUMONT, CATHOLIC DIOCESE OF. The tenth Catholic diocese in Texas, the Diocese of Beaumont, was established on September 29, 1966. On territory now belonging to the diocese occurred some of the earliest Catholic activity in the state. Concerned over French exploration of eastern Texas in the 1680s, Spain sent a series of expeditions to strengthen the Spanish presence there. Catholic missionaries, including Francisco Casañas de Jesús María,[qv] accompanied these forces. Casañas founded Santísimo Nombre de María Mission on the edge of the Neches River, roughly five miles north of the site of modern-day Weches, Texas. Accounts differ as to whether the mission lay on the east or west bank. If the former, it would stand as the first mission within what, in time, would be the original boundaries of the Diocese of Beaumont, though the area was later assumed into the Catholic Diocese of Tyler.[qv] The first Mass was celebrated there on September 8, 1690. A flood destroyed the mission in 1692.

As the French presence waned and Indians grew increasingly hostile to the Spanish, missionary activity in East Texas was suspended, in 1693. Beginning in 1716, however, Franciscans[qv] returned to establish a string of East Texas missions. In 1718 San Antonio de Valero Mission was begun in San Antonio as a supply center for the network. War between the French and Spanish temporarily halted activity, but missionary efforts were resumed after 1721 and continued for over 100 years. In 1834, however, Padre José Antonio Díaz de León,[qv] the last of the Franciscan friars in the area, was killed in Polk County, and more than 140 years of Spanish Catholic activity in Texas came to an end.

Traditionally the Catholic Church[qv] in Texas had been under the direction of bishops in Mexico. Mexican independence and the establishment of the Republic of Texas,[qv] however, weakened this structure, and the Texas church came increasingly under the influence of French Catholics in Louisiana. In 1840 John Timon[qv] was appointed prefect apostolic of Texas; he was raised to vicar apostolic in 1842. On May 4, 1847, all of Texas became the Diocese of Galveston. Many new dioceses were established over the subsequent years as the original diocese was divided again and again. Beaumont was among these.

During the tenure of Galveston bishop Claude Marie Dubuis[qv] (appointed in 1861), the Sisters of Charity (*see* SISTERS OF CHARITY OF THE INCARNATE WORD, SAN ANTONIO) came to Texas, where they established a number of hospitals, including St. Mary's in Port Arthur and St. Elizabeth's (formerly Hotel Dieu) in Beaumont. During the administration of Bishop Nicholas A. Gallagher[qv] (appointed in 1882) church ministry to blacks increased significantly, especially under the Josephite Fathers (*see* BLACK CATHOLICS). Bishop Christopher E. Byrne,[qv] appointed in 1918, continued these efforts and initiated others to serve Hispanics, especially those who migrated to East Texas in the wake of the Cristero Revolt in the 1930s. The Spanish Augustinian Fathers continued this ministry.

In 1966 the Diocese of Beaumont was formed from the Catholic Diocese of Galveston-Houston.[qv] It included thirteen counties (Angelina, Cherokee, Hardin, Jasper, Jefferson, Nacogdoches, Newton, Orange, Polk, Sabine, San Augustine, Shelby, and Tyler) and the parts of Chambers and Liberty counties lying east of the Trinity River and Galveston Bay. The area covered 11,790 square miles of the Sabine region of East Texas. Bishop Vincent M. Harris[qv] was appointed to lead the new diocese, which had a Catholic population of some 83,000, most of it concentrated in the Beaumont–Port Arthur–Orange area. The diocese comprised thirty-two parishes and fifteen missions; seventy priests and 278 nuns staffed its various units. Warren L. Boudreaux served as the second bishop, from 1971 to 1978, then was transferred to a Louisiana diocese. The resettlement program "The Vietnamese," produced by the Diocese of Beaumont, won the praise of Pulitzer Prize author Frances Fitzgerald in the New York *Times* and was the cover feature in *Texas Monthly*[qv] in June 1976. Beaumont received its third bishop, Bernard J. Ganter, on December 13, 1978; Bishop Ganter died in 1994 and was replaced on May 9 of that year by Joseph A. Galante.

Over the years the diocese has continued to grow. On December 12, 1986, the Vatican established the Diocese of Tyler. Transferred to the new see were six northern counties previously in the Beaumont diocese: Angelina, Cherokee, Nacogdoches, Sabine, San Augustine, and Shelby. Afterward, the Diocese of Beaumont included an area of 7,080 square miles with a Catholic population of nearly 84,000. Major ethnic groups and nationalities of Catholics in the area include African Americans, Germans, Hispanics, Irish, Italians, Vietnamese,[qqv] and Cajuns. In 1994 eighty priests, sixty sisters, thirty-two permanent deacons, and four brothers served in a variety of ministries. The diocese ran forty-three parishes, ten missions, and two pastoral centers. Eight schools in the diocese enrolled 2,785 students on the elementary and secondary levels, and St. Mary's and St. Elizabeth's hospitals continued to provide health care in Port Arthur and Beaumont. The Beaumont edition of the *Texas Catholic* was replaced by the Diocesan paper, the *East Texas Catholic,* first published on February 12, 1982. In 1994 the paper's circulation was 15,000. (*See* CATHOLIC HEALTH CARE, CATHOLIC JOURNALISM). At the time, the Catholic population of the diocese numbered 89,124.

BIBLIOGRAPHY: Catholic Archives of Texas, Files, Austin. *East Texas Catholic,* August 8, 1986. History of the Beaumont Diocese (MS, Catholic Archives of Texas, Austin). *Texas Catholic,* December 19, 1986. *Texas Catholic Herald,* January 6, 1967. *Texas Monthly,* June 1976.

Steven P. Ryan, S.J.

BEAUMONT, TEXAS. Beaumont, the county seat of Jefferson County, is in the northeast part of the county, at 30°05′ north latitude, and 94°06′ west longitude, on the west bank of the Neches River and Interstate Highway 10, eighty-five miles east of Houston and twenty-five air miles north of the Gulf of Mexico. With nearby Port Arthur and Orange, it forms the Golden Triangle, a major industrial area on the Gulf Coast. Beaumont developed around the farm of Noah and Nancy Tevis, who settled on the Neches in 1824. The small community that grew up around the farm was known as Tevis Bluff or Neches River Settlement. Together with the nearby community of Santa Anna, it became the townsite for Beaumont when, in 1835, Henry Millard[qv] and partners Joseph Pulsifer and Thomas B. Huling[qqv] began planning a town on land purchased from the Tevises. The most credible account of how the town was named is that Millard gave it his wife's maiden name, Beaumont. At Millard's urging, the First Congress of the Republic of Texas[qv] made Beaumont the seat of the newly formed Jefferson County and granted it a charter in 1838. Under a second charter municipal government was organized in 1840, but it was soon abandoned. Another attempt at municipal government in 1860 was short-lived. Continuous municipal government dates from incorporation under a general statute in 1881. Beaumont was a small center for cattle raisers and farmers in its early years, and, with an active riverport by the late 1800s, it became an important lumber and rice-milling town. The Beaumont Rice Mill, founded in 1892, was the first commercial rice mill in Texas. Beaumont's lumber boom, which reached its peak in the late 1800s, was due in large part to the rebuilding and expansion of the railroads after the Civil War.[qv] By the early 1900s the city was served by the Southern Pacific, Kansas City Southern, Atchison, Topeka, and Santa Fe, and Missouri Pacific railroad systems. The population grew from 3,296 in 1890 to 9,427 in 1900.

The Spindletop oil gusher of 1901 produced a boom that left Beaumont with a doubled population (20,640 in 1910), great wealth, and a petroleum-based economy that expanded as refineries and pipelines were built and new fields discovered nearby (*see* SPINDLETOP OILFIELD). Three major oil companies—the Texas Company (later Texaco[qv]), Gulf Oil Corporation,[qv] and Humble (later Exxon[qv])—were formed in Beaumont during the first year of the boom. The Magnolia Refinery (*see* MOBIL OIL COMPANY) became the city's largest employer; by 1980 it was Mobil's largest manufacturing plant. Beaumont became a major seaport (variously second or third in tonnage in Texas in the 1970s) after the Neches was channelized to Port Arthur in 1908. By 1916 the channel was deepened, a turning basin dredged, and a shipyard constructed. The Gulf States Utilities Company, which serves southeast Texas and southwest Louisiana, made its headquarters in Beaumont. Discovery of a new oilfield at Spindletop in 1925 brought another burst of growth. The population of Beaumont was 40,422 in 1920 and 57,732 in 1930. This era also had its darker side: in the 1920s the Ku Klux Klan[qv] gained strength in Beaumont, and from 1922 to 1924 it controlled local politics. By the end of the 1920s, however, it had lost much of its membership and consequently its power. Though stagnant through the Great Depression,[qv] Beaumont's economy prospered during World War II[qv] with shipbuilding and oil refining. With the new boom came overcrowding, which may have contributed to the Beaumont race riot of 1943,[qv] in which interracial violence led to the declaration of martial law and the virtual shutdown of the city in June.

Beaumont's economy grew with petrochemicals and synthetic rubber in the post-war era and reached a plateau about 1960, when the growth slowed. In the mid-1950s the city, which had been segregated since Reconstruction,[qv] saw the civil rights movement begin to gain momentum, as the local chapter of the NAACP won two consecutive desegregation suits, one of them at Lamar State College. In the early 1960s an inquiry by the General Investigating Committee of the Texas House of Representatives resulted in three days of public hearings on Beaumont's illegal prostitution and gambling district, a boomtown byproduct; the police department was subsequently reorganized. Beaumont had 94,014 residents in 1950 and 119,175 in 1960; by 1964 it was the sixth-largest city in Texas. By 1970 its population had fallen to 115,919, in part because of the automation of the petrochemical industry that had begun in the early 1960s. Though by 1980 Beaumont's population had risen to 118,102, the city had fallen to the twelfth-largest in the state. The 1980 population was 61.2 percent white and 36.6 percent black and included large Italian and Cajun and small Hispanic and Asian elements. Religious groups include Catholics (*see* BEAUMONT, CATHOLIC DIOCESE OF), various Protestant denominations, and Jews. In the early 1980s major cultural organizations included a symphony orchestra, a civic opera, a ballet, several art museums, and a community playhouse. Medical facilities included one neurological and at least three general hospitals. The main campus of Lamar University is in Beaumont. The city's two independent school districts were united in 1983. In 1985 Beaumont had one newspaper, the Beaumont *Enterprise,*[qv] two television stations, and several local radio stations. Under its present charter (1947) Beaumont has a council-manager government. The Ninth Court of Civil Appeals, the federal district court, and the Lower Neches Valley Authority are located in Beaumont. Jefferson County Airport in Nederland provides the area with commuter and general aviation facilities; Beaumont is also served by its own municipal airport. Annual events in Beaumont include the South Texas State Fair, the Neches River Festival, and the Kaleidoscope Arts and Crafts Festival. The city park system comprises over thirty community and neighborhood parks and the Babe Didrikson Zaharias[qv] Museum. Major historical restorations include the John J. French Museum, the Tyrell Historical Library, and the McFaddin-Ward House.[qv] Among the city's museums are the Gladys City Boom Town Museum, a full-scale replica of the Spindletop boomtown, and the Texas Energy Museum. Beginning in the early 1980s the Beaumont area, because of its reliance on the depressed heavy-industry and petrochemical markets, became the slowest-growing in the state and consistently had the highest unemployment on the Texas Gulf Coast. In 1990 Beaumont had a population of 114,323, and the early 1990s witnessed a number of important revitalization projects in the downtown area.

BIBLIOGRAPHY: W. T. Block, ed., *Emerald of the Neches: The Chronicles of Beaumont from Reconstruction to Spindletop* (Nederland, Texas: Nederland Publishing, 1980). W. T. Block, A History of Jefferson County, Texas, from Wilderness to Reconstruction (M.A. thesis, Lamar University, 1974; Nederland, Texas: Nederland Publishing, 1976). James Anthony Clark and Michel T. Halbouty, *Spindletop* (New York: Random House, 1952). Judith Walker Linsley and Ellen Walker Rienstra, *Beaumont: A Chronicle of Promise* (Woodland Hills, California: Windsor, 1982). John H. Walker and Gwendolyn Wingate, *Beaumont, a Pictorial History* (Virginia Beach, Virginia, 1981).

Paul E. Isaac

BEAUMONT *ENTERPRISE*. The Beaumont *Enterprise* was first published as a weekly by John W. Leonard from November 6, 1880, until some time in 1889. A daily paper of the same name, published by the Beaumont Enterprise Publishing Company, began in 1897. The paper also appeared as the Daily *Enterprise*, Sunday *Enterprise*, Beaumont Sunday *Enterprise Journal*, and Beaumont *Enterprise Journal*. In the 1990s the paper was published by Aubrey L. Webb, edited by Ben Hansen, and had a circulation of 70,810.

BIBLIOGRAPHY: Paul Isaac, "Laissez-Faire to National Planning," *East Texas Historical Journal* 3 (October 1965). *Diana J. Kleiner*

BEAUMONT AND GREAT NORTHERN RAILROAD. The Beaumont and Great Northern Railroad was chartered on June 22, 1905, to connect Trinity in Trinity County with Livingston, thirty-seven miles to the southeast in Polk County. The capital stock was $370,000. The principal place of business was Onalaska, Polk County. The members of the first board of directors were William Carlisle and George W. Pennell, both of Atchison, Kansas; L. O. Jackson of Onalaska; James E. Hill[qv] and L. T. Sloan, both of Livingston; A. C. Bird of Chicago, Illinois; R. C. Fyfe of Tyler; H. E. Farrell of St. Louis, Missouri; and W. F. Davis of Groveton. Between August 1905 and May 1908 the company built thirty-three miles of track from Trinity through Onalaska to Livingston. In 1908 the B&GN was sold to R. C. Duff to become part of his proposed line from Waco to Port Arthur. Carlisle bought the road back in 1910 and by August 1911 had completed an additional fifteen miles between Trinity and Weldon. Shortly thereafter, Duff repurchased the line and sold it to the Missouri, Kansas and Texas (Katy). In 1913 the Katy asked the Texas legislature for authority to consolidate the B&GN. Permission was granted over the governor's veto, and the attorney general secured an injunction against the consolidation. The controversy was settled in 1914, when the Katy leased the B&GN for ninety-nine years and agreed to expend $6 million to extend the line from Weldon to Waco. However, the Katy entered receivership in 1915 and, when reorganized in 1923, left the B&GN out of the new company. The B&GN reverted to its original owners, who renamed it Waco, Beaumont, Trinity and Sabine Railway Company when independent operation resumed on April 1, 1923. *S. G. Reed*

BEAUMONT *INDUSTRIAL ERA*. The Beaumont *Industrial Era*, a black newspaper, was published between 1903 and 1947 in Beaumont.

BIBLIOGRAPHY: WPA Writers' Program, *Texas: A Guide* (New York: Hastings House, 1940; rev. ed. 1969). *Diana J. Kleiner*

BEAUMONT PLACE, TEXAS. Beaumont Place is on the Southern Pacific Railroad and U.S. Highway 90 two miles southwest of Sheldon Reservoir in east central Harris County. State highway maps in the 1980s showed two churches, a school, and numerous dwellings at the site. Beaumont Place was listed as a community in 1990, but without census figures. *Diana J. Kleiner*

BEAUMONT RIOT OF 1943. On June 15 and 16, 1943, whites and blacks clashed in Beaumont, Texas, after workers at the Pennsylvania shipyard in Beaumont learned that a white woman had accused a black man of raping her. On the evening of June 15 more than 2,000 workers, plus perhaps another 1,000 interested bystanders, marched toward City Hall. Ultimately the leaderless and disorganized crowd may have reached 4,000. Even though the woman could not identify the suspect among the blacks held in the city jail, the workers dispersed into small bands and began breaking into stores in the black section of downtown Beaumont. With guns, axes, and hammers, they proceeded to terrorize black neighborhoods in central and north Beaumont. Many blacks were assaulted, several restaurants and stores were pillaged, a number of buildings were burned, and more than 100 homes were ransacked. More than 200 people were arrested, fifty were injured, and two—one black and one white—were killed. Another black man died several months later of injuries received during the riot.

Mayor George Gary mobilized the Eighteenth Battalion of the Texas State Guard[qv] late that night, and acting Texas governor A. M. Aiken, Jr.,[qv] declared Beaumont to be under martial law. (Governor Coke Stevenson and Lt. Governor John Lee Smith[qqv] were both out of the state on official business.) A force of 1,800 guardsmen came to Beaumont, as did 100 state police and 75 Texas Rangers.[qv] Most arrived after the violence had subsided. A curfew of 8:30 P.M. was placed on the entire city, and the Texas Highway Patrol quickly sealed off the city by closing all roads. Beaumont was placed off-limits to all military personnel. Local bus services were halted, and all intrastate bus lines were rerouted around the town. Mayor Gary closed all liquor dispensaries in the city and also closed parks and playgrounds. All public gatherings were cancelled, including Juneteenth[qv] celebrations. Black workers were not allowed to go to work. The Jefferson County Fairgrounds was turned into a stockade to accommodate the overflow of prisoners from the city and county jails. By June 20 a military tribunal had reviewed the cases of the 206 arrested. Twenty-nine were turned over to civil authorities on charges of assault and battery, unlawful assembly, and arson. The remainder were released, mostly because of lack of evidence. Also on June 20, Aiken ended the period of martial law.

The Beaumont riot had its roots in the tensions of World War II.[qv] Beaumont had become a war boomtown when people moved there in 1941 to take jobs in the shipyards and war plants. The population of Jefferson County increased by 56,671 between 1941 and 1948; more than 18,000 of those settled in the city in 1942 and 1943. Rapid population growth brought about forced integration because service facilities were not abundant enough to permit complete segregation. Housing shortages were severe, and the races were forced to live in close proximity. In the factories, blacks began to have access to semi-skilled and skilled jobs, a situation that put them in competition with white workers. Tensions between whites and blacks were serious enough that early in June 1943 separate commuter transportation had been put into service to end racial violence on overcrowded buses. There were also food shortages. Food allotments and ration cards had been issued in 1941 in Beaumont. Although the population had drastically increased by 1943, wholesalers' quotas were still based on 1941 population figures—a situation that caused severe shortages of meats and canned goods. Three days before the riot, J. H. Kultgen, head of the regional food administration, wired Washington, D.C., with the message that the food shortages in Beaumont were "conducive to riot."

In addition to these factors, a chapter of the Ku Klux Klan[qv] was active in the city and was planning to host a regional convention of the Klan on June 29. They hoped to bring 15,000 to 20,000 Klansmen from all over the South to hear William Simmons, "imperial emperor" of the KKK, offer the keynote address. The proposed meeting received an enormous amount of media attention and helped intensify racial tensions. At the same time, the black community was preparing for its annual Juneteenth celebration, scheduled for Saturday, June 19, when hundreds of East Texas blacks were expected to come to Beaumont.

Finally, exacerbating these problems, a rape was alleged to have occurred on June 5. A black man was accused of assaulting an eighteen-year-old Beaumont telephone operator, the daughter of a Louisiana shipyard worker then working in a Beaumont plant. The black man was subsequently shot and killed by Beaumont police while resisting arrest. The incident had elevated racial tensions. When a second alleged rape occurred on June 15, it triggered the violence. Beaumont then joined Detroit, New York, Los Angeles, Mobile, Philadelphia, Indianapolis, Baltimore, St. Louis, and Washington, D.C., as sites of bloody race riots in the summer of 1943.

BIBLIOGRAPHY: James A. Burran, "Violence in an 'Arsenal of Democracy'," *East Texas Historical Journal* 14 (Spring 1976). James S. Olson and Sharon Phair, "Anatomy of a Race Riot: Beaumont, Texas, 1943," *Texana* 11 (1973).

James S. Olson

BEAUMONT AND SARATOGA TRANSPORTATION COMPANY. The Beaumont and Saratoga Transportation Company, chartered on February 13, 1905, was a unique facility in that it was chartered, not as a railroad common carrier, but as a transportation company. Its twelve miles of track, located in northern Jefferson County, ran from a pine timber stand to a mill owned by the Keith Lumber Company in Voth. At Voth the line connected with the Texas and New Orleans and the Gulf, Colorado and Santa Fe. The Beaumont and Saratoga Transportation Company was sold to the Kirby Lumber Company in 1922. Its track was abandoned in 1935.

BIBLIOGRAPHY: S. G. Reed, *A History of the Texas Railroads* (Houston: St. Clair, 1941; rpt., New York: Arno, 1981).

Julianne Johnston

BEAUMONT, SOUR LAKE AND WESTERN RAILWAY. The Beaumont, Sour Lake and Western Railway Company was chartered on August 8, 1903, as the Beaumont, Sour Lake and Port Arthur Traction Company; the name was changed on June 30, 1904. R. C. Duff and other financial backers from Columbus, Ohio, and Beaumont, Texas, organized the Traction Company to build an electric line between Port Arthur and Sour Lake. However, as Port Arthur seemed increasingly unlikely to overtake Houston as a major shipping center, and as Sour Lake oilfield[qv] production declined, some of the original investors lost heart. Duff nonetheless determined to complete at least part of the venture and retained enough financial support to complete a steam-powered railroad from Beaumont to Sour Lake in 1904. The members of the first board of directors were G. W. Meeker, Duff, Emory J. Smith, William Wiess, T. S. Reed, Hugh E. Smith, J. M. Richards, W. A. Smith, and B. R. Norvell. The renamed railroad amended its charter to allow it to connect Beaumont with Port Arthur, Sour Lake, Batson, and Houston, and to transport freight, passengers, mail and express. Duff sold the line to Benjamin Franklin Yoakum[qv] in 1905 at a tremendous profit for the remaining investors. As part of Yoakum's Gulf Coast Lines, the BSL&W was extended from Grayburg to Houston in December 1907 despite high water and the threat of yellow fever along the Trinity River. In 1916 the BSL&W reported passenger earnings of $180,000 and freight earnings of $604,000. The eighty-five-mile line became part of the Missouri Pacific[qv] system in 1924, but continued to operate as a separate company until merged with the MP on March 1, 1956.

Robert Wooster

BEAUMONT WHARF AND TERMINAL COMPANY. The Beaumont Wharf and Terminal Company was incorporated by John Henry Kirby[qv] and other businessmen on March 26, 1897, to build wharves along the Neches River and tracks to connect them with outside rail interests. The company laid between three and four miles of track. It was subsequently owned by the Atchison, Topeka and Santa Fe Railway Company and connected with city tracks at the Port of Beaumont. Other railroads serving Beaumont ran over portions of the BW&T to reach the port. The BW&T opened in 1898; in 1903 it reported total earnings of $52,000 and owned one locomotive and eighty-eight cars. In 1935 it had a four-mile belt railway at Beaumont plus terminal tracks. In 1937 the project was reclassified as a terminal operation. The properties of the company were merged into the Gulf, Colorado and Santa Fe Railway Company, effective at the close of business on June 30, 1957.

Robert Wooster

BEAUXART GARDENS, TEXAS. Beauxart Gardens, originally a federal subsistence homestead colony, is between U.S. Highway 69/96/287 and Farm Road 823 six miles southeast of Beaumont in eastern Jefferson County. Once the site of intensive rice farming by residents of Nederland and Viterbo, the area was developed by the federal government during the Great Depression[qv] and named for its location between Beaumont and Port Arthur. The town plat was filed in 1934 and approved by the Resettlement Administration the following year. Fifty families were located on the 205-acre tract. The houses, of three to six rooms, also included 3½ acres for each family to cultivate for its own use. Inhabitants worked part-time at nearby refineries and spent the remainder of their working hours on the government truck farm at Beauxart Gardens. A voting precinct was established at Beauxart Gardens on August 10, 1942. The community now lies slightly west of the Jefferson County airport.

BIBLIOGRAPHY: Beaumont *Enterprise*, May 31, 1936. WPA Federal Writers' Project, *Port Arthur* (Houston: Anson Jones, 1939).

Robert Wooster

BEAVER CREEK (Anderson County). Beaver Creek rises five miles northeast of Montalba in northwestern Anderson County (at 31°58′ N, 95°42′ W) and runs southwest for fifteen miles, through northwestern Anderson County, to its mouth on Catfish Creek, three miles northwest of Tennessee Colony (at 31°52′ N, 95°53′ W). The stream, intermittent in its upper reaches, traverses nearly level to moderately steep terrain surfaced by sandy and clayey upland soils. The banks are heavily wooded in places with oak, hickory, gum, and pine trees. Beavers live in the area. Otter Creek is the principal tributary of Beaver Creek.

—— (Burnet County). Beaver Creek rises between Lookout and Long mountains fourteen miles northwest of Burnet in northwestern Burnet County (at 30°55′ N, 98°20′ W) and flows southwest for eight miles to its mouth on Lake Buchanan (at 30°52′ N, 98°25′ W). The surrounding terrain is generally flat with local deep dissections and surfaced by shallow, stony soil that supports oak, juniper, and mesquite.

—— (Cherokee County). Beaver Creek rises two miles northeast of Central High in southeastern Cherokee County (at 31°43′ N, 95°03′ W) and runs southeast for 5½ miles to its mouth on the Angelina River, one mile north of the State Highway 21 bridge (at 31°41′ N, 94°58′ W). The stream is intermittent in its upper reaches. It traverses flat to gently rolling terrain surfaced by sandy and clay loam that supports grasses and mixed hardwoods and pines.

—— (Clay County). Beaver Creek rises two miles southwest of Ringgold in extreme eastern Clay County (at 33°45′ N, 97°59′ W) and flows northeast for fourteen miles, through eastern Clay and western Montague counties, before joining Belknap Creek two miles northwest of Belcherville (at 33°50′ N, 97°52′ W). The stream, intermittent through most of its course, traverses flat to rolling land surfaced by sandy and clay loams that support scrub brush, mesquite, live oak, post oak, conifers, and grasses. For most of its history the Beaver Creek area has been used as crop and range land. At times minerals have been extracted near the banks.

—— (Foard County). Beaver Creek, also known as Eutaw or Utah

Creek, rises two miles southwest of Dixie Mound and five miles west of Crowell in western Foard County (at 33°58′ N, 99°50′ W) and runs southeast for ninety miles, through Wilbarger County, to its mouth on the Wichita River, three miles north of Kadane Corner in Wichita County (at 33°53′ N, 98°49′ W). The creek is dammed in southwest Wilbarger County to form Santa Rosa Lake and in the southeastern part of the county to form Lake Electra. It is joined by Middle Beaver Creek and South Beaver Creek. Beaver Creek is intermittent in its upper reaches. It crosses an area of steeply to moderately sloping hills and flat to rolling terrain with local escarpments, surfaced by shallow and stony to deep sandy and clay loams that support mesquite, oak, grasses, hardwoods, conifers, and brush. The stream was first called Rio Eutaw or Utah; it was known by this name to members of the Texan Santa Fe expedition.[qv] It was given the name Beaver Creek by Randolph B. Marcy,[qv] perhaps for his Indian guide, a Delaware Indian named Black Beaver.

——— (Leon County). Beaver Creek, a spring-fed perennial stream, rises three miles west of Centerville in central Leon County (at 30°16′ N, 96°04′ W) and flows east for ten miles to its mouth on Keechi Creek, four miles east of Centerville (at 31°15′ N, 95°56′ W). It traverses gently sloping to nearly level terrain surfaced by sandy loam that supports post oak, black hickory, pecan, elm, water oak, and hackberry trees along the creekbed. Settlement in the vicinity began during the 1840s. By 1848 Centerville had been established on the north bank of the creek's upper course; it became the seat of Leon County in 1850. During Reconstruction[qv] two companies of Union troops were stationed on the north bank south of Centerville. Redland has been located on the south bank of the middle creek since the 1850s.

BIBLIOGRAPHY: James Young Gates and H. B. Fox, *A History of Leon County* (Centerville, Texas: *Leon County News*, 1936; rpt. 1977). Frances Jane Leathers, *Through the Years: A Historical Sketch of Leon County and the Town of Oakwood* (Oakwood, Texas, 1946).

——— (Mason County). Beaver Creek begins at the convergence of Threadgill and Squaw creeks, 3½ miles east of the Hilda church and cemetery in southeastern Mason County (at 30°32′ N, 99°05′ W). The stream, fed by numerous artesian springs, flows north for twelve miles to its mouth on the Llano River, a mile southeast of the Hedwig Hill community (at 30°40′ N, 99°06′ W). Beaver Creek rises in limestone hills on the eastern edge of the Edwards Plateau and traverses flat to rolling terrain with local escarpments. The land surface is shallow, stony, and clayey, with some areas of deep sandy loam. Grasses and open stands of live oak, mesquite, and Ashe juniper predominate in the area flora. Early German settlers from Fredericksburg began to settle along the banks of Beaver Creek around 1855. The community of Hilda later grew out of these settlements.

BIBLIOGRAPHY: Kathryn Burford Eilers, A History of Mason County, Texas (M.A. thesis, University of Texas, 1939). *Mason County News*, Centennial Edition, June 19, 1958.

BEAVER DAM, TEXAS. Beaver Dam is a small, predominantly black community fourteen miles northwest of DeKalb in northeastern Bowie County. The town, named for a large beaver dam on a nearby creek, has never had a post office. In 1933 it reported one rated business and a population of ten. In the 1940s and 1950s the reported population was twenty-five. In 1984 Beaver Dam comprised a church, a cemetery, and a few scattered houses.

BIBLIOGRAPHY: J. J. Scheffelin, *Bowie County Basic Background Book.*

Cecil Harper, Jr.

BEAVER DAM CREEK. Beaver Dam Creek, a perennial stream, rises eight miles northeast of Centerville in northeast Leon County (at 31°23′ N, 95°56′ W) and flows southeast for nineteen miles to its mouth on the Trinity River, on the Houston county line sixteen miles east of Centerville (at 31°17′ N, 95°42′ W). About five miles above its mouth, in an ancient segment of Trinity River bed, the stream fans into an extensive marsh of 4,000 acres. Terraces surrounding the marsh contain prehistoric Caddo archeological sites. The stream traverses steeply sloping to nearly level terrain, surfaced by sandy and clay loam that support dense woods of loblolly pine, sweet gum, post oak, black hickory, pecan, elm, water oak, and hackberry woods along the creekbed. Settlement of the area began during the early 1840s. Thomas H. Garner, one of the first settlers in the county, established a sawmill on a tributary of the creek. Since the mid-nineteenth century Eunice has been located on the north bank of the creek; Hopewell and Russell are also on the north bank. Pleasant Springs and Old Midway lie on the south bank of the upper creek.

BIBLIOGRAPHY: James Young Gates and H. B. Fox, *A History of Leon County* (Centerville, Texas: Leon County *News*, 1936; rpt. 1977). Leon County Historical Book Survey Committee, *History of Leon County* (Dallas: Curtis Media, 1986).

BEAVER LAKE. Beaver Lake, a natural reservoir, was located three miles northeast of Juno in northern Val Verde County (at 30°10′ N, 101°05′ W). It was a well-known landmark among Indians and early settlers. It was destroyed in the 1950s, after overgrazing on the upper hills allowed floodwaters to sweep gravel into the lake until it became an intermittent water hole. The surrounding terrain is sharply dissected canyonland cut from massive limestone with large wash deposits. The soils of the area are dark, calcareous stony clays and clay loams. The vegetation consists primarily of oak, juniper, grasses, mesquite, and water-tolerant hardwoods and conifers. Among the wildlife of the area is the broad-tailed or Mexican beaver, for which the lake was named. Indians came to Beaver Lake for water in the eighteenth and nineteenth centuries. By 1849 the United States Army was stationing soldiers there to protect travelers who stopped for water. The expedition of Lt. William Henry Chase Whiting[qv] came to Beaver Lake and found abandoned Comanche lodges in May 1855. Before the railroad arrived in South Texas, cattlemen drove their herds from Laredo to Beaver lake for watering before trailing them to northern markets. In the 1880s local cattlemen gathered their herds at the lake for branding. The town of Juno, three miles southwest of Beaver Lake, made use of its water. The Hurman Benteley family was among the first to settle near the lake.

BIBLIOGRAPHY: Roy L. Swift and Leavitt Corning, Jr., *Three Roads to Chihuahua* (Austin: Eakin Press, 1988). Whitehead Memorial Museum et al., *La Hacienda* (Norman: University of Oklahoma Press, 1976).

BEAZLEY, WILLIAM HERBERT (1837–1919). William Herbert Beazley, Confederate Army and Navy officer, physician, and advisor to the Coushatta Indians, was born on October 30, 1837, six miles east of Vicksburg, Mississippi, to A. G. A. and Mary Herbert (Washington) Beazley. When he was three years old, in 1840, the family moved to Texas. They lived in Smithfield, in what is now Polk County, across the Trinity River from the Logan league (*see* ACE, TEXAS). Beazley spent many of his early years working on his family's Logan-league plantation and operating a sailing vessel based at the site of present La Porte on Galveston Bay. On the Logan league he served as clerk, agent, and business manager for his uncle, Alexander Hamilton Washington,[qv] who operated the plantation.

After Texas entered the Confederacy in 1861, Beazley volunteered for service in the Confederate Navy and was attached, later in 1861, to the command of W. W. Hunter, the superintendent in charge of works for defense of the Texas coast. One of Beazley's principal duties was to operate his sailing vessel, the Fanny Morgan, as a dispatch boat and courier for guard duty on Galveston Bay and in staking channels. In 1862 he and Hunter and the local Alabama and Coushatta Indians cooperated with Major Washington in erecting obstructions in the Trinity River to prevent the ascent of Union gunboats; they also constructed flatboats to transport supplies down the Trinity to Confederate forces along the Texas coast. A Confederate naval station was established on the Logan league, and Beazley served as clerk and secretary to Commander Hunter.

Gen. John B. Magruder[qv] recaptured Galveston from federal forces on New Year's Day, 1863, and the naval station on the Logan league was abandoned in April 1863. Hunter and his command were ordered to Richmond, Virginia, for new assignments. Beazley requested a transfer to land forces and returned in the summer of 1863 to Texas, where he was authorized to organize the Alabama and Coushatta Indians and other recruits into a unit to build flatboats and transport supplies down the Trinity River to Confederate forces in the Texas coastal areas. This unit was listed in military records as Company A, Beazley's Unattached Cavalry, and in December 1863 was designated also as Company K and assigned on a standby basis to Morgan's Regiment of cavalry. In March 1864 Beazley's company moved to Magnolia, a Trinity River port in Anderson County, where they were joined by Capt. B. F. Lilley's company of Pardoned Deserters. Beazley received his parole in Houston on July 15, 1865, with the rank of captain, K Company, Morgan's Regiment.

After the war he attended the New Orleans School of Medicine (later Tulane University) and graduated in 1867. In 1868 he married Mary Virginia Carr of Smithville, Polk County, Texas; they eventually had twelve children. Mrs. Beazley died in 1893, and Beazley married Eugenie Sarah Jones of Leggett on January 16, 1895. Six children were born to this marriage.

The members of Coushatta chief Colita's[qv] village had continued to live on the Logan league, and Beazley served as their advisor and physician. He also helped to have the remainder of this group transferred to the Alabama Indian reservation in Polk County. A few of the Coushattas remained on the Logan league until 1906, when they moved to the Polk County reservation.

In 1878 Beazley joined the Methodist Church in Shepherd, Texas. He was a charter member of the Dick Dowling Camp of United Confederate Veterans of Houston and was awarded the Confederate Cross of Honor by the San Jacinto Chapter, United Confederate Veterans, at Cold Spring, Texas, in 1909. He died on May 18, 1919, and was buried in the cemetery adjoining the Shepherd Methodist Church.

BIBLIOGRAPHY: W. H. Beazley Collection, Polk County Museum, Livingston, Texas. Emma Haynes, The History of Polk County (MS, Sam Houston Regional Library, Liberty, Texas, 1937; rev. ed. 1968). Howard N. Martin, "Texas Redskins in Confederate Gray," *Southwestern Historical Quarterly* 70 (April 1967). *Official Records of the Union and Confederate Navies* (Washington: Department of the Navy, 1894–1927). *The War of the Rebellion: A Compilation of the Official Records of the Union and Confederate Armies* (Washington: GPO, 1880–1901).

Howard N. Martin

BEBE, TEXAS. Bebe, a rural community on Texas Highway 97 in southwestern Gonzales County, was originally called Stroman; two men named Perry and Stroman owned a general store in that location. In 1896–97, the area had tri-weekly mail service. When, on August 10, 1900, a post office was to be established, officials requested a name change. Presumably another Texas settlement already had that designation. The new name supposedly derived from the B. B. Baking Powder signs that lined the road into the place. H. R. Oakes established a general store soon after the post office opened. In 1914–15 Bebe had daily mail service and a population of twenty. Y. H. Stroman continued his merchandising operation and H. L. Whitten had opened a blacksmith shop. In time there were several stores, a barbershop, a combination garage and mercantile store, and a cotton gin that operated until 1948. In 1916 several small schools were consolidated into the Bebe school, which, in turn, was annexed to the Nixon school system in the mid-1940s. A Methodist church functioned in the community prior to 1941, when it was closed. Initially cotton was the economic foundation of the Bebe community. It was later superseded by poultry and livestock farming and the raising of feed grains. As farming became more mechanized and required less labor, and as transportation improved, Bebe and neighboring Monthalia and Cost saw their base eroded, and they began to contract. The 1990 population was approximately fifty-two, and the only business was the combination store and post office.

BIBLIOGRAPHY: Leonard Gandre and Estelle Froehner, *A Century of Methodism, 1886–1986: A History of the Monthalia United Methodist Church* (Gonzales, Texas: Quality Print Shop, 1986). Gonzales County Historical Commission, *History of Gonzales County* (Dallas: Curtis, 1986).

Estelle K. Froehner and Leonard A. Gandre

BECCERRO CREEK. Beccerro (Becerra) Creek, also known as Parida Creek, rises ten miles northeast of Laredo in south central Webb County (at 27°36′ N, 99°17′ W) and runs northeast for twenty-nine miles to its mouth on Salado Creek, twenty-seven miles northeast of Callaghan (at 27°58′ N, 98°58′ W). It traverses low-rolling and flat terrain with locally shallow depressions, surfaced by sandy and clay loams that support grasses, mesquite, chaparral, and water-tolerant hardwoods.

BECERRA CREEK. Becerra (Becerro) Creek, an intermittent stream, rises four miles southeast of Laredo in southwestern Webb County (at 27°26′ N, 99°22′ W) and runs southwest for eleven miles to its mouth on the Rio Grande, eleven miles south of Laredo (at 27°17′ N, 99°29′ W). The stream is consecutively dammed to form San Ramon Lake, O'Keefe Lake, and Zachary Lake. It traverses flat terrain with locally shallow depressions, surfaced by clays that support water-tolerant hardwoods, conifers, and grasses.

BECERRO CREEK. Becerro Creek begins two miles southeast of Bigfoot in far northeastern Frio County (at 29°01′ N, 98°51′ W) and runs southwest for ten miles to its mouth on San Miguel Creek, twelve miles northeast of Pearsall (at 28°56′ N, 98°55′ W). Becerro is Spanish for "yearling calf." The upper stream traverses an area of low-rolling hills and prairie; the downstream terrain is flat with locally shallow depressions. The land surface is clay and sand. Grasses, dwarf evergreen oaks, mesquite, water-tolerant hardwoods, and conifers grow in the area.

BECK, CARL (1850–1920). Carl (Karl) Beck, choir, orchestra, and band conductor, was born in Ilmenau, Thuringia, on April 26, 1850. He was educated as a musician in Germany, came to the United States as part of a music group in 1875, and settled in New Orleans. In May 1884 he moved to San Antonio to become conductor of the Beethoven Männerchor and the Mendelssohn Mixed Chorus. An energetic and progressive leader, Beck conducted excerpts from Richard Wagner's *Tannhäuser* and *Lohengrin* at the 1885 State Sängerfest in Houston. This may have been the first performance of Wagner in Texas. When San Antonio hosted the festival in 1887 Beck organized a forty-six-member orchestra that performed Felix Mendelssohn's Italian Symphony, possibly the first complete symphony to be heard in Texas.

Beck had an orchestra of more than two dozen players to complement his choruses and also to perform independently. The orchestra played a subscription series of six concerts at Muth's Garden in 1894, with concertmaster Wilhelm Marx as soloist. The need for a concert hall was satisfied in 1895, when the Beethoven Männerchor built the 1,200-seat Beethoven Hall on South Alamo Street. Beck programmed the music of Wagner whenever he could muster the forces necessary. During the 1896 State Sängerfest, hosted by the Beethoven Männerchor, Beck presented four concerts that included six Wagnerian works, in addition to music by Giuseppe Verdi, Ludwig van Beethoven, Camille Saint-Saëns, Karl Maria von Weber, and Edvard Grieg. The combined forces united to perform the "Spring" section of Joseph

Haydn's oratorio *The Seasons.* By the 1890s Beck had also developed an accomplished band, an addition that enabled him to promote popular music. Even with the band, Beck programmed Wagner in potpourri arrangements, and a wider audience than usual came to hear the performances.

In 1904, after twenty years in San Antonio, he moved to Odessa, where he organized a band of fourteen members that played from Toyah to Abilene. When enthusiasm waned, Beck moved to Pecos and later to Kingsville. In July 1919, after Arthur Claassen[qv] had left San Antonio, Beck again accepted conductorship of the Beethoven Männerchor and returned to the Alamo City, where he died on October 2, 1920. See also GERMAN MUSIC.

BIBLIOGRAPHY: Theodore Albrecht, "101 Years of Symphonic Music in San Antonio," *Southwestern Musician/Texas Music Educator,* March, November 1975.

Theodore Albrecht

BECK, FANNIE DAVIS VEALE (1861–1956). Fannie Beck, writer, daughter of William and Maria Lavenia (Cresswell) Veale, was born in Dresden, Texas, on October 15, 1861. In about 1863 the family moved to the vicinity of Palo Pinto, then on to the extreme western frontier of the state, where they were frequently attacked by Indians. At first the Veales lived in a large, rectangular, stone building that had been used for a fort. They later moved into a four-room, double log cabin. In *On the Texas Frontier,* a vivid, first-hand account of her life in Texas published in 1937, Fannie recalls the thirteen years of living in fear of the Indians before they were confined to reservations in 1875. Although she had only three years of formal education, Fannie was also taught by her father, who was a teacher, lawyer, judge, and state legislator. In about 1877 the Veales moved to Breckenridge. There, on March 3, 1885, Fannie married Henry Harrison Beck, a cattleman and merchant, who had founded the community's first church. The Becks first settled on a ranch in Bosque County. In 1888 they moved to the Gulf Coast, where they lived for two years in Rockport and twelve years in Aransas Pass. In 1903 they moved to Corsicana, where they lived for one year before moving to Morning Sun, Iowa, Henry's childhood home. Fannie and Henry Beck had eleven children; nine were born in Texas and two in Iowa.

Fannie Beck was a civic leader in Morning Sun. She was president of Sorosis Club National, a member of the board of directors of the Morning Sun Public Library, and a Sunday school teacher at the Presbyterian church. She was a Democrat and was keenly interested in politics. In 1937, so that her children would know about their Texas heritage, she published her historical memoir *On the Texas Frontier.* She died in St. Louis, Missouri, in 1956.

BIBLIOGRAPHY: Fannie Davis Veale Beck, *On the Texas Frontier: Autobiography of a Texas Pioneer* (St. Louis: Britt, 1937). Mary Whatley Clarke, *The Palo Pinto Story* (Fort Worth: Manney, 1956). Jo Ella Powell Exley, ed., *Texas Tears and Texas Sunshine: Voices of Frontier Women* (College Station: Texas A&M University Press, 1985).

Jo Ella Powell Exley

BECK, THOMAS (ca.1819–?). Thomas Beck, who represented Walker, Madison, and Grimes counties in the Texas House of Representatives during the Fourteenth, Sixteenth, and Seventeenth legislatures, was born in Kentucky about 1819, the son of black and white parents. He came to Texas around 1842 and was a farmer in Navasota when he was first elected to the legislature in 1874. During the Fourteenth Legislature Beck served on the Privileges and Elections and the Agriculture and Stock Raising committees. He was also elected to the Sixteenth Legislature, which met in 1879; in it he served on the Roads, Bridges, and Ferries Committee. During the Seventeenth Legislature of 1881 Beck sat on the Agricultural and the Roads, Bridges, and Ferries committees. He successfully sponsored a bill designed to prevent individuals from employing children without their parents' consent and expressed interest in legislation that would increase the authority of local courts and fund Prairie View State Normal School (now Prairie View A&M University). According to the United States census report, Beck lived with his wife Martha, three children, and two grandchildren in 1880.

BIBLIOGRAPHY: Merline Pitre, *Through Many Dangers, Toils and Snares: The Black Leadership of Texas, 1868–1900* (Austin: Eakin, 1985).

Paul M. Lucko

BECK BRANCH. Beck Branch rises two miles west of Cutoff Mountain in eastern Hamilton County (at 31°45′ N, 97°56′ W) and runs southwest for eight miles to its mouth on the Leon River (at 31°39′ N, 97°56′ W). It crosses flat to steeply sloping terrain surfaced by shallow, stony, clay loam that supports juniper, oak, grasses, chaparral, and cacti.

BECKER, TEXAS. Becker, three miles southwest of Anderson in southwestern Grimes County, was founded about 1869, when Christian Becker, an immigrant from the Rhineland, established a cotton gin in the vicinity of Holland Creek. Over the next several decades Christian Becker assisted in the settlement of more than twenty families of Germans[qv] in the Grimes County area and employed several of them at the gin. Mail service to the community was provided over a rural route from Navasota. The settlement appears to have been abandoned before the turn of the century.

BIBLIOGRAPHY: Grimes County Historical Commission, *History of Grimes County, Land of Heritage and Progress* (Dallas: Taylor, 1982).

Charles Christopher Jackson

BECKHAM, ROBERT H. (?–1916?). Robert H. Beckham, army officer, became a private in the Fourth Infantry, Texas Volunteer Guard, in 1890. He advanced through the ranks to a captaincy in 1898. During the Spanish-American War he was captain and commissary under Brig. Gen. S. S. Sumner and was brevetted major for gallantry at San Juan Hill and Santiago de Cuba. Beckham reentered the state service in July 1903, and became assistant quartermaster general in December 1909. He was adjutant general of Texas from December 15, 1910, to January 23, 1911, when he retired with the rank of brigadier general. He is believed to have died in 1916.

BIBLIOGRAPHY: *Biennial Report of the Adjutant General of Texas,* 1913.

Seymour V. Connor

BECKHAM, TEXAS. Beckham, six miles north of Sulphur Springs and two miles west of State highways 19 and 154 in north central Hopkins County, was named for early settlers Riley and John Beckham. John Barker settled at the site in 1864. A post office operated there from 1899 until 1904 with John S. Haggard as postmaster. In the mid-1930s Beckham had a church, a school, and a number of scattered dwellings. The school later was consolidated with the North Hopkins school district, and by the late 1980s only the church marked the site of the community. *J. E. Jennings*

BECKMAN, TEXAS. Beckman (Beckmann) was near the junction of Interstate Highway 10 and Loop 1604, fourteen miles northwest of downtown San Antonio in northwestern Bexar County. The site was settled before 1900 and named for John Beckmann, artist and recluse, who spent his last years there. In the mid-1930s Beckman was a flag stop on the Texas and New Orleans Railroad. The chief industry was a limestone quarry. In 1940 the settlement had a store, a church, and a population of twenty-five. After World War II[qv] most of the residents moved away, but as late as 1984 Beckmann was still shown on maps. *Minnie B. Cameron*

BECKMANN, ALBERT FELIX (1855–1900). Albert Felix Beckmann (Beckman), architect, was born in San Antonio, Texas, on September 16, 1855. After receiving his early education in San Antonio, he traveled to Germany, where he studied architecture. He returned to San Antonio around 1880 and in 1883 formed a partnership with James Wahrenberger,[qv] another German-trained architect. Among their most notable works in San Antonio were the White Elephant Saloon on Alamo Plaza, Dr. Kalteyer's Drug Store on Military Plaza, the City-County Hospital on San Fernando Hill (1886), and the original Joske's[qv] Store (1887, now demolished) at Alamo and Commerce streets. They also designed houses for many of the city's well-to-do residents, including Carl Hummel (1884), Edward Steves, Jr. (1884), Mrs. A. Elmendorf, E. Elmendorf, A. Nette, J. Minter, R. Pereida, S. Brewer, and others. In addition, Wahrenberger and Beckmann collaborated on jails in Brackettville and Eagle Pass, a courthouse in Eagle Pass, and a customs and warehouse building and a federal office building in Piedras Negras, Coahuila (1891). Beckmann spent eighteen months in Piedras Negras overseeing the construction.

He married Marie (Mary) Guenther on October 18, 1886. He was a member of the San Antonio Opera Club and the Turn-Verein (*see* TURNVEREIN MOVEMENT) and served as San Antonio city alderman from 1891 to 1896. Around 1891 Beckmann and Wahrenberger ended their partnership. Beckmann opened his own office but subsequently served with Wahrenberger as local architect for the St. Louis firm of E. Jugenfeld and Company for the construction of the Lone Star Brewery after 1895. He continued his practice until his death in 1900.

BIBLIOGRAPHY: Chris Carson and William B. McDonald, eds., *A Guide to San Antonio Architecture* (San Antonio Chapter, American Institute of Architects, 1986). Files, Architectural Drawings Collection, Architecture and Planning Library, University of Texas at Austin. San Antonio *Express*, October 25, 1881, July 24, 1889, June 11, 1890, February 4, 1891, April 3, 1892, July 23, 1893. *Christopher Long*

BECKMANN, JOHN CONRAD (1815–1907). John (Johann) Conrad Beckmann, ironwork craftsman, was born on June 13, 1815, in Rülle, near Osnabrück, Westphalia, the son of Johann Heinrich and Katarina Maria (Kohmöller) Beckmann. He immigrated to New York in 1839 and traveled to Baltimore and Cincinnati. He then returned to Zurich, Switzerland, and brought his betrothed, Regina Mueller, to New York, where they were married in 1841. His brothers Joe and Bernhart were already in New York.

Beckmann had been trained in Zurich as a locksmith, as a woodworking craftsman, and as a blacksmith. He moved to San Antonio, Texas, in 1846. Later he was employed by the United States government to set up three forges in the Alamo[qv] for blacksmith work for the army and for the renovation of the Alamo. His first home, built in 1849, was behind the Alamo on Crockett Street. Later he built a home and blacksmith shop on the southwest corner of Commerce and Casino streets. With the urging of Dr. Ferdinand Herff,[qv] Beckmann fashioned hand-wrought iron bedsteads for his German friends.

He was a charter member of Alamo Masonic Lodge Number 44. As a founder of the German-English School,[qv] he took part in the cornerstone laying in 1859, the hundredth anniversary of the birth of German poet Friedrich Schiller. Beckmann was a founder and charter member of early San Antonio German organizations: the Casino Club,[qv] the Turnverein (*see* TURNVEREIN MOVEMENT), the Krankenkassenverein (hospitalization insurance association), Arbeiter Verein (workers association), the Beethoven Männerchor, and the Teutonia Mixed Chorus (*see* GERMAN MUSIC). Beckmann died on April 12, 1907, in San Antonio and was buried in the Alamo Masonic Cemetery. He was survived by one son, although the Beckmanns had been the parents of seven children; several died in a cholera epidemic. Beckmann's portrait, painted by artist Edward Grenet[qv] in the early 1880s, is said to have encouraged the young artist in his career as a portrait painter.

BIBLIOGRAPHY: Frederick Charles Chabot, *With the Makers of San Antonio* (Yanaguana Society Publications 4, San Antonio, 1937). San Antonio *Express*, April 13, 1907. San Antonio *Light*, April 1, 1973. *A Twentieth Century History of Southwest Texas* (2 vols., Chicago: Lewis, 1907). *S. W. Pease*

BECKNELL, WILLIAM (1787/88–1856). William Becknell, known as the "Father of the Santa Fe Trade," son of Micajah and Pheby (Landrum) Becknell, was born in Amherst County, Virginia, in 1787 or 1788. He married Jane Trusler there in 1807 and was living near St. Louis, Missouri, by 1810. He saw extensive service on the frontier during the War of 1812. He joined Daniel Morgan Boone's company of United States Mounted Rangers as first sergeant in May 1813. He was promoted to the rank of ensign in July 1814, shortly after Boone's nephew, James Callaway, assumed command of the company. Becknell participated in Maj. Zachary Taylor's[qv] campaign against British-backed Indians that culminated in the battle of Credit Island, at the site of present-day Davenport, Iowa, in September 1814. He commanded the defense of Fort Clemson, Missouri, when Captain Callaway was killed by Indians in March 1815.

Becknell moved to central Missouri after the war and engaged in ferrying, freighting, and the salt trade. By 1817, after the death of his first wife, he had married Mary Cribbs, a Methodist from Pennsylvania, and had moved to Franklin, Missouri. William and Mary had three children. Becknell was an unsuccessful candidate for the Missouri House of Representatives in 1820. Motivated by financial problems, he organized a trading party that crossed the Great Plains to New Mexico in 1821. His party was welcomed to the previously forbidden province, and he returned to Franklin with encouraging profits. He took the first wagons across the trail in 1822 on his second journey to New Mexico, and led a party of trappers into Colorado on his third visit in 1824–25. He participated in the federal grading and marking project of the Santa Fe Trail[qv] in 1825 and 1826. He was appointed justice of the peace of Saline County, Missouri, in 1827, and was elected to the Missouri House of Representatives in 1828 and 1830 as a Jacksonian Democrat. He commanded a company of militia during the Black Hawk War.

In 1835 Becknell moved to Red River County, Texas. He mustered a company of mounted volunteers known as the Red River Blues in July 1836. The unit served along the Lavaca River until October. In that month Becknell reported to the capital of the Republic of Texas,[qv] believing that he had been elected to the House of Representatives, but relinquished his place when Collin McKinney[qv] arrived from Red River County with a greater number of votes. Becknell subsequently commanded Red River militia companies in 1838, 1841, and 1842. Though he entered regional folklore as the foolish farmer who traded 1,000 acres of fertile land for a supply of antifever pills, he amassed a sizable estate in land and livestock in Red River and Lamar counties. He also owned a bridge spanning the Sulphur River. He was appointed to supervise the Texas congressional elections of 1845, and the United States congressional elections of 1846. Becknell died on April 25, 1856, and was buried near Clarksville.

BIBLIOGRAPHY: Larry M. Beachum, *William Becknell, Father of the Santa Fe Trade* (El Paso: Texas Western Press, 1982).
Larry Mahon Beachum

BECK'S CHAPEL, TEXAS. Beck's Chapel was off Farm Road 59 eleven miles south of Athens in southern Henderson County. It was founded in the late 1840s by David A. Anding and his family and was evidently named for an early church. A local school was operating by 1906, when it had an enrollment of forty-three. In the mid-1930s the settlement had a church, a vacant school building, and a number of houses. After World War II[qv] many of the residents moved out of the area, and in the early 1990s only a church, a cemetery, and a few houses remained. *Christopher Long*

BECKUM CREEK. Beckum Creek rises two miles east of Woodlawn in north central Harrison County (at 32°40′ N, 94°18′ W) and runs northeast for 6½ miles through northeastern Harrison County to its mouth on Big Cyprus Bayou, near Baldwin (at 32°43′ N, 94°14′ W). It is intermittent in its upper reaches. The surrounding gently undulating to hilly terrain is surfaced by loam and clay and is heavily wooded in places with pine and hardwood trees. The land is used predominantly for agriculture.

BECKVILLE, TEXAS. Beckville, at the junction of State Highway 149 and Farm roads 124 and 959, eight miles northeast of Carthage in northeastern Panola County, was established a mile east of the present site and named for Matthew W. Beck, who settled in the area around 1850. A local post office opened in 1857, and by 1885 the community had two churches, two steam gristmills, three general stores, a hotel, a blacksmith, and an estimated population of seventy-five. When the Texas, Sabine Valley and Northwestern Railway was built through the county in 1886, the townspeople demanded such high prices for their property that railroad officials bypassed it a mile to the south. Joe Biggs, who owned the land in that area, sold it to the railroad and laid out a new townsite. Within a short time most of the businesses were moved to the railroad and the old Beckville was completely deserted. The first Beckville school was built in 1889, and by 1897 the town had a three-teacher school with a total enrollment of 151. In 1914 the population reached 750. In 1917 a fire destroyed a part of the business district. Beckville was incorporated by 1929, when it had a population of nearly 880. A drought in 1927 and the onset of the Great Depression,[qv] however, halted the town's growth. By the mid-1930s the population had dropped to 453, and many businesses were closed. After World War II[qv] the population remained steady; in 1965 Beckville had a population of 423 and twelve businesses. In 1990 the population was 783, and in the early 1990s the community had fifteen rated businesses.

BIBLIOGRAPHY: *History of Panola County.* (Carthage, Texas: Carthage Circulating Book Club, 1935?). Leila B. LaGrone, ed., *History of Panola County* (Carthage, Texas: Panola County Historical Commission, 1979). John Barnette Sanders, *Index to the Cemeteries of Panola County* (Center, Texas, 1964). John Barnette Sanders, *Post-offices and Post Masters of Panola County, Texas, 1845–1930* (Center, Texas, 1964).

Christopher Long

BECKWORTH, LINDLEY GARRISON (1913–1984). Lindley Garrison Beckworth, United States representative, judge, and lawyer, was born on June 30, 1913, in Kaufman County, Texas, to Otis Jefferson and Josie (Slaughter) Beckworth. He attended several common schools in Upshur County and in 1928 enrolled in Gilmer High School, from which he graduated in 1931. Like both of his parents, Beckworth became a teacher. After attending Southern Methodist University in 1931–32, he taught at Shady Grove in Upshur County during 1932–33. He attended Sam Houston State Teachers College (now Sam Houston State University) the first summer term of 1933 and the University of Texas from July 1933 to June 1934. In the spring of 1934 he worked for the Civil Works Corps and took correspondence courses from Abilene Christian College. He taught during the 1934–35 and 1935–36 school years, attended the University of Texas law school during the summer of 1935, and attended Baylor University law school in the summer of 1936.

In January 1936 Beckworth, a Democrat, announced his candidacy for the state legislature. He later defeated five candidates in the first primary, but did not receive a majority of the votes. In the runoff he was nominated by a 3,343-vote margin. After representing the Fourth District in the Texas House of Representatives for one term, he was one of five candidates who ran against incumbent Morgan G. Sanders[qv] in 1938 for the Third Congressional District seat. With his father as campaign manager, Beckworth led in the first primary. He defeated Brady Gentry[qv] in the second primary and went on to become, at twenty-five, the youngest person elected to the United States House of Representatives in the twentieth century. He served seven terms in the House and in 1952 announced his candidacy for the Senate seat that Thomas T. Connally[qv] was vacating. Despite a three-month, 20,000-mile campaign, Beckworth lost to Price Daniel, Sr.,[qv] by a three-to-one margin. After losing the 1954 election for his old House seat by less than 1,000 votes, he recaptured it in 1956. In the United States House of Representatives Beckworth was an advocate of small farmers and businessmen, servicemen and veterans, and education. His House committee memberships included Interstate and Foreign Commerce, Post Office and Civil Service, and Foreign Affairs. He was the chairman of the Texas congressional delegation in 1952.

The 1965 Reapportionment of Congressional Districts Act eliminated Beckworth's district and placed him in the Fourth Congressional District, represented by Ray Roberts. He lost to Roberts in the 1966 primary. President Lyndon B. Johnson[qv] appointed him to the United States Customs Court on March 14, 1967, and he served until August 1968. He then practiced law in Longview with the firm of Whitehead and Whitehead. In November 1970 he was elected to the Texas Senate from the Second Senatorial District. As a state senator, he worked for the establishment of the University of Texas at Tyler and the University of Texas Health Center at Tyler.[qv] He served one term and returned to his law practice.

Beckworth married Eloise Carter of Tyler on June 27, 1942; they had two daughters and three sons. Two of the sons subsequently practiced law with their father. During and after his congressional career, Beckworth lived in Upshur County. He was admitted to the State Bar of Texas[qv] in 1937, was a member of the Forum Law Society, the Masons, and the Odd Fellows. He was a Baptist. He died on March 9, 1984, at the University of Texas Health Center in Tyler and is buried in Rose Hill Cemetery, Tyler.

BIBLIOGRAPHY: Lindley Garrison Beckworth Papers, Barker Texas History Center, University of Texas at Austin. Billie Bundick Kemper, Lindley Beckworth: Grassroots Congressman (M.A. thesis, Stephen F. Austin State University, 1980). Tyler *Courier-Times-Telegraph,* March 11, 1984. Vertical Files, Barker Texas History Center, University of Texas at Austin.

Lawrence A. Landis

BECTON, EDWIN PINCKNEY (1834–1901). Edwin Pinckney Becton, physician and legislator, son of Eleanor (Sharpe) and John May Becton,[qv] was born in Gibson County, Tennessee, on June 27, 1834. In 1841 the family moved to San Augustine, Texas. Becton attended Austin College and an academy in Rusk County and studied medicine in private offices in New Danville, Texas, and Nashville, Tennessee, before entering the medical department of the University of Nashville, where he graduated on March 2, 1857. He did postgraduate work at the University of Louisville, 1873–74, the University of Maryland, 1879–80, and Tulane University, 1885–86. In 1862 he entered the Confederate Army as a private in the company of Capt. J. F. Pegue of the Waterhouse Regiment. He became assistant surgeon in the army and served with the Twenty-second Regiment, Texas Infantry, under Richard B. Hubbard.[qv] After the war Becton practiced at Tarrant (Hopkins County) and Sulphur Springs and also represented Hopkins County in the Texas Legislature, 1870–71. He was president of the Medical Association of Texas (later the Texas Medical Association[qv]) in 1886. In 1895 he was appointed superintendent of the Texas School for the Blind[qv] at Austin. Becton married Mary Eliza Dickson on November 17, 1857. After her death, he married Mrs. Olivia L. Smith in 1867. He died in Austin on January 14, 1901.

BIBLIOGRAPHY: Lewis E. Daniell, *Types of Successful Men in Texas* (Austin: Von Boeckmann, 1890). George Plunkett [Mrs. S. C.] Red, *The Medicine Man in Texas* (Houston, 1930). *Transactions of the State Medical Association of Texas,* 1901.

Jeanette H. Flachmeier

BECTON, JOHN MAY (1806–1853). John May Becton, Presbyterian minister and teacher, was born in Craven County, North Carolina, on January 9, 1806, to Frederick Edwin and Fannie (May) Becton. Soon after John's birth, the Bectons sold their farm and moved to Rutherford County, Tennessee, where the boy attended Pebble Hill Academy. John married Eleanor Sharp on January 18, 1827. They lived on their farm in Rutherford County, Tennessee, until 1831, when they sold the farm and moved to Gibson County, Tennessee. After being converting from the Baptist faith to Presbyterianism in 1832, Becton was ordained at Mount Carmel Presbyterian Church in Tennessee, in April 1840.

He arrived in San Augustine County, Texas, in the fall of that year, and his family came in 1841. Becton became pastor of the Goodlaw Schoolhouse Congregation, which he moved to San Augustine. There he became a schoolteacher. On February 11, 1843, he met with Marcus A. Montrose and Phanuel W. Warriner[qqv] in the San Augustine Presbyterian Church to organize the Presbytery of Eastern Texas, which was absorbed into the Presbytery of the Brazos shortly thereafter and became the establishing source of support for San Augustine University. The men obtained a subscription of 4,500 acres, and during the second term of the university Becton served as head teacher of the Introductory Department. In addition to his ministry and teaching, he also organized a chapter of the Sons of Temperance in San Augustine. Because of ill health, however, he resigned his pastorate and his teaching position in December 1843. In 1844 he was living in Nacogdoches County, Texas. Thereafter, he asked to return to missionary work and was encouraged by the church to do so. Becton organized Douglas (Emmaus) Presbyterian Church in 1844. In 1845 he also joined James H. Starr and Thomas J. Rusk[qqv] to establish Nacogdoches University.

In 1845 Becton organized the Presbyterian church in Henderson and became a teacher at Rusk Academy. He also organized churches at Rusk and Larissa and reported that he was in charge of five churches and eight mission stations. He organized numerous other churches, including those at Palestine, Church Hill, Mount Bethel, and Gum Springs. In 1852 he founded Church Hill Academy in northern Rusk County, and in 1851 he, Warriner, and W. H. Singletary were appointed to organize the Presbytery of Eastern Texas. Becton died on July 14, 1853, at Danville and was buried there.

BIBLIOGRAPHY: George L. Crocket, *Two Centuries in East Texas* (Dallas: Southwest, 1932; facsimile reprod., 1962). William Stuart Red, *A History of the Presbyterian Church in Texas* (Austin: Steck, 1936).

Carl L. McFarland

BECTON, TEXAS. Becton is on the Burlington Northern Railroad just east of Farm Road 400 and twenty-four miles northeast of Lubbock in northeastern Lubbock County. It was first named for W. E. Bledsoe of the Three Circle Ranch, but in 1917, when E. H. Moody applied for a post office, there was already a Texas town named Bledsoe, so he used the name Becton, after Abner M. Becton, an early settler who donated land for a new school building. Moody then became the first and only postmaster. Mail reached Becton by way of Lorenzo Star Route until the Fort Worth and Denver Railway began operation in 1928. According to old-timers, the post office operated until 1949; other sources indicate that it closed by 1943. The first school was a one-room building constructed by W. E. Bledsoe, where students attended for two terms. The school also housed local church services. It was moved to a new location in 1910 but later burned. In 1924 a new brick building was built. The Bledsoe Independent School District is one of the oldest in Lubbock County; at one time it was incorporated with the Estacado school district. In the summer of 1936 Bledsoe School became a part of the Idalou school district. The Bledsoe Church of Christ was established in 1917 and served the community until the early 1970s. The Baptist church in Bledsoe was first organized in 1915 as the Bethany Baptist Church, and the group had its own building. In the 1920s the Baptist group built a new building named Becton Baptist Church. Because of declining membership the small remaining congregation disbanded in 1973.

The community was located in a rich farming area and was increasingly prosperous with the advent of irrigation. In 1936 Becton had three businesses, two schools, a church, and a population of twenty-five. In 1945–46 there were still three businesses, and the population had jumped to 150. In 1974 Becton had no businesses and a population of 125. In 1978 the community had three churches and a factory. In 1990 it had no businesses and 125 residents.

Jeanne F. Lively

BEDDOE, EARL PERCY (1822–1876). Earl Percy Beddoe, pioneer civil engineer, was born on January 30, 1822, in eastern Tennessee, son of Philip Tolbert and Catherine (Parr) Beddoe. He married Martha Caroline Hembree on October 12, 1843, in Tennessee, and they had nine children. In 1845, after an education in civil engineering, Beddoe moved to Texas, lived in Marshall, where he built a tanyard, then in 1850 settled in Sabinetown, where he established a saddle and harness business. He served for a while there as school principal; he was named county surveyor of Sabine County and laid out the town of Hemphill as the new county seat in 1859. Beddoe acted as a courier during the Civil War,[qv] and as a civil engineer he figured in the planning of fortifications at Sabine Pass in 1863 (*see* SABINE PASS, BATTLE OF). He helped plan and execute the embankments or breastworks fortifying Sabinetown in 1864. In 1869 or early 1870 the family moved to Sabine Parish, Louisiana, but soon after 1871 they moved to Navarro County, Texas, where Beddoe died on November 27, 1876, in Chatfield.

BIBLIOGRAPHY: Robert Cecil McDaniel, *Sabine County, Texas* (Waco: Texian, 1987). Helen Gomer Schluter and Blanche Finley Toole, *1850 Sabine County Census* (Westminster, Colorado, 1979). Virgie Speights, *Old Timers of Sabine County* (Nacogdoches, Texas: Ericson, 1983).

Helen Gomer Schluter

BEDFORD, TEXAS. Bedford, bisected by State Highway 121, is northeast of Fort Worth in the northeast quadrant of Tarrant County, north of the West Fork of the Trinity River. The first settlers arrived in the late 1840s in the Bedford area, located strategically between Fort Worth and Grapevine. Milton Moore of North Carolina established the community's first school in his log cabin in 1861 with a dozen or more students. A settlement developed in the 1870s, after Weldon Bobo moved from Tennessee and established a general store and gristmill to serve area farmers. Bobo and a group of farmers agreed to name their community Bedford, after the county in Tennessee from which many of them had come. Bobo, Moore, and others founded New Hope Christian Church in 1874, and the first official post office opened in Bobo's home in 1877. In the 1880s and 1890s Bedford was a booming town, with a population of 1,000 or possibly even 2,000 that surpassed that of all other Tarrant County towns except Fort Worth. In addition to the alleged twenty-eight businesses that served the town, the community was also the home of Bedford College, founded in 1882. The college, which was something of a combination high school–junior college, survived until fire gutted the building in 1893.

Shortly after 1900 the prosperity ended. In 1901 the Dallas–Fort Worth Interurban rail line was built south of the Trinity, and, closely paralleling it, U.S. Highway 80 was also soon completed through Arlington and Grand Prairie. The two new arteries diverted traffic away from Bedford Road. In 1903 the Rock Island Railroad also bypassed Bedford. Businesses and residents moved, and the post office closed in 1909. Though only Bobo's store and perhaps fifty residents were left in the business district, in 1912 the town built a new two-story brick school on the site of the old college. Truck farming and dairying were prevalent from 1910 through the 1930s, and there were no more than eighty residents in Bedford as late as 1940. The community's general store was maintained by the related Bobo and Fitch families from the 1870s to the 1960s.

World War II[qv] and the construction of nearby military bases and defense plants caused Bedford's population to swell to something over 400 by 1953; 100 of the residents lived at Bedford Boys Ranch, a home for wayward boys aged ten to fourteen. The post office reopened in 1950. In fear of being swallowed up by burgeoning Hurst or Euless, the town voted 55 to 20 to incorporate in 1953. In 1955 Bedford voted against merging with the new Hurst-Euless School District, but in 1958 residents narrowly approved the school merger by 212 to 189. Between 1955 and 1960 Bedford increased its size from two square miles to just over ten, and the population increased to more than 2,700. But the 1961 master plan zoned everything as residential or agricultural, presaging painful political clashes in the 1960s between newcomers demanding services and old-line settlers resisting suburbanization and taxes. Newcomers launched a movement to merge Bedford with the more populous Euless in 1967. It passed in Euless, but was beaten in Bedford by 975 to 422. Bedford apartment zoning, however, began in 1968, and in 1969 the Bedford Chamber of Commerce merged with the Hurst-Euless chamber and the three towns established a hospital district.

By 1970 Bedford had more than 10,000 residents. In 1974 the old Boys Ranch became the town's biggest park. The decade of the 1970s saw the establishment of an industrial park, shopping centers, and restaurants, as well as the completion of the nearby Dallas–Fort Worth International Airport.[qv] There was a tremendous growth spurt from the late 1970s through the mid-1980s. Thousands of urbanites were seeking a small-town life; most were professionals and Republicans, and many were northerners. Battles over apartment and commercial zoning marked the 1970s and 1980s. The population increased to some 20,800 in 1980 and about 44,000 in 1990, with 400 businesses. The town was split in the 1990s over proposed city involvement in the development of a central business district, an effort to create a downtown in a suburban community. The old Bedford School, complete with museum, was scheduled for restoration in 1994.

BIBLIOGRAPHY: Clippings File, Bedford Public Library. *Historic Resources Survey: Selected Tarrant County Communities* (Fort Worth: Historic Preservation Council for Tarrant County, 1990). Vertical Files, Barker Texas History Center, University of Texas at Austin (Bedford, Texas, Peters' Colony).

George N. Green

BEDIAS, TEXAS. Bedias is at the intersection of State Highway 90 and Farm roads 1696 and 2620, twenty-nine miles northeast of Navasota in northeast Grimes County. The community was named for the Bidai Indians, whose Caddo name means "brushwood." The town in turn has given its name to the distinctive tektites[qv]—called Bediasites—found in Texas, most of which have been discovered within Grimes County. Settlement of the area began in 1835, when Thomas Phiney Plaster[qv] established a plantation a few miles west of the present townsite; earliest reports of the community refer to it as Plasterville. In 1844 Archelaus B. Dodson[qv] took up residence on the northern edge of the settlement; his wife, Sarah Bradley Dodson,[qv] reportedly designed the first Lone Star flag. A post office was established at Bedias in 1846, 1847, or 1867, according to various sources. A Baptist church was organized in 1848, and the first Methodist congregation in the community was formed by a circuit rider from Palestine in 1871. By 1885 the population had grown to 300 residents, who supported four gristmill-gins, three churches, and four privately operated schools.

In 1903 the International–Great Northern Railroad line reached Bedias. By 1907 the town had five general stores, two banks, two hotels, two gins, and sundry additional businesses; by 1915 a population of 500 was reported. Most of the town's business section was destroyed by fire in 1927 but was soon restored. In 1936 the town reported twenty-five rated businesses and an estimated population of 500. The community's fortunes declined during the 1960s. By 1967 its population had fallen to an estimated 290 and its businesses to five. In 1990 Bedias had a population of 301 and six rated businesses.

BIBLIOGRAPHY: Grimes County Historical Commission, *History of Grimes County, Land of Heritage and Progress* (Dallas: Taylor, 1982). Adele B. Looscan, "Harris County, 1822–1845," *Southwestern Historical Quarterly* 18–19 (October 1914–July 1915).

Charles Christopher Jackson

BEDIAS CREEK. Bedias Creek, a spring-fed perennial stream, rises four miles southeast of North Zulch in far southwestern Madison County (at 30°51′ N, 96°06′ W) and flows east for forty-seven miles to its mouth on the Trinity River, at the Houston county line (at 30°56′ N, 95°37′ W). The creek's lower course forms the border between Madison and Walker counties. The stream traverses gently sloping to nearly level terrain surfaced by loam and clay that support post oak, black hickory, pecan, elm, water oak, willow oak, black gum, hackberry, sweet gum, and loblolly pine trees along the banks. Settlement in the vicinity began during the 1830s. In the late nineteenth century Bullard was established on the north bank of the middle creek. Cross was founded on the south bank of the upper creek about 1900. The stream derives its name from that of the Bidai Indians, who inhabited land that is now in northern Grimes and southern Madison counties in the early nineteenth century.

BIBLIOGRAPHY: Grimes County Historical Commission, *History of Grimes County, Land of Heritage and Progress* (Dallas: Taylor, 1982). Madison County Historical Commission, *A History of Madison County* (Dallas: Taylor, 1984).

BEDIAS ROAD. The Bedias Road or Bedias Trail, an Indian trail of the time of Spanish and French exploration, connected the Bidai Indian village on Bedias or Santo Tomás Creek with another settlement at or near the site of present Nacogdoches. The trail crossed the Trinity River at Paso Tomás, the site of Bucareli,[qv] passed the Bidai village at the Don Joaquín crossing of the Angelina River, ten miles south of Nacogdoches, and then turned north toward Nacogdoches. This is one of the roads called El Camino Real by the Spaniards, but it was not the same as the Old San Antonio Road,[qv] the principal *camino real* of Texas.

BIBLIOGRAPHY: A. Joachim McGraw, John W. Clark, Jr., and Elizabeth A. Robbins, eds., *A Texas Legacy, the Old San Antonio Road and the Caminos Reales: A Tricentennial History, 1691–1991* (Austin: State Department of Highways and Public Transportation, 1991).

Robert Bruce Blake

BEDICHEK, ROY (1878–1959). Roy Bedichek, writer and folklorist, was born in Cass County, Illinois, on June 27, 1878, the son of James Madison and Lucretia Ellen (Craven) Bedichek. In 1884 the family moved to Falls County, Texas. Bedichek attended rural schools and Bedichek Academy, established at Eddy by his father. In February 1898 he entered the University of Texas. Soon he began to work in the office of the registrar, John A. Lomax,[qv] who became his friend for life. In 1903 he received a B.S. degree and in 1925 an M.A. He was a reporter for the Fort Worth *Record* (1903–04) and taught in high schools in Houston (1904–05) and San Angelo (1905–08). He served as secretary of the Deming, New Mexico, Chamber of Commerce (1908–13) and edited the Deming *Headlight* (1910–12). In 1910 he married Lillian Lee Greer; they had three children. In 1913 Bedichek returned to Austin and became secretary of the Young Men's Business League, which later merged with the chamber of commerce. In 1915–16 he was executive secretary of Will C. Hogg's[qv] Organization for Promoting Interest in Higher Education in Texas. He served as city editor of the San Antonio *Express* for a year; then in the fall of 1917 he began work in Austin with the University Interscholastic

League,[qv] a part of the Bureau of Extension. As director of the league he shaped its policies and made it a success. He ceased direction in 1948 at the age of seventy. In visiting schools over the state he formed the habit of camping out because suitable lodging was often unavailable. Camping stimulated his interest in wildlife, especially in birds. Urged by his close friends, J. Frank Dobie and Walter Prescott Webb,[qqv] he took a leave of absence for a year beginning in February 1946 and went into seclusion at Friday Mountain Ranch,[qv] Webb's retreat southwest of Austin, to write *Adventures with a Texas Naturalist* (1947), which is included in John H. Jenkins's[qv] *Basic Texas Books. Karánkaway Country* (1950) won the Carr P. Collins[qv] Award for the best Texas book of the year, as did *Educational Competition: The Story of the University Interscholastic League of Texas* (1956). A fourth book, *The Sense of Smell* (1960), appeared posthumously. Bedichek liked to rise several hours before daybreak and study or write in a separate building beside his home. Every day he worked in his garden, swam, or walked. Without ever having been seriously ill, he died suddenly of heart failure on May 21, 1959. He was an excellent storyteller, a fine conversationalist, and a delightful correspondent.

BIBLIOGRAPHY: Roy Bedichek, *Letters of Roy Bedichek,* ed. William A. Owens and Lyman Grant (Austin: University of Texas Press, 1985). Eleanor James, *Roy Bedichek* (Austin: Steck-Vaughn, 1970). William A. Owens, *Three Friends: Roy Bedichek, J. Frank Dobie, Walter Prescott Webb* (Garden City, New York: Doubleday, 1969). San Antonio *Light,* July 5, 1959. *Saturday Evening Post,* October 16, 1948. *Texas Observer,* June 27, 1959.

Wilson M. Hudson

BEE, BERNARD ELLIOTT, SR. (1787–1854). Bernard E. Bee, attorney, soldier, and statesman, was born in Charleston, South Carolina, in 1787, the son of Thomas B. Bee, member of the Royal Privy Council in colonial South Carolina and of the Continental Congress, lieutenant governor of South Carolina, and justice of the United States Circuit Court of South Carolina during the administration of George Washington. Bernard Bee studied law in Charleston, served on the staff of his brother-in-law and Governor James Hamilton of South Carolina,[qv] and became a primary influence upon Hamilton's interest in Texas. As Hamilton's aide, Bee was a prominent advocate of nullification in South Carolina in 1832. In 1836, however, shortly after the battle of San Jacinto,[qv] he moved to Texas and settled near Houston. He joined the Army of the Republic of Texas[qv] but resigned to serve first as secretary of the treasury and later as secretary of state in David G. Burnet's[qv] ad interim government.[qv] When Antonio López de Santa Anna[qv] was sent to Washington after the battle of San Jacinto, George W. Hockley, Reuben M. Potter,[qqv] and Bee accompanied him. Bee lent Santa Anna $3,000 in return for a draft on the Mexican general's Mexico City bank. When Bee attempted to cash the draft, however, Santa Anna refused to honor it, insisting that he had signed the draft under duress as a prisoner of war. Bee served as secretary of war under Sam Houston[qv] and later as secretary of state in the first administration of Mirabeau B. Lamar.[qv]

When the Mexican Federalists seemed friendly to the idea of Texas independence, Bee resigned as secretary of state in order to enter diplomatic service. On February 20, 1839, the new republic dispatched him to Mexico City as minister and agent to the government of Mexico. Texas officials did not believe that he would be recognized as minister, since recognition would constitute a de facto recognition of Texas independence. Nevertheless, as agent Bee hoped to negotiate a peace and secure that recognition. He was authorized to offer Mexico $5 million for the recognition of Texas independence, with the Rio Grande as the republic's southern boundary. Finally, if his other proposals failed, he was authorized to "propose a compromise by negotiating for the purchase of all that portion of [Texas] which is not within the original boundaries."

Bee arrived at Veracruz on the French frigate *La Gloire* in early May but remained on board until he received permission to come ashore. He was eventually allowed to land despite avidly unfavorable public sentiment. He stated his government's proposals to Gen. Guadalupe Victoria, who forwarded them to the Mexican Council of State, which rejected them unanimously. At the same time Bee was privately threatened with imprisonment. Santa Anna was by then back in control of the Mexican government and refused to meet with Bee. The mission came to naught. On May 24, 1839, Bee informed Texas authorities of Mexico's rejection and sailed for the United States by way of Havana.

On April 20, 1840, Bee, who was already in the United States, replaced Richard G. Dunlap[qv] as Texas minister plenipotentiary in Washington. Soon after assuming his duties, however, in ill health, he went to visit his family in South Carolina, and he did not return to Washington until the following December. On February 21, 1841, he accepted his government's instructions to attempt to negotiate a general treaty of amity and commerce with Spain and its West Indies possession, Cuba. In a letter to the Chevalier d'Argaiz, the Spanish minister at Washington, Bee observed that "a natural bond of Union and sympathy between Texas and Cuba is found in the great dependence of both countries upon slave labor, both regarding with extreme regret, the spirit of fanaticism abroad in certain portions of the world ready to despoil by the manumission of slaves, without indemnity to the holder, honest citizens of the right guaranteed to them by the laws under which they live." Although Spain declined to enter into open treaty negotiations with Texas, it did allow free trade between Texas and Cuba. Bee also took up the question of Indian raids out of the United States into the Republic of Texas.[qv] The administration of Martin Van Buren proved hostile to Texas interests, however, and Bee decided after suffering several rebuffs to curtail his business until William Henry Harrison was inaugurated. Harrison's untimely death further delayed Bee's mission, but on April 12, 1841, after the inauguration of John Tyler, the Texas minister reopened the questions of Indian depredations, a treaty of commerce, and the extradition of criminals. After initial positive meetings with United States secretary of state Daniel Webster, Bee again stalled negotiations by departing for South Carolina. He returned to Washington in June, however, and formalized the treaty with the United States. On July 27, 1841, he submitted it to Webster, but not until January 16, 1843, was the treaty ratified. By that time, however, Bee was no longer minister. Sam Houston had been inaugurated president of the Republic of Texas on December 13, 1841, and, thinking that Bee's many absences from his Washington post were "injurious to the interests of this Government and disrespectful to that of the United States," recalled him on December 27 and replaced him with James Riley. Bee retorted lamely that his actions had been in the best interests of Texas.

On March 15, 1842, after Rafael Vásquez[qv] captured San Antonio, Bee was elected chairman of a meeting of Harris County citizens that advocated war against Mexico. A unit was raised under Bee, Moseley Baker,[qv] and A. C. Allen to report to Alexander Somervell,[qv] but was never called to active service. Bee was opposed to annexation[qv] and returned to South Carolina in 1846. He died there in 1854. He was the father of Confederate generals Hamilton P. Bee and Bernard E. Bee, Jr.[qqv] Bee County was named in his honor in 1857. His papers are in the Barker Texas History Center,[qv] University of Texas at Austin.

BIBLIOGRAPHY: Dudley Goodall Wooten, ed., *A Comprehensive History of Texas* (2 vols., Dallas: Scarff, 1898; rpt., Austin: Texas State Historical Association, 1986).

Thomas W. Cutrer

BEE, BERNARD ELLIOTT, JR. (1824–1861). Bernard Elliott Bee, Jr., Confederate general, was born on February 8, 1824, in Charleston, South Carolina, the son of Anne and Bernard E. Bee, Sr.[qv] In the summer of 1836 the family moved to the Republic of Texas,[qv] where Bee's father served as secretary of state. The young man was appointed to the United States Military Academy at West Point with an "at large" status on July 1, 1841, and he graduated thirty-third in the class of 1845. He was brevetted a second lieutenant in the Third United States Infantry regiment on July 1, 1845, and was confirmed in that grade on September 21, 1846. In the Mexican War[qv] he was brevetted to the rank of first lieutenant on April 18, 1847, "for gallant and meritorious conduct" at the battle of Cerro Gordo and to captain on September 13, 1847, for his role in the storming of Chapultepec. He was also presented with a sword by the state of South Carolina for his services. Bee served as adjutant in the Tenth United States Infantry regiment from July 25, 1848, through March 3, 1855, and was promoted to first lieutenant on March 5, 1851, and to captain on March 3, 1855. After resigning his United States Army commission on March 3, 1861, Bee was elected lieutenant colonel of the First South Carolina Regulars, a Confederate regiment of artillery. On June 17, 1861, he was appointed brigadier general and assigned to the command of a brigade in Gen. Pierre G. T. Beauregard's Army of Virginia at Manassas Junction. There, on July 21, 1861, his men sustained the brunt of the federal assault on the Confederate left wing in the first battle of Manassas, or Bull Run, and Bee is said to have ordered his men to "Rally behind the Virginians! There stands Jackson like a stonewall!" thus giving Gen. Thomas J. Jackson his famous sobriquet. Leading by example, Bee was constantly at the head of his brigade and fell mortally wounded just as the enemy assault began to recede. He died on July 22, 1861, in the small cabin near the battlefield that had been his headquarters. The Confederate congress confirmed his rank as brigadier general more than a month after his death. He is buried in Pendleton, South Carolina. He was the brother of Hamilton P. Bee.[qv]

BIBLIOGRAPHY: Francis B. Heitman, *Historical Register and Dictionary of the United States Army* (2 vols., Washington: GPO, 1903; rpt., Urbana: University of Illinois Press, 1965). Ezra J. Warner, *Generals in Gray* (Baton Rouge: Louisiana State University Press, 1959).

Thomas W. Cutrer

BEE, CARLOS (1867–1932). Carlos Bee, lawyer, politician, and legislator, the son of Mildred (Tarver) and Hamilton P. Bee,[qv] was born on July 8, 1867, at either Saltillo, Coahuila, or Monterrey, Nuevo León. His parents were temporarily residing in Mexico after the collapse of the Confederacy, but they returned to San Antonio, Texas, in 1874. Bee attended San Antonio schools and the Agricultural and Mechanical College of Texas (now Texas A&M University). He studied law while working as a railway mail clerk in the judge advocate's office at Fort Sam Houston, was admitted to the bar in 1893, and began to practice law in San Antonio. For two years he served as United States commissioner for the Western District of Texas, and he was district attorney of the Thirty-seventh District for six years, 1898–1905. He was a member of the Bexar County school board for two years, 1906–08. In 1904 Bee was chairman of the state Democratic convention and a delegate to the national Democratic convention at St. Louis. As a member of the Texas Senate for two terms, 1915–19, he introduced a compulsory school bill and a fifty-four-hour work week for women. He was elected to the Sixty-sixth Congress (1919–21) and subsequently resumed his law practice in San Antonio. Bee married Mary Kyle Burleson of Austin. He died in San Antonio on April 20, 1932, and was buried in the City Cemetery. He was survived by his second wife, Mary Elizabeth.

BIBLIOGRAPHY: *Biographical Directory of the American Congress* (Washington: GPO, 1859–). Norman Kittrell, *Governors Who Have Been and Other Public Men of Texas* (Houston: Dealy-Adey-Elgin, 1921).

Anne W. Hooker

BEE, HAMILTON PRIOLEAU (1822–1897). Hamilton P. Bee, Confederate brigadier general, the son of Anne and Bernard E. Bee,[qv] was born in Charleston, South Carolina, on July 22, 1822. The family moved to Texas while he was still a youth. In 1839 he served as secretary for the commission that established the boundary between the Republic of Texas[qv] and the United States, and in 1843 Texas president Sam Houston[qv] dispatched Bee, with Joseph C. Eldridge and Thomas S. Torrey[qqv] to convene a peace council with the Comanches. On August 9, 1843, the commissioners obtained the promise of the Penatekas to attend a council with Houston the following April. The meeting culminated in the Treaty of Tehuacana Creek. In 1846 Bee was named secretary of the Texas Senate.

During the Mexican War[qv] he served briefly as a private in Benjamin McCulloch's[qv] famed Company A—the "Spy Company"—of Col. John Coffee Hays's[qv] First Regiment, Texas Mounted Rifles, before transferring in October 1846, as a second lieutenant, to Mirabeau B. Lamar's[qv] independent company of Texas cavalry. Bee volunteered for a second term in October 1847 and was elected first lieutenant of Lamar's Company, now a component of Col. Peter Hansborough Bell's[qv] Regiment, Texas Volunteers.

After the war Bee moved to Laredo and was elected to the Texas legislature, where he served from 1849 through 1859. From 1855 through 1857 he was speaker of the House. He was elected brigadier general of militia in 1861 and appointed brigadier general in the Confederate Army to rank from March 4, 1862. His brigade was composed of August C. Buchel's[qv] First, Nicholas C. Gould's Twenty-third, Xavier B. Debray's[qv] Twenty-sixth, James B. Likin's Thirty-fifth, Peter C. Woods's[qv] Thirty-sixth, and Alexander W. Terrell's[qv] Texas cavalry regiments. Given command of the lower Rio Grande district, with headquarters at Brownsville, Bee expedited the import of munitions from Europe through Mexico and the export of cotton in payment. On November 4, 1863, he was credited with saving millions of dollars of Confederate stores and munitions from capture by a federal expeditionary force under Gen. Nathaniel P. Banks.[qv] After transfer to a field command in the spring of 1864, Bee led his brigade in the Red River campaign[qv] under Lt. Gen. Richard Taylor.[qv] Having had only slight training or experience in the art of war and having served only in an administrative capacity to that time, he was less than skillful in handling troops. While he was leading a cavalry charge at the battle of Pleasant Hill, two horses were shot from beneath him, and he suffered a slight face wound. Though he was afterward the object of some heavy criticism, he was assigned to the command of Thomas Green's[qv] division in Gen. John A. Wharton's[qv] cavalry corps in February 1865 and was later given a brigade of infantry in Gen. Samuel Bell Maxey's[qv] division.

After the war Bee went to Mexico for a time. In 1876 he returned to San Antonio, where he remained until his death, on October 3, 1897. He is buried in the Confederate Cemetery in San Antonio. Bee was married to Mildred Tarver of Alabama in 1854, and they had six children. He was the brother of Gen. Bernard Elliott Bee, Jr.[qv]

BIBLIOGRAPHY: Hamilton Prioleau Bee Papers, Barker Texas History Center, University of Texas at Austin. Clement Anselm Evans, ed., *Confederate Military History* (Atlanta: Confederate Publishing, 1899; extended ed., Wilmington, North Carolina: Broadfoot, 1987–89). Fredericka Meiners, Hamilton Prioleau Bee (M.A. thesis, Rice University, 1972). Fredericka Meiners, "Hamilton P. Bee in the Red River Campaign," *Southwestern Historical Quarterly* 78 (July 1974). Charles D. Spurlin, comp., *Texas Veterans in the Mexican War: Muster Rolls of Texas Military Units* (Victoria, Texas, 1984). Ezra J. Warner, *Generals in Gray* (Baton Rouge: Louisiana State University Press, 1959). Marcus J. Wright, comp., and Harold B. Simpson, ed., *Texas in the War, 1861–1865* (Hillsboro, Texas: Hill Junior College Press, 1965).

Thomas W. Cutrer

BEE BRANCH. Bee Branch rises in northwestern Gonzales County (at 29°46′ N, 97°22′ W) and runs southwest for seven miles to its mouth on Sandy Fork (at 29°40′ N, 97°23′ W). It traverses flat to rolling prairie surfaced by clay that supports mixed hardwoods and pines.

BEE CAVE CREEK. Bee Cave Creek rises four miles northeast of Lometa in northern Lampasas County (at 31°16′ N, 98°22′ W) and extends northeast for 7½ miles to its mouth on Simms Creek, 5½ miles southeast of Moline (at 31°19′ N, 98°17′ W). It crosses an area of the Grand Prairies characterized by steep slopes and limestone benches, which often give a stairstep appearance to the landscape along streams. Soils in the area are generally thin clay loams, and vegetation consists primarily of grasses and open stands of live oak, mesquite, and juniper.

BEE CAVES, TEXAS. Bee Caves (Beecaves or Bee Cave) is at the intersection of State Highway 71 and Farm roads 620 and 2244, twelve miles west of Austin in west central Travis County. It was named by early settlers for a large cave of wild bees found near the site. A post office opened there in 1870 with Martin V. Lackey as postmaster. By 1871 Wiley Johnson was operating a trading post at the settlement. In the mid-1880s the Bee Caves community had a steam gristmill, a cotton gin, a general store, a church, a school, and twenty residents. The population fell to ten in the early 1890s but rose to fifty-four by 1914. The post office at Bee Caves was discontinued in 1915, and mail for the community was sent to Cedar Valley. The Bee Caves school was consolidated with the Teck common school district in the 1940s and with the Dripping Springs Independent School District in Hays County in 1951. The population was reported at fifty from the 1940s through the 1980s. In 1990 it was 241.

BIBLIOGRAPHY: Mary Starr Barkley, *History of Travis County and Austin, 1839–1899* (Waco: Texian Press, 1963). John J. Germann and Myron Janzen, *Texas Post Offices by County* (1986).

Vivian Elizabeth Smyrl

BEE CAVES CREEK. Bee Caves Creek rises three miles south of the Kerr Wildlife Management Area[qv] in west central Kerr County (at 30°00′ N, 99°29′ W) and runs northeast for five miles to its mouth on the North Fork of the Guadalupe River (at 30°04′ N, 99°27′ W). It traverses an area of the Edwards Plateau characterized by loamy soils and rocky outcrops. The vegetation in the area consists primarily of dense stands of live oak and Ashe juniper.

BEECHAM BRANCH. Beecham Branch rises just southeast of Mallard in southeast Montague County (at 33°34′ N, 97°38′ W) and flows south for four miles to its mouth on Denton Creek, 1½ miles northeast of Jackson (at 33°32′ N, 97°41′ W). It traverses flat to rolling terrain surfaced by deep to shallow sandy loams that support brush and grasses. For most of the county's history the Beecham Branch area has been used as rangeland.

BEECH CREEK (Nacogdoches County). Beech Creek rises just west of Looneyville in northwestern Nacogdoches County (at 31°46′ N, 94°51′ W) and runs west for five miles to its mouth on the Angelina River, one mile west of Farm Road 1648 (at 31°46′ N, 94°56′ W). It crosses flat terrain with local shallow depressions, surfaced by sandy and clay loam that supports water-tolerant hardwoods, conifers, and grasses along the banks.

—— (Tyler County). Beech Creek rises seven miles east of Woodville in east central Tyler County (at 30°46′ N, 94°16′ W) and flows south for thirty-three miles to its mouth on Village Creek, five miles northeast of Kountze in Hardin County (at 30°26′ N, 94°16′ W). The stream is intermittent in its upper reaches. Near it, hardwood forests and conifers grow from sandy and clay loams.

BEECH GROVE, TEXAS. Beech (Beach) Grove is south of U.S. Highway 190 and Science Hall, six miles southwest of Jasper in western Jasper County. A post office was established there in 1890. The local school had thirty pupils and one teacher in 1897; by 1905 the community had three schools for white children with 128 pupils and four teachers, and four schools for black children with 207 pupils and four teachers. Beech Grove had a general store and cotton gin in 1914. George W. Smyth[qv] lived in the community. A population of seventy-five remained in 1930. Three businesses operated in Beech Grove in 1932, and state highway maps in 1936 showed two cemeteries at the townsite. Beech Grove School was moved six miles northeast to a highway junction in 1937, and the post office moved in 1944 to a new location at Curtis, to the northwest. In the 1980s a town hall, two schools, and a campground remained. *Diana J. Kleiner*

BEE COUNTY. Bee County (Q-14) is in the Rio Grande plain of south central Texas, fifty miles northwest of Corpus Christi and 146 miles southeast of Austin. It is bordered on the north by Karnes and Goliad counties, on the east by Refugio County, on the south by San Patricio County, and on the west by Live Oak County. Beeville is the county's largest town and seat of government. The center point of the county is 28°25′ north latitude and 97°45′ west longitude. Several important thoroughfares cross the county, including U.S. highways 59 and 181 and State highways 202 and 359. The county's transportation needs are also served by the Southern Pacific Railroad. An airport built in 1966 serves Beeville and the surrounding region.

Bee County covers 866 square miles that slope gently to the coast. The elevation ranges from 200 to 300 feet. Geologically northern Bee County is in the Rio Grande embayment; the Lissie and Beaumont formations extend into the southern part of the county to form a broad, flat, and fertile plain. Blanco, Medio, and Aransas creeks and their tributaries, which flow in a southeasterly direction, drain the county. The southwest corner of the county has cracking clayey soils or loamy surfaces with cracking clayey subsoils. The northern two-thirds of the county has dark, alkaline soils, with loamy surface layers and cracking clayey subsoils, while the remainder of the county has light-colored acidic soils, with loamy surface layers and cracking clayey subsoils. Between 41 percent and 50 percent of the land in the county is considered prime farmland.

Most of the area is in the South Texas Plains vegetation region, characterized by open grasslands and scattered shrubs and cacti. Buffalo, antelopes, deer, bears, panthers, and wolves once roamed the region; early records indicate that the area also supported wildcats, coyotes, and jackrabbits. Many small mammals are currently found in the county, including foxes, squirrels, opossums, mice, rats, gophers, skunks, moles, and bats.

The climate is subtropical and humid, with mild winters and warm summers. Temperatures range in January from an average low of 42° F to an average high of 65°, and in July from 73° to 96°. The average annual rainfall is thirty inches. There is no snowfall. The growing season averages 275 days per year, with the last freeze in late February and the first freeze in early December. Hurricanes[qv] are likely to occur during the late summer.

Bee County has been the site of human habitation for several thousand years. Artifacts recovered in the region suggest that the earliest human inhabitants arrived around 6,000 to 10,000 years ago and camped along the creek valleys. At the time of the first contact with Europeans, various Karankawa bands inhabited the eastern part of the future county, while Lipan Apaches and Borrados roamed the northwest and southwest sections. The Skidi Pawnees left arrowheads in Sulphur Creek near the site of present Pawnee.

The first Spanish grant in the area was made to Carlos Martínez in 1789 for his services in the king's army at La Bahía and his father's deed of killing an Apache chief at San Antonio de Béxar Presidio.[qv] The first permanent settlers, Jeremiah O'Tool, his sons Martin and Michael, and James O'Reilly, sailed from Ireland in 1826. Women and children arrived in 1829 and helped to established the community of Corrigan, named for Ellen O'Tool Corrigan's husband. In 1828 William and Patrick Quinn settled in the Power and Hewetson colony[qv] at Papalote Creek, and in 1834 settlers from Tipperary, Ireland, landed at Copano Bay and went to the headwaters of the Aransas River (near the site of present Beeville), in the McMullen-McGloin colony.[qv] Other early residents included Martín De León,[qv] who established a ranch east of the Aransas in 1805, and the Castillo, Santos, and Moya families, who received Mexican land grants in the area in the early 1830s.

Eleven Bee County landowners, including Timothy Hart, William Quinn, James O'Conner, and James and William St. John, were among the signers of the Texas Declaration of Independence.[qv] During the Texas Revolution[qv] many of the settlers fled to New Orleans, but most returned, and in the 1840s and 1850s a small but steady stream of settlers moved to the area. Most took up ranching, which was ideally suited for the broad open expanses of grasslands.

Bee County was established shortly after the settlement of the Cart War,[qv] which originated ten miles east of the site of Beeville. The county, named for Barnard E. Bee, Sr.,[qv] was formed from San Patricio, Goliad, Refugio, Live Oak, and Karnes counties on December 8, 1857, and officially organized on January 25, 1858, when the first officers were elected. Beeville, the first county seat, was on Medio Creek, near Medio Hill, where the first post office had been established in 1857. In 1860 Maryville became county seat; this community was later designated Beeville-on-the-Poesta to distinguish it from the former county seat.

In antebellum Texas[qv] the Bee County economy was based almost exclusively on cattle ranching. By 1860 cattle in the county numbered 33,376. Some families grew small crops of corn and other grains, but farming remained on the subsistence level until well after the Civil War.[qv] Because of the emphasis on ranching, on the eve of the war only seventy-nine slaves lived in the county, out of a total population of 910, most of whom were evidently cowherds and drovers. During the war cattle were driven to the Mississippi and to Mexico. The cowmen organized home guards at Papalote and Beeville under captains William P. Miller and Allen Carter Jones,[qqv] and some Bee County men served with Confederate forces elsewhere. Although the local economy experienced a marked downturn as a result of the conflict, Bee County as a whole was spared the worst effects of the war. By the early 1870s its fortunes began to recover.

The most important economic event in the early postwar period was the great cattle boom. Many postwar cattle drives to the north followed the Chisholm Trail[qv] until about 1877, when that route was replaced by the Dodge or Western Trail.[qv] During the 1870s and early 1880s many Bee County ranchers drove their cattle to the Rockport-Fulton area, where a large number of hide and tallow plants had sprung up. In 1880 the census counted 25,030 cattle in the county, and in 1890 the total was more than 32,000. During the decade of the 1870s sheep ranching[qv] also enjoyed a brief heyday. Between 1870 and 1880 the number of sheep in the county grew from 1,860 to 61,130, and a for a time it appeared that sheep might supplant cattle as the county's most important export. But during the 1880s the sheep declined sharply; by 1910 fewer than 1,000 sheep were kept on Bee County ranches.

The 1880s saw the beginnings of large-scale agriculture, with corn and oats as the principal crops. In 1870 the county had only twenty-five farms; by 1890 it had 264; and by 1900 the farms numbered 628. In 1895 a state Agricultural Experimental Station was opened near Beeville, which assisted local farmers in selecting appropriate crops and introducing modern farming methods. Corn, flax, peanuts, fruits, vegetables, and onions became the principal products.

The railroads contributed to the rise of the farming economy. The San Antonio and Aransas Pass Railway was completed from San Antonio to Pettus and Beeville in 1886. The following year the railroad extended south to Skidmore and Papalote. In 1888 the Gulf, Western Texas and Pacific Railway was built from Victoria to Beeville. The railroads not only opened up new markets outside the county, but also brought large numbers of new settlers. Between 1870 and 1890 the population of the county nearly quadrupled, from 1,082 to 3,720. Over the course of the next twenty years it almost quadrupled again, reaching 12,090 in 1910. Many of the new settlers were recent immigrants, drawn to the area by its mild climate and abundant land. By 1910 nearly a quarter of the county's population was foreign born, with new residents from Mexico (1,381) and Germany (188) forming the largest contingents. The growth in population encouraged dramatic growth in agriculture. Between 1900 and 1920 the number of farms in Bee County increased from 628 to 1,497, and agricultural receipts grew nearly fivefold. Cotton, which had been introduced during the 1890s, became a leading crop, and by 1930 the county was producing some 15,000 bales annually.

Despite the impressive growth of farming, livestock raising continued to play a central role in the county's economy. The number of ranches and cattle continued to increase steadily after the turn of the century. Commercial-scale poultry raising was introduced during the early 1900s. By 1930 county farms raised 73,236 chickens, and turkeys and geese were also being raised in significant numbers (*see* POULTRY PRODUCTION). Horse ranching also played an important role in the economy during the first three decades of the century. In 1920 there were more than 5,000 horses on Bee County's ranches, and buyers came from all over South Texas to attend horse auctions in Beeville.

The growing population and expanded farming activity combined to drive up land prices, and during the early 1920s large-scale tenant farming was introduced. By 1930 more than half (1,182) of the county's 1,731 farms were operated by tenants, who came from all strata of society, though, in contrast to tenants in some other areas of the state, the majority were white. Most were recent arrivals unable to buy land. During the Great Depression[qv] of the 1930s, many fell victim to falling prices for agricultural products and to the reluctance of banks to extend credit. By 1940 fewer than half (629) of the tenants who had farmed a decade before were still on the land.

In 1929 oil and gas were discovered at Pettus, and revenues and jobs from the oilfields helped to offset some of the affects of the depression. But the economy did not begin to recover until World War II,[qv] when several military installations were opened in and around Beeville. Despite the downturn in the county's economy, the population continued to grow steadily. In 1940 it was 16,481, up nearly 1,000 since 1930, and in 1950 it reached 18,110.

In 1954 the first United States Navy all-jet base opened at Naval Auxiliary Air Station (now Chase Naval Air Station[qv]) in Beeville; the base continues to contribute a significant part of the county's payroll. Several small industries—most of them relating to agribusiness—have opened in Beeville and Pettus in the late twentieth century, but the mainstay of the economy remained farming and ranching. In 1982, 93 percent of the land in the county was in farms and ranches, 17 percent of the farmland was under cultivation, and 5 percent was irrigated. Bee County ranked 139th among the 254 Texas counties in agricultural receipts, with 63 percent coming from livestock and livestock products, primarily from cattle. Principal crops included grain sorghums, corn, and wheat. Cotton culture,[qv] which declined sharply during the depression, had made a comeback and become a leading cash crop.

Oil and gas extraction form the other mainstay of the local economy. In the early 1990s oil production averaged some 800,000 barrels annually; between 1930 and 1991 crude production was 99,091,271 barrels. A number of petroleum industries and oilfield-service firms are located in Pettus.

The total number of businesses in the county in the early 1980s was 491. In 1980, 8 percent of laborers were self-employed, 21 percent were employed in professional or related services, 4 percent in manufacturing, 20 percent in wholesale and retail trade, and 19 percent in agriculture, forestry, fishing, and mining; 13 percent worked in other counties, and 1,507 retired workers lived in Bee County. Nonfarm earnings in 1981 totaled $206,200,000.

The first schools in the county were opened in 1858. Two of the earliest were located in Papalote and Beeville. In the early 1990s Bee County had four school districts with eight elementary, two middle, and four high schools. The average daily attendance in 1981–82 was 4,884, with expenditures per pupil of $2,299. Forty-two percent of the 307 high school graduates planned to attend college. In 1983, 39 percent of the school graduates were white, 59 percent Hispanic, 2 percent black, and 0.7 percent Asian. Bee County College (est. 1965), a vocational and academic two-year college under local and state control, is located in Beeville. In 1992 the enrollment was 2,250.

Politically, Bee County has been staunchly Democratic; although Republican presidential candidates won majorities in most late-twentieth-century elections, Democratic officials continued to maintain a virtual monopoly on countywide offices. In the mid-1980s Bee County had forty-five organized churches, with a estimated combined membership of 15,748. The largest denominations were Catholic, Southern Baptist, and United Methodist. The county population was 23,775 in 1960, 22,737 in 1970, 26,030 in 1980, and 25,135 in 1990. In the 1970s and 1980s came a marked influx of new Hispanic residents. In the early 1990s the county ranked forty-ninth among all United States counties in the percentage of persons of Hispanic origin, and persons of Hispanic descent (46 percent) form the largest ancestry group, followed by English (16 percent) and German (16 percent). In 1990 only 2.7 percent of the population was African American; Asians (.09 percent) and American Indians (0.4 percent) were the other leading minority groups. Rural Bee County grew in population by 24 percent between 1970 and 1980. The age groups with the largest increases were those between twenty-five and twenty-nine and from birth to five years. The jobless rate in the early 1990s was around 6.5 percent. Hunting leases and camping draw numbers of tourists to the area. Among the leading attractions are the Beeville Art Gallery and Museum, the annual Western Week held in October, the Diez y Seis de Septiembre (one of the fiestas patrias[qv]) and nearby Choke Canyon State Park and Lake Corpus Christi.[qqv]

BIBLIOGRAPHY: Grace Bauer, *Bee County Centennial, 1858–1958* (Bee County Centennial, 1958). Grace Bauer (Lillian Grace Schoppe), The History of Bee County, Texas (M.A. thesis, University of Texas, 1939). Camp Ezell, *Historical Story of Bee County, Texas* (Beeville: Beeville Publishing, 1973). Mrs. I. C. Madray, *A History of Bee County* (Beeville, Texas: *Bee-Picayune*, 1939). Robert J. Marshall, An Administrative Survey and Proposed Plan of Reorganization for the Public Schools of Bee County, Texas (M.A. thesis, University of Texas, 1939). Joseph Gustav Rountree, *History of Bee County, Texas* (Beeville?, Texas, 1960).

Grace Bauer

BEE COUNTY COLLEGE. Bee County College, a two-year state college at Beeville, Texas, began when the Bee County Junior College District was established in November 1965. In December of that year voters approved a tax to support the college and the issuance of bonds to erect buildings. The board of trustees and President Grady C. Hogue began the college program in September 1967, with an enrollment of 790 students taught by twenty-four full-time and eleven part-time instructors. The campus, donated by the A. C. Jones family, is about a mile north of Beeville. The library holdings totaled 13,500 volumes in 1969. The school provided the first two years of college degree programs; it offered technical courses leading to associate's degrees in electronic data processing, drafting and design, electronics, and mid-management in business; it also provided vocational courses leading to certificates in automotive mechanics, business and accounting, general business, data processing, secretarial work, clerk-typist tasks, and nursing. The college was approved by the Texas Education Agency[qv] and the Texas College and University System Coordinating Board (later the Texas Higher Education Coordinating Board[qv]). It is a member of the American Association of Junior Colleges and the Texas Association of Public Community/Junior Colleges, as well as numerous other professional and academic organizations. In 1974 the enrollment was 1,670. That year Norman E. Wallace became the school's second president. The institution had thirteen divisions: Distribution and Marketing, Health Services, Industrial, Kinesiology and Health Sciences, Language, Mathematics and Physics, Office Occupations, Performing Arts, Public Services, Science and Agriculture, Social Sciences, Technology, and Visual Arts. A faculty of ninety-five served an enrollment of 2,338 in 1991. Investment and physical-plant resources totaled $17,196,650 in 1991. Off-campus programs were offered in Alice and Kingsville. Beeville County College offered A.A., A.S., and A.A.S. degrees, as well as certificates of achievement in various technological and vocational fields.

BEE CREEK (Bosque County). Bee Creek rises 4½ miles west of Meridian in west central Bosque county (at 31°54′ N, 97°44′ W) and flows south for nine miles to its mouth on Meridian Creek, in the southwestern section of the county (at 31°48′ N, 97° 39′ W). The stream is intermittent in its upper reaches. It flows through Meridian State Recreation Area,[qv] where a dam with a spillway impounds a small lake. A short waterfall is located farther downstream, three miles above the mouth.

____ (Brazos County). Bee Creek rises in the southwestern section of the Texas A&M University campus in College Station, Brazos County (at 30°37′ N, 96°20′ W), and runs east for 5½ miles to join Carters Creek (at 30°37′ N, 96°16′ W). The stream runs through what became, in the 1970s and 1980s, a heavily populated residential area of southwest College Station. Before development, the flat to rolling area along the streambed was vegetated by grasses and hardwood and pine forest. The soils are shallow to deep sandy and clay loams. Bee Creek has become synonymous with recreation in College Station, since one of the city's largest parks is named for it.

____ (Caldwell County). Bee Creek begins just southwest of Elm Grove in western Caldwell County (at 29°53′ N, 97°28′ W) and runs north for 8½ miles to its mouth on Walnut Creek, four miles northwest of Red Rock in Bastrop County (at 29°58′ N, 97°30′ W). It traverses rolling prairie surfaced by shallow, clay loams that support mesquite, mixed hardwoods, and grasses.

____ (Cass County). Bee Creek rises 2½ miles south of Douglassville in north central Cass County (at 33°10′ N, 94°21′ W) and flows southeast for 5½ miles to its mouth on Johns Creek, six miles west of Atlanta (at 33°07′ N, 94°16′ W). The stream is intermittent in its upper reaches. It traverses a gently undulating to gently rolling area surfaced by sandy and loamy soils that predominantly support pines and hardwoods.

____ (Ellis County). Bee Creek rises four miles northwest of Italy in southwestern Ellis County (at 32°12′ N, 96°59′ W) and runs north for 4½ miles. It traverses rolling terrain surfaced with clays and clay loams that support oak, juniper, and grasses. For most of the county's history the Bee Creek area has been used as range and crop land. Bee Creek empties into Chambers Creek 5½ miles north of Italy (at 32°16′ N, 96°57′ W).

____ (Fort Bend County). Bee Creek rises just south of Paw Paw Lake in southern Fort Bend County (at 29°22′ N, 95°40′ W) and flows southeast for 4½ miles to its mouth on Cow Creek (at 29°19′ N, 95°37′ W). The vegetation along its banks consists of mixed hardwoods interspersed with various prairie grasses. The area's variable terrain is surfaced by highly impermeable soil and calcareous clay.

____ (Robertson County). Bee Creek rises five miles south of Wheelock in south Robertson County (at 30°51′ N, 96°25′ W) and runs southeast for eleven miles to its mouth on Cedar Creek in Brazos County, 3½ miles northeast of Cottonwood (at 30°51′ N, 96°18′ W). It crosses nearly level to gently sloping terrain surfaced by clay and sandy loam that support post oaks and grasses.

____ (Travis County). Bee Creek rises in West Lake Hills just east of Farm Road 2244 in central Travis County (at 30°18′ N, 97°50′ W) and runs east for three miles to its mouth on Lake Austin, just above Tom Miller Dam (at 30°18′ N, 97°47′ W). It flows beneath steep slopes and benches surfaced by shallow clay loams that support juniper, live oak, mesquite, and grasses.

____ (Travis County). Bee Creek begins six miles northwest of the Round Mountain community in the northwestern corner of Travis County (at 30°36′ N, 98°02′ W) and runs south for three miles to its mouth on Cow Creek (at 30°34′ N, 98°03′ W). It crosses an area of steep slopes and benches surfaced by shallow clay loam that support juniper, live oak, mesquite, and grasses.

BEEDE, JOSHUA WILLIAM (1871–1940). Joshua William Beede, geologist, was born on September 14, 1871, in Raymond, New Hampshire, to Hiram Pratt and Lydia Marie (Brown) Beede. While he was young the family moved to Kansas, where he attended local schools and eventually received his B.S. from Washburn College, Topeka, in 1896. By 1899 Beede received both his M.A. and Ph.D. from the University of Kansas, where Professor C. S. Prosser introduced him to the Pennsylvanian and Permian rocks of Kansas, Oklahoma, and Texas. From 1897 to 1899 Beede worked as an assistant in paleontology and geology at the University of Kansas and from 1899 to 1901 taught science at Atchison County High School, Effingham, Kansas. He was invited to Indiana University in 1901 as an instructor of geology and by 1909 had risen to the rank of associate professor. In 1917 he accepted a position with the Bureau of Economic Geology and Technology of the State of Texas. He resigned this position in 1922 to become a geologist for the Empire Gas and Fuel Company.

While working in Texas Beede published several articles on the geology and paleontology of the upper Paleozoic formations of Texas. Working in conjunction with other geologists, he was able to identify the presence of the Permian system in America. Furthermore, this research "fixed the lower boundary of this important succession of rocks, and determined the faunal succession and the remarkable evolutionary changes that swept over the faunas of these late Paleozoic times." In 1928 Beede returned to Indiana University to serve as professor of geology. He stayed until 1931, when he moved to Oklahoma. From 1896 to 1902 he served on geological surveys in Kansas and Oklahoma and in the United States Geological Survey. Beede was active in a number of professional organizations, including the American Association of Petroleum Geologists and the Geological Society of America. He was a founding member of the Indiana chapter of Sigma XI. He died in Tulsa, Oklahoma, on February 27, 1940. *See also* PERMIAN BASIN.

BIBLIOGRAPHY: E. R. Cumings, "Joshua William Beede (1871–1940)," *Bulletin of the American Association of Petroleum Geologists* 24 (October 1940).

Kris Ercums

BEEF CANYON (Brewster County). Beef Canyon rises eight miles west of Bullis Gap in eastern Brewster County (at 29°51′ N, 102°43′ W) and runs northeast for ten miles to its mouth on San Francisco Creek six miles north of Bullis Gap (at 29°54′ N, 102°36′ W). In the upper reaches of Beef Canyon steep to gentle slopes are surfaced by variable soils that support scrub brush and grasses; in its lower reaches flat terrain with local shallow depressions is surfaced by clay and sandy loams that support water-tolerant hardwoods, conifers, and grasses.

—— (Kinney County). Beef Canyon is a break in the Anacacho Mountains in southeastern Kinney County. It originates in the southwestern side of the mountains (at 29°12′ N, 100°12′ W) and runs southwest for six miles to its mouth on Stricklin Creek (at 29°08′ N, 100°15′ W).

BEEF CREEK. Beef Creek rises two miles south of the junction of U.S. Highway 96 and Recreational Road 255 in northern Jasper County (at 31°02′ N, 93°59′ W) and extends west for eight miles to its mouth on the Angelina River, just south of Sam Rayburn Reservoir (at 31°04′ N, 94°05′ W). The stream runs through woodlands characteristic of Jasper County, with pines predominating. The terrain is gently undulating to hilly at the source of the creek but levels out near its mouth.

BEEF HOLLOW. Beef Hollow is a narrow canyon in east central Dickens County. The usually dry creekbed rises six miles east of Dickens (at 33°42′ N, 100°42′ W) and runs south for seven miles to its mouth on Little Croton Creek, seven miles east of Dickens (at 33°37′ N, 100°43′ W). It traverses an area of moderately steep slopes with locally high relief, surfaced by sand and silt loam that support mesquite and grasses. As a creekbed, the canyon is sometimes called Beef Hollow Creek. The hollow was probably named by cattle rustlers.

BIBLIOGRAPHY: Fred Arrington, *A History of Dickens County: Ranches and Rolling Plains* (Quanah, Texas: Nortex, 1971).

BEEF TRAIL. The Beef Trail, or Beef Road, as surveyed by John R. Bevil, ran from Orcoquisac, or Liberty, Texas, to a junction with the La Bahía Road.[qv] Running northeast through the site of present Jasper, it crossed the Sabine River near that of Belgrade, Newton County. After crossing the Sabine, one branch went to Alexandria, Louisiana, and the other to Natchitoches, Louisiana. The name came from the fact that the road was used for driving cattle from Texas into Louisiana. The trail, which is supposed to have been surveyed about 1823, was abandoned soon after the Texas Revolution.[qv]

Robert Bruce Blake

BEE HOUSE, TEXAS. Bee House is on Farm Road 183 eleven miles west of Gatesville in western Coryell County. The community was established in the 1850s as Boyd's Cove, named for James Boyd. In 1884 residents applied for a post office to be called Bee Hive, for the many bees in local cliffs and caves, but the postal service issued the name of Bee House. By the mid-1890s Bee House had a general store, a corn mill, four churches, and 150 residents. From the mid-1880s until 1916 a Masonic lodge held meetings on the upper floor of the community's two-story schoolhouse; in 1904 the Bee House school had seventy-eight students and two teachers. Bee House declined during the late 1930s, and the population fell to fifty by 1940. A church and a post office marked the community on county highway maps in the 1980s. The reported population was forty in 1990.

BIBLIOGRAPHY: Coryell County Genealogical Society, *Coryell County, Texas, Families, 1854–1985* (Dallas: Taylor, 1986). Zelma Scott, *History of Coryell County* (Austin: Texas State Historical Association, 1965).

Vivian Elizabeth Smyrl

BEE HOUSE CREEK. Bee House Creek, in western Coryell County, is formed by the confluence of North Bee House and South Bee House creeks. North Bee House Creek rises two miles south of Evant in the northwestern corner of the county (at 31°25′ N, 98°09′ W) and flows southeast for fifteen miles. South Bee House Creek rises five miles northeast of Adamsville in northeastern Lampasas County (at 31°21′ N, 98°07′ W) and flows southeast for ten miles. The two streams run together fifteen miles southeast of Evant (at 31°19′ N, 97°59′ W), and the stream thus formed, Bee House Creek, continues southeast for ten miles to its mouth on Cowhouse Creek, ten miles north of Copperas Cove (at 31°17′ N, 97°53′ W). The area's flat to rolling terrain is surfaced by sandy and clay loams that support water-tolerant hardwoods, conifers, and grasses.

BEE INDUSTRY. Although the honeybee is not native to North America, European settlers brought bees with them into every colonial area. Most authorities agree that Spanish missionaries brought in the original Texas stock, for bees were already numerous in Texas at the beginning of Anglo-American colonization. Wilhelm Brukish, who moved to Texas in 1842 as a member of the German colony of Prince Carl of Solms-Braunfels,[qv] was probably the first person in Texas to become interested in the commercial possibilities of bees. He wrote a book on beekeeping and introduced the box hive with removable frames that replaced the pioneer log gum hive. Beekeeping was further facilitated by the invention of foundation comb in 1857, the extractor in 1865, and the bee smoker in 1870. Beginning in the early 1860s stock was gradually improved by importing gentler Italian queen bees; by 1945 that effort had been so successful that 97 percent of the bees in Texas were of that strain.

In pioneer days bees were kept only for home honey consumption and the use of beeswax for church and household candles. Beekeeping as an industry developed in the later part of the nineteenth century, was greatly stimulated by World War I,[qv] and has shown continuing progress since that time. Commercial beekeeping is a migratory operation, in which beekeepers move hives of bees from one source of honey to another. Colonies moved both into and out of Texas produce honey from wildflowers and cultivated crops. Much of the honey produced in Texas has come from one or more of the 5,000 nectar-bearing wild plants native to various areas of the state, including horsemint, mesquite, huajilla, guayacan, white brush, gaillardia, sumac, and ratan. The leading cultivated honey-producing plants include cotton, white and yellow sweet clover, and fruit trees, especially the citrus fruits in the lower Rio Grande valley.

Although honey is still used chiefly as a food, it is also employed in making cosmetics, toothpaste, shoe polish, and vinegar, and in treating tobacco and tobacco pipes. Beeswax is used to waterproof fabrics and to make candles, foundation comb, small castings for foundries, dental impressions, and floor and furniture polish. The raising of queen and worker bees for national and foreign markets is also an important branch of the Texas bee industry. Between 1930 and 1948 the estimated number of colonies of bees in Texas rose from 200,000 to 300,000. During the same period the return to producers from the sale of honey increased from $20,000 to $1 million. The return from the sale of queen and worker bees averaged one-third the amount received from the sale of honey. By 1954 honey production had decreased two million pounds from its 1953 total. The value of the 7,560,000 pounds produced by the state's 280,000 bee colonies was estimated at $1.1 million. By 1964, although the number of colonies had declined to 252,000, production had risen to 12,096,000 pounds valued at $1,887,000. Texas ranked eighth in the United States in honey production in 1963. In 1966 a total of 12,189,000 pounds of honey produced by 239,000 colonies was valued at $1,914,000.

Texas ranked among the ten leading states in honey production in 1970 and produced a decade high of 236,000 pounds of beeswax, valued at $185,000, in that year. In the early 1970s queen bee production was valued annually at one million dollars, and queen bees were shipped to England, France, Sweden, Finland, Australia, New Zealand, and Iran. A high for the decade of 13,000,000 pounds of honey valued at $6 million was produced in 1975 by 208,000 colonies of bees. By 1978 Texas ranked fourth nationally in colonies of bees behind California, Florida, and North Carolina. Bees added to the state's agricultural production by cross-pollinating vegetable, fruit, nut and legume crops, particularly, cucumbers, cantaloupes, and alfalfa. From 1970 to 1990 honey production fluctuated from a low of 7,000,000 pounds in the mid-1980s to a high of 11,400,000 pounds, valued at $6,657,600, in 1981, when 239,000 pounds of beeswax valued at $442,400 was also produced from only 190,000 colonies. Between 1980 and 1986 Texas produced packaged bees worth over $3 million and queen bees valued at over $1 million. Colonies of bees declined to a low of 110,000 by 1988 and rose to only 140,000 by 1990.

In the 1990s Africanized honeybees arrived from Mexico. Known as "killer bees," the invading honeybees were the offspring of Africanized bees that had escaped from a research project in Brazil in 1956 and mated with domesticated European honeybees. Though their sting was no more potent than that of other honeybees, killer bees more vigorously and aggressively defended their colonies. The first killer bees arrived in Hidalgo County in 1990, and the community of Hidalgo subsequently came to be known as the "Killer Bee Capital of Texas." By 1991 a total of twenty-five colonies were reported in Texas, and by 1992 killer bees had arrived in Travis County. In that year eighteen counties in South Texas were placed under quarantine to prevent further spread of the bees. By 1994 one death had been attributed to killer bees, and over 190 stinging accidents had been reported.

BIBLIOGRAPHY: Thelma Burleson, The Origin and Development of the Bee Industry in Texas (M.A. thesis, University of Texas, 1938).

Thelma Burleson and Diana J. Kleiner

BEE-LÓPEZ AGREEMENT. Along the Texas-Mexico border during the Civil War,[qv] peace and stability were prime concerns. When Confederate officials moved toward formal agreement with Mexican border officials, the need for law and order, more than for trade, supplied the chief motivation. Incidents of lawlessness abounded. The first Regiment of the Union, for instance, a band of men commanded by an Antonio Zapata,[qv] was accused of entering Texas at will and carrying out crimes. On December 26, 1862, a group of armed Mexicans crossed into Texas, attacked a Confederate wagon train, and killed three teamsters. The same day another group crossed the Rio Grande and murdered Isidro Vela, chief justice of Zapata County.

Early in 1863 Brig. Gen. Hamilton H. Bee,[qv] Confederate commander of the West Sub-District of Texas, approached Albino López, civil and military commandant of Tamaulipas and a subordinate of Mexican president Benito Juárez, to negotiate an agreement for border regulation. Bee presented himself as "specially charged by my government with the maintenance of friendly relations with the Republic of Mexico." In February 1863 an agreement was reached and signed. Certain classes of criminals would be extradited; Mexican officials agreed to surrender counterfeiters who had been operating through Matamoros. Some of these were United States agents who were attempting to discredit Confederate currency. General border turmoil was to be regulated cooperatively. José Agustín Quintero,[qv] Confederate agent in northern Mexico, attended the meeting and acted as observer and advisor for both sides. He also reported to the Confederate State Department.

The Bee-López agreement was not a binding international treaty. After it was signed, the Confederate government cautioned Quintero to avoid demanding extradition since "we have no right, in the absence of treaty stipulations, to demand the extradition."

Late in 1864 the expulsion of Juárez supporters by French and Mexican imperial forces under the command of Gen. Tomás Mejía nullified the Bee-López agreement. But Quintero soon discovered that Mejía was prepared to enter informal negotiations about border control. In December 1864 Gen. James E. Slaughter, who replaced Bee as Confederate commander of the West Sub-District of Texas, signed an extradition agreement with Mejía. The final clause of the agreement expressed the mutual expectation that the agreement would "be formally accepted by their respective governments, elevating them to solemn treaties."

Although not technically treaties, both the Bee-López and the Slaughter-Mejía pacts had the effect of international agreements since they were enforced equally upon the citizens of both nations. Both agreements, motivated not by trade concerns but by the need to keep law and order on the border, are significant because they demonstrate the recognition of the Confederate government by Mexico.

BIBLIOGRAPHY: Thomas Schoonover, *Dollars over Dominion: The Triumph of Liberalism in Mexican–United States Relations, 1861–1867* (Baton Rouge: Louisiana State University Press, 1978). Jorge L., Tamayo, ed., *Benito Juárez: Documentos, Discursos y Correspondencia* (14 vols., Mexico City: Editorial Libros de México, 1972). Ronnie C. Tyler, *Santiago Vidaurri and the Southern Confederacy* (Austin: Texas State Historical Association, 1973). *The War of the Rebellion: A Compilation of the Official Records of the Union and Confederate Armies.*

Thomas Schoonover

BEEMAN, JAMES J. (1816–1888). James J. Beeman, pioneer settler, the son of James Beeman, was born on December 21, 1816, in Calhoun

County, Illinois. On December 6, 1840, he arrived in Texas and settled near Dalby Springs in Red River County. In 1846 he was elected justice of the peace in Dallas County. After an unsuccessful gold venture in California in 1849, he returned to Dallas County. He settled in 1855 in what later became Parker County, worked as a cabinetmaker, and set up a small store on the Fort Worth–Fort Belknap road five miles north of the site of present Weatherford. The first county court in Parker County was held in a post oak grove at his home on June 2, 1856. On February 17, 1858, he moved his store to Weatherford and became postmaster. Beeman again moved to Dallas County in 1864. He died in Lampasas County on December 7, 1888. In Illinois he married Sarah Crawford, who came with him to Texas; after her death he married Elizabeth Baker, a teacher in Dallas County.

Fred R. Cotten

BEE MOUNTAIN (Bosque County). Bee Mountain is in the Kimball Bend area of the Brazos River, fifteen miles northeast of Morgan in northeastern Bosque County (at 32°08′ N, 97°30′ W). It rises 850 feet above sea level in a portion of the Grand Prairies characterized by flat to rolling terraces and surfaced with clay and sandy loams. Juniper, oak, mesquite, and grasses grow in the area.

—— (Bosque County). Bee Mountain is a mile south of Meridian by the North Bosque River in the central part of the county (at 31°52′ N, 97°37′ W). It rises 960 feet above sea level in a level to hilly portion of the Grand Prairies. Soils in the area vary from shallow, stony clay loams to deep, cracking clays, and the local vegetation generally consists of grasses, oak, juniper, chaparral, cacti, and some mesquite.

—— (Brewster County). Bee Mountain, sometimes called Dee Mountain, is located about a mile north-northwest of the community of Study Butte in southwestern Brewster County (at 29°21′ N, 103°32′ W). The elevation of its summit is 3,452 feet above sea level. The mountain rises in sheer cliffs several hundred feet high on its southern and western exposures, towering over the desert flats. Remnants of mining activity around Bee Mountain, particularly to its south and west, bespeak its location in the historic Terlingua quicksilver district (see MERCURY MINING). The mountain and surrounding area are covered with sparse, arid vegetation characteristic of Chihuahuan Desert scrub. The name Bee Mountain is said to derive from the numerous bee hives that could once be found in the rocky crevices and pockets on the sides of the mountain. The small black honey bees native to this region commonly build their hives in such locations. The intensive harvesting of honey from these wild hives by settlers, who would burn out the bees in order to take the honey, greatly reduced the bee colonies in the region. Some of the native colonies have been replaced, however, by domestic bees brought into the area that subsequently escaped their apiaries and colonized in the wild.

BIBLIOGRAPHY: Clifford B. Casey, *Soldiers, Ranchers and Miners in the Big Bend* (Washington: Office of Archeology and Historic Preservation, U.S. Department of the Interior, 1969). Virginia Madison and Hallie Stillwell, *How Come It's Called That? Place Names in the Big Bend Country* (Albuquerque: University of New Mexico Press, 1958). Ross A. Maxwell, *The Big Bend of the Rio Grande* (Bureau of Economic Geology, University of Texas at Austin, 1968). Kenneth B. Ragsdale, *Quicksilver: Terlingua and the Chisos Mining Company* (College Station: Texas A&M University Press, 1976).

—— (Brewster County). Bee Mountain is four miles northeast of Castolon in Big Bend National Park,[qv] southern Brewster County (at 29°11′ N, 103°29′ W). It rises to an elevation of 3,310 feet above sea level. The vegetation in the area is characteristic of Chihuahuan Desert scrub, which includes various semisucculents such as lechuguilla, sotol, and yucca, and arid-habitat shrubs such as creosote bush and ocotillo. Numerous bee hives could once be found in the rocky crevices and pockets on the mountain's sides.

BEERS, IOLA BARNS (1852–1925). Iola Barns Beers, civic leader, the daughter of Thomas and Antoinette Barns, was born in New Orleans on December 17, 1852. She moved to Galveston with her parents in 1875 and in 1879 or 1880 married William Francis Beers, a Galveston insurance agent and civic leader. They had one son. Iola Beers is best known for founding two prominent women's organizations in Galveston. In 1890 she founded the Girl's Musical Club, which, with the aid of trained musicians, educated talented young women and assisted them in their musical studies regardless of income. The club presented concerts and held biweekly meetings to study the history of music and the work of great composers. Galveston's example became the model for the Girl's Musical Club of Houston, founded by a Galveston member. Iola Beers also served on the executive committee of the Ladies' Musical Club of Galveston.

In 1893 she represented Texas at the Chicago World's Fair and later was on the Texas committee at the St. Louis World's Fair. She raised $2,000 for the Galveston public school's representation at the Chicago fair. In addition she raised $5,000 for equipment for the Galveston public schools through such productions as *H.M.S. Pinafore*, performed at the Grand Opera House.

After the Galveston hurricane of 1900,[qv] she joined the relief efforts of the American Red Cross Association. Clara Barton appointed her chairman of the Eleventh Ward distribution committee. She continued her Red Cross work during World War I.[qv]

Iola Beers joined many progressive women's organizations and was on the board of directors of the Galveston Orphan's Home and the Galveston Art League. She belonged to the Wednesday Club and the Galveston Equal Suffrage Association. Perhaps her greatest civic contribution came through helping to found, with Anna Maxwell Jones, the Women's Health Protective Association[qv] in 1901. Within the first year she and sixty-five other women had the bodies of hastily buried storm victims moved to a gravesite at the west end of the island and began beautifying the area. Throughout her years of association with the WHPA she demonstrated her commitment to music and public education by chairing the Education and Art Committee, the Public Schools Committee, and the School Hygiene Committee of the WHPA. She died in Galveston on November 13, 1925.

BIBLIOGRAPHY: Galveston *Daily News*, November 14, 15, 1925. S. C. Griffin, *History of Galveston, Texas* (Galveston: Cawston, 1931). Elizabeth Hayes Turner, Women's Culture and Community: Religion and Reform in Galveston, 1880–1920 (Ph.D. dissertation, Rice University, 1990).

Elizabeth Hayes Turner

BEESON, BENJAMIN (?–ca. 1837). Benjamin Beeson (or Beason), one of Stephen F. Austin's[qv] Old Three Hundred[qv] colonists, received title to his land in Colorado County on August 7, 1824. He operated a ferry on the Colorado River at the site of present Columbus, where his wife, Elizabeth, kept an inn. In April 1836 the Beeson family was at Harrisburg, where Mrs. Beeson operated a boarding house. Benjamin Beeson died before March 9, 1837; the *Telegraph and Texas Register*[qv] of March 14, 1837, carried a notice that William B. DeWees, Leander Beeson,[qqv] and Abel Beeson were administrators of his estate.

BIBLIOGRAPHY: Sam Houston Dixon and Louis Wiltz Kemp, *The Heroes of San Jacinto* (Houston: Anson Jones, 1932). Amelia W. Williams and Eugene C. Barker, eds., *The Writings of Sam Houston, 1813–1863* (8 vols., Austin: University of Texas Press, 1938–43; rpt., Austin and New York: Pemberton Press, 1970).

Seymour V. Connor

BEESON, LEANDER (1817–1858). Leander Beeson (or Beason), farmer and Texas militiaman, was born in Tennessee about 1817, the son of Benjamin and Elizabeth Beeson. In 1822 he moved to Texas with his father. He served as a private in Capt. William J. E. Heard's[qv] Company F of Col. Edward Burleson's[qv] First Regiment, Texas Volunteers, from February 25 to May 25, 1836. For his service in the battle of San Jacinto[qv] Beeson received a bounty of 320 acres in Colorado

County in December 1839. By 1840 he had acquired 2,580 acres on the east bank of the Colorado River four miles northeast of Columbus in central Colorado County, where, with his wife Rebecca and son Leander, he raised cattle. Beeson died in Colorado County in 1858; his wife served as executor of his estate.

BIBLIOGRAPHY: Colorado County Historical Commission, *Colorado County Chronicles from the Beginning to 1923* (2 vols., Austin: Nortex, 1986). Sam Houston Dixon and Louis Wiltz Kemp, *The Heroes of San Jacinto* (Houston: Anson Jones, 1932).

Charles Christopher Jackson

BEESON, WILLIAM E. (1822–1882). William E. Beeson, first president of Trinity University, was born in Berkley County, Virginia, on October 21, 1822. He obtained his early training in Logan County, Kentucky, and in April 1840 joined the Logan Presbytery of the Cumberland Presbyterian Church. He graduated from Cumberland University (Lebanon, Tennessee) in 1849 and taught at Bowling Green, Kentucky, until 1852, when he became president of Chapel Hill College at Daingerfield, Texas. In 1851, while teaching at Bowling Green, he married Margaret E. Fleming. During the Civil War,[qv] Beeson closed the school and joined the Daingerfield Grays as a first lieutenant. After the war, he returned to Chapel Hill and stayed until 1869, when he left to become the first president of Trinity University, then located at Tehuacana. Besides his duties as president he also taught mental and moral science. In 1877 he took a leave of absence and traveled in the interest of an endowment of a chair in theology. He returned to the presidency in 1878 and also taught theology. He continued as president at Trinity until his death, near Hillsboro on September 5, 1882.

BIBLIOGRAPHY: Thomas H. Campbell, *History of Cumberland Presbyterian Church in Texas* (Nashville: Cumberland Presbyterian Publishing House, 1936). S. M. Templeton, "A Paper on Early Cumberland Presbyterian History in Texas" (Joint Session of the Synods of Texas, Fort Worth, September 23, 1931). *Claudia Hazlewood*

BEESON'S FORD. Beeson's (Beason's) Ford was located on the Colorado River at the site of present Columbus in Colorado County. It was named after Benjamin Beeson,[qv] who operated a ferry at the crossing. Beeson's wife, Elizabeth, ran an inn there. In 1836 Sam Houston's[qv] army camped at the crossing from March 19 to March 26. The ford had to be abandoned as the Mexican army approached.

BIBLIOGRAPHY: Amelia W. Williams and Eugene C. Barker, eds., *The Writings of Sam Houston, 1813–1863* (8 vols., Austin: University of Texas Press, 1938–43; rpt., Austin and New York: Pemberton Press, 1970).

Anthony S. Powers

BEEVILLE, TEXAS. Beeville, the county seat of Bee County, is on Poesta Creek at the intersection of U.S. Highway 181, State Highway 59, and the Southern Pacific Railroad, in central Bee County. The site of the community was settled by the Burke, Carroll, and Heffernan families in the 1830s. Several of the settlers were killed by Indians during the early years of the settlement. When Bee County was organized in 1858, the county seat was founded at a site on the east bank of Medio Creek seven miles east of the current site of the community. This first county seat was known as Beeville-on-the-Medio. This location proved inconvenient, and in 1859 Ann Burke Carroll, Patrick Carroll, and Patrick Burke donated land for a townsite at the current location of Beeville. The first name for the new community was Maryville, after a member of the Heffernan family who had survived the Indian massacre. Eight months later the county commissioners changed the name to Beeville, and for some time the court's minutes referred to Beeville-on-the-Medio and Beeville-on-the-Poesta. In 1857 G. B. McCollom operated an inn in the new community. George W. McClanahan opened the first store, and a post office was established in 1859. In 1860 the first courthouse was erected and the Beeville Masonic Lodge built a second story for its meetings. The community contributed a company of men to the Confederate Army during the Civil War.[qv] In 1878 a second courthouse was built, which burned down in 1911. A third, brick building was erected in 1912 and was subsequently remodeled in 1942 and 1948–50. The first jail was built in 1874; a second was built in 1893 and renovated in 1979. Beeville's growth was spurred by the arrival of two railroads in the 1880s. In 1880 the community was still small, with an estimated 300 inhabitants, two general stores, two hotels, a gin and gristmill, and a blacksmith shop. In 1886 the San Antonio and Aransas Pass Railway built through the community, connecting it with Corpus Christi and San Antonio, and in 1889 this railroad was joined by the Gulf, Western Texas and Pacific, building southwest from Victoria. By 1890 Beeville had an estimated 1,000 inhabitants. William O. McCurdy launched the first newspaper, the Beeville *Bee,* in 1886, and the *Picayune* joined it in 1890. The two papers were combined to form the *Bee-Picayune* in 1928.

Beeville incorporated for the first time in 1890, but the corporation was dissolved the following year. In 1900 the population had grown to 2,311. The town received electricity and municipal water in 1903 and sewerage in 1910. Beeville was incorporated for the second time in 1908, with a mayor-aldermanic government. Residents opted for a commission government in 1912, then changed to a council-manager government in 1951. The town continued to grow during the early decades of the twentieth century. In 1920 the population reached 3,062, and the following year the streets were paved. The discovery of oil and gas in the county in 1929 led to the building of several large office buildings in Beeville; the Union Producing Company had its district offices there from 1930 until the 1970s. Between 1920 and 1930 the population increased by more than 60 percent, reaching 4,806. In spite of the boost given the local economy by the oil industry, Beeville was hard hit by the Great Depression[qv] in the 1930s. A WPA office was opened in the community, and government-funded projects improved city streets. The population grew to 6,789 in 1940, the year the Beeville Chamber of Commerce was chartered. During World War II[qv] Beeville benefited from the construction of the Naval Auxiliary Air Station at Chase Field, which eventually became the Naval Air Station, Beeville.[qv] The base trained naval aviators from 1943 through 1946, then was temporarily deactivated. In response to the demands of the Korean War the field was reopened in 1952 and continued to train pilots until its closing in 1992. Beeville continued to grow, reaching 9,348 inhabitants in 1950 and 13,811 in 1960. Thereafter, the population remained relatively constant—13,506 in 1970, 14,574 in 1980, and 13,547 in 1990. The first school in Beeville was held in a private home in 1860, and the first school building was built in 1877. The Beeville school district had ten schools in the mid-1980s. The first parochial school was Saint Mary's Academy, built in 1896 and destroyed by fire in 1930. St. Joseph's School was built on the same location, and seven other parochial or private schools existed in 1984. Bee County College opened in 1967. The earliest church services were held in the homes of the Irish Catholic settlers of the area in the 1840s. The first Methodist church was organized in 1861, and the first Baptist church in 1869. The community had thirty-two churches in the mid-1980s. In 1990 the town's economy was focused on county government, oilfield services, and agribusiness. Western Week was held every October in the city coliseum. Beeville had a senior citizen's center and a hospital and was home to Bee County College.

BIBLIOGRAPHY: Grace Bauer, *Bee County Centennial, 1858–1958* (Bee County Centennial, 1958). Grace Bauer (Lillian Grace Schoppe), The History of Bee County, Texas (M.A. thesis, University of Texas, 1939).

Grace Bauer

BEEVILLE RIOT OF 1894. The Beeville Riot was one of many incidents of inter-ethnic conflict in late-nineteenth-century Texas. Numerous Mexicans immigrated into central and eastern Texas in the 1880s and 1890s, became a source of cheap labor for farmers and businessmen, and began to compete with liberated African Americans[qv] and unskilled whites. White employers increased the friction among the three groups, especially between blacks and Mexican Americans,[qv] by hiring more of the latter at lower wages as Mexican immigrants increased in numbers in the Beeville area in the 1890s. The heightened antagonism came to a boil and ended with a raid on the Mexican section of the community in August 1894. Blacks, with the assistance of some "wild white boys," pelted the Mexicans and their homes with rocks, beat a few, and told them to leave the area or suffer greater punishment. At least three Mexicans were seriously injured. Most whites sided with the Mexicans, who were viewed as more reliable, better workers, and less antagonistic. The Beeville *Bee* noted that the Mexicans were more tranquil, not as unruly, more industrious, and less expensive to hire. The incident is of unique interest, as it did not threaten white social and economic dominance. White interest in the riot, implied in the newspaper coverage, reflects a desire to keep wages low by fostering competition between the two minority groups involved.

BIBLIOGRAPHY: Beeville *Bee,* June 7, 1888, August 17, 1894. Arnoldo De León, *They Called Them Greasers: Anglo Attitudes Toward Mexicans in Texas, 1821–1900* (Austin: University of Texas Press, 1983).

Juan O. Sanchez

BEHAMON, TEXAS. Behamon was near the Trinity River in southern Angelina County. The settlement was named for Frank Behamon, who moved to the area in the 1870s. Some lumbering was done there before 1900. In the early 1990s only a few scattered houses remained in the area.

BIBLIOGRAPHY: Angelina County Historical Survey Committee, *Land of the Little Angel: A History of Angelina County, Texas,* ed. Bob Bowman (Lufkin, Texas: Lufkin Printing, 1976).

Claudia Hazlewood

BEHRENS, TEXAS. Behrens was a school community just east of State Highway 386 and four miles northeast of Mason in central Mason County. It was named for Henry Julius Behrens, one of the first German settlers to move there from Fredericksburg (*see* GERMANS). He arrived in January 1880, and he and his neighbors soon built a school on his land, with Miss Ellen C. Hill as the first teacher. No population has been listed for Behrens since 1904. The Behrens family cemetery is located at the site, and the rock Behrens house was still standing as late as 1976. *Alice J. Rhoades*

BEHRENVILLE, TEXAS. Behrenville (or Behrnville) is eleven miles northeast of Georgetown in northern Williamson County. It was named after H. T. Behrens, an early settler. German, Austrian, Moravian, Bohemian, and Silesian immigrants settled in the Behrenville area in the 1880s and 1890s. The locality had its own post office from 1901 to 1906 and is closely associated with the nearby community of Theon. Behrenville had an estimated population of thirty-five from 1933 to 1946. From 1947 to 1965 the population was estimated at sixty. From 1966 to 1990 the population estimate remained steady at thirty.

BIBLIOGRAPHY: Clara Stearns Scarbrough, *Land of Good Water: A Williamson County History* (Georgetown, Texas: Williamson County Sun Publishers, 1973). *Tim Davis*

BEHRING STORE, TEXAS. Behring Store, seven miles east of Seguin on a road that later became U.S. Highway 90A in eastern Guadalupe County, was built in 1913 by Henry Behring, who had immigrated from Germany in 1872. Earlier settlers in the area had come from the southern United States shortly after the Texas Revolution.[qv] Three miles west of the store is the site of the battle of Plum Creek.[qv] Three miles east is a well-preserved rock house that was a stage stand at a pre–Civil War racetrack. The Behring Store community had three businesses, several houses, and a population of twenty in 1946. There was no evidence of the community in 1987 maps.

Willie Mae Weinert

BEHRNS, FRANCIS MARION (1863–1942). Francis Marion Behrns, school founder and civic leader, was born in Llano, Texas, on October 9, 1863, the son of John H. L. Behrns. He took over the management of a small store that his father had purchased in the late 1870s and directed the store for four years before leaving to attend school in Liberty Hill. In the late 1880s, Behrns began teaching in Llano and at Cherokee. He chartered West Texas Normal and Business College at Cherokee in 1889. For many years, while the predominant trend was for urban families to send their children to colleges in small towns, the school enjoyed prominence in the region. Eventually, though, larger institutions in larger cities became popular, and Behrns sold the school to Southwestern University in Georgetown in 1901–02. He was a past master of the Masonic lodge of Llano and a member of the Llano chapter of Royal Arch Masons, Council of Royal and Select Masters, the Llano Commandery of Knights Templars, the Scottish Rite, and the Ben Hur Shrine of Austin. Behrns contributed to the construction of the Masonic Temple at Llano, which he planned and supervised; he designed the interior. Behrns died a bachelor on June 10, 1942, in Austin and was buried in Llano.

BIBLIOGRAPHY: Vertical Files, Barker Texas History Center, University of Texas at Austin. *Jill Seeber*

BEITONIJURE INDIANS. The Beitonijure Indians were one of twenty Indian groups that joined Juan Domínguez de Mendoza[qv] on his expedition from El Paso to the vicinity of present San Angelo in 1683–84. Since Mendoza did not indicate at what point the Beitonijures joined his party, it is impossible to determine their range or affiliations. However, Indians between the Pecos River and the San Angelo area were being hard pressed by Apache Indians at that time, and it seems likely that the Beitonijures ranged between these two localities.

BIBLIOGRAPHY: Herbert Eugene Bolton, ed., *Spanish Exploration in the Southwest, 1542–1706* (New York: Scribner, 1908; rpt., New York: Barnes and Noble, 1959). *Thomas N. Campbell*

BELCHER, EDWARD (1799–1877). Edward Belcher, a leader of the Colony of Kent,[qv] the son of Andrew Belcher of Halifax, Nova Scotia, was born in 1799. He entered the Royal Navy in 1812 and was knighted in January 1843. The same year he published his *Narrative of a Voyage around the World Performed in H.M.S. Sulphur during the Years 1836–1842.* Sometime during the period between 1848 and 1852 Belcher was in Texas to make arrangements for the English settlers of the Colony of Kent. This included supervising the survey of the colony made by Maj. George B. Erath and Neil McLennan.[qqv] Belcher became an admiral in the British navy on October 20, 1872, and died on March 18, 1877.

BIBLIOGRAPHY: *Dictionary of National Biography.* Dorothy Waties Renick, "The City of Kent," *Southwestern Historical Quarterly* 29 (July 1925). *Karen Yancy*

BELCHERVILLE, TEXAS. Belcherville is at the intersection of U.S. Highway 82 and Farm Road 1816, fifteen miles northwest of Montague in northwestern Montague County. The settlement was first called Belcher, after John and Alex Belcher, area ranchers and landowners, but was renamed Belcherville by 1858. The community, however, was nothing more than the headquarters of the Belcher Ranch until 1887, when, anticipating the extension through the area of the tracks of the Gainesville, Henrietta and Western Railway, the Belchers purchased 27,000 acres of land and plotted a townsite. A post office was opened that year. The rail connection, combined with the almost complete destruction by tornado of nearby Red River Station in 1890, contributed to Belcherville's growth and development as an area cattle and cotton shipping point. By 1893 it had been incorporated, and more than twenty businesses operated there. By 1900 Belcherville had 305 residents, thirty businesses, and two schools.

During the twentieth century the community declined, and residents voted to repeal the act of incorporation in 1908. Just after World War I[qv] two fires destroyed much of the local business district, and many merchants apparently moved to nearby Nocona. Belcherville had a population of 192 in the mid-1920s and eighty-five in the mid-1930s, when five businesses were in operation there. The post office closed sometime after 1930. Belcherville's population subsequently fluctuated, rising to ninety-four by the mid-1940s, declining to thirty-one by the mid-1950s, and rising to ninety by the late 1960s, when no businesses were reported. The community may have incorporated again in the first half of the twentieth century, since it was reported to be the smallest incorporated town in the United States in 1958. From the 1960s to 1990 Belcherville reported a population of thirty-four.

BIBLIOGRAPHY: T. Lindsay Baker, *Ghost Towns of Texas* (Norman: University of Oklahoma Press, 1986). Bowie *News,* July 24, 1958. John Clements, *Flying the Colors: Texas, a Comprehensive Look at Texas Today, County by County* (Dallas: Clements Research, 1984). Guy Renfro Donnell, The History of Montague County, Texas (M.A. thesis, University of Texas, 1940). Jeff S. Henderson, ed., *One Hundred Years in Montague County, Texas* (St. Jo, Texas: Ipta Printer, 1978).

Brian Hart

BELCO, TEXAS. Belco, in northwestern Gray County, was established as an oil camp in 1929, during the height of the local boom. It sprang up around the refinery erected by the Bell Oil and Gas Company a mile east of Pampa. Mail came through the Pampa post office. During the 1930s Belco reported four businesses but had no population listings until 1945 and 1947, when the *Texas Almanac*[qv] recorded a population of eighty. In 1932 Danciger Oil and Refineries, manufacturer of Roadrunner Gasoline, took over the plant and hired as many as 200 people. A year after the takeover the capacity of the refinery was increased by 4,000 barrels. During World War II[qv] Danciger produced high-octane gasoline as aviation fuel for area bases. The refinery also was known as the sponsor of the Pampa Road Runner baseball team, which included Sammy Baugh of subsequent football fame. The Phillips Petroleum Company bought the refinery in 1946 and later closed it. That move, in addition to the growth of Pampa, resulted in Belco's rapid demise.

BIBLIOGRAPHY: Gray County History Book Committee, *Gray County Heritage* (Dallas: Taylor, 1985). *H. Allen Anderson*

BELDING, TEXAS. Belding is on the Atchison, Topeka and Santa Fe tracks ten miles southwest of Fort Stockton in Pecos County. The community was named for A. N. Belding, director of the Kansas City, Mexico and Orient Railway. The proposed town was laid out in April 1913 by Horace H. Stevens and John Brooks, trustees of the Davenport Irrigation and Land Associates Company. Lots in the townsite were reserved for a town square, a hotel, a general store, a pump company, a lumberyard, a hardware store, and stockyards. Track construction of the Kansas City, Mexico and Orient reached Belding in the same year. After the hotel was built, plans to develop Belding were abandoned because it became apparent that the limited water supply could be utilized only with expensive electrical pumping. The hotel was later moved to Leon Lake. Nevertheless, in 1986 Belding remained a quiet farming community.

BIBLIOGRAPHY: Pecos County Historical Commission, *Pecos County History* (2 vols., Canyon, Texas: Staked Plains, 1984). Charles P. Zlatkovich, *Texas Railroads* (Austin: University of Texas Bureau of Business Research, 1981). *Glenn Justice*

BELFALLS, TEXAS. Belfalls is at the intersection of Farm roads 935 and 438, nine miles northeast of Temple in northeastern Bell County. Its name is a combination of county names, Bell and Falls. It once had a double voting box, one for Falls County and one for Bell County. A Belfalls post office was opened in 1891, and by 1896 the community had 260 inhabitants, a hotel, a Baptist church, a mill and gin, two general stores, and two "capitalists." The Belfalls school had sixty-nine pupils and two teachers in 1903. In 1907 the post office was discontinued, and mail service was routed through Oenaville. Around 1915 mule power was used to dig the lake that supplies water to Belfalls Water Company. The population of Belfalls had dropped to eighty-four by 1933, but in 1947 the town had six businesses and 200 inhabitants. A second decline followed in the 1950s, and the population fell to fifty in 1964 and twenty in 1988 and 1990.

BIBLIOGRAPHY: Bell County Historical Commission, *Story of Bell County, Texas* (2 vols., Austin: Eakin Press, 1988). *Mark Odintz*

BELFRAGE, GUSTAVE W. (1834–1882). Gustave W. Belfrage, entomologist, the son of Axel and Margareta Sophie (Leijonhujucid) Belfrage, was born in Stockholm, Sweden, on April 12, 1834. In 1854 he became a student in the high school of forestry in Stockholm, and in 1857 he was made steward of the forest. He immigrated to America in 1859 or 1860, lived for a time in New York, and then moved to Chicago, where he began collecting insect specimens. On January 4, 1867, he moved to Texas to continue that work. A fire destroyed all of his books and many of his collections in 1868, but by the end of that year he was selling large exhibits of insects to the Swedish Academy of Science at Stockholm. He moved to Clifton in 1870. In 1879 he built a small hut near Norse, where he died on December 7, 1882.

BIBLIOGRAPHY: S. W. Geiser, *Naturalists of the Frontier* (Dallas: Southern Methodist University, 1937; 2d ed. 1948).

Lura N. Rouse

BELGRADE, TEXAS. Belgrade is on Farm Road 1416 in east central Newton County, about one mile west of the Sabine River and sixty miles northeast of Beaumont. Indians who called the place Biloxi, either in memory of a visit to the Mississippi town of that name or in reference to their group name, once occupied the surrounding area, which lay at the Sabine River crossing of the old Coushatta Trace.[qv] Belgrade was founded by William McFarland in 1837. It was the first organized town in what was to become Newton County and was named after a more famous riverport, the capital of Serbia. Early settlers had high hopes for their new community; McFarland's son Thomas called the site "the most beautiful I had ever seen for a town." Numerous town lots sold at $100 each. During the 1840s and 1850s Belgrade became a center for agriculture and trade and a busy riverport served by several steamboats. The presence of a large raft two miles above the town undoubtedly aided early growth by concentrating river traffic at Belgrade. The town had a post office by 1840; its name was changed to Biloxi in 1853 and back to Belgrade in 1860. Belgrade made an unsuccessful bid to become the county seat during the mid-1850s. The town, although reportedly the site of one store and a sawmill in the 1880s, never realized the hopes of its founders. The expansion of railroads into East Texas in the early 1900s hurt the river trade. Belgrade also never became a major center for the lumber industry,[qv] which sparked growth in much of Newton County during the early twentieth century. The Belgrade post office was closed from 1866 to 1879 and again from 1906 to 1910; it was permanently removed in 1936. The original townsite is now abandoned and the buildings dismantled. A few persons still live in nearby communities, now called Upper and Lower Belgrade.

BIBLIOGRAPHY: Frederick Charles Chabot, ed., *McFarland Journal* (Yanaguana Society Publications 8, San Antonio, 1942). Madeleine Martin, "Ghost Towns of the Lower Sabine River," *Texas Gulf Historical and Biographical Record* 2 (1966). Newton County Historical Commission, *Glimpses of Newton County History* (Burnet, Texas: Nortex, 1982). Miriam Partlow, *Liberty, Liberty County, and the Atascosito District* (Austin: Pemberton, 1974). Texas Surveyors Association Historical Committee, *Three Dollars Per Mile: Accounts of Early Surveying in Texas* (Burnet, Texas: Eakin Press, 1981).

Robert Wooster

BELK, TEXAS. Belk is at the intersection of Farm Roads 197 and 1499, three miles south of the Red River in extreme north central Lamar County. The site, settled in the 1840s by herders who ran their livestock on the open range of Round Prairie, remained sparsely settled after the railroads of the 1880s chose other settlements as rail stops. A post office was established in 1899 but closed six years later. In 1933 the settlement had thirty residents and one business. Maps for 1936 showed a store, a church, a school, and a cluster of houses. In 1949 Belk had a population of fifty and two businesses. In 1957 the children of Belk were attending school in the Chicota Independent School District, and in 1970 the community had no businesses. Maps of 1980 showed the United Methodist Church, Midway Church, and a few dwellings along Farm Road 197. The population in 1990 was fifty-five.

BIBLIOGRAPHY: Thomas S. Justiss, An Administrative Survey of the Schools of Lamar County with a Plan for Their Reorganization (M.A. thesis, University of Texas, 1937). *We Share Our Heritage: Post Oak–Belk Old Settlers Reunion, 1975* (Barker Texas History Center, University of Texas at Austin). *Vista K. McCroskey*

BELKNAP, AUGUSTUS (1841–1889). Augustus Belknap, San Antonio civic leader and founder of the Belknap Rifles,[qv] was born on March 19, 1841, in Newburgh, New York, the son of Augustus Belknap. He was educated in private military schools and worked in the hardware business from 1856 to 1861, when, at the beginning of the Civil War,[qv] he entered the Seventh Regiment of the New York National Guard, on April 19, 1861. After his term of duty expired he reenlisted with what later became the Sixty-seventh Regulars, New York Volunteers. He was severely wounded at the battle of Fair Oaks, Virginia, and he saw action at Seven Pines and Fredericksburg. He was mustered out of service on February 9, 1863, with the rank of captain. He married a Miss Pickard on December 9, 1863; they had three daughters and one son. Belknap joined the Old Guard Metropolitan Regiment in New York City after the war, and he became a junior partner in the hardware firm of William S. Dodge and Company.

In 1877 he moved to San Antonio, where he became founder and president of the company that operated the city's only streetcar system. He was president and director of the Opera House Company and a director of the San Antonio Fair Association. He was elected alderman of the Second Ward in 1883 and 1885 and alderman-at-large in 1887, but he resigned later that year when he became the Republican candidate for Congress from the Tenth District; he was defeated in that race. Belknap was the founder and sponsor of the Belknap Rifles, which he organized in October 1884. He died on a visit to Santa Barbara, California, on June 22, 1889, and his body was taken to the Belknap family vault in Greenwood Cemetery, Brooklyn, New York, where an honor guard of six members of the Belknap Rifles was in attendance.

BIBLIOGRAPHY: Frederick Charles Chabot, *With the Makers of San Antonio* (Yanaguana Society Publications 4, San Antonio, 1937). San Antonio *Express*, June 24, 25, 1889. *A Twentieth Century History of Southwest Texas* (2 vols., Chicago: Lewis, 1907). *S. W. Pease*

BELKNAP, CHARLES (?–?). Charles Belknap, one of Stephen F. Austin's[qv] Old Three Hundred[qv] colonists, was a partner of George Brown.[qv] On May 22, 1827, the two men received title to a sitio[qv] now in Fort Bend County. The census of 1826 listed Belknap as a farmer and stock raiser aged between twenty-five and forty. He died before October 31, 1829, when the Texas Gazette[qv] carried a notice of a public sale of his real estate.

BIBLIOGRAPHY: Lester G. Bugbee, "The Old Three Hundred: A List of Settlers in Austin's First Colony," *Quarterly of the Texas State Historical Association* 1 (October 1897).

BELKNAP, WILLIAM GOLDSMITH (1794–1851). William Goldsmith Belknap, soldier, was born on September 7, 1794, in Newburgh, New York. He was commissioned a third lieutenant in the Twenty-third Infantry on April 5, 1813, and served in the War of 1812. He was promoted to captain of the Third Infantry in 1822 and to major of the Eighth Infantry in 1842. He was brevetted to lieutenant colonel on March 15, 1842, for "general good conduct" against the Florida Indians. With the annexation[qv] of Texas to the Union, Belknap accompanied Gen. Zachary Taylor's[qv] army of observation to Corpus Christi and on May 1, 1846, was given command of one of Taylor's brigades. At the battle of Resaca de la Palma[qv] Belknap led his new brigade with great distinction, riding ahead of it and seizing a Mexican flag. On May 9, 1846, he was brevetted to colonel "for gallant and distinguished service" at the battles of Palo Alto[qv] and Resaca de la Palma, and to brigadier general on February 23, 1847, for his role in the battle of Buena Vista. He was subsequently made inspector general on Taylor's staff. On September 26, 1847, he was appointed lieutenant colonel of the Fifth Infantry. After the Mexican War[qv] Belknap served as commandant of Fort Gibson, Indian Territory, from December 1848 through May 1851. He also served as commander of Military Department Number Seven, the area west of the Mississippi River, south of the thirty-seventh parallel, and north of Texas and Louisiana. He died at Fort Belknap, a post named in his honor, on November 10, 1851. Gen. Belknap was married to Ann Clark. The couple were the parents of William Worth Belknap, secretary of war in the administration of Ulysses S. Grant.

BIBLIOGRAPHY: Francis B. Heitman, *Historical Register and Dictionary of the United States Army* (2 vols., Washington: GPO, 1903; rpt., Urbana: University of Illinois Press, 1965). Raphael P. Thian, comp., *Notes Illustrating the Military Geography of the United States, 1813–1880* (Washington: GPO, 1881; rpt., with addenda ed. John M. Carroll, Austin: University of Texas Press, 1979). *Thomas W. Cutrer*

BELKNAP, TEXAS. Belknap was a half mile east of Fort Belknap and three miles south of the site of present Newcastle in Young County. The nearby fort was named for Gen. William G. Belknap,[qv] who selected the site and established Camp Belknap in 1851. During the early 1850s a small settlement grew up near the fort and was named for it. In 1856 Young County was organized, and Belknap became the first county seat, although the town was little more than a trading post and a post office, the latter established on August 14, 1856. Graham became county seat in 1874. With the army providing frontier security, however, Belknap rapidly grew by 1859 to comprise five general stores, two blacksmith shops, a hotel, a billiard parlor, a school that met at the fort, and 150 people. The community became a stop on the Butterfield Overland Mail[qv] route to California. In Belknap on September 14, 1859, Indian agent Robert S. Neighbors[qv] was shot and killed by opponents of his policy.

The coming of the Civil War[qv] and removal of United States troops from the fort brought Belknap's prosperity to an end. Although Confederate soldiers occasionally camped in the area, the few families that stayed mainly lived in the fort for protection against Indians. Little community activity was evident when federal troops returned to Fort Belknap in 1867, but by 1874 the settlement had recovered enough to reestablish the post office, which had been discontinued in

1866. In 1892 the town had a hotel, several stores, and 125 people. But it consolidated with the new settlement of Newcastle in 1908, when the discovery of coal prompted the Wichita Falls and Southern Railway to build into Young County. The Belknap post office was discontinued and moved to Newcastle on March 3 of that year. Only an unmarked cemetery remained near the original site by the 1980s.

BIBLIOGRAPHY: T. Lindsay Baker, *Ghost Towns of Texas* (Norman: University of Oklahoma Press, 1986). Earl Burk Braly, "Fort Belknap of the Texas Frontier," West Texas Historical Association *Yearbook* 30 (1954). Carrie J. Crouch, *Young County: History and Biography* (Dallas: Dealey and Love, 1937; rev. ed., *A History of Young County, Texas*, Austin: Texas State Historical Association, 1956). Kenneth F. Neighbours, *Robert Simpson Neighbors and the Texas Frontier, 1836–1859* (Waco: Texian Press, 1975). *Charles G. Davis*

BELKNAP CREEK. Belknap Creek rises at the confluence of Middle Belknap Creek and West Belknap Creek, three miles north of Stoneburg in east central Montague County (at 33°44′ N, 97°56′ W), and runs northeast for 18½ miles to its mouth on the Red River, three miles north of Belcherville (at 33°52′ N, 97°50′ W). The stream, intermittent in its upper and middle reaches, traverses generally flat terrain surfaced by clay and sandy loams that support water-tolerant hardwoods, conifers, and grasses. The area has served as crop and range land. Belknap Creek is joined by East Belknap Creek four miles southeast of Ringgold and by Rattlesnake Creek 5½ miles south of Ringgold.

BELKNAP RIFLES. The Belknap Rifles, a San Antonio military company, was named for Augustus Belknap,[qv] who helped some twenty or thirty young men to organize and finance their own company after they were refused admission to the San Antonio Rifles. Robert B. Green,[qv] a graduate of the Agricultural and Mechanical College of Texas (later Texas A&M University), was chosen captain when the group was organized, on October 14, 1884. Aided by friends, families, and employers in securing uniforms and traveling expenses, the group participated in drills in nearby cities and on the San Antonio plazas. In competitive drills with similar groups the Belknap Rifles won more prizes on the drill field than any other militia company in the United States and made the highest score ever made in competition, at the Interstate Drill at Galveston in June 1889. In 1889 Samuel A. Maverick[qv] took the group by water to New York to the centennial of the founding of Manhattan. Their last official appearance as the Belknap Rifles was at the San Antonio fairgrounds in 1897.

With the outbreak of the Spanish American War, the Rifles volunteered in a body and enlisted as Company F, First Texas Volunteer Infantry, under Capt. Solon L. McAdoo, 1st Lt. W. B. Hamilton, and 2d Lt. Raymond Keller. A few of the original members of the group then organized the Belknap Cavalry and enlisted as Troop I, First Volunteer Cavalry, under Capt. John F. Green,[qv] 1st Lt. Hal L. Howard, and 2d Lt. John W. Tobin.[qv]

BIBLIOGRAPHY: Charles Merritt Barnes, *Combats and Conquests of Immortal Heroes* (San Antonio: Guessaz and Ferlet, 1910). Vertical Files, Barker Texas History Center, University of Texas at Austin (Augustus Belknap, Robert B. Green). *Rena Maverick Green*

BELL, CHARLES KEITH (1853–1913). Charles Keith Bell, state attorney general, was born in Chattanooga, Tennessee, on April 18, 1853. He moved to Texas in 1871; two years later he returned to Tennessee, where he read law. After he was admitted to the bar in 1874, he began the practice of law in Hamilton. Bell was county attorney of Hamilton County in 1876. He served the Twenty-ninth District as district attorney, 1880–82; state senator, 1884–88; and district judge, 1888–90. He was elected as a Democrat to the Fifty-third and Fifty-fourth congresses; he served from March 4, 1893, to March 3, 1897, but was not a candidate for renomination in 1896. He practiced law in Fort Worth until May 1901, when he was appointed attorney general by Governor Joseph D. Sayers.[qv] Bell served in that post until 1904, when he again resumed his practice of law. He ran unsuccessfully for governor in 1906 and at the close of the campaign ceased to take an active part in politics. At one time Judge Bell served as chairman of the Anti-State-Wide Prohibition Association and as chairman of the YMCA of Fort Worth. He married Florence Smith in 1906; they had a son. Bell died on April 23, 1913, and was buried under Masonic auspices in East Oakwood Cemetery, Fort Worth.

BIBLIOGRAPHY: *Biographical Directory of the American Congress* (Washington, D.C.: GPO, 1859–). Lewis E. Daniell, *Personnel of the Texas State Government, with Sketches of Representative Men of Texas* (Austin: City Printing, 1887; 3d ed., San Antonio: Maverick, 1892). *Anne W. Hooker*

BELL, JAMES G. (1832–1867). James G. Bell, trail driver and diarist, the son of Samuel Bell, was born in Tennessee in 1832. The family moved to Indianola, Texas, in 1852, and later the father opened a jewelry store in San Antonio. In 1854 Bell decided to join in driving a herd of cattle to California for John James,[qv] a San Antonio surveyor. Rather than write letters back to his family, Bell kept a diary of his experiences and observations, a chronicle of a little-known trail to the West. He joined his brother, Edward C. Bell, in California and died there in 1867.

BIBLIOGRAPHY: James G. Bell, "A Log of the Texas-California Cattle Trail, 1854," ed. J. Evetts Haley, *Southwestern Historical Quarterly* 35–36 (January–July 1932).

BELL, JAMES HALL (1825–1892). James Hall Bell, lawyer and justice, the son of Mary Eveline (McKenzie) and Josiah Hughes Bell,[qv] was born at Bell's Landing (now Columbia) on January 2, 1825. In 1837 he entered St. Joseph's College at Bardstown, Kentucky, but returned to Texas on the death of his father in 1838. He attended Centre College, Danville, Kentucky, from 1839 to 1842, when he returned to Texas and served under Alexander Somervell[qv] in repelling the Mexican invasions of 1842.[qv] Bell studied law with William H. Jack[qv] and entered Harvard University in 1845. He returned to Texas in 1847 and formed a partnership with Robert J. Townes[qv] to practice law at Brazoria. From 1852 to 1856 Bell was district judge, and from August 2, 1858, to August 1864 he served as associate justice of the Texas Supreme Court. He was secretary of state under A. J. Hamilton[qv] from August 7, 1865, to August 17, 1866. At the time of the Coke-Davis controversy[qv] in 1873, Bell interviewed President U. S. Grant and is said to have persuaded Grant not to intervene in Texas in behalf of Edmund J. Davis.[qv] After Reconstruction,[qv] Bell engaged in mining in Mexico. He died in Austin, Texas, on March 13, 1892.

BIBLIOGRAPHY: Austin *Statesman*, March 15, 1892. Harbert Davenport, *History of the Supreme Court of the State of Texas* (Austin: Southern Law Book Publishers, 1917). Andrew Phelps McCormick, *Scotch-Irish in Ireland and America* (1897).

BELL, JOHN S. (?–?). John S. Bell, early legislator, probably moved to Texas in the late 1830s. He was granted a conditional land certificate in San Augustine on December 23, 1839. He represented Shelby County in the House of the Fifth Congress, 1840–41, where he served on the Indian affairs, education, and engrossed bills committees. On November 1, 1844, he filed a claim against the Republic of Texas[qv] for provisions supplied the Sabine troops in August 1844. The claim was paid in 1852, when Bell was living at Shelbyville.

BIBLIOGRAPHY: Texas House of Representatives, *Biographical Directory of the Texan Conventions and Congresses, 1832–1845* (Austin: Book Exchange, 1941). *Jeanette H. Flachmeier*

BELL, JOSIAH HUGHES (1791–1838). Josiah Hughes Bell, Brazoria county planter, founder of East and West Columbia, Texas, and one of Stephen F. Austin's[qv] Old Three Hundred[qv] colonists, was born on August 22, 1791, in Chester District, South Carolina, the son of John and Elizabeth (Hughes) Bell. His father died when he was five, and at age eleven the young man was apprenticed to two uncles in the hat business in Tennessee. He later moved to Missouri Territory, where he became justice of the peace of Bellevue Township in 1813 and served in the Indian wars growing out of the War of 1812. He was discharged from service by 1815 and manufactured hats and dealt in pelts for a time. In 1818 he sold his farm in Missouri and on December 1 of that year married Mary Eveline McKenzie of Kentucky, with whom he had eight children. Bell's son, Thaddeus C. Bell, was the second white child born in Austin's colony.

After a period in Natchitoches, Louisiana, Bell came to Texas with Austin in 1821. He brought with him a family of slaves and settled on New Year Creek, near old Washington. There he served as *síndico procurador*[qv] in 1821 and alcalde[qv] in 1822. From 1822 until August of 1823, when Austin was in Mexico, Bell took charge of Austin's colony. Horatio Chriesman[qv] made the colony's first survey on February 10, 1823, to locate Bell's land grants on the west side of the lower Brazos. Bell moved to what became known as Bell's Creek in January 1824, was made a militia lieutenant the same year, and was joined by his family in the fall. By 1829 a community known as Bell's Landing or Marion, which became an important inland port, grew up around a landing he constructed near his home. Bell developed a sugar plantation along the creek's banks and subsequently laid out the two towns that came to be known as East Columbia and West Columbia. He built the area's first hotel in 1832, constructed a school, and as an innovative town planner provided garden plots for new residents.

In 1834 he called a meeting of the colonists to draw up representations to Mexico for Austin's release from prison. He was Austin's friend and dependable agent in settling differences and publicizing new regulations among the colonists. He followed Austin's conservative policy in dealing with Mexico before the Texas Revolution,[qv] but he was loyal to the Texas cause during the war. Bell sold the tract embracing both Marion and East Columbia to Walter C. White and James Knight[qqv] in October 1837 and moved to West Columbia, where he died on May 17, 1838; he was buried there. The value of his estate was estimated at $140,000.

BIBLIOGRAPHY: James A. Creighton, *A Narrative History of Brazoria County* (Angleton, Texas: Brazoria County Historical Commission, 1975). Andrew Phelps McCormick, *Scotch-Irish in Ireland and America* (1897). Vertical Files, Barker Texas History Center, University of Texas at Austin. *Merle Weir*

BELL, PAUL CARLYLE (1886–1952). Paul Carlyle Bell, Baptist minister and school founder, son of W. C. and Minerva (Kelly) Bell, was born at Rio Frio, Texas, on December 9, 1886. He attended Baylor University, where he studied three years in the academy and completed a B.A. degree in classical studies in 1914. While in Waco he worked with Mexican missions under the supervision of Mrs. A. J. Barton, wife of the pastor of the First Baptist Church. Bell served the Mexican church at Bridgeport, Texas, from December 1912 to June 1913, then became pastor of the Mexican Baptist Church in Bastrop. He was married to Ida Perle Elliott of Bridgeport on June 3, 1914; they had six girls and a boy.

In fall 1914 Bell and his wife enrolled as students at Southwestern Baptist Theological Seminary, where they remained for just a short time before returning to Bastrop. Bell served from 1919 to 1923 as pastor of the First Mexican Baptist Church, Austin. He returned to Bastrop and served as a pastor there from 1923 to 1935 and from 1937 to 1941. He pastored simultaneously the Bastrop Baptist Church (1925–28) and the Mexican Baptist Church. From 1935 to 1937 the Mexican church was pastored by Pascual Hurtiz, from Mexico, while Bell directed the school he had established there.

Bell's first educational endeavor at Bastrop was an elementary school for Mexican children. He subsequently built buildings and founded an industrial school for theological and ministerial training in Bastrop known as the Mexican Baptist Institute. The same building served as the church and the school, which began in 1926 with one student and continued to operate until May 1941. Even though the institute lasted for only fifteen years, it filled an important need for theological preparatory training for Mexican ministerial students. An orphanage housed in the school was begun about 1927 and lasted until 1936, when Bell was forced to close it.

Ida Perle Bell died in 1940, and Bell married Gladys Harmon of South Carolina on November 14, 1941. He was invited by the Home Mission Board of the Southern Baptist Convention to direct Baptist work in Panama. He accepted the invitation, went there in late 1941, and served until his retirement in January 1952. He then returned to Lufkin, Texas, where his oldest daughter, Ida Ruth, lived. Bell died on July 24, 1952, after a number of operations for a brain tumor. He was buried at Fairview Cemetery, Bastrop, beside his first wife.

BIBLIOGRAPHY: *Baptist Standard*, October 30, 1930. Bastrop *Advertiser*, November 11, 1926. *Ernest E. Atkinson*

BELL, PETER HANSBOROUGH (1812–1898). Peter Hansborough Bell, governor of Texas, was born on May 12, 1812, in Spotsylvania County, Virginia. He engaged in business in Petersburg until he left Virginia to fight for the independence of Texas. As a private in the cavalry company of Henry W. Karnes,[qv] he fought in the battle of San Jacinto,[qv] for which service, on June 6, 1838, he was issued a donation certificate for 640 acres of land. For serving in the army from May 1, 1836, to January 23, 1839, he was granted another 1,080 acres. He was also issued a headright certificate, dated June 7, 1838, for one-third league of land for army service before May 1, 1836. Bell was appointed assistant adjutant general on May 10, 1837, and inspector general on January 30, 1839. He joined the Texas Rangers[qv] under John C. (Jack) Hays[qv] in 1840 and held the rank of major in the Somervell expedition[qv] of 1842. In 1845 Bell was captain of a company of rangers but resigned that commission to enter the United States Army at the outbreak of the Mexican War.[qv] Under the command of Gen. Zachary Taylor,[qv] Bell won distinction at the battle of Buena Vista. As lieutenant colonel he commanded the part of Hays's regiment designated for service in Texas on the Rio Grande. He was experienced in frontier affairs, and the operations of his battalion inspired confidence in the people so that the line of settlement pushed southwestward rapidly.

Bell was elected governor of Texas in 1849 and again in 1851. A few months before the expiration of his second term in 1853 he resigned to fill the vacancy in the United States Congress caused by the death of David S. Kaufman.[qv] He remained in Congress from 1853 to 1857.

On March 3, 1857, Bell married Mrs. Ella Reeves Eaton Dickens, the daughter of a wealthy North Carolina planter, William Eaton, and the widow of Benjamin Dickens. Bell moved to her home at Littleton, North Carolina. At the outbreak of the Civil War[qv] he was offered a commission as colonel of Confederate forces by Jefferson Davis,[qv] but he refused to serve and spent the war years on his wife's plantation. In 1891 the Texas legislature voted Bell a donation and a pension in appreciation for his services to the republic and the state. Bell County was named in his honor. Bell died on March 8, 1898, and was buried in the cemetery at Littleton. His and his wife's remains were removed to Texas in 1930 and reinterred in the State Cemetery[qv] at Austin. In 1936 the state of Texas erected a memorial to Bell, which stands at the southwest corner of the courthouse grounds in Belton.

BIBLIOGRAPHY: Sam Houston Dixon and Louis Wiltz Kemp, *The Heroes of San Jacinto* (Houston: Anson Jones, 1932). Norman Kittrell, *Governors Who Have Been and Other Public Men of Texas* (Houston: Dealy-Adey-Elgin, 1921). Notes and Fragments, *Southwestern Historical Quarterly*, April 1910. *Anne W. Hooker*

BELL, THOMAS B. (?–?). Thomas B. Bell, one of Stephen F. Austin's[qv] Old Three Hundred[qv] colonists, received title to a league of land now in Brazoria County from the Baron de Bastrop[qv] on August 16, 1824. On October 3, 1825, he headed a committee at Cedar Lake that wrote to Austin about the best means of contending with the Karankawa Indians. The Colorado District census of 1825 listed Bell, and the 1826 Texas census described him as a farmer and stock raiser aged between twenty-five and forty, with a wife and three children. While petitioning for additional land in 1829, Bell gave his wife's name as Prudencio and his residence as Austin Municipality. Noah Smithwick[qv] visited him in 1835 at his pole cabin on the San Bernard River. Bell is probably the Thomas Bell who served in Capt. John York's[qv] company of volunteers for the revolutionary army[qv] from about September 1835 to December 1835, participated in the siege of Bexar,[qv] and received donation and bounty land grants for his military service. He received a donation certificate for 640 acres in Archer County and a bounty warrant for 320 acres in the same county in summer 1857. Bell may have been the Thomas Bell who was a bearer of a Lone Star flag in the battle of Concepción[qv] in 1835. A Thomas B. Bell served on the committee that printed the Goliad Declaration of Independence,[qv] which was distributed in December 1835. A Thomas Bell lived with his family in Austin County in February 1844.

BIBLIOGRAPHY: Eugene C. Barker, ed., *The Austin Papers* (3 vols., Washington: GPO, 1924–28). Lester G. Bugbee, "The Old Three Hundred: A List of Settlers in Austin's First Colony," *Quarterly of the Texas State Historical Association* 1 (October 1897). Daughters of the Republic of Texas, *Muster Rolls of the Texas Revolution* (Austin, 1986). Adele B. Looscan, "Harris County, 1822–1845," *Southwestern Historical Quarterly* 18–19 (October 1914–July 1915). Thomas L. Miller, *Bounty and Donation Land Grants of Texas, 1835–1888* (Austin: University of Texas Press, 1967). Noah Smithwick, *The Evolution of a State, or Recollections of Old Texas Days* (Austin: Gammel, 1900; rpt., Austin: University of Texas Press, 1983). *Telegraph and Texas Register*, February 28, 1844. *Texas State Gazette*, August 28, 1852.

BELL, WILLIAM (1831–1921). William Bell, early settler, Confederate soldier, and legislator, son of Robert and Belinda (Scott) Bell, was born on February 13, 1831, in Rhea County, Tennessee. In 1839 the family moved to Texas and settled south of Mount Enterprise. For about three years Bell carried the mail from Minden to Monroe, Louisiana, then moved to Lamar County, worked in a drugstore, and hauled freight between Gainesville and Jefferson. He spent 1853 to 1856 in California. In 1859 he lost about three-fourths of his herd while driving cattle to California. He subsequently returned to Lamar County and entered the stock business. On January 8, 1861, he married Sarah Lord Van Wey at Rosalie and settled on a farm. The family later moved to Honey Grove. Bell served three years in the Trans-Mississippi Department of the Confederate Army. In 1878 he represented Lamar County in the Sixteenth Legislature. He was a member of the Honey Grove Masonic Lodge. The Bells had four children and celebrated their golden wedding anniversary at Paris, Texas, in 1911. Bell died at the home of his daughter in Paris on July 14, 1921.

BIBLIOGRAPHY: Dallas *Morning News*, February 3, 1911. E. W. Swindells, *A Legislative Manual for the State of Texas* (2 vols., Austin, 1879, 1883).

Jeanette H. Flachmeier

BELL, WILLIAM MADISON (1899–1983). William Madison (Matty) Bell, football coach, was born in Fort Worth, Texas, on February 22, 1899, the son of Mr. and Mrs. R. E. Bell. He graduated in 1916 from North Fort Worth High School, where he played on the Steers' unofficial state championship team in 1915. He attended Centre College in Danville, Kentucky, from 1916 to 1920, and received his B.S. degree. He was head coach at Haskell Indian Institute in Lawrence, Kansas (1920–21), at Carroll College in Waukesha, Wisconsin (1922–23), and at Texas Christian University (1923–28). He coached at Texas A&M from 1929 to 1933, when he moved to Dallas to coach at Southern Methodist University. His tenure at SMU was interrupted in 1941 by World War II,[qv] during which he served as a commander in the United States Naval Reserve (Aviation) from 1942 to 1945. In 1945 he returned to SMU, where he continued as head coach until 1949. He also served as director of athletics there from 1945 to 1964. He retired in 1964.

In Centre College Bell was a member of the "Praying Colonels" of World War I[qv] vintage. He helped establish this small Kentucky school's reputation as a "killer." At TCU he played a significant role in guiding the school through its fledgling years in the Southwest Conference.[qv] He also coached some of TCU's first nationally renowned players, such as Raymond (Raggs) Mathews. During his first year at SMU he took the Mustangs to the Rose Bowl with a 12–0 record and lost to Stanford, 0-7. In 1940 he tied Texas A&M for the championship of the Southwest Conference. In his last game at SMU, in the Cotton Bowl[qv] on December 3, 1949, he brought the seriously undermanned Mustangs, who were twenty-four-point underdogs, to a near-defeat of Notre Dame, which won the game by a late touchdown, 27 to 20. At SMU Bell coached such star players as Kyle Rote, Ewell Doak Walker, Jr., Paul Gage, Gil Johnson, and Johnny Champion. He was known as a great defensive coach and renowned for his wide-open style of game. To his players at SMU, he was known as "Moanin' Matty." He was remembered for the respect he gave each of them and for never using a word of profanity. In 1950 he was succeeded as head coach by his assistant, H. N. (Rusty) Russell.

Bell was a Methodist and a member of the Dallas Athletic Club and the Shrine and Hella temples. He was president of the American Football Coaches Association in 1943–44 and was inducted into the National Football Hall of Fame in 1955 and the Texas Sports Hall of Fame[qv] in 1960. He and his wife, Peggy (Kendrick), had a daughter. He died on June 30, 1983, and was buried at Restland Memorial Park, Dallas.

BIBLIOGRAPHY: John Holmes, *Texas Sport: The Illustrated History* (Austin: Texas Monthly Press, 1984). *Texas Sports Hall of Fame: Its Members and Their Deeds* (Grand Prairie: Texas Sports Hall of Fame, 1981). Vertical Files, Barker Texas History Center, University of Texas at Austin. *Who's Who in Texas Today*, 1st ed. (Austin: Pemberton Press, 1968).

Andrew Blifford

BELLAIRE, TEXAS. Bellaire, on Interstate Loop 610, is surrounded by Houston, West University Place, and Southside Place in southwest Harris County. William Wright Baldwin, acting as president of the South End Land Company, founded Bellaire and Westmoreland Farms after purchasing the 9,449-acre Rice Ranch in 1908. Baldwin was a native of Iowa and nationally known as vice president of the Burlington Railroad. The development was six miles from Houston on the eastern edge of the Rice Ranch, so named for former owner William Marsh Rice.[qv] Promotional advertising in 1909 explained that Bellaire was named for the area's Gulf breezes, but Baldwin may have named it for Bellaire, Ohio, a town served by his railroad. By 1910 Baldwin had invested over $150,000 in capital improvements to turn the treeless prairie into an attractive location for residences and small truck farms. From the site to Main Street in Houston he constructed Bellaire Boulevard. He also incorporated the Westmoreland Railroad Company to build an electric streetcar line down the center of the boulevard. The streetcar, known as the "Toonerville Trolley," operated from December 12, 1910, until bus service replaced it on September 26, 1927. In 1910 horticulturist Edward Teas was induced to move his nursery from Missouri to Bellaire Boulevard to implement landscaping plans drawn by landscape architect Sid Hare. A Bellaire post office opened in 1911.

The South End Land Company advertised nationwide to attract Midwestern farmers and others who were eager to escape harsh winters. Bellaire was promoted as an exclusive residential neighborhood and agricultural trading center with the conveniences of city living and reliable access to Houston. On June 24, 1918, with a population of about 200, Bellaire obtained a general-law city charter. The population reached 1,124 by 1940. Houston's expansion after World War II[qv] transformed Bellaire into a popular suburb, but geographical growth was halted when Houston annexed the surrounding land on December 31, 1948. In April 1949 Bellaire adopted a home-rule charter with a council-manager government. The city had 10,173 residents in 1950. The Swedish general consul's office has been located in Bellaire since 1953.

Bellaire is zoned for residential, commercial, and light industrial sections. High-rise office buildings are located along Loop 610, but Bellaire is largely known as a residential city. Zoning and land-use controversies, long the stuff of Bellaire politics, led to a recall of the mayor and three councilmen in 1977. A resurgence in new residential construction began in the late 1980s.

By 1968 Bellaire had fifteen churches and one synagogue. Leading community organizations include the Bellaire–Southwest Houston Chamber of Commerce, the Bellaire Historical Society, Friends of the Bellaire Library, Friends of Bellaire Parks, and the Bellaire Women's Civic Club. City management is noted for its police and fire protection, library, public works, parks and recreation facilities, recycling center, and an office on aging. The population was 19,872 in 1960, 16,331 in 1987, and 13,842 in 1990.

BIBLIOGRAPHY: Bellaire *Texan*, November 25, 1971, June 5, 1974. Mrs. Robert N. Gay and Mrs. J. W. Hawks, *Bellaire's Own Historical Cookbook* (Bellaire, Texas: Bellaire Women's Civic Club, 1969). *A History of Bellaire* (Bellaire, Texas: Greater Bellaire Chamber of Commerce, 1971). Vertical Files, Barker Texas History Center, University of Texas at Austin.
Jeffrey D. Dunn

BELL BOTTOM, TEXAS. Bell Bottom is on Caney Creek and Bell Bottom Road sixteen miles southeast of Bay City in southeastern Matagorda County. The settlement is named for A. C. Bell, who in the late 1800s bought land to develop in what was then a thickly overgrown area. The site was settled by around 1905 by two black families from Gainesmore and Brazoria who purchased small tracts from Bell. The settlement gradually developed and by around 1927 was served by a one-classroom black elementary school, Mable Kennedy School. During the 1930s at Bell Bottom around twenty families were engaged in vegetable farming, and at least as late as the late 1940s the community had a church, though the school was probably gone by that time. A successful gas well was drilled in the area in the mid-1970s, though additional drilling did not pay off. In the mid-1980s a few small ranches, vegetable farms, and sod farms remained in the community of around forty-three families. Though Bell Bottom was unlabeled on county highway maps, a cemetery and St. Mark Church were shown at the site in 1990.

BIBLIOGRAPHY: Frank J. Balusek, Survey and Proposed Reorganization of the Schools of Matagorda County, Texas (M.Ed. thesis, University of Texas, 1939). Matagorda County Historical Commission, *Historic Matagorda County* (3 vols., Houston: Armstrong, 1986).
Rachel Jenkins

BELL BRANCH (Ellis County). Bell Branch rises three miles west of Italy in southwestern Ellis County (at 32°12′ N, 96°59′ W) and flows northeast for 4½ miles, across flat land surfaced with clay and sandy loams that support water-tolerant hardwoods, conifers, and grasses. For most of the county's history, the area has been used as range and crop land. Bell Branch joins Chambers Creek two miles northwest of Italy (at 32°15′ N, 96°55′ W).

—— (Erath County). Bell Branch begins two miles northwest of Dublin in southern Erath County (at 32°07′ N, 98°22′ W) and extends east for seven miles to its mouth on Green Creek, five miles east of Dublin (at 32°06′ N, 98°16′ W). It first traverses flat to rolling terrain, then an area of steep slopes and benches. The surrounding soil surface of sandy and clay loams supports brush, juniper, live oak, mesquite, and grasses.

—— (Fayette County). Bell Branch rises a mile northeast of Warrenton in north central Fayette County (at 30°02′ N, 96°44′ W) and extends east, passing under State Highway 237, to its mouth on Cummins Creek (at 30°02′ N, 96°41′ W). The stream traverses low-rolling hills and prairies surfaced by sandy loam over firm clay. The area is vegetated primarily with mesquite and grasses and, though considered fair for agriculture, is used primarily as unimproved pasture.

BELL BRANCH, TEXAS (Atascosa County). Bell (Belle) Branch was a rural community three miles south of Fashing in eastern Atascosa County. The settlement was a stage stop on the San Patricio Trail[qv] in the 1870s. A local post office opened in 1871, but service was removed to Campbellton in 1879. Bell Creek, which runs through the area, is probably the source of the name. By 1936 Bell Branch was no longer indicated on highway maps, and by 1963 only ruins marked the site.

BIBLIOGRAPHY: *Atascosa County History* (Pleasanton, Texas: Atascosa History Committee, 1984). Margaret G. Clover, The Place Names of Atascosa County (M.A. thesis, University of Texas, 1952).
Linda Peterson

BELL BRANCH, TEXAS (Ellis County). Bell Branch was just west of Farm Road 876 on Bell Branch, ten miles southwest of Waxahachie in southwestern Ellis County. Bell Branch Lake was built as a water reservoir for the International–Great Northern Railroad when it came through the community in 1903, but by the 1950s the area surrounding the lake was used as a private country club. In the 1930s and 1940s the community was in a cattle-raising area and had a population of twenty and one business. In 1980 Bell Branch was still listed as a community.
Lisa C. Maxwell

BELL CHAPEL, TEXAS. Bell Chapel is on Farm Road 353 eighteen miles southeast of Center in southern Shelby County. The predominantly black community was evidently established after the Civil War[qv] and was named for a local church. In the mid-1930s Bell Chapel had a church, a school, and a number of houses. The school closed around the time of World War II,[qv] but in the early 1990s a church and a few scattered houses still remained in the area.

BIBLIOGRAPHY: Charles E. Tatum, *Shelby County: In the East Texas Hills* (Austin: Eakin, 1984).
Christopher Long

BELL COUNTY. Bell County (J-17), in east central Texas, is located along the Balcones Escarpment approximately forty-five miles north of the Capitol[qv] in Austin and is bordered by Coryell, McLennan, and Falls counties on the north, on the east by Falls and Milam counties, on the south by Milam and Williamson counties, and on the west by Lampasas and Burnet counties. Belton, the third largest town in the county, serves as the county seat and is sixty-five miles north of Austin. The county's center lies at approximately 31°02′ north latitude and 97°30′ east longitude. Interstate Highway 35 and State highways 195, 95, and 317 are the major north–south roads in the county; U.S. Highway 190 and State Highway 36 cross the county east and west. Bell County is also served by Amtrak, the Atchison, Topeka and Santa Fe, the Union Pacific, and the Belton railroads.

Bell County comprises some 1,055 square miles and is divided into regions by the Balcones Escarpment, which runs through the approximate center of the county from southeast to northwest. The eastern part of the county, on the Blackland Prairie, consists of comparatively level prairieland, mainly undulating to gently rolling. The western half of the county belongs to the Grand Prairie region of Texas, and includes undulating to rolling uplands, deeply cut with stream valleys that, in places, have stony slopes and steep bluffs. Bell County ranges in elevation from about 450 feet above sea level in the southeast to about 1,200 feet above sea level on the western boundary. The county is drained chiefly by the Little River and its tributaries, especially the Leon, Lampasas, and Salado rivers, which come together at historic Three Forks to form the Little River. Soils in the eastern part of the county are mostly dark, loamy to clayey "blackland" soils; the rich Houston black clay is the most common type and the most suitable for farming. The soils west of the Balcones fault are light to dark and loamy and clayey, with limy subsoils; shallow, stony soils in places have encouraged ranching and hardwood and pine production. Vegetation west of the fault is characterized by tall grasses and oak, juniper, pine, and mesquite trees, while the eastern part of the county, which has been extensively utilized for farming, is still wooded along its streams with a variety of hardwood trees. Between 41 and 50 percent of the land in Bell County is considered prime farmland. Mineral resources include limestone, oil, gas, sand and gravel, and dolomite.

In the mid-nineteenth century, early settlers found a rich wildlife population of, deer, wild turkeys, wolves, bear, buffalo, antelope, wild horses, ducks, geese, wild hogs, and an occasional alligator. While the buffalo, bear, and hogs were hunted to extinction in the county in the nineteenth century and the last alligator was killed in 1908, Bell County still provides habitat for many wild species, including deer, antelope, and numerous birds; Belton Lake and Stillhouse Hollow Lake[qqv] provide a refuge for Bell County wildlife. Temperatures range from an average high of 96° in July to an average low of 36° in January. Rainfall averages thirty-four inches a year; the average relative humidity is 82 percent at 6 A.M. and 52 percent at 6 P.M., and the growing season averages 258 days annually.

The area currently comprising Bell County has been the site of human habitation since at least 6000 B.C. Evidence of Archaic Period (ca. 7000 B.C.–A.D. 500) and possibly Paleo-Indian Period (pre-7000 B.C.) inhabitants has been recovered from archeological sites at the Stillhouse Hollow Site, Lake Belton, and Youngsport. Numerous campsites, kitchen middens and burial mounds from the late prehistoric era have been found along the watercourses of the county, and rockshelters for burials have been discovered in the western part of the county. The earliest known historical occupants of the county, the Tonkawas, were a flint-working, hunting people who followed the buffalo[qv] on foot. During the eighteenth century they made the transition to a horse culture and began to use firearms. Lipan Apaches, Wacos, Anadarkos, Kiowas, and Comanches also frequented the land that become Bell County. The Lipans camped by the rivers and streams, and early white settlers had friendly relations with them. Early settlers also recorded that the Indians fired the prairie each spring to burn off the matted winter grass and facilitate new growth. But by the late 1840s the Lipans, Tonkawas and other groups who had customarily camped and hunted in the Bell County area had been decimated by European diseases and driven away by white settlement. Comanche raiding parties continued to strike into the county until 1870.

While the Spanish had explored the Little River to the east in what would become Milam County and had established missions along the San Gabriel to the southeast in the eighteenth century, there is no evidence that they traversed the future Bell County area. Anglo settlement began in the 1830s, when the area was part of Robertson's colony[qv] and, somewhat later, part of old Milam County. The area was first settled in 1834 and 1835 by the families of Goldsby Childers, Robert Davidson, John Fulcher, Moses Griffin, John Needham, Michael Reed, William Taylor, and Orville T. Tyler, who settled as colonists along the Little River. The settlements were deserted during the Runaway Scrape,[qv] reoccupied, and then deserted again after the Indian attack on Fort Parker in June 1836. In their retreat from the fort several of the settlers were overtaken by Indians and killed. The area was reoccupied in the winter of 1836–37. In November 1836 George B. Erath[qv] established a fort on the Little River about a mile below the Three Forks, which has been variously known as Smith's Fort, the Block House, Fort Griffin, and Little River Fort.[qv] The settlements along the river were considerably troubled by marauding Indians. The more important engagements of 1837 were the Elm Creek Raid[qv] on January 7 and the Post Oak Massacre in June. Little River Fort was abandoned, and by 1838 all settlers had left the Bell County area. On May 26, 1839, the Bird's Creek Indian fight,[qv] a bloody but indecisive skirmish between Texas Rangers[qv] and Comanches, took place about 1 ½ miles northwest of the site of present Temple.

Settlers began to return to the Bell County area after the peace treaties of 1843–44, and Indian raids into the county became less frequent. By the census of 1850, the population of what would shortly become Bell County was approximately 600 whites and sixty black slaves. Bell County was formed on January 22, 1850, and named for Peter H. Bell.[qv] The election held to organize the county took place in April at the "Charter Oak," near the center of the county at the military crossing on the Leon River. Nolan Springs was chosen as the county seat and named Nolanville. On December 16, 1851, the name was changed to Belton. In 1854 Coryell County was marked off from Bell County, and in 1856 the legislature attached a six-mile-wide strip of Falls County to Bell County. In 1860, when a resurvey of the line between Bell and Milam counties was made and recognized by the legislature, Bell County assumed its present boundaries.

The last serious Indian raid occurred in March 1859. The Independent Blues, a company of volunteer rangers led by John Henry Brown,[qv] was organized in the immediate aftermath of the raid to protect the frontier. This group functioned for about two months. It was succeeded by several other volunteer units that operated into the summer of 1860. Bell County had a population of 3,794 whites and 1.005 blacks in 1860. Most of the settlers had come to the county either from the older settled counties of lower and eastern Texas, or from the southern United States. The county was not really part of the plantation economy like the eastern part of antebellum Texas;[qv] two-thirds of the 179 slaveholders in 1860 owned seven or fewer slaves, and only four county residents owned twenty slaves or more. Belton, Aiken, and Salado, the only towns, were on a stage route running north from Austin. Salado College was established in 1859 and flourished in the second half of the nineteenth century. Early settlement in the county was along the creeks and rivers, but by 1860 most of the county land, some 462,884 acres, was divided into farms. A series of drought years in the mid-1850s hindered the development of farming in the area, and Bell County farmers still operated in a frontier economy on the eve of the Civil War.[qv] Due to the uncertain supply of water, much of the land in the county was considered worthless for anything but undeveloped pasture, and county residents raised large herds of cattle and sheep. The 42,037 cattle enumerated by the 1860 census was not equalled again until the 1950s. There were only 21,196 cleared acres in the county in 1860, and the large number of oxen in the county, 2,132, when compared to the relatively small number of mules, 646, indicates that many farmers were still doing the heavy work of breaking the land to the plough. Corn and wheat were the main crops, though cotton was introduced into the county along the Little River in the mid-1850s and 514 bales of cotton were harvested in 1860.

A significant minority of Bell County residents were Unionists during the secession[qv] crisis. A Whig newspaper, the *Independent,* was published in Belton, and, in the election of 1859, Bell County strongly supported Sam Houston.[qv] In 1861, however, the county voted 495 to 198 in favor of secession, and many of the former Unionists loyally supported the Confederacy during the Civil War. Out of a white population of some 4,000 at the beginning of the war, one source claims that more than 1,000 Bell County men served in Confederate or state military units. Companies organized in the county served in the First, Fourth, Sixth, and Eighteenth Texas Cavalry regiments, and the Sixth, Sixteenth, and Seventeenth Texas Infantry regiments. Bell County civilians established a variety of rural industries to provide shoes, saddles, and other goods for themselves and the forces. Unionist sentiment never entirely disappeared, however, and from 1862 to 1865 some Union sympathizers and Confederate deserters congregated in northern Bell County at what locals called "Camp Safety."

Reconstruction[qv] in Bell County was a troubled and violent period. Federal troops were quartered in Belton in 1865–66 to support Hiram Christian, newly appointed chief justice of the commissioners' court, but they were powerless to prevent a series of feuds between political factions that resulted in murders and lynchings. Horse and cattle thieves thrived in the unsettled conditions of the time and contributed to the anarchy that prevailed in the county. During the brief return to self-government under Governor James W. Throckmorton[qv] in 1866–67, Bell County sent X. B. Saunders[qv] to the Constitutional Convention of 1866,[qv] and a Belton mob helped to discredit Throckmorton's administration by lynching several pro-Union men who were being held prisoner for feud-related murders. Bell County whites chafed under the imposition of congressional Reconstruction in 1868, and a Ku Klux Klan[qv]–like organization was established in the county. Due to the small number of black voters in the county, Radical Republicans were dependent on military assistance for local control, and the election of December 1869 returned Bell County to Democratic party[qv] rule. The pattern of lawlessness continued into the mid-1870s; and the worst example of vigilante violence occurred on the evening of May 25, 1874, when a mob of men from Bell and other counties broke into the Belton jail and killed nine men, eight members of a gang of accused horse thieves and an accused murderer. One of the most interesting cultural movements of the period in Texas was the Belton Woman's Commonwealth,[qv] a celibate commune of "sanctificationists" that flourished in Belton from the 1870s through the 1890s.

Before the Civil War, African Americans[qv] had formed some 21 percent of the county population. The difficulties they faced in finding a niche in Bell County society in the postwar period can be glimpsed in an 1868 description of the county's blacks by a former Confederate officer: "The negroes behave as well as any one expected, though a large majority of them...are inclined to shift from place to place without having any settled employment." Most of the immigration to the county after the Civil War was white; the black population fell to 11 percent of the total in 1870 and fluctuated between 8 and 12 percent until the 1970s, when it increased to about 16 percent. As in other areas of Texas, blacks were relegated to segregated and inferior housing and educational facilities until the 1960s. Though racial violence was not as common in Bell County as it was in some areas of the state, there were at least two lynchings, in 1911 and 1915, and the Klan was revived in the county in the 1920s.

The Civil War and Reconstruction had a dramatic, if temporary, impact on the county economy. In 1870 the value of Bell County farms was only half of what it had been in 1860. Recovery was fairly rapid, aided by the growth of the cattle and sheep industries and, in the 1870s, by a dramatic expansion of cotton farming. From 1866 to the mid-1870s, stock raising was the chief county industry. One of the main feeder routes to the Chisholm Trail[qv] entered the county near Prairie Dell, extended through the center of Salado and the eastern edge of Belton, and left the county in the direction of Waco. Many cattle drives passed through or originated in the county from the 1860s to the early 1880s. Cattle raising, after declining somewhat in importance in the early twentieth century, was again a major part of the county agricultural economy by 1950, and in 1969 ranchers owned a record 56,101 cattle. Sheep and goat raising also followed a similar pattern in the county. The number of sheep grew from 9,718 in 1870 to 21,224 in 1880, and nearly doubled again to 42,063 sheep producing 198,665 pounds of wool in 1890. The sheep industry declined dramatically in the late nineteenth and early twentieth centuries to some 7,859 sheep producing 31,245 pounds of wool in 1920, but revived in the 1930s and reached a new high of 50,141 sheep and 270,311 pounds of wool in 1940. Mohair became a significant agricultural product by 1930, and reached a peak in 1959, when some 32,269 goats were raised in the county (*see* WOOL AND MOHAIR INDUSTRY).

Cotton, the second boom industry in Bell County, also developed after the Civil War. Cotton culture[qv] in the county, which had been relatively insignificant before the war, rose to successive heights of 9,217 bales in 1880, 37,473 bales in 1890 and a peak of 58,050 bales in 1910. The number of improved acres increased more than sevenfold between 1870 and 1880, and nearly doubled again to some 378,355 acres by 1890. While much of the land was used to grow wheat, corn, oats, and other food crops in 1880, cotton was grown on 26 percent of the cropland in 1890, 45 percent in 1900, 55 percent in 1910, and 61 percent as late as 1930.

Attracted by economic opportunities in ranching and farming, large numbers of immigrants swelled the population of Bell County in the later nineteenth century. The number of residents doubled between 1860 and 1870, from 4,799 to 9,771, more than doubled again to 20,517 in 1880, and had reached 45,535 by the turn of the century. Many immigrants came either from the older counties of Texas or from other southern states, particularly Arkansas, Alabama, Mississippi, and Tennessee. Population pressure and the shift to cotton production after 1870 adversely affected the economic position of the growing number of county farmers. Increasingly concerned over marketing and credit issues, Bell County citizens pioneered the Grange[qv] movement in Texas in the 1870s, and Salado became one of the state centers of Grange activities. Nevertheless, as early as 1880, 41 percent of the county's farms were worked by tenants. The number increased to 58 percent by 1900 and remained at about 60 percent until the 1920s, when it increased still further to a maximum of 68 percent by 1930. Tenancy rates began to decline during the Great Depression[qv] with the shift away from cotton and other staple crops, and by 1959 had dropped to approximately 24 percent of the county's farmers.

Both the cotton and cattle booms were aided by the improved communications available in the county in the later nineteenth century. The Gulf, Colorado and Santa Fe, the first railroad to be built in Bell County, reached Belton in 1881 and established Temple as its headquarters that same year. Temple quickly surpassed Belton to become the largest town in the county by 1890. In 1882 the Missouri, Kansas and Texas crossed the county, and Belton secured a branch line of this railroad from Echo. The Belton and Temple Interurban, an electric line, was constructed in 1905 (*see* ELECTRIC INTERURBAN RAILWAYS). Roads were generally poor throughout the county in the early twentieth century. There were 11,748 automobiles in the county by 1935, and extensive improvements, including blacktopping, of all major roads took place in the 1930s, as highway development[qv] continued throughout the state.

In 1870 only eighty-four foreign-born inhabitants out of a population of 9,771 lived in Bell County. Significant numbers of Germans,[qv] Austrians, and Czechs[qv] moved to the county between 1880 and 1920. Though foreign-born residents never exceeded 5 percent of the county population, these groups and their descendents formed distinctive cultural enclaves, particularly in the southern and eastern parts of the county. For the most part these groups seem to have coexisted peacefully with the Anglo majority of Bell County citizens, but they were harassed by the County Council of Defense during World War I[qv] and by the county Klan in the 1920s. The Hispanic population never exceeded 3 percent of the county total until the second half of the twentieth century, when it rose to some 11 percent of the whole.

By 1930 Bell County had an ethnically mixed population of 50,030. The county economy was still overwhelmingly agricultural, with only 41 manufacturing establishments employing some 565 workers in operation that year. While cotton production was near its peak in terms of percentage of cropland, the cotton industry was already undergoing a rapid transformation. The combined effects of soil depletion, overproduction, and the boll weevil[qv] had already damaged the industry by the mid-1920s, and the situation of cotton growers was further worsened by the depression. The county population dropped to 44,863 in 1940, as many residents left to find jobs elsewhere. Among the county farmers who remained, the depression encouraged diversification and a shift away from staple crops to livestock. Between

1930 and 1940 the number of acres used for cotton growing fell by more than half, and cotton production shrank from 57,574 bales to 30,435. Acres used for corn production increased over the same period by almost half, and wool and mohair production almost doubled, to 137,434 pounds and 75,827 pounds respectively. Though cotton continued to be an important crop in eastern Bell County, the county's farmers increasingly turned to such other crops as sorghum and wheat and to livestock raising in the later twentieth century. Poultry production[qv] also grew in significance in the county economy, and in 1970 Bell County ranked first in the state in turkey raising.

The two world wars had a major impact on Bell County. The community enthusiastically threw itself into the war effort in 1917, providing twice its draft quota on one occasion and forming a variety of citizens' organizations to assist in rationing, in maintaining morale, and in providing services for the armed forces. A more permanent change in county life brought about by World War II[qv] was the establishment of the military base at Fort Hood in the western part of the county; this large installation continues to function as a military training center. In the 1980s much of western Bell County lay within the boundaries of the military reservation, and the fort's estimated 160,000 military personnel, dependents, military retirees, and civilian employees exerted a tremendous economic and social influence on the civilian communities bordering the base. Neighboring Killeen was the largest city in the county, and the contiguous communities of Killeen, Harker Heights, and Nolanville, with an estimated combined population of 50,949 in 1980, were home to almost a third of the county's inhabitants.

The growth of the Fort Hood–Killeen area has been matched by developments in the rest of the county. Bell County's population shot up to 73,824 in 1950, and increased by 27 to 32 percent every decade thereafter, to reach 157,820 in 1980 and 191,088 in 1990. The county also became increasingly urbanized: by 1980, 81 percent of the population lived in urban areas, and Bell County was one of the most densely populated counties in the state. Population growth benefited from and contributed to economic diversity in Bell County. In 1982 approximately 6,900 county residents were employed in factories, more than three times as many as in 1963; other major areas of employment in the 1980s were construction, agribusiness, retail trade, and services. Among the noteworthy educational and medical institutions in the county are the University of Mary Hardin-Baylor, Central Texas College, Temple Junior College, the University of Central Texas, Scott and White Memorial Hospital,[qv] and the Olin E. Teague Veterans Center.[qv]

Politically, Bell County remained solidly Democratic for a century after Reconstruction, though there were sizable minorities of Greenbackers in 1880, Populists in 1892, and supporters of James Ferguson,[qv] a Temple man, in 1920. Independent farm movements attracted supporters in the county in 1880s and 1890s, and county prohibitionists achieved their goal of a dry county in a local-option vote in 1915. The county went Republican by a narrow margin in the 1928 presidential election rather than vote for the Catholic Al Smith, and went Republican again in the presidential election of 1972. County voters chose Jimmie Carter in 1976 and then supported Republican presidential candidates through the election of 1992.

Recreation and tourist attractions in Bell County include Belton and Stillhouse Hollow lakes, the Central Area Museum in Salado, the Belton Independence Day celebration and rodeo (July), the Central Texas State Fair in Belton (September), and the Salado Art Fair (August) and gathering of the Scottish clans (November).

BIBLIOGRAPHY: Bertha Atkinson, The History of Bell County, Texas (M.A. thesis, University of Texas, 1929). Bell County Historical Commission, *Story of Bell County, Texas* (2 vols., Austin: Eakin Press, 1988). Oscar Lewis, *On the Edge of the Black Waxy: A Cultural Survey of Bell County* (Washington University Studies, St. Louis, 1948). George Tyler, *History of Bell County* (San Antonio: Naylor, 1936).

Seymour V. Connor and Mark Odintz

BELL CREEK. Bell Creek rises three miles west of Fashing in southeastern Atascosa County (at 28°47′ N, 98°10′ W) and runs south for five miles to its mouth on West Weedy Creek, seventeen miles north of Three Rivers in northern Live Oak County (at 28°42′ N, 98°08′ W). It crosses flat to rolling prairie with local depressions, surfaced by dark clay and sandy loams that support water-tolerant hardwoods, conifers, mesquite, cacti, and grasses. The land in the area is primarily used for dry-land farming and grazing. Bell Creek may have been named either for an early settler, Sebastian Bell, or because a family living near the creek hung a bell on the neck of a pet doe so that she wouldn't be shot.

BIBLIOGRAPHY: Margaret G. Clover, The Place Names of Atascosa County (M.A. thesis, University of Texas, 1952).

BELLE PLAIN, TEXAS (Callahan County). Belle Plain, six miles southeast of Baird in Callahan County, was established in 1876. Nelson M. Smith purchased state school land for the site in 1875 and laid out a town with wide streets and a designated business district. The site was intended to become a commercial center for the county. Some attribute the name of the community to some bell-shaped contour in the surrounding country, but more likely it was the name of the first child born at the townsite, Katie Belle Magee. By the summer of 1876, the town had three businesses, including a saloon operated by J. W. Cheatham. After Callahan County was formally organized in 1877, voters selected Belle Plain over nearby Callahan City as the first county seat. The new county seat prospered, drawing citizens from Callahan City and other smaller towns as well as new settlers. It eventually had several stores and saloons, a stone jail, two fraternal lodges, eleven lawyers, and four physicians. A newspaper, the *Callahan County Clarendon*, was begun in 1879. The population was never large (about 400 in 1884), but the town served as a regional supply center and exporter of wool, hides, and cotton.

The pride of Belle Plain was Belle Plain College, and both college and community declined simultaneously. When the railroad was built through Baird, some citizens moved there. In 1883 Baird became the county seat, and the population of Belle Plain diminished further. The town's newspaper moved to Baird that year, and the stone jail was eventually disassembled and rebuilt in the new county seat. The region was also damaged by the hard winter of 1884–85 and the drought of 1886–87. After a financial struggle, the college closed in 1892. With the college gone, the county government lost, and most of the population moved away, Belle Plain was doomed. In 1897 only four families and one small store remained in the area. The post office was belatedly discontinued in October 1909.

BIBLIOGRAPHY: T. Lindsay Baker, *Ghost Towns of Texas* (Norman: University of Oklahoma Press, 1986). Brutus Clay Chrisman, *Early Days in Callahan County* (Abilene, Texas: Abilene Printing and Stationery, 1966). Thomas Robert Havins, *Belle Plain, Texas: Ghost Town in Callahan* (Brownwood, Texas: Brown Press, 1972). Russell F. Webb, History of Early Colleges of Callahan County, Texas (M.A. thesis, Hardin-Simmons University, 1949).

Larry Wolz

BELLE PLAIN, TEXAS (Moore County). Belle Plain was east of Dumas in eastern Moore County. The site was settled in 1927, when certain of the lawless element, who had been driven out of Borger by the Texas Rangers,[qv] fled Hutchinson County and set up shop just across the county line. The development consisted mostly of crude, hastily built shacks and quickly became a booming, bawdy settlement that specialized in bootleg beer and whiskey, gambling dens, and brothels. Almost as quickly as it had grown, the town shrank, as its temporary residents moved away to escape the law again. By 1929 only the school, a store, and a filling station remained. The post office was closed and mail routed to Stinnett in 1930. Many buildings were either torn down or allowed to fall apart, while others were moved to Altman (now Sunray). By the time prohibition[qv] was repealed in 1933, Belle Plain had ceased to exist.

BIBLIOGRAPHY: Myrna Tryon Thomas, *The Windswept Land: A History of Moore City* (Dumas, Texas, 1967). *H. Allen Anderson*

BELLE PLAIN COLLEGE. Belle Plain College was established in 1881 by the Northwest Conference of the Methodist Church.[qv] John Day gave the new school ten acres of land in Belle Plain, Callahan County, and local citizens donated generously in the beginning. During its first year (1881–82) the college operated in conjunction with the public school. F. W. Chatfield served as its first president. After a state charter was granted to the institution in the spring of 1882, Rev. J. T. L. Annis took over as president for two years. During his administration enrollment reached 122. Other presidents at Belle Plain College were John W. McIllhenny (1884–85), C. M. Virdel (1885–87), and I. M. Onins (1887–92). From the beginning the college advertised a department of music. By the end of the decade the school had fifteen pianos, a brass band, and an orchestra. By 1885 the institution had two buildings on its land, but the entire plant had been mortgaged to pay for classroom furnishings and musical instruments. Funds for the operation of the school came only from the local school district, a fact that hastened the institution's demise. The railroad skipped Belle Plain, Baird became the Callahan county seat in 1883, and the population declined. Two years of bad weather further eroded the college's financial base. By 1887 the trustees of Belle Plain College were unable to make mortgage payments. Judge I. M. Onins took over the school with its debts in 1887, after a successful school year, but the mortgage company foreclosed on the property in 1889. The company allowed the school to continue to operate until the president's death in 1892.

BIBLIOGRAPHY: Brutus Clay Chrisman, *Early Days in Callahan County* (Abilene, Texas: Abilene Printing and Stationery, 1966). Thomas Robert Havins, *Belle Plain, Texas: Ghost Town in Callahan* (Brownwood, Texas: Brown Press, 1972). Russell F. Webb, History of Early Colleges of Callahan County, Texas (M.A. thesis, Hardin-Simmons University, 1949). *Larry Wolz*

BELLEVUE, TEXAS. Bellevue is on U.S. Highway 287 seventeen miles southeast of Henrietta in southeastern Clay County. Although there were a few settlers in the area in the late 1870s, the community developed in 1882, when the officials of the Fort Worth and Denver City Railway selected the site as a shipping point for its rail line. A surveyor named the new community after Bellevue Hospital of New York City. Postal service to the community began that same year. The presence of the railroad established the town as a farm-market center for southeastern Clay County. In 1902 the 300 residents voted to incorporate. The community's promising future was almost swept away by a tornado that hit the town on April 26, 1906. Fourteen residents died, and the destructive winds left only three or four buildings standing. But within a year or two the Bellevue *News* claimed that the town was rebuilt. The population subsequently renewed its growth and surpassed 700 by the middle 1920s. But in the Great Depression[qv] residents left in search of work. In the early 1930s the discovery of oil on nearby Worsham Ranch did little for the town. Over the next three decades the population continued to decline, from 546 in 1936 to 289 in the middle 1960s. Over that same period the number of businesses also decreased, from twenty-six to ten. Bellevue had a population of 378 in the late 1980s and 333 in 1990.

BIBLIOGRAPHY: Katherine Christian Douthitt, ed., *Romance and Dim Trails* (Dallas: Tardy, 1938). William Charles Taylor, *A History of Clay County* (Austin: Jenkins, 1972). *David Minor*

BELL HOLLOW. Bell Hollow begins two miles northwest of Brokeleg Mountain in southeastern Sutton County (at 30°33′ N, 100°11′ W) and runs southeast for three miles to its mouth on the North Llano River, just east of the site of old Camp Allison (at 30°29′ N, 100°09′ W). The surrounding gently rolling limestone terrain of the western Edwards Plateau is surfaced with loams broken by rock outcrops. Range grasses and scattered small stands of oak, juniper, and mesquite grow in the area.

BELLINGER, CHARLES (1875–1937). Charles Bellinger, black political leader, was born in Caldwell County, Texas, on April 15, 1875. He grew up in a farming family and in his teens became an employee of a saloon owned by Jeff Howard in Lockhart. With his savings and with loans from Howard and the Pearl Brewing Company, he established his own saloon in San Antonio by 1906 and developed a reputation as an exceptional gambler. He expanded his activities to include a pool hall, a cafe, a cab company, a real estate and construction company, a theater, a barbershop, a private lending service for blacks, a lottery, and a bootlegging operation during Prohibition.[qv]

Bellinger entered local politics in 1918 and, with the aid of black ministers, developed support among black voters for John W. Tobin,[qv] who served as sheriff and mayor, and later for the Quin family. In return the city government provided the black neighborhood with paved and lighted streets, plumbing, a meeting hall, and a branch library, as well as improved recreation facilities and schools. Black political participation set San Antonio apart from most Texas and southern cities and stimulated the state legislature to require a white primary[qv] in the 1920s, a move that led to court decisions in the 1930s and 1940s declaring such voter exclusion unconstitutional.

In 1936 Bellinger was convicted of failure to pay income tax, a conviction that resulted in a fine and an eighteen-month sentence at Leavenworth penitentiary. Illness led to his transfer to a government hospital and to a parole granted by President Franklin D. Roosevelt at the request of San Antonio city government leaders and Bellinger's son, Valmo.

Charles Bellinger and his first wife, Celestine (Pelliman), had twelve sons and daughters, but only two boys and three girls survived childhood. After his divorce, he married Addie Scott. He was a Methodist and Mason. He died on June 14, 1937, and was buried at East View Cemetery, San Antonio.

BIBLIOGRAPHY: Audrey Granneberg, "Maury Maverick's San Antonio," *Survey Graphic*, July 1939. Houston *Informer*, June 16, 1937. Andrew Webster Jackson, *A Sure Foundation and a Sketch of Negro Life in Texas* (Houston, 1940). Owen P. White, "Machine Made," *Collier's*, September 18, 1937. *Alwyn Barr*

BELLISLE, FRANÇOIS SIMARS DE (1695–1763). François Simars de Bellisle was born in France in 1695. In autumn 1719, like Álvar Núñez Cabeza de Vaca[qv] almost two centuries earlier, he was marooned near Galveston Bay. His ensuing struggle for survival in some ways parallels that of the noted Spaniard.

On August 14, 1719, Bellisle sailed as an officer on the French West Indies Company ship *Maréchal d'Estrée*, bound for Louisiana. When it entered the Gulf of Mexico, the ship became lost, sailed past the Mississippi River, and ran aground near Galveston Bay. Bellisle and four companions asked to be put ashore to ascertain their position and seek help. The ship, having floated free, sailed away without them. Seeking some familiar landmark, the castaways walked east, perhaps as far as the Sabine River, and ascended a river believed to have been the San Jacinto. Having crossed the bay, Bellisle alone reconnoitered westward, possibly as far as the Brazos River. That winter the Frenchmen were unable to kill enough game to sustain themselves. One by one, Bellisle's companions died of starvation or exposure. Out of ammunition, Bellisle ate oysters, boiled grass, and huge yellow worms pried from driftwood. When he at last encountered Indians on an island in the bay, they stripped him of his clothing and robbed him of his possessions. But they fed him, and he remained with the wandering Atákapan band throughout the summer of 1720, while it hunted for deer and buffalo and dug "wild potatoes," traversing "the most beautiful country in the world."

Treated as a slave, Bellisle was forced during the following winter constantly to carry burdens. He was kept naked and was often subjected to beatings, without recourse. When a group of Bidai Indians came to the Atákapa camp, he managed to write a letter and give it to the visitors with instructions to deliver it to "the first white man." The letter, passed from tribe to tribe, at last reached the Hasinais, who took it to Louis Juchereau de Saint-Denis[qv] at Fort Saint-Jean-Baptiste (Natchitoches, Louisiana). Saint-Denis sent the Hasinais to rescue the French castaway.

Bellisle remained among the Hasinais more than two months and was taken into the lodge of a young widow, Angélique (Angelina to the Spaniards), whose name appears several times in French and Spanish records. Guided by her two children, he reached the French post at Natchitoches on February 10, 1721, and arrived at Biloxi in early April.

He then entered the service of Jean Baptiste Le Moyne, Sieur de Bienville, and the following summer returned to the Texas coast. He sailed on August 21, 1721, aboard the ship *Subtile* with Jean Baptiste Bénard de La Harpe,[qv] who had orders to occupy "the Baye Saint-Bernard" (Matagorda), site of La Salle's[qv] landing in 1685. The captain of the ship was Jean Béranger,[qv] who the previous year had sought to reconnoiter the same bay but had entered Aransas Pass instead. This time he erred again and landed in Galveston Bay. As La Harpe explored the bay, Bellisle served as interpreter among the natives, "who were quite surprised at seeing their slave again." finding the Indians hostile to his intent, La Harpe ordered withdrawal. From nine of Bellisle's former captors taken back to Biloxi as prisoners, Béranger compiled an Atákapan vocabulary, which helps to define the bay explored as Galveston Bay rather than Matagorda.

Bellisle, who remained in the Louisiana colony until 1762, served at various outposts and on expeditions to the interior. He acquired a plantation near New Orleans. In 1753 he became a member of the Superior Council of Louisiana and served as town commander of New Orleans. He died in Paris on March 4, 1763.

BIBLIOGRAPHY: Henri Folmer, "De Bellisle on the Texas Coast," *Southwestern Historical Quarterly* 44 (October 1940). Jean-Baptiste Bénard de La Harpe, *The Historical Journal of the Establishment of the French in Louisiana*, trans. Joan Cain and Virginia Koenig (Lafayette: University of Southwestern Louisiana, 1971). Pierre Margry, ed., *Découvertes et établissements des Français dans l'ouest et dans le sud de l'Amérique septentrionale, 1614–1754* (6 vols., Paris: Jouast, 1876–86). Frank Wagner, ed., and William M. Carroll, trans., *Béranger's Discovery of Aransas Pass* (Friends of the Corpus Christi Museum, 1983). Mildred Mott Wedel, *La Harpe's 1719 Post on Red River and Nearby Caddo Settlements* (Austin: Texas Memorial Museum, 1978).

Robert S. Weddle

BELLMEAD, TEXAS. Bellmead is on State Highway 31 two miles northeast of Waco in east central McLennan County. The community began in the mid-1920s, when the Missouri, Kansas and Texas Railroad chose the site for its locomotive shops. Several hundred people were employed at the shops, and families began moving to the area. The first school was called Bellmead in honor of Belle Meade Farms, a prominent horse farm in Tennessee. Area schools were consolidated to form the La Vega Independent School District in 1927. A post office was established at Bellmead in 1937 with A. L. Gilliam as postmaster. Residents of the community voted to incorporate in 1939, but the incorporation was soon dissolved for lack of water, sewerage, and fire services. In the mid-1940s the Bellmead post office was discontinued and replaced by branch service from Waco.

The Bellmead economy revived in 1942, when Waco Army Air Field (later called James Connally Air Force Base[qv]) opened just northeast of town. The population was reported at twenty-five in the early 1940s, but it increased rapidly after World War II,[qv] rising to 800 by 1949. The community was reincorporated in 1954 with a mayor-alderman government. By 1960 Bellmead had 5,127 residents and

Charles Bellinger. From A. W. Jackson, A Sure Foundation *(Houston? 1940?), p. 584. Courtesy Alwyn Barr, Lubbock.*

eighty-five businesses. When the air force base was closed in 1965 Texas A&M University established the James Connally Technical Institute at the facility (*see* TEXAS STATE TECHNICAL INSTITUTE). Although Bellmead developed some retail businesses and service industries of its own, its proximity to Waco enabled residents to commute to work or shop in the larger city. The population of Bellmead was 7,698 in 1970, 7,569 in 1980, and 8,336 in 1990.

BIBLIOGRAPHY: William Robert Poage, *McLennan County Before 1980* (Waco: Texian, 1981). Vertical files, Barker Texas History Center, University of Texas at Austin. Vertical file, Texas Collection, Baylor University. *Vivian Elizabeth Smyrl*

BELLMONT, L. THEODORE (1881–1967). L. Theodore (Theo) Bellmont, athletic director and professor at the University of Texas, son of Leo and Mary (Lutz) Bellmont, was horn in Rochester, New York, on September 24, 1881. He attended schools in Rochester and then the University of Tennessee, from which he received an LL.B. degree in 1908. While there, he was active in athletics, college politics, and fraternal organizations. From 1908 until 1913 he was secretary of the YMCA in Houston. In 1913 he was employed by the University of Texas as director of athletics, a post that included the supervision of intercollegiate athletics, physical training, and intramural sports. He later became professor and director of physical training for men. During his career at UT he pulled the athletic program out of debt and in three years had it showing a profit; helped organize the Southwest Conference[qv] in 1914–15; started the annual football series at the State Fair of Texas,[qv] now the Texas-Oklahoma game; inaugurated the blanket tax for student admission to UT athletic contests; was cofounder of the Texas Relays; organized an intramural sports program; organized the T Association to honor UT athletes; and was a major force in raising the money with which to build Memorial Stadium.

In 1910 he married Freda Alice (Fritz) Jucket in Chicago. They had two children and seven grandchildren. In 1917 Bellmont went to the School of Military Aeronautics in Austin as a first lieutenant and became a captain. He was sent as a pilot to Kelly Field (*see* KELLY AIR FORCE BASE) in San Antonio, where he was a flight instructor. He returned to his duties at UT in the fall of 1919. In 1957 he retired as professor and director emeritus. Bellmont was a member of the Rotary Club and served two years as the local president, was a vestryman at All Saints Episcopal Church for twenty-five years, organized and led the Capital City American Legion Post, was a YMCA director for many years, headed the Travis County chapter of the American Red Cross for a period, and was a Scottish Rite Mason and a member of Pi Kappa Alpha fraternity. He also served on grand juries, the local tax-appraisal board, and the board of equalization. Bellmont Hall on the campus of the University of Texas was named for him in 1972. He was one of the first four named to the Longhorn Hall of Honor in 1957. Bellmont died on December 27, 1967, and was buried in Austin Memorial Park.

BIBLIOGRAPHY: Austin *American-Statesman*, December 28, 1967. Richard Pennington, *"For Texas I Will": The History of Memorial Stadium* (Austin: Historical Publications, 1992). Vertical files, Barker Texas History Center, University of Texas at Austin.

Margaret C. Berry

BELL MOUNTAIN (Gillespie County). Bell Mountain, with an elevation of 1,956 feet, is two miles north-northeast of Eckert in northeastern Gillespie County (at 30°27′ N, 98°43′ W).

BELLOWS, WARREN SYLVANUS (1889–1967). Warren Sylvanus Bellows, civil engineer, was born in Kansas City, Missouri, on August 15, 1889, to Dr. George E. and Stella (Ferris) Bellows. In 1911 he received his degree in civil engineering from the University of Kansas and by 1921 had established a general contracting firm in Houston, the W. S. Bellows Construction Corporation. This firm was responsible for many major constructions in Houston, in addition to several buildings in other Texas cities and on the campuses of the University of Texas, Texas A&M University, Southern Methodist University, and the University of Houston. The Houston buildings include the Auditorium Hotel, one of the first of Bellows's constructions, completed in the 1920s, the Humble Headquarters Building, the American General Insurance Company and Prudential Insurance Regional Headquarters buildings, the First City National Bank, and the Bank of the Southwest. One of the late Houston constructions was the Alley Theatre.[qv] Bellows's firm participated in the building of the Naval Air Station, Corpus Christi,[qv] built hotels in Galveston, Fort Worth, and Mobile, Alabama, and constructed the administration buildings on the campuses of the University of Texas and the University of Houston. Probably his most famous construction was the San Jacinto Monument, at 570 feet the tallest monument in the world when it was completed in 1939 (*see* SAN JACINTO MONUMENT AND MUSEUM).

Bellows was a member of the American Society of Civil Engineers, president of the Associated General Contractors of America (1946), chairman of the Houston Port Commission from 1950 to 1954, president of the Houston Chamber of Commerce in 1948–49, member of the board of governors of the University of Houston, and member of the Texas Board of Corrections (*see* PRISON SYSTEM). He was also an industrial member of the War Labor Board during World War II,[qv] director of the Gulf, Colorado and Santa Fe Railway, and director of the YMCA. He was a trustee of the M. D. Anderson Foundation, Texas Medical Center, Southwest Research Institute,[qqv] Southwest Legal Foundation, and Board of Visitors of the University of Texas Cancer Foundation. Bellows was chairman of the Houston Symphony Society and belonged to the Philosophical Society of Texas,[qv] the Sons of the Republic of Texas[qv] (which in 1967 made him a knight of the Order of San Jacinto), and the Sons of the American Revolution, which awarded him the 1955 Good Citizens Award. His several awards include the Royal Order of Vasa from King Gustav VI of Sweden in 1956, the Distinguished Service Award from the University of Kansas, and the First Annual Meritorious Award of the San Jacinto Chapter of Texas Professional Engineers. On February 3, 1967, Bellows died in Houston; he was survived by his wife, Anna (Williams), and four children.

BIBLIOGRAPHY: Joseph L. Clark, *Texas Gulf Coast: Its History and Development* (4 vols., New York: Lewis Historical Publishing, 1955). Houston *Chronicle*, February 5, 1967. Houston *Post*, February 5, 1967. *Houston*, March 1951.

BELLS, TEXAS. Bells is on U.S. Highway 82 ten miles east of Sherman in east central Grayson County. The first settlers in the area arrived in the mid-1830s. Community development, however, did not occur until the early 1870s. At first the site was called Gospel Ridge because of its numerous churches. Sometime after the Civil War[qv] the name became Bells, again with reference to the area churches. The increase in the number of farms, combined with the arrival of the tracks of the Texas and Pacific and Missouri, Kansas and Texas railways, established the community as an shipping and retail center. The growth prompted the incorporation of Bells in 1881. In 1893 a post office branch opened. By 1900 the community had 400 residents, twenty businesses, two schools, a number of churches, and a weekly newspaper, the *North Texas Courant*. By the mid-1920s the number of residents had grown to just over 600; businesses numbered thirty, including a bank. The community supported a high school and a grade school. The depression and World War II[qv] slowed the growth. Beginning in the 1950s, however, a steady increase in population resumed. In 1955 the population was just over 600; in 1990 it was 962.

David Minor

BELL'S FERRY, TEXAS. Bell's Ferry was about eighty miles north of Beaumont in northwestern Jasper County. It crossed the Angelina River above its confluence with the Neches. The Bell's Ferry post office was open from 1889 to 1891. *Robert Wooster*

BELLVILLE, TEXAS. Bellville, the county seat of Austin County, is at the junction of State highways 36 and 159 and Farm roads 529, 1456, and 2429, in central Austin County. The town was named for Thomas B. Bell,[qv] one of Stephen F. Austin's[qv] Old Three Hundred,[qv] who came to Texas in 1822 and built a residence in the Bellville vicinity in 1838. In 1846 voters decided to replace San Felipe as county seat with a new community near the geographic center of the county. Bell offered to donate 108 acres from the Nichols league for the new town. His offer, plus 37½ acres from his brother James Bell, was officially accepted the following year, and the site was surveyed and laid out in 1848. A post office was opened in 1849, and a temporary log courthouse was erected around the same time. In 1850 this courthouse was replaced by a larger structure in the central square. During the early 1850s several merchants, including Hermann Miller and a man named Strother, opened stores around the square. A new brick courthouse was begun in 1854, and other businesses opened in the late 1850s.

The town grew slowly until the Gulf Coast and Santa Fe Railroad reached it in the winter of 1879–80. In four months the population increased from 300 to 522. Brick structures replaced wooden ones, and opulent Victorian homes were erected. Bellville became a transporting point for the region's cotton crop. In 1898, at the peak of the county's cotton boom, 8,626 bales of cotton were shipped from the town. By 1884 Bellville had two churches, two hotels, a bakery, a lumberyard, three saloons, twelve general stores, a public school, and two weekly newspapers, the Bellville *Standard* and the *Austin County Times.* Other signs of the town's rapidly growing prosperity included a library in 1886, the construction of a new courthouse in 1887, and the opening of the first bank in the early 1890s.

The population, which reached 1,000 in the mid-1880s, was heavily German, and the town's schools provided instruction in both English and German. The local Turnverein (*see* turnverein movement) opened an opera house in 1889, and a decade later it built a large music pavilion on the outskirts of town. Other German institutions included a German singing society—the Concordia Gesangverein—the Harloff Beer Hall, the Germania Hotel, and German Methodist and Lutheran churches. In 1891 a German-language weekly, the Bellville *Wochenblatt,* began publication. Another newspaper was published by a black schoolteacher for several years before 1900.

In 1914 Bellville had two banks, a creamery, an ice plant, and telegraph and telephone connections. Oil was discovered in the county in 1915, and the development of the local oilfields further spurred the town's growth. By 1928 the population was 2,000. It fell during the Great Depression[qv] to 1,300 by the eve of World War II,[qv] but subsequently grew slowly. By the early 1950s the population once again reached 2,000, and in the late 1980s it surpassed 3,000. The number of businesses similarly declined during the years of the depression, from ninety-five in 1931 to seventy-five in 1940. After the war, however, the town's economy also recovered, and despite occasional drops, the number of businesses gradually increased. In 1991 Bellville had 100 businesses; the largest share of receipts came from retail sales, light manufacturing, and oil production. The population in 1990 was 3,378.

bibliography: *Austin County: Beilage zum Bellville Wochenblatt, den alten Texanern gewidmet und den jungen Texanern zu Nutz' und Frommen* (Bellville, Texas: Bellville *Wochenblatt,* 1899).

Christopher Long

BELLVILLE *COUNTRYMAN.* The Bellville *Countryman,* founded on July 28, 1860, was a semiweekly newspaper published by W. S. Thayer for editor and proprietor John P. Osterhout.[qv] Though the paper's motto was "Independent in All Things—Neutral in None," it favored the Southern wing of the Democratic party.[qv] The paper regularly carried a column in German. Osterhout continued publication throughout the Civil War,[qv] publishing the paper on halfsheets. The Bellville *Countryman* ceased on August 21, 1865, but was subsequently continued by the *Texas Countryman.*

bibliography: Marilyn M. Sibley, *Lone Stars and State Gazettes: Texas Newspapers before the Civil War* (College Station: Texas A&M University Press, 1983).

Diana J. Kleiner

BELLWOOD, TEXAS. Bellwood is on Lake Bellwood and the St. Louis and Southwestern Railway just west of Tyler and south of State Highway 31 in western Smith County. It was supposedly named for Frances Marion Bell, who owned a store in Tyler in the early 1850s. By 1936 the lake had been impounded by a dam built across Indian Creek. The lake, originally privately owned, served as a water source for Tyler and was later bought by the city. In 1936 a gauging or pumping station, accessed by a graded and drained road, was located on the lake. In 1976 the community had a few scattered dwellings, some water tanks, and one business. In 1985 the Bellwood Country Club and Briarwood Country Club were nearby.

bibliography: "Pictures from Our Past," *Chronicles of Smith County,* Fall 1968. Albert Woldert, *A History of Tyler and Smith County* (San Antonio: Naylor, 1948).

Vista K. McCroskey

BELLWOOD LAKE. Bellwood Lake is just west of Tyler in central Smith County (at 32°20′ N, 95°22′ W). It lies north of Greenbriar Lake and is bordered by Tyler Loop 323 on the east and State Highway Spur 164 on the west. The lake was named for the surrounding community, Bellwood. The dam was constructed across Indian Creek to form Bellwood Lake before 1936 and served as a source of water for Tyler. The city later bought the facility from the Cain interests. Maps for 1936 showed a small community, a gauging or pumping station, and a small park on the eastern shores. In 1966 recreational facilities included a golf course and a picnic area. The Briarwood Country Club had been completed, and a water tank had also been set up on the eastern shore. By 1981 the Bellwood Country Club had been added. The crest of the spillway is 426 feet above mean sea level, and the lake has a capacity of 1,391 acre-feet. It is popular for fishing and boating.

bibliography: John Clements, *Flying the Colors: Texas, a Comprehensive Look at Texas Today, County by County* (Dallas: Clements Research, 1984). "Pictures from Our Past," *Chronicles of Smith County,* Fall 1968.

BELMENA, TEXAS. Belmena is on Farm Road 485 five miles northeast of Cameron in north central Milam County. A post office operated there from 1900 until 1906. A school and several businesses and houses marked the community's location on county highway maps in 1941. Belmena had a population of fifteen in 1990.

bibliography: Lelia M. Batte, *History of Milam County, Texas* (San Antonio: Naylor, 1956).

Vivian Elizabeth Smyrl

BELMONT, TEXAS. Belmont, between Gonzales and Seguin on U.S. Highway 90A in western Gonzales County, was established in the 1840s as a stage stop called Centerville. The Galveston, Harrisburg and San Antonio Railway built through the community. When citizens applied for a post office they had to choose a new name because another Centerville in Texas already had a post office. Residents selected Belmont, supposedly for the Belmont family of horse-racing fame. In 1885 the town had a steam sawmill, a cotton gin, a district school, two churches, daily mail service, and a population of 100. A stage made daily runs to Luling; tickets were $1.50 each. In 1896 the population reached its apex at 125. That year the town had three general stores, a grocer, a hotel, and a blacksmith.

On June 14, 1901, a shoot-out, which the newspapers labeled the "Battle of Belmont," occurred when lawmen attacked the home of Martín and Refugia Robledo,[qv] who where giving refuge to fugitive Gregorio Cortez.[qv] The early twentieth century witnessed a gradual decline in Belmont's population. In 1904 Belmont reported one school with forty-eight students. In 1914 the town had a physician and a telephone connection. In 1936 a school and a hotel served the community. In the 1940s Belmont had a church, a gin, a general store, a garage, and a population of around 100. By the 1980s the population had dwindled to sixty-five. It was sixty in 1990, when, held together by the church and a community hall, the rural community was a gathering point for local farmers. A nearby gravel pit contributed to Belmont's economy.

bibliography: Américo Paredes, *With His Pistol in His Hand: A Border Ballad and Its Hero* (Austin: University of Texas Press, 1958).

Stephen L. Hardin

BELO, ALFRED HORATIO (1839–1901). Alfred Horatio Belo, newspaper publisher and Confederate army officer, was born at Salem, North Carolina, on May 27, 1839, the son of Edwin Belo. He grew up in a devout Moravian community and attended Bingham School. Later he graduated from the University of North Carolina. With North Carolina's secession, Belo raised and was commissioned captain of a company from Forsythe County assigned to the Fifty-sixth North Carolina Infantry. During the Civil War[qv] he served in every major engagement of Robert E. Lee's[qv] Army of Northern Virginia from Manassas to Appomattox. For his conduct at the first battle of Manassas (Bull Run) he was promoted to major. In 1862 he further endeared himself to his regiment by fighting a duel against an officer of another regiment. Belo resented an aspersion against the North Carolinians' courage and challenged the calumniator to an exchange of fire with Mississippi rifles. Neither principal was injured in the exchange. Largely as a result of this affair of honor, Belo was elected lieutenant colonel and later colonel of his regiment. He was severely wounded at Gettysburg on July 2, 1863, and his left arm was shattered at the battle of Cold Harbor, Virginia, on June 3, 1864.

In 1865 Belo rode horseback to Texas and joined the staff of the Galveston *News*[qv] just before it was returned from Houston to Galveston, and presently he acquired a partnership with Willard Richardson,[qv] its publisher. With this partnership the paper began a great expansion of its facilities. In that year the Galveston *Daily News* was launched as an outgrowth of the daily war extras that the historic *Weekly News* had issued during the closing days of the war. The *Texas Almanac*,[qv] which had been suspended during the war, was revived in 1867. On June 30, 1868, Belo married Nettie Ennis, daughter of Cornelius Ennis.[qv] They had two children, one of whom, Alfred Horatio Belo, Jr., succeeded his father to the presidency of the *News*. After Richardson's death in 1875, Belo became principal owner of the newspaper and continued in that capacity until his death.

On October 1, 1885, Belo established the Dallas *Morning News*.[qv] He was with the *News* for thirty-six years and directed the policy of its publication for more than a quarter of a century. He became widely known as a liberal in the development of Texas and instituted many of the policies that continued to control the Dallas *News* well into the mid-twentieth century. His two newspapers became a standard pattern for other newspapers, notably the New York *Times*. Both the Galveston and Dallas papers passed into other hands, but the Dallas *News* perpetuated his name under its corporate designation of A. H. Belo Corporation.[qv] Alfred H. Belo died at Asheville, North Carolina, on April 19, 1901, and was buried near his boyhood home at Salem. Upon hearing of Belo's death, President Grover Cleveland said, "I feel it to be a personal loss, as he was a friend to whom I was warmly attached, as a chivalrous, high-minded man, and an exceptionally able, fearless and conscientious journalist. His death is a loss to the entire country."

BIBLIOGRAPHY: Sidney S. Johnson, *Texans Who Wore the Gray* (Tyler, Texas, 1907).

George B. Dealey

BELOTT, TEXAS. Belott, a farming community on Farm Road 1733 twelve miles northeast of Crockett in east central Houston County, was probably established around the time of the Civil War.[qv] It was named for Andrew J. Belott, a prominent early settler buried in nearby New Energy Cemetery. A local school was built in the 1870s, and a post office operated in the community from 1890 to 1908. In the mid-1930s the settlement had a church, a school, four stores, and an estimated population of fifty. The school was consolidated with that of Glover in 1936; in 1968 the Glover school became part of the Kennard school district. After World War II[qv] many residents moved away, and by the mid-1960s only a church and a single store remained; the estimated population in 1965 was twenty. In the early 1990s Belott was a dispersed rural community.

BIBLIOGRAPHY: Houston County Historical Commission, *History of Houston County, Texas, 1687–1979* (Tulsa, Oklahoma: Heritage, 1979).

Eliza H. Bishop

BELTON, TEXAS. Belton, the county seat of Bell County, is on Nolan Creek at the junction of Interstate 35 and U.S. highways 81 and 190, near the geographic center of the county. The area was first settled in the late 1840s. When Bell County was established in 1850 the small settlement of Nolan Springs, named for adventurer Philip Nolan,[qv] was chosen as county seat and renamed Nolanville. Col. Henry B. Elliot surveyed the area, and E. Lawrence Stickney made a plat of the town. The town was laid out on the Shelbyville plan, with a large courthouse square as its focus. The first sale of town lots was held on August 26, 1850. Joe Townsend and A. T. McCorcle were among the first merchants to build stores. W. H. Tichenal is reported to have sold goods from his wagon on the square, and John C. Henry, with a barrel of whiskey and a tin cup, is supposed to have operated a saloon under a tree just east of the site of the later Main Street bridge. The post office was established as Nolanville in October 1850. In December 1851 the Texas legislature incorporated the town and changed the name to Belton, after Bell County. A small log courthouse was erected on the courthouse square in 1852. Weekly stagecoach service began the same year, and the town became an stop on the mail route from Little Rock, Arkansas, to San Antonio.

By the mid-1850s numerous merchants had opened stores on or near the courthouse square, and Belton emerged as a regional trading center. The original log courthouse was sold at auction in 1855, and a new two-story limestone building was constructed in 1859. In 1860 Belton, with a population of 300, was the largest town in the county.

During the secession[qv] crisis there was some pro-Union sentiment in Belton. A Whig newspaper, the *Independent*, was published there, and in the election of 1859 Bell County residents voted overwhelmingly for Sam Houston.[qv] Nonetheless, in 1861 the county voted for secession by a wide margin. A large number of men from Belton served in the Confederate forces, and local residents established several small industries to support the war effort, including a complex of stock pens and slaughterhouses to process dried beef.

After the war Belton experienced a protracted period of violence and lawlessness. Federal troops were stationed in the town to protect federal judge Hiram Christian but were unable to stop a series of political murders and lynchings. Several pro-Union sympathizers being held prisoner for political murders were lynched by a Belton mob in 1866, and by the late 1860s the Ku Klux Klan[qv] and several other similar organizations had grown up. The Republicans proved powerless to stop the growing tide, and by the early 1870s conservative Democrats were once again firmly in control.

After Reconstruction[qv] the town continued to grow as a business center for the surrounding agricultural area. One of the main feeder routes of the Chisholm Trail[qv] ran along the eastern edge of the town, and numerous cattle drives originated in or passed through the area during the 1870s and 1880s. In 1867 the town's first bank was organized by Josephus Zacharias Miller and others, and Belton soon developed into a regional banking center. The late 1860s and 1870s also witnessed the beginning of a religious and social experiment, the Belton Woman's Commonwealth[qv] or Belton Sanctificationist movement. Led by Martha White McWhirter[qv] and several other prominent Belton women, the Sanctificationists broke away from the town's established Protestant churches and formed an economic cooperative. In 1887 they opened the three-story Central Hotel, for many years the town's largest and most modern, and in later years operated a steam laundry and several nearby farms. The group also founded the town's first library in a room in the hotel.

In 1879 a fire destroyed much of the town's central business district, but the stores were quickly rebuilt. A new Renaissance Revival courthouse, designed by architect Jasper N. Preston,[qv] was constructed in the late 1870s, and by the mid-1880s Belton had a population of 4,000, daily mail and stagecoach service, three newspapers, an opera house, five schools, steam grist and flour mills, two hotels, thirteen grocery stores, and three banks. During this period Belton also developed into a processing and shipping center for the region's growing cotton crops. The first cottonseed oil mill was built in the town in 1879, and a number of cotton gins began operating.

In the early 1880s the first railroad, the Gulf, Colorado and Santa Fe, reached the town, and the Missouri, Kansas and Texas was built through in 1882. Nevertheless, Temple, established by the Santa Fe eight miles to the northeast in 1881 and aggressively promoted by the railroad, quickly surpassed Belton as the county's largest town. Some Belton businesses moved to Temple, but Belton's importance as a county seat and cotton center ensured its survival. An electric interurban line was constructed linking the two towns in 1905, and commerce developed between them. The late nineteenth century also saw other important developments: a public water system was built in the mid-1880s, a fire department was organized in 1884, and the town received electricity in 1889. In 1885 Baylor Female College, later the University of Mary Hardin-Baylor, was moved to Belton. Belton Academy, founded in 1886, operated until 1911. A large cotton yarn factory opened in 1901, and by 1904 the town reported a population of 3,700. In December 1913 much of the downtown was flooded when Nolan Creek overflowed its banks, but the town continued to prosper until the early 1930s, when falling cotton prices and the onset of the Great Depression[qv] forced many businesses to close. The population, which reached a peak of 6,500 in 1928, fell to 3,779 in 1931. The economy only began to recover in the early 1940s with the development of nearby Fort Hood.[qv]

After World War II[qv] the population grew steadily. In 1950 Belton reported a population of 6,246 and 180 business establishments. By 1990 the town had a population of 12,476; about 67 percent of the inhabitants were white, 17 percent were black, and 12 percent were Hispanic. The largest employers were the city of Belton, Bell County, and the University of Mary Hardin-Baylor.

BIBLIOGRAPHY: Bertha Atkinson, The History of Bell County, Texas (M.A. thesis, University of Texas, 1929). Bell County Historical Commission, *Story of Bell County, Texas* (2 vols., Austin: Eakin Press, 1988). Oscar Lewis, *On the Edge of the Black Waxy: A Cultural Survey of Bell County* (Washington University Studies, St. Louis, 1948). George Tyler, *History of Bell County* (San Antonio: Naylor, 1936).

Christopher Long

BELTON ACADEMY. Belton Academy, in Belton, was established in 1886 by Charles Wedemeyer. The school offered advanced preparatory training and operated until 1911. Walton Harris Walker[qv] was a student at Belton Academy.

BIBLIOGRAPHY: George Tyler, *History of Bell County* (San Antonio: Naylor, 1936).

BELTON LAKE. Belton Lake (Belton Reservoir) and Belton Dam are on the Leon River, part of the Brazos River basin, three miles north of Belton in northwestern Bell County (at 31°07′ N, 97°28′ W). The project is owned by the United States government and operated by the United States Army Corps of Engineers, Fort Worth District. Construction began in July 1949; the main structure was completed in April 1954, and deliberate impoundment began on March 8, 1954. In 1966 the reservoir had a capacity of 210,600 acre-feet and a surface area of 7,400 acres at the top of the conservation storage space (elevation 569 feet above mean sea level). The reservoir provided 887,000 acre-feet of flood-control storage capacity. The drainage area above the dam was 3,560 square miles. The United States government leased for fifty years all facilities to the Bell County Water Control and Improvement District in January 1956. This district supplies Fort Hood, Killeen, and other areas with water. An additional 113,700 acre-feet of conservation storage space was sold to the Brazos River Authority[qv] for $1,602,822 plus operational costs. The authority retained the right to purchase additional storage capacity from the federal government if the conservation storage capacity is enlarged.

BIBLIOGRAPHY: C. L. Dowell, *Dams and Reservoirs in Texas: History and Descriptive Information* (Texas Water Commission Bulletin 6408 [Austin, 1964]).

Seth D. Breeding

BELTON RAILROAD. The Belton Railroad Company was chartered on April 14, 1960. The capital was $50,000, and the business office was at Belton. Members of the first board of directors included C. V. Griggs, Fred Guffy, Glen H. Jones, V. R. Means, and Roy Sanderford. In February 1961 the company purchased about seven miles of railroad between Smith and Belton from the Missouri-Kansas-Texas Railroad Company (Katy), and the Belton began operation on June 1, 1961. This line had originally been built by the Katy in 1882. Fred H. Guffy was president of the company, and the Guffy family controlled the majority of the stock. In 1963 the Belton owned one locomotive and two cars and handled $36,896 in freight. By 1972 the company had two locomotives and one freight car, but earnings were down to $19,582. On June 3, 1991, certain assets of the Belton were sold to the Georgetown Railroad Company, and in 1993 the line continued operation as the Belton Subdivision of the Georgetown. Fred Guffy, Jr., retained rights to the Belton name as well as the station and other property located west of Interstate Highway 35 in Belton.

George C. Werner

BELTON WOMAN'S COMMONWEALTH. The Belton Woman's Commonwealth, a commune based on the doctrines of religious perfectionism, celibacy, and Wesleyan sanctificationism, grew out of a small group of middle-class Protestant women that began to form in the late 1860s under the leadership of Martha McWhirter,[qv] a prominent figure in Belton's nonsectarian Union Sunday School, who organized a women's Bible study and prayer group that met weekly in the members' homes. After she professed to have been sanctified, she urged her followers to seek divine revelations and to share them with the group. At the same time, the women prayed about the trials in their everyday lives, especially for guidance to deal with authoritarian husbands sometimes given to unscrupulous business practices, intemperate drinking, and physical abuse. The wives increasingly sought personal, that is, religious and financial, autonomy.

Gradually an alternative communal life evolved, which replaced the unsatisfactory situations of these women. A number of developments took place concurrently in the 1870s. The religious separatism of the Sanctificationist women provided a sheltered environment for the development of idiosyncratic religious practices; the women believed themselves to be the recipients of prophetic dreams and direct revelations from God. Further, by a revelation for which McWhirter claimed Pauline scriptural authority, the sanctified were required to separate themselves from the undevout; sanctified wives were to live in their marital homes and perform their household duties, but with no sexual and as little social contact as possible with their unsanctified spouses.

Following McWhirter's example, the women began to make money by marketing eggs and dairy products and by taking in laundry, hauling wood, and working as domestic servants and home nurses. Much of the work was collective, and in 1879, having become financially independent, the women started a common treasury. Because some of the husbands reacted angrily or violently, McWhirter's home began to fill with sanctified sisters seeking refuge. Her husband moved into rooms over his store, and the women began to live communally by making use of their various homes and by building houses on properties owned or claimed by members. Job rotation reinforced communal values, allowed each member a variety of tasks and responsibilities, and provided leisure to pursue various other educational and financial enterprises. Thus, individual members were able to educate themselves in such useful trades as dentistry, blacksmithing, and shoemaking. Authority was shared by all members in principle, although in practice McWhirter exerted much influence.

At first the property owned and inherited by various women

served only to provide them with shelter. Eventually it became the basis for more ambitious economic efforts; one home became a boardinghouse, and a commercial laundry was started. From these and their other work the women profited financially. In 1886 they bought one hotel and began building another by expanding the boardinghouse. Title to property was held in individual names for some time, but in 1891 the group incorporated as the Central Hotel Company. By this time they owned a large amount of property in town as well as three farms.

Though Woman's Commonwealth had successfully established itself economically and administratively by the early 1880s, community hostility remained. Belton citizens blamed Martha McWhirter and the Sanctificationists for separations and divorces. When two immigrant Scottish brothers sought out the group for religious reasons they were kidnapped, whipped, warned to leave town, and briefly committed to the state asylum. No other males tried to join. The hotel had become successful by 1887, and hostility gradually dissipated. Throughout the decade the Belton Woman's Commonwealth became increasingly respected and accepted. The sisters' book collection, housed in a small room in their hotel, became so popular that it was moved to a larger facility outside the commune, and in 1903 it formally became the city's public library.

In 1898 or 1899 the women decided to retire from business and move to Washington, D.C., so that they might pursue their growing interest in cultural activities. Using their savings of perhaps as much as $200,000, they bought a house in Mount Pleasant, Maryland. In Washington, where they incorporated in 1902 as the Woman's Commonwealth of Washington, D.C., they became more visible to the national press, and a number of articles were published describing their history and life. In both the Belton and Washington communities membership averaged about thirty, most of whom were women and their children.

After Martha McWhirter died in 1904, Fannie Holtzclaw took over as the commune's leader. By 1906 only eighteen adult women were left in the Commonwealth, but they continued to be successful in operating a farm in Maryland and a boardinghouse in Washington. The Woman's Commonwealth gradually expired as aging and death reduced its numbers, but some members continued to live at the Maryland farm as late as 1918.

bibliography: Eleanor James, "Martha White McWhirter (1827–1904)," in *Women in Early Texas,* ed. Evelyn M. Carrington (Austin: Jenkins, 1975). Eleanor James, "The Sanctificationists of Belton," *American West,* Summer 1965. Melissa Johnson, "Sanctified Sisters," *Texas Historian,* November 1974. Jayme A. Sokolow and Mary Ann Lamanna, "Women and Utopia: The Woman's Commonwealth of Belton," *Southwestern Historical Quarterly* 87 (April 1984). George Tyler, *History of Bell County* (San Antonio: Naylor, 1936).

Mary Ann Lamanna and Jayme A. Sokolow

BELVIEW, TEXAS. Belview is a church community thirteen miles northeast of Jefferson and two miles northeast of the intersection of State highways 49 and 43 in northeastern Marion County. The Belview school had seventy-two black pupils and one teacher in 1899. In 1938 the community had a two-room schoolhouse with twenty-nine elementary students. By 1955 the school had consolidated with the Jefferson schools, and in 1962 all that remained at the site of Belview was a church, which was still shown on state highway maps in 1983.

bibliography: Jack Reed Harvey, Survey and Proposed Reorganization of the Marion County Schools (M.A. thesis, University of Texas, 1940). *Mark Odintz*

BELZORA, TEXAS. Belzora was at a ferry crossing where Farm Road 14 now crosses the Sabine River in extreme northern Smith County. The site, originally part of the Juan Santos Coy survey, was settled in 1850 and named for Belle Ham of Tyler. On May 12, 1852, though only a ferry station, Belzora was granted a post office, with Radford Berry as postmaster. Berry had also owned the ferry for at least two years. In 1850 the county commissioners' court had allowed him to charge 2 ½ cents for ferrying sheep and hogs, five cents for a person or loose cattle and horses, ten cents for a person on horseback, and forty cents for a two-horse wagon. Because it was situated on the heavily traveled Dallas-Shreveport road, the town also included a combination stagecoach stop and store, owned by Thomas R. Swann.

Though the post office was discontinued in 1856, Belzora seemed ripe for development. In 1861 Swann and F. M. Bell bought all the land in the area and laid out town lots, but none was ever sold. Bell later sold his property to Swann. Efforts to open the port to major navigation also failed. The steamer *Ben Henry* made an unsuccessful attempt to journey downriver with local cotton and freight, and light steamers could maneuver upstream only six months of the year. Even the *Patent,* a flat-bottomed boat, was stranded at Belzora for ten days because of low water. Such navigational difficulties led natives to refer to the crossing humorously as the "Head of Navigation on the Sabine River."

During the Civil War[qv] a carding plant was located nearby, and according to local lore a Confederate commissary operated in Belzora. In the 1870s the Galveston *News*[qv] listed Belzora as a port, and area farmers often used flatboats and canoes to transport goods downstream from there when the river was high. Business ambitions proved futile, however, and Belzora began to decline with the construction of the International–Great Northern Railroad in Smith County. The settlement appeared on county maps as late as 1903 but by 1936 had disappeared from county records. Over the subsequent years a few houses, a church, and even an occasional business have been located in the area, but there has been no further settlement at the site.

bibliography: Gladys Peters Austin, *Along the Century Trail: Early History of Tyler, Texas* (Dallas: Avalon Press, 1946). Howard O. Pollan, "1849–1850, Smith County's Formative Years: Abstract of the Commissioner Court Minutes," *Chronicles of Smith County,* Spring 1969. Smith County Historical Society, *Historical Atlas of Smith County* (Tyler, Texas: Tyler Print Shop, 1965). Donald W. Whisenhunt, comp., *Chronological History of Smith County* (Tyler, Texas: Smith County Historical Society, 1983). Albert Woldert, *A History of Tyler and Smith County* (San Antonio: Naylor, 1948).

Vista K. McCroskey

BEN ARNOLD, TEXAS. Ben Arnold (Benarnold) is on U.S. Highway 77 seven miles north of Cameron in northern Milam County. The community began as a stop on the San Antonio and Aransas Pass Railway in 1890 and was named for Bennie Arnold, B. I. Arnold's three-year-old daughter, who was mascot on the first train to pull into the new station. A local post office was opened in 1892, and by 1896 the community had three churches, a district school, and 125 residents. In 1903 the school had two teachers and eighty students. In the 1920s the population of Ben Arnold rose to 250; it remained fairly stable until the late 1960s, when it fell to 148. The Ben Arnold school system was consolidated with the Cameron Independent School District by the early 1970s. In 1977 the Southern Pacific abandoned the section of track connecting Ben Arnold with Cameron to the south and Rosebud to the north. The community had 148 residents and several businesses in 1990.

bibliography: Lelia M. Batte, *History of Milam County, Texas* (San Antonio: Naylor, 1956). Milam County Heritage Preservation Society, *Matchless Milam: History of Milam County* (Dallas: Taylor, 1984).

Vivian Elizabeth Smyrl

BEN-ASH (?–1844). Ben-Ash was chief of Battise Village[qv] of the Coushatta Indians during the first half of the nineteenth century.

This village was on the west bank of the Trinity River at the Coushatta Trace[qv] crossing of the Trinity, near the site of present Point Blank in San Jacinto County. Land in this area proved to be desirable for agricultural activities, and George T. Wood,[qv] who was elected governor of Texas in 1847, established a plantation bordering the Trinity a half mile downriver from Battise Village. Ben-Ash lived on a hill two miles from the Trinity, and this location in San Jacinto County is still called Ben-Ash Hill.

Records of the Republic of Texas[qv] indicate that Ben-Ash participated in various types of this nation's activities relating to Indian affairs. The ledger sheet of the republic's Indian commissioners for 1843 includes a list of gifts for Ben-Ash. On May 13, 1844, the Indian commissioners called a meeting with Texas tribes on the council ground at Tehuacana Creek (*see* TEHUACANA CREEK COUNCILS) for the purpose of establishing a boundary, regaining horses stolen from the white settlements, and distributing presents to the groups assembled. The minutes for this meeting show that Ben-Ash was present for the conference.

Ben-Ash died sometime in 1844. A passport written by Republic of Texas President Sam Houston[qv] on October 17, 1844, states: "Know Ye that the bearer hereof, the widow of Ben-Ash who died lately at this place (Washington-on-the-Brazos), is on her way home to the Coshattee tribe of Indians . . . near Smithfield on the Trinity river; and they are hereby recommended to the hospitality and kind treatment of the good people of the Republic on the road."

BIBLIOGRAPHY: Louella Styles Vincent, "Governor George Thomas Wood," *Southwestern Historical Quarterly* 20 (January 1917). Amelia W. Williams and Eugene C. Barker, eds., *The Writings of Sam Houston, 1813–1863* (8 vols., Austin: University of Texas Press, 1938–43; rpt., Austin and New York: Pemberton Press, 1970). Dorman H. Winfrey and James M. Day, eds., *Texas Indian Papers* (4 vols., Austin: Texas State Library, 1959–61; rpt., 5 vols., Austin: Pemberton Press, 1966). *Howard N. Martin*

BENAVIDES, ALONSO DE (ca. 1578–1635). Father Alonso de Benavides, custos of the Franciscan missions in New Mexico from 1626 to 1629, the son of Pedro Alonso Nieto and Antonia Murato de Benavides, was born on the island of San Miguel in the Azores about 1578. He is noted for his memorials, which comprise one of the basic sources for Southwest history. He arrived in New Spain in 1598 and took vows with the Franciscans[qv] some three years later in Mexico City. Benavides filled the office of novice master at Puebla for a time and was later associated with the Inquisition, while residing at the friary of Cuernavaca. He was appointed custos in New Mexico in 1623 while serving as guardian at Temanatla. He did not reach New Mexico to assume his new duties until January 24, 1626.

Although his work was handicapped by a shortage of priests, Benavides was able to extend missionary activity in the province with ten new missions. When Fray Esteban de Peréa came to succeed him in April 1629, he brought twenty-nine new missionaries. Benavides returned to Mexico City in March 1630 and proceeded forthwith to Spain. He arrived the following August to present his 1630 memorial to King Philip IV. He then went to Agreda to interview Mother María de Jesús de Agreda[qv] about her relationship with Indians of the American Southwest, who claimed to have been instructed in the Catholic faith by the mysterious "Lady in Blue." Madre María told him that through spiritual translocation she had visited among the Indians many times to take them the divine message.

From 1633 to 1635 Benavides was in Rome as confessor to Francisco de Melo. During that time he presented to Pope Urban VIII his "Memorial of 1634," a revision and expansion of his 1630 treatise. On returning to Spain, Benavides received royal appointment as auxiliary bishop of Goa, India. He sailed for his new assignment on April 4, 1635, and died on the voyage. The two Benavides memorials, which complement rather than duplicate each other, are rich in geographical detail, descriptions of mission life, and ethnographic information, some of it pertaining to the Apaches and Jumanos of the Texas plains.

BIBLIOGRAPHY: Alonso de Benavides, *Benavides' Memorial of 1630*, trans. Peter P. Forrestal (Washington: Academy of American Franciscan History, 1954). *Robert S. Weddle*

BENAVIDES, BASILIO (1800–1863). Basilio Benavides, the second of five Tejanos (*see* TEJANO) known to have served in the Texas House of Representatives during the nineteenth century, was born in Laredo on April 15, 1800. His family was originally from Revilla in what is now Tamaulipas, Mexico. He married Encarnación García, also of Laredo. Benavides entered public life at the age of sixteen, when he became postmaster of Laredo, a position he held until 1827. From 1827 until 1848, when Laredo experienced some of its most troublesome times, Benavides was either the mayor of the city or a military commandant. During this period he also fought on the Federalist side to establish the Republic of the Rio Grande,[qv] a brief union of Coahuila, Nuevo León, and Tamaulipas, along the Texas-Mexico border in 1840.

In December 1842, during his tenure as mayor, soldiers with the Somervell expedition,[qv] which was dispatched to avenge Mexican raids in Texas earlier that year, pillaged the city. Eight years later Laredo citizens, under Benavides's leadership, unsuccessfully sought payment for their losses from the Texas Senate. After the Mexican War[qv] Benavides, along with other Tejanos, unsuccessfully petitioned American authorities to return control of the city to Mexico.

In the 1850s he served as chief justice of Webb County and managed his family's sheep and cattle ranch. In 1859 he was elected to represent Webb County in the Texas House of Representatives for one term. As a member of the Eighth Legislature he was appointed to the Committee on Public Lands and the Committee on Joint Indian Affairs. During the Civil War[qv] Benavides, who had joined the secessionist movement in the legislature, was involved in the May 1861 battle of Carrizo in which Santos Benavides,[qv] his nephew, defeated Juan N. Cortina.[qv] Benavides died in 1863.

BIBLIOGRAPHY: Gilberto Miguel Hinojosa, *A Borderlands Town in Transition: Laredo, 1755–1870* (College Station: Texas A&M University Press, 1983). *Members of the Legislature of the State of Texas from 1846 to 1939* (Austin: Texas Legislature, 1939). *Teresa Palomo Acosta*

BENAVIDES, CRISTÓBAL (1839–1904). Cristóbal Benavides, son of José Jesús Benavides and Tomasa Cameros, was born on April 3, 1839, in Laredo. He was also the great-great-grandson of Tomás Sánchez de la Barrera y Garza,[qv] who had established the village of Laredo in 1755. Benavides received his education in Laredo and Corpus Christi, and before the Civil War[qv] was a stockman who built up a sizable ranch. With the coming of the Civil War he enlisted as a sergeant in a company of local Tejanos being raised by his half-brother, Santos Benavides.[qv] Within a year he had achieved the rank of lieutenant. The company commanded by Santos was then reorganized into a unit called Benavides' Regiment. Cristóbal Benavides was promoted to captain and given command of a company in his brother's regiment. On March 19, 1864, he fought to defend Laredo against Union forces that had advanced upriver from Brownsville intent on seizing or destroying some 5,000 bales of cotton stacked in St. Augustine Plaza in Laredo. Benavides later served under Col. John S. Ford[qv] in the 1864 Confederate Rio Grande expedition to drive Union forces out of the lower Rio Grande valley. On June 23, 1864, in the lower Valley at Las Rucias, he led an attack against a Union outpost. After having his horse shot from under him in the daring charge, he was singled out for bravery. At the end of the war, Benavides, along with his brothers, were among the last to surrender.

After the war Benavides married Lamar Bee, daughter of Confederate general Hamilton P. Bee.[qv] Six daughters and four sons were born of the marriage. Although his brother Santos served in the

Texas legislature and another half-brother, Refugio Benavides,qv was elected several times as mayor of Laredo, Cristóbal Benavides concentrated more on his sheep and cattle ranch and on his mercantile business than on politics. By 1890 he had become one of the wealthiest men in Webb County. He died on September 2, 1904. In the late 1930s his remains were removed from the Old Laredo Cemetery and interred in the Laredo Catholic Cemetery, where family members erected an impressive monument in his honor.

bibliography: Jerry D. Thompson, *Warm Weather and Bad Whiskey: The 1886 Laredo Election Riot* (El Paso: Texas Western Press, 1991). *A Twentieth Century History of Southwest Texas* (2 vols., Chicago: Lewis, 1907). *Jose Francisco Segovia*

BENAVIDES, PLÁCIDO (?–1837). Plácido Benavides, a native of Reynosa, Tamaulipas, Mexico, was renowned for his contribution to the settlement of Victoria, Texas, and to the Texas Revolution.qv He was a godson of Capt. Henrique Villareal, who had him educated and later sent to Texas in 1828 as secretary to Fernando De León,qv commissioner of De León's colony and son of Martín De León.qqv For three years Benavides issued land titles and recorded the business transactions of the settlement. In 1831 he married Agustina De León, daughter of the empresario,qv and settled on a league and a labor of land on Zorillo Creek, which was renamed Placido Creek in his honor. The ranch was near the grants of his brothers, Eugenio, Isidro, and Nicolás.

Benavides was elected alcaldeqv of Guadalupe Victoria in 1832 and again in 1834. He was one of the important "Ten Friends" for whom the town's main street was named Calle de los Diez Amigos. After the death of his father-in-law in 1833, the Mexican government authorized him to continue the settlement contract and recruit colonists. As captain of the colony's militia he built a fort, the Round Top House, for the defense of Guadalupe Victoria, and with his brother-in-law Silvestre De Leónqv led several attacks against the Comanches and Tonkawas.

Benavides continued his prominent role during the Texas Revolution. In October 1835 he successfully led the resistance against surrendering to Mexican forces a cannon and another De León son-in-law, José M. J. Carbajal,qv who was sought for arrest by Col. Domingo de Ugartecheaqv for his participation in the Coahuila and Texasqv legislature. With John J. Linnqv Benavides went to Gonzales to train the volunteers amassing there after the battle of Gonzales.qv The two proposed to intercept Gen. Martín Perfecto de Cos,qv who had landed at Copano and, after marching to Goliad, was en route to reinforce Ugartechea at Bexar; but finding most at Gonzales unwilling, Benavides and Linn joined Benjamin Fort Smith'sqv company, which set out to liberate Goliad. Benavides arrived in Guadalupe Victoria ahead of the company and became one of many Victorians joining George M. Collinsworth'sqv Matagorda volunteers, who were on the way to liberate Goliad themselves. He became leader of a company of about thirty Mexican rancheros in Collinsworth's force, which captured Goliad on October 9–10, 1835 (see goliad campaign of 1835). On October 14 he and his rancheros left with Smith's men, following Gen. Stephen F. Austin'sqv orders, and marched to San Antonio, where they fought against Cos in the siege of Bexar.qv Benavides received notice for his gallantry and efficiency, especially as part of the division under Francis W. Johnsonqv that assaulted the house of Juan Martín Veramendi.qv

In early 1836 Benavides was warned by the alcalde of Matamoros that Antonio López de Santa Annaqv planned to draw Texans to Matamoros in order to defeat them from the rear while Santa Anna simultaneously attacked Goliad and Bexar. Benavides traveled to San Patricio and informed Robert C. Morrisqv of the plot; Morris enclosed Benavides's warning in a letter dated February 6 to James Walker Fannin,qv who was then at Refugio planning to carry out the provisional government'sqv campaign against Matamoros. Benavides's message caused Fannin instead to remove his headquarters to Goliad.

Later in February Benavides, appointed by the General Councilqv as a first lieutenant in the regular cavalry, was with Morris and Reuben R. Brownqv as part of Dr. James Grant'sqv party of twenty-six men who were procuring horses near San Patricio for Grant's and Francis W. Johnson's own Matamoros expedition (*see* matamoros expedition of 1835-36). Grant's men were surprised by Mexican general José de Urrea'sqv forces, and in the ensuing battle of Agua Dulce Creek,qv Grant dispatched Benavides to Goliad to warn Fannin of Urrea's advance.

Though Benavides was an ardent foe of Santa Anna, like many colonists he remained loyal to Mexico and therefore could not support the move toward Texas independence that he found at Goliad. He returned to Guadalupe Victoria after carrying Grant's message to Fannin and attempted to isolate himself and his family on his ranch, only to find himself later rendering aid to Isaac D. Hamilton,qv quartermaster of Jack Shackelford's Red Rovers,qqv who had escaped the Goliad Massacre.qv Confronted by lancers of Urrea's army looking for stragglers, Benavides was compelled to surrender his severely wounded companion. Hamilton was later saved by Francita Álavez,qv the "Angel of Goliad," and then escaped.

After the battle of San Jacintoqv Benavides was ostracized with most other Mexican Texans for his supposed sympathy with Mexico and forced to flee with the De León family to New Orleans. He died in Opelousas, Louisiana, in 1837. His widow died five years later in Soto la Marina, Tamaulipas, where she had fled with her mother, Patricia De León.qv In 1838 Benavides's brothers returned to Victoria to claim what they could of their lands, which had been taken over by Anglo settlers. Plácido and Agustina Benavides had three daughters, Pilar and Martinita, who settled in Rio Grande City, and Librada, who married Patricio De León, grandson of the empresario, and settled in the Mission Valley area.

bibliography: Joe Tom Davis, *Legendary Texians* (3 vols., Austin: Eakin Press, 1982–86). Roy Grimes, ed., *300 Years in Victoria County* (Victoria, Texas: Victoria *Advocate*, 1968; rpt., Austin: Nortex, 1985). A. B. J. Hammett, *The Empresario Don Martín de León* (Waco: Texian Press, 1973). *Craig H. Roell*

BENAVIDES, REFUGIO (1821–1899). José del Refugio Benavides, politician and Confederate officer, was born on July 6, 1821, at Laredo, Texas, the oldest child of José Jesús and Margarita (Ramón) Benavides. He was also the great-great-grandson of Tomás Sánchez de la Barrera y Garza,qv who had founded Laredo in 1755. Benavides first rose to political prominence in Laredo politics in the decade following the Mexican War.qv In one of the first municipal elections under American rule, on June 28, 1850, he was elected alderman. The Benavides family also played an important role in secession and the Civil Warqqv in South Texas. John S. (Rip) Fordqv wrote that the Benavides family "broke ground in favor of secession" and "did the Confederacy an immense favor by declaring for her." During the war on the border, Refugio Benavides rose to the rank of captain in command of a company in the Thirty-third Texas Cavalry. Later, a regiment raised by Col. Santos Benavidesqv was simply known as Benavides' Regiment.

Refugio Benavides first saw action in the battle of Carrizo (at the site of modern-day Zapata) on May 22, 1861, when he joined Santos in an attack on the forces of the Mexican revolutionary Juan Cortina.qv Benavides had raced sixty miles through the night down the Mexican side of the river and was able to avoid Cortina's pickets at the crossing near Carrizo and to tell Santos that reinforcements were on the way from Laredo. After the arrival of the Laredo reinforcements, the Benavides brothers led an attack on Cortina that drove the revolutionaries across the river into Mexico. In April 1862 Benavides mustered into the Confederate States Army an eighty-five-man company of Mexican Texans. In December 1862 three of his men were killed by Mexican revolutionaries near Roma. Other raiders attacked a Confederate wagontrain near Rio Grande City and even raided into Zapata County, where they hanged the county judge, Ysidro Vela. With fifty-five men, Benavides went in pursuit of the Mexican raiders. They crossed the Rio Grande into Mexico and tracked them to Mesquital Lealeño, near Camargo, where they were camped in a large corral. Without hesitation, the captain ordered an attack. With Benavides in front, the Tejanos were said to have "boldly stormed" the enclosure, "tearing down the gate amid a hail of bullets, in the midst of which three horses were killed and two men wounded." In the fight eighteen of the raiders were killed, fourteen were wounded, and several were taken captive. Benavides lost two of his men. He and Santos Benavides helped defend Laredo on March 19, 1864, from a Union cotton raid in what became known as the battle of Laredo. A federal expedition from the lower Rio Grande valley had pushed upriver to Laredo hoping to burn the 5,000 bales of cotton stacked in St. Augustine Plaza. After three hours of fighting, the bluecoats were "repulsed by the vigorous fire of my gallant men," Santos Benavides wrote. Refugio Benavides next saw action with Rip Ford in the Confederate Rio Grande expedition. Moving downriver from Laredo, Benavides's company was utilized on a number of occasions by Ford for scouting purposes because of the Tejanos' familiarity with South Texas. On June 25, 1864, Benavides was in the battle at Las Rucias, upriver from Brownsville. Ford, by using an "obscure trail through the chaparral" was able to "get within a few hundred yards of the enemy before being discovered." Benavides was sent in a flanking movement to attack the federal force but was stopped twice by a small lagoon. He was able, however, to join Ford for a final attack that overran the federals. In his report of the battle, Ford singled out Benavides for his gallant conduct during the battle.

On December 8, 1873, Refugio was elected mayor of Laredo once again. His administration provided one of the first public schools, the Esquela Amarilla, constructed the first sewers in the city, established a number of ordinances in an effort to maintain law and order, and helped rewrite the Laredo city charter. He easily led an entire slate of candidates to victory in the next year's election and was elected for a third time in 1875, although this last election was unsuccessfully contested in court. In 1876 Benavides decided not to seek reelection. In 1874 he raised a company of rangers at Laredo to combat the growing bandit and Kickapoo Indian threat on the border. When he was given authority to cross the Rio Grande into Mexico, if necessary, the Mexican government filed a formal protest with Washington. Although it remains unclear whether Benavides did cross into Mexico, the matter was never successfully resolved.

Benavides was married twice, to Teresa Pizaña, with whom he had five children, and to Anastacia García, with whom he had one son. He died of chronic diarrhea at the home of his son in the Heights section of Laredo on June 29, 1899, and was buried in the Old Catholic Cemetery. During World War II[qv] his remains were moved to the Herrera family plot in the newer Catholic Cemetery.

BIBLIOGRAPHY: Stanley Cooper Green, *Laredo, 1755–1920* (Laredo: Nuevo Santander Museum Complex, 1981). Gilberto Miguel Hinojosa, *A Borderlands Town in Transition: Laredo, 1755–1870* (College Station: Texas A&M University Press, 1983). John Denny Riley, Santos Benavides: His Influence on the Lower Rio Grande, 1823–1891 (Ph.D. dissertation, Texas Christian University, 1976). Jerry Don Thompson, *Laredo: A Pictorial History* (Norfolk: Donning, 1986). Jerry Don Thompson, *Sabers on the Rio Grande* (Austin: Presidial, 1974). Jerry Don Thompson, *Vaqueros in Blue and Gray* (Austin: Presidial, 1976).

Jerry Thompson

BENAVIDES, SANTOS (1823–1891). Santos Benavides, the highest ranking Mexican American to serve the Confederacy, the son of José Jesús and Margarita (Ramón) Benavides, was born in Laredo, Texas, on November 1, 1823. He was the great-great-grandson of Tomás Sánchez de la Barrera y Garza,[qv] the founder of Laredo. Benavides married Augustina Villareal in 1842, and the couple eventually adopted four children. As a political and military leader in Laredo, Benavides brought a traditionally isolated region closer to the mainstream of Texas politics while preserving a sense of local independence. His prominence in Laredo resulted initially from the influence of his uncle, Basilio Benavides,[qv] who was three times elected alcalde[qv] under Mexican rule, then mayor and state representative after annexation.[qv] Santos Benavides's success as a merchant and rancher also contributed to his selection as *procurador* in 1843, then to his election as mayor of Laredo in 1856 and chief justice of Webb County in 1859. He won further distinction as the leader of several campaigns against the Lipan Apaches and other Indians. Under both Mexican and American rule, his politics remained consistent. During the Federalist-Centralist wars that swept the Rio Grande frontier in the 1830s and 1840s, geographically isolated northern Mexico supported the Federalist cause of local autonomy against the Centralists, who wanted power focused in distant Mexico City. As a young man Benavides fought for the Federalists. Frustrated with the Mexican government, he cooperated with the forces of Mirabeau B. Lamar,[qv] which occupied Laredo during the Mexican War.[qv] Benavides joined his uncle in opposing the annexation of the Laredo area by the United States, as called for by the Treaty of Guadalupe Hidalgo,[qv] because he feared it would compromise the independent character of northern Mexico. When Texas seceded, Benavides and his brothers supported the Confederacy, whose states'-rights principles were so close to their regionalism.

Commissioned a captain in the Thirty-third Texas Cavalry (or Benavides' Regiment) and assigned to the Rio Grande Military District, Benavides quickly won accolades as a fighter. He drove Juan Cortina[qv] back into Mexico in the battle of Carrizo on May 22, 1861, and quelled other local revolts against Confederate authority. In November 1863 Benavides was promoted to colonel and authorized to raise his own regiment of "Partisan Rangers," for which he used the remnants of the Thirty-third. His greatest military triumph was his defense of Laredo on March 19, 1864, with forty-two troops against 200 soldiers of the Union First Texas Cavalry,[qv] commanded by Col. Edmund J. Davis,[qv] who had, ironically, offered Benavides a Union generalship earlier. Perhaps Benavides's most significant contribution to the South came when he arranged for safe passage of Texas cotton along the Rio Grande to Matamoros during the Union occupation of Brownsville in 1864.

During Reconstruction[qv] he continued his mercantile and ranching activities with his brother Cristóbal Benavides[qv] and remained active in politics. In support of his son-in-law, Gen. Lázaro Garza Ayala, and Sebastian Lerdo de Tejada, he was accused of using his rancho, Charcos Largo, as a supply depot for filibustering expeditions against Mexican president Porfirio Díaz. He served three times in the Texas legislature from 1879 to 1884 and twice as an alderman of Laredo. He was instrumental in the formation of the Guarache or citizen's party in South Texas, a faction of the Democratic party opposed to the powerful Botas (*see* BOTAS AND GUARACHES). His political affiliations indicated his continued belief in regional independence from national authority. His leadership built Democratic support among Hispanics in Webb County and contributed to the eclipse of the Republican party in the region. Benavides's friendship with the followers of Benito Juárez and his kinship ties to Manuel Gonzales prompted Porfirio Díaz to select him as an envoy to the United States during the reciprocity controversy in 1880. In recognition of his political achievement, he was appointed Texas delegate to the World Cotton Exposition in 1884. Benavides died at his home in Laredo on November 9, 1891.

BIBLIOGRAPHY: Evan Anders, *Boss Rule in South Texas: The Progressive Era* (Austin: University of Texas Press, 1982). John Denny Riley, Santos Benavides: His Influence on the Lower Rio Grande, 1823–1891 (Ph.D. dissertation, Texas Christian University, 1976). Jerry Don Thompson, "A Stand along the Border: Santos Benavides and the Battle for Laredo," *Civil War Times Illustrated,* August 1980. Jerry Don Thompson, *Vaqueros in Blue and Gray* (Austin: Presidial, 1976). *The*

War of the Rebellion: A Compilation of the Official Records of the Union and Confederate Armies. J. B. Wilkinson, *Laredo and the Rio Grande Frontier* (Austin: Jenkins, 1975). *Jerry Thompson*

BENAVIDES, TEXAS. Benavides is at the intersection of State highways 339 and 359 and Farm Road 2295, on Las Animas Creek and the Texas Mexican Railway eighteen miles southwest of San Diego in Duval County. It is the third most populous town in the county. The community is named after Plácido Benavides, whose uncle, also named Plácido Benavides,qv was called by one writer "the 'Paul Revere' of South Texas." The younger Plácido Benavides was a Confederate Army veteran, who in the 1870s built his Rancho Palo Alto into one of the biggest ranches in Duval County. In 1880 the county asked his permission to locate a railroad depot on his property. He agreed and then in 1881 donated eighty acres to the community that was growing up around the railroad station. A post office was established in Benavides in 1881 with Jacob William Toklas as postmaster. By far the most significant event of the decade, however, was the arrival in 1882 of a twenty-two-year-old former ranchhand and schoolteacher named Archer Parr,qv who later became the boss of Duval County and founded the most notorious political dynasty in Texas (*see* BOSS RULE).

By 1884 only San Diego had more than Benavides's estimated 300 residents among Duval County towns, and Benavides had a church, a school, two groceries, two meat markets, and one saloon. A number of the town's leading citizens were of Mexican-American descent. In addition to Plácido Benavides and his brother Isidro, who were among the first to plant cotton in Duval County, these included horse breeder Daniel Gonzales, cotton planter Don Vicente Vera, and Francisco Carrillo, principal of the Spanish Academy, who spoke six languages and also worked as a court interpreter.

The town grew to an estimated 500 inhabitants during the 1890s, and 110 pupils attended the Benavides school during the 1906–07 school year. By 1914, when Parr sought unsuccessfully to increase the patronage and tax revenues at his disposal by establishing a new county, Pat Dunn County,qv with Benavides as its seat, the town had six general stores, two grocers, a cotton gin, a lumber company, and telephone service. The estimated population had dropped to 250 but by the mid-1920s had risen to 1,897. A bank was established by 1928, and in the early 1930s, when the estimated population was 1,200, Benavides had thirty-five businesses. By the late 1930s and early 1940s the town had grown to an estimated population of 3,081, fueled by proximity to many of Duval County's most productive oilfields; among the town's eighty businesses were a branch of the Southern Alkali Corporation, which produced salt; the J. C. Products Manufacturing Company, which made perfume and cosmetics; and the Duval Gasoline Company.

In 1950 the town's sixty-three retail and ten service establishments had a combined $2,084,000 in sales. The estimated population had already begun a gradual decline that lasted for the next three decades, however, dropping to 3,016 in the mid-1950s, 2,250 in the mid-1960s, and 1,897 in the late 1970s, with an accompanying drop in business activity. In the early 1980s the population began to rise again, and by the latter part of the decade had reached an estimated 2,005. In 1990 it was 1,788.

BIBLIOGRAPHY: Arnoldo De León, *Benavides: The Town and Its Founder, 1880* (Benavides, Texas: Benavides City Council–Benavides Centennial Committee, 1980). Arnoldo De León, *A Social History of Mexican Americans in Nineteenth Century Duval County* (San Diego, Texas: Duval County Commissioners Court, n.d.). Vertical files, Barker Texas History Center, University of Texas at Austin. *Martin Donell Kohout*

BEN BOLT, TEXAS. Ben Bolt is on Farm Road 2508 off U.S. Highway 281, seven miles south of Alice in south central Jim Wells County. Mexican herders were residents of the ranching area before the building of the railroad. The town was laid out in 1904 by L. B. Collins. When he named the town, which is right down the road from Alice, he did so under the influence of a popular song, "Ben Bolt," the first line of which is "Don't you remember sweet Alice, Ben Bolt?" A post office was established at Ben Bolt in 1906. By 1914 the town had fifty residents, a cotton gin, a general store, and a cattle breeder. That year the San Antonio and Aransas Pass Railway built a line through the community. By 1947 Ben Bolt had a population of 120 and four businesses. In 1950 the population was estimated at seventy-five and in 1966 at 138. From 1974 to 1990 it was 110.

BIBLIOGRAPHY: Vertical files, Barker Texas History Center, University of Texas at Austin. *Alicia A. Garza*

BEN BRANCH. Ben Branch rises a mile southeast of Hickston in northern Gonzales County (at 29°34′ N, 97°12′ W) and runs 4½ miles northwest to its mouth on Valley Branch, two miles southeast of Nickel (at 29°35′ N, 97°16′ W). The surrounding moderately rolling terrain is surfaced by fine sandy loam that supports hardwoods, pines, mesquite, and prairie grasses.

BENBROOK, TEXAS. Benbrook is at the intersection of Interstate Highway 20 and U.S. Highway 377, ten miles southwest of Fort Worth in southwestern Tarrant County. It was established by settlers from Tennessee and other southern states about 1857 and originally called Miranda. In 1876 the Texas and Pacific Railway extended its tracks through the area. The community was renamed for James M. Benbrook, a native of Indiana, who had come to Tarrant County about 1874 and played an important part in persuading the Texas and Pacific officials to build their line through the site. Benbrook opened a post office in 1880. The local school registered sixty-four students and employed one teacher during the 1905–06 term. By the middle 1920s, when its first population statistics were reported, only twenty persons lived in Benbrook, a number that remained constant through the following decade. The onset of the World War IIqv brought an increase in the population, which was 100 in the late 1940s and 617 a decade later. By 1957 the town had twenty businesses. The completion of Benbrook Reservoirqv in the early 1950s contributed to the community's development. Benbrook grew along with the Dallas–Fort Worth area. In 1965 the population was 3,300; it reached 9,900 by 1976 and in 1990 stood at 16,564.

BIBLIOGRAPHY: Janet L. Schmelzer, *Where the West Begins: Fort Worth and Tarrant County* (Northridge, California: Windsor, 1985). Ruby Schmidt, ed., *Fort Worth and Tarrant County* (Fort Worth: Texas Christian University Press, 1984). Kathleen E. and Clifton R. St. Clair, eds., *Little Towns of Texas* (Jacksonville, Texas: Jayroe Graphic Arts, 1982). *Brian Hart*

BENBROOK FIELD. Benbrook Field, at Benbrook, was initially known as Taliaferro No. 2 and was part of a complex of three Taliaferro fields near Fort Worth. It was also called Carruthers Field. After the beginning of World War Iqv it was renamed Benbrook Field by the United States Army. The field was used during that war as an aerial gunnery school for American and Canadian students and was afterward deactivated.

BIBLIOGRAPHY: Robert Hays, "Military Aviation in Texas," *Texas Military History* 3 (Spring 1963). *Art Leatherwood*

BENBROOK RESERVOIR. Benbrook Reservoir is an artificial lake in the Trinity River basin ten miles south of Fort Worth and just south of Benbrook in southwestern Tarrant County (at 32°39′ N, 97°27′ W). It is owned by the United States government and operated by the Fort Worth District of the United States Army Corps of Engineers. Construction of the dam on the Clear Fork of the Trinity River began in

May 1947 and was completed in December 1950. Water impoundment began in September 1952. The reservoir, which meets area flood control, conservation, navigation, and recreational needs, has a capacity of 88,250 acre-feet and a surface area of 3,770 acres at an elevation of 694 feet above mean sea level. It drains an area of 429 square miles above its dam. It is in an area of variable terrain surfaced by shallow, stony, clay loams that support juniper and oak trees, chaparral, cacti, and grasses. Six public parks are located on the reservoir's forty miles of shoreline, many offering picnic, camping, boating, and swimming facilities. Some residential development has taken place around Benbrook Reservoir.

BENCHLEY, TEXAS. Benchley, the first community in Robertson County, is on U.S. Highway 190 in southwestern Robertson County. Irish[qv] immigrants originally settled the area between 1829 and 1834 and named it Staggers Point, but many left because of Indian depredations and the Runaway Scrape.[qv] William Henry held the original title to the land. By the 1840s the community had three stores, a racetrack, and a gun club. A local tale tells of a band of desperados who arrived in the town purporting to be preachers. While the leader preached a sermon, his associates made off with a number of horses. Residents pursued the horse thieves, killed several, including the reverend imposter, and recovered their stock. Robert Henry established the first cotton gin at Staggers Point in 1850. By the 1860s the community had several businesses, including perhaps the first saddletree shop in Texas and a beef-pickling plant. The Old Irish Church, a Presbyterian church, and a school were functioning. The Houston and Texas Central Railway reached the site in 1868, and as the settlement developed into a town the citizens gave it the name Benchley, in honor of the first freight conductor, Henry Benchley. A telegraph station established at the depot was operated by a one-armed man named Squires, and a post office provided the community with mail service from 1882 into the 1950s. The first postmaster was John Chatham; the last was Clara Wallin Bowman. Until 1940 the population never exceeded 150 residents; it dropped to 100 by 1950, then increased to 270 by 1960. From 1968 through 1990 it was reported as 110.

BIBLIOGRAPHY: J. W. Baker, *History of Robertson County, Texas* (Franklin, Texas: Robertson County Historical Survey Committee, 1970). Mary K. T. Galloway et al., The Irish of Staggers Point (MS, Barker Texas History Center, University of Texas at Austin, 1973).

James L. Hailey

BEND, TEXAS. Bend, on Ranch Road 580 at a horseshoe-shaped bend in the Colorado River fourteen miles southeast of San Saba in southeastern San Saba and western Lampasas counties, developed in the nineteenth century as a supply and processing center for farmers. The area was originally settled in 1854 by three Low brothers from Tennessee, David Donald, James Milton, and William, and first named Schleicher's Bend, after Gustav Schleicher.[qv] By 1856 it was called McAnelly's Bend, for Robert Daugherty McAnelly, a landowner on the Lampasas side of the river. A post office under the latter name opened on the east side of the river in 1858 but was discontinued sometime after 1861. When application for a post office on the San Saba side of the river was made in the late 1870s, the names Little Breeches and Bend were submitted; the Bend post office opened in 1879 in the home of Seth Martin Moore, the local ferry operator, and has operated continuously since.

The town developed in the 1870s and 1880s, as a gristmill, cotton gin, and general store were established to meet the needs of local farmers and cattlemen. The first school on the San Saba side of the Colorado River was organized in 1872 near the mouth of Cherokee Creek, and by the 1880s Baptist, Methodist, and Christian churches had opened. In 1890 the community had a reported 400 residents, a justice of the peace precinct, a constabulary, craft shops, mercantile stores, and a hotel. For most of the twentieth century, however, Bend has recorded 100 to 125 residents. Corn, cotton, and cattle provided the initial basis for local commerce. In the late nineteenth century the pecan industry[qv] also became commercially important. After 1920 extensive pecan orchards were planted, and by midcentury the Hollis native pecan had become the region's primary cash crop. Bend boosters consider the Jumbo Hollis, which stands near the banks of the Colorado River, to be the world's most productive pecan tree. It is claimed that the tree yields nuts of extraordinary size and that in 1919 it produced more than 1,000 pounds. The tree is named for its first known owner, Thomas I. Hollis. In 1990 Bend reported a population of 115 and two businesses.

BIBLIOGRAPHY: Jonnie Ross Elzner, *Relighting Lamplights of Lampasas County, Texas* (Lampasas: Hill Country, 1974). Alma Ward Hamrick, *The Call of the San Saba: A History of San Saba County* (San Antonio: Naylor, 1941; 2d ed., Austin: Jenkins, 1969). *San Saba County History* (San Saba, Texas: San Saba County Historical Commission, 1983).

Daniel P. Greene

BENDESTSEN, TEXAS. Bendestsen is on U.S. Highway 59 forty-five miles northeast of Houston in northwestern Liberty County. The heavily forested area was opened to extensive logging by the construction of the Houston, East and West Texas Railway during the late 1870s. One of a number of sawmills in northern Liberty County was established at Bendestsen, just south of Cleveland. The old sawmill community later became the site of the Champion Paper Company lumberyards. It is often considered part of Cleveland.

BIBLIOGRAPHY: Barbara Smith, comp., "Cleveland's History," *Cleveland Area Pioneer*, June 1978.

Robert Wooster

BENEDICT, HARRY YANDELL (1869–1937). Harry Yandell Benedict, tenth president of the University of Texas, was born in Louisville, Kentucky, on November 14, 1869, the son of Joseph and Adele (Peters) Benedict. In 1877 his mother, with Yandell and his brother Carl, moved to Texas to occupy land acquired during the Republic of Texas[qv] era by her grandfather, S. W. Peters, on the Brazos River in Young and Stephens counties; with them came Adele Benedict's father, H. J. Peters. Young Yandell was taught by his well-educated mother at home except for eight months when he attended schools in Graham and Weatherford. The family had a library of 1,000 books brought by the Peters family from Kentucky.

Benedict entered the University of Texas on examination in February 1889 and graduated with a B.S. with first honors in civil engineering in 1892. He received his M.A. in 1893. While completing his work at the university, he was a fellow (1891–92) and a tutor (1892–93) in pure mathematics. From 1893 to 1895 he served as an assistant at the McCormick Observatory at the University of Virginia. For the next three years (1895–98), he studied at Harvard, where he received his Ph.D. in mathematical astronomy in 1898. He was in charge ad interim of mathematics and astronomy at Vanderbilt University in 1899. In 1900 he married Ada Stone of Henderson, Texas. They had two sons.

Benedict joined the faculty of the University of Texas at the beginning of the 1899–1900 session as instructor of mathematics. He rose rapidly in rank until he became professor of applied mathematics and astronomy in 1907. He served as director of extension from 1909 to 1911. In 1911 he was made dean of the College of Arts and Sciences, a position he kept until 1927, when he was elected president. From 1913 until 1920 he also served as dean of men. He was president from 1927 until his death. During his presidency an extensive building program added fifteen new buildings to the campus. His dream was to see the completion of the University of Texas McDonald Observatory,[qv] but he died two years before it opened. He wrote *Book of Texas* with John A. Lomax[qv] (1916), *Unified Mathematics* with two other mathematicians (1915), *A Source Book of Legislative History of the University of Texas* (1917), *Peregrinusings* (1924), and numerous articles.

He was a fellow of the American Association for the Advancement of Science, a president of the Texas Academy of Science,[qv] and a member of the American Mathematical Society, the American Astronomical Society, the National Education Association, the Texas State Teachers Association,[qv] the Society for the Promotion of Engineering Education, the American Statistical Association, Phi Beta Kappa, Tau Beta Pi, the Fortnightly Club, Town and Gown, the Rotary Club, the University Club, and Sigma Alpha Epsilon fraternity. He was a Democrat. Benedict was granted honorary doctor of laws degrees by Baylor in 1920 and Southwestern in 1929. He died suddenly of a cerebral hemorrhage on May 10, 1937. At the time, he was working on a history of the University of Texas; the unfinished manuscript is in the university archives. Benedict was buried in Oakwood Cemetery. Benedict Hall, on the UT campus, named in his honor, was dedicated in April 1953.

BIBLIOGRAPHY: Roy Bedichek, "President H. Y. Benedict In Memoriam," *Alcalde*, June 1937. Carl John Eckhardt, *One Hundred Faithful to the University of Texas at Austin* (197-?). T. H. Shelby, "H. Y. Benedict," *Texas Outlook*, October 1927. Vertical files, Barker Texas History Center, University of Texas at Austin. *Margaret C. Berry*

BENEDICTINE SISTERS. The Benedictine Sisters, whose origin goes back to the sixth century in Italy, first came to Texas in 1919. Mother Ledwina and another nun first left the motherhouse at St. Mary's, Pennsylvania, in 1911 and established a small group at the Isle of Pines, Cuba. Mother Ledwina headed a group of eight sisters in 1919, when they left Cuba for Texas and settled in Leming, a small town in Atascosa County, south of San Antonio. There they operated a convent and school (Mother Ledwina died there), before moving to San Antonio in 1926. From 1926 to 1963 the Benedictine Sisters operated a nursing home in San Antonio. In 1961 they bought twenty-seven acres of Hill Country[qv] land at Boerne, Kendall County. From 1961 to 1963 they improved the land, on which already stood three substantial rock houses. In August 1963 the sisters moved to the new location in Boerne and trained additional sisters there. In 1968 they opened a day and boarding school for girls, which had an average annual enrollment of forty-five girls until 1972, when it was converted to a coeducational institution with a kindergarten and grades one through twelve. By the 1975–76 term there were 210 boys and girls in attendance. The boarding school was subsequently phased out. The acreage of the facility had increased to 47.5 acres by 1976 and many new buildings had been constructed, including five classroom buildings, a learning center, a gym, and a chapel. In 1983 the school was closed because of lack of funding. In its place an "early learning" and after-school daycare center was established in 1987. The motherhouse building, one of the old rock houses, was enlarged in 1976. In 1983 the Sisters established the Benedictine Resource Center in San Antonio. The center administers the three components of the Benedictine Sisters' Ministries. These components are the Pastoral Outreach in Boerne, which includes the Health and Wholeness Center for Senior Citizens, the Omega Retreat Center, the Hispanic Outreach program, and the Children's Inn, a children's shelter; the Public Policy and Priorities program in Austin, which does legislative work focusing on poverty and children in Texas; and the Community Organization Effort which serves high-risk children of parents in the criminal justice system and victims of domestic violence. In 1994 there were twenty-five Benedictine Sisters in Texas, and the prioress was Sister Frances Brisenio. *Eldon S. Branda*

BENEFIELD, JOHN BARRY (1877–1971). Barry Benefield, journalist, author, and novelist, was born on May 12, 1877, in Jefferson, Texas, to Benjamin Harrison and Harriet Adelaide (Barry) Benefield. He grew up studying the travelers that stopped to spend the night at his father's combination wagonyard and feed store in Jefferson. As he swept the floor in the store, he began gathering information for his many short stories and novels, often about his native East Texas. As a boy, his mother, herself a writer, encouraged him to write about people. In 1898 he entered the University of Texas. Benefield financed his years at the university by teaching at Smithland, thirty miles from Jefferson. During this four-year period he won the *Cactus* short story prize in 1900–01 and was editor-in-chief of the *University of Texas Magazine* in 1901–02, an English student assistant the same year, and secretary of the *Cactus* in 1902. He graduated as class historian in 1902 and was a member of Phi Gamma Delta fraternity. After graduation he worked for the Dallas *Morning News*[qv] for a year and then moved to New York, where he worked for the New York *Times*. In June 1913 he married Lucille Stallcup of Smithville, Texas. In 1914 he retired to the New Jersey hills for a rest and recuperation of his health. During this time he began writing some of the short stories later published in *Short Turns* (1926). He became an advertising writer during World War I[qv] and later a book editor for the Century Company.

He published his first novel, *The Chicken-Wagon Family*, in 1925. The Fox film company bought the movie rights before the manuscript was offered for publication. The *Woman's Home Companion* offered him $10,000 for the serial rights to the next novel, *Bugles in the Night* (1927). During the Great Depression[qv] he lost almost all of his money, but he was able to make enough on short stories he submitted to magazines to survive. Reynal and Hitchcock, a publishing company, offered him a job if he would write a new novel for them. He wrote *Valiant is the Word for Carrie*, which they published in 1935. He received $17,500 from Paramount for the movie rights. In 1947 he retired to Peekskill, New York. When his wife died in 1960 he sold the house and everything in it and moved back to Jefferson to live with his sister in the house where he grew up. He died on September 22, 1971. His short stories have often appeared in such magazines as the *Century*, *Collier's Weekly*, and *Ladies Home Journal*. His novels include *Little Clown Lost* (1928), *Eddie and the Archangel Mike* (1943), and *April Was When It Began* (1939).

BIBLIOGRAPHY: *Alcalde* (magazine of the Ex-Students' Association of the University of Texas), January 1926. Vertical files, Barker Texas History Center, University of Texas at Austin. *David Littlefield*

BEN FICKLIN, TEXAS. Ben Ficklin (Benficklin), seat of Tom Green County from 1875 to 1882, was located five miles south of Fort Concho on the east bank of the South Concho River. In 1868 Maj. Benjamin F. Ficklin[qv] bought from John O. Meusebach[qv] 640 acres on the South Concho near the spring from which Fort Concho hauled its drinking water. There Ficklin built headquarters for his San Antonio–El Paso Mail[qv] line. Francis Corbett Taylor, a close friend of Ficklin, came from Alabama to take charge of the Concho mail station. After Ficklin's sudden death in Washington, D.C., on March 10, 1871, Taylor carried on the prospering stage line. In 1873, with William Stephen Kelly and Charles B. Metcalfe,[qv] he laid out a town a mile up the river and named it Ben Ficklin in honor of his friend. Kelly, also from Alabama, built the first house. The post office was established on August 27, 1873, with Henry M. Taylor as postmaster.

Taylor and Kelly were among the commissioners appointed to organize Tom Green County in 1874. In January 1875 they led a successful campaign to make Ben Ficklin the county seat, against the stiff challenge of San Angela (now San Angelo). Taylor had the support of stage line employees, Fort Concho officers, area ranchmen, and the growing numbers of business and professional men who, with their families, had been attracted to the new town. San Angela's saloons, gambling houses, and prostitutes were popular with soldiers, cowboys, and buffalo hunters. Ben Ficklin's first courthouse was donated by Taylor and Sheriff James Spears. An adobe[qv] building housed a subscription school, and lots were donated for future church buildings. Three stores and a hotel were soon erected. Around 600 people were living in Ben Ficklin when Taylor died in 1879. A two-story stone courthouse was completed in February 1882.

Heavy rains the night of August 23, 1882, swelled Dove Creek, Spring Creek, the Middle Concho, and the South Concho, already high because of a wet summer, out of their banks. Their combined waters roared down on Ben Ficklin at midmorning on August 24, and the town was destroyed. On the flat, only the courthouse, the jail, and two houses remained standing. Up the hill, fifteen houses and the schoolhouse remained. Sixty-five people were drowned. County offices and the post office were moved to San Angela, which became the county seat in 1883 with the new name San Angelo. Some survivors moved to Sherwood; others found jobs and free homesites in San Angelo. Two families continued to live at Ben Ficklin, a favorite swimming and picnicking spot, into the new century. The Ben Ficklin cemetery, on a hill overlooking new residences, holds the graves of flood victims and of F. C. Taylor and his wife, reinterred there after the flood dislodged their coffins. The Texas Historical Commission[qv] erected a marker at the townsite in 1965.

BIBLIOGRAPHY: Mrs. S. C. Autry, *Tom Green County* (San Angelo: Fort Concho Museum, n.d). Gus Clemens, Jr., *The Concho Country* (San Antonio: Mulberry Avenue, 1980). Mary Bain Spence and Susan Miles, "Major Ben Ficklin," West Texas Historical Association *Yearbook* 27 (1951).

Katherine T. Waring

BENFORD, TEXAS. Benford was on the Missouri, Kansas and Texas (Katy) Railroad between Corrigan and Stryker in eastern Polk County. In the mid-1880s construction of the Trinity and Sabine Railway through northern Polk County opened the virgin forests of the area to major lumbering interests. The Trinity and Sabine, acquired and extended by the Katy, spawned a large number of sawmills near Corrigan. Among these was the mill at Benford, which was established in 1889 and named for its founders, Bennett and Stanford. A post office was opened in 1905, and Benford eventually became a station on the Katy line. The lumber plant was operated by a variety of firms, including the West Lumber Company, the Burkett and Barnes Lumber Company, the Mardez Lumber Company, the Glynn Lumber Company, the Ragley Lumber Company, and the Lynch Davidson Company. When the timber was gone, the sawmill community faded; the post office closed in 1924.

BIBLIOGRAPHY: *A Pictorial History of Polk County, Texas, 1846–1910* (Livingston, Texas: Polk County Bicentennial Commission, 1976; rev. ed. 1978).

Robert Wooster

BEN FRANKLIN, TEXAS. Ben Franklin is on the Atchison, Topeka and Santa Fe Railroad and Farm roads 38 and 128 four miles northeast of Pecan Gap in northwestern Delta County. The settlement was located on Benjamin Simmons's land grant and named for his son. The Simmons family, along with the Birdwells and Hogues, arrived in the area in 1835 and were among the first settlers. The first post office was established by Isaac B. Nelson in 1853 at his one-room cabin on the crossroads. The community, at that time in Lamar County, supported cotton gins, the Greenville Smith sawmill, and the Wynn and Donaldson distillery. In 1854 Taliaferro B. Chaffin donated two acres for a Methodist Episcopal church. Citizens built the structure from materials provided by Smith's sawmill. Funds raised from the sale of whiskey supplied by the distillery paid the pastor's $190 annual salary. The post office was closed in 1859 but reopened in 1867.

Mary Dinnie taught the first school in the settlement, probably established shortly after the Civil War[qv] in the vacant side of a double log feed crib. A new facility, though not much more elaborate, was constructed two years later, and a man named Moore taught classes there. In 1870 B. F. Nidever opened the first livery stable and began a stage line to the county seat. By 1884 Ben Franklin was a school district; the community had a population of 200 and thrice-weekly mail service. Cotton ginning and shipment were the major businesses, but others included three sawmills, a shingle manufacturer, two flour mills, and a feed mill. The town also had three general stores, the McGinnis and Company saloon, a restaurant, an apothecary shop, and a blacksmith shop.

The Gulf, Colorado and Santa Fe Railway built a track just north of Ben Franklin in 1886, and the settlement became a stop on the line by 1889. In 1890 it had a population of 1,000, two hotels, two livery stables, and a telegraph office. John McFall had opened a grocery, and P. H. Snodgrass worked as a sign painter. Citizens could attend new Baptist, Christian, and Adventist churches. In 1892 Ben Franklin supported two new hotels, a doctor had opened an office, and a barber had moved to town. The municipal government consisted of Harvey McIntyre, constable, and J. N. Carroll, justice of the peace. E. Hammond was school principal. The Methodist Episcopal church was moved to a new site donated by John W. Jackson and his wife in 1898.

In 1895 the Texas-Midland Railroad built through Cooper, the county seat, with stops at Enloe, Klondike, and Horton. These more centrally located towns drew much of the traffic from Ben Franklin. By 1904 the population had decreased to 343. In 1912 only two businesses remained. Records for 1918 indicated two schools, one for white and one for black children. The town had 300 people and no businesses in 1925. In 1929 it had 500 residents and a bank. By 1936 the railway had become part of the Gulf, Colorado and Santa Fe system, and the town had seven businesses, a school, three churches, and a population of 300. In 1945 there were 250 residents and seven businesses. In 1964 Ben Franklin had a water tank, two churches, two cemeteries, one business, the post office, and 150 inhabitants. The Ben Franklin school district had been consolidated into the Fannindel system, in Fannin County, by 1970. That year there was a Ben Franklin Community Center. The only business in 1976 was Fremman's Grocery. In 1990 the community had seventy-five residents.

BIBLIOGRAPHY: Paul Garland Hervey, A History of Education in Delta County, Texas (M.A. thesis, University of Texas, 1951). Wilma Ross and Billie Phillips, *Photos and Tales of Delta County* (1976).

Vista K. McCroskey

BEN HUR, TEXAS. Ben Hur (Benhur) is near the intersection of Farm roads 339 and 2489, eight miles northwest of Groesbeck in western Limestone County. The area was first settled after the Civil War[qv] when Joseph Nussbaum started selling acreage to farmers. The town was originally called Cottonwood, but according to local legend the name was changed in 1895 to Ben Hur by A. T. Derden, a resident of the town who was an admirer of Lew Wallace's best-selling book of the same name. A school and a post office were established that year with James A. Parker as postmaster. In 1900 the town had a population of 127 and several businesses. Since it was located off the railroad, most of the business activity moved to nearby Mart. In 1906 the post office was closed. The population grew to about 200 by 1947 but declined again to 100 by the mid-1960s. The population decline forced the consolidation of the school with that of Mart in 1957. Subsequently, the remaining businesses and churches closed. The population of the community was listed as 100 in 1990.

BIBLIOGRAPHY: *Memorial and Biographical History of Navarro, Henderson, Anderson, Limestone, Freestone, and Leon Counties* (Chicago: Lewis, 1893). Ray A. Walter, *A History of Limestone County* (Austin: Von Boeckmann–Jones, 1959).

Ray A. Walter

BENINA, TEXAS. Benina was twenty miles south of San Augustine in southeastern San Augustine County. The settlement was granted a post office named Ashton in 1871, and the name was changed to Boren's Mills in 1874. The community had an estimated 100 inhabitants, three cotton gin–gristmill combinations, and a blacksmith shop in 1884. The name was changed again to Benina in 1889. F. C. Powell was running a general store in the town in 1890. In 1896 Benina had a population of thirty and Methodist and Baptist churches. In 1914 the population had dropped to twenty-five inhabitants. The post office closed

in 1920, and by the 1940s Benina was no longer listed on state highway maps.
Mark Odintz

BENJAMIN, TEXAS. Benjamin, county seat and first town organized in Knox County, is located at the intersection of U.S. Highway 82 and State Highway 6, eighty-three miles southwest of Wichita Falls. Hilory H. Bedford, president and controlling stockholder in the Wichita and Brazos Stock Company, founded the town in 1885 and named it for his son Benjamin, who had been killed by lightning. To encourage settlement in the region, Bedford gave each of his twelve fellow stockholders a fifty-acre tract of land and set aside forty additional acres for a town square. He was instrumental in the organization of Knox County in 1886, with Benjamin as the county seat. The town received its first mail service in 1884; Bedford was postmaster. In 1886 the Benjamin school was organized with R. P. Dimmitt, Mrs. Oliver, and Mrs. M. S. Berry as first teachers. Other early residents included W. P. Lane, who opened a saddle shop in 1885, Tom Isbell, the first sheriff of Knox County, and Dr. G. H. Beavers.

The courthouse was constructed in 1938 and the school buildings for the independent school system in 1942; both projects were built with Work Projects Administration[qv] labor. Other establishments in the county seat in 1986 included four churches, four service stations, a cafe, and the Knox County Museum. The museum, located at the courthouse, has an excellent barbed wire[qv] exhibit and numerous other frontier artifacts. Benjamin is the site of the colorful Moorhouse Park, dedicated by the state highway department in 1965. Four miles east of town is another popular tourist attraction known as the Narrows,[qv] a picturesque crest that separates the drainage basins of the Wichita River. The town, which was incorporated in 1928, is located on the Atchison, Topeka and Santa Fe Railroad and derives most of its income from farming, ranching, and oil. Benjamin had a population of 600 in 1940. It recorded 257 residents in 1980 and 225 in 1990.

BIBLIOGRAPHY: Mrs. R. D. Gray, *Early Days in Knox County* (New York: Carleton, 1963). Knox County History Committee, *Knox County History* (Haskell, Texas: Haskell Free Press, 1966). Kathleen E. and Clifton R. St. Clair, eds., *Little Towns of Texas* (Jacksonville, Texas: Jayroe Graphic Arts, 1982).
Edloe A. Jenkins

BENNET, VALENTINE (1780–1843). Valentine Bennet, soldier and pioneer, was born in Massachusetts in 1780 to a Puritan family. He fought in the War of 1812, lived for a time in New York, Louisiana, and Ohio, and married in 1817. Shortly after the death of his wife he made provision for his children and set out for Texas, where he settled at Velasco in November 1825. In 1832 he took a leading part in the battle of Velasco,[qv] where he was severely wounded in the face and hip. He moved to Gonzales in 1834 and in 1835 was one of the eighteen men who defied Domingo de Ugartechea's[qv] order in the battle of Gonzales.[qv]

Bennet was elected lieutenant when the Gonzales militia was organized, and from that time on he was in the thick of the Texas Revolution.[qv] He participated in the battle of Concepción[qv] in October 1835 and the siege of Bexar[qv] in December. He held the rank of assistant quartermaster and received honorable mention from Gen. Edward Burleson[qv] for efficiency in keeping the army well supplied. Later, as quartermaster of the revolutionary army,[qv] he was kept busy supplying beef for Sam Houston's[qv] growing forces as the general retreated from Gonzales to the battleground of San Jacinto. After the battle of San Jacinto[qv] Bennet remained with the army. Early in 1838, after a three-month furlough, he brought his son back to Texas with him. On December 25, 1838, he brought his daughter to live in his home in Gonzales.

In 1841 he was commissioned a major in the quartermaster's department of the Army of the Republic of Texas[qv] and was sent on the Texan Santa Fe expedition.[qv] Among the other Santa Fe prisoners he suffered many indignities and cruelties at the hands of his Mexican guards; in August 1842 the prisoners were released, and Bennet returned to Texas. He reentered the Texas army when Gen. Adrián Woll[qv] invaded Texas; subsequently, he took part in the Somervell expedition.[qv] He died at the home of his daughter on July 24, 1843, and was buried in the old cemetery at Gonzales.

BIBLIOGRAPHY: *Biographical Encyclopedia of Texas* (New York: Southern, 1880). Gonzales *Inquirer*, June 4, 1953. Marie Bennet Urwitz, "Valentine Bennet," *Quarterly of the Texas State Historical Association* 9 (January 1906). E. W. Winkler, ed., *Secret Journals of the Senate, Republic of Texas* (Austin, 1911). Dudley Goodall Wooten, ed., *A Comprehensive History of Texas* (2 vols., Dallas: Scarff, 1898; rpt., Austin: Texas State Historical Association, 1986).
Amelia W. Williams

BENNETT, GWENDOLYN BENNETTA (1902–1981). Gwendolyn Bennett, black writer and artist, was born in Giddings, Texas, on July 8, 1902, the only child of Joshua Robin and Mayme Frank (Abernathy) Bennett. She spent only one year in Texas. Her paternal grandfather, R. B. Bennett, had come from North Carolina on a wagon train and was a small rancher and then a barber in Giddings. Her father had been a principal in a Gonzales, Texas, black high school from 1901 to 1903. In 1903 he moved his family to Wadsworth, Nevada, where he and his wife taught in the Indian Service for the Bureau of Indian Affairs. Gwen Bennett's earliest memories were of life on this Paiute Indian reservation. In 1906 the Bennetts moved to Washington, D.C., where he worked as a clerk for the Bureau of Indian Affairs and enrolled in the Howard University School of Law. He obtained his law degree in 1908. His wife filed for divorce in 1910 and was awarded custody of Gwendolyn. Joshua subsequently kidnapped Gwendolyn and took her with him as he moved from Washington to Pennsylvania and, finally, to Brooklyn, New York. There, Gwendolyn Bennett came of age at the start of the Harlem Renaissance.

In her childhood she had recited long poems to appreciative adults and painted well. She attended Girls' High School in Brooklyn, where she became the first African American in the school's literary and drama societies; she also won first place in an art contest. Subsequently, she attended Columbia University (1921) and then Pratt Institute (1922–24), studying art education. During this time she began publishing. In December 1923 *Opportunity*, the official organ of the National Urban League, accepted her poem "Heritage," and *The Crisis*, the official organ for the National Association for the Advancement of Colored People,[qv] carried her cover illustration. From 1923 to 1931 Bennett's poetry periodically appeared in *The Crisis, Opportunity, Psalms*, and *The Gypsy*, and several anthologies. During this same period she produced five journal cover illustrations. In 1926 *fire!!*, a small arts magazine begun by African-American artists Langston Hughes, Wallace Thurman, Bruce Nugent, and Gwen Bennett, among others, carried "Wedding Day," her first published story. Her second story, "Tokens," appeared in Charles S. Johnson's *Ebony and Topaz* (1927).

She accepted a position as instructor at Howard University in 1924, teaching design, watercolor, and crafts. She received a fellowship to study art in Paris in 1925 and at the Barnes Foundation in Marion, Pennsylvania, in 1927. Also in 1927 she married Dr. Alfred Joseph Jackson, who had been an intern at Freedman's Hospital, Howard University. The young couple moved to Eustis, Florida, where they resided until the early 1930s, when they returned to New York.

Jackson died in 1936 and Bennett remarried in 1940, when she met Richard Crosscup, a literature teacher and social activist. Their interracial marriage was not a socially accepted union. In 1935 Bennett joined the Harlem Artists Guild; from 1939 to 1944 she directed the Harlem Community Art Center but was suspended for her political convictions. In the early 1940s she served on the board of the Negro Playwright's Guild, and she directed the development of the George Washington Carver Community School. She was one of the most versatile figures to participate actively both in the 1920s arts movement known as the Harlem Renaissance and in the 1930s arts alliance formed among African-American graphic artists called the Harlem Artists Guild.

Gwendolyn Bennett never returned to Giddings. She retired from public life in the 1940s but remained in New York until 1968. Through the 1950s to the mid-1960s she worked for the Consumers Union. When she retired from this agency, she and her husband moved to Kutztown, Pennsylvania, where she had established an antique store. On January 9, 1980, Richard Crosscup died of sudden heart failure. His wife died on May 30, 1981, in the Reading County Hospital.

BIBLIOGRAPHY: *Dictionary of Literary Biography*, Vol. 51. Jessie Carney Smith, ed., *Notable Black American Women* (Detroit: Gale Research, 1992). *Sandra Y. Govan*

BENNETT, JOSEPH L. (?–1848). Joseph L. Bennett, military officer, moved to Texas in the spring of 1834 and settled in what is now Waller County. At the outbreak of the Texas Revolution[qv] he joined the army. About March 1, 1836, he set out with his company for San Antonio, planning to march to the relief of the beleaguered garrison at the Alamo, but learned of the fall of the fort at the Colorado River. Thereupon Bennett joined Sam Houston's[qv] army at Beeson's Crossing and was commissioned captain on March 12. With the reorganization of the army on April 8 he was elected lieutenant colonel of Col. Sidney Sherman's[qv] Second Regiment of Texas Volunteers. Bennett fought with distinction at the battle of San Jacinto.[qv] According to his account in a letter to Houston he actually led the regiment of which Sherman was the nominal commander, while Sherman skulked in "a small island of timber." On May 27, 1837, Bennett received Houston's commission as colonel and appointment as commander of a regiment of "mounted gunmen" for the protection of the frontier.

Bennett served in the House of Representatives of the Third and Fourth congresses of the Republic of Texas, November 5, 1838, through February 3, 1840. He represented Montgomery County as a stout supporter of the policies of Sam Houston. During this period he also held the government contract for the delivery of mail between Houston and Montgomery.

In 1842 Bennett raised a battalion for the Somervell expedition,[qv] but when most of his men returned to their homes soon after the expedition reached the Rio Grande, he joined the battalion commanded by Maj. Bartlett Simms.[qv] When Alexander Sommervell[qv] ordered the command back into Central Texas, however, Bennett agreed to return and not take part in what became known as the Mier expedition.[qv]

In 1848 he moved from Montgomery to Navarro County and settled on his headright, located partly in Navarro County and partly in Freestone County. The present town of Streetman is within three miles of the old Bennett home, where Bennett died in the fall of 1848. He was survived by his wife, Elizabeth, and five children.

BIBLIOGRAPHY: John H. Jenkins, ed., *The Papers of the Texas Revolution, 1835–1836* (10 vols., Austin: Presidial Press, 1973). Texas House of Representatives, *Biographical Directory of the Texan Conventions and Congresses, 1832–1845* (Austin: Book Exchange, 1941). Amelia W. Williams and Eugene C. Barker, eds., *The Writings of Sam Houston, 1813–1863* (8 vols., Austin: University of Texas Press, 1938–43; rpt., Austin and New York: Pemberton Press, 1970).

Thomas W. Cutrer

BENNETT, MILES (1816–1887). Miles Bennett, son of Armstead and Faith Bennett, was born on July 26, 1816, in Indiana. He was the fourth of seven children, all of whom moved with their parents to Texas in 1834 and settled in an area now in the north part of Houston County. The sons bought land and moved into what is now Anderson County. Miles served in the Texas army from June 1 to September 1, 1836, as a private and was in the battle of San Jacinto.[qv] He also served in the Mexican War and one year in the Civil War.[qqv] His early land grants date from a Class 3 certificate in March 1839 and include a land patent in Anderson County, dated November 14, 1849, but not filed until July 17, 1874. His first wife was Rachel Parker, daughter of Daniel Parker.[qv] Rachel, born September 27, 1821, died on December 23, 1843, soon after the birth and death of their first child. They are buried in the same grave in Pilgrim Cemetery, the first persons interred there. Miles married Laura Jordan (Jerdon, Jourdon) on May 29, 1848. They had five children. The Bennetts were prosperous farmers; his real estate was valued at $8,000 and his personal property at $3,500 in 1860. Bennett died at his home in Anderson County, Texas, on November 28, 1887. There are grave markers for Bennett (a Texas Centennial[qv] marker) and his wives in the Pilgrim Cemetery.

This man is not to be confused with Miles S. Bennett, son of San Jacinto veteran Valentine Bennett (1780–1843).

BIBLIOGRAPHY: Pauline Buck Hohes, *A Centennial History of Anderson County, Texas* (San Antonio: Naylor, 1936). Gifford E. White, *1840 Citizens of Texas* (2 vols., Austin, 1983–84). *Mrs. Harmon Watts*

BENNETT, STEVEN L. (1946–1972). Steven L. Bennett, Medal of Honor recipient, was born at Palestine, Texas, on April 22, 1946, son of Elwin Bennett. He received a bachelor of science degree from the University of Southwestern Louisiana and was a member of the Air Force Reserve Officer Training Corps. He was commissioned in the United States Air Force on August 12, 1968, and served on active duty until his death in Vietnam on June 29, 1972. He was assigned to the Twentieth Tactical Air Support Squadron at DaNang Air Base, with primary duty as a forward air controller. On June 29, 1972, he was the pilot of a light aircraft flying an artillery-adjustment mission along a heavily defended area over a large concentration of enemy troops massing to attack friendly forces. He requested tactical air support but was told that none was available. Determined to aid the endangered troops, he strafed the enemy positions four times, and the enemy began a retreat. Bennett continued his attack, and as he completed his fifth pass, his aircraft was struck by a surface-to-air missile. The plane was severely damaged in the left engine and the left main landing gear. With the aircraft on fire, he realized that a landing at a friendly airfield was impossible. He instructed his observer to prepare to eject, but was informed that the observer's parachute had been shredded during the attack. Bennett chose to ditch in the nearby Gulf of Tonkin, with the full knowledge that this type of aircraft had never been successfully ditched in water. When the plane struck the water it cartwheeled and was damaged so that escape from the cockpit was impossible. The observer escaped and was rescued, thanks to the selfless action of Captain Bennett. Bennett's wife, Linda, of San Antonio, received the posthumous award from Vice President Gerald Ford at the White House in Washington, on August 8, 1974. Bennett is buried in Lafayette Memorial Cemetery at Lafayette, Louisiana. In addition to his wife, he was survived by one child.

BIBLIOGRAPHY: Donald K. Schneider, *Air Force Heroes in Vietnam* (Washington: GPO, 1979). *Art Leatherwood*

BENNETT, TEXAS (Frio County). Bennett, also known as Bennett Settlement and Hamlin, was on the Leona River a half mile west of the intersection of Interstate Highway 35 and the Frio River in southwest Frio County. The settlement was named for one of the community's first settlers, Hamilton Bennett, who came to the area in 1876. Between 1876 and 1877 an irrigation project consisting of a dam, water wells, and a canal system, funded by the state of Texas with a large land grant, was brought near completion in Bennett before a flood of the Leona River destroyed the dam. According to local tradition the dam was never rebuilt because the volume of water in the river dropped. Between 1878 and 1881 a post office by the name of Hamlin operated in the community. Although the community disappeared from maps after 1885, local people continued to refer to the site as

Bennett or Bennett Settlement. Around 1908 a well was drilled at the site that provided continuous irrigation water for local farmers as late as 1990. The site of Bennett was within the Cory and McWilliams Ranch in 1936. Remains of the canal and several wells were said to be visible aboveground as late as 1971.

BIBLIOGRAPHY: Mrs. W. A. Roberts, "Frio County Has a Colorful History," *Frontier Times*, June 1936. *Ruben E. Ochoa*

BENNETT, TEXAS (Parker County). Bennett is near Farm Road 113 fifteen miles southwest of Weatherford in southwestern Parker County. Settlement of the area, which originally was known by the Indian name Lakota, began in the middle to late 1880s. In 1890 George E. Bennett established the Acme Brick Company at the town's present site, and the community that gradually developed around the company was called Bennett. After his father's death, Walter R. Bennett assumed the responsibilities of running the company. The younger Bennett built Acme Brick into one of the largest plants in the Southwest. The company employed over 100 men who lived in Acme Brick homes, making Bennett essentially a company town. The Mineral Wells and Northwestern Railroad carried the bricks from Bennett to retail points throughout the Southwest. A church, a public school, and a general store served the Acme employees. In 1990 the population was eighty-five.

BIBLIOGRAPHY: John Clements, *Flying the Colors: Texas, a Comprehensive Look at Texas Today, County by County* (Dallas: Clements Research, 1984). Gustavus Adolphus Holland, *History of Parker County and the Double Log Cabin* (Weatherford, Texas: Herald, 1931; rpt. 1937). Weatherford *Democrat*, August 11, 1939. *David Minor*

BENNETT, TEXAS (Trinity County). Bennett, on State Highway 94 eleven miles northeast of Groveton in northeastern Trinity County, was established in the late nineteenth century. During the first decades of the twentieth century the area was the site of intensive logging. Many of the residents subsequently moved away, but in the 1990s a church, a cemetery, and a few scattered houses were still at the site.

BIBLIOGRAPHY: Patricia B. and Joseph W. Hensley, eds., *Trinity County Beginnings* (Groveton, Texas: Trinity County Book Committee, 1986). *Christopher Long*

BENNETT, TEXAS (Yoakum County). Bennett was a ranch community six miles northeast of Denver City in Yoakum County. It developed as an oilfield-supply center after the discovery of oil in 1936. At that time there was a church in Bennett, but the post office was in Denver City. In 1948 Bennett had a school and a few businesses, but by 1964 the town no longer appeared on maps.

BIBLIOGRAPHY: Vertical files, Barker Texas History Center, University of Texas at Austin. Yoakum County Historical Commission, *Yoakum County* (Dallas: Taylor, 1985).

BENNETT CREEK (Llano County). Bennett Creek rises five miles west of Oxford in southwestern Llano County (at 30°36′ N, 98°47′ W) and flows north for nine miles to its mouth on Hickory Creek, nine miles west of Llano (at 30°42′ N, 98°50′ W). It traverses an area of the Llano basin characterized by flat to rolling terrain with local escarpments and a surface of thick, fine, sandy soils that support open stands of live oak and mesquite.

——— (Mills County). Bennett Creek begins two miles southeast of Goldthwaite in southeastern Mills County (at 31°28′ N, 98°25′ W) and runs southeast for twenty-three miles to its mouth on the Lampasas River, in northern Lampasas County (at 31°24′ N, 98°12′ W). The stream is probably named for Charles H. Bennett, who had a large land grant on its banks in the northern corner of Lampasas County. It is dammed in its upper reaches. It crosses variable terrain surfaced by stony and clayey loam that supports grasses, cacti, brush, scattered post oak, and Spanish oak.

BENNINGFIELD, HUDSON POSEY (ca. 1810–ca. 1885). Hudson Posey Benningfield, pioneer Red River County settler, was born near Nashville, Tennessee, around 1810. Around 1816 he moved with his family to the Red River valley in Arkansas. Around 1820 they crossed the river with Charles Burkham[qv] and settled in what became known as the Burkham Settlement[qv] in northeastern Red River County, Texas. In 1833 Benningfield married Susannah Burkham Baker, widow of James Baker. During the Mexican War[qv] Benningfield served in Capt. Samuel W. Simms's company of Texas volunteers along with his brother-in-law Ahijah Burkham. In the 1860 census Benningfield is listed as a farmer, age fifty, with personal property valued at $3,000 and six children. After the Civil War[qv] he moved to Atascosa County, where he evidently died around 1885.

BIBLIOGRAPHY: Pat B. Clark, *The History of Clarksville and Old Red River County* (Dallas: Mathis, Van Nort, 1937). Claude V. Hall, "Early Days in Red River County," *East Texas State Teachers College Bulletin* 14 (June 1931). *Red River Recollections* (Clarksville, Texas: Red River County Historical Society, 1986). Rex W. Strickland, Anglo-American Activities in Northeastern Texas, 1803–1845 (Ph.D. dissertation, University of Texas, 1937). *Christopher Long*

BENOIT, TEXAS. Benoit was on U.S. Highway 67 and the Santa Fe Railroad twelve miles northeast of Ballinger in east central Runnels County. The community was started in 1886 and named Norwood, but with the establishment of a local post office in 1906 it was renamed for J. Benoit, an early settler. W. F. Hill opened the first store in 1912 and was the last postmaster. At its peak Benoit had two stores, a gin, a blacksmith shop, and a one-room schoolhouse. The population was 100 in 1940, but by 1950 the settlement had disappeared.

BIBLIOGRAPHY: Charlsie Poe, *Runnels Is My County* (San Antonio: Naylor, 1970). *William R. Hunt*

BENONINE, TEXAS. Benonine is on Interstate Highway 40 near the Oklahoma state line, a mile west of Texola in southeastern Wheeler County. G. W. Burrow built the first homestead near the site in 1900. The town was platted by C. B. Harbert in 1909, when the Chicago, Rock Island and Gulf Railway built through the area, and named after the local Benonine Oil and Gas Company. The Benonine post office existed by October 1909. For a short time Benonine had a printing office, a bank, and high hopes of prospering as a shipping point. Burrow, who later served as a deputy sheriff, opened a general store in 1909. However, growth faltered, mainly because of the emergence of Shamrock as the county's leading business center. By 1918 the post office had been discontinued and mail rerouted through Texola, and by 1920 the bank and other businesses had been moved away, leaving only the railroad switch and loading pens. The nearby Brooks Ranch became noted, however, for its experimental buffalo[qv] herd.

BIBLIOGRAPHY: Sallie B. Harris, comp., *Hide Town in the Texas Panhandle: 100 Years in Wheeler County and the Panhandle of Texas* (Hereford, Texas: Pioneer, 1968). Millie Jones Porter, *Memory Cups of Panhandle Pioneers* (Clarendon, Texas: Clarendon Press, 1945). Fred Tarpley, *1001 Texas Place Names* (Austin: University of Texas Press, 1980). *H. Allen Anderson*

BEN'S HOLE CREEK. Ben's Hole Creek rises in the Christmas Mountains nine miles northeast of the community of Study Butte in south central Brewster County (at 29°26′ N, 103°27′ W) and flows southwest for twelve miles to its mouth on Terlingua Creek, just above the Ranch Road 170 crossing (at 29°'20 N, 103°'33 W). The upper reaches of the stream traverse the Christmas Mountains, from which the creek descends some 2,000 feet through a rugged and broken desert landscape. Local plant life, rubricated in the scientific literature as Chihuahuan Desert scrub, features such sparse, xerophytic plants as lechuguilla, ocotillo, and the ubiquitous creosote bush. The creek detours around the towering cliffs of Wildhorse Mountain, its route paralleled by State Highway 116. The name Ben's Hole Creek probably derives from that of Ben's Water Hole, at one time a well-known watering spot on the streamcourse. The water hole lay on the route between Terlingua to the south and Alpine far to the north. Ben's identity is lost.

BENSON, ELLIS (1808–1892). Ellis (sometimes Elias) Benson, soldier and legislator, was born in Vermont in 1808 and moved to Texas in January 1836. At the outbreak of the Texas Revolution[qv] he joined Capt. John Hart's[qv] company of volunteers (later commanded by Lt. Richard Roman[qv]) at Velasco, on January 30, 1836. On February 13 Benson accepted a bounty of twenty-four dollars and joined the regular army "for two years or the duration of the war." At the battle of San Jacinto[qv] he served as a gunner in Capt. Henry Teal's[qv] company of Lt. Col. James Clinton Neill's[qv] "artillery corps." In December 1836 Benson was a private in Capt. John Smith's[qv] Company A of the First Regiment, Regular Infantry, stationed on Galveston Island, but was detached to garrison duty at Anahuac. By February 28 he was still in the army and back at his regular duty station at Galveston. Benson was a member of William Ryon's company on the Somervell expedition.[qv] He was also one of the vice presidents of the convention that met on the San Jacinto battlefield on April 21, 1860, to nominate Sam Houston[qv] for president. On July 26, 1881, the Texas Veterans Claims Commission approved his application for a veteran's pension. Benson was an active member of the Texas Veterans Association.[qv] He died in Houston in 1892.

BIBLIOGRAPHY: Dallas *Weekly Herald*, July 28, 1881. Daughters of the Republic of Texas, *Defenders of the Republic of Texas* (Austin: Laurel House, 1989). Daughters of the Republic of Texas, *Muster Rolls of the Texas Revolution* (Austin, 1986). Sam Houston Dixon and Louis Wiltz Kemp, *The Heroes of San Jacinto* (Houston: Anson Jones, 1932).

Thomas W. Cutrer

BENSON, NETTIE LEE (1905–1993). Nettie Lee Benson, historian, teacher, and librarian, the fourth of ten children of Jasper William and Vora Ann (Reddell) Benson, was born in Arcadia, Galveston County, Texas, on January 15, 1905. The family moved in 1908 to Sinton, where her father established a vegetable-shipping business. Nettie Lee graduated from Sinton High School in 1922 as valedictorian. A voracious reader, she studied Spanish, played competitive tennis, and participated in numerous school and church activities. She was a lifelong member of the Sinton Presbyterian Church (her parents were founding members); in later years she was a benefactor of the Presbyterian Children's Home and Service Agency.

Miss Benson's involvement with Mexico and with teaching began early in her life. She considered a course by Professor Charles W. Hackett[qv] on Spanish North America that she took in 1925 at the University of Texas her prime motivation for studying Mexico. Shortly after taking the course, she moved to Monterrey, Nuevo León, and taught from 1925 to 1927 at the Instituto Inglés-Español, a school run by the Methodist Church. She earned a bachelor's degree with honors at UT in 1929, and began graduate work the following year. She left in 1931 to teach fifth grade in Hartley and returned to Sinton the next year to care for an ailing mother and to teach Spanish and English at Ingleside High School. For the next ten years she sponsored field trips to Monterrey for the high school senior class. She was also instrumental in gaining admittance of Hispanic students to the previously all-white high school. By continuing graduate study during the summers, Miss Benson earned a master's degree in 1935 from UT with majors in Latin-American history and government.

She returned to UT on a leave of absence in 1941 to take what she thought would be refresher courses, but stayed to complete her doctorate in 1949. In 1942 she began her lifelong association with the library that now bears her name, the Latin American Collection. Miss Benson quickly became an authority on Latin-American library acquisitions and bibliography. She began an aggressive acquisition program for the library that included trips to Mexico, South America, and the Caribbean, and developed an innovative acquisition methodology adapted to conditions in the Latin-American book-publishing trade. From a respectable 30,000 volumes in 1942, the Latin American Collection grew to 305,000 volumes by 1975, the year of her retirement. The Nettie Lee Benson Latin American Collection[qv] became one of the most comprehensive and distinguished Latin-American libraries in the world. Miss Benson's expertise was recognized by her library colleagues when she was chosen as the representative for the Latin American Cooperative Acquisitions Project, a consortium of major United States research libraries, for which she collected books in South America and Central America from 1960 to 1962.

At UT her teaching career took a new direction. In 1962 she began to teach Mexican and Latin-American history for the history department, and in 1964 she initiated with Ford Foundation funding a Latin-American library-studies program in the Graduate School of Library Science. She retired from teaching in the library school in 1975, but continued her popular graduate seminars in Mexican history until 1989. One of her first history seminars resulted in a classic book of essays written by her students, *Mexico and the Spanish Córtes, 1820–1834*, published by the University of Texas Press[qv] in 1966 and reprinted in Spanish by the Mexican congress in 1985. Miss Benson directed numerous master's and doctoral theses over her twenty-six years of teaching.

Complementing her library and teaching activities, she presented countless papers and published many articles and books on nineteenth-century Mexican history and on the holdings of the Latin American Collection. A Spanish translation of her doctoral dissertation, *The Provincial Deputation in Mexico: Precursor of the Mexican Federal State*, was published in Mexico in 1952 and again in 1980. Augmented by additional research on the topic, an expanded English version of the dissertation was published by the University of Texas Press in 1992. An essay, "Texas as Viewed from Mexico, 1820–1834," appeared in the January, 1987, issue of the *Southwestern Historical Quarterly*, which was dedicated to her.

Nettie Lee Benson was an active member of many professional historical, archival, and library organizations. She was a founding member of the Seminar on the Acquisition of Latin American Library Materials in 1956 and of the Latin American Studies Association in 1966. She held a number of offices in several organizations, serving as president of the Seminar (1970–71) and as chairperson (1970) of the Bolton Prize Committee of the Conference on Latin American History. She was elected to the editorial board of the *Hispanic American Historical Review* (1974–79). In 1992 she was elected an honorary life member of the Texas State Historical Association.[qv] The highest recognition of her achievements was the renaming in 1975 of the Latin American Collection in her honor by the University of Texas Board of Regents shortly after her retirement. At this time, she began the endowment of the Nettie Lee Benson Library Fund for the purchase of rare materials for the Benson Collection. Miss Benson was also president of the Fourth International Conference of United States and Mexican Historians (1973) and a recipient of the Order of the Aztec Eagle (1979), the highest official decoration given to non-Mexicans by Mexico. She received honors from the Southwestern Council on Latin American Studies (1968-69), the UT-Austin Institute of Latin American Studies (1973), the Casa de Cultura Americana (1974), the Conference on Latin American History (1976), the Seminar on the Acquisition of Latin American Library Materials (1977), the Texas House of Representatives (1977), the UT-Austin Ex-Students' Association (1981), the UT-Austin Graduate School (1984), the office of the UT president (1986), and the UT College of Liberal

Arts (1990). She died of natural causes at age eighty-eight in Austin on June 23, 1993.

BIBLIOGRAPHY: Austin *American-Statesman,* June 25, 1993. "Nettie Lee Benson: A Legend in Her Time," *ILAS Newsletter,* Winter 1990. Vertical Files, Barker Texas History Center, University of Texas at Austin. *Laura Gutiérrez-Witt*

BENT CREEK. Bent Creek rises in northeastern Hutchinson County (at 35°58′ N, 101°16′ W) and flows south for eight miles to its mouth on the Canadian River, eleven miles northeast of Plemons (at 35°'54 N, 101°'07 W). It crosses an area of flat to rolling plains and sandy and clayey soils, where the vegetation consists mainly of mesquite shrubs and grasses. Bent Creek was named for William Bent, of the Bent, St. Vrain, and Company trading firm, which operated from 1832 until 1849 and in 1843 built the short-lived trading house that gave Adobe Walls its name. It was also the site of the first battle of Adobe Walls[qv] in November 1864. The creek is on the Turkey Track Ranch.[qv]

BIBLIOGRAPHY: Pauline D. and R. L. Robertson, *Cowman's Country: Fifty Frontier Ranches in the Texas Panhandle, 1876–1887* (Amarillo: Paramount, 1981).

BENTON, BENJAMIN FRANKLIN (1827–1862). Benjamin Franklin Benton, editor and soldier, was born on April 29, 1827, in Carrol County, Tennessee, the son of Mary (Hunter) and Samuel L. Benton, Sr.[qv] At about the age of eleven he moved to Texas with his parents and settled in Sabine County. After his father's term as a representative in the Fourth Congress (1839–40), the Bentons moved into neighboring San Augustine County. Benton received his degree at the Wesleyan Male and Female College on July 31, 1845. In 1850 he and B. F. Price became copublishers of the Redland *Herald,* and in 1857 and 1858 they published the *East Texian.* Benton received his Masonic degrees in the Redland Lodge No. 3, where he served as junior warden in 1854 and worshipful master in 1855. He was a three-term elected district clerk of San Augustine from 1854 until 1861. At the outbreak of the Civil War[qv] in 1861, he organized a company of 114 volunteers and became captain of Company K, First Texas Infantry, in Hood's Brigade,[qv] known as the Texas Invincibles and attached to the Army of Northern Virginia. The war took a heavy toll on Company K; in addition to battle casualties, many men, including Benton's brother Jesse, died of measles or chicken pox. On June 27, 1862, Captain Benton fell at the head of his command in the battle of Gaines' Mill, in defense of Richmond, at Cold Harbor, Virginia. He was buried on the battlefield and reinterred on January 18, 1867, with Masonic honors, in the San Augustine City Cemetery near the graves of his parents and brother.

BIBLIOGRAPHY: George L. Crocket, *Two Centuries in East Texas* (Dallas: Southwest, 1932; facsimile reprod., 1962). O. T. Hanks, *History of Captain B. F. Benton's Company, Hood's Texas Brigade, 1861–1865* (Austin: Morrison, 1984). *McXie Whitton Martin*

BENTON, SAMUEL L., SR. (1786–1846). Samuel Benton, Sr., Republic of Texas[qv] congressman, was born in 1786 in Hillsboro, Orange County, North Carolina, the son of Jesse and Ann "Nancy" (Gooch) Benton. He was the brother of Thomas Hart Benton, United States Senator from Missouri from 1821 to 1851, and the father of Benjamin Franklin Benton.[qv] Samuel Benton was married March 21, 1808, to Mary Hunter, born in 1792. The ceremony was performed in Williamson County, Tennessee, the place of her birth. Benton served in the War of 1812 as a first sergeant in the Tennessee Militia. He returned to Williamson County at the end of the war in 1815 and remained there until 1826, when he moved his family to Carroll County, Tennessee.

He moved to Texas in January 1836 from Missouri. He and his wife, four of their children, and his brother Jesse, Jr., settled in San Augustine. Samuel Benton received a headright certificate for a league and a labor now in Sabine County. In the fall of 1836 he joined Capt. Thomas H. Barron's[qv] Company B, Texas Rangers,[qv] which was commissioned on November 1 and discharged on December 31, 1836. Benton represented Sabine County in the House of Representatives of the Fourth Congress, where he served on the finance, public lands, public printing, and claims and accounts committees. In 1840 the census listed him as owner of eight slaves and 4,615 acres. By 1841 the Bentons were residents of San Augustine County, Texas. Benton died on September 28, 1846, and was buried in the San Augustine City Cemetery. He was survived by his wife and nine children. Six of their sons served in the Civil War,[qv] and only two survived. Mary died in 1865 and was buried beside her husband.

BIBLIOGRAPHY: Daughters of the Republic of Texas, *Muster Rolls of the Texas Revolution* (Austin, 1986). Mary Smith Fay, *War of 1812 Veterans in Texas* (New Orleans: Polyanthos, 1979). Louis Wiltz Kemp Papers, Barker Texas History Center, University of Texas at Austin. Alma Cheek Redden, *A Chronicle of Pioneer Families: The Bentons and the Taylors of the North Carolina Backcountry* (Greensboro, North Carolina: Acme Printing and Typesetting Company, 1969). Harriet Smither, ed., *Journals of the Fourth Congress of the Republic of Texas, 1839–1840, to Which Are Added the Relief Laws* (3 vols., Austin: Von Boeckmann–Jones, n.d.). Texas House of Representatives, *Biographical Directory of the Texan Conventions and Congresses, 1832–1845* (Austin: Book Exchange, 1941). Gifford E. White, ed., *The 1840 Census of the Republic of Texas* (Austin: Pemberton, 1966; 2d ed., Vol. 2 of *1840 Citizens of Texas,* Austin, 1984). *McXie Whitton Martin*

BENTON, TEXAS. Benton, also known as Benton City, was on Atascosa Creek twenty-five miles northwest of Jourdanton in Atascosa County. Its site is within the current city limits of Lytle. Benton was settled in 1876 and had a post office from that year to 1929. The community may have been named for Thomas Hart Benton, a senator from Missouri and friend of Sam Houston,[qv] or for Samuel L. Benton,[qv] who fought in the Texas Revolution,[qv] or for one of his sons, who settled on land inherited from his father in the area. In 1878 Benton had a Masonic hall, a newspaper called the Benton City *Era,* and a school called Benton City Institute. In 1879 the residents tried to form their own county, but were thwarted by the residents of Medina and Bexar counties whose land they wanted to appropriate. The town was bypassed by the International–Great Northern Railroad in 1881, and the population dropped to fifty by 1884. By 1904 it had rebounded to 308, and in 1914 it had dropped to 200. A gristmill–gin, three churches (Baptist, Methodist, and Christian), at least one general store, a blacksmith shop, and several cattle-breeding services operated in the town and surrounding ranch community during those years. In 1904 the local public school had seventy-five students and two teachers. In 1914 the school had 104 students. The high school was consolidated with the Lytle school district in 1919, and by 1925 the population of Benton had dropped to fifty. The elementary school closed in 1934. After 1956 only the ruins of the Benton City Institute and the Masonic hall marked the site.

BIBLIOGRAPHY: *Atascosa County Centennial, 1856–1956* (Jourdanton, Texas: Atascosa County Centennial Association, n.d). *Atascosa County History* (Pleasanton, Texas: Atascosa History Committee, 1984). Margaret G. Clover, The Place Names of Atascosa County (M.A. thesis, University of Texas, 1952). *Linda Peterson*

BENTON CITY INSTITUTE. Benton City Institute, originally known as Benton City Normal Institute, was founded in 1876 and located on the ground floor of the Masonic building in Benton. The school, first run by Col. John D. Morrison, offered accounting, law, music, and surveying, plus basic academic subjects. It was funded partially by the state, though it was a private institution. The remainder of its funding came from tuition. By 1878 the institute was coeducational and owned and run by Professor and Mrs. Bernard C. Hendrix, formerly of Kentucky. When the Masons moved to Lytle in 1909, the institute expanded to utilize the entire building. The school was renamed Benton School in 1889 and Old Rock School in 1910. The institution ceased to exist when the Benton schools were consolidated with those of Lytle in 1919. A state historical marker was erected at the ruins of the building in 1971.

BIBLIOGRAPHY: *Atascosa County History* (Pleasanton, Texas: Atascosa History Committee, 1984). Margaret G. Clover, The Place Names of Atascosa County (M.A. thesis, University of Texas, 1952).

Linda Peterson

BENTON CREEK. Benton Creek rises six miles north of Medina in north central Bandera County (at 29°53′ N, 99°14′ W) and runs south for five miles across an area of the Edwards Plateau characterized by steep slopes and limestone benches to its mouth on the Medina River, a mile north of Medina (at 29°49′ N, 99°16′ W). Forests of live oak and Ashe juniper become interspersed with open areas of varied grasses and prickly pear as the stream descends toward its junction with the river.

BENTONVILLE, TEXAS. Bentonville is on State Highway 44 seven miles east of Alice in east central Jim Wells County. A post office established there in 1910 operated until 1932. Bentonville was named for an early settler. By 1914 the community had a population of fifty, two general stores, a cotton gin, and a blacksmith. A stop on the Texas-Mexican Railway was also established there that year. By 1936 the town had only scattered dwellings and farm units. In 1949 it had a population of twenty and one business. The population remained constant in the 1950s and 1960s and decreased to fifteen in 1974. In 1979 the community had scattered dwellings, a windmill, an oil well, and was a stop on the Texas-Mexican Railway. In 1990 the population was still fifteen. *Alicia A. Garza*

BENTSEN, LLOYD MILLARD, SR. (1894–1989). Lloyd M. Bentsen, Sr., businessman, one of six children born in a 7½-year period to Niels Peter and Tena (Peterson) Bentsen, was born on November 24, 1894, in Argo Township, near White and Brookings, South Dakota, just west of the Minnesota state line. His father had immigrated from Denmark to farm. The family experienced many typical adversities of homesteading on the prairie frontier—fire, which destroyed their first dwelling and belongings, crop failure, harsh winters, sparse medical care, and hostility against Scandinavian immigrants. Lloyd Bentsen lived on the family homestead until World War I.[qv] He ceased schooling at thirteen years and worked for local farmers at harvesting and roping and taming mustangs.[qv] He also cultivated a youthful dedication to motorcycles and high-speed adventure thereon. He survived a cycle accident on a muddy farm road that left him with a partially severed foot and severe body lacerations, but sufficiently well to enlist at the beginning of World War I in the United States Signal Corps for aviator training at Kelly Field, San Antonio. His brother Elmer enlisted in the navy and went through the war on the second battleship *Texas.*[qv] In Texas during training Lloyd met and married Edna Ruth Colbath, known thereafter as Dolly. Bentsen and his wife joined his parents, who heeded medical advice and moved from South Dakota to Sharyland, Texas, an irrigated citrus and vegetable utopia envisioned by John H. Shary[qv] and developed by him near Mission. On November 5, 1918, the Bentsens left their homestead and began driving the 1,675 miles to the Rio Grande valley by car. They drove for seventeen days. The family arrived penniless. Peter Bentsen rented a place in Mission and began working as a land agent for John Shary. He also began a nursery-seedling business and sent out a call to the family for help. Lloyd, Sr., and Elmer mustered out of the military after the Armistice and responded to that message. A Bentsen beachhead was thus established in Texas. All saved diligently and invested in Valley[qv] land as soon as they could.

Lloyd and Elmer Bentsen became the premier colonizers and developers of Hidalgo County, which led all counties of the United States in cotton production and raised a good part of the Valley's 1948 $100 million citrus and vegetable crop. In 1952 the county centennial program described the contribution of Lloyd and Elmer's stake in the county's economic development. The Pride O Texas citrus trademark contributed substantially to the fortune that the Bentsen family began amassing. Elmer and Lloyd were principals in the Elsa State Bank, Elmer a president and director and Lloyd on the board of directors. Lloyd was also a principal in the First National banks of McAllen, Mission, Edinburg, Raymondville, and Brownsville. He served as president of the Rio Grande Valley Chamber of Commerce from 1944 to 1946 and was instrumental in uniting and developing Cameron, Hidalgo, Starr, and Willacy counties. Later in life he became sensitive to preserving the natural environment of the Valley and donated land that became the Bentsen–Rio Grande Valley State Scenic Park.[qv]

Bentsen did not accumulate land and monetary fortunes without problems. In 1952–55 he had courtroom difficulties in Texas and Washington, D.C., over land sales. He was accused by five plaintiffs of conspiracy and fraud in the sale of Ramsmeyer Gardens, supposedly irrigated land fit for citrus, and one plaintiff wanted back acreage in Minnesota that he had traded to Bentsen for his share in the land venture. Bentsen himself testified that he had sold the land in question to Homer F. Ramsmeyer, and that all sales thereafter were not of his doing. Federal district judge James Allred[qv] ruled that the Bentsen Group, consisting of the Bentsen Brothers, G. F. Dorn, Bentsen Brothers, Incorporated, and the Rio Grande Development Company, having been cleared by jury of a conspiracy, were derivatively clear of fraud. In another land dispute, buyers of Valley lands from the Bentsen Group claimed that the sellers had failed to maintain and tend citrus plantings, as they were required to do by the original purchase transaction. In 1951 a severe freeze had wiped out many Valley orchards. "This freeze did produce a bumper crop of litigation," said Paul A. Porter, attorney for Bentsen before the Supreme Court of the United States. Bentsen later recalled that there were "15, 16, 17 suits altogether, a lot of them." No fraud was ever found, although damages of $5,000 to one plaintiff were later mandated by the court. Bentsen gradually moved out of Valley land development and invested $7 million in organizing an insurance and financial holding company in Houston. Lloyd Bentsen, Jr., was the chief executive of this Houston entity until he ran for the United States Senate in 1971, at which time it was sold for $22 million.

In 1959 Bentsen was promoted to major general in the Texas State Guard[qv] Reserve Corps by Governor Allan Shivers.[qv] If the Texas National Guard were called to duties outside the Texas borders, Bentsen's units were to replace the absent guardsmen.

The Bentsen family was a tightly knit group, as first-generation immigrant families tended to be. The men disdained publicity, especially personal publicity. They respected the past, particularly the sacrifices of the earliest Bentsens. In the Hidalgo County Centennial Historical Program a full-page tribute to Peter and Tena Bentsen read, "Like many others, they pioneered in another section and then came here to repeat a venture that began with a vision and demanded fortitude, self reliance and enterprise to complete." Bentsen and his wife had four children, one of whom, Lloyd Bentsen, Jr., was a congressman, a United States senator, a vice-presidential candidate, and secretary of the treasury. Lloyd Bentsen, Sr., died at the age of ninety-five on January 17, 1989, in an automobile accident in Edinburg.

BIBLIOGRAPHY: Lloyd M. Bentsen Papers, Barker Texas History Center, University of Texas at Austin. Fort Worth *Star-Telegram,* February 27, 1952. Hidalgo County Centennial Corporation, *The Centennial Celebration of the Organization of Hidalgo County in Texas* (Mission, Texas: Times Publishing Company, 1952). Joan R. Sloan Johnson, *The Bentsen Family: From Denmark to Texas* (Austin: Hart Graphics, 1985). New York *Times,* January 18, 1989. Vertical Files, Barker Texas History Center, University of Texas at Austin.

Howard Lackman

BENTSEN–RIO GRANDE VALLEY STATE SCENIC PARK. Bentsen–Rio Grande Valley State Scenic Park, a 588-acre park on the Rio Grande six miles west of Mission in Hidalgo County, was acquired by the state in 1944. The park is a favorite spot for bird watchers. It has many rare specimens, including Lichenstein's oriole, hooded oriole, gray hawk, pauraque, groove-billed ani, longbilled thrasher, green jay, kiskadee flycatcher, and red-eyed cowbird.

BIBLIOGRAPHY: Vertical files, Barker Texas History Center, University of Texas at Austin.

BENVANUE, TEXAS. Benvanue was on the banks of Bailey Creek near the Jefferson county line in northeastern Clay County. The settlement began at a ferry in 1869, and the community became a focal point for nearby settlers. Within the next few years a semiweekly newspaper, a number of businesses, a school, and a stage line connecting Benvanue with Henrietta, seventeen miles to the south, served the fifty residents. In 1876 postal service to the community began. By the late 1890s the population of the town was estimated to be 100. Just after the turn of the twentieth century officials of the Texas and Oklahoma Railroad decided to bypass Benvanue and run the rail line through Byers, three miles to the west. Once the decision was announced, residents and businesses abandoned Benvanue and moved to Byers. Postal service to Benvanue was transferred to Byers in 1904. By 1910 there were few buildings and fewer residents in Benvanue. The school building remained standing until the 1940s, but by 1984 no trace of the community remained on county maps.

BIBLIOGRAPHY: William Charles Taylor, *A History of Clay County* (Austin: Jenkins, 1972).

David Minor

BEN WHEELER, TEXAS. Ben Wheeler is on State Highway 64 and Farm roads 279 and 858 twelve miles southeast of Canton in southeast central Van Zandt County. The community is surrounded by springs in rich farming country that was originally part of Henderson County. The site, probably settled in the 1840s, had a post office by 1876 and was named for Kentucky native Benjamin F. Wheeler, who arrived from New Orleans around 1847 and obtained a grant of 640 acres at Creagleville, near Grand Saline. Wheeler carried the mail from Tyler to Buffalo by Jordan's Saline, and residents submitted his name when they made application for a post office in 1878. In the early 1880s George Claugh built a general store, a schoolhouse, and a church one mile east of the present townsite and applied to move the post office and change the name to Georgetown. The effort failed. The community is sometimes called Clough, probably an error for Claugh. In 1888 Ben Wheeler had three churches, a district school, saw and grist mills, two syrup mills, cotton gins, and a general store.

The Alamo Institute, a local coeducational boarding school established by J. F. Davidson in 1891, had an enrollment of 142 in 1903. Before 1893, when a fire destroyed most of its structures, Ben Wheeler had seven stores, three gin-and-mill combinations, boarding houses, two churches, and the Berry Resort Hotel. In 1896 the population was 500, but a smallpox epidemic reduced the residents to 238 by 1904, when school enrollment was 163. A grocery store was established at Ben Wheeler in 1905, and in 1919 the town had a bank, a school, two churches, two cotton gins, a corn mill, the weekly *Headlight,* and an annual fair. With the growth of the nearby Van oilfield, hotels and dance halls opened. The population reached 375 in 1933. During the 1930s the cotton market fell, and many local farmers turned to truck farming. Businesses expanded to eighteen by 1943, dwindled to nine by 1972, and rose to twenty-two by 1988. Many farmers turned to cattle raising in the 1960s. The community was incorporated with 400 residents in 1962, and the school was consolidated with the Van Independent School District in 1966. The reported 1964 and 1990 population was 400. In 1984 Ben Wheeler had two churches, a school, several businesses, and a population of 250. The Prairie Springs and Asbury cemeteries are located nearby.

BIBLIOGRAPHY: Wentworth Manning, *Some History of Van Zandt County* (Des Moines, Iowa: Homestead, 1919; rpt., Winston-Salem, North Carolina: Hunter, 1977). William Samuel Mills, *History of Van Zandt County* (Canton, Texas, 1950). Van Zandt County History Book Committee, *History of Van Zandt County* (Dallas, 1984). Victoria *Advocate,* July 14, 1984.

Diana J. Kleiner

BÉRANGER, JEAN (1685–?). Jean Béranger, a Breton sea captain in service of Governor Jean Baptiste Le Moyne de Bienville and of the French Company of the Indies, was born at La Rochelle in 1685. Bienville was master of the *Neptune* in 1716 and sailed up the Mississippi as far as the site of New Orleans before turning back because of dangerous flooding and floating logs. Each year fleets of warships were sent from France to defend Louisiana from Spain. War broke out in early 1719, and Béranger participated in the assault and taking of Pensacola on May 14. The Spaniards counterattacked in August 1719, captured the small French garrison, and took them to Havana as prisoners. Pensacola was recaptured by the French on October 16. Béranger was ordered to take the Spanish prisoners to Havana because the French had insufficient food to feed them. In some manner unattested by documentary sources, Béranger was able to unload the Spanish prisoners at Havana and depart with his ship without being captured by the Spaniards.

When the French found the war was over in May 1720, Bienville ordered Béranger to explore the Bay of St. Bernard and look for a suitable site for colonization. Béranger took an old Spanish ship, renamed *St. Joseph,* that had been captured at Pensacola for the expedition, and his voyage resulted in the discovery of Aransas Pass, Texas. His description of St. Joseph and Mustang islands, Live Oak Point, and the language and customs of the Karankawa Indians remains the most authentic, definitive published account.

BIBLIOGRAPHY: Hubert Howe Bancroft, *History of the North Mexican States and Texas* (2 vols., San Francisco: History Company, 1886, 1889). Benjamin Franklin French, *Historical Collections of Louisiana* (New York: Wiley and Putnam, etc., 1846–53; rpt., New York: AMS Press, 1976). Marcel Giraud, *Histoire de la Louisiane Français* (Paris: Presses Universitaires de France, 1953; trans. by Joseph C. Lambert, rev. and corr. by the author, Baton Rouge: Louisiana State University Press, 1974). Jack D. L. Holmes, "Dauphin Island in the Franco-Spanish War, 1719–22," in *Frenchmen and French Ways in the Mississippi Valley,* ed. John Francis McDermott (Urbana: University of Illinois Press, 1969). Pierre Margry, ed., *Découvertes et établissements des Français dans l'ouest et dans le sud de l'Amérique septentrionale, 1614–1754* (6 vols., Paris: Jouast, 1876–86). *Memoire des Cognoissances que de Sieur Béranger . . .* (MS, Archives Nationales de France). Frank Wagner, ed., and William M. Carroll, trans., *Béranger's Discovery of Aransas Pass* (Friends of the Corpus Christi Museum, 1983).

Frank Wagner

BERCLAIR, TEXAS. Berclair, on U.S. Highway 59 sixteen miles from Goliad in southwestern Goliad County, was established as a shipping point on the Gulf, Western Texas and Pacific rail line to serve an already well-populated ranching area. On December 10, 1889, Joseph Blackburn paid the railroad company $100 as a bonus for building through Goliad County and donated right-of-way through the southern corner of his ranch. A post office was established in 1889, along with a depot and stock pens. A hotel built at the site in 1887 to board the railroad workers later accommodated passengers from the daily train between Victoria and Beeville. In 1892 Berclair had a steam cotton gin, a saloon, a weekly newspaper called the *Blossom,* and eighteen other businesses serving an estimated 200 residents. For a while the Baptist church building was used by other Protestant groups, but by 1914 Methodist and Catholic churches had been built. The population and number of businesses declined in the early twentieth century; the saloon was closed by local law in 1910. By the 1920s, however, about 300 people were living in Berclair, which had twenty businesses and was designated a banking town in 1929 and 1931. The number of businesses began to dwindle; the population remained stable for a while at 350, until the 1970 census recorded a decline to sixty-one residents and two businesses. Berclair was named either by the railroad surveyor after his home in Virginia or after the given names of Bert and Clair Lucas, owners of a nearby ranch. In the mid-1980s the settlement still supplied surrounding ranches. In 1986 the post office served sixty-one residents. In 1990 the population was seventy.

BIBLIOGRAPHY: Goliad County Historical Commission, *The History and Heritage of Goliad County,* ed. Jakie L. Pruett and Everett B. Cole (Austin: Eakin Press, 1983). *Craig H. Roell*

BEREA, TEXAS (Bell County). Berea was a post office and school community on Farm Road 2483 five miles north of Belton in central Bell County. The settlement, named for a biblical Middle Eastern city, began in 1868 when pioneers from Georgia purchased land and built log cabins in the fertile area on Pepper's Creek. A one-room house provided a place for the community gatherings, school, and worship. Rev. Roder Bauchman was the first teacher and preacher. The post office opened in 1895, was consolidated with Belton for a time in 1897, and was consolidated permanently with Belton in 1902. The Berea school had sixty-four pupils and one teacher in 1903. In 1948 the community consisted of a school, a church, and scattered dwellings, but Berea had disappeared from the state highway map by 1988.

BIBLIOGRAPHY: Bell County Historical Commission, *Story of Bell County, Texas* (2 vols., Austin: Eakin Press, 1988). *Mark Odintz*

BEREA, TEXAS (Houston County). Berea (Beria), at the junction of State Highway 7 and Farm Road 232 eight miles east of Crockett in east central Houston County, was established before 1900. In the mid-1930s the settlement had two churches, several stores, a cemetery, and a number of houses. After World War II[qv] many of the residents moved away, but in the mid-1960s the community still had a church, a cemetery, and a number of houses. In the early 1990s Berea was a dispersed rural community.

BIBLIOGRAPHY: Houston County Historical Commission, *History of Houston County, Texas, 1687–1979* (Tulsa, Oklahoma: Heritage, 1979). *Houston County Cemeteries* (Crockett, Texas: Houston County Historical Commission, 1977; 3d ed. 1987). *Christopher Long*

BEREA, TEXAS (Marion County). Berea is on Farm Road 728 four miles northwest of Jefferson in central Marion County. It was founded as a Seventh-Day Adventist colony about 1914. In 1962 the community had a Seventh-Day Adventist church, a cemetery, a number of dwellings, and the Jefferson Rural Academy, an Adventist school. Berea had a population of 142 in the 1960s and seventy-four in the 1970s. In 1989 Jefferson Seventh-Day Adventist Academy had approximately forty pupils, and the community had a grocery store, a church, an elementary school, a number of homes, and a population estimated by one local resident at 250. The official count in 1990 was seventy-four. *Mark Odintz*

BERETTA, SALLIE WARD (1873–1964). Sallie Ward Beretta, clubwoman and civic leader, was born in 1873 in Austin, Texas, to John R. and Louisa (Hartsook) Ward, who were originally from Virginia. After attending Beechcroft College in Tennessee (1888–90) and the University of Texas (1891–93), she married banker John King Beretta of San Antonio, on December 9, 1896. The couple had one child.

Mrs. Beretta's official involvement in public affairs began in 1912, when she was appointed by President Woodrow Wilson to a four-year term as state chairman of the High Cost of Living Campaign. In World War I[qv] she volunteered for the Red Cross and worked at army hospitals. Throughout the 1920s and 1930s she held numerous San Antonio civic positions, including the presidencies of the City Federation of Women's Clubs and the San Antonio Council of Girl Scouts. Her involvement in these two groups led to her collecting bluebonnet seeds with Girl Scouts and then launching a campaign through the federated clubs to distribute them for planting on Texas roadsides and areas outside the state. This endeavor earned her the nickname "Bluebonnet Lady." Also as president of the Federation of Women's Clubs she pushed for improving the quality of motion pictures for children while making the prices more affordable. Later, when she served as state chairman of the Texas Federation of Women's Clubs[qv] Motion Pictures Committee, she organized a Woman's Day that featured benefit shows at theaters across the state. The visibility and success of her work through the federated clubs led to her being asked to run for mayor and senator, offers that she declined. She did, however, accept a position as president of the board of directors of the Witte Museum[qv] Association in San Antonio; she was the first woman to hold this position. She also served on the San Antonio planning board and charter-revision committee in the 1920s. She was vice president of the Broadway National Bank for a number of years and served on the board of directors of the First National Bank.

Mrs. Beretta was named to the board of regents of state teachers' colleges in 1933 and served for eighteen years, during which she was usually the only woman on the board. She was selected to chair the committee overseeing Southwest Texas State Teachers College (now Southwest Texas State University) in San Marcos for twelve years. In 1947 her fellow members voted to name a women's dormitory at Southwest Texas in her honor. She presented the school with a gift of 125 acres on the Blanco River near Wimberley in 1951.

Sallie Beretta's other civic work included membership in the Colonial Dames of America,[qv] the San Antonio History Club, the Housewives League of San Antonio, the United Daughters of the Confederacy,[qv] the National Board of the Girl Scouts, the Women's Democratic Committee, and the Daughters of the Republic of Texas.[qv] In 1950 she contributed money to the DRT to assist in establishing a library at the Alamo. She lived in San Antonio throughout her adult life and died there on November 27, 1964.

BIBLIOGRAPHY: San Antonio *Express,* November 28, 1964. San Antonio *Light,* May 3, 1981. "Texas Women: A Celebration of History" Archives, Texas Woman's University, Denton. Vertical files, Barker Texas History Center, University of Texas at Austin. Who's Who of American Women. *Debbie Mauldin Cottrell*

BERGER BLUFF. Berger Bluff is a sandy bluff, 8.7 meters high, on the Goliad County side of Coleto Creek west of Victoria. The entire bluff (now inundated by Coleto Creek Reservoir) apparently has stratified prehistoric Indian occupations, although the middle 4.5 meters has never been sampled. The upper deposits were excavated in 1977, 1979, and 1983, the lower deposits in 1979–80. Most excavation in the upper deposits was concentrated in a three-by-four-meter block about 2.5 meters deep. Here, chiefly in the upper forty-five centimeters, Late Prehistoric artifacts and animal remains from the Toyah Phase (radiocarbon dated elsewhere in south Texas at A.D. 1300–1600) and the Austin Phase (about A.D. 800–1300) were found. Toyah Phase artifacts include Perdiz arrow points and preforms, a few pieces of plain bone-tempered pottery, a core, and preforms for thinned bifaces. Austin Phase artifacts include Scallorn arrow points, Darl points, thinned bifaces, and a core. Snail and freshwater mussel shells are found throughout but are especially abundant in the Austin

Phase midden, where at least seven species of mussels and nine of land snails were found. Most of the mussel shells are atypically small, suggesting that frequent washouts due to flooding of Coleto Creek may have prevented mussels from reaching maturity. Vertebrates (about four dozen kinds) are also abundant in both of these Late Prehistoric phases and include gar, white-tailed deer, pocket gopher, eastern mole, eastern cottontail, cotton rat, soft-shell turtle, wood rat, red-eared turtle, jackrabbit, opossum, Western diamondback rattlesnake, bison, and many other kinds of mammals, reptiles, birds, and fish.

Below these Late Prehistoric occupations, samples were taken from two meters of Archaic sediments. The upper part, apparently Late Archaic, contains a few Ensor (dated elsewhere at about 200 B.C. to A.D. 600) and Morhiss dart points, along with other thinned bifaces, biface preforms, cores, hammerstones, ground sandstone, modified flakes, chipping debris, snails, and mussel shells. Very little animal bone survives in these older deposits, only white-tailed deer and fish having been recognized. Features of probable Archaic age include two small clusters of fire-cracked sandstone and a small pit with dark fill. The lower part of the excavation block has sparse cultural debris and mussel and snail shell of unknown age, perhaps Middle Archaic.

Separated from the bottom of the bluff-top excavation block by 4.5 meters of unexcavated sediments and exposed at the foot of Berger Bluff in the form of a prominent ledge or bench were 2.25 meters of cyclically bedded early Holocene Coleto Creek floodplain deposits, apparently cemented by alkaline groundwater from a nearby spring (though no actual spring conduit was located). By the Late Prehistoric, the creek began rapidly incising the several meters of floodplain deposits that had accumulated, leaving a resistant ledge when it encountered these locally cemented deposits. The weighted average of eight radiocarbon assays from the bench deposits is 9564 ± 43 B.P. (B.P. = before A.D. 1950), but it is likely that the span of time represented by the bench deposits is much longer than implied by this single average age.

The bench excavations, consisting of eight one-square-meter units of varying depth, produced sparse cultural evidence: chipping debris (including that from a chipping area), cores, a few introduced pebbles, a small triangular biface reject, and three cultural features (two small pits and the hearth mentioned above), but no diagnostic artifacts. These deposits, however, provide an early Holocene paleoenvironmental record unequaled in the region. The record suggests that by about 8000–10000 B.P., the upland landscape between the drainages in this part of the coastal plain had already taken on an essentially Holocene biotic composition. Coleto Creek, however, retained vestiges of its cooler and wetter Pleistocene ecology and served as a refuge for fauna (especially invertebrates), and possibly for flora as well.

Three species of very small snails now extirpated in South Texas were extracted by flotation and identified. *Valvata tricarinata*, an aquatic snail now ranging from Oklahoma or Nebraska north to Canada, prefers such deep, cool water as Nebraska springwaters (15° C; modern Coleto Creek water ranges from 17° C in February to 30° in July). *Pomatiopsis lapidaria*, an amphibious snail, prefers marshes with grass, sedges, and cattails in the eastern United States and plains as far south as Kansas. *Gastrocopta armifera* is a land snail that in North Texas lives in decaying logs and under leaf litter. Altogether over thirty taxa of snails, many of them microscopic in size, were identified in the bench deposits; some species tolerate well-drained open woodlands or savanna habitats, but many inhabit leaf litter in wooded floodplains or are wetland or aquatic species. In contrast to the upper deposits, few mussel shells were found in the lower. Most were *Amblema plicata* valves lying flat on a buried floodplain surface. All of the bench mussels, however, were conspicuously larger than their Late Prehistoric counterparts from the upper deposits, a fact that suggests flash flooding was not yet common in the very early Holocene. Particle-size, carbonate, and organic-carbon analyses of a column of twenty-eight sediment samples suggest that the early Holocene creek was very different from its modern counterpart. flowing in a broader, flatter, more heavily vegetated floodplain, it was narrower, deeper, more sinuous, and muddier than the modern creek, and lacked its contemporary propensity for flash flooding.

Next to the small hearth already mentioned, a remarkable deposit of several thousand bone fragments from small animals was found. Some of the bone was found on the hearth surface, but only a few fragments were charred. The deposit consists of the remains of various small animals: eastern mole, frog, gopher, smallmouth salamander, small perching birds, pocket mouse, fish (perch-sized), prairie vole or pine vole, kangaroo rat, least shrew, rabbit, wood rat, field mouse, northern grasshopper mouse, toad, small snakes, and lizards. A juvenile rabbit is the largest animal. Nothing approaching this density of bone was found elsewhere in the bench deposits. Laboratory extraction of lipids from sediment samples showed that the hearth was much higher in fatty acids, especially those characteristic of animal tissue. Extreme clustering of the bone indicates the fauna was concentrated in the digestive tract of a predator. At least two distinct assemblages occur: aquatic-riparian species that probably collected in or around the creek and spring itself; and a sandy grassland (upland or floodplain) assemblage featuring fossorial rodents. Two behavioral groups are evident: the first, active both day and night (usually living in burrows, sometimes in thickets or debris), would be vulnerable to all kinds of predators. The second is nocturnal and fossorial. Venturing out at night to forage, these would be vulnerable to owls but not hawks, and especially to humans, since they are confined to burrows during the day. The mole, for example, rarely ventures above ground and is only occasionally taken by owls. In general, this is a cryptic or reclusive fauna, composed of small and inconspicuous animals with a wide range of adaptations; aquatic, aerial, terrestrial, and terrestrial-fossorial habits are represented, indicating that the Berger Bluff predator foraged successfully in a diversity of habitats and coped with a diversity of prey habits. This kind of flexibility is distinctly human. The vertebrate fauna is typically Holocene, although there are a few species not found in the immediate vicinity today.

The concentration of this bone deposit suggests fecal remains. The diversity of prey behaviors and habitats, the extensive breakage (indicating mastication), proximity to the hearth, and partial charring of some of the bones all seem to indicate the predator was human. The deposit may well represent a very early broad-spectrum foraging pattern exemplified at Baker Cave and Horn Shelter No. 2[qqv] (Texas), Medicine Lodge Creek (Wyoming), the Stigenwalt site (Kansas), and perhaps Shawnee Minisink (Pennsylvania). Similar prey were often captured by task groups of women and children in ethnographically known societies.

BIBLIOGRAPHY: David O. Brown, *The Berger Bluff Site (41GD30A): Excavations in the Upper Deposits* (University of Texas at San Antonio Center for Archaeological Research, Archaeological Survey Report 115, 1979). Kenneth M. Brown, *Archaeological Survey and Backhoe Testing for Flume No. 3 Right-of-Way at Coleto Creek Reservoir, Goliad County, Texas* (University of Texas at San Antonio Center for Archaeological Research, Archaeological Survey Report 128, 1986). Anne A. Fox et al., *Intensive Survey and Testing of Archaeological Sites on Coleto Creek, Victoria and Goliad Counties, Texas* (University of Texas at San Antonio Center for Archaeological Research, Archaeological Survey Report 67, 1979).

Kenneth M. Brown

BERGHEIM, TEXAS. Bergheim ("Mountain Home"), a German immigrant community, is on State Highway 46 and Farm Road 316 ten miles northeast of Boerne in far southeastern Kendall County. Austrian-born Andreas Engel immigrated to Texas in 1885 to avoid military service. In 1887 Casper Seltenfuss (Sültenfuss) hired Engel to cut the native cedars on his property on the Guadalupe River. At this time cedar was used for fence building and was burned to produced charcoal. Engel and his new wife purchased land from Seltenfuss and built their first general store. In 1900 Engel sold his store and bought three acres of land at the site of present Bergheim. A cotton gin was erected and began operation on September 15, 1900. The post office opened, and Engel became postmaster in 1901. The Bergheim post office became a rural branch of the Boerne post office in 1965 and was still operating in 1990. Cotton, charcoal, cedar, and corn were the means of livelihood for Bergheim and the surrounding area. A new store was built from limestone quarried nearby in 1903. In 1907 a house was built adjoining the store. In 1916 Rudolph and Alfred Engel succeeded their father in the business; Rudolph managed the cotton gin, and Alfred handled the store and post office. Cotton ginning came to an abrupt end with the onslaught of the boll weevil.[qv] The gin was afterward used to grind cornmeal. At this time cedar again became the chief source of income for the area, and Bergheim was said to operate the largest cedar yard in the state. Cedar posts were traded for groceries, and many cedar choppers were employed there. The sheep, goat, and cattle industries supported the community by 1950 and in 1990 were the economic backbone of the area. The store and post office have remained in the Engel family and were owned and operated by Andreas Engel's great-grandson in 1990, when the business provided fence-building supplies, feed, and dry goods, as well as the necessary grocery staples for the local ranchers. Bergheim General Store and Post Office received a state historical marker in 1983. Bergheim's population was listed as twenty-two in 1980 and 1990.

BIBLIOGRAPHY: Kendall County Historical Commission, *A History of Kendall County, Texas* (Dallas: Taylor, 1984). *Joyce M. Gass*

BERGMANN, JOSEF ARNOŠT (1797–1877). Josef Arnošt Bergmann, Czech pioneer, was born on August 13, 1797, in the village of Západov near Mladá Boleslav (Jungbunzlau) in what is now the Czech Republic, the son of Josef and Katerina (Sindelar) Bergmann. He dropped the name Josef early, perhaps to avoid conflict with his father, and used the name Arnošt or Ernst for the remainder of his life. Bergmann began training for the Catholic priesthood at Litomysl, but he left the Catholic Church to study in the Protestant theological department at Breslau, Prussia, and was ordained a minister in 1830. His first assignment was at Stroužný (today Pstražna) in the Glatz district in Poland (then called Silesia).

Bergmann married Marie Berndt on December 15, 1830, and their first six children were born at Stroužný. On October 2, 1849, he preached his last sermon there and announced his plan to move to Texas. The family embarked on the *Alexander* at Hamburg on December 20, 1849, and arrived at Galveston on March 2, 1850. They went by coastal and river steamers to San Felipe and then by oxcart to Cat Spring. The German colonists hired Bergmann as their schoolteacher and preacher. He preached their Easter service in March 1850 at Cat Spring. Bergmann bought the tract of land currently called Kollattschny Cemetery, and there preached and taught school in a small log building. A fifth Bergmann daughter was born and died in 1853, and two daughters died of yellow fever in 1855 or 1856.

Bergmann wrote a long letter back to Stroužný soon after his arrival in 1850. This letter told of the freedom to be found in Texas, the large amount of land available at cheap prices, and how he had already acquired many chickens, hogs, cows, and a horse. His letter was eventually published in the *Moravské Noviny* (*Moravian News*), and people in Moravia began to discuss plans for following the Bergmann family to the great free state of Texas. Groups of Czech families came in 1852, 1853, and 1854, and this started the waves of migration of Czech and Moravian people to Texas. Bergmann, credited by many Czech immigrants and their descendants as their reason for immigrating to Texas, was the father of the Czechs[qv] in Texas.

Bergmann preached and taught school at Cat Spring until 1871, when he moved to Corsicana to be nearer his daughters, who had married German men and moved there with the railroad. In the evening of April 6, 1877, he told his wife that he was going to die and asked her to bring his Bible, gather the family, and light the lamp. He died quietly at midnight and was buried at the Oakwood Cemetery, Corsicana. His wife died in Hempstead on September 14, 1888, and was buried alongside her husband.

BIBLIOGRAPHY: Dorothy Klumpp and Albert J. Blaha, Sr., *The Saga of Ernst Bergmann* (Houston, 1981). Clinton Machann and James W. Mendl, *Krásná Amerika: A Study of the Texas Czechs, 1851–1939* (Austin: Eakin Press, 1983). *Albert J. Blaha, Sr.*

BERG'S MILL, TEXAS. Berg's Mill (Mills) was on the San Antonio and Aransas Pass Railway near San Juan Capistrano Mission, eight miles south of downtown San Antonio in southern Bexar County. The settlement grew up around the ruined buildings of the first wool-washing mill in the area. It was named for L. S. Berg, a San Antonio promoter. A post office opened there in 1887, closed in 1890, and reopened in 1892 under the name Hellemans, after a local family. Both names were used for a time, but in later years the original name was preferred. In 1940 Berg's Mill was at the center of the Median Irrigation Project and had a population of 100. With the growth of San Antonio after World War II[qv] the community lost its separate character, and by the 1960s it was no longer shown on maps.

Minnie B. Cameron

BERGSTROM AIR FORCE BASE. Bergstrom Air Force Base, on State Highway 71 seven miles east of Austin in Travis County, was activated on September 19, 1942, as Del Valle Army Air Base. It was constructed in the summer of 1942 on 3,000 acres leased from the city of Austin. The Chisholm Trail[qv] ran through the tract. The name of the base was changed to Bergstrom Army Air Field on March 3, 1943, in honor of Capt. John A. E. Bergstrom, who was killed at Clark Field, Philippine Islands, on December 8, 1941. He was the first Austinite killed in World War II.[qv] The base was renamed Bergstrom Field on November 11, 1943, and became Bergstrom Air Force Base in December 1948. Initially, Bergstrom was the home of troop-carrier units. It was declared a permanent base after World War II and was at various times assigned to the Strategic Air Command and the Tactical Air Command. After July 1966 it was under the control of the Tactical Air Command and housed the headquarters for the Twelfth Air Force, which was responsible for all Tactical Air Command reconnaissance, fighter, and airlift operations west of the Mississippi River. The economic contribution of the base in fiscal 1989 on a fifty-mile radius was estimated to be $343 million and on Central Texas, $533 million. On September 30, 1993, Bergstrom was officially closed. That year voters approved a bond issue for the construction of an Austin airport at the base.

BIBLIOGRAPHY: *Air Force Bases: A Directory of U.S. Air Force Installations both in the Continental U.S. and Overseas, with Useful Information on Each Base and Its Nearby Community* (Harrisburg, Pennsylvania: Stackpole, 1965). Robert Mueller, *Air Force Bases*, Vol. 1: *Active Air Force Bases within the United States of America on 17 September 1982* (Washington: Office of Air Force History, 1989).

Art Leatherwood

BERING, TEXAS. Bering is on U.S. Highway 59 in central Polk County, about ninety miles north of Houston. Conrad, E. J., and W. G. Bering built a sawmill at the site in the early 1880s, after the construction of the Houston, East and West Texas Railway through Polk County opened up the area to large-scale lumber interests. A post office was established in 1906. The Bering plant, one of the long-running sawmills in the region, was managed by W. D. Winston for much of the time and operated until about 1920. After the mill closed, most of the community's residents drifted away, although about fifty remained through the 1930s.

BIBLIOGRAPHY: *A Pictorial History of Polk County, Texas, 1846–1910* (Livingston, Texas: Polk County Bicentennial Commission, 1976; rev. ed. 1978).

Robert Wooster

BERKLEY CREEK. Berkley Creek rises near U.S. Highway 287 in southeastern Donley County (34°48′ N, 100°36′ W) and flows southeast for about eight miles to its mouth on Parker Creek, just south of Memphis in northeastern Hall County (at 34°42′ N, 100°32′ W). It extends through an area of moderately steep slopes and locally high relief, surfaced with silt loams that support mesquite and grasses.

BIBLIOGRAPHY: Pauline D. and R. L. Robertson, *Cowman's Country: Fifty Frontier Ranches in the Texas Panhandle, 1876–1887* (Amarillo: Paramount, 1981).

BERLANDIER, JEAN LOUIS (ca. 1805–1851). Jean Louis Berlandier, early naturalist, was born before 1805 between Fort de l'Ècluse, France, and Geneva, Switzerland. He studied botany at the academy in Geneva and at the same time probably served an apprenticeship to a pharmacist. In 1824 his article on the gooseberries, "Grossulariaciae," was published in the *Mémoires* of the Society of Natural History of Geneva; in 1826 it was included in Auguste Pyrame DeCandolle's *Prodromus*, a book on the plants of the world.

Chosen by DeCandolle to make botanical collections in Mexico, Berlandier arrived at Pánuco, Vera Cruz, on December 15, 1826. He collected plants in that vicinity before continuing his journey to Mexico City, where he joined, as botanist, the Mexican Boundary Commission, which left Mexico City on November 10, 1827, under the command of Manuel de Mier y Terán.[qv] Berlandier made botanical collections around Laredo, Texas, in February 1828 and around San Antonio, Gonzales, and San Felipe in March, April, and May 1828. He fell ill with malaria on May 17 near the site of present Anderson and was sent back to Matamoros, Tamaulipas. He subsequently returned to San Antonio and from November 19 to December 18 accompanied an expedition under José Francisco Ruiz[qv] to explore the silver mines on the San Saba River. On February 3, 1829, he accompanied Antonio Elosúa to put down an uprising against the presidio commander at Goliad. The commission was dissolved in November 1829, and Berlandier settled at Matamoros, where he married and became a physician.

He made further botanical and animal collecting trips in Mexico and Texas, one in 1834 to Goliad. He and Rafael Chovell published *Diario de viaje de la Comisión de Límites* (1850). During the Mexican War[qv] Berlandier was in charge of the hospitals in Matamoros and served as an interpreter. He drowned in the San Fernando River near Matamoros in 1851.

BIBLIOGRAPHY: Jean Louis Berlandier, *Journey to Mexico during the Years 1826 to 1834*, trans. Sheila M. Ohlendorf et al. (2 vols., Austin: Texas State Historical Association, 1980). S. W. Geiser, *Naturalists of the Frontier* (Dallas: Southern Methodist University, 1937; 2d ed. 1948). Ohland Morton, *Terán and Texas: A Chapter in Texas Mexican Relations* (Austin: Texas State Historical Association, 1948)

Clinton P. Hartmann

BERLIN, TEXAS. Berlin is on County Road 30 three miles south of Brenham in central Washington County. The area was first settled in 1848 by the Valentin Hoffmann family, who emigrated from Hesse, Germany, in 1846. In 1851 Hoffmann purchased 156 acres of land. Three of his sons served in the Confederate Army, and after the war two of them established a cotton gin–gristmill in Berlin. Among the early settlers were F. W. Schürenberg, who came to Washington County from Germany in 1848 and engaged in farming and blacksmithing in Berlin, and Herman Knittel, born in Silesia, who operated a mercantile business and served as postmaster of Berlin after his return from Confederate service. On December 24, 1854, Rev. Johann G. Ebinger, a Lutheran pastor, came to preach to the German settlers in the county at Berlin and held the first Lutheran services in the county. Ludwig Lehmann, who was born in Vienna, Austria, in 1794, and emigrated from Brandenburg, Prussia, in 1849, donated eleven acres for a school and church building, and plans to organize a congregation were made. The first church in Berlin was built of logs in 1855, the second was a frame building, and another frame building was erected in 1880. A county public school formed the nucleus of this German settlement until it was consolidated with the Brenham Independent School District in 1956. In the late 1980s the site of Berlin was marked by a church building constructed in 1955, a parsonage, and the cemetery, which dates to the late 1850s. A three-community (Berlin, Zionsville, Mill Creek) fire-department building in the vicinity was used for community gatherings. Eben-Ezer Lutheran Church received a state historical marker in 1974.

BIBLIOGRAPHY: Annie Maud Avis, ed., *History of Burton* (Burton, Texas, 1974). Rudolph L. Biesele, *The History of the German Settlements in Texas, 1831–1861* (Austin: Von Boeckmann–Jones, 1930; rpt. 1964). Elizabeth A. J. Lehmann, *From Hesse, Germany to Texas, 1846: The Valentin Hoffmann Family* (Brenham, Texas, 1981). Mrs. R. E. Pennington, *History of Brenham and Washington County* (Houston, 1915). Charles F. Schmidt, *History of Washington County* (San Antonio: Naylor, 1949).

Elizabeth Lehmann

BERMUDA, TEXAS (Dimmit County). Bermuda, first known as Bermuda Colony, was a farming community and real estate development six miles east of Carrizo Springs on the north side of the Nueces River in north central Dimmit County. The town takes its name from the Bermuda onion, one of the area's principal crops and for a time a source of profit for local farmers. Bermuda was largely established by "Colonel" J. S. Taylor, an audacious land developer who had helped to establish Del Mar, California. In 1899 Taylor initiated construction of a dam across the Nueces River. He also drilled a deep artesian well. By 1903 the completed thirty-foot dam had formed a reservoir ten miles long. Taylor's planting of onions and strawberries on a large scale was an early financial success and became the model for the future development of Dimmit County. Settlers moved to the area, and by 1902 E. M. Cobb opened a store on the site. In 1904 a post office opened, and by 1915 the settlement had forty-eight residents. Drought and low prices between 1916 and 1918, however, devastated the small farmers. No population statistics are available for Bermuda after 1915. In 1919 the post office and the Baptist Church closed. A map compiled in the mid-1940s showed an unnamed cluster of ten dwellings in the area, but a 1972 map showed only two buildings on the site.

BIBLIOGRAPHY: Laura Knowlton Tidwell, *Dimmit County Mesquite Roots* (Austin: Wind River, 1984). Vertical files, Barker Texas History Center, University of Texas at Austin.

John Leffler

BERMUDA, TEXAS (Shelby County). Bermuda was nine miles north of Center and two miles southwest of Tenaha in northern Shelby County. The settlement received a post office in 1880, with Peter N. Bentley as postmaster. In 1884 the population was reported as twenty. The post office was discontinued in 1891, and the mail was sent to Center. In 1897 the settlement had a one-room, one-teacher school with forty-eight pupils. By 1938 the school had closed.

Cecil Harper, Jr.

BERNARDI, PROSPERO (1794–ca. 1837). Prospero Bernardi, participant in the Texas Revolution,[qv] was born in Italy in 1794 and was a notary by trade. He arrived in Texas aboard the schooner *Pennsylvania* on January 28, 1836, as a member of Capt. Amasa Turner's[qv] volunteer company, raised in New Orleans. Bernardi enlisted in the Texas army on February 13, 1836, and distinguished himself in the battle of San Jacinto.[qv] He remained in the army until January or February 1837, when he was medically discharged from John Smith's company at Galveston because of a spinal injury sustained during combat. Bernardi received a bounty grant and a first-class headright grant for his military service, but both were assigned to other parties. Bernardi's whereabouts by 1838 were unclear. In February of that year two former fellow soldiers testified that they understood he was deceased. A bust of the Italian soldier stands in front of the Hall of State,[qv] Fair Park, Dallas, to commemorate his participation in the battle of San Jacinto.

bibliography: Sam Houston Dixon and Louis Wiltz Kemp, *The Heroes of San Jacinto* (Houston: Anson Jones Press, 1932). San Jacinto Notebooks, L. W. Kemp Papers, Barker Texas History Center, University of Texas at Austin. *Valentine J. Belfiglio*

BERNARDO, TEXAS. Bernardo is at the intersection of Farm Road 949 and Bernardo Road, on the south bank of the San Bernard River twelve miles northeast of Columbus in Colorado County. The earliest settlers were German immigrants who came to Texas about 1845 as colonists of the Adelsverein[qv] and were followed by other Germans. They preferred to remain where a good number of Germans had established themselves and where frontier conditions were not as trying as in the Fisher-Miller land grant[qv] in west central Texas, the area designated for colonization. Bernardo was originally known as Bernardo Prairie because of the local terrain. It was also earlier called Braden; several families by that name were among the early settlers. The community was on the main road from Houston to towns and settlements inland. During the Civil War[qv] it served as a dumping station for cotton being hauled to Mexico. However, it never became a large settlement but remained a farming and ranching community with scattered homes and farms.

Bernardo had its own post office from 1898 to 1917. As early as 1872 there was a local Catholic school staffed by the Sisters of Divine Providence.[qv] In 1911 it was merged with the Mentz Catholic school, which was in turn replaced by a public school that later became part of the Columbus Independent School District. In 1986 Bernardo had a general store and a volunteer fire department and was a voting precinct with 187 registered voters. Some descendants of the original settlers still lived in the area, although land was being purchased by people from Houston and surrounding areas. In 1990 the population was 155.

bibliography: Rudolph L. Biesele, *The History of the German Settlements in Texas, 1831–1861* (Austin: Von Boeckmann–Jones, 1930; rpt. 1964). *Arliss Treybig*

BERNARDO PLANTATION. Bernardo Plantation, one of the plantation homes of Jared E. Groce,[qv] was located on a high bluff on the Brazos River four miles south of the site of present Hempstead in Waller County. In 1822 Groce, the first large planter in Texas, built a rambling story-and-a-half house of cottonwood logs, hewn and counterhewn, at the site. When completed, it had four large rooms downstairs, two rooms and a hall upstairs, and a house-length gallery supported by polished walnut columns. The other plantation buildings included a kitchen, the doctor's house, Bachelor Hall for entertaining guests, a dairy, and quarters for the house slaves. Removed near a lake were quarters for the field slaves, an overseer's house, a kitchen and dining hall, and a day nursery for children of the field workers. Cotton was planted in 1822, and a gin was in operation in 1825.

About 1833 Groce divided his plantation property, and Bernardo fell to Leonard Waller Groce.[qv] Jared Groce, Sr., was back at Bernardo from March 31 to April 15, 1836, when the Texas army under Sam Houston[qv] camped near Groce's Ferry.[qv] A hospital was set up for the soldiers; all plantation facilities were at their disposal. Bernardo was filled with refugees of the Runaway Scrape.[qv] There the women made sandbags for the army, and Groce melted his lead pipes for bullets. On April 12 the Twin Sisters[qv] were unloaded and placed in front of Bernardo. The army crossed the river on the *Yellow Stone*[qv] on April 12–14.

Jared E. Groce died in Grimes County on November 20, 1836, and was buried at Bernardo. Leonard Groce lived at Bernardo from 1833 until 1853, when he moved his family to a new home at Liendo Plantation,[qv] although he continued to own and plant Bernardo until his death in 1873. Several of his relatives occupied the house in the years following his move to Liendo. A son, William Wharton Groce, tore the log house down in 1865 in order to build a new home a few miles from Bernardo. After Leonard Waller Groce's death in 1873, another son, Dr. Leonard Waller Groce, bought Bernardo from other heirs and constructed a frame dwelling. He later sold the plantation, which subsequently had a number of owners. A historical marker at a rest area on U. S. Highway 290 three miles east of Hempstead commemorates the Groce family plantations.

bibliography: Abigail Curlee, "History of a Texas Slave Plantation," *Southwestern Historical Quarterly* 26 (October 1922). Laura Hale, The Groces and Whartons in the Early History of Texas (M.A. thesis, University of Texas, 1942). Mary Groce Mackey, "The Groce Family of Texas," *Frontier Times*, October 1948. Waller County Historical Survey Committee, *A History of Waller County, Texas* (Waco: Texian Press, 1973). Frank E. White, History of the Territory that Now Constitutes Waller County, Texas, from 1821 to 1884 (M.A. thesis, University of Texas, 1936). *Claudia Hazlewood*

BERROTERÁN, JOSÉ DE (?–?). José de Berroterán was commander of the presidios of Mapimí and Conchos in Mexico for thirty-five years. While captain of Presidio de Conchos he was ordered to command an expedition to explore the territory from San Juan Bautista[qv] up the Rio Grande to the mouth of the Río Conchos. This area was part of what was known as the Despoblado, a refuge for groups that preyed on the frontier settlements of Nueva Vizcaya and Coahuila. Berroterán left Conchos on January 13, 1729, with fifty-eight soldiers, six Indian guides, and more than 500 horses and mules, and arrived at San Juan Bautista on March 15. There, joined by another fifteen soldiers and forty Indians, he began his exploration on March 29. The group traveled west of the Rio Grande to the Río San Antonio, twenty-five miles west of the site of present Eagle Pass, where Berroterán received orders to divide his troops into three parts; two groups were to fend off attacks of roving tribes at Presidio de Coahuila (Monclova) and Santa Rosa de Nadadores, and one was to proceed to Cuatro Ciénagas. After holding a meeting with his officers, Berroterán decided not to follow the orders because the tribes would be gone before his troops could reach the places attacked and the third group would not be large enough to continue the mission. The expedition continued along the west bank of the Rio Grande and reached the site of present Ciudad Acuña on April 12. Unable to continue along the river because of the canyon, the group made a long detour to the west and finally crossed the Rio Grande near the site of present Langtry on April 19. On April 28 in another meeting with his officers, Berroterán decided that it was too difficult to continue the march with the limited supplies on hand. He ordered the detachment from Coahuila to return to its presidio by way of Santa Rosa de Nadadores; the remaining groups left the following day, and arrived at Nueva Vizcaya on May 16. In his report, submitted to the viceroy, Berroterán states, "The gulf or pocket [the Despoblado] . . . contains steep places, dry places, few waterholes, and great distances. . . . For this reason it cannot be inhabited nor populated by rational Christians." He was severely criticized by Brigadier Pedro de Rivera y Villalón,[qv] who said the mission was a failure because Berroterán made too much of the hardships and depended too much on his Indian guides. The *auditor*, Juan Manuel de Oliván Rebolledo,[qv] agreed, although he allowed that one purpose—to open communications between Nueva Vizcaya and Coahuila—had been accomplished. Berroterán was charged with "laxity of duty" in a report to the governor of Parral on June 17, 1730.

bibliography: Hubert Howe Bancroft, *History of the North Mexican States and Texas* (2 vols., San Francisco: History Company, 1886, 1889). Carlos E. Castañeda, *Our Catholic Heritage in Texas* (7 vols., Austin: Von Boeckmann–Jones, 1936–1958; rpt., New York: Arno, 1976). Donald E. Chipman, *Spanish Texas, 1519–1821* (Austin: University of Texas Press, 1992). James M. Daniel, "The Spanish Frontier in West Texas and Northern Mexico," *Southwestern Historical Quarterly* 71 (April 1968).

John G. Johnson

BERRY, ANDREW JACKSON (1816–1899). Andrew Jackson (Jack) Berry, ranger, soldier, and rancher, the son of Betsy (Smothers) and John Berry,[qv] was born in Monroe County, Indiana, on May 16, 1816. The family moved to Texas in late 1826 and settled in the Atascosito District. In 1834 Andrew moved with the family to Mina, later named Bastrop. He enlisted as a private in the Mina Volunteers on February 28, 1836, and fought at San Jacinto as a member of Company C, First Regiment, commanded by Capt. Jesse Billingsley.[qv] After the victory he extended his service until June. He was living in Houston when the town was first laid out. In 1838 he was living in what later became Caldwell, Burleson County, where the Berry family had moved after San Jacinto. With his brothers Joseph and Bate Berry[qqv] he fought in the battle of Plum Creek[qv] on August 12, 1840, under the command of Col. Edward Burleson.[qv] In 1843 he enlisted in Capt. Jack (John C.) Hays's[qv] Texas Rangers,[qv] and in 1846 he served at Goliad under Lt. John T. Price.[qv] Berry moved his family in 1847 to the future Williamson County, where the family was gathering on the Berry league on Berry Creek and the San Gabriel River. He served as a member of the first grand jury after that county was organized. He enlisted as a private in the Confederate Army and later served as captain in Archie Hart's company, Twenty-seventh Brigade. He joined the Texas Veterans Association[qv] when it was organized at Houston in 1873. He left Williamson County and was ranching in Lampasas County in 1876, but moved in 1881 to a ranch he purchased south of Baird in Callahan County, where he spent the rest of his life. Jack Berry married Rhoda Jane Hughes (1824–ca. 1866) on July 29, 1839; they had nine children. He married Mary Catherine Sloan on September 3, 1872; eight children were born of this marriage. In 1936 Mary Catherine was honored at the Texas Centennial[qv] celebration in Dallas as the last surviving widow of a San Jacinto veteran. Berry died on July 31, 1899, in Baird when his team of mules, frightened by a train, ran away and he was thrown from his wagon. He is buried in the Ross Cemetery at Baird, where the state of Texas placed a marker for him as a veteran of San Jacinto.

bibliography: Sam Houston Dixon and Louis Wiltz Kemp, *The Heroes of San Jacinto* (Houston: Anson Jones Press, 1932). William Moses Jones, *Texas History Carved in Stone* (Houston: Monument, 1958). W. K. Makemson, *Historical Sketch of First Settlement and Organization of Williamson County* (Georgetown, Texas, 1904). Jack Pope, ed., *John Berry and His Children* (Austin, 1988). Clara Stearns Scarbrough, *Land of Good Water: A Williamson County History* (Georgetown, Texas: Williamson County Sun Publishers, 1973).

Jack Pope

BERRY, JOHN (1786–1866). John Berry, pioneer colonist, gunsmith, and blacksmith, was born in Louisville, Kentucky. He fought in the War of 1812. He moved from Christian Settlement, Illinois, to Blue Spring, Indiana, in 1816. Berry had three sons by his first wife, Betsy (Smothers), daughter of William Smothers,[qv] whom he married about 1810 and who died in Indiana; three daughters by Gracie Treat, whom he married on July 13, 1819; and twelve children by Hannah Devore, whom he married in Liberty, Texas, on May 8, 1831. In late 1826 he moved his family to the Atascosito District on the lower Trinity River in Texas. Mexico awarded him a lot in Liberty when it organized the municipality in May 1831. As a gunsmith, blacksmith, knifesmith, and furniture builder Berry qualified for the lot as an artisan. Sometime before 1834 he moved to Mina, later called Bastrop, where Mexico awarded him two town lots and a twelve-acre farm lot as an artisan. David Crockett,[qv] traveling on the Old San Antonio Road[qv] toward the Alamo,[qv] stopped at Mina while Berry repaired Crockett's famous rifle, Old Betsey. Berry's three sons by his first wife were Joseph, John Bate, and Andrew Jackson Berry.[qqv] All three sons were Texas Rangers[qv] before and after the Texas Revolution,[qv] all served in the Army of the Republic of Texas,[qv] and all fought in the battle of Plum Creek.[qv] Berry, his wife Hannah, and their small children took refuge at Fort Parker during the revolution, and upon returning to Bastrop found their home burned to the ground. In 1840 the family moved to the settlement that later became Caldwell in Burleson County, where they lived for the next ten years. The Texas Congress named Caldwell as the county seat in 1840, but the county was not organized until 1846. The Berry family was living there at the time. Berry applied to be a Robertson colonist on November 6, 1835, but did not settle on his league of land, located about three miles northeast of Georgetown, until the winter of 1846. He built a spring-driven gristmill, later called Gann's Mill, on Berry Creek. In 1848 he served as a commissioner, named by the Texas legislature, to organize Williamson County. For the fourth time, he was living in a Texas county seat when the county was organized. Berry was a member of the Church of Christ; his third wife, Hannah, was a faithful Baptist. Their home at Berry Creek was regularly used for Baptist services. Berry died on December 24, 1866, and is buried in a small family cemetery on the Berry league. His grave is marked by a plaque placed by the Daughters of the War of 1812. Five of Berry's sons and three of his sons-in-law served in the Confederate Army. His most distinguished direct descendant was his great-grandson Audie Murphy.[qv] On the grounds of the Williamson County Courthouse, the buhrstone from the Berry Mill is preserved beneath a state historical marker placed for Berry, whose descendants meet annually to commemorate the Berry family's service to Texas.

bibliography: John Holland Jenkins, *Recollections of Early Texas*, ed. John H. Jenkins III (Austin: University of Texas Press, 1958; rpt. 1973). Malcolm D. McLean, comp. and ed., *Papers Concerning Robertson's Colony in Texas* (19 vols., Arlington: University of Texas at Arlington Press, 1974–93). Miriam Partlow, *Liberty, Liberty County, and the Atascosito District* (Austin: Pemberton, 1974). Jack Pope, ed., *John Berry and His Children* (Austin, 1988). Andrew Jackson Sowell, *Early Settlers and Indian Fighters of Southwest Texas* (Austin: Ben C. Jones, 1900; rpt., Austin: State House Press, 1986). Virginia H. Taylor, *The Spanish Archives of the General Land Office of Texas* (Austin: Lone Star, 1955).

Jack Pope

BERRY, JOHN BATE (1813–1891). John Bate Berry, often known as Bate Berry, son of Betsy (Smothers) and John Berry,[qv] was born in Indiana on May 8, 1813, the oldest of three sons of this marriage. His mother died soon after the birth of her third child, Joseph Berry.[qv] John Berry and his three sons moved to Texas in 1826 with the intention of settling in Robertson's colony,[qv] but instead settled for a while near the mouth of Buffalo Bayou in what is now Harris County. Bate received a grant of a league of land on April 7, 1831, in Austin's colony on the east side of the Colorado River adjoining Ira Ingram's[qv] grant. He served as a private for fifty days in the Permanent Volunteer Company of Texas Militia in Capt. Robert McAlpin Williamson's[qv] company of Col. John Henry Moore's[qv] battalion, from July 26 to September 13, 1835. On February 28, 1836, he and his brother Andrew Jackson Berry[qv] joined the Texas army as privates, and although Andrew Jackson fought in the battle of San Jacinto,[qv] Bate, it has been reported, was among those detailed on April 21, 1836, to guard the baggage train and the camp of the sick opposite Harrisburg and did not take part in the battle. It seems that on February 28, 1836, Bate was appointed to drive a team and served until June 1, 1836, and thus was a part of the baggage train itself at the time of the battle. He was discharged from Capt. Jesse Billingsley's[qv] service on the latter date, after which he served as a private in Capt. William W. Hill's[qqv] company from July 3 to October 3, 1836. He enrolled for three months in the ranging service of Texas on January 6, 1838, but he served only until February 20, when he was discharged. Bate and Andrew Jackson Berry both fought under Col. Edward Burleson[qv] in the battle of Plum Creek[qv] on August 12, 1840, against the Comanches. Bate and Joseph Berry each received land grants in Robertson's colony.

After the capture of San Antonio in September 1842 by Gen. Adrián Woll,[qv] Bate joined Capt. William P. Rutledge's company of Jackson County, on October 17, 1842. The company was transferred to the command of Capt. Jerome B. Robertson[qv] on November 15, and to that of Capt. Charles K. Reese[qv] on December 19, when Robertson's company returned home from the Rio Grande with Gen. Alexander Somervell.[qv] Joseph and Bate had enrolled in the Brazoria company under Capt. John Shelby McNeill for the Somervell expedition,[qv] and when Somervell started for home from the Rio Grande on December 19, 1842, he, too, transferred to Reese's company. Thus both brothers became members of the Mier expedition.[qv] Joseph was killed in the battle of Mier, and Bate was captured and imprisoned in Mexico until September 16, 1844. During the Mexican War[qv] he served in Col. John C. Hays's[qv] regiment as a scout under Capt. Creed Taylor[qv] for Gen. Zachary Taylor[qv] in northern Mexico, and on one occasion was strongly admonished by General Taylor to discontinue his practice of scalping Mexican soldiers whom he had killed in battle.

After the Mexican War Berry received a first-class headright certificate and selected his land in Williamson County, where he resided until the end of the Civil War.[qv] Shortly thereafter, probably influenced by his brother-in-law, James Bradberry (husband of Bate's half-sister, Elizabeth), he moved to the upper Llano valley. He settled on the river two miles above the mouth of Red Creek in Kimble County. There he built a log house surrounded by a stockade of tall pickets to afford protection from the Indians and raised cattle. Some five or six miles to the southwest, on Gentry Creek in Kimble County, lived the Raleigh Gentry family, including Nancy Frazier Gentry, widow of William Gentry (son of Raleigh Gentry), who was killed during the Civil War, and her young son. After John Bate and Nancy agreed to be married they rode horseback to Fredericksburg, a distance of sixty miles, where they were married on March 9, 1867. In 1871 they moved to Willow Creek in Mason County, where, on March 2, 1878, Bate purchased 160 acres of land from Gustav Schleicher[qv] and, on December 28, 1881, bought from William Koock three acres of land a mile or so west of Mason at a settlement known as Koockville. In those days Berry was often involved in helping to defend the frontier against Indians. In Mason County he farmed and ranched until his death at his home near Koockville, on December 20, 1891. Berry was a devout member of the Church of Christ. He was buried in the Grit Cemetery in Mason County. His wife died in 1928 at the age of eighty-three and was buried beside him.

BIBLIOGRAPHY: Sam Houston Dixon and Louis Wiltz Kemp, *The Heroes of San Jacinto* (Houston: Anson Jones, 1932). Ovie Clark Fisher, *The Texas Heritage of the Fishers and the Clarks* (Salado, Texas: Anson Jones Press, 1963). *Joseph Milton Nance*

BERRY, JOHN G. (1805–1871). John G. Berry, born in 1805 in North Carolina, was a merchant and trader in the Ayish Bayou District (later San Augustine County) of Texas in the 1830s. His steamboat, the *Big Ben,* made regular trips up the Sabine River to deliver goods and collect cotton for export to New Orleans. He first married Harriett Carolina Clark, and eight children were born to their union; his second marriage was to Cornelia Price Sossaman, widow of Charles Sossaman. Berry was San Augustine postmaster in 1840 and 1841. In February 1842 he and John T. Mason[qv] were mail contractors for Route 3, from Nacogdoches to Cincinnati, Texas. In 1844 Berry was appointed collector of customs at San Augustine; that year he also served on the first board of trustees of Wesleyan College. In April 1845 he called a meeting in San Augustine to urge the annexation[qv] of Texas to the United States. In the early 1840s he built the Berry Hotel on the corner of Columbia and Harrison streets in San Augustine. The lower story was occupied by a saloon on one side and a general store on the other, while above were hotel rooms and a ballroom and stage. For many years the hotel was a popular gathering place. Berry died on December 16, 1871, and is buried in the San Augustine City Cemetery.

BIBLIOGRAPHY: George L. Crocket, *Two Centuries in East Texas* (Dallas: Southwest, 1932; facsimile reprod., 1962). William Seale, *San Augustine in the Texas Republic* (Austin: Encino, 1969). *Telegraph and Texas Register,* April 23, 1845. Amelia W. Williams and Eugene C. Barker, eds., *The Writings of Sam Houston, 1813–1863* (8 vols., Austin: University of Texas Press, 1938–43; rpt., Austin and New York: Pemberton Press, 1970). *McXie Whitton Martin*

BERRY, JOSEPH (ca. 1819–1842). Joseph Berry, victim of the battle of Mier, third son of Betsy (Smothers) and John Berry,[qv] was born in Monroe County, Indiana, about 1819 and named after his father's brother. With his father and brothers, John Bate and Andrew Jackson Berry,[qqv] he moved to Texas in 1826 and settled near the mouth of Buffalo Bayou in what is now Harris County. In 1834 John Berry, with his third wife and children, moved to Mina (Bastrop), where Joseph Berry, a gunsmith like his father, joined John Jackson Tumlinson's[qv] rangers, composed largely of citizens of Bastrop County. Joseph aided in the construction of a fort near Liberty Hill in 1835 and later served as second in command of that outpost. He was listed on the tax rolls of Liberty County in 1840 as the administrator of Thomas Nesbet's estate of 640 acres. Berry and his brother John Bate received grants of land in the Robertson colony.[qv] Joseph's grant was patented in what is now Williamson County. In 1840 the Berrys were living in Burleson County. After the seizure of San Antonio in September by the Mexican army under Gen. Adrián Woll,[qv] Berry rallied to the defense of the frontier by joining the Brazoria Company under Capt. John Shelby McNeill for the Somervell campaign, and when Brig. Gen. Alexander Somervell[qv] started home from the Rio Grande on December 19, 1842, he transferred to Capt. Charles K. Reese's[qv] company, to which his brother Bate also transferred, and thus became a member of the Mier expedition.[qv] As the Texan forces advanced against Mier in the late afternoon of December 25, Joseph fell down the wet, slippery bluff of the Alcantro River and broke his thigh. With a Texan doctor and a small guard, including his brother, he was placed in a hut near the Alcantro River opposite Mier, where, the next day around eleven o'clock in the morning, the small party of Texans was discovered by the enemy, and Joseph was killed.

BIBLIOGRAPHY: Ovie Clark Fisher, *The Texas Heritage of the Fishers and the Clarks* (Salado, Texas: Anson Jones Press, 1963). Joseph Milton Nance, ed., *Mier Expedition Diary: A Texas Prisoner's Account by Joseph D. McCutchan* (Austin: University of Texas Press, 1978).

Joseph Milton Nance

BERRY, KEARIE LEE (1893–1965). Military officer Kearie Lee Berry, the son of Thomas Eugene and Viola (Riley) Berry, was born in Denton, Texas, on July 6, 1893. After graduating from Denton High School, he attended the University of Texas (1912–16), where he established a reputation as one of the best college athletes in the Southwest. Although he lettered four times in football and three times in track, his favorite sport was wrestling. He won the Southwest Conference[qv] heavyweight wrestling championship in 1915 and 1916. In the latter year he left the university to enlist in the Texas National Guard,[qv] thus beginning ten months' service on the Mexican border with the Second Texas Infantry.

Though he was commissioned a second lieutenant in the officer reserve corps in 1917, Berry remained in the United States during World War I.[qv] In 1919, however, he participated in the combined American and British military action in the Soviet Union. His unit spent a year and a half near Vladivostok. Berry was promoted to captain in 1921 and returned to the United States to become an infantry company commander at Fort Sam Houston, San Antonio. In 1924 he returned to Austin as a War Department student, and at the age of thirty-one he was an All Southwest Conference guard on the University of Texas football team. After graduating in 1925 he received further military training at Fort Benning, Georgia. Four years later the army assigned him to teach military science and tactics at the University of Vermont, where he also coached football and basketball. In recognition of his athletic achievements, Berry was inducted into the University of Texas Longhorn Hall of Fame in 1930.

After his assignment in Vermont, he was promoted to major and traveled to China with instructions to act as a military advisor to that country's army. He was transferred to the Philippines a month before the bombing of Pearl Harbor and, now a colonel, participated in the defense of Bataan Peninsula. After the fall of Bataan on April 9, 1942, he survived the infamous Bataan Death March and spent the remainder of the war, forty months, as a prisoner of war.

Berry was released in 1945 and received the Purple Heart, the Distinguished Service Cross, the Distinguished Service Medal, the Silver Star, the Bronze Star, and the (Philippine) Legion of Honor award. He was promoted to brigadier general in 1946 and retired the following year. He was appointed an adjutant general in the Texas National Guard in June 1947 and continued in this capacity until he resigned in 1961. He lived in Austin for four years with his wife, Alice, with whom he had a son and daughter. On April 25, 1965, he suffered a heart attack. Two days later he died at Fort Sam Houston Medical Center in San Antonio.

BIBLIOGRAPHY: Dallas *Morning News*, April 28, 1965. San Antonio *Express*, April 28, 1965.
David Minor

BERRY, M. (?–?). M. (possibly Manders or Mandus) Berry was a partner of M. M. Battle and John Williams, Sr.,[qqv] as one of Stephen F. Austin's[qv] Old Three Hundred.[qv] The partners received title to a sitio[qv] of land on Linnville Bayou in what is now Matagorda County from the Baron de Bastrop[qv] on August 10, 1824. A Mandus Berry voted in an alcalde[qv] election on December 1824 at San Felipe de Austin, and an 1826 census of Austin's colony lists Mandus Berry as a single man and carpenter aged between sixteen and twenty-five. Berry and Battle were contractors at San Felipe. In 1832 Mandus Berry served under Aylett C. Buckner or John Austin[qqv] at the battle of Velasco,[qv] which Berry survived.

BIBLIOGRAPHY: Eugene C. Barker, ed., *The Austin Papers* (3 vols., Washington: GPO, 1924–28). Lester G. Bugbee, "The Old Three Hundred: A List of Settlers in Austin's First Colony," *Quarterly of the Texas State Historical Association* 1 (October 1897). Charles Adams Gulick, Jr., Harriet Smither, et al., eds., *The Papers of Mirabeau Buonaparte Lamar* (6 vols., Austin: Texas State Library, 1920–27; rpt., Austin: Pemberton Press, 1968). Matagorda County Historical Commission, *Historic Matagorda County* (3 vols., Houston: Armstrong, 1986). Texas General Land Office, First Census of Austin's Colony, 1826 (MS, Barker Texas History Center, University of Texas at Austin).

BERRY CREEK (Burleson County). Berry Creek begins two miles east of Caldwell in central Burleson County (at 30°33′ N, 96°37′ W) and runs southeast for eleven miles to its mouth on Davidson Creek (at 30°26′ N, 96°33′ W). It crosses gently sloping to nearly level terrain surfaced by loam that supports post oak, blackjack oak, elm, hackberry, water oak, and pecan trees along the banks. Settlement in the area began during the early 1830s. New Tabor, one of the oldest and largest communities in the county, was established near the headwaters by Czech-Moravian and German immigrants about 1870. The stream is named for Burleson County pioneer Radford Berry, a resident of Fort Tenoxtitlán in 1832, who seems to have lived in the vicinity of the creek sometime thereafter.

BIBLIOGRAPHY: Burleson County Historical Society, *Astride the Old San Antonio Road: A History of Burleson County, Texas* (Dallas: Taylor, 1980).

—— (Burnet County). Berry Creek rises 1½ miles southwest of Briggs in northeastern Burnet County (at 30°53′ N, 97°57′ W) and flows southeast for thirty-two miles to its mouth on the San Gabriel River, about four miles northeast of Georgetown in Williamson County (at 30°40′ N, 97°36′ W). The stream, intermittent in its upper reaches, was named for John Berry,[qv] who was granted the land near the mouth of the creek and settled on its banks in 1846. The banks are heavily wooded for much of the creek's course, mainly with mesquite, juniper, and oak. The surrounding terrain is gently rolling and surfaced with clayey soils used predominantly for agriculture.

BIBLIOGRAPHY: Clara Stearns Scarbrough, *Land of Good Water: A Williamson County History* (Georgetown, Texas: Williamson County Sun Publishers, 1973).

—— (Frio County). Berry Creek rises a mile south of Farm Road 57 and sixteen miles west of Pearsall in central Frio County (at 28°56′ N, 99°22′ W) and runs southeast for twelve miles before joining Cattail Creek (at 28°49′ N, 99°17′ W) a mile above the latter stream's confluence with the Leona River in west central Frio County. The stream is named for Tillman Berry, an early settler of the area. Area vegetation includes various grasses and a scattering of pecan and willow trees. The creek crosses flat to rolling terrain with steep margins, surfaced by sand and gravel.

BIBLIOGRAPHY: Mrs. W. A. Roberts, "Frio County Has a Colorful History," *Frontier Times*, June 1936.

BERRY HILL, TEXAS. Berry Hill is on a country road just east of Farm Road 142 near the Ivy oilfield in the northwest corner of Shackelford County. In 1938 the Berry Hill school served thirty-nine pupils and three teachers, and in 1940, when it was identified as Bern Hill on county maps, the community had the school and scattered dwellings. Though the school had been consolidated with the Lueder school by the 1960s, the school building was still standing in 1985; the Berry Hill community was still identified on county maps in 1992.
Mark Odintz

BERRYMAN, HELENA DILL (1804–1888). Helena Dill Berryman, pioneer settler and philanthropist, daughter of Helena (Kimble) and James Dill,[qv] was born in Nacogdoches on September 8, 1804. Her family believed her to be the first Anglo child born in Texas. While attending school in Natchitoches, Louisiana, she met and married Capt. Henry Berryman in 1823 and moved with him to Virginia. She inherited the southwest league of the Helena Kimble land grant near Alto, and the couple returned to Texas to live. In 1847 the Berrymans built a log mansion called Forest Hill Plantation.[qv] After the death of her husband in 1859 Mrs. Berryman continued to live at Forest Hill, which was the home not only of the three Berryman children but also of thirty orphan children. Mrs. Berryman was the first contributor to Buckner Orphans Home (*see* BUCKNER BAPTIST CHILDREN'S HOME). She died on March 13, 1888, and was buried in the family cemetery on the plantation. In 1969 the Texas Historical Commission[qv] placed a marker at the site.

BIBLIOGRAPHY: Marker files, Texas Historical Commission, Austin. Vertical files, Barker Texas History Center, University of Texas at Austin.
Lessie Carlton

BERRY'S CREEK. Berry's Creek begins three miles southeast of Patilo in northeastern Erath County (at 32°27′ N, 98°07′ W) and runs southeast for nine miles to its mouth on Paluxy Creek, near the Hood county line (at 32°21′ N, 98°01′ W). The surrounding terrain is fairly level and surfaced by stony gravel that supports some grass.

BERRY'S CREEK, TEXAS. Berry's Creek, also known as Johnsonville, was on Berry Creek five miles northeast of Georgetown in central Williamson County. John Berry,[qv] one of the earliest settlers in the county, founded a gristmill on Berry Creek in 1846, on a league of land granted him by the Republic of Texas.[qv] By the 1860s the Berry grant was also the site of a store-tavern-stagecoach stop called Berry's Creek, and the scattered community also had, at various times, a blacksmith shop and a gin. The Berry's Creek school, also called Boatner's School, had forty-five pupils and one teacher in 1903. Swedish emigrants came to the area in the late nineteenth century and about 1915 built the Free Mission Evangelical Church. The community had a population of fifty and two businesses in 1941. The school was consolidated with the Georgetown district in 1949. In 1988, though the *Texas Almanac*[qv] still listed the community as having a population of fifty, Berry's Creek no longer appeared on the county map. A population of fifty was reported again in 1990.

BIBLIOGRAPHY: Clara Stearns Scarbrough, *Land of Good Water: A Williamson County History* (Georgetown, Texas: Williamson County Sun Publishers, 1973).
Mark Odintz

BERRYVILLE, TEXAS. Berryville is off State Highway 155 twenty-two miles southeast of Athens in the southeastern corner of Henderson County. The settlement, on Lake Palestine (the Neches River), grew up after the Civil War.[qv] A post office opened in 1871, and by 1885 the community had Methodist, Baptist, and Christian churches, a district school, two general stores, two grocers, a gristmill-gin, and a reported population of 500. During the late 1890s, however, the town began to decline. The post office closed in 1905, and by the mid-1930s only a church and a number of houses remained in the area. In the early 1960s Lake Palestine was constructed nearby. In 1980 the population reached 362. The community incorporated during the 1980s, and in 1990 the largely residential area had 749 inhabitants.
Christopher Long

BERTNER, ERNST WILLIAM (1889–1950). Ernst William Bertner, physician and hospital administrator, son of Gustave and Anna (Miller) Bertner, was born at Colorado City, Texas, on August 18, 1889, to a German immigrant family. He graduated from the New Mexico Military Institute in Roswell in 1906 and returned to Colorado City, where, with his father's assistance, he opened a drugstore. After a year as a businessman Bertner left Colorado City for Galveston to enroll in the University of Texas School of Pharmacy. Once there, he decided to study medicine rather than pharmacy, and in 1911 he received his medical degree from the University of Texas Medical Branch. He then traveled to New York City, where he served as an intern and resident at Willard Parker Hospital, Saint Vincent's Hospital, and Manhattan Maternity Hospital. Among the many patients he saw in New York was Jesse H. Jones,[qv] a prominent Texas businessman and future New Deal government official. Jones offered Bertner a position as house physician in his new multimillion-dollar Rice Hotel in Houston and encouraged the young doctor to open his practice in the Bayou City. Bertner moved into the Rice Hotel in 1913 and lived there most of the rest of his life.

He practiced medicine in Houston until 1917, when he became one of the first physicians in the city to volunteer for military service. He served as a lieutenant with the British Army Medical Corps in Europe until 1918 and then transferred to the American Expeditionary Force. He was discharged with the rank of major in 1919. During World War II[qv] he commanded the Harris County Emergency Medical Service of the Office of Civilian Defense and received a presidential citation for his service. After his discharge he practiced medicine in Houston until 1921, when he moved to Baltimore, Maryland, for a year of postgraduate study in surgery, gynecology, and urology at Johns Hopkins University. Bertner's interest in the treatment of cancer began at Johns Hopkins, where he studied with Dr. Thomas Cullen, an authority on gynecologic cancer. In 1922 Bertner returned to private practice in Houston. He built a successful practice and in 1935 became chief of staff at Hermann Hospital,[qv] a position he also held at Jefferson Davis Hospital. He served on the surgical staffs of Memorial Hospital and Southern Pacific Hospital. During the 1930s he became increasingly influential in state and local medicine. He was elected president of the Texas Association of Obstetricians and Gynecologists, the Harris County Medical Society, the Texas Surgical Society, the Postgraduate Medical Assembly of South Texas, and the Texas Medical Association.[qv]

In 1942 negotiations between the M. D. Anderson Foundation[qv] and the University of Texas brought the M. D. Anderson Hospital for Cancer Research to Houston; the university regents appointed Bertner acting director of the hospital until a permanent director could be found. He served for four years and donated his salary to the new hospital. Perhaps more than anyone else, Bertner saw M. D. Anderson Hospital as the first step toward the development of a major medical center in Houston. The center Bertner envisioned needed broad-based support; to that end the trustees of the Anderson Foundation established the Texas Medical Center[qv] in 1946 and deeded the property in the center to the new corporation. Bertner served as the first president. After the regents of the University of Texas appointed Dr. R. Lee Clark director and surgeon-in-chief at M. D. Anderson Hospital later that year, Bertner devoted himself to planning and developing the medical center, which moved ahead rapidly. By 1948 M. D. Anderson Hospital was well established, Baylor University College of Medicine had moved into its new home in the medical center, and Hermann Hospital, Methodist Hospital,[qv] and the Shriners Hospital for Crippled Children were under construction.

Bertner served as a member of the executive committees of the Central Association of Obstetricians and Gynecologists and the Texas Social Hygiene Association. He was state counselor and fellow of the American College of Surgeons, vice president of the American Cancer Society, and chairman of the executive committee of the society's Texas division. In 1949 the society presented Bertner its award for distinguished service in cancer research. He was a fellow of the American Medical Association and a member in 1944 of its House of Delegates. He served as vice president of the Southern Medical Association and was a member of the Texas Railway and Traumatic Surgical Association, the American Urological Association, the American Gynecological Association, and the Interurban Gynecological Society. He was professor and chairman of the Department of Gynecology at Baylor College of Medicine and also served as lecturer in gynecology and oncology at the University of Texas Medical Branch in Galveston. He was vice chairman of the Houston Board of Health, a member of the Houston Chamber of Commerce, and a member of the national Citizens Committee for the Hoover Report. He was a Presbyterian and a Mason, a Knight Templar, a Shriner, and a knight commander of the court of honor of the Scottish Rite. His distinguished career brought him many honors. In Bertner's name the Houston Endowment gave Jesse H. Jones fellowships totaling $25,000 to M. D. Anderson Hospital. A building at the Ochsner Institute in New Orleans, Louisiana, was named for Bertner, and a street in the Texas Medical Center carries his name. In June 1950 Baylor University awarded him an honorary doctor of laws degree.

Bertner married Julia Williams of St. Louis, Missouri, on November 20, 1922. They had no children. Although Bertner spent much of his professional life in a struggle against cancer, he himself succumbed to the disease in Houston on July 18, 1950.

BIBLIOGRAPHY: N. Don Macon, *Mr. John H. Freeman and Friends:*

A Story of the Texas Medical Center and How It Began (Houston: Texas Medical Center, 1973). Walter H. Moursund, *A History of Baylor University College of Medicine* (Houston, 1956). *Texas State Journal of Medicine*, September 1950. *Randy J. Sparks*

BERTRAM, TEXAS. Bertram is at the junction of Farm roads 243 and 1174 and State Highway 29, ten miles west of Burnet in eastern Burnet County. The town was established in 1882, when the community of San Gabriel in Williamson County was moved two miles northwest to the newly constructed Austin and Northwestern Railroad. The new community was named for Austin merchant Rudolph Bertram, the largest stockholder in the Austin and Northwestern. A post office opened in 1882, and by 1891 the town had an estimated population of 150, a cotton gin–gristmill, three general stores, a grocer, a blacksmith, a shoemaker, and two wagonmakers. After 1900 Bertram was a shipping point for cotton, cattle, and wool. In 1928 a record 11,624 bales of cotton were ginned in the town. In the early 1930s plummeting cotton prices and the Great Depression[qv] caused the town's population to decline from a high of 1,000 in 1929 to 550 by 1931. It was 600 in 1949 and by 1966 stood at 1,205. In 1989 the town had a population of 1,002 and nineteen businesses. At that time Bertram's principal industries included the manufacture of ceramic floor tiles, paving tiles, marble fixtures, and vacuum-formed and molded plastic products. In 1990 the population was 849.

BIBLIOGRAPHY: Darrell Debo, *Burnet County History* (2 vols., Burnet, Texas: Eakin, 1979). *Tommye Dorbandt Potts*

BERWICK, TEXAS. Berwick, originally Jeannette, was ten miles west of Jacksboro in central western Jack County. The first settlers arrived in the area in the mid-1880s, and by 1885 the community had its own post office. Jeannette was renamed Berwick by 1910, when the Gulf, Texas and Western Railroad arrived. Berwick was intended to serve as a flag stop for the railroad and developed into a retail point for area ranchers. A general store, blacksmith shop, and cotton gin served the estimated thirty-five residents in 1914. That year the post office was discontinued, and the mail was brought in from Jacksboro. Berwick was unable to compete with Jacksboro after the construction of U.S. Highway 281 and State Highway 66. By the late 1940s the community was abandoned.

BIBLIOGRAPHY: Jack County Scrapbook, Barker Texas History Center, University of Texas at Austin. *David Minor*

BESS, FORREST CLEMENGER (1911–1977). Forrest Bess, artist, the son of Arnold and Minta (Lee) Bess, was born in Bay City, Texas, on October 5, 1911. His father was an itinerant oil worker, and Bess spent his childhood in various oil towns throughout Texas and Oklahoma. Probably inspired by the fantasy painting of his maternal grandmother, he became interested in painting at an early age. In 1924 he took his first art lessons from a neighbor in Corsicana. In 1929 he entered the Agricultural and Mechanical College of Texas (now Texas A&M University), where he began to study architecture. He became interested in English literature, Hinduism, Greek mythology, and the works of Darwin and Freud. In 1931 he transferred to the University of Texas. After dropping out of school in 1933, he worked for a short time as a roughneck in various oilfields to earn money to go to Mexico. There he began to paint in a style that he identified as post-impressionist, modeled upon that of Vincent Van Gogh and Maurice Vlaminck. He returned to the United States in 1934 and set up a studio in Bay City. He had his first exhibition in a Bay City hotel lobby in 1936. During World War II[qv] he served with the United States Army Corps of Engineers in the camouflage division and received a commendation for his services. In 1946 he suffered a mental breakdown; after spending some time in the Veterans Administration Hospital in San Antonio (now the Audie L. Murphy Memorial Veterans Hospital[qv]) he obtained a job giving art lessons there. A few years later, when his father's health was failing, he returned to Bay City to manage the family bait camp in Chinquapin. He lived there the rest of his life selling bait, building frames, designing visual aids for the public school, giving private art lessons, and occasionally selling his paintings.

In 1948 he made a trip to New York City, where he met Betty Parsons, a prominent New York City gallery owner who represented leading Abstract Expressionist and Color field painters Barnett Newman, Clyfford Still, Jackson Pollock, and Mark Rothko. Parsons mounted the first major exhibition of Bess's work in 1949; it was followed by shows in 1954, 1957, 1959, 1962, and 1967. Critic Meyer Schapiro championed Bess's work and wrote an essay for the 1962 retrospective exhibition of his paintings at the Betty Parsons Gallery. Bess's work was included in the Corcoran Gallery Biennial (1939), and he was featured in solo exhibitions at the Witte Museum[qv] in San Antonio (1938, 1967), the Museum of Fine Arts, Houston[qv] (1951), the Oklahoma Art Center, Oklahoma City (1951), the André Emmerich Gallery, Houston (1958), the Contemporary Arts Museum, Houston[qv] (1962), and the New Arts Gallery, Houston (1963), among others. His work was featured at the M. H. de Young Memorial Museum, San Francisco (1958), and in 1962 some of his works were included in "Wit and Whimsy in 20th Century Art," an exhibition organized by the American Federation of Arts in New York.

Bess was a visionary abstract artist whose small oil paintings featured personal symbolic images, such as crescents, eyes, crosses, lines, and simple geometric forms, which he saw in his dreams. He kept a notebook by his bed in which he drew the visions. He claimed to have had his first vision, a Dutch village guarded by a lion and a tiger, in 1915, and he later recorded this in one of his paintings. He was inspired by Carl Jung's theories to study mythology, alchemy, archeology, and religion; he became convinced that his ideograms, as he called them, could end human suffering, including death, by aiding the physical transformation of the male and female bodies into an androgynous being. Bess wrote to several psychologists and anthropologists, including Jung, and kept a notebook of sketches, clippings, and quotations to develop his thesis. In 1960 he had himself surgically altered in an effort to become androgynous.

During the 1960s his work attracted the interest of Texas artists Jim Love and Roy Fridge and such collectors as Dominique and John de Menil,[qv] Nina Cullinan,[qv] Stanley Marcus, Houston architect Howard Barnstone,[qv] and New York architect Philip Johnson. Bess's theory on hermaphroditism alienated many, however, and his career waned after his last show at Parsons's gallery in 1967. During the 1970s Bess became increasingly eccentric. In 1974 he suffered a mild stroke and was admitted to the San Antonio State Hospital,[qv] where he was diagnosed a paranoid schizophrenic. Later that year he entered a nursing home in Bay City. At that time he stopped painting. He died in Bay City on November 11, 1977.

The Whitney Museum of American Art mounted a solo exhibition of Bess's paintings in 1981, and in 1987 a retrospective of his work was exhibited at the Butler Gallery in Houston. In 1988 a solo exhibition of his work was organized by the New York gallery Hirschl and Adler Modern, and the show subsequently traveled to the Museum of Contemporary Art in Chicago. Bess's paintings were also shown at the Museum Ludwig, Cologne, Germany, in 1989. His work is represented in the permanent collections of the Museum of Fine Arts, Houston, and the Menil Collection. His correspondence has been collected by the Houston branch of the Smithsonian Institute's Archives of American Art.

BIBLIOGRAPHY: Michael Ennis, "His Name was Forrest Bess," *Texas Monthly*, June 1982. Barbara Haskell, *Forrest Bess* (New York: Whitney Museum of American Art, 1981). John Money and Michael De Priest, "Three Cases of Genital Self-Surgery and Their Relationship to

Transsexualism," *Journal of Sex Research* 12 (November 1976). Vertical files, Houston Museum of Fine Arts.

Kendall Curlee and Rebecca H. Green

BESS, TEXAS (Dallas County). Bess was fourteen miles northeast of Dallas on Duck Creek; the site is now in Richardson, northern Dallas County. The settlement was started in the 1850s by members of the Peters colony[qv] and named for Lemuel Bess, who received a certificate for 320 acres that included the site. The land was patented in Dallas County in his name after he sold it. In 1949 Bess was served on a rural mail route from Garland. *Lisa C. Maxwell*

BESS, TEXAS (Duval County). Bess was sixteen miles north of San Diego in northeastern Duval County. A post office under the name of Mindiette operated there for less than a year in 1879, with Fabian Favela as postmaster. A second post office named Shaeffer after a local rancher opened in 1883 with John F. Leo Phelan as postmaster. In the 1890s a general store operated in Shaeffer, and by 1914 the town had a cotton gin. The local school was still known as the Mindiette school when forty-one pupils were registered in 1906–07. In 1917 the community was renamed Bess. In 1925 its estimated population was twenty. Two years later the count was 100, but by the mid-1930s it was again twenty, where it remained through 1990. Bess had two businesses during the 1930s, but by the early 1940s only one was still in operation. In the late 1940s the community had a few dwellings, a church, a cemetery, and a school. By 1955 the latter was known as the Bess school, but by the mid-1960s it had been consolidated with the San Diego Independent School District. At that time the community, which had a few scattered dwellings and the García and San José cemeteries, was called Mendiates on maps. In the mid-1970s the church was still identified as the Bess church. *Martin Donell Kohout*

BESSER, JOHN SLATER (1802–1893). John Slater Besser, explorer, prison administrator, and public servant, the son of Jacob and Susannah (Tinsley) Besser, was born on August 13, 1802, in Northumberland County, Pennsylvania. His father was a native of Heidelberg, Germany, and his mother a native of London, England. When Besser was two, his family moved to Philadelphia, where he attended the public school. In 1818 he left Philadelphia for the West. In St. Charles, Missouri, he spent three years learning the trade of a tailor. He accompanied William H. Ashley and his partner, Andrew Henry, in 1822 on a trapping and trading expedition up the Missouri River to the Yellowstone.

Subsequently, until November 1840, Besser was a resident of Missouri, where he served in the state militia and rose through the ranks to general. He was elected a justice of the county court of Lincoln County in 1830 and served in that capacity for four years. In 1834 he was elected as a Democrat to the Missouri legislature. After his terms he set out for the Republic of Texas.[qv] He settled near Huntsville in February 1841. In 1849 he moved into Huntsville, where he lived the remainder of his life. He served as a member of the commissioners' court of Montgomery County for two years, until the county was divided in 1846 into Montgomery, Grimes, and Walker counties.

Besser built the first jail in Walker County and was appointed purchasing agent, later known as financial agent, for the Texas State Penitentiary at Huntsville,[qv] a position he held from 1852 to 1863. For twenty months during Sam Houston's[qv] administration he was out of office; in retaliation for Besser's failure to support his gubernatorial candidacy, Houston relieved Besser of his duties, an act that Houston later claimed was the only mistake of his administration. Besser is credited with having drafted rules for the regulation of the penitentiary, and during his administration a revenue-producing factory was instigated there. During Governor Francis R. Lubbock's[qv] administration Besser was investigated by the Texas legislature for mismanagement, possibly an event motivated by his Union sympathies. He was not accused of wrongdoing, but neither was doubt thoroughly erased. In 1863, after Confederate soldiers took cloth from the prison factory at gunpoint and fired shots into his office, Besser resigned.

He was a Mason, a Presbyterian elder, and a lifelong Democrat. He was one of two persons in Lincoln County, Missouri, who voted in 1824 for Andrew Jackson for president. In Texas he opposed annexation[qv] to the United States. Although he was an anti-Houston "Southern Rights" Democrat in 1859, he considered secession[qv] from the Union unwise and in 1861 voted against it. In 1878 he was county judge of Walker County, although he was not a lawyer. His administration of county affairs and his economical management of the public money won him praise from his peers.

Besser was married four times, but had children only with his first wife, Julia Hampton, daughter of Thomas Hampton, an American Revolutionary War soldier and relative of Gen. Wade Hampton. The couple married in Lincoln County, Missouri, in June 1825 and had nine children, of whom six grew to majority. Besser died on May 19, 1893, in Huntsville and is buried in Oakwood Cemetery there.

BIBLIOGRAPHY: William S. Speer and John H. Brown, eds., *Encyclopedia of the New West* (Marshall, Texas: United States Biographical Publishing, 1881; rpt., Easley, South Carolina: Southern Historical Press, 1978). *Allie Mae Whitley*

BESSIE, TEXAS. Bessie, in southwestern Gaines County, was the site of the first school recognized by the state of Texas in Gaines County in the early 1900s. A post office operated there from 1905 to 1910, with James C. Dean as postmaster. The town, however, never developed, and the site was dropped from maps.

BIBLIOGRAPHY: Ed Ellsworth Bartholomew, *The Encyclopedia of Texas Ghost Towns* (Fort Davis, Texas, 1982). *Charles G. Davis*

BESSIES CREEK. Bessies Creek, also known as Best Creek, Best's Creek, or Besses Creek, rises 1½ miles northeast of Monaville in central Waller County (at 29°58′ N, 96°01′ W) and flows southeast for thirty miles, through northern Fort Bend County, to its mouth on the Brazos River, three miles south of Fulshear (at 29°39′ N, 95°54′ W). It crosses an area of moderate to steep slopes surfaced by sandy loam and clay that support hardwoods and crops. The creek was probably named for Isaac Best, an early settler of Waller County.

BESSMAY, TEXAS. Bessmay is on U.S. Highway 96 one mile north of Buna and thirty-seven miles north of Beaumont in south central Jasper County. The construction of the Gulf, Beaumont and Kansas City Railway from Silsbee to Kirbyville in 1895 and the Orange and Northwestern from Orange to Newton between 1902 and 1906 opened the area to extensive lumbering operations. Bessmay is named for the daughter of John Henry Kirby,[qv] whose mill opened at the site in the early 1900s. The Bessmay post office began operations in 1903. By 1904 Kirby inspectors called the Bessmay facility, with planer, sawmill, and kiln, "the best owned by the company." Mill R, as the plant was called, was equipped with modern conveniences, including an electric light plant, and was valued at $350,000 in 1907. In 1914 a Kirby manager noted that the sawmill, which could cut 130,000 board feet in a single ten-hour shift, was "running day and night." As forests were depleted and lumbering operations consolidated at Silsbee, the old sawmill town of Bessmay lost some of its population, from 600 in 1949 to 400 by the mid-1960s. However, logging remained important in the local economy. The Bessmay election precinct was consolidated with that of Buna in 1956.

BIBLIOGRAPHY: Kirby Lumber Corporation Papers, Steen Library, Stephen F. Austin State University. S. G. Reed, *A History of the Texas Railroads* (Houston: St. Clair, 1941; rpt., New York: Arno, 1981).

Robert Wooster

BEST, ISAAC (1774–1837). Isaac Best, one of Stephen F. Austin's[qv] Old Three Hundred[qv] colonists, the son of Stephen Best, was born in 1774, possibly in Pennsylvania. He married Mary Margaret Wilkins, and the couple had nine children. After spending his early years in Pennsylvania and Kentucky, Best and his wife left Garrard County, Kentucky, and moved to Montgomery County in southern Missouri in 1808. There he built a mill and an outpost known as Best's Fort, which served as a refuge from Indian attacks during the War of 1812. The family and several slaves moved to Texas in 1824. On August 19 of that year Best received title to a sitio[qv] east of the Brazos River in what is now Waller County. He increased his landholdings and built a home near the site of present Pattison. The 1826 census described Best as a farmer and stock raiser between forty and fifty years of age. His household consisted of his wife, three sons, two daughters, and four slaves. Best may have lived at San Felipe in 1833, when William B. Travis[qv] issued a subpoena for him as a witness in a case against Isaac Clower. Best died near Pattison in 1837. On August 29, 1974, the Texas Historical Commission[qv] dedicated a marker to him on Farm Road 1458 1 ½ miles west of Pattison.

BIBLIOGRAPHY: Lester G. Bugbee, "The Old Three Hundred: A List of Settlers in Austin's First Colony," *Quarterly of the Texas State Historical Association* 1 (October 1897). Waller County Historical Survey Committee, *A History of Waller County, Texas* (Waco: Texian, 1973).

BEST, TEXAS. Best, on the Santa Fe Railroad in southwestern Reagan County, was started in 1924 as an Orient Railroad switch, reputedly named for an English stockholder, Tom Best. After the discovery of oil in 1923, Best was developed as a supply center for the county's expanding production. By 1925 its population was an estimated 3,500. Although boosters envisioned a model town, undesirable oil-boom followers gave Best a wild reputation, as portrayed in Clyde Ragsdale's novel *The Big Fist* (1946). The reputation seems to have been deserved. There were enough murders, knifings, shootings, and brawls that the slogan became "the town with the Best name in the world and the Worst reputation." The town declined rapidly after 1925. By 1945 only a few businesses and 300 people remained. In 1983 there were two families and a service station-post office. In 1990 the population was twenty-five.

BIBLIOGRAPHY: Carl Coke Rister, *Oil! Titan of the Southwest* (Norman: University of Oklahoma Press, 1949). Martin W. Schwettmann, The Discovery and Early Development of the Big Lake Oil Field (M.A. thesis, University of Texas, 1941). *Jane Spraggins Wilson*

BETHANY, TEXAS (Collin County). Bethany, in southwestern Collin County, was started about 1876 and named for an early settler. In 1990 a cemetery remained, and the site had become part of Plano. *Brian Hart*

BETHANY, TEXAS (Panola County). Bethany is on the Louisiana state line and U.S. Highway 79 twenty-two miles northeast of Carthage in northeastern Panola County. The site was first settled around 1840. The community, which grew up as a stopping point for settlers moving to Texas from the Old South, was originally known as Vernon, but the name was changed to Bethany around 1849 when a post office was established. In the 1840s the town had a log store, a tavern, a water-powered grain mill, and a tannery. In 1860 the post office was relocated to Caddo Parish, Louisiana. After the Civil War[qv] Bethany began to decline, and by the late 1890s the local school had only nine students. The development of the Bethany gas field, which opened in the 1920s, brought a resurgence of the economy, and by the mid-1930s the community had two churches, five stores, an elementary school, and a number of houses. After World War II[qv] Bethany began to decline again. In the mid-1960s it supported a church, a community center, and several businesses. In the early 1990s Bethany was a dispersed rural community with a church and a few stores. One of the stores, bisected by the state line, was built in 1889 by a barkeeper who wanted to take advantage of the differences in state laws; in half of the store drinking was legal, in the other gambling was legal.

BIBLIOGRAPHY: *History of Panola County.* (Carthage, Texas: Carthage Circulating Book Club, 1935?). John Barnette Sanders, *Postoffices and Post Masters of Panola County, Texas, 1845-1930* (Center, Texas, 1964). *Christopher Long*

BETHEL, GEORGE EMMETT (1894–1935). George Emmett Bethel, physician and teacher, was born on November 2, 1894, in Garland, Texas, the son of Simpson and Virginia Marcia (Soule) Bethel. After attending Garland High School and the University of Texas, he taught in 1914 at Lockhart. In 1923 he graduated with honors from the Medical Branch of the University of Texas (now the University of Texas Medical Branch at Galveston), where he was elected to Alpha Omega Alpha, a national honorary scholastic fraternity, and, as an undergraduate, served as assistant instructor in the anatomy department. After a year's internship in St. Mary's Infirmary (now St. Mary's Hospital[qv]) in Galveston, he spent two years in Philadelphia General Hospital, one of them as assistant chief resident physician. He returned to the University of Texas medical school as associate professor of anatomy in 1926, but in September of that year he was asked to serve as director of the University of Texas health services. He was also professor of therapeutics in the UT School of Pharmacy. In 1928 Bethel was appointed dean of the University of Texas medical school. Under his stewardship the institution raised its standards and expanded its facilities. He was a member of the Texas Medical Association[qv] and the Southern Medical Association, a fellow of the American College of Physicians, and a member of Alpha Kappa medical fraternity. He was director of the Galveston YMCA, the Rosenberg Library,[qv] and the Red Cross board. He was a Rotarian, a Baptist, and a Mason. Dr. Bethel died on April 17, 1935, after an extended illness and was buried at Gorman, Texas.

BIBLIOGRAPHY: *Who Was Who in America*, Vol. 2. *Albert O. Singleton*

BETHEL, TEXAS (Anderson County). Bethel is on U.S. Highway 287 eight miles southeast of the Trinity River in northwest Anderson County. Most of the land at the site was granted to José de Jesús Grande on October 28, 1828. In his grant application he agreed to populate and cultivate the land, but little colonization was done until the earliest Anglo-American settlement about 1833, part of a Baptist migration to the area. By the early 1850s the community had a general store and a blacksmith shop. A Bethel post office operated from 1852 until 1914; Charles Gilmore was the first postmaster. The 1860 census of Anderson County showed 300 inhabitants at Bethel.

The local cemetery was begun, and a church building was erected, on five acres of land donated by Henry Rampy on July 13, 1859. The deed was made to F. S. Jackson, Thomas Hudson, and Isaiah King for church and cemetery purposes for Baptists, Methodists, and Cumberland Presbyterians. Rampy had come to the area in 1848. The church was used for about forty years, after which it was abandoned and the building was torn down. The cemetery was still in use in 1990 and was maintained by a voluntary association including descendants of the original grantor. Until recent years the cemetery was marked by a grove of huge cedar trees. Local legend says that during the Civil War[qv] the Confederacy had a campground at the cemetery. While bivouacked there, a large number of soldiers died; since it was not prudent to mark their graves and leave evidence of the encampment, the cedar trees were planted so that after the war people could return and place markers.

The economy of the area has always been largely agricultural. During the Great Depression[qv] of the 1930s the population dropped to thirty. It rose to ninety when major oil discoveries after World War II[qv] temporarily improved the economy. Bethel's population stayed around ninety until the 1970s, when it declined again to thirty. The Bethel school district was consolidated with the Cayuga Independent School District in the 1950s, and in 1990 all that remained of Bethel was the cemetery and the facilities of the Cayuga school district. The 1990 population was thirty-one.

BIBLIOGRAPHY: Kathleen E. and Clifton R. St. Clair, eds., *Little Towns of Texas* (Jacksonville, Texas: Jayroe Graphic Arts, 1982). Michael J. Vaughn, *The History of Cayuga and Cross Roads* (Waco: Texian Press, 1967). *Michael J. Vaughn*

BETHEL, TEXAS (Burnet County). Bethel is on Farm Road 963 eight miles northeast of Burnet in north central Burnet County. A school was established there in 1869. The settlement was closely linked with nearby Sage, which had a post office and a store but used the Bethel school. The school had one teacher and twenty-five students in the mid-1890s; it closed in 1941, when the area was consolidated with the Burnet Independent School District. Several houses and a cemetery marked the community on county highway maps in the late 1940s. Bethel had a community center and a few scattered houses in 1990.

BIBLIOGRAPHY: Darrell Debo, *Burnet County History* (2 vols., Burnet, Texas: Eakin, 1979). *Vivian Elizabeth Smyrl*

BETHEL, TEXAS (Freestone County). Bethel is six miles east of U.S. Highway 84 and thirteen miles southeast of Fairfield in southeast Freestone County. Bethel School had thirty-one white pupils in 1891 and thirty-eight in 1903. Little Bethel School had nineteen black pupils in 1891 and thirty-nine in 1899. By the 1930s the community had only three or four scattered dwellings. In the 1960s only one dwelling and a cemetery remained.

BIBLIOGRAPHY: Freestone County Historical Commission, *History of Freestone County, Texas* (Fairfield, Texas, 1978).

Chris Cravens

BETHEL, TEXAS (Gregg County). Bethel, 1½ miles northeast of Gladewater in northwestern Gregg County, was established in the mid-1840s and grew up around the Bethel Baptist Church. A local school was founded later and continued to operate until the early twentieth century. The community, however, began to decline after the Civil War[qv] and disappeared around the 1870s. The church became the present First Baptist Church of Gladewater. In the 1990s the site was located on the northeastern edge of Gladewater.

BIBLIOGRAPHY: Eugene W. McWhorter, *Traditions of the Land: The History of Gregg County* (Longview, Texas: Gregg County Historical Foundation, 1989). *Christopher Long*

BETHEL, TEXAS (Henderson County). Bethel is on State Highway 19 six miles north of Athens in north central Henderson County. The settlement was evidently founded around the time of the Civil War.[qv] In the mid-1930s it had a church, a school, and a number of houses. After World War II[qv] the school closed, and in the early 1990s only a church, a cemetery, and a few houses remained.

Christopher Long

BETHEL, TEXAS (Hopkins County). Bethel, also known as Askew, eleven miles southeast of Sulphur Springs and two miles west of Farm Road 269 in southeastern Hopkins County, was settled in 1853 by R. E. Matthews and John and R. S. Askew. In 1860 John Askew gave land for a church that continued to be used until 1948. A post office under the name Askew operated in Mary Harden's store from 1901 to 1906, when the store closed. A local school was conducted after the turn of the century and in 1905 had an enrollment of thirty-one. In the mid-1930s the community comprised a church, a school, and a few scattered dwellings. By the early 1950s the church and school had closed. In the early 1960s the area was known as Bethel. In the late 1980s the site was marked only by Bethel Church.

J. E. Jennings

BETHEL, TEXAS (Houston County). Bethel, a rural community off Farm Road 227 two miles west of Tadmore in eastern Houston County, was established before 1900. A local school had an enrollment of fifty-four in 1897. In the mid-1930s the community had a church, a store, a cemetery, and a number of houses. After World War II[qv] many of the residents moved away, but in the mid-1960s a church, a cemetery, and a few widely scattered houses still remained in the area. In the early 1990s Bethel was a dispersed rural community.

Christopher Long

BETHEL, TEXAS (Rusk County). Bethel is a scattered community of rural residences on an unimproved road five miles south of Henderson in Rusk County. In 1903–04 a school there had one teacher and twenty-seven students and in 1907–08 fifty-six students and one teacher. Bethel is shown on 1936 maps as Bethel School. At that time a cemetery and a church were also located there. On 1965 maps only the church and cemetery are shown. Bethel is a farming and stock-raising community now in the Henderson Independent School District.

BIBLIOGRAPHY: Dorman H. Winfrey, *A History of Rusk County* (Waco: Texian, 1961). *John G. Johnson*

BETHEL, TEXAS (San Saba County). Bethel, formerly known as Velma and Lone Hand, is beside the Cottonbelt Road five miles northeast of the community of Richland Springs in central San Saba County. W. C. Locker and his family settled in this cotton-producing area in the early 1890s and constructed a cotton gin. Lone Hand School, built in 1894, gave the community its first name. Baptist services were held either in the school building or under a brush arbor until a separate structure was built for the church. W. J. Crouch opened his general store in 1897, and on July 5, 1899, he opened the post office under the name of Velma, in honor of Miss Velma Whitehead. After the post office closed in 1906, the community was called Bethel. The school building had been replaced by a new one named Bethel School. After the boll weevil[qv] devastated the cotton industry, farmers in the community turned to melon and berry production and pecan and fruit orchards. The farmers continued to diversify by producing peanuts, cattle, and swine. A church and cemetery were located at the townsite in 1984.

BIBLIOGRAPHY: *San Saba County History* (San Saba, Texas: San Saba County Historical Commission, 1983). *Karen Yancy*

BETHEL, TEXAS (Tarrant County). Bethel was a railroad community on the Missouri, Kansas and Texas Railroad in southern Tarrant County. It was established sometime during or after the late 1870s and served area farmers and ranchers as a community center for twenty or thirty years, then disappeared. The Bethel station appeared on county highway maps as late as 1936. Bethel never had a post office. According to some sources, a second Bethel, originally part of the Peters colony[qv] grant, existed in eastern Tarrant County during the 1850s.

BIBLIOGRAPHY: Janet L. Schmelzer, *Where the West Begins: Fort Worth and Tarrant County* (Northridge, California: Windsor, 1985).

David Minor

BETHEL, TEXAS (Van Zandt County). Bethel, near Farm Road 1651 eight miles southwest of Canton in southwest Van Zandt County, dates to October 27, 1858, when William F. Palmer and his wife deeded acreage for a Methodist Episcopal Church, South, and a cemetery nine miles southwest of Canton. In 1936 Bethel comprised a school, a church, a cemetery, and scattered dwellings, but by the 1950s the school had been consolidated with the Canton Independent School District. In 1965 the church, the cemetery, a single business establishment, and several dwellings marked the townsite, but population figures were unavailable. By 1984 only the church and scattered dwellings remained.

BIBLIOGRAPHY: Van Zandt County History Book Committee, *History of Van Zandt County* (Dallas, 1984). *Diana J. Kleiner*

BETHEL BAPTIST CHURCH. Bethel Baptist Church was organized in an area referred to as the "dark corner" of Sabine County, between the settlements of Milam and Sexton. It was constituted on February 7, 1841, in the home of Theophilus Harris as a Predestinarian Regular Baptist Church of Jesus Christ under the authority of Daniel Parker[qv] and his Pilgrim Church at Elkhart, Anderson County. The Bethel group had met earlier and asked to be aligned with the Union Association of the Pilgrim Church, but it appears that it never did in fact join the association. Bethel Church was among the five East Texas Missionary Baptist churches that met at Union (Old North) Church four miles north of Nacogdoches on November 11, 1843, and organized the Sabine Baptist Association. They were the Union and Mount Zion, Nacogdoches County; Border and Bethel, Harrison County; and Bethel, Sabine County. The action of the Bethel Church in aligning itself with the Sabine Association naturally aroused the ire of Daniel Parker, his Predestinarian brethren in the Pilgrim Church, and the Union Association, who were opposed to missionary societies and boards, Bible societies, Sunday schools, and secret organizations, all of which were claimed to be purely devices of man with no scriptural authority for their existence. Parker's Pilgrim Church, in regular conference on August 17, 1844, called upon the Bethel Church to surrender its authority as a church, since it had "departed from the faith and order." At a meeting held at Bethel Church from October 6 to 13, 1845, thirty-six persons were baptized into the Missionary Baptist belief. The site of the old Bethel Baptist Church was deeded to the church on November 17, 1878, by Mrs. Julie R. Mason, widow of William Mason, who had obtained the land from the Republic of Texas[qv] in 1838. The white frame building and old cemetery are located in an opening of a heavily wooded forest. The oldest Baptist church in Sabine County, it has remained in continuous operation since it was founded, although the name has been changed to New Hope Baptist Church.

BIBLIOGRAPHY: Zenos N. Morrell, *Flowers and Fruits from the Wilderness* (Boston: Gould and Lincoln, 1872; rpt. of 3d ed., Irving, Texas: Griffin Graphic Arts, 1966). William Tellis Parmer, *A Centennial History of Sexton Lodge* (Milam, Texas: Sexton Lodge, 1960). Papers of the Pilgrim Predestinarian Regular Baptist Church of Jesus Christ, Barker Texas History Center, University of Texas at Austin. "Records of an Early Texas Baptist Church," *Quarterly of the Texas State Historical Association* 11, 12 (October 1907, July 1908). Sabine Baptist Association Collection, Texas Collection, Baylor University. San Augustine *Red-Lander*, October 26, 1844.

Helen Gomer Schluter

BETHLEHEM, TEXAS (Limestone County). Bethlehem, a predominantly black community west of Mexia in north central Limestone County, grew up around a Primitive Baptist church. Around 1900 the school at Bethlehem was merged with the schools at Sardis and Smith Chapel to form Woodland School. This institution was consolidated with the school at Rocky Crossing in the 1930s. Bethlehem was not marked on county highways maps by the 1940s.

BIBLIOGRAPHY: Walter F. Cotton, *History of Negroes of Limestone County from 1860 to 1939* (Mexia, Texas: Chatman and Merriwether, 1939). James Cecil Moore, Reorganization of School Districting in Limestone County, Texas (M.A. thesis, University of Texas, 1935).

Vivian Elizabeth Smyrl

BETHLEHEM, TEXAS (Marion County). Bethlehem was a school community fourteen miles northwest of Jefferson in northwestern Marion County. The Bethlehem school had eighty-nine black pupils and one teacher in 1899. In 1938 the community had a one-room schoolhouse that accommodated thirty-five elementary students. The school was consolidated with the Lassater schools by 1955, and in 1962 Bethlehem was not shown on government survey maps.

BIBLIOGRAPHY: Jack Reed Harvey, Survey and Proposed Reorganization of the Marion County Schools (M.A. thesis, University of Texas, 1940). *Mark Odintz*

BETHLEHEM, TEXAS (Milam County). Bethlehem was three miles north of Rockdale in central Milam County. It became a voting precinct in 1880. The settlement, which was named for the biblical city, had a one-teacher school with forty-two students in 1903. The school was consolidated with the Rockdale Independent School District in 1954. No evidence of the community appeared on 1988 county highway maps.

BIBLIOGRAPHY: Lelia M. Batte, *History of Milam County, Texas* (San Antonio: Naylor, 1956). Milam County Heritage Preservation Society, *Matchless Milam: History of Milam County* (Dallas: Taylor, 1984).

Vivian Elizabeth Smyrl

BETHLEHEM, TEXAS (Smith County). Bethlehem is a church community a mile east of Saline Bay and three miles west of Flint in extreme southwestern Smith County. The church and cemetery lie just north of Farm Road 346. In 1936 a local school employed two teachers for fifty-eight black students in grades one through seven, and the vicinity supported three churches. By 1952 the school had been consolidated with the Bullard Independent School District. Maps for 1973 show a large church, a cemetery, and a few scattered farms at the site of Bethlehem. The area was still sparsely settled in 1981. The Wheeler Rodeo Grounds were located to the west and Julia Drew Temple to the north.

BIBLIOGRAPHY: Edward Clayton Curry, An Administrative Survey of the Schools of Smith County, Texas (M.Ed. thesis, University of Texas, 1938). *Vista K. McCroskey*

BETHLEHEM, TEXAS (Upshur County). Bethlehem is on Farm Road 1650 eleven miles southeast of Gilmer in southeastern Upshur County. The site was settled in the early 1850s. A school began operating there around 1900. In the mid-1930s the community had a church, a school, a store, a cemetery, and a number of scattered houses. During the 1950s Bethlehem and nearby Omega formed an independent school district with a high school. The school and church were later moved a mile south to New Bethlehem, and in 1958 the school was consolidated with the East Mountain school district. In the mid-1960s Bethlehem had a church, a cemetery, a store, and a few houses. In 1990 the church and cemetery were still maintained, and Bethlehem reported a population of twenty-five.

BIBLIOGRAPHY: Doyal T. Loyd, *History of Upshur County* (Waco: Texian Press, 1987). *Christopher Long*

BETHLEHEM, TEXAS (Van Zandt County). Bethlehem was near Farm Road 1504 eight miles northwest of Canton in northwest Van Zandt County. It had one white and one black school; the enrollment was forty-one in 1903 at the black school, which existed by 1890, and seventy-two at the white school in 1905. By the 1950s the school population was divided between the Edgewood and Wills Point school districts. New Hope Cemetery is located near the site. The 1936 state highway maps showed a school and scattered dwellings there, but by 1965 Bethlehem had disappeared.

BIBLIOGRAPHY: Van Zandt County History Book Committee, *History of Van Zandt County* (Dallas, 1984). *Diana J. Kleiner*

BETO, GEORGE JOHN (1916–1991). George John Beto, criminal-justice expert, teacher, and Lutheran minister, was born in Hysham, Montana, on January 19, 1916, the son of Margaret (Witsma) and Louis Beto, a circuit riding Lutheran minister. When he was a year old he moved with his parents to New Rockford, North Dakota. Two years later the family moved to Lena, Illinois, where Beto lived until 1930, when he enrolled in Concordia College, a Lutheran boys' boarding school in Milwaukee, Wisconsin. After completing a six-year college-preparatory curriculum in five years, Beto studied for the ministry at Concordia Seminary in St. Louis, Missouri, from 1935 to 1937. He transferred to Valparaiso University in Indiana during 1937 and received his bachelor of arts degree there in 1938. Beto returned to the seminary in 1938 and completed his theological studies in 1939; the school awarded him a doctor of divinity degree in 1989. From 1939 until 1949 he taught history at Concordia Lutheran College in Austin, Texas. From January 1949 to June 1959 he served as the college's president. Beto was ordained a minister of the Lutheran Church (Missouri Synod) at St. Paul's Church in Austin in 1944 and served for a time as the congregation's assistant pastor. Also in 1944 he earned a master of arts degree in medieval history from the University of Texas. In 1955 he completed a Ph.D. in educational administration at UT.

Beto began a lengthy involvement with criminal justice when in 1953 Governor Allan Shivers[qv] appointed him to the Texas Prison Board (renamed Texas Board of Corrections in 1957). Until July 1959 Beto served on the administrative agency of the Texas prison system, performing the duties of board secretary for three of those years. He played a crucial role in the establishment of perhaps the first General Education Development testing program for prisoners in the nation in 1956 and the following year received a medal from the Texas Heritage Foundation in recognition of his contributions to that project. Beto resigned from the Board of Corrections and Concordia College to become president of Concordia Theological Seminary at Springfield, Illinois, on July 1, 1959. He remained in that position until 1962. During these years he visited and surveyed prisons in Germany, France, England, Denmark, and Holland. He also served as chairman of the Committee to Evaluate the Illinois Youth Commission and was a member of the Illinois Parole and Pardon Board.

After the death of Oscar Byron Ellis[qv] in November 1961, Beto became director and chief of chaplains for the Texas Department of Corrections, on March 1, 1962; he held those positions through August 31, 1972. Prisoners often called him "Walking George" because he unexpectedly visited inmates and employees at the various prison properties. Beto, who observed that "the poor, the stupid, and the inept" composed the majority of the prison population, also believed in the possibility of rehabilitation. Although many inmates admired him for his willingness to communicate with them, they also regarded him as a stern disciplinarian, a "preacher" with "a baseball bat in one hand and a Bible in the other."

Like Ellis, Beto mastered the use of favorable publicity and media support for his administration. Cooperating with board chairman H. H. Coffield to promote a positive image, he secured legislative approval and appropriations for the prison system and successfully shielded his department from the scrutiny of potential critics. He persuaded the legislature and Governor John Connally to enact a state's-use law in 1963, which required state government agencies to purchase manufactured goods from the state's prisons. That law resulted in a tremendous expansion of industrial activity and employment and training for prisoners; the sale of prison-manufactured goods increased from less than $600,000 in 1964 to more than $6 million annually by 1972. As the prisoner population increased from 12,000 to 16,000 during these years, Beto supervised the opening of two new prison units at Huntsville and won legislative approval and funding for a large facility in Anderson County. Although fewer prisoners worked in agriculture than in earlier years, the farm program, under Byron W. Frierson, assistant director for agriculture, continued to produce income from cash sales as well as allow prisoners to raise most of the food consumed by the institution.

George Beto (third from left) leading a tour of a Texas prison, ca. 1970 (the others, left to right: unidentified, Barbara Jordan, Beto, R. M. Cousins, William S. Heatly, A. G. McKain, Byron W. Frierson). Courtesy Mrs. Byron W. Frierson, Sugar Land. Prisoners called Beto "Walking George" because of his regular tours of prison facilities.

Through Beto's urging, the Board of Corrections in 1963 converted the Harlem Farm (*see* JESTER STATE PRISON FARM) into a prerelease facility to provide an eight-week program of counseling and education for state prisoners prior to their release. In 1969 the department began a special work-release program that allowed selected prisoners, with less than a year remaining before discharge, to work as paid employees for private employers and return to prison after completing their shifts. Also during 1969, at Beto's instigation, the Texas legislature authorized a nongeographical public school district for inmates housed at all prison units. Financed by the state Foundation School Program Fund, the Windham school district was possibly the first educational system of its kind established at any state prison in the nation. Beto also expanded college-education programs at prison facilities and cooperated with Sam Houston State University to develop a criminology program for research and the training of prison employees and others interested in pursuing criminal justice careers. In 1965, probably for the first time in the history of the Texas prison system, Beto hired African-American employees. During his years as director he received national and international recognition for his abilities; his peers in the American Correctional Association elected him president for 1969–70. From 1966 to 1969 he served on the National Advisory Council on Correctional Manpower and Training; in 1970 he was a delegate to the Fourth United Nations Conference on Prevention of Crime and Treatment of the Offender in Kyoto, Japan.

Despite the prestige enjoyed by Beto among penologists and political leaders, he also attracted a number of critics. Considered by some reformers as "enlightened" but "reactionary," he received much criticism for his use of authoritarian disciplinary policies and methods of control that allowed certain prisoners to supervise and discipline other inmates. Many prisoners complained that Beto and his staff harassed and threatened those who attempted to file civil-rights suits against prison officials. A federal court ruled in favor of prisoners and their attorney, Frances Jalet Cruz, who charged that Beto had denied them access to legal services. The court found Beto liable for "unlawful intimidation," and "unlawful punishments" and awarded monetary damages valued at $10,000 to twelve prisoners and Jalet. On June 29, 1972, near the end of Beto's tenure as director, prisoner David Ruiz filed a handwritten petition against conditions of confinement in Texas prisons that began the most enduring prisoners'-rights suit in the nation's history.

Beto's reputation among most criminal justice experts remained intact, however, for the remainder of his life. After he retired as director of the Texas Department of Corrections, he served as a professor of corrections at Sam Houston State University from 1972 until 1991. Beto was a member of the Texas Constitutional Revision Commission, 1973–74, and a member of the Texas Youth Commission[qv] board, 1975–78. Federal District Judge Frank Johnson in 1976 selected him to monitor conditions in Alabama prisons during class-action litigation by prisoners in that state. Beto served with the American Bar Association Commission on Correctional Facilities and Services, 1971–78, and the National Advisory Commission on Criminal Justice Standard and Goals, 1972–73. He represented the United States at United Nations Conferences on Prevention of Crime and Treatment of the Offender at Geneva, Switzerland, in 1975 and Milan, Italy, in 1985 and evaluated correctional facilities in Poland, Egypt, and Qatar in 1976. As a consultant, he also surveyed United States military correctional sites in West Germany in 1974 and at Fort Leavenworth, Kansas, in 1984.

Beto received a Distinguished Alumnus award from the University of Texas in 1971; the state of Texas opened two prison units in Anderson County in 1980 and 1981 and named them for him. He and his wife, the former Marilyn Knippa, whom he married on March 5, 1943, were the parents of four children. Following his retirement from Sam Houston State University in 1991, Beto moved to Austin, where he served as chief of chaplains for the Texas Youth Commission from September until he died of an apparent heart attack on December 4 of that year. He was buried in the State Cemetery[qv] in Austin. *See also* PRISON SYSTEMS.

BIBLIOGRAPHY: George John Beto Papers, Gresham Library, Sam Houston State University. Ronald Craig Copeland, The Evolution of the Texas Department of Corrections (M.A. thesis, Sam Houston State University, 1980). Ben M. Crouch and James W. Marquart, *An Appeal to Justice: Litigated Reform of Texas Prisons* (Austin: University of Texas Press, 1989). Steve J. Martin and Sheldon Ekland-Olson, *Texas Prisons: The Walls Came Tumbling Down* (Austin: Texas Monthly Press, 1987). Vertical files, Barker Texas History Center, University of Texas at Austin. *Paul M. Lucko*

BETSADA, TEXAS. Betsada was probably near the eastern bank of Tres Palacios Bay four miles across the bay from what is now Palacios, in southwestern Matagorda County. In 1895 the community received a post office, and A. P. Logan was postmaster until it closed the following year. In 1896 Betsada, described in that year's Texas State Gazetteer and Business Directory as "a northern colony," reported a population of seventy-five. The community does not appear on more recent maps.

BIBLIOGRAPHY: Matagorda County Historical Commission, *Historic Matagorda County* (3 vols., Houston: Armstrong, 1986).
Rachel Jenkins

BETTER SCHOOLS AMENDMENT. The Better Schools Amendment to the Constitution of 1876[qv] was passed by Texas voters in 1920. It removed limitations on tax rates allowable by local school districts for support of their public schools. The constitution designated local taxes, public lands, occupation taxes, and poll taxes as funding sources for Texas public schools. In 1908 voters approved a limit on the rate of local taxation, which educational leaders in 1920 considered an obstacle to progress. A vigorous campaign for the Better Schools Amendment was led by State Superintendent of Public Instruction Annie Webb Blanton,[qv] who was assisted by such education advocates and leaders as Jane Y. McCallum, Alexander Caswell Ellis, Robert E. Vinson, Samuel Palmer Brooks, and Frederick Eby.[qqv] The campaign was headquartered in Austin and patterned after the big war drives. It utilized county organizations, songs, slogans, posters, automobile stickers, and speaking tours. May 1, 1920, was designated "Tag Day" by campaign leaders, and more than $20,000 was raised as teachers, schools, colleges, parent-teacher groups, and businesses purchased tags to show support and help finance the amendment. The amendment, approved by the Thirty-sixth Legislature in 1919, was sent to voters for ratification on November 2, 1920. It was approved by a vote of 221,223 to 126,282.

Passage of the Better Schools Amendment was significant not only for its removal of local tax limitations but also for its effort at easing the state's burden of school financing by making it possible for local support to increase. Educators also hoped the amendment would increase equality in school conditions by opening an opportunity for each district to improve its facilities. The results of the amendment were mixed. According to Annie Blanton, it brought a 51 percent increase in local support for public schools before she left office in 1923. Some school personnel, however, were disappointed that many local districts moved slowly to increase taxation while continuing to rely on the state as their primary source of financing. The Better Schools Amendment, still part of the Texas Constitution, offered a mechanism for funding public education, along with additional taxes and the Permanent School Fund.[qv]

BIBLIOGRAPHY: Frederick Eby, *The Development of Education in Texas* (New York: Macmillan, 1925). Frederick Eby Papers, Texas Collection, Baylor University. Cecil Eugene Evans, *The Story of Texas Schools* (Austin: Steck, 1955). *Texas Outlook*, September 1920, January 1921. Vertical files, Barker Texas History Center, University of Texas at Austin (Annie Webb Blanton). *Debbie Mauldin Cottrell*

BETTIE, TEXAS. Bettie, at the junction of U.S. Highway 271 and Farm Road 2088, six miles north of Gilmer in north central Upshur County, was established in the early 1880s as a stop on the newly constructed Texas and St. Louis Railway. During the antebellum period (*see* ANTEBELLUM TEXAS) the area had been a lumbering center. The town was named for Mary Elizabeth (Aunt Bettie) Anderson, an early settler. A Bettie post office opened in 1882 with Neri Anderson, owner of the local general store, as postmaster. By 1885 the community had a steam lumber and shingle mill, Baptist and Methodist churches, a district school, and an estimated population of 100. Much of the town's economy was based on lumbering, but after 1890 Bettie also became an important center for shipping sweet potatoes. The first area school was established at nearby Rocky Point but was moved to Bettie in 1894. By 1906 two local schools were operating, with a total enrollment of 128. A bank was organized at Bettie in 1913 but was closed in 1921, when the county's banks were consolidated. The population continued to grow during the 1920s, to a peak of 400 in 1929. During the 1930s, however, it began to decline, partly as a result of the Great Depression[qv] and the flight to the larger cities. In the mid-1930s Bettie comprised ten businesses and a number of scattered houses; the population in 1933 was estimated at 284. After World War II[qv] the town continued to decline; the population was 150 in 1958 and 100 by the mid-1960s. The post office and most of the businesses closed. In the mid-1960s Bettie consisted of several stores and a large number of houses. In 1990 it was a small rural community with three stores and an estimated population of 110.

BIBLIOGRAPHY: G. H. Baird, *A Brief History of Upshur County* (Gilmer, Texas: Gilmer *Mirror*, 1946). Doyal T. Loyd, *History of Upshur County* (Waco: Texian Press, 1987). *Christopher Long*

BETTINA, TEXAS. Bettina, a short-lived commune on the north bank of the Llano River in western Llano County, was settled in 1847 by a fraternity of highly educated German communitarian freethinkers influenced by the writings of Étienne Cabet[qv] and Charles Fourier. Bettina was the seventh, and last, of the Adelsverein[qv] colonies in Texas. It was one five settlements attempted by the Adelsverein within the Fisher-Miller Land Grant[qv] after John O. Meusebach[qv] concluded a treaty with the Comanches in the spring of 1847. It was named for Bettina Brentano von Arnim, a German liberal and writer. The first building was a thatched common house forty feet long by twenty-two feet wide. An adobe[qv] house, with a shingled roof and a massive fireplace, was built next. Crops were planted, and the first harvest was satisfactory. However, cooperation gradually foundered because of dissention over work details and the role of a young woman cook, a Hispanic captive presented as a gift by a Comanche chief who underwent successful eye surgery while visiting Bettina. The utopian venture lasted less than a year, but many of the members of this group went on to make major contributions to Texas life. Notable were Dr. Ferdinand von Herff,[qv] an eminent San Antonio physician and surgeon; Gustav Schleicher,[qv] an engineer who helped to expand the state's rail system and who thereafter became a member of Congress; and Jacob Kuechler,[qv] a vocal Unionist who became commissioner of the General Land Office[qv] in Austin. Others, such as Christoph Flach and Johannes Hoerner, founded large and prominent Hill Country[qv] families that for four or five generations retained vestiges of freethinking liberalism and ethics. The writings of Louis Reinhardt and Friedrich Schenck,[qv] two members, illustrate the everyday experiences of the group in Texas; Herff wrote a political treatise in which he touches on the colony and generalizes on the founding principles. The journalist Emma F. Murck Atgelt, the geologist Ferdinand von Roemer, the editor Ferdinand J. Lindheimer,[qqv] and others not directly associated with the fraternity also wrote about the settlement and its individual members. Vera Flach wrote a moving twentieth-century account of the acculturation of one of the Bettina families. The former commune is commemorated, along with the nearby Adelsverein settlements of Castell and Leiningen, by a state historical marker placed in 1964 on the north side of the Llano River across from Castell.

BIBLIOGRAPHY: Rudolph L. Biesele, *The History of the German Settlements in Texas, 1831–1861* (Austin: Von Boeckmann–Jones, 1930; rpt. 1964). Vera Flach, *A Yankee in German-America: Texas Hill Country* (San Antonio: Naylor, 1973). Ferdinand von Herff, *The Regulated Emigration of the German Proletariat with Special Reference to Texas,* trans. Arthur L. Finck (San Antonio: Trinity University Press, 1978). H. T. Edward Hertzberg, trans., "A Letter from Friedrich Schenck in Texas to His Mother in Germany, 1847," *Southwestern Historical Quarterly* 92 (July 1988). Glen E. Lich and Dona B. Reeves, eds., *German Culture in Texas* (Boston: Twayne, 1980). Glen E. Lich, *The German Texans* (San Antonio: University of Texas Institute of Texan Cultures, 1981). Louis Reinhardt, "The Communistic Colony of Bettina," *Quarterly of the Texas State Historical Association* 3 (July 1899).

Glen E. Lich

BETTIS, VALERIE ELIZABETH (1919–1982). Valerie Elizabeth Bettis, modern dance and theatrical choreographer, daughter of Roy and Valerie (McCarthy) Bettis, was born on December 19, 1919, in Houston, Texas. She received training in ballet and Wigman modern dance technique during her youth in Houston. After attending the University of Texas for a year, she went to New York in 1937 to study with choreographer Hanya Holm. She performed with the Hanya Holm and Dance Group from 1937 to 1940. Beginning in 1941 she directed her own modern dance ensemble and performed in various theatrical productions. Her dance works emphasized character studies and often incorporated the spoken word. One of her best-known pieces, *The Desperate Heart,* was inspired by John Malcolm Brinnin's poem of the same title. In 1943 she married Bernardo Segall, her company's musical director.

Valerie Bettis often choreographed for companies other than her own. With *Virginia Sampler,* a dance she made for the Ballet Russe de Monte Carlo in 1947, she became the first modern dancer to provide a work for a classical company. In 1952 she choreographed *A Streetcar Named Desire,* based on Tennessee Williams's play, for the Slavenska-Franklin Ballet. The American Ballet Theater acquired the piece two years later, and the Dance Theater of Harlem revived it in 1981.

Bettis taught on the faculty of the Connecticut College School of Dance and performed at the American Dance Festival in 1949, 1950, and 1954. During the 1950s she took on assignments in theater, film, and television. Theatrical director Lee Strasberg's 1951 presentation of *Peer Gynt* included choreography by Bettis, as did the Columbia Pictures films *Affair in Trinidad* (1952), *Salome* (1953), and *Let's Do It Again* (1953), all with Rita Hayworth. Bettis choreographed musical programs for NBC-TV and CBS-TV and had acting roles in several television dramas. In 1955 in New York she replaced Lotte Lenya in the lead role in Kurt Weill's *Threepenny Opera* (New York). She and Segall were divorced that year.

Bettis married Arthur A. Schmidt in 1959, after which the pace of her career slowed. She started the Dance Studio Foundation in New York in 1964, "for dancers who act and actors who dance." In 1969 the studio produced a new performance group, the Valerie Bettis Theater/Dance Company, which continued presenting her works into the mid-1970s. Arthur Schmidt died in 1969. The National Endowment for the Arts awarded Bettis a fellowship to adapt for dance W. H. Hudson's novel *Green Mansions*; she was preparing the work for the Omega Liturgical Dance Company when she died in New York on September 26, 1982. Her remains were cremated there.

BIBLIOGRAPHY: Barbara Naomi Cohen-Stratyner, *Biographical Dictionary of Dance* (New York: Schirmer, 1982). New York *Times,* June 9, 1969, September 28, 1982. Herbert M. Simpson, "Valerie Bettis: Looking Back," *Dance Magazine,* February 1977.

Sherilyn Brandenstein

BETTS, JACOB (?–1837). Jacob Betts, one of Stephen F. Austin's[qv] Old Three Hundred[qv] colonists, came to Texas from Georgia as early as 1822 and voted in an alcalde[qv] election in August 1823. As one of the Old Three Hundred he received title to a sitio[qv] now in Matagorda County on August 19, 1824. In May 1825 he wrote to Austin stating that he had spent three years "in poverty and misery" in Texas, where he had come looking for better times, and that he was dissatisfied with "soft words and fair promises" and wanted more land. In 1826 he sold half a league to James Grant (possibly Dr. James Grant[qv]). Thomas M. Duke[qv] wrote Austin from Bay Prairie on January 3, 1827, that the Karankawa Indians had destroyed the Betts homestead, and on May 13, 1827, Betts was among those signing a treaty with the Karankawas at La Bahía.[qv] In 1836 Betts was among the men serving in Albert Clinton Horton's[qv] company, the Matagorda Volunteers, under James W. Fannin.[qv] He died on October 31, 1837, and his daughter Mary Betts Kincheloe was administrator of his estate.

BIBLIOGRAPHY: Eugene C. Barker, ed., *The Austin Papers* (3 vols., Washington: GPO, 1924–28). Lester G. Bugbee, "The Old Three Hundred: A List of Settlers in Austin's First Colony," *Quarterly of the Texas State Historical Association* 1 (October 1897). Matagorda County Historical Commission, *Historic Matagorda County* (3 vols., Houston: Armstrong, 1986). Harriet Smither, ed., "The Diary of Adolphus Sterne," *Southwestern Historical Quarterly* 30 (October 1926, January, April 1927). William Barret Travis, *Diary,* ed. Robert E. Davis (Waco: Texian Press, 1966).

BETTS CHAPEL, TEXAS. Betts Chapel, a small black farming community, is on a county road known as old Highway 44 six miles northwest of Giddings in southwestern Lee County. Abram Betts, the founder, came from Virginia to Fayette County after emancipation and subsequently settled in Lee County. The town was named for his son Wright. Betts Chapel had a community store, Missionary Baptist and Methodist churches, and a one-teacher school. The school held classes in the Methodist church on Abram Betts's land; this church may have been named Betts Chapel. In 1898 the school had thirty-three students. The Rosenwald Fund provided for a new school some years later, officially named Willy Branch No. 21 but commonly known as Betts Chapel School. The only trace of the community in 1990 was the Betts Chapel cemetery, which was partially covered by plants in 1973 and had around forty-five graves.

BIBLIOGRAPHY: Lee County Historical Survey Committee, *A History of Lee County* (Quanah, Texas: Nortex, 1974). *Nolan Thompson*

BEULAH, TEXAS (Angelina County). Beulah was on Farm Road 58 eleven miles southwest of Lufkin in southern Angelina County. In the 1930s the settlement had a church, a store, and a number of houses; many of the residents worked in the nearby Ginter oilfield. After World War II[qv] the population declined, and in the early 1990s only two churches and a few scattered houses remained.

Christopher Long

BEULAH, TEXAS (Johnson County). Beulah was on Mustang Creek eighteen miles northwest of Cleburne. Settlement of the site occurred in 1853. A post office operated there from 1882 until 1890. The population grew from thirty in 1885 to ninety-four in 1892. Area farmers raised and shipped livestock. Beulah was bypassed by the railroads and by 1910 was all but abandoned. *David Minor*

BEULAH, TEXAS (Lee County). Beulah is six miles north of Lexington in extreme northern Lee County. The settlement flourished briefly around the turn of the century as a community center for the surrounding farms. A church and school were built there sometime before 1900 and, during the 1905–06 school year, enrolled twenty-two students. The community began to decline a short time later. By the mid-1930s it no longer appeared on state highway maps. In the 1980s only a cemetery marked the site.

BIBLIOGRAPHY: Lee County Historical Survey Committee, *A History of Lee County* (Quanah, Texas: Nortex, 1974). *Christopher Long*

BEULAH, TEXAS (Limestone County). Beulah is five miles southwest of Groesbeck in south central Limestone County. In 1896 it was a common school district with fifty-five students. The school and several houses marked the community on county highway maps in the 1940s, but in 1949 the Beulah school was divided between the Groesbeck and Thornton independent school districts. Little remained in the community by the 1980s. The community was listed, though without statistics, in 1990. *Vivian Elizabeth Smyrl*

BEVERLY, TEXAS. Beverly was on the Lampasas-to-Belton stage line midway between Copperas Cove and Killeen in southern Coryell County. Arthur Whipple Beverly, a local rancher, served as postmaster when a post office opened in 1875. The office was discontinued in 1883, and mail for the community was sent to Sugar Loaf. The site of Beverly became part of Fort Hood in the 1940s.

BIBLIOGRAPHY: Coryell County Genealogical Society, *Coryell County, Texas, Families, 1854–1985* (Dallas: Taylor, 1986). John J. Germann and Myron Janzen, *Texas Post Offices by County* (1986).

Vivian Elizabeth Smyrl

BEVERLY HILLS, TEXAS. Beverly Hills is an incorporated town on State Highway 6 four miles south of downtown Waco in south central McLennan County. By the early 1940s the community of 237 had voted to incorporate. Afterward, the population of Beverly Hills grew rapidly, from 703 in the early 1950s to 2,670 in the late 1970s; many residents chose to live there and commute to work in Waco. Waco eventually grew to surround Beverly Hills, leaving the community unable to expand its boundaries. The smaller community was dependent on Waco for its water supply and sewage disposal, and although it had its own business district, its economy was closely linked with that of Waco. In 1989 the population of Beverly Hills was estimated at 2,364.

BIBLIOGRAPHY: William Robert Poage, *McLennan County Before 1980* (Waco: Texian, 1981). *Vivian Elizabeth Smyrl*

BEVIL, JOHN (1784–1862). John Bevil, early Jasper County settler and developer, son of John Randolph and Laodicea (Burton) Bevil, was born in Mecklenburg County, Virginia, on August 24, 1784. He moved to Jasper County, Georgia, where he married Frances Boynton, a native of New York, then lived in Ohio, Tennessee, and Louisiana before moving to Texas in the mid-1820s. Bevil's Settlement, the region comprising the approximate territory of Bevil Municipality and, later, modern Jasper and Newton counties, was named for him. Most writers credit Bevil with being the first settler in what later became Jasper County. In 1834 he became alcalde[qv] of the municipality. He served as a delegate from Bevil to the Consultation[qv] in 1835. He was elected chief justice of Jasper County in 1839 and resigned the position the following year. As a land speculator, he developed the townsites of Jasper and Bevilport, as well as the unsuccessful City of the Pass, downstream from Sabine City (now Sabine Pass) in Jefferson County. His propensity for land deals occasionally got him into trouble, and he was reportedly forced to leave Jasper County for a time as a result of disputes over property titles. By 1850 Bevil had amassed over $6,500 in real property. He and his first wife had eight sons. She died in 1855, and he moved to Tyler County and subsequently remarried, this time to Mrs. Clarissa Miles, a native of South Carolina. By 1860 Bevil and his wife were living in Jefferson County. He died on November 10, 1862, in Tyler County and was buried in Jasper County.

BIBLIOGRAPHY: Madeleine Martin, *More Early Southeast Texas Families* (Quanah, Texas: Nortex, 1978). *Robert Wooster*

BEVIL OAKS, TEXAS. Bevil Oaks is on State Highway 105 six miles west of Beaumont in northern Jefferson County. The community was named after two subdivisions, Bevil Acres and River Oaks. The residential area of some 370 persons was incorporated in July 1963 by a 60-0 vote. In 1970 the federal census set the population at 663. By 1980 that figure had grown to 1,306. The community's economy depends largely on that of Beaumont and the heavily industrialized Golden Triangle (Beaumont–Orange–Port Arthur). In 1990 the population was 1,350. *Robert Wooster*

BEVILPORT, TEXAS. Bevilport (Bevelport) is on Farm Road 2799 and the east bank of the Angelina River nine miles west of Jasper in northwestern Jasper County. It was named for John Bevil,[qv] but it should not be confused with the Bevil, Texas, that became Jasper. Bevilport was a river-navigation point from 1830 to 1860. Sam Houston[qv] purchased the first lot in the townsite. The community had a population of 140 by 1831 and was noted for bustling docks, which shipped East Texas cotton and hides to New Orleans. A mail station operated at Bevilport in 1835, and the community was incorporated by the Congress of the Republic of Texas[qv] on June 5, 1837. The town had a hotel and main street by the 1850s and served as a business and social center until the Civil War.[qv] It was a freight depot for northern Jasper County during high-water seasons. In the 1870s the town declined when logging for the Beaumont sawmills impeded river transportation on the Neches River below its confluence with the Angelina. A post office, established in 1854, was discontinued in 1866, reopened in 1897, and closed permanently in 1899. In the 1890s the community had a general store and a population of 100. A historical marker was erected at the site in 1936, but by 1948 only two old store buildings and the home of Randolph C. Doom,[qv] built in 1852, were still standing. In the 1980s two nearby churches and scattered dwellings remained to mark the townsite.

BIBLIOGRAPHY: William Seale, *Texas Riverman: The Life and Times of Captain Andrew Farney Smyth* (Austin: University of Texas Press, 1966). Marie Smith, comp., *Historically Marked Sites in Jasper County* (Jasper, Texas: Jasper County Historical Commission, 1979).

Diana J. Kleiner

BEVIL'S SETTLEMENT. Bevil's Settlement was a loosely defined community of pre–Republic of Texas settlers who settled between the Neches and Sabine rivers on land that was eventually organized as Jasper and Newton counties. The settlement was named for John Bevil,[qv] who moved there before 1829. Additional immigration was somewhat facilitated by Lorenzo de Zavala's[qv] grant to settle 500 families in Southeast Texas in 1829. The next year George W. Smyth[qv] found about thirty families scattered between the Sabine and Neches rivers. The area received a form of recognition when Juan Antonio Padilla[qv] was appointed comisario[qv] of the Bevil's Settlement precinct as part of Nacogdoches Municipality. Several residents participated in the Anahuac Disturbances and the battle of Nacogdoches.[qqv] The municipality, established in 1834, was renamed Jasper in 1835. Though most of the residents of Bevil's Settlement were apparently clustered near the site of present-day Jasper, a few early settlers established roots to the east, in what later became Newton County. In 1836 Mary Austin Holley[qv] described Bevil's Settlement as being on the Sabine River within the jurisdiction of the Department of Nacogdoches. "It is a populous neighborhood," she wrote, "but cannot be called a town." Newton County secured its separation from Jasper County in 1846.

BIBLIOGRAPHY: Mary Austin Holley, *Texas* (Lexington, Kentucky: J. Clarke and Company, 1836; rpts., Austin: Steck, 1935; Texas State Historical Association, 1985). James M. McReynolds, A History of Jasper County, Texas, Prior to 1874 (M.A. thesis, Lamar State College of Technology, 1968).

Robert Wooster

BEWLEY, ANTHONY (1804–1860). Anthony Bewley, abolitionist Methodist minister, was born on May 22, 1804, in Tennessee, the son of John Bewley, a Methodist preacher. While still a young man he decided to enter the ministry. From 1829 to 1834 he served the Methodist Church[qv] as a circuit-riding member of the Holston Conference of Virginia. Around 1834 he married Jane Winton of Roane County, Tennessee. They had five sons and three daughters. In 1837 the Bewleys moved to Polk County, Missouri, and six years later Bewley resumed his circuit-riding ministry and joined the Missouri Conference of the Methodist Episcopal Church. When the church divided over the issue of slavery[qv] in 1845, the Missouri Conference voted to join the Methodist Episcopal Church, South. Bewley was among the antislavery members of the conference who refused to accept this decision and chose instead to remain in what they considered to be the true Methodist Church. By 1848 these Methodists had reorganized into the Missouri Conference of the Northern Church, though many still referred to themselves simply as members of the Methodist Episcopal Church.

By 1858, after serving for ten years in Northern Arkansas, Texas, and Missouri, Bewley had moved his family to Johnson County, Texas, and established a mission sixteen miles south of Fort Worth. Although he was considered to be weak on the slavery issue by some northern Methodists, his antislavery views were threatening to southerners. Thus, when vigilance committees alleged in the summer of 1860 that there was a widespread abolitionist plot to burn Texas towns and murder their citizens, suspicion immediately fell upon Bewley and other outspoken critics of slavery (*see also* TEXAS TROUBLES). Special attention was focused on Bewley because of an incendiary letter, dated July 3, 1860, addressed to a Rev. William Bewley and supposedly written by a fellow abolitionist, William H. Bailey. Many argued that the letter, which urged Bewley to continue with his work in helping to free Texas from slavery, was a forgery. The letter was widely published, however, and taken by others as evidence of Bewley's involvement with the John Brownites in Texas.

Recognizing the danger, Bewley left for Kansas in mid-July with part of his family. En route he stopped for eleven days in Indian Territory to wait for the remainder of his family and later visited with friends in Benton County, Arkansas. On September 3, 1860, a Texas posse caught up with him near Cassville, Missouri. His captors returned him to Fort Worth on September 13. Late that night vigilantes seized Bewley and delivered him into the hands of a waiting lynch mob. His body was allowed to hang until the next day, when he was buried in a shallow grave. Three weeks later his bones were unearthed, stripped of their remaining flesh, and placed on top of Ephraim Daggett's storehouse, where children made a habit of playing with them. After Bewley's death the Northern Methodists ended their activities in Texas.

BIBLIOGRAPHY: *Dictionary of American Biography.* Charles Elliott, *South-Western Methodism: A History of the M. E. Church in the South-West, from 1844 to 1864* (Cincinnati: Poe and Hitchcock, 1868). Macum Phelan, *History of Early Methodism in Texas, 1817–1866* (Nashville: Cokesbury, 1924); *A History of the Expansion of Methodism in Texas, 1867–1902* (Dallas: Mathis, Van Nort, 1937).

Donald E. Reynolds

BEWLEY, MURRAY PERCIVAL (1884–1964). Murray Percival Bewley, painter, son of Murray P. and Hallie C. (Samuel) Bewley, was born in Fort Worth, Texas, on June 19, 1884. His first art teacher was Mrs. W. J. Lennin of Fort Worth. His mother, a patron of art, inspired him to develop his skills. He studied with Henry Read at the Denver Art School, for two years at the Chicago Art Institute, and subsequently at the Pennsylvania Academy of the Fine Arts with Cecilia Beaux. In New York, while studying with Robert Henri and William Merrit Chase, Bewley was awarded a scholarship that enabled him to accompany Chase to Florence, Italy. Afterward, he lived in Paris from 1906 until 1913, continued to study, and exhibited regularly at the Salon.

That year he returned to Fort Worth and set up a studio. In 1916 he married Bernice Wren of Fort Worth, and they moved to New York, where they stayed until 1924. In New York Bewley had his first one-man show at Ferargils Gallery. He won first prize at the Salmagundi Club in 1921 and from then until the early 1930s exhibited regularly at the Metropolitan Studio and at the Macbeth, Babcock Grand Central, and Milch galleries in New York. In 1930, after the death of his wife, he returned to Europe. Thereafter he only occasionally visited Fort Worth, to paint portraits of family and friends. He took up residence in Paris, where he married Mireille Laurent in 1933. In 1939 he returned to Fort Worth, and in 1940 he painted the last of his Fort Worth portraits. The Bewleys moved to Beverly Hills, California, in the early 1940s. During this period Bewley continued to exhibit in New York and Los Angeles galleries. In 1956 he returned to France. He died in Lyons in September 1964 after an operation. The Fort Worth Art Center mounted a memorial exhibition of his work that October.

The majority of Bewley's subjects are portraits and nudes. However, the works completed near the end of his life are primarily still lifes and flower compositions. His work is characterized by a soft, loose brush stroke, and his palette often consists of violets and opalescent colors. Bewley was a member of the Paris-American Artists Association, the Allied Artists of America, the New York Society of Artists, and the Salmagundi Club. His work is represented in the Dallas Museum of Art, the Modern Art Museum of Fort Worth, the Museum of Fine Arts, Houston,[qqv] and the Pennsylvania Academy of the Fine Arts.

BIBLIOGRAPHY: Frances Battaile Fisk, *A History of Texas Artists and Sculptors* (Abilene, Texas, 1928; facsimile rpt., Austin: Morrison, 1986). Esse Forrester-O'Brien, *Art and Artists of Texas* (Dallas: Tardy, 1935). Fort Worth Art Center, *Memorial Exhibition: Murray Bewley (1884–*

1964) (October 1964). Vertical files, Barker Texas History Center, University of Texas at Austin. Vertical files, Dallas Museum of Art.

Rebecca H. Green

BEXAR. The name Bexar was commonly applied to the presidio of San Antonio de Béxar[qv] and the villa of San Fernando de Béxar,[qv] which developed into the present city of San Antonio, as well as to the municipality from which modern Bexar County evolved.

BEXAR, SIEGE OF. The siege of Bexar (San Antonio) became the first major campaign of the Texas Revolution.[qv] From October until early December 1835 an army of Texan volunteers laid siege to a Mexican army in San Antonio de Béxar. After a Texas force drove off Mexican troops at Gonzales on October 2, the Texan army grew to 300 men and elected Stephen F. Austin[qv] commander to bring unity out of discord. The Texans advanced on October 12 toward San Antonio, where Gen. Martín Perfecto de Cos[qv] recently had concentrated Mexican forces numbering 650 men. Cos fortified the town plazas west of the San Antonio River and the Alamo,[qv] a former mission east of the stream.

By the time the Texans camped along Salado Creek east of San Antonio in mid-October their numbers had grown to over 400 men, including James Bowie and Juan N. Seguín,[qqv] who brought with him a company of Mexican Texans. Bowie and James W. Fannin, Jr.,[qv] led an advance to the missions below San Antonio in late October, while Cos brought in 100 reinforcement men. On October 25 the democratic Texans conducted a debate over strategy. Sam Houston,[qv] who had come from the Consultation[qv] government, urged delay for training and for cannons to bombard the fortifications. Austin and others won support to continue efforts at capturing San Antonio.

From San Francisco de la Espada Mission on October 27, Austin sent Bowie and Fannin forward to Nuestra Señora de la Purísima Concepción de Acuña Mission with ninety men to locate a position nearer the town for the army. There on the foggy morning of the twenty-eighth Cos sent Col. Domingo de Ugartechea[qv] with 275 men to attack the advance force. The Texans drove off the assault from a position along the bank of the San Antonio River, inflicting over fifty casualties and capturing one cannon. Austin arrived after the battle of Concepción[qv] to urge an attack on San Antonio but found little support among his officers.

Cos then resumed defensive positions in San Antonio and the Alamo, while the Texans established camps on the river above and below the town and grew to an army of 600 with reinforcements from East Texas led by Thomas J. Rusk.[qv] After discussion among the Texan officers produced little support for an attack, some volunteers went home for winter clothes and equipment. Yet the arrival of more East Texans in early November offset the departures.

Texas and Mexican cavalry skirmished from time to time as the Texans scouted to capture Mexican supplies and to warn of any reinforcements for Cos. After a lack of early success, William Barret Travis[qv] led the capture of 300 Mexican mules and horses grazing beyond the Medina River on November 8. Four days later Ugartechea left San Antonio with a small cavalry force to direct the march of reinforcements from below the Rio Grande. Austin sent cavalry to intercept him, but the Mexican troops evaded them. Both armies suffered morale problems as a result of colder weather and limited supplies.

When three companies with over a hundred men arrived from the United States in mid-November, Austin again planned an attack. Officers still expressed doubts, however, and it was called off. Austin then left to assume diplomatic duties in the United States. The Texas troops selected Edward Burleson[qv] as their new leader.

When Erastus (Deaf) Smith[qv] reported approaching Mexican cavalry on November 26, Burleson ordered out troops to cut them off. Skirmishing followed near Alazán Creek west of town, with attack and counterattack by both sides. Finally the Mexican troops withdrew into San Antonio. The engagement became known as the Grass Fight[qv] because captured Mexican supply animals carried fodder for horses rather than the rumored pay for Mexican soldiers.

Because of limited supplies and approaching winter, Burleson considered withdrawing to Goliad at the beginning of December. Information on Mexican defenses from Texans who were allowed to leave San Antonio led to new attack plans. But fears that the Mexican army had learned of the assault brought a near breakup of the Texan army. When a Mexican officer surrendered with news of declining Mexican morale, Benjamin R. Milam and William Gordon Cooke[qqv] gathered more than 300 volunteers to attack the town, while Burleson and another 400 men scouted, protected the camp and supplies, and forced Cos to keep his 570 men divided between the town and the Alamo.

James C. Neill[qv] distracted the Mexican forces with artillery fire on the Alamo before dawn on December 5, while Milam and Francis W. Johnson[qv] led two divisions in a surprise attack that seized the Veramendi and Garza houses north of the plaza in San Antonio. Mexican cannon and musket fire kept the Texans from advancing farther during the day and silenced one of their cannons.

That night and the next day the Texans destroyed some buildings close to them and dug trenches to connect the houses they occupied. On the seventh the Texans captured another nearby house, but Milam died from a sharpshooter's bullet. Johnson then directed another night attack that seized the Navarro house. On December 8 Ugartechea returned with over 600 reinforcements, but only 170 were experienced soldiers. Untrained conscripts formed the other 450 men, who brought with them few supplies. Burleson sent 100 men into town to join the Texan force that captured the buildings of Zambrano Row in hand-to-hand fighting. Cos ordered his cavalry to threaten the Texan camp, but they found it well defended. That night Cooke with two companies seized the priest's house on the main plaza, but they seemed cut off from the Texas army.

When Cos sought to concentrate his troops at the Alamo, four companies of his cavalry rode away rather than continue the struggle. Cos then asked for surrender terms on the morning of December 9. Burleson accepted the surrender of most Mexican equipment and weapons, but allowed Cos and his men to retire southward because neither army had supplies to sustain a large group of prisoners.

Texas casualties numbered thirty to thirty-five, while Mexican losses, primarily in the Morelos Infantry Battalion, which defended San Antonio, totaled about 150; the difference reflected the greater accuracy of the Texans' rifles. Most of the Texas volunteers went home after the battle, which left San Antonio and all of Texas under their control.

BIBLIOGRAPHY: Alwyn Barr, *Texans in Revolt: The Battle for San Antonio, 1835* (Austin: University of Texas Press, 1990).

Alwyn Barr

BEXAR, TEXAS. Bexar was off a road that is now U.S. Highway 81 two miles west of Somerset and eighteen miles southwest of downtown San Antonio in southwestern Bexar County. It was established after the Civil War[qv] and had a post office from 1883 to 1907. The settlement declined after 1900, but as late as the 1930s it still had a church, a cemetery, a store, and a number of houses. The church and store were closed after World War II,[qv] and in the early 1990s only a few scattered houses remained in the area.

Christopher Long

BEXAR ARCHIVES. The Bexar Archives are the Spanish and Mexican records of Texas, assembled in San Antonio during its long history as the capital and principal community of Texas. Both in their volume and breadth of subject matter the Bexar Archives are the single most important source for the history of Hispanic Texas up to 1836. The Archives, housed at the University of Texas since 1899, constitute more than eighty linear feet of materials, in a quarter million pages. The documents are rich in sources about the administrative, legal, military, religious, economic, and social life of Texas and surrounding areas from the founding of the presidio of San Antonio de Béxar in 1718 to the independence of Texas from Mexico in 1836.

The Bexar Archives reflect the growth and development of Spanish Texas and Mexican Texas.[qqv] Earlier documents deal with the affairs of settlers from the Canary Islands, and relations between the military, civil, and missionary communities that constituted San Antonio. Major topics during the eighteenth century include Indian policy and relations, military affairs, cattle raising, trade, legal proceedings, and exploration and communications. After 1803, the documentation also reflects a growing Anglo-American presence in the area, the development of trade and colonization, and currents of political unrest and revolution. As the affairs of Texas and the region grew in complexity, so does the volume of documentation in the Bexar Archives. Fully half of the collection represents the Mexican period (1821 to 1836).

The University of Texas received the Bexar Archives in 1899 through the efforts of university history professor Lester G. Bugbee.[qv] By agreement with the Bexar County Commissioners Court, the university undertook to house, organize, calendar, and translate the collection. Certain land and legal documents were retained in San Antonio for use in county business. Since much of the original order of the Bexar Archives had been disturbed over the years, University of Texas librarians and historians arranged all the documents—whether provincial, municipal, military, or private—into chronological order in the following series:

1. Coahuila y Texas Official Publications, 1826–1835
2. General Governmental Publications, 1730–1836
3. Non-governmental Publications, 1778, 1811–1836
4. General Manuscript Series, 1717–1836
5. Undated and Undated Fragments

The physical arrangement and a corresponding calendar provided easy access to the Bexar Archives for such scholars as Eugene C. Barker and Carlos E. Castañeda,[qqv] who began to make ample use of the Bexar Archives in their research. By the 1930s a systematic translation program had also begun. By the mid-1990s, translations existed for the following portions of the archives:

Series I: 1717–1790 (162 volumes)
Series II: 1804–1808 (38 volumes)
Series III: Printed Decrees, 1803–1812 (4 volumes)

The University of Texas greatly expanded access to the Bexar Archives when it microfilmed the entire collection between 1967 and 1971. That project produced 172 reels of film and a corresponding set of published guides. Copies of the microfilm are now available at major educational institutions nationwide. Translations done to date are also available on microfilm. More recently, scholar Adán Benavides has compiled a comprehensive name guide to the Bexar Archives, based on all substantive documents as they are entered in the microfilm edition.

BIBLIOGRAPHY: Henry Putney Beers, *Spanish and Mexican Records of the American Southwest: A Bibliographic Guide to Archive and Manuscript Sources* (Tucson: University of Arizona Press, 1979). Adán Benavides, Jr., comp. and ed., *The Béxar Archives, 1717–1836: A Name Guide* (Austin: University of Texas Press, 1989). Chester V. Kielman, *Guide to the Microfilm Edition of the Bexar Archives, 1717–1836* (3 vols., Austin: University of Texas Library, 1967–71). *John Wheat*

BEXAR COUNTY. Bexar County (M-15), in the interior belt of the Coastal Plain of South Central Texas, is crossed by the Balcones Escarpment.[qv] The area northwest of the escarpment, about one-eighth of the county, lies on the Edwards Plateau[qv] in high, hilly country, the source of numerous springs and artesian and underground wells. The San Antonio River and San Pedro Creek originate in such springs. The San Antonio is the county's principal river, and into it flow a number of smaller streams, including the Medina River and Medio, Leon, Helotes, Salado, and Calvares creeks. Cibolo Creek forms the boundary between Bexar and Comal counties on the north and Guadalupe on the east.

The county is bounded on the north by Kendall and Comal counties, on the east by Guadalupe and Wilson counties, on the south by Atascosa County, and on the west by Medina and Bandera counties. The county seat and largest city is San Antonio. Other large population centers include Alamo Heights, Balcones Heights, Castle Hills, Converse, Lytle, Olmos Park, Terrell Hills, Timberwood Park, Universal City, and Windcrest. Several major highways serve the county, including Interstate highways 10, 37, 35, and 410, and U.S. highways 81, 87, 90, 181, and 281. The county's transportation needs are also served by the Missouri Pacific, the Missouri, Kansas and Texas, and the Southern Pacific railroads, as well as San Antonio International Airport.

Bexar County comprises 1,248 square miles. The altitude varies from 600 to 1,200 feet. In the far northwestern corner of the county are the Glenrose Hills, in which the highest elevations of the county are found. To the southeast lie the somewhat lower Edwards Flint Hills. The northern third of the county has undulating to hilly terrain, with alkaline soils over limestone and limy earths with shallow to deep loamy soils. The remainder of the county has very dark, loamy soils with some clayey subsoils and gray to black, cracking clayey soils with a high shrink-swell potential. In the far south is a narrow strip of nearly level to gently rolling terrain with loamy surface layers and loamy to clayey subsoils. The northern quarter of the county has Edwards Plateau vegetation of tall and medium-height grasses, live oak, juniper, and mesquite. A central strip is Blackland Prairie with vegetation consisting of tall grasses. The remainder of the county has South Texas Plains vegetation, including grasses, live oak, mesquite, thorny bushes, and cacti. Mineral resources include sulfur springs, limestone, kaolin, clay, fuller's earth, greensand, lignite, petroleum, and natural gas.

The climate is subtropical-subhumid, with mild winters and hot summers. Temperatures in January range from an average low of 39° F to an average high of 62° and in July from 73° to 96°. The average annual rainfall is thirty-one inches; the average relative humidity is 84 percent at six A.M. and 52 percent at six P.M. The growing season averages 265 days a year, with the last freeze in early March and the first freeze in late November. Crops include oats, sorghum, hay, corn, wheat, and a variety of fruits and vegetables.

Bexar County is located in an area that has long been the site of human habitation. Archeological artifacts from the Clovis culture recovered in the region suggest that hunting and gathering peoples established themselves in the region more than 10,000 years ago. During historic times, the area was occupied by the Coahuiltecans, Tonkawas, and Lipan Apaches.

The first Europeans to explore the region came with an expedition in 1691 led by Domingo Terán de los Ríos and Fray Damián Massanet,[qqv] who evidently reached the San Antonio River near where San Juan Capistrano Mission was later founded. Nearby they found a group of Payayas living on the riverbank. The Indians, as Massanet recorded in his diary, called the place Yanaguana; he, however, renamed the site San Antonio de Padua to celebrate the memorial day of St. Anthony, June 13. The next group of Spanish explorers, an expedition led by two Franciscans,[qv] fathers Antonio de San Buenaventura y Olivares and Isidro Félix de Espinosa, and a military officer, Pedro de Aguirre,[qqv] did not reach the area until April 1709. Much impressed by the setting and the availability of water, they noted that the area might make a promising site for future settlement. In 1714 Louis Juchereau de St. Denis[qv] crossed the region on his way to San Juan Bautista.[qv] Espinosa again visited the site in 1716 on his way to East Texas with the expedition of Domingo Ramón[qv] and this time recommended San Pedro Springs[qv] as a mission site. Near that spot, in May 1718, Martín de Alarcón [qv] led the expedition that founded San Antonio de Valero Mission and San Antonio de Béxar (or Béjar) Presidio, named for Viceroy Balthasar Manuel de Zúñiga y Guzmán Sotomayor y Sarmiento, second son of the duke of Bexar. By the end of the winter of 1718 numerous Indians of the Jamrame, Payaya, and Pamaya groups had joined the mission. In 1720 Fray Antonio Margil de Jesús [qv] founded San José y San Miguel de Aguayo Mission a short distance to the south. Another mission, San Francisco Xavier de Naxara,[qv] was established in 1722, but proved unsuccessful and was merged with San Antonio de Valero in 1726. In 1724 the San Antonio de Valero mission compound, which had originally been located at the site of the present-day Chapel of Miracles south of San Pedro Springs, was moved to Alamo Plaza. In 1731, after the removal of the missions from East Texas, three additional missions—Nuestra Señora de la Purísima Concepción de Acuña, San Francisco de la Espada, and San Juan Capistrano—were founded along the San Antonio River.

During the 1720s the Spanish population of the area was about 200, including fifty-three soldiers and their families and four civilians with their families. On March 9, 1731, fifty-five Canary Islanders [qv] arrived at Bexar, and the villa of San Fernando de Béxar [qv] became the first municipality in the Spanish province of Texas. The five missions, together with the presidio and the villa of San Fernando, constituted the most important Spanish concentration in Texas. By the mid-1730s the total population of the area was some 900, including 300 Spanish and 600 Indian converts. An epidemic in 1738–39 devastated the missions, killing perhaps three-fourths of the Indian population. At Mission San Antonio de Valero alone, only 182 of 837 Indians who had been baptized survived. By 1740, however, the missions' populations began to recover. The number of converts at the five missions reached more than 500, as many of the indigenous Coahuilatecan peoples living in the region fled to them as a refuge from the Apaches and Comanches.

The missions developed as self-supporting communities, each ringed with farmland irrigated by a comprehensive system of acequias,[qv] or irrigation ditches. Crops included grain, cotton, flax, beans, sugarcane, and vegetables. Each of the missions also maintained sizable herds of cattle, sheep, and goats on extensive ranchlands located around Bexar. Governor Manuel M. de Salcedo [qv] described Mission Concepción's ranch in 1809 as comprising some thirty-eight square miles and extending east and northeast from the mission to Cibolo Creek. An inventory in 1756 recorded that the Concepción ranch had 700 cattle, 1,800 sheep, and large herds of goats and horses.

Both the missions and the villa of Bexar were subject to sporadic attacks of Apaches and Comanches; nearly a quarter of the Spanish who died between 1718 and 1731 were reportedly victims of Apache attacks. A truce was signed with the Apaches in August 1749, but occasional attacks by Comanches and Apaches continued well into the nineteenth century.

In 1772 the government offices of Spanish Texas were moved from Los Adaes [qv] to Bexar, and some of the East Texas settlers also moved. Nonetheless, Bexar remained a small frontier outpost, as Father Juan A. Morfi [qv] described in a report of the late 1770s, with "fifty-nine houses of stone and mud, seventy-nine of wood, all poorly built without a preconceived plan. The whole town," he continued, "resembles a poor village rather than the capital of a province."

After the secularization of the missions in 1793–94, they gradually became satellite civilian communities under the authority of the town of Bexar. The mission lands were distributed to the few remaining Indians and the increasing number of Spanish settlers; most of the better land nearest the settled areas was controlled by the town's elite, which was made up of the descendants of the original Canary Islanders and presidial soldiers. The complex network of irrigation systems that had been operated by the missions was partially abandoned, and by 1815 the amount of irrigated farmland had declined markedly.

Despite the downturn brought on by the secularization of the Spanish missions,[qv] San Antonio de Béxar continued to be an overwhelmingly agricultural community. Subsistence farming was the rule. The largest number of cultivators worked small family plots, though many farms were also worked by tenant farmers or day laborers. The elite landowners increased the size of their holdings after the secularization of the missions, and some of the largest ranchers exported horses and cattle to Coahuila or Louisiana.

During the late colonial period, Bexar continued to serve as the capital of the province of Texas as well as the main shipping point for supplies headed for Nacogdoches and La Bahía. Between 1811 and 1813 the city was also center of revolutionary activity against Spanish rule. In 1811 a former militia captain, Juan Bautista de Las Casas (*see* CASAS REVOLT) following the lead of Miguel Hidalgo y Costilla [qv] in Mexico, mounted an insurrection in Bexar that quickly spread throughout the province of Texas. Las Casas's band of followers, which included the poorer soldiers and civilians of the lower social stratum who resented the rule of the Spanish elite, scored early successes, arresting the governor and his military staff and seizing the property of the most ardent royalists. On March 1, 1811, however, some of the conservative military officers and clergy supported by the *isleños* (aristocratic decedents of the original Canary Island settlers), staged a counterrevolution. Las Casas was captured in Chihuahua and executed, and his head was salted and shipped in a box to Bexar for display on Military Plaza in an attempt to dissuade others from taking up his cause.

After Las Casas's death, the leadership of the insurrectionists fell to Bernardo Gutiérrez de Lara,[qv] who led an army of Mexican revolutionaries and sympathetic Americans from Louisiana that seized San Antonio in the spring of 1813 and proclaimed Texas an independent state (see Gutiérrez-Magee expedition). But in August, royalist forces commanded by José Joaquín Arredondo [qv] succeeded in routing the insurrectionists and restoring order. Arredondo's victory was followed by a period of reprisals that included confiscation, detentions, and executions; in San Antonio alone, loyalists shot 327 supporters of the rebellion.

In the wake of the rebellion, the population of Bexar and the surrounding region fell markedly and did not begin to grow again until the end of the decade. By 1820, however, Bexar had some 2,000 inhabitants, with slightly more females (1,021) than males (973); several hundred more lived on ranches in the outlying countryside. During the 1830s the population again increased slightly, although the number of inhabitants in Bexar declined as more town dwellers moved out to adjoining farms and ranches.

Soon after the first Anglo-American colonists came to Texas in 1821, San Antonio became the western outpost of settlement. In 1824 Texas and Coahuila [qv] were united into one state with the capital at Saltillo; a Department of Bexar was created with a political chief to have authority over the Texas portion of the state. During the late 1820s and early 1830s increasing numbers of American settlers began moving to San Antonio, though the city remained preponderantly Mexican at the beginning of the Texas Revolution.[qv]

In late October 1835, Texas volunteers laid siege to the city, which was garrisoned by the Mexican army under Martín Perfecto de Cos.[qv] On December 10, after fierce hand-to-hand fighting, it was occupied by Texan forces (*see* BEXAR, SIEGE OF). San Antonio was retaken by government forces commanded by Antonio López de Santa Anna [qv] during the battle of the Alamo [qv] on March 6 of the following year. After the subsequent defeat of Santa Anna's army in the battle of San Jacinto,[qv] the city was reoccupied by Texan forces, but the area, claimed by both sides, continued to be fought over. In March 1842, six years after Texas independence, Mexican general Rafael Vásquez [qv] briefly occupied San Antonio, and in September of the same year, Adrián Woll [qv] led another Mexican invasion force that seized the city.

Because of the uncertainty posed by the frequent invasions, San Antonio and the surrounding area were largely depopulated. Many settlers fled during the Runaway Scrape [qv] of 1836 or during subsequent attacks, and did not return in large numbers until after Texas joined the Union. As late as 1844, San Antonio had only some 1,000 residents, nine-tenths of whom were of Mexican descent.

The first Protestant churches in what became Bexar County were not organized until 1844, when two circuit riders, Methodist John Wesley DeVilbiss[qv] and Presbyterian John McCullough formed congregations. In 1847 the Presbyterians built a small adobe[qv] church, and the Methodists constructed their own building in 1852. Trinity Mission of the Episcopal Church was founded in 1850, an Evangelical Lutheran church was organized in 1857, and the Baptists organized their first church in 1861.

The newly formed Bexar County covered much of the western edge of settlement in Texas. During the late Mexican period, Texas had been divided into four departments, with the department of Bexar stretching from the Rio Grande to the Panhandle[qv] and as far west as El Paso. With the winning of Texas independence, the departments became counties, and on December 20, 1836, Bexar County was established, with San Antonio as county seat. Since 1860, when the partitioning of Bexar County began, 128 counties have been carved from the original county, leaving the present county at 1,248 square miles.

Despite the steady growth of the population in the late 1840s, fueled by large numbers of immigrants from the Old South and from Germany, Bexar County was still a sparsely populated region during the early years of statehood. In 1850 the county had a total population of 5,633, 3,488 of whom lived in San Antonio. The economy, as during the Spanish and Mexican periods, was still based on ranching and subsistence agriculture. Livestock accounted for the most important agricultural product in the county's early years. The census of 1850 reported 5,023 cattle, 1,025 oxen, 3,241 milk cows, 2,715 swine, 633 horses, and 7,007 sheep. Corn constituted the most important crop, followed by oats, beans, and other vegetables. The amount of farmland actually in use was very small: less than 5 percent of the total land in farms (5,062 of 135,182 acres) had been tilled, and as late as 1858 three-fourths of the county's terrain was still prairie. Most of the farms were also small; on the eve of the Civil War[qv] only one farm in the county was larger than 1,000 acres, and most were smaller than fifty.

The main source of revenue for the county was trade carried on by team trains between San Antonio and Mexico and New Orleans. A number of German and Anglo immigrants opened mercantile establishments in the city, but there was little in the way of industry. In 1860 the county had only twenty-eight manufacturing establishments, with 135 employees.

In contrast to many other areas of Texas, slaves played only a minor role in the Bexar County economy. In 1850 there were only 419 African Americans[qv] living in the county, thirty of whom were free. By 1860 the number of slaves had grown to 1,395, or slightly less than 10 percent of the county's total population. Most of the county's 294 slaveholders owned five or fewer slaves; only two owned more than forty.

Bexar County, with its large German population, was a center for antislavery sentiment. Nevertheless, county residents voted for secession[qv] 827 to 709 (54 percent for, 46 percent against). On February 16, 1861, Gen. David E. Twiggs,[qv] commander of the federal Department of Texas, which was headquartered in San Antonio, surrendered all United States forces, arms, and equipment to a committee of local secessionists backed by a large force of Texas Rangers[qv] under Major Benjamin McCulloch.[qv] Although Bexar County escaped the destruction that devastated other parts of the South, the war years were difficult for the county's citizens, who were forced to deal with the lack of markets and wild fluctuations in Confederate currency, as well as with concern for those on the battlefield. With many of the men away fighting, the county and the surrounding region experienced an upsurge of cattle rustling and other crimes, and a committee of vigilantes organized "necktie parties" for bandits, cattle thieves, and Union sympathizers.

After the war San Antonio was occupied by Union soldiers, but the county was spared much of the political violence that consumed other parts of Texas. The war and its aftermath, however, had a serious effect on the county's economy. Land prices fell significantly—by as much as half—and most of the county's businesses suffered. Many of the county's farms also fell idle. The amount of improved farmland declined by more than 60 percent between 1860 and 1870, from 13,697 to 5,546 acres. With little tax money coming in, San Antonio and county officials were unable to fund many services. Public sanitation suffered, and as a result the county had a serious cholera outbreak in 1866.

Except for San Antonio, which continued to be a commercial and military center, the county remained scantily settled and undeveloped. Most of the population continued to be concentrated in the San Antonio River valley, with only a few small settlements in the northern, eastern, and western parts of the county. Economic recovery did not begin until the late 1860s and early 1870s with the start of the great cattle drives. Because Bexar County was located at the northern apex of the diamond-shaped area that was the original Texas cattle kingdom, it became an increasingly important center for the ranching industry. By 1870, the number of beef cattle in the county reached 55,325, nearly double the figure for 1860. A sharp increase in the price of wool and the large amount of free range west and south of the city also spurred the development of sheep ranching,[qv] particularly in the decade between 1870 and 1880.

The economic recovery, however, found its most important stimulus with the arrival of the first railroad, the Galveston, Harrisburg and San Antonio Railway, which reached San Antonio in February 1877. The completion of the rail link with the coast made the shipment of local products far easier and helped to fuel a rapid growth in population. The number of inhabitants in the county, which had grown by less than 2,000 between 1860 and 1870, nearly doubled over the next decade, increasing from 16,043 in 1870 to 30,470 in 1880. Many of the new residents were recent immigrants from Europe and Mexico. Of the total population in 1880, 7,912 were foreign-born, with the largest numbers coming from Mexico (3,498), Germany (2,621), Ireland (471), England (334), and France (293). After the Civil War the county's black population also grew dramatically as many freed slaves settled in and around San Antonio. By 1880 the number of African-American inhabitants had reached 3,867, nearly three times what it had been in 1860.

In 1881 a second railroad, the International–Great Northern, reached the city from the northeast. The completion of the two railroads not only brought new prosperity, but helped to change the physical face of the county. Before the 1870s most visitors had been struck by the fact that San Antonio and environs, despite relatively large numbers of English, Irish, and Germans,[qqv] still more resembled a Mexican community than an American one. The influx of new settlers and manufactured building products gradually transformed the city and county, altering its appearance to more closely resemble that of other communities in Texas. The changing character of Bexar was perhaps most tellingly revealed in 1890, when for the first time the number of the county's inhabitants born in Germany (4,039) actually outnumbered those who had been born in Mexico (3,561).

The construction of the railroads also stimulated the establishment or greatly spurred the growth of numerous new communities, particularly along their route, including Macdona, Von Ormy, Cassin, Atascosa, Thelma, Beckman, Luxello, Converse, and Kirby. But despite the growth of the new communities, in 1890 the overwhelming majority of the county's inhabitants, 37,673 of 49,266, lived in San Antonio.

The 1880s also saw many new industries. By 1887 San Antonio listed among its businesses three bookbinderies, four breweries, three carriage factories, four ice factories, three tanneries, one wool-scouring plant, and an iron foundry. Between 1880 and 1890 employees in manufactures in the county grew from 362 to 2,518. After the turn of the century the manufacturing sector continued to show impressive growth. By 1920 the county had 328 factories employing 6,860 persons.

During the late nineteenth and early twentieth centuries the agricultural economy, too, grew markedly. Between 1880 and 1920 the number of farms grew from 1,136 to 3,205, and the amount of land in farming increased from less than 400,000 acres to more than 800,000. Soon after World War I,[qv] a colony of Belgian immigrants began truck farming on a large scale just south and west of the city. The principal crops during the early years of this century included corn, milo, hegari, cane, oats, vegetables, and fruits. Prior to World War II [qv] Bexar County also remained an significant source of beef cattle, and poultry raising and dairying took an increasingly important place in the county's economy. By the late 1940s more than half of the county's agricultural receipts came from livestock and livestock products. In addition, large amounts of wool and mohair were shipped to the Midwest and to New England for manufacture. Oil was first discovered in the county in 1889, and since World War II has represented a significant part of the area's economy. In 1990 county wells produced 550,793 barrels. Total production up to January 1, 1991, amounted to 32,548,292 barrels.

Another important spur to the county's economy was tourism. By the turn of the century, Bexar County and San Antonio began to attract increasing numbers of tourists, drawn by the Alamo, the missions, and the area's mild winter climate. A spa and hotel opened in the 1890s at Hot Sulphur Wells, just south of the city, drew guests from as far away as the Midwest and the East Coast. And for a short time just after 1900 San Antonio vied with Hollywood as a center for the infant movie industry.

Beginning in the second half of the nineteenth century San Antonio also developed as an important military center. The San Antonio Arsenal [qv] was opened in 1858, and in 1878 the city deeded ninety acres to the federal government for what eventually became Fort Sam Houston.[qv] During World War I Kelly and Brooks fields (which later became Kelly Air Force Base and Brooks Air Force Base [qqv]) were established to train pilots, and Camp Bullis and Camp Travis [qqv] were opened. At the end of the war, a part of Kelly Field became Duncan Field,[qv] and in 1931 Randolph Field [qv] was established as a primary flight training base. During World War II [qv] Duncan Field was reintegrated with Kelly, and Camp Normoyle,[qv] a motor base, was added.

Between 1910 and 1930 cotton, which had previously been grown only on small quantities, became one of the county's most important cash crops. The 1880 census reported that only 1,543 bales of cotton had been produced in the county that year; by 1906 the number had grown to 19,499; and in 1926 the figure reached 27,505. During the same period the amount of land given to cotton production grew steadily, and by the mid-1920s nearly a third of the improved farmland was used for cotton culture.[qv]

The same period also saw a steady rise in the number of tenant farmers in the county. Before 1880 fewer than 10 percent of the farmers were tenants; in 1910 some 40 percent of the farms were worked by tenants; and by 1930 more than half, 1,580 of 3,205 farms, were operated by nonowners. The majority of the leaseholders were Anglos, but much of the labor was performed by persons of Mexican descent, who were poorly paid and frequently lived in poverty.

During the 1920s Bexar County experienced the beginnings of agricultural mechanization. Tractors and other machines appeared in the county in increasing numbers, and by the eve of World War II, Bexar County farms were among the most mechanized in the state. The onset of the Great Depression,[qv] falling agricultural prices, and the arrival of the boll weevil [qv] brought hardships for many of the farmers of Bexar County. Many were forced to leave the land and move to the city or to turn to other occupations. Cotton production, which peaked in the mid-1920s, fell dramatically during the 1930s and 1940s. Farmers who remained in the area began to devote more of their resources to truck farming and to growing feed for livestock.

Despite the area's relatively diversified economy, the depression hit Bexar County hard. By the mid-1903s many people were out of work and very glad of the New Deal programs that gave them work paving streets and building bridges, sewers, and parks. Among the largest projects of the period were the renovation of La Villita [qv] and the San Antonio missions, and the construction of the Paseo del Rio [qv] along the San Antonio River in the center of the city.

During World War II, Bexar County's already large military presence grew even more, as the area's bases became an important center for the training of army air corps cadets under the auspices of the San Antonio Aviation Cadet Center. At the height of the war, more than 21,000 civilian war workers were employed at Kelly Field alone. After the war, the presence of so many military personnel continued to bring changes to the county. Thousands of returning veterans enrolled in local colleges and universities, and many others, attracted by the area during their service years, moved to the city. San Antonio also developed into a major retirement center for military families, drawn by the relatively low cost of living and the access to the two large area military medical centers, Wilford Hall and Brooke Army Medical Center.[qv] Since the end of the Second World War, the economy of the area has continued to depended heavily on a large federal payroll from the various military bases and research facilities, and from the large number of retired military residents.

During the twentieth century Bexar County developed into a major educational center. The earliest mention of a school in the county occurred in 1789, when José de la Mata asked the cabildo [qv] or town council to grant official standing to his private school. There were several private or free schools in the late Spanish and Mexican period, usually meeting in private homes. By 1828 there was also a school for Anglo-American children in San Antonio called McClure's School. During the revolution most of these schools closed, but by the early 1850s two private schools were in operation, one for boys and one for girls, run by the Brothers of Mary (Marianists [qv]) and the Ursuline Sisters [qv] respectively. In the late 1850s and 1860s several additional schools were opened, including the German-English School, St. Mary's Hall, and a Freedmen's Bureau [qqv] school for the children of newly liberated slaves. Several public elementary schools followed, and in 1879 the first public high school was founded. Since then a number of institutions of higher learning have opened, including Incarnate Word College, chartered in 1881; Our Lady of the Lake University, founded as a two-year college in 1912; St. Mary's University, which started as a junior college in 1924; Trinity University, which moved to its present site in San Antonio in 1952; and the University of Texas at San Antonio, which was established in 1969. The county is also served by two community colleges, San Antonio College, which opened in 1925; and St. Philip's College, which became a junior college in 1927. In the early 1980s Bexar County had fifteen community school districts with 184 elementary, 55 middle schools, 35 high schools, and 19 special-education schools. Fifty-five percent of the 12,382 high school graduates planned to attend college. In 1982–83, 35 percent of the school graduates were white, 58 percent Hispanic, 7 percent black, 0.9 percent Asian, and 0.1 percent American Indian.

Politically, from the time of the annexation [qv] of Texas to the Union until the 1950s, Bexar County was staunchly in the Democratic camp. Republican presidential candidates Warren G. Harding and Herbert Hoover received a narrow majority of the county's votes in the 1920 and 1928 elections respectively, but Democrats prevailed in every other election until Dwight D. Eisenhower's [qv] first campaign in 1952. Since that time Republicans have won the majority of the elections, the exception being those of John F. Kennedy in 1960, Lyndon Baines Johnson [qv] in 1964, Hubert Humphrey in 1968, and Jimmy Carter in 1976.

The number of businesses in Bexar County in the early 1980s was 18,747. In 1980, 6 percent of the labor force were self-employed, 21 percent were employed in professional or related services, 11 percent in manufacturing, 24 percent in wholesale and retail trade, 10 percent in public administration, and 2 percent in other counties; 60,392 retired workers lived in the county. Leading industries included oil and gas extraction, brewing of beer, general and heavy construction, soft-drink canning and bottling, commercial printing, bookbinding, lumber milling, iron and steel milling, and the manufacture of men's and women's clothing, household furniture, curtains and draperies, cardboard boxes, pharmaceuticals, shoes, ready-mix concrete, construction machinery, aircraft and aircraft parts, and electronic components. Nonfarm earnings in 1981 totaled $9,609,598,000.

In 1982, 66 percent of the land in the county was in farms and ranches, with 27 percent of the farmland under cultivation and 14 percent irrigated. Bexar County ranked fifty-third among counties in the state in agricultural receipts, with 61 percent coming from livestock and livestock products. Principal crops included oats, sorghum, hay, corn, wheat, pecans, and vegetables; primary livestock products included cattle, milk, sheep, wool, and hogs.

Tourism, now the number one nongovernmental provider of jobs in Bexar County, has played an increasingly important role in the county's economy. The construction of two large theme parks, Sea World of Antonio and Fiesta Texas, combined with the areas other attractions, including the annual Fiesta San Antonio, the Texas Folklife Festival, San Antonio Missions National Historical Park,[qqv] the zoo, and the many museums, have made San Antonio and the surrounding area a prime tourist destination.

The area has also developed into a major regional medical center in the past few decades. Facilities include the University of Texas Health Science Center at San Antonio,[qv] the South Texas Medical Center, Santa Rosa Hospital (*see* CATHOLIC HEALTH CARE), Wilford Hall Medical Center, and Brooke Army Medical Center.

During the second half of the twentieth century the population of Bexar County grew rapidly. According to the 1940 census the county had a population of 333,176; in 1960 it had reached 687,151; in 1980 it was 988,800; and in 1990 for the first time it topped the one million mark. As in previous times, the overwhelming majority of the inhabitants lived in the city of San Antonio, the tenth largest city in the United States; of the 1,185,394 residents in the county in 1990, 935,933 lived in the city, and many of the remainder lived in the surrounding suburbs. Other large communities included Alamo Heights (6,502), Universal City (13,057), Converse (8,887), Terrell Hills (4,592), Castle Hills (4,198), and Balcones Heights (3,022). Persons of Hispanic descent made up the largest group, 49.7 percent or 589,180; 7.1 percent were black, 1.3 percent were Asian, and 0.4 percent were American Indian.

During the 1980s and 1990s, as a result of attempts to diversify the area's economy, San Antonio and Bexar County became the site of a number of electronics and biotechnology companies. The increasing volume of trade with Mexico and Central America also promised to help bolster the economy. Environmental matters—the preservation of the Edwards Aquifer, the source of San Antonio's water supply, as well as preservation of other fragile features of the western hills—were among the area's most prominent concerns. *See also* SPANISH TEXAS, MEXICAN TEXAS, RANCHING, RANCHING IN SPANISH TEXAS.

BIBLIOGRAPHY: Frederick Charles Chabot, *With the Makers of San Antonio* (Yanaguana Society Publications 4, San Antonio, 1937). Jesús F. de la Teja and John Wheat, "Bexar: Profile of a Tejano Community, 1820–1833," *Southwestern Historical Quarterly* 89 (July 1985). Leah Carter Johnston, *San Antonio: St. Anthony's Town* (San Antonio: Librarians Council, 1947). Gerald E. Poyo and Gilberto M. Hinojosa, eds., *Tejano Origins in Eighteenth-Century San Antonio* (San Antonio: Institute of Texan Cultures, 1991). Charles W. Ramsdell, *San Antonio: A Historical and Pictorial Guide* (Austin: University of Texas Press, 1959). San Antonio Bicentennial Heritage Committee, *San Antonio in the Eighteenth Century* (1976). Marker files, Texas Historical Commission, Austin. WPA Federal Writers' Project, *San Antonio: An Authoritative Guide to the City and Its Environs* (San Antonio: Clegg, 1938).

Christopher Long

BEYER, TEXAS. Beyer, on the north bank of the San Antonio River in southern Bexar County, was the site of a gristmill established by August Beyer before 1877. With the growth of the city of San Antonio the site was incorporated, and by the 1930s was no longer shown on maps.

Claudia Hazlewood

BEYERSVILLE, TEXAS. Beyersville is on Farm Road 619 thirty-five miles northeast of Austin in east Williamson County. The area was first settled shortly after the Civil War[qv] and was originally known as Dacus or Dacus Crossing. Beyersville became the town's official name in 1893, when Gustav Beyer established a post office, which remained in operation until 1909. The Dacus school opened in 1889, adopted the name Beyersville in 1897, and was consolidated with the Taylor schools in 1950. In 1896 Beyersville had an estimated population of only fifteen, but soon grew to include several retail stores and gins, two blacksmith shops, a garage, a tavern, and a molasses mill. The Order of Sons of Hermann[qv] hall served as a center for community activities. Beyersville's population was estimated at 100 from 1933 to 1970. From 1970 to 1990 it remained around seventy-five. At some time the community was moved one mile south of its original site, to a location known earlier as Happy Hill. In 1986 Beyersville had two taverns, a diesel and equipment repair shop, and a Czech fraternal hall.

BIBLIOGRAPHY: Clara Stearns Scarbrough, *Land of Good Water: A Williamson County History* (Georgetown, Texas: Williamson County Sun Publishers, 1973).

Clara Stearns Scarbrough

BIARD, JOHN WILSON (1841–1913). John Wilson Biard (Baird), early Lamar County settler, was born in Limestone County, Alabama, on October 31, 1841, the son of William Washington and Amanda Menifee (Finn) Biard. When he was five, his family moved to Texas and settled nine miles southeast of Paris in Lamar County, on a headright granted to Robert H. Wheat, a relative of the family. Biardstown was named for William Washington Biard, who built the first house in the community. John W. Biard married Elizabeth (Lizzie) Holbrook on August 31, 1865; the couple had seven children. In 1867 he and his wife donated land for the Biardstown school. Biard also lived in Jones County, Texas, in Hugo, Oklahoma, and in Sulphur, Oklahoma, where he died on March 14, 1913. He was buried in the family cemetery in Biardstown.

BIBLIOGRAPHY: Maud Biard Smith, *The Biard Family* (Paris, Texas: Peerless, 1929). Marker files, Texas Historical Commission, Austin.

Christopher Long

BIARDSTOWN, TEXAS. Biardstown is on Farm Road 1497 six miles south of Paris in south central Lamar County. It was originally called Baird in honor of a founder, John W. Biard,[qv] whose name was miswritten Baird. The post office opened in 1880 as Baird but was renamed Biard later that year. In 1883 the name was changed to Biardstown. The following year postmaster W. A. Milling, who also served as justice of the peace, reported a population of 100. The town had become important in cotton shipping, and its businesses included a cotton gin, two flour mills, a general store, two blacksmith shops, a cobbler's establishment, and two doctor's offices. In 1890 a new carpenter shop had opened. Two years later the mail was arriving on a daily basis, and a district school had been organized. Another general store had opened, and four new physicians had moved to town. Municipal officials were Sheriff James W. Biard, Justice of the Peace W. C. Gross, and Constable J. R. Scott. In 1896 the school enrolled seventy-seven students and employed one teacher.

The number of residents had increased to 163 in 1904, and in 1914 residents had access to a telephone exchange. From 1925 through the 1940s the population was 163; the postal service was discontinued during this period. Maps for 1936 identified two businesses, a school, and a cluster of dwellings. The population peaked in 1950, when the town had 250 residents and eight businesses. By 1957 local students attended school in the Delmar Independent School District. No businesses were reported in 1970, although residents still numbered 250.

The population fell by 1974 to seventy-five. Most of these residents were part-time farmers who worked in nearby Paris. In 1984 Biardstown had several dwellings and one church. In 1990 the population was seventy-five.

BIBLIOGRAPHY: Thomas S. Justiss, An Administrative Survey of the Schools of Lamar County with a Plan for Their Reorganization (M.A. thesis, University of Texas, 1937). Fred I. Massengill, *Texas Towns: Origin of Name and Location of Each of the 2,148 Post Offices in Texas* (Terrell, Texas, 1936).

Vista K. McCroskey

BIBB, TEXAS. Bibb, also known as Bibb Mission, was twelve miles northwest of Comanche in northwestern Comanche County. It was established in the 1870s. The Bibb post office opened in 1878, and by 1884 the community had an estimated population of fifty, a school, and a church and shipped cotton and livestock. The following year a small store was established in Bibb. In 1896 the settlement had two grocery stores, a cotton gin, a flour mill, and Christian and Methodist churches. Bibb reached its peak population of 176 in 1900. The community declined rapidly in the next decade, and the post office closed in 1909. By the 1930s it was no longer listed on county maps.

BIBLIOGRAPHY: Comanche County Bicentennial Committee, *Patchwork of Memories: Historical Sketches of Comanche County, Texas* (Brownwood, Texas: Banner Printing, 1976).

Mark Odintz

BIBIT INDIANS. The Bibit (Bibi, Mabibit) Indians were one of the many Coahuiltecan groups of the late seventeenth century that lived in northeastern Coahuila and also ranged across the Rio Grande into the southwestern part of the Edwards Plateau.[qv] The Bosque-Larios expedition[qv] of 1675 encountered the chief of a small group of Bibits who were hunting in what is now the vicinity of Kinney County. This leader reported that his band had recently declined in numbers because of a smallpox epidemic. The Bibits probably ranged evenfarther north into the Edwards Plateau, since in 1683–84 Juan Domínguez de Mendoza[qv] listed the Bibis among the groups that he expected to see on the Colorado River east of present San Angelo.

BIBLIOGRAPHY: Herbert Eugene Bolton, ed., *Spanish Exploration in the Southwest, 1542–1706* (New York: Scribner, 1908; rpt., New York: Barnes and Noble, 1959). Charles W. Hackett, ed., *Pichardo's Treatise on the Limits of Louisiana and Texas* (4 vols., Austin: University of Texas Press, 1931–46). Vito Alessio Robles, *Coahuila y Texas en la época colonial* (Mexico City: Editorial Cultura, 1938; 2d ed., Mexico City: Editorial Porrúa, 1978).

Thomas N. Campbell

BIBLE, DANA XENOPHON (1891–1980). Dana Bible, football coach and athletic administrator, was born to Jonathan and Cleopatra Bible in Jefferson City, Tennessee, on October 8, 1891. He graduated from Jefferson City High School in 1908 and subsequently received a B.A. from Carson-Newman College, in his home state. In 1912 he started his coaching career at Brandon Prep in Shelbyville, Tennessee. The following year he moved to Mississippi College, where Texas A&M recruited him in 1916 to coach its freshman team. In 1917 the school promoted Bible to head coach, and the team won the first of five Southwest Conference[qv] championships under Bible's leadership.

In 1922 in the Dixie Classic, the precursor of the Cotton Bowl,[qv] Bible made his most visible and lasting impression in his A&M career when he began what became known as the Twelfth Man Tradition. Bible had a roster of only eighteen players, who had to play both defense and offense against the heavily favored Praying Colonels of Centre College. He lost three players to injuries early in the game, but the Aggies took the lead. Fearing more injuries and a possibility of having to forfeit the game for lack of men, Bible called upon a reserve halfback, E. King Gill, who was in the press box running stats for the team, to suit up and be ready if needed. The Aggies beat the Colonels without Gill's help, but since then A&M students stand throughout football games to show their willingness to play if needed.

Bible left A&M in 1929 to coach the University of Nebraska Cornhuskers. During his eight seasons at Nebraska he won six conference championships and had a record of forty-nine wins, fifteen losses, and seven ties. He returned to Texas in 1936 to coach A&M's main rival, the University of Texas Longhorns. Upon his arrival at UT the coach initiated the "Bible Plan" to rebuild and sustain the football team. The plan had two parts. First, Bible and his coaching staff divided the state into fifteen recruitment districts; prominent UT alumni in each district played a major role in persuading high school players to go to Austin. Bible believed that native Texans would play harder for the school than players from out of state. Alumni were crucial to the second part of the Bible Plan, as well. The coach devised an innovative scholarship and financial-aid program to assist players in getting their education. For those players who demonstrated a need, campus jobs were provided during the long term and in the summer; alumni supplied jobs, and a portion of the players' wages were dedicated to tuition and fees for the following year.

In five seasons Bible took the Longhorns from last place to first place in the Southwest Conference. His team also won the SWC title in 1943 and 1945. Before he retired from coaching in 1946, his UT record stood at sixty-three wins, thirty-one losses, and three ties. From 1947 to 1956 Bible served as UT's athletic director. He also published a book, *Championship Football: A Guide for Player, Coach and Fan*, in 1947. After he left football he and his wife, Dorothy, operated Camp Mystic,[qv] a summer camp for girls.

Bible was a charter member of the National Football Hall of Fame and the 1954 recipient of the Amos Alonzo Stagg Award. In 1959 he was elected to the Texas Sports Hall of Fame.[qv] During the 1960s each of the three of the schools where he had coached placed him in its hall of fame. Bible was on the National Collegiate Football Rules Committee for twenty-five years and served as a president of the American Football Coaches Association.

He married Rowena Rhodes on December 19, 1923; the couple raised two children. Rowena died in 1942, and Bible married Agnes Stacy in 1944, but the union ended in divorce in 1950. He married Dorothy Gilstrap on February 2, 1952. He was a member of the Delta Kappa Epsilon Fraternity, a Shriner, and a Baptist. Bible died on January 19, 1980, and was buried at Memorial Park in Austin.

BIBLIOGRAPHY: Wilbur Evans and H. B. McElroy, *The Twelfth Man: A Story of Texas A&M Football* (Huntsville, Alabama: Strode, 1974). John D. Forsyth, *The Aggies and the Horns* (Austin: Texas Monthly Press, 1981). Denne H. Freeman, *Hook 'Em Horns: A Story of Texas Football* (Huntsville, Alabama: Strode, 1974). James W. Pohl, "The Bible Decade and the Origin of National Athletic Prominence," *Southwestern Historical Quarterly* 86 (October 1982). Vertical files, Barker Texas History Center, University of Texas at Austin.

David S. Walkup

BIBRA, BARON AUGUST LUDWIG KARL GEORG FRIEDRICH VON (1808–1894). August von Bibra, who as director of the business affairs of Hermann, sovereign prince of Wied, became general manager of the Verein zum Schutze Deutscher Einwanderer in Texas (later the Adelsverein[qv]), was born in Germany on January 30, 1808, a lesser member of an old line of the German nobility. He was privy from its inception to the development of the verein, the emigration enterprise first organized by a group of German noblemen in 1842 that resulted in the founding of New Braunfels, Fredericksburg, and other German communities in Texas. The prince of Wied purchased a share in the society against his and Bibra's better judgment because he was engaged to the sister of the Duke of Nassau, the protector of the society; but he took no active part in the society until 1847, when debts and dissension made it apparent that, if the noblemen hoped to save the honor of their names and possibly some of their investment, a new approach must be taken by more businesslike minds. From that point on Bibra was intimately involved in the affairs of the verein; and in 1851, when the prince was elected president, he took over complete management. For more than ten years thereafter, he struggled to repay the verein debts and to revitalize the emigration program, always with the thought that what had been accomplished had been of great value to Texas and to the Germans who had gone there. In 1864, when he drafted a pro memoria entitled "The Texas Enterprise with Reference to Its Results," he still held the faint hope that the land the verein had controlled might eventually prove valuable to its members. Little else is known about Bibra. He died in Germany in 1894.

BIBLIOGRAPHY: *Gothaisches genealogisches Taschenbuch der freiherrlichen Häuser*, Vol. 9 (Gotha: Perthes, 1859). Wied Archives, Barker Texas History Center, University of Texas at Austin.

Jeanne R. Willson

BICKETT, JOHN HAMILTON, JR. (1892–1947). John Hamilton Bickett, Jr., judge, was born at Cameron, Texas, on July 29, 1892, son of John Hamilton and Minnie (Muse) Bickett. He attended public school at Cameron and later at Dallas and San Antonio, after which he entered the University of Texas. He was awarded B.A. and LL.B. degrees in 1914 and in the same year was admitted to the state bar. When the United States entered World War I,[qv] Bickett enlisted as a private; by the end of the war he was regimental sergeant major. From 1924 to 1934 he served on the state Board of Law Examiners. He resigned when Governor Miriam A. Ferguson[qv] appointed him chief justice of the Fourth Court of Civil Appeals in San Antonio. Bickett was reelected, but in 1935 he resigned to serve as general counsel of Southwestern Bell Telephone Company. He was appointed to the board of regents of the University of Texas in 1942 and served as chairman in 1943–44. He retired in 1944. Bickett was president of the State Bar of Texas[qv] in 1945–46. He was also a member of the Philosophical Society of Texas[qv] and a Presbyterian. In 1924 he married Lula Wright Styles. He died on May 1, 1947, in Dallas and was buried at Mission Burial Park, San Antonio.

BIBLIOGRAPHY: *Alcalde* (magazine of the Ex-Students' Association of the University of Texas), May 1942, January 1943, June 1947. *Proceedings of the Philosophical Society of Texas*, 1947. Ocie Speer, *Texas Jurists* (Austin, 1936). Texas Legislature, *House Journal*, April–June 1947. Vertical files, Barker Texas History Center, University of Texas at Austin.

BICKLER, JACOB (1849–1902). Jacob Bickler, teacher and school administrator, son of Peter and Katherine (Schöffling) Bickler, was born in Sobernheim, now in the Rhineland-Palatinate, Germany, on November 20, 1849. At the age of fourteen, he went to Milwaukee, Wisconsin, to live with his father and stepmother. There he attended public school and Markham's Milwaukee Academy. He received a B.A. from the University of Wisconsin in 1870 and an M.A. in 1871. In 1871–72 he was principal of the La Crosse, Wisconsin, public school.

Bickler moved to Austin in 1872 and was associated with his uncle, Philip Bickler, as a teacher in Bickler German-English Academy until April 1, 1873, when he was appointed assistant draftsman and calculator in the General Land Office[qv] of Texas. There he met Martha Lungkwitz, eldest daughter of artist Hermann Lungkwitz.[qv] They were married on January 24, 1874, in Austin, and eventually became the parents of nine children. In 1877 in Austin Bickler founded the Texas German and English Academy, a boys' school, which he successfully operated for ten years. He accepted the superintendency of Galveston public schools in 1887, returned to Austin in 1892, and founded Bickler Academy, a coeducational school, which flourished until his death. The curricula of his schools included many languages as well as music and liberal arts courses.

Bickler was fluent in six languages, his lectures were erudite and

Dana Bible. Courtesy Texas A&M University Archives.

animated, and he was known as an outstanding teacher in preparing students for college work. Many graduates of his schools became leaders in professions and business. A school in Austin was named for him. He was a member of the National Teachers Association and the Texas State Teachers Association,[qv] of which he was president in 1887. He wrote and presented a resolution at the 1891 association meeting calling upon the board of regents of the University of Texas in Austin to establish a chair of pedagogy (later the School of Education) at the university, and this was accomplished within a few months. Bickler was a member of the summer faculty at the University of Texas. He also conducted summer classes at Fredericksburg and Mason. He died in Austin on April 30, 1902, and was buried in Oakwood Cemetery.

BIBLIOGRAPHY: Lewis E. Daniell, *Types of Successful Men in Texas* (Austin: Von Boeckmann, 1890).

Ralph A. Bickler

BIDAI INDIANS. The Bidai (Beadeye, Bedias, Biday, Viday) Indians lived between the Brazos and Trinity rivers in southeastern Texas. Although at times they ranged a larger area, their main settlements were in the vicinity of present Grimes, Houston, Madison, Walker, and Trinity counties, and a number of place names record their former presence in this area. The earliest reference to the tribe was in a Spanish document of 1691 which noted that a group of "Bidey" lived in proximity of the Hasinais. In 1718 and 1720, François Simars de

Bellisle[qv] reported that an agricultural people by the name of Bidai lived near the Trinity in eastern Texas. In 1748–1749 some of the Bidais were briefly at San Francisco Xavier de Horcasitas Mission before San Ildefonso Mission was built nearby for the Bidai, Deadose, and Akokisa Indians. These missions, which were established on the San Gabriel River near the site of present Rockdale, were abandoned by 1755. In 1756–57 Nuestra Señora de la Luz Mission was established on the lower Trinity River for the Akokisas and Bidais, and some of the Bidais settled near this mission for a short time. It was the grouping of the Bidais with these other groups that has caused some confusion as to the origins and language of the tribe. It was typically thought that the Spanish grouped natives on missions because they spoke common or similar languages. Thus, the Bidais were believed to have had some kinship to the Atakapa people. Upon further study, scholars have concluded that diverse languages were spoken by mission residents but that they might have spoken a second common language in dealing with one another. In the 1770s, the Bidais were reported to have been in league with the French to sell guns to the Lipan Apaches, enemies of the Spanish. In 1776–77 the Bidai population was reduced by about 50 percent in a single epidemic, and by 1820 only a few small groups of Bidais survived. Some of these joined the Akokisas; others joined the Koasati, who were living nearby; and still others were taken in 1854 to the Brazos Indian Reservation[qv] in what is now Young County. The last group eventually ended up in Indian Territory, now Oklahoma, where their identity was soon lost. In 1830 Jean Berlandier[qv] wrote that the tribe was dependent on hunting for their existence and that they were very poor. He also described their customs as resembling those of the Caddos. He believed them to be one of the "oldest of the native people." While later studies associated the Bidai with Atákapa customs and rituals, conclusive evidence concerning their culture is not known.

BIBLIOGRAPHY: Lawrence E. Aten, *Indians of the Upper Texas Coast* (New York: Academic Press, 1983). Jean Louis Berlandier, *Indians of Texas in 1830*, ed. John C. Ewers and trans. Patricia Reading Leclerq (Washington: Smithsonian, 1969). William W. Newcomb, *The Indians of Texas* (Austin: University of Texas Press, 1961). Andre Sjoberg, The Bidai Indians of Southeastern Texas (M.A. thesis, University of Texas, 1951).

Thomas N. Campbell

BIEGEL, TEXAS. Biegel was on Baylor and Cedar creeks in the Joseph Biegel league, eight miles east of La Grange in central Fayette County. Biegel, a German immigrant from Alsace-Lorraine, received his league, originally granted to F. W. Johnson, from the Mexican government on November 29, 1832. He sold one-quarter of the league to Bernard Scherrer, 1,872 acres to Christian Wertzner, and smaller parcels to others. By 1845 Biegel owned only 400 acres of his original 4,428. As the earlier landowners divided their holdings, an agricultural community of German, Swiss, and Alsatian families developed. Many were related, and all considered themselves part of one large family. In 1866 Helmuth Kroll opened a general store that became the post office and polling place in 1875. A commercial area developed around Kroll's store, including two cotton gins, sugar and corn mills, a sawmill, and a blacksmith shop. The Schützen Verein operated a dance hall and public school. In 1882 the *Texas State Gazetteer and Business Directory* reported the population as 250, but by 1896 it had declined to fifty. The commercial area, located on the old road from La Grange to San Felipe, declined after the railroad passed to the south in 1888.

In 1974–75 the Biegel league was acquired by the Lower Colorado River Authority,[qv] and a coal-fired generating plant and reservoir were constructed there. Several buildings and family cemeteries were moved to various locations in Texas. The Biegel home, built of twenty-foot logs, was moved to the Winedale Historical Center,[qv] and the Biegel-December cemetery was moved to higher ground within the confines of the LCRA property. By the end of 1975 the site of the first German settlement in Fayette County had been inundated.

BIBLIOGRAPHY: Emily Suzanne Carter and Crystal Sasse Ragsdale, *Biegel Settlement: Historic Sites Research, Fayette Power Project, Fayette County* (Texas Archeological Survey Research Report 9, University of Texas at Austin, 1976). Frank Lotto, *Fayette County: Her History and Her People* (Schulenburg, Texas: Sticker Steam Press, 1902; rpt., Austin: University of Texas Press, 1981).

Daphne Dalton Garrett

BIERSCHWALE, EDNA HELEN (1907–1975). Edna Bierschwale, an Impressionist painter, was born on July 4, 1907, in Comfort, Texas, the daughter of Robert and Martha (Flach) Bierschwale. After an education in Comfort, Fredericksburg, and San Antonio, she enrolled at Sophie Newcomb College in New Orleans, where she engaged in formal art studies. In 1931 she returned to Texas, joined the San Antonio artists' colony, and pursued a career in art. Her principal media were watercolors and clay; her style ranged from impressionistic in the former to art deco in the latter. Though not widely known today because her works remain in private collections, Bierschwale combined as well as if not better than any of her contemporaries the style of international impressionism with the idiom of the Hill Country.[qv] Her paintings are lyrical and nuanced. A woman of striking beauty and refinement who spent her last decades in her ancestral home in Comfort, Bierschwale was the subject of compelling portraits by Etienne Ret and Xavier Gonzales, among others. She died on January 20, 1975, in Comfort and is buried in the Comfort cemetery.

Glen E. Lich

BIERSCHWALE, MARGARET BROTHERTON (1894–1973). Margaret Bierschwale, historian and librarian, was born to Charles and Mamie (Brotherton) Bierschwale on October 3, 1894, in Mason, Texas. She was the eldest of three daughters. After early education in Mason, she continued high school studies at the Whitis School in Austin. She received her diploma from Ward-Belmont School, Nashville, Tennessee, in 1914. The next year she entered Randolph Macon Woman's College in Lynchburg, Virginia. After earning the A.B. degree in 1918, she went to Columbia University in New York, where she received an M.A. degree in English in 1920.

From 1921 to 1923 Bierschwale headed the English Department at John Tarleton Agricultural College (now Tarleton State University) in Stephenville, Texas. She left to attend Columbia University again and earned a B.S. in library science there. She worked at the New York Public Library for several years. She returned to John Tarleton in 1931 to become the head librarian. Under her administration the library's holdings, especially reference materials, serials, and rare Texana, grew significantly. In 1935 she was granted a year's leave to pursue doctoral studies in library science at Columbia. She resigned from John Tarleton in 1944 and spent most of the next four years in Mason conducting local historical research. In 1948 she joined the library staff and library science faculty at Southwestern University in Georgetown, Texas.

Bierschwale moved back to Mason to care for her mother in 1950. She wrote articles on Mason and Mason County for the *Handbook of Texas*. She produced the article "Mason County, Texas, 1845–1870" for the April 1949 issue of the *Southwestern Historical Quarterly*[qv] as a portion of a longer unpublished history of Mason County that she continued developing during the 1950s and 1960s. In 1966 Anson Jones Press of Salado published her book, *Fort McKavett, Texas: Post on the San Saba*. Bierschwale remained in Mason until her death in an automobile accident on December 9, 1973. Her remains were buried in the Gooch Cemetery at Mason.

BIBLIOGRAPHY: *J-Tac* (newspaper of John Tarleton Agricultural College), December 7, 1943. *Mason County Historical Book* (Mason, Texas: Mason County Historical Commission, 1976).

Sherilyn Brandenstein

BIESELE, LEOPOLD (1827–1905). Leopold Biesele, German revolutionary who became a rural school teacher in Guadalupe County, was born in the grand duchy of Baden in 1827, perhaps in Bruchsal or possibly in Lörrach, near Basel. At the time of the democratic uprising in Baden in 1849, Lt. Biesele was stationed in Kehl. The soldiers of his company deposed their captain and elected Leopold in his stead. Insurgent forces were besieged in Fortress Rastatt by Prussian troops invited into Baden by Grand Duke Leopold to quell the revolt. After the rebels surrendered, court-martial proceedings were brought against insurgent officers. The military trial of Leopold Biesele for high treason resulted in his being turned over to the civil courts, which had him incarcerated. He escaped from the Bruchsal prison and was understood by his relatives to have swum the Rhine to France and freedom. Biesele was included, with rank of major, in a list of fugitive rebel officers published in 1855. He never let himself be photographed, possibly because he did not hear of the general amnesty of 1862.

He traveled to Texas in 1851 and settled on York Creek in Guadalupe County. On January 9, 1853, he married Babette Vogel, also from Baden; they had at least eleven children. Biesele helped to organize the Blum school, in which he taught from 1863 until 1876. Thereafter, he taught nearer his home until he retired from teaching in 1883. He deeded land to the York Creek Gesangverein and organized an orchestra made up of his relatives. His son Julius, father of Rudolph L. Biesele,[qv] played the violin. At a family reunion in 1899, Biesele presented a poem on his experiences as a revolutionary Forty-eighter, in the style of the poems of political satire common in nineteenth-century Germany. It was printed in the *Neu Braunfelser Zeitung*[qv] in 1906, about a year after his death in Guadalupe County on June 3, 1905.

BIBLIOGRAPHY: Wolfgang Dressen, ed., *1884–1849: Bürgerkrieg in Baden: Chronik einer verlorenen Revolution* (Berlin: Wagenbach, 1975). Guadalupe *Gazette Bulletin*, July 28, August 4, 1927. New Braunfels *Zeitung*, April 19, 1906. *John J. Biesele*

BIESELE, RUDOLPH LEOPOLD (1886–1960). Rudolph Leopold Biesele, historian, was born on January 29, 1886, at York's Creek in Guadalupe County, Texas, one of three children of Julius and Hedwig (Bading) Biesele, a farming couple who were the children of German immigrants. He attended public schools in Guadalupe County. In 1905 he received a teacher's certificate from Southwest Texas State Normal School (now Southwest Texas State University), after which he attended the University of Texas (B.A., 1909; M.A., 1910). He taught high school German and civics in Corsicana and high school history in Waco. Around the time of the outbreak of World War I[qv] he shifted from German studies to history because of anti-German sentiment.

In 1924 Biesele moved his family to Austin and began graduate studies toward the Ph.D. in history. He taught in the University of Texas history department from 1925 to 1928, when he received his Ph.D. In 1928–29 he taught history at the University of Alabama; in 1929–30 he substituted for Professor C. W. Hackett[qv] in the University of Texas history department; in 1930–31 he was chairman of the Department of History and Social Science at Louisiana Polytechnical Institute; from 1931 to 1941 he was associate professor of history at the University of Texas; from 1941 to 1957 he was professor of history there; and from 1957 until his death he was professor emeritus. He was remembered by many for his record of service to the history department at the University of Texas and for his warm dedication to his students over a lifetime of teaching.

Biesele's most outstanding accomplishment was *The History of the German Settlements in Texas, 1831–1861* (1931). Also of note were his supervision of more than 100 master's theses in history and his service as associate editor of the *Southwestern Historical Quarterly*[qv] from 1937 to 1957. He served on the editorial board of the *Journal of Southern History* from 1943 to 1946. He belonged to the Southwest Social Science Association and the Texas State Teachers Association,[qv] and was a member of the executive council of the Texas State Historical Association.[qv]

Biesele was awarded a Hermannssöhne Stipendium by the New Braunfels lodge of the Order of Sons of Hermann[qv] to support his study of German literature, a university advanced fellowship in history for 1926–27, and a posthumous plaque of appreciation by the New Braunfels Conservation Society in 1969. He was married on September 3, 1910, to Anna Emma Jahn; they had four children. Biesele was a founding member of the Westminster Presbyterian Church in Austin, in which he served as elder and taught Sunday school classes. He died in Austin on January 4, 1960.

BIBLIOGRAPHY: *Mississippi Valley Historical Review*, September 1960. Report of the Special Rudolph L. Biesele Memorial Resolution Committee (Documents and Minutes of the General Faculty, University of Texas, June 17, 1960). *Megan Biesele*

BIG AGUJA CANYON. Big Aguja Canyon begins three miles south of Black Mountain and nine miles northwest of Fort Davis in central Jeff Davis County (at 30°41′ N, 103°59′ W) and extends northeast for twenty-eight miles to meet Madera Canyon and form the channel of Toyah Creek two miles southwest of Toyahvale and Balmorhea State Park in southwestern Reeves County (at 30°56′ N, 103°49′ W). The area's rugged terrain is surfaced by shallow, stony soils that support scrub brush, grasses, creosote bush, and cacti. The canyon is named for Big Aguja Mountain.

BIG AGUJA MOUNTAIN. Big Aguja Mountain is located fourteen miles north of Fort Davis in northeastern Jeff Davis County (at 30°47′ N, 103°51′ W). The higher of the mountain's twin peaks rises to an elevation of 5,722 feet above sea level, eighty feet higher than its neighbor and some 1,800 feet higher than Farm Road 1832, two miles to the north. The area's shallow, stony soils support live oak, piñon, juniper, and grasses. *Aguja*, Spanish for "needle" or "spire," refers to the mountain's shape.

BIG BEAR CREEK. Big Bear Creek rises about three miles west of Keller in north central Tarrant County (at 32°57′ N, 97°19′ W) and runs southeast about twenty miles to join Little Bear Creek to form Bear Creek, near the Dallas–Fort Worth International Airport[qv] in northeastern Tarrant County (at 32°52′ N, 97°04′ W). The creek traverses low-rolling to flat terrain with deep to shallow sandy and clayey loam soils that support scrub brush, cacti, and grasses.

BIG BEE ROCK. Big Bee Rock, also known as Bee Mountain and Big Bee Mountain, is near Meridian Creek 3½ miles west of Clifton in southwestern Bosque County (at 31°48′ N, 97°39′ W). Its elevation is 949 feet. The area is flat to rolling and locally dissected. The land surface is of stony clays and loams that support oak, juniper, mesquite, and grasses. On February 12, 1978, at 2:40 P.M., a nearby rancher heard a loud blast and, upon investigating, found that an end had broken off Big Bee Rock.

BIBLIOGRAPHY: Bosque County History Book Committee, *Bosque County, Land and People* (Dallas: Curtis Media, 1985).

BIG BEND NATIONAL PARK. Big Bend National Park, the first national park in Texas, comprises more than 1,250 square miles (about the size of Rhode Island) in the Big Bend of the Rio Grande along more than 100 miles of the Texas-Chihuahua-Coahuila border southeast of El Paso in Brewster County. It has been described as a land of "killing heat and freezing cold; deadly drought and flash flood; arid lowland and moist mountain woodland; and a living river winding its way across the desert." The Rio Grande flows for 107 miles on the park's southern boundary, through Santa Elena, Mariscal, and Boquillas canyons, the deepest gorges on the river. In 1978 the United States Congress designated a 191-mile section of the Rio Grande a Wild and Scenic River, sixty-nine miles of which lie on the park boundary. Most Big Bend acreage is arid alluvial plains, the most representative example of the Chihuahuan Desert in North America. The Chisos Mountains,[qv] the southernmost range in the continental United States and completely enclosed in the park, rise over 7,800 feet above sea level. They support relict forests from the late Pleistocene era of ponderosa pine, Douglas fir, Arizona cypress, quaking aspen, and bigtooth maple. The popular Basin, a topographic depression in the Chisos range, offers visitors a cool respite from the desert heat and spectacular panoramic vistas. Annual precipitation in the arid to semiarid climate ranges from five inches in the desert to twenty inches in the mountains. The National Park Service considers Big Bend "one of the outstanding geological laboratories and classrooms of the world." Geological processes readily visible at the park are sedimentation, deformation, and volcanism. Recovered fossil forms of ancient plants and animals include a bivalve three feet wide and four feet long, the largest known pterosaur (a flying dinosaur), and the skull of a chamosaurus, a horned dinosaur, all of which help make Big Bend an invaluable resource for paleontological research and preservation.

The topographical and climatic extremes provide habitats for a varied flora and fauna, including over 1,000 species of plants, 78 mammals, 56 reptiles, 10 amphibians, 35 fish, and 434 birds (more than any other United States park and more than half the species of birds in North America). Endangered species found at Big Bend are the peregrine falcon, black-capped vireo, Mexican long-nosed bat, and Big Bend gambusia (a tiny fish found only in the park). There are several species in the United States that can only be found in Big Bend: Del Carmen white-tail deer, colima warbler, Mexican drooping juniper. The Chisos agave lives nowhere else in the world. In 1976 the United Nations Educational, Scientific, and Cultural Organization designated Big Bend a "Man and the Biosphere" international reserve, one of only twenty-eight in the United States. Cooperative research and educational programs subsequently began with Mexico. Although human beings came late, the park contains archeological and historical sites representing more than 10,000 years of inhabitants, including Jornado Mogollón, Jumanos, Chisos, Mescalero Apache, and Comanche Indians; Spanish explorers and missionaries; and farming, ranching, mining, and military activities of the last two centuries. Nine National Register archeological and historic sites or districts document the Indian and Anglo-Mexican presence at Castolon Historic District (trading post), Hot Springs Historic District (recreational and therapeutic springs), Mariscal Mining District, Homer Wilson Ranch Site, Rancho Estelle, Luna's Jacal (a Mexican goatherd's abode), Burro Mesa Archaeological Site, and two additional archeological sites. There are also exhibits in the visitor centers as well as recreational opportunities, including hiking, river rafting, horseback riding, birding, and back-country camping. Park Service staff schedule interpretive programs throughout the year.

The legislative history of the park began in 1933, when the Texas legislature inaugurated Texas Canyons State Park on fifteen sections of land in the vicinity of Santa Elena, Mariscal, and Boquillas canyons on the Rio Grande in southern Brewster County. Later that year the name was changed to Big Bend State Park and the Chisos Mountains were added to the park acreage. The National Park Service investigated the site in January 1934 and recommended establishment of both a Civilian Conservation Corps[qv] camp and a national park. The NPS regarded Big Bend as "decidedly the outstanding scenic area of Texas." President Franklin D. Roosevelt took a personal interest in Big Bend because of a proposed international, or companion, park in Mexico (still being discussed decades later). The United States Congress passed the enabling legislation on June 20, 1935, stipulating that acquisition of the park acreage "shall be secured . . . only by public and private donations." By 1942 most of the land was purchased with a $1.5 million appropriation from the Forty-seventh Texas Legislature. Although several thousand acres remained in private hands, the park opened to the public in 1944. In 1972 the Congress appropriated $300,375 for the last 8,561.75 acres, finally placing the entire original park area of 708,118.40 acres in federal ownership. Subsequent additions have increased the park acreage to 801,163.02 acres, of which 776,693.22 acres are federal land.

In 1944 the park had a staff of five and received a modest appropriation of $15,000. That first year only 1,409 people visited Big Bend. Visitors averaged more than 230,000 annually from 1981 to 1990; in 1976, a record 456,201 visited Big Bend. The appropriation likewise has increased. In the 1990s it exceeded $2.5 million annually. The park has more than 100 full-time staff positions supplemented by temporary employees, interns, and volunteers. Development of the isolated desert park has evolved slowly. Mission 66, a decade-long project begun in the 1950s to upgrade a neglected national-park system that had suffered through inadequate funding during World War II[qv] and the Cold War, pumped $14 million into Big Bend for roads, bridges, trails, campsites, and a lodge, restaurant, and cabins in the Chisos Basin. The NPS, however, has never advocated extensive improvements. The vast majority of the park acreage is managed as natural zones to "remain largely unaltered by human activity."

BIBLIOGRAPHY: Arthur R. Gomez, *A Most Singular Country: A History of Occupation in the Big Bend* (Santa Fe: National Park Service; Salt Lake City: Charles Redd Center for Western Studies, Brigham Young University, 1990). John Jameson, *Big Bend National Park: The Formative Years* (El Paso: Texas Western Press, 1980). John Jameson, *Big Bend on the Rio Grande: Biography of a National Park* (New York: P. Lang, 1987). Ross A. Maxwell, *Big Bend Country: A History of Big Bend National Park* (Big Bend Natural History Association, 1985). Ross A. Maxwell, *The Big Bend of the Rio Grande* (Bureau of Economic Geology, University of Texas at Austin, 1968). Ronnie C. Tyler, *The Big Bend* (Washington: National Park Service, 1975). Roland H. Wauer, *Naturalist's Big Bend* (Santa Fe: Peregrine, 1973; rev ed., College Station: Texas A&M University Press, 1980). *John Jameson*

BIG BEND RANCH STATE NATURAL AREA. Big Bend Ranch State Natural Area in southwestern Brewster County and southeastern Presidio County is the largest park in the state system; it comprises nearly 265,000 acres, although in 1992 some 40,000 acres remained under private ownership. At one time the Big Bend Ranch was among the ten biggest working ranches in Texas. The first known ranchers in the area were Andrés Madrid, who began running sheep north of the site of present Lajitas in the 1870s, and the Carrasco family. In the 1910s the brothers Woodworth, Gus, and Gallie Bogel began buying and consolidating small stock outfits in the vicinity; they went bankrupt during the Great Depression,[qv] however, and their holdings were purchased by Mannie and Edwin Fowlkes, who continued the process of consolidation begun by the Bogels.

The property changed hands several more times before Robert O. Anderson, chairman of Atlantic Richfield Corporation, offered it to the state for $8 million, or about $36 an acre. The price was well under market value, but land commissioner Robert Armstrong could not persuade the legislature to approve the sale at that time. A few years later Governor William Clements attempted to arrange a land-swap deal whereby Anderson would receive state lands elsewhere in exchange for the ranch, but the plan was defeated amid charges of cronyism. In 1986 Anderson announced that he would sell oil leases on eighty-six acres of Big Bend Ranch, but on July 21, 1988, the Texas Parks and Wildlife Commission formally approved the purchase of the ranch by the state for $8.8 million. The title to the ranch was at that time held by the Hondo Oil and Gas Company, owned by Anderson and Walter Mischer of Houston.

Big Bend Ranch State Natural Area was opened to the public on January 19, 1991. Visitor centers have been constructed near each end of the park: at Fort Leaton State Historic Site,[qv] four miles southeast of Presidio, and at the Barton Warnock Environmental Education Center, just east of Lajitas. The two are connected by Ranch Road 170, known as the Camino del Río, which winds some sixty miles between Lajitas and Presidio. The natural area encompasses a vent crater of the defunct Bofecillos Volcano; a collapsed volcanic laccolith along its eastern boundary; picnic tables at Madera Canyon; Colorado Canyon, popular with rafters and canoeists; the thirty-mile unimproved Rancherías Canyon–Leon (Panther) Canyon Trail; a one-half mile trail into Cloud Canyon; one unimproved primitive campground; and all-day guided bus tours from both visitor centers.

The area has been declared an international biosphere reserve, a nature area recognized under a United Nations program, by the United States government. It is home to eleven endangered species of plants and animals and ninety major archeological sites. Vegetation in the area, of the Chihuahuan Desert variety, includes grama, silver bluestem, tanglehead, and tobosa grasses; mesquite, acacia, creosote, mariola, lechuguilla, ocotillo, and candelilla bushes; scrub oak, cottonwood, ash, willow, and the endangered Hinckley's oak; and the Big Bend or Harvard bluebonnet. Almost 400 species of birds either live in or migrate to the area; the Western mastiff bat, cactus wren, zone-tailed hawk, white-winged dove, great blue heron, beaver, golden eagle, peregrine falcon, deer, mountain lion, javelina, canyon tree frog, Couch's spadefoot toad, Trans-Pecos copperhead, monarch butterfly, Chihuahuan horse-lubber grasshopper, and tarantula belong to the local fauna.

In 1992 the future of the area became the focus of some controversy as the Texas Parks and Wildlife Department[qv] sought to develop a master plan for managing the area's resources. Some wanted to open the area to hunters, while others argued that hunting should be prohibited or allowed only on a very limited scale. Other issues involved the area's name, which some thought should be changed to avoid confusion with neighboring Big Bend National Park,[qv] and whether or not grazing cattle should be allowed on natural area land (the Parks and Wildlife Department maintained a small herd of cattle, with a maximum of 150 head, in the area).

BIBLIOGRAPHY: *Big Bend Ranch State Natural Area Visitor Guide* (Austin: Texas Parks and Wildlife Department, 1990). Jerry Sullivan, "The Gate's Open at Big Bend Ranch," *Texas Parks and Wildlife*, March 1991.
Martin Donell Kohout

BIG BLUE CREEK. Big Blue Creek rises in two branches in southwestern Moore County. North Big Blue Creek rises four miles southwest of Dumas (at 35°49′ N, 102°03′ W) and joins the main branch just west of U.S. Highway 287 near the Beauchamp Ranch (at 35°47′ N, 101°58′ W). The main branch originates eight miles southwest of Dumas (at 35°45′ N, 102°03′ W) and, fed by several tributaries, flows southeast for twenty-eight miles, through a vast, broken ranching and mineral area, to its mouth on Lake Meredith in the southeast corner of the county (at 35°43′ N, 101°40′ W).

BIG BLUFF CREEK. Big Bluff Creek rises three miles north of U.S. Highway 377 in western Mason County (at 30°49′ N, 99°26′ W) and runs southeast for thirteen miles to its mouth on the Llano River, 2½ miles north of Ranch Road 1871 (at 30°41′ N, 99°23′ W). The stream rises in the limestone hills on the eastern edge of the Edwards Plateau[qv] and traverses a section of the Llano basin characterized by flat to rolling terrain surfaced by loam, clay, and shallow, stony soils that support grasses and open stands of live oak, mesquite, and Ashe juniper. Early settlers established themselves on the creek around 1855. The settlements on Big Bluff, Little Bluff, and Honey creeks eventually became known as Streeter.

BIBLIOGRAPHY: J. Marvin Hunter, "Brief History of Mason County," *Frontier Times*, November, December 1928; January, February, March 1929.

BIG BOGGY CREEK. Big Boggy Creek rises three miles southwest of Bay City and two miles west of the Colorado River in the Bay Prairie of Matagorda County (at 28°55′ N, 95°59′ W) and runs southeast for twenty-three miles to its mouth on the Gulf Intracoastal Waterway,[qv] just off East Matagorda Bay (at 28°44′ N, 95°50′ W). The stream is intermittent in its upper reaches. Before the construction of the waterway the creek emptied directly into the bay. Big Boggy Creek forms Boggy Lake about a mile before its mouth. As it nears the coast it forms the western border of Big Boggy National Wildlife Refuge.[qv] Upstream the terrain is low-rolling to flat and locally dissected, surfaced by deep to shallow sandy and clay loams that support grasses and hardwoods. Near the coast the terrain changes to a saltwater marshland that supports diverse plant and animal species including waterfowl, shrimp, and numerous grasses.

BIG BOGGY NATIONAL WILDLIFE REFUGE. Big Boggy National Wildlife Refuge is on East Matagorda Bay just south of Lake Austin and twenty-one miles south of Bay City in southern Matagorda County. It is bordered on the west by Big Boggy Creek, on the east by a county road leading to the small fishing community of Chinquapin, and on the south by the Gulf Intracoastal Waterway.[qv] It provides winter habitat for migratory waterfowl. In 1990 it had 4,113 acres of coastal prairie and salt marsh. It is accessible only by way of Chinquapin Road or by boat. Dotted by numerous small lakes, including Lake Kilbride and Pelton Lake, the refuge, along with other such refuges on the Texas Gulf Coast, provides essential winter habitat for birds on the Central Flyway, one of four major migratory routes over the continental United States. Big Boggy Refuge is administered from the Brazoria National Wildlife Refuge[qv] by the United States fish and Wildlife Service, Department of the Interior. It was established in July 1983 with 1,410 acres purchased from the LeTulle estate, which also sold the refuge most of its additional land with the exception of Dressing Point Island in East Matagorda Bay, which was purchased from the Bear estate. The island provides a breeding ground for such colonial birds as pelicans, herons, and spoonbills; the endangered brown pelican has nested there also. In 1990 two wildlife easements (partially protected habitat not owned by the refuge) totaling 258 acres adjoined the mainland refuge. In the late 1980s Big Boggy National Wildlife Refuge was one of thirteen national wildlife refuges in Texas, which together total some 250,000 acres, and one of 420 in the United States. Though Big Boggy is generally closed to visitors, fishing and waterfowl hunting are permitted in season. Those interested in area wildlife are encouraged to try nearby San Bernard National Wildlife Refuge,[qv] a few miles to the east, or Brazoria National Wildlife Refuge.
Rachel Jenkins

BIG BOW (1833–?). Big Bow (Zepko-ette or Za-ko-yea), Kiowa chief, was born in 1833 on Elk Creek, Indian Territory. He was descended from a line of prominent war chiefs and inherited his name from his father and grandfather. From his father he learned at an early age to be a warrior, and by the time he was eighteen he had been on two raids into Mexico. In 1851 Big Bow was made a war chief but lost popularity that winter after eloping with the wife of another warrior. What was more, he offended many Kiowas with his scornful attitude toward the tribal religion. He was especially skeptical of medicine men, particularly the prognostications uttered by Maman-ti[qv] through his inflatable "medicine owl." Often Big Bow asserted that his own strength and courage, not the aid of a bird, would ensure him success in war. Consequently, he frequently went on raids either solo or accompanied only by one or two others. On a foray into New Mexico in 1855, he almost single-handedly captured several ponies and took a Navajo scalp. The following spring, after other tribal leaders expressed doubt about his boasts, he took another chief, Stumbling Bear, back with him to the scenes of his escapades in New Mexico. He frequently rode with the Quahadi band of Comanches on the Llano Estacado[qv] and became familiar with the areas between the Pecos River and the Rio Grande.

Big Bow's high rank was indicated by the fact that his leggings were fringed with human hair. He took part in raids into Texas and New Mexico during the 1860s and led one against the Utes in southern Colorado in the summer of 1869. Although he reportedly was an accomplice at the Salt Valley attack on May 17, 1871, he evaded arrest at Fort Sill. With his friend and fellow chief White Horse[qv] he staged the attack on the government wagon train at Howard's Wells on April 20, 1872, and the attack on Abel Lee and his family near Fort Griffin on

June 9. Thomas Battey, a Quaker missionary, later recalled Big Bow's "treacherous and ferocious countenance." At the outbreak of the Red River War[qv] in June 1874, Big Bow attempted to talk the Kiowa war faction, led by Lone Wolf[qv] and Maman-ti, into staying holed up in the canyons along Elk Creek. But when Maman-ti's "medicine" predicted complete safety for the group in Palo Duro Canyon, they voted to go there. Big Bow thus participated in the siege of Lyman's wagon train[qv] on September 9–14 and fought a brief battle with Col. Ranald S. Mackenzie's[qv] Fourth Cavalry at Palo Duro on September 27.

Sometime before Mackenzie's attack, Big Bow had disappeared briefly into the Llano Estacado, accompanied by Maman-ti's adopted son, the white captive Tehan.[qv] He then reappeared with Black Horse's[qv] band of Quahadis after killing and scalping a cavalry soldier. When defeat was inevitable, Big Bow was among the first of the Kiowa leaders to surrender in February 1875. It was reported that just before coming to the agency he killed Tehan because he was part white, but Big Bow and his family declared that Tehan had died of thirst on the plains. Big Bow readily submitted to the federal authorities and through the influence of Kicking Bird[qv] was enlisted as a scout to help bring in other bands. His cooperation kept him from going to prison in Florida with other Kiowa chiefs.

He subsequently emerged as a leader in his tribe's difficult adjustment to reservation life. On occasion he made friendly visits to the Utes and Pueblos in New Mexico. He and his braves often bargained with white traders and ranchers, including James A. Whittenburg,[qv] whose son George he once tried to adopt for a price of seventy-five horses. In 1886, with agent Jessie Lee Hall's[qv] permission, Big Bow led three Kiowas west to recover horses stolen by rustlers. He and a companion named Pay-kee overtook the thieves, killed one of them, and successfully recovered the stock, even though they had only a few rounds of ammunition with them. With his family Big Bow settled in the Rainy Mountain community and during his later years was converted to Christianity. One of his sons, Dom-ai-te, was noted in the tribe as a horse racer. The date and place of Big Bow's death are unknown. Several of his descendants still resided in the Anadarko area in the late twentieth century.

BIBLIOGRAPHY: Amarillo *Daily News*, October 20, 1936. Mildred P. Mayhall, *The Kiowas* (Norman: University of Oklahoma Press, 1962; 2d ed. 1971). James Mooney, *Calendar History of the Kiowa Indians* (Washington: GPO, 1898; rpt., Washington: Smithsonian Institution Press, 1979). Wilbur Sturtevant Nye, *Bad Medicine and Good: Tales of the Kiowas* (Norman: University of Oklahoma Press, 1962). Wilbur Sturtevant Nye, *Plains Indian Raiders* (Norman: University of Oklahoma Press, 1968).

H. Allen Anderson

BIG BRANCH. Big Branch, which is dammed in its upper reaches, rises two miles northwest of Gunsight and just west of U.S. Highway 183 in southwest Stephens County (at 32°33′ N, 98°54′ W) and runs northeast for six miles to its mouth on Lake Daniel, nine miles south of Breckenridge (at 32°37′ N, 98°52′ W). It crosses an area of rolling hills surfaced by clay and sandy loam that supports scrub brush, mesquite, cacti, and grasses. Toward the mouth the terrain becomes flat with local shallow depressions and a surface of clay and sandy loam from which grow water-tolerant hardwoods, conifers, and grasses.

BIG BRIARY CREEK. Big Briary Creek rises three miles north of Rosebud in southern Falls County (at 31°07′ N, 96°58′ W) and runs southeast for ten miles to its mouth on Pond Creek, twelve miles northeast of Cameron in Milam County (at 31°01′ N, 96°53′ W). It traverses flat to rolling prairie surfaced by dark, calcareous clays that support mesquite, cacti, and grasses.

BIG BROWN CREEK. Big Brown Creek begins three miles southwest of Fairfield in central Freestone County (at 31°42′ N, 96°06′ W) and runs northeast for thirteen miles to its mouth on Tehuacana Creek, four miles east of Fairfield Lake (at 31°50′ N, 96°00′ W). The stream is dammed in its middle reaches to form Fairfield Lake. It crosses flat to rolling prairies with local shallow depressions, surfaced by clay and sandy loams that support hardwoods, mesquite, conifers, and grasses. The area is used primarily for dry-land farming.

BIG BRUSHY CREEK (Kaufman County). Big Brushy Creek rises at the confluence of Brushy and Berry creeks eight miles northwest of Terrell in Kaufman County (at 32°48′ N, 96°23′ W) and runs southeast for 27½ miles, across flat to rolling terrain surfaced with dark calcareous clays that support mesquite and cacti. For most of the county's history, this area has been used as range and crop land. Big Brushy Creek joins King Creek three miles southwest of Kaufman (at 32°34′ N, 96°20′ W).

—— (Lavaca County). Big Brushy Creek rises 5½ miles northwest of Yoakum in far western Lavaca County (at 29°21′ N, 97°12′ W) and flows southeast, entering DeWitt County and skirting Yoakum on the west and south, then reentering Lavaca County and continuing for 30 ½ total miles to its mouth on Clarks Creek, 2½ miles northeast of the intersection of U.S. Highway 77 and State Highway 111 (at 29°11′ N, 96°56′ W). The stream passes the Yoakum sewage-disposal plant and the South Yoakum and Brushy Creek oil and gas fields, then flows through poorly drained sandy upland prairie used primarily as rangeland for cattle. Across this generally rolling terrain, vegetation consists of a fairly dense cover of scrub oak and mesquite that provides excellent habitat for wildlife.

BIG CANYON. Big Canyon begins on the WB Flats one mile northwest of the Dimple Hills in southwestern Pecos County (at 30°21′ N, 102°58′ W) and runs southeast for 106 miles to its mouth on Meyers Canyon, six miles northeast of the Southern Pacific tracks in east central Terrell County (at 30°05′ N, 101°55′ W). Its steep to gentle slopes are surfaced by variable soils that support scrub brush and sparse grasses.

BIG COW CREEK. Big Cow Creek rises eight miles southeast of Browndell in northwestern Newton County (at 31°05′ N, 93°53′ W) and flows south-southeast for fifty-six miles to its mouth on the Sabine River, ten miles southeast of Kirbyville (at 30°34′ N, 93°44′ W). The stream, intermittent in its upper reaches, traverses gently undulating to hilly terrain where loblolly, shortleaf, and longleaf pines grow.

BIG CREEK (Bowie County). Big Creek, also known as Langum Creek, rises a mile east of New Boston in central Bowie County (at 33°28′ N, 94°23′ W) and flows southeast for sixteen miles to its mouth on Wright Patman Lake, ten miles south of Hooks (at 33°20′ N, 94°17′ W). The stream, intermittent in its upper reaches, flows through Red River Army Depot.[qv] The soils are loamy in the upper and middle reaches and clayey around the mouth. The downstream area is heavily wooded, with pines and various hardwoods predominating.

—— (Brazos County). Big Creek rises near Allenfarm in southern Brazos County (at 30°24′ N, 96°15′ W). Weaving its way eastward for 24½ miles, it travels through the flatlands of the Brazos River valley and empties into the Navasota River at the Brazos-Grimes county line (at 30°23′ N, 96°08′ W). The stream traverses flat terrain with local shallow depressions, surfaced with clay and sandy loams. The area has been highly cultivated with crops, but where native vegetation remains it consists mainly of post oaks.

—— (Delta County). Big Creek, also known as Richland Creek, rises in a pool a mile southeast of Ben Franklin in northwest Delta County (33°28′ N, 95°46′ W) and runs southeast for 14½ miles to its mouth on the South Sulphur River, six miles southeast of Cooper (at 33°21′ N, 95°36′ W). East Fork and Cedar creeks are tributaries. Upstream, Big Creek traverses rolling prairies with high slopes and a surface of dark gray clay that supports oak, juniper, mesquite, and grasses; the low-lying floodplains at the mouth are surfaced by sand, gravel, and mud that support water-tolerant hardwoods, conifers, and grasses.

____ (Fort Bend County). Big Creek rises where Coon and Cottonwood creeks converge in south central Fort Bend County (at 29°29′ N, 95°50′ W) and flows southeast for twenty-five miles to its mouth on the Brazos River (at 29°22′ N, 95°35′ W). It crosses variable terrain surfaced by highly impermeable soil and calcareous clay that support mixed hardwoods and prairie grasses.

____ (Franklin County). Big Creek rises six miles southwest of Mount Vernon in western Franklin County (at 33°06′ N, 95°17′ W) and runs northeast for thirteen miles to its mouth on White Oak Creek, six miles northwest of Mount Vernon (at 33°16′ N, 95°16′ W). Loamy alluvial soils flank the stream, and the surrounding wooded area, which is frequently flooded, is used mainly as pasture.

____ (Houston County). Big Creek, also known as Caney Bayou, rises four miles southwest of Crockett in west central Houston County (at 31°18′ N, 95°31′ W) and flows southwest for eighteen miles to its mouth on the Trinity River, near the Fort Trinidad oilfield (at 31°04′ N, 95°39′ W). It crosses flat terrain surfaced by clay and sandy loam that supports water-tolerant hardwoods, conifers, and grasses.

____ (Jack County). Big Creek rises in north central Jack County (at 33°27′ N, 98°00′ W) and runs southeast for twenty-one miles to its mouth on Lake Bridgeport, four miles west of Chico in western Wise County (at 33°17′ N, 97°52′ W). The stream is intermittent in all but its lowest reaches. It traverses generally flat terrain surfaced by clay and sandy loams that support water-tolerant hardwoods, conifers, and grasses.

____ (Jasper County). Big Creek rises six miles south of Jasper in central Jasper County (at 30°51′ N, 93°59′ W) and flows southwest for fifteen miles to its mouth on the Neches River, four miles south of Town Bluff Dam (at 30°46′ N, 94°08′ W). The stream, intermittent in its upper reaches, runs through gently undulating terrain surfaced by deep loam that supports pines and grasses. A nineteenth-century observer described Big Creek as "a beautiful stream of clear-running water."

BIBLIOGRAPHY: W. T. Block, ed., *Emerald of the Neches: The Chronicles of Beaumont from Reconstruction to Spindletop* (Nederland, Texas: Nederland Publishing, 1980).

____ (Limestone County). Big Creek rises four miles southwest of Prairie Hill in northwestern Limestone County (at 31°38′ N, 96°51′ W) and runs southwest for six miles before its name changes to Mussel Run Creek (at 31°14′ N, 96°51′ W). Under the latter name it empties into the Brazos River two miles west of Highbank in south central Falls County (at 31°10′ N, 96°52′ W). The stream is intermittent in its upper reaches. It crosses low-rolling to flat prairie with local shallow depressions, surfaced by clay and sandy loams that support mesquite, scrub brush, cacti, grasses, water-tolerant hardwoods, and conifers.

____ (Limestone County). Big Creek rises four miles north of Kosse in southern Limestone County (at 31°21′ N, 96°38′ W) and runs east for six miles to its mouth on Steele Creek, five miles south of Thornton (at 31°21′ N, 96°34′ W). It crosses generally flat terrain with local shallow depressions and a surface of clay and sandy loams that support water-tolerant hardwoods, conifers, and grasses.

____ (San Jacinto County). Big Creek rises five miles west of Shepherd in central San Jacinto County (at 30°31′ N, 95°06′ W) and flows southeast for twenty-two miles to its mouth on the Trinity River, two miles west of Romayor in Liberty County (at 30°28′ N, 94°53′ W). The stream is intermittent in its upper reaches, which are now part of the Big Creek Scenic Area,[qv] designated by the United States Forest Service in 1963 as a nature preserve. The scenic area includes excellent examples of loblolly pine, yaupon, and dogwood, representative of the formerly vast Big Thicket[qv] of East Texas. While still in San Jacinto County, Big Creek flows north of Shepherd before cutting southward to form a marshy bottomland known as the Break.

BIG CREEK, TEXAS. Big Creek is off Farm Road 2666 eight miles southeast of Coldspring and sixty miles north of Houston in southern San Jacinto County. It originally developed around a Methodist church known as Farley's Chapel and was established before the 1890s; Bill Lovett, George Howard, and John Jagers were among the early inhabitants. The little farming community did not have a post office or stores, but numerous tram lines in the vicinity and the fact that extensive lands were acquired or leased there by the Texas Long Leaf Lumber Company indicate that logging was important in the area. Although the tram lines have been abandoned, two churches and scattered buildings remained in the mid-1980s. The settlement is just east of Big Creek Scenic Area.[qv]

BIBLIOGRAPHY: Ruth Hansbro, History of San Jacinto County (M.A. thesis, Sam Houston State Teachers College, 1940).

Robert Wooster

BIG CREEK SCENIC AREA. Big Creek Scenic Area is on Forest Service Road 217 six miles west of Shepherd in east central San Jacinto County. The scenic area, which is maintained by the Texas Forestry Association,[qv] features a 3½-mile hiking trail in four loops that partially follows Big Creek. Camping, picnicking, swimming, and showers are available at nearby Double Lake Recreation Area.

Christopher Long

BIG CYPRESS, TEXAS. Big Cypress was on the Texas and St. Louis Railway near the banks of Big Cypress Creek five miles from Pittsburg in northern Camp County. A post office was established there in 1889 and closed in 1891. According to a publication of in 1892, the community had a gristmill, a gin, and a store, all operated by the postmaster, M. C. Davis, who was also a photographer. The community also had a Mason, a carpenter, a shoemaker, and an estimated population of seventy-five, but that estimate probably included the nearby black community of Harvard, or Harvard Switch. By 1910 Big Cypress had ceased to exist.

BIBLIOGRAPHY: Artemesia L. B. Spencer, *The Camp County Story* (Fort Worth: Branch-Smith, 1974). *Cecil Harper, Jr.*

BIG CYPRESS CREEK (Franklin County). Big Cypress Creek rises near the Hopkins county line in southeastern Franklin County (at 33°03′ N, 95°21′ W) and flows southeast for sixty miles to its mouth on Big Cypress Bayou, three miles west of Jefferson in southern Marion County (at 32°45′ N, 94°30′ W). The stream forms the boundary lines between Camp and Titus, Camp and Morris, and Morris and Upshur counties. Big Cypress Creek is intermittent in its upper reaches. It runs through flat to rolling terrain surfaced by sandy and clay loams that support water-tolerant hardwoods, conifers, and grasses. The fact that Big Cypress Creek formed the last link in a chain of navigable waters contributed to Jefferson's rise as a commercial center in the days before the railroads. Between 1842 and 1872 the town was the principal riverport in Texas, serving as a distribution point for much of North and East Texas. Boats brought goods from New Orleans and St. Louis and returned laden with cotton and other agricultural products. With the coming of the railroads in the early 1870s, river traffic declined. Since World War II[qv] Big Cypress Creek has been dammed in two locations: on the border of Camp and Titus counties to form a series of lakes including Lake Cypress Springs, Lake Bob Sandlin, and Monticello Reservoir; and in Marion County to form Lake O' the Pines. Once the conduit of early settlement, the creek's waters now serve as an important source of recreation and tourist dollars.

BIBLIOGRAPHY: Fred Tarpley, *Jefferson: Riverport to the Southwest* (Austin: Eakin Press, 1983).

____ (Tyler County). Big Cypress Creek, also known as Cypress Creek, rises five miles south of Chester in northwestern Tyler County (at 30°51′ N, 94°35′ W) and flows southeast for twenty-seven miles to its mouth on Turkey Creek, a mile southeast of Hillister (at 30°38′ N, 94°21′ W). The stream is intermittent for much of its course. Its major tributary is Little Cypress Creek, which rises five miles southwest of

Colmesneil in west central Tyler County (at 30°51′ N, 94°29′ W). The smaller stream, also intermittent in its upper stages, flows south for eleven miles to its juncture with Big Cypress Creek, seven miles northwest of Warren (at 30°42′ N, 94°29′ W). The surrounding terrain is flat to rolling with local escarpments. The soil surface is mostly deep sandy loam. Hardwood forests and conifers predominate in the heavily wooded area.

BIG DIE-UP. In the early 1880s the Panhandle[qv] and South Plains regions of West Texas were beginning to be crowded with ranchers. Before long the ranges were overstocked, and the depletion of grasses threatened the cowmen's livelihood. During the northers and blizzards of harsh Panhandle winters, cattle tended by instinct to drift southward, sometimes for over 100 miles, to seek shelter in various canyons and river valleys. Range outfits often had a hard time separating their cattle. Barbed wire[qv] fencing seemed to be an answer. Accordingly, drift fences, fences intended to keep cattle from drifting, were built. In 1882 the Panhandle Stock Association ranchers erected a drift fence that ran from the New Mexico line east through Hartley and Moore counties to the Canadian River breaks in Hutchinson County. Over the next few years more sections were added, so that by 1885 barbed wire drift fences stretched across the entire northern Panhandle, from thirty-five miles deep in New Mexico to the Indian Territory. These formed an effective barrier for northern cattle attempting to drift onto the southern ranges.

Beginning in late December of 1885, a series of blizzards struck the southern plains. Cattle retreating to the south were stalled by the drift fences and unable to go any farther. They huddled against each other along the fence line in large bunches, some of them 400 yards across. Unable to stay warm or escape the crush, these cattle either smothered or froze to death in their tracks within a short while. Others bogged down in icy creek beds and draws. Many, caught in open areas without sufficient food, water, or shelter, either died of thirst or afterward fell victim to wolves or coyotes. When the storms dissipated in January 1886, thousands of dead cattle were found piled up against the Panhandle drift fences, and hundreds more along lesser, but similar, man-made barriers on other rangelands. The Cator brothers' Diamond C herd was almost wiped out, and others like Henry Cresswell's[qv] Bar CC and the Seven K[qv] suffered staggering losses.

The following winter, 1886-87, brought more such blizzards to the Panhandle, and again the corpses of cattle trapped by the fences were appallingly numerous. Ranchers in Wheeler County estimated many herd losses to be as high as 75 percent along the cooperatively built barrier that followed the course of Sweetwater Creek near Mobeetie. An LX Ranch[qv] employee reportedly skinned 250 carcasses a mile for thirty-five miles along one section of drift fence. The "Big Die-up" was followed by prolonged summer droughts, and many cowmen went broke. Though some, like James Cator[qv] and Hank Cresswell, eventually recovered, others sold out at a loss, and several ranches changed hands.

BIBLIOGRAPHY: Henry D. and Frances T. McCallum, *The Wire That Fenced the West* (Norman: University of Oklahoma Press, 1965). David L. Wheeler, "The Blizzard of 1886 and Its Effect on the Range Cattle Industry in the Southern Plains," *Southwestern Historical Quarterly* 94 (January 1991). David L. Wheeler, "The Texas Panhandle Drift Fences," *Panhandle-Plains Historical Review* 55 (1982).

H. Allen Anderson

BIG EDDY. Big Eddy rises a half mile south of San Jacinto Dam on Lake Houston in northeast Harris County (at 95°07′ N, 29°54′ W) and flows southeast for 1½ miles to its juncture with the San Jacinto River (at 95°07′ N, 29°53′ W). The stream is located in the eastern part of Dwight D. Eisenhower Park. It traverses flat swampland where pines and hardwoods grow.

BIG ELKHART CREEK. Big Elkhart Creek rises a mile west of Salmon in southwestern Anderson County (at 31°34′ N, 95°30′ W) and runs southwest for 22½ miles, through southwestern Anderson County and northwestern Houston County, to its mouth on the Trinity River, 1 ½ miles northwest of Halls Bluff in Houston County (at 31°22′ N, 95°41′ W). The stream is intermittent in its upper reaches. It traverses gently sloping to moderately steep terrain surfaced by sand, clay, and loam that support occasional heavy woods of mixed pine and hardwoods. The major tributaries of Big Elkhart Creek include Little Elkhart Creek and Moccasin Branch.

BIG ELM CREEK (Limestone County). Big Elm Creek rises two miles north of Lavender in east central Limestone County (at 31°33′ N, 96°39′ W) and runs southwest for sixteen miles to its mouth on Big Creek, ten miles east-northeast of Marlin in Falls County (at 31°24′ N, 96°44′ W). The creek crosses flat to rolling prairie with local shallow depressions and a surface of dark, calcareous clays and sandy loams that support water-tolerant hardwood and conifers near the creek and mesquite, cacti, and grasses in the surrounding area.

—— (McLennan County). Big Elm Creek rises a mile east of Moody in southwestern McLennan County (at 31°19′ N, 97°21′ W) and flows southeast for forty-nine miles, through McLennan, Bell, and Milam counties, to its mouth on the Little River, about three miles north of Cameron in Milam County (at 30°54′ N, 96°56′ W). The stream, intermittent in its upper reaches, crosses nearly level to sloping terrain surfaced by clayey and loamy soils used predominantly for agriculture and occasionally dotted with big elms.

BIGELOW, HORATIO (?–?). Horatio Bigelow, a member of the Long expedition,[qv] was one of the eleven men of the supreme council of the provisional government,[qv] which, on June 22, 1819, declared the province of Texas a free and independent republic. Sometime in August 1819, with Eli Harris,[qv] he edited the Nacogdoches *Texas Republican*.[qv] Apparently Bigelow was captured with James Long[qv] and other members of the expedition in 1821, but by 1829 he had returned to Nacogdoches, where he was associated with the Nacogdoches *Mexican Advocate*.[qv]

BIBLIOGRAPHY: Douglas C. McMurtrie, "Pioneer Printing in Texas," *Southwestern Historical Quarterly* 35 (January 1932). *Quarterly of the Texas State Historical Association*, Notes and Fragments, January 1904. Dudley Goodall Wooten, ed., *A Comprehensive History of Texas* (2 vols., Dallas: Scarff, 1898; rpt., Austin: Texas State Historical Association, 1986).

L. W. Kemp

BIG FIELDERS CREEK. Big Fielders Creek rises five miles west of Big Hackberry Canyon in eastern Terrell County (at 30°14′ N, 101°52′ W) and runs southeast for thirty miles to its mouth on the Pecos River, a mile below Cash Canyon in northwestern Val Verde County (at 30°08′ N, 101°34′ W). The creek joins Henderson Draw two miles above the Pecos River. The path of Big Fielders Creek sharply dissects massive limestone that underlies flat terrain, forming a rugged and winding valley. Wash deposits of sand, gravel, and mud cover the canyon floor. The soils of the area, generally dark, calcareous, stony clays and clay loams, support oaks, junipers, grasses, and mesquites.

BIG FIVEMILE CREEK. Big Fivemile Creek rises in Flatonia, southwestern Fayette County (at 29°41′ N, 97°07′ W), and flows 13½ miles, first north, under bridges on U.S. Highway 90 and Interstate Highway 10; then west, past the State Highway 95 bridge; then southwest, back under U.S. 90 and I-10, then beneath the Southern Pacific railroad bridge. It empties into Peach Creek in Gonzales County (at 29°39′ N, 97°13′ W). Throughout its course the stream flows over sandy clay loams with cracking clayey subsoils, of middling agricultural value. Although there are some fields and orchards downstream, the area is used primarily for pasture. The vegetation in the area ranges from open pasture and cultivated fields with some encroaching mesquite and cedar to densely timbered bottomlands of mixed oak, cedar, sycamore, and hackberry with a yaupon understory. These undisturbed bottomlands interspersed with cleared uplands provide good wildlife habitat. The creek's name is possibly derived from its crossing of the Southern Pacific five miles east of Waelder.

BIGFOOT, TEXAS. Bigfoot is at the intersection of Farm roads 462 and 472, eighteen miles northeast of Pearsall in northeastern Frio County. The site was settled about 1865 and during its early years was known as Connally's Store, for Bob Connally. D. T. Winters established a gin and mill there by 1880. When James Connally secured a post office for the community in 1883, he named it Bigfoot, for William A. A. (Bigfoot) Wallace,[qv] a resident of the community. A Baptist church was organized there in the 1880s, and by 1890 Bigfoot had a general store and an estimated population of twenty-five. During the 1890s citizens opened a public school, which in 1907 had three teachers and 105 pupils. The community had a population of 146 in 1900, but much of the town's business section burned in 1903. Bigfoot's population fell to an estimated 100 by the 1930s, and in the 1940s the community had a church, a school, a row of five businesses, and a number of scattered dwellings. The Bigfoot school consolidated with that of Devine in 1949. With the development in the 1950s of the Bigfoot oilfield to the south, the community grew, and in 1964 it had a population of 210, three churches, two businesses, and a number of dwellings. During the 1970s its population diminished again, and was estimated at seventy-five from 1972 to 1992. In the 1980s Bigfoot still had the post office, two businesses, and three churches. The Bigfoot Wallace museum is in the community.

BIBLIOGRAPHY: Frances Bramlette Farris, *From Rattlesnakes to Road Agents: Rough Times on the Frio*, ed. C. L. Sonnichsen (Fort Worth: Texas Christian University Press, 1985). *Mark Odintz*

BIG FOSSIL CREEK. Big Fossil Creek, also known as Fossil Creek, rises 4½ miles northwest of Saginaw in southwestern Tarrant County (at 32°57′ N, 97°24′ W) and runs southeast for nineteen miles to its mouth on the West Fork of the Trinity River, just east of Haltom City (at 32°47′ N, 97°14′ W). The stream is intermittent in its upper reaches and is dammed five miles south of Haslet. It traverses flat to rolling terrain surfaced by clay and sandy loams that support water-tolerant hardwoods, conifers, grasses, chaparral, and cacti. The area is heavily urbanized.

BIGGERS, DON HAMPTON (1868–1957). Don H. Biggers, newspaper editor, satirist, and historian, the son of Samuel Washington and Elizabeth A. Biggers, was born in Meridian, Texas, on September 27, 1868. His boyhood on a small cattle ranch near Breckenridge and visits to the buffalo range gave Biggers a lifelong love of the land and of those who settled and farmed it. He learned the printing trade in Colorado City in 1884. In 1889 he published his first booklet, *A Handbook of Reference . . . of Eastland County,* a glowing account of the county's many advantages. On October 5, 1890, he married Nettie Lee Cox. They were married for sixty-seven years and had five sons and a daughter. In 1890 Biggers purchased the Midland *Gazette.* When its offices burned a few months later, the restless editor took up a wandering and prolific career of writing and publishing in various West and Central Texas towns. He published the Ranger *Atlas* (1891), the Clayton (New Mexico) *Union-Democrat* (1897), the *West Texas Stockman* (1898–1900), the *Colorado Spokesman* (1900), and the Rotan *Advance* (1907–09). In 1901 he published *History That Will Never Be Repeated,* about the development of ranching in West Texas (this work was reprinted in 1961 by Seymour V. Connor under the title *A Biggers Chronicle*), and in 1902 *Pictures of the Past,* a collection of old-timers' reminiscences about the great buffalo[qv] slaughter of the 1870s (this work was not reprinted and is a rare and expensive item of Texana). Articles that Biggers wrote about West Texas for the Dallas *Morning News*[qv] in 1904 were published as a book, *From Cattle Range To Cotton Patch,* in 1905. By 1935 Biggers had published at least ten other books. He also issued several satirical papers, *The Josher* (1899–1902), *The Texas Cleaver* (1902–05), and *Billy Goat Always Buttin' In* (1908). In 1909 he moved his family to Lubbock, where he farmed and wrote articles. He served in the Texas House of Representatives for Lubbock in 1915. In 1918 he started the *Oil Belt News* in Eastland. The following year he sold the paper and wrote articles on the state prison system[qv] for the Fort Worth *Record.* In 1920 Biggers served again in the Texas House, representing Eastland. He ran for the office of commissioner of agriculture and promised to abolish the office if elected. He lost. Also in 1920 he wrote about corruption in the Eastland County oilfields for the Ranger *Record.*

In 1921 Biggers started the *Independent Oil News and Financial Reporter,* mainly to expose fraudulent promotion schemes; his success brought threats on his life, since files he gave the federal district attorney in Fort Worth helped send fraudulent promoters to prison. In 1922 in Fort Worth Biggers issued several short-lived publications dedicated to opposing the Ku Klux Klan.[qv] Again, he endured physical threats but refused to stop his anti-Klan campaign. In 1925 he published *German Pioneers in Texas,* a history of German settlement. He helped Louis Wiltz Kemp[qv] expose highway scandals in the administration of Miriam Ferguson[qv] and published *Our Sacred Monkeys,* a satirical account of James E. Ferguson's[qv] political career, in 1933.

Biggers spent his later years roaming the Southwest with his wife, writing letters to politicians and editors to protest hypocrisy and injustice wherever he saw it. He died in Stephenville on December 11, 1957.

BIBLIOGRAPHY: Don Hampton Biggers Papers, Southwest Collection, Texas Tech University. Seymour V. Connor, *A Biggers Chronicle* (Lubbock: Texas Technological College, 1961). James McEnteer, *Fighting Words: Independent Journalists in Texas* (Austin: University of Texas Press, 1992). *James McEnteer*

BIGGERS, TEXAS. Biggers was five miles east of the site of present McKinney in central Collin County. Settlement occurred sometime in the early 1890s, after the construction of the Biggers-Allen Mill in the late 1880s. By 1899 a general store and post office operated at the site with Wade Biggers as postmaster. The population of the settlement never exceeded twenty-five, however, and the post office closed in 1903. The community continued to exist until sometime in the early 1950s.

BIBLIOGRAPHY: Roy Franklin Hall and Helen Gibbard Hall, *Collin County: Pioneering in North Texas* (Quanah, Texas: Nortex, 1975).
David Minor

BIGGS, TEXAS. Biggs was 3½ miles northwest of Carthage in north central Panola County. It was established in the early 1880s and had a post office from 1884 to 1895, when the mail was rerouted through Delray. By the 1890s Biggs had two general stores, a gristmill, and a population of twenty-five. During the second decade of the twentieth century the settlement was dropped from maps.

BIBLIOGRAPHY: John Barnette Sanders, *Postoffices and Post Masters of Panola County, Texas, 1845–1930* (Center, Texas, 1964).
Christopher Long

BIGGS ARMY AIR FIELD. Biggs Army Air Field in El Paso County was originally named Biggs Field for Lt. James A. Biggs, an El Paso pilot killed in France in 1918. Though after World War I[qv] Biggs Field became the station of the First Surveillance Group, it was little more than a refueling stop until the outbreak of World War II,[qv] when it was greatly expanded by a $10 million construction program. In the summer of 1942 it became headquarters of the Twentieth Bomber Command and the Sixteenth Bombardment Operational Training Wing; B-17, B-24, and B-29 crews trained there. With the foundation of the United States Air Force in 1947 the field was renamed Biggs Air Force Base. Both the Tactical Air Command and the Strategic Air Command operated from the base until it was turned over the United States Army in 1966 and designated Biggs Army Air Field. In the early 1990s the field continued to serve as a support base for nearby Fort Bliss.

BIBLIOGRAPHY: Harriot Howze Jones, comp. and ed., *El Paso: A Centennial Portrait* (El Paso, 1972). Robert Mueller, *Air Force Bases*, Vol. 1 (Maxwell Air Force Base, Alabama: Simpson Historical Research Center, 1982).

Art Leatherwood

BIG HEAD MOUNTAIN. Big Head Mountain is 22 ½ miles northwest of New Braunfels in northwestern Comal County (at 29°59′ N, 98°19′ W). It rises 153 feet above Carper's Creek, on its east side, to an elevation of 1,473 feet. The surrounding area of the Balcones Escarpment is flat to rolling and, in places, deeply and densely dissected. The loam land surface, broken with rock outcrops, primarily supports live oak and Ashe juniper woods.

BIG HEAD VILLAGE, TEXAS. Big Head (Bighead) Village, one of the earliest settlements in Gregg County, was located east of Big Head Creek near the site of the later Presbyterian church at New Danville, on the northeastern edge of the site of present Kilgore. The name of the community is believed to have come from a Cherokee word, but it is unclear whether Big Head was established by Indians. Maps show a settlement at the site as early as the mid-1840s, and the community is mentioned in a document as late as 1850. By the 1860s the settlement had disappeared, and no trace remains.

BIBLIOGRAPHY: Eugene W. McWhorter, *Traditions of the Land: The History of Gregg County* (Longview, Texas: Gregg County Historical Foundation, 1989).

Christopher Long

BIG HILL, TEXAS. (Gonzales County). Big Hill, a rail stop eight miles east of Gonzales in northeastern Gonzales County, had a post office from 1857 to 1873. In 1889, when the San Antonio and Aransas Pass Railway built a spur from Shiner to Lockhart, a sign reading "Big Hill" marked a stopping point on the line. In 1932, however, the company abandoned the line, and afterward the rails were taken up. Big Hill remained a small farming and ranching community for a while. By 1936 only a rural schoolhouse marked the townsite, and by 1965 the site was no longer named on state highway maps.

Stephen L. Hardin

BIG HILL, TEXAS (Jefferson County). Big Hill, ten miles southeast of Hamshire in southwestern Jefferson County, is named after a hill that rises about thirty feet above the low-lying marshy prairies of the Southeast Texas coast. In 1909 the area became a site for development, and many tracts were sold to second-generation Swedish Americans from Illinois, Michigan, Wisconsin, and New York. The new settlers grew fig and citrus orchards until a hurricane destroyed most of their houses and barns in 1915 (*see* HURRICANES). The residents subsequently moved the remnants of their houses to Winnie and Hamshire. Many of the Swedes[qv] retained their property rights, however, a decision that proved extremely profitable when oil and gas were found at the Big Hill Fields in the late 1940s and early 1950s.

Robert Wooster

BIG HILL, TEXAS (Limestone County). Big Hill (Bighill), on Farm Road 2489 seven miles west of Thornton in western Limestone County, was named for an elevation used by the Indians as a lookout point. Settlement began there in the 1880s with the opening of the blacklands for farming. Big Hill Methodist Church, which served as the focus of the community for many years, was organized in 1879. A post office was opened in 1894 with Bailey A. Garrett as postmaster, and in 1896 a Big Hill school district was organized. The town's population reached a peak of about 100 in 1915 but began to decline by the 1920s as business grew in nearby Groesbeck. The Big Hill post office was closed in 1924, and by 1949 the population had declined to twenty. After World War II[qv] the church disbanded, and the school was consolidated with that of Groesbeck. By 1985 only the abandoned church and cemetery were left to mark the site of the town.

BIBLIOGRAPHY: *Memorial and Biographical History of Navarro, Henderson, Anderson, Limestone, Freestone, and Leon Counties* (Chicago: Lewis, 1893). Ray A. Walter, *A History of Limestone County* (Austin: Von Boeckmann–Jones, 1959).

Ray A. Walter

BIG HILL BAYOU. Big Hill Bayou rises four miles southeast of LaBelle in southern Jefferson County (at 29°50′ N, 95°05′ W) and flows northeast for ten miles to its mouth on Taylor Bayou, south of Port Acres (at 29°53′ N, 94°02′ W). It cuts through the marshy terrain that characterizes most of the upper Texas Gulf coastline. For much of its course it runs through the J. D. Murphee Wildlife Management Area, which provides habitat for coastal waterfowl, shrimp, blue crab, and finfish.

BIBLIOGRAPHY: Texas General Land Office, *Areas of Particular Concern: Upper Texas Coastal Region* (map, Austin, 1975).

BIG HOLLOW CREEK. Big Hollow Creek begins nine miles southwest of Divot in southwest Frio County (at 28°44′ N, 99°23′ W) and runs northeast for four miles to its mouth on Todos Santos Creek, two miles northwest of Divot (at 28°46′ N, 99°21′ W). It traverses rolling prairie upstream, then flat terrain with locally shallow depressions. The caliche and clay land surface supports dwarf evergreen oak, juniper, mesquite, grasses, water-tolerant hardwoods, and conifers.

BIG INCH AND LITTLE BIG INCH. The Big Inch and Little Big Inch were two pipelines laid during World War II[qv] from East Texas to the northeast states. Secretary of the Interior Harold Ickes realized as early as 1940 that shipment of petroleum to the northeast by tanker ships would be impossible in time of war because of German submarines. In 1941, at Ickes's urging, oil industry executives began to plan the building of two pipelines—one, twenty-four inches in diameter, called the Big Inch, to transport crude oil, and another, twenty inches in diameter, called the Little Big Inch, to transport refined products. Although Ickes asked the Federal Allocation Board for steel to build the pipelines, he was turned down in September and again in November 1941. After the attack on Pearl Harbor another request, now to the War Production Board, was rejected, but Ickes still persuaded Jubal Richard Parten[qv] to head the Petroleum Administration for War transportation department. On June 10, 1942, the WPB gave approval for the first section of the Big Inch, which stopped in Illinois. Construction was through a private company, War Emergency Pipelines, Incorporated, but the pipelines were owned by the federal government through its Defense Plant Corporation, a subsidiary of the Reconstruction Finance Corporation.

Work began on the Big Inch on August 3, 1942. The WPB approved the second leg of the pipeline on October 26, 1942. A ditch four feet deep, three feet wide and 1,254 miles long was to be dug from Longview across the Mississippi River to Southern Illinois and then east to Phoenixville, Pennsylvania, with twenty-inch lines from there to New York City and Philadelphia. Crude oil was delivered to the end of the first leg, Norris City, Illinois, on February 13, 1943. By August 14, 1943, the Big Inch had been completed. In January 1943 approval was given for the first half of the Little Big Inch; approval for the entire line was given on April 2. This line, beginning in the refinery complex between Houston and Port Arthur and ending in Linden, New Jersey, was completed on March 2, 1944. Cost of the two lines was $146 million, financed entirely by the RFC. Together the pipelines carried over 350 million barrels of crude oil and refined products to the East Coast before the war in Europe ended in August 1945.

After the war, the pipelines became the focus of a clash of interest groups, with the oil and gas industry wanting to convert them to natural-gas pipelines and the railroad and coal industries opposing this. The Surplus Property Administration, given the task of determining future use, hired an engineering firm to study options; this study recommended that the pipelines be converted to natural-gas transmission. At the same time the United States Senate held hearings on their future use. In January 1946 the SPA recommended that first preference should be to continue use as in the war to ensure availability of the lines in a national emergency. However, by June 1946 the War Assets Administration announced an auction for the lines. All bids were ultimately rejected because no defined use preference had been established. After a strike by coal miners in November 1946 the WAA solicited bids to lease the lines, with Tennessee Gas and Transmission Company awarded a lease for natural-gas use to run from December 3, 1946, to April 30, 1947. Once it was established that the lines were viable for natural-gas transmission, the WAA again offered them for auction. The high bid of $143,127,000 came from a new corporation, Texas Eastern Transmission Corporation, formed by George Rufus and Herman Brown[qv] and their partners. The purchase was final on November 14, 1947. As of 1993, Texas Eastern had its headquarters in Houston.

BIBLIOGRAPHY: Christopher J. Castaneda, "The Texas–Northeast Connection: The Rise of the Post–World War II Gas Pipeline Industry," *Houston Review* 12 (1990). James Anthony Clark and Michel T. Halbouty, *The Last Boom* (New York: Random House, 1972).

Jerrell Dean Palmer and John G. Johnson

BIG ISLAND SLOUGH. Big Island Slough rises near the intersection of State Highway 225 and Miller Road in southeast Harris County (at 29°42′ N, 95°05′ W) and flows south seven miles to its mouth on Armand Bayou, three miles northwest of Clear Lake (at 29°36′ N, 95°06′ W). It traverses flat, flood-prone grasslands.

BIG JIM (?–1900). Big Jim, a Shawnee chief, grandson of Tecumseh and son of one of the chiefs who signed the Indian treaty of February 23, 1836, was born in the Sabine reservation in Texas in 1834. His native name was Wapameepto ("Gives Light as He Walks"), and his popular name, Big Jim, was a mistake for his English name, Dick Jim. In 1872 he became chief of his band, often called Big Jim's band of Absentee Shawnees. He resented the encroachments of settlers, never became Christianized, and made efforts to move his people away from white men. In 1900, while in Mexico to investigate possibilities of moving his people there, he died of smallpox.

BIBLIOGRAPHY: Frederick Webb Hodge, ed., *Handbook of American Indians North of Mexico* (2 vols., Washington: GPO, 1907, 1910; rpt., New York: Pageant, 1959).

Seymour V. Connor

BIG LAKE (Anderson County). Big Lake is a natural lake on Lake Creek two miles east of the Trinity River in southwestern Anderson County (at 31°43′ N, 95°50′ W). In 1964 there was a housing development on its eastern shore.

—— (Reagan County). Big Lake is on Farm Road 137 a mile southwest of the community of Big Lake in south central Reagan County (at 31°10′ N, 101°29′ W). It is fed by Big Lake Draw and lies in a floodplain. It covers an estimated 1,000 acres. The shores of Big Lake are composed of sand, silt, gravel, and mud, with limestone and dolomite substrata. Scrub brush, grasses, and water-tolerant hardwoods grow around the lake.

BIG LAKE, TEXAS. Big Lake is on State Highway 137, U.S. Highway 67, and the Atchison, Topeka and Santa Fe Railway seven miles north of the Crockett county line in south central Reagan County. In 1905 the Coates family settled on the west side of the water-filled depression called Big Lake, a landmark holding the only fresh water between the Concho rivers and Comanche Springs at Fort Stockton. The Taylor family took up land on the east side of the water. In 1911 T. H. Taylor sold 320 acres of land to the Kansas City, Mexico and Orient Railway of Texas for a townsite and station. The townsite, named for the lake located two miles to the south, was laid out, and a stock pen was built to hold cattle for railroad shipment. A boxcar became the depot, and a hotel with family-style dining was established. The Nairn family opened a grocery store near the tracks, and the Anderson family began a general mercantile store. W. W. Coates and A. H. Garner installed a line from Stiles, the county seat, to Big Lake to give the community telephone service. A public school was started with fifteen students in a small building that later became the Methodist parsonage. The town was ready for the arrival of the railroad. In 1912 the KCM&O built tracks from Mertzon to Girvin by way of Big Lake, and a post office was established. By fall of 1915 forty to fifty people lived in the community.

On May 28, 1923, oil was discovered in Reagan County near the town of Big Lake (*see* BIG LAKE OILFIELD). That summer, oil leases sold for quick profits for local landowners and out-of-town speculators. Several new cafes, a hardware store, and a lumberyard opened to profit from the expected Big Lake boom; the hotel was expanded by a twelve-room addition; and Big Lake citizens voted to incorporate on August 15. In 1925, when a population of 100 was reported and when Big Lake appeared to be the most important town in the county, it became the county seat. The town grew to a population of 1,500 by 1927 and to 2,000 by the next year.

But the Great Depression[qv] brought the population down to 832 in 1931, when the number of businesses was reported at sixty. Throughout the 1930s and 1940s Big Lake settled into the role of a supply town for the local oil industry; the population dropped as low as 763, and the number of businesses varied between twenty-five and sixty-five. On May 23, 1951, the Spraberry Trend area was brought into production in Reagan County. Big Lake experienced another modest but sustained oil boom. Its population increased to 2,140 in 1952, to 2,600 in 1956, to 2,668 in 1961, and to 3,098 in 1966. The number of businesses during these years was about seventy-five. During the 1970s the population remained between 2,345 and 2,942, and the number of businesses bounced between fifty and seventy-eight. From 1982 to 1991 Big Lake had a population of more than 3,400 and between seventy-five and 100 businesses. In 1990 the population was 3,672.

BIBLIOGRAPHY: Julia Cauble Smith, The Early Development of the Big Lake Field, Reagan County, Texas (M.A. thesis, University of Texas of the Permian Basin, 1988). Vertical files, Barker Texas History Center, University of Texas at Austin. J. L. Werst, Jr., ed., *The Reagan County Story* (Big Lake, Texas: Reagan County Historical Survey Committee, 1974).

Julia Cauble Smith

BIG LAKE OIL COMPANY. The Big Lake Oil Company was chartered under the laws of Delaware by Michael L. Benedum in Pittsburgh, Pennsylvania, on October 5, 1923, to acquire and develop a 10,000-acre lease on University of Texas land in Reagan County, in what became the Big Lake oilfield.[qv] The land, which included the Santa Rita Oil Well,[qv] had been owned by Frank T. Pickrell and associates, who had formed the Texon Oil and Land Company in 1919. Pickrell sold tracts of Texon's oilfields to Benedum for $200,000 and a quarter share in the Big Lake Oil Company. The new company operated with Levi Smith[qv] as president and Pickrell as vice president. On

October 19, 1923, Benedum and his associates formed the Plymouth Oil Company[qv] as a parent company that managed BLOC. Walter S. Hallanan was president of Plymouth, and Jerome G. Farquaher was vice president. The BLOC immediately assumed operation of Santa Rita No. 1 and the Texon Company's test wells two and three. By late 1923, four more wells were underway, and the BLOC opened an office in San Angelo. In February 1924, ten wells were being drilled, and in March, a well was begun using rotary tools, a first for West Texas, where cable tools had dominated. In May a rig burned and was replaced with the first steel derrick. After several dry holes, well number 9 began flowing at seventy barrels an hour and assured the field. By May 1926, BLOC had sixty producing wells. As the BLOC expanded, it also built Texon, a town for its employees, including a water system and an ice plant. Pipelines, tank-loading racks, a tank farm for oil storage, and an oil-treating plant were built. Electrification of the field was started immediately, and by 1927, with current furnished by the Pecos Valley Power and Light Company, the BLOC field was among the nation's earliest to be fully electrified. In 1941, the BLOC built its own power plant for the field and Texon. In April 1925 the BLOC completed a casing-head gasoline plant to convert wellhead gas to gasoline, all of which was snipped to the Humble refinery at Baytown. In 1930 the plant was enlarged and a gas line built to supply San Angelo; in 1936, it was converted to recycling. An explosion and fire ended operations in 1951.

Lack of an outlet for the steadily increasing production of the field caused the BLOC and the adjoining Texon Company to conclude, in October 1924, an agreement with the Marland Oil Company to join in organizing the Reagan County Purchasing Company to transport the bulk of its crude to market. The BLOC continued its drilling program through the 1930s and 1940s, and although a few wells were drilled in the 1950s, by 1954 the field was primarily a pumping operation. The Big Lake field was unique in that never before had one company ever held all the leases on such a large area. Throughout its existence, the BLOC applied the most modern business and conservation practices. Because of its concern for the welfare of its workers and their families, the company enjoyed the reputation of being an ideal employer. Opening of the Santa Rita well and development of the BLOC field brought growth to several towns within a hundred-mile radius, opened the Permian Basin[qv] for exploration, and produced immense wealth for the University of Texas. In 1962 Plymouth Oil Company was sold to Marathon Oil Company, which continued to operate the Big Lake oilfield.

bibliography: Sam T. Mallison, *The Great Wildcatter* (Charleston, West Virginia: Education Foundation of West Virginia, 1953). Samuel D. Myres, *The Permian Basin: Petroleum Empire of the Southwest* (2 vols., El Paso: Permian, 1973, 1977). Martin W. Schwettmann, The Discovery and Early Development of the Big Lake Oil Field (M.A. thesis, University of Texas, 1941). Martin W. Schwettmann, *Santa Rita: The University of Texas Oil Discovery* (Austin: Texas State Historical Association, 1943; rpt. 1958). *Jane Spraggins Wilson*

BIG LAKE OILFIELD. Big Lake Oilfield, located in the southwest corner of Reagan County on University of Texas land, opened the Permian Basin[qv] to oil production and endowed the Permanent University Fund[qv] with $4 million by 1926, the year of its peak production. The field grew from a large tract oil promotion attempted by Reagan County lawyer Rupert P. Ricker.[qv] In January 1919, when West Texas was considered oil-barren, Ricker initiated mineral leasing on university lands by filing on 431,360 acres in Reagan, Upton, Irion, and Crockett counties. He tried selling leases from the tract to raise the filing fee of $43,136, due the General Land Office[qv] in thirty days, but had no luck promoting wildcat leases located hundreds of miles from known oil production. Just before the deadline, he sold his preliminary leases for $2,500 to an old army friend, Frank T. Pickrell, of El Paso.

The ambitious, energetic Pickrell and his partner, Haymon Krupp,[qv] a prosperous El Paso merchant, also attempted unsuccessfully to sell leases from the tract, then determined to develop the acreage themselves. Krupp organized Texon Oil and Land Company and invited several New York investors to join him in forming a Delaware corporation in April 1919. To help fund the drilling program, the new corporation divided its acreage into tracts ("groups") of 10,240 acres and offered certificates of interest for sale in Group No. 1. For $200 the investor was promised a .0004882 percent undivided interest in the sixteen-section block. After completion of the first oil test on Group No. 1, however, Texon converted each certificate of interest to stock in the newly formed Group No. 1 Oil Corporation, rather than allowing the investors to collect the more profitable overriding royalty interest.

The first oil test drilled on Group No. 1, called Santa Rita No. 1 (see santa rita oil well) was spudded on August 17, 1921. Driller Carl Cromwell[qv] and various tool dressers worked on the cable tool rig for 646 days, drilling on average only 4.7 feet per day. On May 25, 1923, the crew drilled into the "Big Lime" near 3,050 feet and discovered gas bubbles rising from the casinghead. Cromwell and toolie Dee Locklin shut down the well to keep reports tight while they leased surrounding acreage for themselves.

Early on May 28, with no further drilling, the well blew in. Oil sprayed over the derrick and flowed intermittently until it was controlled at the end of June. Although Texon had an oil well, however, the company had neither drilling capital to prove the extent of the field nor oil-experienced management to direct its drilling program. Pickrell tried unsuccessfully to find a company to buy part of the field. Major companies were uninterested because they owned flush production near their coastal refineries, and production from isolated West Texas presented a 500-mile transportation obstacle. But in the fall of 1923 Pickrell found an investor.

On October 5, 1923, Pickrell, representing Texon management, contracted with an agent of Michael L. Benedum, a successful Pittsburgh independent oilman. Pickrell transferred blocks 1, 2, and 9, Reagan County (including the Santa Rita No. 1 and two drilling offsets), to Benedum for $200,000 and one-fourth interest in a new company—Big Lake Oil. Benedum and his friends organized Plymouth Oil Company on October 19, 1923, for oil exploration in West Texas and as a parent company for Big Lake Oil, which would drill the contracted Texon leases.

When the first four wells proved unproductive and Big Lake's drilling fund was depleted, Benedum persevered in the field's development. He lent the company $800,000 to continue drilling, and his determination was rewarded. The No. 9 well's initial daily production was 1,400 barrels, on June 24, 1924. The No. 10 came in with 1,840 barrels on July 11. But the No. 11, which began producing 3,600 barrels daily on July 31, proved the field's productivity.

The Big Lake Field, which covers an area of about 4½ square miles, produced oil and gas from two main horizons. Its shallow field tapped the Big Lime (later designated San Andrés) of the Upper Permian at about 3,000 feet, and its deeper field drew from the Ellenburger Lime of the Ordovician at depths between 8,200 and 8,800 feet. The deeper field was discovered on December 1, 1928, when Group No. 1 Oil Corporation's University 1-B was extended to 8,525 feet and became the world's deepest well. By the fall of 1929 University 1-B's daily production was nearly 3,000 barrels of oil and more than 25.6 million cubic feet of gas. The significance of University 1-B's discovery, like that of Santa Rita No. 1, was the evidence offered of vast oil and gas reserves in West Texas from both shallow and deep horizons.

In February 1929, shortly after University 1-B was discovered, Texon's management sold controlling interest in the field to Marland Oil Company for $9.5 million. On June 18, 1929, Marland merged with Continental Oil Company. In 1962 Plymouth Oil, along with its subsidiary Big Lake Oil, sold out to Marathon Oil Company. Continental and Marathon currently operate the original field; they reported fourteen wells, 495,432 barrels of oil, and 411,103 million cubic feet of gas for 1986.

Secondary recovery in Big Lake Field employed two methods. Gas from lower horizons was injected into the upper field in the 1930s. Continental injected salt water into the San Andrés at 2,900 feet in 1965 and 1972.

What began as a large-tract lease promotion by Ricker and continued as a wildcat-drilling promotion under Pickrell and Krupp became a large and profitable oilfield under Benedum. The cumulative production for the field at the beginning of 1987 was 129,089,783 barrels of oil and 10,246,580 million cubic feet of gas. From Big Lake Field, oil exploration spread into other areas of the Permian Basin, which became one of the largest oil-producing regions of Texas and of the United States.

BIBLIOGRAPHY: Nora Locklin, "Santa Rita: An Eyewitness to a Great Discovery," *Permian Historical Annual* 24 (1984). Samuel D. Myres, *The Permian Basin: Petroleum Empire of the Southwest* (2 vols., El Paso: Permian, 1973, 1977). David F. Prindle, "Oil and the Permanent University Fund: The Early Years," *Southwestern Historical Quarterly* 86 (October 1982). Crawford K. Stillwagon, *Rope Chokers* (Houston: Rein, 1945). *Julia Cauble Smith*

BIG LUMP, TEXAS. Big Lump was a lignite-mining community on the International–Great Northern Railroad four miles west of Milano in southeastern Milam County. A post office opened there in 1912. In 1914 Big Lump had a cotton gin, a general store, and as many as 400 residents, as well as the lignite mine. The increase in oil and gas production in Texas nearly eliminated the lignite market in the 1920s. The post office at Big Lump was discontinued in 1924, and most residents moved away. No evidence of the community remained on county highway maps in 1988. *See also* COAL AND LIGNITE MINING.

BIBLIOGRAPHY: Lelia M. Batte, *History of Milam County, Texas* (San Antonio: Naylor, 1956). *Vivian Elizabeth Smyrl*

BIG MINERAL CREEK. Big Mineral Creek rises at the junction of its northern and southern branches two miles north of Whitesboro in western Grayson County (at 33°41′ N, 96°54′ W) and runs east for ten miles to its mouth on the Big Mineral arm of Lake Texoma, seven miles northwest of Southmayd (at 33°43′ N, 96°46′ W). The surrounding terrain is generally flat with occasional shallow depressions, surfaced by clay and sandy loams that support water-tolerant hardwoods, conifers, and various grasses. The region has served as range and cropland.

BIG MOUNTAIN. Big Mountain is five miles northeast of Uvalde in south central Uvalde County (at 29°16′ N, 99°45′ W). With an elevation of 1,143 feet above sea level, its summit rises 150 feet above the nearby intersection of Farm Road 2369 and U.S. Highway 90 West.

BIG MUSH (?–1839). Big Mush, known to early settlers also as Hard Mush and among his people as Gatunwali, was a principal diplomat or "war chief" of the Cherokee Indians. His village in Texas, established at an unknown date, was one of several Cherokee communities. In 1827, when the Cherokees backed out of the abortive Fredonian Rebellion,[qv] Big Mush succeeded Richard Fields[qv] as chief diplomat, or war chief of the Cherokees' intervillage council. The next year, 1828, he headed the diplomatic team that hosted members of Terán's expedition visiting in Texas. In February 1836 Big Mush was a signatory of the Cherokee Treaty negotiated by Sam Houston.[qv] The treaty's rejection by the Texas Senate in 1837 subsequently led Big Mush and Chief Bowl[qv] to ally with Mexican agents preparing for invasion of Texas. As a result of this action, President Mirabeau B. Lamar[qv] ordered the Cherokees to leave Texas. Refusing to acquiesce in the expulsion of their people, Big Mush, Bowl, and the Cherokee council prepared people for war. Both met death in the battle of the Neches[qv] on July 16, 1839.

BIBLIOGRAPHY: Mary Whatley Clarke, *Chief Bowles and the Texas Cherokees* (Norman: University of Oklahoma Press, 1971). Dianna Everett, *The Texas Cherokees: A People between Two Fires, 1819–1840* (Norman: University of Oklahoma Press, 1990). Frederick Webb Hodge, ed., *Handbook of American Indians North of Mexico* (2 vols., Washington: GPO, 1907, 1910; rpt., New York: Pageant, 1959). E. W. Winkler, "The Cherokee Indians in Texas," *Quarterly of the Texas State Historical Association* 7 (October 1903). Albert Woldert, "The Last of the Cherokees in Texas and the Life and Death of Chief Bowles," *Chronicles of Oklahoma* 1 (June 1923). *Dianna Everett*

BIG ONION CREEK. Big Onion Creek rises five miles southwest of Waxahachie in northeastern Ellis County (at 32°21′ N, 96°56′ W) and flows southeast for fourteen miles over generally flat terrain surfaced with clay and sandy loams that support water-tolerant hardwoods, conifers, and grasses. For most of the county's history, the Big Onion Creek area has been used as range and crop land. Big Onion Creek joins Little Onion Creek to form Onion Creek a mile northeast of Avalon (at 32°14′ N, 96°45′ W).

BIG PINE CREEK. Big Pine Creek is formed by the junction of Little Pine and Tanyard creeks 1½ miles south of Kanawha in northwestern Red River County (at 33°51′ N, 95°14′ W). The stream winds northeast for fourteen miles to its mouth on the Red River, about a mile west of Albion in north central Red River County (at 33°52′ N, 95°03′ W). The soils along the creek are clayey, and the area is heavily wooded, with various hardwoods predominating.

BIG ROCK, TEXAS. Big Rock, just off Farm Road 1861 thirteen miles southwest of Canton in southwest Van Zandt County, was at or near the site of an undershot water mill built by W. W. Stirman in 1848. A post office operated there from 1856 until 1868. A black school was in existence by 1890 and had an enrollment of fifty-five in 1904. In the 1930s the community had a school for blacks and one for whites, and two churches, a business, and numerous residences. By 1965, however, two churches, and scattered dwellings were all that remained, and by 1984 the churches were gone.

BIBLIOGRAPHY: Van Zandt County History Book Committee, *History of Van Zandt County* (Dallas, 1984). *Diana J. Kleiner*

BIG ROCK SHELTER. The ancient hieroglyphics and etchings at Big Rock Shelter, located in northern Henderson County, have held the interest of amateur and professional archeologists for many years. Big Rock is the only known rockshelter in the Caddoan area of East Texas. Because the shelter has protected the archeological deposits, materials such as floral and faunal remains have been well preserved. Excavations by archeologists from Southern Methodist University indicate that the shelter was first occupied about A.D. 600 by prehistoric Indians. The designs carved into the surface of the shelter were made, at least in part, by these people. Later, prehistoric Caddo Indians occupied the shelter.

The site is located on a high ridge that forms the divide among the Trinity, Neches, and Sabine rivers. The shelter overlooks a vast area of hickory and oak uplands that is transitional from the East Texas pine forests to the prairies. The sand hills of the ridge are the site of permanent springs that supplied water for the occupants of the shelter.

The shelter was most likely never a permanent residence but a place for occasional overnight stays that may have had religious significance. It opens to the north and therefore provides poor protection from winter weather. However, during the rest of the year it forms a cool, protected location.

Petroglyphs were carved on both the ceiling and back wall of the rockshelter and to the east of the shelter's drip line. The carvings are of two general categories, representations of animal footprints and clusters of abstract geometrical designs; the latter consist of both rectilinear and curvilinear motifs. The recognizable animal prints, all of which occur outside the shelter, are deer, turkey, and raccoon.

Faunal remains from the shelter indicate that the Caddoan occupants made use of deer, rabbits, turtles, and mussels, the latter two from the permanent springs located only a few hundred feet away. Remains of hickory nuts were also found. Stone tools found at the site were made of pebbles probably brought in from the gravel deposits on the Trinity and Sabine rivers. The most common arrowheads were Scallorn and Alba points. The few prehistoric ceramic fragments recovered in the Caddoan deposits seem to be representative of the Saunders Focus, a prehistoric Caddoan unit.

BIBLIOGRAPHY: J. J. Faulk, *History of Henderson County* (Athens, Texas: Athens Review Printing, 1926). Thomas H. Guderjan, "Big Rock: A Woodland and Caddoan Rock-Shelter in East Texas," *Bulletin of the Texas Archeological Society* 55 (1984). A. T. Jackson, *Picture Writing of Texas Indians* (Austin: University of Texas Press, 1938). *A Memorial and Biographical History of McLennan, Falls, Bell, and Coryell Counties* (Chicago: Lewis, 1893; rpt., St. Louis: Ingmire, 1984).

Thomas H. Guderjan

BIG ROCKY CREEK. Big Rocky Creek rises in a tank just east of State Highway 95 and three miles south of Flatonia in southwestern Fayette County (at 29°39′ N, 97°07′ W); it flows southeast for 23½ miles to its mouth on the Navidad River (at 29°34′ N, 96°49′ W). The stream has several named tributaries. It crosses a land surface of many different soil types that support the production of hay and corn and provide pasture for cattle and horses. Until the 1960s cotton was grown in the area in abundance. The vegetation along the stream is a mixture of oak, hackberry, pecan, sycamore, and cedar, with an understory of yaupon. Wildlife, particularly deer and squirrel, is abundant along the stream's lower reaches. During the Runaway Scrape[qv] Sam Houston's[qv] troops crossed Big Rocky Creek near where U.S. Highway 77 now crosses it, about 7 ½ miles south of Schulenberg.

BIG SALINE CREEK. Big Saline Creek begins thirteen miles south of Menard in southern Menard County (at 30°45′ N, 99°46′ W) and runs southeast for twenty-two miles to its mouth on the Llano River, six miles southeast of London in Kimble County (at 30°38′ N, 99°31′ W). It crosses flat to rolling prairie with local escarpments and deep dissections, surfaced by shallow and stony to fine sandy loam that supports oak, juniper, mesquite, and grasses upstream and hardwood forests downstream.

BIG SANDY, TEXAS. Big Sandy, also known as Big Sandy Switch, at the junction of State Highway 155, U.S. Highway 80, and Farm Road 2911, fourteen miles southwest of Gilmer in extreme southwestern Upshur County, was established in the early 1870s. In 1873 the Texas and Pacific Railway was built through the area, and around 1880 the Tyler Tap, a narrow-gauge railroad, intersected the Texas and Pacific just south of Big Sandy Creek. A switch was constructed at the junction of the two railroads and came to be known as Big Sandy Switch, after the creek. By the early 1880s a small settlement, also known as Big Sandy Switch, began to grow up. A post office was established in 1875, and two merchants named Arenson and Yesner opened stores around the same time. By 1885 the community, now known as Big Sandy, had several stores and saloons, Baptist and Methodist churches, a school, and an estimated population of 500. Several hotels and restaurants opened by 1900, and by the eve of World War I[qv] Big Sandy had two banks, a weekly newspaper named the *Times*, and a cotton market. The town's principal products included lumber, cotton, potatoes, and livestock. The community incorporated on June 21, 1926. The estimated population was 850 in 1929. By 1933 the population had fallen to 579, and the community had twenty businesses, several churches and schools, and a large number of houses. After World War II[qv] Big Sandy again began to grow. The population increased from 609 in 1945 to over 1,000 by 1958, when the number of businesses was twenty-eight. In the mid-1960s Big Sandy had five or six churches, a high school, and twenty businesses. In 1990 the town was a regional commercial and shipping center with twenty-eight businesses and a population of 1,185.

BIBLIOGRAPHY: G. H. Baird, *A Brief History of Upshur County* (Gilmer, Texas: Gilmer *Mirror*, 1946). Doyal T. Loyd, *History of Upshur County* (Waco: Texian Press, 1987). Vertical files, Barker Texas History Center, University of Texas at Austin. *Christopher Long*

BIG SANDY CREEK (Clay County). Big Sandy Creek rises a mile northwest of Newport in southern Clay County (at 33°30′ N, 98°04′ W) and flows east for just under forty miles, through southwestern Montague County and central Wise County. The stream is impounded in southwestern Montague County to form Lake Amon G. Carter. Below the lake, six miles west of Sunset, the creek resumes its course, then passes within two miles of Alvord and joins the West Fork of the Trinity River five miles east of Bridgeport in central Wise County (at 33°12′ N, 97°40′ W). Big Sandy Creek flows over mostly flat land surfaced by clay and sandy loams that support water-tolerant hardwoods, conifers, and grasses. Throughout the county's history the area has been used as range and crop land.

—— (Donley County). Big Sandy Creek rises in two main branches that meet five miles south of Clarendon in southwestern Donley County (at 34°53′ N, 100°54′ W). The stream flows southwest for twelve miles to its mouth on Mulberry Creek, in the northeastern corner of Briscoe County (at 34°43′ N, 100°05′ W). Sandy Camp, one of the JA Ranch's[qv] twelve winter camps, was located near this stream. Big Sandy Creek flows through an area of moderately steep slopes with locally high relief and a surface of deep silt loams that support mesquite and grasses.

—— (Falls County). Big Sandy Creek begins three miles northeast of Perry in northern Falls County (at 31°28′ N, 96°54′ W) and runs southeast for seventeen miles to its mouth on Big Creek, four miles southeast of Marlin (at 31°17′ N, 96°50′ W). The stream, which has been dammed a few miles northeast of Marlin, forms both the Old Marlin City Lake and the New Marlin Reservoir. It traverses flat to rolling prairie surfaced by dark, calcareous clays that support mesquite, cacti, and grasses.

—— (Hopkins County). Big Sandy Creek rises just east of Harmony in extreme southeastern Hopkins County (at 33°01′ N, 95°21′ W) and runs southeast for eighteen miles, across eastern Wood County and the southwestern corner of Upshur County, to its mouth on the Sabine River, a mile southeast of Big Sandy (at 32°33′ N, 95°04′ W). The stream, which is intermittent in its upper reaches, is dammed southwest of Winnsboro to form Lake Winnsboro. It traverses generally flat terrain with local shallow depressions, surfaced by clay and sandy loam that supports water-tolerant hardwoods, conifers, and grasses.

—— (Lamar County). Big Sandy Creek, also known as Sandy Creek, rises in south central Paris, in central Lamar County (33°39′ N, 95°33′ W), and flows southeast for five miles, then south for sixteen, to its mouth on the North Sulphur River, just north of the Delta county line (at 33°26′ N, 95°25′ W). It crosses low-lying floodplains surfaced by poorly drained clay that floods several times a year and supports water-tolerant hardwoods, conifers, and grasses.

—— (Lee County). Big Sandy Creek rises 2½ miles west of Lawhon Springs in extreme western Lee County (at 30°23′ N, 97°16′ W) and flows southwest for twenty-one miles, through northwestern Bastrop County, before emptying into the Colorado River nine miles northwest of Bastrop (at 30°10′ N, 97°21′ W). The stream, which is intermittent in its upper reaches, flows through rolling prairie surfaced with clay loams that primarily support hardwood and pine forest, mesquite, and grasses.

——— (Newton County). Big Sandy Creek rises just west of Weeks Settlement in northwestern Newton County (at 31°05′ N, 93°51′ W) and flows northeast for twenty-two miles to its mouth on Sixmile Creek, in the Sabine National Forest[qv] in Sabine County (at 31°15′ N, 93°42′ W). the stream, intermittent in its upper stages, traverses generally hilly woodlands. Downstream, several abandoned tram railroad lines indicate the former presence of lumbering operations.

——— (Polk County). Big Sandy Creek rises four miles southeast of Moscow in central Polk County (at 30°52′ N, 94°48′ W) and flows southeast for forty-seven miles, through Polk County and into Hardin County, to its juncture with Kimball Creek, just northwest of Village Mills (at 30°30′ N , 94°26′ W). The stream has also been called Alabama Creek by residents of Polk County and Village Creek by residents of Hardin County. It was given its current name in 1960 by the United States Geological Survey. It flows through the Alabama-Coushatta Indian Reservation and is protected for about sixteen miles in Polk County as part of the Big Sandy Creek Corridor of the Big Thicket[qv] National Preserve. Numerous tram railroad lines on both banks of the Big Sandy indicate that the region was once used by lumbermen for logging and sawmilling operations. In Hardin County the stream runs through the West Village Mills oilfield before joining with Kimball Creek to form Village Creek.

——— (Stephens County). Big Sandy Creek begins sixteen miles southwest of Breckenridge in southwest Stephens County (at 32°32′ N, 98°57′ W) and extends north for twenty-one miles to its mouth on Hubbard Creek Reservoir, six miles northwest of Breckenridge (at 32°49′ N, 98°58′ W). It crosses flat terrain with local shallow depressions, surfaced by clay and sandy loam that supports water-tolerant hardwoods, conifers, and grasses.

——— (Travis County). Big Sandy Creek, sometimes called Sandy Creek, begins two miles northeast of the Round Mountain community in northwestern Travis County (at 30°36′ N, 97°55′ W) and runs south for twelve miles to its mouth on Lake Travis, just east of Jonestown (at 30°30′ N, 97°55′ W). It crosses an area of steep slopes and benches surfaced by shallow clay loams that support juniper, live oak, mesquite, and grasses.

BIG SATAN CREEK. Big Satan Creek rises 2½ miles west of U.S. Highway 277/377 in east central Val Verde County (at 29°44′ N, 100°51′ W) and runs southwest for thirteen miles to its mouth on the Devils River, here part of Amistad Reservoir (at 29°40′ N, 100°57′ W). The last part of the streamcourse passes through Satan Canyon. Bluff Creek is a tributary. The path of Big Satan Creek sharply dissects massive limestone that underlies flat terrain, forming a deep and winding canyon. The area's generally dark, calcareous, stony clays and clay loams support oaks, junipers, grasses, and mesquites.

BIG SILVER CREEK. Big Silver Creek rises six miles north of the Nolan-Coke county line and nine miles southwest of Maryneal in southwest Nolan County (at 32°09′ N, 100°33′ W) and flows northwest, then southwest, for thirty-five miles before emptying into the Colorado River eighteen miles southeast of Colorado City in southeast Mitchell County (at 32°08′ N, 100°48′ W). The flora along the streambed includes juniper, live oak, mesquite, and various grasses in the upper reaches; hardwoods, scrub brush, and grasses in the mid-section; and water-tolerant hardwoods, conifers, and grasses in the lower reaches. The creekbed begins in steeply sloping terrain with benches, continues through flat to rolling terrain with local scarps, and ends in flat terrain with locally shallow depressions and an expansive clay surface.

BIG SKID CREEK. Big Skid Creek rises seven miles south of Olney in north central Young County (at 33°16′ N, 98°44′ W) and runs south for six miles until it enters the Brazos River three miles west of Newcastle (at 33°12′ N, 98°46′ W). Its drainage area comprises ranch and oil lands, including the Lairmore oilfield. Little Skid Creek, a small, intermittent tributary of Big Skid Creek, runs two miles before joining with the larger branch two miles above the Brazos River confluence. The area terrain is surfaced by clay and sandy loams that support water-tolerant hardwoods and grasses.

BIG SLOUGH WILDERNESS AREA. Big Slough Wilderness Area is near the northeastern tip of Davy Crockett National Forest,[qv] fifteen miles from Alto in Houston County. The 3,040-acre area, set aside by an act of Congress in 1964, is the state's smallest wilderness area. Nevertheless, Big Slough contains an unusual diversity of plant and animal life, including four distinctly different plant associations: short leaf pine and southern red oak; loblolly pine, white oak, and shagbark hickory; water oak, willow oak, and loblolly pine; and overcup oak, mayhaw, and planer tree. Black oak, a species rare in Southeast Texas, also grows in the upland regions. Most of Big Slough lies within the floodplain of the Neches River, which forms eleven of the twelve miles of its eastern boundary. The northern half of the wilderness is covered by a sluggish watercourse named Big Slough, a partly abandoned channel of the Neches. The slough is rich in channel catfish and other marine life. To its southeast is a marshy area of several hundred acres that contains a series of beaver and alligator ponds. Bottlebrushes surrounding the ponds attract a profusion of butterflies and other insects. Part of the area has never been forested, and no logging has been permitted in it since 1968. During wet periods much of the area is covered by water, and it is then possible to canoe along a four-mile loop from the Neches to Big Sough and back.

BIBLIOGRAPHY: Edward C. Fritz, *Realms of Beauty: The Wilderness Areas of East Texas* (Austin: University of Texas Press, 1986).

Edward C. Fritz

BIG SOUS CREEK. Big Sous Creek rises three miles southwest of Riomedina in eastern Medina County (at 29°26′ N, 98°49 W) and runs southeast for eight miles to its mouth on the Medina River, three miles west of Macdona in western Bexar County (at 29° 23' N, 98° 47' W). It traverses rolling terrain surfaced by clay loam that supports mesquite, live oak, and grasses.

BIG SPRING, TEXAS. Big Spring, the county seat of Howard County, is at the intersection of Interstate Highway 20, U.S. highways 80 and 87, State Highway 350, Farm Road 700, and the Missouri Pacific line in southwest central Howard County. The city is in a rocky gorge between two high foothills of the Caprock[qv] escarpment in West Texas. It derives its name from the nearby "big spring" in Sulphur Draw, which was a watering place for coyotes, wolves, and herds of buffalo,[qv] antelope, and mustangs;[qv] the spring was a source of conflict between Comanche and Shawnee Indians and a campsite used by early expeditions across West Texas. Signal Mountain, ten miles southeast of Big Spring, was a landmark used by early cattlemen. In 1849 Capt. Randolph B. Marcy's[qv] expedition reached Big Spring on the return trip from Santa Fe and marked it as a campsite on the Overland Trail to California. The spring was also a campsite on the Santa Fe Trail[qv] from Fort Smith, Arkansas, to El Paso. Early ranchers, among them Adolph Miller and C. C. Slaughter,[qv] reached the area in the late 1870s, and after the ranchers came four-section plots with squatters' dugouts. In the late 1870s the community of Big Spring began near the spring as a settlement of hide huts and saloons for buffalo hunters. In 1880 the Texas and Pacific built through the area, following the line of Sulphur Draw several miles north of the spring. The community moved to the tracks, and Big Spring became the site of railroad shops and a station. When Howard County was organized in 1882 Big Spring became the county seat. That same year a post office started operating in the community, and its first general store opened. By 1884 Big Spring had an estimated population of 1,200, six saloons, four general stores, and a weekly newspaper (the *Pantagraph*). Several private schools were operating in the community by 1890, and the town had a public school by 1898.

By 1900 Big Spring had a population of 1,255. The Big Spring *Herald* was founded as a weekly in 1904 and became a daily in 1928. In 1905 an opera house opened, and in 1907 the city incorporated with an aldermanic form of city government. Big Spring installed a waterworks in 1913. In 1914 the city had a hotel, three banks, and Baptist, Catholic, Episcopalian, Christian, and Methodist churches. In 1920 Big Spring was a small city of 4,273 that served as a shipping point for livestock, cotton and small grains. Oil was discovered in the vicinity in 1926, and the city experienced a boom over the next ten years. In 1927, in response to rapid growth, Big Spring switched to a council-manager form of city government.[qv] The population of Big Spring had grown to 13,375 by 1930. By 1936 there were 810 wells in production in the surrounding oilfields. The Big Spring State Hospital[qv] for the mentally ill was opened in 1939. The city's growth was halted briefly in the late 1930s, and its population fell to 12,604 in 1940 but then revived again during World War II.[qv] Big Spring Army Air Corps Bombardier School was opened on land southwest of the city in 1942 and during the war graduated more than 5,000 bombardiers. After the school was closed as a military installation in 1945, its airfield served as the municipal airport for a number of years. Howard County Junior College opened in 1946. In 1950 the city reported 650 businesses and 17,258 inhabitants.

Big Spring again grew dramatically during the 1950s, when its population increased by 80 percent—to 31,230. It flourished through its petrochemical industries and as a banking and distribution center for the county. Part of this growth was also due to a renewed military presence: the airfield was reactivated as a military base in 1951, and in 1952 it was renamed Webb Air Force Base.[qv] Over the next several decades the city's population began a slow decline, falling to 28,735 by 1970, 24,804 by 1980, and 23,093 by 1990. Webb Air Force Base was deactivated in 1977, and its site became part of Big Spring Industrial Park. In the 1990s the community remained an important agribusiness and petrochemical center and was the site of a number of local events, including the annual county fair and several rodeos.

BIBLIOGRAPHY: *History of Howard County, 1882–1982* (Big Spring, Texas: Howard County Historical Commission, 1982).

Claudia Hazlewood and Mark Odintz

BIG SPRING DRAW. Big Spring Draw rises in Cosden Lake on the south side of Big Spring in south central Howard County (at 32°13′ N, 101°29′ W) and runs northeast for 4½ miles to its mouth on Beal's Creek, a mile southeast of the intersection of Farm Road 700 and Interstate Highway 20 (at 32°15′ N, 101°25′ W). It crosses terrain scored with red gullies. Mesquite and grasses are the predominant vegetation.

BIG SPRING STATE HOSPITAL. Big Spring State Hospital, on State Highway 87 two miles northwest of Big Spring, is a psychiatric facility that the Texas legislature voted to establish in 1937. Previously, patients from the vast region of West Texas had to be transported many miles away from their homes. Big Spring was selected partly because the city agreed to donate the land on which to build the hospital and partly because a permanent water supply was guaranteed. The hospital began receiving patients in June 1939.

The original complex had eight buildings. In 1990 it had grown to forty-three buildings, including an all-faith chapel, a school building, an outpatient clinic, a workshop, an enclosed swimming pool, a gymnasium, a four-building work village, a rehabilitation therapy building, a central kitchen, and a volunteer building. The hospital staff numbered over 900 employees. It once housed a maximum of 1,100 patients and now averages 324; about 1,800 admissions and discharges occur each year. The average length of stay is between thirty and ninety days. Emphasis is placed on quality treatment to shorten the period of illness. Treatments have expanded to include a full range of rehabilitation therapies, education, individual and group psychotherapy, and family intervention, in addition to medication. The new focus is on community-based programs, and in 1990 ten outreach clinics of the hospital operated throughout West Texas.

Big Spring State Hospital was the first Texas mental hospital to have its doors unlocked during the daylight hours. In cooperation with the local school district, it was first in the state to pilot an on-campus educational program; in 1990 it had a fully accredited school program on campus. It was the first to have a public-awareness program, specialty units for the treatment of adolescents and alcoholics, and both male and female patients in the same unit. The hospital was a pioneer in developing aftercare programs for the mentally ill. It was one of the first in the state to have an organized volunteer program. Big Spring State Hospital is financed through the Texas Department of Mental Health and Mental Retardation[qv] and accredited by the Joint Commission of Accreditation of Healthcare Organizations and Medicare.

BIBLIOGRAPHY: *History of Howard County, 1882–1982* (Big Spring, Texas: Howard County Historical Commission, 1982).

Lorene Burns Barbee

BIG SPRING STATE RECREATION AREA. Big Spring State Recreation Area is on Farm Road 700 and Big Spring Mountain on the southern edge of Big Spring in Howard County. The 344-acre park was once an Indian campground. The site was a city park until Big Spring turned it over to the State Parks Board in 1934. During the late 1930s the Civilian Conservation Corps[qv] added a number of facilities, including a stone dance pavilion. Among the major attractions is a large prairie dog[qv] town. Facilities include a scenic drive, a lookout point at the edge of the mesa, and tables for picnicking.

BIBLIOGRAPHY: Ray Miller, *Texas Parks* (Houston: Cordovan, 1984).

Christopher Long

BIG SPRING VETERANS ADMINISTRATION MEDICAL CENTER. The Big Spring Veterans Administration Medical Center was established in 1950 as the Veterans Administration Hospital. It offers general medical and surgical services with additional programs in acute psychiatry, alcohol treatment, and nursing-home care. It is located on a thirty-one acre tract in southern Big Spring. The main building, a six-story structure, has light buff-faced brick exterior walls. In 1989 a 4,900-square-foot addition was built to house the new computer and telephone systems. By this time the facility was known as Big Spring Veterans Administration Medical Center. The Big Spring VA is managed by Conrad Alexander, Medical Center director, David Keith, associate director, and Darryl H. Powell, M.D., chief of staff. It is fully accredited by the Joint Commission on Accreditation of Healthcare Organizations. The Medical Center also has affiliations with the Texas Tech University Health Science Center, Lubbock; Howard College, Big Spring; Texas Tech University, Odessa; Angelo State University, San Angelo; Amarillo Community College; Texas Woman's University, Denton; Scenic Mountain Medical Center, Big Spring; and Our Lady of the Lake University, San Antonio. The institution affords training in ophthalmology, nursing, dental hygiene, medical laboratory technology, radiologic technology, physical therapy, social work, clinical and counseling psychology, and dietetics. Ophthalmology residents and other students work at the facility as part of their education. More than 79,000 veterans are served by the Big Spring VA Hospital. It is charged with providing both primary and secondary health care for former service men and women in one New Mexico County and forty-six West Texas counties. The center's mission has expanded over the years to allow it to serve its patients better. Through Department of Defense sharing agreements with Goodfellow Air Force Base[qv] in San Angelo and Dyess Air Force Base[qv] Hospital in Abilene, the Big Spring VA provides services for veterans in those areas. In Midland the Veterans Readjustment Counseling Center assists veterans having difficulty in readjusting to civilian life as a result of their military service. In 1993 the Medical Center had 249 authorized beds, including 40 nursing-home-care beds. Its 1992 average daily census was 102 patients. In the fiscal year 1992, the center logged 2,660 inpatient and 30,752 outpatient visits. In 1993, twenty-two full-time and two part-time physicians provided comprehensive health care at the center. They were assisted by a nursing staff of seventy-eight RNs, twenty-five LVNs, and eleven nursing assistants. Administrative, clerical, and maintenance personnel increased the total number of employees to 439.

Lorene Burns Barbee

BIG SQUARE, TEXAS. Big Square is on Farm Road 145 fifteen miles southwest of Dimmitt in southwestern Castro County. It was settled in 1908 by the M. L. Stiles family, who moved to the area from Iowa. The Will Wyler family came the next year. The community had a post office from 1910 to 1920. Stiles built the first schoolhouse, which was replaced in 1920 by a two-room brick structure. A larger school was opened in 1939, and in 1945 the school district was merged with the schools of Springlake and Dimmitt. Big Square acquired its name from the large, two-story houses built by various members of the Stiles family.

BIBLIOGRAPHY: Castro County Historical Commission, *Castro County, 1891-1981* (Dallas: Taylor, 1981). *H. Allen Anderson*

BIG STINKING CREEK. Big Stinking Creek rises six miles southwest of Aspermont in central Stonewall County (at 33°08′ N, 100°25′ W) and flows northeast for sixteen miles to join the Salt Fork of the Brazos River in the northern part of the county (at 33°15′ N, 100°11′ W). The stream is fed by sulphur springs, the smell of which accounts for its name. It traverses an area of moderately steep slopes with locally high relief, surfaced by silt loams. In addition to mesquite, swamp grasses and algae grow in the area. Hawks and dragonflies hover overhead.

BIBLIOGRAPHY: Gunnar Brune, *Springs of Texas*, Vol. 1 (Fort Worth: Branch-Smith, 1981).

BIG SUNDAY CREEK. Big Sunday Creek rises four miles south of Sapoak Cemetery in northern Erath County (at 32°25′ N, 98°16′ W) and runs northeast for fifteen miles to its mouth on Palo Pinto Creek, one mile northeast of Santo in southeastern Palo Pinto County (at 32°37′ N, 98°12′ W). It crosses flat terrain with local shallow depressions, surfaced by clay and sandy loam that supports water-tolerant hardwoods, conifers, and grass.

BIG THICKET. The Big Thicket of Southeast Texas is difficult to define geographically. The early explorers thought of it as the heavily wooded area south of the Old San Antonio Road,[qv] east of the Brazos, north of the coastal prairie and the La Bahía Road,[qv] and west of the Sabine. As pioneers began penetrating and settling the area the size became more tightly defined, but to this day it has never been absolutely delineated. Some scientists identify the thicket by soil types and vegetation and stretch it across Southeast Texas from Grimes to Newton counties. The federal government established the Big Thicket National Preserve in twelve different units in Polk and Tyler counties and the counties to their south. The old people and old families, however, who have always known that they lived in the Big Thicket, define it as a much smaller area. This is frequently called the bear hunters' thicket.

This traditional Big Thicket—the bear hunters' thicket—is about forty miles long and twenty miles across at its widest. It is flat land, grey clay and sand, part of the Pine Island Bayou[qv] drainage system. It is a thickly wooded area that begins in the southern parts of Polk and Tyler counties, where the creeks flow out of the red dirt hills. It ends in the south below Sour Lake, where the dense woods thin out in stands of pine and in the rice farms of the coastal prairie. The eastern and western boundaries were easier to define in the old days before the loggers got hold of it, but east of Cypress Creek the elevation is higher, the land is sandy, and there used to be great climax stands of yellow pine five and six feet in diameter. The western boundary of the thicket was marked by big open pine stands along the spoil banks of the Trinity River and by Batson Prairie on the southwest. Before the incursion of the lumber and oil industries, this heart of the thicket was characterized by dense vegetation and by large numbers of deer, bear, panthers, and wolves, as well as the common varieties of mammals, birds, reptiles, and amphibians.

The history of the Big Thicket goes back to the time when it was covered with water. In the last sixty million years, "recent times" according to geologists, the Gulf shoreline of Southeast Texas submerged and emerged time after time, in unison during the Pleistocene Age with periodic glaciations to the north. The shore line that contained the thicket rose above the waters of the Gulf during the Ice Age, and was built up by silt washed down and deposited by some ancestral Trinity River. The woods of the thicket grew, and ten thousand years ago the thicket dwellers included mastodons, elephants, the American horse, Taylor's bison, camels, tapirs, and giant sloths, beavers, and armadillos. Preying on these animals were the sabre-toothed tiger and the dire wolf. Their day ended around 8,000 years ago. The time of the glaciers established varieties of soils and vegetation in the thicket that remained after the glaciers retreated, and produced a unique biological crossroads of at least eight different kinds of plant communities. The Big Thicket is possibly the most biologically diverse area in the world. Cactus and ferns, beech trees and orchids, camellias and azaleas and four carnivorous plants all occupy what is called the thicket, along with the pines, oaks, and gums common to the rest of East Texas. The thicket also supports a wide variety of animal life and is especially noted for the many species of birds, around 350, that either live in the area or visit annually. The abundant rainfall and the long growing season, around 246 days, ensure that vegetation and all the animal life that depends on it thrive.

Three groups of Indians are historically associated with the early history of the thicket. They are the Atakapas, the Caddos, and the Alabama-Coushattas. In the historical beginning only the Caddo and the Atakapas moved through the thicket with any regularity. Other tribes from as far away as Oklahoma, Colorado, and Kansas made periodic hunting trips into the thicket for bear meat, skins, and tallow. The Tonkawas, Lipans, and Wichitas met in peace at the medicinal spring around what is now called Sour Lake. But primarily the thicket was the meathouse of the mound-building Caddos, who occupied the fertile rolling hills to the north, and the cannibalistic Atakapas, who bounded the thicket on the Gulf Coast and on the Trinity bottoms. At the end of the eighteenth century the Alabamas and Coushattas began to settle on the northern and western fringes of the thicket, and the woods became theirs. The first man to lay a personal claim to the area was Lorenzo de Zavala,[qv] whose 1829 Mexican land grant included the Big Thicket. No Mexicans came, however, and the first settlers to move into the thicket area were Anglo-Americans who began moving into Southeast Texas in the 1830s. The first settlers stopped on the eastern edge of the Thicket, but soon the Thicket itself was spotted here and there with log cabins and with people who lived off the land as naturally as their Indian neighbors. These are the people who are still there, in blood and genes if not in the flesh. The core of the Thicket population is still white, Anglo-Saxon, and Protestant. The black population within its boundaries is small. The thicket did not lend itself to plantation farming and the slaves and field hands that went with it. There are a few Cajuns on the southwestern edge, in the Batson Prairie area. There are a few Slavonians left over from the days of tie cutting and stave making, and some "foreigners" stayed behind after they drifted in to work for the big sawmills or during the oil boom. But the natives, the ones whose roots are generations deep in the thicket soil, are Southerners by sympathy and migration; they are conservative politically and socially, and they are Protestant fundamentalist in religion.

The economic history of the thicket is much the same as that of the rest of East Texas. Until the 1880s the inhabitants dwelt scattered through the woods and lived off what they raised on subsistence farms. They ran hogs and cattle on a relatively free range and hunted small game, deer, and bear. The lumber industry[qv] brought a new economy in the 1880s, cut the virgin pine, and opened up more land to farm and graze. The Sour Lake oilfield[qv] in 1901, then the Saratoga and other thicket oilfields brought about a period of frantic activity. After the booms, life settled back to its normal, rural pace and remained so through the 1930s. World War II[qv] and the shipyards of the Gulf Coast brought about the major change in the thicket way of life. Many of those who went to war or the shipyards never returned to the thicket country. After the war the increasing number of paved roads and cars and power lines funneled in massive doses of the outside world. Except for the most confirmed woodsmen, the bulk of the population is now located in Kountze, Honey Island, Sour Lake, Saratoga, and Batson.

Formal efforts to save the Big Thicket from the devastation of the lumber and oil industries began with the founding of the East Texas Big Thicket Association by R. E. Jackson in 1927. Early conservationists joined the association, which hoped to preserve 400,000 acres as a national forest. One result was a biological survey in 1936 by H. B. Parks and V. L. Cory of the Texas Agricultural Experiment Station.[qv] The East Texas Big Thicket Association gained considerable political support during the thirties, but the war economy at the end of the decade demanded pine lumber and hardwoods, and the conservation movement fell into neglect. In the early 1960s conservationists again began their drive to save parts of the thicket for a state park. They were led by Lance Rosier, a long time thicket guide and naturalist, and Dempsie Henley, mayor of Liberty, who on October 4, 1964, founded what became the Big Thicket Association. By 1966 the Big Thicket Association had decided to push for national-park status. Senator Ralph Yarborough was its most powerful proponent in Congress. In 1974 a bill by Charles Wilson and Bob Eckhardt to establish an 84,550-acre Big Thicket National Preserve was passed by Congress and signed by President Gerald Ford. The preserve now consists of twelve protected units scattered through Hardin, Liberty, Polk, Tyler, and Jasper counties. Some of these units are in the heart of the old bear hunters' thicket.

Bibliography: Francis E. Abernethy, ed., *Tales from the Big Thicket* (Austin: University of Texas Press, 1966). Pete Addison Gunter, *The Big Thicket: A Challenge of Conservation* (Austin: Jenkins; Riverside, Connecticut: Chatham, 1971). Pete A. Y. Gunter, *The Big Thicket: An Ecological Reevaluation* (Denton: University of North Texas Press, 1993). Campbell and Lynn Loughmiller, *Big Thicket Legacy* (Austin: University of Texas Press, 1977). Howard Peacock, *The Big Thicket of Texas: America's Ecological Wonder* (Boston: Little, Brown, 1984).

Francis E. Abernethy

BIG THICKET LIGHT. The Big Thicket light (or the Saratoga light) is a ghostly light that periodically appears at night on the Old Bragg Road that runs through the heart of the Big Thicket in Hardin County. Bragg Road was originally a seven-mile bed for a Santa Fe branchline from Bragg Station, on what is now Farm Road 1293, to Saratoga. The rails were laid in 1901 and pulled in 1934, but the bed remained and became a well used road through some of the densest woods in the Big Thicket. The Big Thicket light was reported while the tracks were still down. In summer 1960 Archer Fullingim,[qv] editor and publisher of the Kountze *News*, began running front page stories speculating on the nature of the light; these stories were picked up and carried in metropolitan newspapers in Texas and elsewhere. Light seers visited Bragg Road by the hundreds. They described the light, disagreeing as to its color or characteristics, but agreeing that a ghostly light of some sort frequented the road. The lights were variously rationalized as the reflections of car lights going in to Saratoga, patches of low-grade gas, a reflection of foxfire or swamp fire, or the figment of hysterical imaginations.

More romantic explanations produced stories about local history. The light was a mystical phenomenon that typically frequented areas where treasure was buried, and some early Spanish conquistadors had cached a golden hoard in the thicket but had failed to return for it. The light was a little bit of fire that never was extinguished after the Kaiser Burnout or the ghost of a man shot during the burnout, when the Confederate soldiers fired part of the thicket to flush out Jayhawkers who did not choose to fight for the South. Another story tells of a railroad man who was decapitated in a train wreck on this part of the Saratoga line; they found his body but never could locate his head, and the body continues to roam up and down the right-of-way looking for the lost member. And one tale tells that the light comes from a spectral fire pan carried by a night hunter who got lost in the Big Thicket years ago. He still wanders, never stopping to rest, always futilely searching for a way out of the mud and briars.

The story of the Mexican cemetery tells of a crew of Mexicans who were hired to help cut the right-of-way and lay the tracks. But, rumor has it that the foreman of the road gang, rather than pay them a large amount of accumulated wages, killed the men and kept the money. They were hurriedly interred in the dense woods nearby, from whence come their restless, uneasy souls, clouded in ghostly light to haunt that piece of ground that cost them their lives. And there is the story of a man who sold his farm and parted with everything that he couldn't pack in a suitcase, to work on the railroad. He was devoted to the line and became a brakeman on the "Saratoga." When the Santa Fe began to cut down on its runs, he found himself without a job or prospects. He died soon after, and his lonesome and troubled spirit still walks the road bed with its brakeman's lantern, the Big Thicket light, looking for the life that left him behind.

Bibliography: Francis E. Abernethy, ed., *Tales from the Big Thicket* (Austin: University of Texas Press, 1966). Vertical files, Barker Texas History Center, University of Texas at Austin.

Francis E. Abernethy

BIG TIMBER CREEK. Big Timber Creek rises in two forks thirteen miles southwest of Lipscomb in southern Lipscomb County (at 36°06′ N, 100°24′ W) and flows south for twenty miles to its mouth on the Canadian River, three miles northwest of Canadian in northwestern Hemphill County (at 35°56′ N, 100°25′ W). It was once part of the Cresswell (Bar CC) Ranch[qv] properties. The stream crosses flat to rolling country with moderate relief and local escarpments, surfaced with sand and sandy loam that support mesquite brush and grasses.

Bibliography: Pauline D. and R. L. Robertson, *Cowman's Country: Fifty Frontier Ranches in the Texas Panhandle, 1876–1887* (Amarillo: Paramount, 1981).

BIG TREE (ca. 1850–1929). Big Tree (Ado-Eete), Kiowa warrior, chief, and cousin of Satanta,[qv] was born somewhere in the Kiowa domain at the time when pressures from the expanding Caucasian population were threatening the tribe's traditional way of life. By the late 1860s the embattled Kiowas were forced to seek an accord with whites. The agreement, arrived at during the Medicine Lodge Treaty Council in 1867, forced Big Tree and the Kiowas to move to a reservation in southwestern Oklahoma. Frustrated by the confinement, Big Tree came under the sway of leaders of the tribal war faction at an early age. He joined Satank, Lone Wolf,[qqv] and Satanta in raids on settlements inside Indian Territory and across the Red River in Texas. He reputedly was involved in an abortive attack on Fort Sill in June 1870 but really gained notoriety as a result of his participation in the Warren Wagontrain Raid,[qv] or Salt Creek Massacre, of May 18, 1871. After this incident, at the urging of Gen. William T. Sherman,[qv] the army moved to suppress the Kiowas.

Army activity proved to be unnecessary, however, because, within days of the raid, Satanta, Satank, and Big Tree arrived at Fort Sill to collect their rations. There Satanta boasted of his role in leading the Warren raid and implicated Big Tree and Satank. Sherman had the three chiefs arrested. Big Tree attempted unsuccessfully to escape by diving through a window. He was transferred with the others chiefs, in handcuffs and leg irons, to Jacksboro, Texas, to stand trial for murder. At Jacksboro, in the first instance where Indian chiefs were tried before a civil court, Satanta and Big Tree (Satank had been killed on the way to Jacksboro) were convicted of murder and sentenced to hang. However, the federal government, fearing Indian reprisals following the scheduled executions, pressured Texas governor Edmund J. Davis[qv] to commute the death sentences to life imprisonment. Davis took that action despite vocal opposition from General Sherman and large segments of the Texas population, and in September 1871 Big Tree and Satanta were transferred to the state prison at Huntsville (*see* TEXAS STATE PENITENTIARY AT HUNTSVILLE).

The principal effect of this sequence of events was to divide the tribe more firmly between war and peace factions. In Indian Territory federal agents recognized the danger and, hoping to control what promised to be a volatile situation, promised the tribe that the two chiefs would be released and returned upon promises of good behavior. On August 19, 1873, after two years of serving as "hostages" to ensure Kiowa passivity, Big Tree and Satanta were paroled. Their continued freedom, however, was conditional and could be revoked by any hostile acts committed by the Kiowas, even if the two chiefs were not involved.

Yet, despite the stiff parole terms, the Kiowas, allied with Quahadi Comanches, resumed raiding in the winter of 1873–74, and by the next summer Big Tree and Satanta seem to have joined in the attacks. On August 22, 1874, a number of Kiowas, led by Satanta and Big Tree, combined with Quahadis and skirmished with troops during ration distribution at Anadarko Agency, Indian Territory. From there the Indians moved onto the Llano Estacado[qv] in Texas, where, on September 9, 1874, a party of 200 Kiowas, including Lone Wolf, Satanta, and Big Tree, attacked Gen. Nelson A. Miles's[qv] supply train, some thirty-six wagons escorted by a company of the Fifth Infantry and a detachment of the Sixth Cavalry. For three days the army held off the Indians until, unable to overwhelm the soldiers, the Kiowas drew off and returned home.

This was to be Big Tree's last military venture. The latest series of confrontations convinced the army to step up its patrols across the Llano Estacado, an effort that made life miserable for the constantly fleeing fugitives. Satanta and Big Tree turned themselves in at the Cheyenne Agency in Darlington, Indian Territory, in late September. From there they were transferred in chains to Fort Sill, and on October 6 Satanta was returned to Huntsville, where he committed suicide in 1878.

Big Tree remained imprisoned at Fort Sill until the Kiowas were finally defeated in December 1874. After his release, he spent the remainder of his life counseling peace and acceptance of the white man's ways. His new direction was especially manifested in his drive to discredit the revivalist doctrine preached by the prophet P'oinka in 1887 and in his decision not to participate in the Kiowa Ghost Dance of 1890. He was among those who requested a missionary and was instrumental in establishing the first Baptist mission on the Kiowa reservation. By 1897 Big Tree's conversion was complete; he became a member of the Rainy Mountain Baptist Church and served as a deacon for thirty years. He died at his home in Anadarko on November 13, 1929, his last act of leadership being his unsuccessful opposition to

Kiowa chief Big Tree. Photograph by William S. Soule. Probably at Fort Sill, Indian Territory, ca. 1867–74. Prints and Photographs Collection, Indians—W. Soule, Photographer file, CAH; CN 00080.

the allotment of Kiowa lands in 1901. He was buried near his home in the Rainy Mountain Cemetery.

BIBLIOGRAPHY: Hugh Corwin, *The Kiowa Indians: Their History and Life Stories* (Lawton?, Oklahoma, 1958). Allen Lee Hamilton, "The Warren Wagontrain Raid: Frontier Indian Policy at the Crossroads," *Arizona and the West* 28 (Autumn 1986). Mildred P. Mayhall, *The Kiowas* (Norman: University of Oklahoma Press, 1962; 2d ed. 1971). Wilbur Sturtevant Nye, *Carbine and Lance: The Story of Old Fort Sill* (Norman: University of Oklahoma Press, 1937; 3d ed. 1969). Robert M. Utley, *Frontier Regulars: The United States Army and the Indian, 1866–1891* (New York: Macmillan, 1973). John Edward Weems, *Death Song: The Last of the Indian Wars* (Garden City, New York: Doubleday, 1976).

Brian C. Hosmer

BIG TRESTLE DRAW. Big Trestle Draw, a shallow valley, begins on the southern edge of the Davis Mountains in north central Presidio County (at 30°24′ N, 104°07′ W) and runs south for fourteen miles to its mouth on Draw Creek, three miles west of U.S. Highway 67 (at 30°14′ N, 104°07′ W). Its course crosses alluvial fans and wash deposits of sand and gravel and passes over weathered igneous rock. The soil in the area is generally sand and clay loam, often rough and stony. The local vegetation consists primarily of sparse grasses, cacti, and desert shrubs.

BIG WELLS, TEXAS. Big Wells is on State Highway 86 seventeen miles northeast of Carrizo Springs in northeastern Dimmit County. It was named for the artesian wells once found in the area; water from the first well supposedly jetted higher than thirty feet out of the ground. Big Wells was one of several land-development projects in Dimmit County between 1909 and 1917. The town began as a 480-acre parcel of the Big Four Colony, an ambitious, 56,000-acre development project that may have grown out of efforts to promote the Bermuda Colony, another Dimmit County development scheme.

In 1908 the Hurst and Brundage Company began to promote the town. Actual settlement at the site apparently began in 1910, and the town grew rapidly, partly because it was situated on the San Antonio, Uvalde and Gulf tracks. In 1911 a local post office opened; by the next year Big Wells had two schools, and a new, three-story high school was added in 1914. By 1915 the town had 800 residents, a bank, a newspaper, four general stores, a lumber company, and at least one hotel.

Big Wells suffered through a difficult period of drought, low crop prices, and marketing problems between 1916 and 1918. Businesses failed and many people left. The newspaper folded in 1919. By 1925 the population of Big Wells had reportedly dropped to 300. By 1929, however, it had rebounded to 700, and by 1944 the town had 866 residents and sixteen businesses. Big Wells has mostly depended for survival on oil operations in the area. The artesian wells have required pumps to produce water since World War II.[qv] In 1955 the town had 1,077 people and fifteen businesses, but its school closed that year. In 1973 Big Wells had 711 people and six businesses. In 1989 it had 833 people and three businesses; the use of new horizontal drilling techniques had brought old oilfields back to life. In 1990 the population was 756.

BIBLIOGRAPHY: Austin *American-Statesman*, December 18, 1989. Paul S. Taylor, "Historical Note on Dimmit County, Texas," *Southwestern Historical Quarterly* 34 (October 1930). Laura Knowlton Tidwell, *Dimmit County Mesquite Roots* (Austin: Wind River, 1984). Vertical files, Barker Texas History Center, University of Texas at Austin.

John Leffler

BIG WILLOW CREEK. Big Willow Creek begins in southeast Falls County (at 31°13′ N, 96°39′ W) and enters northern Robertson County three miles northeast of Bremond. It runs south, then east, for a total of nine miles, to its mouth on Walnut Creek, four miles southeast of Bremond (at 31°06′ N, 96°38′ W). It traverses level to gently sloping terrain surfaced by sandy loams that support post oaks and grasses.

BILINGUAL EDUCATION. On June 3, 1973, Governor Dolph Briscoe signed into law the Bilingual Education and Training Act (S.B. 121) enacted by the Sixty-third Texas Legislature. This event marked a historic turning point in the education of Mexican-American students in the state. The bilingual-education aspects of the law were new and unprecedented. The centerpiece was the mandate that all Texas elementary public schools enrolling twenty or more children of limited English ability in a given grade level must provide bilingual instruction. That a language other than English could be used in the instruction was especially significant because it abolished the English-only teaching requirement imposed by state laws dating as far back as 1918. The law dealt a serious blow to the notorious "no Spanish rule" institutionalized by the measures. For decades Texas teachers had used English-only laws to sanction punitive actions against Mexican-American students who violated the no-Spanish requirement. In the early 1970s, the United States Commission on Civil Rights reported that Mexican-American students caught speaking Spanish faced fines (a penny for every Spanish word), had to stand on a "black square," or were made to write "I must not speak Spanish." School personnel rationalized these actions as pedagogical measures.

Tensions between Anglos and Mexican Americans[qv] had existed in Texas since the earliest settlements. Anglos saw Tejanos as "culturally dissimilar" and unassimilable. Because of their Mexican culture, Tejanos also complacently accepted social inequality. The nationwide xenophobia and nativism at the turn of the century exacerbated the ethnic rift in Texas. The segregated Mexican schools that operated in the 1920s and into the 1960s reflected these tensions. Educators insisted that segregated schools were needed for the benefit of Mexican-American children. But the "language handicap" in Mexican schools was an excuse to isolate the children. Indeed, school authorities often assigned Mexican-American students to segregated schools purely on the basis of surname, although their first language was English. Mexican schools became socializing instruments for cleansing the "Latin" children of their linguistic and cultural baggage before mixing with Anglo peers. A statement of the Texas Department of Education (later renamed the Texas Education Agency[qv]) in 1923 illustrated this view. It extended a welcome to Mexican-American parents, but advised that the Mexican language and customs were unacceptable. Mexican children must learn the English language and shed their cultural habits. The "melting pot" dictums were rigidly followed and often forced Mexican-American children to spend two to three years in the first grade to learn English. Furthermore, Mexican schools often had run-down facilities and equipment, shortened school terms, and large classes taught by underpaid, ill-trained teachers. The case *United States v. Texas* (1981) affirmed "pervasive, intentional discrimination throughout most of this century" against Mexican-American students. Prejudice and deprivation, District Judge William W. Justice stated, blocked equal educational opportunities for these children and produced a "deep sense of inferiority, cultural isolation, and acceptance of failure." Through their segregated schooling, Mexican Americans had suffered de jure discrimination from the state of Texas and the Texas Education Agency, whose actions were found to violate the Equal Protection Clause of the Fourteenth Amendment.

Between 1971 and 1974 the United States Commission on Civil Rights documented the effects of separate and unequal education, the no-Spanish rule, and other culturally exclusionary acts on the education of Mexican Americans. The commission reported that traditional monolingual schools had fostered poor academic performance, demeaning influences, and alienation among Mexican-American students. In a 1967 conference, Sévero Gómez, a TEA official, reported on the consequences of sub-par education. He said that about 89 percent of the children with Spanish surnames, and those with Spanish as their primary language, dropped out of school. More specifically, he said that in one of the five largest Texas cities 15 percent of the children had Spanish surnames but provided 90 percent of the dropouts.

Before the passage of S. B. 121 in 1973, both educators and private citizens in Texas had supported projects to improve the education of Mexican-American children. In the 1920s *escuelitas* offered home-based reading and writing instruction in Spanish for preschoolers. These barrio "schools," found mainly in South Texas, operated as late as 1965. In the late 1920s the League of United Latin American Citizens[qv] established the "First 100 (English) Words" program for Spanish-speaking preschoolers. In 1958 LULAC, in cooperation with the American G.I. Forum,[qv] organized the community-based "Little School of the 400."[qv] These schools taught basic English vocabulary considered essential for success in the formal school setting. In 1959 the TEA launched "Little Schools of the 400" summer preschool programs. By 1964 these programs had enrolled some 20,000 students in 173 school districts. Programs in English as a second language also promoted English skills among Mexican-American students with limited English proficiency. In 1964 Texas had the highest concentration of Mexican-American students enrolled in elementary and secondary ESL programs in the Southwestern states. The federal Elementary and Secondary Education Act of 1965 and other legislation sparked a flurry of compensatory measures for "disadvantaged" students. Head Start, Title I, Migrant Education, and Follow Through programs employed varying approaches and techniques to promote English skills. These programs concentrated on language teaching and learning and affirmed that the "language barrier" was primarily a symptom of incompatibilities between the school and learner. In the 1960s the civil-rights movement[qv] and the Great Society programs of the Johnson administration caused a major change in the perception of ethnic minorities. Institutionally segregated schooling ended, political mechanisms obstructing minority group voting collapsed, and it became unpopular to be publicly racist. Equal educational opportunities for linguistically and culturally atypical learners became a desirable goal. Bilingual schooling emerged as an alternative approach.

In 1964 Superintendent Harold Brantley of the Laredo United Consolidated School District launched the first bilingual program in Texas. He built on the experience of the first bilingual program in the nation, initiated in the Coral Way school in Dade County, Florida. At Coral Way federal funds supported bilingual education for Cuban immigrants and inspired similar ventures elsewhere in the nation. Brantley made the initial effort in the first grade of the Nye Elementary School, and expanded the program into the second and third grades. The idea spread to schools in San Antonio, McAllen, Edgewood, San Marcos, Harlandale, Zapata, Del Rio, Edinburg, Bandera, El Paso, La Joya, Mission, Corpus Christi, and Del Valle. The programs fostered the transition of Spanish-speaking children from instruction in their native language to English-only teaching and learning. The program ranged from exclusive instruction in Spanish with gradual integration of ESL, to thirty minutes a day in Spanish with the rest of the instruction in English. District funds financed the initial programs and later were supplemented with federal subsidies available under Title I or Title III of the 1965 Elementary and Secondary Education Act. By May 1969, Texas had sixteen school districts with bilingual programs serving 10,003 students.

Before the passage of the Texas Bilingual Education and Training Act in 1973, TEA officials had faced an interesting dilemma when asked to review proposals that violated the English-only law. At first they circumvented the law by reporting these programs as experimental. In 1967, TEA developed an accreditation standard that allowed school districts, on a voluntary basis, to offer non-English-speaking children an instructional program using two languages. In 1969, with support from Representative Carlos Truan and Senator Joe Bernal, the Sixty-first Texas Legislature legalized this permissive standard and permitted bilingual instruction when such instruction was educationally advantageous to pupils. In 1971 Representative Truan presented a bill in the legislature for stronger bilingual programs, but was unable to muster support because the Sharpstown Stock-Fraud Scandal[qv] dominated the proceedings. In the next legislature Truan, Senator Chet Brooks, and other supporters won the needed support. The passage of the federal Bilingual Education Act in 1968 helped their cause. This law, originally approved as Title VII to the Elementary and Secondary Education Act of 1965, addressed the problems of those children who were educationally disadvantaged because of their inability to speak English. Title VII provided competitive grants directly to school districts. Districts were obligated to finance their bilingual projects after a period of five years. By the spring of 1973, nineteen Texas school districts with Title VII programs had to seek local or state funding. They looked to the state for help. Title VII funds also had helped support students deficient in English, but this money could not accommodate the 243,185 limited-English-ability children needing instruction. School districts with the highest proportion of Mexican-American students historically have been the poorest funded because of insufficient property taxes. These local districts have been severely hampered in maintaining regular programs.

Chicano[qv] activists were able to persuade the United States Office for Civil Rights to investigate violations against "national-origin minority" children. This helped to fortify the argument for bilingual legislation in Texas. OCR broadened its enforcement policies beyond reviews involving discriminatory acts against African Americans.[qv] On May 25, 1970, OCR director J. Stanley Pottinger issued a memorandum stipulating that those school districts with more than 5 percent national-origin minority children were obligated under Title VI of the Civil Rights Act of 1964 to provide equal educational opportunity for language-minority students. Specifically, school districts had to take action where "inability to speak and understand the English language" excluded national-origin minority children from participation in the educational programs. The OCR outlined three criteria: 1) school districts could not assign students to classes for the mentally retarded, or exclude them from taking college courses on the basis of tests measuring only English language skills; 2) ability grouping for the purpose of dealing with special language needs was permissible if temporary; and 3) parents of national-origin minority children must be informed of school activities in a language other than English, if necessary.

The Texas Bilingual Education Act (S.B. 121) required that school districts use native-language instruction to promote learning and facilitate the transfer of the language-minority child to the English-only mainstream program. English literacy skills were to be developed through ESL teaching. State funds from the Foundation School Program could be used to support these special programs. The allocation for the first biennium (1973–75) of the program was $2.7 million.

The *Lau v. Nichols* decision of the United States Supreme Court (1974) assured the survival of the bilingual program. The court declared that children who could not understand the language of instruction were denied access to a quality education. On August 11, 1975, Education Commissioner Terrel Bell announced guidelines for identifying and evaluating children with limited English skills and for planning appropriate bilingual education and ESL education. *United States v. Texas,* filed by the G.I. Forum and LULAC, reinforced legal support for bilingual education. It criticized state efforts to address the needs of children. Judge Justice ordered the TEA to initiate additional bilingual instruction, if needed, to satisfy "their affirmative obligation" and guarantee linguistically deprived children an equal educational opportunity. The decisions in *United States v. Texas* and *Lau v. Nichols* were prime catalysts for the expansion of bilingual and ESL programs in the state. Also, increased immigration of non-English speakers has required more language programs to include children from Latin America and Asia.

Reportedly, the Texas population will grow four times as fast as the nation's during the next fifty years. Hispanics will rival Anglos as the state's dominant population group early in the twenty-first century. In 1990, in Texas, of 3.5 million children ages 5–17, 28.2 percent did not speak English at home, and 25.8 percent of the same age group spoke Spanish. The 1973 legislative mandate to increase learning opportunities for Mexican Americans heralded a new era in Texas education. The legislation recognized the political feasibility of requiring instruction in a language other than English, thereby effectively nullifying the infamous no-Spanish rule. However, native-language instruction has been provided for only a fraction of the students who need it, due in large measure to the dearth of qualified teachers. These limitations, notwithstanding, the past twenty years have brought about changes. Though bilingual education has provoked controversy during its short history, it has gained legitimacy as an appropriate and pedagogically sound way to educate language-minority students in the public schools of Texas.

BIBLIOGRAPHY: Thomas P. Carter, *Mexican Americans in School: A History of Educational Neglect* (New York: College Entrance Examination Board, 1970). James Crawford, *Bilingual Education: History, Politics, Theory, and Practice* (Trenton, New Jersey: Crane, 1989). Dallas *Morning News,* December 17, 1986, March 5, 1988. Arnoldo De León, *They Called Them Greasers: Anglo Attitudes Toward Mexicans in Texas, 1821–1900* (Austin: University of Texas Press, 1983). J. W. Edgar, "Programs in Texas for Improving Educational Opportunities for Mexican-Americans," in *Improving Educational Opportunities for the Mexican-American,* ed. D. M. Estes et al. (San Antonio: Southwest

Educational Development Laboratory, 1967). Jose Esteban Vega, The Enactment of Bilingual Education Legislation in Texas, 1969–1973 (Ph.D. dissertation, University of Michigan, 1980).

Rodolfo Rodríguez

BILLIAMS CREEK. Billiams Creek (also known as Billam's, Billiam's, Billiums, Billums, and Billum's Creek) rises seven miles southwest of Colmesneil in northwest central Tyler County (at 30°52′ N, 94°32′ W) and runs northeast for thirteen miles to its mouth on the Neches River, between Best Bend and Sheephead Bend, not far from the site of old Fort Terán, in the extreme north of Tyler County (at 31°00′ N, 94°26′ W). Billiams Creek, the water and power source for a thriving pioneer settlement established about 1840, is said to have been named for Chief Billiams of the Billiams Indians, a group of Cherokees that the early settlers found living along Billiams and Wolf creeks. The Billiams Creek area provided cypress and pine lumber and excellent cotton-growing blackland, and was the site of the Billiams Creek community.

BIBLIOGRAPHY: *It's Dogwood Time in Tyler County* (Woodville, Texas), March 1953, 1954, 1956, 1963.

BILLIAMS CREEK, TEXAS. Billiams (Billum) Creek was established about 1840 on Billiams Creek in north central Tyler County. It was at the intersection of the two mail routes across Tyler County before the Civil War[qv] and had not only a water mill (combined cotton gin, gristmill, and sawmill) but also a post office and a blacksmith shop. Nearby was one of the earliest churches in Tyler County, the Philadelphia Primitive Baptist Church. Prominent early settlers included Josiah Wheat, Robert Cummins Fulgham,[qv] Argulus Parker, Abe Willson, Ben Enloe, and Harmon Frazier. After the Civil War a skirmish known locally as the battle of Billiams Creek occurred when federal authorities indicted six residents for not releasing their slaves and sent soldiers to arrest them. The Billiams Creek men shot all the federal soldiers from ambush and buried them, and their bodies are said never to have been found. The post office was closed in 1866, though the area remained the focus of a dispersed farming community until the 1940s. By the 1980s only a few residents remained in the area, most of whom raised cattle and timber.

BIBLIOGRAPHY: Lou Ella Moseley, *Pioneer Days of Tyler County* (Fort Worth: Miran, 1975). *It's Dogwood Time in Tyler County*, March 1953, 1954, 1956, 1963.

Megan Biesele

BILLINGSLEY, JESSE (1810–1880). Jesse Billingsley, San Jacinto soldier, ranger, and legislator, was born on October 10, 1810, in Rutherford County, Tennessee, the son of Jeptha and Miriam (Randolph) Billingsley. In 1834 he moved to Mina, Texas. On November 17, 1835, he joined Capt. Robert M. Coleman's[qv] company of Mina Volunteers—forty-nine Bastrop County men, including George B. Erath.[qv] Billingsley served until December 17. When this unit mustered into Sam Houston's[qv] army at the beginning of the Texas Revolution,[qv] it was designated Company B of Col. Edward Burleson's[qv] First Regiment, and on March 1, 1836, Billingsley was elected its captain. He commanded the company at the battle of San Jacinto,[qv] where he received a wound that crippled his left hand for life. The company disbanded at Mina on June 1. Billingsley thereafter served as a private in John C. Hunt's ranger company, from July 1 through October 1, 1836.

He was elected from Bastrop County to the House of Representatives of the First Congress of the Republic of Texas and is said to have "furnished his own grub, slept on his own blanket, and wor[n] a buckskin suit that he took from a Comanche Indian whom he killed in battle." Billingsley was reelected to the House of the Second Congress in 1837. In February 1839 he commanded a company of volunteers under Edward Burleson that pursued and engaged the band of Comanche raiders who had killed the widow of Robert Coleman and their son Albert and kidnapped their five-year-old son, Thomas. In 1842 Billingsley recruited volunteers to aid in the repulse of the invasion of Adrián Woll[qv] and fought with John C. Hays[qv] at the battle of Salado Creek.[qv] After annexation[qv] he served as a senator in the Fifth (1853–54) and Eighth (1859–61) legislatures. Billingsley died on October 1, 1880, and was buried in the front yard of his house near McDade. On September 3, 1929, he was reinterred in the State Cemetery[qv] at Austin.

BIBLIOGRAPHY: John Henry Brown, *Indian Wars and Pioneers of Texas* (Austin: Daniell, 1880; reprod., Easley, South Carolina: Southern Historical Press, 1978). Daughters of the Republic of Texas, *Muster Rolls of the Texas Revolution* (Austin, 1986). Andrew Jackson Sowell, *Early Settlers and Indian Fighters of Southwest Texas* (Austin: Ben C. Jones, 1900; rpt., Austin: State House Press, 1986). Texas House of Representatives, *Biographical Directory of the Texan Conventions and Congresses, 1832–1845* (Austin: Book Exchange, 1941). Vertical files, Barker Texas History Center, University of Texas at Austin.

Thomas W. Cutrer

BILLINGSLEY, VIRGINIA CATHERINE SHAW (ca. 1843–ca. 1920). Virginia Billingsley, plantation businesswoman, was born about 1843, the daughter of D. C. and Amaryllis Shaw of Wayne County, Mississippi. She married James Bolivar Billingsley of Hinds County, Mississippi, on November 28, 1850, and moved with him in 1865 to settle on land that Billingsley had inherited from Willis Lang,[qv] near Marlin in Falls County, Texas. The couple had six children. Virginia Billingsley apparently took an active role in running the family estate after her husband's death in 1882. In 1889 she leased forty-eight acres of her land to former slave Dolly Lang in exchange for three bales of cotton yearly. She also was routinely involved in buying and selling working animals for the estate and was successful enough in her plantation management to be approached for loans on farm property. In 1903 she filed a lawsuit over damage done to her crops by neighboring stock. In all of her business dealings she was known as V. C. Billingsley. In addition to her plantation, she maintained a home in Waco between 1894 and 1901. She was an avid writer of personal essays and used them to express her strong religious beliefs. She also supported prohibition.[qv] She died around 1920.

BIBLIOGRAPHY: James Bolivar and Virginia Catherine Billingsley Papers, Barker Texas History Center, University of Texas at Austin. *A Memorial and Biographical History of McLennan, Falls, Bell, and Coryell Counties* (Chicago: Lewis, 1893; rpt., St. Louis: Ingmire, 1984). Ruthe Winegarten, *Texas Women* (Austin: Eakin Press, 1985).

Debbie Mauldin Cottrell

BILLINGTON, TEXAS. Billington, three miles west of Farm Road 936 and twenty-four miles northwest of Groesbeck in Limestone County, was initially called Antioch. It was renamed in honor of Ezekiel Jackson Billington, a Baptist minister and early settler, when the post office was established in 1886. In 1890 the town had a population of twenty-five, a physician, a cattle dealer, and a justice of the peace, as well as Billington, who remained the only local preacher until at least 1896. In 1892 the population was still twenty-five, and a general store had been added. In 1896 the number of residents peaked at forty-five, and a blacksmith shop, a corn and gin mill, and an additional cattle dealership were listed in the town's businesses. The post office closed in 1904, and the mail was routed through Mount Calm. Billington school was consolidated with the Axtell school, and the church was disbanded. Population figures for the 1930s list a low of six residents and a high of twenty. In 1984 Billington was listed as an unincorporated community, but the population was last recorded in 1948 as an estimated twenty. A cemetery and church building marked the location.

BIBLIOGRAPHY: Carmen Weempe, *History of Billington* (Billington, Texas, Cemetery Association, 1978).

Ray A. Walter

BILLS CREEK. Bills Creek begins in southwest Palo Pinto County (at 32°37′ N, 98°34′ W) and runs southeast for seven miles to its mouth on the North Fork of Palo Pinto Creek, 1½ miles west of Strawn (at 32°33′ N, 98°30′ W). It traverses relatively flat terrain surfaced by stony, clay loams that support shrubs and live oaks.

BILOXI, TEXAS. Biloxi is at the junction of Farm roads 1416 and 2460, forty-five miles northeast of Beaumont in east central Newton County. Indians from east of the Mississippi River, probably Biloxi, settled the area sometime before 1822. They called the site Biloxi, either in reference to the Mississippi town of that name, which they had visited, or simply in reference to their group designation. In either case, the area was one of three known sites of Indian occupation in the area that become Newton County. The Biloxis continued to visit the region until after the Civil War.[qv] In 1829 Lorenzo de Zavala[qv] acquired the region including Biloxi from the Mexican government as part of a large grant to which he was to sponsor the immigration of 500 families. Settlers entered the Biloxi region shortly thereafter and established sizable plantations. Most of the newcomers eventually concentrated at nearby Belgrade, although Biloxi maintained its post office from 1853 to 1860. Despite setbacks, Newton County at one time licensed ferry operations at the Biloxi crossing of Big Cow Creek. As of the 1960s a few persons still inhabited the area just west of the site of Biloxi.

BIBLIOGRAPHY: Madeleine Martin, "Ghost Towns of the Lower Sabine River," *Texas Gulf Historical and Biographical Record* 2 (1966). Archie P. McDonald, "'Westward I Go Free': Some Aspects of Early East Texas Settlement," *East Texas Historical Journal* 4 (October 1966). Newton County Historical Commission, *Glimpses of Newton County History* (Burnet, Texas: Nortex, 1982). Fred Tarpley, *1001 Texas Place Names* (Austin: University of Texas Press, 1980). Texas Surveyors Association Historical Committee, *Three Dollars Per Mile: Accounts of Early Surveying in Texas* (Burnet, Texas: Eakin Press, 1981). *Robert Wooster*

BILOXI CREEK. Biloxi (Balaxy) Creek rises 1½ miles east of Lufkin in central Angelina County (at 31°20′ N, 94°38′ W) and runs south for 20½ miles to its mouth on Buck Creek, a mile above the latter's confluence with the Neches River (at 31°04′ N, 94°36′ W). Biloxi Creek crosses low to moderately rolling terrain surfaced by sandy clay loam that supports pine, oak, and other hardwoods, as well as mesquite and grasses. The stream was named either for the town of Biloxi, Mississippi, or for the Biloxi Indians, some of whom moved westward to Louisiana and eventually to the Neches River area of Texas.

BIBLIOGRAPHY: Frederick Webb Hodge, ed., *Handbook of American Indians North of Mexico* (2 vols., Washington: GPO, 1907, 1910; rpt., New York: Pageant, 1959).

BILOXI INDIANS. The Biloxi Indians (also written Baluxa, Beluxi, Bilocchi, Bolixe, Paluxy, and many other names by European chroniclers) were Siouan speakers who were first recorded living near present Biloxi, in southern Mississippi. Since they were the southernmost speakers of the Sioux language and were surrounded by Muskhogean-speaking groups, it is believed that they migrated from the north at an earlier unknown date. The Biloxis were matrilineal. While they probably lived in tents in the North, a French observer reported that in Mississippi they lived in long houses with mud walls and bark roofs; they made pottery, baskets, wooden bowls, and bone and horn implements. About 1763 some of the Biloxis moved westward to western Louisiana. In 1828 there were twenty families on the east bank of the Neches River in what is now Angelina County, Texas, in the area of present Biloxi Creek. The Biloxis were never numerous. Their westward movements, like those of many migratory Gulf Coast groups in early historical times, are attributed to pressure from Europeans. Like the Alabama, Coushatta, and Caddoan tribes with which the Biloxis allied themselves in East Texas, the Biloxis were reputed to have "no pretensions to soil, and were on friendly terms with the people of the Republic." However, in 1836 the Biloxis appeared as associates of the Cherokees in the treaty of February 23 at Chief Bowl's[qv] village. In 1837 a committee report of the Texas Senate located the Biloxis and their allies together in the Nacogdoches and Liberty counties, estimating their strength at "150 warriors." When Albert Sidney Johnston and President Mirabeau B. Lamar[qqv] declared war on the Cherokees and killed Bowl, the rout was easily extended to other East Texas tribes such as the Biloxis, many of whom were harried from Texas into Arkansas by July 25, 1839. In 1843, however, other Biloxis who had moved westward signed the treaty of September 29 with the Republic of Texas[qv] at Bird's Fort on the Trinity River. In 1846 Butler and Lewis found a Biloxi camp on Little River in Bell County. Other Biloxis moved farther west, and were encountered later as associates of the Seminoles as far west as Brackettville, Texas, and as far south as Nacimiento, Coahuila. Families and individuals also lived with the Choctaws and Creeks in Indian Territory and among the Alabama-Coushattas near Livingston, Texas.

BIBLIOGRAPHY: Jean Louis Berlandier, *Indians of Texas in 1830*, ed. John C. Ewers and trans. Patricia Reading Leclerq (Washington:: Smithsonian, 1969). James O. Dorsey and John R. Swanton, *A Dictionary of the Biloxi and Ofo Languages* (Washington: Smithsonian Institution, Bureau of American Ethnology, 1912). Dianna Everett, *The Texas Cherokees: A People between Two Fires, 1819–1840* (Norman: University of Oklahoma Press, 1990). M. R. Haas, "The Last Words of Biloxi," *International Journal of American Linguistics* 23 (1968). Frederick Webb Hodge, ed., *Handbook of American Indians North of Mexico* (2 vols., Washington: GPO, 1907, 1910; rpt., New York: Pageant, 1959). Anna Muckleroy, "The Indian Policy of the Republic of Texas," *Southwestern Historical Quarterly* 25–26 (April 1922–January 1923). Joseph Milton Nance, *After San Jacinto: The Texas-Mexican Frontier, 1836–1841* (Austin: University of Texas Press, 1963).

Megan Biesele

BILSING, SHERMAN WEAVER (1885–1954). Sherman Weaver Bilsing, teacher and researcher in entomology, was born on December 8, 1885, near Crestline, Ohio. He completed study at Martin Boehm Academy, Westerville, Ohio, in 1908 and in 1912 received both a B.S. from Otterbein College and a B.A. from Ohio State University. The latter awarded him an M.S. in 1913. He spent the summer of 1915 at the University of California, Berkeley. Bilsing went to the Agricultural and Mechanical College of Texas (now Texas A&M University) in 1913 as instructor of entomology. He became acting head of the entomology department in 1915 and head in 1918. He returned to Ohio State University for graduate study in 1923 and received a Ph.D. from that institution in 1924. His research and publications were mainly on insects that attack pecan trees. He was the leading authority on biology and control of the pecan-nut casebearer and published some basic works on this species. He took an active role in the American Association for the Advancement of Science, the Entomological Society of America, and the Texas Academy of Science[qv] and served in various offices of these organizations. He was also instrumental in establishing the Texas Entomological Society[qv] and was its president for the first six years of its existence. Bilsing was married to Alma Merwin of Mount Vernon, Iowa, and they had two sons. He retired from Texas A&M in 1952 and died on July 23, 1954.

BIBLIOGRAPHY: *Journal of Economic Entomology*, December 1954. V. A. Little, *A Brief History of Entomology at the Agricultural and Mechanical College of Texas* (College Station: College Archives, 1960). Marjorie Ann Merwin, The Life of Sherman Weaver Bilsing (M.A. thesis, Southern Methodist University, 1961). *Horace R. Burke*

BINFORD, PAULINE LARIMER (1893–1966). Pauline Larimer Binford, poet, daughter of Charles A. and Elizabeth (Wanamaker)

Larimer, was born on June 17, 1893, near Library, Allegheny County, Pennsylvania, on a homestead owned by her family since the time of the American Revolution. Her father, a Presbyterian minister, died before her birth. She moved to Texas with her mother in 1912 and enrolled at Baylor College in Belton (now the University of Mary Hardin-Baylor), from which she graduated in 1916. She taught in Texas high schools for several years. On September 1, 1923, she married Benjamin Bryan Binford of Dallas, where she resided the rest of her life. Mrs. Binford started her writing career early. Her first published poem appeared in the Pittsburgh *Sun* when she was thirteen. Through the years she contributed to a wide range of magazines, including religious periodicals, and received numerous honors for her work. She wrote two volumes of verse, *My Heart Knows a Song* (1948) and *Keep the Wonder* (1966), the latter of which was published only a few weeks before her death. She was a life member of the Poetry Society of Texas.[qv] She died on August 28, 1966.

BIBLIOGRAPHY: Dallas *Morning News*, August 29, 1966.

William E. Bard

BINGHAM, FRANCIS (ca. 1777–1851). Francis Bingham, pioneer settler, was born about 1777. He was one of Stephen F. Austin's[qv] Old Three Hundred[qv] and came to Texas from Perry County, Mississippi, as early as October 1822. In November 1823 he subscribed twenty bushels of corn towards paying the expenses of the Baron de Bastrop[qv] as deputy to the legislature of Coahuila and Texas.[qv] Bingham's title to two leagues and a labor of land now in Wharton, Brazoria, and Waller counties was granted on July 10, 1824. By January 1825 he returned to Monroe, Louisiana, to move his family to Texas, but illness in the family prevented his returning until after August 1827, when he wrote Austin that his wife might not come with him because she had heard unpleasant things about the country and the Indians. Bingham ultimately established on Oyster Creek, on the line between Brazoria and Fort Bend counties, a plantation that remained in the hands of the family for over a century. A visitor to Texas in 1835 wrote that Bingham's place had been in operation only three or four years but had 200 acres of cleared canebrake land in cultivation and about 600 cattle. The house, in a grove of China trees, was a one-story log structure, with the board planed at Bingham's mill. The furniture had been brought from the United States, where Bingham made an annual visit. Mrs. Bingham, who said she had become reconciled to Texas, had numerous servants, four or five children, and could visit neighbors within twenty miles. In 1845 Bingham attended a Brazoria mass meeting in favor of annexation.[qv] He died on July 22, 1851.

BIBLIOGRAPHY: Eugene C. Barker, ed., *The Austin Papers* (3 vols., Washington: GPO, 1924–28). Lester G. Bugbee, "The Old Three Hundred: A List of Settlers in Austin's First Colony," *Quarterly of the Texas State Historical Association* 1 (October 1897). *Telegraph and Texas Register*, April 30, 1845. *Texas State Gazette*, August 2, 1851. Abner J. Strobel, *The Old Plantations and Their Owners of Brazoria County* (Houston, 1926; rev. ed., Houston: Bowman and Ross, 1930; rpt., Austin: Shelby, 1980). *Visit to Texas* (New York: Goodrich and Wiley, 1834; rpt., Austin: Steck, 1952).

BINGHAM BRANCH. Bingham Branch rises at the juncture of North and South Bingham creeks, four miles southeast of Forestburg in southeast Montague County (at 33°31′ N, 97°30′ W), and flows southeast for two miles to its mouth on Clear Creek in Cooke County (at 33°30′ N, 97°28′ W). It crosses flat to rolling terrain surfaced by sandy and clay loams that support water-tolerant hardwoods, conifers, and grasses. For most of the county's history the Bingham Branch area has been used as rangeland. Henry Bingham once owned the land that the stream crosses.

BINGHAM CREEK. Bingham Creek rises just west of Douglass in western Nacogdoches County (at 31°41′ N, 94°54′ W) and runs southwest for 4½ miles to its mouth on the Angelina River, one mile south of State Highway 21 (at 31°39′ N, 94°57′ W). It traverses flat terrain with local shallow depressions, surfaced by clay and sandy loam that supports water-tolerant hardwoods, conifers, and grasses along the streambed.

BINKLEY, WILLIAM CAMPBELL (1889–1970). William Campbell Binkley, historian and teacher, was born on April 30, 1889, at Newbern, Tennessee. He studied history at the University of California, where he received a B.A. (1917), an M.A. (1918), and a Ph.D. (1920). Binkley began teaching history at Colorado College in 1921 and became a full professor in 1925. He was a student of the history of the West and the frontier, but his special interest was Texas history. From 1930 to 1953 he was professor and chairman of the Department of History at Vanderbilt University. In 1953 he was named professor of history at Tulane University and editor of the *Mississippi Valley Historical Review*, positions he held until his retirement in 1963; he was given an honorary LL.D. degree by Tulane in 1964.

During his long teaching career Binkley spent many summers in Austin teaching at the University of Texas and doing research. He was looked upon there as an ex officio member of the history department and worked with those who were also interested in his special field, notably Eugene C. Barker and Walter Prescott Webb.[qqv] After his retirement from Tulane, where he was named professor emeritus, Binkley lived in Austin for a year working on the official correspondence of the Republic of Texas.[qv] He taught in 1965–66 at the University of Houston, where he was distinguished professor of American history. He returned to New Orleans and taught history at University College, a part of the adult continuing-education division of Tulane University, until February 1970.

In addition to editing the *Mississippi Valley Historical Review*, Binkley edited the *Tennessee Historical Quarterly* and the *Journal of Southern History*. He was a founder of the Southern Historical Association and was active in that organization as well as in the Mississippi Valley Historical Association and the American Historical Association. He became a member of the Philosophical Society of Texas[qv] in 1940. Binkley wrote numerous articles for historical journals. His three major works were *The Expansionist Movement in Texas, 1836–1850* (1925), *Official Correspondence of the Texas Revolution, 1835–1836* (1935), and *The Texas Revolution* (1952). He died on August 19, 1970, and was survived by his wife, Vera (McGlothlin), and two daughters. He was buried in Lake Lawn Park and Mausoleum, New Orleans.

BIBLIOGRAPHY: New Orleans *Times-Picayune*, August 20, 1970. Vertical files, Barker Texas History Center, University of Texas at Austin.

BIPPUS, TEXAS. Bippus is on an unnumbered graded country road eleven miles south of the Oldham county line and eleven miles east of the New Mexico state line in northwestern Deaf Smith County. About 1910 several families purchased and fenced small tracts on a former XIT Ranch[qv] pasture within a ten-mile radius of each other. In 1914 George Bippus, a Russian immigrant farmer, donated land for a school building. Over the next few years the school was enlarged and used as a church and for other community functions. After the Bippus school district was consolidated with that of Walcott in 1950, the building was converted into a private farm home. A small area church was utilized off and on until 1978, when regular services were discontinued. A community clubhouse, however, was still used for various functions in 1985.

BIBLIOGRAPHY: *Deaf Smith County: The Land and Its People* (Hereford, Texas: Deaf Smith County Historical Society, 1982).

H. Allen Anderson

BIRCH, TEXAS. Birch, on Farm Road 60 and Birch Creek eight miles northwest of Somerville in southern Burleson County, has been a farming community since the first half of the nineteenth century.

Settlement in the vicinity began in the mid-1830s, but the first record of a community appears in the records of the newly organized Burleson County Commissioners Court in 1846. In the mid-1880s a number of Czechoslovakian immigrants reached Burleson County; they settled in Caldwell and also pushed several miles to the southwest. Some of them help to found Frenstat, and others proceeded to Birch. A post office operated in Birch from 1891 until 1908, and a school operated in the town for several years until it was consolidated with the Somerville Independent School District in 1948. In 1941 Birch had a population estimated at twenty-five and two accredited businesses. Population estimates remained at the same level until 1948, the last year for which figures are available. In 1961 a Birch congregation of the United Church of Christ was consolidated with a church in Lyons. By the early 1960s only a tiny cluster of houses remained at the site.

BIBLIOGRAPHY: Burleson County Historical Society, *Astride the Old San Antonio Road: A History of Burleson County, Texas* (Dallas: Taylor, 1980). *Charles Christopher Jackson*

BIRCHAM CREEK. Bircham Creek begins in northwestern Montague County a half mile west of the Cooke county line (at 33°43′ N, 97°30′ W) and runs north for 4½ miles to its mouth on Mountain Creek, three miles southwest of Bulcher in northwestern Cooke County (at 33°47′ N, 97°29′ W). It traverses flat to rolling terrain surfaced by deep, fine, sandy loam that supports hardwood forests and conifers along its banks.

BIRCH CREEK (Burleson County). Birch Creek rises six miles southwest of Caldwell in southwestern Burleson County (at 30°25′ N, 96°44′ W) and runs southeast for ten miles to its mouth on Lake Somerville (at 30°19′ N, 96°37′ W). It traverses gently sloping to nearly level terrain surfaced by loam that supports post oak, blackjack oak, elm, and hackberry trees on the banks. Anglo-American habitation in the vicinity began in the early 1830s. Birch, one of the oldest settlements in the county, was established during the 1840s.

—— (Hopkins County). Birch Creek rises a mile southeast of downtown Sulphur Springs in south central Hopkins County (at 33°07′ N, 95°38′ W). The stream, which is intermittent in its upper reaches, formerly flowed fourteen miles to the south to empty into Lake Fork Creek three miles west of Yantis in northwestern Wood County (32°54′ N, 95°39′ W). In the late 1970s the lower streambed was inundated by Lake Fork Reservoir, so that the creek now flows into the reservoir two miles southeast of Seymore in extreme southern Hopkins County. The stream crosses generally flat terrain with local shallow depressions and sandy and clay loam soils. The area vegetation consists primarily of water-tolerant hardwoods, conifers, and grasses.

—— (Leon County). Birch Creek rises four miles west of Jewett in western Leon County (at 31°22′ N, 96°13′ W) and runs southwest for twelve miles to its mouth on the Navasota River, the Robertson county line (at 31°20′ N, 95°14′ W). The stream crosses sloping to nearly level terrain surfaced by sandy loam that supports post oak, black hickory, pecan, elm, water oak, and hackberry on its banks. Newby, on the east bank of the upper creek, was established in the early twentieth century. Friendship lies on the west bank of the lower creek.

BIBLIOGRAPHY: James Young Gates and H. B. Fox, *A History of Leon County* (Centerville, Texas: Leon County *News*, 1936; rpt. 1977).

—— (Leon County). Birch Creek rises four miles south of Oakwood in northeastern Leon County (at 31°31′ N, 95°50′ W) and runs south for six miles to its mouth on Upper Keechi Creek, fourteen miles east of Buffalo (at 31°27′ N, 95°50′ W). Two and a half miles below its source the stream feeds Lake Leon, which is a mile long. The stream traverses sloping to nearly level terrain surfaced by sandy loam that supports post oak, black hickory, pecan, elm, water oak, and hackberry along its banks. Settlement in the vicinity began in the 1840s. About 1850 the Mount Pisgah community was established on the west bank of the upper creek near the headwaters of the tributary Red Branch.

BIBLIOGRAPHY: Frances Jane Leathers, *Through the Years: A Historical Sketch of Leon County and the Town of Oakwood* (Oakwood, Texas, 1946).

BIRCHES CREEK. Birches Creek rises at the confluence of Hetty Branch and Wallace Branch, two miles west of Taylors Chapel in north central Cherokee County (at 32°02′ N, 95°14′ W), and runs northeast for five miles to its mouth on Mud Creek, two miles east of Gould (at 32°03′ N, 95°10′ W). The stream, intermittent in its upper reaches, crosses flat to gently rolling terrain surfaced by sandy and clay loam that supports grasses and mixed hardwoods and pines.

BIRD, CHARLIE DAVID (1866–1961). Charlie David Bird, rancher, banker, and civic leader, was born on October 31, 1866, on Pumpkin Creek in Canton, Georgia, to Thomas M. and Mary Ann (Stephens) Byrd. Thomas Bird, a Confederate veteran, moved the family to Arkansas, then to Erath County, Texas. They changed the spelling of their name upon their arrival. Charlie and his brother and sisters went to school three months of the year. Bird ran away as a youth and in 1884 went to work for the Pitchfork Ranch[qv] in Dickens County. He hired on in 1885 as a line rider for the Matador Ranch[qv] in Motley County and remained with that operation for fifteen years. At twenty-one he helped drive 2,000 three-year-old steers through Indian Territory to the railhead at Kiowa, Kansas. At various times he also punched cows for the flying V, Frying Pan,[qv] Double N Bar, and F ranches, while working his own ranch between periods of employment. In 1888 his pay for a season's work was a broomtail pony and a worn saddle. He lived in a dugout[qv] with a horse, a rooster, a speckled hen, and a brood of chicks for companions. By signing petitions Bird helped organize Motley, Floyd, and Dickens counties. He voted in the first election of Motley County in 1891 and served as a county commissioner for ten years. On December 8, 1891, he married Daisy Blair of Erath County at Duffau, Texas. They had six children. Bird and his family lived in a dugout on the Tongue River, two miles south of the site of present-day Roaring Springs, until 1900. Quanah Parker[qv] and his Comanche band camped near their home once a year, and in a gesture of friendliness Bird often gave them beef.

Besides establishing the Bird Ranch, which was still operated by heirs near the end of the twentieth century, Charlie Bird helped build the first church, the First Baptist, in Plainview in 1884. He was a charter member of the First Baptist Church in Matador, a stockholder, director, president, chairman of the board, and charter member (1907) of the First State Bank of Matador, a charter member (1898) of Masonic Lodge No. 824 in Matador, and a member of Khiva Temple in Amarillo. He served as the first president of the Motley-Dickens County Old Settlers Association. Mrs. Bird died in March 1948, and Charlie subsequently married a childhood friend, Mrs. Ada Black, of Colorado Springs. She died in December 1957. Bird died on February 22, 1961, at the age of ninety-four.

BIBLIOGRAPHY: Fred Arrington, *A History of Dickens County: Ranches and Rolling Plains* (Quanah, Texas: Nortex, 1971). Eleanor Traweek, *Of Such as These: A History of Motley County and Its Families* (Quanah, Texas: Nortex, 1973). *Marisue Potts*

BIRD, JOHN (1795–1839). John Bird, soldier and Indian fighter, was born in Perry County, Tennessee, in 1795, the son of William Bird. After service under Andrew Jackson in the War of 1812 he returned to Tennessee, where he married Sarah Denton. The couple had four children. The Bird family moved to Stephen F. Austin's[qv] Texas colony in June 1830 and the next year received a league of land in what later became Burleson County. Bird was elected captain in the colony's militia and in 1832 led a column of volunteers up the Brazos River on an expedition against the Comanches. During the Texas Revolution[qv] he commanded a unit of Texas cavalry against the Mexicans near San Antonio in 1835, and in March 1836 he commanded sixty volunteers in defense of the western frontier on the Brazos.

On April 2, 1839, Bird was elected captain of a company of rangers, which he led to Fort Milam on the Texas frontier. He and a single companion, N. Brookshire, set out on the morning of April 20, 1839, scouting for Indians. After crossing the Little River on the morning of May 25, the two encountered a party of Comanches skinning buffalo. The Indians fled but returned on the following morning, May 26, heavily reinforced, and stampeded a herd of buffalo thorough the rangers' camp. Bird and his men pursued the retreating Indians for four miles before discovering that they had ridden into a trap laid by an estimate 300 warriors. The rangers attempted to fall back to Fort Milam but were overtaken and attacked after about a quarter of a mile, at about 3:00 P.M. The rangers repulsed several mounted charges by the Comanches but were severely beset by Indians on foot, who approached Bird's position by way of a sheltered ravine. At sunset, however, the Indians withdrew, "yelling like devils," according to one survivor of the fight. Five of the rangers had been killed, including Bird, who was shot through the heart by an arrow. "He was the bravest of the brave," according to one of the rangers, "and died encouraging his men to fight like heroes." Comanche deaths were variously estimated at between thirty and seventy-five.

Despite having successfully defended themselves in what is now known as the Bird's Creek Indian Fight,[qv] the rangers were too badly weakened to sustain their position any longer and immediately began their retreat toward Fort Smith, which they reached at 2:00 A.M. on May 27. Reinforced at Nashville and commanded by N. Brookshire, they returned to the field to bury their dead and found that Bird and the others had been mutilated by the Comanches. The rangers set out in pursuit of their enemies but were unable to catch them. They took revenge on the body of a Comanche chief who had been killed in the battle and buried near the Indians' abandoned camp.

At the time of his death Bird owned 354 acres of land in Austin County. Blair Alexander was named administrator of his estate. A marker commemorating the Bird's Creek Fight was erected near Temple by the Texas Historical Commission.[qv]

BIBLIOGRAPHY: Daughters of the Republic of Texas, *Muster Rolls of the Texas Revolution* (Austin, 1986). Charles Adams Gulick, Jr., Harriet Smither, et al., eds., *The Papers of Mirabeau Buonaparte Lamar* (6 vols., Austin: Texas State Library, 1920–27; rpt., Austin: Pemberton Press, 1968). Frances Terry Ingmire, comp., *Texas Ranger Service Records, 1847–1900* (St. Louis, 1982). *A Memorial and Biographical History of McLennan, Falls, Bell, and Coryell Counties* (Chicago: Lewis, 1893; rpt., St. Louis: Ingmire, 1984). New Orleans *Daily Picayune*, June 17, 1839. George Tyler, *History of Bell County* (San Antonio: Naylor, 1936). Gifford E. White, ed., *The 1840 Census of the Republic of Texas* (Austin: Pemberton, 1966; 2d ed., Vol. 2 of *1840 Citizens of Texas*, Austin, 1984). Gifford E. White, *1830 Citizens of Texas* (Austin: Eakin, 1983). *Thomas W. Cutrer*

BIRD, STEPHEN MOYLAN (1897–1919). Stephen Moylan Bird, poet, was born on October 12, 1897, in Galveston, Texas, the son of John Moylan and Alice Otis (Jones) Bird and a direct descendent of Revolutionary War general Stephen Moylan. He completed high school at the age of sixteen and wished to become a naturalist but was forced by straitened circumstances to work instead in railroading and as a clerk on the cotton exchange. In leisure moments he began to write brief lyrics, using streetcar transfers and the backs of envelopes for his manuscript paper. In the winter of 1917–18 he submitted some poems that were accepted for *Contemporary Verse* by the editor, Charles Wharton Stork, who described the young poet as an "American Keats" with poetic gifts that still needed to mature. Bird enlisted in 1918 as a naval recruit during World War I[qv] and was sent to the Great Lakes for training. In October 1918 he became a cadet at West Point but felt the environment to be oppressive, and on January 1, 1919, he was found dead in his room, apparently a suicide. A posthumous collection of his verses, *In the Sky Garden*, was published in 1922 by Yale University Press; it contained a number of imaginative lyrics on nature and one or two realistic poems.

BIBLIOGRAPHY: Leonidas Warren Payne, *Survey of Texas Literature* (New York: Rand McNally 1928). *Sonja Fojtik*

BIRD CREEK (Bell County). Bird Creek rises in the middle of Temple, in north central Bell County (at 31°07′ N, 97°21′ W), and extends southwest for four miles to its mouth on the Leon River, just south of Temple (at 31°03′ N, 97°25′ W). The stream was named for John Bird,[qv] a captain in the Texas Rangers[qv] who was killed in an Indian fight on its banks in 1839. Most of the creek is in Temple.

—— (King County). Bird Creek rises near Bateman in northeastern King County (at 33°42′ N, 100°10′ W) and runs southeast for seven miles to its mouth on Ox Yoke Creek, a tributary of the South Wichita River (at 33°40′ N, 100°02′ W). It flows beneath rolling to steep slopes surfaced by locally stony, shallow sandy and clay loams that support juniper, cacti, and sparse grasses.

BIRD POUROFF CANYON CREEK. Bird Pouroff Canyon Creek begins ten miles northwest of Gilpin in southeast Dickens County (at 33°29′ N, 100°34′ W) and extends southwest for five miles before merging with Croton Creek (at 33°28′ N, 100°35′ W). Close to its mouth it descends almost 300 feet through a steep, narrow canyon. The area is characterized by densely dissected gullies and low hills; the soils are shallow to fairly deep loams. Bird Pouroff Canyon is one of many drains of the Croton Breaks, an area of broken terrain in southeastern Dickens County.

BIRDS. No other state in the United States has such a remarkable variety of birds as Texas. By 1991 the number of species recorded from the state totalled 594, including extinct, extirpated, and introduced species. An additional six species were listed as historical and eleven species were considered to hypothetically occur in Texas. There are several reasons for the great number of species; aside from being the largest state, Texas is also one of the most diversified so far as its surface is concerned; moreover, the state extends north into the Great Plains, east into the humid lowlands of the southeastern United States, south into the almost tropical lower Rio Grande region, and west into the desert country. Thus the state has attracted species from east and west, north and south, from the sandy gulf coastal islands, the wide open plains of the north, the deserts and desert mountains of the west. This situation applies not only to the permanently resident birds, of which Texas has a greater proportion than any other state with the possible exception of California; but it also means that migrants from other areas of the United States visit some part of Texas. Perhaps the greatest variety of birds is to be found along parts of the coast and in the region of the lower Rio Grande.

In the humid, heavily forested river bottoms of East Texas one of the most spectacular as well as most famous of birds, now extirpated from Texas, was the ivory-billed woodpecker. Its retiring habits, even where it was in the more inaccessible swamps, made it difficult to study this bird in its native haunts. Its nest, an excavation in a tall tree, was watchfully guarded by the parent birds. This woodpecker is sometimes confused with another inhabitant of the lowland forests, the pileated woodpecker, which, however, is somewhat smaller and has less white on the wing, lacking also the conspicuous whiteness of bill that has suggested the name ivory-billed woodpecker. The pileated woodpecker is much more numerous, although it is by no means a conspicuous bird, being also more or less shy and at times difficult to approach. It, too, lives in the forest and rears its young in a similar hole in a large tree. The mortise-like holes that it makes in the trees in search of insect food are a good means of identification. When actively employed in digging these holes it makes the chips fly, and sometimes the noise that results resembles not a little that of a distant wood chopper. Some of the humid river bottom lands and forests attract an almost unbelievable population of small birds, and among them one of the most beautiful is the yellow-trimmed hooded warbler, the black mask on the head suggesting the name. This warbler is an inhabitant chiefly of the lower parts of the trees and of the undergrowth, where, particularly in the canebrakes, its song is one of the outstanding bird melodies.

The upland park-like forests do not have so many bird inhabitants as the deciduous areas of the stream valleys. These fragrant pineries, however, attract several interesting birds that are found much less frequently, if at all, in other kinds of country. Among these is the appropriately named pine warbler. It is an inconspicuous olive-green bird which behaves somewhat like an injured creeper and entertains its mate with a monotone song singularly suggestive of that of the chipping sparrow. Another characteristic inhabitant of the pine forests is the brown-headed nuthatch, a cousin of the common white-breasted nuthatch and a smaller, much less conspicuous bird with a voice that sounds like a miniature cracked tin horn. In cultivated lands, and particularly about human dwellings, one of the most conspicuous of all the birds is the Texas state bird, the northern mockingbird.[qv] Its almost unlimited vocal repertoire is notorious, and its imitative ability has, of course, suggested the bird's name. Around the lakes of the interior of Texas are the snowy egret and the great egret, the white pinions of which make them conspicuous features of the landscape. Other herons, particularly the great blue heron, together with the elusive king rail, inhabit the marshes and borders of these bodies of water, while the surface is frequently dotted with various kinds of ducks, particularly in the region of the Great Plains. On the prairies of the interior, as well as on the coast and in other bushy areas, the scissor-tailed flycatcher is conspicuous. This bird, one of the best known of all the land birds of Texas, has gray, black, and white plumage with a dash of red and pink to relieve the monotony, together with long tail feathers, which make it easily distinguishable.

The Llano Estacado of the northwestern part of the state has a relatively sparse bird population. The slate-gray Mississippi kite is one of the most characteristic; its soaring flight makes it an attractive bird. It nests in the trees of the narrow fringe of vegetation along the streams, as well as in the tall bushes of the chaparral. Another bird of the high open areas is the burrowing owl, so called because it makes its nest in a hole in the ground, often adapting to its use an abandoned prairie dog burrow, which has given rise to the story that it inhabits these burrows along with the prairie dog and rattlesnake, a story long since disproved. In the mesquite and other chaparral of the southern and middle parts of Texas, one of the most conspicuous and intriguing birds is the greater roadrunner, or "paisano," as it is known to the Mexicans. Its habit of running on the ground to escape its enemies, and the many stories that are told of its prowess in fighting rattlesnakes, have made it almost a legendary character in folklore. Its speed on foot is really remarkable, although this has been often somewhat exaggerated.

In the marshes of the Gulf coast one finds blackbirds and grackles of various kinds in abundance. Their great flocks sometimes resemble clouds of smoke. Hidden away in the grass, reeds, or grain are the long-billed marsh wren, the wary clapper rail, and the brilliantly colored purple gallinule, along with other water and shore birds. On the coastal beaches, both of the islands and the mainland, one of the outstanding birds is the black skimmer, which has received its name from its habit of flying close to the water and dipping its bill frequently into the surface. It sometimes appears in large flocks that range themselves along the sand or on the mud flats like great platoons of soldiers. Another inhabitant of the shores is the red-billed, black and white plumaged American oystercatcher, a bird which has acquired its name from its habit of feeding on bivalves. Perhaps the most conspicuous bird, as it is the largest along the shore, is the brown pelican, which breeds in sometimes extensive colonies not far back from the waters of the Gulf of Mexico. This bird, apparently clumsy on land, is marvelous on the wing, for not only can it soar indefinitely, but it has the uncanny ability to skim over the water, even when waves are running, so close to the surface that it seems almost impossible for it not to touch the water with its wings, yet it never does. To obtain its food it dives from on high with a great splash into the water and disappears, soon coming up again but facing in the opposite direction. Perhaps the most spectacular of Texas's birds on the wing is the magnificent frigatebird, or, as it is sometimes called, the man-o'-war bird, so named because it is a pirate and obtains a large part of its food by robbing the gulls and other water birds. Its black or black and white plumage makes it a conspicuous figure as it sails for long periods with wings and long forked tail expanded, and with very little or no motion of the wings. On the coastal prairie there lives one of the most attractive game birds of all Texas, Attwater's greater prairie-chicken. Unfortunately, this bird has been greatly reduced in relatively recent years, since over-shooting and lack of proper protection caused it to be practically exterminated from many of its former haunts.

In the semi-tropical valley of the lower Rio Grande there are many birds that are found in practically no other area in the United States, these being tropical species that extend up from northeastern Mexico. Among them no bird is more bizarre than the northern jacana. This bird, with a peculiar comb-like fleshy appendage on top of its head and bright yellow-green wings, is a strange apparition as it flies low over the water, or with its long, slender, unwebbed toes stalks about over the lily pads.

Out on the edge of the arid region in the deep canyons, the remarkable black-capped vireo lives. In addition to its own regular song, it has notes which in many respects remind one of the mockingbird. Like many of the other vireos it inhabits the bushes along the canyons, and, like them, builds a pendant nest in the horizontal fork of a bush. The canyon wren also holds a high place among the songsters of the west. Its remarkable melody, starting high and descending through more than an octave, resounds from the canyon walls until it seems to come from a bird two or three times its size. It lives in the crevices of the rocky walls of the canyons, where it is easily completely hidden from sight. The dry regions of central western Texas harbor such birds as the black phoebe, which places its nest on a little shelf of rock in a canyon or even in an abandoned well. Here, too, lives one of the most remarkable birds of all Texas, the white-throated swift. It is well-named, because it is one of the most rapid fliers in the world. When it really is in haste, it dashes down through the canyons at such speed that the eye finds it difficult to follow. There are also in the desert area other attractive birds, such as the vermilion flycatcher, which draws attention not only because of its brilliant plumage but also because of its intriguing nesting and other habits. Here, too, is the cactus wren, well-named because it is so fond of building its coconut-shaped nest in the most forbidding cacti as well as in other bushy vegetation, leaving only a very small opening at the side for an entrance. The tiny verdin, although barely half the size of the cactus wren, sometimes builds a thorny castle almost as large with the entrance being from below at one end, which effectively keeps out most of its enemies.

So many remarkable birds occur in the picturesque Chisos Mountains that it is difficult to pick out the most important. The gray-breasted jay, which is common throughout this range, is found in no other area in the United States and is a noisy, conspicuous inhabitant of the woodland. Here, also, lives the Colima warbler, a very small bird whose color makes it obscure. It breeds in these mountains but nowhere else in the United States. In the Chisos, as well as in other mountains, there are also many birds that have come down from the more northern Rocky Mountains. Such are the zone-tailed hawk, a marvelous flyer that lives in canyons and the forests of the mountains; the Hutton's vireo; the mountain chickadee, which is similar in appearance to the Carolina chickadee of eastern Texas; and the noisy, mischievous, Sleller's jay.

In addition to the great variety of remarkable birds that are to be found in Texas, there are two famous birds that were formerly common in the state, but which now unfortunately, have been exterminated throughout their ranges in the United States. These are the well-known Carolina parakeet, whose taste for food runs to cocklebuts, and the still more widely known passenger pigeon. This bird was at one time so abundant at certain seasons of the year in parts of eastern Texas that it broke down the branches of the trees in some of its roosts.

BIBLIOGRAPHY: *A Checklist of Texas Birds* (Austin: Texas Parks and Wildlife Department, 1984). Edward A. Kutac, *Birders Guide to Texas* (Houston: Lone Star, 1989). Harry Church Oberholser, *The Bird Life of Texas* (2 vols., Austin: University of Texas Press, 1974). Roger Tory Peterson, *A Field Guide to the Birds of Texas* (Boston: Houghton Mifflin, 1960). John H. Rappole and Gene H. Blacklock, *Birds of Texas: A Field Guide* (College Station: Texas A&M University Press, 1994). John L. Tveten, *The Birds of Texas* (Fredericksburg, Texas: Shearer, 1993). *Harry C. Oberholser*

BIRDSALL, JOHN (1802–1839). John Birdsall, judge and attorney general in the Republic of Texas,[qv] son of Maurice and Ann (Pixley) Birdsall, was born in Greene, Chenango County, New York, in 1802. He received his legal training in New York and was appointed circuit court judge of the Eighth District by New York governor DeWitt Clinton. Birdsall served in the New York Senate in 1832 and 1833. In 1837 he moved to Texas and became the law partner of Thomas J. Gazley[qv] in Houston. President Sam Houston[qv] appointed Birdsall attorney general of the Republic of Texas on August 15, 1837, and the Senate of the Second Congress unanimously confirmed him. Houston then appointed Birdsall chief justice pro tempore as successor to James Collinsworth.[qv] He served briefly, but the Senate refused to confirm him in this post. On January 8, 1839, he became the law partner of Sam Houston. The partnership lasted until Birdsall's death. Birdsall was a charter member of the Philosophical Society of Texas.[qv] He and his first wife, Ann (Whiteside), had two sons. In 1836 Birdsall married Sarah Peacock. He died of yellow fever on July 22, 1839, and was buried in Glendale Cemetery, Harrisburg (now Houston).

BIBLIOGRAPHY: George A. Birdsall, *The Birdsall Family* (Annandale, Virginia, 1958; rev. ed. 1964). Amelia W. Williams and Eugene C. Barker, eds., *The Writings of Sam Houston, 1813–1863* (8 vols., Austin: University of Texas Press, 1938–43; rpt., Austin and New York: Pemberton Press, 1970). E. W. Winkler, ed., *Secret Journals of the Senate, Republic of Texas* (Austin, 1911). Andrew White Young, *History of Chautauqua County* (New York, 1875). *Edward C. Breitenkamp*

BIRDS CREEK. Birds Creek rises just north of the DeWitt county line and two miles northwest of Westhoff in southern Gonzales County (at 29°11′ N, 97°30′ W) and runs east for 4½ miles to its mouth on Sandies Creek, two miles northwest of Westhoff (at 29°12′ N, 97°26′ W). The stream is intermittent in its upper reaches. It traverses an area of low-rolling hills and prairies surfaced by highly expansive clay that supports grass and some mesquite. Water-tolerant hardwoods grow near the mouth. The stream was named for James Bird, who obtained the original land grant in the area.

BIRD'S CREEK INDIAN FIGHT. The Bird's Creek Indian Fight occurred on May 26, 1839, near the site of present Temple, when a ranger force of thirty-four men under the command of Capt. John Bird[qv] came in contact with more than 200 Caddo, Kickapoo, and Comanche Indians. The Texans were victorious but suffered several casualties, including Captain Bird. A Comanche chief was killed in the fight. The creek on which the battle was fought became known as Bird's Creek. Two markers near Temple commemorate the event.

BIBLIOGRAPHY: Rupert N. Richardson, *The Comanche Barrier to South Plains Settlement* (Glendale, California: Clark, 1933; rpt., Millwood, New York: Kraus, 1973). Harold Schoen, comp., *Monuments Erected by the State of Texas to Commemorate the Centenary of Texas Independence* (Austin: Commission of Control for Texas Centennial Celebrations, 1938). Temple *Daily Telegram*, April 17, 1936. George Tyler, *History of Bell County* (San Antonio: Naylor, 1936).

BIRDSDALE, TEXAS. Birdsdale was on Bird's Creek two miles northwest of the site of present Temple in northern Bell County. The post office, named for John Bird,[qv] opened in January 1873 with Louis C. Allen as postmaster. At its peak the community had a school, a church, and several stores. When the Gulf, Colorado and Santa Fe Railway Company began to establish the community of Temple in 1880 and 1881, many Birdsdale residents were drawn away. The post office at Birdsdale was discontinued in May 1881, and the remaining residents gradually dispersed.

BIBLIOGRAPHY: Martha Bowmer, *Temple: Backtracking 100 Years, a Centennial Journey* (N.p.: Temple Centennial Commission, 1981). John J. Germann and Myron Janzen, *Texas Post Offices by County* (1986). *Vivian Elizabeth Smyrl*

BIRDSTON, TEXAS. Birdston was on Farm Road 416 two miles northeast of Streetman in extreme south central Navarro County. It was probably established before the Civil War.[qv] In 1866 a Birdston post office opened, and by 1885 the town had two steam gristmill and cotton gin combinations, a sawmill, five churches, and a public school. The estimated population in 1892 was 250. After 1900 the town began to decline; many residents moved to Streetman, on the railroad. In 1909 the Birdston post office closed, and by the mid-1930s the community no longer appeared on highway maps. In 1990 the former townsite was marked only by a cemetery and a few scattered houses.

BIBLIOGRAPHY: Annie Carpenter Love, *History of Navarro County* (Dallas: Southwestern, 1933). *Christopher Long*

BIRDVILLE, TEXAS. Birdville, in central Tarrant County, developed from Fort Bird, the first settlement in the county. It was established in 1841 and named for Capt. Jonathan Bird. Birdville was a functioning settlement by 1848, and its earliest residents were farmers and cattle ranchers. It was selected by the state legislature as the county seat when Tarrant County was established in 1849. A local post office open in 1851 and served as a mail distribution point for a number of communities to the west. Birdville lost by seven votes to Fort Worth in a county seat election in November 1856. In 1870 Birdville had four general stores and a blacksmith shop. During the 1896–97 term, the local black school enrolled fourteen pupils and employed one teacher, and the white school registered seventy-seven students and employed two teachers. The post office closed in 1906, when the community's population was reported at 107. The same population was reported through 1940. In the late 1940s the community had a population of 200 and five businesses, and in the middle 1950s it had 400 residents. By 1990 it had been annexed by Haltom City.

BIBLIOGRAPHY: Janet L. Schmelzer, *Where the West Begins: Fort Worth and Tarrant County* (Northridge, California: Windsor, 1985). Ruby Schmidt, ed., *Fort Worth and Tarrant County* (Fort Worth: Texas Christian University Press, 1984). *Brian Hart*

BIRDWELL, ALTON WILLIAM (1870–1954). Alton William Birdwell, teacher and college administrator, oldest son of George Preston and Adelaide (Kilgore) Birdwell, was born near Elkhart, Texas, on September 18, 1870. In 1899 he enrolled at the University of Texas; he attended the University of Missouri in the summer of 1900 and the University of Chicago in the summers of 1910, 1912, and 1914. He received his M.A. degree from George Peabody College for Teachers in August 1915. In 1940 Southwestern University conferred on him an honorary LL.D. degree. Birdwell began teaching in Smith County in 1892, and in 1899 he became principal of North Side Elementary School in Tyler. In 1904 he was made the first county school superintendent of Smith County. In 1906 he became principal at Tyler High School. At Southwest Texas Normal School (now Southwest Texas State University) he became professor of history in 1910, head of the history department in 1911, and dean of the college in 1915. When Stephen F. Austin State Teachers College (now Stephen F. Austin State University) was established in 1921, Birdwell was president, a position he held until 1942. From 1925 through 1933 he spent a part of each summer teaching public school administration at George Peabody College for Teachers. He was president of the Texas State Teachers Association,[qv] a trustee of George Peabody College for Teachers, director of a bank, and a member of several professional associations. He was in great demand as a speaker and spoke in cities throughout the United States. Some 200 of his speeches are in the Birdwell Collection in the Stephen F. Austin State University Library. Birdwell married Margaret Shipe in 1915. He died on October 25, 1954, and was buried in Sunset Memorial Cemetery, Nacogdoches.

BIBLIOGRAPHY: Bettye Herrington Craddock, *The Golden Years* (Waco: Texian Press, 1973). Polly A. R. Mallow, The Life and Work of Alton William Birdwell (M.A. thesis, Southern Methodist University, 1945). Patricia Ann Townsend, The Speeches of Doctor Alton W. Birdwell (M.A. thesis, Stephen F. Austin State University, 1956).

C. K. Chamberlain

BIRDWELL, JOHN E. II (1929–1991). John Birdwell, rancher and cattleman, was born on July 8, 1929, in Ralls, Texas, to John Lowry and Cordelia (Golden) Birdwell. He was named Joe Earnest, but he later changed his name to John E. Birdwell II. He attended grade school in Ralls and in Lubbock, where his family moved in 1939. He attended Lubbock High School and then the high school at Jacksonville Baptist College, where he received his diploma in 1947. He attended Texas Technological College briefly in 1947. From 1945 to 1949 he managed his father's ranch near Justiceburg before leasing the Connell Ranch of some 100,000 acres near Post. In 1949 he married Genene Lee Bateman in Clovis, New Mexico. They had four sons and a daughter. In 1945 Birdwell and his father leased the VVN Ranch, the southernmost camp of the XIT Ranch[qv] in Bailey County. A year later they drove to New York City to buy the ranch from Stone-Webster Investment Company. Birdwell moved to Lubbock in 1966 and continued ranching in Garza, Throckmorton, Haskell, and Bailey counties. He was chairman of Birdwell Cattle Feeders, a ranching and cattle-feeding operation in Bailey County, until his retirement in 1989, when Governor Bill Clements appointed him to the Texas Water Commission.[qv]

Birdwell was president of the Texas and Southwestern Cattle Raisers Association[qv] and a member of the board of directors of the National Cattlemen's Association, the Beef Industry Council, the Southwestern Exposition and Fat Stock Show, and the Texas Hereford Association. He was also a board member of the Brazos River Authority.[qv] He received the Gerald W. Thomas Outstanding Agriculturist Award from the Texas Tech College of Agricultural Sciences. He served on the Texas Tech Board of Regents from 1981 to 1987 and as its chairman in 1986. He died at his home in Lubbock on August 6, 1991, after a lengthy illness from a brain tumor. Funeral services were held at Central Baptist Church in Lubbock. He was buried in the State Cemetery[qv] in Austin.

BIBLIOGRAPHY: Lubbock *Avalanche-Journal*, August 9, 1991. Vertical Files, Barker Texas History Center, University of Texas at Austin.

Lawrence L. Graves

BIRKHEAD, CLAUDE V. (1880–1950). Claude V. Birkhead, Texas jurist and soldier, was born on May 27, 1880, in Phoenix, Oregon. His family moved to Texas during his youth, and he attended Waco public schools and Fort Worth University. He was admitted to the State Bar of Texas[qv] in 1899 and moved to San Antonio. In 1910 he was appointed to the bench of the Seventy-third District Court; after his election to that post in 1912, he resigned to resume law practice. He was recognized as a leader of the bar of Southwest Texas.

He enlisted in 1899 as a private in Company K, First Texas Infantry, and his long military record ended only with his death. He was a colonel of field artillery in the Texas National Guard[qv] at the outbreak of World War I.[qv] He entered federal service as a colonel of the Thirty-first Field Artillery and served in the American Expeditionary Force in France until the end of the war. He stayed in the Texas National Guard after the war and received numerous promotions. In 1923 he was brigadier general of field artillery of the Thirty-sixth Division.[qv] In 1936 he was promoted to major general and made commanding general of the division, which was federalized on November 25, 1940. In September 1941 Birkhead was placed in command of the internal security force of the Third Corps area, with headquarters at Baltimore. He was placed on the retired list, effective May 27, 1948. On December 6, 1947, he was appointed major general of the Texas State Guard[qv] Reserve Corps and assigned to be its commanding general. On August 2, 1948, he was promoted to lieutenant general. With an indefatigable interest in the welfare of veterans, he served as first department commander of Texas of the American Legion.[qv] He was also president of the National Guard Association of the United States. He was on the board of directors of Peacock Military Academy[qv] for many years, and one of its dormitories was named in his honor. Birkhead died on November 19, 1950, in San Antonio.

BIBLIOGRAPHY: San Antonio *Express*, November 20, 1950. Vertical Files, Barker Texas History Center, University of Texas at Austin.

Hobart Huson

BIRKMANN, GOTTHILF (1854–1944). Gotthilf Birkmann, Lutheran pastor and amateur entomologist, was born on June 4, 1854, at Waterloo, Illinois. He graduated from Concordia College in Fort Wayne, Indiana, in 1873 and from Concordia Theological Seminary, St. Louis, Missouri, in 1876. He assumed his first pastorate in 1876 in West Yegua (now Fedor), Lee County, Texas. He served the Trinity Lutheran Church at this rural locality for three years and then moved to Dallas in 1879 to serve three years at the Zion Lutheran Church there. While at Zion, Birkmann organized a parish school. In 1882 he returned to Fedor, where he remained as pastor of Trinity Lutheran Church until he retired in 1922. Birkmann served as secretary of the Southern District of the Lutheran Church, Missouri Synod, in 1882–83. He also served as vice president from 1884 to 1889. In 1889 he was interim president of the district but returned to the vice presidency in 1891. He was also president of the Texas District of the Lutheran Church, Missouri Synod, from 1912 to 1920. He was an avid, lifelong student of Hebrew and Greek. Birkmann published numerous articles on the early history of the Lutheran Church in Texas. They appeared in newspapers (mostly in the Giddings *Deutsches Volksblatt*,[qv] but also in the Giddings *News*) and Lutheran periodicals (the *Texas Distriktsbote, Texas Lutheran Messenger, Missions-Taube, Lutheraner*), and have been an important source for historians. He was awarded an honorary doctorate of theology by Concordia Lutheran Theological Seminary in 1936. A chapel at Concordia College in Austin is also named in his honor.

Birkmann began collecting insects about 1885 and continued to do so until 1920, when his eyesight began to fail. He apparently became interested in entomology when he visited Ludolph Heilingbrodt of neighboring Bastrop County and viewed the latter's collection at an exposition in New Orleans. Birkmann first started collecting butterflies but later changed his interests to wasps and bees, since they took up less space. Many of his specimens were studied by professional entomologists. In 1899 he published a list of 307 species and varieties of bees and wasps collected at Fedor. Many of his specimens were purchased by the Museum of Comparative Zoology of Harvard University. Birkmann attended the Sixth Annual meeting of the Texas Entomological Society[qv] in 1934, at nearly eighty years of age, and in 1936 his name was added to the honorary list of members. A considerable number of the bees and wasps he collected at or near Fedor proved to be new species, and others represented significant extensions of known ranges for species. Most of these specimens are safely housed in major collections. Birkmann died at Giddings on May 17, 1944.

BIBLIOGRAPHY: William Henry Bewie, *Missouri in Texas: A History of the Lutheran Church–Missouri Synod in Texas, 1855–1941* (Austin: Steck, 1952). R. W. Strandtman, "Rev. G. Birkmann," *Texas Journal of Science* 2 (1950). *Horace R. Burke*

BIROME, TEXAS. Birome is on Farm Road 308 fifteen miles south of Hillsboro in south central Hill County. The town was established in 1910 as a shipping point on the International–Great Northern Railroad, which had recently extended its tracks across the county, and given a portmanteau name derived from the given names of Bickham and Jerome Cartwright. The two brothers owned the 4,800-acre Cartwright Ranch, on which Birome was located. The settlement reached its height during the first decade of the twentieth century. By 1910 Birome had a school, a general store, a cotton gin, a blacksmith shop, a doctor, a barbershop, and an ice cream parlor. A Birome post office began operating in 1912. Fifty persons lived in Birome by the mid-1920s. Though its reported population remained unchanged between that time and the mid-1960s, the community experienced considerable decline, no doubt affected by the Great Depression[qv] and the dislocations resulting from World War II.[qv] The school closed in 1952, and the railroad tracks were abandoned. By the mid-1970s the population had fallen to thirty-one, a number still reported in 1990. In the early 1980s the community had a number of residences, a church, a community center, a grocery store, a cotton gin, and a post office.

BIBLIOGRAPHY: Hill County Historical Commission, *A History of Hill County, Texas, 1853–1980* (Waco: Texian, 1980).
David Minor

BIRTHRIGHT, TEXAS. Birthright, also known as Lone Star, on Farm Road 71 ten miles northeast of Sulphur Springs in north central Hopkins County, began about 1870 as a store in the ranchhouse of E. C. Birthright. A post office was established in 1871 in the store with Edward McLaughlin as postmaster. Lone Star School was a mile west of the store; the Lone Star Methodist Church met in the school until its building was erected in 1892. In 1885 the widely dispersed town, by then known as Birthright, had four steam mill-gins, three churches, a school, and an estimated population of 150. In 1890 the population had grown to 250, and a weekly paper named the Lone Star *Appeal* was being published. By 1893 the post office had been moved to the farm home of G. C. McCauley, a half mile northwest of the school. Around 1894 Randolph Reed opened a store 1½ miles west of the original site and became postmaster. In 1925 the community reported eighty-five residents. During the mid-1930s Birthright had a post office, a school, two churches, and four stores. By 1948 only the post office, a church, and a store remained. The post office and the stores later closed, and in the early 1960s the town had two churches and a few scattered houses. In the late 1980s Birthright was a dispersed rural farming community. The population in 1990 was forty.

BIBLIOGRAPHY: Florene Chapman Adams, *Hopkins County and Our Heritage* (Sulphur Springs, Texas: 197-?). *J. E. Jennings*

BIRY, TEXAS. Biry, also referred to as Biryville and as Briar Branch, is on Farm Road 173 and Briar Branch Creek, twelve miles southeast of Hondo in Medina County. The settlement was situated within empresario Henri Castro's[qv] original land grant and was established, under the name Briar Branch, around 1888 by the sons of Castro's initial European grantees. The first school was built there in 1892, and 1896 school records show thirty-nine students attending the Briar Branch School. The community had some 300 people in 1900. Forced to shorten the name to accommodate a new post office in 1907, community residents chose Biry in honor of Jacob Biry, pioneer settler and town founder. The post office, with Joseph Franger as its first postmaster, operated out of the Franger-Schmidt General Store. Also in 1907 a cotton gin was built to serve the community. The Franger-Schmidt business expanded to include a meat market, a cafe, and a saloon and dance hall, but by 1914 the store was out of business. The saloon and cafe ended operations during prohibition,[qv] but dancing continued in the hall well into the 1930s. The population of Biry had declined to twenty by 1948, and this decline continued after Highway 173 bypassed the community in the 1950s. The Biry school was closed in 1952, when it consolidated with the Devine school district. Soon after the highway was completed, Marvin Hass opened what was for a time the last store to operate in the community; the old store building was being used as an oil-well supply warehouse as late as 1983. By the early 1990s Biry was attracting new residents, many of whom commuted to work in San Antonio. Others in the community were engaged in farming, ranching, and the oil business; at this time the majority of the oil-producing wells in Medina County were within ten miles of Biry. Population statistics for Biry were not available in the 1980s and early 1990s.

BIBLIOGRAPHY: Castro Colonies Heritage Association, *The History of Medina County, Texas* (Dallas: National Share Graphics, 1983). John J. Germann and Myron Janzen, *Texas Post Offices by County* (1986). *Ruben E. Ochoa*

BISHOP, CURTIS KENT (1912–1967). Curtis Kent Bishop, newspaperman and author, was born in Bolivar, Tennessee, on November 10, 1912, the son of D. E. and Annie (Cornelius) Bishop. He moved to Texas as a boy, graduated from Big Spring High School in 1934, and attended the University of Texas from 1934 to 1936; at the university he was twice editor of the *Ranger*, the student magazine, and sports reporter for the student newspaper, the *Daily Texan*.[qv] He worked as a reporter for the Austin *Tribune* from 1939 to 1942 and the Austin *American-Statesman*[qv] from the time he was sixteen, a job which he later took permanently. He wrote a column, "This Day in Texas," syndicated throughout the state. During World War II[qv] Bishop was with the Foreign Broadcast Intelligence Service in Latin America and the Pacific Theater. On his return he became widely recognized for his books on sports and for his western novels, at least six of which were made into motion pictures. He wrote other books in the field of teenage sports fiction, among them *Half-Time Hero* (1956) and *Dribble Up* (1956). In the historical field he wrote *The First Texas Ranger: Jack Hays* (1959) and *Lots of Land* (1949), the latter with James Bascom Giles. He wrote hundreds of magazine articles and was given an award by *Look* magazine for a television play. He wrote under several pen names. As a result of the book written with Bascom Giles, the General Land Office[qv] of Texas employed Bishop to examine its archives in order to help prepare the case for Texas in the Tidelands controversy.[qv] He worked at the Land Office for about thirteen years, between 1947 and 1967. At the time of his death he was administrative assistant in the public relations department. From 1954 to 1960 he was a member of the Texas Employment Commission.[qv] Bishop was married to Grace Eyree, and they had four children. He died of a heart attack on March 17, 1967, in Austin and was buried in Austin Memorial Park.

bibliography: Vertical Files, Barker Texas History Center, University of Texas at Austin. *Joe B. Frantz*

BISHOP, TEXAS. Bishop, at the junction of U.S. Highway 77 and State Highway 428 in extreme southwestern Nueces County, was originally on the Driscoll Ranch and was called Julia Siding. In 1910 F. Z. Bishop, a Corpus Christi insurance agent, bought a large parcel of land at the site and established a town. Before the first lots were put on sale on May 30, 1910, the town was laid out with a complete modern sewage system, eight miles of graded streets, and two miles of cement sidewalks. A $35,000 electric light and water plant was established, and a telephone system was installed. A hotel and several residences were erected, and a $16,000 store and office building was opened. In September 1910, when the first school opened in a three-room frame building, sixteen children were enrolled. Enrollment increased to sixty by the end of the term. Within three years the previously undeveloped expanse of brush, cactus, and mesquite was transformed into a new and prosperous agricultural section. In 1923 30,000 bales of local cotton were marketed for more than $4,000,000, and Bishop was referred to as the "Cotton Capital of the Coast." In 1941 the farmers combined 3,000 pounds of grain to the acre, and "Grain Mart of the Coastal Bend" was added to the label.

The town grew rapidly during the 1920s, reaching a high of 2,500 in 1928. With the onset of the Great Depression,[qv] however, many residents left, and by 1936 the population had fallen to 953. After World War II[qv] Bishop once again began to grow, and by the mid-1950s it had a population of 4,000 and eighty-five businesses. In 1968 the town had eight churches, a state bank, a weekly newspaper, and a reported 4,180 residents. The population subsequently declined slowly, falling to 3,337 in 1992. Over the same period the number of businesses fell from sixty to thirty. In the early 1990s Bishop was the site of petrochemical plants and petroleum processing. The major sources of farm income are cotton, grain sorghums, livestock, and poultry.

bibliography: Nueces County Historical Society, *History of Nueces County* (Austin: Jenkins, 1972). *Lillion Effie Wimsatt*

BISHOP BRANCH. Bishop Branch rises just south of Cistern in southwestern Fayette County (at 29°49′ N, 97°13′ W) and extends southeast for 3½ miles to its mouth on Live Oak Creek (at 29°48′ N, 97°11′ W). It runs through several stock tanks and, after crossing State Highway 95, past several strip-mines where clay has been extracted for road construction. The land surface is a very friable, fine, sandy loam with a firm clay subsoil. The area is fair to poor for agricultural purposes and primarily supports pasture for cattle. Vegetation along the branch consists of mixed oaks and cedar with mesquite, willow, sycamore, and yaupon.

BISHOP COLLEGE. Bishop College was founded by the Baptist Home Mission Society in 1881 in Marshall, Texas. The drive to establish a Texas college for black Baptists was originally founded by Nathan Bishop, native of New York, and superintendent of the Providence, Rhode Island, and Boston, Massachusetts, school systems. Ten years earlier Rufus C. Burleson,[qv] then president of Baylor University, had contacted Bishop requesting a contribution of $25,000. Bishop agreed but died before sending the money. Later his wife, Carolina Caldwell Bishop, contributed $10,000 to the American Baptist Home Mission Society in order to initiate construction on the school. A selection committee that included the distinguished pastor from the New Hope Baptist Church in Dallas, Rev. Allen R. Griggs,[qv] visited several East Texas cities and determined that Marshall was the best location for the school. Local Baptist ministers then raised $1,600, purchased a tract of land from the Holcomb family, and temporarily named the new facility South-Western Baptist College. In 1880 forty additional acres was purchased and donated to the school by Mrs. Bishop. The institution was named Bishop College.

The new college's orientation was primarily religious, but the charter stated that it would "give instruction in literature, science, and the arts" as well. Although always plagued with financial difficulties, Bishop expanded its course offerings. In 1925 the school began a two-year training program for ministers. It elected its first black president, Joseph J. Rhoads,[qv] in 1929. That year it discontinued the high school department and received senior rank from the State Board of Education. In 1932 an annual training institute for in-service ministers and lay church workers began. The program was named the Lacy Kirk Williams Institute in 1943. It attracted the attention and attendance of many prestigious clergymen, including Martin Luther King, Jr., and Jesse Jackson. In 1931 Bishop College was given a Class B rating by the Southern Association of Colleges and Secondary Schools and in 1948 was granted Class A accreditation. In 1947 a junior college branch was opened in Dallas, and a graduate program leading to the M.Ed. degree was initiated. The Zale jewelry family (*see* zale jewelry corporation) contributed to the library project, and by the 1980s the Zale Library housed more than 130,000 volumes, in addition to collections of federal publications, clippings, and pamphlets, and over 375 periodicals and newspapers.

M. K. Curry, Jr., assumed the presidency in 1952. Under his administration the graduate program in teacher education was terminated, a minimum endowment of $300,000 was raised, the faculty was strengthened, and the Marshall campus was renovated. Plans to move the college were formulated when, in 1957, the Hoblitzelle Foundation (*see* hoblitzelle, karl st. john) gave ninety-eight acres in south Dallas for a new campus. Four Baptist conventions joined in the purchase of an additional two-acre plot, and an anonymous gift enlarged the campus by 287 acres in 1964. Initial construction in the multimillion-dollar expansion program on the Dallas campus provided an administration-classroom building, a gymnasium-auditorium, housing facilities, and a fine arts building, converted from the junior college branch. The move to the new campus was accomplished in 1961.

Additional construction included a student center (1962); men's dormitory and married-student apartments, classrooms, an infirmary, service buildings, and a stadium (1963); and a library, chapel, and science building (1964). The college further acquired the Sabine Farms Community Center, twelve miles south of Marshall, and cooperated with various other community-service agencies. Rechartered by the state in 1961, the college reduced the number of trustees but strengthened their power.

The church-related college was nonsectarian and interracial in selection of students and faculty. The college program, emphasizing liberal arts education, included summer sessions and an evening division of adult education. B.A. or B.S. degrees were available in twenty major fields. By 1969 the library contained 75,000 volumes. During the 1974–75 term Bishop College had an enrollment of 1,243 students and a faculty of 100. Curry was still president.

The 1970s also brought problems. In early 1970 the American Association of University Professors blacklisted the school because of the firing of a white professor and the arrest of a number of students who demonstrated against the firing. The AAUP stated that the academic freedom of students and faculty had been seriously infringed. Furthermore, criminal charges of embezzlement were filed against the president and two other employees. Although the president and one of the employees were cleared, enrollment dropped, and the college was unable to meet a large debt owed to the federal government. The debt was restructured several times, but financial problems became worse. In December 1986 the Southern Association of Colleges and Schools revoked Bishop's accreditation and membership in the association. Because of this the college lost its right to participate in several government financial programs and access to funds from the

United Negro College Fund. In April 1987 Bishop College filed Chapter 11 bankruptcy in an unsuccessful attempt to restructure its debts and raise money to remain open; it was closed in 1988. At the time it closed the student body was dominated by foreign and out-of-state students; fewer than 10 percent were from Dallas. The grounds and facilities were then occupied by Paul Quinn College, originally from Waco and affiliated with the African Methodist Episcopal Church.[qv]

BIBLIOGRAPHY: Austin *American-Statesman*, August 17, 1988. Michael R. Heintze, A History of the Black Private Colleges in Texas, 1865–1954 (Ph.D. dissertation, Texas Tech University, 1981; published as *Private Black Colleges in Texas, 1865–1954* [College Station: Texas A&M University Press, 1985]). Vertical Files, Barker Texas History Center, University of Texas at Austin. Carl Bassett Wilson, History of Baptist Educational Efforts in Texas, 1829–1900 (Ph.D. dissertation, University of Texas, 1934). *Jack Herman and Peggy Hardman*

BISHOP HOLLOW, TEXAS. Bishop Hollow was a frontier settlement on the Frio River seven miles southwest of the site of present Pearsall in central Frio County. A post office was established in the community in 1878 and called Ireland; it was discontinued in 1881 and moved to the newly established railroad town of Pearsall. According to county sources the site was subsequently known as Bishop Hollow. In 1900 a local school by the name of Bishop had twenty-four students taught by one teacher. Bishop Hollow does not appear on twentieth-century maps.

BIBLIOGRAPHY: Mrs. W. A. Roberts, "Frio County Has a Colorful History," *Frontier Times*, June 1936. *Ruben E. Ochoa*

BISHOPS' COMMITTEE FOR HISPANIC AFFAIRS. The Bishops' Committee for Hispanic Affairs was originally founded as the Bishops' Committee for the Spanish Speaking in January 1945 in San Antonio under the leadership of Archbishop Robert E. Lucey,[qv] to involve the Catholic Church[qv] directly in improving the social and spiritual welfare of Mexican Americans[qv] in the state. Lucey set out to establish BCSS in 1941. He first organized a "summer school of social justice" to teach priests in the Southwest about the church's role in helping workers organize for better working conditions. Then in 1943–44, he called a series of meetings for church leaders who worked with Spanish-speaking Catholics in Texas. These gatherings became the basis for BCSS, which Lucey envisioned as a means to fight for social justice for Hispanics. While these events set up a structure for BCSS, two other elements were just as significant in establishing BCSS: Lucey's reputation as a fighter for working people and the high level of unemployment, poverty, and racism that affected the Mexican Americans of San Antonio, many of whom lived on an annual income of $2,000 in houses with dirt floors and no plumbing or water.

At the time the committee was founded, President Franklin D. Roosevelt's New Deal brought federal efforts against societal ills and provided BCSS with philosophical backing. Roosevelt had sent his congratulations on the prelate's elevation to archbishop, thus indicating his acceptance of Lucey's vision. From its earliest days, the committee reflected Lucey's ideas for attaining equality, and it remained firmly under his control until his retirement in 1969.

To carry out the church's mission among Mexican Americans, the committee set up permanent headquarters in San Antonio under Lucey's executive directorship. Though its original plan called for a rotating system of regional offices throughout the Southwest, Lucey never permitted the committee hierarchy to move outside the state. Once organized, the BCSS set up religion classes for children, child-care programs, clinics, and community centers on the west side of San Antonio, where Tejanos were segregated. In El Paso the committee emphasized public housing and youth work, and in Corpus Christi it participated in the successful unionization of the city's bus drivers, 70 percent of whom were Mexican American.

All in all, activism grounded in the church's treatises on social morality was the strength of BCSS's work. Although its activities received favorable coverage in the national press, anxious San Antonio businessmen decried what appeared to be a church-sponsored social revolution taking place in their midst. But BCSS paid little attention to criticism.

Besides its work in the state's cities during its formative years, BCSS also took up the cause of migratory farm laborers, prompting some to declare that the committee was really a farmworkers' union. In 1950 BCSS became formally involved with the migrant farm laborers. The catalyst for this was Lucey's service on President Harry S. Truman's panel that investigated farmworkers' and braceros' working and living conditions. The panel held public hearings around the state, and Lucey ensured that the committee's executive secretary, Fr. Theodore Radthe, testified about the substandard salaries and exploitation suffered by farmworkers. The testimony, which was not fully endorsed by the entire BCSS, did not succeed in promoting Lucey's efforts to oppose legislation establishing the Bracero program.[qv]

This failure to persuade government authorities to provide protective legislation for farmworkers set the committee on a different course. Lucey decided to organize a voluntary effort among Catholic parishes in the dioceses along the migrant trail. Besides assisting the farmworkers in their area, the volunteers conducted regular inspections of farm labor camps and reported any mistreatment to the authorities. Despite its wholehearted efforts, BCSS was able to provide only temporary relief to the workers along the migrant trail. Indifferent church members and a lack of funds spelled doom for the project. Through the 1950s, the committee continued to fight for farmworkers and oppose the Bracero program, which Lucey condemned as a vehicle that principally served the interests of growers. BCSS charged that the program used "slave laborers" and called for an end to it.

In the 1960s, BCSS initially endorsed the efforts of farmworkers in Texas to strike and gain collective bargaining rights. But that effort mired the committee in controversy that ended only with Lucey's retirement. The conflict erupted in 1967–68 between Lucey, the authoritarian head of BCSS, who did not tolerate dissent, and young BCSS priests. Lucey's transfer of dissident or outspoken priests working with the farmworker cause prompted a call for his resignation as archbishop by some sixty-eight priests under his jurisdiction. In 1969, with Lucey at the end of his career, the committee became part of the National Conference of Catholic Bishops. Its official title was changed to Bishops' Committee for Hispanic Affairs to reflect a broader national involvement with all Hispanic groups in the country. The Secretariat for Hispanic Affairs was made the administrative arm of the reorganized committee. The committee continued its work in the Southwest, focusing on social-justice issues affecting Hispanics. In January 1991 the committee elected Msgr. Enrique San Pedro, auxiliary bishop of the Diocese of Galveston-Houston,[qv] as its new president and organized a three-year plan of action to fulfill its mission to serve Hispanic Catholics.

BIBLIOGRAPHY: Saul E. Bronder, *Social Justice and Church Authority: The Public Life of Archbishop Robert E. Lucey* (Philadelphia: Temple University Press, 1982). *Texas Observer*, July 26, 1957.

Teresa Palomo Acosta

BISHOP'S PALACE. The Bishop's Palace, also known as the Walter Gresham House, is at 1402 Broadway in Galveston. The three-story Châteauesque residence was designed by noted Galveston architect Nicholas J. Clayton[qv] and built for attorney and legislator Walter Gresham[qv] between 1887 and 1893. It is particularly notable for its exterior of sculpted granite, limestone, and sandstone and the elaborate carved woodwork on the interior. The Catholic Diocese of Galveston-Houston[qv] bought the house in 1923, and for many years it served as the seat of the local bishop. The diocese opened the house to the public in 1963. The structure was declared a Recorded Texas Historic

Landmark in 1967 and was added to the National Register of Historic Places in 1970. Since 1975 it has also been included in the East End Historic District.[qv]

BIBLIOGRAPHY: James Wright Steely, comp., *A Catalog of Texas Properties in the National Register of Historic Places* (Austin: Texas Historical Commission, 1984). *Christopher Long*

BISKATRONGE INDIANS. The Biskatronge (Biscatronge, Plañidores, Pleureurs, Weepers) Indians are known from a single document pertaining to the La Salle expedition[qv] in the late seventeenth century. This document, the narrative of Anastase Douay,[qv] indicates that the Biskatronge lived inland well to the north or northeast of Matagorda Bay, probably between the Colorado and Brazos rivers. Douay said that La Salle's party called these people "weepers" because they greeted the French by weeping for a quarter of an hour. Douay's Biskatronge cannot be identified with any Indian group named in Henri Joutel's[qv] journal of the same expedition. A. S. Gatschet equated the Biskatronge with the Coco, but his reasons for doing so were not made explicit. The affiliations of the Biskatronge remain undetermined.

BIBLIOGRAPHY: Isaac Joslin Cox, ed., *The Journeys of René Robert Cavelier, Sieur de La Salle* (2 vols., New York: Barnes, 1905; 2d ed., New York: Allerton, 1922). Albert S. Gatschet, *The Karankawa Indians, the Coast People of Texas* (Cambridge, Massachusetts: Peabody Museum of American Archaeology and Ethnology, 1891). Frederick Webb Hodge, ed., *Handbook of American Indians North of Mexico* (2 vols., Washington: GPO, 1907, 1910; rpt., New York: Pageant, 1959). John Gilmary Shea, *Discovery and Exploration of the Mississippi Valley* (New York: Redfield, 1852). *Thomas N. Campbell*

BISSETT MOUNTAIN. Bissett Mountain is fourteen miles northeast of Alpine in northern Brewster County (at 30°23′ N, 103°25′ W). With an elevation of 5,483 feet above sea level, the summit rises 1,400 feet above U.S. Highway 67, five miles to the northwest. The area's shallow, stony soils support oak, juniper, and some mesquite. The peak was named for Dave Bissett, an early prospector in the vicinity.

BITTER CREEK (Archer County). Bitter Creek, also known as Browns Creek, rises within the Megargel oilfield four miles east of Megargel in southwest Archer County (at 33°27′ N, 98°53′ W) and runs south through southwest Archer and southwest Young counties to its mouth on the Brazos River, just east of the Throckmorton-Young county line (at 33°21′ N, 98°55′ W). It traverses an area of rolling hills surfaced by clay and sandy loam that supports scrub brush, mesquite, cacti, and grasses. The church community of Bitter Creek and the Padgett Cemetery are near the stream in northwest Young County.

—— (Hall County). The East and West forks of Bitter Creek rise in southern Donley County and flow southwest for ten miles before converging a mile north of State Highway 256 in northwestern Hall County (at 34°43′ N, 100°51′ W). Bitter Creek runs southwest for six miles to its mouth on the Prairie Dog Town Fork of the Red River, in northwestern Hall County (at 34°37′ N, 100°53′ W). It traverses an area of moderately steep slopes with locally high relief and a surface of silt loam that supports mesquite and grasses. The creek was probably named for the saline springs downstream. The land upstream was once part of the JA Ranch[qv] horse pasture; this area was later developed as the Bitter Creek Ranch by R. G. Welch of California; in 1959 it became the property of Lawrence R. Hagey, Amarillo businessman and civic leader.

BIBLIOGRAPHY: Virginia Browder, *Donley County: Land O' Promise* (Wichita Falls, Texas: Nortex, 1975).

—— (King County). Bitter Creek, in northeast King County, rises one mile west of the King-Knox county line (at 33°45′ N, 100°01′ W) and runs southeast for six miles to its mouth on the South Wichita River, a mile north of Getaway Canyon (at 33°40′ N, 100°00′ W). It crosses an area of rolling to steep slopes surfaced by clay and sandy loams that support juniper, cacti, and sparse grasses.

—— (Nolan County). Bitter Creek begins a half mile southwest of Nolan in east central Nolan County (at 32°16′ N, 100°16′ W) and runs north for twenty-seven miles to its mouth on Sweetwater Creek, a mile west of Eskota in southeast Fisher County (at 32°32′ N, 100°16′ W). The stream is dammed southeast of Sweetwater to form Sweetwater Lake. Upstream, it runs through steeply sloping terrain with benches; downstream, it crosses flat land with local scarps and locally shallow depressions. Juniper, live oak, mesquite, grasses, hardwoods, scrub brush, water-tolerant hardwoods, and conifers grow in the area.

—— (Taylor County). Bitter Creek begins four miles southeast of Trent in the northwest corner of Taylor County (at 32°28′ N, 100°06′ W) and flows northeast for twenty-three miles before disemboguing into the Clear Fork of the Brazos River in southwest central Jones County (at 32°37′ N, 99°53′ W). At the stream's source the terrain is flat to gently sloping and surfaced with loose sand that supports scrub brush and grasses. Toward the Brazos the terrain remains similar, but the soil surface is silt loam that predominantly supports mesquite.

BITTER CREEK, TEXAS. Bitter Creek was settled in the early 1880s by the Montgomery and Bardwell families. The site, said to have been south of present Sweetwater, was presumably located near Bitter Creek in northeast Nolan County. No community appears there on later maps.

BIBLIOGRAPHY: Ed Ellsworth Bartholomew, *The Encyclopedia of Texas Ghost Towns* (Fort Davis, Texas, 1982). *Charles G. Davis*

BITTER LAKE CREEK. Bitter Lake Creek rises four miles south of Northfield in northeast Motley County (at 34°14′ N, 100°35′ W) and flows north for five miles to its mouth on the North Pease River, near the Motley-Hall county line (at 34°19′ N, 100°35′ W). The stream is north of the Matador Ranch[qv] lands. It crosses an area of moderately steep slopes with locally high relief and a surface of shallow to moderately deep silt loams that support mesquite and grasses.

BIVINS, LEE (1862–1929). Lee Bivins, Amarillo rancher, oilman, and civic leader, son of Oliver C. and Elizabeth Jane (Miller) Bivins, was born on October 7, 1862, in Farmington, a small settlement south of Sherman, in Grayson County, Texas. His father, who came to Texas from Indiana in 1854, ranched, ran a mercantile store, and operated the county's first mill. Bivins showed an early interest in cattle raising; as a boy, he often collected dogies from neighbors, brought them home, and hand-fed them. Before he was twenty he had a sizable herd and had established two general stores in Sherman. On August 18, 1882, he married his childhood sweetheart, Mary Gilbert (*see* BIVINS, MARY ELIZABETH GILBERT), and they settled in Sherman. They had two daughters and two sons; both daughters died in childhood.

Bivins's interest in cattle raising led him to the Panhandle[qv] early in 1882. By 1889 he had built a makeshift shack at Claude, where he lived alone; his family joined him after he had established his new business ventures. He opened a grocery store, a wheat mill, and an elevator in Claude and purchased from the JA Ranch[qv] the Mulberry Pasture, later the Mulberry Ranch, seven miles south of town. Bivins's real estate ventures in Claude resulted in the town's Bivins Addition. In 1890 he was elected county commissioner from his precinct.

A much-publicized feud with the nefarious saloonkeeper Skid Ellis began when Ellis's son Ed embezzled some money Bivins had entrusted to him. Tension between the two heightened as Lee's brother Dick, who had joined him in Claude, began courting Ellis's niece in 1898. Ellis ended the courtship by shooting and killing Dick. Bivins attempted to settle the score when he found himself on the same train with Ellis, although he managed only to wound his adversary. He was charged with attempted murder but acquitted the following year.

Ellis recovered, was tried for killing Dick Bivins, and acquitted. He later left the Panhandle.

Bivins opened a livery stable in Amarillo in 1900. In 1903 he built a magnificent three-story home of brick and stone at 1000 Polk Street. He paid the workmen in cash at the end of each day and never revealed the cost of the house. His cattle holdings grew steadily during this time. During his first years in Amarillo he leased several hundred acres of land for his growing herd. His first big purchase was the Cross Bar Ranch, on the south bank of the Canadian River. On October 6, 1910, Bivins purchased 30,354 acres from the American Pastoral Company. The purchase, which included both the LX Ranch[qv] headquarters built by Henry C. Harding in 1902 and the right to use the LX brand, cost $79,000. Three years later he bought the LIT Ranch[qv] from the Prairie Cattle Company; this property included the townsite of Old Tascosa. On May 19, 1915, Bivins bought an additional 53,329 acres from the American Pastoral Company for about $203,000. In 1918, with Berkeley Dawson, he added another 50,000 acres of LIT land to his holdings. He also purchased the Coldwater Ranch, south of Texhoma, part of the XIT Ranch[qv] properties near Channing, and extensive holdings near Fort Sumner, New Mexico. By the 1920s Bivins was said to be the largest individual cattle owner in the world and the largest landowner west of the Mississippi. His leased lands comprised more than a million acres, and he often ran 60,000 cattle with the LX and X Bar brands. He reportedly once rode a horse the ninety miles from Dalhart to Amarillo without leaving his property. It was said that he cornered the Texas steer beef market in 1918–19. In 1918 natural gas found on his Potter County land proved to be part of the largest field in the world. More oil and gas was discovered on his holdings in several counties along the Canadian River.

Bivins also owned extensive stock in businesses and property in Amarillo, including the Bivins Building, built on the site of the old opera house, which had been destroyed by fire in 1915. He helped establish the Panhandle Aerial Service and Transportation Company, Amarillo's first airport, and served as its president. He served eight years as an Amarillo city commissioner and was elected mayor in 1925. He held that office until his death from a heart attack on January 17, 1929, in Wichita Falls. He was buried in the Llano Cemetery in Amarillo. His sons, Miles and Julian, became operators of the Bivins properties, which were later divided into separate ranches. Julian Bivins donated the Old Tascosa site for the establishment of Cal Farley's Boys Ranch[qv] in 1939. The old courthouse, once the home of Julian and his wife, Berneta, later became the Julian Bivins Museum.

BIBLIOGRAPHY: Gus L. Ford, ed., *Texas Cattle Brands* (Dallas: Cockrell, 1936). Della Tyler Key, *In the Cattle Country: History of Potter County, 1887–1966* (Amarillo: Tyler-Berkley, 1961; 2d ed., Wichita Falls: Nortex, 1972). Margaret Sheers, "The LX Ranch of Texas," *Panhandle-Plains Historical Review* 6 (1933). *H. Allen Anderson*

BIVINS, MARY ELIZABETH GILBERT (1862–1951). Mary Bivins, pioneer and philanthropist, was born on February 12, 1862, in Lebanon, Collin County, Texas, to Miles Green and Lucy Harriett (Williams) Gilbert, Jr. The Gilberts had moved to the area three years earlier from Missouri. Mary was educated at Mary Nash College in Sherman and married Lee Bivins[qv] on August 18, 1882. They became the parents of two sons and two daughters, but only the sons survived childhood. Bivins moved the family to the Panhandle[qv] in 1890; there he acquired his first ranch, the Mulberry Pasture, south of Claude. By the time the family settled in Amarillo, around the turn of the century, Bivins was one of the largest cattle operators in the world. His wife supervised the building of their new home while he was away on business, and the magnificent three-story structure became an Amarillo landmark. For twenty years after Mrs. Bivins left the building to the city, it served as the public library.

The gift of her home capped a lifetime of largesse. Mrs. Bivins's philanthropies ranged from private gifts, such as furnished houses for needy families, to support for a wide range of public charities, including the preventorium of the Amarillo Tuberculosis Association, the School Children's Relief fund, and the American Red Cross. She donated building sites for the Maverick Club, the West Amarillo Christian Church, and the VFW headquarters; she also initiated the building fund and helped purchase the lot for the Social Center for Girls. Mrs. Bivins donated the chapel at Phillips University in Enid, Oklahoma, and financed the education of a number of young Christian ministers. Until the age of eighty-seven, she was the grande dame of the Amarillo Fat Stock Show and patroness of the young stock raisers; she kept the bidding high at the 4-H and Future Farmers of America auctions and donated most of her purchases for resale. Only in advanced age would she finally allow a grandson to dispatch her bids. Her most important philanthropy was the Mary E. Bivins Foundation, established in 1949 to sponsor medical and social programs for the needy elderly. In 1951 the foundation built the Elizabeth Jane Bivins Home, a retirement center later expanded and remodeled into a social care facility. The Bivins Memorial Nursing Home followed in 1968. The foundation cooperates with regional academic and hospital nursing programs to give nursing students experience in nursing-home work. Mrs. Bivins died in Amarillo on December 31, 1951, and was buried in Llano Cemetery.

BIBLIOGRAPHY: Amarillo *Globe-Times*, December 31, 1951. Amarillo *Globe-News*, November 18, 1979. *Cattleman*, February 1952.
Judith N. McArthur

BIVINS, TEXAS. Bivins is on State Highway 43 and the Missouri Pacific Railroad seven miles southwest of Atlanta in southern Cass County. It had its origins in two large sawmills built at the tracks of the Texas and Pacific Railway in 1884. The station that opened there soon became a shipping and gathering place for local farmers. The post office at nearby Wayne was moved to this location in 1889, and the town was named Bivins, in honor of J. K. and Frank H. Bivins, the owners of one of the sawmills. By 1896 it had two churches, a school, numerous businesses, and a population of 300. Although the sawmills in the area closed, the town remained a shipping point, and the population remained stable until the end of World War II.[qv] From 1972 through 1990 the population was reported at 105, and in 1986 Bivins had seven rated businesses.

BIBLIOGRAPHY: Atlanta (Texas) *Citizens Journal*, Sixtieth Anniversary Edition, 1939. *Cecil Harper, Jr.*

BIVINS LAKE. Bivins Lake, also known as Amarillo City Lake, is an artificial reservoir formed by a dam on Palo Duro Creek ten miles southwest of Amarillo in western Randall County (35°02′ N, 102°02′ W). It is owned and operated by the city of Amarillo to recharge the groundwater reservoir that supplies the city's well field. The project was started in 1926, completed a year later, and named for Lee Bivins.[qv] It has a capacity of 5,120 acre-feet and a surface area of 379 acres at the spillway crest elevation 3,634.7 feet above mean sea level. Water is not diverted directly from the lake, but the water in storage recharges, by infiltration, a series of ten wells that are pumped for the city supply. Because runoff is insufficient to keep the lake full, on several occasions there has been no storage. The drainage area above the dam measures 982 square miles, of which 920 square miles are probably noncontributing. The lake is located in flat to rolling country with local escarpments and a surface of fine sandy loams that support brush and grasses.

BIBLIOGRAPHY: Duane F. Guy, ed., *The Story of Palo Duro Canyon* (Canyon, Texas: Panhandle-Plains Historical Society, 1979). Mrs. Clyde W. Warwick, comp., *The Randall County Story* (Hereford, Texas: Pioneer, 1969). *Seth D. Breeding*

BIZZELL, WILLIAM BENNETT (1876–1944). William Bennett

Bizzell, sociologist and university president, son of George McDuffie and Sara Elizabeth (Wade) Bizzell, was born at Independence, Texas, on October 14, 1876. He received his B.S. and Ph.B. degrees at Baylor University in 1898 and 1900 and his LL.M. and D.C.L. degrees from the Illinois College of Law in 1911 and 1912. In 1921 he received his Ph.D. at Columbia University. On August 16, 1900, Bizzell married Carrie Wray Sangster of Navasota, where he was superintendent of schools from 1900 to 1910. From 1910 to 1914 he was president of the College of Industrial Arts (now Texas Woman's University) at Denton, and from 1914 to 1925 he was president of the Agricultural and Mechanical College of Texas (now Texas A&M University). From College Station Bizzell went to Norman, Oklahoma, to become president of the University of Oklahoma. He held that post until 1941, when he became president emeritus and head of the department of sociology. He was a member of the American Association for the Advancement of Science, the American Sociological Society, and the American Political Science Association, as well as a fellow of the Royal Economic Society of England. On November 16, 1936, he was elected to the Oklahoma Hall of Fame. His published works include *Austinean Theory of Sovereignty* (1912), *Judicial Interpretation of Political Theory* (1914), *Social Teachings of Jewish Prophets* (1916), *Farm Tenantry in the United States* (1921), *Rural Texas* (1923), and *The Green Rising* (1927), as well as textbooks in economics. Bizzell died in Norman, Oklahoma, on May 13, 1944.

BIBLIOGRAPHY: *Who's Who in America*, 1943.

BLACK, EUGENE (1879–1975). Eugene Black, congressman and judge, was born on July 2, 1879, in Blossom, Texas, the son of Alexander Wesley and Talula Ann (Shackelford) Black. The family moved from Lamar County to Clarksville in neighboring Red River County in the early 1890s. In 1905, after receiving a law degree from Cumberland University, Lebanon, Tennessee, he was admitted to the Texas bar. He first practiced law in Clarksville, where he and his brother Ernest began a wholesale grocery business. Their firm, Black Brothers Company, was an early bottler of Coca-Cola.

Between 1905 and 1914 Black built a prosperous law practice, and his other businesses also did well. In 1914 he ran as a Democrat for the United States Congress and won election in the First District of Texas. Citizens of the district enjoyed relative prosperity in the years before and after World War I[qv] as demand improved for agricultural commodities and local small-scale manufacturing increased.

Once in the House, Black became a close ally of John Nance Garner,[qv] a friend of the Black family and one of the most influential Democrats in Congress. Though he was never a flamboyant sponsor of legislation, Black was considered a valuable member of the Texas delegation and held several leadership positions in the state's Democratic caucus. In the 1922 election he was opposed by former populist James H. (Cyclone) Davis,[qv] who attacked Black as a friend of big business and enemy of the small farmer. Black's support of private ownership of the railroads was a particular issue. He won this contest but lost to J. Wright Patman[qv] in 1928. Patman had supported Black in the 1922 election, perhaps because Davis was an outspoken member of the Ku Klux Klan.[qv]

By 1928 economic conditions in Black's district, as in the rest of the rural South, had worsened. Texas Democrats had struggled without much success to aid farmers. In this as well as in enforcement of prohibition,[qv] Black had been supportive but not boisterous. In a 1927 letter to Patman, Atticus Webb, superintendent of the Anti-Saloon League of Texas,[qv] praised Black for being a "sincere prohibitionist" but added, "by nature Mr. Black is not a fighter." Patman's more aggressive and combative manner evidently matched the voters' mood in that difficult year. They listened intently as Patman attacked Black's record in the same style and along the same lines as Davis. Ironically Patman, who subsequently served in Congress until the mid-1970s, also gained votes by claiming it was time to give a younger man a chance. Black lost the election by a vote of 17,938 to 20,886. He won only three of the eleven counties in his district, but he had the satisfaction of carrying the two counties where he was best known, Lamar and Red River, by large margins.

He was soon appointed a judge on what became the United States Tax Court, a job for which his kindness and courtly manner suited him. He was well respected by his peers and wrote many closely studied cases. Black served as a regular member of the court until 1953 and on recall basis until he retired in 1966. By then he was in his mid-eighties but still vigorous. He had represented the First District of Texas in the United States House of Representatives from 1915 to 1929 and served as a judge on the Tax Court of the United States from 1929 to 1966.

Black married Maimie Coleman in 1903. They had six children. One daughter, Margaret, never married and served as Black's secretary through much of his career. The family was active in the Methodist Church[qv] and lived primarily in Washington, D.C., after Black's initial election to Congress. There Black died on May 22, 1975.

BIBLIOGRAPHY: Naples *Monitor*, March 30, 1928. Wright Patman Papers, Lyndon Baines Johnson Library, Austin. Washington *Post*, May 27, 1975. *Who's Who in the South and Southwest*, Vol. 10.

Walter L. Buenger

BLACK, HARRY ALFRED (1866–1935). Harry Alfred Black, civic leader, son of John Henry and Julia Emma (Bunce) Black, was born on August 22, 1866, in New York City. He attended public schools and became connected with the lumber industry.[qv] In 1900 he moved to Houston as general manager of the timber department of the Houston Oil Company. In 1910 he moved to Galveston, where he became head of the Black Hardware Company. Black was president of the Galveston Chamber of Commerce and vice president of the United States Chamber of Commerce and of the International Chamber of Commerce. In January 1923 he went to Europe as a member of a committee on the Dawes Reparation Plan. In 1887 in Chicago he married Ella Maude Smith; they had one son. Black died on September 9, 1935, and was buried in Galveston Memorial Park.

BIBLIOGRAPHY: S. C. Griffin, *History of Galveston, Texas* (Galveston: Cawston, 1931). *Who Was Who in America*, Vol 2.

Kaye A. Walker

BLACK, JAMES HARVEY (1884–1958). J. Harvey Black, allergist and professor, the son of John Adam and Nancy (Murphy) Black, was born on March 27, 1884, in Huntington, West Virginia. He grew up in Paris, Texas, and attended Southwestern University, Dallas Campus, from 1900 to 1902 and Atlanta College of Physicians and Surgeons from 1903 to 1905. He received his M.D. in 1907 at Southwestern Medical School in Dallas (*see* UNIVERSITY OF TEXAS SOUTHWESTERN MEDICAL CENTER). In 1906–07 he interned at St. Paul's Hospital in Dallas. Afterward he continued his training at Montreal (Quebec) General Hospital, the research laboratory of the New York Board of Health, and Philadelphia General Hospital.

In 1907 he began his medical career in Dallas by opening a private clinical-pathology practice; he joined the staff of Southwestern University Medical Department as a professor of bacteriology and pathology and remained until 1915. In 1914 he became dean of the medical school, then under the supervision of Southern Methodist University. He married Arlene Patton on September 4, 1913, in Catlettsburg, Kentucky. They had two daughters.

Baylor University College of Medicine in Dallas employed Black as a professor of bacteriology and pathology, preventive medicine, and clinical medicine from 1915 to 1942. In addition to teaching he remained active in his clinical pathology practice, which in 1932 changed from a general practice to one specializing in allergies. He was an author of several articles dealing with allergies, in addition to coauthoring several books, including *Practice of Allergy* in 1948 and *Primer of*

Allergy in 1950. In Dallas he was consultant at Children's Medical Center after 1930 and Parkland Hospital from 1945.

Black was secretary and chairman of the Dallas Advisory Medical Board under the Selective Service System in 1917–18, a diplomate of the American Board of Internal Medicine, a fellow of the American College of Physicians, and a member of the Texas Medical Association,[qv] the Dallas County Medical Society, the American Public Health Association, the American Association for the Advancement of Science, and the American Medical Association. He was also president of a variety of medical associations, including the American Society of Clinical Pathology (1929–30), the American Association for the Study of Allergy (1934–35), and the Texas Pathology Society (1934–35). He was chairman of the Dallas Interracial Committee and of the medical division of various Dallas social agencies. He was active in the Dallas Council on World Affairs, the Dallas Chamber of Commerce, and the Better Business Bureau. His social activities included the Dallas Philosophical, Town and Gown, Athletic, and Rotary clubs. He was a Mason and Democrat. Black died on November 30, 1958, in Dallas, after suffering a heart attack during the service at Highland Park Presbyterian Church, where he was an elder and a Sunday school teacher.

BIBLIOGRAPHY: Dallas *Morning News*, December 1, 1958. *National Cyclopaedia of American Biography*, Vol. 46. *Texas State Journal of Medicine*, January 1959.

Lisa C. Maxwell

BLACK, JOHN S. (1790–1855). John S. Black, early Texas colonist, participant in the Texas Revolution,[qv] and Indian commissioner, was born in Tennessee in 1790 and settled in Grimes County, Texas, in 1830. Like many other settlers who came to Texas during this time, he came from a family that had taken part in the American Revolution. His father, Gavin Black, was a lieutenant in the American army. His grandfather, George Black, signed the Tryon Declaration of Independence in Raleigh, North Carolina, in 1775. Black staked out his claim on the Coushatta Trace,[qv] on an "open picturesque prairie dotted with small groves of timber and covered with a carpet of tall nutritious grass." His title for a league of this land, later known as Black's Prairie, was granted on April 6, 1831. He later received an adjacent quarter league abandoned by his brother Marcus, who returned to Tennessee.

In 1835 Black served as a cavalryman under the command of Stephen F. Austin.[qv] He and his son Monroe took part in the siege of Bexar[qv] on December 5–9, 1835, under the command of Gen. Edward Burleson.[qv] Black went on to participate in the battle of San Jacinto[qv] as a captain in the quartermaster's corps. In 1838 he received two bounty warrants for land for his service in the Texas army. After independence, he remained in the service of the Republic of Texas[qv] in the quartermaster's depot in Houston. After 1842 he was an Indian commissioner. Under the leadership of Sam Houston,[qv] he worked to gather many Indian groups to persuade them to remain at peace and engage in commerce with the white man. Black was one of three Texas Indian commissioners who met with eight Texas Indian groups on Tehuacana Creek on March 8, 1843. This meeting was a preparation for a larger general council to be held in the fall of that year (*see* TEHUACANA CREEK COUNCILS). On April 10, 1843, Houston authorized a payment of $200 to Black for his services as Indian commissioner in the fall and winter of 1842, as well as $175 for his continued service on the Texas frontier.

Black was a devoted Mason who tried to settle his area exclusively by Masons. His name is listed on a monument under the old Masonic Oak in Brazoria. He died in 1855 and was buried on a hill near his land, which is today south of a roadside park. His wife, Mary, was buried next to him in 1868.

BIBLIOGRAPHY: Irene Taylor Allen, *Saga of Anderson—The Proud Story of a Historic Texas Community* (New York: Greenwich, 1957). Grimes County Historical Commission, *History of Grimes County, Land of Heritage and Progress* (Dallas: Taylor, 1982).

Gayla Gressett Nicar-Kemp

BLACK, READING WOOD (1830–1867). Reading Wood Black, merchant, county commissioner, Indian commissioner, and legislator, was born on September 23, 1830, in Springfield Township, Burlington County, New Jersey, the son of Thomas and Mary Grey (Wood) Black. At Springfield he attended the Upper Friends' School. In 1847 he became owner and manager of the 144-acre Clover Hill farm in nearby Northampton Township. Influenced by his cousin, Capt. William Reading Montgomery of the Eighth United States Infantry, who was then assigned to Fort Gates, Black moved to Texas in the spring of 1852. On April 14, in partnership with Nathan L. Stratton, who had accompanied him from New Jersey, Black purchased an undivided half league and labor of land near the head of the Leona River at the site of present-day Uvalde. One of his nearest neighbors was William Washington Arnett.[qv] Black entered into stock raising and acquired a thousand head of sheep. He erected a substantial stone building. With the aid of San Antonio lithographer William C. A. Thielepape,[qv] he then laid out a town that he called Encina (now Uvalde). Black also opened a store, cleared a garden, and operated a limekiln and two rock quarries. On June 12, 1854, he purchased an additional 640 acres in order to accommodate more stock and expand his town. In 1858 he built a gristmill, and by 1860 he owned a wagon train that freighted between San Antonio and Piedras Negras. As Uvalde's population grew between 1856 and 1861, Black prospered, and on January 6, 1859, he married Permilia Jane McKinney.

Black was a Quaker. He was remarkably friendly to local Indians, especially the Tonkawas, and on several occasions helped to formulate treaties with the various groups living on or near the Rio Grande. He was not entirely a pacifist, however, but helped to organize and commanded a militia company for protection against marauding Comanches in 1856. In June of that year his company and one from the Sabinal area defeated a Comanche war party some thirty miles below Uvalde, thus effectively stopping Indian raids for two years.

In September 1855 he established the first school in what is now Uvalde County, and in November he successfully lobbied the state legislature to organize Uvalde County and have his town named the county seat. On April 21, 1856, he was elected county commissioner. On May 12 he and his fellow commissioners completed formal organization and on June 14 named Encina county seat. Black was reelected county commissioner in 1858 and elected county judge in 1860. Although opposed to secession,[qv] he took the oath of allegiance to the Confederate States of America and continued doing business as usual until the murder of a number of prisoners by Confederate militiamen after the battle of the Nueces,[qv] on August 10, 1862. Repulsed by the anti-Unionist activities of Confederate home guards, Black moved to Mexico and remained there until the end of the Civil War.[qv] By then he had amassed $50,000 worth of property in Coahuila. In June 1866 he was the Unionist nominee for Congress from the Seventy-first District. He easily defeated Samuel A. Maverick[qv] and S. C. Thompson, then returned to Uvalde in July 1866 in anticipation of the opening of the legislature in August. In the legislature he strongly supported ratification of the Fourteenth Amendment, arguing that the Texas failure to support the amendment would be interpreted by the Radical Republicans as a sign of disloyalty to the Union. Black did not stand for reelection when his term expired in November 1866. In September 1867 he attempted to form a Union League[qv] in Uvalde. This "act of disloyalty" to Texas and the South so incensed his former friend G. W. (Tom) Wall that on the morning of October 3 Wall murdered Black in his own store in the presence of several witnesses. Wall fled to Mexico and never returned to Texas. Black's papers, preserved in the Barker Texas History Center[qv] at the University of Texas, were edited in 1933 by Ike Moore and published as *The Life and Diary of Reading Wood Black.*

Thomas W. Cutrer

BLACK, RUBY AURORA (1896–1957). Ruby Aurora Black, journalist and biographer of Eleanor Roosevelt, was born on September 14, 1896, in Thornton, Texas, the daughter of George Washington and Cornelia (Long) Black. Her father, a cotton farmer and politician who served a term in the Texas legislature and was the mayor of Thornton, encouraged an interest in politics in his daughter. Ruby attended Sweetwater High School and the University of Colorado, then entered the University of Texas in 1913, but a series of schoolteaching and newspaper jobs prevented her from graduating until 1921. She graduated Phi Beta Kappa. As an undergraduate, she was a reporter for the student newspaper, the *Daily Texan*,[qv] and later became its first female editor in chief. She was president of the Sidney Lanier[qv] Literary Society, and her prominent participation in writing, editing, and campus life earned her the sobriquet "the Colonel House of varsity politics" in the university yearbook.

Her first newspaper job was for the Thornton *Hustler* in 1917, for which she set type, sold advertising, addressed delivery wrappers, and wrote news stories, editorials, and columns. While she was there she became the local leader of supporters for Gov. William P. Hobby[qv] in his reelection bid against former governor James E. Ferguson,[qv] though her editor supported Ferguson. After graduating from college she moved to Chicago to manage the Women's National Journalistic Register, a placement bureau sponsored by the journalism society Theta Sigma Phi. From 1921 to 1923 she taught journalism and completed two years of graduate study in economics and related fields at the University of Wisconsin. In September 1922 she married Herbert Little, a reporter for the United Press syndicate, and the couple moved to St. Louis, where Ruby became the St. Louis *Times*'s labor editor. In 1924 Little's work took them to Washington, D.C., where Ruby found employment difficult to secure. Eventually, she established the Ruby A. Black News Bureau in 1928 and with fewer than five reporters provided news service to approximately twenty papers in Puerto Rico and seven states, including Texas.

A tiny, short-haired woman who was once mistaken for a boy, Ruby Black found that some of her most difficult work was convincing others that a woman could be a good journalist. "The toughest part of a woman's work in Washington journalism," she once said, "is to get a job." She joined the National Woman's Party, the Birth Control League, the Society of Women Geographers, and the Woman's National Press Club, of which she was later president. She also edited *Equal Rights Magazine* and received national attention for her dispute with the United States Department of State to allow her to use her birth name on her passport. She is regarded as the first woman to win such permission. She was also a member of the Texas Folklore Society[qv] and national president of Theta Sigma Phi.

Ruby Black became a White House correspondent for United Press in 1933 and covered Eleanor Roosevelt's activities for the next seven years. Her biography of Roosevelt appeared in 1940 and won the National Headliner award from Theta Sigma Phi in 1941. Researching and writing the book consumed so much of her time and finances that she gave up her news bureau to finish it. "I'm busted," she said when it was over. She then went to work as an information specialist for the Office of Inter-American Affairs, where she pursued her interests in Latin America and served as a liaison to the White House. She retired in ill health, perhaps suffering from epilepsy, in 1947. She and Little were divorced in 1955; the couple had one daughter. Ruby Black died on December 15, 1957, in Washington, the victim of a fire, possibly caused by a cigarette.

BIBLIOGRAPHY: *Alcalde* (magazine of the Ex-Students' Association of the University of Texas), March 1941. Ruby A. Black Papers, Manuscript Division, Library of Congress, Washington. Washington *Post*, December 16, 1957. *Who Was Who in America*, Vol. 3.

Nancy Baker Jones

BLACK, WILLIAM LESLIE (1843–1931). William Leslie (Colonel) Black, soldier, cattleman, author, businessman, adventurer, and promoter of Angora goats, the son of Charles and Agnes (Sewell) Black, was born in New Orleans in 1843. His father was a cotton broker of Scottish and English ancestry. Black left school at an early age to work for his father, joined the Confederate Army, and was wounded at Shiloh. After his recovery he served in the Confederate Navy, in which he ran cotton through the Union blockade to England. He was also part of an expedition against the Union Navy on the Pacific coast, was captured and imprisoned at Fort Alcatraz, and was sentenced to be hanged as a pirate but was pardoned.

After the Civil War[qv] he lived in the Bahamas and New York, grew wealthy, helped to found the New York Cotton Exchange, traveled extensively, married Camilla Bogert in 1869, began raising his family of ten children, and in 1875 moved to St. Louis. The next year he purchased a ranch near Fort McKavett on the San Saba River in Texas. He remained in St. Louis for several years, however, as an absentee landlord while others worked the ranch, on which he grazed cattle and sheep. Annually he made a trip to West Texas to inspect his property. When he learned that his herders preferred goat meat to mutton, he purchased a small flock of goats to supply his men. By 1884, when with his family he moved permanently to the ranch, he had discovered the value of Angoras, a better breed that brought more money than his common species. Knowing that he could upgrade his stock by introducing full-blooded Angora sires, he bought eight males and four females. After a few years of breeding, Black had increased his flock enough to justify shearing the animals to sell the mohair as he sold wool.

In the mid-1890s, goat and mohair growers widely recognized Black as the nation's leading authority on Angoras. Two developments were largely responsible. First, in 1893 he realized that his herd of 8,000 browsing animals had to be reduced or it would overrun his ranch. Accordingly, he contacted an acquaintance with Armour and Company in Chicago, offering to sell 1,000 fat wethers at the company's price. Declining for the company, the friend informed Black that goat meat was not popular among its customers and did not sell. His friend advised slaughtering the goats for their hides and tallow and packing the meat in cans. Thus was born on Black's ranch the Range Canning Company, one of the first meat-packing operations, rendering plants, and tanneries of goat hides in West Texas. The second development was Black's promotion of the Angora goat industry. He studied the goat and its habits and forage, making careful notes about its routines. He read all he could about the animal. He wrote a booklet about Angoras in the 1890s, in which he called upon Texas farmers and ranchers to take advantage of the commercial opportunities offered by goat raising, "this new, and valuable, industry." In response he received scores of inquiries asking all manner of questions. Such spirited response encouraged Black to write more. The result was publication in 1900 of a book on the Angora goat and mohair industry, *A New Industry—or Raising the Angora Goat*, which proved to be a favorite manual and textbook for more than forty years. Black's contributions to the industry helped to make the Edwards Plateau[qv] an economically productive region.

In addition to this more important work, Black invented a cotton picker, patented a "special guide" for windmills, invented his Little Wonder Nut Sheller for use especially on his home-grown pecans, secured with others a futures market for wool trading, and continued his writing. He died four weeks after a paralytic stroke, on May 11, 1931. *See also* WOOL AND MOHAIR INDUSTRY.

BIBLIOGRAPHY: Paul H. Carlson, *Texas Woolybacks: The Range Sheep and Goat Industry* (College Station: Texas A&M University Press, 1982). Edith Black Winslow, *In Those Days: Memoirs of Edwards Plateau* (San Antonio: Naylor, 1950).

Paul H. Carlson

BLACK, TEXAS. Black, on U.S. Highway 60 in northeastern Parmer County, was established in 1898 as a station on the Pecos Valley and

Northern Texas Railway. It was named for E. B. Black, who in 1901 purchased farmland north of the railroad from his brother-in-law, J. E. English. In 1908 the Wright Land Company began selling XIT Ranch[qv] lands, and buyers came in on the company's special excursion trains. In 1910 a school was opened in Black, and a post office was established in 1912, with J. Baker as postmaster. The post office was discontinued twice, in 1914 and 1920, then reestablished in 1926. For a time sweet potatoes were grown commercially around Black. In 1921 Ray Conway opened a grocery store, a portion of which was used for church services and community gatherings. After the Black school district was consolidated with the Friona schools in 1950, the former school building was remodeled into a community center. A mercantile store was also a focal point until it closed in 1981 after owner Les Deaton retired. Nevertheless, the Black community has remained active through various social clubs, youth organizations, and its annual Thanksgiving dinner. Grain elevators dominate the town, which in 1980 reported four businesses and in 1990 a population of 100.

BIBLIOGRAPHY: Parmer County Historical Commission, *Prairie Progress* (Dallas: Taylor, 1981). Parmer County Historical Society, *A History of Parmer County* (Quanah, Texas: Nortex, 1974).

H. Allen Anderson

BLACK ANKLE, TEXAS. Black Ankle is on a country road off Farm Road 3153 six miles east of San Augustine in northeastern San Augustine County. In 1940 the community had the Black Ankle school and a number of scattered dwellings. By 1988 all that remained at the site was a church. *Mark Odintz*

BLACK BAYOU. Black Bayou rises near Springdale Cemetery in northeastern Cass County (at 33°13′ N, 94°10′ W) and runs southeast for twenty-four miles to its mouth on Soda Lake in Caddo Parish, Louisiana, just south of the Louisiana-Arkansas state line (at 32°42′ N, 93°55′ W). The stream is intermittent in its upper reaches. It traverses flat to gently rolling terrain surfaced by sandy and clay loam that supports grasses and mixed hardwoods and pines.

BLACK BEAN EPISODE. The Black Bean Episode, an aftermath of the Mier Expedition,[qv] resulted from an attempted escape of the captured Texans as they were being marched from Mier to Mexico City. After an escape at Salado, Tamaulipas, on February 11, 1843, some 176 of the men were recaptured within about a week. A decree that all who participated in the break were to be executed was modified to an order to kill every tenth man. Col. Domingo Huerta was to be in charge of the decimation. The victims were chosen by lottery, each man drawing a bean from an earthen jar containing 176 beans, seventeen black beans being the tokens signifying death. Commissioned officers were ordered to draw first; then the enlisted men were called as their names appeared on the muster rolls. William A. A. (Bigfoot) Wallace,[qv] standing close to the scene of the drawing, decided that the black beans were the larger and fingered the tokens successfully to draw a white bean. Observers of the drawing later described the dignity, the firmness, the light temper, and general courage of the men who drew the beans of death. Some left messages for their families with their companions; a few had time to write letters home. The doomed men were unshackled from their companions, placed in a separate courtyard, and shot at dusk on March 25, 1843. The seventeen victims of the lottery were James Decatur Cocke, William Mosby Eastland, Patrick Mahan, James M. Ogden, James N. Torrey, Martin Carroll Wing,[qqv] John L. Cash, Robert Holmes Dunham, Edward E. Este, Robert Harris, Thomas L. Jones, Christopher Roberts, William N. Rowan, James L. Shepherd, J. N. M. Thompson, James Turnbull, and Henry Walling. Shepherd survived the firing squad by pretending to be dead. The guards left him for dead in the courtyard, and he escaped in the night but was recaptured and shot. In 1848 the bodies were returned from Mexico to be buried at Monument Hill,[qv] near La Grange, Fayette County.

BIBLIOGRAPHY: John Crittenden Duval, *The Adventures of Big Foot Wallace, the Texas Ranger and Hunter* (Macon, Georgia: Burke, 1870). Thomas J. Green, *Journal of the Texian Expedition Against Mier* (New York: Harper, 1845; rpt., Austin: Steck, 1935). Sam W. Haynes, *Soldiers of Misfortune: The Somervell and Mier Expeditions* (Austin: University of Texas Press, 1990). Harold Schoen, comp., *Monuments Erected by the State of Texas to Commemorate the Centenary of Texas Independence* (Austin: Commission of Control for Texas Centennial Celebrations, 1938). Houston Wade, *Notes and Fragments of the Mier Expedition* (La Grange, Texas: La Grange *Journal*, 1936).

BLACKBERRY CREEK. Blackberry Creek rises in Dundee, in northwestern Archer County (at 33°45′ N, 98°54′ W), and flows north for just over ten miles to its mouth on the Wichita River, near the Wichita county line (at 33°50′ N, 98°54′ W). The stream, intermittent in its upper reaches, traverses gently rolling land surfaced by clay and sandy loams that support scrub brush, mesquite, cacti, and grasses. For most of the county's history, the Blackberry Creek area has been used as range and crop land. Early settlers often referred to the stream as Bobs Creek.

BIBLIOGRAPHY: Glenn A. Gray, *Gazetteer of Streams of Texas* (Washington: GPO, 1919).

BLACKBURN, EPHRAIM (1754–1807). Ephraim Blackburn, a member of Philip Nolan's[qv] botched expedition, son of James and Mary Blackburn, was born in 1754 and reared in West Nottingham Township, Pennsylvania. He was a Quaker but nonetheless commanded a company in the American Revolution. He married Prudence Rich. Blackburn gave his home state as Maryland in 1801, when he entered Texas above Nacogdoches as a member of Nolan's expedition. Blackburn was captured with the Nolan party and imprisoned at Chihuahua. When Spanish authorities decreed that one man of the nine survivors of the expedition should be killed, dice were thrown to determine who should be hanged. Blackburn, the oldest man in the group, cast the dice first and threw the low number. He was hanged in the Plaza de los Urangas in Chihuahua City, Mexico, on November 11, 1807.

BIBLIOGRAPHY: Edward Everett Hale, "The Real Philip Nolan," *Publications of the Mississippi Historical Society* 4 (1901). Edward Everett Hale, *Philip Nolan's Friends: A Story of the Change of Western Empire* (New York: Scribner, Armstrong, 1877). Maurine T. Wilson, Philip Nolan and His Activities in Texas (M.A. thesis, University of Texas, 1932). Maurine T. Wilson and Jack Jackson, *Philip Nolan and Texas: Expeditions into the Unknown Land, 1791–1801* (Waco: Texian Press, 1987). *Kaye A. Walker*

BLACKBURN, JAMES KNOX POLK (1837–1923). James Blackburn, soldier, was born in Maury County, Tennessee, in 1837 and moved with his family to Texas in 1856. He attended Alma Institute[qv] in Lavaca County for two years and then taught school until 1861. He joined the force under Benjamin McCulloch[qv] that accepted the surrender of Gen. David E. Twiggs[qv] in San Antonio. Shortly afterward he enlisted in a company of cavalry drawn from Fayette, Lavaca, and Colorado counties, which became one of the elements of the Eighth Texas Cavalry,[qv] or Terry's Texas Rangers. Blackburn was elected first lieutenant of his company a few weeks after the battle of Shiloh and soon became captain. He served with his command in all major engagements until the battle of Farmington, on October 7, 1863, when he was seriously wounded with a point-blank shot that passed through both thighs. He refused to permit the surgeon to amputate and fell into the hands of the enemy but was paroled for hospitalization. After a severe illness and a long period of recovery, he was finally able to return to the rangers in February 1865, but could not assume command until he had been properly exchanged. His exchange was not validated until the surrender of Joseph E. Johnston's[qv] army. Blackburn had spent his period of recuperation in Tennessee, and he decided to settle there, in Giles County, where he married Mary McMillan Laird. He became the owner of a plantation and for some time also represented the area in the Tennessee legislature. He died on July 6, 1923. Blackburn's *Reminiscences of the Terry Rangers,* one of the few accounts of service in the rangers by a participant, was published in the *Southwestern Historical Quarterly*[qv] in 1918 and reprinted separately in 1979.

BIBLIOGRAPHY: Leonidas B. Giles, *Terry's Texas Rangers* (Austin: Von Boeckmann–Jones, 1911). *Nowlin Randolph*

BLACK CATHOLICS. The first blacks to arrive in what is now the United States came with the Spaniards and were Spanish-speaking members of the Catholic Church.[qv] Estevanico,[qv] the first known black Catholic in Texas, was a guide and interpreter for Álvar Núñez Cabeza de Vaca.[qv] Estevanico came to Texas about 1528, nearly 100 years before the first slaves arrived at Jamestown. When Cabeza de Vaca's ship was wrecked, Estevanico led the survivors inland. One by one they died. Estevanico learned much from the Spanish clergy and was admired for his linguistic and medical skills, which enabled him to live among the Indians for eight years. The Indians killed him, however, in 1539. Though Estavanico's life was short and his immediate influence was not large, his historical role as the first black Catholic in Texas is significant. The area he traversed later comprised the state's busiest slave ports, as well as the port in which emancipation was announced, Galveston (*see* JUNETEENTH).

Estevanico's numerous successors over the next three centuries are largely nameless. Although some black Americans became Catholic under the influence of their owners, it is very likely that many blacks were Catholic in their native Africa and brought their faith with them to this country. The Catholic religion had flourished in Africa since biblical times; the New Testament records an apostolic incursion into sub-Saharan Africa. Though Europeans largely thought of slaves as pagans, some slaves may actually have converted their masters to Catholicism.

Louisiana has been a major source of black Catholics in Texas. Slaves were baptized by the Catholic French in that state as early as 1699. Shortly before the Civil War,[qv] 60 percent of the country's black Catholics resided in Louisiana; in the early 1990s two-thirds of the South's black Catholics still lived there. During the Civil War[qv] large numbers of slaves, many of them Catholic, were brought from Louisiana. Later, other black Catholics migrated from Louisiana, sometimes in large numbers. In 1927 a great flood of the Mississippi River sent blacks fleeing to Crosby, Texas. Because so many of them were Catholic, by 1936 a mission, Blessed Martin de Porres, was established for the former Louisianans in Crosby. In 1951, as industrial opportunities began to increase in Houston, another large influx of black Louisiana Catholics moved to Houston and surrounding areas. That year, the Diocese of Galveston had the fifth-largest black Catholic population among United States dioceses.

Statewide, numerous communities have contributed to the history of black Catholics in Texas. There have been at least thirty-five predominantly black parishes in Texas during the last century. In addition to the Houston-Galveston area, Washington-on-the-Brazos, Corpus Christi, Dallas and Fort Worth, Austin, and several East Texas communities have supported black Catholic parishes and missions. The mission at Washington-on-the-Brazos, the earliest known such group in the state, was founded in 1849. In 1840 plantation owner Malcolm Spain, a Catholic Mississippian, had brought a large group of blacks to the Brazos River country in Washington Country. The mission, now known as Blessed Virgin Mission, is part of the Catholic Diocese of Austin[qv] and serves about forty families.

An emphasis on ministry to black Catholics in Texas coincided with the Third Plenary Council of Baltimore in 1884. The council established annual Negro and Indian missions collections among American Catholics—collections that are still taken—and set up a commission to oversee the distribution of funds. In Houston the first known black parish was established in October 1887 by Bishop Nicholas A. Gallagher[qv] of Galveston. He dedicated a small elementary school in the city's Third Ward for the education of black children. At the time, nearly 10,500 of Houston's estimated 28,000 residents were black. Over 100 years later, on February 19, 1988, Louisiana native Curtis Guillory, the first black Catholic bishop in Texas, was installed as auxiliary bishop of the Catholic Diocese of Galveston-Houston.[qv]

St. Peter Claver Church was founded in San Antonio in 1888 by an Irish priest who disliked the fact that blacks had to sit in the rear of churches. Although black Catholics in San Antonio were not numerous, their number grew until, in 1915, there were three predominantly black churches in the city. In 1889 Holy Rosary Church of Galveston was founded. An important community was established in Ames in 1890, when black Catholics from Louisiana began migrating to this community. Our Mother of Mercy Church was started there in 1910.

From 1900 until the 1950s Catholicism was growing in other parts of the state as well. As the black population of Central and North Texas grew, the number of black Catholics in these areas increased. The older rural black Catholic communities continued to exist, though they were losing numbers. In Austin, Holy Cross Catholic Church was founded in 1936. The parish also included a school and a hospital, the first black Catholic hospital in Texas. The hospital presented an important opportunity that extended beyond the Catholic community of Austin: it provided black women an opportunity to study nursing and gave black doctors a place to practice (*see* CATHOLIC HEALTH CARE).

Catholic schools played a key role in trying to foster integration. In the 1940s San Antonio archbishop Robert E. Lucey[qv] promoted integrated meetings and competitions between black and white schools. By 1954 at least 100 black students went to white Catholic schools in the San Antonio area. During the 1956–57 school year there were over 1,100 blacks in twenty-four integrated Catholic schools in Texas.

Several religious orders have been important in the history of black Catholics in Texas, especially the Dominican Sisters, the Jesuits, the Oblates of Mary Immaculate, the Congregation of Holy Cross,[qqv] the Society of the Divine Word, and the Josephite Fathers. Particularly noteworthy in the earliest years were the Josephites and the Holy Cross order. Black Catholics have also been developed and sustained by the Knights and Ladies of St. Peter Claver. Claver leaders have provided support for black parishes and raised money to help black men and women pursue vocations.

Individuals have also made outstanding contributions. Fr. John Henry Dorsey was the second black Josephite priest in America and the first known black priest in Texas. Fr. Joseph John of the Society of African Missions of Lyons traveled to Corpus Christi in 1926 and returned to his native Trinidad in 1929. In the early 1990s Fr. George Artis, pastor of Holy Cross parish in Austin and a Divine Word priest, was a leader of black Texas Catholics.

Historically, both blacks and Catholics have met stiff opposition from some white Texans, ranging from general aversion to Ku Klux Klan[qv] violence. If this situation had been averted, the antislavery teaching intrinsic to the Catholic faith might have been more influential in Texas culture. Segregation helped to determine where and how black parishes began in Texas. The effect of integration on their development is, however, unknown. Black Catholic ranks in Texas have been gradually supplemented by migration from other parts of the country, particularly the North. The influx was especially heavy from the late 1960s to the early 1980s. The majority of black parishes remain predominantly black and preserve rich traditions. The renewed emphasis in the Catholic Church upon welcoming the cultural gifts of all peoples, together with continued condemnation of racism, offers a propitious climate for growth. In 1993, of the two million black Catholics nationwide, approximately 54,000 lived in Texas. The largest number resided in the Houston-Galveston Area. *See also* AFRICAN AMERICANS.

BIBLIOGRAPHY: Carolyn Arrington, *Black Explorer in Texas: Estevanico* (Austin: Eakin Press, 1986). Alwyn Barr, *Black Texans: A History of Negroes in Texas, 1528–1971* (Austin: Jenkins, 1973). Carlos E. Castañeda, *Our Catholic Heritage in Texas* (7 vols., Austin: Von Boeckmann–Jones, 1936–58; rpt., New York: Arno, 1976). Vertical Files, Barker Texas History Center, University of Texas at Austin. Catholic Church. *Roxanne J. Evans*

BLACK CODES. Black Codes were the laws passed by Southern state legislatures to define the legal place of blacks in society after the Civil War.[qv] In Texas the Eleventh Legislature produced these codes in 1866. The intent of the legislation was to reaffirm the inferior position that slaves and free blacks had held in antebellum Texas[qv] and to regulate black labor. The codes reflected the unwillingness of white Texans to accept blacks as equals and also their fears that freedmen would not work unless coerced. Thus the codes continued legal discrimination between whites and blacks. The legislature, when it amended the 1856 penal code, emphasized the continuing line between whites and blacks by defining all individuals with one-eighth or more African blood as persons of color, subject to special provisions in the law.

A variety of sources provided the pattern of the new codes. Antebellum southern laws that regulated free blacks and the laws of northern states designed to do the same furnished the model for regulation of black civil rights, while directives of the Freedmen's Bureau[qv] and the legislation of other Southern states supplied examples of statutes that attempted to control black labor.

An "Act to define and declare the rights of persons lately known as Slaves, and Free Persons of Color" (1866) functioned as the keystone of the state's civil rights legislation. This law gave blacks, in common, basic property rights. They could make and enforce contracts; sue and be sued; make wills; and lease, hold, or dispose of real and personal property. The state further guaranteed blacks the rights of personal security and liberty and prohibited discrimination against them in criminal law. This act, however, specifically left in effect a variety of earlier legal restrictions. Blacks were not allowed to vote or hold office, they could not serve on juries, and they could testify only in cases involving other blacks. They could not marry whites.

These restrictions were supplemented by other legislation. The state required railroads to provide separate accommodations for blacks, thus establishing the precedent for segregation in public facilities. An education law specifically excluded blacks from sharing in the public school fund. The state's homestead law prohibited the distribution of public land to blacks.

Laws designed to reestablish control over black workers were more complex, since the legislature faced the problem of securing this goal without restoring slavery.[qv] The result was a set of interrelated statutes that gave local authorities and landowners the ability to coerce free labor with the threat of forced labor. Although many of these laws made no specific mention of race, they were primarily aimed at and enforced against blacks. The first law passed to accomplish the legislature's goal was the apprentice law. This act made possible the apprenticing of minors, either with parental consent or through the order of the county court. They required masters to provide food, clothing, medical attention, humane treatment, and education for some trade or occupation, which could include farm labor. In turn, a master had the use of the apprentice's labor and the power to inflict corporal punishment to ensure work. The law allowed masters to pursue runaways and levied heavy fines against persons who interfered with apprentice obligations. Exclusive jurisdiction over enforcement of this law rested with the county court.

The contract law also strengthened the position of local economic interests. Under it, all labor agreements that involved work for more than one month had to be in writing and filed with the county court. Workers were given a lien on half a crop to ensure the payment of wages. Employers, however, were given strong guarantees for the delivery of labor, particularly in the power to deduct wages for such contract violations as disobedience, waste of time, theft or destruction of property, or absence from home without permission. Local control over contract issues was certain, for authority over these matters was given to a court consisting of a local justice of the peace and two landowners.

A vagrancy law allowed local courts to arrest people whom they defined as idle, fine them, and contract their labor if they could not pay the fine. Under this law minor vagrants could be apprenticed. Local courts received the power to put such convicts to work at any type of labor until the fine was paid. Local authorities received even more power by a law that authorized them to put to work at any employment persons sentenced to county jails for any misdemeanor or petty offence. The vagrancy law and the convict-labor law provided the key means of intimidating freedmen into either apprentice or contract labor.

The black codes never fully accomplished their goals. On January 3, 1867, Gen. Joseph B. Kiddoo[qv] of the Freedmen's Bureau declared the contract law biased against freedmen and prevented its enforcement. This made the other labor codes useless. Restrictions on civil rights crumbled with the beginning of congressional Reconstruction[qv] in March 1867 and the registration of blacks as voters. Only segregation survived, despite attacks upon the practice throughout Reconstruction. The most immediate effect of the codes thus had been not to accomplish any of their intended results, but to hasten the end of presidential Reconstruction and lead to new federal intervention under the direction of Congress.

BIBLIOGRAPHY: John P. Carrier, A Political History of Texas during Reconstruction, 1865–1874 (Ph.D. dissertation, Vanderbilt University, 1971). Charles W. Ramsdell, *Reconstruction in Texas* (New York: Columbia University Press, 1910; rpt., Austin: Texas State Historical Association, 1970). James Smallwood, *Time of Hope, Time of Despair: Black Texans during Reconstruction* (London: Kennikat, 1981). Theodore B. Wilson, *The Black Codes of the South* (University, Alabama: University of Alabama Press, 1965). *Carl H. Moneyhon*

BLACK COLLEGES. After the Civil War,[qv] black Texans discovered that the abolition of slavery[qv] did not carry with it any guarantee of social, political, or economic equality. This became painfully evident during the course of Reconstruction[qv] as many white Texans refused to accept African Americans[qv] as equals, and worked systematically to keep them in a segregated, second-class status, as near to slavery as possible. Especially troubling were the actions of Texas lawmakers who, between 1866 and 1900, erected an elaborate network of segregation laws that effectively deprived blacks of their rights as citizens. Beginning with the Constitution of 1866,[qv] laws were written barring blacks from voting, holding public office, and serving on juries. Laws segregating public facilities, such as railroad cars, theaters, restaurants and hotels, also appeared. Not surprisingly, statutes were also passed ensuring that the state's educational system was kept separate and, it was obvious, unequal. During the 1870s and 1880s many white Texans were opposed to the idea of providing extensive educational opportunities for blacks. They also were against the idea of integrating the public schools. Many held strong convictions, reinforced by the works of several popular nineteenth-century social scientists, that blacks were intellectually inferior to whites and unable to master more than the most basic of educational skills. Such individuals argued that providing higher education to the former slaves was a waste of the state's resources. Others feared that education would make blacks difficult to control or would reduce the pool of cheap agricultural and industrial labor. Some were concerned about the social interaction and intermarriage that might result from school integration.

In spite of opposition, however, efforts to further black educational opportunities moved forward. During the initial phase of Reconstruction, the Freedmen's Bureau[qv] took the lead in establishing elementary and secondary schools for the former slaves. By May 1866 the bureau had set up more than 100 schools across the state. Though staffed primarily by white Southerners, bureau schools were an affront to many white Texans and were the object of much criticism and hostility. Where funds and volunteers permitted, white Northern religious denominations also established elementary and secondary schools. Groups such as the Freedmen's Aid Society, the American Missionary Association, and the American Baptist Home Mission Society were in the vanguard of these early efforts. Such black communions as the African Methodist Episcopal Church[qv] and the Colored Methodist Episcopal Church sought to Christianize and educate the former slaves. Northern philanthropists and the churches soon realized, however, that little headway would be made until Texas had a large cadre of black leaders, including teachers. This required that the benefits of higher education be made available to the black population. The 1870s and 1880s were a dramatic and somewhat romantic period in the history of black higher education. Driven by religious and moral zeal, Northern missionary and religious groups established dozens of colleges across the South. In most states, the efforts of these groups predated the establishment of public black colleges. This was the case in Texas, where the first black private college was established in 1872, while the state's first public black college did not appear until 1878.

The first black college established in Texas was Paul Quinn College, founded in Austin in 1872 by a small group of circuit-riding pastors of the AME Church and named for a bishop who served the church on the western frontier from 1844 until his death in 1873. The college was founded to develop ministers and train freedmen to assume the duties and responsibilities of citizenship. After operating unsuccessfully in a church building for five years, the school was moved to Waco, where it struggled to survive as a trade school. There students were offered courses in blacksmithing, carpentry, tanning, saddlery, and other basic skills.

Wiley College was established in Marshall in 1873 by the Freedmen's Aid Society of the Methodist Episcopal Church. Together with the Methodist Episcopal Church, the society sought to prepare African Americans for citizenship through a wide range of educational and relief efforts. By 1869 it had founded fifty-nine elementary schools across nine Southern states. By 1878 the society had founded twenty colleges, seminaries, or medical schools in eleven Southern states. Wiley College was named for one of the society's foremost figures, Bishop Isaac D. Wiley, a Pennsylvanian who gained prominence in the Methodist Episcopal Church as a missionary in China, and as a minister in New York, New Jersey, Pennsylvania. When the Civil War began, Wiley was a vocal supporter of the Union war effort and the drive to abolish slavery. At the end of the war he involved himself in efforts to Christianize and educate the former slaves. Wiley was a charter member of the Freedmen's Aid Society, and went on to serve as its vice president and president.

Tillotson College, established in Austin in 1877, was originally named Tillotson Collegiate and Normal Institute. It opened to students in January 1881. The school was founded by the American Missionary Association and initially offered elementary, secondary, and college training. Tillotson was only one of several educational ventures sponsored by the AMA, which was itself the result of a merger in 1847 of several white Northern missionary groups. Before and after the Civil War, the AMA worked to eliminate caste limitations and was active in the promotion of education. Beginning in 1858, the AMA established eight colleges, including Atlanta University, Fisk University, and Hampton Institute. Tillotson College was named for George Jeffrey Tillotson, a retired Congregationalist minister from Hartford, Connecticut, who raised over $16,000 and purchased several acres of land in Austin for the establishment of a collegiate and normal school.

State-supported higher education for African Americans began in 1878 with the foundation of Prairie View State Normal School (now Prairie View A&M University). The school came about as a result of the Morrill Act of 1866. Prairie View A&M, located between Hempstead and Houston, was established to provide agricultural and vocational training to blacks. As a part of Texas A&M University, it received part of the federal funds designated for land-grant colleges in Texas. In the 1880s, Prairie View expanded its curriculum to include teacher training. Since many whites were opposed to more extensive educational offerings for blacks, Prairie View remained essentially an agricultural, vocational, and normal school until 1901. Before that time Prairie View was hardly the branch university promised in the Constitution of 1876.[qv] Many black leaders thought the constitution had promised a classical university similar to the University of Texas. Although a black university was proposed and authorized by ballot in 1882, no action was taken by the Texas legislature to begin construction. While blacks pressured legislators to found a university, most whites lobbied lawmakers simply to expand the role of Prairie View. In 1897, as pressure increased from such groups as the Colored Teachers State Association of Texas (*see* TEACHERS STATE ASSOCIATION OF TEXAS), the legislature passed a bill authorizing the use of 50,000 acres of public land for the establishment and maintenance of a black state university at Austin. The Texas Supreme Court, however, in *Hogue v. Baker* (1898), invalidated the action by prohibiting the land commissioner from appropriating more land for educational purposes (*see* LAND APPROPRIATIONS FOR EDUCATION). By 1899 it became clear that a separate black university would not be built. In 1901, Prairie View was authorized to begin teaching college courses in classical and scientific studies.

In 1946 state lawmakers began to worry about the implications of a lawsuit involving Heman M. Sweatt,[qv] a graduate of Wiley College who had been denied admission to the law school at the University of Texas. Sweatt filed suit in Texas district court, which ruled that either equal facilities must be provided within six months or Sweatt must be admitted to the University of Texas. The legislature responded by establishing a makeshift law school in Houston. As the famous *Sweatt v. Painter*[qv] case continued to unfold, state leaders decided that a university for blacks was needed to help preserve segregation in higher education. In 1947 the state took over Houston College for Negroes and restructured it as Texas State University for Negroes. In 1951 its name was changed to Texas Southern University.

Bishop College was founded in Marshall in 1881 by the American Baptist Home Mission Society. The society had been founded in 1832 to assist in evangelizing the West. At the beginning of the Civil War the society became interested in the plight of Southern blacks and became a leader in spreading the Gospel and furthering education in the South. By 1881 the society had established five colleges, including Morehouse College, Benedict College, and Bishop College. The drive to found a college for black Baptists in Texas was led by a white educator, Nathan Bishop, a native New Yorker and graduate of Brown University who became an innovator in public education. After his retirement in 1858, Bishop used his wealth and the remaining twenty-two years of his life helping the disadvantaged. In 1872, Rufus C. Burleson,[qv] president of Baylor University, appealed to Bishop for assistance in building a black Baptist college. Several years later, Bishop agreed to help, but died before the funds could be sent. His wife, Carolina Caldwell Bishop, also supported the idea and later contributed $10,000 to the American Baptist Home Mission Society to begin the project. The society sent S. W. Marston, the district secretary, and Allen R. Griggs,[qv] pastor of New Hope Baptist Church in Dallas, to select an appropriate location. After visiting Dallas, Houston, Austin, Marshall, Texarkana, Little Rock, and Shreveport, they settled on Marshall. The decision was prompted by the enthusiasm of the Baptists in East Texas, the dense black population there, and the presence of a black Baptist high school called Centennial College. Local supporters raised $1,600 and purchased ten acres for what was initially called South-Western Baptist College. In 1880, forty more acres were added and the school was renamed Bishop College. The process was completed when Centennial College merged with Bishop, thus giving the new school the nucleus of its first student body.

Guadalupe College, a black-owned and black-operated institution, was founded in 1884 by the Guadalupe Baptist Association. Its first campus was five acres near the county courthouse in Seguin. In 1914 the school was moved to the western edge of town, to a site donated by San Antonio philanthropist George W. Brackenridge.[qv] Guadalupe College sprang from a squabble between the white Baptist Home Mission Society and black Baptist groups in Central and South Texas. Its founding resulted from the society's decision to locate Bishop College in Marshall. Many black Baptists were unhappy that the college had not been founded in their region of the state. In response, black Baptists founded Hearne Academy in 1881, and Houston Academy and Guadalupe College in 1884. Between 1888 and 1893, black Baptists repeatedly asked the Home Mission Society to support both Bishop and Guadalupe College. When the society refused to support more than one college in Texas, black Baptists formed the General Missionary Baptist Convention of Texas and gave their full support to Guadalupe College.

Mary Allen College, in Crockett, was founded in 1886 on ten acres of land provided by local residents. An adjoining 260 acres was later donated by James Snydor of Illinois. The school began in a vacant hotel rented by supporters. The two-year school, originally known as Mary Allen Seminary, was established for the education of black women by the Presbyterian Board of Missions for Freedmen. It was named for Mary E. Allen, wife of the board's secretary. Mrs. Allen had been instrumental in persuading the board to found a school for women in Texas. Largely through the efforts of Samuel Fisher Tenney,[qv] pastor of the First Presbyterian Church in Crockett, the Board of Missions picked Crockett as the site of the college.

Texas College, on 101 acres of land just north of Tyler, was organized in 1894 under the auspices of the Colored Methodist Episcopal Church. In 1909, the college was renamed Phillips University, in honor of the exceptional service of CME bishop Henry Phillips. Supporters objected to the new name, and the college took back its original name in 1917. Texas College became the state's third black-controlled institution to be founded by a black church.

In March 1898 the Episcopal Church established St. Philip's College in San Antonio. St. Philip's was one of only four black colleges founded by the Episcopalians. These schools ultimately fell under the control of the American Church Institute for Negroes, which was established in 1906 to promote educational activities for the church. St. Philip's was unique because its founders did envision it as a center for liberal-arts instruction. Instead, it began as a vocational institution and has remained one for most of its history. The person most closely responsible for the foundation of the school was Rev. James Steptoe Johnston,[qv] bishop of the Missionary District of Western Texas. Concerned that the Episcopal Church had done little to further the education of blacks, Johnston determined to establish an institution in San Antonio. In 1897 he organized a girls' sewing class in the rectory of St. Philip's Church. In 1898 he purchased a lot behind the church and commissioned the construction of a two-room schoolhouse. When completed, St. Philip's Industrial School opened with courses in cooking, sewing, and house-cleaning.

In 1900 the Freedmen's Aid Society founded its second college in Texas. The institution capped a twenty-four-year struggle that began in 1876, when Andrews Normal School was opened in Dallas. After failing to attract sufficient support there, Methodist leaders moved the school to Austin. In 1883, Richard S. Rust, secretary of the Freedmen's Aid Society, purchased six acres of land on the east side of Austin. Shortly afterward, Samuel Huston—a wealthy landowner from Marengo, Iowa, for whom the college was later named—got the enterprise under way by donating $9,000. Another Methodist supporter, H. S. White of Romeo, Michigan, gave a 500-volume library. In the early 1890s work was authorized to begin on the construction of a building. The foundation was completed when funds ran out in 1893. Only sixteen years later could the structure be completed. The basement was enclosed in 1898, and Reuben S. Lovinggood was sent to begin classes two years later. With little money and few students, he managed to develop the school's enrollment and curriculum. By 1905, a few college-level courses were being offered.

Like the establishment of Guadalupe College, the founding of Butler College, in Tyler, resulted from independent action on the part of local black Baptists. The East Texas Baptist Association founded Butler College in 1905. The school was originally named East Texas Normal and Industrial Academy and offered only elementary education and a few classes in sewing. In 1924 it was renamed in honor of its first president, C. M. Butler.

The last of the black denominational colleges to be founded in Texas was Jarvis Christian College. The Christian Women's Board of Missions of the Disciples of Christ established the school in 1912 in the small East Texas town of Hawkins. Like most of the white Northern denominations, the Disciples of Christ sent missionaries into the South with advancing Union armies. Seeing the need for more black clergy, the church decided to establish schools for general and religious education. In all, the Disciples of Christ established five schools across the South. Jarvis Christian College traces its beginnings back to 1910, when James J. and Ida Van Zandt Jarvis[qqv] of Fort Worth donated 456 acres near Hawkins for the establishment of a black college. Mrs. Jarvis's long-time involvement in the Christian Women's Board of Missions led to the gift. The school was named Jarvis Christian Institute in the Jarvises' honor.

In addition to the colleges founded during this period, a number of other so-called colleges offered limited educational opportunities for black Texans. These schools however, never provided college-level work. While it seems certain that they all hoped to rise to such a stature, all of these institutions failed to do so for lack of funding, personnel, or other obstacles. One of the earliest of these was Centennial College, which provided high school training in Marshall from 1875 to 1881 before merging with Bishop College. The black Baptist Missionary and Educational Convention founded Hearne Academy in 1881. In 1909 the academy moved to Fort Worth, where it continued as an elementary and secondary school under the name Forth Worth Industrial and Mechanical College. In 1885, black Baptists founded an elementary and secondary school called Houston Baptist College. From 1901 to 1928 the black General Baptist Convention of Texas provided precollege instruction at Central Texas College in Waco. Similar training was offered at Conroe-Porter Industrial College, which opened in 1903. Black Baptists established Brenham Normal and Industrial College in 1905, but the institution offered mostly elementary courses. R. L. Smith, president and founder of the Farmers' Home Improvement Society, founded a school in 1906 at Ladonia called the Farmers' Improvement Society Agricultural College. In 1913 white Baptist ministers in Austin founded St. John's Industrial Institute and Orphanage, which provided domestic and elementary instruction. In the early 1900s, near Oakwood, black Baptists founded Boyd Industrial Institute. The school operated until 1919, when a fire destroyed the building. In 1925 the Primitive Baptist Church selected Mexia as the site for St. Paul Industrial College. In Palestine, around the turn of the century, the Northeast Texas Christian Convention established an elementary school called the Christian Theological and Industrial College.

Over the years, the curricula of the black colleges in Texas changed significantly. During the 1880s, the course offerings were affected by the prevailing racial attitudes of whites and by the rising tide of vocationalism, popularized by Samuel Chapman Armstrong and Booker T. Washington. The vocational model clashed with the classical or liberal arts model desired by many black teachers and students. While business and government leaders succeeded in pressuring black public colleges to adopt extensive vocational curricula, most private colleges, including those in Texas, developed only limited vocational programs. Besides the costs associated with maintaining vocational courses, many black college leaders feared that if everyone emphasized industrial training, African Americans would be restricted to the status of semiskilled factory and agricultural workers. By the mid-1950s, vocational training had virtually disappeared at the private black colleges. While Prairie View maintained its traditional land-grant emphasis, an increasing number of its students chose degree programs in such areas as education, business, and science.

Throughout their history, the black colleges of Texas struggled to develop adequate financial resources. Since most whites were either apathetic or hostile toward them, state and philanthropic support for these schools remained limited. Consequently, black colleges drew much of their support from the most impoverished segment of Texas society. This support took the form of church gifts and tuition and fees. Black colleges operated in a climate of severe austerity and financial uncertainty. While organized philanthropy helped, the colleges were constantly seeking ways to increase revenue. Every black college president had special fund-raising plans. College choirs and quartets traveled the state recruiting prospective students and soliciting donations. Shortages of funds also prompted colleges to join together in joint ventures. By the 1930s, Bishop, Wiley, Paul Quinn, Prairie View, and Jarvis Christian were sharing the cost of faculty, speakers, and special entertainment. In spite of all their efforts, however, none of the black colleges succeeded in developing a sound financial base or extensive endowments. In most cases these schools managed from one year to the next by juggling a shifting combination of church gifts, tuition revenue, and philanthropic grants. When financial burdens became too great, or when they were faced with a financial crisis, college officials were often compelled to make difficult choices. Financial troubles forced Paul Quinn College, for example, to move from Austin to Waco in 1877. After operating in Waco for 113 years, Paul Quinn moved to Dallas in 1990. In 1937, a fire in the administration building brought about the end of Guadalupe College. St. Philip's College, which had struggled to survive as a two-year vocational school, was finally taken over in 1942 by the San Antonio Board of Education. Between 1945 and 1947 Tillotson College and Samuel Huston College merged. In 1961, Bishop College moved its campus from Marshall to Dallas. With a $20 million dollar debt and only 300 students, Bishop College ceased operations in 1988. Financial problems, caused by declining enrollments, forced the closure of Butler College in 1971 and Mary Allen College in 1972. From the 1960s on, as Texas institutions of higher education became increasingly desegregated, the historically black colleges watched their enrollments decline as black students took advantage of the wider range of educational opportunities.

One of the enduring strengths of these institutions has been the dedicated service of their teachers and administrators. Again and again, these individuals displayed the courage and creativity to help their institutions weather internal as well as external problems. They also left their mark on Texas history by preparing thousands of students to become productive members of society. The lives of such professors such as Melvin J. Banks (Bishop College), J. W. Frazier (Samuel Huston College), Melvin B. Tolson[qv] (Wiley College), Ira Reid (Texas College) and Venita C. Waddleton (Jarvis Christian) were characterized by self-sacrifice and professional dedication. Presidents such as Joseph J. Rhoads[qv] (Bishop College), W. Rutherford Banks[qv] (Texas College and Prairie View A&M), Dominion R. Glass (Texas College), Reuben S. Lovinggood (Samuel Huston College), and Mary E. Branch[qv] (Tillotson College) were legendary for their tireless efforts to advance their institutions. The black colleges in Texas have made and continue to make positive contributions to the enrichment of the state's social, economic and political fabric. During the late nineteenth and early twentieth centuries, these institutions shouldered much of the responsibility for all levels of black education. Had it not been for these institutions, a majority of the state's black youth would have remained illiterate. Though poorly funded and often maligned, these institutions provided educational opportunities very similar to those found at other colleges and universities in the South. They successfully prepared thousands of students to become clergy, teachers, lawyers, physicians, dentists, and other professionals. Many of their graduates went on to make significant contributions, not only in their fields or professions, but also to the black community in general. Examples of prominent graduates include Mildred Jefferson (Texas College), who became the first female graduate of Harvard Medical School; Allen C. Hancock (Texas College), who served as dean of Jarvis Christian College and later president of Texas College; David Abner, Jr.[qv] (Bishop College), who became president of Guadalupe College; J. R. E. Lee[qv] (Bishop College), who became president of Florida A&M University; singer and composer Jules (Julius) Bledsoe[qv] (Bishop College); NAACP activist John H. Wells; folklorist J. Mason Brewer[qv] (Wiley College); civil-rights activist James L. Farmer, Jr. (Wiley College), who helped found the Congress for Racial Equality; Heman Sweatt (Wiley College), whose lawsuit played a central role in desegregating graduate and professional schools; and Barbara Jordan (Texas Southern University), who was the first black graduate of Boston University Law School (1959) and who served during the 1960s and 1970s in the Texas Senate and the United States Congress.

BIBLIOGRAPHY: Alwyn Barr, *Black Texans: A History of Negroes in Texas, 1528–1971* (Austin: Jenkins, 1973). Alwyn Barr and Robert A. Calvert, eds., *Black Leaders: Texans for Their Times* (Austin: Texas State Historical Association, 1981). Michael R. Heintze, A History of the Black Private Colleges in Texas, 1865–1954 (Ph.D. dissertation, Texas Tech University, 1981; published as *Private Black Colleges in Texas, 1865–1954* [College Station: Texas A&M University Press, 1985]). Lawrence D. Rice, *The Negro in Texas, 1874–1900* (Baton Rouge: Louisiana State University Press, 1971). George Ruble Woolfolk, *Prairie View* (New York: Pageant, 1962).

Michael R. Heintze

BLACK COWBOYS. Black cowboys have been part of Texas history since the early nineteenth century, when they first worked on ranches throughout the state. A good many of the first black cowboys were born into slavery[qv] but later found a better life on the open range, where they experienced less open discrimination than in the city. After the Civil War[qv] many were employed as horsebreakers and for other tasks, but few of them became ranch foremen or managers. Some black cowboys took up careers as rodeo performers or were hired as federal peace officers in Indian Territory. Others ultimately owned their own farms and ranches, while a few who followed the lure of the Wild West became gunfighters and outlaws. Significant numbers of African Americans[qv] went on the great cattle drives originating in the Southwest in the late 1800s. Black cowboys predominated in ranching sections of the Coastal Plain between the Sabine and Guadalupe rivers.

A number of them achieved enviable reputations. Bose Ikard,[qv] a top hand and drover for rancher Charles Goodnight,[qv] also served him as his chief detective and banker. Daniel W. (80 John) Wallace[qv] started riding the cattle trails in his adolescence and ultimately worked for cattlemen Winfield Scott and Gus O'Keefe. He put his accumulated savings toward the purchase of a ranch near Loraine, where he acquired more than 1,200 acres and 500 to 600 cattle. He was a member of the Texas and Southwestern Cattle Raisers Association[qv] for more than thirty years. William Pickett[qv] made his name as one of the most outstanding Wild West rodeo performers in the country and is credited with originating the modern event known as bulldogging. He was inducted into the National Cowboy Hall of Fame in 1971.

Black cowboys have continued to work in the ranching industry throughout the twentieth century, and African Americans who inherited family-owned ranches have attempted to bring public recognition to the contributions of their ancestors. Mollie Stevenson, a fourth-generation owner of the Taylor-Stevenson Ranch near Houston, founded the American Cowboy Museum to honor black, Indian, and Mexican-American cowboys. Weekend rodeos featuring black cowboys began in the late 1940s and continue to be popular. These contests owe their existence to the Negro Cowboys Rodeo Association, formed in 1947 by a group of East Texas black businessmen-ranchers and cowboys.

BIBLIOGRAPHY: Arthur T. Burton, *Black, Red, and Deadly: Gunfighters of the Indian Territory, 1870–1907* (Austin: Eakin Press, 1991). Philip Durham and Everett L. Jones, *Negro Cowboys* (New York: Dodd, Mead, 1965). Jack Lowry, "The Forgotten Cowboys," *Texas Highways*, May 1991. Wendy Watriss and Fred Baldwin, "Soul in the Saddle," *Houston City*, February 1981. *Teresa Palomo Acosta*

BLACK CREEK (Cass County). Black Creek rises 7½ miles northeast of Marietta in northwestern Cass County (at 33°14′ N, 94°26′ W), and extends three miles east to its mouth on Wright Patman Lake (at 33°14′ N, 94°24′ W). The area around the creek is flood-prone, and native vegetation includes water-tolerant hardwoods, conifers, and grasses.

—— (Kendall County). Black Creek begins just north of Pleasant Valley in southeastern Kendall County (at 29°49′ N, 98°37′ W) and runs 3½ miles north to its mouth on Spring Creek, four miles east of Kreutsberg (at 29°52′ N, 98°38′ W). It traverses an area of steep slopes and benches and flat terrain with local deep dissections, surfaced by shallow clay loams that support juniper, live oak, mesquite, and grasses.

—— (Medina County). Black Creek begins two miles west of the Southern Pacific Railroad and four miles south of Dunlay in east central Medina County (at 29°17′ N, 98°59′ W) and runs thirty-four miles southeast to its mouth on San Miguel Creek in Frio County (at 28°52′ N, 98°55′ W). It crosses flat terrain with local shallow depressions upstream and flows beneath some low-rolling hills downstream. Water-tolerant hardwoods, conifers, and grasses grow near the source, and grasses, mesquite, and chaparral near the mouth.

—— (Tyler County). Black Creek rises north of Warren and five miles southwest of Hillister in southern Tyler County (at 30°39′ N, 94°25′ W); it runs southeast for thirteen miles, through Lake Hyatt and east of John H. Kirby[qv] State Forest, to its mouth on Hickory Creek, just north of the Tyler-Hardin county line (at 30°32′ N, 94°23′ W). It crosses flat terrain with local shallow depressions surfaced by clay and sandy loam that supports water-tolerant hardwoods, conifers, and grasses.

—— (Webb County). Black Creek, also known as Prieto Creek, rises twelve miles north of Bruni in southeastern Webb County (at 27°37′ N, 98°55′ W) and runs north for thirty-eight miles to its mouth on the Nueces River, thirty-one miles southeast of Cotulla in southeastern La Salle County (at 28°05′ N, 98°53′ W). The stream is intermittent for the first half of its course and is dammed seventeen miles below its source to form Biel Lake. It crosses flat terrain with local shallow depressions, surfaced by expansive clays that support water-tolerant hardwoods, conifers, and grasses.

—— (Wise County). Black Creek rises five miles north of Decatur in north central Wise County (at 33°19′ N, 97°36′ W) and flows southeast for thirteen miles to its mouth on Denton Creek, two miles east of the old Allison community (33°17′ N, 97°25′ W). It crosses flat to rolling terrain surfaced mostly with deep fine sandy loam. The stream is intermittent in its upper reaches. The area around it has been used mostly for range and crop land.

BLACK CREEK, TEXAS. Black Creek is on Farm Road 2200 six miles northwest of Devine in southeastern Medina County. Black Creek flows through the area. The eighth post office established in Medina County began operations in Black Creek in 1877 with John W. Reed as postmaster. The post office was discontinued in 1880. School records showed ninety-nine students attending two schools in 1908. Those schools, New Canaan and Black Creek, remained in the Black Creek school district until 1911 and were then combined in a two-room schoolhouse at the junction of the Devine-Yancey and the Devine-Hondo roads. One of the rooms served as an assembly hall with a piano, drop curtains, and a backdrop on a raised stage. In 1921 the community built another schoolhouse on the Adams Ranch in the western part of the district to serve students in remote areas. The Black Creek Primitive Baptist Church, located a few miles south of Black Creek, was established in 1882 by William S. Dubose. An active Baptist Church and school were all that remained of Black Creek in 1948. The Black Creek Baptist Church continued to serve the sparsely populated community in 1989.

BIBLIOGRAPHY: Castro Colonies Heritage Association, *The History of Medina County, Texas* (Dallas: National Share Graphics, 1983). Houston B. Eggen, History of Public Education in Medina County, Texas, 1848–1928 (M.A. thesis, University of Texas, 1950).

Ruben E. Ochoa

BLACK CYPRESS BAYOU. Black Cypress Bayou is formed by the convergence of Cunningham and Black Cypress creeks seven miles east of Avinger in southern Cass County (at 32°54′ N, 94°26′ W). It flows southeast for nineteen miles, through southern Cass County and central Marion County, to its mouth on Big Cypress Bayou, four miles east of Jefferson (at 32°46′ N, 94°17′ W). The banks of the stream are heavily wooded in places with pine and hardwood trees, and the creek flows through nearly level to gently undulating terrain surfaced by sandy, loamy, and clayey soils used predominantly for timber cultivation and agriculture.

BLACKER, ALLEN (1832–1905). Allen Blacker, legislator, pioneer, and civic leader, was born to Dennis and Rachel (Hotsenviller) Blacker in Ross County, Ohio, on February 5, 1832. He was educated in public schools at Frankfort, Ohio. He studied law under Allen G. Thurman and later joined the law offices of McClintock and Smith, a prominent commercial law firm. In 1859 he moved to Nebraska City to serve as clerk of the territorial court. Blacker married Martha Porter Robinson on January 24, 1861, and they eventually had five children. He assumed military service during the Civil War[qv] with Company D of the First Nebraska Calvary, where he was promoted to the rank of major. Blacker was also a war correspondent with the New York *Herald* and served as judge advocate in St. Louis and Fort Leavenworth, Kansas, during a period of martial law.

In 1865 he resigned his commission and in 1869 moved to El Paso, Texas. He sent for his family in 1873. In 1875 he was elected district judge of El Paso. In 1880 he was a representative to the Texas legislature from the Seventy-fifth District. Blacker was a delegate to the Democratic national convention in 1888. He became city attorney of El Paso in 1866 and held that position through the following year. In 1888 he became an alderman, and in 1890 he was a city judge. When faced with failing health, Blacker moved his family to Cloudcroft, New Mexico, in 1900, where he served as justice of the peace, postmaster, and county commissioner. He returned to El Paso in 1904 and was elected city commissioner. Blacker wrote a treatise on military law that was adopted as the authority on the subject by the United States government. He was also a member of the Grand Army of the Republic. He died on December 26, 1905, in El Paso.

BIBLIOGRAPHY: Buckley B. Paddock, ed., *A Twentieth Century History and Biographical Record of North and West Texas* (Chicago: Lewis, 1906).
Melanie Watkins

BLACK EXTENSION SERVICE. The Cooperative Extension Service, an educational arm of the United States Department of Agriculture, was established by the Smith-Lever Act of 1914. The agency's primary purpose was "to aid in diffusing among the people of the United States useful and practical information on subjects relating to agriculture and home economics, and to encourage the application of the same." Funds were appropriated on a formula basis to state land-grant institutions. In Texas the agency became the Texas Agricultural Extension Service.[qv]

In Texas were two land-grant institutions. The Agricultural and Mechanical College of Texas (later Texas A&M University) was established by the Morrill Act of 1862, and Prairie View College (later Prairie View A&M University) was established for African Americans[qv] by the second Morrill Act (1890). This arrangement was the result of the "separate but equal" practice of providing dual educational facilities for white and black people in the segregated South. The Smith-Lever Act allowed the state legislature to select the institution to administer the new program but specified that the institution established for blacks by the 1890 act should also receive a portion of the funding. Thus what became known as Negro Extension Work in Texas was born.

In 1915 the Texas legislature authorized the establishment of the Texas Agricultural Extension Service and assigned the responsibility for implementation of this new program to Texas A&M. Negro Extension Work was initiated at Prairie View A&M in August 1915. Robert L. Smith,[qv] a native of South Carolina and a successful businessman, teacher, and Texas legislator, was selected to head up the extension team; Mrs. Mary Evelyn V. Hunter,[qv] from Finchburg, Alabama, was hired upon her graduation from Prairie View; and Jacob H. (Jake) Ford, a native Texan, farmer, and teacher from Wharton, was hired as an agronomist. At the end of the first year the report to the state extension director's office at Texas A&M listed 144 clubs organized with 6,013 members, 97 lectures attended by 21,985 people, 89 field demonstrations attended by 3,121 people, 860 winter-garden demonstrations, and 135 poultry demonstrations. Given the mode of travel and communication facilities available at the time, the results showed the first year of Negro Extension Work in Texas to be highly successful.

In the early 1920s, under the leadership of Calvin H. Waller, funds for additional extension staff were secured. By 1940 the service employed forty-six county agricultural agents and thirty-six county home demonstration[qv] agents. Over the years they assisted African-American farmers and farm families, including youth, with such programs as food preservation, housing, health, and sanitation, as well as swine, dairy products, cattle, and poultry production. During the Great Depression,[qv] they assisted farm families with clothing, home improvement, mattress making, and food.

In the 1950s and 1960s the staff grew to a total of 104 professional employees servicing sixty counties in the northeastern third of the state. Emphasis was placed on educating leaders and community development while continuing the assistance farmers had come to expect from their local extension agents. After the passage of the Civil Rights Act of 1964 the structure of the Texas Agricultural Extension Service was no longer the same. The dual organizational system was required to merge into one. The Negro Extension Work ceased to exist on August 31, 1965.

BIBLIOGRAPHY: Lincoln David Kelsey and Cannon Chiles Hearne, *Cooperative Extension Work* (Ithaca, New York: Cornell University Press, 1949; 3d ed., Ithaca: Comstock, 1963). Wayne D. Rasmussen, *Taking the University to the People: Seventy-Five Years of Cooperative Extension* (Ames: Iowa State University Press, 1989).
Dempsey H. Seastrunk

BLACK FILMMAKING. The first Texas-based motion pictures were made as early as 1921 by a black film company, Superior Art productions of Houston. Two black-owned San Antonio film companies, Lone Star and Cotton Blossom, were also active in the early 1920s. Lone Star made four motion pictures in 1922 and one in 1923. Because the films no longer exist and were never copyrighted (the usual source for dating films), which of the four 1922 films was made first is unknown, but we do know their titles: *Stranger From Way Out Yonder, The Wrong Mr. Johnson, You Can't Keep A Good Man Down,* and *The Wife Hunters.* Of the latter film, we know the names of the cast members (Bob White, Jessie Purty, Edward Townsend, V. Stevens, P. Massey, H. C. Grant, J. T. Walton, and J. G. Selby) and that part of the film was shot on locations in Vicksburg, Mississippi. We also know the primary cast members in Lone Star's sole 1923 entry, *Why Worry—* Byron Smith, Mae Morris, and Frank Brown. The M. W. Baccus Films Company, although white-owned, specialized in making films of interest mainly to African Americans[qv] in Dallas in 1922. Its sole known production was entitled *From Cotton Patch To Congress.* Hit by the Great Depression,[qv] the influenza epidemic, and the advent of the more expensive process of making sound films in the late 1920s, the Texas black film companies and producers of what were then called "race movies" went into oblivion, as did the perishable nitrate-based prints and negatives of their films.

From 1941 through 1947 Alfred R. Sack of Dallas and Spencer Williams,[qv] a black screenwriter-actor from Hollywood, produced ten films in and around Dallas, including two comedies (*Juke Joint* and *Dirty Gertie from Harlem, U.S.A.*), two religious films (*Go Down, Death* and *The Blood of Jesus*), two dramas (*Girl in Room 20* and *Of One Blood*), and a musical performance film featuring Dizzy Gillespie and his Orchestra (*Jivin' in Bebop*). The films were produced under various company names, such as Sack Amusement Enterprises, which was the main distributor of black-cast films in the United States between 1920 and 1950, Amergro Films, Sack Attractions, and Harlemwood Studios. Most of the Sack-Williams films have been found and restored by the Southwest Film-Video Archives in Dallas. In the summer of 1983 the last remaining film prints of more than 100 works in the original 35-millimeter format made between the 1920s and the early 1950s were found in a Tyler warehouse. Some of them were intended strictly for black audiences. Though most of the films in the collection, now dubbed the Tyler, Texas, Black Film Collection, were in various stages of deterioration from nitrate decomposition, several were restored. Of the twenty-two titles in the collection, fifteen had a black artist as producer, director, or screenwriter, and the majority of those had a black writer-director or a black producer-director. *See also* FILM INDUSTRY.

BIBLIOGRAPHY: Donald Bogle, *Toms, Coons, Mulattoes, Mammies and Bucks: An Interpretive History of Blacks in American Films* (New York: Viking Press, 1973). Thomas Cripps, *Slow Fade to Black: The Negro in American Film, 1900–1942* (New York: Oxford University Press, 1977). G. William Jones, *Black Cinema Treasures: Lost and Found* (Denton: University of North Texas, 1991). Phyllis Klotman, *Frame By Frame: A Black Filmography* (Bloomington: Indiana University Press, 1978). Henry T. Sampson, *Blacks in Black and White: A Source Book on Black Films* (Metuchen, New Jersey: Scarecrow, 1977).
G. William Jones

BLACKFOOT, TEXAS. Blackfoot is on Farm Road 860 twenty miles from Palestine in northwestern Anderson County. Around 1850 a member of the family of Cynthia Anne Parker[qv] preached in a

Primitive Baptist church located at the site. The first settlers came from South Carolina and Mississippi. They included Abe Hoff, Isaac Brown, and D. M. Crisp. The name of the community supposedly originated in 1870 when Uncle Hamp Hanks, Sr., was told that he was in the "Blackfoot nation." Before the Civil War[qv] Blackfoot had one school, known as the Stillhouse school and taught by Mrs. Eilding. A later, two-room school, the Isabel school, was consolidated in 1942 with the Ward-Blackfoot-Springfield school system. The oldest church, Friendship Baptist, organized in 1860, was located on the line between Ward and Blackfoot. Land was donated by Josh Taylor in 1890 for the construction of the First Christian church in Blackfoot, although the church had been organized a few years earlier. The post office was established in 1886 with William U. Stafford as postmaster. In February 1907 it closed, and the community's mail was routed through Montalba.

Hogs, corn, cattle, and cotton were raised in the Blackfoot area. About 1880 Obe Childress and A. M. Kay built the first cotton gin, which operated for over sixty years. In 1941 the REA New Area Co-op was formed, and Blackfoot received electricity. Telephone service began in 1959. During the East Texas oilfield[qv] strike in 1930, a field was discovered at Blackfoot; it still had producing wells in the late 1950s. At the beginning of the twentieth century Blackfoot had a justice of the peace courthouse that was used until about 1935 for precinct court. The building remained standing on the Isabell farm until 1973, when a windstorm blew it down. The population of Blackfoot before the Civil War[qv] was an estimated forty. In 1896 it had decreased to thirty but by 1936 had increased to 200. In 1988 Blackfoot had a cemetery, the Friendship Baptist Church, and two dairies. The population in 1990 was thirty-three.

BIBLIOGRAPHY: Mrs. Ernest Douglas and Mrs. G. H. Williams, *Anderson County Folklore and Early History* (Palestine, Texas: Sesquicentennial School Project Committee, 1986). Palestine *Daily Herald*, May 29, 1936.
Georgia Kemp Caraway

BLACK FORK CREEK. Black Fork Creek rises in southeast Tyler in central Smith County (at 32°19′ N, 95°16′ W) and runs northwest through Tyler and the surrounding countryside for fourteen miles to its mouth on Prairie Creek, two miles southeast of New Harmony (at 32°24′ N, 95°26′ W). Upstream, it traverses flat to rolling terrain with some local steep slopes, surfaced by loamy, fine sand that supports hardwood and pine forests. Downstream, where the soil is interspersed with gravel and underlain by red clay, water-tolerant hardwoods, conifers, and native grasses grow. The low-lying flood plains at the mouth are surfaced by poorly drained loam over clay. County records for 1903 showed the Black Fork School District located on the creek five miles east of Tyler. It comprised two schools. One employed two teachers and enrolled eighty-two black students; the other had sixty-six white pupils and one teacher. In 1936 one school remained for seventy-seven black students and one teacher. By 1952 it had been consolidated into the Dixie Independent School District.

BIBLIOGRAPHY: Edward Clayton Curry, An Administrative Survey of the Schools of Smith County, Texas (M.Ed. thesis, University of Texas, 1938).

BLACK HILL. Black Hill is twenty-two miles northeast of Terlingua in west central Brewster County (at 29°38′ N, 103°31′ W). With an elevation of 4,004 feet above sea level, it rises 590 feet above State Highway 118, three miles to the west. Its shallow, stony soils support scrub brush and grasses.

BLACK HILL, TEXAS. Black Hill, also known as Loma Prieta, is nine miles northwest of Pleasanton on Farm Road 478 in northeast Atascosa County. It was named for the black rocks that dominate the landscape. In 1920 Black Hill School was built and named by early settler Jack Temple. By 1934 it had twenty-nine students and two teachers. In the 1940s the community had one business and numerous scattered dwellings. In 1953 the Black Hills school was consolidated with that of Pleasanton. In the late 1960s a community center and a few widely scattered dwellings were located at the site, which is no longer shown on maps.

BIBLIOGRAPHY: Margaret G. Clover, The Place Names of Atascosa County (M.A. thesis, University of Texas, 1952). Martin Stroble, Administrative Survey and Proposed Plan of Reorganization for the Public Schools of Atascosa County (M.Ed. thesis, University of Texas, 1936).
Linda Peterson

BLACK HILL BRANCH. Black Hill Branch rises three miles northeast of Lytle in southwestern Bexar County (at 29°16′ N, 98°45′ W) and runs northeast for three miles to its mouth on Live Oak Creek, 1½ miles southwest of Atascosa (at 29°16′ N, 98°43′ W). It traverses rolling land surfaced by clay loam that supports mesquite and grasses.

BLACK HILLS (Brewster County). The Black Hills are eighteen miles northeast of the Persimmon Gap Ranger Station in east central Brewster County (centered at 29°49′ N, 102°59′ W). The highest point in the Black Hills, at an elevation of 3,385 feet above sea level, rises some 585 feet above Dove Mountain Road, a half mile south. The soils in the Black Hills are shallow and stony and support scrub brush and grasses.

—— (Presidio County). The Black Hills are located just east of the Atchison, Topeka and Santa Fe Railway in southwestern Presidio County (at 29°37′ N, 104°08′ W). With elevations of 3,637 and 3,499 feet above sea level, the summits rise an average of 568 feet over Black Hills Creek, which runs along the western edge of the hills. The hills were formed by successive flows of volcanic rhyolite and basalt. They stand in desert mountain terrain cut by numerous rugged canyons. Vegetation in the area consists primarily of sparse grasses, cacti, and desert conifer and oak shrubs.

BLACK HILLS, TEXAS. Black Hills, on Farm Road 1839 eight miles northwest of Corsicana in north central Navarro County, was probably established before 1900. By 1906 a two-teacher school was in operation there with eighty-nine students. At its height just before World War I,[qv] Black Hills had a cotton gin, a store, and a church. The community began to decline during the 1920s, and by the mid-1930s only a cemetery and a few houses remained. In 1990 Black Hills was a dispersed community.

BIBLIOGRAPHY: Annie Carpenter Love, *History of Navarro County* (Dallas: Southwestern, 1933). Wyvonne Putman, comp., *Navarro County History* (5 vols., Quanah, Texas: Nortex, 1975-84). Alva Taylor, *History and Photographs of Corsicana and Navarro County* (Corsicana, Texas, 1959; rev. ed., *Navarro County History and Photographs*, Corsicana, 1962).
Christopher Long

BLACK HILLS CREEK. Black Hills Creek rises near White Springs, seven miles northeast of the Black Hills in southeastern Presidio County (at 20°40′ N, 104°01′ W), and flows southwest for eighteen miles to join Terneros Creek. The united stream subsequently flows a mile to its mouth on the Rio Grande, four miles below Fort Leaton State Historic Site[qv] (at 29°32′ N, 104°16′ W). The stream principally crosses Quaternary alluvium, but it originates in volcanic deposits and terminates in the gravel terrace of the Rio Grande floodplain. The soils are light reddish-brown to brown sands and clay loams, often rough and stony. The vegetation consists primarily of sparse desert shrubs.

BLACK HOLLOW. Black Hollow begins five miles northeast of Muenster in northwestern Cooke County (at 33°42′ N, 97°17′ W) and runs north for four miles to its mouth on South Fish Creek, three miles southeast of Marysville (at 33°45′ N, 97°17′ W). The hollow traverses variable terrain surfaced by shallow, stony, clay loams that support oak, juniper, chaparral, cacti, and grasses.

BLACK HORSE (?–ca. 1900). Black Horse, or Tu-ukumah, was a Comanche war chief known among his people as Pako-Riah (Colt) or Ta-Peka (Sun Rays). He was sometimes called Nigger Horse by John R. Cook[qv] and other buffalo hunters. Black Horse was elevated to second chief in the Quahadi band after the death of Bull Bear in 1874. He was among the first of the Quahadis to surrender to the United States Army at Fort Sill at the end of the Red River War[qv] in early 1875. Although a relatively obscure leader, he won considerable notoriety among the whites in 1876–77 when he led 170 renegade warriors in the short-lived Staked Plains War, or Hunters' War, the last Indian foray in the Panhandle.[qv]

Weary of meager rations and confinement, Black Horse's party left the Fort Sill reservation with their families on December 15, 1876, to hunt buffalo and make war on any white hunters they saw. Two troops of cavalry went after them but lost their trail in a snowstorm. The band camped in Thompson's Canyon, near the site of present Lubbock, and on February 22 attacked several buffalo-hunting groups operating in the vicinity. Among other depredations, they killed and scalped Marshall Sewell, destroyed hides and supplies, and stole horses belonging to Patrick F. Garrett[qv] and Skelton Glenn's hunting party. Black Horse also led the raid on John (Buckskin Bill) Godey's camp, where he stampeded the horses and besieged the hunters for hours before they slipped away in the dark. The hunters' militia from Charles Rath's[qv] store reached Black Horse's camp and engaged in the battle of Yellow House Draw, or Pocket Canyon, on March 18, 1877. Black Horse escaped in the fight and later was reported to have been killed, along with his wife, at Lake Quemado by "buffalo soldiers" of the Tenth United States Cavalry[qv] under Capt. P. L. Lee on May 4. However, that report proved erroneous; the leader killed at Lake Quemado was Ekawakane (Red Young Man), a fearless and reckless warrior who had resisted reservation life to the end. Black Horse lived on peacefully for several years and died at Cache, Oklahoma, about 1900.

BIBLIOGRAPHY: John R. Cook, *The Border and the Buffalo: An Untold Story of the Southwest Plains* (Topeka, Kansas: Crane, 1907; rpt., New York: Citadel Press, 1967). Wayne Gard, *The Great Buffalo Hunt* (New York: Knopf, 1959). James L. Haley, *The Buffalo War: The History of the Red River Indian Uprising of 1874* (Garden City, New York: Doubleday, 1976). Paul I. Wellman, *Death on Horseback: Seventy Years of War for the American West* (New York: Lippincott, 1947). Paul I. Wellman, *Death on the Prairie: The Thirty Years' Struggle for the Western Plains* (New York: Macmillan, 1934).

H. Allen Anderson

BLACK JACK, TEXAS (Cherokee County). Black Jack, on Farm Road 2750 eighteen miles northeast of Rusk in northeastern Cherokee County, was first settled in the 1840s by Robert Graves Stadler,[qv] a native of South Carolina and veteran of the Texas Revolution.[qv] He was joined by a number of relatives, mostly nephews and nieces, who built a small settlement that they named after the numerous blackjack trees in the vicinity. A log schoolhouse was constructed around the time of the Civil War,[qv] and in 1875 the Blackjack Baptist Church was organized. However, the town did not grow until around 1916, when John W. Gray and Tom Upchurch opened a store. At its height just after World War I[qv] the small community had two stores, a cotton gin, a garage, a church, a school, and a population of 100. After World War II[qv] the school was consolidated with the Troup school. The last store closed in 1961, but as late as 1966 the reported population was still seventy-five. In 1990 Black Jack was a dispersed rural community with a church, a few scattered houses, and a population of forty-seven.

BIBLIOGRAPHY: *Cherokee County History* (Jacksonville, Texas: Cherokee County Historical Commission, 1986). Hattie Joplin Roach, *A History of Cherokee County* (Dallas: Southwest, 1934).

James R. Niendorff

BLACK JACK, TEXAS (Henderson County). Black Jack is on Farm Road 1803 nine miles northeast of Athens in eastern Henderson County. The settlement was evidently founded prior to 1900. A local school was operating by 1906, when it had an enrollment of 114. In the mid-1930s Black Jack had a church, a school, and a number of houses. After World War II[qv] the school closed, and in the early 1990s only a church, a cemetery, and a few scattered houses remained.

Christopher Long

BLACKJACK, TEXAS (Smith County). Blackjack is just south of Lake Tyler off Farm Road 346 in southern Smith County. It is bordered on the east by Prairie Creek. The settlement, only a half mile east of the St. Louis and Southwestern Railway (originally the International–Great Northern), had a school, two churches, and a small collection of farms in 1936. By 1952 its school had been consolidated with the Whitehouse Independent School District. In 1973 the center of the scattered farm community was the New Canaan Church and Cemetery, and in 1981 Blackjack was identified as a church community.

BIBLIOGRAPHY: Albert Woldert, *A History of Tyler and Smith County* (San Antonio: Naylor, 1948).

Vista K. McCroskey

BLACK JACK CREEK. Black Jack Creek rises four miles east of Muldoon in south central Fayette County (at 29°48′ N, 97°01′ W) and flows northwest for five miles to its mouth on Pinoak Creek (at 29°50′ N, 97°03′ W). The winding stream, which has many small unnamed tributaries, runs through moderately rolling hills surfaced with sandy loams that support hardwood and pine forest, mesquite, and grasses. The stream is flanked by blackjack trees, for which it is named. The bottom timber bordering the creek helps prevent it from drying out, thus enhancing the surrounding area as range and crop land.

BIBLIOGRAPHY: Frank Lotto, *Fayette County: Her History and Her People* (Schulenburg, Texas: Sticker Steam Press, 1902; rpt., Austin: University of Texas Press, 1981).

BLACK JACK SPRINGS, TEXAS. Black Jack Springs was near Farm Road 609 twelve miles southwest of La Grange in southwestern Fayette County. The community, named for the nearby clear springs and blackjack oak trees, was settled in the mid-1830s by Anglo pioneers. During the early 1850s they were joined by German immigrants, including Johannes Christlieb Nathanael Romberg.[qv] A post office was opened there in 1868, and in 1871 land was donated for separate white and black cemeteries. By 1884 Black Jack Springs reported a population of 400, three general stores, two steam gristmill–cotton gins, a broom factory, a Lutheran church, and a school. In 1896 the community claimed 100 inhabitants and had a Baptist church, a saloon, and a cotton gin. During the early 1900s the town had a dance hall, a church, and a school. Its post office closed in 1910, and by the late 1930s its church had moved to Swiss Alp and its school had been closed. By the 1940s only the cemetery remained to mark the site of the community.

BIBLIOGRAPHY: La Grange High School, *Fayette County: Past and Present* (La Grange, Texas, 1976).

Mark Odintz

BLACK KETTLE NATIONAL GRASSLAND. Black Kettle National Grassland is on Farm Road 2266 twelve miles east of Canadian in Hemphill County, Texas, and Roger Mills County, Oklahoma. The 31,576-acre preserve was purchased during the 1930s by the United States Department of the Interior under the Bankhead-Jones Farm

Tenant Act in an effort to return some of the badly eroded land of the Dust Bowl[qv] to its natural state. The preserve, which includes Lake Marvin, is administered by the United States Department of Agriculture Forest Service under a policy of multiple use for range, watershed, recreation, and wildlife. Open grasslands, marshes, and woodlands provide habitats for wildlife ranging from deer and turkeys to wood ducks and barred owls. Recreational facilities at the grassland include several cabins, hiking trails, and camping and picnicking areas.

BIBLIOGRAPHY: George Oxford Miller, *Texas Parks and Campgrounds: Central, South, and West Texas* (Austin: Texas Monthly Press, 1984).

Christopher Long

BLACKLAND, TEXAS. Blackland is on State Highway 276 four miles southeast of Rockwall in central Rockwall County. The settlement received a post office in 1876. During the 1880s it had a population of 125, three businesses, and a gristmill. Local farmers shipped cotton, wheat, and oats. The population had declined to about fifty by 1900, although the Blackland school employed two teachers and registered seventy-nine students. The post office was closed in 1903. Blackland's population was 114 in 1904, fourteen in 1940, and forty-nine in 1990.

Brian Hart

BLACKLAND ARMY AIR FIELD. Blackland Army Air Field, five miles northwest of Waco, was activated in June 1942. It was initially named China Springs Army Air Field and was also known as Waco Army Air Field No. 2 before being renamed after the local black soil. It was first a glider training school and in October 1942 became an advanced two-engine pilot school. The field became inactive on October 31, 1945, and by 1950 was operating as Waco Municipal Airport. Some buildings were used as a public housing project.

BIBLIOGRAPHY: Patricia Ward Wallace, *Our Land, Our Lives: A Pictorial History of McLennan County* (Norfolk–Virginia Beach, Virginia, 1986).

Art Leatherwood

BLACK MESA. Black Mesa, in southern Brewster County, is southwest of the Chisos Mountains and about 5½ miles north-northeast of Castolon within Big Bend National Park[qv] (at 29°13′ N, 103°29′ W). This mesa, which rises 2,775 feet above sea level, is composed of massive, hard, dense basaltic lava of the Chisos Formation surrounded by softer Cretaceous sedimentary rocks. It derives its name from its dark color. Mammalian tooth and bone fragments that date from the Eocene have been found in tuff deposits on the southeast corner of the mesa. The local vegetation, which includes scattered shrubs such as creosote bush and ocotillo and various semisucculents such as lechuguilla, sotol, and yucca, is characteristic of Chihuahuan Desert scrub.

BIBLIOGRAPHY: Ross A. Maxwell et al., *Geology of Big Bend National Park* (Austin: Bureau of Economic Geology, University of Texas, 1967). A. Michael Powell, "Vegetation of Trans-Pecos Texas," in *New Mexico Geological Society Guidebook* (Socorro, New Mexico: New Mexico Geological Society, 1980).

—— A second Black Mesa is about 6½ miles northeast of Lajitas in southwesternmost Brewster County (at 29°21′ N, 103°43 W). The mesa, a mafic sill in Cretaceous sedimentary rocks, reaches an elevation of 4,286 feet above sea level near the center of its table-top. Mafic rocks are generally dark, hence the mesa's name. Owing to the low resistance of the sedimentary rocks and the near-horizontality of the sill, erosion has left a flat topographic high, or mesa. Black Mesa is covered sparsely with Chihuahuan Desert scrub, including scattered shrubs such as creosote bush and ocotillo, and various semisucculents such as lechuguilla, sotol, and yucca. After mining operations came into the area near the beginning of the twentieth century, Black Mesa marked the northwestern edge of the Terlingua quicksilver district (*see* MERCURY MINING). Both the Lone Star mine and the larger Marfa and Mariposa operation were located just south of Black Mesa.

BIBLIOGRAPHY: Clifford B. Casey, *Soldiers, Ranchers and Miners in the Big Bend* (Washington: Office of Archeology and Historic Preservation, U.S. Department of the Interior, 1969). W. N. McAnulty, "Geology of Cathedral Mountain Quadrangle, Brewster County, Texas," *Bulletin of the Geological Society of America* 66 (1955). A. Michael Powell, "Vegetation of Trans-Pecos Texas," in *New Mexico Geological Society Guidebook* (Socorro, New Mexico: New Mexico Geological Society, 1980). Kenneth B. Ragsdale, *Quicksilver: Terlingua and the Chisos Mining Company* (College Station: Texas A&M University Press, 1976).

BLACK MOUNTAIN (Brewster County). Black Mountain is twenty-five miles southwest of Marathon in west central Brewster County (at 29°53′ N, 103°26′ W). Its peak rises to 4,610 feet above sea level, 760 feet above Chalk Draw, a mile west. Soils on the mountain are shallow and stony and support scrub brush and grasses.

—— (Brewster County). Black Mountain is ten miles west of the Rio Grande and six miles north of the Black Gap Wildlife Management Area in eastern Brewster County (at 29°44′ N, 102°51′ W). With an elevation of 3,642 feet above sea level, it rises some 920 feet above Reagan Canyon, four miles to the east. Shallow, stony soils on Black Mountain support live oak, piñon, juniper, and grasses.

—— (Jeff Davis County). Black Mountain is eleven miles northwest of Fort Davis in central Jeff Davis County (at 30°43′ N, 103°59′ W). A radio tower stands on its summit, which, at 7,544 feet above sea level, rises some 1,900 feet above a nearby spring in Big Aguja Canyon, a mile to the southeast. The shallow, stony soils on Black Mountain support Douglas fir, aspen, Arizona cypress, maple, ponderosa pine, and madrone.

—— (Kinney County). Black Mountain is in far north central Kinney County (at 29°37′ N, 100°20′ W). With an elevation of 2,090 feet above sea level, its summit rises 500 feet above the nearby West Nueces River.

—— (Uvalde County). Black Mountain is five miles west of Knippa in central Uvalde County (at 29°18′ N, 99°43′ W). With an elevation of 1,275 feet above sea level, its summit rises 220 feet above nearby Farm Road 2690.

BLACK MOUNTAINS. The Black Mountains are thirty miles northeast of Sierra Blanca in east central Hudspeth County (their center is at 31°34′ N, 105°09′ W). The range is 4½ miles long from east to west. Its highest elevation is 5,561 feet above sea level. The area's land surface of shallow, stony soils supports scrub brush and grasses.

BLACKOAK, TEXAS. Blackoak (Black Oak), at the junction of Farm roads 69 and 269 in southeastern Hopkins County, was named for its location in a forest of black oak. The area was first settled around 1850. In the mid-1850s David Attaway, an early settler, donated land for a church, and a local post office was established in 1854 under the name Black Oak with David H. Campbell as postmaster. By 1885 the community had a district school, Methodist and Baptist churches, and a population of 100. In 1905 the community had two public schools, one for white children that had forty-eight students that year, and one for black children that had thirty. The post office closed in 1905, and in 1933 the town had a population of twenty-four and one business. In 1936 the community comprised two churches, a cemetery, a school, and a number of scattered dwellings. After World War II[qv] the school was closed, and most of the residents moved away. In the mid-1960s Blackoak had a church, a cemetery, and a number of scattered farmhouses. In 1988 a church and cemetery were still at the site.

Christopher Long

BLACK PEAK (Brewster County). Black Peak, also known as Back Peak, is thirteen miles northwest of the Persimmon Gap Ranger Station in central Brewster County (at 29°43′ N, 103°23′ W). The peak, at an elevation of 4,818 feet above sea level, rises some 1,560 feet above Chalk Draw, a mile east. Shallow, stony soils on Black Peak support scrub brush and grasses.

—— (Brewster County). Black Peak is fifteen miles southwest of Marathon in the Del Norte Mountains in west central Brewster County (at 30°06′ N, 103°28′ W). The summit, at an elevation of 4,964 feet above sea level, rises 965 feet above Maravillas Creek, a mile south. The soils on Black Peak are shallow and stony and support scrub brush, creosote bush, cacti, grasses, oak, and mesquite.

—— (Culberson County). Black Peak is five miles southeast of Plateau in south central Culberson County (at 31°01′ N, 104°29′ W). With an elevation of 4,776 feet above sea level, it rises 600 feet above Interstate 10, two miles to the south.

BLACK POINT, TEXAS. Black Point, an old Spanish landing place, is at the point in Refugio County where the Aransas River flows into Copano Bay. The mouth of the river is quite wide; within it lies a shell reef that was once occupied by Karankawa and Copano Indians. Francis, John, and Thomas Welder landed at Black Point in May 1836 and a few years later established a ranch on the shell reef. They later sold this tract to Philip Dimmitt.[qv] From 1838 to 1841 Black Point was a landing depot for munitions and supplies for the Mexican Federalist armies. The Black Point settlement figured in many Indian raids, including the kidnapping of Jacob Kring. Peter Doren (sometimes cited Doring) built a house on the point and established a ranch; his cattle grazed on the free open range. During the period of the Republic of Texas[qv] a road ran from Black Point to Refugio. There was also a trail that extended from Black Point around the bay and across Live Oak Peninsula. In the 1840s John H. Wood[qv] settled at Black Point. The modern community of Bayside occupies the site.

BIBLIOGRAPHY: Hobart Huson, *Refugio: A Comprehensive History of Refugio County from Aboriginal Times to 1953* (2 vols., Woodsboro, Texas: Rooke Foundation, 1953, 1955). *Hobart Huson*

BLACK RIDGE. Black Ridge is southwest of Agua Fria Mountain and twelve miles north-northwest of Terlingua in southwestern Brewster County (at 29°29′ N, 103°41′ W). It runs from the northwest to the southeast for two miles and includes at least three points higher than 3,950 feet above sea level. The highest point on the ridge, near its southeastern end, is 4,025 feet above sea level and rises more than 400 feet above the surrounding Chihuahuan Desert floor. The relatively less resistant sedimentary rocks around the mafic ridge have eroded away, leaving the harder rock exposed. Mafic rocks are generally dark-colored. Black Ridge supports sparse vegetation characteristic of Chihuahuan Desert scrub, including scattered semisucculents such as lechuguilla, sotol, and yucca, and various shrubs such as creosote bush and ocotillo.

BIBLIOGRAPHY: Ross A. Maxwell, *The Big Bend of the Rio Grande* (Bureau of Economic Geology, University of Texas at Austin, 1968). W. N. McAnulty, "Geology of Cathedral Mountain Quadrangle, Brewster County, Texas," *Bulletin of the Geological Society of America* 66 (1955). A. Michael Powell, "Vegetation of Trans-Pecos Texas," in *New Mexico Geological Society Guidebook* (Socorro, New Mexico: New Mexico Geological Society, 1980).

BLACK SEMINOLE INDIANS. Black Seminole Indians, sometimes known as Indian blacks, black Muscogulges, or Seminole freedmen, emerged as a distinct ethnic group in seventeenth-century Florida. During the early part of that century, the Spanish crown, which controlled Florida, gave land to a group of Lower Creeks hoping to form a buffer zone between themselves and the English settlers in Georgia and the Carolinas. Over time the Creeks were joined by other bands such as the Mikasukis and the Apalachicolas. By 1822 this confederation had adopted the name Seminole and numbered close to 5,000 members. Throughout the history of Spanish Florida the crown had also offered asylum to runaway slaves, i.e., maroons, from the English colonies. Entire free communities of blacks existed under Spanish rule in Florida and other parts of the empire. When the Spanish surrendered Florida to Britain in 1763, the policy of legal manumission ended, but the area's reputation as a sanctuary persisted. Runaways turned to the Seminoles for protection and asylum from slave hunters. During and after the American Revolution, the Seminoles added to the number of maroons through capture and purchase. Although considered slaves by the Seminoles, blacks found life a great deal more tolerable under their new masters, who adopted many of the practices of the lenient Spanish slave system. Seminoles in Florida often refused to sell their slaves or to turn them over to slavehunters or other Indians without being coerced.

Typically, maroons lived in separate communities next to the Seminoles, with their own leaders and political systems. They were allowed to own weapons and had control over their labor. Their culture largely reflected a mixture of Seminole, African, and white customs. The most formal obligation that existed between the two groups was the payment of an annual tribute, usually a percentage of the slave's crop. Seminoles barred the majority of blacks from becoming full members in their clans, but in certain cases they did extend membership or special status to such individual black leaders as John Kibbetts and Juan Caballo.[qqv] Intermarriage between the two ethnic groups occurred, but on a limited basis. Studies also suggest that, unlike the Seminoles, the majority of Black Seminoles practiced monogamy. Although they did not have tribal membership, Black Seminoles played key roles in both political and military matters. The Seminoles began to rely on the maroons, with their knowledge of English, as interpreters and intermediaries in negotiations with whites. When negotiations broke down, Black Seminoles proved to be especially fierce warriors, since they fought not only for the Seminoles' freedom but for their own. During the Seminole Wars of the early nineteenth century, maroons and Seminoles, in separate units, fought the United States Army in an attempt to resist relocation to the West. Both contemporaries and historians attribute much of the persistence of the struggle to the maroons' contributions as fighters, guides, and spies. Despite the efforts of both groups, the end of the wars meant the loss of their homeland and for many blacks, captured during the hostilities, a return to slavery[qv] in the United States. For Black Seminoles, removal also meant the beginning of the dispersal of their people to Oklahoma, Mexico, and Texas.

A major consequence of the Second Seminole War was the deterioration of relations between Seminoles and Black Seminoles. During the conflict, the United States Army initiated a policy, devised by Gen. Thomas S. Jesup, to divide the two races by offering the maroons their freedom if they surrendered. When maroon leaders entered into negotiations with the army, many Seminoles felt not only betrayed but cheated out of their legal property. Due to Seminole protest, the army was unable to fulfill its promises to the Black Seminoles, and when both groups reached Indian Territory problems arose as to the status of the maroons. The confusion surrounding the blacks' independence was further complicated by the subjugation of the Seminoles to Creek rule in Indian Territory, a stipulation of removal treaties that did not sit well with a majority of either Seminoles or Black Seminoles. After the Seminoles agreed to Creek rule in 1845, maroons found themselves subjected to the Creek slave codes, which prohibited them from owning weapons and property and threatened the existence of their independent communities. Black Seminoles found their former allies, the Seminoles, increasingly unwilling to support them in their efforts to resist the oppressive Creek codes. Seminoles believed that the maroons had betrayed them in the removal process. Fearing the loss of their autonomy, the maroons rejected Seminole authority and turned to the army for protection. But the army refused to support the maroons' claims of freedom and insisted that they return to Seminole rule, which often meant being sold to Creek or white slaveowners. Led by Juan Caballo, a substantial number of Black Seminoles went to Mexico in 1849.

In desperate need of people to patrol the Texas-Coahuila border for Comanches and Apaches, the Mexican government offered the maroons and a splinter band of Seminoles, led by Seminole warrior Wild Cat, a joint grant of land at the juncture of Río San Rodrigo and Río San Antonio. The maroons, now referred to as Mascogos, established an independent settlement at El Moral. As was the case in Florida, the maroon communities in Mexico continued to be havens for runaway slaves and freed blacks of mixed blood. Resettlement in Mexico, however, did not mean that the maroons escaped the continual efforts of slave hunters or the antiabolition sentiment that dominated Southern culture. Slaveowners and slave proponents in the United States besieged the Mexican government with requests that blacks within their boundaries be returned to slavery. As raids and hostilities increased, fearing a breach of the Treaty of Guadalupe Hidalgo,[qv] the Mexican government decided to move both the maroons and the Seminoles to a tract of land at the Hacienda de Nacimiento, located in the interior on the Río San Juan Sabinas. Once they were in Nacimiento, the weak alliance that had been formed by the maroons and Wild Cat's Seminoles essentially ended. The maroons proved to be better than their Seminole counterparts at settling the land, while the Seminoles preferred to conduct campaigns against other Indians rather than farm. When Wild Cat's Seminoles returned to Indian Territory in 1861, the Mascogos remained in Mexico.

External and internal pressures throughout the 1860s divided the Mascogos into three groups in Mexico—at Parras, Nacimiento, and Matamoros—and a band, led by Elijah Daniels, across the border in Texas. In 1870 the United States Army entered into negotiations with John Kibbetts, the leader of the group at Nacimiento, to employ Black Seminoles as Indian scouts and fighters in West Texas. Kibbetts agreed to move his people to Texas and to work for the army in exchange for the government's promise to support his people until they were moved to the Seminole Nation in Indian Territory. At Fort Duncan on August 16, 1870, Kibbetts was commissioned a sergeant and ten of his followers enlisted as privates.

The families of the men along with other members of Kibbetts's band established a camp on Elm Creek near the fort. In 1871 Daniels's band and the Matamoros faction arrived at Fort Duncan, increasing the number of Black Seminole Scouts[qv] by eighteen. By late 1875 Juan Caballo had brought his group to the fort as well. Although he refused to enlist as a scout himself, members of his band joined, and Caballo acted as an independent interpreter and negotiator. Other Black Seminoles established villages on military reservations to wait for their relocation to Indian Territory. Though they made some improvements to the land and contributions to construction projects at the forts, the groups were heavily dependent on army rations for their subsistence. After the 1870s the scouts' numbers were also strengthened by American freedmen, Mexican blacks, and blacks from the regular army. Eventually, black scouts were stationed at Fort Duncan and Fort Clark. They served primarily under the command of Col. Ranald S. Mackenzie and Lt. John L. Bullis.[qqv] The scouts' knowledge of English, Spanish, and various Indian dialects proved valuable to the army, as did their years of experience fighting the Indians in Mexico. The scouts distinguished themselves in the Indian wars; four of them—John Ward, Isaac Payne, Pompey Factor,[qqv] and Adam Payne—were awarded the Medal of Honor.

Despite the scouts' service to the United States, the government proved reluctant to fulfill its contract with the maroons concerning land. Originally, the army classified the maroons as Indians and believed that the group could be settled on Indian land. Questions arose from Indian agents, however, about the ethnicity of the group. Despite some mixing between the two groups, the Black Seminoles had maintained their identity as a separate people. What ensued was a battle among the army, the Indian Bureau, and the Department of the Interior over who would assume financial responsibility for the refugees. In the meantime, the material conditions of the group worsened as rations were periodically suspended and the maroons were unable to raise sufficient crops on the military reservations. In 1876 the military ordered all of the Black Seminoles to leave Fort Duncan for Fort Clark. Some of the maroons believed that their move to Indian Territory was in sight, but the army disappointed them as government bureaucrats continued to debate the questions of ethnicity and responsibility.

For their part, the Black Seminoles on military lands were split over moving to the Seminole Nation or returning to Nacimiento in Mexico. In the end some squatters returned to Nacimiento; others found refuge with Seminole freedman communities in the Seminole Nation, while still others remained at Fort Clark. When the United States disbanded the scouts in 1912, the maroons at Fort Clark, who numbered between 200 and 300, moved to nearby Brackettville, where the Seminole Indian Scout Cemetery is located. In the 1990s, communities of Black Seminoles still existed in Brackettville, Oklahoma, and Nacimiento. Reunions and cultural celebrations are held on a regular basis by Black Seminoles from all three communities. Despite the groups' modern differences, Black Seminoles in Texas, Oklahoma, and Mexico take great pride in their common heritage.

BIBLIOGRAPHY: Grant Foreman, *The Five Civilized Tribes* (Norman: University of Oklahoma Press, 1934). Kevin Mulroy, *Freedom on the Border: The Seminole Maroons in Florida, the Indian Territory, Coahuila and Texas* (Lubbock: Texas Tech University Press, 1993). Kenneth Wiggins Porter, *The Negro on the American Frontier* (New York: Arno Press, 1971). Kenneth Wiggins Porter, "The Seminole Negro-Indian Scouts, 1870–1881," *Southwestern Historical Quarterly* 55 (January 1952). Richard Price, *Maroon Societies: Rebel Slave Communities in the Americas* (Baltimore: Johns Hopkins University Press, 1979).

Tracé Etienne-Gray

BLACK SEMINOLE SCOUTS. On August 16, 1870, Maj. Zenas R. Bliss[qv] enlisted a special detachment of thirteen Black Seminole scouts from a group of approximately 100 who had recently arrived at Fort Duncan, Texas, from three main camps in northern Mexico. These people represented part of the mixed-blood Seminole and black population that had migrated to northeastern Mexico during 1849 and 1850 to escape American slave hunters. Originally, they had been well treated by the Mexican government, which employed them as militiamen against Comanche and Lipan Apache raiders, but they had subsequently been neglected by federal officials. In direct response to Capt. Frank W. Perry's offers of scouting jobs and protection, the Black Seminoles under subchief John Kibbetts[qv] resettled at Fort Duncan. During the following three years other kinsmen who had lived at Matamoros, Tamaulipas, and Laguna de Parras, Coahuila, also crossed the border into Texas and raised the total Black Seminole population to approximately 180. The first complement of scouts carried out their tracking duties so well that Bliss raised the number of enlistees to thirty-one by the end of 1871. He also elevated them to permanent military status by supplying them with arms, ammunition, and rations, as well as paying them the standard salary of privates in the regular army. Kibbetts served as company sergeant and received slightly higher pay. Successful operations along the Rio Grande attracted the attention of other officers, and in July 1872 Lt. Col. Wesley Merritt prevailed upon Bliss to transfer some of the scouts and their families north to Fort Clark.

At Fort Clark the scouts finally gained a permanent officer to com-

Black Seminole scouts, ca. 1912. Courtesy ITC. Around 1870 about 500 people descended from both African Americans and Seminole Indians moved back into Texas from Mexico, where they had been living. Some of these "Black Seminoles" served in the United States Army as scouts.

mand their unique group. Lt. John Lapham Bullis[qv] eagerly accepted the assignment in 1873, and despite his inexperience in dealing with Indians, the thirty-two-year-old officer quickly proved his mastery of the situation. Bullis succeeded because he gained the respect of his men by undergoing privations in the field with them and looking out for the needs of their families. Within a few months after Bullis took command of the scouts, they were playing a key role in Col. Ranald S. Mackenzie's[qv] May raid against a hostile Kickapoo camp near El Remolino, Coahuila. Because this village lay forty miles inside Mexico, the expedition relied heavily on the Black Seminoles and other scouts to prevent contact with Mexican soldiers and to assure a speedy withdrawal once the mission was accomplished. In performing this duty the scouts gained Mackenzie's respect, and he employed them a year later in his campaign against Comanche and Kiowa camps in Palo Duro Canyon.[qv] As trackers, couriers, and combatants, they demonstrated their value even beyond the familiar terrain of South Texas and northeastern Mexico. After these events of the Red River War,[qv] Indian threats to West Texas were greatly reduced, but small raiding parties still occasionally left the reservation near Fort Sill, Indian Territory, or crossed the border from their mountain refuges in Mexico. Between 1875 and 1881 the Black Seminole scouts spent much time on the trail of these small raiding parties. One fight at Eagle's Nest Crossing (*see* EAGLE NEST CREEK) on the Pecos River earned the Medal of Honor for scouts John Ward, Isaac Payne, and Pompey Factor.[qqv] The same award had previously gone to Pvt. Adam Payne for his gallantry in the Red River War. Despite their celebrated service record, the scouts suffered several major setbacks during this six-year period. Confrontations with members of John King Fisher's[qv] gang around Brackettville, Texas, resulted in some later killings of scouts. Furthermore, white citizens around Brackettville and Fort Clark began to agitate for the scouts' removal so that the land upon which their families were settled could be opened to public sale. The 1882 transfer of Bullis to Indian Territory likewise weakened the position of the black Indians by causing a large reduction in the complement of fifty scouts and a slashing of the ration issues to their families. Indirect congressional lobbying efforts by Bullis, Mackenzie, Col. Edward Hatch, and even Gen. Philip H. Sheridan,[qv] commander of the Military Division of the Missouri, failed to secure what the Black Seminoles needed most—title to their land near Fort Clark. In August 1912 the last sixteen Black Seminole scouts were mustered out of service, but by this time many of their destitute families had already moved to Del Rio, Eagle Pass, and other border towns to seek employment as ranchhands, laborers, and domestic servants. Their long years of service went virtually unnoticed by the progressive population of the new West. *See also* BLACK SEMINOLE INDIANS.

BIBLIOGRAPHY: Robert G. Carter, *On the Border with Mackenzie, or Winning West Texas from the Comanches* (Washington: Eynon Printing, 1935). John Allen Johnson, "The Medal of Honor and Sergeant John Ward and Private Pompey Factor," *Arkansas Historical Quarterly* 29 (Winter 1970). Kenneth Wiggins Porter, "The Seminole Negro-Indian Scouts, 1870–1881," *Southwestern Historical Quarterly* 55 (January 1952). Frost Woodhull, "The Seminole Indian Scouts on the Border," *Frontier Times,* December 1937.

Michael L. Tate

BLACK'S FORT. Black's Fort, on the South San Gabriel River in eastern Burnet County, was named for William Black, who built it in 1851, reportedly to protect local settlers from Indian raids. It consisted of a thick-walled stone house and a springhouse within a stone and wood stockade and served as a residence and a storage place for supplies and ammunition. It saw little defense service, however, as most of the raids occurred in the western part of the county near Fort Croghan. The building supposedly served as a fort until 1868. Thereafter it continued to be used as a residence. In 1936 the Texas Centennial[qv] Commission placed a marker on the site. In the latter part of the twentieth century there was some speculation that Black's Fort was not, in fact, a fort, but instead simply a residence. Possibly the structure, apparently the only stone house in the area, was called Black's Fort but had never actually served as a defense fort. As of the early 1990s there was no evidence to support or refute the claim, and the 1936 marker remained at the site.

BIBLIOGRAPHY: Malvin George Bowden, History of Burnet County (M.A. thesis, University of Texas, 1940). Marker Files, Texas Historical Commission, Austin.

BLACKSHEAR, EDWARD LAVOISIER (1862–1919). Edward Lavoisier Blackshear, teacher and administrator, was born in Montgomery, Alabama, on September 8, 1862, the son of Adlene Pollard and Abram Vandiver, who were slaves. Because his mother was a maid in the main house, he learned to read and write along with the white children of the Pollard family. He attended the first public school for African-American children in Montgomery and the Swayne School and Academy, established by the American Missionary Society there. In 1875 he entered Tabor College in Iowa, where he graduated in 1881 with Hightower T. Kealing.[qv] Blackshear taught in public schools for a year before joining Kealing in Waco in 1882. Blackshear's health failed during this year, and when he moved to Waco he first worked as a laborer putting up telegraph poles on the Texas-Midland Railroad. He afterwards attributed regaining his health to this labor and believed that physical, as well as intellectual, development was necessary for a well-educated person. He was soon hired to teach at Paul Quinn College, but in early 1883 he moved to Austin to teach at the Eighth Ward School. In the fall of 1883 he became principal of the Wheatsville School, and in May 1884 he was appointed principal of the summer normal school for black teachers to be held in Goliad. In 1888 he became the principal of the Central Grammar School and in 1892 the supervisor of all the African-American schools in Austin, as well as the principal of the high school, where he succeeded Kealing. He served as president of the Teachers State Association of Texas[qv] in 1903–04.

After his first wife died, he married Rachel Works. They had three children. In 1906 Governor James S. Hogg[qv] appointed Blackshear, a Democrat, to succeed Laurine C. Anderson,[qv] a Republican, as principal of Prairie View State Normal and Industrial College. While Blackshear was principal the school prospered. He earned a master's degree from Tabor College in 1902. But his success was not without its price, for the principalship at Prairie View was a political appointment. In the 1914 Democratic gubernatorial primary, Blackshear, a prohibitionist, supported Thomas H. Ball[qv] against the eventual winner, James E. Ferguson.[qv] The following year the newly inaugurated governor demanded that Blackshear be removed. Blackshear's explanation of his political activities failed to save his job. In that same year he was made head of government extension work for three states. He died on December 12, 1919, and is buried in Hempstead. Gregorytown School in Austin was renamed Blackshear School in his honor in 1936, when an extensive renovation and expansion program for the school began.

bibliography: Dallas *Weekly Herald*, May 8, 1884. Vernon McDaniel, *History of the Teachers State Association of Texas* (Washington: National Education Association, 1977). *May Schmidt*

BLACKSHEAR, KATHLEEN (1897–1988). Kathleen Blackshear, artist and teacher, was born in Navasota, Texas, on June 6, 1897, the daughter of Edward Duncan and May (Terrell) Blackshear and the granddaughter of Thomas E. Blackshear.[qv] She attended public schools in Navasota and began studying art and music in her early teens. After graduating from Navasota High School in 1914, she earned a bachelor of arts degree from Baylor University, where she contributed to the idea of establishing the Armstrong Browning Library.[qv] A photograph of Kathleen Blackshear was placed in the cornerstone of the Browning Library in 1950. After college she spent a year studying at the Art Students League in New York City. From 1918 to 1924 she worked in various teaching and design jobs and traveled to Europe and Mexico.

In the fall of 1924 she entered the School of the Art Institute of Chicago, where she studied with John Norton, Charles Fabens Kelley, William Owen, and Helen Gardner. Gardner, the author of Art Through the Ages, one of the first textbook surveys of art history to incorporate non-Western art, inspired in her an interest in African and Asian art that shaped her career. In 1926 Blackshear was hired to teach art history under the direction of Gardner, and the two women thereafter formed a close relationship that lasted until Gardner's death in 1946. Both women took their students to the Oriental Institute and the Field Museum of Natural History, thus affirming the value of African and Asian art at a time when non-Western art was usually studied from an anthropological viewpoint. They have been credited with shaping the distinctive style that emerged among Chicago artists during the 1940s and the 1950s. Blackshear also emphasized visual analysis of the formal properties of art objects, an emphasis that one student described as "teaching art history as art, not as history." She was remembered for the warm support and encouragement that she offered her students, particularly blacks.

Blackshear rejected academicism in her art and teaching. Drawing on memories of her childhood on a Southern farm, she used blacks as her primary subject matter from 1924 to 1940. Influenced by African masks and textiles, Post-Impressionists such as Paul Cézanne and Georges Seurat, and Cubism, she worked in a simplified, geometric style that became increasingly abstract in her later years. She experimented with ceramics, enamels, and batik processes after she earned her master of fine arts degree from the School of the Art Institute in 1940.

She participated in over fifty-five group exhibitions sponsored by such organizations as the Art Students League of Chicago, the Chicago Society of Artists, and the Art Institute of Chicago. The Witte Museum[qv] in San Antonio mounted the first solo exhibition of her work in 1941 and included her in two later exhibitions. She was also included in group exhibitions at the Museum of Fine Arts, Houston[qv] (1930, 1934), the Fort Worth Museum of Art (1935; *see* modern art museum of fort worth), the Dallas Museum of Fine Arts (1936, 1939, 1953; *see* dallas museum of art), and Rice University (1965). She exhibited her work for the last time at the HemisFair,[qv] San Antonio, in 1968. In addition to teaching and exhibiting, Blackshear wrote two plays and provided analytical drawings for Helen F. Mackenzie's *Understanding Picasso: A Study of His Styles and Development* (1940), Katharine Kuh's *Art Has Many Faces: The Nature of Art Presented Visually* (1951), and the revised and third editions of Gardner's *Art Through the Ages* (1936, 1948).

Kathleen Blackshear retired from teaching in 1961 and returned to Navasota with her companion, Ethel Spears. She continued to lecture on art at museums and schools throughout Texas until the early 1970s and received the title professor emeritus from the School of the Art Institute of Chicago in 1968. She died on October 14, 1988, in Navasota, where she was buried in Oakland Cemetery. Her work as an artist and teacher was honored with the 1990 retrospective exhibition "A Tribute to Kathleen Blackshear," organized by the School of the Art Institute of Chicago. Her work is included in the permanent collections of Southwestern University in Georgetown, the Modern Art Museum of Fort Worth, the Museum of Fine Arts in Houston, the Art Institute of Chicago, and a number of private collections in Navasota, Houston, Chicago, and San Diego.

bibliography: Kathleen Blackshear and Ethel Spears Papers, 1920–1990, Archives of American Art, Smithsonian Institution, Washington. Chris Petteys, *Dictionary of Women Artists* (Boston: Hall, 1985). Carole Tormollan, *A Tribute to Kathleen Blackshear* (School of the Art Institute of Chicago, 1990). *Kendall Curlee*

BLACKSHEAR, THOMAS EDWARD (1809–1867). Thomas Edward Blackshear, planter, soldier, and politician, was born in Montgomery County, Georgia, on August 18, 1809, the son of Edward and Emily (Mitchell) Blackshear. During the 1820s he moved with his parents to the vicinity of Thomasville in Thomas County, Georgia, then on the southwestern Georgia frontier. He graduated from the University of Georgia at Athens in 1828 and married Thomas County native Emily Goodwyn Raines (1814–1866) on December 8, 1831; they became the parents of nine children. As a planter of some means and scion of a distinguished Georgia family, Blackshear became a civic leader in the Thomasville area and served in the Georgia House of Representatives during the 1830s and in the Senate during the 1840s. He took time out from his political career to participate in the Creek campaign of 1836 as captain of a scout company of the Sixty-ninth Regiment, Second Brigade, Georgia Militia, and remained in the service during subsequent Indian wars; he eventually attained the rank of major general. On January 9, 1839, he was appointed secretary of the board of directors of the Brunswick and Florida Railway Company, of which he was a stockholder.

During the 1850s, as Thomas County's population increased rapidly, Blackshear grew restless and decided to migrate westward. He sold his property and moved to Texas with a large retinue of slaves in 1858. He took up cotton planting on a tract of bottomland near the Navasota River just east of Navasota in southwestern Grimes County. He soon purchased additional land along the Brazos River south of Navasota. By 1860 he had amassed property valued at $150,000 and was thus one of the two wealthiest men in the county; his estate then included 123 slaves, a number that grew to 152 by 1865. A notable aspect of his plantation management was his utilization of blacks as "drivers" and in other positions of trust. Although Blackshear himself did not serve in the military during the Civil War,[qv] four of his sons fought in the armies of the Confederacy.

Like many other planters Blackshear experienced great difficulties adjusting to the harsh realities of agriculture in Reconstruction[qv] Texas. Dismayed at what he considered the unreliable work habits of freedmen, he resolved to cultivate his property exclusively with white sharecroppers, each farming tracts of from forty to sixty acres. In an effort to recruit the necessary labor, he corresponded with newspaper editors in his native state, including Lucius C. Bryan of the Thomasville *Southern Enterprise*, to enlist their cooperation in advertising the advantages of Texas agriculture to poor white farmers struggling for subsistence on the exhausted soils of Georgia. Blackshear was planning a trip to Georgia to engage tenants when he contracted yellow fever and died on October 20, 1867. His correspondence, diary, memorandum book, and account book are in the Barker Texas History Center,[qv] University of Texas at Austin.

BIBLIOGRAPHY: Randolph B. Campbell, *An Empire for Slavery: The Peculiar Institution in Texas, 1821–1865* (Baton Rouge: Louisiana State University Press, 1989). Maurine Chinski, *The Navasota Bluebonnet: Commemorating One Hundred Years of City Growth and Development, 1854–1954* (Navasota, Texas: Grimes County Chamber of Commerce, 1954). Grimes County Historical Commission, *History of Grimes County, Land of Heritage and Progress* (Dallas: Taylor, 1982). *Members of the Legislature of the State of Texas from 1846 to 1939* (Austin: Texas Legislature, 1939). William Warren Rogers, ed., "From Planter to Farmer: A Georgia Man in Reconstruction Texas," *Southwestern Historical Quarterly* 72 (April 1969). *Marie Giles*

BLACK SPRING BRANCH. Black Spring Branch begins two miles southeast of Purves in southern Erath County (at 31°59′ N, 98°14′ W) and runs northeast for three miles to its mouth on Little Green Creek, two miles south of Alexander (at 32°01′ N, 98°12′ W). The stream is dammed to form Soil Conservation Service Reservoir 13 at its mouth. The area's steep slopes and benches are surfaced by shallow clay loams that support juniper, live oak, mesquite, and grasses.

BLACK STATE CONVENTIONS. Black state conventions were held in Texas on at least ten occasions during the period from Reconstruction[qv] through the 1890s to express the concerns of blacks in an era before the existence of lasting groups that focused upon the economic, political, and civil rights of minorities. Often these state meetings sent delegates to national conventions seeking the same goals. The Texas State Central Committee of Colored Men met in Austin on March 22, 1866, with Jacob Fontaine,[qv] a Baptist minister, presiding. It opposed a request for funds, which presumably would benefit former slaves, by Episcopal bishop Alexander Gregg,[qv] who did not have the trust of the committee. Instead, committee members expressed their preference for the work of the Freedmen's Bureau.[qv]

On July 3–4, 1873, delegates for a Colored Men's State Convention gathered at Brenham with Norris Wright Cuney,[qv] a Republican party[qv] leader, as president. They announced support for friendly race relations, a federal civil rights act, open political meetings, black landholding, internal improvements, immigration to the United States, President U. S. Grant, and the Republican party. The delegates criticized the violence faced by blacks and efforts to repudiate state debts.

When a Colored Men's State Convention, chaired by former legislator Richard Allen,[qv] met on July 4, 1879, in Houston, it focused upon the causes of the black exodus from Texas and the South to Kansas. The members repeated some earlier concerns and objected to the exclusion of blacks from juries, lack of adequate schools, harsh treatment in prisons, inequitable enforcement of laws against intermarriage, and railroad segregation. To solve these problems the delegates generally urged blacks to move out of the state, although some individuals favored acquisition of land on the Texas frontier.

A black convention followed in Dallas on February 16–17, 1880, with delegates from nearby North Texas counties and W. R. Carson, a local minister, presiding. Those attending favored an effort to seek land in West Texas as a solution to problems of discrimination. To promote that goal the convention founded the Texas Farmer's Association, which proved unsuccessful, perhaps because of white Democrats' fears that it would strengthen the Republicans.

On July 10–12, 1883, a State Convention of Colored Men of Texas, chaired by Abraham Grant, a minister in the African Methodist Episcopal Church,[qv] met at Austin in response to the United States Supreme Court decision that declared the Civil Rights Act of 1875 unconstitutional. The delegates took a nonpartisan position on politics and reasserted earlier concerns about various forms of discrimination. The convention called for establishment of a Colored People's Progressive Union to assist in court cases on civil rights, but it did not develop.

Black leaders gathered on August 5–7, 1884, at Houston, with John N. Johnson presiding. The convention supported many positions taken in previous meetings, denied any plots to attack whites, urged equal sentences for black and white criminals, opposed lynching,[qv] and emphasized moral conduct.

On September 8–9, 1886, a Colored Men's State Convention met at Brenham with D. W. Roberts, an Austin minister, in the chair. It focused upon the need for education and economic advancement, an emphasis that resulted in an appeal to the legislature for a black industrial college.

Delegates to a Colored Men's State Convention gathered in Waco on August 20–22, 1889, again under the direction of Roberts. In addition to citing new examples of old problems, they protested lynching and moves toward political disfranchisement of blacks. Yet they also emphasized economic progress, offered thanks for educational advances, and endorsed high moral standards.

Two years later, on September 1–2, 1891, the next Colored Men's State Convention met in Houston, chaired by I. B. Scott, a Methodist minister. The delegates adopted new resolutions in favor of home ownership, a black-owned railroad, black inspectors for state prison camps, membership of black teachers on county examining boards, and the founding by the state of a black university. A further address opposed efforts to segregate black exhibits at the World's Fair to be held in 1893.

The last black state convention came together at Houston on May 23, 1895, with Scott, now serving Wiley College as president, again in the chair. Key issues that aroused the concern of delegates continued to include discriminatory laws, antiblack group violence, and exclusion from juries. The convention also honored Frederick Douglass and sought to found a permanent Colored Men's Union. Although that effort failed, it foreshadowed the establishment of the National Association for the Advancement of Colored People,[qv] to which some former convention leaders later belonged. Through the late nineteenth century the black conventions provided one of the strongest collective voices for the black people of Texas.

BIBLIOGRAPHY: E. W. Winkler, *Platforms of Political Parties in Texas* (Austin: University of Texas, 1916).

Alwyn Barr

BLACKSTOCK, LEO GUY (1899–1972). Leo (Lee) Guy Blackstock, attorney, teacher, and World War II[qv] hero, was born on November 1, 1899, at Whitt, Texas, the son of Rabun A. and Pearl (Mathis) Blackstock. He attended high school in Weatherford and then enrolled in the University of Texas, where he earned a B.A. degree in economics in 1923, an M.A. degree in business administration in 1925, and, while holding a full-time teaching position in the College of Business Administration, a J.D. degree (with highest honors) from the UT law school in 1933. He taught at Trinity University in 1924–25, when the institution was located at Waxahachie, and at Sam Houston State Teachers College (now Sam Houston State University) from 1925 to 1927. With some interruptions he served on the faculty of the University of Texas from 1927 to 1971 in both the College of Business Administration and the School of Law.

Blackstock took a leave of absence from the university from 1937 to 1939 to serve as chief examiner of the gas utilities division of the Railroad Commission[qv] of Texas. In 1936 he was commissioned a captain in the United States Army Reserve and was on active duty in the army from November 1, 1940, to November 30, 1946. He was a graduate of the Command and General Staff School and assistant judge advocate of the Tenth Army Corps; he served in the Pacific Theater, where he participated in the New Guinea campaign of 1944, the initial invasion of the Philippines at Leyte in 1944, and the Mindanao campaign in 1945. He was assigned from October 1945 to November 1946 to the occupation forces in Japan, where he was chief of the prosecution division, legal section, of the Supreme Command of the Allied Powers in Tokyo and was in charge of the prosecution of Japanese war criminals (classes B and C). He received numerous decorations and citations, including the Bronze Star. After he was released from active duty as a colonel, he remained in Japan as a civilian attached to the army, from December 1, 1946, to August 8, 1948, and continued his work in the prosecution of war criminals. His work, however, did not prevent him from enjoying a close and warm relationship with many Japanese friends for the remainder of his life.

Afterward, Blackstock returned to the University of Texas, where he was professor of business law in the College of Business Administration and, from 1953 to 1966, visiting professor of military law in the School of Law. He retired from the university on May 31, 1971, when he became professor emeritus. His book, *Cases on Military Justice* (1954), was a significant contribution in that field. He also wrote several other works and lectured extensively off campus on various aspects of law.

He was married to Harriet L. Barrickman on June 30, 1923, at New Braunfels; they had two sons. On May 26, 1948, he was married to Hannah-Graham Belcher in two ceremonies (official and religious) at Yokohama and Tokyo, Japan. He died on September 4, 1972, and was buried in Fort Sam Houston Cemetery in San Antonio. Several years before his death he gave his fine collection of books on military law to the library of the University of Texas School of Law. In 1973 the Leo G. Blackstock Fund was established to provide an annual scholarship to a prelaw undergraduate in the College of Business at the University of Texas at Austin.

BIBLIOGRAPHY: Vertical Files, Barker Texas History Center, University of Texas at Austin.

Eldon S. Branda

BLACKTAIL CREEK. Blacktail Creek rises at the breaks of the Llano Estacado[qv] in northwestern Briscoe County (at 34°41′ N, 101°21′ W) and flows north for four miles to its mouth on the Prairie Dog Town Fork of the Red River, near the northern county line (at 34°44′ N, 101°20′ W). The creek was once part of the Tule division of the JA Ranch,[qv] and most of it still lies within the ranch's boundaries. The stream crosses terrain surfaced by silt loams that support mesquite and grasses.

BIBLIOGRAPHY: Briscoe County Historical Survey Committee, *Footprints of Time in Briscoe County* (Dallas: Taylor, 1976). Harley True Burton, *A History of the JA Ranch* (Austin: Von Boeckmann–Jones, 1928; rpt., New York: Argonaut, 1966).

BLACK WALNUT CREEK. Black Walnut Creek, also known as Walnut Creek, is a perennial stream that rises four miles east of New Ulm in western Austin County (at 29°53′ N, 96°25′ W) and flows northeast for seven miles through mostly open country to its mouth on West Mill Creek (at 29°57′ N, 96°24′ W). It traverses rolling to nearly level terrain surfaced by sandy loam that supports post oak, blackjack oak, elm, hackberry, water oak, and pecan trees near the banks. Settlement in the vicinity of the stream began during the early 1830s. The sandy soils in this well-timbered region of Austin County, between New Ulm and Cat Spring, render much of the area unsuitable for agriculture and have slowed settlement. During the late 1840s German immigrants established New Bremen near the creek's mouth.

BIBLIOGRAPHY: C. W. Schmidt, *Footprints of Five Generations* (New Ulm, Texas: New Ulm *Enterprise*, 1930).

BLACKWATER DRAW. Blackwater Draw begins at the Texas–New Mexico border in northwestern Bailey County (at 34°19′ N, 103°04′ W) and stretches southeast for sixty-three miles, across Lamb and Hale counties, to its end on Yellow House Draw, in Yellow House Canyon northeast of Lubbock in central Lubbock County (at 33°36′ N, 101°50′ W). A creek that runs through much of the valley is dammed in its upper reaches. The surrounding flat to rolling terrain is surfaced by sandy loam and sand that support hardwood forests and grasses.

BLACKWELL, THOMAS H. (ca. 1804–1851). Thomas H. Blackwell, soldier and civil servant, was born in Kentucky around 1804. In a letter of introduction to Sam Houston[qv] dated January 2, 1836, J. S. Smith of Richmond, Kentucky, characterized "Major" Blackwell as a man who came to Texas "to do or die." At the battle of San Jacinto[qv] Blackwell served as a private in Capt. Henry W. Karnes's[qv] company of Mirabeau B. Lamar's[qv] "cavalry corps." After the Texas Revolution[qv] Blackwell served the Republic of Texas[qv] as recording clerk of the House of Representatives of the First Congress. He was also clerk of the board of land commissioners in Brazoria County and on December 15, 1837, was elected clerk of the Brazoria District Court by both houses of Congress. He was reelected on February 1, 1841. He was one of a committee of twenty-eight men from Brazoria County who, on April 14, 1845, drew up resolutions favoring the annexation[qv] of Texas. In 1850 he was listed as a merchant who owned $5,000 worth of property in Brazoria County. Blackwell never married. He died at his home in Brazoria County in March 1851, and Christopher Stringfellow was named administrator of his estate.

BIBLIOGRAPHY: *Compiled Index to Elected and Appointed Officials of the Republic of Texas, 1835–1846* (Austin: State Archives, Texas State Library, 1981). Daughters of the Republic of Texas, *Muster Rolls of the Texas Revolution* (Austin, 1986). Sam Houston Dixon and Louis Wiltz Kemp, *The Heroes of San Jacinto* (Houston: Anson Jones, 1932). John H. Jenkins, ed., *The Papers of the Texas Revolution, 1835–1836* (10 vols., Austin: Presidial Press, 1973). *Telegraph and Texas Register*, December 6, 1836, January 11, 1837, December 16, 1837, April 14, 1845.

Thomas W. Cutrer

BLACKWELL, TEXAS. Blackwell is on State Highway 70, Farm Road 1170, and the Santa Fe tracks three miles northwest of Oak Creek Reservoir in Nolan and Coke counties. The community was originally called James or Jamestown when the plat was filed in 1906, but it was renamed for an Orient Railroad stockholder when the railroad was built through later that year. A post office was granted to the community in March 1907. The town developed as a trading center for portions of Nolan, Coke, and Taylor counties. Its first school opened in 1907, and in 1929 the Blackwell Rural Consolidated High School was organized. Churches at the community included Methodist, Baptist, and Church of Christ, established in 1903, 1909, and 1928 respectively. In 1945 the town reported a population of 500 and thirteen businesses. In 1980 its population was 286 and in 1990, 339.

bibliography: E. L. Yeats and Hooper Shelton, *History of Nolan County* (Sweetwater, Texas: Shelton, 1975). *William R. Hunt*

BLACKWELL, ENID AND TEXAS RAILWAY. The Blackwell, Enid and Texas Railway Company was chartered on July 2, 1901, to lay track from Vernon, Texas, to the north bank of the Red River, near the east line of Wilbarger County. The initial capital was $20,000, and the business office was in Vernon, Wilbarger County. Members of the first board of directors included C. T. Herring,[qv] L. G. Hawkins, Bismarck Houssels, B. J. Parker, and J. R. Tolbert, all of Vernon; Breckenridge Jones and Eugene Benoist of St. Louis, Missouri; Edward L. Peckham of Oklahoma; and W. C. Robinson of Winfield, Texas. In 1902 twelve miles of track was completed from Vernon to the Red River, where connection was made with the Blackwell, Enid and Southwestern Railway Company. The following year the line received $47,217 in passenger revenue and $152,917 in freight revenue. On June 30, 1904, the road was acquired by the St. Louis, San Francisco and Texas Railway Company, which operated it until the line was abandoned in 1957. *Chris Cravens*

BLAFFER, SARAH CAMPBELL (1885–1975). Sarah (Sadie) Campbell Blaffer, art patron and philanthropist, daughter of William Thomas and Sarah (Turnbull) Campbell, was born in Waxahachie, Texas, on August 27, 1885. Her father was one of the founders of the Texas Company (later Texaco[qv]). She was educated at the Catholic convent in Lampasas and the Boston Conservatory. On April 22, 1909, she married Robert E. Lee Blaffer, one of the founders of Humble Oil and Refining Company, at St. Mary's Episcopal Church in Lampasas. They had four children. Sarah Blaffer's devotion to the visual arts began during a visit to the Louvre on her wedding trip to Europe. Over the years she acquired an extensive art collection ranging from fourteenth-century Old Master paintings to Impressionist and Expressionist works. She became an early benefactor of the Museum of Fine Arts, Houston,[qv] to which she donated original works by Paul Cézanne, Frans Hals, Antonio Canaletto, and Auguste Renoir. In 1964 she established the Sarah Campbell Blaffer Foundation, the primary goal of which is to bring the visual arts to people throughout the state of Texas. The foundation collected art works in two central categories, Old Masters and abstract Expressionism. In order to focus on fourteenth to eighteenth century works, the foundation sold its collection of twenty-eight abstract Expressionist works in 1987. The remaining pieces travel as a study collection throughout the state, free of charge, to towns that might not otherwise have the opportunity to collect or borrow such works. These touring collections have expanded over the years to include specialized collections, such as a first edition of Francisco Goya's "Disasters of War" etchings, Netherlandish and German genre paintings from the sixteenth and seventeenth centuries, Italian paintings from the fourteenth to eighteenth century, and British art from the sixteenth to eighteenth century. In 1973 the University of Houston art museum was named in Sarah Blaffer's honor for the works of art that she and other family members had lent to the institution. She lived in Houston, where she died on May 13, 1975.

bibliography: Hugh Best, *Debrett's Texas Peerage* (New York: Coward-McCann, 1983). Houston *Chronicle,* September 18, 1977, January 20, 1980, July 3, 1989. Houston *Post,* July 3, 1989. Janet Kutner, "Feeding 'the Hunger for Excellent Things'," *ARTnews,* September 1976. Terisio Pignatti, *Five Centuries of Italian Paintings, 1300–1800: From the Collection of the Sarah Campbell Blaffer Foundation* (exhibition catalog, London: White Brothers, 1985). *Nancy S. Hixon*

BLAINE, TEXAS. Blaine was a farming community thirty-three miles southeast of Canton in southeastern Van Zandt County. A Blaine post office was established in 1893 and discontinued in 1907. A black school established at the site by 1890 reached an enrollment of seventeen in 1903. At its height Blaine had a black Methodist church, but the community never appeared on state highway maps and had no recorded population estimates. *Diana J. Kleiner*

BLAIR, JOHN (1803–1836). John Blair, Alamo defender, was born in Tennessee in 1803. On February 19, 1835, he registered as a married man for a league of land in Texas. He may have been one of the volunteers who accompanied James Bowie[qv] to Bexar and the Alamo in early 1836. Louis Rose,[qv] who left the Alamo before the final battle, later testified that he "Left [John Blair] in the Alamo 3 March 1836." Blair died in the battle of the Alamo[qv] on March 6, 1836.

bibliography: Robert Bruce Blake, "A Vindication of Rose and His Story," in *In the Shadow of History,* ed. J. Frank Dobie, Mody C. Boatright, and Harry H. Ransom (Publications of the Texas Folklore Society 15, Detroit: Folklore Association, 1939). Daughters of the American Revolution, *The Alamo Heroes and Their Revolutionary Ancestors* (San Antonio, 1976). Bill Groneman, *Alamo Defenders* (Austin: Eakin, 1990). *Bill Groneman*

BLAIR, SAMUEL (1807–1836). Samuel Blair, Alamo defender and officer of the Alamo garrison, was born in Tennessee in 1807. He registered as a single man for a quarter league of land in the Power and Hewetson colony[qv] on August 4, 1834. On September 10, 1834, he registered for a headright of land in James McGloin's[qv] colony. Blair took part in the siege of Bexar.[qv] He later served in the Alamo garrison as assistant to the ordnance chief, Robert Evans,[qv] with the rank of captain. He died in the battle of the Alamo[qv] on March 6, 1836.

bibliography: Daughters of the American Revolution, *The Alamo Heroes and Their Revolutionary Ancestors* (San Antonio, 1976). Daughters of the Republic of Texas, *Muster Rolls of the Texas Revolution* (Austin, 1986). Bill Groneman, *Alamo Defenders* (Austin: Eakin, 1990). Texas General Land Office, *An Abstract of the Original Titles of Record in the General Land Office* (Houston: Niles, 1838; rpt., Austin: Pemberton Press, 1964). *Bill Groneman*

BLAIR, WILLIAM COCHRAN (1791–1873). William Cochran Blair, Presbyterian missionary, was born in Bourbon County, Kentucky, on March 16, 1791. During the War of 1812 he volunteered in Ross County, Ohio, and served as a private with Maj. Robert Harper's battalion. Blair graduated from Jefferson College, Pennsylvania, in 1818 and from Princeton Theological Seminary in 1821. He was ordained in 1822 and spent eight years among the Chickasaw Indians. During the early years of his ministry he worked under the synods of South Carolina and Georgia and under the Mississippi Presbytery. He married Susan Mueller on June 20, 1827, in Natchez, and they had one daughter. In 1828 he founded the First Presbyterian Church of Memphis, and in 1835 he became the first moderator of the Synod of Mississippi. At some time the family moved from Natchez to East Baton Rouge in Louisiana. Blair visited Texas in 1838, and the following year the Board of Foreign Missions of the General Presbyterian Assembly sent him to Texas as a missionary, primarily to the Mexican population. Blair settled in Victoria in the spring of 1840 to preach, teach, and distribute Spanish-language Bibles and religious tracts. Although one of several ministers authorized by the Mississippi Synod to organize the Presbytery of the Brazos, he was delayed by high water and so was unable to participate in the work at Independence in April 1840. On October 2, 1841, he organized a church in Victoria, where he preached until 1847, when the property was lost in a lawsuit. Blair and his family were forced to flee twice from invading Mexican forces and several times from raiding Comanche Indians. He and his wife cared for Rebecca Jane Fisher[qv] and her brother for some time after the murder of their parents and the children's recovery from Indians in the spring of 1840. Blair moved to Goliad and was principally responsible for the town's donation of land for Aranama College in the early 1850s. He presided over the college for a time and was a member of the board. He also aided in securing funds for Austin College. By 1857 he was living in Green Lake, west of Port Lavaca. He moved to Port Lavaca as he became less active and preached there until his death, on February 13, 1873. He was buried in Port Lavaca.

BIBLIOGRAPHY: Mary Smith Fay, *War of 1812 Veterans in Texas* (New Orleans: Polyanthos, 1979). William S. Red, ed., "Allen's Reminiscences of Texas, 1838–1842," *Southwestern Historical Quarterly* 18 (January 1915). William Stuart Red, *A History of the Presbyterian Church in Texas* (Austin: Steck, 1936). Victor Marion Rose, *History of Victoria* (Laredo, 1883; rpt., Victoria, Texas: Book Mart, 1961). Jessie Guy Smith, *Heroes of the Saddle Bags: A History of Christian Denominations in the Republic of Texas* (San Antonio: Naylor, 1951).

Louise Kelly

BLAIR, WILLIAM FRANKLIN (1912–1985). W. Frank Blair, zoologist, was born on June 25, 1912, at Dayton, Texas, the eldest of the five children of Percy Franklin and Mona Clyde (Patrick) Blair. His family moved to Westville, Oklahoma, in 1916 and to Tulsa, Oklahoma, in 1922. Blair graduated from Tulsa Central High School in 1930 and earned a bachelor's degree from the University of Tulsa in 1934. He married Fern Antell, a librarian at the University of Tulsa, on October 25, 1933; they had no children.

Blair received an M.S. degree from the University of Florida in 1935 and a Ph.D. from the University of Michigan in 1938. He remained at the University of Michigan as a research associate until 1942, when he entered the United States Army Air Corps. He returned briefly to Ann Arbor in 1946 and in the same year accepted a position at the University of Texas, where he remained for the rest of his life. He was the first director of the university's Brackenridge Field Laboratory and chairman of the budget council for the Marine Science Institute. He was promoted to professor in 1955 and to professor emeritus in zoology upon his retirement in 1982. Between 1935 and 1982 Blair published or edited some 162 papers, articles, and books, including *Vertebrates of the United States* (1957), *The Rusty Lizard: A Population Study* (1960), *Evolution in the Genus Bufo* (1972), and *Big Biology: The U.S.-I.B.P. [International Biological Program]* (1977). He supervised forty-nine Ph.D. and fifty-one M.A. studies and was an invited lecturer for ninety presentations worldwide between 1968 and 1982.

He developed an international reputation in the fields of ecology and evolutionary biology and conducted major research projects on subjects such as the genus *Bufo* and its parallels in the faunas of desert regions in North and South America. The latter project led to his involvement in the International Biological Program, a fifty-seven-nation project sponsored by the International Council of Scientific Unions, which had as its major goal the achievement of a better understanding of the world's ecosystems. From 1968 to 1972 Blair was chairman of the United States National Committee of the IBP. He also helped edit the program's fourteen scientific volumes on the global environment. In 1977 he was honored for his work with the IBP as the twenty-fifth recipient of the Joseph Priestly Award, established by Dickinson College in Carlisle, Pennsylvania, to recognize scientific contributions to the welfare of humanity.

Blair was a fellow of the American Association for the Advancement of Science. He served as president of the American Institute of Biological Sciences, the Ecological Society of America, the Southwestern Association of Naturalists, and the Texas Herpetological Society. He was also vice president of the American Society of Ichthyologists and Herpetologists and of the Texas Academy of Science.[qv] He was a member of several environmentally oriented state committees, including the Governor's Colorado River Basin Water Quality Management Study Planning Committee (1972–73) and the Texas Committee on Natural Resources (beginning in 1969).

Blair died on February 11, 1985; his ashes were scattered over the grounds of his ten acres, on the site of Fort Colorado. At his request the land was donated to the Travis Audubon Society, which established the site as a natural preserve for ecological studies.

BIBLIOGRAPHY: Vertical Files, Barker Texas History Center, University of Texas at Austin. *Who's Who in America*, 1980–81.

Art Leatherwood

BLAIR, TEXAS. Blair is a farming community on the Atchison, Topeka and Santa Fe line and Farm Road 126, four miles southwest of Merkel in northwestern Taylor County. The area was settled in the 1890s, and in 1897 it became the center of school district number 32, which included the schools of Patterson and Center Point. In 1904 these schools were consolidated as Blair school, named for Watt Blair, a prominent member of the community. The next year a post office was opened, and in 1910 the Gulf, Colorado and Santa Fe built through the community. The school was moved closer to the tracks soon after the railroad came through. A new two-story schoolhouse was built a few years later; it was also used for Baptist, Methodist and Church of Christ services. By 1914 Blair had telephone service and two general stores, a grocer, and a population of fifty. The population declined to twenty-five in the 1920s, and the post office closed in 1926. Blair's fortunes picked up in the 1930s, and its population had increased to 125 by 1940, when it also had two churches, a school, and eight businesses. The school consolidated with the Merkel system in 1944, and by the 1950s the population was once again estimated at about fifty. From 1968 through the early 1990s Blair had an estimated twenty-five inhabitants. Its last store closed in 1975, and the train station was also shut down. In 1984 the community consisted of a few scattered dwellings. During the early 1990s the annual Blair Reunion was still being held each October; however, like almost everything else of Blair, the reunion had been moved to nearby Merkel.

BIBLIOGRAPHY: Juanita Daniel Zachry, *A History of Rural Taylor County* (Burnet, Texas: Nortex, 1980). *George Strader*

BLAIR CREEK (Fayette County). Blair Creek rises in a tank a mile from the Lee county line in northwest Fayette County (at 30°06′ N, 96°50′ W) and flows southwest for 4½ miles to its mouth on Owl Creek, one mile west of Nechanitz (at 30°03′ N, 96°52′ W). It traverses flat to moderately rolling lands surfaced by sandy loam and mixed sand and gravel that support sparse to dense thickets of oak, cedar, and yaupon. The area is marginal for agriculture. The creek may be named after either William or James Blair, who left the county in 1849 with Joseph Young and others to go to the gold fields of California.

——— (Franklin County). Blair Creek rises eight miles southwest of Mount Vernon in southwestern Franklin County (at 33°05′ N, 95°15′ W) and flows south for three miles to its mouth, on Lake Cypress Springs. The stream is intermittent in its upper reaches. Upstream, the terrain is gently undulating to rolling with a loamy surface; downstream, the soils are sandy. The area is heavily wooded, with pines and various hardwoods predominating. The stream was probably named for James Blair, who patented land near its mouth.

BLAIR'S FORT. Blair's Fort, the largest western family fort, a nonmilitary installation, was west of Desdemona in Eastland County. Only folk stories remain about C. C. Blair, an early rancher, who built the fort in 1860; however, accounts reveal that his ranch had been previously victimized by marauding Comanches and Tonkawas, the presumed reason for the installation's existence. Between 1857 and 1862 the Indians were unusually active along the frontier; although their main objective was to steal horses, they killed and burned residences on the slightest provocation. Settlers were forced to come together for mutual protection, and forted ranches were established. At Blair's Fort twelve log cabins were built; tents were stretched around an open square, and all was enclosed by a fence eight or ten feet high. During the time the fort was used eight families found protection there. The fort was also a frequent stopping place for Texas Rangers[qv] on their journeys; large supplies of food and ammunition were kept on hand. Later a road opened between Stephenville and Fort Griffin, which passed through Blair's Fort. Blair's Fort stood for five years, 1860–65. A Confederate Memorial Marker was placed at the site on July 14, 1965.

BIBLIOGRAPHY: Eastland County Historical Book Committee, *Gateway to the West: Eastland County History,* Vol. 1 (Eastland, Texas, 1989). Carolyne Lavinia Langston, *History of Eastland County* (Dallas: Aldridge 1904).

Jeanne F. Lively

BLAKE, BENNETT (1809–1896). Bennett Blake, jurist, legislator, land dealer, banker, and delegate to the Confederate Congress and the Constitutional Convention of 1875,[qv] the son of Samuel Dow and Abigail (Lee) Blake, was born at Sutton, Vermont, on November 11, 1809. He married Mary Lewis in New Hampshire in 1833, but she died the next year, leaving a son who died at age sixteen in Philadelphia. After the untimely death of his first wife and the failure of his first business venture, Blake moved to Boston, where he lived with a sister for several months before deciding to seek his fortune in Texas. He arrived in Nacogdoches in 1835 with only twenty dollars but ultimately acquired a large farm and began a new life as merchant and farmer. He married Keziah Catherine Harrison, daughter of William Fenley, on December 26, 1850; and on November 24, 1853, he married Ellazina Harris, daughter of Elbridge G. and Mary Hamilton Harris. With his third wife he had three children.

As his financial condition improved, Blake soon began acquiring additional land in Nacogdoches County and over all of East Texas. Some he purchased outright, but much he acquired as a result of his moneylending. For many years, while Texas laws prohibited banks and restricted banking operations, Blake lent varying sums of money to his fellow Texans, the loans usually being secured by land and land titles. In effect, he functioned as a private banker and consequently as a land speculator.

He entered upon a distinguished career in public service shortly after his arrival in Texas. His neighbors first elected him a justice of the peace in 1838 and reelected him until, by 1850, he had served some ten years in that office. Thereafter, he became chief justice of Nacogdoches County, an office he held for twelve years. In these twenty-two years he reportedly heard and decided 7,000 civil suits and 500 criminal cases.

Blake fought in the Texas Revolution.[qv] He also served under Gen. Thomas J. Rusk[qv] in an expedition against the Cherokee Indians in 1839 and engaged in a second Cherokee expedition in 1841. East Texas voters elected him to the state legislature in 1862, and he became one of the Texas delegates to the Congress of the Confederate States of America, where he served during 1863–64. After the Reconstruction[qv] period, voters again chose him to represent them at the Constitutional Convention of 1875, where at age sixty-six he was the second oldest delegate. Thereafter, although his friends and neighbors urged him to continue in service to the public, he declined to accept public office and concentrated instead on his banking and farming. Judge Blake was a Democrat and Mason. He died in Nacogdoches County on March 1, 1896, and is buried in Oak Grove Cemetery in Nacogdoches.

BIBLIOGRAPHY: Bennett Blake Papers, Special Collections, Steen Library, Stephen F. Austin State University. Joe E. Ericson, *Banks and Bankers in Early Texas, 1835–1875* (New Orleans: Polyanthos Press, 1976). Joe E. Ericson, *Judges of the Republic of Texas (1836–1846): A Biographical Directory* (Dallas: Taylor, 1980). *Memorial and Genealogical Record of Texas (East)* (Chicago: Goodspeed, 1895; rpt., Easley, South Carolina: Southern Historical Press, 1982).

Joe E. Ericson

BLAKE, JACOB EDMUND (1812–1846). Jacob Edmund Blake, soldier, was born in Philadelphia in 1812, the son of businessman George Blake. He attended the United States Military Academy at West Point and graduated in 1833. He was posted to the Sixth Infantry and spent the next four years working at various stations in clerk positions. In July 1838 he was transferred to the new Corps of Topographical Engineers as a first lieutenant. He saw service in Florida during the Seminole War (1838–39) as assistant topographical engineer and in 1842 as a member of Gen. William J. Worth's[qv] staff. Blake was also involved in the 1841 survey of the Texas–United States border and did work on Lake Erie, in New Orleans, and in Florida.

In 1845 he was assigned to General Zachary Taylor's[qv] army of observation at Corpus Christi. In October of that year, he was posted to San Antonio de Béxar to survey the roads between there and Corpus Christi–Point Isabel. In San Antonio he made an important rendering of the unrestored Alamo chapel and barracks (1845). The drawing, now preserved at the National Archives, is considered one of the best representations of the Alamo before its repair in 1850. The result of his survey was the map of South Texas in which the Blake drawing was included.

When Taylor moved to the Rio Grande, Blake rejoined the main army. He was mentioned in Taylor's official report for his daring reconnaissance of the Mexican lines just before the battle of Palo Alto.[qv] During the lull between the battles of Palo Alto and Resaca de la Palma[qv] in May 1846, Blake remained in the saddle nearly twenty-four hours before returning to camp at Rancho Viejo. When he unsaddled his horse, his holsters hit the ground and his gun went off. The ball struck him, and he died a few hours later, on May 9, 1846, and was buried on the Palo Alto battlefield. In 1909 his body, having already been moved to Fort Brown, was again transferred when Fort Brown National Cemetery was moved. Blake now rests in a mass grave with other Mexican War[qv] soldiers at the National Cemetery in Alexandria, Louisiana. Camp Blake, at the San Pedro River on the military road between San Antonio and El Paso, was named in honor of Lieutenant Blake.

BIBLIOGRAPHY: George W. Cullum, *Biographical Register of the Officers and Graduates of the U.S. Military Academy at West Point, New York.* S. W. Geiser, "Men of Science in Texas, 1820–1880," *Field and Laboratory* 26–27 (July–October 1958–October 1959). Susan Prendergast Schoelwer, *Alamo Images* (Dallas: DeGolyer Library, 1985).

Kevin R. Young

BLAKE, ROBERT BRUCE (1877–1955). Robert Bruce Blake, historian and compiler of Spanish and Mexican Texas documents, was born in Moscow, Texas, on September 21, 1877, the third child of Robert Bruce and Sarah (Pratt) Blake. While he was still an infant his father purchased a weekly newspaper, the *News Boy,* in Jasper, and moved his family there. As a youth Blake helped his father in the newspaper office. He later owned and published the *News Boy* for many years. On December 21, 1921, he married Belle Patten, with whom he had one son. The family moved in 1925 to Nacogdoches, where Blake took up a position as court reporter and county clerk. He developed a deep interest in the history of the area of Spanish and Mexican Texas,[qqv] bordered by San Antonio on the west and Nacogdoches on the east, and dedicated himself to preparing a definitive documentary of that area. Over the course of the next three decades Blake translated and transcribed an enormous number of documents from the Nacogdoches and Bexar archives[qqv] and various family collections. The documents, spanning the period from 1744 to 1837, included not only letters, financial records, censuses, muster rolls, family papers, and proclamations, but also a wide array of legal papers—jury verdicts, subpoenas, petitions, affidavits, summonses, bills of slave sales, orders, records of civil and criminal proceedings, bonds, minutes, and writs. Blake bound his typewritten transcriptions in large volumes, some ninety-three in all, each of approximately 400 pages. The transcripts, consisting of more than 3,500 pages, provide a unique documentary record of the region; they constitute what historian Charles A. Bacarisse called "the bed-rock for a history of East Texas."

In 1942, in order to continue his research in the Texas State Archives and the Barker Texas History Center[qqv] archives at the University of Texas, Blake moved his family to Austin, where he lived for the rest of his life. He died there on November 30, 1955. After his death, carrying out her husband's bequest, his wife turned his scrapbooks and other work over to Winnie Allen,[qv] archivist at the Barker Center, where they are now housed. Duplicate copies of the books are also available at the Texas State Archives in Austin, Stephen F. Austin State University in Nacogdoches, and the Houston Public Library.[qv]

BIBLIOGRAPHY: Vertical Files, Barker Texas History Center, University of Texas at Austin. *Christopher Long*

BLAKE, THOMAS M. (1810–1836). Thomas M. Blake, early settler, arrived in Texas in August 1830. He was a single man and a blacksmith from Kentucky. In July 1835 he applied to Stephen F. Austin[qv] for a quarter of a league at the head of Bay Prairie in Wharton County. The land was not patented until 1848, long after his death. In his will he had requested that 500 acres be given to Sarah Savage, who was by then the wife of his neighbor, John Huff.[qv] Blake joined George M. Collinsworth[qv] and some forty-seven men from the Bay Prairie area in October 1835 for the ninety-mile march to Goliad. He signed the Pledge of Protection and on the next day, October 9, helped capture the presidio at La Bahía. He stayed in Goliad when Collinsworth and most of his men returned home and was still there in November when Philip Dimmitt[qv] was relieved of his command. Blake signed the Goliad Resolutions[qv] protesting the order. Blake was a first sergeant under Col. James W. Fannin[qv] at Fort Defiance, the new name that Fannin had given to the old presidio at La Bahía. He started on the march to Victoria on March 19, 1836, and was captured at the battle of Coleto.[qv] On March 27, 1836, by order of Gen. Antonio López de Santa Anna,[qv] 380 men were marched out of La Bahía and shot. Blake was one of the 352 men that died. His body was left to rot with the others, and his bones were later buried in the mass grave at Goliad. (*See also* GOLIAD CAMPAIGN OF 1835, GOLIAD CAMPAIGN OF 1836, GOLIAD MASSACRE.)

BIBLIOGRAPHY: Daughters of the Republic of Texas, *Muster Rolls of the Texas Revolution* (Austin, 1986). Hobart Huson, *Captain Philip Dimmitt's Commandancy of Goliad, 1835–1836* (Austin: Von Boeckmann–Jones, 1974). Matagorda County Historical Commission, *Historic Matagorda County* (3 vols., Houston: Armstrong, 1986). Kathryn Stoner O'Connor, *The Presidio La Bahía del Espíritu Santo de Zúñiga, 1721 to 1846* (Austin: Von Boeckmann–Jones, 1966). Villamae Williams, *Stephen F. Austin's Register of Families* (Nacogdoches, Texas: Ericson, 1984). *Barbara L. Young*

BLAKE, TEXAS. Blake, two miles northwest of Williams on Farm Road 563 in north central Brown County, was the location of a tank farm and oil-pumping station. The settlement was on a mail route from May. A rural church served the surrounding farming community but was disbanded in the 1980s. The only remaining community activity is the Blake Cemetery Association.

BLAKENEY, TEXAS. Blakeney, a mile south of the Red River in north central Red River County, was begun in the early 1850s and developed around a store, which was operated by M. C. Albudy in 1890. A local post office was established with M. B. Yarbrough as postmaster in 1904 and replaced by rural delivery in 1918. The population of Blakeney was 100 in 1910; in 1940 one business and a population of twenty-five were reported. In 1984 Blakeney consisted of widely scattered houses and no businesses. *Claudia Hazlewood*

BLALACK, TEXAS. Blalack was on the St. Louis, Brownsville and Mexico Railway near U.S. Highway 83 four miles northwest of Brownsville in southern Cameron County. In 1907 a school at the site had twenty-four students under the instruction of one teacher. The following year the Texas and New Orleans Railroad was built three miles east of the school. Blalack is probably named for P. E. Blalock, an important developer in the area. In 1948 the community comprised several scattered dwellings. By 1983 it no longer existed, and the site was in the Brownsville city limits. *Alicia A. Garza*

BLALOCK, BRYAN (1895–1964). Bryan Blalock, leader in the dairy industry,[qv] son of William Meredith and Willie (Boothe) Blalock, was born on November 16, 1895, on a farm four miles south of Marshall. He finished high school in Marshall, then attended the University of Texas for two years. Before he was twenty-one he was elected tax collector of Harrison County; afterward he assisted in starting the Marshall *Morning News* (later the Marshall *News Messenger*). He was elected manager of the Marshall Chamber of Commerce in 1921 and served until 1930. Then he joined in organizing the Texas Milk Products Company and served as its president until 1943, when the firm was sold to the Borden Company. Blalock expanded the operation from one plant to five and became vice president and public relations director of Borden's southern division. He served for seven terms as president of the Texas Dairy Institute and for many years served on national committees affecting the dairy industry. He organized the East Texas Dairy Finance Corporation, which lent money to farmers to buy dairy cows.

During the last twenty years of his life Blalock became widely known as a speaker. He made more than 2,000 speeches in thirty-eight states and Canada and was noted for his keen sense of humor and his faith in free enterprise. He was a Methodist and a thirty-second-degree Mason. He married Irby Davis on September 18, 1918, and they had two daughters. He died on June 13, 1964, at Marshall, and was buried in Grange Hall Cemetery there.

BIBLIOGRAPHY: Longview *Daily News*, June 15, 1964.
Narcie Moore Crosby

BLALOCK, MYRON GEER (1891–1950). Myron Geer Blalock, politician and soldier, was born on the family farm at Grange Hall, Harrison County, on January 3, 1891, the son of William Meredith and Willie Henry (Boothe) Blalock. While earning his B.A. (1914) and his law degree (1916) from the University of Texas, he entered politics; he served in the Texas House of Representatives for the 126th district from 1913 to 1918. On August 22, 1917, Blalock married Bertha Mary Storey; they had three children. Blalock served in the army in World War I[qv] and rose to the rank of major. After the war he returned to Marshall and opened a law practice there. He continued to be active in the Democratic party[qv] and was appointed chief justice of the Texas Court of Civil Appeals, Sixth District, at Texarkana in 1932.

From the mid-1930s through 1948 he was one of the most important officials of the Democratic party in Texas. He served as Democratic national campaign committee chairman in Texas during the presidential campaigns of 1936 and 1940. At the convention of 1936 he opposed the successful move to repeal the two-thirds rule for making nominations, as he thought the repeal would diminish the role of southern states in the Democratic party. He reentered military service in 1938 and served as finance officer in the Texas National Guard[qv] for the Thirty-sixth Infantry Division[qv] until 1941; he was a colonel in the United States Army Service Forces until a heart attack in 1943 induced him to retire from active service. He resumed his political career and served as Democratic national committeeman for Texas from 1944 to 1948. When the Texas Democratic party split into pro and anti-Roosevelt factions before the convention of 1944, Blalock was the only party official acceptable to both sides as committeeman, and he acted as a peacemaker in the dispute. In the postwar period he steered a middle course, advocating loyalty to the national party while deploring what he called the increasing influence of "northern party machines" at the expense of the southern Democratic party. He also opposed President Harry Truman's civil-rights measures as pandering to northern minority interests. In 1948 Blalock retired from party office and returned to his law practice in Marshall. He belonged to the Masons, the Methodist Church,[qv] and the American Legion.[qv] He died at his home near Marshall on December 28, 1950, and was buried in the family cemetery at Grange Hall.

BIBLIOGRAPHY: Vertical Files, Barker Texas History Center, University of Texas at Austin. Alvin Wirtz Papers, Lyndon Baines Johnson Library, University of Texas at Austin. *Mark Odintz*

BLANCAS CREEK. Blancas Creek, also known as Blanca Creek, begins ten miles southeast of Laredo in southern Webb County (at 27°29′ N, 99°18′ W) and extends southwest for eighteen miles to its mouth on Mesquite Creek, nine miles northeast of San Ygnacio in northern Zapata County (at 27°16′ N, 99°21′ W). It crosses both low-rolling and flat terrain with locally shallow depressions, surfaced by clay and sandy loams that support grasses, mesquite, chaparral, and water-tolerant hardwoods.

BLANCHARD, TEXAS. Blanchard is at the junction of Farm roads 3126 and 2457, eighty-two miles north of Houston in west central Polk County. Early settlers in the area called the community West Tempe after a local creek. Completion of the Beaumont and Great Northern Railway from Onalaska to Livingston in 1908 brought significant change in western Polk County. A railroad stop was established south of the West Tempe cemetery and named Blanchard by William Carlisle, owner of the sawmill at Onalaska, after his brother-in-law, Ben Blanchard, of New York. After the railroad had been finished, a stave mill was built at Blanchard. A post office was established there in 1908. The rail line was acquired by the Waco, Beaumont, Trinity and Sabine Railway in 1923 and abandoned in 1949. When Lake Livingston was constructed in 1968, a series of roads and parks developed in the area. Blanchard's population was estimated at fifty in the mid-1920s, mid-1980s, and early 1990s. *Robert Wooster*

BLANCHETTE, TEXAS. Blanchette was located on the Texas and New Orleans Railroad north of Beaumont in northeastern Jefferson County. The community, one of Beaumont's first residential subdivisions, was named for wealthy Beaumont real estate man and farmer Valery Blanchette. The Blanchette stop was listed on Railroad Commission[qv] maps of Texas for 1901 and 1905, but it does not appear on subsequent versions of this publication. The site is now part of Beaumont. *Robert Wooster*

BLANCO, BEATRIZ (?–?). Beatriz Blanco, journalist, is one of the women of El México de Afuera ("Mexico Abroad"), a group of Mexican exiles who left Mexico during the Mexican Revolution[qv] of 1910. Members of this group saw themselves as foreigners living in the United States only until they were able to return to their mother country. When these exiles, forced to leave Mexico because of their political ideology, arrived in the United States, they started Spanish-language newspapers,[qv] opened bookstores, and started other businesses. Beatriz Blanco was one of the few women who worked at *La Prensa,*[qv] a newspaper founded on February 13, 1913, by Ignacio E. Lozano,[qv] a prominent member of El México de Afuera. Blanco and two other women from Mexico, Hortensia Elizondo and Rosario Sansores, were members of the editorial board of *La Prensa.* In the 1920s and 1930s, Beatriz Blanco edited the Página del Hogar y de las Damas ("Home and Ladies' Page") of *La Prensa.* Like many other members of El México de Afuera, she had strong emotional and cultural ties to Mexico, was Catholic, believed in Our Lady of Guadalupe,[qv] and had a strong commitment to keeping the Mexican culture and Spanish language alive among her compatriots in the United States. She was a short-story writer, essayist, and critic. Her work, which often appeared in her section of the paper, was strongly influenced by her religion. *La Prensa* served as a vehicle to promote the faith and ideology of El México de Afuera. In San Antonio, Blanco was president of the Club Mexicano de Bellas Artes, a social club whose membership was composed predominantly of exiled Mexican women. The club served as a gathering center for women of the *colonia mexicana.* It fostered solidarity among Mexican women in the community, provided emotional support to them, and reinforced their cultural ties to Mexico. In 1940, Beatriz Blanco returned to Mexico. *Juanita Luna Lawhn*

BLANCO, VICTOR (?–?). Victor Blanco, Mexican official and Texas legislator, brother-in-law of Ramón Músquiz,[qv] was a citizen of Monclova. He represented his state as alternate deputy of the provincial deputation on September 8, 1823. Considering the establishment of a colony in Texas on the Trinity River, he appointed Samuel May Williams[qv] as his agent to select a site, but his plans never materialized. Blanco was governor of the state of Coahuila and Texas[qv] from May 30, 1826, to January 27, 1827, during which time he suppressed the Fredonian Rebellion[qv] of 1826. On July 4, 1827, Blanco was elected the first vice governor under the Constitution of Coahuila and Texas.[qv] He represented the state as a senator in the Mexican Congress from 1833 to 1835 and was reelected to the same office in 1835. In the legislature he opposed Stephen F. Austin's[qv] request that Texas be separated from Coahuila. In 1841 Blanco was in Monclova engaged in warfare with Indians. He later participated in the Mexican War.[qv]

BIBLIOGRAPHY: Vito Alessio Robles, *Coahuila y Texas en la época colonial* (Mexico City: Editorial Cultura, 1938; 2d ed., Mexico City: Editorial Porrúa, 1978). Hubert Howe Bancroft, *History of the North Mexican States and Texas* (2 vols., San Francisco: History Company, 1886, 1889). Eugene C. Barker, ed., *The Austin Papers* (3 vols., Washington: GPO, 1924–28). Nettie Lee Benson, *The Provincial Deputation in Mexico* (Austin: University of Texas Press, 1992). Bexar Archives, Barker Texas History Center, University of Texas at Austin.
Winifred W. Vigness

BLANCO, TEXAS. Blanco is on U.S. Highway 281 twelve miles south of Johnson City in south central Blanco County. In 1853 pioneer stockmen built cabins along the Blanco River near the present site of the town and prepared to defend themselves against Indian attack. In 1854 the operators of the Pittsburgh Land Company, including Gen. John D. Pitts,[qv] A. M. Lindsey, F. W. Chandler, William E. Jones, and Capt. James H. Callahan,[qv] purchased the league granted to Horace Eggleston by the government of Coahuila and Texas[qv] in 1835. They laid out the town of Pittsburgh, named for General Pitts, across the river from the site of future Blanco. That same year a Methodist church was organized by circuit rider Daniel Rawls.[qv] The congregation met in a log cabin built to withstand Indian raids, which also served as a school. The Twin Sisters Masonic Lodge, organized at Curry's Creek perhaps as early as 1856, moved to Pittsburgh around 1857.

When Blanco County was organized in 1858, an election located the county seat across the river from Pittsburgh, and named the townsite Blanco for the Blanco River. The Pittsburgh Land Company gave the new town 120 acres of land. In 1858 a post office was established. Mail service was temporarily discontinued with the beginning of the Civil War,[qv] but the citizens raised money to bring mail once a week from New Braunfels in order to receive the war news. The first Baptist church was organized in 1859. In 1860 the first courthouse was built on the public square by A. V. Gates for about $600.

In spite of hardships suffered during the Civil War, the town continued to grow and by 1870 had four stores, a hotel, and a gin. The old union church, built in 1871 at a cost of $1,300, remained for many years the center of town life. It was used as a church by different denominations, as a schoolhouse, and as a community meeting place. In 1874 the Masons drew up a charter for Blanco Masonic University. A foundation was laid, but building was discontinued because of a lack of funds. A new courthouse of native stone was built in 1875 by Frederick E. and Oscar Ruffini,[qqv] architects. In 1876 a fire destroyed the Masonic lodge, the old courthouse, and all of the county records. The same year the residents of Johnson City made their first attempt to have the county seat relocated by petitioning for an election. They were unsuccessful. In 1884 the citizens of Blanco formed a joint stock company to raise the capital necessary to establish a high school. They elected a board of directors and a president and applied for a charter for Blanco High School under the Private Corporations Act. A two-story building was built on the foundation of the Masonic university. It opened in October 1884, and the first class graduated in 1887. In 1890 Johnson City won a county seat election, and Blanco lost its position as county seat; the courthouse records were moved to Johnson City in 1891. The rivalry between the two towns that began with this election is still hot.

Blanco has primarily been a ranch and farm trade center. It had a population of 469 in 1904 and 1,100 by 1939, when the town was incorporated. By 1946 the town had forty businesses, a hospital, and a weekly newspaper, the *Blanco County News*. The population dropped in the 1940s to 453 before increasing again in the 1950s. In 1980 the census reported 1,179 residents in Blanco. There were forty-six businesses. In 1990 the population was 1,238. Christ of the Hills Orthodox Monastery is nearby.

BIBLIOGRAPHY: Austin *American-Statesman*, November 14, 1993. Kathleen E. and Clifton R. St. Clair, eds., *Little Towns of Texas* (Jacksonville, Texas: Jayroe Graphic Arts, 1982). John W. Speer, *A History of Blanco County* (Austin: Pemberton, 1965). *Bessie Brigham*

BLANCO CANYON. Blanco Canyon, on the White River, begins just north of the intersection of Farm roads 37 and 3111 in southwestern Floyd County (at 33°59′ N, 101°29′ W) and runs southeast for a total of thirty miles to its mouth, on the eastern cliffs of the Caprock[qv] some eight miles southeast of Crosbyton (at 33°40′ N, 101°10′ W). At its beginning the canyon is about fifty feet deep, and its elevations range from 3,125 feet above sea level at the river to 3,175 feet on top of the escarpment. Its average width is 1,500 feet. The gorge runs southeast, gradually deepening and widening as it crosses U.S. Highway 62 south of Floydada and enters Crosby County. It extends six miles southwest of Floydada, a mile southwest of the Mount Blanco community, and three miles east of Crosbyton. Crawfish Canyon, labeled Cañón Cangrejo on some early maps, is the only major side-canyon. This five-mile ravine along Crawfish Creek in north central Crosby County enters Blanco Canyon south of the intersection of Farm roads 193 and 651. At its mouth, some eight miles southeast of Crosbyton, Blanco Canyon is six miles wide; its cliff heights average 300 to 500 feet. The soils are loamy up the canyon and clayey and silty near its mouth. Scrub brush and grasses predominate in the area. Blanco Canyon was a favorite campground for wayfarers, including Indians, soldiers, and buffalo hunters. Col. Ranald S. Mackenzie[qv] established a supply camp known as Anderson's Fort near the canyon mouth in 1871; it is now on the National Register of Historic Places. In the 1880s the canyon became the first point of settlement for newcomers to the region because water and wood could readily be found there. The Plains Baptist Assembly[qv] grounds and the Floydada Country Club are located in Blanco Canyon south of Floydada.

BIBLIOGRAPHY: Claude V. Hall, *Early History of Floyd County* (Canyon, Texas: Panhandle-Plains Historical Society, 1947). Wilbur Sturtevant Nye, *Carbine and Lance: The Story of Old Fort Sill* (Norman: University of Oklahoma Press, 1937; 3d ed. 1969). Ernest Wallace, *Ranald S. Mackenzie on the Texas Frontier* (Lubbock: West Texas Museum Association, 1964).

BLANCO CANYON, BATTLE OF. The battle of Blanco Canyon marked the climax of Col. Ranald S. Mackenzie's[qv] initial campaign against Comanche bands in West Texas. In September 1871 Mackenzie received permission from Gen. William T. Sherman[qv] to mount an expedition against the Kotsoteka and Quahadi Comanche bands, which had refused to come into their reservation in the aftermath of the Warren Wagontrain Raid.[qv] Mackenzie gathered eight companies of the Fourth United States Cavalry,[qv] two companies of the Eleventh Infantry, and a group of twenty Tonkawa scouts at the site of old Camp Cooper on the Clear Fork of the Brazos in late September. The column set out in a northwesterly direction on October 3, hoping to find the Quahadi village, including the warriors led by Quanah Parker,[qv] encamped in Blanco Canyon near the headwaters of the Freshwater Fork of the Brazos River, southeast of the site of present Crosbyton. On the fourth night out a base camp was established at the junction of the Salt Fork of the Brazos and Duck Creek, near the site of present Spur. The next day the infantry were left behind at the camp while the scouts and cavalry continued on.

On October 9 the cavalry column reached the White River and Blanco Canyon. Late that evening Quanah Parker and a Comanche force stampeded through the cavalry camp, driving off sixty-six horses. The following morning a detachment of troopers set off down the canyon chasing a small group of Indians who were driving several horses. Topping a hill in the ragged edge of the canyon, the soldiers were confronted with a much larger party of Indians waiting in ambush and suffered the loss of one trooper, the sole white fatality of the campaign. Lt. Robert Goldthwaite Carter[qv] and five men held off the Comanches while the rest of the detachment retreated, an action for which he was eventually awarded the Medal of Honor. The timely arrival of the Tonkawas and Mackenzie's main column saved the detachment from annihilation and forced the warriors to withdraw. The Comanches slowly retreated up the bluffs and walls of Blanco Canyon, sniping at the troopers and taunting their Tonkawa enemies before disappearing over the Caprock[qv] onto the Llano Estacado.[qv] Mackenzie continued pursuing the Indians over the next few days, forcing them to abandon lodge poles, tools, and many of their possessions as they fled. He finally caught up with them on the late afternoon of October 12 but was prevented from attacking them by an unseasonable blue norther,[qv] accompanied by blinding snow and sleet, that halted the cavalry and forced them to camp for the night. The column continued the pursuit the next morning, but the horses and men were becoming increasingly exhausted. After following the Indian trail for about forty miles, nearly to the vicinity of present Plainview, the column turned back. On October 15, as the cavalry descended the wall of Blanco Canyon, their scouts saw two Comanches spying on the column. In the skirmish that followed the two Comanches were killed, and Macenzie and another soldier were wounded. The command continued to the mouth of Blanco Canyon, where they rested for a time. On October 24 Mackenzie attempted to continue the campaign, setting out for the headwaters of the Pease River with the remaining fit men and horses. His wound became worse, and he turned over command to Capt. Clarence Mauck. As the weather worsened and the condition of his command deteriorated, Mackenzie ordered Mauck to end the expedition. By mid-November the troops had returned to their posts at forts Davis and Richardson.

Mackenzie regarded the campaign as less than successful. He and his troops had marched 509 miles with the loss of one man and many horses and had accomplished no more than to frighten one hostile Comanche band. Yet they had penetrated into a hitherto unexplored area of the Llano Estacado and had become more knowledgeable in Plains Indian warfare as a result of the battle of Blanco Canyon. Never again would the vast Llano Estacado be a safe refuge for Comanche bands, as subsequent campaigns clearly demonstrated.

bibliography: Robert G. Carter, *On the Border with Mackenzie, or Winning West Texas from the Comanches* (Washington: Eynon Printing, 1935). Bill Neeley, *Quanah Parker and His People* (Slaton, Texas: Brazos, 1986). Ernest Wallace, *Ranald S. Mackenzie on the Texas Frontier* (Lubbock: West Texas Museum Association, 1964).

H. Allen Anderson

BLANCO COUNTY. Blanco County (K-15) is in the Hill Country[qv] of south central Texas, bordered on the west by Gillespie County, on the north by Burnet and Llano counties, on the east by Hays County, and on the south by Kendall and Comal counties. Johnson City, the county seat, is four miles north of the center of the county, forty miles west of Austin and sixty miles northwest of San Antonio. The county's center lies at 30°23′ north latitude and 98°24′ west longitude. Blanco County comprises 714 square miles of the eastern edge of the Edwards Plateau[qv] and has an elevation range of 800 to 1,850 feet above sea level. The terrain is generally hilly to mountainous, and along some streambeds the landscape has a "stairstep" appearance due to limestone benches and steep slopes. The vegetation consists mainly of stands of live oak and Ashe juniper, with mesquite and grasses. The soils are generally dark, calcareous, stony, clay loams with rock outcrops. Mineral resources include limestone, lead, oil, gas, industrial sand, and dolomite. Most of the county is best suited for rangeland and wildlife habitat. The northern and central part, about two-thirds of the total area, drains into the Colorado River in Travis County through Miller and Cypress creeks and the Pedernales River. The southern third of the county drains into the Guadalupe River through the Blanco and Little Blanco rivers. The temperatures range from an average high of 96° F in July to an average low of 34° in January, the rainfall averages 34.39 inches per year, and the growing season extends an average of 234 days.

There is archeological evidence that Indians camped in the Blanco County area as early as A.D. 1150, and ancestors of the Lipan Apaches, who had migrated from the great Northwest, may have been roaming the area when the Spanish arrived in the sixteenth century. There is not much concrete evidence of Spanish and French exploration of the area at that time, but the fact that there was a proposal for a mission on the Pedernales River submitted by a Father Santa Ana, plus the fact that the Marqués de San Miguel de Aguayo[qv] named the Blanco River in 1721, does suggest that the Spanish knew the area fairly well. Small expeditions continued to cross the territory throughout the eighteenth century, but most of what is now Blanco County had been explored by 1749.

Land agents, empresarios, and Indian fighters began visiting the area about 1821. Land grants, however, were not issued by the Mexican government until 1826, when Benjamin R. Milam[qv] was given a contract to settle 300 families between the Colorado and Guadalupe rivers. The land granted constituted a small part of the early Blanco County area. In 1835 Jesse L. McCrocklin,[qv] Horace Eggleston, Noel Mixon, and Benjamin Williams each received a league of land now in Blanco County, but these tracts remained largely undeveloped until the middle of the nineteenth century.

By 1836 the Comanches had claimed all lands within the present boundaries of Blanco County. This hostile tribe made war on Apaches and white settlers alike, causing them to band together to fight their common enemy. Capt. James Hughes Callahan[qv] first visited the Blanco River area on his way to an Indian battle. He was apparently impressed with the land along the river and so returned in 1853 with his friend, Eli Clemens Hinds. Both men built homes on the Blanco River in 1854, thus becoming the first white settlers in what is now Blanco County. Later that year Joseph Bird established Birdtown, now known as Round Mountain, in the northern part of the county.

Also in 1854 Gen. John D. Pitts,[qv] who had fought in Indian campaigns with Callahan, came to settle in the Blanco County area. Pitts, with Callahan, Judge William S. Jones from Curry's Creek in what was then Comal County, Andrew M. Lindsay of San Marcos, and F. W. Chandler of Travis County, chartered the Pittsburgh Land Company and laid out the town of Pittsburgh between 1854 and 1855. The first church in the county was built in 1854 by a Methodist circuit rider named Daniel Rawls.[qv] As more and more settlers moved into the area, missionaries from various Christian churches also established themselves in Blanco County.

In 1855 settlers in the western part of what was then Comal County began to agitate for a new county. As a result, Kerr County was established in 1856. This, however, did not help the people of northern Comal County. They continued to petition the legislature, and through the efforts of members of the Pittsburgh Land Company, Blanco County was formed on February 12, 1858, from parts of Comal, Hays, Burnet, and Gillespie counties and named for the Blanco River. Some historians believe that Blanco County also acquired two small unattached pieces of Travis County. The total area of the new county was 1,043 square miles.

The act that established Blanco County also stipulated that the county seat should be called Blanco and that an election should be held to determine the location, which should be within five miles of the center of the county. A spot on the north bank of Martin's Fork of the Blanco River, just across from Pittsburgh, was chosen as the site for the new town. The Pittsburgh Land Company donated a 120-acre tract of land there, and Blanco was founded. A courthouse was erected on the town square in 1860. It was replaced in 1885 by a limestone structure that came to be known as the Old Courthouse, which fell into private hands after Johnson City became the county seat; the Old Courthouse was restored in the early 1990s.

Blanco County was settled predominantly by natives of Tennessee and Alabama, mostly Anglo-Saxon Protestants, although about a tenth of the residents were natives of Germany. According to the United States census, 1,218 people, including ninety-eight slaves, lived in the new county by 1860, and 184 farms had been established. Indian corn and wheat were the county's most important crops, but settlers also grew small amounts of rye, tobacco, and cotton on the 6,400 acres classified as "improved." The settlers also had vegetable gardens to supplement their meat-laden diets. Cattle and sheep were central to the local economy. Over 13,000 cattle and 4,179 milk cows were counted in Blanco County in 1860. The same year, large herds of sheep were brought from Missouri; over 19,000 sheep were counted in Blanco County in 1860, and the county produced more than 44,300 pounds of wool.

Though many of the residents of Blanco County in 1860 were native Southerners, and though some owned slaves, the majority apparently had Unionist sympathies. Immigrants from Northern states and from Europe helped to sway opinion toward the Unionist position, and when secession[qv] came to a vote in Blanco County it was voted down 170 to 86. In spite of the county's Unionist sympathies, few former slaves chose to remain in the area after emancipation. In 1870, after the Civil War,[qv] only forty-four blacks lived in the county, most of whom probably settled in Peyton, a freedmen's colony near Blanco.

The war disrupted economic expansion. By 1870 the county's population had dropped to 1,187, and livestock and crop production had declined dramatically. The number of milk cows fell to 1,397 by 1870, and beef cattle dropped to 8,755; most devastating to the county was the loss of over 16,000 sheep during the same period. Though the production of corn actually increased, other crops were severely reduced. Wheat harvests fell from 2,355 bushels in 1860 to 1,391 bushels in 1870. As a result, farm and ranch values plummeted from a total of $576,302 at the onset of the conflict to $90,736 in 1870.

During the Civil War the county lost a large part of the land on its southwestern border when the legislature established Kendall County in 1862. The legislature compensated Blanco County by giving it additional parts of Hays and Burnet counties. When all the changes were complete, Blanco County comprised the 714 square miles of land it occupies today, but the town of Blanco was no longer at its geographical center. By 1875 James Polk Johnson and other settlers on the Pedernales River in the northern part of the county began to agitate for a new county seat. For the next fifteen years Johnson and his friends petitioned that the county seat be moved; in 1879 Johnson City was founded near the new geographical center of the county in hopes that it would become the new county seat. After a number of hotly contested elections the people of the north were successful, and in 1891 Johnson City became the seat of county government.

As elsewhere, education in Blanco County began with one-room schoolhouses. In 1874 the Masons of Blanco chartered Blanco Masonic University. The project literally did not get off the ground, however, for once the foundation of the building was laid, there was no money left. A few years later citizens in the community formed a corporation to raise money to build a high school. Blanco High School was chartered in 1883 and built on the unused university foundation. The first class graduated in 1887. The school system grew slowly, as many of the young men who attended seem to have dropped out, possibly to work on family farms or ranches.

Census reports show livestock and crop production generally increasing from 1870 to 1900. The number of farms in the county increased to 519 by 1880, to 645 in 1890, and to 702 in 1900. Meanwhile the number of cattle almost tripled, to over 31,000 by 1880, and remained at that level in 1900. Similarly, the number of sheep in the county recovered to prewar levels by 1880, when over 19,000 sheep where counted, and in 1890 Blanco County had 30,000 sheep. Angora goats, which were to become a significant aspect of the county's economy in the twentieth century, were counted for the first time in 1900, when 789 goats of all kinds were reported. Crop production increased as well during this period and in 1900 stood at 17,150 bushels of wheat, 24,708 bushels of oats, and 215,230 bushels of corn. The population of Blanco County increased as its economy developed. In 1880 it was 3,583. By 1890 it had risen to 4,649 and by 1900 to 4,703.

During the late nineteenth and early twentieth centuries cotton production rose steadily in the county, and by 1910 the fiber had become one of the county's most important crops. Blanco County's first cotton gin was established in 1870; by 1900 cotton culture[qv] occupied more than 10,300 acres of county land, which that year produced more than 8,951 500-pound bales. By 1910 cotton was grown on 16,000 acres in the county. Between 1900 and 1930 local farmers also diversified considerably, as peanuts, peaches, pecans, pears, plums, grapes, and figs were produced. By 1929 more than 20,000 peach and pecan trees were being harvested.

The land of the county offered only limited possibilities for crop production, however, and was much better suited for livestock. Between 1910 and 1930 the number of cattle remained constant at 20,000, and sheep grazing grew considerably. By 1930 Blanco County had 71,000 sheep and produced 433,473 pounds of wool. Mohair goats also became an important part of the economy during this time, and in 1929 farmers in the county sheared almost 274,000 pounds of mohair. During the period from 1920 to 1930 the number of sheep rose from 9,685 to 71,049, and the number of goats rose from 13,780 to 81,500 (*see* SHEEP RANCHING, GOAT RANCHING, WOOL AND MOHAIR INDUSTRY). Poultry production[qv] also increased in importance during this period. From 1920 to 1930 the number of chickens in the county increased from 29,153 to 43,136 and the number of turkeys from 3,517 to 14,937. The number of farms in Blanco County reached its peak between 1910 and 1920 and declined thereafter. The county had 753 farms in 1910, 713 in 1920, and 708 in 1929. Population figures for the period reflect the same downward trend; residents numbered 4,703 in 1900, 4,311 in 1910, 4,063 in 1920, and 3,842 in 1929.

During the Great Depression[qv] farm and ranch values plummeted and crop production fell. The number of farms in the county continued to drop; by 1940 only 632 farms remained in Blanco County. However, ranchers managed to keep most of their cattle and even substantially increased the number of sheep; in 1940 the county reported 90,000 sheep. The effects of the depression on the county were also tempered by a marked rise in government projects in the area, many of them acquired through the influence of Lyndon Baines Johnson,[qv] who had developed a close relationship with President Franklin D. Roosevelt. Many of the county's roads were paved, and the federal government's Civilian Conservation Corps[qv] worked to improve state parks in the area. Perhaps most importantly, the New Deal introduced full electric power to the area through the Lower Colorado River Authority[qv] and the Pedernales Electric Cooperative. Though many county residents suffered through the years of the depression, these projects help to explain a rise in the population of Blanco County between 1929 and 1940. By 1940 4,264 people were living in the county.

The number of farms continued to drop between World War II[qv] and the 1970s, when their number again began to rise. In 1950 the county had 567 farms, in 1959 it had 516, and by 1969 only 472 remained. By 1982, however, there were 488 farms in the county. Population since World War II followed the same pattern. After the brief increase during the depression, the number of people in Blanco County dropped to 3,780 in 1950, then to 3,657 in 1960 and 3,567 in 1970, before rising to 4,681 by 1980. In 1990, 5,972 people lived in the county.

Farm and ranch supply stores have been the most prominent businesses in the two population centers of the county, Blanco and Johnson City. However, tourism has also become an important part of the local economy since the 1960s, as many visitors are attracted to Blanco State Recreation Area[qv] just south of Blanco, Pedernales Falls State Park[qv] in the northern part of the county, and to the Lyndon Baines Johnson Birthplace, Boyhood Home, and Ranch.[qv] In the 1980s Blanco County ranked 210th of the 254 Texas counties in agricultural receipts. Primary crops included wheat, hay, and oats; peaches and pecans were important. Blanco County continued to raise sheep, cows, cattle, goats, and turkeys and to produce wool, milk, meat, and mohair. Most county residents worked in tourism, agribusiness, or construction, and the county supported two newspapers, the *Record Courier* of Johnson City and the *Blanco County News* of Blanco.

BIBLIOGRAPHY: John Moursund, *Blanco County History* (Burnet, Texas: Nortex, 1979). John W. Speer, *A History of Blanco County* (Austin: Pemberton, 1965). *Mary H. Ogilvie and John Leffler*

BLANCO CREEK (Karnes County). Blanco Creek rises near the intersection of the Bee, Goliad, and Karnes county lines in extreme southern Karnes County (at 28°41′ N, 97°48′ W). It flows southeast for forty-five miles, forming the boundary between Bee and Goliad counties and continuing into west central Refugio County, where its confluence with Medio Creek just west of Refugio forms the Mission River (at 28°19′ N, 97°19′ W). The stream is intermittent in its upper reaches. It traverses flat to rolling terrain with clay loam and sandy loam soils that support water-tolerant hardwoods and grasses.

—— (Uvalde County). Blanco Creek begins a mile south of Farm Road 1050 and five miles southwest of Utopia in northeast Uvalde County (at 29°35′ N, 99°37′ W) and extends fifty-one miles southeast to its mouth on the Frio River, just west of Farm Road 187 (at 29°06′ N, 99°27′ W). Little Blanco Creek is a tributary of Blanco Creek. The stream crosses an area of steep to gently sloping terrain, where the limestone bedrock is locally exposed but generally surfaced by shallow gravelly loam and clay that support scrub brush and grasses. Downstream, the terrain is rolling, and the land surface of clayey loam supports oak, juniper, grasses, and, at the mouth, pecan and other hardwood trees.

BLANCO MASONIC UNIVERSITY. Blanco Masonic University was planned at Blanco in December 1874, when a board of directors was elected, a building committee was appointed, and funds were solicited for the school. In February 1875 officials drew plans for the building, petitioned the Texas legislature for a grant of land, and had stone quarried for the building. But evidently sufficient funds were not raised, for in 1883 the university stock was transferred to another project, Blanco Masonic High School. R. C. Traweek donated a lot for the building site for this institution, G. A. Horlee donated land to be sold for building money, and two teachers were employed. In September 1884 one wing of the building had been completed when the plans were abandoned and the directors decided to merge the Masonic High School with the Blanco public school. The new school opened as a graded high school; it graduated its first class in 1887. It continued to function at least through 1893.

BIBLIOGRAPHY: Blanco Masonic University and High School Papers, Barker Texas History Center, University of Texas at Austin.

BLANCONIA, TEXAS. Blanconia is on State Highway 202 twenty-two miles southeast of Beeville in southeastern Bee County. The town was established in 1834 when John and Michael Keeting acquired a half league of land from the state of Coahuila and Texas.[qv] This land was in Refugio County until Bee County was established in 1857. In the beginning the town was named Kymo and had nicknames including Pull Tight and Dark Corners. In 1888, when Tom McGuill applied for a post office, the town was renamed Blanconia, after Blanco Creek. The community post office was established in 1888 and discontinued sometime after 1930. Many of the earliest settlers at the townsite came from Refugio and Goliad when Texas was still part of Mexico. One settler, Sally Scull,[qv] eventually became a famous "pistol-totin' horse trader." In 1855 a local Baptist church was established and named N-2, after L. R. McDaniel's cattle brand. In 1905 Blanconia had a one-teacher school with twelve pupils. By 1914 the town had its largest recorded population, 200, and was a thriving trade center with three stores and three churches. The community had twenty-five residents and one store during the early 1930s. All that remained at the site by the late 1950s was the N-2 Church, McGuill's store, and St. Catherine's Church. In 1968 the community's population was fifteen, and no businesses were reported there. The population was still reported as fifteen in the early 1990s.

BIBLIOGRAPHY: Grace Bauer, *Bee County Centennial, 1858–1958* (Bee County Centennial, 1958). Camp Ezell, *Historical Story of Bee County, Texas* (Beeville: Beeville Publishing, 1973).

Rebecca Leigh Kendall

BLANCO RIVER. The Blanco River rises from springs three miles south of the Gillespie county line in northeastern Kendall County (at 30°05′ N, 98°42′ W) and flows southeast for eighty-seven miles, through the Hill Country[qv] counties of Blanco and Hays, to its mouth on the San Marcos River, inside the San Marcos city limits (at 29°52′ N, 97°55′ W). The Blanco is part of the Guadalupe River basin and has a drainage area of over 400 square miles. In 1721 members of the Aguayo expedition[qv] named the river for the white limestone along the banks and in the streambed. Other early Spanish expeditions reportedly crossed the Blanco, including those of Pedro Vial[qv] in 1786 and José Mares[qv] in 1788. Indians, including Comanches and Apaches, inhabited the region along the river well into the 1850s. Bartlett Sims[qv] first surveyed the land along the Blanco River in what is now Blanco County in 1835, and land grants were made during the period of the Republic of Texas.[qv] By the mid-1840s the first settlers had come to the region. Blanco County was formed in 1858. The terrain features stairstep limestone benches and moderate to high slopes, surfaced by dark, calcareous stony clays and clay loams that support oak, juniper, mesquite, and grasses in the surrounding area and water-tolerant hardwoods and conifers along the riverbed. The countryside is used principally for ranchland and secondarily for residences. Much of the bank is privately owned. The river is generally shallow and is impounded by a series of low-water dams. Springs from Glenrose limestone in the Middle Trinity Aquifer support the Blanco River in its upper reaches. Two major tributaries in Blanco County, Callahan Branch and Flat Creek, join the main (or north) fork (once known as Martin's Fork) of the river. In western Hays County the Little Blanco River adds volume to the Blanco. Cypress Creek, another major tributary, rises from Jacob's Well and flows into the Blanco River at Wimberley.

Some unique features along the Blanco River include the Narrows in western Hays County and the Devil's Backbone near Wimberley. Dinosaur tracks are embedded in the limestone riverbed about three miles downstream from Blanco State Recreation Area[qv] in Blanco. Indian mounds and related archeological sites can be found along the river downstream from the Little Arkansas Springs, east of Wimberley. The Blanco River also flows underground along several spots in its course. In its lower reaches it flows beneath moderate slopes surfaced by acid sandy and clay loam that supports pecans, hardwoods, and grasses. During the 1960s a major reservoir was proposed at Cloptin's Crossing, two miles southwest of Wimberley. The dam was never built, however, and in 1990 the Cloptin Reservoir still remained the subject of debate. Excessive pumping of the Trinity and Edwards aquifers has reduced spring-flow in the area and caused some concern for the quality of water in the Blanco River. Several recreational areas, including Blanco State Recreation Area in Blanco, private parks and resorts in Wimberley, and Dudley Johnson (Five-Mile Dam) Park near San Marcos, operate on the Blanco.

BIBLIOGRAPHY: *An Analysis of Texas Waterways* (Austin: Texas Parks and Wildlife Department, 1974). Gene Kirkley, *A Guide to Texas Rivers and Streams* (Houston: Lone Star, 1983). John Moursund, *Blanco County History* (Burnet, Texas: Nortex, 1979). U.S. Geological Survey, *Water Resources Data: Texas, Water Year 1983* (3 vols., Washington: GPO, 1984).

Laurie E. Jasinski

BLANCO STATE RECREATION AREA. Blanco State Recreation Area is just off U.S. Highway 281 on the south side of Blanco in Blanco County. The 105-acre park covers about a mile-long strip of land on both sides of the Blanco River. Private landowners deeded the land to the state in 1933. On June 20, 1933, Company 854 of the Civilian Conservation Corps[qv] made improvements on the land. Capt. John L. Hill was commander of the camp, which included 177 CCC workers and a corps of engineers. The men built two seven-foot-high dams of stone from the riverbed, roads, two concrete bridges, and a concession house with eighteen-inch stone walls and pine timbers and shingles. Facilities also included a bathhouse, seven campsites, and a seventy-foot table. The work group included a tree army responsible for pruning trees and shrubs and planting shade and fruit trees. The workmen completed their job in May 1934, and Blanco State Park (as it was called then) became one of the earliest parks in the Texas park system.

Glenrose limestone in the park gives the terrain a stairstep appearance. The riverbed contains layers of limestone and softer marl formed since prehistoric times, when a shallow sea covered the area that is now the Hill Country;[qv] outcroppings of a fossil zone with ancient clams and oysters can be seen. Dinosaur tracks have been preserved in the streambed a mile upriver from the park and three miles downstream from the park, on private property. Local vegetation includes juniper, live oak, mesquite, and grasses that grow from dark calcareous stony clays and clay loams. Some water-tolerant hardwoods and conifers are present along the streambed. Area wildlife includes deer, armadillos, squirrels, and a variety of birds.

In 1982 renovations began in the park with the addition of more facilities and the first solar-heated water system in a Texas state park. The system included 240 gallons of thermal storage for showers and restrooms and resulted in savings in the cost of electricity. The renovated park opened on July 30, 1983. Its facilities included thirty-seven picnic sites, twenty-one campsites, ten trailer hookups, and a trailer dump station. The park is used by local citizens and tourists, many from Austin and San Antonio. Fishing, swimming, boating, and camping are popular park activities.

BIBLIOGRAPHY: Ross A. Maxwell, *Geologic and Historic Guide to the Texas State Parks* (Bureau of Economic Geology, University of Texas at Austin, 1970). John Moursund, *Blanco County History* (Burnet, Texas: Nortex, 1979). James Wright Steely, *The Civilian Conservation Corps in Texas State Parks* (Austin: Texas Parks and Wildlife Department, 1986). *Texas Parks and Wildlife*, March 1985.

Laurie E. Jasinski

BLANCPAIN, JOSEPH (?–1756). Joseph Blancpain was a French trader of Natchitoches, Louisiana, whose activities in Texas heightened bad feeling between France and Spain in the middle of the eighteenth century. In 1754 Blancpain, Elias George, Antonio de la Fara (Antonio Dessars), and two black men from Louisiana were caught by Lt. Marcos Ruiz[qv] trading among the Orcoquiza Indians in Spanish territory. The Frenchmen's stock of goods was confiscated and divided among their captors; their huts were given to Chief Calzones Colorados;[qv] and they were taken to Mexico City and imprisoned. Blancpain testified that he lived on a plantation near New Orleans and that he had been licensed by Jean Baptiste Le Moyne de Bienville, governor of Louisiana, to trade for horses among the Attacapa Indians. A list of his goods showed him to be furnishing the Indians with firearms, and his diary caused the Spanish to believe him to be an agent for the French government. On February 6, 1756, Blancpain died in prison in Mexico City. His companions were sent to Cádiz, Spain, and imprisoned for life. As a result of this incident, the king of Spain issued an order that any Frenchman found in Spanish domains without a permit would be sent to Acapulco and shipped to the island of Juan Fernández or the presidio of Valdivia in South America.

BIBLIOGRAPHY: Herbert E. Bolton, "Spanish Activities on the Lower Trinity River, 1746–1771," *Southwestern Historical Quarterly* 16 (April 1913). Carlos E. Castañeda, *Our Catholic Heritage in Texas* (7 vols., Austin: Von Boeckmann–Jones, 1936–58; rpt., New York: Arno, 1976).

Kaye A. Walker

BLAND, TEXAS. Bland was ten miles northwest of Belton on Owl Creek and Farm Road 184 in northwestern Bell County. The community was founded about 1880 by John Atkerson, who opened a store on the site. His name for the community, Pokerville, was supposedly derived from his fondness for playing poker with his customers. In 1894, when a post office was granted to the community, a more seemly name, Bland, was chosen; the name was possibly from that of D. T. Bland, an early settler in the area. Twenty people lived in the community in 1896. In 1925 Bland had sixty-three residents, but by 1949 its population had declined to twenty, and the community had one business. In the mid-1950s the site was inundated by Lake Belton.

BIBLIOGRAPHY: Belton *Journal*, April 6, 1950. *Mark Odintz*

BLANDLAKE, TEXAS. Blandlake is beside Bland Lake at the intersection of Farm roads 1279 and 3230, on the Atchison, Topeka and Santa Fe Railway four miles north of San Augustine in northern San Augustine County. It started in 1901 as a station on the Gulf, Colorado and Santa Fe and was granted a post office with the name Stop in that year. In 1903 the name was changed to Blandlake, after the local lake, which was once owned by the Bland family. In 1907 the community had two schools serving seventy-six black pupils and one school serving fifty white pupils. By 1914 Blandlake had fifty inhabitants, the Bland and Fisher Lumber Corporation, a second lumber company, a grocer, and a general store. In 1940 the community had twenty-five inhabitants, a church, a business, and a number of scattered dwellings. In 1990 the community had three businesses and an estimated twenty-five inhabitants. *Mark Odintz*

BLAND MOUNTAIN. Bland Mountain is beside Belton Lake in western Bell County (at 31°13′ N, 97°30′ W), near the mouth of Owl Creek and the eastern boundary of Fort Hood. With an elevation of 715 feet above sea level, its summit rises 100 feet above the lake.

BLANKENSHIP, MARY ALMA PERRITT (1878–1955). Mary Alma (Allie) Blankenship, pioneer and writer, the daughter of William Wallace and Mary Ann (Richards) Perritt, was born on May 4, 1878, in Meridian, Texas. In 1883 her mother died; two years later her father died. Allie and her younger brother and sister were reared by grandparents, Hampton and Elander Caroline Richards. The Richardses had lost their plantation after the Civil War,[qv] so Hampton became a traveling Baptist minister, and Elander worked as a midwife and pharmacist.

On December 15, 1895, Allie married Andrew Wesley Blankenship at the Alarm Creek community in Erath County. They eventually had a son and daughter. For a time the Blankenships were sharecroppers near Stephenville. In 1901 James W. Jarrott, a lawyer, land agent, and friend of Allie's, told them about some land in the Panhandle[qv] that would soon be available for homesteaders. The Blankenships traveled by wagon to an uninhabited prairie on the border of Hockley and Terry counties about twenty miles southwest of Lubbock. Allie, her infant son, and an eight-year-old boy named Brock Gist stayed on the land alone while Andrew went to Lubbock to file a claim on four sections of land. At first the ranchers were hostile to the homesteaders. On August 28, 1902, James Jarrott was murdered at a lonely windmill in the pasture of the Lake Tomb Cattle Company.

The Blankenships' first permanent home in the Panhandle was a half dugout (*see* DUGOUT). They had a herd of cattle and some land under cultivation. With their prairie neighbors, they built a one-room schoolhouse on their land around 1907 or 1908. In 1909 this school became Lubbock School District 13. The Blankenships also built an interdenominational church that Allie, a Baptist, attended.

In 1917 Andrew and Allie rented a house in Lubbock, and Allie and the children subsequently lived in town during the school years. In the Great Depression[qv] the Blankenships were forced to convert their 2,560-acre combination farm and ranch into a cotton farm. As automobiles became more common they stopped raising horses. They traded the last of their horses and mules for forty acres of land two miles from Lubbock (*see also* HORSE BREEDING and MULE RAISING). After Texas Tech University was built on the adjacent land, the Blankenships built the Town and Country Shopping Center.

After Blankenship died on December 8, 1952, Allie moved in with her daughter, Doyle, and her husband, James Goodwin Thornhill. Allie and Doyle began compiling Allie's memoirs for a special exhibit called Saga of the South Plains, which was to be mounted at the Museum of Texas Tech University.[qv] Allie died suddenly in Lubbock on September 11, 1955, a few days before the exhibition opened. In 1958 her memoirs were published as *The West Is for Us* by the West Texas Museum Association.

BIBLIOGRAPHY: Jo Ella Powell Exley, ed., *Texas Tears and Texas Sunshine: Voices of Frontier Women* (College Station: Texas A&M University Press, 1985). *Jo Ella Powell Exley*

BLANKET, TEXAS. Blanket is on U.S. Highway 67/377 ten miles northeast of Brownwood in eastern Brown County. According to some accounts Blanket Creek was named in 1852 by a group of surveyors who came upon a band of Tonkawa Indians who had been caught in a downpour and had spread their blankets over sumac bushes near the creek for protection. Later the name was transferred to the community that developed on its banks. Two of the earliest settlers in the area were F. M. Cross and Dan Pinkard, who arrived in 1862. Pinkney Anderson established a store in 1873 and was the first postmaster when a post office was established in 1875. When the Fort Worth and Rio Grande Railroad was extended from Comanche to

Brownwood in 1891, Blanket was moved from its former site to its present location. It had a population of 304 in 1904 and 472 in 1929. In the 1930s it had twenty businesses and a population of more than 300. By 1970 it had seven businesses and its population remained at around 300. In the late 1980s Blanket had five businesses and 388 residents, and in 1990 its population was 381. Artist Harold O. Kelly[qv] lived for a while in Blanket.

BIBLIOGRAPHY: Thomas Robert Havins, *Something about Brown: A History of Brown County, Texas* (Brownwood, Texas: Banner Printing, 1958). Fred Tarpley, *1001 Texas Place Names* (Austin: University of Texas Press, 1980). *Jeanne F. Lively*

BLANKET CREEK (Brown County). Blanket Creek begins five miles north of Blanket in eastern Brown County (at 33°54′ N, 98°50′ W) and runs southeast for thirty miles, through southwestern Brown County and western Mills County, to its mouth on Pecan Bayou, four miles southwest of Mullin in west central Mills County (at 31°31′ N, 98°45′ W). It traverses generally flat terrain with local shallow depressions and a surface of clay and sandy loam that supports water-tolerant hardwoods and grasses.

——— (Real County). Blanket Creek, an intermittent, spring-fed stream, rises on the eastern edge of the Frio canyon in southeastern Real County (at 29°39′ N, 99°38′ W) and flows south, then southwest, for a total of thirteen miles, to its mouth on the Frio River (at 29°35′ N, 99°40′ W). It is joined by Bear Creek seven miles below its origin. It descends into the Frio canyon over a bed of limestone, gravel, and calcareous soil. The surrounding heavily dissected canyonlands of the Balcones Escarpment[qv] are forested with open stands of live oak, Ashe juniper, and mesquite.

BLANTON, ANNIE WEBB (1870–1945). Annie Webb Blanton, teacher, suffragist, and the first woman in Texas elected to statewide office, was born on August 19, 1870, in Houston, one of seven children of Thomas Lindsay and Eugenia (Webb) Blanton. Her twin sister, Fannie, died as a girl. A brother, Thomas Lindsay Blanton,[qv] represented central West Texas in the United States Congress from 1917 to 1936. Annie Blanton attended school in Houston and La Grange. After graduating from La Grange High School in 1886, she taught in a rural school in Fayette County. After her father's death in 1888, she moved to Austin, where she taught in both elementary and secondary schools. She supported herself by teaching while studying at the University of Texas, where she graduated in 1899.

From 1901 to 1918 Blanton served on the English faculty of North Texas State Normal College (now the University of North Texas) in Denton, where she became active in the Texas State Teachers Association.[qv] Because she established herself as a strong believer in equal rights for women and also was known for having written a series of grammar textbooks, she was elected president of the association in 1916. She was the first woman to hold this position.

In 1917 Texas suffragists found a sympathetic leader in Gov. William P. Hobby,[qv] after the impeachment of Gov. James Ferguson.[qv] In Hobby's first called legislative session in February 1918 women obtained the right to vote in Texas primaries. The suffragists offered their support to Hobby in his 1918 bid for the Democratic gubernatorial nomination and asked Annie Blanton to run for state superintendent of public instruction. In a bitter campaign, she was accused of being an atheist and of running as a tool for others, but she fought back and charged the incumbent with close associations with the impeached former governor and the breweries. In the July 1918 primary, when Texas women exercised their voting rights for the first time, Blanton defeated incumbent Walter F. Doughty[qv] and Brandon Trussell by a large margin. Her victory in the general election in November made her the first woman in Texas elected to statewide office.

During her tenure as state superintendent a system of free textbooks was established, teacher certification laws were revised, teachers' salaries were raised, and efforts were made to improve rural education. Blanton was reelected in November 1920, when voters also passed the Better Schools Amendment, which she had proposed as a means of removing constitutional limitations on tax rates for local school districts. She served as state superintendent through 1922, when she did not seek a third term but ran unsuccessfully for the United States Congress from Denton County. She subsequently returned to the University of Texas, where she received her master's degree in 1923. She taught in the UT education department until 1926, then took a leave of absence to earn her Ph.D. from Cornell University. After returning to the University of Texas in 1927, she remained a professor of education there for the rest of her life.

Annie Webb Blanton, ca. late 1920s. Prints and Photographs Collection, Annie Webb Blanton file, CAH; CN 03545.

Blanton published several books during her career, including *Review Outline and Exercises in English Grammar* (1903), *A Handbook of Information as to Education in Texas* (1922), *Advanced English Grammar* (1928), and *The Child of the Texas One-Teacher School* (1936). In 1929 she founded the Delta Kappa Gamma Society,[qv] an honorary society for women teachers, which in 1988 had an international membership of 162,000. She also was active in national educational groups and served as a vice president in the National Education Association in 1917, 1919, and 1921. Throughout her career she was especially interested in the needs of rural schools.

Blanton, who never married, was a Methodist. She died in Austin on October 2, 1945, and was buried in Oakwood Cemetery. Public schools are named for her in Austin, Dallas, and Odessa, and a women's dormitory at the University of Texas at Austin bears her name.

BIBLIOGRAPHY: Debbie Mauldin Cottrell, *Pioneer Woman Educator: The Progressive Spirit of Annie Webb Blanton* (College Station: Texas

A&M University Press, 1994). Dallas *Morning News*, July 28, 30, 1918, May 14, 1922. Eunah Temple Holden, *Our Heritage in the Delta Kappa Gamma Society* (Austin: Delta Kappa Gamma Society, 1960; rpt. 1970). *Proceedings and Addresses of the Texas State Teachers' Association*, 1916. Vertical Files, Barker Texas History Center, University of Texas at Austin.

Debbie Mauldin Cottrell

BLANTON CREEK. Blanton Creek rises 5½ miles northeast of Detroit in western Red River County (at 33°41′ N, 95°10′ W) and runs northeast for seven miles to its mouth on Pecan Bayou, nine miles northwest of Clarksville (at 33°44′ N, 95°06′ W). The soil around the creek is loamy, and the area is heavily wooded, with pines and various oaks predominating.

BLANTON, THOMAS LINDSAY (1872–1957). Thomas Lindsay Blanton was born in Houston, Texas, on October 25, 1872, a son of Thomas Lindsay and Eugenia (Webb) Blanton and brother of Annie Webb Blanton.[qv] He attended the public schools of Houston and La Grange and graduated from the law school of the University of Texas in 1897. He married May Louise Matthews, daughter of John A. and Sallie (Reynolds) Matthews,[qqv] in 1899, and they had five children. Blanton began the practice of law in Cleburne but soon moved to Albany. There he practiced until 1908, when he was elected district judge. He was reelected to that office in 1912. In 1916 he was elected to the United States Congress as a Democrat; his first tenure ran from 1917 to 1929. In 1928 he did not seek reelection but ran unsuccessfully for the United States Senate. Upon the death of his successor, Robert Q. Lee,[qv] in 1930, he again won election to Congress. He remained in the House until 1937. He served on the committees on claims, education, irrigation[qv] and arid lands, railways and canals, woman suffrage,[qv] Indian affairs, and the District of Columbia. In 1932 he moved to the appropriations committee, where he remained until 1937.

Early in his career Blanton incurred the wrath of Samuel Gompers and the labor leadership. In World War I[qv] he favored a "work or fight" amendment to the draft law. He opposed the railroad strike of 1921. He received many threats, and his car was once fired upon near Washington. In 1924 he proposed to stop all immigration for five years. In 1926 he forced the resignation of a District of Columbia commissioner for overcharging veterans in guardian fees. He caused an investigation at St. Elizabeth's Hospital that resulted in the court's declaring forty-five inmates sane and releasing them. In 1928 he introduced a bill to stop immigration for seven years, to require all aliens to register, and to deport those who did not become citizens. In 1935 he introduced a bill to outlaw Communists in the United States. In his long career he consistently opposed extravagance. On May 28, 1919, he introduced a resolution calling upon all government departments to furnish a list of employees earning money outside the government and the names of all relatives on the payroll. All his fellow Texans voted against the resolution. His opposition to all congressional junkets and fringe benefits voted for themselves by Congressmen caused ill feeling toward him among his colleagues.

After being defeated in 1936, Blanton practiced law in Washington until 1938, when he returned to Albany to practice there. During World War II[qv] he urged President Franklin D. Roosevelt to ask Congress to pass promptly a law fixing the death penalty for strikers in wartime. In 1954 he withdrew at his wife's request from a race for Congress against Omar Burleson, who was seeking a fifth term.

The Dallas *Morning News*[qv] once observed that every delegation needed one Tom Blanton. In Congress he had a record of near perfect attendance and offered more objections to appropriations than any other member. Upon his retirement, the Washington *Post* said that he had saved the government millions of dollars and would be missed. He died in Albany on August 11, 1957, and was buried in the Albany Cemetery.

BIBLIOGRAPHY: Abilene *Reporter-News*, August 12, 1957. Frank Carter Adams, ed., *Texas Democracy: A Centennial History of Politics and Personalities of the Democratic Party, 1836–1936* (4 vols., Austin: Democratic Historical Association, 1937). *Biographical Directory of the American Congress*. San Angelo *Standard Times*, April 6, 1924. Vertical Files, Barker Texas History Center, University of Texas at Austin.

Thomas Lloyd Miller

BLASDEL, EUGENE SHERWOOD (1878–1930). Eugene Sherwood Blasdel, the son of Judson Sherwood and Anna (Jenness) Blaisdell, was born on November 16, 1878, in Champaign, Illinois. He was stricken with infantile paralysis at the age of nine and received only limited formal schooling. He developed an insatiable appetite for books and a love for recreation and the outdoors, and was able to walk again by the time he was twelve. In 1890 he moved with his family to Des Moines, Iowa, where his father established a grain business. He soon learned the financial aspects of agribusiness and in 1896 succeeded his father as manager of the Charles Counselman and Company grain elevator at Gowrie, Iowa. In 1898 he enrolled at Doane Academy, a branch of Denison University at Granville, Ohio. A year later he started his own business selling gasoline engines, then an innovation. In anticipation of joining the Klondike gold rush Blasdel moved in January 1901 to Seattle, where he worked as an engineer on fishing vessels. Both of these business ventures were curtailed by bouts with typhoid fever. After his second recovery in Seattle, Blasdel worked briefly as a reporter for the San Francisco *Examiner* and the *Mercury*. He returned to Iowa in November 1901 and became a traveling auditor for the Counselman firm. Acquaintance with Gov. Henry G. Blasdel in San Francisco motivated Eugene to modify his surname. He married Libbie Howard, a high school principal from Jefferson, Iowa, on May 2, 1904, and settled briefly in Chicago, where he worked at the Neola Elevator Company headquarters.

In October 1904 the Blasdels decided to move to Texas after noticing a land company's ad pushing the "golden opportunities" of the Panhandle.[qv] Upon arrival at Groom, Carson County, Blasdel established a lumberyard and with John Walter Knorpp as a partner opened the town's first bank. After Libbie's death on May 28, 1905, Blasdel sold out his interest in the bank to Knorpp. A year later he sold his lumberyard to A. C. Morgan, a lumber salesman from Elk City, Oklahoma. Blasdel then began speculating in land leases and built a small house in town for himself and his parents. For a time he worked for the National Bank of Commerce in Amarillo and in 1908 purchased a quarter-section farm three miles northwest of Groom, on which he built a granary.

To learn more about banking and the nature of Wall Street, particularly in relation to the recent panic of 1907, Blasdel took courses in composition and economics at the University of Chicago and business courses at the New York University School of Commerce, Accounts, and Finance. While in New York he worked briefly as a reporter for the *Wall Street Journal* and made several influential contacts, including one with John D. Rockefeller. He also visited several grain operations throughout the Midwest and Canada. On the train from Milwaukee to Chicago he met Kathleen Meiklejohn, a speech teacher. They were married at Waupun, Wisconsin, on June 2, 1909. They had six children, the oldest of whom died as a child.

The newlyweds returned to the farm near Groom, where Blasdel began raising wheat and kafir by a new method then called dry-tillage farming. This method proved fairly successful during a poor season, and in 1911 he sold the farm and started his own grain elevator in town. The following year he moved his family and business to Amarillo, where he established the Plains Grain Company and purchased an interest in several other elevators. Through his contacts in the outside market Blasdel sold a considerable amount of wheat abroad, particularly after the outbreak of World War I[qv] in 1914. He was said to have had the world corner on red top cane seed in 1916–17. In 1918, however, when the federal government ordered all domestic grain in storage to be moved to ports for shipment abroad, he liquidated his business in protest.

After a severe bout with influenza Blasdel began searching out the natural resources of the Panhandle, looking for possible deposits of clay for brick, sand for glass, gravel, copper, gold, oil, and gas. After the discovery of gas on the Masterson ranch in December 1918, Blasdel purchased Grover C. Bishop's interest in an expiring oil and gas lease on Samuel Burk Burnett's[qv] Four Sixes Ranch.[qv] With W. H. Fuqua[qv] and Pat H. Landergin (*see* LANDERGIN BROTHERS) as partners, Blasdel secured a new contract with Burnett, hired Charles N. Gould[qv] to locate sites for wells, and brought in the Gulf Production Company to do the drilling. Their efforts paid off in 1920, when Gulf No. 1 Burnett began producing fifty million cubic feet of gas daily, and again on March 20, 1921, when Gulf No. 2 became the Panhandle's first successful oil well. The latter date coincided with the birth of Blasdel's youngest child, whom he named James Gulf in honor of the occasion.

With his new fortune Blasdel bought stock in various oil companies, obtained more oil leases, and invested in Amarillo real estate. Still maintaining an interest in the Groom Elevator Company, he also planned to resume his role as a grain dealer and erect more elevators. In addition he became a member of the Chicago Athletic Club and envisioned buying a seat on the Chicago Board of Trade. Often he took his family on extended vacations and camping trips. Blasdel was appointed United States food and fuel administrator for the Texas Panhandle and was president of the Amarillo School Board from 1919 to 1921. He also served a term (1923–24) as mayor of Amarillo and was a member of the Central Presbyterian Church there.

In the fall of 1929 a severe attack of bronchitis left Blasdel's health even more delicate, and the wishes of his family to remain in Amarillo influenced his decision not to reenter the grain business. On October 16, 1930, he died of a heart attack while he was hunting deer on a vacation with his wife and four of his children in the Blue Mountains near Springerville, Arizona. He was buried in Llano Cemetery, Amarillo.

BIBLIOGRAPHY: Henry E. Hertner, ed., *Three Questions, Three Answers: A Story from the Life of Dr. Charles Newton Gould* (Amarillo: Potter County Historical Survey Committee, 1967). Jo Stewart Randel, ed., *A Time to Purpose: A Chronicle of Carson County* (4 vols., Hereford, Texas: Pioneer, 1966–72). *H. Allen Anderson*

BLASIG, ANNE JUSTINE (1900–1971). Anne Justine Blasig, author of *The Wends of Texas* (1954), was born on July 25, 1900, in Sealy, Texas, the daughter of Hermann and Caroline (Mennicke) Schmidt. The family moved to Galesburg, Illinois, in 1901, then in 1908 to Dexter, Iowa. Anne worked her way through the University of Iowa, where she received a B.A. in history. In 1951 she received an M.A. in history from the University of Texas. She taught in the public schools of New Braunfels, Brady, and Mercedes for twelve years. In Brady she helped establish the McCulloch County Library. She subsequently taught school in Harlingen for twenty-one years and was named outstanding teacher of the year before retiring in 1970. Hermann Schmidt was the last Wendish-speaking Lutheran minister in Serbin, Texas, from 1922 to 1947. Anne Blasig's book, *The Wends of Texas,* was first an M.A. thesis. She wrote numerous stories and articles and translated into English materials relating to the Wends[qv] in Texas, including an old ship's register of Wendish immigrants. She contributed to the Wendish exhibit at the University of Texas Institute of Texan Cultures[qv] during HemisFair[qv] in 1968. She was married to Carl A. Blasig on July 1, 1924, and the couple had one daughter. Mrs. Blasig died on August 30, 1971, in San Benito and was buried in Mount Meta Cemetery there.

BIBLIOGRAPHY: Anne Blasig Papers, Barker Texas History Center, University of Texas at Austin. Austin *American,* September 2, 1971. Vertical Files, Barker Texas History Center, University of Texas at Austin. Vertical Files, University of Texas Institute of Texan Cultures, San Antonio. *Mrs. Milton Walther*

BLAYLOCK, LOUIS (1849–1932). Louis Blaylock, publisher, civic leader, and mayor of Dallas, was born in Sevier County, Arkansas, on October 21, 1849, the son of Willis and Irene (Gibs) Blaylock. His family moved to Texas in 1852 and settled in Austin. In 1866 he began work as a typesetter for the *Texas Christian Advocate,* a Methodist paper (now the *United Methodist Reporter*[qv]). Blaylock and William A. Shaw eventually took over the paper, which by 1876 had a circulation of 13,000, supposedly the largest circulation of any contemporary paper in Texas. By 1887 the paper claimed a circulation of 18,000. Blaylock moved the *Advocate* to Dallas and formed the Blaylock Publishing Company in 1887. He left the paper in 1922 after being with it for fifty-six years. Blaylock served as Dallas police commissioner from 1901 to 1904 and was both police and fire commissioner from 1913 to 1915. He served as city administration and finance commissioner from 1919 until 1923, when he was elected mayor. Since he was seventy-four at the time of his election, he was soon nicknamed "Daddy" Blaylock. While in office he was noted for kissing every gorgeous movie star, festival queen, or other prominent female who visited Dallas, as an official welcome to the city. Blaylock was also known as one of the most able and conservative mayors in the city's history. In 1871 he married Georgia Darton, and they eventually had five children. He was active in the First Methodist Church in Dallas, as a member of the building committee and as president of the board of trustees. He was publisher of the daily paper for the Methodist General Conference when it met in Dallas in 1902. He was also a prominent Mason. Blaylock died on December 4, 1932, and was buried in Oakland Cemetery, Dallas.

BIBLIOGRAPHY: John D. Barron, A Critical History of the *Texas Christian Advocate,* 1849–1949 (M.A. thesis, University of Missouri, 1952). Dallas *Morning News,* August 3, 1970. *Walter N. Vernon*

BLAZEBY, WILLIAM (1795–1836). William Blazeby, defender of the Alamo, was born in England in 1795. He traveled to Texas from New York by way of New Orleans as a second lieutenant in Capt. Thomas H. Breece's[qv] company of New Orleans Greys.[qv] Blazeby took part in the siege of Bexar[qv] and remained in Bexar afterward as captain and commander of the Greys under Lt. Col. James C. Neill.[qv] Blazeby died in the battle of the Alamo[qv] on March 6, 1836.

BIBLIOGRAPHY: Daughters of the American Revolution, *The Alamo Heroes and Their Revolutionary Ancestors* (San Antonio, 1976). Daughters of the Republic of Texas, *Muster Rolls of the Texas Revolution* (Austin, 1986). Bill Groneman, *Alamo Defenders* (Austin: Eakin, 1990). John H. Jenkins, ed., *The Papers of the Texas Revolution, 1835–1836* (10 vols., Austin: Presidial Press, 1973). *Bill Groneman*

BLEAKWOOD, TEXAS. Bleakwood is at the junction of Farm Road 363 and U.S. Highway 87, forty-five miles north of Beaumont in west central Newton County. One of the first settlers in the area was Thomas S. McFarland,[qv] who established a plantation home. The post office that served the area from 1850 to 1860 was called Cotland, presumably after a San Augustine County residence sold by McFarland in 1838. The post office was moved a short distance in 1867 and renamed Bleakwood by T. L. McDonald, in honor of his former home in Scotland. In 1883 officials again moved the post office, this time to the community that had grown up around Jessie Lee's grist and saw mills. The area's rich forests attracted the interest of large lumber industries, which began to penetrate Newton County in the late 1890s. The Jasper and Eastern Railway between Kirbyville and the Sabine River was completed in 1905, and the Orange and Northwestern linked Newton to Orange by 1906. These lines gave Bleakwood early railroad connections to move timber to processing plants. In its heyday just after 1900, Bleakwood had the post office, two general stores, sawmills, and a railroad depot. At least one small lumber company seems to have been based there in 1910. From 1928 to 1942 the E. E. McDonald Lumber Company operated a large plant at Bleakwood. Despite the company's departure and a major flood that temporarily severed Bleakwood's railroad links in the early twentieth century, the community remained a shipping point for logs, ties, staves, and pulpwood. The Bleakwood post office closed in 1943. An 1890 estimate set the population at fifty-eight; subsequent figures through 1950 range from fifty to 150. By 1966, however, the community's population had increased to about 300, and it remained at that level in the early 1990s.

BIBLIOGRAPHY: Newton County Historical Commission, *Crosscuts: An Anthology of Memoirs of Newton County Folk* (Austin: Eakin, 1984). Newton County Historical Commission, *Glimpses of Newton County History* (Burnet, Texas: Nortex, 1982). *Robert Wooster*

BLEDSOE, ALBERT A. (?–1882). Albert A. Bledsoe, pioneer settler, state comptroller, and county judge, moved to Dallas County, Texas, from Kentucky in 1847. He purchased the headright of Roderick Rawlins,[qv] who later became his son-in-law. Bledsoe subdivided the tract and surveyed a townsite that he called Lancaster. He was elected chief justice of Dallas County in 1865 but lost a reelection bid the following year. He also failed in an attempt to represent the county at the Constitutional Convention of 1866.[qv] During Reconstruction[qv] he was appointed county judge, a position he held until 1869. He was elected to represent Dallas County at the Constitutional Convention of 1868–69,[qv] where his political views aligned him with the Radical Republican faction. He was nicknamed "Iron-clad" after he publicly took the "Iron-clad" oath of loyalty to the United States. He served on the committee that recommended the establishment of the controversial and unpopular State Police[qv] to curb lawlessness and violence.

Bledsoe returned to Dallas after the convention and remained county judge until he was appointed comptroller of public accounts.[qv] He gained notoriety in this position for his refusal to allow the transfer of $500,000 worth of state bonds to the International Railroad Company and for filing fraud charges—of which the rail line was found innocent—against the company in state district court in Austin in February 1873. Bledsoe contended that the rail company had arranged to pay a number of state legislators in return for their votes in favor of 1870 legislation authorizing the transfer of $10,000 in bonds for each mile of track constructed by the railroad. Upon the completion of fifty miles of track, the company had demanded $500,000 in bonds, which Governor E. J. Davis[qv] signed but which Bledsoe, as state comptroller, refused to sign. The company filed a writ of mandamus in state district court to force Bledsoe to sign and deliver the bonds. The matter eventually reached the state Supreme Court, which, by a three-to-two vote, voided the writ, thereby siding with Bledsoe. The end of Reconstruction[qv] in Texas hastened the end of Bledsoe's public career. He died at his home in Dallas on October 8, 1882.

BIBLIOGRAPHY: Ann Patton Baenziger, "The Texas State Police during Reconstruction: A Reexamination," *Southwestern Historical Quarterly* 72 (April 1969). James R. Norvell, "The Railroad Commission of Texas: Its Origin and History," *Southwestern Historical Quarterly* 68 (April 1965). *Semi-Weekly Farm News* (Dallas), June 1, 1934.

Brian Hart

BLEDSOE, JESSE SAUL (1776–1836). Jesse Saul Bledsoe, lawyer and politician, was born in Culpeper County, Virginia, on April 6, 1776, the son of Joseph and Elizabeth (Miller) Bledsoe. He moved to Kentucky with his brother, Robert Emmett Bledsoe, and eventually graduated from Transylvania Seminary at Lexington. Around 1800 he married the oldest daughter of Col. Nathaniel Gist. Bledsoe entered law school and was admitted to the bar about 1800. He took part in Kentucky politics from 1808 to the 1830s, holding offices as secretary of state, state legislator, state senator, and United States senator. As an attorney, he instructed his nephew, Robert Emmett Bledsoe Baylor,[qv] in his law office, and one of his clients was John Peter Schatzell.[qv] In 1822 Bledsoe was appointed circuit judge of the Lexington District and became professor of law at Transylvania University. In 1831 he left the office to become a minister. He traveled to Mississippi in 1833, moved to Nacogdoches, Texas, in 1835, and died there on June 25, 1836. He is supposed to have amassed a large collection of Texas historical documents with the intention of writing a definitive Texas history. Shortly after his death, his papers were sold at an auction in Nacogdoches. Robert E. B. Baylor possessed some of the collection, but most of the documents have disappeared since Bledsoe's death.

BIBLIOGRAPHY: Mann Butler, *A History of the Commonwealth of Kentucky* (Louisville: Wilcox, Dickerman, 1834). George W. Ranck, *History of Lexington, Kentucky* (Cincinnati: Clarke, 1872).

Laurie E. Jasinski

BLEDSOE, JOSEPH (1827–ca. 1906). Joseph Bledsoe, soldier and jurist, was born in Bourbon County, Kentucky, on February 15, 1827, the son of Hiram M. and Susan T. (Hughes) Bledsoe. In 1839 the family moved to Lafayette County, Missouri, where young Bledsoe attended high school at Lexington. He graduated from Bethany College in West Virginia in 1850 and was admitted to the bar. Before establishing a practice, however, he taught school for a year in Hinds County, Mississippi, and then accepted a position as chief engineer of the Texan Emigration and Land Company (*see* PETERS COLONY). A letter of introduction from George S. Walton dated March 13, 1854, describes Bledsoe as "a gentleman and a scholar" and asks the addressee's assistance in "furthering him along in your *golden state*."

After spending a year surveying the Peters Colony beyond the frontier on the upper Brazos River, Bledsoe moved to Austin, where he practiced law. On March 25, 1857, he married Miranda Sneed, the daughter of Judge Sebron Graham Sneed[qv] of Austin. The ceremony was performed by his friend Chief Justice John B. Costa of the state Supreme Court. In 1858, when Bledsoe moved his practice to Denton, he became a leader of the secession[qv] movement. He moved to McKinney in 1860 and was living there at the outbreak of the Civil War.[qv] He was elected first lieutenant in Capt. Joseph M. Bounds's[qv] company of Col. William C. Young's[qv] Eleventh Texas Cavalry regiment. He saw duty in Indian Territory and under Gen. Ben McCulloch[qv] at the battle of Elkhorn Tavern (Pea Ridge), where he was wounded by a charge of grapeshot on March 10, 1862. After his regiment was reassigned east of the Mississippi River, he took part in the battle of Corinth before returning to Texas to recruit an artillery company, the Bledsoe Battery. As captain of the battery he saw action at the battles of Newtonia, Prairie Grove, Cave Hill, Bayou Meta, and Helena, all in Arkansas. Late in 1864 Bledsoe was reassigned to command of a company on the Rio Grande, twenty-five miles from Brownsville, with "plenty to eat and nothing to do." He wrote in December 1864, "This is a easier place to soldier than any I have been in and as I have seen a pretty rough time since war commenced I would like to stay here a while at least to rest."

With the breakup of the Confederacy, Bledsoe wrote to his friend Edward Pearsall Gregg[qv] that he was stranded in Austin "without means" and "doing nothing." "I have returned like nearly all other soldiers without *a dollar*," he related, and since the courts seemed unlikely to reopen in the near future he was considering going into business. He returned to McKinney, however, and reestablished his practice. On December 28, 1868, he married Florence L. Davis, the niece and ward of Horace Clark[qv] and an early female instructor at Baylor University. The couple had five children. On September 1, 1869, Bledsoe joined Samuel Bell Maxey, John J. Good,[qqv] and forty-seven other prominent men of the Second Congressional District in urging Capt. John C. Conner[qv] of the United States Army to run for the House of Representatives.

Bledsoe became comptroller of public accounts in February 1870 and for a time lived again in Austin. He was elected judge of the Twenty-seventh Judicial District in 1876 and reelected in November 1880. On August 9, 1884, he was elected chairman of the executive committee of the Grayson County Democratic party, and on August 18 in Houston he was elected a vice president of the state Democratic party[qv] convention. Bledsoe was still on the bench as late as 1885 and was spoken of as living as late as 1906.

bibliography: *Biographical Encyclopedia of Texas* (New York: Southern, 1880). Joseph Bledsoe Papers, Barker Texas History Center, University of Texas at Austin. Dallas *Times Herald,* March 6, 1861, June 19, 1861, September 11, 1869, February 12, 1870, August 24, 1872, August 14, 1884, August 21, 1884. Clement Anselm Evans, ed., *Confederate Military History* (Atlanta: Confederate Publishing, 1899; extended ed., Wilmington, North Carolina: Broadfoot, 1987–89). Buckley B. Paddock, ed., *A Twentieth Century History and Biographical Record of North and West Texas* (Chicago: Lewis, 1906). William S. Speer and John H. Brown, eds., *Encyclopedia of the New West* (Marshall, Texas: United States Biographical Publishing, 1881; rpt., Easley, South Carolina: Southern Historical Press, 1978). *Texas State Gazette,* March 28, 1857.
Thomas W. Cutrer

BLEDSOE, JULIUS LORENZO COBB (1897–1943). Julius (Jules) Bledsoe, black baritone and composer, was born on December 29, 1897, in Waco, Texas, the son of Henry L. and Jessie (Cobb) Bledsoe. He attended Central Texas Academy in Waco from about 1905 until his graduation as class valedictorian in 1914. He then attended Bishop College in Marshall, where he earned a B.A. in 1918. He was a member of the ROTC at Virginia Union University in Richmond in 1918–19 and studied medicine at Columbia University in New York City between 1920 and 1924. While attending Columbia, he studied voice with Claude Warford, Luigi Parisotti, and Lazar Samoiloff. He was sponsored by the impresario Sol Hurok for his professional singing debut on April 20, 1924, at Aeolian Hall in New York. As a concert artist Bledsoe performed in the United States and Europe. He was praised for his ability to sing in several languages, for his vocal control and range, and for his power to communicate through music.

His best-known achievement was his portrayal of Joe in Florenz Ziegfeld's 1927 production of Jerome Kern's *Showboat.* His interpretation of "Ol' Man River" made the song an American classic. In his versatile career of nearly twenty years Bledsoe performed with such distinguished musical organizations as the Boston Symphony Chamber Players (1926), the BBC Symphony in London (1936), and the Concertgebouw Orchestra of Amsterdam (1937). He also sang for vaudeville and radio and in opera. He sang the role of Amonasro in Giuseppe Verdi's *Aïda* with the Cleveland Stadium Opera (1932), the Chicago Opera Company at the Hippodrome in New York (1933), and the Cosmopolitan Opera Company, also at the Hippodrome (1934). A highlight of his career was his performance in the title role for the European premiere, in Amsterdam, of Louis Gruenberg's opera *The Emperor Jones* (1934). In 1940 and 1941 Bledsoe worked in films in Hollywood. He played the part of Kalu in *Drums of the Congo,* and, although his name did not appear in the credits, he probably played in *Safari, Western Union,* and *Santa Fe Trail.*

He wrote several patriotic songs and songs in the style of spirituals and folk songs. Some of his compositions were "Does Ah Luv You?" (1931); "Pagan Prayer" (date unknown), on a poem by Countee Cullen; "Good Old British Blue" (1936); and "Ode to America" (1941). He wrote an opera, *Bondage* (1939), based on Harriet Beecher Stowe's novel *Uncle Tom's Cabin.* Bledsoe's *African Suite,* a set of four songs for voice and orchestra, was featured with the Concertgebouw Orchestra, directed by Wilhelm Mengelberg. After a war bond tour Bledsoe died, on July 14, 1943, in Hollywood, from a cerebral hemorrhage. He is buried in Greenwood Cemetery in Waco.

bibliography: *Baker's Biographical Dictionary of Musicians.* Jules Bledsoe Papers, Texas Collection, Baylor University. Maud Cuney-Hare, *Negro Musicians and Their Music* (Washington: Associated Publishers, 1936). Lynnette Geary, The Career and Music of Jules Bledsoe (M.Mus. thesis, Baylor University, 1982). Dayton Kelley, ed., *The Handbook of Waco and McLennan County, Texas* (Waco: Texian, 1972).
Lynnette Geary

BLEDSOE, WILLIAM HARRISON (1869–1936). William Harrison Bledsoe, attorney, politician, and investor, one of six children of Willis Scott and Susan (Harrison) Bledsoe, was born at Cleburne, Texas, on December 23, 1869. After attending public schools in Cleburne, he attended the University of Texas briefly and was admitted to the State Bar of Texas[qv] in 1890. He returned to Cleburne to practice and joined his brother Albert for a time in a partnership. In 1908, lured by opportunities farther west, he moved to Lubbock and set up his practice. Although he first worked alone, he soon acquired partners, and he eventually helped to form Bledsoe, Crenshaw, and Dupree, a leading law firm in Lubbock. Bledsoe primarily handled cases involving land titles and ownership disputes. He also helped establish the South Plains Bar Association (1910), served as Lubbock City Attorney (1911), and was a member of the Lubbock School Board (1912).

Following the lead of his father in Johnson County, Bledsoe served in the Texas legislature. He was first elected in 1915 to the House of Representatives. He was chairman of two important house committees—that which investigated Governor James E. Ferguson[qv] in 1917 and voted to impeach him, and that which moved to reform the Texas Rangers[qv] in 1919. After serving two terms in the lower house, Bledsoe moved to the Senate in 1919. His most noteworthy accomplishment there was Senate Bill 103, which established Texas Technological College (now Texas Tech University). The Locating Board selected Lubbock, Bledsoe's adopted hometown, as the site for the new college. Bledsoe, who was mentioned several times as a possible candidate for higher statewide office, was seriously injured in an automobile accident in 1927. As a result, he withdrew from the campaign for reelection and never again sought elective office.

In addition to his legal and political career, he found time to invest in land, not only in Lubbock but in neighboring counties and in Ohio. He also owned an interest in a Virginia railroad. Bledsoe was a Mason and a member of the Woodmen of the World and the Knights of Pythias. During World War I[qv] he was chairman of the Lubbock chapter of the Four Minute Men. He also served on the legal advisory board for the draft. Bledsoe was married to Alice Mathews, who died in 1915. They had three children. He married Emma K. Boone, an attorney, and they had one son. Bledsoe was a member of the First Christian Church. He died on March 30, 1936, in Lubbock and was buried there.

bibliography: William H. Bledsoe Papers, Southwest Collection, Texas Tech University. Jane Gilmore Rushing and Kline A. Knall, *Evolution of a University: Texas Tech's First Fifty Years* (Austin: Madrona, 1975). Vertical File, Southwest Collection, Texas Tech University. Homer Dale Wade, *Establishment of Texas Technological College, 1916–1923* (Lubbock: Texas Tech Press, 1956).
Michael Q. Hooks

BLEDSOE, TEXAS. Bledsoe is at the junction of Farm roads 595, 769, and 2182 and the terminus of a branch line of the Atchison, Topeka and Santa Fe tracks in west central Cochran County, 1½ miles from the Texas–New Mexico state line. The town was established by the Panhandle and Santa Fe Railway when the line was built west from Lubbock in 1925; the community was named for Samuel T. Bledsoe, an official of the company, who later became president. The railroad's plans to extend from Bledsoe into New Mexico never materialized. The Panhandle and Santa Fe completed the rail line in 1925, and on December 1, 1925, the first scheduled train ran from Lubbock to Bledsoe. The community's first settlers were Mr. and Mrs. R. C. Strickland. Bledsoe was in a good location to serve as a shipping point for local ranchers, so it grew rapidly and quickly became a cattle-shipping center. The first school there opened in November 1925. The first business building was occupied by a firm that printed the *Cochran County News*, the county's first newspaper. In 1926 a post office was established, with James M. Lackey as postmaster; his wife taught at the first school in Bledsoe. By 1929 Bledsoe had a population of 400, several stores, four filling stations, three lumberyards, two hotels, a church, a cafe, an electric plant, an ice plant, a barbershop, a movie theater, and a dance hall. By 1936 the population had declined to 150, and only ten businesses remained. The primary reasons for this decline were the lack of water and the decreasing need for the railroad. By 1970 the population level at Bledsoe had stabilized at 125, where it remained in the early 1990s, when about four businesses were operating there.

BIBLIOGRAPHY: Elvis Eugene Fleming, *Texas' Last Frontier: A History of Cochran County* (Morton, Texas: Cochran County Historical Society, 1965). James Marshall, *Santa Fe: The Railroad That Built an Empire* (New York: Random House, 1945). Kathleen E. and Clifton R. St. Clair, eds., *Little Towns of Texas* (Jacksonville, Texas: Jayroe Graphic Arts, 1982). *Leoti A. Bennett*

BLEIBLERVILLE, TEXAS. Bleiblerville, on Farm Road 2502 four miles northeast of Industry in northwestern Austin County, was named for Robert Bleibler, who established a general store at the site in the late 1880s. By the late nineteenth century, successive waves of German immigration into northwestern Austin County had produced a large German population in the vicinity. A post office was established in Bleiblerville in 1891. By 1900 Theodore Wehring operated a cotton gin in the community. An active Red Cross chapter, organized locally during World War I,[qv] included ten black residents on its sixty-eight-member roster. The nearby Welcome School is a mile northwest of town on Farm Road 2502. In 1904 the town reported a population of 101. The population rose to an estimated 150 by 1925. In 1931 four businesses were reported in the community. The population climbed to an estimated 225 by 1966 as oil exploration increased in the area. By 1972, however, it had fallen to an estimated seventy-one, its level in 1990. *Charles Christopher Jackson*

BLESSING, TEXAS. Blessing is west of the junction of State Highway 35 and Farm Road 616 and twenty miles west of Bay City in northwestern Matagorda County. The town was promoted by Jonathan Edwards Pierce,[qv] on whose land it was established. In 1903, when Pierce gave the right-of-way to the Galveston, Harrisburg and San Antonio Railway, the future of the unnamed settlement seemed assured. A grateful Pierce hoped to designate the place "Thank God," but the United States Postal Department rejected his proposal. As a compromise, the place was named Blessing, and a post office opened in 1903, with James H. Logan as first postmaster. Between 1903 and 1905 a library building was attached to the train station. In 1905 the St. Louis, Brownsville and Mexico Railway also built through Blessing. D. A. Wheeler's hotel soon followed. On September 1, 1907, residents platted the townsite, and the townsite company made provisions for school and church sites. In 1909 P. Ansley established a local newspaper. By 1914 Blessing had 500 inhabitants, two churches, a bank, a hotel, a telephone connection, and a weekly newspaper, the Blessing *News*. In 1925 Blessing's population was still recorded at 500. In 1931 the town had a population of 450 and twenty-two businesses. During the 1937–38 school year, nine teachers instructed 251 white students in eleven grades, and two teachers instructed thirty-eight black students in seven grades. By 1949 the Blessing district had been consolidated with the Tidehaven Independent School District. In 1945 Blessing's population had risen to 600, served by thirteen businesses. Though in 1966 the population was reported as 1,250; in 1968 it had dropped to 405. In 1990 the town had 571 residents and twelve businesses.

BIBLIOGRAPHY: Frank J. Balusek, Survey and Proposed Reorganization of the Schools of Matagorda County, Texas (M.Ed. thesis, University of Texas, 1939). Matagorda County Historical Commission, *Historic Matagorda County* (3 vols., Houston: Armstrong, 1986). Kathleen E. and Clifton R. St. Clair, eds., *Little Towns of Texas* (Jacksonville, Texas: Jayroe Graphic Arts, 1982). *Stephen L. Hardin*

BLESSING BROTHERS. Samuel T. Blessing (ca. 1832–1897), John P. Blessing (ca. 1833–1882), and Solomon T. Blessing (born ca. 1840), pioneer Texas photographers and dealers in photographic supplies, were all natives of Maryland; at least two of them were brothers. In 1856 Samuel opened a daguerreotype gallery in New Orleans with Samuel T. Anderson. By 1859 Anderson and Blessing, "daguerrean artists," had an office on Twenty-third Street in Galveston, Texas, but the Union blockade during the Civil War[qv] apparently shut down the Texas trade.

Immediately after the war John P. and Solomon T. Blessing advertised as artists and operated photographic galleries in both Houston and Galveston. They offered photographs made by many processes, including paper prints finished in oil, pastel, or watercolor, and a large assortment of photographic supplies, which they attempted to keep up to date with the rapid technological advances in the field. Among their Galveston employees were P. H. Rose and portrait artist Louis Eyth.[qv]

In 1870 the Blessings opened Blessing's Photographic Temple, a new portrait gallery in Galveston. Their establishment included a copying and enlarging department, from which they could produce all sizes of portraits, from miniatures to life-size. In addition they offered portraits in oil, painted from photographs to reduce the traditional lengthy sittings. In the 1872 Galveston City Directory they boasted that they operated "the best equipped gallery in the state." They exhibited chromos, stereoscopic views of Galveston, albums, and portraits of famous people. In addition to their artistic interests, Solomon was a retail merchant, and the brothers sold Wilson's sewing machines and operated the dry-goods firm of Foster and Blessing. They are last listed as Blessing and Bro. in Galveston in 1882–83, when John resided in Baltimore, Maryland.

Around 1886 or 1887 Solomon moved to Dallas and opened a store at 461 Elm Street. Samuel T. Blessing of New Orleans was evidently an important associate of this enterprise, if not its head. When he died in 1897, Solomon succeeded him as manager of the business. John did a number of views of Houston buildings that were lithographed by W. H. Rease of Philadelphia and included as vignettes around W. E. Wood's map of Houston, published in 1869.

BIBLIOGRAPHY: Richard Pearce-Moses, *Photographic Collections in Texas: A Union Guide* (College Station: Texas A&M University Press, 1987). Margaret Denton Smith and Mary Louise Tucker, *Photography in New Orleans: The Early Years, 1840–1865* (Baton Rouge: Louisiana State University Press, 1982). *Ben W. Huseman*

BLEVINS, TEXAS. Blevins is on Farm Road 1239 twenty miles west of Marlin in western Falls County. A school was built there in 1885, and the next year a post office was established. By the mid-1890s the community had a cotton gin, two general stores, and 100 residents. Its post office was discontinued in 1904, but the Blevins school continued to operate until the district was divided between the Troy Independent School District in Bell County and the Bruceville-Eddy district in McLennan County. The population of Blevins was 130 in the 1940s. It fell to thirty-six by the mid-1960s, and remained at that level through 1990.

BIBLIOGRAPHY: Lillian S. St. Romain, *Western Falls County, Texas* (Austin: Texas State Historical Association, 1951).

Vivian Elizabeth Smyrl

BLEWETT, TEXAS. Blewett, a mining community originally known as Carbonville, is on Farm Road 1022 and Turkey Creek five miles southeast of Cline in far southwestern Uvalde County. Outcroppings of limestone rock asphalt cover 50,000 to 60,000 acres in the area. The Lathe Carbon Company, formed, according to one source, by a group of New York capitalists, opened a bitumen mine at the site in 1888. Failure to sell its bitumen, in a market limited to the paint and varnish industry, forced the company to close before its second year. Beaumont capitalist John Blewett Smyth, for whom the community was probably named, used bituminous limestone to develop a new road-paving material in 1912. The first production of limestone rock asphalt for street and road surfacing began at the Blewett location in 1912. A post office opened at the community in 1928, two years after it had become the terminus of a spur line from the Texas and New Orleans Railroad at Cline. The township is often designated as Mine No. 2 to distinguish it from Smyth Mine No. 1, a mile distant. High-grade commercial asphalt was produced at an average annual rate of 1,250,000 tons during peak production in 1927, and 125,000 tons during the 1930s. By 1940 many of Blewett's buildings had been abandoned, though a school and a commissary were still in operation there. Although the community reported an estimated population of only fifty in 1940, some evidence suggests that it had as many as 500 residents during periods of peak operation at the mines. In 1948 Blewett had the asphalt mine, a nine-section group dwelling, a hotel or tourist camp, one additional business, a school, and a scattering of residences. Although the Missouri Pacific rail service to Uvalde was discontinued in April 1966, the railroad continued service to the Uvalde Rock Asphalt Company and White's Uvalde Mines near Blewett. By 1988 Blewett had an estimated population of twenty-five and two businesses, one of which housed the post office. The population was still reported as twenty-five in 1990.

BIBLIOGRAPHY: *A Proud Heritage: A History of Uvalde County* (Uvalde, Texas: El Progreso Club, 1975). WPA Writers' Program, *Texas: A Guide* (New York: Hastings House, 1940; rev. ed. 1969).

Ruben E. Ochoa

BLIN, JOSEPHINE (?–1852). Josephine (Mother Ste. Arsene) Blin, foundress of the Ursuline Sisters[qv] in Galveston, was a native of Paris, France. At the age of sixteen she entered the Sisters of the Infant Jesus, a congregation founded for the instruction of girls. When, shortly thereafter, Bishop Dubourg of New Orleans returned to France in search of priests and religious to work in his diocese, Sister Ste. Arsene volunteered; she sailed from Le Havre in April 1817 and, upon arrival in New Orleans, lived in the Ursuline convent and was professed as an Ursuline. On January 16, 1847, Bishop J. M. Odin[qv] of Galveston instituted a new Ursuline Academy.[qv] Seven volunteers, with Mother Ste. Arsene as superior, came from New Orleans. After six years of service at the head of the foundation, the mother superior died, on October 10, 1852.

BIBLIOGRAPHY: S. M. Johnston, *Builders by the Sea: History of the Ursuline Community of Galveston, Texas* (New York: Exposition, 1971). *Souvenir of the Diamond Jubilee and Yearbook, 1847–1922* (Galveston: Ursuline Academy, 1922).

BLINN COLLEGE. Blinn College, at Brenham, originally Mission Institute, was founded in 1883 by the Southern German College of the Methodist Episcopal Church to train ministers for the mission conference. President Carl Urbantke[qv] and the original class of three students met in the German Methodist Church. After four years of operation the struggling school received a boost when Christian Blinn of New York pledged financial support, including funds for a two-story building. In gratitude, the Methodist annual conference for 1889 changed the name of the institution to Blinn Memorial College. In its early years the college served as an academy, with preparatory, normal, theological, and music departments and instruction beginning at the third grade. The school became coeducational in 1888. Through the fifty years that it was sponsored by the Methodist Church,[qv] the institution enrolled more than 7,000 students and trained nearly 100 ministers. The highest enrollment was 239, in the 1907–08 school year. In 1906 the building now termed Old Main was erected, with Andrew Carnegie contributing almost half of the $28,000 cost.

With the growth of public high schools, academies declined, and Blinn was made a junior college in 1927. In 1930 the college was merged with Southwestern University. In 1933 the Methodist Church discontinued its support, and in 1934 Blinn Memorial College was again a separate institution. From 1934 to 1937 the residents of Brenham operated the college as a private institution. In the latter year Washington County voters established a junior college district, and Blinn College became the first county-district junior college in the state. Charles Frank Schmidt[qv] was its first president after it became tax-supported. The 1907–08 enrollment figure was not surpassed until after World War II.[qv] In 1950 the college received additional funding from Washington County voters and began a construction program that included a library and fine arts building. By the early 1950s the enrollment had risen to over 1,100 students, as veterans enrolled in twelve evening schools, eleven of which were off campus.

By 1957, when James H. Atkinson assumed the presidency, the off-campus program had dwindled to one school, but construction continued on the fifteen-acre main campus as school officials anticipated the effect of the post–World War II baby boom on enrollment. Students numbered 1,350 by 1966–67. By 1974–75 additional dormitories had brought housing capacity to over 750, and the enrollment was 1,642. The school offered both vocational-terminal and academic-transfer programs. In the 1970s the college again began extending its programs, with off-campus operations in Bryan, College Station, Grimes County (at the Texas Department of Corrections), and Bastrop (at the Federal Correctional Institute). By 1983 the main campus had grown to over 100 acres, and the physical plant was valued at over $11 million. In 1990 the student enrollment was 7,098.

BIBLIOGRAPHY: Arthur A. Grusendorf, The Social and Philosophical Determinants of Education in Washington County, Texas, from 1835 to 1937 (Ph.D. dissertation, University of Texas, 1938). Charles F. Schmidt, *History of Blinn College* (San Antonio, 1935?; 2d ed., Fort Worth, 1958).

James H. Atkinson

BLISS, DON ALFONSO (1854–1939). Don Alfonso Bliss, lawyer, judge, and legal scholar, son of Joseph F. Bliss, was born in Artesia, Mississippi, on December 14, 1854. He graduated from King's College, Bristol, Tennessee, in 1873. On April 22, 1874, he married Myra Maud Hampton; they had six children. The family moved to Texas, where Bliss conducted the Van Alstyne Institute from 1881 to 1885, then entered the law school of the University of Texas. He was admitted to the bar in 1886 and practiced in Sherman until 1892, when he was appointed judge of the Fifteenth Judicial District. In 1906, at the insistence of Jot Gunter,[qv] with whom he had practiced in Sherman, he moved to San Antonio, where he served on the board of education. As an authority on land-title cases, he wrote on the establishment of Texas law in regard to public charities and represented Adina de Zavala[qv] in the case to save the Alamo in 1907. He also published a legal work, *The Nature of the Title Held by the Heirs of a Deceased Wife to One-half of the Ganancial Property under the Spanish Law* (n.d.). When irrigation[qv] projects opened the Rio Grande valley for citrus-fruit growing and truck farming, Judge Bliss represented several purchasers and became an authority on irrigation law. He practiced in San Antonio until shortly before his death there, on December 3, 1939.

BIBLIOGRAPHY: Emory A. Bailey, *Who's Who in Texas* (Dallas: John B. McCraw Press, 1931). Frank W. Johnson, *A History of Texas and Texans* (5 vols., ed. E. C. Barker and E. W. Winkler [Chicago and New York: American Historical Society, 1914; rpt. 1916]). Vertical Files, Barker Texas History Center, University of Texas at Austin.

BLISS, ZENAS RANDALL (1833–1900). Zenas Randall Bliss, United States army officer, was born in Rhode Island and was appointed from his native state to the United States Military Academy at West Point on July 1, 1850. He graduated forty-first in his class and was assigned to duty as a brevet second lieutenant in the First Infantry on July 1, 1854. He was posted to Texas and served at Fort Duncan until 1855, when he was promoted to second lieutenant and transferred to an Eighth Infantry assignment at Fort Davis. In 1858 he served briefly at Camp Hudson and forts Inge and Mason and in 1859 at forts Mason and Clark. Back at Camp Hudson he was promoted to first lieutenant in 1860 and to captain in 1861. Secession[qv] found Bliss at Fort Quitman. After Gen. David E. Twiggs[qv] surrendered the federal forts in Texas, Bliss attempted to march his garrison to the Texas Gulf Coast, but was intercepted by Confederate troops under Gen. Earl Van Dorn[qv] just west of San Antonio and held prisoner until April 5, 1862. In May 1862 he was commissioned as colonel of the Tenth Rhode Island Infantry, and in August he was transferred to the Seventh Rhode Island Infantry. Bliss was brevetted to major in the regular army in 1862 for "gallant and meritorious service" at the battle of Fredericksburg, Virginia, and to lieutenant colonel in 1864 for his service at the battle of the Wilderness. At the battle of Fredericksburg Bliss led his regiment, which had never before been under fire, to within a few yards of the Confederate lines before being repulsed, thereby winning the Medal of Honor. With the end of the Civil War[qv] he was mustered out of volunteer service on June 9, 1865.

In the postbellum army Bliss was assigned as major of the Thirty-ninth Infantry on August 6, 1867, and transferred to the all black Twenty-fifth United States Infantry[qv] on March 15, 1869. Subsequently appointed commander of the Department of Texas, Bliss made his headquarters at San Antonio and served at forts Bliss, Clark, Davis, and Duncan between 1871 and 1879. He was appointed lieutenant colonel of the Nineteenth Infantry in 1879 and promoted to colonel of the Twenty-fourth Infantry[qv] in 1886. He was promoted to brigadier general in 1895 and to major general in 1897. He retired from active duty on May 22, 1897, and died in Washington, D.C., on January 2, 1900. A copy of his unpublished memoirs, Reminiscences of Zenas R. Bliss, is housed in the Barker Texas History Center[qv] at the University of Texas at Austin.

BIBLIOGRAPHY: George W. Cullum, *Biographical Register of the Officers and Graduates of the U.S. Military Academy at West Point, New York* (8 vols., New York [etc.]: D. Van Nostrand [etc.], 1868–1940). Francis B. Heitman, *Historical Register and Dictionary of the United States Army* (2 vols., Washington: GPO, 1903; rpt., Urbana: University of Illinois Press, 1965). Houston *Post*, January 3, 1900.

Thomas W. Cutrer

BLISS CREEK. Bliss Creek, a perennial stream, rises three miles southwest of Buffalo in west central Leon County (at 31°23′ N, 96°06′ W) and flows northeast for twelve miles to its mouth on Buffalo Creek, six miles east of Buffalo (at 31°29′ N, 95°58′ W). It crosses sloping to nearly level terrain surfaced by sandy loam that supports post oak, black hickory, pecan, elm, water oak, and hackberry trees along its banks. Settlement in the vicinity began during the 1840s. The community of Buffalo, on the north bank of the stream, was founded as a station on the International and Great Northern line in 1872.

BIBLIOGRAPHY: James Young Gates and H. B. Fox, *A History of Leon County* (Centerville, Texas: Leon County *News*, 1936; rpt. 1977).

BLOCK, HARLON HENRY (1924–1945). Harlon Henry Block, soldier, the first of four sons of Edward Frederick and Ada Belle Block, was born on November 6, 1924, at Yorktown, Texas. After graduating from Weslaco High School, he entered the marines, on February 18, 1943, in San Antonio. He completed basic training in San Diego, California, attended parachute training school, and was assigned to the First Marine Parachute Regiment. As a member of this unit he experienced his first combat duty during the Bougainville campaign. He subsequently appeared in one of the most famous battle photographs ever taken: the raising of the flag atop Mount Suribachi on the island of Iwo Jima during World War II.[qv] After his parachute regiment was disbanded, on February 29, 1943, he was transferred to Company E, Second Battalion, Twenty-eighth Marines, Fifth Marine Division. This company landed on Iwo Jima on February 19, 1945. Mount Suribachi, the 550-foot-high extinct volcano on the southern end of the island, was assaulted by the Twenty-eighth Marines on February 20. By mid-morning of February 23 they had reached the top of Suribachi and defeated the last Japanese defenders. Six marines raised a small flag to signal their victory to their fellow soldiers below. Later, a second, larger flag (ninety-six by fifty-six inches) was raised. Corporal Block helped with the second flag by stooping and guiding the base of the pole into the volcanic ash while the other five men heaved the flag upward. As the flag rose Associated Press photographer Joe Rosenthal snapped the Pulitzer Prize-winning photograph. Corporal Block, however, never saw the famous picture. He was killed in action on March 1, 1945, when his unit advanced in the direction of Mishi Ridge. He was buried in the Fifth Marine Division Cemetery near the base of Mount Suribachi; in January 1949 his body was taken home for private burial in Weslaco.

BIBLIOGRAPHY: Bernard C. Nalty, *The United States Marines on Iwo Jima* (Washington: U.S. Marine Corps, 1967). Richard F. Newcomb, *Iwo Jima* (New York: Holt, 1965). *David V. Stroud*

BLOCK CREEK. Block Creek rises six miles southwest of Bankersmith in northwestern Kendall County (at 30°06′ N, 98°55′ W) and runs southeast for fourteen miles to its mouth on the Guadalupe River, four miles east of Comfort (at 29°59′ N, 98°50′ W). It crosses an area of steep slopes and benches surfaced by shallow clay loams that support juniper, live oak, mesquite, and grasses.

BLOCK CREEK, TEXAS. Block Creek was a small community on the east bank of Block Creek and the old Comfort to Fredericksburg road, 2½ miles north of Farm Road 473 and some eight miles northeast of Comfort in western Kendall County. It was settled, in part, by Freethinkers. A post office opened at Block Creek in 1884 and closed in 1895. In 1890 the community had fifteen residents. The Block Creek school had opened by around 1900 and remained the focus of a common school district until 1949, when it became part of the Comfort Independent School District. In 1913 the Fredericksburg and Northern Railway established a flag stop in Block Creek to benefit nearby Hillingdon Ranch. Two or three houses marked the community on county highway maps in the late 1940s, but by the 1980s these were no longer shown on maps of the area.

BIBLIOGRAPHY: Kendall County Historical Commission, *A History of Kendall County, Texas* (Dallas: Taylor, 1984).

Melissa G. Wiedenfeld

BLOCKER, ABNER PICKENS (1856–1943). Abner (Ab) Pickens Blocker, trail driver, youngest of the three sons of Abner Pickens and Cornelia Randolph (Murphy) Blocker, was born on January 30, 1856, on the family ranch near Austin, Texas. He spent his youth in farm and ranch work and in 1876 joined his older brothers, William B. and John R. Blocker,[qqv] on their range in Blanco County. In 1877 he helped deliver 3,000 steers to John Sparks in Wyoming. Over the next seventeen years he drove longhorn cattle[qv] up the trails from Texas to various buyers in Oklahoma, Kansas, Colorado, Wyoming, and Montana, and as far north as the Canadian border. In the summer of 1885 he delivered 2,500 head from Tom Green County to B. H. (Barbecue) Campbell, manager of the Capitol Syndicate's Buffalo Springs division in Dallam County. Campbell had contracted to buy cattle for the newly established XIT Ranch,[qv] and this was the first herd from South and West Texas to arrive. Blocker devised the XIT brand, for which the syndicate's ranch was named. Afterward he was involved in the dispute at Fort Supply, Oklahoma, resulting from the attempts of Kansas ranchers to quarantine the herds of his brother and other South Texas cattlemen and keep the Texans from crossing their land (*see* TEXAS FEVER).

Beginning in 1887 Blocker tried cotton farming for two years, but a period of drought soon put him back in the saddle. In 1890 he was made range boss of his brother's Chupadero Ranch, near Eagle Pass. His last overland trail drive was to Deadwood, South Dakota, with Harris Franklin's herd in 1893. In 1896 he married Florence Baldwin; they had a daughter. The family resided on a ranch in La Salle County, fifteen miles southeast of Cotulla, until a prolonged drought ruined them financially. In 1903, after living in Oklahoma for a year, the Blockers returned to Eagle Pass and subsequently took up residence again at the Chupadero Ranch. There they remained until 1912, when Blocker began working for the Texas Cattle Raisers Association (later the Texas and Southwestern Cattle Raisers Association[qv]). He died in San Antonio on August 9, 1943, and was buried in Dignowity Cemetery.

BIBLIOGRAPHY: *Cattleman*, September 1943. J. Evetts Haley, *The XIT Ranch of Texas and the Early Days of the Llano Estacado* (Chicago: Lakeside, 1929; rpts., Norman: University of Oklahoma Press, 1953, 1967). J. Marvin Hunter, *Trail Drivers of Texas* (2 vols., San Antonio: Jackson Printing, 1920, 1923; 4th ed., Austin: University of Texas Press, 1985). Jimmy M. Skaggs, *The Cattle-Trailing Industry: Between Supply and Demand, 1866–1890* (Lawrence: University Press of Kansas, 1973).
H. Allen Anderson

BLOCKER, DAN (1928–1972). Dan Blocker, television actor, was born on December 10, 1928, in DeKalb, Texas, the son of Ora Shack and Mary (Davis) Blocker. His delayed birth certificate, filed by a doctor on March 22, 1929, recorded his name as Bobby Don Blocker. When he was six years old the family moved to O'Donnell, in West Texas, where his father operated a general store. Dan attended local schools before entering Texas Military Institute[qv] in San Antonio at the age of twelve. He studied at Hardin-Simmons University and then entered Sul Ross State Teachers College (now Sul Ross State University) in Alpine in 1947. He was always big—fourteen pounds at birth, reportedly the largest baby ever born in Bowie County. He stood over six feet and weighed 200 pounds as a youth of twelve; by the time he became a star football player at Sul Ross he was six feet, four inches tall and weighed over 275 pounds.

At college Blocker became interested in acting. When he graduated with a B.A. degree in speech and drama, he refused offers of professional careers in both football and boxing. He acted in summer stock in Boston and soon afterward was drafted for combat duty in Korea, where he served as an infantry sergeant with the Forty-fifth Division. In 1952 he returned to Sul Ross, where he earned an M.A. degree. There he married his college sweetheart, Dolphia Lee Parker, on August 25, 1952; they had four children. Blocker taught school in Sonora, Texas, and Carlsbad, New Mexico, before moving to California in 1956 to work on a Ph.D. degree at the University of California at Los Angeles. During this time he also worked as a substitute teacher at Glendale and began his career as a professional actor in Los Angeles. In 1959 he was cast in the role of "Hoss" Cartwright on the NBC network television production, "Bonanza," one of the longest-running and most popular TV series. Blocker was an enormously popular actor and successful businessman; he was co-owner of a nationwide chain of steak houses called Bonanza. He received the Texan of the Year Award in 1963 from the Texas Press Association,[qv] and in 1966 he served as honorary chairman of the Texas Cancer Crusade. He played the role of Hoss Cartwright for thirteen seasons on national television, until his death on May 13, 1972, from complications following an operation. The television series was terminated soon after his death. Blocker was buried in Woodmen Cemetery, DeKalb, Texas.

BIBLIOGRAPHY: San Antonio *Express*, May 15, 1972. Vertical Files, Barker Texas History Center, University of Texas at Austin.

BLOCKER, JOHN RUFUS (1851–1927). John Rufus Blocker, trail driver and rancher, second of the three sons of Abner Pickens and Cornelia Randolph (Murphy) Blocker, was born in the Edgefield district of South Carolina on December 19, 1851. The family moved to Texas in 1852 and settled near Austin. During the Civil War[qv] John helped drive ox teams to Mexico to avoid the Union blockade. He attended the Swan Coats School and Texas Military Institute, Austin,[qv] before 1871, when he entered the cattle business in Blanco County with his brother Bill. Seeing the demand for beef in the North, Blocker made his first trail drive to Ellsworth, Kansas, in 1873. Over the next twenty years he took longhorn cattle[qv] to buyers in Colorado, Nebraska, Wyoming, the Dakotas, and Montana, and was said to know every waterhole from the Rio Grande to the Yellowstone River. On the trail he used an inverted seven brand, and his peculiar but effective mode of roping cows with a large loop came to be known among cowmen as the "Blocker loop." During one trip in 1885 with 25,000 steers, he and his brother Ab, who had joined the family business in 1876, were detained at Fort Supply (or Camp Supply) by Oklahoma and Kansas ranchers who would not allow them to go on to market because of the fear of Texas fever.[qv] After several appeals to the United States government, Blocker and George W. West,[qv] whose herd was also affected, finally obtained a cavalry escort to their destination. Soon afterward, the cow trails through Kansas were closed to prevent the disease from spreading.

In 1881 Blocker married Annie Lane of Austin; they had four children. At one time or another, and with various partners, Blocker owned ranches in Tom Green, Coke, Maverick, and Dimmit counties, including the Chupadero Ranch near Eagle Pass, and also land in northern Mexico. In 1893 the Blocker brothers made their last trail drive north when they delivered Harris Franklin's herd of 9,000 cattle to a buyer in Deadwood, South Dakota. In later years Blocker made his home in San Antonio, where he joined the Texas and Southwestern Cattle Raisers Association.[qv] He also helped organize the Old Time Trail Drivers Association and was elected its first president. He died at San Antonio on December 1, 1927, and was buried in Dignowity Cemetery.

BIBLIOGRAPHY: *Cattleman*, January 1928. Gus L. Ford, ed., *Texas Cattle Brands* (Dallas: Cockrell, 1936). *History of the Cattlemen of Texas* (Dallas: Johnson, 1914; rpt., Austin: Texas State Historical Association, 1991). J. Marvin Hunter, *Trail Drivers of Texas* (2 vols., San Antonio: Jackson Printing, 1920, 1923; 4th ed., Austin: University of Texas Press, 1985). Jimmy M. Skaggs, *The Cattle-Trailing Industry: Between Supply and Demand, 1866–1890* (Lawrence: University Press of Kansas, 1973).
H. Allen Anderson

BLOCKER, TRUMAN GRAVES, JR. (1909–1984). Truman G. Blocker, Jr., surgeon, teacher, and administrator, was born in West Point, Mississippi, on April 17, 1909, to Truman Graves and Mary Ann (Johnson) Blocker. He attended public schools in Sherman, Texas, and graduated from Austin College in 1929. After receiving his M.D. degree from the University of Texas Medical Branch at Galveston in 1933, he interned at the Graduate Hospital of the University of Pennsylvania, Philadelphia, then devoted a year to residency training in surgery at John Sealy Hospital[qv] in Galveston. He then served as an instructor in surgery at the Presbyterian Hospital affiliated with Columbia University in New York City until 1936, when he returned to UTMB as an assistant professor of surgery. Blocker received certification from the American Board of Surgery in 1940 and from the American Board of Plastic Surgery in 1942.

From the summer of 1942 until the summer of 1946 he served as a military surgeon, first in the United States Air Force, then in the United States Army. He became chief of plastic surgery and later chief of surgery at Wakeman General Hospital in Camp Atterbury, Indiana. He was particularly interested in maxillofacial injuries, especially those requiring extensive repair of soft-tissue defects and bone grafting. When he was discharged Colonel Blocker was awarded the Legion of Merit.

He returned to UTMB in 1946 and became professor and chief of a new division of plastic and maxillofacial surgery. After ships anchored in Texas City exploded in 1947, injuring and burning some 3,000 persons (*see* TEXAS CITY DISASTER), Blocker and his wife, Dr. Virginia Howard (Irvine) Blocker, published a survey of the casualties. For this and other research studies involving trauma and burns the Blockers received the Harvey Allen Award from the American Burn Association in 1971.

While continuing a full schedule of surgical operations, guiding an extensive program of research in plastic and reconstructive surgery, and teaching numerous students and residents, Blocker accepted increasingly more complex administrative assignments at UTMB. Between 1946 and 1964 he was variously director of postgraduate studies, director of the special surgical unit, director of hospitals, dean of the clinical faculty, chairman of the interim executive committee, and chairman of the department of surgery. He served as chief administrative officer of UTMB for ten years, first as executive director and dean (1964–67), then as president (1967–74). He encouraged the Shriners of North America to choose UTMB as the site of one of their three hospitals for the care of burned children. The Shriners Burns Institute[qv] opened in 1966 and is recognized as one of the outstanding facilities of its kind in the world. Blocker's diligence, vision, and persuasive powers occasioned unprecedented growth and expansion of UTMB's facilities and academic programs, transforming the medical school into an internationally recognized academic health-sciences center.

Blocker held numerous consultant positions with the Veterans Administration and the offices of the surgeons general of the United States Army and the United States Air Force. In 1953 he inspected medical installations in Korea and Japan. While he was in Hiroshima he lectured to medical students and performed plastic surgery on atomic bomb victims. His experience with burn therapy, his devotion to military medicine, and his interest in the treatment of mass casualties resulting from nuclear attacks led to his appointments to the Subcommittee on Burns (later Trauma) of the National Research Council, to the Surgery Study Section of the United States Public Health Service, and to the Advisory Panel on Medical Sciences of the Department of Defense.

Between 1937 and 1973 Blocker authored or coauthored 182 publications, most of which dealt with the care of burn victims. He was an active member of more than thirty professional groups. He received numerous awards from local, state, national, and international associations, including Distinguished Service awards from the American Society of Maxillofacial Surgeons and the American Board of Surgery. In 1983 former students established the Truman G. Blocker, Jr., Distinguished Chair in Plastic Surgery at UTMB. Dr. Blocker died at John Sealy Hospital in Galveston on May 17, 1984, from the effects of a stroke that he had suffered on New Year's Day. He was survived by his wife and four children. After his death the collections of rare books and historical artifacts in the Moody Medical Library[qv] at UTMB were renamed the Truman G. Blocker, Jr., History of Medicine Collections.

BIBLIOGRAPHY: William C. Levin, "Truman G. Blocker, Jr.," *The Bookman*, July–August 1984. *Chester R. Burns*

BLOCKER, WILLIAM BUTLER (1850–1921). Bill Blocker, rancher and trail driver, the oldest of the three sons of Abner Pickens and Cornelia Randolph (Murphy) Blocker, was born on May 28, 1850, in Mobile, Alabama, where his father owned a cotton plantation. In 1852 the family moved to Texas, settled on a tract south of Austin, and established a cattle ranch. Blocker attended a private school. At the age of ten he began accompanying his father on roundups. He soon proved himself an adept cowhand and quickly mastered the techniques of the trade. Although his father had planned to send him to law school, Blocker went into the cattle business for himself at the age of nineteen. Thomas F. McKinney[qv] advanced him $3,000 to buy and round up cattle and make his first drive up the Chisholm Trail[qv] to Abilene, Kansas. In 1871, after gathering more herds in Blanco, Hays, Travis, and Caldwell counties, Blocker and his brother John bought their first ranch in Blanco County; their youngest brother, Ab, joined this family enterprise as a drover in 1876. Although Blocker made fewer trail drives than his brothers did, he was an expert cowman and soon gained several backers. In 1874 he married Elizabeth Eleanor Irving, whose father owned a ranch on the Pedernales in Blanco County. Eight children were born to the couple. Blocker purchased a second ranch between Lockhart and Austin and later ran cattle near Kyle, in Hays County. He built a home in Austin for his family, although he preferred the open range. When automobiles became available he purchased one for the family but continued to drive his horse-drawn buggy. He died on October 28, 1921, and was buried in the family lot in Austin.

BIBLIOGRAPHY: Ruth Hunicutt, "Bill Blocker, Pioneer Cattleman," *Cattleman*, December 1946. J. Marvin Hunter, *Trail Drivers of Texas* (2 vols., San Antonio: Jackson Printing, 1920, 1923; 4th ed., Austin: University of Texas Press, 1985). Jimmy M. Skaggs, *The Cattle-Trailing Industry: Between Supply and Demand, 1866–1890* (Lawrence: University Press of Kansas, 1973). *H. Allen Anderson*

BLOCKER, TEXAS (Harrison County). Blocker, on Farm Road 2625 six miles southeast of Marshall in southeastern Harrison County, is the site of the brick plantation home of Henry Ware,[qv] who moved to the county in the early 1840s. Ware is said to have introduced new stock, machinery, and farm implements to the section; he grew wheat and operated a flour mill and a woolen mill, said to be the first in Texas and perhaps in the South. He operated a tannery and manufactured boots and shoes. During the Civil War[qv] he ran his machinery full-time until the Confederate surrender closed his industries. When the Marshall and East Texas Railway was built, Blocker became a thriving settlement with a mill, a commissary, and over 400 voters. The community seems to have been named for Dr. Eugene Blocker, a member of the prominent Blocker family of Marshall, who married Ware's oldest daughter, Fannie Asbury Ware, in 1861. The Blocker community had a post office from 1910 to 1927 and in 1914 had an estimated 300 inhabitants. The town declined after the mill was partially destroyed by fire and the railroad was discontinued. In 1946 there were some thirty-five voters left at the community. In 1983 Blocker consisted of a cemetery and several scattered dwellings.

BIBLIOGRAPHY: Randolph B. Campbell, *A Southern Community in Crisis: Harrison County, Texas, 1850–1880* (Austin: Texas State Historical Association, 1983). Carol Morris Little, *Historic Harrison County* (Longview, Texas, 1984). *Sallie M. Lentz*

BLOCKER, TEXAS (Harrison County). Blocker was south of the Louisiana and Arkansas Railway on a site near where present Farm roads 9 and 1999 intersect, four miles west of the Louisiana state line and sixteen miles northeast of Marshall in northeastern Harrison County. The community was presumably named for William J. Blocker, who owned the land grant it was on. The town had a post office from 1884 to 1901. In 1890 Blocker had a population of twenty-five, a steam gristmill, a cotton gin, and a general store. By 1892 it had a population estimated at fifty and two churches. In 1896 Blocker had a voting box, and the following year the Blocker district school enrolled thirty-three students. In 1900 a railroad, which became part of the Missouri, Kansas and Texas the following year, was built through the area. In 1901 Blocker's post office and the general store were moved to a new community three miles to the west, named Leigh, that grew up along the railroad. Blocker did not appear on the state highway map of 1948, and in 1984 all that remained at the townsite was a cemetery.

BIBLIOGRAPHY: Jerome McCown, Scraps of the Early History of Marshall and Harrison County (MS, Barker Texas History Center, University of Texas at Austin). Charles P. Zlatkovich, *Texas Railroads* (Austin: University of Texas Bureau of Business Research, 1981).

Mark Odintz

BLOCKER CREEK. Blocker Creek rises three miles east of the Montague county line in southwestern Cooke County (at 33°35′ N, 97°26′ W) and runs southeast for 16½ miles to its mouth on Clear Creek, in extreme northwestern Denton County (at 33°25′ N, 97°20′ W). It crosses flat to rolling terrain with a surface of expansive clays and clay loams and deep, fine sandy loam that supports oak, juniper, brush, and grasses.

BLODGETT, TEXAS. Blodgett is at the junction of Farm roads 21 and 127, ten miles southwest of Mount Pleasant in southwestern Titus County. John F. Blodgett operated the community's only post office from 1903 to 1905. In 1945 the town had one business and about twenty-five residents. In 1984 Blodgett had two churches and a cemetery.

BIBLIOGRAPHY: Wright Patman, *History of Post Offices—First Congressional District of Texas* (Texarkana, Texas, 1946?).

Cecil Harper, Jr.

BLOODGOOD, WILLIAM (1800?–?). William Bloodgood, one of Stephen F. Austin's[qv] Old Three Hundred[qv] colonists, a native of either New York or New Jersey, was born around 1800 and traveled to Texas in 1824 with the Enoch Brinson[qv] family. Bloodgood's wife, the former Lucy Ballow, and Mrs. Brinson were sisters. Bloodgood received title to a sitio[qv] of land now in Chambers and Harris counties on August 10, 1824. The census of March 1826 listed him as a carpenter aged between twenty-five and forty, with a wife and a son. Brinson and Bloodgood had a disagreement over the boundary between their land on Cedar Bayou in 1827. In June 1834 William B. Travis[qv] was employed by Bloodgood to write a deed of land to W. D. Smith. By June 1835, when Bloodgood made out a character certificate and application for land at Nacogdoches, he had three children. On March 21, 1838, he received a bounty warrant for 320 acres from the secretary of war or the republic for his military service from May 8 to August 8, 1836. On October 16, 1867, 320 acres in Refugio County was patented to Henry Smith, Bloodgood's assignee. Bloodgood served on a Harrisburg grand jury in March 1838. In January 1846 he was present at a Harris County meeting to nominate a sheriff. He was still living in Harris County in 1850, when he was fifty years old.

BIBLIOGRAPHY: Eugene C. Barker, ed., *The Austin Papers* (3 vols., Washington: GPO, 1924–28). Lester G. Bugbee, "The Old Three Hundred: A List of Settlers in Austin's First Colony," *Quarterly of the Texas State Historical Association* 1 (October 1897). Daughters of the Republic of Texas, *Founders and Patriots of the Republic of Texas* (Austin, 1963–). Charles Adams Gulick, Jr., Harriet Smither, et al., eds., *The Papers of Mirabeau Buonaparte Lamar* (6 vols., Austin: Texas State Library, 1920–27; rpt., Austin: Pemberton Press, 1968). Andrew Forest Muir, ed., "Diary of a Young Man in Houston, 1838," *Southwestern Historical Quarterly* 53 (January 1950). *Telegraph and Texas Register*, March 31, 1838, January 28, 1846. William Barret Travis, *Diary*, ed. Robert E. Davis (Waco: Texian, 1966).

BLOOM, SAM R. (1904–1983). Sam R. Bloom, advertising executive, was born on January 28, 1904, in Clarksville, Red River County, Texas. His father, a merchant who had immigrated from Germany, had married Fannie Solomon, a native of Fort Worth, and Sam grew up in Fort Worth, where he attended high school. At age seventeen he became a traveling salesman for Marshall Field and Company, Montgomery Ward, and several wholesale companies. He subsequently became an advertising solicitor for the Fort Worth *Record* (later the Fort Worth *Star-Telegram*[qv]) and several Scripps-Howard and Hearst newspapers in El Paso and San Antonio; then in 1924 he took a position at the Dallas *Times Herald*.[qv] He rose in 1941 to the position of advertising director there. He was with the *Herald* almost thirty years and served on the board of directors of the *Herald* and its radio and television properties.

When he started his own firm around 1952, Zale Jewelry[qv] was one of his primary accounts. He named his new company Sam Bloom Advertising. In 1961 President John F. Kennedy summoned Bloom to Washington to serve with the White House Conference on Equal Employment and the National Advisory Committee on Desegregation. When he returned to Dallas, Bloom called on merchant Stanley Marcus and others to help begin the integration process (*see* CIVIL-RIGHTS MOVEMENT) and also produced a film, *Dallas at the Crossroads*, which was shown all over the South by the Dallas Citizens Council. In these efforts Bloom worked closely with C. A. Tatum, Jr., Robert B. Cullum,[qqv] Jim Chambers, and John Stemmons. Bloom married Evelyn Goldstein of Fort Worth; the couple had two children. He was an active civic leader and was twice president of Temple Emanu-El.[qv] His service as president included the era when the majestic temple on Hillcrest in Dallas was built. The Dallas Advertising League named him Ad Man of the Year in 1972 and presented him with the Bill Kerss Award in 1981 for his service to the community. When Sam Bloom died on July 17, 1983, his son Robert assumed the agency's presidency. At the time, Bloom Advertising had billings of $150 million and 350 employees. Bloom was posthumously named to the Advertising Hall of Fame in New York in December 1990.

BIBLIOGRAPHY: Natalie Ornish, *Pioneer Jewish Texans* (Dallas: Texas Heritage, 1989). Vertical Files, Barker Texas History Center, University of Texas at Austin. *Natalie Ornish*

BLOOMBURG, TEXAS. Bloomburg is on the Kansas City Southern Railway six miles east of Atlanta and less than a half mile from the Arkansas state line in northeastern Cass County. Settlement in this area began before the Civil War,[qv] but Bloomburg did not begin to develop as a community until the Texarkana and Fort Smith Railway was built through the area in 1895. When the post office was opened in 1896 it was named for an official of the railroad company. Since the town was the last station on the railroad line before it left the state, it soon became a shipping point for area farmers. In 1898 the Texas, Arkansas and Louisiana Railway was constructed between Atlanta and Bloomburg; until it was abandoned in 1920 it gave residents of Bloomburg access to the Texas and Pacific Railway. By 1900 the town had a population of 198. It was incorporated in 1911 and by 1914 had a small bank, a hotel, a restaurant, several stores, and a population estimated at 600. Between 1914 and the 1960s the population fluctuated between a high of 600 and a low of 433; in the 1960s it fell from 500 to 231. In 1980 the population was 419, and in 1986 the town had three rated businesses. In 1990 the population was 376.

Cecil Harper, Jr.

BLOOMFIELD, TEXAS. Bloomfield was on a road that is now Farm Road 372, fifteen miles southeast of Gainesville in southeastern Cooke County. The community was reportedly settled in 1876 and had a post office from 1877 to 1907. Mrs. Angeline Jackson, sister of the first postmaster, named the community for a field of yellow wildflowers. The first settler was probably Alfred Robison, a widower who moved with his children to Texas from Tennessee before the Civil War.[qv] Crockett Robison operated a store and served as first postmaster at Bloomfield, and Claude Robison established the first cotton gin in the community. Other early settlers were Perry Pierce,

Jeff Montgomery, Reason Jones, Louis Jordan, Robert Jones, Pat and Steve Sanders, Parson Boling, Alex Davis, and Tom Wooten. Dr. John S. Riley, who settled two miles west of Bloomfield in 1871, was an uncle of the poet James Whitcomb Riley.

Methodist, Baptist, and Church of Christ congregations were organized and met in the school building; no church building was ever erected. The Old Union School, the first school to serve the area, was a small, one-room log structure on Reason Jones's land. John Shipley was the teacher. The first school closer to Bloomfield was established in 1879 and taught first by E. E. Runion (Runyon). Some years later two other schools were built, in the eastern and western parts of the school district. After these two buildings were destroyed by a tornado in 1888, a single school was rebuilt on the west side of Bloomfield. In 1929 the Bloomfield school district was incorporated with the new Union Grove district.

Bloomfield reached the zenith of its development in the 1880s. By 1884 it had four stores, steam gristmill–cotton gins, Methodist and Baptist congregations, and a population of 300. By 1890 the population stood at 350, but by 1892 it had declined to 100, and in 1896 to thirty-five. The flour mill closed down in 1890, and the last gin was moved to Burns City around 1902. Bloomfield continued as a dispersed settlement through the first half of the twentieth century; it recorded a population of forty-seven from 1933 to 1948 and of twenty from 1949 to 1962. During the 1960s it reported around 100, although the 1963 county map showed only a cemetery at the site. From 1968 through 1987 a population of thirty was reported. The project area of Lake Ray Roberts, a reservoir under construction in the late 1980s, included the site of Bloomfield. The old Bloomfield schoolhouse was moved to the grounds of the University of North Texas in Denton for preservation.

BIBLIOGRAPHY: Gainesville *Daily Register and Messenger,* August 30, 1948. Oral Histories Concerning Bloomfield, Cooke County Library, Gainesville, Texas. A. Morton Smith, *The First 100 Years in Cooke County* (San Antonio: Naylor, 1955). *Odessa Morrow Isbell*

BLOOMFIELD BRANCH. Bloomfield Branch rises three miles northwest of Crystal Falls in northwest Stephens County (at 32°55′ N, 98°57′ W) and runs northeast for three miles to its mouth on the Clear Fork of the Brazos River, near the Young county line (at 32°57′ N, 98°56′ W). The stream extends beneath steep to moderately sloping hills surfaced by shallow soils that support oak, mesquite, and grasses, to a rolling prairie surfaced by clay loams that support mesquite and grasses.

BLOOMING GROVE, TEXAS. Blooming Grove, also known as Gradyville, is on State Highway 22 and Farm Road 55 ten miles west of Corsicana in northwestern Navarro County. The town originated in a store established by R. J. Grady and Sam Andrews shortly after the Civil War.[qv] When a post office was established there in 1871, citizens met at the White Church Cemetery to choose a name for the community. The town was named either for a grove of blooming trees or for the son—Blooming Davis—of a Doctor Davis. After 1881 the community moved a mile north to be on the Cotton Belt rail line (officially known as the St. Louis Southwestern Railway) and merged with the community of White Church. The new town grew rapidly from a population of 200 in 1884 to 800 in 1890, when townspeople sought incorporation. The city limits and boundaries were officially set on March 31, 1890. The oldest church in town, the White Church, began as the Methodist Mission in 1869. In 1887 the community's first public school was established. Central Texas College, a junior college, was opened at Blooming Grove under the auspices of the Corsicana Methodist Conference in 1902 but closed in 1912 because of mismanagement. The first newspaper, the Blooming Grove *Enterprise,* was published briefly in 1888. It was followed in 1890 by the *Rustler,* which later became the *Times,* which was still being published in 1990. By 1900 Blooming Grove was a shipping and trade center for the surrounding area and depended mainly on agriculture for its economy. At that time the town had four gins, four churches, several grocery stores, several independent cotton buyers, two gristmills, two lumberyards, two restaurants, two hotels, and a community fair. The town declined in the mid-1930s due to falling cotton prices and the onset of the Great Depression.[qv] Railroad service to the community was discontinued in 1931. Many stores and gins closed, and banks failed. Farmers were unable to borrow money and moved away. The town's population dropped from a high of 1,500 in 1933 to 821 in 1936. After World War II[qv] some residents left to work in nearby factories and cities. In 1990 the town had a population of 847 and eight businesses.

BIBLIOGRAPHY: Annie Carpenter Love, *History of Navarro County* (Dallas: Southwestern, 1933). Wyvonne Putman, comp., *Navarro County History* (5 vols., Quanah, Texas: Nortex, 1975–84). Alva Taylor, *History and Photographs of Corsicana and Navarro County* (Corsicana, Texas, 1959; rev. ed., *Navarro County History and Photographs,* Corsicana, 1962). *Carol M. Rushing*

BLOOMINGTON, TEXAS. Bloomington, the second principal city in Victoria County, is on State Highway 185 in a major oilfield fifteen miles southeast of Victoria. The town was established as a station on the St. Louis, Brownsville and Mexico Railway (built in 1906) and laid out in 1910 by developers Burton, Wharton, and Wilson. The site was named for Bloomington, Illinois, the original home of many of the first settlers. The post office was established in 1907. When the railway completed a branch from Victoria to Port O'Connor in 1912, Bloomington became an important crossroads. The next year the town was incorporated, and its population grew to 600 by 1925. The corporation was dissolved in 1929 to enable the county to build a road through the site from Placedo to Victoria. The discovery of oil in April 1947 added to the area's rich agricultural and ranching assets, primarily the Patrick H. Welder and Traylor estate properties. The community's population reached 1,756 in 1960. The number of businesses declined, however, from thirty-five to nineteen as the divided highway afforded easy access to Victoria. The Bloomington Independent School District, founded in 1919, originated from the rural school that was first held in a lumberyard there in 1908. The district covers 111 square miles, takes in the Placedo and Dacosta areas, and in 1986 was the only system in Victoria County operating its own buses. Though Bloomington's population declined slightly during the 1970s, the 1980 census recorded 1,840 residents there. Many worked at the nearby Dupont and Union Carbide plants, which were built in the early 1950s and contributed significantly to the area's growth. Eight churches and five businesses were listed at the community in 1984. The population in 1990 was 1,888.

BIBLIOGRAPHY: Victoria *Advocate,* Progress Edition, March 10, 1963. *Craig H. Roell*

BLOSSOM, TEXAS. Blossom is on the Missouri Pacific Railroad and at the intersection of Farm Road 196 and U.S. Highway 82, nine miles east of Paris in eastern Lamar County. The site was occupied by 1849, when the post office opened under the name Blossom Prairie. In 1876 the settlement became a stop on the Texas and Pacific Railway and was soon a shipping point for lumber, railroad ties, livestock, and grain. By 1884 the population reportedly had grown to 1,000. Businesses included five steam-operated gristmill–cotton gins, four sawmills, five grocery stores, two drugstores, three saloons, two dry goods stores, and Mrs. L. E. Jackson's millinery. Citizens also had access to three churches, a district school, a telegraph office, three doctors, a lawyer, a barber, and an undertaker. A newspaper, the *Knights of Honor Sentinel,* was published weekly, and D. G. Flenniken was postmaster.

The town was incorporated in 1886, and two years later citizens shortened its name to Blossom. In 1890 postmaster W. H. Byrn reported 1,200 inhabitants. A new gin and mill, as well as several new sawmills, had been established. William Chester was editor of the Blossom *Bee*, a weekly newspaper that had replaced the *Sentinel*. New businesses included a livery stable, a butcher shop, two confectioneries, the Crockett brothers' photography studio, and Mrs. L. R. Burke's hotel. In 1892 postmaster Green B. Eades had opened a furniture factory, Mollie E. Cross had established a new millinery shop, and the Exchange Bank was in operation with a capital of $30,000. The Blossom school reported four teachers and 259 students in 1896.

During the 1890s the depletion of the local lumber supply led many mills and workers to leave the area, and by 1900 the town population had decreased to 874. Early in the 1900s new businesses and more abundant cotton crops replaced lumberyards in Blossom's economy. In 1914 a cottonseed oil mill, a cotton gin, a brickyard, a produce company, and a broom factory were in operation. A few tourists came for locally produced mineral water that was reportedly effective against digestive problems. Another hotel and another bank, as well as several restaurants and clothing stores, opened, and residents had access to a new telephone exchange. They had also organized a band and an orchestra.

Throughout the 1920s Blossom's population slowly increased, reaching 1,200 in 1929. With the onslaught of the Great Depression,[qv] however, many farmers and stock raisers left the area for cities. Though Blossom had thirty businesses in 1931, the number of residents had plummeted to 650. By 1933 only eighteen businesses remained open. Maps for 1936 showed a small town with 858 inhabitants and a sizable but sparsely settled school district. The town did not share much in the economic relief brought to some parts of Texas by World War II.[qv] Residents left, businesses closed, and farming became the main occupation. In 1955 the population was 780, and fifteen businesses remained in operation. The town had 545 inhabitants in 1962. Maps for 1964 showed the school and four churches. A dam on Cuthand Creek had impounded City Lake. The Blossom Independent School District had been absorbed into the Prairieland Independent School District by 1970. In the 1970s, although businesses continued to close, the population began to grow, as many people chose to live in Blossom and work in nearby Paris. By 1980 the number of residents had reached 1,133, and eleven business were in operation. Blossom had 1,487 residents in 1983 and 1,737 in 1989, when the town supported nine businesses. In 1990 the population was 1,440.

BIBLIOGRAPHY: Thomas S. Justiss, An Administrative Survey of the Schools of Lamar County with a Plan for Their Reorganization (M.A. thesis, University of Texas, 1937). Fred I. Massengill, *Texas Towns: Origin of Name and Location of Each of the 2,148 Post Offices in Texas* (Terrell, Texas, 1936).

Vista K. McCroskey

BLOUNT, JAMES H. (ca. 1797–?). James H. Blount, soldier and member of the Consultation[qv] (1835), was born in North Carolina about 1797. He left that state about 1830 and in 1831 was principal of Greensburg Academy in St. Helena Parish, Louisiana. He arrived in Bevil Municipality, Texas, in 1835 and acquired a league of land on the east bank of the Neches River in the bounds of present-day Jasper County. The same year Blount married Penelope Williams and was listed as a farmer on census reports. He was one of five delegates from Bevil to the Consultation, although there is no record of his having taken part in the proceedings. Blount joined the Texas army in December 1835 and was brevetted first lieutenant in the artillery by Gen. Thomas J. Rusk[qv] on June 22, 1836. He became a clerk in the paymaster general's office in 1836. He had at least one child. Stephen H. Everitt[qv] administered Blount's Jasper County estate in 1840. In 1863 a James H. Blunt received a 960-acre bounty warrant in McLennan County, for service between December 1835 and October 21, 1836.

BIBLIOGRAPHY: Kirbyville *Banner*, June 2, 1971. Madeleine Martin, *More Early Southeast Texas Families* (Quanah, Texas: Nortex, 1978). Texas House of Representatives, *Biographical Directory of the Texan Conventions and Congresses, 1832–1845* (Austin: Book Exchange, 1941).

Robert Wooster

BLOUNT, JAMES P. (1849–1928). Physician and banker James P. Blount, the son of Jesse M. and Sophia (Caudle) Blount, was born on March 11, 1849, in Carrollton, Mississippi. He spent most of his childhood in Denton, Texas, where his father moved in 1856. After graduating from high school Blount studied medicine and opened his first office in Grand Saline. He returned to Denton and continued to practice medicine, opened a pharmacy, and became active in community affairs. He served on two committees that established North Texas State Normal School (now the University of North Texas) and the Girls Industrial College (now Texas Woman's University) in Denton. He was also a trustee of the public school system and a founding member of the Denton Board of Trade, the forerunner of the Denton County Chamber of Commerce.

Blount's position as a prominent physician and businessman resulted in his nomination as Democratic party[qv] candidate for a seat in the Texas House. He was elected in 1884 and represented the Twentieth District for one term. He declined to stand for reelection because of the time the legislature took away from his medical practice and growing business interests. He did, however, serve as a delegate to the Democratic national convention in 1888 and on the Democratic State Executive Committee in 1896.

The First National Bank of Denton selected him as president in 1891. He resigned in 1892, however, to become president of the Denton County National Bank, which he helped organize. During his twenty-year tenure as president, Blount examined and wrote articles on the Federal Reserve Act and legislation affecting farmers; his writings attracted the interest of university economists throughout the Southwest. Blount remained president of the bank until 1912, when he resigned as a result of poor health. After recuperating, he became president of the First Guarantee State Bank of Denton but served for only two years, since his health faltered again. He subsequently declined offers to serve in an executive capacity with local banks; instead, he concentrated his attention on his medical practice and business interests.

He married Jesse Kearby in 1869. She died in 1900, leaving him with three children. Blount married Mrs. E. K. Fritzlen of Dayton, Ohio, in 1910. By the mid-twenties, his health had deteriorated, and on his doctor's advice he traveled to Savannah, Missouri, in order to recuperate. There he died on October 9, 1928. He was buried in Denton.

BIBLIOGRAPHY: C. A. Bridges, *History of Denton, Texas, from Its Beginning to 1960* (Waco: Texian Press, 1978). *National Cyclopaedia of American Biography*, Vol. 23. E. W. Winkler, *Platforms of Political Parties in Texas* (Austin: University of Texas, 1916).

David Minor

BLOUNT, STEPHEN WILLIAM (1808–1890). Stephen William Blount, signer of the Texas Declaration of Independence,[qv] soldier, and county official, son of Stephen William and Elizabeth (Winn) Blount, was born in Burke County, Georgia, on February 13, 1808. He was elected colonel of the Eighth Regiment of Georgia Militia in 1833, served as deputy sheriff and sheriff of Burke County for four years, and was an aide-de-camp to Brig. Gen. Robert Tootle and Maj. Gen. David Taylor from 1832 to 1834. He arrived in Texas in August 1835 and settled at San Augustine. He was one of the three representatives from San Augustine at the Convention of 1836[qv] at Washington-on-the-Brazos and there signed the Declaration of Independence. On March 17, 1836, when the convention adjourned, he returned to San Augustine and joined the Texas army in the company of Capt. William D. Ratcliff. He reached San Jacinto the day after the battle had been fought. Blount returned to the United States and in Alabama, sometime after February 1, 1838, married Mrs. Mary Landon Lacy; they had eight children. Blount brought his wife to Texas in 1839.

He was the first county clerk of San Augustine County and from

1846 to 1849 was postmaster at San Augustine. He was a delegate to the Democratic state convention in 1850 and to the national Democratic convention at Cincinnati in 1876. He acquired 60,000 acres, on which he raised cotton. During the Civil War[qv] he was fiscal agent for the Confederate States of America. He was a charter member of Redland Lodge No. 3 at San Augustine, and a member of the Episcopal Church. He was vice president of the United Confederate Veterans when he died, on February 7, 1890. He was buried at San Augustine. An oil portrait of Blount by Stephen Seymour Thomas[qv] was presented to the Dallas Historical Society[qv] and placed on exhibit in the Hall of State[qv] in 1950.

BIBLIOGRAPHY: Sam Houston Dixon, *Men Who Made Texas Free* (Houston: Texas Historical Publishing, 1924). Louis Wiltz Kemp, *The Signers of the Texas Declaration of Independence* (Salado, Texas: Anson Jones, 1944; rpt. 1959). Norman Kittrell, *Governors Who Have Been and Other Public Men of Texas* (Houston: Dealy-Adey-Elgin, 1921). Vertical Files, Barker Texas History Center, University of Texas at Austin.

L. W. Kemp

BLOUNT, THOMAS WILLIAM (1839–1934). Thomas William Blount, Confederate Army officer and legislator, the oldest son of Mary (Landon) and Stephen William Blount,[qv] was born during a visit of his parents to Shelby Springs, Alabama, on October 27, 1839. His father was a signer of the Texas Declaration of Independence.[qv] The family returned home to San Augustine, Texas, while Blount was an infant. The Blounts were a family of some means and in addition to their town house in San Augustine owned a plantation on Patroon Creek in the east end of the county. Blount received a primary education in San Augustine and graduated from Kentucky Military Institute at age eighteen. The next year he "took a course in literature," and at age twenty he began to read law.

After secession[qv] Blount spent three weeks in Montgomery, Alabama, the temporary capital of the Confederate States, where John H. Reagan[qv] introduced him to Jefferson Davis,[qv] who appointed him a lieutenant in the Confederate Army. Blount was ordered to report to Pensacola, Florida, as a member of Gen. Braxton Bragg's quartermaster staff. Bragg's mother had been a Blount, a circumstance that no doubt hastened his preferment. Among his duties in the early months of the war was the escort of $2.5 million in specie and banknotes from the Treasury Department in Montgomery to Pensacola to pay Bragg's troops. After about a month in the quartermaster corps, Blount requested and received transfer to the staff of Gen. Adley Hogan Gladden, whom he served as aide-de-camp, instructor in artillery, and inspector general. Blount commanded a battery during the bombardment of Fort Pickens in November 1861 and until April 1862 supervised the fortification of Mobile Bay. In April he was reassigned to Bragg's command at Corinth, Mississippi, and appointed chief of ordnance. He participated in the defense of Fort Pillow, Tennessee, and served as its last commandant prior to its evacuation by the Confederates at the end of May 1862. Thereafter he served for a time on the staff of Gen. Earl Van Dorn[qv] before transferring to the staff of Gen. Henry Watkins Allen as inspector general and participating in the battle of Baton Rouge, in August 1862. He was captured at Baton Rouge, placed on the gunboat USS Essex, and interviewed by Commodore David Dixon Porter and later, in New Orleans, by Gen. Benjamin F. Butler. Blount was shortly exchanged and returned to the army as ordnance officer under Col. William R. Miles during the siege of Port Hudson, Louisiana. When Port Hudson was surrendered on July 9, 1863, he once again became a prisoner and ate "old rotten beans and rancid bacon" at Johnson Island until February 1, 1865, when he was transferred to Fortress Monroe. From there he was moved to Fort McHenry and then to Fort Delaware before being paroled on June 12, 1865. He returned to San Augustine on July 4.

Although the ill effects of prison caused him to give up the study of law, in 1866 Blount was elected to represent the Fifth District in the Eleventh Texas Legislature—the so-called "Bloody Eleventh"—composed almost entirely of former Confederate officers. He served but a single term before returning to his plantation about four miles west of San Augustine. Blount was married to Mary Rather of Shelby County and was the father of four children. In 1929 he dictated his memoirs to an amanuensis, Lois Foster Blount, who edited them for publication in the *Southwestern Historical Quarterly*[qv] (July 1935). In 1910 he returned to San Augustine, where he died on May 6, 1934.

BIBLIOGRAPHY: Frank W. Johnson, *A History of Texas and Texans* (5 vols., ed. E. C. Barker and E. W. Winkler [Chicago and New York: American Historical Society, 1914; rpt. 1916]).

Thomas W. Cutrer

BLOUNT INDIANS. The Blount Indians, a Seminole tribe originally from Florida, migrated to Texas about 1800 and finally settled on the Alabama-Coushatta Indian Reservation.

Margery H. Krieger

BLOW, GEORGE W. (?–?). George W. Blow, early settler and Republic of Texas[qv] congressman, a native of Virginia, moved to Texas probably after the revolution and before June 1839, when he received a conditional headright certificate. In October 1839 he was prosecuting attorney of the Fourth Judicial District, the area from Bexar to San Patricio counties, and in July 1840 was commissioner for examining land records in Bexar County. From November 2, 1840, to February 5, 1841, he represented Bexar County in the House of the Fifth Congress of the republic. He was living in Norfolk, Virginia, on February 18, 1847, when he was appointed commissioner of deeds in Virginia.

BIBLIOGRAPHY: Texas House of Representatives, *Biographical Directory of the Texan Conventions and Congresses, 1832–1845* (Austin: Book Exchange, 1941).

John L. Sims

BLOWOUT COMMUNITY, TEXAS. Blowout Community, a settlement fifteen miles northwest of Johnson City in northwestern Blanco County, dates back to 1854. That year a party of two dozen homesteaders from Kentucky settled on the east side of Comanche Creek near Comanche Spring, about three miles below the creek's origin. As more settlers moved into the area the small community of Blowout developed upstream from the spring. The name came from Blowout Cave, located in a hillside east of Comanche Creek about a mile above Comanche Spring. The cave was at one time home to thousands of bats, and a great deposit of guano accumulated in it. Supposedly, ammonia and other gases from the decomposing guano built up in the cave, and when lightning struck at the cave mouth the gases exploded—hence the name Blowout. Today there is little trace left of Blowout Community or the settlement at Comanche Spring. Only isolated ranchhouses remain at those sites, and only scattered ranches can now be found among the rocky hills along Comanche Creek.

BIBLIOGRAPHY: Gunnar Brune, *Springs of Texas,* Vol. 1 (Fort Worth: Branch-Smith, 1981).

Richard Bruhn

BLOX, TEXAS. Blox was on a small rise four miles north of Jasper and seventy-seven miles north of Beaumont in north central Jasper County. The settlement was named for Charles or E. D. Bloxsom, officers with the Kirby Lumber Company, which had established a logging camp at the site by 1919. That same year a post office was opened there. To house the new workers the Kirby company moved in numerous vacant buildings from Kirbyville. At the height of the local logging activity Blox had a population of some 1,200, about a third of whom were black. Most Blox residents went to Jasper for entertainment. As the locally available hardwoods and pines were cut out, lumbering operations were gradually shifted to New Blox, a logging camp twenty miles to the northwest. The Blox election precinct, established in 1922, was abolished in 1926. In 1931 the community's post office was discontinued, and the old town was completely torn down and moved to New Blox.

BIBLIOGRAPHY: Jasper County Scrapbook, Barker Texas History Center, University of Texas at Austin. Kirby Lumber Corporation Papers, Steen Library, Stephen F. Austin State University.

Robert Wooster

BLOYS, WILLIAM BENJAMIN (1847–1917). William Benjamin Bloys, Presbyterian minister and founder of the Bloys Camp Meeting,[qv] was born on January 26, 1847, in McClemoresville, Tennessee, the second of seven children, to Mordecai Dowel and Amelia Patterson (Yergan) Bloys. The elder Bloys was a farmer and saddlemaker. Since they were Unionists, the Bloyses moved to Illinois in 1862. William attended an academy in Salem and then worked for ten years as a teacher and farmer. In 1876 he entered Lane Theological Seminary in Cincinnati to become a Presbyterian minister and foreign missionary. He graduated on May 7, 1879, and was ordained shortly thereafter. He married Isabelle Catherine Yeck on May 22, 1879. They had seven children.

Bloys's missionary desires were thwarted by a lung ailment that disqualified him for assignment overseas. He applied to the Presbyterian Home Mission Program of the Northern Presbyterian Church and was accepted. His first assignment was in Coleman, Texas. In 1879 he established several churches there and in the surrounding communities. In 1888, upon his doctor's advice, he moved to Fort Davis, Jeff Davis County. There he soon established Presbyterian congregations throughout the Davis Mountains and in the Big Bend. He served voluntarily as chaplain to the army post at Fort Davis until it was closed in 1891. He regularly conducted services in churches, homes, and even cow camps for all who requested them, regardless of religious affiliation. In 1890, with the encouragement and aid of people from the area, Bloys founded the Cowboy Campmeeting at Skillman's Grove; its annual meetings continue. In 1910 Bloys helped to petition for and found the Presbytery of El Paso. He served as its clerk-treasurer from 1910 until 1917, except for the year 1914, when he served as moderator. He died on March 22, 1917, at Fort Davis. After his death the Cowboy Campmeeting was renamed Bloys Camp Meeting, and a marble monument was erected there in his honor. Nearly a century later, Bloys is remembered and revered as the "Little Shepherd of the Hills."

BIBLIOGRAPHY: Clifford B. Casey, *Mirages, Mysteries and Reality: Brewster County, Texas, the Big Bend of the Rio Grande* (Hereford, Texas: Pioneer, 1972). William F. Evans, *Border Skylines: Fifty Years of "Tallying Out" on the Bloys Round-up Ground* (Dallas: Baugh, 1940). Carlysle Graham Raht, *The Romance of the Davis Mountains and Big Bend Country* (Odessa, Texas: Rahtbooks, 1963).

Deborah Bloys Hardin

BLOYS CAMP MEETING. Since 1890 the Bloys Camp Meeting (or Bloys Cowboy Campmeeting) has met annually at Skillman's Grove in the Davis Mountains of the western Big Bend area. The encampment is sixteen miles southwest of Fort Davis, Jeff Davis County. It comes alive for only five days of the year, usually from the second Tuesday of August to the following Sunday. All religious denominations are welcomed, but the event is sponsored by the Presbyterians, Methodists, Baptists, and Disciples of Christ, each of which participates in the five-day meeting. Four religious services are held each day in addition to children's Bible classes, youth meetings, Bible studies, and prayer meetings. The camp is organized and operated by the Bloys Campmeeting Association, the members of which are either descendents of the founding families or elected by members. The camp is on a section of land bought by the association in 1902 and is supplied with electricity and running water. Nothing can be bought or sold on the grounds; all food, water, and amenities are free to the guests, who may make contributions to help cover expenses. Costs not covered by the generosity of guests are assumed by the members.

The camp meetings were begun in 1890 by William Benjamin Bloys,[qv] a Presbyterian home missionary serving in Fort Davis. Because the ranches of the region were widely separated by vast, uninhabited areas, it was virtually impossible for frontier families to worship with their neighbors and friends. Bloys rode to many of the outlying ranches from Fort Davis, but he was rarely able to minister to the whole community at one time. In October 1890, while visiting the family of John Z. Means, Bloys devised a plan to bring local families together annually for religious services. An old-style camp meeting was organized, and on October 10, 1890, forty-three people gathered in Skillman's Grove for the first time. The two-day meeting included Bible instruction and sermons as well as a great deal of socializing. The meetings were first held under a brush arbor and then for many years in a canvas tent. A permanent tabernacle was built in 1912 and expanded as attendance grew. It still serves as the central meeting place. As more people attended the camp meetings, the camp was divided into five areas where families gathered and ate. These evolved into the five eating sheds that now feed the entire camp. Cooking is still done ranch-style on open fires. The average number attending was more than 3,000 by 1988.

Joe Evans, one of the original members, in conjunction with Everett King, Ralph Hall, and Roger Sherman, started a chain of camp meetings at sites in New Mexico and other western cattle states, including Nogala Mesa, New Mexico, Valentine, Nebraska, Willcox and Prescott, Arizona, and Elko, Nevada. The Hill Country Cowboy Campmeeting near Ingram, Texas, was also patterned after the Bloys encampment and still meets each August during the week following the Bloys meeting.

BIBLIOGRAPHY: Minnie D. Clifton, "A History of the Bloys Camp Meeting," *Sul Ross Teachers College Bulletin* 27 (June 1, 1947). William F. Evans, *Border Skylines: Fifty Years of "Tallying Out" on the Bloys Round-up Ground* (Dallas: Baugh, 1940). Carlysle Graham Raht, *The Romance of the Davis Mountains and Big Bend Country* (Odessa, Texas: Rahtbooks, 1963). Inez Dudley Rogers, *"Not Made with Hands": The Story of the First Bloys Cowboy Camp Meeting* (Barstow, Texas, 1952). Cecilia Thompson, *History of Marfa and Presidio County, 1535–1946* (2 vols., Austin: Nortex, 1985). Vertical Files, Barker Texas History Center, University of Texas at Austin (W. B. Bloys).

Deborah Bloys Hardin

BLÜCHER, ANTON FELIX HANS HELLMUTH VON (1819–1879). Anton Felix von Blücher, interpreter, surveyor, and engineer, the grand nephew of Waterloo hero Gerhard Leberecht von Blücher, was born in Prussia on November 15, 1819. His education at the University of Berlin (M.A. degree) included civil engineering, law, and languages. In 1844 he left Berlin for New Orleans, where he worked as a draftsman in a shipyard. There he changed his name to Felix A. von Blücher. In 1845 he joined Prince Carl of Solms-Braunfels[qv] in Texas as an interpreter and engineer. He acted as interpreter at New Braunfels in the signing of John O. Meusebach's[qv] treaty with the Comanche chiefs. In 1847 he was in Mexico serving Gen. Winfield Scott as interpreter. He settled in Corpus Christi in 1849, after a visit to Germany, where he married Maria Augusta Imme. He was surveyor of Nueces County school lands and city alderman. In 1853 he surveyed the army road to Eagle Pass. He was an officer in the Confederate engineers and artillery during the Civil War[qv] and later served as a military engineer in Mexico. He returned to civilian life to practice law but soon accepted a position as consulting engineer for the Corpus Christi and

Rio Grande Railroad Company. Two years later, in 1875, he was made deputy county surveyor of Zapata County and began resurveying Spanish grants as required by the Texas constitution. He died at Tresquilas Ranch in Cameron County on February 6, 1879, and was survived by his widow and five children.

BIBLIOGRAPHY: Mrs. Frank DeGarmo, *Pathfinders of Texas, 1836–1846* (Austin: Von Boeckmann–Jones, 1951). Edna Weedon Tobias, The History of Education in Nueces County (M.A. thesis, Sul Ross State College, 1936). *Hortense Warner Ward*

BLUE, TEXAS. The site of Blue, on Farm Road 696 eight miles west of Lexington in northwestern Lee County, was first settled around 1846 by three brothers, Joseph, William, and Isaac Jackson, who received a one-third league grant for service in the Mexican War.[qv] The settlement was originally named Blue Branch after a nearby stream. A local post office was established in 1878 with Dr. S. J. Williams as postmaster. The same year, a Methodist church was organized there, and a cotton gin was operating at about the same time. William Jackson operated a small chair factory. The community's post office closed in 1895 but was reopened in 1897, and the name of the settlement was shortened to Blue. In 1906 a one-room school at Blue had thirty-three students. The settlement began to decline after 1910. Its post office closed in 1913, and its school was consolidated with the Lexington Independent School District in 1941. In the mid-1930s the town comprised a school, a business, and several scattered dwellings. In 1945 its reported population was twenty-five. In the early 1980s the town was a dispersed rural community with a church and one business.

BIBLIOGRAPHY: Lee County Historical Survey Committee, *A History of Lee County* (Quanah, Texas: Nortex, 1974). *Christopher Long*

BLUE BELL CREAMERIES. Blue Bell Creameries, a limited partnership with headquarters in the rural town of Brenham, Texas, and more than twenty branch offices, is a manufacturer of ice cream and frozen dessert products that distributes to southwestern states including Texas, Oklahoma, Louisiana, Mississippi, Arkansas, Kansas, Missouri, and New Mexico. The company began in 1907 as a Washington County dairy-farmers' cooperative called the Brenham Creamery Company, when the founders converted a nearby abandoned cotton gin into a creamery and made butter from their excess supplies of cream. Ice cream production began in 1911, and the firm took its name from a native Texas wildflower in 1930. E. F. Kruse, who took over as general manager in 1919, is credited with reversing the creamery's declining fortunes after two early managers failed to expand the business. Chairman and chief executive officer Ed Kruse and President Howard Kruse, both sons of E. F. Kruse, succeeded their father in heading the firm. Initially, Blue Bell produced ice cream at the rate of two gallons a day in wooden tubs filled with ice. Refrigerated trucks for distribution to retail food outlets replaced horse-drawn delivery wagons in 1936, and in 1958 the company discontinued making butter in order to specialize in ice cream production. Its most popular ice cream flavor, Homemade Vanilla, was introduced in 1969 and, with a new continuous freezer, production increased to 15,000 gallons an hour by 1993.

In 1977 the company adopted its familiar logo depicting a young girl leading a cow. By 1992 Blue Bell was the nation's number-two ice cream, behind Breyer's. Blue Bell dominated the regional ice cream market with sales of $170 million—a 57 percent market share in Texas and a 32 percent share in Oklahoma and Louisiana. With its 300,000-square-foot plant, the firm is Brenham's largest private employer. At tours of its Brenham production facility and new corporate headquarters and visitor center, completed in 1988, Bluebell hosted roughly 117,000 people each year.

Over the years, Blue Bell has diversified its products with the development of frozen dietary desserts, nonfat frozen yogurt, and frozen snacks, including Blue Bell Ice Cream Sandwiches, Snickers, Nestle's Crunch, and Eskimo Pie. Responding to demands for lower calorie confections, the company began using NutraSweet, and holds the distinction of being the first major United States ice cream manufacturer to make a "lite" product in 1986. Bluebell continues to obtain its raw materials, including milk and cream, from large cooperatives of dairy farmers, primarily in Texas.

Company expansion began with the construction of temporary production facilities in Houston in 1960. A branch was opened in Austin in 1965, at Beaumont in 1973, and at Dallas in 1978. Between 1980 and 1986 manufacturing plants were opened in Alvin, Fort Worth, San Antonio, Longview, and Waco, and in 1989 Blue Bell opened out-of-state distribution branches in Oklahoma City, Oklahoma, and Baton Rouge, Louisiana. Though it controls all shipping and handling of its products, Blue Bell, unlike Baskin-Robbins and other ice cream chains, does not maintain its own sales outlets, but sells its products through retail grocery chains. Since it is located in the heart of dairy country, the company has never needed to own its sources of raw materials, but continues to depend on farmers in the surrounding area. In 1990 it began distributing products in Mexico through Manhattan Paletas, and in 1992 it opened a production facility in Broken Arrow, Oklahoma.

Blue Bell grew from 650 employees in 1955 to 1,300 workers in 1987. In the latter year the company established Blue Bell Advertising Associates, an in-house advertising agency, to produce seasonal radio and television spots to air between February and October. With well-placed media advertising, Blue Bell effectively reinforced its image as the "little creamery in Brenham" that makes "the best ice cream in the country." In 1990 the original Brenham plant, which incorporated building elements from the American Cotton Gin Company and included a one-story main building in the Art Moderne style, was listed in the National Register of Historic Places for its role as an agricultural processing facility. *See also* DAIRY INDUSTRY *and* DAIRY PRODUCTS.

BIBLIOGRAPHY: Austin *American-Statesman*, May 25, 1991. Charles F. Schmidt, *History of Washington County* (San Antonio: Naylor, 1949). Vertical Files, Barker Texas History Center, University of Texas at Austin. *Rajni Madan*

BLUEBONNET. On March 7, 1901, the Twenty-seventh Texas Legislature adopted the bluebonnet, flower of the annual legume *Lupinus subcarnosus*, as the state flower. The flower's popular name derives from its resemblance to a sunbonnet. It has also been called buffalo clover, wolf flower, and, in Spanish, *el conejo* ("the rabbit"). On March 8, 1971, the legislation was amended to include *L. texensis* and "any other variety of bluebonnet not heretofore recorded." At least four other species of bluebonnet grow in Texas: *L. havardii, L. concinnus, L. perennis,* and *L. plattensis.* Contrary to various folk stories and legends claiming that the plant originated outside the state, *L. texensis* and *L. subcarnosus* are native to Texas. In 1933 the legislature adopted a state flower song, "Bluebonnets," written by Julia D. Booth and Lora C. Crockett. Also in the 1930s the Highway Department began a landscaping and beautification program and extended the flower's range. Due largely to that agency's efforts, bluebonnets now grow along most major highways throughout the state. The flower usually blooms in late March and early April and is found mostly in limestone outcroppings from north central Texas to Mexico. Its popularity is widespread. Although early explorers failed to mention the bluebonnet in their descriptions of Texas, Indian lore called the flower a gift from the Great Spirit. The bluebonnet continues to be a favorite subject for artists and photographers, and at the peak of bloom, festivals featuring the flower are held in several locations.

BIBLIOGRAPHY: Jean Andrews, *The Texas Bluebonnet* (Austin: University of Texas Press, 1986). Donovan Stewart Correll and Marshall Conring Johnston, *Manual of the Vascular Plants of Texas* (Renner, Texas: Texas Research Foundation, 1970). Billie Lee Turner, *The Legumes of Texas* (Austin: University of Texas Press, 1959). *Jean Andrews*

BLUEBONNET BOWL. The Bluebonnet Bowl, an annual post-season football classic, was initiated in Houston in 1959 as a result of the efforts of a civic group composed of Elvin Smith, Lou Hassell, and Eddie Dyer, who were appointed by the Houston Chamber of Commerce Athletics Committee in 1958. In the one year between the inception of the idea for a Bluebonnet Bowl and its actual realization, the group managed to secure NCAA sanction, obtain Southwest Conference[qv] approval, and procure the use of Rice Stadium. The first game, on December 19, 1959, matched Clemson University against Texas Christian University. In the first eight years of the Bluebonnet Bowl's existence the television contract improved from $16,000 to the 1967 contract of $180,000. The proceeds from the bowl games have been distributed to various Harris County charitable organizations. Beginning in 1968 the annual football game was played in the Astrodome,[qv] and the event was referred to as the Astro-Bluebonnet Bowl. Games were played at Rice Stadium in 1985 and 1986. Unable to continue after a drop in ticket sales and failure to attract a corporate sponsor, the Bluebonnet Bowl ceased after its game on December 31, 1987, at the Astrodome. *Lou Hassell*

BLUEBONNET GIRLS' STATE. Bluebonnet Girls' State, an American Legion[qv] program similar to Lone Star Boys' State,[qv] was instituted as part of the Americanism program of the American Legion Auxiliary in 1940 to counter certain imported un-American activities identified by the American Legion before World War II.[qv] The program's intent is to train high-school-age girls in becoming better citizens, with emphasis on American democratic principles and the American system of government. Program objectives also include teaching participants to live together as a self-governing group and informing them about the duties, privileges, rights, and responsibilities of American citizenship. Meetings were held at Baylor University in 1941 and 1942 but were then canceled until the end of World War II.[qv] They began again in 1946 and continued annually into the mid-1990s at Texas Lutheran College. Participants set up fictitious cities and a state, electing officials to govern each. Bluebonnet Girls' State is overseen by the Girls' State Committee, its policy-making body. Two girls each year are selected as members of Girls' Nation, held in Washington, D.C.

BIBLIOGRAPHY: Harold M. Branton, *The American Legion Department of Texas, 1919–1986: An Official History* (Waco: American Legion Department of Texas, 1987). *John G. Johnson*

BLUE BRANCH (Coryell County). Blue Branch begins a mile south of Arnett in west central Coryell County (at 31°26′ N, 97°53′ W) and runs east for seven miles to its mouth on the Leon River, five miles northwest of Gatesville (at 31°'28 N, 97°'49 W). The terrain is generally flat to rolling, with local steep slopes and a surface of shallow clay loam that supports juniper, live oak, mesquite, and grasses.

—— (Lee County). Blue Branch rises five miles northeast of McDade in northwestern Lee County (at 30°21′ N, 97°10′ W) and flows northeast for 5½ miles to its mouth on Middle Yegua Creek, two miles northeast of Blue (at 30°25′ N, 97°10′ W). The stream flows through rolling prairie with clay loam soils. Mesquite and grasses predominate in the region.

BLUE CREEK (Brewster County). Blue Creek rises from a spring in the Chisos Mountains about three-quarters of a mile southwest of Emory Peak in Big Bend National Park[qv] (at 29°14′ N, 103°19′ W) and runs west-southwest for eighteen miles, descending from the Chisos through rugged and beautiful Blue Creek Canyon, then issuing onto the Rio Grande floodplain, and finally running into the Rio Grande about 6½ miles below the mouth of Santa Elena Canyon (at 29°08′ N, 103°32′ W). Downstream, the creek crosses gravel and silt deposits where have been found a number of mammalian tooth, skull, and skeleton fragments, and also a sizable quantity of skeletal turtle remains, all dating from around the late Eocene. Blue Creek, the major drainage system in this area, drains the southwestern Chisos Mountains and the lands between the mountains and the Rio Grande. Much evidence suggests that the area was occupied for thousands of years by Indians, who depended upon the creek as a water supply. In recent years the water table has dropped because deforestation in the mountains and heavy grazing by domestic livestock at lower elevations have reduced the ability of the ground to absorb and hold rain. The springs that once fed Blue Creek have dried up, and it is now a dry channel except in rainy weather. The earliest settlement of the area began in the late 1890s, when mercury mining[qv] began in the Terlingua mining district to the northwest. The subsequent increase in population resulted in part from an influx of Mexican-American families onto the Rio Grande floodplain, where they herded goats and cattle and took up irrigated farming. The most significant settlement to emerge from this development was Castolon, which was built just below the confluence of Blue Creek and the Rio Grande.

BIBLIOGRAPHY: Clifford B. Casey, *Mirages, Mysteries and Reality: Brewster County, Texas, the Big Bend of the Rio Grande* (Hereford, Texas: Pioneer, 1972). Clifford B. Casey, *Soldiers, Ranchers and Miners in the Big Bend* (Washington: Office of Archeology and Historic Preservation, U.S. Department of the Interior, 1969). Ross A. Maxwell, *The Big Bend of the Rio Grande* (Bureau of Economic Geology, University of Texas at Austin, 1968). Ross A. Maxwell et al., *Geology of Big Bend National Park* (Austin: Bureau of Economic Geology, University of Texas, 1967).

—— (Cherokee County). Blue Creek rises just north of Mount Selman in north central Cherokee County (at 32°04′ N, 95°17′ W) and runs northwest for five miles to its mouth on Flat Creek, two miles northwest of Old Larissa (at 32°06′ N, 95°20′ W). The stream is intermittent in its upper reaches. It crosses flat to gently rolling terrain surfaced by clay and sandy loam that supports mixed hardwoods and pines and grass.

—— (Guadalupe County). Blue Creek rises a mile south of New Berlin in southwestern Guadalupe County (at 29°27′ N, 98°06′ W) and flows south for 4½ miles to its mouth on Elm Creek, a mile north of the Guadalupe-Wilson county line (at 29°24′ N, 98°05′ W). The surrounding terrain is flat to rolling with local shallow depressions and a surface of sandy and clay loam that supports mesquite, water-tolerant hardwoods, and conifers.

—— (Wharton County). Blue Creek rises one mile north of El Campo and twelve miles west of Wharton in west central Wharton County (at 29°14′ N, 96°17′ W) and runs southeast for twenty-four miles to its mouth on the Colorado River, a mile south of the county line in northern Matagorda County (at 29°04′ N, 96°01′ W). It crosses flat to rolling prairie with some shallow depressions, surfaced by calcareous clays and sandy and clay loams that support mesquite, cacti, grasses, water-tolerant hardwoods, and conifers.

BLUE CROSS AND BLUE SHIELD OF TEXAS. Blue Cross and Blue Shield of Texas began in 1929, the year of the stock market crash that inaugurated the Great Depression,[qv] when Justin Ford Kimball,[qv] a former Dallas school superintendent, became the Baylor University official in charge of Dallas hospital units. Kimball devised a plan that would allow teachers to contribute fifty cents a month to a fund that would guarantee them up to twenty-one days of hospital care at Baylor Hospital. After the "Baylor Plan" appeared, planners began to consider the idea of offering community-wide plans to fund members. The prepaid health-care plan received its name in 1933, when E. A. van Steenwyk, head of a Minnesota hospitalization plan, designed a poster using the blue Geneva cross, known as a universal symbol of health care, and a Latin motto meaning "Without the Lord We Can Do Nothing." Eventually, the plan came to be known as the Blue Cross plan. The crest of the American Hospital Association, which set national standards for plans, appeared in the center of the blue cross until 1972, by which time the Blue Cross concept had become independent of the hospital system.

The Texas plan came into being in 1942 when the American Hospital Association approved a group chartered in 1939 as Group Hospital Services, Incorporated, as the Blue Cross Plan of Texas. In 1944 the Baylor Plan dissolved, and its members were transferred to Group Hospital Service. Meanwhile, a California plan that paid physicians instead of hospitals had been introduced in 1939. Its symbol, which became the trademark of the new plan, was a blue shield bearing the ancient medical symbol of a caduceus. In 1945 Group Hospital Service purchased a mutual insurance company and restructured it as Group Medical and Surgical Service, thereby establishing a companion Blue Shield plan to offer benefits for physician care in addition to its other service.

The fully formed Texas Plan expanded rapidly during the 1950s, adding major medical and other types of coverage. In 1960 it was the first plan in the nation to offer life insurance through a comprehensive group-insurance package. This component developed from an earlier enterprise known as the American Savings Life Insurance Company of Houston, a limited-stock life-insurance company, which became a Blue Cross and Blue Shield of Texas subsidiary known as Group Life and Health Insurance Company in 1960. The company later offered individual life, permanent life, short and long term disability coverage, and accidental death coverage, in addition to group term life insurance. By the 1990s Group Life and Health had more than $14 billion worth of life insurance in force. Also in 1960 Blue Cross moved its home office to Dallas, and the enterprise entered the Federal Employee Program, which provided health coverage for Texas government workers. In 1966, with the instigation of Medicare, Blue Cross and Blue Shield of Texas became an intermediary organization. In 1986 the enterprise incorporated a third-party administrator known as HealthCare Benefits and in 1992 established BlueChoice, a network of physicians and health-care professionals offering quality cost-effective care throughout the state. In 1993 a network of dentists known as DentaBlue was first offered to subscribers.

Betty N. Momanyi

BLUE GAP, TEXAS. Blue Gap was near the Coleman county line twenty-five miles northeast of Ballinger in extreme northeastern Runnels County. A log post office, established there in February 1878 with James K. Paulk as postmaster, was the first in the county; it was, in fact, founded before the county was organized in 1880. The townsite was named for a pass through nearby Table Mountain. For a brief period Blue Gap was a stop on the Round Rock–Buffalo Gap stage line. The community was short-lived, however, and its post office was discontinued in March 1881. The old post office building was restored in the 1960s, and a Texas Historical Commission qv marker was dedicated at the site in 1966.

BIBLIOGRAPHY: Frank D. Jenkins, ed., *Runnels County Pioneers* (Abilene, Texas: R&R Reproduction, 1975). A. E. Skinner, *The Rowena Country* (Wichita Falls: Nortex, 1973). Leonard Glenn Smith, A History of Runnels County (M.A. thesis, Trinity University, 1963).

Charles G. Davis

BLUEGROVE, TEXAS. Bluegrove is on Farm Road 172 eleven miles south of Henrietta in central Clay County. Settlement of the community began in 1882, primarily through the efforts of E. A. Copp, L. B. Brown, and E. M. Childs. The community's name comes from its location near a grove of post oak trees that look blue from a distance. A. W. Flynn's general store at Bluegrove became a center for area farmers and ranchers. In 1895 postal service to the community began. The community's population grew slowly but steadily, reaching its peak in the 1920s, when Bluegrove had a reported 240 residents. After the 1940s, however, the population declined. From the mid-1950s through 1990 the population of Bluegrove was reported at 125. The JAC Electric Cooperative, headquartered at Bluegrove, serves Jack, Archer, and Clay counties.

BIBLIOGRAPHY: Katherine Christian Douthitt, ed., *Romance and Dim Trails* (Dallas: Tardy, 1938). William Charles Taylor, *A History of Clay County* (Austin: Jenkins, 1972).

David Minor

BLUE HILLS. The Blue Hills, a three-peak range also known as Blue Mountain, are three miles west of Farm Road 1024 on the edge of Lewis Canyon in north central Val Verde County (at 30°03′ N, 101°20′ W). The tallest peak, with an elevation of 2,155 feet above sea level, rises 255 feet above the surrounding countryside. The hills are formed of sharply dissected massive limestone and are surrounded by wash deposits. They stand in flat terrain dotted with shallow depressions. Area vegetation includes oak, juniper, grasses, some mesquite, and water-tolerant hardwoods and conifers.

BIBLIOGRAPHY: *Geology of the Val Verde Basin and Field Trip Guidebook* (Midland: West Texas Geological Society, 1959).

BLUE HOLE CREEK. Blue Hole Creek rises three miles east of Mary's Peak and two miles north of U.S. Highway 70 in northwestern Foard County (at 34°06′ N, 99°57′ W) and runs south for fifteen miles to its mouth (at 33°58′ N, 99°56′ W) on Good Creek, fourteen miles west of Crowell. Although Vivian lies just to the east, the creekbed mainly traverses remote rangelands. The stream originates from several large waterholes known as Blue Hole Springs. Before irrigation qv seriously reduced their flow, these springs produced plentiful water and were frequented by Indians, hunters, and settlers. In the late 1970s the springs continued to flow. The surrounding rolling to steep slopes are surfaced by stony clay and sandy loams that support juniper, cacti, and sparse grasses.

BIBLIOGRAPHY: Gunnar Brune, *Springs of Texas*, Vol. 1 (Fort Worth: Branch-Smith, 1981).

BLUE HOLLOW. Blue Hollow begins in northwestern Cooke County (at 33°49′ N, 97°18′ W) and runs north for two miles, through the southwest corner of Warrens Bend valley, to its mouth on the Red River (at 33°52′ N, 97°18′ W). A levee was built on the east bank of the hollow in the early 1900s to prevent the creek or the Red River from changing course. Local sources indicate that the hollow was named after one or both of the Blue brothers, Orasmus and William, who arrived at Warrens Bend before 1850.

Jordan E. Pybas

BLUE MOUND. Blue Mound, two miles south of Haslet in northwestern Tarrant County (at 32°57′ N, 97°21′ W), is 864 feet high.

BLUE MOUND, TEXAS (Denton County). Blue Mound, a scattered rural community on Interstate Highway 35 six miles northwest of Denton in Denton County, was founded by German-speaking people in the last quarter of the nineteenth century. The site was originally called Indian Mound but was renamed Blue Mound for the local blue prairie flowers. In 1876 Herman Christian Barthold, Sr., and his family traveled by covered wagon from Springfield, Illinois, to begin the settlement. Later, many more Germans qv journeyed through the Midwest to Blue Mound, while still others immigrated to the community directly from Germany, most of them through the agency of John B. Schmitz. qv Community residents established a school, a German Baptist church, and a German Methodist church. In the early 1900s a Lutheran church in nearby Krum also served Blue Mound residents. Blue Mound's Methodist church, which conducted worship services in German until 1938, has survived since the 1890s. The Blue Mound community furnished the native limestone for the outer walls of the Denton County Courthouse, constructed in 1896. Although in the 1980s perhaps three-fourths of the residents in the Blue Mound area were descendants of the original German community, only limited aspects of German culture survived there. During the 1980s the former school building was still used as a community center.

BIBLIOGRAPHY: Denton *Record–Chronicle*, December 23, 1975.
Olga Borth Sauls

BLUE MOUND, TEXAS (Tarrant County). Blue Mound is on Farm Road 156 eight miles north of Fort Worth in north central Tarrant County. In 1920 John Kennedy, an immigrant from Scotland, established Globe Laboratories, Incorporated, to produce serum to immunize cattle against black leg. In 1933 he purchased several hundred acres near the intersection of Blue Mound and Watauga roads in order to expand his serum business and to begin a new operation, the Globe Aircraft Company. Over the next decade a settlement grew up around the Kennedy businesses and was called Blue Mound because of its proximity to the hill of the same name. During the 1950s Bell Helicopter used the Kennedy facility to develop its new helicopters. In 1960, however, Bell left the facility, and the Kennedy building has remained vacant ever since. Blue Mound, however, survived and incorporated in 1960. The population steadily increased thereafter, surpassing 2,000 in the mid-1970s. During the 1980s the town became a bedroom community for residents employed in Fort Worth or at Dallas–Fort Worth International Airport.[qv] In 1990 the population was 2,133. *David Minor*

BLUE MOUNTAIN (Jeff Davis County). Blue Mountain is eight miles southwest of Fort Davis in south central Jeff Davis County (at 30°34′ N, 104°01′ W). With its elevation of 7,286 feet above sea level, it rises some 1,800 feet above the Point of Rocks roadside park on State Highway 166, three miles to the southwest. Blue Mountain is composed mainly of volcanic rocks thirty-five million years old. Its shallow, stony soils support Douglas fir, aspen, Arizona cypress, maple, ponderosa pine, and madrone.

—— (Uvalde County). Blue Mountain is two miles west of Knippa in east central Uvalde County (at 29°18′ N, 99°40′ W). With an elevation of 1,268 feet above sea level, its summit rises 290 feet above nearby U.S. Highway 90 West, where the road crosses the Dry Frio River.

—— (Winkler County). Blue Mountain is fourteen miles northeast of Kermit and forty-two miles northwest of Odessa in northeastern Winkler County. It is part of the southern escarpment of the Llano Estacado and the Caprock,[qqv] and its summit rises 3,392 feet above sea level. The mountain has a long history of human occupation. In 1938 an archeological study of two rockshelters there revealed numerous projectile points, some awls, beads, scrapers, and a knife, and some pottery thought to be of Pueblo origin. The study noted about thirty pictographs in the shelters and more than 100 rare boat-shaped mortar holes similar to those found in Garza and Coke counties. Archeologists have been unable to determine precisely the cultures that lived at Blue Mountain. According to Jim Cook, a former Comanche captive living in Odessa in 1932, the Blue Mountain rockshelters were occupied by Comanches in the nineteenth century. In the 1970s most of the pictographs at Blue Mountain were destroyed by smoke when people built fires in the rockshelters.

BIBLIOGRAPHY: William Curry Holden, "Blue Mountain Rock Shelter," *Bulletin of the Texas Archeological and Paleontological Society* 10 (1938). Odessa *News–Times*, September 9, 1932.

BLUE MOUNTAINS. The Blue Mountains stand between the James and Llano rivers and extend from eastern Kimble County to southwestern Mason County. Their summit elevations range from 1,800 to 2,176 feet above sea level. Monument Mountain, with a height of 2,160 feet above sea level, is within this range in Mason County (at 30°34′ N, 99°27′ W). The range runs from the southwest to the northeast in the limestone hills of the northeastern edge of the Edwards Plateau.[qv] The local countryside is generally flat and surfaced with stony, clayey, and loamy soils that support grasses and open stands of live oak, mesquite, and Ashe juniper.

BLUE NORTHER. The term *blue norther* denotes a weather phenomenon common to large areas of the world's temperate zones—a rapidly moving autumnal cold front that causes temperatures to drop quickly and that often brings with it precipitation followed by a period of blue skies and cold weather. What is peculiar to Texas is the term itself. The derivation of *blue norther* is unclear; at least three folk attributions exist. The term refers, some say, to a norther that sweeps "out of the Panhandle under a blue-black sky"—that is, to a cold front named for the appearance of its leading edge. Another account states that the term refers to the appearance of the sky after the front has blown through, as the mid-nineteenth-century variant "blew-tailed norther" illustrates. Yet another derives the term from the fact that one supposedly turns blue from the cold brought by the front. Variants include *blue whistler,* used by J. Frank Dobie,[qv] and, in Oklahoma, *blue darter* and *blue blizzard.* Though the latter two phrases are found out-of-state, *blue norther* itself is a pure Texasism. The dramatic effects of the blue norther have been noted and exaggerated since Spanish times in Texas. But that the blue norther is unique to Texas is folklore.

BIBLIOGRAPHY: *Dictionary of American Regional English,* Vol. 1 (Cambridge, Massachusetts: Harvard University Press, 1985).
Roy R. Barkley

BLUE RIDGE, TEXAS (Collin County). Blue Ridge is at the intersection of State Highway 78 and Farm Road 981, in northeastern Collin County. The town is on land originally owned by Matthiss Mowry, who received a land grant from the Republic of Texas[qv] for his service in the Texas Revolution.[qv] Blue Ridge was established in 1876 and named for its hilltop location and the blue-flowering grass that grows in the area; from a distance the grass looks like a blue haze. In 1876 a post office was established at Blue Ridge, and the next year a cotton gin, sawmill, and gristmill were constructed there. By 1900 the community had an estimated population of just under 400, which increased to 600 by 1915. That same year the Greenville and Whitewright Northern Traction Company (later the Greenville and Northwestern Railway) built a railroad line from Blue Ridge to Anna, twelve miles northeast. The line was abandoned five years later. On October 8, 1919, a tornado struck Blue Ridge, killing seven people and destroying over $100,000 worth of property. The town recovered, however, and by 1930 its 450 residents had electric and natural gas utilities, a telephone exchange, paved roads, a high school, and more than twenty businesses. Blue Ridge incorporated in 1936, and by 1940 it had thirty businesses serving more than 400 residents. Although Blue Ridge weathered the Great Depression[qv] better than most Texas towns, after the 1930s the number of businesses there steadily declined. Mechanization of farming and job opportunities in the Dallas area after World War II[qv] contributed to this decline. In 1960 Blue Ridge had 350 residents served by sixteen businesses. During the 1970s it served as a retail market for the few but prosperous farmers in the heart of the Blackland Prairie near Pilot Grove Creek. The community in 1984 had an estimated 442 residents and five reported businesses; in 1990 its population was 521.

BIBLIOGRAPHY: Roy Franklin Hall and Helen Gibbard Hall, *Collin County: Pioneering in North Texas* (Quanah, Texas: Nortex, 1975). J. Lee and Lillian J. Stambaugh, *A History of Collin County* (Austin: Texas State Historical Association, 1958). *David Minor*

BLUE RIDGE, TEXAS (Falls County). Blue Ridge, on Farm Road 1771 about ten miles east of Marlin in eastern Falls County, takes its name from a series of low hills in the area. In 1850 residents of the community objected to the boundaries of the new Falls County; they thought that the Brazos River should form the western county line and the Navasota River should form the eastern one. They also wanted Blue Ridge to be the county seat. But they succeeded only in delaying the organization of the county until the following year. A post office was established at Blue Ridge in 1854 and discontinued in 1857. The railroads that built through eastern Falls County in the early 1870s bypassed Blue Ridge, eliminating any chance it had of developing as a commercial center. Part of the widely dispersed community was known as Harlanville for a number of years. The Blue Ridge school had fifty-five students in 1933; it was annexed by the Marlin Independent School District in 1948. A few scattered houses marked the community's location on county highway maps in the late 1940s, but only one business remained on maps in the 1980s. No population estimates were available.

BIBLIOGRAPHY: Lillian S. St. Romain, *Western Falls County, Texas* (Austin: Texas State Historical Association, 1951).

Vivian Elizabeth Smyrl

BLUE RIDGE, TEXAS (Fort Bend County). Blue Ridge is sixteen miles east of Richmond on a ridge of Oyster Creek in northeastern Fort Bend County. Though part of Stephen F. Austin's qv first colony, the site was not permanently occupied until the late 1880s. Blue Ridge never had a post office or school. The W. Allen Robinson family built a ranch headquarters there in the 1890s. The Robinsons, among the first families to settle in the vicinity, had arrived from Arlington, Texas, in 1894. In 1919 oil was discovered nearby. Soon after, a salt mine opened, and in 1925 gas was discovered. During this time Blue Ridge (also known as Hobby) became a boomtown with gambling houses and a bank. By 1936 the site had been incorporated by the Blue Ridge State Prison Farm, and most residents were prison system qv personnel. In 1958 the Texas Board of Corrections voted to sell the 4,348 acres of prison land at Blue Ridge for private development. No population figures were registered for Blue Ridge until 1970, when the settlement listed fifty inhabitants and no businesses. The area developed phenomenally beginning in the early 1970s, when parts of it were annexed by Houston and several elementary schools were opened in Blue Ridge, including the Briargate, Ridgegate, Ridgemont, and Blue Ridge elementary schools of the Fort Bend Independent School District. In 1979, on the site that once housed convicts, Willowridge High School opened. In 1986 Christa McAuliffe Middle School, named for schoolteacher and astronaut Christa McAuliffe, opened near Willowridge High School. Residents support numerous ethnically and religiously varied churches. *Peggy Isbell and Charles Woodson*

BLUES. The earliest reference to what might be considered blues in Texas was made in 1890 by collector Gates Thomas, who transcribed a song titled "Nobody There." Thomas doesn't mention whether the singing was accompanied by an instrument, but he does indicate that it was a pentatonic tune containing tonic, minor, third, fourth, fifth, and seventh chords, all of which combined to produce something similar to a blues tune. Later Thomas published other song texts that he had collected from African Americans qv in South Texas. Some of these included verses that had been noted by other writers in different areas of the South. The song "Baby, Take a Look at Me," for example, was transcribed both by Thomas and Charles Peabody in Mississippi. And "Alabama Bound" and "C. C. Rider" are variants of blues songs that Jelly Roll Morton sang in New Orleans. Geographically diffuse sources suggest that blues musicians were itinerant and that blues was part of an oral tradition that developed in different areas of the South. By all accounts, the blues was widespread in the early 1900s. Thousands of blacks during this period were migratory, looking for work and escape from all too prevalent racism. Blues singers were often migrant workers who followed the crop harvests or lived in lumber camps and boom towns. Some settled down and labored as sharecroppers, leasing small tracts of land controlled by white landowners. Others continued roving from town to town, working odd jobs in the growing urban centers—Dallas, Houston, Shreveport, and Atlanta—cities where black migrant populations were crowded into neighborhoods of shotgun shacks and pasteboard houses.

Blues music expresses the hardships of newly freed black slaves. The freedoms offered by Reconstruction qv were hard-won—racism, Jim Crow laws, and the Ku Klux Klan qv were major obstacles to economic independence and self-determination. Still, leisure, even under the most desolate circumstances, was vitally new and served as a catalyst in the development of the blues. Early blues answered the need for a release from everyday life. The blues is an intensely personal music; it identifies itself with the feelings of the audience—suffering and hope, economic failure, the break-up of the family, the desire to escape reality through wandering, love, and sex. In this way, blues is somewhat different from African songs, which usually concern the lives and works of gods, the social unit (tribe and community), and nature. With its emphasis on individual experience blues reflects a Western concept of life. Yet, as a musical form it shows little Western influence. The traditional three-line, twelve-bar, *aab* verse form of the blues arises from no apparent Western source, although some blues does incorporate Anglo-American ballad forms that have six, ten, or sixteen bar structures. Early blues drew from the music of its time: field hollers and shouts, which it most closely resembles melodically; songster ballads, from which it borrows imagery and guitar patterns; spirituals and Gospel, which trained the voices and ears of black children. These, with exception of the ballad, were the descendants of African percussive rhythms and call-and-response singing. Although blues drew from the religious music of both African and Western cultures, it was often considered sinful. Blues singers were stereotyped as "backsliders" in their own communities. In many areas blues was known as the devil's music. As historian Larry Levine points out, blues blended the sacred and the secular. Like the spirituals and folktales of the nineteenth century, blues was a plea for release, a mix of despair, hope, and humor that had a cathartic effect upon the listener. The blues singer had an expressive role that mirrored the power of the preacher, and because of this power, blues was both embraced and rejected by blacks and their churches. In Texas, blues musician Lil Son Jackson explained to British blues aficionado Paul Oliver that it was, in effect, the spiritual power of the blues that made the music sinful. "If a man hurt within and he sing a church song then he's askin' God for help. . . . if a man sing the blues it's more or less out of himself. . . . He's not askin' no one for help. And he's really not really clingin' to no one. But he's expressin' how he feel. He's expressin' to someone and that fact makes it a sin, you know. . . . you're tryin' to get your feelin's over to the next person through the blues, and that's what make it a sin." Because of the frequent lack of centralized authority in black churches, however, community opposition to the blues varied from place to place. Rarely were blues singers completely ostracized. They lived on the margins of what was acceptable and derived their livelihood from itinerant work at house parties and dances.

With the growth of the recording industry during the 1920s the audience for blues expanded among blacks nationwide. For example, demographic studies indicate that Blind Lemon Jefferson's qv records sold thousands of copies to blacks in the urban ghettos of the North, but in Dallas Jefferson was recognized primarily as street singer who performed daily with a tin cup at the corner of Elm Street and Central Avenue. Despite his limited commercial success in Dallas, he had a great influence on the development of Texas blues. Huddie (Leadbelly) Ledbetter qv credited him as an inspiration, as did Aaron Thibeaux (T-Bone) Walker. qv What distinguishes Jefferson from the other blues performers of his generation was his singular approach to the guitar, which established the basis of what is today known as the Texas style. He strummed or "hammered" the strings with repetitive bass figures and produced a succession of open and fretted notes, using a quick release and picking single-string, arpeggio runs. T-Bone Walker later applied this technique to the electric guitar and, combined with the influences of the jump and swing blues of the regional or "Territory" jazz bands of the 1920s and 1930s, produced the modern sound.

In the Territory jazz bands of the Southwest, the guitar was used as a rhythm instrument to underlie the voice and horn sections. The introduction of the electric guitar occurred first in these bands and was pioneered by Eddie Durham [qv] of San Marcos and Charlie Christian [qv] of Fort Worth. By using electric amplification jazz guitarists were able to increase the resonance and volume of their sound. Charlie Christian is credited with teaching T-Bone Walker about the electric guitar and its potential as a solo instrument. In the rhythm and blues of T-Bone Walker the electric guitar assumed a role that superseded the saxophone, which had until then been the prominent solo instrument in jazz. The interplay between the saxophone and the guitar remained important in rhythm and blues, but the relationship between the instruments was transformed. The rhythm and blues band sound became tighter and depended more on the interplay of the electric guitar with the horn section, piano, and drums.

In Texas, blues has developed a unique character that results not only from the introduction of the electric guitar, but also from the cross-pollination of musical styles—itself a result of the migratory patterns of blacks—as well as the impact of the recording industry and mass-media commercialization. Not only is the black population of Texas less concentrated than that of other states in the South, but blues music in Texas also evolved in proximity to other important musical traditions: the rural Anglo, the Cajun and Creole, the Hispanic, and the Eastern and Central European. The white crossover to blues in Texas began in the nineteenth century, when black fiddlers and guitar songsters played at white country dances. Eddie Durham recalled in interviews that his father was a fiddler who played jigs and reels as well as blues. Mance Lipscomb's [qv] and Gatemouth Brown's fathers were songsters who played fiddle and guitar. White musicians were exposed to blues at country dances and minstrel shows and among black workers in the fields, road gangs, turpentine camps, and railroad yards. Country singer Bill Neely [qv] said that he first heard blues when he picked cotton in Collin County north of Dallas in the 1920s, but he learned to play blues by listening to Jimmie (James Charles) Rodgers.[qv] Though known as a country singer, "Jimmie Rodgers was a bluesman," Neely maintained. "A lot of those songs Jimmie Rodgers didn't write. He got them from the blacks he heard when he was growing up in Mississippi and when he worked as a brakeman on the railroad." The influence of blues and jazz is also apparent in the early western swing bands of Bob (James Robert) Wills and Milton Brown, where the horn sections of the Territory jazz bands were imitated and developed through different instrumentation. In addition, blues and jazz influenced Hispanic as well as Anglo-European popular music.

In the 1920s Dallas became a recording center primarily because it is a geographical hub. The major race labels, those catering to an African-American audience, held regular sessions in Dallas. Okeh, Vocalion, Brunswick Columbia, RCA, and Paramount sent scouts and engineers to record local artists once or twice a year. Engineers came into the city, set up their equipment in a hotel room, and put the word out. Itinerant musicians found their way to Dallas, among them the legendary Delta bluesman Robert Johnson, who recorded there in 1937 (but was also recorded in San Antonio). In part, the intense recording activity in Dallas was spurred by the commercial success of Blind Lemon Jefferson, who was discovered by a Paramount record company executive on a Deep Ellum [qv] sidewalk and invited to Chicago to make race records. Between 1926 and 1929 Blind Lemon made more than eighty records and proved to be the biggest-selling country bluesman of his generation. As a result of his huge commercial success, blues singers from around the south flocked to Dallas with the hope of being recorded. Generally, these musicians lived and worked in the area around Deep Ellum and Central Tracks. Deep Ellum was the area of Dallas, north and east of downtown, where black newcomers to the city flocked. Branching off from Elm Street was Central Tracks, a stretch of railroad near the Union Depot, where the Texas and Pacific line crossed the Houston and Texas Central line. Lying east of the downtown business district and north of Deep Ellum, Central Tracks was the heart of the black community. In the area were Ella B. Moore's Park Theater, with vaudeville, minstrel, and touring blues and jazz shows, the Tip Top, Hattie Burleson's dance hall, the Green Parrot, and the Pythian Temple, designed by the black architect William Sidney Pittman.[qv] In addition to Blind Lemon Jefferson, there were other important blues musicians, who recorded in Dallas during the heyday of Deep Ellum and Central Tracks. These included Lonnie Johnson, Lillian Glinn, Little Hat Jones, Alger (Texas) Alexander, Jesse Thomas, Willard (Ramblin) Thomas, Sammy Hill, Otis Harris, Willie Reed, Oscar (Buddy) Woods, Babe Kyro (Black Ace) Turner, and the young T-Bone Walker. With the Great Depression [qv] of the 1930s, race recording declined, but the Dallas area remained a center of blues activity. In the 1940s the railroad tracks on Central Avenue were torn up to make room for Central Expressway, which was built in the 1950s, and for R. L. Thornton Freeway in the 1960s. These changes choked Deep Ellum off from downtown and the area became a warehouse district with industrial suppliers and small businesses mixed in. In the 1980s the redevelopment of Deep Ellum stimulated commercial activity, street life, and a club scene that has become an important venue for contemporary blues. Among blacks in Dallas, the locus of blues activity in the 1940s and 1950s shifted from Central Tracks to North and South Dallas. The Rose Ballroom, opened by T. H. Smith in March 1942 and reopened as the Rose Room in April 1943, became a showplace for the best of the local and nationally known blues artists. T-Bone Walker performed there, as did Big Joe Turner, Pee Wee Crayton, Lowell Fulson, Eddie Vinson, Jimmy Nelson, and Henry (Buster) Smith.[qv] The Rose Room was renamed the Empire Room in 1951 and continued to feature the most popular rhythm and blues of the day: ZuZu Bollin, Lil Son Jackson, Clarence (Nappy Chin) Evans, Mercy Baby, Frankie Lee Sims, and Smoke Hogg. In the 1960s Chris Strachwitz of Arhoolie Records worked in earnest to release contemporary recordings of these and other blues musicians in Dallas and elsewhere in Texas. Since 1985, Documentary Arts, a nonprofit organization in Dallas, has been involved in the documentation and preservation of Texas blues through the production of radio features, films, videos, audio cassettes, and compact discs. The Dallas Blues Society has also worked to heighten public knowledge of the blues through the promotion of concerts and the production of audio recordings. In 1987 Dallas pianist Alex Moore became the first African-American blues musician from Texas to receive a National Heritage Fellowship from the Folk Arts Program National Endowment for the Arts.

African Americans in Houston settled mostly in four segregated wards: the Third, Fourth, Fifth, and Sixth. It was in the Third Ward that Sam (Lightnin) Hopkins [qv] accompanied his cousin Alger (Texas) Alexander in the late 1920s, and where Hopkins returned by himself in the 1940s to play on Dowling Street. The Santa Fe Group gathered in the Fourth Ward.[qv] They were a loosely knit association of itinerant black pianists in the 1920s and 1930s that included Robert Shaw,[qv] Black Boy Shine, Pinetop Burks, and Rob Cooper, who played in the roadhouses and juke joints along the Santa Fe tracks, playing their distinctive style of piano that combined elements of blues with the syncopation of ragtime. In the Fifth Ward [qv] also there were black blues pianists, but their style of performance was even more eclectic. Probably the most well-known of these were members of the George W. Thomas family. The eldest, George Thomas, Jr., was born about 1885, followed by his sister, Beulah, better known as the classic blues singer Sippie Wallace, and her brother, Hersal. In Houston there were fewer opportunities for recording than in Dallas until after World War II,[qv] when several independent labels were started. The earliest to record blues was Gold Star, founded by Bill Quinn in 1946 as a hillbilly label to record Harry H. Choates.[qv] In 1947 Quinn decided to enter the race market by recording Lightnin' Hopkins. By the early 1950s competition among independent record labels in Houston was intense. Macy's, Freedom, and Peacock (as well as Bob Shad's New York–based Sittin-In-With label) were all involved in recording local and regional blues musicians, including Lightnin' Hopkins, Goree Carter, Lester Williams, Little Willie Littlefield, Peppermint Harris, Grady Gaines, and Big Walter Price. Of the Houston-based independent labels, Peacock emerged as the most prominent. Houston businessman Don Robey founded Peacock Records in 1949 to record Gatemouth Brown, who was the headliner at Robey's Bronze Peacock club. The first rhythm and blues singer with whom Robey made the charts was Marie Adams, whose song "I'm Gonna Play the Honky Tonks" was a hit in 1952. With this success, Robey expanded his recording interests by acquiring the Memphis label Duke Records. Through this acquisition Robey secured the rights to the musicians who were then under contract to Duke. These included Johnny Ace, Junior Parker, and Bobby Blue Bland. In addition to Peacock and Duke, Robey started the Songbird and Back Beat labels, as well as the Buffalo Booking Agency, which was operated by his associate, Evelyn Johnson. Robey's business began to wane in the early 1960s, but benefited greatly from the influx of British rock 'n' roll and the revival of interest in rhythm and blues. In 1973 Robey sold his recording and publishing interests to ABC/Dunhill. Concurrent with the growth of Peacock Records, a new generation of Houston-bred rhythm and blues musicians began their careers, but were not recorded by Don Robey. These musicians included Albert Collins, Johnny Copeland, Joe Hughes, Johnny Watson, Clarence and Cal Green, and Pete Mayes. Playing at the Club Matinee, Shady's Playhouse, the Eldorado Ballroom, and other nightspots around Houston, these musicians emulated the music of T-Bone Walker and eventually developed their own distinctive performance styles.

Austin was slower to develop as a recording center than Dallas or Houston, although there is a long history of blues in Central Texas. The relatively small black population of Austin made the capital unappealing for record producers until the 1960s, when the "Austin Sound" began to attract national attention. With the influx of white musicians, including Jimmie Vaughan, Stevie Ray Vaughan,[qv] Joe Ely, Angela Strehli, and Kim Wilson, the enthusiasm for blues has grown significantly. The success of these musicians has also benefited many older African-American blues musicians who gained a larger audience outside of their own community and performed at Antone's, the Continental Club, and other venues near the University of Texas campus. In Austin, T-Bone Walker clearly had the biggest influence upon aspiring black blues musicians, including Dooley Jordan, Jewel Simmons, and T. D. Bell. Bell himself has also inspired younger blues artists, such as Herbert (Blues Boy) Hubbard and W. C. Clark. In the 1950s the Victory Grill on East Eleventh Street was an important venue for local musicians as well as for nationally touring acts. In addition to rhythm and blues, Austin has also been the home of barrelhouse blues pianists Grey Ghost, Robert Shaw, and Lavada Durst, and for country blues guitarist Alfred (Snuff) Johnson. In recent years, Texas Folklife Resources in Austin has presented some of these performers in touring programs. John Wheat, of the Center for American History at the University of Texas at Austin, has been building an important sound archive, including the Texas Music Collection, the John A. Lomax[qv] Family Papers, the Mance Lipscomb/Glen Alyn Collection, the William A. Owens Collection, and other blues recordings, posters, and memorabilia.

BIBLIOGRAPHY: William Barlow, *"Looking Up at Down": The Emergence of Blues Culture* (Philadelphia: Temple University Press, 1989). Lawrence Cohn, *Nothing but the Blues: The Music and the Musicians* (New York: Abbeville Press, 1993). Francis Davis, *The History of the Blues* (New York: Hyperion, 1995). Alan B. Govenar, *The Early Years of Rhythm and Blues: Focus on Houston* (Houston: Rice University Press, 1990). Alan B. Govenar, *Meeting the Blues* (Dallas: Taylor, 1988). Paul Oliver, *The New Grove Gospel, Blues and Jazz: With Spiritual and Ragtime* (London: Macmillan, 1986). *Alan Govenar*

BLUE SKY LAW. The Blue Sky Law, enacted by the Thirty-eighth Legislature as House Bill 177 on May 15, 1923, was designed to stop the flow of worthless stock certificates into Texas and was directed largely at oil companies. The statute required concerns offering stock for sale in Texas to file applications with the secretary of state for permits to sell the securities. Each application was to give the previous business of the officers of the company and to have attached a financial statement of the company's resources. The law remained in force until it was superseded by the Securities Act passed by the Forty-fourth Legislature in 1935.

BIBLIOGRAPHY: *General Laws of the State of Texas Passed by the Thirty-eighth Legislature at Its First, Second and Third Sessions, 1923* (Austin: Secretary of State, 1923). *Elmer W. Flaccus*

BLUE SPRINGS, TEXAS (Nacogdoches County). Blue Springs was on Farm Road 226 twenty-five miles southeast of Nacogdoches in extreme southeastern Nacogdoches County. It was named for a nearby spring. A Blue Springs school was in operation by 1904, when it had an enrollment of fifty-four. During the 1930s the settlement comprised the school, a church, and a number of houses. The school was closed during the 1940s, and by the early 1990s only a cemetery and a few scattered houses remained in the area. *Christopher Long*

BLUE SPRINGS, TEXAS (Van Zandt County). Blue Springs, a farming community on State Highway 64 two miles northwest of Canton in northwest Van Zandt County, had a school by 1890; its enrollment reached thirty-one in 1905. State highway maps of 1936 showed a church and scattered dwellings at the townsite. The school was consolidated with the Canton Independent School District in the 1950s. By 1987 only a single business remained at the site, which was no longer listed as a community. *Diana J. Kleiner*

BLUE STAR ART SPACE. The Blue Star Art Space, a nonprofit, noncollecting institution dedicated to exhibiting contemporary art, is in a 137,000-square-foot complex of old warehouses at 116 Blue Star, on the southern edge of downtown San Antonio. The Blue Star Art Space, characterized in national art publications as a "galvanizing force" for San Antonio's art community, was founded in 1986 by a group of artists and businessmen. The Blue Star project began in a climate unfriendly to contemporary art: three galleries devoted to modern art had just closed, leaving San Antonio artists no place to show their work. Artists Jeffrey Moore, Richard Thompson, Kent Rush, Richard Mogas, Adair Sutherland, and Lewis Tarver subsequently teamed up with a group of businessmen to establish an organization called Contemporary Art for San Antonio, which succeeded in raising $40,000. Developers Hap Veltman and Bernard Lifshutz donated the use of a 12,000-square-foot space in an empty warehouse complex they had bought for an arts community. The first Blue Star exhibition opened on July 1, 1986, featuring fifty-six works by twenty-seven local artists, both unknowns and established artists such as Richard Thompson, James Cobb, and John Tweddle. The exhibition drew over 3,500 visitors during the following month and has since become an annual event.

The first exhibition was followed by a number of such successful shows as Dead Days '86, organized to coincide with the November 1 Día de los Muertos celebration. Curated by University of Texas at San Antonio graduate student Maureen O'Malley, the exhibition featured over 200 works on the theme of death by Texas artists Sharon Kopriva, Earl Staley, Benito Huerta, and others, as well as New York artists Sue Coe, Alex Grey, and Robert Morris. Blue Star has also organized solo exhibitions and hosted shows planned by other alternative exhibition venues, such as Sculpture: The Spectrum organized by the Lawndale Art and Performance Center[qv] in Houston.

The Blue Star Art Space presents six exhibitions a year and is run by a board of thirty artists and art professionals. Blue Star was run by volunteers until November 1988, when director Jeffrey Moore and an assistant, Heather Edwards, were hired to coordinate programming, publicity, and fund-raising efforts. Blue Star has received funds from the National Endowment for the Arts, the Texas Commission on the Arts,[qv] the city of San Antonio, and numerous private foundations and donors. The Brown Foundation and and H-E-B[qqv] make substantial annual contributions to Blue Star's operating budget, which was $200,000 in 1991. Lifshutz has continued to provide rent-free space for the center.

Within two years after Blue Star opened, a thriving arts community had developed in the warehouse complex, which housed over two dozen artists' studios and living quarters, a conservation center for works on paper, architects' offices, two theatrical companies, and a multimedia space called the Filmhaus. Two other galleries settled in the Blue Star project: Blue Collar Gallery, codirected by artists Holly Moe and Gary Schafter, featured work by young artists who work with challenging concepts and styles; and Locus Gallery, run by Ralph G. Mendez, exhibited work by contemporary artists from around the country. By 1991 the complex had entered into a period of transition. Renovations to add forty-six living and working units for artists forced the Filmhaus and both galleries to close and other groups to relocate.

The Blue Star complex has drawn a diverse group of artists, working in styles that range from Beth Eidelberg's traditional watercolors to Holly Moe's drawings, executed with cigarette and gunpowder burns on low-pile carpet. Artists closely involved with Blue Star Art Space include the sculptors Gail Kline, Stephen Daly, and Ken Little; painter James Cobb; and painter and printmaker Anita Valencia. Blue Star and its various satellites have prompted interaction between artists and art professionals from such institutions as the San Antonio Art Institute, the San Antonio Museum Association,[qqv] the University of Texas at San Antonio, and the Southwest Crafts Center, thus fostering a more fertile environment for contemporary art in San Antonio.

Bibliography: Jamey Gambrell, "Texas: State of the Art," *Art in America* 75 (March 1987). Katherine Gregor, "Shaking Things Up," *ARTnews*, January 1988. New York *Times*, December 20, 1987.

Kendall Curlee

BLUETOWN, TEXAS. Bluetown is a dispersed rural community on the Missouri Pacific tracks off the junction of U.S. Highway 281 and Farm Road 506, six miles south of La Feria in southwestern Cameron County. A rail line connecting Fernando to Santa Maria was built through the area in 1913 by the San Benito and Rio Grande Valley Railway. The Bluetown community was established in the early 1940s as a local market for citrus fruit and various other crops. In 1945 Bluetown had three stores and a population of seventy-five, and by 1950 it had an estimated population of 100, a few dwellings, a church, and a cemetery. Its population continued to be reported at 100 until 1972, when it dropped to forty. Bluetown in 1984 had scattered dwellings, three businesses, a church, and a cemetery. In the early 1990s its population was still estimated at forty. A colonia[qv] developed in the area during the 1960s, and by 1976 it had eighty dwellings and an estimated population of 396. In 1986 the colonia, also known as Bluetown, had ninety-one homes and an estimated population of 410.

Bibliography: *Colonias in the Lower Rio Grande Valley of South Texas: A Summary Report* (Policy Research Project Report No. 18, Lyndon B. Johnson School of Public Affairs, University of Texas at Austin, 1977).

Alicia A. Garza

BLUEWATER, TEXAS. Bluewater is on an unnumbered road south of Farm Road 943 in southwestern Polk County, sixty-five miles north of Houston. The community was presumably named after Blue Branch Creek, which runs through the area. The settlement was started in the late 1890s by settlers including Daniel Rick Bush, Jim Geldard, and E. Dowden. Early residents built a log church and established the Blue Branch school, a cotton gin, a sawmill, and a blacksmith shop. The post office, called Dowden after its first postmaster, was open from 1904 to 1915. A few scattered buildings and residences, including a church and a cemetery, remained in the area in the late 1980s.

Bibliography: *A Pictorial History of Polk County, Texas, 1846–1910* (Livingston, Texas: Polk County Bicentennial Commission, 1976; rev. ed. 1978).

Robert Wooster

BLUE WING LAKE. Blue Wing Lake is on a small tributary of the San Antonio River six miles west of Elmendorf in southeastern Bexar County (at 29°16′ N, 98°26′ W). The artificial lake was built after 1900 and is owned and operated by the private Blue Wing Club for irrigation purposes. The lake has a maximum capacity of 1,600 acre-feet and a normal capacity of 1,000 acre-feet. The surrounding terrain is flat to gently rolling and is surfaced by clay loam that supports mesquite, cacti, and grasses.

BLUFF, TEXAS (Bandera County). Bluff is on Wallace Creek and State Highway 16 nineteen miles northwest of Bandera in north central Bandera County. Among the earliest settlers in the area was W. A. A. (Bigfoot) Wallace,[qv] for whom the creek was named. In 1873 J. A. Chamberlain built a sawmill on the creek near the site of the community. By 1896 Wallace Creek School had been built near the Chamberlain mill, and that year the school had fifty pupils and one teacher. When the school burned down in 1899, it was rebuilt at a site by a nearby bluff overlooking the creek. In 1906 a post office was opened in a general store by the bluff, and the small settlement took the name Bluff. In 1925 the community had a store and an estimated twenty residents. Its post office closed in 1930, and that same year its school was consolidated with that of Medina. In 1948 Bluff reported a population of twenty-five and consisted of a single business and a number of scattered dwellings. The community was still shown on the 1983 county highway map; at that time the Medina Children's Home was located at a site just east of Bluff.

Bibliography: Bandera County History Book Committee, *History of Bandera County, Texas* (Dallas: Curtis, 1986).

Mark Odintz

BLUFF, TEXAS (Fayette County). Bluff is on the south side of the Colorado River directly across from La Grange in central Fayette County. Its primary features are a high bluff and the Monument Hill–Kreische Brewery State Historic Site,[qv] located just west of U.S. Highway 77 on an extension of Farm Road 155. The area was granted by the Mexican state of Coahuila and Texas[qv] to David Berry on November 20, 1832. During the late 1840s the land was purchased by Carl George Willrich, one of a number of well-off German immigrants known as Forty-eighters, who came to Texas to escape civil war in Germany. H. L. Kreische acquired the title to the top of the bluff in about 1849 and began construction of his brewery, which for many years served as the focal point of the community. He also provided a burial place on his land for those Texans, including David Berry, who had died in the Dawson massacre[qv] or after drawing black beans as Mier expedition[qv] members. Bluff had a post office from 1869 to 1903, after which mail was delivered from La Grange. The Bluff voting precinct was established in 1876. Around 1900 the settlement had two stores, a blacksmith shop, a cotton gin, and a post office. Improved transportation across the Colorado River to La Grange led to the economic decline of the town. By 1960 cotton was gone as a crop, and the gin had ceased to function. Cotton fields were replaced by cow pastures and, on the bluff itself, by a large residential development overlooking La Grange. In 1987 at the site were two businesses and a large country club.

BIBLIOGRAPHY: Frank Lotto, *Fayette County: Her History and Her People* (Schulenburg, Texas: Sticker Steam Press, 1902; rpt., Austin: University of Texas Press, 1981). *Jeff Carroll*

BLUFF CREEK (Briscoe County). Bluff Creek rises in eastern Briscoe County (at 34°27′ N, 101°01′ W) and runs east for five miles to its mouth on the Little Red River, where that stream intersects with the western line of Hall County (at 34°30′ N, 100°56′ W). The streambed is on the former JA and Quitaque[qqv] (Lazy F) ranches and is still the site of ranching activities. Burson Lake, a small reservoir on Bluff Creek, has concessions and other lake-resort facilities. The creek crosses terrain surfaced by silt loams that support mesquite and grasses.

—— (Collin County). Bluff Creek rises in the southeast corner of Collin County (at 33°35′ N, 96°23′ W) and flows southwest for two miles to Moores Lake. From the dam at the west end of the lake, the stream flows west for a half mile and then turns southwest again to run an additional 1½ miles to its mouth on Camp Creek, near the northern border of Rockwall County (at 33°00′ N, 96°26′ W). Bluff Creek traverses flat to rolling terrain surfaced by dark clays that support prairie grass, mesquite, and cactus. *Elizabeth Lee Bass*

—— (Coryell County). Bluff Creek rises two miles due west of Osage in eastern Coryell County (at 31°31′ N, 97°37′ W) and flows to the east for about twelve miles, then drains into the Middle Bosque River two miles north of Crawford in northwestern McLennan County (at 31°34′ N, 97°28′ W). The creek's drainage area is range and crop land of variable topography; the vegetation is mostly juniper, live oak, grasses, and chaparral, well adapted to the region's thin, stony, clay loam land surface. *Sylvia Edwards*

—— (Edwards County). Bluff Creek begins two miles northeast of Goode Triangulation Station in south central Edwards County (at 29°43′ N, 100°19′ W) and runs northwest for seven miles to its mouth on the West Nueces River, two miles east of Ellis Triangulation Station (at 29°45′ N, 100°23′ W). It crosses flat terrain with local deep and dense dissection, surfaced by shallow, stony soils that support oak, juniper, and mesquite.

—— (Knox County). Bluff Creek rises east of the Alexander Ranch and three miles southwest of Truscott in Knox County (at 33°44′ N, 99°53′ W) and runs northeast for ten miles to its mouth on the North Wichita River (at 33°49′ N, 99°49′ W). It crosses an area of steeply to moderately sloping hills surfaced by shallow, stony, sandy and clay loams that support mesquite, oak, and grasses.

—— (McCulloch County). Bluff Creek begins four miles west of Rochelle in northeast central McCulloch County (at 31°15′ N, 99°18′ W) and runs north for 18½ miles to its mouth on the Colorado River, four miles northeast of Fife (at 31°25′ N, 99°18′ W). It traverses flat to rolling terrain with local shallow depressions and a surface of sandy and clay loams that support water-tolerant hardwoods, conifers, and grasses in the upper and middle reaches of the creek and scrub brush and mesquite near the mouth.

—— (Motley County). Bluff Creek rises in east central Motley County (at 33°59′ N, 100°35′ W) and runs northeast for seven miles to its mouth on the Tongue or South Pease River, a mile north of U.S. Highway 62/70 and west of the Motley-Cottle county line (at 34°00′ N, 100°31′ W). The headwaters of the creek are near Summit, a switch on the Quanah, Acme and Pacific Railroad. The area is characterized by sloping terrain surfaced by shallow silt loams that support mesquite and grasses.

—— (Palo Pinto County). Bluff Creek, also known as Wolf Creek, rises a mile north of Brad in northwest Palo Pinto County (at 32°48′ N, 98°32′ W) and runs northeast for five miles to its mouth at Johnson Bend on Possum Kingdom Lake (at 32°51′ N, 98°29′ W). In the upper reaches it crosses an area of rolling hills surfaced by sandy and clay loam that supports scrub brush, mesquite, cacti, and grasses. Downstream, the terrain becomes flat and the soils more clayey and stony; oak, juniper, and some mesquite grow there.

—— (Scurry County). Bluff Creek rises eight miles northwest of Snyder in western Scurry County (at 32°47′ N, 101°02′ W) and runs south for nineteen miles to its mouth on the Colorado River, twelve miles southwest of Snyder and just south of Farm Road 1606 (at 32°34′ N, 101°03′ W). The stream is intermittent in its upper and middle reaches. It runs beneath moderately steep slopes with locally high relief, surfaced by silt loams from which grow mesquite and grasses.

—— (Shackelford County). Bluff Creek rises just north of U.S. Highway 180 in west central Shackelford County (at 32°43′ N, 99°26′ W) and runs sixteen miles northwest to its mouth on the Clear Fork of the Brazos River (at 32°51′ N, 99°34′ W). It crosses flat terrain with local shallow depressions and a surface of sandy and clay loam that supports water-tolerant hardwoods, conifers, and grasses.

—— (Taylor County). Bluff Creek rises a mile southeast of U.S. Highway 277 and six miles northeast of Shep in southeast Taylor County (32°12′ N, 100°03′ W) and extends southeast for thirty-nine miles before emptying into Elm Creek 2½ miles east of Hatchel in north central Runnels County (at 31°51′ N, 99°54′ W). Bluff Creek rises in steeply sloping terrain with benches, flows through flat to rolling terrain with local scarps, and ends in flat land with locally shallow depressions. Juniper, live oak, mesquite, and grasses predominate in the upper reaches, scrub brush and grasses in the midsection, and water-tolerant hardwoods, conifers, and grasses in the lower reaches.

—— (Val Verde County). Bluff Creek rises a mile west of the junction of U.S. highways 277 and 377 in east central Val Verde County (at 29°44′N, 100°50′ W) and runs southwest for eight miles to its mouth on Big Satan Creek, a mile north of Slaughter Bend on the Devils River (at 29°41′ N, 100°56′ W). Its short course dissects flat terrain of massive limestone, forming a deep and winding canyon. Soils in the area are generally dark, calcareous stony clays and clay loams that support oaks, junipers, grasses, and mesquites. The creek, named for the steep cliffs that form its banks, is a relatively insignificant part of the area drainage system.

—— (Wilbarger County). Bluff Creek rises in east and west forks that meet eighteen miles southeast of Vernon in southeastern Wilbarger County (at 33°58′ N, 98°57′ W). The creek then flows southeast for six miles, crossing the county line into Wichita County, where it joins Rough Creek about eighteen miles south of Electra (at 33°55′ N, 98°55′ W). The stream runs through an area of moderately steep slopes surfaced with silt loams that support mesquite and grasses.

BLUFF DALE, TEXAS. Bluff Dale, on U.S. Highway 377 and the North Paluxy River in northeastern Erath County, was originally called Bluff Spring by the pioneers who settled near the site's artesian wells. Bluff Dale became the name when the post office was granted in 1877. When the Fort Worth and Rio Grande Railway was constructed in 1889, Jack Glenn donated land for a new townsite on the line a short distance to the east. The relocated town prospered for the next two decades and was incorporated in 1908. By 1915 it had its own bank, as well as a newspaper, the Bluff Dale *Sun*. Bluff Dale reported 680 residents in 1936, 500 in 1940, and 123 in 1980. By 1989, however, the population had grown to 300. By that year the school had expanded to more than seventy students from only twenty in 1983 and had reinstituted competitive sports. In 1989 the town also had three churches, a volunteer fire department, a Study and Garden Club, a beautification committee, and five historical markers.

bibliography: Vallie Eoff, A History of Erath County, Texas (M.A. thesis, University of Texas, 1937). *Cathey Yarbrough Sims*

BLUFF SPRINGS, TEXAS. Bluff Springs is on Onion Creek eight miles south of Austin and two miles east of Interstate Highway 35 in southern Travis County. It was settled in the early 1850s, and a post office opened there in 1853 with William S. Smith as postmaster. By the mid-1880s Bluff Springs was a thriving community with steam gristmills–cotton gins, a church, a district school, and 250 residents; daily stage service provided residents with access to Luling, Lockhart, and Austin. The principal crops grown for shipment by area farmers were cotton, corn, oats, and sweet potatoes. The population of Bluff Springs fell to fifty by 1892. Its post office was discontinued in 1902, and mail for the community was sent to Buda. The community's population fell to twenty-five by the early 1930s but rose to fifty by 1939. A church and a few businesses and scattered houses marked the community on county highway maps in the 1940s. Bluff Springs reported a population of fifty in 1990.

bibliography: John J. Germann and Myron Janzen, *Texas Post Offices by County* (1986). *Vivian Elizabeth Smyrl*

BLUFFTON, TEXAS. Bluffton, also known as New Bluffton, is on Farm Road 2241 near the western shore of Lake Buchanan twelve miles northeast of Llano in northeastern Llano County. One of the earliest settlements in the region that was to become Llano County, Bluffton originated when Billy Davis settled on the west bank of the Colorado River in 1852. He was followed by a relative, I. B. Maxwell, in 1853. Maxwell reportedly named the settlement for his hometown, Bluffton, Arkansas, perhaps because of the bluffs facing the new community on the east bank of the Colorado River. Bluffton grew to some significance because it was near an early saltworks operated by Davie Cowan and was also near several Colorado River crossings between Burnet and points west. In 1873 a post office was established there with John O. Brown as postmaster. By 1883 Bluffton was a stage stop between Burnet and Llano, with a blacksmith shop, a cotton gin, a hotel, saloons, and other enterprises. In that year a fire, allegedly started by drunken cowboys, destroyed the town. It was rebuilt a half mile north. Although at one time more prosperous than the county seat, Llano, Bluffton was bypassed by the railroad and subsequently declined. When Buchanan Dam (which originally was to be called Bluffton Dam) was completed in 1937, Lake Buchanan[qv] inundated the townsite, and Bluffton moved again, this time five miles west. The new Lake Buchanan also caused the relocation of State Highway 29 between Burnet and Llano, further isolating Bluffton. In 1986 the local economy focused on ranching, tourism, and retirement, and the community had seventy-five residents, a post office, and a store. The population was still reported as seventy-five in 1990.

bibliography: Tillie Badu Moss Fry, A History of Llano County (M.A. thesis, University of Texas, 1943). Wilburn Oatman, *Llano, Gem of the Hill Country: A History of Llano County* (Hereford, Texas: Pioneer, 1970). *James B. Heckert-Greene*

BLUITT, BENJAMIN R. (1865–1918). Benjamin R. Bluitt, the first black surgeon in Texas, was born in December 1865 in Freestone County, Texas. He grew up and was educated in Limestone County. He continued his education at Wiley College in Marshall and Meharry Medical School in Nashville, Tennessee. Before opening a practice in Dallas in 1888 he practiced in Illinois, Pennsylvania, and New York. In 1900 he was living in Dallas with his wife of ten years, Cornelia, his mother, Maria, and a niece. His business office was in the Pythian Temple. Bluitt was an executive committee member of the Negro Business League of Dallas and served as an officer of the first black bank in Dallas, the Penny Savings Bank, and as a trustee at St. James African Methodist Episcopal Church. He opened the first black hospital in Dallas in 1905, the Bluitt Sanitarium, on Commerce Street. As a hobby he raised and trained thoroughbred horses. In 1918 he moved his practice to Chicago, where he died and was buried.

bibliography: Dallas *Morning News*, February 17, 1987. *Lisa C. Maxwell*

BLUM, LEON (1837–1906). Leon Blum, businessman and philanthropist, son of Isaac and Julie Blum, was born in Gunderschoffer, Alsace, in 1837. He served an apprenticeship with a tinsmith before he immigrated to the United States in 1854. He first opened a mercantile business in Richmond, Texas, but moved his business to Galveston in 1869 and soon enlarged his operations to reach throughout Texas and the Southwest and into foreign countries. Blum was said to be the largest Texas importer of dry goods at the time, as well as an exporter of cotton and other commodities. His firm, Leon and H. Blum, was one of the stockholders in the Gulf, Colorado and Santa Fe Railway, and the town of Blum, in Hill County, was named for him when the townsite was developed on the line. In 1903 he was president of Blum Land Company. He was a contributor to Bayland Orphans' Home for Boys[qv] and to various schools. Blum married Henrietta Levy of Corpus Christi in 1862; they had two children. He died at Galveston on April 28, 1906, and was buried there in the Hebrew Cemetery.

bibliography: John Henry Brown, *Indian Wars and Pioneers of Texas* (Austin: Daniell, 1880; reprod., Easley, South Carolina: Southern Historical Press, 1978). Lewis E. Daniell, *Types of Successful Men in Texas* (Austin: Von Boeckmann, 1890). Galveston *News*, April 28, 1906. *Jeanette H. Flachmeier*

BLUM, TEXAS. Blum is on Farm roads 933 and 67 and the Atchison, Topeka and Santa Fe tracks near the northern edge of Lake Whitney, fifteen miles northwest of Hillsboro in the northwestern corner of Hill County. Philip Nolan[qv] reportedly captured mustangs[qv] in the area, and settlers moved into the region before 1880. The community was established in 1881, when the tracks of the Gulf, Colorado and Santa Fe Railway were extended through the county. The railroad company, in planning the line's route through Hill County, had designated a station in the Nolan River valley on the edge of a farm owned by W. H. Taylor. Taylor surveyed a townsite on his property and sold lots. The resulting community was named for Leon Blum,[qv] a railroad official and prominent Galveston merchant. The new town grew rapidly. A post office opened there in 1882, and in 1883 a school subscription drive was successful. By 1890 Blum had 315 residents, and by 1908 it had 1,000 residents, four dry-goods stores, four grocery stores, two banks, and two hotels. In addition, that year local cotton gins processed over 5,000 bales and the Blum Independent School District was established. Blum incorporated in 1913. In 1925 it had a population of 550 and thirty businesses. By the mid-1930s its population had fallen to 403, served by twelve businesses. In 1977 Blum had 382 residents and eighteen businesses, and by 1990 it had 358 residents and twenty-one businesses.

bibliography: Hill County Historical Commission, *A History of Hill County, Texas, 1853–1980* (Waco: Texian, 1980). *A Memorial and Biographical History of Johnson and Hill Counties* (Chicago: Lewis, 1892). *Brian Hart*

BLUMENTHAL, TEXAS (Colorado County). Blumenthal, meaning "valley of flowers," was close to Redgates Creek and about seventeen miles south of Industry in northern Colorado County. The settlement was established before 1840 by German immigrants and was a farming community with indefinite boundaries. The land where the settlement was situated was originally granted to Peter Piper. In 1840 Louis Cachand Ervendberg,[qv] the first known German Protestant missionary in Texas, established a congregation in the area, in addition to congregations in nearby Frelsburg, Biegel, Cummins Creek, Industry, and Cat Spring. Blumenthal never became a commercial center and never had a post office. Dr. Joseph A. Fischer, an associate of Pastor Ervendberg, agreed to teach school in the communities that had active congregations.

BIBLIOGRAPHY: Frelsburg Historical Committee, *The History of Frelsburg* (New Ulm, Texas: Enterprise, 1986). *Jeff Carroll*

BLUMENTHAL, TEXAS (Gillespie County). Blumenthal is on U.S. Highway 290 nine miles southeast of Fredericksburg in southeastern Gillespie County. The community is said to have been established around 1900. In the early 1940s the population was reported at ten, but the number of residents increased to twenty-five by 1945. Two businesses and a few scattered houses marked the community on county highway maps in the late 1940s, but by the late 1980s most of these had disappeared. *Vivian Elizabeth Smyrl*

BLUM ROCKSHELTER. Blum Rockshelter, an archeological site near Blum in Hill County, was discovered by George Benson in 1951. Because it was to be covered by the flood-control pool of Lake Whitney, it was excavated in 1952 by Edward B. Jelks as part of a salvage program to save archeological evidence in danger of being destroyed. The rockshelter was formed as Nolan's River cut into a soft limestone bank. Eventually the course of the river shifted slightly to the east, leaving a shelter on the west bank. During floods the river deposited sediments on the floor of the shelter, thus producing a stratigraphic separation of the artifacts left there. Several chipped stone knives, scrapers, drills, and arrow points were found, as well as some bone tools and a few Caddoan-style pottery fragments. Excavation of these artifacts provided the first evidence of a clear temporal separation between two divisions of the Central Texas Aspect. Scallorn-type arrow points, which are a defining feature of the Austin Focus, were found mainly in the lower levels of the excavation. Perdiz-type points, diagnostic of the Toyah Focus, were found only in the upper levels. This suggested that the Toyah Focus was the later of the two divisions and possibly developed out of the Austin Focus. The chronology was corroborated by a substantially larger sample of artifacts subsequently found at the Kyle Rockshelter.[qv] The artifacts and field notes from Blum are stored at the Texas Archeological Research Laboratory, J. J. Pickle Research Center,[qv] University of Texas at Austin.

BIBLIOGRAPHY: Edward B. Jelks, "Excavations at the Blum Rockshelter," *Bulletin of the Texas Archeological Society* 24 (1953). Edward B. Jelks, *The Kyle Site* (Austin: University of Texas Department of Anthropology, 1962). Dee Ann Suhm, "A Review of Central Texas Archeology," *Bulletin of the Texas Archeological Society* 29 (1958).
Edward B. Jelks

BLUNDELL CREEK. Blundell Creek rises three miles south of Mount Vernon in central Franklin County (at 33°08′ N, 95°14′ W). It originally ran southeast for fifteen miles to join Big Cypress Creek (at 33°04′ N, 95°02′ W) 3½ miles southeast of Monticello in Titus County. During the late 1960s the Dallas Power and Light Company constructed a dam across the creek near its mouth to form Lake Monticello. The stream, which is intermittent in its upper and middle reaches, crosses a gently undulating to rolling area with loamy topsoil. The land is heavily wooded, with pines and various hardwoods predominating.

BLUNTZER, TEXAS. Bluntzer is at the junction of Farm roads 624 and 666, some twenty-four miles west of Corpus Christi in northwestern Nueces County. It was named for an early ranching family. Nicholas Bluntzer came to the area in 1860 and settled near an area formerly known as Santa Margarita Crossing, one of the principal stopping points on the San Antonio–Brownsville stagecoach line. The Bluntzer school was opened in the 1870s on W. W. Wright's Rancho Seco. After the school building was inundated during the 1919 hurricane, the school was moved to a site, donated by Justice Bluntzer, on a nearby hill. The community reported a population of twenty-five from 1900 to 1950. By the 1970s Bluntzer was the only remaining common school in Nueces County. In 1971 the school was annexed to the Banquete Independent School District. In the early 1990s Bluntzer reported a population of 150.

BIBLIOGRAPHY: Nueces County Historical Society, *History of Nueces County* (Austin: Jenkins, 1972). *Christopher Long*

BLY, TEXAS. Bly was six miles north of Mount Pleasant in northern Titus County. A post office opened there in 1893, with George W. Bistline as postmaster. In 1896 the settlement had a gin, a mill, a blacksmith shop, and a population of twenty-five. Its post office was closed in 1908, and by 1936 Bly no longer existed.

BIBLIOGRAPHY: Wright Patman, *History of Post Offices—First Congressional District of Texas* (Texarkana, Texas, 1946?).
Cecil Harper, Jr.

BLYDEN, LARRY (1925–1975). Larry Blyden, stage and television actor, was born Ivan Lawrence Blieden on June 23, 1925, in Houston, Texas, the son of Adolph and Marian (Davidson) Blieden. He attended Wharton Elementary School, Sidney Lanier Junior High School, and Lamar High School in Houston. He was a student at Southwestern Louisiana Institute in 1943–44 and graduated from the University of Houston with a B.S. in 1948. There he worked for KPRC radio and did theatrical work with the Houston Little Theater and with the Community Players. Blyden joined the United States Marine Corps in World War II. After his discharge, he went to New York, where he worked in radio and studied acting with Stella Adler. He changed his name because he thought Blieden had too many letters for a stage name. His big break came in 1957, when he secured a part in Joshua Logan's production of *Mr. Roberts.* He later performed in such Broadway plays as *Flower Drum Song* (1958), *The Apple Tree, Blues for Mr. Charlie, Luv, You Know I Can't Hear You When the Water's Running* (1969), and *Oh Men, Oh Women* (1953). Blyden appeared in TV plays, including *What Makes Sammy Run* and *Harvey.* He appeared as a host on "Personality," a daytime game show, and as John Daly's successor on "What's My Line?" Blyden arrived in Hollywood only after proving himself on professional TV and Broadway. His first movie was *The Bachelor Party,* written by Paddy Chayefsky. He won a Tony award as an actor in and coproducer of a revival of *A Funny Thing Happened on the Way to the Forum.* Two weeks before his death, he left the Broadway hit *Absurd Person Singular* after 250 performances. He received a Tony nomination for his work in the British farce. On April 17, 1954, Blyden married actress Carol Haney. They had two children and were divorced in 1961. Blyden died on June 7, 1975, in Agadir, Morocco, from injuries received in a car crash.

BIBLIOGRAPHY: Vertical Files, Barker Texas History Center, University of Texas at Austin. *Jeny Rydell*

BLYTHE CREEK. Blythe Creek rises eight miles southwest of DeKalb in southwestern Bowie County (at 33°28′ N, 94°44′ W) and extends southeast for fifteen miles before joining Weaver Creek to form Bassett Creek about twelve miles southeast of DeKalb (at 33°20′ N, 94°36′ W). The soils over which Blythe Creek flows are loamy in the upper reaches and clayey downstream. The land is generally heavily wooded, predominantly with post oak, blackjack oak, and elm.

B'NAI ABRAHAM SYNAGOGUE, BRENHAM. The B'nai Abraham congregation in Brenham was organized in 1885. Original Jewish settlers in the county included B. Levinson, who arrived in 1861, and the Alex Simon family, which arrived in 1866. These men became active in the business community of Brenham, and as other

Jewish settlers arrived, the need for a synagogue grew. The first building, constructed in 1892, burned; a second was built in 1893. L. Fink served as first president, F. Susnitsky as vice president, L. Z. Harrison as treasurer, and J. Lewis and Abe Fink as secretaries. The twenty charter members were led by Rabbi Israel. In the 1990s the synagogue was believed to be the oldest Orthodox synagogue to have been in continuous use in Texas.

bibliography: W. O. Dietrich, *The Blazing Story of Washington County* (Brenham, Texas: Banner Press, 1950; rev. ed., Wichita Falls: Nortex, 1973). Robert A. Hasskarl, Jr., *Brenham, Texas, 1844–1958* (Brenham: Banner-Press, 1958). Charles F. Schmidt, *History of Washington County* (San Antonio: Naylor, 1949). Vertical Files, Barker Texas History Center, University of Texas at Austin (Washington County). Ruthe Winegarten and Cathy Schechter, *Deep in the Heart: The Lives and Legends of Texas Jews* (Austin: Eakin Press, 1990).

James L. Hailey

BOALES, CALVIN (ca. 1800–1853). Calvin Boales, ranger officer and colonist in Sterling C. Robertson's[qv] colony, son of James and Elizabeth (Bradshaw) Boales, was born in Christian County, Kentucky, around 1800. His father was a native of Ireland. In January 1835 Boales left for Texas from Lawrence County, Mississippi. He, his wife, Frances Ann, and their three children were sworn as colonists in Robertson's colony on December 27, 1835. They settled on a labor of land on the Brazos River 1½ miles below the Nashville settlement in what is now Milam County. There Boales and his sons farmed. His headright league later became part of Collin County.

Boales served as fourth sergeant in Sterling C. Robertson's company of rangers, mustered into service on January 17, 1836. The company was organized at Viesca and headquartered at the falls of the Brazos River during 1836 to protect the colony from Indian depredations. Boales was captain of this company, a ranging detachment under Col. Edward Burleson,[qv] from July 1836 to January 1837. For his service he received a bounty land grant of 320 acres on the Little River in what is now Bell County. On February 20, 1836, Boales and sixty-seven other settlers in Robertson's colony (Milam Municipality) signed a memorial addressed to the Convention of 1836[qv] at Washington-on-the-Brazos. The petition stated that the signers were determined to assist the Texas government in conducting the war to a successful conclusion by defending the country from both Indian depredation and Mexican attack. They recommended the establishment of a separate "Register's Office," with records in English, so that they could obtain legal titles to their land and other settlers would be encouraged to come to Texas. This recommendation resulted in the establishment of the General Land Office[qv] of Texas on December 22, 1836.

As a citizen of Milam County, Boales signed a petition addressed to the Senate and House of Representatives of the Republic of Texas[qv] on April 20, 1838, requesting protection against Indians. He then served in a ranging company on the frontier of Milam County from March to June 1839 under Capt. George B. Erath.[qv] Boales further supported the Army of the Republic of Texas[qv] by providing food supplies to Col. Wheeler's troops on their march to the frontier in 1840.

He married Frances Ann Tandy of Virginia on June 22, 1826, in the Bethel Baptist Church, Christian County, Kentucky. In addition to the children that immigrated with them, they had four children in Texas. Boales died in February 1853 in Austin.

bibliography: Malcolm D. McLean, comp. and ed., *Papers Concerning Robertson's Colony in Texas* (19 vols., Fort Worth: Texas Christian University Press, 1974–76; Arlington: University of Texas at Arlington Press, 1977–92). *Caroline B. Bass*

BOARD, TEXAS (Navarro County). Board, a farming community on Board Creek three miles south of Pursley in southwestern Navarro County, was probably established in the early 1880s. A post office opened there in 1886, and by the turn of the century a school was in operation; in 1906 the school enrolled eighty-eight. The town, however, was in decline. The post office closed in 1904, and by the mid-1930s Board no longer appeared on highway maps.

Christopher Long

BOARD, TEXAS (Van Zandt County). Board was twelve miles northeast of Canton in northeastern Van Zandt County. When resident Jim Board met with the county judge and others to establish a local school on land donated by early settlers, the school was named in his honor. Enrollment reached twenty-six in 1905. The Board school was consolidated with the Wills Point Independent School District in 1949. Jones Cemetery, located in Board north of Farm Road 1395, dates to the 1870s and is all that remains of the Board and Jones communities.

bibliography: Van Zandt County History Book Committee, *History of Van Zandt County* (Dallas, 1984). *Diana J. Kleiner*

BOARD OF CONTROL. The Board of Control was established by the Texas legislature in 1919 and was composed of three members appointed by the governor for six-year, overlapping terms. The major duties of the board were to purchase supplies for the departments and eleemosynary and educational institutions of the state; control the state's public buildings and grounds; rent extra buildings and offices for state agencies; prepare the biennial appropriation budget and submit it to the governor; and control the state historical parks.

The Board of Control was responsible for the administration of the state's eleemosynary institutions until 1949, when administration was transferred to the new Board for Texas State Hospitals and Special Schools.[qv] In 1951 the Budget Division of the Board of Control was transferred to the governor's office. In 1953 the old Board of Control was reorganized, and a new one, composed of three part-time gubernatorial appointees, was established. The agency's functions included serving as the chief purchasing office for state departments and institutions, auditing and certifying to the comptroller of public accounts[qv] all claims for goods sold to the state, and operating and maintaining the Capitol[qv] and other state office buildings, grounds, the State Cemetery,[qv] and other state property in Austin. After the State Building Commission was established in 1954, that agency assumed the duties carried out by the Engineering Section of the Board of Control. The Sixty-fifth Legislature later abolished the State Building Commission and transferred duties back to the board.

In the 1970s the board's responsibilities included managing a system of telecommunications services for state agencies. It maintained a central office-supply store, messenger service, and telephone service, as well as an office-machine repair service. The agency was organized into six divisions: Central Purchasing, Centralized Services, Automated Services, Building and Property Services, Security, and Telecommunications Services. In 1979 the Board of Control was abolished and replaced by the State Purchasing and General Services Commission.

bibliography: Wilbourn E. Benton, *Texas: Its Government and Politics* (Englewood Cliffs, New Jersey: Prentice-Hall, 1961; 4th ed. 1977). Stuart MacCorkle and Dick Smith, *Texas Government* (New York: McGraw-Hill, 1964). Dick Smith, *A Layman's Guide to the Texas State Administrative Agencies* (Austin: Bureau of Municipal Research, University of Texas, 1945). Texas Research League, *Purchasing, Warehousing, and Distribution* (Report No. 10 in a survey of the Board for Texas State Hospitals and Special Schools, May 1955). *Dick Smith*

BOARD CREEK. Board Creek rises two miles northwest of Eldorado Center in southwestern Navarro County (at 31°52′ N, 96°40′ W) and flows northeast for fifteen miles before entering Richland Creek four miles west of Richland (at 31°55′ N, 96°30′ W). The stream crosses flat to rolling terrain surfaced with clayey and sandy loams that support water-tolerant hardwoods and grasses.

BOARD OF MANSION SUPERVISORS. The Board of Mansion Supervisors, established in 1931 to make plans and designs for repairs on the Governor's Mansion,[qv] including the grounds, furniture, fixtures, and interior decoration, consisted of three members appointed by the governor for six-year overlapping terms. Along with the Board of Control[qv] its consent was needed for any changes in furniture, fixtures, and equipment belonging to the state. The board was abolished in 1965, and its powers and functions were given to the Texas Commission on the Arts.[qv]

BOARD OF MEDICAL CENSORS. The Board of Medical Censors, a forerunner of the Board of Medical Examiners, was established on December 14, 1837, by the Congress of the Republic of Texas[qv] for the purpose of granting licenses to practice medicine and surgery in the republic. The law required that the board be composed of one physician from each senatorial district and that the members be graduates of medicine and surgery from authorized colleges and universities. A twenty-dollar fee was collected from those who passed an examination. Without a license, physicians could not collect unpaid fees in court. The first board was composed of Ashbel Smith[qv] from Harrisburg and Liberty, A. C. Hoxey[qv] from Washington-on-the-Brazos, George W. Hill[qv] from Milam, J. M. Neil Stuart from Brazoria, J. P. B. January[qv] from San Patricio, Refugio, and Goliad, R. A. Irion[qv] from Nacogdoches and Houston, Joel Johnson from Austin and Colorado, Isaac Jones from the Red River district, Thomas Anderson[qv] from Mina and Gonzales, A. M. Levy[qv] from Matagorda, Victoria, and Jackson, and H. Bissell from Bexar. The board was scheduled to meet once each year, but difficulty of transportation over long distances and Indian attacks frequently prevented annual meetings. The board was discontinued by a state legislative act of February 2, 1848.

BIBLIOGRAPHY: Sylvia Van Voast Ferris and Eleanor Sellers Hoppe, *Scalpels and Sabers* (Austin: Eakin Press, 1985). Pat Ireland Nixon, *The Medical Story of Early Texas, 1528–1853* (Lancaster, Pennsylvania: Lupe Memorial Fund, 1946). *John Q. Anderson*

BOARD OF PARDONS AND PAROLES. The Board of Pardons and Paroles releases inmates from the prison system[qv] and recommends clemency decisions to the governor of Texas. Board structure, powers, and responsibilities have altered since the institution's inception. In 1929 the Texas legislature abolished the two-member Board of Pardon Advisors, which had existed since 1893, and established a three-person body to advise the governor on clemency matters. Board members, who served for six-year terms, received their positions through gubernatorial appointment subject to state senatorial confirmation. The governor designated one member as chairman, and the board selected another as supervisor of paroles. Stanhope Henry, James R. Hamilton, and J. O. Woodward served as the first members of a board that functioned in a purely advisory capacity; governors could grant clemency without board approval or advice.

Clemency consists of such measures as full pardons, conditional pardons, paroles, reprieves, furloughs, and the restoration of citizenship rights for those convicted of crimes. A full pardon essentially forgives offenders for their crimes and restores all of their civil rights. A conditional pardon releases offenders from prison and extends forgiveness as long as individuals comply with certain conditions, such as good behavior. Failure to adhere to those conditions voids the clemency and subjects the offender to reimprisonment. Parole, also a conditional release, permits certain prisoners freed at the discretion of designated officials to serve their sentences outside of the prison under state supervision. Parolees who fail to comply with supervision or commit new offenses usually return to prison after the board revokes their parole. A reprieve suspends the execution of a sentence for a temporary period; at various times in the board's existence the terms *reprieve, furlough,* and *emergency parole* have all referred to temporary releases from prison for a specified time, followed by a return at the end of the time period. On numerous occasions, however, governors have extended temporary releases and granted conditional pardons to those initially freed for only brief periods. Clemency has also included such actions as the remission of fines and bond forfeitures, the restoration of driver's licenses, and the commutation or reduction of sentences, including the change of a death penalty to life imprisonment.

Parole was regarded during the 1930s as the most desirable release method because it required convicts to meet criteria associated with length of time served, offense category, behavior while confined, and rehabilitation potential. Equally important, parole enabled authorities to supervise the return of prisoners into the free world by counseling them and monitoring their behavior. Texas law from 1930 until 1947 authorized parole consideration for first time prisoners serving the minimum terms of a sentence for an indeterminate or indefinite number of years and at least one-third of a sentence for a determinate or definite period of time. State laws also permitted prison officials to deduct a certain amount of time from the sentences of prisoners who displayed exemplary behavior. However, statutes required that all prisoners serve a minimum of one calendar year in order to attain parole eligibility. Despite the parole law, most prisoners completed their full sentences, though often with reduced time due to good behavior. At least one governor, Ross S. Sterling[qv] (1931–33), attempted to permit early releases only through parole and furlough without granting pardons. His successor, Miriam A. Ferguson[qv] (1933–35), however, released some prisoners through parole and furlough, but chiefly granted full and conditional pardons. Texas governors, state release laws, and the board received extensive criticism during the early 1930s. Investigation reports from criminal-justice specialists decried the lack of social-welfare expertise among board members, all of whom were attorneys trained to make parole decisions from a strictly judicial approach unrelated to prisoners' potential for coping outside of prison. Investigators also complained about low salaries, the absence of adequate clerical assistance, the lack of formal procedural rules, and the failure by board members to interview individual prisoners. Above all, parole experts criticized the state's failure to provide supervision for those released on parole. Although some parolees complied with board reporting requirements through correspondence, most prisoners apparently failed to maintain contact with members. Parole revocations thus only occurred when law enforcement officials notified the board of new offenses committed by parolees.

Governor James Allred[qv] (1935–39), who had campaigned against the excessive leniency and alleged corruption of the Ferguson clemency policies, took several steps to improve the performance of the Board of Pardons and Paroles. In 1935, to provide supervision for parolees and prisoners released through conditional pardons, Allred established a system of voluntary county parole boards. Composed of representatives of various civic organizations, voluntary boards helped conditionally released prisoners obtain employment and otherwise readjust to free society. Allred required the volunteers to submit reports to the Board of Pardons and Paroles and to inform the governor concerning any violations of release conditions. By 1938 nearly 1,100 volunteers sat on boards of one to ten members in 243 counties. Voluntary boards existed in 250 counties by 1946; Allred's volunteer system remained the only supervisory agency for Texas parolees until 1957. Allred also supported passage of a successful 1936 state constitutional amendment that reorganized the Board of Pardons and Paroles and reduced the governor's role in the clemency process. The restructured board began operations in 1937 and consisted of three members: one appointed by the governor, another by the chief justice of the Texas Supreme Court, and a third by the presiding judge of the Texas Court of Criminal Appeals.[qv] Following state senatorial confirmation, board members held their positions for six-year overlapping terms. J. B. Keith, T. C. Andrews, and Bruce W. Bryant were the first members to serve under the new law. The board chose one member as its chairman, usually for a two-year term. Until 1947 one person retained an office in Huntsville, the headquarters of the Texas prison system, while the others worked in Austin. The new law required board recommendation for gubernatorial pardons, reprieves, commutations, and remissions of fine and forfeitures but allowed only the governor to revoke paroles and conditional pardons. The amendment gave the legislature authority to enact parole laws but did not expressly authorize parole powers for the governor. Allred, however, followed board recommendations and issued paroles subject to terms included in the 1930 eligibility law, granting conditional pardons in certain cases where prisoners might not meet parole criteria.

Governors who followed Allred issued conditional pardons rather than paroles. A Texas attorney general's opinion in 1946 determined that the 1936 amendment had not given governors the power to grant paroles; since the legislature had not provided for board issuance of paroles either, the attorney general decided that all past parole releases were in fact conditional pardons, and not subject to parole eligibility requirements. State officials nevertheless continued to refer to all persons released conditionally as parolees. The restructured board and Allred granted 650 conditional pardons and 50 paroles in 1937 while releasing another 195 prisoners through reprieves and furloughs. In 1942 and 1943 the board freed more than 2,000 individuals annually through conditional pardons and reprieves; in 1943 alone the county parole boards supervised nearly 3,500 parolees whom the board and governor had released over a period of years. Perhaps influenced by military and civilian personnel shortages associated with World War II, the number of prisoners freed by the board and the governor exceeded the number who completed their full sentences from 1942 through 1946.

Despite the initial political success and acclaim received by the voluntary county parole boards, the system attracted a growing number of critics who decried the shortcomings of volunteer officers. Observers cited the lack of professional training on the part of volunteers, inadequate time devoted to supervision, the failure of the state to provide adequate resources, and, in some instances, incompetent and inconsistent administration by a number of the volunteer boards. In 1947 the legislature passed a probation and parole law designed to establish a statewide system of professional officers to supervise parolees and probationers, certain offenders whom courts exempted from prison under suspended sentences contingent upon their good behavior. The legislature, however, refused to appropriate funds to implement the new law. This same law also altered parole eligibility by requiring prisoners to serve one-third of the maximum term of both determinate and indeterminate sentences; the measure established a fifteen-year ceiling as the maximum period necessary to attain parole consideration, regardless of sentence length. By 1950 the board was considering more than 10,000 prison cases and more than 2,000 other clemency cases; that year, members successfully recommended the issuance of more than 900 conditional pardons while supervising more than 2,400 parolees through the county volunteer boards. The following year Texas became the last state to join the Interstate Compact for the Supervision of Parolees and Probationers. This agreement allowed the board to supervise parolees and probationers who moved to Texas from other states and to arrange for the supervision of Texas parolees and probationers who desired to leave their state. During 1956 the board considered more than 13,000 prison cases and more than 2,000 other requests for executive clemency. The board granted more than 1,000 conditional pardons between August 31, 1955 and September 1, 1956.

Starting in September 1956, the board and the governor began issuing certificates of parole rather than conditional pardons. The board hoped the new documents would clarify the distinction between such terms as *parole* and *conditional pardon* and avoid confusion in other states under the Interstate Parole Compact. As the state's prisoner population expanded during the 1950s, prison officials urged the legislature to fund parole supervisors as a means for reducing overcrowding; prison director Oscar Byron Ellis[qv] suggested that expert supervision would permit the safe release of large numbers of prisoners. In 1957, the legislature, persuaded by the urgings of Ellis and other criminal justice observers, enacted a new probation and parole law that funded the hiring of paid parole supervisors. Texas was one of the last three states to adopt a professional parole system. The law separated probation and parole functions and required counties to supervise probationers. Vincent O'Leary, former chief of paroles and probations for the state of Washington, became director of the Texas system and hired the first seventeen officers in December 1957; by the end of August 1958 the board had employed the remaining twenty-three officers. Voluntary county boards remained to supervise parolees in remote areas of the state. The forty parole officers and their five supervisors, along with the voluntary boards, were overseeing almost 4,000 cases by 1960; the legislature authorized an additional thirty officers in 1961, when for the first time since 1946 the number of parolees almost equaled those who completed their full sentences.

The 1957 probation and parole law also exempted some prisoners from the 1947 rule that required them to serve a third of their sentence before attaining parole eligibility. According to the new, somewhat confusing, provisions, prisoners who had served minimum terms of indeterminate sentences, where the maximum number of years was less than four times as great as the minimum, could receive parole consideration. Also, in those instances where the maximum sentence exceeded the minimum terms by four times, prisoners could attain parole after serving one-fourth of the maximum sentence periods. In 1965 the legislature again revised eligibility laws, effective January 1, 1966, by providing that all prisoners need only serve one-fourth rather than one-third of their sentences in order to achieve parole consideration. In 1967, however, the legislature returned parole eligibility to the one-third requirement that had existed prior to the 1965 law and the 1957 modifications. In 1966 the board considered more than 28,000 prison cases and more than 2,000 other clemency cases; the governor approved more than 2,000 board recommendations; parole officers supervised approximately 2,600 Texas parolees and more than 600 parolees from other states, but only 38 percent of Texas prisoners received their releases through parole that year. Under the Interstate Compact, the board also supervised 400 out-of-state probationers through voluntary county parole officers and county probation offices. Board activity increased throughout the 1960s. By 1970 the board was considering more than 23,000 prison cases and paroling more than 2,000 inmates; another 3,000 prisoners completed their sentences without parole or conditional release.

During the 1970s the legislature enacted a number of measures designed to help the board deal with an increasing volume of activity. A 1975 act provided for the appointment of six parole commissioners to assist the board with prison cases. The measure authorized the governor, the chief justice of the Texas Supreme Court, and the presiding judge of the Court of Criminal Appeals each to appoint, with senatorial confirmation, two commissioners for six-year terms. Parole commissioners did not consider nonprison clemency cases, nor did the new law involve them in administrative matters. Board members and parole commissioners sat together in three-member panels to grant, deny, and revoke paroles. The law mandated that three commissioners live near Huntsville, where they could interview prisoners eligible for parole. The legislature authorized an additional three commissioners during 1982. The board began contracting for halfway houses to serve certain released prisoners in 1976. The following year, the legislature tightened parole eligibility requirements for certain offenses. Those convicted of aggravated sexual assault, aggravated robbery, aggravated kidnapping, or any felony involving the use or exhibition of a deadly weapon, were to serve at least one-third (the measure required a minimum of at least two years and a twenty-year maximum) of their sentence in calendar time, irrespective of any possible reduction of time for good behavior. Also in 1977 the legislature expanded the activities of parole officers. All prisoners convicted after August 29, 1977, who did not make parole but instead completed their sentences due to reduced time for good behavior, would receive mandatory supervision from parole officers during the time remaining on their original sentences.

Federal court orders against overcrowding and a reluctance to construct new penal facilities, despite an increasing prisoner population, greatly expanded board activity in the 1980s. By 1980 the agency employed more than 230 parole officers, although state laws permitted the board to use volunteers to supplement the professional staff. Two years later the board was reviewing more than 24,000 cases and successfully recommending the parole of more than 7,000 prisoners; the board also contracted for thirty-seven halfway houses in 1982 and assumed responsibility for more than 4500 prisoners through mandatory supervision. In 1983 Texas voters approved a constitutional amendment that significantly altered the board's structure and powers. The amendment removed the governor from the parole process, although the governor retained clemency powers for nonprison cases and could grant full and conditional pardons, reprieves, commutations of sentences and fines, remissions of bond forfeitures, and the restoration of civil rights and driving privileges. A related statute authorized the board to grant and revoke paroles without gubernatorial approval and increased the board to six members, all appointed by the governor subject to senatorial confirmation; the governor named the chairman and vice chairman, while the board received authorization to hire nine parole commissioners. In 1984 the board implemented specialized caseloads to enable officers to oversee certain categories of released prisoners requiring intensive supervision, such as sex offenders, mentally retarded persons, and potential repeat offenders. By the following year the board was supervising more than 35,000 former prisoners statewide; for the first time following enaction of the 1977 law, the number of individuals under mandatory supervision exceeded those released through parole. Parole officers in six counties began electronic monitoring of some high-risk offenders in 1987. The board and parole commissioners considered more than 49,000 cases, paroled more than 25,000 prisoners, and released 7,000 individuals through mandatory supervision in 1988. More than 1,500 agency employees, including about 700 parole officers, supervised approximately 52,000 released prisoners in the state's 254 counties. More than 9,500 individuals resided in halfway houses. In 1989, to alleviate overcrowding in state jails, the board contracted with a private security company for the establishment of a parole-violator facility in San Antonio.

The legislature significantly reorganized state criminal-justice institutions in 1989 by merging the prison system, the Adult Probation Department, and the administrative and parole-supervision duties of the Board of Pardons and Paroles into a new Texas Department of Criminal Justice, effective in 1990. However, a separate Board of Pardons and Paroles remained to consider prison releases and to revoke parole and mandatory supervision violators. The new law abolished the parole commissioners, increased the number of board members to eighteen gubernatorial appointees serving six-year terms, gave the governor authority to appoint the board chairman, and removed the board from Austin, placing members at five different locations in close proximity to various state prison facilities. The board continued to make gubernatorial clemency recommendations for reprieves, commutations, and restoration of civil rights. In 1990 the board considered more than 71,000 prison cases and released more than 42,000 prisoners to the Parole Division of the Texas Department of Criminal Justice. Numerous changes in parole and release laws occurred in 1987. Legislation adopted that year relaxed parole eligibility by requiring persons convicted for offenses on or after September 1 of that year to serve one-fourth of their sentences rather than the one-third required by the previous law. Persons convicted of "capital" murder, aggravated offenses, and those involving the use or display of a deadly weapon were to serve the one-fourth minimum, but not more than fifteen years of their sentence in calendar time in order to qualify for parole consideration. Another 1987 act prohibited release under mandatory supervision for those guilty of aggravated offenses, capital murder, use of a deadly weapon, deadly assault on law enforcement or corrections officers, injury to a child or elderly person, arson, or certain categories of robbery and burglary.

Following publicity surrounding the release of infamous criminals during the late 1980s, the legislature tightened parole eligibility standards. A 1991 law mandated that persons sentenced to life for "capital" murder serve a minimum of thirty-five years before they could receive parole consideration; two years later, the legislature raised the minimum period to forty years. Also in 1993 the legislature replaced earlier parole laws for violent offenders with measures that raised eligibility requirements to the highest levels in the state's history. Those convicted of aggravated offenses, including acts involving the use of deadly weapons, were to serve the shorter time equal to one-half of the maximum sentence (thirty years). Another 1993 law required a two-thirds vote from the entire Board of Pardons and Paroles, rather than a majority vote from a three-person panel, before prisoners serving time for "capital" murder could receive parole.

Although the board has sometimes been criticized for slow release when prisons were overcrowded, it has more often been the object of public ire for releasing parolees who subsequently committed heinous crimes. Major controversies have especially ensued in instances where parolees have paid individuals to assist their release by the board. The influence exerted by consultants, legislators, or others with close ties to board members and governors has precipitated accusations of favoritism, injustice, and corruption from prisoners, state officials, the media, and private citizens. Recognizing the potential for conflicts of interest, Governor Allred during 1937 asked the legislature to prohibit its members from practicing before the board, but the state's lawmakers denied his request. A former board chairman who served during the 1950s remembered "extreme pressure from some state senators" who would "threaten to cut our salary to $1 a year if we didn't go along with them on paroles." In 1947 a Texas Senate committee report castigated the board for "gross abuse of discretion" in relation to numerous clemency recommendations. The committee determined that the board had irresponsibly suggested gubernatorial clemency for many repeat offenders and prisoners who displayed poor behavior, such as attempting to escape. Noting inconsistent decisions, the committee also faulted the board for disregarding formal procedures and for the close relationship that existed between one board member and "professional clemency seekers." Irrespective of sentence lengths or the nature of their crimes, prisoners able to pay parole consultants often received favorable treatment from board members. Although the committee criticized Governor Coke R. Stevenson's[qv] (1941–47) acceptance of board recommendations without proper study, the report called for the board's abolition and suggested that the governor's office handle all future clemency policies. The legislature rejected the proposal but in 1947 adopted a law that required individuals testifying before the board to file signed affidavits stating whether or not they had received a fee for their services. The board, however, did not implement the affidavit requirements until 1953.

Prisoners seeking release continued to hire consultants to expedite their cases before the board. As during the 1940s, publicity surrounding the release of notorious criminals who had retained paid parole representatives and then committed serious crimes prompted public outrage in the late 1980s and early 1990s. Legislative investigators in 1989 and 1992 discovered that certain parole consultants solicited prisoners and their families and contacted board members and employees to request "special" reviews as well as favorable release and revocation decisions. The investigators located other instances in which consultants exploited inmates with exorbitant and often unrefundable fees, though they provided few actual services. Some former board members and agency employees, including a former chairman, had even acted as parole consultants after terminating their board employment. Though the legislature did not specifically enact measures in 1989 to regulate parole consultants, it did write a general state ethics law that prohibited former board members and regulatory-agency employees for two years from practicing before the agency that had employed them. As controversies concerning parole consultants and poor parole decisions intensified, however, the legislature adopted a number of new laws in 1993 that strictly regulated parole consulting for the first time in the board's history. The prohibition against practice by board members and agency employees extended to ten years after leaving the board or terminating employment. Only attorneys licensed in Texas could represent prisoners for compensation; representatives were required to reveal any business associations with current and former board members and employees. On August 10, 1994, a federal court issued a five year probated perjury sentence to former board chairman James Granberry. Granberry had cast a favorable vote that paroled former death row inmate Kenneth McDuff, whom law enforcement officials later suspected of killing as many as nine women after his release. After resigning from the board in 1991, Granberry had worked as a parole consultant, representing individual prisoners before the board he had formerly chaired. He admitted that he had given false testimony to a federal magistrate about the number of prisoners he had represented after leaving the board. Granberry's punishment consisted of an order to perform 150 hours of community service and a requirement that he reside for six months in a halfway house.

Between 1990 and 1994, as the state embarked upon a massive prison-expansion program, the board sharply curtailed parole releases; whereas the board had approved 79 percent of all parole cases in 1990, it approved only 39 percent in 1993. A special report prepared by the Texas comptroller of public accounts in 1994 characterized parole as "the least understood and least popular aspect of the criminal justice system" and urged the legislature to transfer parole supervision from the Texas Department of Criminal Justice to community supervision and corrections departments throughout the state. Such a proposal suggested a system that at least partly resembled the decentralized county parole board supervision that had existed prior to the employment of paid parole supervisors beginning in 1957.

BIBLIOGRAPHY: James Allred Papers, Special Collections, University of Houston. Gary Cartwright, "Free to Kill," *Texas Monthly,* August 1992. Price Daniel Papers, Sam Houston Regional Library and Research Center, Liberty, Texas. Stuart A. MacCorkle, "Pardoning Power in Texas," *Southwestern Social Science Quarterly* 15 (December 1934). *The Prison Labor Problem in Texas* (Washington: Prison Industries Reorganization Administration, 1937). Jack Ross, *Parole and Executive Clemency in Texas* (Austin: Board of Pardons and Paroles, 1966). Vertical Files, Barker Texas History Center, University of Texas at Austin.

Paul M. Lucko

BOARD FOR TEXAS STATE HOSPITALS AND SPECIAL SCHOOLS. The Board for Texas State Hospitals and Special Schools was established by the Fifty-first Legislature in the spring of 1949 to govern the state hospitals and state schools formerly under the jurisdiction of the Board of Control.[qv] A nine-member board, of which no more than three could be physicians, was appointed by the governor, with concurrence by the Senate, to six-year overlapping terms. The board approved budgets for the central office and each individual institution. In 1956 the board exercised oversight of twenty-two hospitals and special schools. It was abolished in 1965 and its duties transferred to other departments, primarily the Texas Department of Mental Health and Mental Retardation.[qv]

BOARDTREE CREEK. Boardtree Creek rises west of the Illinois Bend oilfield in northeastern Montague County (at 33°51′ N, 97°33′ W) and runs north for three miles to its mouth on the Red River, west of Illinois Bend on the Texas-Oklahoma border (at 33°54′ N, 97°33′ W). It crosses flat terrain with local shallow depressions surfaced by clay and sandy loam that supports water-tolerant hardwoods, conifers, and grasses.

BOARD OF WATER ENGINEERS. The Board of Water Engineers, established by the Texas legislature in 1913, was composed of three members appointed by the governor for six-year terms. One of the members was then made chairman and served as the chief administrative officer. The major duties of the board were to approve plans concerning the organization of irrigation[qv] and water-supply districts, approve the issuance of bonds by such districts, issue permits for storage and diversion of water, and make plans for storage and use of floodwater. In 1949 the legislature gave the board the power to define and designate underground water reservoirs and authorize underground water-conservation districts. In 1955 the board was granted the authority to approve federal projects requiring the governor's approval. This included any related construction done by the United States Army Corps of Engineers. The board was also required to employ a chief engineer at that time. The Board of Water Engineers dealt with matters concerning state surface-water appropriation and the collecting of related data. It conducted groundwater examinations and studied the effects of silt in streams, water runoff, and evaporation. In 1956 the board employed eighty-five full-time employees who worked within the various divisions of the agency: administrative, statistical and publications, permits and appropriations, surface water, and ground water. In 1962 the title of the Board of Water Engineers was changed to the Texas Water Commission,[qv] and the agency was reorganized three years later to become the Texas Water Rights Commission.[qv] *Laurie E. Jasinski*

BOATRIGHT, ELIZABETH KEEFER (1899–1989). Elizabeth Keefer Boatright, etcher and watercolorist, the daughter of James Blair and Estelle (Cherry) Keefer, was born in Houston, Texas, on November 4, 1899. She decided that she would pursue a career in art after she won second place in a nationwide art contest for children when she was seven. She attended the Southern Seminary in Virginia from 1915 to 1917 and then began studying art under a Mrs. Creager, whom she accompanied to Washington, D.C. Always a person of independence and strong opinion, Elizabeth decided she was being taught in the wrong way and returned to Houston, but was more determined than ever to learn to paint. In 1920 she enrolled at the Art Institute in Chicago where she studied until 1924. That year she went to New York to study at the Art Students League. She left because of the death of her mother but returned the next year at the request of Joseph Pennell, the etcher, to become his assistant. In the fall of 1926 she joined the faculty of Sul Ross State College in Alpine, Texas, as art instructor. There she became interested in western themes, particularly Indians. She visited reservations in northern New Mexico and was the first white woman given permission to sketch there. She married Mody C. Boatright[qv] in 1931 but did not join him in Austin until the end of the 1931–32 school year; they had two children. She continued to work in Indian materials, doing graphic arts and etchings from 1929 to 1937 and watercolors from 1927 to 1947. She worked in Taos, Idelfonso, and Conchiti Pueblo. She became known as the "Etcher of Indians." Some of her more notable etchings include *The Sand Painter* (Navajo), *Storm Cloud on Wind* (1927, Navajo), *Black Eagle Dance* (Pueblo), and *Singing in the Moonlight* (Taos). This last item was selected as one of the hundred best etchings of 1934. She developed a technique for making etchings with color. No other etcher in the country had used the process. The United States Museum of Graphic Arts in Washington in 1934 invited her to send a solo show of thirty etchings, and from that show her *Hurrying Lady* was selected to become part of the permanent collection.

Elizabeth Boatright gave up etching when she saw her young son perilously close to a container of acid she used in her work. After that she devoted her energies almost entirely to watercolor painting, although she occasionally worked in oil. As an opponent to the abstract painting taught by the art faculty at the University of Texas she was challenged by a faculty member, who suggested that she was incapable of producing abstract art; she proceeded to paint a 45″-by-60″ abstract that was highly successful. She then returned to doing watercolor landscapes. In the late 1940s and into the 1960s she organized art classes in towns in the Austin area. These classes resulted in art clubs and an increased interest in art that still continues. After the death of her husband in 1970 she moved to Corpus Christi and began painting seascapes. Her *Fisherman's Wharf* was selected to go on tour in Mexico with a show of American art. Except for an interim in Georgetown, she lived in Corpus Christi for the rest of her life. Early on she was elected to the Pen and Brush Club in New York (1925) and the Chicago Society of Etchers (1930). She later became a member of the Texas Fine Arts Association [qv] and the Texas Watercolor Society. The list of shows in which her work was displayed covers some twelve typed pages. In 1936, for example, her work was displayed in Dallas, Buffalo, New York (on two occasions), Santa Fe, Philadelphia, Fort Worth, and Austin. Her work is in the permanent collections of the Southwestern Museum of Art, Los Angeles; the Museum of New Mexico, Santa Fe; the United States National Museum of Graphic Arts, Washington; the Feldman Collection, Dallas; the Texas Memorial Museum [qv] and the Texas Fine Arts Association, Austin; and the Museum of the Big Bend, [qv] Alpine. She was known primarily as Elizabeth Keefer to the art world. Her own selection of her most outstanding works includes *The Sand Painter* (a good example of her use of color in etchings), *Storm Cloud on Wind, Black Eagle Dance,* and *Singing in the Moonlight.* Elizabeth Keefer Boatright died on February 20, 1989, in Corpus Christi.

BIBLIOGRAPHY: Doris Dawdy, *Artists of the American West* (3 vols., Athens, Ohio: Swallow, 1974–86). Peter Haskins Falk, ed., *Who Was Who in American Art* (Madison, Connecticut: Sound View, 1985). Mantle Fielding, *Dictionary of American Painters, Sculptors and Engravers* (New York: Struck, 1945; rev. ed., ed. Glenn B. Opitz, Poughkeepsie: Apollo, 1983). Esse Forrester-O'Brien, *Art and Artists of Texas* (Dallas: Tardy, 1935). Vertical Files, Barker Texas History Center, University of Texas at Austin.

Ernest B. Speck

BOATRIGHT, MODY COGGIN (1896–1970). Mody Boatright, folklorist and educator, the son of Eldon and Frances Ann (McAuley) Boatright, was born in Mitchell County, Texas, on October 16, 1896. He was the youngest of ten children in a ranching family and the grandnephew of pioneer cattlemen and merchants Mody and Sam Coggin of Brownwood. In early years he was educated alternately by a governess on the ranch and at school in town. He finished his high school education at West Texas State Teachers College (now West Texas A&M University), where he earned a delayed bachelor's degree in 1922, after serving two years in the army in 1917–19. He received his master's degree at the University of Texas in 1923 and his Ph.D. there in 1932. He taught at Sul Ross State Teachers College from 1923 until 1926, when he joined the staff of the University of Texas. Except for one year, 1934–35, when he was at the College of Mines and Metallurgy (now the University of Texas at El Paso), he remained at the University of Texas until he retired in 1968, rising through the ranks from junior instructor to full professor and chairman of the English department. Boatright began his career as a folklorist in 1925, when sJ. Frank Dobie [qv] asked him to contribute a tale, "The Devil's Grotto," to the next publication of the Texas Folklore Society. [qv] In 1934 Boatright published *Tall Tales from Texas Cow Camps,* a collection of stories he had learned in his youth and later from cow-country students. *Gib Morgan: Minstrel of the Oil Fields* (1945), Boatright's second collection of tall tales, moved from the ranch to the oil patch. It presented the career and stories of a folk character comparable to Mike Fink or Johnny Appleseed. The book won him national recognition as a folklorist.

Unlike many of his contemporaries who embellished folk tales with literary touches, Boatright retold stories in an unadorned and concise style much closer to true folk narration and recognized that in oral performance these tales were very molded by the immediate situation of their telling. His work stressed the importance of studying folklore in its total cultural context and of relating it to the lives of those who practiced it. Boatright published *Folk Laughter on the American Frontier* in 1949. In this book he delineated the nature of the tall tale, explored many areas of folk humor, and demonstrated that frontier humor was not born of despair but was a manifestation of the buoyancy and optimism of the frontiersmen. This work, like *Tall Tales from Texas Cow Camps,* was innovative in suggesting that folklore may arise out of conflict between different social groups, a view at variance with the then-common notion that folklore was the result of the shared experiences of an isolated "folk."

In 1937 Boatright joined Dobie in editing the annual collections published by the Texas Folklore Society. In 1943 he became secretary and editor of the society; he edited annual publications until 1964. As principal editor, often with coeditors such as Donald Day, [qv] Allen Maxwell, and especially Wilson M. Hudson, he edited thirteen volumes of folklore in addition to the five volumes he worked on with Dobie. He was elected a fellow of the American Folklore Society in 1962 and was also a vice president of the society in the same year. He was chosen a fellow of the Texas Folklore Society in 1968, an honor previously accorded only Leonidas W. Payne, Jr., John A. Lomax, [qqv] and J. Frank Dobie. *The Family Saga and Other Phases of American Folklore,* a collection of lectures delivered by Boatright, Robert B. Downs, and John T. Flanagan, appeared in 1958. In it Boatright points out that family stories are often a fertile source of folklore. In 1963 Boatright published *Folklore of the Oil Industry,* the fruition of some twenty years of research. The book explores the introduction of traditional character stereotypes and motifs into the oil fields. Boatright was among the first American folklorists to study the traditions of an emerging modern industry. His investigations into folk activities in the oil fields continued, and in 1970 he published, with William A. Owens, *Tales from the Derrick Floor,* a pioneer work in oral history. Boatright also wrote on such topics as folklore in a literate society, the relationship between popular literature and national folk heroes, and myth in the modern world, studies which attested his belief that individuals in complex, industrialized societies are not so different from "folk" or "primitive" ones as is sometimes supposed. Three years after his death *Mody Boatright, Folklorist,* a collection of his essays, was published. In 1925 Boatright married Elizabeth Reck, with whom he had a daughter. His first wife died in 1929, and in 1931 he married Elizabeth E. Keefer (*see* BOATRIGHT, ELIZABETH K.), with whom he had a son. Elizabeth, an artist, illustrated his first two books. Boatright was a lifelong Democrat and a member of the Texas Institute of Letters [qv] and of the Writers Guild. He died in Abilene on August 20, 1970, after a heart attack.

BIBLIOGRAPHY: Ernest B. Speck, ed., *Mody Boatright, Folklorist: A Collection of Essays* (Austin: University of Texas Press, 1973). Ernest B. Speck, *Mody C. Boatright* (Austin: Steck-Vaughn, 1971).

Ernest B. Speck

BOATWRIGHT, THOMAS (1760–ca. 1830). Thomas Boatwright, early Texas settler, was born in Virginia, moved to Illinois, and by 1819 was living in old Miller County, Arkansas. In the early fall of 1821 he and his wife, Amy, and their ten children traveled with the Gilleland, Kuykendall, Williams, and Gates families down Trammel's Trace [qv] to Nacogdoches. In early December they left for Austin's Spanish land grant and arrived at the La Bahía [qv] Crossing on the Brazos River on December 31, 1821. They immediately crossed over into Austin's land grant, traveled ten miles beyond the crossing, and on the last day of 1821 camped beside a flowing stream, now known as

New Year Creek, in Washington County, Texas. Here, the families of Thomas Boatwright and Abner Kuykendall[qv] settled until they received their land grants in 1824.

On July 27, 1824, Boatwright was granted a league of land now in Austin County, Texas, fronting upon the Brazos River. His son-in-law, Daniel Gilleland,[qv] received a grant of a labor in the southeast corner of Boatwright's grant. Neither the Boatwright nor the Gilleland families ever lived on these grants. About 1825 Boatwright and his family returned to Miller County, Arkansas, with numerous other families who had settled in Austin's colony, to protest the United States agreement with the Choctaw Indians that gave to the Indians all of the property owned by these settlers in Miller County, Arkansas. They were unsuccessful in their protests, and the Boatwrights moved to Pope County, Arkansas, where Boatwright died; he was still listed in the 1830 census, but by 1833 his wife was a widow. In 1833 Amy Boatwright and three of her sons, Thomas, Friend, and Richard, were back in Texas making applications for land grants. Mrs. Boatwright was seventy-two. On October 24, 1835, she received a grant of a league then in Montgomery County and now part of Madison County. She died by 1839.

bibliography: Worth Stickley Ray, *Austin Colony Pioneers* (Austin: Jenkins, 1949; 2d ed., Austin: Pemberton, 1970).

John G. Gilleland and Thomas R. Underwood, Jr.

BOAZ, HIRAM ABIFF (1866–1962). Hiram Abiff Boaz, Methodist bishop and college administrator, was born in Murray, Kentucky, on December 18, 1866, the son of Peter Maddox and Louisa Ann (Ryan) Boaz. In 1873 his family moved to Tarrant County, Texas. After his graduation from Sam Houston Normal Institute (now Sam Houston State University), he taught in Fort Worth. He received B.S. (1893) and M.A. (1894) degrees from Southwestern University, the latter with highest honors. After ordination to the Methodist ministry, he served churches in Fort Worth, Abilene, and Dublin. In 1902 he became president of Polytechnic College (later Texas Wesleyan University) in Fort Worth, where he remained for nine years. After a brief period as vice president of Southern Methodist University during its formation, he returned to Polytechnic College and stayed for five years.

Following two years as secretary of the Methodist Board of Church Extension in Louisville, Kentucky, in 1920 Boaz became the second president of Southern Methodist University, where he served until his election as bishop in the Methodist Episcopal Church, South, in 1922. After four years as bishop in the Far East, he returned to the United States to serve as bishop in Arkansas, Oklahoma, Texas, and New Mexico. After retiring in 1938 he initiated and continued to help with the sustentation campaign for Southern Methodist University, through which Dallas citizens contributed to the university. Boaz was given honorary degrees by several institutions. He was a trustee of Southern Methodist and Southwestern universities. His publications include an autobiography, *Eighty-four Golden Years* (1951). Boaz was married to Carrie Odalie Brown on October 4, 1894; they had three daughters. He died in 1962 at the age of ninety-five and was buried in Dallas.

bibliography: *Mustang* (publication of the Southern Methodist University Alumni Association), January–February 1962. *Who's Who in the South and Southwest,* Vol. 2. *Howard Grimes*

BOAZ, TEXAS. Boaz was between Brown's and Wolf creeks sixteen miles south of Gatesville in southeastern Coryell County. It was sometimes called Dunn's House, after John C. Dunn, who served as postmaster when the post office opened there in 1885. The community, presumably named for the biblical Boaz, in 1890 had a mill, a gin, a Baptist church, and thirty residents. By 1896 its population had risen to fifty. The Boaz post office was discontinued in 1912, and mail for the community was sent to Tama. The site became part of the Fort Hood military reservation in the early 1940s.

bibliography: Coryell County Genealogical Society, *Coryell County, Texas, Families, 1854–1985* (Dallas: Taylor, 1986). John J. Germann and Myron Janzen, *Texas Post Offices by County* (1986).

Vivian Elizabeth Smyrl

BOBCAT HILLS. The Bobcat Hills begin three miles southwest of McCamey in the southwest corner of Upton County and extend across the county line into Crockett County. They are flanked by U.S. Highway 385, Farm Road 1901, and the Pecos River. Their summit (at 31°06′ N, 102°16′ W) has an elevation of 2,695 feet. The hills are composed of a limestone and calcareous clay substrate surfaced with shallow, stony clay loams in which grow juniper, oak, grasses, chaparral, and cacti.

BOB CREEK. Bob Creek rises four miles west of U.S. Highway 83 in southern King County (at 33°27′ N, 100°21′ W) and runs south for five miles to its mouth on the Salt Fork of the Brazos River, in northern Stonewall County (at 33°23′ N, 100°20′ W). It passes steep slopes surfaced by clay and sandy loams in which grow juniper, cacti, scrub brush, and sparse grasses.

BOBIDA INDIANS. In 1683–84 Juan Domínguez de Mendoza[qv] led an exploratory expedition from El Paso eastward as far as the junction of the Concho and Colorado rivers east of the site of present San Angelo. In his itinerary he listed the names of thirty-seven Indian groups, including the Bobidas, from whom he expected to receive delegations. This name does not appear in later documents. It is possible that Mendoza's Bobidas were the same as the Boboles (Babeles), who at the same time lived in northeastern Coahuila but ranged northward across the Rio Grande into the southwestern part of the Edwards Plateau,[qv] but this identity has yet to be demonstrated. If there is no relationship between the two, then it seems likely that the Bobidas were one of many groups in north central Texas that were swept away by the Lipan Apache and Comanche advance of the eighteenth century.

bibliography: Vito Alessio Robles, *Coahuila y Texas en la época colonial* (Mexico City: Editorial Cultura, 1938; 2d ed., Mexico City: Editorial Porrúa, 1978). Herbert Eugene Bolton, ed., *Spanish Exploration in the Southwest, 1542–1706* (New York: Scribner, 1908; rpt., New York: Barnes and Noble, 1959). Charles W. Hackett, ed., *Pichardo's Treatise on the Limits of Louisiana and Texas* (4 vols., Austin: University of Texas Press, 1931–46). *Thomas N. Campbell*

BOBO, TEXAS. Bobo is on U.S. Highway 84 twelve miles northwest of Center in northwestern Shelby County. The settlement grew up in the mid-1880s as a stop on the newly built Houston, East and West Texas Railway. A post office operated there from 1893 to 1898. In 1896 the community reported a general store and a population of ten. In the mid-1930s Bobo had a church, a sawmill, and a number of houses. After World War II[qv] many of its residents moved away, but in the early 1990s a church, two cemeteries, and a few scattered houses still remained there.

bibliography: Charles E. Tatum, *Shelby County: In the East Texas Hills* (Austin: Eakin, 1984). *Christopher Long*

BOBOLE INDIANS. This was one of the more important groups of Indians of northeastern Coahuila during the latter half of the seventeenth century. At times the Boboles (Babeles), who spoke a Coahuiltecan language, were in settlements on or near the Rio Grande in the present Eagle Pass area, and they also crossed into Texas to hunt bison in the southwestern part of the Edwards Plateau, particularly in the area of present Kinney and Edwards counties. Bobole males also accompanied various Spanish exploratory and military expeditions that crossed the Rio Grande into Texas. In 1665 about 300 Bobole warriors were with Fernando de Ascué when he penetrated southern Texas and decisively defeated the Cacaxtles. Later, in 1675, twenty-two Boboles were with the Bosque-Larios expedition,[qv] which crossed the Rio Grande near modern Eagle Pass. It is possible that the Boboles were the same people as the Bobidas on the list of tribes made by Juan Domínguez de Mendoza.[qv] This list was made when Domínguez was at the junction of the Colorado and Concho rivers east of the site of present San Angelo in 1684. If the two are identical, then the Boboles ranged much farther north in the western Edwards Plateau region than has been realized. Another Indian group with a similar name, Bobori, lived somewhere between Durango, Mexico, and Presidio, Texas, in 1693, but the relationship of these Boboris to the Boboles of northeastern Coahuila remains undetermined.

BIBLIOGRAPHY: Vito Alessio Robles, *Coahuila y Texas en la época colonial* (Mexico City: Editorial Cultura, 1938; 2d ed., Mexico City: Editorial Porrúa, 1978). Herbert Eugene Bolton, ed., *Spanish Exploration in the Southwest, 1542–1706* (New York: Scribner, 1908; rpt., New York: Barnes and Noble, 1959). Charles W. Hackett, ed., *Historical Documents Relating to New Mexico, Nueva Vizcaya, and Approaches Thereto, to 1773* (3 vols., Washington: Carnegie Institution, 1923–37).

Thomas N. Campbell

BO BRANCH. Bo Branch rises in a tank two miles west-northwest of Bylers Point Church in west central Fayette County (at 29°54′ N, 97°07′ W) and runs southwest for 3½ miles to its mouth on Buckners Creek (at 29°51′ N, 97°08′ W). It crosses land with a fine, friable sandy loam surface and firm clay subsoil that primarily support grass for cattle. Among other plants in the area are mixed oaks and cedars with an understory of yaupon that provides good wildlife habitat.

BOBVILLE, TEXAS. Bobville is at the crossing of Bobville Road and the Atchison, Topeka and Santa Fe Railway, a mile south of Dobbin and twenty miles west of Conroe in western Montgomery County. In 1878 the Central and Montgomery Railway line from Navasota to Montgomery was built through the Bobville area. A man named Glen, who worked for the Santa Fe line, named the water tank and depot. The community was established sometime after 1887 as a lumber-shipping point on the Gulf, Colorado and Santa Fe. Around 1906–07 the Trinity and Brazos Valley Railway came through a mile east of Bobville, and some businesses and residents moved to Bobbin, later called Dobbin, on the railroad junction. By 1910 Bobville had a population of 100. A post office operated there from 1911 to 1919. By 1915 Bobville had a population of 200, a telephone connection, and three general stores. The town had a church and several scattered dwellings during the mid-1940s. Though a 1986 map showed Bobville with a railroad switch and several houses near the rail line, by 1990 the Bobville switch and depot were gone, and only a few ranches off Bobville Road and a few stores east of town remained.

BIBLIOGRAPHY: Montgomery County Genealogical Society, *Montgomery County History* (Winston-Salem, North Carolina: Hunter, 1981).

Will Branch

BOCA CHICA BAY. Boca Chica Bay is five miles southeast of Port Isabel and three miles northeast of the mouth of the Rio Grande off the extreme southeastern part of Cameron County (centered at 26°00′ N, 97°09′ W). It is two miles long and is bounded on the north by Brazos Island, on the east by Del Mar Beach, on the southeast by Boca Chica Beach, and on the southwest and west by Mesa del Gavilán. *Boca Chica* is Spanish for "little mouth."

BOCHERETE VILLAGE. Bocherete (Bocrettes, Tserabocherete) was an Indian village mentioned to Henri Joutel[qv] in 1687. It was said to be north or northwest of the Colorado River in a region occupied mainly by the Tonkawa Indians. The precise site has not been identified.

BIBLIOGRAPHY: Frederick Webb Hodge, ed., *Handbook of American Indians North of Mexico* (2 vols., Washington: GPO, 1907, 1910; rpt., New York: Pageant, 1959). Henri Joutel, *Joutel's Journal of La Salle's Last Voyage* (London: Lintot, 1719; rpt., New York: Franklin, 1968).

Margery H. Krieger

BODAN CREEK. Bodan Creek (Boden Creek, Bodane Bayou), rises just west of Central in northwest Angelina County (at 31°27′ N, 94°49′ W) and flows southwest for 12½ miles to its mouth on the Neches River (at 31°23′ N, 94°57′ W). The surroundings are typical of the East Texas piney woods, where the flat to moderately rolling land is surfaced with red sandy clays and loams that support pine and hardwood forests.

BODANSKY, MEYER (1896–1941). Meyer Bodansky, medical scientist, was born at Elizabetgrad, Russia, on August 30, 1896, one of seven children of Phineas and Eva Bodansky. He immigrated to the United States with his family in 1907. He received his B.A. degree from Cornell University in 1918, his M.A. from the University of Texas in 1922, his Ph.D. from Cornell in 1923, and his M.D. from the University of Chicago in 1935. He married Eleanor Abbott, and they had two daughters.

Bodansky began his research in metabolism immediately after he finished his undergraduate work at Cornell. He was an instructor in biological chemistry at the University of Texas Medical Branch from 1919 to 1923 and an adjunct professor from 1923 to 1925. He left Galveston in 1925 to teach for a year at Stanford University and returned to UTMB as an associate professor in 1926. In 1930 he became a full professor of pathological chemistry. He also directed the laboratories at John Sealy Hospital[qv] and John Sealy Memorial Research Laboratory. In 1932–33 he served as visiting professor of physiological chemistry at American University in Beirut, Lebanon. During this productive period he wrote *Introduction to Physiological Chemistry* (1937) and *Laboratory Manual of Physiological Chemistry* (1939), both standard textbooks in biochemistry. With his brother, Dr. Oscar Bodansky, who served as chief of biochemistry at Sloan-Kettering Institute for Cancer Research, he wrote *Biochemistry of Disease* (1940), which was translated into several languages and used worldwide in medical schools. He published over 100 scientific articles and papers as well. Bodansky pioneered chemical investigation into calcium absorption, vitamin deficiencies, kidney diseases, and endocrine functions. In 1937 the Texas Pathological Society presented him its award for outstanding work in medical research, proclaiming his monograph on "The Chemistry of Heart Action" the "greatest contribution to medical science by a Texan during the preceding year." Bodansky died of a pulmonary infection on June 14, 1941, at the height of his career.

BIBLIOGRAPHY: Galveston *Daily News*, June 15, 1941. *The University of Texas Medical Branch at Galveston: A Seventy-five Year History* (Austin: University of Texas Press, 1967).

Natalie Ornish

BODIE, TEXAS. Bodie, a farming community just southwest of Longview in east central Gregg County, was established around 1900 as a station on the International–Great Northern Railroad. It was named for Gabriel Augustus (Bodie) Bodenheim, long-time mayor of Longview. In the mid-1930s the settlement had a church, several stores, a mill, and a number of houses. In the early 1990s Bodie was a dispersed rural community, and many of the area's residents worked in nearby Longview.

BIBLIOGRAPHY: Eugene W. McWhorter, *Traditions of the Land: The History of Gregg County* (Longview, Texas: Gregg County Historical Foundation, 1989).

Christopher Long

BOERNE, TEXAS. Boerne, the county seat of Kendall County, is located on Cibolo Creek, Interstate Highway 10, and U.S. Highway 87 thirty miles northwest of San Antonio in the southern part of the county. In 1849 a group of German colonists from Bettina[qv] camped on the north side of Cibolo Creek, about a mile west of the site of present Boerne. They called their new community Tusculum, after Cicero's home in ancient Rome. In 1852 Gustav Theissen and John James laid out the townsite and changed the name to Boerne in honor of Ludwig Boerne, a German poet and publicist. A post office was established in 1856 with August Staffell as postmaster. The community had only ten houses in 1859, but it was chosen as county seat by a margin of sixty-seven votes after the county was established in 1862. A courthouse was built in 1870 and was still in use in the 1990s; it was thus the second-oldest courthouse in the state. Boerne developed the reputation of having a very healthful environment and quickly became known as a health resort. By 1884 it had five hotels, assorted businesses, and 250 residents. Cotton, wool, and grain were the principal shipments, but timber, cedar posts, and building stone were also profitable commodities. The arrival of the San Antonio and Aransas Pass Railway in 1887 brought increased economic opportunity, and by 1890 the population of Boerne had risen to 800.

Boerne residents voted to incorporate in 1909 and established a mayor-alderman form of city government. Also in that year they established the Boerne Independent School District. The population was reported at 950 in 1914, and the community prospered through the 1920s. The Great Depression[qv] of the 1930s, however, all but put an end to the tourism and cotton farming that had been staples of the local economy. The population fell from an estimated 2,000 in 1928 to 1,117 in 1931; it had risen to only 1,271 by the 1940s. In the 1950s, however, many residents turned to nearby San Antonio for employment, and Boerne became a bedroom community. The population grew at a slow but steady rate, reaching 2,169 in 1960. In the 1960s construction in neighboring Bexar County of the San Antonio Medical Center and the University of Texas at San Antonio, as well as the completion of Interstate Highway 10, made Boerne even more attractive as a town from which to commute. Its population rose to 2,400 by 1970, 3,254 by 1980, and 4,274 by 1990.

In spite of the influx of different ethnic groups, the German cultural tradition has dominated the community in many ways. The Boerne Gesangverein, or singing society, which was established in 1860, was an important social and recreational organization until it disbanded in 1977; German community organizations still active in 1990 included the Boerne Schuetzen Verein (shooting club), which was formed in 1864, and the Boerne Village Band, which was formed about the same time as the singing society. Boerne has also held an annual celebration, the Berges Fest, since 1967.

BIBLIOGRAPHY: Kendall County Historical Commission, *A History of Kendall County, Texas* (Dallas: Taylor, 1984). Garland A. Perry, *Historic Images of Boerne, Texas* (Boerne: Perry Enterprises, 1982). Vertical Files, Barker Texas History Center, University of Texas at Austin.

Vivian Elizabeth Smyrl

BOERNE VILLAGE BAND. The Boerne Village Band was organized in 1860 by Karl Dienger in Boerne, the county seat of Kendall County. Having previously organized the Boerne Gesang Verein (singing club), Dienger organized the band to complement the singing festivals in Boerne with band music. He coordinated both musical groups from 1860 to 1885. Ottmar von Behr, who moved with his family to Sisterdale in the 1840s, was a strong influence in the band. Two of his children, Jennie and Ottmar, played with the group, and Jennie's husband, Fritz Fisher, taught his nephews, Ottmar, Jr., Arthur, and Oscar, to play musical instruments. In time, both Oscar and Ottmar Behr became directors of the band. Later, Oscar's daughter, Roma, married Alvin Herbst, and their son Kenneth, a veterinarian in Boerne, became the band director. His sons Kenneth, Jr., and Clint also became members. In all, the descendants of the Behr family have included four generations of musicians and three generations of directors for the Boerne Village Band.

The Boerne Village Band managed to stay organized and practiced in barns during the difficult Civil War[qv] period. After the war it continued to practice and play at various events in and around Boerne. During World War I and World War II[qqv] the band was less active but remained organized. After World War II Ottmar Behr, despite losing his son Calvin in Normandy, reassembled the group, with Erhard Ebner, Henry Schrader, Eugene Ebell, Alvin Grosser, Fritz Grosser, Harry Grosser, and others participating.

In 1988 the Federal Republic of Germany recognized the Boerne Village Band for its contribution to the German heritage in Texas and America by donating to it much traditional German music and a magnificent tenor horn. For the band's 130th anniversary in 1990, Peter Fihn, a noted German composer, dedicated and presented his march, "Grüsse an Texas" ("Greetings to Texas"), to the band. In 1991 the Texas Legislature adopted a resolution to recognize the Boerne Village Band for "keeping alive German music as part of our heritage." The City of Boerne and the Boerne Area Historical Preservation Society have also recognized the band for its contribution to the German heritage of Boerne. Additionally, in 1988 the Federal Republic of Germany presented Dr. Kenneth C. Herbst, director of the band since 1972, with its Friendship Award. Otto Schicht, a special friend in Bavaria, helped obtain authentic uniforms for the band, which were first worn during its 1986 Texas Sesquicentennial performances. On May 2, 1992, Dr. and Mrs. Herbst and other invited guests attended a luncheon given by the president of Germany, Richard von Weizsaeker, during his state visit to Houston, where he commended the German musical tradition in Boerne.

Acclaimed as "the Oldest Continuously Organized German Band in the World outside Germany Itself," the Boerne Village Band continued in 1993 to practice weekly. With sixteen members and several associates, the band continued to perform regularly at the Texas Folklife Festival,[qv] the New Braunfels Wurstfest, the Kendall County Fair, the Boerne Berges Fest, Boerne Abendkonzerte (summer evening concerts), and many other events.

BIBLIOGRAPHY: Garland A. Perry, *Historic Images of Boerne, Texas* (Boerne: Perry Enterprises, 1982). *Robert H. Thonhoff*

BOFECILLOS CANYON. Bofecillos Canyon, in southern Presidio County, begins on the north side of Elephant Mountain (at 29°28′ N, 104°02′ W) and runs west for ten miles to its mouth on the Rio Grande, eight miles southeast of Fort Leaton State Historic Site[qv] (at 29°29′ N, 104°12′ W). It crosses the eroded volcanic terrain of the Bofecillos Mountains area and terminates in the gravel terrace of the Rio Grande floodplain. The soils in the area are generally sands and clay loams, often rough and stony. The vegetation consists primarily of sparse desert shrubs.

BOFECILLOS MOUNTAINS. The Bofecillos Mountains are surrounded by Bofecillos Canyon on the north, Tapado Canyon on the southeast, and Redford Bolson on the south and southwest, in southern Presidio County (at 29°27′ N, 104°05′ W). Their elevations range from 4,922 feet above sea level (Panther Mountain) to 5,137 (Oso Mountain). The Bofecillos are composed of conglomerate, sandstone, tuff, and basalt. Loose rubble covers their surface. The surrounding desert mountain terrain is cut by numerous rugged canyons. Sparse grasses, cacti, and desert conifers and oak shrubs grow in the area. In 1852 the boundary survey expedition of Maj. William H. Emory[qv] passed through the Bofecillos Mountains.

BOGATA, TEXAS. Bogata, at the junction of U.S. Highway 271, State Highway 37, and Farm Road 909 in southwestern Red River County, serves a farming and ranching area and houses employees of firms in Paris, Clarksville, and Mount Pleasant. Oil and gas are produced in the vicinity but not in bonanza quantities. The town's population, which grew slowly through the decades when most of the area was losing ground, reached 1,508 in 1980, when Bogata had a 154-bed nursing home, medical and dental clinics, a locally owned bank, and thirty business establishments.

Bogata may be the oldest Anglo-American settlement in North Texas. William and Mary McGill Humphries settled near springs on Little Mustang Creek in 1836 and called the settlement that grew up around them Maple Springs. Humphries had come to the area as a teenager in 1818 with the Nathaniel Robbins[qv] party. After his father's death in 1821 he accompanied his mother "back east" but eventually returned to Texas with his young family on learning of Sam Houston's[qv] victory at San Jacinto. Mary Humphries's life was a paradigm of the westward movement. She was born in Carolina in 1809 and was four times moved to new frontiers—as an infant to Tennessee, as a child to Alabama, as a young woman to Mississippi, and finally to Texas, where she lived until 1899.

By 1844 the Maple Springs community comprised enough families to support a school. A post office followed in 1851. Commercial development began after the Civil War[qv] with the opening of a store selling goods freighted from Jefferson. In 1880 the settlement divided, apparently as a result of increasing growth. The old Maple Springs post office adopted the name of Rosalie, and in 1881 a second post office opened a few miles to the west, slightly north of the site of present Bogata. When the United States government refused to accept Maple Springs as the new post office's name, postmaster James E. Horner submitted an alternative. Horner, who had a romantic enthusiasm for Latin-American republican revolutions against Spanish rule, suggested the name Bogotá, after the Colombian capital, which was the scene of his hero Simón Bolívar's victory in 1814. The suggestion was accepted, but, perhaps owing to Horner's penmanship, the name was misspelled Bogata. The town inhabitants accepted the official spelling but pronounce the name "Buh-góh-ta."

During the 1880s both communities sent their children to a school taught by Sorg Scales; among Scales's students was future vice president John Nance Garner.[qv] By 1885 Bogata had two churches, four cotton gins, six gristmills, and a population of 400. In 1910 the town's second newspaper, the *News*, replaced its predecessor, the *Reformer*. The Paris and Mount Pleasant Railway arrived in 1910, causing the town to move its commercial establishments to a new main street nearer the railroad tracks. Train service was discontinued in 1956. In 1990 the population was 1,421.

BIBLIOGRAPHY: Travis Hale, The History of Bogata (MS, Archives, East Texas State University, 1950). Iva Lassiter Hooker, *History of Bogata* (1982). Red River County Historical Association Files, Red River County Public Library, Clarksville, Texas. Jack Rogers, History of Bogata (MS, Archives, East Texas State University, 1930). Kathleen E. and Clifton R. St. Clair, eds., *Little Towns of Texas* (Jacksonville, Texas: Jayroe Graphic Arts, 1982). Rex W. Strickland, "Miller County, Arkansas Territory," *Chronicles of Oklahoma* 18 (March 1940).

John M. Howison

BOG CREEK. Bog Creek, also known as Hog Creek, rises two miles north of East Mountain in southeastern Upshur County (at 32°37′ N, 94°52′ W) and flows northeast for seven miles to its mouth on Clear Creek, two miles northwest of Bethlehem (at 32°41′ N, 94°49′ W). The stream is intermittent in its upper reaches. It traverses rolling terrain surfaced by moderately deep to deep clayey sand that supports mixed hardwood and pine forests and grasses.

BOGGIE CREEK. Boggie Creek rises five miles northwest of Westhoff in central DeWitt County (at 29°15′ N, 97°24′ W) and runs southwest for five miles to its mouth on Sandies Creek, four miles east of Westhoff (at 29°11′ N, 97°24′ W). It crosses flat to rolling prairie surfaced by calcareous clay that supports mesquite, prairie grass, and scrub brush. The streambed is known for quicksand.

BOGGY BRANCH (DeWitt County). Boggy Branch rises seven miles south of Cuero in central DeWitt County (at 28°59′ N, 97°21′ W) and runs southeast for seven miles to its mouth on Five Mile Creek (at 28°56′ N, 97°17′ W). It traverses flat to rolling terrain surfaced by highly permeable soil that supports scrub brush and grasses.

____ (Fayette County). Boggy Branch rises in a wooded area a mile northwest of Round Top High School in northern Fayette County (at 30°05′ N, 96°42′ W) and runs southeast for about 2½ miles, past the school and the north side of Round Top, to its mouth on Rocky Creek (at 30°04′ N, 96°41′ W). Throughout most of its meandering course its banks are steeply sloping and wooded with a mixture of oak and cedar and an understory of yaupon. The sandy loam topsoil in the area overlies firm clay. Slopes render the land better for unimproved pasture and wildlife habitat than for agriculture.

BOGGY CREEK (Colorado County). Boggy Creek rises near the right-of-way of the Missouri, Kansas and Texas Railroad in northern Colorado County (at 29°56′ N, 96°32′ W) and runs southwest seven miles to its mouth on Cummins Creek, four miles east of Fayetteville (at 29°54′ N, 96°36′ W). The stream was originally named Andrews Creek, in honor of John Andrews, who received a land grant nearby in July 1824. Much of the creek's course parallels the MKT tracks. The local terrain is gently sloping and is surfaced with loamy silt or clay topsoils over a mottled clay subsoil. In 1887 the MKT completed its line from Denison to Boggy Tank on its way to Houston. Boggy Tank was a swampy area that gave the creek its current name. The railroad built a turntable there. The town of Pisek was moved to its site on the creek and remained active until the 1940s. The lowlands along the creek are covered with oaks, cedar, yaupon, wild grape, and sumac.

____ (Leon County). Boggy Creek, a spring-fed perennial stream, rises eight miles southwest of Centerville in southwestern Leon County (at 31°12′ N, 96°07′ W) and flows east for twenty-three miles to its mouth on the Trinity River, twelve miles east of Leona (at 31°07′ N, 95°47′ W). Midway down its course the creek forms Hayden Lake. It traverses nearly level terrain surfaced by sandy and loamy soils that along the creek banks support post oak, black hickory, pecan, elm, water oak, and hackberry. The first settlers' building in the county was a two-story blockhouse constructed on the north bank of the upper creek in 1840. The structure, known as Fort Boggy because of the marshy condition of the creek bottom, was intended to protect settlers in the region between the Navasota and Trinity rivers north of the Old San Antonio Road.[qv] Since the 1880s Flynn has been located on the south bank of the upper creek. Cairo and Middleton are on the north bank of the lower creek.

____ (Throckmorton County). Boggy Creek is formed by the confluence of North and South Boggy creeks in north central Throckmorton County (at 33°17′ N, 99°09′ W). North Boggy Creek rises about five miles south of the Baylor county line (at 33°20′ N, 99°17′ W) and flows southeast for ten miles. The south fork begins ten miles northwest of Throckmorton (at 33°18′ N, 99°15′ W) and runs east for about seven miles. After the confluence, Boggy Creek continues eastward through Elbert, then flows into western Young County. Its mouth on the Brazos River is three miles north of Proffitt (at 33°14′ N, 98°54′ W). The stream crosses an area of rolling hills surfaced by clay and sandy loams that support scrub brush, mesquite, cacti, grasses, live oak, and juniper.

BOGUS SPRINGS, TEXAS. Bogus Springs was in the Rodessa oilfield a mile east of McLeod in southeastern Cass County. The community had ten residents and one rated business in the mid-1930s and twenty residents and one business in the mid-1950s. By 1986 Bogus Springs no longer existed as a named community. In the early 1900s there was a community in Cass County named Baugus Springs, after the local Baugus family. This was probably an earlier name for the same settlement.

BIBLIOGRAPHY: Atlanta (Texas) *Citizens Journal*, August 4, 11, 1904. *Cass County Cemeteries: Texas Records* (Atlanta, Texas: Cass County Genealogical Society, 1976). *Cecil Harper, Jr.*

BOHEMIA, TEXAS. Bohemia was on the banks of the Main (Middle) Concho River south of the road from San Angelo to Arden and on the old road from San Angelo to Sherwood in west central Tom Green County. George Hagelstein, who owned 12,000 acres of land on the Middle Concho River, began dividing it into farms for sale early in 1906, and plans were made for a townsite to be called Twin Mountain City. When the plat for the town was filed in March, the name had been changed to Bohemia. The settlement comprised thirty families when William Limbrugger was appointed postmaster there on March 27, 1907. Bohemia soon had a general store, a school, at least one saloon, a livery stable, and a cemetery. As many as 100 people, mostly Czech immigrants from farther east, lived there from 1906 to around 1909. The land, however, was not well-suited to agriculture. The community's post office was discontinued on June 30, 1909. By 1910 most of the farmers, after trying to supplement their incomes by gathering pecans and cutting wood, had decided to move. Most of them either went back to East Texas or moved to the Lipan Flats area of Tom Green County and the Rowena area of Runnels County. After major highways and the railroad bypassed the town, the site was completely abandoned.

BIBLIOGRAPHY: Julia Grace Bitner, The History of Tom Green County, Texas (M.A. thesis, University of Texas, 1931).
Betty Jane Smith

BOHEMIAN. The *Bohemian*, published quarterly from 1899 to 1905 by a Fort Worth club called Our Literary Club in Bohemia, claimed to be the "first and only literary magazine, not of Texas alone, but of the South." The club and magazine were founded in 1898 by Mrs. Henrie C. L. Gorman and others for self-improvement and the development of Southern literature. Business and professional men, teachers, and other amateur writers contributed factual articles, fiction, and poetry. The World's Fair Edition in 1904 featured articles on Texas history. The magazine collapsed for lack of funds. *Elizabeth Woodcock*

BOHEMIAN, TEXAS. Bohemian, also known as Bohemian Community, was off State Highway 94 four miles northeast of Groveton in northeastern Trinity County. The settlement was formed around 1920 by immigrants from Czechoslovakia. Many of the settlers originally lived in Cedar Rapids, Iowa, before moving to Trinity County. The group was led by Augustin (August) Dolezal, who operated a bakery in Groveton. Some Czechs settled in Groveton; others established farms northeast of the town. Most residents, however, moved out of the area after World War II.[qv] In the 1980s few traces of the community remained; a cemetery built by the first settlers was overgrown, and most of the graves had been removed.

BIBLIOGRAPHY: Patricia B. and Joseph W. Hensley, eds., *Trinity County Beginnings* (Groveton, Texas: Trinity County Book Committee, 1986). Trinity County Historical Commission, *Trinity County Cemeteries* (Burnet, Texas: Nortex, 1980). *Christopher Long*

BOHLS, SIDNEY WILLIAM (1898–1969). Sidney William Bohls, pathologist and public health researcher, was born on April 12, 1898, in Pflugerville, Texas, the son of Emil H. and Julia (Pfluger) Bohls. After serving in the United States Army during World War I,[qv] he entered the University of Texas in Austin; he graduated in 1921 and received an M.D. degree from the University of Texas Medical Branch in 1926. Bohls completed an internship at Santa Rosa Hospital in San Antonio and did postgraduate study at the Rockefeller Institute and Harvard Medical School.

When the Pasteur Institute, the Laboratory of the Pure Food Commission, and the Bacteriological Laboratory were consolidated in 1928, Bohls was appointed director of laboratories for the Texas Department of Health.[qv] Under his direction, the first production of typhoid vaccine and diphtheria toxoid was made available to Texans. His state laboratory was the fifth in the country to be licensed for the manufacture of biological products for use in immunization activities. Bohls was also a pioneer in research on relapsing fever, typhus, and smallpox vaccines. During World War II[qv] the services of the laboratory were extended to include the processing of blood plasma for civilian emergency use.

Bohls was a leader in rabies research and control. He published more than thirty scientific papers in state and national journals. Under his direction, the accredited schools of medical technology were organized at Brackenridge and Austin State hospitals.[qqv] He entered private practice in clinical pathology in 1959 and was consulting pathologist for hospitals in Austin and throughout the state at the time of his death.

Bohls was a member of the Texas Medical Association,[qv] the American Medical Association, the Southern Medical Association, the Travis County Medical Society, and the American Public Health Association. He was a fellow of the College of American Pathologists, a diplomate of the American Board of Pathology, and president of the Texas Society of Pathologists and of the Texas Public Health Association. He was a founding member of the First English Lutheran Church in Austin. He was married to the former Claryce Manning Pitts. They had no children. Bohls died on June 24, 1969, in an Austin hospital.

BIBLIOGRAPHY: Austin *American-Statesman*, June 27, 1969. Howard E. Smith, *History of Public Health in Texas* (Austin: Texas State Department of Public Health, 1974). *Texas Medicine*, September 1969.
Patricia L. Jakobi

BOICE, HENRY S. (1860–1919). Henry S. Boice, rancher and manager of the XIT Ranch,[qv] was born in Las Vegas, New Mexico, in 1860, the son of a local physician. He began working as a cowboy at age fifteen for fifteen dollars a month. Since his contemporaries were mostly native New Mexicans, he spoke mainly Spanish throughout his youth. Beginning in 1878 Boice worked for Henry W. Cresswell's[qv] ranch near Pueblo, Colorado, where he became foreman at age twenty-one and subsequently Cresswell's partner. Boice also ran his own cattle, branded LK connected. When Cresswell drove his herd down to the Panhandle[qv] of Texas, he put Boice in touch with David Berry, a New York financier, who also owned a herd in Pueblo County. The result was the formation of the Berry-Boice Cattle Company, in which Boice managed the range and supervised the buying and selling of cattle.

In 1881 Boice moved the company herd, branded with three sevens, to a choice range along Palo Duro Creek in Ochiltree and Hansford counties. The Three Sevens Ranch was mainly a steer operation, and Boice contracted for steers throughout the Southwest, purchasing 25,000 a year. Most of these were shipped from the Panhandle to ranges in North Dakota. Because of his extensive travels, he gained perhaps the widest knowledge of ranchers and cattle among his contemporaries. Cresswell and other Panhandle ranchers were counted among his circle of friends. In 1885 Boice trailed the remainder of his Three Sevens cattle to North Dakota and closed out his Panhandle operation. By that time the Berry-Boice Company was operating on a grand scale, mostly in the badlands along the Little Missouri River. There Boice became acquainted with Theodore Roosevelt and Gregor Lang, whose ranches bordered his own. By 1896 Boice was the leading shipper of grass-fed young steers through the Chicago commission firm of Clay, Robinson and Company.

Boice was among the first to buy purebred bulls and breed up his stock. The Kansas firm of Gudgell and Simpson, established in 1879 to import bulls for breeders, sold him several prize bulls, especially Herefords. Boice went to Independence, Missouri, to do business with Charles Gudgell, and met Gudgell's daughter LuBelle, whom he married in 1891; they had three sons and two daughters.

When the Berry-Boice Company closed out in 1897, Boice formed the H. S. Boice Cattle Company and purchased the Beatty brothers' ranch, with headquarters at Point of Rocks on the Cimarron River, near the point where the Oklahoma, Kansas, and Colorado boundaries meet. The firm shipped from the railroad towns of Texhoma and Arkalen, Oklahoma, a fact that necessitated a drive of more than a hundred miles to load the cattle. Since only Hereford bulls were used, Boice's herd grew in both quality and quantity during the decade of the ranch's existence. Although his family resided at Kansas City most of the year, they spent summers at Point of Rocks, where the sons gained valuable ranching experience. During this period Boice and several partners formed a livestock loan and commission company in Kansas City, but this enterprise soon fell into financial straits, and the partners lost everything. Boice accepted the general managership of the XIT Ranch in 1905 and moved his family to Channing, in Hartley County, Texas. By 1906 he had closed out the H. S. Boice Cattle Company, and two years later he began investing in the Block Ranch, in the Carrizozo-Roswell area of New Mexico, and the Chiricahua Cattle Company in southern Arizona. Boice remained with the XIT until it closed out its cattle operations in 1912. As the Capitol Freehold Land and Investment Company's[qv] last general manager, he won a reputation for his refusal to smoke, drink, or swear and for possessing "a will like a rock." R. L. Duke was among the range foremen who worked under him.

After 1912 Boice and his family settled at the Chiricahua (CCC) Ranch, which he and his partners reorganized as the Boice, Gates, and Johnson Cattle Company. Boice died on the ranch in December 1919. His two oldest sons, Henry and Frank, and their sons continued Boyce's successful efforts at improving their stock of purebred Herefords.

BIBLIOGRAPHY: Cordia Sloan Duke and Joe B. Frantz, *6,000 Miles of Fence: Life on the XIT Ranch of Texas* (Austin: University of Texas Press, 1961). J. Evetts Haley, *The XIT Ranch of Texas and the Early Days of the Llano Estacado* (Chicago: Lakeside, 1929; rpts., Norman: University of Oklahoma Press, 1953, 1967). Pauline D. and R. L. Robertson, *Cowman's Country: Fifty Frontier Ranches in the Texas Panhandle, 1876–1887* (Amarillo: Paramount, 1981).

H. Allen Anderson

BOILING MOUNTAIN. Boiling Mountain is on the Uvalde county line twenty-four miles northeast of Brackettville in far northeastern Kinney County (at 29°31′ N, 100°07′ W). With an elevation of 1,981 feet above sea level, its summit rises 700 feet above Montell, six miles to the east. The mountain is named for a nearby spring.

BOIS D'ARC, TEXAS. Bois d'Arc is at the intersection of Farm Road 860 and State Highway 19, fifteen miles northwest of Palestine in northwestern Anderson County. In the 1930s the settlement had a church, a single business, a number of dwellings scattered along the road, and a district school. In 1932 the Bois d'Arc school enrolled forty-five. By 1955 it had been consolidated with the Montalba school. In 1985 Bois d'Arc was a small crossroads community with two businesses, a church, and several homes.

BIBLIOGRAPHY: Thomas Paul Jones, The Reorganization of the Public Schools of Anderson County, Texas (M.Ed. thesis, University of Texas, 1934).

Mark Odintz

BOIS D'ARC CREEK (Collin County). Bois d'Arc Creek rises three miles east of Copeville in southeast Collin County (at 33°05′ N, 96°21′ W) and runs southeast for eight miles through moderate to gently rolling land with clayey soils. It is crossed by Farm Road 1778 and the St. Louis, Southwestern and Missouri, Kansas, and Texas railroads before joining the Sabine River a mile from Royce City in northeast Rockwall County (at 32°59′ N, 96°19′ W). In the late nineteenth century the trees along the banks of the creek provided a source of timber for the city of Dallas.

BIBLIOGRAPHY: J. Lee and Lillian J. Stambaugh, *A History of Collin County* (Austin: Texas State Historical Association, 1958).

—— (Grayson County). Bois d'Arc Creek rises two miles northwest of Whitewright in southeastern Grayson County (at 33°32′ N, 96°26′ W), runs northeast across Fannin County, and eventually forms a natural boundary between Fannin and Lamar counties before its confluence with the Red River (at 33°50′ N, 95°51′ W). The stream, intermittent in its upper reaches, is sixty miles long. It flows over the permeable, clayey soils of Grayson County and the highly calcareous Catalpa clay of Fannin County. South of Bois d'Arc Creek in Fannin County is a cove, part of a chalk escarpment. As a sizable tributary to the Red River, Bois d'Arc Creek was significant to the early history of Fannin County. Along it the settlement of the county progressed rapidly after the arrival of Daniel Rowlett[qv] and six families in early 1836. En route to the Alamo, David Crockett[qv] wrote to his family about "Bodark Bayou," the richness of the area, and the possibility that he would settle in the vicinity. Fort Inglish,[qv] which provided protection for the early settlers of Fannin County, was located on Bois d'Arc Creek. The stream also provided the original name of the county seat, which was called Bois d'Arc at its establishment in 1843 but renamed Bonham in 1844.

BIBLIOGRAPHY: R. L. Jones, "Folk Life in Early Texas: The Autobiography of Andrew Davis," *Southwestern Historical Quarterly* 43 (October 1939, January 1940). Rex Wallace Strickland, "History of Fannin County, Texas, 1836–1843," *Southwestern Historical Quarterly* 33, 34 (April, July 1930).

Donna J. Kumler

BOIS D'ARC AND SOUTHERN RAILWAY. The Bois d'Arc and Southern Railway was constructed in the mid-1920s by the East Texas Road and Gravel Company in order to exploit the gravel deposits in Kaufman County. The line, considered a tram road at first, ran seven miles between Bois d'Arc station on the Texas and New Orleans line in Dallas County and the Byron station in Kaufman County. The gravel company chartered the road on July 9, 1934. The capital was $10,000, and the business office was located at Randol, two miles south of Bois D'Arc in Kaufman County. Members of the first board of directors included Edmund P. Gaines, Jr., J. Fred Schoellkopf, Jr., Wilson Schoellkopf, G. O. Moore, G. A. Nettleton, Hugo Schoellkopf, and E. E. Newcomer, all from Dallas.

In 1935 the line was designated a common carrier by the Railroad Commission.[qv] This decision was met with bitter protest from large Texas railroads on the grounds that it would open a legal door through which other Texas gravel companies could earn a division of rates for their freight. After a lengthy legal dispute a compromise was reached in 1938 whereby the Bois d'Arc and Southern was recognized as a common carrier on intrastate traffic. The road was abandoned in 1946.

Mark Howard Atkins

BOISE, TEXAS. Boise is on the Chicago, Rock Island and Pacific Railroad just south of Interstate Highway 40, twenty miles west of Adrian in southwestern Oldham County. It emerged as a shipping point for area ranchers and farmers, and mail was routed through Adrian. The depot was used until the 1980s, when the Rock Island discontinued its services in the Panhandle.

H. Allen Anderson

BOLD SPRINGS, TEXAS. Bold Springs is on Farm roads 350 and 942 eighty-five miles north of Houston in west central Polk County. One of a series of small communities known collectively as the Louisiana Settlement,[qv] Bold Springs was established during the 1840s and named after the springs in the area. A Baptist church was organized there in 1849. The community subsequently had a small turpentine distillery. The Bold Springs post office was known as Nettie, after the postmistress, Nettie Burgess, and operated from 1903 to 1923. A few scattered residences and a church remained in 1984. In 1990 the population was 100.

BIBLIOGRAPHY: *A Pictorial History of Polk County, Texas, 1846–1910* (Livingston, Texas: Polk County Bicentennial Commission, 1976; rev. ed. 1978). *Robert Wooster*

BOLES, JOHN (1895–1969). John Boles, stage and screen star, the son of John Monroe and Mary Jane (Love) Boles, was born on October 27, 1895, at Greenville, Hunt County, Texas. In early childhood he demonstrated an affection and talent for acting and singing. After graduating from the University of Texas in 1917, he returned to Greenville, where he was one of many "locals" selected by an out-of-town producer to act in an opera at the King Opera House. This experience convinced him that he preferred music and the stage to the preference of his parents, a medical degree and a doctor's practice. On June 21, 1917, Boles married Marielite Dobbs and, submitting to his parents wishes, decided to attend medical school.

For two years in World War I[qv] he served in the army intelligence service. After the war Boles studied music in New York. His voice, physique, and handsome face led to his selection as the lead in the 1923 Broadway musical *Little Jesse James*. He quickly became an established star of Broadway and attracted the attention of Hollywood producers and actors. Gloria Swanson persuaded him to travel to Hollywood and star in the film *Loves Of Sunya* (1926). After portraying Capt. Jim Stewart in *Rio Rita* (1929) he accepted the lead of Red Shadow in the *The Desert Song* (1930) and became a matinee idol.

His arrival in Hollywood coincided with the introduction of talkies. Unlike many of his colleagues, Boles made the transition from silent to sound films with few problems. He acted in over a dozen films during the 1930s, normally playing a successful, sophisticated, urban businessman. He played opposite Barbara Stanwyck in *Stella Dallas* (1937), Rosalind Russell in *Craig's Wife* (1936), and Shirley Temple in *Curley Top* (1935), *Littlest Rebel* (1935), and *Stand Up and Cheer* (1934). He also had roles in *Frankenstein* (1931) and *Back Street* (1932). By the end of the decade, however, Boles's fame waned, and he left movie-making for eleven years. Over the decades he had saved his money and invested it in the oil business in Texas. In 1943 he starred with fellow Texan Mary Martin[qv] in *One Touch of Venus* on Broadway. He returned to the screen in *Babes in Baghdad* in 1952. From the mid 1950s, however, he lived and worked in San Angelo, Texas. There on February 27, 1969, he suffered a stroke and died. He was survived by his wife and two daughters.

BIBLIOGRAPHY: San Angelo *Standard Times*, February 28, 1969. Vertical Files, Barker Texas History Center, University of Texas at Austin. *David Minor*

BOLES HOME. Boles Home is one of the largest children's homes supported and maintained by the Church of Christ. The institution, originally Boles Orphans' Home, was funded by William Foster and Mary Barnhart Boles. In 1923 the couple donated 436 acres of land near Quinlan to the Church of Christ and requested that the church make improvements to the site at a value of at least $10,000 before January 1, 1925. Through the efforts of church officials of the Pearl and Brown Street Church of Christ in Dallas and under the direction of A. O. Colley, the money was collected, and a home for ten orphans was opened on November 24, 1924. Colley, the minister of the Greenville Church of Christ, served as the institution's first superintendent. He oversaw the construction of a boys' dormitory and organized the beginnings of a successful farm. During the mid-1930s superintendent J. B. Nelson added more buildings. By 1940 the home had sixteen buildings, room for 237 children. On November 23, 1939, Mr. and Mrs. Boles provided a gift of an additional 321 acres. Between 1943 and 1949 twenty-three buildings and 818 acres of land were added to the home. Over the next four decades the acreage decreased. By the mid-1970s the institution was surrounded by more than 100 acres located near the banks of Lake Tawakoni. A public elementary school and high school were located on the campus. In 1990 Boles Home had eight cottages. Each cottage housed a maximum of eight children needing out-of-home care, including counseling and other professional services.

BIBLIOGRAPHY: W. Walworth Harrison, *History of Greenville and Hunt County, Texas* (Waco: Texian, 1976). Elizabeth Mary Bonner, A Study of the Church of Christ in Texas (M.A. thesis, University of Texas, 1941). *David Minor*

BOLING, TEXAS. Boling is on Farm roads 1301 and 442 and the west bank of Caney Creek, nine miles southeast of Wharton in southeastern Wharton County. The community was established in 1900, when the New York, Texas and Mexican Railway built through the area. Robert E. Vineyard had a town plat surveyed and named it Bolling in honor of his six-year-old daughter, Mary Bolling Vineyard. The post office listing altered the spelling. Before the arrival of the railroad, the site was known as Floyd's Lane and was on the trail that led to crossings on the San Bernard and Colorado rivers. Until after the railroad was built, no major road, only a trail along Caney Creek, led to Wharton from the site. The railroad brought in a few settlers, but the area remained largely in the hands of large landowners, remnants from the plantation era. In 1907 Boling had a school for black students, with four teachers and an enrollment of 104. These children were primarily the descendants of former slaves whose families still lived in the area, working as tenant, sharecropper, or salaried agricultural workers on the large land tracts. In 1907 the community had a store, a blacksmith shop, and fewer than a dozen families.

Beginning in 1925, sulfur, oil, and gas were discovered at Boling Dome,[qv] and Boling became a boomtown. Its population grew from twenty in 1920 to 450 in 1930. One of the new Boling subdivisions named all its streets after oil companies operating on Boling Dome. Vineyard's platted town became a residential section, rather than a business district as he had hoped. A post office established at the community in 1926 had one rural-route service in the 1980s. A Boling Chamber of Commerce was established in 1935, and the town was incorporated in 1940; by 1944 its population reached 800. The Boling Independent School District was organized in 1941, bringing in schools in Iago and Newgulf to help form the district. In 1973 part of the Hungerford Independent School District was consolidated into the Boling district. The high school campus was in Boling, the junior high campus in Iago, and the elementary campus in Newgulf. In the early 1990s the town's economy was based largely on oil, gas, and sulfur production. Its population was reported as 700 from the mid-1940s to the mid-1960s and declined to 521 by 1972. Thereafter the number of residents began to increase again, to 1,297 by 1990. The closure of the sulfur plant at Newgulf in December 1993 adversely affected the Boling economy. *Merle R. Hudgins*

BOLING DOME. Boling Dome, an underground rock structure that contains petroleum, sulfur, and salt, is on the western bank of the San Bernard River almost entirely in Wharton County (at 29°18′ N, 95°56′ W). It is oval in shape and ranges five miles east-west and three miles north-south, encompassing 5,500 acres. The Boling Dome caprock mantle of minerals is shallow, 383 feet below the surface. Another 120 feet through caprock, at the center of Boling Dome, is the salt dome itself, about 500 feet below the surface. Its outer edge requires up to 5,000 feet of drilling before reaching salt. The entire Boling Dome area is seventy-five feet above sea level. Salt domes in Texas have been of particular geologic significance because of their mineral production. Most of them are located on the Gulf Coast between the lower Colorado and Neches rivers. They have also been used for product storage and disposal.

Sulfur production at the Boling Dome is from the crest of the caprock to deep down the southeast flank of the cap. The first well went into production in March 1929, using the Frasch method for removal (pumping steam into the ground to melt the sulfur, then pumping the liquid sulfur out). The sulfur reserve covers more than 1,500 acres. This reserve, owned by Texasgulf, Incorporated, has produced more sulfur than any other sulfur mine in the world. As of 1990, 80.5 million long tons of sulfur had been removed. The first oil well at the dome went into production in December 1925. As of 1989 the Boling field had produced 6,246 million cubic feet of natural gas and 25,635,836 barrels of oil. Over 8,000 wells had been drilled to mine the sulfur reserve, and 12,000 wells for oil and gas. In addition, at the Boling Dome, Valero, Incorporated, operates three gas-storage caverns in the salt stock, with a combined volume of 7.5 million barrels.

Spacing between the boreholes for sulfur wells is about 100 feet; the sulfur holes, with the 12,000 additional injection wells for oil and gas, produce a highly porous zone that affects the integrity of the dome. On August 12, 1983, a sinkhole approximately 250 feet in diameter and twenty-five feet deep, formed suddenly over the crest of the Boling Dome on Farm Road 442 three miles north of Boling, collapsing the roadway. Water filled the ditch. In early drilling records such as those that the Gulf Production Company kept for a well drilled near the middle of the sinkhole in 1927, there is evidence that an underground cavern once extended over 100 feet vertically but apparently collapsed. Several other sinkholes have occurred over the Boling Dome, a condition that is becoming common at other salt dome sites where sulfur and oil are produced.

Two communities, Boling and Newgulf, are located at the Boling Dome. Their existence is due directly to the production of sulfur and oil from the dome. Newgulf is a Texas Gulf Sulphur company town, and Boling is located at the intersection of State Farm roads 1301 and 442.

BIBLIOGRAPHY: Michel Thomas Halbouty, *Salt Domes, Gulf Region, United States and Mexico* (Houston: Gulf, 1967; 2d ed. 1979). William F. Mullican III, *Subsidence and Collapse of Texas Salt Domes* (Geological Circular 88-2, Bureau of Economic Geology, University of Texas at Austin, 1988).

Merle R. Hudgins

BOLIVAR, TEXAS (Brazoria County). Bolivar, on the east bank of the Brazos River at the northwest corner of Harris Reservoir in northwestern Brazoria County, was the site of the plantation of Henry Austin, first cousin of Stephen F. Austin.[qqv] Soon after his arrival in the county in 1830 Austin established a cotton plantation on the Brazos River twenty-five miles south of San Felipe, named it Bolivar, and set up one of the first gins in the county. In 1837 he began promoting the community of Bolivar, which had already had a population of fifty by 1835. According to a contemporary account, "the land around Bolivar is the best in the colony; clothed with heavy timber, with peach and cane undergrowth to the distance of six miles from the river. The bank of the river in front of the town is a high bluff of stiff red clay. At Bolivar, the timber tract is five or six miles wide and the road to the prairie is walled in with tall cane filling all the space between the trees." A Bolivar post office was established by 1838 and discontinued by 1843. The town failed to develop after preliminary sales because of continued pressure for money. Plans to make Bolivar the western terminus of the proposed Galveston Bay and Brazos Railroad were never completed. In April 1839 Austin sold his plantation home for conversion to a public house, and the town was abandoned.

BIBLIOGRAPHY: Juan N. Almonte, "Statistical Report of Texas," *Southwestern Historical Quarterly* 28 (January 1925). James A. Creighton, *A Narrative History of Brazoria County* (Angleton, Texas: Brazoria County Historical Commission, 1975). William Ransom Hogan, "Life of Henry Austin," *Southwestern Historical Quarterly* 37 (January 1934). Andrew Forest Muir, "Railroad Enterprise in Texas, 1836-1841," *Southwestern Historical Quarterly* 47 (April 1944).

Diana J. Kleiner

BOLIVAR, TEXAS (Denton County). Bolivar, at the intersection of Farm roads 2450 and 455, fourteen miles northwest of Denton in Denton County, was founded in 1859. William Crawford sold the site to Hiram Daily, a Methodist minister and doctor, who opened a general store, laid out the town, and called it New Prospect. In 1861 Ben Brown, a farmer, who had moved from Bolivar, Tennessee, suggested the renaming of the town and persuaded residents to vote for the name Bolivar by providing them free drinks. John Simpson Chisum[qv] ranched near Bolivar but moved his herds in 1863 to West Texas. Bolivar was only three miles east of the Chisholm Trail,[qv] which ran through the Wilson, Forester, Chisum, and Waide ranches. Cowboys on the trail came to Bolivar to stay at its hotel and patronize its saloons. Development of the community was slow but steady until 1886. In that year Bolivar merchants moved their businesses to Sanger, on the Gulf, Colorado and Santa Fe Railway. From 1900 until 1940 Bolivar remained a small community of farmers. The economy received a slight boost from oil production during the 1940s and early 1950s. At one time forty oilfields were in and around the community. In 1947 Bolivar had 115 residents. As the production of oil declined, however, so did the population. In 1980 a post office, a convenience store, and forty residents remained. In 1990 the population was still recorded as forty.

BIBLIOGRAPHY: Edward Franklin Bates, *History and Reminiscences of Denton County* (Denton, Texas: McNitzky Printing, 1918; rpt., Denton: Terrill Wheeler Printing, 1976). Harwood P. Hinton, Jr., "John Simpson Chisum, 1877–84," *New Mexico Historical Review* 31–32 (July 1956–January 1957). E. Dale Odom and Bullitt Lowry, *A Brief History of Denton County* (Denton, Texas, 1975). Denton *Record-Chronicle*, June 13, 1948, August 13, 1950, August 2, 1953.

Eunice Sullivan Gray

BOLIVAR LIGHTHOUSE. The Bolivar Lighthouse is on State Highway 87 near the west end of Bolivar Peninsula[qv] in the easternmost part of Galveston County. In 1852 the United States Coast Survey map advised using "Sanderson's House" on the Gulf side of Point Bolivar and a nearby lightboat to navigate the entrance to Galveston Bay, though in that year the federal government built a lighthouse on the point to prevent shipwrecks. An 1855 survey lined up the lighthouse with Fort Point at the tip of Galveston Island for the purposes of navigation. Confederates destroyed the original lighthouse to avoid assisting the enemy during the Civil War.[qv]

A new lighthouse was built by the federal government in 1872. The 52,000-candlepower beacon guided ships through the undredged ship channel from the Gulf of Mexico into the port of Galveston. The tall brick lighthouse, which extends 117 feet above sea level, was sheathed in cast-iron plates riveted together, anchored to a nine-foot concrete foundation, and originally painted with black and white stripes. It withstood the storms of 1900 and 1915, provided shelter for residents, and saved many lives. In 1917 soldiers at Fort San Jacinto accidentally shelled the lighthouse during target practice in a dense fog, shaking up the lighthouse keeper and his family. Bolivar Lighthouse was retired in 1933, when the South Jetty Light replaced it. Plans to convert the tower and grounds into a public park failed, and in 1947 the government sold the lighthouse as surplus property to the E. W. Boyt interests, which closed it to the public. The lighthouse appeared on television in the 1970 drama "My Sweet Charlie," and in 1977 the Texas Historical Commission[qv] registered it as a historic landmark. The lighthouse journal is housed at the Rosenberg Library[qv] in Galveston.

BIBLIOGRAPHY: A. Pat Daniels, *Bolivar! Gulf Coast Peninsula* (Crys-

tal Beach, Texas: Peninsula, 1985). Galveston *Daily News*, May 13, 1983. Houston *Chronicle*, December 8, 1968. Houston *Post*, June 26, 1960.
A. Pat Daniels

BOLIVAR PENINSULA. Bolivar Peninsula, named for Simón Bolívar (1783–1836), the first president of Bolivia, is a narrow strip of eroding land or "barrier island" stretching twenty-seven miles along the Texas Gulf Coast in a northeasterly direction to form eastern Galveston County (the center of the peninsula is at 29°26′ N, 94°41′ W). At its widest point between Crystal Beach and Caplen, the peninsula is three miles wide. At its narrowest point—where Rollover Pass[qv] divides the community of Gilchrist—the peninsula is a quarter of a mile wide. Water separates the peninsula from Galveston Island[qv] by a distance of less than three miles. The sheltered Gulf Intracoastal Waterway,[qv] which extends the length of the peninsula on the north side, is used primarily for transporting freight; at Bolivar Roads,[qv] it forms a water passageway that serves as the marine entrance from the Gulf of Mexico to Galveston Bay. The Bolivar portion of the waterway belongs to the Galveston District and is maintained by the United States Army Corps of Engineers. Bolivar Peninsula is accessible by land from the Texas mainland only through southern Chambers County. Towns on the peninsula, in addition to Crystal Beach (the only incorporated community), Caplen, and Gilchrist, include Port Bolivar and High Island; independent school districts serving the peninsula include Galveston and High Island. At the southwestern tip of the peninsula at Point Bolivar[qv] stands old Fort Travis, named for Alamo hero Col. William B. Travis.[qv]

Although Galveston Island has been generally considered the most likely site of the shipwreck of Álvar Núñez Cabeza de Vaca[qv] on November 6, 1528, in recent years speculation has developed that the explorer might have arrived on Bolivar Peninsula, near High Island. Indians occupied parts of the peninsula during the eighteenth and nineteenth centuries, and probably much earlier. Atakapas established a burial ground near Caplen, where flint artifacts have been excavated; Orcoquisas occupied the coastal prairie and passed across the peninsula to Galveston Island; and Karankawas roamed the Texas Gulf Coast in the nineteenth century. According to legend, Jean Laffite's[qv] entire pirate crew from Galveston Island sometimes held parties on the peninsula. At least one former pirate, Laffite's cabin boy, Charles Cronea, made his home there at Highland, where he is buried.

In 1815 former Gutiérrez-Magee expedition[qv] members Warren D. C. Hall and Henry Perry[qqv] explored the area, and by 1816 the peninsula served as a "highway" for the overland slave trade between Galveston and Louisiana. Privateer Louis Michel Aury[qv] transported slaves across the peninsula along this route. According to various sources, the peninsula was named by either Hall, Perry, Aury (who had a commission from Simón Bolívar), or one of the men accompanying Francisco Xavier Mina,[qv] who built an earthwork at Point Bolivar in 1816. Dr. James Long[qv] built a mud fort called Fort Las Casas at the same site in 1820, and here Jane Wilkinson Long[qv] spent the winter of 1821–22. In 1836 the peninsula served as a refuge for Galveston Island settlers during the Runaway Scrape,[qv] and when provisional president David G. Burnet[qv] and his staff moved to Galveston Island, many Galvestonians moved eastward up Bolivar Peninsula. Probably the first permanent settler on the peninsula was Samuel D. Parr, who arrived in 1838 and claimed a league of land beginning at Bolivar Point and extending five miles eastward, but by 1850 fifteen families lived between Point Bolivar and High Island, and by 1885 the peninsula's population had grown to 500.

The North Jetty, at the southwestern end of the peninsula, is one of twin restraining walls built into the Gulf of Mexico to provide a deepwater channel to Galveston. The South Jetty extends into the Gulf from Galveston Island. Work on the jetties began as a construction experiment in 1874, and the major portion was completed only after Congress appropriated funds for the work in 1890. Completion of the system in 1898 made Galveston a deep-sea port for world commerce. The jetties now protect shipping to various cities along the Houston Ship Channel,[qv] and are used as fishing spots by many sportsmen.

The Gulf and Interstate Railway, which began operation between Port Bolivar and Beaumont in 1896, hastened area development before going into receivership in 1900, and Port Bolivar became an important freight terminal for the Santa Fe Railway, which acquired assets of the rebuilt Gulf and Interstate in 1908. Though destruction of rail lines in the Galveston hurricane of 1900[qv] prevented the growth of Port Bolivar and further damage resulted from the hurricane of 1915, the Santa Fe provided rail service from Port Bolivar to High Island until 1942. Later, the Gulf, Colorado and Santa Fe leased track on the peninsula. Ferries and barges moved cargo-filled freight cars from Point Bolivar across Bolivar Roads to Galveston Island and the Galveston wharves and transported people on excursions every weekend. Free public ferries between Galveston Island and the peninsula operated under the auspices of the State Highway Department after 1933.

Once an important agricultural and ranching area known as the "breadbasket of Galveston" and the "watermelon capital" of Texas, Bolivar Peninsula also enjoyed a brief oil boom centered near High Island. In the 1990s it had an estimated permanent population of 4,000, increased by hundreds of vacation-home owners and summer and weekend visitors seeking recreational activities, which included swimming, sunbathing, fishing, hunting, beachcombing, shell hunting, and bird watching. Though many workers were employed on the peninsula, others commuted to jobs in Galveston, Beaumont, Port Arthur, and other cities to the east.

Important man-made features on the peninsula include Bolivar Lighthouse,[qv] near its western end, and Rollover Fish Pass, reopened by the Texas Game and Fish Commission (later merged into the Texas Parks and Wildlife Department[qv]) in 1955 to reintroduce sea water in East Bay to increase salinity and help marine life to and from the bay's spawning and feeding areas. Two areas of national significance to birdwatchers—the Houston Audubon Society's Louis Smith Bird Sanctuary in High Island and Bolivar Flats near Port Bolivar—offer migrating birds their first landfall as they reach North America from homes in Central and South America. The area is also home to tens of thousands of native shore birds. Bolivar Peninsula Habitat Development Site, a seventeen-acre tract, was developed by the United States Army Corps of Engineers and Texas A&M University.

BIBLIOGRAPHY: A. Pat Daniels, *Bolivar! Gulf Coast Peninsula* (Crystal Beach, Texas: Peninsula, 1985). Dermont H. Hardy and Ingham S. Roberts, eds., *Historical Review of South-East Texas* (2 vols., Chicago: Lewis, 1910). S. C. Griffin, *History of Galveston, Texas* (Galveston: Cawston, 1931).
A. Pat Daniels

BOLIVAR ROADS. Bolivar Roads is the strip of water enclosed by the North and South jetties between Galveston Island and Bolivar Peninsula. The channel provides an entrance from the Gulf of Mexico to Galveston Bay (at 29°21′ N, 94°45′ W).

BOLL, JACOB (1828–1880). Jacob (Jakob) Boll, naturalist, was born in Bremgarten, Aargau, Switzerland, on May 29, 1828. He received his education in Switzerland and Germany and married Henriette Humbel in 1854. He bought a pharmacy in Bremgarten, collected specimens of the flora of his canton, and published a book on his findings in 1869. The same year Boll came to Texas, stopping on his way at Harvard to visit Louis Agassiz, who suggested that Boll go to Texas to collect animals for the Harvard Museum of Comparative Zoology. He collected in Texas during 1870 and returned to Harvard to be assistant custodian in the museum. In the spring of 1871 he returned to Switzerland, taking species of American wild silkworm for experimentation, and while there his cantonal government commissioned him to collect mollusks and seeds of woody plants of Texas. In October he returned to Harvard, made a collection of insects of New

England, and was elected a member of the Boston Society of Natural History on January 3, 1872. Back in Switzerland in March, he made a botanical exploration of the Albula Pass, for which he was elected to membership in the Academia Caesarea Leopoldino–Carolina Naturae Curiosorum of Germany. After his wife's death in August 1873 Boll returned to the Harvard museum and in the spring of 1874 settled in Dallas, Texas.

In 1876, while on a field trip collecting specimens of the Colorado potato beetle for his cantonal government, he discovered fossil animals in the rocks of the Wichita River country. In 1877 he was appointed to work with the United States Entomological Commission for the study of the Rocky Mountain locust. Between 1877 and 1880, while collecting for Edward D. Cope,[qv] Boll found thirty-two new, rare species of Permian vertebrates, including stegocephalian amphibians and theromorph reptiles, land forms that were embedded in deltas of Texas rivers. At the same time he made an extensive collection of tiny butterflies and moths (*microlepidoptera*), as well as Texas reptiles, batrachia (tailless amphibians), and fish. In an article for the *American Naturalist* of September 1880, he first identified scientifically the Permian rocks of Texas. Boll died on an expedition in Wilbarger County on September 29, 1880.

BIBLIOGRAPHY: *Dictionary of American Biography* (New York: Scribner, 1929). S. W. Geiser, *Naturalists of the Frontier* (Dallas: Southern Methodist University, 1937; 2d ed. 1948). *Clinton P. Hartmann*

BOLLAERT, WILLIAM (1807–1876). William Bollaert, writer, chemist, geographer, and ethnologist, son of Andrew Jacob Bollaert, was born at Lymington, England, on October 21, 1807. After training in chemistry, he took a position as a laboratory assistant at the Royal Institution while only thirteen years old and worked for several eminent scientists, including Michael Faraday. He made several original discoveries about benzoic acid and published articles in the *Journal of the Royal Institution* before the sudden blindness of his father forced him to seek a more lucrative career. At age eighteen he sailed for Peru, where he worked as an assayer in the silver-mining province of Tarapacá. The young adventurer subsequently surveyed the vast mining district for the Peruvian government and became one of the first Englishmen to cross the treacherous Atacama Desert. Failure to secure an assistantship at King's College, London, in 1830, ended Bollaert's aspiration for an academic career. Afterward, he devoted his life to worldwide travel. During 1833 he used his talents in artillery and engineering to assist Maria II of Portugal to retain her throne. For this service he received the Portuguese War Medal and was made a Knight of the Order of the Tower and Sword. After a six-year life of intrigue in Spain, Bollaert journeyed to the Republic of Texas[qv] at the behest of his friend William Kennedy,[qv] who was subsequently appointed British consul at Galveston. He reached the coastal town in February 1842 and began to prepare a report for the British Admiralty. During the next two years he traveled extensively throughout Texas and wrote not only his formal report but also a very detailed journal, which he hoped to use someday as material for a commercial book. Troubled with fevers and the dimmed prospects of Britain's future in Texas (because of British opposition to annexation[qv] of Texas), he left Galveston on July 10, 1844.

Bollaert returned broke to London and decided to settle down for the first time since leaving the Royal Institution. In August 1845 he married Susannah McMorran of Stamford, England. They subsequently had a son and four daughters. After several years of financial difficulties, Bollaert became able to provide a comfortable middle-class life for his family. In 1854 business took him again to South America, where he visited Panama, Ecuador, Peru, and Chile. Later ventures in the Ecuadoran Land Company failed to yield a profit. Throughout his life, he steadily produced publications about history, ethnology, science, and travel. By 1865 he had published eighty articles in a variety of journals, ranging from the popular *Colburn's United Service Magazine* to the scholarly *Transactions of the Linnaean Society*. He published three books: *Antiquarian, Ethnological and Other Researches in New Granada, Ecuador, Peru and Chile* (1860); a translation entitled *The Expedition of Pedro de Ursa and Lope de Aguirre in Search of Eldorado and Amagua in 1560–1* (1861); and *The Wars of Succession in Portugal and Spain, from 1826 to 1840* (1870). He also wrote an "Essay on Salt," which won him a bronze medal from the Society of Arts in 1853. Despite his prolific publication, his writing about the Texas years was limited to a few scattered articles published in popular journals. His original "Texas Manuscript," consisting of six diaries and two volumes of journals, was purchased in 1902 by Edward E. Ayer and presented nine years later to the Newberry Library in Chicago. In 1956 editors W. Eugene Hollon and Ruth Lapham Butler published the original manuscript under the title *William Bollaert's Texas*. It remains one of the most important sources of information on the Republic of Texas and its people. Bollaert died in London on November 15, 1876,

Michael L. Tate

BOLL WEEVIL. The boll weevil is a snout beetle (*Anthonomus grandis*) first named by Carl H. Boheman, a Swedish systematist. He assumed that the specimens came from Cuba, but modern research indicates that they were collected near Veracruz in 1840. Ancient specimens have been found from the earliest times in the valley of Mexico. The ravages of the insect have been known in Mexico for at least two millenia. American entomologists became aware of the boll weevil as a cotton pest as early as 1880, but its first introduction to Texas seems to have been announced by Charles W. DeRyee,[qv] a druggist of Corpus Christi, in a letter dated October 3, 1894. The insect, which proved to be one of the most devastating pests ever introduced to American agriculture, was definitely identified by Dr. Eugene A. Schwarz. The boll weevil is about one-fourth inch in length and changes from white to black as it matures. The beetles are susceptible to winter freezes, and those that survive hibernation emerge in the spring to feed for five or six weeks on the tender growth of young cotton plants. As the season progresses, they eat and lay eggs in the cotton buds and new bolls. Each punctured bud or boll falls to the ground and becomes food for the eggs that hatch in two or three days. The boll weevil migrated across the Rio Grande and had spread from the Valley to the Sabine and Red rivers by the beginning of the twentieth century. By 1903 it covered all of eastern Texas to the Edwards Plateau[qv] and by the 1920s had reached north and west to the High Plains,[qv] then encompassing all the geographic areas of Texas cotton production. Boll weevil infestation caused a steady drop in cotton yields over a thirty-year period. The greatest destruction was in the South Texas fields. In 1904 an estimated 700,000 bales were lost to the boll weevil, at a cost of $42 million. Damage that resulted in about a 6 percent yield reduction in 1910 leaped to a 34 percent reduction in 1921. Fifty-three years later the per-acre yield reduction due to boll weevils still hovered at 7 percent and cost an estimated $260 million.

Unlike many other insects, the boll weevil was resistant to conventional insecticides, poisons, and then-known antipest practices. Its spread from Mexico depended on a combination of appropriate weather conditions and cultivation practices, coupled with a shortage of cotton gins. Cotton bolls with seed were often transported from the lower Rio Grande valley to gins as far north as Alice, and this practice may have contributed to the spread of the weevil. Basic information on the relationship of the boll weevil to the cotton plant and other cultivated plants was explored by C. H. Tyler Townsend, one of the many colorful personalities involved in the early fight against the boll weevil. Townsend was an official of the United States Department of Agriculture who traveled through southern Texas in 1894 and reported as much as 90 percent crop damage in that area. In 1899 the state appointed Frederick W. Mally,[qv] an entomologist, to direct state efforts to combat the insect. Mally launched a cultivation plan intended to produce crops early, before the weevils multiplied.

But record freezes that delayed early planting, heavy rainfall, and the great Galveston hurricane of 1900[qv] all combined to help spread the boll weevil in spite of Mally's brilliant but seriously underfunded labors.

In 1901 E. Dwight Sanderson succeeded Mally as state entomologist. He continued many of Mally's programs, but in addition the Texas legislature chose to offer a $50,000 prize for discovery of a way to rid Texas of the boll weevil. The proclamation was made from the Capitol[qv] steps on July 13, 1903. A Boll Weevil Commission was appointed by Gov. S. W. T. Lanham[qv] to evaluate the claims and claimants to the prize. But no one really expected the contest to work. The prize offered by the legislature made both themselves and the boll weevil a figure of fun for newspapers throughout the nation, and this episode is sometimes found in civics or government texts as an illustration of the foolishness of lawmaking bodies. A more meaningful effort to control the boll weevil occurred on Walter C. Porter's demonstration farm at Terrell, where Seaman A. Knapp[qv] led the work that later served as a model for the National Extension Service. The boll weevil continued to spread year by year through Louisiana, Arkansas, Mississippi, Alabama, the Carolinas, Tennessee, and Virginia. By World War I,[qv] calcium arsenate had been found reasonably effective in poisoning the insect, and during the 1920s fluorides were introduced. Mally's cultivation practices continued to be a sensible and important way to manage boll weevil infestations. Organic pesticides and traps depending on synthetic sex pheromones have not been so effective with the boll weevil as they have been with other insects. The possibility of eradication of the organism simply by suspending cotton culture for two or more years over a broad region has not been disproved, but neither has it been fully tested. Since the boll weevil does not survive well on the High Plains of Texas, this region seems to be more favorable to future cotton production than the coastal areas. *See also* COTTON CULTURE.

BIBLIOGRAPHY: Samuel Lee Evans, Texas Agriculture, 1880–1930 (Ph.D. dissertation, University of Texas, 1960). Frank Wagner, *The Boll Weevil Comes to Texas* (Friends of the Corpus Christi Museum, 1980).

Frank Wagner

BOLT, TEXAS. Bolt, on lower Simpson Creek in eastern San Saba County, was named for William James Bolt, who operated a saloon and store at the site from 1854 to 1857. There James Barnet had a blacksmith shop operated by slave labor. *Alice Gray Upchurch*

BOLTON, HALE WILLIAM (1879–1920). Hale William Bolton, artist, was born on September 27, 1879, in Fredericksburg, Iowa, the son of George W. and Alice Lucy (Hale) Bolton. The family moved to Honey Grove, Texas, in 1896. By 1905 Bolton was in the Oak Cliff section of Dallas earning his living as a piano tuner for the Jesse French Piano and Organ Company. He was also a violinist. He studied art with Frank Reaugh,[qv] exhibited in Nashville, Tennessee, and won gold medals at the Tri-State Exhibition in Memphis in 1907, 1910, and 1913. In 1909 he studied at the St. Louis School of Fine Arts, after which he traveled in Europe for several years and studied with William Orowelt in Holland and William Rueloup and Paul Abram in Paris. Bolton returned to Oak Cliff in 1914 and was employed by the Dallas Piano Works. He entered exhibitions in both Dallas and Fort Worth. In 1915 he won a medal for a painting exhibited in Galveston. He specialized in western subjects and worked in oils or pastels. In 1916 he became a member of the American Federation of Arts and moved to California. The following year he returned to Texas and lived with his parents in Oak Cliff. He exhibited at the Dallas Woman's Forum in 1916 and 1918. Shortly before his death, he was awarded a grand prize by the California Society of Art. He died at Rusk, Texas, on October 10, 1920.

BIBLIOGRAPHY: Diana Church, *Guide to Dallas Artists, 1890–1917* (Plano, Texas, 1987). Peter Haskins Falk, ed., *Who Was Who in American Art* (Madison, Connecticut: Sound View, 1985). Esse Forrester-O'Brien, *Art and Artists of Texas* (Dallas: Tardy, 1935).

Diana Church

BOLTON, HERBERT EUGENE (1870–1953). Herbert Eugene Bolton, historian, was born in Wilton, Wisconsin, on July 20, 1870, to Edwin Latham and Rosaline (Cady) Bolton. He attended the University of Wisconsin, where he graduated with a bachelor's degree in 1895. That year he also married Gertrude James; they eventually had seven children. Bolton continued studies under Frederick Jackson Turner in 1896–97. From 1897 to 1899 he was Harrison Fellow at the University of Pennsylvania, where he studied American history under John Bach McMaster. Bolton received his Ph.D. at the University of Pennsylvania in 1899 and for the next two years taught at Milwaukee State Normal School. In 1901 he went as instructor of history to the University of Texas, where he remained until 1909. Though he taught medieval and European history at UT, he soon developed a lively interest in the history of Spanish expansion in North America. Beginning in the summer of 1902, he made a series of pioneering forays into archives in Mexico. At the invitation of the Carnegie Institution he prepared a report on materials for United States history in Mexican archives, and this was published in 1913. Bolton was an associate editor of the *Quarterly of the Texas State Historical Association* (now the *Southwestern Historical Quarterly*[qv]). In 1904 he and his colleague Eugene C. Barker[qv] published a textbook, *With the Makers of Texas: A Source Reader in Texas History.* Beginning in 1906 Bolton studied the history of Indians in Texas for the United States Bureau of Ethnology and wrote more than 100 articles for the *Handbook of American Indians North of Mexico.* His interest in Texas history was reflected in more than a dozen learned articles as well as in his published volumes on *Athanase de Mézières and the Louisiana-Texas Frontier, 1768–1780* (1914), and *Texas in the Middle Eighteenth Century: Studies in Spanish Colonial History and Administration* (1915). Although his later research and writing were more concerned with the Pacific coast, Bolton retained a strong interest in Texas history. He declined the presidency of the University of Texas in 1914 but continued to look back with affection to his years there.

From 1909 to 1911 Bolton was professor of American history at Stanford University, and from 1911 until his retirement in 1940 he was professor of history at the University of California, Berkeley. From 1919 to 1940, except for two years, he served as chairman of the history department, and for the same twenty-two years he was director of the Bancroft Library. At the University of California he inaugurated a course called "History of the Americas," in which he emphasized the need to study the Americas as a whole. He outlined this thesis in his presidential address to the American Historical Association at Toronto in 1932, under the title "The Epic of Greater America." Although he became professor emeritus in 1940, Bolton taught as lecturer in history from 1942 to 1944.

He was tireless and enthusiastic in his research, in the exploration of old trails and historic sites, and in putting the results of his research and travel on paper. His bibliography consists of ninety-four entries, including nearly two dozen books written or edited. His concept of the Spanish Borderlands, the crescent-shaped area from Georgia to California, as a fruitful field for study and interpretation was an important addition to historical thought. He is also remembered as a great teacher. He lectured to large undergraduate classes and conducted research seminars for graduate students. More than 300 master's theses and 100 doctoral dissertations were written under his supervision. As a teacher, scholar, and writer, he was an individual of lasting influence. Bolton died of a stroke at Berkeley, California, on January 30, 1953.

BIBLIOGRAPHY: John Francis Bannon, *Herbert Eugene Bolton: The Historian and the Man, 1870–1953* (Tucson: University of Arizona

Press, 1978). Wilbur R. Jacobs et al., *Turner, Bolton, and Webb: Three Historians of the American Frontier* (Seattle: University of Washington Press, 1965; rpt. 1979).

John Haskell Kemble

BOLTON, JOHN THOMAS (1840–1915). John Thomas Bolton, soldier, physician, and politician, was born near Washington, Georgia, on March 22, 1840 (March 27, 1839, according to some sources), the son of Charles L. and Mary (Nolan) Bolton. In February 1846 his father purchased 1,000 acres of land in Wharton County, Texas, for $10,000. Bolton earned a medical degree in New Orleans and in 1856 joined his family in Wharton County. With the outbreak of the Civil War[qv] he enlisted in July 1861 as first corporal in Capt. J. F. Roberts's Reserve Cavalry company of the Wharton County Home Guards, Texas State Troops; he later joined the regular Confederate service as a private in Company C of Col. Reuben R. Brown's[qv] Thirty-fifth Texas Cavalry. He was soon promoted to assistant surgeon. With Brown's regiment he served in Texas and in the Red River campaign[qv] in Louisiana in 1864. After the war Bolton resumed his medical practice but spent most of his time as a cotton planter. He also served as a Wharton county commissioner for eight years, as county treasurer, and on the Wharton City Council. In 1869 he married Mary Rogers, the daughter of William P. Rogers.[qv] The couple had three children. Bolton was a member of the United Confederate Veterans. He died at Wharton on March 29, 1915. His correspondence, diary, and plantation records are preserved in the Barker Texas History Center[qv] at the University of Texas at Austin.

BIBLIOGRAPHY: John Thomas Bolton Papers, Barker Texas History Center, University of Texas at Austin. Clement Anselm Evans, ed., *Confederate Military History* (Atlanta: Confederate Publishing, 1899; extended ed., Wilmington, North Carolina: Broadfoot, 1987–89). Frank W. Johnson, *A History of Texas and Texans* (5 vols., ed. E. C. Barker and E. W. Winkler [Chicago and New York: American Historical Society, 1914; rpt. 1916]). *Thomas W. Cutrer*

BOMARTON, TEXAS. Bomarton, on U.S. Highway 277 near the Knox county line in southwest Baylor County, was founded in 1906, when the Wichita Valley Railroad was extended from Seymour to Abilene. It was named for W. H. Bomar, an early settler. Tom McClure established a post office in 1906 in his store. B. B. Calfee and J. R. Snyder ran another early store. A school was started in 1907, churches were constructed between 1908 and 1910, and two cotton gins were operating in 1914. Marketing and baseball games made Bomarton a lively center on Saturdays. Another amenity was a large open grazing area for milk cows and calves. The population in the community was 580 in 1920, 600 in 1930, and 598 in 1940. During and after World War II[qv] Bomarton declined. The population was 150 in 1960, twenty-seven in 1980, and twenty-three in 1990.

BIBLIOGRAPHY: Baylor County Historical Society, *Salt Pork to Sirloin*, Vol. 1: *The History of Baylor County, Texas, from 1879 to 1930* (Quanah, Texas: Nortex, 1972); Vol. 2: *The History of Baylor County, Texas, from 1878 to Present* (1977). *William R. Hunt*

BONAMI, TEXAS. Bonami is on the Atchison, Topeka and Santa Fe Railway sixty miles north of Beaumont in east central Jasper County. It was established in 1901 when the Lee-Irvine Lumber Company built a sawmill on the rail line, then named the Gulf, Beaumont and Kansas City. The site was first called Leeton for one of the partners, D. J. Lee, but was renamed Bonami in 1902 by the first postmaster, R. J. Cooper, for a Louisiana town of the same name. The sawmill, which had a daily capacity of 25,000 board feet, was sold to the Bleakwood Lumber Company the following year. L. S. Bean managed the Bonami mill. The Bonami post office closed in 1914, and the following year Bean sold an edger, saw, and engine in storage at Bonami to J. J. and V. S. Bean. Presumably using this equipment, the Bonami mill resumed operations that lasted until 1929, when the installations were removed. A rural community remained, and in 1948 the population was 200. In 1986 Bonami had no apparent community center but was marked by an abandoned sawmill and the Freewill Baptist Church. Logging, a sand and gravel operation, and chicken and stock raising were the chief economic activities.

Robert Wooster

BONANZA, TEXAS. Bonanza is off State Highway 19 thirteen miles south of Sulphur Springs in southwestern Hopkins County. The site was settled in the late 1860s or early 1870s. The community was originally known as Fowler's Store when M. W. Fowler secured a post office there in 1879. The post office was renamed Cold Hill in 1883 and Bonanza in 1898. By 1885 the town had a gristmill and cotton gin, Baptist and Presbyterian churches, a hotel, a blacksmith, two grocers, and a population of 100. A local public school opened around 1900, and during the 1905–06 school year it had an enrollment of sixty. In 1906 the post office was closed. The census of 1940 gave the population as forty. In 1948 the community had a store, a church, and a two-teacher school. The school was later closed, and in the late 1980s the site of the town was marked only by a number of scattered dwellings.

BIBLIOGRAPHY: Sylvia M. Kibart and Rita M. Adams, eds., *Pioneers of Hopkins County, Texas*, Vol. 1 (Wolfe City, Texas: Henington, 1986).

Christopher Long

BONAPARTE, JEROME NAPOLEON, JR. (1830–1893). Jerome Napoleon Bonaparte, Jr., was born in Baltimore, Maryland, on November 5, 1830, the son of Jerome Napoleon and Susan May (Williams) Bonaparte. He was the grandson of Jerome Bonaparte, the younger brother of the Emperor Napoleon I of France. While serving as a lieutenant in the French navy Jerome Bonaparte met and married Elizabeth Patterson of Baltimore, "a reigning belle of that city," and the couple had one child. The emperor took exception to his brother's marrying a commoner, however, and the marriage did not last. On July 1, 1852, Jerome N. Bonaparte, Jr., graduated from the United States Military Academy at West Point, eleventh in his class. He was brevetted a second lieutenant in C Troop of the Regiment of Mounted Rifles and was assigned to duty at Fort Inge. On August 30, 1853, he was promoted to the substantive rank of second lieutenant. His letters from Fort Inge and Fort Ewell, now at the Maryland Historical Society, shed considerable light on the life of a junior officer on the Texas frontier in the 1850s. On August 16, 1854, after two years of frontier duty, he resigned from the United States Army when Napoleon III summoned him to Paris to commission him into the French army. Bonaparte served in Algiers, the Italian campaign, the Crimean War, and the Franco-Prussian War and eventually rose to the rank of colonel. In 1871 he returned to the United States to marry Mrs. Caroline Edgar. With the exception of a prolonged stay in Paris from 1873 through 1879, he spent the rest of his life in America. He died at Pride's Crossing, Massachusetts, on September 3, 1893. Gen. Dabney H. Maury wrote that Bonaparte's "commanding appearance, the grace and gentleness of his demeanor, and his fine intelligence win him the admiration of all who know him." Bonaparte was said to have been held high in the esteem of his kinsman, the emperor Louis Napoleon.

BIBLIOGRAPHY: Francis B. Heitman, *Historical Register and Dictionary of the United States Army* (2 vols., Washington: GPO, 1903; rpt., Urbana: University of Illinois Press, 1965). Dabney Herndon Maury, *Recollections of a Virginian in the Mexican, Indian, and Civil Wars* (New York: Scribner, 1894). *William D. Hoyt, Jr.*

BONAVÍA Y ZAPATA, BERNARDO (?–1812). Bernardo Bonavía y Zapata, Knight of Alcántara and corregidor of Mexico, entered the service of the king of Spain in 1758. In 1788 he was appointed governor of Texas but, because his services were needed elsewhere, did not serve. Bonavía was appointed governor-intendant of Durango in 1796 and served in that capacity until 1809, when he was appointed military commander of Texas. He had previously been ordered to Texas in 1806 with the governors of Nuevo León and Coahuila but was unable to join them since he was urgently needed in Durango. Bonavía had played an important role in putting the liberal reforms of Charles III in trade and commerce into effect in Mexico and worked to see those reforms placed in operation in the provinces, especially in Texas.

On his arrival in Texas he requested all ranking officials to present written statements of their views on defense and development of the province. On the basis of these reports and his own observations he recommended to Nemesio Salcedo y Salcedo, commandant general of the Provincias Internas,[qv] that frontier defenses be strengthened immediately. Bonavía also called a meeting of the governors of Coahuila, Nuevo León, and Texas to discuss measures for the development of Texas; he forwarded the recommendations of the group, particularly for free trade and immigration, to the commandant general on June 28, 1809. On July 20, 1809, Bonavía called a second meeting to consider establishing direct water communication between Texas and Veracruz and the opening of a free-trade port. When Salcedo did not approve their plan to open the Port of San Bernard,[qv] Bonavía warned that if conditions of trade and commerce in Texas were not remedied, the time would soon come when the colonists would take things into their own hands. He also recommended, unsuccessfully, that the decree of May 30, 1804, calling for the reorganization of presidios[qv] into provincial regiments for defense, be put into effect.

In late 1810 Bonavía returned to Durango to suppress a revolt. He commanded the royalists forces in Oaxaca in 1812 during the uprising of Miguel Hidalgo y Costilla[qv] and was defeated. Bonavía was captured and shot on December 2, 1812.

BIBLIOGRAPHY: Hubert Howe Bancroft, *History of Arizona and New Mexico, 1530–1888* (San Francisco: History Company, 1889; facsimile ed., Albuquerque: Horn and Wallace, 1962). Hubert Howe Bancroft, *History of the North Mexican States and Texas* (2 vols., San Francisco: History Company, 1886, 1889). Carlos E. Castañeda, *Our Catholic Heritage in Texas* (7 vols., Austin: Von Boeckmann–Jones, 1936–58; rpt., New York: Arno, 1976).

Frank Goodwyn

BOND, GEORGE D. (1860–1924). George D. Bond, radiologist, the son of Thomas B. and Ann (McLemore) Bond, was born at Spring Hill, Tennessee, in 1860. He completed his medical training at Vanderbilt University in Nashville in 1880, at a time when the faculty consisted of thirty-five professors. After practicing three years in Spring Hill, Bond moved his practice to Hillsboro, Texas. He served as the president of the Hill County Medical Society in 1905. In 1907 he moved to Fort Worth and established his practice in the Flat Iron Building.[qv] He specialized in X ray and electrotherapeutics and pioneered machines and techniques in the field of radiology. Bond continued his practice and joined the staff of the Fort Worth School of Medicine as a demonstrator under the chairman of obstetrics in 1911. He established the radiology departments at John Peter Smith Hospital and St. Joseph Hospital[qv] in Fort Worth. Eventually, he was joined in the practice by his son, Thomas B. Bond, who had begun his medical service by turning the crank of his father's static machine, a device used before the development of an effective generator or common electric current.

George Bond was an active member of the American Medical Association, the State Medical Association of Texas (now the Texas Medical Association[qv]), and the Tarrant County Medical Society. Along with several other pioneer radiologists, he established the Texas Roentgen Association, later known as the Texas Radiological Society. He also served on the Cancer Committee of the Texas Medical Association. He published an article on cancer in the *Texas State Medical Journal* in 1916. Bond was also a member of the Methodist Episcopal Church, South. He was married to Lucy Guthrie. They had two children. Bond died in Fort Worth on December 6, 1924, and was buried in Hillsboro, Texas.

BIBLIOGRAPHY: Fort Worth *Star-Telegram,* December 8, 1971. Buckley B. Paddock, *History of Texas: Fort Worth and the Texas Northwest Edition* (4 vols., Chicago: Lewis, 1922).

Kenneth E. Austin

BONE BUSINESS. The best years of the Texas bone business were 1870 to 1937. Freighters returning to Kansas from Texas forts loaded their empty wagons with old, brittle, ash-colored buffalo bones and piled them along the right-of-way of the Atchison, Topeka and Santa Fe Railway. A good report on their industrial use reached Kansas at about the same time that the AT&SF rails arrived. The railroad therefore set off a boom of bone picking, hauling, and shipping north of the Arkansas in 1872. As it died down in 1874, the slaughter of the Texas buffalo herd began. When the latter ended in 1878, it had added many thousands of fresh bones to the old from the Cross Timbers[qv] to the upper Panhandle[qv] to below the Colorado River and up the Pecos River and other streams into New Mexico.

Half a dozen bone roads ran northward to points along the AT&SF and other lines, and at least as many went eastward to the rail heads built in Northeast and Central Texas in the 1870s. The Fort Griffin–Dodge City road was the best known of the first group. Those going eastward reached heads at Austin, Dallas, Denison, Fort Worth, Gainesville, Round Rock, Sherman, and San Antonio. The Old Buffalo Road ran from Cottle and Foard counties to Henrietta and Wichita Falls. Several bone roads came off the Caprock,[qv] and another from Glasscock and Sterling counties went down the North Concho River to San Angelo.

As many as 100 bone wagons traveled together. A king-sized wagon drawn by oxen or mules, plus its two trailers, could carry 10,000 pounds of bones. When the panic of 1873 stopped rail construction, bone pickers rushed into the field and raised hundreds of "little mountains" of bones along the right-of-ways. Freighters hauled out army, merchant, and ranch supplies and brought back bones. Agents, brokers, buyers, and speculators bought piles, and freighters hauled them to the rails or to intermediate points like Doans, Griffin, Henrietta, San Angelo, and Wichita Falls. San Antonio shipped 3,333 tons between July 1877 and November 1878.

Resumption of rail construction extended the Texas and Pacific from Fort Worth across the bone lands in 1880–81, the Southern Pacific to the Pecos by 1882, and the Fort Worth and Denver City to Henrietta, Wichita Falls, Harrold, Vernon, Quanah, Childress, Washburn, and Texline between 1880 and 1888. For several years in the early eighties Texas led the world as a source of bones. Prices climbed from three or four dollars a ton in the early seventies to as high as twenty-two or twenty-three dollars briefly in the eighties, then settled around eight dollars by the end of the century. Texas bones went to Baltimore, Boston, Detroit, Harrisburg, New Orleans, New York, Philadelphia, St. Louis, and Europe. Old bones were ground into meal, fresh ones supplied refineries with calcium phosphate to neutralize cane-juice acid and decolor sugar, choice bones went to bone-china furnaces for calcium phosphate ash, and firm bones went to button factories.

Abilene, Sweetwater, Colorado City, Big Spring, and Midland had their great bone piles. Several are described as stretching half a mile along the tracks and being thirty feet wide and sixteen high. From Abilene 109 cars of fifteen tons each, or 1,635 tons, were sent to New Orleans after mid-1881. Colorado City became the largest Texas and Pacific shipping point. Hundreds of families beat droughts, debts, and famine by picking and selling bones. Huge piles of bones were built by men like James Kilfoile and his crews, who worked ahead of the rail gangs laying railroad tracks. One picker piled up eighty tons at Big Spring and sold the heap for $4,000. To avoid "bone wars" pickers recognized the unwritten law of right of discovery, preemption, and priority to a reasonable area.

Cattle bones supplanted buffalo bones before 1900. By the 1920s each county had several bone men, who would keep pastures clean of bones for them. In the 1930s "boning" temporarily returned to popularity to ease woes of the Great Depression.[qv] But with economic recovery and the discovery of a new process of making bone meal, it passed out. The bone business had contributed greatly to the freight and rail business and saved many families from being forced back East in the early days. One source estimates that Texas alone shipped out a half million tons of buffalo bones, worth $3 million at six dollars a ton. *See also* BUFFALO, BUFFALO HUNTING.

BIBLIOGRAPHY: Ralph A. Smith, "The West Texas Bone Business," West Texas Historical Association *Yearbook* 55 (1979).

Ralph A. Smith

BONEO Y MORALES, JUSTO (?–1744). Justo Boneo y Morales, governor of Texas and knight of the Order of Santiago, held the rank of lieutenant colonel in the Spanish army. He was ordered on July 15, 1740, to investigate the French boundary near Los Adaes[qv] and the charges made by Carlos Franquis de Lugo[qv] against former governor Manuel de Sandoval[qv] and the missionaries in Texas. Boneo y Morales was at Nuestra Señora del Pilar de los Adaes Presidio[qv] on December 17, 1743, when he assumed the office of governor of Texas. He had been appointed by the king himself. He attended the funeral of Louis Juchereau de St. Denis[qv] in June 1744 and thanked God that the irritating Frenchman was gone. Boneo y Morales died in September of the same year, while still in office.

BIBLIOGRAPHY: Herbert Eugene Bolton, *Texas in the Middle Eighteenth Century* (Berkeley: University of California Press, 1915; rpt., Austin: University of Texas Press, 1970). Bexar Archives, Barker Texas History Center, University of Texas at Austin. Charles W. Hackett, ed., *Pichardo's Treatise on the Limits of Louisiana and Texas* (4 vols., Austin: University of Texas Press, 1931–46). Juan Agustín Morfi, *History of Texas, 1673–1779* (2 vols., Albuquerque: Quivira Society, 1935; rpt., New York: Arno, 1967).

BONER, MARIAN OLDFATHER (1909–1983). Marian O. Boner, first director of the Texas State Law Library and authority on Texas legal history, was born in Cleburne, Texas, on June 25, 1909, the daughter of Henry and Berta Oldfather. She received her B.A. (1930) and M.A. (1931) in physics from the University of Texas. While at the university she was a member of Phi Beta Kappa, Sigma Chi, and Kappa Beta Pi. She dedicated herself for many years to raising her family before deciding to return to the university and begin a second career. In 1955 she was awarded her LL.B. with honors by the university law school and was admitted to the Texas bar. In law school she was a member of the *Texas Law Review*, graduated second in her class, and was awarded the Order of the Coif, the highest honor that can be earned by a law student in the United States. After graduation from law school, Mrs. Boner worked for Judge Robert Stayton before becoming reference librarian and assistant professor at Tarlton Law Library, a position she held from 1960 to 1965. She was promoted to associate librarian and assistant professor in 1965 and to associate professor of law in 1968. At the university she taught courses in legal research and writing. In recommending her for promotion to associate professorship, W. Page Keeton, dean of the University of Texas School of Law, stated, "As a scholar she has established herself quantitatively and qualitatively. Her article on the doctrine of *Erie v. Tompkins* [*Texas Law Review*, 40 (1960)], a jurisprudential issue of monumental proportions, is regarded as definitive." Among her other publications, her book *A Reference Guide to Texas Law and Legal History* is also a definitive legal reference source.

In 1972 Mrs. Boner was appointed first director of the Texas State Law Library; she served until her retirement in 1981. She was a member of the State Bar of Texas[qv] and served on the Committee on Legal Publications and the Committee on the History and Traditions of the State Bar. She was president of the Southwest Association of Law Libraries in 1969–70, secretary to the national organization of the American Association of Law Libraries from 1970 to 1973, and president of that association in 1974–75. She was a member of All Saints Episcopal Church. She married Charles Paul Boner on September 9, 1930. They had three sons. Marian Boner died in Austin on April 2, 1983.

BIBLIOGRAPHY: Austin *American-Statesman*, February 1, 1970. *Texas Bar Journal*, March 1984.

Roy M. Mersky

BONFIRE SHELTER. Bonfire Shelter, the oldest mass bison-kill site in the New World, lies in a deeply entrenched canyon one kilometer above its juncture with the Rio Grande near Langtry, Texas. This large rockshelter, hidden behind a massive roof fall, holds three bone deposits and at least two occupational levels, each stratum separated from the others by sterile cave fill. The lowest bone deposit contains the scattered skeletal remains of now-extinct large game animals, such as elephant, camel, horse, and bison. These species ranged the lower Pecos region at the end of the Pleistocene, about 14,000 to 12,000 years ago. The intermingling of the bones of so many species, the cut marks and breakage patterns on the bones, and the presence of large, anvil-like limestone blocks indicate that this site was used as a butchering station. The second, younger bone bed contains only bison bones of the now extinct species *Bison antiquus*. About 120 animals are represented by body parts. Stone tools, including Paleo-Indian arrowheads such as Folsom and Plainview, and radiocarbon assays of charcoal from small hearths date this level to 10,000 years ago, when herds of the giant bison were driven over the cliff above, killed on the rocks below, and either rolled or dragged into the shelter for butchering. Over 7,000 years later the site was again used for the same purpose, the stampeding of herds of modern bison to their death (*see* BUFFALO). The discarded bones, meat, and fat, the residue from butchering, apparently ignited spontaneously and reduced this bone deposit to ash and burned and brittle bone.

In the third level, among the remains of an estimated 800 bison, numerous stone tools were found, including projectile points similar to the Montell and Castroville types more common in Central Texas. Pollen (*see* PALYNOLOGY) and other environmental indicators support the theory that during a short mesic interlude about 2,600 years ago the grasslands of the Southern Plains extended into the lower Pecos, bringing the bison herds and their attendant hunters into the region until a return to arid conditions forced their retreat. Bonfire Shelter is thus both the oldest and the southernmost example of the jump technique of bison hunting and the only site of this type yet recorded on these margins of the Southern Plains. Its preservation can be attributed to the massive roof fall, which diverted the falling bison into the shelter rather than into the canyon, where their remains would have been washed away by flood.

Bonfire Shelter was excavated in 1963–64 and 1983–84 by the Texas Archeological Survey. Faunal remains are curated at the Vertebrate Paleontological Laboratory, and artifacts, notes, and photographs are stored at the Texas Archeological Research Laboratory and the Texas Memorial Museum[qv] at the University of Texas at Austin.

BIBLIOGRAPHY: Vaughn Motley Bryant, Late Full-Glacial and Post-glacial Pollen Analysis of Texas Sediments (Ph.D. dissertation, University of Texas at Austin, 1969). David S. Dibble, "On the Significance of Additional Radiocarbon Dates from Bonfire Shelter, Texas," *Plains Anthropologist* 15 (1970). David S. Dibble and Dessamae Lorrain, *Bonfire Shelter: A Stratified Bison Kill Site, Val Verde County, Texas* (Texas Memorial Museum Miscellaneous Papers 1 [Austin: University of Texas, 1968]).

Solveig A. Turpin

BONHAM, DORA DIETERICH (1902–1973). Dora Dieterich Bonham, businesswoman and historian, daughter of Roy Ferguson and Annie (Fulkes) Dieterich, was born in Watters, Texas, on May 19, 1902. She attended schools in Fiskville and Austin before entering the University of Texas in 1921. She was employed in the Bureau of Child Hygiene of the Texas Department of Health[qv] from 1924 to 1937. She married Eugene Bonham on October 2, 1937, and with him became associated with Rauscher, Pierce, and Company in San Angelo. In addition to developing a successful business career, Mrs. Bonham was also especially active in promoting Texas history programs throughout her adult life. She was a member of the Daughters of the Republic of Texas, the Texas State Historical Association,[qqv] the Tom Green County Historical Association, the Austin Heritage Society, the American Association of University Women,[qv] and the Fort Concho Museum Board; she was a special consultant on Texas history with the San Angelo and Lake View public schools for many years. Her biography of her grandfather, Francis Dieterich,[qv] *Merchant to the Republic* (1958), is an insightful study of Austin and Texas during the days of the republic. She bequeathed most of her estate to the University of Texas at Austin, designating the University Archives (*see* BARKER TEXAS HISTORY CENTER), the Texas Memorial Museum,[qv] the Department of History, and the College of Business Administration as specific beneficiaries. She was a member of the First Christian Church, San Angelo. She died on June 22, 1973, and was buried in Walnut Creek Cemetery, near Austin.

BIBLIOGRAPHY: Dora Dieterich Bonham Papers, Barker Texas History Center, University of Texas at Austin. Austin *American,* July 29, 1958. San Angelo *Standard Times,* April 6, 1968, June 24, 1973.

Chester V. Kielman

BONHAM, JAMES BUTLER (1807–1836). James Bonham, officer of the Alamo garrison, son of James and Sophia Butler (Smith) Bonham, was born at Red Banks (present-day Saluda), Edgefield County, South Carolina, on February 20, 1807. Recent evidence indicates that he was a second cousin of William B. Travis.[qv] Bonham entered South Carolina College (later the University of South Carolina) about 1824 but never graduated. During his senior year he led a student protest against the poor food served at the college and the obligation of students to attend class in bad weather. He and a number of other students, perhaps the entire senior class, were expelled. Bonham took up the study of law and began practicing in Pendleton, South Carolina, in 1830. On one occasion he caned an opposing lawyer who insulted Bonham's female client. When ordered to apologize by the judge, Bonham threatened to tweak the judge's nose and was promptly sentenced to ninety days for contempt of court.

In 1832, during the nullification crisis, Bonham served as an aide to South Carolina governor James Hamilton, a position that brought him the rank of lieutenant colonel. At the same time he served as captain of a Charleston artillery company. By April 1834 he was practicing law in Montgomery, Alabama. On October 17, 1835, he led a rally of support for the Texan cause at the Shakespeare Theater in Mobile. Three days later he was elected by citizens of Mobile to carry their resolutions of support to Sam Houston.[qv] In another two weeks he was organizing a volunteer company, the Mobile Grays,[qv] for service in Texas.

Bonham reached Texas in November 1835 and quickly involved himself in political and military affairs. On December 1, 1835, he wrote to Sam Houston from San Felipe volunteering his services for Texas and declining all pay, lands, or rations in return. On December 20, 1835, he was commissioned a second lieutenant in the Texas cavalry, but apparently was not assigned to any specific unit. He had time to set up a law practice in Brazoria and was advertising the fact in the *Telegraph and Texas Register*[qv] by January 2, 1836.

Bonham and Houston quickly developed a mutual admiration. After being in Texas for only one month Bonham recommended to Houston that William S. Blount of North Carolina be granted a commission as a captain in the Texas cavalry. On January 11, 1836, Houston recommended to James W. Robinson[qv] that Bonham be promoted to major, for "His influence in the army is great—more so than some who 'would be generals'." Bonham probably traveled to San Antonio de Béxar and the Alamo with James Bowie[qv] and arrived on January 19, 1836. On January 26 he was appointed one of a committee of seven to draft a preamble and resolutions on behalf of the garrison in support of Governor Henry Smith.[qv] On February 1 he was an unsuccessful candidate in the election of delegates to represent the Bexar garrison at the Texas constitutional convention.

He was sent by Travis to obtain aid for the garrison at Bexar on or about February 16, 1836. He returned to the Alamo on March 3, bearing through the Mexican lines a letter from Robert M. Williamson[qv] assuring Travis that help was on its way and urging him to hold out. Bonham died in the battle of the Alamo[qv] on March 6, 1836. He is believed to have died manning one of the cannons in the interior of the Alamo chapel.

Bonham's life and role in the siege and battle of the Alamo have been romanticized more than that of any other defender. He has often been portrayed as a colonel and one of the commanders of the Alamo garrison. He is called "Colonel" by Travis in two letters from the Alamo, but this was only a title of respect dating back to his days with the South Carolina militia. His actual rank was second lieutenant, and he had no standing in the Alamo's chain of command. He was present sporadically at the Alamo. Bonham is wrongly remembered as bringing the news that Colonel Fannin was not coming to Travis's aid, when he actually brought word from Williamson that help was coming. In 1956 the Texas Centennial[qv] Commission erected a statue of Bonham on the courthouse square of the town of Bonham, named in his honor.

BIBLIOGRAPHY: Milledge L. Bonham, "James Butler Bonham: A Consistent Rebel," *Southwestern Historical Quarterly* 35 (October 1931). Wallace O. Chariton, *100 Days in Texas: The Alamo Letters* (Plano, Texas: Wordware, 1990). Daughters of the American Revolution, *The Alamo Heroes and Their Revolutionary Ancestors* (San Antonio, 1976). Bill Groneman, *Alamo Defenders* (Austin: Eakin, 1990). John H. Jenkins, ed., *The Papers of the Texas Revolution, 1835–1836* (10 vols., Austin: Presidial Press, 1973). Thomas R. Lindley, "James Butler Bonham," *Alamo Journal,* August 1988. Walter Lord, *A Time to Stand* (New York: Harper, 1961; 2d ed., Lincoln: University of Nebraska Press, 1978). Stephen B. Oates, ed., *The Republic of Texas* (Palo Alto, California: American West, 1968). Phil Rosenthal and Bill Groneman, *Roll Call at the Alamo* (Fort Collins, Colorado: Old Army, 1985). Vertical Files, Barker Texas History Center, University of Texas at Austin.

Bill Groneman

BONHAM, TEXAS. Bonham, county seat and commercial center of Fannin County, is on U.S. Highway 82 and State highways 78 and 121 on the northern edge of the Blackland Prairie twelve miles south of the Red River. Settlement began with the arrival in 1836 of Bailey Inglish[qv] from Butler County, Kentucky. In 1837 he built Fort Inglish, a blockhouse and stockade, on 1,250 acres of land located on Bois d'Arc Creek near timber and water supplies. John P. Simpson[qv] came soon thereafter, and Inglish and Simpson donated the original townsite, known as Bois d'Arc, as an inducement to settlement. Inglish also secured the town's first post office, which served an area of several hundred miles, including what is now Collin and Grayson counties. When Bois d'Arc became the Fannin county seat on January 26, 1843, the county extended into the Panhandle[qv] and Greer County, Oklahoma Territory; the area later became twenty Texas counties. Bois d'Arc was renamed Bonham on February 26, 1844, in honor of James B. Bonham,[qv] who died at the Alamo. By the early 1840s, C. C. Alexander of Cumberland County, Kentucky, established a business house to supply Fort Worth and nearby forts, and Bonham became a resting and supply base for homeseekers in northeastern Texas. During the Civil War[qv] the town was an agricultural center located at a strategic point near the state's northern border, though few people lived there between 1855 and 1870. Bonham was the site of Gen. Henry E. McCulloch's[qv] Confederate military headquarters for the northern subdistrict of Texas, and local merchants sold supplies to the government. After the Civil War an influx of settlers from the upper South increased the population and contributed to the town's educational, financial, and industrial development. Bonham incorporated on February 2, 1848, obtained a charter to incorporate land within a mile of the courthouse in 1873, and in 1990 operated under a charter granted in 1911.

The Masonic Female Institute, a young ladies' seminary, opened in 1855. Carlton College began in 1867, consolidated with Carr-Burdette College in Sherman in 1914, and affiliated with Texas Christian University in 1916. Fannin College for men opened in 1883. Public schools opened in 1890, and new brick buildings were constructed for both black and white schools in 1928. Bonham Independent School District later absorbed thirty-two consolidated districts covering 230 square miles and five campuses. The Bonham *News*, the county's first newspaper, was founded in 1866 by B. Ober. The Fannin County National Bank opened in 1874, the Steger Opera House (built in 1890) brought touring companies of performers, and major church denominations were represented by 1900. Bonham women founded numerous service and cultural institutions, among them the Current Literature Club (1898), the Bonham Public Library (1901), and a Mother's Club that became affiliated with the national Parent-Teacher Association in 1924. Allen Memorial Hospital was built in 1903.

Bonham was a division point on the Texas and Pacific railroad in 1873. The Dennison, Bonham and New Orleans branch of the Missouri, Kansas and Texas line was built from Bonham to Denison by 1887. By 1888 the town produced row crops including grain and cotton and had 117 businesses, three colleges, three papers, a furniture factory, a sawmill, gristmills, and gins. The Bonham Cotton Mill,[qv] once the largest west of the Mississippi, was chartered in 1900. The Bonham Free Kindergarten opened in 1907 to benefit mothers working in the mill. The mill was sold for profit in 1920 but retained its workforce and local manager. Work Projects Administration and Civilian Conservation Corps[qqv] efforts during the Great Depression[qv] built the high school auditorium, gym, and other projects. World War II[qv] construction included a prisoner of war camp and Jones Airfield for pilot training (1941). Subsequently, row crops were replaced with pastures and small-grain farming, and Bonham farmers raised rabbits, poultry, beef, and dairy cattle. The Southwest Pump Company, General Cable plant, a Coca Cola bottling works, a cucumber-receiving station, and factories for ice, mattresses, brooms, mops, and ice cream employed local workers. In 1988 Bonham had 286 businesses, thirteen industries, a daily paper, an airport, an industrial park, the sixty-five-bed Northeast Medical Center, and a library facility completed in 1976. In 1990 Bonham had a population of 6,686.

Bonham is famous as the home of Sam (Samuel T.) Rayburn,[qv] national Democratic party[qv] minority leader and speaker of the House from 1940 to 1947. The Sam Rayburn House and Sam Rayburn Library[qqv] and the county museum of history are open to the public. Singer Roberta Dodd Crawford[qv] is also from Bonham. During the Texas Centennial[qv] celebration in 1936 federal funds were used to build a replica of Fort Inglish; a second replica was built in 1976. Bonham is the site of the annual Fannin County Fair. Bonham State Recreation Area[qv] and Lake Bonham are three miles southeast of the town.

BIBLIOGRAPHY: Bonham *Daily Favorite*, January 8, 1986. Bonham High School, *History of Bonham* (Dallas: Harben-Spotts, 1929?). Beverly Christian, "Bonham Cotton Mills," *East Texas Historical Journal* 26 (Fall 1988). Will A. Evans, *Bonham 52 Years Ago* (Bonham, Texas: Fannin County Genealogical Quarterly, 1984). *Fannin County Folks and Facts* (Dallas: Taylor, 1977). Juanita C. Spencer, *Bonham—Town of Bailey Inglish* (Wolfe City, Texas: Henington, 1977). Pat Stephens, ed., *Forgotten Dignity: The Black Community of Bonham . . . 1880–1930* (Bonham, Texas: Progressive Citizens, 1984). Vertical Files, Barker Texas History Center, University of Texas at Austin.

Diana J. Kleiner

BONHAM COTTON MILL. The Bonham Cotton Mill, organized on May 12, 1900, by nine Bonham directors acting for the 192 local stockholders, became by 1950 the largest light sheeting mill west of the Mississippi River, with 17,200 spindles and 426 looms, capital stock valued at $600,000, and an annual payroll of $780,000 for 380 employees. It was for decades the major employer in Bonham.

Its textile operations started in 1900 with 5,000 spindles and 150 looms. Capital stock was valued at $150,000 and shares at $100 each; by 1906 the value of stock had risen to $200,000. By 1910 the company employed 196 workers. Consolidated Textile Corporation, an eastern company, bought the mill and forty-six tenant houses for $575,000 in 1920. The onset of the Great Depression[qv] sent Consolidated into bankruptcy, and all its plants closed early in 1930. Bonham businessmen raised the $100,000 purchase price to return ownership to Texas in January 1931, but Dallas investors had assumed control by 1933. Employment stabilized at about 190, and production was geared to light sheeting for tomato frames. During World War II[qv] orders for drill, a heavy fabric, dramatically expanded production and required twenty-four-hour operation. By 1950 employment peaked at 380, and the mill marketed light sheeting and drill for tents, awnings, and sporting goods through a nationwide network of sales offices.

After 1956 lower tariffs undercut the domestic market for cotton textiles, and the company struggled to survive. A merger with the Brenham Cotton Mill in 1958 was dissolved in 1962. Employment dropped to 285 in 1962, at a weekly payroll of $16,500. The mill was reorganized as Red River Textile Mills, and a local drive raised $250,000 to save it. It was mortgaged in 1966 and 1968 before declaring bankruptcy in 1970.

John C. Saunders, a pharmacist, was the first director and managed the mill until his death in 1934. H. A. Burow managed the mill from 1934 until the 1958 merger with Brenham Cotton Mill. The work force at the mill was about 50 percent female at any given time, with the exception of World wars I and II,[qqv] when the percentage probably rose significantly. A 1950 celebration of the mill's fiftieth anniversary revealed that nearly 60 percent of the employees who had been at the mill for over forty years were women. Three women had worked there since its first day. Perhaps because of this, the mill operated a free kindergarten for fifty years. The kindergarten, begun in 1907 by members of the First Methodist Church, was conducted in a private home. Mill manager Saunders was credited with getting a permanent building constructed and for assuming mill responsibility for the kindergarten. Although the first free kindergarten in Texas had been established in Galveston fifteen years earlier, the cotton mill's school was unusual for a town the size of Bonham. The kindergarten was controlled and operated by women. Children from throughout the town were accepted, and tuition was charged those who could afford it. Despite the mill's responsibility for the kindergarten, finances were a problem, and it was eventually supported by the Community Chest. Children were awarded a diploma after two years of lessons in manners, health, cleanliness, and the Bible. One teacher served the school for over forty years, assisted by several aides. In 1950 she estimated that 2,000 children had been students there. The kindergarten was governed by a board composed of two women from each church in Bonham. It closed in 1957.

BIBLIOGRAPHY: Bonham *Daily Favorite*, December 27, 1930, January 24, 1931, May 8, 1950. Beverly Christian, "Bonham Cotton Mills," *East Texas Historical Journal* 26 (Fall 1988). Floy Crandall Hodge, *A His-*

tory of Fannin County (Hereford, Texas: Pioneer, 1966). *Texas Industry*, October 1940. *Beverly M. J. Christian*

BONHAM *DAILY FAVORITE*. The Bonham *Daily Favorite* was founded on May 2, 1910. The paper is an outgrowth of the weekly *Fannin County Favorite*, which was founded by Dr. J. M. Terry sometime around 1880 and absorbed the Bonham *Democrat*. According to some sources, Terry began to publish a daily edition of the paper known as the *Daily Favorite* in addition to the weekly in the 1890s, and this paper subsequently passed through a series of owners, including the Farm Labor Union. In 1922 the *Fannin County Favorite* merged with the Bonham *News* to form the Bonham *News and Fannin County Favorite*. The Bonham *News*, a weekly and semiweekly successor to the weekly *Texas News*, published from 1866 to 1873 by William T. Gass, Jr., had been published beginning in 1874 by editors J. W. Piner and A. D. Chisholm. The Bonham *Daily Favorite* is recalled for the writings of columnist R. M. Cantrell, who contributed to the paper from 1939 until 1976, and for its record of the public career of Samuel T. (Sam) Rayburn,[qv] Fannin County Congressman and longtime speaker of the United States House of Representatives. In 1990 the *Daily Favorite* was published by Dennis Arterburn and had a circulation of 2,833.

BIBLIOGRAPHY: *Texas Newspaper Directory* (Austin: Texas Press Service, 1991). *Diana J. Kleiner*

BONHAM STATE RECREATION AREA. Bonham State Recreation Area, four miles southeast of Bonham on Farm Road 271, was established in 1934 on 261 acres of land donated by the city of Bonham to the State Parks Board. The National Park Service drew up the plans for the park, and Civilian Conservation Corps[qv] workers carried out the construction. Like most CCC-built parks, Bonham State Recreation Area includes a small lake surrounded by shelters, a bathhouse, and a swimming beach. Fishing and low-speed boating are allowed on the lake. The park is less heavily wooded than many other state parks in East Texas. Its flora includes oak, cedar, cottonwood, black willow, and green ash trees, and part of its area is grassy prairie. Park facilities include lakeside campsites, some with electrical outlets, picnic sites, and a group picnic shelter, barracks, and mess hall.

BIBLIOGRAPHY: Mildred J. Little, *Camper's Guide to Texas Parks, Lakes, and Forests* (Houston: Pacesetter, 1978; 2d ed., Houston: Lone Star, 1983). Ray Miller, *Texas Parks* (Houston: Cordovan, 1984). *Brian Hart*

BONILLA, ANTONIO (?–?). Antonio Bonilla, Spanish administrator and historian of early Texas, was an officer of the Secretaría de Cámara in Mexico in October 1772, when the viceroy of New Spain ordered a written history of Texas. Bonilla had never been to Texas, and few historical accounts of the province then existed. He relied largely on original sources, including hundreds of royal statutes and forty volumes of government archives, in compiling his *Breve Compendio* of Texas history. This work recounts government and military activities in Texas between 1685 and 1772 and summarizes recommendations for reorganizing the Texas presidial system. Bonilla completed the work in fifteen days.

In 1773 he became an assistant to Hugo Oconór,[qv] inspector general of the Provincias Internas[qv] of New Spain, who directed military affairs on the northern frontier. Oconór and his two assistants were responsible for annual inspections and reports to the viceroy on the defense of the presidios. As adjutant-inspector and secretary of the commandancy general of the Internal Provinces, Bonilla took part in a seven-member conference convened by the commandant general, Teodoro de Croix,[qv] in San Antonio de Béxar in January 1778 to consider an alliance with various North Texas tribes against the Apaches. In 1784 the government was considering a reorganization of the Spanish mission system,[qv] which had become a drain on the royal treasury. Bonilla, by this time secretary of the viceroyalty, compiled individual reports to the viceroy from every frontier office and mission in the province.

BIBLIOGRAPHY: Herbert Eugene Bolton, "The Spanish Abandonment and Re-occupation of East Texas, 1773–1779," *Quarterly of the Texas State Historical Association* 9 (October 1905). Carlos E. Castañeda, *Our Catholic Heritage in Texas* (7 vols., Austin: Von Boeckmann–Jones, 1936–58; rpt., New York: Arno, 1976). Charles W. Hackett, ed., *Pichardo's Treatise on the Limits of Louisiana and Texas* (4 vols., Austin: University of Texas Press, 1931–46). Elizabeth Howard West, trans., "Bonilla's Brief Compendium of the History of Texas, 1772," *Quarterly of the Texas State Historical Association* 8 (July 1904).
Timothy Palmer

BONILLA, FRANCISCO LEYVA DE (?–?). Francisco Leyva de Bonilla, a Portuguese captain in the service of Spain, was dispatched in 1594 by Governor Diego de Velasco of Nueva Vizcaya to pursue beyond the frontiers of that state a rebellious band of Indians that had committed acts of theft. Once across the border, Bonilla and his party determined to explore New Mexico and the plains beyond and to search for Quivira (*see* CORONADO, FRANCISCO VÁSQUEZ DE, and CÍBOLA, SEVEN CITIES OF). Six soldiers refused to participate in this unauthorized expedition, and Capt. Pedro de Cazorlá warned Bonilla that to make such a move was to commit treason. Nevertheless Bonilla and his followers marched to the upper Rio Grande pueblos and spent about a year there, making Bove (San Ildefonso) their principal headquarters. In 1599 they wandered northeast via Cicuye (Pecos) onto the Great Plains, where they found large herds of buffalo.[qv] They arrived at the real Quivira, an agricultural Indian village of grass huts on what was probably the Arkansas River in present Kansas. After a few days there, the expedition continued on toward a larger stream, believed to have been the Platte in what is now Nebraska, some twelve days' journey beyond the Arkansas. According to Jusepe, a Mexican Indian who was with the party, Bonilla was stabbed to death after a quarrel with his lieutenant, Antonio Gutiérrez de Humaña,[qv] who then assumed command.

BIBLIOGRAPHY: Herbert Eugene Bolton, ed., *Spanish Exploration in the Southwest, 1542–1706* (New York: Scribner, 1908; rpt., New York: Barnes and Noble, 1959). Charles W. Hackett, ed., *Pichardo's Treatise on the Limits of Louisiana and Texas* (4 vols., Austin: University of Texas Press, 1931–46). *Frank Goodwyn*

BONITA, TEXAS (Comal County). Bonita, five miles northeast of New Braunfels in eastern Comal County, was established in 1853–54 when Duncan McBryde, Thomas J. Haley, and J. S. Craft settled on lands in the Nancy Kenner and Orilla Russell leagues. Haley had his slaves seal crevices in a sinkhole on the Balcones Escarpment to make a waterhole for the livestock of the first families. In 1876 Peter Triesch donated land on the east side of Alligator or San Geronimo Creek for the school.

BIBLIOGRAPHY: New Braunfels *Herald*, July 6, 1954.
Oscar Haas

BONITA, TEXAS (Montague County). Bonita is on Farm Road 1815 nine miles northeast of Montague in northeastern Montague County. It was established in 1886, when the Gainesville, Henrietta and Western Railway extended its tracks through the area and was named either for Bonita Hansen, the daughter of an engineer on the rail line, or for the Spanish word *bonita*, reportedly suggested by a surveyor who was taken with the area's beauty. In 1887 the community received a post office. By 1900 the population was 300, and Bonita had become a shipping point for cattle and cotton. In 1906 a bank was chartered locally. Several fires destroyed much of the community, and U.S. Highway 82 bypassed Bonita when it built from St. Jo to Nocona. The post office ceased operations sometime after 1930. Bonita declined from a population of 218 and seven businesses in the 1930s to eighty residents and three businesses by the late 1950s. In 1990 the population was fifteen.

BIBLIOGRAPHY: John Clements, *Flying the Colors: Texas, a Comprehensive Look at Texas Today, County by County* (Dallas: Clements Research, 1984). Guy Renfro Donnell, The History of Montague County, Texas (M.A. thesis, University of Texas, 1940).

Brian Hart

BONITA CREEK (Nacogdoches County). Bonita Creek, also known as Bayou Bonita, rises just south of Central Heights in north central Nacogdoches County (at 31°43′ N, 94°41′ W) and flows southeast for nine miles, through central Nacogdoches, to its mouth on La Nana Bayou, just south of downtown (at 31°35′ N, 94°39′ W). The stream is intermittent in its upper reaches. It crosses flat terrain with local shallow depressions, surfaced by clay and sandy loam that supports water-tolerant hardwoods, conifers, and grasses along the banks.

—— (Potter County). Bonita (Bonillo) Creek rises in eastern Potter County (at 35°19′ N, 101°43′ W) and flows northwest for ten miles to its mouth on the Canadian River, in the east central part of the county (at 35°28′ N, 101°47′ W). The surrounding flat to rolling terrain has some escarpments in the north and local depressions towards the south and is surfaced by deep, fine, sandy to clay loam that supports hardwoods, especially water-tolerant ones, brush, and grasses. The stream, located on land that formerly belonged to the LX Ranch,[qv] crossed the site of the second ranch headquarters. Its junction with the Canadian is now in the Sanford Recreation Area, which includes Lake Meredith.

BONITO CREEK. Bonito Creek rises seventeen miles south of Carrizo Springs in south central Dimmit County (at 28°16′ N, 99°55′ W) and runs east for sixteen miles to its mouth on Velenzuela Creek, eight miles southwest of Catarina (at 28°15′ N, 99°41′ W). Upstream, it flows through rolling hills surfaced by sandy and clay loam that supports scrub brush, mesquite, grasses, and cacti; downstream, hardwoods and grasses grow on flat land with local shallow depressions.

BONNELL, GEORGE WILLIAM (?–1842). George W. Bonnell, journalist and soldier, a native of Onondaga County, New York, was an editor in Alabama for a time and moved by 1829 to Columbus, Mississippi, where he worked as an editor. He traveled to Texas in the summer of 1836 with a company of volunteers from Columbus that he had recruited for the Texas war of independence. In December 1837 he was living in Houston, where he was a charter member of the Philosophical Society of Texas.[qv] During Sam Houston's[qv] first term as president of the republic, Bonnell was commissioner of Indian affairs. In April 1838 he reported efforts of Manuel Flores[qv] and other Mexican emissaries to stir up the Indians in Texas against the whites. In June 1838 Houston assigned Bonnell to prepare a report for the Bureau of Indian Affairs on the status of relations with the Indians. Bonnell advocated a harsh policy against them. In November 1838, with rank of major, he was campaigning against the Indians. In 1839 he moved to Austin, where he and Jacob W. Cruger[qv] were selected as government printers on December 6. On January 15, 1840, Bonnell started publication of the first Austin *Texas Sentinel.*[qv] He sold the *Sentinel* on December 26, 1840, the year he printed his *Topographical Description of Texas, to Which is Added an Account of the Indian Tribes.* That year he was also a charter member of the Texas Patriotic and Philanthropic Society and sometimes worked as a Spanish translator in the General Land Office.[qv] In January 1841 he was involved with the Texas Trading, Mining, and Emigrating Company. On February 4, 1841, he became a charter member of the Austin Lyceum. He took part in the Texan Santa Fe expedition[qv] and was released from prison in Mexico in the summer of 1842, in time to return to Texas to join the Mier expedition[qv] as a lieutenant in Company F. On December 26, 1842, Bonnell was left with a camp guard on the Texas side of the Rio Grande. When the guard was ordered to retreat, he and a companion returned to the camp for horses, and Bonnell was captured and shot by a Mexican soldier, probably on December 27, 1842. Mount Bonnell, on the Colorado River near Austin, was named for him, probably by Gen. Edward Burleson[qv] in 1838.

BIBLIOGRAPHY: Austin History Center Files. George B. Erath, "The Memoirs of George B. Erath, 1813–1891," *Southwestern Historical Quarterly* 26–27 (January–October 1923; rpts., Austin: Texas State Historical Association, 1923; Waco: Heritage Society of Waco, 1956). Thomas J. Green, *Journal of the Texian Expedition Against Mier* (New York: Harper, 1845; rpt., Austin: Steck, 1935). William S. Speer and John H. Brown, eds., *Encyclopedia of the New West* (Marshall, Texas: United States Biographical Publishing, 1881; rpt., Easley, South Carolina: Southern Historical Press, 1978). Houston Wade, *Notes and Fragments of the Mier Expedition* (La Grange, Texas: La Grange *Journal,* 1936). John Melton Wallace, George W. Bonnell, Frontier Journalist in the Republic of Texas (M.A. thesis, University of Texas, 1966).

L. W. Kemp

Bucking Broncos, *by Mary Bonner, ca. 1924. Copperplate etching.* $5\frac{7}{8}'' \times 9\frac{15}{16}''$. *Courtesy Witte Museum, San Antonio, Texas.* Bucking Broncos *is one of three etchings in a series called* Texas *that hung in the Salon d'Automne in Paris in 1924.*

BONNER, MARY ANITA (1887–1935). Mary (Polly) Bonner, artist and printmaker, daughter of Dr. Samuel Lafayette and Carrie Ann (Hill) Bonner, was born at Bayou Bartholomew Plantation near Bastrop, Louisiana, on March 31, 1887. She and her older sister and brother, Emma Jane and William Feuilleteau, spent their formative years on the plantation. In 1897, six years after Samuel Bonner's death, the widow Bonner moved the family to San Antonio, Texas, in search of superior educational opportunities for the children. In 1901 Mary enrolled at San Antonio Academy, and after graduation she attended the University of Texas from 1904 to 1906. She also subsequently traveled in Europe and probably studied in Switzerland and Germany.

Her serious commitment to art began when she spent the summer of 1922 at the Woodstock art colony in upstate New York. There she decided to devote the rest of her life to the art of etching. Serious artists received scant encouragement in Texas at that time; indeed, the University of Texas had no art department until 1938. As Mary spoke French fluently, she chose to study in France; she set sail in the fall of 1922 and found lodging in a pension in Paris, where she lived part of every year for the next seven years. She searched among Parisian printmakers for a master from whom to learn the craft. She spent six weeks going from studio to studio before deciding that print maker Édouard Henri Léon offered the kind of instruction she sought. Léon was a product of the École des Beaux-Arts, the classical stronghold of French academic art, and from him she received superb technical instruction. As early as 1923, Mary Bonner began entering work in juried exhibitions such as the conservative Salon des Artistes Français favored by her master. Her etchings often received official recognition by this group: honorable mention, 1925, to *Notre Dame, Paris;* bronze medal, 1926, to *Portrait of a Princess of the House of Este after Pisanello;* silver medal, 1931, to *Sunflower Girl.*

Bonner asserted her independence, however, when in 1924 she exhibited three etchings in the Salon d'Automne, "where the most daring members of the avant-garde were welcome." Her entries, based on ranch life in Texas and titled *Bucking Broncos, Cowboys,* and *Mesquites,* attracted the notice of Parisian art critics. In the fall of 1925 she submitted another etching inspired by memories of South Texas. *Les Cowboys,* a three-part frieze, was one of the sensations of the salon and was reproduced by three French newspapers to illustrate their coverage of the exposition.

Édouard Léon and his wife journeyed to the United States early in 1927, accompanied by their hostess and guide, Mary Bonner. Léon served as a juror for the second Texas Wildflower Exhibition, held at the Witte Museum[qv] in San Antonio and sponsored by Edgar B. Davis.[qv] The artists did not let this duty infringe on their work schedule, however; Bonner and Léon spent most of their days painting and etching Spanish missions and other picturesque subjects in south central Texas.

By 1928 she had taken up the causes of art and conservation in San Antonio to the extent that she devoted less time to her own work. She was especially active in the San Antonio Art League, the San Antonio Conservation Society,[qqv] and the Southern States Art League.

Mary Bonner spent the last years of her life quietly at the family residence in San Antonio. She was recovering from surgery when a blood clot caused her death on June 26, 1935, at the age of forty-eight. Funeral services were held at St. Mark's Episcopal Church, and her ashes were buried at Mission Burial Park.

BIBLIOGRAPHY: Mary Carolyn Hollers George, *Mary Bonner: Impressions of a Printmaker* (San Antonio: Trinity University Press, 1982). *Mary Carolyn Hollers George*

BONNER, MICAJAH HUBBARD (1828–1883). Micajah Hubbard Bonner, lawyer and state Supreme Court justice, son of William N. Bonner, was born in Greenville, Alabama, on January 25, 1828. In 1836 the family moved to Holmes County, Mississippi. Bonner attended LaGrange College in Kentucky, studied law, and began practice at Lexington, Mississippi, in 1848. In 1849 he moved to Marshall, Texas, where he practiced law and married Elizabeth Patience Taylor. Later he moved to Rusk and formed a partnership with James Pinckney Henderson,[qv] which lasted until Henderson was elected to the United States Senate in 1857. Bonner then practiced law with his brother, F. W. In 1873 he was appointed judge of the Seventh District and moved to Tyler. In 1878 he was appointed associate justice of the Texas Supreme Court by Governor R. B. Hubbard.[qv] Bonner became chief justice in 1878 and served in that capacity until his retirement in 1882. He returned to Tyler, where he died on November 28, 1883.

BIBLIOGRAPHY: James D. Lynch, *The Bench and Bar of Texas* (St. Louis, 1885). Wentworth Manning, *Some History of Van Zandt County* (Des Moines, Iowa: Homestead, 1919; rpt., Winston-Salem, North Carolina: Hunter, 1977). Hattie Joplin Roach, *A History of Cherokee County* (Dallas: Southwest, 1934). *Jeanette H. Flachmeier*

BONNER, THOMAS REUBEN (1838–1891). Thomas Reuben Bonner, son of William N. and Martha Ellen (Wade) Bonner, was born in Holmes County, Mississippi, on September 11, 1838. He moved with his parents to Rusk, Texas, in February 1850. At twelve years of age he became an apprentice printer on the *Cherokee Sentinel.* He began at that time to educate himself by reading and self-directed study. He left the *Sentinel* to take charge of his father's farm in 1854 and was a farmer at the outbreak of the Civil War.[qv] He entered Confederate service in April 1862 as captain, Company C, of Col. William B. Ochiltree's[qv] Eighteenth Texas Infantry. He was subsequently major, lieutenant colonel, and colonel of that regiment, which served in the Trans-Mississippi Department as an element of Walker's Texas Division.[qv] After the war Bonner farmed until 1866, when he began reading law at Rusk in the office of his older brothers, F. W. and M. H. Bonner.[qv] He was admitted to the bar in 1867 and practiced law at Rusk until September 1872, then moved to Tyler, where he entered the banking business with E. C. Williams. Bonner became a leading East Texas banker, railroad director, and financier. He was apparently married twice, first to Cynthia A. Madden of Cherokee County and, later, to Mary Davenport. With Mary he had two sons. In 1866 Bonner represented Rusk County in the state legislature. In 1876 he was elected to the legislature from Smith County and was speaker of the House during the ensuing session. He was a Methodist and a high-ranking Mason. He died in 1891.

BIBLIOGRAPHY: Sidney S. Johnson, *Texans Who Wore the Gray* (Tyler, Texas, 1907). William S. Speer and John H. Brown, eds., *Encyclopedia of the New West* (Marshall, Texas: United States Biographical Publishing, 1881; rpt., Easley, South Carolina: Southern Historical Press, 1978). *Lester Newton Fitzhugh*

BONNER, WILLIAM (1783–1877). William Bonner, early settler and planter, was born in Abbeville District, South Carolina, on April 16, 1783, the son of James and Mary (Laird) Bonner. As a young man he worked as a wagoner hauling goods between Abbeville and Charleston. During the War of 1812 he served in the South Carolina militia and rose to the rank of lieutenant. On March 27, 1816, he married Ann Lee Joel of Charleston, with whom he had eleven children. In 1818 Bonner and his family moved to Monroe County, Alabama, and later to Wilcox County. During this period he began accumulating considerable wealth and put his younger siblings through school. In the early 1850s he moved to Texas and settled on Tehuacana Creek in Freestone County. Between 1854 and 1858 he and his brother, Dr. John Bonner, acquired large tracts of land in the area. By 1860 he owned 112 slaves and $104,920 in real property and was reportedly the wealthiest man in Freestone County. That year his plantation produced 900 bushels of corn and ninety-eight bales of cotton. Bonner was a devout Presbyterian who played an important role in the affairs of the church and was one of the organizers of the Harmony Hill Church at Steward's Mill in October 1876. He and his large extended family were also prominent in local affairs and helped build many of Freestone County's early roads. Bonner died at his home in Freestone County on July 1, 1877, and was buried in the Bonner family cemetery near Steward's Mill. In 1970 a Texas historical marker was placed at the gravesite.

BIBLIOGRAPHY: Randolph B. Campbell, *An Empire for Slavery: The Peculiar Institution in Texas, 1821–1865* (Baton Rouge: Louisiana State University Press, 1989). Marker Files, Texas Historical Commission, Austin. *Christopher Long*

BONNER'S FERRY, TEXAS. Bonner's (Bonner) Ferry was an early settlement near the site of the present State Highway 21 bridge on the Neches River in southeast Cherokee County. The site, located where the Rusk-to-Crockett road crossed the river at Matthews Bluff, had probably long been known as a place to cross the river; during the Spanish Colonial period it may have been one of several places where the Old San Antonio Road[qv] crossed the Neches, though the evidence is not clear. In November 1846 the Cherokee County Commissioners Court granted a permit to John Stinson to establish a ferry there. In 1851 William N. Bonner assumed the ferry operation, and during the next few years a small settlement grew up known as Bonner's or Bonner Ferry. A local post office operated from 1862 to 1873.

The community, however, evidently declined with the coming the railroads, and by the 1880s it no longer appeared on maps. No vestiges of the settlement remained in 1990.

BIBLIOGRAPHY: *Cherokee County History* (Jacksonville, Texas: Cherokee County Historical Commission, 1986). A. Joachim McGraw, John W. Clark, Jr., and Elizabeth A. Robbins, eds., *A Texas Legacy: The Old San Antonio Road and the Caminos Reales* (Austin: Texas State Department of Highways and Public Transportation, 1991). Hattie Joplin Roach, *A History of Cherokee County* (Dallas: Southwest, 1934).

Christopher Long

BONNERS MILLS, TEXAS. Bonners Mills was a short-lived settlement on the Neches River in southwestern Angelina County. A post office opened there in 1876 but was closed the next year. The community was evidently named for W. H. Bonner, who operated a mill and served briefly as postmaster in 1877. The settlement had apparently been abandoned by the early 1880s.

BIBLIOGRAPHY: Angelina County Historical Survey Committee, *Land of the Little Angel: A History of Angelina County, Texas,* ed. Bob Bowman (Lufkin, Texas: Lufkin Printing, 1976).

Christopher Long

BONNEY, TEXAS. Bonney is on Farm Road 521 six miles north of Angleton in Brazoria County. The town was established on the International–Great Northern Railroad in 1873 and named for a conductor on the Columbia Tap Railroad. By 1889 a local post office had been established, and in 1890 Bonney had a general store. The next six years brought a school and three more businesses, including another general store, a cotton gin, and an express and telegraph agent. In 1895 the town reported a population of seventy-five. By 1906 there was a school with one teacher and twenty students. The post office was discontinued in 1920. In 1955 the town had one business and twenty-five inhabitants. In 1988 the population was ninety-nine. In 1990 it was 339.

BIBLIOGRAPHY: James A. Creighton, *A Narrative History of Brazoria County* (Angleton, Texas: Brazoria County Historical Commission, 1975).

Lori Allbright

BONNIE VIEW, TEXAS. Bonnie View is on Farm Road 629 in southern Refugio County, on acreage formerly a part of the Bonnie View Ranch of John Howland Wood.[qv] The area was colonized by settlers primarily of German and Bohemian descent. In 1907–08, when the ranch was divided into farm lots, local farmers established a trading community that included a store, a gin, and a school. In 1948 Bonnie View had several farms clustered around two businesses. By 1988 the population had dwindled to twenty-five, where it remained in 1990.

BIBLIOGRAPHY: Hobart Huson, *Refugio: A Comprehensive History of Refugio County from Aboriginal Times to 1953* (2 vols., Woodsboro, Texas: Rooke Foundation, 1953, 1955).

Hobart Huson

BONO, TEXAS. Bono is on Farm Road 2331 a mile west of U.S. Highway 67 in southwestern Johnson County. The site was settled in the early 1870s with the arrival of the families of Calvin L. Jones and B. H. Williamson, who donated twenty acres each for a townsite. Sixteen acres were set aside as a church and school site; the remaining acreage was free to individuals who would build homes there. The church and school community attracted a number of families to the new community, named Bono by Jones. In 1879 a local post office opened. By 1900 the population reached seventy-five, and the town had become the site of a Baptist revival meeting. Unlike other Johnson County communities that the railroads bypassed, Bono continued to thrive until the Great Depression.[qv] The settlement had a gin, two stores, two churches, and a school. The population was seventy-five in 1938. Beginning in the 1940s, however, the population declined, the post office closed, and the number of area farmers decreased as the region switched from cotton to dairy production. A community building and Baptist church remained in the area in 1971, and the state highway map showed a cemetery at Bono in 1984.

BIBLIOGRAPHY: Frances Dickson Abernathy, The Building of Johnson County and the Settlement of the Communities of the Eastern Portion of the County (M.A. thesis, University of Texas, 1936). Viola Block, *History of Johnson County and Surrounding Areas* (Waco: Texian Press, 1970). Johnson County History Book Committee, *History of Johnson County, Texas* (Dallas: Curtis Media, 1985).

David Minor

BONUS, TEXAS. Bonus, near the junction of Farm roads 102 and 2614, fifteen miles north of Wharton in northern Wharton County, was established in the mid-1890s, when the construction of the Cane Belt Railroad (chartered by William Thomas Eldridge,[qv] W. L. Dunovant, and others) terminated at the plantation site owned by Eldridge and Dunovant in Wharton County. An extension of this line ran to another plantation owned by Eldridge and Dunovant just a few miles south and west of Bonus. In 1896 the community applied to the postal department for a post office and requested the name Alamo, but that name was not approved. Reportedly the name Bonus was chosen instead because the railroad owners were promised a bonus for building a line into the area. The Bonus post office opened in 1896. Bonus initially had relatively few white residents. Little mail was received at the community, and its post office was discontinued three times before being permanently discontinued in 1940, when local mail was routed through Eagle Lake or Egypt.

The syndicate and partnership of Eldridge and Dunovant encompassed land in the area running from Eagle Lake to Garwood in Colorado County and to Bonus in Wharton County. In the early 1900s a prison camp was established of Bonus, and prisoners were contracted to work the land and perform other agricultural jobs. The Dunovant-Eldridge partnership dissolved in 1901; Dunovant took the lands in the Eagle Lake area, and Eldridge took the Bonus plantation. In 1902, Eldridge shot and killed Dunovant.

Eldridge and Dunovant had brought black families to Bonus to work the large fields of sugarcane, cotton, corn, and rice. By 1905 a local school black children had fifty-seven pupils and one teacher. Nedra School, a small black school east of Bonus, eventually merged with Bonus to form the Bonus-Nedra district. In 1926 the district had four schools, four teachers, seventy-five white pupils, and 110 black pupils. In 1958 the district was consolidated with the Hungerford Independent School District, and in 1973 this area became part of the East Bernard ISD.

In 1936 Bonus had two businesses and a population of fifty, which declined to a population of forty-two by the 1980s, when no businesses were reported. The Eldridge-to-Bonus rail link was abandoned in 1940, and the rail bed was converted into a county road. In 1992, the main Cane Belt service line was terminated; the tracks, ties, and gravel bed were removed.

BIBLIOGRAPHY: J. O. Graham, *The Book of Wharton County, Texas* (Wharton?: Philip Rich, 1926). Annie Lee Williams, *A History of Wharton County* (Austin: Von Boeckmann–Jones, 1964).

Merle R. Hudgins

BON WIER, TEXAS. Bon Wier is at the junction of Farm roads 1416 and 363 and U.S. Highway 190, in eastern Newton County. The town was established in 1905 as a station on the Jasper and Eastern Railway, which linked Kirbyville to the Sabine River, and was named for B. F. Bonner and R. W. Wier, manager and surgeon, respectively, of the Kirby Lumber Company (*see* KIRBY, JOHN HENRY). The company built Bon Wier to take advantage of the lush forests in the vicinity as part of its huge expansion program. Specifically, the town was to serve Trotti and Lee's Mill. Bon Wier opened a post office in 1906. Logging camps operated there from 1918 to 1924, again from 1927 to 1929, and finally from 1932 to 1935. The Gulf, Colorado and Santa Fe Railway acquired the 17½-mile Jasper and Eastern in 1948, before becoming the Atchison, Topeka and Santa Fe the same year. Several sawmills still operated in Bon Wier in 1990. Its population, estimated to be about 300 in 1936, reached an apparent high of 500 during the late 1940s before dropping slightly in the 1960s to an estimated 475, a level it maintained in 1990.

bibliography: Newton County Historical Commission, *Glimpses of Newton County History* (Burnet, Texas: Nortex, 1982). Charles P. Zlatkovich, *Texas Railroads* (Austin: University of Texas Bureau of Business Research, 1981). *Robert Wooster*

BOOK CLUB OF TEXAS. The Book Club of Texas was formed by Stanley Marcus in Dallas in 1929 to foster the production of fine books and to sponsor exhibitions and lectures about book making, printing, and binding and typographical design. After study at Harvard, where the Widener Library impressed him, Marcus returned to Texas determined to produce twentieth-century parallels to the Widener's fifteenth and sixteenth century exemplars. Influenced by his familiarity with the Book Club of California, an organization of bibliophiles who mined the rich printing talent in the San Francisco area, Marcus persuaded four others to join him: folklorist and banker John A. Lomax, architect David R. Williams, Fannie E. Ratchford,[qqv] librarian of the University of Texas Wrenn Collection, and lawyer John Hackler. Hackler incorporated the Book Club of Texas as a nonprofit organization, Ratchford proposed titles for publication, Lomax located material worthy of publication, and Williams and Marcus became the project's artistic directors. After Williams designed a colophon representative of the club's southwestern focus—a circle of Texas ranch brands surrounding a BCT branding iron—the group solicited members by mailing a quarto-sized invitation printed on handmade Italian paper to bibliophiles throughout the state.

The club was governed by a board of eleven directors who ensured that it remained noncommercial as well as nonprofit. The club's publications were limited editions, sold to its membership of 300. Members had no responsibility other than to pay yearly dues of ten dollars, although the club's board hoped that they would also purchase each of its publications. The plan was to issue an annual volume devoted to history or literature, with a preference for indigenous or previously unpublished literature. The club stressed the tasteful and appropriate format. The typeface, paper, ink, page layout, illustration, and binding were to blend in a way that enhanced the prose. Prices ranged from two to fifteen dollars. The seven titles the club published were Ellis Bean's[qv] *Memoir of Col. Ellis P. Bean* (1930), Harry Stillwell Edwards's *Eneas Africanus* (1930), Virginia Quitman McNealus's *Code Duello: Letters Concerning the Prentiss-Tucker Duel of 1842* (1931), William Faulkner's *Miss Zilphia Gant* (1932), Alexander Watkins Terrell's[qv] *From Texas to Mexico and the Court of Maximilian in 1865* (1933), J. Frank Dobie's[qv] *Tales of the Mustang* (1936), and Fannie Ratchford's *The Story of Champ d'Asile* (1937). Of the seven, only three were actually produced in Texas; one was produced in New York by a former Texan, Hal Marchbanks. Two came from the Lakeside Press of Chicago and one from the Rydal Press, Santa Fe. Three—*Code Duello, Miss Zilphia,* and the Terrell memoir—won inclusion in the Fifty Books of the Year competition of the American Institute of Graphic Arts. Today, Dobie's *Tales of the Mustang* and Faulkner's *Miss Zilphia Gant* are the rarest and most eagerly sought. The publication of Faulkner's work earned the club attention when the chairman of the Southern Methodist University English department attempted unsuccessfully to have Henry Nash Smith,[qv] an SMU professor, fired for writing the book's introduction.

In 1938, troubled by the economic uncertainty of the Great Depression[qv] and the possibility of war, the club's managers felt compelled to abandon publication. In 1941 the remaining stock of books was transferred to the Texas Folklore Society,[qv] which used the sales proceeds to initiate its Range Life Series under J. Carl Hertzog's[qv] supervision.

In 1988 the Book Club of Texas was reestablished, with seventeen interim directors, an executive director, and Marcus serving as honorary president. Its three goals were to promote excellence in bookmaking, encourage fellowship among Texas book lovers, and educate a wider audience by sponsoring lectures and exhibitions around the state. Membership was limited to 750, and dues were thirty-five dollars annually. The new club's first two publications were John Graves's *Goodbye to a River,* which included previously unpublished photographs by Graves, and Gertrude Beasley's *My First Thirty Years,* both published in 1989. In 1991 the club published Don Hampton Biggers's *Buffalo Guns and Barbed Wire* and Carolyn Osborn's *The Grands: A Short Story.* Bruce Cheeseman's *Perfectly Exhausted with Pleasure: An Account of the Richard King–Mifflin Kenedy Excursion Train to Laredo* was published in 1992.

bibliography: Dallas *News,* July 15, 1962. *Stanley Marcus*

BOOKER, SHIELDS (?–1843). Shields Booker, physician and surgeon of the Army of the Republic of Texas,[qv] was born in South Carolina. He moved on the eve of the battle of San Jacinto[qv] to Texas and served in that battle as assistant surgeon of Col. Sidney Sherman's[qv] Second Regiment, Texas Volunteers, under surgeon Anson Jones.[qv] For his services in the Texas Revolution[qv] Booker received land near Brazoria. On April 30, 1836, he was appointed a surgeon in the Texas army. On leave from the army on April 8, 1837, he left New Orleans on the American schooner *Julius Caesar,* bound for his home in Brazoria County. On April 12 the schooner was overtaken and captured by the Mexican brig-of-war *General Terán.* He was made a prisoner and transported to Matamoros, from where he escaped on May 13. This incident was linked with the capture of the Texas warship *Independence*[qv] and the imprisonment of William H. Wharton.[qv] A year later Booker filed a petition in the Congress of the republic for compensation for his property lost aboard the *Julius Caesar.* He returned to active duty on January 23, 1839, and served as surgeon on the staff of Col. Edward Burleson[qv] at the battle of the Neches[qv] on July 16, 1839. On January 14, 1840, the Republic of Texas[qv] Senate confirmed President Mirabeau B. Lamar's[qv] reappointment of his friend Booker as surgeon in the army. On April 5 of that year, as part of an expedition commanded by Capt. George T. Howard,[qv] Booker attempted to negotiate an exchange of captives with the Comanches, but was able to ransom only a Mexican girl, an American boy, and one other prisoner. He resigned from the Texas army on July 31, 1840, and soon thereafter joined the Federalist army in Mexico in its attempt to establish a Republic of the Rio Grande.[qv] In March 1841 he reported that Gen. Mariano Arista[qv] had assembled an army of 4,000 troops and eighteen pieces of artillery to invade Texas and was already marching toward the Rio Grande. The report, however, proved false.

On September 10, 1842, Judge Anderson Hutchinson[qv] of the San Antonio District Court heard the case of *Shields Booker v. the City of San Antonio,* wherein Booker was suing the city for a fee of fifty pesos promised him by former mayor Juan N. Seguín.[qv] Booker was represented by Samuel A. Maverick.[qv] On that day Mexican general Adrián Woll[qv] captured San Antonio and the fifty-two men in the courtroom. Booker, Maverick, Hutchinson, and the rest of the litigants, spectators, and officers of the court were marched to Mexico City and from there to Perote Prison.[qv] Although Mexican authorities refused to allow Booker to treat fellow prisoner John R. Cunningham, who died of malaria on the Leona River, he did treat a Mexican soldier for snakebite a few days later, and the man recovered. At Perote, where the prisoners were chained in pairs and forced to labor on castle repairs, Booker was shot by a drunken Mexican soldier on March 19,

1843. James L. Trueheart[qv] recorded in his diary that the soldier was actually attempting to shoot one of his own officers who had earlier that day reprimanded him and who was then sharing a bench with Booker; but neither Maverick nor R. A. Barkley, who also wrote of the incident, believed that the shooting was accidental. On being struck Booker is reported to have exclaimed, "The rascal has shot me at last." The musket ball entered near his neck, shattered his collar bone, and exited near his spine. He died on March 21 and was buried in the castle moat. His San Antonio lawsuit was continued through March 4, 1845, when it was dismissed for lack of prosecution; the order stated that "the plaintiff had failed to appear."

bibliography: Daughters of the Republic of Texas, *Defenders of the Republic of Texas* (Austin: Laurel House, 1989). Sam Houston Dixon and Louis Wiltz Kemp, *The Heroes of San Jacinto* (Houston: Anson Jones, 1932). Joseph Milton Nance, *Attack and Counterattack: The Texas-Mexican Frontier, 1842* (Austin: University of Texas Press, 1964). Pat Ireland Nixon, *The Medical Story of Early Texas, 1528–1853* (Lancaster, Pennsylvania: Lupe Memorial Fund, 1946). *Telegraph and Texas Register,* May 26, June 13, 1837, April 18, 25, 1838, November 2, 1842. *Texas Sentinel,* April 15, 1840, March 25, 1841.

Thomas W. Cutrer

BOOKER, TEXAS. Booker, at the intersection of State highways 15 and 23, in northwestern Lipscomb County, originated seven miles to the northwest in 1909 as La Kemp, Oklahoma. The town, including the post office, was moved piecemeal from Oklahoma to Texas in 1919, when the Panhandle and Santa Fe Railway was extended from Shattuck, Oklahoma, to Spearman, Texas. The new townsite was platted in August 1917 by Thomas C. Spearman and named for B. F. Booker, a civil engineer with the line. By 1920 the town had grain elevators, cattle-shipping pens, a bank, a school, three churches, and a population of 600. By 1929 modern utilities had been installed. Due to the Great Depression and Dust Bowl,[qqv] Booker's population decreased from 495 in 1930 to 386 in 1940. But by 1949 agricultural recovery, new farming techniques, and oil exploration had caused the population to increase to 1,500. In 1984 the town had 1,219 residents and fifty-two businesses. In addition to its farm and ranch economy, after 1956 Booker greatly benefited from local oil and gas production. A new sewage plant was completed in 1966, and a new hospital and clinic were built in 1973. The town is incorporated. In 1990 it had a population of 1,236 and reached into Ochiltree County.

bibliography: Mrs. Lowell Bowdle and Mrs. Mason Lemons, eds., *Dimensions of Progress: Fiftieth Anniversary of Booker, Texas, 1919–1969* (1969). *A History of Lipscomb County, Texas, 1876–1976* (Lipscomb, Texas: Lipscomb County Historical Survey Committee, 1976).

H. Allen Anderson

BOONE, HANNIBAL HONESTUS (1834–1897). Hannibal Honestus (Honostus) Boone, lawyer, Confederate Army officer, and Texas attorney general, one of two sons of Joseph Green(e) and Harriet N. (Latham) Boone, was born in Tipton County, Tennessee, on February 24, 1834. By 1842 the family had moved to De Soto County, Mississippi. In 1852, after his mother's death, Boone's family moved to a site in Austin (now in Waller) County, Texas. Boone attended Mountain Academy in Tipton County, Tennessee. He then studied law at Austin College in Huntsville, Texas. He quit school four months before graduation when his father became ill, but he did eventually obtain his license to practice law. For the next four years Boone managed his father's plantation; in 1859 he began his legal practice at Hempstead. Sometime before December 1861 he married Harriet Rebecca Fullinwieder, with whom he had one daughter.

In February 1861 Boone enlisted as a private in Col. John S. Ford's[qv] regiment of the Confederate Army and served for a time on the Rio Grande frontier. Upon his return from that campaign, he enlisted in Capt. W. A. McDade's company, with which he served at Dickinson's Bayou and around Galveston. On July 4, 1862, he left Hempstead for Louisiana with five companies under Maj. Edwin Waller.[qv] Though he entered Waller's unit as a second lieutenant, he was shortly promoted to major and with Waller's Thirteenth Texas Cavalry was attached to Green's (formerly Sibley's) Brigade, with which he saw action along the Louisiana-Texas-Arkansas border. As Waller's executive officer Major Boone led Waller's Thirteenth Texas Cavalry Battalion (which became Waller's Cavalry Regiment around December 1864) in the commander's absence. Boone was wounded on September 29, 1863, at Fordoche, Louisiana, and lost his right arm and the first two fingers and thumb of his left hand. He was subsequently transferred back to Texas, where he served post duty under Gen. John Bankhead Magruder,[qv] commander of the Department of Texas, for the remainder of the war. Boone became engaged to Susan H. Gordon in 1863, and they were married in November of that year.

After the war they moved to Anderson, Texas, where Boone practiced law in partnership with Isham G. Searcy.[qv] Boone was elected attorney general of Texas on the Democratic ticket in 1876 and served one term. When that ended in 1878, he moved to Navasota and resumed his law practice. He organized one of the first camps of Confederate veterans there and was elected commander of the Division of Texas at the reunion of the United Confederate Veterans in May 1895. Boone and his wife had a large number of children. He continued to practice law in Navasota until his death there, on May 23, 1897.

bibliography: E. L. Blair, *Early History of Grimes County* (Austin, 1930). Hannibal Honestus Boone Papers, Barker Texas History Center, University of Texas at Austin. John Henry Brown, *Indian Wars and Pioneers of Texas* (Austin: Daniell, 1880; reprod., Easley, South Carolina: Southern Historical Press, 1978). Norman Kittrell, *Governors Who Have Been and Other Public Men of Texas* (Houston: Dealy-Adey-Elgin, 1921). Charles Spurlin, comp., *West of the Mississippi with Waller's 13th Texas Cavalry Battalion* (Waco: Texian Press, 1971).

Alice J. Rhoades

BOONE, THEODORE SYLVESTER (1896–?). Theodore Sylvester Boone, black attorney, pastor, author, and editor, was born in Winchester, Texas, on December 28, 1896, the son of Alexander and Lillian (Chaney) Boone. He attended Terrell High School in Terrell, Texas, and a series of universities including Prairie View A&M and Bishop College in Texas. From 1918 to 1920 he studied at Des Moines University and the University of Iowa. In 1921 he wrote a book entitled *Paramount Facts in Race Development.* The next year he attended the University of Chicago and the Chicago Law School and published *Laws of Trusts and Trustees.* He practiced law in Indianapolis, Indiana, and was admitted to the Supreme and the United States district courts of that state. Boone married Ruby Beatrice Alexander in December 1921. In 1924 he attended Arkansas Baptist College in Little Rock, Arkansas, and later that year began serving as pastor of Eighth Street Baptist Church in Temple, Texas. He was also the editor-in-chief of the *Western Star,* a black Baptist church publication, and wrote another book, *Race Migration, It's Cause and Cure* (1924). He was the secretary of the Texas delegation to the National Baptist Convention in 1924 and 1925. In 1926 Boone wrote *History of Negro Baptists in Texas* and edited *Flaming Sword,* a monthly magazine published in Indianapolis. Boone was a Republican, a Mason, and a member of Kappa Alpha Psi and the Odd Fellows. He retired in Temple, Texas.

bibliography: *Who's Who in Colored America,* 1930–32.

Kharen Monsho

BOONE PRAIRIE, TEXAS. Boone Prairie, also known as Hayes, is just south of Farm Road 979 and eight miles north of Franklin in extreme northeast Robertson County. The community was settled in 1872. By 1880 it had a post office with A. A. Hayes, who owned a general store, as postmaster. By 1885 the settlement had a population of thirty, three churches, a district school, and a combined gristmill and cotton gin. By 1891 it had a population of fifty, two physicians, and another gin and gristmill. The next year it had three general stores and three physicians. By 1900 the area had become known as Boone Prairie and was divided into East Boone Prairie and West Boone Prairie, though maps continued to label the area Hayes up to the 1940s. In 1904 the East Boone Prairie school had an enrollment of ninety-seven pupils and two teachers, and the West Boone Prairie school had an enrollment of thirty-six and one teacher. The post office closed in 1906. The town is shown with one store, three churches, two cemeteries, and a population of twenty-five on a 1942 map that refers to it as Hayes. On 1969 and 1983 revised maps the community was shown divided into East and West Boone Prairie. A few scattered dwellings, two cemeteries, and the Hayes Church were at the site.

BIBLIOGRAPHY: J. W. Baker, *History of Robertson County, Texas* (Franklin, Texas: Robertson County Historical Survey Committee, 1970). *Richard Allen Burns*

BOONETOWN, TEXAS. Boonetown (Boontown) was off State Highway 94 seven miles west of Groveton in west central Trinity County. It was founded around the time of the Civil War[qv] by Whitnall Alston Boone, said to have been the great-nephew of Daniel Boone. Most of its residents moved out of the area after World War II.[qv] In the early 1990s only a cemetery remained.

BIBLIOGRAPHY: Patricia B. and Joseph W. Hensley, eds., *Trinity County Beginnings* (Groveton, Texas: Trinity County Book Committee, 1986). Trinity County Historical Commission, *Trinity County Cemeteries* (Burnet, Texas: Nortex, 1980). *Christopher Long*

BOONS CREEK (Jack County). Boons Creek rises north of Gibtown in extreme southeastern Jack County (at 33°02′ N, 97°59′ W) and runs thirteen miles northeast to its mouth on Hunt Creek, at Lake Bridgeport in western Wise County (at 33°09′ N, 97°53′ W). The surrounding flat to rolling terrain is surfaced by clay and sandy loam that supports water-tolerant hardwoods, conifers, and grasses.

___ (Lee County). Boons Creek rises in pastureland near the Fayette county line in southeastern Lee County (at 30°04′ N, 96°56′ W) and runs southeast for five miles to its mouth on Piney Creek, four miles south of Warda in Fayette County (at 30°01′ N, 96°55′ W). It traverses nearly level to undulating land surfaced by sandy loam interspersed with surface deposits of sand and gravel and heavy subsoils of clay mixed with gravel that support grasses, oak forests, water-tolerant hardwoods, conifers, yaupon, and hackberry. The area is marginal for pasture and is occasionally used as a source of sand and gravel. Local sources generally credit the creek's name to a family that settled in the area shortly before the Civil War.[qv]

___ (Leon County). Boons (Boon's, Boon) Creek, a perennial stream, rises at the confluence of Northwest Fork and Ringgold Creek, three miles southeast of Oakwood in northeastern Leon County (at 31°33′ N, 95°48′ W) and flows southeast for six miles to its mouth on the Trinity River, at the Houston-Leon county line nine miles southeast of Oakwood (at 31°30′ N, 95°44′ W). The stream traverses nearly level terrain surfaced by clay that supports intermittent woods of post oak, black hickory, pecan, elm, water oak, and hackberry in its lower course. Settlement in the vicinity began in the mid-nineteenth century. Pilgrim's Rest, Shiloh, and Timesville are located on the west bank of the lower creek. The stream is probably named for James N. Boone, an original grantee of land along the creek's upper course.

BOON SLOUGH. Boon Slough rises in a small impoundment known as Willingham Lake eight miles northwest of Uvalde in central Uvalde County (at 29°19′ N, 99°50′ W) and runs south for seven miles to its mouth on Cooks Slough, two miles northwest of the intersection in Uvalde of U.S. Highway 83 and U.S. Highway 90 West (at 29°14′ N, 99°49′ W). It rises in flat terrain with local shallow depressions surfaced by shallow, stony gravel that supports water-tolerant hardwoods, conifers, and grasses and crosses into flat to rolling prairie with local scarps surfaced by deep clay that supports oak, juniper, grasses, and mesquite.

BOONSVILLE, TEXAS. Boonsville is on Farm Road 920 twenty miles southwest of Decatur in southwestern Wise County. By the mid-1870s an estimated thirty farmers were settled near the banks of Boon's Creek, named for Stephen Boon, a pioneer settler of the county. In 1878 a post office was established with Joseph Roth as postmaster. Two years later Charlie Miller built a cotton gin near the banks of South Willow Creek. Three stores were operating by 1881. The following year the town was moved from Boon's Creek to its present site. By 1914 Boonsville had a population of 200, two general stores, a school, a bank, and a steam gristmill. Residents expected to get a railroad connection in the early 1890s but were disappointed. The failure to obtain a railroad and the decline in cotton production in the surrounding area between 1900 and 1910 effectively stalled the town's growth. From 1914 until the mid-1970s the population hovered around 150. It declined sharply in the early 1970s to fifty-two, where it remained in 1990. The school was consolidated with the Bridgeport district in 1950, and the post office closed in 1969.

BIBLIOGRAPHY: Rosalie Gregg, ed., *Wise County History* (Vol. 1, n.p: Nortex, 1975; Vol. 2, Austin: Eakin, 1982). *David Minor*

BOONVILLE, TEXAS. Boonville, the first county seat of Brazos County, was on Farm Road 158, which is also known as Boonville Road, two miles northeast of the site of what is now Bryan. The Republic of Texas[qv] Congress appointed a committee—made up of J. H. Jones, Eli Seale, William T. Millican,[qv] Joseph Ferguson, and Mordecai Boon, Sr.—that selected for the county seat a tract of 150 acres from the John Austin[qv] league. The committee purchased the land, which was originally an unbroken post oak forest, from Elizabeth and William Pierpont[qv] for $150 and conveyed it in a deed to Brazos County on July 30, 1841. The town was built around a public square, with space in the square reserved for a courthouse. In 1841 Boonville was the county seat of Navasota County, but the county name was changed to Brazos in 1842. The town was probably named in honor of Mordecai Boon, Sr., whose uncle was Daniel Boone. In 1843 Boonville residents built a jail, and in 1846 they acquired a post office and built a courthouse. The Boonville courthouse, known as the "board shanty," served many purposes: there Gen. Sam Houston[qv] and other prominent statesmen made speeches, and circuit preachers such as William Tryon and Robert Alexander[qqv] gave sermons. A stage line went from Houston through Boonville in 1850; its drivers and passengers would stop at the Boonville hotel overnight. The town enjoyed prosperity from 1842 to 1866. However, when the Houston and Texas Central Railway was extended from Millican to Bryan in 1866, Boonville residents elected, on October 15, 1866, to make Bryan the county seat. In December 1866 the Boonville mail was rerouted through the Bryan post office. In the 1990s all that remained of Boonville was the cemetery on Boonville Road. The townsite is marked by a Texas Centennial[qv] monument.

BIBLIOGRAPHY: Glenna Fourman Brundidge, *Brazos County History: Rich Past—Bright Future* (Bryan, Texas: Family History Foundation, 1986). Elmer Grady Marshall, History of Brazos County (M.A. thesis, University of Texas, 1937). Margaret Lips Van Bavel, *Birth and Death of Boonville* (Austin: Nortex, 1986). *Christina L. Gray*

BOOS-WALDECK, COUNT LUDWIG JOSEPH VON (1798–1880). Count Ludwig Joseph von Boos-Waldeck, cofounder of the Adelsverein[qv] and one of its first representatives in Texas, the son of Count Clemens of Boos-Waldeck and Montfort and Lady Johanne of

Bibra, was born in Koblenz, on the Rhine River in what later became Germany, on November 26, 1798. He was descended from a line of Rhenish knights and nobles dating back to the thirteenth century. Little is known about his youth and education, but he began his military career in the Prussian army. He left that service in 1832, however, to become aide-de-camp, with the rank of major, to Duke Adolf of Nassau. In 1837 the duke promoted him to the rank of lieutenant colonel.

In April 1842 Boos-Waldeck and a few other nobles met at Biebrich on the Rhine, near Mainz, to organize a society, which they called the Adelsverein, to promote German emigration to Texas. In Mainz, on May 19, Boos-Waldeck was appointed the society's authorized agent and was ordered to proceed to Texas in the company of another member, Count Victor August of Leiningen,[qv] on a mission to obtain land for the society in Texas. Shortly after their arrival in Galveston in late August 1842, the two visited President Sam Houston[qv] briefly in Houston and presented to him the society's plans. In October the two agents traveled to Columbia, to San Felipe de Austin, to the German settlement of Rödersmühl (now Shelby), on Mill Creek in Austin County, and finally, in November, in the company of Secretary of State Anson Jones,[qv] to Washington-on-the-Brazos, where the Congress of the Republic of Texas[qv] was in session. In the temporary capital Boos-Waldeck and Leiningen met a second time with Houston and Jones to discuss a land grant to the society for the settlement of German emigrants. Although Houston and Jones offered to extend the society such a grant, Boos-Waldeck and Leiningen declined the offer when they learned that the grant would be in territory west of Austin that was still subject to Indian depredations. Mindful of the expenses to the society of settling immigrants on a large and distant grant, Boos-Waldeck conceived the plan of establishing, in the more settled region near Austin's colony, a limited settlement that could serve later as a base for colonization farther to the west. In January 1843 he purchased a tract of land now in Fayette County, the William H. Jack[qv] league near Industry, the home of Friedrich Ernst.[qv] Boos-Waldeck named the land Nassau Farm[qv] in honor of his friend and sovereign and the protector of the society, Duke Adolf of Nassau. For a year after its purchase Boos-Waldeck worked to develop the plantation's resources and its value to the society as a center for future German settlement in Texas. In his first written report to the society, presented at a general meeting in June 1843; in his correspondence with the society's business manager and secretary, Count Carl Frederick Christian of Castell-Castell;[qv] and finally upon his return to Germany in March 1844, Boos-Waldeck counseled resolutely against immediate colonization on a large scale. His views were supported by Duke Adolf, but the other members failed to heed his advice and warnings. Consequently, in April 1844 Count Joseph and his brother, Count Anton of Boos-Waldeck, withdrew from the society.

In April 1843, during his visit to Texas, Boos-Waldeck was promoted by Duke Adolf to the position of chief equerry, which he assumed upon his return to Germany, in addition to his former post as the duke's aide-de-camp. In 1846, at his own request, he was retired from active military service. In 1850 the duke awarded Boos-Waldeck a lifetime annual pension of 4,000 gulden, in recognition of the count's faithful and superior service. During the 1860s Boos-Waldeck maintained a lively correspondence with Duke Adolf from his home in the Bavarian town of Pielenhofen, near Regensburg. On October 1, 1880, he died at Aschaffenburg, a Bavarian city on the Main River east of Frankfurt.

BIBLIOGRAPHY: Rudolph L. Biesele, *The History of the German Settlements in Texas, 1831–1861* (Austin: Von Boeckmann–Jones, 1930; rpt. 1964). Solms-Braunfels Archives (transcripts, Sophienburg Museum, New Braunfels, Texas; Barker Texas History Center, University of Texas at Austin). *Louis E. Brister*

BOOT CANYON. Boot Canyon is a deep, rugged valley cut by an intermittent stream high in the Chisos Mountains of Big Bend National Park[qv] in southern Brewster County. The headwaters of its drainage are near the South Rim of the Chisos Mountains, south of Emory Peak (at 29°14′ N, 103°17′ W). The stream is fed by Boot Spring. The canyon runs northeast for four miles to its mouth near the upper end of Juniper Canyon (at 29°15′ N, 103°16′ W). Boot Canyon descends rapidly some 2,500 feet. Near its midpoint stands a giant rock spire called the Boot, for which the canyon was named. Just below the Boot the canyon deepens over 1,000 feet in less than half a mile, between massive cliffs. With the exception of a few scattered grassy meadows, the greater part of Boot Canyon is wooded. The vegetation throughout the drainage includes a mixture of oak-juniper-piñon woodland and conifer forest, with the former predominant in most areas. Boot Canyon also shelters the only native stand of Arizona cypress in Texas.

BIBLIOGRAPHY: Alpine *Avalanche,* September 14, 1951. A. Michael Powell, "Vegetation of Trans-Pecos Texas," in *New Mexico Geological Society Guidebook* (Socorro, New Mexico: New Mexico Geological Society, 1980).

BOOTH, TEXAS. Booth is on the Atchison, Topeka and Santa Fe Railway and Farm Road 2759, eight miles southeast of Richmond in eastern Fort Bend County. The site was originally a part of the Henry Jones[qv] league in the Stephen F. Austin[qv] colony. Freeman Irby Booth founded the settlement in the 1890s, giving it his name. Booth was a major landowner in the county and operated a general store, a lumberyard, a cotton gin, and a syrup mill in the community. The town of Booth was granted a post office in 1894 and had a Baptist church, a school, and an estimated 150 inhabitants in 1896. In 1914 the community had an estimated 300 inhabitants, a bank, and telephone service. In 1926 the Booth schools served eighty-five white and 177 black students. The population of the community stayed an estimated 100 from 1925 through 1948, and in the 1940s Booth had two churches, a school, a cemetery, and a number of dwellings. Booth's population fell to forty in 1949. In 1980 the community comprised a collection of dwellings and two businesses. Its population was estimated at sixty in 1990.

BIBLIOGRAPHY: S. A. McMillan, comp., *The Book of Fort Bend County* (Richmond, Texas, 1926). *Mark Odintz*

BOOTHE CREEK. Boothe Creek rises four miles northwest of Dalby Springs in southwestern Bowie County (at 33°26′ N, 94°44′ W) and runs south for ten miles to its mouth on the Sulphur River, three miles west of the Red River county line (at 33°19′ N, 94°42′ W). The creek crosses an area of low-rolling hills surfaced by loam that supports dense woods of post oak, blackjack oak, and elm. The stream may have been named for Benjamin Boothe, an original grantee of land in the area.

BOOTLEG, TEXAS. Bootleg (Bootleg Corner) is in southwestern Deaf Smith County. There are two stories about the origin of its name. One associates the name with Moonshine Sheep Camp, where a moonshine still was once located; the campground was for cowboys and others traveling from La Plata to Endee, New Mexico. Another story has it that the community was named for a "bootleg school"—a small school building that was moved to various locations by agents selling land for the Capitol Syndicate (*see* XIT RANCH) so that prospective customers would believe there was a school near the land they were buying. The first real school in the area was probably that at Messenger, begun in 1909 by J. N. Messenger, a local farmer. It was near an old XIT Ranch campsite four miles west of Bootleg Corner and south of Garcia Lake. For that reason, the farming community around it is often called Garcia. During the 1930s Bootleg Corner experienced a boom of sorts after Louis Woodford converted the abandoned "bootleg school" building into a general store, which became a trading center for the western part of the county. In 1942 Woodford bought a rival store across the road that had been erected in 1936 by

Phineas Short. Although these buildings were later torn down and hauled away, the Precinct 3 County Barn retains the name Bootleg Corner. In 1914 the Walcott school was built thirteen miles northwest of Hereford in the middle of the Walcott, Piatt, Arnold, and O'Brien ranches. It changed locations several times before 1950, when the original Walcott, Bippus, and Messenger districts were consolidated as the Walcott district and a modern brick school building was erected north of Bootleg Corner. The school is also used for various community functions, as is the Garcia community building, which is on the site of the old Messenger school.

BIBLIOGRAPHY: *Deaf Smith County: The Land and Its People* (Hereford, Texas: Deaf Smith County Historical Society, 1982).

H. Allen Anderson

BOOT ROCK. Boot Rock is a mile east of Emory Peak in the Chisos Mountains of Big Bend National Park[qv] in southern Brewster County (at 29°15′ N, 103°17′ W). It is a slender stone tower that stands isolated between massive cliffs in a high, heavily wooded canyon. It resembles an inverted cowboy boot and is referred to in some sources as the Cowboy Boot; local residents call it the Boot. Boot Rock is an erosional remnant, a surviving portion of what was once probably a dike cutting through the Chisos Formation.

BIBLIOGRAPHY: Ross A. Maxwell, *The Big Bend of the Rio Grande* (Bureau of Economic Geology, University of Texas at Austin, 1968).

BOQUILLAS, TEXAS. Boquillas, also known as Rio Grande Village, was on the Rio Grande eighteen miles southeast of Panther Junction in Big Bend National Park[qv] in southeastern Brewster County. Boquillas means "little mouths" in Spanish, presumably a reference to the numerous small streams or arroyos draining the Sierra del Carmen into the Rio Grande. The first American explorers of the region were surveyors who came under the command of Maj. William H. Emory[qv] in the summer of 1852. Emory's report made no mention of any settlement in the area, and the first development there did not occur for another three decades. On January 16, 1882, surveyors John T. Gano, E. L. Gage, and E. M. Powell traveled down the Rio Grande on flat-bottomed boats and arrived near the mouth of Boquillas Canyon. They were escorted by Texas Rangers[qv] under Capt. C. L. Nevill. According to local legend, they discovered a number of horses on the north side of the river near the mouth of the canyon. As they lacked the means to bring the horses with them, and because they believed that the animals would be used by hostile Indians, Nevill ordered all the horses killed; thus the canyon was called Dead Horse Canyon, and eventually the mountains to the north became known as the Sierra del Caballo Muerto, which means "dead horse mountains" in Spanish.

In the following year silver and lead mining began in Boquillas del Carmen, just across the Rio Grande in Mexico. When the railroad built through Marathon, that northern Brewster County town became the nearest railhead for the output of the Del Carmen mines. The Consolidated Kansas City Smelting and Refining Company built a cable tramway to transport ore from Mexico to the United States side, where it built a processing plant.

For the next twenty years various speculators bought and sold land on the Texas side of the river, but the first permanent resident of Boquillas, Texas, was Dennis Edward (Ed) Lindsey, who was appointed by the United States Customs Service to inspect ore shipments from the Del Carmen mines in 1894. The enterprising Lindsey also opened a store that served the population on both sides of the river; graded a crude road from Boquillas to Marathon, which the Consolidated Company later upgraded to a second-class highway at a cost of $75,000; and became the unofficial local postmaster. When the residents of Boquillas, Coahuila, discovered that the mail service via the railroad to Marathon was much quicker than the Mexican mail, Lindsey began picking up mail for them whenever he went into Marathon for supplies. When he finally applied for an official post office in July 1896, he estimated the local population as 300 on the Texas side of the river, including San Vicente, and 1,000 on the Mexican side. The application was approved, and the post office was opened in Lindsey's store.

The development of Boquillas continued to depend heavily on the mining operation across the river. In 1897 La Villa de Boquillas del Carmen in Coahuila was declared an official villa, and in 1899 Robert T. Hill[qv] reported that its population was 2,000. In that year Daniel Guggenheim of New York set up the American Smelting and Refining Company (ASARCO[qv]), which took over Consolidated KSARCO's cable tram and processing plant in Boquillas. In 1900 Lindsey sold his store and moved to Lajitas. Shortly thereafter the rancher Martín Solís, who had been leasing land in the area since 1893, bought his own land and opened a store to replace Lindsey's. Another local entrepreneur was Jesse Deemer, who had arrived in the Boquillas area in the 1880s. With the backing of Marathon merchant C. W. Hess, Deemer opened a second store in competition with Solís's.

But the most enterprising of all may have been the German immigrant Max A. Ernst, who settled eight miles northwest of Boquillas at a place called La Noria (the well). Ernst was a rancher, notary public, justice of the peace, and county commissioner and opened a small schoolhouse at La Noria. In 1901 he was named the postmaster, a fact that suggests he had already unofficially moved the Boquillas post office there, although he did not formally apply for such a move until 1903. He also provided more competition for the Solís family by opening the Big Tinaja Store, a business move that may have led to his murder. On September 27, 1908, Ernst was shot three times by an unknown assailant. Before he died he wrote a note that suggested a Solís had been responsible. Several members of the Solís family, including Martín's son Benito, who ran the store, were suspected, but never convicted. Around 1911, perhaps due to the persistent rumors about his role in Ernst's death, Benito Solís sold the store and moved away. Also in 1911 ASARCO closed the Boquillas smelter.

With the death of Ernst and the departure of Lindsey and Solís, María Sada,[qv] who had moved to Boquillas in 1906, became the leading local entrepreneur. She ran a store and cafe there until 1936, when her husband died and she moved to Del Rio. In October 1913 W. K. Ellis, who owned a candelilla wax factory at McKinney Spring, ten miles northeast of Ernst's store, was named postmaster, and the post office's name was changed from Boquillas to McKinney Spring. The McKinney Spring office was discontinued in 1921.

In 1914 a group of San Antonio and Houston businessmen renewed interest in the Boquillas mining district. The Mexican-owned Puerto Rico Mining Company was operating in the Sierra del Carmen, but the closing of the Boquillas smelter meant that the ore had to be shipped to Marathon and carried by railroad to the ASARCO smelter in El Paso, the only such facility in West Texas. The Texas investors built a second and more elaborate cable tramway across the Rio Grande, a few miles downstream from the old KSARCO tram. This new tramway terminated at La Noria and necessitated the construction of a road from that village to the Boquillas-Marathon highway. The tramway was briefly successful, but the Puerto Rico mine closed before the end of World War I.[qv] The Glenn Spring raid[qv] occurred on May 5, 1916, twelve miles west of Boquillas. Shortly thereafter, whether from fear of future raids or because of lingering suspicions about his link to the bandits, Deemer sold his store and moved to California.

The estimated population of Boquillas grew from twenty-five in the late 1930s to thirty in the mid-1940s and forty by the end of the decade, but by the early 1960s had dwindled to six. In 1990 Boquillas had a campground and a few scattered buildings, including a ranger station, a United States Customs post, and a Sul Ross State University research station.

BIBLIOGRAPHY: Clifford B. Casey, *Mirages, Mysteries and Reality: Brewster County, Texas, the Big Bend of the Rio Grande* (Hereford, Texas: Pioneer, 1972). Arthur R. Gomez, *A Most Singular Country:*

A History of Occupation in the Big Bend (Santa Fe: National Park Service; Salt Lake City: Charles Redd Center for Western Studies, Brigham Young University, 1990). *Martin Donell Kohout*

BOQUILLAS CANYON. Boquillas Canyon, on the Rio Grande in southeastern Brewster County, is one of the most famous canyons in Big Bend National Park[qv] and is a favorite site for float trips down the river. Though its walls are more open and eroded than those in Santa Elena and Mariscal canyons, they still rise as high as 1,500 feet above the river below. They were carved out of thick layers of limestone originally deposited as sediments in a shallow sea, between 60 million and 130 million years ago. The actual length of Boquillas Canyon is a matter of some debate. According to the United States Geological Survey, it begins three miles northeast of the community of Boquillas (at 29°12′ N, 102°55′ W) and winds four miles east to its mouth five miles northeast of Boquillas (at 29°13′ N, 102°53′ W). Other estimates put its length at seventeen miles, longer than Santa Elena and Mariscal canyons, and place its endpoint eight miles upstream from Stillwell Crossing just west of the mouth of Heath Creek. The river is somewhat calmer in Boquillas Canyon than in Santa Elena and Mariscal canyons, but Boquillas Canyon is still an imposing sight. M. T. W. Chandler, the leader of a surveying expedition that was to explore the Rio Grande from El Paso to the mouth of the Pecos in 1852, aborted his mission at the canyon, which he called Cañón de Sierra Carmel. Instead, he and his men, their boats wrecked and their supplies low, struck eastward across Mexico to Fort Duncan, near Eagle Pass. Boquillas means "little mouths" in Spanish, perhaps a reference to the canyon's narrow mouth.

BIBLIOGRAPHY: Ronnie C. Tyler, *The Big Bend* (Washington: National Park Service, 1975).

BOQUILLAS HOT SPRINGS. Boquillas Hot Springs is a group of hot (41°C, 106°F) springs about two miles west of Rio Grande Village and five miles north of Boquillas in Big Bend National Park,[qv] southern Brewster County. An ancient people dug out a pit for bathing here, and bedrock mortars as well as rock paintings and smoke-blackened cliffs indicating the lengthy presence of native peoples may be seen in the area. When the Spaniard Pedro de Rábago y Terán[qv] visited the springs in 1747, he found the Apaches living in villages and growing squash plants. The Comanche Trail[qv] later passed the springs. For a time early in the twentieth century they were a popular bathing resort, and the water from the springs still flows into a walled-up pool. The springs are probably fed by surface-recharged water that circulates to a depth of about 700 meters, where it is heated; it then returns to the surface along faults and emerges from the Boquillas limestone on the bank of the Rio Grande. The rate of flow has been falling since the early twentieth century.

BIBLIOGRAPHY: Gunnar Brune, *Springs of Texas,* Vol. 1 (Fort Worth: Branch–Smith, 1981). *Gunnar Brune*

BORACHO, TEXAS. Boracho was on U.S. Highway 80 and the Texas and Pacific Railway ten miles west of Kent and twenty-six miles east of Van Horn in south central Culberson County. It was apparently founded around the time that the railroad was built through the area in the early 1880s. Its name is probably a misspelling of *borracho,* Spanish for "drunk." One source says the town got its name during the construction of the railroad, when the crew for the Texas and Pacific, building west through Culberson County, was outpacing the competing Galveston, Harrisburg and San Antonio crew, which was building east from Hudspeth County. The GH&SA crew donated several wagonloads of whiskey to their rivals and took the lead while the T&P crew was sleeping off the booze. Another source, however, says that the name is Spanish for "violet-covered" and is derived from the name of nearby Boracho Peak in Jeff Davis County. A local post office operated from 1908 until 1912 with Mary E. Glenn as postmistress. Maps of the area from the mid-1950s showed just one dwelling at the site. By 1970 a cemetery was all that remained there.

Martin Donell Kohout

BORACHO PEAK. Boracho Peak, thirty-nine miles northwest of Fort Davis in northwestern Jeff Davis County (at 30°56′ N, 104°23′ W), rises to an elevation of 5,647 feet above sea level, some 1,000 feet above the Culberson county line, a half mile north. Its shallow, stony soils support live oak, piñon, juniper, and grasses. Various explanations of the name have been offered, including the suggestion that it is Spanish for "violet-colored" or a misspelling of *borracho,* Spanish for "drunk."

BORDELON, WILLIAM JAMES (1920–1943). William James Bordelon, Medal of Honor recipient, the son of M. J. Bordelon, was born in San Antonio, Texas, on December 25, 1920. He entered military service at San Antonio on December 10, 1941. On November 20, 1943, Staff Sgt. Bordelon was attached to the Second Marine Division in action against the Japanese on the atoll of Tarawa in the Gilbert Islands. After landing under enemy fire that killed all but four men in his tractor, he remained in action even after he was hit. He provided cover fire for a group scaling a seawall and, disregarding his own injuries, went to the aid of two wounded men in the water. While attacking a Japanese machine-gun position by himself, he was killed. Sergeant Bordelon's personal valor was a contributing factor in the ultimate occupation of the island. He is buried at Oahu, Hawaii.

BIBLIOGRAPHY: Committee on Veterans' Affairs, United States Senate, *Medal of Honor Recipients, 1863–1973* (Washington: GPO, 1973).

Art Leatherwood

BORDEN, GAIL, JR. (1801–1874). Gail Borden, Jr., inventor, publisher, surveyor, and founder of the Borden Company, son of Gail and Philadelphia (Wheeler) Borden, was born in Norwich, New York, on November 9, 1801. In 1816 the family moved to New London, Indiana, where Borden obtained his only formal schooling, totaling not more than a year and a half. He is thought to have been captain of the local militia when barely twenty years old. In 1822 he was a principal figure in rescuing a freedman from rustlers. Shortly afterward he moved to Mississippi in search of a milder climate to cure a persistent cough. In Mississippi Borden surveyed and taught school. In 1826 he was official surveyor for Amite County as well as deputy federal surveyor.

After arriving at Galveston Island on December 24, 1829, he farmed and raised stock in upper Fort Bend County and spent some time in surveying. By February 1830 he had succeeded his brother, Thomas H. Borden,[qv] as surveyor for Stephen F. Austin's[qv] colony. In 1832 Borden was named one of three members of the San Felipe committee of correspondence. In the Convention of 1833[qv] he represented Lavaca District . He also assumed many of the duties of colonial secretary for Austin in the absence of Samuel M. Williams.[qv]

As early as January 1835 Borden made plans to found a newspaper, but it was October 10 before the first issue of his *Telegraph and Texas Register,*[qv] published in partnership with his brother Thomas and Joseph Baker,[qv] appeared in San Felipe. In the meantime he had prepared the first topographical map of Texas and had resumed his responsibilities on the committee of correspondence. Borden published the *Telegraph* in San Felipe until March 1836, in Harrisburg in April 1836, in Columbia from August 1836 to April 1837, and in Houston in May and June 1837. In October 1835 he was appointed collector for the Department of Brazos, a post he held until 1837. In October and November 1836 he helped lay out the site of Houston.

On June 20, 1837, Borden sold his partnership in the *Telegraph* to Jacob W. Cruger[qv] and became the first collector of the port of Galveston under the Republic of Texas.[qv] His first term as collector lasted from June 1837 to December 1838, when Mirabeau B. Lamar[qv] removed him for political reasons. His second term lasted from December 1841 to April 1843; he resigned after a dispute with President Sam Houston[qv] over evaluation of exchequers.

From 1839 to 1851 Borden was secretary and agent for the Galveston City Company (*see* galveston, texas), which owned most of Galveston Island and for which he helped sell 2,500 lots. He invented a "locomotive bath house" for Galveston women who wished to bathe in the Gulf of Mexico. As an alderman he helped to rid the island temporarily of gamblers. He and his first wife reputedly became the first Anglo-Americans to be baptized in the Gulf west of the Mississippi River. He became Sunday school missionary to the poor and to travelers. He was a trustee of the Texas Baptist Education Society, which founded Baylor University. And he was an officer in the local temperance society and deacon and clerk of the local Baptist church. In 1842 Borden directed insular defenses against an expected Mexican invasion.

In the middle 1840s he began inventing. He is supposed to have experimented with large-scale refrigeration as a means of preventing yellow fever and with a terraqueous machine, a sort of prairie schooner that would go on land or water. In 1849 he perfected a meat biscuit, made of dehydrated meat compounded with flour, which he tried to market on a worldwide scale in partnership with Ashbel Smith.[qv] Although this project left him deeply in debt, for seven years Borden struggled to sell meat biscuits. For this purpose he moved to New York in 1851 to be nearer trade centers.

In 1853 he sought a patent on a process for condensing milk in vacuum, but it was 1856 before he received American and British patents. He then dropped the meat biscuit to devote himself to condensing milk. He opened a factory in Connecticut in 1856 but failed, then tried and failed again in 1857. Through Jeremiah Milbank, a New York financier, he received new backing and opened another factory in Connecticut in 1858. When the Civil War[qv] brought intensified demand for condensed milk, sales grew so much that Borden's success was assured. He opened another factory in Connecticut, two in New York, and one in Illinois and licensed other concerns in Pennsylvania and Maine. He also invented processes for condensing various fruit juices, for extract of beef, and for coffee. After the Civil War he established a meat-packing plant at Borden, Texas, twelve miles west of Columbus, and a sawmill and copperware factory at Bastrop.

After 1871 he spent his winters in Texas because of the milder climate. In 1873 he built a freedmen's school and a white children's school, organized a day school and a Sunday school for black children, aided in constructing five churches, maintained two missionaries, and partially supported numerous poorly paid teachers, ministers, and students. Borden married Penelope Mercer in Mississippi in 1828; they had seven children. In 1845 he married Augusta Stearns, and in 1860 he married Emeline Eunice Church. He died in Borden, Texas, on January 11, 1874; his body was shipped by private car to New York to be buried in Woodlawn Cemetery.

bibliography: Joe B. Frantz, *Gail Borden: Dairyman to a Nation* (Norman: University of Oklahoma Press, 1951). Hattie Borden Weld, *Historical and Genealogical Record of the Borden Family* (Los Angeles, 1899?). Clarence R. Wharton, *Gail Borden, Pioneer* (San Antonio: Naylor, 1941).

Joe B. Frantz

Gail Borden, Jr., and son John. Courtesy Rosenberg Library, Galveston.

BORDEN, JOHN PETTIT (1812–1891). John P. Borden, participant in the Texas Revolution[qv] and the first commissioner of the General Land Office[qv] of Texas, was born in Norwich, New York, on December 30, 1812, the son of Gail and Philadelphia (Wheeler) Borden, Sr. He came to Texas with other family members in December 1829, and he received 1,102 acres on November 20, 1832, in Stephen F. Austin's[qv] second colony, located on the Colorado River in the area that later became Wharton County. Borden enrolled in Capt. George Collinsworth's[qv] company on October 7, 1835, and participated in the taking of Goliad two days later (*see* goliad campaign of 1835). He helped write a resolution to Austin informing him that the Goliad men reserved the privilege of naming their own company commander. He then enrolled in Capt. Philip Dimmitt's[qv] company and took part in the siege of Bexar[qv] in December 1835. Borden was discharged on January 11, 1836, but reenlisted a few weeks later and served as first lieutenant in Moseley Baker's[qv] company at the battle of San Jacinto.[qv]

In late 1836 he and his brother Gail Borden, Jr.,[qv] surveyed and laid out the town of Houston. He married sometime around 1837, but his wife, Elizabeth, died on May 10, 1838, in Richmond, Texas. Sam Houston[qv] appointed Borden the first land commissioner of Texas, an office he held from August 23, 1837, to December 12, 1840. Starting out in his office in Houston, Borden faced the enormous task of acquiring and protecting numerous Mexican and Spanish land titles issued before the republic. The records provided valuable evidence to validate land ownership. Borden began with no money, supplies, or employees to undertake his job, and at one time he had to store the records at friends' houses. Yet in 1837 he reported the successful acquisition of land documents from all over Texas, with the exception of records from three eastern and two southern colonies.

In 1839 Borden moved the land archives from Houston to Austin. He received $1,200 for the transportation by wagon of almost 5,000 pounds of documents. In October of that year, with a small group of assistants, he worked on making recommendations for land patents by comparing surveyors' notes. The office, underfunded and understaffed, faced growing pressure from the public to speed the patent process. Borden tried to increase public and government awareness of the need for more funding, manpower, and authority for the land office that was responsible for administering 216 million acres of Texas lands. Frustrated, he resigned in December 1840; his efforts, however, helped demonstrate the importance of the land office.

Borden was a member of the Somervell expedition[qv] in 1842 but did not go on to Mier. He subsequently moved to Galveston, studied law, and was an agent for the Galveston City Company (*see* galveston, texas). He entered a law practice at Richmond and married Mary Susan Hatch in 1843. They had nine children. In 1844 he was elected county judge of Fort Bend County and in 1846 was elected chief justice of the county. The family moved to McGloin's Bluff in San Patricio County. Borden established the Ingleside Seminary, a boys academy which he operated until 1873. In the mid-1870s he moved to Borden, Texas, in Colorado County. He died on November 12, 1891.

bibliography: Sam Houston Dixon and Louis Wiltz Kemp, *The Heroes of San Jacinto* (Houston: Anson Jones, 1932). Galveston *Daily News,* November 14, 1891. Garry Mauro, *Land Commissioners of Texas* (Austin: Texas General Land Office, 1986). Homer S. Thrall, *A Pictorial History of Texas* (St. Louis: Thompson, 1879). Vertical Files, Barker Texas History Center, University of Texas at Austin.

William N. Todd IV and Gerald Knape

BORDEN, PASCHAL PAVOLO (1806–1864). Paschal Pavolo Borden, soldier, merchant, and surveyor, brother of Gail, Jr., Thomas H., and John P. Borden[qqv] and son of Gail and Philadelphia (Wheeler) Borden, Sr., was born in Norwich, New York, in December 1806. The family moved to Kentucky, to Indiana, and, in 1829, to Texas. Borden served as an official surveyor for the state of Coahuila and Texas.[qv] On March 4, 1831, he received 1,102 acres of land in Stephen F. Austin's[qv] second colony, on Mill Creek in what is now Washington County. From 1831 to 1835 he farmed and helped in his father's blacksmith shop in San Felipe. During the Texas Revolution[qv] Borden was a member of Capt. John Bird's[qv] company from October 24 to December 13, 1835. He then served as a private in Moseley Baker's[qv] company until June 1, 1836. He fought in the battle of San Jacinto[qv] and was therefore granted 3,306 acres of land by the Fort Bend county board. In late 1836 at Columbia, he opened a general store with H. F. Armstrong, and in December 1837 he began a term as Fort Bend county surveyor, a position he combined with a private real estate enterprise. In September 1846 he was named administrator of the estate of Moses Lapham.[qv] By 1854 he was farming at Seclusion, near Egypt. Borden was married on February 3, 1838, to Frances Mary Heard, sister of William J. E. Heard;[qv] after Frances's death he married Martha Ann Stafford, on July 19, 1842. By his second wife Borden had three sons. He died on April 28, 1864.

bibliography: Sam Houston Dixon and Louis Wiltz Kemp, *The Heroes of San Jacinto* (Houston: Anson Jones, 1932). Joe B. Frantz, *Gail Borden: Dairyman to a Nation* (Norman: University of Oklahoma Press, 1951). Virginia H. Taylor Houston, "Surveying in Texas," *Southwestern Historical Quarterly* 65 (October 1961). Hattie Borden Weld, *Historical and Genealogical Record of the Borden Family* (Los Angeles, 1899?). *Joe B. Frantz*

BORDEN, SIDNEY GAIL (1846–1908). Sidney Gail Borden, businessman and local official, son of Mary Susan (Hatch) and John Pettit Borden,[qv] was born on March 15, 1846, in Richmond, Texas, moved to San Patricio County as a youth with his family, and settled in the Ingleside area. His mother was the daughter of George Hatch.[qv] John P. Borden, a brother of Gail Borden, Jr.,[qv] registered the brand J6 on August 26, 1856, in San Patricio County. Sidney joined the Confederate forces at nineteen and served on the Rio Grande with Capt. A. C. Jones in local skirmishes.

After the war Borden returned to San Patricio County and engaged in a number of ranching and business enterprises. He founded the riverport of Sharpsburg in the early 1870s. With D. C. Rachal[qv] he purchased a schooner, the *Nueces Valley,* to transport merchandise to his store, S. G. Borden Mercantile, at Sharpsburg. Wool, hides, cotton, and wine were shipped out of the port. Borden developed vineyards near Hart's Lake and shipped a white wine, Sharpsburg's Best, and a red wine, Rachal's Choice, throughout South Texas. Borden and Rachal built the first cotton gin in the area in the early 1880s. In addition to his wine, gin, ranch, and shipping businesses Borden operated a Nueces River ferry that was the primary link for Nueces County travelers heading north. He also operated a meat packery on the river near Sharpsburg. In partnership with two other men, he developed town and farm lots in Sharpsburg, which became the largest community in the county.

Borden was elected justice of the peace in 1871 and named county judge in 1881. He served through 1888 and again for a short time in 1897–98. He was appointed county surveyor in 1895 and was postmaster at Sharpsburg from 1883 until the post office was moved to Angelita in 1908. He built the first telephone line in the county, from Sharpsburg to Corpus Christi, a distance of twenty miles; this line served the entire area, especially to summon medical aid. Borden married Mary G. Sullivan on December 28, 1876. He died at his home in Sharpsburg on January 31, 1908, and is buried in the Rose Hill Cemetery in Corpus Christi. The Bordens had six children.

bibliography: Corpus Christi *Caller-Times,* January 18, 1959. Keith Guthrie, *History of San Patricio County* (Austin: Nortex, 1986). Rachel Bluntzer Hébert, *The Forgotten Colony: San Patricio de Hibernia* (Burnet, Texas: Eakin Press, 1981). *San Patricio County News,* September 29, 1938. *Keith Guthrie*

BORDEN, THOMAS HENRY (1804–1877). Thomas Henry Borden, early settler, soldier, and inventor, son of Gail and Philadelphia (Wheeler) Borden, Sr., was born in Norwich, New York, on January 28, 1804. After a boyhood in New York, Kentucky, and Indiana, he joined Stephen F. Austin's[qv] colony in Texas in 1824 as one of the Old Three Hundred.[qv] In 1830 he was Austin's official surveyor, a post he later resigned in favor of his brother, Gail Borden, Jr.[qv] In 1833 T. H. Borden was farming near Tenoxtitlán, but by 1835 he had moved to Fort Bend.

During November and December 1835 he participated with the Texas army in the Grass Fight[qv] and the siege of Bexar[qv] under Benjamin R. Milam.[qv] In October 1835 he helped Gail Borden and Joseph Baker[qv] found the *Telegraph and Texas Register.*[qv] He remained with that paper until March 14, 1837, when he sold his interest to Dr. Francis Moore, Jr.[qv] In October 1836 Borden helped lay out the city of Houston, and the following year he entered the real estate business in Columbia, sometimes in partnership with Erastus (Deaf) Smith and sometimes with Robert D. Johnson.[qqv] He was active in founding the town of Richmond, and as late as 1873 still owned much land in Fort Bend and Brazoria counties.

In 1840 Borden was living in Galveston, engaged principally in surveying and butchering. He constructed the first windmill on Galveston Island and ran it in combination with the first local gristmill. At his home the first Baptist church in Galveston was organized, on January 30, 1840. Like his brother Gail he had a gift for invention; he is sometimes credited with inventing the terraqueous machine often attributed to his brother. In Galveston he invented a steam gauge, or manometer, for use on river steamboats. In 1849 he moved to New Orleans, where he had an excellent business. According to tradition, he did not believe in the principle of patents; so other gauge manufacturers patented his product and eliminated him from competition.

On June 4, 1829, Borden married Demis Woodword, who bore him two sons before her death in Houston on September 16, 1836. He married Louisa R. Graves of New York in 1838. Loss of his steam-gauge business, Civil War[qv] losses, and the protracted illness of his wife reduced Borden to comparative poverty in the late 1860s and necessitated his moving back to Galveston, where he died on March 16, 1877.

bibliography: Joe B. Frantz, *Gail Borden: Dairyman to a Nation* (Norman: University of Oklahoma Press, 1951). Galveston *Daily News,* March 17, 1877. Hattie Borden Weld, *Historical and Genealogical Record of the Borden Family* (Los Angeles, 1899?).

Joe B. Frantz

BORDEN, TEXAS. Borden is between Interstate Highway 10/U.S. Highway 90 and the Southern Pacific Railroad, four miles northeast of Weimar in southwestern Colorado County. Before the Civil War[qv] the area was known as Harvey's Creek Settlement. Soon after the war, however, Gail Borden, Jr.,[qv] founder of the Borden Milk Company, returned to Texas and after building homes for himself, his sons, and his brother, John P. Borden,[qv] on the hills above the creek, named the settlement Bordenville. In 1872 the Galveston, Harrisburg and San Antonio Railway completed its line through the area. Borden invested $125,000 in the Borden Meat Preserving Company there in 1872. In 1873 the company built a slaughterhouse capable of handling twenty-five head daily and the facilities for preparing "extract of beef," roast beef, and beef hash. Borden also built a school for white children and a freedmen's' school for black children. Prospective residents, drawn by the railroad, available jobs, and land that sold for five to fifty-seven dollars an acre, flocked to the new community. On January 19, 1874, a post office was established with John P. Borden as postmaster. It continued in operation until 1905, when mail was rerouted through Weimar.

Although the processing plant operated for several years after Gail Borden's death in 1874, the higher rates charged by the railroad for shipping processed meat instead of live cattle ultimately forced the plant to close. By then, however, the community was well established, with a depot, a hotel, a gin, several stores, schools, and a resident population of more than 100. It was described in 1878 as a "snug little town" surrounded by lands that produced cotton, cane, and grain. During the 1930s the highway was moved about one-half mile south of the community, and some businesses moved to the new site. Most residences and the headquarters for a railroad section remained in the old location. The highway department built a two-acre impoundment beside the new U.S. 90, named it Borden Lake, and installed roadside picnic facilities. Schools in the area were consolidated with the Weimar Independent School District in 1948, and by that time all but one business in Borden had closed. The construction of I-10 during the late 1950s routed even more traffic away from the area, and the Old San Antonio Road[qv] became Colorado County 217. By the 1980s most of the land in the area had reverted to pasture, and a resident population of less than fifty and one business remained.

BIBLIOGRAPHY: *Colorado County Sesquicentennial Commemorative Book* (La Grange, Texas: Hengst Printing, 1986). Joe B. Frantz, *Gail Borden: Dairyman to a Nation* (Norman: University of Oklahoma Press, 1951). Mary Hinton, *Weimar, Texas: First 100 Years, 1873–1973* (Austin: Von Boeckmann–Jones, 1973). *Jeff Carroll*

BORDEN COUNTY. Borden County (D–10), at the edge of the Llano Estacado,[qv] is bounded on the east by Scurry County, on the south by Howard County, on the west by Dawson County, and on the north by Lynn and Garza counties. The rolling, broken land of the county drains to the Colorado River and its tributaries and to Lake J. B. Thomas. The Caprock,[qv] Gail Mountain, and Muchakooga Peak are notable physical features. The soils are loams, sandy loams, and clay. The county center is at 32°45′ north latitude and 101°25′ west longitude, seventy miles southeast of Lubbock. The county comprises 907 square miles at 2,400–3,000 feet elevation. The annual rainfall is 18.2 inches. The average minimum temperature in January is 32° F; the maximum in July is 96°. The 214-day growing season produces an average annual agricultural income of $12.5 million from beef cattle, sheep, cotton, wheat, sorghums, and other grains. There is no manufacturing, but 7,620,366 barrels of oil produced in 1982 earned almost $245 million.

Comanches hunted buffalo in the region before white settlement. It was within the range of the Penateka band, also called the Honey-Eaters or Wasps, the largest and best-known Comanche band. The Penatekas led the advance into the southern plains in the eighteenth century after the people, a segment of the northern Shoshones, learned the use of Spanish horses and transformed themselves from impoverished root and plant gatherers to hunters. Settlers were not attracted to the area that is now Borden County until the end of the nineteenth century. It was too distant from the United States Army's frontier outposts to be safe even after the Civil War,[qv] and it seemed too dry to sustain ranching and farming. The county was marked off in 1876 from Bosque County and named for Gail Borden, Jr.,[qv] a newspaper publisher and organizer of the Republic of Texas,[qv] and a surveyor who helped lay out the site of Houston and prepared the first topographical map of Texas.

In 1876 ranchers from Howard County extended their range into Borden County. By 1880 there were thirty-five residents who, unlike most pioneers, resisted intrusions of railroads and other settlers who might disrupt their use of the open range. As late as 1890, only 222 people lived in the county on twenty-five farms and ranches; only 1,146 acres in the county were classified as "improved" by the United States census that year. At this time the local economy revolved completely around the cattle industry, and in 1890 over 71,000 cattle were counted in Borden. The county was organized in 1891, and Gail was made the county seat.

More farmers moved into the area between 1890 and 1910. In 1900 there were 129 ranches and farms in Borden County, and the population had increased to 776. A small boom occurred in 1902, when state school lands became available for leasing. New arrivals, mostly farmers, were not welcomed by the established ranchers, and many left. Nevertheless, by 1910 there were 228 farms and 1,386 residents in the county; thirty-six of the farms were worked by tenants. For the scattered population of the county, isolated rural life brought its own rewards. As young Mary Blankenship,[qv] who passed through the area in 1901 to settle with her husband somewhat to the north, reflected: "We had plenty of time to be still and know God. He was our nearest neighbor." The farms in the county dropped to 197 by 1920, but by 1930 the number had increased to 292 and the population was 1,505.

Many of the newcomers grew cotton, which by 1930 had become the county's most important crop. Cotton was first planted in the area during the 1890s; in 1900, it was grown on 137 acres of Borden County land. Cotton farming in 1910 comprised 2,206 acres, and in 1920, 3,820 acres; by 1929 more than 20,000 acres of county land was planted in cotton, while only 28,000 acres of cropland was harvested in the entire county.

The Great Depression[qv] of the 1930s put an end to the budding development of the county. By 1940 only about 12,000 acres of county land was planted in cotton, and only 233 farms remained in Borden; only 1,356 residents were counted that year. The discovery of considerable oilfields in 1949 did not arrest the decline of Borden County population, although it did provide fortunate ranchers and farmers with another source of income. Oil production in the county was more than 3,150,000 barrels in 1950, almost 9,819,000 barrels in 1960, and more than 10,876,000 barrels in 1974. Production decreased during the 1980s, however, and in 1990 amounted to only 5,679,658 barrels. By 1991, more than 340,003,000 barrels of petroleum had been taken out of Borden County since discovery in 1949.

The population of the county continued to decline after World War II.[qv] Only 1,106 people lived in Borden County in 1950, and only 1,076 in 1960, 888 in 1970, 859 in 1980, and 799 in 1990. Tourists, mostly hunters and fishermen at Lake J. B. Thomas,[qv] contribute to the economy. Gail, the county seat and only town of note, had an estimated population of 202 in 1991. The highway system includes U.S. Highway 180 (west–east) and Farm Road 669 (north–south).

William R. Hunt and John Leffler

BORDENTOWN, TEXAS. Bordentown was a proposed township on the Brazos River about a mile below Thompson's Ferry in Fort Bend County. Sometime after 1837 Paschal Pavolo Borden[qv] surveyed the area for the projected settlement. He secured a license to operate a ferry across the Brazos, which he did for several years, but there is no evidence that a community ever materialized.

Stephen L. Hardin

BORDER, JOHN PELHAM (1819–1873). John Pelham Border, public official and Confederate soldier, was born in Lincolnshire, England, on February 19, 1819, the son of William and Sarah (Mell) Border. He immigrated with his parents to the United States in 1823 and lived for a time in New York before moving to Texas in 1835 as a surveyor. He first served in the Texas army from October to December 1835, and participated in the successful Goliad Campaign of 1835.[qv] Border enlisted again on April 1, 1836, and joined Capt. William Kimbro's[qv] company at the battle of San Jacinto.[qv] In 1837 he settled in San Augustine as a merchant. He was elected county clerk on January 4, 1841, appointed postmaster of San Augustine in 1842, and made a lieutenant colonel of militia in 1847. He married Catherine Elizabeth Harding on March 5, 1844; they had six children. At the outbreak of the Civil War[qv] Border raised seven companies in San Augustine, Nacogdoches, Sabine, and Shelby counties. They were formed together as Border's Battalion, and he was appointed lieutenant colonel of the unit. The battalion was later joined to another battalion to form Thomas Scott Anderson's[qv] regiment, of which Border was lieutenant colonel. In May 1864 Border assumed command of Camp Ford, the stockade for federal prisoners. In several postwar memoirs, he was characterized by former prisoners as a harsh and brutal commandant. After the war he and his family settled in New Iberia, Louisiana, where he died on June 12, 1873, and was buried in the Protestant Cemetery. In 1887 his widow married Oran Milo Roberts,[qv] governor of Texas from 1879 to 1883. Catherine Elizabeth Border Roberts died on July 21, 1920, and was buried in the State Cemetery,[qv] Austin.

BIBLIOGRAPHY: Louis Wiltz Kemp Papers, Barker Texas History Center, University of Texas at Austin. Leon Mitchell, Jr., "Camp Ford, Confederate Military Prison," *Southwestern Historical Quarterly* 66 (July 1962).

Kate Harding Bates Parker and Clara Elisabeth Bates Nisbet

BORDER PACIFIC RAILROAD. The Border Pacific Railroad Company was chartered on February 1, 1984, to acquire thirty-two miles of track from the Missouri Pacific between Mission in Hidalgo County and Rio Grande City in Starr County. The initial capital was $80,000. The principal place of business was Rio Grande City. The incorporators were Sam Vale, Linda Vale, Lloyd M. Bentsen, Sr.,[qv] and George Cantrell, all of McAllen; A. J. Vale, Miriam Vale, Gustavo Pérez, and Yolanda Pérez, all of Rio Grande City; and Trinidad Guillen and Dora Guillen, both of Fort Worth. In 1990 the railroad reported revenues under $5 million and hauled waste, scrap, nonmetal minerals, and farm products. *Nancy Beck Young*

BORDERSVILLE, TEXAS. Bordersville, a black community on Farm Road 1960 and State Highway 184 in northeast Houston, less than a half mile northeast of Houston Intercontinental Airport, began in 1927 when the sawmill at Humble closed and blacks who had worked there were forced to leave. Edgar Borders opened a mill nearby, hired some of the unemployed, and provided wooden shacks as housing. In 1940 the community had one store and a population of 100 but remained at least five miles from the nearest schools, in the Aldine Independent School District; thirty-five miles from the nearest public health care at Ben Taub Hospital in Houston; and an equal distance from grocery stores and libraries. In 1941 Borders closed the mill and rented or sold the land that became Bordersville to the people living there. When Borders died in 1963, most residents did not own the land they lived on, but no one asked them to leave. In the 1960s local men organized a civic club that became the Bordersville Neighborhood Council, joined the Houston Junior Chamber of Commerce, dug a deep water well, and painted local houses.

In 1965 Houston annexed the community, then considered the worst pocket of poverty in the city, characterized by dilapidated houses and a lack of paved streets, running water, and sewers. Though residents were expected to pay city taxes, no provision was made for city utilities. In 1974 a community center, the Three H Service Center (standing for Houston, Humble, and Harris County, since it served people within a twenty-mile radius) was built with the help of a grant from the federal Economic Development Administration of the Department of Commerce. The center was designed by architect John Zemanek, who won an award for his cluster of nine low buildings. The center, funded by city and federal agencies and local churches and staffed by volunteers, provided day care, tutoring, employment for elderly and youth, a senior-citizen center, food assistance, literacy classes, a health clinic, public baths for the homeless, summer recreation, and other services. In 1975, when the population was 550, water for bathing, cooking, and drinking was delivered twice a week by Houston Fire Department trucks and stored in barrels outside homes. The average annual income of residents was between $2,500 and $3,500. In 1983 the center helped to organize funding to install sink, bathtub, and commode modules for each home and, to convince the city to extend water lines, collected the city fee for connecting front-yard water faucets. The center later built porches on each house. Federal funds were used to install water service in 1981, but as late as 1985, 700 people lived in 120 homes in the community, cooking on woodstoves or outdoors, lacking access to transportation, and depending on Social Security. Reluctance to aid the community was attributed to the fact that the land was expected to be sold to commercial or industrial developers in the near future. State highway maps in the 1980s showed four churches and multiple dwellings in Bordersville.

BIBLIOGRAPHY: Houston Metropolitan Research Center Files, Houston Public Library. James Martin SoRelle, The Darker Side of 'Heaven': The Black Community in Houston, Texas, 1917–1945 (Ph.D. dissertation, Kent State University, 1980). Fred R. von der Mehden, *The Ethnic Groups of Houston* (Houston: Rice University, 1984). *Diana J. Kleiner*

BOREGAS CREEK. Boregas Creek rises 1½ miles northeast of Geneva in northern Sabine County (at 31°30′ N, 93°55′ W) and runs southeast for ten miles to its mouth on Palo Gaucho Bayou (at 31°23′ N, 93°50′ W), less than a half mile from that bayou's mouth on Toledo Bend Reservoir. The area around the streambed is gently sloping to moderately steep and lies mostly within Sabine National Forest. The name of the stream is most likely a misspelling of the Spanish *borregas,* meaning "lambs less than a year old." The creek forms the eastern boundary of the Juan Ignatio Pifermo land grant, which, confirmed in September of 1794, is the oldest land grant in the county. That grant was also the site of Antonio Gil Ibarvo's[qv] ranch, El Lobanillo, in the 1770s. The first white to settle on the banks of the creek was Jack Cedars, who came to the area sometime around 1790. When Stephen F. Austin[qv] made his first trip to the province of Texas in 1821, he spent his first night on Boregas Creek, which he referred to in his journal as "Boreg Creek."

BIBLIOGRAPHY: Robert Cecil McDaniel, *Sabine County, Texas* (Waco: Texian, 1987). Edna McDaniel White and Blanche Findley Toole, *Sabine County Historical Sketches and Genealogical Records* (Beaumont, 1972).

BOREN, JAMES MINUS (1870–1937). James Minus (Bud, Judge) Boren, cowboy, judge, and banker, son of George and Jane (Hodges) Boren, was born in Berryville, Arkansas, on February 14, 1870. He moved with his parents and two brothers to Williamson County, Texas, in 1877 in a two-horse wagon with one extra horse. The journey took three months, during which the family was delayed in Dallas by Mrs. Boren's illness and the death of her infant son. In 1879 the elder Boren traded his farm for cattle and rangeland at Coleman, and Bud and his brother John drove the herd there. Since there were no fences, the boys loose-herded the cattle all winter. The Boren children attended various one-room schools for a limited formal education. During the extremely cold winter of 1880 the family lost most of their herd, sold out all the remaining animals except for seven milk cows and two yokes of oxen, and moved to Bell and eventually to Fisher County.

In 1890 Bud and John went to work for their uncle, Andrew J. Long, on the OS and OB ranches in Borden County, for a monthly salary of twenty-five dollars. Boren did extra trail work as foreman and earned an extra two dollars a day by driving herds of up to 2,000 steers to Amarillo, a thirty to forty day trip. After his marriage to Ella Bridges on October 3, 1899, he left the OS, bought the lease, and filed claim for a ranch. He was awarded the land on February 7, 1900, and moved onto the ranch. When the commissioners of Borden County granted a petition to form a separate county, the citizens of the area held an election on the OS Ranch, location of the only voting box, named the county Garza, and elected Boren county judge, even though he was on a cattle drive at the time. The county seat was named Post City (now Post), after C. W. Post,[qv] who had donated the land for the town. The Borens moved to Post and in 1908 built a home in which their heirs still lived more than eighty years later. Boren was a Mason and a charter director of the First National Bank. He drilled the first producing oil well in the county and served on the school board. He and Ella had two children, who took over the operation of the original ranch. Boren died on November 17, 1937.

BIBLIOGRAPHY: Garza County Historical Survey Committee, *Wagon Wheels: A History of Garza County,* ed. Charles Didway (Seagraves, Texas: Pioneer, 1973). Post City *Post,* November 17, 1937.

Mildred B. Boren

BOREN, SAMUEL HAMPSON (1811–1881). Samuel Hampson Boren, soldier and businessman, son of Capt. James and Jane (Blair) Boren, was born in Giles County, Tennessee, on December 3, 1811. The family moved to Marshall County, Tennessee, where Boren was educated and later taught school. In 1838 he moved to Nacogdoches in the Republic of Texas,[qv] where he acquired land and became a prosperous planter. He served under Gen. Thomas J. Rusk[qv] in the militia of the republic. In 1846, upon the annexation[qv] of Texas to the United States and the outbreak of war with Mexico, he joined the Second Texas Cavalry regiment, part of the brigade commanded by Gen. James Pinckney Henderson.[qv] During the war he fought in the battles of Monterrey and Buena Vista and was promoted to lieutenant. In 1854 Boren moved with his family to Tyler, where he began a cotton and general-merchandise business and became a business leader and large landowner. He was active in the early development of Tyler and an incorporator and stockholder in numerous enterprises of great aid to East Texas. He helped buy the lot for the First Christian Church in 1859 and later served on the building committee. He was married at Nacogdoches on October 21, 1839, to Sarah Dickson Long. Eight children were born to them. Boren died on September 28, 1881, and was buried in Oakwood Cemetery, Tyler.

BIBLIOGRAPHY: Sid S. Johnson, *Some Biographies of Old Settlers* (1900; facsimile, Tyler, Texas: Smith County Historical Society, 1965). William S. Speer and John H. Brown, eds., *Encyclopedia of the New West* (Marshall, Texas: United States Biographical Publishing, 1881; rpt., Easley, South Carolina: Southern Historical Press, 1978).

Hampson Gary

BOREN, TEXAS. Boren was on Sixmile Creek two miles southeast of Carthage in south central Panola County. It grew up around a mill established in the 1880s. For a time a railroad spur connected Boren to the main rail line in Carthage. A Boren post office operated from 1893 until 1905, when the mail was sent to Carthage. In 1896 Boren had a general store, a number of scattered houses, and an estimated population of 200. A school was in operation there by 1900. Most of the residents apparently moved to Carthage, however, and by the mid-1930s Boren was no longer shown on county highway maps.

BIBLIOGRAPHY: Leila B. LaGrone, ed., *History of Panola County* (Carthage, Texas: Panola County Historical Commission, 1979). John Barnette Sanders, *Postoffices and Post Masters of Panola County, Texas, 1845–1930* (Center, Texas, 1964).

Christopher Long

BORGER, ASA PHILLIP (1888–1934). Asa Phillip (Ace) Borger, town builder, was born to Phillip and Minnie Ann (West) Borger on April 12, 1888, on the family farm near Carthage, Missouri. His father, a veterinarian, died when Ace was six, and the Borger children were raised by their mother and two grandmothers. Borger attended school in Carthage and graduated from business college. Around 1907 he married a classmate, Elizabeth Willoughby. The couple spent their first years in a rented farmhouse near Carthage, where Borger opened a lumberyard; they had three children.

Borger began his career as a town promoter when World War I[qv] broke out in Europe. In 1915 he and his younger brother Lester Andrew (Pete) sold real estate in the mining town of Picher, Oklahoma, in the center of valuable lead and zinc deposits. Much lead was produced from Picher for the war effort. In 1917 the Borgers, in company with the noted wildcatter Tom Slick, laid out the oil town of Slick near Bristow, Oklahoma. At each town the Borgers and their associates built hotels, filling stations, and lumberyards, sold real estate, and pushed for the building of railroad lines to the sites. In 1922 they successfully launched Cromwell, Oklahoma, as a boomtown. Though Borger and his family maintained a home for a time in each of these towns, he continued to use Carthage as his main base.

Borger became interested in the discovery of the Panhandle oilfield. Early in 1926, after personally checking out the reports, he purchased 240 acres from rancher John Frank Weatherly at fifty dollars an acre. He next obtained a grant from Texas secretary of state Emma Grigsby Meharg[qv] to organize the Borger Townsite Company, with capital stock of $10,000 divided into 100 shares of $100 each. In addition to Borger himself, the company's stockholders included C. C. Horton of the Gulf Oil Company and John R. Miller, an old friend from Oklahoma boom days who became the new town's first mayor. The company proceeded to lay out the town and opened the sale of lots on March 8, 1926. By the end of that first day, it had grossed between $60,000 and $100,000, and after six months Borger sold out completely, for more than a million dollars.

He established a lumberyard in the town named for him and opened its first bank. Often he took out full-page ads in area papers promoting settlement in Borger and other oil-rich sites throughout West Texas and eastern New Mexico in which he had bought an interest. He also owned a string of Panhandle wheat elevators and 19,000 acres of farmland in Hansford County. In 1927 Ace and Pete Borger, in association with Albert S. Stinnett,[qv] established the towns of Stinnett and Gruver and were influential in making Stinnett the Hutchinson county seat. In 1929 Borger built a spacious two-story family home, the first brick residence in Borger. From the start he had set aside building sites for churches and schools. His wife, Elizabeth, became active in community affairs; her love for beauty and culture was reflected in the antiques with which she decorated their home. Visiting dignitaries were lavishly entertained there.

Borger's overt generosity with friends and acquaintances caused hard feelings among certain of the town's populace, however, particularly Arthur Huey, the Hutchinson county treasurer. Huey's dislike for Borger intensified after the Borger State Bank, which Borger had established in June 1930 with himself as president and his son Phillip as vice president, failed, causing a minor panic among local businessmen and small depositors. The elder Borger was later convicted of receiving deposits in the insolvent bank and assessed a two-year prison term, a judgment that he appealed. Meanwhile, Huey was jailed for embezzlement and reportedly asked Borger to help bail him out.

When Borger refused, Huey made threats against his life. On August 31, 1934, Borger was getting his mail at the city post office when, according to witnesses, Huey walked in with a Colt .45, shouted obscenities, and shot him five times. Huey then took Borger's own .44 and fired four more shots with it. Lloyd Duncan, farm boss for the Magnolia Petroleum Company,[qv] was severely wounded by the shots and died five days later. At his trial, which was held in Canadian, Huey claimed that he had shot in self-defense, arguing that Borger was gunning for him. The jury believed him and acquitted him. Three years later, however, he was sent to the state penitentiary for theft of county funds. Funeral services for Ace Borger were held in Borger, and his body was shipped back to Missouri for burial in the family plot at Carthage.

Borger's sons, Phillip and Jack, left the area soon after their father's death. However, their sister, Helen, remained and occupied the brick house with her husband, Fritz Thompson. Ace Borger's dream house, now a Texas historical landmark, has remained a family treasure.

BIBLIOGRAPHY: Hutchinson County Historical Commission, *History of Hutchinson County, Texas* (Dallas: Taylor, 1980). Jerry Sinise, *Black Gold and Red Lights* (Burnet, Texas: Eakin Press, 1982).

H. Allen Anderson

BORGER, TEXAS. Borger, at the junction of State highways 136, 152, and 207, in south central Hutchinson County, was established by and named for A. P. (Ace) Borger,[qv] who was reputed throughout Oklahoma and Texas to be a shrewd town promoter. In March 1926, after the discovery of oil in the vicinity, Borger and his partner, attorney John R. Miller, purchased a 240-acre townsite near the Canadian River in the southern part of the county. Within ninety days of its founding, sensational advertising and the lure of "black gold" brought over 45,000 men and women to the new boomtown. In October the charter incorporating the city of Borger was adopted, and Miller was elected mayor. By that time the Panhandle and Santa Fe Railway had completed a spur line to Borger, a post office had opened, and a school district had been established. J. D. (Big Heart) Williams set up the first hamburger stand in Borger on the three-mile-long Main Street, where a hotel and a jail had also been erected. Telephone service and steam-generated electricity were available by the end of 1926. Before wells were drilled, drinking water was provided in tank wagons. The ranchers John R. Weatherly and James A. Whittenburg,[qv] hoping to cash in on the boom, established two rival townsites, Isom and Dixon Creek, next to that of Borger. Later these were incorporated into the Borger city limits, as was the oil camp of Signal Hill to the northeast. In November 1927 a fire destroyed the Dixon Creek Oil Company refinery, causing more than $60,000 worth of damage. One noted visitor to Borger during this time was the artist Thomas Hart Benton, whose painting *Boom Town* depicts his impression of Borger's Main Street.

Within a matter of months, oilmen, prospectors, roughnecks, panhandlers, fortune seekers, card sharks, bootleggers, prostitutes, and dope peddlers descended on Borger. "Booger Town," as it was nicknamed, became a refuge for criminals and fugitives from the law. Before long the town government was firmly in the hands of an organized crime syndicate led by Mayor Miller's shady associate, "Two-Gun Dick" Herwig. The center of this vice was Dixon (now Tenth) Street, notorious for its brothels, dance halls, gambling dens, slot machines, and speakeasies. Murder and robbery became commonplace. Illegal moonshine stills (*see* MOONSHINING) and home breweries flourished with the blessings of Herwig and his henchmen, including W. J. (Shine) Popejoy, the king of the Texas bootleggers. Acting on petitions and investigative reports, in the spring of 1927 Governor Daniel J. Moody[qv] sent a detachment of Texas Rangers[qv] under captains Francis Augustus Hamer and Thomas R. Hickman[qqv] to remedy the situation. Although the rangers proved a stabilizing force and compelled many undesirables to leave town, Borger's wave of crime and violence continued intermittently into the 1930s and climaxed with the murder of District Attorney John A. Holmes by an unknown assassin on September 18, 1929. This episode prompted Moody to impose martial law for a month and send state troops to help local authorities rid the town of the lawless element. This goal was eventually achieved, but not before Ace Borger was shot to death by his longtime enemy Arthur Huey on August 31, 1934.

The Great Depression[qv] also helped to propel Borger from one era into another by the late 1930s. Although Phillips Petroleum and other companies profited from the fields around Borger, prices in oil and gas dropped, ending the boom. "Black dusters," augmented by soot from carbon black plants, turned day into night (*see* DUST BOWL). "Okie" migrants, tractored off their foreclosed farms, were sometimes able to find jobs in the Borger plants and refineries. With the aid of the Work Projects Administration,[qv] streets were improved, and the boom shacks were replaced with permanent buildings. During World War II[qv] synthetic rubber and other petroleum products became important in the Borger area. The Hutchinson County Airport was constructed north of town in 1949. By the 1960s Borger was one of the largest centers for oil, carbon black (*see* CARBON BLACK INDUSTRY), and petrochemical production and supplies in the state. In 1969 Borger was designated an All-American city. The advent of Lake Meredith also added to the town's economy. The population was listed at 14,000 in 1943, 17,949 in 1950, 20,911 in 1960, 14,195 in 1970, and 15,837 in 1980. By 1980 Borger had 488 businesses, including several manufacturers. In 1990 the population was 15,675.

Borger remains an important shipping point for agricultural produce as well as for the petroleum products manufactured there. The community supports eight schools, fifty churches, two banks, two radio stations, twenty-four city parks, a library, a hospital, and Frank Phillips College,[qv] a junior college. The city's newspaper, the Borger *News-Herald* (formerly the *Hutchinson County Herald*), has been in business since 1926. The Hutchinson County Museum, opened in 1977, houses artifacts of the county's pioneer past. Borger is especially noted for its scale models of the buildings at Adobe Walls at the time of the 1874 battle (*see* RED RIVER WAR). The annual World's Largest Fish Fry is held in Borger each June.

BIBLIOGRAPHY: Hutchinson County Historical Commission, *History of Hutchinson County, Texas* (Dallas: Taylor, 1980). H. Gordon Frost and John H. Jenkins, *"I'm Frank Hamer": The Life of a Texas Peace Officer* (Austin: Pemberton Press, 1968). John H. White, *Borger, Texas* (1929?; rpt., Waco: Texian Press, 1973). *H. Allen Anderson*

BORGLUM, JOHN GUTZON DE LA MOTHE (1867–1941). Gutzon Borglum, painter and sculptor, was born in Idaho on March 25, 1867, the son of Danish immigrants James and Ida (Michelson) Borglum. He first studied art in California under William Keith and Virgil Williams. There the large painting *Stagecoach,* now in the Menger Hotel[qv] in San Antonio, was completed. In 1890 Borglum went abroad to study for two years in Paris at the Académie Julien and the École des Beaux Arts and also under individual masters, the most important of whom was Auguste Rodin. Borglum exhibited in the Old Salon in 1891 and 1892 as a painter and in 1891 in the New Salon as a sculptor with *Death of the Chief,* for which he was awarded membership in the Société des Beaux-Artes.

After a year of work in Spain he returned to California, in 1893, and from there went to England in 1896. In England he painted portraits and murals, illustrated books, and produced sculpture. *Apache Pursued,* executed at this time, is owned in replica by the Witte Museum[qv] in San Antonio. Sculpture became Borglum's prime artistic medium; examples of his work include the head of Lincoln (1908) at the Capitol in Washington, D.C., a seated bronze sculpture of Lincoln (1911) in Newark, New Jersey, two equestrian statues of Philip H. Sheridan[qv] (1907, 1924), and the Wars of America group (1926). The most famous and monumental of his works are the sculptures at

Mount Rushmore National Memorial, South Dakota, of Washington, Jefferson, Lincoln, and Theodore Roosevelt. These were dedicated on August 10, 1927, and completed, after Borglum's death, by his son Lincoln.

In 1925 the sculptor moved to Texas to work on the monument to trail drivers commissioned by the Trail Drivers Association.[qv] He completed the model in 1925, but due to lack of funds it was not cast until 1940, and then was only a fourth its originally planned size. It stands in front of the Texas Pioneer and Trail Drivers Memorial Hall next to the Witte Museum in San Antonio. Borglum lived at the historic Menger Hotel, which in the 1920s was the residence of a number of artists. He subsequently planned the redevelopment of the Corpus Christi waterfront; the plan failed, although a model for a statue of Christ intended for it was later modified by his son and erected on a mountaintop in South Dakota. While living and working in Texas, Borglum took an interest in local beautification. He promoted change and modernity, although he was berated by academicians.

Borglum was married to Mrs. Elizabeth Putnam in 1889; the marriage ended in divorce in 1908. On November 6, 1941, Borglum died in Chicago, Illinois, survived by his wife, Mary (Montgomery), and his two children. He was buried in Forest Lawn Memorial Park, Glendale, California.

BIBLIOGRAPHY: Lincoln Borglum, *My Father's Mountain: Mt. Rushmore and How It Was Carved* (Rapid City, South Dakota: Fenwinn Press, 1966). Robert Joseph Casey and Mary Borglum, *Give the Man Room: The Story of Gutzon Borglum* (Indianapolis: Bobbs-Merrill, 1952). Frances Battaile Fisk, *A History of Texas Artists and Sculptors* (Abilene, Texas, 1928; facsimile rpt., Austin: Morrison, 1986). Gilbert C. Fite, *Mount Rushmore* (Norman: University of Oklahoma Press, 1952). Esse Forrester-O'Brien, *Art and Artists of Texas* (Dallas: Tardy, 1935). Willadene Price, *Gutzon Borglum: Artist and Patriot* (New York: Rand McNally 1962). San Antonio *Light,* June 20, 1937.

Caroline Remy

BORLAND, MARGARET HEFFERNAN (1824–1873). Margaret Borland, Victoria rancher, daughter of John and Julia Heffernan, was born in Ireland on April 3, 1824. The Heffernans were among the Irish colonists who arrived in Texas in 1829 with John McMullen and James McGloin[qqv] and settled at San Patricio. Margaret's elder sister, Mary, was also born in Ireland; two younger brothers, John and James, were born in San Patricio. Margaret was thrice married and widowed. Her first husband, Harrison Dunbar, was killed in a private argument in Victoria soon after she bore their only child, a daughter. Margaret Dunbar married Milton Hardy several years later; Hardy died of cholera in 1855, leaving two more children with Margaret. Mrs. Hardy married Alexander Borland about 1858, a marriage that produced four children. Borland died in 1867; several of Margaret's children and grandchildren died the same year in a yellow fever epidemic. She had assisted Borland in his cattle business and, after his death, assumed full responsibility for the estate. Though she left the physical labor to her hired hands, she bought and sold livestock. By 1873 she owned a herd of more than 10,000 cattle. She was said to be the only woman known to have led a cattle drive. She left her Victoria home in the spring of 1873 with two sons, both under fifteen, a seven-year-old daughter, an even younger granddaughter, a group of trail hands, and about 2,500 cattle. But after successfully reaching Wichita, Kansas, she died, on July 5, 1873, of an illness variously described as "trail fever" and "congestion of the brain." Her body was returned to Texas and buried in Victoria Cemetery.

BIBLIOGRAPHY: Margaret Borland Papers, Barker Texas History Center, University of Texas at Austin. Sue Flanagan, *Trailing the Longhorns* (Austin: Madrona, 1974). C. Richard King, "Margaret Borland," *Texana* 10 (1972). Victor Marion Rose, *History of Victoria* (Laredo, 1883; rpt., Victoria, Texas: Book Mart, 1961).

James C. McNutt

BORN, HENRY (1849–1921). Henry Born (Dutch Henry), outlaw, was born to German immigrant parents on July 2, 1849, in Manitowoc, Wisconsin. In the 1860s he moved with his family to Montague, Michigan, where he worked as a lumberjack. The most reliable accounts indicate that Born moved to Kansas about 1869 and for the next six years engaged in buffalo hunting[qv] and freighting in Kansas and eastern Colorado. He was one of the hide men who entered the Panhandle[qv] of Texas from Dodge City in the spring of 1874, and was among the participants in the second battle of Adobe Walls (*see* RED RIVER WAR) on June 27. At the time of the Indian attack, Born was in the Myers and Leonard store, along with Fred Leonard, Charley Armitage, Bartholomew (Bat) Masterson,[qv] and several others. One account of the battle credits him with killing the black bugler who was fighting with the Indians. Afterward Born served briefly as a civilian scout for the army. He was reportedly assigned to Gen. George A. Custer[qv] but soon quit, declaring that Custer was the "meanest man" he ever knew.

The story of how Born became the outlaw known as Dutch Henry is filled with legend. According to W. M. Tilghman, Born began working in the early 1870s as a cook for Mark Bedell, who bought hides and ran a warehouse at Kit Carson, near Fort Lyon, Colorado. Tilghman related how Born filed a claim in Kansas and with his savings bought a team and wagon, hired a helper, and began his own hide-hunting operation, intending to go back for his sweetheart in Michigan after the season was over. However, a party of Cheyennes raided his camp and stole the horses, leaving Born and his helper wounded and on foot. After taking his companion to town, Born told the commandant at Fort Lyon about his loss and asked to borrow a team to bring in his hides. The commandant refused and reportedly threatened arrest when Born persisted. Subsequently, Born helped himself to several army mules and the commandant's best horse, hauled his hides, sold the mules, and declared in a letter that he was going to "collect one hundred Indian ponies and one scalp." Although Tilghman implies that the episode took place before Adobe Walls, other sources agree that it occurred sometime after the battle.

Soon after the close of the Red River Indian War in 1875, Dutch Henry emerged as the leader of a horse-stealing ring operating in a vast area from Kansas to eastern Colorado and New Mexico and including the Texas Panhandle. Although the actual number of Born's followers is disputed, Charles A. Siringo[qv] claimed that he had as many as 300, including several who acted merely as fences. W. E. Payne, a member of a military surveying party from which Dutch Henry's gang stole horses near Fort Elliott in the fall of 1875, recalled that six men committed the theft. Bill Tilghman claimed that Born "played a lone hand" and "specialized in Indian ponies and government mules," for which he found a lucrative market. Indeed, Born once declared that he had never taken "a white man's horse." Nevertheless, newspaper reports embellished his reputation as a "road agent and murderer." In 1877, after establishing the JA Ranch,[qv] Charles Goodnight[qv] met with Dutch Henry and eighteen members of his band camped on Commission Creek near Fort Elliott. They made a pact, sealed with a drink, that bound the outlaw leader not to raid below the Salt Fork of the Red River, the northern boundary of Goodnight's range. Born remained true to his word, and Goodnight left him alone.

Demands that Dutch Henry be brought to justice increased. More than once he had managed to escape from jails and elude law officers, but in December 1878 the Las Animas county sheriff, R. W. Wootton, arrested him at Trinidad, Colorado. There Born was tried for stealing mules and ordered transferred to the Bent County Jail. Instead, Masterson took him to Dodge City under warrant as a fugitive from justice to stand trial for grand larceny. Although Born was acquitted in January 1879, he was subsequently arrested by a deputy United States marshal and taken to Arkansas to finish a prison term. Though his time behind bars apparently was brief, Born declared that he was "even with the Indians and the Government."

In the 1880s he took up prospecting and lived for a time at Summitville, Colorado. Later he opened the successful Happy Thought Mine at Creede. In the 1890s he filed on 160 acres on the West Fork of the San Juan River twenty miles from Pagosa Springs. He successfully disputed a rival claim and was issued a patent in 1903. The place subsequently became known as Born's Lake.

Born married Ida Dillabaugh in July 1900 and fathered four children. In his later years he talked little about his past and for seven years did not even keep a gun in his house, claiming that he had "had all of the killing that he wanted." Charles Siringo and Bill Tilghman were among the old friends who had a standing invitation to come and fish with Born at the lake. Born died of pneumonia on January 10, 1921, and was buried at Pagosa Springs.

BIBLIOGRAPHY: T. Lindsay Baker and Billy R. Harrison, *Adobe Walls: The History and Archaeology of the 1874 Trading Post* (College Station: Texas A&M University Press, 1986). Zoe A. Tilghman, *Marshal of the Last Frontier: Life and Services of William Matthew Tilghman* (Glendale, California: Clark, 1949). *H. Allen Anderson*

BOROBAMO INDIANS. The Borobamo Indians are known from a single Spanish document of 1683 that does not clearly identify their area. They may have lived somewhere in west central Texas. Their affiliations are unknown.

BIBLIOGRAPHY: Charles W. Hackett, ed., *Pichardo's Treatise on the Limits of Louisiana and Texas* (4 vols., Austin: University of Texas Press, 1931–46). *Thomas N. Campbell*

BORRADO INDIANS. Borrado is a misspelled Spanish name that was used to refer to Indians who practiced body painting, usually in stripes. In Texas this name was applied to Indian groups in two separate areas, one in western Texas, the other in southern Texas and adjoining northeastern Mexico. In western Texas an early reference (1693) mentions "Borrados" and "other Borrados" who lived somewhere north of the Rio Grande and "between Texas and New Mexico." Today these Borrados still cannot be more precisely identified or located. In the seventeenth and eighteenth centuries the second group of Borrados ranged over a large area that extended from Saltillo, in southeastern Coahuila, eastward across Nuevo León into Tamaulipas. In the eighteenth century they appeared in southern Texas, particularly along the coast and in the lower Rio Grande area. At various times during the second half of the eighteenth century, groups of these Borrados entered three of the missions at San Antonio—Nuestra Señora de la Purísima Concepción de Acuña, San José y San Miguel de Aguayo, and San Juan Capistrano. These Borrados spoke a Coahuiltecan language.

BIBLIOGRAPHY: Herbert Eugene Bolton, *Texas in the Middle Eighteenth Century* (Berkeley: University of California Press, 1915; rpt., Austin: University of Texas Press, 1970). Jack Autrey Dabbs, trans., *The Texas Missions in 1785* (Preliminary Studies of the Texas Catholic Historical Society 3.6 [January 1940]). Charles W. Hackett, ed., *Historical Documents Relating to New Mexico, Nueva Vizcaya, and Approaches Thereto, to 1773* (3 vols., Washington: Carnegie Institution, 1923–37). Frederick Webb Hodge, ed., *Handbook of American Indians North of Mexico* (2 vols., Washington: GPO, 1907, 1910; rpt., New York: Pageant, 1959). J. R. Swanton, *Linguistic Material from the Tribes of Southern Texas and Northeastern Mexico* (Washington: Smithsonian Institution, 1940). *Thomas N. Campbell*

BORREGO, TEXAS. Borrego was on the south bank of the San Antonio River sixteen miles southeast of downtown San Antonio in southeastern Bexar County. It was established around 1900, and by the mid-1930s it had a school, a church, a store, and a number of houses. With the growth of San Antonio after World War II[qv] Borrego gradually lost its separate identity, and by the 1950s it was no longer shown on maps. *Christopher Long*

BORREGO CREEK. Borrego Creek rises two miles west of Fairview in western Wilson County (at 29°07′ N, 98°21′ W) and runs southeast for twenty-six miles to its mouth on the Atascosa River, 1½ miles northwest of Campbellton in southeastern Atascosa County (at 28°46′ N, 98°18′ W). It crosses flat to rolling terrain with clay loam and sandy loam soils that support water-tolerant hardwoods and grasses.

BÖSE, EMIL (1868–1927). Emil Böse (Boese), geologist, was born to Johann Heinrich and Johanna (Karutz) Böse on June 8, 1868, in Hamburg, Germany. He took his doctorate in Munich in 1893 under Karl von Zittel, after which he spent several years studying the Triassic rocks of the Italian Alps. In 1898 he accepted a position as geologist with the Instituto de Geología de México. Böse, one of several outstanding geologists who worked in northern Mexico and Texas in the early part of the twentieth century, is best known for outlining the basic stratigraphy of northern Mexico. He remained at the institute until 1915 and was responsible for the preparation of many of the guidebooks for the excursions and meetings of the International Geological Congress in Mexico City and environs in 1906. Although he published many articles and monographs during this period, probably one of the most important was "Monografía Geológica y Paleontológica del Cerro de Muleros cerca de Ciudad Juárez, Estado de Chihuahua, y descripción de la fauna Cretácea de la Encantada, Placer de Guadalupe, Estado de Chihuahua, México" (1910).

In 1915 Böse joined the Bureau of Economic Geology of the University of Texas under the direction of Johan A. Udden.[qv] He worked for the bureau for two years, first with Charles Laurence Baker[qv] and Wayne Bowman in Trans-Pecos Texas, and later in North Texas and other parts of the state. With Udden and Baker he wrote *Review of the Geology of Texas* (1916). He decided to return to Mexico during the latter part of World War I,[qv] but since he was a reserve colonel in the German army he was temporarily detained in San Antonio by United States authorities.

From 1917 to 1922 he was engaged as a consulting geologist in various parts of Texas, Oklahoma, New Mexico, and Mexico. He subsequently joined O. A. Cavins and others in exploratory geology for the Richmond Petroleum Company of Mexico, a subsidiary of the Standard Oil Company of California. Böse traveled much in Mexico, and his letters describing desert life in western and northern Coahuila during and following the period of Francisco (Pancho) Villa[qv] are fascinating.

Böse's publications on the geology of Texas included several bulletins at the University of Texas, papers in the *American Journal of Science,* numerous bulletins and papers for the Instituto de Geología de México, and articles in the International Geological Congress journals and in various scientific bulletins. His last papers, published posthumously, were "Cretaceous Ammonites from Texas and Northern Mexico" and, with O. A. Cavins, "The Cretaceous and Tertiary of Southern Texas and Northern Mexico." Böse was the first to describe the Jurassic and Cretaceous peninsula in northern Mexico now known as the Coahuila Peninsula or Coahuila Island.

He married Helene Miller on October 2, 1900. They had five children. Early in 1924 his family moved to Munich, where the children could get what the Böses considered a proper education. Böse continued to work for Richmond Petroleum Company, mostly in Mexico, though he visited his family in Germany in the summer of 1926. On November 8, 1927, he died as a result of injuries received in an automobile accident west of Sabinal, Texas.

BIBLIOGRAPHY: Emil Böse Papers, Barker Texas History Center, University of Texas at Austin. *Who Was Who in America,* Vol. 1.
Keith Young

BOSMAN, TEXAS. Bosman (Bozman, Bozemann's) was just south of Farm Road 837 and twenty miles northwest of Palestine in northwestern Anderson County. In 1898 its district school had one teacher and some thirty-one black pupils. In the 1960s there was a school building on the site, but by 1982 nothing remained of Bosman.

Mark Odintz

BOSQUE, FERNANDO DEL (?–?). On May 15, 1674, the Audiencia of Guadalajara appointed Antonio Balcárcel as *alcalde mayor* (governor) of Coahuila for five years. The new official was charged with exploring and colonizing the province at his own expense. In November 1674 on a march to the north of Saltillo, Balcárcel chose Fernando del Bosque, an experienced and trustworthy soldier, as his standard bearer. That expedition founded the settlement of Nuestra Señora de Guadalupe near the site of present Monclova on December 8, 1647. Associated with the new outpost were two missionaries, fathers Juan Larios and Dionisio de San Buenaventura, who wished to expand their Christianization efforts to include Indians north of the Rio Grande.

In 1675 Barcárcel chose Bosque to accompany an expedition that crossed the Rio Grande on May 11 of that year. The site of the crossing is in dispute, but it was perhaps Paso de Francia (*see* SAN ANTONIO CROSSING), near the future site of mission San Juan Bautista.[qv] The Bosque-Larios expedition[qv] traveled forty-one leagues (about 110 miles) beyond the Rio Grande and gave names to six localities. During the journey Bosque wrote an extensive report describing the topography that they encountered. At several sites Indians indicated their willingness to accept religious instruction in the Christian faith. This undertaking and an earlier reconnaissance of the same general area by Brother Manuel de la Cruz is notable in that they are the earliest well-authenticated missionary enterprises to cross the Rio Grande below the Pecos junction.

After completion of the entrada in June 1675, Bosque suggested that three mission districts, including lands and Indians north of the Rio Grande, be established. Internal conditions in Coahuila delayed action on the proposal for a decade. By then the focus of attention had shifted to East Texas to counter the threat posed by René Robert Cavelier, Sieur de La Salle.[qv] The French challenge in many respects served to short-circuit early missionary activity in extreme south central Texas. In the late 1670s Fernando del Bosque disappears from known historical records.

BIBLIOGRAPHY: Herbert Eugene Bolton, ed., *Spanish Exploration in the Southwest, 1542–1706* (New York: Scribner, 1908; rpt., New York: Barnes and Noble, 1959). Carlos E. Castañeda, *Our Catholic Heritage in Texas* (7 vols., Austin: Von Boeckmann–Jones, 1936–58; rpt., New York: Arno, 1976). Donald E. Chipman, *Spanish Texas, 1519–1821* (Austin: University of Texas Press, 1992). Robert S. Weddle, *San Juan Bautista: Gateway to Spanish Texas* (Austin: University of Texas Press, 1968).

Donald E. Chipman

BOSQUE COLLEGE AND SEMINARY. Bosque College and Seminary was a nonsectarian school in Bosque (later Bosqueville), about five miles north of Waco. It succeeded Bosque Academy and also Waco Female Seminary,[qv] which held its last term in 1856–57. The same faculty and virtually the same board of trustees that had managed the Waco seminary were involved in establishing the school at Bosque, which received its charter on February 16, 1858. John C. Collier,[qv] a Cumberland Presbyterian minister who had headed Bosque Academy in 1854 and taught at the Waco Female Seminary during its last year, became president of the college. Among the trustees who served both institutions were Herman Aiken, Noah T. Byars, George Bernard Erath, and Amos Morrill.[qqv] The prospectus for the female division announced an annual session extending from September 1 to July 1, with the only break being a one-week holiday at Christmas. The school would encompass primary and preparatory departments, in addition to the "regular course" (freshman through senior levels). Classes would include Latin, Greek, French, Spanish, German, and Italian; music (melodeon and piano); drawing and painting; and lessons in wax, fruit, flowers, and embroidery. Other studies included algebra, trigonometry, chemistry, astronomy, rhetoric, logic, political economy, and mental and moral philosophy. By 1858 Hebrew and the guitar, violin, and flute had been added to the curriculum. Although the school was nonsectarian, tuition was to be free for daughters of full-time clergymen, or clergy of limited means.

The Bosque school was the first coeducational college in McLennan County, though the male and female departments were originally located a mile apart. In 1860 Collier sold the Bosque Male College to the trustees but continued to teach and serve as president. The school prospered and had as many as 400 students in 1861, but the Civil War[qv] thinned its ranks: that year a company of 100 male students left to enlist, and in 1863 Collier resigned to become a scout in Ross's Brigade.[qv] In late 1863 or in 1864 Solomon G. O'Bryan took over as president of Bosque Male and Female College, a position he held for two years. (O'Bryan had taught in either the Bosque academy or the college while he was pastor of the First Baptist Church, Waco,[qv] in the 1850s.) The school, also known as Bosqueville Male and Female College, apparently closed about 1865.

BIBLIOGRAPHY: Robert Douglas Brackenridge, *Voice in the Wilderness: A History of the Cumberland Presbyterian Church in Texas* (San Antonio: Trinity University Press, 1968). William Franklin Ledlow, History of Protestant Education in Texas (Ph.D. dissertation, University of Texas, 1926). Vertical Files, Barker Texas History Center, University of Texas at Austin (Bosque College).

Vivian Elizabeth Smyrl and Mary M. Standifer

BOSQUE COUNTY. Bosque County (F–16) is located in Central Texas. The county seat, Meridian, is situated in the center of the county at latitude 31°56′ N and longitude 97°39′ W. The county lies approximately sixty miles south of Dallas–Fort Worth and forty miles north of Waco. Bosque County is bordered by Erath and Somervell counties to the north, Johnson and Hill counties to the east, McLennan and Coryell counties to the south, and Hamilton County to the west. State Highways 174, 144, 22, and 65 traverse the county, along with numerous county and farm-to-market roads; the public road system comprises 1,106 miles.

Bosque County is an agrarian area that covers 989 square miles. As a part of the Grand Prairie subdivision of the North Central Plains, the land is primarily an area of shallow to deep, well-drained soils underlain by limestone. Around the streams are deep, well-drained and moderately well-drained soils. Many believe that the soil is the most important natural resource of the county because the life of the livestock and the flora and fauna depend heavily upon it. Much sand, gravel, and limestone are mined in the county for construction. The alluvial soils of the riverbottoms promote the growth of elm, cottonwood, river birch, sycamore, ash, pecan, and a variety of oak trees. The area is also distinguished by clusters of flat-topped hills separated by low areas of flat grassland. Although many grasses cover the prairie areas of Bosque County, Johnson grass is the most common. Numerous livestock graze in the county, where sudden outcroppings of white limestone form tall, steep hills or cliffs. Throughout the plains areas, cedars, oaks, and mesquites are prevalent. The only commercial mineral found in Bosque County is limestone. In this region of rolling hills, the altitude ranges from 480 to 1,200 feet.

Bosque County is considered a "well-watered" area. The Brazos River borders the eastern edge of the county, and the Bosque River cuts through the center of the county north to south. Besides the major rivers, there are numerous smaller watercourses or tributaries, such as Mesquite, Grass, Hill, Duffan's, Fall, Honey, Meridian, Spring, Turkey, and Mill creeks. Near the northeast corner of the county lies the well-known Kimball's Bend in the Brazos River. In

1951 Lake Whitney was constructed on the Brazos River at the southeastern edge of Bosque County. This reservoir is used for recreation, flood control, and power generation. Throughout the county, the supply of water is adequate for domestic use, livestock, and irrigation.

Bosque County is very hot in the summer and cool in the winter, with occasional cold surges that cause sharp drops in otherwise mild temperatures. In the winter, the average low temperature is 47° F. The lowest temperature on record, however, is 23°, recorded at Whitney Dam on February 2, 1951. During the summer, the average daily high temperature is 95°. A record 111° was recorded on July 26, 1954. Rainfall is uniformly distributed throughout the county with an average of 33 inches a year. The heaviest one-day rainfall was 6.22 inches, measured at Whitney Dam on October 19, 1971. The average growing season lasts 243 days; the last freeze usually occurs in late March and the first freeze around late November. Along the North Bosque River in the southmost corner of the county, where the impermeable bedrock is most widely extended, serious floods occur. Intensive cultivation of the land has been a problem throughout the history of the county. Since the survival of the area depends on the soil, governmental agencies attempt through management to guard against flooding or erosion and exhaustion of the soil.

Tonkawa, Waco, and Tawakoni Indians roamed Central Texas long before settlement by European Americans. The Tonkawas were the most predominant in number, and they proved to be quite peaceable. They are said to have claimed that they never took a scalp. They were a small group, and the only complaint that the settlers registered against them was stealing. The Comanches, who lived nearby, occasionally raided travelers or settlers in the Bosque territory to steal horses and property or to take scalps. When whites followed them in attempts to regain their property, the Tonkawas often acted as their guides.

The first exploring expedition that recorded travel in this area was made in 1721 by the Marqués de San Miguel de Aguayo,[qv] a Spaniard who established many missions in Texas. In one trip from San Antonio de Béxar to an East Texas mission, he ventured away from the regular road, the Old San Antonio Road,[qv] and wandered north. During this time he camped near the Brazos River and a major tributary. He named this tributary Bosque, Spanish for "woods." The county, therefore, derives its name from the Bosque River.

Settlement of the area began in 1825 when Sterling C. Robertson[qv] obtained a grant from the Mexican government in order to colonize the area along the Brazos River. Very few of the homesteaders chose to live within the current boundaries of Bosque County; however, the grant did prompt travel through the area. The land granted was later transformed into districts, one being the Milam District. George B. Erath,[qv] a surveyor for both the Republic of Texas[qv] and the state of Texas, is credited with naming many of the streams and landmarks in Texas. In the late 1830s he named Meridian Creek and the Meridian Knobs for the fact that they were near the ninety-eighth meridian. In 1841 the botched Texan–Santa Fe expedition[qv] passed through the region, and many of the travelers chose to stay. In 1847, a prominent banker from New York, Richard B. Kimball, obtained a grant of land from the state of Texas along the west bank of the Brazos river fourteen miles north of the mouth of the Paluxy River. Soon, Kimball formed a partnership with Jacob De Cordova[qv] in order to develop this land. They planned to establish a town so that they could lure prospective settlers to move to the area. A site was chosen along the Brazos River where there was a shallow ford. They named the town after Kimball. Since this was the best spot to cross the river for miles, many east-to-west travelers came through town. At this point the Chisolm Trail[qv] crossed the waterway. The location of Kimball, therefore, made it a good stopping place for settlers, ranchers, and cowboys. Following a somewhat prosperous start, however, Kimball was missed by the railroads that were built in the county later in the decade; therefore, the town quickly declined, and only a few people remain there today.

In 1850, McLennan County was carved out of the Milam District. The same year the Universal Immigration Company of England purchased 27,000 acres of land from Richard Kimball and laid out a townsite on the west bank of the Brazos. In the late 1850s, the company sent over thirty families, comprising approximately 120 people. They settled in an area between the present-day towns of Kopperl and Kimball under a massive rock formation called Solomon's Nose. They named their idealistic colony Kent. Unfortunately, the citizens of Kent fell to the same fate that their predecessors did more than a century before in Jamestown, Virginia. The first harsh winter caused many hardships that led to a high number of fatalities. During the following spring, in their last attempts to survive as a community, they bought several cattle and some seed corn; however, they failed to build a fence around the crop and the cows ate all of the corn before it could be harvested. The settlement quickly broke up, and the colonists migrated separately to other areas. Some moved back to England.

Bosque County was officially formed in February 1854 from McLennan County. Soon a site was chosen at which to locate the county seat. Erath laid out the town of Meridian in the center of the county on land donated by Dr. Josephus M. Steiner. Town lots were sold at a public auction on the Fourth of July 1854. Soon thereafter, the first courthouse, a one-story log cabin, was erected in the middle of town. This building served the needs of the residents until 1869, when a larger frame structure was built. In 1871 this second courthouse burned. For four years the business of the county was conducted in a tent. In 1875 the third, and present, courthouse was completed, a three-story structure of native stone.

Also in 1854, Norwegian immigrants began to move to the area. Ole Canuteson, the first, believed that the land was much like that in Norway. The state of Texas offered 320 acres to each family that would settle in the new county, and the Norwegians took advantage of the offer. Cleng Peerson,[qv] the "father" of Norwegian immigration to America, led the settlers to the region. The bulk of them settled in a triangular area bound by the present-day towns of Clifton, Norse, and Cranfills Gap. Peerson was sixty-seven years old when he moved to Bosque County, and he lived the remainder of his life in the area. Many descendants of the Canutesons, Ringnesses, Dahls, Questads, and other Norwegian settlers still live in Bosque County.

The first county election took place on August 7, 1854. The turnout was small, but county officials were chosen and the local government began to function. The next significant election took place on February 23, 1861, when secession[qv] was the issue. The citizens voted for it by 233 to 81; the Norwegians voted against secession by 52 to 42. Like many other European immigrants in Central Texas, the Norwegians of southern Bosque County maintained Union sentiments throughout the conflict, though they did not join in the fighting.

The history of the Civil War[qv] era in Bosque County is sketchy because of skimpy record keeping. Between 1861 and 1865 many men from the county served in the military. The most significant contributions were to the Second Frontier District, the Nineteenth Texas Infantry, and Company H of Col. T. C. Hawpe's[qv] regiment. The latter two units saw action in the Louisiana and Arkansas campaigns, and a few of the members fought with the Army of Northern Virginia. The majority of the soldiers, however, guarded the area against Indians. In January 1865 many of them fought in the famed battle of Dove Creek[qv] battle against the Kickapoos. Although the battle took place in what it now Tom Green County, many Bosque County fighters participated; about ten of them died. Probably the most significant impact of the Civil War in Bosque County was that it slowed, and in some places halted, development. Few people moved to new counties at the time, and the Norwegians stopped coming.

The county began to make progress in the decades following the Civil War. During Reconstruction[qv] the county population grew, from 4,981 in 1870 to 11,216 in 1880. Additionally, the black population increased from 293 in 1860 to 528 in 1870. But lawlessness, including the killing of freedmen, flourished. In early 1870 the situation was so bad that the Austin *Daily State Journal* reported Bosque County was averaging two killings each week. Bosque County whites blamed the Republican government for these problems; the Democratic party[qv] has dominated the county ever since.

By 1880 the population had grown to 11,216, and the value of the farms in the county had finally surpassed the $1 million mark. New communities were established. Furthermore, in 1881 the Texas Central and the Santa Fe railroads came to the area, and several towns began to thrive. The number of manufacturing establishments increased from eleven in 1880 to eighty-five in 1900. The county, however, did not sustain this surge of growth, and by 1920 only twenty-one manufacturers remained; the number was the same in 1977.

At the turn of the century the population had increased to 17,390, but growth fell off subsequently in livestock production, crop production, and manufacturing. There were several reasons for the local depression. The soil was exhausted and eroding. Declining prices, spring floods, summer droughts, unseasonable weather, and onslaughts of insects plagued farmers. During the second decade of the twentieth century, Bosque County witnessed its first decline in population, decreasing from a peak of 19,013 in 1910 to 18,032 in 1920. The downward trend continued until 1980. During the decade before the Great Depression,[qv] Bosque County farmers and ranchers witnessed noticeable losses in agriculture. From 1920 to 1930, the value of all farms decreased from $26,308,381 to $17,255,955. The production of wheat alone dropped by more than 500,000 bushels. Manufacturers were down to eleven by 1930. When the depression hit the entire nation in 1929, Bosque countians were already suffering very hard times.

The residents of the county had remained faithful followers of Democratic politics from 1876 to 1932. The only break occurred in 1928, when they opposed Democratic candidate Alfred Smith because he was a Catholic with New York mannerisms. In November 1932 the county joined the voters of Texas and the rest of the nation to give Franklin D. Roosevelt an overwhelming victory at the polls. On March 25, 1933, when citizens in need of aid were required to assemble at the city hall in Clifton to register for assistance, 107 residents applied. Within a few days, half of them were employed clearing the municipal park under the Federal Emergency Relief Act. The Civilian Conservation Corps[qv] opened Camp Clifton on the banks of the Bosque River on June 21, 1933. The corps was assigned to beautify the city park and to construct low-water dams on nearby streams. Merchants of Clifton welcomed the workers with open arms. In June, articles in the local paper called for cotton growers to plow under a portion of their crops. Reportedly, at least 90 percent of the cotton farmers of the county supported the program; county farmers received an estimated $125,831 cash for the destroyed cotton. When Congress passed the National Industrial Recovery Act, "blue eagles" began to appear in store windows throughout the county. But though the New Deal assisted Bosque County residents, it they could not stop the downward trend that had begun in the 1920s.

A succession of dry years in the late 1940s and 1950s forced many farmers to abandon their farms. The total number of farms dropped from 2,229 in 1930 to 1,558 in 1950. Only 1002 farms were registered in 1982. During the mid-twentieth century, agricultural production and some livestock production also decreased. Fortunately for the county, when agriculture dropped off, manufacturing picked up the slack. Manufacturing establishments steadily increased in number and value every census year after 1947. After 1970, employment opportunities increased due to industrial growth in lumber, stone products, limestone, and, most significantly, apparel and textiles.

During the 1980s, Bosque County grew in population and economy. In the late 1970s and 1980s residents of Clifton, the largest town, carried out "Operation Comeback." The town grew by 40 percent in population and more than 100 percent in businesses. The town renovated old buildings in order to open a modern home for senior citizens, established Goodall–Witcher Hospital, and opened a 150-employee garment factory, an oilfield-tool manufacturing plant, and a 100-employee lime plant.

In 1990, the population of Bosque County reached 13,924, of which 91 percent were Anglo; the peak of 1920 was still unattained. Bosque County ranks fourteenth among all United States counties in the percentage of its population that is sixty-five years of age or older. In addition to Clifton, Meridian, and Valley Mills, the county has numerous small towns. As of 1982, there were 7,420 registered voters in the county. Voter turnout ranged remarkably between 58 and 73 percent in the 1980s; 97 percent voted Democratic and three percent voted Republican in the 1982 primaries. About half of those registered cast a ballot. Voting in presidential elections has varied. Since supporting Franklin Delano Roosevelt for four terms, county voters switched to the Republican candidates in 1952, 1972, and 1980 through 1992. The education level in the county has steadily increased. In 1850, 22 percent of the population had graduated from high school; in 1980, 44 percent.

Several prominent persons have hailed from Bosque County. Among them were Calvin M. Cureton,[qv] state attorney general and a member of the state Supreme Court; Earle B. Mayfield,[qv] United States senator; James E. and Miriam A. Ferguson,[qqv] governors of Texas; and the Tandy family, who formed the Tandy Corporation.[qv]

BIBLIOGRAPHY: Bosque County History Book Committee, *Bosque County, Land and People* (Dallas: Curtis Media, 1985). *Bosquerama, 1854–1954: Centennial Celebration of Bosque County, Texas* (Meridian, Texas: Bosque County Centennial Association, 1954). William C. Pool, *A History of Bosque County* (San Marcos, Texas: San Marcos Record Press, 1954). William C. Pool, *Bosque Territory* (Kyle, Texas: Chaparral, 1964).

Kristi Strickland

BOSQUE-LARIOS EXPEDITION. On April 30, 1675, Fernando del Bosque, Fray Juan Larios, Fray Dionisio de San Buenaventura, ten Spanish soldiers, Lázaro Agustín, governor of the Indian pueblo of San Miguel de Luna, Capt. Juan de la Cruz, and twenty Bobole Indians set out from the mission of Nuestra Señora de Guadalupe, at the site of present Monclova, Coahuila, to convert the Indians of the Coahuila. On the Nadadores River they were joined by a hundred Guyquechale Indians. The expedition reached the Río Sabinas (Coahuila) on May 5, erected a cross, and took formal possession of the river. On May 11 it reached the Rio Grande, probably a little below the present site of Eagle Pass. Bosque took formal possession of the river, erected a wooden cross, and renamed the river the San Buenaventura del Norte. On May 15 the expedition was met by several Indian chiefs, who asked the missionaries to come to teach and baptize their followers. The oath of allegiance to the king was administered to all the Indians, a portable altar was set up, and Mass was celebrated.

In all, the Spaniards traveled forty leagues past the Rio Grande and made six halts in south central Texas. On May 25 they reached a site in present Edwards County that they called San Pablo Hermitano. They returned by a northerly route to Guadalupe, where they arrived on June 12; there Bosque made a formal report to Antonio de Balcárcel. The latter recommended that three mission districts be established, including land and Indians north of the Rio Grande. Indian hostilities and disputes with Nuevo León about the jurisdiction of the area, however, delayed implementation of the plan for more than a decade, and by that time the focus of efforts had shifted to East Texas to counteract French incursions.

BIBLIOGRAPHY: Vito Alessio Robles, *Coahuila y Texas en la época colonial* (Mexico City: Editorial Cultura, 1938; 2d ed., Mexico City: Editorial Porrúa, 1978). Carlos E. Castañeda, *Our Catholic Heritage in Texas* (7 vols., Austin: Von Boeckmann–Jones, 1936–58; rpt., New York: Arno, 1976). Donald E. Chipman, *Spanish Texas, 1519–1821* (Austin: University of Texas Press, 1992).

Kaye A. Walker

BOSQUE RIVER. The Bosque River rises in four main branches, the North, East, Middle, and South Bosque rivers, at Lake Waco, on the northwest edge of Waco in central McLennan County (at 31°34′ N, 97°12′ W), and flows south for four miles to its mouth on the Brazos River, in Cameron Park in the city limits of Waco (at 31°35′ N, 97°09′ W). The North Bosque River, the longest branch of the river, rises in north central Erath County and cuts through Hamilton County into Bosque County, where it is joined by the East Bosque River, which rises in Erath County. From their confluence the North Bosque continues into central McLennan County, where it is joined by the South and Middle Bosque rivers as it flows into Lake Waco. The Bosque River flows through rolling hills where the dominant vegetation includes post oak and cedar. The upper branches, in Erath, Hamilton, and Bosque counties, are relatively narrow, free-flowing, and scenic, with clear water and heavily vegetated banks.

The word *bosque* is Spanish for "woods" or "woody lands," and, according to some accounts, the name was applied to the stream by the Marqués de San Miguel de Aguayo[qv] in 1719. Other authorities say that the river was named for a French trader, Juan Bosquet, who was living with the Tawakoni Indians in the 1770s. George B. Erath[qv] explored the river on an expedition in 1837, and the Texan Santa Fe expedition[qv] of 1841 crossed the area. Bones of Ice Age mammoths that lived 17,000 years ago have been located near the river's junction with the Brazos. Indians who lived along the river included Caddo, Tonkawa, Tawakoni, Towash, and Waco.

BIBLIOGRAPHY: *An Analysis of Texas Waterways* (Austin: Texas Parks and Wildlife Department, 1974).

BOSQUEVILLE, TEXAS. Bosqueville is four miles northwest of downtown Waco near the intersection of Farm roads 1637 and 3051 in north central McLennan County. Settlement of the area was well underway by the 1850s, and the community may have served as an early voting site. Little Berry White donated ten acres of land for a school and cemetery in 1850. In 1854 the Bosque Academy was established by Cumberland Presbyterian minister John C. Collier.[qv] As the community's Methodist population began to grow, that denomination also used the academy's facilities for its gatherings. The school, which eventually added a conservatory of music, by 1860 had 180 students and two institutions: the Bosqueville Academy for Boys and the Seminary for Young Ladies. The school closed when the Civil War[qv] began, but was later reorganized as the Bosque College and Seminary,[qv] a nonsectarian school that purported to be the country's first coeducational institution. A townsite was laid out in 1858, and the Bosqueville post office was established in April 1860 with Cornellius P. Petit as postmaster. By the mid-1880s Bosqueville had three churches, a general store, and 100 residents. Cotton and wheat were the principal cash crops grown by area farmers. In the 1890s Bosqueville was on a daily stage route between Waco and China Spring. The post office was discontinued in 1907, and mail for the community was routed through Waco. The population of Bosqueville was reported at seventy-five in 1910 and at ninety-four in 1930; it rose to 100 by the late 1940s. Two schools and several scattered houses marked the community on county highway maps in the 1940s. The Bosqueville schools were consolidated with the China Springs rural high school district in 1959; Bosqueville became the focus of an independent school district in 1965. Its population was estimated at seventy-two from the 1970s through the early 1990s.

BIBLIOGRAPHY: Dayton Kelley, ed., *The Handbook of Waco and McLennan County, Texas* (Waco: Texian, 1972). William Robert Poage, *McLennan County Before 1980* (Waco: Texian, 1981). Vertical File, Texas Collection, Baylor University. *Vivian Elizabeth Smyrl*

BOSSOM, ALFRED CHARLES (1881–1965). Alfred Charles Bossom, architect, author, and member of Parliament, son of Alfred Henry and Amelia Jane (Hammond) Bossom, was born in Islington, London, England, on October 16, 1881. He took his architectural training at Regent Street Polytechnic and at the Royal Academy schools. In 1903 he traveled to the United States to design a housing scheme at Allegheny, Pennsylvania, for the Carnegie Steel Mills, Pittsburgh. He undertook the restoration of Fort Ticonderoga in New York state in 1908. His marriage to Emily Bayne, daughter of Samuel Bayne, president of National Seaboard Bank, New York, and owner of the second oil well drilled in the United States, undoubtedly influenced Bossom's evolving specialty in bank design and buildings for the petroleum industry, usually in the form of the skyscraper.

America was booming, and skyscraper construction had reached maturity. Bossom's contribution was to implement existing technologies with maximum efficiency. His theories, philosophy and work methods are summarized in his book, *Building to the Skies: The Romance of the Skyscraper* (1934). By 1918 his burgeoning architectural practice, which occupied offices at 680 Fifth Avenue in New York, was handling a flood of commissions in various parts of the county, primarily along the eastern seaboard and in Texas. The firm's work in Dallas includes the American Exchange National Bank (1918, associate architects Lang and Witchell), and the Magnolia–Mobil Petroleum Building (1922). Maple Terrace Apartments (1924–25) and alterations and extensions to the Adolphus Hotel were both done in collaboration with architects Thomson and Swaine. Bossom's major work in Houston is the Petroleum Building (1925–26), done in association with architects Briscoe, Dixon, and Sullivan. Bossom designed the United States National Bank in Galveston (1924). While he was working in Texas, he and his wife, both inveterate travelers, roamed the Southwest and traveled into Mexico. Alfred's sketches and commentary and Emily's photographs were published by Charles Scribner's in 1924 as *An Architectural Pilgrimage in Old Mexico,* which included the eighteenth-century missions in San Antonio.

The family returned to England in 1926, at the height of Bossom's professional career, determined that their three sons should be educated there. Bossom began a new life in public service, entirely detached from architectural practice. He was elected to Parliament as Conservative member for Maidstone, Kent, in 1931 and served for twenty-eight years. He was made a baronet in 1953, was elected chairman of the Royal Society of Arts (1957–59), and in 1960 was made life peer, taking as his title Lord Bossom of Maidstone. His enthusiasm for Texas was manifested in his leadership of the Anglo-Texan Society,[qv] of which he served as president from the mid-fifties until his death in London in 1965 at age eighty-three.

BIBLIOGRAPHY: Dennis Sharp, ed., *Alfred C. Bossom's American Architecture, 1903–1926* (London: Book Art, 1984).

Mary Carolyn Hollers George

BOSS RULE. During the second half of the nineteenth century and the first part of the twentieth, boss rule became a prevalent pattern of political organization in the big cities of the United States. Typically, a clique of politicians dominated the political life of a city by manipulating the votes of large numbers of immigrants. The bosses resorted to bribery and coercion, but they also won the support of the hard-pressed newcomers by providing informal welfare services and limited opportunities for upward mobility. Businessmen as well often embraced the systems to secure special favors from city government. Some historians have even argued that the centralization of authority resulting from boss rule was an essential step in solving social problems growing out of rapid urban growth.

The concentration of political power in the hands of a few has not been uncommon in Texas cities during the twentieth century. In cities like Dallas and Houston, powerful business interests have prevailed. For example, the Citizens' Council and its sister organization, the Citizens' Charter Association, not only promoted the economic growth of Dallas but also, beginning in the mid-1930s, determined the character of city government. Corporate executives participating in these Dallas organizations recruited candidates for public office, arranged newspaper support, and provided generous financial backing. Their candidates usually carried the city elections. The corporate leaders also directly decided such basic social issues as the pace of racial integration in Dallas.

Despite the concentration of power and the limits on the political choices open to the public, however, this form of business government did not conform to the basic features of Texas boss rule. The truest and most notorious application of machine politics took root in South Texas during the closing decades of the nineteenth century and was still visible in some counties ninety years later. Stephen Powers and James B. Wells, Jr.,[qqv] oversaw the establishment of a Democratic political machine in Cameron County during the 1870s and 1880s. The ring retained control of Cameron County politics until 1920 and contributed to the formation of similar organizations in Hidalgo, Starr, and Duval counties.

All of the South Texas Democratic machines followed the same pattern of operation. While manipulating the vote of the Hispanic majority and engaging in varying degrees of graft, the bosses and their cohorts served the interests of their diverse constituencies. In the courts and the state legislature, lawyer-politicians defended the ambiguous and sometimes suspect land claims of local ranchers. The politicos held land taxes to a minimum and lobbied for the deployment of Texas Rangers[qv] to maintain order and intimidate the Mexican masses, who had shown signs of rebelliousness against white domination during an earlier era. The bosses catered to the needs of land speculators, developers, bankers, and merchants by promoting the extension of railroad lines to this remote section of the state. To the Mexican-American laborers the South Texas politicians offered paternalistic services modeled after the feudalistic obligations of Mexican *patrones* to their *peones.* In return for relief during hard times and the financing of weddings, funerals, and other special occasions, lower-class Mexicans submitted to the political control of the bosses. Anglo politicians also reached an accommodation with the well-to-do Mexican families who were able to retain their lands and businesses in the face of the American onslaught after the Civil War.[qv] In fact, Manuel Guerra[qv] acted as the political boss of Starr County from 1905 until his death in 1915.

Thousands of white settlers came to South Texas, especially when large-scale irrigation was introduced in the lower Rio Grande valley. Racial hatred intensified during the border violence accompanying the Mexican Revolution.[qv] These influences fueled a widespread rebellion against boss rule in South Texas after 1900. The white challengers to the Democratic machines expressed both a commitment to honest, businesslike public administration and a racist contempt for Hispanic involvement in politics. Still the machines displayed remarkable resilience. Although the Wells machine of Cameron County collapsed in 1920, the Hidalgo County organization under John Closner and later Anderson Y. Baker[qv] survived until 1930. The Guerra family continued to rule Starr County until 1946, when another Hispanic-controlled organization established its dominance.

The most notorious of all the South Texas rings, the Duval County structure headed by Archer Parr[qv] from 1908 until his death in 1942 and then by his son George Parr,[qv] lasted until 1975. The rule of the Parr family weathered public outcries over apparent political murders, repeated state and federal investigations into blatant acts of graft and election fraud, and even the imprisonment of George Parr in 1936 for income-tax evasion. The Parr machine gained nationwide attention in 1948 when late and allegedly fraudulent election returns from Duval County and neighboring Jim Wells County gave Lyndon B. Johnson[qv] a narrow primary victory over Coke R. Stevenson[qv] in the United States Senate race.

At different times, political machines dependent on Hispanic support have existed in Corpus Christi, Laredo, and El Paso, but Texas-style boss rule left its most enduring imprint on the rural counties of South Texas. Not even the suicide of George Parr and the collapse of his organization in 1975 brought this political phenomenon to an end.

bibliography: Evan Anders, *Boss Rule in South Texas: The Progressive Era* (Austin: University of Texas Press, 1982). Dudley Lynch, *The Duke of Duval: The Life and Times of George B. Parr* (Waco: Texian Press, 1976). Mario T. García, *Desert Immigrants: The Mexicans of El Paso, 1880–1920* (New Haven: Yale University Press, 1981).

Evan Anders

BOSTICK, SION RECORD (1819–1902). Sion Record Bostick (Bostwick), soldier of the Republic of Texas[qv] and the Confederate States of America, son of Caleb R. Bostick,[qv] was born in Alabama on December 7, 1819. The elder Bostick was a farmer and stock raiser and one of the ten original Texas Rangers.[qv] He was granted a sitio[qv] in what became Matagorda County by Stephen F. Austin[qv] on July 24, 1824. Sion joined his father there in 1828. In 1829 the family moved to San Felipe and in 1832 to the site of Columbus.

Sion Bostick was present for the battle of Gonzales in the company of Capt. P. R. Splane and took part in the siege of Bexar.[qv] When Antonio López de Santa Anna[qv] marched into Texas, Bostick reenlisted, on March 21, 1836, as a private in Capt. Moseley Baker's[qv] company of Col. Edward Burleson's[qv] First Regiment, Texas Volunteers; he fought in the battle of San Jacinto.[qv] A Sion Bostick is also listed as a member of Capt. William H. Patton's[qv] Columbia Company at the time of the battle. With two other scouts, Joel Robinson and James A. Sylvester,[qqv] Bostick captured and brought in Santa Anna on April 22. After San Jacinto he reenlisted as a private in the army, first for the term from March 11 through May 25 and then from July 1 to October 1, in the company of Capt. B. F. Ravill.

In 1840 Bostick was living in Colorado County and owned two slaves. He took part in the battle of Plum Creek[qv] that year and later claimed to have served during the Mexican War[qv] in Capt. Claborne C. Herbert's[qv] Company E of Col. John Coffee Hays's[qv] First Texas Mounted Rifles. This company was recruited in Columbus, but Bostick's name does not appear on its muster roll. On March 21, 1862, the forty-one-year-old Bostick enlisted in Capt. John C. Upton's[qv] Company B of Col. James J. Archer's Fifth Texas Infantry regiment of the famed Hood's Texas Brigade.[qv] He served for a time in Virginia but was discharged by the order of the Confederate secretary of war on September 22 as over age. "During the war with Spain I was very much troubled because I was too old to go," he later wrote.

Bostick died of cancer at his home in San Saba on October 15, 1902. He was a member of the Texas Veterans' Association.[qv] His not entirely reliable memoir of the Texas Revolution,[qv] dictated when he was past eighty years of age, was published in the *Southwestern Historical Quarterly*[qv] in 1901.

bibliography: Donaly E. Brice, *The Great Comanche Raid* (Austin: Eakin Press, 1987). Lester G. Bugbee, "The Old Three Hundred: A List of Settlers in Austin's First Colony," *Quarterly of the Texas State Historical Association* 1 (October 1897). Daughters of the Republic of Texas, *Muster Rolls of the Texas Revolution* (Austin, 1986). Frances Terry Ingmire, comp., *Texas Ranger Service Records, 1847–1900* (St. Louis, 1982). C. W. Raines, *Year Book for Texas* (2 vols., Austin: Gammel-Statesman, 1902, 1903). Harold B. Simpson, *Hood's Texas Brigade: A Compendium* (Hillsboro, Texas: Hill Junior College Press, 1977). Gifford E. White, *1830 Citizens of Texas* (Austin: Eakin, 1983).

Thomas W. Cutrer

BOSTON, TEXAS. Boston, the county seat of Bowie County, is just south of U.S. Highway 82 and the Missouri Pacific Railroad and twenty-two miles east of Texarkana in central Bowie County. In the mid-1880s citizens of Texarkana and eastern Bowie County succeeded in a campaign to mark Texarkana the county seat (*see* old boston, texas). About five years later the citizens of western and central Bowie County were able to get a new election to choose another county seat; they proposed locating the geographic center of the county and building the courthouse there. Their campaign succeeded, and in 1890 construction of a new courthouse began at a site a mile south of New Boston and three miles north of the older city named Boston. Residents applied for a new post office under the name Center, but because a town by that name already existed, the request was denied; the names Hood and Glass were not accepted for the same reason. Because the law required a post office at every county seat, the post office was moved from the original Boston community. The name was transferred also, and the original Boston site became known as Old Boston. The new county seat had a population of 175 by 1896, and its population remained at around that level through the early 1990s. Because of its proximity to the much larger town of New Boston, Boston never developed a substantial commercial base. Through the mid-1980s it had never reported more than five rated businesses; in 1982 it had only two. In 1984, though the city limits of Boston and New Boston touched, the two towns maintained their separate identities and post offices. In 1986 a new Bowie County Courthouse was built in New Boston, but Boston remained the official county seat. The population of Boston was reported at 200 in the early 1990s.

BIBLIOGRAPHY: Dallas *Morning News,* March 6, 1938.

Cecil Harper, Jr.

BOSTWICK, CALEB R. (?–1837?). Caleb R. Bostwick (Bostick, Bostic), one of Stephen F. Austin's[qv] Old Three Hundred[qv] colonists, may have originally been from Columbia County, New York. He moved to Texas as early as 1820 or 1821, when he traveled from Arkansas with John Ingram[qv] and the Thomas Williams[qv] family. In 1822 Bostwick and Williams helped move newly arrived settlers up the Colorado from the landing at its mouth. A census of the Colorado District in March 1823 listed Bostwick as a twenty-eight-year-old carpenter who owned one horse. By May of that year he had enlisted in a scouting company, headed by Moses Morrison,[qv] that had been raised to control Karankawa Indians in the area around the Colorado River and Tres Palacios Creek, and in June 1823 Bostwick, Williams, Morrison, and Thomas Jamison[qv] cut a path south to Bay Prairie in what later became Matagorda County, then over to the rich lands of the Caney Creek bottom and to Cedar Lake. In November 1823 Bostwick subscribed ten bushels of corn toward paying the expenses of the Baron de Bastrop[qv] as Texas delegate to the Mexican congress. Bostwick was a partner of Robert Brotherton[qv] as one of the Old Three Hundred colonists. The partners received title to a sitio[qv] now in Matagorda County on July 24, 1824. In October 1825 Bostwick joined Daniel DeCrow[qv] and other colonists at Cedar Lake in petitioning Austin to treat with the Karankawa Indians. The census of 1826 listed Bostwick as a single farmer and stock raiser. He eventually married Martha DeMoss, daughter of Martha and Charles DeMoss,[qv] and they had at least one child. In November 1830 Bostwick and Morrison were among the commissioners appointed by the ayuntamiento[qv] of San Felipe to report on the best route for a road from Jennings Crossing on the Colorado River to Brazoria. Bostwick fought in Aylett C. Buckner's[qv] company at the battle of Velasco[qv] in June 1832. The exact date of his death is unknown. In March 1837 Isaac Van Dorn[qv] applied to be administrator of his estate.

BIBLIOGRAPHY: Eugene C. Barker, ed., *The Austin Papers* (3 vols., Washington: GPO, 1924–28). Lester G. Bugbee, "The Old Three Hundred: A List of Settlers in Austin's First Colony," *Quarterly of the Texas State Historical Association* 1 (October 1897). Dan E. Kilgore, *A Ranger Legacy: 150 Years of Service to Texas* (Austin: Madrona, 1973). Matagorda County Historical Commission, *Historic Matagorda County* (3 vols., Houston: Armstrong, 1986). *Texas Gazette,* November 6, 1830. Leonie Rummel Weyand and Houston Wade, *An Early History of Fayette County* (La Grange, Texas: La Grange *Journal,* 1936). E. W. Winkler, comp., *Manuscript Letters and Documents of Early Texians* (Austin: Steck, 1937).

Rachel Jenkins

BOSWELL, MARGIE BELLE (1875–1963). Margie Belle Boswell, poet, was born in Pueblo, Colorado, on June 20, 1875, the daughter of A. G. and Mary Isabel (Whiteside) Huffmaster, who moved to Texas when she was an infant. She studied at Parker Institute,[qv] Whitt, Texas, from 1889 to 1892, then taught in the Fort Worth public schools until 1897, when she married W. E. Boswell. They had eleven children. Mrs. Boswell conducted a poetry program over Station KFJZ in Fort Worth, taught verse technique, contributed poems to literary journals, and published eight books of poetry: *The Mockingbird and Other Poems* (1926), *Scattered Leaves* (1932), *The Upward Way* (1937), *Wings Against the Dawn* (1945), *The Light Still Burns* (1952), *Starward* (1956), *Sunrise in the Valley* (1959), and *Selected Poems and Little Lines* (1962). She wrote feature articles as well as verse and, beginning in 1937, contributed a column to the Fort Worth *Press.* She was president of the American Poetry League and a member of several poetry societies, including the Poetry Society of Texas.[qv] She won several poetry prizes and established the Boswell Poetry Prize at Texas Christian University. She was a member of the University Christian Church in Fort Worth. She died in Fort Worth on May 29, 1963, and was buried in Greenwood Cemetery there.

BIBLIOGRAPHY: Florence Elberta Barns, *Texas Writers of Today* (Dallas: Tardy, 1935). Fort Worth *Star-Telegram,* May 30, 1963. *Notable Women of the Southwest* (Dallas: Tardy, 1938). *Who's Who of American Women,* 1958–59.

Sonja Fojtik

BOSWELL, TEXAS. Boswell is on Boswell Creek and a country road off Farm Road 1375, thirteen miles southeast of Huntsville in southeastern Walker County. In 1881 community residents organized the Boswell Creek Baptist Church. Members met in a nearby log schoolhouse until 1883, when a church building was constructed on donated land. In 1896 a post office opened at Boswell, and by 1914 the community had ten residents and a general store–post office operated by J. M. Baird. The post office closed in 1921. By 1940 Boswell had the church, a cemetery, and a number of scattered dwellings. The community's Baptist church was rebuilt several times, and the structure built in 1928 still stood in 1982, when the church received a Texas Historical Commission[qv] marker. In 1990 the community was still named on the county highway map. *Mark Odintz*

BOTAS AND GUARACHES. In 1884 two political factions in Laredo and Webb counties designated themselves as Botas and Guaraches. The Botas ("Boots"), led by Raymond Martin,[qv] a powerful political patron and one of the wealthiest men on the border, and incumbent county judge, José María Rodríguez,[qv] were essentially the "wealthy" class, although they drew much support from the less fortunate. The reform club, which adopted the slogan Guaraches ("Sandals") to symbolize the lower class, included Santos Benavides,[qv] who had previously served as county judge and as a colonel in the Confederate Army.

The Guaraches, with the small but vocal contingent of Republicans in Laredo, turned the general election of 1884 into a referendum on the dominance of city and county governments by Martin-controlled Bota politicians. Most of the attention that year centered around the race for county judge between Rodríguez and Juan V. Benavides, the son of Santos Benavides. The constant flow of alcohol before the election, a cherished custom on the border, led to several violent confrontations. Tension was heightened by James Sanders Penn,[qv] owner and editor of the Laredo *Times,* whose editorials strongly criticized the Botas. The election saw the usual accusations of illegal voting, including paying Mexican aliens to vote. In a record vote Rodríguez was reelected as county judge, and the Botas took four of five county precincts.

By 1886, with the usual meetings, parades, accusations, and alcohol, quick tempers and itchy trigger fingers were added to an already tense political scene. But except for the usual complaints of unqualified voters and arrests for drunkenness, the city election on April 6, 1886, was peaceful. Although the vote was close, the Botas won. In their celebration the following day, they paraded the streets of Laredo promising to bury a Guarache in effigy. When the Guaraches attacked the Bota parade, one of the biggest gun battles in the history of the American West developed. As many as 250 men were involved in the fighting at one time or another. It took two companies of the Sixteenth United States Infantry and one company of the Eighth Cavalry to restore peace. Although the official number of dead in what was called the Laredo Election Riot was placed at sixteen, unofficial reports placed the number as high as thirty, with as many as forty-five wounded.

Although the bitter rivalry between the two parties continued, the Botas and Guaraches joined forces against the Texas Prohibition party in 1887. In 1888 a few leaders from the two parties joined to form the Laredo Immigration and Improvement Society. After the Guaraches elected their first mayor, Andrew H. Thaison,[qv] in 1895, factions from both the Botas and Guaraches came together to form the Independent Club.[qv] The Independent party or "Partido Viejo" as it came to be called on the border, dominated Laredo and Webb County politics under the *patrón* system until 1978. In the last decade of the nineteenth century, political factions in Duval and La Salle counties were also known from time to time as either Botas or Guaraches.

BIBLIOGRAPHY: C. L. Sonnichsen, *Ten Texas Feuds* (Albuquerque: University of New Mexico Press, 1957; rpt. 1971). Jerry Don Thompson, *Laredo: A Pictorial History* (Norfolk: Donning, 1986). Seb S. Wilcox, "The Laredo City Election and Riot of April, 1886, " *Southwestern Historical Quarterly* 45 (July 1941).

Jose Francisco Segovia

BOTELLA CREEK. Botella Creek rises fourteen miles southwest of Carrizo Springs in western Dimmit County (at 28°23′ N, 100°01′ W) and runs southwest for five miles to its mouth on Rosita San Juan Creek, nineteen miles southwest of Carrizo Springs in eastern Maverick County (at 28°21′ N, 100°07′ W). It traverses flat to rolling terrain with local escarpments, surfaced by deep, fine, sandy loam that supports brush and grasses; toward the creek's mouth the land is flat with locally shallow depressions and a surface of sandy and clay loam that supports water-tolerant hardwoods and grasses.

BOTELLO, JOSÉ MARÍA (?–?). José María Botello, Presbyterian evangelist, was born in Santander Jiménez, Tamaulipas, Mexico, between 1840 and 1850. He lived in Matamoros. He was converted from Catholicism to Presbyterianism and served as an elder in the Matamoros Presbyterian congregation. Another convert, Leandro Garza Mora, introduced Botello to Rev. J. W. Graybill, pastor of the Presbyterian congregation in Brownsville. In 1883 Botello helped Graybill move to San Marcos and was impressed with the living conditions there. Botello returned for his family and set up residence on a farm outside of San Marcos. Shortly after his arrival a death occurred in the Spanish-speaking community, and no priest was available for a graveside ceremony. Botello offered his services and preached a stirring sermon that attracted a small group of followers. Within a year ten converts ready for baptism and membership in the local Presbyterian church were received. In the same year the Presbytery of Western Texas licensed Botello "to preach the gospel to his people." Primarily through his efforts, the Mexican Presbyterian Church of San Marcos, the first Mexican-American Presbyterian church in Texas to be affiliated with the Presbyterian Church (U.S.A.), was formally organized, on November 2, 1887, with twenty-six members. After Botello had returned to Mexico to live after his wife's death, he was ordained a minister by the Presbytery of Tamaulipas, on April 10, 1887. Although he returned to San Marcos for a brief stay (1890–92), his influence as a group leader was diminished, and he completed his ministry in Mexico. He was reportedly ninety-seven when he died.

BIBLIOGRAPHY: Robert Douglas Brackenridge and Francisco O. García-Treto, *Iglesia Presbiteriana: A History of Presbyterians and Mexican Americans in the Southwest* (San Antonio: Trinity University Press, 1974; 2d ed. 1987). *R. Douglas Brackenridge*

BOTTOM, TEXAS. Bottom (Bottoms) was six miles north of Temple and six miles southeast of Troy in northeastern Bell County. The community was named for Chatham Bottoms, who arrived in the county in 1888 with his family and settled on Elm Creek. In 1891 Robert Childers gave land for a school and church. The land was deeded to the Methodist Episcopal Church, South. The first school term was 1894–95. Eventually a grocery store, gin, drugstore, and five churches were located at the community. Bottom had a population of thirty in 1896 and a post office from 1895 to 1901, when its mail was routed through Temple. In 1936 the local school contracted to Troy Independent School District and in 1940 was consolidated with it. Bottom was not shown on the 1948 county highway map.

BIBLIOGRAPHY: Bell County Historical Commission, *Story of Bell County, Texas* (2 vols., Austin: Eakin Press, 1988). *Mark Odintz*

BOUCHU, FRANCIS (1829–1907). Francis Bouchu, a Catholic priest described in 1890 as a lawyer, bricklayer, stonemason, photographer, printer, and historian, was born in Ste. Colombe-Vienne, Department of Isère, France, on April 15, 1829. He moved to Texas as a young man and was ordained in Galveston on March 19, 1855, one of the first priests ordained in Texas. The same year Father Claude Marie Dubuis,[qv] who later became bishop of Galveston, assigned Bouchu to the Church of San Fernando (*see* SAN FERNANDO DE BÉXAR CATHEDRAL) in San Antonio as assistant pastor. Bouchu served as itinerant priest for the outlying settlements and ranches in the largely Spanish-speaking areas south of the city.

In 1858 he was appointed pastor of the former Spanish missions of San Francisco de la Espada and San Juan de Capistrano. In addition to fulfilling his duties as priest, he worked tirelessly to restore the old missions; he is remembered chiefly for this work. When he moved to Espada in 1858, he found the complex in ruins. Most of the outbuildings and walls had collapsed, and the stones had been carried off for building materials. Only the façade and rear wall of the chapel were still standing. Working largely by himself, Bouchu rebuilt the side walls of the chapel on the old foundations. He constructed a new roof and regilded the surviving statues of St. Francis, the Virgin Mary, and Christ on the Cross, which he mounted on the altar in the sanctuary. He also restored the two-story colonial convent that served as his residence. It was renovated between 1955 and 1958. Although less well known than his work at Espada, Bouchu's restoration of San Juan Capistrano, which was in a similar state, was equally as important. He restored the church and a postcolonial house in the compound and rebuilt portions of the old walls. His work came at a critical time for the missions, which had been threatened for years and might have disappeared completely. Because of his restoration work, Espada and San Juan Capistrano were spared the extensive damage suffered by San José y San Miguel de Aguayo and San Antonio de Valero missions.

Finding that there was no adequate catechism in Spanish, Bouchu wrote one in 1872 and printed several thousand copies himself on a hand printing press. In 1896 his catechism became the official catechism of the diocese of San Antonio, and by 1897 it had gone through four editions. It was used throughout South Texas and New Mexico for many years. Bouchu died in San Antonio on August 19, 1907, and is buried there. *See also* SAN ANTONIO MISSIONS NATIONAL HISTORICAL PARK *and articles on individual missions.*

BIBLIOGRAPHY: William Corner, *San Antonio de Bexar: A Guide and History* (San Antonio: Bainbridge and Corner, 1890). Marion A. Habig, *The Alamo Chain of Missions* (Chicago: Franciscan Herald Press, 1968; rev. ed. 1976). *James T. Escobedo, Jr.*

BOUGHTON, IVAN BERTRAND (1893–1974). Ivan B. Boughton, expert on sheep and goat diseases and the fourth dean of the School of Veterinary Medicine at the Agricultural and Mechanical College of Texas (now Texas A&M University), was born on January 5, 1893, in Defiance, Ohio. He received his D.V.M. from Ohio State University in 1916, served two years in the United States Army, and was discharged as a first lieutenant in 1919. That year he joined the staff of the University of Illinois as a researcher and teacher in pathology. In 1925 he was appointed chief of service of Technique d'Agriculture for the Republic of Haiti, where he served for six years. In 1931 he returned to the United States to enroll as a graduate student at Ohio State.

In 1932 he moved to Texas. For sixteen years he worked as a veterinarian for the Texas Agricultural Experiment Station, Substation Fourteen, in Sonora. There Boughton, through his writings, established his reputation as one of the foremost researchers into the diseases of sheep and goats. On September 1, 1948, he was appointed dean of the School of Veterinary Medicine at A&M, at a time when the administration was emphasizing coordination among the teaching, research, and extension activities at the institution. Boughton played a major role in coordinating these areas. He was also active in organized veterinary medicine. He was a member of the American Veterinary Medical Association Council on Education from 1950 until 1958 and was elected an honor-roll member of the AVMA in 1971, after fifty years of active membership. He served as president of the Texas State Veterinary Medical Association in 1951. Ill health forced him to resign his deanship in 1953. In 1961 he retired from modified service as a professor of veterinary pathology. He died on May 21, 1974.

BIBLIOGRAPHY: Vertical Files, Barker Texas History Center, University of Texas at Austin. *J. D. McCrady*

BOULTINGHOUSE MOUNTAIN. Boultinghouse Mountain is near Smithwick in southeastern Burnet County (at 32°34′ N, 98°05′ W). Its summit reaches an elevation of 1,300 feet above sea level. The mountain was named for Daniel Boultinghouse, who settled nearby in 1853 and reportedly killed a large number of bears on the mountain. The surrounding area is gently sloping and surfaced with shallow dark clays in which grow primarily juniper, mesquite, and grasses.

BIBLIOGRAPHY: Darrell Debo, *Burnet County History* (2 vols., Burnet, Texas: Eakin, 1979). *Madolyn Frasier*

BOUNDARIES. In the middle of the twentieth century the boundaries of Texas were 2,845.3 miles long, counting the great arc of the Gulf Coast line and only the larger river bends. If the smaller meanderings of the rivers and the tidewater coast line were followed, the boundary was 4,137 miles long and enclosed 263,644 square miles of land and 3,695 square miles of water surface. The location of Texas boundaries has been the subject of international and interstate conflict resulting in treaties, litigation, and commissions from 1736 to the present. Controversy over details continues, as the tidelands controversy and the Chamizal dispute[qqv] illustrate. In 1995 the state legislature authorized a Red River Boundary Commission to fix the boundary between Oklahoma and Texas, where the still-shifting Red River[qv] has frequently changed course and muddied the issue for two centuries.

The eastern boundary was the first to become the subject of controversy and the first to be marked definitely. Both Spain and France claimed the area of present Texas, and by 1716 Spanish presidios at Los Adaes[qv] and French trading posts at Natchitoches were separated by only a few miles. In 1736 the commanders at the two outposts agreed on the Arroyo Hondo, a Red River tributary between the Sabine River[qv] and Natchitoches, as the boundary between Louisiana and New Spain. After Louisiana was ceded to Spain in 1762, the Arroyo Hondo continued to be regarded as the boundary between the province of Louisiana, a subdivision of the captaincy-general of Cuba, and the province of Texas, a subdivision of the commandancy-general of the Provincias Internas.[qv] When the United States purchased Louisiana in 1803, the boundary of the purchase was not defined, but early in 1804 President Thomas Jefferson decided that the territory extended to the Rio Grande.[qv] To refute this claim Spain began to investigate her historic claim to the Texas area; Father Melchor de Talamantes and later José Antonio Pichardo[qqv] made detailed studies of the limits of Louisiana and Texas. While they made academic investigations of the historic boundaries, Spanish forces, in 1806, moved east of the Sabine River to repel an anticipated invasion by Aaron Burr.[qv] In order to avert a clash, James Wilkinson and Simón de Herrera,[qqv] the United States and Spanish military commanders, entered into an agreement that established the Neutral Ground,[qv] the area between the Arroyo Hondo and the Sabine River, as a buffer. The makeshift arrangement lasted until 1819, when the Adams-Onís Treaty[qv] between Spain and the United States defined the eastern boundary of Texas as beginning at the mouth of the Sabine River, continuing along the west bank of the river to its intersection with the thirty-second parallel, and running due north from that intersection to the Red River. Spain delayed ratification of the Adams-Onís Treaty until 1821. By that time Mexico had declared her independence of Spain and refused to recognize the treaty boundary line. In 1828, after repeated efforts by the United States, the Mexican administration agreed to a survey of the 1819 line, but the Mexican congress refused to confirm the survey treaty until 1832, and then the line remained unsurveyed. Meanwhile, between 1819 and 1836 the Neches River[qv] was occasionally advanced as the eastern boundary of Texas. In 1840–41 a survey was made of that portion of the line between the Republic of Texas[qv] and the United States from the Gulf of Mexico[qv] to the Red River by a joint commission representing the two countries.

On July 5, 1848, the United States Congress passed an act giving its consent to the state of Texas to move its eastern boundary from the west bank of the Sabine River (including Sabine Pass and Sabine Lake[qqv]) to the middle of that stream, and on November 24, 1849, the Texas legislature enacted a law to that effect. The boundary was unchallenged from that time until November 27, 1941, when Louisiana governor Sam Jones wrote Texas governor Coke Stevenson,[qv] asserting that Louisiana's western border was the west bank of the Sabine River. Louisiana's claim rested on United States treaties of 1819 with Spain, 1828 with Mexico, and 1838 with the Republic of Texas, all of which designated the west bank of the Sabine as the boundary of the United States. However, the boundary of the United States at the west bank of the Sabine River was not identical to that of the Louisiana boundary, which extended only to the middle of the river. The state of Louisiana contended that the United States was negotiating on Louisiana's behalf and consequently had no authority to grant Texas the western half of the river in the act of 1848. It was more than twenty-seven years after Governor Jones's letter to Governor Stevenson before Louisiana participated in any legal proceedings. United States district judge Robert Van Pelt, special master for the United States Supreme Court, heard the claims and recommended to the court, in a report filed in May 1972, that the boundary between Texas and Louisiana should be the geographic middle of the Sabine River, Sabine Lake, and Sabine Pass. He also recommended that Louisiana be awarded all islands that existed in the river on April 8, 1812 (the date Louisiana was admitted to the Union), subject, however, to any claims that Texas might make to any such islands by reason of acquiescence and prescription; that all islands formed in the eastern half of the Sabine River since 1812 be awarded to Louisiana; and that all islands formed in the western half of the river since 1812 be awarded to Texas. Sixty-one square miles of the river and lake was involved in the dispute; at stake were more than 35,000 acres of land, four producing oil wells, and $2.6 million in oil lease bonuses collected by Texas. Both states filed exceptions to the recommendations by the special master in July 1972, and after answers to each state's exceptions the Supreme Court was to rule on the master's report. The case was argued before the court in December 1972; the court's ruling came early in March 1973, saying, in effect, that the boundary was the geographic middle of the Sabine River. However, the case was sent back to the special master for further study in regard to the ownership of islands and also to determine the extension of the boundary into the Gulf of Mexico.

Except for the possible claim of the Rio Grande as the western boundary for the Louisiana purchase, the western boundary of Texas had no significance in international relations and practically no mention in Mexican interstate relations before Texas independence. In 1721 the Medina River was considered the boundary between Texas and Coahuila; in 1811 the Nueces River[qv] was the boundary between Texas and Tamaulipas. Provisions of the secret treaty of Velasco, which bound the Mexican army to retreat beyond the Rio Grande and Texas not to claim land beyond that river, was the beginning of the Texas claim to the Rio Grande as the western boundary. On December 19, 1836, the First Congress of the republic declared the southern and western boundary of Texas to be the Rio Grande from its mouth to its source and thence a line due north to the forty-second parallel. The Texan Santa Fe expedition[qv] of 1841 was an unsuccessful attempt to assert Texas authority in the New Mexico area embraced in that land claim. Texas claimed the same western limits after annexation.[qv] The treaty of Guadalupe Hidalgo[qv] (1848) affirmed the Rio Grande boundary[qv] to El Paso as the international boundary, but the Texas claim to New Mexico, then occupied by United States troops, remained in dispute. Texas decreed a county, Santa Fe County, to include the area, but the people of New Mexico protested the Texas claim. After prolonged debate in Congress and the Texas newspapers and near-armed dispute, an adjustment was reached in the Compromise of 1850.[qv] The compromise line ran the Texas western boundary from El Paso east along the thirty-second parallel to the 103d meridian, up that meridian to 36°30′ latitude, and along that line to the 100th meridian, thence down the 100th meridian to the Red River. The thirty-six-thirty line was chosen since Texas was a slave state and that line had been established in 1820 as the Missouri Compromise[qv] line between slave and free territory in the Louisiana Purchase. After 1850 the line was apparently fixed, but the boundary was not. An error in the surveying of the western line gave Texas a strip about two miles wide west of the 103d meridian; Congress confirmed the boundary, as surveyed, in a joint resolution of February 16, 1911. Shifts in the channel of the Rio Grande necessitated other changes. In 1929 the Supreme Court assigned to Texas 25,000 acres of former New Mexican land lying on the western side of the channel of the river. The Rio Grande Rectification Project,[qv] authorized in 1933, provided for the exchange of 3,500 acres of land, part of it in the El Paso area, between the United States and Mexico. The International Boundary and Water Commission[qv] is a permanent agency with jurisdiction over the boundary questions on the Rio Grande.

As defined in the Adams-Onís Treaty of 1819, the northern and northwestern boundary of Texas followed the course of the Red River westward to the 100th meridian and north along that meridian to the Arkansas River, the whole line as depicted in the Melish map[qv] of 1818. Then the Compromise of 1850 placed the north line of the Panhandle[qv] at 36°30′. No problem arose over this boundary until 1858, when A. H. Jones and H. M. Brown, who had been employed to locate the 100th meridian in making surveys of grants to various Indian tribes, discovered that the Melish map had erroneously located that meridian 100 miles too far east. In 1852 Randolph B. Marcy[qv] discovered that there were two main branches of the Red River lying between the Melish line and the 100th meridian. The supposedly correct meridian was surveyed in 1860, the same year that the Texas legislature decreed Greer County.[qv] Because of the Civil War and Reconstruction,[qqv] Greer County was not organized until 1886 and was in process of being settled when the United States land commissioner protested the Texas claim to the land north of the Prairie Dog Town Fork of the Red River. The controversy went to the United States Supreme Court, which ruled on March 16, 1896, that the Texas boundary was the south or Prairie Dog Town Fork of the Red River and the astronomical 100th meridian.

The northern boundary again became controversial in 1919, when Texas drillers discovered oil in the bed of the Red River just north of Burkburnett. Oklahoma claimed the bed of the river and sued Texas for title in the Supreme Court. The Greer County case had defined the Texas boundary as the south bank of the Red River, but Texas claimed that the south bank in 1919 was not the same as the south bank at the time of the Melish map and the treaty of 1819. The contest became a three-cornered suit, with Oklahoma claiming the entire riverbed, Texas claiming title to the south half, and the United States disputing both claims and asserting ownership of the south half as trustee for the Indians. The decision in the four-year suit was rendered on January 15, 1923. In it the Supreme Court defined a riverbank as the bank cut by the normal flow of water, or where vegetation stopped, gave Oklahoma the north half of the bed and political control of the entire bed, and gave the United States the south half of the bed as trustee for the Indians, but allowed Texas to retain control of the oil wells in the floodplain between the riverbanks. To prevent further dispute, the court ordered a survey of the south bank as it was in 1819 and the placing of concrete markers along the survey line. The report of Arthur Kidder and Arthur H. Stiles, the commissioners who made the survey, was accepted on April 25, 1927.

In the meantime, in 1920 Texas sued Oklahoma on the grounds that the surveys of the 100th meridian made in 1858 and 1860 had erroneously placed that meridian a half mile too far west. Surveys made in 1892 and 1902 had not solved the problem of ownership of an area 134 miles long and between 3,600 and 3,700 feet wide. One Oklahoma resident complained that she had not moved a foot in forty-five years but had lived in one territory, two states, and three counties. In 1927 the Supreme Court ordered Samuel S. Gannett to survey the meridian. He worked from 1927 to 1929, largely at night to avoid the aberrations of heat waves, and placed concrete markers at every two-thirds of a mile. The court ruled in 1930 that the Gannett line was the true meridian. Oklahoma tried unsuccessfully to buy back the strip that the Texas legislature incorporated in 1931 in Lipscomb, Hemphill, Wheeler, Childress, and Collingsworth counties. Higgins was the only town in the ceded area. *See also* NECHES RIVER BOUNDARY CLAIM, TREATIES OF VELASCO.

BIBLIOGRAPHY: Bunyan H. Andrew, "Some Queries Concerning the Texas-Louisiana Sabine Boundary," *Southwestern Historical Quarterly* 53 (July 1949). Jacqueline Eckert, International Law and United States–Mexican Boundary Relations (Ph.D. Thesis, University of Texas, 1939). Grant Foreman, "Red River and the Spanish Boundary in the Supreme Court," *Chronicles of Oklahoma* 2 (March 1924). Herbert P. Gambrell and Lewis W. Newton, *A Social and Political History of Texas* (Dallas: Southwest Press, 1932). Charles W. Hackett, ed., *Pichardo's Treatise on the Limits of Louisiana and Texas* (4 vols.,

Austin: University of Texas Press, 1931–46). J. Evetts Haley, *The XIT Ranch of Texas and the Early Days of the Llano Estacado* (Chicago: Lakeside, 1929; rpts., Norman: University of Oklahoma Press, 1953, 1967). Webb L. Moore, *The Greer County Question* (San Marcos, Texas: Press of the San Marcos *Record*, 1939).

BOUNDS, JOSEPH MURPHY (1822–1863). Joseph Murphy Bounds, soldier and hotelman, was born in Missouri in 1822. Before July 1, 1845, he arrived in McKinney, Texas where he worked as a "floating trader." During the Mexican War[qv] Bounds was a first lieutenant in Company C until the company was disbanded, on September 5, 1846. On May 24, 1849, he married Eliza S. Hurt, the fifteen-year-old daughter of Mrs. Ann Hurt, who arrived in Collin County accompanied only by her daughter. Bounds received a land certificate from the Peters colony[qv] in 1850, which he sold unlocated. By 1860 he had become the first hotelkeeper in McKinney and had $6,000 in personal property. At that time he and Eliza had three children. In 1861 Bounds raised a cavalry company in the county and by February 1862 had been promoted to lieutenant colonel of the Eleventh Texas Cavalry. Though he led the regiment in the battle of Murfreesboro, Tennessee, his promotion to colonel was never approved. He was murdered on October 27, 1863.

BIBLIOGRAPHY: Confederate Service Records, 1861–1865, National Archives, Washington. Seymour V. Connor, *The Peters Colony of Texas: A History and Biographical Sketches of the Early Settlers* (Austin: Texas State Historical Association, 1959). Roy Franklin Hall and Helen Gibbard Hall, *Collin County: Pioneering in North Texas* (Quanah, Texas: Nortex, 1975). Charles D. Spurlin, comp., *Texas Veterans in the Mexican War: Muster Rolls of Texas Military Units* (Victoria, Texas, 1984).

Lisa C. Maxwell

BOUNTY CERTIFICATES. Bounty certificates were issued to soldiers and to families of deceased soldiers by the republic and the state of Texas in payment for military service. The size of the grant varied according to circumstances from 160 to 1,280 acres. *See* LAND GRANTS.

BIBLIOGRAPHY: Reuben McKitrick, *The Public Land System of Texas, 1823–1910* (Bulletin of the University of Wisconsin, Economics and Political Science Series 10.1 [February 1918]).

BOURGEOIS D'ORVANNE, ALEXANDER (?–?). Alexander Bourgeois d'Orvanne and Armand Ducos[qv] received colonization contracts from the Republic of Texas[qv] on June 3 and July 6, 1842, permitting 1,700 families to be located in Texas. Apparently they secured no immigrants before the expiration of the contracts. On September 19, 1843, Bourgeois negotiated with the Adelsverein[qv] for the transfer of the Bourgeois-Ducos grant on the Uvalde, Frio, and Medina rivers to the verein and served as colonial director for the society for four months in 1844.

BIBLIOGRAPHY: E. D. Adams, *British Diplomatic Correspondence Concerning the Republic of Texas, 1836–1846* (Austin: Texas State Historical Association, 1918?). Moritz Tiling, *History of the German Element in Texas* (Houston: Rein and Sons, 1913).

Rudolph L. Biesele

BOURKE, JOHN GREGORY (1846–1896). John Gregory Bourke, army officer, author, ethnologist, and folklorist, was born to Irish Catholic parents Edward Joseph and Anna (Morton) Bourke in Philadelphia, Pennsylvania, on June 23, 1846. He lied about his age in order to enlist in the Fifteenth Pennsylvania Volunteer Cavalry in 1862 and saw action at the battle of Murfreesboro, where he earned the Medal of Honor. He fought at the battle of Chickamauga, endured the Confederate siege of Chattanooga, and witnessed the destruction of Atlanta. In the summer of 1865 he was mustered out of volunteer service and entered West Point. He graduated eleventh in a class of thirty-nine in 1869 and received his commission in the Third Cavalry. He married Mary F. Horbach of Omaha, Nebraska, on July 25, 1883; the couple had three daughters.

Bourke was a well-known Indian fighter, writer, crusader for Indian rights, and anthropologist before he reported to Fort Ringgold, Rio Grande City, Texas, in 1891. He had already fought Indians in the Southwest and on the Great Plains and had served on the staff of Gen. George Crook from 1871 until 1886. He wrote several articles and six books on military history and ethnology, including his best-known work, *On The Border with Crook* (1891), before his arrival in South Texas.

Bourke's two-year tour of duty along the lower Rio Grande established his significance in Texas history. He became pivotal in the suppression of Catarino Garza's[qv] effort against the government of Porfirio Díaz in Mexico. The Mexican government demanded that the United States act because Garza had based his force in Texas. In turn, the federal government instructed the state of Texas, federal marshals, and the United States Army to stop the Garzistas. Initially Bourke noted that many South Texans—Mexican Americans and Anglos—openly supported Garza and that Fort McIntosh in Laredo and Fort Ringgold together mustered only two troops of cavalry and two companies of infantry with which to patrol an area of 500 square miles. Nonetheless, Bourke followed orders, and his raids on ranches suspected of harboring Garzistas earned him the undying enmity of many South Texans. During his attack on a Garzista camp at Retamal on December 22, 1891, brisk fighting occurred and a soldier was killed. County, state, and federal officials and army officers began to side openly with various political factions in South Texas, and their bitter bickering and feuds broke into the Texas and national press. Before leaving Texas in 1893, Bourke became deeply involved in the rancorous imbroglio surrounding Garza. Bourke's diaries remain a valuable source on the Garza movement.

Bourke was also a pioneer scholar of the Hispanic folk culture of South Texas and northeastern Mexico. His fluency in Spanish, his experience among the Hispanics of New Mexico and Arizona, and his background as an ethnologist prepared him to research Mexican lore, folk customs, and the utilization of plants and animals in the local materia medica. He also studied Mexican plays of the Nativity along the lower Rio Grande. His work in Texas resulted in a series of monographs, including articles in the *American Anthropologist* and the *Journal of American Folk-Lore*. His contributions to the study of Texas further enhanced his reputation as a scholar, and he was elected president of the American Folk-Lore Society in 1895. Bourke suffered an aneurysm and died in Philadelphia on June 8, 1896; he was buried at Arlington National Cemetery.

BIBLIOGRAPHY: Joseph C. Porter, John Gregory Bourke, Victorian Soldier-Scientist: The Western Apprenticeship, 1869–1886 (Ph.D. dissertation, University of Texas at Austin, 1980). Joseph C. Porter, *Paper Medicine Man: John Gregory Bourke and His American West* (Norman: University of Oklahoma Press, 1986).

Joseph C. Porter

BOURLAND, JAMES G. (1801–1879). James G. Bourland, soldier and state senator, was born in South Carolina on August 11, 1801, to Benjamin and Nancy Bourland. He was married twice, to Catherine Wells and Nancy Salina, and had seven children. He lived in Kentucky and Tennessee, where he traded in slaves and horses, before he moved to what is now Lamar County, Texas, in 1837. He led a volunteer company against Indians in 1841. Later that year he served as second-in-command to William C. Young[qv] in another campaign and stayed when Young organized the Third Regiment, Texas Mounted Rifles, for the Mexican War.[qv] After serving as a deputy surveyor, he became the collector of customs for the Red River District in 1842 and was elected to the Senate of the First and Second state legislatures. A clash over customs duties with the crew of a United States ship in 1843 led to his being awarded a substantial sum of money by a United States court five years later. After his father, who had also settled in Texas, died in 1851, Bourland invested in a mercantile enterprise and founded a plantation on land now in Cooke County.

During the late 1850s he again led a volunteer company against Indians. When the Civil War[qv] began, he served as provost marshal for the region in which he resided and in that role directed the investigation that climaxed with the Great Hanging at Gainesville[qv] in 1862. Afterward, he was authorized to organize and lead the "Border Regiment," which remained in North Texas although it was in Confederate service, and was later given control of all troops on the northwestern frontier. He was accused of atrocities, in addition to the Great Hanging, but Confederate officials ignored the accusations. After the war ended he received a presidential pardon and was acquitted by a civil court. He subsequently lived in seclusion until his death, on August 20, 1879.

BIBLIOGRAPHY: Bourland Family File, Sherman Municipal Library, Sherman, Texas. Richard B. McCaslin, Tainted Breeze: The Great Hanging at Gainesville, Texas (Ph.D. dissertation, University of Texas at Austin, 1988). William S. Speer and John H. Brown, eds., *Encyclopedia of the New West* (Marshall, Texas: United States Biographical Publishing, 1881; rpt., Easley, South Carolina: Southern Historical Press, 1978). Rex Wallace Strickland, "History of Fannin County, Texas, 1836–1843," *Southwestern Historical Quarterly* 33, 34 (April, July 1930).

Richard B. McCaslin

BOURLAND, JOSEPH W., SR. (1872–1960). Joseph W. Bourland, Sr., obstetrician and gynecologist, the son of Hillen Armour and Priscilla (Howland) Bourland, was born on October 21, 1872, in Hannibal, Missouri. He received his bachelor's degree at Baylor University in Waco, Texas, and his medical degree at the Columbia University College of Physicians and Surgeons in New York. He served his internship at Elizabeth General Hospital and Dispensary in Elizabeth, New Jersey, and completed his residency at the New York Infant Asylum in New York. He established a private practice in Dallas in 1897.

In 1915 Bourland became one of the first doctors in Dallas to specialize in obstetrics and gynecology and is credited with the invention of the incubator for premature infants. He served as a captain in World War I[qv] in the medical corps of the United States Army. After the war he served ten years as chief of obstetrical services at Florence Nightingale Maternity Hospital, a division of Baylor University Hospital, and ten years as a member of the board of governors at Parkland Hospital. In addition to his private practice he taught at both Baylor College of Medicine and Southwestern Medical School, after Baylor moved to Houston in 1943.

Bourland belonged to the American Board of Obstetrics and Gynecology, the American Medical Association, the Southern Medical Association, and the Texas Medical Association.[qv] In 1935 he was a president of the Texas Association of Obstetricians and Gynecologists. He was also a member of the American College of Surgeons and the Dallas Southern Clinical Society and the founder and director of the Dallas Medical and Surgical Clinic before his retirement in 1954. He was a member of the First Methodist Church, where his father had been pastor, and was a member of the board of stewards for twenty years. He was married to Virgie Bookhout, and they had three children. On February 20, 1960, Bourland died at the home of his son in Dallas. He is buried at Oakland Cemetery.

BIBLIOGRAPHY: Dallas *Morning News,* February 21, 1960. *Texas State Journal of Medicine,* May 1960.

Lisa C. Maxwell

BOURLAND, WILLIAM H. (1811–1860). William H. Bourland, early settler, soldier, and legislator, was born in Kentucky in 1811 and immigrated to Texas in December 1840. He enlisted in the Texas Rangers[qv] in 1841 and led a contingent of men in the battle of Village Creek[qv] in May of that year. From 1843 to 1845 he represented Lamar County in the House of the Eighth and Ninth congresses of the republic. On September 2, 1844, he was issued an unconditional certificate for land in Lamar County. In 1845 he introduced a bill to incorporate the town of Paris, the county seat of Lamar County. After annexation[qv] he served in the First and Second legislatures from Lamar County and in the Fifth Legislature from Grayson County. He was a major in the Mexican War[qv] and after it moved to the Chickasaw Nation, from which his wife had come. He died there on April 2, 1860.

BIBLIOGRAPHY: La Grange *True Issue,* May 4, 1860. Texas House of Representatives, *Biographical Directory of the Texan Conventions and Congresses, 1832–1845* (Austin: Book Exchange, 1941).

Todd Lowry

BOURNE, DANIEL (1810–1836). Daniel Bourne, Alamo defender, was born in England in 1810. He and his brothers immigrated to America, and Bourne moved on to Gonzales, Texas. He took part in the siege of Bexar[qv] as a member of Capt. T. F. L. Parrott's[qv] artillery company. He later served in the Bexar garrison in Capt. William R. Carey's[qv] artillery company. Bourne died in the battle of the Alamo[qv] on March 6, 1836.

BIBLIOGRAPHY: Daughters of the American Revolution, *The Alamo Heroes and Their Revolutionary Ancestors* (San Antonio, 1976). Daughters of the Republic of Texas, *Muster Rolls of the Texas Revolution* (Austin, 1986). Bill Groneman, *Alamo Defenders* (Austin: Eakin, 1990).

Bill Groneman

BOUZIER CREEK. Bouzier Creek, also known as Brushy Creek, rises in northeastern Coke County (at 32°04′ N, 100°28′ W) and runs east for nine miles before reaching its mouth on Oak Creek Reservoir, also in the northeastern part of the county (at 32°03′ N, 100°19′ W). The stream crosses flat terrain, where sandy and clay loams support a variety of grasses.

BOVINA, TEXAS. Bovina is on U.S. Highway 60 between two forks of Running Water Draw in western Parmer County. Originally the community was the Hay Hook Line Camp of the XIT Ranch,[qv] and the ranch headquarters was one of the county's earliest buildings. When the Pecos and Northern Texas Railway was built through the ranch in 1898 a switch was placed at the site to be used by cowboys to unload cottonseed shipped in as feed. Some of this feed was invariably spilled along the tracks, causing XIT cattle to gather at the unfenced right-of-way. Often they lay down, compelling railroad workers to get off their trains and prod them off the tracks. As a result the site was labeled Bull Town, a name replaced by the more elegant Bovina when the post office was established on January 31, 1899. Bovina soon experienced a boom and for a time shipped a larger volume of cattle than any other shipping point in the world.

By the time settlers began moving into the area around 1905, two churches had been organized and a school started. In addition Bovina had a general store, a livery barn, a barbershop, and a boardinghouse where travelers, most of whom brought their own bedding, were accommodated with meals. As land sales increased, a bank, a second hotel, and numerous residences were built. The South and West Land Company established its headquarters at Bovina, and school facilities were enlarged to meet the needs of a rapidly growing populace. By 1915 the town had about 200 residents.

Although the boom leveled off after World War I,[qv] Bovina remained an important agricultural and livestock marketing center. In 1948 it was incorporated, with J. W. Kimbrow as mayor. At the same time the residents organized a volunteer fire department and voted for bonds to install a modern water system. Previously, water had been obtained from tanks rented from the Santa Fe Railroad. A weekly newspaper, the Bovina *Blade,* was established in 1955, and during the 1960s ambulance service was started. A medical clinic was established in 1966 with funds from the Sears Foundation. In the mid-1980s Bovina had twenty-eight businesses, four churches, and a three-acre city park. Its high school girls' track team won notice as the 1978 Class A state champions. Annual events included a Chamber of Commerce and Agriculture Banquet in March and the Fourth of July Celebration. A historic marker, featuring a longhorn bull statue, recalls the Bull Town era. Bovina's population was 1,029 in 1960, 1,499 in 1980, and 1,549 in 1990.

BIBLIOGRAPHY: J. Evetts Haley, *The XIT Ranch of Texas and the Early Days of the Llano Estacado* (Chicago: Lakeside, 1929; rpts., Norman: University of Oklahoma Press, 1953, 1967). Parmer County Historical Commission, *Prairie Progress* (Dallas: Taylor, 1981). Parmer County Historical Society, *A History of Parmer County* (Quanah, Texas: Nortex, 1974). Fred Tarpley, *1001 Texas Place Names* (Austin: University of Texas Press, 1980). *H. Allen Anderson*

BOW CREEK. Bow Creek rises three miles northwest of the Davis triangulation station in west central Throckmorton County (at 33°11′ N, 99°23′ W) and runs north for seventeen miles to its mouth on Millers Creek, at the south end of Millers Creek Reservoir (at 33°22′ N, 99°26′ W). The stream traverses flat terrain with local shallow depressions, surfaced by clay and sandy loams that support water-tolerant hardwoods, conifers, and grasses.

BOWDEN, ARTEMISIA (1879–1969). Artemisia Bowden, black school administrator and civic leader, was born in 1879 in Albany, Georgia, the daughter of Milas and Mary Bowden. She graduated from St. Augustine's Normal School in Raleigh, North Carolina, in 1900. After teaching for two years in North Carolina, she moved to San Antonio, Texas, in 1902 to take over as principal of St. Philip's Normal and Industrial School, an Episcopal day school for black girls (*see* ST. PHILIP'S COLLEGE). Under her guidance the school added a boarding department, outgrew its original facilities, and by 1926 had achieved private junior college status, with Bowden as president.

During the Great Depression,[qv] when the Episcopal Church and the Diocese of West Texas would no longer accept financial responsibility for the college, Bowden refused to let the school die. She assumed the obligation of keeping St. Philip's open and began a campaign to have the San Antonio Independent School District take over the institution. Although she argued that the city owed blacks a publicly supported junior college as long as it continued to operate a white junior college out of public funds, the board of education repeatedly refused to accede. Finally, in 1942, it reluctantly incorporated St. Philip's into the municipal junior college system, and Artemisia Bowden continued to direct it as dean. In 1954, after fifty-two years as head of St. Philip's, she retired and became dean emerita.

She did graduate work during the summers at Columbia University, Cheney State Teachers' College, the New York School of Social Work, and the University of Colorado. She was granted a B.A. degree in 1935 by St. Augustine's College, her alma mater, after it was upgraded from a normal school, and received honorary degrees from Wiley and Tillotson colleges. She was president of the San Antonio Metropolitan Council of Negro Women, founder and president of the city's Negro Business and Professional Women's Club, and a member of the executive committee of the Coordination Council on Juvenile Delinquency of the Texas Social Welfare Association. She held memberships in the National Association of College Women's Clubs and several state and national associations for professional educators. She was named to the Texas Commission on Interracial Relations in 1947.

Bowden gave her time outside St. Philip's to civic and welfare projects for the blacks of San Antonio. She was primarily responsible for the introduction of a black nursing unit in Robert B. Green Hospital, for securing Lindbergh Park for black residents, and for establishing the East End Settlement House. She also helped establish the State Training School for Delinquent Negro Girls at Brady (*see* CROCKETT STATE SCHOOL).

The National Council of Negro Women cited Artemisia Bowden as one of the ten most outstanding woman educators in the country. Many local organizations also recognized her lifetime of service, including Zeta Phi Beta Sorority, which named her woman of the year in 1955. Bowden Elementary School in San Antonio and Bowden Administration Building at St. Philip's College are named in her honor. She was a member of the Southern Conference of Christians and Jews and of St. Philip's Episcopal Church in San Antonio. She died in San Antonio on August 18, 1969.

BIBLIOGRAPHY: Jo Eckerman, "Artemisia Bowden: Dedicated Dreamer," *Texas Passages,* Winter 1987. Vertical Files, Barker Texas History Center, University of Texas at Austin. Vertical Files, University of Texas Institute of Texan Cultures, San Antonio.

Judith N. McArthur

BOWEN, JOHN (?–1867). John Bowen, merchant and city official was born Ralph William Peacock to one of the early families of Philadelphia. He attended the University of Pennsylvania. He and his brother George Steinmetz Peacock may have traveled through Texas in the late 1820s on their way to South America. It is claimed that the two brothers acquired a large cattle ranch in Argentina, which they lost in a revolution. They are also said to have owned a wholesale commission business in Rio de Janeiro as well as large landholdings and other business interests in Brazil. The brothers made their way back to the United States. In Philadelphia, George married and became a father. He moved with his family to Texas but contracted cholera and died in Indianola or Port Lavaca; he was buried in San Antonio. Ralph traveled to San Antonio from Philadelphia by way of South America in the early or mid-1840s. In 1845 he purchased a five-acre tract of land, a peninsula formed by the San Antonio River that he called Bowen's Island, for $300. On the "island" was the old homestead La Quinta, part of the original Spanish land grant of the Curbelo family; the Curbelos were Canary Islanders.[qv] The house became the first United States post office in San Antonio, with Bowen as postmaster. In 1848, by act of the Texas legislature, Peacock changed his name to that of his half-brother, John Bowen, of Philadelphia and of Bowen's Hall, Kingston, Jamaica, upon the request of Bowen, who had no heirs. The act was signed by Governor George T. Wood.[qv] Peacock served as an alderman in 1848–49, and after legally changing his name he served as city treasurer from 1849 to 1854, in 1856–57, and 1857–58. During the years of the republic and early statehood he operated a store for hides, wool, and pecans, as well as a general store on Main Plaza. George Peacock had left a widow and child, and John Bowen married the widow, Mary Elizabeth Peacock, in San Fernando Church on August 29, 1850. They built a seven-room cottage on the banks of the San Antonio River and raised seven children. Bowen was a Unitarian. He died on December 13, 1867, and was eulogized in the San Antonio *Express* "as a man of great firmness of character [who] stood firm through all the dark days of the [Civil War], as a loyal citizen to the United States." He was buried alongside his brother George on Bowen's Island. When the San Antonio River channel was changed, their remains were removed to San Fernando Cemetery No. 1. A state historical marker identifying John Bowen and his island is located at the site. Bowen should not be confused with the John S. Bowen who fought at the siege of Bexar.[qv]

BIBLIOGRAPHY: Frederick Charles Chabot, *With the Makers of San Antonio* (Yanaguana Society Publications 4, San Antonio, 1937). *A*

Twentieth Century History of Southwest Texas (2 vols., Chicago: Lewis, 1907). *Mary Ann Noonan Guerra*

BOWEN, REUBEN DEAN (1859–1939). Reuben Dean Bowen, agricultural promoter, the son of William Abraham and Clementine Dalmatia (Richards) Bowen, was born in Montgomery County, Texas, on December 18, 1859. He attended St. Mary's University, Galveston, and the Agricultural and Mechanical College of Texas (now Texas A&M University), 1877–78. On May 15, 1890, he married Bonnybel Wright of Paris, Texas. By 1895 he had become active in agricultural promotion in the Southwest. He was president of the Kiomatia Planters Company of Red River County. He began the movement to popularize the use of cotton in manufacturing and was chairman of the Farmers' Union committee to study greater consumption of cotton. He was instrumental in securing competition from other states in bidding for cottonseed in Texas. Bowen helped organize the Mississippi Valley Association, the American Farm Bureau, and the Farmers Manufacturing Association. He died at New Orleans on August 27, 1939.

BIBLIOGRAPHY: *Who Was Who in America,* Vol. 2.

BOWEN, WILLIAM ABRAHAM (1856–1921). William Abraham Bowen, newspaper editor and author, the son of William A. and Clementine D. (Richards) Bowen, was born at Bagdad, Florida, on April 14, 1856. He attended Southwestern University in Georgetown, Texas, from 1875 to 1877 and on December 12, 1877, married Ada DeBardeleben of Bastrop. Bowen was owner and editor of the *Advance Guard* at Decatur, 1873–74. In 1874 he founded the Montague *News.* From 1880 to 1908 he held correspondent and editorial positions with the Houston *Daily Post* (*see* HOUSTON *POST*), the San Antonio *Daily Express* (*see* SAN ANTONIO *EXPRESS-NEWS*), the Chicago *Times,* and the *Texas Christian Advocate* (now the *United Methodist Reporter*[qv]). In 1908 he founded the Arlington Printing Company and the *Farmers' Fireside Bulletin,* which became the official paper for the Farmers' Union in Texas, Louisiana, and Oklahoma. He wrote *Chained Lightning* (1883), *Why Two Methodist Churches in the United States?* (1901), and *Uncle Zeke's Speculation* (1910). He died on April 14, 1921.

BIBLIOGRAPHY: Frank W. Johnson, *A History of Texas and Texans* (5 vols., ed. E. C. Barker and E. W. Winkler [Chicago and New York: American Historical Society, 1914; rpt. 1916]). *Who Was Who in America,* Vol. 2. *Kaye A. Walker*

BOWER, JOHN WHITE (1808–1850). John White Bower, early settler, soldier, and judge, son of Isaac and Frances Ann (Cuthbert) Bower, was born in Talbotton, Georgia, on December 7, 1808. The family moved to Arkansas Territory in 1819. Bower traveled to Texas after May 2 and before November 28, 1835, when his certificate of election to the Consultation[qv] was presented to the General Council[qv] of the provisional government[qv] by Lewis T. Ayers,[qv] although Bower himself did not attend. He operated a ferry on the San Antonio River opposite Carlos Rancho. He was one of the two representatives from San Patricio in the Convention of 1836[qv] at Washington-on-the-Brazos and there signed the Texas Declaration of Independence.[qv] Bower was also in charge of James W. Fannin, Jr.'s,[qv] spy system during the Goliad campaign. Fannin was leading the Goliad garrison to reinforce William B. Travis[qv] and his command inside the Alamo when Bower brought news that Gen. José de Urrea[qv] was quickly advancing on Goliad at the head of a large Mexican force. Bower's information influenced Fannin to abandon his plans to relieve the Alamo and return to Goliad (*see also* GOLIAD CAMPAIGN OF 1836).

In 1838 Bower married Bridget O'Brien. Their daughter Frances Elizabeth married James Power, Jr., son of the empresario[qv] James Power.[qv] Bower represented Refugio County in the House of the Sixth and Seventh congresses of the Republic of Texas,[qv] 1841–43, and was elected chief justice (i.e., county judge) of Refugio County on October 4, 1843, and again in 1847. He died on January 13, 1850, and was buried near the San Antonio River ferry he had operated years before. In 1936 the Texas Centennial[qv] Commission placed a monument at Bower's grave.

BIBLIOGRAPHY: Hobart Huson, *Refugio: A Comprehensive History of Refugio County from Aboriginal Times to 1953* (2 vols., Woodsboro, Texas: Rooke Foundation, 1953, 1955). *L. W. Kemp*

BOWERS, HERBERT EDMUND (1868–1910). Herbert Edmund Bowers, Episcopal Church official, son of John and Elizabeth (Savage) Bowers, was born in Southampton, England, on May 2, 1868. He received his B.A. and M.A. degrees at Hertford College, Oxford, in 1887 and 1889. He moved to America in 1889 and on July 15, 1892, married Emilie Blundell-Blake in Toronto, Ontario. He received a D.D. degree at Rutherford College, North Carolina, and an LL.D. at Chaddock College, Illinois. He taught at St. John's College in Canada in 1892, was rector at St. Paul's Church, Vancouver, in 1895–96, served as general missionary for the Episcopal diocese of Spokane, Washington, in 1896–97, and later was assistant at Trinity Church, Newport, Rhode Island. In Texas he was rector of the Episcopal churches at Bryan and Navasota, 1898–1901; Marshall, 1901–06; and Grace Church, Galveston, 1906–08. He was dean of the Northern Texas Convention in 1903 and deputy to the General Convention in 1904. After leaving Texas he was rector at All Saints Church, Los Angeles, and dean of Arkansas Theological College. He died at Santa Monica, California, on March 12, 1910, and was buried at Woodlawn Cemetery on March 16.

BIBLIOGRAPHY: *Who Was Who in America,* Vol. 1.

BOWERS, JOHN HENRY (1817–1907). John Henry Bowers (Bauers) was born near Colmar, Alsace, on November 6, 1817. He attended the University of Mühlhausen before 1835, when he went on a cruise to China and India and, observing how the English Army doctors treated cholera, became interested in medicine. Bowers landed in New York in January 1836, took a boat for Galveston, Texas, and was en route from Columbia to join the Texas army at the time of the battle of San Jacinto.[qv] In ministering to the wounded he attended and befriended the captive Mexican general Antonio López de Santa Anna.[qv] Bowers also attended Gen. Sam Houston[qv] and became his close friend. Houston gave him a painting of himself, which later burned in Bowers's home. Bowers joined the army and served in a military hospital at Houston in the late 1830s. He became a protégé of Dr. Ashbel Smith,[qv] with whom he studied medicine and who sent him to the University of Louisiana (later Tulane University), where he received a degree in medicine.

Bowers practiced at Houston and around Galveston and cared for Smith's patients in the latter's absence. He became part owner of the first drugstore in the Republic of Texas,[qv] which opened in Columbus in 1844. During a yellow fever epidemic in 1844 he used the vessels *Dayton* and *Scioto Belle*[qqv] as hospitals. He joined the Texas troops for service in the Mexican War[qv] and in February 1849 opened his practice at Brownsville. He practiced there until 1851, when he moved to Columbus and married Anne Griffith. During a cholera epidemic in 1851 and 1852 he used medicines he had secured years before in India. He was among the first to diagnose a yellow fever epidemic in 1873.

He died on September 4, 1907, at Columbus and was buried there in the Odd Fellows Cemetery. His manuscript observations on epidemic disease in Texas and collections of his letters are in the Texas State Library and the Barker Texas History Center.[qqv]

BIBLIOGRAPHY: Colorado County Historical Commission, *Colorado County Chronicles from the Beginning to 1923* (2 vols., Austin: Nortex,

1986). George Plunkett [Mrs. S. C.] Red, *The Medicine Man in Texas* (Houston, 1930).

BOWERS, MARMION HENRY (1829–1872). Marmion Henry Bowers, attorney and state legislator, son of Henry J. Bowers, was born on April 29, 1829, at Moore's Hill, Indiana. In 1851 he obtained a law degree from Indiana University, Bloomington. After practicing law in Indiana for a short time he moved to Burnet (then called Hamilton Valley), Texas, in March 1853, with $4.25 in his pocket and no prospects. He organized a school where he taught briefly before developing a law practice in Burnet. Bowers was narrowly defeated in an election for district judge in the fall of 1856. By November 15, 1856, he was practicing law in Austin, where he was at different times in partnership with Joseph J. Dennis and Alexander Stuart Walker.[qqv] During the summer after his move to the Texas capital, Bowers had a severe attack of what he called hemorrhage of the lungs. After marrying Mary M. Batterton in Indiana on September 16, 1858, he considered moving to Cincinnati to set up a law practice but decided it would be wiser to stay where he had an established business. On January 20, 1862, he enlisted in the Confederate service. He served with the Travis County Infantry in Flournoy's regiment, where he held the rank of captain. After his military service, Bowers was elected to the Tenth Texas Legislature (1863–64). In 1869 he was elected to the Texas Senate, where he served until his death. During the troubled days of Reconstruction[qv] he delivered a speech in the Senate, on June 20, 1870, that opposed Governor Edmund J. Davis's[qv] newly legislated right to declare martial law. That speech was said to have helped overthrow the Radical Republican regime in Texas. Bowers was a devout Baptist and a Mason. He died in Austin on March 3, 1872, of consumption, after having suffered from the disease for much of his life. He and his wife had five children.

BIBLIOGRAPHY: *State Journal Appendix* (Austin: Tracy, Siemering, 1870). Texas Legislative Council, *Members of the Texas Legislature, 1846–1980* (Austin, 1980?). *Linda Cheves Nicklas*

BOWERS, TEXAS (Milam County). Bowers, four miles northwest of Buckholts in western Milam County, was a switch on the Gulf, Colorado and Santa Fe Railway. The 1941 county highway map showed a business and two houses at the site.

BIBLIOGRAPHY: Lelia M. Batte, *History of Milam County, Texas* (San Antonio: Naylor, 1956). *Vivian Elizabeth Smyrl*

BOWERS, TEXAS (Polk County). Bowers was on an unnamed road off Farm Road 352 northeast of Pluck in northeastern Polk County. The community was established when A. W. Morris moved his sawmill there from Morrisville in 1885 and may have been named in honor of the mill's construction supervisor. Morris used the Trinity and Sabine tap route of the Missouri, Kansas and Texas rail system to get his lumber to market. A fire destroyed his mill in 1887, but he rebuilt his plant, and by 1889 it was capable of sawing 65,000 board feet of lumber a day. The Bowers facilities also included five miles of tram roads, two small locomotives, a planer, and dry kilns. In 1889 a large general store served the community's 300 residents. The local post office was called Clevilas from 1886 to 1887, when its name was changed to Bowers. The mill was sold to W. T. Carter and Brother after their plant at nearby Barnum burned in 1897, and the Carter company moved it to a new site at Camden. Although Bowers continued to be shown on railroad maps for two decades, its post office was discontinued in 1898.

BIBLIOGRAPHY: W. T. Block, ed., *Emerald of the Neches: The Chronicles of Beaumont from Reconstruction to Spindletop* (Nederland, Texas: Nederland Publishing, 1980). *A Pictorial History of Polk County, Texas, 1846–1910* (Livingston, Texas: Polk County Bicentennial Commission, 1976; rev. ed. 1978). *Robert Wooster*

BOWERS AND PINEY CREEK RAILWAY. The Bowers and Piney Creek Railway Company was chartered on March 28, 1889, to build from a point on the line of the Trinity and Sabine Railway in Polk County to the mouth of Piney Creek, on the Neches River in Tyler County, about ten miles total. The initial capitalization was $50,000, and the business office was in Bowers. Members of the first board of directors included A. W. Morris (president) and W. P. McComb from Montgomery; C. W. Putnam (vice president) from Kansas City, Missouri; William Wise of Beaumont; W. T. Carter of Barnum; G. H. Morris of Bowers; and William Dawson of Trinity. By 1890 the company completed thirteen miles from the junction of the Trinity and Sabine track to Piney Creek as a logging railroad. Its charter was revoked by the Texas legislature on April 1, 1891.

Chris Cravens

BOWIE, JAMES (1796–1836). James Bowie was born near Terrapin Creek (now Spring Creek) where it crosses Bowie's Mill Road (Turnertown Road), nine miles northwest of Franklin, Logan County (now Simpson County), Kentucky, probably on April 10, 1796. He was the son of Reason (or Rezin) and Elve Ap-Catesby Jones (or Johns) Bowie. In 1794 Reason Bowie had moved his family from Tennessee to Logan County, where he farmed and operated a gristmill with the help of eight slaves. In February 1800 he moved to Madrid, in what is now Missouri. On May 2, 1801, at Rapides, Louisiana, Reason Bowie and his brothers David, Rhesa, and John swore allegiance to the Spanish government. In October the families settled on farms in what is now Catahoula Parish. There Reason's sons, James, John J., Stephen, and Rezin P. Bowie,[qv] grew to manhood. The family took an active part in community affairs and the elder Bowie reportedly became the largest slaveowner in his locale, with twenty slaves. About 1809 the Bowie clan moved to the Atakapa country in southeastern Louisiana; there Reason purchased 640 acres on the Vermilion River near the mouth of Little Bayou. He then developed a plantation near Opelousas, where he grew cotton and sugarcane, raised livestock, and bought and sold slaves. He died there around 1821.

In his teens James Bowie worked in Avoyelles and Rapides parishes, where he floated lumber to market. He invested in property on the Bayou Boeuf and traded in 1817–18 at what is now Bennett's Store, south of Cheneyville. He was fond of hunting and fishing, and family tradition says that he caught and rode wild horses, rode alligators, and trapped bears. When grown, Bowie was described by his brother John as "a stout, rather raw-boned man, of six feet height, weighed 180 pounds." He had light-colored hair, keen grey eyes "rather deep set in his head," a fair complexion, and high cheek-bones. Bowie had an "open, frank disposition," but when aroused by an insult, his anger was terrible. During the War of 1812, James and Rezin joined the Second Division, Consolidated, a unit that contained the Seventeenth through Nineteenth regiments, drawn from Avoyelles, Rapides, Natchitoches, Catahoula, and Ouachita parishes. In January 1815 the brothers were on their way to join Andrew Jackson's forces at New Orleans when the war ended.

After the war they traded in slaves. They bought them from the pirate Jean Laffite,[qv] who captured slave shipments in the Caribbean and Gulf of Mexico and ran a slave market on Galveston Island. Laffite landed slaves at Bowie's Island in Vermilion Bay, and the Bowies took the slaves up the Vermilion and sold them in St. Landry Parish. When they had $65,000 they quit the business. James and Rezin also dabbled in land speculation and developed friendships with local wealthy planters. James became engaged to Cecelia Wells (b. 1805), who died on September 7, 1829, in Alexandria, two weeks before their wedding was to take place.

He also made enemies. Norris Wright, Rapides parish sheriff and local banker, refused to make a loan that Bowie sorely needed. In 1826 Bowie met Wright in Alexandria, where tempers flared and Wright fired point-blank at Bowie; but the bullet was deflected. After this encounter, Rezin gave his brother a large butcher-like hunting knife to carry. On September 19, 1827, near Natchez, Jim Bowie participated in the Sandbar Fight, which developed at a duel between Samuel Levi Wells III and Dr. Thomas Maddox. After the principals had exchanged shots without effect, two observers continued the affair. Alexander Crain fired at Samuel Cuny, and when Cuny fell, Bowie fired at Crain but missed. Wright shot Bowie through the lower chest, and Bowie, said an eyewitness, "drew his butcher knife which he usually wears" and chased Wright. The Blanchard brothers shot Bowie in the thigh, and Wright and Alfred Blanchard stabbed him in several places. As Wright bent over him, Bowie plunged the knife into his assailant's breast, then raised himself and slashed Blanchard severely. All the witnesses remembered Bowie's "big butcher knife," the first Bowie knife.[qv] Reports of Bowie's prowess and his lethal blade captured public attention, and he was proclaimed the South's most formidable knife fighter. Men asked blacksmiths and cutlers to make a knife like Jim Bowie's.

During the late-1820s, Bowie lived in New Orleans, enjoying its excitement and pleasures. In 1824 he had met and become a fast friend of Edwin Forrest, a rising actor who later achieved international fame. Bowie had his portrait painted about this time. When Forrest played Natchez in 1829, Bowie apparently gave him the Sandbar knife. The actor kept the knife in a glass case in his mansion in Philadelphia until his death. In 1987 the knife, complete with sheath, was still in the possession of Forrest's trustees. James and his brothers Rezin and Stephen established the Arcadia sugar plantation of some 1,800 acres near the town of Thibodaux, Terrebonne Parish, where they set up the first steam-powered sugar mill in Louisiana. Rezin was elected to the Louisiana state legislature. James spent little time at Arcadia, however; in the late 1820s he traveled to the eastern cities, as well as Arkansas and Mississippi. On February 12, 1831, the brothers sold Arcadia and other landholdings and eighty-two slaves to Natchez investors for $90,000.

When Bowie first entered Mexican Texas[qv] is unknown. He possibly was recruited in 1819 in New Orleans with Benjamin R. Milam[qv] and others for the Long expedition.[qv] On January 1, 1830, Bowie and a friend left Thibodaux for Texas. They stopped at Nacogdoches, at Jared E. Groce's[qv] farm on the Brazos River, and in San Felipe, where Bowie presented a letter of introduction to empresario[qv] Stephen F. Austin[qv] from Thomas F. McKinney,[qv] one of the Old Three Hundred[qv] colonists. On February 20 Bowie and his friend Isaac Donoho took the oath of allegiance to Mexico. Bowie, age thirty-four, was at his prime. He was convivial, loved music, and was generous. He also was ambitious and scheming; he played cards for money, and lived in a world of debt. He reached San Antonio with William H. Wharton[qv] and Mrs. Wharton, Isaac Donoho, Caiaphas K. Ham,[qv] and several slaves. They carried letters of introduction to two wealthy and influential Mexicans, Juan Martín de Veramendi and Juan N. Seguín.[qqv] Bowie's party continued on to Saltillo, the state capital of Coahuila and Texas.[qv] There Bowie learned that a Mexican law of 1828 offered its citizens eleven-league grants in Texas for $100 to $250 each. (A league was 4,428.4 acres.) Bowie urged Mexicans to apply for the eleven-league grants, which he purchased from them. He left Saltillo with fifteen or sixteen of these grants, and continued to encourage speculation in Texas lands. His activities irritated Stephen F. Austin, who hesitated to approve lands Bowie wanted to locate in the Austin colony but eventually allowed the tracts there.

In San Antonio Bowie posed as a man of wealth, attached himself to the wealthy Veramendi family, and was baptized into the Catholic Church,[qv] sponsored by the Veramendis. In the autumn of 1830 he accompanied the family to Saltillo, and on October 5 officially became a Mexican citizen. The citizenship was contingent on his establishing wool and cotton mills in Coahuila. Through his friend Angus McNeill[qv] of Natchez, he purchased a textile mill for $20,000. On April 25, 1831, in San Antonio, Bowie married Ursula de Veramendi. He had appeared before the mayor, declared his age as thirty-two (he was actually thirty-five), and pledged to pay Ursula a dowry of $15,000.

James Bowie, after George P. A. Healy. Courtesy TSL.

He valued his properties at $222,800. But the titles to his 60,000 arpents of Arkansas land, valued at $30,000, were fraudulent. Walker and Wilkins of Natchez owed Bowie $45,000 for his interest in Arcadia Plantation, and had given McNeil $20,000 for the Saltillo mill. Bowie borrowed $1,879 from his father-in-law and $750 from Ursula's grandmother for a honeymoon trip to New Orleans and Natchez. The Bowies settled in San Antonio.

Veramendi family tradition says Bowie spent little time at home. He apparently became fascinated by tales of the "lost" Los Almagres Mine,[qv] said to be west of San Antonio near the ruin of Santa Cruz de San Sabá Mission. Bowie obtained permission from Mexican authorities for an expedition into Indian country financed by the Veramendis, and on November 2, 1831, he left San Antonio with his brother Rezin and nine others. On the nineteenth they learned that a large Indian war party was following them, and six miles from San Saba, Bowie camped in an oak grove. An attempt to parley failed. Bowie's men fought for their lives for thirteen hours. The Indians finally drew off, reportedly leaving forty dead and thirty wounded. Bowie lost one man killed and several wounded. The party returned to San Antonio. On January 23, 1832, Bowie made another foray to the west. He now carried the title of "colonel" of citizen rangers. He left Gonzales with twenty-six men to scout the headwaters of the Colorado for Tawakonis and other hostile Indians. After a fruitless search of 2½ months, he returned home.

In July, in Natchez, he learned that José de las Piedras,[qv] Mexican commander at Nacogdoches, had visited the towns of Anahuac and

Velasco to quiet the antagonisms between the government and the mainly Anglo citizens. Upon his return, Piedras demanded that all citizens in his jurisdiction surrender their arms. The colonists rejected the demand. Bowie hurried to Nacogdoches, and on August 1 accompanied James W. Bullock[qv] and 300 armed men in their siege of the garrison there. Piedras chose to fight. During the night he evacuated his men and marched south, having lost thirty-three killed. Bowie and eighteen men ambushed the Mexican column, and Piedras fled. Bowie marched the soldiers back to Nacogdoches (*see* NACOGDOCHES, BATTLE OF). On March 9, 1833, Monclova replaced Saltillo as the state capital. When the two towns raised small armies to contest the change, Bowie favored Monclova. On one occasion when the forces confronted each other, he rode out and tried to precipitate a battle. He believed that the fortunes of Texas land speculators lay with Monclova.

In September, Veramendi, his wife Josefa, and Ursula Bowie died of cholera at Monclova. Ursula died on the tenth. A Bowie relative and Veramendi family tradition say Ursula and one child died in the epidemic. A Bowie family friend reported that Ursula had two children, but both died young. Bowie was ill with yellow fever in Natchez and unaware of the deaths. On October 31 he dictated his last will, in which he bequeathed half of his estate to his brother Rezin and half to his sister Martha Sterrett and her husband.

Mexican laws passed in 1834 and 1835 opened the floodgates to wholesale speculation in Texas lands, and Texas-Coahuila established land commissions to speed sales, since the state treasury was empty. Bowie was appointed a commissioner to promote settlement in John T. Mason's[qv] purchase. The governor also was empowered to hand out 400-league parcels for frontier defense. The sale of these large tracts angered some colonists, who also resented a rumored plan by speculators to make San Antonio the capital. They questioned Bowie's handling of Mason's 400-league purchase. One traveler met Bowie and Mason en route from Matamoros to Monclova with $40,000 in specie to pay the last installment on Mason's land. Bowie also sold Mason land certificates to his friends in Natchez. In May 1835, however, Santa Anna abolished the Coahuila-Texas government and ordered the arrest of all Texans doing business in Monclova. Bowie fled the capital for Texas. On June 22 he wrote a friend in Nacogdoches that all communication between Mexico and Texas had been cut, that troops were boarding ships at Matamoros for the Texas coast, and that Mexican forces were en route from Saltillo toward the Rio Grande. By July, Bowie and others in San Felipe and Nacogdoches were beating the drum for war.

On July 31, 1835, William B. Travis[qv] wrote Bowie that Texans were divided and that the Peace Party[qv] appeared the stronger. Travis was a leader of the War Party.[qv] Bowie had hired Travis as early as 1833 in San Felipe to prepare land papers, and in June 1834 Travis represented Bowie and Isaac Donoho in a case filed by Francis W. Johnson.[qv] Travis also did legal work for Bowie's friend Jesse Clifft, who made the first Bowie knife. The War Party sought military support among the Indian tribes in East Texas. On August 3, Bowie reported on a recent tour of several villages where he found many of the Indians on drunken sprees and all reluctant to cooperate. Within a week Bowie took a small group of Texas "militia" to San Antonio and seized a stack of muskets in the Mexican armory there.

On September 1, Austin arrived home from a long imprisonment in Mexico City. On October 3, Santa Anna abolished all state legislatures in Mexico. After being elected to command the volunteer army, Austin issued a call to arms. On October 16 his forces camped on Cibolo Creek twenty miles from San Antonio. Bowie arrived with a small party of friends, principally from Louisiana, and Austin placed him on his staff as a colonel. Travis and others joined the army. Gen. Sam Houston,[qv] in command of the Texas regular army, arrived and condemned the idea of attacking Bexar. He maintained that Austin's army, weak and ill-trained, should fall back to the Guadalupe or Colorado river. Bowie and Capt. James W. Fannin,[qv] at Austin's orders, scouted south of Bexar for a new campsite. On their way, Bowie drove off a Mexican patrol. On October 26, Austin moved 400 men to San Francisco de la Espada Mission. Bowie took ninety-two horsemen and inspected area of Nuestra Señora de la Purísima Concepción de Acuña Mission, near Bexar. At dawn on the twentieth-eighth, in a heavy fog, the Mexicans attacked Bowie with 300 cavalry and 100 infantry. Bowie fought for three hours. "Bowie was a born leader," Noah Smithwick[qv] wrote years later of the battle of Concepción,[qv] "never needlessly spending a bullet or imperiling a life. His voice is still ringing in my old deaf ears as he repeatedly admonished us. Keep under cover boys and reserve your fire; we haven't a man to spare." Bowie captured a six-pounder cannon and thirty muskets. He lost one man, while the Mexicans left sixteen on the field and carried off as many. Austin moved the Texan army to Concepción.

Three days after the battle Austin sent Travis and fifty men to capture some 900 horses being driven south to Laredo, and asked Bowie to create a diversion to cover the escape of Mexican soldiers who wanted to desert. Bowie made a display of force while the soldiers came out and fled into the countryside. On October 31 Bowie notified Gen. Martín Perfecto de Cos[qv] that he would join Austin in an attack on Bexar. On November 1 Austin demanded that Cos surrender; he refused. Austin hesitated. On November 2, Bowie asked to be relieved of command. He had tried to resign on October 9 and join Fannin's company. Bowie had earlier served in a volunteer ranger group, fought Indians, and was the type of officer who served the community in time of need. He apparently had little interest in a formal command. Provisional governor Henry Smith[qv] and Houston wanted him to raise a volunteer group and attack Matamoros, but the General Council[qv] declared that Bowie was not "an officer of the government nor army." On November 2, Austin's officers voted 44 to 3 against storming Bexar. Bowie did not vote.

On November 24, Austin, appointed a commissioner to the United States, held an election to determine his successor. Bowie received 5 votes, Edward Burleson[qv] 361, Fannin 68, F. W. Johnson 10, and a man named Wallace 83. Burleson immediately took over the army and appointed Bowie his adjutant and inspector general. On the twenty-sixth Bowie and thirty horsemen rode out to check on a Mexican packtrain near town, and Burleson followed with 100 infantry. Bowie met the train and charged its escort, fought briefly, then saw his adversaries retire, having lost sixty men. As the train was loaded with bales of grass for the garrison livestock, the clash was called the Grass Fight.[qv] Bowie subsequently proceeded to Goliad to determine conditions there. During his absence, Burleson attacked Bexar on December 5 and forced the Mexican garrison to surrender and retire to the Rio Grande. The volunteers left for home. Bowie received a letter from Houston dated December 17, suggesting a campaign against Matamoros. If that was impossible, Houston suggested, Bowie could perhaps organize a guerilla force to harass the Mexican army. The Matamoros expedition[qv] was approved, but Col. F. W. Johnson was placed in charge.

On January 19, 1836, Bowie arrived in Bexar from Goliad with a detachment of thirty men. He carried orders from Houston to demolish the fortifications there. The situation was grim. Col. James C. Neill,[qv] commander of a contingent of seventy-eight men at the Alamo,[qv] stated that his men lacked clothing and pay and talked of leaving. Mexican families were leaving Bexar. Texas volunteers had carried off most of the munitions and supplies for the Matamoros expedition. On February 2 Bowie wrote Governor Smith, urging that Bexar be held because it was a strategic "frontier picqet guard." Travis, promoted to lieutenant colonel, arrived with thirty men on February 3; David Crockett[qv] rode in with twelve men on the eighth. The garrison had some 150 men. On February 11, Neill gave his command to Travis and left. The volunteers preferred Bowie as commander. Travis held an election that split the command: Bowie was chosen a full colonel of volunteers, and Travis retained his command as lieutenant colonel of regulars. They would sign all general orders as co-commanders. Travis soon complained of Bowie's drunkenness and erratic conduct, however. Bowie ordered certain prisoners set free, and while drunk paraded the volunteers under arms in Bexar. Travis took his regulars from the Alamo to the Medina River to escape implication in the disgraceful affair.

On February 20 Bowie and Travis learned that some 1,500 Mexican cavalrymen were advancing on Bexar, and sent a dispatch to Goliad asking Fannin for help. Within hours the Mexicans marched into Bexar. On February 23 they requested a parley. Without consulting Travis, Bowie asked for and received terms: the Texans must surrender. On February 24 Bowie fell from a platform while attempting to position a cannon and broke several ribs. He was confined to a cot and urged the volunteers to follow Travis. He was occasionally carried outside to visit with his men. He also apparently had a disease "of a peculiar nature," which has been diagnosed as pneumonia or typhoid-pneumonia, but probably was advanced tuberculosis.

On March 6 the Mexicans attacked before dawn, and all 188 defenders of the Alamo perished. Santa Anna asked to see the corpses of Bowie, Travis, and Crockett, and Bexar mayor Francisco Ruiz identified the bodies. Bowie lay on his cot in a room on the south side. He had been shot several times in the head. During his lifetime he had been described by his old friend Caiaphas K. Ham as " a clever, polite gentleman . . . attentive to the ladies on all occasions . . . a true, constant, and generous friend . . . a foe no one dared to undervalue and many feared." Slave trader, gambler, land speculator, dreamer, and hero, James Bowie in death became immortal in the annals of Texas history. *See also* ALAMO, BATTLE OF.

BIBLIOGRAPHY: James L. Batson, *James Bowie and the Sandbar Fight* (Madison, Alabama: Batson Engineering and Metalworks, 1992). William Campbell Binkley, ed., *Official Correspondence of the Texan Revolution, 1835–1836* (2 vols., New York: Appleton-Century, 1936). Walter W. Bowie, *The Bowies and Their Kindred: A Genealogical and Biographical History* (Washington: Cromwell Brothers, 1899). J. Frank Dobie, "James Bowie," *American West,* Spring 1965. John S. Ford, Memoirs (MS, John Salmon Ford Papers, Barker Texas History Center, University of Texas at Austin). *Heroes of Texas: Featuring Oil Portraits from the Summerfield G. Roberts Collection* (Waco: Texian Press, 1964). John H. Jenkins, ed., *The Papers of the Texas Revolution, 1835–1836* (10 vols., Austin: Presidial Press, 1973). A. R. Kilpatrick, "Early Life in the Southwest—The Bowies," *DeBow's Southern and Western Review* 1 (October 1852). Walter Lord, *A Time to Stand* (New York: Harper, 1961; 2d ed., Lincoln: University of Nebraska Press, 1978). Raymond W. Thorp, *Bowie Knife* (Albuquerque: University of New Mexico Press, 1948).

William R. Williamson

BOWIE, REZIN PLEASANT (1793–1841). Rezin P. Bowie, son of Reason (or Rezin) and Elve Ap-Catesby (Jones or Johns) Bowie, was born on September 8, 1793, on a farm one mile west of Gallatin, Sumner County, Tennessee. In 1909 the standing chimney was the only testimony that remained of the Bowie cabin. Neither Rezin P. nor his brother James Bowie,[qv] of Alamo[qv] fame, was born at Elliott's Springs, Tennessee, as some sources claim. In 1794 Reason Bowie moved his family to a farm he acquired by grant on Terrapin Creek in Logan County, Kentucky. There the family farmed, operated a gristmill, and likely distilled bourbon whisky. The Logan County property was sold in 1800. After a short stay in Livingston County, Kentucky, the family moved to the Spanish-held District of New Madrid, now in Missouri, and remained until 1802. That year they sold the Missouri property and established themselves in the future Catahoula Parish, Louisiana. Reason Bowie, according to Rezin's brother John J., fled "the refinements of civilization" and "retired to wilder regions, where he could enjoy those sports and stirring adventures peculiar to a frontier life." The Catahoula region was wild country, and the Bowie boys, especially Rezin and Jim, gloried in the life. They acquired the survival skills of an Indian and developed expertise in use of weapons. The Bowies lived on Bushley Creek; Reason's twin brother Rhesa and brother David developed land grants nearby. The Bowies' first economic endeavor was a whiskey still that garnered needed cash and trade until it was abandoned in favor of cotton cultivation. Reason had some twenty slaves, more than any other man in the Catahoula area. In 1809 the family moved to the Atakapa country of southeastern Louisiana. Rezin was sixteen, James thirteen, and Stephen twelve. They settled on a 640-acre property, Bowie's Woods, purchased from John Grecian years before on the Vermilion River. The family's last move was to St. Landry Parish, where Reason purchased a large tract of land, a portion of which is in Opelousas today. There the Bowies engaged in land speculation, farming, lumbering, sawmilling, and the slave trade.

Rezin Bowie married Margaret Nevil (Nevill, Neville) on September 15, 1814, at St. Landry's Catholic Church in Opelousas. At this time he adopted Catholicism and chose the name James for the ceremony. The name "James Rezin Bowie" in the church records has been the source of some confusion. War of 1812 rolls list Rezin and James as privates and volunteers in the Second Division Consolidated. The Second Division was composed of the Seventeenth through the Nineteenth regiments, which represented Avoyelles, Rapides, Natchitoches, Catahoula, and Ouachita parishes in 1814 and 1815. Bowie family records state that Rezin and James were en route to the battle of New Orleans and were bitterly disappointed that it ended before they arrived. Rezin was commissioned captain of the Mounted Rifles in the Avoyelles Battalion in 1825 and later became a colonel. The Bowie brothers were involved for a time with the pirate Jean Laffite[qv] in the illegal importation and sale of slaves in Louisiana. In 1852, John J. Bowie described the operation: "James, Rezin and myself fitted out some small boats at the mouth of the Calcasieu and went into the trade on shares. We first purchased forty negroes from Laffite at the rate of one dollar per pound, or an average of $140 for each negro; we brought them into the limits of the United States, delivered them to a custom house officer, and became the informers ourselves; the law gave the informer half of the value of the negroes, which we put up and sold by the United States Marshall, and we became the purchasers of the negros, which entitled us to sell them within the United States. We continued to follow this business until we made $65,000, when we quit and soon spent all our earnings." Laffite delivered slaves from Galveston Island by ship to the river mouths. The bayou waterways, at the time, allowed transportation from the Calcasieu River into Rapides Parish. Another route was to deliver the slaves to Bowie Island in Vermilion Bay, where they were received and brought up the Vermilion River and then overland to St. Landry. Both Rezin and James Bowie moved north up Bayou Boeuf from Opelousas and acquired property in St. Landry, Avoyelles, and Rapides parishes. Land speculation in Louisiana properties and land titles became their occupation. Both acquired numerous holdings in various areas and became well established and successful in their endeavors. Their young brother Stephen bought property and farmed in Avoyelles.

Rezin Bowie was best known in the nineteenth century, perhaps in this, as the inventor of the famous Bowie knife.[qv] His brother James brought fame to himself and notoriety to the knife when he killed Maj. Norris Wright with it in the noted Sandbar Fight on September 19, 1827. In 1838 Rezin wrote concerning the Bowie knife, "The improvement in its fabrication, and the state of perfection which it has since acquired from experienced cutlers was not brought about through my agency." Rezin's actions belie his words, however, for he had a number of superior Bowie knives made by experienced cutlers that he carried himself and gave to friends. Several of these have been located and documented. Were it not for Rezin's continuing interest and pride, precious little would be known concerning the origin, features, and appearance of the first Bowie knives.

With his brothers James and Stephen, Rezin established Arcadia, a sugar plantation of some 1,800 acres near the town of Thibodaux

(Terrebonne Parish). There the Bowies established the first steam-powered sugar mill in Louisiana. Rezin was elected to the Louisiana legislature three times. On February 12, 1831, the Bowie brothers sold Arcadia and other holdings to investors from Natchez for $90,000.

By 1830, James Bowie had moved to Texas. He soon became interested in the "lost" Los Almagres Mine,qv said to be near the Santa Cruz de San Sabá Mission ruin west of San Antonio. James obtained permission from Mexican authorities for an expedition into Indian country. Rezin rode in from Louisiana, and on November 2, 1831, James, Rezin, and nine others left San Antonio. On the nineteenth, learning that a large Indian war party was following them, they camped in an oak grove six miles from the ruin. Rezin Bowie and David Buchanan sought to compromise with the Indians, but they were fired upon. A thirteen-hour fight known as the San Saba Indian fight ensued. The Indians finally retreated, and the party returned to San Antonio. In 1832 Rezin and James traveled to New York, Philadelphia, and Washington. Rezin was seeking expert medical treatment for his eyes. In Philadelphia Samuel C. Atkinson, publisher of the *Saturday Evening Post* newspaper induced Rezin to write an account of the San Saba battle. "An Indian Fight" was reprinted in a book entitled *Atkinson's Casket or Gems of Literature, Wit and Sentiment* in 1833. Rezin's version, the only one in public print, became the only widely read account of the subject.

Following the sale of Arcadia, Bowie and his wife moved for the last time to a plantation on the west bank of the Mississippi River in Iberville Parish. The location was south of Plaquemine across the river from San Gabriel Catholic Church. While living there Bowie and Gen. John Wilson acquired the Pintado papers. Capt. Vicente Sebastián Pintado, the royal surveyor for the Spanish government, took these important surveys and record of deeds and grants to Havana as his personal property, and the Spanish government supported him. From there he sold needed land information and confirmations back into Louisiana, parts of Mississippi, and Alabama. Pintado told his wife to continue selling the valuable data after his death, but not the documents. The United States government wanted the papers, but Pintado would not sell. After Pintado's death his widow set a price of $20,000 and then $24,500 on the papers. The United States decided not to purchase them. Access to the Pintado papers gave a land speculator like Rezin Bowie a trump card. But Rezin's health was poor, and his eyesight had continued to deteriorate. Whether he derived the expected benefits from the Pintado papers is unknown. He died in New Orleans on January 17, 1841, leaving his wife and three daughters. He was buried in the San Gabriel Catholic Church graveyard. In the early 1850s his body was disinterred and moved to St. Joseph Catholic Cemetery in Port Gibson, Mississippi. St. Joseph, also known as the Bowie Church, was financed by funds raised by Rezin's daughter Elve and her husband, John Taylor Moore. Margaret Bowie purchased property and donated it for the cemetery.

BIBLIOGRAPHY: Walter W. Bowie, *The Bowies and Their Kindred: A Genealogical and Biographical History* (Washington: Cromwell Brothers, 1899). Jay Guy Cisco, *Historic Sumner County, Tennessee* (Nashville: Folk-Keelin, 1909). A. R. Kilpatrick, "Early Life in the Southwest—The Bowies," *DeBow's Southern and Western Review* 1 (October 1852). Raymond W. Thorp, *Bowie Knife* (Albuquerque: University of New Mexico Press, 1948). Vertical Files, Barker Texas History Center, University of Texas at Austin. *William R. Williamson*

BOWIE, TEXAS. Bowie is an incorporated community on U.S. Highway 81 fifteen miles southwest of Montague in southwestern Montague County. In 1882, when the tracks of the Fort Worth and Denver Railway were built through the area, local settlers who had been there since the early 1860s moved to the site of the construction camps, and soon businesses appeared in canvas tents. A townsite was laid out on August 15, 1882, and residents applied for a post office to be named for James Bowie.qv On July 22, 1884, residents voted to incorporate the new town. Bowie became a market and financial center for farmers and ranchers between Fort Worth and Wichita Falls. In 1885 it had a population of 1,000, three hotels, a bank, a weekly newspaper, schools, and a number of churches. The Chicago, Rock Island and Texas Railway came to Bowie in 1893, and by 1900 the community had an estimated 2,600 residents. By the mid-1920s Bowie had a population of 3,000 and about 100 businesses, including four banks, two weekly newspapers, a hospital, and a business college (opened in 1912). During the mid-1950s the population was 6,796, and by the late 1980s the town reported 5,818 residents and 160 businesses. By then Bowie was the largest town in Montague County. In 1990 its population was 4,990.

BIBLIOGRAPHY: Guy Renfro Donnell, The History of Montague County, Texas (M.A. thesis, University of Texas, 1940). Jeff S. Henderson, ed., *One Hundred Years in Montague County, Texas* (St. Jo, Texas: Ipta Printer, 1978). Vertical Files, Barker Texas History Center, University of Texas at Austin. *David Minor*

BOWIE COUNTY. Bowie County (B–22) is in the far northeastern corner of the state, bordered by the Red River on the north, with Arkansas and Oklahoma across its northern boundary and Arkansas to the east. Boston, the county seat, is located near the center of the county at 33°27′ north latitude and 94°25′ west longitude, twenty-one miles west of Texarkana, the county's largest town. The county occupies 891 square miles of the East Texas Timberlands. The terrain is level to gently rolling; its elevation ranges from 200 to 450 feet above mean sea level. The county is drained by the Red and Sulphur rivers, which form its northern and southern boundaries. Most of the soils are either loamy or clayey. Mineral resources include oil, gas, lignite, and ceramic clay. The county also has abundant forest lands, and in 1981 its timber production totalled 10,292,035 cubic feet. Temperatures range from an average high of 94°F in July to an average low of 30° in January. Rainfall is abundant, averaging forty-seven inches a year, and the growing season is long, an average of 235 days annually. At first European contact, wildlife native to the area included buffalo, deer, bear, beaver, and turkey.

Archeological evidence in contiguous Red River County indicates that this portion of Texas was occupied by Indians as early as the Late Archaic Period, ca. 1500 B.C. At the time of first European contact, the area was occupied by the Caddo Indians, an agricultural people with a highly developed culture. During the last decade of the eighteenth century, due to epidemics and problems with the Osages, the Caddos abandoned the villages they had occupied for centuries. During the early 1820s bands of Shawnee, Delaware, and Kickapoo Indians immigrated to the area, but they had abandoned their settlements by the mid-1830s. Although white settlement of the county had already begun when these later bands of Indians arrived, relations between the Indians and settlers were relatively peaceful.

The time of the earliest European exploration of the county cannot be conclusively determined. The northernmost of the numerous routes attributed to the Moscoso expeditionqv in 1542 crosses Bowie County; if the expedition actually took this route, the area was among the earliest explored parts of the state. The first European contact with this region more likely occurred, however, between 1687, when Henri Joutelqv traveled north in search of Henri de Tonti,qv and 1690, when Tonti returned to Texas in search of survivors of the La Salle expedition.qv Prolonged European activity in the area began in 1719, when Le Poste des Cadodaquiousqv was founded by Jean Baptiste Bénard de La Harpe.qv American exploration of the area began in 1806, when President Thomas Jefferson, eager to strengthen the American claim to the area, dispatched Thomas Freeman and Dr. Peter Custisqv to explore the area. Following the Red River, the Freeman and Custis expedition reached Spanish Bluff,qv almost due north of the site of present New Boston, before being forced to turn back by Spanish soldiers.

Because the area of Northeast Texas encompassing present Bowie County was considered by many to be part of Arkansas, it was the site of some of the earliest white settlement in Texas. Hunters and traders were active in the area by 1815, and in contiguous Red River County permanent settlement was underway by 1818. Although the details of earliest settlement in Bowie County are not clear, the area was probably settled around 1820, when Miller County, Arkansas,[qv] was organized. This county encompassed not only what is now Bowie County, but all of the Red River settlements.

Although the early settlers seem to have regarded the area as part of the United States, when the United States government refused to issue them land titles many of these settlers turned first to the Mexican government and then to Arthur G. Wavell's agent, Benjamin R. Milam,[qqv] in an attempt to obtain valid land titles. While doing so, they continued to send representatives to the Arkansas legislature. When the Convention of 1836[qv] met at Washington-on-the-Brazos, the Red River settlements were represented by Richard Ellis, Samuel P. Carson, Robert Hamilton, Collin McKinney, and Albert H. Latimer.[qqv] Three of these men—Ellis, Carson, and McKinney—were living within the confines of the future Bowie County. That year Red River County, which included all the territory now in Bowie County, was established.

Bowie County was demarked in December of 1840 and named for James Bowie.[qv] As originally delineated, the county included all or part of the territories of present Cass, Titus, and Morris counties. In 1846 the county was reduced to its present size and boundaries with the establishment of Cass and Titus counties. DeKalb, in the western part of the county, was designated temporary county seat, while a commission was appointed to choose a more appropriate permanent site. The commission chose the town then named Boston (*see* OLD BOSTON, TEXAS), which became the county seat in 1841. In the mid-1880s the citizens of Texarkana conducted a successful campaign to make Texarkana the county seat. About five years later residents of the western and central parts of the county campaigned successfully for yet another county seat, this one to be at the geographic center of the county. The new courthouse was constructed in 1890, and the town that grew up around it was named Boston. The county seat has remained at this location. Shortly before Texarkana ceased being the county seat, the courthouse burned and almost all the county records were destroyed.

In antebellum Texas[qv] Bowie County was overwhelmingly rural and agricultural. At the time of the Civil War,[qv] Boston, the county's largest town, had a population of only 300 or 400. Most county residents were employed in agriculture, and cotton was the county's most important cash crop. The production of cotton began in the 1830s and expanded steadily. The county's farmers reported a crop of 1,113 bales in 1849 and 6,874 bales in 1859. Although cotton was clearly predominant, livestock was also important to the county's economy. In 1860 Bowie County farmers reported a total of 12,819 swine, 3,281 milk cows, 1,160 working oxen, 7,601 other cattle, and 1,331 sheep. Even though cotton was the principal cash crop, the largest crop was corn; the harvest amounted to 218,289 bushels in 1859. The self-sufficient county raised more than enough corn and hogs for subsistence.

Bowie County was largely settled by Southerners, and, as in most other areas in the cotton South, slavery[qv] was a vitally important economic and social institution. Throughout the antebellum years slaves outnumbered free inhabitants. In 1850 there were 1,641 blacks in the county and 1,271 whites. During the 1850s, although the white population grew at a slightly faster rate than the black, in 1860 slaves outnumbered whites 2,651 to 2,401. Of the county's 145 slaveholders in 1850, twenty-two (15 percent) owned more than twenty slaves each. These planters owned more than half of all the slaves in the county. During the 1850s slaveholding became more concentrated. While the free population of the county grew by 89 percent between 1850 and 1860, the number of slaveholders in the county increased by only 30 percent. Within the slaveholding class the distribution of slaves remained about the same. Roughly 23 percent of the slaveholders present in 1860 were of the planter class, and they owned 65 percent of all slaves in the county.

Bowie County's white population overwhelmingly supported the secession[qv] movement during the winter of 1860–61. When the Ordinance of Secession was voted on in February 1861, Bowie County residents approved it by a vote of 208 to 15. They also wholeheartedly supported the war effort of the Confederacy.

Bowie County was never invaded, and it thus escaped the physical destruction that devastated other parts of the South. Nonetheless, the war years were trying times for the county's citizens. In addition to concern for loved ones on the battlefield, citizens were forced to deal with disruptions to the local economy caused by the unstable Confederate currency and the lack of a market for their cotton. The end of the war brought wrenching changes in the county's economic foundation. While the end of slavery meant freedom for the black, to the white slaveholder it was a serious loss of capital. In 1859 Bowie County slaveholders had paid taxes on 2,269 slaves appraised at $1,167,139, a sum that represented 64 percent of all taxable property in the county. After the war economic loss, the widespread belief that free blacks would not work, and the uncertain status of the South in the nation led to a loss of confidence that caused property values to plummet in 1865.

Two events occurring almost simultaneously in the summer of 1867 turned the bitterness of many of the county's discouraged white citizens into rage. First, it became obvious that the Radical Republicans were intent on providing blacks in the South a measure of legal and political equality. Second, in July 1867 federal troops were stationed in the county for the first time. Although local sources claim that the garrison in the county was composed of some eighteen to twenty men, federal records indicate that it never comprised more than twelve men. The soldiers were under the direction of William G. Kirkman, a former Union Army captain who was to act as an agent of the Freedmen's Bureau[qv] for the district. The number of troops in the county was just large enough to provide a galling reminder of the legal authority vested in the army of occupation, but not large enough to provide protection for area African Americans[qv] or Unionists. This was made evident during the army's first month in the county, when Kirkman and his men attempted to arrest the notorious killer Cullen Baker.[qv] Baker escaped the encounter, leaving one soldier dead and others wounded. As Baker and his gang increasingly restricted their killing to federal soldiers and freedmen, he gained the sympathy of many whites in Bowie County. Although few in the county would ever have ridden with Baker, many were willing to help him elude capture. A local writer stated years after the event that "this man Cullen Baker was hailed as a hero, and by many, even as a Moses who had appeared, to lead them out of the wilderness of Northern Political Tyranny and oppression." About a year after Kirkman and his men clashed with Baker they tried a second time, and one of Baker's men was killed. Shortly thereafter, Kirkman was indicted for murder by the civil authorities in the county. A local Unionist wrote army headquarters saying that events had left Kirkman "partially deranged and not capable of knowing what course to pursue." Kirkman was ordered to close his office and report to headquarters. The day he was to leave Bowie County he was murdered, and though Baker boasted of having committed the crime, the act was officially ruled "murder by person or persons unknown." The soldiers who had been stationed in the county to support Kirkman were removed, and no other agent of the Freedmen's Bureau was stationed in Bowie County.

In addition to the activities of Baker and his gang, armed bands of a county organization resembling the Ku Klux Klan[qv] patrolled the county killing or expelling blacks who were intent on exercising their political rights. At the same time, they worked to prevent most blacks from leaving the county, thus preserving a labor force to work the cotton fields. The operation of these bands, coupled with the failures of the Union military, made Reconstruction[qv] of short duration in the county. Whereas in Harrison County, a county with roughly the same proportion of slaves in 1860 located about eighty miles to the south, the Southern Democrats were unable to regain control of the county until 1878, Bowie County Democrats regained control of the county at the first election after the radical Constitution of 1869[qv] was promulgated.

After the election of 1869, Bowie County remained solidly Democratic. In presidential politics the county voted Democratic in every presidential election until 1968, when its vote went to George Wallace in a close three-way race. Subsequently the county voted for Republican presidential candidates, with the exception of Jimmy Carter in 1976 and William J. Clinton in 1992.

The turmoil of Reconstruction[qv] was probably largely responsible for the decline in the county's total population between the censuses of 1860 and 1870. In 1870, though the county's white population had risen slightly, from 2,401 to 2,434, the county's black population had dropped from 2,651 to 2,249. For the first time since annexation,[qv] whites were in a majority in the county. The census of 1870 registered what was the beginning of a long-term trend. With some exceptions, though the number of blacks in the county grew larger every ten years, as a percentage the black population declined. By 1980 the 16,498 blacks living in the county constituted a little less than 22 percent of the county's 75,301 residents.

For sixty years after Reconstruction the economic base of Bowie County remained largely agricultural. Cotton was still the principal crop, and following the disastrous 1869 harvest of 2,990 bales, production of the staple expanded steadily, to a high of 30,520 bales in 1929. The production of corn, the principal food crop, ranged from the 1869 low of 104,805 bushels to a high of 929,954 bushels in 1909. For many of the county's residents, cotton provided a livelihood but not prosperity. Beginning in 1880, when the statistics were first compiled, each census recorded a higher percentage of farmers who did not own the land they farmed. In 1880, 36 percent of all farmers in the county were tenants, the largest portion of whom farmed on shares. By 1930, 64 percent of the farmers in the county were tenants.

Though agriculture was the foundation of the county's economic base, the county was never exclusively agricultural. Manufacturing provided jobs for a small portion of the labor force in 1850, when fourteen persons were employed to make products valued at $12,100. Between 1880 and 1890 the county experienced a small boom in manufacturing. In 1880, 185 people were employed to make products valued at $417,840. By 1890 the number of people employed had jumped to 1,157, and the annual product was valued at $1,757,425. The depression of the 1890s was probably responsible for a serious decline during the next ten years, as the number of people employed dropped to 500. Afterward, manufacturing expanded steadily; in 1930, 1,583 people were employed at wages totalling $1,568,500 to make products valued at $11,919,153.

In addition to an expansion in manufactures, the county was also becoming more urban. This change was largely due to the coming of the railroad. When the Texas and Pacific Railway was constructed through the county, beginning in 1873, towns along its route began to garner an increasingly larger share of the market activities of area farmers. The railroad also was responsible for a new town, Texarkana, which, almost from its founding, served as a major market center and shipping point for farmers in the surrounding three-state area. By 1900 the 5,256 people who lived on the Texas side of Texarkana comprised almost 20 percent of the population of the county. By 1930 the 16,602 people in that part of the town amounted to 34 percent of the population of the county. In 1930 the county's four largest towns had a population of 19,071, a little over 39 percent of the county's total population.

Like most other areas of the country, Bowie County was hit hard by the Great Depression.[qv] For the agricultural sector of the county the effects of the depression were becoming apparent by 1930, when the average value of county farms fell from the 1920 value of $3,498 to $2,373. The effect of the depression on manufacturing is not so obvious because that segment of the county's economy was not really depressed until after the census of 1930 had been taken, and by the census of 1940 recovery was underway. Still, the census of 1940 registered a drop in number of employees (from 1,583 to 1,536), wages paid (from $1,568,500 to $1,041,528), and value of products (from $11,919,153 to $7,175,535).

World War II[qv] brought the same trauma to residents of the county that other wars had brought, as hundreds of the county's citizens fought overseas. But it was also the beginning of more positive and lasting changes in the county's economy. In 1941 two massive military installations were constructed in the county, the Lone Star Army Ammunition Plant and Red River Army Depot.[qqv] These two installations, which occupy almost 40,000 acres, employed thousands of people in building and storing war supplies. By 1945, 769,977 tons of matériel had been shipped from these two locations. After the war, operation of the plant and depot continued; in 1992 more than 8,000 people, civilian and military, were employed at them.

The opportunities for employment off the farm accelerated changes in agriculture that had begun during the depression. Federal payments to farmers who withdrew a part of their land from cultivation had caused some landlords to drive the tenants off their land. The number of farms in the county fell from 5,451 in 1930 to 3,890 in 1940, and the percentage of tenant farmers in the county fell to 46. During the 1940s, as tenants left for better jobs in the cities, the number of farms in the county continued to fall. By 1950 tenants operated just 21 percent of the 3,127 farms in the county. As tenants left the land, farms became larger and increasingly mechanized, a change registered in the census. In 1930 one of the chief power sources for farmers was the mule (*see* HORSE AND MULE INDUSTRY). The census that year counted 8,527 mules in the county. By 1950, the last year for which figures are available, the number had fallen to 2,214.

Changes in consumer products also led to decreasing demand for cotton, and production of the staple declined to 20,168 bales in 1940 and to 9,015 bales in 1950. Cotton remained a major crop for Bowie County farmers through the 1960s; the 1968 crop was reported as 8,938 bales. But Bowie County farmers gradually abandoned cotton in the 1970s, so that by 1981 no production was reported. By 1982 livestock was the most important agricultural commodity, with county farmers reporting a total of 62,528 cattle. Wheat, soybeans, and hay were the largest crops in 1981, when production was reported as 391,955 bushels, 201,163 bushels, and 61,385 tons, respectively. Ninety-seven percent of the farmers in Bowie County owned all or part of the land they farmed, and the 1,130 farms in the county were worth an average of $176,125 each.

During the period after World War II, though agriculture remained vital, it was replaced as the cornerstone of the county's economy by manufacturing and wholesale and retail trade. These two industries employed 48 percent of the county's labor force and headed a list of nonfarm occupations that generated almost $683 million in earnings in 1981. Agricultural receipts in 1982 were $30,491,000.

The changes in the county's economic base were reflected in other areas. The proportion of urban residents in the county continued to increase through the census of 1980, when 64 percent of the county's residents lived in urban areas as defined by the United States Census Office. Texarkana, situated on Interstate Highway 30 and U.S. Highway 82, remained a major market center and the county's largest city. The changing nature of employment opportunities had led to an emphasis on the importance of formal education. In 1950 only 26 percent of all residents of the county over twenty-five had completed high school. By 1980 that figure had risen to almost 60 percent.

Bowie County is home to various types of recreation and entertainment. The Bowie County Courthouse and Jail in Boston is listed in the National Register of Historic Places, along with seven sites in and around Texarkana, including the Draughn-Moore House, the

Offenhauser Building, the Saenger Theater, the Hotel McCartney, the Rialto Building, the Whitaker House, and the Roseburough Lake Site. There are seven major lakes in the county, the largest being the 20,300-acre Wright Patman Lake.[qv] Game and fur animals include deer, squirrel, quail, muskrat, beaver, otter, opossum, mink, ring-tailed cat, badger, fox, raccoon, skunk, and civet cat (*see* FURBEARING MAMMALS). Texarkana supports a museum and a zoo as well as various cultural events sponsored by Texarkana College. Finally, the county serves as a major point of entry into the state of Texas because of its location on Interstate 30. In 1990 the population of Bowie County was 81,665.

BIBLIOGRAPHY: Bowie County Historical Commission, *Bowie County, Texas, Historical Handbook* (Texarkana, Texas: Smart Printing Company, 1976). Barbara S. Overton Chandler, A History of Bowie County (M.A. thesis, University of Texas, 1937). Barbara Overton Chandler and J. E. Howe, *History of Texarkana and Bowie and Miller Counties, Texas-Arkansas* (Texarkana, Texas-Arkansas, 1939). Emma Lou Meadows, *DeKalb and Bowie County* (DeKalb, Texas: DeKalb *News,* 1968). Rex W. Strickland, Anglo-American Activities in Northeastern Texas, 1803–1845 (Ph.D. dissertation, University of Texas, 1937). Vertical Files, Barker Texas History Center, University of Texas at Austin. Tom Wagy, comp., *An Historical Bibliography of Bowie County, Texas and Miller County, Arkansas* (East Texas State University at Texarkana, 1987). *Cecil Harper Jr.*

BOWIE CREEK. Bowie Creek rises in the Brady Mountains six miles south of Lohn in west central McCulloch County (at 31°15′ N, 99°27′ W) and runs southeast for 12½ miles to its mouth on Brady Creek, two miles west of Brady (at 31°09′ N, 99°23′ W). It crosses generally flat terrain with local shallow depressions, surfaced by sandy and clayey loams that support water-tolerant hardwoods, conifers, and grasses.

BOWIE KNIFE. In 1838 Rezin P. Bowie, brother of Alamo hero James Bowie,[qqv] claimed that he made the first Bowie knife while the Bowies lived in Avoyelles Parish, Louisiana. He designed it as a hunting knife and gave it to James for protection after his brother had been shot in a fight. Blacksmith Jesse Clifft, who lived on Bayou Boeuf and was a close friend and neighbor of the Bowies in the 1820s, forged the knife according to Rezin Bowie's design. The original Bowie knife was like a butcher knife in profile, with a thin blade but no silver mounts. Bowie wore it in a silver-mounted black-leather sheath. The Bowie knife gained widespread notoriety after the celebrated Sandbar Fight on September 19, 1827, near Natchez. On that date Samuel Levi Wells and Dr. Thomas Maddox engaged in a duel on the first large sandbar above Natchez on the Mississippi state side of the river. After firing pistols at each other without effect, Wells and Maddox shook hands and started off the field. But members of the Maddox group suddenly fired at Wells's followers, who included James Bowie. Bowie fell, shot through a lung. An archenemy, Norris Wright, along with Alfred Blanchard, stabbed him repeatedly with swordcanes. Bowie raised himself, grabbed Wright, and sank the big knife into his assailant's heart, killing him instantly. Combatants and eyewitnesses described the "large butcher knife" in letters and interviews, and a legend began. Newspapers across the nation printed lurid and detailed stories of the Sandbar Fight. The public reveled in the prowess of James Bowie and his lethal weapon. In a day when pistols frequently misfired, the Bowie knife was a perfect backup. As its popularity spread, schools were established, especially in the old Southwest, to teach the arts and dodges of Bowie knife fighting. Later, W. W. Bowie, a kinsman, wrote that James Bowie gave his Sandbar Fight knife, the first Bowie knife, to the famous actor Edwin Forrest, whom Bowie had met in New Orleans in February 1824.

In 1828, some months after the Sandbar Fight, James Bowie made a trip to the East. In Philadelphia he apparently placed his knife in the hands of Henry Schively, a cutler. His brother Rezin wanted a high-quality knife drawn on the lines of the first, complete with a fancy silver sheath. Rezin wore the knife for several years, his initials R. P. B. engraved on the pommel cap. In 1831 he gave the knife to a friend, Jesse Perkins, of Jackson, Mississippi. The Clifft knife is the immediate progenitor of the classier Schively knife. Rezin Bowie basked in the glory surrounding his brother James and the knife. He regularly wore a silver-mounted Bowie, which he eventually presented to a friend, usually an important individual. He had several knives made by Daniel Searles of Baton Rouge, Louisiana, in the 1830s. Rezin presented the Searles knife now displayed in the Alamo to H. W. Fowler, United States Dragoons. Fowler's name is engraved on the sheath.

Early Bowie knives do not fit the popular image of the weapon. One thinks of a blade with a concave arch (clip point) cut into the end of the blade, and a cross-guard to protect the hand. Early examples, however, had a thick, heavy butcher-knife-like blade, with a straight back (top) and no clip point or hand guard. The blade varied in length from 8½ to 12½ inches and was sharpened on the true edge. Wooden handles were attached with silver pins and washers. The Searles knives of the 1830s were one-piece ebony, checkered, and decorated with small silver nails. Blacksmiths fashioned most of the subsequent Bowie knives and added rudimentary crossguards to keep the hand from sliding onto the blade. Eventually, they lengthened the guards as protection from an opponent's blade, but the owner often found the extended guards clumsy and cut them off. The clip point, a curve on the top of the blade back of the point, became popular. The clip was often sharpened so that a backstroke would inflict a serious wound. Spear-point Bowie blades also were forged, dagger-shaped, with both edges sharpened. Blacksmith-made Bowies were generally plain and unsigned, had iron (or brass) mountings, and hardwood, bone, or horn handles. The knife was both a hunting knife and a tool. With it, one could clear a path, hack a sapling, dig a hole, or butcher game. In the siege of Bexar[qv] in 1835, Texans used Bowie knives to dig through roofs and walls and engage in hand-to-hand combat with the Mexicans. The knife was not designed or balanced for throwing.

Southerners replaced their swordcanes with Bowie knives, and sought expert cutlers, North and South, to craft fine blades. The cutlers usually were surgical and dental instrument makers in large cities. Most signed their works; Peter Rose and John D. Chevalier were prominent in New York, English & Huber and Clarenbach & Herder in Philadelphia, Reinhardt in Baltimore, Thomas Lamb in Washington, Dufilho in New Orleans, Alfred Hunter in Newark, Marks and Rees in Cincinnati, Daniel Searles in Baton Rouge, and Rees Fitzpatrick in Natchez. Henry Schively also made improved versions in various styles. English cutlers in Sheffield, who had dominated the American cutlery market since colonial times, took advantage of the fascination with the Bowie knife. They capitalized on vivid reports by English journalists of murder and mayhem in America involving the weapon. A trickle of Sheffield Bowie knives in the early 1830s developed into a flood before the Civil War.[qv] Bowie knife collections indicate that only about one in ten was American made. English cutlers applied clever motifs and blade etchings that appealed to American tastes and patriotic spirit. Examples include such labels as "American Bowie Knife," "Texas Ranger Knife," "Arkansas Toothpick," "Patriot's Self Defender," "Death to Abolition," "Death to Traitors," "Americans Never Surrender," "Rio Grande Camp Knife," and "I'm A Real Ripper." Handle and guard mountings also carried symbols and slogans with American appeal. Cutlers attached handles of ivory, pearl, tortoise shell, black and gray buffalo horn, India stag horn, and fine woods. Handle pommels of nickel silver featured horseheads, shells, and geometric designs. Manufacturers generally signed their blades and added such distinctive trademarks as I*XL, B4ANY, and XCEED. At the outbreak of the Mexican War[qv] in 1846, the Bowie knife was a popular weapon in Texas. Texas Rangers[qv] under Jack (John Coffee) Hayes and Ben McCulloch[qqv] carried Bowie knives and Colt dragoon pistols into battle. Knife blades stamped and etched with Mexican War motifs appeared. Zachary Taylor,qv mounted on Old Whitey, was a favorite subject. Bust etchings included "Old Zach," "General Taylor Never Surrenders," "Palo Alto," and "Buena Vista." Pommels featured a Taylor bust with a patriotic slogan.

In the late 1830s an alarmed public in several Southern states demanded stringent laws to curtail the increasing "rule of the Bowie knife." In January 1838 the Tennessee legislature passed "An Act to Suppress the Sale and Use of Bowie Knives and Arkansas Toothpicks in this State." However, the sale of the knives continued to accelerate, reaching a peak after the Civil War. During that war, crude Bowie knives were popular among Confederate soldiers. Some had large, wide blades, like those of artillery shortswords; most were unmarked. The Confederates considered the knife an essential accoutrement in the early months of the war, but as the conflict wore on the knife was replaced with the bayonet. The knives had hickory or hardwood handles and iron mounts, and were worn in heavy leather sheaths with throats and tips of tin, iron, or brass. Blades had scratch engravings and crude acid etchings, with such patriotic motifs as "Sunny South," "Confederate States Defender," or "Death to Yankees." A few Confederate Bowie knives were made by experienced cutlers and exhibited excellent workmanship. Union soldiers generally wore Sheffield-made Bowie knives.

"In the history of American arms," wrote historian Harold L. Peterson (1958), "three weapons stand out above all the rest: the Kentucky rifle, the Colt's revolver, and the Bowie knife." Each became a part of the "great American Legend." The popularity of the Bowie was established in the 1830s, expanded during the 1840s, and reached its peak in the 1850s. After the Civil War the knife diminished in favor, and by the mid-1870s was relegated to use as a hunting knife. The efficiency, reliability, and wide distribution of Colt revolversqv retired the Bowie knife from its prominent role in the nation's history.

BIBLIOGRAPHY: Avoyelles Parish Courthouse Records, Marksville, Louisiana. James L. Batson, *James Bowie and the Sandbar Fight* (Madison, Alabama: Batson Engineering and Metalworks, 1992). Walter W. Bowie, *The Bowies and Their Kindred: A Genealogical and Biographical History* (Washington: Cromwell Brothers, 1899). Harold Leslie Peterson, *American Knives: The First History and Collectors' Guide* (New York: Scribner, 1958). Vertical Files, Barker Texas History Center, University of Texas at Austin. William R. Williamson, *Bowie Knife, Dirk and Dagger: Articles* (1979).

William R. Williamson

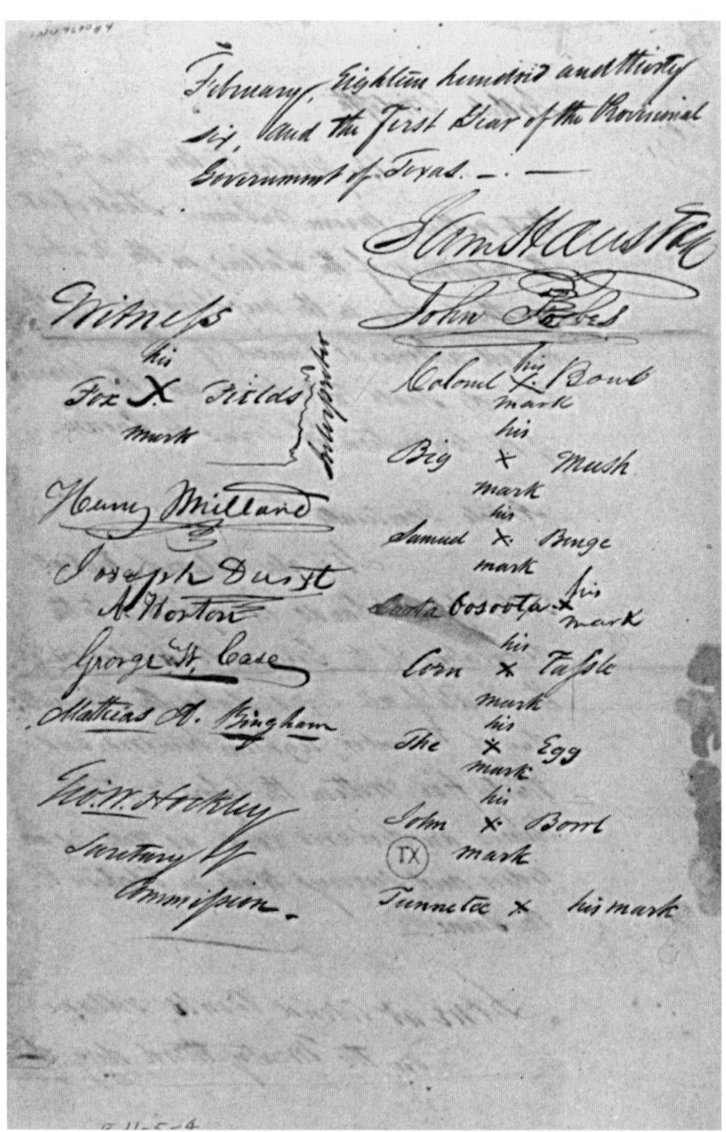
February, Eighteen hundred and thirty six, and the First Year of the Provisional Government of Texas. —

Sam Houston

John Forbes

Witness

his Fox X Fields mark — interpreter

Colonel his X Bowl mark

his Big X Mush mark

his Samuel X Benge mark

Henry Millard

Joseph Durst

A. Horton

George W. Case

Mathias A. Bingham

Geo. W. Hockley Secretary of Commission

[illegible] Bosorota his X mark

his Corn X Tassle mark

his The X Egg mark

his John X Bowl mark

Tunnetee X his mark

Treaty of February 23, 1836, signed by Sam Houston, Cherokee chief Bowl, and others at Bowl's village on Caney Creek, about nine miles north of Henderson. Courtesy TSL. This treaty gave Bowl's tribe and others the right to live and farm between the Angelina and Sabine Rivers.

BOWIE MOUNTAIN. Bowie Mountain, 5½ miles southwest of Oxford in southern Llano County (at 30°32′ N, 98°44′ W), has an elevation of 1,483 feet above sea level and rises 200 feet above Ranch Road 965 to the southeast. The surrounding terrain is flat to rolling to steep and is surfaced with soils ranging from deep sandy and clay loams to shallow and stony cover. Open stands of live oak, mesquite, and juniper grow in the area.

BOWIEVILLE, TEXAS. Bowieville was a farming community on Farm Road 457 twelve miles southeast of Bay City in eastern Matagorda County. It was probably named for nearby Lake Bowie. In 1936 Bowieville had about ten dwellings but no businesses. By 1949 the community was within the Van Vleck Independent School District, and by 1978 Bowieville was no longer shown on the county highway map.

BIBLIOGRAPHY: Matagorda County Historical Commission, *Historic Matagorda County* (3 vols., Houston: Armstrong, 1986).

Stephen L. Hardin

BOWL (ca. 1756–1839). Chief Bowl (also known as Duwali, Diwal'li, Chief Bowles, Colonel Bowles, Bold Hunter, and the Bowl), the principal chief of the Cherokees in Texas, was born in North Carolina around 1756. He was the son of a Scottish father and a full-blooded Cherokee mother. Duwali was leader of a village at Little Hiwassee (in western North Carolina). In 1791 he signed the Treaty of Holston, and in 1805 he signed an unauthorized cession treaty, a move that proved unpopular with the majority of Cherokees. In early 1810, to access better hunting ground and to escape growing pressures of settlement in the southern states, he and his band moved across the Mississippi River and settled in the St. Francis River valley, near New Madrid, Missouri. In 1812–13 his people moved into northwestern Arkansas, south of the Arkansas River, and in 1819 they once more moved on, stopping briefly in southwestern Arkansas and at the three forks of the Trinity River before settling north of Nacogdoches. In Texas Chief Bowl became the primary "civil" chief or "peace chief" of a council that united several Cherokee villages. In 1822 he sent diplomatic chief Richard Fieldsqv to Mexico to negotiate with the Spanish government for a land grant or title to land occupied by Cherokees in East Texas. In 1827 he cooperated with the Mexican government in putting down the Fredonian Rebellion.qv In 1833 he made another attempt to secure from the Mexican government land on the Angelina, Neches, and Trinity rivers, but negotiations were interrupted by political unrest in Texas. In February of 1836 Sam Houston[qv] negotiated a treaty with Bowl's council, guaranteeing the tribe possession of lands occupied in East Texas. After the Texas Revolution,[qv] however, the treaty was invalidated by the Senate of the Republic of Texas.[qv] In desperation, Bowl briefly allied with agents soliciting allies for a Mexican reinvasion of Texas. Shortly thereafter, President Mirabeau B. Lamar[qv] ordered him and his people to leave Texas. After negotiations failed, Bowl mobilized his warriors to resist expulsion. On July 16, 1839, Chief Bowl was killed in the battle of the Neches.[qv] On this site, the scene of the last engagement between the Cherokees and whites in Texas, the state of Texas erected a marker in 1936.

BIBLIOGRAPHY: Mary Whatley Clarke, *Chief Bowles and the Texas Cherokees* (Norman: University of Oklahoma Press, 1971). Dianna Everett, *The Texas Cherokees: A People between Two Fires, 1819–1840* (Norman: University of Oklahoma Press, 1990). Dorman Winfrey, "Chief Bowles and the Texas Cherokees," *Chronicles of Oklahoma* 32 (Spring 1954). E. W. Winkler, "The Cherokee Indians in Texas," *Quarterly of the Texas State Historical Association* 7 (October 1903). Albert Woldert, "The Last of the Cherokees in Texas and the Life and Death of Chief Bowles," *Chronicles of Oklahoma* 1 (June 1923).

Dianna Everett

BOWLES, WILLIE DEE (1912–?). Willie Bowles, teacher and early historian of the woman suffrage[qv] movement, was born on February 4, 1912, to Gordon and Beatrice (Cosper) Worley in Piedmont, Alabama. She attended school in Auburn, Alabama, and Rock Hill, South Carolina. She matriculated at Sam Houston State Teachers' College (now Sam Houston State University), Huntsville, Texas, in 1926 and received her bachelor of arts degree in 1931. From 1931 to 1934 Mrs. Bowles taught English and Spanish at the high school in Alief, Texas. Between 1934 and 1939 she taught history at the Senior High School in Harlingen, Texas. In 1934 she enrolled in the graduate school at the University of Texas at Austin, where she received her master's degree in 1939. Her thesis, History of the Woman Suffrage Movement in Texas, was one of the first to be written on the subject.

Alicia A. Garza

BOWLES CREEK (Cherokee County). Bowles Creek rises two miles southeast of Rusk in south central Cherokee County (at 31°47′ N, 95°06′ W) and runs southwest for fifteen miles to its mouth on the Neches River, two miles southwest of Weeping Mary (at 31°35′ N, 95°10′ W). The stream, which is intermittent in its upper reaches, traverses flat to gently rolling terrain surfaced by clay and sandy loams that support mixed hardwoods and pines. The creek was probably named for Chief Bowl,[qv] a leader of the Cherokees in East Texas.

___ (Rusk County). Bowles Creek, intermittent in its upper reaches, rises a mile south of Overton in a marshy area of northwestern Rusk County (at 32°15′ N, 94°59′ W) and flows south twelve miles to its mouth on Johnson Creek, four miles south of Price (at 32°01′ N, 94°59′ W). It repeatedly crosses the Cherokee-Rusk county line. It was probably named for Chief Bowl,[qv] a Cherokee leader. The stream traverses flat terrain with local shallow depressions, surfaced by sandy and clay loams in which pine and hardwood forests grow.

BOWLES SPRINGS. Bowles Springs is three miles northwest of Alto in southern Cherokee County (at 31°41′ N, 95°06′ W). The springs were named for Chief Bowl, the leader of a band of Cherokees who lived in the area from 1819 to 1839. A treaty that assigned the land along the Angelina River to the Cherokees was signed by Sam Houston[qv] and Chief Bowl at the springs in 1837. The treaty, however, was rejected by the Republic of Texas[qv] Senate, and shortly thereafter President Mirabeau B. Lamar[qv] ordered the Indians to leave Texas. When the Cherokees chose to fight rather than leave, many of them were killed, including Bowl. A granite monument now marks the site of the Indian village. The flow from the springs was measured at a rate of 1½ quarts per second in November 1979. The surrounding terrain is rolling to flat and is surfaced by sandy and clay loams that support mixed hardwoods and pines.

BIBLIOGRAPHY: Gunnar Brune, *Springs of Texas,* Vol. 1 (Fort Worth: Branch-Smith, 1981).

Gunnar Brune

BOWLING, CHARLES TAYLOR (1891–1985). Charles T. Bowling, painter and lithographer active in the pre–World War II group of Regionalist artists known as the Dallas Nine,[qv] was born in June 1891 in Quitman, Texas, the fifth of eight children born to Robert W. and Grace Elizabeth (Long) Bowling. Shortly after Robert Bowling's death in 1900, the family moved to Dallas, where Charles attended public schools and worked part-time. Although he never completed high school, he cultivated his artistic skills through a series of sign-painting and draftsman jobs and began a forty-nine-year career as a draftsman and civil engineer for Texas Power and Light Company in 1916. He and Sadie Britt were married in Dallas around 1915; they had three sons and a daughter.

Bowling began studying fine art at age thirty-five, when a long convalescence at home left him with free time to sketch and paint. He subsequently studied with Olin H. Travis[qv] at the Dallas Art Institute[qv] and then pursued independent studies with Frank E. Klepper and Alexandre Hogue.[qqv] Bowling developed a highly finished, realistic style that featured rural landscapes and urban scenes; he favored a subtle palette of grey, ochre, rust, and cool blue-green. He exhibited his work at the Dallas County Allied Arts Exhibition from 1930 to 1943, winning numerous purchase prizes and awards. During the Great Depression[qv] he befriended the Dallas circle of Regionalist artists and helped such artists as Otis M. Dozier and William Lester[qqv] get drafting jobs. Bowling exhibited his work at the Texas Centennial[qv] Exposition (1936), the New York World's Fair (1939), and the Golden Gate Exposition (1939) and was honored with solo exhibitions at the Hockaday Junior College (1939) and the Dallas Museum of Fine Arts (1941).

Bowling was a charter member and president of the Lone Star Printmakers, a print circuit operated from 1938 to 1942 by a number of Dallas Regionalist artists. Bowling found his métier in lithography, and he quickly emerged as one of the dominant talents in the group. In 1941 he acquired a lithographic press and began printing his own and other artists' work. He mastered a technique characterized by compositional clarity, rich textural range, and skillful gradation of tones that reinforced the lonely, somber mood of many of his landscape prints, which generally included just one or two figures, if any. Frequently he invested inanimate objects such as the twisting limbs of a tree or a telephone pole with expressive pathos. He also favored urban scenes that focused on the "side where the seams are," featuring Dallas Little Mexico in such prints as *Industrial Encroachment* (1939).

Bowling exhibited his work in Pennsylvania, in New York, and throughout the South and Southwest during the following years. He was a member of the Dallas Art Association, the Dallas Print Society, the Klepper Art Club, the Texas Fine Arts Association,[qv] and the Southern States Art League; he served on the board of directors of the TFAA. He continued to produce art until 1959, when his failing vision forced him to stop. He retired from Texas Power and Light in 1965 and died of a heart attack at the C. C. Young nursing home in Dallas on July 27, 1985. He was buried at Restland Memorial Park. In recognition of his friendship with Jerry Bywaters,[qv] Bowling's family donated twenty-six of his lithographs to the Jerry Bywaters Collection of Art of the Southwest at Southern Methodist University, which organized an exhibition of his work, The Lithographs of Charles T. Bowling (1891–1985), in 1991. Bowling's works are also included in the

Trailerville, *by Charles T. Bowling, 1940. Lithograph.* $12\frac{3}{8}'' \times 14\frac{3}{4}''$. *Photograph by George Holmes. Courtesy Archer M. Huntington Art Gallery, University of Texas at Austin; gift of Charles and Dorothy Clark, 1982.*

collections of the Witte Museum,[qv] San Antonio, the Archer M. Huntington Art Gallery[qv] at the University of Texas at Austin, the Museums of Abilene,[qv] and the Dallas Museum of Art.[qv]

BIBLIOGRAPHY: Dallas *Morning News,* July 29, 1985. Rick Stewart, *Lone Star Regionalism* (Austin: Texas Monthly Press, 1985). Texas Artists File, Bywaters Collection, DeGolyer Library, Southern Methodist University.
Kendall Curlee

BOWMAN, JESSE (1785–1836). Jesse Bowman, Alamo defender, was born in Tennessee in 1785. By 1811 he was in Illinois, where he made his living as a trapper and hunter. His son Joseph was born in Illinois. Bowman, his wife, and three children became the first known settlers of Camden, Ouachita County, Arkansas, in 1824. Four years later they moved to Hempstead, Arkansas. In the 1830s Bowman, his son, and his brother and nephews immigrated to Texas and received land in Red River County. Bowman and his son served in the Texas army during the Texas Revolution.[qv] As a member of the Alamo garrison, Bowman died in the battle of the Alamo[qv] on March 6, 1836.

BIBLIOGRAPHY: Daughters of the American Revolution, *The Alamo Heroes and Their Revolutionary Ancestors* (San Antonio, 1976). Files, Daughters of the Republic of Texas Library, San Antonio. Bill Groneman, *Alamo Defenders* (Austin: Eakin, 1990).
Bill Groneman

BOWMAN, JOHN J. (1807–1890). John J. Bowman, a member of Stephen F. Austin's[qv] Old Three Hundred,[qv] was born in Rutherford County, Tennessee, on August 15, 1807, the eldest of four children of Joseph and Mary (Richmon) Bowman. The family moved to New Madrid, Missouri, and lived there until their home was destroyed by an earthquake in 1811. From there they moved to Natchez, Mississippi. In the spring of 1822, Bowman and his father arrived in the Matagorda Bay area of Texas with the Austin colonists. He and Henry Williams,[qv] both single men, were paired together and granted a league of land on the east bank of the Colorado River about five miles above its mouth. Due to the hardships of the country, Joseph Bowman returned to his home in Natchez.

On October 3, 1835, John Bowman joined a company commanded by George M. Collinsworth[qv] in Matagorda County. They marched to Goliad and assisted in its capture (*see* GOLIAD CAMPAIGN OF 1835). Bowman remained there three months under the command of Philip Dimmitt[qv] and was later appointed a first lieutenant in the artillery under the command of James W. Fannin, Jr.[qv] While stationed at Goliad, Bowman signed the Goliad Declaration of Independence.[qv] At the end of the revolution, he was honorably discharged from the army and awarded 320 acres of land for his services.

He was married before 1831 to Amanda Eliza Rawls, a daughter of Amos Rawls.[qv] After she died he married her cousin Eliza, a daughter of Daniel Rawls,[qv] on September 13, 1840, in Nacogdoches. The couple moved to Tensas Parish, Louisiana, in the mid-1840s and purchased a 2,800-acre plantation, where they raised ten children and remained until the Civil War.[qv] After the fall of Vicksburg, Bowman burned his cotton, left with his family and slaves, and eventually moved to Cherokee County, Texas. He died on March 30, 1890; his wife died on December 23 of the same year. Both were buried in Mount Hope Cemetery, near Wells, Texas. Bowman was a member of the Methodist Episcopal Church and was instrumental in building the first church building in southern Cherokee County.

BIBLIOGRAPHY: DeWitt Clinton Baker, comp., *A Texas Scrap-Book* (New York: Barnes, 1875; rpt. 1887; facsimile rpt., Austin: Steck, 1935). Harvey Frost Bowman, The Joseph Bowman Family (MS, Genealogy Department, Texas State Library, Austin, 1976). Original Land Grant Collection, Texas General Land Office, Austin. *Frost Bowman*

BOWMAN, JOHN TIBAUT (1883–1937). John Tibaut Bowman, government official and businessman, the son of Mollie (Tibaut) and Thornton Hardie Bowman,[qv] was born in Belton, Texas, on September 8, 1883. He attended public schools in Belton. He served as private secretary for Oscar B. Colquitt[qv] before Governor Colquitt appointed him secretary of state in 1912, a position he held for less than a year. In 1915 Bowman was awarded a medal for distinguished service with the Pan American exposition in San Francisco. He married Gladys Greenless in Corsicana in 1916. They had three sons. During the later years of his life he owned a successful municipal bond business, Bowman-Roche and Company. He was a director of American National Bank, Acme Life Insurance Company, and Union Standard Life Insurance Company of Dallas. He was also the first president of the Texas Investment Bankers Association. Bowman was active in numerous civic organizations. He was a Methodist. He died on May 9, 1937, and was buried in Austin Memorial Park.

BIBLIOGRAPHY: Austin *American*, May 10, 1937. Austin History Center Files. Ellis A. Davis, and Edwin H. Grobe, comps., *The New Encyclopedia of Texas*, 4-vol. ed. *Laurie E. Jasinski*

BOWMAN, JOSEPH WYLIE (1887–1943). Joseph Wylie Bowman, transportation developer, one of five children of Joseph Strong and Annie (Brakebill) Bowman, was born on January 16, 1887, near Knoxville, Tennessee. The family moved to Texas in 1895, and young Joe attended country schools near Greenville in Hunt County and Rotan in Fisher County. He was assistant cashier of the Cowboy State Bank in Rotan for three years, after which he operated a grocery store and then established the Bowman Automobile Company, which sold Studebakers, in Greenville. In 1923 Bowman and his partner, Jess C. Levens, were among the first to bring busses to Texas; they bought the chassis in Detroit and had the bodies mounted on them in Bellefontaine, Ohio, before driving them to Texas. Two years later Bowman sold his automobile business and bought rights to operate busses on five schedules between Fort Worth and Dallas. In 1929 he moved to Lubbock and bought South Plains Coaches, a bus line that traveled on the unpaved roads from Lubbock to Sweetwater. From four drivers on this line eventually grew Texas, New Mexico, and Oklahoma Coaches, Incorporated, which operated fourteen lines over more than 10,000 miles a day, from Western Oklahoma to Carlsbad, New Mexico. Bowman was a member and director of the Texas Motor Transportation Association and a member of the National Bus Owners' Association. He was a Methodist and member of the Lions Club, the Elks, the Knights of Pythias, the Lubbock Chamber of Commerce, and the Lubbock Board of City Development. He helped build the Milam Home for Orphans in Lubbock and was active in other charities. He was an avid sportsman and was recognized as one of the leading horse trainers in the Southwest. His saddle horses and trotters won many trophies and ribbons at shows in West Texas. Bowman married Bula Birdsong in 1909. The couple had no children. He died on December 19, 1943, and is buried at Greenville, Texas.

BIBLIOGRAPHY: Seymour V. Connor, ed., *Builders of the Southwest* (Lubbock: Southwest Collection, Texas Technological College, 1959). Reference File, Southwest Collection, Texas Tech University.

Lawrence L. Graves

BOWMAN, SARAH (ca. 1812–1866?). Sarah Bowman, commonly known as the Great Western or the Heroine of Fort Brown, legendary camp follower of the Mexican War,[qv] hotelkeeper, and sometime prostitute, was born Sarah Knight in 1812 or 1813, but whether in Tennessee or Clay County, Missouri, is unclear. She acquired several husbands during the course of her travels, many without benefit of clergy, so there is considerable confusion about her surname. In various sources and at different times she is referred to as Mrs. Bourjette, Bourget, Bourdette, Davis, Bowman, Bowman-Phillips, Borginnis, and possibly Foyle. A mountain of a woman who stood six feet two inches tall, she picked up the nickname Great Western, probably in a reference to the contemporary steamship of that name, which was noted for its size. John Salmon Ford[qv] wrote that she "had the reputation of being something of the roughest fighter on the Rio Grande and was approached in a polite, if not humble, manner." Little is known about Sarah before the Mexican War. Rumors claim that she was with Zachary Taylor's[qv] forces during the Seminole Wars, but her

The "Great Western" as Landlady, *by Samuel E. Chamberlain. From Chamberlain's manuscript My Confession, in the West Point Museum, United States Military Academy. Courtesy Summerlee Foundation, Dallas. This is the only known likeness of Sarah Bowman, the "Great Western."*

first substantiated appearance occurred in 1845, when she accompanied her husband, a soldier in the Eighth United States Infantry qv and a member of Taylor's army of occupation, to Corpus Christi. At that time the wives of enlisted men could enroll with the army as cooks and laundresses and follow their husbands into the field. Among these camp followers was the Great Western, who cooked for appreciative officers. Sarah first distinguished herself as a fighter at the crossing of the Arroyo Colorado in March 1846, when she offered to wade the river and whip the enemy singlehandedly if Gen. William Jenkins Worth qv would lend her a stout pair of tongs. The legends surrounding her exploits grew during the bombardment of Fort Brown in May 1846, when she refused to join the other women in an underground magazine but calmly operated her officers' mess uninterrupted for almost a week, despite the fact that a tray was shot from her hands and a stray shell fragment pierced her sunbonnet. Her fearlessness during the siege earned her another nickname, the Heroine of Fort Brown. She traveled with the army into the interior of Mexico and opened a hotel in Saltillo, the American House, where she again demonstrated her bravery during the battle of Buena Vista by loading cartridges and even carrying some wounded soldiers from the battlefield to safety. During this period she was married to her second husband, known variously as Bourjette, Bourget, and Bourdette, a member of the Fifth Infantry. Sarah apparently remained in Saltillo as a hotelkeeper until the end of the war, but in July 1848 she asked to join a column of dragoons that had been ordered to California. By this time her husband was probably dead, and she was told that only married women could march with the army. Undaunted, she rode along the line of men asking, "Who wants a wife with fifteen thousand dollars and the biggest leg in Mexico? Come, my beauties, don't all speak at once. Who is the lucky man?" After some hesitation a dragoon named Davis, probably David E. Davis, stepped forward, and the Great Western once again marched with the army.

In 1849 Sarah arrived in El Paso and briefly established a hotel that catered to the flood of Forty-niners traveling to the gold fields. She leased the hotel to the army when she left for Socorro, New Mexico, with a new husband, Albert J. Bowman, an upholsterer from Germany. When Bowman was discharged on November 30, 1852, the couple moved to Fort Yuma, where Sarah opened another restaurant. She lived first on the American, then the Mexican, side of the river, to protect her adopted children. By the mid-1860s she was no longer married to Bowman, but she served as company laundress and received an army ration. In 1856 she traveled to Fort Buchanan to set up a hotel ten miles below the fort. She had returned to Fort Yuma by 1861. Although Sarah was well known as a hotelkeeper and restaurateur, she probably had other business interests as well. One chronicler referred to her as "the greatest whore in the West," and Lt. Sylvester Mowry, a soldier stationed at Fort Yuma in 1856, wrote of Sarah that "among her other good qualities she is an admirable 'pimp'." The date of Sarah's death, reportedly caused by a tarantula bite, is unclear, though one contemporary source indicates that she died in 1863. She was buried in the Fort Yuma post cemetery on December 23, 1866, with full military honors. In August 1890 the Quartermaster's Department of the United States Army exhumed the 159 bodies buried at the Fort Yuma cemetery and moved them to the presidio at San Francisco, California. Among these bodies was that of Sarah Bowman.

BIBLIOGRAPHY: J. F. Elliott, "The Great Western: Sarah Bowman, Mother and Mistress to the U.S. Army," *Journal of Arizona History* 30 (Spring 1989). Brantz Mayer, *History of the War between Mexico and the United States,* Vol. 1 (New York and London: Wiley and Putnam, 1848). Ronald Dean Miller, *Shady Ladies of the West* (Los Angeles: Westernlore, 1964). Brian Sandwich, *The Great Western: Legendary Lady of the Southwest* (Southwestern Studies 94, El Paso: Texas Western Press, 1990). Edward S. Wallace, *The Great Reconnaissance: Soldiers, Artists, and Scientists on the Frontier, 1848–1861* (Boston: Little, Brown, 1955). Edward S. Wallace, "The Great Western," *The Westerners: New York Brand Posse Book* (1958). *Regina Bennett McNeely*

BOWMAN, THORNTON HARDIE (1843–1905). Thornton Hardie Bowman, the son of James and Caroline (Dougherty) Bowman, was born at Clinton, Louisiana, on May 29, 1843. He was educated at Collegiate Institute in Louisiana, Southern University in Alabama, and the Lycée Impérial in Tours, France. During the Civil War qv he joined Company A, William Wirt Adams's regiment of Mississippi Cavalry, as a private and participated in battles in Kentucky and Tennessee, where he was taken prisoner but later exchanged. In 1866 he worked as a law student in the office of a judge in Baton Rouge. Sometime in the late 1860s he married Mary Hall; they had two children. In 1871 Bowman moved to Belton, Texas, where he taught school, practiced law, and entered politics. In January 1874 he became a clerk in the Department of State under Richard Coke qv and on April 21, 1874, was promoted to chief clerk in the secretary of state's office. In 1881, after the death of his first wife, he married Mollie Tibaut of Austin and, accompanied by his bride, went as representative of Texas to the Cotton Exposition in Atlanta, Georgia. The couple eventually had four children. From 1881 to 1883 Bowman was secretary of state under Governor Oran M. Roberts. qv He served as a member of the state printing board and the state board of education. For his health he moved to a ranch in West Texas. During the 1890s he was twice elected county judge of Howard County and once as county attorney of Howard, Glasscock, and Dawson counties. He also lectured throughout Texas emphasizing the concerns of Confederate veterans. In January 1899 he was appointed superintendent of the State Orphans' Home in Corsicana (*see* CORSICANA STATE HOME). Bowman was a Methodist and a Democrat. He died on November 7, 1905, and was buried in Austin.

BIBLIOGRAPHY: Thornton Hardie Bowman, *Reminiscences of an Ex-Confederate Soldier, or Forty Years on Crutches* (Austin: Gammel-Statesman, 1904). *Annabyrd Bowman Davis*

BOWMAN CREEK. Bowman Creek rises 1½ miles south of Sand Creek and 1½ miles northwest of Kurten in Brazos County (at 30°48′ N, 96°17′ W) and runs southeast for twelve miles to its mouth on the Navasota River, which there forms the Brazos-Grimes county line, 4½ miles southeast of Reliance (at 30°43′ N, 96°10′ W). The creek rises in flat to rolling terrain; downstream, the land is a flat floodplain with shallow depressions. The local vegetation, growing in sandy and clayey loams, changes from pine and hardwood forest upstream to water-tolerant hardwoods downstream.

BOWSER, OLIVER P. (1842–1915). Oliver P. Bowser, businessman and legislator, son of David and Mary A. (Bookwalter) Bowser, was born in Montgomery County, Ohio, on March 21, 1842. The family moved to Dallas County, Texas, in 1856. Bowser enlisted as a private in Company E, Eighteenth Texas Cavalry, in 1861, and rose to lieutenant; he fought in the battles of Franklin and Nashville under John Bell Hood. qv In 1873 he and W. H. Lemmon became partners in an implement company, acquired considerable land, and developed the Oak Lawn section of Dallas. Beginning in 1892 Bowser served one term in the Texas House of Representatives, one four-year and two two-year terms in the state Senate, and another term as representative. He wrote the Dallas County road law, the county auditor law, and a Texas house-insurance measure. He was president of the Texas Good Roads Association and the Texas Manufacturers Association. qv In July 1866 he married Virginia L. Murray. He died in Dallas on December 15, 1915, and was buried in Grove Hill Cemetery.

BIBLIOGRAPHY: Frank W. Johnson, *A History of Texas and Texans* (5 vols., ed. E. C. Barker and E. W. Winkler [Chicago and New York: American Historical Society, 1914; rpt. 1916]). *Memorial and Biographical History of Dallas County* (Chicago: Lewis, 1892; rpt., Dallas:

Walsworth, 1976). William S. Speer and John H. Brown, eds., *Encyclopedia of the New West* (Marshall, Texas: United States Biographical Publishing, 1881; rpt., Easley, South Carolina: Southern Historical Press, 1978).

BOWSER, TEXAS. Bowser is near the intersection of Farm roads 45 and 765, nine miles north of Richland Springs in northwestern San Saba County. The community was established by residents who got flooded out of the nearby community of Bowser Bend. The Bowser post office operated from 1892 to 1921. The Martin gin began operating in Bowser in 1891 and continued to run there for about fifty years. Bowser had a population of 100 in 1896, when it also had a cotton gin, a school, a gristmill, and Methodist, Baptist, and Christian churches. By the early 1930s Bowser had two businesses and a population of twenty-four, and by the late 1940s its population had risen to fifty. The Bowser Community Church was still at the site in 1983.

BIBLIOGRAPHY: *San Saba County History* (San Saba, Texas: San Saba County Historical Commission, 1983). *Karen Yancy*

BOWSER BEND, TEXAS. Bowser Bend was in a bend of the Colorado River twenty-four miles northwest of San Saba in northwestern San Saba County. The community, founded about 1875, developed around a gin owned by James Monroe Locker and a store managed by his sons. A post office, named in honor of A. Bowser, was established there in 1887 by Simeon Whitted in his home. In the late 1880s a fire destroyed the Bowser school. It was soon rebuilt, this time on higher ground to avoid the floods that occasionally struck the community. By 1892 Bowser Bend had a population of 150 and a general store, a mill-gin, a physician, a justice, and a constable. In 1893 its post office was discontinued. After the local gin was moved, Bowser Bend residents began to move to nearby Bowser. A church and various school buildings remained at the townsite in the 1980s, when the school, then the focus of a restoration project, served as headquarters for an annual summer homecoming celebration.

BIBLIOGRAPHY: *San Saba County History* (San Saba, Texas: San Saba County Historical Commission, 1983). *Karen Yancy*

BOX, JOHN ANDREW (1803–1874). John Andrew Box, Methodist preacher and soldier in the Texas Revolution,[qv] was born in Franklin County, Tennessee, on July 2, 1803, a son of Stephen F. and Keziah Box. He was married twice, first to a Miss Allbright, with whom he had four children, and then to Lucenda Yarbrough, with whom he had nine children. Box moved to Texas in 1834 and received a league of land in Joseph Vehlein's[qv] colony, in what is now Houston County. He enlisted in Capt. Hayden S. Arnold's[qv] First Company of Col. Sidney Sherman's[qv] Second Regiment, Texas Volunteers, on March 5, 1836, and served at the battle of San Jacinto.[qv] He was discharged on May 30, 1836. Box was an early circuit rider for the Methodist Church[qv] but discontinued his preaching after San Jacinto. On April 22, 1837, he, his father and brothers, and 102 others from Mustang Prairie petitioned Congress to establish a constitutional county, and Houston County became the first county formed by the Republic of Texas.[qv] In 1861 Box served as a delegate to the Secession Convention.[qv] He died on August 2, 1874.

BIBLIOGRAPHY: Armistead Albert Aldrich, *The History of Houston County, Texas* (San Antonio: Naylor, 1943). Sam Houston Dixon and Louis Wiltz Kemp, *The Heroes of San Jacinto* (Houston: Anson Jones, 1932). E. W. Winkler, ed., *Journal of the Secession Convention of Texas* (Austin, 1912). *Edna Box Riley*

BOX, JOHN CALVIN (1871–1941). John Calvin Box, judge, legislator, and Methodist minister, was born near Crockett, Texas, on March 28, 1871. He attended rural schools in Houston County and subsequently studied law at the Alexander Institute (*see* LON MORRIS COLLEGE) in Kilgore. He was admitted to the bar in 1893 and practiced law in Lufkin for a time before moving to Jacksonville in 1897. From 1898 to 1901 he was county judge of Cherokee County, and from 1902 to 1905 he served as mayor of Jacksonville. Box was active in Democratic party[qv] affairs and for a number of years was Democratic committee chairman for Cherokee County and a member of the Democratic State Executive Committee; he also served as a delegate to the Democratic state conventions in 1908 and 1910. In 1918 he was elected to the House of Representatives, where he served from 1919 to 1931 and gained recognition for his work to uphold the national-origins quota system of the 1924 immigration law. Box was appointed to the first board of trustees of Southern Methodist University. He married Mina Hill of Lufkin on June 1, 1893; the couple had two children. After his retirement from Congress, he returned to Jacksonville and practiced law. He died there on May 17, 1941.

BIBLIOGRAPHY: Sam Hanna Acheson, Herbert P. Gambrell, Mary Carter Toomey, and Alex M. Acheson, Jr., *Texian Who's Who,* Vol. 1 (Dallas: Texian, 1937). *Biographical Directory of the American Congress.* Dallas *News,* May 18, 1941. Vertical Files, Barker Texas History Center, University of Texas at Austin. *Anne W. Hooker*

BOX, NELSON A. (1808–ca. 1849). Nelson A. Box, settler and soldier, was born in 1808 in Franklin County, Tennessee, a son of Stephen F. and Keziah Box. He moved from Tennessee to Blount County, Alabama, and then to Texas in 1834. He and his wife, Elizabeth (Garner), had several children. After coming to Texas, Box enlisted in the revolutionary army[qv] and fought at the battle of San Jacinto[qv] in Capt. Hayden Arnold's[qv] company. In 1837 he and his father and brothers, along with other citizens of Mustang Prairie, organized Houston County, the first county of the republic. Box died about 1849 and was buried in Box-Beeson Cemetery, three miles south of Crockett.

BIBLIOGRAPHY: Sam Houston Dixon and Louis Wiltz Kemp, *The Heroes of San Jacinto* (Houston: Anson Jones, 1932). Houston County Historical Commission, *History of Houston County, Texas, 1687–1979* (Tulsa, Oklahoma: Heritage, 1979). *Edna Box Riley*

BOX, THOMAS GRIFFIN (1817–1859). Thomas Griffin Box, early settler and soldier, son of Stephen F. and Keziah Box, was born in Franklin County, Tennessee, on January 12, 1817. He was married three times, first to Rachel Wilkerson, then to Amanda Georgia Alexander, and then to Sarah Crowson Massingale. He became a Methodist minister and moved to Texas in 1835. He enlisted in the Texas army as a member of Capt. Hayden S. Arnold's[qv] First Company of the Second Regiment, Texas Volunteers, and fought at the battle of San Jacinto.[qv] In 1837 he and his father and brothers petitioned Congress to establish Houston County, the first county formed by the republic. He died on February 18, 1859.

BIBLIOGRAPHY: Sam Houston Dixon and Louis Wiltz Kemp, *The Heroes of San Jacinto* (Houston: Anson Jones, 1932). Houston County Historical Commission, *History of Houston County, Texas, 1687–1979* (Tulsa, Oklahoma: Heritage, 1979). *Edna Box Riley*

BOX, TEXAS. Box was four miles southeast of the site of what is now Vernon in central Wilbarger County. The settlement was named for the surrounding five-mile-square school district. The school, established there about 1893, became the community center for nearby residents. In 1916 the school's name was changed from Box to East Vernon. A grocery store was built nearby in 1925 but closed in 1931. The school was divided between the Vernon and Oklaunion school districts in 1949. Reunions were held at the old school building, near the intersections of Farm roads 1949 and 433, until 1981.

BIBLIOGRAPHY: Wilbarger County Historical Commission, *Wilbarger County* (Lubbock, 1986). *Charles G. Davis*

BOX CHURCH, TEXAS. Box Church is in the timbered region along McKenzie Creek four miles south of Groesbeck in central Limestone County. It was named for a church established in the community in the 1890s. One of the first schools there was established by Joseph H. Powell in the early 1850s. In 1886 Oscar Williams built the first store at the site. Dwindling population forced the school to consolidate with that of Groesbeck in 1950. In 1988 Box Church had two stores, a trailer-manufacturing plant, and a population of forty-five. The population was still forty-five in the early 1990s.

BIBLIOGRAPHY: Ray A. Walter, *A History of Limestone County* (Austin: Von Boeckmann–Jones, 1959). *Ray A. Walter*

BOX COLONY. Michael James Box, at times a member of the Texas Rangers,[qv] heard a story that a man could make $25,000 a day from the gold in "Red Mountain" near Durango, Mexico. Counterreports did not prevent him from collecting more than 300 followers, including women, children, and his aged parents and leaving Laredo, in March 1861, in search of riches. During the next five months the colonists experienced thirst, extreme fatigue, and the tyranny of Box's leadership. As they neared their destination, the little mining town of Corneta, smallpox broke out, and Box had to obtain medical assistance through the governor of Durango. None of the colonists could speak Spanish, a factor that contributed to their delusion. Box and ten men departed on a fruitless two-week search for Red Mountain. Upon the return of the party, the angry colonists attempted to have the governor of Durango prosecute Box, but the Mexican official refused. Thereafter the colonists broke into confused groups—one man was killed at a fandango, some were too poor to return to Texas, and a dozen went to work in the nearby mines, but most of the Texans returned home. Some of these were murdered en route. Box remained at Corneta as a miner, although other members of his family returned to Texas.

BIBLIOGRAPHY: James P. Newcomb, *Secession Times in Texas* (San Francisco, 1863). *Donald E. Everett*

BOX CREEK (Anderson County). Box Creek rises three miles northeast of Elkhart in southern Anderson County (at 31°40′ N, 95°33′ W) and runs southwest for 16½ miles to its mouth on the Trinity River, just east of Titi Lake (at 31°33′ N, 95°43′ W). The stream is intermittent in its upper reaches. Its banks are heavily wooded in places with mixed pine and hardwood trees, and the surrounding nearly level to moderately steep terrain is surfaced by sandy, clayey, and loamy upland soils. The stream was named for Roland W. Box, who was granted land on its banks in 1835.

___ (Cherokee County). Box (Boxes) Creek rises at the confluence of Bean's Creek and Dement Creek, four miles southwest of Rusk in south central Cherokee County (at 31°45′ N, 95°13′ W), and runs southeast for sixteen miles to its mouth on the Neches River, two miles southwest of Weeping Mary (at 31°35′ N, 95°11′ W). The stream is intermittent in its upper reaches and runs through flat to gently rolling terrain with clay and sandy loam soils in which grow mixed hardwoods and pines.

BOX CREEK, TEXAS. Box (Box's) Creek was an early settlement on Box Creek southeast of Rusk in east central Cherokee County. It was first settled around 1835 by Roland W. Box, who purchased a third of a league of land that had been granted to Stephan Burnham. Box built a small log fort on a bluff west of Box Creek about a half mile from the southeast corner of the Zaccheus Gibbs survey. Box's Fort, as the stockade was called, became the center of a settlement; Box's father, John M. Box, and his brothers—Samuel C., William, James, and John A.—built houses nearby. A local post office operated from 1851 to 1866, and the county's first Grange[qv] was organized at Box Creek in 1874. Over the years there were several churches and stores in the area, but a permanent settlement was never established, and by 1900 the community was no longer shown on maps. In the early 1990s only a few scattered houses remained in the area.

BIBLIOGRAPHY: *Cherokee County History* (Jacksonville, Texas: Cherokee County Historical Commission, 1986). Hattie Joplin Roach, *A History of Cherokee County* (Dallas: Southwest, 1934).

Christopher Long

BOXELDER, TEXAS. Boxelder is 7½ miles south of Annona in southeastern Red River County. The town was named for the trees found along the bottoms of Shawnee and Crooked Branch creeks. Planters started a scattered community at the site between 1840 and 1860. Henry A. Sloan became postmaster when the office was established there in 1885. The community's population was fifty in 1910, and in 1940 it reported two businesses and a population of seventy-five. By 1956 its post office had been closed. In 1986 the population of Boxelder was estimated at seventy-five, and the community reported no businesses. During the early 1990s Boxelder reported a population of more than 250. *Claudia Hazlewood*

BOX QUARTER, TEXAS. Box Quarter, on a mail route from Calvert in western Robertson County, was a supply point for an agricultural community on Walnut Creek. The one-store settlement had a population of twenty in 1940.

BOX AND STRIP CONSTRUCTION. Box and strip construction is an efficient method of erecting small wooden buildings without elaborate frameworks. It consists of using standard-dimension lumber to build houses or other structures in the manner in which a large wooden box was constructed. Box and strip is a simple technique. Supported upon rocks, wooden piers, or a concrete foundation, a floor platform is first assembled with joists, usually two-by-sixes spaced about two feet apart, and wooden flooring. Nailed vertically (rarely horizontally) to the sides of this platform are one-by-twelve boards forming the walls; there are no studs. Then strips, ordinarily one-by-threes or one-by-fours, sometimes with molded edges, are nailed over the cracks between the boards. A two-by-four plate nailed to the top of the boards forming the walls supports the rafters and ceiling joists, also of two-by-fours. Shingles nailed to strips supported by the rafters complete the roof. Openings for doors and windows are framed with two-inch members. A hammer, saw, level, and square are all the tools required for construction.

The historical origins of box and strip construction are presently uncertain, but the technique probably comes from England, where whip-sawn or pit-sawn boards on simple frameworks were used in buildings. In colonial America barns, shops, and other service buildings also had board walls. Eventually box and strip construction was greatly facilitated by mass production techniques of the Industrial Revolution. The efficient manufacture of dimension lumber by power sawmills and the mass production of nails greatly increased the economy of this type of construction. With the extension of the railroads over the treeless prairies and plains, lumber buildings replaced adobe[qv] or sod houses. Although balloon or platform framing with studded walls was generally employed for large houses, box and strip was used for small houses and service buildings.

In Texas box and strip buildings are particularly noteworthy in the treeless Panhandle[qv] and on the South Plains and other westerly regions. While the railroads economically transported lumber to numerous towns, it had to be hauled laboriously by wagon to rural areas; hence the need for efficiency in the use of materials. Often the interiors of box and strip houses were lined with either center-matched siding or beaded ceiling material, installed horizontally, which produced both a more attractive and more air-tight building.

Numerous buildings of many sorts, including churches, have been built with box and strip technique. It was used for a jail erected about 1890 in Floydada and a courthouse built in Leakey about the same time. Several examples of circa 1900 can be seen at the Ranching Heritage Center[qv] in Lubbock, where the Harrel House and the Box and Strip House exemplify the technique. It was also used in the Reynolds-Gentry Barn and the Barfield School, although in the latter the strips were removed, building paper installed, and weatherboards applied on the exterior to decrease drafts.

BIBLIOGRAPHY: Andrew Jackson Downing, *The Architecture of Country Houses* (New York and Philadelphia: Appleton, 1850; rpt., New York: Da Capo Press, 1968). William H. Pierson, Jr., *American Buildings and Their Architects* (Garden City, New York: Doubleday, 1978). Willard B. Robinson, *Gone from Texas: Our Lost Architectural Heritage* (College Station: Texas A&M University Press, 1981). Willard B. Robinson, *The People's Architecture: Texas Courthouses, Jails, and Municipal Buildings* (Austin: Texas State Historical Association, 1983).

Willard B. Robinson

BOX T RANCH. The operation that later evolved into the Box T Ranch began in 1879 when James Monroe Day[qv] arrived from Austin and began grazing cattle on Camp Creek, a tributary of Wolf Creek in southeastern Lipscomb County. His brother Tony had a homestead on Wolf Creek near Fort Supply, Oklahoma, and a brother-in-law, Alexander Young, started the YL Ranch in Beaver County, Oklahoma. In the 1880 census the Day brothers were listed as large operators in Lipscomb County, with livestock valued at $100,000, including 10,000 cattle and 100 horses. Their hired cowhands were paid a total of $6,000 that year. In addition to the Wolf Creek range, the Days also owned grazing land in the disputed Greer County,[qv] Oklahoma. Cattle on both of these ranges carried their DAY brand.

In the summer of 1882 the Days sold their Wolf Creek holdings, including 18,000 cattle, to the Dominion Cattle Company of Canada for $450,000. The new owners moved the headquarters to the Cherokee Outlet in what is presently Ellis County, Oklahoma, and began using the Box T brand and running cattle on range leased from the Indians. That arrangement continued until 1885, when President Grover Cleveland ordered all white ranchers out of Indian Territory. A new headquarters was then constructed on Camp Creek, but until fences were erected grazing continued across the line into the territory. The twin brothers John and Sam Douglas were among the first to arrive and work for the Dominion Company. Lishe Stevens, Gaston Smith, James F. Bryson, and Frank Biggers served successively as foremen. The Box T employees helped sponsor the organization of Lipscomb County in 1886 and attempted to make their proposed townsite of Dominion, in the heart of their range, county seat. That honor went instead to Lipscomb, near the boundary of the neighboring Seven K Ranch. Higgins became the Box T's railhead and supply center. By 1887 the Dominion Company owned roughly 30,000 cattle and 400 horses.

In 1888, after settlers began coming into the area, the Dominion Company sold the Box T to a man named Dameron, who hired Patrick Doyle as range manager. Doyle purchased an interest in the ranch the following year and brought his bride, Harriet, back from his native Canada. By 1900 the Doyles had purchased the remainder of the Box T; they continued to run it on a reduced scale. Their most famous cowhand was George Sennitt, who became legendary for his wild shenanigans. A favorite story with the Doyles' three sons was that Sennitt once challenged Will Rogers, who was working for Perry Ewing's Little Rob Ranch in Oklahoma, to a horse race in Higgins. Bets were quickly made and exchanged among cowboys and townspeople; Rogers won the race by a head. Later, Rogers immortalized Sennitt as the "Irish Lad" in his newspaper columns and radio broadcasts.

After her husband's death, Harriet Doyle married John A. May, who managed the ranch until 1940, when he was killed in an accident in Amarillo. Her sons, Frank and Robert Doyle, then took over management of the Box T. In 1955 Vester L. Smith and Willis Price bought most of the ranch, and Smith became the manager. In 1986 the Doyle family still owned a share of the Box T, the only pioneer ranch extant in Lipscomb County.

BIBLIOGRAPHY: Gus L. Ford, ed., *Texas Cattle Brands* (Dallas: Cockrell, 1936). Laura V. Hamner, *Short Grass and Longhorns* (Norman: University of Oklahoma Press, 1943). *A History of Lipscomb County, Texas, 1876–1976* (Lipscomb, Texas: Lipscomb County Historical Survey Committee, 1976).

H. Allen Anderson

BOXWOOD, TEXAS. Boxwood, on Farm Road 1649 twelve miles northeast of Gilmer in eastern Upshur County, was probably founded in the 1880s or early 1890s. A post office operated there from 1895 to 1906. Around 1900 Boxwood had a population of thirty. In the mid-1930s the community comprised a school, a store, and a number of scattered houses. After World War II[qv] its school was consolidated with the Ore City school, and by the mid-1960s all that remained of Boxwood was a few widely scattered houses.

BIBLIOGRAPHY: Doyal T. Loyd, *History of Upshur County* (Waco: Texian Press, 1987).

Christopher Long

BOY, TEXAS. Boy, originally known as Japan, was on State Highway spur 494 and the Southern Pacific Railroad eighteen miles southeast of Conroe in southeastern Montgomery County. In 1979 the settlement consisted of a railroad station, a school, several churches, and numerous businesses. By that date, however, the community had been overtaken by suburban development between Porter and Humble, four miles to the south.

Will Branch

BOYCE, ALBERT GALLATIN (1842–1912). Albert Gallatin Boyce, general manager of the XIT Ranch,[qv] was born on May 8, 1842, near Austin in Travis County. He served in the Confederate Army throughout the Civil War[qv] and was wounded at the battle of Chickamauga in September 1863. After the war he began rounding up wild, unbranded cattle in Central Texas, and in 1867–68 he drove a herd to California. On December 20, 1870, he married Annie Elizabeth Harris; they had five children.

Boyce began his career with the XIT in 1885, when he served as trail boss for the herds purchased by the Capitol Syndicate from J. W. and D. H. Snyder.[qv] These cattle, which he drove to the Buffalo Springs division, were among the first to arrive at the XIT. Boyce succeeded B. H. Campbell as the ranch's general manager in June 1887 and remained in that position for eighteen years, during which time he made his own fortune. He put his Methodist principles into action by forbidding the cowboys to gamble and carry six-shooters and insisting on the strict observance of Sundays. He was a charter member of the Cattle Raisers Association of Texas (now the Texas and Southwestern Cattle Raisers Association[qv]) and later served as its vice president and on its executive committee. After his retirement from the XIT in 1905, Boyce moved to Amarillo, where, with Benjamin T. Ware,[qv] he helped organize the Amarillo National Bank and became one of its biggest stockholders. At one time he was president of the bank and maintained a palatial residence on Polk Street. Later he organized the Midway Bank and Trust Company at Dalhart and was president of this institution until his death.

He was shot to death on January 13, 1912, in the lobby of the Metropolitan Hotel in Fort Worth by John B. Sneed, an Amarillo rancher whose wife, Lena, had eloped with Boyce's son Al. His body was brought back to Amarillo for interment in Llano Cemetery. Sneed was arrested and subsequently tried in Vernon for the killing, but the jury acquitted him; later, on the night of September 14, 1912, Sneed murdered Al Boyce in Amarillo. Since both the Sneed and Boyce families had friends and relatives in high places, the affair resulted in a bitter feud that simmered on for several years (*see* BOYCE-SNEED FEUD).

BIBLIOGRAPHY: Carl L. Duaine, *The Dead Men Wore Boots: An Account of the Thirty-Second Texas Volunteer Cavalry, CSA, 1862–1865* (Austin: San Felipe, 1966). J. Evetts Haley, *The XIT Ranch of Texas and the Early Days of the Llano Estacado* (Chicago: Lakeside, 1929; rpts., Norman: University of Oklahoma Press, 1953, 1967).

H. Allen Anderson

BOYCE, TEXAS. Boyce, on Farm Road 879 four miles east of Waxahachie in central Ellis County, was named for W. A. Boyce, who settled there in 1872. The settlement was first served by a stagecoach service that operated between Waxahachie and Ennis. In 1878 the Southern Pacific Railroad was constructed through the area, and settlers moved there. By December 1883 a post office was in operation in Boyce, and within ten years the settlement had grown to support five businesses and three churches. By 1925 Boyce's population had reached its recorded high of 250, but the community began to decline soon after. Its post office closed sometime after 1930. The town reported 150 residents and three businesses in 1945 and eighty residents and no businesses in 1964. Its population remained seventy-five, with no reported businesses, from 1977 through 1990.

BIBLIOGRAPHY: Edna Davis Hawkins, et al., *History of Ellis County, Texas* (Waco: Texian, 1972).

Brian Hart

BOYCE-SNEED FEUD. In October 1911, John Beal Sneed, the son of Joseph Tyre Sneed, Sr., placed his wife of twelve years, Lenora (Lena) Snyder Sneed, in Arlington Heights Sanitarium in Fort Worth after Lena confessed her infatuation with Al Boyce, Jr., to him. Sneed and Boyce had vied for Lena's affection when all three were students at Southwestern University[qv] in Georgetown. Sneed's action set off a bizarre series of events that symbolized the tenacity of frontier justice in West Texas in the early twentieth century. Less than a month after her incarceration, with the aid of Al Boyce, Lena escaped from the sanitarium and the pair eloped to Canada. Discovered in Winnipeg, Canada, the two were arrested by the authorities, who released Lena into the custody of her husband and her father, Tom Snyder. Initially, Lena returned to Clayton, New Mexico, with her father. She later returned to her husband. After abduction charges against Boyce were dismissed by a Fort Worth court in early January 1912, Sneed fatally shot Boyce's father, Albert G. Boyce, Sr.,[qv] alleging that the man had assisted his son in breaking up Sneed's home. Sneed's murder trial generated intense interest all over the United States and parts of Canada. Newspapers carried the day-by-day developments. In Fort Worth, the trial produced controversy that led to violence. Four men were killed outside the courthouse, and women fought with hatpins in the courthouse halls and even in the courtroom. After failing to reach a verdict, the jury was dismissed and a mistrial was declared. The jury was split 7 to 5 for acquittal. After the murder of his father in March by a tenant farmer believed to be associated with the Boyces, Beal Sneed shot and killed Al Boyce, Jr., as Boyce was walking in front of Polk Street Methodist Church in Amarillo. Sneed had lain in wait for two weeks in a cottage across from the church, waiting to catch Boyce unaccompanied by his brother Lynn. After firing three blasts of his twelve-gauge shotgun into Boyce, Sneed walked to the courthouse and surrendered himself and his weapon to the Potter County sheriff. Juries acquitted Sneed for both murders, declaring that they were justifiable homicides. A flood of congratulatory letters and telegrams greeted news of the verdicts. But reporters from papers outside of Texas regarded the shootings as cold-blooded murder. When reporters demanded a reason for the acquittal in the murder of Al Boyce, Jr., the jury foreman, James D. Crane, responded by saying, "The best answer is because this is Texas. We believe in Texas a man has the right and the obligation to safeguard the honor of his home, even if he must kill the person responsible."

Sneed, reunited with Lena, moved to Paducah, where he owned a ranch and a cotton farm. He also engaged in land speculation that resulted in further troubles for him. In October 1922, a federal court found him guilty of bribing a juror in a lawsuit concerning a land deal. Judge James C. Wilson sentenced Sneed to two years in Leavenworth Federal Penitentiary. In Sneed's absence, C. B. Berry, a Paducah groceryman and cotton raiser, shot and killed Wood Barton, Sneed's son-in-law, over a money dispute. Sneed, out of prison and dissatisfied with Berry's acquittal, retaliated by shooting Berry five times. Amazingly, Berry survived. Berry then responded by attempting to kill Sneed. Both men were found not guilty at their trials. Despite the acquittal, the Sneeds had worn out their welcome in Paducah, and their fortunes were low when they moved to Dallas. But Sneed recovered by investing in the East Texas oilfield.[qv] He and Lena lived in style in Dallas for more than thirty years. Sneed died of bone cancer on April 22, 1960. Lena died of heart failure on March 6, 1966. They are buried side by side in Hillcrest Cemetery in North Dallas.

BIBLIOGRAPHY: Dallas *Morning News,* January 14, February 8, 1912.

Thomas H. Thompson

BOYD, FRANCES ANNE MULLEN (1848–1926). Frances (Fannie) Boyd, writer, was born in New York City on February 14, 1848. Her father owned a bakery there, and the family was well-to-do. Her mother died when she was quite young, and her father remarried. Frances married Lt. Orsemus Bronson Boyd on October 9, 1867, in New York City. For the next eighteen years she followed her officer-husband, a graduate of West Point, from one duty station to another, making a home for themselves and, eventually, their three children, at frontier posts in Nevada, Arizona, New Mexico, and Texas. Boyd's military career spanned the post–Civil War[qv] Indian wars, years when travel was dangerous and living conditions primitive.

In December 1875 Mrs. Boyd and their daughter and son accompanied Lieutenant Boyd to a new assignment at Fort Clark, Texas. The post, located forty miles from the Rio Grande near the site of present-day Brackettville, guarded the San Antonio–El Paso road. For six months in 1879–80 the Boyds lived at Fort Duncan, a small garrison at Eagle Pass, where troops patrolled the international boundary. After two of the children were stricken with malaria in 1881, Frances Boyd took them all back to New York. The family remained separated while Boyd served at various stations. In 1885 Frances returned to Fort Clark, her husband's current post. Boyd was soon ordered to New Mexico, where he died, on July 23, 1885.

Left a widow at age thirty-seven, Frances Boyd took up residence in Washington, D.C., where she had social connections, and later lived in New York City. Her descendants remember that she traveled extensively in Europe. Her *Cavalry Life in Tent and Field,* a tribute to her husband that describes her experiences in the West as an officer's wife, was published in 1894. It is considered one of the finest of the genre. Early in the new century, perhaps in 1908, she bought a house and land in Boonton, New Jersey, where she lived for the rest of her life. She died in Elizabeth, New Jersey, on May 2, 1926.

BIBLIOGRAPHY: Orsemus B. Boyd File, United States Military Academy Library, West Point, New York. Veterans Administration, Pension Application File, National Archives, Washington.

Darlis A. Miller

BOYD, FRANK DOUGLAS (1867–1929). Frank Douglas Boyd, physician, son of John A. and Amy E. (Harrison) Boyd, was born on Christmas Eve, 1867, at Rusk, Texas. He demonstrated an interest in medicine while attending public school in Cherokee County. After completing his undergraduate work at the Agricultural and Mechanical College of Texas (now Texas A&M University), he left for Kentucky to study medicine at the University of Louisville. He received his degree in 1890 and left for New York, where he did additional study before leaving for San Antonio, Texas. There he established his first medical practice and, on April 21, 1892, married Mattie E. Callaban. The couple had three children, but their two sons did not survive childhood.

In 1897 Boyd moved to Fort Worth and opened an office with Dr.

Charles Head. The two men quickly established a reputation as leading eye, ear, nose, and throat specialists. In addition to his medical practice Boyd lectured on hygiene and physical diagnosis at the medical school of Fort Worth University (now Texas Wesleyan University). Later he joined the staff of Baylor Medical College in Dallas as professor of otolaryngology. To keep abreast of his field he did postgraduate work in Vienna, Berlin, and London. He also found time to volunteer his services as an oculist for the State Masonic Orphans Home in Fort Worth.

Boyd was a member of the American Medical Association and the American Academy of Ophthalmology and Otolaryngology; he was a fellow of the American College of Surgeons. He chaired the Board of Council of the State Medical Association and in 1914 was president of the Texas State Medical Association (*see* TEXAS MEDICAL ASSOCIATION). During the last two decades of his medical practice he was the senior member of Boyd and Boyne Hospital in Fort Worth. In addition, he was a Scottish Rite Mason and Baptist deacon. He continued to practice medicine until he died, after a brief illness, on January 4, 1929. He was buried in Fort Worth.

BIBLIOGRAPHY: Fort Worth *Star-Telegram,* January 5, 1929. Frank W. Johnson, *A History of Texas and Texans* (5 vols., ed. E. C. Barker and E. W. Winkler [Chicago and New York: American Historical Society, 1914; rpt. 1916]). *Memorial and Genealogical Record of Southwest Texas* (Chicago: Goodspeed, 1894; rpt., Easley, South Carolina: Southern Historical Press, 1978). Buckley B. Paddock, *History of Texas: Fort Worth and the Texas Northwest Edition* (4 vols., Chicago: Lewis, 1922). George Plunkett [Mrs. S. C.] Red, *The Medicine Man in Texas* (Houston, 1930). *Texas State Journal of Medicine,* February 1929.

David Minor

BOYD, HENRY ALLEN (1876–1959). Henry Allen Boyd, the first black to hold a clerkship in the San Antonio post office, manager and cofounder of the Nashville *Globe,* was born in Grimes County, Texas, on April 15, 1876, one of nine children of Richard Henry (born Dick Gray) and Hattie (Moore) Boyd. His father, a former slave and Texas cowboy turned Baptist minister, inspired young Henry with an "aggressive concern for race achievement and personal initiative." Henry Allen Boyd began working in the San Antonio post office while still a teenager. He remained there until leaving Texas with his wife and daughter around 1896. The family settled in Nashville, Tennessee, where Boyd's father was secretary of the National Baptist Convention's Home Mission Board and had founded a publishing firm. Boyd joined his father in Nashville and began working for the National Baptist Publishing Board. He became an ordained Baptist minister in 1904. When the elder Boyd died in 1922, Henry carried on the work of the publishing facility.

An unsuccessful black boycott against the Nashville streetcars in 1905 inspired men such as Boyd to establish the Nashville *Globe,* the "only secular black newspaper" in the city. The editorial tone of the *Globe* combined "Booker T. Washington economic self-help philosophy, and an uncompromising sense of black pride." Boyd's concern with the progress of African Americans led to other business ventures. The National Baptist Church Supply Company manufactured and marketed church furniture from the publishing facility's physical plant. The National Negro Doll Company produced dolls with the plant's machinery. Boyd noted in the *Globe,* "When you see a Negro doll in the arms of a Negro child then you know that the child is being taught a lesson in race price and race development which will not result in race suicide."

Boyd's efforts resulted in the founding in 1911 of the Tennessee Agricultural and Industrial State Normal School with money from the Morrill Act. The Tennessee Normal, Agricultural, and Mechanical Association was formed to lobby for Tennessee A&I (now Tennessee State University) in Nashville. The school emphasized industrial education, although teacher training soon became a significant part of the program. Boyd's father founded the One Cent Savings Bank and Trust Company (now Citizens Savings Bank and Trust Company), the original black bank in Nashville. Boyd took over control of the institution upon his father's death, and from his position as chairman entered into a variety of business enterprises, including the purchase of stock in Jacksonville, Florida, real estate. He also bought stock in the Standard Life Insurance Company of Atlanta and the Supreme Liberty Life Insurance Company of Chicago, which he served as a director and director emeritus. After two major surgeries Boyd succumbed to pneumonia, on May 23, 1959, leaving behind a daughter, two sisters, and a brother. His funeral was held on June 3 in Mount Olive Baptist Church, Nashville; the burial followed at Greenwood Cemetery.

BIBLIOGRAPHY: Lester C. Lamon, *Black Tennesseans, 1900–1930* (Knoxville: University of Tennessee Press, 1977). Rayford W. Logan and Michael R. Winston, eds., *Dictionary of American Negro Biography* (New York: Norton, 1982). *Peggy Hardman*

BOYD, ISABELLE (1844–1900). Isabelle (Belle) Boyd, actress and Confederate spy, was born on May 9, 1844, in Martinsburg, Virginia (now West Virginia), to Benjamin Reed and Mary Rebecca (Glenn) Boyd. Her varied career brought her to Texas at least twice—first to perform in Houston and Galveston theaters, and later to settle temporarily in Dallas. She graduated from Mount Washington Female College at the age of sixteen in 1860. The following year, after shooting a Union soldier who broke into her home and gleaning information from the sentries who temporarily guarded her, she began smuggling notes to Confederate officers. Later she served as a courier for generals Pierre G. T. Beauregard and Thomas J. (Stonewall) Jackson and their subordinates. Belle was apprehended aboard ship in May 1864, while carrying dispatches to Confederate agents in England, and banished to Canada. But she subsequently reached England, where, in August of the same year, she married Samuel Wylde Hardinge, the Union naval ensign assigned to guard her after her capture. In 1865 she published an account of her wartime activities, *Belle Boyd in Camp and Prison.*

Soon widowed and left with a small daughter, she went on stage in England in 1866. That same year she made her United States debut in St. Louis and soon afterward adopted the stage name Nina Benjamin. In fall 1868 she performed in several plays in Houston, having contracted with Maurice and Henry Greenwall[qv] to appear at their stock houses in Houston and Galveston. However, a disagreement between Henry Greenwall and members of the acting company led to cancellation of the bookings. With new manager Thomas P. Ochiltree,[qv] Belle proceeded to Austin, where she gave a series of dramatic readings. When the new year arrived, she left the state.

On March 17, 1869, she retired from the stage to marry John Swainston Hammond. They moved to California, where she suffered a mental collapse and gave birth to a son in a Stockton insane asylum. At Mount Hope, near Baltimore, she was treated, recovered, and was discharged in 1870. She had three more children with Hammond, a traveling salesman, and the family moved to various cities around the country before settling in 1883 in Dallas.

The marriage was dissolved on November 1, 1884. Two months later Belle married twenty-four-year-old Nathaniel Rue High of Toledo, Ohio, a stock-company actor, and in order to support her family she returned to the stage with High as her business manager. She debuted in Toledo on February 22, 1886, with a dramatic narrative of her own exploits as a Confederate spy. Until her death she toured the country, performing her show in a Confederate uniform and cavalry-style hat. Belle Boyd died at the Hile House in Kilbourn (now Wisconsin Dells), Wisconsin, on June 11, 1900, and was buried there at Spring Grove Cemetery. Her fashionable house on Pocahontas Street in Dallas, which she sold on July 29, 1887, was razed in 1963.

BIBLIOGRAPHY: *Dictionary of American Biography.* Ruth Scarborough, *Belle Boyd: Siren of the South* (Macon, Georgia: Mercer University Press, 1983). Louis A. Sigaud, *Belle Boyd* (Richmond, Virginia:

Dietz, 1944). *Webster's American Military Biographies* (Springfield, Massachusetts: Merriam-Webster, 1978). *Joan J. Perez*

BOYD, JOHN (1796–1873). John Boyd, legislator, the son of Abram Boyd, was born near Nashville, Tennessee, in 1796. The family moved to Kentucky, but Boyd returned as a young man to Tennessee, where he married Elizabeth McLean in Maury County and settled in Trigg County. The couple had nine children, six of whom died in childhood. Boyd and his family moved to Texas in the fall of 1835 and settled in Sabine County. Though no record of his military service is extant, he is said to have participated in the Texas Revolution.[qv] From October 1836 through May 1838 he represented Sabine County in the House of the First and Second congresses of the Republic of Texas.[qv] He moved from Sabine to Robertson County in 1845 and then to Limestone County, where he located a claim near the Tehuacana Hills. Boyd was a strong supporter of secession[qv] and represented the Nineteenth Senatorial District in the Ninth Legislature (1862–63). He was a Cumberland Presbyterian. He gave 1,100 acres and a cash donation for the founding of Trinity University at Tehuacana. Boyd died in Limestone County in 1873.

BIBLIOGRAPHY: *Memorial and Biographical History of Navarro, Henderson, Anderson, Limestone, Freestone, and Leon Counties* (Chicago: Lewis, 1893). Texas House of Representatives, *Biographical Directory of the Texan Conventions and Congresses, 1832–1845* (Austin: Book Exchange, 1941). *Cecil Harper, Jr.*

BOYD, RICHARD HENRY (1843–1922). Richard Henry Boyd, Baptist leader, publisher, and entrepreneur, was born into slavery as Dick Gray on March 5, 1843, at the B. A. Gray plantation in Noxubee County, Mississippi. His mother, Indiana Dixon, had six other boys and three girls. In 1849 Gray began a plantation near Brenham in Washington County, Texas. Boyd worked there until the outbreak of the Civil War[qv] and then accompanied Gray as a servant in one of the Confederate armies fighting around Chattanooga, Tennessee. After Gray and his two eldest sons were killed near Chattanooga, Boyd carried the youngest son, who was badly wounded, back to the Texas plantation. Boyd took charge of the plantation and became an efficient manager in the production and sale of cotton. He traded cotton successfully in Mexico. After emancipation (*see* JUNETEENTH) he continued to trade cotton, then began work as a cowboy. He later worked as a laborer at a sawmill in Montgomery County. In 1867 he changed his name from Dick Gray to Richard Henry Boyd.

He began to educate himself after emancipation with Webster's *Blue-Backed Speller,* McGuffey's *First Reader,* and the assistance of white friends. In 1869 he entered Bishop College at Marshall, married Hattie Moore, and in the latter part of the year was ordained a Baptist minister. He did not remain at Bishop College long enough to complete his degree. In 1870 he organized six churches into the first black Baptist association in Texas. In 1876 black Texas Baptists selected Boyd as their representative to the Centennial Exposition in Philadelphia. He also served as secretary of the Missionary Baptist General Convention in Texas and as its superintendent of missions in Texas. While serving in these positions he promoted the idea of publishing literature for black Baptist Sunday schools. He brought out his first pamphlets in 1894 and 1895. During Boyd's residence in Texas he established churches at Waverly, Old Danville, Navasota, Crockett, Palestine, and San Antonio.

In 1896 participants at the National Baptist Convention in St. Louis elected Boyd secretary of home missions in the United States. In this position he fostered the development of four Panamanian churches during the construction of the Panama Canal. He served as secretary of home missions until 1914. In 1905 he served as a delegate to the World Baptist Alliance meeting at London. He moved to Nashville, Tennessee, in 1896 and founded the National Baptist Publishing Board in January 1897. The board issued the first series of Baptist literature for blacks ever published. Boyd and his followers received the assistance of influential white friends to finance the venture. The National Baptist Publishing Board soon developed into the main source of religious literature for black Baptists throughout the world. In its first eighteen years, the publishing board issued more than 128 million periodicals. Its physical plant was valued at over $350,000 in 1912.

Boyd was also an organizer of the Citizens Savings Bank and Trust Company of Nashville and served as its first president, from 1904 until 1922. In 1906 he became the first president of the Nashville Globe Publishing Company and financed the publication of the Nashville *Globe.* He also founded the National Baptist Church Supply Company and the Negro Doll Company, which were housed at the plant of the National Baptist Publishing Board. The National Baptist Church Supply Company manufactured and sold church furniture. The Negro Doll Company began distributing black dolls in 1911. The National Negro Business League listed Boyd as a member for life.

In 1915 the National Baptist Convention split over the question of whether to incorporate. E. C. Morris led the move for incorporation, while Boyd opposed it. Boyd feared that incorporation would alter the voluntary nature of Baptist organizations and give the convention legal control over all entities identified with it, including his own enterprises. Morris's faction formed an incorporated convention, while Boyd's followers formed an unincorporated convention and retained control of the National Baptist Publishing Board. The incorporated convention filed an unsuccessful suit to take control of the publishing board.

Boyd wrote or edited fourteen books, including *Baptist Catechism and Doctrine* (1899), *National Baptist Pastor's Guide* (1900), *National Jubilee Melody Songbook* (n.d.), and, at the request of the National Baptist Convention, *The Separate or "Jim Crow" Car Laws, or Legislative Enactments of Fourteen Southern States* (1909). Boyd's compilation of Jim Crow legislation included an introduction that urged blacks to make legal protests wherever separate accommodations were not equal as provided by law.

Richard and Hattie Moore Boyd had nine children. Their most prominent child was Henry Allen Boyd,[qv] who managed almost all of his father's ventures and was an influential teacher, civic leader, and businessman in Tennessee. Boyd suffered a cerebral hemorrhage on August 19, 1922, and died at his Nashville home on August 2. Masonic rites were held for him on August 26. On August 27, 1922, 6,000 people attended a public service for him in the Ryman Auditorium at Nashville. He is buried in Greenwood Cemetery, Nashville, Tennessee.

BIBLIOGRAPHY: *The Afro-American Texans* (San Antonio: University of Texas Institute of Texan Cultures, 1975). Andrew Webster Jackson, *A Sure Foundation and a Sketch of Negro Life in Texas* (Houston, 1940). Rayford W. Logan and Michael R. Winston, eds., *Dictionary of American Negro Biography* (New York: Norton, 1982). Charles H. Wesley and Patricia W. Romera, eds., *International Library of Negro Life and History* (11 vols., New York: Publishers Company, 1968). *Nolan Thompson*

BOYD, WILLIAM RUFUS, JR. (1885–1959). William Rufus Boyd, Jr., banker and chairman of the War Council of the Petroleum Industry during World War II,[qv] the son of Judge William R. and Lizzie (Self) Boyd, was born in Fairfield, Freestone County, Texas, on January 7, 1885. He attended Fairfield public schools and after high school was employed as a printer at the Fairfield Recorder. He then attended Metropolitan Business College in Dallas and later studied law at George Washington University in Washington, D.C. He received his law license at age nineteen. Boyd was subsequently appointed secretary to Congressman Scott Field,[qv] who represented Freestone and Limestone counties. He served for two years in Washington before moving in 1906 back to Freestone County, where he became the first mayor of Teague at the age of twenty-one. He soon moved to Eddy, McLennan County, where he organized the Farmers and Merchants State Bank and was its president for two years. He was the Texas representative of the National Citizens League for the Promotion of a Sound Banking System and later served as a member of the Dallas investment firm of Philip, Boyd, and Company. At the outbreak of World War I[qv] he served in Chicago as the regional manager of the Chamber of Commerce of the United States. After the war he was the national campaign manager for the League to Enforce Peace, an organization led by former President William Howard Taft, which sought support for United States membership in the League of Nations.

Boyd joined the American Petroleum Institute in 1920 and served as vice president from 1928 to 1941 and as president from 1941 to 1949. During World War II he was chairman of the War Council of the Petroleum Industry, a national war service agency that delegated petroleum resources to the war effort. In 1946 President Harry S. Truman conferred upon Boyd Presidential Medal of Merit, the highest government decoration possible for a civilian, for his service during the war.

Boyd married Gertye Watson of Fairfield on May 17, 1906, and they had one child. From 1950 to 1959 he devoted his time to civic, patriotic, charitable, and religious organizations. He was a member of the Texas Turnpike Authority from 1955 to 1959 and founded the Methodist Men's Club in Teague. Boyd died on November 6, 1959, in Teague and was buried in Arlington National Cemetery. In 1969 a Texas state historical marker was erected for Boyd in Teague.

BIBLIOGRAPHY: Freestone County Historical Commission, *History of Freestone County, Texas* (Fairfield, Texas, 1978). Vertical Files, Barker Texas History Center, University of Texas at Austin.

Chris Cravens

BOYD, TEXAS. Boyd is on State Highway 114 seven miles south of Decatur in southern Wise County. In the early 1890s farmers settled at the site, in the curve of the North Fork of the Trinity River. The community was originally referred to as Greasy Bend because the area was used to fatten hogs. After the Rock Island line reached the town in 1893, the settlement was renamed Parkhurst in honor of a railroad official. The community received a post office branch in September 1893. Sometime later, railroad officials complained that Parkhurst might become confused with Park Springs, a town just down the line, and Parkhurst citizens selected the name Boyd for their town, in honor of H. S. Boyd, another railroad executive. The Boyd community incorporated in 1895 and soon became a retail point for area farmers. Until the 1940s cotton and livestock were the area's principal agricultural products; afterward Boyd became a center for melons. In the late 1950s the town began to serve as a bedroom community for citizens working in Fort Worth. Its population increased from 496 to 525 between 1940 and 1960 and grew steadily thereafter. In 1990 Boyd reported a population of 1,041 and forty-five businesses.

BIBLIOGRAPHY: Rosalie Gregg, ed., *Wise County History* (Vol. 1, n.p: Nortex, 1975; Vol. 2, Austin: Eakin, 1982). *David Minor*

BOYD RANCH, TEXAS. Boyd Ranch was a dispersed rural community of black farmers about two miles south of Cheapside, Gonzales County, and fourteen or fifteen miles north of Cuero in north central DeWitt County. Its residents worked as sharecroppers on a large ranch belonging to a Mr. Boyd. During the 1920s the community had a school but no church. Residents attended Mount Enon Baptist Church in Dement, four miles north of Cheapside in Gonzales County. The community had a cemetery close to the Guadalupe River. Boyd Ranch was not shown on the 1936 county highway map.

Mary M. Standifer

BOYDS CHAPEL, TEXAS. Boyds Chapel is at the intersection of U.S. Highway 180 and Farm Road 126, in west central Jones County. The site was settled in the early 1890s and named for Alex Boyd. A school was built there in 1895. Various faiths met in a church built by the Methodists until the Baptists also built a church. A local school district was established in 1927, but some years later the school closed. Boyds Chapel had a store from 1916 until sometime after 1947.

BIBLIOGRAPHY: Hooper Shelton and Homer Hutto, *The First 100 Years of Jones County* (Stamford, Texas: Shelton, 1978).

William R. Hunt

BOYDSTON, TEXAS. Boydston, near Interstate Highway 40 and the Donley county line twenty-four miles south of Pampa in southwestern Gray County, began in northern Donley County. Henry S. Boystun was the first settler in the area. A post office named Boydston opened in 1891. In 1903 the Chicago, Rock Island and Gulf Railway built through the area and constructed a siding just across the county line from the settlement; the community's post office was subsequently moved to the new Gray County location. Sources disagree upon whether the town was named for Boystun or for H. S. Boyd, an official of the railroad. John Fraser had opened a general store in Boydston by 1910. In 1930 the community had a store and a population of ten. By 1941 it reported two businesses and a population of forty, figures that remained stable through 1964. After 1940 local residents' mail was sent through Groom. The completion of Interstate Highway 40 led to the community's demise. By 1980, when the railroad ceased operations there, only a cow shed and two abandoned grain elevators remained at the site.

BIBLIOGRAPHY: Arthur Hecht, comp., *Postal History in the Texas Panhandle* (Canyon, Texas: Panhandle-Plains Historical Society, 1960). *H. Allen Anderson*

BOYLAN, JAMES D. (?–?). James D. Boylan became commander of the *Passaic* on August 28, 1836, and used the ship in defensive operations with the Texas Navy,[qv] which bought it, recommissioned it, and renamed it the *Viper.* Boylan was commissioned captain on November 12, 1836. On May 22, 1837, he was nominated for commandant of the Texas Navy, but the nomination was postponed and, on June 1, 1837, was rejected. In July 1837 he was with the fleet off the Yucatán coast and on July 24 went ashore at Chilbona. He explored the main islands in the Alacráns, hoisted the Texas flag, and took possession in the name of the government. In September he was commended for his services by Samuel Rhoads Fisher,[qv] secretary of the navy. On October 4, 1837, the Senate, hearing that Boylan, then captain of the *Brutus,*[qv] had been authorized to depart on a cruise, ordered his arrest. In December, President Sam Houston[qv] explained that he had retained Boylan because he had recruited the crew for the *Brutus* and his dismissal would occasion too much unrest in the navy. On April 10, 1839, Boylan applied to President Mirabeau B. Lamar[qv] for appointment to the navy, but apparently his request was not granted, for he went to Yucatán and was commander of the Yucatán flotilla in May 1842 when it cooperated with the Texas fleet against Mexico.

BIBLIOGRAPHY: William Campbell Binkley, ed., *Official Correspondence of the Texan Revolution, 1835–1836* (2 vols., New York: Appleton-Century, 1936). Jim Dan Hill, *The Texas Navy* (New York: Barnes, 1962). Amelia W. Williams and Eugene C. Barker, eds., *The Writings of Sam Houston, 1813–1863* (8 vols., Austin: University of Texas Press, 1938–43; rpt., Austin and New York: Pemberton Press, 1970). *L. W. Kemp*

BOYLE, ANDREW MICHAEL (1818–1871). Andrew Michael (Andrew A.) Boyle, settler and soldier, was born Andrew Michael O'Boyle, the son of Hugh and Maria (Kelly) O'Boyle, in County Mayo, Ireland, on September 29, 1818. At his confirmation he changed his name to Aloysius, and later in life he dropped the O' from O'Boyle. After his mother's death his father deserted the family.

He and his siblings immigrated to New York in 1832, and in 1834 the family moved to Texas and helped found San Patricio. On January 7, 1836, Boyle joined Ira J. Westover's[qv] battery of the first company of regular artillery in the Texas army. He fought with James W. Fannin, Jr.,[qv] and was wounded at Goliad and taken prisoner. He was spared from the Goliad Massacre[qv] by order of Gen. Francisco Garay[qv] because of the kindness of Boyle's sister to Garay at San Patricio. Boyle was given a passport and a parole, taken to Matamoros, and released to go the United States. After the Texas Revolution[qv] he traded on the Gulf of Mexico for four years and then started a store near Red River, Louisiana. In 1846 he married Elizabeth Christi in New Orleans. Evidently he joined the gold rush to California, for in 1851 he was in Boston to buy boots and shoes for his store in San Francisco. In 1858 he moved to Los Angeles, where he operated a shoe store and bought land for his home and a vineyard. Boyle Heights, in East Los Angeles, was named for him. He died in Los Angeles on February 9, 1871.

BIBLIOGRAPHY: Andrew A. Boyle, "Reminiscences of the Texas Revolution," *Quarterly of the Texas State Historical Association* 13 (April 1910). Harbert Davenport, Notes from an Unfinished Study of Fannin and His Men (MS, Harbert Davenport Collection, Texas State Library, Austin; Barker Texas History Center, University of Texas at Austin). Daughters of the Republic of Texas, *Muster Rolls of the Texas Revolution* (Austin, 1986). Rachel Bluntzer Hébert, *The Forgotten Colony: San Patricio de Hibernia* (Burnet, Texas: Eakin Press, 1981).

Jeanette H. Flachmeier

BOYNTON, BENJAMIN LEE (1898–1963). Ben Boynton, football player, was born on December 6, 1898, in Waco, Texas, the son of Charles Albert and Laura Bassett (Young) Boynton. He began his football career as quarterback at Waco High School, where he was an all-round sports star (1913, 1914, 1915).

At a time when the sports focus was on eastern collegiate football, Boynton attended Williams College, where during his sophomore year his kickoff returns placed him high among top contenders for national recognition. He played quarterback on an undefeated Williams team and was selected as one of the members of the All-Eastern eleven. At the close of the 1917 season the International News Service placed him on its All-American team. He thus became the first Texan named to an All-American team. He left school in 1918 and became a gunnery sergeant in the marine aviation corps during World War I.[qv] In 1919 he returned to Williams, where he achieved legendary status in eastern collegiate football. Harvard, Yale, and Princeton all lost to Williams College in 1917, 1919, and 1920.

Boynton was named to Frank Menke's All-American teams for three seasons. He was one of the few players listed as three-time All-American by the Official Football Guide in 1919 and 1920. He was described as one of the best drop-kickers ever and a fine field general and open-field runner. He tied an all-time record for the longest scoring run by any method (110 yards) when he ran out a long punt return in the 1920 game against Hamilton College. He was also classed as one of the first great passers in football.

After graduation Boynton worked for Bethlehem Steel Company in Steeltown, Pennsylvania, and was on the professional football circuit for four years with five different teams. At one time he played on two teams at the same time—the Frankfort Yellow Jackets on Saturdays and the Buffalo All-Americans on Sundays. In professional football he was considered second only to Jim Thorpe in all-round football ability; he was also described as a "brainy" fellow who could do anything.

Boynton organized the Southwest Football Officials Association in 1926 and officiated at college and high school games until 1939, when he became a sportscaster for Southwest Conference[qv] games. He served as a navy lieutenant commander during World War II.[qv] He was a longtime president of the Texas Golf Association and a Dallas insurance executive. He died in Dallas on January 23, 1963, and was survived by his wife, Katherine. Boynton was elected to the College Football Hall of Fame in 1962. He was also named to the Texas Sports Hall of Fame.[qv]

BIBLIOGRAPHY: Dallas *Morning News,* January 24, 1963. Dallas *Times Herald,* January 23, 24, 1963. Vertical Files, Barker Texas History Center, University of Texas at Austin.

BOYNTON, CHARLES ALBERT (1867–1956). Charles Albert Boynton, Republican party[qv] leader and judge, the son of Alpheus S. and Jane Grannis (Cook) Boynton, was born on November 26, 1867, in East Hatley, Quebec, Canada. He received a B.S. degree from Glasgow (Kentucky) Normal University in 1888 and an LL.B. degree from the University of Michigan in 1891, the year he was admitted to the State Bar of Texas[qv] and began practice in Waco. He married Laura Bassett Young on November 1, 1897; they had three sons. Boynton was a delegate to the Republican national convention of 1900 and in 1904 was chairman of the Texas delegation to the national convention in Chicago. He was appointed a United States district attorney by Theodore Roosevelt in June 1906 to succeed Edwin H. Terrell,[qv] of San Antonio, and was reappointed by William H. Taft in 1910. Boynton had supported Taft at the 1908 Republican national convention. He was the Texas Republican gubernatorial candidate against William P. Hobby[qv] in 1918. In 1924 President Calvin Coolidge appointed Boynton to the federal bench at El Paso, where he served until he retired in 1947. He lived in Dallas from 1947 until his death in 1956. Judge Boynton was an Episcopalian and had been active in Waco civic affairs until his elevation to the bench.

BIBLIOGRAPHY: Sam Hanna Acheson, Herbert P. Gambrell, Mary Carter Toomey, and Alex M. Acheson, Jr., *Texian Who's Who,* Vol. 1 (Dallas: Texian, 1937). Paul D. Casdorph, *A History of the Republican Party in Texas, 1865–1965* (Austin: Pemberton Press, 1965). E. W. Winkler, *Platforms of Political Parties in Texas* (Austin: University of Texas, 1916).

Paul D. Casdorph

BOYNTON, CHARLES MILTON (1836–1901). Charles Milton Boynton, teacher and editor, son of William and Harriet (Curtis) Boynton, was born on April 25, 1836, on the St. Francis River near Sherbrooke, Quebec, Canada. He lived for a time in Iowa, Illinois, and Kentucky before he moved to Texas, where he taught school in Rusk and Houston counties before the Civil War.[qv] During the war he returned to Kentucky and entered into a mercantile business with his brother at Millersburg, where, on March 12, 1862, he married Sarah Louise Irvin; the couple had three sons and three daughters. Boynton later taught in Carlisle and London, Kentucky, and in Atlanta, Illinois. In August 1875 he moved to Hamilton, Texas, and in January 1877 he and J. S. Sparkman bought the Hamilton *Herald,* which Boynton eventually owned alone and he continued to edit throughout his life. In 1881 Boynton became assistant to the secretary of the Senate; he was later secretary. He also served as examiner of candidates for admission to the state normal schools for his district. He died at Hamilton on March 8, 1901, and was buried there; his wife died on January 4, 1902. His son, George H. Boynton, took over management of the Hamilton *Herald.*

BIBLIOGRAPHY: Lewis E. Daniell, *Texas—The Country and Its Men* (Austin?, 1924?). Frank W. Johnson, *A History of Texas and Texans* (5 vols., ed. E. C. Barker and E. W. Winkler [Chicago and New York: American Historical Society, 1914; rpt. 1916]).

Jeanette H. Flachmeier

BOYNTON, EDWIN CURTIS (1871–1949). Edwin Curtis Boynton, minister, son of Julius Nelson and Maria (Irvin) Boynton, was born at Millersburg, Kentucky, on February 6, 1871. The family moved to Hamilton County, Texas, in 1881 and engaged in sheep raising. Boynton attended Add-Ran Christian College at Thorp Spring and returned to Kentucky to study in the College of the Bible of Transylvania University. On December 27, 1891, he delivered his first formal sermon in the Old Cane Ridge Meeting House, which had been the site of a great religious revival in 1801. Boynton began his Texas ministry at Seymour, where he married Alice Lewis on December 26, 1896. Their son, Paul Lewis Boynton, was born during his pastorate at Llano. In March 1899 Boynton became pastor of the First Christian Church at Huntsville and was later the minister at Whitewright and at the University Church of Texas Christian University, located at that time in Waco. He did graduate work at the University of Chicago and held pastorates at Huntsville, at North Dallas Christian Church, and at Belton before entering YMCA work during World War I.[qv] Boynton was State Prelate of Knights Templar of Texas, a director of the Huntsville-Walker County Hospital, and a trustee of the Juliette Fowler Homes[qv] for Orphans and Aged. After World War I he returned to preach at Huntsville. He was given a Doctor of Divinity Degree by Texas Christian University on June 1, 1936, and was pastor emeritus of the First Christian Church there at the time of his death on February 28, 1949.

BIBLIOGRAPHY: Texas Legislature, *Senate Journal* (Austin, 51st Legislature, 1949). Walker County Genealogical Society and Walker County Historical Commission, *Walker County* (Dallas, 1986).

J. L. Clark

BOYNTON, TEXAS. Boynton was on the Texas and New Orleans Railroad ten miles southeast of Huntington in southeastern Angelina County. The settlement was founded in 1904 by the Boynton Lumber Company, which built a sawmill at the site. The mill had a daily capacity of 25,000 board feet and at its height employed seventy-five men. The company closed the mill in 1908, and within a short time the town was abandoned. In the early 1990s only a few scattered houses remained in the area.

BIBLIOGRAPHY: Angelina County Historical Survey Committee, *Land of the Little Angel: A History of Angelina County, Texas,* ed. Bob Bowman (Lufkin, Texas: Lufkin Printing, 1976).

Christopher Long

BOY SCOUTS. Texas and the Southwest projected the idea of its rugged, picturesque frontier life on the imaginations of the Boy Scout movement's founders, who relayed it to the youth they hoped to influence. In the serialized book that introduced scouting in 1908, *Scouting for Boys,* British lieutenant general R. S. S. Baden-Powell told tales of Red Indians and army scouts. As a child playing in a London park, he dreamed of living with the Indians on the Texas plains and shooting buffalo.[qv] American author, illustrator, and naturalist Ernest Thompson Seton wrote to a Panhandle[qv] Scout troop in 1915, "Some of my best days were spent riding in the Panhandle. It is a glorious country, one of the best in the World for Scouting." The boys of Texas (and adults interested in their well-being) responded eagerly to the new movement. Based solely on the popularity of Baden-Powell's book, and before a national organization had been started, groups of boys began Scout activities in troops and small groups in 1908, 1909, and 1910. The claims of several troops to be the first organized in Texas, whether before or after the incorporation of the Boy Scouts of America on February 8, 1910, are difficult to verify. BSA archives do show that the thirty-seventh registered scoutmaster in the country was a Texan, Rev. George W. Sheafor, of Comanche, in 1910. Community leaders recognized the benefits of scouting and organized local councils throughout the state. By 1928 Scout councils in the following cities, organized in the years shown, covered Texas: San Antonio and Austin, 1912; Houston and Colorado City, 1913; El Paso, 1917; Paris and Port Arthur, 1918; Beaumont, Corpus Christi, Dallas, Fort Worth, Galveston, and Texarkana, 1919; Wichita Falls, 1920; Amarillo and Brownwood, 1921; Abilene, Lubbock, Sweetwater, and Tyler, 1922; Sherman and Waco, 1924; Eastland, Harlingen, San Angelo, and Uvalde, 1926; Pampa, 1928.

From earliest days, boys of all races and creeds found scouting available to them in Texas. Black youth formed a troop in Port Arthur as early as 1916. The BSA report to Congress for 1930 named Dallas as one of the southern cities in which scouting was growing in the black community. A special training course for Scout leaders was held that year at Prairie View. Hispanic boys were also active in scouting, often in units with non-Hispanic boys. Jewish youth had been active in scouting in San Antonio for many years before a synagogue sponsored a troop for them in 1924. Texas business and civic leaders have strongly supported Scouting, including Frank W. Wozencraft[qv] (the "Boy Mayor" of Dallas), Lloyd Bentsen, Dolph Briscoe, H. Ross Perot, and Harold Hook. Long one of the most active Scouting states in the nation, Texas had 308,179 youth and 81,573 adult members in Texas as of 1994. The BSA national office, employing some 550 people, was moved to Irving in 1979. Camp Strake, near Conroe, is the most used Scout camp in the world; more than 40,000 people spent at least one night there in 1994.

BIBLIOGRAPHY: Minor Huffman, *History of Region Nine, Boy Scouts of America, 1920–1967* (1968). Minor Huffman, *Sam Houston Scouts* (1985). Frank Hilton, *Panjandrum: A History of Scouting in the Concho Valley Council, 1911–1941* (1990). Robert W. Peterson, *The Boy Scouts: An American Adventure* (New York: American Heritage, 1984).

Nelson R. Block

BOYS PEAK. Boys Peak, formerly known as Yates Peak and as Potters Peak, is 7½ miles northwest of Lampasas and three miles west of U.S. Highway 281 in south central Lampasas County (at 31°10′ N, 98°14′ W). Its summit, with an elevation of 1,491 feet above sea level, rises 350 feet above nearby Lucy Creek. The peak is in an area of the Grand Prairies region characterized by steep slopes and limestone benches, which give a stairstep appearance to the landscape. The local soils are chiefly shallow clay loams that support grasses and open stands of live oak, mesquite, and Ashe juniper.

BOZ, TEXAS. Boz is on Farm Road 1493 five miles southwest of Waxahachie in southwestern Ellis County. Its settlement occurred sometime in the late 1880s or early 1890s. It had a post office from 1891 to 1906. Throughout much of its history Boz was a school and church community of area farmers. In the mid-1930s it had seventy-five residents and three businesses. Its school closed in 1943. In 1986 the community reported fifteen residents, but probably more resided in the immediate vicinity. The Bethel Methodist Church in Boz was the set for several scenes in the movie *Places in the Heart* (1984). In 1989 the community's remaining residents feared their town's ultimate destruction since the federal government had selected Ellis County as the site for the proposed superconducting supercollider. In 1990 the population of Boz was still reported as fifteen, but by 1992, as plans for the supercollider continued, eighty-four-year-old Monnie Bratcher was the only remaining resident. The superconductor project was canceled not long afterward.

BIBLIOGRAPHY: Dallas *Morning News,* December 6, 1992. Houston *Chronicle,* February 19, 1989.

David Minor and Paul M. Lucko

BOZAR, TEXAS. Bozar was on U.S. Highway 183 midway between Mullin and Goldthwaite in northern Mills County. As late as 1936 it was a one-store ranching community with a station on the Gulf, Colorado and Santa Fe Railway.

Claudia Hazlewood

BOZEMAN'S CORNER, TEXAS. Bozeman's Corner, north of Gladewater in northwestern Gregg County, grew up during the oil boom of the 1930s. At its height in the mid-1930s the settlement had several stores and a number of houses. It began to decline around the time of World War II,[qv] and after the war the area was annexed by Gladewater. *Thelma Hall*

BRACE, DAVID KINGSLEY (1891–1971). David Kingsley Brace, a pioneer in the field of physical education testing, was born on September 4, 1891, in Lincoln, Nebraska, the son of David L. and Eleanor (Kingsley) Brace. He attended high school in Portland, Oregon, where he lettered in football and was captain of the track team. In 1915 he received his B.A. degree from Reed College (as a member of that school's first graduating class) in Portland, where he again took part in football and track. At Teachers College, Columbia University, he received an M.A. degree in 1921 and a Ph.D. in 1927. After a year as general science and physical education teacher in a junior high school in Salem, Oregon (1915–16), he spent four years in China, directing physical education at Chihli Provincial Higher Normal College, Paotingfu, and Tsing Hua College, Peking. From 1920 to 1926 he taught at Columbia University. In 1926 Brace moved to the University of Texas and established the Department of Physical and Health Education, of which he was chairman from 1926 to 1958. He retired from active teaching in 1962, after thirty-six years on the faculty of the University of Texas.

Brace's interests were in safety, motor-learning studies, tests and measurements, and techniques and skills in sports. He developed the Brace Motor Ability Test to test physical skills, one of the first tests to use modern scientific methods. In 1915 his study *The Family and Socialized Play* won the Municipal League Prize in Portland, Oregon. In 1924 he published the first achievement tests for football and basketball. He was the author of, or contributor to, ten books published between 1924 and 1958. In 1937 he wrote *Measuring Motor Ability*. His publications from 1922 to 1961 included pamphlets, booklets, and more than 100 articles. He was a member of the Austin Parks and Recreation Board from 1955 to 1968, and during his chairmanship of that board (1957–64), he, with other board members, pursued a policy of acquiring land for city parks. At various times he served as president of the American Academy of Physical Education, as principal specialist in physical education for the United States Office of Education, and as a member of the President's Council on Youth Fitness.

He was married to Dorothy Walton on December 25, 1915, in Portland, Oregon. After her death in 1935 he married Mary Elizabeth Bulbrook, on July 12, 1936, in Fort Worth; they had two daughters. Brace died in Austin on December 27, 1971.

BIBLIOGRAPHY: Austin *American*, December 28, 1971. Austin *Statesman*, December 29, 1971. *TAHPER Journal*, May 1963. Vertical Files, Barker Texas History Center, University of Texas at Austin. *Who's Who in Texas Today* (Austin: Pemberton Press, 1968).

BRACERO PROGRAM. On August 4, 1942, the United States government signed the Mexican Farm Labor Program Agreement with Mexico, the first among several agreements aimed at legalizing and controlling Mexican migrant farmworkers along the southern border of the United States. Managed by several government agencies, including the Department of Agriculture, as a temporary, war-related measure to supply much-needed workers during the early years of World War II,[qv] the Bracero (Spanish for "arm-man"—manual laborer) program continued uninterrupted until 1964. The agreement guaranteed a minimum wage of thirty cents an hour and humane treatment (in the form of adequate shelter, food, sanitation, etc.) of Mexican farmworkers in the United States. During the first five years of the program, Texas farmers chose not to participate in the restrictive accord. In 1943 the Texas growers, through the American Farm Bureau Federation, lobbied in Washington to weaken the terms of the agreement, since they suspected that the accord would eventually apply to seasonal workers in other areas, domestic service, and other related fields of temporary employment. Texas farmers, in the meantime, opted to bypass the Bracero program and hire farmworkers directly from Mexico. These "wetbacks" entered the United States illegally.

It has been estimated that in the 1950s the United States imported as many as 300,000 Mexican workers annually. This abundant supply of labor finally enticed Texans to participate fully in the program. By the end of the 1950s, Texas was receiving large numbers of *braceros*. The majority of the workers complied with the requirements of the agreement; many, however, remained illegally in the United States after their work time expired. Concurrently, the Immigration and Naturalization Service began Operation Wetback, a plan designed to round up illegal Mexicans, particularly in Texas and California. Government data indicate that in 1954 Operation Wetback repatriated to Mexico more than 1.1 million *mojados* ("wetbacks"). By the middle of the 1950s the INS expulsions reached a high of 3.8 million. The necessity of additional manpower in agriculture during the Korean War encouraged Mexico to squeeze as many favorable modifications into the agreement with the United States as possible. In 1951 the Mexican migration program was revised under the "temporary" Public Law 78. The United States government included in the amended version several clauses pertaining to expenses of transportation from Mexico to reception centers in the United States, guaranteed burial expenses, assistance in negotiation of labor contracts, and a guarantee that employers would return workers to reception centers at the expiration of the contract. Public Law 78 was extended in 1954, 1956, 1958, 1961, and 1964.

Mexican agricultural workers, considered an unlimited supply of cheap labor, have been pawns to a host of economic, political, social, and humanitarian interests. Poor wages, lack of educational opportunities for the children, malnutrition, poor sanitation, and discrimination have contributed to continued sources of friction between Texas growers and migrant laborers and the federal government. Migrant workers have nonetheless continued to walk to the United States, legally or illegally. Between 1942 and 1964 more than 4.5 million *braceros* entered the United States. Most never returned. After the end of the Bracero program, the number of illegal immigrants in this country may have increased. Though the Immigration Reform Control Act of 1986 gave legal status, or amnesty, to those who resided and worked in this country by January 1, 1982, illegals continue to be hired and often exploited.

BIBLIOGRAPHY: Howard L. Campbell, Bracero Migration and the Mexican Economy, 1951–1954 (Ph.D. dissertation, American University, 1972). Richard B. Craig, *The Bracero Program: Interest Groups and Foreign Policy* (Austin: University of Texas Press, 1971). Arnoldo De León, *Mexican Americans in Texas: A Brief History* (Arlington Heights, Illinois: Harlan Davidson, 1993). Ernesto Galarza, *Merchants of Labor: The Mexican Bracero Story* (Charlotte, California: McNally and Loftin, 1964). John McBride, *Vanishing Bracero: Valley Revolution* (San Antonio: Naylor, 1963). M. Otey Scruggs, "Texas and the Bracero Program, 1942–1947," *Pacific Historical Review* 32 (1963).

Fred L. Koestler

BRACHES, CHARLES (1813–1889). Charles Braches, teacher, merchant, Indian fighter, and public official, was born on February 25, 1813, at Gaulkhausen, Prussia. He sailed for America on April 3, 1834, and landed at Baltimore, Maryland, from where he later traveled through St. Louis, Missouri, to Sharon, Mississippi. There he organized and operated a literary and music school. In 1840 he moved to Texas and settled in Gonzales, where, in partnership with Dr. Caleb S. Brown, he opened a merchandising business. Braches represented Gonzales County in the House of the Seventh Congress of the Republic of Texas, from November 14, 1842, until January 16, 1843. He participated in several Indian fights, including the battles of Plum Creek, Medina,[qqv] and Hondo. His eleemosynary gifts to schools and churches reportedly ran into thousands of dollars. Braches married Sarah Ann McClure on March 2, 1843. He was a member of the Cumberland Presbyterian Church. He died in his Gonzales County home on July 7, 1889.

BIBLIOGRAPHY: John Henry Brown, *Indian Wars and Pioneers of Texas* (Austin: Daniell, 1880; reprod., Easley, South Carolina: Southern Historical Press, 1978). Texas House of Representatives, *Biographical Directory of the Texan Conventions and Congresses, 1832–1845* (Austin: Book Exchange, 1941). *Stephen L. Hardin*

BRACHFIELD, CHARLES LOUIS (1871–1947). Charles Louis Brachfield, lawyer and jurist, was born in Vicksburg, Mississippi, on January 10, 1871, the oldest son of Benjamin and Yetta (Baruch) Brachfield. In 1877 the family moved to Texas and settled in Henderson, where Benjamin Brachfield worked as a merchant. Charles attended Henderson College and subsequently clerked in the law office of Judge W. H. Wood in Waco. He was admitted to the bar in 1890 at the age of nineteen and set up a law practice in Henderson. He was elected county judge in 1897 and reelected in 1898 and 1902. He served in the Texas Senate for eight years, from January 1903 through September 1910, and was appointed District Court judge by Governor W. P. Hobby[qv] in 1918; he held this post until 1928. In 1926 Brachfield ran for attorney general, thus becoming the first Jew to seek statewide office. He lost the election, in part because of his strong prohibition[qv] views and the large slate of candidates, but came within 3,600 votes of forcing a runoff—a remarkable feat in view of the power and influence of the Ku Klux Klan[qv] at the time. Brachfield never married. He was active in the Masons and Odd Fellows and was a director of the First National Bank of Henderson. His law practice, which he continued until his death, included independent oil producers, Gulf Oil, and the Methodist church in Old London, Texas. He was widely respected in the community. After he died on June 6, 1947, a rabbi and a Methodist minister jointly conducted services.

BIBLIOGRAPHY: Natalie Ornish, *Pioneer Jewish Texans* (Dallas: Texas Heritage, 1989). Texas Jewish Historical Society Collection, Barker Texas History Center, University of Texas at Austin. Vertical Files, Barker Texas History Center, University of Texas at Austin. Ruthe Winegarten and Cathy Schechter, *Deep in the Heart: The Lives and Legends of Texas Jews* (Austin: Eakin Press, 1990).
Christopher Long

BRACHFIELD, TEXAS. Brachfield is five miles southwest of Pinehill in far eastern Rusk County. The community was called Murvall, for its location on Murvall Creek, when it was settled in the 1860s. It was preceded by a settlement called Gibson Town. Gibson Creek runs through the land survey on its way to Murvall Creek. Early settlers in the area included the Watkins, Miller, Brown, Welch, Hannah, and Debard families. In 1853 Archibald H. Watkins was appointed postmaster at Murvall. The old Trammel's Trace[qv] from Mount Enterprise to Pinehill may have come right through the site, and the trail probably contributed to the town's settlement. From 1892 to 1905 the *Rusk County News* called the place Needmore, for the community was said to need more of everything. Needmore had a sulfur springs and spa called Welch Springs, and Nathaniel Johnston built a hotel and store there about 1896, the year he was appointed postmaster. The community was renamed again when it was discovered that there was another Needmore in Texas. In 1900 Charles L. Brachfield[qv] stood on a stump and made his first political speech for election as county judge; hence the town's new name. The community had a post office from 1900 to 1906. The highest population recorded for the town was eighty during the 1950s and 1960s, and its residents declined afterward to thirty or fewer. The population in 1990 was thirty.

BIBLIOGRAPHY: *Rusk County History* (Henderson, Texas: Rusk County Historical Commission, 1982). *Megan Biesele*

BRACHT, VIKTOR FRIEDRICH (1819–1887). Viktor Bracht, businessman, explorer, and railroad agent, was born in Düsseldorf, Germany, on September 17, 1819. Sent by the government to represent the interests of German colonists in Texas, he landed at Galveston on June 19, 1845, and proceeded to New Braunfels, where he lived for a year. He was back in Germany in 1846–47 but returned to Texas in 1848, worked as a merchant at New Braunfels until 1855, and then became a wholesale grocer in San Antonio. In 1848 Bracht wrote a history entitled *Texas im Jahre 1848;* the book was translated into English by Charles Frank Schmidt in 1931. Bracht made extensive explorations along the Medina, Colorado, Guadalupe, San Antonio, Pedernales, and Llano rivers. He left Texas for New York in 1860 and subsequently spent several years in Mexico as general agent of a railroad company. In 1869 he moved to Rockport to be bookkeeper for J. M. and Thomas H. Mathis.[qv] Bracht became deputy collector of customs at Rockport in 1871, held the same position at Carrizo in Zapata County for a time, and then became postmaster at Rockport. He married Sebilla Shaefer at Indianola in 1848 and died in Rockport on January 26, 1887.

BIBLIOGRAPHY: Corpus Christi *Caller,* February 5, 1887. S. W. Geiser, "Men of Science in Texas, 1820–1880," *Field and Laboratory* 26–27 (January 1958–October 1959).

BRACKEN, TEXAS (Comal County). Bracken, on the International–Great Northern Railroad 13½ miles southwest of New Braunfels in southern Comal County, was named for William Bracken, who acquired land in the area in 1849. The townsite on the new railroad was named Davenport for James G. Davenport, who settled there in 1868. With the growth of the community and the building of a gin and stores, residents applied for a post office. The name was changed from Davenport to Bracken in 1883 because a Davenport post office had already been established in the state. In 1940 the post office had been discontinued, and the population was reported as fifty. After World War II[qv] the Davenport school was consolidated with the schools of Solms and Danville to form Comal Elementary School. The population of Bracken stabilized around seventy-five in the 1970s. In 1990 it was still seventy-five.

BIBLIOGRAPHY: Oscar Haas, *History of New Braunfels and Comal County, Texas, 1844-1946* (Austin: Steck, 1968). *Oscar Haas*

BRACKEN, TEXAS (Panola County). Bracken (Brackens) was a farming community off Farm Road 31 fifteen miles northeast of Carthage in northeastern Panola County. The site was first settled between 1835 and 1838 by the Thomas Bracken family, and in 1900 the settlement had a blacksmith shop, a gristmill, and a syrup mill. By the mid-1930s only a few scattered houses and a cemetery remained in the area. In the early 1990s the site was still marked by a cemetery.

BIBLIOGRAPHY: John Barnette Sanders, *Index to the Cemeteries of Panola County* (Center, Texas, 1964). Marker Files, Texas Historical Commission, Austin. *Christopher Long*

BRACKENRIDGE, GEORGE WASHINGTON (1832–1920). George Washington Brackenridge, businessman and philanthropist, son of John Adams and Isabella (McCullough) Brackenridge, was born in Warwick County, Indiana, on January 14, 1832. He attended Hanover College, the University of Indiana, and Harvard University. He moved to Texas with his parents in 1853, settled at Texana, and was surveyor of Jackson County from about 1857 to 1860. Although his three brothers served in the Confederate Army, Brackenridge became a war profiteer in the Matamoros cotton trade and with his family and a friend formed the cotton firm of Brackenridge, Bates, and Company. Among his business contracts was trader Charles Stillman.[qv] Sometime during the Civil War, Brackenridge was forced to leave Texas after claiming Union sympathies. He was appointed United States Treasury agent on July 30, 1863, and worked for the Treasury Department in New Orleans after the capture of that city by Union forces. After the war he became a Republican and a prohibitionist. In 1866 he organized the San Antonio National Bank. From 1883 to 1906 he was president of the San Antonio Water Works Company. He was president of a trust company, director of the Express Publishing Company, and president of the San Antonio school board. He became a regent of the University of Texas in November 1886 and continued as such until January 1911. He was again a regent from August 1917 to January 1919. As chairman of the committee on university land from 1889 to 1911, he aided in collecting back rents on university properties and placing them on a paying basis.

Brackenridge's benefactions to educational institutions included four school buildings in San Antonio, Guadalupe College in Seguin, B Hall on the campus of the University of Texas, University Hall for women medical students at Galveston, money for the founding of the school of home economics at the University, a loan fund for women students in architecture, law, and medicine, and a gift of 500 acres on the Colorado River in Austin to the University of Texas. He also supported the employment of women as instructors in the university system. His proposal that the main campus of the university be moved to the land on the Colorado was defeated. At the time that Governor James E. Ferguson[qv] vetoed the university appropriation bill for 1917–19, Brackenridge agreed, if necessary, to underwrite the expenses of the university for the next biennium out of his own private funds. He donated Brackenridge Park to the city of San Antonio. The Brackenridge home, Head of the River, was purchased by Incarnate Word College. Brackenridge was a life member of the Texas State Historical Association.[qv] He was never married. He died in San Antonio on December 28, 1920, and was buried with Masonic rites in the family cemetery near Edna, Jackson County. The bulk of his fortune went to the George W. Brackenridge Foundation for education.

BIBLIOGRAPHY: Nugent E. Brown, *B Hall, Texas: Stories of and about the Famous Dormitory, Brackenridge Hall, Texas University* (San Antonio: Naylor, 1938). Basil Young Neal, George Washington Brackenridge, Citizen and Philanthropist (M.A. thesis, University of Texas, 1939). Marilyn M. Sibley, *George W. Brackenridge* (Austin: University of Texas Press, 1973). *A Twentieth Century History of Southwest Texas* (2 vols., Chicago: Lewis, 1907). Robert E. Vinson, "The University Crosses the Bar," *Southwestern Historical Quarterly* 43 (January 1940).

Mary Eleanor Brackenridge and brother George W. Brackenridge, 1920. Andrew W. George Papers, CAH; CN 08128. This photograph was taken two years after Miss Brackenridge became the first woman to register to vote in San Antonio.

BRACKENRIDGE, JOHN THOMAS (1828–1906). John Thomas Brackenridge, Confederate veteran and bank president, was born in Warwick County, Indiana, on September 3, 1828, the son of John Adams and Isabella Helena (McCulloch) Brackenridge. He attended Indiana State University and Bloomington Law School before being admitted to the bar in 1851. He practiced law at Boonville until 1854, when he moved to Texana, Texas, where he was a merchant until 1861. In 1862 he joined the Confederate Army; he served as a captain of cavalry in Texas and Indian Territory until 1863, then was promoted to major in the Thirty-third Cavalry under John B. Magruder[qv] for coast picket duty. In 1866 Brackenridge became cashier of the San Antonio National Bank; in 1877 he was president of First National Bank of Austin. His first marriage was to E. R. Smith of Boonville, Indiana; his second, to Mary E. Dupuy in Jackson County, Texas. Brackenridge died in San Antonio on March 3, 1906, and was buried in Oakwood Cemetery, Austin.

BIBLIOGRAPHY: Austin *Statesman,* March 4, 1906. *Biographical Encyclopedia of Texas* (New York: Southern, 1880).

BRACKENRIDGE, MARY ELEANOR (1837–1924). Mary Eleanor Brackenridge, clubwoman and advocate of women's rights, daughter of John Adams and Isabella Helena (McCulloch) Brackenridge, was born in Warwick County, Indiana, on March 7, 1837. George W. Brackenridge[qv] was her brother. She spent her childhood in Indiana and, upon graduating from Anderson Female Seminary in New Albany in 1855, joined her family, who had moved to Jackson County, Texas. She remained in Jackson County until 1866, when she and her mother went to San Antonio to live with George. John A. Brackenridge had died in 1862.

In San Antonio, Eleanor became a champion of civic and social betterment. She was active in the Texas Federation of Women's Clubs, the Daughters of the American Revolution,[qqv] the Texas Mothers' Congress, the Order of the Eastern Star, and the Presbyterian Church.[qv] She was a firm believer in prohibition[qv] and a strong supporter of the Woman's Christian Temperance Union.[qv] She founded the Woman's Club of San Antonio and served as its president for seven years. Under her guidance the club turned its attention from literary subjects to such issues as the need for police matrons, female probation officers, industrial and vocational education, and the general welfare of women and children. She made a study of the state's legal code and published a pamphlet entitled *The Legal Status of Texas Women* in 1911.

In February 1912 Brackenridge was elected president of the newly organized San Antonio Equal Franchise Society. The formation of this society stimulated interest throughout the state, and delegates from seven Texas cities met in San Antonio and organized the Texas Woman Suffrage Association in April 1913. Eleanor Brackenridge held the office of president for one year and then became honorary president. Though no longer an active officer, she continued to support the movement, and when the Texas legislature granted primary suffrage to women in 1918 she was the first woman in Bexar County to register to vote (*see* woman suffrage).

She was one of a group of citizens instrumental in securing the establishment of a state-supported college for women, the College of Industrial Arts (now Texas Woman's University). In 1902 she became a member of its first board of regents, and she served in that capacity until her death more than twenty years later. As a regent she took an active interest in the affairs of the institution and often assisted students in financial need. She urged the legislature to give the woman's college adequate support and sometimes chided its members for failing to vote for requested appropriations. In 1916 a dormitory was named in her honor.

Eleanor Brackenridge traveled widely, often to places not readily accessible to Americans in her time. She was also one of the first women in the nation to serve as a bank director. She was a member of the board of directors of the San Antonio National Bank and the San Antonio Loan and Trust Company, institutions founded by her brother.

Neither Eleanor nor George ever married. They shared the same residence, Fern Ridge, until George died in 1920. After his death Eleanor continued to live at Fern Ridge, where she died after a cerebral hemorrhage, on February 14, 1924. When reporting her death, the San Antonio *Express* called her "in many respects the foremost woman citizen of Texas." She was buried in the Brackenridge family cemetery near Edna in Jackson County.

bibliography: Johnowene B. C. Menger, M. Eleanor Brackenridge (M.A. thesis, Trinity University, 1964). San Antonio *Express,* February 15, 1924. A. Elizabeth Taylor, "The Woman Suffrage Movement in Texas," *Journal of Southern History* 17 (May 1951; rpt., in *Citizens at Last: The Woman Suffrage Movement in Texas,* ed. Ruthe Winegarten and Judith N. McArthur, Austin, 1987). Joyce Thompson, *Marking a Trail: A History of the Texas Woman's University* (Denton: Texas Woman's University Press, 1982). *Woman's Who's Who of America* (New York: American Commonwealth, 1914).

A. Elizabeth Taylor

BRACKENRIDGE, ROBERT J. (1839–1918). Robert J. Brackenridge, businessman and Confederate soldier, son of John Adams and Isabella (McCulloch) Brackenridge, was born in Boonville, Indiana, on December 28, 1839. The family moved to Texas in 1853. Brackenridge was a cowboy and laborer on his father's farm as a boy and attended common schools. In 1860 he entered Hanover College, in Indiana. At the outbreak of the Civil War[qv] he returned to Texas and entered Confederate service under his brother John Thomas Brackenridge.[qv] At Aransas Pass he was captured by Gen. Nathaniel P. Banks's[qv] command, but was paroled through the influence of his brother George W. Brackenridge and Governor A. J. Hamilton,[qqv] both Texas Union men. During his parole he studied medicine in Mankato, Minnesota, and fought in a few skirmishes against the Sioux Indians. He graduated from Rush Medical College, Chicago, in 1867, then settled in Jackson County, Texas. He moved to Austin in 1874 and gave up the active practice of his profession. He held the position of cashier of the First National Bank of Austin until the sale of all the stock of the bank held by his family. In 1885 he married Mary T. Lyons; they had one child. Brackenridge was president of the Frontier Telephone and Telegraph Company for some years. He was active in the First Presbyterian Church, U.S.A., and in many religious endeavors. In 1886 he helped originate an organization known as the Seven Churches, which had as its object the promotion of practical and everyday religion, and for many years he served as president of the Austin Bible Society. He was an active worker in the bond election in 1914 to build a new city hospital, which about 1930 was renamed Brackenridge Hospital[qv] in his honor. He died in Austin on June 26, 1918.

bibliography: Austin *Statesman,* June 26, 1918. LaPrelle Brackenridge Papers, Austin History Center, Austin. Vertical Files, Barker Texas History Center, University of Texas at Austin.

Elizabeth N. Kemp

BRACKENRIDGE HOSPITAL. Brackenridge Hospital, in Austin, the oldest public hospital in Texas, opened on July 3, 1884. The City-County Hospital, as it was called, was jointly owned by the city of Austin and Travis County until 1907, when the county withdrew its support. The two-story stone building was built at a cost of $10,000 on a city block in the northeast corner of Austin set aside for a hospital when the town was laid out in 1839. It had a maximum capacity of forty patients. Austin doctors had tried for fifteen years to provide Austin residents with hospital care, but financial problems had forced their establishments out of business.

In 1915 a new forty-five-bed facility was completed, and between 1929 and 1941 the addition of wings on the south, west, and north sides raised the bed capacity to 208. The size of the hospital gradually increased until a $43 million, 363-bed structure was built in several phases during the 1970s, just west of the site of the original building. City Hospital—its name after 1907—became Brackenridge Hospital in 1929, when the city council renamed it in honor of Dr. Robert J. Brackenridge,[qv] who had served as chairman of the hospital board, led the campaign to finance the 1915 hospital building, and worked for many years toward improving medical care in Austin.

Brackenridge Hospital offered Austin's first intercranial and open-heart surgery in 1948 and 1961. The city's first intensive-care unit opened there in 1960, its first cardiac-care unit in 1971, and its first alternative birth center in 1978. In addition, the Brackenridge Emergency Room, the regional trauma center for a ten-county area, treated an average of 70,000 patients annually during the early 1990s. Brackenridge also housed the area's first nursing school, which was established in 1915 and operated by the hospital until 1984, when Austin Community College assumed responsibility for the program. After beginning an education program for interns and residents after World War II,[qv] Brackenridge became a fully accredited teaching hospital in the mid-1950s.

As a public hospital, Brackenridge has always sustained a good deal of public scrutiny and has always had financial difficulties. As the hospital grew in the twentieth century, problems grew with it, and the administration of the hospital became increasingly politicized. When Brackenridge lost over $6 million in the 1975–76 fiscal year, the city council considered selling the hospital or leasing it to a management firm. After months of debate, however, the city council voted in 1978 to retain ownership and control of Austin's only public hospital. In 1993 there were 399 beds in the general hospital and 82 beds in a free-standing children's hospital, attended by a staff of approximately 1,900. In 1992 the hospital's average daily census was 253, and outpatient visits numbered 107,000.

bibliography: Lisa Fahrenthold and Sara Rider, *Admissions: The Extraordinary History of Brackenridge Hospital* (Austin: Brackenridge Hospital, 1984).

James A. Marten

BRACKETT, OSCAR BERNADOTTE (1812–1857). Oscar Bernadotte Brackett, merchant, was born on March 22, 1812, in Salina, Onondaga County, New York. He inherited a fortune in a salt works, then lost it in speculation. He married Emily Wood on May 16, 1832, then finished college in 1833. Brackett came to Texas in 1844 from Syracuse with $20,000 in cash and some merchandising experience. His wife joined him two years later. With Peter Gallagher[qv] he purchased goods in New Orleans for a mercantile store in downtown San Antonio. Brackettville was named for him after he set up a supply settlement on the site of that town in 1852 for nearby Fort Clark. His business enterprises included ownership of land in the Fort Clark and Las Moras Creek area and operation of a line of freight wagons between San Antonio and Mexico. Despite the danger of Indians, Brackett and his wife often drove back and forth between San Antonio and Brackettville. Brackett served as an alderman in San Antonio (1847–48) and was a Whig until the party dissolved in 1855, after which he was said to have "cooperated with democracy." He died in San Antonio on December 2, 1857, and was buried in City Cemetery No. 1. He was survived by his wife and four daughters.

BIBLIOGRAPHY: John Henry Brown, *Indian Wars and Pioneers of Texas* (Austin: Daniell, 1880; reprod., Easley, South Carolina: Southern Historical Press, 1978). Frederick Charles Chabot, *With the Makers of San Antonio* (Yanaguana Society Publications 4, San Antonio, 1937). San Antonio *Ledger,* December 5, 12, 1857. *S. W. Pease*

BRACKETTVILLE, TEXAS. Brackettville, the county seat of Kinney County, is on U.S. Highway 90 twenty-two miles northeast of the Rio Grande and 125 miles west of San Antonio, near the geographic center of the county. It is named after Oscar B. Brackett,[qv] who established the first general dry goods store near the site of Fort Clark[qv] in 1852. Brackett, as it was called originally, was established on the San Antonio–El Paso Road, and by 1857 its Sargent Hotel and small restaurant run by Mr. Sheedy were a regular stop for the San Antonio–San Diego stage line. The settlement was six miles south of Las Moras Mountain near the prolific Las Moras Springs. Roving bands of Indians, who had historically hunted and camped at Las Moras Springs, harassed early settlers.

The community experienced a period of steady growth after the Civil War,[qv] attracting cattle rustlers, buffalo hunters, gamblers, and businessmen. In 1868 Brackett had ten homes and a population of fifty. Kinney County's school was started by Mrs. Margaret Martin Ballantyne around 1870 and housed in Brackett's home. Rev. Eggling-ton Barr, a chaplain at Fort Clark, held Protestant services. The community was known as Brackett or Brackett City when it received a post office in 1873; another Texas community was named Brackett, however, so the postal service changed the community's name to Brackettville. It was designated the county seat of Kinney County when the county was established in 1876.

St. Mary Magdalene's, Brackettville's first church, was established in 1875; the Gilead Church, a Seminole Indian church, sometime in the late 1870s; St. Andrew's Episcopal in 1884; the Church of Christ in 1899; the Baptist Church in 1904; the Methodist Church in 1920; a second Baptist Church in 1921; St. John's Baptist Church in 1926; Jerusalem Temple Apostolic Church in the mid-1960s; and the Frontier Baptist Church in 1977.

Brackettville enjoyed a period of exceptional prosperity during the period between 1878 and 1882, as nearby Fort Clark swelled with thousands of soldiers. The town grew rapidly, and many businesses, constructed of limestone blocks quarried nearby, were established. Devastating floods in 1880 and 1899 caused considerable damage and persuaded many of Brackettville's residents to move to higher elevations about the community.

The Gulf, Harrisburg and San Antonio Railway originally planned to route its westward track through Brackettville but in 1882 followed an alternate path ten miles south of the community. In 1884 Brackettville had an estimated population of 1,400, two churches, three schools, a private bank, a weekly newspaper known as the *Brackett News,* a Masonic and Odd Fellows lodge, and a daily stage to Spofford. By this time the community was an established shipping point for wool and hides. In 1896 Brackettville had an estimated population of 1,000 and four teachers for 207 students. In 1914 the community had an estimated population of 800, a bank, a cotton gin, and a weekly newspaper called the Brackettville *News-Mail,* which had been established by W. W. Price in 1906. Each year between 1921 and 1926 the Brackettville school children were treated to four days of Chautauqua theatrical performances. In 1927 Brackettville had an estimated population of 2,000, a grade school, and a high school. Many residents of the community owned or worked on ranches in the area; sources of income included livestock, wool and mohair, pecans, and hay. Brackettville was incorporated on July 28, 1930, to ensure funding for a new water-distribution plant.

In 1936 the town had an estimated population of 1,822, of which an estimated 75 percent were of Mexican or Seminole-Negro descent. The commercial viability of the community at this time was highly dependent on business with nearby Fort Clark, sheep and goat ranching, truck farming, and the tourist industry. In 1936 Brackettville had an elementary school for black and Hispanic children and another for white children.

Brackettville reached its highest population in 1943 at an estimated 3,500. A federally funded brick high school for local black students was completed in April 1944; officially classified as a four-year high school, it is believed to the only one of its kind between San Antonio and El Paso at that time. The community had an estimated population of 2,653 in 1947. From 1952 to 1982 Brackettville had thirty to forty businesses and an estimated 1,700 people. During that time the town was Kinney County's principal market and shipping point. In addition to ranching, some income was derived from tourism, centered mainly on Fort Clark, which has been restored and opened as a guest ranch, and on Alamo Village,[qv] a replica of the Alamo used in several motion pictures. In the 1980s Brackettville hosted the Frontier Fair, Fort Clark Cavalry Days, and the Western Horse Races and Barbecue. In 1990 the population was 1,740.

BIBLIOGRAPHY: Agnes Fritter, "Pioneer Days of Kinney County," *Texas History Teachers Bulletin* 13 (1946). *Kinney County: 125 Years of Growth, 1852–1977* (Brackettville, Texas: Kinney County Historical Society, 1977). Vertical Files, Barker Texas History Center, University of Texas at Austin. *Ruben E. Ochoa*

BRAD, TEXAS. Brad, on U.S. Highway 180 and State Highway 16 twenty miles west of Mineral Wells in west central Palo Pinto County, was named for its founder, Bradford Fitzgerald. In 1940 Brad had twenty-eight residents and three stores. After the completion of the Possum Kingdom dam in 1945, Brad became one of the entry points to Possum Kingdom Reservoir[qv] and its recreational facilities. The community's population was reported as twenty-six in 1980 and 1990.

BIBLIOGRAPHY: J. C. Koen, A Social and Economic History of Palo Pinto County (M.A. thesis, Hardin-Simmons University, 1949).
William R. Hunt

BRADBURN, JOHN DAVIS (1787–1842). John (Juan) Davis Bradburn was born in Virginia in 1787, moved with his family to Christian County, Kentucky, by 1810, and became a trader at Springfield, Tennessee. He was probably a member of the Gutiérrez-Magee expedition[qv] in 1812. He was elected third lieutenant of Buard's company, Eighteenth Regiment of Louisiana volunteers, by the returned filibusters in 1814, when the British attacked New Orleans. The Natchitoches regiment failed to arrive at the Crescent City before January 8, 1815, when Andrew Jackson defeated the British.

After the war Bradburn joined Henry Perry,[qv] a veteran of the Gutiérrez-Magee endeavor, who was planning a second attack on Spanish Texas.[qv] Stationed in the Nacogdoches area, Bradburn funneled men and equipment to Perry at Bolivar Peninsula and Perry's Point (Anahuac) in 1816. Perry and Bradburn joined Luis Michel Aury,[qv] who had recently been appointed governor of Texas by the Mexican revolutionary government in exile on Galveston Island, a staging area for a descent on La Bahía.[qv] Before Aury's plans matured, Francisco Xavier Mina[qv] arrived with funds, men, and a new plan to attack Soto la Marina, Tamaulipas, and join Mexican guerrillas. The group sailed in April 1817 and easily took the Spanish fort. Upon joining the patriots at Fort Sombrero in Guanajuato in July, Bradburn became second in command of the American volunteers. A successful siege by the royalists forced the insurgents to evacuate, and Bradburn was one of the few to escape. He managed to join Vicente Ramón Guerrero[qv] near Acapulco and served the cause until December 1820, when he defected to Agustín de Iturbide,[qv] commander of the Spanish army. Iturbide, a native Mexican, was secretly planning a coup to expel the Spaniards, and Bradburn apparently served as intermediary between Iturbide and Guerrero in uniting the diverse Mexican factions in order to defeat the Spanish. The union of the two allowed the promulgation of the Plan de Iguala in February 1821, and the Spanish soon admitted defeat.

Once independence from Spain was achieved, Bradburn remained in the Mexican army as a lieutenant colonel and an aide to Iturbide. He married a titled heiress, María Josefa Hurtado de Mendoza, whose family owned property on the Zócalo, the House of Tiles. Bradburn survived the numerous political changes of the 1820s and in 1830 was appointed commander of a new garrison on Galveston Bay. Commandant Gen. Manuel de Mier y Terán[qv] ordered him to locate a site for the fort, a military town, and a customhouse, to be named Anahuac. Bradburn chose Perry's Point, overlooking the mouth of the Trinity.

The Law of April 6, 1830,[qv] endeavored to "Mexicanize" Texas by limiting future immigration from the United States and to encourage native Mexicans to populate Texas. Bradburn encountered hostility from his fellow Anglo-Americans when he tried to carry out Mier y Terán's orders, which included inspecting land titles, issuing licenses to Anglo lawyers, and enforcing the customs laws of the nation. The exemption from paying tariffs granted to Austin's colonists had expired, and the federal government expected the revenue to pay for the six new military posts guarding the entrances to Texas.

William B. Travis[qv] was among the leaders opposing Bradburn, and he violated the military laws governing the post by words and deeds calculated to stir a rebellion. When Bradburn arrested him and other leaders of the movement, emotional outcries on the Brazos started a force marching to attack Anahuac. The rebels invaded the village on June 10, 1832, and Bradburn agreed to an exchange of prisoners—Travis and the other Anglos in exchange for nineteen cavalrymen ambushed by the insurgents the previous day—and withdrawal of the insurgent force. The cavalrymen were released, but when Bradburn later discovered that a number of rebels had remained in town overnight, he refused to free his prisoners and began firing on the town.

The insurgents then withdrew to Turtle Bayou, where they drew up a series of resolutions explaining their action in light of news that the Federalist faction under Antonio López de Santa Anna[qv] was defeating the Centralist administration supported by Bradburn. An uneasy peace lasted while the rebels sent to the Brazos for cannons and Bradburn appealed for help from other military commanders in Texas. Col. José de las Piedras[qv] marched from Nacogdoches, but fearing that he was outnumbered he met with Anglo insurgents near Liberty and agreed to their demands—remove Bradburn from command and free Travis and the others.

After Bradburn was relieved of command on July 2, he feared plots against his life and on July 13 fled to New Orleans. He returned to the Rio Grande and continued his career with the waning Centralist army until its defeat in December 1832. He then lived in retirement at his home near Matamoros until 1836, when he was ordered against his wishes to join José de Urrea's[qv] command of the port of Copano, where he saw none of his old adversaries. The defeat of Santa Anna at San Jacinto caused the rest of the Mexican army to retreat, and Bradburn made his way back to Matamoros and retirement. He was briefly called back to duty during the Federalist Wars, but ill health prevented him from attacking San Antonio in the Mexican invasions of 1842.[qv] Bradburn died at Matamoros on April 20, 1842, and was buried on his ranch, Puertas Verdes, in what is now Hidalgo County, Texas. His only son, Andrés, became a priest; he disposed of his maternal inheritance in the 1880s. The widow Bradburn sold the ranch, which eventually became La Lomita Seminary near Mission (*see* LA LOMITA MISSION).

See also ANAHUAC DISTURBANCES, TURTLE BAYOU RESOLUTIONS, TEXAS REVOLUTION.

BIBLIOGRAPHY: Margaret S. Henson, *Juan Davis Bradburn: A Reappraisal of the Mexican Commander of Anahuac* (College Station: Texas A&M University Press, 1982). *Margaret Swett Henson*

BRADFORD, CHARLES M. (1826–?). Charles M. Bradford, Confederate soldier, was born in Pennsylvania in 1826. He moved to Louisiana on the eve of the Civil War[qv] and joined the Louisiana military service for a four-month period that began in January 1861. By early April he had become a major in James Strawbridge's First Louisiana Infantry. Shortly afterward, when the unit was transferred to Pensacola, Florida, Bradford resigned his commission. In September 1861 he became a lieutenant colonel in command of the Third Battalion, Louisiana Infantry. Soon his eight-company battalion was moved to Virginia, where it was active in the Norfolk-Portsmouth area throughout the fall of 1861. In mid-1862 Bradford became lieutenant colonel of the Fifteenth Louisiana Infantry when his battalion was enlarged by two additional companies and converted into a regiment. He was, however, court-martialed for conduct prejudicial to good order and military discipline and for disrespect toward his superior. After being sentenced to loss of pay and suspension of rank for six months, he chose to resign his commission.

He moved to Owensville, Texas, in January 1864, and sought permission of Gen. John Bankhead Magruder[qv] to raise a volunteer mounted regiment from state troops and from those subject to conscription (*see* CONSCRIPTION UNDER THE CONFEDERACY). He was appointed major and served in quartermaster functions for several months before he finally gained command of what became known as Bradford's Battalion. The early summer of 1864 saw his companies chasing deserters and overawing disloyal elements in Bastrop, Austin, and Fredericksburg. Then, in July 1864, he was named colonel and placed in command of Bradford's Regiment (a consolidation of his battalion, Mann's Battalion, Hoxey's Battalion, and Poole's Company of Texas Cavalry). The new regiment was mustered into Confederate service in mid-1864 and took up defensive positions in the Galveston area for the duration of the war.

BIBLIOGRAPHY: Service Records, National Archives, Washington. *The War of the Rebellion: A Compilation of the Official Records of the Union and Confederate Armies* (Washington: GPO, 1880–1901).
Allan C. Ashcraft

BRADFORD, TEXAS. Bradford is at the intersection of Farm Road 837 and State Highway 19, eighteen miles northwest of Palestine in northwestern Anderson County. The community was settled about 1879, and the Bradford post office, probably named for the first postmaster, B. L. Bradford, operated from 1882 to 1907. In 1884 the community had an estimated population of 150, a Presbyterian church, a district school, a general store, and steam cotton gins-gristmills. Bradford reached a peak estimated population of 200 in 1896, and in the early 1900s J. B. and D. D. Hanks established a sawmill and gin there. The community began to decline soon thereafter. In 1900 it had 125 inhabitants, and by 1933 its population had fallen to about twenty. In the 1930s Bradford had a factory, one additional business, and a number of dwellings scattered along the road. In the mid-1940s the population of the community was estimated at fifty. The population had declined to twenty-five by 1949 and from 1974 to 1990 was estimated at twenty-two. In 1985 Bradford had a business, a cemetery, and several homes. *Mark Odintz*

BRADLEY, EDWARD R. (?–?). Edward R. Bradley, one of Stephen F. Austin's[qv] Old Three Hundred[qv] colonists, received title to a league of land now in Brazoria County on August 10, 1824. The March 1826 census reported that he lived with his wife, Elizabeth, four sons, and two daughters and was over fifty years old. He may have been the E. R. Bradley of Gonzales County who was delinquent in taxes owed the Republic of Texas[qv] in 1840.

BIBLIOGRAPHY: Lester G. Bugbee, "The Old Three Hundred: A List of Settlers in Austin's First Colony," *Quarterly of the Texas State Historical Association* 1 (October 1897). *Texas Sentinel*, June 17, 1841.

BRADLEY, JOHN (?–?). John Bradley, one of Stephen F. Austin's[qv] Old Three Hundred[qv] colonists, arrived in Texas before April 20, 1824, when he took his oath of allegiance in the home of James B. (Brit) Bailey.[qv] Bradley, who had known the family of Moses Austin[qv] in Missouri around 1820, received title to a league of land in what is now Brazoria County on July 8, 1824. The 1826 colonial census showed him as a farmer and stock raiser aged between twenty-five and forty, with a wife, Betsy, a son, and a daughter. He wrote S. F. Austin on June 30, 1826, that he had settled on the east side of the Brazos River and asked for a labor of land at the mouth of the river. He may have been the same John Bradley whose name appeared on the Colorado County tax rolls in 1840 and the Lavaca County rolls in 1846. A John Bradley of Fayette County also was among those captured with Nicholas Dawson[qv] in October 1842 and held at Perote Prison[qv] in Mexico until September 22, 1843.

BIBLIOGRAPHY: Eugene C. Barker, ed., *The Austin Papers* (3 vols., Washington: GPO, 1924–28). Paul C. Boethel, *The History of Lavaca County* (San Antonio: Naylor, 1936; rev. ed., Austin: Von Boeckmann–Jones, 1959). Lester G. Bugbee, "The Old Three Hundred: A List of Settlers in Austin's First Colony," *Quarterly of the Texas State Historical Association* 1 (October 1897). Leonie Rummel Weyand and Houston Wade, *An Early History of Fayette County* (La Grange, Texas: La Grange *Journal*, 1936).

BRADLEY, JOHN M. (ca. 1800–1844). John M. Bradley, soldier, was born about 1800 in North Carolina. In February 1832 he arrived in Texas as a widower with his four children. He was captain of the Tenaha Militia at the battle of Nacogdoches,[qv] August 2, 1832, and in the fall he represented the Tenaha District at the Convention of 1832[qv] in San Felipe. In October 1835 Bradley raised a company in San Augustine and Tenaha that he commanded as captain. He participated in the Grass Fight[qv] on November 26 and distinguished himself at the siege of Bexar.[qv] On May 15, 1836, a company of volunteers under Captain Bradley, the San Augustine Cavalry, joined the Texas army at Fort Bend on the Brazos and participated in expelling the Mexican army from Texas. The company was discharged at Victoria on July 23. During the Regulator-Moderator War,[qv] Bradley, a Moderator sympathizer, left his home on Patroon Creek and went to San Augustine in search of Charles Watt Moorman,[qv] leader of the Regulators, and attempted to assassinate him. In July 1844 Moorman followed Bradley to a Baptist revival meeting at the Masonic Hall and shot him to death as he left the building. Bradley is buried in the Old Texan Cemetery between San Augustine and Shelbyville in Shelby County.

BIBLIOGRAPHY: George L. Crocket, *Two Centuries in East Texas* (Dallas: Southwest, 1932; facsimile reprod., 1962). John W. Middleton, *History of the Regulators and the Moderators* (Fort Worth: Loving, 1883). Thomas L. Miller, *Bounty and Donation Land Grants of Texas, 1835–1888* (Austin: University of Texas Press, 1967). Mildred Cariker Pinkston, *People, Places, Happenings: Shelby County* (Center, Texas: Pinkston, 1985). Texas House of Representatives, *Biographical Directory of the Texan Conventions and Congresses, 1832–1845* (Austin: Book Exchange, 1941). Gifford E. White, *Character Certificates in the General Land Office of Texas* (1985).

McXie Whitton Martin

BRADLEY, PALMER (1894–1968). Palmer Bradley, attorney and businessman, was born in Tioga, Texas, on December 12, 1894, the son of Robert L. and Mary (Boxley) Bradley. About 1900 the family moved to Roswell, New Mexico, where Bradley attended public schools before entering the University of Texas in 1912; he received a B.A. degree from there in 1916. He served as a first lieutenant in the Forty-second Field Artillery during World War I,[qv] then returned to the University of Texas and received a law degree in 1919. The following year he moved to Houston to join the law firm that later became Andrews, Kurth, Campbell, and Jones. Except for military service in World War II,[qv] when he served as commanding officer of the pilot school at the Pre-Flight Training School in Santa Ana, California, Bradley practiced law with this firm until his death.

In 1929 Bradley, an authority on oil and gas law, helped organize the parent company of the General Crude Oil Company in Houston; for many years he served as one of its directors. He also helped organize the Southern National Bank of Houston in 1960 and was chairman of its board for several years. He was a director of Trans-World Airlines for a number of years after World War II.

He won a number of tennis titles in Texas and New Mexico and in 1931 helped found the River Oaks Tennis Tournament, an annual event that grew to international significance. Bradley was an avid collector of books and had a wide-ranging knowledge of Civil War[qv] history. He acquired an excellent collection of books on this period. He was a member of the Texas State Historical Association[qv] and contributed numerous articles to the *Handbook of Texas.* He served for many years as chairman of the Houston chapter of the Civil War Round Table. He married Genevra Harris in Nacogdoches, Texas, on February 24, 1921; they had two children. He died on June 13, 1968, and was buried in Glenwood Cemetery in Houston.

BIBLIOGRAPHY: *Texas Bar Journal*, September 22, 1968.

Robert L. Bradley

BRADLEY, THOMAS W. (?–?). Thomas W. Bradley, one of Stephen F. Austin's[qv] Old Three Hundred,[qv] came to Texas in partnership with Samuel T. Angier and George B. Hall[qqv] in 1824, and the three were issued a league and a labor of land in what is now Brazoria County in August of that year. On June 4, 1835, Bradley was among the signers of a petition protesting the enforcement of Mexican customs laws at Anahuac and was third in command of William Barret Travis's[qv] party that had stormed the fort there in 1832 (*see* ANAHUAC DISTURBANCES). This is apparently the same Thomas Bradley who, on November 17, 1838, with partners A. Garner and James Morgan,[qv] advertised town lots for sale in the new town of Swartwout on the Trinity River in Liberty County. On June 21, 1842, he was listed as a first-class militiaman in the company of Capt. Thaxton Epperson of Beat Four at Swartwout.

BIBLIOGRAPHY: Lester G. Bugbee, "The Old Three Hundred: A List of Settlers in Austin's First Colony," *Quarterly of the Texas State Historical Association* 1 (October 1897). Daughters of the Republic of Texas, *Muster Rolls of the Texas Revolution* (Austin, 1986). *Telegraph and Texas Register*, November 17, 1838.

Thomas W. Cutrer

BRADLEY, TEXAS (Angelina County). Bradley was a short-lived settlement near Homer in southeastern Angelina County. A post office opened there in 1881 but was suspended the next year, and by the late 1880s the community was no longer shown on maps.

BIBLIOGRAPHY: Angelina County Historical Survey Committee, *Land of the Little Angel: A History of Angelina County, Texas*, ed. Bob Bowman (Lufkin, Texas: Lufkin Printing, 1976).

Christopher Long

BRADLEY, TEXAS (Johnson County). Bradley, sixteen miles northeast of Cleburne in extreme northeastern Johnson County, was established in 1855, when Jackson Bradley built a school near the banks of Mountain Creek on land that was then in Ellis County. In 1881 the county line was moved east and the school and settlement became part of Johnson County. In 1900 the local school had eighty-seven pupils and one teacher, but by 1905 it had been consolidated with nearby schools. That year Bradley was a switch on the International and Great Northern Railroad. In the 1930s and 1940s the community reported a population of twenty-five, with one business. A church and a school served area residents in 1940. The community was abandoned sometime after the 1940s.

bibliography: Johnson County History Book Committee, *History of Johnson County, Texas* (Dallas: Curtis Media, 1985).

Brian Hart

BRADLEY'S CORNER, TEXAS. Bradley's Corner, which originated sometime in 1919 between Springfield and Newton, was one of a dozen or so towns that grew up in Wichita County during the oil boom between 1918 and the early 1920s. After the gusher at Fowler Number 1 on July 28, 1918, the population of the northeastern corner of the county increased by an estimated 65,000 in fourteen months. Tent cities appeared. At Bradley's Corner, a collection of tents and shacks provided shelter for those rushing to the area; also at the boomtown were makeshift dining halls, gambling houses, saloons, and areas where dozens of cots covered by huge canvases acted as hotels. The Bradley's Corner community quickly became known as the "wickedest place in existence." By 1921, however, the noise of such saloons as Buckets of Blood had ended, and the settlement had been abandoned.

bibliography: Louise Kelly, *Wichita County Beginnings* (Burnet, Texas: Eakin Press, 1982). Wichita Falls *Times,* May 15, 1957.

David Minor

BRADSHAW, AMZI (1824–1885). Amzi Bradshaw, lawyer, legislator, and soldier, the son of Elias and Kiziah (Kimmons) Bradshaw, was born in Hickman County, Tennessee, on January 13, 1824. He received a limited education and taught in various schools in Tennessee before moving to Texas in 1849. He settled first at Enterprise in Rusk County and taught school there, then removed to Quitman, where he studied law and was admitted to the bar in 1852. He subsequently moved to Waxahachie and opened a law practice. In 1860 he was elected district attorney, and in 1861 he represented Ellis County in the Secession Convention,[qv] where he voted in favor of secession. He resigned his position as district attorney to enlist as a private in Company C, Nineteenth Texas Cavalry, C.S.A., and participated in the battle of Cape Girardeau, Missouri. He was discharged on May 25, 1863, but then recruited his own company, which became Company D, Showalter's Texas Cavalry. He was made captain on August 7, 1863. Bradshaw and his unit were a part of John S. Ford's[qv] Cavalry of the West and campaigned in 1864 to rid the Rio Grande valley of Union troops from Laredo to Brownsville. Bradshaw continued his law practice in Waxahachie after the war. He was a delegate to the Constitutional Convention of 1866[qv] and served a term in the state Senate during the Fourteenth Legislature (1874–75). He married Martha S. Bishop on January 16, 1867. He died on January 23, 1885, and was buried in the Waxahachie City Cemetery.

bibliography: William S. Speer and John H. Brown, eds., *Encyclopedia of the New West* (Marshall, Texas: United States Biographical Publishing, 1881; rpt., Easley, South Carolina: Southern Historical Press, 1978).

J. L. Bryan

BRADSHAW, TEXAS. Bradshaw is on U.S. Highway 83 some 1½ miles from the Runnels county line in southern Taylor County. It was founded when the Santa Fe rail line was constructed through the area in 1909. After the railroad bypassed Audra, two miles west of the site of Bradshaw, Audra residents moved to be closer to the railroad. C. M. Bradshaw is believed to have given a portion of his land for the railroad and for the development of a town, which was named for him. In 1910 the town had two gins, two grocery stores, a general mercantile store, a butcher shop, a drugstore, a blacksmith shop, a hardware store, and a Methodist church. By 1914 it had added Baptist and Christian churches, a bank, and a hotel. Bradshaw flourished in the 1920s, and in 1929 its population reached 450. In the 1930s, as local transportation improved and gave the population readier access to Abilene, twenty-eight miles to the north, Bradshaw declined as a center of commerce. In 1988 Bradshaw's population was reported as twenty-five. Its young people attended school in nearby Tuscola, and local mail was routed through Winters. Bradshaw's businesses comprised a gas station and the Audra Mercantile Company, owned by Opal Hunt, the daughter of one of Bradshaw's original settlers. Residents of the surrounding area farmed wheat and milo and raised cattle.

bibliography: Juanita Daniel Zachry, *A History of Rural Taylor County* (Burnet, Texas: Nortex, 1980).

Charla Birchum and Jennifer Kaaikala

BRADY, JOHN THOMAS (1830–1890). John Thomas Brady, lawyer, legislator, newspaperman, and Houston city promoter, the son of John and Mary (Davis) Brady, was born in Charles County, Maryland, on October 10, 1830. He attended Charlotte Hall Academy and taught in the county's public schools for three years. He was admitted to the bar at Port Tobacco, Maryland, about 1855 and practiced law briefly. He then moved to Westport, Missouri, where he edited the *Frontier News* for two years. When troubles developed in Kansas, Brady moved there to assist in organizing the new territorial government. He was elected public printer, a position in which he published the journals and laws of the state's first legislature, and became district attorney for the Third Judicial District of the territory.

In 1856 he moved to Texas and established a law practice at Houston while living at Harrisburg. In Houston he served as leading counsel for the heirs of Christopher Dart against Elisha M. Pease,[qv] a case involving the recovery of 300 slaves smuggled into Brazoria County by Monroe Edwards.[qv] In 1866 Brady was one of a group of businessmen who established the Texas Transportation Company, which became part of the Southern Pacific Railroad and built a line from Houston to Clinton on Buffalo Bayou. In the 1880s he helped to organize the Houston Belt and Magnolia Park Railway Company, later part of the Missouri Pacific. At different times Brady served as the first president of each railroad. He was also interested in deepening the Houston ship channel[qv] and had the bayou dredged in what became Houston's first turning basin. The new channel cut Brady's Island from his property.

In the Civil War[qv] Brady served the Confederacy on Gen. John B. Magruder's[qv] staff and was a volunteer aide to Commodore Leon Smith on the steamer *Bayou City*[qv] in the capture of the *Harriet Lane*[qv] and the defeat of the federal fleet at Galveston Harbor on January 1, 1863. He received special mention for his courage at the battle of Galveston.[qv] Brady was elected to the Tenth Legislature in 1863 and served as chairman of the committee on finance. In 1866 he was chairman of the committee on internal improvements in the Eleventh Legislature, and he was an advocate of the State Plan for building railroads. As a senator in the Sixteenth Legislature in 1878, he was chairman of the committee on public debt. In 1880 he was nominated for Congress by the National Greenback Labor party.

On March 31, 1858, he married Caledonia Tinsley of Brazoria County. The Brady home, known as the Cedars or the Brady Place, comprised 2,000 acres, from which the Magnolia Park subdivision was later developed. After his first wife's death Brady married Lennie Sherman, the daughter of Sidney Sherman,[qv] on November 24, 1880. When Lennie died, Brady married Estelle Jenkins of Maryland, with whom he had two daughters. Brady bred thoroughbred cattle and served as the first president of the Texas State Fair Association. He died after suffering a stroke on an inspection of the port of Houston on June 26, 1890, and was buried at Glenwood Cemetery.

BIBLIOGRAPHY: Daughters of the Republic of Texas, *Founders and Patriots of the Republic of Texas* (Austin, 1963–). *History of Texas, Together with a Biographical History of the Cities of Houston and Galveston* (Chicago: Lewis, 1895). Houston Metropolitan Research Center Files, Houston Public Library. Marguerite Johnston, *Houston, The Unknown City, 1836–1946* (College Station: Texas A&M University Press, 1991). *Jeanette H. Flachmeier*

BRADY, PETER RAINSFORD (1825–1902). Peter Rainsford Brady, surveyor, soldier, and public servant, was born on August 4, 1825, in Georgetown, Washington, D.C., the son of Peter and Ann (Rainsford) Brady. He entered Georgetown College at the age of twelve and served in the United States Navy (1844–46) and on the United States Coast Survey before moving to San Antonio, Texas. In 1847 he joined the surveying party of J. J. Giddings and surveyed part of the Fisher-Miller Land Grant[qv] designated Giddings District 3, which included almost all of what is now McCulloch County and parts of Concho, Menard, and San Saba counties. According to Thomas Brown, a member of the party, Brady mistakenly identified a creek as the Concho River during the survey, and when the error was discovered the creek was designated "Brady's Creek" (now Brady Creek[qv]). According to family legend, however, Brady found the creek when the party was searching for water, and the stream was named in his honor. Over a quarter of a century passed before McCulloch County was organized and its county seat named Brady City.

Brady was recruited by Lt. Col. Peter Hansbrough Bell[qv] in November 1847 and served in the companies of William B. Crump and Samuel Highsmith[qv] protecting the western frontier of Texas. He was discharged on September 30, 1848, and after joining the California gold rush returned to Texas to serve as first lieutenant in Capt. W. A. A. (Bigfoot) Wallace's[qv] company of Texas Rangers[qv] in 1850–51. In 1853 he joined the surveying party of Andrew B. Gray,[qv] formed to survey for a route from Texas to California for the Thirty-second Parallel Railroad Company. When the expedition ended in 1854, Brady formed the Arizona Mining and Trading Company and settled in Arizona, then a part of New Mexico Territory. With the advent of the Civil War[qv] he found himself a minority in his allegiance to the Union and moved to Sonora, Mexico. From there he traveled, engaging in intelligence activities and locating supplies for the Union forces. During the years following the war he served in many public offices, including treasurer and sheriff of Pima County, Arizona; sheriff, treasurer, school trustee, and surveyor of Pinal County, Arizona; chairman of the Board of Commissioners for the State Prison System at Yuma; special agent of the United States Private Court of Claims; and member of the Eighth, Sixteenth and Nineteenth assemblies of the Arizona Territorial legislature, from which he retired in 1898 as the oldest member at age seventy-three. In addition to his many years of public service Brady was a pioneer in the development of the Arizona mining and cattle industries and, as a charter member and officer of the Arizona Pioneers Historical Society (formed in 1884), was active in preserving the area's heritage.

Brady married Juana Mendivil (Mendibles), and they had four sons and a daughter. Later widowed, he married María Antonia Ochóa, and they had three sons and a daughter. Bearing his name are not only Brady Creek and the city of Brady but Brady Lake, Brady Mountains, and the Brady Bend of the Colorado River in Concho County. He died on May 3, 1902, ten years before Arizona became the forty-eighth state. On July 3, 1993, artist Frederick Hambly presented portraits of Peter R. Brady (his great-great grandfather) and Ben McCulloch[qv] to the Heart of Texas Museum at the Heritage Days celebration in Brady.

BIBLIOGRAPHY: Jessie Laurie Barfoot, History of McCulloch County, Texas (M.A. thesis, University of Texas, 1937). Jessie Laurie Barfoot, "The Early History of McCulloch County," West Texas Historical Association *Year Book* 26 (1950). Francis P. Brady, "Portrait of a Pioneer," *Journal of Arizona History* 16 (Summer 1975). *Reminiscences of Peter R. Brady, Who Accompanied the Expedition* (Los Angeles: Westernlore Press, 1963). *Marilyn Carroll Smiland*

BRADY, TEXAS. Brady, the county seat of McCulloch County, is located on U.S. highways 87, 283, and 190, 115 miles northwest of Austin, near the geographic center of Texas. When the area was settled in the 1870s, the community was named Brady City after Brady Creek, which runs through town. The name was shortened to Brady when the town was incorporated in 1906. In 1787–88 Spanish explorer José Mares[qv] crossed the creek near the site of present Brady. Henry and Nancy Fulcher, the first settlers on Brady Creek, donated land for the townsite in the mid-1870s. Allison Ogden and his father-in-law, Ben Henton, built a store in 1875. A post office opened in 1876. After residents of McCulloch County chose Brady as county seat on May 15, 1876, the town grew fairly quickly. Brady had about fifty residents in 1877, and a stone courthouse was completed in 1878. Thomas Maples began weekly publication of the Brady *Sentinel* in 1880; by 1884 Brady had two churches, a district school, three stores, two hotels, and 300 residents.

Stock raising was the primary occupation in the Brady area before 1900. In the 1870s and 1880s local ranchers drove their cattle to markets in Kansas. Most other trade was with Brownwood and Lampasas. The number of farms and fences increased with the influx of immigrants in the late 1880s and 1890s. Poultry, sheep, goats, cotton, and pecans joined cattle as important sources of income for area residents. When the Fort Worth and Rio Grande Railway arrived in 1903, Brady became a principal shipping point for Central Texas. The Gulf, Colorado and Santa Fe came to Brady in 1912. By 1914 the town had grown to include four churches, two schools, two banks, several processing plants, manufacturing and supply outlets, and 2,669 residents.

In 1926 Brady residents celebrated the building of forty-two-acre Richards Park by holding a two-day barbecue on the Fourth of July weekend; it was such a success that the celebration was labeled the "July Jubilee" and became an annual event. Curtis Field[qv] opened just north of Brady in 1942 as a pilot-training school. Also during World War II[qv] a German prisoner-of-war camp was built three miles east of the town; it housed more than 300 Germans, most of them members of Rommel's Afrika Korps (*see* GERMAN PRISONERS OF WAR).

Brady grew slowly from the 1920s through the 1950s, with population estimates reaching a peak of 6,800 in 1958. In 1959 the Gulf, Colorado and Santa Fe Railway abandoned the section of track between Brownwood and Brady, thereby reducing Brady's access to outside markets. The population fell to 5,338 by 1961 and subsequently stabilized. Brady Reservoir[qv] was completed in 1963 for flood control, municipal and industrial water needs, and recreation. The Atchison, Topeka and Santa Fe abandoned the track between Brady and Eden in 1972, leaving the town with only a branch track to connect it with the main line at Lometa, in Lampasas County.

Brady had 5,925 residents and 142 businesses in 1988. It was principally a farming and ranching community. Its industry included a mohair-combing plant and sand-mining operations. The Francis King Art Gallery and Museum houses works by King, a painter and sculptor, and a collection of restored antique cars. Brady celebrates an annual band festival and goat cook-off every Labor Day. The stone courthouse, built in 1900, was renovated in 1974. In 1989 G. Rollie White Downs, one of the first horse racetracks in Texas after the passage of pari-mutuel laws in 1989, operated briefly in Brady but was unprofitable and closed by 1990. Brady's population in 1990 was 5,946.

BIBLIOGRAPHY: Jessie Laurie Barfoot, History of McCulloch County, Texas (M.A. thesis, University of Texas, 1937). Wayne Spiller, comp., *Handbook of McCulloch County History* (Vol. 1, Seagraves,

Texas: Pioneer, 1976; Vol. 2, Canyon, Texas: Staked Plains Press, 1986). Vertical Files, Barker Texas History Center, University of Texas at Austin. *Vivian Elizabeth Smyrl*

BRADY BEND. Brady Bend is a bend on the Colorado River at the northeastern Concho county line, a quarter mile west of the Concho–McCulloch county line and ten miles northeast of Millersview (at 31°29′ N, 99°37′ W). It curves through flat to rolling terrain surfaced by clay and sandy loams that support grasses, scrub brush, mesquite, and cactus.

BRADY CREEK. Brady Creek rises thirteen miles southwest of Eden in southwestern Concho County (at 31°06′ N, 100°02′ W) and flows ninety miles eastward, through McCulloch County and into west central San Saba County, to its mouth on the San Saba River, twenty-one miles southwest of San Saba (at 31°08′ N, 98°59′ W). The creek, which has flowing water throughout most of its course, is dammed in its upper reaches at Camp Billy Gibbons, a Boy Scout camp belonging to the Comanche Trail Council, and again at the Brady Reservoir, three miles west of Brady in McCulloch County. It traverses flat to rolling terrain surfaced in some places by shallow, stony soil and in others by clay loams that support grasses, oaks, junipers, and mesquite. In the scout camp the creek's south bank is a high bluff. Tributaries of the stream in Concho County include Live Oak Creek, Fitzgerald Creek, Harden Branch, Kelly Creek, and Maverick Creek, and in McCulloch County, South Brady Creek, Bowie Creek, Live Oak Creek, Post Oak Creek, Onion Creek, and Little Brady Creek.

BRADY MOUNTAINS. The Brady Mountains extend from west to east across Concho and McCulloch counties (their center point is 31°16′ N, 99°35′ W). The highest elevation in these mountains is 2,021 feet above sea level. The surrounding terrain is flat to rolling and surfaced by shallow, stony soils or clay loams that support oak, juniper, mesquite, and grasses.

BRADY RESERVOIR. Brady Reservoir is in the Colorado River basin three miles west of Brady in central McCulloch County (at 31°07′ N, 99°24′ W). The project is owned and operated by the city of Brady as a municipal and industrial water supply. Construction began on December 27, 1961, and was completed on May 14, 1963; impoundment of water began on May 22, 1963. The reservoir has a conservation storage capacity of 30,430 acre-feet and a surface area of 2,020 acres at the service spillway crest elevation of 1,743 feet above mean sea level. At the emergency spillway crest elevation of 1,762 feet the reservoir capacity is 90,480 acre-feet, and the surface area is 4,464 acres. This additional capacity provides 60,050 acre-feet of surcharge space for temporary retention of floodwaters. The drainage area of Brady Creek above the dam is 508 square miles.

BIBLIOGRAPHY: C. L. Dowell, *Dams and Reservoirs in Texas: History and Descriptive Information* (Texas Water Commission Bulletin 6408 [Austin, 1964]). Wayne Spiller, comp., *Handbook of McCulloch County History* (Vol. 1, Seagraves, Texas: Pioneer, 1976; vol. 2, Canyon, Texas: Staked Plains Press, 1986). *Seth D. Breeding*

BRAGG, TEXAS. Bragg is on Farm Road 1293 ten miles west of Kountze in northwestern Hardin County. The site was named for former Confederate general Braxton Bragg and was a flag stop on the Gulf, Colorado and Santa Fe Railway, which was built through the area in 1901. A small community grew up around the stop when John Henry Kirby,[qv] seeking to harvest the rich forests of the Big Thicket,[qv] built a sawmill there in 1901. Although the mill was not rebuilt after a 1903 fire, Bragg became an important railroad junction when the Santa Fe system extended a branch line to the oil boomtown of Saratoga in 1904. A hotel, a depot, and a post office were built at Bragg to serve railroad and oil men in the region. The community's post office was closed in 1914. The other railroad installations were dismantled when the Saratoga trunk line was abandoned in 1934. Scattered oil and gas wells were drilled north of Bragg during the 1950s. A small agricultural community remained there in 1990.

BIBLIOGRAPHY: Aline House, *Big Thicket: Its Heritage* (San Antonio: Naylor, 1967). Mary Lou Proctor, A History of Hardin County (M.A. thesis, University of Texas, 1950). *Robert Wooster*

BRAHMAN CATTLE. The Brahman, *Bos indicus*, is thought to have originated in India more than 4,000 years ago. Brahman cattle were introduced to Texas in the mid-1800s and have since been bred with Hereford[qv] and shorthorn cows to produce animals more resistant to disease and insects. Over the years southeastern Texas has become the major breeding center for the American Brahman. There are more than thirty breeds of *Bos indicus*, but only four—Guzerat, Gir, Nellore and Krishna valley (all named for place names in India except for the last, which is named for a river there)—have figured in the development of the distinct American Brahman. Two of the earliest importations to America were to South Carolina, where a Dr. Campbell and Campbell R. Bryce brought two Indian bulls and four cows from Egypt in 1835 and Dr. James Bolton Davis imported some Brahmans in 1849. The breeding records of Davis's first two bulls was lost during the Civil War.[qv] In 1854 two to four bulls were shipped by the British government to a Richard Barrow in Louisiana. As early as 1860 Brahman crosses that probably originated from the Barrow cattle were shipped to Hays County, Texas, and a Brahman bull was included in a bankruptcy transfer in Comal County in 1862. In 1871 rancher Mifflin Kenedy[qv] bought 120 cattle that were part Brahman and part Durham. In 1874 he and Richard King[qv] purchased fifteen Brahman bulls in New Orleans that were then transported to Rockport, Texas. Brahman herds were also developed in Galveston and at the ranches of James A. McFaddin[qv] and John David Miller at Victoria. John N. Keeran and Abel H. "Shanghai" Pierce[qqv] bought five Brahmans at Indianola in 1878. In 1885, J. M. Frost and Albert Montgomery imported two Brahman bulls, named Khedive and Richard III, from India to New Orleans, where they were bred with the offspring of Barrow's four bulls. Frost-Montgomery Brahmans were subsequently sold for cattle-improvement programs in coastal areas of Texas, Florida, and Louisiana. Allen M. McFaddin of Victoria and F. B. Wood of Refugio purchased the remaining herd of the Montgomery cattle after Montgomery's death in 1894. Another group of Brahmans was brought to the United States by the Hagenbeck Circus for show at the St Louis World's Fair of 1904. Al McFaddin probably brought one of those bulls, Prince, to Texas. The largest early importation was financed by Thomas M. O'Connor and the estate of Shanghai Pierce. A. P. Borden toured India for the Pierce estate and selected fifty-one Brahman cattle, which were quarantined in 1906 in New York harbor, where about eighteen died of surra. As a result of the surra outbreak the Department of Agriculture forbade importation of cattle from India until 1946. From 1906 until 1946 any Brahman cattle that entered the United States came through Brazil and Canada. The Brazilian Brahman was called a zebu. In 1924 ninety of these were brought across the Rio Grande into Texas by Dr. Ferdinand Ruffier at Eagle Pass and distributed throughout South Texas. In 1946 eighteen more zebu bulls were brought to Texas from Brazil.

Apparently little has been done to breed purebred Brahmans for meat production. Instead, their desirable characteristics have been used to improve other breeds for production in Texas, principally Herefords and shorthorns. Several cattle breeds have been developed in Texas from crossbreeding with the Brahman. The famous Santa Gertrudis of the King Ranch[qv] is three-eighths Brahman and five-eighths shorthorn, and the Brangus is three-fourths Brahman and one-fourth Angus. Other Brahman crossbreeds are the beefmaster, a mix of 50 percent Brahman and roughly equal percentages of shorthorn and Hereford; the Braford, which is three-eighths Brahman and five-eighths Hereford; the Charbray, which is three-eighths Brahman and five-eighths Charolais; and the Simbrah, which consists of three-eighths Brahman and five-eighths Simmental. The most distinguishing characteristic of the Brahman is a large hump over the shoulders. Bulls weigh 1,600 to 2,200 pounds at maturity and cows 1,000 to 1,400. Most are varying shades of grey or red with a black muzzle, hoofs, and switch. They also have a well-developed dewlap extending in folds from the lower jaw to the chest. The Brahman has several traits that suit it for the hot Texas climate. It has sweat glands throughout the body that enable it to withstand more heat than other breeds, and a muscular membrane under the skin that enables it to shake off insects. Because they can travel long distances from water, Brahmans have greater grazing range than other cattle. They are highly resistant to ticks, which indirectly cause the death of many beef animals (*see* TEXAS FEVER), and are practically immune to pinkeye and cancer eye. They seldom seek shelter from the sun, so are out grazing when other breeds are lying in the shade.

In February 1924, mainly through the efforts of cattleman James W. Sartwelle, a group of Brahman breeders met at the Rice Hotel in Houston and founded the American Brahman Breeders Association for the purpose of registering worthy animals. A. M. McFaddin served as the first president, and the association formally adopted "Brahman," as opposed to other versions of the name, including Brahma, Bramah, Brahmin, and Bremmer. (Regardless of its spelling, the term is often pronounced "Braymer" in Texas.) The first animal registered was a bull named Sam Houston, a descendant of McFaddin's Prince. Members of the association established standard characteristics required for registration and formed committees to inspect every animal before it could be recorded. By 1942 more than 33,000 American Brahman animals had been registered. In 1964, after Governor John Connally[qv] proclaimed a Brahman bull, Bobo, a "Texan Ambassador of Goodwill," Jerry D. Cotten rode the bull to the World's Fair in New York City. His journey covered more than 2,000 miles and took seven months. In 1982 more than 350,000 Brahmans were registered and the breeders association, headquartered in Houston, enrolled about 300 American Brahman breeders from Texas.

BIBLIOGRAPHY: Joe A. Akerman, *American Brahman* (Houston: American Brahman Breeders Association, 1982). Charles Schreiner III, "The Background and Development of Brahman Cattle in Texas," *Southwestern Historical Quarterly* 52 (April 1949).

Art Leatherwood

BRAINARD, EDWARD HENRY (1860–1942). Edward Henry Brainard, early Panhandle[qv] rancher, the son of Mr. and Mrs. Peter H. Brainard, was born on July 4, 1860, in Otis, Massachusetts, and moved with his parents to Sparrowbush, New York, in 1868. There he completed high school at the age of fifteen and did such various odd jobs as clerking in local stores and rafting on the Delaware River. In the spring of 1880 he went to Colorado to work for the Pollard and Piper cattle firm. He accompanied the Pollards to the Texas Panhandle and worked for a time on Robert Moody's[qv] PO Ranch. After a brief return trip to New York in the fall of 1882 Brainard went to work for Joseph Morgan's[qv] Triangle Ranch, northeast of the site of present Canadian. He always recalled Morgan's beneficence; when Morgan was fatally stricken with smallpox Brainard rode thirty-five miles to Mobeetie to get a doctor. After Henry W. Cresswell[qv] added the Triangle to his Bar CC range Brainard went to work for him, and in 1887 Cresswell promoted him to range foreman. The following year Brainard acquired a 480-acre tract on John's Creek in Roberts County. His parents and sister Mary, who later became the first schoolteacher in Canadian, moved from Sparrowbush to Canadian to be near him. Although he had begun purchasing land and cattle of his own, Brainard continued as foreman of the Bar CC until 1895. He afterwards made his home in Canadian, where he became involved in banking. In 1901 he married Kittie Belle Fullerton, daughter of a family of Dutch and Irish extraction from Sparrowbush. They had two children. Over the next several years Brainard took pride in his high-grade Hereford cattle, which bore his Lazy B brand. He served on the executive committee of the Texas Cattle Raisers Association (now the Texas and Southwestern Cattle Raisers Association[qv]) and for eight years was a member of the Canadian City Commission. By 1940 the Brainard family had acquired 50,000 acres of ranchland. Brainard died on August 20, 1942, and was buried in the Canadian cemetery. Decades later the family continued to operate the Lazy B. The old Brainard home remained a landmark in Canadian.

BIBLIOGRAPHY: Sallie B. Harris, *Cowmen and Ladies: A History of Hemphill County* (Canyon, Texas: Staked Plains, 1977). John M. Hendrix, "Ed Brainard: 60 Years a Cowman," *Cattleman*, July 1940. Lester Fields Sheffy, "Edward Henry Brainard," *Panhandle-Plains Historical Review* 19 (1946). F. Stanley [Stanley F. L. Crocchiola], *Rodeo Town (Canadian, Texas)* (Denver: World, 1953). *H. Allen Anderson*

BRALLEY, FRANCIS MARION (1867–1924). Francis Marion Bralley, college administrator, was born at Honey Grove, Texas, on March 6, 1867. He attended county schools and, after graduating from Wilcott Institute in 1885, enrolled in Methodist College, where he graduated two years later. During the next five years he taught in the public schools of Fannin and Lamar counties. On March 17, 1892, he married Melida Meade. The couple had four sons. In 1882 Bralley became superintendent of Fannin County schools. Six years later he returned to his hometown to serve as superintendent of the Honey Grove school system.

In 1905 he began a three-year appointment in Austin as the chief clerk in the State Department of Education (later part of the Texas Education Agency[qv]). He resigned in 1908 to become the general agent of the Texas Conference for Education. Although he served in this position for only one year, Bralley is credited with the success of an amendment to the Texas Constitution that allows school districts to levy local taxes for construction and needed repairs. In 1909 he accepted the presidency of the Texas School for the Blind.[qv] In November of the same year Governor Thomas Campbell[qv] appointed him to complete the term of R. B. Cousins[qv] as state superintendent of public transportation. The following year Bralley ran unopposed for the elective office. He was reelected in 1912 and resigned on September 1, 1913, to become head of the University of Texas extension department. He resigned that post the next year to accept the presidency of the College of Industrial Arts (now Texas Woman's University) at Denton. Bralley served as president of the college for eleven years. During his tenure the school's academic reputation increased. Its enrollment grew from 700 in 1913 to 2,000 in 1924, and the school property increased in value from $325,000 to just over $2 million.

Bralley was president of the chamber of commerce and the Rotary Club and chairman of the board of the Christian church of Denton. He was a Mason and Knight of Pythias and president of the board of regents of the State Teachers College (now the University of North Texas). On August 23, 1924, he died in Dallas of a bronchial infection. He was buried in the Odd Fellows Cemetery in Denton.

BIBLIOGRAPHY: Dallas *Morning News*, August 24, 1924. Vertical Files, Barker Texas History Center, University of Texas at Austin.

David Minor

BRAMAN, DON EGBERT ERASTUS (1814–1897). Don Braman, public official, the oldest child of Andrew and Nancy (Hawes) Braman, was born in Norton, Bristol County, Massachusetts, on September 21, 1814. He attended the common schools of Providence, Rhode Island. In 1833 he visited an uncle, Don Carlos Hawes, in Macon, Georgia, and in 1835 participated in a raid against the Cherokee Indians in what is now Eufaula. In 1836 he traveled to New Orleans, and the following year he headed to Texas with a large number of volunteers for the Texas army. He enlisted at Camp Johnson in Jackson County on March 9, 1837, and was discharged on June 30,

1838, from Captain Miles, Company E, Second Regiment, Texas Volunteers. He received payment of land in Baylor County for his service.

Braman received a second class headright of 640 acres in Matagorda County and served as a customs officer at Matagorda. He was appointed clerk of the First Judicial District Court in 1847 and served in that office until 1866. He studied law while he was district clerk and was admitted to the bar in 1853. He served as mayor of Matagorda for several years and was appointed county judge in 1867 by Governor Elisha M. Pease.[qv] Braman was the author of *Braman's Information About Texas* (1857), which gave a description of counties and information for emigrants. He was a pro-Union Southerner, but he had a few slaves. In 1860 he was listed as a lawyer with $8,200 worth of land and $7,300 in personal property. He financed cattle drives to northern markets. After the 1886 hurricane he moved to Victoria. On April 28, 1844, he married Mary Elizabeth Burkhart; they had eleven children, who were all baptized at Christ Episcopal Church, Matagorda. Braman died on February 17, 1897, and his funeral was conducted at St. Mary's Catholic Church, where he had been confirmed in 1893. He was buried in Evergreen Cemetery.

BIBLIOGRAPHY: John Columbus Marr, History of Matagorda County (M.A. thesis, University of Texas, 1928). Matagorda County Historical Commission, *Historic Matagorda County* (3 vols., Houston: Armstrong, 1986).
Zia Crowell Miller

BRAMLETTE, EDGAR ELLIOTT (1860–1929). Edgar Elliott Bramlette, teacher, foreign minister, and school administrator, the son of William and Adelia (Bates) Bramlette, was born in Paris, Texas, on November 19, 1860. He took his B.A. degree at Vanderbilt University in 1883 and from 1883 to 1886 was instructor in classical languages at the University of Texas, where he received the first M.A. degree awarded by the school (1886). In 1884 he married Louise Linn in Austin. Bramlette was United States consul in Germany from 1886 to 1889. There he helped break up a system of undervaluation by which some importers had gained a monopoly on goods. He also wrote an informative report on trichinosis with regard to an American pork embargo. His import investigation led to his appointment as special expert of the United States Treasury Department. From 1889 to 1891 he studied at Leipzig University. He was superintendent of schools at Fort Worth, Texas, from 1893 to 1898, taught languages at the Agricultural and Mechanical College of Texas (now Texas A&M University) from 1898 to 1900, was president of John Tarleton College (now Tarleton State University) from 1900 to 1906, and taught at Texarkana and Huntsville from 1906 to 1911, when he became superintendent of the Texas School for the Blind[qv] in Austin. From 1923 to 1929 he was superintendent of the American Publishing House for the Blind at Louisville, Kentucky. He was a member of Kappa Alpha, the Knights of Pythias, and the Masons. He was a Methodist and a Democrat. Bramlette died in Louisville on March 6, 1929, and was buried at Oakwood Cemetery, Austin.

BIBLIOGRAPHY: Austin *Statesman,* March 9, 1929. Lewis E. Daniell, *Texas—The Country and Its Men* (Austin?, 1924?). Vertical Files, Barker Texas History Center, University of Texas at Austin.

BRAMMER, WILLIAM LEE (1929–1978). William Lee (Billy, Bill) Brammer, journalist and political novelist, son of H. L. and Kathleen Brammer, was born at Dallas (Oak Cliff), Texas, on April 21, 1929. He graduated from North Texas State College (now the University of North Texas) and worked in the late 1940s and early 1950s as sports editor of the Denton *Record Chronicle*[qv] and on the staffs of the Corpus Christi *Caller-Times*[qv] and Austin *American.* Later in his career he was a writer for *Time* magazine and a contributing editor to *Texas Monthly* magazine and the *Texas Observer.*[qqv] From 1955 to 1959 Brammer worked as press aide in Washington, D.C., to Lyndon B. Johnson,[qv] when Johnson was Senate majority leader. During that period he wrote a 1950s era novel, *The Gay Place* (1961), which was set in an unnamed state capital that clearly was Austin. The novel's central figure was a crude and ruthless political progressive, Gov. Arthur Fenstemaker, who was a master of solving political crises and imposing order on the legislative process. The fictional governor, while depicted as an earthy but sympathetic and charming character, shared some of the personal traits and the political acumen of Lyndon Johnson. LBJ did not appreciate the book. *The Gay Place* was published by Houghton-Mifflin in March 1961 and won critical acclaim in literary circles but did not sell well. Pulitzer Prize-winning author and journalist David Halberstam called *The Gay Place* "an American classic that will be on reading lists a hundred years from now." Brammer had an excellent literary mind and a knack for the absurd that made him a master of the political lampoon. The novel earned him the Houghton-Mifflin Literary Fellowship Award for 1960 and was believed to be front-runner for the 1962 best book of fiction award of the Texas Institute of Letters,[qv] which went instead to Katherine Anne Porter's[qv] *Ship of Fools.* In 1963 *The Gay Place* was scheduled to be made into a movie starring Paul Newman, but a change in studio management caused the plans to be canceled.

Brammer covered the 1960 Democratic national convention as a correspondent for *Time* magazine. In 1961 he worked in the unsuccessful United States Senate campaign of Congressman James Wright of Fort Worth, who later served as speaker of the House. Brammer continued to write and received an advance from Random House to do a biography of Johnson while LBJ was serving in the White House. But Brammer developed "writer's block" and never completed another book. He lived in Austin and supported himself by holding numerous menial jobs (short-order cook, waiter, house-painter) until January 1970, when he was named to the faculty of the School of Journalism at Southern Methodist University in Dallas. That position was short-lived. Brammer returned to Austin, where he continued to write and work at odd jobs. Friends said his eccentric work habits and drug use, coupled with frequent moves and self-imposed pressure to produce a novel to match *The Gay Place,* caused physical deterioration and eventual loss of his drive to write. He lived in Austin in a room supplied by a friend, where he suffered cardiac arrest on February 11, 1978. He had been working an another novel, *Fustian Days,* when he died. *The Gay Place* has been reissued several times, including a paperback edition by Texas Monthly Press in 1978, and was reprinted in 1995 by the University of Texas Press.[qv] Brammer and his first wife, Nadine, were divorced in the 1950s. He married Dorothy Vance while in Washington. They were divorced in 1969. He was not married when he died. Brammer was survived by two daughters and one son. The funeral service for Brammer, a Protestant, was at the Wilke-Clay Funeral Home Chapel in Austin, and interment was in Laurel Land Memorial Park, Dallas.

BIBLIOGRAPHY: Vertical Files, Barker Texas History Center, University of Texas at Austin.
Walter H. Gray

BRANCH, ANTHONY MARTIN (1823–1867). Anthony Martin Branch, Confederate congressman, was born in Buckingham County, Virginia, on July 16, 1823, one of ten children of Winnifred (Guerrant) and Samuel Branch III. He graduated from Hampden-Sidney College in 1842 and in 1847 moved to Huntsville, Texas, where he formed a law partnership with Henderson Yoakum[qv] and became closely associated with Sam Houston.[qv] (When Houston died Branch served as executor of his will and guardian of his children.) On March 18, 1849, Branch married Amanda Smith.

In 1850 he was elected district attorney of the Seventh Judicial District. In 1859 he represented his district in the House of Representatives of the Eighth Texas Legislature, where, according to a contemporary biographer, he "well sustained his reputation for eloquence and ability." In November 1861 he was elected as a Democrat to the state Senate. Although a Unionist, he resigned from the Senate and on March 20, 1862, enlisted in the Confederate Army. A month later he was elected captain of Company A in Col. George Washington

Carter's[qv] Twenty-first Texas Cavalry. On August 3, 1863, Branch defeated Peter W. Gray[qv] in the race to represent the Third District of Texas in the Second Confederate Congress. In Richmond he served as a member of the Elections, Military Affairs, and Territories and Public Lands committees and was vitally interested in the exportation of cotton through Mexican ports. Although a staunch political ally of President Jefferson Davis,[qv] Branch was an uncompromising exponent of states' rights. As such he fought to keep Texas troops in Texas and opposed Confederate interference with the Texas economy. After the war he returned to Texas and was elected to the United States House of Representatives in both the Thirty-ninth and Fortieth congresses but was denied his seat by the Radical Republican majority. He returned to Huntsville and helped to incorporate the Central Transit Company in 1866. Branch practiced law until his death during a yellow fever epidemic, on October 3, 1867. He is buried in Oakwood Cemetery near the grave of Sam Houston.

BIBLIOGRAPHY: Clement Anselm Evans, ed., *Confederate Military History* (Atlanta: Confederate Publishing, 1899; extended ed., Wilmington, North Carolina: Broadfoot, 1987–89). Jon L. Wakelyn, *Biographical Dictionary of the Confederacy* (Westport, Connecticut: Greenwood, 1977). Ezra J. Warner and W. Buck Yearns, *Biographical Register of the Confederate Congress* (Baton Rouge: Louisiana State University Press, 1975).

Thomas W. Cutrer

Mary Elizabeth Branch, ca. 1930–44. Courtesy Huston-Tillotson College, Austin. Photograph courtesy ITC.

BRANCH, EDWARD THOMAS (1811–1861). Edward Thomas Branch, early Texas legislator and judge, was born in Richmond, Virginia, on December 6, 1811. After moving to Jackson, Mississippi, he arrived in 1835 in Texas, reportedly having been hijacked en route to Cuba, robbed, and put ashore at Anahuac; he settled in Liberty. He was defeated in the election of delegates to the Consultation[qv] but remained in Liberty as a teacher until the spring of 1836. At the outbreak of the Texas Revolution,[qv] he joined the revolutionary army.[qv] He served as first sergeant of William M. Logan's[qv] company from March 6 to June 6, 1836, and saw action at the battle of San Jacinto.[qv] He later reenlisted and served from July 7 to October 7, 1836, as first lieutenant in a company led by Benjamin Franklin Hardin.[qv]

After the government of the Republic of Texas[qv] was organized, Liberty County residents elected Branch a representative to the First and Second congresses (October 3, 1836–May 24, 1838), where he chaired the House Ways and Means Committee. In 1838 a joint session of the legislature appointed him judge of the Fifth Judicial District, a position that constitutionally made him an associate justice of the Texas Supreme Court as well. However, his active service on the bench was brief. The court did not meet until January 1840, and Branch left office on August 12 of that year, before the end of his term. In 1843 he was postmaster in Liberty and in 1846 was elected to the House of Representatives of the First Legislature of the newly annexed state. Branch was a slaveowner who at one time owned 3,343 acres of land. When he was not occupied by public business he divided his time between farming and the practice of law in Liberty County. He was a Methodist and a Mason. He married Annie Cleveland Wharton, an adopted child of Texas patriot and diplomat William Harris Wharton,[qv] on August 15, 1838. They had five children. Branch died on September 24, 1861, and is buried in a family cemetery in Liberty.

BIBLIOGRAPHY: Joe E. Ericson, *Judges of the Republic of Texas (1836–1846): A Biographical Directory* (Dallas: Taylor, 1980). Texas House of Representatives, *Biographical Directory of the Texan Conventions and Congresses, 1832–1845* (Austin: Book Exchange, 1941).

Patricia L. Duncan

BRANCH, MARY ELIZABETH (1881–1944). Mary Elizabeth Branch, college president, was born near Farmville, Virginia, on May 20, 1881, the daughter of Tazewell and Harriett Branch. Although few African Americans[qv] received a public education in the late nineteenth century, the Branch children attended Farmville's elementary school. Their parents, born slaves but now members of a developing black middle class, also taught their children at home. After completing high school studies in the normal school at Virginia State College, Petersburg, Mary Branch became an English teacher in the elementary school at Blackstone, Virginia. Later she joined the faculty of her alma mater, where she remained for twenty years. She was a challenging and popular instructor and also served as the college's housing director. During summers she attended the University of Pennsylvania, Columbia University, and the University of Chicago. The last granted her a bachelor's degree in 1922 and a master's degree in English in 1925. She also began studies there towards a doctorate in education. Towards the end of her career she received honorary degrees from Virginia State College and Howard University.

Branch began teaching social studies at Sumner Junior College in Kansas City, Kansas, in 1927. In 1928 she became dean of women at Vashon High School in St. Louis, which was then the largest school for black girls in the country. In 1930 the American Missionary Association appointed her president of Tillotson College in Austin, Texas. A troubled institution, Tillotson had been forced by declining enrollments and poor administration to reorganize as a junior college for women in 1929. As president, Branch sought to make Tillotson a successful and respected four-year college once more. Under her direction the college's facilities were improved. The library expanded. Old buildings underwent renovation, and new buildings, including a men's dormitory and a gymnasium, were constructed. In order to attract new students and strengthen the educational program, Branch abolished the high school program and increased the college budget. She also doubled the size of the faculty and raised education requirements for instructors. She recruited students throughout the Southwest and offered scholarships to the most needy. In an effort to give Tillotson a more contemporary atmosphere, Branch abolished mandatory chapel, permitted the organization of fraternities and sororities, and encouraged the formation of academic and athletic clubs. Throughout her tenure she also worked to improve the college's relationship with the community by participating in civic affairs and establishing contacts with faculty at the University of Texas and Samuel Huston College, as well as with public school teachers and administrators. She also worked towards a merger with Samuel Huston College, although the two institutions did not join until after her tenure.

During the Branch administration enrollment steadily grew. Moreover, in 1935, Tillotson reorganized as a coeducational, four-year institution. In 1936 the college was admitted to membership in the American Association of Colleges, and in 1943 it received an "A" rating from the Southern Association of Colleges and Secondary Schools. While in Austin, Mary Branch became active in the civil-rights movement. She became president of the Austin chapter of the National Association for the Advancement of Colored People[qv] in 1943. She also served on the State Interracial Commission of Texas. During the Great Depression[qv] she devoted much time to the National Youth Administration.[qv] In 1935 Lyndon B. Johnson[qv] appointed her to the NYA Negro Advisory Board for Texas. In 1944 Branch helped to establish the United Negro College Fund. She died in Baltimore, Maryland, on July 6, 1944, at the height of her career.

BIBLIOGRAPHY: Olive D. Brown and Michael R. Heintze, "Mary Branch: Private College Educator," in *Black Leaders: Texans for Their Times*, ed. Alwyn Barr and Robert A. Calvert (Austin: Texas State Historical Association, 1981). Mary Jenness, *Twelve Negro Americans* (New York, 1936). Chrystine I. Shackles, *Reminiscences of Huston-Tillotson College* (Austin, 1973).

Olive D. Brown and Michael R. Heintze

BRANCH, TEXAS. Branch is on the shoreline of Lavon Lake eleven miles southeast of McKinney in southern Collin County. The settlement was named for J. T. Branch, who operated a general store there. A post office operated at the community from 1901 until 1903, when mail was routed through nearby Clear Lake. In 1960 the population of Branch was twenty-five; in 1980 and 1990 it was estimated at 447.

BIBLIOGRAPHY: Roy Franklin Hall and Helen Gibbard Hall, *Collin County: Pioneering in North Texas* (Quanah, Texas: Nortex, 1975). J. Lee and Lillian J. Stambaugh, *A History of Collin County* (Austin: Texas State Historical Association, 1958). *David Minor*

BRANCHVILLE, TEXAS. Branchville is on Farm Road 485 thirteen miles east of Cameron in eastern Milam County. The town may have received its name when W. B. Easterwood, a store owner in Port Sullivan, opened a branch store in the area. Branchville was the name given to the community's post office when it opened in 1878. The population grew from twenty in 1884 to eighty-five in 1896, at which time the community had a Baptist church, a district school, and two general stores. In 1903 Branchville had a one-teacher school for thirty white students and two one-teacher schools for 133 black students. The post office closed in 1908, but in the 1940s the community had two schools, four churches, several businesses, and 100 residents. Its schools were consolidated with the Cameron Independent School District by the early 1970s. Branchville had 200 residents in 1990.

BIBLIOGRAPHY: Lelia M. Batte, *History of Milam County, Texas* (San Antonio: Naylor, 1956). *Vivian Elizabeth Smyrl*

BRANDEN BRANCH. Branden Branch rises 2½ miles northwest of Forestburg in southeastern Montague County (at 33°34′ N, 97°35′ W) and runs south for 8½ miles to its mouth on Denton Creek, a mile north of the county line and a mile west of New Harp (at 33°27′ N, 97°36′ W). It crosses generally flat to rolling terrain surfaced by sandy and clay loams that support water-tolerant hardwood trees, conifers, brush, and grasses. The area has served as crop and range land.

BRANDON, TEXAS. Brandon is at the intersection of State Highway 22 and Farm Road 1243, ten miles east of Hillsboro in eastern Hill County. In 1840–41 a road was surveyed on the banks of Pecan Creek several miles from the site of Brandon. Elisha S. and Martha Wyman settled on this road in 1846. In 1851 a voting box was placed across the road in a grove of trees near Wyman Spring, when the area was still in Navarro County. All seventeen men in what would become Hill County voted there in the election. In 1852 a post office known as White Rock was established on White Rock Creek in the home of Henry Harlos (or Hollis) in Navarro County. In 1853, when Hill County was established, the Brandon area was in the new county. Joseph M. Martin built White Rock Mill on the creek before 1855, and by 1861 the Woods home in the community was used as an overnight stagecoach stop; it hosted such famous guests as Cynthia Ann Parker.[qv] In 1868 the name of the post office was changed to Jackson, probably to avoid confusion between the numerous White Rock communities in Texas. It had a post office only five months before it was withdrawn. The community received a post office in 1873 and was named Brandon. Dr. J. R. Harrington, a dentist, named the settlement and served as its first postmaster. The community was known as a health resort, and people camped near its several sulfur springs. Brandon was a prosperous community on the major road from Corsicana to Hillsboro. At one time it had a hotel, three churches, a school, a blacksmith shop, a cotton gin, and grocery, hardware, and drug stores.

In 1888 the St. Louis, Arkansas and Texas Railway of Texas, which became the St. Louis Southwestern of Texas in 1891 and was known as the "Cotton Belt," was constructed through the county but missed Brandon. The citizens decided to move the community one mile northeast to be on the railroad. The new location was on the Calvin Parker and James McGee surveys, and the community was originally to be called Ferguson, for R. A. (Bob) Ferguson, who donated much of the townsite, but instead it took the name of the old townsite, Brandon. The town was laid out in 1888 and by 1890 had a population of seventy-five. By 1892 it was incorporated with W. N. Harris as mayor. Later that year a new school was built. In 1905 it had two teachers and ninety-three students. By 1914 Brandon had a population of 450 and two banks. In 1934 the population was 260, and State Highway 22 had been constructed through the community. With the removal of the railroad in 1936, the business population declined still further. In 1980 and 1990 the population was eighty. The community still had several active churches, a grocery store, a gas station, a cotton gin, and a grain elevator. "Old Brandon" still had a cemetery.

BIBLIOGRAPHY: Hill County Historical Commission, *A History of Hill County, Texas, 1853–1980* (Waco: Texian, 1980).

Lisa C. Maxwell

BRANIFF, THOMAS ELMER (1883–1954). Thomas Elmer Braniff, businessman and aviation pioneer, was born on December 6, 1883, in Salina, Kansas, to John A. and Mary Catherine (Baker) Braniff. In 1891 the family moved to Kansas City, Missouri, where Braniff at-

Thomas Braniff, Fort Worth, 1935. Courtesy Braniff Collection, History of Aviation Collection, University of Texas at Dallas. The new Lockheed L-10A had just arrived at Meacham Field in Fort Worth when Braniff posed with it in 1935.

tended public school until the end of the 1901 term, when he followed his family to the Oklahoma City area. There he joined his father's insurance business but soon opened his own office in partnership with Frank Merrill. On October 26, 1912, he married Bess Thurman; they had two children, who predeceased them.

Braniff built his company into one of the leading mortgage and insurance businesses in the Southwest and gained industry-wide attention by his development of a plan using surety bonds to guarantee first-mortgage indebtedness. He bought out Merrill in 1916 to form the T. E. Braniff Company, and in 1924 he bought out a partner in a loan firm and incorporated the business as Braniff Investment Company. He built Oklahoma City's first skyscraper, the T. C. Braniff Company headquarters, founded Prudential Fire Insurance Company with Ed Overholser in 1928, and in 1929 was one of the incorporators of Kansas City Fire Insurance Company.

In 1927, in partnership with several others, Braniff purchased a second-hand airplane. He and E. E. Westerfelt soon bought out the others. The following year Braniff joined his brother Paul in operating an airline between Oklahoma City and Tulsa, thus instituting the first airline in the Southwest, which became Braniff Airways,[qv] Incorporated, on November 3, 1930. Braniff moved the administrative headquarters to Love Field[qv] in Dallas on June 1, 1942, and took up residence in Dallas himself. At its peak, Braniff International was one of the largest airlines in the world, with 12,000 employees. It was the only major airline to retain the name of its founder.

Tom Braniff received honors from all over the world. He was a devout Catholic and was honored by his church as a Knight of Malta and a Knight of the Order of the Holy Sepulchre; in 1944 he was granted the title Knight Commander of the Order of St. Gregory the Great by Pope Pius XII, the highest honor that can be bestowed on a layman. Braniff was Catholic cochairman of the National Conference of Christians and Jews from 1946 until his death and helped found the World Organization for Brotherhood, from which he later received the first American citation. He served as a director of the American-Korean Foundation and as chairman of the Transportation and Commerce Committee of the United States Inter-American Council on Commerce and Production. Oklahoma City University and Southern Methodist University awarded him honorary degrees; he was also an honorary member of Delta Phi Epsilon, a foreign service fraternity. With his wife he set up the Braniff Foundation to support worthy religious, educational, and scientific undertakings. In 1952 the University of Denver selected him Aviation Man of the Year. Two years later, on January 10, 1954, he died in the crash of a private plane in Louisiana.

BIBLIOGRAPHY: Dallas *Morning News,* January 11, 1954, May 13, 1982. Dallas *Times Herald,* January 11, 1954, May 13, 1982. *Time,* May 24, 1982. *Who Was Who in America,* Vol. 4. *Joan Jenkins Perez*

BRANIFF AIRWAYS. Braniff Airways was once the world's sixth largest airline. Oklahoma City insurance man and financier Thomas Elmer Braniff[qv] and four friends founded the Oklahoma City–Tulsa Airline, beginning with partial payment on a five-seat Stinson Detroiter airplane. On June 20, 1928, this aircraft made its maiden voyage between the two cities, piloted by the founder's brother Paul. Three months later a group of Oklahoma businessmen invested in the company and changed its name to Paul R. Braniff, Incorporated, despite the fact that Thomas Braniff was in charge of the fledgling carrier.

Universal Air Lines, a St. Louis conglomerate seeking to develop an air-rail network in the center of the country to compete with Transcontinental Air Transport, a forerunner of Trans World Airlines, bought the company in 1929 and renamed it Braniff Air Lines. In 1930 Braniff Airways was incorporated and went public as a subsidiary of the Universal Air Lines System, with Paul Braniff as secretary-treasurer and Thomas Braniff as president. Universal sold its Braniff division to Aviation Corporation, the holding company that became American Airlines in 1934 (*see* AMR CORPORATION). Within two years Braniff adopted the advertising slogan "The World's Fastest Airlines" and began using Lockheed Vega aircraft to add routes to Chicago, Kansas City, St. Louis, and Wichita Falls, Texas.

Braniff was close to insolvency when the United States Post Office awarded it an airmail route between Dallas and Chicago in 1934. At the time airmail routes were the lifeblood of many small airlines, since they guaranteed a source of revenue in an unpredictable business climate. The same year Braniff moved company operations and maintenance facilities to Love Field,[qv] Dallas, from Oklahoma City. In 1935 the company bought Long and Harmon Air Service and gave it mail contracts connecting Dallas–Fort Worth and the Panhandle[qv] with Mexico through connections in Brownsville. As the first airline to offer service between Chicago and the Mexican border, Braniff adopted the advertising slogan, "From the Great Lakes to the Gulf."

During World War II[qv] Braniff surrendered over half its fleet to the United States military and trained military pilots, radio operators, and mechanics. It flew to the Panama Canal Zone and for the Air Transport Command. At the same time it continued to expand and in 1942 moved its administrative offices from Oklahoma City to Dallas. The Civil Aeronautics Board granted approval to serve South America in 1943, and the company was renamed Braniff International Airways. Braniff acquired Bowen Air Lines and operated it in 1935–36; it owned and operated Aerovias Braniff in Mexico from 1943 to 1946. By 1948 Braniff routes were opened to Ecuador, Panama, and Cuba, and in 1952 Braniff International merged with Mid-Continent Airlines, thus adding thirty-two routes to the twenty-nine domestic and nine international routes the company operated at the time.

T. E. Braniff was killed in a private plane crash near Shreveport, Louisiana, in 1954. Charles E. Beard,[qv] an air-transport expert who joined the firm as general traffic manager in 1935, was named president of the airline. Beard guided the airline to continued growth, particularly in South America. By 1957 Braniff's annual payroll had increased to over $22 million, and the company operated maintenance facilities in Dallas, Minneapolis–St. Paul, Chicago, Kansas City, San Antonio, and Lima, Peru. The company moved into a new ten-story headquarters building in Dallas and new terminal facilities at Love Field in 1958. Revenue passenger miles increased from 550 million in 1953 to 1.5 billion in 1964; during the same time the company's one-cent-per-share earnings increased to $2.03.

In August 1964 the Dallas-based Greatamerica Corporation, an insurance company, acquired 57.5 percent of Braniff stock. Troy Post, Greatamerica's Texas-born chairman, had decided to purchase Braniff after his senior vice president in charge of finance, C. Edward Acker, concluded a study of poorly managed companies and listed Braniff among the worst. To lead Braniff, Post recruited Harding L. Lawrence, former executive vice president of Continental Airlines. In 1965 Lawrence replaced Beard as president and chief executive officer of the airline and reincorporated Braniff Airways in Nevada in 1966. From that time until 1990, despite subsequent changes, Post and his administration dominated the firm. Lawrence brought a flamboyant style to the airline and oversaw Braniff's greatest period of growth. Declaring that "sameness is boring," he announced an "end of the plain plane" by painting company aircraft in seven bright solid colors, hiring an interior decorator to redesign cabins and terminals, and having world-renowned Italian fashion designer Emilio Pucci design revealing uniforms for company flight attendants. In November 1967 Post sold Greatamerica and a controlling interest of Braniff stock to Ling-Temco-Vought, Incorporated (*see* LTV CORPORATION). Friction arose when Braniff executives blamed LTV for bleeding the airline of cash during the late 1960s to finance other acquisitions. In 1971, on the orders of the United States Department of Justice, LTV was forced to divest itself of Braniff to purchase a steel company. Braniff International Corporation was formed in 1972 as a holding company with Braniff Airways.

By 1969 the company had become an exclusively jet airline using the advertising slogan, "If You've Got It, Flaunt It!" After his "Jellybean Airline" acquired South American competitor Panagra Airways (Pan American–Grace Airways) in 1967, Lawrence commissioned artist Alexander Calder to paint a DC-8, "to focus international attention on South America as a vacation destination." Calder also painted a Braniff Boeing 727 red, white, and blue in 1976 to commemorate the United States Bicentennial. By 1978 the airline was flying to destinations in the mainland United States, Hawaii, South America, and London, Paris, Frankfurt, and Amsterdam.

The Airline Deregulation Act of 1978 prompted Lawrence to embark on what was then the greatest expansion in airline history; acting on the conviction that survival in a deregulated environment was dependent on size, he added thirty-one destinations to Braniff service over the next two years. Long-term debt increased over $305 million from 1978 to the end of 1979, exacerbated by higher fuel prices and interest rates and a countrywide recession that led to decreased air travel in mid-1979. In the third quarter of 1979, generally the industry's most profitable quarter, Braniff lost $9.8 million, its first loss since early 1975. By 1980 interest payments rose to more than $92 million, and between 1978 and 1980 Braniff's net worth fell from roughly $250 million to just over $66 million. In 1979 Braniff withdrew from ten unprofitable routes, citing high fuel prices and low traffic levels. To raise cash the company began selling its more modern planes and relying on older, less fuel-efficient planes. Layoffs in 1979–80 reduced employees from a high of 15,000 to 11,500, and in 1980 the company withdrew from its unprofitable routes in the Far East. That year Braniff lost $131 million, an industry record at the time.

In December 1980 Lawrence resigned, and in January 1981 John J. Casey, executive vice president since 1968, was named chairman, president, and CEO. Casey, a former Seaboard World Airlines and American Airlines executive, refocused the company on its shorter routes and obtained a 10 percent pay cut agreement from union employees, but he was unable to stop the red ink and was shortly forced to lay off another 1,000 employees and discontinue all routes to Europe except the London route. In late 1981 Casey hired Howard D. Putnam, former president and chief executive officer of Dallas-based Southwest Airlines,[qv] to assume similar duties at Braniff. Putnam and Philip Guthrie, the executive vice president of finance, reduced the number of fares from 582 to fifteen and removed first-class seats from domestic flights. By the end of 1981 Braniff had a negative net worth estimated at $90 million. Unable to meet its payroll, Braniff International Corporation ceased operations in May 1982, recalled its sixty-two aircraft, fired all but 225 of its 9,000 employees, and filed for Chapter 11 protection from creditors.

Two attempts to resurrect the airline failed. In 1983 the Pritzker family of Chicago obtained bankruptcy-court approval for a $70 million offer to revive the airline. In 1984 a new Braniff, Incorporated, launched its first flight with a fleet of thirty planes under the direction of president William Slattery, formerly chief of European operations for Trans World Airlines. Of the company's 2,200 employees, 98 percent had worked for the old Braniff and agreed to return to work for lower wages. The low-cost airline, headquartered in Dallas, operated routes out of Dallas–Fort Worth International Airport[qv] to twenty-one cities. In 1988 Philadelphia investors Jeffrey W. Chodorow and Arthur G. Cohen bought the company, but increased price competition forced the airline to declare bankruptcy again in 1989 and ground its jets in November of the same year. Chodorow and Cohen started flights again under the Braniff name in 1991, using the assets of Emerald Airlines, a Houston charter airline they purchased in 1990. Under new chief executive officer Gregory B. Dix, the company attempted to carve a niche for itself in the leisure travel market by offering $79 one-way fares from Dallas–Fort Worth to Newark and Los Angeles. In 1992 the company ceased operations, again citing increased fare wars. By 1993 all that remained of the former airline was Dalfort Aviation, a training enterprise associated with Love Field in Dallas.

BIBLIOGRAPHY: Charles E. Beard, *Thomas E. Braniff, 1883–1954, Southwest Pioneer in Air Transportation* (New York: Newcomen Society, 1955). George Walker Cearley, Jr., *Braniff—With a Dash of Color and a Touch of Excellence* (Dallas: Airline Historical Publications, 1980). John J. Nance, *Splash of Colors: The Self Destruction of Braniff International* (New York: Morrow, 1984). Vertical Files, Barker Texas History Center, University of Texas at Austin (Airlines—Braniff).

Jon Kutner, Jr.

BRANN, WILLIAM COWPER (1855–1898). William Cowper Brann, journalist, was born on January 4, 1855, in Coles County, Illinois, the son of Noble J. Brann, a Presbyterian minister. After his mother's death in 1857, he was placed in the care of a neighboring farm couple, William and Mary Hawkins. In 1868, when he was thirteen and in the third grade at school, he slipped away one night, with his few belongings in a small carton he could carry. He never returned, nor did he receive any further formal schooling. He worked as a hotel bellboy, then as a house painter's helper, and finally as a printer's devil and cub reporter. On March 3, 1877, he married Carrie Belle Martin at Rochelle, Illinois. They had two daughters and a son. In Houston in 1890 his daughter Inez took her own life, an event for which Brann blamed himself.

He moved from St. Louis to Galveston to Houston and then to San Antonio and gained a reputation as a brilliant though vitriolic editorialist. He worked for the St. Louis *Globe Democrat* from 1883 to 1886, then for the Galveston *Evening Tribune* and the Galveston *News*.[qv] He moved to Austin in 1891, worked briefly for the Austin *Statesman* (*see* AUSTIN *AMERICAN-STATESMAN*), and, staking all of his limited savings, launched the first issue of his "journal of personal protest," the *Iconoclast*.[qv] It failed. Brann disposed of his Austin press to writer William Sydney Porter,[qv] later famous as O. Henry, and left Texas. He returned in October 1892 as editor of the San Antonio *Express* (*see* SAN ANTONIO *EXPRESS-NEWS*). Later in the year he moved to Houston as chief editorial writer for the Houston *Post*,[qv] and in 1894 he moved to Waco as chief editorialist for the Waco *Daily News*. In February 1895 he revived publication of the *Iconoclast*. This time it was successful and eventually attained a circulation of 100,000.

Brann took obvious relish in directing his stinging attacks upon institutions and persons he considered to be hypocritical or overly sanctimonious. He by no means confined his distaste to Baptists, but directed it generously to Episcopalians, anything British, women, and, perhaps with the greatest harshness, blacks. Among his targets was Baylor University, a Baptist institution that he scourged as "that great storm-center of misinformation." On October 2, 1897, Brann was kidnapped by student-society members and taken to the Baylor campus, where he was asked to retract his statements about the university. On October 6, having failed to leave town, he was beaten by a Baptist judge and two other men.

In November 1897 occurred a street gunfight between one of Brann's supporters, McLennan county judge G. B. Gerald, and the pro-Baylor editor of the Waco *Times-Herald* (*see* WACO *TRIBUNE-HERALD*), J. W. Harris, and his brother W. A. Harris. Both Harrises died, and the judge lost an arm. On April 1, 1898, on one of Waco's main streets, Brann was shot in the back by a brooding supporter of Baylor University named Tom E. Davis. Before the editor died he was able to draw his own pistol and kill his assailant. Brann was buried in Oakwood Cemetery, Waco.

Before his death he had gained popularity as a lecturer and tried his hand as a playwright. In 1889 he registered three plays at the Library of Congress: *Cleon, That American Woman,* and *Retribution,* the last of which was staged in 1893 in San Antonio.

BIBLIOGRAPHY: William C. Brann, *Complete Works of Bran, the Iconoclast* (New York: Brann, 1919). Charles Carver, *Brann the Iconoclast* (Austin: University of Texas Press, 1957). Edward G. Fletcher and Jack L. Hart, *Brann the Playwright* (University of Texas Publication 4121, Austin, 1941). Susan Nelle Gregg, Waco's Apostle (M.A. thesis, University of Texas at Austin, 1986). Cathy Howard, "Brann's *Iconoclast* and the Fight Against Baylor University," *Texas Historian,* September 1980. Andy Kopplin, "W. C. Brann, a Texas Iconoclast," *Texas Historian,* May 1981. Vertical Files, Barker Texas History Center, University of Texas at Austin. Gary Cleve Wilson, "Bane of the Baptists," *Texas Monthly,* January 1896.

Roger N. Conger

BRANNIN, CARL PHILIP (1888–1985). Carl Philip Brannin, social reformer and journalist, was born in Cisco, Texas, on September 22, 1888, the second son of seven children born to Lewis E. and Catherine (Bacon) Brannin. After graduating as valedictorian from Cisco High School, he enrolled at the Agricultural and Mechanical College of Texas (now Texas A&M University), became editor of the student newspaper, took part in his first protest when students demonstrated against the college president, and in 1909 graduated with a bachelor of science degree in textile engineering.

Brannin took a job as an apprentice at a textile mill in Dallas but found the work unsatisfactory. He then sold life insurance and real estate, both similarly unfulfilling. In 1911 he read a book that greatly influenced not only him but an entire generation of reformers—Henry George's *Progress and Poverty.* This work inspired in Brannin a lifelong zeal to improve conditions in society through political and economic reform. After finding work as a desk clerk at the Dallas YMCA, he began organizing classes to study George's single-tax theory, the socialism of Upton Sinclair, and the social gospel of Walter Rauschenbusch. His energy led him into other activities at the YMCA as well, especially that of helping young people find employment in the city.

In 1914 he accepted an offer from Rev. Herbert S. Bigelow in Cincinnati to become his assistant at the nondenominational People's Church, where Brannin edited a weekly paper, the *People's Press.* As editor he advocated a single tax, pacifism, civil liberties, old-age pensions, and unemployment insurance. He arranged for a variety of speakers on these and other topics, and became secretary and organizer of the People's Power League, a lobby group.

On March 2, 1918, he married Laura Haeckle of Cincinnati, herself a dedicated reformist whom Brannin met at the People's Church. The couple involved themselves in social activism in a number of cities over the next fifteen years before settling permanently in Dallas in 1933. These cities included Kansas City, Missouri, where Brannin joined a group of socialists that included Earl Browder in opposing

American involvement in World War I;[qv] Washington, D.C., where Brannin worked as a publicist for the Plumb Plan and from where he traveled through the East to seek support for public ownership of the railroads; and Seattle, Washington, where the couple worked at odd jobs for two years and associated with the radical community. Meanwhile, oil had been discovered on a small, generally worthless peanut farm left to Brannin ten years earlier by his aunt. The income derived did not represent a fortune, but for years it provided the Brannins with a steady, moderate source of income that freed them from the daily job of earning a living and permitted them to travel widely.

During a three-month trip to Mexico in 1922 Brannin began what became a long-time association with the Federated Press, a labor news service. In the San Francisco area he worked for a while as assistant editor of *Labor Unity*. In 1925 the Brannins toured Europe and the Soviet Union, making contact with radicals wherever they went. Afterwards the couple returned once more to Seattle, where Brannin became director of Seattle Labor College. In 1933 they moved with their adopted son, Robert, to Dallas. There they continued for the next several decades to involve themselves on a grass-roots level with causes and politics. They joined the Socialist party,[qv] and in 1936 Brannin was the party's unsuccessful nominee for governor. He became state secretary of the party and was involved especially in efforts to organize labor. In 1938 he resigned this post; thereafter the Brannins aligned themselves with the liberal side of the Democratic party[qv] in Texas.

The Brannins joined the First Unitarian Church in Dallas in 1947. During the 1950s and 1960s their attention turned more and more to the civil rights movement. Brannin became a member of the executive committee of the local National Association for the Advancement of Colored People.[qv] The couple participated in efforts in Dallas to desegregate various facilities, often joining picket lines when they were in their seventies.

Laura Brannin died of cancer in 1965. Brannin continued to speak for liberal causes before local government bodies, to work with the local chapter of the American Civil Liberties Union (the founder of which, Roger Baldwin, was an old friend), to write letters to editors on current topics, and to join antiwar picket lines as well as desegregation efforts. On March 18, 1977, Brannin was honored at an appreciation dinner at Eastfield College, Dallas, sponsored by a wide range of friends. He died on June 16, 1985.

BIBLIOGRAPHY: Clipping File, Texas-Dallas History and Archives Division, Dallas Public Library. Miriam Allen DeFord, *On Being Concerned: The Vanguard Years of Carl and Laura Brannin* (Dallas, 1969). Darwin Payne, *Dissenting Opinion: Carl Brannin's Letters to the Editor, 1933–1976* (Austin: American Civil Liberties Union Foundation of Texas, 1977). Vertical Files, Barker Texas History Center, University of Texas at Austin.

Darwin Payne

BRANNIN, LAURA HAECKL (1888–1965). Laura Haeckl Brannin, social activist, was the daughter of Joseph and Elizabeth Haeckl of Cincinnati, Ohio, where she was born on February 8, 1888. Her paternal grandfather had fled the draft in the German states by immigrating to America; her father was a skilled cabinetmaker, active member of the carpenter's union, and a religious skeptic. Laura and her three siblings were able to complete high school, but extensive college courses were beyond their financial reach. Laura graduated from Hughes High School in Cincinnati and took a few business-college courses and night courses at the University of Cincinnati. She encountered Herbert Bigelow's People's Church in Cincinnati and immediately accepted its Unitarian creed, free-wheeling discussion groups, and interracial membership. She was an active participant in the Church's People's Power League, a political organization concerned with a variety of municipal issues. It was through the church that she met her future husband, Carl P. Brannin,[qv] a native Texan. Brannin had gone to Cincinnati to be the editor of the *People's Press*, the newspaper published by the People's Church. When Brannin quit the paper in 1917, Laura succeeded him as editor. In March of 1918 they were married.

Laura often worked at clerical and social work jobs and generally served as Carl's alter ego. She traveled abroad with him, moved to Dallas in 1933 with him, wrote her own letters to the editors of the Dallas newspapers, and actively participated in Socialist affairs in Texas in the mid-1930s. Laura organized a series of lectures in Dallas for the League for Industrial Democracy. She joined Carl in the Unitarian Church of Dallas in 1947, and in the civil-rights battles of the 1950s and 1960s in the city. The Brannins were feted by the state's liberal community in 1963 for their "selfless" dedication to progressive causes. In one of Laura's last letters, in the Dallas *Morning News* of January 28, 1965, she wrote, "The sensible thing to do is to admit that China exists, then to be ready to talk to her and trade with her. Trade—it is a magic word—one of the most powerful deterrents to war." Just prior to her death, she and her husband established the Laura and Carl Brannin Collection of Religion in Social Action at the Bridwell Library of the Perkins School of Theology, Southern Methodist University. Laura Brannin died of cancer of the liver on August 11, 1965. In May of 1966 the Catholic Interracial Group awarded the Brannins the Father John LaFarge Award for the couple's civil-rights work. The Brannins had one adopted son, Robert.

BIBLIOGRAPHY: Carl and Laura Brannin Papers, Manuscripts and Archives Division, University of Washington Libraries, Seattle. Carl P. Brannin Papers, Texas Labor Archives, University of Texas at Arlington. Miriam Allen DeFord, *On Being Concerned: The Vanguard Years of Carl and Laura Brannin* (Dallas, 1969). Darwin Payne, *Dissenting Opinion: Carl Brannin's Letters to the Editor, 1933–1976* (Austin: American Civil Liberties Union Foundation of Texas, 1977).

George N. Green

BRANNUM, WILLIAM THOMAS (1816–1842). William Thomas Brannum, naval agent of the Republic of Texas,[qv] was born around 1816 in Georgia, traveled to Texas as a bachelor in December 1835, and was awarded a first-class headright certificate dated January 25, 1838, for one-third of a league of land. He was initiated into Holland Lodge No. 1 of the Masonic order in Houston on February 13, 1837. Brannum married Elizabeth Tritton Shelton in New Orleans on July 13, 1840, and they had one daughter, who married John Miller Haden.[qv]

Brannum joined the Texas Navy[qv] in 1836 under Commodore Charles E. Hawkins as clerk to Capt. George Washington Wheelwright[qv] on the flagship *Independence*,[qv] where he rose to the position of purser. Brannum then served as agent for the second Republic of Texas Navy under Edwin Ward Moore.[qv] As navy agent he made on-the-spot investigations and reported on the condition of foreign vessels, their armament, and their munitions; inventoried and divided the spoils of captured ships; and recruited men and arranged for all payrolls and supplies. He was also responsible for selling Texas treasury notes at the highest market price available in New Orleans and other places in the United States. Brannum served as enrolling clerk for the Republic of Texas Senate from November 5, 1838, to January 24, 1839. On September 25, 1839, he was responsible for the purchase for the Texas Navy of the ninety-five-ton schooner *Louisville*.[qv]

Commodore Moore dispatched the schooner *San Antonio*[qv] to Yucatán on August 27, 1842, in an effort to collect enough money to keep the Texas fleet afloat and to pay bills already incurred. Brannum signed on as purser. The *San Antonio* never reached Campeche and was never again heard from.

BIBLIOGRAPHY: Alex Dienst, "The Navy of the Republic of Texas," *Quarterly of the Texas State Historical Association* 12–13 (January–October 1909; rpt., Fort Collins, Colorado: Old Army Press, 1987). Navy of the Republic Service Records, Adjutant General's Record

Group, Texas State Archives, Austin. Tom Henderson Wells, *Commodore Moore and the Texas Navy* (Austin: University of Texas Press, 1960). *Mary Smith Fay*

BRANOM, TEXAS. Branom, in western Hopkins County, was named for Merrett Branom, who settled in the area before the county was established in 1846. A school opened there around 1900, and during the school year 1905–06 it had an enrollment of thirty-eight. In 1915 the Pecan and Greenwood schools united to form the Branom school district, and the Willow Oak and Faulk Grove schools were later added. In the late 1940s Branom was a dispersed rural community. The Ray's Chapel Methodist Church was located on the corner of the school campus, and the Mount Zion Presbyterian Church was a quarter mile west. In the 1980s Branom was no longer shown on the county highway map. *J. E. Jennings*

BRANSFORD, TEXAS. Bransford was a mile west of State Highway 121 in northeastern Tarrant County. The settlement was probably established around 1870 and by 1877 had a few houses clustered around a general store and post office operated by Felix G. Bransford. The site was abandoned in 1888 when the tracks of the St. Louis Southwestern Railway were extended through the nearby settlement of Red Rock. The Bransford post office and store resumed operations in Red Rock, which adopted the name of the abandoned community. In the early 1900s Bransford had four general stores, four physicians, two blacksmiths, a livery stable, and a post office. The local school enrolled 117 students and employed two teachers during the 1905–06 term. Bransford soon declined as rapidly as it had grown, due largely to the development of nearby Coleysville. The Bransford post office closed in 1913. A 1936 map shows two churches and scattered dwellings at the townsite. Bransford was reported as an agricultural settlement and railroad station in 1940. Since then, however, it has ceased to exist as an organized community.

BIBLIOGRAPHY: *Historic Resources Survey: Selected Tarrant County Communities* (Fort Worth: Historic Preservation Council for Tarrant County, 1990). *Brian Hart*

BRASHEAR, WILLIAM C. (ca. 1812–1849). William C. Brashear, naval officer of the Republic of Texas,[qv] the son of Sarah Brashear, was born about 1812. He came to Texas from Kentucky during the Texas Revolution[qv] and served as a second lieutenant in Capt. James Pope Price's company of Kentucky Volunteers, but his company arrived too late to fight in the battle of San Jacinto,[qv] and on August 6, 1836, Brashear was detached for duty aboard the brig *Hope.* In an undated document apparently written later in 1836, Thomas Jefferson Chambers[qv] referred to Brashear as "a very respectable young officer" attached to Col. C. S. Harrison's battalion.

Brashear was placed in command of the steam warship *Zavala*[qv] in October 1841 while she lay in ordinary. In March 1842 he was faced with the unpleasant duty of running his ship aground in Galveston harbor to keep her from sinking, after the government refused to appropriate funds to patch her leaks. With the loss of his ship, Brashear was appointed to command of the Galveston Navy Yard in the autumn of 1842.

Soon thereafter he resigned from the Texas Navy[qv] and, by the end of 1842, was contemplating leaving Texas to seek service in the Russian navy. This prompted President Sam Houston[qv] to write his regrets to Brashear on January 7, 1843, that Texas had not provided "a theater of action worthy of your generous emulation." On July 19, 1843, Houston nominated Brashear as a lieutenant in the Texas Navy, and the Senate confirmed the nomination on the same day. At the same time, he was appointed naval commissioner in place of Col. James Morgan,[qv] a close friend of Commodore Edwin Ward Moore,[qv] whom President Houston relieved of command on July 19, 1843. In that capacity Brashear presided over the dismantling of the first navy of the Republic of Texas and, despite his personal distaste for Houston's treatment of his former commander, was summoned to testify against Moore at his court-martial. In February 1844, when Texas was negotiating with the United States for a treaty of annexation,[qv] Houston instructed J. Pinckney Henderson[qv] in Washington, D.C., to attempt to secure a commission in the United States Navy for Brashear if the treaty were confirmed. Houston described Brashear and three of his fellow officers as "worthy of their rank and gentlemen who will obey orders." On September 24, 1844, Brashear was promoted to commander.

He died in Beltsville, Maryland, on October 31, 1849. His mother petitioned the Texas Committee on Naval Affairs, on April 28, 1858, for the five years' pay granted to naval officers of the Republic of Texas upon annexation. Sam Houston responded that Brashear had always conducted himself in such a way as to win "my approval and admiration."

BIBLIOGRAPHY: Alex Dienst, "The Navy of the Republic of Texas," *Quarterly of the Texas State Historical Association* 12–13 (January–October 1909; rpt., Fort Collins, Colorado: Old Army Press, 1987). C. L. Douglas, *Thunder on the Gulf: The Story of the Texas Navy* (Dallas: Turner, 1936; rpt., Fort Collins, Colorado: Old Army Press, 1973). Jim Dan Hill, *The Texas Navy* (New York: Barnes, 1962). John H. Jenkins, ed., *The Papers of the Texas Revolution, 1835–1836* (10 vols., Austin: Presidial Press, 1973). *Texas State Gazette,* November 24, 1849. Tom Henderson Wells, *Commodore Moore and the Texas Navy* (Austin: University of Texas Press, 1960). Amelia W. Williams and Eugene C. Barker, eds., *The Writings of Sam Houston, 1813–1863* (8 vols., Austin: University of Texas Press, 1938–43; rpt., Austin and New York: Pemberton Press, 1970). *Thomas W. Cutrer*

BRASHEAR, TEXAS. Brashear, on Interstate Highway 30 and Farm Road 2653 in west central Hopkins County, was named for Joseph Brashear, who surveyed the townsite. The area was part of the Wise Ranch in 1898, when G. W. Mahoney bought the ranch, divided it into small farms, laid out the townsite, and donated land for a school, a church, and a cemetery. A post office was established at Brashear in 1899, with W. G. Crain as postmaster. A school opened the same year, and in 1905 it had an enrollment of 149. By 1914 the town had Baptist, Christian, and Methodist churches, a bank, a newspaper, a telegraph connection, and a reported population of 400. Its population was estimated at 300 in the mid-1920s and 350 in the late 1940s. In 1948 the town had six stores, four churches, a two-teacher school, and a cotton gin. The population declined during the 1960s to 280 and continued to be reported at that level in 1990. In the late 1980s Brashear had four churches, a factory, a post office, and a number of scattered houses. *Christopher Long*

BRASWELL, RADFORD O. (1873–1932). Radford O. Braswell, physician, son of D. B. and Jane (Barrith) Braswell, was born near Decatur, Alabama, on September 19, 1873. He attended the Southern University of Alabama and the Physio-Medical College of Indiana, where he graduated in 1896. He did graduate work at the College of Medicine and Surgery in Chicago, New York Polyclinic, Mayo Clinic, and Tulane University. In 1894 he moved to Dallas and began his medical practice. On July 12, 1900, he married Mamie McKinnon of Dallas. He established the Braswell Sanitarium in Mineral Wells, where he remained from 1900 to 1907. He then moved to Fort Worth and established another Braswell Sanitarium in 1921. He was a member of the Tarrant County Medical Society, the American Medical Association, and the Texas Medical Association.[qv] He was for six years a member of the Texas State Board of Medical Examiners, under the administration of Thomas M. Campbell,[qv] and for several years was examiner for the Industrial Accident Board (now the Texas Workers'

Compensation Commission[qv]). He was a specialist in orthopedic surgery and performed many operations for charity. He was chief surgeon at Braswell Sanitarium and chief of staff at St. Joseph Hospital[qv] in 1931. He died at Fort Worth on May 5, 1932.

BIBLIOGRAPHY: Buckley B. Paddock, *History of Texas: Fort Worth and the Texas Northwest Edition* (4 vols., Chicago: Lewis, 1922). *Texas State Journal of Medicine,* July 1932. *Jeanette H. Flachmeier*

BRAVO, MANUEL BOX (1901–1984). Manuel Box Bravo, county judge and civil-rights advocate, the son of David and Emma (Box) Bravo, was born at El Ambrado Ranch in Hidalgo County, Texas, on May 2, 1901. His mother came from the distinguished Box family, pioneers who settled in Houston County during the mid-1830s. Manuel, the oldest of eight children, lived and went to school near his birthplace on the banks of the Rio Grande. Though hard economic conditions forced him to quit school after completing the eighth grade, he graduated from McAllen High School in 1924. On October 24, 1919, he married Josefa Villarreal Pérez in Edinburg; they had three sons and one daughter. He worked in the Hidalgo County courthouse tax collector's office and later earned promotion to chief deputy in the delinquent tax department. In 1921 Bravo, a devout Catholic, became a charter member of the Knights of Columbus,[qv] an affiliation he maintained until his death. In the late 1920s he helped establish and served as president of the Edinburg Council of the League of United Latin American Citizens.[qv]

In 1932 he won the primary election of the Democratic party[qv] for district clerk of Hidalgo County. A year later he and his family moved to Zapata, where he engaged in several self-employed business ventures. In the November 3, 1936, general election, Bravo won by an overwhelming majority as a write-in candidate for county judge from the Partido Viejo (as supporters called the Democratic party). On January 1, 1937, he became the new county judge. He ordered county officials to begin the practice of keeping minutes of school board meetings, records of expenditures, inventories of school supplies and equipment, and auditable accounts. Despite the fact that the county was economically very poor and the educational system was in a state of neglect, his fiscal management of the school budget allowed for improvements in school facilities, approved accreditation standards for all grade levels, more certified teachers, and better playground facilities. He purchased school buses and established a veterans vocational training school with classes in vocational agriculture, distributive education, trade and industrial training, and basic preparatory courses. In 1952 Bravo successfully campaigned to get the taxpayers to approve the first bond election in the history of Zapata County.

Bravo supported Lyndon B. Johnson's[qv] farm bill of 1949, a bill that provided for telephone service to rural communities. He also solicited government assistance during droughts; in 1952 he lobbied for the establishment of a Soil Conservation Service Office for Zapata County. During the 1940s Bravo became actively involved in civil rights when he joined Alonso S. Perales and José T. Canales[qv] in condemning racial discrimination in Texas. On September 13, 1943, the Zapata County Commissioners Court approved a resolution endorsing the Good Neighbor Policy. In 1949, during the Felix Longoria affair,[qv] Bravo brought the incident to Johnson's attention. During World War II[qv] Bravo was chairman of the War Fund in Zapata County, which exceeded the established goal by 45 percent. For his loyalty, patriotism, and public spirit in a time of national crisis, the American Red Cross and the United States Treasury War Finance Committee honored him with awards.

In the 1950s the construction of the International Falcon Reservoir meant the inundation of the entire town of Zapata (the county seat of Zapata County) and other neighboring communities. Bravo fought the government for just compensation for the people. Throughout Johnson's political career Bravo was a personal friend and confidant. He retired from public office on October 1, 1957. In 1973 he served as a member of the local citizens' advisory committee to the Texas Constitutional Revision Committee. He died in Zapata on September 18, 1984, and is buried in the Zapata County Cemetery family plot.

BIBLIOGRAPHY: Ronnie Dugger, *The Politician: The Life and Times of Lyndon Johnson* (New York: Norton, 1982). Edinburg *Valley Review,* April 8, 1932. Virgil N. Lott and Mercurio Martinez, *The Kingdom of Zapata* (San Antonio: Naylor, 1953). *Juan Gilberto Quezada*

BRAY, WILLIAM L. (1865–1953). William Bray, botanist, forest ecologist, and teacher, son of William and Martha Ann (Foster) Bray, was born at Burnside, Illinois, on September 19, 1865. He graduated from Cornell University in 1891 and took his B.A. degree from Indiana University in 1893 and his Ph.D. from the University of Chicago in 1898. He also spent a year (1896–97) working under Heinrich Gustav Adolf Engler at the Royal Botanical Garden in Berlin. On December 28, 1899, he married Alice Weston; they had three children.

In 1897 Bray started his tenure at the University of Texas. There he was the first botanist, though some instruction in the subject had been offered by Frederick W. Simonds.[qv] From his early work, completed in Berlin and printed in Engler's *Botanische Jahrbücher* (1897), on the worldwide distribution of the Frankenia family and the comparison, suggested by Engler, of the Sonoran Desert flora with that of arid Chile and Argentina (1898), there is a clear line to Bray's Texas studies. In January 1899 the university established a School of Botany by separating botany from the School of Biology. Under Bray's direction the special assignment of the new school was to make a "Botanical Survey of the State for the purpose of studying the flora in its relation to the environmental factors of climate, rainfall, heat, geological structure and topography." A few months later Bray published his careful outline, "The Flora of Texas as a Field for Botanical Study," followed by the shorter "Some Practical Phases of the Study of Botany" (1900). His own professional works then followed in quick succession: "The Ecological Relations of the Vegetation of Western Texas" (1901), *Forest Resources of Texas* (1904), *The Timber of the Edwards Plateau of Texas* (1904), "Vegetation of the Sotol Country in Texas" (1905), *Distribution and Adaptation of the Vegetation of Texas* (1906), and *The Mistletoe Pest in the Southwest* (1910). Hoping to achieve a balance between exploitation and conservation, Bray also wrote "A Forest Working Plan for the Long Leaf Pine Lands of Texas" (1903). For the Louisiana Purchase Exposition in St. Louis (1904), Bray, in collaboration with W. F. Blair of Dayton, Texas, prepared an exhibit of some 130 specimens of Texas trees, which received the grand prize from the international jury. This exhibit later became the property of the university.

In 1907 Bray went to Syracuse University as professor of botany; there he was dean of the graduate school from 1918 until his retirement in 1943. Notable among his later work is *Development of the Vegetation of New York State* (1915). He died in Syracuse, New York, on May 25, 1953. He was a Methodist.

BIBLIOGRAPHY: Vertical Files, Barker Texas History Center, University of Texas at Austin. *Who's Who in America,* 1950–51. *Who Was Who in America,* Vol.3. *Anders S. Saustrup*

BRAY'S BAYOU. Bray's Bayou rises just northeast of Clodine in northern Fort Bend County (at 29°43′ N, 95°41′ W) and runs southeast for fourteen miles to its mouth on Buffalo Bayou (at 29°44′ N, 95°17′ W). The stream is intermittent in its upper reaches. It traverses variable terrain surfaced by impermeable soils and, downstream, by calcareous clay. Mixed hardwoods and prairie grasses grow in the vicinity.

BRAZORIA. The schooner *Brazoria,* commanded by William J. Russell,[qv] was a small vessel that took part in the battle of Velasco[qv] in

1832. She was anchored at Brazoria when preparations were being made for the Texans' attack on the town, then was commandeered to carry a company of soldiers and two or three small cannons taken from the *Ariel*[qv] to support the ground troops under John Austin.[qv]

BIBLIOGRAPHY: James Lewellyn Allhands, *Gringo Builders* (Joplin, Missouri, Dallas, Texas, 1931). *Velasco in Texas History* (Angleton, Texas: Brazoria County Centennial Club, 1936).

BRAZORIA, TEXAS. Brazoria, on Farm Road 521, State Highway 36, and the Brazos River eight miles southwest of Angleton in west central Brazoria County, was established in 1828, when John Austin[qv] laid out the town on land granted by Stephen F. Austin.[qv] Austin chose the name "for the single reason that I know of none like it in the world." Six Masons met in March 1835 under a giant oak in the town, the "Masonic Oak," to organize what was reportedly the first Masonic lodge in Texas. Brazoria was virtually deserted in the Runaway Scrape.[qv] H. M. Shaw opened a school at the community in April 1838. A post office was established there in 1846, and by 1884 Brazoria was described as a "stirring village" of 800. It had several steam cotton gins and grist and sugar mills, twelve general stores, three hotels, five churches, and "excellent schools." Area farmers shipped crops on the river. By 1890 Brazoria had 900 residents and was the county seat of Brazoria County. By 1892 the *Velasco World*, a weekly newspaper, had been established there, and by 1914, the *Banner*. After the railroad bypassed Brazoria, it began to decline as its neighbor, Angleton, grew. Angleton became county seat in 1897. The local school at Brazoria had three teachers and an enrollment of 142 in 1906. The population was 633 in 1904 and 1,050 in 1929. By 1939 the discovery of oil and a sulfur field nearby and the building of a traffic bridge began to revive the town. Its population reached 1,291 by 1962 and 3,025 by 1987, when Brazoria had some fifty businesses. The Clemens Unit, a prison where inmates raise livestock and crops, is on 8,116 acres of land just south of the townsite. Each October Brazoria hosts a Bluegrass and Gospel Fall Festival, and its old town area is of historic interest. In 1990 the community reported a population of 2,717.

BIBLIOGRAPHY: Brazoria County Federation of Women's Clubs, *History of Brazoria County* (1940). James A. Creighton, *A Narrative History of Brazoria County* (Angleton, Texas: Brazoria County Historical Commission, 1975). *Anna Hallstein*

BRAZORIA *ADVOCATE OF THE PEOPLE'S RIGHTS*. The *Advocate of the People's Rights*, a weekly newspaper published in Brazoria by Oliver H. Allen and John A. Wharton,[qv] was possibly printed on a press belonging to Daniel W. Anthony.[qv] It was opposed to Stephen F. Austin.[qv] Wharton soon withdrew from the venture because of lack of popular support. The earliest known issue of the paper is dated November 23, 1833; on March 27, 1834, it was announced that the paper would resume publication when Allen returned from the United States. Two issues of the paper, those of February 22, 1834, and of March 27, 1834, are in the Barker Texas History Center[qv] at the University of Texas at Austin.

BIBLIOGRAPHY: Eugene C. Barker, "Notes on Early Texas Newspapers," *Southwestern Historical Quarterly* 21 (October 1917). James A. Creighton, *A Narrative History of Brazoria County* (Angleton, Texas: Brazoria County Historical Commission, 1975). Douglas C. McMurtrie, "Pioneer Printing in Texas," *Southwestern Historical Quarterly* 35 (January 1932). Marilyn M. Sibley, *Lone Stars and State Gazettes: Texas Newspapers before the Civil War* (College Station: Texas A&M University Press, 1983). John Melton Wallace, *Gaceta to Gazette: A Checklist of Texas Newspapers, 1813–1846* (Austin: University of Texas Department of Journalism, 1966).

BRAZORIA COUNTY. Brazoria County (G-18), on the prairie of the Gulf Coast at the mouth of the Brazos River in Southeast Texas, is bordered by Matagorda, Fort Bend, Harris, and Galveston counties. It covers an area of 1,407 square miles. Its highest altitude is sixty feet above sea level. The center of the county lies at approximately 29°10′ north latitude and 95°26′ west longitude, near the county seat, Angleton. Other principal towns include Alvin, Amsterdam, Brazoria, Damon, Pearland, Rosharon, Holiday Lake, Old Ocean, Bailey's Prairie, Iowa Colony, Bonney, Hillcrest Village, Brookside Village, Danbury, Liverpool, Manvel, and Sweeny; the towns that constitute Brazosport include Clute, Freeport, Quintana, Oyster Creek, Jones Creek, Lake Jackson, Richwood, and Surfside Beach. Key county roads include State highways 6, 35, 36, and 288, and railroad service is provided by the Atchison, Topeka and Santa Fe and Southern Pacific railroads. The annual rainfall is fifty-two inches, and the mean annual temperature is 69° F. Hurricanes[qv] and floods are common in the region, among the most notable being the hurricanes of 1854, 1900, 1909, 1915, 1932, 1941, Hurricane Carla in 1961, and the floods of 1899, 1913, 1915, 1929, and 1940. Soils in the county are chiefly alluvial loams and clays, and are highly productive when well drained. The growing season averages 309 days a year. In 1982, between 61 and 70 percent of the land was considered prime farmland. The principal streams flowing through Brazoria County into the Gulf of Mexico include the Brazos and San Bernard rivers, Oyster Creek, Bastrop Bayou, and Chocolate Bayou. The Gulf Intracoastal Waterway[qv] crosses Brazoria County near the coast. The Brazos River divides the county into two sections; the western one-third is covered by hardwoods, and the rest is generally prairieland. Abundant groves of pin oak, cedar, live oak, mulberry, hackberry, ash, elm, cottonwood, and pecan trees grow in the river and creek bottoms, while cordgrasses, bunchgrasses, and sedges predominate in the coastal marshes. When settlers first arrived, wildlife was abundant, including deer, bear, turkey, and fish. Two major national wildlife refuges, the Brazoria and San Bernard, are close to the Gulf Coast in Brazoria County. In 1947 the county ranked fourth in state timber production. More recently, the petrochemical industry and mineral resources including oil, gas, sulfur, salt, lime, sand, and gravel, concentrated in the Damon Mound–West Columbia–Freeport area, have dominated the county economy. Magnesium is also extracted locally from seawater.

Before Anglo-American colonization,[qv] the region was occupied by Karankawa Indians. Archeological excavations have revealed some of the shell middens and campsite refuse of this nomadic people, who exploited maritime and mainland resources on a seasonal basis as early as A.D. 450. Skirmishes with colonists, including the battle of Jones Creek[qv] in 1824, resulted in expulsion of most of the Indian population to the area south of the Rio Grande by 1850.

In 1528 Spanish explorer Álvar Núñez Cabeza de Vaca[qv] landed on the Isle of Mal Hado (Island of Evil Destiny), possibly San Luis Island. Scholars agree that his party probably crossed Oyster Creek, Old Caney Creek, and the Brazos and San Bernard rivers, roaming the area that became Brazoria County looking for provisions. Spanish soldiers under Alonso De León,[qv] governor of Coahuila, passed through the region in search of the La Salle expedition[qv] in 1689, and Joaquín de Orobio y Basterra came in 1727 searching for possible French intruders in the Trinity River area. In an effort to forestall French or English incursions, the Spanish began to occupy Texas in the eighteenth century, but entered the future Brazoria County chiefly to trade with Indians or search for stolen horses. Though expeditions on the Trinity probably traveled through for missionary purposes in the 1750s, the area was not settled by the Spanish. Similarly, early American military expeditions did not reach the future county, though a popular tradition suggests that pirate Jean Laffite[qv] used the mouth of the Brazos as a rendezvous and buried treasure along its banks.

Though the alluvial bottomlands of the county's rivers attracted settlement by Americans as early as 1820, the passengers of the schooner *Lively* who landed at the mouth of the Brazos in December

1821 passed on to Richmond. The area was first populated when Stephen F. Austin[qv] selected it for his proposed settlement, and eighty-nine of Austin's Old Three Hundred[qv] had grants in what is now Brazoria County by 1824. The earliest communities were Velasco (at the site of present Surfside), East Columbia (originally known as Bell's Landing or Marion), Columbia (later West Columbia), and Brazoria. Quintana and Liverpool were also settled before 1832. In 1835 Mary Austin Holley[qv] observed, "The rage is now for making towns," but many new towns, including George L. Hammeken's[qv] thriving community on San Luis Island, failed to survive.

Brazoria County became part of the Victoria district when Austin's original San Felipe district was divided in two in 1826. In 1832 the legislature of Coahuila separated Brazoria Municipality from San Felipe and made Brazoria its capital. Brazoria Municipality was the scene of the battle of Velasco[qv] on June 26, 1832, and witnessed other agitation against Mexican rule. In 1833 county residents suffered both flood and cholera, but in 1834 population in the municipality reached 2,100, and prosperity returned. A decision was made to change the name of the municipality from Brazoria to Columbia, to make Columbia the seat of government, and transfer some territory to Matagorda Municipality. At the time, the largest settlements in the future county were Brazoria, with 500 residents, Velasco with 100, and Bolivar with fifty. As early as the mid-1830s, cotton farms produced more than 5,000 bales annually, and plantation owners in the area became some of the wealthiest in Texas. On March 1, 1835, a meeting near Brazoria led to the establishment of the first Masonic lodge in Texas, Holland Lodge No. 36 (*see* FREEMASONRY).

When Stephen F. Austin declared against Santa Anna at another meeting in Brazoria on September 8, 1835, Texans began to prepare for a revolution. Agitation for independence led to the formation of committees of public safety and public meetings to discuss the impending break. After the convention at San Felipe and engagements at Gonzales, Goliad, and Bexar, volunteer companies were organized and a provisional government[qv] approved on November 13, 1835. Henry Smith[qv] of Brazoria County served as the first provisional governor. Formation of a permanent council soon thereafter brought the inauguration of mail routes throughout the area. Rebellion grew in 1835 and 1836, culminating in the Texas Declaration of Independence.[qv]

Citizens of the county contributed men and means to the Texas Revolution[qv] and participated in the Runaway Scrape.[qv] After his capture at the battle of San Jacinto[qv] on April 21, 1836, Santa Anna and members of his army were taken to Velasco, then the location of the provisional government. Here Santa Anna signed the Treaties of Velasco[qv] with the Republic of Texas[qv] on May 14, 1836. Columbia, the seat of the ad interim government,[qv] served as the capital of the republic when sessions of the first Texas Congress met in October 1836. During the first session Stephen F. Austin died and was buried at Peach Point. Houston became the capital.

Under the provisional government, Texas accepted the constitution that made its first counties from former municipalities. Brazoria County, among the first, took its name from the Brazos River when the Congress of the republic established it on March 24, 1836. Brazoria, which became county seat when the county was organized on December 20, 1836, served until 1896, when Angleton replaced it. The establishment of Fort Bend County in 1837 and of Galveston County in 1838 drew the present county boundaries, and the towns of Columbia, Velasco, and Brazoria were incorporated by the Congress of the republic in 1837.

According to some sources, the last shipment of African Americans[qv] brought as slaves into North America arrived at the mouth of the San Bernard River in 1840. At the time, the community of Brazoria had an estimated population of 800 and Columbia of 300; 80 slaveholders in the county owned a total of 1,316 slaves. Yellow fever and flooding in 1843 and 1844 slowed growth, but the annexation[qv] of Texas to the United States in 1845 and the Mexican War[qv] had little effect on residents of Brazoria County, mostly farmers. By 1847 Brazoria County had 1,623 white inhabitants and 3,013 slaves. In 1852 the county produced 7,329 hogsheads of sugar, the most of all Texas counties.

During pioneer days, the Brazos River was the chief artery by which immigration, communication, and commerce penetrated Texas from the Gulf. Small boats regularly navigated as far as East Columbia, and customhouses were located at Brazoria and Velasco. By 1840, Buffalo Bayou and the growing town of Houston had begun to draw commerce away from the Brazos, but freight and passenger service between Brazoria, other Brazos River ports, and Galveston was established by 1842, and a canal from the Brazos mouth to West Galveston Bay was completed by 1857 (*see* GALVESTON AND BRAZOS NAVIGATION COMPANY).

Between 1849 and 1859 plantation life in Brazoria County flourished, and the county became the wealthiest in Texas, with a typically Southern society based on slavery.[qv] Agriculture was the foundation of the county's early economy, and some of the state's largest and most prosperous sugar and cotton plantations grew up along the rivers and deeper creeks on which crops could be shipped by barges. Plantations in the county between 1850 and 1860 numbered forty-six, including nineteen sugar, sixteen cotton, and three that produced both sugar and cotton. Before the war, these plantations produced an average of 7,000 to 8,000 hogsheads of sugar annually, and up to three-fourths of the state's output in 1857. Many planters raised cattle, and some cultivated oranges, lemons, and other fruits. Each of twenty-six county residents owned more than $100,000 in property by the year 1860; the foremost planter was John H. Herndon,[qv] whose real property was valued at more than $1.6 million and personal property at more than $106,000. In that year Brazoria County had 2,027 white, 5,110 black slave, and six free black residents; by 1864, when slaves numbered 5,125, their value was only slightly less than the county's 283,151 acres of land. Town life was subordinated to plantation life, and Old Velasco and Quintana served as Gulf seaports and resort centers for antebellum plantation society. Later, the two towns declined in importance as plans for an intracoastal canal to divert trade developed, and in 1875 and 1900 both were almost destroyed by hurricanes. Other transportation in the period was provided by the Houston Tap and Brazoria Railroad, chartered in 1856 and built by planters to connect East Columbia with Houston markets and with the Buffalo Bayou, Brazos and Colorado Railroad at Pierce Junction. After the Civil War,[qv] this railroad became the property of the International–Great Northern.

Residents of Brazoria County cast more than 99 percent of their votes for secession,[qv] 527 for and two against. During the Civil War, the Dance Brothers[qv] gun works manufactured weapons, companies were organized for the Confederate Army, and women were left to run the plantations. Fortifications built at Velasco and Quintana weathered Union attacks in 1862. Confederate blockade runners operated along the coast, and some cotton was shipped overland by mule and wagon to Mexico. Though the county suffered little physical damage in the war, the presence of federal troops and loss of profit from cotton crops in 1864 brought increasing hardship. Some plantations were destroyed, and agricultural production declined sharply with the freeing of the slaves. David G. Mills[qv] alone lost 313 slaves as a result of emancipation. County land was valued at more than $3 million in 1860, but its value had declined to less than $2 million by 1866. During the same period, total property value in the county fell from almost $7 million to less than $3 million. Many plantations were divided into smaller farms or turned into pastures; others eventually became part of the Ramsey, Retrieve, Clemens, and Darrington state prison farms (*see* PRISON SYSTEM). In 1870 only a single Brazoria County resident, farmer William Bryan, had a prewar level of wealth, with real property valued at $100,000 and personal property worth $20,000. As conditions worsened, some Brazoria countians moved to Mexico, where they organized settlements in the Tuxpan River valley in Vera Cruz.

Brazoria County had been primarily Democratic in politics from annexation to the Civil War, but voted Republican throughout Reconstruction[qv] because the majority of voters were newly franchised freedmen. The county supported Rutherford B. Hayes, James A. Garfield, James G. Blaine, Benjamin Harrison, and William McKinley in the national elections from 1876 to 1900. During Reconstruction, federal troops were stationed at Brazoria and Sandy Point. A Freedmen's Bureau[qv] agent arrived in the county in 1865, the Union League[qv] organized and registered black voters by the mid-1870s, and voters elected black legislator George T. Ruby[qv] as early as 1870 and Nathan H. Haller[qv] as late as 1894. Such organizations as the Ku Klux Klan,[qv] San Bernard Rifles, and Prairie Rangers attempted to maintain the supremacy of whites in the county in opposition to Reconstruction measures, though some former slaves succeeded in attaining positions of wealth and leadership. The White Man's Union ultimately disfranchised black voters, however, and removed local politics from the hands of carpetbaggers and freedmen. From 1895 until the 1950s, the Taxpayers Union worked to assure "the fact that this is a white man's country and that white supremacy must obtain," and held primaries in which only whites could vote (*see* WHITE PRIMARY). Leaders posted notices that African Americans elected to office could not serve, and in the 1890s placed guards around the courthouse to enforce their edict. From 1900 to 1988 voting was predominantly Democratic; the county supported Republicans Theodore Roosevelt, Warren G. Harding, Herbert Hoover, Dwight D. Eisenhower,[qv] Richard M. Nixon, Ronald Reagan, and George H. W. Bush. Third-party candidates received little assistance from Brazoria County, though in 1944, 1948, and 1980 they won a significant percentage of the vote. In 1990 half the county's residents were registered voters.

Between 1870 and 1880 the population in Brazoria County grew from 7,527 to 9,774, largely due to the arrival of federal soldiers and other Northerners, foreign immigrants, and Confederate soldiers from Texas and the Old South. S. A. Hackworth, a white Republican, bought land in Wharton, Fort Bend, and Brazoria counties and sold it to blacks in the 1870s and 1880s. By the 1890s Columbia was the largest town in the county, followed by Brazoria, Velasco, Quintana, Sandy Point, and Liverpool, and new towns had been founded—Alvin, Angleton, and Pearland. In 1898, at the end of the Spanish-American War, Adm. George Dewey acquired 65,000 acres of land in Brazoria County.

Economic recovery came slowly in the post–Civil War era. The principal crops were corn, grains, sweet and Irish potatoes, fruits, wild grapes, and cotton and sugar for export. Sugar production, reduced in the early years of Reconstruction, burgeoned with the use of convict labor by 1871, but never again reached earlier levels. By 1867 the value of livestock, chiefly cattle, nearly equalled that of agriculture. When cattlemen found northern markets shut off in the late 1860s, hide and tallow factories were established along the Brazos River; Brazoria County packed $100,000 worth of canned beef in 1870. Figs were introduced in the Alvin area around the turn of the century and became an important crop. Four canneries were later built in the community. Live oak moss was ginned at Angleton.

Though the Galveston and Brazos Navigation Company was chartered as early as 1850, major improvements in transportation began only in the 1870s, starting with a canal across Galveston Bay, completed with the help of the federal government. By 1905 workers completed jetties to deepen the water in the harbors at Velasco and Quintana, and in part of what became the Gulf Intracoastal Waterway. The Brazos River Harbor Association was founded in 1925, and by 1929 Brazos River diversion reduced the problem of sanding in the channel and opened the harbor at Freeport. Railroad transportation improved. The Houston and Brazos Valley Railroad reached Velasco by 1907, the Sugar Land Railroad was serving plantations along Oyster Creek by 1916, and the St. Louis, Brownsville, and Mexico Railway established service to Brazoria by 1937. All were later acquired by the Missouri Pacific system, and more recently by the Southern Pacific. Major state highway construction in the county was done in the 1920s and 1930s, though State Highway 288 was not completed until later.

The value of Brazoria County agriculture rose steadily after Reconstruction, and the majority of residents earned their livelihood from the soil until the late 1930s. The use of mules declined with widespread use of tractors after 1925, and the number of farms increased steadily to a maximum of 3,065 in 1940. Houston Lighting and Power service reached the county in 1927. But by 1930 the effects of the Great Depression[qv] were obvious. Whereas fewer than a third of county farmers were tenants in 1880, by 1930 tenants constituted a majority, a condition that lasted until the 1950s. Between 1900 and 1930 Brazoria County was described as a cattle-raising area, with some oil and sulfur production, dairying, and diverse farming. The dairy industry,[qv] centered around Alvin, peaked between 1910 and 1930, and cotton culture[qv] in 1920. Corn culture[qv] concentrated near Sweeny, Brazoria, Damon, Danbury, and Angleton, stock farming around Alvin, truck farming in the Sweeny area, figs and poultry near Alvin and Angleton, and pecans around Sweeny and East Columbia.

Rice culture[qv] enhanced the economy. Farmers near Danbury and elsewhere started planting rice after 1900 and began to dig rice canals in 1935. From a total of 6,000 acres planted in the crop in 1903, planting grew to 16,000 acres by 1940. In 1948 favorable growing conditions made Brazoria County the nation's number-one rice producing area, with a crop valued at more than $10 million. The average yield per acre almost doubled between 1956 and 1970; an average of 53,000 acres was planted during those years. Rice and grain exports comprised 65,000 tons in 1968; American Rice, Incorporated, at Brazosport, shipped 350,000 tons of rice in 1990.

Brazoria County mineral development began at West Columbia oilfield[qv] as early as 1901. Oil production started at Brazoria in 1902, reached 12,500,000 barrels in 1921, declined during the depression, and then resumed. Brazoria County ranked fourth among Texas counties in 1946, with 29,308,106 barrels produced. Sulfur deposits at Bryan Mound, Hoskins Mound, and Stratton Ridge Dome were first mined in 1912, and soon made the county first in United States production of sulfur. The Freeport Sulphur Company employed 800 persons at Bryan and Hoskins Mound in 1930 and extracted 2,000 tons of sulfur daily. By 1944 the firm had extracted 552,000 long tons of ore (*see* SULFUR INDUSTRY). The county's contribution to World War I[qv] came from factories at Brazoria, Sweeny, and Hasima that produced live oak nails for shipbuilding.

Brazoria County manufacturing was relatively unimportant as late as 1940, when it employed only 166 persons. During the 1940s, however, the number of manufacturing jobs increased rapidly. As the depletion of Bryan Mound sulfur deposits brought an end to the area's principal industry, Dow Chemical Company, drawn to natural resources at Freeport, came in 1939 and soon gave rise to the Brazosport[qv] industrial and port community. After the Japanese attack on Pearl Harbor in 1941, members of the Texas National Guard[qv] manned newly established Dow facilities, while the company constructed 2,300 dwelling units in less than two months for its workers. By 1945 exports from Brazosport amounted to 117,610 tons. Another effect of World War II[qv] on the county took the form of camps for prisoners of war,[qv] which housed German soldiers and members of Rommel's Afrika Corps for a time. A second phase of industrialization began in the 1950s as "customer companies," including Monsanto and processors of chemical fertilizers, established operations nearby to make use of Dow products. Industrial development attracted more workers, including people from East Texas and some African Americans from nearby communities, while real estate developments produced such new Brazosport communities as Lake Jackson. Transportation, meanwhile, included by 1949 the Gulf, Colorado and Santa Fe Railway and the Missouri Pacific, which operated the Houston and Brazos Valley, the St. Louis, Brownsville and Mexico, the International—Great Northern, and the Texas and New Orleans.

The county population grew from 27,069 in 1940 to 46,413 in 1950, and continued to expand. By 1982, at which time 17,800 persons were employed in 2,785 business establishments in Brazoria County, three decades of further growth had more than tripled the population to 185,244.

Small farms in Brazoria County increased through the 1930s and 1940s, and farmers increasingly raised crops as tenants rather than landowners. By 1945 agribusiness had appeared; fewer than 7 percent of all farms accounted for almost 70 percent of farm income, and more than 50 percent of farms made less than $1,000 annually. At the same time, the county ranked eighth in Texas cattle production, with 69,437 head, and farmers turned to the Brahman breed. Overall farm production peaked in the 1950s, with 130,000 acres of cropland harvested. County farmers owned almost 82,000 cattle by 1960, and by 1968 cattle outnumbered people. Roughly 60 percent of the county's agricultural income derived from rice in the 1970s, and 40 percent from livestock and poultry; cotton, soybeans, and grain increased in importance by the latter part of the decade. By 1976 the county had forty-eight oil and gas fields, including Old Ocean, Chocolate Bayou, Damon Mound, Hastings,[qv] Bryan Mound, Danbury, Manvel, and West Columbia. In the late twentieth century petroleum and mineral production and marketing, together with other extraction and manufacturing and the chemical industry, continued to shape the county's development and the lives of local farmers and ranchers. Magnesium from sea water, which ranked Brazoria County first in the nation's production, along with oyster shell, sulfur, and salt, was manufactured at Freeport and Velasco. The shrimping industry[qv] grew at Freeport after World War II. In 1967, 610 boats harvested 14,000,000 pounds of shrimp; the 1971 catch was 160 times larger than that in 1970, and the harvest doubled again by 1972. Both fishing and the recreation industry, which grew up after 1960, fostered ongoing development on the Gulf Coast.

By the 1980s the county had 186 manufacturing establishments that employed almost 18,000 workers. In the 1990s, when the county had more than 41,000 acres of rice in production, the chief agricultural products were rice, cattle, cotton, corn, small grains, forage, and truck crops, with some sorghum, soybeans, and horses. The Brazoria-Galveston Soil Conservation District promoted adequate drainage to allow cultivation.

The population of Brazoria County has become more homogeneous during the twentieth century. After 1900 the white population grew steadily. By 1920, as blacks began to leave for employment in northern cities, the county had twice as many white as black residents. A typical county resident at the turn of the century was born either in the lower South or within the state of Texas. Native whites comprised 62.9 percent of the total population in 1930, and grew to 71.4 percent in 1940. Mexican Americans[qv] increased in the 1930s, especially around Alvin, where they were employed as farm laborers. The county population, 23,114 in 1930, increased steadily but predominantly in urban areas after 1940, and rose almost 57 percent between 1970 and 1980. Of a total population of 182,244 in 1982, almost 68 percent were native Texans, 13,152 were African American, and 22,679 Hispanic.

Brazoria County's first school was established in 1827, Brazoria Academy in 1839, Alvin Normal School in 1890, and the University of South Texas in 1897. By 1900 eight independent school districts with 200 teachers and forty school buildings served the county's 6,000 pupils. Alvin Community College, founded in the late 1940s, enrolled 3,900 students in 1990. Brazosport College began in 1968. Common-school districts expanded significantly around 1920, suffered declining enrollments during the Great Depression, but grew again by 1940 as the northern county population increased with the rapid growth of Houston, and the southern and central parts of the county grew through the influence of increasing industrialization. New independent school districts became necessary. In 1935 the county had twenty-seven schools for whites and twenty-eight for blacks, and in 1940 Pearland had the only first-class high school among the common-school districts. In 1950 only 23 percent of the county population had completed high school, but by 1982 more than 65 percent had done so. College graduates numbered almost 14 percent that year.

Brazoria County offers water sports, fishing, hunting, and other recreation, along with historic sites including Varner-Hogg Plantation State Historical Park.[qv] The county celebrates a San Jacinto Festival at West Columbia and the Spring Fling at Clute in April; a Mexican Fiesta at Pearland and Youth Rodeo and Frontier Days at Alvin in May; a Fishing Fiesta at Freeport, a Fireworks Display at Alvin, and the Great Texas Mosquito Festival and Parade at Clute in July; a Founders Day Celebration at Pearland in September; and a County Fair and Rodeo at Angleton and the Bluegrass and Gospel Fall Festival at Brazoria in October.

BIBLIOGRAPHY: Brazoria County Federation of Women's Clubs, *History of Brazoria County* (1940). Brazosport *Facts*, June 28, 1964. Abigail Curlee, A Study of Texas Slave Plantations, 1822–1865 (Ph.D. dissertation, University of Texas, 1932). Freeport *Facts*, July 16, 1942. Frank W. Johnson, *A History of Texas and Texans* (5 vols., ed. E. C. Barker and E. W. Winkler [Chicago and New York: American Historical Society, 1914; rpt. 1916]). Edwin C. Mason, General Survey of the Rural Schools of Brazoria County, Texas (M.A. thesis, University of Texas, 1940). William Otho Morris, Proposed Plan of Reorganization of the Public Schools of Brazoria County, Texas (M.A. thesis, University of Texas, 1937). Abner J. Strobel, *The Old Plantations and Their Owners of Brazoria County* (Houston, 1926; rev. ed., Houston: Bowman and Ross, 1930; rpt., Austin: Shelby, 1980).

Diana J. Kleiner

BRAZORIA NATIONAL WILDLIFE REFUGE. Brazoria National Wildlife Refuge is five miles east of Freeport and eleven miles southeast of Angleton and is bordered to the north and east by Bastrop Bayou and to the south by Bastrop, Christmas, and Drum bays. In accord with federal migratory bird conservation acts, it provides winter habitat for migratory waterfowl. By the late 1980s the refuge comprised 12,000 acres of saline and nonsaline prairies and marshes in southern Brazoria County and offered habitat to more than 425 species of wildlife, including some 270 bird species. The refuge is dotted with numerous small lakes, including Nicks, Wolf, Salt, and Cox lakes, and is bisected by the Gulf Intracoastal Waterway[qv] and the freshwater Big Slough, which hosts a small American alligator population. The upland prairies support wildlife including sandhill cranes, coyotes, and bobcats, and the shore area hosts herons, sandpipers, avocets, and stilts. More uncommon marsh and water birds, including roseate spoonbills, double-crested cormorants, and yellow rails, make seasonal appearances, and the endangered American peregrine falcon has occasionally been seen there. Brazoria National Wildlife Refuge, along with other such refuges on the Texas Gulf Coast, provides essential winter habitat for birds on the Central Flyway, one of four major migratory routes over the continental United States. During the winter months duck and goose populations reach peaks as high as 30,000 and 40,000, respectively, and birders at the Audubon Society's December Freeport Christmas Bird Count often identify more than 200 different bird species, one of the highest counts in the country, in the vicinity of the refuge.

The refuge was established in 1966 with 6,398 acres, half of which was bought from rancher Jack Phillips. It gradually expanded with numerous smaller purchases from various landholders and in 1986 began managing the Slop Bowl addition, which it acquired from the Nature Conservancy. In the late 1980s refuge management included dikes and controlled burns and also allowed cattle grazing from October to April. In March 1991 an additional 28,655 acres, known as the

Hoskins Mound Marsh, was added to the refuge, for a total of 40,854 acres. Fishing and waterfowl hunting were allowed in season. Brazoria National Wildlife Refuge is administered by the United States Fish and Wildlife Service, Department of the Interior. Its offices are based at Angleton and also serve as headquarters for the nearby San Bernard and Big Boggy National Wildlife refuges.[qqv] *Rachel Jenkins*

BRAZORIA RESERVOIR. Brazoria Reservoir, an off-channel reservoir, is in the Brazos River basin six miles southwest of Angleton in central Brazoria County (at 29°03′ N, 95°32′ W). The project, owned and operated by Dow Chemical Company, is used for industrial water supply. It was designed by engineers Lockwood and Andrews, constructed by general contractor Gulf Bitulithic, and completed on May 1, 1954. Diversion of water from the Brazos began in April 1954. The storage reservoir has a capacity of 21,970 acre-feet and a surface area of 1,865 acres at a crest elevation of 31.07 feet above mean sea level. The reservoir level is maintained by water pumped from the Brazos River.

BRAZORIA *TEXAS REPUBLICAN.* The Brazoria *Texas Republican,* a weekly newspaper, began publication on July 5, 1834. Franklin C. Gray[qv] and A. J. Harris were publishers until Harris retired in December 1834. The paper began as a three-column, four-page sheet but changed to five columns by November 14, 1835. Publication probably ceased in March 1836 with the Mexican attack. According to some sources, Gray was accused of trying to effect the escape of Antonio López de Santa Anna[qv] after San Jacinto, and this accusation destroyed the paper's influence.

BIBLIOGRAPHY: James A. Creighton, *A Narrative History of Brazoria County* (Angleton, Texas: Brazoria County Historical Commission, 1975). Joe B. Frantz, Newspapers of the Republic of Texas (M.A. thesis, University of Texas, 1940). Mary Glasscock Frazier, Texas Newspapers during the Republic (March 2, 1836–February 19, 1846) (M.Journ. thesis, University of Texas, 1931). Marilyn M. Sibley, *Lone Stars and State Gazettes: Texas Newspapers before the Civil War* (College Station: Texas A&M University Press, 1983). WPA Historical Records Survey Program, *Texas Newspapers* (Houston: San Jacinto Museum of History Association, 1941).

BRAZOS, TEXAS. Brazos, on Farm Road 129 and the Missouri Pacific Railroad in southeastern Palo Pinto County, was established when the Texas and Pacific Railway reached the area in 1880. The community was named for the Brazos River, which the railroad crossed at its site. The town had a population of 113 and four stores by 1940. Its population was reported as forty-seven in 1980 and 1990.

BRAZOS BEND STATE PARK. Brazos Bend State Park is on the Brazos River near Farm Road 762 in Fort Bend County seven miles west of Rosharon. The 4,897-acre park was originally part of the Abner Harris and William Barrett[qqv] land grants and for many years served as a ranch and hunting preserve. The state acquired the site from private owners in 1976, and the park officially opened in 1984. The park is heavily wooded with a wide variety of trees, including oak, elm, pecan, sycamore, and cottonwood. It is home to squirrels, white-tailed deer, bobcats, raccoons, opossums, grey foxes, coyotes, feral hogs, and alligators, as well as a wide range of birds. Park facilities include a group dining hall, fishing piers, restrooms, showers, campsites, and picnic tables. The George Observatory is located in the park woods, and its largest telescope is available for public use.

BIBLIOGRAPHY: Ray Miller, *Texas Parks* (Austin: Cordovan, 1984).
Christopher Long

BRAZOS COUNTY. Brazos County (J-19), between the Navasota and Brazos rivers in southeast central Texas, is bounded on the northwest by Robertson County, on the east by Madison and Grimes counties, on the south by Washington County, and on the southwest by Burleson County. The center point of the county is at 30°40′ north latitude and 96°18′ west longitude. The county was named for the nearby Brazos River.[qv] Bryan is the county seat, and College Station is the other major community in the county. Brazos County is crossed by U.S. Highway 190 and State highways 6, 21, and 30, as well as the Missouri Pacific and the Southern Pacific railroads. It comprises 588 square miles of rolling prairie and woodland with elevations that range from 200 to 350 feet above sea level. The average annual rainfall is thirty-nine inches. The average minimum temperature in January is 39° F; the average maximum in July, the hottest month, is 95°. The county has a growing season of 268 days, its soils are alluvial to sandy, and between 11 and 20 percent of the land is considered prime farmland. The northern third of the county is in the Blackland Prairie area and is vegetated by elm, oak, pecan, and mesquite trees along streams. The remainder of the county is in the Post Oak Savannah vegetation area, which features post oak, walnut, and pecan trees.

Brazos County has been the site of human habitation for more than 12,000 years. Evidence of Paleo-Indian inhabitants in the area has turned up in the form of spearpoints, and the remains of a butchered mammoth have been found at the Duewall-Newberry Site on the Brazos River. Archaic hunters and gatherers in the future county lived on deer, bison, roots, and nuts. Within the historic period, Spanish explorers reported Bidai and Tonkawa Indians in the area, and there is evidence that groups related to the Apaches and Comanches occasionally hunted buffalo[qv] as far east as Brazos County. Spanish travelers on the Old San Antonio Road[qv] passed along the northwest boundary of the future county, but there was no Spanish settlement in the area.

The territory that is now Brazos County was included in Stephen F. Austin's[qv] second colony and became part of Washington Municipality under the Mexican government. Colonists who sought plantation sites on the Brazos between 1821 and 1831 included Elliot McNeil Millican, Richard Carter,[qqv] James H. Evetts, Melvan Lanham, Lee C. Smith, and Mordecai Boon. In 1837 most of the area of present-day Brazos County was included in Washington County. The Brazos River, which bisected the latter, proved a serious obstacle to county government, and a new county, Navasota, was formed in January 1841. The first court, with Judge R. E. B. Baylor[qv] presiding, was held later that year in the home of Joseph Ferguson, fourteen miles west of the site of present Bryan. The county seat, named Boonville for Mordecai Boon, was located on John Austin's[qv] league and was surveyed by Hiram Hanover[qv] in 1841. In January of the following year Navasota County was renamed Brazos County. The 1850 census showed 466 whites and 148 black slaves in the county. Of the approximately 176,000 acres in farms at that time, less than 2,000 acres was cleared for crops. Farmers concentrated on growing corn and a bit of cotton. The county remained overwhelmingly rural in the 1850s; only two families lived in the county seat in 1852, and only two post offices, Boonville and Millican, operated in the county in 1856.

In 1860 growth in the county was speeded by the arrival of the Houston and Texas Central Railroad, with Millican as its terminus. By that year the county had some 14,509 acres under cultivation, and cotton production had increased from 142 bales in 1850 to 2,269 bales. On the eve of the Civil War,[qv] Brazos County had a mixed economy of small farms and a few larger plantations, with a population of 1,713 whites and 1,063 slaves. Of the 118 slaveholders in the county, seventy-seven owned fewer than five slaves, and only four owned more than fifty. The county voted 215 to 44 for secession[qv] in 1861 and mobilized its inhabitants for the war. The railhead at Millican became an important transportation center for the Confederate war effort, and a training camp was established nearby in 1861. Local men formed companies or parts of companies in the Twenty-first and Twenty-fifth Texas Cavalry regiments, the Tenth Texas Infantry regiment, and other army units, and participated in various home and state guard units. During the war the Brazos County Commissioners Court acted to gather supplies for the Confederacy and assist the indigent families of men serving in the armed forces.

Federal troops arrived in Millican in June 1865, when Brazos County began almost eight years of Reconstruction[qv] turmoil. County blacks and white landowners struggled to work out their new economic and social relations, and a series of Freedmen's Bureau[qv] agents, occasionally backed by small numbers of federal soldiers, attempted to mediate between the groups. While black children attended school for the first time at Millican and at Wilson's Plantation, whites and blacks quarreled constantly over labor contracts, and interracial violence became increasingly common. This strife reached its peak in the Millican race riot of 1868. The Ku Klux Klan[qv] made its first appearance in the county in June of that year, when a group of masked men paraded through the black neighborhood in Millican. Armed blacks fired at the Klan members, drove them off, and organized a militia company under the leadership of George Brooks, a black clergyman who had also been active in registering black voters and was much hated by some white county residents. In July false rumors spread among the black community of Millican that a local black leader, Miles Brown, had been lynched by whites. Escalating tensions on both sides eventually led to several armed confrontations between groups of whites and blacks that left at least six blacks dead, including Brooks.

Brazos County politics was also tumultuous in the postwar period. Immediately after the war, during the presidential phase of Reconstruction, former Confederates were allowed to hold local office and the prewar political structure of the county remained unchanged. At the end of 1867 many officeholders were removed from office by federal authorities as part of the new policies of congressional Reconstruction, and by the following year the county was dominated by the Republican party.[qv] Powerful local families like the Millicans, who were leaders in the Democratic party,[qv] and the Myerses, who were prominent Republicans, engaged in questionable voting practices and occasional violence in the struggle to control county politics. By the time of the gubernatorial election of 1873, Brazos County was once again Democratic by a slim majority. Blacks continued to hold office on the county commissioners' court through the 1880s, and one county black, Elias Mayes,[qv] served in the Texas House of Representatives in 1879 and 1889. In 1890 local white Democrats instituted a "White Man's Campaign" similar to the white primary[qv] movement in other counties, which acted to disfranchise black voters. The Republican party remained a force in county elections for a time, and Brazos County voted for Republican presidential candidates in 1888 and 1896. From the election of 1900 until the 1950s, however, the county remained solidly Democratic. Subsequently, county voters supported Republican presidential candidates in 1952 and 1956, and from 1968 through 1992.

While county residents worked out the social and political problems left by the Civil War, the county prospered and grew. In 1866 the Houston and Texas Central Railroad resumed construction past Millican, and county citizens voted to make a site on the railroad line, the new community of Bryan, their county seat. Both Millican and the former county seat, Boonville, declined rapidly as their inhabitants moved themselves, their goods, and in some cases, the lumber from their homes and stores to Bryan. By 1870 Brazos County had 9,205 inhabitants, more than a three-fold increase since 1860. Cotton production had also tripled since 1860, and for the first time county ranchers raised cattle and hogs in substantial numbers. Sheep ranching[qv] reached an all-time county record in 1870, when 8,565 sheep were counted, in contrast to only 219 in 1860.

Population growth continued at a more modest rate in the next few decades, reaching 13,576 in 1880 and 16,650 in 1890. The black population of the county increased more rapidly than the white, growing from 3,759 in 1870 to 6,250 in 1880. In 1890 the number of African Americans[qv] reached 8,845, and for the only time in its history the county had a black majority. Beginning in the 1870s substantial numbers of Germans, Austrians, and Czechs[qqv] (Bohemians) migrated to the county, and Italians[qv] began arriving in the 1880s. In 1900 the county population reached 18,859. Of the 10,005 white residents that year, 1,403, or 14 percent, were foreign born, including 553 from Italy, 239 from Germany, and 223 from Bohemia. Settlement and economic growth were hastened in the county by transportation developments in the last decades of the nineteenth century. In the 1880s the Gulf, Colorado and Santa Fe Railway built through the southern part of the county and the Hearne and Brazos Valley Railway built through the northwest. In 1900 the International–Great Northern built through to Bryan, and in 1910 the Bryan and College Station Interurban Railway was started between Bryan and Texas A&M College.

In the last decades of the nineteenth century and the early years of the twentieth century cotton increasingly dominated county agriculture. Acres planted with cotton grew from 28,044 in 1880 to almost 44,000 in 1890 and to an all-time high of 72,275, about a third of all improved acres in the county, in 1910. About half the cotton acreage was usually allotted to corn, the second major crop in the county. The county also followed the general Southern pattern of large numbers of small farms, many of them worked by tenants and sharecroppers. The number of farms increased from 666 in 1870 to 1,630 in 1880 and 2,088 in 1890. In 1900, of the 2,613 farms in the county, 1,576, or 60 percent, were worked by tenants and sharecroppers. Black farmers were much less likely to own land than their white counterparts. In 1900 more than half of the white farmers owned their own farms, while only 20 percent of black farmers were owners. In 1920 the number of farms reached a peak of 3,023, and the number of tenant farmers reached its zenith at 1,939, or 64 percent. As a percentage of the total cropland harvested, cotton land probably reached its peak in 1930, when more than 64,000 of the 88,224 acres harvested was used to grow cotton. Thereafter, county farming began to change in response to changing technologies and opportunities. During the Great Depression[qv] much of the rural workforce left the county to seek work in the cities of Texas or left the state entirely. By 1940 the number of farms had fallen to 1,773, comparable to the number of farms back in 1880. Mechanized farming began in the bottomlands of the county along the rivers in the late 1920s and slowly spread to other parts of the county. With the loss of even more of the rural labor supply after World War II,[qv] farmers consolidated their holdings and turned to tractors, mechanical cotton harvesters, and other machines to work their fields.

During the twentieth century, Bryan and College Station played an increasingly important role in the life of the county. After its founding as a railroad town in 1866, Bryan slowly grew to a community of 3,589 in 1900, when approximately one-fifth of county residents lived there. The nearby community of College Station, which grew around Texas A&M after its founding in the 1870s, numbered only 391 inhabitants in 1900. Both communities grew steadily, and by 1940 they had a combined population of 14,026; at that time more than half of the county population lived in the two communities. As the county population continued to grow—to 38,390 in 1950, 57,978 in 1970 and 93,588 in 1980—the urban population continued to grow both absolutely and with relation to the rural population. In 1980 the 81,506 inhabitants of Bryan–College Station were 87 percent of the residents of Brazos County. Significant industries that developed in the two-city area in the later twentieth century included defense electronics and varied manufacturing.

At the same time that the county was becoming more urban, the building of a network of rural roads in the 1930s and 1940s transformed the Brazos County countryside. As late as 1930 the great majority of the county's farms, 2,100 of 2,439, were located on dirt roads. Twenty years later only 538 were still on dirt roads. Similarly, though only forty-eight farms had electricity in 1930, rural electrification[qv] brought power to most of the county's farms by the early 1960s. Starting in the 1960s, as Texas A&M University embarked on a major expansion program, much of the rural land in the vicinity of Bryan–College Station was brought into the suburban orbit of the two cities. By the mid-twentieth century, county farmers had increasingly turned away from the old agricultural staples of corn and cotton and had moved on to cattle ranching. In the 1980s cotton was generally grown on approximately 12,000 acres, only 15 percent of the acreage used for cotton in 1925. The number of cattle in the county increased from 25,354 in 1940 to 42,545 in 1950 and fluctuated between 45,000 and 57,000 through the 1980s. As part of the shift to cattle, feed crops of hay, oats, and wheat became more important in the county in the decades following 1950. Oil, first discovered in the county in 1942, became an important part of the county economy in the 1970s, and by 1990 a total of 73,427,789 barrels had been produced.

In 1982, 67 percent of the land was in farms and ranches, with 18 percent of the farmland under cultivation and 20 percent irrigated. Primary crops were hay, cotton, sorghum, oats, and wheat, and primary livestock and products were cattle, hogs, and milk. The industries with the most employment were agribusiness, oil and gas extraction, and construction. In 1980 Brazos County was one of the most densely populated counties in the state. Of its 94,492 inhabitants, the largest ancestry groups were English and German. The black population of the county, which had remained relatively static at about 9,000 for most of the century, began to increase in the 1970s and was 10,350 in 1980. Significant Hispanic migration to the county began in the second half of the twentieth century; by 1980 Hispanic residents numbered 9,455. In 1990 the county had 121,862 residents. The incorporated towns were Bryan (55,002), College Station (52,456), and Wixon Valley (186). Brazos County hosts a number of fall, spring, and summer festivals. The Texas Brazos Trail, which offers tourists scenic views of wildflowers and forests, passes through the county, and there are recreational parks for boating and fishing on several of the county's lakes and reservoirs. The Texas World Speedway, which opened in 1969, is a local venue for auto racing.

BIBLIOGRAPHY: Glenna Fourman Brundidge, *Brazos County History: Rich Past—Bright Future* (Bryan, Texas: Family History Foundation, 1986). Elmer Grady Marshall, History of Brazos County (M.A. thesis, University of Texas, 1937). *Mark Odintz*

BRAZOS COURIER. The *Brazos Courier*, published in Brazoria by R. L. Weir from February 17, 1839, until December 1840, was a five-column, four-page newspaper that resembled in appearance the *People*,[qv] a paper printed at Brazoria in 1838. The *Courier* was published weekly on Tuesday and sold for five dollars a year. Advertisements occupied most of the paper until April 1840, when it began publication of the laws of the Republic of Texas.[qv]

BIBLIOGRAPHY: James A. Creighton, *A Narrative History of Brazoria County* (Angleton, Texas: Brazoria County Historical Commission, 1975). Mary Glasscock Frazier, Texas Newspapers during the Republic (March 2, 1836–February 19, 1846) (M. Journ. thesis, University of Texas, 1931). John Melton Wallace, *Gaceta to Gazette: A Checklist of Texas Newspapers, 1813–1846* (Austin: University of Texas Department of Journalism, 1966). WPA Historical Records Survey Program, *Texas Newspapers* (Houston: San Jacinto Museum of History Association, 1941).

BRAZOS FLOOD OF 1899. Between June 17 and June 28, 1899, rainfall averaging 8.9 inches fell over 66,000 square miles, causing the Brazos River to overflow its banks and inundate an estimated 12,000 square miles. Damage to property was estimated at more than $9 million and 284 persons were known to have perished in the floodwaters; thousands of others were left homeless. The flood's highest recorded stage was at Hearne, where, as at many points, the waters rose above all available flood gauges. *Curtis Bishop*

BRAZOS AND GALVESTON RAILROAD. The Brazos and Galveston Railroad Company was chartered by the Republic of Texas[qv] on May 24, 1838. The capital stock was $500,000, divided among 5,000 shares. W. G. Cooke and Asa Brigham[qqv] subscribed to 2,000 shares for Galveston; James F. Perry and George L. Hammeken[qqv] took out 1,500 shares for Austinia; and Edmund Andrews and Frederick A. Sawyer[qv] received the remaining 1,500 shares for Brazoria. The railroad originated because Galveston wanted a shorter route to the planters along the Brazos and Colorado rivers to circumvent the competition from Houston, Harrisburg, and San Luis. The railroad secured permission in its charter to use boats, vehicles, wagons, or carriages and to improve bays, rivers, and harbors. Congress reserved the right to regulate the charges, and in January 1840 it amended the charter to substitute canals for turnpikes and to provide a maximum freight rate of 2½ cents a mile per 100 pounds. Men and munitions for the army and navy were to be transported free. The enterprise failed, but it stimulated railroad projects in Houston.

BRAZOS INDIAN RESERVATION. In the summer of 1854 Gen. Randolph B. Marcy,[qv] under orders of the United States Department of War and Interior and in accordance with an act of the Texas legislature of February 6, located two Indian reservations in West Texas. The Brazos Reservation originally comprised four leagues, or 18,576 acres, twelve miles south of Fort Belknap, where the Brazos River makes three big bends. The size was doubled when an adjacent tract of equal size, intended for the western Indians, was added to it. The main building was three miles east of the site of Graham, where a few scattered stones mark the remains of the agency.

Under the direction of Maj. Robert S. Neighbors,[qv] the general supervisor of all Indians in Texas, Capt. Shapley P. Ross[qv] was made the Brazos agent. J. J. Strum was agriculturist, and Zachariah Ellis Coombes[qv] was educational instructor. About 2,000 Indians took up life on the Brazos Reservation; Caddo, Anadarko, Waco, and Tonkawa Indians had their own villages, and these shrinking groups were glad to have protection from the Comanches. Supplies for the Indians cost the government $80,000 annually. Contracts were made with ranchers for beef, and on an average thirty-four cattle were delivered each week. The federal government had control of the reservation and a ten-mile surrounding area, to prevent the sale of liquor to the Indians. Texas, however, reserved the right of jurisdiction over persons other than Indians for offenses committed upon the person or property of anyone in the state.

About 600 acres was put in cultivation, mostly in corn, wheat, vegetables, and melons. The Indians were good farmers, and many white settlers recognized and respected the reservation dwellers, did not interfere with them, and were not molested by them. Rangers and military officers enlisted the Indians as scouts against the warring tribes. The braves were eager to take part and were so helpful that between fifty and 100 were on regular duty. However, this pleased neither the anti-Indian white men nor the wild Indians. It also incited a spirit of envy among the friendly Penateka Comanches on the Upper Reserve, who were not permitted to fight against other Comanche groups.

The situation grew worse. Small depredations took place and were always attributed to reservation Indians, so that a lone Indian off the reserve was not safe. A little newspaper published in Jacksboro called the *White Man*[qv] added fuel to the flame of hatred. By 1858 this antagonism verged on warfare. Feeling ran so high that Governor H. R. Runnels and Gen. Sam Houston[qqv] appealed to the federal government to move the Indians out of the state.

The government, therefore, ordered a survey of land in Indian Territory, but before a suitable location could be secured two incidents brought the issue to a climax. In December 1858 Choctaw Tom and his party of seventeen received permission for a week's hunt in Palo Pinto County. They camped on Ioni Creek a few miles above Golconda, the principal settlement and trading post. On the night of

December 26 an attack was made on the party. Seven Indians were found dead in their blankets and four others were wounded.

The commander at Fort Belknap ordered a company of troops to the Brazos reserve. Capt. J. B. Plummer, commander of the troops, fortified the agency building with skins and poles, and made a stockade to protect the women and children. Major Neighbors arrived for an investigation. On January 9, 1859, Governor Runnels issued a proclamation warning all Texans against engaging in hostilities against the Indians. He ordered Col. John Henry Brown[qv] to the frontier with 100 men. Major Neighbors learned that the attack on Choctaw Tom's party was made by white men from Erath County. Their names were secured, and an examining trial was set to take place in Waco, but no indictments were made.

On May 23, 1859, several hundred whites led by John R. Baylor[qv] appeared on the Brazos reserve. Baylor stated that he had come for certain Indians and that if the United States troops opened fire on his party, he would treat them as Indians. The agency prepared for battle. Captain Baylor retreated for consultation with his men; while so doing he killed an Indian woman working in her garden and an old man. Then the party hurried from the reserve, pursued by Indians. A few miles beyond stood the Marlin Ranch, which Baylor and his men reached by noon. The men asked Mrs. Marlin to prepare a meal, but before she could comply with their demands, Indians were sighted. The Baylor men took to the cabins on the ranch. United States troops from Fort Belknap had followed, but, having no jurisdiction over the Indians when they were off the reserve, did not intervene. The battle lasted all afternoon. Chief John Hatterbox was killed, two of Baylor's men lost their lives, and others were wounded. The Baylor men were buried on the ranch, and the next morning the wounded were taken to Fort Belknap.

Neighbors promptly ordered the removal of the Indians from both reservations to Indian Territory. As there was no land allotted there for Texas Indians, it was decided to place them with the Wichita Indians in the Washita valley. The Brazos reservation was abandoned on July 31, 1859, and two weeks of traveling brought the caravan of Indians to the valley of the Washita, where on September 1 they were delivered by Neighbors to the Wichita agency officials. Captain Ross resigned his position after seeing his charges safely located, and expressed regret in parting.

Although the Texas Indians set up their villages among the peaceable Wichita Indians, their days of peace and life were short. In 1862 a group of pro-Union Indians from Kansas attacked the pro-Confederate Tonkawas and killed a number of them. The few Tonkawas who escaped wandered back into Texas. Others, generally pro-Union, fled to Kansas.

bibliography: Lena Clara Koch, "The Federal Indian Policy in Texas, 1845–1860," *Southwestern Historical Quarterly* 28 (January, April 1925). Virginia Pink No'l, The United States Indian Reservations in Texas, 1854–1859 (M.A. thesis, University of Texas, 1924). Joseph B. Thoburn and Muriel H. Wright, *Oklahoma* (4 vols., New York: Lewis Historical Publishing, 1929). *Carrie J. Crouch*

BRAZOS INSTITUTE. Brazos Institute, located in Golconda (later Palo Pinto) in Palo Pinto County, was organized by representatives from twelve Baptist churches, called the Brazos River Association, in 1858. The group met with representatives of Providence Church in Parker County and subscribed $7.20 toward forming a Baptist school. A committee to raise further money was appointed, including Rev. G. W. Slaughter, John Hittson, William (Choctaw Bill) Robinson, and Noah T. Byars.[qqv] Within a year $1,500 had been raised, and the school had a stone building. Courses were offered for only one term, taught by three teachers, one of whom was Mrs. Byars. More than seventy students were enrolled. There are two versions of why the school closed. One says that the building was defective, the other that the chaos attendant upon the Civil War[qv] forced abandonment of the school in 1861. The building was torn down in 1867.

bibliography: Mary Whatley Clarke, *The Palo Pinto Story* (Fort Worth: Manney, 1956). *Thomas Robert Havins*

BRAZOS ISLAND. Brazos Island is a barrier island south of Padre Island, at the south end of the Laguna Madre (at 26°01′ N, 97°09′ W). The lower Rio Grande valley was largely ranching country when Mexican independence opened the port of Brazos Santiago on Brazos Island. A lively trade in specie, wool, and hides in exchange for cloth, hardware, and machinery developed. Gen. Zachary Taylor[qv] set up his headquarters on Brazos Island in 1845. During the Civil War[qv] the port was occupied by both Union and Confederate forces. It was an important avenue of trade and supply. The last shot of the Civil War is reported to have been fired on Brazos Island on May 12, 1865. Most of the buildings on the island were destroyed by the hurricane of 1867 (*see* hurricanes). The port and settlement have long ceased to exist.

bibliography: Writers' Roundtable, *Padre Island* (San Antonio: Naylor, 1950).

BRAZOS ISLAND STATE SCENIC PARK. Brazos Island State Scenic Park, also known as Brazos Island State Recreation Area, is off State Highway 4 (Boca Chica Road) just north of the mouth of the Rio Grande and twenty-four miles east of Brownsville in Cameron County. The park has 217 undeveloped acres and offers ocean fishing, surfing, swimming, camping, and nature study. It was established by legislative act in 1957 from lands held by the General Land Office.[qv] Nearby are three battlegrounds: the sites of the Mexican War[qv] battles of Palo Alto and Resaca de la Palma[qqv] and the battle of Palmito Ranch,[qv] the last land engagement in the Civil War.[qv] The park takes its name from Brazos Santiago Island, on which it is located.

BRAZOS LARGOS INDIANS. These Coahuiltecan Indians are known through a single missionary report (1794) from Nuestra Señora del Espíritu Santo de Zúñiga Mission[qv] near Goliad. In this report they are identified as a subdivision of the Aranamas, and at that time only nine remained. When Governor Manuel Muñoz[qv] visited the Goliad mission in 1794 during his study of the feasibility of enforcing the secularization decree, he determined that none of the 125 mission Indians, including the nine Brazos Largos, were able to manage their own affairs. The name, which is Spanish for "long arms" or perhaps "big arms," suggests that the Spaniards observed a physical difference between these and other Aranama groups. The original territory of the Brazos Largos was probably the same as that of the Aranamas.

bibliography: Carlos E. Castañeda, *Our Catholic Heritage in Texas* (7 vols., Austin: Von Boeckmann–Jones, 1936–58; rpt., New York: Arno, 1976). Esteban L. Portillo, *Apuntes para la historia antigua de Coahuila y Texas* (Saltillo: Tipografía "El Golfo de México" de Severo Fernández, 1886). *Thomas N. Campbell*

BRAZOS PLANTER. The *Brazos Planter*, a Brazoria newspaper, was published in 1845 by Samuel J. Durnett.[qv] The La Grange *Intelligencer*[qv] referred to the *Planter* in its issues of March 30 and September 23, 1845.

bibliography: Marilyn M. Sibley, *Lone Stars and State Gazettes: Texas Newspapers before the Civil War* (College Station: Texas A&M University Press, 1983). Ben C. Stuart, "Hamilton Stuart: Pioneer Editor," *Southwestern Historical Quarterly* 21 (April 1918).

BRAZOS POINT, TEXAS. Brazos Point is on Farm Road 56 eleven miles northeast of Walnut Springs and fifty miles northwest of Waco in northeastern Bosque County. It was founded by Charles Walker

Smith and Tom Willingham when they built a store, cotton gin, and mill beside the Brazos River. A school was erected for the settlement in 1860. The Brazos Point Community Church was located near the school. A post office was established in 1873. During the mid-1880s the town supported a steam cotton gin, a gristmill, a general store, a physician, and a population of 200. However, by 1896 the population had decreased to seventy-five and the post office had closed. The community moved to Farm Road 56 for better business opportunities. Population estimates remained at fifty between 1933 and 1947, after which no figures were recorded.

BIBLIOGRAPHY: Bosque County History Book Committee, *Bosque County, Land and People* (Dallas: Curtis Media, 1985). William C. Pool, *Bosque Territory* (Kyle, Texas: Chaparral, 1964).

Karen Yancy

BRAZOSPORT, TEXAS. Brazosport is on State Highway 288 where the Brazos River meets the Gulf of Mexico, sixty miles south of Houston in southern Brazoria County. It is a 214-square-mile urbanized industrial and port area. According to some sources the popular name was first used in eighteenth-century nautical charts. Brazosport shares a chamber of commerce with local economically linked municipalities—Clute, Freeport, Lake Barbara, Richwood, and Lake Jackson—and small towns—Jones Creek, Oyster Creek, Quintana, Surfside, Gulf Park, Bryan Beach, Perry's Landing, and Bastrop Bayou.

Port facilities, sulfur mines, and the chemical industry were largely responsible for rapid growth in the community after Dow Chemical Company arrived in 1939. By 1990 the firm employed almost 11,000 people. The Brazos River Harbor Navigation District was established in 1925 to govern development of the Port of Freeport; it opened the harbor on December 11, 1954. The nation's first seawater conversion plant was established in Brazosport in 1959, and in the 1970s Bryan Mound Salt Dome provided strategic oil reserves for the United States government. The Brazosport resort industry promotes forty-four miles of beaches and sport and commercial fishing. It is responsible for annual events, including the April Blessing of the Texas Gulf Fleet, the June Sandcastle and Sand Sculpture Contest and Fort Velasco Day, July Fishin' Fiesta and Shrimp Festival, September Shrimp Boil and Auction, and October Sausage Festival. In 1988 a Foreign Trade Zone opened by the Port of Freeport provided access to worldwide markets. Local pacemaker manufacturer Intermedics merged with Sulzer Brothers of Switzerland in that year, bringing new industry to the area.

In 1944 the Brazosport communities consolidated to form a single school district, and by 1957 a high school, five junior high schools, nine elementary schools, and a community college served the area. Brazosport College, originally Brazosport Junior College, opened in March 1968 with an enrollment of 879. It was later moved to a site two miles from Lake Jackson. Brazoria Memorial Hospital was dedicated in 1988, and two new county parks, Quintana and Stahlman, opened in the 1990s. In 1945 Brazosport had 23,000 residents. The population rose to 35,000 by 1954, declined briefly in 1956, then rose steadily, despite severe damage done by Hurricane Carla in 1961 (*see* HURRICANES). The population in 1990 was 52,258.

BIBLIOGRAPHY: Brazosport Chamber of Commerce, *An Overview of the Brazosport Area* (Lake Jackson, Texas: First Port Group, n.d.). James A. Creighton, *A Narrative History of Brazoria County* (Angleton, Texas: Brazoria County Historical Commission, 1975). Vertical Files, Barker Texas History Center, University of Texas at Austin.

Diana J. Kleiner

BRAZOSPORT COLLEGE. Brazosport College, a junior college, serves the Brazosport area, which includes Clute, Lake Jackson, and Freeport, and the surrounding areas of West Columbia, Sweeny, Brazoria, and Angleton. It was voted into being by the citizens of the Brazosport Independent School District in 1948, but several factors delayed its establishment. These included the rapid growth of the Brazosport Independent School District, the Korean War, and Hurricane Carla (*see* HURRICANES). A maintenance tax for the college was authorized by voters, and the Brazosport Junior College District was officially established on August 1, 1967. J. R. Jackson was appointed president of the new district in 1967 and held the position until March 1, 1978. W. A. Bass, who was the first employee hired by the junior college in 1968, replaced Jackson.

The college opened in the fall of 1968. Classes were held at the Brazosport Education Extension Center in Freeport. Enrollment was 868 in the first semester—637 in credit courses and 231 in noncredit courses. The college had forty-five employees. Brazosport Junior College was renamed Brazosport College in October 1970 to reflect the growing educational role of the school.

In 1968 plans were drawn up for a new permanent campus. A $5 million college bond election for construction of the facility was passed, and a permanent structure was built on 156 wooded acres in Lake Jackson near historic Oyster Creek. The entire college structure, over 300,000 square feet, was built under one roof in order to integrate the academic and occupational facilities and encourage interaction between vocational and academic students. The building was designed to be expanded for future growth.

Student enrollment increased steadily during the 1970s and early 1980s. In 1985 the 50,000th student enrolled. In 1990 the college enrolled 3,850 students in credit courses. Brazosport College offers academic preparation for four-year colleges, technical-vocational-occupational training, and continuing education courses. The college also has programs for inmates in area prisons to encourage prisoners to attend college as a rehabilitation tool. The college is accredited by the Southern Association of Colleges and Schools, and courses and programs in technical and vocational education have been approved by the Texas Education Agency.[qv] Brazosport College also grants associate degrees or certificates to vocational students. Originally, the occupational programs were secondary. However, since the late 1970s the number of vocational students enrolled in the college has exceeded that of academic students.

BIBLIOGRAPHY: Brazosport College, *Southern Association Self-Study Report, 1983–1984* (Brazosport, Texas, 1985). Brazosport *Facts*, August 22, 1967, February 21, 22, 1968, January 6, 1984, August 29, 1985.

Karen Gillenwaters

BRAZOS RIVER. The Brazos River rises at the confluence of its Salt Fork and Double Mountain Fork[qqv] near the eastern boundary of Stonewall County (at 33°16′ N, 100°01′ W) and runs 840 miles across Texas to its mouth on the Gulf of Mexico, two miles south of Freeport in Brazoria County (at 28°53′ N, 95°23′ W). The two forks emerge from the Caprock[qv] 150 miles above the confluence, thus forming a continuous watershed 1,050 miles long, which extends from New Mexico to the Gulf of Mexico and comprises 44,620 square miles, 42,000 of which are in Texas. It is the longest river in Texas and the one with the greatest discharge. It has all of the varied characteristics of a trans-state stream, from the plains "draw" drainage through canyons at the breaks of the Llano Estacado,[qv] the West Texas rolling plains, and the Grand Prairie hill region, to its meandering course through the Coastal Plain. The elevation of the streambed at the confluence of the two forks is 1,500 feet above sea level. From this point the Brazos descends to the Gulf at a rate diminishing from 3½ feet a mile to one-half foot a mile.

Below the Caprock escarpment the Brazos traverses an area of rolling topography in the vicinity of Palo Pinto County, where low escarpments cross the watershed and the basins of the Brazos and its tributaries are deeply trenched and confined in narrow valleys with steep sides or bluffs. The floodplains are narrow, and improvements came slowly and comparatively late. When the river reaches the escarpment that crosses the watershed on a line from Georgetown to Waco, the topography changes to gently rolling, then to an almost featureless plain down to the coast. In this portion the river and its tributaries flow through much less rugged terrain, and stream valleys are wide and flat. Here the floodplain became highly developed rather early in Texas history. The Brazos has seven principal tributaries, including the Salt and Double Mountain forks. The others are the Clear Fork, the Bosque and Little rivers, Yegua Creek, and the Navasota River. In addition, there are fifteen subtributaries within the watershed, the most important being the Leon River, a tributary of the Little.

The Brazos is probably the river that Indians of the Caddoan linguistic group called Tokonohono. This name is preserved in the narratives of the expedition led by René Robert Cavelier, Sieur de La Salle,[qv] and the Brazos is widely identified as the river that La Salle named the Maligne. The name Brazos was probably first applied to the Colorado River, and there is considerable evidence that several early explorers got the Colorado and the Brazos rivers confused. In 1716 Isidro Félix de Espinosa and Domingo Ramón[qqv] probably called the Brazos "la Trinidad," but the present names were established well before the end of the Spanish period. The full name of the river, often used in Spanish accounts, is Los Brazos de Dios, "the arms of God." Many legends have grown up explaining the name. Probably the earliest is that Francisco Vázquez de Coronado[qv] and his men wandering up the Llano Estacado were about to perish from lack of water when the Indians guided them to a small stream, which the men then named Brazos de Dios. Another account tells of a Spanish ship tossed about by a storm in the Gulf of Mexico that had exhausted its supply of drinking water. The sailors were parched with thirst, lost, and unable to determine which direction they should go to find land, when one of the crew noticed a muddy streak in the waters. The ship followed the streak's current to the mouth of a wide river on a great rise. The ship sailed up the river, and the sailors drank fresh water and were saved. In gratitude they christened the unknown stream Brazos de Dios. Another account fixes the naming of the stream in the 1760s, when an extreme drought made it impossible for the Spanish miners on the San Saba to work. They had heard that the drought was even worse toward the south. They headed toward the Waco Indian village where, according to reports, there was a never-failing stream. Many of the men and beasts died en route, and the precious bullion was buried, but the few who finally reached the stream named it Brazos de Dios. The last story, told to Albert Pike[qv] in 1831, accounts for the reversal of the names of the Colorado and the Brazos.

Although the Brazos was well known to Spanish explorers and missionaries who described the Indians along its banks, the first permanent settlements on the river were made by Anglo-Americans. John McFarland,[qv] one of the Old Three Hundred,[qv] founded San Felipe de Austin at the Atascosito Crossing[qv] of the Brazos. The town became the colonial capital of Texas. The river acquired further significance as being, at Velasco, the scene of the first colonial resistance to Mexican authority, and, at Columbia and at Washington-on-the-Brazos, the site of two of the first seats of government of the republic. Cotton and sugar plantations established along the Brazos in pre–Civil War days were showplaces of Texas and homes of some of the wealthiest men in the state.

The climate of the Brazos watershed varies considerably from temperate to subtropical. The average annual temperature is 59°F in its upper reaches and 70° in the coastal region. Normally, the winters are mild and short, even in the upper reaches, but severe weather is not unknown. Temperatures of zero and even lower have been recorded. The average annual rainfall is 29.5 inches, ranging from sixteen in the northwest to forty-seven in the southeast. Soil types along the Brazos vary from sandy loams to deep clay. A variety of natural vegetation ranges from scattered oak mottes and bunch grasses in drier areas to conifers and hardwoods in areas where rain is plentiful. Virtually the entire area of the watershed is suitable for some form of farming or ranching activity. The most important products of the region have been cotton, cattle, and oil.

Originally, the Brazos was navigable for 250 miles from the Gulf to Washington. It was an important waterway before the Civil War,[qv] and efforts to improve it for navigation continued until the early twentieth century. The most important cities in the Brazos watershed are Lubbock, Graham, Waco, Temple, Belton, Freeport, and Galveston. Houston abuts the region along the Fort Bend and Brazoria county lines.

The waters of the Brazos basin are administered by the Brazos River Authority,[qv] an autonomous state agency established by the legislature in 1929. In later years the Brazos has maintained its importance as a source of water for power, irrigation, and other services. The river has been dammed in several places to form reservoirs for flood control, municipal use, and recreation, the most important of these man-made lakes being Possum Kingdom and Whitney reservoir.[qqv] In *Goodbye to a River* (1976), John Graves gave an account of his journey in a canoe down the Brazos in the mid-1970s, with historical sketches of Indians and pioneers.

BIBLIOGRAPHY: James M. Day, "The Mississippi of Texas, 1821–1850," *Texana* 3 (Spring 1965). Glenn A. Gray, *Gazetteer of Streams of Texas* (Washington: GPO, 1919). Kenneth E. Hendrickson, Jr., *The Waters of the Brazos: A History of the Brazos River Authority, 1929–1979* (Waco: Texian Press, 1981). Pamela A. Puryear and Nath Winfield, Jr., *Sandbars and Sternwheelers: Steam Navigation on the Brazos* (College Station: Texas A&M University Press, 1976). Rupert N. Richardson, *Texas: The Lone Star State* (New York: Prentice-Hall, 1943; 4th ed., with Ernest Wallace and Adrian N. Anderson, Englewood Cliffs, New Jersey: Prentice-Hall, 1981). Vertical Files, Barker Texas History Center, University of Texas at Austin. Charles Albert Warner, *Texas Oil and Gas Since 1543* (Houston: Gulf, 1939).

Kenneth E. Hendrickson, Jr.

BRAZOS RIVER AUTHORITY. The Brazos River Authority was established in 1929 by the Texas legislature as a public agency of the state of Texas. The 1929 act, a pioneering step in the history of water-resource management, marked the first time anywhere in the United States that development and management of the water resources of an entire major river basin had been entrusted to a single public agency organized for that purpose. The authority was originally known as the Brazos River Conservation and Reclamation District; in 1953 its name was changed to the Brazos River Authority by the Texas legislature. It has statutory responsibility for developing and conserving the surface water resources of the Brazos River[qv] basin in Texas and for putting these resources to use in the best interest of the people of Texas. The Brazos River basin covers some 42,000 square miles in Texas, about one-sixth of the area of the state; the boundaries of the river authority include all or part of sixty-five Texas counties. The authority is governed by a board of twenty-one directors appointed by the governor and confirmed by the Texas Senate. The directors serve staggered six-year terms. In the early 1990s the Brazos River Authority had some 160 employees and comprised eight divisions: General, Possum Kingdom, Possum Kingdom Hydroelectric, Lake Granbury, Lake Limestone, Federal Reservoirs, Pollution Control, and Water Treatment.

The authority in the early 1930s developed its first master plan for control, conservation, and development of the surface-water resources of the Brazos basin. The original master plan proposed the construction of thirteen major dams on the Brazos and its tributaries. The first reservoir project built by the river authority was Possum Kingdom Reservoir, a conservation and power project completed in 1941 on the main stem of the Brazos River northwest of Fort Worth. Financing of this project was obtained by a combination of state tax remissions and a federal grant from the Works Progress Administration (*see* WORK PROJECTS ADMINISTRATION). Two further reservoirs have been constructed by the authority: Lake Granbury, completed in 1969, and Lake Limestone, completed in 1978.

In the 1940s the Brazos authority began working closely with the United States Army Corps of Engineers after the corps was given responsibility by Congress for federal flood-control activities throughout the nation. The Brazos authority contracted with the federal government for inclusion of conservation storage space in nine corps of engineers reservoirs throughout the Brazos basin. These nine federal reservoirs, in addition to the three reservoirs owned and operated entirely by the Brazos authority, are integrated into the authority's basin-wide system of reservoirs in accordance with its master plan for water-resource development. The nine relevant corps of engineers reservoir projects in the Brazos basin are lakes Aquilla (construction completed in 1983), Belton (1954), Georgetown (1980), Granger (1980), Proctor (1963), Somerville (1967), Stillhouse Hollow (1968), Waco (1965), and Whitney (1951).

Additional water needs in the Gulf Coast area south of Houston were met through two canal systems acquired in 1967 by the Brazos River Authority. These two systems provided 130 miles of mainline canals that enabled the authority to supply water from the Brazos basin directly to water users throughout this industrial region as far east as Texas City and Galveston. Water was also supplied through these systems for irrigation of more than thirty thousand acres of rice.

Water quality is an increasingly important aspect of water-resource management, and the authority is continually expanding its activities in this field. For many years the authority's primary concern was the natural salt pollution in the upper Brazos basin. The authority spent considerable effort and money in the 1950s investigating this problem and defining the principal source of pollution. More recently it has also become concerned with problems of man-made pollution, and has developed several regional sewerage systems to prevent the development of potentially serious pollution problems. Although the Brazos River Authority is a public agency of the state, the authority carries out all of its activities without levying taxes. With the exception of occasional government grants for specific projects, it is entirely self-supporting, using revenues from its operations to pay all its costs.

BIBLIOGRAPHY: Kenneth E. Hendrickson, Jr., *The Waters of the Brazos: A History of the Brazos River Authority, 1929–1979* (Waco: Texian Press, 1981).

BRAZOS SANTIAGO, TEXAS. The port of Brazos Santiago was located on Brazos Island in what is now Cameron County. According to a United States Coast Survey map in 1867 it was across Brazos Santiago Pass from the south end of Padre Island (at 26°02′ N, 97°09′ W). Before 1848 the port was wharves on the lagoon side of Brazos Island. Goods destined for ports up the Rio Grande had to be offloaded at Brazos Santiago because the bars at the mouth of the Rio Grande were too shallow for ships capable of plying the Gulf. Trade for Matamoros and interior Mexico was landed at the harbor on Brazos Island and then transported to Matamoros by oxcart. During the Mexican War[qv] Gen. Zachary Taylor[qv] established a supply depot on Brazos Island, which handled all American and north Mexico supplies, and several thousand American troops debarked from the port. After 1848 Richard King[qv] developed shallow-draft steamboats that could negotiate the shallow bars at the mouth of the Rio Grande. His boats could then offload in the lee of Brazos Island, go around to the Gulf side, and cross the bars and travel up the Rio Grande to their destination. By 1867 the north end of Brazos Island was a well-developed military port with three wharves on Brazos Santiago Pass, a railroad south to Boca Chica and on to Whites Ranch on the Rio Grande, four barracks, a hospital with four outbuildings, two gun emplacements, numerous warehouse buildings, and a lighthouse. After the Civil War[qv] the troops left Brazos Island, and the small town of Brazos faded away; most of the buildings were destroyed by the storm of 1867.

BIBLIOGRAPHY: *Southwestern Historical Quarterly*, Texas Collection, July 1943, January 1945. Writers' Roundtable, *Padre Island* (San Antonio: Naylor, 1950).

Art Leatherwood

BRAZOS SANTIAGO PASS. Brazos Santiago Pass is the water passage between Padre Island and Brazos Island, just southeast of Port Isabel in Cameron County (at 26°04′ N, 97°07′ W). It provides entry to the Gulf Intracoastal Waterway[qv] and to the Brownsville Ship Channel. The name Brazos Santiago is often mistakenly said to have been given the inlet by Francisco de Garay,[qv] though he never came to the area.

BIBLIOGRAPHY: Writers' Roundtable, *Padre Island* (San Antonio: Naylor, 1950).

BRAZOS, SANTIAGO AND RIO GRANDE RAILROAD. Low water over the bar at the mouth of the Rio Grande frequently delayed boats taking supplies to the large federal force that occupied the Texas side of the river in 1865. In order to reduce transportation delays, Bvt. Maj. Gen. Edward R. S. Canby and, later, Maj. Gen. Philip H. Sheridan[qqv] authorized the use of military labor and materials to construct a nine-mile railroad that was completed in December 1865. The line, commonly called the Brazos Santiago and Rio Grande, ran from Brazos Santiago along the beach on Brazos Island to White's Ranch on the river.

As conditions in Texas and Mexico stabilized after the Civil War,[qv] the military presence along the Rio Grande was reduced. The BS&RG was offered for sale in April 1866. On July 7 of that year it was sold to Gen. J. R. West and Richard Chenery, who operated it as the Brazos Santiago and Brownsville. However, the railroad, which was built as a military expediency, was poorly located to serve civilian needs. West and Chenery failed to make the payment due in November 1866, and the BS&RG reverted to military operation. Considerable track damage resulted from the devastating hurricane that hit the lower Texas coast in October 1867 (*see* HURRICANES), and the line was not returned to service. The remains were sold to the Indianola Railroad and moved to Indianola in late 1868. The BS&RG was the only railroad in Texas built to a track gauge of five feet.

BIBLIOGRAPHY: Brownsville *Ranchero*, October 16, 1868. J. Lee and Lillian J. Stambaugh, *The Lower Rio Grande Valley of Texas* (San Antonio: Naylor, 1954).

George C. Werner

BRECKENRIDGE, TEXAS. Breckenridge, the county seat of Stephens County, is at the intersection of U.S. highways 180 and 183, four miles east of Hubbard Creek Reservoir in west central Stephens County. It originated about 1854 as Picketville, named either for the post and clay structure of the early homes or for early rancher Bill Picket. When the county was organized in 1876, the town was made county seat and renamed Breckenridge after John C. Breckinridge, United States senator from Kentucky and vice president, although the spelling of the name was altered. That year the first courthouse was built, and a post office was opened. The *Northwest Texian*, the town's first newspaper, began publication in 1877. Among early publishers were B. B. Greenwood and E. W. Davenport. Davenport later started the *Democrat*, a weekly which survived until 1924. In the early 1880s a two-story school building was erected, and the upper floor, referred to as the "Opera House," was used for church services. By 1884 Breckenridge had an estimated 500 inhabitants, Methodist, Baptist, and Presbyterian churches, a district school, a bank, and five general stores. The population reached 531 in 1900, a new school building was erected in 1906, and by 1914 Episcopalian and Christian churches had joined the others.

Breckenridge served as the court and local trading center for several quiet decades until 1916–17, when oil discoveries at Ranger occurred. Drilling started at the Breckenridge field in 1918, but the boom did not really get underway until 1920, when the town saw the arrival of thousands of workers and speculators, who threw up acres of tents and shacks in the classic oil boomtown manner. From a population estimated at 1,500 in January 1920 the town grew to 30,000 within a year. Activity was frenzied as some 200 wells were put down inside the city limits; hoards of gamblers, liquor sellers, and prostitutes were on hand to provide recreation. By July the town acquired its first railroad, the Wichita Falls, Ranger and Fort Worth, which was soon joined by the Cisco and Northeastern. After three exciting years, oil production slowed, and the town lost much of its population, although it held its place as a commercial and oil production center. By 1930 the population had fallen to 7,569, and the town had 480 businesses. The Great Depression[qv] brought the population down further to 5,826 in 1940. The population was 6,605 in 1950, 5,944 in 1970, and 5,665 in 1990. In the 1980s Breckenridge was still a center for petroleum-related industries and was a retail and shipping center for the county. It is the home of the Breckenridge Aviation Museum. Just northwest of the city is Hubbard Creek Reservoir,[qv] and Possum Kingdom Lake is to the east in Palo Pinto County.

BIBLIOGRAPHY: Betty E. Hanna, *Doodle Bugs and Cactus Berries: A Historical Sketch of Stephens County* (Quanah, Texas: Nortex, 1975). Loy W. Hartsfield, A History of Stephens County (M.A. thesis, University of Texas, 1929). *Stephens County* (Breckenridge, Texas: Stephens County Sesquicentennial Committee, 1987). *William R. Hunt*

BRECKINRIDGE, TEXAS. Breckinridge is north of the intersection of Lyndon B. Johnson Freeway and Greenville Avenue, a mile east of Restland Cemetery and ten miles northeast of downtown Dallas in Dallas County. In the 1840s families from Kentucky and Tennessee began arriving in the area. Early families included the Jacksons, Prigmores, Rouths, and Campbells. The settlement was on the road from Dallas to what was then Indian Territory. In 1853 Spring Creek Baptist Church was built. The first store was built about 1857, and soon after, a blacksmith shop was established. The Floyd Inn served as a stop for the stage from Dallas to Denton. In 1858 Mont Vale Academy, the first school, was built. A local post office was established in 1858 with postmaster Charles Shane and named for the Kentucky statesman John C. Breckinridge, elected vice president under James Buchanan in 1856. Several stores and a Grange[qv] were located in Breckinridge. In 1867 a tornado caused considerable damage in the town. In 1873 the Houston and Texas Central Railway built nearby and established Richardson a few miles north of Breckinridge. Most Breckinridge businesses, including the post office and the Grange store, moved to the new town. Until June 1874 the post office retained the name Breckinridge. The Grange kept the name for several more years.

BIBLIOGRAPHY: Barbara Braithwaite, comp., *A History of Richardson* (Richardson, Texas: Richardson Historical Society, 1973). John H. Cochran, *Dallas County: A Record of Its Pioneers and Progress* (Dallas: Arthur S. Mathis Service, 1928). David S. Switzer, *It's Our Dallas County* (Dallas: Switzer, 1954). *A. C. Greene*

BREECE, THOMAS H. (?–ca. 1851). Thomas H. Breece, soldier of the Republic of Texas,[qv] joined a company of New Orleans Grays[qv] in New Orleans and marched with his comrades to San Augustine and Nacogdoches, where the battalion was officially organized. Breece was elected captain. His lieutenants were John J. Baugh[qv] and George Washington Main. According to a circular printed in Nacogdoches during the time of their visit, the men of Breece's company were "mostly athletic mechanics, who have abandoned their homes and lucrative employments for the disinterested purpose of sustaining the righteous cause of freedom. Their very appearance must convince every Texian that they will either 'do or die.'"

Breece and his fifty-four-man company served at the siege of Bexar,[qv] December 5–10, 1835, where they took part in the capture of the Veramendi Palace (*see* VERAMENDI, JUAN MARTÍN). After the battle the company was disbanded, and the men were dispersed into other companies. Many of them were killed with William B. Travis[qv] at the Alamo, James W. Fannin[qv] at Goliad, or Francis W. Johnson and James Grant[qqv] on the Matamoros expedition.[qv] Breece was saved, however, by Sam Houston's[qv] order of December 21, 1835, from Washington-on-the-Brazos, to proceed "to whatever point you may deem best for the interest of the service & there recruit as many men as you possibly can." Breece was then to report to Copano or Matagorda by March 1, 1836.

For his service Breece received a bounty warrant for 640 acres, which he apparently sold to Jacob De Córdova.[qv] A Thomas H. Breeze, probably the same man, was elected justice of the peace of the Sixth District at Harrisburg on February 4, 1839. The 1840 census of the Republic of Texas listed Breece as a resident of Harris County and the possessor of one watch and one clock. By February 1, 1851, he had died, and a Henry J. Breece had been named executor of his estate.

BIBLIOGRAPHY: *Compiled Index to Elected and Appointed Officials of the Republic of Texas, 1835–1846* (Austin: State Archives, Texas State Library, 1981). Daughters of the Republic of Texas, *Muster Rolls of the Texas Revolution* (Austin, 1986). John H. Jenkins, ed., *The Papers of the Texas Revolution, 1835–1836* (10 vols., Austin: Presidial Press, 1973). Thomas L. Miller, *Bounty and Donation Land Grants of Texas, 1835–1888* (Austin: University of Texas Press, 1967). *Telegraph and Texas Register*, December 2, 26, 1835. *Texas State Gazette*, February 1, 1951. *Thomas W. Cutrer*

BREEDEN, CHARLES GOODWIN (1860–1925). Charles Goodwin Breeden, businessman, son of Paul Hamilton and Mary (Kibbe) Breeden, was born in Victoria, Texas, on January 27, 1860. His father was a captain in the Confederate Army. Charles was named for a noted physician in early Victoria, Dr. Sherman Goodwin. As a boy he worked for the Victoria *Advocate*[qv] as a printer. In 1875, on his fifteenth birthday, he moved to the new town of Cuero to work in the printing office of the Cuero *Weekly Star*, then published by J. H. Tucker. In 1876 Breeden resigned from newspaper work to work for Otto Buchel, a merchant and banker in Cuero. After twelve years in Buchel's employ, Breeden became associated with the business firm of P. J. Willis and Brother. In 1889 he joined his eldest brother, Walter Kibbe Breeden and his brother-in-law, Robert Henry Wofford, to establish the firm of Breeden Brothers, merchants in cotton, wool, pecans, sugar futures, agricultural implements, and groceries, both wholesale and retail. This firm occupied a leading position in the economic life of South Texas for the next half century.

The Breeden Brothers firm merged in 1911 with Henry Runge's[qv] company to form the Breeden-Runge Wholesale Company. C. G. Breeden assumed the presidency, a position he held until his death. Breeden-Runge developed branches in Kenedy, Alice, Yorktown, and for a short time in San Antonio. The Texas counties served by the company included Lavaca, Gonzales, DeWitt, Karnes, Wilson, Victoria, Jackson, Calhoun, Bee, Nueces, San Patricio, Jim Wells, Kleberg, Duval, Brooks, Jim Hogg, Live Oak, and Goliad. Breeden was a director and vice president of the First State Bank and Trust Company of Cuero and held interests in the Cuero Packing Company and other DeWitt County enterprises. He served two terms as a director of the Cuero Chamber of Commerce and was a charter member of the Cuero Rotary Club, a member of the Jewel Lodge of the Knights of Pythias, and an Episcopalian. He was also a member of the first fire-fighting company established in Cuero, known as the Stonewall Fire Brigade, and of the Council of Defense during World War I.[qv] He was married to Mabel Claire Hall on December 15, 1915. They had two daughters. He died on December 30, 1925, and was interred in Hillside Cemetery, Cuero.

BIBLIOGRAPHY: Cuero *Record*, December 30, 1925, January 24, 1926. DeWitt County Historical Commission, *History of DeWitt County, Texas* (Dallas: Curtis, 1991). *W. Lamar Fly*

BREEDING, BENJAMIN WILKENS (1820–1902). Benjamin Wilkens Breeding, the son of David W. and Sarah (Davis) Breeding, was born in Christian County, Kentucky, in 1820 and moved with his family to Colorado County, Texas, in February 1833. According to his pension application, in 1836 he served in Moseley Baker's[qv] company, which fought a detachment of Antonio López de Santa Anna's[qv] troops at the San Felipe ferry. Breeding and Thomas Chaudoin later brought the "Twin Sisters"qv cannons, which had bogged down near Harrisburg, to Sam Houston'sqv army at Bernardo Plantation.qv Because he was on leave to transport his parents beyond the Trinity River, Breeding missed the battle of San Jacinto.qv But he later fought in battles against the Mexicans and Indians. He obtained a first-class headright certificate in 1838 for a third of a league of land in Fayette County, but his claim was disallowed until April 1847. He served as a private under Col. John H. Mooreqv in an 1840 campaign against the Comanches and was honorably discharged. In 1842 he participated in the campaigns against Rafael Vásquez and Adrián Woll,qqv and in 1843 he was a member of the Snively expedition.qv He enlisted in the Confederate Army in June 1861 and served as a captain with the Texas state troops during the Civil War.qv In December 1874 he moved to San Marcos. Breeding married Catherine Jane Mayhar in Colorado County on February 2, 1852, and they had seven children. He was a charter member of the Fayette Masonic Lodge and in 1875 joined the San Marcos lodge. He died in San Marcos in 1902 and is buried there.

BIBLIOGRAPHY: Vertical Files, Barker Texas History Center, University of Texas at Austin.
Cari Thomas

BREEDING, DAVID W. (ca. 1778–1843). David W. Breeding, early settler, was born about 1778 in Virginia and moved to Christian County, Kentucky, by 1810. He married Sarah Davis; they had six sons, including John V., Napoleon B., Fidelio S., and Benjamin W. Breeding.qqv In February 1833 Breeding, with his family and two brothers, John and Richard Landy Breeding (not to be confused with David's sons by the same name), moved to Colorado County, Texas. In 1838 the part of Colorado County where he settled became Fayette County. Breeding was a member of the first board of land commissioners of the new county. He was also a juror at the first district court session held in Fayette County early in 1838. He died on December 28, 1843, and was buried at the Breeding family cemetery, five miles northeast of Fayetteville.

BIBLIOGRAPHY: Marker Files, Texas Historical Commission, Austin. Vertical Files, Barker Texas History Center, University of Texas at Austin.
Seth D. Breeding and Betty Porter

BREEDING, FIDELIO SHARP (ca. 1818–1849). Fidelio Sharp Breeding, soldier at San Jacinto, son of Sarah (Davis) and David W. Breeding,qv was born about 1818 in Christian County, Kentucky, and came to Texas with his parents in February 1833. He received a headright certificate for one-third league of land in Fayette County on January 19, 1838, and later he received 640 acres for participating in the battle of San Jacintoqv in Capt. William J. E. Heard'sqv company of "Citizen Soldiers." He seems to have been the only one of the brothers who actually participated in the battle. He joined the United States Army during the Mexican Warqv and marched with the army from Veracruz to Mexico City during October and November 1847. Breeding never married. He died in San Antonio in 1849, en route to the California gold mines with his brother Benjamin W. Breeding.qv

BIBLIOGRAPHY: Daughters of the Republic of Texas, *Muster Rolls of the Texas Revolution* (Austin, 1986). Sam Houston Dixon and Louis Wiltz Kemp, *The Heroes of San Jacinto* (Houston: Anson Jones, 1932). Vertical Files, Barker Texas History Center, University of Texas at Austin.
Seth D. Breeding and Betty Porter

BREEDING, JOHN V. (1807–1869). John V. Breeding, early settler, soldier, and sheriff, was born on October 16, 1807, in Virginia and came to Texas with his parents David W. and Sarah (Davis) Breeding in February 1833. He was in the Ranging Corps from November 24, 1835, to September 13, 1836. He served in the Texas army from February 1 to May 10, 1836, and was in Capt. William J. E. Heard'sqv company under Sam Houstonqv in the San Jacinto campaign, although he did not participate in the battle. Breeding received a bounty warrant for 320 acres for service from February 1 to May 10, 1836, and a donation certificate for 640 acres for being on the baggage detail at San Jacinto. He was the first sheriff of Fayette County after its organization in 1838 and also served under Col. John Henry Mooreqv on a campaign against the Comanche Indians from September to November 1840. In 1840, for tax purposes, he declared title to 380 acres with 738 under survey, two town lots at La Grange, one gold watch, ten cattle, and two saddle horses. Breeding married Louisa Parks Ware on February 10, 1842, in Colorado County, and they had eight children. He died in 1869 in Fayette County and was buried in the Breeding family cemetery near Fayetteville.

BIBLIOGRAPHY: Thomas L. Miller, *Bounty and Donation Land Grants of Texas, 1835–1888* (Austin: University of Texas Press, 1967). Vertical Files, Barker Texas History Center, University of Texas at Austin. Gifford E. White, ed., *The 1840 Census of the Republic of Texas* (Austin: Pemberton, 1966; 2d ed., Vol. 2 of *1840 Citizens of Texas*, Austin, 1984).
Seth D. Breeding and Betty Porter

BREEDING, NAPOLEON BONAPARTE (1815–1861). Napoleon Bonaparte Breeding, early settler and soldier, one of six sons of Sarah (Davis) and David W. Breeding, was born in Kentucky in 1815.qv In February 1833 he came to Texas with his family and settled in Mina Municipality, which later became Fayette County. He served as a second sergeant and fought in Thomas Alley'sqv company in the siege of Bexarqv in December 1835. From February to May 1836 he served in the Texas army. He was a member of Capt. William J. E. Heard'sqv company with the baggage detail at Harrisburg during the battle of San Jacinto.qv In 1836 Breeding was a member of Stephen Townsend's company, and in 1843 he traveled with the Snively expedition.qv He married Charlotte O'Bar on January 19, 1838; theirs was the first marriage recorded in Fayette County. They had six children and lived in Fayette County until Breeding's death, on February 22, 1861.

BIBLIOGRAPHY: Comptroller's Records, Texas State Archives, Austin. Daughters of the Republic of Texas, *Founders and Patriots of the Republic of Texas* (Austin, 1963–). Louis Wiltz Kemp Papers, Texas State Archives, Austin.
Cari Thomas

BREEDLOVE, TEXAS. Breedlove, sometimes called Needmore, was fifteen miles south of Gainesville in southern Cooke County. It was established in the early 1880s by a man named Fuqua and one named Breedlove. J. S. Riley donated land for a school in 1885. Before a school was built in nearby Hemming in 1890, children from that community also attended the Breedlove school. Though never very large, Breedlove began to decline around 1900. A cotton gin was built next to the school in the late 1880s or 1890s but ceased operating around 1900. By 1936 the community no longer appeared on highway maps.

BIBLIOGRAPHY: Gainesville *Daily Register*, Centennial Edition, August 30, 1948. A. Morton Smith, *The First 100 Years in Cooke County* (San Antonio: Naylor, 1955).
Odessa Morrow Isbell

BREEN, CHARLES (1787–?). Charles Breen, one of Stephen F. Austin'sqv Old Three Hundredqv colonists, received title to a league of land now in Brazoria County on May 24, 1824. His character certificate stated that he was born in Georgia in 1787 and that he came from Alabama to Texas with his wife, two sons, and two daughters. He may have been living in Williamson County in 1850.

BIBLIOGRAPHY: Lester G. Bugbee, "The Old Three Hundred: A List of Settlers in Austin's First Colony," *Quarterly of the Texas State Historical Association* 1 (October 1897).

BREMOND, PAUL (1810–1885). Paul Bremond, railroad builder, financier, and entrepreneur, was born in New York City on October 11, 1810, to Paul Barlie and Catherine (Green) Bremond of Fishkill, New York. The elder Bremond was a French émigré physician. The younger Bremond left school at the age of twelve to become apprentice to a firm of hatters. He engaged in the hat business in New York and Philadelphia but suffered large losses in the panic of 1837. In 1839 he moved to Galveston, Texas, where he opened an auction and commission house. About 1842 he moved to Houston and expanded his interests, along with the circle of businessmen that included William Marsh Rice, Thomas William House,[qqv] and William A. Van Alstyne.

Bremond helped to incorporate the Galveston and Red River Railroad, which began construction in 1855. In 1856 the legislature changed the name of the road to Houston and Texas Central, and Bremond, as president, built it north through Hempstead. It was later built through Dallas to Sherman and became one of the major rail lines in the state. Bremond was also involved in the incorporation of the Brazos Plank Road.

He married Harriet Martha Sprouls of New York and with her had a son and two daughters, one of whom, Margaret, was the first wife of William Marsh Rice. Harriet died in 1846, and Bremond then married Mary E. Van Alstyne (daughter of his business partner), by whom he had five daughters. After her death he married the Viscountess Mary Louise de Valernes.

Although most of his family were Episcopalians, Bremond, a spiritualist, organized a Houston society for the study of spiritualism. He believed that he was spiritually guided by Moseley Baker,[qv] a soldier of the Texas Revolution.[qv] According to Bremond's own story, the spirit of Baker prodded him to build another railroad. He secured a charter in 1875 for the Houston, East and West Texas Railway, to run from Houston to Shreveport through the East Texas piney woods. Though the Houston and Texas Central and most railroads were standard gauge (4' 8"), Bremond now favored a narrow-gauge (3') road, which he thought would be more economical to build and operate. Construction began in 1876 and proceeded slowly. The line reached Livingston in 1879, the site of Lufkin in 1882, and Nacogdoches in 1883. Because local funds and the state land grant did not provide sufficient capital, Bremond mortgaged the railroad to borrow large sums from eastern bankers. The road continued to build north and east to the Sabine River and eventually to a junction with a sister railroad, the Houston and Shreveport, in January 1886. Bremond, however, did not live to see the completion of his work. He died on May 8, 1885, while visiting in Galveston and was buried in Glenwood Cemetery, Houston. The town of Bremond in Robertson County and Bremond streets in Houston, Lufkin, and Nacogdoches are named for him.

BIBLIOGRAPHY: Robert S. Maxwell, *Whistle in the Piney Woods: Paul Bremond and the Houston, East and West Texas Railway*, Texas Gulf Coast Historical Association Publication Series 7.2 (November 1963). S. G. Reed, *A History of the Texas Railroads* (Houston: St. Clair, 1941; rpt., New York: Arno, 1981).

Robert S. Maxwell

BREMOND, TEXAS. Bremond is at the junction of State Highway 14 and Farm roads 46, 2413, 2954, and 2293, ten miles east of the Brazos River in northwestern Robertson County. It received its name from Paul Bremond.[qv] The site was part of the original 1841 land grant of Mary Peterson, widow of John Peterson, who died in the Texas Revolution.[qv] Peterson's heir sold the property to William Keigwin in 1850. In 1869 Keigwin transferred the land to William Baker and a group of investors, among them William M. Rice,[qv] who surveyed and subdivided the tract. The investors granted a right-of-way through Bremond to the Houston and Texas Central Railway Company in 1869. Articles of incorporation were forwarded to the secretary of state on August 12, 1869. The first train pulled into Bremond on June 15, 1870, with over 1,000 well-wishers present for the occasion. The town was incorporated on August 13, 1870. A post office opened in 1870 with Sam Morehead as postmaster. The community had several churches, merchants, and a newspaper named the *Central Texan* and owned by R. H. Purdom. Purdom sold the paper to B. W. Cramer in 1874, and it became the *Sentinel*. In September 1870 a school was established under the direction of G. W. Holland. By 1871 Bremond had six hotels, several merchants, three physicians, a drugstore, a law firm, and a population exceeding 1,000.

In the 1870s a large number of Polish immigrants arrived. The community assisted in building a Catholic church in 1878. Encouraged by J. C. Roberts, a leading citizen of the community, these immigrants began growing cotton. In 1885 the population of Bremond numbered 800; it declined to 387 in 1890 and was 650 in 1900. In the 1920s and 1930s Bremond had just over 1,200 residents and fifty businesses. In the 1940s and 1950s the population was just over 1,100, and the number of businesses had dropped. In 1948 Bremond was served by State highways 6 and 14 and the Texas and New Orleans Railway. It had two cemeteries, several churches, a school, and many businesses. By 1978–79 the population had dropped to 815, but it began to increase in the 1980s. In 1990 Bremond had a population of 1,110 and fourteen businesses.

BIBLIOGRAPHY: J. W. Baker, *History of Robertson County, Texas* (Franklin, Texas: Robertson County Historical Survey Committee, 1970).

James L. Hailey

BREMOND BLOCK HISTORIC DISTRICT. The Bremond Block, a National Register historic district in Austin, is one of the few remaining upper-class Victorian neighborhoods of the middle to late nineteenth century in Texas. The individual homes have been preserved intact in almost unaltered form. Large live oaks and lush planting frame these residences at the edge of a bluff a short walk from Congress Avenue. Six of these houses were built or expanded for members of the families of brothers Eugene and John Bremond, who were prominent in late-nineteenth-century Austin social, merchandising, and banking circles. They are located within the square block bordered by West Seventh, West Eighth, Guadalupe, and San Antonio streets. The district also includes several houses on the west side of San Antonio and the south side of West Seventh, at least three of which were built or altered by the North family.

The two earliest houses are on Guadalupe. The Hale Houston house was built before 1860 and later was the home of the son-in-law of John Bremond, Jr. The B. J. Smith house at 610 Guadalupe dates from the 1850s. Both houses are nicely proportioned, one-story Texas examples of the Greek Revival style with full-width front porches. Both have later additions to the rear. The Walter Bremond house, on the corner of San Antonio and West Eighth, was originally a one-story limestone building but was given a 1½-story addition in 1887 with a wide second-story balcony and a crested mansard roof in the Second Empire style. Its next-door neighbor, the Catherine Robinson house, was owned by Eugene Bremond's sister, Pauline Bremond Robinson, then by her daughter Catherine. It was begun before 1860 and enlarged sometime between 1870 and 1890 by the addition of a Classical Revival two-story front gallery.

Across San Antonio Street from these is the large North-Evans Château, built originally in 1874 of limestone rubble, with a simple two-story porch. In 1894 architect Alfred Giles[qv] remodeled and expanded it into a late Victorian castle, with crenellation, Romanesque arcades in many galleries, a tower, and high terraces with huge buttressed retaining walls. The building has been the meeting place of the Austin Woman's Club for a number of years. At the south corner of the same street, the Eugene Bremond house (enlarged in 1877) is a large, rambling, one-story Victorian frame residence. Its porches have scroll saw brackets, paired slender columns, and bracketed eaves. Across the street on the opposite corner and on the bluff at 700 San Antonio is an 1877 apartment building of stuccoed rubble with a two-story porch and several additional stories behind and below on the steep bluff.

Two other two-story houses, on West Seventh, complete the Bremond Block's significant buildings. Though both are of the local tan brick, they are of quite different character. The Pierre Bremond house (1898) in the center of the block, the last of the series to be built, is subdued late Victorian with a low-pitched hip roof, a double gallery, and an unobtrusive tower on the west side. The 1886 Second Empire style John Bremond house on the corner of Seventh and Guadalupe is the most outstanding of all of the buildings and has been pictured in textbooks as a graceful and exuberant example of Texas Victorian architecture. Its crested mansard roof has elaborate dormers, polychrome slate shingles, and concave bracketed curves on the front gable. The cast-iron work on the wrap-around gallery is outstanding. This house and several of the others were built by George Fiegel. All the buildings within the Bremond Block are beautifully maintained.

BIBLIOGRAPHY: Drury Blakeley Alexander and (photographs) Todd Webb, *Texas Homes of the Nineteenth Century* (Austin: University of Texas Press, 1966). Building Files, Austin History Center. James Wright Steely, comp., *A Catalog of Texas Properties in the National Register of Historic Places* (Austin: Texas Historical Commission, 1984).

Roxanne Williamson

BRENAN, WILLIAM (?–1839). William Brenan, soldier and legislator of the Republic of Texas,[qv] was born in Ireland and immigrated to Texas, probably by way of Nacogdoches, in the fall of 1835. On October 25, 1835, he enlisted as a private in Capt. Samuel O. Pettus's[qv] company of New Orleans Grays.[qv] He saw action at the siege of Bexar[qv] and the disastrous battle of Coleto.[qv] He survived the infamous Goliad Massacre,[qv] however, and was discovered at Goliad by doctors J. H. Barnard and John Shackelford.[qqv] He thereupon joined Capt. William H. Patton's[qv] company—the so-called Columbia Company—of Col. Sidney Sherman's[qv] Second Regiment, Texas Volunteers, in time to participate in the battle of San Jacinto.[qv] At least six others of Patton's men—Daniel Murphy, Nathaniel Hazon, Charles Shane, N. J. Devinneyr, Thomas Heny, and Thomas Hope—were likewise survivors of Fannin's command. On October 9, 1836, Brenan was indemnified twenty-five dollars for the loss of his rifle at Goliad. For his service in the Texas Revolution[qv] he was issued a bounty warrant for 1,280 acres, which he sold to Benjamin Fort Smith.[qv]

After the war Brenan moved to San Patricio County, where he was elected to the House of Representatives of the Second Congress of the Republic of Texas. He served from September 25, 1837, until May 24, 1838. At the end of the session he moved to Victoria. During this time he was proprietor of the Western Land Agency, which operated in Bexar, Refugio, San Patricio, and La Bahía. This is apparently the same William Brenan who was captured by Mexican soldiers near San Patricio and imprisoned at Matamoros until he escaped early in February 1839. He was reelected to the House and planned to return to San Patricio to build a home. He and a friend left Victoria in July 1839, in route to San Patricio. His badly decomposed body was discovered on the road between the two towns some three months later, and he is supposed to have been murdered.

BIBLIOGRAPHY: Joseph H. Barnard, *Dr. J. H. Barnard's Journal: A Composite of Known Versions*, ed. Hobart Huson (Refugio?, Texas, 1949). Daughters of the Republic of Texas, *Muster Rolls of the Texas Revolution* (Austin, 1986). Harbert Davenport, Notes from an Unfinished Study of Fannin and His Men (MS, Harbert Davenport Collection, Texas State Library, Austin; Barker Texas History Center, University of Texas at Austin). Sam Houston Dixon and Louis Wiltz Kemp, *The Heroes of San Jacinto* (Houston: Anson Jones, 1932). Richmond *Telescope and Register*, October 9, 1839. *Telegraph and Texas Register*, March 20, October 20, 1838. Texas House of Representatives, *Biographical Directory of the Texan Conventions and Congresses, 1832–1845* (Austin: Book Exchange, 1941).

Thomas W. Cutrer

BRENHAM, RICHARD FOX (ca. 1810–1843). Richard Fox Brenham, physician and member of the Texan Santa Fe expedition[qv] and the Mier expedition,[qv] was born to Robert and Mary M. (Fox) Brenham about 1810 in Woodford County, Kentucky. He attended Transylvania College, then moved to Texas before the revolution. He served in the Texas army from June 15 to September 15, 1836, and received a 320-acre tract in Cooke County for his services. He may have never taken possession of this land, however. He lived part of the time between the revolution and 1841 in Austin, where he practiced medicine. In 1841 President Mirabeau B. Lamar[qv] selected Brenham to serve as one of the civil commissioners of the Texan Santa Fe expedition, which sought to bring the city of Santa Fe and at least a portion of the trade along the Santa Fe Trail[qv] under the control of the Republic of Texas.[qv] Upon the failure of this mission in September and October 1841 Brenham and his fellow "Santa Fe Pioneers" were arrested by Mexican authorities and imprisoned in Mexico City. Brenham was released in April 1842 and returned to Austin, where he joined the Somervell expedition[qv] against Mexico. When William Somervell[qv] ordered his volunteers to disband and return to Texas despite their success in capturing Laredo, Texas, and Guerrero, Tamaulipas, Brenham joined with others who were unwilling to return home and set out on the Mier expedition. On December 26, 1842, Brenham took part in a rebellion and escape attempt at Salado, on the route from Matamoros toward Mexico City. Though many of the Texans temporarily escaped, Brenham was killed in the fighting, on February 11, 1843. In 1844 the town of Brenham in Washington County was named in his honor.

BIBLIOGRAPHY: Mrs. R. E. Pennington, *History of Brenham and Washington County* (Houston, 1915).

Kaye A. Walker

BRENHAM, TEXAS. Brenham, the county seat of Washington County, is on U.S. Highway 290 seventy-two miles northwest of Houston. The Hickory Grove community changed its name in 1843 to Brenham in honor of Republic of Texas[qv] hero Dr. Richard Fox Brenham,[qv] who had practiced medicine in the vicinity. In February 1844 Brenham became the county seat through the electoral efforts of Jabez D. Giddings[qv] and Jesse Farral's and James Hurt's offer of 100 acres as a townsite. A post office was established in 1846. In 1858 the new county seat, a rapidly growing supply center for a prosperous agricultural area, was incorporated. With the construction of the Washington County Railroad in 1860, Brenham, the rail terminus, served as a distribution point for the state's interior until 1871, when the Houston and Texas Central was extended to Austin.

Despite the 1867 yellow fever epidemic, the burning of commercial buildings by federal occupation troops during Reconstruction,[qv] and destructive fires in 1873 and 1877, Brenham's economy expanded to include banking (1866), silk and cigar manufacturing (1880s), and other light industry. Jewish merchants helped stimulate the town's extensive retail and wholesale trade. Arrival of the Gulf, Colorado and Santa Fe Railway in 1880 augmented Brenham's significance as a regional marketing center. Immigration, primarily of Germans, peaked in the early 1880s.

By the 1890s cottonseed oil, mattress manufacturing, food and fiber processing, and metal fabricating were significant economic activities. In 1905 the Washington County State Bank, in 1988 the oldest surviving state bank in Texas, was organized. Black professionals and black-owned stores served their own community during the first half of the twentieth century. Brenham's population doubled every decade between 1860 and 1900. Despite a brief reign of terror by the Ku Klux Klan[qv] in the 1920s, merchandising, marketing, and processing industries enabled the town to preserve its position as a regional economic center between 1910 and the 1950s. Brenham's population briefly declined around 1910 and then increased slowly through the 1950s.

The annual Maifest in Brenham, begun in 1881, originated from German immigrants' Volksfests (1874–79). The annual Juneteenth[qv] celebration, initiated in the late 1870s and revived in 1983, attracted blacks from Texas cities in the 1920s and 1930s. A black church was organized in Camptown, Brenham's first black neighborhood, by 1872.

Jewish residents founded an Orthodox congregation in 1885. St. Paul's Evangelical Lutheran Church (1890), St. Mary's Catholic Church (1870), the German Methodist Church (1873), and the Presbyterian church (1877) were formed as a result of European immigration. Brenham's Fortnightly Club, still in existence, established Brenham Public Library in 1899. the *Southern Enquirer* (1866) became the Brenham *Banner-Press*[qv] in 1913 and is still being published. From 1873 to 1919 the German-language *Texas Volksbote* was published in Brenham.

Brenham has served as a regional educational center since Reconstruction, when a large freedmen's school was established there. In 1875 the town began operating the first tax-supported school system in Texas, including a school for blacks. One of six Texas school systems to receive Peabody Funds, Brenham schools achieved a reputation as one of the state's best educational organizations. German Methodists of Brenham founded Mission Institute (1883), later renamed Blinn Memorial College (now Blinn College) in appreciation of financial support from Rev. Christian Blinn (1889). The Lutheran College (1891) and a black female college also provided higher education in later nineteenth-century Brenham.

The population rose rapidly, from 7,740 in 1960 to 12,796 in 1988. The population increase was triggered by the influx of Houston-area and rural Washington County residents, expansion of processing and light industry, and the advent of new manufacturers, encouraged by the Brenham Industrial Foundation, established in 1953. Brenham State School,[qv] established in 1974, is a leader in the field of managing mental retardation. Blue Bell Creameries,[qv] which began as Brenham Creamery Company in 1907, became the biggest ice cream producer in Texas in 1970 and by 1987 had annual sales of over $100 million. Firemen's Park, established in 1884, and Henderson Park, established in the 1920s to serve the black community, are Brenham's oldest parks. Several Victorian residences in town have been restored, and the Main Street Program has renovated downtown Brenham to encourage tourism. This effort has been supported by the Washington County Heritage Society. In 1990 the population was 11,952.

BIBLIOGRAPHY: Brenham *Banner-Press*, Centennial Edition, January 1, 1965. Robert A. Hasskarl, Jr., *Brenham, Texas, 1844–1958* (Brenham: Banner-Press, 1958). Mrs. R. E. Pennington, *History of Brenham and Washington County* (Houston, 1915). "Special Report: Brenham," *Texas Business*, November 1983. Vertical Files, Barker Texas History Center, University of Texas at Austin (Bluebell Creamery). Washington County Scrapbook, Barker Texas History Center, University of Texas at Austin. *Carole E. Christian*

BRENHAM *BANNER-PRESS*. The Brenham *Banner-Press* began publication in Washington County in 1866 as the *Southern Banner*. It reflected the political controversy that developed during Reconstruction[qv] and was published as a weekly until 1913. It served as an organ of the resurgent Democratic party.[qv] Between 1871 and 1876 the paper was known as the Brenham *Banner* and appeared in weekly and semiweekly editions published by John G. Rankin. From 1877 until 1907 it was a weekly published by Rankin and McCrimmon as the Brenham *Weekly Banner*. In 1876 the paper became a daily published by Rankin and Levin. The Brenham *Daily Press* was published by George Tucker from around 1893 until 1913, when it merged with the Brenham *Daily Banner* to form the Brenham *Daily Banner Press*, which appeared from 1913 until 1926 in both daily and weekly editions. In 1917 the paper became the first Texas daily to hire a female editor. After 1926 the paper was called the Brenham *Banner-Press* and appeared daily. In the 1990s the *Banner-Press* was published and edited by Charles Moser and had a circulation of 5,611.

BIBLIOGRAPHY: *Texas Newspaper Directory* (Austin: Texas Press Service, 1991). *Diana J. Kleiner*

BRENHAM STATE SCHOOL. Brenham State School is one of thirteen residential institutions for the mentally retarded operated under authority of the board of the Texas Department of Mental Health and Mental Retardation,[qv] a nine-member board appointed by the governor. It was established through the General Appropriations Act of the Sixty-first Legislature in 1969 and was the culmination of efforts by Speaker of the House Gus F. Mutscher and members of the Brenham Industrial Foundation headed by Paul F. La Roche. As a legislator, Mutscher had long been a champion of handicapped Texans, and La Roche and the Industrial Foundation were interested in having a state facility in Washington County for economic reasons. Thus, an alliance was formed that expanded state services for mentally retarded citizens and offered a substantial economic boon to the area. Brenham was considered an acceptable location for a state school by the Board of Mental Health and Mental Retardation because of its proximity to the populous Gulf Coast. The Industrial Foundation offered an additional incentive by pledging a site. A 211-acre property inside the city limits was purchased by the Industrial Foundation from the Linda Giddings Anderson family, and Washington County Judge Otis Tomachefsky assisted with transfer of the property to the state in 1970. Initial construction was begun in February 1971 by general contractor K. A. Sparks.

Brenham State School opened in January 1974 with a residential bed capacity of 384 and staff numbering 214. Major expansion projects started in 1974 and 1980 increased the capacity to 552. In 1992 the workforce stood at 1,043. The facility was accredited in 1976 by the Joint Commission on Accreditation of Hospitals, using standards for residential facilities for the mentally retarded published in 1971. It was the first residential facility in Texas to achieve accreditation and because of this distinction has continuously been viewed as a model. The Community Services Division of Brenham State School was established in 1972 and has been accreditated since 1984. It was the first community-services program in the state to affiliate with a local Housing and Urban Development–funded project to provide low-rent housing to the mentally retarded. Col. H. T. Ray, executive director of the Brenham Housing Authority, was instrumental in obtaining approval from HUD to use this method of funding to construct the first new residential dwellings in the nation designed specifically for the mentally retarded. The first two homes built are still in use. The 1992 book value of state-owned buildings at Brenham State School was $10,002,776, and property was valued at approximately $400,000. The operating budget for fiscal year 1992 was $21,060,555. Turnover in personnel has historically remained below 15 percent a year. Recruitment and retention of professional and paraprofessional staff has been accomplished with relative ease because of the many amenities of the community and its geographic relationship to Houston, Austin, and Bryan–College Station. The current trend in the United States is towards community-based services for the mentally retarded. Two of the present state schools (Fort Worth and Travis) are scheduled for closure by 1999. However, the prospect for continued operation of Brenham seems good because of its outstanding record of service delivery, operational efficiency, and community support.

BIBLIOGRAPHY: *Future Directions, 1988–1993* (Austin: Texas Department of Mental Health and Mental Retardation, 1988). *Turning Points: History of the Texas Department of Mental Health and Mental Retardation, 1856–1989* (Austin: Texas Department of Mental and Mental Retardation, 1989). *Jimmy R. Haskins*

BRENNAN, THOMAS FRANCIS (1855–1916). Thomas F. Brennan, first bishop of the Catholic Diocese of Dallas,[qv] the son of James and Margaret (Dunne) Brennan, was born at Bally Cullen, Tipperary, Ireland, on October 10, 1855. His family immigrated to the United States when he was eight years old. Brennan began his studies for the priesthood at St. Bonaventure's in Allegheny, New York, subsequently went to the University of Rouen, France and, from there, to the University of Innsbruck in Austria, where he was awarded a doctor of divinity degree in 1876. He was ordained a priest on July 4, 1880, in Brixen, Austria, by the local bishop, John de Leiss. Soon afterward Brennan began studies in canon law. His early career included a number of pastoral assignments in the Diocese of Erie, Pennsylvania. In July 1890 the Vatican established Dallas as the third diocese in Texas. The new diocese covered 109 counties in northern and northwestern Texas and El Paso and Culberson counties in the far west—a total area of 118,000 square miles. Brennan was named the first bishop of the new see, and on April 5, 1891, Tobias Mullen, bishop of Erie, consecrated him to the episcopacy. At age thirty-five, Brennan was the youngest Catholic bishop in the United States at the time.

A dynamic, handsome gentleman, Brennan was blessed with gifts for conversation, languages, and public speaking. Various reports tally the number of languages at his command from seven to twenty. During his early months as bishop he traveled widely, spoke publicly at every opportunity, and established himself as an exceptional orator. His addresses were often reprinted in major newspapers. In his brief tenure he built churches in Texarkana, Forney, Pilot Point, Muenster, Windthorst, Lindsay, Wichita Falls, Clarendon, Fort Worth, Waxahachie, and Denton. He also began publication of the *Texas Catholic.* He had inherited, however, the taxing responsibility of an extensive diocese, short on personnel and in considerable debt. While on a visit to the Vatican in 1892, Bishop Brennan was relieved of his Dallas post and transferred to St. John's, Newfoundland, where he spent several years. In 1904 he went to Rome, where he retired to the monastery of Grottoferrata and remained until his death, on March 21, 1916. He is buried at Frescati.

BIBLIOGRAPHY: Carlos E. Castañeda, *Our Catholic Heritage in Texas* (7 vols., Austin: Von Boeckmann–Jones, 1936–58; rpt., New York: Arno, 1976). Catholic Archives of Texas, Files, Austin.

Steven P. Ryan, S.J.

BRESLAU, TEXAS. Breslau is on Farm Road 957 seven miles northwest of Hallettsville in north central Lavaca County. In the early days of the Republic of Texas,[qv] James Lyons received a headright certificate and located a one-half league tract there on the east side of the Lavaca River. Between 1845 and 1848 the Lyons tract became the property of Walter Hinkley, a prosperous lawyer and planter from Harrison County, who occupied the area and in 1850 purchased the tract granted to Horace Eggleston on the west side of the river. The Hinkley plantation was relatively self-sufficient and was worked by the second largest force of slaves in Lavaca County. Following Hinkley's death in 1854, the plantation remained in the ownership of his widow until much of it was sold by a subsequent husband to pay debts.

During and after the Civil War[qv] German immigrants moved into the area and established small farms to grow cotton. In the 1870s Fritz Ladewig acquired the land surrounding the old Hinkley crossing on the Lavaca River, established a store and cotton gin, and donated land for a school and a Lutheran church. The community, named in honor of the Prussian city of Breslau (now Wrocław, Poland), prospered, and in 1880 a post office was established. Although the post office closed in 1911, the predominantly Protestant German community remained relatively self-sufficient during the opening years of the twentieth century. By 1915 enough Czech Catholic immigrants had arrived to support a church of their own. The economy of Breslau rose and fell with the supply and demand for cotton. By 1948 the community had six stores, two schools, a gin, a community hall, and a population of about seventy-five. Subsequent school consolidation sent the students to Hallettsville or Schulenburg. The discovery of oil and the decline of cotton production caused the gin and most of the small businesses to close during the 1950s and 1960s. Most of the farmland reverted to range for cattle, and, although in 1987 two stores remained, the sixty-five residents conducted most of their business in Hallettsville. In 1990 the population was still sixty-five.

BIBLIOGRAPHY: Paul C. Boethel, *Colonel Amasa Turner, the Gentleman from Lavaca, and Other Captains at San Jacinto* (Austin: Von Boeckmann–Jones, 1963).

Jeff Carroll

BRÉTAULT, JEAN BAPTISTE (1843–1934). Jean Baptiste Brétault (Padre Juanito, Padre Juan de la Costa), early South Texas Catholic missionary, the son of Pierre Jean Charles and Anne Marie (Audoin) Brétault, was born at La Tournerie de Fief-Sauvin, near Angers, France, on October 22, 1843. After joining the Oblates of Mary Immaculate[qv] in 1869, he was ordained a priest and sent to the Texas missions in 1872, despite the loss of a lung to tuberculosis. He arrived at Point Isabel on August 11 and was stationed at Immaculate Conception Church, Brownsville, where he took up the pastoral circuit of Father Pierre Keralum[qv] upon the latter's mysterious disappearance on November 12. Brétault's huge mission field, known as La Costa (the lower Coastal Plains), comprised today's Hidalgo, Willacy, Kenedy, and Kleberg counties. It was arid, brushy, and almost empty land, about which were scattered some 150 ranchos that averaged one to ten families each. By his own account, during thirty-nine years of active ministry Brétault traveled 23,400 leagues (about 70,000 miles) on horseback, performed 927 weddings, and baptized 6,406 infants. The rough conditions of early South Texas come to life in his remark, "I believe that a sixth of the children I baptized died before reaching the light of reason, which means that I have 1,077 little angels praying for me." During the course of his travels Brétault was lost in the desert twice and pinned down six times by snowstorms and five times by hurricanes.

From 1896 to 1901 he rode the mission circuit out of Rio Grande City (Starr, Jim Hogg, and Brooks counties); afterward he rode La Costa again until, his health broken, he retired in 1908 to the Oblates' La Lomita Mission, after which the city of Mission was later named. Brétault passed his last years in quiet prayer at La Lomita, tending a garden and regaling Oblate novices with tales of early Texas. Once a year John G. Kenedy, son of Capt. Mifflin Kenedy,[qv] sent a special train to bring the old missionary to visit La Parra Ranch and King Ranch,[qv] where for decades Brétault had been padrecito to the cowhands and their families. Brétault died on May 31, 1934.

BIBLIOGRAPHY: Archives of the Missionary Oblates of Mary Immaculate, Southern United States Province, San Antonio. James Talmadge Moore, *Through Fire and Flood: The Catholic Church in Frontier Texas, 1836–1900* (College Station: Texas A&M University Press, 1992).

William L. Watson, O.M.I.

BREWER, JOHN MASON (1896–1975). John Mason Brewer, black folklorist, son of J. H. and Minnie T. Brewer, was born in Goliad, Texas, on March 24, 1896. His sister, Stella Brewer Brooks, an authority on Joel Chandler Harris and the Uncle Remus tales, shared his interest in folklore. Brewer attended the black public schools in Austin and in 1917 received a B.A. from Wiley College in Marshall. He joined the army in 1918, became a corporal, and spent a year in France as an interpreter (he spoke French, Spanish, and Italian). He then returned to a career as a teacher and principal in Fort Worth. He eventually moved from secondary schools to colleges. He was working for an oil company in Denver, Colorado, when he began writing stories and poems, first for the company trade journal and later for a monthly journal called *The American Negro.* In 1926 he was a professor at Samuel Huston (now Huston-Tillotson) College in Austin, where he met University of Texas professor J. Frank Dobie,[qv] who influenced him to turn from publishing his own poetry to collecting and publishing black folklore. In 1950 Brewer received an M.A. from Indiana University, and in 1951 an honorary doctorate from Paul Quinn College in Waco. He was a Methodist and Democrat, with political friends as diverse as Governor Allen Shivers and President Lyndon B. Johnson.[qqv]

Brewer's list of "firsts" is impressive. As the first black member of the Texas Folklore Society[qv] he addressed its meetings and published in six of its annual volumes. He became the first black member of the Texas Institute of Letters[qv] in 1954, after being chosen one of twenty-five best Texas authors by Theta Sigma Phi, for *The Word on the Brazos: Negro Preacher Tales from the Brazos Bottoms of Texas.* He was the first black to serve as vice president of the American Folklore Society. He received grants for research in Negro folklore from the American Philosophical Society, the Piedmont University Center for the Study of Negro Folklore, the Library of Congress, the National Library of Mexico, and the National University of Mexico. He has been compared to Zora Neale Hurston, a black writer who was part of the Harlem Renaissance. Like her, he was noted for his use of black dialects. He eventually became nationally known as a folklorist and popular lecturer and was included in *Who's Who in America* the year after he died.

Brewer's major books are *The Word on the Brazos, Aunt Dicy Tales* (1956), *Dog Ghosts and Other Negro Folk Tales* (1958), *Worser Days and Better Times* (1965), and an anthology, *American Negro Folklore* (1968), for which he won the Chicago Book Fair Award in 1968 and the Twenty-first Annual Writers Roundup award for one of the outstanding books written by a Texas author in 1969. Notable among several early volumes of poetry and history are *Negrito* (1933) and *Negro Legislators of Texas* (1936); both were reprinted in the 1970s.

After ten years of teaching at Livingston College in North Carolina, Brewer returned to Texas and finished his career at East Texas State University in Commerce, where he was distinguished visiting professor from 1969 until his death. He died on January 24, 1975, and was buried in Austin, leaving his second wife, Ruth Helen, of Hitchcock, Texas, and a son by his first wife. A short film on Brewer's life was made in 1980 by the Texas Folklore Society and the Texas Commission on the Arts and Humanities.

BIBLIOGRAPHY: James W. Byrd, *J. Mason Brewer: Negro Folklorist* (Austin: Steck-Vaughn, 1967). *Who's Who in America*, 39th ed.).

James W. Byrd

John Mason Brewer. Courtesy Austin History Center, Austin Public Library; photo no. PICB 01060.

BREWING INDUSTRY. Describing the early years of the brewing industry in Texas is difficult since few records are available that detail Texas industries before the end of the Civil War.[qv] The breweries that were in operation were home breweries or small, local operations, generally in areas inhabited by large numbers of Germans.[qv] Before 1840 the beers produced in the United States were principally top-fermented brews that did not need aging or maturing. These were ales, porters, and stouts and were brewed mainly by British immigrants with recipes they brought to America. About 1840, German immigrants in Texas and throughout the United States had begun expressing their preference for lager beer, which was brewed with a bottom-fermenting yeast that used secondary fermentation. It had to be aged at a cool temperature for four weeks to nine months. The majority of the Texas breweries built during this period brewed only lager beer. Since there was little artificial refrigeration or mechanization in Texas before 1860, almost all beer was brewed in the cool months. It was usually stored in some form of cool cellar until the aging was completed. The small breweries used only hand-operated brewing equipment. The limited capabilities of these breweries usually required no more than four workers. The 1850 census population schedule listed nineteen brewers and distillers in Texas. However, the 1850 manufacturing schedule did not list any. This indicates there were people who considered themselves to be in the brewing business, even though they operated only small home breweries.

William A. Menger's Western Brewery (1855–78), located on Alamo Square in San Antonio, is usually considered the first commercial Texas brewery. By its last year of business in 1878, it was the largest operating brewery in Texas. In 1859, Menger also opened a very popular hotel next to his brewery. The Menger Hotel[qv] still contains the large cellar, constructed of three-foot-thick stone walls, that was used to chill the beer produced by the brewery. The cellars were cooled by the Alamo Madre ditch that flowed through what is now the patio of the hotel. Menger hired Charles Degen as his brewmaster. When Menger died in 1871, Degen continued with the brewery until it closed in 1878. The 1860 population census listed eleven breweries in Texas. Houston had three that were producing an estimated total of 4,300 barrels of beer annually, and two of the three were powered by steam engines. One of the San Antonio breweries was producing both a lager and a bock beer, and was probably doing its own malting. All of the breweries were located in areas of sizable German population, except for those in El Paso and Nacogdoches. The number of Texas breweries had increased to twenty-seven by 1870. They were all small and continued to be in areas with large German populations. Dallas, La Grange (Fayette County), and Brenham each had two breweries; others were located in Jefferson, Paris, Sherman, Austin, Industry, Hallettsville, High Hill, Waco, Marlin, Bastrop, Bellville, Victoria, San Antonio, Castroville, Fredericksburg, and New Braunfels. Houston was the leader in the state with three breweries. The 1870 census also indicated a total of seventy-seven employees in the breweries. Only four of the breweries were equipped with steam engines.

The period between 1870 and 1890 witnessed a rapid growth and decline in the Texas brewery industry. In 1875 the Brewers License Tax Records of the Internal Revenue Service indicated that there were forty-four breweries licensed to sell beer. The number of breweries increased to fifty-eight in 1876, with a production of 16,806 barrels. Beginning in 1877, however, the number of Texas breweries steadily declined. In 1879 there were twenty-seven, with a total production of 7,749 barrels. The decline continued throughout the 1880s. By June 1889 the state had only eight breweries operating. The largest in 1878 was Menger's Western Brewery of San Antonio with a production of 1,666 barrels a year. It was followed by the G. F. Giesecke and Brothers Brewery of Brenham (1,137 barrels), the H. L. Kreisch Brewery of La Grange (774), and the Lorenz Zeiss Brewery of Brenham (722). The smallest documented brewery, owned by W. F. Both and Company of Weatherford, sold forty-nine barrels in 1878. Total production for all of the breweries in the state that year was 10,050 barrels. The decline of the industry was caused by a combination of factors of the free enterprise system. National breweries, such as Anhaeuser-Busch of St. Louis, came to Texas with a superior product that sold at a competitive price. The national breweries could afford improved brewing and packaging techniques and massive advertising campaigns. In addition, Texas breweries were undercapitalized and did not have the financial or production capabilities to compete with the national breweries.

The year 1883 proved to be the turning point for a competitive Texas brewery industry when Adolphus Busch took his technology to San Antonio and with a group of San Antonio businessmen built the first large, mechanized brewery in Texas. The Lone Star Brewery (1884–1918) produced its first beer in 1884, when the total Texas production increased to 3,083 barrels. Production had an even larger increase in 1885, when it jumped to 17,246 barrels. The Lone Star Brewery used the same principles as the national breweries, which forced some smaller breweries out of business. Lone Star built a modern plant with the latest equipment. It had its own bottling plant; and it transported beer by wagon and railroad throughout most of Texas, into Mexico, and as far west as California. The Lone Star Brewery prospered until Prohibition[qv] with sales of as much as 65,000 barrels of lager beer annually, marketed under the labels Buck, Erlanger, Cabinet, Alamo, and Standard. The brewery did not reopen its doors after Prohibition. The name, Lone Star, however, was used taken up by another San Antonio brewery in 1940. The only other large brewery to start in Texas in the 1880s was the San Antonio Brewing Association. A group of San Antonio businessmen purchased the existing J. B. Behloradsky Brewery (1881–83) and started producing Pearl Beer in 1886. In 1916 Pearl was the largest brewery in Texas, with a capacity of 110,000 barrels a year. Otto Koehler managed the brewery until his death in 1914, when his wife, Emma, took over management and guided the brewery through the lean Prohibition years of 1918 to 1933. Besides the Pearl and Lone Star Breweries, the only other breweries in operation in Texas in 1890 were a few small, locally operated enterprises that were sustained by loyalty, low prices, and fresher products. These breweries included the Herman Frank Home Brewery in Belleville (1882–1918), the Simon Mayer Brewery in Dallas (1895–1900), the Dallas Brewing Company in Dallas (1889–93), the Texas Brewing Company in Fort Worth (1890–1918), the Frederick Probst Brewery in Fredericksburg (1874–95), the Gustave Franke Brewery in Meyersville (1884–1903), the Felix Bachrach Brewery in San Antonio (1890), the Charles Degen Brewery in San Antonio (1879–1911), the Alamo Brewing Association in San Antonio (1888–93), the Lorenz Ochs and George Aschbacher Brewery in San Antonio (1890–1904), and the Michael Cellmer Brewery in Yorktown (1878–91). Of the thirteen Texas breweries that were operating in 1890, only Lone Star, the San Antonio Brewing Association (Pearl), Herman Frank, the Dallas Brewing Company, and the Texas Brewing Company in Fort Worth survived intact until Prohibition in 1919. Of those five, only the San Antonio Brewing Association and the Dallas Brewing Company made beer after Prohibition. The breweries that did managed to survive until 1918 concentrated on serving local markets, maintaining low overhead, and producing superior beers.

Between 1890 and 1918, Texas had as many as forty-three breweries; many, however, started and ended within a few years. They either suffered from lack of capital, produced an inferior product, or could not compete with the national or large San Antonio breweries. Of the forty-three, seventeen were in San Antonio. Many were operated in the same plants under successively different names. One brewery in San Antonio changed names and owners five times in six years.

On January 16, 1919, national Prohibition forced thirteen Texas breweries to stop the legal production of beer. Of these, eight were large, regional breweries, and the other five were small breweries that served a local market. Breweries either closed their doors or switched to the production of nonalcoholic beverages such as sodas or "near beers." The Galveston Brewing Company (1895–1918) was one of the few regional breweries that survived Prohibition. Adolphus Busch and William J. Lemp of St. Louis were both major stockholders of the corporation that raised $400,000 to found the Galveston Brewing Company in 1895. The brewery formally began operations on February 3, 1896. The pre-Prohibition physical plant consisted of a large ice plant that could produce seventy-five tons of ice, and a modern brewery that could produce 75,000 barrels of beer a year. The plant also had cold-storage rooms and railroad tracks on two sides of the building. The company dug several wells that gave a water supply of two million gallons a day. The Galveston brewery was so well constructed that it survived the Galveston hurricane of 1900[qv] with only minor damage. The major product of the Galveston brewery before Prohibition was a beer called High Grade. The other popular brand produced by the Galveston brewery was Seawall Bond. The majority of the Galveston beer was consumed in Galveston and Harris counties. After Prohibition forced the legal production of beer to cease, the brewery turned to a "nonintoxicating cereal beverage" called Galvo. When this proved unsuccessful, the company removed the brewing equipment and produced soft drinks under the name XXX Company. The Galveston brewery changed owners three more times before it opened again in 1934 as Galveston-Houston Breweries, Incorporated (1934–55).

After Prohibition the number of small speciality brewers like the Galveston Brewing Company continued to decline, as national chains such as Anhaeuser-Busch and Miller moved into Texas. The decline in number of breweries had little to do, however, with the level of consumption or production of beer. In 1940 the per capita consumption of malt beverages, including beer, in Texas was 7.5 gallons. In 1980 it was 30.1 gallons, approximately a 300 percent increase. In 1994 per capita beer consumption was at 27.8 gallons. Texas progressed from a production rank of twenty-eighth among the states in 1878, when it had roughly thirty-seven breweries, to second place in 1983, when it had only six breweries. Those six were Anhaeuser-Busch, Miller, Schlitz, Lone Star, Pearl, and Spoetzl. The industry consolidation in Texas reflected a larger national trend. In 1876 the United States had more than 2,685 breweries. By 1947 that number had dropped below 500, and by 1980 there were only 90 plants operating in the United States.

In Houston, the Anhaeuser-Busch brewery opened its doors in 1966 with the capacity to produce 900,000 barrels a year. With the rise in consumption, the plant increased its facilities and its production levels. In 1982 it was producing 3.5 million barrels a year. The brewery, on a 126-acre site, achieved its enormous output through the use of automated equipment. In 1983 it employed about 500 people and produced such brands as Budweiser, Budweiser Light, Michelob, and Michelob Light for the Texas and Southern Louisiana market. In 1994 Anhaeuser-Busch employed about 1,100 people at its Houston facility. The Miller Brewing Company bought the Carling Brewing Company in Fort Worth in 1966. After a $12 million expansion, Miller began brewing its own brands in 1969. In 1975 it was the largest brewery in Texas, with an output of six million barrels. By 1979 it was producing eight million barrels. In 1983, Miller's Fort Worth plant employed around 1,600 workers. Its brands included Miller High Life, Miller Lite, Löwenbräu, and Magnum Malt Liquor. Its products were distributed to twelve states, including Alabama,

Kansas, Missouri, and Hawaii. In 1995 Miller employed 1,000 people. In 1966 the Joseph Schlitz brewing company began producing a million barrels a year in its newly opened Longview facility. In conjunction with the brewery the company also opened an aluminum-can plant in 1974. The combined payroll of the two in 1981 was over $24.3 million. Stroh Brewery bought out Schlitz in 1982 but continued to produce beer under the Schlitz label. The Lone Star Brewing Company, which opened its doors in 1940, began producing the "national beer of Texas" after owners acquired the Lone Star Beer copyright. They produced 39,000 barrels in their first year of production. Lone Star is currently marketed in Texas, Louisiana, Arkansas, and New Mexico. The brewery is noted for developing the milipore filter system, which made nonrefrigerated draft beer feasible. In 1976, the Olympia Brewing Company of Washington state bought the brewery. In 1983, Olympia sold Lone Star to Heileman Brewing Company of LaCrosse, Wisconsin. In 1981 the brewery produced 1.5 million barrels of Lone Star, Lone Star Light, and Buckhorn. In 1995 Lone Star had 230 employees. The Pearl Brewing Company,[qv] originally the San Antonio Brewing Association, is one of the oldest breweries in Texas. In the 1960s and 1970s the company acquired Goetz Brewing of Missouri and Southdown Corporation of Houston. The acquisitions allowed Pearl to move into national markets. It expanded its product line by buying the formula and label of Jax beer, a popular New Orleans product. In 1981, Pearl's 1.8 million barrels of beer was distributed in forty-five states. The company employed 535 people at its San Antonio facility. As of 1995 Pearl employees numbered 350 and production was 1.1 million barrels. In 1995 S&P Company of Mill Valley, California, owned Pearl, which makes Pearl, Pearl Light, Jax, Falstaff, and 900 Malt Liquor. The Spoetzl Brewery,[qv] started in 1909 by the Shiner Brewing Association in Shiner, was operated by the Spoetzl family from 1914 to 1966, when it was sold to William Bigler of San Antonio. It was sold again in 1984 to a consortium of native Texans. In the 1970s and 1980s the brewery's Shiner Beer and Shiner Bock had less than 1 percent of the Texas market. Following the tradition of its founders, Spoetzl continued to utilized more manual labor than the larger plants. In 1983 Spoetzl produced 60,000 barrels of beer. The fortunes of the company took a downturn in the late 1980s; production was only 36,000 barrels in 1990. Sales and production improved after Carlos Alvarez of San Antonio purchased the brewery in 1989. Improved marketing techniques and changes in consumer tastes brought production to 100,000 barrels in 1994. Spoetzl brands include Shiner Premium, Shiner Bock, and Kosmos Reserve Lager. Spoetzl beers are distributed in Texas and fourteen other states.

In addition to these large breweries, Texas also has several "microbreweries," i.e., businesses that produce less than 75,000 barrels a year. In 1995, they included Frio Brewing and Yellow Rose Brewing in San Antonio, Saint Arnold Brewing Company in Houston, and the Texas Brewing Company in Dallas. The Dallas plant operated on the site of the historic Dallas Brewing Company (1890). Hill Country Brewing was in Austin, as was the Celis Brewery, which distributed their beers in more than thirty states and in Europe. In the 1990s, a revival of small, regional breweries was initiated with the passage in 1993 of a law that allowed restaurants and bars to produce and sell on their premises their own brews. The eighteen brew pubs operating in 1995 were legally classified as retail businesses rather than breweries. Brew pubs are allowed to sell up to 5,000 barrels a year. Though they may sell it at their establishments, they may not distribute it through retail outlets.

BIBLIOGRAPHY: Stanley Baron, *Brewed in America: A History of Beer and Ale in the United States* (Boston: Little, Brown, 1962). *Brewers and Texas Politics* (2 vols., San Antonio: Passing Show Printing Company, 1916). Donald Bull et al., *American Breweries* (Trumbull, Connecticut: Bullworks, 1984). Mike Hennech, *Encyclopedia of Texas Breweries: Pre-Prohibition (1836–1918)* (Irving, Texas: Ale Publishing, 1990). Linda Johnson and Sally Ross, *Historic Texas Hotels and Country Inns* (Austin: Eakin Press, 1983). Joseph Pluta, "Regional Change in the United States Brewing Industry," Bureau of Business Research, University of Texas at Austin, 1983). Moritz Tiling, *History of the German Element in Texas* (Houston: Rein and Sons, 1913).

Michael C. Hennech and Tracé Etienne-Gray

BREWINGTON CREEK. Brewington Creek rises twelve miles northwest of Medina in south central Kerr County (at 29°56′ N, 99°25′ W) and flows southeast, through Kerr and Bandera counties, for 7½ miles to its mouth on the North Prong of the Medina River, eight miles northwest of Medina (at 29°53′ N, 99°21′ W). The stream is intermittent in its upper reaches. It flows through Edwards Plateau, characterized by flat limestone formations with localized dissection surfaced by shallow, stony soils to clay loam that support open stands of live oak, Ashe juniper, and mixed grasses.

BREWSTER, FEW (1889–1957). Few Brewster, attorney and legal scholar, was born in Williamson County, Texas, on May 10, 1889, the son of V. B. and America (Seymour) Brewster. After graduating from Killeen High School, he attended Baylor University and Howard Payne College (now Howard Payne University), which later awarded him an honorary doctorate. He transferred to the University of Texas, where he became a quizmaster and belonged to the Order of Chancellors while in the law department. After receiving his B.A. in 1913, Brewster completed work for the LL.M. in 1916. Later he was initiated into Phi Delta Phi fraternity. He practiced law in Temple from 1916 to 1929, except while he was a second lieutenant in the infantry in World War I.[qv] He remained active in the American Legion.[qv] In 1918 he married Myra Kilpatrick of Temple; they had three children.

Brewster was county attorney of Bell County from 1919 to 1923. Then he served as district attorney until 1929, when he became district judge of the Twenty-seventh District. After several terms he resigned to accept appointment in November 1941 to the Supreme Court Commission of Appeals. When the state Supreme Court was enlarged to nine members in 1945, he became an associate justice. He was elected in 1948 and reelected in 1954.

While Brewster was president of the Bell County Bar Association he served as an officer of the Texas Bar Association, first as head of the judicial section (1937–38), then as secretary (1938–39), and subsequently as vice president (1939–40). He became vice president of the new State Bar of Texas[qv] in April 1940 and served as president in 1940–41. Besides being a frequent speaker, he published several articles, including "Benefit of Clergy" (1939) and "Prime Obligation" (1954) in the *Texas Bar Journal;* in the latter article he urged acceptance of a racially integrated bar. His success as an administrator and judge was enhanced by his "tension-breaking humor," and he was a legal scholar whose work was carefully planned and executed. One outstanding example was his 400-page manuscript to serve as "a ready reference to the more important phases of the law relating to prohibited liquor and searches and seizures as declared in the Texas statutes and decisions." This study included digests of cases, forms, and an overall index for ready reference. The work was revised and ready for publication in 1930, but after some delay and condensation it was published under the title *Search and Seizure* (1931).

Brewster served as an associate justice of the Supreme Court of Texas from 1945 to 1957, when he resigned because of ill health. He died at home of a heart attack on October 12, 1957, and was buried at the State Cemetery[qv] in Austin.

BIBLIOGRAPHY: Vertical Files, Barker Texas History Center, University of Texas at Austin. Clarence R. Wharton, ed., *Texas under Many Flags* (5 vols., Chicago: American Historical Society, 1930). *Who's Who in America,* 1952–53. *Robert C. Cotner*

BREWSTER, HENRY PERCY (1816–1884). Henry Percy (Persy) Brewster, lawyer and personal secretary of Sam Houston,[qv] was born on November 22, 1816, in the Laurens District, South Carolina, where he studied and began the practice of law. He learned of the Texas Revolution[qv] while on a trip to Alabama and traveled to New Orleans, where Lt. Meriwether Woodson Smith[qv] recruited him for service in the Texas army. There he and his fellow recruits "remained two days without anything to eat except a box of rotten Fish." Brewster landed at Velasco on April 2, 1836. In Austin county he joined Capt. Henry Teal's[qv] Company A of Lt. Col. Henry Millard's[qv] First Regiment of Regular Infantry but was detached for duty as Sam Houston's private secretary. Brewster was subsequently reassigned to his old company, then to the command of Capt. Andrew Briscoe[qv] for a single day of duty at the battle of San Jacinto.[qv] Afterward he accompanied Houston to New Orleans for treatment of the general's wound.

Brewster returned to Texas in August and on October 1 was appointed acting secretary of war and navy, to succeed John A. Wharton,[qv] in the administration of David G. Burnet.[qv] In the fall of 1836 he established a legal practice at Brazoria. In 1840 he was appointed district attorney of the Second Judicial District, a post he held until 1843. On March 16 of that year he married Ann Elizabeth Royal at Matagorda. In 1849 he was appointed attorney general by Governor George T. Wood,[qv] to succeed John W. Harris,[qv] who had resigned. In 1855 Brewster moved to Washington, D.C., to practice international law. At the outbreak of the Civil War[qv] he returned to Texas and was commissioned a captain and appointed adjutant general to Gen. Albert Sidney Johnston[qv] on September 11, 1861. On March 17, 1862, he became Johnston's chief of staff and was with the general when he was killed at the battle of Shiloh in April 1862. Thereafter Brewster served on the staff of Gen. John Bell Hood,[qv] where he rose to the rank of colonel. At the close of the war he returned to Texas and practiced law in San Antonio. In 1881 Governor John Ireland[qv] appointed him commissioner of insurance, statistics, and history, a position he held until his death. Brewster died in Austin on December 28, 1884. His body was taken to Galveston and buried in the Gulf of Mexico. Brewster County was named in his memory in 1887.

BIBLIOGRAPHY: Sam Houston Dixon and Louis Wiltz Kemp, *The Heroes of San Jacinto* (Houston: Anson Jones, 1932). Zachary T. Fulmore, *History and Geography of Texas As Told in County Names* (Austin: Steck, 1915; facsimile, 1935). Galveston *Daily News*, December 29, 1884. C. L. Greenwood Collection, Barker Texas History Center, University of Texas at Austin. John H. Jenkins, ed., *The Papers of the Texas Revolution, 1835–1836* (10 vols., Austin: Presidial Press, 1973). James D. Lynch, *The Bench and Bar of Texas* (St. Louis, 1885). Marcus J. Wright, comp., and Harold B. Simpson, ed., *Texas in the War, 1861–1865* (Hillsboro, Texas: Hill Junior College Press, 1965).

Thomas W. Cutrer

BREWSTER COUNTY. Brewster County (L-7), the largest county in Texas, is located in the Trans-Pecos region of West Texas, and is the site of Big Bend National Park,[qv] the largest park in the state. Brewster County is bordered by Presidio County to the west, Jeff Davis County to the northwest, Pecos County and Terrell County to the east, and the Rio Grande to the south. Alpine, the county seat and largest town, is 220 miles southeast of El Paso in northwestern Brewster County. The county's center lies about fifty miles southeast of Alpine at approximately 29°51′ north latitude and 103°01′ west longitude. U.S. Highway 90 and the Southern Pacific Railroad cross the northern part of the county; U. S. Highway 385 and State Highway 118 enter Brewster County from the northeast and northwest, respectively, and run south to Big Bend National Park; and the South Orient Railroad crosses the northwestern part of the county.

Brewster County comprises 6,169 square miles of largely rough and mountainous terrain, with elevations ranging from 1,700 to 7,825 feet above sea level; the latter elevation, the tenth highest in the state, is at Emory Peak.[qv] Most of Brewster County drains into the Rio Grande, although the northern part drains into the Pecos River. Soils are generally shallow and stony, with some loamy to sandy soils and clayey subsoils. Vegetation at lower elevations in the county is drought resistant; sparse grasses, desert shrubs such as ocotillo, lechuguilla, sotol, acacias, tarbrush, and creosote bush, some mesquite, and cactus predominate. At intermediate elevations vast grasslands occur in mountain basins; white oak, juniper, and piñon woodlands dominate the slopes. Douglas fir, aspen, Arizona cypress, maple, Arizona pine, oaks, and madrone are found at the higher elevations. The fauna in Brewster County includes the pronghorn antelope, mule deer, white-tail deer, bobcat, mountain lion, desert bighorn sheep, black bear, coyote, raccoon, badger, prairie dog, pack rat, kangaroo rat, skunk, ringtail cat, porcupine, jackrabbit, cottontail, golden eagle, roadrunner, quail, dove, rock wren, white-winged dove, mourning dove, Canyon Wren, painted bunting, zone-tailed black hawk, and Colima warbler. Mineral resources include mercury, silver, lead, fluorspar, nonceramic clay, and lignite coal. Of these, the most important to the historical development of Brewster County was mercury; for most of the first half of the twentieth century the Terlingua Mining District in southern Brewster County was among the nation's leading producers (*see* MERCURY MINING). The climate is subtropical-arid. The average minimum temperature in January is 34° F, and the average maximum temperature in July is 95°. The growing season averages 239 days a year, and the average annual precipitation is twelve inches. Less than 1 percent of the land in the county is considered prime farmland.

The area of southern Brewster County now in Big Bend National Park has long fascinated man, who has lived there for more than 9,000 years. The first human beings in the Big Bend were probably nomadic hunters and gatherers moving south ahead of the great ice sheets of the North American glaciers. When a prolonged period of drought ensued, the large game animals disappeared, and so did the people. When the drought ended, between 4000 and 3000 B.C., man reappeared. By around A.D. 1000 residents of the area were practicing rudimentary agriculture and could no longer be considered nomadic; and by the time the Spanish began to arrive, in the sixteenth century, pueblo culture had begun in the Big Bend.

The first European to set foot in what is now Brewster County may have been álvar Núñez Cabeza de Vaca[qv] in 1535; more certain is the presence in August 1583 of Antonio de Espejo's[qv] expedition, which probably passed the future site of Alpine en route to La Junta de los Ríos.[qv] Juan Domínguez de Mendoza[qv] is believed to have camped at Kokernot Spring,[qv] just northeast of Alpine, in 1684. But there was no extensive European presence in the Big Bend until the middle of the eighteenth century, when the Spanish began to explore the area in an effort to combat Indian raids into Mexico from the north. In 1747 Governor Pedro de Rábago y Terán[qv] of Coahuila led an expedition into the Chisos Mountains, and in 1772 Lt. Col. Hugo Oconór[qv] led an expedition to locate sites for forts along the Rio Grande. Oconor placed Capt. Francisco Martínez[qv] in command of the presidio at San Vicente, on the Comanche Trail[qv] on the Mexican side of the river. Between 1779 and 1783 Col. Juan de Ugalde[qv] organized four assaults on the Mescalero Apaches who had settled in northern Mexico, the last of which drove them back across the Rio Grande and into the Chisos Mountains, where the Spanish pursuit halted. The Mescaleros reemerged, and in January 1787 Ugalde launched a new campaign against them. When the Indians again sought refuge in the Chisos Mountains, Ugalde decided to follow them with forty men. In the ensuing battle the Spanish killed hundreds of Indians and captured many more, while suffering only one death of their own. In the face of such defeats, the three leading Mescalero chiefs, Patula Grande, Quemado, and Zapato Tuerto, agreed in March 1789 to submit to Spanish rule.

For much of the nineteenth century the presence of Comanche raiding parties on their way to and from Mexico combined with the forbidding local topography to discourage European exploration of the Big Bend. The first Mexican and American explorers of the area, who arrived after the Mexican War,[qv] found harsh country indeed. In October 1851 Col. Edvard Emil Langberg,[qv] a Swedish soldier of fortune who was the Mexican commandant of Chihuahua, traversed what is now southern Brewster County. In the autumn of 1852 M. T. W. Chandler, assigned by the United States–Mexico boundary survey to work down the Rio Grande from Presidio del Norte to the mouth of the Pecos River, led a party into what is now the heart of Big Bend National Park. Chandler explored Santa Elena Canyon, the Chisos Mountains (where he named the highest peak after his boss, William H. Emory[qv]), Mariscal Canyon, and Boquillas Canyon[qqv] before giving up due to a shortage of supplies and the weakened condition of his party.

In the summer of 1859 a camel expedition under 2d Lt. Edward L. Hartz set out from Fort Davis to explore the Comanche Trail and recommend a possible site for a fort on the Mexican border to protect against Indian raids. Hartz went through Persimmon Gap and down Tornillo Creek to the Rio Grande. A year later, a second camel expedition under 2d Lt. William Echols also explored along the Rio Grande, with the same goal as the Hartz expedition (*see* CAMELS). Before a fort could be built, however, the outbreak of the Civil War[qv] put an end to those plans.

After the war, three interrelated factors led to white settlement of what later became Brewster County: the presence of the United States Army, the development of the cattle industry, and the arrival of the railroad, all of which happened more or less simultaneously. Taking advantage of the Civil War, Indian cattle-rustling raids via the Comanche Trail rose sharply during the early 1860s and greatly reduced the number of cattle in northern Mexico. The high prices consequently paid by Mexican ranchers for imported cattle convinced Central Texas cattlemen to chance the long drive across the Big Bend country.

The revival of trade between Texas and Mexico along what has been called the Chihuahua Trail brought freighters and other transients to the future Brewster County. Kokernot Spring, where Mendoza had camped two centuries earlier, became a principal stopping place on the trail, renamed Burgess Waterhole after pioneering freighter John D. Burgess, whose wagon train was attacked by Indians there. In response to such threats, officials at Fort Davis[qv] established Camp Peña Colorado[qv] a few miles south of the future site of Marathon in 1879. Burgess and such other freighters as August Santleben[qv] helped spread the word about the open rangeland available in the Big Bend, and in the 1870s many ranchers from other parts of the state made plans to come west and investigate the area. Among them were Beverly Greenwood, from the Del Rio area, who came in 1878 and spent several months exploring northern Brewster County; Mayer and Solomon Halff,[qqv] San Antonio merchants who leased to the government the land on which Camp Peña Colorado was located and who later became the first men to ship cattle into what is now Brewster County; and John Beckwith, who in 1879 drove a herd of cattle to the vicinity of Peña Colorado Springs[qv] and later contracted to supply meat to Camp Peña Colorado.

The burgeoning cattle industry got a major boost in 1882, when the Galveston, Harrisburg and San Antonio Railway[qv] built through the area. Suddenly the gradual influx of cattlemen became a veritable flood, as a number of surveyors who had come with the railroad, and the Texas Rangers[qv] who had been assigned to protect them, elected to stay. Among them were such men as Alfred S. Gage, James B. Gillett, and Joseph D. Jackson,[qqv] who soon became the leading citizens of Brewster County.

Initially, at least, ranchers generally settled in the northern part of what is now Brewster County, for ease of shipping their cattle via the railroad; the Gage Ranch and the G4 Ranch,[qv] started in the mid-to-early 1880s, were the first major cattle operations in what is now southern Brewster County, and Gage soon moved north to be nearer the railhead. Several towns sprang up along the rails, the most significant of which were Alpine, then called Murphyville, and Marathon.

These two quickly became shipping points and important supply centers for the booming cattle industry. Five years after the coming of the railroad, in 1887, Brewster County was marked off from Presidio County, as were Jeff Davis, Buchel, and Foley counties. Brewster County was named for Henry P. Brewster,[qv] secretary of war under David G. Burnet.[qv] Buchel and Foley counties[qqv] were not organized and were attached to Brewster County for judicial purposes. The first Brewster County elections were held on February 4, 1887, when Murphyville was selected as county seat; on March 14 of that year a contract was let for the construction of the Brewster County courthouse and jail. In 1890 Brewster County had just 710 residents, while Buchel and Foley counties had only 298 and 25 residents respectively. By 1897 Buchel and Foley counties had still not been organized, and in that year their territory was officially added to that of Brewster County, making the latter the largest county in Texas.

About this time the mercury-mining industry exploded in southern Brewster County. Scattered agricultural communities had existed for years on both sides of the Rio Grande, but had been largely ignored by the county government in Alpine, due to their isolated position and relatively small and heavily Hispanic populations. In 1884, however, a Presidio merchant named Ignatz Kleinman made the first significant discovery of mercury in the Big Bend, setting off a mining boom that made the Terlingua Mining District one of the leading sources of mercury in the nation in the first half of the twentieth century.

The dominant personality in the development of mercury mining in Brewster County was Chicago shoe manufacturer Howard E. Perry, whom the local Mexican Americans[qv] punningly nicknamed "El Perrito" (the little dog) for his tenacity. Perry built his Chisos Mining Company, established in 1903, into one of the largest mercury mines in the nation; by 1905, it was supplying 20 percent of the mercury in the United States.

The population of Brewster County increased more than 700 percent between 1890 and 1910. The rise from 710 in 1890 to 2,356 in 1900 was due in part to the addition of Buchel and Foley counties, but between 1900 and 1910 the population more than doubled, to 5,220. This increase resulted largely from the development of mercury mining and other industries that exploited natural resources. Southern Brewster County became an important source of wealth for the northern rail towns from which various products were shipped. Mercury mined at Terlingua and on Mariscal Mountain was shipped north, as was the silver and lead from mines on the Mexican side of the river in the Boquillas area, the candelilla wax produced at factories at Glenn Spring and Mariscal, and the guayule rubber from a factory in Marathon. By 1910 the residents of Alpine decided that their town deserved to be the site of a summer normal institute; this school eventually grew into Sul Ross State University.

The isolated position of many of the mining and industrial settlements that grew up in southern Brewster County made them tempting targets for raiders from Mexico, especially during the turbulent early years of the Mexican Revolution.[qv] As early as the spring of 1912, J. O. Langford, who owned a resort at Hot Springs, on the Rio Grande, was asking for military protection from bandits from across the river. In response to such needs, troops were stationed at several locations in the Big Bend. The mere presence of a handful of troops, however, did not eliminate the threat. Perhaps the most famous incursion from across the Rio Grande was the Glenn Spring Raid[qv] of May 5, 1916, in which bandits overwhelmed nine cavalrymen posted at Glenn Spring to protect against just such an event.

After World War I[qv] raiders from Mexico became less of a problem, at least in part because many of the mines and wax factories that had tempted them were played out. The population of Brewster County dropped from 5,220 to 4,822 between 1910 and 1920. Cattle ranching remained an important local industry, however, and the Highland Hereford Breeders Association was organized in 1918 to promote the cattle ranched in Brewster and Jeff Davis counties. Brewster County ranchers had 99,671 cattle in 1900, all but 125 of them beef cattle. In 1910 and 1920 the number of cattle dropped to 59,671 and 57,543 respectively, but by 1930 had climbed back to 91,143. The rise was paralleled by an increase in the number of people, from 4,822 in 1920 to 6,624 in 1930. In the 1930s, however, the local cattle industry was hit hard by depression and drought, and the population of Brewster County dropped from 6,624 to 6,478. Despite the efforts of the Federal Emergency Relief Administration, most Big Bend ranchers were forced to shoot their stock because they could neither feed nor move them, and the number of cattle dropped from 91,143 to 39,488 by the end of the decade. By 1936 many local cattlemen had given up ranching and moved away, and much of their land eventually ended up in Big Bend National Park.

The history of the park begins in February 1933, when State Representative Everett Ewing Townsend[qv] cosponsored a bill for the establishment of Texas Canyons State Park. On October 27, 1933, Governor Miriam A. Ferguson[qv] signed legislation establishing a greatly expanded Big Bend State Park. In May 1934 the Civilian Conservation Corps[qv] established a camp in the Chisos Mountains basin. The camp, eighty-five miles from the nearest town, was the temporary home of more than 200 laborers, mostly Hispanic. Their first project was to build a seven-mile road into the mountains using no power equipment.

The federal presence in the Big Bend led the citizens of Brewster County to press for the establishment of a national park, and in June 1935 Congress passed legislation founding Big Bend National Park. Acquiring the land for the park was a long and often frustrating process, but it finally opened to the public in June 1944. Since then the park has become one of the best-known tourist attractions in Texas, with 214,982 overnight visits and 258,400 daily visits in 1990.

Cattle ranching and mining have never regained the prominence in Brewster County that they had in the late nineteenth and early twentieth centuries. The county population rose from 6,478 in 1940 to 7,309 in 1950; dropped to 6,434 in 1960; and climbed again, to an all-time high of 7,780, in 1970, before declining slightly to 7,573 in 1980. The number of people employed in agriculture, however, steadily declined, from 712 in 1930 to 507 in 1950 and only 202 in 1970. Similarly, the number of people employed in mining dropped from 206 in 1930 to 147 in 1940 and 11 in 1950. In subsequent years, when the mercury mines enjoyed a brief renaissance, that figure rose again, to 32 in 1970 and 80 in 1980.

In the early 1980s Brewster County was fifty-third among United States counties in land area, and one of the most sparsely populated in Texas. The largest ancestry groups were Hispanic and English, both at 43 percent. In 1990 the population was 8,681. The largest town, Alpine, had 5,637 residents. The Brewster County economy has become increasingly dependent on tourism. In 1952 Houston oilman Walter M. Mischer began buying land around Lajitas, in southwestern Brewster County, and in 1976 he began "reconstructing" a Wild West town that had never existed, complete with condominiums, motels, restaurants, and shops, next to old Lajitas, the true ghost town. The World Championship Chili Cookoff at Terlingua began as a tongue-in-cheek challenge between Wick Fowler and humorist H. Allen Smith in 1967 and has become a November tradition, celebrated across the state and nation. In 1988 the state of Texas doubled the size of its state park system when it bought the Big Bend Ranch, in southwestern Brewster and southeastern Presidio counties; the resulting Big Bend Ranch State Natural Area[qv] opened to the public in January 1991.

BIBLIOGRAPHY: Clifford B. Casey, *Mirages, Mysteries and Reality: Brewster County, Texas, the Big Bend of the Rio Grande* (Hereford, Texas: Pioneer, 1972). Arthur R. Gomez, *A Most Singular Country: A History of Occupation in the Big Bend* (Santa Fe: National Park Service; Salt Lake City: Charles Redd Center for Western Studies, Brigham Young University, 1990). *Martin Donell Kohout*

BREWSTER CREEK (Bell County). Brewster Creek rises two miles northwest of Buckhorn in northern Bell County (at 31°18′ N, 97°26′ W) and runs southeast for 2½ miles, through northern Bell County, to its mouth on Stampede Creek (at 31°15′ N, 97°26′ W), a mile above the latter's juncture with the Leon River. Brewster Creek flows through nearly level to gently sloping terrain surfaced by clayey soils used predominantly for agriculture.

____ (Cooke County). Brewster Creek rises three miles south of Sivells Bend in extreme north central Cooke County (at 33°49′ N, 97°15′ W) and runs southeast for two miles to its mouth on Bear Head Creek, four miles southeast of Sivells Bend and ½ mile west of the Red River (at 33°47′ N, 97°12′ W). The surrounding rolling terrain is surfaced by deep to shallow expansive clays and clay loams that support oak, juniper, and grasses.

BRIAR, TEXAS. Briar is on Farm Road 730 twenty-two miles northwest of Weatherford in the northeast corner of Parker County, the southwest corner of Wise County, and the northwest tip of Tarrant County. The community's development began in the late 1870s and early 1880s. A local post office operated from 1884 until 1904. By the late 1890s the community had thirty residents and two businesses. For much of its history Briar has served area farmers as a school and church community. Until the late 1960s its population remained well under fifty. In the early 1970s, however, the community began to grow rapidly as a result of the growth of nearby Fort Worth. In 1980 the population was estimated at 1,810: 349 in Parker County, 642 in Wise County, and 819 in Tarrant County. In 1990 the population was 3,899.

BIBLIOGRAPHY: John Clements, *Flying the Colors: Texas, a Comprehensive Look at Texas Today, County by County* (Dallas: Clements Research, 1984). *David Minor*

BRIAR BRANCH (Milam County). Briar Branch rises five miles east of Rockdale in southeastern Milam County (at 30°38′ N, 96°55′ W) and runs southwest for eight miles to its mouth on East Yegua Creek and the Burleson-Lee county line, fifteen miles west of Caldwell (at 30°33′ N, 96°57′ W). It crosses rolling to flat terrain surfaced by clay and sandy loams that support mesquite, scrub brush, cacti, and grasses.

____ (Wise County). Briar Branch rises a mile east of Alvord in north central Wise County (at 33°23′ N, 97°38′ W) and runs south for six miles to its mouth on Big Sandy Creek, one mile east of Lone Star (at 30°17′ N, 97°42′ W). The stream crosses mostly flat terrain with a deep surface of fine sandy loam that supports brush and grasses. The land has been used as range and crop land.

BRIARCLIFF, TEXAS. Briarcliff is on Lake Travis and Farm Road 2222, twenty miles northwest of Austin in western Travis County. It was developed as a resort area in the 1960s, with summer homes, country clubs, and water sports providing the main attractions. The population was reported as 129 in 1988 and 335 in 1990.

BIBLIOGRAPHY: Austin History Center Files.

Vivian Elizabeth Smyrl

BRIAR CREEK (Cooke County). Briar (Brier) Creek rises in extreme northeastern Cooke County (at 33°53′ N, 96°57′ W) and runs four miles northeast to its mouth on Lake Texoma, near the Sheppard Air Force Base[qv] Recreation Area in northwest Grayson County (at 33°53′ N, 96°54′ W). It crosses variable terrain surfaced by shallow, stony clay loam that supports juniper, oak, grasses, chaparral, and cacti.

____ (Navarro County). Briar Creek rises a mile northeast of Barry in western Navarro County (at 32°07′ N, 96 38' W) and runs southeast for fourteen miles to its mouth on Richland Creek, a tributary of the Trinity River, ten miles south of Corsicana (at 31°58′ N, 96 32' W). At the source the surrounding flat to rolling prairie is surfaced by calcareous clay that supports mesquites and grasses; the flat terrain near the mouth is surfaced by sandy and clay loam that supports water-tolerant hardwoods, conifers, and grasses. Briar Creek passes under State Highway 22, Farm Road 744, State Highway 31, and the St. Louis and Southwestern Railway.

____ (Navarro County). Briar Creek rises two miles west of Elmhouse in northwestern Navarro County (at 32°08′ N, 96°39′ W) and flows east for eighteen miles to its mouth on Chambers Creek, five miles east of Corsicana (at 32°07′ N, 96°22′ W). The surrounding flat to rolling terrain is surfaced by moderately deep to deep sandy and clay loams that support water-tolerant hardwoods, conifers, and grasses. The creek is crossed by the tracks of the Chicago, Rock Island and Pacific Railroad.

____ (Young County). Briar Creek rises near Loving in northeast Young County (at 33°14′ N, 98°30′ W) and runs southwest for thirteen miles to its mouth on Salt Creek, one-half mile north of Lake Graham (at 33°12′ N, 98°39′ W). It traverses rolling prairie surfaced by clay loams that support mesquite and grasses.

BRIARY, TEXAS. Briary (Briary Church) was thirteen miles northeast of Cameron in northern Milam County. It was named for nearby Big Briary Creek. Two churches, a school, and several businesses and houses marked its location on county highway maps in the 1940s.

BRICE, TEXAS. Brice, on State Highway 70 in northwestern Hall County, was named for C. R. Brice, the county attorney from 1896 to 1900. The post office was first located in Briscoe County in March 1899 and then moved to the present site in February 1903 with Arthur E. Benson as postmaster. The townsite was situated on the Horn and Dickson properties. George Dickson gave the land for church and school purposes, and Horn opened the first store. At its peak in the 1920s the community served a fertile farm area that produced cotton, grains, and alfalfa. It had three stores and filling stations, two churches, a blacksmith shop, a gin, a garage, and a five-teacher brick schoolhouse for eleven grades. For several years the community was divided into two parts, known as North and South Brice. In 1986 a gin was located on the South Brice site at the junction of State highways 70 and 256. The main community, which included a combination filling station and store and two churches, was two miles north. The school was consolidated with that of Lakeview in 1952, and the post office was closed in 1954, when mail was routed through Clarendon. In 1990 the population was thirty-seven.

BIBLIOGRAPHY: Inez Baker, *Yesterday in Hall County* (Memphis, Texas, 1940). Virginia Browder, *Hall County Heritage Trails, 1890–1980* (2 vols., Canyon, Texas: Staked Plains, 1982, 1983).

H. Allen Anderson

BRICK HOUSE GULLY. Brick House Gully rises near the intersection of Gessner and Clay roads, two miles east of Addicks Dam in northwest Harris County (at 95°33′ N, 29°50′ W) and flows southeast through flat, sandy terrain for five miles to its mouth on White Oak Bayou in the Heights subdivision of Houston (at 95°26′ N, 29°50′ W).

BRIDGE CITY, TEXAS. Bridge City is at the junction of State Highway 73/87 and Farm Road 1442, twenty-two miles southeast of Beaumont in southern Orange County. It was originally called Prairie View for its location on the coastal prairie and became known as Bridge City after the construction of a notable highway bridge over the Neches River linking Orange County to Port Arthur. The Bridge City post office was established in 1946, and by 1952 the estimated population had reached 3,000. Industrial growth was aided by the channelization of Cow Bayou, the completion of a private electric plant in 1962, and the presence of nearby oilfields and petrochemical plants. Despite Bridge City's rapid growth, voters proved reluctant to incorporate their community. Although the population was 4,677 in 1960, two incorporation attempts in 1961 failed to secure a majority of voters. In 1970 Bridge City electors finally agreed to incorporate by a margin of 677 to 466. By that time, the population had increased to 8,164. In 1980 the population was 7,667, and in 1990 it was 8,034.

BIBLIOGRAPHY: Faye Farley, "A History of the Post Offices in Orange County from 1848," *Las Sabinas: The Official Quarterly Publication of the Orange County Historical Society* 2 (Spring 1976).

Robert Wooster

BRIDGE CREEK. Bridge Creek rises three miles south of Snook in southeastern Burleson County (at 30°26′ N, 96°27′ W) and flows south for eight miles, through mostly wooded country, to its mouth on Yegua Creek, the Burleson-Washington county line (at 30°21′ N, 96°25′ W). The stream traverses gently sloping to nearly level terrain surfaced by loamy and clayey soils. Dense stands of post oak, blackjack oak, elm, hackberry, water oak, and pecan trees line the banks along much of the creek's length. Settlement in the vicinity began in the early 1830s, and Merle was established near the headwaters of the creek during the 1880s.

BIBLIOGRAPHY: Burleson County Historical Society, *Astride the Old San Antonio Road: A History of Burleson County, Texas* (Dallas: Taylor, 1980).

BRIDGEPORT, TEXAS. Bridgeport is on State Highway 114 eight miles west of Decatur and two miles east of Lake Bridgeport in western Wise County. It originated in February 1860 when a group organized by William H. Hunt[qv] secured a charter from the West Fork Bridge Company to build a bridge across the West Fork of the Trinity River. The bridge was to be part of the Butterfield Overland Mail[qv] route. Pierce Woodward suggested the name. A year later, however, the Civil War[qv] began, the mail route was abandoned, and the wooden bridge collapsed. Bridgeport remained a small, rural community until 1873, when a new iron bridge was constructed for transporting supplies from Decatur to Fort Richardson. In May of that year a post office was established. In the 1880s coal was discovered near the town, and for the next forty years the Wise County Coal Company was one of the state's chief producers of bituminous coal. Competition from oil and gas forced the coal mines to close in 1929.

In 1893, when Rock Island tracks reached within two miles of Bridgeport, the town moved a mile east to take advantage of the rail line. The railroad established Bridgeport as an retail center for area cattle ranchers and dairy farmers. The town incorporated in 1913 and in 1920 had a population of 1,872. By the end of the decade Bridgeport was producing crushed stone for road construction and was the site of a brick factory. The completion of Lake Bridgeport in 1931 further diversified the economy; Bridgeport became a tourist center for visitors to the lake. The population of Bridgeport grew steadily after the 1920s and surpassed 2,000 in the mid-1950s. In 1986 it had an estimated 3,737 residents and 153 businesses and was the second largest town in Wise County. In 1990 the population was 3,581.

BIBLIOGRAPHY: Cliff D. Cates, *Pioneer History of Wise County* (Decatur, Texas: Old Settlers Association, 1907). Rosalie Gregg, ed., *Wise County History* (Vol. 1, n.p: Nortex, 1975; Vol. 2, Austin: Eakin, 1982).

David Minor

BRIDGES, WILLIAM B. (?–?). William B. Bridges, early Texas farmer and public official and one of Stephen F. Austin's[qv] Old Three Hundred,[qv] immigrated from Arkansas to Texas as early as April 1824 and received a sitio[qv] of land now in Jackson County on July 21 of that year. In April 1831 Mexican officials filed a character certificate and a land application under his name, listing him as a single farmer from Arkansas who was twenty-three years of age. In 1838 Bridges received a headright certificate for a labor of land in Gonzales County. W. B. Bridges was listed in the July 17, 1841, issue of the Austin *Texas Sentinel*[qv] as being delinquent in paying his 1840 taxes in Gonzales County. Bridges may have served as justice of the peace in Fayette County in 1843. On September 17, 1871, the Columbus *Citizen* reported the burial of a William Bridge, who had come to Texas "around 1825."

BIBLIOGRAPHY: Lester G. Bugbee, "The Old Three Hundred: A List of Settlers in Austin's First Colony," *Quarterly of the Texas State Historical Association* 1 (October 1897). Louis Wiltz Kemp Papers, Barker Texas History Center, University of Texas at Austin.

Stephen L. Hardin

BRIDGES CHAPEL, TEXAS. Bridges Chapel is on U.S. Highway 271 8½ miles northwest of Mount Pleasant in northwestern Titus County. It grew around a Methodist church constructed at the site sometime around the Civil War[qv] and named Bridges Chapel, after Relious Bridges, who donated the land for the church and the adjacent cemetery. In 1870 the members of the community built a school named Stonewall that initially offered a high school program, but by 1932 offered only nine grades. By 1932 the community had a school for black children that offered instruction through grade seven. Improvements in transportation and a decline in the rural population of the county, however, forced the consolidation of the Stonewall school with the Mount Pleasant Independent School District. In 1984 Bridges Chapel had a church, a cemetery, a community center, and a few widely scattered houses.

BIBLIOGRAPHY: John Marion Ellis II, *The Way It Was: A Personal Memoir of Family Life in East Texas* (Waco: Texian Press, 1983). Traylor Russell, *History of Titus County* (2 vols., Waco: Morrison, 1965, 1966; rpt., Walsworth, Texas, 1975).

Cecil Harper, Jr.

BRIDGETOWN, TEXAS. Bridgetown is on a rural road off State Highway 240 seventeen miles northwest of Wichita Falls in north central Wichita County. It developed with the northwest extension of the Burkburnett oilfield[qv] in 1920 and derived its name from its location at the south end of a mile-long wooden toll bridge across the Red River, connecting Wichita County with Tillman County, Oklahoma. As Bridgetown was born during the county's oil boom, it naturally attracted residents more interested in profit than in the establishment of a permanent community. The settlement was little more than a collection of tents sprawled along a stretch of the Red River bounded by a mission and a "notorious dive." Liquor, although prohibited by law in Bridgetown, could be obtained with ease almost anywhere in town.

The population of Bridgetown reportedly varied between 3,500 and 10,000 during the early years. A local post office opened in 1920, and soon afterward two motion picture theaters, a bank, a jail, and a church were constructed. When the oil boom in Wichita County ended during the middle 1920s, however, the boomtown rapidly dwindled in size and activity; its population fell to 100 by 1926. In 1936 the population was still reported at 100, and the town had two businesses. The post office had closed. Bridgetown had a population of eighty and two businesses in the late 1940s. Since then no statistics have been available.

BIBLIOGRAPHY: Louise Kelly, *Wichita County Beginnings* (Burnet, Texas: Eakin Press, 1982).

Brian Hart

BRIDGE VALLEY, TEXAS. Bridge Valley is near the crossing of Farm Road 609 and Buckner's Creek, three miles southwest of La Grange in Fayette County. Most of the site was land granted to John Dancy and Edward Manton[qqv] in the early 1830s. The settlement never became more than a farming community with an economy based on cotton and corn grown along the creek. During the 1880s many of the original settlers were replaced by the second big wave of German and Czech immigrants to Fayette County. In 1898 the business community consisted of a store and post office combination, a saloon, a blacksmith shop, and a school. Voters went to nearby La Grange to cast ballots. In 1903 the post office closed. Soon the other businesses closed too. By 1987 nothing remained except the farms, which concentrate on cattle raising, and Cedar Cemetery, just south of the creek.

BIBLIOGRAPHY: Frank Lotto, *Fayette County: Her History and Her People* (Schulenburg, Texas: Sticker Steam Press, 1902; rpt., Austin: University of Texas Press, 1981). Leonie Rummel Weyand and Houston Wade, *An Early History of Fayette County* (La Grange, Texas: La Grange *Journal*, 1936).

Jeff Carroll

BRIDWELL, JOSEPH STERLING (1885–1966). Joseph Sterling Bridwell, oil and cattle man, was born on March 23, 1885, in Northview, Missouri. He completed public school at Marshfield, Missouri, and moved to Wichita Falls, Texas, in January 1909, after a short stay in Oklahoma. He sold a peculiar type of barbed wire[qv] stretcher. Not one of the gadgets has ever been found. He became interested in the oil business and in 1921 leased some lands on William T. Waggoner's[qv] ranch and a block north of Nocona. At every location on the latter place was a productive well. In 1927 he founded the Bridwell Oil Company, which at one time owned over 700 wells in Texas, Oklahoma, Colorado, Wyoming, Nebraska, and Montana. With these as "nest eggs," he became the largest independent oil operator in the state during the 1940s and 1950s. He served with the American Petroleum Institute, the largest association representing the entire petroleum industry. He was a member and president of North Texas Oil and Gas Association and a member of the National Petroleum Council, the Texas Mid-Continent Oil and Gas Association, the Independent Petroleum Association of America, and the General Gas Committee. Bridwell purchased ranches in Archer County in 1932 and in Clay County in 1935. His total acres grew to more than 160,000 by 1952, and he had more than 100 employees. These ranches carried 6,000 head of livestock, of which some 1,200 were registered. He had many champion cattle; the most famous was Larry Domino, the 1939 world champion bull. Bridwell established the Bridwell Soil Builders Award program in Wichita, Clay, and Archer counties. He was a founder and president (1940–41) of the West Texas Chamber of Commerce[qv] and president (1935) of the Wichita Falls Chamber of Commerce, and was a member of the boards of the Texas and Southwestern Cattle Raisers Association, the Southwestern Exposition and Livestock Show, the Texas Research Foundation[qqv] in Renner, and the Southwest Foundation for Research and Education in San Antonio. He was for a while president of the American Hereford Association and the Independent Producers Equity Association. He was a member of the American Quarter Horse Association, the American National Cattleman's Association, the Archer County Farm Bureau, the Friends of the Land of Columbus, Ohio, and the Wichita Falls Farm and Ranch Club. Bridwell served on the boards of the Methodist Home in Waco, the Texas Research League,[qv] and Southern Methodist University. Bridwell was a member of the American Bible Society. He built several homes for the Methodist Orphanage at Waco and financed the construction of the Bridwell Library[qv] in the Perkins School of Theology at Southern Methodist University in Dallas. He donated the land for Bridwell Park in Wichita Falls. In 1941 he persuaded Gen. Rush B. Lincoln, then commander of the Army Air Corps Technical Training Command, to establish Sheppard Field in Wichita Falls. The field later became Sheppard Air Force Base.[qv] He sold the original 300-acre site for the training installation to the government for one dollar. In the 1950s, Bridwell started a nonsmoking plan for his employees, offering them a fifty-dollar bonus each year for both not starting and quitting. This program was heralded worldwide. Bridwell was married and had two daughters. He died May 9,

1966, in Wichita Falls. In 1972 the Archer County Historical Commission placed a historical marker for Bridwell in Bridwell Park, on U.S. highway 281 south of Windthorst.

bibliography: *Cattleman,* June 1966. Mary Basham Loggie, Joseph Sterling Bridwell (M.A. thesis, Midwestern University, 1967). *Sheep and Goat Raiser,* June 1966. Vertical Files, Barker Texas History Center, University of Texas at Austin. *Jack O. Loftin*

BRIDWELL LIBRARY. The Bridwell Library at Southern Methodist University in Dallas is the university's primary resource for theological and religious studies. It was established in 1950 and named for its benefactor, Joseph Sterling Bridwell.[qv] The library is primarily responsible for supporting the needs of faculty and students in the Perkins School of Theology. It is primarily funded by the J. S. Bridwell Foundation. The original Georgian building, designed by Dallas architect Mark Lemmon,[qv] was expanded in 1967. It underwent renovation in 1988 under the direction of the architectural firm of Hellmuth, Obata, and Kassabaum and was rededicated in October 1989. The library holds one of the finest collections of theological manuscripts in the Southwest, indeed in the nation. The Special Collections contain more than 25,000 printed books dating from the fifteenth to the twentieth century, manuscript correspondence by John Wesley and other important figures in early Methodism, archival collections of American Methodism and private presses, and a small group of medieval and Renaissance manuscripts. Most of the printed works, often in first and early editions, are in the fields of theology, church history, scripture, liturgy, and philosophy. Many of these editions are distinguished by the arts of illustration and typography, and by notable provenances and historically significant bindings. Nearly 700 incunabula (books printed before 1501), often in their original bindings, are housed in the Special Collections. Among them is a thirty-one-leaf fragment of the Gutenberg Bible. The largest groups of incunabula are editions of the Bible, of theological and devotional works, and of the Greek and Roman classics. Special Collections also houses approximately 5,000 sixteenth-century imprints, including most of the textually significant Protestant editions of the English and German Bible, of Protestant and Catholic liturgical texts, of early Reformation tests, and of the classics. Bridwell's large Bible holdings are supplemented by the on-deposit rare Bible and Bibliana collection of Elizabeth Prothro of Wichita Falls. Seventeenth and eighteenth century holdings include numerous works of English church history, theology, liturgy, hymnology and religious polemic. Most of the works of John Wesley (1703–1791), the founder of Methodism, and of his colleagues and critics are present in first and early editions. Special Collections includes a Special Reference section composed of bibliographies, catalogs, monographs, and journals that support research in the subjects and genres described above, and in the history of the book. The Bridwell Library houses a Methodist Reference Collection containing important nineteenth and twentieth century editions of Methodistica, and the Journals and Minutes of the Methodist Church[qv] and its historical antecedents, American and British. The Elizabeth Perkins Prothro Galleries hosts major exhibitions drawn from the library's special collections as well as from the collections of other institutions and collections. The Gill Room, adjacent to the Prothro Galleries, is distinguished by two engraved stone carvings by book designer and sculptor Eric Gill (1882–1940). Though the work is formally named *Alleluia,* the artist referred to it as *Hijinks in Paradise.* The room is used for receptions and book signings. The Bridwell Library is available to all with a nominal deposit. It hosts three major exhibits each year and arranges group tours upon request.

bibliography: *The Ferguson Collection of Bridwell Library, SMU* (Dallas: Bridwell Library, 1960). Lewis Howard Grimes, *A History of the Perkins School of Theology* (Dallas: Southern Methodist University Press, 1993). *Incunabula in Bridwell Library* (Dallas: Bridwell Library, 1979). James F. White, *Architecture at SMU: 50 Years and Buildings* (Dallas: Southern Methodist University Press, 1966).

Stephen Earl Comer

BRIENT, ELLEN LOUISE (1882–1958). Ellen Louise Brient, pioneer organizer of Texas nurses, daughter of Alfred and Louisa Brient, was born in West Drayton, England, in 1882. The family moved to San Antonio, Texas, when she was sixteen months old. Ellen attended public schools and Trinity Methodist Church. After a brief study in a Fort Worth University, she enrolled as a student at John Sealy Hospital[qv] School of Nursing in 1902 in Galveston. At that time this school was the only one in the state with a nursing department at the university level. After completing the two-year program, she returned to San Antonio in 1904.

She did private-duty nursing for six years. Subsequently, working with a small group of other graduate nurses in the early 1900s, she organized what became District 8 of the Texas Graduate Nurses' Association. Nineteen nurses from over the state met in Fort Worth on February 22, 1907, to formulate a bill for the Texas legislature. Ellen Brient attended a meeting on June 3 in Houston, at which time a nurse-practice act was developed. This bill was accepted in a nurses' meeting in San Antonio on April 20, 1908, and introduced to the state legislature in 1909; it was passed without amendments, and Texas became one of the first states to obtain protective nurse legislation.

After a stay in El Paso to care for her mother, Miss Brient returned to San Antonio to find that the local nurses' organization had been discontinued. Many times she and Margerie M. Taylor, superintendent of Physicians and Surgeons Hospital, were the only two who attended the monthly meetings. But they kept at it, the nurses' association grew, and the work on nursing issues continued. Ellen Brient was among the first 3,000 nurses in the nation to enroll in the American Red Cross. She served as chairman of the Red Cross Nursing Service for her district in World War I.[qv] Later she taught Red Cross classes in hygiene and home care. She served as operating-room supervisor and later as the superintendent of nurses at the Physicians and Surgeons Hospital, where she became aware that a small hospital without teaching facilities could not give nursing students the education they needed. She prepared to close the school and launched her idea of an all-graduate nursing staff, but then was forced to resign again to care for her mother.

The Revised Nurse's Registration Bill was passed by the legislature in 1923, after vigorous opposition. Only by great effort on the part of several nursing leaders, particularly Miss Brient, did the bill pass. As a result a number of small, inadequate training schools, where female students were exploited as cheap labor and were poorly trained, were closed.

Brient became superintendent of nursing at Nix Memorial Hospital in San Antonio in 1929 and was director of nurses for that 150-bed private hospital for seventeen years. During the Great Depression[qv] the school was near bankruptcy, but it nevertheless became one of the first hospitals with an all-graduate nursing staff. Ellen Brient attended all of the meetings of the Texas Nurses Association,[qv] some years serving as member of the board of directors or on some important committee. She was president in 1914–15, 1919–20, 1926–27, and 1931–32, the only one to serve four terms. In April 1932 she gave the welcoming address for her state group at the Biennial Convention of Nurses, held in San Antonio. This meeting was attended by 2,670 graduate nurses from forty states, including members from the American Nurses Association, the National League of Nursing, and the National Organization for Public Health Nursing. Ellen Brient retired in 1946 and was honored by Nix Hospital doctors and nurses. She died in San Antonio on January 28, 1958, and was buried in the family plot in City Cemetery No. 4. Many nurses who trained or worked under her attended in uniform and served as honorary pallbearers at her funeral. The Ellen Louise Brient Scholarship Loan Fund was established by District 8, Texas Nurses Association, in her memory.

BIBLIOGRAPHY: Eleanor McElheny Crowder, *Nursing in Texas: A Pictorial History* (Waco: Texian Press, 1980). A. Louise Dietrich et al., *History of the Texas Graduate Nurses' Association* (El Paso: Hughes-Buie, 1932). San Antonio *Express*, January 29, 1958. Texas Graduate Nurses' Association *Bulletin*, March 1958. *Arvella B. Vowell*

BRIER CREEK (Montague County). Brier Creek rises five miles northeast of Lake Amon G. Carter in southwestern Montague County (at 33°34′ N, 97°52′ W) and runs south for 5½ miles to its mouth on the lake, five miles south of Bowie (at 33°29′ N, 97°52′ W). It traverses generally flat terrain surfaced by clay and sandy loams that support water-tolerant hardwood trees, conifers, and grasses.

—— (Young County). Brier Creek rises ten miles east of Olney in northeast Young County (at 33°22′ N, 98°36′ W) and flows north for six miles to its mouth on the West Fork of Curtis Creek, twelve miles southeast of Archer City in southeast Archer County (at 33°26′ N, 98°34′ W). Turkey Springs was probably located on the creek in Young County. The springs were an important water source in the 1850s but have been dry for a considerable time. The creek's drainage area encompasses ranch and oil-field lands surfaced by shallow, stony clay and sandy loams in which grow oak, mesquite, and grasses.

BRIGADE DISTRICTS. Thirty-two brigade districts were established by the Texas legislature on February 14, 1860, to facilitate the organization of the state militia. After the outbreak of the Civil War,[qv] a special law of December 25, 1861, organized the state into thirty-three districts, corresponding generally to the thirty-three senatorial districts. Each district was headed by a brigadier general appointed by the governor. After organization each brigade elected its own commanding officer. A general law of the Tenth Legislature on December 16, 1863, reduced the number of districts to six, and the organization of the districts was suspended with the end of the Civil War.

BIBLIOGRAPHY: Hans Peter Nielsen Gammel, comp., *Laws of Texas, 1822–1897* (10 vols., Austin: Gammel, 1898).

Clinton P. Hartmann

BRIGGS, CLAY STONE (1876–1933). Clay Stone Briggs, lawyer, judge, and congressman, the son of George Dempster and Olive (Branch) Briggs, was born in Galveston, Texas, on January 6, 1876. After attending the University of Texas, Harvard University, and the law department of Yale University, he was admitted to the bar in 1899 and began to practice in Galveston. He was a member of the Texas House of Representatives in the Thirtieth Legislature and served as judge of the Tenth Judicial District of Texas from 1909 until 1919. That year he was elected as a Democrat to the United States Congress, where he served until his death from a heart attack in his Washington apartment on April 29, 1933. Judge Briggs was survived by his second wife, the former Mrs. Lois Slayton Woodworth, and their two children. He was buried in Syracuse, New York.

BIBLIOGRAPHY: Dallas *Morning News*, April 30, 1933. *Biographical Directory of the American Congress*. Vertical Files, Barker Texas History Center, University of Texas at Austin. *Anne W. Hooker*

BRIGGS, ELISHA ANDREWS (1820–1906). Elisha Andrews Briggs, Texas Ranger, merchant, and Baptist minister, the son of Dea Isaac Briggs, was born at Amherst, Massachusetts, on August 19, 1820. Because of ill health he left college at Gull Prairie, Michigan, and went to live with his father, a government agent on an Indian reservation. In 1841 he started for Texas on a log raft on the Mississippi River, worked his way on a steamboat to New Orleans, and studied law and Spanish there for a year with his uncle, Thomas B. Andrews. The uncle sent him to Texas as manager of his land in Fort Bend County. A flood on the Brazos River ruined the buildings and plantation, and Briggs moved to Austin in the summer of 1843.

He became a Texas Ranger in 1844 and recruited men for a special detail to protect Castroville and Quihi in Castro's colony.[qv] He scouted, trailed, and fought Indians in the San Antonio area for two years under John Coffee (Jack) Hays and William A. A. (Bigfoot) Wallace.[qqv] In 1846, under Maj. Samuel Highsmith,[qv] he joined the United States Army in Mexico. When he left ranger service, he bred fine horses and became manager of the Vance ranch. In the summer of 1848 he married Frances Weber of Castroville. In 1859 he moved to San Antonio, where he opened a mercantile business in 1861. During the Civil War[qv] he opened the first direct road between San Antonio and Matamoros to carry the Confederate mail between those cities. He was appointed by Governor Pendleton Murrah[qv] to receive and record claims of ranchmen for stock stolen by Indians. In 1866 he moved twenty miles from San Antonio to a homestead where he farmed and raised stock while serving as justice of the peace and notary public. In 1874 he entered the Baptist ministry. He assisted in reorganization of the Medina Baptist Church at Somerset and helped organize the Rio Grande Baptist Association at Frio Town. He traveled as a missionary over his trails of Indian fighting and preached in Spanish and English. He died at his home on December 29, 1906.

BIBLIOGRAPHY: Andrew Jackson Sowell, *Early Settlers and Indian Fighters of Southwest Texas* (Austin: Ben C. Jones, 1900; rpt., Austin: State House Press, 1986). *Jeanette H. Flachmeier*

BRIGGS, GEORGE WAVERLEY (1883–1957). George Waverley Briggs, journalist and banker, was born at Burford's Landing, near Camden, Alabama, on February 27, 1883, son of Alice (Burford) and Ritchie Jones Briggs, a Methodist, and later Congregationalist, minister. He attended public and private schools and the academy of Jacob Bickler[qv] in Austin. After studying at the University of Texas, Briggs became a reporter on the Austin *Tribune* (1905–06). At later times he held the positions of staff correspondent of the San Antonio *Express* (1906–10) and Dallas *Morning News*[qqv] (1911–13) and managing editor of the Austin *Statesman* (1910–11) and the Galveston *News*[qqv] (1913–18). For the San Antonio *Express* he wrote a series of articles that became, in book form, *The Texas Penitentiary* (1909). As a result he was appointed a penitentiary commissioner of Texas. His work on the Dallas *Morning News* included a study of city and state housing, resulting in *The Housing Problem in Texas* (1911). Governor W. P. Hobby[qv] appointed Briggs commissioner of insurance and banking, 1918–20. Briggs later became vice president and trust officer of the City National Bank and its successor, the First National Bank, Dallas. He wrote the *Digest of Texas Insurance and Banking Laws*. Briggs was responsible for three major legislative acts: the Texas trust act, the common trust fund act, and the Texas probate code. He held office in many organizations: the American Red Cross, national and Dallas chambers of commerce, National Committee on Prisons and Prison Labor, Texas Tax League, Southwestern Legal Foundation, Texas Centennial[qv] Exposition, Dallas Historical Society,[qv] and the Philosophical Society of Texas.[qv] He was awarded, by George VI, the King's Medal for civilian service to the Allies in World War II.[qv] At the time of his death he was director of the Dallas *Morning News*. In 1912 Briggs married Lorena May Foster, for many years a member of the board of regents of Texas State College for Women, Denton (now Texas Woman's University). Briggs died in Dallas on July 16, 1957, and was buried in Oakwood Cemetery, Austin.

BIBLIOGRAPHY: Sam Hanna Acheson, Herbert P. Gambrell, Mary Carter Toomey, and Alex M. Acheson, Jr., *Texian Who's Who*, Vol. 1 (Dallas: Texian, 1937). *Proceedings of the Philosophical Society of Texas* (1957).

BRIGGS, TEXAS. Briggs is at the intersection of U.S. Highway 183 and Farm Road 2657 in northeastern Burnet County. The site is part of the Aaron F. Boyce survey patented to Boyce's heirs on September 30, 1850. The Boyce land is on the headwaters of Berry Creek, where a number of permanent springs provided constant water. Settlers first called the area Springs, then Gum Springs. The land on which Briggs stands was purchased by Stephen Taylor from W. T. (Bill) Gann, who came to Texas from Missouri in 1855. Taylor arrived from Tennessee around 1880. Between 1870 and 1890 many new settlers arrived from Kentucky, Tennessee, Mississippi, the Carolinas, Alabama, and other states to establish homes and farms in this blackland section of Burnet County. Taylor built a cotton gin and sold it in 1882; he then erected the first general store in the area that became known as Taylors Gin.

In 1888 a petition was circulated among the citizens and sent to Washington, D.C., requesting a post office for Taylor's Gin; the request was granted on March 27, 1888. William Hazelwood, a physician who set up practice in the community, passed a petition to get the name changed to Briggs, in honor of his mother-in-law, Mrs. Henry D. Briggs. The community was renamed on June 21, 1898. By 1900 a site had been platted into lots and blocks, land had been donated for a new school, and the population had reached 100. Businesses thrived, cotton was king, and two gins operated in Briggs; the town had doctors, a drugstore, and two general stores. Telephones and electricity came in the early 1900s. A bank was chartered in 1909. From 1906 to 1928 business prospered. On April 12, 1906, a tornado demolished the school. A new building was built, and in 1915 a high school was organized. The population reached about 300 in the 1920s.

In 1928 devastating fires took their toll of homes and businesses, most of which were never rebuilt. The Great Depression[qv] brought on a farming decline; the remaining gin and businesses closed. With the arrival of U.S. Highway 183 many citizens began commuting to shop and to work in nearby communities, including Killeen, Copperas Cove, and Camp Hood (now Fort Hood). Briggs's population reached its height of 520, served by twenty business, in 1936. The population subsequently fluctuated between 250 and 300 until the late 1960s, when it declined to ninety-six. In 1969 the Briggs school was consolidated with the Burnet district. In the late 1980s Briggs had two churches, a post office, two service stations, and scattered residences. The population was ninety-two in 1990.

BIBLIOGRAPHY: Darrell Debo, *Burnet County History* (2 vols., Burnet, Texas: Eakin, 1979). Vertical Files, Barker Texas History Center, University of Texas at Austin. *Estelle Bryson*

BRIGHAM, ASA (ca. 1790–1844). Asa Brigham, signer of the Texas Declaration of Independence,[qv] first treasurer of the Republic of Texas,[qv] and mayor of Austin, was born in Massachusetts about 1790. With his wife, Elizabeth S., two sons, a daughter, and a son-in-law, he arrived in Texas from Louisiana in April 1830. In December the ayuntamiento[qv] of San Felipe de Austin announced his election as *síndico procurador*[qv] for the precinct of Victoria (Brazoria), and in December 1831 he was elected *comisario*[qv] for the same precinct. He was one of those who signed a document on June 20, 1832, indicating readiness to participate in military operations in the interest of Texas independence. On October 6, 1832, he was elected treasurer for the Brazoria district. Brigham was appointed a member of the Brazoria board of health in 1831. After 1832 he kept a ferry at Brazoria, where he ran a mercantile business with his son-in-law, and later he was a stockholder in the San Saba Colonization Company and receiver of stock for the Brazos and Galveston Railroad. He acquired leagues of land at Hall's Bayou in Brazoria County and in Galveston and Bastrop counties, and raised sugar, cotton, corn, and cattle. By 1833 his daughter, wife, and son-in-law had all died. Though he held slaves for a time, Brigham later signed petitions for free blacks. As one of those instrumental in establishing a Masonic lodge at Brazoria, he served as junior warden there and was also a charter member of the Masonic Grand Lodge of Texas, organized at Houston on December 20, 1837.

Brigham was elected Brazoria alcalde[qv] in 1835. He served as one of four representatives from Brazoria to the Convention of 1836[qv] at Washington-on-the-Brazos and was a signer of the Texas Declaration of Independence. He remained at the convention until at least March 16, 1836. David G. Burnet[qv] appointed him auditor of the Republic of Texas,[qv] and President Sam Houston[qv] named him treasurer on December 20, 1836. He was the first to hold the latter office and was reappointed by Mirabeau B. Lamar[qv] in January 1839. On February 16, 1839, Brigham became a Houston alderman while serving as national treasurer. He left the treasury on April 12, 1840; later that year he was charged with using state funds for private purposes but was cleared. Houston reappointed him treasurer on December 31, 1841, and in 1842 Brigham became mayor of Austin.

After the death of his first wife he married Mrs. Ann Johnson Mather, on July 8, 1839. He died on July 3, 1844, at Washington, Texas, where he is buried. A monument was erected by the state of Texas at the burial site in 1936, and Brigham's remains were removed to a site in Washington-on-the-Brazos State Historical Park[qv] sometime later.

BIBLIOGRAPHY: Eugene C. Barker, ed., "Minutes of the Ayuntamiento of San Felipe de Austin, 1828–1832," 12 parts, *Southwestern Historical Quarterly* 21–24 (January 1918–October 1920). Joseph W. Hale, "Masonry in the Early Days of Texas," *Southwestern Historical Quarterly* 49 (January 1946). Andrew Forest Muir, "The Free Negro in Harris County, Texas," *Southwestern Historical Quarterly* 46 (January 1943). Andrew Forest Muir, "Railroad Enterprise in Texas, 1836–1841," *Southwestern Historical Quarterly* 47 (April 1944). Levonne Durham Rochelle, Life and Times of Asa Brigham: Treasurer of the Republic of Texas (M.A. thesis, University of Texas, 1956). Sam A. Shuler, "Stephen F. Austin and the City of Austin," *Southwestern Historical Quarterly* 69 (January 1966). Texas House of Representatives, *Biographical Directory of the Texan Conventions and Congresses, 1832–1845* (Austin: Book Exchange, 1941). Vertical Files, Barker Texas History Center, University of Texas at Austin. *L. W. Kemp*

BRIGHT, DAVID (?–?). David Bright, one of Stephen F. Austin's[qv] Old Three Hundred[qv] colonists, came to Texas from Illinois in 1822 and landed near the mouth of the Colorado River. On December 20, 1823, he voted in the alcalde[qv] election at San Felipe. He was one of the electors in the Colorado District in April 1824, when the Baron de Bastrop[qv] was chosen Texas delegate to the state convention of Coahuila and Texas.[qv] On May 10, 1824, Bright and his wife agreed that their daughter Betsy might marry Noel Roberts.[qv] One daughter had already married Eli Hunter,[qv] another of the Old Three Hundred. On July 15, 1824, Bright received title to a league of land on Oyster Creek in what is now eastern Fort Bend County and a labor of land that later became part of Austin County. The census of 1826 classified Bright as a farmer and stock raiser aged over fifty. His household then included his wife, a son, and a daughter. That daughter evidently married Patrick Reels,[qv] also of the Old Three Hundred. In April 1836 the Bright family and the Reels family camped near Liberty during the Runaway Scrape.[qv]

BIBLIOGRAPHY: Eugene C. Barker, ed., *The Austin Papers* (3 vols., Washington: GPO, 1924–28). Lester G. Bugbee, "The Old Three Hundred: A List of Settlers in Austin's First Colony," *Quarterly of the Texas State Historical Association* 1 (October 1897). *Southwestern Historical Quarterly*, Notes and Fragments, April 1923. "Reminiscences of Mrs. Dilue Harris," *Quarterly of the Texas State Historical Association* 4, 7 (October 1900, January 1901, January 1904). Clarence Wharton, *Wharton's History of Fort Bend County* (San Antonio: Naylor, 1939).

BRIGHT, TEXAS. Bright, eight miles north of Dawson in western Navarro County, was probably established in the late 1890s. A post office opened there in 1900 and operated until 1904. At its height around 1900 the community had a store, a gin, and a number of houses. By the mid-1930s Bright was no longer shown on highway maps. *Christopher Long*

BRIGHTMAN, JOHN CLAVER (1819–1867). John Claver Brightman, doctor and soldier, was born in Floyd County, Indiana, on May 21, 1819, the son of George Claver and Nancy (Moore) Brightman. He received a high school education before the family moved to Galveston, Texas, in March 1843. They then moved in the spring of 1844 to Port Lavaca and subsequently to Seguin, Victoria, and Kemper's Bluff, and finally in 1845 to Goliad. Brightman studied medicine in these various communities. About 1855 he was in Karnes County, where he was elected chief justice (county judge). About 1858 he went to Houston to practice medicine but left there in September 1859 because of an outbreak of yellow fever. In the Confederate Army he took the place of a man named Chambers and participated in fighting around Galveston. He died of yellow fever at Harrisburg in 1867. He had never married.

BIBLIOGRAPHY: John Claver Brightman Papers, Barker Texas History Center, University of Texas at Austin.

BRIGHT STAR, TEXAS (Rains County). Bright Star is on Farm Road 2795 six miles southeast of Emory in eastern Rains County. It was founded around the time of the Civil War.[qv] During the 1930s it had a church, a school, two businesses, and a population of fifty. The school and both of the businesses closed after World War II.[qv] In the early 1990s the church and a community center still remained, and in 1990 the reported population was seventy-five.

Christopher Long

BRIGHT STAR, TEXAS (Van Zandt County). Bright Star, at the intersection of Farm roads 47 and 1395, eighteen miles northwest of Canton in northwest Van Zandt County, had a school in 1890 that reached an enrollment of 102 in 1905 and was consolidated with the Wills Point Independent School District by the 1950s. State highway maps of 1936 showed a business, a cemetery, and scattered dwellings at the townsite, but by the 1980s only the church, the cemetery, and residences along the highway remained. *Diana J. Kleiner*

BRIGHT STAR EDUCATIONAL SOCIETY. The Bright Star Educational Society was chartered on February 14, 1860, to promote a nondenominational, coeducational school to be located in Hopkins County. Apparently the outbreak of the Civil War[qv] interfered with building plans, and the school did not open. A community called Bright Star existed for some time in Hopkins County, and between 1854 and 1871 a post office operated under that name. Nothing else, however, is known about the community.

BRILEYTOWN, TEXAS. Brileytown, also known as Old Brileytown, was an early settlement just off U.S. Highway 59 fifteen miles northeast of Nacogdoches in northeastern Nacogdoches County. Sources suggest that the area was settled prior to the Civil War.[qv] At one time there were several stores at the site. By 1880, however, Brileytown was deserted. Subsequently, a public school began operating there before 1900; in 1904 it had an enrollment of twenty-five. The school later closed, and in the early 1990s only a church and a few scattered houses remained in the area. *Christopher Long*

BRINDLEY, GEORGE VALTER (1886–1970). George Valter Brindley, surgeon and administrator of Scott and White Memorial Hospital[qv] in Temple, was born in Auburn, Texas, on January 8, 1886, the son of George Goldthwaite and Mattie (Haines) Brindley. He attended Grandview Junior College in Texas from 1903 to 1906, then went on to earn his M.D. at the University of Texas in 1911. He began his association with Scott and White Hospital in 1911, when he joined the staff of what was then called Temple Sanitarium. During his long career at the hospital, he served as a surgeon and as head of the surgery unit and was one of the chief administrators of the institution for over half a century. In 1917, on the death of Dr. Raleigh R. White,[qv] one of the founders of the hospital, Brindley was appointed to the board of directors of Scott and White and received shares in the private corporation. He assisted in the hospital's shift from a partnership structure to a group practice and helped preside over the dramatic expansion of the institution from the 1920s to the 1940s. In 1949 Brindley, along with A. C. Scott, Jr., and M. W. Sherwood, donated $1.5 million in stock and assets to convert the hospital from a private institution to a public one. He became a cofounder of the Scott, Sherwood, and Brindley Foundation, which owned and administered the hospital's physical assets, and served on the board of trustees of the foundation.

Brindley was a lecturer at the University of Texas medical school from 1945 to 1949, and in 1951, as assistant dean of the university's Temple facility, he directed the training of surgeons at Scott and White. He also published a number of articles in medical journals. He was president of the Texas Medical Association[qv] in 1949 and of the American Cancer Society in 1956. He married Arabella Owens in 1913; they had three sons, all of whom became physicians. Brindley was a Baptist and a long-time board member of the University of Mary Hardin-Baylor. He died on October 7, 1970, and is buried in Temple.

BIBLIOGRAPHY: Austin *American-Statesman*, October 8, 1970. Dayton Kelley, *With Scalpel and Scope: A History of Scott and White* (Waco: Texian Press, 1970). Vertical Files, Barker Texas History Center, University of Texas at Austin. *Who's Who in the South and Southwest*, Vol.2. *Mark Odintz*

BRINDLEY, PAUL (1896–1954). Paul Brindley, pathologist and professor, was born near Maypearl, Texas, on December 27, 1896, the last of the seven children of George Goldthwaite and Mattie (Hanes) Brindley. He acquired his premedical education at the University of Texas, Austin. He received his M.D. from the University of Texas Medical Branch in 1925 and did postgraduate work at the Mallory Laboratory of Boston City Hospital and the Mayo Clinic. Brindley became instructor of pathology at UTMB in 1925 and was promoted to associate professor in 1927. In 1929 he was appointed professor and chairman of the Department of Pathology, positions he held until his death. For twenty-five years he also served as a consultant in pathology for St. Mary's Hospital[qv] and the United States Public Health Hospital in Galveston and at Lackland Air Force Base in San Antonio. Brindley was responsible for establishing the Galveston chapter of the American Cancer Society and in 1948 was the society's first president. During his career Brindley published over twenty papers in his specialty, many focusing on his interests in aneurysms, malignant diseases, and Madura foot, a tropical disease. After World War II[qv] the surgeon general of the Army invited Brindley to visit several Central American countries, including Costa Rica, Guatemala, and Honduras, as a teacher and consultant on Madura foot.

Brindley was preceded at UTMB by his brother, George Valter Brindley,[qv] who graduated in 1911. Over the years that Paul Brindley taught at UTMB, eleven of his nephews graduated from the medical branch, ten of them as M.D.'s and one with an M.S. in anatomy. Their presence on the campus led to his being known fondly as "Uncle Paul" among his students. Brindley married Anne Ammons on July 2, 1929. They had no children. Brindley, an accomplished photographer, recorded many of their travels through Mexico, Canada, and the United States. He died in Galveston, while reading in bed, on December 28, 1954.

Brindley became a fellow of the American College of Physicians in 1934 and of the American College of Pathologists in 1947. He was twice president of the Texas Society of Pathologists, which posthumously awarded him its first Caldwell Memorial Award in January 1955. After his death, the sophomore class of 1954–55 erected a plaque in his honor in the Keiller Building at UTMB. In 1982 his wife established the Paul Brindley Distinguished Professorship and Scholarship

Fund in UTMB's Department of Pathology. Income from this fund enables the department to bring outstanding pathologists, of whom many are UTMB graduates, to the campus for a week of lectures and seminars with faculty and students.

BIBLIOGRAPHY: Galveston *Daily News*, September 5, 1965. *Texas State Journal of Medicine*, February 1955. *The University of Texas Medical Branch at Galveston: A Seventy-five Year History* (Austin: University of Texas Press, 1967). *Who's Who in America*, 1950–51.

Patricia L. Jakobi

BRINGHURST, ANTOINETTE POWER HOUSTON (1852–1932). Nettie Bringhurst, poet, was born in Huntsville, Texas, in 1852, one of eight children of Sam and Margaret Lea Houston.[qqv] She attended Baylor Female College at Independence and Austin Female College. She began writing poetry at an early age; her poems appeared in Scribners and in the New York *Evening Post.* On February 28, 1877, at the Governor's Mansion[qv] in Austin she was married to W. L. Bringhurst, a professor at Texas Military Institute, Austin,[qv] and later at the Agricultural and Mechanical College of Texas (now Texas A&M University). The couple had five children, four of whom died in childhood. In 1904 Mrs. Bringhurst was awarded first prize by the *Bohemian,* a Fort Worth magazine, for the best poem on the Alamo. She was state historian of the Daughters of the Republic of Texas[qv] from 1906 to 1908 and was elected poet laureate for life in 1908. Her best known poems include "The Lone Star Flag of Texas," "A Garnered Memory," "My Father's Picture," and "The Veterans' Reunion." In 1925 she unveiled a statue of her father in Houston. She died on December 5, 1932, as the result of an automobile accident. Funeral services were held at the Alamo. She was buried in Mission Burial Park, San Antonio.

BIBLIOGRAPHY: Austin *Daily Democratic Statesman*, March 2, 1877. Daughters of the Republic of Texas, *Fifty Years of Achievement: History of the Daughters of the Republic of Texas* (Dallas: Banks, Upshaw, 1942). San Antonio *Express*, December 5, 7, 1932. *Texaco Star*, July–August 1933.

John Q. Anderson

BRINKER, MAUREEN CATHERINE CONNOLLY (1934–1969). Maureen (Little Mo) Catherine Connolly Brinker, tennis champion, was born on September 17, 1934, in San Diego, California, the daughter of Martin and Jessamine (Gillan) Connolly; her father was a lieutenant commander and athletics officer in the United States Navy. Although not a native Texan, Maurine spent the later years of her brief life in Dallas, where she was an active leader in the development of junior tennis programs. The Connollys divorced when Maureen was a young child, and her mother later married and divorced a musician, August Berste. Maureen grew up with and was raised by her mother and a great-aunt. At her mother's urging, she studied singing and dancing as a child and also enjoyed horseback riding. In 1944 she began playing tennis on municipal courts in San Diego. Her first coach, Wilbur Folsom, instructed the talented ten-year-old to switch from playing left-handed to right and coached her through her first tournament, in which she was a runner-up.

Maurine's career continued to advance under the direction of Eleanor "Teach" Tennant, who had coached such tennis stars as Bobby Riggs and Alice Marble. With Tennant's instruction, Maurine won the girls-fifteen-and-under division of the Southern California Invitational Tennis Championship in 1947. As she continued her tournament career, she quickly won more than fifty championships and in 1949 became the youngest person ever to win the national junior title. By 1950 she was the tenth-ranked woman player in the United States, and in 1951, the year she graduated from high school, she was selected to play on the United States Wightman Cup team, the youngest player ever chosen. From 1951 to 1954 Maureen Connolly dominated women's tennis worldwide. She won the United States Women's Singles Championship in 1951, 1952, and 1953; the French Singles Championship in

Maureen Connolly Brinker. Courtesy Maureen Connolly Brinker Tennis Foundation, Dallas.

1953 and 1954; and Wimbledon in 1952, 1953, and 1954. In 1953 she became the first woman to win the grand slam of tennis, with victories at the national championship tournaments of Australia, France, Great Britain, and the United States. This feat was not repeated by a woman tennis player until Margaret Court in 1970. The Associated Press named Connolly female athlete of the year in 1952, 1953, and 1954. She earned her nickname "Little Mo" from sportswriters who likened her explosiveness on court to the powerful battleship USS *Missouri*, which was based in her hometown of San Diego in the 1950s. During her time of tennis stardom she also worked occasionally as a copy girl and columnist for the San Diego *Union.*

She was frequently compared to such tennis greats as Helen Wills and Suzanne Lenglen, and in later years such stars as Chris Evert evoked memories of Connolly. She was described as a calm but fierce competitor with legendary mental concentration, though she was a friendly teenager with interests in music, dancing, and movies when she was not playing tennis. She was a baseline specialist with an especially strong backhand.

Maureen Connolly's amateur tennis career was cut short in July 1954, when she injured her right leg in a horse-riding accident. After realizing she would never return to her previous level, the twenty-year-old announced her retirement from tennis, in February 1955. Shortly thereafter she became engaged to Norman E. Brinker, a

United States Navy officer and former member of the United States Olympic equestrian team. They married in June 1955, and the couple had two daughters. After her retirement from tennis Maurine Brinker spent much of her time coaching younger players. In 1963 the Brinkers moved to Dallas, where they opened a new restaurant chain called Steak and Ale. In Dallas, in an effort to acknowledge the assistance she had received as a junior player, Mrs. Brinker and Mrs. Frank Jeffet established the Maureen Connolly Brinker Tennis Foundation to advance achievement among junior tennis players in Texas. This foundation has remained an active organization for junior tennis through its tournaments, awards, and financial support. It also sponsored a women's tournament in Dallas for many years. Maurine Brinker was active in equestrian sports in Dallas. In 1968 the city honored her as Woman of the Year for her work with its youth, and in that same year she was elected to the International Tennis Hall of Fame.

Maureen Connolly Brinker was diagnosed with stomach cancer in 1966. She died in Dallas on June 21, 1969, survived by her mother, husband, and two daughters. She was buried in Hillcrest Memorial Park in Dallas. The year before her death the Maureen Connolly Brinker annual tennis tournament was started in Dallas in her honor. An award in her name was established shortly after her death by the foundation and the United States Lawn Tennis Association to honor outstanding junior girl players. The foundation has since established many other programs and awards bearing Maurine Brinker's name.

BIBLIOGRAPHY: Dallas *Morning News*, June 22, 23, 1969. Owen Davidson and C. M. Jones, *Great Women Tennis Players* (London: Pelham Books, 1971). *Dictionary of American Biography*. Virginia Wade and Jean Raferty, *Ladies of the Court: A Century of Women at Wimbledon* (New York: Atheneum, 1984).

Debbie Mauldin Cottrell

BRINKER, TEXAS. Brinker, on Farm Road 69 seven miles east of Sulphur Springs in eastern Hopkins County, was settled around 1845 and named for a pioneer family. A school was built there in 1872, financed by private donations. Church services were held in the school until 1880, when a Baptist church building was erected. Smith Bromley opened a local cotton gin in 1882. A Brinker post office opened in 1901 with Susan W. Coppedge as postmistress; it operated until 1906. In the mid-1930s Brinker had a school, a church, and a number of scattered dwellings. In 1940 the reported population was twenty. In the late 1980s the community had a meeting hall, a church, and a cemetery.

BIBLIOGRAPHY: Sylvia M. Kibart and Rita M. Adams, eds., *Pioneers of Hopkins County, Texas*, Vol. 1 (Wolfe City, Texas: Henington, 1986).

J. E. Jennings

BRINKLEY, JOHN ROMULUS (1885–1942). John Romulus (changed to John Richard) Brinkley, controversial medical charlatan, broadcaster, and political candidate, the only son of John and Candice (Burnett) Brinkley, was born near Beta, Jackson County, North Carolina, on July 8, 1885. He was orphaned at an early age and was raised by an aunt. He married Sally Wike in 1908, and they had three daughters. In 1913 that marriage ended in divorce, and Brinkley married Minnie Telitha Jones. They had a son.

Brinkley was educated in a one-room school at Tuckasiegee, North Carolina, but never earned a diploma. From 1907 through 1915 he attended several diploma mills such as Bennett Medical College of Chicago and Eclectic Medical University of Kansas City. In spite of dubious credentials he was licensed by the state of Arkansas and set up a medical practice in Milford, Kansas. In 1918 he began performing his controversial "goat gland operation," designed to restore male virility and fertility by the implantation of goat glands. Before long more than 100 customers a week were receiving the $750 rejuvenation operation. As a result of the operations and a large patent medicine business, "Doc" Brinkley became extremely wealthy. In 1923 he constructed the first radio station in Kansas, KFKB, a powerful station that carried country music and fundamentalist preaching.

In 1928 the American Medical Association's executive secretary, Dr. Morris Fishbein, attacked Brinkley for diagnosing illnesses and prescribing medicines over the radio. Consequently, in 1930 the Kansas State Medical Board revoked Brinkley's medical license, and the Federal Radio Commission refused to renew his broadcasting license. Brinkley responded by entering the governor's race, hoping to appoint new members to the medical board. Running as an independent, write-in candidate, he came extremely close to winning—his loss coming only because thousands of votes were thrown out on technicalities. Subsequent bids for the governorship in 1932 and 1934 also failed.

In 1931 he received authority from Mexican officials to build a powerful transmitter at Villa Acuña, Mexico, across the river from Del Rio, Texas. In 1933 he moved his entire medical staff and facilities to the Roswell Hotel in Del Rio. He used his station, XER, to entice his listeners to visit his clinic or buy an array of gimmicks, among them ampules of colored water, at a price of six for $100. In Texas he rarely implanted goat glands, but substituted what he described as "commercial glandular preparations." He also performed numerous prostate operations and instituted the use of Mercurochrome shots and pills to help restore youthful vigor. Estimates are that he earned $12 million between 1933 and 1938. During this period his conspicuous display of wealth—a lavish mansion, expensive cars, planes, yachts, and diamonds—was second to none. In 1938 he moved his medical activities to Little Rock, Arkansas, but maintained his residence in Texas. About that time he lost a libel suit against Fishbein, fought numerous malpractice suits, and battled the Internal Revenue Service over back taxes. In 1941 he was forced to file for bankruptcy. The following year circulatory problems led to the amputation of one of his legs, and on May 26, 1942, he died in San Antonio of heart failure. He was buried in Memphis, Tennessee.

BIBLIOGRAPHY: Gerald Carson, *The Roguish World of Doctor Brinkley* (New York: Rinehart, 1960). *Dictionary of American Biography*. Gene Fowler and Bill Crawford, *Border Radio* (Austin: Texas Monthly Press, 1987). New York *Times*, May 27, 1942. Frank Wardlaw, "The Goat-Gland Man," *Southwest Review* 66 (Spring 1981).

Keith D. McFarland

BRINKLEY CREEK. Brinkley Creek rises four miles southeast of Turlington in east central Freestone County (at 31°41′ N, 96°01′ W) and runs northeast for three miles to its mouth on an unnamed marsh two miles southeast of Indian Creek Lake (at 31°43′ N, 95°59′ W). It crosses flat to rolling terrain with local escarpments, surfaced by deep, fine sandy loams that support hardwood and conifer forests. Developed parts of the land in the area are used primarily for farming.

BRINKMANN, ALEXANDER (1868–1947). Alexander Brinkmann, lumber merchant and Texana collector, was born in a log cabin at Comfort, Texas, on March 26, 1868, the eldest child of Otto and Marie (Ochse) Brinkmann. He attended the six-grade Comfort school and took a business course in San Antonio. In 1890 he married Emmie Bodemann; they had four sons and two daughters. Brinkmann and his father had a lumber business in Comfort. Later Brinkmann formed a partnership with Edward Steves[qv] and Sons of San Antonio. In the early 1940s he sold his interest. Brinkmann is best known for his collection of Texana. In 1928 he acquired the library of Carl Assmann of Austin. Brinkmann collected pictures of early settlers of the Hill Country,[qv] letters, documents, muster rolls, membership lists, and minutes of various groups and organizations, many of which are displayed in the Comfort Historical Museum, which he helped found in 1933. His library of Texana and western Americana consisted of more than four thousand items at the time of his death in Comfort, on August 29, 1947.

bibliography: Guido E. Ransleben, *A Hundred Years of Comfort in Texas* (San Antonio: Naylor, 1954; rev. ed. 1974).

Guido E. Ransleben

BRINSON, ENOCH (?–?). Enoch Brinson, one of Stephen F. Austin's[qv] Old Three Hundred[qv] colonists, moved from Louisiana to Texas before August 7, 1824, when he received title to a sitio[qv] now in Harris County. The census of 1826 classified him as a farmer and stock raiser aged between twenty-five and forty, with a wife, Eliza. Brinson was living on San Jacinto Bay in October 1826, when he protested Dr. Johnson C. Hunter's[qv] charges for surveying. Brinson was at one time a surveyor for the Coahuila and Texas[qv] government. By April 1827 he had bought part of the William Bloodgood[qv] league, and on July 10, 1830, the *Texas Gazette*[qv] carried an announcement that Enoch Brinson had opened a blacksmith shop and a house of private entertainment. In 1835 C. C. Cox described Brinson as a hospitable Baptist who had lost an eye and wore a tuft of hair over where the eye had been. At that time Mrs. Brinson was milking thirty or forty cows and selling produce in Galveston. On March 23, 1838, Brinson and a woman named Delilah Sharr were indicted for fornication; Brinson married a Delilah Bell, possibly the same person, in Harrisburg County (later Harris County) on September 22, 1838. In March 1839 he was administering the Page Balow estate, and in 1844 he served on a grand jury in Houston.

bibliography: Eugene C. Barker, ed., *The Austin Papers* (3 vols., Washington: GPO, 1924–28). Lester G. Bugbee, "The Old Three Hundred: A List of Settlers in Austin's First Colony," *Quarterly of the Texas State Historical Association* 1 (October 1897). C. C. Cox, "Reminiscences of C. C. Cox," *Quarterly of the Texas State Historical Association* 6 (October 1902, January 1903). Virginia H. Taylor Houston, "Surveying in Texas," *Southwestern Historical Quarterly* 65 (October 1961). Louis Wiltz Kemp Papers, Barker Texas History Center, University of Texas at Austin. Adele B. Looscan, "Harris County, 1822–1845," *Southwestern Historical Quarterly* 18–19 (October 1914–July 1915). *Telegraph and Texas Register*, March 27, 1839, April 20, 1844.

BRISBANE, ALBERT (1809–1890). Albert Brisbane, a socialist and founder of La Réunion,[qv] a utopian community in Dallas County, was born on August 22, 1809, in Batavia, New York, the only son of James and Mary (Stevens) Brisbane. His father was a wealthy businessman and landowner and provided him with a life free of financial concerns. At eighteen Brisbane moved to Europe, where he studied philosophy under Victor Cousin in Paris and G. W. F. Hegel in Berlin. During this youthful sojourn he discovered Charles Fourier's *Traité de l'Association Domestique-Agricole* and became interested in the Fourierist search to discover "a just and wise organization of human society." After two years of study with Fourier, Brisbane returned to the United States in 1834 to popularize his mentor's ideas. The publication of *Social Destiny of Man; or, Association and Reorganization of Industry* (1840) and *Association; or, A Concise Exposition of the Practical Part of Fourier's Social Science* (1843) established Brisbane as one of the leading proponents of communal socialism. He also maintained close contact with the leading French Fourierist of the period, Victor P. Considérant.[qv]

By the early 1850s domestic problems in France had persuaded Considérant to adopt Brisbane's idea of founding a utopian model community in the United States with European and American participants. Throughout the spring of 1853 the two men toured southwestern America and, impressed by the climate, soil, and inexpensive land of the area around the site of present-day Dallas, determined that north central Texas would be the ideal location for the community. La Réunion was financed by a joint-stock company, the European Society for the Colonization of Texas, with an operating budget of 5.4 million francs. Once the site was selected, however, Brisbane was not actually involved in the colony, which did not succeed and ended by 1859.

Afterward, Brisbane's interest in a utopian community declined. He spent most of the remainder of his life in Europe, devoting his time to scholarly and artistic pursuits. He was married first to Sarah White, with whom he had three children, and then to Redelia Bates. He died in Richmond, Virginia, on May 1, 1890.

bibliography: Rondel V. Davidson, "Victor Considérant and the Failure of La Réunion," *Southwestern Historical Quarterly* 76 (January 1973). *Dictionary of American Biography* (New York: Scribner, 1928–81).

Christopher E. Guthrie

BRISCOE, ANDREW (1810–1849). Andrew Briscoe, merchant, patriot, judge, and railroad promoter, was born on November 25, 1810, on the plantation of his father, Parmenas Briscoe, in Claiborne County, Mississippi. He made several trips on horseback between Mississippi and Texas before settling in Texas, where he registered in 1833 as a citizen of Coahuila and Texas.[qv] With a shipment of goods he opened a store in Anahuac in 1835. Briscoe opposed the irregular collection of customs dues by Mexican authorities at Anahuac and presented resolutions of protest at a mass meeting there and later at Harrisburg. When he attempted to trade to DeWitt Clinton Harris[qv] goods with unpaid duties, both he and Harris were arrested by Mexican officials. They were released when William B. Travis[qv] and his volunteers came to drive Antonio Tenorio[qv] out of office (*see also* anahuac disturbances). In July Briscoe wrote to the editor of the Brazoria *Texas Republican*[qv] justifying the action taken. In August he received a congratulatory letter from Travis. Briscoe was captain of the Liberty Volunteers at the battle of Concepción[qv] and followed Benjamin R. Milam[qv] in the siege of Bexar.[qv] He was elected a delegate from his municipality with Lorenzo de Zavala[qv] and attended the Convention of 1836[qv] at Washington-on-the-Brazos, but evidently because of the urgency of reentering military service he did not remain until its close. At the battle of San Jacinto[qv] he was captain of Company A, Infantry Regulars.

In 1836 Briscoe was appointed chief justice of Harrisburg by Sam Houston.[qv] When his term ended in 1839, he began dealing in cattle and trying to promote a railroad. In 1839 he planned a road from Harrisburg to the Brazos River. In 1840, when the project was abandoned, about two miles had been graded and laid with ties. That year, in a paper entitled "California Railroad," he gave a complete plan for building a railroad from Harrisburg to San Diego via Richmond, Prairieville, Austin, and El Paso. In 1841 he secured a charter from the Republic of Texas[qv] for the Harrisburg Railroad and Trading Company, of which he was president. In the spring of 1849 Briscoe moved his family to New Orleans, where he engaged in banking and brokerage until his death, on October 4, 1849. He was survived by his wife, Mary Jane Harris Briscoe,[qv] and four children.

bibliography: Adele B. Looscan, "Harris County, 1822–1845," *Southwestern Historical Quarterly* 18–19 (October 1914–July 1915).

Lewis W. Newton

BRISCOE, BIRDSALL PARMENAS (1876–1971). Birdsall P. Briscoe, architect, was born on June 10, 1876, in Harrisburg, Texas, the son of Andrew Birdsall and Annie Frances (Paine) Briscoe. He was the grandson of Andrew Briscoe[qv] and the great-grandson of John R. Harris,[qv] founder of Harrisburg. He grew up on his parents' ranch near Goliad and attended San Antonio Academy,[qv] Texas Agricultural and Mechanical College (now Texas A&M University), and the University of Texas. During the Spanish-American War Briscoe served in the United States Army Infantry as a sergeant; he subsequently served as a major in the army during World War I.[qv]

He learned architecture through apprenticeships with the Houston architects C. Lewis Wilson and Lewis Sterling Green. After a brief partnership with Green (1909–11), Briscoe began independent practice in 1912. From 1922 until 1926 he was in partnership with Sam H. Dixon, Jr. From 1919 until his retirement in 1955, Briscoe shared an office with Maurice J. Sullivan.[qv] Although from time to time he collaborated with both Dixon and Sullivan on nonresidential commissions, Briscoe was best known for his elegantly composed and detailed houses.

He established his reputation as an exceptional designer at the outset of his career. His aptitude for disciplined formal composition and correct, scholarly rendition of historic detail placed him at the forefront of the eclectic trend in Houston architecture during the second decade of the twentieth century. Briscoe's finest houses, designed between 1926 and 1940, exhibit the array of historical architectural styles characteristic of American eclectic architecture and are distinguished by the architect's gift for harmonious proportion and full-bodied ornamental detail.

He worked extensively in the Houston neighborhoods of Courtlandt Place, Shadyside, Broadacres, and River Oaks. Among his clients for houses were William Lockhart Clayton (1917), W. T. Carter (1920), R. Lee Blaffer[qqv] (1920), Walter H. Walne (1925), Burdine Clayton Anderson (1928), Robert W. Wier (1928), Milton R. Underwood (1934), Wirt A. Paddock (1936), I. H. Kempner, Jr. (1936), and Dillon Anderson[qv] (1938). Outside Houston, Briscoe's best-known project was the remodeling of the Patton-Varner House near West Columbia (*see* VARNER-HOGG PLANTATION STATE HISTORIC PARK) for Ima and William Clifford Hogg[qqv] in 1920.

Briscoe married Ruth Dillman in 1927. He joined the American Institute of Architects in 1921 and was elected a fellow of the institute in 1949. From 1934 until 1941 he served as district officer for South Texas of the Historic American Buildings Survey. He was the author of two western adventure novels, *In the Face of the Sun* (1934) and *Spurs from San Isidro* (1951). He was a parishioner of Christ Church. He died in Houston on September 18, 1971, and is buried at Oak Hill Cemetery in Goliad.

BIBLIOGRAPHY: James Charles Susman, The Architecture of Birdsall Parmenas Briscoe (M.A. thesis, University of Texas at Austin, 1979).

Stephen Fox

BRISCOE, DOLPH, SR. (1890–1954). Dolph Briscoe, Sr., cattleman, was born on September 1, 1890, in Fulshear, Texas, one of four children of Judge Lee Adolphus and Lucy (Wade) Briscoe. His father was a planter, jurist, rancher, and descendant of Andrew Briscoe.[qv] His mother was a granddaughter of Randolph Foster.[qv] On October 1, 1913, Briscoe married his cousin Georgie Briscoe, who resided in Fulshear, and a year later the couple moved to Uvalde. Their son, Dolph Briscoe, Jr., became the fortieth governor of the state of Texas. Briscoe, Sr., started in his youth tending cattle at the periphery of his family's plantation. He worked beyond the bordered cultivated fields and quickly became a natural at roping, culling, and driving cattle. His entrepreneurial talents also emerged early. Already mounted by dawn, he began a newspaper route around Fulshear and won a Houston *Post*[qv] competition for increased subscriptions, as well as a scholarship to Peacock Military Academy.[qv] But Briscoe naturally gravitated toward the range life. "I had my chance at college," he wrote, "but I didn't want college. My father wanted me to attend the State University and study law, but I liked horse trading better." Briscoe ran mules and horses from Bee, Wilson, and Dimmit counties to the farmers on the coastal prairies, and business was profitable, especially soon after the harvest. He expanded operations and began selling in Arkansas and Missouri. He partnered with Leo Byrd and ranched along the Leona River. He traded cattle, formed a partnership with J. M. Patton and Albert Finley, and by 1919 was buying cattle by the thousands. He "went broke," he recalled, in 1921 and again in 1932. He next became a commission agent for Humble Oil and Refining Company for the Uvalde territory, and in the course of distributing for Humble (later Exxon[qv]), he made friends with Ross Sterling,[qv] president of Humble and Briscoe's next partner in the cattle business. After buying the Chupadera Ranch in Dimmitt and Webb counties the two men went broke.

In 1932 the cattle business, like many other businesses in the nation, went sour. Beef at two cents a pound would not even pay the freight costs. Briscoe faltered but did not quit. He leased in subsequent years the Catarina Ranch, then bought 35,000 acres of it. He ran the Margarito Ranch and put 5,000 Hereford cattle[qv] on it in northern Coahuila. He became a partner of Albert Finley in a 10,000-acre spread named the Gato and acquired the Rio Frio Ranch, 14,000 acres north of Uvalde. His O6 (Open Six) brand was an adaptation of the original Sterling-Briscoe O9 brand, which Dolph Briscoe, Jr., later used. The O6 rapidly spread across several counties as the indefatigable Briscoe began to build his cattle fortunes for a third time. In 1933 he founded the Uvalde Wool and Mohair Company, which became his official office when he was not out on his land. In 1973, in the midst of a school-tax dispute over the Briscoe holdings, the Dallas *Morning News*[qv] estimated that the Briscoe family owned 303,125 acres in five counties, and that with additional leased acreage they controlled a million acres worth $40 million. The Briscoes were consequently the state's largest landholders.

By this time Briscoe hobnobbed with prominent Texans who came to socialize and to hunt at his ranches, particularly at the Chupadera, while he owned it with Ross Sterling and before it went belly up. Jesse Jones,[qv] millionaire and lumber baron of Houston, R. M. Farrar,[qv] president of the Union National Bank of Houston, former governor W. P. Hobby,[qv] Frank E. Clarity, former vice president of the Fort Worth and Denver Railway, Walter W. Fondren,[qv] Houston investor, John Mobley, general counsel of the Missouri Pacific Railroad, Duval West,[qv] a federal judge, Judge C. A. Goeth of San Antonio, and Edward W. Kilman[qv] of the Houston *Post Dispatch* were visitors to Briscoe's ranches. He was also active in Governor Daniel J. Moody's[qv] campaign for office, and he helped extensively when his old friend Sterling ran for governor. During James Allred's[qv] term Briscoe was chairman of the Texas Racing Commission.[qv] Indeed, Briscoe himself was considered by others as a possible candidate for office. He declined to run, however.

He gained recognition among ranchers for his successful crossbreeding programs. He used Brahman bulls on registered Herefords with successful weight increases during the early ranching years. Later, under the guidance of Robert J. Kleberg, Jr.,[qv] he turned to Santa Gertrudis and became a charter member of the Santa Gertrudis Breeders International. At age forty-one Briscoe was the youngest president-elect of the Texas and Southwestern Cattle Raisers Association.[qv] He was reelected for a second term. During his tenure he led the association's protest against the weighing of cattle in intrastate shipments, promoted cattle-theft protection, and lobbied for lower commission costs and more field inspectors. He also served on the Uvalde City Council, was a director of the Federal Reserve Bank of Dallas,[qv] and was a vice president of the National Finance Credit Corporation of Texas, as well as a vice president of the Texas Livestock Marketing Association. Briscoe was a Mason, a Shriner, and a parishioner at St. Phillips Episcopal Church in Uvalde. Recollections of him by friends and neighbors, including John Nance Garner,[qv] invariably dealt with his personal warmth, his unvarnished friendliness, and his forthrightness in human relationships. Briscoe died unexpectedly on July 15, 1954, in Uvalde.

BIBLIOGRAPHY: Dolph Briscoe, Jr. Papers, Barker Texas History Center, University of Texas at Austin. Mary Whatley Clarke, "Dolph Briscoe of Uvalde," *Cattleman*, January 1953.

Howard Lackman

BRISCOE, MARY JANE HARRIS (1819–1903). Mary Jane Harris Briscoe, Houston civic leader and founder of the Daughters of the Republic of Texas,[qv] the daughter of John Richardson and Jane (Birdsall) Harris,[qqv] was born at Ste. Genevieve, Missouri, on August 17, 1819. She was raised in New York and remained to attend finishing school there when members of her family immigrated to Texas. She joined her brother, DeWitt Clinton Harris,[qv] in Harrisburg in the fall of 1836. She knew Sam Houston[qv] and other Texas leaders, became known as the "Belle of Buffalo Bayou," and was one of four of John R. Harris's children to become shareholders in the Harrisburg Town Company, which established that community. On August 17, 1837, she married Andrew J. Briscoe;[qv] they had five children. Her husband died in 1849, after which she managed his estate. Mrs. Briscoe lived for a time at her father-in-law's plantation in Claiborne County, Mississippi, before returning to Texas in 1852 to live at Anderson, Galveston, and Harrisburg before moving to Houston in 1874. On July 18, 1881, as a widow of a signer of the Texas Declaration of Independence,[qv] she received a donation grant of 1,280 acres. The Daughters of the Republic of Texas was organized at the Briscoe home in 1891, and she served as vice president of the organization until 1897. She was founder and first president of Sheltering Arms, a home for women in Houston. She wrote sketches and reminiscences and was a charter member of the Texas State Historical Association,[qv] of which she was elected an honorary life member in 1897. Mary Briscoe died in Houston on March 8, 1903, and was buried in Glenwood Cemetery.

BIBLIOGRAPHY: John Henry Brown, *Indian Wars and Pioneers of Texas* (Austin: Daniell, 1880; reprod., Easley, South Carolina: Southern Historical Press, 1978). Marguerite Johnston, *Houston, The Unknown City, 1836–1946* (College Station: Texas A&M University Press, 1991). Adele B. Looscan, "Mrs. Mary Jane Briscoe," *Quarterly of the Texas State Historical Association* 7 (July 1903). Thomas L. Miller, "Texas Land Grants to Veterans of the Revolution and Signers of the Declaration of Independence," *Southwestern Historical Quarterly* 64 (January 1961). Andrew Forest Muir, "Railroad Enterprise in Texas, 1836–1841," *Southwestern Historical Quarterly* 47 (April 1944). C. W. Raines, *Year Book for Texas* (2 vols., Austin: Gammel-Statesman, 1902, 1903). Vertical Files, Barker Texas History Center, University of Texas at Austin. *Seymour V. Connor*

BRISCOE, TEXAS. Briscoe, on Farm Road 1046 just off U.S. Highway 83 in northern Wheeler County, was platted by the Lone Star Townsite Company and named for J. B. Briscoe, an official of the Panhandle and Santa Fe Railway, in 1929. That same year A. V. Airington was granted in court a fifty-year telephone franchise for both Briscoe and nearby Allison. The Wiley Gas Company furnished the town its fuel, and Panhandle Power and Light brought in electricity. In 1930 the Briscoe post office opened. The Briscoe school district increased in size and enrollment during the 1930s, when it absorbed the Gageby schools. In 1939 Briscoe had six businesses and an estimated population of 150. In 1961 the population was estimated at 270. From 1974 to 1980 the estimated population was 210, and in 1984 Briscoe had four businesses. In 1990 the population was 135.

BIBLIOGRAPHY: William Coy Perkins, A History of Wheeler County (M.A. thesis, University of Texas, 1938). Millie Jones Porter, *Memory Cups of Panhandle Pioneers* (Clarendon, Texas: Clarendon Press, 1945). *H. Allen Anderson*

BRISCOE COUNTY. Briscoe County (D-9) is on the edge of the Texas High Plains along the eastern Caprock[qv] escarpment, which separates the Llano Estacado[qv] from the rolling plains. It is bordered on the east by Hall County, on the west by Swisher County, on the north by Armstrong County, and on the south by Floyd and Motley counties. Briscoe County was separated from the Bexar District in 1876, organized in 1892, and named for Andrew Briscoe,[qv] a soldier in the Texas Revolution,[qv] who during the period of the republic became a judge and railroad promoter. The county comprises 887 square miles of irregular terrain ranging up to 3,300 feet in altitude; the elevation drops in Tule Canyon as low as 1,000 feet. The annual precipitation averages 10.5 inches, and the growing season averages 214 days a year. The average annual minimum temperature is 26° F in January, and the annual maximum is 94° in July. Silverton, the county seat, is five miles southwest of the center of the county, which is at 101°15′ west longitude and 34°30′ north latitude, sixty miles southeast of Amarillo.

Soils vary from gray and chocolate loams to light sand in the valleys of the Prairie Dog Town Fork of the Red River and its tributaries, including Tule Creek. These streams have formed the canyons and breaks crossing the county's northern and eastern portions. Abundant native grasses grow in the broken areas, as do mesquite and cedar trees; cotton, wheat, and grain sorghums are raised on the arable lands above the Caprock.

Geologists have found evidence of occupation by pre-Columbian people throughout Briscoe County; ruins of irrigation canals or of stockades attest to a high degree of civilization. Plains Apaches followed these Indians and were displaced around 1700 by the Comanches, who found the canyon recesses abundant with buffalo, antelope, and other wild game. José Mares and Pedro Vial[qqv] led trading expeditions through the vicinity in the late 1780s, as did Francisco Amangual[qv] in 1808. The advance party of the Texan Santa Fe expedition[qv] passed by the Quitaque country in 1841, and in 1852 captains Randolph B. Marcy and George B. McClellan[qqv] followed the Prairie Dog Town Fork through the area of the present county. Since the breaks west of the site of present Quitaque contained springs, that area became a favorite haunt of Comanchero[qv] traders. White captives of Comanche raiders were often separated and traded to other Indian bands or Comancheros in the notorious Valley of Tears.[qv] That ended after Col. Ranald S. Mackenzie's[qv] Fourth United States Cavalry[qv] crisscrossed the county in pursuit of the "Mongols of the West" in 1872, and again after they battled the Indians at Tule Creek on September 25–27, 1874. On September 29 Mackenzie's troops slaughtered over 1,000 Indian horses at Tule Canyon after their crucial victory at Palo Duro Canyon the day before (*see* RED RIVER WAR).

With the power of the Comanches broken, Briscoe County was open for white settlement. Although the "dean" of Comancheros, José Piedad Tafoya,[qv] had maintained a trading post at Los Lenguas Springs (Los Lingos Creek) between 1865 and 1867, no real settlement occurred until open-range cattle raising came to the area. In 1878 the Baker brothers and O. J. Wiren established the Quitaque (Lazy F) Ranch,[qv] which was added to the JA Ranch[qv] properties in 1882 and fenced the following year. The Quitaque, owned by Charles Goodnight[qv] and L. R. Moore after the former terminated his partnership with Cornelia Adair[qv] in 1887, was a primary influence on the county's early economy. The JA and Shoe Bar[qv] ranches owned land in the northeastern part of the county. By 1890 a few stock farmers and small ranchers had begun taking up lands on the periphery of the Lazy F.

The town of Quitaque began in 1890 as a stage stop. Merchants and other businessmen also trickled in; in 1891 Thomas J. Braidfoot laid out the townsite of Silverton and led the movement for the organization of the county. By the spring of 1892 enough settlers had arrived to bring Braidfoot's plan to fruition. A petition was circulated, and on March 15, 1892, the electorate officially organized the county and chose Silverton as its seat. J. N. Stalbird was elected the first county judge, F. D. Fisher county attorney, R. I. Hanna treasurer, T. L. Anderson clerk, and Miner Crawford sheriff. By 1900 the population had grown to 1,253, and six school districts had been established. Immigrant farmers introduced various crops to the region before World War I,[qv] the most promising of which were wheat, sorghum, and cotton. Cotton was first grown in Briscoe County on an experimental basis but became one of the county's most important crops by 1930. In 1900 only eight acres of Briscoe County land was planted in cotton; in 1910 over 3,400 acres were devoted to the fiber, then 7,535 acres in 1920, and over 36,000 acres in 1929. The county's first gin was built in 1912.

Between 1900 and 1930 ranches gave way to farms, until most of the arable lands were under cultivation by the early 1930s. The number of farms in the county grew from 170 in 1900 to 307 in 1910, then to 397 in 1920 and 679 in 1930. As farming expanded, the population grew, from 2,162 in 1910 to 2,948 by 1920 and to 5,590 by 1930.

Agricultural growth in the South Plains finally brought a railroad into the county. Until the 1920s all freight came in wagons, and later in automobiles, from Amarillo or Estelline. In 1925, however, the Fort Worth and Denver Railway decided to build into the region. A branch line was completed from Estelline westward to Quitaque and Silverton by 1927, then southward from Quitaque to Plainview and Lubbock in 1928. Also during this time graded auto roads replaced many of the old wagon routes; State Highway 86 was completed from Tulia via Silverton and Quitaque to Turkey, in Hall County. Later, State Highway 256 linked Silverton with Memphis and Clarendon.

During the Great Depression [qv] the agricultural economy suffered and contracted. The number of farms in the county dropped from 679 to 516 between 1929 and 1940, and cotton production dropped by more than 30 percent. Losses associated with the depression were also responsible for a drop in the county's population; 5,590 people lived in Briscoe County in 1930 but only 4,056 in 1940. The consolidation and mechanization of agriculture after World War II [qv] resulted in further dislocation of the farm populace, and the county's population dropped to 3,528 by 1950. A slight rise to 3,577 in 1960 was followed by sharp declines to 2,794 in 1970, 2,579 in 1980, and 1,971 in 1990. By the early 1990s Silverton and Quitaque had populations of 779 and 513 respectively; the remainder of the Briscoe County population resided on farms and ranches.

In the early 1990s Briscoe County continued to rely heavily on agriculture as a major source of revenue; its irrigated land comprised 40,000 acres. Cotton, grain sorghums, and wheat continued to be of prime importance, though vegetables and melons were beginning to be introduced. Ranching in the county was almost entirely limited to cattle. The Haynes Boy Scout and Girl Scout camps, named for N. W. (Mammie) Haynes, an area hotel owner and civic leader, are located in the breaks east of Silverton. Recreation facilities are available at Lake Theo, built in 1962 and named for rancher Theo Geissler, and at Mackenzie Reservoir and Caprock Canyons State Park,[qqv] both opened in the 1970s.

BIBLIOGRAPHY: Briscoe County Historical Survey Committee, *Footprints of Time in Briscoe County* (Dallas: Taylor, 1976). S. G. Reed, *A History of the Texas Railroads* (Houston: St. Clair, 1941; rpt., New York: Arno, 1981). Vertical File, Southwest Collection, Texas Tech University. Ernest Wallace, *Ranald S. Mackenzie on the Texas Frontier* (Lubbock: West Texas Museum Association, 1964).

Donald R. Abbe and H. Allen Anderson

BRISTOL, TEXAS. Bristol is on Farm Road 660 eighteen miles northeast of Waxahachie in northeastern Ellis County. Among the first settlers in the area in the early 1840s was Joshua W. Brock; from 1854 to 1869 a post office operated under the name of Brocksville. Dancing was a popular diversion in the area's early social life, and for a time the community was unofficially called Heelstring. Community development revolved around a steam gristmill, a sawmill, and a cotton gin constructed by the Sparkman family in the late 1860s. The first community building, a log church, school, and lodge room, was constructed in 1870. The Bristol post office opened in 1872. By 1890 Bristol had 200 residents served by a half dozen businesses, a bank, two churches, and an elementary school. The population reached a high of 300 in 1933 but dropped to 200 by 1950 and below 200 in the mid-1960s. From 1972 through 1990 the community reported ninety-four residents. In the late 1980s Bristol continued to serve as a supply and service center for area farmers and as a school and church community.

BIBLIOGRAPHY: Edna Davis Hawkins, et al., *History of Ellis County, Texas* (Waco: Texian, 1972).

David Minor

BRITE, LUCAS CHARLES II (1860–1941). Luke Brite, pioneer Presidio County rancher and philanthropist, son of Lucas Charles and Nancy Caroline (Carr) Brite, was born in Caldwell County, Texas, on July 29, 1860. He had two brothers and a sister. Their father died when Brite was three years old, and while still a boy he began working on ranches in La Salle and Frio counties. In 1879 he went to work in Coleman and Tom Green counties with his brother Robert. In 1885 Robert Brite died, and Luke trailed a small herd of 166 cattle from Frio County to Capote Peak in Presidio County. After spending several years camped alone in the pristine wilderness, he had a substantial ranch. He married schoolteacher Edward (Eddie) McMinn Anderson on June 24, 1896, in Schell City, Missouri. The couple lived on the ranch at Capote Peak the first six years of their marriage and in 1902 moved into Marfa. They had a son and a daughter.

Brite developed a ranch of 125,000 acres in Presidio County and became the breeder of champion Herefords. By March 1920 he had managed to ship 1,000 bulls of his own breeding for each of the preceding fourteen years. His cattle-breeding received several honors. He took greatest pride in the Cudahy Trophy for Grand Champion Carload of Feeder Cattle, which he won in 1922 and 1925. In 1918 he helped to organize the Highland Hereford Breeders Association in Marfa. That same year he was elected president of the Panhandle and Southwestern Stockmen's Association. He became president of the American National Live Stock Association in 1927. In July 1928 Brite helped organize the Highland Fair Association in Presidio County and served as chairman of the livestock committee.

The Brites were devoted members of the First Christian Church in Marfa, which they joined in August 1897, when Addison Clark [qv] held a meeting and organized the church. In 1911 and in 1914 the Brites gave a total of nearly $60,000 to establish the Chair of English Bible and to build the Bible College building at Texas Christian University. Luke Brite became chairman of the board of trustees of Brite College of the Bible at TCU in 1926.

In 1941 in El Paso he was stricken with appendicitis. He died from complications from surgery on September 4, 1941. After her husband's death, Eddie Brite served the remainder of his term on the board of trustees of Brite College. She was the first woman to serve on that board. In 1942 she was received as an honorary member of the Beta Iota chapter of Delta Kappa Gamma, a national educational society. She was given a life membership in the Texas Federation of Women's Clubs [qv] in 1945. In 1948 TCU awarded her an honorary doctor of laws degree.

BIBLIOGRAPHY: Noel Leonard Keith, *The Brites of Capote* (Fort Worth: Texas Christian University Press, 1950). Cecilia Thompson, *History of Marfa and Presidio County, 1535–1946* (2 vols., Austin: Nortex, 1985). Vertical Files, Barker Texas History Center, University of Texas at Austin. Clayton W. Williams, *Texas' Last Frontier: Fort Stockton and the Trans-Pecos, 1861–1895* (College Station: Texas A&M University Press, 1982).

Julia Cauble Smith

BRITE, TEXAS. Brite is 3½ miles north of Capote Peak and three miles east of the Sierra Vieja Mountains in the highlands of northwestern Presidio County. It grew up around the store on the ranch of Lucas Charles Brite [qv] and was sometimes called Brite's Store. The settlement established a school before 1911, when Brite's Ranch Precinct No. 7 reported seventy-eight students and a population of

468 in the county scholastic census. By 1914 it was selected as a county voting precinct. The store housed a post office from 1916 until 1926. Mexican bandits robbed the store twice. The first attack, known as the Brite Ranch Raid,[qv] occurred on Christmas Day, 1917, when about forty-five raiders sacked the store and killed postman Mickey Welch and two passengers on his mail stage. On March 3, 1933, Mexican bandits looted the store. In 1933 Brite listed a population of ten, and as late as 1939 the Brite school was maintained as part of the Marfa district. After World War II[qv] the population in Brite grew to twenty-five. In 1966 it was twenty-one, and the store was closed.

BIBLIOGRAPHY: Cecilia Thompson, *History of Marfa and Presidio County, 1535–1946* (2 vols., Austin: Nortex, 1985). Ronnie C. Tyler, *The Big Bend* (Washington: National Park Service, 1975).

Julia Cauble Smith

BRITE DIVINITY SCHOOL. Brite Divinity School is the theological seminary of Texas Christian University. It has a separate board of trustees and its own dean but is administered by the TCU system. The seminary, like its parent institution, has formal and informal ties to the Christian Church (Disciples of Christ).[qv] In its mission statement, Brite defines itself "as an intellectual center of the church." The school dates back to 1895, when J. B. Sweeny, a religion instructor, led a reorganization of TCU's Department of Bible into a separate school called the Bible College. Despite Sweeny's strong leadership and a new name, it was difficult to distinguish the Bible College from the original religion department. Lucas Charles Brite II's[qv] endowment of a chair in English Bible in 1911 and donation of additional funds in 1914 provided the stimulus for the college's growth into Brite College of the Bible, renamed for its benefactor. The newly incorporated school offered one and two year graduate degrees. In 1941 the American Association of Theological Schools extended accreditation after the school increased its requirement for a divinity degree to a three-year program. The school also holds accreditation from the Southern Association of Colleges and Secondary Schools.

The years following World War II[qv] proved to be a boom for the seminary; its faculty doubled and its student body grew. In 1952 the school moved into the south wing of TCU's newly built Religion Center. The new location was in close proximity to the Robert Carr Chapel, which is also housed in the center. In the early 1950s Brite College integrated its student body, an action TCU did not take campus-wide until 1964. Black students were still not allowed to live in seminary housing or eat in the university cafeteria. In 1963 a renewal of the school's charter brought a change in its name from Brite College of the Bible to Brite Divinity School. The school also changed its basic degree from a bachelor of divinity to a master of divinity in 1967. By 1970 it offered the doctor of ministry as well. Since its inception, the school has had seven deans: Colby D. Hall (1914–47), D. Ray Lindley (1947–50), Roy C. Snodgrass (1950–55), Elmer D. Henson (1955–71), William E. Tucker (1971–76), M. Jack Suggs (1976–89) and Leo G. Perdue (1989–). In the early 1990s the school offered the following graduate programs: master of divinity, master of theological studies, certificate of theological studies, doctor of ministry in homiletics, and doctor of ministry in pastoral theology and pastoral counseling. In 1994 enrollment in the school was 242.

BIBLIOGRAPHY: *Brite Divinity School: A Historical Sketch* (Fort Worth: Brite Divinity School, Texas Christian University, 1989). Colby D. Hall, *History of Texas Christian University* (Fort Worth: Texas Christian University Press, 1947). Noel Leonard Keith, *The Brites of Capote* (Fort Worth: Texas Christian University Press, 1950). *Texas Christian University Bulletin*, May 1993.

Tracé Etienne-Gray

BRITE RANCH RAID. The ranch of Lucas Charles Brite,[qv] at Capote Peak in western Presidio County, was attacked by about forty-five Mexicans, possibly supporters of Francisco (Pancho) Villa,[qv] on Christmas Day 1917. The raid was well planned. The attackers cut the ranch's telephone lines to prevent any call for help. They chose a holiday, when most of the ranch workers were away and the Brites were at their Marfa home. The family of T. T. Van Neill, ranch foreman, was at the ranch. The first awareness of the assault came when the foreman's father saw riders dismounting in the yard and scattering for cover. He fired on the evident leader of the attackers, and a gunfight developed between the Neills and the raiders. The bandits captured two ranch workers and sent one, José Sánchez, to tell the Neills that the other would be killed if they did not surrender. The Neills knew they were outnumbered and gave the raiders the key to Brite's Store to appease them. After looting the store of clothes, canned goods, and cash, the raiders rounded up the best horses and stole all the ranch's saddles. During the looting of the store, postman Mickey Welch arrived at the ranch in his mail stage with two Mexican passengers. The robbers shot the passengers and hanged Welch in the store.

The bandits stayed at the ranch several hours and were still there when Rev. H. M. Bandy and his family arrived at the ranch to visit the Neills. The raiders allowed the Bandys to reach the Neill home, where the reverend led a prayer and took up a rifle to defend the ranch. The Bandys and the Neills were rescued eventually when a large number of armed neighbors and soldiers arrived in automobiles. James L. Cobb, a neighbor of the Brites, had heard the shots and investigated without being detected. Cobb then drove twelve miles to telephone Luke Brite in Marfa. Brite called Col. George Langhorne of the Eighth Cavalry for help. Although a large posse arrived in automobiles, the raiders escaped down the rimrock, where cars could not follow. Langhorne's soldiers borrowed horses from local ranchers and joined the troops from Ruidosa in pursuit of the robbers. On the morning of December 26 the raiders crossed the Rio Grande at the Los Fresnos ford into Mexico. Later that day some 200 members of troops M and G of the Eighth Cavalry crossed at the same point and pursued them. The American forces engaged in a running fight with about fifteen of the raiders and killed ten of them in a canyon not far from Pilares, Chihuahua. They recovered some of the stolen goods, but most of the horses were lost or in such poor condition that they had to be shot. The other raiders escaped into the mountains. Only one United States soldier, Private John F. Kelly, was wounded in the conflict. Fiske and his men returned to Texas with the recovered property that evening.

BIBLIOGRAPHY: El Paso *Times*, December 27, 1917, January 4, 1918. Noel Leonard Keith, *The Brites of Capote* (Fort Worth: Texas Christian University Press, 1950). Virginia Madison, *The Big Bend Country of Texas* (Albuquerque: University of New Mexico Press, 1955; rev. ed., New York: October House, 1968). Ronnie C. Tyler, *The Big Bend* (Washington: National Park Service, 1975). U.S. Senate, *Investigation of Mexican Affairs: Preliminary Reports and Hearings* (66th Cong., 2d Sess.; 2 vols., Washington: GPO, 1920). Harry Warren Papers, Archives of the Big Bend, Sul Ross State University.

Julia Cauble Smith

BRITO, SANTIAGO A. (?–1892). Santiago Brito, county sheriff and city marshall in Brownsville, was probably born in the Rio Grande valley. He was married and had a family of five children. He was owner of *El Demócrata*, a Spanish-language newspaper in Brownsville, before he was elected Cameron county sheriff in 1884. Newspaper accounts of Brito's accomplishments as a lawman regularly appeared in regional newspapers during the 1880s. In 1890 Matthew L. Browne won the office of sheriff, and, on December 1, 1890, Brito applied for and received the post of Brownsville city marshall. Some time before, he had been made a special Texas Ranger by order of Governor Lawrence Sullivan Ross.[qv]

On January 19, 1891, the Rio Grande Railroad was robbed of some $75,000 as well as government mail. Brito succeeded in capturing José

Mosqueda,[qv] the leader of the outlaws, and thus became part of the folklore of the Texas Mexican community. Brito's involvement in the investigation was initially the idea of Simón Celaya, the general manager of the railroad, who was financially responsible for the stolen goods. He was later sued by a Mexican company for the loss of 10,500 silver pesos and gold worth $9,110. The territorial authority brought Brito in conflict with Sheriff Browne, in whose jurisdiction the crime occurred. Browne and Brito both organized posses to hunt the outlaws and apparently argued about their power over the case. Brito solved the case in nine days. He and a posse made up of his former deputies searched the scene of the robbery and combed the surrounding area for the criminals. He found two witnesses, a boy whose uncle was involved in the crime and a vaquero who had found the tool used to derail the train. Uncovering the "home-made spike-puller" led Brito to the blacksmith who had forged it and ultimately to José Mosqueda and his accomplices. When Brito refused to hand his prisoners over to Browne, John M. Haynes, a United States marshall, had to intervene and place the prisoners in the only available jail, which was in Brownsville, thus landing them in Browne's custody. Much of the money was apparently never recovered. Mosqueda and one other conspirator were sentenced to life and ten-year sentences, respectively. Both reportedly died in jail. Browne was shot on a cattle drive less than a year after the train robbery, and Brito was shot and killed in August 1892.

"El Corrido de José Mosqueda" was composed in the 1890s to commemorate the event. A version of almost a half century later presents Brito as a coward fleeing from Mosqueda after a skirmish and Mosqueda as a hero. *See also* CORRIDOS.

BIBLIOGRAPHY: Milo Kearney, ed., *Studies in Brownsville History* (Pan American University at Brownsville, 1986). Carlos Larralde, *Mexican-American Movements and Leaders* (Los Alamitos, California: Hwong, 1976). Américo Paredes, "José Mosqueda and the Folklorization of Actual Events," *Aztlán* 4 (Spring 1973).

Teresa Palomo Acosta

BRITTON, FORBES N. (1812–1861). Forbes N. Britton, soldier, businessman, and legislator, was born in 1812 in Clarkesville, Virginia, and is thought to have attended Kenyon College in Ohio. He was appointed from Virginia to the United States Military Academy at West Point and graduated thirty-third in his class on July 1, 1834. He was brevetted a second lieutenant, Seventh Infantry, on July 1, 1834. He was appointed a second lieutenant on November 18, 1835, promoted to first lieutenant on July 7, 1838, and made a captain on February 16, 1847, after serving in the Mexican War.[qv] For most of his army career he moved Indians from the southeastern United States to sites in Indian Territory.

He resigned his commission on July 16, 1850, and moved to Corpus Christi to practice law and speculate in real estate. With Cornelius Cahill, Britton began a profitable commission business in 1850. In 1852 he was one of the incorporators of the Corpus Christi Navigation Company, formed for the purpose of dredging a ship channel into Corpus Christi Bay. He lobbied for construction of a road between Corpus Christi and El Paso and joined with William L. Cazneau, James Power, Henry L. Kinney,[qqv] and others in forming the Texas Western Railroad Company on February 16, 1852; the company laid no track. Britton incorporated the Western Artesian Well Company with Charles Stillman, Henry Redmond, Frederick Belden,[qqv] D. S. Howard, and H. Clay Davis on November 14, 1857. He was elected senator from the Nueces district in the Seventh (1857–58) and Eighth (1859–60) Texas legislatures, where as a moderate and a Unionist he supported Gov. Sam Houston.[qv] While serving in the legislature he was commissioned chief of staff to General Houston, on February 25, 1860, with the rank of brigadier general.

Britton married Rebecca Millard of Washington, D.C., on March 13, 1836, and they had two sons and two daughters; their daughter Elizabeth married Edmund J. Davis.[qv] Britton died in Austin on February 14, 1861, while attending a special session of the legislature, and was buried in the State Cemetery,[qv] the third person to be interred there.

BIBLIOGRAPHY: Corpus Christi *Ranchero*, February 25, 1860, February 23, April 6, 1861. Francis B. Heitman, *Historical Register and Dictionary of the United States Army* (2 vols., Washington: GPO, 1903; rpt., Urbana: University of Illinois Press, 1965). Amelia W. Williams and Eugene C. Barker, eds., *The Writings of Sam Houston, 1813–1863* (8 vols., Austin: University of Texas Press, 1938–43; rpt., Austin and New York: Pemberton Press, 1970).

Frank Wagner

BRITTON, FRANK L. (?–?). Frank L. Britton, attorney and adjutant general of Texas under Edmund J. Davis[qv] from November 15, 1872, to January 15, 1874, also served as Davis's private secretary. He was probably a nephew of Davis's wife, Anne Britton Davis. At one time he served as city attorney of Austin. A Texas legal directory listed him as a member of the Davis and Britton law firm in Austin in 1876–77. On August 9, 1877, he was accused of shooting United States marshal Thomas F. Purnell in Austin. Britton was jailed but released without bail by August 20. Conflicting testimony in court as to whether both men pulled guns made a case for self-defense.

BIBLIOGRAPHY: Austin *Daily Democratic Statesman*, August 10, 20, 1877. H. L. Bentley and Thomas Pilgrim, *Texas Legal Directory for 1876–77* (Austin: Democratic Statesman Office, 1877). Clarence P. Denman, "The Office of Adjutant General in Texas, 1835–1881," *Southwestern Historical Quarterly* 28 (April 1925).

BRITTON, TEXAS. Britton is on Farm Road 661 and the Texas Central Railroad in the northwest corner of Ellis County. It was called Hellandville when the post office was established in 1895. The name was changed to Britton in 1896. At one time the town had a bank, a school, a church, and several businesses, including an egg processing center and a grain elevator. Britton had five businesses and 300 citizens in 1925. In 1932 it had a population of 200 and seven businesses. The school closed, and the district and the mail route were divided between Mansfield and Midlothian. In 1980 and 1990 only thirty people lived in Britton. In 1990 the area produced grain crops such as maize and corn. Britton Methodist Church remained the focal point of the community. Britton Grocery Store and Farmers Supply still operated in the town. Joe Pool Lake is near Britton between Grand Prairie and Cedar Hill.

BIBLIOGRAPHY: Edna Davis Hawkins, et al., *History of Ellis County, Texas* (Waco: Texian, 1972).

Jeffrey Pilchiek

BROADDUS, TEXAS. Broaddus is at the intersection of Farm roads 1277 and 83 and State Highway 147, seventeen miles southwest of San Augustine in southwestern San Augustine County. It was founded around 1904 as a station on the St. Louis Southwestern Railway and that year was granted a post office with the name Broaddus. The town prospered on its shipments of lumber and by 1914 had five general stores, a drugstore, and the Lufkin Land and Lumber Company. By 1925 the population of Broaddus was estimated at 400. Rail service to the community was discontinued in the 1930s, and in 1940 Broaddus had ten businesses, two churches, and a school. Its population fell to 300 by 1950 and to 231 by 1960, then fluctuated between 180 and 240 through the 1980s. It reported a population of 212 in 1990. For most of the twentieth century it has been the second most populous town in San Augustine County.

Mark Odintz

BROADMOOR, TEXAS. Broadmoor was sixteen miles northwest of Brady in western McCulloch County. A post office operated there from 1907 to 1921. The Harris or Broadmoor school opened in 1908.

In 1914 Broadmoor had two general stores, a cotton gin, and 100 residents. Its school was moved to Lohn in the early 1930s. There was no evidence of the community shown on the 1948 county highway map.

BIBLIOGRAPHY: Jessie Laurie Barfoot, History of McCulloch County, Texas (M.A. thesis, University of Texas, 1937).

Vivian Elizabeth Smyrl

BROADVIEW, TEXAS. Broadview is on U.S. Highway 84 and the Atchison, Topeka and Santa Fe Railway, within a mile of the northwestern city limit of Lubbock in Lubbock County. A small settlement grew up around a Santa Fe switch, named Broadview by railroad company officials, when the line built through the area in 1913. The rural school of North West Ward existed for a time near the switch and also served as a church for various denominations. A man named Watson established the Broadview gin in 1932. Although businesses and expanding developments have all but enveloped the area, the Broadview gin and railroad switch operated into the mid-1980s. In 1978 the Broadview Baptist Church was established on Farm Road 2528, about two miles southwest of the rail switch. Church membership in the mid-1980s was some 400. *Charles G. Davis*

BROADWAY, TEXAS (Crosby County). Broadway is near the junction of U.S. Highway 82 with Farm Road 836, in eastern Crosby County forty-five miles east of Lubbock. The name of the community, which refers to the breadth of the prairie, was suggested by "Uncle" Shorty Reynolds, who built the first general store in the area about 1924. Ira Benton delivered mail to the gin that R. A. Crausbay built at the crossroads about 1926. Though by the mid-1980s the gin and store were closed, the buildings were still standing.

BIBLIOGRAPHY: Crosby County Pioneer Memorial Museum, *A History of Crosby County, 1876–1977* (Dallas: Taylor, 1978).

Edloe A. Jenkins

BROADWAY, TEXAS (Lamar County). Broadway is on Farm Road 1184 seven miles south of Paris between Robertson and Auds creeks in south central Lamar County. The settlement was founded in 1885, when F. E. Hutchins (sometimes Hutchings) opened a general store there. A post office opened at the community in 1890, and Hutchins suggested the name Broadway because of the townsite's prairie location. In 1892 the community had the general store, a cotton gin, and a blacksmith shop. Its population was reported as 127 from 1904 through the mid-1940s. In 1931 the community reported four businesses. The 1936 county highway map also identified a school at the site. After World War II[qv] and with the decline in farm prices, many residents began to leave the vicinity in search of jobs in the cities. The local school closed, and in 1957 area students were attending classes within the Delmar Independent School District. By 1970 the population of Broadway had decreased to twenty-five. A few scattered dwellings still marked the townsite on a 1983 map of the area. In 1990 the community's population was still reported as twenty-five.

Vista K. McCroskey

BROADWAY JUNCTION, TEXAS. Broadway Junction is at the intersection of Farm Road 1184 and State Highway 24, seven miles south of Paris in south central Lamar County. The settlement developed in the twentieth century with the road systems in the area and was probably named for its proximity to the community of Broadway. The 1936 county highway map shows it as an unidentified cluster of dwellings with two businesses. In 1983 Broadway Junction had a school, a cemetery, and three businesses. *Vista K. McCroskey*

BROCK, TEXAS. Brock is on Farm Road 1543 eleven miles southwest of Weatherford in southwestern Parker County. In 1876 James M. Maddux moved from Arkansas and settled in the area. By the mid-1880s a cotton gin and gristmill had been built there, and postal service began for the community in 1888. In the early 1890s the town added a flour mill and the Olive Branch Collegiate Institute. By 1900 Brock had an estimated 100 residents. Its post office was discontinued in 1919. Its population was reported as more than 100 until the 1940s, when it was ninety-five; it later dropped to twenty-five. In 1980 and 1990 Brock reported fifty-one residents.

BIBLIOGRAPHY: Gustavus Adolphus Holland, *History of Parker County and the Double Log Cabin* (Weatherford, Texas: Herald, 1931; rpt. 1937).

David Minor

BRODBECK, JACOB FRIEDRICH (1821–1910). Jacob Friedrich Brodbeck, pioneer school supervisor and sometimes considered the first man to fly in an airplane, was born in the duchy of Württemberg on October 13, 1821. He attended a seminary in Esslingen and taught school for six years in Württemberg before sailing for Texas with his brother George on August 25, 1846. He reached Fredericksburg in March 1847, became the second teacher at the Vereins Kirche,[qv] where he replaced Johann Leyendecker, and later taught at the Grape Creek school and other Gillespie County schools. He became a United States citizen in 1852, and in 1858 he married Maria Christine Sophie Behrens, a former student at Grape Creek; they eventually had twelve children.

Brodbeck served as Gillespie county surveyor and district school supervisor in 1862 and was a county commissioner from 1876 to 1878. He is best remembered, however, for his attempts at powered flight almost forty years before the famous success of Orville and Wilbur Wright. Brodbeck had always had an interest in mechanics and inventing; in Germany he had attempted to build a self-winding clock, and in 1869 he designed an ice-making machine. His most cherished project, however, was his "air-ship," which he worked on for twenty years. In 1863 he built a small model with a rudder, wings, and a propeller powered by coiled springs. That year he also moved to San Antonio, where he became a school inspector. Encouraged by the success of his model at various local fairs, Brodbeck set about raising funds to build a full-sized version of his craft that would be capable of carrying a man. He persuaded a number of local men, including Dr. Ferdinand Herff[qv] of San Antonio, H. Guenther of New Braunfels and A. W. Engel of Cranes Mill, to buy shares in his project, promising to repay them within six months of selling the patent rights to his machine.

There are conflicting accounts of what happened next. One says that Brodbeck made his first flight in a field about three miles east of Luckenbach on September 20, 1865. His airship, which featured an enclosed space for the "aeronaut," a water propeller in case of accidental landings on water, a compass, and a barometer, and for which Brodbeck had predicted speeds between 30 and 100 miles per hour, was said to have risen twelve feet in the air and traveled about 100 feet before the springs unwound completely and the machine crashed to the ground. Another account, however, says that the initial flight took place in San Pedro Park, San Antonio, where a bust of Brodbeck was later placed. Yet another account reports that the flight took place in 1868, not 1865. All the accounts agree, however, that Brodbeck's airship was destroyed by its abrupt landing, although the inventor escaped serious injury.

After this setback, his investors refused to put up the money for a second attempt, so he embarked on a fund-raising tour of the United States. His papers were stolen in Michigan, however, and he failed to persuade his audiences to invest in his scheme. Brodbeck returned to Texas and lived on a ranch near Luckenbach until his death, on January 8, 1910, six years after the Wright brothers' first flight at Kitty Hawk. No drawings or blueprints of Brodbeck's craft have survived, and his aviation achievements remain shrouded in doubt. He was buried on his farm near Luckenbach.

BIBLIOGRAPHY: Roger Bilstein and Jay Miller, *Aviation in Texas*

(Austin: Texas Monthly Press, 1985). Anne Marie Lindig, "Gillespie County's Bird-Man," *Junior Historian*, March 1949.

Martin Donell Kohout

BROGADO, TEXAS. Brogado is on Sandia Creek and U.S. Highway 290 a mile northeast of Balmorhea in southwestern Reeves County. It was founded before 1880 by Mexican farmers who were drawn to the area by the abundant springwater. A Brogado post office operated in an adobe[qv] building from 1894 until 1918. A public school with twenty-four students and one teacher was in session in 1897. The settlement was named for a visiting priest, Father Brogado, who was revered by the people of the parish. In the 1990s Brogado remained a farming community with a store. At the heart of the settlement stood its old Catholic church and cemetery. Brogado reported a population of 122 in 1990.

BIBLIOGRAPHY: Alton Hughes, *Pecos: A History of the Pioneer West* (Seagraves, Texas: Pioneer, 1978). Pecos County Historical Commission, *Pecos County History* (2 vols., Canyon, Texas: Staked Plains, 1984).

Julia Cauble Smith

BRONCO, TEXAS. Bronco is on U.S. Highway 380 and the New Mexico border, seventy miles southwest of Lubbock in western Yoakum County. Just two miles west of the town lies old Pueblo Springs, a watering place for Indians before Europeans came to the plains. Sulphur Draw, the headwaters of the Colorado River, originates near Bronco. In 1903 a cowpuncher, H. (Gravy) Fields, started a store at the site of the town. He succeeded in procuring a post office, but because the postal authorities rejected his first choice of a name the town remained nameless until some months later, when a traveling salesman suggested Bronco after seeing a local cowboy ride a bucking horse. K. T. Manning served as the first postmaster. By 1912 Bronco had a population of twenty-five and a store that served surrounding ranches. In 1915 L. W. Walker had established a flour mill there. A cotton gin was built at the town in 1947. Bronco's growth, like that of other Yoakum County towns, was hindered by the lack of a railroad. The reported population peaked in 1961 at an estimated 180, then by the mid-1960s fell to thirty, where it remained in 1990.

BIBLIOGRAPHY: Frank P. Hill, "Plains Names," *Panhandle–Plains Historical Review* 10 (1937). Texas Industrial Commission, *General Community Profile on Plains* (Austin, 1976). Texas State Highway Department, *A Guide to the South Plains of Texas* (Lubbock, 1935).

Leoti A. Bennett

BRONSON, TEXAS. Bronson is at the junction of State Highway 184 and U.S. Highway 96, nine miles west of Hemphill in western Sabine County. It is served by the Atchison, Topeka and Santa Fe Railway. As early as 1895 settler and developer John H. Kirby[qv] came to the area and bought large tracts of land, most of which was covered with virgin pine timber. Bronson, named for Samuel Bronson Cooper,[qv] was laid out on 200 acres on the course of the Gulf, Beaumont and Great Northern Railway, which was being built through the county in the spring of 1902. Merchants moved in, bought lots and land, and began construction with imported lumber. In 1902 Kirby built the Kirby Lumber Company. That year the Bronson *Bulletin*, a weekly newspaper, began publication under the direction of William A. Fields, and a post office opened with Nathan Pratt as postmaster. A number of businesses operated in Bronson, including Hamilton-Pratt Mercantile, Dean Mercantile, and Toole Mercantile, a boardinghouse for railroad and sawmill workers, and a restaurant. A Masonic lodge was established in 1904, and an independent school district was formed in 1905. By 1910 the town had a population of 1,000.

Throughout the early part of the twentieth century Bronson continued to grow. Baptist and Methodist churches were established. Bronson State Bank opened in 1907. By 1916 the Lufkin, Hemphill and Gulf Railway had constructed a line from Bronson to Hemphill, and the community served as a major shipping point. A second bank opened in 1919; the two banks were consolidated in 1921. Major highway construction began in the area during the 1920s, when the town's population peaked at 1,200. During the 1930s the population declined due to economic hardships and a diminishing timber supply. The bank closed in 1931. By 1941 the population was an estimated 800; it decreased to 300 by 1949. In 1962 the Bronson Independent School District was consolidated with the Pineland district. During the next two decades the population fluctuated between 500 and 600, but by the 1980s it was an estimated 254. In 1992 Bronson had a population of 259.

BIBLIOGRAPHY: Robert Cecil McDaniel, *Sabine County, Texas* (Waco: Texian, 1987).

Essie Walton Martin

BRONTE, TEXAS. Bronte, on U.S. Highway 277 at its junction with State Highway 158 in east central Coke County, was founded in the late 1880s and named for the English novelist Charlotte Brontë. J. B. McCutchen drove a herd of cattle into the area from Santa Anna in 1889, and other settlers followed, including Dr. W. F. Kay, who started the town. Lumber was hauled from Ballinger for the community's early buildings. Oso and Bronco were the town's original names, but the post office rejected Bronco to avoid confusion with another town. Bronte had a post office by 1890, when it also had two churches and a school. Its population was 213 in 1900. The Kansas City, Mexico and Orient Railway was completed through the area in 1907, and around this time Bronte was moved a mile to be near the track so it could become a shipping point on the railroad. The first train, however, reportedly did not run until 1909. In 1910 the town had a population of 635 and a number of businesses, including two cotton gins, a bank, and a newspaper (the *Enterprise*, established in 1906). When Kickapoo Creek flooded in 1953, it led to the founding in 1959, with federal support, of the Kickapoo Coke County Water Control and Improvement District. Bronte's population was reported as 999 in 1960, some 925 in 1970, 983 in 1980, and 962 in 1990. Local tourist attractions include Old Fort Chadbourne on Oak Creek nearby. Recreation areas in the vicinity include Oak Creek and Lake Spence, a 14,950-acre site for water sports.

BIBLIOGRAPHY: Jewell G. Pritchett, *From the Top of Old Hayrick: A Narrative History of Coke County* (Abilene, Texas: Pritchett, 1980). Kathleen E. and Clifton R. St. Clair, eds., *Little Towns of Texas* (Jacksonville, Texas: Jayroe Graphic Arts, 1982). Fred Tarpley, *1001 Texas Place Names* (Austin: University of Texas Press, 1980).

William R. Hunt

BRONTÉ CLUB. Viola Case, a pioneer schoolteacher in Victoria, organized the Bronté Club, the oldest women's literary club in Texas, in 1855. The organization, originally named the Victoria Literary Club, was a literary society for the girls of her school, the Victoria Female Academy.[qv] The members collected eleven volumes of current literature, which were kept in a dry goods box under Mrs. Case's bed. On a certain day of each week the books were taken out and distributed to the girls. This embryonic lending library was the beginning of the Bronté Library, the predecessor of the Victoria Public Library. Until 1975, when it was placed under the management of the city and county of Victoria, the library was governed by the Library Committee of the Bronté Club.

During the 1860s the Bronté Club is said to have devoted more time to war relief than to literary study. The club was probably generally dormant until 1868, when the Sorosis Club was organized in New York City in protest against the all-male Press Club of New York City, which gave a banquet for the visiting Charles Dickens and invited no women. This event seems to have stirred up women's club spirit across the country. Though started as a school society, the Bronté Club was reorganized as a community club in 1873, became a school society again in 1878, and in 1880 was changed to a community club again. In 1880, because the literary club needed new members and wanted a more distinctive name, it accepted for the first time older girls and young married women and changed its name to Brontë Literary Club, in honor of Charlotte Brontë.

When the national movement for federation of women's clubs began, the Brontë Club sent a delegate, Mrs. A. B. Peticolas, wife of Alfred Brown Peticolas,[qv] to the first meeting of the Texas Federation of Women's Clubs,[qv] held in Tyler in 1898. The club's calendar for that year shows it as a member of this state organization, which joined the national General Federation of Women's Clubs in 1899. On May 9, 1884, the Brontë Club had authorized the Junior Brontë Literary Club, a new group that was reorganized as the Currer Bell Study Club, named after the pseudonym of Charlotte Brontë, on May 1, 1951.

The Brontë Club dropped "literary" from its title in its *Year Book* of 1901–02, although it continued to emphasize literature in its programs. The *Year Book* of 1905–06 stated that the club's objectives were to promote the "mental and social culture of its members," an "altruistic spirit," and philanthropic endeavors, as well as "the interests of State and Fifth District Federation." Due to its broadened purposes, the club offered a wide variety of programs through the years about subjects ranging from civics to philosophy. Among the Brontë Club's civic projects was the sponsorship of a lecture by Eleanor Roosevelt in December 1940, which a crowd of 2,500 attended. Mrs. Roosevelt subsequently wrote in her column "My Day" about her visit to Victoria and "one of the oldest women's clubs in the country." The club continued to contribute both funds and books to its original civic work, the Victoria Public Library. It was made an honorary member of the library, and an appointed club member serves on the library's advisory board. The Brontë Club celebrated its centennial on April 3, 1973.

bibliography: Brontë Club Files, Victoria, Texas. Leopold Morris, *Pictorial History of Victoria and Victoria County* (San Antonio, 1953). Victoria *Advocate*, April 6, 8, 1923, December 5, 1940. Texas Federation of Women's Clubs *Year Book*, 1935.

Geraldine F. Talley

BROOCKS, JOHN HENRY (1829–1901). John Henry Broocks, Confederate Army officer, was born in Jackson, Tennessee, on October 12, 1829, the son of Elizabeth A. and Travis G. Broocks.[qv] In 1837 the family moved to San Augustine, Texas, where Broocks attended Wesleyan College and San Augustine University. He then worked in his father's mercantile business until the outbreak of the Mexican War,[qv] when he enlisted as a private in Capt. Otis M. Wheeler's Company A of Col. George T. Wood's[qv] Second Regiment of Texas Mounted Rifles. After returning from Mexico, Broocks engaged in the mercantile business until 1852, then moved to California to try his hand first at mining and farming and then at merchandising at Shaw's Flat. After succeeding in these efforts, he returned to San Augustine in July 1854 to marry Elizabeth J. Polk; the couple had eight children. In 1855 Broocks moved to his farm.

Soon after secession[qv] he raised a company of cavalry in San Augustine County that became Company C of Whitfield's Legion,[qv] or the Twenty-seventh Texas Cavalry. Broocks was elected major. As part of Gen. Ben McCulloch's[qv] Army of the West during the first year of the war, this regiment fought at Elkhorn Tavern, Arkansas. In Mississippi the following year it saw action at Iuka, Yazoo Pass, and Spring Hill. When Whitfield was promoted to brigadier general on March 9, 1863, Broocks became lieutenant colonel. Edwin R. Hawkins, the new regimental commander, was often ill, and Broocks frequently served in his place, so well that he won, according to one his troopers, "the love of his men and the confidence and respect of his superiors in rank."

Commanding Whitfield's Legion on March 5, 1863, Broocks distinguished himself in the defeat and capture of a strong Union reconnoitering expedition at Thompson's Station, Tennessee. In this engagement Broocks's brother, a captain of the legion, was killed in action. Broocks's command met with disaster in April 1864 near Spring Hill, Tennessee, when a cavalry detachment under Union general Gordon Granger[qv] surprised it in camp and captured more than a hundred men of the regiment as well as its horses, mules, wagons, and camp equipage. Broocks was among those who escaped capture, but, as Samuel Barron[qv] of Ross's Brigade[qv] wrote, "no officer in the army would have felt more mortification at such an occurrence than the brave, gallant John H. Broocks. It was said that he was so haunted by the sounds and scenes of the capture of his regiment that he was almost like one demented, and that for days and days afterwards he would sit away off alone on some log, with his head down, muttering, 'Halt! you d----d rebel, halt!'"

After the war Broocks retired to his San Augustine County farm. Although he was repeatedly called upon to run for the state Senate, he declined to do so; he did serve as chairman of the Democratic Congressional District Committee. He died on April 16, 1901.

bibliography: Samuel Barron, *The Lone Star Defenders: A Chronicle of the Third Texas Cavalry, Ross' Brigade* (New York: Neale, 1908; rpt., Waco: Morrison, 1964). Victor Marion Rose, *Ross' Texas Brigade* (Louisville, Kentucky: *Courier-Journal*, 1881; rpt., Kennesaw, Georgia: Continental, 1960). A. W. Sparks, *The War between the States* (Tyler, Texas: Lee and Burnett, 1901; rpt., Longview, Texas: D&D, 1987).

Thomas W. Cutrer

BROOCKS, LYCURGUS WATTERS (1840–1873). Lycurgus Watters Broocks, soldier and editor, was born in San Augustine, Texas, in 1840, the son of Elizabeth Ann (Morris) and Travis Gustavus Broocks.[qv] He was associated with his father and brothers in the mercantile business. During the Civil War[qv] he enlisted in the Confederate Army when he was twenty-one and served as a private in Capt. Daniel McDowell Short's[qv] Company, South Kansas–Texas Regiment, Mounted Volunteers. On May 2, 1863, he was appointed second lieutenant and ordnance officer in the Department of Mississippi and Louisiana. Broocks was a planter and had extensive landholdings. He was also an editor of the *South East Texan*, published in San Augustine. In 1866 he married Emma Alston Border, and the couple had two daughters. Broocks died in 1873 and was buried in the Broocks family cemetery five miles east of San Augustine.

bibliography: *The War of the Rebellion: A Compilation of the Official Records of the Union and Confederate Armies.*

Kate Harding Bates Parker and C. Elisabeth Bates Nisbet

BROOCKS, MOSES LYCURGUS (1864–1908). Moses Lycurgus Broocks, son of Col. John Henry and Elizabeth Jerome (Polk) Broocks, was born near San Augustine, Texas, on November 1, 1864. He graduated from the law department of the University of Texas in 1891 and began law practice in San Augustine. He was elected to the House of Representatives of the Twenty-third Texas Legislature in 1892. After moving to Beaumont, he was elected district attorney of the First Judicial District in 1896 but served only one term before his election to the Fifty-ninth Congress in 1905. After one session in Congress he resumed practice in San Augustine. Broocks died in San Antonio on May 27, 1908, and was buried in the Broocks Cemetery, four miles east of San Augustine.

bibliography: *Biographical Directory of the American Congress.*

BROOCKS, TRAVIS GREENE (1808–1864). Travis Greene Broocks, early San Augustine civic leader, son of Bibulous and Isabel (Ashworth) Broocks, was born in Charlotte County, Virginia, on August 20, 1808. He was reared in Bedford County, Tennessee, where he married Elisabeth Ann Morris on July 7, 1827. To this union six children were born. In 1838 the family moved to San Augustine, Texas, where Broocks established a mercantile business, first in partnership with Bernard Reilly and later with his sons. During the Córdova Rebellion in 1838, Broocks was captain of the San Augustine Volunteer

Militia; his first lieutenant was James Howard Hopkins. Broocks was elected justice of the peace in 1840 and served as postmaster of San Augustine from 1842 to 1846. In 1844 President Sam Houston[qv] ordered Broocks to Shelby County with 600 men to assist in putting down the Regulator-Moderator War.[qv] His men arrested Charles Watson (Watt) Moorman[qv] and quelled the troubles, while Broocks won the title "General." In 1846 he constructed the first brick building in San Augustine. He became a member of the Redland Masonic Lodge No. 3, of which he was senior warden in 1847, worshipful master in 1849, and treasurer in 1855. Broocks died at his home about four miles east of San Augustine in January 1864 and was buried in the nearby Broocks family cemetery.

bibliography: George L. Crocket, *Two Centuries in East Texas* (Dallas: Southwest, 1932; facsimile reprod. 1962). Daughters of the Republic of Texas, *Founders and Patriots of the Republic of Texas* (Austin, 1963–). James M. Day, comp., *Post Office Papers of the Republic of Texas* (2 vols., Austin: Texas State Library, 1966–67). McXie Whitton Martin, *1850 Citizens of San Augustine County, Texas* (1984). Mrs. Harry Joseph Morris, comp. and ed., *Citizens of the Republic of Texas* (Dallas: Texas State Genealogical Society, 1977). Amelia W. Williams and Eugene C. Barker, eds., *The Writings of Sam Houston, 1813–1863* (8 vols., Austin: University of Texas Press, 1938–43; rpt., Austin and New York: Pemberton Press, 1970).

McXie Whitton Martin

BROOKE, GEORGE MERCER (?–1851). George Mercer Brooke, United States Army officer, was born in Virginia and was commissioned first lieutenant in the Fifth United States Infantry on May 3, 1808. He was promoted to captain on May 1, 1810, and to major of the Twenty-third Infantry on May 1, 1814. On August 15, 1814, he was brevetted lieutenant colonel for his gallant defense of Fort Erie, Upper Canada; on September 17, 1814, he was brevetted colonel for "distinguished and meritorious service" in leading an attack on the British siege lines. On May 17, 1815, he was transferred to the Fourth Infantry and on January 27, 1819, to the Eighth. He was promoted to the substantive grade of lieutenant colonel on March 1, 1819, and transferred back to the Fourth on August 13 of the same year. He was brevetted brigadier general on September 17, 1824, for "ten years' faithful service in one grade," and was promoted to colonel commanding the Fifth Infantry on July 15, 1831. On August 1, 1844, he was appointed to the command of Military Department Number Four with responsibility for the states of Ohio, Indiana, Michigan, Wisconsin, Illinois, Iowa, and Missouri. And on June 10, 1846, he was appointed commander of the Western Division of the United States Army—the territory of the United States west of the Mississippi River—which he took over from Gen. Edmund P. Gaines,[qv] who had overstepped his authority by calling up thousands of militiamen for the Mexican War[qv] that the government could not use. Brooke, from his headquarters in New Orleans, was responsible for forwarding reinforcements and supplies to the field armies of generals Zachary Taylor[qv] and Winfield Scott in Mexico. Except for a time in November 1847 when he presided at the court-martial of Lt. Col. John Charles Frémont, Brooke continued in this capacity until July 1, 1848, when he was superseded by General Taylor. Thereafter Brooke briefly commanded Military Department Number One, which comprised Alabama, Mississippi, Louisiana, Tennessee, Kentucky, and Florida. On May 30, 1848, he was brevetted to major general for his service in the Mexican War, and on July 7, 1849, he was appointed to the command of Military Department Number Eight—roughly the eastern two-thirds of Texas—and served at that post until his death, on March 9, 1851.

bibliography: K. Jack Bauer, *The Mexican War, 1846–1848* (New York: Macmillan, 1974). Francis B. Heitman, *Historical Register and Dictionary of the United States Army* (2 vols., Washington: GPO, 1903; rpt., Urbana: University of Illinois Press, 1965). Raphael P. Thian, comp., *Notes Illustrating the Military Geography of the United States, 1813–1880* (Washington: GPO, 1881; rpt., with addenda ed. John M. Carroll, Austin: University of Texas Press, 1979).

Thomas W. Cutrer

BROOKE, ROGER (1878–1940). Roger Brooke, military physician, was born at Sandy Springs, Maryland, on June 14, 1878, the son of Roger and Louisa (Thomas) Brooke. He graduated from the University of Maryland medical school in 1900 and entered the Medical Corps of the United States Army on June 29, 1901. He was married in 1905 to Grace M. Macomb. He became a specialist in infectious diseases, especially tuberculosis. His early tours of duty included the Philippine Islands, Fort Bayard, New Mexico, and Fort Leavenworth, Kansas. During World War I[qv] Brooke was senior instructor and later commanding officer of the Medical Officers' Training Camp, Camp Greenleaf, Georgia. For this service he was awarded the Distinguished Service Medal. Later tours of duty included the office of the surgeon general, Washington; the division of medicine of the Veterans Bureau, Gorgas Hospital, Canal Zone; and Fort Sam Houston, Texas, where he was chief of the medical service and from 1928 to 1933 commanding officer of the station hospital. In 1935 Brooke was ordered to Washington in charge of the Professional Service Division. His next tour was at Letterman General Hospital, San Francisco, where he was in command when he received his promotion to brigadier general. He was transferred to the Medical Field Service School, Carlisle Barracks, Pennsylvania, where he remained on duty as commandant until his death. Brooke was a fellow of the American College of Surgeons and of the American College of Physicians and a member of the American Medical Association, the American Society of Tropical Medicine, the National Tuberculosis Association, and the Association of Military Surgeons. Station Hospital, Fort Sam Houston, was designated Brooke General Hospital on September 4, 1942, in recognition of the outstanding manner in which Roger Brooke identified himself with community interests while in command of the hospital. In 1946 the unit was expanded to become Brooke Army Medical Center.[qv] General Brooke died on December 18, 1940.

bibliography: Eldon Cagle, Jr., *Quadrangle: The History of Fort Sam Houston* (Austin: Eakin Press, 1985). *Military Surgeon*, February 1941.

BROOKE ARMY MEDICAL CENTER. Brooke Army Medical Center, at Fort Sam Houston in San Antonio, one of the health facilities under the United States Army Health Services Command, provides primary, secondary, and tertiary health care to its eligible population in a 450-bed facility, which also includes clinics in most medical specialties and subspecialties. Activities at Brooke cover almost every aspect of health care, postgraduate medical education, medical training, and medical research. Located within Brooke is the Army Burn Center, operated by the United States Army Institute of Surgical Research.

In 1870, when the Post of San Antonio was established on the Texas frontier, Brooke began as a small medical dispensary in a log cabin. Two temporary buildings served as the post hospital until 1886, when the first permanent hospital was built on what is now Staff Post Road. That structure still stands and is used as quarters for visiting dignitaries. In 1903 the army decided to enlarge the hospital and in 1907 completed a new hospital with eighty-four beds. During the next decade an additional 1,000 beds were added in fifty temporary wooden ward structures, but after World War I[qv] these buildings fell into disuse.

During ensuing years Brooke was called the post hospital and was housed in a variety of buildings, all of which led up to the construction in 1936–37 and grand opening in 1938 of the main hospital. The facility was named Brooke General Hospital in 1942 in honor of one of its previous commanders, Brig. Gen. Roger Brooke.[qv] Other units were added as the years progressed. Beach Pavilion was used primarily for convalescent purposes during and after World War II,[qv] and

Chambers Pavilion was added as a psychiatric facility. Brooke has been a medical center since 1946 and at one time was responsible for all of the medical training in the army. In 1990 Brooke was one of the top medical centers in the nation for treatment, teaching, and research. Construction of a new Brooke Army Medical Center began in 1987. As part of its mission Brooke supports the Army Burn Center, the Fort Sam Houston Dental Activity, and the Area Dental Laboratory, all three also located at Fort Sam Houston.

BIBLIOGRAPHY: Corpus Christi *Caller*, September 12, 1976. San Antonio *Express*, May 15, 1977. San Antonio *Express News*, October 10, 1965. San Antonio *Light*, November 2, 1945. Vertical Files, Barker Texas History Center, University of Texas at Austin (Fort Sam Houston, San Antonio Hospitals). *Ray Dery*

BROOKEEN CREEK. Brookeen Creek rises a mile north of Abbott in south central Hill County (at 31°54′ N, 97°03′ W) and runs southeast for ten miles to its mouth on Tehuacana Creek, twelve miles northwest of Hubbard (at 31°47′ N, 96°58′ W). It crosses generally flat to rolling terrain surfaced by dark, commonly calcareous clays that support mesquite and cacti. The area has served as crop and range land.

BROOKELAND, TEXAS. Brookeland is on U.S. Highway 96 thirteen miles south of Bronson in southwestern Sabine County. The town was named for John C. Brooke, who served as first postmaster when the community received a post office in 1866. The population of Brookeland was estimated at 300 in 1884, when it had a steam cotton gin, two general stores, and a lumber and grist mill powered by water from Mill Creek. By 1896 the community's population had fallen to an estimated 150 residents. In 1902 the Gulf, Beaumont and Great Northern Railway was constructed through the county and passed about a mile from Brookeland. A new town, to be named Weed after a railroad official, was laid out by the tracks. Although the Weed townsite was used, its name was not, and gradually the site on the tracks became known as Brookeland. In 1914 Brookeland's population was estimated at 800. By the 1920s businesses in the town included a bank, a hotel, and a Ford automobile agency. Brookeland was hard hit by the Great Depression.[qv] Its bank failed in 1933, and its population began to decline. By 1970 the population had fallen to an estimated 189, though in that decade the town began to grow again, largely because of its proximity to Sam Rayburn Reservoir,[qv] which attracted 2.6 million visitors in 1980. Although the *Texas Almanac*[qv] consistently reported Brookeland's population as 220 from 1974 through 1990, by the mid-1980s local sources indicated that the population of the community was growing, and by 1986 it had probably exceeded 300.

BIBLIOGRAPHY: Robert Cecil McDaniel, *Sabine County, Texas* (Waco: Texian, 1987). *Cecil Harper, Jr.*

BROOKESMITH, TEXAS. Brookesmith, between Clear Creek and Spring Branch in southwestern Brown County, was named by David Smith in 1902, in honor of Brownwood banker Brooke Smith. A post office was established at Brookesmith in 1903. The community's early settlers included David Smith and Brooke and Aaron Lee. The town had three cotton gins and several other businesses until cotton farming declined in the 1950s. In the 1980s Brookesmith had the post office, a store, a gas station, and a twelve-grade school. In 1980 and 1990 the community reported a population of sixty-one.

BIBLIOGRAPHY: Kathleen E. and Clifton R. St. Clair, eds., *Little Towns of Texas* (Jacksonville, Texas: Jayroe Graphic Arts, 1982).
William R. Hunt

BROOKHAVEN, TEXAS. Brookhaven was on Oak Branch twelve miles northwest of Belton in northwestern Bell County. Before 1882 the community was loosely known as Post Oak Branch and was the site of numerous revivals and camp meetings. In the summer of 1882, when a local school was constructed, the community's name was changed to Brookhaven at the suggestion of Charlie and Ed Oswalt, who named it for the town in Mississippi where they had previously lived. A post office served Brookhaven from 1884 to 1913. In 1896 Brookhaven had a population of seventy-five and a Masonic hall, a district school, a cotton gin, two general stores, two drugstores, and three churches (Baptist, Methodist, and Presbyterian). The Brookhaven school enrolled 132 pupils in 1903. The community's population had dropped to fifty by the mid-1940s, when the town had two businesses. By 1949 the Fort Hood military reservation had subsumed the site of Brookhaven, and the community was not listed in that year's *Texas Almanac*.[qv]

BIBLIOGRAPHY: Bell County Historical Commission, *Story of Bell County, Texas* (2 vols., Austin: Eakin Press, 1988). *Mark Odintz*

BROOKLYN, TEXAS. Brooklyn was sixteen miles northeast of Center in northeastern Shelby County. A post office was established in the community in 1872, with Wiett S. Childress as postmaster; the office was discontinued in 1883, and local mail was sent to Tomday. The community had a one-room school in 1903.

Cecil Harper, Jr.

BROOKS, BLUFORD (?–?). Bluford (Beauford?) Brooks, one of Stephen F. Austin's[qv] Old Three Hundred[qv] colonists, received title to a sitio[qv] of land on August 10, 1824. On December 15, 1830, the ayuntamiento[qv] of San Felipe de Austin declared that Brooks had abandoned the country in 1825 and that his land, which lay west of the Brazos River near the Old San Antonio Road,[qv] was vacant and the title void. A Beauford Brooks was justice of the peace at Washington-on-the-Brazos in 1856, and another of the same, born in South Carolina about 1797, was living in Jasper County in 1850.

BIBLIOGRAPHY: Eugene C. Barker, ed., *The Austin Papers* (3 vols., Washington: GPO, 1924–28). Eugene C. Barker, ed., "Minutes of the Ayuntamiento of San Felipe de Austin, 1828–1832," 12 parts, *Southwestern Historical Quarterly* 21–24 (January 1918–October 1920). Lester G. Bugbee, "The Old Three Hundred: A List of Settlers in Austin's First Colony," *Quarterly of the Texas State Historical Association* 1 (October 1897). Worth Stickley Ray, *Austin Colony Pioneers* (Austin: Jenkins, 1949; 2d ed., Austin: Pemberton, 1970).

BROOKS, CARRIE JANE SUTTON (1903–1964). Carrie Jane Sutton Brooks, black physician, was born in San Antonio, Texas, in 1903. She graduated from Riverside High School as valedictorian, after which she entered Howard University. There she was president of the Alpha chapter of Delta Sigma Theta sorority for one term and received her medical degree in the 1920s. She was among the first black interns at Freedman's Hospital in Washington, D.C. Dr. Brooks practiced medicine for a few years in San Antonio, specializing in women and children, and helped establish the first YWCA branch for blacks there. She married a physician, John Hunter Brooks, and they both practiced medicine in New Jersey until her health failed. She died in January 1964.

BIBLIOGRAPHY: San Antonio *Register*, January 17, 1964.
Ruthe Winegarten

BROOKS, JAMES (1906–1992). James Brooks, muralist and abstract painter, was born on October 18, 1906, in St. Louis, Missouri, one of four children of William Rodolphus and Abigail F. (Williamson) Brooks. His father was a traveling salesman, and the Brooks family moved frequently until 1916, when they settled in Dallas. Following his graduation from Oak Cliff High School in 1922 Brooks studied art at Southern Methodist University for two years. He then studied with James A. Waddell at the Dallas Art Institute[qv] and took private lessons with Martha Simkins.[qv] In 1926 he moved to New York City, where he worked as a commercial artist to fund his night classes with

Boardman Robinson and Kimon Nicolaides at the Art Students League.

Brooks began exhibiting paintings and prints in a social realist style in various group shows around New York in the early 1930s. He executed three murals for the WPA Federal Art Project between 1936 and 1942, during which time he met the painters Jackson Pollock and Philip Guston. His best-known mural, *Flight*, runs 235 feet around the rotunda of the Marine Air Terminal at La Guardia Airport in Queens. The mural was painted over without explanation in the 1950s, possibly because some saw left-wing symbolism in it, but following the protests of art historians and curators it was fully restored in 1980. Brooks enlisted in the United States Army in 1942 and served as an art correspondent in Egypt and the Near East. He spent the last few months of the war at the Office of Special Services in Washington, D.C.

Upon his return to New York in September 1945 he renewed his friendships with Guston, Pollock, and Bradley Walker Tomlin and began to solicit criticism from Wallace Harrison. Brooks developed an abstract style influenced by the synthetic Cubism of Pablo Picasso and Georges Braque. In the summer of 1948 he developed a more fluid abstract style after being inspired by the random shapes that occurred on the back of canvases to which he had glued paintings with black paste. He subsequently executed a series of stained and dripped canvases that were featured at his first solo exhibition the following year at the Peridot Gallery in New York City.

Many of Brooks's early works in the Abstract Expressionist style retained vestiges of the Cubist grid. He experimented with enamels, gouache, and thinned oils over various backgrounds such as crayon; his palette generally alternated between browns, grays, or blacks and more vivid colors. Later in his career Brooks introduced more assertive forms, but shied away from developing any dominant method or style, wishing to avoid "nausea with one's own pictorial clichés." In the late 1960s he switched from oils to acrylics, a change that prompted the use of a wider range of colors, broader strokes, and simpler compositions with larger color areas. He used numbers and letters to identify his paintings. He frequently added nonsense syllables to the letters as a mnemonic device, forming such titles as *Pask, Burwak,* and *Jondol.*

Although Brooks's service in the army excluded him from participation in ground-breaking exhibitions at Peggy Guggenheim's Art of This Century gallery, he has nevertheless been considered by critics to be a member of the first generation of Abstract Expressionists. He participated in many group exhibitions around the country, among the most important being the historic, artist-organized Ninth Street Exhibition (1951), which included the work of Pollock, Hans Hofmann, Franz Kline, Willem de Kooning, and Robert Motherwell, and two influential exhibitions organized by the Museum of Modern Art in New York City, Twelve Americans (1956) and New American Painting (1959). His work has been featured in many solo exhibitions; retrospectives of his work were organized by the Whitney Museum of American Art in New York (1963) and the Dallas Museum of Fine Arts (1972).

Throughout his career Brooks supplemented his income from painting with teaching posts at various institutions, including Columbia University, New York (1946–48); Pratt Institute, New York (1948–58); Yale University, New Haven, Connecticut (1955–60); New College, Sarasota, Florida (1965–67); Miami Art Center, Miami, Florida (1966); Queens College, Queens, New York (1966–69); Southampton College of Long Island University, Southampton, New York (1968); and the University of Pennsylvania, Philadelphia (1971–72). He was the artist-in-residence at the American Academy in Rome, Italy, in 1963. Brooks was awarded a Guggenheim Fellowship in 1969 and in 1973 was elected to membership in the National Institute of Arts and Letters.

James Brooks married Mary MacDonald in 1938 and in 1947 married Charlotte Park. He developed Alzheimer's disease in 1985 and died on Long Island on March 9, 1992. Examples of his work are at the Brooklyn Museum, the Detroit Institute of Art, the Solomon R. Guggenheim Museum and the Museum of Modern Art in New York, the Tate Gallery in London, the Whitney Museum of American Art in New York, the Museum of Fine Arts, Houston,[qv] the Art Institute of Chicago, the Boston Museum of Fine Arts, the Dallas Museum of Art,[qv] the Metropolitan Museum of Art, New York, Southern Methodist University, Dallas, and the Archer M. Huntington Art Gallery,[qv] Austin.

BIBLIOGRAPHY: Sam Hunter, *James Brooks* (exhibition catalog, New York: Frederick A. Praeger, 1963). *James Brooks: Paintings, 1952–1975; Works on Paper, 1950–1975* (exhibition catalog, New York: Martha Jackson Gallery, 1975). New York *Times*, March 12, 1992.

Kendall Curlee

BROOKS, JOHN ABIJAH (1855–1944). John Abijah Brooks, Texas Ranger captain, state legislator, and county judge of Brooks County, son of Dr. John and Mary Jane (Kerr) Brooks, was born in Bourbon County, Kentucky, on November 20, 1855. He is known in the annals of the Texas Rangers[qv] as one of the "Four Great Captains," the others being John R. Hughes, William J. McDonald, and John H. Rogers.[qqv] Brooks had a lean frame, angular features, a mustache, a soft voice, and kindly yet determined manners. He worked as a cowboy and miner after he moved to Collin County, Texas, about 1876. He joined the service as a private at the beginning of 1883 and rose through the ranks—corporal, sergeant, and lieutenant—to become captain in 1889 of Company F in the Frontier Battalion.[qv] Of the "Four Great Captains" Brooks and Rogers received the least publicity, but they were said to be "dependable, intelligent, and wise in the ways of criminals." As the head of a ranger company in the field, Brooks had to recruit and fire personnel, order supplies, assign men to cases, and report to his superiors in Austin. From East Texas to the Rio Grande, Brooks and the rangers under his command, including Anderson Yancey Baker[qv] and Winfred Bates, tried to combat violent crime and disorder, such as the Catarino Garza[qv] troubles and the Reese–Townsend feud at Columbus. One incident, the killing of ranch owner Ramón de la Cerda by Baker in 1902, led to hostilities between political factions and ranger supporters and opponents. Brooks was commended for keeping the various factions under control. In addition, he and his rangers took part in policing oil-boom towns and stopping prizefights in El Paso in 1896 and Galveston in 1901. In his early ranger career, Brooks became involved in shootouts with fence cutters (*see* FENCE-CUTTING) in Brown County and with the Conner gang in the piney woods of East Texas. In the latter gunbattle one ranger was killed and three wounded, including Brooks, who lost several fingers on his left hand. He resigned his commission as head of Company A in the ranger force on November 15, 1906. After leaving the rangers and moving to Falfurrias, Brooks remained a faithful public servant. He was a Democrat. He served in the House of Representatives in the Thirty-first and Thirty-second legislatures and was instrumental in establishing the new county named in his honor. He then became engrossed in his duties as county judge of Brooks County, being first elected on September 2, 1911, and serving until February 1939. He was preceded in death by his wife, Virginia (Wilburn), whom he married on September 16, 1890. They had two children. Brooks died on January 15, 1944, and was buried in Falfurrias.

BIBLIOGRAPHY: William Warren Sterling, *Trails and Trials of a Texas Ranger* (Norman: University of Oklahoma Press, 1968). Walter Prescott Webb Papers, Barker Texas History Center, University of Texas at Austin. Walter Prescott Webb, *The Texas Rangers* (Boston: Houghton Mifflin, 1935; rpt., Austin: University of Texas Press, 1982).

Harold J. Weiss, Jr.

BROOKS, JOHN SOWERS (1814–1836). John Sowers Brooks, soldier, son of Absalom H. Brooks, was born in Staunton, Virginia, on

January 31, 1814. He worked in the office of the Staunton *Spectator* and served in the United States Marine Corps eleven months before leaving New York for Texas on November 5, 1835, to volunteer for the Texas army. After arriving at Velasco on December 20, 1835, he became adjutant of the Georgia Battalion[qv] and accompanied that group under command of James W. Fannin, Jr.,[qv] to undertake the Matamoros expedition of 1835–36.[qv] In February 1836 Brooks resigned as adjutant and became aide to Fannin. He served as chief engineer and had charge of ammunition and artillery. His letters from Texas to his family in Virginia are valuable expressions of the sentiments of the volunteer soldiers and portray their activities and hardships. In those letters he gave Goliad the name "Fort Defiance." Brooks was wounded and captured at the battle of Coleto[qv] and died in the Goliad Massacre[qv] on March 27, 1836.

BIBLIOGRAPHY: John E. Roller, "Capt. John Sowers Brooks," *Quarterly of the Texas State Historical Association* 9 (January 1906).

BROOKS, MICAJAH MADISON (1856–1934). Micajah Madison Brooks, attorney and judge, was born near Macon, Mississippi, in 1856. After graduating from the University of Virginia law school, he moved to Texas in 1879 and settled first at Forney and later at Greenville. He practiced law at Greenville for nine years and was appointed associate justice of the Court of Criminal Appeals in 1889. He held the position until 1910; in the meantime he moved to Dallas in 1902 and ran unsuccessfully for governor in 1906. Brooks drew up the charter for Southern Methodist University, served as attorney for the school, and became the first president of its board of trustees. After he retired from the bench in 1910, he engaged in private practice in Dallas until 1921. He and his wife, the former Mattie Jenkins, were the parents of four children. Brooks died at his home in Dallas on January 10, 1934, and was buried in Greenville.

BIBLIOGRAPHY: Dallas *Morning News*, January 11, 1934. Vertical Files, Barker Texas History Center, University of Texas at Austin.

Claudia Hazlewood

BROOKS, SAMUEL PALMER (1863–1931). Samuel Palmer Brooks, university president, was born in Milledgeville, Georgia, on December 4, 1863, the son of Samuel Erskine and Aurelia Elizabeth (Palmer) Brooks. About 1868 he and his family moved to Johnson County, Texas. Brooks entered the high school department of Baylor University at the age of twenty-four and graduated with an A.B. degree in 1893. He received a second A.B. degree from Yale in 1894, returned to Texas to teach in the Baylor history department, and completed an M.A. degree at Yale in 1902. He married Mattie Sims of Cleburne on December 24, 1895; they had two children.

From 1902 to 1931 Brooks served as president of Baylor University. During his administration he added to the university the college of medicine, the college of dentistry, the school of nursing, the school of law, the school of commerce and business, and the theological department; the university's endowment grew by $2 million, and several new buildings were built, including the Carroll Library, Brooks and Waco halls, a women's dormitory, and a heating plant. Enrollment rose from 783 in 1902 to 3,039 in 1930.

Brooks organized the Texas Association of Colleges in 1916 and served as president of the college section of the Texas State Teachers' Association[qv] in 1901 and 1919. He was corresponding secretary of the Texas Baptist Education Commission in 1905, president of the Baptist General Convention of Texas from 1914 to 1917, and vice president of the Southern Baptist Convention in 1910 and 1917. He served as vice president of the Texas State Peace Society and organized the Texas State Peace Congress in 1907; he was president of that body from 1907 to 1915. He was appointed by President Woodrow Wilson to an international peace commission and served in 1915–16. Brooks received honorary degrees from Richmond College in 1903, Mercer University in 1922, Austin College in 1924, and Georgetown College (Kentucky) in 1929. He was a Mason, a trustee of the Southern Baptist Theological Seminary, and a member of the Southern Baptist Education Association. He died in Waco after a lengthy illness, on May 14, 1931, and was buried in Oakwood Cemetery.

BIBLIOGRAPHY: Dallas *Morning News*, May 15, 1931. *National Cyclopaedia of American Biography*, Vol. 51. James B. Renberg, Samuel Palmer Brooks: President of Baylor University, 1920–1931 (M.A. thesis, Baylor University, 1961). Vertical Files, Barker Texas History Center, University of Texas at Austin.

John B. Wilder

BROOKS, SAMUEL W. (1829–1903). Samuel W. Brooks, architect, engineer, and builder, was born in Pennsylvania in 1829. At the age of seven his family took him to Ohio. About 1850 he moved to New Orleans, where he established a lumber business in 1853 and worked as a builder and architect. Brooks left New Orleans in 1863 and moved to Matamoros, Tamaulipas, where he remained until 1878, when he moved across the Rio Grande to Brownsville. During the last quarter of the nineteenth century, he was the foremost architect, engineer, and builder in the Brownsville area. He served eight terms as city engineer of Brownsville, was superintending architect for the United States Courthouse, Custom House, and Post Office (1892, demolished), and built levees along the Rio Grande at Fort Brown in Brownsville and at Hidalgo. Brooks built the post hospital at Fort Brown (1869), a set of buildings at Fort Ringgold at Rio Grande City, the Church of the Advent in Brownsville (1877, demolished), and the first Cameron County Courthouse in Brownsville (1883). He was the architect of the superintendent's lodge at the National Cemetery at Fort Brown (demolished); the First Presbyterian Church, Brownsville (1870, demolished); the Melitonio H. Cross house, Matamoros (1885); the first Hidalgo County Courthouse, Hidalgo (1886); the Vivier Opera House, Brownsville (1891, demolished); the Louis Kowalski house, Brownsville (1893); the Josephine G. Browne house, Brownsville (1894); the Frank B. Armstrong[qv] house, Brownsville (1896, demolished); and the Starr County Courthouse, Rio Grande City. Brooks's own house survives in Brownsville, although it has been moved from its original location. Reflecting the cultural isolation of South Texas during the late nineteenth century, the buildings Brooks designed were stylistically conservative. He often adapted a simplified rendition of mid-nineteenth-century picturesque eclectic architectural detail to prevailing Creole typologies and construction techniques.

Brooks married twice. After the death of his first wife, he married a widow, Inez Falgot. He had two children by his first marriage, both of whom he outlived. Brooks was a parishioner of the Church of the Advent. He died in Brownsville on February 15, 1903.

BIBLIOGRAPHY: Betty Bay, *Historic Brownsville: Original Townsite Guide* (Brownsville, Texas: Brownsville Historical Association, 1980). W. H. Chatfield, *The Twin Cities of the Border and the Country of the Lower Rio Grande* (New Orleans: Brandao, 1893; rpt., Brownsville: Brownsville Historical Association, 1959).

Stephen Fox

BROOKS, VICTOR LEE (1870–1925). Victor Lee Brooks, attorney and judge, son of David and Beatrice (Houghton) Brooks, was born at Rutledge, Alabama, on September 25, 1870. The family moved in 1881 to Austin, Texas, where he attended both private and public schools. Upon graduation from Austin High School in 1888, he enrolled at the University of Texas. After two years as an undergraduate, Brooks entered the University of Texas law school, where he graduated in 1892 at the top of his class. He then began a law practice in Austin, which was interrupted when he was chosen by Judge Robert S. Gould and Robert L. Batts[qqv] to fill a temporary vacancy on the law faculty at the University of Texas. He taught in 1895–96; Batts said Brooks's knowledge of law and his use of the English language made him an excellent teacher. Nevertheless, he was not made a permanent faculty member because the board of regents thought he was too young. From 1898 to 1903 he was Austin city attorney under Mayor Emmett White. The two were credited with saving Austin from bankruptcy after the Austin Dam broke in 1900. On August 16, 1904, Brooks married Grace S. Harrison of Austin, and they eventually had three sons.

Brooks was appointed judge of the Twenty-sixth Judicial District, composed of Travis and Williamson counties, in 1903. His best-known case was an antitrust suit brought against the Waters-Pierce Oil Company (*see* WATERS-PIERCE CASE). The case, in the courts from 1897 to 1909, became one of the most famous in Texas judicial history, perhaps because of the company's connection with Joseph Weldon Bailey,[qv] then a United States senator. The oil company was found guilty of violating the antitrust laws and fined more than $1,623,000. Judge Brooks's judgment was sustained in appeals all the way to the United States Supreme Court. He resigned from the bench in 1907 to resume his private practice after serving one appointed term and one elected term. He was a member of the firm Gregory, Batts, and Brooks until Thomas W. Gregory[qv] was appointed attorney general of the United States. Brooks then became a partner in Brooks, Hart, and Woodward. In 1924 the practice of Batts and Brooks was established. Brooks served as special council to the University of Texas Board of Regents in 1925 in leasing university lands for oil. He died on a fishing trip with his son, Henry, near Fort McKavett on September 1, 1925, and was buried in Oakwood Cemetery.

BIBLIOGRAPHY: *Alcalde* (magazine of the Ex-Students' Association of the University of Texas), July 1926. Austin *American-Statesman*, September 1, 1925. Vertical Files, Austin History Center. Vertical Files, Barker Texas History Center, University of Texas at Austin.

Mary Jayne Walsh

BROOKS AIR FORCE BASE. Brooks Air Force Base is on State Loop 13 seven miles southeast of San Antonio, just west of Interstate Highway 37 in Bexar County. The site occupies about 1,300 acres. After the United States entered World War I[qv] in 1917, the army established the facility to train flying instructors in the Gosport System. According to that method, developed by the Royal Air Force, an instructor spoke to a student pilot through a tube and corrected the trainee in flight. The army initially called the training site Gosport Field; the name was changed to Signal Corps Aviation School, Kelly Field No. 5, on December 5, 1917. After the death of Cadet Sidney Johnson Brooks, Jr., in a training accident, the army renamed the facility Brooks Field, on February 4, 1918. By the end of that year the field had sixteen hangars. Hangar 9, now the Edward H. White II Memorial Museum, is a national historic landmark and is reputedly the oldest existing hangar in the United States Air Force.

In 1919 the army replaced the pilot school with a balloon and airship school. Following a series of accidents, however, the army closed this school, on June 26, 1922. From 1922 until 1931 Brooks served as the primary flying school for the army air corps; more than 1,400 pilots were trained there. Notable instructors and students included such aviation figures as Charles Lindbergh, Claire L. Chennault,[qv] Lester Maitland, and Jimmy Doolittle. The School of Aviation Medicine was transferred from Hazlehurst Field in New York to Brooks on August 1, 1926. In 1928 Brooks began training paratroopers; on Thanksgiving Day, 1929, the first mass paratroop drop in United States Armed Forces history took place at Brooks. The experiments at Brooks confirmed the practicality of tactical paratrooper warfare, which was used on many occasions during World War II.[qv] Both the flying school and the aviation medicine school were moved to nearby Randolph Field (now Randolph Air Force Base[qv]) in 1931.

Brooks served as a center for aerial-observation training in the 1930s. A special school for combat observers started there on July 1, 1940. The army established an Air Corps Advanced Flying School at Brooks on January 1, 1941, to teach pilots of single-engine aircraft aerial observation skills. Observation training was discontinued in 1943, when Brooks began training pilots of the new B-25 bomber for use in World War II. Brooks's training function ceased in 1945 when a tactical unit under the Third Air Force joined the facility. In 1948, after the air force was separated from the army, the Department of Defense changed the name of the base to Brooks Air Force Base. From 1949 until 1958 operating units at the base included the 259th Air Base, 2577th Air Force Reserve Flying Training Center, the 2577th Air Base Group, and the 3790th Air Base Group.

Starting in the summer of 1959, Brooks began a transition from a flight-training base to a center for medical research, development, and education. The School of Aviation Medicine returned to Brooks from Randolph, and the base became headquarters for the Aerospace Medical Center on October 1, 1959. On June 23, 1960, all flying at the facility ceased. With the growth of the United States space program, the aviation medicine school received the new title United States Air Force School of Aerospace Medicine, in May 1961; in November 1961 the center and school became part of the Aerospace Medical Division, which received the title Human Systems Division on February 6, 1987. The medical center has played a major role in the national space program; its accomplishments include the development of the capsule that carried the monkey Sam into outer space on December 4, 1959. President John F. Kennedy's final official act was the dedication of four buildings in the complex that housed the Aerospace Medical Division headquarters and the School of Aerospace Medicine.

Researchers at Brooks continue to study space medicine and have contributed to the advancement of manned flight. Brooks also houses the Air Force Human Resources Laboratory, the Air Force Occupational and Environmental Health Laboratory, the Air Force Drug Testing Laboratory, and the Air Force System's Command Systems Acquisition School. In November 1987 Sidney J. Brooks, Jr., Memorial Park was dedicated on the base. In 1995 the Department of Defense decided to close the base.

BIBLIOGRAPHY: Charles A. Dempsey, *Air Force Aerospace Medical Research Laboratory: 50 Years of Research on Man in Flight* (Wright-Patterson Air Force Base, Ohio: U.S. Air Force, 1985). Robert Mueller, *Air Force Bases*, Vol. 1 (Maxwell Air Force Base, Alabama: Simpson Historical Research Center, 1982). Vertical Files, Barker Texas History Center, University of Texas at Austin. Green Peyton Wertenbaker, *Fifty Years of Aerospace Medicine* (Brooks Air Force Base, Texas, 1968).

Edward B. Alcott

BROOKS CHAPEL, TEXAS. Brooks Chapel, on Farm Road 1251 twelve miles west of Carthage in western Panola County, was settled before the 1850s and named for a church built by early settler John Fletcher Brooks. The community's first school was built around 1878 on land donated by Brooks a mile west of the present Brooks Chapel church. The school was later moved to a site just east of what is now the community center. In 1902 the school burned and was rebuilt next to the Brooks Chapel church. In the mid-1930s the community had a church, a school, a cemetery, and a number of houses. Its school was closed in 1942, and local students were transferred to the Carthage or Beckville school. By the mid-1960s a church, a cemetery, a community center, and a few scattered dwellings remained in the area. During the early 1990s Brooks Chapel was a dispersed community.

BIBLIOGRAPHY: Leila B. LaGrone, ed., *History of Panola County* (Carthage, Texas: Panola County Historical Commission, 1979).

Christopher Long

BROOKS COUNTY. Brooks County (R-14) is in the Rio Grande Plain region south of Corpus Christi on U. S. Highway 281. It is bounded on the north by Duval and Jim Wells counties, on the east by Kleberg and Kenedy counties, on the south by Hidalgo and Starr counties, and on the west by Jim Hogg County. The center of the county lies at approximately 27°03′ north latitude and 98°14′ west longitude. Falfurrias, the county's largest town and county seat, is in northeastern Brooks County at the junction of U.S. Highway 281,

State highway 285, and Farm roads 2191 and 1418. Other communities include Encino, Flowella, and Rachal.

Brooks County comprises 942 square miles of brushy mesquite land. The elevation ranges from 100 to 400 feet. The nearly level to undulating soils are poorly drained, dark and loamy or sandy; isolated dunes are found. In the northeast corner of the county the soils are light-colored and loamy at the surface and clayey beneath. The vegetation, typical of the South Texas Plains, includes live oaks, mesquite, brush, weeds, cacti, and grasses.

In the early 1990s, 95 percent of the land was devoted to farming and ranching; 3 percent was under cultivation and 2 percent irrigated. Only 1 to 10 percent of the land is considered prime farmland. Mineral resources include caliche, gypsum, salt domes, oil, and gas. Gas production from gas wells totaled 90,434,098 thousand cubic feet in 1982; 520,482 barrels of condensate, 739,581 barrels of crude oil, and 2,392,340 thousand cubic feet of casinghead gas were also produced. Temperatures in Brooks County range from 44° F to 69° in January and from to 73° to 97° in July. The average annual temperature is 73°. The average annual rainfall is twenty-five inches, and the growing season averages 310 days.

Artifacts dating from the Paleo-Indian period (9,200 B.C. to 6,000 B.C.) suggest that human beings have lived in the Brooks County area for approximately 11,000 years. During the historical era the Indians of the region belonged to the Coahuiltecan linguistic group.

In the sixteenth century the Spanish made various explorations of the area; however, because of its distance from the coast, the lack of a major river, and wide stretches of deep sand that made travel difficult, the area remained unsettled. Although land grants in the Trans-Nueces region were made as early as 1767, it was not until the 1800s that an effort was made to introduce colonists into the territory that became Brooks County. About twenty-five land grants were made in the Brooks County area by the Spanish and Mexican governments. The earliest, the San Salvador del Tule grant, was given to Juan José Ballí on November 8, 1797. Other important early grants included El Encino en el Poso, made to Luciano Chapa around 1827, and El Paisano, made to Ramón de la Garza around the same time. But because of its isolation most of the families receiving grants settled along the Rio Grande rather than in the Brooks County area and only sporadically brought their cattle to the region.

Between the Texas Revolution[qv] and the end of the Mexican War,[qv] Brooks County lay in the disputed territory between the Rio Grande and the Nueces River. During these conflicts many of the original grantees fled to Mexico, and much of the area was occupied only by wandering vaqueros. Gradually, with the cessation of hostilities, some families returned, but frequent droughts and lack of transportation discouraged permanent settlement.

After Texas independence the area was made part of San Patricio County. In 1846 San Patricio County was divided to form Nueces County, which in 1848 was divided to form Cameron, Webb, and Starr counties; from the latter two counties Brooks County was later formed.

The number of Anglo settlers in the region was initially very small, but began to increase after the Civil War.[qv] Initially, the advent of these settlers did not alter the region's economic or social character. Most of the newcomers were ranchers, and many of them married into the most prominent families and adopted the existing social code. As a result, the Brooks County area remained largely Hispanic in character, and many of the original Hispanic rancheros were able to hold on to all of their land and to dominate the local political scene into the early 1890s. The situation began to change with the arrival of Edward C. Lasater,[qv] who moved to the area in the early 1890s and quickly emerged as the dominant figure in the county. In 1895 Lasater set up headquarters a few miles south of the present site of Falfurrias at the north entrance to the lower Rio Grande valley and gradually accumulated more than 350,000 acres in the area, including much of what became Brooks County. The same year he purchased 7,000 cows from the Kenedy Pasture Company and soon built up his herd to one of the state's leading cattle breeders.

With the extension of the San Antonio and Aransas Pass Railway from Alice to his ranch in 1904, Lasater founded the town of Falfurrias and subdivided a large portion of his ranchland for sale to farmers. Lured by prospects of abundant land, numerous settlers arrived to farm around Falfurrias. Within the span of a few years the character of economy changed markedly, from large-scale ranching to a mixture of farming and ranching, and Anglos increasingly dominated local politics.

During the latter half of the nineteenth century, the area that was to become Brooks County was part of Starr County. However, Lasater, a Republican, had a number of run-ins with Starr County's political boss, Manuel Guerra,[qv] who sought to maintain his control of the area. In 1911, after several years of effort, Lasater, with the help of State Representative James Abijah Brooks,[qv] succeeded in having Brooks County separated from Starr County, with Falfurrias as the county seat. The initial plans were to name the new county Falfurrias County, but in the end it was decided to name it Brooks in honor of James Brooks, who worked diligently for its formation. Upon organization of the county Amado de la Garza was elected sheriff and tax collector, Brooks was elected county judge, E. R. Rachal tax assessor, Rufino García, Sr., county and district clerk, and Lázaro López county treasurer. Ironically, in the early 1910s, a different faction of ranchers in western Brooks County lobbied to have its own county formed to break free of Lasater's influence. As a result, in 1913 Jim Hogg County was carved out of 990 square miles of Brooks County, and Brooks County assumed its present dimensions.

Between 1900 and 1940 the economy of Brooks County was predominantly based on ranching. In 1906 E. R. Rachal planted the first citrus trees, marking the introduction of the citrus industry into Brooks County. Freezes, droughts, and other pests, however, kept the industry from growing, and citrus fruit has remained of minor importance. Farming also failed to take hold. Despite Lasater's attempts to introduce commercial farming at the turn of the century, the emphasis remained on livestock raising, principally of cattle, and the small amount of farming was geared toward growing cattle feed. But rather than beef cattle, many ranchers focused on dairying, particularly of Jersey cows, which produced milk with a high fat content; already by the 1920s the high quality of Falfurrias butter and other dairy products[qv] was widely recognized.

The period 1920 to 1930 saw a marked increase in agriculture in the county. In 1920 there were 394 farms in Brooks County; by 1930 the number had grown to 513, and the number of cattle had reached nearly 40,000. During the Great Depression[qv] of the 1930s most of the area's farmers suffered hard times, but because of their reliance on meat, milk, butter, and other livestock products they fared somewhat better than farmers in other areas of the state who raised cotton and similar crops. Oil, discovered in the county in 1935, helped some cash-poor farmers to settle longstanding debts and survive the depression years, but not until the early 1940s did the economy began to recover fully.

The agricultural scene changed little between 1940 and 1970. The principal industry remained cattle raising, with the main emphasis on breeding and dairying. Although farming occupied 796,388 acres in 1959, only 8,321 acres was used for crops, mostly cattle feed. Cotton farming was introduced on a small scale during the 1950s, and in the 1960s commercial truck farming began to grow in importance. Subsequently, truck farming became one of the leading generators of revenue. In the early 1990s Brooks County was among the leading producers of watermelons and honeydew melons in the state, and it was a major source of fresh market vegetables. The main emphasis in the early 1990s, however, remained on cattle raising; at that time fully 80 percent of agricultural receipts came from cattle and cattle products.

The population of Brooks County grew rapidly during its early years, from 4,560 in 1920 to 9,195 in 1950, before declining slightly to 8,005 in 1970. In 1980 the population again showed modest growth, reaching 8,428, but nearly half of the residents (4,164) were retirees. Between 1970 and 1980 the rural population grew by nearly 41 percent, largely as a result of a growing influx of retired persons attracted by the warm climate. Many Mexican Americans[qv] were also moving to the area, and in 1980 Brooks County ranked seventh among all United States counties in percentage of residents of Hispanic origin. In 1990 the population was 8,204.

Like many other South Texas counties, Brooks County has remained staunchly Democratic over the years. From the county's inception through 1992 the majority of county residents voted Democratic in every presidential election, and Democrats continued to exercise a virtual stranglehold on local offices. In the 1982 primary 100 percent of those who went to the polls voted Democratic, with a total of 3,314 votes cast.

The first school in the county opened in 1912. In 1982 the county had one school district with three elementary schools, one middle school, and one high school. Sixty-nine percent of the 109 high school graduates planned to attend college. In 1982–83, 8 percent of the students were Anglo and 92 percent were Hispanic. The county had two doctors, two dentists, a hospital with facilities for thirty-one, ambulance service, a mental-health clinic, and a nursing home with a capacity for 100 residents. The county also had two weekly newspapers, Falfurrias *Facts* and *Paisano Press.* In the early 1980s Brooks County had seventeen churches with an estimated combined membership of 6,694; the largest denominations were Catholics, Southern Baptists, and United Methodists.

Recreation facilities in the county include the Heritage Museum of Falfurrias and four municipal parks with a total of sixty-six acres. The Texas Tropical Trail runs through Brooks County. Hunting opportunities abound. Special events in Brooks County include the Fiesta Ranchera in May, the Watermelon Roundup and Mexican Village Celebration, both in June, and the Fourth of July Rodeo.

BIBLIOGRAPHY: James Lewellyn Allhands, *Gringo Builders* (Joplin, Missouri, Dallas, Texas, 1931). Evan Anders, *Boss Rule in South Texas: The Progressive Era* (Austin: University of Texas Press, 1982). Lloyd Dyer, The History of Brooks County (M.A. thesis, Texas A&I College, 1938). Falfurrias *Facts,* June 15, 1934. Jovita González, Social Life in Cameron, Starr, and Zapata Counties (M.A. thesis, University of Texas, 1930). Thomas Hester, *Digging into South Texas Prehistory: A Guide for Amateur Archaeologists* (San Antonio: Corona Press, 1980). Dale Lasater, *Falfurrias: Ed C. Lasater and the Development of South Texas* (College Station: Texas A&M University Press, 1985). David Montejano, *Anglos and Mexicans in the Making of Texas, 1836–1986* (Austin: University of Texas Press, 1987). Marker Files, Texas Historical Commission, Austin. John R. Wunder, *At Home on the Range: Essays on the History of Western Social and Domestic Life* (Westport, Connecticut: Greenwood Press, 1985). *Alicia A. Garza*

BROOKS CREEK. Brooks Creek, sometimes called Lick Creek, rises four miles north of Bassett in southern Bowie County (at 33°23′ N, 94°32′ W) and runs south for eleven miles to its mouth on Anderson Creek, twelve miles south of New Boston (at 33°18′ N, 94°26′ W). It is intermittent in its upper reaches. The creek traverses an area of loamy soils upstream and clayey soils downstream. The area is for the most part heavily wooded, predominantly with hardwoods.

BROOKSHIRE, NATHEN (1793–1853). Nathen (Nathan) Brookshire, early settler, was born to James and Mary Brookshire of Rutherford County, Tennessee, in 1793. Before he moved to Texas in 1832, he served in both the Creek War and the War of 1812. On October 5, 1835, he received a league of land in Stephen F. Austin's[qv] fifth colony. He and his wife, the former Mary Ann Hooks, settled with three of their six children on land now in Waller and Fort Bend counties. Brookshire fought with Capt. John Bird's[qv] company in the Bird's Creek Indian Fight[qv] near the site of Temple. During the bloody battle against hundreds of Indians, Bird was killed, and Brookshire was chosen to succeed him. In return for his service he received 640 acres of land. In 1850 Captain Brookshire listed his occupation as farmer. At his death on January 10, 1853, his estate was valued at $2,900. It included almost 2,000 acres in Harris, Fort Bend, and Austin counties. He is buried in the Brookshire Cemetery.

BIBLIOGRAPHY: Corrie Pattison Haskew, *Historical Records of Austin and Waller Counties* (Houston: Premier Printing and Letter Service, 1969). Waller County Historical Survey Committee, *A History of Waller County, Texas* (Waco: Texian, 1973). *William Reed*

BROOKSHIRE, TEXAS. Brookshire is on U.S. Highway 10 in southern Waller County thirty miles west of Houston. The town is named for Capt. Nathen Brookshire,[qv] who received title to a league of land as a member of Stephen F. Austin's[qv] fifth colony in 1835. Many skeptics thought that the area, which was surrounded by coastal prairies, was unfit for settlement. Detractors were surprised when—because of the rich alluvial soil of the Brazos riverbottom and the arrival of the Missouri, Kansas and Texas Railroad—Brookshire developed into a thriving agricultural community. The railroad and Brookshire's proximity to Houston made the town an ideal shipping point for crops such as cotton, melons, corn, and pecans. By 1893 a post office had been established at the community. With agriculture as its basis, the economy of Brookshire flourished. By 1897 the Brookshire *Times* noted that the town had some thirty businesses and had shipped 10,000 bales of cotton that year. Although cotton remained king in Brookshire in 1900, the crop's economic significance diminished over the next three decades because of falling cotton prices and the demand for farm labor in the lucrative war industries. The community's economy, however, was not devastated, as rice became a major cash crop that increased in production every decade after 1900. Brookshire's population was 1,250 in 1920, then fluctuated over the next two decades, then steadily increased through the 1980s. In 1980 Brookshire, with a population of 2,244, was a center for rice, peanut, soybean, and cattle production. The town had a number of churches, a sizable consolidated school district, two banks, and several large businesses. The Waller County Museum, in the home of former resident Dr. Paul Donigan, is located in Brookshire. Each October the town is host to the Waller County Festival, which celebrates diverse ethnic backgrounds. In 1990 the community's population was 2,922.

BIBLIOGRAPHY: Mildred W. Abshier, ed., *Waller County Whatnots* (Hempstead, Texas: Waller County Historical Commission and Waller County Historical Society, 1986). Waller County Historical Survey Committee, *A History of Waller County, Texas* (Waco: Texian, 1973). *William Reed*

BROOKSHIRE BROTHERS. During the fall of 1921 Austin and Tom M. Brookshire of Lufkin pooled their resources to open a grocery business named Brookshire Brothers on the courthouse square. By 1928 eight brothers and sisters had invested in the partnership. Brookshire Brothers No. 2 was opened in Nacogdoches, No. 3 in Tyler, and No. 4 in Henderson. By 1939 all but four family members had left the partnership to enter other enterprises. In 1962 the partnership converted itself to a corporation, and officers of the next generation of the Brookshires, along with their children, assumed managerial positions. The corporation introduced an employee profit-sharing plan and in 1991 offered study courses to personnel interested in modern merchandising and sales innovations. By 1990 Brookshire Brothers, Incorporated, had grown to sixty-one diversified stores, five of which were in Louisiana. The network of stores extended north to Carthage, south to Clute, west to Rockdale, and east to De Ridder, Louisiana. The corporate complex occupied ninety-seven acres on Lufkin Loop 287 and included a distribution center, offices, bakery, and service buildings. The delivery fleet had thirty-six tractors and eighty-six semi-trailers that traveled an average of 4,160,000 miles yearly. In 1986 the business added nine Budget Chopper stores, a warehouse-style operation with fewer amenities and lower prices.

BIBLIOGRAPHY: Angelina County Historical Survey Committee, *Land of the Little Angel: A History of Angelina County, Texas*, ed. Bob Bowman (Lufkin, Texas: Lufkin Printing, 1976). "Top of the Market," *Texas Monthly*, April 1988. Vertical Files, Barker Texas History Center, University of Texas at Austin. *Anne Brookshire Hinton*

BROOKSHIRE GROCERY COMPANY. The Brookshire Grocery Company was founded in 1939 by Wood T. Brookshire after his involvement in a number of family-owned stores, including Brookshire Brothers.[qv] For his interest in the Brookshire Brothers partnership he took three Tyler stores and renamed them Brookshire's Food Stores. He soon added a store in Longview. His self-service and air-conditioning were firsts for the area. He established a profit-sharing program for the store managers. The business continued to expand through the 1950s and increased nonfood lines, offered free parking and check cashing, added more frozen foods, increased the self-service meat department, and provided more fresh produce. Two sons, Bruce G. and Shirley (Woody), joined the family business and in 1969 assumed control of the enterprise; Wood Brookshire was chairman of the board.

By 1991 Brookshire Grocery Company operated seventy-eight conventional supermarkets under the trade name Brookshire's Food Stores, eleven warehouse-style stores under the trade name Super 1 Foods, and 1 "superstore" under the trade name Brookshire's Supercenter. Among the specialty departments in the stores were bakeries, delicatessens, floral departments, in-store film-processing centers, pharmacies, and video rentals. The firm employed more than 7,500 personnel that year. The corporate offices and wholesale distribution center were in Tyler. The company had 275 vehicles in its fleet and handled 10,734 items regularly in its warehouses. Two bakeries, one in Tyler and one in Shreveport, Louisiana, supplied the stores.

In 1977 The Brookshires established the World of Wildlife and Country Store Museum in the corporate complex. The museum featured educational dioramas and artifacts for children. A rose garden at the corporate headquarters on Loop 323 in Tyler is maintained as a memorial to Wood T. Brookshire.

BIBLIOGRAPHY: Dallas *Morning News*, January 1, 1965, November 16, 1990. Archie P. McDonald, *Notable East Texans* (Austin: Eakin Press, 1986). "Top of the Market," *Texas Monthly*, April 1988. Vertical Files, Barker Texas History Center, University of Texas at Austin.
Anne Brookshire Hinton

BROOKSIDE VILLAGE, TEXAS. Brookside Village, an incorporated residential community on Clear Creek twenty-six miles north of Angleton in extreme north central Brazoria County, is just south of the Houston city limits and the Harris county line. The community was at one time served by the Atchison, Topeka and Santa Fe Railway. The 1936 county highway map showed only scattered dwellings at the townsite, but by 1961 the community's population numbered 560. In 1982 Brookside Village had two churches and a school, and South Park Cemetery lay a mile to its east. The community's population reached a new high of 1,671 in the early 1980s and declined to 1,538 by 1988. In the early 1990s Brookside Village's population was reported as 1,535. *Diana J. Kleiner*

BROOKSTON, TEXAS. Brookston is at the intersection of Farm roads 38, 1506, 1509, and the Missouri Pacific Railroad, just south of U.S. Highway 82 and five miles west of Paris in west central Lamar County. The town, originally part of the Zachariah Westfall survey, was established in 1870; it became the temporary terminus of the Texas and Pacific Railway when completion of the road was delayed during the panic of 1873. The post office was established that year and named for A. D. Brooks, owner of the land. By 1884 the population had reached 100, and Brookston was an important cotton-shipping point. Contemporary businesses included two general stores, a steam-powered cotton gin, a corn mill, a saloon, and a Western Union telegraph office. Mail arrived daily. Citizens numbered 500 in 1890. A new cotton gin was soon opened, as well as two more general stores, four groceries, a blacksmith shop, a butcher shop, a drugstore, a candy emporium, and a wagonmaking establishment. Within two years three churches were established, and residents acquired access to a telephone exchange. The major new commercial enterprise was Mrs. M. Hemphill's hotel. Municipal officials included Constable A. R. Bryant and Justice of the Peace C. G. Hunt. The school had been organized by 1896, when ninety-nine students were enrolled. It had two teachers.

The early railroad years were the most successful for Brookston, however, and by 1904 the population had decreased to 237. In 1914 the town had 225 citizens, a new hardware store, and a life insurance company, but some businesses were closing. Though the number of inhabitants had increased to 300 by 1925, the economic boom of the early days never returned. The town was also hard hit by the Great Depression.[qv] In 1930 only 130 people lived in Brookston. Many local residents moved away to metropolitan areas in search of work. Some of these had returned by 1933, but the number of businesses had decreased from twelve in 1931 to eight. Maps for 1936 showed three churches and two school buildings. By 1957 the school system had been consolidated with the West Lamar Independent School District, and residents numbered 250. In 1970 the number of businesses had dropped to two, and the population had decreased to 200. Maps for 1984 identified two churches, a small school building, and a cluster of dwellings. In 1990 Brookston had seventy inhabitants, three stores, and the post office.

BIBLIOGRAPHY: Thomas S. Justiss, An Administrative Survey of the Schools of Lamar County with a Plan for Their Reorganization (M.A. thesis, University of Texas, 1937). *Vista K. McCroskey*

BROOME, TEXAS. Broome, on the North Concho River and U.S. Highway 87 ten miles southeast of Sterling City in east central Sterling County, was founded in 1924 as a station on the Panhandle and Santa Fe Railway and was named for early rancher C. A. Broome. The community acquired a post office that was discontinued in 1939. In 1947 the settlement had a combination store and filling station and a population of twenty-five. Its population was eighteen in 1980, and by 1990 no population figures were reported for the community.
William R. Hunt

BROTHERHOOD OF TIMBER WORKERS. The Brotherhood of Timber Workers was an industrial union of sawmill workers in East Texas and western Louisiana organized by Arthur Lee Emerson and Jay Smith in December 1910. The union grew out of discontent on the part of sawmill workers and poor farmers—sharecroppers and tenant farmers—who worked in the mills on a seasonal basis. The demands of the "timber barons" in the southern pine region imposed an unwanted regimentation that disrupted the way of life of these workers. Deplorable housing and working conditions, as well as complaints typical of company towns, dominated the workers' everyday lives. These conditions intensified with the rapid depletion of the yellow pine stands after 1900. Worker reactions to sudden and sometimes unannounced pay cuts and irregular paydays led to sporadic work stoppages in the Texas-Louisiana pine region from 1902 to 1907. These labor disorders led to the formation in 1906 of the Southern Lumber Operators' Association, whose primary concern was to prevent organized labor from gaining any foothold in area lumber mills. The labor efforts suffered from a lack of effective leadership, and the Operators' Association achieved relatively easy victories, which led to complacency and inactivity. In the years after 1907 corporate abuse continued to result in worker frustration and occasional resistance. By the winter of 1910 sawmill workers responded to a call to address employer regimentation of their lives, in what one historian described as "a radical, collective response to industrial capitalism."

Emerson and Smith organized the first local of the BTW at Carson, Louisiana, in December 1910; others in East Texas and western Louisiana soon followed, and delegates from these locals met in Alexandria, Louisiana, in June 1911 and formally established the Brotherhood of Timber Workers. The BTW's constitution espoused moderation, listed employer abuses, and stated willingness to meet with employers to discuss employee concerns at any time. In addition, the constitution welcomed women and black members, as well as those performing any sawmill job, earmarks of a true industrial union. The document also demanded union recognition, a just consideration of workers' grievances, and a living wage. In response the Operators' Association characterized the BTW as "socialistic" and "anarchistic" and imposed a lockout of "infected" mills with the purpose of destroying the union.

C. B. Sweet, of the Long-Bell mills, declared his workers to be "loyal" and threatened to ignore the lockout. This lack of solidarity among operators resulted in a meeting in which the Operators' Association agreed to require "yellow dog" contracts of existing and new employees in order to determine their status. These contracts required employees to documents stating that they were not and would not become members of the BTW. Nonsigners were dismissed and blacklisted. "Infected" mills would close indefinitely on August 7, 1911. John Henry Kirby,[qv] head of the Kirby Lumber Company, which operated a number of mills in East Texas, held antiunion rallies and barbecues in Kirbyville, Texas, and De Ridder, Louisiana, the latter a BTW stronghold. The union's influence, however, continued to grow, and the Operators' Association suffered a severe setback when Sam Park of the American Lumber Company at Merryville, Louisiana, broke ranks by signing a contract with the BTW, thereby keeping his mill open. Battle lines were drawn.

Subsequently, an intensified antiunion campaign by the Operators' Association, which featured the use of lockouts, strikebreakers protected by Burns and Pinkerton detectives, and labor spies throughout the remainder of 1911 failed to break the Brotherhood. These tactics caused Emerson and Smith to integrate blacks and whites in the BTW; they understood that the operators would seek to utilize any nonunionized blacks as scab labor. Gradually, however, the cumulative effects of the lockouts and blacklists, followed by a hard winter in 1911–12, began to take their toll.

Rumors circulated after a trip by Emerson to Chicago in early 1912 that the Brotherhood might affiliate with the militant Industrial Workers of the World. In May at their second annual convention BTW delegates did vote to affiliate with the IWW, and in September the seventh annual convention of the IWW consummated the merger. The BTW, now officially the Southern District of the National Industrial Union of Forest and Lumber Workers, and reenergized by the merger with the IWW, called another strike; the Operators' Association answered with new lockouts and a lengthened blacklist. Additional strikebreakers, protected by gunmen, were imported, and on July 7, 1912, at Graybow, Louisiana, as Emerson prepared to speak to nonunion workers of the Galloway Lumber Company, a ten-minute gun battle, during which an estimated 300 shots were fired, left three men dead, another dying, and over forty wounded. Emerson and sixty-four BTW men were arrested, along with the mill owner and three guards; a subsequent grand jury indicted all of the union men, but none of the company men. Expenses for the defense of Emerson and eight other union men depleted union resources. The murder trial, held in Lake Charles, finally resulted in acquittal of the union men, but the operators, after forcing out Sam Park from the leadership of the American Lumber Company at Merryville, imposed a new lockout. Operations resumed with the aid of imported strikebreakers. The BTW's effectiveness was over by the spring of 1913, although a few holdouts remained until early 1916.

Although some historians have argued that the merger with the militant IWW led to the Brotherhood's downfall, most contend that the operators had already determined to destroy the BTW before its affiliation with the IWW because of its success in achieving union solidarity among the sawmill workers. The BTW demonstrated that downtrodden, unskilled, and racially mixed rural sawmill workers could be effectively unionized. Their history also demonstrates that the lumber barons, like other industrialists, polarized communities in the pine belt and isolated and repressed the workers, especially the blacks, thereby smashing the union. *See also* LUMBER INDUSTRY.

BIBLIOGRAPHY: James R. Green, "The Brotherhood of Timber Workers, 1900–1913: A Radical Response to Industrial Capitalism in the Southern U.S.A.," *Past and Present* 60 (August 1973). Charles R. McCord, A Brief History of the Brotherhood of Timber Workers (M.A. thesis, University of Texas, 1959). George T. Morgan, "The Gospel of Wealth Goes South: John Henry Kirby and Labor's Struggle for Self-Determination," *Southwestern Historical Quarterly* 75 (October 1971). George T. Morgan, "No Compromise—No Recognition: John Henry Kirby, the Southern Lumber Operators' Association, and Unionism in the Piney Woods, 1906–1916," *Labor History* 10 (Spring 1969).

James C. Maroney

BROTHERS, ROBERT LEE, JR. (1908–1979). Robert Lee Brothers, Jr., the "Poet of Peach Creek," son of Robert Lee and Alma (Kokernot) Brothers, was born on December 29, 1908, at Big Hill, on the old Kokernot ranch in Gonzales County, Texas. He graduated from Gonzales High School and studied one year at Baylor University. When his father died the following June (1929), he returned to the land he had inherited to become a cattleman. Though his roots were in the cattle business, he published three books of poetry and won many poetry awards. His first collection, *Democracy of Dust,* was published in 1947. The themes in this and subsequent works revolve around ranching, the outdoors, and human nature. His second book, *The Hidden Harp* (1952), won the Texas Institute of Letters[qv] award for 1953. His poem "Requiem for a Foundling" won the Reynolds Lyric Award in Virginia. Among the other awards Brothers received was a special citation given during the semicentennial of *The Lyric* in 1970 to "poets . . . who have diligently served the cause of traditional poetry throughout the years." Mabel Major[qv] describes his work as "distinguished by precision of phrase and by a keen ironic insight into human character." He was an active member of the Poetry Society of Texas[qv] and served as a judge for many poetry contests. Brothers was born a Southern Baptist and a Southern Democrat. Though he never fitted the fundamentalist mold, much of his poetry is deeply spiritual. In the last ten or fifteen years of his life he developed an affinity for the Republican party.[qv] He was politically active on the local and county level, where he registered the poor to vote as a part of a campaign to remove corrupt local politicians from office. He was married briefly to Julia Cobb, then divorced. In June 1936 he married Docia Azilea Barfield, an old sweetheart he had known since she was sixteen; they had two daughters. Docia died on October 4, 1955. Brothers died of a heart attack on Mothers' Day, May 13, 1979, at his home in Gonzales.

BIBLIOGRAPHY: Mabel Major et al., *Southwest Heritage: A Literary History with Bibliography* (Albuquerque: University of New Mexico Press, 1938; 3d ed. 1972). Vertical Files, Barker Texas History Center, University of Texas at Austin.

Barbara Jo Brothers

BROTHERS OF THE CHRISTIAN SCHOOLS. The Brothers of the Christian Schools, also known as the Christian Brothers, are a Catholic teaching order founded by St. John Baptiste de la Salle in seventeenth-century France. They first came to the United States in 1845, when they established a school in Baltimore, and by 1918 they had established five provinces in the United States: Baltimore, New York, St. Louis, San Francisco, and New Orleans–Santa Fe. The brothers first came to Texas in January 1861, when they took over the operation of St. Mary's University in Galveston. This school survived the bombardment of the city by Union forces in January 1863, but the yellow fever epidemic of 1867 forced it to close. From 1869 to 1871 the brothers operated St. Joseph's College in Brownsville but thereafter did not return to Texas until 1925, when they took over the two-year-old St. Patrick's High School in El Paso, which had previously been under the direction of the Sisters of Loretto.[qv]

On September 8, 1925, the renamed Cathedral High School opened with forty-five boys; its first graduating class, in 1927, had seven students. By 1933 the enrollment had grown to 200, but Cathedral shared the El Paso Community Center with a separate grade school until 1940. In that year the community center closed, the grade school moved, and the high school took over the entire facility. In 1972 El Paso's Jesuit High School closed, and Cathedral's enrollment reached 400 for the first time. By 1981, when the brothers of the Christian Schools celebrated their tercentenary, Cathedral was the only private religious school for boys in El Paso. In 1992 the enrollment was 530.

The brothers returned to Galveston in 1931 and took over Kirwin High School, which had been staffed by Ursuline and Dominican sisters.[qqv] Eleven years later a new building was erected on the site of the original Moody home, where the school had been located since 1927. The brothers ran Kirwin until 1968, when it was combined with Dominican High School and the Ursuline Academy to form O'Connell High School. The brothers continued to work in the new school until 1975.

The third Christian Brothers educational endeavor in Texas was Price College in Amarillo. Amarillo Bishop Rudolph A. Gerken[qv] established a boys' school known as St. George's College in 1928, and for ten years the school was run by diocesan priests. Its name was changed to Price Memorial College in 1930 at the request of Katherine E. Price, the widow of merchant Lucien B. Price. The word *Memorial* was dropped from its title when the Christian Brothers took over the school in 1938. Two years later Price added an eighth grade to the four high school years, and in 1964 the school was renamed Price Catholic High School, to avoid confusion caused by the word *College.* The brothers withdrew from the school sometime after the mid-1960s.

The Christian Brothers have also operated several other Texas schools, including La Salle High School in San Antonio from 1957 to its closing in 1968; Antonian High School in San Antonio from 1964 to 1971; and Marian Christian High School in Houston from 1978 to its closing in 1989.

BIBLIOGRAPHY: Carlos E. Castañeda, *Our Catholic Heritage in Texas* (7 vols., Austin: Von Boeckmann–Jones, 1936–58; rpt., New York: Arno, 1976). Catholic Archives of Texas, Files, Austin.

Martin Donell Kohout

BROTHERTON, ROBERT (?–1839). Robert Brotherton (Brotherington) was one of the original settlers of the Colorado District and an official in Colorado County in the Republic of Texas.[qv] He arrived in Texas from Missouri in the summer of 1822, bringing with him a letter of introduction addressed to Stephen F. Austin[qv] from Missouri governor Alexander McNair, who promised that Brotherton would be an "industrious farmer." Brotherton was one of the Old Three Hundred[qv] settlers of the Austin colony. He was wounded in the back during an Indian raid in July 1822, shortly after arriving in Texas. The incident, along with an Indian attack on three other men the following day, motivated colonist Robert H. Kuykendall[qv] to lead a punitive expedition that culminated in a successful ambush of the Karankawa Indians at Skull Creek.

On July 24, 1824, Brotherton and his partner, Caleb R. Bostic, received a sitio[qv] of land in Austin's colony, where they farmed and raised stock. A census report of 1826 lists Brotherton as a farmer and stockman, aged between twenty-five and forty years. He was not recorded as having a wife or family. He began to take part in local politics early in 1825. In January of that year he acted as a judge in the election of James Cummings as alcalde[qv] of the Colorado District. In 1836 Brotherton sat on the committee that designated Columbus the seat of the newly formed Colorado County. He became county clerk in April 1837. In December of the same year the Congress of the Republic of Texas[qv] appointed him clerk to the board of land commissioners in Colorado County. The Brotherton house was named a stock subscription site for the Colorado Navigation Company in 1838. Brotherton died early in 1839. His probate petition is dated March 25 of that year. He left only a modest estate and debts accrued in farming.

BIBLIOGRAPHY: Eugene C. Barker, ed., *The Austin Papers* (3 vols., Washington: GPO, 1924–28). Lester G. Bugbee, "The Old Three Hundred: A List of Settlers in Austin's First Colony," *Quarterly of the Texas State Historical Association* 1 (October 1897). Jesse Burnam, "The Reminiscences of Captain Jesse Burnam," *Quarterly of the Texas State Historical Association* 5 (July 1901). J. H. Kuykendall, "Reminiscences of Early Texans," *Quarterly of the Texas State Historical Association* 6–7 (January, April, July 1903). William Barret Travis, *Diary*, ed. Robert E. Davis (Waco: Texian Press, 1966).

Ken Hendrickson

BROUSSARD, JOSEPH ELOI (1866–1956). Joseph Broussard, pioneer rice grower and miller, son of Eloi and Mary Azema (Hebert) Broussard, was born on December 18, 1866, in the home of his maternal grandparents on Hillebrandt Bayou in the site that is now Beaumont, Texas. Mary Hebert's father had moved to Texas from Louisiana in 1842. After Eloi Broussard's early death, Mary married Lovan Hamshire, and the young Broussard was reared on the family ranch near the site of present Hamshire, Texas. After three years' schooling in Galveston, Broussard worked cattle and delivered mail on horseback in the lower Taylor's Bayou area of Jefferson County. When a post office was established in 1885, he became its first postmaster and named it La Belle for his fiancée, Mary Belle Bordages. They were married in 1889 and moved to Beaumont, where Broussard bought one-third interest in a gristmill. In 1892 he converted the gristmill to a rice mill, which, as Beaumont Rice Mills, became the first commercially successful rice mill in Texas. The mill continued in operation in the late 1980s under the founder's grandson.

Less than 1,500 acres was planted with rice in Texas in 1892. To foster rice production, in 1898 Broussard cofounded the Beaumont Irrigation Company, whose initial canal led to the formation of the Lower Neches Valley Authority.[qv] The system is now capable of irrigating 50,000 acres of rice while supplying the area's industrial requirements for water. At the time of Broussard's death, acres planted with rice in Texas annually reached well over 400,000, and production had spread to twenty-three counties. Through family landholdings and the advancement of credit to farmers, the mill, under Broussard's management, farmed some 10,000 acres of rice in peak years. On this acreage rice growing was rotated with cattle raising, a lifelong interest of Broussard.

From 1907 to 1918 Broussard was president of the Rice Millers' and Dealers' Association, forerunner of the present Rice Millers' Association of America. In 1909, when the industry faced a financial crisis, Broussard was a member of a two-man team that successfully marketed American rice in Europe. In 1950 the International Rice Festival at Crowley, Louisiana, was dedicated to him. As an exemplary Catholic, Broussard was knighted in 1938 by Pope Pius XI.

On October 6, 1956, he died. He was survived by his wife and nine children. Two new varieties of rice, developed at the China, Texas, Rice-Pasture Experiment Station and planted worldwide, were named

Bella Patna and LaBelle in honor of the rice pioneer's widow and in recognition of his continuous support of the station's research programs. *See also* RICE CULTURE.

BIBLIOGRAPHY: Genevieve Broussard Dutton, "Pioneer Rice Industrialist and Man of Faith: Joseph Eloi Broussard (1866–1956)," *Texas Gulf Coast Historical and Biographical Record* 15 (1979). *Rice Mill: 50 Years (1892–1942)* (Beaumont, Texas: Beaumont Rice Mill, 1942). John H. Walker and Gwendolyn Wingate, *Beaumont, a Pictorial History* (Virginia Beach, Virginia, 1981).
Gerry Doyle

BROWDER'S SPRINGS. Browder's (Browder) Springs, located a mile southeast of the Dallas County Courthouse (at 32°43′ N, 96°45′ W), played two important roles in the early history of Dallas: as the first public water supply for the town and subsequently as a ruse by which Dallas captured the Texas and Pacific Railway. The artesian springs were named for Lucy Jane Browder and her two sons, Edward and Isham, who acquired the property before 1850. They served as a source of fresh water for residents in the vicinity, while the picturesque location, which included Mill Creek, was a popular site for picnics; it later became the city's first public park, City Park. In 1878 the privately owned Dallas Water Supply Company purchased Browder's Springs and two surrounding acres and expanded the pumping facilities it had inaugurated two years earlier on Mill Creek. Relations between the company and the city became increasingly strained because of poor service, and in 1881 the city bought the entire system, including the land, engines, boiler, pumps, standpipes, machinery, hydrants, hoses, and fire plugs, for $65,000. This first public station was closed in 1886 because water consumption was surpassing the capacity of the springs. A well was drilled from which residents could draw their own water. The station was reopened during droughts in 1909–10 and 1937 and then closed permanently. The springs disappeared when Mill Creek became a sewer in the 1930s, and the location was buried under R. L. Thornton Freeway in the 1960s.

In 1871, when the state legislature was debating a bill granting right of way to the Texas and Pacific, the T&P was planning a line west from Marshall along the thirty-second parallel, intended to cross the Houston and Texas Central near Corsicana. Representative John W. Lane of Dallas managed to attach a rider to the bill specifying that the T&P must cross the H&TC "within one mile of Browder's Springs." The bill passed before it was discovered that Browder's Springs was only a mile from the Dallas County Courthouse. Dallas leaders mollified the outraged railroad officials by raising a large bond issue ($100,000) for the benefit of the railroad and donating a right-of-way through town, now Pacific Avenue. Dallas thus became the first rail crossroads in the state and the shipping center for north central Texas.

BIBLIOGRAPHY: M. E. and Eric H. Bolding, *Origin and Growth of the Dallas Water Utilities* (Dallas, 1981). William L. McDonald, *Dallas Rediscovered: A Photographic Chronicle of Urban Expansion, 1870–1925* (Dallas: Dallas County Historical Society, 1978).
Michael V. Hazel

BROWER, JOHN (?–?). John Brower, New York merchant, succeeded August W. Radcliff as consul for the Republic of Texas[qv] in New York City. He was recommended by Morgan L. Smith,[qv] and his appointment by David G. Burnet[qv] was confirmed by the Texas Senate on January 18, 1841. Brower took charge of the consular office on March 27 and during his incumbency worked to effect ratification of the commercial treaty between Texas and the United States, reported to the Texas government attempts by Mexican agents to equip and man ships in New York harbor, and between November 1844 and March 1845 made a trip to Europe in the interest of Texas. His term ended with annexation[qv] on February 16, 1846.

BIBLIOGRAPHY: Alma Howell Brown, "The Consular Service of the Republic of Texas," *Southwestern Historical Quarterly* 33 (January, April 1930). *Diplomatic Correspondence of the Republic of Texas*, ed. George Pierce Garrison (3 parts, Washington: GPO, 1908–11).
Claudia Hazlewood

BROWN, AARON B. (1830–1884). Aaron B. Brown, bridge builder and Houston civic leader, the son of Aaron B. and Rachel Brown, was born in Springdale, Ohio, on May 4, 1830. He attended the Farmer's Academy until the age of sixteen, ran away briefly to run a canal boat between Cincinnati and Dayton, and worked for a time in his father's carriage factory. In 1851 he went to Missouri and was contractor for construction of the Hannibal and St. Joseph Railroad. He returned to railroad work in Ohio in 1853 and married Jane F. Lamb; they had seven children, only one of whom survived to adulthood. In 1857 Brown moved to Texas, where he was superintendent of bridges for the Texas and New Orleans Railroad. He built bridges between Waco and Albany and between Garret and Terrell for the Houston and Texas Central Railway and across White Oak and Buffalo bayous to connect the Houston and Texas Central with the Galveston, Houston and Henderson Railroad. In Houston he acquired real estate, became a Mason, and served on the board of aldermen. When his health failed, he stayed for a while in Ripley County, Indiana, but returned to Houston, where he died on July 7, 1884. He was buried in Glenwood Cemetery, Houston.

BIBLIOGRAPHY: *History of Texas, Together with a Biographical History of the Cities of Houston and Galveston* (Chicago: Lewis, 1895).
Diana J. Kleiner

BROWN, CARRIE BERTHA PFEIFFER (1886–1977). Carrie Brown, clubwoman, the daughter of John and Sophie Pfeiffer, was born in Carrizo Springs, Texas, on August 8, 1886. When she was five years old she and her family moved to Encinal; later they settled in San Antonio. Carrie was educated in the San Antonio public schools and at the University of Texas in Austin, where she was active in the student council and received her B.A. in 1906. Two years later she married Alexander A. Brown, a young physician with a practice in general medicine. They had three children. The Browns surrounded themselves with an outstanding library of fine books and collections of art, china, and antique furniture. Carrie worked with the San Antonio Kindergarten Association, the nonsectarian Immigrant Night School established by the National Council of Jewish Women, the City Federation of Women's Clubs, the Crippled Children's Association, the Bexar County Medical Auxiliary, the PTA, and the Texas Children's Home-Finding Society. She served as president or board member in each of these associations. The state chapter of the American Association of University Women[qv] was organized in San Antonio in her home. She served as a charter member, as secretary, and three times as president. From 1941 to 1943 she was president of the Texas State Division of AAUW. Those were the war years, and the organization was involved in war-connected activities.

Her involvement in such educational matters as women on college faculties, child labor bills, education for dependent children, and teacher recruitment resulted in her election to honorary membership in the Delta Kappa Gamma Society.[qv] When a vacancy occurred on the University of Texas Board of Regents, Mrs. Brown's many friends urged Governor Coke Stevenson[qv] to appoint her. She would have been the first woman to hold the position, but the time was not yet ripe for such an action.

Carrie Brown was a charter member and president of the San Antonio Section of the National Council of Jewish Women. She was a member of Congregation Temple Beth-El and a director of its Sisterhood. She died on June 1, 1977, in San Antonio of a heart attack.

BIBLIOGRAPHY: Ruthe Winegarten and Cathy Schechter, *Deep in the Heart: The Lives and Legends of Texas Jews* (Austin: Eakin Press, 1990).
Betty B. Cohen

BROWN, ED (ca. 1840–?). Ed Brown, black state representative, was born around 1840 in Alabama. He was a carpenter who apparently lived in Rusk County. He won election to the legislature in 1874 and served a single term. He was one of six black legislators elected to the Fourteenth Legislature and served on the Agriculture and Stock Raising Committee. In the legislature he opposed efforts to dilute African-American voting strength by redrawing county boundaries.

BIBLIOGRAPHY: J. Mason Brewer, *Negro Legislators of Texas and Their Descendants* (Dallas: Mathis, 1935; 2d ed., Austin: Jenkins, 1970). Randolph B. Campbell, *A Southern Community in Crisis: Harrison County, Texas, 1850–1880* (Austin: Texas State Historical Association, 1983). Merline Pitre, *Through Many Dangers, Toils and Snares: The Black Leadership of Texas, 1868–1900* (Austin: Eakin, 1985).

Paul M. Lucko

BROWN, EDGAR WILLIAM, SR. (1859–1917). E. W. Brown, physician, lumberman, and mayor of Orange, was born in Ringgold, Georgia, on November 22, 1859, to Dr. Samuel Moore and Georgia (Malone) Brown. After the Civil War[qv] the family moved to Texas: first to Jasper, then to Magnolia Springs, and in 1871 to Orange. He graduated with honors from Tulane University at New Orleans in 1882 and began his medical practice in Orange.

On November 28, 1888, he was married to Carrie Launa Lutcher, daughter of Henry Jacob Lutcher,[qv] one of the richest lumbermen in the United States. Three children were born to them: E. W. Brown Jr.,[qv] Lutcher Brown, and Fannie Brown Moore (Mrs. Rucie). In the late 1880s, with the expansion of the Lutcher lumber business, Brown was urged by Lutcher to join with him and W. H. Stark, Brown's brother-in-law, in operating the growing industrial empire. Brown gave up his medical practice to devote full time to lumbering. He took charge of the newly established Dibert, Stark, and Brown Cypress Company at Donner, Louisiana, and for twelve years commuted weekly by train to Donner from his home at Orange. The original investment of $60,000 in this plant came to be worth a vast fortune.

The company opened another cypress operation at Lutcher, Louisiana, with Brown as president, but he withdrew from active management, leaving L. W. Gilbert to manage the plant under Brown's direction. Brown shared with Stark the general supervision of the great yellow pine and cypress interests of their organization. Brown also was president of the Lutcher and Moore Cypress Lumber Company, vice president of the Lutcher and Moore Lumber Company of Orange, and a partner in the Yellow Pine Paper Mill. He became one of the wealthiest and most successful manufacturers in the United States. He helped to secure a deepwater channel from Orange to the Gulf during the development of the Gulf Intracoastal Waterway,[qv] and to replace a ferry on the Sabine River with an iron bridge to connect Orange to Louisiana. Brown and Stark used their own money to build the dump for the bridge approach on the Louisiana side.

Brown acquired large landholdings in Orange County and became a famous farmer, building water canals for rice growing, and clearing and cultivating many acres. He invested in the development of the area oil industry. On June 16, 1917, he died of cancer at his home at Green and Sixth streets. Mrs. Brown subsequently moved into John W. Link's[qv] mansion at Green and Ninth streets, bought for Link's daughter, Fannie B. Moore. Mrs. Moore died of pneumonia on October 12, 1918, but Mrs. Brown continued to live in the home until her death on October 3, 1941. All the family are buried in Evergreen Cemetery.

BIBLIOGRAPHY: *Gulf Coast Lumberman*, July 1, 1917. Howard Williams, ed., *Gateway to Texas: The History of Orange and Orange County* (2d ed., Orange, Texas: Heritage House Museum, 1988).

Jeanette Heard Robinson

BROWN, EDGAR WILLIAM, JR. (1894–1976). Edgar W. Brown, Jr., Orange County banker, shipbuilder, financier, and philanthropist, was a native and lifelong resident of Orange, born on February 10, 1894, to Carrie (Lutcher) and Dr. Edgar William Brown, Sr.[qv] He was the grandson of Henry Jacob Lutcher,[qv] one of the wealthiest lumbermen in the United States. Brown attended Princeton, but in 1917, in his junior year, his father died, and he returned to Orange to look after his family's business interests. He was married on July 23, 1915, to Gladys Slade, daughter of Mr. and Mrs. Charles Slade of Monroe, Louisiana. Four sons were born to them. After Gladys died on September 17, 1959, Brown married Elizabeth Smith Hustmyre of Orange, on November 20, 1960.

He was director and officer of the First National Bank, organizer and chairman of the County National Bank, and chairman of the board of the Orange National Bank. In 1933 he became the principal owner of Levingston Shipbuilding Company, which during World War II[qv] built many vessels for the war effort and was awarded the "E" award for outstanding service to the United States Navy. Later Brown acquired the Gulfport Shipbuilding Company in Port Arthur and the Higman Towing Company, which he sold to his son L. Slade Brown in 1969. He was president of the Lutcher-Moore Cypress Lumber Company and vice president of the Dibert, Stark, and Brown Cypress Lumber Company. With his brother, B. Lutcher Brown, and his mother, he organized the Brown Paper Mill Company in Monroe, Louisiana, in 1923 and acquired vast holdings of timber for its supply. In 1959 this property was sold for a substantial fortune to the Olin Corporation. Brown was a founder of the Sabine River Water Shed Association, which later became the Sabine River Authority,[qv] and ultimately developed Toledo Bend Reservoir.[qv] After World War II he was a founder, with H. J. Lutcher Stark,[qv] his cousin, of the Industrial Development Committee, which led to the development of Chemical Row with its many petrochemical plants.

Brown was known in Houston as a director and life member of the Houston Fat Stock Show. The 1974 show and rodeo were dedicated to him in recognition of his years of support. He was named Man of the Year in 1967 by the Variety Club of Houston in recognition of his philanthropies. He served many years in the management of the Bill Williams Charity Capon Dinners in Houston. Among his other philanthropies, he supported the American Red Cross and Salvation Army in Orange and provided new facilities for them. He and Gladys supported and donated funds to the Bancroft School library in their Pinehurst home district, and they founded and supported Girls Haven in Orange. They gave the Slade Chapel to the First Methodist Church of Orange and set up a foundation to provide for its maintenance; they also contributed a parsonage. To the First Presbyterian Church they gave a manse and a protective dome for the church's priceless stained-glass windows. The Browns gave the First Baptist Church of Orange money toward the building of the McCorquodale Education Building and a recreational building. Brown donated a building to the Orange Community Players and funds to assist with many of their productions. In his memory each year the troupe presents a "Mr. Edgar" award to outstanding achievers.

Brown gave his former residence on Green Avenue to the city of Orange for a city hall and left his fine mansion, Lindenwood, and its sixty-two acres on Old Highway 90, in Pinehurst, to the First Methodist Church. When that church was unable to accept it, the estate was given to Lamar University at Orange as an educational center. Edgar Brown died on January 8, 1976, and was buried in the Brown family vault in Evergreen Cemetery, Orange.

BIBLIOGRAPHY: *Who's Who in the South and Southwest*, Vol. 10. Howard Williams, ed., *Gateway to Texas: The history of Orange and Orange County* (2d ed., Orange, Texas: Heritage House Museum, 1988).

Jeanette Heard Robinson

BROWN, EDWY ROLFE (1868–1942). Edwy Rolfe Brown, oilman, son of John A. and Isabel (Shaw) Brown, was born in Little Hocking, Ohio, on December 4, 1868. He attended Marietta Academy and received a B.A. degree from Marietta College in 1894. From 1894 to 1898 he worked for the Standard Oil Company of New York, first as yardman and later as superintendent of the refinery. He moved to Texas with Joseph Stephen Cullinan[qv] in April 1898 and established a refinery at Corsicana. In 1901 or 1902 Brown became general manager of the Corsicana Refining Company, the Corsicana Pipe Line Company, and the Corsicana Petroleum Company; in 1911 he became vice president of the Magnolia Petroleum Company[qv] and in 1914 moved to Dallas as general manager. He was director and vice president of Standard Oil Company of New York from 1925 to 1929 and chairman of the board after 1932. He was a director of the Federal Reserve Bank of Dallas[qv] from 1930 to 1935 and was city commissioner of Dallas in 1931–32. He served as president of the Dallas Chamber of Commerce, as a director of the Southwestern Life Insurance Company and of the Gulf Insurance Company, and as trustee of the University of Dubuque and of Marietta College in Ohio. He was one of the organizers of the Texas Centennial[qv] Central Exposition in Dallas in 1936. On November 14, 1900, Brown married Nelle Loraine Hamilton; they had one daughter. Nelle died in 1911. On April 30, 1913, Brown married Florrie Bess McCrery. He died in New York City on January 25, 1942, and was buried in Grove Hill Cemetery, Dallas.

BIBLIOGRAPHY: *Who's Who in America*, 1938–39. Dallas *Morning News*, January 28, 1942.

Jeanette H. Flachmeier

BROWN, FRANK (1833–1913). Frank Brown, county official, son of John D. and Sarah (Wade) Brown, was born on June 26, 1833, in Nashville, Tennessee. When he was two years old, he came to Texas with his parents, who were settlers in the Sterling C. Robertson[qv] colony at Old Nashville. In the winter of 1839–40 the family moved to Washington-on-the-Brazos, where the father died and Frank was carrier boy for the *National Register*. Mrs. Brown and her five children moved to Austin in 1846. From October 1848 to February 1849 Brown worked in the office of the *Western Texian* in San Antonio. He married Georgiana McLemore in Austin on January 1, 1856. Their family came to include twelve children, Brown's mother, an invalid sister, and an orphaned niece and nephew. Brown was elected county clerk of Travis County, probably in 1856, and was reelected in 1858 and 1862. He enlisted in the Confederate Army as a private, was honorably discharged as a captain of home guards at the end of the war, and was paroled early in July 1865. The same year he was appointed clerk of the district court and city alderman of Austin. From July 1865 until January 1867 he was associated with James A. Foster as publishers of the Austin *Southern Intelligencer*.[qv] Brown was commissioned clerk of the district court in 1866 and later elected to the post. He resigned in 1869, was reappointed, and resigned again the same year. He was clerk of the district court in 1873 and of the county court in 1876 and was reelected for each term through 1892. According to his own statement, in his old age he had served continuously for forty years. After Brown's retirement he compiled his annals of Travis County and the city of Austin. His manuscript is a storehouse of information about the history of the Austin area in the second half of the nineteenth century. He died at Austin at the home of his daughter, Mrs. Henry Hutchings, on January 27, 1913.

BIBLIOGRAPHY: Austin *American*, January 20, 1924. Austin *Statesman*, October 29, 1899, January 28, 1913. Frank Brown, Annals of Travis County and the City of Austin (MS, Frank Brown Papers, Barker Texas History Center, University of Texas at Austin). Galveston *News*, October 8, 1895.

Frances K. Hendricks

BROWN, GEORGE (1801–1836). George Brown, Alamo defender, was born in England in 1801. He immigrated to America and lived in Yazoo, Mississippi, before settling in Gonzales, Texas. He was one of four George Browns in the Texas army during the Texas Revolution.[qv] He died in the battle of the Alamo[qv] on March 6, 1836.

BIBLIOGRAPHY: Daughters of the American Revolution, *The Alamo Heroes and Their Revolutionary Ancestors* (San Antonio, 1976). Bill Groneman, *Alamo Defenders* (Austin: Eakin, 1990).

Bill Groneman

BROWN, GEORGE (?–?). George Brown, early settler, was in Texas at the time of the census of March 1826, when he was classified as a farmer and stock raiser, a single man aged between sixteen and twenty-five. He was a partner of Charles Belknap[qv] as one of Stephen F. Austin's Old Three Hundred[qv] colonists. The partners received title to a sitio[qv] of land now in Fort Bend County on May 22, 1827. Brown was possibly a partner of Jacob Eberly in running races at Columbia in October and November 1836. They dissolved their partnership on September 9, 1837.

BIBLIOGRAPHY: Lester G. Bugbee, "The Old Three Hundred: A List of Settlers in Austin's First Colony," *Quarterly of the Texas State Historical Association* 1 (October 1897). *Telegraph and Texas Register*, October 25, November 9, 1836, September 23, 1837.

BROWN, GEORGE RUFUS (1898–1983). George Rufus Brown, businessman, civil engineer, and philanthropist, son of Riney Louis and Lucy Wilson (King) Brown, was born in Belton, Texas, on May 12, 1898. After studying at Rice University he graduated from the Colorado School of Mines in 1922. He joined the marines in the final months of World War I[qv] and later worked briefly as a mining engineer in Butte, Montana. After suffering a serious injury in a mining accident, he returned to Texas to join a small construction firm founded by his brother, Herman Brown.[qv] The firm later became Brown and Root, Incorporated, after Herman's brother-in-law, Dan Root, a prosperous Central Texas cotton farmer, made an investment in the firm. The paving of dirt roads and building of steel bridges for municipal and county governments in Central Texas led the firm to successful joint bids to construct the Marshall Ford (now Mansfield) Dam on the Colorado River. In 1940, the company won a $90 million joint bid to build the Naval Air Station at Corpus Christi. By the late 1950s Brown and Root became one of the largest engineering and construction companies in the world. In the 1960s and 1970s the firm completed jobs world-wide, including Guam, Spain, the United Kingdom, Iran and the Persian Gulf. In 1942 the brothers formed the Brown Shipbuilding Company on the Houston Ship Channel,[qv] which built 359 ships during World War II,[qv] employed 25,000 people, and was awarded the Army-Navy "E" and a presidential citation. Soon after the war, George and Herman Brown and a group of other investors purchased the Big Inch and Little Inch[qv] pipelines with a high bid of $143 million and founded Texas Eastern Transmission Corporation. After the death of his brother Herman in 1962, George became president of Brown and Root. Later that year the corporation was sold to the Halliburton Company. Brown served as a director of the Halliburton Company, Armco Steel Corporation, Louisiana Land and Exploration Company, International Telephone and Telegraph Corporation, Trans-World Airlines, Southland Paper Company, First City Bancorporation, and Highland Oil Company.

He served on important commissions for presidents Truman, Eisenhower, Kennedy, and Johnson, and was appointed to commissions for the state of Texas, from the 1930s under Governor James Allred[qv] to the 1970s under Governor Dolph Briscoe. He was a well-known friend and visible supporter of Lyndon B. Johnson[qv] throughout his political career. He was the recipient of many honors during his lifetime, including Awards from Rice University, Colorado School of Mines, Southwestern University, and the University of Texas. He received several awards in construction and engineering, including the John Fritz Medal in 1977 from the five national engineering societies, and the American Petroleum Institute Gold Medal. Brown served as chairman of the board of trustees of Rice University for fifteen years of his twenty-five years of service on the board. In 1951 the Brown brothers and their wives established the Brown Foundation,[qv] through which they pursued a strong and generous interest in philanthropy. By June 30, 1994, the foundation had granted more than $381 million to charitable institutions, primarily in higher education and the arts. In 1925 Brown married Alice Nelson Pratt of Lometa, Texas, who became well-known for her support for the arts at the local, state, and national levels. They had three children. Brown died on January 22, 1983, and was buried in Glenwood Cemetery, Houston.

BIBLIOGRAPHY: *Houston Business Journal,* March 19, 1979. Houston *Post,* January 23, 1983.
James C. Martin

BROWN, GEORGE WILLIAM (?–1847). George William Brown, a lawyer from Henrico County, Virginia, traveled to Galveston, Texas, in 1842 as a result of a call for volunteers for a proposed expedition against Mexico after the invasion of San Antonio by Rafael Vásquez.[qv] In 1844 he was district attorney of the Second Judicial District. He represented Colorado County at the Convention of 1845,[qv] in which he served on the judiciary committee. Brown died of tuberculosis in 1847.

BIBLIOGRAPHY: Texas House of Representatives, *Biographical Directory of the Texan Conventions and Congresses, 1832–1845* (Austin: Book Exchange, 1941).

BROWN, HARRY WYSE (1827–1907). Harry Wyse Brown, physician, was born in Savannah, Georgia, on October 20, 1827, the son of Robert Cuthbert and Mary Lowe (Clark) Brown. He studied medicine under Robert A. T. Gridley at La Grange, Georgia, at the College of Physicians and Surgeons in New York from 1845 to 1847, and at the University of New York in 1847–48. He graduated from Bellevue Hospital Medical College in May 1848. He practiced in Griffin and Atlanta, Georgia, before 1856, when he became professor of chemistry and anatomy in the Atlanta Medical College. He became a surgeon in the Confederate Army in 1861 and served in hospitals in Columbus, Mississippi, and in Atlanta, Macon, Augusta, and Madison, Georgia. At the end of the war he moved to Belton, Texas, and in 1868 to Waco. He was president of the Waco Medical Society, vice president of the American Medical Association, and president of the Texas State Medical Association in 1875–76 (*see* TEXAS MEDICAL ASSOCIATION). Brown married Mary Eaton Smith of Gallatin, Tennessee, in 1849, and they had four children. He died in Waco at the home of one of his daughters on November 26, 1907.

BIBLIOGRAPHY: Lewis E. Daniell, *Types of Successful Men in Texas* (Austin: Von Boeckmann, 1890). Dayton Kelley, ed., *The Handbook of Waco and McLennan County, Texas* (Waco: Texian, 1972). *A Memorial and Biographical History of McLennan, Falls, Bell, and Coryell Counties* (Chicago: Lewis, 1893; rpt., St. Louis: Ingmire, 1984).
Jeanette H. Flachmeier

BROWN, HENRY STEVENSON (1793–1834). Henry Stevenson Brown, early settler, trader, and Indian fighter, was born in Madison County, Kentucky, on March 8, 1793, the son of Caleb and Jemima (Stevenson) Brown. In 1810 he moved to St. Charles County, Missouri, where he was later sheriff. He volunteered for the War of 1812 and participated in the battle at Fort Clark, Illinois, in 1813. He married Mrs. Margaret Kerr Jones about 1814, moved to Pike County, Missouri, in 1819, and carried on trading via flatboat between Missouri and New Orleans. In December 1824, accompanied by his brother John (Waco) Brown,[qv] he landed at the mouth of the Brazos River equipped to trade with the Mexicans and Indians. In 1825 he was in command of a party of settlers that attacked and destroyed a band of Waco Indians at the site of present Waco. Brown was in Green DeWitt's[qv] colony in 1825 and in 1829 was in command of a company from Gonzales on a thirty-two-day campaign against the Indians. From 1826 to 1832 he engaged in the Mexican trade from headquarters in Brazoria, Gonzales, and San Antonio. At the time of the Anahuac Disturbances[qv] of 1832, Brown carried the information on the Turtle Bayou Resolutions[qv] from Gonzales to the Neches and Sabine River settlements and under John Austin[qv] commanded a company of eighty men in the battle of Velasco.[qv] He was a delegate from Gonzales to the Convention of 1832[qv] at San Felipe de Austin and in 1833 was a member of the ayuntamiento[qv] of Brazoria. He died in Columbia on July 26, 1834. Brown County was named for him.

BIBLIOGRAPHY: DeWitt Clinton Baker, comp., *A Texas Scrap-Book* (New York: Barnes, 1875; rpt. 1887; facsimile rpt., Austin: Steck, 1935). Texas House of Representatives, *Biographical Directory of the Texan Conventions and Congresses, 1832–1845* (Austin: Book Exchange, 1941). Mrs. C. A. Westbrook, "Captain Henry S. Brown, Pioneer," *Frontier Times,* June 1925.
John Q. Anderson

BROWN, HERMAN (1892–1962). Herman Brown, business founder and executive, was born in Belton, Texas, on November 10, 1892, the son of Riney Louis and Lucy Wilson (King) Brown. His Texas roots went back two generations to 1839; his mother's grandfather, Hugh B. King, and his mother's father, Rufus Y. King, were county judges of Milam and Lee counties, respectively. After studying briefly at the University of Texas in 1911, Brown was employed by a contractor in Belton. In 1914 he was given eighteen mules in lieu of back wages and went into the construction business. In 1919 his brother-in-law, Dan Root, advanced him money for working capital, and the company was named Brown and Root, Incorporated. In 1922 Herman's younger brother, George Rufus Brown,[qv] joined the firm. Dan Root, a prosperous Central Texas cotton farmer, died in 1929. The paving of dirt roads and building of steel bridges for municipal and county governments in Central Texas led the firm to a successful joint bid in 1936 to construct the Marshall Ford Dam (now Mansfield Dam) on the Colorado River. A 1940 contract to construct the Corpus Christi Naval Air Station was the first of their big federal war projects. The brothers formed the Brown Shipbuilding Company in 1942 and constructed more than 350 vessels for the navy. The shipyard had a labor force of 25,000 and won the Army-Navy E and a presidential citation. After World War II[qv] the Brown brothers and other investors purchased the Big and Little Inch[qv] pipelines from the government with the winning high bid of $143 million and organized a new company, Texas Eastern Transmission Company, which is now a part of Pan-

George Rufus Brown (left) and Herman Brown at the Greens Bayou Marine Fabrication Yard, 1957. Courtesy Isabel Brown Wilson, Houston. Brown and Root, Inc., pioneered in the construction of platforms for offshore oil and gas production.

handle Eastern Corporation. Brown and Root was widely known during the 1950s and 1960s for constructing United States air and naval bases (in Spain, France, and Guam) and roads, dams, bridges, petrochemical plants, and large offshore drilling platforms. In 1961 the company won the planning contract for the $200 million Manned Spacecraft Center in Houston. In December 1962 the Halliburton Company[qv] of Dallas purchased Brown and Root, which continues to operate under its own name. In 1917 Brown married Margarett Root; they later adopted two children. Brown died on November 15, 1962, and was buried in Glenwood Cemetery, Houston. Margarett Root Brown died on January 25, 1963, and is buried by his side. Brown was a cofounder of the Brown Foundation.[qv] He was a member of the board of directors of First City National Bank of Houston, Texas Eastern Transmission Corporation, Southwestern University, Armco Steel Corporation, and Texas Children's Hospital[qv] in Houston. He was also active in oil and gas exploration and ranching.

BIBLIOGRAPHY: Houston *Chronicle,* November 16, 1962. Houston *Post,* November 16, 1962.

BROWN, INA CORINNE (1896–1984). Ina Corinne Brown, teacher, was born in Gatesville, Texas, on May 27, 1896, the daughter of John Dayton and Corinne (Wells) Brown. She was a descendant of Orceneth Fisher,[qv] prominent pioneer Methodist preacher in Texas. Her great-grandfather Fisher's second wife was Rebecca Jane Fisher.[qv] Ina attended Southern Methodist University from 1919 to 1921. She then moved to Nashville, Tennessee, where she served on the educational staff of the Methodist Church[qv] until 1934. The University of Chicago granted her a B.A. degree in 1936 and a Ph.D. in anthropology in 1942. She also studied at the London School of Economics and, in 1937–38, at the British Museum on a Rosenwald Fellowship. From 1939 to 1941 she worked for the federal government's National Survey of Higher Education for Negroes. Her duties there included assisting black colleges throughout the United States to develop their curricula. She also traveled extensively in Europe, Asia, and Africa to study racial problems. She was professor of social anthropology at Scarritt College, Nashville, from 1942 to 1966; after her retirement she was professor emeritus there. She was a special lecturer at Peabody College, Vanderbilt University, and Fisk University, all in Nashville. She was the author of three books on race relations: *The Story of the American Negro* (1936), *Race Relations in a Democracy* (1949), and *Understanding Other Cultures* (1963). *Understanding Other Cultures* was once required freshman English reading at the University of Texas and has been used in Japanese colleges for students learning English. Brown contributed to the *Encyclopedia of Black America* (1981), and she was a consultant in behavioral sciences to *World Book Encyclopedia* from 1963 to 1966.

Ina Brown was a member of Phi Beta Kappa, Sigma Xi, the International Federation of University Women, and the American Association of University Women.[qv] She was a fellow of the American Anthropological Association, the American Geographical Society, the American Association for the Advancement of Sciences, and the Society for Applied Anthropology. She served as a consultant to city public school systems involved in desegregation in Alabama, Tennessee, Mississippi, Georgia, and Florida, a service sponsored by Peabody College.

In 1929–30 she and a woman companion crossed Central Africa from the mouth of the Congo on the west coast to Mombasa in British East Africa (now Kenya) on the east coast, a distance of 1,700 miles. It was a journey that probably no woman had made before that time. The two traveled by boat and train, were carried in hammocks, and walked. On her trip to Asia Brown interviewed Mahatma Gandhi and Toyohiko Kagawa. In her later years her health was poor, but she continued her reading and writing—especially letters to the Nashville daily papers. She was chosen in 1984 as a distinguished alumna of Southern Methodist University. Ina Brown died in Hermitage, Tennessee, near Nashville, on May 12, 1984.

BIBLIOGRAPHY: *Contemporary Authors. Who's Who of American Women,* 1958–59.

Walter N. Vernon

BROWN, JACOB (?–1846). Jacob Brown, United States Army officer, was born in Massachusetts and enlisted as a private in the Eleventh United States Infantry on August 3, 1812. By the time of his commissioning as an ensign in the Eleventh Infantry on April 15, 1814, he had risen to the rank of sergeant. Promotion to third lieutenant came on May 1 and to second lieutenant on September 1, 1814. On May 17, 1815, he was transferred to the Sixth Infantry, where he served as regimental quartermaster from April 16 to June 1, 1821. He was promoted to first lieutenant on August 18, 1819, to captain on April 7, 1825, and to major on February 27, 1843.

With the outbreak of the Mexican War[qv] Brown and his regiment were ordered to the Rio Grande with Gen. Zachary Taylor's[qv] army of occupation. When Mexican general Mariano Arista's[qv] army crossed the Rio Grande on April 1, 1846, Taylor ordered the strengthening of Fort Texas, on the north bank opposite Matamoros. By May 1 the fortification was complete, and Taylor marched the bulk of his army toward Point Isabel to protect his supply line, leaving Brown in command of Fort Texas. Brown's garrison consisted of elements of the Seventh Infantry, Capt. Allen Lowd's four eighteen-pounder cannons, and Capt. Braxton Bragg's battery of field artillery, about 500 men in all. At 5:00 A.M. on May 3, Arista began his attack on Fort Texas with a bombardment from Matamoros and investment by Gen. Pedro Ampudia's[qv] infantry brigade. Lowd's eighteen-pounders quickly silenced the Mexican artillery, but a second battery downriver and out of range of the lighter American guns soon took up the bombardment. Hearing the sound of the guns, Taylor dispatched Texas Ranger Samuel H. Walker[qv] with instructions to Brown to defend Fort Texas to the last man. Although he outnumbered Brown's garrison by several thousand men, Ampudia determined that his artillery could not breach the fort's dirt walls and that an assault would be too costly and so settled into a formal siege. He posted Gen. Antonio Canales's[qv] irregular cavalry on the road to Point Isabel to block American reinforcements and supplies, then continued his bombardment and waited for starvation to compel Brown's surrender. At about 10:00 A.M. on May 6, 1846, Brown was mortally wounded by an enemy shell; he died on May 9. Command of the fort devolved upon Capt. Edgar S. Hawkins, who refused Ampudia's surrender demand on the afternoon of the sixth and held his lines until Arista withdrew Ampudia's command beyond the Rio Grande on May 8. Major Brown was one of the only two American fatalities in the siege. Fort Texas was renamed Fort Brown in his honor, and the city of Brownsville derived its name from that of the fort.

BIBLIOGRAPHY: K. Jack Bauer, *The Mexican War, 1846–1848* (New York: Macmillan, 1974). Francis B. Heitman, *Historical Register and Dictionary of the United States Army* (2 vols., Washington: GPO, 1903; rpt., Urbana: University of Illinois Press, 1965).

Thomas W. Cutrer

BROWN, JAMES MADISON (1839–1892). James Madison Brown, lawman and horseman, son of John Humphrey and Jane Ann Brown, was born in Alabama in 1839. The Browns, with several other families, settled permanently in what is now San Saba County, Texas, where John Brown helped establish the town of San Saba. James, the eldest son, grew up to be an excellent judge of horses and in his later years became wealthy from winning on the turf. During the Civil War[qv] he served as a minuteman under the command of W. R. Wood and later under his father's command. In 1869 he was probably one of the trail hands that drove a large herd from the San Saba region to Roswell, New Mexico Territory. In 1870 he resided in Washington County, where he had already established a reputation as a gambler. In 1872–73 he served as a private in the state police force. He joined Washington County Volunteer Militia Company A, commanded by Capt. Leander H. McNelly,[qv] and served from April 30 to November 30, 1875. During this time he also was establishing a reputation as a horseman; he raced successfully in Gonzales County as well as Travis County.

Lee County, separated from Washington County in 1874, was still a frontier area and needed strong law enforcement officials. James McKeown was the new county's first sheriff, and on February 15, 1876, Brown was elected to take his place. He served in that office during a very lawless era and established a reputation for being an energetic sheriff. But his years were not without controversy. He was involved in several personal feuds as well as several killings. His most notable act in office was the legal hanging of noted outlaw William P. Longley.[qv]

After his career as sheriff, Brown developed his racing stables and raced on tracks in cities outside of Texas, including St. Louis, Nashville, and Chicago. On September 6, 1892, while at the Garfield Park in Chicago, police attempted to arrest him on an old murder charge from Texas. Brown resisted, and in the ensuing gunfight he was killed, along with two members of the Chicago police force. Chicago newspapers described him as a millionaire but also alleged that he may have murdered as many as fourteen men while he was sheriff. It was surmised that his position and the fear he engendered among his contemporaries protected him from prosecution. Brown was buried in Fort Worth. He was survived by his wife and five children.

BIBLIOGRAPHY: Ed Ellsworth Bartholomew, *Wild Bill Longley: A Texas Hard-Case* (Houston: Frontier Press of Texas, 1953). Lee County Historical Survey Committee, *A History of Lee County* (Quanah, Texas: Nortex, 1974). *San Saba County History* (San Saba, Texas: San Saba County Historical Commission, 1983).

Chuck Parsons

BROWN, JAMES MOREAU (1821–1895). James Moreau Brown, businessman, was born in Orange County, New York, on September 22, 1821, the son of John M. and Hannah (Krantz) Brown. The family moved to New York City when Brown was a child. As a teenager he drove a canal boat along the Erie Canal, working with Charley Mallory, later of the Mallory Steamship Lines. He also served an apprenticeship as a brickmason and plasterer and developed ability as an architect. After his apprenticeship Brown traveled in the South. He stayed for a while in New Orleans and then lived for several years in Vicksburg, where he prospered financially.

In 1843 he moved to Galveston, Texas, where he influenced the building of first brick jail and the old market. In 1848 he was elected an alderman. He entered the hardware business in 1847, then formed a partnership in 1850 with Stephen Kirkland, a blacksmith. Kirkland reportedly built the first hook and ladder truck in Texas. Brown was an original member of the first Galveston volunteer fire brigade, organized in October 1843. When Kirkland died in 1859, Brown closed the business and became president of the Galveston, Houston and Henderson Railroad. For his help in transporting men from Houston to help recapture Galveston from Union troops, Gen. John B. Magruder[qv] rewarded him with the honorary title of colonel. Brown also served the Confederacy as a purchasing agent in Mexico. After the war he resigned from the presidency of the railroad and engaged in the wholesale hardware business in partnership with J. W. Lang. In 1875 Lang sold out to Brown, who then admitted his son J. S. Brown to full partnership in the firm, the name of which was changed to J. S. Brown and Company. The firm became one of the largest enterprises of its kind in the South. After the war Brown also designed and supervised the construction of the First National Bank of Galveston, which was organized in 1866.

By 1870 he was one of the wealthiest men in Texas, with $175,000 in real property and $100,000 in personal property. In 1871 Governor Edmund J. Davis[qv] appointed him to the Galveston board of aldermen. Brown also served as a director and president of the First National Bank of Galveston, director and president of the Galveston Wharf Company (*see* GALVESTON WHARVES), director of the Union and Marine Fire Insurance Company, and president of the board of the Life Association of America. In addition, he promoted the Galveston gas and light companies and served as chairman of the committee for construction of the city waterworks.

Brown married Rebecca Ashton Stoddart of Philadelphia in 1846. In 1859 he built what was reputed to be the first brick house in Galveston, known as Ashton Villa.[qv] He also reportedly donated generously, as well as anonymously, to individuals in need. He was a member of the Knights Templar and the Odd Fellows. He died on December 24, 1895. His funeral was held in Trinity Church (Episcopal), and he was buried in Galveston Cemetery. He was survived by his wife and five children.

BIBLIOGRAPHY: Drury Blakeley Alexander and (photographs) Todd Webb, *Texas Homes of the Nineteenth Century* (Austin: University of Texas Press, 1966). John Henry Brown, *Indian Wars and Pioneers of Texas* (Austin: Daniell, 1880; reprod., Easley, South Carolina: Southern Historical Press, 1978). Galveston *Daily News*, December 26, 1895. Dermont H. Hardy and Ingham S. Roberts, eds., *Historical Review of South-East Texas* (2 vols., Chicago: Lewis, 1910). Charles Waldo Hayes, *Galveston: History of the Island and the City* (2 vols., Austin: Jenkins Garrett, 1974). Ray Miller, *Ray Miller's Galveston* (Houston: Cordovan Press, 1983).

Jeanette H. Flachmeier

BROWN, JAMES MURRY (1800–1836). James Murry Brown, Alamo defender, was born in Pennsylvania in 1800. He moved to Texas in 1835 and registered in De León's colony[qv] on April 17, 1835. He took part in the siege of Bexar[qv] and later served in the Alamo garrison. Brown died in the battle of the Alamo[qv] on March 6, 1836.

BIBLIOGRAPHY: Daughters of the American Revolution, *The Alamo Heroes and Their Revolutionary Ancestors* (San Antonio, 1976). Daughters of the Republic of Texas, *Muster Rolls of the Texas Revolution* (Austin, 1986). Bill Groneman, *Alamo Defenders* (Austin: Eakin, 1990).

Bill Groneman

BROWN, JEREMIAH (?–?). Jeremiah Brown, naval officer of the Republic of Texas,[qv] was given command of the schooner-of-war *Invincible*[qv] on March 12, 1836. Although Commodore Charles E. Hawkins[qv] is said to have placed Brown in irons immediately after taking command of the Texas fleet at Matagorda, he nevertheless retained command of what was reckoned the finest ship in the Texas Navy.[qv] As captain of the *Invincible,* Brown was dispatched by Hawkins to patrol off Matamoros to prevent Mexican reinforcements and supplies from reaching Antonio López de Santa Anna's[qv] army in Texas and in particular to engage or drive off the Mexican ship *Moctezuma.* Brown encountered and engaged the Mexican brig-of-war, then rechristened *Bravo,* at the mouth of the Rio Grande on April 10, 1836. The *Bravo,* fighting without her rudder, was run aground and wrecked by a broadside from the *Invincible.* Later that same day Brown captured the American-owned brig *Pocket,*[qv] out of New Orleans, en route from Matamoros to Santa Anna's army in Texas with a contraband cargo of flour, rice, lard, biscuit, and 300 kegs of powder. Brown arrived on April 8 with his prize at Galveston, and there he learned from captured documents that Santa Anna had plans to capture all Texas ports and to station 1,000 men on Galveston Island. Thus forewarned, the Texas government hastily fortified the island. The provisions captured aboard the *Pocket* ultimately were consigned to Sam Houston's[qv] army. Brown, then aboard the *Invincible* at Galveston, was the first Texas naval officer to receive word of the Texas victory at San Jacinto. Overjoyed, he began firing the midship gun until he reflected, "Hold on boys or old Hawkins will put me in irons again."

The *Invincible* sailed to New Orleans to refit, and the crew was charged with piracy. Forty-six of the crew members left the city abruptly to avoid arrest, leaving Brown ashore. When his ship was returned to New Orleans on May 1, under the escort of the United States ship *Warren*, however, Brown surrendered to federal authorities on May 20. On the same day he was released on bail provided by Thomas Toby,[qv] a merchant friendly to the Texas cause, and he was later acquitted of the charge. After being rearrested on the same charge, Brown was again aided by Toby, who purchased the *Pocket* and paid all of the claims against the crew of the *Invincible*. Brown was then personally sued by the *Pocket*'s insurer for the cost of its cargo, but no record of the suit's outcome has come to light. The United States government concluded a convention with Texas, whereby Texas paid $11,750 for damage claims filed by passengers and crew of the *Pocket*, plus $705 in interest.

The *Invincible* was released from New Orleans and went back on patrol in the Gulf. On June 1 she took aboard the captured Mexican general Santa Anna and was at first ordered to sail with him to Veracruz. On June 5, however, volunteers under Gen. Thomas J. Green[qv] forbade the *Invincible* to sail. Thus relieved of that responsibility, Brown and his ship rode at anchor off Velasco until July 4, when they came to the aid of the *Brutus*,[qv] menaced off Matagorda by the powerful *Vencedor del Álamo*, and succeeded in frightening away the Mexican ship and chasing it as far as Veracruz. After blockading the harbor for several days, Brown returned to New Orleans, where his ship took on passengers Branch T. Archer and William H. Wharton[qqv] and sailed on July 13 for Galveston. Brown then returned to Velasco and received orders to blockade Matamoros. The *Invincible* was ordered to New York for refitting on August 4 and arrived there in September. Brown returned his ship to Galveston on March 14, 1837. That month he was relieved of duty, and the *Invincible* was placed under the command of Commodore H. L. Thompson by order of the new president, Sam Houston. Jeremiah Brown was the elder brother of William S. Brown,[qv] also a captain in the Texas Navy.

BIBLIOGRAPHY: Alex Dienst, "The Navy of the Republic of Texas," *Quarterly of the Texas State Historical Association* 12–13 (January–October 1909; rpt., Fort Collins, Colorado: Old Army Press, 1987). C. L. Douglas, *Thunder on the Gulf: The Story of the Texas Navy* (Dallas: Turner, 1936; rpt., Fort Collins, Colorado: Old Army Press, 1973). Jim Dan Hill, *The Texas Navy* (New York: Barnes, 1962). C. T. Neu, "The Case of the Brig *Pocket*," *Quarterly of the Texas State Historical Association* 12 (April 1909). Amelia W. Williams and Eugene C. Barker, eds., *The Writings of Sam Houston, 1813–1863* (8 vols., Austin: University of Texas Press, 1938–43; rpt., Austin and New York: Pemberton Press, 1970).

Thomas W. Cutrer

BROWN, JOHN (?–?). John Brown, one of Stephen F. Austin's[qv] Old Three Hundred[qv] colonists, was born in Kentucky and came to Texas from Arkansas before August 19, 1824, when he received title to a league and a labor of land now in Waller and Harris counties. According to the census of 1826 he was a single man, thirty-seven years old, and had six slaves. The *Texas Gazette*[qv] of August 29, 1830, ran a notice that John Brown had opened a house of entertainment at San Antonio de Béxar. In January 1836 Thomas Barnett[qv] was administrator for the estate of John Brown, deceased. It is uncertain whether or not the man who was dead in 1836 was the original colonist, because several men named John Brown were members of the Austin colony.

BIBLIOGRAPHY: Eugene C. Barker, ed., *The Austin Papers* (3 vols., Washington: GPO, 1924–28). Lester G. Bugbee, "The Old Three Hundred: A List of Settlers in Austin's First Colony," *Quarterly of the Texas State Historical Association* 1 (October 1897). *Telegraph and Texas Register*, January 30, 1836.

BROWN, JOHN (1786?–1852). John (Red) Brown, Democratic county and state official, was born in Ireland on October 30, 1786, although sources differ about his year and place of birth. He moved to Texas in 1836 and settled near Nacogdoches, where he practiced law and farmed. He was listed as an Irishman and a farmer on the Nacogdoches County census records of 1839, 1840, and 1845. A John Brown who claimed residence from 1836 and was able to prove residence from 1838 was granted 640 acres on January 22, 1846. He represented Nacogdoches County in the House of the Sixth Congress of the republic (1841–42), and he may have helped form a citizens' patrol on August 3, 1841, to help control the black population in Nacogdoches County. Brown helped organize the state Democratic party[qv] in Austin on April 27, 1846. He was one of three commissioners appointed on June 15, 1848, to locate the state penitentiary.

Brown was one of the founders of Henderson County when it was formed from Nacogdoches County in 1846. He was notary public in 1848, and by 1849 he operated a ferry across Kickapoo Creek. He received a license from the state of Texas to build a toll bridge near Brownsboro, or Old Normandy, as the location was called at that time. A bridge was in place during the Civil War,[qv] but it is not known if Brown actually constructed it. He was appointed on July 6, 1850, as one of the county commissioners assigned to locate the county seat of Henderson County. Athens was their choice. Brown was also elected a county commissioner for the 1850–52 term. Old Brownsboro, one-half mile southeast of the site of present-day Brownsboro, was named for him. He had that site surveyed on the proposed Southern Pacific rail route. Brown was married first to Margaret Hodges Brooks, who died in 1849, and subsequently, on March 20, 1851, to Elizabeth Holland in Henderson County. He probably died in 1852.

BIBLIOGRAPHY: Mrs. Claude Corder, comp., *1850–1860 Census of Henderson County, Texas, Including Slave Schedule and 1846 Tax List* (Chicago: Adams, 1984). Daughters of the Republic of Texas, *Founders and Patriots of the Republic of Texas* (Austin, 1963–). Carolyn Reeves Ericson, *Nacogdoches, Gateway to Texas: A Biographical Directory* (2 vols., Fort Worth: Arrow-Curtis Printing, 1974, 1987). Carolyn Reeves Ericson, *Nacogdoches Headrights: A Record of the Disposition of Land in East Texas and in Other Parts of that State, 1838–1848* (New Orleans: Polyanthos, 1977). J. J. Faulk, *History of Henderson County* (Athens, Texas: Athens Review Printing, 1926). *Old Homes of Henderson County* (Athens, Texas: Henderson County Historical Commission, 1982). Texas House of Representatives, *Biographical Directory of the Texan Conventions and Congresses, 1832–1845* (Austin: Book Exchange, 1941).

Linda Sybert Hudson

BROWN, JOHN (1796–1833). John (Waco) Brown, early settler, was born in Kentucky on September 9, 1796. He married Nancy Ann Howell in Missouri in 1820 and came to Texas with his brother, Henry S. Brown,[qv] in December 1824. He was captured by the Waco Indians in 1825 and held prisoner for more than a year, thereby acquiring his sobriquet. He brought his wife and two sons from Missouri in 1829 and settled at San Felipe. In April 1833 he furnished supplies for José de las Piedras[qv] to move his troops west to Mexico. Brown was a legal client of William B. Travis[qv] in San Felipe shortly before his death in 1833. He is sometimes confused with another John Brown,[qv] one of Stephen F. Austin's[qv] Old Three Hundred[qv] colonists.

BIBLIOGRAPHY: Homer S. Thrall, *A Pictorial History of Texas* (St. Louis: Thompson, 1879).

BROWN, JOHN DUFF (ca. 1823–1908). John Duff Brown, physician, son of Nancy Ann (Howell) and John (Waco) Brown,[qv] was born in Lexington, Kentucky, about 1823. He was brought to San Antonio, Texas, by his parents in 1827 or 1828. After his father's death in 1833, he lived for a time at Gonzales with his uncle, Henry Stevenson Brown,[qv] and at Brazoria, where his mother operated a hotel. He returned to Kentucky to attend a seminary in Lexington and, after graduating from Collier College, began the practice of medicine at

Jackson, Kentucky. Brown returned to Texas in 1847 and practiced medicine with his uncle C. S. Brown at Gonzales until he entered John C. (Jack) Hays's[qv] western regiment for service in the Mexican War.[qv] In 1848 Brown married Mary Anna Mayes of Tuscumbia, Alabama. He reentered the army early in 1849 to serve as assistant surgeon for the company under Henry E. McCulloch.[qv] From 1849 until the Civil War,[qv] Brown practiced medicine and operated a plantation at Oakland in Colorado County. Although over age, Brown volunteered for the Confederate Army, first in Ebenezar B. Nichols'[qv] regiment at Galveston and then in Company D of Waul's Legion.[qv] He was serving in Mississippi in 1864, when he was discharged because of disability. Brown moved to Llano County, where he continued to practice medicine while farming and ranching. His reminiscences, written in 1907, were published in the *Quarterly of the Texas State Historical Association* in 1909. Brown died in Llano on May 10, 1908.

BIBLIOGRAPHY: John Duff Brown, "Reminiscences of Jno. Duff Brown," *Quarterly of the Texas State Historical Association* 12 (April 1909). Frank W. Johnson, *A History of Texas and Texans* (5 vols., ed. E. C. Barker and E. W. Winkler [Chicago and New York: American Historical Society, 1914; rpt. 1916]). *Texas State Journal of Medicine*, September 1928.

BROWN, JOHN HENRY (1820–1895). John Henry Brown, pioneer historian, newspaper editor, soldier, and legislator, was born on October 29, 1820, in Pike County, Missouri, to Margaret (Jones) and Henry S. Brown.[qv] Although Henry S. Brown was involved in Texas affairs from 1824 till his death in 1834, his family remained in Missouri, where John Henry began working in a printing office at age twelve. The younger Brown spent most of his adolescence working on newspapers in Pike County and St. Louis and received little formal schooling. In November 1837 he moved to Texas to live with his uncle, James Kerr,[qv] on the Lavaca River. Two years later Brown moved to Austin and began working on the Austin *Texas Sentinel*.[qv] He was soon drawn into skirmishes with Indians on the Texas frontier and participated as a private in the battle of Plum Creek[qv] in August 1840. By 1841 he had been elected first sergeant of a company of minutemen. He moved to Victoria the same year, but he remained active in frontier warfare. In the spring of 1842, in the wake of the Mexican invasions,[qv] he joined John C. Hays's[qv] company. In September of that year he suffered a hip injury in the battle of Salado.[qv] He then took part in the Somervell expedition[qv] and afterward returned to San Antonio, on January 7, 1843.

In April of the same year Brown returned to Missouri, where he married Marion (Mary) F. Mitchel on July 9. He remained in his home state working as a journalist for almost two years, then returned to Texas with his wife in April 1845 and settled in a small community near Rock Spring. In late 1846 he moved again to Victoria, where he gained employment on the Victoria *Advocate*[qv] and became a major of the newly formed state militia. In 1848 he and his family, now including two sons, moved to Indianola. There Brown founded and edited the Indianola *Bulletin*, contributed a series of articles on "Early Life in the Southwest" to *De Bow's Review*, and published a pamphlet on Texas history.

In 1854 Brown became associate editor of the *Civilian and Galveston Gazette* (*see* GALVESTON *CIVILIAN*) and gained such popularity in Galveston that he was elected to the state legislature. After his legislative service he was elected mayor of Galveston, in 1856. He began a second term as mayor in 1857, but it was cut short by his reelection to the legislature.

Tired and suffering from ill health, Brown moved in 1858 to Belton. He was appointed to a committee to study problems with placing Indians on reservations and became captain of two military companies formed in 1859 to enforce the committee's recommendations. In this capacity he again saw action as an Indian fighter. He also again took on editorial duties, this time for the Belton *Democrat*. He edited the *Democrat* until 1861, when he became a delegate to the Secession Convention,[qv] where he served as chairman of the committee that prepared the articles of secession. With the outbreak of the Civil War[qv] he became a member of Brig. Gen. Benjamin McCulloch's[qv] staff; he advanced from private to major and published the War Bulletin from McCulloch's camp in Arkansas. When the general was killed in 1862 Brown was transferred to the staff of Gen. Henry E. McCulloch,[qv] where he served as assistant adjutant general. But poor health forced him in 1863 to rejoin his family, then in Austin. During the remainder of the war Brown served with the Texas militia and commanded the Third Frontier District. He participated with Col. John S. Ford[qv] in the last engagement of the war, the battle of Palmito Ranch,[qv] on May 13, 1865.

In June 1865 Brown and his family emigrated to Mexico, along with a number of other disaffected Southerners. The Browns settled in the Tuxpan River valley, and Brown surveyed areas for settlement as assistant commissioner of immigration for the Mexican government of Maximilian. In 1869 he visited Texas and the East on behalf of the Mexican government, and the next year he made a lecture tour of the northern states for the Evangelical Church in Mexico. After a brief period in New Orleans the family returned to Texas to live in 1871; they finally settled in Dallas. In 1872 Brown was again elected to the state legislature, and three years later he became a member of the state Constitutional Convention of 1875.[qv]

During the last fifteen years of his life he divided his time primarily between political duties and historical writing and editing. In 1880–81 he served as the revising editor of the *Encyclopedia of the New West*. In 1881 he was also appointed state commissioner for the surveying, marking, and locating of school lands. He served as a Dallas alderman in 1884 and from 1885 to 1889 as the city's mayor. From 1888 to 1890 he also held a post as justice of the peace. Meanwhile, he found time to write and publish two historical books, *The History of Dallas County, 1837–1887* (1887) and *The Life and Times of Henry Smith* (1887). These were followed by his two most ambitious works, *Indian Wars and Pioneers of Texas* (ca. 1896) and *The History of Texas from 1685 to 1892* (1892), both considered standards.

Brown and his wife had five children, including a daughter, Marion Brown Taylor, who studied under San Antonio artist Julian Onderdonk[qv] and illustrated her father's *History of Texas from 1685 to 1892* and her mother's *A Condensed History of Texas for Schools* (1895). Brown died of a bronchial ailment on May 31, 1895, in Dallas. His voluminous papers are preserved in the Barker Texas History Center,[qv] University of Texas at Austin.

BIBLIOGRAPHY: John Henry Brown Papers, Barker Texas History Center, University of Texas at Austin. Lawrence E. Honig, *John Henry Brown, Texian Journalist, 1820–1895* (El Paso: Texas Western Press, 1973). *Memorial and Biographical History of Dallas County* (Chicago: Lewis, 1892; rpt., Dallas: Walsworth, 1976). *Erma Baker*

BROWN, LEONARD BENJAMIN (1901–1968). Leonard Benjamin Brown, founder of Texas-based common carriers, the son of Robert Benjamin and Emma Pearce Brown, was born in 1901 at Beeville. He went to Beeville High School and attended Morris Business School for a year, but as a youth also drove a mule team and worked for the Praeger Hardware Company and the Missouri Pacific Railroad in McAllen. He joined the Texas infantry, served as a field agent for the United States Census Bureau in 1920, and later managed a tailor shop before joining his father's R. B. Brown Transfer Company in 1921. In 1924 he founded the Robstown Transportation and Storage Company, which transported cotton and later evolved into a common carrier. Brown overcame hurricanes[qv] and the lack of paved roads to reach local, and then statewide, destinations. He expanded into Oklahoma and finally across the nation, before regulation by the Texas Railroad and Interstate Commerce commissions was established, and integrated his business by putting sales representatives at each of the company's terminal areas. In 1927 Brown moved to Corpus Christi, where he founded the Port City Transport Company. He consolidated his businesses in 1930 and sold them in 1944.

He continued to found businesses in the 1940s. At Kerrville he organized the Leonard B. Brown and Brother Insurance Agency and built KEVT. In 1941 at Dallas he organized a company that in 1948 became Best Motor Lines, another common carrier, which he sold in 1955. As a director of the Houston and Kerrville chambers of commerce, he also made numerous real estate investments. After a truck strike of American Federation of Labor workers in 1950, Brown founded Transport Insurance, and in 1958 he established the Transport Life Insurance Company. He also organized the Howard Electric Company and Bromac Corporation in 1956 and Texas Oklahoma Express at Dallas in 1957. In 1960 he organized the First Business Investment Corporation, and in 1963 helped organize the Commercial National Bank of Dallas. By the 1980s Brown's Red Arrow trucking firm had 867 employees, Best Motor Lines employed 1,374, Texas Oklahoma Express 117, and Transport Insurance 180. On April 10, 1937, Brown married Virginia Holloway. He died at Beeville on April 17, 1968. *Diana J. Kleiner*

BROWN, MONTAGUE KINGSMILL (1878–1964). Montague Kingsmill Brown, cattleman, entrepreneur, and civic leader in Pampa, was born on May 22, 1878, near London, England. His father was a broker with the London Stock Exchange and, as Brown later quipped, "went broker, by Jove!" After leaving school at the age of fifteen, Brown worked in a lumber company and bank, starting at two dollars a week. When the Boer War broke out in 1899 he enlisted in the British army and saw action in South Africa, where he worked his way up from trooper to regimental sergeant major. After the war he considered returning to Africa to make his fortune. However, in 1902 Brown's uncle Andrew Kingsmill, manager of Lord Rosebery's London bank, was sent by his employer to investigate the property of the White Deer Lands (*see* FRANCKLYN LAND AND CATTLE COMPANY) in the Panhandle[qv] of Texas. On returning to England, Kingsmill persuaded his nephew to go to Texas and work for the syndicate.

Accordingly, Brown arrived on April 27, 1903, at the boxcar depot and the two or three stores that composed the new rail town of Pampa. He entered the employ of the White Deer Lands, then managed by George Tyng.[qv] When Timothy Dwight Hobart[qv] succeeded Tyng as manager in 1903, Brown ably assisted him in promoting and surveying the lands being sold to small ranchers and farmers. In all, Brown helped dispose of some 600,000 acres. Over the years he successfully branched out into cattle raising, railroads, and later into oil. Impressed with the Panhandle environment, he obtained his naturalization papers in 1914 and in 1922 married Josye Barnes, a native of Oklahoma. After Hobart resigned as manager of the White Deer Lands in 1924, Brown and C. V. P. Buckler[qv] were appointed comanagers of the properties. Brown retired from that position in 1935 but continued to build up his fortune through investments in various businesses. In 1957, when the White Deer Corporation was liquidated, Brown bought the remaining properties with a $70,000 bid.

As a civic leader he devoted his efforts to promoting Pampa as a townsite. He played the drums in Alex Schneider's band, since that was "the only instrument he could play and talk at the same time." He preached the town's first funeral rites, using his Anglican prayer book, and was mayor of Pampa when the town became the Gray county seat in 1928. Brown also served on the school board for sixteen years, was president of the Rotary Club, helped organize the country club, and was a senior warden of St. Matthew's Episcopal Church. In addition, he was a director of Pampa's First National Bank and Southwestern Investment Company and was president of the Security Federal Savings and Loan Association. Brown was a Scottish Rite Mason, generously supported both the Boy and Girl Scouts, and also chaired the Gray County selective service board for six years. Along with C. P. Buckler and Walter Purviance, he was appointed a trustee for the Lovett Estate. In 1952 Brown served as program chairman for the county's fiftieth anniversary celebration. In addition, he was a vice president of the Panhandle-Plains Historical Society[qv] and with Buckler was instrumental in donating the White Deer Land Company records to the Panhandle-Plains Museum[qv] in Canyon.

Among his many honors, Brown was named man of the year by the Pampa Chamber of Commerce in 1958 and adult leader of the year by the city's Key Club in 1963. In January 1964 he was awarded an honorary doctor of laws degree by Incarnate Word College in San Antonio. He sponsored the M. K. Brown Range Life series of historical books, published by the University of Texas Press.[qv] Brown was robust and was said to have "a ready laugh and a story to tell." He contributed much of his fortune to Pampa's businesses and cultural advancements and helped send many young people through college. On September 10, 1964, he died from injuries received in a car collision in Pampa. Portions of his huge bequest were used to construct the M. K. Brown Memorial Civic Auditorium and to renovate the old White Deer land-office building into a county museum.

BIBLIOGRAPHY: Bill Cherry, "White Deer Land Company Records," *Panhandle-Plains Historical Review* 32 (1959). *Gray County Bicentennial Observance, 1776–1976: Souvenir Program* (Pampa, Texas: Gray County Bicentennial Committee, 1976). Sylvia Grider, "'He's for Progress': C. P. Buckler and the White Deer Land Company," West Texas Historical Association *Yearbook* 43 (1967). Lester Fields Sheffy, *The Francklyn Land & Cattle Company* (Austin: University of Texas Press, 1963). Lester Fields Sheffy, *The Life and Times of Timothy Dwight Hobart* (Canyon, Texas: Panhandle-Plains Historical Society, 1950). *H. Allen Anderson*

BROWN, REUBEN H. (1851–1875). Reuben H. Brown, city marshal of Cuero during the Sutton-Taylor Feud,[qv] son of Palestine T. and Miriam Brown, was born in Texas on November 28, 1851. His family was from Tennessee. The extent of his formal education may have been well above the average. He was described by historian Victor M. Rose[qv] as "liberally educated, and almost a perfect specimen of physical manhood." Brown grew up on his parents' farm and is listed in the 1870 census as a farm hand. The earliest newspaper account to mention him identifies him as city marshal of Cuero. In January 1874 he shot and killed James Gladney McVea in McGanan's Bar in Cuero.

In the early 1870s Brown was considered a leader of the Sutton-Tumlinson forces, who were waging a feud against the Taylor-Pridgen forces. Authorities were able to get members of both factions to sign a treaty of peace on August 12, 1873, and Brown was one of forty men who signed. But the document was broken not long after the signing. On March 11, 1874, William E. Sutton, leader of the Sutton forces, and his friend Gabriel Webster Slaughter, were killed by cousins William and James C. Taylor on the deck of the steamer *Clinton* at Indianola. A reward of $500 was offered for each of the Taylors. On April 3, 1874, Brown arrested William Taylor on the charge of murdering Sutton; for this Brown received the reward. The press treated the action as a major accomplishment, and Marshal Brown received wide recognition. For unspecified reasons he resigned his office on June 8, 1874.

During the destructive hurricane of September 15–17, 1875, which nearly destroyed Indianola (*see* HURRICANES), William Taylor escaped from jail. He sent word to Brown that he would kill him. On November 17, 1875, Reuben H. Brown was shot and killed while gambling in a Cuero saloon. First reports stated that five unknown men entered the saloon and fired at him, although a later account identified the man who fired first as Mason "Winchester Smith" Arnold. Although no one was ever brought to trial for the killing, it would seem that the cousins William and James C. Taylor had a hand in it. Brown died without having married. He was buried in the family cemetery seven miles south of Clinton. For many years the grave was lost, but it was relocated in 1990. Brown rests today in what is known as the Epperson Cemetery, on private land.

BIBLIOGRAPHY: Cuero *Weekly Star*, January 23, April 8, 15, June 11, 1874. Victor Rose, *The Texas Vendetta, or the Sutton-Taylor Feud* (New York: Little, 1880; rpt., Houston: Frontier, 1956). C. L. Sonnichsen, *I'll Die Before I Run—The Story of the Great Feuds of Texas* (New York: Devin-Adair, 1962). Robert C. Sutton, Jr., *The Sutton-Taylor Feud* (Quanah, Texas: Nortex, 1974). *Chuck Parsons*

BROWN, REUBEN R. (ca. 1808–?). Reuben R. Brown, soldier of the Republic of Texas[qv] and the Confederate States of America, was born in Georgia around 1808 and moved to Texas in November 1835 in company with Hugh and John Love, both also of Georgia. They traveled by way of Nacogdoches to Bexar, where they arrived at the Alamo the day after Col. Edward Burleson[qv] had received the surrender of Gen. Martín Perfecto de Cos.[qv] Brown thereupon joined Capt. B. L. Lawrence's company to participate in the Matamoros expedition of 1835–36.[qv] According to his own account, his escape from the massacre of James Grant's[qv] command at the battle of Agua Dulce Creek[qv] was as miraculous as any on record. On March 2, 1836, according to Brown's account, Grant led some fifteen men in a raid on Gen. José de Urrea's[qv] horse herd at the Camargo ranches, which was being guarded by the troops of a Captain Rodríguez. Brown was chosen to lead the attack and claimed to have personally captured Rodríguez, but Urrea counterattacked and surrounded all of the insurrectionists except Brown, Grant, and Plácido Benavides,[qv] who were riding in the lead of the raiders. Seeing the desperate nature of the situation, Grant dispatched Benavides to inform James W. Fannin[qv] at Goliad of the fate of his command and then followed Brown's recommendation that they "Go in and die with the boys." Brown's horse was shot from under him, and he remounted on the horse of Maj. Robert C. Morris,[qv] who had been killed in the fighting. Thereafter Brown was lanced through the arm and again unhorsed. On March 8, 1836, a Thomas B. Rees wrote to a friend in Georgia that "Rubin Brown & Coln. Grant with about twenty men was attacked in a open perary & Both of them fel and all of there men that was not killed was taken prisoners." According to Brown's claim, he was lassoed and beaten senseless but allowed to live because Urrea wanted to question him. He was taken to Urrea's headquarters at San Patricio, where he was offered his freedom if he would go to Goliad and persuade Fannin to surrender. After declining, Brown was marched to Matamoros, where he was confined and forced to work as a street cleaner by day and sleep in a foul jail at night for eleven months. Then, according to his story, he escaped from prison with the aid of a local Irishman who had been retained by Brown's parents in Georgia, and rejoined the Army of the Republic of Texas by way of Mier and Victoria. Brown received his discharge from Gen. Felix Huston[qv] and departed for North Carolina for the summer.

On returning to Texas he established a plantation at the mouth of the Brazos River with twenty-four slaves. By 1850 he was a prosperous planter with twenty-one slaves, and by 1860 he had amassed real estate valued at $14,250 and personal property, including slaves, valued at $40,335, and employed a French gardener named Pierre. His hospitality was well known. In January 1847 the St. Louis *Spirit of the Times* published "A Texas Hunting Song," composed on Brown's plantation on the eve of a great hunt. With his wife, Jane E., who was also a Georgia native, he had five children.

On April 14, 1845, Brown attended an annexation[qv] meeting at Brazoria and was appointed to a committee to prepare "an Address to the People of Texas" on the subject. When the Civil War[qv] broke out he was elected lieutenant colonel of Col. Joseph Bates's[qv] Thirteenth Texas Infantry and saw service on the Texas coast between Galveston and Matagorda Island, primarily near Brown's home at the mouth of the Brazos. In 1862 he was given command of an independent cavalry battalion, the Twelfth, made up of companies from Bates's regiment. Toward the end of 1863 Brown was promoted to colonel and organized and commanded the Thirty-fifth Texas Cavalry, a consolidation of his own and Maj. Lee C. Rountree's battalions. This regiment served in Texas until it was transferred to Louisiana in the spring of 1864 and saw action in Brig. Gen. Henry E. McCulloch's[qv] brigade of Walker's Texas Division[qv] during the Red River Campaign.[qv] Brown's was one of two regiments named the Thirty-fifth Texas Cavalry, the other being that of Col. James B. Likens. On July 19, 1881, the Texas Veterans' Board approved Brown's application for a pension. Pioneer Texas historian John Henry Brown[qv] referred to Reuben R. Brown as "a brave and intelligent man."

BIBLIOGRAPHY: Harbert Davenport, Notes from an Unfinished Study of Fannin and His Men (MS, Harbert Davenport Collection, Texas State Library, Austin; Barker Texas History Center, University of Texas at Austin). James M. Day, comp., *Texas Almanac, 1857–1873: A Compendium of Texas History* (Waco: Texian Press, 1967). Phineas Jenks Mahan, *Reminiscences of the War for Texas Independence* (Houston, 1872). William S. Speer and John H. Brown, eds., *Encyclopedia of the New West* (Marshall, Texas: United States Biographical Publishing, 1881; rpt., Easley, South Carolina: Southern Historical Press, 1978). Vertical Files, Barker Texas History Center, University of Texas at Austin. *Thomas W. Cutrer*

BROWN, RICHARD (1808–1893). Richard Brown, soldier of the Republic of Texas,[qv] was born in Philadelphia, Pennsylvania, on November 16, 1808, the son of William Brown, a prominent Philadelphia physician. While Richard was one, the family moved to Charleston, South Carolina, in a vain attempt to improve his mother's health. She soon died, however, and Richard's father lived only until the boy was three years old. Thereafter Brown lived with his father's sister, Mrs. William McKee, of Mecklenburg County, North Carolina.

Upon hearing of the war in Texas, Brown sold his small farm, his cotton gin, and his two slaves and moved west. At New Orleans he joined the Texas army on October 19, 1836, by enlisting in Capt. David Sample's Company E of the First Regiment of Texas Infantry. The unit arrived in Texas on November 10. According to his enlistment papers Brown was then twenty-six years old and had light skin, blue eyes, and brown hair. He served through January 1, 1837. For his service he received a bounty warrant for 1,280 acres of land that he sold to N. H. Watrous.

Upon the expiration of his enlistment period Brown returned briefly to North Carolina but by 1838 was back in Texas, where he settled in Robertson County. During the next few years he was a member of what was said to be the first surveying crew on Galveston Island and taught school for a time in Walker County. In response to the incursion of Adrián Woll,[qv] however, Brown enlisted at San Antonio as a private in Capt. William M. Barrett's[qv] company of Col. Joseph L. Bennett's[qv] First Regiment of the Southwestern Army on October 1, 1842. As a member of the Somervell expedition[qv] he marched to the Rio Grande. When Alexander Somervell[qv] ordered the expedition to disband, Brown chose with the majority of his comrades to continue the campaign under the leadership of William S. Fisher.[qv] He saw action at the subsequent battle of Mier and was imprisoned with the rest of the Texans who were captured there. After drawing a white bean in the notorious Black Bean Episode,[qv] Brown was chained to A. B. Hanna and forced to work on the streets of Mexico City. He was subsequently removed to Perote Prison and incarcerated until September 16, 1844, when he and Hanna were released, having been manacled together for sixteen months, according to family sources. The two returned to Texas together by way of Veracruz and New Orleans, and together they settled on Murval Creek in Rusk County, where Brown was employed as overseer on the Reasonover plantation.

In 1849 he married seventeen-year-old Nancy Jane Cook. They had twelve children. In 1850 Brown's real estate was valued at $400. In 1852 he bought a farm six miles east of Henderson, where he lived the rest of his life. On April 21, 1879, he became a founding member of the Mier Prisoners Association at Belton. He was also a Mason. Brown died on his farm on August 24, 1893, and was buried some ten miles east of Henderson at the Pine Grove Presbyterian Church, which he had helped to found. In 1971 the Texas Historical Commission[qv] placed a marker at his gravesite.

BIBLIOGRAPHY: Daughters of the Republic of Texas, *Muster Rolls of the Texas Revolution* (Austin, 1986). Thomas L. Miller, *The Public Lands of Texas, 1519–1970* (Norman: University of Oklahoma Press, 1972). Joseph Milton Nance, *Attack and Counterattack: The Texas-Mexican Frontier, 1842* (Austin: University of Texas Press, 1964). Vertical Files, Barker Texas History Center, University of Texas at Austin.

Thomas W. Cutrer

BROWN, ROBERT (ca. 1818–?). Robert Brown, Alamo defender, was born around 1818 and arrived in Texas in October 1835, a single man. He is mentioned by William Barret Travis[qv] in a letter of February 25, 1836, as being one of the men who sallied forth from the Alamo to La Villita[qv] to burn huts that were affording cover to Mexican troops. Brown was sent out of the Alamo, probably as a courier, sometime later in the siege. He continued to serve the Texan forces during the revolution and guarded baggage and supplies at Harrisburg.

BIBLIOGRAPHY: Daughters of the American Revolution, *The Alamo Heroes and Their Revolutionary Ancestors* (San Antonio, 1976). John H. Jenkins, ed., *The Papers of the Texas Revolution, 1835–1836* (10 vols., Austin: Presidial Press, 1973). Bill Groneman, *Alamo Defenders* (Austin: Eakin, 1990).

Bill Groneman

BROWN, ROBERT T. (1873–1952). Robert T. Brown, judge, was born in 1873 at Brown's Lake, three miles north of Henderson, Texas, the son of Taylor Brown, Jr. His mother was the daughter of Robert W. Smith,[qv] a Texas army officer who fought at San Jacinto. Brown was educated in public schools and at Rock Hill Institute,[qv] near Minden. He read law in the offices of John Arnold and W. C. Buford. Brown said that he received his training "in the field with chain and compass," and since most of the estimated 25,000 cases he tried during his twenty-seven years on the bench involved boundaries and titles, it was to his advantage that he knew the territory. He was admitted to the bar in 1898 and served two terms as county attorney. In 1924 he became district judge of the Fourth Judicial District, which at that time included Rusk, Panola, and Shelby counties. The East Texas boom produced thousands of lawsuits, and many important ones came to Brown's court. He sat on the case against Columbus M. Joiner[qv] to put the oil well Daisy Bradford No. 3 into receivership. He sat on Joiner's cases against Ed Laster and H. L. Hunt,[qv] both of which resulted in Joiner's withdrawing his complaint. Brown's court decided in favor of Parade Gasoline Company when its residue gas was involved in the New London School Explosion.[qv]

Judge Brown became known for his dry wit. His judgment in the case against Joiner has become famous: "I believe that when it takes a man three and a half years to find a baby he ought to be able to rock it for a while. This hearing is postponed indefinitely." About the attraction of oil: "If you want a successful gathering of long-lost kinfolks, just manage to find oil on the old homestead." And about the failure to find it: "Nothing, not even the facts, can settle a lawsuit as quickly and as thoroughly as a dry hole." Brown was a Mason. He died of a heart attack in his courthouse office on October 24, 1952, and was buried at Lakewood Memorial Cemetery in Henderson.

BIBLIOGRAPHY: James Anthony Clark and Michael T. Halbouty, *The Last Boom* (New York: Random House, 1972). Dallas *News*, October 14, 1951, October 25, 1952. Vertical Files, Barker Texas History Center, University of Texas at Austin.

Jerrell Dean Palmer

BROWN, THOMAS JEFFERSON (1836–1915). Thomas Jefferson Brown, chief justice of the Texas Supreme Court, son of Ervin and Matilda (Burdett) Brown, was born in Jasper County, Georgia, on July 24, 1836. At the age of ten he moved with his family to Washington County, Texas. After attending county schools he received an LL.B. degree from Baylor University in 1856 and passed the bar exam in 1857. He established his first law office at McKinney, where, on August 7, 1859, he married Louise T. Estes. The couple had seven children. Brown quickly established his legal reputation among county residents, partly because of his partnership with McKinney lawyer and future governor James W. Throckmorton.[qv]

During the Civil War[qv] Brown served as an officer in Col. Robert H. Taylor's[qv] regiment of the Twenty-second Texas Cavalry. In 1865 he returned to McKinney and his law practice. Seven years later, however, he moved his practice to Sherman, where he practiced law for the next sixteen years in partnership with Don A. Bliss.[qv] His sympathies with the Grange and the Farmers' Alliance[qqv] led him in 1888 to campaign for a seat in the Texas House. He served in the Twenty-first and Twenty-second legislatures and in a special session held March 14 through April 12, 1892. In the legislature he introduced a bill to establish a Railroad Commission.[qv] Although this initial effort failed, Brown publicized the need for such a regulatory agency by writing twelve articles that detailed what he believed to be unreasonable rate schedules, inflationary pricing, and undue influence in Texas politics by the railroads. The articles appeared in 1890 in the *Southern Mercury*,[qv] a Farmers' Alliance publication printed in Dallas. The articles, combined with Attorney General James Stephen Hogg's[qv] well-publicized legal attacks against the railroads, helped bring about the commission. In 1891, with Hogg as governor, the Texas legislature established the commission.

The following year Brown was appointed district judge of Grayson and Collin counties. In 1893 he left Sherman to take a seat as associate justice of the Texas Supreme Court at Austin. For the next decade and a half he served as associate justice and as an unofficial advisor to Texas Democrats, among whom his status increased so much that in 1901 Edward M. House[qv] suggested that Brown run for governor. He declined, however, comfortable with his position on the bench. His loyalty to the court was rewarded in 1911, when he became chief justice. But stomach cancer marred his tenure at the head of the court. On May 26, 1915, he died at Greenville, where he had gone for treatment.

BIBLIOGRAPHY: Alwyn Barr, *Reconstruction to Reform: Texas Politics, 1876–1906* (Austin: University of Texas Press, 1971). Dallas *Morning News*, May 27, 1915. *National Cyclopaedia of American Biography*, Vol. 18.

David Minor

BROWN, WILLIAM LAUNCELOT (1873–1942). William Launcelot Brown, surgeon, was born in Coffeyville, Kansas, on September 23, 1873, the son of W. V. and Sarah Brown. He received his early education in public schools in Missouri and Iowa and was granted a medical degree by Rush Medical College (Chicago) in 1896. After two years of postgraduate training at Cook County Hospital in Chicago, he established a practice in Unionville, Missouri. In search of a drier climate because of impaired health, Brown moved to Phoenix, Arizona, in 1900. He and his brother, Dr. C. P. Brown, were employed as surgeons by the Phelps-Dodge Corporation, which managed the Copper Queen Mining Company in Bisbee, Arizona. After the corporation built a railroad between Bisbee and El Paso, Texas, the two brothers became railway surgeons and moved to El Paso, in September 1902. Brown served as chief railway surgeon until the El Paso and Southwestern Railroad was bought by the Southern Pacific. He then became consulting surgeon of the western division of the Southern Pacific, a post he retained until his death.

During his years as railway surgeon, Brown specialized in orthopedic injuries and became internationally recognized for his achievements in that specialty. He was one of a handful of surgeons west of the Mississippi River invited to present papers at the North American Congress of Surgery held in Toronto, Ontario, in 1931. He contributed more than thirty publications to the literature of surgery. He was the founder of the *El Paso County Medical Society Bulletin* and one of the founders of *Southwestern Medicine.* Brown was a member of the House of Delegates of the American Medical Association in 1911 and chairman of the section on surgery of the Texas Medical Association[qv] in 1920. In 1934 he was named honorary life president of the Southwest Medical Association. He was a fellow of the Western Surgical Association, the American College of Surgeons, and the American Medical Association. He served for many years as a member of the board of directors of the Hotel Dieu Sisters Hospital in El Paso and was a founder of the Associated Charities of El Paso (later named the Family Welfare Association) and of the first junior college in El Paso, which later became the College of Mines and then the University of Texas at El Paso. Brown married Katherine Murphy on June 2, 1906, and they had a daughter. He was a Presbyterian but had been converted to Catholicism by the time of his death in El Paso on December 28, 1942.

BIBLIOGRAPHY: El Paso *Times*, December 29, 1942. *Texas State Journal of Medicine*, March 1943.
Chester R. Burns

BROWN, WILLIAM M. (1838–1902). William M. Brown, politician, was born in Wilmington, North Carolina, in 1838. While he was still an infant the family moved to Augusta County, Virginia. He graduated from Washington College in the late 1850s. In 1861 he enlisted in the Confederate Army and served as a lieutenant in the Rock Bridge Artillery company. He was wounded in two battles, the latter being Gettysburg in July 1864, where he was captured and then imprisoned on Johnson's Island. After his release at the end of the war he moved to Marlin, Texas, where he had a cotton commission business. In 1876 he was elected to represent the Twenty-first District in the Texas Senate; he served in the Fifteenth and Sixteenth legislatures. During his term he married Mamie Dill of Austin; they had four children. Brown was comptroller of public accounts from 1880 until January 1883. He was one of the organizers of the John Bell Hood[qv] Camp of Confederate Veterans in Austin in 1884 and was instrumental in the establishment of the Confederate Home for Men (*see* TEXAS CONFEDERATE HOME). Brown was state oil inspector from 1887 to 1891. He was a Presbyterian and a Democrat. He died in Austin on August 2, 1902.

BIBLIOGRAPHY: *Biographical Encyclopedia of Texas* (New York: Southern, 1880). C. W. Raines, *Year Book for Texas* (2 vols., Austin: Gammel-Statesman, 1902, 1903). E. W. Swindells, *A Legislative Manual for the State of Texas* (2 vols., Austin, 1879–83).

BROWN, WILLIAM S. (?–1838?) William S. Brown, Texas Navy[qv] officer, a resident of Velasco, joined the revolutionary army[qv] in 1835 and took part in the siege of Bexar.[qv] After Martín Perfecto de Cos[qv] capitulated, Brown proceeded to Goliad, where he was said to have designed a revolutionary flag displaying a bloody arm, stripes of red and white, and the motto "Independence." The flag may have been hoisted at Velasco in January 1836 (*see* FLAGS OF THE TEXAS REVOLUTION). Brown was made captain of the schooner *Liberty*[qv] in January 1836; he was a brother of Jeremiah Brown,[qv] captain of the *Invincible.*[qv] On March 3, 1836, William Brown captured the Mexican trading vessel *Pelicano* near Sisal and got its cargo safely to Matagorda Bay. Because of a quarrel with Charles E. Hawkins,[qv] commodore of the Texas Navy, Brown was superseded in command of the *Liberty* on March 12, 1836. In July he was given another navy commission and was put in charge of the *Comanche* and the *Fanny Butler,* two captured Mexican vessels. Later he was commissioned captain of the privateer *Benjamin R. Milam,* but he died in New Orleans before the ship was ready for service. A eulogy appeared in the *Telegraph and Texas Register*[qv] for August 18, 1838.

BIBLIOGRAPHY: William Campbell Binkley, ed., *Official Correspondence of the Texan Revolution, 1835–1836* (2 vols., New York: Appleton-Century, 1936). Alex Dienst, "The Navy of the Republic of Texas," *Quarterly of the Texas State Historical Association* 12–13 (January–October 1909; rpt., Fort Collins, Colorado: Old Army Press, 1987). *Southwestern Historical Quarterly,* Texas Collection, April 1947. Dudley Goodall Wooten, ed., *A Comprehensive History of Texas* (2 vols., Dallas: Scarff, 1898; rpt., Austin: Texas State Historical Association, 1986).

BROWN, WILLIAM S. (?–?). William S. Brown, one of Stephen F. Austin's[qv] Old Three Hundred[qv] colonists, received title to a sitio[qv] now in Washington County on July 29, 1824. He was commissioned first lieutenant in the colonial militia on November 26, 1824. The census of 1826 classified him as a farmer and stock raiser, a single man aged between twenty-five and forty. He had three servants. The William S. Brown of the Old Three Hundred may have been the William S. Brown who designed the Goliad flag and who later served in the Texas Navy,[qv] or he may have been the second lieutenant under Ira Westover[qv] who was killed in the Goliad Massacre[qv] in March 1836.

BIBLIOGRAPHY: Eugene C. Barker, ed., *The Austin Papers* (3 vols., Washington: GPO, 1924–28). Lester G. Bugbee, "The Old Three Hundred: A List of Settlers in Austin's First Colony," *Quarterly of the Texas State Historical Association* 1 (October 1897). Harbert Davenport, "Men of Goliad," *Southwestern Historical Quarterly* 43 (July 1939). *Telegraph and Texas Register,* November 9, December 22, 1836.

BROWN, TEXAS. Brown, on Farm Road 2212 in northeastern Martin County, was probably named for Bain Brown, who settled in the area in 1905. A rural school district was organized there in 1917, and the first school building was constructed in 1922. It was consolidated with the Flower Grove school during the late 1940s. For a time a cotton gin was at a site across the street from the school. Lutisia Nichols served the community as midwife and doctor. A church was built at the community in 1936, and the grocery store was torn down in 1978.

BIBLIOGRAPHY: Vernen Liles, Pioneering on the Plains: The History of Martin County, Texas (M.A. thesis, University of Texas, 1953). Martin County Historical Commission, *Martin County, Texas* (Dallas: Taylor, 1979).
Noel Wiggins

BROWN COLLEGE, TEXAS. Brown College is on Doe Run, a half mile from the Brazos River and sixteen miles northeast of Brenham in northeastern Washington County. The agricultural community was developed by 1961. In the 1980s Mount Cavalry Church was in the vicinity. *Carole E. Christian*

BROWN COUNTY. Brown County (F-14), near the geographic center of Texas, is bordered on the north by Eastland County, on the west by Coleman County, on the south by McCulloch and San Saba counties, and on the east by Comanche and Mills counties. The center of the county lies at 31°45′ north latitude and 99°00′ west longitude, sixty-five miles southeast of Abilene. The county is named for Capt. Henry Stevenson Brown,[qv] a company commander in the battle of Velasco,[qv] a delegate to the Convention of 1832,[qv] and one of the first Anglo-Americans in the area. Elevation over this rolling country varies from 1,200 to 2,000 feet. Soils vary from heavy loam to sand, clay, and shales over the county's 936 square miles. Local waterways are Pecan Bayou and its tributaries and the Colorado River, which forms the southern boundary of the county. The average low temperature in January is 33° F; the average high in July is 96°. The growing season lasts 242 days. Rainfall averages 27.42 inches annually, and 6,000 acres are under irrigation. The county produces $30.5 million annually from agriculture, including cattle, hogs, sheep, goats, grain sorghums, wheat, and pecans.

Comanches of the Penateka band (Honey-Eaters or Wasps) roamed the region in the nineteenth century; they were the southernmost Comanche band and apparently led the advance into the southern plains.

Like other plains people they were mounted warriors and splendid hunters of buffalo.

The first whites in the area were Spanish soldiers under Capt. Nicolás Flores y Valdez,[qv] who in 1723 pursued Apaches to recover stolen horses and captives. After a similar Spanish expedition in 1759, a group of Anglo-Americans, led by Capt. Henry Stevenson Brown, entered the region in 1828 to recover livestock stolen by Comanches. Land surveys were made in 1838. In 1856 Welcome W. Chandler,[qv] John H. Fowler, and others settled in the valleys of Pecan Bayou and Jim Ned Creek.

The county was formed on the western frontier in 1856 from Comanche and Travis counties and organized in 1858, with Brownwood designated as the county seat; the town was also awarded the county's first post office that year with Wiley B. Brown as postmaster. In 1860 the United States census found 244 people living in the county, none of them slaveholders. The census also counted 2,070 cattle in the area, and ninety-one acres of land was classified as "improved." The county developed slowly between its founding and the 1870s, primarily because conditions were not secure for settlement until the late 1870s or early 1880s, as settlers were harassed by Indians and white predators for twenty years after the county was formed. The original settlers had to resist Comanches who entered the region from the north at Mercer's Gap or from the west along Pecan Bayou, near Elkins. White desperados caused problems too; in 1875 the Fort Worth–Brownwood stage was robbed five times in two months. Much of the criminal activity during the 1870s was attributed to John Wesley Hardin's[qv] gang; in 1874 Brown County citizens were among those who lynched suspected gang members at Comanche, and Hardin himself was forced to flee.

Though increasing numbers of farmers moved into the area in the 1870s, 1880s, and 1890s, the county's economy was dominated by cattle ranching throughout most of the nineteenth century. The number of cattle in the county rose from 2,070 in 1860 to 40,000 in 1880 and remained at about the same level until 1900. County ranchers joined the main cattle trail to Abilene and Dodge City in north Coleman County and fought with local farmers attempting to fence off their lands. Strife between ranchers and farmers over the fencing of open range raged for several years until 1886, when the Texas Rangers[qv] killed two fence cutters (*see also* fence cutting). Meanwhile, the number of farms in the area increased steadily, rising from only twenty-two in 1870 to 1,206 in 1880 and 1,396 in 1890.

Development of the county was accelerated in the 1890s and early 1900s when two railroads built tracks into the area, providing a stimulus to area farmers and helping maintain an atmosphere favorable to experiments in crop diversification. The Fort Worth and Rio Grande Railway reached the county in 1892; the Gulf, Colorado and Santa Fe line built into Brownwood in 1895, and by 1903 had extended its tracks to Menard. The new railroad connections helped Brownwood to prosper, since the absence of railroad facilities in southern Eastland and Callahan counties led farmers from those areas to Brownwood to do their marketing.

Political affairs were volatile in Brown County in the 1880s and 1890s. The Greenback party[qv] was active there during the 1880s and was championed by two newspapers, the *Investigator*, published by Judge Charles H. Jenkins,[qv] and the *Age of Reason*, published by the Mikel brothers. In the late 1880s and early 1890s the Populists were supported by the Brownwood *Bulletin*, first published by J. H. Byrd and later by William H. Mayes.[qv] Most residents during this period, however, were Democrats and read the *Pecan Valley News*, first published in 1894 (a weekly newspaper named after this one was published in the 1970s by Tevis Clyde Smith). Prohibition[qv] caused discord until the county voted itself dry in 1903. It remained dry until the late 1950s, when the sale of beer for off-premises consumption was made legal.

Between 1870 and 1900 citizens of the county also developed a school system and centers of higher education. The first school in the county opened in 1860, when Judge Greenleaf Fisk,[qv] a large landowner, volunteered to teach the children. By the 1874–75 school term a number of communities maintained schools on a regular basis. Altogether, 514 pupils in the county were enrolled for the four-month term. Brownwood established its own school system in 1876, and other communities soon followed suit. By 1885 the county had 2,000 students and sixty-four teachers in small rural schools and community school systems. In 1888 the Presbyterians established Daniel Baker College, the county's first center of higher learning, and in 1890 a group of Baptists established Howard Payne College. Daniel Baker struggled financially until 1894, when it passed to the Southern Synod of the Presbyterian Church. Howard Payne granted degrees until 1897, then operated as a junior college until 1913, when it was again upgraded to senior college status. In 1953 the two schools were combined under the name of Howard Payne College (now Howard Payne University).

By 1900 the county was much more settled than it had been twenty years before, and farming had become the chief mainstay of the local economy. The United States census counted 2,044 farms and ranches in the county that year, 823 of them operated by tenants; and the county's population had risen to 16,019. Although farmers planted oats, wheat, and other crops, corn and cotton were the favorites. In 1900 29,000 acres of county land were planted in corn and 46,000 were planted in cotton.

The county's agricultural economy boomed during the first ten years of the twentieth century, primarily because of a rapid expansion of cotton culture.[qv] Cotton had been Brown County's most important crop since 1890, when a total of more than 16,000 acres was devoted to producing the fiber. In the early 1900s, however, cotton acreage in the county expanded more rapidly and became even more important for the local economy. In 1908, the peak year for cotton in the county, 43,574 bales were ginned, and in 1910 county farmers planted almost 83,000 acres in to cotton. By this time fruits and pecans had also become an important part of the local agricultural economy. By 1910 Brown County farmers were raising 74,300 peach trees and 46,400 pecan trees. During these boom years the number of farms in the county increased 35 percent, to 2,741; tenants operated 1,160 of the farms in the county in 1910. By 1910 the population was 22,935.

The boll weevil[qv] appeared in the county about 1909, however, and production of cotton quickly declined. By 1920 only 7,335 acres was planted in cotton, and in 1929 only 7,281 bales were produced; in 1940 12,400 acres was devoted to the crop. Some local farmers turned to other crops, especially wheat and oats; others, however, were driven off their farms. By 1920 the number of farms in the county had dropped to 2,303, and by 1930 only 2,158 remained. The population of the county dropped to 21,682 in 1920. By 1930 it had risen again to 26,382, partly thanks to a brief oil boom.

Oil was discovered in Brown County in 1879, and a small producing well was drilled on the H. M. Barnes farm near Grosvenor in 1900. Later, several other wells were drilled, but the first commercial production came from the efforts of Jack Pippen in 1917 at Brownwood. The first large field began producing from a depth of 1,100 feet in 1919 near Cross Cut. In 1926 a boom followed the success of the White well on Jim Ned Creek; some 600 wells were drilled in several fields in the county during this time.

The Great Depression[qv] of the 1930s ended the oil boom, as prices dropped and production fell off. The agricultural sector was also hammered; between 1929 and 1940 cropland harvested in the county dropped from 146,129 acres to 118,000, and the number of farms dropped to 2,119. Hardship was widespread during the 1930s, but conditions were alleviated somewhat by the state's "bread bonds" and New Deal relief programs. Among the federal projects that employed workers and improved county facilities were road and school construction. The construction of a dam during the early 1930s also helped to alleviate some of the effects of the depression.

Interest in an irrigation dam below the confluence of Pecan Bayou and Jim Ned Creek first arose during a serious drought that afflicted the area in 1894 and 1895. Initial attempts to fund the project failed, but in 1928 voters of the Brownwood Water District approved bonds for $2.5 million to construct the dam, which was completed in 1932. Depression conditions made local bond funding for canals impossible, but the federal government granted $450,000 to carry water from Lake Brownwood[qv] to thirsty land. It was predicted that several years of normal rainfall would be required to fill the lake behind the dam, but an almost unprecedented storm in July 1932 filled it in six hours. In spite of projects such as these, the depression further damaged a local economy that in some respects had been already struggling. By 1940 only 2,119 farms remained in the county, and the population had dropped to 25,924.

The beginning of America's involvement in World War II[qv] helped to resurrect the local economy. Between 1941 and 1943 military needs led to the construction of Camp Bowie,[qv] an infantry and cavalry training center that covered 122,000 acres south of Brownwood and cost $35 million to build. The facility affected the county both socially and economically; over 10,000 construction workers were hired to build the camp, and eventually 30,000 troops were assigned there; German prisoners of war[qv] were also confined there. The influx of people into the county caused a housing shortage in greater Brownwood and around the camp that lasted through the war despite the army's construction of a 200-unit housing project.

The war also helped to revive the local oil industry; in 1944 Brown County lands produced more than 400,000 barrels of crude. The industry fully revived after the end of World War II, when large fields were discovered at greater depths, and water flooding of old fields was begun. In 1958 production totaled 542,132 barrels, and in 1960 more than 516,000 barrels. Production dropped during the early 1960s but picked up again during the late 1970s. The county produced 418,000 barrels of oil in 1978, 452,648 barrels in 1982, and 498,000 barrels in 1989. In 1990 production dropped to 349,400 barrels. By 1991 more than 50,561,000 barrels of oil had been taken from Brown County lands since 1917.

Though the revival of the oil industry during the 1940s had helped to raise the county's population to 28,607 by 1950, the county experienced an extended drought between 1950 and 1957; rainfalls during this period fell to as low as twelve inches a year, forcing some farmers to move to Brownwood and other cities. By 1960 the population of the county had dropped to 24,728. The county revived somewhat during the 1960s, however, and by 1970 the population had risen again to 25,877. It was 33,057 in 1980 and 34,371 in 1990.

After the 1950s the Republican party[qv] carried the county in five of nine presidential elections, including 1980 and 1984. The party did less well in gubernatorial and senatorial races during the same period, winning just one of the former (1984), and three of the latter (1966, 1972, 1984).

By the 1980s Brown County's economy was stable and becoming more diversified. In 1982 the county reported 59,495 cattle and an income of over $4.5 million from dairy products, 17,056 goats, 11,009 sheep, and 8,031 hogs; major crop production included 251,437 bushels of wheat, 167,493 bushels of oats, 47,256 bushels of sorghum, and 5,910,819 pounds of peanuts.

In 1984 Brown County had 937 businesses employing 11,660 people, with annual wages of over $186 million; the majority of these businesses were located in Brownwood. County businesses in the mid-1980s were chiefly linked to agribusiness, brick and tile, and oil products, though industries also included a 3M plant, a Superior Cable factory, and a Kohler toilet factory. County income in 1984 from agribusiness, oil products, and brick and tile concerns totalled $110,800,000.

The county is served by an adequate transportation system, with U.S. highways 67 and 84 crossing from east to west, and 377 and 183 from northeast to southwest. A state highway crosses from northwest to southeast. The Atchison, Topeka and Santa Fe Railroad crosses the state from the northeast to the west through Brownwood. Communities in Brown County include Early, Bangs, Blanket, Brookesmith, Cross Cut, Grosvenor, Indian Creek, May, and Zephyr. Brownwood, the largest city in the county, had a 1990 population of 18,387. The county is the birthplace of author Katherine Ann Porter,[qv] who was born on a farm at Indian Creek; her family moved to Hays County in 1892. Robert Ervin Howard,[qv] a pulp fantasy writer who attended school in Brownwood and published his first writings there, achieved considerable popularity during his lifetime and still has a considerable following. Recreation in the county centers around Lake Brownwood State Recreation Area.[qv] Brownwood also has a youth festival in January.

BIBLIOGRAPHY: Thomas Robert Havins, *Something about Brown: A History of Brown County, Texas* (Brownwood, Texas: Banner Printing, 1958). Tevis Clyde Smith, *Frontier's Generation* (Brownwood, Texas, 1931; 2d ed. 1980). James C. White, *The Promised Land: A History of Brown County* (Brownwood, Texas: Brownwood *Banner*, 1941).

John Leffler

BROWN CREEK (Cass County). Brown Creek rises in the Cusseta Mountains six miles east of Marietta in northwestern Cass County (at 33°11′ N, 94°29′ W) and runs northeast for 6½ miles to its mouth on Powell Creek, just west of the mouth of Powell Creek on Wright Patman Lake (at 33°13′ N, 94°24′ W). The stream is intermittent in its upper reaches. It traverses hilly land with loamy soils upstream, then enters gently undulating to gently rolling terrain. The land is heavily wooded, with pines and various hardwoods predominating.

BROWNDELL, TEXAS. Browndell is at the junction of Farm Road 1007 and U.S. Highway 96, in extreme northeastern Jasper County eighty-five miles north of Beaumont. The area, in the vast East Texas piney woodlands, became accessible to large-scale lumbering operations with the construction of the Gulf, Beaumont and Great Northern Railway north of Roganville in the early 1900s. The Kirby Lumber Corporation built a sawmill in northeastern Jasper County shortly thereafter, and the mill site was called Browndell in honor of Dell Brown, the wife of one of John Henry Kirby's[qv] financial backers. The Browndell post office opened in 1903 and was discontinued in 1928. By 1904 an enthusiastic Kirby Corporation official dubbed the Browndell plant, with kilns, planer, and sawmill, "one of the company's most successful and economic mills." Ten years later the facility, known as Mill S, could reportedly cut 75,000 to 80,000 board feet of lumber every ten hours. The 1925 fire that destroyed the mill threatened the continued existence of the Browndell community. Its population, once estimated to be about 900, fell to below 200 by the mid-1940s. The community's economy was revitalized, however, after the completion of the Sam Rayburn Reservoir[qv] opened up new recreational opportunities in the area. Browndell residents voted to incorporate in 1968. By the mid-1980s the community's population had increased to more than 225; in 1990 it was reported as 192.

Robert Wooster

BROWNFIELD, MARION VIRGIL (1854–1929). Marion Virgil Brownfield, West Texas cattleman, banker, and philanthropist, the oldest of nine children of Joseph Collins and Martha (Schipps) Brownfield, was born in Iowa in January 1854. The Brownfields had migrated from Uniontown, Pennsylvania. Later the family moved to Texas, where they settled near Smithfield, in Tarrant County north of Fort Worth. There Brownfield received a common school education. During the Civil War[qv] his father served in the Confederate Army and was taken prisoner by Union forces. Brownfield became a cowboy. After 1871 he trailed herds north to the Kansas markets and soon acquired land and stock of his own. In 1876 he married Elizabeth Ann Hornbeck. They had four sons and a daughter; the daughter later married Roscoe Wilson.[qv]

In 1886 Brownfield moved his herd to Nolan County and acquired ranch holdings south of Sweetwater, where he established his headquarters. His wife died in 1894. In 1896 he leased 100 sections in Terry and Lynn counties, onto which he moved his herd by 1898, in partnership with Sam Singleton. By 1900 the partnership had been dissolved; Singleton took the land in Lynn County. Brownfield subsequently acquired title to fifty-two sections in southeastern Terry County, on which he ran his cattle bearing the Saucer Block brand, a half-circle over a square. He placed his headquarters on Lost Draw, near the center of this spread. He was joined in 1901 by his oldest son, Dick, who purchased from his father the western part of the ranch holdings, brought in his own cattle, and built a small house for himself and his bride. When W. G. Hardin and A. F. Small bought a section of Dick's land for a townsite in 1903, the Brownfields helped lay out the new settlement, which was named for them, and led in the successful effort to designate it the county seat when Terry County was organized in 1904.

From that time on Brownfield was a leading booster of the town that bears his name. He established the Brownfield State Bank in 1905 and was its first president. He also financed the first mercantile store and donated land for the community cemetery and a lot for the Masonic lodge, of which he became a charter member. Although he was a Lutheran, he contributed to every church and school in the community. In 1909 he "drug out" the county's first auto road, which ran from Brownfield through his ranch to Lamesa in Dawson County. As a charter member of the Texas and Southwestern Cattle Raisers Association,[qv] Brownfield became acquainted with several high officials of the Santa Fe Railroad, whom he convinced to lay track through his town in 1917. In 1912, after his wife died, Brownfield married Augusta Youngblood; they had a daughter.

By the mid-1920s Brownfield had ranchland in both Terry and Yoakum counties, which his son Ray managed after his retirement. He often enjoyed hunting, and although he never ran for public office, he maintained a strong interest in state and regional politics. On February 11, 1929, he suffered a heart attack while driving home, and although he was able to guide his car to a filling station, he died before medical aid could be rendered. He was buried in the Brownfield Cemetery after Masonic rites. His sons Dick and Ray continued to operate the family's West Texas ranches. Dick donated the old Brownfield home to the city as a tribute to his father, and it is now used for the Terry County Museum.

BIBLIOGRAPHY: Kyle Martin Buckner, "The History of Brownfield, Texas," West Texas Historical Association *Yearbook* 19 (1943). *Cattleman*, March 1929. Lubbock *Daily Journal*, February 12, 1929. "The Peter Hurd Mural," *Museum Journal* 1 (1957). Terry County Historical Survey Committee, *Early Settlers of Terry* (Hereford, Texas: Pioneer, 1968).

H. Allen Anderson

BROWNFIELD, TEXAS. Brownfield is at the junction of U.S. highways 62, 82, 380, and 385 and State Highway 137, forty miles southwest of Lubbock in central Terry County. In 1903 town promoters W. G. Hardin and A. F. Small arrived in Terry County planning to turn Small's few hundred dollars into thousands. The two men bought the county's center lot from A. M. (Dick) Brownfield and began to plat the site, giving every voter in the county a lot in order to enhance the town's chances of becoming the county seat; they named the town after a prominent ranching family. The founders donated one block each for the courthouse, the school, and churches. J. R. Hill, the first to arrive with his family, built Hill's Hotel, the first business establishment, on the north side of the square. On April 1, 1903, Hill opened the first post office in his hotel building and became the first postmaster. The settlers lived in tents, covered wagons, or dugouts (*see* DUGOUT) until construction materials for houses could be hauled from Big Spring or Colorado City. A school was built, and since there was no money for a teacher or equipment it served as a dance hall, church, and general gathering place until 1905, when the first school term began.

On June 28, 1904, Brownfield was voted county seat by a slim margin over the larger and older town of Gomez. The *Terry County Voice* (later *Herald*) moved to Brownfield from Gomez a few weeks after the election. The Brownfield State Bank was established on October 7, 1905, to serve Gaines, Terry, and Yoakum counties, as well as parts of eastern New Mexico, since the area had no convenient banking services. With the coming of the automobile in 1910 and the railroad in 1917, the town and county experienced rapid growth. To encourage the building of a railroad from Lubbock to Seagraves, the citizens donated the right-of-way and station grounds to the South Plains and Santa Fe Railroad Company. The town was incorporated in October 1920 with a population of 1,200. During the Great Depression[qv] the William Randolph Hearst interests moved into Brownfield, then in the best corn-producing area of West Texas, and 10,000 cattle were finished for market that same year. For a number of years cattle were shipped to Brownfield from Mexico to be fattened.

Agricultural development was the major source of population growth until 1937, at which time 3,100 people lived in the town. By 1940 Brownfield was the leading grain center on the South Plains and an important part of the economic development of the northern Permian Basin.[qv] By 1941 four oil wells were in operation, and more were expected. In 1950 diversified agriculture was still the main occupation, but oilfields had attracted petroleum industries as well. The town's population increased from 6,160 in 1950 to 10,286 in 1960. It dropped to 9,647 during the next ten years, as agricultural production—mainly in field crops—and income decreased 30 percent from 1964 to 1969. In 1986 the county remained one of the leading cotton-producing counties in the state. In 1988 Brownfield had a population of 10,846. In 1990 it was 9,560.

BIBLIOGRAPHY: Kyle Martin Buckner, "The History of Brownfield, Texas," West Texas Historical Association *Yearbook* 19 (1943). Kathleen E. and Clifton R. St. Clair, eds., *Little Towns of Texas* (Jacksonville, Texas: Jayroe Graphic Arts, 1982).

Leoti A. Bennett

BROWN FOUNDATION. The Brown Foundation, in Houston, Texas, was established in 1951 by Margarett and Herman Brown[qv] and Alice and George R. Brown as a nonprofit charitable foundation. In 1962 the Browns gave additional resources to the foundation; in 1963, after their deaths, the estate of Margarett and Herman Brown was given to the Brown Foundation. All funds donated to the foundation and income generated from these funds are to be used for public charitable purposes, principally for support, encouragement, and assistance to the arts and education. From 1951 to 1985 the Brown Foundation awarded grants in excess of $185 million to artistic, educational, medical, and other charitable organizations. The affairs of the foundation are managed by a board of trustees composed of ten members, nine of whom are related either by blood, adoption, or marriage to one of the four original donors.

BIBLIOGRAPHY: *The Hooper Directory of Texas Foundations.*

Katherine B. Dobelman

BROWNING, DAVID GREIG, JR. (1931–1956). David Greig (Skippy) Browning, champion springboard diver, was born in Boston, Massachusetts, on June 5, 1931, the son of David G. and Martha (Hollingsworth) Browning, Sr. He was taken to Texas by his parents when he was three and began diving when he was four, under the direction of his father. The family lived for a time in Corpus Christi before moving to Dallas, where Browning in 1941 entered his first competition in swimming and diving contests.

After a brilliant high school diving career at Dallas Highland Park, where he was three times state diving champion, he enrolled at Wayne State University in Detroit, but after one semester he transferred to the University of Texas at Austin. He had studied with coach Clarence Pinkston at the Detroit Athletic Club and came within one-fifth point of making the 1948 Olympic team before he was seventeen. In April

1949 he made his first national Amateur Athletic Union bid at Daytona Beach, Florida, but was edged out by the 1948 Olympic champion, Bruce Harlan of Ohio State. At their next competition four months later in Los Angeles, Browning beat Harlan and won his first national title. At the University of Texas he was named All-American diver in 1950, 1951, and 1952. In all three years he won the Southwest Conference[qv] diving championship on both the one-meter and three-meter boards. He dominated Southwest Conference diving for three years and was undefeated in dual meets during his collegiate career. He received a long list of diving awards, among which were eight AAU national diving titles and four National Collegiate Athletic Association titles. In the spring of 1952 at the intercollegiate competition at Yale he was given a perfect score of ten on a cutaway 1½ pike, rated one of the most difficult of dives. He made up his own special dives and the AAU rules committee officially adopted some of them. The University of Texas yearbook, *Cactus,* listed Browning as a Goodfellow in 1951 and 1952.

At the 1952 summer Olympics in Helsinki, Finland, Browning, in his senior university year, was acknowledged as the world's diving champion when he was awarded the Olympic gold medal. The following August he won the championship of the National AAU outdoor meet at Newark, New Jersey. In 1952 he accomplished what no other diver ever had by winning the Amateur Athletic Union, National Collegiate Athletic Association, and Olympic diving championships in all springboard events, both one-meter and three-meter. In 1954 he won his last AAU championship; he was sixty-five points ahead of his nearest competitor, something unheard of in that caliber diving competition.

He was married to Corinne (Cody) L. Couch on September 7, 1950, and graduated from the University of Texas with a degree in business administration in January 1953. He received his wings as a naval pilot at Pensacola, Florida, in June 1955. Browning was in training for the 1956 Olympics and favored to win another gold medal, when he was killed in the crash of his AFJS Fury, a jet carrier fighter, on March 13, 1956, on a training flight near Rantoul, Kansas. In 1957 he was named to the Helms Athletic Foundation Hall of Fame. In 1960 he was selected for the University of Texas Longhorn Hall of Honor, and in 1962 he was named to the Texas Sports Hall of Fame.[qv]

BIBLIOGRAPHY: Vertical Files, Barker Texas History Center, University of Texas at Austin.

BROWNING, GEORGE WASHINGTON (1806–1879). George Washington Browning, soldier and judge, was born in Scotland in 1806 and in April 1835 immigrated to Texas, where he enlisted in Capt. John Hart's[qv] company at Velasco on January 30, 1836. He was subsequently transferred to Capt. Amasa Turner's[qv] Company B, First Regiment, Regular Infantry, and mustered out of service on October 27, 1836. Browning later served as a private in Capt. John Smith's[qv] Company A, First Regiment, Infantry, in which he enlisted on December 31, 1836. His name appears on a Velasco muster roll of February 13, 1836, and a Galveston muster roll of February 28, 1837. Browning was a lawyer of some prominence. He served as justice of the peace in San Augustine County from 1836 to 1838. He was elected justice of the peace in Houston County on February 4, 1839, and chief justice of Burnet County, a defunct judicial county (*see* DEFUNCT COUNTIES), on April 24, 1841. He died in Austin on May 14, 1879.

BIBLIOGRAPHY: *Compiled Index to Elected and Appointed Officials of the Republic of Texas, 1835–1846* (Austin: State Archives, Texas State Library, 1981). Amelia W. Williams and Eugene C. Barker, eds., *The Writings of Sam Houston, 1813–1863* (8 vols., Austin: University of Texas Press, 1938–43; rpt., Austin and New York: Pemberton Press, 1970).

Thomas W. Cutrer

BROWNING, JAMES NATHAN (1850–1921). James Nathan Browning, attorney and lieutenant governor of Texas, son of William F. and Mary L. (Burke) Browning, was born on a farm near Arkadelphia, Clark County, Arkansas, on March 13, 1850. His father died when James was four, and his mother later married J. F. Stegall. The Civil War[qv] ended early school advantages for Browning, but he educated himself during his spare time. In 1866 the family moved to Cooke County, Texas. After working as a cowboy in Stephens County for a year, Browning went into partnership with his brother Joe in the cattle business at Fort Griffin, a venture that often brought the partners in contact with Indian warfare.

While ranching at Fort Griffin, Browning studied law under C. K. Stribling. He was admitted to the bar at Albany in 1876 and served for a while as justice of the peace, then as Shackelford county attorney for two years. He turned reforming zeal against gambling and other frontier vices and taught a Sunday school class. He married Cornelia E. Beckham, who died in childbirth two years later. He subsequently married Virginia Bozeman, on March 9, 1897; they had five sons and four daughters. In 1881 Browning resigned as county attorney and moved to Mobeetie, where he was appointed attorney of the Thirty-fifth Judicial District by Governor Oran M. Roberts.[qv] He was elected to four terms as representative in the Texas legislature from the Forty-third District, in 1882, 1884, 1886, and 1890. As a legislator he led the "free grass" elements in opposition to the leasing of large tracts of school lands to big cattle raisers in Northwest Texas. He also served as a member of the committees on penitentiaries and irrigation and was chairman of the judiciary committee. Browning's honesty and fairness won the respect of his constituents, who bestowed upon him the nickname "Honest Jim."

In 1888 he declined to run again for the legislature and moved his law practice from Mobeetie to Clarendon. In February 1896 he moved to Amarillo and formed a law partnership with W. H. Madden, with whom he remained for the next sixteen years. In 1898, after nomination by the Texas Democratic convention, Browning was elected to his first term as lieutenant governor. Before he took office, his son Fred was fatally injured by a fall from a horse. Browning was reelected lieutenant governor on the Democratic ticket with Governor Joseph D. Sayers.[qv] After leaving office in 1903 he was appointed to the University of Texas Board of Regents by Governor S. W. T. Lanham.[qv] In 1904 Browning opened his own law firm in Amarillo. He was elected district judge in 1906 and served for eight years. Throughout his later years he was active in his community as a Mason, a Shriner, and a member of the local Methodist church. He died at Amarillo on November 9, 1921, and was buried there in Llano Cemetery.

BIBLIOGRAPHY: J. Evetts Haley, *Charles Goodnight* (Norman: University of Oklahoma Press, 1949). Della Tyler Key, *In the Cattle Country: History of Potter County, 1887–1966* (Amarillo: Tyler-Berkley, 1961; 2d ed., Wichita Falls: Nortex, 1972). Buckley B. Paddock, ed., *A Twentieth Century History and Biographical Record of North and West Texas* (Chicago: Lewis, 1906). Millie Jones Porter, *Memory Cups of Panhandle Pioneers* (Clarendon, Texas: Clarendon Press, 1945). Glenn Shirley, *Temple Houston* (Norman: University of Oklahoma Press, 1980). Thomas F. Turner, "Prairie Dog Lawyers," *Panhandle-Plains Historical Review* 2 (1929).

H. Allen Anderson

BROWNING, TEXAS. Browning (Browning's) is on Farm Road 2767 and the eastern edge of the Chapel Hill oilfield nine miles southeast of Winona in eastern Smith County. The town was named for its earliest settlers. Around 1850 Isaiah Browning traveled to the area from Oxford, Mississippi, and early in the 1870s built the first large house there; the house was still standing in 1990. The Browning's community was granted a post office in 1879, with William A. Owens as first postmaster. In 1884 I. W. Browning owned the local gin and gristmill, and the partnership of Browning and Bradshaw owned the town's general store. In 1898 the community's post office was moved to Starrville, but it operated again in Browning from 1899 to 1902, when it was again transferred to Starrville. During the 1890s the population stabilized at around fifty, and the community had a sawmill, a church, a district school, and a saloon. In 1903 it had two one-teacher schools, one with fifty-one white students and the other with forty-seven black students. By 1933 the town reported a population of twenty-five and one business. Records for 1936 show no school at the community, and by 1952 local students attended classes in the Holts Independent School District. A 1966 map showed a few scattered dwellings in the area, near Corinth Church and just south of Prairie Creek. In 1990 the community reported a population of twenty-five.

BIBLIOGRAPHY: "The Browning House," *Chronicles of Smith County*, Spring 1964. "Post Offices and Postmasters of Smith County, Texas: 1847–1929," *Chronicles of Smith County*, Spring 1966. "School Sights," *Chronicles of Smith County*, Fall 1969. Donald W. Whisenhunt, comp., *Chronological History of Smith County* (Tyler, Texas: Smith County Historical Society, 1983). *Vista K. McCroskey*

BROWNING CREEK. Browning Creek rises 1½ miles northwest of Ben Wheeler and south of State Highway 64 in southeastern Van Zandt County (at 32°27′ N, 95°43′ W) and runs east for nine miles to its mouth on the Neches River, a half mile southeast of Rhine Lake (at 32°30′ N, 95°40′ W). It crosses flat to rolling terrain with local escarpments, surfaced by deep, fine sandy loam that supports hardwood forests, brush, and grasses. Toward the creek's mouth, the land is flat to rolling and surfaced by dark calcareous clays in which grow mesquite, grasses, and cacti.

BROWNING-FERRIS INDUSTRIES. Browning-Ferris Industries, with headquarters in Houston, provides waste management, recycling, and sanitation services to commercial, industrial, residential, and governmental clients in the United States and international markets. Under a decentralized management structure, its numerous subsidiaries and affiliates collect, transport, treat, and dispose of commercial and industrial solid wastes and facilitate resource recovery, hazardous-waste treatment, municipal and commercial sweeping, medical-waste services, portable-restroom services, asbestos removal, and public transportation, including city and charter bus services, shuttles, and on-call van service. In 1988 BFI was the industry's second largest publicly held company, serving 4.5 million households, 544 municipal contracts, and 522,000 commercial and industrial customers. In 1992 the company had 26,000 employees, operated in the United States, Canada, Hong Kong, Kuwait, the Netherlands, Puerto Rico, Saudi Arabia, Spain, the United Kingdom, and Venezuela and had sales of $3.25 billion. BFI owned, leased, or operated more than ninety sanitary landfills, had fifty-five transfer stations for urban waste consolidation and shipment to distant disposal sites, and carried out initial resource recovery through its American Ref-Fuel Company, jointly owned with Air Products and Chemicals, Incorporated.

The company was founded as American Refuse Systems, Incorporated, in 1967 when accountant Tom Fatjo, Jr., began residential waste collection in his Houston suburb. By 1968 he had expanded into shopping malls and small factories and won a Houston landfill contract that allowed him to enter the disposal business. Fatjo entered into a partnership with Louis A. Waters, then vice president of corporate finance for a New York securities brokerage, and acquired controlling interest in Browning-Ferris Machinery Company, a publicly traded firm that distributed, serviced, and leased heavy equipment for construction and maintenance. In 1970 the partners incorporated Browning-Ferris Industries.

As the business grew, national regulation regarding the environment put new restrictions on collection and disposal services, toughened sanitation standards, curtailed incineration, mandated landfill burial, and increased costs. Competitors failed, and Fatjo bought them out, keeping many on as managers. Harry Phillips, Sr., of Patterson Waste Control, joined BFI when it acquired his firm; became BFI president in 1970. In 1976 he became chief operating officer, a post he held until 1988. The company entered recycling in 1972 with the acquisition of Consolidated Fibres, Incorporated, a processor of waste fibers, and by the mid-1970s owned a nationwide wastepaper company. BFI provided sanitation services in Spain through its first overseas contract in 1973. By 1975 revenues totalled $256 million. At this time the firm operated 2,800 trucks in 131 cities, had 7,700 employees, and owned sixty landfills.

Passage of the 1976 Resource Conservation and Recovery Act and the establishment of the Environmental Protection Agency Superfund caused new problems for BFI, leading to litigation over environmental violations and accusations of price fixing. In 1988 William D. Ruckelshaus, former Environmental Protection Agency chief and deputy attorney general during Watergate, assumed the office of chairman and chief executive. In 1991 Harry Phillips returned to top management. In 1983 CECOS International, a BFI subsidiary, had established a new Chemical Services Division to treat hazardous wastes along with BFI's Newco Waste Systems, and in 1988 BFI had acquired W. T. Stephens Contracting Incorporated, an asbestos-removal business. In 1990, however, BFI withdrew from the toxic-waste business after a series of legal and financial problems. Subsequently, BFI developed facilities for treatment of infectious medical wastes.

BIBLIOGRAPHY: *The International Directory of Company Histories* (Chicago: St. James Press, 1988–). *Diana J. Kleiner*

BROWNLEE, TEXAS. The now-deserted community of Brownlee was on State Highway 137 in central Martin County. In 1908 a townsite was laid out there, and lots were sold in the expectation that a railroad to be built from Lamesa to Sterling City would pass through the town. A man named Allen built a grocery store, and when a post office was established, he became postmaster. Brownlee acquired a second grocery store and a school, which was moved from nearby Sulphur Valley. The town even made a bid to take the place of Stanton as county seat. But the planned railroad was never built, the bid failed, and in 1915 the Brownlee school was consolidated with the Plainview school.

BIBLIOGRAPHY: Martin County Historical Commission, *Martin County, Texas* (Dallas: Taylor, 1979). *Noel Wiggins*

BROWN PEN MOUNTAIN. Brown Pen Mountain, eleven miles southeast of Breckenridge in southern Stephens County (at 32°35′ N, 98°52′ W), has an elevation of 1,528 feet.

BROWNSBORO, TEXAS (Caldwell County). Brownsboro is on Farm Road 1322 eight miles southeast of Lockhart in south central Caldwell County. Soon after the area began to be settled in the 1850s, the Clear Fork Baptist Church was established there. The community that grew up around the church was named for R. A. Brown. In the 1920s the community's economy received a boost from the discovery of oil in nearby fields. Brownsboro had a store, a gin, and a school, in addition to the church, to serve about fifty families. In the 1930s the community had a semiprofessional baseball team. Brownsboro began to fade in the 1940s, when the population fell to twenty-five. Area children attended the nearby Oakland school until it was consolidated with the Lockhart Independent School District in 1949. A few scattered houses remained at the site of Brownsboro in the 1980s.

BIBLIOGRAPHY: Mark Withers Trail Drive Museum, *Historical Caldwell County* (Dallas: Taylor, 1984). *Vivian Elizabeth Smyrl*

BROWNSBORO, TEXAS (Henderson County). Brownsboro is at the intersection of Farm roads 607 and 314 and State Highway 31, seventeen miles northeast of Athens in northeast Henderson County. It was settled in 1849 by John (Red) Brown,[qv] who operated a toll bridge across Kickapoo Creek on the road to Jordan's Saline and Tyler. Several Norwegians[qv] immigrated to the area between 1849 and 1857.

By 1860 Henry Cade had erected a sawmill and a cotton gin. With the construction of the St. Louis Southwestern Railway through the county in 1880, the town moved to the railroad. In 1885 Brownsboro had six general stores and a population of 100. It had four churches, a hotel, a grocer, a saloon, and a blacksmith in 1892, when a post office was opened. The population was 500 in 1914. State highway maps of 1936 showed two schools, a church, several buildings, and scattered dwellings at the townsite. In 1989 the population was 710. In 1990 it was 545.

BIBLIOGRAPHY: J. J. Faulk, *History of Henderson County* (Athens, Texas: Athens Review Printing, 1926). Kathleen E. and Clifton R. St. Clair, eds., *Little Towns of Texas* (Jacksonville, Texas: Jayroe Graphic Arts, 1982). *L. Michael Davis*

BROWNSBORO, TEXAS (Kendall County). Brownsboro was on the north bank of the Guadalupe River and River Bend Road, just southeast of Farm Road 473 and three miles east of Comfort in western Kendall County. The settlement, one of the county's earliest, had a public school from 1848 to 1944 and its own post office. The Nichols Ranch was about 1½ miles north of the community. The Fredericksburg and Northern Railway built through the area in 1913 and later established a flag stop at the ranch. During the 1980s the Brownsboro cemetery and a few scattered houses were all that remained of the community. *Melissa G. Wiedenfeld*

BROWNS CREEK (Coryell County). Browns Creek rises in southern Coryell County (at 31°18′ N, 97°48′ W) and flows south for eight miles to its juncture with Cowhouse Creek, near Sugarloaf Mountain two miles from the southern county line (at 31°13′ N, 97°44′ W). The stream is entirely within the borders of Fort Hood.[qv] It descends from an area of low ridges to one of steep slopes surfaced by shallow clay that supports juniper, mesquite, live oak, and grasses. The stream was named for John M. Brown, a Coryell County pioneer who settled on its banks in 1855.

BIBLIOGRAPHY: Frank E. Simmons, *History of Coryell County* (Gatesville, Texas: *Coryell County News*, 1936). *Sylvia Edwards*

——— (Freestone County). Browns Creek rises in south central Freestone County (at 31°36′ N, 96°08′ W) and runs southeast for 9½ miles to its mouth on Buffalo Creek, three miles northeast of Buffalo in Leon County (at 31°30′ N, 96°02′ W). Browns Creek is intermittent in its upper reaches. It traverses flat to rolling terrain with local escarpments and shallow depressions, surfaced by sandy and clay loams that support hardwoods, conifers, and grasses. The developed land in the area is used primarily for dry-land farming.

——— (Lampasas County). Browns Creek rises just south of Knight Mountain and 5½ miles southeast of Lometa in southwestern Lampasas County (at 31°09′ N, 98°21′ W) and runs southwest for 5½ miles to its mouth on Lynch Creek, three miles west of Nix (at 31°08′ N, 98°26′ W). It crosses an area of the Grand Prairie region characterized by steeply to moderately sloping hills, with some sections displaying the steep slopes and limestone benches that often give a stairstep appearance to the landscape along streams. The shallow, stony sandy and clay loams support grasses and open stands of live oak, Ashe juniper, and mesquite.

——— (Mills County). Browns Creek rises in central Mills County (at 31°36′ N, 98°34′ W) and runs south for fourteen miles to its mouth on Pecan Bayou, in the southern part of the county (at 31°27′ N, 98°42′ W). The terrain is flat with local shallow depressions and a surface of sandy and clay loams that support water-tolerant hardwoods, conifers, and grasses.

BROWN'S CREEK, TEXAS. Brown's Creek, a farming and ranching community with a one-room school, was twelve miles south of Gatesville in southern Coryell County. In 1855 John M. Brown settled on the creek, which was named for him. Residents received their mail at Boaz from 1875 until 1912. The community was in decline when the area was appropriated for Camp Hood (later Fort Hood[qv]) in 1942.

BIBLIOGRAPHY: Coryell County Genealogical Society, *Coryell County, Texas, Families, 1854-1985* (Dallas: Taylor, 1986). *Sylvia Edwards*

BROWN'S FERRY, TEXAS. Brown's Ferry, also known as Brown's, was an early riverport on the Angelina River near its confluence with Attoyac Bayou in southeastern Nacogdoches County. A settlement seems to have been at the site as early as 1849, when Robert Patton's riverboat, the *Angelina*, began plying the waters between Pattonia and Sabine Pass. During the 1850s Brown's Ferry was a shipping point for neighboring cotton plantations, and several stores operated there around the time of the Civil War.[qv] In the 1870s the settlement became a regular stopping point for the *Laura*[qv] and other riverboats. A one-way ticket from Brown's Ferry to Sabine Pass, which included meals, cost fifteen dollars; the trip took an average eighteen to twenty-two days. The construction of the railroads in late 1870s and 1880s brought an end to river traffic on the Angelina, and Brown's Ferry declined rapidly. By 1900 the settlement was a ghost town. Sam Rayburn Reservoir has inundated much of the area.

BIBLIOGRAPHY: Richard W. Haltom, *The History of Nacogdoches County, Texas* (Nacogdoches, 1880; rpt., Austin: Jenkins, 197-). Nacogdoches County Genealogical Society, *Nacogdoches County Families* (Dallas: Curtis, 1985). *Christopher Long*

BROWN'S VALLEY, TEXAS. Brown's Valley, near Farm Road 636 four miles northwest of Kerens in southeastern Navarro County, was probably established before 1900. At one time it had a church, a store, and a gin. By the mid-1930s only a few scattered houses remained. Children in the area attended school in Kerens or Bazette. In the early 1990s Brown's Valley was a dispersed rural community.

BIBLIOGRAPHY: Annie Carpenter Love, *History of Navarro County* (Dallas: Southwestern, 1933). *Christopher Long*

BROWNSVILLE, CATHOLIC DIOCESE OF. The Catholic Church[qv] in the four future counties composing the Diocese of Brownsville began in 1548, when the Spanish monarchy decreed, and Pope Paul III confirmed, the Diocese of Guadalajara. These mission lands, part of the northern provinces of New Spain, were within the jurisdiction of the Franciscan colleges for the Propagation of the Faith at Querétaro and Zacatecas. In 1777 the Diocese of Linares was formed; in 1792, when the see (episcopal seat) was moved, it became the Diocese of Monterrey. Subsequent church-state tensions in Mexico resulting from the decade-long Mexican war of independence[qv] left the Diocese of Monterrey with no resident bishop. The Mexican War[qv] also disrupted life in the lower Rio Grande area. However, there were scattered priests who ministered to Catholics on both sides of the Rio Grande (*see* CATHOLIC DIOCESAN CHURCH OF SPANISH AND MEXICAN TEXAS). With the establishment of the Prefecture Apostolic of Texas in 1840, the Brownsville region came under American administration.

The French-speaking Oblates of Mary Immaculate[qv] were the first order of religious to arrive in the lower Rio Grande region after the establishment of the Diocese of Galveston in 1847. They were recruited by Jean Marie Odin,[qv] its first bishop. Upon their arrival in 1849 they found most of the Catholics in the area living on ranchos. Thus began the horseback ministry of the Oblates at Santa Rita and more than 100 other ranchos and communities along the river. La Lomita ranch, south of the site of present-day Mission, became an important way-station for the "Cavalry of Christ" (*see* LA LOMITA MISSION). The Galveston diocese included the entire state of Texas. Odin's successor, Claude Marie Dubuis,[qv] found the area too large to administer as a unit and appealed to Rome for some division of the territory. The resulting Vicariate Apostolic of Brownsville, established in 1874 by act of Pope Pius IX, included the land between the Nueces River and the Rio Grande, an area that later became the dioceses of Corpus Christi and Brownsville. By the same act Immaculate Conception Church in Brownsville (built under the direction of the Oblates and completed in 1859) was selected as cathedral. Catholics in the area numbered between 30,000 and 40,000. Those who resided in the four counties that make up the present Diocese of Brownsville were mostly all Mexican Americans[qv] who could trace their lineage to early settlers brought by José de Escandón's[qv] colonization of the region in the mid-eighteenth century. Many of the oldest towns in the present diocese originated with these early Catholic settlements. Laredo was the oldest city in the vicariate and is the site of the oldest parish in South Texas, San Agustín, built in 1789. The first bishop of the vicariate was Dominic Manucy,[qv] a priest from the Diocese of Mobile. He had only about twenty priests: fourteen Oblates in Brownsville, Rio Grande City, and Roma, and others in Corpus Christi, Laredo, Refugio, San Patricio, and San Diego.

In 1875 Manucy moved the see to Corpus Christi, built a new church there to replace the original worn-out structure that had served the community since 1854, and kept the name of St. Patrick's for the new church, completed in 1881. When Manucy requested a transfer and was appointed bishop of the Diocese of Mobile in 1884, he appointed Father Claude C. Jaillet[qv] as vicar general of Brownsville. From 1885 to 1890 Jaillet handled the administration, and the vicariate had no bishop.

From 1852 on, the Oblates consistently accounted for half of the clergy in the vicariate. Notable orders of women serving in the vicariate were the Sisters of the Incarnate Word and Blessed Sacrament,[qv] who came from Lyons, France, and arrived in Brownsville in 1853; the Ursuline Sisters,[qv] who came to Laredo in 1868; and the Sisters of Mercy,[qv] who arrived in Refugio in 1875. The Brownsville convent and school of the IWBS sisters were demolished by the hurricane of 1867 but soon reconstructed. Peter Verdaguer,[qv] made second bishop in 1890, moved the see to Laredo, where most of the Catholic population lived. He was highly esteemed by the people, who affectionately called him "Padre Pedro." He continually traveled throughout the vicariate for the twenty years of his assignment, and died on a tour of confirmation near Mercedes in 1911. Provincial bishops meeting in New Orleans later that year requested that Rome elevate the vicariate to a diocese. Pope Pius X did so in 1912 and made Corpus Christi the see city. The following year Paul J. Nussbaum[qv] was named bishop. With an area of 88,000 square miles, the new diocese had a total population estimated at 158,000; 83,000 of these were Catholics, and 70,000 of these were Hispanic. Bishop Emmanuel B. Ledvina[qv] succeeded to the see in 1921. He became a great builder of churches in the diocese before resigning for reasons of health in 1949 and being succeeded by Mariano S. Garriga.[qv]

The Diocese of Brownsville was established on July 10, 1965, composed of four counties in the lower Rio Grande valley—Cameron, Hidalgo, Starr, and Willacy—an area of 4,226 square miles, taken from the Catholic Diocese of Corpus Christi.[qv] Its first bishop was Adolph Marx, who had been auxiliary bishop in Corpus Christi. Marx was installed in September 1965; he soon left for Europe to attend meetings of the Second Vatican Council, and died on November 1 in his birthplace, Cologne, Germany. His successor, Humberto Medeiros,[qv] was appointed and installed in 1966. Medeiros left Texas to become archbishop of Boston in 1970 and was made a cardinal in 1973. John J. Fitzpatrick served as bishop of Brownsville from 1971 until his retirement in 1991. An important feature of his tenure was attention to the migrant farmworkers of South Texas. In a 1977 publication, Fitzpatrick noted that "70 per cent of the 400,000 people in the Valley [were] Catholics; 83 per cent of the Catholics speak Spanish as their first language. . . . Only 112 priests serve almost 300,000 Catholics, the lowest ratio of priests to Catholics in any diocese in this country." A 1976 survey of the diocese showed that 57 percent of the 61 parishes had Sunday Masses in Spanish. Of all Masses each week, 56 percent were in Spanish. Fitzpatrick was succeeded by Enrique San Pedro, a native of Cuba who had served five years as the first Hispanic auxiliary bishop of the Diocese of Galveston-Houston.[qv] San Pedro died in 1994, and Raymundo Peña was appointed to succeed him.

In 1994 the Catholic population of the diocese was 652,214 (of a total population of 805,203), served by sixty-one parishes and forty-six missions. Fifty-nine of the parishes had resident pastors. The diocese had two homes for the aged, two retreat houses, one health-care center, and nine social-service agencies. Men's religious orders represented in the diocese numbered ten; women's, thirty-six. There were seven monastery-residences for priests and brothers and sixty-six convent-residences for sisters. Catholic student centers were located at the campuses of the University of Texas at Brownsville and U.T–Pan American at Edinburgh. Catholic elementary and secondary schools enrolled 3,238 students.

BIBLIOGRAPHY: Carlos E. Castañeda, *Our Catholic Heritage in Texas* (7 vols., Austin: Von Boeckmann–Jones, 1936–58; rpt., New York: Arno, 1976). Donald E. Chipman, *Spanish Texas, 1519–1821* (Austin: University of Texas Press, 1992). Gilbert R. Cruz, "The Vicariate Apostolic of Brownsville, 1874–1912: An Overview of Its Origins and Development," in *From the Mississippi to the Pacific: Essays in Honor of John Francis Bannon*, ed. Russell M. Magnaghi (Marquette: Northern Michigan University Press, 1982). Bernard Doyon, *The Cavalry of Christ on the Rio Grande, 1849–1883* (Milwaukee: Bruce, 1956). James Talmadge Moore, *Through Fire and Flood: The Catholic Church in Frontier Texas, 1836–1900* (College Station: Texas A&M University Press, 1992). *New Catholic Encyclopedia* (16 vols., New York: McGraw-Hill, 1967–74). Robert E. Wright, O.M.I., "Pioneer Religious Congregations of Men in Texas before 1900," *Journal of Texas Catholic History and Culture* 5 (1994).

Jana E. Pellusch

BROWNSVILLE, TEXAS. Brownsville, the county seat of Cameron County, is across the Rio Grande from Matamoros, Tamaulipas, at the southernmost tip of Texas. The city is at the southern terminus of U.S. highways 77 and 83 and the Missouri Pacific and Southern Pacific railroads, as well as a major port of entry to Mexico. Although the site was explored as early as the seventeenth century, the first settlers did not arrive until the latter part of the eighteenth century. In 1765 the community of San Juan de los Esteros (present-day Matamoros) was established across the Rio Grande. In 1781 Spanish authorities granted fifty-nine leagues of land on the northern bank of the river, including all of the site of Brownsville, to José Salvador de la Garza, who established a ranch about sixteen miles northwest of the site. During the early nineteenth century a small number of squatters, most of them herders and farmers from Matamoros, built huts in the area. A small settlement had formed by 1836, when Texas declared her independence from Mexico, but the region was still only sparsely settled when United States troops under Gen. Zachary Taylor[qv] arrived in early 1846. After taking up a position across from Matamoros, Taylor's forces began the construction of a defensive position near the settlement. Their temporary fort was originally called Fort Texas, but was renamed Fort Brown a short time later, in honor of Maj. Jacob Brown, who died during a Mexican attack on the stronghold. After the Mexican War,[qv] at the signing of the Treaty of Guadalupe Hidalgo[qv] in 1848, the area became part of the state of Texas and fell within the jurisdiction of San Patricio County. The same year Charles Stillman[qv] purchased a large part of the Garza grant north and northwest of Matamoros, including part of the city's common landholdings, from the children of the first wife of José Narciso Cavazos. Cavazos had remarried, however, and the heirs of his second wife, led by the eldest son, Juan N. Cortina,[qv] had been given legal title to the property, a fact that later led to a long series of legal battles over ownership. Stillman and his partner, Samuel Belden, laid out a town that they called Brownsville. George Lyons, deputy surveyor of Nueces County, surveyed a townsite of 4,676 acres. In December

1848, Stillman, Belden, and Simon Mussina[qv] formed the Brownsville Town Company and began selling lots for as much as $1,500 each.

Brownsville was made county seat of the new Cameron County on January 13, 1849, and a post office went into operation on February 3. Within a short time the town's population—swollen by refuges from Matamoros and Forty-niners taking the Gila route to the gold fields of California—had increased to more than 1,000. Despite a cholera epidemic in the spring of 1849 that reportedly killed nearly half the population, the town continued to boom. Brownsville soon replaced Matamoros as the leading trade center for northern Mexico. Merchants on both sides of the border quickly recognized the advantage of shipping goods to Brownsville and then smuggling them across the Rio Grande to avoid paying high Mexican duties. During the Mexican War, Richard King, Mifflin Kenedy[qqv] and Charles Stillman had set up a transport company to haul American troops and supplies up the river. After the war the three men managed to establish a virtual monopoly on Rio Grande transportation, thus ensuring the Anglo dominance of trade in the area and helping to spur the town's growth. As a result of the flourishing commerce, numerous stores sprang up along the riverfront. A city market opened in 1850, when the first regular newspaper, the *Sentinel,* began publication. The 1850 census showed a population of 519, two-thirds of whom were from the states along the Atlantic seaboard; most of the remainder were Mexican, Irish, French, English, and German. The culture of the town reflected the cosmopolitan character of its inhabitants: a large number of the early residents had previously lived in Mexico and many had absorbed Mexican customs and practices. Because of Brownsville's extensive trade network and large European contingent, a large percentage of the residents were fluent in several languages, including Spanish, English, French, and German.

Efforts were made to incorporate the town in the early 1850s, but a protracted series of legal battles over who had actually owned the land—Stillman or Cavazos's heirs—complicated matters. The Third Texas Legislature passed a measure on January 24, 1850, incorporating the town and relinquishing all state's rights and title to the area, but the Fourth Legislature repealed the law as of April 1, 1852, because of claims made by the Cavazos heirs. After a series of special sessions the following year, the legislature reincorporated the city on February 7, 1853. But the title issue was not completely settled until 1879, when the United States Supreme Court ruled in favor of the Stillman group. Despite recurring epidemics of cholera and yellow fever, Brownsville prospered and grew. Already by 1853 S. P. Moore, the surgeon of Fort Brown, estimated the population to be 3,500. The first Catholic church was founded by the Oblates of Mary Immaculate[qv] in 1854, and by 1856 the Episcopalians, Methodists, and Presbyterians had established churches. The first school, Villa María School for girls, was opened by four Sisters of the Incarnate Word and Blessed Sacrament[qv] in 1853, and the following year Melinda Rankin[qv] established the Rio Grande Female Institute[qv] with Presbyterian support. The first public school was established in 1855 with an enrollment of eight students.

The Civil War[qv] years were a period of prosperity for Brownsville and Matamoros. After the Union Navy succeeded in blockading most Southern ports, the Confederates looked for other avenues to ship cotton to Europe in return for ammunition, medicines, and other war supplies. The Confederates initially shipped their goods overland to the Brazos Santiago Pass[qv] at the mouth of the Rio Grande and from there to the neutral port of Bagdad in Mexico. But after Union forces captured Port Isabel the trade was moved inland to Brownsville. In November 1863 federal troops under Gen. Nathaniel P. Banks[qv] marched on Brownsville seeking to interrupt the trade. The outgunned Confederates abandoned Fort Brown, blew it up with 8,000 pounds of explosives, and withdrew. On July 30, 1864, Confederate troops commanded by John S. (Rip) Ford[qv] reoccupied the town and held it until May 1865, a month after the surrender of Gen. Robert E. Lee.[qv] Despite pleas of Union commanders to end the

Miller Hotel, Brownsville, ca. 1865–66. Photograph attributed to Louis de Planque. Courtesy Lawrence T. Jones III Collection, Austin. An early social center in Brownsville, the Miller Hotel offered a barroom and a noted restaurant and served as a terminus for several stage lines.

conflict, the Confederates in the area refused to surrender, and on May 13, 1865, they fought a skirmish with Union troops just outside of Brownsville. The battle of Palmito Ranch[qv] was the last battle of the Civil War. A few days later the Confederates in Brownsville agreed to a truce.

After the war Union armies reoccupied Brownsville and launched a massive construction effort to repair war-damaged Fort Brown. By 1869 army engineers had completed seventy new buildings at the fort and stationed army, infantry, and cavalry units there. The Brownsville economy, which had been buoyed up by the smuggling trade during the war years, however, was slower to recover. Despite the construction of the narrow-gauge Rio Grande Railroad from Brownsville to Port Isabel in 1872, the town grew only modestly during the early 1870s and did not fully rebound until the middle of the decade. In 1875 authorities reestablished the Brownsville public school system, and by 1884 the town had two banks, three churches, two ice houses, a cotton gin, and a population of nearly 5,000. In 1892 the *Cosmopolitan,* a local newspaper, was purchased by Jesse O. Wheeler,[qv] who renamed it the Brownsville *Herald.* The paper was still serving the city in the early 1990s. Among the chief local concerns voiced in the *Herald's* editorial pages was the need for a railroad connection to the north and a bridge to link the city with Matamoros. Several attempts were made to attract a railroad, but not until 1904 did the St. Louis, Brownsville and Mexico Railway reach the town. In 1910 a railroad bridge was constructed between Brownsville and Matamoros and regular service between the two towns began.

The introduction of the rail link to Brownsville opened the area for settlement of northern farmers, who began arriving in the lower Rio Grande valley in large numbers after the turn of the century. The new settlers cleared the land of brush, built extensive irrigation[qv] systems and roads, and introduced large-scale truck farming. In 1904 H. G. Stillwell, Sr., planted the first commercial citrus orchard in the area, thus opening the way for citrus fruit culture,[qv] one of the Valley's leading industries. The expansion of farming in the area and the railroad link to the North brought new prosperity to Brownsville and spurred a host of civic improvements. In 1908 work on a city-owned electric-lighting system, waterworks, and sewerage system was launched, and in 1910 the first international car bridge connecting Brownsville and Matamoros was completed. During the next two decades, a large influx of whites from the North served to reshape Brownsville's ethnic structure. Before 1900 nearly half of all those born in the city were the products of interracial marriages, and both Anglo and Mexican customs were widely practiced and respected. The town's new residents, mostly Protestant and white, however, were more reluctant to assimilate, and as a result ethic divisions began to widen. Racial tensions, however, did not confine themselves to Anglos and Mexicans. The Brownsville Raid of 1906 qv involved black troops stationed at Fort Brown. The soldiers went on a rampage in the city and killed or wounded a number of townspeople. Relations between persons of Mexican descent and the Anglo populace also began to deteriorate; many of the new Anglo immigrants saw their Mexican neighbors as "racial inferiors" ignorant of the American way of life, while Mexican Americans,qv the majority of whom worked as common laborers, became increasingly resentful of their situation. The animosities grew even worse during the Mexican Revolution,qv when border raids by Mexican bandits wrecked havoc among the Valley's populace.

The decades after the turn of the century also saw a profound shift in the political structure of the city and its environs. Before the arrival of the farm settlers, politics in South Texas was dominated by cliques of merchants, lawyers, and large landowners. In Brownsville the political scene was controlled by Democratic political boss James B. Wells,qv whose power eventually extended across much of South Texas. Although Wells occasionally resorted to intimidation, his power rested largely on meeting the needs of his constituents, from both the Anglo elite and the Hispanic majority. He welcomed the participation of Mexican Americans in his political organization and the municipal government, and he provided modest, informal support for his most impoverished constituents, much like a Mexican *patrón* or big-city boss. With the changing demographic make-up of the city and surrounding region and the rising tide of racial hostility between Anglos and Hispanics, however, Wells could no longer maintain his position, and he lost control of Brownsville in 1910. A new Anglo elite, made up mostly of recent arrivals, emerged, and a new social order, based on de facto segregation, became the rule.

During the 1920s Brownsville underwent a new period of prosperity as the area experienced a prolonged land boom. Enterprising agents went to the midwestern and northern states boosting the abundant cheap land in and around Brownsville. Special trains were dispatched to bring prospective buyers to the area, and during the height of the boom in the early 1920s as many as 200 landseekers a day were being brought into the environs. The population of Brownsville, which was just over 6,000 in 1900, grew nearly four-fold during the next three decades, reaching 22,021 in 1930. During the Prohibition qv years Brownsville became a popular port of entry into Mexico, attracting numerous tourists who wanted to have a drink in Matamoros. Smuggling, always an important industry, had a brief heyday as the town became an important crossing point for illegal liquor. The 1920s also witnessed a series of civic improvements: roads were paved, a new international bridge was opened, and the first airport was constructed. Efforts were also begun to build a ship channel from Brazos Santiago Pass, so that deepwater vessels could dock in Brownsville. In December, 1928, voters approved a measure establishing the Brownsville Navigation District and provided $2 million in bonds to build the channel. The work initially went slowly, but after a major hurricane hit the area in 1933 the Public Works Administration lent money to the district to complete the seventeen-mile-long channel and build a turning basin and terminal facilities. The port of Brownsville, located five miles northeast of the city, was officially opened on May 15, 1936. State Highway 48 runs alongside the seventeen-mile-long ship channel that connects the port to the Gulf Intracoastal Waterway.qv The port was originally 32 feet deep and 200 feet wide, while the turning basin was 36 feet deep by 1,000 feet wide and handled five million tons of cargo annually. The port of Brownsville is on the Brownsville Ship Channel, and the turning basin is about seventeen miles (14.5 nautical miles) inland from Brazos Santiago Pass. During the 1970s the southern side of the port was enlarged to 350 feet wide and 1,900 feet long. By 1980 the port had forty-eight piers, wharfs, and docks, with seventeen facilities in the Brownsville Ship Channel, seventeen in the fishing harbor, and fourteen on the Brownsville Turning Basin. The port was connected by rail to the Missouri Pacific Railroad, the Southern Pacific Transportation Company, and the National Railways of Mexico. Dry and cold storage warehouses, oil bunkering, bulk liquid storage, marine repair plans, dry-docking facilities, and a grain elevator were also available at the port.

The completion of the port made Brownsville the shipping center for the lower Rio Grande valley and northeastern Mexico and helped the city to weather the worst effects of the Great Depression.qv By the late 1930s the economy began to recover, and on the eve of World War II qv Brownsville stood poised to begin another era of prosperity. During the war Fort Brown served as training base for the 124th Cavalry, and large numbers of servicemen passed through the town. The fort was deactivated in 1945; the grounds were eventually turned over to the city. After the war, Brownsville once again experienced a period of growth. Shrimpers from Texas and Louisiana moved into the area and established the town as one of the leading shippers of shrimp in the country. The port of Brownsville also saw a growing volume of agricultural produce as vegetable and citrus farming in the Valley expanded. In 1949 the Gulf Intracoastal Waterway was extended to Brownsville and the ship channel was expanded to accommodate larger vessels. Cotton, introduced to the area on a large scale in the late 1940s, saw a marked upswing in the early 1950s, and for a time the port of Brownsville became the world's leading exporter of cotton. Union Carbide began construction of a plant near Brownsville in 1959, and the same year an immigration and customs building was constructed at the International Gateway Bridge.

The 1960s and 1970s saw a continued period of growth. Between 1950 and 1960 the population increased from 36,066 to 48,040, and by 1970 the town had 52,522 inhabitants. In 1966 the Industrial Development Council was formed to encourage new industries, and the following year the Border Industrialization Program was instituted by the Mexican government to attract Mexican businesses and laborers to the border area. The results were impressive. Between 1966 and 1978 the Brownsville area attracted more than 100 industrial firms that offered 13,600 jobs. Major industries in the early 1990s included petrochemicals, frozen foods, canned fruits and vegetables, and the manufacture of paper bags, beverages, mill work, garments, mattresses, hats, and metal products. From the 1970s to the mid-1990s Brownsville grew rapidly. One estimate suggests that as many as 37 percent of household heads in 1980 entered the city between 1969 and 1979. Much of the population growth came from immigration from Mexico, but the area has also seen growing numbers of retirees from the North and Midwest. In 1980 the population of the city was 84,997; by 1990 it had increased to 98,962. Although approximately 80 percent of the population in the early 1990s was of Mexican decent, Anglos still own most of the city's wealth. The last several decades, however, have witnessed a growing Hispanic middle class, and Hispanics have begun to play a larger part in political and community affairs. City leaders have been particularly interested in expanding educational opportunities in the area to promote future development. After considerable lobbying from local leaders the University of Texas System took over Pan American University at Brownsville and renamed it the University of Texas–Pan American–Brownsville in 1989. In September 1991 the name was changed to the University of Texas at Brownsville, and at that time the institution began a partnership with Texas Southmost College. Despite the recent wave of growth the city is faced with a variety of problems including substandard housing in *colonias*qv and high unemployment. Nonetheless, Brownsville continues to be a mecca for tourists year round. Points of interest in and around the city include Fort Brown, the Charles Stillman home, the sites of the battles of Palo Alto,qv Resaca de la Palma,qv and Palmito Ranch, the Gladys Porter Zoo,qv South Padre Island,qv and Matamoros.

BIBLIOGRAPHY: Evan Anders, *Boss Rule in South Texas: The Progressive Era* (Austin: University of Texas Press, 1982). Betty Bay, *Historic Brownsville: Original Townsite Guide* (Brownsville, Texas: Brownsville Historical Association, 1980). Helen Chapman, *The News From Brownsville: Helen Chapman's Letters from the Texas Military Frontier, 1848–1852,* ed. Caleb Coker (Austin: Texas State Historical Association, 1992). W. H. Chatfield, *The Twin Cities of the Border and the Country of the Lower Rio Grande* (New Orleans: Brandao, 1893; rpt., Brownsville: Brownsville Historical Association, 1959). Garna L. Christian, "The Brownsville Raid's 168th Man: The Court-Martial of Corporal Knowles," *Southwestern Historical Quarterly* 93 (July 1989). Charles Daniel Dillman, The Functions of Brownsville, Texas and Matamoros, Tamaulipas: Twin Cities of the Lower Rio Grande (Ph.D. dissertation, University of Michigan, 1968). Henry N. Ferguson, *The Port of Brownsville: A Maritime History of the Rio Grande Valley* (Brownsville: Springman-King, 1976). Milo Kearney and Anthony Knopp, *Boom and Bust: The Historical Cycles of Matamoros and Brownsville* (Austin: Eakin Press, 1991). Milo Kearney, ed., *A Brief History of Education in Brownsville and Matamoros* (University of Texas–Pan American–Brownsville, 1989). Milo Kearney, ed., *Studies in Brownsville History* (Pan American University at Brownsville, 1986). Milo Kearney, ed., *Still More Studies in Brownsville History* (University of Texas at Brownsville, 1991). *The Ports of Freeport, Port Lavaca, Port Isabel and Brownsville, Texas* (Port Series 26, Fort Belvoir, Virginia: U.S. Army Corps of Engineers, 1980). Robert B. Vezzetti and Ruby A. Wooldridge, *Brownsville: A Pictorial History* (Virginia Beach, Virginia: Donning, 1982). John D. Weaver, *The Brownsville Raid* (New York: Norton, 1970).

Alicia A. Garza and Christopher Long

BROWNSVILLE AND GULF RAILROAD. The Brownsville and Gulf Railroad was chartered on May 10, 1883, to connect the ferry landings in Brownsville, Cameron County, with the Rio Grande Railroad, a distance of five miles. The capital stock was $25,000. The principal place of business was Brownsville. The members of the first board of directors were B. W. Thacker, F. A. Lister, and A. R. Woolston, all of Laredo; D. M. Murphy of Corpus Christi; M. Quin of Galveston; Walter Hinchman of New York City; and Charles S. Hinchman of Philadelphia. In 1883 the Brownsville and Gulf built a mile of three-foot-gauge track in Brownsville. Reported gross earnings in 1891 were $3,000. The company was recognized as a common carrier by the Railroad Commission[qv] until 1902, when it was reclassified as a tram road. The BGR held a franchise granted by the United States that authorized the construction of a bridge across the Rio Grande. On March 14, 1906, the line was sold to interests backing the St. Louis, Brownsville and Mexico Railway Company, and the franchise was later used by the Brownsville and Matamoros Bridge Company. Although the BGR was reported to have had one steam locomotive in 1899, mules were normally used to move the rail cars between the station and the ferry landing. *Nancy Beck Young*

BROWNSVILLE AND MATAMOROS BRIDGE COMPANY. The Brownsville and Matamoros Bridge Company, incorporated in Arizona Territory on August 25, 1909, is owned equally by the Missouri Pacific (as successor to the St. Louis, Brownsville and Mexico) and the National Railways of Mexico. The company owns and operates a bridge across the Rio Grande between Brownsville and Matamoros that was constructed between April 1909 and January 1, 1911, under a franchise originally granted to the Brownsville and Gulf Railway Company. The company also has 1.24 miles of track connecting the two cities. *S. G. Reed*

BROWNSVILLE RAID. The Brownsville Raid of August 13–14, 1906, an alleged attack by soldiers from companies B, C, and D of the black Twenty-fifth United States Infantry[qv] stationed at Fort Brown, resulted in the largest summary dismissals in the annals of the United States Army. The First Battalion, minus Headquarters and Company A, arrived at Brownsville, a community of 6,000, from recent duty in the Philippines and Fort Niobrara, Nebraska, on July 28. The soldiers immediately confronted racial discrimination from some businesses and suffered several instances of physical abuse from federal customs collectors. A reported attack on a white woman during the night of August 12 so incensed many townspeople that Maj. Charles W. Penrose, after consultation with Mayor Frederick Combe, declared an early curfew the following day to avoid trouble. The evening passed peacefully until around midnight, when a brief shooting spree claimed the life of bartender Frank Natus and destroyed the arm of police lieutenant M. Y. Dominguez. Various residents claimed to observe soldiers running through the streets shooting, despite the darkness of the hour and vantage points of considerable distance.

Several sets of civilian and military investigations presumed the guilt of the soldiers without identifying individual culprits. A citizens' committee, cooperating with Penrose's own inquiry, successfully demanded the removal of the troops but failed to receive white replacements. Maj. Augustus P. Blocksom, of the army's Southwestern Division, deemed the soldiers uncooperative and urged their dismissal if they refused to turn evidence. The men denied any knowledge of the shooting, while officers and a sentry reported hearing pistol fire outside the reservation. Texas Ranger captain William Jesse McDonald[qv] pursued the trail to twelve enlisted men, whom he arrested for holding positions key to a conspiracy. However, a Cameron County grand jury failed to return any indictments. Inspector General Ernest A. Garlington charged a "conspiracy of silence" against the companies and urged implementation of Blocksom's suggestion. Accordingly, on November 5 President Theodore Roosevelt summarily discharged "without honor" all 167 enlisted men previously garrisoning Fort Brown.

The action of Roosevelt, who had served with black troops in the Spanish-American War and conspicuously appointed African Americans[qv] to office, shocked his black constituency and moved the controversy to the national stage. The Constitution League, a civil-rights organization, decried the lack of due process accorded the soldiers and impugned the timing of the order, which followed the congressional elections. Amid signs of alienation that could jeopardize the presidential ambitions of Secretary of War William Howard Taft, Senator Joseph B. Foraker (R-Ohio) urged a Senate investigation.

Foraker, a nemesis of Roosevelt and an aspiring presidential candidate in his own right, kept the issue alive through speeches and writings over the next several years. He and Roosevelt clashed in addresses to the Gridiron Club in 1907 and hired private detectives to enhance their investigations. The Senate Military Affairs Committee, which included Foraker, conducted hearings while courts-martial cleared Penrose and officer-of-the-day Capt. Edgar A. Macklin of alleged negligence. The majority report, issued in March 1908, concurred with the official White House decision, while a minority of four Republicans found the evidence inconclusive. Yet another minority report, submitted by Foraker and Morgan G. Bulkeley (R-Connecticut), asserted the soldiers' innocence. It assailed alleged contradictory, insufficient, and contrived evidence and bias of witnesses and investigators. The report suggested that townspeople or outsiders had staged the raid to banish the black troops or to avenge customs enforcement.

Submitting to pressure, the administration appointed a board of retired army officers to review applications for reenlistment. After interviewing somewhat over half the applicants, the Court of Military Inquiry in 1910 inexplicably approved only fourteen of the men. The decision, in conjunction with Taft's presidential victory, Roosevelt's retirement, and Foraker's failure to win renomination, effectively closed the matter for more than sixty years.

In 1972, convinced by recent research critical of the government's handling of the affair, Representative Augustus Hawkins

(D-California) urged justice for the debarred soldiers. The Nixon administration concurred and awarded honorable discharges without back pay. Still maintaining the battalion's innocence, Dorsie Willis, the only surviving veteran, received a $25,000 pension.

BIBLIOGRAPHY: Garna L. Christian, "The Brownsville Raid's 168th Man: The Court-Martial of Corporal Knowles," *Southwestern Historical Quarterly* 93 (July 1989). Ann J. Lane, *The Brownsville Affair: National Crisis and Black Reaction* (Port Washington, New York: National University Publications, Kennikat Press, 1971). New York *Times*, September 29, 1972. Vertical Files, Barker Texas History Center, University of Texas at Austin (Brownsville, Texas–Riot). John D. Weaver, *The Brownsville Raid* (New York: Norton, 1970).

Garna L. Christian

BROWNSVILLE AND RIO GRANDE INTERNATIONAL RAILROAD. The Brownsville and Rio Grande International Railroad, chartered in 1984, was the successor to the Missouri Pacific Railroad. The road ran fifteen miles in south Cameron County, through Brownsville. By 1988 the company had fourteen employees. The top commodities shipped over the road were nonmetal materials and metal products. The range of revenue that year was under $5 million.

Chris Cravens

BROWNSVILLE WHARF CASE. The Brownsville Wharf Case, an incident in the history of the boundary between the United States and Mexico, arose in August 1871, when Francisco Palacio, acting chargé d'affaires of Mexico, called the attention of Secretary of State Hamilton Fish to certain construction work on the left bank of the Rio Grande by the Wharf Company of Brownsville. Points involved were interference with the free and safe navigation of the river, invasion of Mexican territory by water, and the danger of altering the dividing line between the two countries. After investigation the United States government reported that the works did not hinder navigation or occasion appreciable destruction of the Mexican bank.

BIBLIOGRAPHY: *Chamizal Arbitration: Appendix to the Case of the United States before the International Boundary Commission*, Vol. 2 (Washington: GPO, 1911).

Jacqueline E. Timm

BROWNTOWN, TEXAS. Browntown was between White Oak Creek and the Sulphur River nine miles northwest of Omaha in northwestern Morris County. In 1900 the Sullivan Sanford Lumber Company bought 20,000 acres in northwestern Morris and northeastern Titus counties. The company built a railroad from Naples north across White Oak Creek and then northwest through the timberland. By 1917 they had cut most of the usable timber and torn up the railroad. They then sold the land to Clayton D. Browne, a Dallas real estate developer who planned to build a community there. Browne divided the land into tracts of eighty to 100 acres and had twelve three-room box houses built along the abandoned railroad grade. He was willing to sell the land on easy terms, making it possible for poor sharecroppers to obtain land of their own. The residents were to have use of the entire 20,000 acres for raising stock and cutting timber.

Many families moved into the area. Some bought the land, some entered into contracts to buy the land, and some simply occupied the land without making any such arrangement with Browne. The small community along the road was named Browntown. By 1921 there were enough families in the area to begin a school, and in 1922 the residents floated a bond and built a white clapboard building with two classrooms. The Great Depression,[qv] however, ruined most of the settlers' hopes of paying off their debts and becoming landowners. In financial difficulty himself, Browne sold the land to Columbus Marion (Dad) Joiner[qv] in 1932. Although Joiner was able to sell leases on the land to individuals throughout the nation, all of the wells he drilled on the land were dry.

In 1942 Joiner sold the land to Paul Pewitt, who wished to use it as a cattle ranch. As Pewitt began to fence and clear the land, those settlers who had depended on the open range for their subsistence faced difficult choices. Some resorted to violence, cutting miles of fence, burning barns, and killing stock. Pewitt retaliated by driving off those who did not have clear title. He rounded up horses and cattle that roamed his land and sold or killed them. The few settlers who had actually obtained clear title to their land gradually sold their holdings to Pewitt and moved away. By the 1970s only one small farm remained, sitting in the middle of the vast modern ranch as a reminder of Browntown and of the hopes and dreams of its founder and residents.

BIBLIOGRAPHY: Deborah Brown and Katharine Gust, *Between the Creeks: Recollections of Northeast Texas* (Austin: Encino, 1976).

Cecil Harper, Jr.

BROWNWOOD, TEXAS. Brownwood is on Pecan Bayou at the intersection of U.S. highways 64, 87, and 377, Farm Road 2524, and the Atchison, Topeka and Santa Fe Railway in south central Brown County. The city and the county are named for Henry Stevenson Brown.[qv] The area was settled by farmers and cattle ranchers like Welcome W. Chandler[qv] and J. H. Fowler. When the sparsely populated county was organized in 1857, the hamlet of Brownwood was chosen as county seat. A post office was opened in the town the following year. The town was originally located on the east side of Pecan Bayou, but in the late 1860s a land-title dispute and problems with an inadequate water supply induced the residents to move to a sixty-acre site on the west side of the bayou donated by Greenleaf Fisk.[qv] Brownwood Masonic Lodge was chartered in 1865. As late as 1872 Brownwood was a small community of two stores, a log courthouse, and about five dwellings. In 1873 John Y. Rankin purchased land around the business district and began to build homes in what became known as the Rankin Addition. In 1876, when the town had an estimated 120 inhabitants and Cumberland Presbyterian, Presbyterian, and Baptist churches, the first bank was opened and a schoolhouse was built that also served as a town hall and a church. Because Brownwood lay on a feeder line of the Western Trail,[qv] stores and saloons served the needs of the cowboys who drove the herds through town. A cotton gin was built in town in 1877 as the state of Texas began to offer the land to farmers.

The 1880s and 1890s were decades of dramatic growth for the community, as the population increased from 725 in 1880 to 2,176 in 1890 and 3,965 in 1900. The town became a center of the Farmers' Alliance[qv] with the building of the West Texas District Alliance Cotton Yard and the establishment of an alliance paper, the weekly *Freemans Journal.* Other newspapers that have been published in the community include the Brownwood *Gazette, Bulletin,* and *Appeal,* the *Pecan Valley News,* the *Texas Immigration and Stock Farmer, Living Issues,* and the *Brown County Banner.* In 1885 the Brownwood *Daily Bee* became the town's first daily paper. The courthouse burned in 1880, and a new one was completed in 1884. In 1884, when Brownwood incorporated, the town had two banks, nine general stores, five saloons, two hotels, and steam cotton and grist mills. The following year the Gulf, Colorado and Santa Fe Railroad built through Brownwood, and in 1886 the town built its first waterworks. An opera house was built in the late 1880s. By 1890 the town had five churches, an icehouse, a fire department, and a sanitarium. A second railroad, the Fort Worth and Rio Grande, built through Brownwood in 1891. There were also significant developments in education during these years. Several local schools were consolidated to form the Brownwood Independent School District in 1883. In 1889 two colleges opened their doors in Brownwood—Daniel Baker College, founded by the Presbyterians, and Howard Payne College, a Baptist institution. Daniel Baker closed, and its campus became part of Howard Payne College in 1953.

By 1900, the city was dominated by the cotton industry. It supported the West Texas Compress Company, the Brownwood Cotton

Oil Mill, and sixteen cotton gins. Severe flooding that year covered parts of the town with up to ten feet of water. Prohibition[qv] became popular in the town in the 1890s, and in 1903, after a series of violent incidents, the town's saloons were closed. Equally rowdy drinking clubs sprang up in response to the saloon closings, and a stretch of one street became known as "Battle Row." The population of Brownwood continued to climb, reaching 6,967 in 1910 and 8,223 in 1920, and in spite of the boll weevil[qv] infestation and other problems in the cotton industry, the city was the largest cotton-buying center west of Fort Worth by 1920. A third railroad, the Brownwood North and South, was built in 1912 to connect Brownwood with the Brown County community of May, but the short-lived railroad lost money and was abandoned in 1927. Brownwood went through two boom periods in the first half of the twentieth century, the first stimulated by the oil industry, the second by the building of a military installation during World War II.[qv] Oil was first discovered near Brownwood in 1917, but the town did not become a major oil-industry site until the 1920s. The population of the city shot up from 8,223 in 1920 to 12,789 in 1930, and estimates from the late 1920s indicate it might have been as high as 15,000. At one time during the boom the city had twenty-five manufacturing and industrial plants in operation. Brownwood's growth was also reflected in the changing percentage of county residents who lived in the town; though fewer than a quarter of Brown County residents lived in Brownwood in 1900, almost half lived in the city by 1930. The pace of development slowed in the 1930s, though the city benefited from the completion of Lake Brownwood[qv] in 1933 and several area WPA projects. In 1940 Brownwood had 13,398 inhabitants, some 52 percent of the Brown County population.

In the fall of 1940, as part of the military buildup associated with the peacetime draft, a military-training installation, Camp Bowie,[qv] was built to the south and southwest of town. The camp eventually became the largest military training center in Texas, and had a major impact on the city of Brownwood. By December 1940 the 13,500 workers at the camp exceeded the 1940 population of the city; by March 1941 Brownwood's population was counted at 22,479, and by some estimates the wartime population eventually reached considerably more than 50,000. The massive influx of workers, the families of military personnel, and soldiers seeking off-base housing created a severe housing shortage in Brownwood, which started the boom in September of 1940 with a mere 200 vacant dwelling units. City residents coped by turning a skating rink into a dormitory, by allowing patrons to bed down in a movie theater after the final show, by subdividing the existing housing stock, and by the building of additional housing units. Though much of the development in town was ephemeral, the wartime boom left the city with better roads and streets, improved sanitation and medical facilities, a municipal airport, and a supply of new housing and business units.

With the closing of Camp Bowie in 1946 Brownwood's wartime gains began to slip away. Attempts to sustain the growth rate of the war years were blocked by the seven-year drought of the late 1940s and early 1950s and its deleterious impact on the agribusiness of the region. In spite of the postwar depression, the city numbered 20,140 inhabitants, 71 percent of the county population, in 1950. Business revolved around wool, oil, poultry, livestock, peanuts, and pecans. Part of the business district burned down in 1953. Brownwood's population declined during the 1950s by more than 15 percent to 16,974 in 1960, and has remained relatively static over the next thirty years, with 17,368 inhabitants in 1970, 19,203 in 1980, and 18,387 in 1990. The growth of nearby Early, located at the old site of Brownwood on the east side of Pecan Bayou has kept the combined population of the two cities at around 20,000; they comprised almost three-quarters of the county inhabitants in 1970. After the old city auditorium, the Memorial Hall, burned in 1960, the city built Brownwood Coliseum in 1963. In the 1970s Brownwood manufactured industrial and transportation equipment, furniture, clothing, woolen goods, crushed stone, livestock drenches, feeds, and also food, glass, plastic, and leather products. In the 1980s important businesses included meat packing, commercial printing, and the manufacture of plumbing fixtures, leather gloves, oilfield machinery and construction equipment. In 1990, with the development of other county communities, the Brownwood-Early area held only 60 percent of Brown County's population, but the city remained an important distributing center for the county and the region. Area attractions included Lake Brownwood State Recreation Area,[qv] Camp Bowie Memorial Park, and the Brown County Museum of History.

BIBLIOGRAPHY: Tessica Martin, "Brownwood, Texas, in World War II," West Texas Historical Association *Year Book* 43 (1967). Tevis Clyde Smith, *From the Memories of Men* (Brownwood, Texas, 1954). Tevis Clyde Smith, *Frontier's Generation* (Brownwood, Texas, 1931; 2d ed. 1980). Tevis Clyde Smith, *Pecan Valley Days* (Brownwood, Texas, 1958). *Mark Odintz*

BROWNWOOD NORTH AND SOUTH RAILWAY. The Brownwood North and South Railway Company was chartered on January 29, 1910, by the citizens of Brown County to build a road eighteen miles from Brownwood, the county seat, north to May. Brooke Smith was the main promoter and president of the company, and he and other Brownwood businessmen hoped to extend the line eventually to Cisco, to link the cotton-producing regions of northern Brown and southern Eastland counties. The capital was $30,000, and the business office was located in Brownwood. Members of the first board of directors included Smith, J. A. Walker, Y. C. Yantis, A. L. Self, G. N. Harrison, R. B. Rogers, Will H. Mays, Henry Ford,[qv] and J. J. Timmins, all of Brownwood. The company made an agreement to use the tracks of the Fort Worth and Rio Grande Railway Company from a half mile east of Pecan Bayou into Brownwood. Work began on the construction of the road but was stopped when some of the subscribers to its stock failed to pay. At that time B. L. Winchell, then president of the St. Louis and San Francisco Railroad Company (Frisco), agreed to complete the line and was given all of the Brownwood North and South assets and liabilities. The eighteen miles to May was placed in operation in November 1911. The line went into receivership along with the other Frisco properties in 1913. In 1916 its earnings included $3,160 in passenger revenue and $5,222 in freight revenue. By 1926 the BN&S was listed as a Class III railroad by the Railroad Commission[qv] and owned no equipment. Earnings for that year included $858 in passenger revenue and $8,652 in freight revenue. The road never was a financial success and was abandoned by 1927.

BIBLIOGRAPHY: Thomas Robert Havins, *Something about Brown: A History of Brown County, Texas* (Brownwood, Texas: Banner Printing, 1958). *Jeanne F. Lively and Chris Cravens*

BROXSON, TEXAS. Broxson was eight miles northeast of Lovelady in south central Houston County. It was established in the late 1880s, and a post office opened there in 1890 with G. W. Broxson, after whom the community was named, as the postmaster. Around 1900 the settlement had a general store, a school, and a number of houses. The post office closed in 1902. By the mid-1930s Broxson no longer appeared on highway maps. *Christopher Long*

BRUCE, ANDREW DAVIS (1894–1969). Andrew Davis Bruce, officer in the United States Army and chief administrator of the University of Houston, the son of John Logan and Martha Washington (Smith) Bruce, was born in St. Louis, Missouri, on September 14, 1894, and grew up in Texas. He graduated from the Agricultural and Mechanical College of Texas (now Texas A&M University), which awarded him a doctorate of laws, and in 1917 entered the army. He returned from combat duty in France in 1918 as a lieutenant colonel after action with the Second Division in France and service with occupation forces in Germany. He married Roberta Linnell Kennedy in 1920 and taught military science and tactics at Allen Academy[qv] in Bryan. The couple had three children. Between the wars Bruce did tours of duty at the Infantry School, foreign duty in Panama, historical work at the Army War College, and service on the War Department general staff, where he revised textbooks on military doctrine. In the early 1940s he organized and commanded the Tank Destroyer Center at Fort Hood. In 1943 he assumed command of the Seventy-seventh Infantry, which he led through heavy fighting in the Guam, Leyte, and Ryukyu campaigns. He and his men buried war correspondent Ernie Pyle on Ie Shima, Ryukyu Islands, in 1945. After Japan surrendered, Bruce served as military governor of Hokkaido. In 1947 he returned to the United States, where he filled various staff positions. He later commanded the Seventh Division in Korea. Bruce, who received medals and decorations for his service from both the United States and other governments, retired in 1954 to serve as president of the University of Houston. The university became state-supported during his term of office, and in 1956 he was made its first chancellor. He was a Mason and a Shriner and served as president of the Houston Chamber of Commerce. Bruce Memorial Hall, a housing complex at Fort Hood, is named in his honor. He died on July 28, 1969, and was buried at Arlington National Cemetery.

BIBLIOGRAPHY: New York *Times*, July 28, 1969. Vertical Files, Barker Texas History Center, University of Texas at Austin. *Who's Who in America*, 1950–51.

Diana J. Kleiner

BRUCE, WILLIAM HERSCHEL (1856–1943). William Herschel Bruce, college president and mathematician, son of Hilery S. and Catherine (Pruitt) Bruce, was born in Troup County, Georgia, on April 8, 1856. He spent most of his childhood in Alabama, where the family moved in 1861. After graduating from high school, Bruce, at the age of nineteen, began his teaching career in a rural school in Alabama. For the next eight years he taught school and attended Alabama A&M College (now Auburn University), where he graduated in 1883 with a B.A. in mathematics. That year he moved to Milltown, Georgia, where he continued to teach and began work on a Ph.D. at Mercer University in nearby Macon. The following year he accepted the position of head of the faculty of Blanco High School in Texas, where, in addition to his teaching and administrative duties, he practiced law. He continued to work on his Ph.D. and became Mercer University's first doctoral graduate in 1890.

During Bruce's nine years in Blanco, his reputation as a teacher and administrator attracted requests from eight school districts inviting him to be their superintendent. In 1893, over the objections of students and residents of Blanco, he accepted the position of superintendent in Marble Falls. He was so popular in Blanco that a number of the high school faculty and many students followed Bruce to his new post. He succeeded in gaining accreditation for the Marble Falls schools, as he had at Blanco. Three years later he did the same for Athens. In 1899 Athens residents financed a private school, which they named Bruce Academy in his honor. In 1899 Bruce left Athens to become president of the newly organized John Tarleton College (now Tarleton State University) in Stephenville, but he resigned in late 1900 because the college trustees refused to grant him a long-term contract.

Bruce returned to Athens for the 1900–01 school year, then accepted an invitation from North Texas State Normal College (now the University of North Texas) to become head of the mathematics department. From 1901 to 1905 he worked in this capacity and, beginning in 1902 or 1903, served as President Joel S. Kendall's[qv] primary assistant. Following Kendall's death in 1905, Bruce, in October 1906, became president of the small, sixteen-year-old school. For the next seventeen years he devoted his energy to establishing North Texas State as the leading teacher-training institution in Texas. By raising admission standards to meet the requirements established by major colleges, increasing the number of faculty members who held graduate degrees, and enlarging course offerings, he had, by 1916, changed North Texas State from a three-year preparatory school to a four-year college. By 1923 the Association of Texas Colleges and Universities[qv] and the American Association of Teachers Colleges had admitted North Texas State as a member. Student enrollment increased during Bruce's presidency from 1,028 to 4,700, while the number of faculty members grew from fourteen to 118. The size of the campus also grew, from ten to twenty-five acres; and eight new buildings, including the school's first dormitory, were added. As a result of these achievements, Bruce was able to persuade Governor Pat Neff[qv] and the state legislature to change the name of the institution to North Texas State Teachers College.

In 1905 Bruce served as president of the Texas State Teachers Association,[qv] and from 1912 to 1923 he was president of the Council of Texas Normal College Presidents. He also served as chairman of the Texas State Board of Examiners from 1905 to 1910. As a result of his first publication, *Some Noteworthy Properties of a Triangle and Its Circles* (1904), he was included in *Men of Science* in 1906. He also coauthored the textbooks *Elements of Plane Geometry* and *Elements of Solid Geometry* in 1910. In 1916 he published *Principles and Processes of Education* for summer-school use. In 1932 *The Nine Circles of the Triangle* received considerable notice from fellow mathematicians. Bruce also published two collections of poetry, *The Charms of Solitude* and *Emergent Man*, in the mid-1920s.

He and Lillie Ora Hart were married in 1879 and had three sons and one daughter. Bruce and his wife were leaders in community affairs and in the Denton Baptist Church until Mrs. Bruce was paralyzed by a stroke in 1923. As a result, on May 28 of that year, Bruce retired from the presidency of North Texas State and was made president emeritus. For the next fourteen years he divided his residence between Denton and Opelika, Alabama, where his wife lived in a clinic run by their son and daughter. After his wife's death in 1937, Bruce returned to Denton. He died on December 30, 1943, while visiting his children in Opelika, where he was interred.

BIBLIOGRAPHY: C. A. Bridges, *History of Denton, Texas, from Its Beginning to 1960* (Waco: Texian Press, 1978). James Lloyd Rogers, *The Story of North Texas* (Denton: North Texas State University, 1965). C. M. Mizell, Dr. W. H. Bruce: His Contribution to Public Education (M.A. thesis, Southern Methodist University, 1926).

David Minor

BRUCE, TEXAS. Bruce was fifteen miles northwest of Cleburne in western Johnson County. The site was settled in the early 1880s and named for early settler Horatio Gates Bruce. By the mid-1880s the community had two churches, a school, and a general store. Between 1885 and 1891 it had a post office. In 1892 it had four businesses and a population of fifty. During the first three decades of the twentieth century most of the families moved to nearby Godley. By 1930 Bruce was no longer an organized community.

BIBLIOGRAPHY: Johnson County History Book Committee, *History of Johnson County, Texas* (Dallas: Curtis Media, 1985).

David Minor

BRUCE FIELD. Bruce Field, a contract primary flying school at Ballinger, was named for R. E. Bruce, a member of the Ballinger Aviation Committee. It was operated under government contract by the San Marcos Flying Service from June 1941 to June 1944.

BIBLIOGRAPHY: Robert E. Hays, Jr., Military Aviation Activities in Texas, World Wars I and II (M.A. thesis, University of Texas, 1963).

Art Leatherwood

BRUCEVILLE-EDDY, TEXAS. Bruceville-Eddy is on Interstate Highway 35 eighteen miles southwest of Waco in southern McLennan County. It began as two separate communities, Bruceville and Eddy, both of which became stations on the Missouri, Kansas and Texas Railroad in 1882. Bruceville was named for Lucien N. Bruce, who donated land for the railroad station. Much of the town's early population came from Mastersville, a community two miles north that the railroad had bypassed. By 1900 Bruceville's population had grown to 289. Among the businesses that developed in the community were a lumber and hardware store, two general stores, and a grocery; Bruceville also had a hotel, two churches, and a school. The Bruceville Independent School District was established in 1904. A state bank opened in 1907, but it overextended its resources during World War I.[qv] A severe local drought in 1925 prevented many area farmers from meeting loan obligations, and although the bank borrowed money to increase its available funds, its directors decided to close the bank in 1927. Bruceville reported 500 residents during the 1930s and early 1940s, but estimates fell steadily in the years after World War II,[qv] as many residents moved to take advantage of job opportunities in larger towns. The number of residents reported was 250 in 1949, 175 in 1964, and twenty-five in 1970.

Bruceville formed a joint city government with nearby Eddy in the mid-1970s. Eddy, on Interstate Highway 35 two miles southwest of Bruceville on the McLennan-Falls county line, was known as Marvin until the Katy Railroad was built through the area in 1882. The post office, which was established that year, was named in honor of Everett B. Eddy, a division superintendent of the railroad. In the mid-1880s the community had a gristmill, three general stores, two churches, a district school, and 150 residents. By the early 1890s Eddy also had two hotels and a weekly newspaper, the *News and Messenger*. Population estimates for that period ran as high as 700. A private bank opened in Eddy in 1901 and was incorporated as the Eddy State Bank in 1906. The bank received a national charter in 1915 and began operating as the First National Bank of Eddy. In 1928 the schools at Bruceville and Eddy were joined to form the county's first consolidated rural high school district. Eddy's population in the late 1920s was estimated at 450. The bank at Eddy survived the Great Depression[qv] but closed in 1942. As some area residents moved away and those who remained began to do more of their trading in larger towns, business activity in Eddy declined. By the mid-1940s the population had fallen to 350. In the late 1950s and early 1960s, however, Interstate Highway 35 was built along the U.S. Highway 81 route, bringing more business to the area and making it easy for residents to commute. Population estimates rose to 600 in the 1960s. After Bruceville-Eddy incorporated in the mid-1970s the number of residents increased rapidly, to 1,038 by the early 1980s and to 1,075 by 1990.

BIBLIOGRAPHY: Charles Leroy Hinkle, A History and Analysis of Rural Banking in McLennan County (M.S. thesis, Baylor University, 1959). Dayton Kelley, ed., *The Handbook of Waco and McLennan County, Texas* (Waco: Texian, 1972). William Robert Poage, *McLennan County Before 1980* (Waco: Texian, 1981). *Vivian Elizabeth Smyrl*

BRUCKISCH, WILHELM (?–1877). Wilhelm Bruckisch, apiarist, was born at Postelwitz, Silesia. In 1847 he founded and presided over the Silesian beekeepers' society and became an associate of Pastor Johann Dzierzon, a European authority on bees. In 1853 Bruckisch came to Texas and settled on the Guadalupe River at Hortontown, where he established an apiary and did horticultural work. He published numerous works on bees, including six editions of the *Bienenbuch* (1847–61), and *Besste Bienenzuchts-Methode nach Pfarrer Dzierzon* (1866); he and edited and published *Die Preussischen Bienennachrichten* (1850). Bruckisch died at Hortontown in 1877.

BIBLIOGRAPHY: S. W. Geiser, "A Century of Scientific Exploration in Texas," *Field and Laboratory* 7 (January 1939).

Clinton P. Hartmann

BRUFF, SAMUEL (ca. 1793–?). Samuel Bruff, early settler and legislator, came to Texas from Tennessee in 1830 and took the oath of allegiance to the Mexican government on March 13. He was a delegate from the district of Alfred (present Colorado County) to the Convention of 1832[qv] in San Felipe. In 1836 he ran unsuccessfully for Congress from Harrisburg. On August 3, 1838, he was issued a headright certificate to one-third league of land in the Milam District.

BIBLIOGRAPHY: Texas House of Representatives, *Biographical Directory of the Texan Conventions and Congresses, 1832–1845* (Austin: Book Exchange, 1941).

BRULAY, GEORGE PAUL (1839–1905). George Paul Brulay, planter, son of Ambroise and Eliza (Vernon) Brulay, was born on December 6, 1839, in Paris, France. He was educated at home and at local schools until he was fourteen, when he boarded a merchant vessel and was shipwrecked off Colombia. After being stranded in Cartagena, he worked his way through the interior of the country for three years, then returned to Paris, where he worked for a commission merchant. At eighteen he shipped out to Tampa, Florida, and from there to the Rio Grande valley of Texas. With his brother Arthur, Brulay opened a business handling merchandise between Matamoros and Monterrey by mule caravans. They also used sailboats to deliver goods to coastal towns, and on one of these trips Arthur was lost at sea. In Brownsville Brulay operated a mercantile business under the firm name of Colon, Brulay, and Company until about 1876. On March 11, 1876, he married Marie E. Boesch; they had five children. In the early 1870s Brulay bought about 400 acres of land, which he named Rio Grande Plantation, east of Brownsville. He first planted cotton and experimented with other produce, including sugarcane. He became a successful cane producer and built a mill, commissary, residences, a schoolhouse, and other buildings as the industry grew. Small rail cars ran from the fields to the mills, and hundreds of laborers were employed. Brulay began irrigating his fields on one of the first irrigation permits on the Rio Grande. The Brulay plantation home became a gathering place not only for local people but for state and foreign travelers as well. In 1891 the Brulay family also maintained a home in Brownsville. The sugarcane plantation was operated for several years after Brulay's death, on March 29, 1905. He was buried in Buena Vista Park, Brownsville.

BIBLIOGRAPHY: W. H. Chatfield, *The Twin Cities of the Border and the Country of the Lower Rio Grande* (New Orleans: Brandao, 1893; rpt., Brownsville: Brownsville Historical Association, 1959). Lewis E. Daniell, *Texas—The Country and Its Men* (Austin?, 1924?).

Grace Edman

BRUMBERG, TEXAS. Brumberg was on State Highway 19 and the International–Great Northern Railroad, four miles south of Crockett in south central Houston County. It was established around 1900. In the mid-1930s it had several stores, a sawmill, and a number of houses. After World War II[qv] many of the residents moved away, and by the mid-1960s Brumberg was no longer shown on highway maps. In the early 1990s only a few widely scattered houses remained in the area.

Christopher Long

BRUMBY, WILLIAM MCDUFFIE (1866–1959). William McDuffie Brumby, public health pioneer, was born in Delhi, Louisiana, in 1866, the son of George McDuffie Brumby, a physician. He attended public schools in Louisiana and the University of Alabama before entering Tulane University Medical School, where he obtained an M.D. in 1889. In 1896, after practicing with his father for seven years, he moved to Houston, Texas. In 1900 he was appointed city health officer for Houston, a position he held until 1907, when he became president of the State Board of Health (*see* TEXAS DEPARTMENT OF HEALTH). During his first year in office he wrote the first statewide sanitary code. Besides his work in fighting smallpox and yellow fever epidemics, he helped found the Texas Tuberculosis Association in 1908 and was one of the first health officers in the country to test dairy herds for tuberculosis. Brumby once stated that his greatest achievement was inducing the International Congress on Tuberculosis in Washington, D.C., to persuade officials in eastern states to establish local tuberculosis-treatment facilities rather than send their residents to the supposedly healthful climate of West Texas. After leaving Austin in 1911, Brumby returned to Houston, where he practiced until his retirement in 1955. He joined the State Medical Association of Texas (now the Texas Medical Association[qv]) in 1904 and served as chairman of the sections on state medicine and public hygiene. He was a member of the Harris County Medical Society, the American College of Surgeons, the American College of Chest Physicians, and the American Medical Association. He died on November 29, 1959, at his home in Houston. He was survived by his wife, Lila (Kirby), three daughters, and a son. He was an Episcopalian.

BIBLIOGRAPHY: Houston *Post*, November 30, 1959. *Texas State Journal of Medicine*, January 1960. Vertical Files, Barker Texas History Center, University of Texas at Austin. *Patricia L. Jakobi*

BRUMLEY, TEXAS. Brumley, on Farm Road 2454 eleven miles northwest of Gilmer in northern Upshur County, was settled before 1900. A school was operating there around 1900, and in 1906 it had an enrollment of eighty-three. In the mid-1930s the community had a school, a store, and a number of scattered houses; the estimated population in 1940 was twenty. After World War II[qv] the Brumley school was consolidated with that of Union Hill, and by the mid-1960s all that remained of Brumley was a church and a few widely scattered houses. In 1990 the church was still there.

BIBLIOGRAPHY: Doyal T. Loyd, *History of Upshur County* (Waco: Texian Press, 1987). *Christopher Long*

BRUMMET, TEXAS. Brummet, also known as Brummet Settlement, was a frontier community on Siestadero Creek four miles northeast of Bigfoot in the extreme northeast corner of Frio County. Early accounts indicate that the settlement was located between the Old Fort Ewell Road and the Old Laredo Road. It is believed to be the first settlement in Frio County; the oldest legible gravestone in the Brummet Cemetery dates back to 1860. Brummet Settlement may have been the home of Joseph W. Gardner[qv] or members of his immediate family in the late 1850s. A school by the name of Centerville operated in the area in 1929. In 1989 the Brummet Cemetery was all that remained. *Ruben E. Ochoa*

BRUNDAGE, TEXAS. Brundage is on State Highway 85 six miles west of Big Wells in northeastern Dimmit County. S. P. Brundage platted the town in 1909, and the community grew quickly after it became a stop on the San Antonio, Uvalde and Gulf Railroad around 1910, the year it was granted a post office. The settlement shipped onions, strawberries, and other crops. By 1915 Brundage had over 100 residents, two general stores, and a telephone connection. The town also had a school at least as early as 1918.

Extended drought and low crop prices, however, drove many Dimmit County farmers off their land by that year. By 1925 the population of Brundage had dropped to fifty. In 1936 the community was still a railroad depot and had a post office, one business, and seven houses. In 1944 the post office closed, and by 1953 the school had been consolidated with the Big Wells district. By the mid-1980s the old school building had been converted to Coomb's Country Steakhouse, but nothing else remained of the town except a cemetery and a few dwellings.

BIBLIOGRAPHY: Paul S. Taylor, "Historical Note on Dimmit County, Texas," *Southwestern Historical Quarterly* 34 (October 1930). Laura Knowlton Tidwell, *Dimmit County Mesquite Roots* (Austin: Wind River, 1984). *John Leffler*

BRUNE CREEK. Brune Creek, named for pioneer settler George Brune, rises four miles northwest of Mentz in northeastern Colorado County (at 29°47′ N, 96°29′ W) and flows south for 5½ miles to its mouth, where it and Piney Creek enter Cummins Creek, two miles northeast of Columbus (at 29°44′ N, 96°30′ W). The stream flows primarily through a gently sloping area with loamy fine sand surfaces and gray sandy clay subsoil that support oak and cedar with a dense understory of yaupon and wild grape. The land is used primarily as unimproved range for cattle.

BRUNI, ANTONIO MATEO (1856–1931). Antonio M. Bruni, entrepreneur and rancher, the son of Mateo and Dominica (Bogales) Bruni, was born on September 19, 1856, in Bozzi, Emilia-Romagna, Italy. His parents died when he was a young boy. In 1872 he moved to San Antonio to live with his uncle Antonio Bruni. Five years later he moved to Laredo and opened a mercantile store with his brother Luigi. The two also had a store in Nuevo Laredo. His mercantile business took him into Webb and Zapata counties, where he acquired an interest in the sheep and cattle industries. In 1882 Bruni was appointed tax assessor of Webb County and in 1892 was elected a county commissioner. He was appointed county treasurer four years later and held this position until his death. Among other business activities, he was vice president of the First National Bank of Laredo, director of the Texas-Mexican Railway, and director of the Border Gas Company. He owned land in Webb and Zapata counties. He established a town on one of his ranches and named it Bruni. Bruni married Consolación Henry in 1879, and the couple had nine children. Consolación was a descendant of José de Urrutia.[qv] They were devout Catholics, prominent local philanthropists, and staunch supporters of the Democratic party.[qv] Bruni died on August 18, 1931. When he died, his ranch holdings came to over 200,000 acres. Bruni Park in Laredo is named for him.

BIBLIOGRAPHY: Ellis A. Davis and Edwin H. Grobe, comps., *The New Encyclopedia of Texas*, 4-vol. ed. *The Italian Texans* (San Antonio: University of Texas Institute of Texan Cultures, 1973). Laredo *Times*, August 18, 19, 1931. *A Twentieth Century History of Southwest Texas* (2 vols., Chicago: Lewis, 1907). *Valentine J. Belfiglio*

BRUNI, TEXAS. Bruni is on State Highway 359 fifty miles southeast of Laredo in Webb County. The site was probably occupied in 1860 by Mexican settlers. The town was named after Antonio Bruni,[qv] an Italian immigrant who arrived in the area around 1877 and owned a general store and a ranch. Bruni became a station on the Texas-Mexican Railway about 1881; a Bruni post office began service in 1900. The community had sixty residents, a general store, and four cattle-breeding businesses in 1914. A 1936 map showed three churches and a school in the town. By 1939 the discovery of the South Bruni oilfield had increased the population to 800 and the business community to thirty. The number of residents declined to 350 in 1943 and remained near that level until 1964, when it was 275. From 1972 through 1984 the population was 214. In 1990 Bruni had 698 residents and twelve businesses.

BIBLIOGRAPHY: J. B. Wilkinson, *Laredo and the Rio Grande Frontier* (Austin: Jenkins, 1975). *Paul M. Lucko*

BRUNNER, TEXAS. Brunner was on the Houston and Texas Central Railway three miles west of Houston in west central Harris County. It had a post office as early as 1888. In 1894 the population was 200. The post office was discontinued in 1905, and mail was delivered from Houston. In 1895 a Baptist college, a German school, and a public school were in operation in Brunner, and the town had two churches, a saloon, and a population of 500. As late as 1905 the population remained at 482, but by 1915, with the expansion of Houston, Brunner was no longer considered a separate community.

Diana J. Kleiner

BRUNSWICK, TEXAS. Brunswick, sixteen miles southeast of Rusk in southern Cherokee County, was established in 1903 by the Cherokee Orchard Company and the St. Louis Southwestern Railway, which developed a demonstration farm there for the scientific cultivation of orchard and garden plants. The farm was supervised by Edward Body, who named the new community after his native town in Canada. A Presbyterian church was built at Brunswick, but no school. Unfortunately, the location proved to be in a "frost pocket," where fruit buds were often nipped. In 1931 the St. Louis Southwestern abandoned the farm, the depot, and the packing plants. One store and a population of forty-five were reported in 1940. In the early 1990s Brunswick was a dispersed rural community with an estimated fifty residents.

BIBLIOGRAPHY: *Cherokee County History* (Jacksonville, Texas: Cherokee County Historical Commission, 1986). Hattie Joplin Roach, *A History of Cherokee County* (Dallas: Southwest, 1934).

E. W. Cole

BRUSH, ELKANAH (1796–?). Elkanah Brush, soldier and legislator of the Republic of Texas,[qv] was born in New York and moved to the Power and Hewetson colony[qv] at Refugio, Texas, in October 1834. He and his two sons, Gilbert Russell and Bradford, received headrights. On November 28, 1835, Brush was appointed by the General Council[qv] at San Felipe de Austin as a commissioner to organize the Refugio militia. He was a member of Ira J. Westover's[qv] party that joined George M. Collinsworth's[qv] command in the capture of Goliad in October 1835, and periodically between October 10, 1835, and January 16, 1836, he served under Capt. Philip Dimmitt[qv] in the Goliad garrison and on the Lipantitlán Expedition.[qv] On December 20, 1835, Brush signed the Goliad Declaration of Independence,[qv] and on July 1, 1836, he enlisted as a private in Capt. Louis P. Cooke's[qv] company of Col. Edwin Morehouse's[qv] First Regiment, First Brigade, Army of the Republic of Texas.[qv] He was mustered out on September 30. For his military service Brush received a bounty warrant for 1,280 acres, which he sold to Robert Peebles.[qv]

Brush was elected to the House of Representatives of the First Congress of the Republic of Texas and fought a closely contested election for the Second. He was the apparent victor and was present at Houston at its first session, on September 25, 1837. But on October 2 William E. Walker[qv] of Victoria claimed the seat. Brush protested on the following day, and a recount showed that Walker had won by two votes. Walker was disqualified on October 7, however, as he was neither a citizen nor a resident. A special election was then called, and James Power[qv] was chosen to fill the vacant seat. In January 1839 Brush, his wife, Sarah, and their four-year-old daughter were farming near Bray's Bayou between Houston and Richmond in Fort Bend County, and in July 1841 Brush's name was published in the Austin *Texas Sentinel*[qv] as a tax delinquent in Fort Bend County. He owed one dollar. He continued to reside in Fort Bend County, where he owned $2,216 worth of real estate, until at least 1850.

BIBLIOGRAPHY: John H. Jenkins, ed., *The Papers of the Texas Revolution, 1835–1836* (10 vols., Austin: Presidial Press, 1973). Texas House of Representatives, *Biographical Directory of the Texan Conventions and Congresses, 1832–1845* (Austin: Book Exchange, 1941).

Thomas W. Cutrer

BRUSH CREEK (Colorado County). Brush Creek rises on the south slope of Rocky Hill twelve miles northwest of Columbus in northwestern Colorado County (at 29°51′ N, 96°39′ W) and flows south for 7½ miles to its mouth on Crier Creek, just above the latter's confluence with the Colorado River (at 29°46′ N, 96°40′ W). It crosses level to sloping terrain surfaced by pale brown loamy sand over a silty clay subsoil. These soils are suited to agriculture and produce good pasture and hay crops. The surrounding scattered to dense stands of scrub oak mixed with cedar also provide excellent wildlife habitat.

—— (Motley County). Brush Creek rises two miles northwest of the site of old Tee Pee City in eastern Motley County (at 35°07′ N, 100°42′ W) and flows east for three miles before entering the Middle Pease River, four miles west of the Motley-Cottle county line (at 35°06′ N, 100°35′ W). The area was once included within the Matador Ranch[qv] lands. The surrounding gently rolling hills have some moderately steep slopes and are surfaced by shallow to moderately deep silt loams that support mesquite and grasses.

BRUSH PEN HOLLOW CREEK. Brush Pen Hollow Creek rises eleven miles north of Oakville in southwestern Live Oak County (at 28°37′ N, 98°06′ W) and runs southwest for nine miles to its mouth on the Atascosa River, six miles northwest of Three Rivers (at 28°33′ N, 98°13′ W). It runs through Brush Pen Hollow. The surrounding terrain is low-rolling to flat upstream and flat downstream and is surfaced by sandy and clay loam that supports scrub brush, cacti, and grasses in the creek's upper reaches and water-tolerant hardwoods and grasses in its lower.

BRUSH PRAIRIE, TEXAS. Brush Prairie, also known as Brushy Creek, is off Farm Road 1280 eleven miles northwest of Groveton in northwestern Trinity County. It was founded around 1900. In the early 1990s the Zion Hill Church and cemetery and a number of scattered houses still remained in the area.

BIBLIOGRAPHY: Patricia B. and Joseph W. Hensley, eds., *Trinity County Beginnings* (Groveton, Texas: Trinity County Book Committee, 1986). Trinity County Historical Commission, *Trinity County Cemeteries* (Burnet, Texas: Nortex, 1980). *Christopher Long*

BRUSHY CREEK (Baylor County). Brushy Creek rises eight miles east-northeast of Mabelle in Baylor County (at 33°42′ N, 98°59′ W) and flows north for seven miles before entering a diversion reservoir on the Wichita River (at 33°46′ N, 98°58′ W). It runs through flat land with local shallow depressions and a surface of sandy and clay loams that support hardwoods, conifers, and grasses.

—— (Baylor County). Brushy Creek rises four miles north of Seymour in northwest Baylor County (at 33°39′ N, 99°18′ W) and runs north for six miles before entering Lake Kemp on the Wichita River (at 33°43′ N, 99°17′ W). It traverses an area of steep to moderately sloping hills surfaced with shallow stony clay and sandy loams in which grow oak, mesquite, and grasses. At the creek's mouth the land is flat with shallow depressions, and hardwoods, conifers, and grasses predominate in the flora.

—— (Brazos County). Brushy Creek rises in fertile farmland a half mile north of Farm Road 60 and one mile west of College Station in Brazos County (at 30°36′ N, 96°23′ W) and flows south for five miles to its mouth on the Brazos River, the Brazos-Burleson county line (at 30°32′ N, 96°24′ W). The area is flat to rolling and marked with steep margins. The clayey and sandy loams support post oak, pecans, willow, mesquite, and grasses, and, in the lower reaches, hardwood and pine forest.

—— (Burleson County). Brushy Creek rises six miles southwest of Caldwell in southwestern Burleson County (at 30°26′ N, 96°44′ W) and runs east for seven miles to its mouth on Davidson Creek, in south central Burleson County (at 30°'27 N, 96°'39 W). It traverses gently sloping to nearly level terrain surfaced by loam that supports post oak, blackjack oak, elm, and hackberry trees along the banks. Settlement in the area began during the early 1830s. In 1872 James L. Dean established a general merchandise store near the headwaters of Brushy Creek on a branch of the Chisholm Trail.[qv] By the late 1870s Deanville had been founded in the vicinity.

BIBLIOGRAPHY: Burleson County Historical Society, *Astride the Old San Antonio Road: A History of Burleson County, Texas* (Dallas: Taylor, 1980).

____ (Callahan County). Brushy Creek rises just south of Farm Road 2228 and ten miles northwest of Cross Plains in southeast Callahan County (at 32°15′ N, 99°14′ W) and runs thirteen miles north to its mouth on Deep Creek, a mile north of Interstate Highway 20 and ten miles east of Baird (at 32°24′ N, 99°15′ W). Among its principal tributaries are two forks, East and West. The East Fork rises five miles east of Admiral (at 32°17′ N, 99°12′ W) and runs five miles northwest to its mouth on the main creek (at 32°20′ N, 99°13′ W); the West Fork rises two miles east of Admiral (at 32°18′ N, 99°16′ W) and runs five miles north to its mouth (at 32°21′ N, 99°15′ W). The main stream's upper reaches pass through variable slopes surfaced by shallow, stony clay loams that support juniper, oak, grasses, chaparral, and cacti; its lower reaches enter flood-prone flat terrain with local shallow depressions, surfaced by clay and sandy loams that support water-tolerant hardwoods, conifers, and grasses. Both forks run through rolling hills surfaced by clay and sandy loams in which grow scrub brush, mesquite, cacti, live oak, juniper, and grasses.

____ (Collin County). Brushy Creek, once known as Hell Creek, rises three miles northeast of Farmersville in east central Collin County (33°12′ N, 96°20′ W). It received its name from a group of surveyors who lost their way while searching for possible routes for a road from Dallas to the Red River. The stream flows southeast for 18½ miles, through a slightly rolling area surfaced with loamy and clayey soils that support mesquite, grasses, and cacti. Brushy Creek is intermittent in its upper reaches. In areas where development has occurred, native vegetation has been replaced by cultivated row or cover crops. Brushy Creek passes within a mile of Josephine and under the tracks of the Atchison, Topeka and Santa Fe Railway before emptying into the Caddo Fork of the Sabine River, four miles southwest of Silva in Hunt County (at 33°00′ N, 96°11′ W).

____ (Colorado County). Brushy Creek rises seven miles northeast of Columbus in northeastern Colorado County (at 29°50′ N, 96°29′ W) and flows southwest for eight miles to its mouth on Cummins Creek (at 29°46′ N, 96°33′ W). The area's thick topsoil of pale brown, loamy, fine sand overlies mottled clay and scattered beds of construction-grade gravel. Vegetation along Brushy Creek is a dense mixture of oak, cedar, and yaupon with scattered pines. Oil and gas wells dot the area, and pipelines cross unimproved pastures with abundant wildlife.

____ (Cooke County). Brushy Creek rises 2½ miles southeast of Dexter in extreme northeastern Cooke County (at 33°48′ N, 96°57′ W) and runs east for ten miles to its mouth on the Big Mineral Arm of Lake Texoma, 2½ miles southeast of Gordonville in northwestern Grayson County (at 33°47′ N, 96°50′ W). The stream is intermittent in all but its lower reaches. It traverses flat to low-rolling terrain surfaced by sandy and clay loams that support water-tolerant hardwoods, conifers, scrub brush, cacti, and grasses along the streambed.

____ (Delta County). Brushy Creek rises just northwest of Enloe in north Delta County (at 33°27′ N, 95°40′ W) and runs southeast for twelve miles to its mouth on the South Sulphur River, two miles east of State Highway 19 (at 33°21′ N, 95°33′ W). Post Oak Creek and Greenbriar Branch flow into Brushy Creek near its mouth. Brushy Creek traverses an area of rolling prairies surfaced by dark gray clay that supports mesquite and grass. County records for 1867 showed Brushy Creek School on the creek several miles south of the site of present Enloe, near Post Oak. Maps for 1964 identified Brushy Creek Cemetery on the southern banks just south of Post Oak.

BIBLIOGRAPHY: Paul Garland Hervey, A History of Education in Delta County, Texas (M.A. thesis, University of Texas, 1951).

____ (Dickens County). Brushy Creek rises seventeen miles northeast of Spur in east central Dickens County (at 33°34′ N, 100°36′ W) and runs east for ten miles to its mouth on Salt Creek, ten miles southwest of Guthrie in western King County (at 33°34′ N, 100°29′ W). It begins in a shallow canyon on mesquite-brush plains and descends over 300 feet through a gradually tapering canyon with loamy topsoil that supports dense undergrowth.

____ (Donley County). Brushy Creek rises twelve miles west of Clarendon in southwestern Donley County (at 45°50′ N, 100°52′ W) and flows south for eight miles to its mouth on Mulberry Creek, twenty miles west of Lakeview in northwestern Hall County (at 34°40′ N, 100°52′ W). The stream was once part of the JA Ranch[qv] horse pasture and is now on Bitter Creek Ranch property. A small reservoir is impounded upstream near State Highway 70 in southern Donley County. The creek flows through terrain with moderately steep slopes and locally high relief, surfaced with silt loams in which grow primarily mesquite and grasses.

____ (Ellis County). Brushy Creek rises near the tracks of the Missouri, Kansas and Texas Railroad a half mile northeast of Red Oak in far north central Ellis County (at 32°31′ N, 96°47′ W) and runs southeast for 11½ miles. It traverses flat to rolling prairie with occasional steep slopes. Soils vary from dark calcareous to expansive clays and clay loams. On the banks grow oak, juniper, and mesquite trees, as well as various grasses and cacti. Historically, this area has functioned largely as range and crop land. Brushy Creek is crossed by Interstate Highway 45 before emptying into Red Oak Creek in the central part of the county a mile northeast of Palmer (at 32°28′ N, 96°39′ W).

____ (Fannin County). Brushy Creek rises in central Fannin County (at 33°37′ N, 96°24′ W) 2½ miles southeast of Dodd City and runs southeast for 5½ miles to its mouth on the North Sulfur River, two miles east of Gober (at 33°41′ N, 96°21′ W). The surrounding flat to rolling prairie has locally steep slopes and is surfaced by shallow to deep clays and clay loams that support oak, juniper, mesquite, and various grasses.

____ (Fannin County). Brushy Creek rises just east of Valley Lake in northwestern Fannin County (at 33°27′ N, 96°21′ W) and flows north for 4½ miles before emptying into the Red River 1½ miles northeast of Valley Lake (at 33°28′ N, 96°16′ W). It traverses flat land surfaced by clay and sandy loams that support water-tolerant hardwoods, conifers, and grasses. For most of the county's history the Brushy Creek area has been used as crop and range land.

____ (Fayette County). Brushy Creek rises in partially wooded pastureland just south of U.S. Highway 90 and halfway between Engle and Praha in southwest Fayette County (29°41′ N, 97°03′ W) and flows east and then southeast for 6½ miles to its mouth on Mulberry Creek, two miles southwest of Schulenburg (at 29°40′ N, 96°57′ W). It is the only major tributary of Mulberry Creek. Brushy Creek, so named for the thick stands of yaupon and cedar that grow on its banks, crosses a surface of loamy clay topsoils that are fair for agriculture but highly erodible on slopes. The terrain is marked by gullies. Most of this land was formerly used for cotton production. After cotton farming ceased in the 1960s, the land reverted to pasture, and in some areas vegetation has returned to provide wildlife habitat.

____ (Franklin County). Brushy Creek rises just north of Winnsboro in southern Franklin County (at 32°58′ N, 95°17′ W) and at one time ran northeast for fifteen miles before disemboguing into Big Cypress Creek, which forms the border between Titus and Camp counties (at 33°02′ N, 95°07′ W). In the mid-1970s, however, when Fort Sherman Dam was built on Big Cypress Creek to form Lake Bob Sandlin, a large portion of the former streamcourse, which had made up part of the Franklin and Camp county line, was inundated. The stream is intermittent in its upper reaches. It crosses generally flat to rolling terrain surfaced by sandy and clay loam that supports conifers. Brushy Creek is joined by the South Fork of Brushy Creek, which rises six miles southeast of Winnsboro in northeastern Wood County (at 32°53′ N, 95°13′ W) and was probably formerly known as Dry Cypress Creek. The South Fork, intermittent in its upper reaches, runs northeast for 6½ miles, briefly forming part of the Wood-Franklin county line, to its mouth on Brushy Creek south of Lake Bob Sandlin (at 32°59′ N, 95°10′ W). The combined streams continue the line between Wood and Franklin counties.

____ (Guadalupe County). Brushy Creek rises four miles northwest of Kingsbury in northeastern Guadalupe County (at 29°42′ N, 97°52′ W) and flows east for five miles to its mouth on the San Marcos River, seven miles northeast of Kingsbury (at 29°43′ N, 97°45′ W). It crosses mostly flat terrain with local shallow depressions, surfaced by sandy and clay loams that support water-tolerant hardwoods, conifers, and grasses.

____ (Harrison County). Brushy Creek rises two miles south of Jackson in northwestern Harrison County (at 32°42′ N, 94°35′ W) and runs northeast for three miles through northwestern Harrison County and southwestern Marion County to its mouth on the Lake O' The Pines, near Jackson (at 32°45′ N, 94°33′ W). The creek was five miles long and emptied into Big Cypress Bayou until the 1950s, when Lake O' The Pines[qv] was impounded by Ferrell's Bridge Dam. The surrounding gently undulating to gently rolling terrain is surfaced by loam and clay. The banks of the stream are heavily wooded in places with pine and hardwood trees, and the land is used in timber cultivation and agriculture.

____ (Hays County). Brushy Creek rises two miles southeast of Buda in eastern Hays County (at 30°05′ N, 97°49′ W) and flows southeast for 14½ miles to its mouth on Plum Creek, five miles northwest of Lockhart in Caldwell County (at 29°'56 N, 97°'44 W). The stream is intermittent in its upper reaches and is dammed a mile above its mouth. It traverses a land surface of clays and shales that principally support grasses.

____ (Henderson County). Brushy Creek rises near Pharris Lake in southeastern Henderson County (at 32°04′ N, 95°41′ W) and runs southeast for 22½ miles, through northeastern Anderson County, to its mouth on the Neches River, by the Neches River oilfield (at 31°55′ N, 95°26′ W). The stream is intermittent in its upper reaches. Its main tributaries are Little Brushy, Indian, Hardshell, and Norwegian creeks. The banks of Brushy Creek are heavily wooded in places with oak, hickory, gum, and pine trees; the terrain is nearly level to moderately steep and surfaced by sandy and clayey soils. The area is used as forest land and for agriculture.

____ (Jackson County). Brushy Creek rises near the Jackson-Wharton-Colorado county line in extreme northern Jackson County (at 29°14′ N, 96°39′ W) and runs southeast for seventeen miles to its mouth on Sandy Creek, at the northern end of Lake Texana just west of Ganado near the Sandy Creek oilfield (at 29°04′ N, 96°34′ W). It crosses flat terrain with local shallow depressions surfaced by clay and sandy loam that supports water-tolerant hardwoods, conifers, and grasses.

____ (King County). Brushy Creek, once known as Hackberry Creek, rises six miles northeast of Haystack Mountain in southwestern King County (at 33°27′ N, 100°21′ W) and flows north for five miles to its mouth on North Croton Creek, a mile west of Interstate Highway 38 (33°32′ N, 100°19′ W). It crosses an area of moderately steep slopes with locally high relief, surfaced by silt loams that support mesquite and grasses.

____ (Lamar County). Brushy Creek rises just northeast of Byrdtown and two miles northeast of Pattonville in extreme eastern Lamar County (at 33°36′ N, 95°21′ W) and flows south for eighteen miles to its mouth on the North Sulphur River, the Delta county line, one mile west of Dawson Lake (at 33°23′ N, 95°17′ W). The creek traverses flat to rolling terrain surfaced by dark loam over gray clay in which grow grasses and water-tolerant hardwoods and conifers. Downstream, the land is a low-lying flood plain with a sand and gravel surface.

____ (Lavaca County). Brushy Creek rises three miles northeast of Hallettsville in north central Lavaca County (at 29°29′ N, 96°54′ W) and flows southeast for eleven miles to its mouth on the Navidad River, 2½ miles south of Sublime (at 29°'25 N, 96°'48 W). It crosses gently rolling terrain with a clay loam surface over a dense clay subsoil. Brushy Creek is prone to flood, but the runoff is rapid. Areas surrounding the stream are mixed open and forested and are used primarily as range and pasture land, with some production of corn and grain sorghum. Wildlife is abundant in the wooded areas, where a mixture of oak, sycamore, pecan, yaupon, and wild grape provide wildlife habitat.

____ (Lee County). Brushy Creek rises two miles northwest of Lexington in northern Lee County (at 30°26′ N, 97°02′ W) and runs northeast for ten miles to its mouth on East Yegua Creek, the Lee-Burleson county line, six miles southeast of Lexington (at 30°28′ N, 96°54′ W). Brushy Creek traverses generally flat terrain with local shallow depressions, surfaced by clay and sandy loam that supports water-tolerant hardwoods and grasses.

____ (Leon County). Brushy Creek, a spring-fed perennial stream, rises a mile west of Jewett in western Leon County (at 31°22′ N, 96°10′ W) and flows southwest for twenty-three miles to its mouth on the Navasota River, in southwestern Leon County (at 31°08′ N, 96°17′ W). It traverses gently sloping to nearly level terrain with sandy to loamy topsoil in which post oak, black hickory, pecan, elm, water oak, and hackberry trees grow along the banks. Settlement in the vicinity began in the nineteenth century. In 1871 the International Railway simultaneously laid out the towns of Jewett, on the east bank near the headwaters of the creek, and Marquez, on the west bank of the middle creek, as stations on its new line through western Leon County. Koch is located on the east bank of the upper creek, and Old Bowling lies on the west bank of the lower creek.

BIBLIOGRAPHY: Frances Jane Leathers, *Through the Years: A Historical Sketch of Leon County and the Town of Oakwood* (Oakwood, Texas, 1946).

____ (McLennan County). Brushy Creek rises four miles west of Mart in eastern McLennan County (at 31°32′ N, 96°54′ W) and flows south-southeast for twenty miles to its mouth on Big Creek, eight miles east of Marlin in Falls County (at 31°20′ N, 96°46′ W). The terrain is flat to rolling prairie with local shallow depressions and a surface of sandy and clay loams in which grow mesquite and grasses upstream and water-tolerant hardwoods and conifers downstream.

____ (Madison County). Brushy Creek rises two miles southeast of Normangee in northwestern Madison County (at 31°01′ N, 96°05′ W) and runs southeast for eight miles to its mouth on Caney Creek (at 30°59′ N, 95°58′ W). It crosses gently sloping to nearly level terrain surfaced by sandy loam that supports pecan, elm, water oak, hackberry, post oak, and black hickory trees on the banks. Settlement in the vicinity of the stream began during the mid-nineteenth century. Laceola is on the south bank of the lower creek.

____ (Montague County). Brushy Creek rises a mile north of Bowie in southwestern Montague County (at 33°35′ N, 97°50′ W) and runs southeast for twenty-two miles to its mouth on Sandy Creek, two miles west of Alvord in northern Wise County (at 33°21′ N, 97°43′ W). It crosses flat to rolling terrain with local escarpments and shallow depressions, surfaced by clay and sandy loams that support hardwoods, conifers, brush, and grasses.

____ (Rains County). Brushy Creek rises just west of Prospect Cemetery in central Rains County (at 32°54′ N, 95°48′ W) and flows southwest for eight miles to its mouth on Little Slough, two miles south of Dunbar Union Cemetery (at 32°47′ N, 95°49′ W). It traverses flat to rolling terrain surfaced by sandy and clay loams that support water-tolerant hardwoods, conifers, and grasses.

____ (Robertson County). Brushy Creek rises ten miles north of Wheelock in southeastern Robertson County (at 30°58′ N, 96°23′ W) and runs southeast for nine miles to its mouth on Cedar Creek, 1½ miles north of Wheelock (at 30°55′ N, 96°23′ W). It crosses nearly level to gently sloping terrain with sandy loam topsoil in which grow post oaks and grasses.

____ (San Augustine County). Brushy Creek rises seven miles southwest of San Augustine in western San Augustine County (at 31°30′ N, 94°13′ W) and runs southwest for seven miles to its mouth on Speer Creek, near Goodwin (at 31°25′ N, 94°16′ W). The stream is intermittent in its upper reaches. Its banks are heavily wooded for most of its length with pine and hardwood trees, and the nearly level to moderately steep terrain is surfaced by loam and clay. The land is used predominantly for agriculture and as forest.

____ (Shelby County). Brushy Creek rises five miles southeast of Joaquin in northeastern Shelby County (at 31°57′ N, 94°08′ W) and flows southeast for six miles to its mouth on Flat Fork Creek (at 31°53′ N, 94°06′ W). It crosses nearly level to moderately steep, heavily wooded terrain with sandy to clayey and loamy topsoils. Pines and various hardwoods predominate in the flora.

____ (Stephens County). Brushy Creek rises in extreme west central Stephens County (at 32°42′ N, 99°05′ W) and runs northeast for five miles to its mouth on Hubbard Creek Lake, three miles southwest of Breckenridge (at 32°45′ N, 99°01′ W). The surrounding terrain exhibits resistant ledges and low cuestas surfaced by shallow, stony soil that supports live oak, juniper, and grasses.

____ (Trinity County). Brushy Creek rises two miles northeast of Chita in south central Trinity County (at 30°58′ N, 95°10′ W) and runs southeast for eleven miles to its mouth on Livingston Reservoir, just south of the Polk county line (at 30°50′ N, 95°09′ W). Before the construction of the reservoir in the 1970s the stream joined the Trinity River near Onalaska. The stream is intermittent throughout most of its course. It crosses flat to rolling terrain surfaced by clay and sandy loam in which grow conifers, water-tolerant hardwoods, and grasses.

____ (Uvalde County). Brushy Creek rises six miles east of Garner State Park and three miles south of Farm Road 1050 in north central Uvalde County (at 29°34′ N, 99°38′ W) and runs eleven miles south to its mouth on the Frio River, four miles southeast of Concan (at 29°27′ N, 99°40′ W). It crosses flat terrain with locally deep and dense dissection, surfaced by gravelly loam and clay that support grasses, oak, juniper, and some mesquite; downstream, the land is flatter and pecans and other hardwoods grow.

____ (Waller County). Brushy Creek rises two miles south of West Magnolia Forest in northeastern Waller County (at 30°12′ N, 95°55′ W) and runs southeast for ten miles, through mostly wooded country, to its mouth on Spring Creek in southwestern Montgomery County (at 30°05′ N, 95°45′ W). The surrounding gently sloping to nearly level terrain is surfaced by sandy loam that supports elm, hackberry, loblolly pine, and shortleaf pine trees on the banks. On February 13, 1687, the French explorer René Robert Cavelier, Sieur de La Salle,[qv] crossed the lower creek heading north toward the Trinity River on one of his many forays into the Texas interior in search of the Mississippi River. Settlement in the vicinity began in the early 1830s when Abraham Roberts patented a league of land near the confluence of Brushy and Spring creeks and established a settlement.

BIBLIOGRAPHY: Robin Navarro Montgomery, *The History of Montgomery County* (Austin: Jenkins, 1975).

____ (Washington County). Brushy Creek rises three miles southeast of Burton in southwest Washington County (at 30°08′ N, 96°34′ W) and runs ten miles south to its mouth on the West Fork of Mill Creek in Austin County (at 30°03′ N, 96°34′ W). It crosses an area of low-rolling hills and prairies surfaced by clay and sandy loam that support grasses, mesquite, and chaparral.

____ (Williamson County). Brushy Creek rises three miles northwest of Leander in southwestern Williamson County (at 30°35′ N, 97°51′ W) and flows east for sixty-nine miles, through southern Williamson County and southwestern Milam County, to its mouth on the San Gabriel River, five miles north of Rockdale (at 30°43′ N, 97°03′ W). The stream is intermittent in its upper reaches. It was named Arroyo de las Ánimas Benditas (Creek of the Blessed Souls) by explorers Louis Juchereau de St. Denis and Domingo Ramón[qqv] in 1716 and was known by variations of that name throughout the Spanish colonial period. It was the site of several of the earliest communities in the county. The battle of Brushy Creek[qv] occurred near its banks in 1839. The banks of the stream are heavily wooded for much of its length with mesquite and hardwood trees, and the creek flows through nearly level to gently rolling terrain surfaced by clayey and loamy soils used predominantly for agriculture.

BIBLIOGRAPHY: Clara Stearns Scarbrough, *Land of Good Water: A Williamson County History* (Georgetown, Texas: Williamson County Sun Publishers, 1973).

____ (Young County). Brushy Creek rises near State Highway 114 a mile west of Loving in northeastern Young County (at 33°15′ N, 98°31′ W) and flows sixteen miles northeast, across the southeastern corner of Archer County, to its mouth on West Fork of the Trinity River, four miles southwest of Antelope in northwestern Jack County (at 33°25′ N, 98°24′ W). Though ranchland makes up some of the creek's drainage area, the stream flows near or through several oilfields, including the Prideaux and Garvey holdings. It crosses an area of rolling prairie where mesquite and grasses grow.

BRUSHY CREEK, BATTLE OF. The battle of Brushy Creek, between Texas Ranger and militia units and Comanche marauders, occurred in late February 1839 a few miles from the site of present Taylor in Williamson County. It was a running affair along Battleground (present Cottonwood) and Boggy creeks and culminated north of Brushy Creek. In January 1839 Chief Cuelgas de Castro,[qv] traveling with a friendly Lipan party, reported to the settlers on the Colorado River that a Comanche band, their enemies, had entered the settlements and were encamped on the San Gabriel River north of Austin. Col. John H. Moore[qv] called out two companies of thirty men each. Joined by the Lipans, they rode to the campsite and found that the Indians had moved upstream. A snowstorm delayed pursuit. Moore tracked the intruders west to the mouth of the San Saba River and skirmished with the Indians, who, under the pretense of surrendering, made off with all his men's horses. About February 18 the Comanches returned east and swept through Travis County into Bastrop County. At Webber Prairie, twelve miles above Bastrop, they killed Mrs. Elizabeth Coleman and her son Albert. They captured her five-year-old son Tommy and seven of Dr. James W. Robertson's slaves.

About February 24 Jacob Burleson, elected a captain of a group of twenty-five mounted men, began scouting the area. Capt. James Rogers, his brother-in-law, joined him with an additional twenty-seven men. A day later, at ten o'clock in the morning, they came upon a Comanche camp near Post Oak Island, some three miles north of Brushy Creek. As most of the Indians fled on foot, Burleson ordered an attack to prevent them from reaching a nearby thicket. Historian J. W. Wilbarger[qv] wrote that the Texans flinched, Burleson was killed, and the command fell back that evening to Brushy Creek. Edward and Aaron B. Burleson[qv] and all their brothers—Jacob, John, and Jonathan—were in the Brushy Creek fight. Jacob Burleson ordered his men, twelve in number, to dismount and charge. Winslow Turner and Samuel Highsmith[qv] did so, but the others, seeing they were outnumbered, took cover. Jacob Burleson was shot in the back of the head while trying to help a young friend untie his horse. Within hours of the debacle, Gen. Edward Burleson and ranger captain Jesse Billingsley[qv] reached Brushy Creek with thirty-two men. Burleson began an immediate pursuit of the Comanches and overtook them shortly after noon. They found the Indians in a strong defensive position. Although his men were outnumbered, Burleson ordered an attack that became a running fight along Battleground Creek. After dark the Comanches departed. They left a wounded black slave who said the Indians lost at least thirty dead and wounded. Besides Jacob Burleson, the Texans lost Edward Blakey and John Walters. Rev. James Gilleland[qv] died ten days later.

In 1925 the schoolchildren of Taylor raised money for a red granite marker to mark the battle site. It was dedicated on November 5, with Walter P. Webb[qv] as featured speaker. The marker is on private property 1.4 miles south of Taylor on the west side of Highway 95.

BIBLIOGRAPHY: John Holland Jenkins, *Recollections of Early Texas*, ed. John H. Jenkins III (Austin: University of Texas Press, 1958; rpt. 1973). Kenneth Kesselus, *History of Bastrop County, Texas, Before Statehood* (Austin: Jenkins, 1986). David Nevin, *The Old West: The Texans* (New York: Time-Life Books, 1975). Noah Smithwick, *The Evolution of a State, or Recollections of Old Texas Days* (Austin: Gammel, 1900; rpt., Austin: University of Texas Press, 1983). J. W. Wilbarger, *Indian Depredations in Texas* (Austin: Hutchings, 1889; rpt., Austin: State House, 1985). *Karen R. Thompson*

BRUSHY CREEK, TEXAS. Brushy Creek is at the intersection of Farm roads 315 and 837, on a tributary of Brushy Creek thirteen miles northeast of Palestine in northeastern Anderson County. The area was settled about 1840 and was originally considered part of the Frankston and Montalba settlements. A wagon train of settlers from South Carolina ended its journey at the site in 1873. A Brushy Creek post office opened that year, and the community and post office were probably named for the nearby creek, though an alternative version states that one of the early settlers, Charles Murphy, named the town for his old home in South Carolina. By 1884 the community had three churches, a district school, steam gin-gristmills, and an estimated 300 inhabitants and shipped grain and livestock. In 1890 the population was estimated at 100, a sawmill had been built, and two coal mines were operating just west of Brushy Creek. The community had a population of 131 in 1900, a Masonic lodge by 1901, and telephone service by 1914. The population was estimated at 100 from 1925 through 1948. The post office closed in 1925. In 1932 the district schools at Brushy Creek enrolled 102 white pupils and eighty-two black pupils. In the 1930s and 1940s the community had two churches, two district schools, two to four businesses, and a number of dwellings. The population dropped to thirty in the late 1940s and 1950s, but Brushy Creek revived in the early 1960s, possibly due to the development of several oilfields in the vicinity. The town had an estimated 200 inhabitants in 1964. The boom appears to have been temporary, however, and the population of Brushy Creek was estimated at seventy from 1970 through 1988. In 1982 the community had Pisgah Church, Brushy Creek Church, and a number of scattered dwellings. The churches were still standing in 1985. In 1990 the population was fifty.

BIBLIOGRAPHY: *Anderson County Herald*, June 21, 1901. Frankston Bicentennial Committees, *The Story of Frankston, Texas, and Neighboring Communities, 1900–1976* (Frankston: Jayroe Graphic Arts, 1976). Pauline Buck Hohes, *A Centennial History of Anderson County, Texas* (San Antonio: Naylor, 1936). Thomas Paul Jones, The Reorganization of the Public Schools of Anderson County, Texas (M.Ed. thesis, University of Texas, 1934). *Mark Odintz*

BRUSHY ELM CREEK. Brushy Elm Creek rises six miles northwest of Muenster in northwestern Cooke County (at 33°43′ N, 97°28′ W) and runs southeast for sixteen miles to its mouth on the Elm Fork of the Trinity River, two miles southeast of Myra (at 33°36′ N, 97°17′ W). It crosses rolling terrain surfaced by expansive clays and clay loams that support oak, juniper, and grasses.

BRUSHY KNOB (Hill County). Brushy Knob, near Derden in northwestern Hill County (at 32°11′ N, 97°20′ W), rises 775 feet above sea level and sixty-five feet above the surrounding landscape. Derden was originally named Brushy Knob. The knob was for years the highest elevation in the county and was a landmark and Indian lookout point and campground. The original Derden cemetery lies at the foot of Brushy Knob.

BIBLIOGRAPHY: Hill County Historical Commission, *A History of Hill County, Texas, 1853-1980* (Waco: Texian, 1980).

—— (Johnson County). Brushy Knob is two miles southwest of Joshua in north central Johnson County (at 32°27′ N, 97°26′ W). It rises to a height of 1,042 feet above mean sea level.

—— (Tom Green County). Brushy Knob, south of Farm Road 2084 five miles southeast of Christoval in southern Tom Green County (at 31°09′ N, 100°27′ W), rises to an elevation of 2,351 feet, or 60 to 180 feet above the surrounding terrain. Resistant ledges and low cuestas surround Brushy Knob, where shallow, stony soils support live oak, juniper, and grasses.

BRUSHY LAKE. Brushy Lake is a natural lake in a former channel of the Red River seven miles north of New Boston in northern Bowie County (at 33°34′ N, 94°26′ W).

BRUSHY PRAIRIE, TEXAS. Brushy Prairie, on Farm Road 1578 eighteen miles west of Corsicana in northwestern Navarro County, was established before 1900. Two schools were in operation there by the early 1900s—a school for whites with an enrollment of sixty-five and one for blacks with an enrollment of fifty-four. In the mid-1930s Brushy Prairie had a church, a gin, a blacksmith shop, a school, a cemetery, and several stores. After World War II[qv] many of the residents moved away, the school was consolidated with that of Frost, and most of the businesses closed. By the mid-1970s only a church, a cemetery, and scattered houses remained. In 1990 Brushy Prairie was a dispersed rural community.

BIBLIOGRAPHY: Annie Carpenter Love, *History of Navarro County* (Dallas: Southwestern, 1933). Alva Taylor, *History and Photographs of Corsicana and Navarro County* (Corsicana, Texas, 1959; rev. ed., *Navarro County History and Photographs*, Corsicana, 1962).

Christopher Long

BRUTON CREEK. Bruton (Brutons) Creek rises 1½ miles north of Bagwell in northwestern Red River County (at 33°41′ N, 95°10′ W) and flows southeast for nine miles to its mouth on McCoy Creek, five miles southwest of Clarksville in southwestern Red River County (at 33°34′ N, 95°07′ W). The soils along the creek are clayey and loamy, and the land is used to grow grain and sorghum or for pasture. The stream was probably named for Elisha Bruton, who had an original grant of land on its banks.

BRUTONS CREEK. Brutons Creek, locally also called Ellison's Creek, rises 3½ miles north of Daingerfield in central Morris County (at 33°05′ N, 94°42′ W) and flows south for eight miles to its mouth on Ellison Creek Reservoir, 2½ miles northwest of Lone Star (at 32°55′ N, 94°44′ W). The stream is intermittent in its upper reaches. The alluvial soils along the banks once made the area prized agricultural land, when settlement came in the late 1830s. The creek was named for David Bruton, an early land grantee. Today the area is one of the most densely populated areas in the county.

BRUTUS. The *Brutus*, a schooner of about 160 tons displacement, was purchased in New Orleans for the Texas Navy,[qv] and Capt. William A. Hurd,[qv] former commander of the *San Felipe*[qv] and the *William Robbins* (later renamed *Liberty*[qv]), was appointed as her captain. She carried a crew of forty men. In New Orleans she was fitted with a long eighteen-pound swivel gun and nine "short guns." After considerable overhauling to accommodate crew and armament and a great deal of legal difficulty concerning payment for repairs, the *Brutus* put to sea and arrived in Texas waters in early February 1836. The ship was said to sail poorly. After the battle of San Jacinto[qv] she was sent to New Orleans for supplies and refitting and then returned to Texas waters, only to be blockaded at Matagorda by the heavily armed Mexican brig *Vencedor del Álamo*. Rescued by the *Invincible*[qv] and the privately owned *Union* and *Ocean*,[qv] the *Brutus* sailed for New York for refitting in September and was there in October 1836. This voyage was apparently undertaken with neither the knowledge nor the permission of Charles E. Hawkins,[qv] the commander of the Texas Navy, for upon his return Hurd was immediately relieved of his command.

Under the command of J. D. Boylan, the *Brutus* convoyed the supply ship *Texas* from Galveston to Matagorda and returned by midnight, June 10, 1837. Within an hour she was back at sea. She sailed first to the mouth of the Mississippi River, where she hoped to intercept Mexican merchant vessels, and then to the Yucatán coast, where she arrived by way of Cuba on July 8. In consort with the *Invincible*, the *Brutus* cruised down to Cozumel, which its crew claimed for the Republic of Texas,[qv] and then, on July 16, turned back up the coast. The two Texas schooners made prizes of the *Union*, the *Telégrafo*, and the *Adventure* off Sisal and on July 26 engaged the batteries defending the city's harbor. Sailing north, the tiny flotilla captured the *Obispo* and the *Eliza Russel* off the Alacranes and then doubled back down the Yucatán coast and took the *Correo de Tabasco* on August 12. The *Brutus* had captured the *Rafaelita* off Veracruz by August 17 and then ran farther up the coast to blockade Matamoros. With their water supply dangerously low, however, the *Brutus* and *Invincible* made for their home port, Galveston; the *Brutus* crossed the bar on August 27. With the approach later that day of two Mexican brigs of war, the *Iturbide* and *Libertador*, the *Brutus* attempted to rejoin the *Invincible* in open water and to engage the enemy. She ran aground in shoal water, however, and the steamer *Branch T. Archer*'s attempt to render assistance resulted only in the unshipping of her rudder. Minutes later the *Invincible*, too, ran aground, where she was pounded to pieces by the surf. A few weeks later the *Brutus*, still held fast by the sands off the tip of Galveston Island, was battered to pieces by a storm. Thus was lost the last effective ship of the Texas Navy until the purchase of a second fleet in 1839.

BIBLIOGRAPHY: Alex Dienst, "The Navy of the Republic of Texas," *Quarterly of the Texas State Historical Association* 12–13 (January–October 1909; rpt., Fort Collins, Colorado: Old Army Press, 1987). C. L. Douglas, *Thunder on the Gulf: The Story of the Texas Navy* (Dallas: Turner, 1936; rpt., Fort Collins, Colorado: Old Army Press, 1973). Jim Dan Hill, *The Texas Navy* (New York: Barnes, 1962). Tom Henderson Wells, *Commodore Moore and the Texas Navy* (Austin: University of Texas Press, 1960). *Thomas W. Cutrer*

BRYAN, BEAUREGARD (1862–1918). Beauregard Bryan, lawyer, was born in Brazoria County, Texas, on January 16, 1862, the son of Moses Austin and Cora (Lewis) Bryan and the great-grandson of Moses Austin.[qv] He attended Baylor University and studied law at the University of Texas. In 1883 he moved to Wichita Falls, where he published the *Herald* for a year before returning to Washington County. He practiced law in Brenham from January 1885 until he moved to El Paso in 1902. Bryan married Lillian A. Lyles at Mobile, Alabama, on December 23, 1886, and they had three children. He was active in Democrat party[qv] politics. He was elected district attorney in Brenham and served in that position for eight years. Subsequently he was a district judge. Governor James Stephen Hogg[qv] appointed him a regent of the University of Texas, and he remained on the board for twelve years, under governors Sayers, Culberson, and Lanham. During the Hogg administration Bryan sat on the state executive committee. He participated in the organization of the Texas State Historical Association[qv] and held various offices in that organization. He was for four years a member of the El Paso school board and a member of the Knights of Pythias. He was an Episcopalian. Bryan died at El Paso on March 4, 1918. A collection of his papers is housed at the Barker Texas History Center,[qv] University of Texas at Austin.

BIBLIOGRAPHY: "Archives Collection," *Library Chronicle of the University of Texas*, Summer 1944. Frank W. Johnson, *A History of Texas and Texans* (5 vols., ed. E. C. Barker and E. W. Winkler [Chicago and New York: American Historical Society, 1914; rpt. 1916]). Vertical Files, Barker Texas History Center, University of Texas at Austin.

James L. Hailey

BRYAN, FRANCIS THEODORE (1823–1917). Francis Theodore Bryan, soldier and engineer, the son of John H. Bryan, was born at New Bern, North Carolina, on April 11, 1823. In 1842 he graduated with honors from the University of North Carolina and in July 1842 was appointed from that state to the United States Military Academy, where he graduated sixth in his class in 1846. As a lieutenant in the Topographical Engineers, he served during the Mexican War[qv] on the staff of Gen. Zachary Taylor,[qv] was wounded at Buena Vista, and was decorated and brevetted first lieutenant for gallant and meritorious conduct. In 1849 Bryan was sent to Texas to explore a northern route from San Antonio to El Paso via Fredericksburg, the San Saba River, and the Guadalupe Mountains. Upon reaching El Paso on July 29, 1849, he reported on the feasibility of the route and recommended sinking wells along the road. In the next few months he made numerous reconnaissance tours between San Antonio and Fort Belknap, Fort Belknap and Fort Graham, and San Antonio and Dona Ana and opened a wagon road between Austin and Fort Mason. He was promoted to first lieutenant in July 1851 and to captain in July 1860. With the outbreak of the Civil War[qv] he resigned his commission, on June 10, 1861, and started to return to North Carolina but was arrested so that he could not join the Confederate Army. After the war Bryan went into business in St. Louis. In 1891 he presented to the University of North Carolina a collection of rare books on engineering, architecture, and biblical and classical literature. He died in St. Louis on October 24, 1917.

BIBLIOGRAPHY: Kemp Plummer Battle, *History of the University of North Carolina* (2 vols., Raleigh: Edwards and Broughton, 1907–12; rpt., Spartanburg, South Carolina: Reprint Company, 1974). A. B. Bender, "Opening Routes Across West Texas, 1848–1850," *Southwestern Historical Quarterly* 37 (October 1933); continued as "The Texas Frontier, 1848–1861: Government Explorations in Texas, 1851–1860," ibid. 38 (October 1934). Francis B. Heitman, *Historical Register and Dictionary of the United States Army* (2 vols., Washington: GPO, 1903; rpt., Urbana: University of Illinois Press, 1965). Raleigh *News and Observer*, October 26, 1917. Vertical Files, Barker Texas History Center, University of Texas at Austin. *William S. Powell*

BRYAN, GUY MORRISON (1821–1901). Guy Morrison Bryan, legislator, Confederate officer, and judge, son of James and Emily Austin Bryan, was born at Herculaneum, Jefferson County, Missouri, on January 12, 1821. His mother was the sister of Stephen F. Austin.[qv] James Bryan died in 1822, and Emily married James F. Perry[qv] in 1824 (*see* PERRY, EMILY MARGARET AUSTIN). In 1831 the family moved to Texas and lived at San Felipe and at Pleasant Bayou until December 1832, when they located at Peach Point Plantation[qv] in Brazoria County. Bryan was boarding with Josiah H. Bell[qv] to attend a school taught by Thomas J. Pilgrim[qv] in March 1836, when he was selected as a courier to carry the William B. Travis[qv] letter written at the Alamo from Bell's Landing to Brazoria and Velasco. Bryan accompanied his mother on the Runaway Scrape[qv] and after her return home visited the battlefield at San Jacinto and enlisted in the Texas army as orderly for Alexander Somervell.[qv] Bryan attended school at Chocolate Bayou in 1836 and 1837 and in May 1837 entered Kenyon College, where he graduated in 1842. He returned to Texas and studied law in the Brazoria law office of William H. Jack[qv] until failing eyesight ended his law studies. Soon after the outbreak of the Mexican War,[qv] Bryan enlisted in a Brazoria volunteer company and was in service under John C. (Jack) Hays[qv] east of the Rio Grande until he had to return home with his brother, Stephen S. Perry, who had become ill. In 1847 Bryan was elected to the Texas legislature. He served six years in the House (1847–53) and four years in the Senate (1853–57). On October 20, 1858, he married Laura H. Jack, daughter of William H. Jack. She accompanied him to Washington, D.C., where he represented the Western District of Texas in the Thirty-fifth Congress, 1857–59. His testimony before the House probably caused the collapse of the impeachment case against John C. Watrous.[qv] Bryan moved to Galveston in 1860 and operated ranches in Galveston and Brazoria counties. He was a delegate to the Democratic National Convention at Charleston, South Carolina, in 1860, and as chairman and spokesman for the delegation led in the split from the convention.

A leader in the movement for secession,[qv] Bryan associated himself with Oran M. Roberts. George M. Flournoy, John F. Marshall, and Williamson S. Oldham qqv in calling for the election of delegates to the Secession Convention.qv During the Civil War,qv early in 1862, Jefferson Davis qv sent Bryan to visit the governors of the Trans-Mississippi Department to reconcile the clash between civil and military authorities. When Bryan requested active field duty in May 1863, General Edmund Kirby Smith qv made him confidential adjutant general. Later Bryan helped organize the Texas Cotton Bureau. He was offered a place on Davis's staff and was later appointed by Pendleton Murrah qv as Texas representative at the headquarters of the Trans-Mississippi Department. After the war, Bryan lived at Galveston except for a time spent in Hot Springs, Arkansas. He was elected to the Texas House of Representatives in 1873, 1879, and 1887, serving as speaker of the Fourteenth Legislature in 1874. In May 1873 he was a charter member of the Texas Veterans Association qv and from 1892 until his death served as its president. He was also a charter member and vice president of the Texas State Historical Association.qv He moved to Austin in 1898 and died there on June 4, 1901. He was buried in the State Cemetery.qv

BIBLIOGRAPHY: John Adriance Papers, Barker Texas History Center, University of Texas at Austin. Guy Morrison Bryan Papers, Barker Texas History Center, University of Texas at Austin. Moses Austin Bryan Papers, Barker Texas History Center, University of Texas at Austin. George P. Garrison, "Guy Morrison Bryan," *Quarterly of the Texas State Historical Association* 5 (October 1901). James Franklin and Stephen Samuel Perry Papers, Barker Texas History Center, University of Texas at Austin. Fannie B. Sholars, Life and Services of Guy M. Bryan (M.A. thesis, University of Texas, 1930). Vertical Files, Barker Texas History Center, University of Texas at Austin. E. W. Winkler, ed., "The Bryan-Hayes Correspondence," *Southwestern Historical Quarterly* 25 (October 1921–April 1922).

BRYAN, JOHN NEELY (1810–1877). John Neely Bryan, Indian trader, farmer, lawyer, and founder of Dallas, son of James and Elizabeth (Neely) Bryan, was born on December 24, 1810, in Fayetteville, Tennessee. He attended Fayetteville Military Academy and after reading law was admitted to the Tennessee bar. Around 1833 he moved to Arkansas, where he became an Indian trader. According to some sources, he and a partner laid out the town of Van Buren, Arkansas. Bryan made his first trip to the future site of Dallas, Texas, in 1839. He returned to Van Buren temporarily to settle his affairs, and in November 1841 he was back in Texas. He settled on the east bank of the Trinity River, not far from the present location of downtown Dallas. In the spring of 1842 he persuaded several families who had settled at Bird's Fort to join him. On February 26, 1843, Bryan married Margaret Beeman, a daughter of one of these families. The couple had five children. Bryan served as postmaster in the Republic of Texas qv and operated a ferry across the Trinity where Commerce Street crosses the river today. In 1844 he persuaded J. P. Dumas to survey and plat the site of Dallas and possibly helped him with the work. Bryan was instrumental in the organizing of Dallas County in 1846 and in the choosing of Dallas as its county seat in August 1850. When Dallas became the county seat, Bryan donated the land for the courthouse.

He joined the California gold rush in 1849 but returned to Dallas within a year. In January 1853 he was a delegate to the state Democratic convention. In 1855, after shooting a man who had insulted his wife, Bryan fled to the Creek Nation. The man recovered, but although Bryan was surely informed of that fact within months of his flight, he did not return to his family in Dallas for about six years. He traveled to Colorado and California, apparently looking for gold, and returned to Dallas in 1860 or early 1861. He joined Col. Nicholas H. Darnell's qv Eighteenth Texas Cavalry regiment in the winter of 1861 and served with that unit until late 1862, when he was discharged because of his age and poor health. When he returned to Dallas in 1862, he became active once more in community affairs. In 1863 he was a trustee for Dallas Male and Female Academy. In 1866 he was prominent in efforts to aid victims of the flood that occurred that year. He also chaired a citizens' meeting that pressed for the completion of the Houston and Texas Central Railway and presided at a rally seeking full political rights for all ex-Confederates. In 1871–72 he was one of the directors of the Dallas Bridge Company, the company that built the first iron bridge across the Trinity. He was also on the platform at the welcoming ceremonies for the Houston and Texas Central train when it pulled into town in mid-July 1872.

John Neely Bryan and his wife, Margaret Beeman Bryan. From the collections of the Dallas Historical Society.

By 1874 Bryan's mind was clearly impaired. He was admitted to the State Lunatic Asylum (later the Austin State Hospital qv) in February 1877, and he died there on September 8 of that year. He was a Presbyterian.

BIBLIOGRAPHY: John William Rogers, *The Lusty Texans of Dallas* (New York: Dutton, 1951; enlarged ed. 1960; expanded ed., Dallas: Cokesbury Book Store, 1965). Lucy C. Trent, *John Neely Bryan* (Dallas: Tardy, 1936).
Cecil Harper, Jr.

BRYAN, LEWIS RANDOLPH, SR. (1858–1938). Lewis Randolph Bryan, lawyer, son of Cora (Lewis) and Moses Austin Bryan,qv was born in Brazoria County, Texas, on October 2, 1858. He graduated from Baylor University in 1877, took a law degree in 1880, was admitted to the bar on April 9 of that year, and established his practice in Angleton. After the Galveston hurricane of 1900 qv he moved to Houston. He became president of the state bar association on July 3,

1902, and was president of the Houston Bar Association in 1911. He married Martha J. Shepard on October 15, 1891; they had three children. Austin College conferred an honorary doctorate on Bryan in 1925. He died on February 11, 1938.

BIBLIOGRAPHY: Houston *Post*, February 12, 1938. *Who Was Who in America*, Vol. 2.

BRYAN, LEWIS RANDOLPH, JR. (1892–1959). Lewis Randolph Bryan, Jr., was born in Quintana, Texas, on August 17, 1892, the son of Martha Jane (Shepard) and Lewis Randolph Bryan.[qv] After the Galveston hurricane of 1900,[qv] his family moved from Velasco to Houston, where he attended public school. Thereafter, he attended Virginia Military Institute and received a law degree from the University of Texas in 1913. He practiced law in Houston until the United States entered World War I, at which time he was commissioned a captain in the army and assigned to the Thirty-sixth Division.[qv] While serving in France he gained promotion to major. In the postwar years Bryan was a lieutenant colonel in the Texas National Guard[qv] and was made brevet colonel upon retirement in 1939.

In 1919 he returned to Houston and joined the Lumberman's National Bank (renamed Second National Bank in 1923) as assistant cashier. He rose to the presidency of the bank in 1944. He became vice chairman of the board in January 1956 when the bank took the name Bank of the Southwest. Bryan was an Episcopalian and active in the religious and cultural affairs of Houston. As a great-grandson of Emily Austin Bryan Perry, sister of Stephen F. Austin,[qqv] he acquired and nurtured an interest in Texas history. He was president of the San Jacinto Museum of History Association (see SAN JACINTO MONUMENT AND MUSEUM) and the Philosophical Society of Texas[qv] in 1958. He was also a trustee of the Texas Gulf Coast Historical Association,[qv] which, beginning in 1961, has offered an annual prize in his honor for historical writing. Bryan was a member of the Sons of the Republic of Texas[qv] and was made a Knight of San Jacinto in 1956.

He was married in San Antonio on November 1, 1924, to Katharine McGown, and they had two sons. At the time of his death on January 30, 1959, Bryan was also a director of the Fort Worth and Denver Railway Company and the Federal Reserve Bank of Dallas,[qv] Houston Branch.

BIBLIOGRAPHY: Vertical Files, Barker Texas History Center, University of Texas at Austin. *James A. Tinsley*

BRYAN, MOSES AUSTIN (1817–1895). Moses Austin Bryan, soldier, son of James and Emily (Austin) Bryan (*see* PERRY, EMILY AUSTIN BRYAN), was born in Herculaneum, Missouri, on September 25, 1817. After the death of James Bryan, Emily Bryan, sister of Stephen F. Austin,[qv] married James F. Perry,[qv] and the family moved to Texas in 1831. Bryan was employed for a time in the store of W. W. Hunter and Stephen F. Austin and then went to Saltillo, Mexico, as Austin's secretary. In 1835 Bryan clerked in the land office. He again became Austin's secretary when Austin became commander of the Texas army in the fall of 1835. After Austin retired from the army, Bryan joined as a private. He served in the battle of San Jacinto[qv] as third sergeant in Moseley Baker's[qv] company, as aide-de-camp on the staff of Thomas J. Rusk,[qv] and as interpreter for the conference between Sam Houston and Antonio López de Santa Anna.[qqv] In 1839 Mirabeau B. Lamar[qv] appointed Bryan secretary of the legation to the United States under Anson Jones.[qv] Bryan was a member of the Somervell expedition[qv] in 1842. During the Civil War[qv] he was a major in the Third Texas Regiment. He helped organize the Texas Veterans Association[qv] in 1873 and served as its secretary until 1886. Bryan married Adaline Lamothe of Rapides Parish, Louisiana, in 1840; she died in 1854. In 1856 he married Cora Lewis, daughter of Ira Randolph Lewis;[qv] they had four sons and a daughter. Bryan died in Brenham on March 16, 1895, and was buried at Independence.

BIBLIOGRAPHY: Beauregard Bryan Papers, Barker Texas History Center, University of Texas at Austin. Sam Houston Dixon and Louis Wiltz Kemp, *The Heroes of San Jacinto* (Houston: Anson Jones, 1932). Homer S. Thrall, *A Pictorial History of Texas* (St. Louis: Thompson, 1879). Vertical Files, Barker Texas History Center, University of Texas at Austin.

BRYAN, OLLIE LOUISE (1871–1932). Ollie Louise Bryan, the first African-American woman to become a practicing dentist in the South, was born in Tennessee on December 28, 1871, the daughter of Anderson and Anna Louise (Smith) Bryant. As a young woman she entered Meharry Medical College in Nashville, Tennessee, where she graduated in 1902, the first woman to do so. By 1906 she had married Dr. F. A. Bryan and moved to Dallas, Texas, where she began practicing as a dentist no later than 1909. She was an active participant in women's social clubs in Dallas, such as the Priscilla Art Club. She was also one of the seventeen women who organized the Royal Art and Charity Club. In 1916 she retired from dentistry and remained a housewife. After being widowed by her husband, she died on November 23, 1932, in Dallas, where she was buried at Woodland Cemetery.

BIBLIOGRAPHY: James Summerville, *Educating Black Doctors: A History of Meharry Medical College* (University, Alabama: University of Alabama Press, 1983). Vertical Files, Barker Texas History Center, University of Texas at Austin. *Sergey Gordeev*

BRYAN, WILLIAM (?–?). William Bryan, Texas diplomat, was influential in the formation of the Republic of Texas[qv] as one of a group of United States citizens who secretly supported the Texas cause and provided Texas with financial assistance, supplies, and services such as transporting and outfitting volunteers and chartering and fitting out vessels for the Texas Navy.[qv] Documentation regarding his birth, marriage, and death has not been discovered.

The initial days of the provisional government[qv] were filled with many difficulties. One major problem was that the country lacked resources to conduct a protracted and vigorous war against Mexico. Texas was forced to seek outside assistance from its only supporter, the United States. To fill this need, Bryan and his mercantile firm appeared in Texas history for the first time. Bryan provided the Texas government with numerous reports and several financial records, which document his activity. On January 14, 1836, he was appointed general agent for Texas in New Orleans. After a few months of providing goods and services to Texas, mostly on credit, he began to worry that Texas and his business would not be able to meet their financial commitments because no cash was coming from the government or Texas commissioners. Unfortunately for him, the Texas government never provided the necessary funds to pay outstanding bills, so Bryan was compelled to borrow cash or use his own capital to delay bill collectors and attempt to maintain good credit. By July 1836 the Texas government owed Bryan's firm $77,468, which was later repaid to him in slow-moving land scrip.

Bryan also orchestrated a clandestine operation that provided Texas with valuable intelligence about Mexico. In New Orleans publications he conducted propaganda campaigns to maintain favorable public opinion about Texas. He provided legal assistance to Texas and its military personnel. His ability to assess and react to critical situations is evident in his handling of the *Pocket* and *Brutus*[qqv] affairs. By his actions, Bryan avoided a possible international confrontation between Texas and the United States. He also made Texas aware of its international duties to other nations upon the seas.

Bryan's reward, however, was not a just one. The administration of David Burnet[qv] replaced his agency with Toby and Brother,[qv] leaving him with an enormous personal debt and damaged credit. During Mirabeau B. Lamar's[qv] presidency, the republic realized its mistake and appointed Bryan consul to New Orleans. He then provided valuable assistance to the second Texas Navy. He remained consul to New Orleans until annexation,[qv] then suddenly disappeared from history.

BIBLIOGRAPHY: Alma Howell Brown, "The Consular Service of the Republic of Texas," *Southwestern Historical Quarterly* 33 (January, April 1930). Robert W. Kesting, William Bryan and the Navy from Abroad (M.A. thesis, St. Mary's University, 1985).

Robert W. Kesting

BRYAN, WILLIAM JOEL (1815–1903). William Joel Bryan, son of James and Emily (Austin) Bryan (*see* PERRY, EMILY AUSTIN BRYAN), was born at Hazel Run in Ste. Genevieve County, Missouri, on December 14, 1815. He attended school at Potosi until 1830. In 1831 he moved to Texas with his mother and stepfather, James F. Perry.[qv] He lived in the eastern part of Brazoria County before moving in 1832 to Peach Point Plantation,[qv] where Bryan was instructed by a governess at home while his father looked after the plantation, cattle, and property of Stephen F. Austin.[qv]

Bryan served in the Texas Revolution[qv] in 1835 with the Brazoria County Volunteers and was with his uncle, Stephen F. Austin,[qv] during the siege of Bexar.[qv] He was with Sam Houston[qv] in the retreat of the army across Texas, but was ill with measles at the time of the battle of San Jacinto.[qv] He served as an overseer at Peach Point between 1836 and 1839, for which he received $800. In April 1840 he married Lavinia Perry, his cousin by marriage, and settled at Durazno (Spanish for "peach") Plantation, an extension of Peach Point Plantation given to the couple on the occasion of their marriage. There the couple's seven children, four of whom later joined the Confederate Army, were born. The death of Bryan's daughter Eliza at the age of five or six occasioned the opening of Gulf Prairie Cemetery. Durazno Plantation raised cotton, cattle, and, by the 1850s, sugar, but made only a single sugar crop between 1852 and 1858. By 1860 Bryan had real property valued at $176,000, personal property valued at $62,320, and thirty-eight slaves. During the Civil War[qv] he fed Confederate troops stationed at the mouth of the Brazos at his own expense. In 1865 he granted the Houston and Texas Central a right-of-way through his land in Brazos County, and a projected townsite, later called Bryan, was named in his honor. Bryan gave the town financial assistance and helped to establish its bank. He dreamed of the development of a deepwater port at the mouth of the Brazos and was involved with George L. Hammeken[qv] in promoting the Brazos and Galveston Railroad from Galveston Bay to the Brazos River and in developing municipal real estate at Austinia, near the site of present Texas City. Emily M. Perry deeded fifty-five of the 122 blocks of the town to Bryan and Hammeken on January 16, 1839, and the remainder on February 1. Bryan was a member of the Texas Veterans Association[qv] and a Presbyterian after 1894. He died on March 3, 1903, and was buried in Gulf Prairie Cemetery at Peach Point.

BIBLIOGRAPHY: Nanetta Key Burkholder, *The 1860 Census of Brazoria County* (Brazosport, Texas: Brazosport Genealogical Society, 1978). Abigail Curlee, "History of a Texas Slave Plantation," *Southwestern Historical Quarterly* 26 (October 1922). C. W. Raines, *Year Book for Texas* (2 vols., Austin: Gammel-Statesman, 1902, 1903). *Southwestern Historical Quarterly*, Texas Collection, July 1953.

Lillian Childress

BRYAN, TEXAS. Bryan, the county seat of Brazos County, is located in west central Brazos County and is crossed by State highways 6 and 21, U.S. Highway 190, Farm roads 158, 1179, 1687, and 1688, and the Missouri Pacific and Southern Pacific railroads. Along with College Station, the home of Texas A&M University, which adjoins Bryan to the south, the city is the urban center of Brazos County. The area around the future site of Bryan was settled by members of Stephen F. Austin's[qv] colony in the 1820s and 1830s. In 1859, when the Houston and Texas Central Railroad graded a railroad bed through the area, a nephew of Austin, William Joel Bryan,[qv] donated land for a townsite to the railroad company. The townsite was named in his honor and was platted that same year. Construction of the railroad was halted at Millican, eighteen miles southeast of Bryan, during the Civil War,[qv] but a community of some 300 inhabitants grew up at the townsite. A post office was opened in Bryan in 1866, and that same year the county voted for Bryan to replace Boonville as the county seat. The railroad reached the community in 1867. That year also saw the arrival of telegraph service and the first general store. Many residents of Millican and Boonville moved to the new county seat in the 1860s, and the first courthouse was built in 1871. Though the city voted to incorporate in 1867, it was not formally incorporated until 1872, when it adopted an aldermanic government.

The Bryan *News-Letter* became the first newspaper in the community in 1868, followed in 1869 by the *Brazos Eagle*, the weekly *Brazos Pilot* in 1877, and the Bryan *Weekly Eagle* in 1889. The *Eagle* became a daily in 1913. A number of other newspapers have been published in the community over the years. The Bryan Independent School District was established in 1877, though the first school was not ready until 1880. The first black public school was also opened in 1880. Several colleges and seminaries flourished for a time in the city in the late nineteenth century, including the Bryan Male and Female Seminary, the Texas Odd Fellows University and Orphanage, Bryan Academy, and Allen Academy.[qv] Texas A&M College, which was eventually of great importance to Bryan, was opened in neighboring College Station in 1876. By 1884 Bryan had an estimated 3,000 inhabitants, who supported Baptist, Methodist, Presbyterian, Christian, and Episcopal churches, two schools, two banks, an opera house with a seating capacity of 500, a cotton gin, an Odd Fellows hall, two planing mills, and two wagon and buggy factories. In 1889 the city obtained electric lighting and a waterworks, and in 1900, when Bryan had a population of 3,589, a second railroad, the International–Great Northern, was built through the community. A Carnegie Library was founded in 1902. The Villa Maria Ursuline Academy was moved to Bryan in 1901, and two Baptist educational institutions, Texas Women's College in 1902 and Bryan Baptist Academy[qv] in 1909, followed soon after.

In 1910, when Bryan's population reached 4,132, the city built an interurban railroad to College Station, which operated until it was replaced by bus service in the 1920s. In the early decades of the twentieth century the community was a major cotton-shipping point for the region. In 1917 Bryan adopted the commission form of city government.[qv] The city continued to grow, reaching 6,307 inhabitants in 1920, 7,814 in 1930, and 11,842 in 1940. In the 1930s the North Oakwood subdivision, lying between Bryan and College Station, voted to incorporate with Bryan and established the boundary between the adjoining communities. Though some local businesses were hard hit by the Great Depression,[qv] the community received some economic stimulation when State Highway 6 was completed through Bryan and College Station in 1936. Bryan Army Air Field, built during World War II[qv] as an aviation-training center, brought further growth to the community. By 1950 the population of Bryan was 18,072. In the 1950s and 1960s shopping centers began to attract business away from the central business district. Stimulated in part by the dramatic growth of Texas A&M since the 1960s, Bryan's population increased rapidly, from 27,542 in 1960 to 33,141 in 1970, 44,337 in 1980, and 55,002 in 1990. Many Bryan businesses moved to the south to take advantage of College Station's growth. In partnership with College Station, Bryan developed various university-related businesses. Local industries include defense electronics, high-tech manufacturing, and agribusiness. Among the local attractions are the Brazos Valley Museum of Natural Science, the Messina Hof Winery, and many turn-of-the-century homes, a number of which are on the National Register of Historical Places or are registered Texas historical landmarks. *See also* CARNEGIE LIBRARIES, ELECTRIC INTERURBAN RAILWAYS.

BIBLIOGRAPHY: Glenna Fourman Brundidge, *Brazos County History: Rich Past—Bright Future* (Bryan, Texas: Family History Foundation, 1986). *Mark Odintz*

BRYAN AIR FORCE BASE. Bryan Air Force Base, six miles west of Bryan in Brazos County, was originally Bryan Army Air Field. The base was activated in 1943 as an instructors' school assigned the task of developing a standardized system of instrument flying. The Full Panel Attitude System developed at the base was one of the most significant contributions the base made to pilot training. The instrument-training school at Bryan AAF was the only one of its kind in the United States Army Air Forces. The base became Bryan Air Force Base upon separation of the air force from the army in 1947. It was deactivated in May 1961. The land and buildings were deeded to the Agricultural and Mechanical College of Texas (now Texas A&M University) in 1962.

BIBLIOGRAPHY: Robert E. Hays, Jr., "Air Force Pilot and Instructor Training in Texas, 1940–45," *Texas Military History* 4 (Summer 1964). *Art Leatherwood*

BRYAN BAPTIST ACADEMY. Bryan Baptist Academy, originally called Texas Woman's College, was proposed by Dr. George B. Butler, pastor, and T. R. Batte, layman, and sponsored by the First Baptist Church of Bryan. A charter for the college was filed in the Texas secretary of state's office on July 13, 1905, naming Butler, Rev. E. Ammons, and Rev. Matthew T. Andrews[qv] as incorporators. The college, on the corner of East 26th Street and Washington Avenue, opened in September 1905 in a two-story, brick structure that served as an administration building and girls' dormitory. The school was to furnish a Christian education for women and girls in music, art, and languages. A. W. Buchanan served as president of the board of directors. Butler took care of administration for the first two or three years, and R. J. H. Simmons, a layman, assumed Butler's duties and became president of the school in 1907 or 1908.

By 1909 the name of the college had been changed to Bryan Baptist Academy for Girls. At that time the institution had five faculty members and a student body of about sixty-five. The school applied on December 6, 1909, for membership in the association of Baptist schools under the Education Board of the Baptist General Convention of Texas and was accepted. The following year boys were admitted to the school. At that time the citizens of Bryan raised $5,600 to pay off one of the academy's notes, and again in the summer of the same year they raised money for a boys' dormitory that housed about thirty students. Professor Richard McDonald was president of the school during this addition. Enrollment was 118 in 1911. A new charter was filed with the secretary of state on February 2, 1912. In 1914 M. E. Weaver, pastor of the First Baptist Church of Bryan, was elected president of the academy. The school had two buildings, 154 pupils, and six teachers in 1915, but enrollment fell to sixty-seven in 1917. More efficient transportation to the nearby Agricultural and Mechanical College of Texas (now Texas A&M University) brought an end to Bryan Baptist Academy in 1918, and the property was sold to Eugene Edge.

BIBLIOGRAPHY: *Annual of the Baptist General Convention of Texas* (1886–). Milton R. Maloney, comp., *History: First Baptist Church, Bryan, Texas* (1941?). *A Better Day is Dawning: History of the First One Hundred Years of the First Baptist Church of Bryan, Texas* (Austin: Von Boeckmann–Jones, 1966). Lois Alyne Wilcox, The Early History of Bryan (M.A. thesis, University of Texas, 1952). *Samuel B. Hesler*

BRYAN BEACH STATE RECREATION AREA. Bryan Beach State Recreation Area is off County Road 723 just outside Freeport in Brazoria County. The 878-acre park was acquired by purchase from private owners in 1973 and named for James Perry Bryan, who built a home there in 1881 and operated a store at nearby Peach Point. Covered with dunes, some up to ten feet in height, the undeveloped park is home to a wide variety of coastal vegetation, including various grasses, shrubs, and forbs. Native animals include ground squirrels, gophers, grasshopper mice, rice rats, cotton rats, rabbits, and opossums. Shorebirds are common, and waterfowl and other migratory birds can be observed.

BIBLIOGRAPHY: Ray Miller, *Texas Parks* (Houston: Cordovan, 1984). *Christopher Long*

BRYAN AND CENTRAL TEXAS INTERURBAN RAILWAY. The Bryan and Central Texas Interurban Railway Company was chartered on April 11, 1913. By 1915 the company, with the encouragement of the Houston and Texas Central, had completed eleven miles between Bryan and Bryan Junction and slightly over twelve miles from Interurban Junction to Whittaker. The B&CTI entered receivership in January 1915. Available records indicate that the B&CTI did not operate its railroad as the company contracted with the Houston and Texas Central to provide freight service and with Mr. S. S. Hunter to handle the passenger business. The line was out of service during 1922 and was abandoned the following year.

Nancy Beck Young

BRYAN AND COLLEGE INTERURBAN RAILWAY. The Bryan and College Interurban Railway Company was chartered on March 21, 1910. In 1911 the road built five miles of track between Bryan and College Station, and in 1916 an additional 1½ miles was constructed between Bryan and Villa Maria. Although primarily a passenger carrier, the line also handled express. The company did not exercise its authority to carry freight. Competition from private automobiles led to the abandonment of the interurban in 1923.

Nancy Beck Young

BRYAN MOUND. During the first decade of the twentieth century a young mining engineer by the name of Bernard Baruch discovered a sulfurous mound some twenty feet above the flat shoreline on the Gulf of Mexico in Brazoria County (at 28°55′ N, 95°23′ W). He tried unsuccessfully to encourage J. P. Morgan to go into partnership to develop the sulfur mine, but Morgan thought the venture too much of a gamble. Later other investors became interested and began a mining process, using the Frasch method for the first time in Texas. In 1912 the first sulfur was mined, and thus began the development of Freeport, Texas, which took its name from that of the Freeport Sulphur Company. Later, oil and gas were also found in the dome. The original operation closed in 1935 after having produced five million tons of sulfur.

In the late 1970s the United States Strategic Petroleum Reserve began to examine the possibilities of oil storage in large vaults left underground by the removal of the sulfur. The reserve they started in Bryan Mound and the Hackberry dome in Lake Charles, Louisiana, are the two main reserves for the nation. In April 1989 another 839,000 barrels of crude oil was added to the Bryan Mound Complex, bringing the total to 219.2 million barrels of oil for reserve. The plant is located off County Road 242, 2½ miles south of Freeport.

BIBLIOGRAPHY: Brazosport *Facts*, November 4, 1962. James A. Creighton, *A Narrative History of Brazoria County* (Angleton, Texas: Brazoria County Historical Commission, 1975). U.S. Department of Energy, *Strategic Petroleum Reserve: Phase III Development* (New Orleans: Strategic Petroleum Reserve Project Management Office, 1981). *W. G. McAlexander*

BRYANS MILL, TEXAS. Bryans Mill is at the junction of Farm roads 994 and 1766, seventeen miles northwest of Linden in northwestern Cass County. In 1873 W. C. Bryan and W. T. Stewart constructed a sawmill at the site. In 1879 the two men applied for a post office, asking that it be designated as Bryan-Stewart Mill. Postal officials in Washington, however, named the office Bryan's Mill and appointed W. T. Stewart the first postmaster. The site became a gathering place and supply point for area farmers. By 1884 the town had a gin, grist and saw mills, two churches, a school, and an estimated population of 250. Toward the end of the nineteenth century the population began to decline and by 1900 had fallen to 109. The post office was closed in the 1950s, and in 1990 the town had a population of 71 with no rated businesses.

BIBLIOGRAPHY: Atlanta (Texas) *Citizens Journal*, 60th Anniversary Ed., 1939.

Cecil Harper, Jr.

BRYANT, BENJAMIN FRANKLIN (1800–1857). Benjamin Franklin Bryant, early settler and participant in the battle of San Jacinto,[qv] was born in Georgia on March 15, 1800. He moved to Texas in 1834 and, with his family, settled on Palo Gaucho Bayou in Sabine County. In March 1836 he recruited and was elected captain of a company of volunteers that joined the main Texas army at Bernardo on March 29, 1836. After participating in the battle of San Jacinto,[qv] Bryant built a fort called Bryant Station on Little River, where he spent his life protecting the frontier from the Indians. In 1845 he built a home near the fort; in it he and his second wife, Roxana (Price), lived the remainder of their lives. Bryant died on March 4, 1857. His body was reinterred in the State Cemetery[qv] at Austin in 1931.

BIBLIOGRAPHY: Charles Adams Gulick, Jr., Harriet Smither, et al., eds., *The Papers of Mirabeau Buonaparte Lamar* (6 vols., Austin: Texas State Library, 1920–27; rpt., Austin: Pemberton Press, 1968).

L. W. Kemp

BRYANT, CHARLES GRANDISON (1803–1850). Charles Bryant, architect and military adventurer, was born in 1803 in Belfast, Maine, the only son of Charles and Elizabeth Hatch (Lowden) Bryant, Jr. Bryant's family moved several times in his youth, but eventually settled in 1806 in Belfast, where his father worked as a shipwright. After his father's death around 1812, Bryant learned the trade of house builder, probably from a local craftsman or during a stay in Boston. By 1825 he had established himself as a builder in Bangor, Maine, where he adopted the middle name Grandison (from Samuel Richardson's novel *Sir Charles Grandison*). In October 1827 Bryant married Sarah Getchell; the couple had seven children.

By 1830 Bryant had a flourishing building practice and had begun to call himself an architect, evidently the first man in Maine to do so. During the 1830s he designed and built a wide variety of structures in Bangor, many of them in the reigning Greek Revival style, and in 1834 he produced a development plan for the city. He also joined the local militia and rose quickly through the ranks. Buoyed by his success, he began speculating in real estate but lost heavily in the panic of 1837. By September of that year he had abandoned his architectural practice and, with two Bangor militia officers, Col. Richard Bartlett and Maj. Joshua Norwood, opened a military school for "instruction in the different branches of the *Science of War*." The school soon developed into a center for recruiting and training volunteers for the Canadian Rebellion of 1837. Bryant, who supported the Canadian separatists, was arrested in July 1838 for breaking the newly passed neutrality law, but he jumped bail to help prepare for a scheduled invasion of Canada in November of that year. When the invasion began, however, Bryant, who had begun to call himself the "Grand Eagle," held his small force back. After the invasion failed, he returned to Bangor in disgrace.

Deeply in debt and hounded by creditors, he closed his military school and went to Texas with his oldest son, Andrew Jackson Bryant. They arrived in Galveston in the fall of 1839, and by 1840 Bryant had been hired by the San Luis Development Company as an architect and builder. He constructed a Greek Revival house for Charles K. Rhodes (1840) in San Luis, but after the company failed in the summer of 1841 he returned to Galveston. During this time he joined the Galveston Fusiliers and spread the story that during the invasion of Canada he had been captured and sentenced to death but had managed to escape. He served in the Fusiliers during the invasion of Rafael Vásquez[qv] (March 1842), then returned to Galveston in the fall of 1842. Unemployed and destitute, he worked at chopping cedar for a time at Hall's Bayou. In 1847 Bryant once again returned to the practice of architecture. He designed St. Mary's Cathedral, Galveston[qv] (1847–48, listed in the National Register of Historic Places 1973), and the Galveston County Prison and Court Room (1847–48, razed). The two buildings, both executed in the Gothic Revival style, were among the first large, architect-designed structures in postcolonial Texas.

By 1849 Bryant, now a major in the Texas Rangers,[qv] was mustering officer and commissary for three companies called to respond to Indian depredations on the western frontier. On January 12, 1850, after crossing Chocolate Bayou ten miles from Nuestra Señora del Refugio Mission, the rangers encountered a raiding party of Lipan Apaches. In the skirmish that followed, Bryant was killed. In recognition of his service, the Texas legislature awarded his heirs 640 acres of land in Montague County.

BIBLIOGRAPHY: John Henry Brown, *Indian Wars and Pioneers of Texas* (Austin: Daniell, 1880; reprod., Easley, South Carolina: Southern Historical Press, 1978). Charles G. Bryant Papers, Barker Texas History Center, University of Texas at Austin. James Mundy and Earle Shettleworth, Jr., *The Flight of the Grand Eagle: Charles G. Bryant, Maine Architect and Adventurer* (Augusta: Maine Historic Preservation Commission, 1977).

Christopher Long

BRYANT, CHARLES W. (ca. 1830–?). Charles W. Bryant, who represented Harris County at the state Constitutional Convention of 1868–69,[qv] was born a slave in Kentucky around 1830. He arrived in Texas after the Civil War[qv] and served as a Freedmen's Bureau[qv] agent and a minister before winning election to the convention. Though he was a Radical Republican who supported Governor Edmund J. Davis[qv] in most instances, Bryant nevertheless opposed the *ab initio* proposal (*see* AB INITIO QUESTION), which would have invalidated all legislative enactments that occurred after the state's secession[qv] from the Union. Bryant also favored the division of Texas into two or more states and supported constitutional provisions designed to prevent voter intimidation and fraud. He introduced resolutions that would have repealed railroad land grants and charters and prohibited convicted murderers from holding office in the state. He also secured a constitutional provision that legitimated black children born to slave parents. During the convention a mother accused Bryant of raping her eleven-year-old daughter. Although most Radicals supported Bryant's denial, contending that moderate Republicans led by Andrew Jackson Hamilton[qv] fabricated the charges, the convention voted by a margin of three to expel Bryant. He was jailed briefly, but the child's mother later dropped the charges against him.

BIBLIOGRAPHY: J. Mason Brewer, *Negro Legislators of Texas and Their Descendants* (Dallas: Mathis, 1935; 2d ed., Austin: Jenkins, 1970). Harrel Budd, The Negro in Politics in Texas, 1867–1898 (M.A. thesis, University of Texas, 1925). Merline Pitre, *Through Many Dangers, Toils and Snares: The Black Leadership of Texas, 1868–1900* (Austin: Eakin, 1985). James Smallwood, *Time of Hope, Time of Despair: Black Texans during Reconstruction* (London: Kennikat, 1981). Ernest Wallace, *The Howling of the Coyotes: Reconstruction Efforts to Divide Texas* (College Station: Texas A&M University Press, 1979).

Paul M. Lucko

BRYANT, DAVID E. (1849–1910). David E. Bryant, attorney and judge, the son of Anthony Bryant, was born in LaRue County, Kentucky, on October 19, 1849. His family moved to the area of Whitewright, Texas, in 1851, and Bryant received his primary and secondary education in local schools. He attended Trinity College (now Duke University) at Durham, North Carolina, and graduated with honors in 1871. He subsequently studied law at a firm in McKinney, Texas, which included among its partners former governor J. W. Throckmorton and future Texas chief justice T. J. Brown.[qqv] Bryant was admitted to the state bar in 1873 and entered a partnership with Brown, when the latter moved to Sherman. Bryant later established the firm of Bryant and Dillard, with Frank Clifford Dillard.[qv] From 1873 until 1890 he served on the board of directors of the Merchants and Planters Bank of Sherman. He married a Miss Thompson in 1879, and he and his wife raised four children. In 1890 President Benjamin Harrison appointed Bryant district judge of the United States court for the eastern district of Texas. He remained on the federal bench until his death in a St. Louis, Missouri, hospital on February 5, 1910.

BIBLIOGRAPHY: Dallas *Morning News*, February 6, 1910. *Who Was Who in America*, Vol. 1.
Brian Hart

BRYANT, IRA BABINGTON, JR. (1904–1989). Ira B. (I. B.) Bryant, Jr., black teacher, historian, author, and lecturer, son of Ellen (Starks) and Ira B. Bryant, Sr., was born in Crockett, Texas, on October 18, 1904. In 1905 the family moved to Caldwell, where Ira, Sr., became principal of Caldwell Colored High School and Ellen taught. The family moved to Houston in 1920 and I. B., Jr., entered Colored High School. There the principal, James D. Ryan,[qv] insisted that he give himself a name for his middle initial. Bryant chose the name Babington, after Thomas Babington McCaulay, whom he had been studying in English literature. After his mother died and his father remarried and moved to Alabama, Bryant and his two brothers were left in Houston to complete their education. He graduated from high school in January 1924 and worked on a ship to provide money for college as well as an opportunity to travel. During the fall of 1924 he entered Fisk University in Tennessee, where he graduated with a B.A. in 1928. He then completed an M.A. from the University of Kansas in 1934 and an Ed.D. from the University of Southern California in 1948. He attended postdoctoral summer workshops at Harvard, Rutgers, Michigan, Washington, and Stanford.

In 1929 Bryant became a social science teacher at Phillis Wheatley High School in Houston. He began advocating the inclusion of the study of black history in the curriculum of Texas public schools. His efforts to preserve "authentic records" of black history began as early as 1935, when he published *The Development of the Houston Negro Schools*. This book is now rare and in demand by historians researching Houston's black history. In 1936, during the Texas Centennial,[qv] he wrote a "Study Guide of Negro History" to be used in the Houston public schools. He published two paperback books: *The Texas Negro Under Six Flags* (1936) and the *Negro Church in Houston, Its Past, Present and Future* (1935). Bryant taught the techniques and provided opportunities for his students to become involved in research projects. One project in particular was a survey by his eleventh-grade civics class at Phillis Wheatley on conditions of Negro housing in the community. The results were printed and bound by the school in 1936. In 1938 Bryant became principal of Booker T. Washington High School (formerly Colored High School), where he remained until 1957. Then he was reassigned as principal at the new Kashmere Gardens High School until 1968, when he resigned. During his principalship he focused on educational leadership and increased new teaching skills among his teachers.

Bryant took an early retirement from the Houston Independent School District in 1968 and taught at Dillard University in New Orleans, Louisiana, as a professor of education for two years. He also served as a director of educational workshops there and served as a part-time instructor at Bishop, Prairie View, and Houston College for Negroes, the forerunner of Texas Southern University. In 1948 he was dean of students and professor of education at Texas State University for Negroes. He was also professor of education and director of workshops of Texas Southern University summer sessions from 1949 through 1955. He served for forty years as a part-time instructor at colleges.

Through his articles for workshops, educational journals, and newspapers, Bryant focused on the inadequacy of educational provisions and health problems in the black community. He also wrote on secondary principals, supervision, instruction, team teaching, Fisk alumni, and sit-ins. His writing skills, his professionalism as a teacher, his expertise in academic research, his continuous efforts to preserve the black heritage, and his courage to raise his voice against social injustices put Bryant in demand as a lecturer and public speaker. In 1963, when he was one of four speakers at a conference on the "Present Employment Picture" held at Rice University, his opinions on the weaknesses of the vocational program for black students in the Houston public school caused criticism.

Bryant resigned from his professorship at Dillard University in 1970 and returned to Houston. He again taught at Texas Southern University as a part-time instructor, then decided to finalize his retirement and devoted his time to writing three books: *Texas Southern University, Its Antecedents, Political Origin and Future* (1975); *Barbara Charline Jordan—From the Ghetto to the Capitol* (1977), the best biography of Barbara Jordan written during that time; and *Andrew Young—Mr. Ambassador* (1979), a documented narrative.

He served on the Houston board of directors for the NAACP during the *Smith v. Allwright* case (1942–44), in which the decision granted blacks the right to vote in primary elections. Bryant was a board member of the Citizens Chamber of Commerce and a trustee of Good Hope Baptist Church. In 1957 he was named Houston chairman of the United Negro College Fund. He was a president of the Southern Association of Colleges and Secondary Schools and of the Fisk University General Alumni Association. In 1966 he became a trustee at Fisk University. As a life member of the National Education Association, he represented the organization at a World Conference on Education in Alsilomar, California, March 5–14, 1970. Two years later he was selected as a delegate to attend the World Council of Organizations of the Teaching Profession in London, England. During his retirement years he was active in the Harris County Retired Teachers Association and was appointed to the Legislative Committee of the Texas State Retired Teachers.

Bryant received numerous awards for service to education, religion, and the community. He was inducted into the Alpha Epsilon Chapter of Phi Delta Kappa at the University of Southern California as the first black member in June 1946 and served as the first black jury foreman in the 208th District of Harris County in January 1974. For fifty-seven years Bryant was married to Thelma Scott Bryant, the niece of Emmett J. Scott. They had no children. Bryant's health began to decline rapidly around 1984, and he died at home on December 16, 1989. A Texas Southern University Scholarship Fund, the Bryant-Johnson Fund, was established by B. A. Turner in 1990.

BIBLIOGRAPHY: Ira B. Bryant Collection, Houston Metropolitan Research Center, Houston Public Library. *Who's Who in the South and Southwest*, Vol. 8.
Willie Lee Gay

BRYANT STATION, TEXAS. Bryant Station was on the Little River twelve miles west of the site of present Cameron in northwestern Milam County. It was established by Benjamin F. Bryant[qv] in 1840 as a fort to protect settlers from Indians. The village that grew up around the fort thrived because of its location on the Marlin-to-Austin stage line and gradually became a commercial center for the region. The post office at Bryant Station was established and discontinued several times between 1848 and 1876; it was known as the Blackland post office from 1874 to 1876. When the Gulf, Colorado and Santa Fe Railway was built through the area in 1881, it missed the community by three miles. Bryant Station faded, and Buckholts became the new social and commercial center. A historical marker was erected at the Bryant Station site in 1936. By the 1940s two cemeteries and a few scattered houses were all that marked the community on county highway maps. The Bryant Station school was consolidated with the Buckholts district in 1941.

BIBLIOGRAPHY: Lelia M. Batte, *History of Milam County, Texas* (San Antonio: Naylor, 1956). Milam County Heritage Preservation Society, *Matchless Milam: History of Milam County* (Dallas: Taylor, 1984).

Vivian Elizabeth Smyrl

BRYARLY, TEXAS. Bryarly, in northeastern Red River County, was named for R. T. Bryarly, who settled in the area before 1840. The settlement was a landing point for steamboats on the Red River as early as 1854. It was called Mound City until Joseph L. Bryarly became postmaster in 1892. Its population was fifteen in 1910 and twenty-two in 1920. In 1940 the community had two stores, two churches, a post office, and a population of fifty. By 1956 the post office had been closed. In 1986 Bryarly reported a population of thirty-two and no businesses. In 1991 the population was recorded as five.

Claudia Hazlewood

BRYCE, TEXAS. Bryce is three miles north of Caledonia and nine miles east of Mount Enterprise in southeastern Rusk County. It was established as a lumbering community in the 1880s and originally named Eulalie. The first postmaster was Henry H. Moreland, appointed in 1893. By 1896 the community had an estimated population of 150, two churches, a physician, at least three businesses, and possibly a school. However, the post office was permanently discontinued in 1907, and the mail rerouted to Timpson. By 1910 the population had fallen to seventy-five; throughout the 1930s it was recorded as forty. By 1984 the community was known as Bryce.

BIBLIOGRAPHY: Dorman H. Winfrey, *A History of Rusk County* (Waco: Texian, 1961).

Megan Biesele

BRYCE BUILDING. The Bryce Building, at 909 Throckmorton Street in Fort Worth, a small five-sided brick office building, was built in 1910 by William J. Bryce. The two-story, 2,500-square-foot structure employs an adaptation of Classical Revival style. It conforms to the shape of its site, wedged in the shadow of adjacent taller structures. Three of the five façades have decorative embellishments, while the north and east sides face other buildings and have little ornamentation. The exterior brick, undoubtedly furnished by Bryce's Denton Press Brick Company, is hard fired with iron ore. An incised panel of cast stone, with the inscription "Bryce Building" in Roman style letters is positioned below the copper cornice and cast-stone coping. The second-story bay above the entry is composed of multipaned panels that serve as doors to the small balcony, which rests on stone consoles. The building's southeast corner is truncated at the first story to enable vehicles to make the narrow turn. Offices of the Bryce Building Company and its subsidiaries occupied the first floor; the second floor was leased out.

William Bryce served the city as builder, civic leader, and mayor from 1927 to 1935. His work as contractor for Camp Bowie, Tarrant County (1917), a major World War I[qv] training facility, earned him an army commendation. He and Marshall R. Sanguinet[qv] were builder and architect for many prominent commercial buildings and residences, including Bryce's office and his home, Fairview (1893).

In 1982 a fire severely damaged the interior of the Bryce Building. The structure was abandoned for several months and was eventually "saved from the wrecking ball" and painstakingly restored to its original use as an office building by Joe and Betty Ambrose. An interior stairway and elevator were added to enable a single tenant to occupy the building. The Bryce Building was listed on the National Register of Historic Places in 1984 and is a Recorded Texas Historical Landmark.

BIBLIOGRAPHY: Janan Cull-Acree, "Hidden Treasure: The Bryce Building," *Dallas–Fort Worth Home and Garden*, March 1985. Fort Worth *Star-Telegram*, September 19, 1983. Oliver Knight, *Fort Worth, Outpost on the Trinity* (Norman: University of Oklahoma Press, 1953). Buckley B. Paddock, *History of Texas: Fort Worth and the Texas Northwest Edition* (4 vols., Chicago: Lewis, 1922). James Wright Steely, comp., *A Catalog of Texas Properties in the National Register of Historic Places* (Austin: Texas Historical Commission, 1984).

Betty B. Ambrose

BRYSON, JAMES GORDON (1884–1968). James Gordon Bryson, physician and author, the son of Joseph Goodson and Elizabeth (Anderson) Bryson, was born on October 6, 1884, in Liberty Hill, Williamson County, Texas. He graduated from the University of Texas medical school in Galveston in 1910 and married Lily Clara Shuddemagen at Christmas of that year; they had six children. Bryson established his medical practice in Pearsall and soon moved to Bastrop; he received training in surgery in Austin in 1918 but after a brief stay in Marlin returned to Bastrop. During his thirty-seven-year career he became one of the best-known general practitioners in Central Texas. He was a member of the Texas Medical Association.[qv] He retired in 1947 and spent much of his time working his Bastrop County farm. He also served as mayor of Bastrop from 1946 to 1950, as well as school board president for several terms between 1923 and his youngest child's graduation from public schools. Bryson returned to the University of Texas at the age of seventy-two to study history. Two books resulted: *Reminiscences of a Country Doctor,* first published in 1963 and reissued in 1965 under the title *One Hundred Dollars and a Horse;* and *Shin Oak Ridge* (1965). Bryson was a Mason, a Democrat, and a Methodist. He died in Bastrop on August 2, 1968, and was buried at Liberty Hill Cemetery.

BIBLIOGRAPHY: Austin *American*, August 3, 1968. Vertical Files, Barker Texas History Center, University of Texas at Austin.

BRYSON, TEXAS. Bryson, on U.S. Highway 380 fourteen miles southwest of Jacksboro in southwestern Jack County, was known until the early 1880s as Mount Hecla, then renamed in honor of Henry Bryson, who built the first residence, a log house, in 1878 and later became a county commissioner. Postal service to Mount Hecla began in 1878; the name of the post office was changed to Bryson in 1884. The tracks of the Chicago, Rock Island and Texas Railway reached the community in 1903, and Bryson had its own bank by 1907. For the first fifty years of its history Bryson was mainly a business and school community of area cattlemen. Though oil was discovered in the county in 1898, not until the mid-1920s did Bryson become the processing center for local oil producers. Oil increased the town's population until Bryson became the second largest town in the county. By 1931 it was incorporated, and in 1947 it had an estimated 806 residents, the largest number in the town's history. As oil production declined, so did the population, which by the late 1970s was 450. In the early 1980s population growth resumed, and by 1988 Bryson had an estimated 690 residents served by seven businesses. In 1990 the population was 520.

BIBLIOGRAPHY: Thomas F. Horton, *History of Jack County* (Jacksboro, Texas: Gazette Print, 193-?). Ida Lasater Huckabay, *Ninety-Four Years in Jack County* (Austin: Steck, 1949; centennial ed., Waco: Texian Press, 1974).

David Minor

BRYSON HILL. Bryson Hill, five miles east of Brady in eastern McCulloch County (at 31°08′ N, 99°35′ W), has an elevation of 1,731 feet above mean sea level, thirty to fifty feet higher than the surrounding countryside. It was probably named for H. N. Bryson, an early landowner in the area.

BUCARELI. Bucareli was a Spanish settlement on the Trinity River, probably near the Robbins Ferry crossing of the river in Madison County, north of Midway. Dissatisfied Spanish colonists ordered from their East Texas homes as a result of the report of the Marqués de Rubí qv lived for a brief time in San Antonio until they could persuade Viceroy Antonio María de Bucareli y Ursúa qv to permit them to return to East Texas. Permission was granted for a settlement at the site where the Old San Antonio Road crossed the Trinity. The settlement, named Nuestra Señora del Pilar de Bucareli, was founded in September 1774, and soon had a a plaza, a church, a guardhouse, twenty houses of hewn wood, and numerous huts. It was to be exempt from civil taxation and church tithes for ten years. For a time the community prospered, reportedly because of illicit trade with the French,qv but an epidemic in 1777 was followed by Comanche raids in 1778. Led by Antonio Gil Ibarvo,qv the settlers, without official permission, deserted Bucareli and moved back to East Texas, where, before April 1779, they established what is now Nacogdoches. *See also* SPANISH TEXAS.

BIBLIOGRAPHY: Herbert Eugene Bolton, *Texas in the Middle Eighteenth Century: Studies in Spanish Colonial History and Administration* (Berkeley: University of California Press, 1915; rpt., Austin: University of Texas Press, 1970). Carlos E. Castañeda, *Our Catholic Heritage in Texas* (7 vols., Austin: Von Boeckmann–Jones, 1936–1958; rpt., New York: Arno, 1976).

BUCARELI Y URSÚA, ANTONIO MARÍA DE (1717–1779). Antonio María de Bucareli y Ursúa, forty-sixth viceroy of New Spain, was born in Seville on January 24, 1717, the son of Luis Bucareli, Marqués de Vallehermoso, and Ana Ursúa Laso de la Vega, Condesa de Gerena. There is no record or indication of his having married. At age fifteen, he answered a military calling by enlisting as a cadet in the brigade of Royal Carabineers. His military service included campaigns in Italy and Portugal, and he rose to the rank of lieutenant general while serving as inspector of coastal fortifications in Granada.

In 1766 Bucareli entered colonial administration as governor and captain general of Cuba, and his excellent record there earned him appointment as viceroy of New Spain in 1771. His relatively long (eight-year) tenure as chief executive, during which he established himself as one of the colony's better viceroys, coincided with significant changes on the northern frontier. The New Regulations for Presidios, flowing from the Marqués de Rubí'sqv inspection, were first printed in Mexico in 1771 and issued in Spain the next year. In 1773 Spanish settlers were compelled to leave East Texas and the capital of Texas was transferred to San Antonio—although the viceroy permitted the Adaesaños (occupants of Los Adaes qv) to return the following year. The entire northern frontier was reorganized into the Provincias Internas qv in 1776. And Nacogdoches was permanently settled in 1779, after the failure of Bucareli,qv a settlement named in part for the viceroy.

In his final years as viceroy, Bucareli was often at loggerheads with Teodoro de Croix,qv commandant general of the Provincias Internas. The two men differed over the placement of presidios along a line from the Gulf of California to Matagorda Bay; they disagreed over the requisite number of troops and attendant expenses required for frontier defenses; and they lacked accord on the most appropriate response to massive Indian attacks on frontier settlers and their possessions.

Controversy surrounded Antonio María de Bucareli to the time of his death. He was under investigation for his handling of sensitive ecclesiastical matters in Puebla when he died in Mexico City on April 9, 1779. However, in recognition of his distinguished service to the crown, Charles III waived posthumous *residencia* (judicial review) proceedings against the deceased viceroy—a rare concession made to colonial administrators and their estates.

BIBLIOGRAPHY: Bernard E. Bobb, *The Viceregency of Antonio María Bucareli in New Spain, 1771–1779* (Austin: University of Texas Press, 1962). Alfred Barnaby Thomas, trans., *Teodoro de Croix and the Northern Frontier of New Spain, 1776–1783* (Norman: University of Oklahoma Press, 1941).

Donald E. Chipman

BUCHANAN, JAMES (1813–1836). James Buchanan, Alamo defender, was born in 1813. He and his wife, Mary, registered as colonists of Stephen F. Austin qv in 1834. As a member of the Alamo garrison, Buchanan died in the battle of the Alamo qv on March 6, 1836.

BIBLIOGRAPHY: Daughters of the American Revolution, *The Alamo Heroes and Their Revolutionary Ancestors* (San Antonio, 1976). Bill Groneman, *Alamo Defenders* (Austin: Eakin, 1990).

Bill Groneman

BUCHANAN, JAMES PAUL (1867–1937). James Paul Buchanan was born in Midway, Orangeburg County, South Carolina, on April 30, 1867. That year his parents moved to Washington County, Texas, where he attended school and grew to manhood. He completed his education in law at the University of Texas in 1889. After graduation, he returned to Washington County, began practicing law, and became involved in politics. He was elected justice of the peace in 1889 and served as the county prosecuting attorney from 1892 to 1899, when he became district attorney for the Twenty-first Judicial District. Buchanan was elected to the state legislature in 1906 and was reelected continuously to state office until 1913, when he won the seat in the United States House of Representatives vacated by Albert Sidney Burleson,qv who had accepted a cabinet position in the Wilson administration. Buchanan became chairman of the Committee on Appropriations and held that post until his death, on February 22, 1937. His seat was taken by Lyndon Baines Johnson.qv Buchanan Dam, near Burnet, was named for him.

BIBLIOGRAPHY: *Alcalde* (magazine of the Ex-Students' Association of the University of Texas), March 1937. Bryan *Eagle*, February 2, 1937. P. A. Grant, "East Texas Congressmen during the New Deal," *East Texas Historical Journal* 11 (Fall 1973). United States Congress, *Biographical Directory of the United States Congress, 1774–1989* (Washington: GPO, 1989). Vertical Files, Barker Texas History Center, University of Texas at Austin.

Anne W. Hooker

BUCHANAN, SARAH ELIZABETH (1840–1939). Sarah Elizabeth Buchanan, writer, was born in Wilkes County, Georgia, on October 18, 1840, the daughter of a Methodist minister. After attending Andrew Female College, Cuthbert, Georgia, she moved to Texas with her husband, John Brown Buchanan, and their growing family in 1883. Buchanan, a veteran of the Fifth Georgia Regiment of Infantry, C.S.A., was an architect and land agent. Of the couple's ten children seven reached adulthood and careers in business, education, and medicine. Mrs. Buchanan published journalism and short stories. About 1896 she joined the staff of *Farm and Ranch*qv magazine as editor of the women's section ("Household") and sections for young people ("Cousin's League") and young children ("Our Juniors"). *Farm and Ranch,* which sought to improve the lives of rural people, circulated widely in the South and Southwest. Known as "Aunt Sallie," Mrs. Buchanan stressed health standards and crusaded against alcohol in her writing. After some years of commuting or mailing her copy from Waxahachie, she moved with her family to Dallas, where she remained the rest of her life. John Brown Buchanan died January 26, 1917. "Aunt Sallie" Buchanan continued her editorship in *Farm and Ranch* until she was ninety-five. For about half a century she belonged to the Texas Press Association;qv she was one of the organizers and a president of the Dallas Pen Women; she was eventually made honorary president for life. After three weeks of illness, she died on March 21, 1939, and was buried in Dallas.

BIBLIOGRAPHY: *Farm and Ranch,* April 1939. Vertical Files, Barker Texas History Center, University of Texas at Austin.

Deolece M. Parmelee

BUCHANAN, WILLIAM (1849–1923). William Buchanan, businessman and philanthropist, was born on September 14, 1849, in Franklin County, Tennessee. He operated sawmills at Leadville, Colorado, and Forest City, Arkansas, before moving to the site of Texarkana, Texas, in 1873, shortly before the town was organized. Beginning with a small sawmill with which he cut into timber the tall pines felled to make way for streets in the new city, he eventually built what was said to be the largest lumber business in the Southwest. His holdings consisted of seven great mills and vast amounts of timberland. As his business began to expand he built a railroad track to connect his timberlands with his mill at Stamps, Arkansas. He extended his road from time to time to reach his timber holdings and finally chartered it in 1898 as the Louisiana and Arkansas Railway Company. The company grew until it included 300 miles of track. On October 9, 1923, Buchanan established the William Buchanan Foundation, "for charitable purposes and the alleviation of suffering and distress," and endowed it with a million dollars. Under the direction of his son-in-law, Stanley Seeger, the foundation worked in cooperation with the University of Texas Medical Branch at Galveston.[qv] On June 19, 1879, Buchanan married Hannah Ferguson. The couple had four children. Buchanan died on October 26, 1923.

BIBLIOGRAPHY: Barbara Overton Chandler and J. E. Howe, *History of Texarkana and Bowie and Miller Counties, Texas-Arkansas* (Texarkana, Texas-Arkansas, 1939). *Cecil Harper, Jr.*

BUCHANAN, TEXAS. Buchanan, five miles northwest of Cleburne in central Johnson County, was established in 1856 and selected as the second county seat in a special election held on October 4 of that year, after the discovery that the original county seat, Wardville, was more than six miles from the county's geographic center. Buchanan was named for Democratic presidential nominee James Buchanan. Following the completion of a log courthouse, the first term of the county court met at Buchanan on February 16, 1857, by which time James Buchanan had been elected president. The county court continued to meet in Buchanan for just over ten years. A post office opened there in 1857, and during the following year a jail was completed. An inadequate water supply, however, severely hampered growth. In 1866 the state legislature designated a portion of western Johnson County for inclusion in the newly established Hood County. This shift of territory reduced Johnson County's size and relocated its geographic center so that Buchanan was no longer within six miles of it. In a special election on March 23, 1867, county voters chose a new county seat, Camp Henderson, which became Cleburne. Buchanan lost its post office in 1868 and was abandoned by 1892.

BIBLIOGRAPHY: Viola Block, *History of Johnson County and Surrounding Areas* (Waco: Texian Press, 1970). *Brian Hart*

BUCHANAN COUNTY. Buchanan County, established in 1858, was named for President James Buchanan. In 1861 the name was changed to Stephens County.

BIBLIOGRAPHY: Hans Peter Nielsen Gammel, comp., *Laws of Texas, 1822–1897* (10 vols., Austin: Gammel, 1898). *Seymour V. Connor*

BUCHANAN DAM, TEXAS. Buchanan Dam is on the south shore of Lake Buchanan and on State Highway 29 eighteen miles from Llano in Llano County. It was initially the site of a construction camp established to build the first of the major flood-control and power-generation facilities on the Colorado River. The project was originally known as Bluffton Dam for the nearby town of Bluffton, but the name was changed to Hamilton Dam, perhaps because its location had been surveyed in 1926 by an engineer named Hamilton. Some say it was named after G. W. Hamilton, vice president of the Middle West Utility Company of Chicago, a company that represented the Insul interests active in developing electrical power distribution in Texas. The Emery-Peck and Rockwood Development Company undertook the construction of the dam in 1931 and established a post office and a settlement of several hundred workers supported by commercial, medical, and recreational facilities. In 1932 bankruptcy forced the closing of the project. United States Congressman James Paul Buchanan[qv] secured federal funds to revive the project in 1934, whereupon the dam, post office, and town were renamed in his honor. The dam was dedicated on October 16, 1937. The town grew steadily as a recreational center, reaching a population of over 1,000 in 1974, when it had numerous businesses. In 1990 the population was 1,099.

BIBLIOGRAPHY: Walter E. Long, *Flood to Faucet* (Austin: Steck, 1956). *James B. Heckert-Greene*

BUCHEL, AUGUSTUS CARL (1813–1864). Carl Buchel, soldier, was born at Guntersblum, Hesse, on October 8, 1813. He dropped the umlaut from his original surname, Büchel, when he moved to Texas. He entered the military academy at Darmstadt at the age of fourteen and at eighteen was commissioned a second lieutenant of volunteers in the First Infantry Regiment of Hesse-Darmstadt. His next military training was at L'école Militaire in Paris, following which he served as a lieutenant in the Foreign Legion of France and participated in the Carlist War in Spain. He was decorated and knighted by Queen Maria Christina in 1838 for his bravery at the battle of Huesca the year before. Subsequently, he was for several years an instructor in the Turkish army and attained the rank of colonel, the highest allowed a Christian. He was offered the rank of general on the condition that he become a Moslem, but he refused and subsequently resigned. There is some indication that he was designated a pasha, a title of respect given officers of high rank.

Buchel had a reputation for dueling and, according to family tradition, is said to have gone to Texas because he killed a man in a duel after his return to Germany. He sailed with the Adelsverein[qv] in 1845 and arrived late that year at Carlshafen, later known as Indianola, where he established residence. In 1846, during the Mexican War,[qv] he raised a company in the First Regiment of Texas Foot Rifles and served as its captain. He was present at the battle of Buena Vista, where he served as aide-de-camp on the staff of Gen. Zachary Taylor.[qv] After the war President Franklin Pierce appointed him collector of customs at Port Lavaca, a position he held for many years. He also sold lumber and building materials in Corpus Christi in partnership with M. T. Huck. In 1859, during the Cortina Wars, he organized the Indianola Volunteers to combat the depredations of Mexican bandits under Juan N. Cortina.[qv] Buchel served until 1860, but the volunteers never actually fought Cortina.

At the outbreak of the Civil War[qv] Buchel joined the Texas militia; late in 1861 he was made lieutenant colonel of the Third Texas Infantry and served in South Texas. He became colonel of the First Texas Cavalry in 1863 and saw extensive service on the Texas Gulf Coast but was transferred to Louisiana when the threat of an invasion of Texas by Union troops became imminent. He was mortally wounded while leading his troops in a dismounted charge at Pleasant Hill, Louisiana, on April 9, 1864. He was taken to Mansfield, where he died and was buried. The generally accepted date of his death is April 15, but Gen. Hamilton P. Bee,[qv] Buchel's commander, related in his official report of the battle that he died two days following the battle, on April 11.

Earlier that year Buchel had been appointed a brigadier general, but the appointment was never confirmed. Later, his body was taken by a detachment of his cavalry to Austin, and he was reinterred in the State Cemetery,[qv] where a eulogy was delivered by Lieutenant Governor Fletcher S. Stockdale.[qv] The state of Texas erected an impressive stone at his grave. Buchel, who never married, was described by his contemporaries as a small, quiet man and is said to have been unassuming, courteous, and gentlemanly in manner. He spoke seven languages. In his honor the state legislature designated an area as Buchel County in 1887, but the county was never organized and eventually became part of Brewster County.

BIBLIOGRAPHY: Louis Lenz Collection, Barker Texas History Center, University of Texas at Austin. Robert W. Stephens, *August Buchel* (Dallas, 1970). Fletcher S. Stockdale, *Eulogy Delivered by Lieut. Gov. F. S. Stockdale . . . at the Obsequies of the Late Col. August Buchel* (Austin: Brown and Foster, 1865). Vertical Files, Barker Texas History Center, University of Texas at Austin. *The War of the Rebellion: A Compilation of the Official Records of the Union and Confederate Armies.*

Robert W. Stephens

BUCHEL, TEXAS. Buchel is on U.S. Highway 183 five miles north of Cuero in eastern DeWitt County. The Buchel school, named for Otto Buchel, on whose land it was built, was established in 1894 and operated until 1950. The Oakville Sunday school, organized in 1894, met in the school building. The 1936 county highway map shows a church at the site, and the 1965 map shows a community center and cemeteries as well. A San Antonio and Aransas Pass Railway depot ten miles southwest of Buchel, midway between Cuero and Yorktown, was also named Buchel and was used for shipping cattle between 1880 and 1930.

BIBLIOGRAPHY: Nellie Murphree, *A History of DeWitt County* (Victoria, Texas, 1962).

Nellie Murphree

BUCHEL COUNTY. The Texas legislature passed an act making Buchel, Foley, and Jeff Davis counties out of Presidio County on March 15, 1887, shortly after passing a similar act making Brewster County out of part of Presidio County. The original Brewster County occupied the northwestern portion of what is now Brewster County, and Buchel County occupied the northeastern part, including the town of Marathon, which was selected as the county seat. Buchel and Foley counties were not organized, however, and on March 22, 1889, the legislature passed an act attaching them to Brewster County for surveying purposes. Buchel County had 298 residents, all but eleven of whom were white, in 1890. Seven years later the legislature passed a bill abolishing Buchel and Foley counties and attaching their territory to Brewster County; this bill was presented to Governor Charles A. Culberson[qv] on April 9, 1897, but he neither signed it nor returned it with his objections to the Senate within the constitutional time limit, so it became law without his signature. With the abolition of Buchel and Foley counties, Brewster County became the largest in Texas. Buchel County was named for A. Carl Buchel.[qv]

BIBLIOGRAPHY: Hans Peter Nielsen Gammel, comp., *Laws of Texas, 1822–1897* (10 vols., Austin: Gammel, 1898).

Martin Donell Kohout

BUCK, BEAUMONT BONAPARTE (1860–1950). Beaumont Bonaparte Buck, army officer, was born in Mississippi on January 16, 1860. He was brought to Texas by his parents about 1870, attended school in Dallas, and joined the Texas militia in 1878. He graduated from the United States Military Academy on February 16, 1885, was assigned to the infantry on June 14, and was stationed at Fort McIntosh. There, on November 20, 1886, he married Kate Bernard, the daughter of his commanding officer, Col. R. F. Bernard. They had three children. Buck was stationed at Fort Ringgold in December 1886, was promoted to first lieutenant in the Nineteenth Infantry in May 1892, and in February 1898 was stationed at Fort Sherman, Idaho, on recruiting duty. In May 1898 he was sent back to Texas as a major in the Second Texas Volunteers. After an honorable discharge on November 9, 1898, he reentered the service as a captain in the Sixteenth Infantry in March 1899 and spent eight months in the Philippine Islands. In 1900–01 he conducted army personnel to the Philippines and Egypt. He was stationed at Fort William McKinley at Manila from 1907 to 1913. He was married a second time on December 30, 1908, and became the father of four children. Buck was promoted to major in 1908 and to lieutenant colonel in 1914. He was sent to France with the Twenty-eighth Infantry in 1916 and became a major general in August 1918. He had received the Distinguished Service Cross in 1909 and after his World War I[qv] service was awarded the Medal of the French Legion of Honor, the Croix de Guerre, and other honors. He retired on June 10, 1925, and made his home in San Antonio. He headed the San Antonio Bicentennial Commission in 1932 and was a founder and president of the State Association of Texas Pioneers. In 1935 he wrote his reminiscences under the title *Memories of Peace and War.* He married Mrs. Virginia Rodgers in September 1949. Buck died in San Antonio on February 10, 1950, and was buried in the Fort Sam Houston National Cemetery. He was survived by his widow, two sons, and four daughters.

BIBLIOGRAPHY: George W. Cullum, *Biographical Register of the Officers and Graduates of the U.S. Military Academy at West Point, New York.* San Antonio *Express,* February 12, 1950. Seb S. Wilcox, "The Laredo City Election and Riot of April, 1886," *Southwestern Historical Quarterly* 45 (July 1941).

BUCK, FRANK (1884–1950). Frank Buck, hunter, author, and filmmaker, son of Howard D. and Ada (Sites) Buck, was born on March 17, 1884, in a wagonyard owned by his father at Gainesville, Texas. When he was five, his family moved to Dallas, where his father, who was distantly related to the Studebaker family, went to work for their Dallas agency dealing in wagons and carriages. After attending public schools in Dallas, Buck left home at the age of eighteen to take a job handling a trainload of cattle being sent to Chicago. In 1911 he made his first expedition to South America. He eventually also traveled to Malaya, India, Borneo, New Guinea, and Africa. From these and other expeditions he brought back many exotic species that he sold to zoos and circuses, and he ultimately acquired the nickname "Bring 'Em Back Alive." Buck was author of *Bring 'Em Back Alive* (with E. Anthony, 1930), *Wild Cargo* (with Anthony, 1931), *Fang and Claw* (with F. L. Fraser, 1935), *Jim Thompson in The Jungles* (1935), *On Jungle Trails* (with Fraser, 1937), *Animals Are Like That!* (with C. Weld, 1939), and his autobiography, *All in a Lifetime* (1941). He was a contributor to the *Saturday Evening Post* and *Colliers,* and for some time he had a radio program. He was president of Frank Buck Enterprises, Incorporated, and Jungleland, Incorporated, and produced several motion pictures, including *Bring 'Em Back Alive, Wild Cargo,* and *Fang and Claw* (made from his books), and *Jungle Menace, Jungle Cavalcade,* and *Jacare.* Buck married Amy Leslie in the early 1900s, but they separated in 1911. He married Muriel Riley in 1928, and they had one daughter. Buck died on March 25, 1950, at Houston.

BIBLIOGRAPHY: Houston *Post,* March 26, 1950. Vertical Files, Barker Texas History Center, University of Texas at Austin. *Who's Who in America* (Chicago: Marquis, 1946–47).

BUCK, TEXAS. Buck was on State Highway 116 seventy-eight miles north of Houston in west central Polk County. The community was named for H. D. (Buck) Reynolds, who moved south from Arkansas and bought the Livingston Lumber Manufacturing Company about 1903. Reynolds built a town around the sawmill, near the Houston, East and West Texas Railway. Buck eventually had a store, a church, a hotel, a school, and homes for the mill workers. Once local timber was cut, about 1920, the mill was sold and moved to Honey Island. The Buck post office, established in 1904, was discontinued in 1930. Only about twenty-five persons remained in the early 1940s, and more recent lists of Texas towns do not include the old sawmill community.

BIBLIOGRAPHY: *A Pictorial History of Polk County, Texas, 1846-1910* (Livingston, Texas: Polk County Bicentennial Commission, 1976; rev. ed. 1978).

Robert Wooster

BUCK BRANCH (Caldwell County). Buck Branch rises six miles southwest of Delhi in southwestern Caldwell County (at 29°47′ N, 97°24′ W) and runs south for nine miles to its mouth on Sandy Fork, six miles west of Waelder in Gonzales County (at 29°40′ N, 97°24′ W). It crosses low-rolling to flat terrain with local dissections, surfaced by sandy and clay loams that support scrub brush, mixed hardwoods, pine, and grasses.

____ (Erath County). Buck Branch rises north of Dublin in southwestern Erath County (at 32°10′ N, 98°22′ W) and runs southeast for five miles to its mouth on Green Creek, southwest of Stephenville (at 32°08′ N, 98°17′ W). It crosses an area of flat to rolling terrain with a surface of deep, fine sandy loam in which brush and grasses grow.

____ (Montague County). Buck Branch rises just west of St. Jo in eastern Montague County (at 33°41′ N, 97°34′ W) and runs east for 3½ miles to its mouth on the Elm Fork of the Trinity River, south of St. Jo (at 33°41′ N, 97°31′ W). It crosses flat to rolling terrain surfaced by deep, very fine sandy loams that support brush and grasses. The Buck Branch area has been used primarily as rangeland.

BUCK CREEK (Angelina County). Buck Creek rises 4½ miles east of Lufkin in north central Angelina County (at 31°20′ N, 94°37′ W) and flows south for 24½ miles to its mouth on the Neches River (at 31°05′ N, 94°36′ W). The surroundings are typical of the East Texas piney woods, characterized by flat to moderately rolling terrain surfaced with red sandy clay and clayey sandy loams that support pine and hardwood forest.

____ (Callahan County). Buck Creek rises six miles southeast of Elmdale oilfield in northwestern Callahan County (at 32°23′ N, 99°34′ W) and runs northwest for twelve miles to its mouth on Cedar Creek in northeastern Taylor County (at 32°31′ N, 99°42′ W). The surrounding flat to gently sloping terrain is surfaced upstream by shallow, stony soil and downstream by shallow to moderately deep silt loams. The area's flora comprises live oak, juniper, grasses, and mesquite.

____ (Cooke County). Buck Creek rises three miles south of Era in southwestern Cooke County (33°28′ N, 97°18′ W) and runs southeast for six miles to its mouth on Clear Creek, in north central Denton County (at 33°23′ N, 97°16′ W). It traverses variable terrain surfaced by shallow, stony clay loams that support oak, juniper, chaparral, cacti, and grasses. Buck Creek has been dammed in its extreme lower reaches.

____ (Donley County). Buck Creek, also known as Spiller Creek, rises in two branches in southeastern Donley County. The North Fork rises four miles east of Hadley (at 34°52′ N, 100°37′ W), and the South Fork three miles southwest of Hadley (at 34°50′ N, 100°41′ W). Both branches flow southeastward into Collingsworth County, where they join fifteen miles west of Wellington (at 34°50′ N, 100°31′ W). The main stream flows seventy miles, through northeastern Childress County and into Harmon County, Oklahoma, to its mouth on the Prairie Dog Town Fork of the Red River (at 34°50′ N, 100°41′ W). William Riley Curtis[qv] established his Diamond Tail Ranch[qv] headquarters on Buck Creek in 1879 and later obtained the Morrisons' Doll Baby range upstream, where the town of Giles was later established. Sam and Joe White ran their OM cattle by the creek in 1880. Buck Creek flows through flat to rolling terrain with local escarpments to moderately steep slopes with locally high relief. Fine sandy or silt loam supports mesquite shrubs and grasses.

BIBLIOGRAPHY: Pauline D. and R. L. Robertson, *Cowman's Country: Fifty Frontier Ranches in the Texas Panhandle, 1876-1887* (Amarillo: Paramount, 1981).

____ (Erath County). Buck Creek rises five miles south of the Palo Pinto county line in northeastern Erath County (at 32°27′ N, 98°11′ W) and runs north for fourteen miles to its mouth on Palo Pinto Creek, near Brazos in southern Palo Pinto County (at 32°38′ N, 98°08′ W). It crosses rolling prairie with clay loam topsoil that supports oak, juniper, mesquite, and grasses.

____ (Frio County). Buck Creek rises a mile northwest of the intersection of U.S. Highway 81 and Farm Road 76 in north central Frio County (at 29°03′ N, 99°03′ W) and runs southwest for twenty-eight miles to its mouth on the Frio River, two miles west of Derby (at 28°46′ N, 99°10′ W). It crosses an area of flat terrain and low rolling hills with steep margins, surfaced by clay and sandy loams in which grow grasses, dwarf evergreen oaks, mesquite, pecan, willow, water-tolerant hardwoods, and conifers.

____ (Grayson County). Buck Creek rises three miles southwest of Dorchester in southwestern Grayson County (at 33°31′ N, 96°42′ W) and runs southwest for twelve miles to its mouth on an arm of Lake Ray Roberts, two miles southeast of Tioga (at 33°26′ N, 96°52′ W). Before the lake was formed in 1987, the stream was joined by Pierce Spring Branch in southeastern Cooke County and ran southwest for seventeen miles to its terminus on Isle du Bois Creek, three miles southwest of Tioga in southeastern Cooke County. Buck Creek crosses generally flat to rolling prairie with occasional steep slopes, surfaced by deep to shallow expansive clays, clay loams, and dark, commonly calcareous clays that support oak, juniper, mesquite, cacti, and grasses. The area has served as crop and range land.

____ (Johnson County). Buck Creek rises a mile southwest of Cleburne State Recreational Park[qv] in southwestern Johnson County (at 32°17′ N, 97°35′ W) and runs south for six miles, crossing under State Highway 200 three miles east of Glen Rose in Somervell County before reaching its mouth on the Brazos River, three miles southeast of Glen Rose (at 32°13′ N, 97°38′ W). The surrounding variable terrain is surfaced by shallow, stony clay loams that support grasses, chaparral, and cacti, as well as juniper and oak trees. The area has been used primarily as range and crop land.

____ (Leon County). Buck Creek rises seven miles west of Centerville in west central Leon County (at 31°16′ N, 96°08′ W) and runs six miles west to disembogue in Brushy Creek three miles northeast of Marquez (at 31°16′ N, 96°13′ W). The stream traverses steeply sloping to nearly level terrain surfaced by sandy and loamy soils. Beside the creek grow post oak, black hickory, pecan, elm, water oak, and hackberry trees. Settlement of the area began in the second half of the 1800s. Concord is on the creek's north bank near its headwaters.

____ (Newton County). Buck Creek rises eight miles north of Burkeville in northern Newton County (at 31°08′ N, 93°39′ W) and once ran northeast for four miles to its mouth on Indian Creek, about 1½ miles west of the Sabine River (at 31°10′ N, 93°36′ W). The creekbed, however, was by the 1980s almost completely submerged in Toledo Bend Reservoir. Several dismantled railroad tracks indicate that lumbering activities once reached the area.

____ (Nolan County). Buck Creek, formerly known as Doyle Creek, rises eleven miles southwest of Maryneal in southwestern Nolan County (at 32°11′ N, 100°37′ W) and runs southwest for ten miles to its mouth on Big Silver Creek, seventeen miles southeast of Colorado City in southeastern Mitchell County (at 32°11′ N, 100°44′ W). It crosses flat terrain with locally shallow depressions, surfaced by expansive clay and sandy and clay loam topsoils that support water-tolerant hardwoods, conifers, and grasses.

____ (Terrell County). Buck Creek rises two miles northeast of the Rose Ranch headquarters in south central Terrell County (at 30°07′ N, 102°14′ W) and runs southeast for fourteen miles to its mouth on Thurston Canyon, three miles north of U.S. Highway 90 (at 30°03′ N, 102°03′ W). Its course crosses steep to gentle slopes on wash deposits and sharply dissects massive limestone to form a winding canyon. The local soils of generally dark, calcareous stony clays and clay loams support scrub brush, oaks, junipers, grasses, and mesquites.

BUCKER CREEK. Bucker Creek rises near Lenz in southwestern Karnes County (at 28°49′ N, 97°58′ W) and runs northeast for seven miles to its mouth on Escondido Creek, three miles west of Kenedy (at 28°50′ N, 97°54′ W). The stream traverses flat to rolling terrain with clay loam and sandy loam soils that support water-tolerant hardwoods and grasses.

BUCKEYE, TEXAS. Buckeye is on Farm Road 1468 and the Missouri Pacific Railroad, nine miles southwest of Bay City and four miles south of Markham in central Matagorda County. It was named by J. W. Stoddard and A. A. Plotner for their native Ohio (the Buckeye State). They purchased the land from Wylie M. Kuykendall[qv] in

1902 and established the Plotner-Stoddard Irrigation Canal headquarters there. The head gate and the pumping station for the company were on the Colorado River and served 30,000 acres. Buckeye had a company store and a boardinghouse. In 1905 thirty-five students were taught in a nearby one-room school that had been donated by Plotner and Stoddard. The community secured a post office in 1907 and in 1908 became a stop on the St. Louis, Brownsville and Mexico Railway spur to Tres Palacios Pumping Plant. In 1914 the community had 100 residents and a canning company, a truck-farming association, a general store, a lumberyard, a hotel, a telegraph agent, and a telephone connection. In 1936 a church, several dwellings, and three businesses were there. In 1940, however, only one business was reported for the community, and its population had dwindled to twenty-five. By 1949 the Buckeye school had been consolidated with the Tidehaven Independent School District. In 1952 Buckeye had about twenty-one dwellings. Its post office closed in 1971. In 1990 its population was reported as twenty-five.

BIBLIOGRAPHY: Matagorda County Historical Commission, *Historic Matagorda County* (3 vols., Houston: Armstrong, 1986).

Stephen L. Hardin

BUCKEYE RANGERS. The Buckeye Rangers, a volunteer company of so-called "emigrants," was recruited for service in the Texas Revolution[qv] in the spring of 1836 around Cincinnati, Ohio, by James C. Allen[qv] and an organization called the Friends of Texas. A series of mass meetings and benefit theatrical performances raised funds and supplies. The arms and military accoutrements appear to have been lent for one year by the quartermaster of the Cincinnati militia district. By June 5 the company of seventy-five to 100 men was recruited and designated the Buckeye Rangers. The volunteers left Cincinnati on the steamboat *Farmer* on June 6, 1836, under the escort of the Cincinnati Greys. They arrived at New Orleans about June 15 and some days later sailed for Texas, apparently on the *Ocean*,[qv] which arrived at Galveston in late June and then proceeded to Velasco, where the company disembarked. The men were welcomed by David G. Burnet[qv] and served as his bodyguard when a plot was disclosed to kidnap and depose him because of the government's protection of Antonio López de Santa Anna[qv] after the treaty of Velasco.[qv] The rangers served under Thomas J. Rusk[qv] until the danger of a threatened Mexican invasion had passed. Most of the volunteers remained to become citizens of Texas.

BIBLIOGRAPHY: William Campbell Binkley, ed., *Official Correspondence of the Texan Revolution, 1835–1836* (2 vols., New York: Appleton-Century, 1936). Louis Wiltz Kemp Papers, Barker Texas History Center, University of Texas at Austin. Houston Wade, *David G. Burnet Letters* (La Grange, Texas: La Grange *Journal*, n.d.). Louis J. Wortham, *A History of Texas* (5 vols., Fort Worth: Wortham-Molyneaux, 1924).

Hobart Huson

BUCK HILL. Buck Hill is thirty-two miles north of Terlingua in west central Brewster County (at 29°46′ N, 103°36′ W). Its summit, with an elevation of 4,184 feet above sea level, rises 280 feet above State Highway 118, a mile to the east. Buck Hill is a small, faulted, sill-like intrusion of igneous rock. Its shallow, stony soils support scrub brush and grasses.

BUCKHOLTS, TEXAS. Buckholts is at the intersection of Farm Road 1915, State Highway 36, and U.S. Highway 190, by the Atchison, Topeka and Santa Fe Railway nine miles northwest of Cameron in northwestern Milam County. The community, established in 1881 when the Gulf, Colorado and Santa Fe Railway built through the area, was named for John A. Buckholts, who donated land for the site. A post office opened there in 1882, and by 1884 Buckholts comprised sixty-one residents, two general stores, two hotels, a dry-goods store, and a lumber dealer. Farmers, including a number of immigrants from Germany, Austria, and Czechoslovakia, were attracted to the blackland soils of the area; cotton became the community's principal shipment in the 1880s and 1890s. The Hope Lutheran Church was organized at Buckholts in 1890, and the congregation erected a building in 1899. Methodist and Baptist churches were also built in the community during the 1890s. A school was built by 1896. In 1900 Buckholts reported a population of 182. In 1903 the Buckholts school had two teachers and eighty-five pupils. By 1914 the community had a bank, telephone service, and a newspaper, the weekly *Bulletin*. The population of Buckholts was estimated at 800 from the 1920s through the 1940s. In 1948 the community had a school, three churches, three factories, and some thirty other businesses. Though exact estimates vary, the population of the town has slowly declined after the 1960s, reaching 362 in 1980 and 335 in the early 1990s.

BIBLIOGRAPHY: Milam County Heritage Preservation Society, *Matchless Milam: History of Milam County* (Dallas: Taylor, 1984).

Mark Odintz

BUCKHORN, TEXAS (Austin County). Buckhorn is on Farm Road 1456 seven miles northeast of Bellville in far northeastern Austin County. Settlement in the vicinity began during the 1830s. Buckhorn was founded in 1873 when H. S. Smith constructed a cotton gin and gristmill on the banks of a small tributary of Caney Creek. A post office was established there in 1874, with N. Cochran as the first postmaster. By 1880 the town had a school, several churches, and a semiweekly stage to Bellville. Buckhorn reported a population of 200 in 1885. In 1901 its post office was discontinued. The Buckhorn school enrolled twenty-one pupils in 1918. The community's population dropped below 100 by 1910 and had dwindled to an estimated ten by 1933. In 1939 the town had two businesses and an estimated population of fifty. From 1974 to 1990 its population was estimated at twenty. Samuel Chapel and Washam Chapel were at the site in the late 1980s.

Charles Christopher Jackson

BUCKHORN, TEXAS (Frio County). Buckhorn was a frontier community a half mile north of what is now Farm Road 1582 and eight miles southeast of Pearsall in southeast central Frio County. In 1913 Frio County school trustees formed a 3,200-acre school district in the southeastern part of the county. The eight-grade school at Buckhorn served the western half of this district, and the school at Shallow Wells its eastern half. Later the school district was parceled into 300-acre farms. Purchasers of the farms joined the families in the area to form the nucleus of Buckhorn. Longtime resident R. F. Foster provided three acres near the school as a site for a Methodist church. By 1929 three dwellings were near the church and school, and the site was surrounded by numerous farms. All that remained of Buckhorn in 1948 was a cemetery and a few dwellings. In 1964 only its cemetery remained. During the early 1990s several descendants of Foster and of John Wesley Devilbiss[qv] lived in the area. *Ruben E. Ochoa*

BUCKHORN CREEK. Buckhorn Creek rises a mile south of Bebe in southwestern Gonzales County (at 29°24′ N, 97°39′ W) and runs southeast for seven miles to its mouth on Salty Creek, 1½ miles southwest of Wrightsboro (at 29°20′ N, 97°36′ W). It traverses flat to rolling prairie with sandy loam topsoils that support grasses and mesquite.

BUCKHORN DRAW. Buckhorn Draw, a valley through which runs an intermittent stream, rises 2½ miles east of State Highway 163 in northeastern Crockett County (at 31°02′ N, 101°12′ W), and runs southeast for forty-two miles to its mouth on Granger Draw, a mile north of Interstate 10 in northwestern Sutton County (at 30°39′ N, 100°52′ W). The draw crosses Schleicher County. Its tributaries include Puckett, Double Mill, Bailey, and Burn draws. Buckhorn Draw sharply dissects massive limestone and crosses flat terrain on alluvial deposits of sand, gravel, and mud. Local soils are generally dark, calcareous stony clays and clay loams. The area vegetation comprises water-tolerant hardwoods and conifers, as well as oaks, junipers, grasses, and mesquites. The draw was named for the Buckhorn Ranch, which is located on its banks.

BUCKHORN SALOON. Albert Friedrich of San Antonio began his exotic horn collection in 1881, three years before the founding of the Lone Star Brewery, which has housed the Buckhorn Saloon since 1957. Friedrich, whose father made horn furniture, began to display his collection at a saloon that he acquired on Dolorosa Street. He moved his business to what became the Buckhorn Saloon, at Soledad and West Houston streets, in 1896. There he maintained one of the most respectable saloons in San Antonio during one of the city's rowdiest eras and acquired the antler collection of a famed hunter, Capt. Ernest Dosch. As a result of prohibition,[qv] in 1922 Friedrich moved his business to 400 West Houston Street, where it was first known as Albert's Curio Store and subsequently as the Buckhorn Curio Store and Cafe. Three decades later the Buckhorn Saloon, with its mirrored back bar intact and a facsimile of the main bar, was restored at the Lone Star Brewery. Quaint machines and trick mirrors were brought from the old Buckhorn, along with the Friedrich collection, which was housed in the adjacent Hall of Horns. The collection includes trophies of big game hunts throughout North America, Europe, Asia, and Africa. The Texas Room, crowned by a chandelier composed of over 4,000 horns from the old Buckhorn Saloon, features such world champions as a longhorn with an eight-foot spread (*see* LONGHORN CATTLE) and a deer head with seventy-eight-point antlers. Stuffed freaks of the animal world can be found alongside a huge gorilla and memorabilia of the "world's greatest" sharpshooting team, San Antonians "Plinky" and Adolph Toepperwein.[qqv] A number of unusual framed artistic designs at the saloon were made by Friedrich's wife, who was a rattlesnake-rattle artist.

BIBLIOGRAPHY: Charles W. Ramsdell, *San Antonio: A Historical and Pictorial Guide* (Austin: University of Texas Press, 1959). Fritz A. Toepperwein, comp., *Footnotes of the Buckhorn: A Lone Star State Landmark* (Boerne, Texas: Highland, 1960). *Donald E. Everett*

BUCKINGHAM, TEXAS. Buckingham is located in northern Dallas County near the Collin county line and is completely surrounded by the city of Richardson. The community was incorporated around 1958 and, as Richardson grew up around it, remained a small semirural enclave with about 150–200 inhabitants. In 1983 developers began purchasing the homes of the sixty-four families that lived in Buckingham, intending to convert the area to apartments, condos, and businesses. By 1985 most of the property in the community belonged to the Buckingham Development Venture. Before the residents moved away they cooperated with the developers to pass a liquor ordinance that made Buckingham a wet community in the middle of dry Richardson. Initial attempts to develop the town were squashed by the real estate crisis of the mid-1980s, and the Buckingham Development Venture went bankrupt in 1987. There were 102 residents in the community in 1990. In the mid-1990s development of Buckingham as an apartment and business district was finally underway, with several apartment buildings, liquor stores, a supermarket, and strip malls. These developments were contested by residents in the surrounding neighborhoods who were concerned about the commercial zoning given to Buckingham and the nature of some of the businesses located in the town.

BIBLIOGRAPHY: Dallas *Morning News*, November 14, 1988.
Mark Odintz

BUCKLER, CECIL VICTOR PAYNE (1885–1967). C. P. Buckler, Panhandle[qv] ranch manager and civic leader, was born in England in 1885 and educated in English private schools. His father was a member of the London Stock Exchange. Buckler moved to the Texas Panhandle at the age of nineteen, after his parents had died and his younger brother had gone to Egypt. He began working as a ranchhand for the White Deer Land Company in 1905, but his ability to type and take shorthand soon earned him the job of company bookkeeper. In 1909 he married Annie Thut; they had three daughters. Buckler gradually lost his distinctive British accent, dropped the Victor from his name, and in 1914 became a United States citizen. In addition to his role as stenographer for British-owned White Deer Lands, he served as justice of the peace, played the baritone in Alex Schneider's town band, and worked to promote the growth of Pampa. In 1935 Buckler became sole manager of White Deer, after comanaging it with M. K. Brown since 1924. He was among the American citizens who purchased most of the British interests in White Deer Corporation when it was reorganized in 1949. He served as its vice president and Texas agent until its liquidation in 1957.

Buckler was a member of the board of the Pampa Independent School District for sixteen years, was a charter member and president of the Pampa Rotary Club, and helped establish the Pampa Country Club. He was one of three appointed trustees of the Lovett estate, a senior warden at St. Matthew's Episcopal Church, a Mason, and a director of the Fairview Cemetery Association of Pampa. He also served as a director of the First National Bank and was president of Security Federal Savings and Loan Association. He was a member of the Panhandle-Plains Historical Society,[qv] served on its board of directors, and was its president in 1960–61. He and M. K. Brown donated the old Francklyn Land and Cattle Company[qv] records to the Panhandle-Plains Historical Museum[qv] in 1959. In his lifetime Buckler saw Pampa grow from a frontier community of fewer than fifty persons to a progressive industrial center. He died on December 27, 1967, and was buried in Fairview Cemetery. Buckler Street, where his home was located, is named for him.

BIBLIOGRAPHY: Sylvia Grider, "'He's for Progress': C. P. Buckler and the White Deer Land Company," West Texas Historical Association *Yearbook* 43 (1967). *H. Allen Anderson*

BUCKLEY, CONSTANTINE W. (1815–1865). Constantine W. Buckley, businessman, attorney, and public official, was born in Surrey County, North Carolina, on January 22, 1815. He moved to Georgia in 1828 and worked as a store clerk until 1834, when he opened his own mercantile establishment, in Columbus. He lost this business in the panic of 1837. He moved destitute to Texas early in 1838, settled in Houston, and served as a clerk in the State Department until September 1839. Under the tutelage of Attorney General John Birdsall[qv] Buckley studied law. In November 1839 he was admitted to the Texas bar and established his practice. He married in 1840 and had two sons and a daughter. In 1847 James Pinckney Henderson[qv] appointed him judge of the Seventh Judicial District. He was elected to that position in 1852 but resigned in 1854 to return to private practice and farming. By this time his first wife had apparently died, for he married Mrs. Ann R. Nibbs in 1852. In 1857 Buckley was elected to the Texas House of Representatives from Austin and Fort Bend counties. The next year he was defeated in his bid for the post of associate justice of the Texas Supreme Court. He was reelected to the legislature in 1859 and served as chairman of the judicial committee. He drowned in the Brazos River near Columbia on December 19, 1865.

BIBLIOGRAPHY: William DeRyee and R. E. Moore, *The Texas Album of the Eighth Legislature, 1860* (Austin: Miner, Lambert, and Perry, 1860). *Stephen L. Hardin*

BUCKLEY, SAMUEL BOTSFORD (1809–1884). Samuel Botsford Buckley, geologist and naturalist, was born at Torry, New York, on May 9, 1809. He graduated from Wesleyan University, Middletown, Connecticut, in 1836. In 1837–38 he gathered botanical collections in Virginia and Illinois. He served as principal of Allenton Academy in Alabama in 1839–40. In the early 1840s he collected twenty-four new plant species in North Carolina, South Carolina, and Tennessee. This resulted in the naming of a new genus, Buckleya, for him. He also obtained the seventy-foot skeleton of a zeuglodon in Alabama. He studied medicine at the College of Physicians and Surgeons in 1842–43. In 1843 he discovered thirteen new species of shells on a collecting trip in Florida. He worked on a farm in New York and in a bookstore in Ohio until 1858, when he returned to Tennessee and North Carolina to do work in geology.

In 1860–61 Buckley was assistant geologist and naturalist in the Texas Geological Survey under Benjamin F. Shumard[qv] and subsequently under Francis Moore.[qv] He lived in the North during the Civil War[qv] and from 1862 to 1865 was chief examiner in the Statistical Department of the United States Sanitary Commission. In 1871–72 he was agricultural and scientific editor of the Austin *State Gazette*.[qv] He received a Ph.D. degree from Waco University in 1872 and, when a second Texas Geological Survey was organized in 1874, became state geologist, a post he held until 1877. Buckley's *Preliminary Report of the Geological and Agricultural Survey of Texas* was published in 1866. He also contributed several articles to the 1867 *Texas Almanac*.[qv] He published a first and second *Annual Report of the Geological and Agricultural Survey of Texas* (1874, 1876). In 1881 he prepared several articles for the Library of Universal Knowledge. Buckley prepared a natural history of Texas, but it was never published; nor, apparently, were accounts of his botanical trips in Texas. Some contemporaries criticized his research as careless, partisan, and unscientific. Texas geologist Anton R. Roessler,[qv] in his published rebuttal to accusations made in Buckley's geological survey report, charged that Buckley took false credit for several geological discoveries and that some of his collections were merely reassembled existing ones.

Buckley was married four times. Charlotte Sullivan of Naples, New York, whom he married in 1852, died in 1854. In 1855 he married Sarah Porter of Naples, who died in 1858. Probably during the early 1860s he married Mary Huttner. In 1864 he married Libbie Meyers of Elbridge, New York. Sources indicate that Buckley fathered three children. According to his will, one daughter survived him. Buckley died in Austin on February 18, 1884.

BIBLIOGRAPHY: *Dictionary of American Biography*. Clark A. Elliott, *Biographical Dictionary of American Science: The Seventeenth through the Nineteenth Centuries* (Westport, Connecticut: Greenwood Press, 1979). *Southwestern Historical Quarterly*, Texas Collection, April 1944. Vertical Files, Barker Texas History Center, University of Texas at Austin.

BUCKLEY, WILLIAM FRANK (1881–1958). William Frank Buckley, lawyer and oil entrepreneur, was born in Washington-on-the-Brazos, Texas, on July 12, 1881, the fourth of eight children of John and Mary Ann (Langford) Buckley, of Irish ancestry. In the fall of 1882 the family moved to San Diego, Duval County, where John Buckley engaged in merchandising, politics, and sheep raising; he also served several elective terms as Duval County sheriff.

Growing up in a Spanish-speaking community, William Buckley became proficient in the language and a close friend of Spanish-speaking peoples, a quality he retained all of his life. One of his early influences was the widely educated parish priest, Father John Pierre Bard, of the Church of San Francisco de Paula in San Diego. After finishing school in San Diego, Buckley taught at a country school near Benavides, where all but a few of the students used the Spanish language. According to records at the University of Texas at Austin, he enrolled there in 1899 and was a student at the university until 1905, when his picture appeared with the law class of 1905. Because of his command of the language he received advanced credit in Spanish in his first years there and was an assistant to a professor in the Romance-languages department. During this time he was also, along with his sister, Priscilla, a Spanish translator in the General Land Office.[qv] With others he initiated the Austin chapter of the Delta Tau Delta national college fraternity and later became one of its most liberal financial supporters. He was a devout Catholic and, along with others, purchased property near the university for the Newman Club. When his father died in 1904 he was the oldest surviving son, and he undertook the care of his mother, whom he moved to Austin, along with his two brothers and two sisters, to a small house on the corner of Lavaca and Nineteenth streets; Buckley later built a large house there (now the site of Cambridge Tower), where his mother lived until her death in 1930. He received a B.S. degree in 1904 and an LL.B. degree in 1905, was quizmaster in the School of Law, and was a member of the John C. Townes[qv] Law Society. In 1905 he was elected editor of the University of Texas yearbook, *The Cactus* (1906). Buckley received his license to practice law in Texas on June 8, 1906, and he was elected a member of the Texas Bar Association (*see* STATE BAR OF TEXAS) in 1909.

He went to Mexico City in 1908 and passed law examinations there, and he and his brother Claude, also a lawyer, acted as counsel for many of the most important American and European oil companies doing business in Mexico. In 1911 they established their own law office with another brother, Edmund, in Tampico, Vera Cruz. By 1914 William F. Buckley had turned his law practice over to his brothers so that he might engage in real estate and the leasing of oil lands. He acquired, improved, and sold land around the city of Tampico, and he founded the Pantepec Oil Company of Mexico. The Mexican Revolution[qv] was at its height in 1912, 1913, and 1914, and after the invasion and takeover of Veracruz by the United States Marines in April 1914, President Woodrow Wilson offered the post of civil governor to Buckley, who indignantly refused the appointment because he was not in sympathy with Wilson's Mexico policy. Later that year Buckley served as counsel for the Mexican government at the ABC Conference at Niagara Falls, where Argentina, Brazil, and Chile acted as mediators between the United States and Mexico. In December 1919 he testified before the United States Senate Subcommittee on Foreign Relations as an expert witness on conditions in Mexico. Knowing the language, the people, and the nature of revolutionary activities there, Buckley believed that internal Mexican policies such as those approved of by American "specialists" would destroy American investments in Mexico. In 1920 he assisted in the foundation of the American Association of Mexico, with offices in Washington and New York, which lobbied for the interests of United States businessmen in Mexico. Because of Buckley's opposition to the government of Gen. Álvaro Obregón and his support of the antigovernment revolution of Manuel Peláez, Buckley was expelled from Mexico in 1921. In January 1922 he gave a full report of his expulsion to the secretary of state of the United States and urged that his country not recognize the Obregón government until certain agreements had been reached between the two countries.

In 1924 Buckley was invited back to Mexico by President Plutarco Calles and returned for a visit, but in that year he transferred his Pantepec Oil Company to Venezuela. There, in a largely undeveloped oil region, he fully committed himself to oil exploration. As one of the first to use the "farm-out" system, Buckley made agreements with some of the largest oil companies, whereby the companies would take over the cost of exploring, drilling, and developing and would in turn share the profits from oil and gas produced on his concessions. He made his first major deal, with Standard Oil, in the 1930s when a large oilfield was found on Pantepec's Venezuelan concessions. Other major producers followed. During his entire career Buckley was primarily interested in unexplored territory, and in 1946 he began a diversification of his oil holdings with the forming of separate companies. Operations assumed an international scale with the leasing of land in Canada, Florida, Ecuador, Australia, the Philippines, Israel, and Guatemala.

In 1922 Buckley gave to the University of Texas his extensive files covering the tumultuous years of Mexican history from the time of his stay in that country. Included in the gift were thirty-five scrapbooks of newspaper clippings and 300 folders containing copies of Buckley's confidential reports, annotated letters, statements, interviews, and other papers. In 1925, over the opposition of the university's librarian, Ernest W. Winkler,[qv] the entire collection was sent to Washington, D.C., for use by the State Department's Mixed Claims Commission (United States and Mexico). It was finally returned at the request of the University of Texas in 1929. The papers are housed in the Nettie Lee Benson Latin American Collection.[qv]

Buckley was married to Aloise Steiner of New Orleans in 1917. A widely read man and always concerned with learning, he closely supervised the trilingual education of their ten children during the years the family lived in Paris, London, and the United States. In the 1920s he purchased the family estate, Great Elm, in Sharon, Connecticut, and later, for a winter home, the estate Kamschatka in Camden, South Carolina. Several of William and Aloise Buckley's children became national figures: James Buckley was elected to the United States Senate, and William F. Buckley, Jr., became a nationally known writer, editor, and speaker for the conservative view in politics. Fergus Reid Buckley, another son, is a journalist and novelist. Priscilla Buckley pursued a career in journalism and was managing editor of the *National Review* for decades. Patricia Buckley was a free-lance book editor in 1986. Members of the family also continued in active operation of the Buckley oil business.

After a stroke on board the *S.S. United States*, between Paris and New York in late September 1958, William F. Buckley was given the last rites of the Catholic Church; he died in Lenox Hill Hospital in New York on October 5, 1958, and was buried in the Quaker Cemetery near his winter home in Camden, South Carolina.

BIBLIOGRAPHY: Priscilla L. Buckley and William F. Buckley, Jr., eds., *W. F. B.—An Appreciation by His Family and Friends* (New York, 1959).

Eldon S. Branda

BUCKLEY DRAW. Buckley Draw (also known as Buckley Creek, Buckleys Creek, and Buckley Drain), a valley through which runs an intermittent stream, begins two miles south of State Highway 189 in southern Sutton County (at 30°18′ N, 100°42′ W) and runs southwest for twenty-three miles to its mouth on the Devils River, a mile northeast of Threemile Canyon in north central Val Verde County (at 30°11′ N, 101°00′ W). The draw sharply dissects massive limestone that underlies flat terrain, forming a deep and winding canyon. Part of its course crosses wash deposits of sand, gravel, and mud. The area topsoils are generally dark, calcareous stony clays and clay loams. Local vegetation includes water-tolerant hardwoods and conifers, as well as oaks, junipers, grasses, and mesquites. The draw was named for Renard Buckley, who filed claim in 1877 on a 160-acre tract of land that included the head of the stream.

BUCK MOUNTAIN. Buck Mountain, about seven miles southwest of Breckenridge in southern Stephens County (at 32°40′ N, 98°59′ W), has an elevation of 1,342 feet above sea level. The surrounding terrain is predominantly rolling prairie and is surfaced with clay loams that support mesquite and grasses.

BUCKNER, AYLETT C. (1794?–1832). Aylett(e) C. (Strap) Buckner, filibuster, Indian fighter, Old Three Hundred[qv] colonist, and folklore hero of colonial Texas, was the son of Aylett and Elizabeth (Lewis) Buckner of Louisa County, Virginia. Red-headed, of Irish and Scottish ancestry, he was supposedly nicknamed "Strap" because of his prodigious size and strength. He traveled to Texas as early as 1812 as a member of the Gutiérrez-Magee expedition[qv] and returned in 1816 under Francisco Xavier Mina[qv] and in 1819 with Dr. James Long.[qv] He probably spent some of the intervening years in the Natchez, Mississippi, area. With Peter Powell[qv] and Oliver Buckner he settled around 1821 on Buckner's Creek in the area that later became Fayette County. In his letters to Stephen F. Austin,[qv] Buckner said that he had been one of the first to build a cabin on the Colorado River, that he had kept an open house ever since he came, and that he had lost more property to Indian depredations than anyone else on the river. He was listed in the March 1823 census of the Colorado district as a twenty-nine-year-old farmer. Buckner became one of Austin's Old Three Hundred settlers when he received title to one sitio[qv] of land on July 24, 1824, and two labores on August 24, 1824, all later in Matagorda County. In the summer of 1824 he was probably among those sent by Austin to make a treaty with Waco and Tawakoni Indians near the site of present Waco. The census of March 1826 listed Buckner as a single man with four servants and one slave.

In 1825 he had some conflict with Austin over the location and amount of his land and attempted to hold a meeting to protest against Austin, who consequently ordered Andrew Rabb[qv] to arrest Buckner for seditious conduct. After consulting with Jared E. Groce[qv] and John P. Cole, Austin was able to work out a better understanding with Buckner. After a quarrel with James Cummins,[qv] Buckner wrote Austin that he wanted to be buried under his own soil and that he wanted to buy a thousand acres of land. In January 1826 Austin selected Moses Morrison, William Kincheloe,[qqv] and Buckner as judges for an election for alcalde[qv] for the district of Mina. In 1826 Buckner made a trip to Matamoros, Tamaulipas, to find out whether or not he could claim land as compensation for his services in the Mina and Gutiérrez expeditions.

As early as May 1826 Buckner was named by Austin as a commander of the militia against local Indians, and in the winter of 1826 he was part of a retaliatory expedition against a band of Karankawas believed to have killed the families of Elisha Flowers[qv] and Charles Cavanagh. Probably because of Buckner's disagreements with Austin, Benjamin W. Edwards[qv] solicited his aid in the Fredonian Rebellion[qv] in December 1826, but Buckner signed resolutions of protest against the rebellion and ultimately became a faithful member of the colony and a close friend of Austin. He was in command of an attack against the Karankawa Indians at Live Oak Bayou in 1831, and in 1832 he led a company of volunteers from the area of present Fayette and Matagorda counties at the battle of Velasco.[qv] There, on June 25 or 26, 1832, he was killed.

Though legend has it that the Indians (who, impressed by his strength, reportedly nicknamed Buckner the "Red Son of Blue Thunder") offered him marriage with Indian princess Tulipita, Buckner never married. One historian has suggested that perhaps it was in part this lack of heirs which allowed the growth of ever-more outlandish legends of his strength and size. Notable among these are the tales of how with one blow he turned back the huge black bull Triste Noche, which had been terrorizing the colony, and how after this feat he was emboldened to challenge the devil himself to a duel. The best account of the latter legend appears in Nathaniel Alston Taylor's 1877 travelogue, *The Coming Empire; Or, Two Thousand Miles in Texas on Horseback*.

BIBLIOGRAPHY: Eugene C. Barker, ed., *The Austin Papers* (3 vols., Washington: GPO, 1924–28). Eugene C. Barker, *The Life of Stephen F. Austin* (Nashville: Cokesbury Press, 1925; rpt., Austin: Texas State Historical Association, 1949; New York: AMS Press, 1970). Eugene C. Barker, ed., "Minutes of the Ayuntamiento of San Felipe de Austin, 1828–1832," 12 parts, *Southwestern Historical Quarterly* 21–24 (January 1918–October 1920). Florence Elberta Barns, "Building a Texas Folk-Epic: The Materials and the Process Which Formed the Saga of Strap Buckner, " *Texas Monthly*, October 1929. Lester G. Bugbee, "The Old Three Hundred: A List of Settlers in Austin's First Colony," *Quarterly of the Texas State Historical Association* 1 (October 1897). J. H. Kuykendall, "Reminiscences of Early Texans," *Quarterly of the Texas State Historical Association* 6–7 (January, April, July 1903). Matagorda County Historical Commission, *Historic Matagorda County* (3 vols., Houston: Armstrong, 1986). Worth Stickley Ray, *Austin Colony Pioneers* (Austin: Jenkins, 1949; 2d ed., Austin: Pemberton,

1970). Nathaniel Alston Taylor and H. F. McDanield, *The Coming Empire, or Two Thousand Miles in Texas on Horseback* (New York: Barnes, 1877; rev. ed., Dallas: Turner, 1936). Vertical Files, Barker Texas History Center, University of Texas at Austin. Leonie Rummel Weyand and Houston Wade, *An Early History of Fayette County* (La Grange, Texas: La Grange *Journal*, 1936).

BUCKNER, ROBERT COOKE (1833–1919). Robert Cooke Buckner, Baptist minister and founder of Buckner Baptist Children's Home,[qv] son of Rev. Daniel and Mary (Hampton) Buckner, was born on January 3, 1833, in Madisonville, Tennessee. He attended Somerset Seminary in Cleveland, Tennessee, and Georgetown College in Kentucky. He was ordained a Baptist minister at the age of seventeen. He pastored churches in Albany, Owensboro, and Salvisa, Kentucky, before moving to Paris, Texas, in 1859. While in Albany, he married Vienna Long, on June 7, 1854. The couple had seven children.

For fourteen years after his arrival in Texas, Buckner was pastor of the Paris Baptist Church. During his last year in Paris, he began a newspaper, the *Religious Messenger*, the title of which was later changed to *Texas Baptist* (*see* TEXAS BAPTIST AND HERALD). He continued to edit the paper until he sold his interest in it in 1883. In 1875 he moved to Dallas, where he began to work toward the establishment of a Baptist orphanage. He secured the approval of the Baptist General Association for Buckner Orphans Home, wrote its original charter, and opened the home in 1879 with three children. He served as president and general manager of the home until his death in 1919, when an estimated 12,000 children had been residents at the home. In 1900 Buckner was part of a group of prominent Baptists, both black and white, who founded the Dickson Colored Orphanage in Gilmer, Upshur County. Buckner served as president of the board of that home from 1900 to 1905 and continued as a member of the board for several years thereafter.

In addition to his activities on behalf of orphans, Buckner was president of the Baptist General Association of Texas for twenty years and helped in founding Texas Baptist Memorial Sanitarium (now Baylor University Medical Center[qv]), which he served from 1904 to 1907 as president of the board. He was a trustee of Baylor University, a member of the National Prison Congress, and frequently a delegate to the national Convention for Charities and Corrections. He was an enthusiastic Mason and a member of Hella Temple of the Shrine. "Father" Buckner, as he was called by thousands young and old, died in Dallas on April 9, 1919, and was buried in Grove Hill Cemetery.

BIBLIOGRAPHY: J. B. Cranfill and J. L. Walker, *R. C. Buckner's Life of Faith and Works* (Dallas: Buckner Orphans Home, 1915; 2d ed. 1916). Dallas *Morning News*, April 10, 1919. *Cecil Harper, Jr.*

BUCKNER, THOMAS ADDISON (1873–1950). Thomas Addison Buckner, newspaperman and civic leader, was born in Bandera County, Texas, on December 24, 1873, the second son of Thomas L. and Martha (Buckelew) Buckner. He married one of his pupils, Harriet Caroline Mayfield, in 1892. During the early years of their marriage he taught school, was justice of the peace in Bandera, and was deputy district and county clerk of Bandera County, where both his grandfather and his father had served as county officials. Buckner began his newspaper career in the office of the Bandera *Enterprise* about 1896 and later owned the newspaper. Subsequently, he owned or managed newspapers at Comfort, Center Point, Ozona, Kerrville, and San Marcos, where he operated the San Marcos *Record* from 1921 until his death. His two sons purchased interests in the paper in 1922 and 1932. Buckner also had two daughters. He was a Baptist and a member of the Texas Press Association,[qv] which he served as director on several occasions, as well as the Texas Editorial Association. He was an early president of the local Kiwanis Club. While the San Marcos *Record* was under his management, Buckner received many awards for excellence. He died on January 23, 1950.

BIBLIOGRAPHY: Vertical Files, Barker Texas History Center, University of Texas at Austin. *Babe Zimmerman*

BUCKNER, TEXAS (Collin County). Buckner, the original county seat of Collin County, was three miles northwest of the site of present McKinney. Settlement began in the early 1840s when John McGarrah arrived from Arkansas to claim a headright of 640 acres. McGarrah opened a trading post to serve the growing number of settlers who began to arrive in the area in the mid-1840s and donated fifty acres of land for a townsite. Later a blacksmith shop was built near the store. On April 3, 1846, the Texas legislature established Collin County and appointed a five-member commission to select two sites within three miles of the center of the county and to supervise an election to choose one of the sites as the county seat, to be called Buckner. On July 4, 1846, about seventy-five persons attended a meeting, probably held at McGarrah's store, and selected that site as the county seat. In 1846 the town received a post office. Because two sites had not been offered to the voters in the election of 1846, and because Buckner was not within three miles of the center of the county, the state legislature called for a new election in 1848. McKinney, three miles southwest of Buckner, was chosen as the new county seat. In May 1848 mail to Buckner was discontinued, and within a year its residents and businesses had moved to McKinney. By the early 1850s the first county seat of Collin County was deserted. In the 1980s, however, activity resumed in the Buckner area, under the influence of a "Third Monday Trade Day" at the site and a nearby Texas Instruments[qv] plant.

BIBLIOGRAPHY: Roy Franklin Hall and Helen Gibbard Hall, *Collin County: Pioneering in North Texas* (Quanah, Texas: Nortex, 1975). Dick King, *Ghost Towns of Texas* (San Antonio: Naylor, 1953). J. Lee and Lillian J. Stambaugh, *A History of Collin County* (Austin: Texas State Historical Association, 1958). *David Minor*

BUCKNER, TEXAS (Parker County). Buckner is on a spur off Farm Road 1189 and on the south side of the Brazos River, fifteen miles southwest of Weatherford in southwestern Parker County. It was originally called Big Valley and later renamed in memory of J. M. Buckner, who drowned with his son in the Brazos. In 1881 a cotton gin–gristmill was established there, and the town became a retail point for area farmers. A post office opened at the community in 1884. By the mid-1890s Buckner had seventy-five residents. Its post office was discontinued in 1919. Buckner was still listed as a community in 1990.

BIBLIOGRAPHY: Gustavus Adolphus Holland, *History of Parker County and the Double Log Cabin* (Weatherford, Texas: Herald, 1931; rpt. 1937). *David Minor*

BUCKNER BAPTIST BENEVOLENCES. Buckner Baptist Benevolences developed out of the Buckner Orphans Home, a children's home in Dallas, which opened in 1879. In 1961 the home's charter was changed to reflect its expanding network of services, and the new entity was named Buckner Baptist Benevolences. In the preceding decades the Buckner home had expanded to include additional locations. In 1918 at Goodnight, Buckner opened a Panhandle Department for the care of destitute children, with B. H. Warren as principal. It was closed in 1920 after a fire destroyed the main building. In 1949 Buckner assumed responsibility for a special unwed mothers' unit, Bethesda Home, in San Antonio, a project of Baptist churches of that city. In August of the same year a groundbreaking ceremony was held near Burnet, Texas, for a 2,000-acre boys' ranch, for school-age boys who needed an encouraging, structured environment. This unit, Buckner Boys' Ranch, soon cared for seventy boys in five cottage dormitories, a church, a central dining hall, and a gymnasium. In 1951 the home purchased forty-five acres of land in residential Houston for the location of Texas Baptist Haven, a new Buckner home for the aged. Ellis L. Carnett was elected as Buckner's new president on March 7, 1952. Under his tenure the home further expanded its ministries with the Trew Home for the Aged in Dallas (1953–54), a new Teacherage addition (1953), and Foster Care, Adoption Services, Mother's Aid, and Homemaker's Service programs in several Texas cities. In 1957 Buckner opened a Girls' Home in Lubbock, later for both girls and boys. The same year Buckner took a major step forward when it formed the Department of Social Services and named Bill Baker as director, responsible for coordinating all the units of Buckner's benevolences. By 1960 the board of directors began selling portions of Buckner's 3,000-acre Dallas holdings, in accordance with the provision of the founder, to invest all proceeds in endowment funds. The directors retained the campus and its immediate environs, the interest from which became the "seed corn" for Buckner's future financial stability. Thus the foundation was set for the formal change in the home's charter to the title of Buckner Baptist Benevolences and its encompassing directives.

The young R. C. Campbell replaced Carnett as president on January 15, 1963. Campbell's tenure of more than thirty years has been marked by growth and by Buckner's ability to adopt programs to meet the needs of society's most vulnerable persons. By 1965 Buckner had opened a remedial learner–vocational preparation school on its Dallas campus. In 1966 the Lubbock Home moved to a new campus located on Fourth Street, designed as a regional social service center to provide for child care, marriage and family counseling, maternity care, adoption, and aging services. The Frank Ryburn Home for the Aging also opened that year, as well as a new maternity home, both in Dallas. Buckner-sponsored foster group homes, a pioneering venture in the area of social work, cosponsored by Baptist churches or associations, sprang up in San Antonio, Tyler, Vernon, Brownsville, and Kerrville. The decade of the 1970s brought greater responsibility to Buckner when, during the spring of 1975, an entire Vietnamese orphanage fled from the Communists to take up residence at the Buckner Home in Dallas. Two Austin nursing homes, Villa Siesta and Monte Siesta, were added in 1970, as well as the Beaumont Children's Home, which moved to a new campus in 1979. In time, the maternity homes in San Antonio and Dallas were replaced by homes for children and seniors, respectively. Treatment centers for the emotionally disturbed, drug rehabilitation facilities, day-care programs, emergency shelters, and abandoned and abused women's and children's programs were developed.

Buckner celebrated its centennial year in 1979 with extensive planning for future service. The 1980s and 1990s were decades of fine-tuning existing programs as well as addressing the needs of growing numbers of homeless mothers with a new program of residential care and vocational-educational guidance. As of 1992, Buckner provided more than forty programs in seventeen Texas cities: residential and foster care, emergency shelters, juvenile centers and rehabilitation programs, adoption services for children of all ages, therapeutic centers for emotionally disturbed and abused children, substance-addiction treatment centers, a Christian camp, maternity care, and a homeless mothers' and children's program. Senior citizens receive care in residential facilities, hospitals, retirement villages, and Alzheimer's and related illness centers. In 1992, with total net assets reaching $97,659,000, Buckner cared for 3,518 children and adolescents and 1,021 seniors.

BIBLIOGRAPHY: Archives, Buckner Baptist Benevolences, Dallas. James Milton Carroll, *A History of Texas Baptists* (Dallas: Baptist Standard, 1923). J. B. Cranfill and J. L. Walker, *R. C. Buckner's Life of Faith and Works* (Dallas: Buckner Orphans Home, 1915; 2d ed. 1916).

Karen O'Dell Bullock

BUCKNER BAPTIST CHILDREN'S HOME. Robert Cooke Buckner,[qv] a Baptist pastor from Tennessee, provided the motivation and leadership that resulted in the establishment of Buckner Orphans Home in 1879. He promoted the home through his newspaper, the *Texas Baptist.* At his encouragement, the Baptist Deacons' Convention passed a resolution at its annual meeting in Paris, Texas, in 1877 to start an orphan's home as soon as $2,000 had been raised. Buckner was named fund-raising agent. Two days later he initiated the first fund-raising effort during a Baptist Sunday school convention, also in Paris. Passing a hat among his fellow brethren under an oak tree, he collected the first twenty-seven dollars. Buckner wrote the charter and filed it with the state of Texas on April 9, 1879. The home was opened in a rented house in Dallas the following December with three children. In September 1880 Buckner purchased the permanent site, a forty-four-acre tract in east Dallas, priced at seventeen dollars an acre. Members of the board knelt in a log cabin on the property two days later and dedicated the home. Six children were moved to a new residence on the site in 1881. The home still operated at this location in 1989. By the turn of the century the home cared for almost 500 children. In 1914 Buckner asked the Baptist General Convention of Texas to take over operation in order to assure its future. He died on April 9, 1919, still serving as general manager. When leadership was passed to his two sons, there were around 600 children in the home. The two new leaders launched one of the largest building campaigns in Buckner's history to modernize and update the campus. In the next twenty years a completely new campus emerged—including twenty fire-proof buildings and paved streets. The home's junior and senior high schools were upgraded and accredited in the 1920s. Forty years later the children began attending public schools in the community.

In 1948 Buckner began enlarging its boundaries and services. Its first expansion was to San Antonio, where it took over the operation of a home for unwed mothers. Three years later it opened Buckner Boys Ranch in the Hill Country.[qv] In 1953 it opened its first retirement home in Dallas, followed two years later by a second home in Houston. A home for girls was established in Lubbock the following year.

In 1961 Buckner Orphans Home was rechartered as Buckner Baptist Benevolences,[qv] a name more appropriate for its expanding services, and the home was renamed Buckner Baptist Children's Home. The home periodically alters its services to meet the critical needs of the day. In addition to basic care, it has added an emergency shelter, an educational and vocational training program for male juvenile delinquents, probated through the court system, and a residential substance-abuse aftercare program for males up to age eighteen. In 1989 the Children's Home annually cared for more than 600 children, and helped another 380 children through programs of foster care and mother's aid. Its budget was $4.2 million. Buckner Children's Home is located on South Buckner Boulevard in Dallas. Operation of the home is directed through a twenty-seven-member board of trustees elected annually by the Baptist General Convention of Texas. In 1995 the home cared for an average of 160 children throughout the year.

BIBLIOGRAPHY: James Milton Carroll, *A History of Texas Baptists* (Dallas: Baptist Standard, 1923). J. B. Cranfill and J. L. Walker, *R. C. Buckner's Life of Faith and Works* (Dallas: Buckner Orphans Home, 1915; 2d ed. 1916). B. F. Fuller, *History of Texas Baptists* (Louisville, Kentucky: Baptist Book Concern, 1900).

Betty Ensminger Patterson

BUCKNERS CREEK. Buckners Creek rises four miles southeast of Rosanky in southeastern Bastrop County (at 29°54′ N, 97°14′ W) and winds gradually southeast, then northeast, for a total of about thirty-three miles before reaching its mouth on the Colorado River, just south of La Grange in Fayette County (at 29°54′ N, 96°53′ W). It crosses loamy uplands in Bastrop and Fayette counties before entering clayey soil near its mouth. Post oak woods grow in the area. The stream is named for early settler Aylett C. Buckner,[qv] who arrived in the La Grange area in 1819.

BUCKS BAYOU. Bucks Bayou rises in the Bay Prairie two miles north of Bay City in northeastern Matagorda County (at 29°02′ N, 95°57′ W) and runs southeast for twelve miles to its mouth on Peyton Creek, three miles east of State Highway 60 (at 28°54′ N, 95°54′ W). The stream is intermittent in its upper reaches and is banked by levees east of Bay City. It traverses rolling to flat, flood-prone terrain with sandy and clay loam topsoils that support water-tolerant hardwoods and grasses.

BUCKS BAYOU, TEXAS. Bucks (Buck) Bayou was on Bucks Bayou Creek and an unpaved road three miles southeast of Bay City in east central Matagorda County. By 1898, with the aid of local resident Henry Tobeck, this German settlement had completed a new schoolhouse, and the next year plans were being made to organize a Sunday school in the new school. In 1904 the Bucks Bayou school enrolled twenty-one students, and around 1909 it became part of the Sexton common school district. During the 1920s Lutheran services were conducted monthly in Louis and Karolina Arnold's house. Possibly also during the 1920s a church for black residents of the area was built on the banks of a nearby creek. By the mid-1930s the community comprised two schoolhouses and a cluster of farms by the road. A schoolhouse had been torn down by the late 1930s, and the community was no longer shown on a 1952 map. In the 1980s the area where Bucks Bayou once stood remained rich farmland, where cattle grazed and rice, grass, milo, and cotton were grown. At that time the townsite was marked by the old cemetery.

BIBLIOGRAPHY: Matagorda County Historical Commission, *Historic Matagorda County* (3 vols., Houston: Armstrong, 1986).

Rachel Jenkins

BUCKSNORT, TEXAS. Bucksnort, originally Jarrett Menefee's Supply Station, was located on a 320-acre prairie owned by Thomas J. Chambers[qv] in what is now east central Falls County. The settlement, about five miles northeast of the falls on the Brazos River below the rebuilt Fort Milam, which provided protection for the settlers, was bounded on the west by a bayou that flowed into Musselrun Creek and on to the Brazos River. When John and Mary Menefee Marlin and James and Nancy Taylor Marlin returned with their families to their land near the Falls of the Brazos in 1837 after the Runaway Scrape,[qv] they found some of their Menefee relatives at the Angelina River. The families of the brothers Laban and Jarrett Menefee accompanied the Marlins and others to the east side of the river, where they formed a little settlement, later called Bucksnort. John Marlin's fort-like home lay three miles south and Dr. Allensworth Adams's home a mile directly north. Supplies were freighted from lower settlements, and the community grew until it had enough children to form a school.

The name Bucksnort, said to have been suggested by an inebriated customer of the saloon, was first recorded in 1844 by William Howe of Ellis County: "Bucksnort is the only supply station between Nashville and Dallas where a man can go to buy food and supplies." When Robertson County was organized in 1838, elections ordered by the county court were held at or near Jarrett Menefee's place. In January 1842 Menefee was one of three men appointed by the Robertson County Commissioners Court to consider a road from Franklin to a place near the falls, or to Menefee's place, and in October of that year five men were ordered to study the route and lay out the road. In 1843 Capt. J. B. Smith recruited a company of eighty men from the surrounding country who eventually joined John Coffee Hays's[qv] Texas Rangers[qv] and served in the Mexican War.[qv]

Movement to the area was steady in the 1840s, and the settlement grew until it had a school, a general store, a blacksmith shop, a saloon, a racetrack with a stable, and a stagecoach stop that served as a post office. On February 8, 1845, Jarrett Menefee purchased the 320-acre tract he had improved as overseer for Chambers. When Menefee died sometime before 1849, his heirs sold the property to J. E. Francks, who in turn sold it to three prominent brothers, David G., John, and James B. Barton. The three men operated the Barton Ranch on the property until their deaths. In 1846, when Limestone County was marked off from Robertson County, Bucksnort became part of Precinct 2 of Limestone County. Four years later, the site became part of Falls County. The name of the settlement was first officially recognized when the Robertson County Commissioners Court ordered an election to be held at the usual place in Bucksnort at the time of annexation[qv] to the United States. Bucksnort residents, however, had already begun to scatter to other communities as the area became safer, and more settlers left as new lands were made available. The community became extinct by about 1852.

BIBLIOGRAPHY: Dallas *Morning News*, March 21, 1971. James T. DeShields, *Border Wars of Texas*, ed. Matt Bradley (Tioga, Texas, 1912; rpt., Waco: Texian Press, 1976). *A Memorial and Biographical History of McLennan, Falls, Bell, and Coryell Counties* (Chicago: Lewis, 1893; rpt., St. Louis: Ingmire, 1984). Mildred Cariker Pinkston, *People, Places, Happenings: Shelby County* (Center, Texas: Pinkston, 1985). Lillian S. St. Romain, *Western Falls County, Texas* (Austin: Texas State Historical Association, 1951).

Marian Garrett Gibbs

BUDA, TEXAS. Buda, on Interstate Highway 35 seventeen miles south of downtown Austin in eastern Hays County, was formally established on April 1, 1881, when Cornelia Trimble donated land for a townsite at an International–Great Northern Railroad depot there. The area, originally a part of the Mexican land grant to Stephen B. von Eggleston, had been settled as early as 1846 by Phillip J. Allen. The first community center in this part of the county, Mountain City, developed before the Civil War,[qv] but it was rapidly depopulated as its residents and businesses flocked to the new rail depot, which took the name of Du Pre. Folklore has it that this name originated in 1880, when, as the railroad pushed into Hays County, the postmaster at Mountain City approached a railroad official and requested, "Do, pray, give us a depot." In 1887, at the request of the post office department, the name was changed to Buda. The common explanation for the new name is that it derives from Spanish viuda, "widow." The town had gained a reputation as a popular eating stop for rail travelers, and the name may refer to a pair of widows who cooked at the Carrington Hotel in the 1880s. The provision of supplies and services to surrounding dairy farms and ranches was the basis of the local economy, and at different times the community supported mills, hotels, banks, a lumberyard, two newspapers, a cheese factory, a movie theater, and a skating rink. In 1928 local businesses organized a chamber of commerce. Buda remained an active commercial center and railroad depot until the Great Depression.[qv] In 1929 its population was estimated at 600, but by 1933 it fell to 300. Only in the mid-1980s, as the growth of Austin began to be felt in Buda, did its population once again approach predepression levels. The town was incorporated in 1948, and in 1967 Buda, Kyle, and Wimberley formed the Hays Consolidated Independent School District (only Buda and Kyle remained in the district after 1986). By the mid-1980s Buda had attracted a cement plant and some craft industry, but the community was still primarily rural and residential. Its population in 1990 was 1,795.

BIBLIOGRAPHY: Mary Starr Barkley, *A History of Central Texas* (Austin: Austin Printing, 1970). Dudley Richard Dobie, *A Brief History of Hays County and San Marcos, Texas* (San Marcos, 1948). Vertical Files, Barker Texas History Center, University of Texas at Austin.

Daniel P. Greene

BUDCONNOR, TEXAS. Budconnor, on the Beaumont, Sour Lake and Western Railway in extreme southwestern Hardin County, was named for one of the railroad's claim agents. The community was established as a logging camp by the Kirby Lumber Company (*see* KIRBY, JOHN HENRY) shortly after the railroad built its extension from Grayburg to Houston in 1908. A local post office opened in 1910. The Kirby operations, which included logging for the Thompson and Ford

Lumber Company, continued until 1918, when the camp was abandoned. The community's post office was discontinued the next year.
Robert Wooster

BUDDHISM. Buddhist organizations arose in Texas in the second half of the twentieth century as a result of missionary activity and immigration. Nichiren Shoshu of America, with national headquarters in Santa Monica, California, is the largest and oldest of the organizations represented in Texas that owes its expansion primarily to missionary activity. Though not denying an afterlife, Nichiren Shoshu emphasizes the promotion of world peace, prosperity, and happiness in this life, a pursuit closely related to the Lotus Sutra, a Buddhist scripture widely revered in the Far East. Nichiren Shoshu originated in Japan and gained a number of converts among American servicemen stationed there following World War II.[qv] The national headquarters for this branch of Buddhism in America was established in 1963 by Masayasa Sadanaga, who later changed his name to George M. Williams in order to emphasize the American nature of the organization in this country. Largely due to seminars conducted by Williams, Nichiren groups started to appear in Texas during the early 1960s. As of 1985 Nichiren Shoshu claimed approximately 15,000 members in Texas, the majority of whom are native to the United States.

A number of publications are produced by the organization, two of the most important throughout the United States being *World Tribune* and *Seikyo Times*. The organization's major center in Texas is in Dallas; chapters also operate in Houston and El Paso. On the local level, activities for members and inquirers center around daily home meetings under the direction of experienced lay leaders. Members are also encouraged to attend national conventions and, when possible, to make a pilgrimage to the organization's major temple at the foot of Mount Fuji in Japan.

The introduction of Tibetan forms of Buddhism to Texas during the 1970s was partly an outgrowth of the Chinese occupation of Tibet in 1950. A center for meditation and study in Boulder, Colorado, founded by a Tibetan refugee, is the home of the Vajradhatu (Realm of the Indestructible), the parent organization of many subgroups throughout the United States. Larger and more established local Vajradhatu centers are called Dharmadhatus, while newer groups are referred to as Dharma Study Groups. Dharmadhatu, founded in 1974, is located in Austin, and Dharma Study Groups meet in Houston, Dallas, and San Antonio. As of 1985 the number of members claimed by Vajradhatu in Texas was about seventy, the majority United States natives. In addition to meditation sessions for members and inquirers, the Dharmadhatu provides cultural programs (art, dance, poetry), weekend seminars, and special lectures presented by visiting scholars who represent Tibetan and non-Tibetan Buddhist traditions. In the smaller Dharma Study Groups, advanced students provide guidance in meditation and study in weekly home meetings.

In an attempt to promote the serious study and practice of Zen Buddhism, two informal meditation groups were formed in the Dallas–Fort Worth area in the summer of 1983; the groups later merged to form the Dallas–Fort Worth Zen Center. In April of 1985, the first sesshin (period of intensive meditation) was held at the center, the practice of Zen by this time being enhanced by the presence of Roshi (Zen Master) Sasaki. By the summer of 1985 the center was holding meditation sessions three times a week and claimed about thirty-six active members, all of whom were native to the United States.

Immigrants to the United States have laid the foundation in Texas for Buddhist organizations that minister primarily to specific ethnic groups under the leadership of monks. In the late 1980s the Khuon-Viet Buddhist Monastery of America at Grand Prairie and the Vietnamese Buddhist Pagoda Phat-Quang at Houston together had more than 800 members, mostly Vietnamese immigrants. Zen meditation as well as devotion to Quan The Am (a Bodhisattva or Savior figure) play an important part in these two communities, which have arisen primarily to meet the needs of refugees who made their way from Vietnam to the United States in the 1970s. Korean immigrants established the Won Buddhist Church of Houston in 1978, and by 1985 the congregation claimed fifty members. The Won Church has its national headquarters in Los Angeles, California. The Texas Buddhist Association, established in 1979 with headquarters in Houston and a branch in Dallas, consists of members from Taiwan, Hong Kong, Vietnam, Singapore, the Philippines, and the United States.

All of these groups represent various aspects of Mahayana, the dominant form of Buddhism among the Chinese, Japanese, Tibetans, Mongolians, Koreans, and Vietnamese. Theravada (or Hinayana), the dominant form of Buddhism in Thailand, Burma, Sri Lanka, Laos, and Kampuchea, has also established a foothold in the Lone Star State with the founding of the Texas Cambodian Buddhist Society at Houston in 1982. The Houston congregation, which claimed 206 members in 1985, is a branch of the Cambodian Buddhist Society, with national headquarters in Washington, D.C.

BIBLIOGRAPHY: Emma McCloy Layman, *Buddhism in America* (Chicago: Nelson-Hall, 1976). Charles S. Prebish, *American Buddhism* (North Scituate, Massachusetts: Duxbury, 1979).
James Breckenridge

BUENA CREEK. Buena Creek rises four miles south of U.S. Highway 90 in southern Terrell County (at 29°57′ N, 102°03′ W) and runs southeast for five miles to its mouth on Indian Creek, a half mile above the junction of Deer and Indian creeks (at 29°52′ N, 102°00′ W). It crosses rolling prairies overlying chalk deposits and variable terrain overlying limestone and limy mud. The area's topsoils are generally dark, calcareous stony clays and clay loams in which oaks, junipers, and grasses grow.

BUENA VISTA, TEXAS (Bexar County). Buena Vista is on Farm Road 1947 and Blue Wing Road eleven miles southeast of downtown San Antonio in southeastern Bexar County. It was settled around 1900. In the mid-1930s Buena Vista had a school, a store, and a number of houses. The school had five teachers for grades one through eight until the early 1950s, when it was consolidated with the Southside Independent School District. *Christopher Long*

BUENA VISTA, TEXAS (Ellis County). Buena Vista was on Farm Road 1446 six miles west of Waxahachie in western Ellis County. Its name, Spanish for "good view," derives from its hilltop location. By 1894 it had a school with eighty-six pupils. From 1915 to 1945 its school offered grades one through nine. In 1947 Buena Vista had a population of eighty, a church, and a school. The Buena Vista school was consolidated with the Waxahachie Independent School District in 1951. The town was no longer shown on county highway maps by the 1970s. *Lisa C. Maxwell*

BUENA VISTA, TEXAS (Pecos County). Buena Vista was near Farm Road 11 six miles southeast of Imperial in northern Pecos County. The settlement was originally called Fruitdale. In 1909 land promoters advertised town lots there and promised easy access to markets upon the arrival of the Kansas City, Mexico and Orient Railway, then under construction. That same year the Orient Hotel was built at the community. A Buena Vista post office was established in 1910. In 1913, however, the railroad bypassed the town on a more direct route from Girvin to Fort Stockton. Buena Vista had a bank, a school, and a church in 1917. Its estimated population in 1925 was fifty. Farming declined in the area because of irrigation problems, and by the 1950s Buena Vista was abandoned.

BIBLIOGRAPHY: Pecos County Historical Commission, *Pecos County History* (2 vols., Canyon, Texas: Staked Plains, 1984).
Glenn Justice

BUENA VISTA, TEXAS (Shelby County). Buena Vista is near the junction of Farm roads 1645 and 2026, twelve miles northwest of

Center in northwestern Shelby County. The community was originally called Bucksnort when it began to form in the early 1830s; it was renamed Buena Vista when it received a post office in 1848. Local accounts suggest that the town was either named for the beautiful local scenery or in honor of the battle of Buena Vista, Gen. Zachary Taylor's[qv] victory in the Mexican War.[qv] The townsite was on the John Richards land grant and was donated by a relative of Richards, known locally as "Granny" Richards. There were some beautiful oak trees on the property, and one of the provisions of the deed was that these trees were never to be cut. In 1884 the town comprised a population estimated at 300 and a gin, a gristmill, a school, and two churches. The next year the Houston, East and West Texas Railway bypassed Buena Vista after the town refused to donate $85,000 to the railroad to have the track's route altered. The town subsequently began to decline, as Timpson to the northeast began to grow. In 1988 Buena Vista consisted of a church and a few widely scattered houses.

BIBLIOGRAPHY: Center *Champion*, August 7, 1952. Charles E. Tatum, *Shelby County: In the East Texas Hills* (Austin: Eakin, 1984).

Cecil Harper, Jr.

BUESCHER, TEXAS. Buescher was on the Galveston, Harrisburg and San Antonio Railway from Alleyton to Smith Point, four miles north of Columbus in Colorado County. The area surrounding Buescher included lands originally granted to James Cummins and James Tumlinson,[qqv] members of Stephen F. Austin's[qv] first colony. Beginning before the Civil War[qv] and continuing throughout the remainder of the 1800s, immigrants from Germany moved into the area, and many of the original large land grants were subdivided into smaller farms. During the 1880s a community grew around a store and saloon operated by Henry Buescher at a junction on the Galveston, Harrisburg and San Antonio line. By 1899 the close-knit community had seven businesses, a popular dance hall, and the sobriquet Ax Handle Junction because of Mr. Buescher's propensity to keep the peace with an ax handle. Children in the area attended several successive schools, the last of which, Pin Oak School, was consolidated with the Columbus schools in 1924. When the railroad bridge over the Colorado River was destroyed by a flood and the line rerouted to the west, most of the Buescher businesses either moved or closed. Later, complete abandonment of the railroad line hastened the demise of the town. During the 1950s, cotton, from the beginning the area's staple crop, was also phased out, and most of the land reverted to pasture. By the 1980s the community was gone.

BIBLIOGRAPHY: *Colorado County Sesquicentennial Commemorative Book* (La Grange, Texas: Hengst Printing, 1986). *Jeff Carroll*

BUESCHER STATE PARK. Buescher State Park is on Farm Road 153 and Park Road 1, three miles north of Smithville in eastern Bastrop County. The state acquired the park's original 1,730 acres in the mid-1930s from the city of Smithville and from private owners. The park featured part of the Lost Pine Forest[qv] and offered excellent opportunities for camping, fishing, picnicking, hiking, and bird-watching. The scenic park road that connected the Buescher and Bastrop state parks was popular among motorists and cyclists. Buescher State Park was reduced in size to 1,013 acres in the early 1970s, when part of its property was transferred to the University of Texas M. D. Anderson Cancer Center[qv] for use as an environmental science park. About 250,000 people visited Buescher State Park in 1990.

BIBLIOGRAPHY: Ross A. Maxwell, *Geologic and Historic Guide to the State Parks of Texas* (Bureau of Economic Geology, University of Texas at Austin, 1970). A. Gayland Moore, "Woodland Parks," *Texas Parks and Wildlife*, March 1989. *Vivian Elizabeth Smyrl*

BUESING, TEXAS. Buesing was a German community at the junction of Farm roads 952 and 2656, seven miles west of Yorktown in western DeWitt County. The community center was the Buesing School, organized in 1914 and named for Henry Buesing, who donated the land. A store was built near the school in 1931 and was still shown on the 1965 county highway map. The Buesing school operated until 1950. In the 1980s the locale was called Cotton Patch.

BIBLIOGRAPHY: Nellie Murphree, *A History of DeWitt County* (Victoria, Texas, 1962). *Craig H. Roell*

BUFFALO. The first reports of the animals popularly called buffalo (a genus of American bison) in Texas were written by Álvar Núñez Cabeza de Vaca[qv] in his description of his journey from Florida to Mexico (1528–36). The buffalo occupied about a third of the North American continent, from latitude 63° north in Canada to about latitude 25° north in Mexico, and from the Blue Mountains of Oregon to the western parts of New York, Pennsylvania, Virginia, and the Carolinas. Authorities disagree about their range in Texas because of the migratory nature of the animals and the shifting of the herd during the period of buffalo hunting[qv] by white men, but it is generally agreed that they roamed the western and central plains of Texas in great numbers. The four main herds in Texas migrated from northern Montana and entered Texas between the 99th and 101st meridians on established trails. The main buffalo trails in Texas were east of the Trans-Pecos and Llano Estacado[qqv] and west of the Western Cross Timbers. At the height of the buffalo population in Texas these trails could be several miles wide. The buffalo usually did not range farther than the Concho River valley, but during certain seasons they migrated as far east and south as the Gulf Coastal Plains.

What was known as the "great slaughter" took place in the early 1870s, and by 1878 the so-called southern herd was practically exterminated. There have been several attempts to protect the buffalo. In 1875 the Texas legislature considered a measure to protect the animals from wholesale slaughter, but Gen. Philip H. Sheridan[qv] protested the bill, contending that peace with the Indians could be maintained only if their food supply was eliminated; the bill failed to pass. Preservation of a few animals was due to the efforts of such men as Charles Goodnight[qv] and Charles J. (Buffalo) Jones, who preserved small herds on their ranches. In 1949 buffalo were found in several city zoos in Texas and on a few ranches in Armstrong and Nolan counties. In the late twentieth century various ranches throughout Texas continued to maintain buffalo herds; the animal had rebounded from near-extinction from the Midwest to the Southwest and West.

BIBLIOGRAPHY: John R. Cook, *The Border and the Buffalo: An Untold Story of the Southwest Plains* (Topeka, Kansas: Crane, 1907; rpt., New York: Citadel Press, 1967). James M. Day, "A Preliminary Guide to the Study of Buffalo Trails in Texas," West Texas Historical Association *Year Book* 36 (1960). *Dictionary of American History*, Vol. 1 (New York: Scribner, 1940). Martin S. Garretson, *The American Bison* (New York: New York Zoological Society, 1938). C. C. Rister, "The Significance of the Destruction of the Buffalo in the Southwest," *Southwestern Historical Quarterly* 33 (July 1929).

BUFFALO, TEXAS (Henderson County). Buffalo, the first county seat of Henderson County, was built on a high bluff on the Trinity River. During the Republic of Texas[qv] era, a group of hunters killed buffalo[qv] in what is now Navarro County and dragged and rafted them down to the site of Buffalo. John P. Moore was operating a ferry there by 1846. That year the legislature established Henderson County from the Nacogdoches district. That area became Henderson, Kaufman, Van Zandt, Rockwall, Wood, and most of Rains counties. In 1847 Henry Jeffries donated 188 acres of land for the town of Buffalo and paid John H. Reagan[qv] to survey the townsite. A store, the county clerk's office, and several homes were built by men lured there by prospects of a port thriving on river traffic. But in 1848 the legislature reduced the size of the county and ordered a survey to determine the new center. That proved to be several miles east of Buffalo between

North and South Twin creeks, and the new site was named Centerville. Voters chose it as the new county seat, but reduction of the county to its present size in 1850 and relocation of the county seat to Athens, near a new geographical center, caused both Buffalo and Centerville to wither and die.

BIBLIOGRAPHY: J. J. Faulk, *History of Henderson County* (Athens, Texas: Athens Review Printing, 1926). *Theo S. Daniel III*

BUFFALO, TEXAS (Leon County). Buffalo is on the Missouri Pacific tracks at the intersection of U.S. highways 79 and 75 and Interstate Highway 45, fourteen miles north of Centerville in northern Leon County. It was established in 1872 on the International–Great Northern Railroad and named for the herds of buffalo[qv] that had roamed the area. The last link of the railroad was completed four miles from the town in April or May 1872. Before the railroad arrived Buffalo residents had shipped cotton by river and driven livestock to market. The Buffalo post office was established in 1876. The community's first school was a two-story structure that later served as the community center—named the "Opera House"—and subsequently until the late 1940s as a hotel. Between 1890 and 1892 Buffalo's reported population grew from 200 to 500; during the 1890s the town had a general store, saloons, cotton gins, a milliner, druggists, a constable, the county commissioner, the notary, and churches established by the Baptists, the Methodists, and the Presbyterians. In 1913 the town was incorporated and had an area of four square miles. Buffalo lost its charter in 1917, but was later reincorporated. It reported a population of 650 in 1929, 470 in 1931, 850 in 1939, and 737 in 1941 and 1950. In 1927 the Concord Common School District consolidated with the Buffalo school district. Seven other districts were consolidated with Buffalo between 1929 and 1970. In 1938 the Buffalo schools had a combined enrollment of 510 students, 342 white and 168 black. Railroad passenger service to the community was discontinued in 1970. In the 1990s Buffalo had an annual watermelon festival and a regular Labor Day–weekend festival known as the Buffalo Stampede. In 1990 Buffalo reported a population of 1,555.

BIBLIOGRAPHY: Leon County Historical Book Survey Committee, *History of Leon County* (Dallas: Curtis Media, 1986).
Maria Elena Kruger

BUFFALO BAYOU. Buffalo Bayou rises at the juncture of Willow Fork and Cane Branch west of Katy near the Waller county line in extreme northern Fort Bend County (at 29°46′ N, 95°50′ W) and flows sixty-five miles east, across southern Harris County, to its mouth on the San Jacinto River, at Lynchburg (at 29°46′ N, 95°05′ W). The stream is tidal from its junction with Whiteoak Bayou at Houston, eighteen miles above its mouth, and has been widened and deepened to form the Turning Basin and the Houston Ship Channel.[qv] Barker Dam, owned by the city of Barker and constructed by the United States Army Corps of Engineers in 1945, impounds Buffalo Bayou to form Barker Reservoir near Addicks. The lake serves primarily as a means of flood control and has a capacity of 135,800 acre-feet. In the 1990s Buffalo Bayou was extremely polluted. It flows from flat terrain with local shallow depressions surfaced by clay loam and sandy loam that support water-tolerant hardwoods, conifers, and grasses into the Houston metropolitan area and the industrial sector surrounding the Houston Ship Channel.

BIBLIOGRAPHY: *An Analysis of Texas Waterways* (Austin: Texas Parks and Wildlife Department, 1974).

BUFFALO BAYOU, BRAZOS AND COLORADO RAILWAY. The construction of the Buffalo Bayou, Brazos and Colorado Railway marked the beginning of the railroad age in Texas. It was the first railroad to begin operating in the state, the first component of the present Southern Pacific to open for service, and the second railroad west of the Mississippi River. In addition, the Houston Tap was built under provisions of the BBB&C charter.

On February 11, 1850, a group that included Gen. Sidney Sherman[qv] received a charter for the BBB&C. Construction began from Buffalo Bayou at Harrisburg in 1851; the first locomotive, which was named for Sherman, arrived in late 1852; and the first twenty miles of track, from Harrisburg to Stafford's Point, opened in August 1853. By January 1, 1856, the BBB&C or Harrisburg Railroad, as it was commonly called, had been extended an additional 12½ miles to East Richmond on the bank of the Brazos River across from Richmond. Construction resumed in 1858, and in late 1860 the tracks extended eighty miles to Alleyton, near the east bank of the Colorado River opposite Columbus. Due to the debilitating effect of the Civil War[qv] and its aftermath on the BBB&C, the company built no new mileage after 1860. However, it extended its service to Columbus in 1867 over the Columbus Tap track. The CT was chartered in 1860 to connect Columbus with the BBB&C and in November 1867 completed its three-mile line and a permanent bridge over the Colorado River.

By 1868 the BBB&C was in financial difficulties and unable to pay a series of judgments rendered against the company. On July 7, 1868, the sheriff of Harris County sold the railroad to Col. William Sledge for $13,000. Sledge retained a 25 percent interest in the line and sold the balance to a group that included Thomas W. Peirce.[qv] The new owners rehabilitated the BBB&C, replacing many crossties and acquiring the first new locomotives and cars since before the war.

To cross the Brazos the railroad first used a ferry and inclined planes on each side of the river. This system was replaced in October 1858 by a low-water crossing. Trains had to cross at a high rate of speed in order to gain the momentum necessary to overcome the steep grade on the opposite side. This bridge presented numerous problems to the BBB&C and prevented efficient operation of the railroad, as it was out of service for extended periods of time when freshets hit the river. In April 1867 a separate company, the Brazos Iron Bridge Association, was organized to finance and build a permanent bridge across the Brazos River; the job was completed on July 8, 1869.

On January 24, 1870, the company was sold for $25,000 under provisions of the 1860 mortgage on the property. A new company with the same name was organized with Peirce as president. In July the charter was amended, the Columbus Tap and the Brazos Iron Bridge Association merged into the BBB&C, and the name of the road changed to Galveston, Harrisburg, and San Antonio Railway.

Although Harrisburg did not develop into the major city on Buffalo Bayou as a result of the construction of the BBB&C, the railroad otherwise fulfilled the expectations of its early backers. The first railroad in Texas, now a part of Southern Pacific's transcontinental Sunset Route between New Orleans and Los Angeles, handles heavy freight traffic as well as Amtrak's Sunset Limited west of Houston.

BUFFALO CAMP BAYOU. Buffalo Camp Bayou, formerly known as Buffalo Creek, rises six miles southwest of Angleton in south central Brazoria County (at 29°04′ N, 95°31′ W) and flows five miles southeast to its mouth on the Brazos River (at 29°02′ N, 95°29′ W). In 1954 Dow Chemical Company impounded sources of the creek for industrial use. The stream traverses flat terrain with local shallow depressions, surfaced by clay and sandy loam that supports water-tolerant hardwoods, conifers, and grasses.

BUFFALO CREEK (Blanco County). Buffalo Creek rises a half mile north of Buffalo Peak in north central Blanco County (at 30°23′ N, 98°25′ W) and runs southwest for 5½ miles to its mouth on the Pedernales River, 3½ miles from Johnson City (at 30°19′ N, 98°27′ W). The stream traverses an area of eroded limestone hills and the southeasternmost outcroppings of Paleozoic rock of the Llano Uplift. Local vegetation comprises live oak, post oak, cedar, and wild grasses; scattered areas have been made barren by timber eradication and overgrazing.

——— (Freestone County). Buffalo Creek rises two miles south of Donie in the southwestern corner of Freestone County (at 31°27′ N, 96°13′ W) and runs southeast for thirty-six miles to its mouth on Upper Keechi Creek, four miles south of Lake Leon in Leon County (at 31°26′ N, 95°49′ W). It crosses flat lands with local shallow depressions, surfaced by sandy and clay loams that support hardwoods, conifers, and grasses. The area is used primarily for dryland farming.

——— (Johnson County). Buffalo Creek, in central Johnson County, is formed by East and West Buffalo creeks. East Buffalo Creek rises five miles northwest of Keene in north central Johnson County (at 32°27′ N, 90°22′ W) and runs southwest for ten miles to Cleburne, where it joins West Buffalo Creek (at 32°20′ N, 97°23′ W). West Buffalo Creek rises two miles west of Joshua (at 32°28′ N, 97°25′ W). The consolidated stream runs southwest for five miles to its mouth on the Nolan River, 5½ miles south of Cleburne in southwestern Johnson County (at 32°16′ N, 97°24′ W). Buffalo Creek crosses low-rolling to flat terrain with sandy and clay loam and dark calcareous clay topsoils that support scrub brush, cacti, mesquite, and grasses.

——— (Lipscomb County). Buffalo Creek rises twenty miles south of Booker in southwestern Lipscomb County (at 36°07′ N, 100°32′ W) and runs north for about six miles to its mouth on Wolf Creek, eleven miles west of Lipscomb (at 36°14′ N, 100°28′ W). The Jones and Plummer Trail[qv] followed the course of the stream to its mouth, near where the Barton brothers first settled in 1878, an area later included in the Cresswell and Seven K ranch[qqv] ranges. Buffalo Creek traverses terrain that varies from flat to rolling, with local escarpments. Native vegetation comprises mesquite brush and grasses in deep, fine sandy loam.

BIBLIOGRAPHY: *A History of Lipscomb County, Texas, 1876–1976* (Lipscomb, Texas: Lipscomb County Historical Survey Committee, 1976). Clinton Leon Paine, The History of Lipscomb County (M.A. thesis, West Texas State College, 1941).

——— (Mills County). Buffalo Creek rises near the Brown county line in southwestern Mills County (at 31°33′ N, 98°55′ W) and runs five miles south to its mouth on the Colorado River, the southern county line (at 31°26′ N, 98°54′ W). It crosses an area of rolling hills and steep slopes surfaced by shallow clays and locally stony sandy loams that support juniper, cacti, and sparse grasses.

——— (Rockwall County). Buffalo Creek rises three miles southeast of Rockwall in southwestern Rockwall County (at 32°55′ N, 96°25′ W) and runs southwest for thirty miles to its mouth on the East Fork of the Trinity River, three miles west of Forney (at 32°45′ N, 96°31′ W). The stream traverses flat to rolling land surfaced by dark, calcareous clays that support mesquite and cacti. For most of the county's history the Buffalo Creek area has been used as range and cropland.

——— (San Saba County). Buffalo Creek rises eight miles northwest of Cherokee in southern San Saba County (at 31°00′ N, 98°52′ W) and runs northeast for twenty miles to its mouth on Cherokee Creek (at 31°02′ N, 98°40′ W). The creek is intermittent in its upper reaches. It crosses an area of flat to gently rolling uplands with clayey and sandy loam soils in which grow live oak, Ashe juniper, mesquite, and grasses.

——— (Scurry County). Buffalo Creek, also known as Buffalo Draw, rises near the Atchison, Topeka and Santa Fe Railway fourteen miles southeast of Snyder in southeastern Scurry County (at 32°35′ N, 100°42′ W) and runs northeast for twenty miles to its mouth on the Clear Fork of the Brazos River, eleven miles west of Roby in west central Fisher County (at 32°46′ N, 100°34′ W). It crosses an area of moderately steep slopes with locally high relief, surfaced by shallow to moderately deep silt loams that support mesquite and grasses. Downstream, the terrain is flat and flood-prone; its surface of loose sand supports scrub brush and grasses.

——— (Tarrant County). Buffalo Creek rises four miles southeast of Haslet in north central Tarrant County (at 32°56′ N, 97°21′ W) and runs northeast for four miles to its mouth on Henrietta Creek, a mile south of the Denton county line (at 32°59′ N, 97°18′ W). It traverses variable terrain surfaced by shallow, stony, clay loams that support oak and juniper trees, chaparral, cacti, and grasses.

——— (Wichita County). Buffalo Creek, formerly called Buffalo Head Creek, rises in North and South forks three miles west of Iowa Park in northwest central Wichita County (at 33°58′ N, 98°44′ W). The South Fork rises near Electra (at 34°01′ N, 98°55′ W) and runs southeast for ten miles to join the North Fork. The North Fork rises three miles northeast of Electra (at 34°02′ N, 98°52′ W) and runs southeast for nine miles before joining the South Fork. In 1964 the North Fork was impounded by the construction of the North Fork of Buffalo Creek Reservoir just over a mile from its juncture with the South Fork (at 35°59′ N, 98°45′ W). The consolidated Buffalo Creek runs southeast for nine miles to its mouth on the Wichita River, two miles southeast of Iowa Park (at 33°55′ N, 98°39′ W). It crosses flat terrain with locally shallow depressions, surfaced by clay and sandy loams that support water-tolerant hardwoods, conifers, and grasses.

BUFFALO DRAW. Buffalo Draw begins a mile southeast of the junction of Farm roads 864 and 2597 in northeastern Sutton County (at 30°38′ N, 100°16′ W) and runs south for ten miles to its mouth on the North Llano River (at 30°32′ N, 100°20′ W). The draw traverses the gently rolling limestone terrain of the western Edwards Plateau, which is characterized by shallow and deep loamy soils occasionally broken by rock outcrops. Range grasses and scattered small stands of oak, juniper, and mesquite grow in the area.

BUFFALO GAP. Buffalo Gap is a break in the Callahan Divide[qv] just north of the community of Buffalo Gap in east central Taylor County (at 32°17′ N, 99°49′ W). It was named for the herds of buffalo[qv] that trampled a well-defined trail through the gap before the area was settled. The gap, with an elevation of 1,898 feet above sea level, is 400 feet below the nearby summits of the Callahan Divide.

BUFFALO GAP, TEXAS. Buffalo Gap, an incorporated community, is at the intersection of Farm roads 89 and 1235, thirteen miles southwest of Abilene in central Taylor County. It was founded in 1857 and has had a post office since 1878. The Callahan Divide,[qv] the topographic boundary between the Brazos and Colorado basins, crosses Buffalo Gap from east to west. Elm Creek passes through and once served as a watering hole for buffalo.[qv] The present Buffalo Gap highway (Farm Road 89) follows the old Center Line Trail, which was surveyed in 1874 and ran from Texarkana to El Paso. Another major road entered the county on the south side of the mountains and passed through Buffalo Gap in the direction of Fort Phantom Hill. The road forked at Buffalo Gap; one branch led southwest to Pecos County and the other to Tom Green County. Buffalo traveled through the area on the way to the high plains. The earliest history of Taylor County centers around this gap in the divide, where in the 1860s and 1870s buffalo hunters made winter camp and from there transported their kill to Fort Griffin and other convenient centers of trade.

As it was the only town in Taylor County, Governor Richard B. Hubbard,[qv] acting Texas secretary of state, approved the selection of Buffalo Gap as the temporary county seat of Taylor County, on April 30, 1874. On July 3, 1878, this action was formalized. Twenty days later the judge, sheriff, clerk, and commissioners met. The first general public election was held with eighty-seven voters. By 1800 Buffalo Gap had 1,200 people, a drugstore, a carriage and blacksmith shop, a big hotel, a jail, three or four grocery stores, and a saloon. Buffalo hunting was popular in 1875. The carcasses sold for five to fifteen dollars, and the bones were used to refine sugar (*see also* BONE BUSINESS). In 1895 the Santa Fe Railroad was built through town.

In 1883 the cornerstone of Buffalo Gap College was laid, and documents pertaining to the times were sealed within the rock. Later, vandals tore out the stone and removed the contents. This Presbyterian college, the first formal attempt at higher education in Taylor County, opened in June 1885. Buffalo Gap called itself the "Athens of the West." The Baptist church at Buffalo Gap is the oldest Baptist church in Taylor County. About 1885 Marshall G. Jenkins began a weekly paper, the Buffalo Gap *Live Oak*, and in the mid-1890s the Buffalo Gap *Messenger* was circulated.

When the Texas and Pacific Railway established headquarters in Abilene, a competition to be county seat began, and in 1883 Buffalo Gap lost the battle. By 1884 Buffalo Gap had decreased in population to 600. Presbyterian, Methodist Episcopal, Baptist, and First Christian churches were established in the community, which also had a newspaper, sixteen businesses, and a high school. In 1890 the population had dropped to 300 and the number of businesses to seven. In 1892 Buffalo Gap had a population of 400, eleven businesses, Presbyterian and Methodist churches, and Buffalo Gap College. The college declined, and its charter expired in 1902. In 1914 the town reported 500 residents, ten businesses, and a bank. Between 1925 and 1980 the population fluctuated between 250 and 400 and businesses between two and twelve. In the 1930s Buffalo Gap had five churches, a number of farms and dwellings scattered along the main roads, and a camp and small park. In 1990 it had 409 residents and six rated businesses.

The town has carved out an identity as an "old-time" cultural and commercial center. In the 1920s its Old Settlers Picnic was a well-attended annual event. The Ernie Wilson Museum of the Old West opened in 1959, as a result of the work of family of R. Lee Rode, who purchased the Old Buffalo Gap Jail and Courthouse and restored it with help from the community. The native limestone jail dates from 1879; the sandstone blocks were concave in the center and mortared together with cannonballs to keep prisoners from chiseling their way out. The jail is listed in the National Register of Historic Buildings. The museum is named for its first curator, who was also a lawyer and publisher of the Buffalo Gap *Messenger*. In the 1990s this museum was part of Buffalo Gap Historical Village.

BIBLIOGRAPHY: Abilene *Reporter-News*, April 27, 1954, March 14, 1961, October 29, 1978, March 15, April 24, 1981, April 18, 1982. Buffalo Gap *Messenger*, June 16, 1961. Sam L. Chalk, "Early Experience in the Abilene Country," West Texas Historical Association *Yearbook* 4 (1928). Tommie Clack, "Buffalo Gap College," West Texas Historical Association *Yearbook* 35 (1959). Marshall Jackson, "Organization of Taylor County," *Bulletin of Local Genealogy and History Published by the West Texas Genealogical Society* 6 (April 1964). Vertical Files, Barker Texas History Center, University of Texas at Austin (Buffalo Gap, Buffalo Gap College, Ernie Wilson Museum of the Old West). Juanita Daniel Zachry, *A History of Rural Taylor County* (Burnet, Texas: Nortex, 1980).

Susan J. Nix

BUFFALO GAP COLLEGE. Buffalo Gap College, in Buffalo Gap, was the first institution offering a formal education in Taylor County. Its origins can be traced to a cowboy and part-time student who began in 1878 to push for a public school in the town. The cornerstone of the building was laid in 1883. The school opened that year with a twenty-year charter as Buffalo Gap High School, with William H. White as principal. When Alpha Young and Rev. A. J. Haynes proposed elevating the school into a college, the board of directors agreed, and in the fall of 1885 the name Buffalo Gap College was adopted. White became the college's first president. Initially the General Assembly of the Presbyterian Church of West Texas controlled the school, but sponsorship soon shifted to the Buffalo Gap and San Saba presbyteries of the Cumberland Presbyterian Church. Trinity University was the only other Presbyterian institution of higher learning in Texas at the time. Classes at Buffalo Gap were held in a large red sandstone building with three recreation rooms and two smaller classrooms. A large auditorium was on the second floor. The school also had a chapel and a study hall. Tuition and board for the five-month term was $100. By December 1885, 106 students were enrolled. The school had at least eight presidents and reached an enrollment exceeding 300 students in 1897. It was often plagued with financial troubles, however. Enrollment for 1900–01 was 103. During the school year 1901–02 White returned to the presidency, but by December 1902 the presbytery had instructed the trustees to sell the property, as the school's charter was near expiration. By July 1906 the sale of the college was completed. Eventually the public schools used the building.

BIBLIOGRAPHY: Abilene *Reporter-News*, April 2, 1956. Tommie Clack, "Buffalo Gap College," West Texas Historical Association *Year Book* 35 (1959). Hamilton Wright, "Old Buffalo Gap College," *Frontier Times*, December 1944.

Louise Kelly

BUFFALO HUMP (?–1870). The English name Buffalo Hump is evidently a euphemism for an Indian name represented in written sources in various forms, among them *Pochanaquarhip* and *Ko-cho-naw quoip*. The name had a phallic significance not precisely recorded. There were more Buffalo Humps than one. The famous one was a celebrated war chief of the Penateka Comanches. He first became prominent after the Council House Fight[qv] in San Antonio in March 1840. Outraged at the incident, he carried out a revenge raid across southeastern Texas. In August 1840 he led nearly 400 warriors and an equal number of women and children in raids on Victoria and Linnville, from where he carried off both livestock and human captives (*see* LINNVILLE RAID OF 1840). Texas militiamen intercepted Buffalo Hump's party and administered it a stinging defeat in the battle of Plum Creek[qv] on August 12, but most of the Comanches and their leader escaped to their camps on the upper Colorado River.

After the Linnville raid and the fight at Plum Creek, Buffalo Hump continued to resist the attempts of Texas settlers upon his people's hunting grounds. In 1844 he met with Sam Houston[qv] and demanded that the white men remain east of the Edwards Plateau. Houston tacitly agreed to this proposal, and Texas Indian agents provided Buffalo Hump with gifts to demonstrate their good will. However, the Texas government was unable to stem the flood of settlers onto Comanche lands, and so the Indians resumed their raids. In response to these attacks, Texas Rangers[qv] struck at Penateka camps, but Buffalo Hump managed to hold his own for some time. Finally, in May 1846 he led the Comanche delegation at Council Springs that signed a treaty with the United States.

As war chief of the Penatekas, Buffalo Hump dealt peacefully with American officials throughout the late 1840s and 1850s. In 1849 he guided John S. Ford's[qv] expedition part of the way from San Antonio to El Paso, and in 1856 he led his people to the newly established Comanche reservation on the Brazos River. Threats from horse thieves and squatters, coupled with his band's unhappiness over their lack of freedom and food, forced Buffalo Hump to move his band off the reservation in 1858. While camped in the Wichita Mountains, the Penatekas were attacked by United States troops under the command of Maj. Earl Van Dorn.[qv] Unaware that Buffalo Hump's band had recently signed a treaty of peace with military authorities at Fort Arbuckle, Van Dorn and his men killed eighty Comanches.

In 1859 Buffalo Hump settled his remaining followers on the Kiowa-Comanche reservation near Fort Cobb in Indian Territory. There, in spite of his distress at the demise of the Comanches' traditional way of life, he asked for a house and farmland so that he could set an example for his people. He died in 1870.

BIBLIOGRAPHY: E. W. Henderson, "Buffalo Hump, a Comanche Diplomat," West Texas Historical Association *Yearbook* 35 (1959). John Holland Jenkins, *Recollections of Early Texas*, ed. John H. Jenkins III (Austin: University of Texas Press, 1958; rpt. 1973). Kenneth F. Neighbours, *Robert Simpson Neighbors and the Texas Frontier, 1836–1859* (Waco: Texian Press, 1975). Robert Simpson Neighbors Papers, Barker Texas History Center, University of Texas at Austin. Rupert N.

Richardson, *The Comanche Barrier to South Plains Settlement* (Glendale, California: Clark, 1933; rpt., Millwood, New York: Kraus, 1973). Dorman H. Winfrey and James M. Day, eds., *Texas Indian Papers* (4 vols., Austin: Texas State Library, 1959–61; rpt., 5 vols., Austin: Pemberton Press, 1966).
Jodye Lynn Dickson Schilz

BUFFALO HUNTING. The buffalo,[qv] known to Europeans and Americans since the days of Hernán Cortés and Francisco Vázquez de Coronado,[qv] lived in countless millions on the Great Plains of the United States until the late 1880s. They had been hunted by all who found them, especially by the Indians, to whom they satisfied many necessities of life. When the frontier of the United States extended to the Great Plains, among the obstacles to be overcome were the Indians and the buffalo—the former for well-known reasons and the latter because they existed in such tremendous numbers as to make farming and ranching impossible and also because they represented the commissary of the warlike Indians.

The immediate cause for the tremendous slaughter of buffalo in the 1870s and 1880s was the completion of the transcontinental railroad. When the Union Pacific was completed in 1869, it became possible to ship hides from the Great Plains to eastern markets for a profit. A second result was the division of the buffalo into two great herds, the northern and the southern. The southern herd was the larger and was exterminated first. The slaughter in the south began in earnest in 1874 and was over by 1878. In the north the great hunts began in 1880 and were over by 1884. The rapid destruction can be seen from these figures: in 1882, 200,000 hides were shipped out of the Dakota Territory; in 1883, 40,000; and the following year, only one carload. Even so, it was estimated that for every two hides shipped, three were lost. Except for a few herds protected on government property or maintained on private ranches, the buffalo were exterminated.

The number of hunters involved in the great hunts is not known, but an estimate for the northern range indicated that in 1882 there were at least 5,000 hunters and skinners at work. Only the strong and adventurous were attracted, most being frontiersmen from Kansas and other border states who were interested in recouping their fortunes. Occasionally an adventurous Englishman was found in the camps. It took a hardy man to brave the elements and the Indians and, most of all, to stand up under the back-breaking work involved in hunting and skinning. Hunting camps often numbered about four men. A group of that size, preparing for a three-month hunt, needed a considerable amount of specialized equipment and supplies, including two two-horse teams hitched to light wagons. One of the wagons hauled the provisions and camp outfit, which might consist of one medium and one large-sized Dutch oven, three large frying pans, two coffeepots, camp kettles, bread pans, a coffee mill, tin cups, plates, knives, forks, spoons, pothooks, a meat broiler, shovels, spades, axes, a mess box, and so forth. The other wagon hauled the bedding, ammunition, two extra guns, a grindstone, war sacks, and the like. For the three months' hunt, the amount of ammunition required was 250 pounds of lead in bars done up in twenty-five pound sacks, 4,000 primers, and three twenty-five-pound cans of powder. Of the four men, ordinarily two were hunters and two cooks and skinners. On a normal day's run, the hunters would locate the herd, single out a small group, and approach as near as possible from downwind. Once close to the group, the hunters formed a "stand" if possible, so that the buffalo were shot in such a way that the rest were not frightened away. The hunter shot at a slow rate so that his gunbarrel did not overheat and expand; he shot at the outside buffalo only, or at any that started to walk off; and he would try to drop each one with one good shot, as a wounded buffalo would soon cause the whole group to bolt. Finally, the group would break, and the surviving animals would wander off, the hunter following and shooting stragglers. When it was impossible to form a stand, the hunt progressed on a trail-and-shoot form, the hunter following a wandering band of buffalo, shooting at intervals as the opportunity presented itself. This method was feasible because the buffalo was a notoriously stupid animal that evidently recognized danger only when he could smell it. He also nearly invariably traveled into the wind so that a hunter could follow with little possibility of detection. These two techniques of hunting were the most desirable and common. There were others, of course, such as lying in wait for buffalo to pass a certain concealed point. A good hunter would kill as many as 100 buffalo in an hour or two, and from 1,000 to 2,000 a season. Most hunters killed in the morning and aided with skinning in the afternoon.

Meat for Dinner *(Emil Oberwetter, left, and John Logan).* Buffalo Gap *(Taylor County), 1874. Photograph by George Robertson, from William J. Oliphant's stereograph series "Life on the Frontier." Courtesy TSL. The photographs that Robertson took on this hunt are believed to be the earliest taken of a buffalo hunt in the United States.*

After the hunter had done his work, the skinners entered the picture. The hides were removed from the carcasses with skinning knives, loaded onto a wagon, and taken back to camp. To speed the skinning process, the wagon was rigged with a forked stick to the center of the hind axle, with the end dragging the ground behind. A chain or rope was attached to the same axle; and when a carcass was to be skinned, the wagon was driven up to it and the rope or chain was attached to a front leg. After the upper side of the carcass was skinned, the wagon was moved, pulling the carcass over a bit, the stick suspended from the back axle acting as a brake. In that way, skinning was made considerably swifter and easier. When the green hides were brought to camp, they were stretched and staked or pegged to the ground with the meat side down. After three to five days they were turned, and so alternated every day until they were dry, at which time they were piled. Usually they were placed in four stacks: bull hides, cow hides, robe hides, and kip hides (hides from younger animals). Buyers ordinarily came out to the camp; the hunters received about $2.00 per bull hide with other prices scaled down accordingly. After the deal was made, the buyer generally sent a freight wagon to the camp to pick up the hides and take them to Fort Worth, Texas, Dodge City, Kansas, or some other railhead, where they could be shipped to buyers in the East.

BIBLIOGRAPHY: John R. Cook, *The Border and the Buffalo: An Untold Story of the Southwest Plains* (Topeka, Kansas: Crane, 1907; rpt., New York: Citadel Press, 1967). William Temple Hornaday, *The Extermination of the American Bison* (Washington: GPO, 1889).
David M. Vigness

BUFFALO LAKE. Buffalo Lake is an artificial reservoir impounded by Umbarger Dam, three miles south of Umbarger on upper Tierra Blanca Creek in western Randall County (at 34°55′ N, 102°06′ W). The dam was built by the Federal Farm Securities Administration to store water for recreational purposes. Construction was started in February 1938 and completed on June 15, 1938; impoundment of water began on June 9. The project was operated by the Soil Conservation Service of the United States Department of Agriculture until 1953, when the Forest Service took over. In 1958 operation of the project was transferred to the Fish and Wildlife Service of the United States Department of the Interior, which made the area a national wildlife refuge. The lake's capacity is 18,150 acre-feet at the spillway crest elevation, 3,642.6 feet above mean sea level. The surface area of the lake at this elevation is 1,900 acres. The lake's drainage area is 2,075 square miles, of which 1,500 square miles are probably noncontributing. Several species of waterfowl use the lake as a winter refuge, and facilities for boating, fishing, swimming, skiing, and camping are provided.

BIBLIOGRAPHY: C. L. Dowell, *Dams and Reservoirs in Texas: History and Descriptive Information* (Texas Water Commission Bulletin 6408 [Austin, 1964]). Mrs. Clyde W. Warwick, comp., *The Randall County Story* (Hereford, Texas: Pioneer, 1969). *Seth D. Breeding*

BUFFALO LAKE NATIONAL WILDLIFE REFUGE. Buffalo Lake National Wildlife Refuge is on Farm Road 168 three miles south of Umbarger in Randall County. The 7,667-acre preserve, purchased by the United States Department of the Interior in the mid-1930s, is among the major waterfowl refuges in the Central Flyway, one of four major migratory routes over the continental United States. Some 275 species of birds have been observed in the area, though the refuge's main attraction is the thousands of ducks and geese that winter there. During the mid-1960s, some 800,000 ducks and 40,000 Canada geese spent the winter at Buffalo Lake. The lake, however, began to dry up in the 1970s because it had no regular inflow, and in the 1980s its future value as a waterfowl sanctuary was uncertain. To provide forage for the birds, each year crops were planted on about 1,000 acres in the dry lakebed. In the 1980s efforts were under way to make a marshy area for wildlife. The open grasslands around the lakebed provided habitat for a variety of animal life, including deer, prairie dogs, bobcats, and coyotes. Recreational facilities at the refuge included a hiking trail, campsites, and picnic areas.

BIBLIOGRAPHY: George Oxford Miller, *Texas Parks and Campgrounds: Central, South, and West Texas* (Austin: Texas Monthly Press, 1984). *Christopher Long*

BUFFALO PEAK. Buffalo Peak, six miles north of Johnson City in north central Blanco County (at 30°22′ N, 98°25′ W), rises 1,660 feet above sea level. The surrounding Edwards Plateau area is characterized by level to gently rolling uplands and ridges marked by steep slopes and limestone benches, which give a stairstep appearance to the landscape. The soil surface is shallow, stony, and clayey. The local vegetation comprises grasses and open stands of live oak and Ashe juniper.

BUFFALO SOLDIERS. Buffalo soldiers was the name given by the Plains Indians to the four regiments of African Americans,[qv] and more particularly to the two cavalry regiments, that served on the frontier in the post–Civil War army. More than 180,000 black soldiers had seen service in segregated regiments in the Union Army during the Civil War,[qv] and many units had achieved outstanding combat records. When Congress reorganized the peacetime regular army in the summer of 1866, it recognized the military merits of black soldiers by authorizing two regiments of black cavalry, the Ninth United States Cavalry and the Tenth United States Cavalry,[qqv] and six regiments of black infantry. In 1869 the black infantry regiments were consolidated into two units, the Twenty-fourth United States Infantry and the Twenty-fifth United States Infantry.[qqv] The two cavalry and two infantry regiments were composed of black enlisted men commanded, with a very few exceptions such as Henry O. Flipper,[qv] by white officers. From 1866 to the early 1890s the buffalo soldiers served at a variety of posts in Texas, the Southwest and the Great Plains. They overcame prejudice from within the army and from the frontier communities they were stationed in, to compile an outstanding service record. Often divided into small company and troop-sized detachments stationed at isolated posts, the buffalo soldiers performed routine garrison chores, patrolled the frontier, built roads, escorted mail parties, and handled a variety of difficult civil and military tasks. They also participated in most of the major frontier campaigns of the period and distinguished themselves in action against the Cheyenne, Kiowa, Comanche, Apache, Sioux, and Arapaho Indians. With outstanding officers such as Benjamin H. Grierson, Abner Doubleday, William Rufus Shafter, Joseph A. Mower[qqv] and Edward Hatch, they were an important component of the frontier army. Thirteen enlisted men from the four regiments earned the Medal of Honor during the Indian wars, as did six officers, and a further five enlisted men won that decoration during the Spanish-American War.

After the Indian wars came to an end in the 1890s the four regiments continued in service, with elements participating in the Spanish-American War, the Philippine Insurrection, and John J. Pershing's[qv] 1916 punitive expedition. The buffalo soldiers found themselves facing increasing racial prejudice at the turn of the century. They were cut off from the segregated towns they were stationed near, and were the victims of slurs, beatings, harassment by law officers, and, on several occasions, sniper attacks. As armed veterans of active service, they occasionally responded with violence. The Ninth Cavalry was involved in racial disturbances in Rio Grande City in 1899, the Twenty-fifth regiment rioted in the Brownsville Raid of 1906,[qv] and the Twenty-fourth regiment was involved in the Houston Riot of 1917.[qv] None of the buffalo soldier regiments went to France during World War I,[qv] though they provided a cadre of experienced noncommissioned officers to other black units that did go into combat. In the 1920s and 1930s, as black newspapers and civil-rights groups anxiously monitored the process, soldiers from the four regiments were increasingly used as laborers and service troops. The Ninth and Tenth cavalries were disbanded, and their personnel were transferred into service units during World War II.[qv] The Twenty-fifth saw combat in the Pacific during the war, and was deactivated in 1949. The Twenty-fourth also served in the Pacific during the Second World War, and fought in the opening stages of the Korean War. The Twenty-fourth, the last segregated black regiment to see combat, was deactivated in 1951, and its personnel were used to integrate other units serving in Korea at the time, an important step in the efforts of the United States Army to desegregate its units.

Popular interest in the Buffalo soldiers began to grow in the 1960s, stimulated by a John Ford film, *Sergeant Rutledge,* and the publication of several scholarly histories. In 1965 a reenactment unit, the Tenth Cavalry Buffalo Soldiers, was formed. In the 1990s a reenactment group with the Texas Parks and Wildlife Department[qv] offered a number of interpretive programs on the buffalo soldiers and performed at state parks and other venues.

BIBLIOGRAPHY: John M. Carroll, ed., *The Black Military Experience in the American West* (New York: Liveright, 1971). Garna L. Christian, *Black Soldiers in Jim Crow Texas, 1899–1917* (College Station: Texas A&M University Press, 1995). William H. Leckie, *The Buffalo Soldiers: A Narrative of the Negro Cavalry in the West* (Norman: University of Oklahoma Press, 1967). Bernard C. Nalty, *Strength for the Fight: A History of Black Americans in the Military* (New York: Free Press, 1986). *Mark Odintz*

BUFFALO SPRINGS. Buffalo Springs is near the Oklahoma state line in north central Dallam County (at 36°29′ N, 102°47′ W). The springs originate from numerous openings in sandstone and in the past were a site for Indian campgrounds and also a favorite watering place for herds of buffalo,[qv] mustangs,[qv] and other animals. In 1878 the XIT Ranch's[qv] first division headquarters was established at the springs. The spring flow declined from 142 liters per second in 1907 to 6.5 in 1977 because of irrigation pumping.

BIBLIOGRAPHY: Gunnar Brune, *Springs of Texas*, Vol. 1 (Fort Worth: Branch–Smith, 1981). *Gunnar Brune*

BUFFALO SPRINGS, TEXAS (Clay County). Buffalo Springs is on Farm Road 3077 fifteen miles south of Henrietta in south central Clay County. Settlement of the area began in 1864, when twenty-five families constructed an outpost and attempted to establish a farming community. The settlers, under persistent Indian attacks and unable to survive a lengthy drought, abandoned the site, which remained uninhabited until 1878, when brothers C. O. and J. Q. Burnett settled about three-quarters of a mile from the ruins of the outpost. The community that developed, named for nearby Buffalo Creek, received postal service that year. By the mid-1890s Buffalo Springs had 200 residents, several stores, and two cotton gins; farming and stockraising were its residents' principal occupations. The reported population fell to 125 in 1914 and 115 by the mid-1920s. In the 1930s Buffalo Springs had a school, two churches, and a variety of small businesses. Its post office was discontinued in 1954, and its population fell from 100 in the 1950s to 60 by the mid-1960s and 51 in 1990.

BIBLIOGRAPHY: William Charles Taylor, *A History of Clay County* (Austin: Jenkins, 1972). *David Minor*

BUFFALO SPRINGS, TEXAS (Comal County). Buffalo Springs was a German farming and ranching community on the west bank of the Guadalupe River about 7½ miles northwest of New Braunfels in east central Comal County. The site at the mouth of Turkey Creek, originally settled by the Bremer family in 1848, offered an abundance of timber and water that attracted more German pioneers in the 1850s. By the 1980s Buffalo Springs had been abandoned. Its site was on the road that parallels the Guadalupe River between New Braunfels and Sattler.

BIBLIOGRAPHY: Lillian Penshorn, A History of Comal County (M.A. thesis, Southwest Texas State Teachers College, 1950).

Daniel P. Greene

BUFFALO SPRINGS LAKE. Buffalo Springs Lake, located on Farm Road 835 nine miles southeast of Lubbock in Lubbock County (at 33°32′ N, 101°42′ W), provides a major recreation area for West Texas. The lake comprises 200 surface acres and has a storage capacity of 3,950 acre-feet. Buffalo hunters first used Buffalo Springs in 1874, when they skirmished with Comanche Indians there. The Causey brothers built a half dugout at Buffalo Springs in 1877, and a year later ranchers moved into the area. Picnics and outings were very popular with the early settlers. The springs were then on land owned by the S. I. Johnston ranch. To develop the site as a recreational spot, Sheriff Bud Johnston and his brother Jim initiated simple improvements. In the late 1920s, after the estate was sold, pioneer J. A. (Andy) Wilson formed the Buffalo Lakes Association and put a small dam across the canyon. Memberships were sold, and boating, swimming, fishing, hunting, camping, and picnicking were available. Some members of the association built cabins around the lake. In December 1957 Lubbock County Water Control and Improvement District No. 1 bought 1,612 acres around Buffalo Lake to provide a community recreation center. The surface level of the lake was elevated repeatedly, most recently in 1960; the site of the main springs has been inundated, though the springs still flow. They have, in fact, benefitted by recharge of their aquifer with water from Lake Meredith, by way of Lubbock lawns and gardens.

The lake is surrounded by farmland and grows rife with summer weeds because of nutrients from the watershed. Its fish include largemouth bass, crappie, channel catfish, striped bass, and walleye. Florida bass were first stocked in 1983, and striped bass fishing is good. A rare member of the horsetail family, the bottlebrush plant, occurs only at the lake. Near the lake, residents lease land from the county and pay for their own improvements. A five-member board elected by county voters governs the lake; members serve alternating terms of two years. Areas are provided for waterskiing, fishing, boating, picnicking, horseback riding, hiking, and camping. Many special events are held at the lake each year, including boat races, waterskiing shows, bicycle races, sailboat regattas, marathons, and country music programs. A small entrance fee is charged, and an estimated million people visit the lake each year.

BIBLIOGRAPHY: Gunnar Brune, *Springs of Texas*, Vol. 1 (Fort Worth: Branch-Smith, 1981). Lawrence L. Graves, ed., *A History of Lubbock* (Lubbock: West Texas Museum Association, 1962).

Jeanne F. Lively

BUFFALO WALLOW FIGHT. The Buffalo Wallow Fight was one of the most unusual engagements in the Red River War.[qv] On September 10, 1874, Col. Nelson A. Miles,[qv] whose command was running short of rations, sent two scouts, Billy Dixon and Amos Chapman,[qqv] and four enlisted men, Sgt. Z. T. Woodhall and privates Peter Rath, John Harrington,[qv] and George W. Smith, from his camp on McClellan Creek with dispatches concerning the delay of Capt. Wyllys Lyman's supply train, then under siege by Indians on the upper Washita River (*see* LYMAN'S WAGON TRAIN). The six-man contingent set out on the trail to Camp Supply in Indian Territory. On the morning of September 12, as they approached the divide between Gageby Creek and the Washita River in Hemphill County, they suddenly found themselves surrounded by about 125 Comanche and Kiowa warriors, some of whom had come from the siege of the wagon train. Since retreating Indians had burned off the prairie grass only days before, there was no shelter close by; Dixon and his companions thus decided to dismount and make a desperate stand. In a few minutes George Smith, who took charge of the horses, fell with a bullet through his lungs. The horses then stampeded, carrying with them the men's haversacks, canteens, coats, and blankets. The mounted Indians indulged in a cat-and-mouse game with their intended victims by circling them and firing on a dead run. Soon Harrington and Woodhall were hit, and Chapman's left knee was shattered by a bullet. When the Indians desisted for a few minutes, Dixon, who had a slight wound in the calf, spotted a buffalo wallow a few yards away. He bade his companions take cover in this shallow depression, which was about ten feet in diameter. By noon, all except Chapman and Smith had reached it safely and with their hands and butcher knives began throwing up the sandy loam around the perimeter of the wallow for better protection. In the process, the men managed to keep their adversaries at bay and away from Smith and Chapman.

As the fight progressed, Dixon tried several times to reach Chapman but was forced back repeatedly by a hail of bullets and arrows. Since the crippled scout had lived as a "squaw man" among the Indians for a time and was known to many of the warriors present, they taunted him by shouting, "Amos, Amos, we got you now, Amos!" Finally, early in the afternoon, Dixon made it to Chapman and carried him back amid the gunfire to the safety of the wallow.

As the day wore on, the five men suffered terribly from hunger, thirst, and wounds; but their expert marksmanship continued to hold back the Indians, who could not even capture Smith's guns. Late in the afternoon an approaching thunderstorm brought relief to the parched men and served to break off the Indian attack, but the blue norther[qv] that it heralded resulted in more suffering from a severe drop in temperature. Taking advantage of the lull in the skirmish,

Peter Rath went to recover Smith's weapons and ammunition and was astonished to find Smith still alive. Dixon and Rath carried the unfortunate trooper back to their makeshift fortress, where he died later that night.

At nightfall the Indians disappeared. Dixon and Rath fashioned crude beds for themselves and their wounded comrades out of tumbleweeds they had gathered and crushed. Afterward Rath went to bring help but was unable to locate the trail and returned in two hours. The following morning, September 13, dawned clear with no Indians in sight. Dixon then volunteered to go for help and found the trail less than a mile away. Soon he saw a column of United States Cavalry in the distance and fired his gun to attract their attention. As it turned out, this contingent consisted of four companies of the Eighth Cavalry from Fort Union, New Mexico, about 225 men in all, under the command of Maj. William R. Price. Price's appearance had caused the Indians to withdraw from the wallow and Lyman's wagons.

Price accompanied Dixon back to the wallow but had no ambulance wagon and was running short of supplies himself. What was more, Dixon's companions mistook the approaching column for Indians and, before the scout could stop them, shot the horse of one of the surgeon's escorts. As a result, the piqued surgeon only briefly examined the men, and Price refused them ammunition or reinforcements, although some of his troops did give them hardtack and dried beef. Price then moved on, promising to notify Colonel Miles and send aid immediately. Not until nearly midnight, however, did aid arrive and the beleaguered men receive food and medical attention. George Smith's body was wrapped in an army blanket and buried in the wallow, and the disabled survivors were taken to Camp Supply for treatment. Amos Chapman's leg was subsequently amputated above the knee, and Woodhall and Harrington recovered and continued their military service. After "severely censuring" Price for his failure to render further aid to the survivors, Colonel Miles recommended that they be given the Medal of Honor for bravery under adverse circumstances. The medals were awarded, including a posthumous one to Smith; Dixon personally received his from Miles while they were encamped on Carson Creek near Adobe Walls.

The Buffalo Wallow Fight was widely publicized as a heroic engagement; Richard Irving Dodge presented a somewhat inaccurate narrative of the episode in his book *Our Wild Indians* (1882). While nearly all accounts of the battle, including Dixon's, claimed that the six men killed as many as two dozen warriors, Amos Chapman, who spent his later years in Seiling, Oklahoma, once told George Bent that no Indian actually fell to their guns. Some years later, the medals of Chapman and Dixon were revoked by Congress since they had served the army as civilian scouts. Dixon, however, refused to surrender what he felt he had justly earned. His medal is now on display at the Panhandle-Plains Historical Museum[qv] in Canyon. In 1925, under direction of J. J. Long and Olive King Dixon,[qv] a granite monument was erected on the Buffalo Wallow site, twenty-two miles southeast of Canadian. It bears the names of the six heroes "who cleared the way for other men."

BIBLIOGRAPHY: Olive K. Dixon, *Life of "Billy" Dixon* (1914; rev. ed., Dallas: P. L. Turner Company, 1927; facsimile of original ed., Austin: State House, 1987). James L. Haley, *The Buffalo War: The History of the Red River Indian Uprising of 1874* (Garden City, New York: Doubleday, 1976). George E. Hyde, *Life of George Bent, Written from His Letters* (Norman: University of Oklahoma Press, 1968). John L. McCarty, *Adobe Walls Bride* (San Antonio: Naylor, 1955).

H. Allen Anderson

BUFFINGTON, ANDERSON (1806–1891). Anderson Buffington, soldier at San Jacinto and Baptist minister, was born in South Carolina on February 14, 1806. After being reared by a stepmother, he ran away from home with his brother John and settled in Nashville, Tennessee, where he learned the printing trade. In Nashville he was licensed to preach by the Nashville Baptist Church. Buffington and Parolee Cobler were married on October 1, 1834, and eventually became the parents of two boys and four girls. The Buffingtons left Tennessee in 1835 and crossed the Red River into Texas in an ox wagon on January 10, 1836. They settled at Washington-on-the-Brazos. Two months later Buffington joined Capt. William Kimbro's[qv] company in the Second Regiment of Texas Volunteers as a private. He was discharged on June 15 at San Augustine and received 640 acres of land for fighting in the battle of San Jacinto.[qv]

Buffington and his wife became members of a prayer-meeting group organized at Washington-on-the-Brazos. Later in the year they formed a small church, Washington Baptist Church No. 1, the first missionary Baptist church in Texas. Buffington was on a committee that requested missionaries from the United States. The church dissolved in 1838. During this time Buffington was operating a sawmill at Washington-on-the-Brazos. He also served in the 1839 campaign against the Cherokee Indians and published a newspaper, the *Tarantula*,[qv] at Washington-on-the-Brazos in 1841. On October 19, 1841, he was ordained by Washington Baptist Church No. 2 and appointed by the American Baptist Home Mission Society as a missionary to Montgomery County.

The Buffingtons moved in 1848 to Anderson, where Buffington opened a store with a man named Van Alstyne. They later sold the business, and Buffington opened another store, but it did not last long. He then opened the second hotel in Anderson and operated it for many years. Buffington preached to Negro congregations in Anderson for twenty years. He was also a strong Mason. At the beginning of the Civil War[qv] he was one of the few men in Grimes County who voted for the Union and Sam Houston.[qv] Both his sons fought in the Confederate Army. Buffington served briefly as postmaster in Anderson in 1865–66. He died on December 20, 1891, and was buried in the Odd Fellows Cemetery at Anderson.

BIBLIOGRAPHY: Irene Taylor Allen, *Saga of Anderson—The Proud Story of a Historic Texas Community* (New York: Greenwich, 1957). Grimes County Historical Commission, *History of Grimes County, Land of Heritage and Progress* (Dallas: Taylor, 1982). Zenos N. Morrell, *Flowers and Fruits from the Wilderness* (Boston: Gould and Lincoln, 1872; rpt. of 3d ed., Irving, Texas: Griffin Graphic Arts, 1966).

Samuel B. Hesler

BUFFORD CREEK. Bufford Creek rises in two branches in north central Stephens County. Its West Fork rises four miles northeast of Breckenridge (at 32°48′ N, 98°50′ W) and flows north for almost seven miles; its East Fork rises six miles northeast of Breckenridge (at 32°49′ N, 98°49′ W) and flows north for 6½ miles. The branches meet just south of the Yellow Fork Community (at 32°53′ N, 98°50′ W). The consolidated creek flows north for 3½ miles to its mouth on the Clear Fork of the Brazos River, west of Farm Road 701 (at 32°55′ N, 98°49′ W). It crosses an area of rolling hills surfaced by clay and sandy loams that support scrub brush, mesquite, cacti, and grasses. Toward the creek's mouth the terrain features rugged hills and scarps surfaced by shallow, stony, sandy loams that support post oak, grasses, and chaparral.

BUFORD, TEXAS. Buford, at the junction of State Highway 208 and Farm Road 1982, five miles north of Colorado City in north central Mitchell County, was originally called Armenderez for an old mill located there. Later the community's name was changed to Belen and then to Buford in honor of Buford Orndorff of El Paso. The community had a post office from 1907 to 1913 but was served later from Colorado City. In 1947 Buford had a population of ninety, three businesses, two churches, and a school. Its population was reported as twenty-five in 1980 and 1990. *William R. Hunt*

BUFORD BRANCH. Buford (or Finney) Branch rises seven miles southeast of Dumont in northwestern King County (at 33°45′ N,

100°26′ W) and runs northeast across fifteen miles of isolated rangeland before reaching its mouth on the North Wichita River, twelve miles south of Paducah in south central Cottle County (at 33°51′ N, 100°18′ W). The local terrain ranges from moderately steep slopes with locally high relief to flood-prone flats with occasional shallow depressions. Its silt, clay, and sandy loam soils support vegetation ranging from mesquite and grasses to water-tolerant conifers and hardwoods. The branch flows through Finney in northwestern King County. A source of the creek was Finney Springs, located northeast of the Finney settlement. The springs were home to buffalo hunter S. B. Street during the 1870s. By 1979, however, the springs were only small seeps.

BIBLIOGRAPHY: Gunnar Brune, *Springs of Texas*, Vol. 1 (Fort Worth: Branch–Smith, 1981).

BUG TUSSLE, TEXAS. Bug Tussle is at the junction of Farm Road 1550 and State Highway 34, ten miles south of Honey Grove and five miles north of Ladonia in southeastern Fannin County. The community was initially called Truss, after John Truss, who settled there. It was founded in the 1890s and had a post office in 1893–94. Later the town's name was changed to Bug Tussle. At least three explanations exist for this unusual name. The most popular is that the name commemorated an invasion of bugs that spoiled a church ice cream social. A variation on this anecdote suggests that the relatively isolated spot, long popular as a site of Sunday school picnics, offered little else for picnickers to do after they ate than watch the bugs tussle. A third story tells of an argument between two old-time residents who wanted to change the name of the town. Their attention was diverted by the spectacle of two tumblebugs fighting. "Look at those bugs tussle," one reportedly remarked, thus settling the argument and rechristening the town. More than seventy Bug Tussle highway signs have been stolen over the years, and for a time it was fashionable for couples to come there to be married, just so that they could say they had been wed in Bug Tussle. Bug Tussle reported only six residents by 1962, but experienced a brief renaissance when the David Graham Hall[qv] foundation took a fifteen-year lease on the downtown area in order to restore it. From 1966 to the mid-1980s the renovated town, sometimes called West Bug Tussle, had a population of thirty and capitalized on its unusual name by producing a number of souvenir items under the "Made in Bug Tussle, Texas" logo. In 1990 its population was reported as fifteen.

BIBLIOGRAPHY: Floy Crandall Hodge, *A History of Fannin County* (Hereford, Texas: Pioneer, 1966). Fred Tarpley, *1001 Texas Place Names* (Austin: University of Texas Press, 1980). Vertical Files, Barker Texas History Center, University of Texas at Austin. *Linda Peterson*

BUGBEE, HAROLD DOW (1900–1963). Harold Dow Bugbee, Western painter and illustrator, was born on August 15, 1900, in Lexington, Massachusetts, son of Charles H. and Grace L. (Dow) Bugbee. The family moved to Texas and established a ranch near Clarendon in 1914. Bugbee exhibited an early talent for drawing and determined to record the old-time ranch life then passing into history. Following his graduation from Clarendon High School in 1917, he attended Texas Agricultural and Mechanical College (now Texas A&M University) and Clarendon College. In 1919, acting upon the advice of Taos artist Bert Phillips, Bugbee enrolled in the Cumming School of Art in Des Moines, Iowa, where he studied for two years with portraitist Charles A. Cumming. From 1922 to the mid-1930s he honed his skills with annual visits to the Taos art colony, where he painted and sketched with W. Herbert Dunton, Ralph Meyers, Leon Gaspard, and Frank Hoffman, among others.

In 1921 Bugbee returned to West Texas. The owner of the Amarillo Hotel, Ernest O. Thompson,[qv] helped to launch his career by commissioning fourteen oils for the Longhorn Room and mounting Bugbee's first big show, which was held in the Amarillo Hotel in the mid-1920s. In 1942 Thompson had Bugbee paint eleven murals for the Tascosa Room of his Herring Hotel. Bugbee sold many of his paintings to ranchmen and collectors of western art, and he drew Christmas-card designs that were used internationally. In 1933 he began a career as an illustrator; he primarily did pen and ink sketches for books, pulp magazines (particularly *Ranch Romances*), historical editions of local and regional newspapers, trade publications such as *The Shamrock*, and thirty-four issues of the *Panhandle-Plains Historical Review*. Beginning with the publication of *Charles Goodnight: Cowman and Plainsman* (1936), Bugbee enjoyed a long-term collaboration with West Texas historian J. Evetts Haley. During this period Bugbee exhibited his work in Clarendon and other Texas cities, as well as at galleries in Kansas City, Chicago, Denver, and New York City. He was drafted into the armed forces in 1942, but was discharged due to health problems just one year later. He painted three murals for Amarillo Army Air Field in 1943; two of the three are in the National Museum of American Art, Smithsonian Institution.

In 1951 Bugbee became part-time curator of art for the Panhandle-Plains Historical Society.[qv] This position, which he held until his death, allowed him to devote much of his time to painting, and he sold or donated more than 230 of his paintings, drawings, and prints to the society's museum in Canyon. He completed twenty-two murals on Indian life and ranching for the museum, the most outstanding of which is *The Cattleman* (1934), painted under the Public Works of Art Project. An early trail-driving scene of cattleman R. B. Masterson[qv] that Bugbee painted on wood panels hangs in the Hall of State[qv] in Dallas. Having spent most of his life on the family ranch, Bugbee provided in his work an authentic insight into daily ranch routine in the Panhandle.[qv]

Bugbee's first marriage, to Katherine Patrick in 1935, ended in divorce. He later married Olive Vandruff, who survived him. He died in Clarendon on March 27, 1963. His work was featured in exhibitions at the Panhandle-Plains Historical Museum[qv] in 1953, 1961, 1970, 1987, and 1994; in 1990 the museum installed a reconstruction of Bugbee's studio. Bugbee exhibits were presented at the Nita Stewart Haley Library at Midland in 1992 and the Cattleman's Museum at Fort Worth in 1993. He also exhibited at Dalhart (1929), Amarillo (1930, 1931, and 1938), Abilene (1931), the University Centennial Exposition in Austin (1936), the Forth Worth Frontier Exposition (1936), and the West Texas Art Exhibition at Fort Worth (1939).

BIBLIOGRAPHY: *Branding with Pen and Ink: H. D. Bugbee* (Canyon, Texas: Panhandle-Plains Historical Museum, 1980). Jeff Dykes, *Fifty Great Western Illustrators: A Bibliographic Checklist* (Flagstaff, Arizona: Northland Press, 1975). Frances Battaile Fisk, *A History of Texas Artists and Sculptors* (Abilene, Texas, 1928; facsimile rpt., Austin: Morrison, 1986). Esse Forrester-O'Brien, *Art and Artists of Texas* (Dallas: Tardy, 1935). John L. McCarty, "Some Memories of H. D. Bugbee," *Southwestern Art* 1 (1966–67). C. Boone McClure, "Harold Dow Bugbee: A Biographical Sketch," *Panhandle-Plains Historical Review* 30 (1957).
Caroline Remy

BUGBEE, LESTER GLADSTONE (1869–1902). Lester G. Bugbee was born in Woodbury, Texas, on May 16, 1869, to Almond and Mary Fannie (Nunn) Bugbee. His parents named him L. G. and called him Dutch; Bugbee later adopted the name Lester Gladstone. He spent his boyhood on his father's farm near Pleasant Point and began his formal education at the Pleasant Point school. He attended Mansfield Male and Female College[qv] from 1884 to 1886 and passed the entrance exam for the University of Texas in January 1887. He completed his B.Litt. degree at the university in 1892 and received his M.A. the following year. He won a fellowship to Columbia College, New York, and spent two years there before returning to the University of Texas as a history tutor in 1895. He was promoted to instructor in 1896 and to adjunct professor in 1900. He assisted in the founding of the Texas State Historical Association[qv] in 1897 and served as corresponding secretary and treasurer of that organization until 1901. Between 1897 and 1899 he published several articles about the history of colonization in Texas, one of the most important of these being "Slavery in Early Texas," published in the *Political Science Quarterly* (1898). In 1898 he also began a successful campaign to get the Bexar county commissioners to place the Bexar Archives[qv] in the University of Texas library. Bugbee was known as an inspiring teacher and a promising scholar. He was diagnosed with tuberculosis in 1901 and took a leave from the university to live in El Paso, but the change of environment did not slow the course of the disease. He moved home to his father's farm at Pleasant Point in January 1902 and died there on March 17.

BIBLIOGRAPHY: Eugene C. Barker, "Lester Gladstone Bugbee, Teacher and Historian," *Southwestern Historical Quarterly* 49 (July 1945). Vertical Files, Barker Texas History Center, University of Texas at Austin. *Eugene C. Barker*

BUGBEE, THOMAS SHERMAN (1842–1925). Thomas Sherman Bugbee, cattleman, the third of the five children of John Brewer and Hannah (Sherman) Bugbee, was born on January 18, 1842, in Washington County, Maine. After limited schooling he left home at the age of fourteen to work on a farm and later at a sawmill. In 1860 he secured an eighty-acre homestead in western Maine, but service in the Tenth Maine Infantry during the Civil War[qv] kept him away from home from 1861 through 1864. Since their home state was heavily affected by the postwar recession, Thomas Bugbee and his brother George made their way west, working as teamsters. Hearing of the money to be made in the cattle market, Bugbee visited Fort Worth and formed a partnership with George Miller and M. M. Shea. In 1869 they purchased 1,200 cattle from John A. Knight for $11 a head and sold them in Idaho for $45 a head. The following year Bugbee and Shea bought 1,500 head and drove them to Colorado. In 1871 Bugbee drove 750 steers to Rice County, Kansas, west of Abilene, where he wintered them in order to get a better price. There he met Mary Catherine (Molly) Dunn, whom he married on August 13, 1872. The newlyweds then loaded their wagon and drove the steers farther west. Near Lakin, Kansas, they built their first dugout home and spent four years building up the herd.

In the fall of 1876 the family departed for Texas. After losing half of their herd and possessions to the raging Cimarron River, the Bugbees arrived with their trail hands and 1,800 cattle at the Canadian River breaks in Hutchinson County. There they established the Quarter Circle T Ranch,[qv] the second oldest in the Panhandle,[qv] with headquarters on Bugbee Creek. In 1882 Bugbee sold his land and cattle and moved his family, which eventually included eight children, to Kansas City, where they could live more comfortably. During the next fifteen years, operating out of Kansas City, he established cattle ranches in Texas, Kansas, and Indian Territory. In 1883, in partnership with Orville Howell Nelson,[qv] he established the Shoe Bar Ranch[qv] in Briscoe, Hall, and Donley counties, Texas. At the same time, he formed the Word-Bugbee Cattle Company with Charles W. Word of Wichita Falls. They grazed 26,000 steers on 250,000 acres of fenced range in the Cheyenne country of Indian Territory. Word and Bugbee were forced to sell out at a loss after President Grover Cleveland evicted all white cattlemen from the reservation grasslands in 1885. In addition, Bugbee owned an 800-acre farm near Bonner Springs, Kansas, and, with William States, operated a 6,000-acre ranch near Dodge City. In 1886 he bought out Nelson's interest in the Shoe Bar and with another partner, L. C. Coleman, formed the Bugbee-Coleman Cattle Company. They remained partners until Coleman's death in 1894, at which time Bugbee sold out his own interest to A. J. Snyder. Afterwards he started the 69 Ranch in Knox County with 3,500 cattle for breeding purposes.

In 1897 Bugbee moved his family from Kansas City to Clarendon, Texas, where he continued with his ranching interests and served as president of the Panhandle and Southwestern Stockmen's Association from 1900 to 1908. He introduced maize, kafir, and many other grains and grasses to the Panhandle and also brought in some of the first harvesters and tractors. As a civic leader, Bugbee led in the founding and supporting of schools and other civilizing institutions. He died at his home in Clarendon on October 18, 1925.

BIBLIOGRAPHY: James Cox, *Historical and Biographical Record of the Cattle Industry* (2 vols., St. Louis: Woodward and Tiernan Printing, 1894, 1895; rpt., with an introduction by J. Frank Dobie, New York: Antiquarian, 1959). John Thomas Duncan, "The Settlement of Hall County," West Texas Historical Association *Yearbook* 18 (1942). Helen Bugbee Officer, "A Sketch of the Life of Thomas Sherman Bugbee, 1841–1925," *Panhandle-Plains Historical Review* 5 (1932). Pauline D. and R. L. Robertson, *Cowman's Country: Fifty Frontier Ranches in the Texas Panhandle, 1876–1887* (Amarillo: Paramount, 1981). Lester Fields Sheffy, "Thomas Sherman Bugbee," *Panhandle-Plains Historical Review* 2 (1929). *H. Allen Anderson*

BULA, TEXAS. Bula, on Farm Road 54 in southeastern Bailey County, was established in 1924 and named Newsome, for W. B. Newsome. The Newsome Ranch of W. B. and Tom Newsome was sold and subdivided into farms of 177.7 acres in 1924–25. Since the name Newsome duplicated another post office name, the name Bula was chosen in 1925, in honor of either Bula Maude Oakes, daughter of Methodist preacher Roma A. Oakes, or Bula Thorn, wife of William H. Thorn, the first postmaster. In 1925 Bula also opened a school and in 1929 a cotton gin. Its school later moved and was closed in 1975. Bula remained a farming community with a population of 105 in 1980 and 1990, when it still had its post office.

BIBLIOGRAPHY: Kathleen E. and Clifton R. St. Clair, eds., *Little Towns of Texas* (Jacksonville, Texas: Jayroe Graphic Arts, 1982). Fred Tarpley, *1001 Texas Place Names* (Austin: University of Texas Press, 1980). *William R. Hunt*

BULAH, TEXAS. Bulah, on Farm Road 23 eight miles southwest of Rusk in southwestern Cherokee County, was established before 1900. In 1940 the predominantly black community had a population of twenty-five, a store, and a union church and school. Most of the residents subsequently moved out of the area, but in the late 1980s a school and a few houses were still there.

BIBLIOGRAPHY: *Cherokee County History* (Jacksonville, Texas: Cherokee County Historical Commission, 1986). Hattie Joplin Roach, *A History of Cherokee County* (Dallas: Southwest, 1934).
Claudia Hazlewood

BULCHER, TEXAS. Bulcher is twenty-seven miles northwest of Gainesville in northwestern Cooke County. In 1872 John A. Dennis moved his family to the site, and they are considered the earliest homesteaders in the area. Later settlers included John Scanland, who donated property for the Scanland Cemetery south and east of Bulcher, and Matthew A. Morris, the postmaster when the post office was established in 1874. Another early resident was William H. Cox, who built a cotton gin in Bulcher in 1875. The population remained fairly stable at around 250 until oil was discovered nearby on June 24, 1926. After the resultant boom, Bulcher began to decline. The town reported a population of forty in 1933 and sixty in 1986. By the early 1990s no population figures were available for the community.

BIBLIOGRAPHY: Gainesville *Daily Register*, Centennial Edition, August 30, 1948. A. Morton Smith, *The First 100 Years in Cooke County* (San Antonio: Naylor, 1955). *Robert Wayne McDaniel*

BULER, TEXAS. Buler, on State Highway 70 in south central Ochiltree County, was named for Davis H. Buller, who owned and operated a store there for several years. A local post office was established in June 1922 with Buller as postmaster, but it was discontinued at the advent of rural mail delivery from Perryton in November 1924. In 1940 Buler reported a population of twenty-five, but by 1950 its store had ceased operation, depriving the community of its center. In the 1980s a grain elevator stood about two miles south of the townsite at the intersection of State Highway 70 and Farm Road 281.

BIBLIOGRAPHY: *Wheatheart of the Plains: An Early History of Ochiltree County* (Perryton, Texas: Ochiltree County Historical Survey Committee, 1969). *H. Allen Anderson*

BULGER CREEK. Bulger Creek rises in southern Taylor County (at 99°53′ N, 32°12′ W) and runs south about twelve miles to join Bluff Creek in northern Runnels County (at 99°56′ N, 32°03′ W). The stream is dammed in southern Taylor County to form Graham Lake, which supplies water for irrigation. The flat to gently sloping terrain along the creekbed is surfaced by moderately deep to shallow silt loams that support mesquite and grasses.

BULKLEY, MYRTLE BALES (1899–1990). Myrtle Bales Bulkley, suffragist and women's-rights activist, was born in Colo, Iowa, on August 5, 1899, the daughter of William Franklin and Cora (Morgan) Bales. She attended public schools in this farming and railroad town and then enrolled in Iowa State Teachers College in Cedar Falls. From her youth she was concerned with differences in how men and women were treated; she was especially affected when the sheriff in Colo threatened to arrest women who wore pants instead of skirts to do farm and machinery work during the World War I.[qv] In 1916, as a college student, she supported women's voting rights through letters, speeches, posters, and door-to-door campaigning. After college she taught in a one-room schoolhouse in rural Iowa, worked as a booking agent for the Chautauqua lecture circuit, and sold encyclopedias in Chicago and New York. She wrote one of the first handbooks on encyclopedia sales, which was translated into several foreign languages and used into the 1990s.

Myrtle Bales became a charter member of the League of Women Voters[qv] when it was initially proposed in 1919, before women had been granted nationwide suffrage. Though she never participated in highly publicized suffrage activities, she worked at the grass-roots level for women's voting rights both in Iowa and across the country. After passage of the Nineteenth Amendment to the United States Constitution (1920), which granted suffrage to women, she participated in marches in New York City for improving other aspects of women's legal rights. In 1926 she married Harold F. Bulkley, whom she met while working on the Chautauqua circuit. As a wife and mother of two children, Myrtle Bulkley remained active in the League of Women Voters, the local women's club, and other volunteer organizations in Pelham Manor, New York.

In 1972, shortly after the death of her husband, she moved from New York to Dallas, Texas, where her daughter had lived since 1960. She joined numerous local women's organizations in Texas and was a charter member of the Women's Southwest Federal Credit Union in Dallas. She testified before the Texas House of Representatives in favor of a statewide equal-rights amendment (*see* TEXAS EQUAL RIGHTS AMENDMENT), and later, when an attempt was made to rescind the state legislature's ratification of a national equal-rights amendment, she again appeared before the Texas legislature on behalf of the law. She also presented programs on the history of woman suffrage[qv] and the equal rights amendment that included narratives of her participation in these causes. These efforts by Bulkley, who was often referred to as one of the country's "last surviving suffragists," made her a link between the early twentieth-century suffragists and participants in the post-1960s women's movement. She was recognized in 1983 by the Women's Center of Dallas with an award for her contributions to women's rights. In 1989 the Dallas League of Women Voters named an annual award in her honor; the first award was presented by Bulkley's daughter, a longtime member of the League.

Bulkley, who suffered from Alzheimer's disease later in her life, died in a Dallas nursing home on June 26, 1990. She was survived by her daughter and son, two sisters, and several grandchildren. A memorial service was held at the First Unitarian Church of Dallas, and her body was donated for medical research.

BIBLIOGRAPHY: Dallas *Morning News*, April 20, 1983, June 28, 1990. Dallas *Times Herald*, August 27, 1985, April 29, 1989.

Debbie Mauldin Cottrell

BULLARD, TEXAS. Bullard, also known as Hewsville, is on the St. Louis Southwestern Railway at the intersection of U.S. Highway 69 and Farm roads 2493, 2137, and 344, twelve miles south of Tyler in extreme southern Smith County. The area, originally occupied by Caddo Indians, was later on the line between the William H. Steel and the Vinson Moore surveys. In 1870 John H. and Emma Eugenia Erwin Bullard settled there. Others had arrived by 1881, when Bullard opened the Hewsville post office in his general store. In 1883 he changed the name of the office to Bullard. That same year the Kansas and Gulf Short Line Railroad laid track from Tyler through Bullard to Lufkin. The Bullard railroad station was completed in August 1884. The community soon became a shipping point for cotton, vegetables, and fruits. By 1890 the population was 200, and businesses included a sawmill, two general stores, a physician, a smithy and wagon shop, and a telegraph office. John Bullard owned a cotton gin and gristmill. There was also a local school, a Baptist church, and a Methodist church. At this time the railroad was known as the St. Louis, Arkansas and Texas Railway. By 1892 the rail line had become the Tyler and Southwestern Railway, and the town had one grocer, a constable, a justice of the peace, a druggist, a physician, a feed store, and a new general store. In 1903 the community had a school for white children with two teachers and sixty-eight pupils and two schools for black children with three teachers and 118 students.

In 1914 Bullard had 400 citizens and several new businesses, including a telephone company, a bank, another cotton gin, four more general stores, three groceries, and a hardware store. The local newspaper, the Bullard *Herald*, was published on a weekly basis, and the railroad had become the St. Louis Southwestern Railway. In the 1920s additional businesses included several packing sheds, restaurants, and boarding houses. A movie theater had opened, and a band also provided entertainment. A traveling jail, seven feet in diameter and made of a barred round tank on wheels, held prisoners until the county sheriff could escort them to Tyler. By 1936 the town had twenty-one businesses, and a large residential community had developed to the west. The Bullard Independent School District included two elementary schools for six teachers and 288 black students and a school offering grades one through eleven with ten teachers and 237 white students. The population was 450 in the post–World War II[qv] years, when the town again became a shipping point for fruit and vegetables. In 1948 Bullard elected a city council and the first mayor, Jap Jones. Residents voted for a $50,000 bond that funded one of the few water systems in Texas using spring water. The number of residents declined to 300 by 1964. In 1973 Bullard had 573 inhabitants, only twenty-seven of whom resided below the Cherokee county line, and a cemetery, four churches, a water tank, an athletic field, and clay pits. In 1981 the community was concentrated around the junction of the highways. Most residents worked in nearby Tyler or other larger towns. In 1989 Bullard had twenty-two businesses and a population of 887. In 1990 the population was 890.

BIBLIOGRAPHY: Bullard Community Library Commission, *The Bullard Area—Its History and People, 1800–1977* (Bullard, Texas, 1979?). Smith County Historical Society, *Historical Atlas of Smith County* (Tyler, Texas: Tyler Print Shop, 1965). *The Southland*, October 1902 (facsimile in *Chronicles of Smith County*, Fall 1969). Kathleen E. and Clifton R. St. Clair, eds., *Little Towns of Texas* (Jacksonville, Texas: Jayroe Graphic Arts, 1982). Donald W. Whisenhunt, comp., *Chronological History of Smith County* (Tyler, Texas: Smith County Historical Society, 1983). Albert Woldert, *A History of Tyler and Smith County* (San Antonio: Naylor, 1948).

Vista K. McCroskey

BULLARD CREEK (Fannin County). Bullard Creek rises a mile southeast of Dodd City in central Fannin County (at 33°35′ N, 96°04′ W) and runs north for 9½ miles, passing beneath the Missouri Pacific railroad bridge just east of the city limits of Dodd City before reaching its mouth on Bois d'Arc Creek, two miles southeast of Lamasco (at 33°39′ N, 96°03′ W). The stream is intermittent in its upper reaches. It traverses flat to rolling land surfaced by clays, clay loams, and sandy loams. Mesquite, conifers, and water-tolerant hardwoods and grasses grow throughout the area. For most of the county's history the Bullard Creek area has been used as range and crop land.

____ (Hall County). Bullard Creek rises in central Hall County (at 34°28′ N, 100°39′ W) and runs north five miles to its mouth on the Prairie Dog Town Fork of the Red River (at 34°32′ N, 100°39′ W). It was once part of the old Mill Iron Ranch range (*see* CONTINENTAL LAND AND CATTLE COMPANY). The stream passes through an area of moderately steep slopes with loamy soils in which grow mesquite and grasses. The area around the junction of the Red River, the Little Red River, and Bullard Creek was popular with ancient peoples from 7,000 years ago until historic times. There were once excellent springs on Bullard Creek.

____ (Harrison County). Bullard Creek rises four miles east of Scottsville in east central Harrison County (at 32°33′ N, 94°10′ W) and runs southeast for 9½ miles to its mouth on Paw Paw Bayou, in Caddo Parish, Louisiana, a mile east of the Louisiana state line (at 32°31′ N, 94°02′ W). It crosses nearly level to hilly terrain surfaced by loams and clays that support dense patches of pine and hardwood trees. The land is used predominantly for agriculture.

BULL BRANCH (Young County). Bull Branch rises four miles north of Proffitt and eight miles northwest of Newcastle in northwestern Young County (at 33°15′ N, 98°51′ W) and runs southeast for about three miles before entering California Creek just north of Farm Road 926 (at 33°13′ N, 98°49′ W). Ranchland and oilfields dominate the creek's drainage area. The local terrain is surfaced by clay and sandy loams that support primarily water-resistant hardwoods and grasses.

BULL CREEK (Cherokee County). Bull Creek rises four miles southeast of Maydelle in west central Cherokee County (at 31°45′ N, 95°15′ W) and runs southwest for six miles to its mouth on the Neches River, four miles northwest of Holcomb Store (at 31°41′ N, 95°17′ W). The stream is intermittent in its upper reaches. It crosses flat to gently rolling terrain surfaced by clay and sandy loams that support grasses and mixed hardwoods and pines.

____ (Coleman County). Bull Creek rises in central Coleman County (at 31°42′ N, 99°32′ W) and runs southeast for eighteen miles, through Fisk and Gouldbusk, to its mouth on the Colorado River, the southern county line (at 31°28′ N, 99°25′ W). It crosses flat terrain with local shallow depressions, surfaced by clay and sandy loams that support water-tolerant hardwoods, conifers, and grasses.

____ (Fayette County). Bull Creek rises on Ross Prairie about midway between Fayetteville and the Ross Prairie Church in eastern Fayette County (at 29°53′ N, 96°41′ W) and runs southeast for seven miles to its mouth on Cummins Creek in Colorado County (at 29°52′ N, 96°36′ W). It crosses nearly level to gently sloping terrain with a sandy loam topsoil and a dense clay subsoil. The land is well suited for agriculture and has produced excellent harvests of cotton and grain. Early settlers recognized the value of this land before 1850, and by that time it was already well settled by English, German, and Czech immigrants. Since the 1950s the area has been used primarily as pasture for cattle and horses.

____ (Garza County). Bull Creek, or Aqua de Toro, rises in several small lakes along the southern edge of the Caprock in extreme southwestern Garza County (at 32°59′ N, 101°33′ W) and runs southeast for fifty miles to its mouth on the Colorado River, a mile south of Farm Road 2085 and two miles east of Lake J. B. Thomas in Scurry County (at 32°35′ N, 101°06′ W). It crosses flat terrain with local shallow depressions, surfaced by clay and sandy loams that support water-tolerant hardwoods and grasses. Buffalo hunter Charlie Hart is credited with naming the creek for the numerous buffalo bulls found there. An 1877 expedition of buffalo hunters in pursuit of Chief Black Horse[qv] camped on Bull Creek several miles northeast of Mushaway Peak in Borden County. The headquarters of the Beal family's Jumbo Ranch was located near the headwaters of the creek. The stream runs across several ranches, including the Dennis Ranch, the Flying D, and the 9R.

____ (Grimes County). Bull Creek, a spring-fed intermittent stream, rises a mile south of Iola in northwestern Grimes County (at 30°46′ N, 96°03′ W) and runs southwest for thirteen miles to its mouth on the Navasota River, the Brazos county line (at 30°40′ N, 96°10′ W). It traverses gently sloping terrain surfaced by sandy and clay loams that along the creek banks support water oak, pecan, elm, hackberry, post oak, and blackjack oak. Settlement near the stream began in the mid-1830s. Iola was founded north of the headwaters about 1850. In 1860 the Texas and New Orleans Railroad extended a tap line from Navasota to Iola through the vicinity of the upper creek. The Enon Baptist Church was on the north bank of the middle creek near the site of the Enon Cemetery from the late 1800s until 1928, when it was moved closer to Iola. Both the Trinity and Brazos Valley Railway and the Houston and Texas Central Railway constructed lines through Iola over the headwaters of the stream about 1907. Farm Road 244 was extended across the upper creek from Iola to Keith in 1949.

BIBLIOGRAPHY: Grimes County Historical Commission, *History of Grimes County, Land of Heritage and Progress* (Dallas: Taylor, 1982).

____ (Mills County). Bull Creek rises just south of Goldthwaite in south central Mills County (at 31°24′ N, 98°36′ W) and runs south eight miles to its mouth on the Colorado River (at 31°21′ N, 98°39′ W). It crosses flat terrain upstream and an area of gentle and steep slopes downstream. Juniper, scattered oak, scrub brush, and grasses grow in the local shallow sandy soil.

____ (Polk County). Bull Creek rises two miles southwest of Carmona in northern Polk County (at 30°59′ N, 94°58′ W) and runs six miles northeast, into Trinity County and then back into Polk County, to its mouth on Piney Creek, seven miles northwest of Corrigan (at 31°03′ N, 94°56′ W). The stream crosses terrain ranging from low, to moderately rolling, to steep with local badlands. Area vegetation consists primarily of pine and oak forests in soil that varies from shallow and moderately dark clay loams to sandy and clay loams of variable depths. An abandoned railroad grade extending from Corrigan to a point near Bull Creek indicates that there was once lumbering activity along the creek's eastern bank.

____ (Travis County). Bull Creek begins three miles northwest of Austin in north central Travis County (at 30°24′ N, 97°50′ W) and runs southeast for twelve miles to its mouth on Lake Austin (at 30°21′ N, 97°47′ W). It runs beneath steep slopes and benches surfaced with shallow clay loams that support juniper, live oak, mesquite, and grasses.

BULLETIN OF THE TEXAS ARCHEOLOGICAL SOCIETY. The *Bulletin of the Texas Archeological Society*, published annually since 1929 (except in 1944), is the principal publication of the Texas Archeological Society.[qv] The bulletin, from 1929 to 1952 entitled *Bul-*

letin of the Texas Archeological and Paleontological Society, was published at Abilene under the editorship of Cyrus N. Ray from 1929 to 1946 (volumes 1–17) and at Lubbock under William Curry Holden[qv] from 1947 to 1952 (volumes 18–23). From 1952 to 1965 the bulletin was published at Austin under successive editors Alex D. Krieger, E. Mott Davis, T. N. Campbell, and Dee Ann Suhm. Several special topic volumes have been published, including *An Introductory Handbook of Texas Archeology* (Volume 25), by Dee Ann Suhm, Alex D. Krieger, and Edward B. Jelks; and *The Gilbert Site* (Volume 37), by Edward B. Jelks. The bulletin usually contains papers on Texas archeology and related subjects as well as book reviews and obituaries; earlier volumes also carried society news and notes, which now appear in *Texas Archeology*, the society newsletter. Each volume of the *Bulletin* averages 200 to 300 pages and usually contains at least five papers; most articles are illustrated with photographs or line drawings. An index to Volumes 1–22 was published in 1953. The first two volumes (1929, 1930) used the spelling "Archaeological" rather than "Archeological." In 1987 the *Bulletin* began publishing a series of articles focusing on a particular region of Texas: "The Southern Texas Coast" (1987), "Lower Pecos and Eastern Trans-Pecos" (1988), "Texas Panhandle and Southern Plains" (1989), and "North Central Texas" (1993). In 1994 the editor was Timothy K. Perttula, and the *Bulletin* had a circulation of 1,700. *Michael B. Collins*

BULLHEAD CREEK (Llano County). Bullhead Creek rises a mile east of the town of Prairie Mountain and a mile west of Bullhead Mountain in extreme southwestern Llano County (at 30°33′ N, 98°52′ W) and runs north for thirteen miles through a wide, sandy bed to its mouth on Hickory Creek, nine miles west of Llano (at 30°42′ N, 98°50′ W). It traverses an area of the Llano basin characterized by flat to rolling to steep terrain, with local dissection and escarpments. Soils in the area range from shallow and rocky to deep sandy and clay loams and support open stands of live oak and mesquite.

—— (Real County). Bullhead Creek, a spring-fed stream, rises in the upper elevations of the divide separating the Nueces and Frio canyons in central Real County (at 29°50′ N, 99°51′ W) and runs west for twenty miles, passing to the southeast of Bullhead Mountain, before joining the Nueces River just below Vance, formerly Bullhead (at 29°49′ N, 100°01′ W). The stream is intermittent in its upper reaches. It winds down the eastern side of the Nueces canyon over a bed of limestone, gravel, and calcareous soil. The surroundings are typical of the heavily dissected canyonlands of the Balcones Escarpment on the southern edge of the Edwards Plateau. The region is forested with open stands of live oak, mesquite, and Ashe juniper.

BULLHEAD MOUNTAIN. Bullhead Mountain is a limestone peak north of Vance (formerly Bullhead) and the intersection of Farm roads 335 and 2631 in far western Real County (at 29°49′ N, 100°00′ W). The summit, at an elevation of 2,042 feet above sea level, rises on the southern edge of the Edwards Plateau. Local vegetation includes open stands of live oak, Ashe juniper, and mesquite on the uplands and ridges and live oak and Ashe juniper woods on the hills and escarpments. An almost certainly apocryphal story has it that the peak was named after the head of an old buffalo bull found on the mountain during the early days of settlement. The more likely explanation is that the name derives from the shape of the mountain.

BULL HIDE CREEK. Bull Hide (Bullhide) Creek rises three miles south of Woodway in south central McLennan County (at 31°28′ N, 97°15′ W) and runs southeast for nineteen miles to its mouth on the Brazos River, four miles east of Golinda in Falls County (at 31°23′ N, 97°01′ W). The stream is intermittent in its upper reaches. It was named for a bull hide that was hung on a tree by a hunter. The creek crosses flat to rolling prairie with locally steep slopes, surfaced by expansive clays and clay loams that support juniper, oak, mesquite, and grasses in its upper and middle reaches and water-tolerant hardwoods and conifers downstream.

BIBLIOGRAPHY: John Sleeper and J. C. Hutchins, comps., *Waco and McLennan County* (Waco: Golledge, 1876; rpt., Waco: Kelley, 1966).

BULL HOLLOW (Edwards County). Bull Hollow, a drainage basin, begins seven miles northeast of the intersection of U.S. Highway 277 and State Highway 55 in northern Edwards County (at 30°17′ N, 100°26′ W) and runs northeast for about 12½ miles to its mouth on Eightmile Draw, five miles south of Interstate Highway 10 in southeastern Sutton County (at 30°24′ N, 100°21′ W). The hollow is located in the gently rolling limestone terrain of the western Edwards Plateau. It crosses loamy soils occasionally broken by rock outcrops. The vegetation in the area consists primarily of range grasses with small scattered stands of oak, juniper, and mesquite.

—— (Sutton County). Bull Hollow begins a mile north of the junction of Farm roads 864 and 2597 in north central Sutton County (at 30°39′ N, 100°17′ W) and runs north for 7½ miles to its mouth on the Middle Valley Prong of the North Llano River, just south of Farm Road 864 in southern Schleicher County (at 30°45′ N, 100°19′ W). The stream crosses the gently rolling limestone terrain of the western Edwards Plateau, where loamy soils occasionally broken by rock outcrops support range grasses and small scattered stands of oak, juniper, and mesquite.

BULLINGER'S CREEK. Bullinger's Creek, formerly known as Palmetto Creek and as Arroyo Dulce, is a spring-fed perennial stream that rises three miles northwest of Sealy in south central Austin County (at 29°49′ N, 96°13′ W) and flows east for eight miles to its mouth on the Brazos River, near San Felipe on the Waller county line (at 29°49′ N, 96°06′ W). The stream traverses sloping to nearly level terrain surfaced by sandy loam that along the lower creek banks supports post oak, blackjack oak, elm, and hackberry. The Stephen F. Austin State Historical Park[qv] lies on the lower creek near the Brazos. Settlement near the stream was underway by 1823, when San Felipe de Austin was formed. The stream helped provide the supply of fresh water, independent of the river, that Stephen F. Austin[qv] believed was essential to the security of the site. Austin built his own residence on Bullinger's Creek about a half mile west of the Brazos. This was a log cabin, with two rooms or wings connected by a central passageway in which a cannon was lodged for emergency use in defending the settlement. About 1880 Sealy was established some four miles west of San Felipe as a station on a new line of the Gulf, Colorado and Santa Fe Railway, which spanned Bullinger's Creek about a mile north of the town. In 1895 the Missouri, Kansas and Texas line extended track through Sealy skirting the south bank of the creek.

BIBLIOGRAPHY: Eugene C. Barker, *The Life of Stephen F. Austin* (Nashville: Cokesbury Press, 1925; rpt., Austin: Texas State Historical Association, 1949; New York: AMS Press, 1970). Sallie Glasscock, *Dreams of an Empire: The Story of Stephen Fuller Austin and His Colony in Texas* (San Antonio: Naylor, 1951). Blanche Hoff, *San Felipe de Austin: Capital of Austin's Colony* (Houston?, 1938). Worth Stickley Ray, *Austin Colony Pioneers* (Austin: Jenkins, 1949; 2d ed., Austin: Pemberton, 1970).

BULLINGTON, ORVILLE (1882–1956). Orville Bullington, lawyer, civic leader, and Republican party[qv] leader in Texas, son of William I. and Sarah (Holmes) Bullington, was born in Indian Springs, Missouri, on February 10, 1882. He received his secondary education in a Tennessee academy, then worked his way through Sam Houston Normal Institute, where he graduated in 1901. He taught school for two years before entering the University of Texas law school in 1903; he finished the three-year law course in two years. He opened a law office in Munday in February 1906 and served as county attorney for a term. In June 1909 he moved to Wichita Falls, where he practiced law for the rest of his life. He was a member of the local, state, and national bar associations. He enlisted for service in World War I[qv] as a private and was discharged as a lieutenant colonel in the Eighth United States Infantry.[qv] On June 28, 1911, Bullington married Sadie Kell, daughter of Frank Kell[qv] of Wichita Falls. They had one son. Bullington served as president of the chamber of commerce in 1929 and was active in other movements to advance Wichita Falls. His business investments included the American National Bank, Kemp Hotel Corporation, Wichita Falls and Southern Railroad (he was chairman of the board when the company folded), and oil interests in the Wichita Falls area and the Panhandle.[qv] He also had farm and ranch investments.

He began in politics as a Democrat, then resigned from that party in 1918 and became active in the Republican party.[qv] As the Republican nominee for governor in 1932, he waged a vigorous campaign. Though unsuccessful, he polled the largest number of Republican votes to that time—317,807 to Miriam A. Ferguson's[qv] 528,986. In 1936 he charged that the New Deal was being run by Communists. He was a delegate to eight Republican national conventions and a member of the state executive committee (1947–52), which he served as chairman in 1951–52. In 1948 he was a member of the temporary platform committee for the Republican National Committee. He led the protest demanding that a representative of the Deep South participate in the drafting of the civil-rights plank. As a result Bullington and three other Southerners served on the committee. He was also involved in the battle over the 1952 Republican presidential nomination. To weaken Eisenhower forces in the state, Bullington and the Robert Taft majority among Texas Republicans imposed a party-loyalty pledge for the first time for participants in precinct, county, and state conventions. Later that year he and several others were charged with fraudulently conspiring to defeat Dwight Eisenhower.[qv] However, Bullington wavered in his support of Taft, and as state chairman of the Republican party in 1952 he publicly admitted that his own Taft forces were not being fair to the Eisenhower Republicans in delegate selection.

In January 1941 Governor W. Lee O'Daniel[qv] appointed Bullington a regent of the University of Texas. He and several other regents determined to cut financing for the university, remove alleged Communists from the faculty and students, and limit the teaching of certain subjects. When university president Homer Rainey[qv] denounced the interference, the regents fired him. Bullington was active in the university's B-Hall Association, was a member of the board of the Ex-Students' Association for twenty years and its president (1921–23), and helped formulate plans for the Barker Texas History Center[qv] at the university. During his tenure as regent Lula Kemp Kell presented the Frank Kell Collection of Texana and Western Books to the university. With her, Bullington contributed to the endowment and added some of his own books to the collection. He was a patron of the Texas State Historical Association.[qv] He also served as president of the Sam Houston State College Ex-Students' Association (1928–32). He died on November 25, 1956, in Wichita Falls.

BIBLIOGRAPHY: Paul D. Casdorph, *A History of the Republican Party in Texas, 1865–1965* (Austin: Pemberton Press, 1965). Alice Cox, The Rainey Affair: A History of the Academic Freedom Controversy at the University of Texas, 1938–1946 (Ph.D. dissertation, University of Denver, 1970). George N. Green, *The Establishment in Texas Politics* (Westport, Connecticut: Greenwood, 1979). Roger M. Olien, *From Token to Triumph: The Texas Republicans since 1920* (Dallas: Southern Methodist University Press, 1982). Homer P. Rainey, *The Tower and the Dome: A Free University Versus Political Control* (Boulder, Colorado: Pruett, 1971). Vertical Files, Barker Texas History Center, University of Texas at Austin.
Louise Kelly

BULLIS, JOHN LAPHAM (1841–1911). John Lapham Bullis, military officer and commander of the famed Black Seminole scouts,[qv] son of Dr. Abram R. and Lydia P. (Lapham) Bullis, was born at Macedon, New York, on April 17, 1841. As the eldest of seven children he had significant leadership in the family. He received a standard education at academies in Macedon and nearby Lima. Despite the devout Quaker sympathies of his parents and the revivalistic fervor of the surrounding area, he rarely attended services, but he apparently still remained on good terms with the family.

Bullis enlisted as a corporal in the 126th New York Volunteer Infantry on August 8, 1862, and subsequently participated in several of the most important actions of the Civil War.[qv] At the battle of Harper's Ferry in September 1862 he was wounded and captured. He rejoined his regiment after exchange, was again wounded and captured at the battle of Gettysburg, and spent the following ten months confined to the notorious Libby Prison in Virginia. Having again been exchanged for Confederate prisoners in the spring of 1864, he joined the 118th United States Infantry, Colored, and received the rank of captain. He participated in a number of major combats around Richmond, Virginia, during the remaining months of the war.

Bullis reenlisted in the regular army as a second lieutenant on September 3, 1867, and returned to Texas, where his Civil War regiment had been stationed for Reconstruction[qv] duty following the war's end. Garrison assignments in coastal Texas provided little chance for military action or promotion, and so in November 1869 he was transferred by request to the new Twenty-fourth Infantry, composed of white officers and black enlisted men. Although the initial years of service along the lower Rio Grande border proved fairly routine, Bullis participated in a number of operations against small Indian raiding parties and cattle rustlers. More important, while stationed at Fort Clark in 1873, he received command of a special troop of Black Seminole scouts that had been mustered three years earlier. Because of their intimate knowledge of the terrain in Coahuila, Mexico, the scouts were assigned to Col. Ranald S. Mackenzie's[qv] expedition in 1873 against renegade Kickapoo camps at Remolino. Bullis and his twenty scouts distinguished themselves in battle and played an important role in Mackenzie's withdrawal to Texas. They served again with Mackenzie during the Red River War[qv] of 1874, which was directed against Comanches, Kiowas, and Southern Cheyennes in the Texas Panhandle. Sixteen years later Bullis received brevet citations for his "gallant service" at Remolino, for similar actions on the Pecos River and near Saragosa, Mexico, during 1875 and 1876 respectively, and for a fight in 1881 with Lipan Apaches at the Burro Mountains in Coahuila.

Upon Bullis's transfer in 1882 from command of the Black Seminole scouts to new duties in Indian Territory, the people of Kinney County, Texas, presented him with two ceremonial swords, one silver and one gold, in appreciation of his efforts to protect the border. The swords were later donated by his daughters to the Witte Museum[qv] in San Antonio. The Texas legislature likewise passed a special resolution in his honor. After service at Camp Supply in Indian Territory from 1882 to 1888, Bullis joined his old regiment in Arizona and served as agent for the Apaches at San Carlos Reservation. In 1893 he was transferred to Santa Fe, New Mexico Territory, to act as agent for the Pueblos and Jicarilla Apaches. Four years later he returned to Texas with the rank of major and was appointed paymaster at Fort Sam Houston. During the Spanish-American War and Philippine Insurrection he saw service in Cuba and the Philippines. In 1904 President Theodore Roosevelt promoted him to the rank of brigadier general, and on the following day Bullis retired from service.

Drawing upon knowledge from his scouting experiences across West Texas, Bullis purchased numerous tracts of land as investments. In 1885 he also entered into a lucrative partnership with fellow officer William R. Shafter[qv] and rancher John W. Spencer to open the Shafter silver mines in Presidio County (*see* SHAFTER MINING DISTRICT). The investments made Bullis a wealthy man and helped promote the settlement of West Texas. His marriage in 1872 to Alice Rodríguez of San Antonio ended with her death in 1887. Four years later he married

Josephine Withers, also of San Antonio; they had three daughters. Bullis died in San Antonio on May 26, 1911. He received a final, posthumous, honor when, on the eve of American entry into World War I,[qv] the new military training base near San Antonio was named Camp Bullis.

BIBLIOGRAPHY: Austin *American-Statesman*, March 2, 1989. Robert G. Carter, *On the Border with Mackenzie, or Winning West Texas from the Comanches* (Washington: Eynon Printing, 1935). Michael L. Tate, "Indian Scouting Detachments in the Red River War, 1874–1875," *Red River Valley Historical Review* 3 (Spring 1978). Edward S. Wallace, "General John Lapham Bullis, the Thunderbolt of the Texas Frontier," *Southwestern Historical Quarterly* 54, 55 (April, July 1951). Ernest Wallace and Adrian S. Anderson, "R. S. Mackenzie and the Kickapoos: The Raid into Mexico in 1873," *Arizona and the West* 7 (Summer 1965). Clayton W. Williams, *Texas' Last Frontier: Fort Stockton and the Trans-Pecos, 1861–1895* (College Station: Texas A&M University Press, 1982).

Michael L. Tate

BULLIS, TEXAS. Bullis was on the Southern Pacific Railroad five miles southeast of Holman Ranch, Texas, in southeastern Val Verde County. It was founded in 1882 as a siding and nonagency railroad station. Prehistoric people lived around the site 6,000 years ago and left art and belongings in caves and rockshelters. A settlement called Seminole was inhabited by Seminole Indians at the site of the station before the advent of the railroad. In the 1870s a battle occurred between Black Seminole scouts[qv] under the command of United States army lieutenant John Lapham Bullis[qv] and a band of hostile Indians near the site where the station was later built. Bullis and fewer than fifty scouts defended the southern Texas border west of Fort Clark against Indian attack from 1869 to 1882. When the railroad tracks reached Val Verde County, Lieutenant Bullis was honored by having a station named for him. The Bullis station was abandoned by the railroad after 1944, and the small community vanished.

BIBLIOGRAPHY: Kenneth Wiggins Porter, "The Seminole Negro-Indian Scouts, 1870–1881," *Southwestern Historical Quarterly* 55 (January 1952). Terrell County Heritage Commission, *Terrell County, Texas* (San Angelo: Anchor, 1978). Edward S. Wallace, "General John Lapham Bullis, the Thunderbolt of the Texas Frontier," *Southwestern Historical Quarterly* 54, 55 (April, July 1951).

Julia Cauble Smith

BULLIS GAP RANGE. The Bullis Gap Range is a ten-mile chain of peaks running from the northwest to the southeast and is located fifty miles southeast of Marathon in eastern Brewster County (the range's center point is 29°50′ N, 102°37′ W). The highest point in the range is at its northwest end, where the elevation is 3,073 feet above sea level. From that point the range descends gradually along a series of summits to its southeasternmost peak, with an elevation of 2,500 feet above sea level, then plummets some 1,000 feet to meet the Rio Grande. The Bullis Gap Range consists of Cretaceous (Comanchean) Santa Elena limestone, a thick-bedded gray limestone. Along its western face for its entire length the range is defined by a linear escarpment that rises some 300 to 500 feet above the plain. This may be the topographic expression of one of many northwest-running faults that occur throughout West Texas. The rugged landscape is dominated by vegetation characteristic of Chihuahuan Desert scrub, including several varieties of semisucculents such as lechuguilla, sotol, and yucca, and shrubs such as creosote bush and ocotillo. The range is almost exactly bisected by a deep defile called Bullis Gap. Like several landmarks in the region, the gap and the range bear the name of Gen. John Lapham Bullis[qv] of the United States Army. As a cavalry lieutenant, Bullis commanded a detachment of Black Seminole scouts[qv] in the area during the late 1870s and early 1880s, and he later became a major landowner in the Big Bend region.

BIBLIOGRAPHY: A. Michael Powell, "Vegetation of Trans-Pecos Texas," in *New Mexico Geological Society Guidebook* (Socorro, New Mexico: New Mexico Geological Society, 1980). Clayton W. Williams, *Texas' Last Frontier: Fort Stockton and the Trans-Pecos, 1861–1895* (College Station: Texas A&M University Press, 1982).

BULL LAKE. Bull Lake, sometimes known as Lebo Lake, is eight miles west of Littlefield in southwestern Lamb County (at 33°55′ N, 102°29′ W). The surrounding flat to gently sloping terrain is surfaced by loose sand and some shallow stony clay loams that support scrub brush and grasses. Near the lake grow chaparral, juniper, and oak. The lake is fed by several small streams that are unnamed on county highway maps.

BULLOCK, HENRY ALLEN (1906–1973). Henry Allen Bullock, first black professor appointed to the faculty of arts and sciences at the University of Texas at Austin, was born on May 2, 1906, in Tarboro, North Carolina, the son of Jessie and Aurelia Bullock. He attended local schools and graduated from Virginia Union University in Richmond, Virginia, in 1928, with a B.A. in social sciences and Latin classics; he received from the University of Michigan an M.A. in sociology and comparative psychology in 1929 and a Ph.D. in sociology in 1942. He was an Earhardt Foundation fellow at the University of Michigan and was twice a general-education fellow.

Bullock taught sociology at North Carolina Agricultural and Technical College in 1929–30. He was subsequently head of the Department of Sociology at Prairie View A&M, Waller County, Texas, where he taught from 1930 to 1949. In 1949–50 he was head of the Department of Sociology and chairman of the Division of Social Sciences at Dillard University in New Orleans. From 1950 to 1969 he was director of graduate research, head of the sociology department, and chairman of the Division of Social Sciences at Texas Southern University in Houston. In 1961 he was named a Minnie Stevens Piper Fellow as an outstanding Texas professor.

In the spring of 1969 Bullock became a visiting professor in the University of Texas at Austin history department to teach a new course, "The Negro in America." He was appointed a regular faculty member for the following fall semester. From 1969 to 1971 he was professor of history and sociology and chairman and designer of the university's first ethnic-studies program. Upon his retirement in 1971 he returned to his home in Houston.

In the early 1930s Bullock organized conferences in the South to train black teachers and administrators in more effective teaching techniques. Among his numerous publications were "A Comparison of the Academic Achievements of White and Negro College Graduates" in the *Journal of Educational Research* in 1950 and "Racial Attitudes and the Employment of Negroes" in the *American Journal of Sociology* in 1951, as well as "Urban Homicide in Theory and Fact" in the *Journal of Criminal Law, Criminology, and Police Science* (1955) and "Significance of the Racial Factor in the Length of Prison Sentences" in the same journal in 1961. "The Houston Murder Problem: Its Nature, Apparent Causes, and Probable Cures" was a special study for the office of the mayor of Houston in 1961. Bullock's various economic and ecological studies resulted in the publication of "Consumer Motivations in Black and White" in *Harvard Business Review* (1961) and "Spatial Aspects of the Differential Birthrate" in the *American Journal of Sociology* (1943). In 1957 he also helped produce a series of twelve thirty-minute films, "People are Taught To Be Different," with fellow faculty members of Texas Southern, for the National Educational Television and Radio center, Ann Arbor, Michigan. The film received second place in the world competition, presented by the Institute for Education by Radio-Television, at the Twenty-third American Exhibition of Educational Radio-Television Programs. Bullock did a study of the attitudes of young children toward the television series "Discovery '63" on a grant from the American Broadcasting Company. He believed that black colleges should continue to exist to develop the leadership needed for blacks and for the nation. He served on the Houston Community Council, the Texas Advisory Committee of the United States Civil Rights Commission, and the

Advisory Group for Equal Employment for President Lyndon B. Johnson.qv For a number of years Bullock wrote a weekly column for the Houston *Informer*, a black newspaper. His book, *A History of Negro Education in the South*, won the Bancroft Prize in 1968. Bullock died in Houston on February 8, 1973, and was buried in Paradise Cemetery there. He was survived by his wife, Merle (Anderson), and three children.

BIBLIOGRAPHY: Faculty Publications File, Texas Southern University. Vertical Files, Barker Texas History Center, University of Texas at Austin. *Naomi W. Ledé*

BULLOCK, JAMES WHITIS (1788–1859). James Whitis Bullock, early settler and soldier, was born in North Carolina in 1788. He enlisted in the army in 1809 at Charleston, South Carolina, and served five years under captains Mabson, Levall, and Woodruff. He fought under Gen. Andrew Jackson in Indian campaigns and in the battle of New Orleans (January 8, 1815). He was discharged at Natchez, Mississippi, as a sergeant. He was married about 1817 to Nancy Horton, sister of Alexander Horton.qv They had eleven children. In January 1824 the Bullock family moved from Washington Parish, Louisiana, to the Ayish Bayou district, in what became San Augustine County, Texas. They settled on the island in the Attoyac River. Colonel Bullock commanded the forces that besieged Nacogdoches on August 1, 1832, and sent a commission to José de las Piedrasqv commanding him to declare for the Constitution of 1824.qv Piedras's refusal led to the battle of Nacogdochesqv on August 2. On March 14, 1836, Bullock commanded a company of thirty-five men in the battle of Refugio.qv About 1852 he moved from San Augustine County to Collin County; his wife died there in 1854, after which he married Syntha Brumet. Bullock died on August 12, 1859, and was buried in Millwood, Texas.

BIBLIOGRAPHY: George L. Crocket, *Two Centuries in East Texas* (Dallas: Southwest, 1932; facsimile reprod., 1962). Mary Smith Fay, *War of 1812 Veterans in Texas* (New Orleans: Polyanthos, 1979). Alexander Horton, *A. Horton—Patriot of the Republic of Texas*, ed. Sam Malone (San Augustine, Texas: Malone, 1984). Nacogdoches Archives, Steen Library, Stephen F. Austin State University; Barker Texas History Center, University of Texas at Austin; Texas State Archives, Austin. Gifford E. White, *Character Certificates in the General Land Office of Texas* (1985). *McXie Whitton Martin*

BULLOCK, URIAH IRWIN (1808–1854). Uriah Irwin Bullock, soldier, was born in Georgia in 1808, the son of Batson and Comfort (Turner) Bullock. In 1835 Bullock was living in Macon, Georgia; he helped organize the Georgia Battalionqv for the Texas Revolutionqv and also advanced money to the volunteer unit as it made its way to Texas. When the battalion was officially organized in Refugio in February 1836, Uriah Bullock was listed as a company commander. Most members of the command were killed at the Goliad Massacre,qv but Bullock had fallen ill with the measles and had been left behind in Velasco, thus escaping their fate. He was discharged from the Texas army in May 1836. Bullock had apparently squandered much of his fortune supporting the revolution, and was seriously in debt when he returned to Georgia after the war. He married Sarah Cox around 1840; they had at least five children. After serving one term in the Georgia state legislature, he in 1841 moved to Panola County, Mississippi, to recoup his fortune. In 1851 the Texas state legislature paid Bullock $606 and issued a grant of 320 acres in what would eventually become Coleman County to reimburse him for his expenses and his services. Bullock died in Mississippi in 1854. *Mark Odintz*

BULLOCK, TEXAS. Bullock, a settlement around a station on the Wichita Falls and Southern Railway, was on what is now Farm Road 61 five miles west of Graham in central Young County. The school and railroad switch were named for John Crittendon Bullock, on whose ranch the station was built. During the 1930s the settlement supported a school, but by 1940–41 the nineteen students in grades one to eleven were attending school in Newcastle. The school and switch were gone by 1965, and Bullock was not identified on 1990 county maps.

BIBLIOGRAPHY: L. G. Cook, *The History of Education in Young County, Texas* (N.p., n.d; Barker Texas History Center, University of Texas at Austin). Barbara Neal Ledbetter, *Scrapbook of Young County* (Graham, Texas: Graham *News*, 1966).

BULLOCK HOUSE. Bullock House, the first hotel in Austin, was built in 1839, at the time that the city was being hastily constructed to become the capital of Texas. Hewn logs, probably oak, were used for construction; the second floor of the main building was of cottonwood planks. The hotel, located at the northwest corner of streets that are now Sixth Street and Congress Avenue, occupied half of the block, with a series of smaller log buildings serving as rooms for guests, the family of Richard Bullock, and servants. An upstairs room in the main building served as a dormitory for occasional troops and other visiting groups and as a meeting place when the first Presbyterian church services were held in Austin. China and furnishings from the Bullock home in Tennessee contrasted strangely with handmade hide-bottomed chairs. The Bullock Hotel was the social center of Austin for a number of years, as well as the official entertainment site for government officials; it accommodated early visitors including Alphonse Dubois de Saligny,qv whose quarrel with Bullock became an incident in Texas financial history known as the Pig War.qv In 1841 the main building was weatherboarded with pine. The hostel was known as Swisher's Hotel after 1852 and as Smith's Hotel after 1858.

BIBLIOGRAPHY: William R. Hogan, *The Texas Republic: A Social and Economic History* (Norman: University of Oklahoma Press, 1946; rpt. 1969). Alexander W. Terrell, "The City of Austin from 1839 to 1865," *Southwestern Historical Quarterly* 14 (October 1910).

BULL RUN CREEK. Bull Run Creek rises in Palo Duro Canyon,qv at the edge of the Llano Estacadoqv in southern Armstrong County (at 34°51′ N, 101°15′ W), and runs southwest for eight miles, across the JA Ranch,qv to its mouth on the Prairie Dog Town Fork of the Red River, just south of the Briscoe county line (at 34°45′ N, 101°17′ W). It traverses sloping mesquite plains with loamy soils.

BULLSHEAD CREEK. Bullshead (Bullhead) Creek rises two miles southwest of Skidmore in southwestern Bee County (at 28°14′ N, 97°45′ W) and runs southeast for ten miles to its mouth on Papalote Creek, a mile south of Papalote (at 28°10′ N, 97°36′ W). It crosses flat to rolling terrain with clay loam and sandy loam soils that support water-tolerant hardwoods and grasses.

BULL WAGON CREEK. Bull Wagon Creek rises in four branches in north central Taylor County and from the point of their convergence (at 32°22′ N, 99°58′ W) flows north about ten miles to join Mulberry Creek near the Taylor–Jones county line (at 32°31′ N, 99°53′ W). Upstream, the creek crosses rolling prairie with shallow to moderately deep clay loams in which grow oak, juniper, mesquite, and grasses; downstream, the terrain is flat and surfaced with sandy and clay loams that support water-tolerant hardwoods, conifers, and grasses.

BULVERDE, TEXAS. Bulverde, on Cibolo Creek nineteen miles west of New Braunfels in southwestern Comal County, was settled in 1850 and called Pieper Settlement, after Anton Pieper. For many years the closest post office was at Smithson Valley, and mail was delivered once a week to the house of Carl Koch in Bulverde. A local post office that operated from 1879 to 1919 was named for Luciano Bulverdo, an early area landowner. Since 1959 Bulverde has been served by a community post office that opened in Charles L. Wood's store. The town had a population of nearly 100 until the 1960s, when it fell to twenty-five. The Herrera, Ufnau, Honey Creek, Mustang Hill, and Green Hill schools were consolidated with the Bulverde school district, which had an enrollment of fifty-two in 1947. In more recent decades two residential developments have been built near the historic crossroads community.

BIBLIOGRAPHY: Oscar Haas, *History of New Braunfels and Comal County, Texas, 1844–1946* (Austin: Steck, 1968). *Oscar Haas*

BUNA, TEXAS. Buna is at the junction of Farm roads 253 and 1004, U.S. Highway 96, and State Highway 62, thirty-six miles north of Beaumont in south central Jasper County. The Beaumont Lumber Company mill in southern Jasper County was first called Carrolla for the Carroll family, prominent Beaumont lumbermen and industrialists. The site was subsequently renamed Buna, however, in honor of one of the family's cousins, Buna Corley. A post office was established there in 1893. With substantial operations in Jasper County underway by 1890, the Beaumont Lumber Company built a tram road from Buna to Ford's Bluff, on the Neches River. John Henry Kirby[qv] later bought the ten-mile-long tram line and by 1896 had converted it to a common carrier and extended it to Beaumont in the south and Roganville in the north. The revamped railroad was called the Gulf, Beaumont and Kansas City. Buna's economic position was solidified in 1902, when the Orange and Northwestern Railway linked the logging town with Orange. Four years later the Orange and Northwestern was extended from Buna to Newton. A townsite situated between the two railroad lines was platted on July 21, 1916. Although the region's economy suffered as the virgin forests were reduced, in later years second-growth timber continued to provide local jobs. In addition to logging, farming remains important to local residents. Numerous oilfields, first discovered in 1948, lie to the west and north of Buna and further augment the local economy. The weekly *East Texas News* was founded at Buna in 1967. The population of Buna was estimated at 650 in the early 1940s, 1,650 by the early 1970s, 2,000 in 1985, and 2,127 in 1990.

BIBLIOGRAPHY: S. G. Reed, *A History of the Texas Railroads* (Houston: St. Clair, 1941; rpt., New York: Arno, 1981). *Robert Wooster*

BUNAVISTA, TEXAS. Bunavista, west of Borger in southern Hutchinson County, was established in 1942 to house employees of a federal government synthetic rubber plant. It was allegedly named after the "Buna S" process for manufacturing synthetic rubber. When World War II[qv] cut off the supply of natural rubber, the Phillips Petroleum Company supervised the construction and operation of this plant, which produced butadiene, an essential ingredient of synthetic rubber. Almost overnight a settlement grew up around the enterprise. Local mail came through the post office in Borger. In 1955 Phillips bought the facility, which became its Copolymer Synthetic Rubber Plant. Several types of synthetic rubber for various uses were manufactured there in the 1980s. By 1966 much of the government housing around the premises had been sold and removed. The population in Bunavista was listed at 2,067 in 1960, at 1,402 in 1970, and at 1,410 in 1980. In 1979 part of Bunavista was incorporated into the city of Borger, and by 1990 Bunavista was a named locale in Borger.

BIBLIOGRAPHY: Hutchinson County Historical Commission, *History of Hutchinson County, Texas* (Dallas: Taylor, 1980).
H. Allen Anderson

BUNCOMBE, TEXAS. Buncombe (Bumcomb, Bunkom, Bunkum), off Farm Road 1970 nine miles southwest of Carthage in southwestern Panola County, was probably established after the Civil War.[qv] A school known as Alpine opened there around 1884, and a post office operated at the community from 1891 until 1893. In the mid-1930s the small settlement had the school, a church, a cemetery, and a number of houses. After World War II[qv] the school was consolidated with that of Clayton, and by the mid-1960s only a church, a cemetery, and a few scattered houses remained in the area. In 1990 Buncombe was a dispersed rural community with an estimated population of eighty-seven.

BIBLIOGRAPHY: Leila B. LaGrone, ed., *History of Panola County* (Carthage, Texas: Panola County Historical Commission, 1979). John Barnette Sanders, *Index to the Cemeteries of Panola County* (Center, Texas, 1964). *Christopher Long*

BUNGER, TEXAS. Bunger, on Farm Road 1287 eight miles south of Graham in southeastern Young County, was originally settled in 1872 by W. T. and Sam Bunger. A post office was established there in 1909 but was closed about 1922. In 1940 Bunger comprised twenty-five residents and one store. From 1974 to 1990 its population was estimated at twenty-six. *William R. Hunt*

BUNKER HILL, TEXAS. Bunker Hill, on State Highway 62 in southeastern Jasper County thirty-three miles northeast of Beaumont, was named for the Massachusetts hill of Revolutionary War fame. After the construction of the Orange and Northwestern Railway from Orange to Buna in 1902, a loading switch was laid at Bunker Hill for locally cut timber. A post office was established there in 1910. Although that office was discontinued in 1915, Bunker Hill was also the site of a Western Naval Stores turpentine camp, abandoned in 1918, and a Texas Company (later known as Texaco) pumping station, closed in 1943. The first producing well in the Bunker Hill oilfield was drilled in 1960. Additional small deposits were found during the next two decades. In 1986 scattered buildings and the "Bunker Hill Ranch" marked the rural community. An abandoned sawmill lay slightly to the west. Most of the area was being used as pastureland.
Robert Wooster

BUNKER HILL VILLAGE, TEXAS. Bunker Hill Village is an incorporated suburban community adjacent to Hedwig Village and Piney Point Village on the western edge of Houston, south of U.S. Highway 90, Interstate Highway 10, and the Missouri, Kansas and Texas Railroad in southwestern Harris County. Earlier, German farmers had settled in the area and local residents established sawmills to cut timber. The 1936 county highway map showed scattered dwellings in the area near one of several sawmills. The community incorporated in December 1954 with a mayor-council form of city government[qv] and established restrictions to prohibit businesses. By 1966 Bunker Hill Village was an affluent neighborhood with two public schools and two churches. Its population grew from 2,216 in 1962 to 4,442 in 1981, declined briefly to 3,668 in 1989, and rose to 4,061 in 1990.

BIBLIOGRAPHY: Hedwig Village *Gazette,* July 4, 1986.
Diana J. Kleiner

BUNKER'S MONTHLY. *Bunker's Monthly,* a periodical running through five volumes and one issue of a sixth, was edited by Peter Molyneaux[qv] and published in Fort Worth from January 1928 to June 1929 and in Dallas from August 1929 to July 1930. The title varied; from January to October 1928 it was *Bunker's Monthly, the Magazine of Texas,* and from December 1928 to July 1930 it was *Texas Monthly.* In July 1930 it was absorbed by *Texas Weekly,*[qv] under the same editorship. The magazine was illustrated by pictures, portraits, and maps. It proposed to avoid partisan politics and to publish anything about Texas that would be of interest to the average reader.

BUNNS BLUFF, TEXAS. Bunns Bluff is on the east bank of the Neches River in extreme western Orange County four miles from Beaumont. The bluff was probably named for Joseph Bunn, who owned the land title there and secured a post office in 1854. Although the Bunns Bluff post office was originally in Jefferson County, it was soon transferred to Orange County. Shortly after the Civil War,[qv] Bunns Bluff was a destination point for shingles rafted down the

Neches River. In 1880 the community had some thirty residents. Its post office was discontinued in 1900, and land at the bluff was purchased by the Beaumont Water Works in 1917. The Wiess and Bunns canals marked the site in 1974.

BIBLIOGRAPHY: James E. Johnson, An Economic History of Orange County, Texas, Prior to 1940 (M.A. thesis, Lamar State College of Technology, 1966). *Robert Wooster*

BUNSEN, JOHANN ERNST FRIEDRICH GUSTAV (1804–1836). Gustav Bunsen, soldier in the Texas war for independence, son of Johann Georg Bunsen, was born at Frankfurt am Main on August 25, 1804. The elder Bunsen was master of the Frankfurt mint. Gustav's cousin, Robert Wilhelm Bunsen, was a pioneer in chemistry, and his elder brother, George Bunsen, was a leading proponent of public education in the United States. Bunsen was trained as a physician and assimilated the doctrines of liberalism and nationalism as a university student. In 1831 he participated in the Polish rebellion against Russian domination. Two years later, in his native Frankfurt, he planned and directed an abortive revolt to overthrow the monarchical regimes of the German Confederation and establish a united and democratic national government. After the failure of this Frankfurt Insurrection on April 3, 1833, Bunsen narrowly escaped arrest by fleeing to America. He married Augusta Berchelmann at Belleville, Illinois, and settled briefly in Cincinnati, Ohio.

Shortly after Sam Houston[qv] issued his appeal for volunteers to serve against Antonio López de Santa Anna[qv] in October 1835, Bunsen joined Capt. James Tarlton's company of Louisville volunteers and set out for Texas. When these men arrived in San Antonio late in December, they found the city already in the hands of the Texas rebels. Eager for action, Bunsen then joined the expedition of James Grant and Col. Francis White Johnson[qqv] against Matamoros. With only sixty-four men, Grant and Johnson marched south and arrived at the village of San Patricio on January 22, 1836. Here Bunsen and his comrades spent a month scouring the countryside for horses for the reinforcement troops they hoped to receive. By this time Santa Anna had launched a major offensive against Texas from south of the Rio Grande. Early on the morning of February 27 a troop of Mexican cavalry surprised Bunsen's party at Julian de la Garza's ranch near San Patricio and slaughtered all but five of the Texans. Bunsen was riddled with bullets before he could fire a shot. While the Mexican army drove north to besiege the defenders of the Alamo, Bunsen was buried in the Garza family plot near the banks of the Nueces River. His name is inscribed on a monument in the old San Patricio Cemetery.

BIBLIOGRAPHY: Hermann Ehrenberg, *Texas und Seine Revolution* (Leipzig: Wigand, 1843; abridged trans. by Charlotte Churchill, *With Milam and Fannin*, Austin: Pemberton Press, 1968). Fannin Notes, Louis Wiltz Kemp Papers, Barker Texas History Center, University of Texas at Austin. Douglas Hale, "Gustav Bunsen: A German Rebel in the Texan Revolution," *East Texas Historical Journal* 6 (October 1968). Gustave Philipp Koerner, *Memoirs* (2 vols., Cedar Rapids, Iowa: Torch, 1909). Richard Schwemer, *Geschichte der freien Stadt Frankfurt am Main, 1814–1866* (3 vols., Frankfurt: Baer, 1910–18).

Douglas Hale

BUNTING, ROBERT FRANKLIN (1828–1891). Robert Franklin Bunting, pioneer Texas Presbyterian minister and chaplain of Terry's Texas Rangers, was born on May 9, 1828, at Hookstown, Beaver County, Pennsylvania, the son of John and Margaret (Moody) Bunting. He earned an A.B. degree at Washington College (now Washington and Jefferson College) in 1849, M.A. and B.D. degrees at Princeton and Princeton Theological Seminary in 1852, and a D.D. degree at Hampden-Sydney in 1867. He was appointed a missionary to Texas by the Presbyterian Church[qv] in 1852, and the next year he established churches at La Grange, Columbus, and Round Top. In 1856 he established the present First Presbyterian Church of San Antonio. In 1861 he served as commissioner from the West Texas Presbytery to the general assembly at Augusta, Georgia, which separated from the Northern church and founded the Presbyterian Church of the Confederate States of America. He returned as a commissioner to Southern Presbyterian assemblies in 1862 and 1864.

From 1861 to 1865 Bunting was chaplain and regimental historian of the Eighth Texas Cavalry[qv]—better known as Terry's Texas Rangers. His ninety-five letters written while he was war correspondent for the Houston *Daily Telegraph* and *Tri-Weekly Telegraph* (*see* TELEGRAPH AND TEXAS REGISTER) and the San Antonio *Herald*[qv] provide a history of the regiment. Bunting also operated a private postal service for Texas troops throughout the war and founded and operated the Texas Hospital for Texas soldiers at Auburn, Alabama, in 1864.

After the war he was pastor of the First Presbyterian Church, Nashville, Tennessee. He returned to Texas in 1869 to become pastor at Galveston, where he served until 1882. He founded and, from 1876 to 1880 edited, the synod's weekly newspaper, the *Texas Presbyterian.*[qv] He was moderator of the Texas Synod in 1872 and state clerk from 1872 to 1883. Bunting left Texas to serve as pastor at Rome, Georgia, in 1883–84. He acted as fiscal agent for Southwestern Presbyterian University (Southwestern College at Memphis, Tennessee) from 1885 to 1889 and then returned to the ministry at Gallatin, Tennessee, where he served from 1889 to 1891.

He was a prominent member of the grand lodges of both the Masonic lodge and the Odd Fellows, as well as a member of Sigma Alpha Epsilon. In 1853 he married Nina Ella Doxey of Columbus, but she died of yellow fever within a year. In 1860 he married Chrissinda Sharpe Craig at Steubenville, Ohio; they had six children. Bunting died at Gallatin, Tennessee, on September 19, 1891, and was buried there.

BIBLIOGRAPHY: Paula Mitchell Marks, "The Ranger Reverend," *Civil War Times Illustrated*, December 1985.

Paula Mitchell Marks

BUNTON, JOHN WHEELER (1807–1879). John Wheeler Bunton, patriot and statesman, son of Joseph Robert and Phoebe (Desha) Bunton, was born in Sumner County, Tennessee, on February 22, 1807. He was educated at Princeton College, Kentucky, and studied law in Gallatin, Tennessee. He arrived in Texas in 1833 and settled first in Austin's colony in San Felipe; soon thereafter he moved to Mina (Bastrop), where, on May 17, 1835, he was elected secretary of the local committee of safety. Such committees, newly organized for protection against the Indians, became the first step toward Texas independence. Bunton represented Mina at the Convention of 1836[qv] at Washington-on-the-Brazos, signed the Texas Declaration of Independence,[qv] and was a member of the committee to draft the constitution of the new republic.

Bunton was first sergeant of Robert M. Coleman's[qv] company of Mina Volunteers. For the siege of Bexar[qv] on December 5–10, 1835, he was transferred to Capt. John York's[qv] company. After being honorably discharged, he rejoined the army, on March 28, 1836. At the battle of San Jacinto[qv] he served on the staff of Gen. Sam Houston[qv] in Capt. Jesse Billingsley's[qv] company of Mina Volunteers. Afterward, Bunton returned to his home, and from October 3 to December 21, 1836, he represented Bastrop County in the House of Representatives of the First Congress of the Republic of Texas.

In the spring of 1836 Bunton returned to Gallatin, Tennessee, and married his sweetheart, Mary Howell. In April the Buntons, accompanied by 140 friends and slaves, left for Texas. At New Orleans they boarded the *Julius Caesar* carrying a cargo valued at $30,000. Near the Texas coast on April 12 the vessel was captured by Mexicans and taken to Matamoros, where all of the passengers were imprisoned for three months. After release, the Buntons and other passengers returned to Tennessee. Bunton soon headed another group that traveled by boat and entered Texas at Indianola on Matagorda Bay. While residing in Austin County, he was elected to the House of Representatives of the Third Congress. He is credited for the bill that established the Texas Rangers,[qv] the bill providing postal service, and the bill outlining the judiciary system. In 1840 he settled on a farm on Cedar Creek in Bastrop County, where he resided for seventeen years. In 1857 he moved to Mountain City, where he engaged in the cattle business. Bunton originated the famous Turkey Foot brand, which was registered in Hays County.

He joined the First Christian Church at Lockhart and was baptized in Walnut Creek in Caldwell County. He was a very tall man, and family members said it was necessary to dam the creek to get sufficient water to immerse him. He was a member of the Texas Veterans Association and a charter member of the Philosophical Society of Texas.[qqv] The Buntons had five sons and a daughter. On September 16, 1862, Mary Bunton died. Bunton was married again on July 26, 1965, in Bastrop County to Hermine C. Duval. He died at his home on August 24, 1879, and was buried in the Robinson Cemetery beside his first wife. In recognition of his patriotic services in behalf of Texas, on Texas Independence Day, March 2, 1932, the remains of John Wheeler and Mary Howell Bunton were moved and reinterred in the State Cemetery[qv] in Austin under the auspices of the Daughters of the Republic of Texas.[qv]

BIBLIOGRAPHY: Sam Houston Dixon, *Men Who Made Texas Free* (Houston: Texas Historical Publishing, 1924). James L. Haley, *Texas: An Album of History* (Garden City, New York: Doubleday, 1985). Louis Wiltz Kemp, *The Signers of the Texas Declaration of Independence* (Salado, Texas: Anson Jones, 1944; rpt. 1959). Bill Moore, *Bastrop County, 1691–1900* (Wichita Falls: Nortex, 1977). Annie Doom Pickrell, *Pioneer Women in Texas* (Austin: Steck, 1929). Worth Stickley Ray, *Austin Colony Pioneers* (Austin: Jenkins, 1949; 2d ed., Austin: Pemberton, 1970). Ann Miller Strom, *The Prairie City: A History of Kyle, Texas, 1880–1980* (Burnet, Texas: Nortex, 1981).

Ann Miller Strom

BUNYAN, TEXAS. Bunyan is on Farm Road 219 ten miles west of Stephenville in western Erath County. It was established the 1870s and named, according to some sources, for an early Methodist preacher in the area, Alexander Bunyan. Other sources claim that when the inhabitants gathered to name their first one-room schoolhouse, one early resident called out "John Bunyan's Academy!" Bunyan cemetery has graves dating back to 1879. The first school was built about 1880 with lumber hauled from Dallas. A two-room school was built in 1905, and further rooms were later added on. At one time the Bunyan school served 140 pupils and provided homes for its teachers. Church services were held in private homes and in the old schoolhouse. The first church building was erected by Methodists and called Elkin's Chapel. The first Baptist church was initially called Cow Creek Chapel, for nearby Cow Creek, but eventually changed its name to Bunyan Baptist. In 1888 the Methodist Episcopal church was organized and met in the Elkin's Chapel building. It built its own church in 1903 (rebuilt in 1920). A Nazarene church was built on a hill overlooking Bunyan but was later dismantled. A post office opened in the community in 1891. In 1896 Bunyan had a population of ten, a flour mill, and a cotton gin. The community's first grocery store was built around 1900. The post office closed in 1904. Bunyan also had several blacksmith shops at different times. In 1935 the school had three teachers and sixty-one pupils. In 1940 Bunyan had a school, two churches, and scattered dwellings. The school was consolidated with those of Dublin in the 1940s. In 1965 Bunyan had one church and scattered dwellings, and in 1966 its population was estimated at twenty. In 1988 two churches, one business, a grain elevator, and a cemetery were at the site. In 1990 the population was still estimated at twenty.

BIBLIOGRAPHY: Henry Herbert Miller, A Proposed Consolidation Plan for the Schools of Erath County, Texas (M.A. thesis, University of Texas, 1938). H. Grady Perry, *Grand Ol' Erath* (Stephenville, Texas, 1974).

Mark Odintz

BURCH, VALENTINE IGNATIUS (1813–1892). Valentine Ignatius Burch, soldier at the battle of San Jacinto,[qv] was born near Bardstown, Kentucky, on February 14, 1813, the son of Samuel Lewis and Dorothea (Brown) Burch, both of Maryland Catholic stock. He was educated at nearby St. Mary's College. In 1826 the family moved to Texas, first to the Nacogdoches area and later to the vicinity of San Augustine. Burch and his younger brother James enlisted in Capt. William Kimbro's[qv] company on March 15, 1836, and participated in the battle of San Jacinto,[qv] where they assisted in the capture of Col. Juan N. Almonte.[qv] The brothers reenlisted on June 4, 1836, in Capt. Henry Reed's[qv] company and served until September 4 of that year. After the revolution Burch settled at Colita in Polk County. In 1843 he married Helen Elmira Cauble, the daughter of Peter Cauble,[qv] and settled at Peach Tree Village in Tyler County (*see* PEACH TREE VILLAGE, TEXAS), where he managed the plantation of his father-in-law as well as his own property in several counties. At Peach Tree Village he was one of the charter subscribers for a private academy in 1870. The Burch home was for years a social center and a haven for Catholic missionaries to East Texas. Burch died on November 26, 1892, and was buried in the family cemetery at Peach Tree Village. He was a member of the Texas Veterans Association.[qv]

BIBLIOGRAPHY: Sam Houston Dixon and Louis Wiltz Kemp, *The Heroes of San Jacinto* (Houston: Anson Jones, 1932). Emma Haynes, The History of Polk County (MS, Sam Houston Regional Library, Liberty, Texas, 1937; rev. ed. 1968). Thomas L. Miller, *Bounty and Donation Land Grants of Texas, 1835–1888* (Austin: University of Texas Press, 1967). Aline T. Rothe, History of Education in Polk County (M.A. thesis, University of Texas, 1934).

John P. Landers

BURDETTE WELLS, TEXAS. Burdette Wells (Burditt Well, Burdetts Well, and Burditt) was developed as a resort and health spa in the 1870s by Dr. H. M. Burditt of Luling. It was on the Clear Fork of Plum Creek midway between Luling and Lockhart. In 1880 the resort was becoming quite successful and shipped 1,200 gallons of water out for public consumption. According to Burditt the water contained large quantities of magnesia and sulfuric acid and was capable of "cur[ing] Liver and Spleen derangement, Bilious Fever, Hectic Fever, Debility, Rheumatism, Erysipelas, Scurvy, bad ulcers, Skin Eruptions, Dropsy, Dyspepsia, Yellow Jaundice... and various diseases instituted and perpetuated by a vitiated condition of the biliary secretions ... [including] all Venereal Diseases, Acute or Chronic consumption in the early stage, where recuperative action is sufficient." The water's popularity led to the construction of a two-story hotel and bathhouse and the establishment of a whistle stop and railroad spur on the San Antonio and Aransas Pass. A local post office named Burdett Well operated in 1878–79; for five months in 1894 a post office operated under the name Burditt.

Control of the resort eventually fell into the hands of the J. H. Maulding Land Company of San Antonio, and Capt. T. P. Bishop directed the hotel and bathhouse. At one time there were plans to expand the enterprise and sell up to 1,000 business and residential lots near the wells. Eventually, the facility lost business and began to deteriorate. However, before this occurred Burdette Wells was also the site of camp meetings that drew crowds of people from a thirty-mile radius to listen to evangelical preaching for two to four weeks at a time. In 1990 there were no known remains of the community.

BIBLIOGRAPHY: Francis W. Wilson, "Burditt's Well," *Plum Creek Almanac*, Fall 1987.

Vanessa L. Davis

BURDINE, JOHN ALTON (1905–1967). John Alton Burdine, teacher and university administrator, was born on February 9, 1905, in Smithville, Mississippi, the son of W. B. and Margie (Knight) Burdine. He moved to Texas as a youth with his parents. He graduated from the Paris, Texas, high school in 1921 and received B.A. and M.A. degrees from the University of Texas in 1926. Except for graduate study at Harvard University, where he received an M.A. degree in 1933 and a Ph.D. degree in 1939, and one year in Washington, D.C., he was a continuous resident of Texas.

Burdine was vice president of the University of Texas from 1941 to 1945, when he resigned in protest against the dismissal of Homer Price Rainey[qv] as university president. He resumed his career in the government department, only to return again to administrative functions when he became associate dean of the graduate school and acting dean of the College of Arts and Sciences in 1957. He became dean of the College of Arts and Sciences in 1958 while continuing to play a significant role in the university's graduate program. He served on a large number of committees concerned with various aspects of governmental change in the state. For a time he was a consultant to the administrator of the Federal Security Agency and served the United States Civil Service Commission and the United States Employment Service as a consultant. He held various committee assignments in the National Municipal League and the National Civil Service League. He assisted with the faculty fellowship program of the Fund for the Advancement of Education and was a member of the board of trustees of the College Entrance Examining Board. His activities within his own academic discipline were equally broad. He served as a vice president of the American Political Science Association, as an officer in several of its regional groups, and on committees of the Social Science Research Council. His many publications dealt with problems of administration at all levels of government.

Burdine married Marian Griffith in 1931, and they had one child. At the time of his death on September 15, 1967, he had been associated with the University of Texas for more than forty years. In 1968 the J. Alton Burdine Fund of the Arts and Sciences Foundation was established at the university as a memorial to him. In 1970 a new university building was named in his honor.

BIBLIOGRAPHY: John Alton Burdine Papers, Barker Texas History Center, University of Texas at Austin. Vertical Files, Barker Texas History Center, University of Texas at Austin. *W. Gordon Whaley*

BUREAU, ALLYRE (1810–1859). Allyre Bureau, political writer, Texas colonizer, musician, and composer, was born in Cherbourg, France, in 1810. He studied at the école Polytechnique and the Paris Conservatory, fought against the king in the July Revolution (1830), and was briefly an artillery officer. He was a Fourierist and friend of Victor P. Considérant.[qv] He wrote for *Démocratie pacifique*, a Fourierist publication, urged social changes in other publications, ran unsuccessfully for national office in 1848 and 1849, and spent some time in prison after the Paris riots of June 1848. He also translated English novels into French.

On September 26, 1854, in Brussels, he signed as a director the charter of the Société de Colonisation Europeo-Americaine au Texas, which founded the La Réunion[qv] colony of French and Swiss emigrants near Dallas, an experiment in the practical application of Fourier's theory. Bureau worked as part of the central agency in Paris and served on a subcommittee to initiate the society's operation. When the colony's financial problems became dire, he traveled to America with his wife, three sons, and daughter; they arrived at La Réunion on January 17, 1857. Upon the resignation of François J. Cantagrel[qv] he assumed the directorship of the colony, but, unable to reverse its deterioration, he dissolved the society on January 28, 1857. Bureau remained at the settlement, where his musical talent contributed much to the colony's reputation for good musical entertainment. He brought the first piano to Dallas and composed such songs as "Clang, Clang, Clang," and "Choose a Flower." One of his compositions appeared in a songbook used in the Dallas public schools. While beginning a trip to France with his wife and daughter for an extended visit, he contracted yellow fever and died in a sanitarium at Kellum Springs, about fifty miles north of Houston, in late 1859.

BIBLIOGRAPHY: *Dictionnaire de biographie française* (13 vols., Paris: Letouzey et Ane, 1933–75). George H. Santerre, *White Cliffs of Dallas: The Story of La Reunion* (Dallas: Book Craft, 1955). Lota M. Spell, *Music in Texas* (Austin, 1936; rpt., New York: AMS, 1973).

Joan Jenkins Perez

BURELL, TEXAS. Burell, also known as French Settlement because most of its settlers spoke French, was three miles northwest of Castroville in northeastern Medina County. Many of the original settlers in Castro's colony[qv] settled in French Settlement between 1844 and 1846. The community was probably named for Louis Burell, cattleman and the first Medina county sheriff. Burell helped to establish the Burell school, which in 1906 had twenty-one students and one teacher. Box-supper parties were held at the school in the 1920s. The school was closed in the 1930s, and the building was purchased by Cora Burell for use as a restaurant, Cora's Place. By 1947 Burell had been abandoned.

BIBLIOGRAPHY: Castro Colonies Heritage Association, *The History of Medina County, Texas* (Dallas: National Share Graphics, 1983). Houston B. Eggen, History of Public Education in Medina County, Texas, 1848–1928 (M.A. thesis, University of Texas, 1950).

Ruben E. Ochoa

BURFORD, NATHANIEL MACON (1824–1898). Nathaniel Macon Burford, attorney, judge, and Civil War[qv] soldier, was born on June 24, 1824, in Smith County, Tennessee, to John Hawkins and Nancy (McAlister) Burford. He graduated from Irving College and the law school at Lebanon, Tennessee, and was admitted to the bar in 1845. He volunteered for service in the Mexican War,[qv] but by the time he got to Knoxville the state's quota had been filled. He then worked his way to Shreveport, Louisiana, and walked from there to Jefferson, Texas, in January 1847. There he became deputy clerk of the district court. He found, however, that the bar was too full for his career ambitions, so he pushed on to Dallas in October 1848, carrying five dollars and several letters of recommendation.

In Dallas he soon formed a law partnership with John H. Reagan[qv] and in 1850 and 1852 was elected district attorney. He drafted the charter for Dallas, which the legislature accepted in 1856, and in the same year became judge of the new Sixteenth Judicial District, a post he held until 1861, when he resigned to join, as a private, the First Texas Artillery under Capt. John Jay Good.[qv] In 1862 he received a commission as colonel and raised a regiment from Dallas, Kaufman, Ellis, Hill, Navarro, McLennan, and Parker counties. This regiment, designated the Nineteenth Texas Cavalry, was ordered to Arkansas, where it joined a brigade forming under Col. William Henry Parsons.[qv] The Nineteenth Texas served the entire war in the Trans-Mississippi Department, generally under the command of Lt. Col. Benjamin W. Watson or Maj. John B. Williams rather than Colonel Burford. After the Red River campaign[qv] in 1864 Burford offered his resignation, admitting that he did not possess the ability to lead troops in combat. His commanding officers agreed, commended his patriotism, and accepted the resignation.

After resuming his legal practice, he became president of the Soldiers' Home Association (1864) and was elected to the House of the Eleventh Legislature (1866), where he was chosen speaker. He was removed from his office along with others by Gen. Philip H. Sheridan[qv] as an "impediment to Reconstruction." In 1868 he endorsed the organization of a Conservative party of Dallas County that condemned "Negro supremacy" and supported President Andrew Johnson's pro-South policy. He was elected presiding justice of Dallas County in April 1875 and judge of the Eleventh District in February 1876, only to resign in April 1877 because of bad health. He was appointed United States commissioner in 1879 and served until 1881.

Burford was a charter member of Tannehill Masonic lodge No. 52 and its first master. On January 18, 1854, he married Mary Knight, daughter of a Dallas pioneer family; they had eight children. Burford was a Democrat and a vestryman in the Episcopal Church. He died in Dallas on May 10, 1898, and is buried in Greenwood Cemetery.

BIBLIOGRAPHY: *Biographical Souvenir of the State of Texas* (Chicago: Battey, 1889; rpt., Easley, South Carolina: Southern Historical Press, 1978). Berry B. Cobb, *A History of Dallas Lawyers, 1840 to 1890* (Bar Association of Dallas, 1934). Dallas *Daily Times Herald,* May 11, 1898. George Jackson, *Sixty Years in Texas* (Dallas: Wilkinson Printing, 1908; rpt., Quanah, Texas: Nortex, 1975). *Joan Jenkins Perez*

BURGENTINE CREEK. Burgentine Creek rises two miles south of Austwell in eastern Refugio County (at 28°22′ N, 96°52′ W) and runs southwest for four miles, through the Aransas National Wildlife Refuge,[qv] to its mouth, on St. Charles Bay in northern Aransas County (at 28°16′ N, 96°55′ W). The name, also variously spelled Bergantin, Vergantine, and Brigatine, is supposed to have been given to the stream because a Spanish barkentine, carrying the payroll for the Mexican garrisons at Bexar and Goliad, was caught in a storm and driven up from Aransas Bay to St. Charles Bay and up the stream. The vessel was supposedly left stranded in the prairie, where it was later found by colonists who used the metal and timber in building homes and constructing implements. Early Spanish records refer to present Goose Island as Isla de Bergantin and to St. Charles Bay as El Bergantin. The surrounding flat, marshy terrain is surfaced by dark clays that support mesquite, cacti, and grasses. *Hobart Huson*

BURGES, RICHARD FENNER (1873–1945). Richard Fenner Burges, legislator and conservationist, the son of Bettie (Rust) and William H. Burges, was born in Seguin, Texas, on January 7, 1873. He attended the Agricultural and Mechanical College of Texas (now Texas A&M University) for one year, read law in the offices of his father in El Paso and J. D. Guinn in New Braunfels, and was admitted to the bar in 1894. He made his home at El Paso after 1892. In 1898 he married Ethel Petrie Shelton; they had a daughter. Burges took part in a so-called "clean up" of El Paso in 1904, was city attorney, and in 1907 wrote the charter for the establishment of commission city government in El Paso. In 1908 he represented Texas at President Theodore Roosevelt's conference of governors. As a member of the House in the Thirty-third and Thirty-fourth legislatures, 1913–15, he wrote or influenced the passing of the Texas Irrigation Code, the royalty mining act, a forestry act, a married women's property act, and a compulsory-education act.

In June 1917 Burges organized Company B, Texas National Guard,[qv] which was incorporated into the Thirty-sixth Infantry Division[qv] as Company A, 141st Infantry. He commanded his battalion in the battle of the Argonne and was awarded the Croix de Guerre for distinguished service.

He was associate counsel for the United States in the arbitration on the Chamizal Dispute[qv] with Mexico in 1910–11. He was president of the International Irrigation Congress, 1915–16, and was general counsel for the El Paso County Water Improvement District. In 1923 he was attorney for Texas interests in negotiation with New Mexico on the division of waters of the Pecos River. Burges was also special counsel for the Texas–Rio Grande Compact Commission and from 1935 to 1940 was a special attorney for the United States Department of Justice in the negotiations with Mexico for the Rio Grande rectification project. From 1921 to 1923 he was president of the Texas Forestry Association.[qv] He belonged to the American Forestry Association and helped promote the development of Carlsbad Caverns in New Mexico as a national park. A member of the board of the El Paso Public Library, of the Texas State Historical Association,[qv] and of the Texas History and Library Commission, he was a noted bibliophile of the Southwest and had a Texas history collection of 5,000 items. Burges died at El Paso on January 13, 1945.

BIBLIOGRAPHY: Richard Fenner Burges Papers, Barker Texas History Center, University of Texas at Austin. Buckley B. Paddock, *History of Texas: Fort Worth and the Texas Northwest Edition* (4 vols., Chicago: Lewis, 1922). *Southwestern Historical Quarterly,* Texas Collection, April 1945. Vertical Files, Barker Texas History Center, University of Texas at Austin. Owen P. White, *Out of the Desert: The Historical Romance of El Paso* (El Paso: McMath, 1924). *Who's Who in America,* 1944–45.

BURGES, WILLIAM HENRY (1867–1946). William Henry Burges, lawyer and political and civic leader of El Paso, was born in Seguin, Texas, on November 12, 1867, the son of William Henry and Bettie (Rust) Burges. He received an LL.B. degree from the University of Texas law school in 1889 and moved to El Paso in September of that year seeking a healthier climate for the asthma that plagued him all his life. Burges practiced law in El Paso from 1889 to 1946, except for a brief period (1917–18) as partner in a Chicago firm, and was El Paso city attorney in 1893–94. From the 1890s to the early 1900s, he led the reform group that fought open gambling and other public vices in what was then a rowdy border town. This civic attitude was dangerous, since such notorious gunmen as Bass Outlaw, John Selman,[qv] and especially John Wesley Hardin[qv] frequented El Paso in those years. Burges proposed a "reservation" in the city where prostitutes could ply their trade away from the traffic of polite society. Tillie Howard, famous El Paso madam, retained Burges to represent her in various legal dealings. He was also a champion of El Paso's large Chinese population. Mar Ben Chew, local Chinese leader, was a longstanding friend and client, and Burges often traveled to the federal court in San Antonio to defend El Paso citizens charged under the Chinese Exclusion Act. He also handled various Rio Grande boundary suits and legal disputes growing out of the Mexican Revolution. After 1897 he was associated with William W. Turney[qv] in the law firm of Turney and Burges, and became a dominant figure in the small group that controlled the politics of El Paso.

His most celebrated case was the defense of the copper companies in the civil and criminal prosecutions that arose out of the deportation of striking miners from Bisbee, Arizona, in 1917. On July 12, 1917, the sheriff of Bisbee and 1,200 deputized citizens rounded up more than 1,100 striking copper miners organized by representatives of the Industrial Workers of the World, loaded them on freight cars, and transported them to New Mexico, where they were abandoned in a remote area. Two miners died. Civil damage suits against the copper companies and the town totalled $14,000,000; nearly 400 Bisbee residents, including copper officials, were charged with kidnapping. Burges had moved to Chicago in 1917 to accept a lucrative partnership in a firm there, but found the climate unhealthy and the pace of urban life not to his taste. He had already determined to return to El Paso when Walter Douglas, vice president and general manager of Phelps Dodge Corporation, came to Chicago to ask him to represent the copper company and other defendants in the case. Burges returned to El Paso in 1918 and resumed his place in the firm of Turney, Burges, Culwell, Holliday, and Pollard. *The State of Arizona v. Harry E. Wootton,* popularly known as the Bisbee IWW Deportation Case, was tried in Tombstone, Arizona, in 1920. Burges's argument before the court—that the community, under "the law of necessity," had the right to preserve itself—was apparently convincing: only one man was actually tried on the charge of kidnapping (he was found not guilty), and by 1921 civil suits stemming from the case had been settled for $100,000. At the end of the spectacular trial Burges advised the companies involved to permit the miners to organize a responsible union.

Burges was a charter sponsor of the El Paso Symphony Orchestra, prepared the Women's Club charter when it incorporated in 1910, and was one of the founding members of the city's famous Toltec Club. In 1904 he was a delegate to the Universal Congress of Lawyers and Jurists in St. Louis. He served as president of the Texas Bar Association (*see* STATE BAR OF TEXAS) in 1909–10, and was a regent of the University of Texas from 1911 to 1914. He also served on the executive committee of the American Bar Association from 1912 to 1915, was one of the sponsors of the formation of the second *Texas Law Review*,[qv] and was on the advisory committee of the original edition of *Texas Jurisprudence.* In 1924 he was special assistant to the United States attorney general in charge of postal-fraud prosecutions in northern Texas.

He married Ada Dean in 1892 in El Paso; she died of pneumonia the same year. In 1896 he married Anna Pollard of Fulton, Missouri. Burges had one of the finest private libraries in Texas, and while living in Chicago he negotiated the purchase of the famous Wrenn Library for the University of Texas. After his death on May 11, 1946, his library of more than 15,000 literary and philosophical classics was sold to the University of Houston. The College of Mines (now the University of Texas at El Paso) named Burges Hall for him. A street and school in El Paso are named for him.

BIBLIOGRAPHY: J. F. Hulse, *Texas Lawyer: The Life of William H. Burges* (El Paso: Mangan, 1982). *Proceedings of the Philosophical Society of Texas,* 1946. Vertical Files, Barker Texas History Center, University of Texas at Austin. Owen P. White, *Out of the Desert: The Historical Romance of El Paso* (El Paso: McMath, 1924). *Who Was Who in America,* Vol. 2. *J. F. Hulse*

BURGESS, GEORGE FARMER (1861–1919). George F. Burgess, farmer, lawyer, and public official, son of Dr. C. H. A. Burgess, was born on September 21, 1861, in Wharton, Texas. In 1888 he moved to Fayette County to begin farming near Flatonia. He subsequently worked as a clerk in a country store, studied law after work, and was admitted to the bar in 1882. Soon afterward, he began his practice at La Grange. On December 28, 1888, he married Marie Louise Sims. Burgess moved to Gonzales in 1884 and served as prosecuting attorney from 1886 until 1889. He was a Democratic presidential elector in 1892. He was elected to the Fifty-seventh Congress in 1900 and served for eight consecutive terms, until March 3, 1917. In an address to a Wharton audience in 1902 he lambasted monopolies and Republicans, asserting that the "great trust evil is caused by Republican governmental favoritism." He closed his speech with a ringing pronouncement: "Do not vote for me because I was born in your town and am a Wharton boy! Do not vote for me because you believe I will make you a good representative! But because I am a Democrat, because my victory means the triumph of the party, for whose good we must all put forth our most earnest efforts, because the triumph of democracy means the strongest factor for the nation's welfare." Burgess made an unsuccessful bid for nomination to the United States Senate in 1916, after which he resumed his law practice in Gonzales. He died in Gonzales on December 31, 1919, and was buried in the Masonic Cemetery.

BIBLIOGRAPHY: Vertical Files, Barker Texas History Center, University of Texas at Austin. *Stephen L. Hardin*

BURGESS, TEXAS. Burgess is on the Little River twelve miles southeast of Belton in southeastern Bell County. The community had a post office from 1894 to 1904 and twenty inhabitants in 1896. Nearby Reed's Lake School enrolled thirty-five pupils in 1903. In 1940 Burgess had a population of twenty-five and one business establishment. By 1964 the site was no longer identified on the topographical map, though there were several scattered dwellings there and the population was reported as fifteen. *Mark Odintz*

BURGESS CREEK. Burgess Creek rises three miles southeast of Weatherford in southeastern Parker County (at 32°43′ N, 97°46′ W) and flows east for six miles, passing through nearly level to rolling land with a surface of shallow to deep clayey and loamy soils that principally support grasses. For most of the county's history the Burgess Creek area has been used as rangeland. The stream empties into Willow Creek, just north of Annetta (at 32°43′ N, 97°40′ W).

BURIED CITY. The Buried City is an important pre-Columbian site on Wolf Creek eighteen miles southeast of Perryton in Ochiltree County. It was well known to buffalo hunters and early ranchers in the area by the late 1870s because its impressive ruins were visible aboveground. Large mounds concealed the remains of stone dwellings, and numerous artifacts were found on the ground around them. The first scientific excavation of the ruins was conducted in the spring of 1907 by T. L. Eyerly, who taught science and history at the short-lived Canadian Academy.[qv] With several interested students, among them fifteen-year-old Floyd V. Studer,[qv] Eyerly probed the rock-slab walls and uncovered many evidences of pre-Columbian habitation. In the academy bulletin Eyerly published two brief papers concerning the findings, reportedly the first discovery of pueblo ruins subsequently linked with the Texas Panhandle Pueblo Culture, or Antelope Creek Focus. The largest of these ruins, later named for geologist Charles N. Gould,[qv] was labeled the Temple. Over the next several years Studer brought the buried city to the attention of other archeologists, most notably Warren K. Moorehead of Phillips Academy in Andover, Massachusetts. Moorehead corresponded with Studer extensively and in 1919 and 1920 made trips to the Panhandle[qv] to examine the ruins. In his book *Archaeology of the Arkansas River Valley* (1931) Moorehead explained that the ancient village site, extending over 3,500 feet along Wolf Creek, was the product of a fairly advanced aboriginal culture of unknown origins. At that time the land on which the "city" was located was part of the Shady Nook Ranch, owned by James T. Fryer, for whom Lake Fryer was named.

Although Studer conducted intermittent surveys of the ruins through 1966, no further major excavations were made. In the early 1980s, however, former Perryton mayor Harold D. Courson, president of Courson Oil and Gas and Natural Gas Anadarko, bought the site and surrounding property. Through his efforts the Texas Historical Commission[qv] was given two easements covering about fifty acres; the site was added to the National Register of Historic Places and was also made a state archeological landmark protected by the Texas Antiquities Code. In 1985 and 1986 Courson supplied the funds for archeological excavations directed by David T. Hughes, then a doctoral student at the University of Oklahoma. Beginning in the summer of 1987 annual excavations were done in conjunction with a Texas Archeological Society field school.

About seven areas of the Buried City, consisting of some five ruins of dwellings, none of which is on the conservation easement, were unearthed by 1988. Between thirty and forty ruins along the creek are within a 900-acre block of land surrounding the easement. The surveys seem to reveal a different picture of the Indians who inhabited the site between A.D. 800 and 1500 than Moorehead and Studer had theorized. Hughes argued that the Buried City inhabitants were of a culture distinct from that of the contemporaneous Antelope Creek Focus. Over several centuries these people developed their own society in relative isolation, even though they retained general Plains Indian characteristics. According to Hughes's hypothesis, the Buried City people were of Caddoan linguistic stock and may have been related to the Wichitas or Pawnees.

The architecture, though comparable to that of the Antelope Creek Focus and the modern Pueblo tribes, appears to have been of local development. Many of the dwellings apparently were built on a scale that was massive by prehistoric standards; one house was found to have had up to 650 square feet of floor space. Large caliche boulders mined from nearby valley walls outlined the rectangular structure. After the stones were set in place the dwelling interior was dug out to an average depth of two feet, with the fill being used to erect the thick exterior walls of the structure. A center aisle ten to twelve feet wide included a hearth, and wooden posts twelve to eighteen inches in diameter stood in each corner to form roof supports. The entrances, crawlways eight to ten feet long, always faced east. In addition to excavating dwelling space, the people also dug circular storage pits about three to four feet deep; apparently these were used until rodents infested them, then were filled with trash. Certainly, digging in the hard caliche must have been a task for these people who had only stone and bone tools.

Although Buried City artifacts such as projectile points, stone knives, and bone tools are similar to those of other contemporary Plains people, the pottery of the Buried City folk is considerably different from that of their Antelope Creek neighbors in that it was finished more smoothly and in some cases polished and decorated, in contrast to the cord-marked, conical vessels of the Antelope Creek villages. Buried City pottery closely resembles that known as Geneceo, from southwestern Kansas. Apparently the inhabitants of Buried City engaged in trade for flint, but although some from the Alibates flint quarries[qv] has been unearthed, much of the Buried City flint was from cobbles and pebbles found along the Canadian River. Perhaps relations between the Buried City folk and the Indians who mined the quarries were not always cordial. There is scant evidence of trade with Mexico or the Southwestern tribes. Some of the flint appears to have come from the Niobrara area on the Kansas-Nebraska line and some from a site in Kay County, Oklahoma. Although archeologists early in the century reported stone cairns concealing remains of the dead on the canyon rim near the village, these apparently were disturbed by passing visitors before the recent excavations, since few burial sites have been located.

Corn and probably beans and squash were among the crops cultivated by the Buried City people. They apparently had a two-tiered system of plots. While some crops were planted in the creek's floodplain to take advantage of the moisture retained in the sandy bottoms, others were sown on higher ground; water was diverted along slopes containing brush diversions to distribute the rainfall more widely. These higher plots were effective safeguards against flooding of the lower fields. At the time of its occupation, the area around the village was well watered by several springs fed by the Ogallala Aquifer. These kept Wolf Creek, which cut into the aquifer's upper level, flowing all year long. Such a region of abundant water often attracted bison, ducks, turkeys, and small animals like rabbits and prairie dogs, all of which provided meat and skins for the Indians. Fish and mussels likewise were staple fare in their diet.

Hughes speculated that the ruins composing the Buried City site represent a series of villages or semipermanent farmsteads inhabited over the course of centuries. At least five groups of structures, each containing seven or eight dwellings, have been identified. It is possible that each group, which may have housed as many as 100 people, was occupied for roughly twenty years, until some local resource, such as firewood, was exhausted. Then the Indians would move along the creek to another site, which they inhabited for another generation. This gradual trek up and down the creek continued until the area was abandoned, probably as a result of drought or intrusion from later nomadic tribes around 1500. The influence from southwestern Kansas on the Buried City populace may have come through trade and intermarriage. Hughes concludes that trade contacts could indeed provide an avenue for bringing husbands and wives into the community.

Much interpretive work remains to be done with the information Hughes and others have gleaned. Nevertheless, Buried City is one of the most important and fascinating Texas archeological finds and sheds light on the Panhandle area's Indian past. A historical marker that briefly tells the site's early history is located on Lake Fryer Road four miles east of U.S. Highway 83.

BIBLIOGRAPHY: Claude W. Dooley, comp., *Why Stop?* (Odessa: Lone Star Legends, 1978; 2d ed., with Betty Dooley and the Texas Historical Commission, Houston: Lone Star, 1985). Floyd V. Studer, "Archeology of the Texas Panhandle," *Panhandle-Plains Historical Review* 28 (1955). *Wheatheart of the Plains: An Early History of Ochiltree County* (Perryton, Texas: Ochiltree County Historical Survey Committee, 1969).

H. Allen Anderson

BURKBURNETT, TEXAS. Burkburnett is close to the Red River at the intersection of Interstate Highway 44 and State Highway 240, ten miles north of Wichita Falls in north central Wichita County. The first settler in the area was North Texas pioneer Mabel Gilbert,[qv] who settled there in 1856. Just to the west in 1879 J. G. Hardin and J. P. Hawkins founded a small community, commonly known as Nesterville to cowboys from Samuel Burk Burnett's[qv] nearby Four Sixes Ranch.[qv] By June 1880 the town had a small store and a reported population of 132. In 1882 the local post office was named Gilbert after Mabel Gilbert; it operated until 1903.

In 1906 Burnett sold 16,997 acres of his ranch holdings in northern Wichita County to a group of investors led by Joseph A. Kemp and Frank Kell,[qqv] who planned to extend the Wichita Falls and Northwestern Railway northward from Wichita Falls to connect with other rail lines to the wheat-producing areas of Oklahoma and Kansas. In this way they hoped to increase the production of flour mills in Wichita Falls. A townsite was laid out along the railroad on the former Burnett lands, a mile north of Gilbert. The Red River Land Company, formed for the occasion, auctioned lots in the townsite on June 6, 1907.

A post office named Burkburnett opened in 1907. Apparently President Theodore Roosevelt helped secure permission from the post office authorities to combine Burnett's two names. The town was linked to Wichita Falls and points south and to various towns in Oklahoma and points north by rail. Gilbert moved to the railroad townsite, and its one-room school building became Burkburnett's first school. A depot opened in 1907, and by 1915 the Missouri, Kansas and Texas Railroad, which purchased the Wichita Falls and Northwestern, ran nineteen trains daily to Burkburnett. By 1912 Burkburnett had a bank, a hotel, cotton gins, and a newspaper. By 1913, when the community incorporated, its population had reached 1,000. A municipal water system was constructed in 1918.

In 1912 oil was discovered west of town; larger strikes were made in 1918 and 1925. These strikes drew thousands of people to the area. By late 1918 wells in the Burkburnett oilfield[qv] were producing 7,500 barrels per day, 20,000 persons had poured into the oilfield region, and twenty trains ran daily between Burkburnett and Wichita Falls. In addition, nineteen refineries processed the locally produced oil. The town's unpaved streets reportedly became lined with newly formed stock offices, brokerage houses, and automobiles stuck in the mud. An article published in *Cosmopolitan* magazine, "A Lady Comes to Burkburnett," captured the spirit of the times and later inspired the 1939 film *Boom Town*, starring Spencer Tracy and Clark Gable. By the mid-1920s Burkburnett's population reached 5,300.

The oil boom died out by the late 1920s and, no doubt affected by the Great Depression and World War II,[qqv] Burkburnett's population declined significantly during the 1930s and 1940s. By 1936 the town had 3,281 persons and 160 businesses; in 1946 it had 2,814 people and eighty-four businesses. In 1941 Sheppard Air Force Base[qv] was established nearby. The town's population increased to 4,555 by the mid-1950s, when 115 businesses served the community. The population almost doubled between 1957 and 1967, from 4,555 to 8,750. In 1989 Burkburnett had a population of 11,025 and 125 businesses, including factories producing chemical products, plastics, and machinery. In 1990 the population was 10,145.

BIBLIOGRAPHY: Louise Kelly, *Wichita County Beginnings* (Burnet, Texas: Eakin Press, 1982). Wichita Falls *Times*, May 15, 1957.

Brian Hart

BURKE, DAVID N. (ca. 1809–?). David (Daniel) N. Burke (Burk), soldier, was captain of the Mobile Grays,[qv] a company of Alabama volunteers that took part in the Texas Revolution.qv Gen. Sam Houston qv welcomed Burke to Texas on November 30, 1835, commending "the manly and liberal feelings which have been manifested by you in the tender of your services in behalf of Texas." The company disembarked at Copano and arrived at San Antonio soon after the successful storming of the town by Texas volunteers in December 1835. On December 25 Burke joined John J. Baugh, William Gordon Cooke,qqv Thomas Llewellyn, B. L. Lawrence, and Thomas K. Pearson, all captains of volunteer companies, in protest against being placed under the same regulations as the regular army of Texas. Nevertheless, on December 30 Burke and his company left Bexar with the army of Col. Francis W. Johnson,qv having volunteered for the expedition against Matamoros. In February 1836 Burke and a number of other volunteer officers in Refugio signed a letter protesting a local official's ruling that volunteers, "claiming Texas as [their] adopted country," not be allowed to vote in the constitutional election. That spring Burke and the Mobile Grays accompanied James Grant qv as far as Goliad, where they subsequently became part of the army of James Walker Fannin.qv Most of the company was killed on March 27, 1836, in the infamous Goliad Massacre.qv Burke, however, was absent from his command and was thus spared. Although the company's muster roll dated February 29 indicates that he was on furlough at that date and had "since died," on March 29 Sam Houston reported to William Christy,qv a New Orleans merchant friendly to the Texas cause, that he had dispatched Burke to New Orleans and Mobile to recruit more volunteers. At Galveston, however, Burke encountered Robert Potter,qv who placed him in charge of the brig *Pocket.*qv After the battle of San Jacinto qv Burke rejoined the army and arrived at Houston's headquarters on the *Yellow Stone.*qv

BIBLIOGRAPHY: Daughters of the Republic of Texas, *Muster Rolls of the Texas Revolution* (Austin, 1986). Harbert Davenport, Notes from an Unfinished Study of Fannin and His Men (MS, Harbert Davenport Collection, Texas State Library, Austin; Barker Texas History Center, University of Texas at Austin). John H. Jenkins, ed., *The Papers of the Texas Revolution, 1835–1836* (10 vols., Austin: Presidial Press, 1973). Amelia W. Williams and Eugene C. Barker, eds., *The Writings of Sam Houston, 1813–1863* (8 vols., Austin: University of Texas Press, 1938–43; rpt., Austin and New York: Pemberton Press, 1970).
Thomas W. Cutrer

BURKE, JAMES (?–1880). James Burke, Presbyterian missionary, popularly known as the "Sunday School Man," was born in Edgefield District, South Carolina, and spent his childhood in Tennessee. In 1837 he sold his prosperous business in Natchez, Mississippi, and moved to San Augustine, Texas, where he aided in organizing the Cumberland Presbyterian church and was made a ruling elder. He aided also in organizing the Austin church and a presbytery. While assistant clerk in the House of the first session of the Second Congress of Texas, he edited a small daily that gave reports of the activities of Congress. This apparently was the first daily paper in Texas. After serving as a private in Company B of the Texan Santa Fe expedition qv in 1841, he sought in 1842 to revive the Galveston *Daily Advertiser.*qv in Galveston. He was married, a second time, in Brazoria to Mrs. Catharine B. Dart in 1843. He continued to run businesses at intervals in Austin, Galveston, and Houston, while holding various offices in the Home Missionary Society, the Texas National Bible Society, the Sons of Temperance, and the American Sunday School Union. He was corresponding secretary of the Texas Literary Institute qv in 1847 and for many years sought to introduce more desirable textbooks in the schools. He traveled over Texas for forty years and was given a friendly welcome everywhere. He had, it is said, never been assailed or insulted, never carried a weapon or felt the need of one. He was connected with all the most prominent benevolent and religious efforts in Texas. Burke died in Houston on August 5, 1880.

BIBLIOGRAPHY: William Stuart Red, *A History of the Presbyterian Church in Texas* (Austin: Steck, 1936).
Louise Kelly

BURKE, JOHN (1830–1871). John Burke, Robert E. Lee's qv "favorite spy" and Texas adjutant general, was born in Philadelphia in 1830 and orphaned or abandoned by his parents at age eleven. He grew up on his own in New York City, then moved to Marshall, Texas, where he worked as a cobbler and studied law at night. He was admitted to the bar, entered practice with his brother-in-law Pendleton Murrah,qv and became a prominent criminal defense attorney.

Shortly after the outbreak of the Civil War qv he enlisted as a private in Company E, First Texas Infantry, Hood's Texas Brigade,qv raised in Marshall and commanded by Frederick Bass, also of Marshall. Shortly afterward Burke began a career as a scout and spy for P. G. T. Beauregard, Joseph E. Johnston,qv and other senior officers, including T. J. Jackson during the Valley campaign of 1862. He rode with J. E. B. Stuart around McClellan's army in 1862. Burke traveled behind Union lines as far as New York, Philadelphia, and Washington. He used disguises, frequently the uniform of a Union officer, and would change the color of his artificial eye. He was able to provide Lee with valuable information about Union forces and dispositions. His most daring adventure came after he was apprehended in Philadelphia. He was placed under guard, in irons and handcuffs. As the train to Washington crossed a high trestle, he jumped into the river and made his way back to Lee.

Fatigued by his exertions and now a colonel, Burke resigned and accepted appointment by Governor Murrah as adjutant general of Texas, effective November 1, 1864. General Lee wrote a letter thanking him for his services. Unfortunately, records of the adjutant general's office were lost in the Capitol fire of 1881, and little of Burke's service in that assignment is known.

At the end of the war he joined Murrah in his flight to Mexico. After Murrah died, Burke returned to Marshall and resumed his law practice. He married Jennie Taylor in 1865, and they had two sons and a daughter. His most famous case at the bar was his defense of prisoners held at Jefferson in the Stockade Case qv in 1869. Burke died at Jefferson on January 18, 1871, and is buried there.

BIBLIOGRAPHY: Traylor Russell, *Carpetbaggers, Scalawags, and Others* (Waco: Texian Press, 1973). Harold B. Simpson, *The Marshall Guards: Harrison County's Contribution to Hood's Texas Brigade* (Marshall, Texas: Port Caddo, 1967). Vertical Files, Barker Texas History Center, University of Texas at Austin.
Max S. Lale

BURKE, ROBERT E. (1847–1901). Robert E. Burke, legislator, son of James M. and Narcissa J. (Holmes) Burke, was born near Dadeville, Alabama, on August 1, 1847. Before he was sixteen he enlisted in Company D, Tenth Georgia Regiment, in the Confederate Army. He moved to Texas in 1866, settled at Jefferson, and began the study of law while working as a clerk and teaching school. He was admitted to the bar in 1870 and moved to Dallas, where he began practice. He served as a member of the city council from 1874 to 1875, county judge from 1878 to 1888, and judge of the Fourteenth Judicial District from 1888 to 1896. He was elected as a Democrat to the Fifty-fifth Congress and served from March 4, 1897, until his death. Judge Burke married Mary L. Henderson; they had three children. He died in Dallas on June 5, 1901.

BIBLIOGRAPHY: *Biographical Directory of the American Congress. A History of Greater Dallas and Vicinity*, Vol. 1., by Philip Lindsley; Vol. 2., *Selected Biography and Memoirs*, ed. L. B. Hill (Chicago: Lewis, 1909).
Anne W. Hooker

BURKE, TEXAS. Burke, in southwestern Angelina County, was founded in 1881–82 at the northernmost point to which the Houston, East and West Texas Railway had then been constructed, on the edge of what was called Bradley Prairie. The town was originally named Rhodes for general store owner W. R. Rhodes and postmaster H. R. Rhodes but was renamed about 1885 for Ed Burke, a civil engineer who took part in the railroad survey. In 1885 it had three sawmills, three cotton gins, a church, and a school. From 1886 to 1955 Burke had a post office. By 1888 it had a larger school, three general stores, a drugstore, a sawmill, a dentist and watchmaker, and a Farmers' Alliance[qv] store. In 1897 Burke had an estimated population of 650. The Burke Methodist Church was organized in 1899–1900, and the First Baptist Church of Burke in 1905. The Baptist church grew steadily until its membership reached a high of 302 in 1965. By 1904 Burke's population had plummeted to 161, a loss that may be explained by the rise of Lufkin, eight miles north, as an industrial center for the county. However, by 1915 the population had risen to 200, and by 1925 it stood at 300. In 1964 the Burke school was consolidated with the Diboll Independent School District. However, by 1966 enough new arrivals were building homes to warrant incorporation and the construction of a municipal water system. Burke had a population of 322 in 1980 and 314 in 1990.

BIBLIOGRAPHY: Angelina County Historical Survey Committee, *Land of the Little Angel: A History of Angelina County, Texas*, ed. Bob Bowman (Lufkin, Texas, 1976). Richard W. Haltom, *History and Description of Angelina County, Texas* (Lufkin, Texas, 1888; rpt., Austin: Pemberton, 1969). *Megan Biesele*

BURKE TOWN, TEXAS. Burke Town was an early farming community on Farm Road 2501 six miles north of Apple Springs in northern Trinity County. It was named for Benjamin Burke, who moved to the area from Tyler County about 1859. In 1861 Burke, with the assistance of his slaves, erected a double-pen log house. A small settlement developed nearby in the years after the Civil War[qv] but had disappeared by the 1930s. In the early 1990s all that remained of the community was Burke's original houses and the Burke Cemetery.

BIBLIOGRAPHY: Patricia B. and Joseph W. Hensley, eds., *Trinity County Beginnings* (Groveton, Texas: Trinity County Book Committee, 1986). *Christopher Long*

BURKETT, GEORGE W. (1847–?) George W. Burkett (Burkitt), businessman and politician, was born in County Derry, Ireland, on November 12, 1847. He immigrated to the United States during the Civil War[qv] and went to work for a contracting firm grading the roadbed of the Union Pacific Railroad. After rising to gang foreman he resigned and worked as a grading subcontractor for the Union Pacific in Utah until 1869, and for the Missouri, Kansas and Texas Railroad in Kansas until 1872. He then moved to Texas, where he was a grading subcontractor for the Texas and Pacific and for the Galveston, Harrisburg and San Antonio railways, before becoming a general contractor for the International–Great Northern Railroad. In that capacity he also built sections of line for the Trinity and Sabine, for the Santa Fe, for the Taylor, Bastrop and Houston, and for the Missouri, Kansas and Texas railways—often as a partner in Burkett, Murphy, and Burns.

In the late 1880s Burkett became one of the organizers and a vice president of the First National Bank of Palestine, a director of the Taylor National Bank, and a stockholder in the First National Bank of Stephenville and the First National Bank of Orange. He was also president of the Taylor Water Works and Ice Company, a stockholder in the Palestine Cotton Seed Oil Company, a dealer in land and railroad ties, and president of the Palestine and Dallas Railway in the 1890s.

He made his entry into state politics as a delegate to the Republican national conventions of 1884 and 1888. In 1892 he was a member of the state executive committee of the "Lily White" Republican organization (*see* LILY-WHITE MOVEMENT) and in 1898 was on the executive committee of the Republican party[qv] in Texas. He was the gubernatorial nominee of the Edward H. R. Green[qv] faction but was withdrawn when the national executive committee recognized the opposing faction as representing Texas Republicans. In 1902 Burkett was the party candidate for governor in a harmony move between factions, but he was defeated by S. W. T. Lanham.[qv] In 1904 Burkett was again a leader of one of the factions within the party. He later served the regular party on its executive committee and as a presidential elector in 1908. He then joined the Progressive party as a follower of Theodore Roosevelt and was a presidential elector in 1912, a member of the state executive committee from 1912 to 1916, and a delegate to the national convention of 1916. Burkett married Mary Hartley of Houston in 1880, and they had a son and a daughter.

BIBLIOGRAPHY: John Henry Brown, *Indian Wars and Pioneers of Texas* (Austin: Daniell, 1880; reprod., Easley, South Carolina: Southern Historical Press, 1978). Paul D. Casdorph, *A History of the Republican Party in Texas, 1865–1965* (Austin: Pemberton Press, 1965). Vertical Files, Barker Texas History Center, University of Texas at Austin. E. W. Winkler, *Platforms of Political Parties in Texas* (Austin: University of Texas, 1916).

BURKETT, TEXAS. Burkett, on State Highway 206 in northeastern Coleman County, was named in 1886 for its first postmaster, William Burkett. The original name, Pleasant Valley, was rejected by the post office. The first settlers were cowboys of the McClennan ranch, who secured land in the area and established a community around the store H. H. Sackett had moved from Camp Colorado. The town progressed as a trading center for several decades. In 1940 it had three churches, a school, five businesses, and 200 residents. Subsequently, the region's rural population declined sharply. The school closed in 1953 after consolidation with the Coleman schools. By the 1980s Burkett had a post office, three churches, a community center, a gas station–grocery, and a well-kept cemetery. Farming, ranching, and oil products sustain the community. In 1980 and 1990 the population was thirty.

BIBLIOGRAPHY: Kathleen E. and Clifton R. St. Clair, eds., *Little Towns of Texas* (Jacksonville, Texas: Jayroe Graphic Arts, 1982).
William R. Hunt

BURKEVILLE, TEXAS. Burkeville is at the intersection of State highways 87 and 63, seventy miles northeast of Beaumont in northeast Newton County. John Burke, for whom the town was named, laid out the plots in 1844, although settlers had apparently been in the area for some time. Upon discovering that Quicksand Creek, the place where the court officially first met, was not at the true geographic center of the county as was formerly supposed, Burkeville citizens petitioned in 1847 for their community to become county seat. Burkeville secured the honor in 1848, and an election the following year confirmed its position by a narrow 86-82 margin. The county courthouse, paid for by subscription, was located on a small tract donated by John Burke. The courthouse question was reopened, however, in 1853, when another election made Newton, a newly established settlement at the geographic center of Newton County, county seat. Burkeville citizens refused to allow the transfer without a struggle; indeed, they succeeded in temporarily restoring Burkeville as county seat in 1855. However, county officers refused to leave Newton, and the state legislature ruled in 1856 that Newton should remain county seat. As a center for local agriculture and trade, however, Burkeville remained active. It served as a Confederate arsenal during the Civil War.[qv] It had a newspaper, the *Newton County Record*, and profited from the growth of the lumber industry[qv] in the early 1900s. Some 600 bales of cotton were shipped from Burkeville in 1882. A small school, Blum Male and Female College, was chartered in Burkeville in 1880; it was named for Leon Blum,[qv] a Galveston merchant who owned a majority of stock in the private corporation that established the school. The institution soon became known as Burkeville School. A fire destroyed every business in Burkeville except one in 1906.

Renewed agricultural strength, especially in stock and poultry raising, several small local industries, and employment opportunities offered by the large refineries of the Gulf Coast had enabled the town's economy largely to overcome the effects of the declining lumber industry by about the time of World War II.[qv] Burkeville probably had between 200 and 300 residents before 1900. With the lumber boom of the first quarter of the twentieth century came new residents, and the population grew to as high as 800. In the subsequent economic decline the number of residents dropped below 400 by the mid-1960s. By the mid-1980s the site of the business section had shifted from along State Highway 87 to along State Highway 63. A sub-courthouse was still located in Burkeville. The Burkeville school district encompassed 320 square miles in 1986. While many residents of Burkeville are self-employed, others continue to work in the timber industry or commute to industrial plants in the area. Nearby, the Toledo Bend Reservoir[qv] provides recreational opportunities. The population in 1990 was 515. *Robert Wooster*

BURKHAM, CHARLES (?–1837). Charles Burkham, pioneer Red River County settler, was born in Virginia before 1790. By 1804 he was living in Madison County, Kentucky, where he married Indiana native Nancy Ann Abbet on September 30. The couple had at least six children, including James Burkham.[qv] According to family legend, Burkham served in the War of 1812, though no record of his service has been found. In 1816 he moved with his wife, three oldest children, and several other families to Arkansas Territory, where he settled in the Red River Valley. In March 1820 the group crossed the river and founded a permanent settlement, known later as Burkham Settlement,[qv] on the mouth of Mill Creek near the present border of Red River and Bowie counties. Burkham was particularly interested in gaining title to his land and over the course of the next decade and a half negotiated with authorities in Miller County, Arkansas, and Mexico seeking clear title. In 1836 he and his son Ahijah joined Capt. Thomas Robbins's company of mounted riflemen. Burkham was murdered by a man named Page in the winter of 1837, while hunting for a runaway slave. Page thought the chains and hand irons in Burkham's saddlebag were gold.

BIBLIOGRAPHY: Pat B. Clark, *The History of Clarksville and Old Red River County* (Dallas: Mathis, Van Nort, 1937). Claude V. Hall, "Early Days in Red River County," *East Texas State Teachers College Bulletin* 14 (June 1931). *Red River Recollections* (Clarksville, Texas: Red River County Historical Society, 1986). Rex W. Strickland, Anglo-American Activities in Northeastern Texas, 1803–1845 (Ph.D. dissertation, University of Texas, 1937). George Travis Wright Family Papers, Barker Texas History Center, University of Texas at Austin.
Christopher Long

BURKHAM, JAMES (1805–1880). James Burkham, pioneer settler, was born Clay County, Kentucky, in the late summer of 1805, the son of Charles and Nancy Ann (Abbet) Burkham. In 1816 the family moved to the Red River Valley in Arkansas Territory. Around 1820 the Burkhams and several other families crossed the river into Texas and settled on the mouth of Mill Creek, at what became known as Burkham Settlement.[qv] During the Texas Revolution[qv] Burkham joined Capt. William Becknell's[qv] company, which set out to join Sam Houston's[qv] main army but arrived the day after the battle of San Jacinto.[qv] Burkham served again briefly in the militia in 1841 and in recognition of his service was awarded a first-class land grant in Red River County near Avery, a bounty warrant of 320 acres in Lamar County, and a plot of land now in Hopkins County. After his mother died in 1845, he moved to Hopkins County and settled near Sulphur Bluff. Burkham was a Mason; in Hopkins County he became a member of the newly organized Old Tarrant Lodge No. 91. Around 1853 he is said to have sold his slaves to James L. Latimer.[qv] Burkham and his wife, Mathilda, whom he married in 1830, had five children. He died at the family homestead near Sulphur Bluff on June 4, 1880.

BIBLIOGRAPHY: Pat B. Clark, *The History of Clarksville and Old Red River County* (Dallas: Mathis, Van Nort, 1937). Claude V. Hall, "Early Days in Red River County," *East Texas State Teachers College Bulletin* 14 (June 1931). *Red River Recollections* (Clarksville, Texas: Red River County Historical Society, 1986). Rex W. Strickland, Anglo-American Activities in Northeastern Texas, 1803–1845 (Ph.D. dissertation, University of Texas, 1937). George Travis Wright Family Papers, Barker Texas History Center, University of Texas at Austin.
Christopher Long

BURKHAM SETTLEMENT, TEXAS. Burkham Settlement was among the earliest Anglo-American settlements in Texas. It was founded by Charles Burkham,[qv] his wife, Ann (Abbet), their children, and several other families. According to the 1830 register of the Wavell Red River colony (*see* WAVELL, ARTHUR GOODALL), the Burkham group reached the Red River valley on July 4, 1816. By March 1820 they crossed the Red River to locate permanently at the mouth of Mill Creek, near what became the border of Red River and Bowie counties and a short distance from the Pecan Point settlement. Also among the early settlers were Hudson Posey Benningfield, Henry B. Stout, and Isaac Bateman.[qqv] The settlement served as a foothold for Anglo-American colonization[qv] in the region and paved the way for large-scale settlement of Northeast Texas during the 1820s and 1830s. The area was a stopping point for others entering Texas, including David Crockett, Nathaniel Robbins, and Francis M. Hopkins.[qqv] As late as the 1930s descendents of the original settlers still lived in the area.

BIBLIOGRAPHY: Pat B. Clark, *The History of Clarksville and Old Red River County* (Dallas: Mathis, Van Nort, 1937). Claude V. Hall, "Early Days in Red River County," *East Texas State Teachers College Bulletin* 14 (June 1931). Blewett Barnes Kerbow, The Early History of Red River County, 1817–1865 (M.A. thesis, University of Texas, 1936). *Red River Recollections* (Clarksville, Texas: Red River County Historical Society, 1986). Rex W. Strickland, Anglo-American Activities in Northeastern Texas, 1803–1845 (Ph.D. dissertation, University of Texas, 1937). George Travis Wright Family Papers, Barker Texas History Center, University of Texas at Austin. *Christopher Long*

BURKS, JOHN C. (ca. 1835–1862). John C. Burks, lawyer and soldier, the son of Joseph H. and Winnifred B. Burks, was born in Georgia about 1835. The family moved to Clarksville, Texas, in 1846. By 1856 Burks had graduated from the law department of Cumberland University and had established a law practice in Clarksville. As the son of a prominent regional political figure, he was soon active in the Democratic party[qv] and was often called on to address political gatherings. On October 13, 1857, he married Penelope Donoho, also of Clarksville. In 1858 Burks was one of three commissioners appointed by Governor Hardin Runnels[qv] to investigate the legality of land certificates issued by county and district courts in the area of the Peters colony[qv] grant. In 1859 he announced his candidacy for the position of district attorney of the Eighth Judicial District. Shortly after his announcement he suffered a series of personal losses that prevented an active campaign. His father died in February, his seventeen-year-old wife died after childbirth in April, and his infant son died in June. He lost the four-man race. By the time of the census in the summer of 1860, Burks had apparently remarried and was living with his wife and her daughter. In June of 1861, following the outbreak of the Civil War,[qv] he helped to raise a company of volunteers, who elected him captain. The company became part of Col. William C. Young's Eleventh Texas Cavalry. When Young resigned as a result of ill health in mid-1862, Burks was promoted to colonel, and later to commander of the regiment. On December 31, 1862, he was mortally wounded while leading a charge on a Union battery at the battle of Murfreesboro, Tennessee. Holding his hand on the wound to control the bleeding, he continued at the head of his command, urging his men forward, until he lost consciousness. In his report of the battle, Gen. Mathew D. Ector[qv] said of Burks: "a better friend, a warmer heart, a more gallant leader than he was, never drew the breath of life."

BIBLIOGRAPHY: Clarksville *Standard*, June 18, 1853, June 28, 1856, October 31, 1857, March 27, 1858, February 19, 1859. Sidney S. Johnson, *Texans Who Wore the Gray* (Tyler, Texas, 1907). *Cecil Harper, Jr.*

BURK STATION, TEXAS. Burk Station was a ranching community between Wichita Falls and Electra in northeastern Wichita County. It developed when rancher Samuel Burk Burnett[qv] built cattle pens at the site in the late 1870s. The tracks of the Missouri, Kansas and Texas Railroad reached the area in the early 1880s and acted as a catalyst for growth. Originally the site was referred to as Burke Switch or Station. By 1882 a hotel, a school, a cotton gin, and two stores served area ranchers and their families. In February 1886 the village acquired a post office branch named Ruthford in honor of Burnett's wife, Ruth B. (Lloyd). Three years later Ruthford competed for selection as the county seat but lost, after which most of the residents left for the new county seat, Wichita Falls. In 1889 the post office closed. For the next ten to fifteen years a few residents remained, but the discovery of oil in 1911 in Electra resulted in their departure.

BIBLIOGRAPHY: Louise Kelly, *Wichita County Beginnings* (Burnet, Texas: Eakin Press, 1982). *David Minor*

BURLEIGH, TEXAS. Burleigh is on Farm Road 529 and the west bank of the Brazos River, six miles east of Bellville in far eastern Austin County. Settlement in the vicinity began in the 1820s, but the town itself was not founded until the late nineteenth century. A local post office was established in a general store in 1893 but was discontinued in 1913. Sixty-two pupils were enrolled at the Burleigh school in 1918. In 1968 Burleigh's population stood at an estimated 150. In the early 1980s three churches and two schools operated in the community. By 1972 the population had fallen to an estimated sixty-nine, where it remained through 1990. *Charles Christopher Jackson*

BURLESON, AARON B. (1815–1885). Aaron B. Burleson was born in Alabama on October 10, 1815, the youngest son of James and Elizabeth (Shipman) Burleson. His father was a captain under Andrew Jackson at the battles of Horseshoe Bend and New Orleans. The Burlesons returned to the old family home in Hardeman County, Tennessee, and from there, in 1827, they moved to Bastrop, Texas. Aaron was raised on the frontier and was a frequent companion of his elder brother Edward Burleson[qv] on campaigns against Indians. Aaron served under his brother's command during the siege of Bexar[qv] and saw action at the battle of San Jacinto[qv] as a member of Capt. Jesse Billingsley's[qv] Company C of Edward Burleson's First Regiment, Texan Volunteers. He was one of the party that captured Antonio López de Santa Anna.[qv]

After the Texas Revolution[qv] he lived on the upper Colorado, approximately equidistant between Bastrop and Waterloo, which became the city of Austin. His nearest neighbors on this exposed frontier were his sister Nancy Rogers, his sister and brother-in-law Rachel and James Rogers, and his brother Jacob. On February 25, 1839, Burleson, again under his eldest brother's command, took part in the battle of Brushy Creek,[qv] a decisive defeat of Comanche raiders in the upper Colorado settlements. In this fight Jacob Burleson was killed and his body badly mutilated.

In 1838 Aaron returned to Tennessee to marry Minerva J. Seaton. The couple immediately returned to Texas and settled at the mouth of Walnut Creek in Travis County. They had six children before Minerva's death in 1855. Burleson was married again, on May 15, 1856, to Jane Tannehill and with her eventually had six children.

In 1842 Burleson again served under his brother Edward, then the vice president of the Republic of Texas, in repulsing the raid of Rafael Vásquez[qv] on San Antonio. In December 1860 Governor Sam Houston[qv] commissioned Burleson to raise a company of rangers for frontier defense. Burleson amassed a considerable fortune before his death at his home near Govalle, some two miles east of Austin, on January 13, 1885. He, both of his wives, and several of his children are buried in the Burleson Cemetery, on the Blanco River near Kyle.

BIBLIOGRAPHY: Daughters of the Republic of Texas, *Muster Rolls of the Texas Revolution* (Austin, 1986). Frank W. Johnson, *A History of Texas and Texans* (5 vols., ed. E. C. Barker and E. W. Winkler [Chicago and New York: American Historical Society, 1914; rpt. 1916]). Vertical Files, Barker Texas History Center, University of Texas at Austin. Amelia W. Williams and Eugene C. Barker, eds., *The Writings of Sam Houston, 1813–1863* (8 vols., Austin: University of Texas Press, 1938–43; rpt., Austin and New York: Pemberton Press, 1970). *Thomas W. Cutrer*

BURLESON, ALBERT SIDNEY (1863–1937). Albert Sidney Burleson, attorney, congressman, and United States postmaster general, was born in San Marcos, Texas, on June 7, 1863, the son of Lucy Emma (Kyle) and Edward Burleson, Jr.[qv] He attended Coronal Institute[qv] in San Marcos and the Agricultural and Mechanical College of Texas (now Texas A&M University); he received a B.A. degree from Baylor University in 1881 and an LL.B. degree from the University of Texas in 1884. The following year he joined his uncle Thomas Eskridge Sneed[qv] and George F. Poindexter in their law practice in Austin. Burleson became interested in politics and rose quickly through the ranks of the local Democratic party.[qv] He served as assistant city attorney of Austin from 1885 to 1890, and in 1891 he was appointed attorney of the Twenty-sixth Judicial District. Among the friends he made during this time was Edward M. House,[qv] who later kept Burleson's name in consideration for a position in President Woodrow Wilson's cabinet. Burleson married Adele Lubbock Steiner on December 22, 1889, and they became the parents of three children.

Burleson represented Texas in the Fifty-sixth through the Sixty-third United States congresses (1899–1913); he served on the committees of agriculture, census, foreign affairs, and appropriations. He was the author of considerable legislation affecting the development of agriculture. Woodrow Wilson appointed him postmaster general in 1913, and Burleson held that post until 1921. During his tenure the post office developed the parcel post and air mail service. Burleson was chairman of the United States Telegraph and Telephone Administration in 1918 and chairman of the United States Commission to the International Wire Communication Conference in 1920. He retired from public life in 1921 and returned to Austin to devote his time to agricultural interests. Although he rarely took an active role in politics after his retirement, he voiced support for presidential candidates Alfred Smith in 1928 and Franklin D. Roosevelt in 1932. Baylor University awarded him an honorary LL.D. degree in 1930. Burleson died of a heart attack at his home in Austin on November 24, 1937, and was buried at Oakwood Cemetery.

BIBLIOGRAPHY: Adrian Anderson, Albert Sidney Burleson: A Southern Politician in the Progressive Era (Ph.D. dissertation, Texas Technological College, 1967). Adrian Anderson, "President Wilson's Politician: Albert Sidney Burleson of Texas," *Southwestern Historical Quarterly* 77 (January 1974). Austin *American-Statesman*, November 25, 1937. *Dictionary of American Biography*. Richard Winston Howard, The Works of Albert Sidney Burleson as Postmaster General (M.A. thesis, University of Texas, 1938). *National Cyclopaedia of American Biography*, Vol. 28. Vertical Files, Barker Texas History Center, University of Texas at Austin. *Seymour V. Connor*

BURLESON, DAVID CROCKETT (1837–1911). David Crockett Burleson, a member of the Texas Rangers[qv] and Civil War[qv] officer, the son of Sarah (Owen) and Edward Burleson, Sr.,[qv] was born on September 6, 1837, probably in Bastrop County, Texas. In 1848 the family settled near San Marcos, where Burleson got the early education that prepared him to attend Baylor University. In 1855 he served in James Hughes Callahan's[qv] company of Texas Rangers.[qv] The following year he and his brother Edward Burleson, Jr.,[qv] traveled to

Mexico to clarify some Hays County land titles. They had little success with the title problem and decided to purchase some cattle to drive back to Texas. They were ambushed by a Mexican mob that stole their cattle, and they were jailed for two weeks at Hacienda Potosí. Burleson spent the rest of the pre–Civil War decade as sergeant-at-arms of the Texas Senate. He married Louisa Ware of Manchaca in 1861, shortly before he raised a company for the Confederate Army at Seguin and became a lieutenant in Company B, Thirty-second Texas Cavalry, which served throughout the war in Texas and Louisiana. He purchased land in 1865 in the hills west of San Marcos and operated a horse ranch there before moving to Buda. After his wife died in 1894 he moved to Austin, where he was a member of the capitol police force until his death, on May 17, 1911. He was buried in Live Oak Cemetery at Buda and was survived by four daughters and one son.

BIBLIOGRAPHY: David C. Burleson Papers, Barker Texas History Center, University of Texas at Austin. Amelia W. Williams and Eugene C. Barker, eds., *The Writings of Sam Houston, 1813–1863* (8 vols., Austin: University of Texas Press, 1938–43; rpt., Austin and New York: Pemberton Press, 1970).

BURLESON, EDWARD (1798–1851). Edward Burleson, soldier and statesman, son of Capt. James and Elizabeth (Shipman) Burleson, was born at Buncombe County, North Carolina, on December 15, 1798. He served as a private in the War of 1812 in his father's company, part of Perkin's Regiment, Alabama. He married Sarah Griffin Owen on April 25, 1816, in Madison County, Missouri Territory; they had nine children. On October 20, 1817, Burleson was appointed a captain of militia in Howard County, Missouri; he was commissioned colonel on June 13, 1821, in Saline County, and was colonel of militia from 1823 to 1830 in Hardeman County, Tennessee.

He arrived in Texas on May 1, 1830, and applied for land in March 1831; title was issued on April 4, 1831. On August 11, 1832, at San Felipe de Austin, he was a member of the ayuntamiento[qv] governing the counties of Austin, Bexar, Goliad, and Guadalupe. On December 7, 1832, he was elected lieutenant colonel of the militia of Austin Municipality. In 1833 he was elected a delegate to the Second Convention in Mina. From 1830 to 1842 he defended settlers in numerous engagements with hostile Indians. On May 17, 1835, in Bastrop he was elected to the committee of safety and was therefore unable to attend the Consultation[qv] of 1835, although he had been elected a delegate. On October 10, 1835, in Gonzales he was elected lieutenant colonel of the infantry in Gen. Stephen F. Austin's[qv] army. On November 24, 1835, Burleson became general of the volunteer army and replaced Austin. On November 26, 1835, he fought in the Grass Fight[qv] during the siege of Bexar.[qv] His father was active in this battle, which was won by the Texans.

On December 1, 1835, Burleson was commissioned commander in chief of the volunteer army by the provisional government.[qv] On December 6 he entered Bexar and, with Benjamin R. Milam,[qv] wrote a report to the provisional government. On December 14, 1835, he reported on the success at Bexar to the provisional governor, Henry Smith.[qv] The volunteer army disbanded on December 20, 1835, and Burleson raised a company and rode to Gonzales in February 1836. By March 10, in Gonzales, he was officially elected colonel of the infantry, First Regiment. On April 21, 1836, at the battle of San Jacinto,[qv] he commanded the First Regiment, which was placed opposite Mexican breastworks and was the first to charge them. Burleson accepted the sword and surrender of Gen. Juan N. Almonte.[qv]

From July 12 to December 1836 he was colonel of the frontier rangers. In 1837 he surveyed and laid out roads to Bastrop, La Grange, and other Central Texas places. On June 12, 1837, he became brigadier general of the militia established by the First Congress of the Republic of Texas. As a representative of the Second Congress from September 26, 1837, to May 1838, Burleson served on the Committee on Post Offices and Post Roads, the Committee on Military Affairs, and the

Edward Burleson, 1850. Daguerreotype. Courtesy TSL.

Committee of Indian Affairs, of which he was chairman. In 1838 he was colonel of the First Regiment of Infantry in the new regular army and on April 4, 1838, defeated Mexican insurrectionists under Vicente Córdova.[qv] In the spring of that year Burleson laid out the town of Waterloo, the original settlement of the city of Austin. He was elected to the Senate of the Third Congress but resigned on January 19, 1839, at President Mirabeau B. Lamar's[qv] request, to take command of the Frontier Regiment.[qv] On May 22, 1839, Burleson intercepted a Córdova agent with proof that Mexico had made allies of Cherokees and other Indians. He defeated the Cherokees under Chief Bowl[qv] in July 1839.

On October 17, 1839, Burleson was in command of the ceremonies establishing Austin as the capital of the Republic of Texas.[qv] He defeated the Cherokees on Christmas Day, 1839, at Pecan Bayou, killing Chief Bowl's son John and another chief known as the Egg. Burleson sent Chief Bowl's "hat" to Sam Houston,[qv] who was enraged. On August 12, 1840, Burleson defeated the Comanches in the battle of Plum Creek.[qv]

In 1841 he was elected vice president of the republic. In the spring of 1842, when the Mexican army under Rafael Vásquez[qv] invaded Texas, Burleson met with volunteers at San Antonio, where they elected him to command. Houston sent Alexander Somervell[qv] to take over, and Burleson handed the command to him. Burleson then made his famous speech before the Alamo: "though Thermopolae had her messenger of defeat, the Alamo had none." In the fall of 1842 Mexican general Adrián Woll[qv] invaded Texas. Burleson raised troops for defense and again yielded the command to General Somervell, sent by Houston. In 1844 Burleson made an unsuccessful bid for the presidency against Anson Jones.[qv] In December 1845 he was elected senator from the Fifteenth District to the First Legislature of the state of Texas. He was unanimously elected president pro tem.

During the Mexican War[qv] Burleson and Governor James P. Henderson[qv] went to Monterrey, Nuevo León; Burleson was appointed senior aide-de-camp, held the rank of major, and served as a spy during the siege of Monterrey and at Buena Vista. In 1847 Burleson, Eli T. Merriman,[qv] and William Lindsey surveyed and laid out the town of San Marcos. In 1848 Burleson introduced a resolution to establish Hays County and donated the land for the courthouse. He chaired the Committee on Military Affairs, which awarded a $1,250,000 grant to Texas for Indian depredations.

Burleson died of pneumonia on December 26, 1851, in Austin, while serving as senator from the Twenty-first District. He was still president pro tem. He was given a Masonic burial at the site of the future State Cemetery,[qv] the land for which was purchased by the state of Texas in his honor in 1854. Burleson was a Methodist.

BIBLIOGRAPHY: Eugene C. Barker, ed., *The Austin Papers* (3 vols., Washington: GPO, 1924–28). Mary Starr Barkley, *History of Travis County and Austin, 1839–1899* (Waco: Texian Press, 1963). Edward Burleson, Jr., Papers, Barker Texas History Center, University of Texas at Austin. John H. Jenkins and Kenneth Kesselus, *Edward Burleson: Texas Frontier Leader* (Austin: Jenkins, 1990). Frank W. Johnson, *A History of Texas and Texans* (5 vols., ed. E. C. Barker and E. W. Winkler [Chicago and New York: American Historical Society, 1914; rpt. 1916]). Kenneth Kesselus, *History of Bastrop County, Texas, Before Statehood* (Austin: Jenkins, 1986). Frances Stovall et al., *Clear Springs and Limestone Ledges: A History of San Marcos and Hays County* (San Marcos: Hays County Historical Commission, 1986). Dudley Goodall Wooten, ed., *A Comprehensive History of Texas* (2 vols., Dallas: Scarff, 1898; rpt., Austin: Texas State Historical Association, 1986).

Helen Burleson Kelso

BURLESON, EDWARD, JR. (1826–1877). Edward Burleson, Jr., early settler, soldier, and politician, son of Sarah (Owen) and Edward Burleson,[qv] was born in Tipton County, Tennessee, on November 26, 1826. The family moved to Bastrop County, Texas, in 1830 and to Hays County in 1848. During the Mexican War[qv] Burleson served with Benjamin McCulloch[qv] in the Texas Mounted Volunteers. In 1856–57, while serving in the Texas Rangers[qv] under John S. Ford,[qv] he rose in rank from lieutenant to major. During the Civil War[qv] he was a major in McCulloch's First Regiment of Mounted Rifles. Burleson was a delegate from the Twenty-first District to the Constitutional Convention of 1875[qv] and served on the commission to locate the penitentiary in East Texas. He married Lucy Emma Kyle of Hays County and was the father of ten children. He died at the home of his sister in Austin on May 12, 1877, and was buried in the family cemetery near Kyle.

BIBLIOGRAPHY: Edward Burleson, Jr., Papers, Barker Texas History Center, University of Texas at Austin. Anne Hammond, The West Texas State Constitutional Convention of 1875 (M.A. thesis, Texas Technological College, 1933). John H. Jenkins and Kenneth Kesselus, *Edward Burleson: Texas Frontier Leader* (Austin: Jenkins, 1990). Vertical Files, Barker Texas History Center, University of Texas at Austin. Amelia W. Williams and Eugene C. Barker, eds., *The Writings of Sam Houston, 1813–1863* (8 vols., Austin: University of Texas Press, 1938–43; rpt., Austin and New York: Pemberton Press, 1970).

BURLESON, EMMA KYLE (1869–1941). Emma Kyle Burleson, preservationist, was born in August 1869 near San Marcos, Texas, the daughter of Lucy Emma (Kyle) and Edward Burleson, Jr.[qv] Her father was a Confederate veteran, a Texas Ranger, and a delegate to the Constitutional Convention of 1875.[qv] His father, Gen. Edward Burleson[qv], came to Texas in 1830 and fought in the battle of San Jacinto[qv] before serving as vice president of the Republic of Texas. Emma's maternal ancestors included Hays County pioneers and politicians Claiborne and Fergus Kyle.[qqv] Her parents both died in 1877, leaving her and her nine siblings to be raised by an uncle. She attended St. Mary's Academy[qv] in Austin and Augusta Female Seminary (now Mary Baldwin College) in Virginia. After completing her education and traveling in Europe, she made Austin her home. Maintaining an ongoing interest in Texas history from her family heritage, she closely followed the state's purchase of the Alamo in 1905, carried out at the request of the Daughters of the Republic of Texas[qv] with a bill sponsored in the Texas legislature by Fergus Kyle. The following year Emma Burleson joined the DRT, an organization in which she remained active for the rest of her life.

She was also active in the Daughters of the American Revolution and the United Daughters of the Confederacy[qqv] and served for many years on the Texas Historical Commission.[qv] She helped preserve the old General Land Office[qv] building and was a founding member in 1911 of the Texas Fine Arts Association.[qv] In this organization she was involved in preserving the studio of her friend, artist Elisabet Ney.[qv] During World War I[qv] Burleson served as secretary-treasurer of the State Council of Defense and as a volunteer nurse at Texas army camps. In 1936 she chaired the official historical contest of the Texas Centennial[qv] Central Exposition. She was also a member of the Philosophical Society of Texas.[qv]

Emma Burleson died in Austin on June 16, 1941. Her funeral was held in St. Mary's Catholic Church (now St. Mary's Cathedral[qv]), and she was buried in Kyle. She was survived by one sister; her brother, Albert Sidney Burleson,[qv] postmaster general of the United States in Woodrow Wilson's administration, had died in 1937.

BIBLIOGRAPHY: Austin *American*, June 17, 18, 1941. *Proceedings of the Philosophical Society of Texas*, 1941. Vertical Files, Barker Texas History Center, University of Texas at Austin.

Debbie Mauldin Cottrell

BURLESON, JAMES, SR. (1775–1836). James Burleson, pioneer settler and Burleson clan leader in Austin's Little Colony, son of Aaron and Rachel (Hendricks) Burleson, was born in Washington County, Tennessee, on May 4, 1775. He was married to Elizabeth Shipman on December 25, 1791, in Rutherford County, North Carolina. They had twelve children. Their oldest son was Edward Burleson.[qv] James and his family moved to Lincoln County, Tennessee, in 1807 and then to the Mississippi Territory (later Madison County, Alabama). This large Burleson family group included several who later moved to Texas, including brothers John, Jonathan, Joseph, and James. During the Creek War the Burlesons were involved in many battles; in one of them Edward saved the life of his uncle Jonathan, the father of Rufus C. Burleson,[qv] founder of Baylor University. In 1813 James and Joseph Burleson were appointed commissaries under Gen. Andrew Jackson for the Creek War and served with Lt. Sam Houston[qv] in the battle of Horseshoe Bend. James, as special and confidential commissary to General Jackson, and his son, Edward, served at the battle of New Orleans in 1815.

Difficulty with Indians in Alabama forced the Burlesons to move to the Missouri territory in 1816 and to Hardeman County, Tennessee, in 1825. In 1831 James followed his son Edward, who had immigrated to Coahuila and Texas[qv] in 1830 with several other family members, and obtained a league on the Colorado River below Austin's Little Colony. In 1834, his wife having died, James married Mary Buchanan Christian (*see* BURLESON, MARY R. B. CHRISTIAN); they had a daughter. Under command of his son, Gen. Edward Burleson, commander at the siege of Bexar,[qv] Capt. James Burleson led a decisive charge in the Grass Fight.[qv] He became ill after being discharged and returned to the home of his daughter, Rachael Rogers, north of Bastrop. There he died on January 3, 1836. He is buried in the McDuff Cemetery on the east side of the Colorado River.

BIBLIOGRAPHY: Georgia J. Burleson, comp., *The Life and Writings of Rufus C. Burleson, D.D., L.L.D.* (1901). Charles Adams Gulick, Jr., Harriet Smither, et al., eds., *The Papers of Mirabeau Buonaparte Lamar* (6 vols., Austin: Texas State Library, 1920–27; rpt., Austin: Pemberton

Press, 1968). Kenneth Kesselus, *History of Bastrop County, Texas, Before Statehood* (Austin: Jenkins, 1986). Vertical Files, Bastrop County Museum, Bastrop, Texas. *Byron Howard*

BURLESON, MARY R. B. CHRISTIAN (1795–1870). Mary Randolph Buchanan Christian Burleson, pioneer settler, daughter of John and Nancy (Wright) Buchanan, was born in Wytheville, Virginia, on March 1, 1795. She married Thomas Christian in 1822 in Kentucky, gave birth to three children, and traveled to the Illinois frontier, where she had two more children. In Missouri the family joined immigrants headed to San Felipe de Austin in Texas, where they arrived in April 1832. They settled in Mina (Bastrop), built one of the first houses there, and obtained a grant of a league in Austin's Little Colony. There Mary Christian gave birth to a daughter. In 1833 the Christians moved north to Webbers Fort on the Colorado River. Thomas Christian was scalped and murdered in the Wilbarger Massacre in August 1833 (*see* WILBARGER, JOSIAH PUGH). Christian and her children moved to Reuben Hornsby's[qv] fort, where in 1834 she married James Burleson, Sr.[qv] They had one daughter. At Mina in 1835 Mary Burleson and ten other women, including Cecilie, a slave of the Samuel Craft family, organized what some believe to be the second oldest Methodist Church in Texas. Mrs. Burleson, by then a widow, fled in the Runaway Scrape[qv] with the Jenkins and Burleson families. In 1840 she moved with her seven children to a newly built log house on Thomas Christian's league. Their house at the edge of the settlement was the first at the site of present-day Elgin. They moved back to Bastrop, however, after their house was ransacked during an Indian attack. Mary Burleson returned to the area in 1847 and remained there until her death.

In the 1860s she and her stepson, Jonathan Burleson, granted a right-of-way to the Houston and Texas Central Railway route through their headright leagues and land for the townsite of Elgin (1872). A one-room log schoolhouse called Burleson Branch School operated between Bastrop and Elgin around 1870. With Mary's encouragement, her sons-in-law obtained a charter for the school as the Burleson Male and Female Academy in 1873. In this sparsely settled area, the school was never well attended; it closed when a school was organized in Elgin. Mary Burleson died on May 27, 1870, in Bastrop and was buried at Christian-Burleson Cemetery on the Christian league.

BIBLIOGRAPHY: John Henry Brown, *Indian Wars and Pioneers of Texas* (Austin: Daniell, 1880; reprod., Easley, South Carolina: Southern Historical Press, 1978). Elgin Historical Committee, *Elgin: A History of Elgin, Texas, 1872–1972* (Austin: Von Boeckmann–Jones, 1972). Kenneth Kesselus, *History of Bastrop County, Texas, Before Statehood* (Austin: Jenkins, 1986). Bill Moore, *Bastrop County, 1691–1900* (Wichita Falls: Nortex, 1977). *Byron Howard*

BURLESON, RICHARD BYRD (1822–1879). Richard Byrd Burleson, minister and geologist, son of Jonathan and Elizabeth (Byrd) Burleson, was born near Decatur, Alabama, on January 1, 1822. In 1842 he graduated from State University, Nashville, Tennessee, and was ordained to the Baptist ministry. In 1847 he married Sarah Leigh of Alabama; she died in 1854. He married Mary Halbert of Mississippi in 1857. In 1855 he moved to Austin, Texas, as pastor of the First Baptist Church. Burleson was appointed professor of natural sciences at Baylor University and remained at Baylor until 1874, when he became Texas state geologist. In 1875 he returned to Baylor. He died at Waco on December 21, 1879.

BIBLIOGRAPHY: *A Memorial and Biographical History of McLennan, Falls, Bell, and Coryell Counties* (Chicago: Lewis, 1893; rpt., St. Louis: Ingmire, 1984).

BURLESON, RUFUS COLUMBUS (1823–1901). Rufus C. Burleson, pioneer Baptist minister and college president, the son of Jonathan and Elizabeth (Byrd) Burleson, was born on August 7, 1823, near Decatur, Alabama. His mother was descended from the Byrd family of Virginia. He entered Summerville Academy in 1837 and remained for two years, then spent some time at schools in Danville and Decatur. His desire was to be a lawyer. After a religious conversion in April 1839, however, he felt a call to preach. He matriculated at Nashville University in 1840 to prepare for the Baptist ministry, but ill health forced him to withdraw in 1841. He studied Greek, Hebrew, and Bible history while recuperating at home. After the return of his health he taught until 1845 in Mississippi, where he was ordained and served briefly as pastor of three churches near Starkville. Burleson entered Western Baptist Theological Seminary in Covington, Kentucky, in 1846 and received his diploma the following year.

He was appointed for mission work in Texas by the Southern Baptist Domestic Mission Board and became pastor of the First Baptist Church in Houston in 1848. After a short, successful pastorate, he was elected in June 1851 to be the second president of Baylor University; he succeeded Henry Lee Graves.[qv] By constant advertising, traveling, and speaking over the state, Burleson brought relative strength and stability to Baylor. On January 3, 1853, he married Georgia Jenkins. On November 19, 1854, he baptized Sam Houston.[qv]

Burleson's beginning at Baylor was marred by friction with Horace Clark.[qv] When the female and male departments of Baylor were separated, Clark became principal of the female department and wanted to act independently of Burleson. The conflict over authority eventually degenerated into a personal feud, which, along with an invitation from a more promising area, led Burleson and the faculty of the male department to move to Waco in 1861. Burleson became president of Waco University, and the school flourished under his leadership. In 1865 it became coeducational and by 1868 was receiving support from the Baptist General Association of Texas, which included most of the northern part of the state.

Meanwhile, Baylor and the Independence area, having been bypassed by the railroad, were in economic difficulty, and the schools were merged in 1886 as Baylor University with Burleson as president. Under his leadership Baylor was able to achieve a permanent position of prominence in Texas education, although not without controversy. His battle with William Brann,[qv] editor of the *Iconoclast*[qv] and constant critic of Baylor and Baptists, erupted in 1894, when a young Brazilian girl living with the Burlesons was found to be pregnant. Brann championed the girl and suggested that Burleson was guilty of improprieties. Even after a grand jury found Burleson innocent, Brann continued his attacks on Burleson's attitude toward the girl. The incident resulted in the departure of some thirty-five female students from Baylor and heightened the feud between Brann and Baylor. In 1897 Baylor moved Burleson out of the presidency and made him president emeritus, a demotion he believed was a direct result of the Brann controversy.

Burleson served as pastor in Houston, Independence, and Waco and was guest preacher and revivalist in many Baptist churches and associations over the state. He was elected president of the Baptist General Convention of Texas[qv] for 1892–93. He also made an important contribution to public education in Texas. In 1869, at the request of Barnas Sears, he began to work unofficially for the Peabody Education Fund, established to work for public education. The fund wanted a man who was respected and well known throughout the state as well as one who would be able to promote a system of public schools. Burleson overcame opposition to public schools, partly by proposing ways to improve teaching. He advocated holding teachers' institutes in various cities and establishing a state teacher-training school. He was also instrumental in the founding of Bishop College; while in New York in 1872 he presented the need for a college for blacks to Nathan Bishop, who contributed at least $35,000 to the institution. Burleson died in Waco on May 14, 1901.

BIBLIOGRAPHY: Robert A. Baker, *The Blossoming Desert—A Concise History of Texas Baptists* (Waco: Word, 1970). Georgia J. Burleson, comp., *The Life and Writings of Rufus C. Burleson, D.D., L.L.D.* (1901). *Encyclopedia of Southern Baptists* (4 vols., Nashville: Broadman, 1958–82). Jack Winton Gunn, The Life of Rufus C. Burleson (Ph.D. dissertation, University of Texas, 1951). Harry Haynes, "Dr. Rufus C. Burleson," *Quarterly of the Texas State Historical Association* 5 (July 1901). Lois Smith Murray, *Baylor at Independence* (Waco: Baylor University Press, 1972). *J. A. Reynolds*

BURLESON, TEXAS. Burleson is on Interstate Highway 35W, U.S. Highway 81, State Highway 174, and Farm roads 731 and 3391, fourteen miles south of Fort Worth in northern Johnson and southern Tarrant counties. Shannon and Village creeks run through the community. The Missouri, Kansas and Texas Railroad runs through the community, and the Gulf, Colorado and Santa Fe runs just to the west. Burleson began when the MKT planned a railroad from Fort Worth to Hillsboro in 1881 and established a depot on the townsite. Grenville M. Dodge, representing the railroad, purchased the land, originally part of the J. W. Henderson survey, from Rev. Henry C. Renfro.[qv] As part of the agreement, Renfro was allowed to name the depot and called it Burleson, in honor of Dr. Rufus C. Burleson,[qv] his teacher and later president of Baylor University.

In 1882 Burleson received a post office located in a saloon, with John L. Dickey as the first postmaster. Soon after it opened, several stores and churches were formed. Burleson was a mile south of an earlier community, Brushy Mound, which was bypassed by the railroad. The first school in the area had been founded at Brushy Mound in 1879. In 1885 a new building was constructed and called Alta Vista College. In 1893 it became Red Oak Academy and was run by the Presbyterian Church.[qv] After the school was discontinued the building was moved to Burleson in 1900. The Brushy Mound site is now in the Burleson city limits.

In its first fifty years Burleson was a stable community organized around agriculture and livestock raising. By 1890 it had a population of 200, grocers, druggists, a general store, and several cotton gin–gristmills. Ten years later the community had a newspaper, the Burleson *Banner*, and an artesian well and waterworks that supplied water to area homes and businesses. In 1899 Burleson shipped 2,000 bales of cotton, eighty cars of wheat and oats, and thirty cars of cottonseed.

The population in Burleson was 368 in 1904 but dropped by the 1920s to 241, before beginning a slow climb to 573 in 1940. The community was incorporated before 1930. In 1912 the North Texas Traction Company began service on its Interurban line between Cleburne and Fort Worth with a stop in Burleson. In 1913 Burleson received its first electricity, powered by wires laid for the Interurban, and in 1921 Lone Star Gas began to provide gas service to Burleson. The Interurban service to Burleson made the town more accessible to the outside world. In 1924 State Highway 21 was built from Fort Worth to Alvarado through Burleson. As Burleson grew land was annexed to provide room for new buildings. Before World War II[qv] the Cumming-Clark addition was built, and after the war the Mound, Tarrant, Crestmoor, and Montclair additions were annexed. The population began to grow more rapidly. From 1940 to 1950 it rose 28 percent, from 573 to 795, but in the next decade the population mushroomed from 795 in 1950 to 2,345 in 1960, as Burleson became a suburb of Fort Worth. The community began to rely less on agriculture and more on business and industry. It supported thirty businesses in the 1930s, and sixty-two in the 1960s. In 1950 Burleson had seven manufacturers, including three feed companies and a brass manufacturer.

By 1980 the population of 11,734 supported 196 businesses. Fourteen manufacturers constructed a variety of items, including glass, mobile homes, camper tops, and metal storage sheds. In 1990 three newspapers, the Burleson *Star* (established 1965), the Joshua *Tribune* (established 1970), and the Burleson *Star Review* (established 1969), were published in Burleson, in addition to technical, trade, and church journals. In 1990 the population of Burleson was 16,113. The Burleson Library and a museum were located in the Victorian home of the Clark and Renfro families, built in 1893.

BIBLIOGRAPHY: Burleson History Committee, *Burleson—The First One Hundred Years* (Dallas: Taylor, 1981). *Lisa C. Maxwell*

BURLESON COLLEGE. The resolution for a college in Greenville, Texas, was presented at the Hunt County Baptist Association on October 1, 1894, by Rev. S. J. Anderson, pastor of the First Baptist Church in Greenville. The following February Burleson College, named after Rufus C. Burleson,[qv] was incorporated by the state of Texas as an educational institution with $50,000 in capital stock. The trustees met and elected Anderson president of the college on May 27, 1895. Some of the land that was given to the college was sold to build and furnish it. The institution took the faculty and pupils of Greenville College, which had closed in April, and the eight seniors of that school became the first graduating class of Burleson College in May. Ownership of Burleson College property passed to the Hunt County Baptist Association in September. Since the administration building was not completed by school time, Burleson College was officially opened in September in the Central Public School building.

The five-acre college campus was located one mile from Greenville, and the three-story, brick administration building was completed in October 1895. A group of interested men organized the Dormitory Stock Company in 1895 and built a three-story, wooden dormitory building by early 1896. Anderson resigned the presidency on September 28, 1898, and sold the dormitory, which he had owned, in November 1899. This transaction left Burleson College without a dormitory until late 1900, when the college purchased the dorm from J. S. Hill. The Hunt Association decided to place the college under the Education Commission of the Baptist General Convention in December 1899.

In June 1907 the trustees and the Baptist Educational Commission decided to make Burleson College a junior college. The three-story, brick girls' dormitory was completed in June 1916, and a similar boys' dormitory was completed by the fall semester of 1917. On April 8, 1925, the girls' dormitory was destroyed by fire, and a similar three-story building was completed by the fall semester of 1926. In 1929 Burleson College had 325 students and nineteen teachers. The college closed on December 5, 1930, due to an overburden of debt and competition with tax-supported schools, especially East Texas State College (*now* East Texas State University) at Commerce.

BIBLIOGRAPHY: Ethel Casslles, A History of Hunt County (M.A. thesis, University of Texas, 1935). W. Walworth Harrison, *History of Greenville and Hunt County, Texas* (Waco: Texian, 1976). William Franklin Ledlow, History of Protestant Education in Texas (Ph.D. dissertation, University of Texas, 1926). Carl Bassett Wilson, History of Baptist Educational Efforts in Texas, 1829–1900 (Ph.D. dissertation, University of Texas, 1934). *Samuel B. Hesler*

BURLESON COUNTY. Burleson County (J-18), in east central Texas, lies approximately forty-five miles east of the state capital at Austin and is bordered by Milam County on the north, on the east by Robertson and Brazos counties, on the south by Washington County, and on the west by Lee County. Caldwell, the largest town and the county seat, is sixty miles east of Austin. The county's geographical center lies at approximately 30°30′ north latitude and 96°36′ west longitude. State Highway 36 is the major north–south thoroughfare, and State Highway 21 spans the county east to west. The county is also served by two major railways the Southern Pacific and the Atchison, Topeka and Santa Fe.

Burleson County covers 668 square miles in the Post Oak Belt region of Texas. Most of its area features undulating to hilly terrain except for the broad alluvial valley along its eastern border, covering nearly one-fourth of the county's surface, which is nearly level. Its elevation ranges from 225 feet above sea level in the southeast to 475 feet in the northwest. The entire county lies within the drainage basin of the Brazos River, which marks its eastern border. The western and southern reaches of the county are drained by Yegua Creek and its principal tributary, East Yegua Creek, which form the county's southern and western borders, respectively, and empty into the Brazos at the southeastern corner of the county. Since 1967 Somerville Lake,[qv] an 11,160-acre reservoir on Yegua Creek near the town of Somerville, has provided recreation, tourism revenue, and much-needed flood protection for the residents of Burleson County.

Almost half the county is surfaced by upland soils of a grayish-brown sandy loam and clayey subsoils, while the Brazos bottoms, running the length of the county's eastern border along the Brazos, are surfaced by reddish, loamy to clayey, alluvial soils. The San Antonio Prairie, a strip of open grassland one to four miles in width stretching through the middle of the county from southwest to northeast, features dark, loamy to clayey, blackland soils with stiff clayey subsoils. With the exception of this band of almost treeless Blackland Prairie, most of the county lies within the Post Oak Savannah vegetation zone, characterized by a combination of post oak forest and "mosaic" areas of interspersed grassland, parkland, and woods. In addition to the predominant post oaks, the hardwood forests that mantle three sevenths of the county's area include such species as blackjack oak, hickory, elm, and hackberry. Many streams are fringed by thick stands of water oak, pecan, and walnut. Peat bogs and marshes abound in the bottomlands. The most abundant types of prairie grass include bluestem, Indian grass, tall bunchgrass, and buffalo grass. Between 21 and 30 percent of the land in the county is classified as prime farmland. Burleson County is also situated along the Luling Fault Zone, recently a focus of intensive oil exploration. Large, newly tapped reserves of petroleum and natural gas and considerable deposits of lignite coal—yet to be exploited commercially—are the most significant of the county's limited mineral resources. Although the bear, alligator, and buffalo that once roamed the area disappeared in the nineteenth century, the county is still inhabited by many wild animal species, including white-tailed deer, coyotes, skunks, raccoons, and opossums, and such wild birds as the mourning dove and bobwhite quail; all find haven in the Somerville State Wildlife Management Area. Temperatures in Burleson County range from an average high of 95° in July to an average low of 39° in January. Rainfall averages thirty-seven inches annually, and the average relative humidity is 84 percent at 6 A.M. and 54 percent at 6 P.M. The growing season averages 268 days a year.

The scanty archeological evidence recovered so far suggests that human habitation in the territory composing modern Burleson County began during the middle phases of the Archaic Period (ca. 7000 B.C.–500 A.D.). The earliest historical inhabitants of future Burleson County, the Tonkawa Indians, were probably descended from the Archaic and Neo-American peoples whose stone artifacts and ceramics were unearthed in the county in the mid-1960s. The Tonkawas were a nomadic hunting and gathering people who lived in widely scattered bands, practiced no agriculture, and sometimes traveled hundreds of miles to follow the buffalo.[qv] They camped along the rivers and streams of much of Central Texas, including the future Burleson County. Their numbers were greatly reduced by European diseases over the course of the eighteenth century. Though the Tonkawas were regarded as friendly by the Anglo-Americans who began to settle among them during the early nineteenth century, their petty thievery was a continual source of annoyance to the newcomers.

Hunting parties of Caddo Indians from East Texas, also considered peaceful by the settlers, roved westward through the area as far as the Colorado River in pursuit of buffalo. The territory of the future county also lay within the range of more hostile southern Wichita peoples, such as the Tawakonis and Wacos, and fatal confrontations between members of these groups and white settlers were not uncommon. Raids on the settlements by small parties, typically seeking horses, seemed to become more frequent during the middle and late 1830s, but in the 1840s the Indians were expelled from the Burleson County vicinity. The federal census of 1850 found no Indians in the county.

During the seventeenth and eighteenth centuries the area of the future county was part of a vast arena of imperial competition between the Spanish and French. The first European to set foot within the bounds of future Burleson County was probably the French explorer and trader Louis Juchereau de St. Denis,[qv] who traveled through the area in 1713 en route from Natchitoches, Louisiana, to the Rio Grande. The trail that he blazed between the Trinity River and San Antonio soon became known as the Upper Road of one of the *caminos reales*, or the Old San Antonio Road,[qv] the most important route from San Antonio to the eastern border of Spanish Texas. In 1718, shortly after founding the Villa de Béxar at the site of present San Antonio, Martín de Alarcón,[qv] governor of Texas, traveled the Upper Road through what is now Burleson County to the Spanish missions among the Texas Indians in East Texas. The first American to visit the area of the future Burleson County may have been the explorer Zebulon M. Pike,[qv] who traversed the Old San Antonio Road to Natchitoches upon his release from imprisonment in Chihuahua in 1807. It is likely that Moses Austin[qv] journeyed through the territory of present Burleson County as he traveled the Upper Road from Arkansas to San Antonio de Béxar seeking an empresario[qv] contract in the fall of 1820.

Anglo-American settlement within the bounds of the future Burleson County began some time after the founding of Stephen F. Austin's[qv] first colony in the early 1820s and proceeded very slowly. The Old San Antonio Road was specified as the northern boundary of the colony, yet before the mid-1830s only a handful of settlers had actually taken up residence in the territory south of the road and north of Yegua Creek. Soon after the Mexican government adopted its Law of April 6, 1830,[qv] which prohibited further Anglo-American settlement in Texas, preparations were made for the construction of a fort on the Brazos to help implement the new policy. In October 1830 Fort Tenoxtitlán[qv] was established by Lt. Col. José Francisco Ruiz[qv] on a high bluff on the west bank of the Brazos, about twelve miles above the crossing of the Old San Antonio Road in what is now northeastern Burleson County. In defiance of his instructions, the Texas-born Ruiz permitted a group of more than fifty Tennesseans led by Sterling C. Robertson[qv] to take up residence in the vicinity of the fort in November 1830, while Robertson attempted to validate the settlement contract that his Nashville Company had negotiated with the Mexican government some years earlier. Some of these newcomers took up residence in the settlement that had arisen near the fort; by July 1831 Francis Smith had established a general store in the community. Other settlers, however, scattered through the countryside; many migrated into the Austin colony south of the Old San Antonio Road and awaited confirmation of Robertson's contract.

In August 1832 the garrison was withdrawn from Fort Tenoxtitlán, and the site was abandoned to the nearby American and Mexican settlers. Although the village of Tenoxtitlán in its turn disappeared during the Civil War,[qv] it remained the only settlement and trading post within the bounds of the future Burleson County until 1840. In 1834, when Robertson at last made good his right to direct settlement in what was thenceforth known as Robertson's colony,[qv] he opened a land office in Tenoxtitlán—which served as the capital of the colony until the founding of Nashville in what is now Milam County—and began issuing patents to land above the Old San Antonio Road. Among the prominent early settlers in what is now Burleson County were William Oldham, Alexander Thomson, Jr., Joseph B. Chance,[qqv] John Teal, Isaac Addison, and John W. Porter. Most of these early settlers and their families, like those brought to Texas by Robertson's Nashville Company, came from the Old South, particularly Tennessee, Kentucky, and Alabama. Once in Texas, they set about perpetuating Southern culture and institutions—including slavery.[qv] Many brought with them considerable investments in slave property. Gabriel Jackson of Kentucky, for example, who arrived in Robertson's colony in December 1833 and soon established a large plantation in the Brazos bottoms of the future Burleson County, was the owner of 100 slaves.

In March and April 1836, alarmed by the news of the fall of the Alamo[qv] and by the fugitives streaming eastward on the Old San Antonio Road, the residents of the area joined the mass flight from the advancing Mexican army known as the Runaway Scrape.[qv] As news of the battle of San Jacinto[qv] spread, however, the settlers quickly returned to find their homes untouched. Growth of the area accelerated after the establishment of the Republic of Texas.[qv] But as white inhabitants became more numerous in the sparsely populated territory, Indian raids became more frequent. The settlers often responded to rumors of impending hostilities by taking refuge at Tenoxtitlán or within the fortifications at the home of William Oldham, in what is now southern Burleson County. But Tenoxtitlán itself became a favorite target of Indian attacks. The last fatal raid within the bounds of the present county occurred in May 1841, the final occasion on which the white population repaired to the forts for defense. With settlement expanding westward and northward, Tenoxtitlán became increasingly inaccessible, and its protection grew less important as the Indian menace diminished rapidly during the 1840s.

Population increase soon produced demands for the organization of local government. In 1830 the territory of present Burleson County south of the Old San Antonio Road was included in the Precinct of Viesca, while the area of the future county north of the road, part of Robertson's colony, was incorporated into Viesca Municipality. In 1835 the region north of the road became part, first, of Milam Municipality, and then of Milam County, after the foundation of the republic in 1836. The territory south of the road and north of Yegua Creek was initially included in Washington Municipality, organized in 1835, and then in Washington County in 1836. In 1840 the area of the present county south of the Old San Antonio Road was transferred from Washington to Milam County. A small settlement and trading post established by Lewis L. Chiles by 1840 at the place where the Old San Antonio Road crossed Davidson Creek in what is now Burleson County was chosen to become the seat of the newly constituted Milam County. A new townsite, soon known as Caldwell, was platted in 1840 by George B. Erath.[qv] Finally, on March 24, 1846, the state's First Legislature established Burleson County, named for Gen. Edward Burleson,[qv] and designated Caldwell the county seat. The county acquired its present boundaries in 1874, when its western reaches beyond East Yegua Creek were given to the new Lee County, thus reducing Burleson County by some 31 percent.

With heavy immigration continuing from the southern United States and from the older settled parts of Texas, the county's white and black populations continued to expand rapidly until the end of antebellum Texas.[qv] In 1847 there were 866 whites and 330 slaves in the county. Although no free blacks were enumerated in any of the antebellum censuses, several are believed to have resided in the county. As early as the mid-1830s Hendrick Arnold,[qv] a free black from Mississippi and a veteran of the battle of San Jacinto, lived within the future boundaries of the county. The black settlement on the large estate of William Oldham, who purchased Arnold's property in 1837, was known for many years as the "Free Settlement" and was probably home to a number of free blacks (presumably including Oldham's seven children by a slave mistress). During the final antebellum decade the county began to acquire an unmistakable flavor of the Old South, as many large plantations were established on the fertile alluvial soils of the Brazos bottoms in the eastern part of the county. These plantations accounted for much of the county's agricultural production. Cotton and corn were virtually the only crops raised, aside from fodder crops and vegetables. In 1850, 70,000 bushels of corn and 1,010 bales of cotton were harvested in the county from only 5,182 acres of improved farmland. Stock raising had already become quite extensive by this date in the uplands of the central and western parts of the county; 12,117 cattle, 13,607 hogs, and 376 sheep were produced in Burleson County in 1850.

The decade of the 1850s witnessed a remarkable expansion of both the county's population and its agricultural production, especially livestock production. Total population increased more than threefold, to stand at 5,683 by 1860; the white population tripled in this period to 3,797, while the slave population quadrupled, to 2,003. By 1860 the county's improved agricultural acreage had increased more than 300 percent, to 23,838 acres. Corn production virtually doubled, to 135,631 bushels; the cotton yield jumped more than fourfold, to 4,418 bales. The county's cattle production soared to 42,469 head by 1860, a 350 percent increase over the 1850 future; not until the 1950s would so many cattle again be raised in Burleson County. Hog production almost doubled during the 1850s, to 24,562. The number of sheep raised in the county registered an astonishing eighteenfold increase, to 6,788 animals, by 1860. However, despite the evidence of impressive growth, frontier conditions persisted in Burleson County agriculture on the eve of the Civil War. Although much of the county's area had already been divided into farms, only 23,838 acres had been improved by 1860. The prevailing high ratio of oxen to mules, 2,031 to 456, suggests that farmers were still struggling with the task of breaking the land to the plow.

By 1856 post offices had been established in the communities of Caldwell, Brazos Bottom, Chance's Prairie, Lexington (now in Lee County) and Prospect. Caldwell, near the geographical center of the county, was a transportation hub and by 1856 had attained a population of 300; until the early 1850s all county roads ran through the town, which was the site of one of the region's finest hotels, the Caldwell House. Census returns at the end of the final antebellum decade describe three county residents as holders of property worth at least $100,000 each; a fourth, Judge A. S. Broaddus, immigrated from Virginia in 1854 with 120 slaves.

As the crisis of the Union unfolded in 1860 and 1861 some opposition to secession[qv] developed within Burleson County. T. H. Mundine,[qv] the county's representative in the Eighth Texas Legislature and a member of the Constitutional Union party,[qv] courageously published an address opposing ratification of the secession ordinance. Most county residents, however, supported the secession movement. A chapter of the secret order known as the Knights of the Golden Circle[qv] was formed at Caldwell and agitated for dissolution of the Union. In the referendum of February 23, 1861, the county voted for secession, 422 to 84. Most county Unionists, including Mundine, appear to have loyally supported the Confederacy during the war. Hundreds of Burleson County residents enlisted in Confederate or state military units. State formations to which companies organized in the county were attached included the First, Second,[qv] Third, Fifth, and Seventeenth Texas Infantry regiments, the Eighth Texas Cavalry,[qv] and Waul's Legion.[qv] On the home front, farmers experimented with the cultivation of unfamiliar food crops, such as wheat. To circumvent the Union Navy's blockade of the Texas coast, county planters transported cotton to Mexico in trains of ox wagons. Far from halting immigration, the war in fact generated a new influx of planter refugees from the lower South seeking protection for their slave property. Newly arrived slaveowners who had difficulty obtaining land hired out their workforce to large plantation operators, as did servicemen compelled to leave their farms in the care of wives and children. Between 1860 and 1864, according to local tax rolls, the county's slave population increased by almost 50 percent, to 2,905. Though some blacks entering the county under these circumstances eventually returned to the communities from which they had been uprooted, many others simply began building a new life where they found themselves at the end of the war.

Reconstruction[qv] in Burleson County, as in much of the rest of the state, was a violent and chaotic period. Outlaws and brigands—many of them veterans unwilling to resume a peaceful life—took advantage of the confusion, and several bands of cattle rustlers and horse thieves operated freely in the heavily forested southern and western parts of the county, along the Yegua and its tributaries. The notorious Sam Bass[qv] and his gang reportedly lived in this area for a time. Some communities resorted to vigilante justice in an effort to curb the lawlessness; the citizens of Yellow Prairie, for example, broke up one gang by capturing and lynching five of its members.

Although no federal soldiers were garrisoned within Burleson County, a company of State Police,qv composed almost entirely of blacks, was stationed at Caldwell during this period, charged with protecting the lives, property, and civil rights of all citizens, including freedmen. Their presence did ensure access to polling places and the court system, but their numbers were too few and their resources too limited to enable them to enforce the laws everywhere within the county. The eastern half of the county, in which the black population was concentrated, fell within the twentieth subdistrict of the Freedmen's Bureau,qv variously headquartered in Grimes and Brazos counties. The records of the subassistant commissioner include numerous reports of violent crimes committed by whites against blacks in Burleson County. Although many, perhaps even most, of these crimes were political in nature, some were blatantly so. In July 1868 a freedman named Wilson, a county registrar, was dragged from his bed at night by an armed mob and hanged and his body mutilated before being tossed into the Brazos River. A Ku Klux Klanqv cell emerged in the county to engage in night-riding and other acts of intimidation aimed at freedmen and their allies. Law-enforcement officials were helpless to bring the perpetrators of such crimes to justice.

Though prewar Unionists such as T. H. Mundine were prominent among the county officials appointed during the provisional administration of Governor A. J. Hamilton,qv the election of 1866 saw conservatives return to power in the county. In late 1867, however, the conservative officials were in their turn swept out of office by the military government imposed upon the state under the congressional Reconstruction plan. Yet, even with the State Police to protect freedmen and other Republican voters, the Democratic partyqv emerged triumphant in Burleson County in the election of 1869 and remained in control of the government virtually without interruption for the next 120 years.

The county's black population had expanded steadily throughout the antebellum era and the Civil War, and it continued its growth after the war; by 1870, 3,040 African Americansqv lived in the county, 52 percent more than in 1860. In 1860 blacks had constituted 35 percent of the population; by 1870 their proportion had risen to 37 percent, and it continued to increase until the early twentieth century, cresting at 46 percent in 1910. During World War I,qv however, as industrial jobs in the North began to open to them for the first time, blacks began to leave Burleson County in large numbers. The county's black population fell 24 percent between 1910 and 1920. Although this trend was reversed in the 1920s, which witnessed a 10 percent increase in the county's black population, the black exodus resumed during the Great Depression,qv as agricultural tenancy began to decline, and then accelerated during the 1940s, as new defense-related jobs opened to blacks in urban areas of the North and West. The county's black population declined by 38 percent during the 1940s and continued to fall by an average of more than 13 percent a decade until, by 1980, blacks constituted only 22 percent of the population. Although the wave of violence unleashed against them in the immediate postbellum years gradually subsided, African Americans in the county suffered the same segregation in housing, public education, and public accommodations, and the same pervasive economic and social discrimination inflicted upon blacks elsewhere. During the 1920s Ku Klux Klan organizations reemerged in Caldwell and Somerville to harass not only blacks but the county's numerous foreign-born residents as well.

Economic recovery from the Civil War was slow. By 1870 the value of Burleson County farms had fallen to just 35 percent of their value in 1860. In 1870 no county residents were listed among the owners of property worth $100,000. However, by the end of the nineteenth century the development of cotton farming and the livestock industry had restored much of the county's former economic vitality. From the mid-1860s through the end of the 1870s county stock raisers drove their cattle northward along a branch of the Chisholm Trailqv that passed through the Deanville area in western Burleson County and thence toward Waco, paralleling the Brazos. Although the 16,308 cattle raised in the county in 1870 represented only 38 percent of the 1860 figure, annual-production levels gradually increased to a postbellum high of 30,765 in 1890. The industry declined somewhat over the next several decades, with production falling to a historic low by 1930, when only 23,334 cattle were enumerated. After 1930, however, the county's cattle herds grew steadily, climbing to a pinnacle of 65,137 animals in 1974. Hog raising also remained a significant agricultural activity. Although the 1860 herd size was never regained, postbellum production rose to a peak of 19,974 animals in 1910, before beginning a long gradual decline to 2,136 by 1987. The county's sheep industry, on the other hand, though managing to recover prewar production levels as early as 1870, dwindled to insignificance during the 1890s and has never revived. Poultry became important after 1880 and remained so for a century before declining precipitously in the 1980s.

Cotton cultureqv expanded slowly in Burleson County during the first fifteen years following the Civil War, but began to boom in the 1880s and by the end of the nineteenth century had become the most important economic activity in the county. The 6,423 bales of cotton raised in 1870 represented a 45 percent increase over the modest 1860 figure. Between 1870 and 1880, however, production declined by 7 percent before soaring 169 percent, to 16,062 bales, by 1890 and then climbing a further 64 percent to a postbellum peak of 25,243 bales in 1900. The number of improved acres in the county doubled between 1870 and 1880 and doubled again by 1890, to 99,584; thereafter acreage grew more slowly, reaching a historic maximum of 144,115 acres in 1930. Only 31 percent of the county's cropland was devoted to cotton cultivation in 1880, but that proportion expanded steadily over the next several decades, to 36 percent in 1890, 44 percent in 1900, and 51 percent in 1910, before cresting at 63 percent in 1930. Although wheat, oats, and vegetables were cultivated on a small scale after the Civil War, corn remained the most important food crop, raised on anywhere from 21 to 34 percent of the county's cropland between 1880 and 1960.

As the county economy gradually recovered from the havoc of the war, rapid population growth resumed. Driven mainly by the large influx of war refugees, population grew by 45 percent between 1860 and 1870, to 8,229. The increase slowed to 12 percent during the 1870s, then accelerated to a robust 41 percent in each of the two subsequent decades, to stand at 18,367 in 1900. As before the war, most of the county's postbellum immigration came from older areas of Texas or from the states of the lower South, particularly Alabama, Mississippi, and Tennessee. Many of the newcomers, like most of the county's black population, became tenant farmers as the rapid spread of cotton cultivation produced a rapid expansion of the crop-lien system. By 1880, 37 percent of the county's farmers were tenants. That figure escalated to 53 percent in 1890, climbed to 61 percent by 1910, and reached a maximum of 63 percent in 1930. Thereafter, with the onset of the depression and the curtailment of cotton cultivation, tenancy rates began to decline; just 15 percent of the county's farmers were tenants in 1959.

The economic resurgence was greatly abetted by improvement of the local transportation system in the late nineteenth century. In the 1860s many Burleson County planters began hauling their cotton to the Houston and Texas Central Railway line in neighboring Brazos County. Indeed, several large landowners in the Brazos bottoms of Burleson County took up residence in Bryan, the seat of Brazos County. Traffic between the two counties provided a thriving business for a number of ferry operators on the Brazos River, and the first bridge between the counties, Pitt's Bridge, was erected in 1875. In the late 1860s the commercial and demographic links between Brazos County and eastern Burleson County generated demands by residents of the Brazos bottoms to transfer that prosperous farming district into Brazos County—demands that were firmly rejected by

Burleson County officials. Finally, with the coming of the railroad to Burleson County, these political pressures subsided. In 1880 the Gulf, Colorado and Santa Fe Railway extended the Brenham–Cameron section of its main line through the county, passing through Caldwell. In the early 1880s Somerville was founded as a station on this line just north of Yegua Creek; by the early twentieth century it rivaled Caldwell as a commercial and industrial center, and surpassed it in population after the First World War. In 1883 the GC&SF constructed a spur between Somerville and Navasota that was soon extended into the piney woods of eastern Texas. In 1895 the Hearne and Brazos Valley Railway completed a short line between Hearne and the Brazos bottoms in an effort to capture the trade of the region for the merchants of Robertson County. The Houston and Texas Central extended its Hearne–Giddings branch line through Caldwell in 1912. And in 1918 a short line known as the "Peavine" was constructed between Bryan and Whittaker in the Brazos bottoms. The roads remained in deplorable condition through the 1930s. State Highway 36 became the county's first paved highway in 1939, and Highway 21 was paved a few years later. Construction of a network of paved farm roads was begun in the 1940s and completed during the 1950s (*see* HIGHWAY DEVELOPMENT).

Transportation improvements and economic revival in the late nineteenth century attracted not only large numbers of American-born immigrants but, for the first time, significant numbers of foreign immigrants as well. Although Burleson County had received a trickle of foreign immigration from the beginning, as late as 1870 the foreign-born constituted only 2 percent of the county's population. In the 1870s, however, substantial numbers of Germans and Austrians[qqv] began settling in communities throughout the county, from Cooks Point in the east to Deanville in the west. During the 1880s large numbers of Czechs[qv] began to settle in many parts of the county; like the Germans they often formed distinct enclaves within older communities, but they also founded several all-Czech towns as well, including Frenstat, New Tabor, and Sebesta, later known as Snook. In the 1890s farmers in the Brazos bottoms in need of agricultural labor assisted in settling considerable numbers of Italians,[qv] mostly Sicilians, in eastern Burleson County, where they were initially employed as sharecroppers. Although the foreign-born never constituted more than 8 percent of the population during the nineteenth century, they enriched the county's cultural and social life immeasurably. As the county's black population declined during the era of World War I, shortages of agricultural labor became acute. To help alleviate this condition, increasing numbers of Mexican migrant workers found employment in the county. Many took up residence, so that Mexicans Americans[qv] became the largest foreign-immigrant group to settle in the county during the twentieth century. By 1930 there were 2,024 persons of Hispanic origin in Burleson County, some 10 percent of the population. Although Mexican immigration was sharply curtailed in the early forties, the county's Hispanic population has remained fairly stable and in 1990 still constituted 11 percent of the total population.

The economy into which the successive waves of newcomers blended has remained overwhelmingly agricultural. Aside from lumbermills, gristmills, and cotton gins, virtually the only industrial activity in Burleson County has been that associated with the Santa Fe Railroad, which for many years maintained a division headquarters and extensive shops in Somerville. Until after World War II[qv] the Santa Fe Tie and Lumber Preserving Company in Somerville remained the county's only industrial operation with more than a handful of employees. This lopsided economic development made the county vulnerable after the turn of the century. Between 1900 and 1940 the population failed to grow. After a meager 2 percent increase between 1900 and 1910, population fell by 10 percent in the ensuing decade, as blacks began to move out. Population did manage to expand during the twenties by a respectable 18 percent—aided by heavy Mexican immigration and a temporary halt in black emigration—and reached a maximum of 19,848 in 1930. However, during the thirties, as the depression transformed the county's agriculture—thus curtailing both cotton production and tenancy—the population fell by 8 percent, to 18,334 in 1940. It plummeted a further 29 percent in the 1940s, as the black exodus resumed on an unprecedented scale and thousands of whites also abandoned the county in search of industrial jobs in the state's urban areas. Over the next twenty years the Burleson County population continued to contract by an average of more than 12 percent a decade, falling to 9,999 by 1970.

Major reconfiguration of the county's agriculture began in the 1930s, as cotton acreage began to decline under the impact of continuing low prices, diminishing soil fertility, and New Deal acreage-reduction programs. The 91,021 acres devoted to cotton cultivation in 1930 dropped by almost half by 1940. The decline continued over the next half century, so that by 1987 cotton was grown on only 8,431 acres in the county. Although the yield remained as high as 27,355 bales as late as 1950, by 1987 that figure had fallen to 13,740. As cotton acreage was reduced, the cultivation of alternative crops such as hay and sorghum and, briefly, peanuts and oats, was expanded; wheat growing has become of some significance since the seventies, with as much as 87,435 bushels being produced on 5,572 acres by 1982. However, most of the former cotton land was withdrawn from crop raising altogether and devoted to livestock production, which after World War II became the county's most important industry; by 1982, 75 percent of the county's agricultural revenues were derived from livestock and livestock products. Oddly, dairying had played only a limited role in the stock-raising boom; although it expanded briefly following World War II, it soon began to decline and by the 1980s was no longer of commercial significance. Meanwhile, the county's harvested cropland fell from 122,274 acres in 1930 to 40,551 acres by 1987. Even the production of corn, an important feature of the county's economy throughout its history, fell off after the war, with yields falling from 634,200 bushels in 1940 to 243,878 in 1987 and acres planted in corn plummeting over the same period from 35,791 to 3,489.

Residents of Burleson County participated enthusiastically in the two world wars and contributed their sons unreservedly to both, but the county was not as directly affected by these conflicts as were many other Texas counties. To further the effort on the home front during the First World War, a Burleson County Council of Defense was organized as early as March 3, 1917, a full month before the formal American declaration of war, a circumstance that reflected the rising tide of anti-German sentiment in the county. County officials vigorously promoted conservation and directed the rationing of flour, sugar, and other essential commodities. The county exceeded its quota in the four Liberty Loan and the Victory Loan bond sales by more than $100,000. A Burleson County Chapter of the American Red Cross, with branches in a dozen communities and a membership of more than 3,900, was formed in July 1917 and worked diligently to provide relief and various social services to military personnel and their families. The county's large German-American population fell under suspicion of disloyalty, and non-English-speaking citizens of all ethnic backgrounds were pressured into using English in schools, churches, and elsewhere. Almost 830 county residents served in the armed forces, including 381 blacks. The rationing programs and loan campaigns of the Second World War were as successful as those of the First. The county's economy was boosted during World War II by the proximity of Bryan Air Field (*see* BRYAN AIR FORCE BASE), just east of the Brazos River. In 1942 farm roads in the Snook area were among the first county roads to be paved in order to facilitate access to a temporary air strip, Smith Field, an adjunct of Bryan Field. More than 1,300 county residents—7 percent of the population—served in the military during this conflict.

Under the stimulus of increasing economic diversification and industrial development after World War II, Burleson County at last resumed growth. The number of manufacturing establishments in the county increased from four in 1947 to twelve in 1982, and the number of employees in the manufacturing sector rose over the same period from 260 to 400. Petroleum was discovered in the county in 1938, but until the energy crisis of the 1970s only token quantities were recovered from the deep rock strata, including the Austin Chalk, in which it is embedded. In the late 1970s production of both crude oil and natural gas increased dramatically, and since the early 1980s several million barrels of oil and billions of cubic feet of natural gas have been extracted annually. Much of this new industrial activity arose in the vicinity of Caldwell, which after 1940 regained from Somerville its former position as the county's largest town. In 1940 Caldwell's population stood at 2,165, Somerville's at 1,621. In 1990 Caldwell had 3,181 residents; Somerville, Snook, and Lyons are the only other towns with populations greater than 150. Although agriculture is still the county's preeminent economic activity, significant employment has been produced in other sectors of the economy in the last few decades. By 1982 only 14 percent of the county's labor force remained employed in agriculture, while 17 percent were employed in trade, 17 percent in manufacturing, and 20 percent in services. Almost one-third of the work force, however, continued to find employment outside the county in such communities as Rockdale, Bryan, and College Station. One of the most important aspects of late-twentieth-century development was the construction of Somerville Dam and Reservoir on Yegua Creek in 1967. Somerville Lake became one of the most prominent recreation areas in south central Texas, attracting several hundred thousand visitors annually and providing stimulation for the county's economy. Furthermore, construction of the lake finally helped end the disastrous flooding of Yegua Creek and the Brazos River, which has plagued the county throughout its history; and it at last rendered obsolete such ineffectual flood-control measures as the thirty-mile-long levee on the west bank of the Brazos, first erected by landowners in 1910.

Politically, Burleson County remained steadfastly Democratic after Reconstruction, although there were sizable minorities of Greenbackers in 1880 and Populists in 1892. The Populists, in fact, actually triumphed in the county in the election of 1894, and the Socialist ticket was only narrowly defeated in 1920. Otherwise, the long string of Democratic victories continued, except for the 1972 presidential election, when the county voted for Richard M. Nixon, and the 1984 election, when it voted for Ronald Reagan.

BIBLIOGRAPHY: Malcolm H. Addison, *Reminiscences of Burleson County, Texas* (Caldwell, Texas, 1886; rpt., Caldwell: Caldwell Printing, 1971). Burleson County Historical Society, *Astride the Old San Antonio Road: A History of Burleson County, Texas* (Dallas: Taylor, 1980). Alfred Henry Conrad, Land Economic Study of Burleson County, Texas (M.S. thesis, Agricultural and Mechanical College of Texas, 1949). Roy Sylvan Dunn, "The KGC in Texas," *Southwestern Historical Quarterly* 70 (April 1967). Otto Charles Rode, A History of Burleson County in the World War (M.A. thesis, University of Texas, 1929). Thomas Clarence Richardson, *East Texas: Its History and Its Makers* (4 vols., New York: Lewis Historical Publishing, 1940).

Charles Christopher Jackson

BURLESON COUNTY (Judicial). Burleson County was established for judicial and other purposes on January 15, 1842. It included all of what is now Burleson County and the northwest portion of what is now Lee County. Caldwell was named the county seat. A few weeks afterwards a Texas Supreme Court decision, *Stockton v. Montgomery* (1842), declared all judicial counties unconstitutional. The present Burleson County was established in 1846.

BIBLIOGRAPHY: James Wilmer Dallam, *A Digest of the Laws of Texas* (Baltimore: Toy, 1845). Hans Peter Nielsen Gammel, comp., *Laws of Texas, 1822–1897* (10 vols., Austin: Gammel, 1898).

Seymour V. Connor

BURLESON CREEK. Burleson Creek rises five miles northwest of Lampasas in south central Lampasas County (at 31°07′ N, 98°15′ W) and flows southeast for seven miles to its mouth on Sulphur Creek, within the Lampasas city limits (at 31°04′ N, 98°10′ W). The stream crosses an area of the Grand Prairies characterized by steep slopes and limestone benches, which give a stairstep appearance to the landscape. Generally shallow sandy and clay loams of the area support grasses and open stands of oak, live oak, mesquite, and juniper. The stream was probably named for John Burleson, whose land grant of 1,280 acres at the mouth of the creek became the site of Lampasas. Hannah Springs, which has a heavy sulphur content, is located on Burleson Creek at the northeast corner of Lampasas. The springs, originally used as a watering hole by the Indians, later became noted as a medicinal bathing spot among white settlers, beginning in the mid-1850s. In 1882, when the Gulf, Colorado, and Santa Fe Railway came to Lampasas, the Hannah Springs Company, under the direction of a man named Hannah, built the Hannah Bath and Opera House, a popular tourist attraction.

BIBLIOGRAPHY: Jonnie Ross Elzner, *Relighting Lamplights of Lampasas County, Texas* (Lampasas: Hill Country, 1974). *An Industrial Survey of Lampasas, Texas* (College Station, Texas: Lampasas Chamber of Commerce, 1959). Ralph Kenneth Loy, *An Economic Survey of Lampasas County* (Austin: University of Texas Bureau of Business Research, 1949).

BURLESON FEMALE INSTITUTE. Burleson Female Institute, sponsored by Baptist congregations, was conducted in the old State Capitol in Austin by Richard B. Burleson,[qv] pastor of the Austin Baptist Church. The school operated only from February to December 1856, when Burleson was elected to the faculty of Baylor University.

BIBLIOGRAPHY: William Franklin Ledlow, History of Protestant Education in Texas (Ph.D. dissertation, University of Texas, 1926). Willie Madora Long, Education in Austin Before the Public Schools (M.Ed. thesis, University of Texas, 1952). Carl Bassett Wilson, History of Baptist Educational Efforts in Texas, 1829–1900 (Ph.D. dissertation, University of Texas, 1934).

Claudia Hazlewood

BURLEY, D. W. (ca. 1844–?). D. W. Burley, who represented Robertson, Leon, and Freestone counties in the Twelfth Texas Legislature, was born in Virginia around 1844. He was a free black before the end of slavery[qv] and in 1864 was a captain in a battalion of black soldiers that defended St. Louis from Confederate raiders. He arrived in Texas in 1865 and later organized a debating society for blacks. He won election to the Texas House of Representatives in 1870 and was one of twelve black legislators to serve in that body. Burley was a Radical Republican, but he displeased some other radicals when he supported an effort to subsidize the Southern Pacific Railroad. He served only one term.

BIBLIOGRAPHY: Alwyn Barr, "Black Legislators of Reconstruction Texas," *Civil War History* 32 (December 1986).

Paul M. Lucko

BURLINGTON, TEXAS. Burlington is on U.S. Highway 77 ten miles north of Cameron in northern Milam County. John and Michael Jones, who were among the first settlers in the area, built cabins as early as 1867. The community was first called Irish Settlement. Itinerant priests ministered there until the construction of a Catholic church in the mid-1880s. The name of the town was changed to Waterford when a post office was opened at the home of Timothy Gleason in 1884. In 1889 Gleason renamed the town after Burlington, Vermont. When the San Antonio and Aransas Pass Railway was built through Burlington in 1891, residents got easier access to markets. Stock pens were set up to hold longhorn cattle[qv] for shipment to St. Louis, Chicago, and Kansas City. Cotton and lumber were also important products. The population of Burlington increased from fifty in the mid-1890s to 362 in 1904. The town reached its peak about 1914, when it reported two churches, a bank, a cotton gin, a weekly newspaper, and 600 residents. The population was listed as 200 in the 1930s and 1940s. Burlington reached a postdepression high of 326 residents in the late 1960s, but that number fell to 125 in the 1970s. The town lost its rail service in 1977, when the Southern Pacific abandoned the section of track between Cameron and Rosebud. Burlington had a population of 140 in 1990.

BIBLIOGRAPHY: Lelia M. Batte, *History of Milam County, Texas* (San Antonio: Naylor, 1956). Milam County Heritage Preservation Society, *Matchless Milam: History of Milam County* (Dallas: Taylor, 1984).

Vivian Elizabeth Smyrl

BURLINGTON–ROCK ISLAND RAILROAD. What became the Burlington–Rock Island was chartered on October 9, 1902, as the Trinity and Brazos Valley Railway Company. By January 1904 the company had completed a line from Cleburne to Mexia, but the original backers were unable to secure financing to complete their project. The railroad was acquired by the Colorado and Southern Railway Company on August 1, 1905, with one-half interest subsequently sold to the Chicago, Rock Island and Pacific Railway Company. With the backing of two major railroads, the Trinity and Brazos Valley was completed from Mexia to Houston and from Teague to Waxahachie in 1907. Trackage rights were secured from the Missouri, Kansas and Texas Railway Company of Texas between Waxahachie and Dallas, and from the Gulf, Colorado and Santa Fe between Cleburne and Fort Worth as well as between Houston and Galveston. Chronically unprofitable, the Trinity and Brazos Valley entered receivership in 1914, with John W. Robins named receiver. Robins was replaced by L. H. Atwell, Jr., who was succeeded by Gen. John A. Hulen[qv] in 1919. Hulen continued as receiver until the company was reorganized as the Burlington–Rock Island on July 7, 1930. Hulen also became the first president of the Burlington–Rock Island, which took its name from the two owning systems. During the receivership General Hulen had begun upgrading the property, and the program was continued by the new company. In addition, trackage rights between Waxahachie and Dallas and between Houston and Galveston, which had been canceled in 1914, were reestablished. Trackage rights into Fort Worth, however, were no longer deemed necessary. At that time the company operated 303 miles of track. In 1931 the Burlington–Rock Island owned twenty-six locomotives, 346 freight cars, and nineteen passenger cars, and earned $64,678 in passenger revenue, $1,381,667 in freight revenue, and $43,024 in other revenue.

On June 1, 1931, the track between Teague and Waxahachie was leased jointly to the Fort Worth and Denver City and the Chicago, Rock Island and Gulf for operation as the Joint Texas Division. Management of the entire Burlington–Rock Island was turned over to the parent companies for alternating five-year periods, with the Rock Island managing until December 31, 1935. The original line between Mexia and Cleburne was abandoned in three stages. In 1932 the thirty miles of track from Cleburne to Hillsboro was abandoned; in 1935 the thirty-five miles of track from Hillsboro to Hubbard was abandoned; and in 1942 the twenty-three miles of track from Hubbard to Mexia was abandoned. On October 1, 1936, the Burlington–Rock Island inaugurated the first streamlined passenger train in Texas, the Sam Houston Zephyr, between Houston and Dallas–Fort Worth. In 1937 the line added a second streamliner, the Texas Rocket. The Rocket was replaced in January 1945 by the Twin Star Rocket, which extended streamliner service from Houston to Minneapolis–St. Paul.

A major change occurred on June 1, 1950, when the Fort Worth and Denver and the Rock Island leased the rest of the railroad from Teague to Houston to be operated as the Joint Texas Division. In April 1964 the railroad was purchased at foreclosure by the parent companies, with each company obtaining an undivided half interest in the property. The physical property was merged into the Fort Worth and Denver and the Rock Island in 1965, and the Burlington–Rock Island dissolved. The Rock Island ceased operations on March 31, 1980, leaving the Fort Worth and Denver as the sole operator of the former Burlington–Rock Island. The Fort Worth and Denver was merged into the Burlington Northern Railroad on December 31, 1982. *See also* BURLINGTON SYSTEM.

George C. Werner

BURLINGTON–ROCK ISLAND RAILROAD MUSEUM. The Burlington–Rock Island Railroad Museum, in Teague, was officially opened on October 4, 1970, and is housed in the original Trinity and Brazos Valley Railway depot and office building. The depot was built in 1906–07 and designed by C. H. Page, Jr., an Austin architect, whose father had worked as a stone mason on the state Capitol.[qv] The two-story building combines the round arches and arcades of Romanesque styling with an asymmetrical Italianate tower. Its bichrome façade features red-brick trim on a buff-colored, pressed-brick background. The hipped roof is covered in red tile. When built, the depot was considered one of the most handsome stations in Texas.

The railway itself, the "Boll Weevil," belonged to the Burlington–Rock Island system for most of its existence and continues freight service to Teague. After a new railroad office was constructed in the 1960s, local historians, led by Llewellyn Notley, retired Teague school superintendent, and P. F. Thomas, retired railroad superintendent, acquired the building for the city of Teague from the Fort Worth and Denver Railway and the Chicago, Rock Island and Pacific Railroad for one dollar. The Burlington–Rock Island Railroad Museum Association of Teague was organized and incorporated by the Texas secretary of state in 1969. The museum opened on October 4, 1970, with United States congressman Olin E. Teague[qv] delivering the dedicatory address. Two state historical markers were unveiled at the program.

The exhibits in the museum include a 1925 Baldwin locomotive donated by W. T. Carter and Brother of Camden, a railroad motor car, a baggage wagon, photographs, timetables, and other memorabilia. Other artifacts of local history are also preserved in the museum, including items pertaining to churches, schools, doctors and hospitals, merchants and business firms, clubs and organizations (including a Boy Scout room), civic leaders, and city officials. The Teague Volunteer Fire Department, which dates back to 1907, developed its own exhibit, which includes the department's first motorized pumper engine, a 1920s Seagraves with dual ignition. The local newspaper, the Teague *Chronicle*, published since 1906, has its own display, which features the Cottrell printing press used by the paper from 1906 to 1976, in addition to a copy of its first issue, dated July 27, 1906, which contains a report on the arrival of Teague's first passenger train. A Veterans' Room displays exhibits of all wars; special memorial cases honor those killed in action. The museum also serves as a permanent depository for the Teague Family Genealogical Research Center, founded by Carroll Hudgens Teague of Oklawaha, Florida. Exhibited on the museum grounds is a two-room log house, dog-trot style, built in the early 1850s for Col. B. A. Philpott near Dew and moved to Teague and restored as a United States Bicentennial project in 1976; the house was donated by Mr. and Mrs. Dale McCeig.

On March 21, 1979, the Burlington–Rock Island Railroad Museum building qualified for listing on the National Register of Historic Places by the Texas Historical Commission[qv] and the United States Department of the Interior. It is the only building in Freestone County so honored.

BIBLIOGRAPHY: James Wright Steely, comp., *A Catalog of Texas Properties in the National Register of Historic Places* (Austin: Texas Historical Commission, 1984). Teague *Chronicle*, May 10, 1979. Paula and Ron Tyler, *Texas Museums: A Guidebook* (Austin: University of Texas Press, 1983).

Dorothy McVey

BURLINGTON SYSTEM. The Chicago, Burlington and Quincy Railroad Company, commonly called the Burlington, was a major midwestern railroad system that had its origins in 1849 as the Aurora Branch Railroad. By 1900 the company had important lines radiating from Chicago to Minneapolis–St. Paul, Denver, Kansas City, and St. Louis. Other lines of the Burlington extended as far west as Billings, Montana. In December 1908 the Burlington gained control of a Texas system extending from the Panhandle[qv] through Fort Worth to Houston and Galveston when it acquired the Colorado and Southern

Railway Company. The Colorado and Southern owned several Texas railroads, the oldest of which was the Fort Worth and Denver City Railway Company, chartered on May 26, 1873. The road was promoted by Fort Worth citizens to connect that city with a railroad from Denver. The Panic of 1873 delayed start of construction until November 1881, but the Fort Worth and Denver City reached Wichita Falls in 1882 and the Texas–New Mexico state line in 1888. The Colorado part of the route began on January 25, 1881, with the chartering of the Denver and New Orleans Railroad Company. In April 1881 the Fort Worth and Denver City and the Denver and New Orleans agreed to connect at the Texas–New Mexico border. The Denver and New Orleans built 125 miles of track from Denver to Pueblo that opened in April 1882. However, the line was sold at foreclosure on March 18, 1886, and reorganized as the Denver, Texas and Gulf Railroad Company. A third company, the Denver, Texas and Fort Worth Railroad, was organized on April 12, 1887, to complete the railroad across Colorado and New Mexico. Connection between the Denver, Texas and Fort Worth and the Fort Worth and Denver City was made on March 14, 1888, at Union Park, New Mexico Territory, 528 miles northwest of Fort Worth. Shortly thereafter, the Denver, Texas and Fort Worth acquired stock control of the Fort Worth and Denver City and the Denver, Texas and Gulf, and the three railroads were operated as an integrated system.

The Colorado lines were consolidated in 1891 as the Union Pacific, Denver and Gulf Railway Company and, along with the Fort Worth and Denver City, operated as part of the Union Pacific system. Following the failure of the Union Pacific, Denver and Gulf, the Colorado and Southern Railway Company was chartered on December 19, 1898, and on January 11, 1899, acquired the lines in Colorado and Texas. The Colorado and Southern then embarked on a program of buying or building feeder lines in North Texas. In 1905 the company acquired the Wichita Valley Railway Company. The Wichita Valley had been chartered on February 8, 1890, and had constructed sixty-one miles from Wichita Falls to Seymour. Other railroads promoted and built by local interests were acquired upon completion. These included the Wichita Valley Railroad Company, which had been chartered on October 12, 1905, and by January 1907 had completed fifty-two miles from Seymour to Stamford. The line between Stamford and Abilene, thirty-eight miles, was built by the Abilene and Northern Railway Company. This company had been chartered on February 5, 1906, and completed its line in 1907. To serve the territory north of Wichita Falls, the Wichita Falls and Oklahoma Railway Company was chartered on October 26, 1903, and by June 1904 had built twenty-four miles of track from Wichita Falls to Byers. The only line built under Colorado and Southern auspices was the Stamford and Northwestern Railway, chartered on January 11, 1909, to build between Stamford and Plainview. Only the eighty-three miles to Spur, which opened in October 1909, was built.

In order to extend its system from Fort Worth to Houston and Galveston, the Colorado and Southern bought the Trinity and Brazos Valley Railway Company on August 1, 1905, and subsequently sold one-half interest to the Chicago, Rock Island and Pacific Railway Company. The Trinity and Brazos Valley had been chartered on October 6, 1902, and by early 1904 had a line operating between Cleburne and Mexia. The Trinity and Brazos Valley completed its line from Mexia to Houston and from Teague to Waxahachie in 1907, and via trackage rights over connecting railroads reached Fort Worth, Dallas, and Galveston. To provide terminal facilities at Houston, the Trinity and Brazos Valley acquired a 25 percent interest in the Houston Belt and Terminal Railway Company, while the Galveston Terminal Railway Company was organized to develop a Galveston terminal. The Trinity and Brazos Valley also acquired a one-eighth interest in the Union Terminal Company in order to provide passenger facilities at Dallas. The Trinity and Brazos Valley was reorganized as the Burlington–Rock Island Railroad[qv] Company in 1930.

There were no new extensions or railroads built by the Burlington Route in Texas until the mid-1920s. By that time a rivalry had developed between the Santa Fe and Burlington systems over building into the Texas South Plains. The area was becoming agriculturally developed, especially with cotton and wheat, and the Burlington was eager to compete for the traffic. To serve the area, the Fort Worth and Denver South Plains Railway Company was chartered on March 6, 1925. A line from Estelline to Lubbock with an extension from Sterly through Plainview to Dimmitt, as well as a branch from Sterly to Silverton, was completed by November 1928. The main line of the Fort Worth and Denver South Plains was 206 miles long and included two of the six railroad tunnels built in Texas. The Fort Worth and Denver South Plains was leased to the Fort Worth and Denver City for operation. On May 20, 1929, the Fort Worth and Denver Northern Railway Company was chartered. It built a 110-mile line from Childress to Pampa, which was completed on July 15, 1933. This company was also leased to the Fort Worth and Denver City for operation.

In January 1939 the president of the Burlington-controlled lines in Texas was Ralph Budd, and John A. Hulen[qv] was one of the vice presidents. In 1940 the system operated 1,031 miles of main track in Texas in addition to the Burlington–Rock Island. There were nine separately chartered railroads and two operating companies in the system. The Fort Worth and Denver City leased the Fort Worth and Denver Northern, the Fort Worth and Denver South Plains, and the Fort Worth and Denver Terminal. Four railroads, namely the Wichita Valley Railroad, the Abilene and Northern, the Stamford and Northwestern, and the Wichita Falls and Oklahoma, were leased by the Wichita Valley Railway Company.

In 1944 the Railroad Commission[qv] reported that the Burlington system earned $12,132,515 in freight revenue, $5,839,399 in passenger revenue, and $1,488,095 in other revenue. The Fort Worth and Denver City was renamed the Fort Worth and Denver Railway Company on August 7, 1951. On June 13, 1952, all of the other Colorado and Southern owned properties in Texas, with the exception of the jointly owned Burlington–Rock Island, were merged into the Fort Worth and Denver. The entire Burlington–Rock Island had been leased to the Fort Worth and Denver and the Rock Island in 1950. The Colorado and Southern and the Rock Island absorbed the Burlington–Rock Island in 1965, when each owner received an undivided one-half interest in the property. The Colorado and Southern's interest was sold to the Fort Worth and Denver and merged into that company. For the first time the 1,115 miles of Burlington-owned track in Texas operated under one corporate name. In 1972 the Fort Worth and Denver owned twenty locomotives and 1,520 freight car, but operated at a loss of $1,743,551. Main-line track mileage had been reduced to 1,033 by 1978.

The Chicago, Burlington and Quincy, the Great Northern, the Northern Pacific, and the Pacific Coast merged on March 2, 1970, under the name Burlington Northern, Incorporated. The name was changed to Burlington Northern Railroad the following year. On November 21, 1980, the St. Louis–San Francisco Railway Company was merged into the Burlington Northern, thus adding the Frisco's Texas mileage to that of the Fort Worth and Denver. The Colorado and Southern was merged into the BN on December 31, 1981, and the Fort Worth and Denver became a direct subsidiary of the BN. This lasted until December 31, 1982, when the Fort Worth and Denver, in turn, was merged into the BN. In 1992 the BN owned 1,020 miles of track in Texas and operated over an additional 160 miles via trackage rights. In 1995 Burlington Northern, Incorporated, and Santa Fe Pacific Corporation agreed to a merger that would produce one of the largest railroad systems in the United States. *George C. Werner*

BURNAM, JESSE (1792–1883). Jesse Burnam, pioneer, was born into poverty in Madison County, Kentucky, on September 15, 1792. He was the youngest of seven children; his father died soon after his birth. The family moved to Shelbyville, Tennessee, in 1808, and there Burnam met Marie Temperance Null Baker, whom he married in September 6, 1812. During service with the Tennessee Militia in the War of 1812 Burnam contracted an unspecified illness that eventually drove him to seek a warmer climate. He arrived in Texas in 1821 and led his own and nine other families to a settlement at Pecan Point on the Red River. He remained there for a number of months before traveling farther into the Texas wilderness. He stopped for a time at the site of present-day Independence and finally, in 1823, settled down on the Colorado River in Fayette County.

Burnam, who was a member of the Old Three Hundred[qv] (his name was thirteenth on Stephen F. Austin's[qv] land-grant list), was ceded an area of land now in Fayette and Colorado counties. In 1824 he established a combination trading post and ferry that soon came to be known as Burnam's Crossing or Burnam's Ferry.[qv] The crossing, which Sam Houston[qv] eventually destroyed during the Texas Revolution[qv] in order to prevent its use by the Mexican army, remained for some years the most northerly settlement on the Colorado, where it was exposed to constant attack by the Karankawa Indians. In the early days attacks were so common that Burnam was forced to be ever on guard; but in the end, the white settlers of the area, led by Burnam and others, broke the Indians' resistance. Burnam served for five years as a militia captain and was instrumental in expelling the Karankawas from Fayette and Colorado counties. He participated in numerous raids upon the Indians, especially in 1823 and 1824, and in 1840 he served in John H. Moore's[qv] expedition against the Comanches.

Burnam represented what became Colorado County at the Convention of 1832 and the Consultation of 1835.[qqv] He was a member of the General Council[qv] of the provisional government[qv] of the Republic of Texas[qv] and later became a Colorado County representative in the First Congress.

In May 1833 Mrs. Burnam died, leaving Burnam with nine children. Later that year he married Nancy Cummins Ross, who bore him seven additional children. Burnam and his family moved to Burnet County in 1855, where they established one of the first sheep-raising operations in the area and a large wheat farm. Burnam owned thirteen slaves in 1860. In January 1864 he split his fortune among his surviving children and retired from public life. He died in his home on Double Horn Creek on April 30, 1883, at the age of ninety-one, and was buried in a stone vault on the property.

BIBLIOGRAPHY: "The Reminiscences of Captain Jesse Burnam," *Quarterly of the Texas State Historical Association* 5 (July 1901). Texas House of Representatives, *Biographical Directory of the Texan Conventions and Congresses, 1832–1845* (Austin: Book Exchange, 1941).

F. B. Largent, Jr.

BURNAM'S FERRY. Burnam's Ferry, also known as Burnam's Crossing, was established in 1824 by Jesse Burnam[qv] at the La Bahía Crossing on the Colorado River in Fayette County, near the site of present La Grange. The settlement consisted of a trading post and ferry and was for some years the northernmost outpost on the Colorado. As such it was subject to frequent attack by the Karankawa Indians of the region. On March 17, 1836, the army of Gen. Sam Houston[qv] crossed the Colorado at Burnam's Ferry in retreat from the forces of Antonio López de Santa Anna[qv] in what later became known as the Runaway Scrape.[qv] Two days later Houston ordered the destruction of the ferry to prevent its use by the oncoming Mexican army. In the end, the Burnam family homestead and store were destroyed as well and were never rebuilt.

BIBLIOGRAPHY: Jesse Burnam, "The Reminiscences of Captain Jesse Burnam," *Quarterly of the Texas State Historical Association* 5 (July 1901). Darrell Debo, *Burnet County History* (2 vols., Burnet, Texas: Eakin, 1979). Texas House of Representatives, *Biographical Directory of the Texan Conventions and Congresses, 1832-1845* (Austin: Book Exchange, 1941).

F. B. Largent, Jr.

BURNELL, TEXAS. Burnell, on Farm Road 743 east of U.S. Highway 181 in extreme southern Karnes County, was a rural community that developed for cotton farming in the early 1900s. The settlement was named for Burnell Butler, a pioneer of Karnes County, and had a school, a cotton gin, and several businesses. The discovery of the Burnell oil and gas field resulted in the construction of a gas plant in the 1960s. In 1990 everything was gone except the name.

BIBLIOGRAPHY: Robert H. Thonhoff, History of Karnes County (M.A. thesis, Southwest Texas State College, 1963).

Robert H. Thonhoff

BURNELL SWITCH, TEXAS. Burnell Switch was a switch and loading track on the Texas and New Orleans Railroad at the Karnes-Bee county line. It served the Burnell oilfield, which extended across Medio Creek into Bee County, and reported three businesses and a population of ten in 1940. After World War II[qv] the businesses all closed, and in the early 1990s only a few scattered farmhouses remained in the area. *Christopher Long*

BURNET, DAVID GOUVERNEUR (1788–1870). David G. Burnet, speculator, lawyer, and politician, was born on April 14, 1788, in Newark, New Jersey, the fourteenth child of Dr. William Burnet, and the third of his second wife, widow Gertrude Gouverneur Rutgers. David was orphaned at an early age and raised by his older half brothers. All of his life he strove to achieve the prominence of his father and brothers: Dr. Burnet served in the Continental Congress and as surgeon general. Jacob Burnet (1770–1853), lawyer, ardent federalist, and later a Whig who nominated his friend, William Henry Harrison, for president, served as a member of the territorial council of Ohio, state legislator, Supreme Court judge, and United States senator, and was honored for intellectual achievements including a history of the territory of Ohio. Another brother, Isaac, was mayor of Cincinnati during the 1820s.

Burnet lived with his brothers in Cincinnati, studied law in Jacob's office, and followed the same conservative politics. He wrote proudly in 1859 that he had never been a Democrat and deplored the course of the "ignorant popular Sovereignty." His attitude and politics did not make him popular in Texas, and his entire life was a string of disappointments. After a classical education in a Newark academy, young Burnet wanted to join the navy but instead was placed by a brother as a clerk in a New York commission house in 1805, a position he disliked. On February 2, 1806, he sailed with the unsuccessful filibustering expedition to Venezuela led by Xavier Miranda. Lieutenant Burnet returned to New York at the end of 1806.

His movements between 1806 and 1817 are obscure; he probably lived with relatives seeking success. About 1817 he moved to Natchitoches, Louisiana, and for the next two years traded with the Comanches near the headwaters of the Brazos with John Cotton. He suffered some sort of pulmonary illness at this time, and living a simple, natural life was supposed to be a cure. His health improved but not his finances, and he returned to Ohio, where he studied law.

In May 1826 Burnet passed through San Felipe on his way to Saltillo to petition for an empresario[qv] grant, which he received on December 22. The grant authorized him to settle 300 families north of the Old Spanish Road and around Nacogdoches, part of the area recently replevined from Haden Edwards,[qv] within six years. He was to receive 23,000 acres from the state of Coahuila and Texas[qv] for every 100 families settled.

Burnet spent 1827 in Texas and then returned to Ohio, where he fruitlessly sought colonists and financial backing from prominent men to develop his grant. In desperation he and refugee Lorenzo de Zavala[qv] sold the rights to their colonization contracts in October 1830 to a group of northeastern investors, the Galveston Bay and Texas Land Company.[qv] Burnet received an undisclosed sum of money and certificates for four leagues of land from the new company. Unfortunately, he was not allowed to located the leagues because of the Law of April 6, 1830.[qv] He used the money to buy a fifteen-horsepower steam sawmill and move his bride to Texas. They left New York on the seventy-ton schooner Cull on March 4, 1831, and arrived in Galveston Bay on April 4. Burnet bought seventeen acres on the San Jacinto River from Nathaniel Lynch qv for the mill and an additional 279 acres east of Lynch facing Burnet Bay, where he built a simple four-room home called Oakland. Between 1831 and 1835 Burnet unsuccessfully petitioned the state for eleven leagues of land because of the mill; the mill, however, lost money, and he sold it in June 1835.

The articulate Burnet impressed local residents, and though he took no part in the events at Anahuac in 1832 (*see* ANAHUAC DISTURBANCES), they chose him to represent the Liberty neighborhood at the convention at San Felipe in 1833. He helped draft the plea to sever Texas from Coahuila and made an earnest statement against the African slave trade. He hoped to become chief justice of the newly established Texas Supreme Court in 1834 but was only named to head the Brazos District Court. Instead of his $1,000 per annum allotment, Burnet wanted a handsome stipend in land like that which Chief Justice Thomas J. Chambers qv received.

Burnet was against independence for Texas in 1835, although he deplored the tendency of the national government toward a dictatorship. Thus his more radical neighbors did not choose him as a delegate to either the Consultation or the Convention of 1836.qqv Nevertheless, he attended the session on March 10, where he successfully gained clemency for a client sentenced to hang. The delegates, who were opposed to electing one of their number president of the new republic, elected Burnet by a majority of seven votes.

His ad interim presidency of the Republic of Texas qv lasted from March 17 to October 22, 1836, and was very difficult. His actions angered Sam Houston,qv the army, the vice president, many cabinet members, and the public, and he left office embittered, intending never to return home, where a number of neighbors had turned against him. He lacked legal clients and was forced to turn to subsistence farming. In 1838 he entered the race for vice president and rode Mirabeau B. Lamar's qv coattails to victory. Forced to serve part of the time as secretary of state and acting president, Burnet became more out of step with public opinion. His bid for the presidency in 1841 against his old enemy, Sam Houston, resulted in defeat after a vitriolic campaign of name-calling.

Burnet was against annexation qv to the United States in 1845 but nevertheless applied for the position of United States district judge in 1846. Even with the Whig influence of his brothers, however, he lacked enough political influence. He was named secretary of state by Governor James P. Henderson qv in 1846 and served one term. An application to the Whig administration in 1849 for a position as Galveston customs collector also failed. His only other public office was largely symbolic, a reward for an elder statesman. In 1866 the Texas legislature named Burnet and Oran G. Roberts qv United States senators, but upon arrival in Washington they were not seated because Texas had failed to meet Republican political demands. Although intellectually opposed to secession,qv Burnet had embraced the Southern cause when his only son, William, resigned his commission in the United States Army and volunteered for Confederate service. The son was killed in a battle at Mobile in 1863, a crushing blow to Burnet, who had lost his wife in 1858.

Burnet had married Hannah Este in Morristown, New Jersey, on December 8, 1830. She bore four children, but only William survived, and the doting parents sacrificed for his education. After Hannah's death Burnet had to hire out his slaves and rent his farm in order to have income to pay his room and board in Galveston. He and Lamar intended to publish a history of the republic to expose Sam Houston, and though Burnet furnished Lamar with many articles, Lamar was unable to find a publisher. Burnet burned his manuscript shortly before his death. He was a Mason and a Presbyterian. He outlived all of his immediate family, died without money in Galveston on December 5, 1870, and was buried by friends. His remains were moved from the Episcopal Cemetery to the new Magnolia Cemetery and finally to Lakeview Cemetery in Galveston, where the Daughters of the Republic of Texas qv erected a monument to him and his friend Sidney Sherman qv in 1894. Burnet County was named for him in 1852, and in 1936 the state erected a statue of him on the grounds of the high school in Clarksville.

David G. Burnet. Prints and Photographs Collection, David G. Burnet file, CAH; CN 00450.

BIBLIOGRAPHY: David Gouverneur Burnet Papers, Barker Texas History Center, University of Texas at Austin. *Diary of Col. William Fairfax Gray: From Virginia to Texas, 1835–36* (Houston: Gray, Dillage, 1909; rpt., Houston: Fletcher Young, 1965). Dorothy Louise Fields, "David Gouverneur Burnet," *Southwestern Historical Quarterly* 49 (October 1945). S. W. Geiser, "David Gouverneur Burnet, Satirist," *Southwestern Historical Quarterly* 48 (July 1944). *Telegraph and Texas Register*, July 1, 1840. Texas House of Representatives, *Biographical Directory of the Texan Conventions and Congresses, 1832–1845* (Austin: Book Exchange, 1941). *Margaret Swett Henson*

BURNET, TEXAS. Burnet, the county seat of Burnet County, is one mile west of the divide between the Brazos and Colorado river watersheds near the center of the county, forty-eight miles northwest of Austin. In 1849 people on the frontier sought protection from the Indians at nearby Fort Croghan. The area was commonly called Hamilton or Hamilton Valley for John Hamilton, who had a league and labor of land there. A creek flowing through the league was also named for him. The town was founded as Hamilton in 1852, when

Burnet County was established. In August of that year a post office in Hamilton was named Burnet Courthouse. In 1857 thirty-five residents of the town petitioned the state legislature to change the name of the town to Burnet since there was another town in Texas named Hamilton. The name was changed in 1858.

A major spurt in growth occurred with the arrival of the Austin and Northwestern Railroad in April 1882. Burnet then became the railhead for the area to the west, including the Llano, Mason, and San Saba vicinities. On June 3, 1885, Southern Produce Company shipped 157,000 pounds of wool from Burnet, reportedly the third largest wool shipment made up to that time in Texas. In 1885 Gustav Wilke,[qv] subcontractor building the Capitol[qv] in Austin, constructed a narrow-gauge railroad from Granite Mountain, fourteen miles south of Burnet, to Burnet. At a point just south of the town and within its city limits, Wilke constructed a yard to shape, finish, and fit the granite for placement in the Capitol building. Here some 1,802 railroad carloads, 31,000 tons, of granite were finished and shipped by the Austin and Northwestern to Austin. After the railroad was extended to Llano in 1892, Burnet declined as a supply point and became a farming and livestock center.

In April 1931 the contract was let for the construction of what was then named Hamilton Dam on the Colorado River ten miles west of Burnet. While this construction was under way as many as 800 men were employed, and Burnet was home for many of them and supply base for nearly all of them. Due to the Great Depression[qv] the Insull-owned corporations, including the one owning Hamilton Dam, failed financially, and work ceased. In 1934 the state legislature established the Lower Colorado River Authority,[qv] which, financed by the federal Public Works Administration, acquired and completed the dam and changed the name to Buchanan Dam. Other dams along the Colorado River soon followed, and Burnet was on a sound economic path from that time forward.

In 1989 the town had a population of 3,794 and in 1990, 3,423. The community was incorporated in 1933 and in 1990 had a city manager form of government. Burnet produces stone and various milled products from stone; mining, milling, shipping of graphite, agribusiness, hunting leases, tourism, and recreation contribute to the economy. Many retirees live in Burnet.

BIBLIOGRAPHY: Frank Brown, Annals of Travis County and the City of Austin (MS, Frank Brown Papers, Barker Texas History Center, University of Texas at Austin). Robert C. Cotner, *The Texas State Capitol* (Austin: Pemberton Press, 1968). Darrell Debo, *Burnet County History* (2 vols., Burnet, Texas: Eakin, 1979). W. P. Fry, *Council Creek Calling (Burnet County Heritage)*, comp. Juanita Fry Ragsdale (San Antonio: Naylor, 1976). Joseph Carroll McConnell, *West Texas Frontier* (Vol. 1, Jacksboro, Texas, 1933; Vol. 2, Palo Pinto, Texas, 1939).

Thomas C. Ferguson

BURNET *BULLETIN*. The Burnet *Bulletin*, a weekly newspaper first published in January 1873, was edited until 1874 by George Whitaker. According to other sources, T. A. Stone may have founded and first edited the paper as the *Burnet County Exponent*, then sold it to Whitaker, who changed the name. Subsequent publishers included C. W. Miller, Charles M. Harris and Company (1875), Swift Ogle and Company (1876), S. L. McFarland and James Kibbee (1876), and James Kibbee (1877). C. W. Macune,[qv] Charles M. Harris, and Swift Ogle were successive editors. Ogle became editor and owner in 1878 but disappeared with some of the paper's funds in 1879, after which Capt. T. E. Hammond served as editor with financial assistance from Gen. Adam R. Johnson.[qv] James A. Stevens ran the paper from 1880 to 1898, when it was acquired by L. C. and Hardee (J. H.) Chamberlain, in whose family it remained until 1960. Ward Lowe, D. C. (Chester) Kincheloe, Lowell C. Welch, Ted C. Polk, and Mr. and Mrs. George Puckett of the Bluebonnet Publishing Company published the paper between 1961 and 1975. Another weekly paper known as the *Bulletin and Bertram Enterprise* was published briefly by Mr. and Mrs. Ted Polk and Mrs. Marvin Dodd in 1974. The weekly *Burnet County Bulletin* appeared from 1974 to 1987 and the *Bulletin and Marble Falls Messenger* after February of the latter year. Former Dallas newsman Tom Graham and associates purchased the paper in 1981 but sold it later that year to Mac B. McKinnon. In the 1990s the paper was published by Rick Espitia and had a circulation of 3,550.

BIBLIOGRAPHY: *Texas Newspaper Directory* (Austin: Texas Press Service, 1991).

Diana J. Kleiner

BURNET COUNTY. Burnet County (J-15), in central Texas, is bordered by Lampasas, Bell, Williamson, Travis, Blanco, Llano, and San Saba counties. Burnet, the county seat, is at the intersection of U.S. Highway 281 and State Highway 29 and on the Austin and Northwestern Railroad, about fifty miles northwest of Austin and 150 miles southwest of Fort Worth. The county's center is about three miles northeast of Burnet at 30°47′ north latitude and 98°11′ west longitude. The county, situated on the northeastern edge of the Hill Country,[qv] comprises roughly 1,000 square miles of gentle to broken hills with elevations ranging from 700 to 1,700 feet above sea level. The terrain in the northwestern, western, and southern parts of the county is characterized by rolling hills with local deep and dense dissections; fertile plateaus and valleys are found in the eastern section, and rolling prairies dominate the north and northeast. The land is drained by the Colorado River, which forms most of the western county line before meandering across the southern part of the county; by the San Gabriel River, which rises in three forks in the northern and central parts of the county; and by the Lampasas River, which cuts across the northeastern corner. Wildlife in Burnet County includes deer, coyotes, bobcats, beaver, opossums, ring-tailed cats, foxes, raccoons, turkeys, badgers, weasels, skunks, and squirrels, as well as assorted birds, fish, and reptiles. Among the county's mineral resources are granite, limestone, industrial sand, and graphite. The average minimum temperature is 37° F in January, and the average maximum is 96° in July. The growing season averages 234 days annually, and the rainfall averages about thirty inches.

Central Texas, including Burnet County, has supported human habitation for several thousand years. Although the archeology of Burnet County has not been fully studied, several prehistoric campsites have been found along the rivers and their tributaries. The hunting and gathering peoples who had established themselves in the area by about 4500 B.C. were probably ancestors of the Tonkawa Indians. No evidence of Spanish exploration or settlement has been found in Burnet County, although missions were established in the 1740s and 1750s in neighboring San Saba County. In the early nineteenth century, surveyors found the local Tonkawa and Lipan Apache groups to be friendly, but the Comanches made frequent raids into the area.

The northeastern section of Burnet County was included in the colonization grant obtained by Robert Leftwich[qv] from the Mexican government in 1825, and was later part of Robertson's colony.[qv] No grants were made in the Burnet County area of the colony until 1835. The remainder of the county was part of the Austin-Williams colony, but no grants were made in the county under that contract. Several surveying and Indian-fighting expeditions from the colonies of Stephen F. Austin and Green DeWitt[qqv] ventured into Burnet County in the 1820s and 1830s, but no permanent settlement occurred. At the time of Texas independence, most of the area was still public domain; through the mid-1840s settlers preferred the relative security of communities farther to the east.

In the 1840s, after the annexation[qv] of Texas to the United States, the federal government became responsible for the protection of frontier settlers from Indian raids. Several companies of Texas Rangers,[qv] financed by the federal government, were stationed along the frontier. In December 1847 a company commanded by Henry E. McCulloch[qv] took up a position about three miles south of the site of present

Burnet. Samuel E. Holland[qv] visited McCulloch's station in 1848 and purchased the 1,280-acre John P. Rozier grant, including the land on which the ranger station was located; the residence he built on that land is said to have been the first permanent home in Burnet County. When the Rangers were relieved by a company of United States Dragoons in December, 1848, Holland protested the construction of a fort on his property; as a result, Fort Croghan was established at the site of future Burnet, three miles to the north. The military abandoned Fort Croghan in December 1853, when it was thought that the population of the area was sufficient to hold its own against the remaining Indians.

The presence of troops had encouraged settlers to make their homes in Burnet County. Among these were such county notables as Noah Smithwick, Logan Vandeveer, and Peter Kerr.[qqv] A group of Mormons[qv] led by Lyman Wight[qv] established a colony at the falls of Hamilton Creek in 1851. By December 1851 the population of the region was large enough to warrant petitioning for the foundation of a new county. Burnet County was formed by the Fourth Texas Legislature on February 5, 1852, from parts of Travis, Williamson, and Bell counties. It was named for David G. Burnet,[qv] president of the provisional government[qv] of the Republic of Texas.[qv] The first county officials were elected later that year.

Residents of the new county were divided on the issue of where to locate the county seat. Some thought it should be on Oatmeal Creek, east of the watershed separating the Brazos and Colorado rivers; others wanted it to be on Delaware Creek, just southwest of the site of Burnet. The faction that won included Vandeveer, Holland, and Kerr, who argued that Hamilton should be the county seat. To help convince people, Kerr donated 100 acres to the county for a townsite. The first post office in the county was established at Hamilton in 1853; the name of the town was changed to Burnet in February 1858.

By 1860 Burnet County had 2,487 residents. Aside from Burnet, the earliest settlements in the county were Smithwick, Oatmeal, and the Backbone Valley community. Stock raising and subsistence farming formed the basis of the early economy. In 1860 county farmers reported having more than 30,000 head of cattle and 11,000 hogs; they grew corn and wheat as food crops, producing 23,900 and 10,200 bushels respectively.

The first efforts at education in Burnet County were hampered by the constant threat of Indian attacks. In the 1850s some early schools were conducted under shade trees, the older boys keeping rifles ready for protection. Small community schools, such as those at Hairston Creek, Pool Branch, Hoover's Valley, and Oatmeal, provided basic education in the county until the establishment of a district system in the 1890s. Marble Falls Alliance University was established in 1890, but did not last long as a college. Extensive schooling for most children was a luxury that came second to helping out on the family farm. In 1896 the county superintendent of schools reported a need for a uniform series of textbooks, better enrollment and attendance, better teaching conditions, and more experienced teachers. Improvements in the system came slowly: in 1940 only 10 percent of the county's population over twenty-five years old were high school graduates. Large-scale consolidation of common-school districts into larger, independent school districts took place in the 1930s and 1940s. As the job market expanded during the next forty years, so did the percentage of residents who finished school. By 1960 nearly 18 percent were high school graduates, and by 1980 the number represented more than 60 percent of the population over twenty-five.

Among the earliest churches in the county were a congregation at Mormon Mill in 1851, a Christian church established at Sycamore Springs in 1851, a Baptist church established on Oatmeal Creek in 1854, and a Church of Christ established at Burnet in 1856. Few communities had their own preacher; itinerant ministers held periodic camp meetings to which people came from miles away. One of the first of these was held in the fall of 1855 by Methodists at Sand Springs, south of Burnet. The first land deed specifically for church purposes was executed in 1859 in Backbone Valley. Most often, early church services were held in a building that also served as the schoolhouse. A Catholic church was established at Burnet in 1930; an African Methodist Episcopal church was established there in 1953. In the early 1980s the county's forty-seven churches had an estimated combined membership of 10,329; Southern Baptist, Church of Christ, and United Methodist were the largest denominations.

Although most early residents of Burnet County came from other Texas counties or other Southern states, the slave population was relatively small; the 235 slaves reported in the 1860 census were divided among sixty-nine owners. The greatest concentration of slaves was in the area of Spicewood and Double Horn Creek. Among the factors contributing to the low number of slaves was the fact that Burnet County was relatively new, and residents had not had time to acquire a great deal of property; also, the soil in the county did not lend itself well to large-scale farming. There were several big ranches in the county, but no plantation-like operations.

Thomas Moore[qv] represented Burnet County at the Secession Convention[qv] in January 1861 and voted for secession; county voters, however, rejected the ordinance of secession later that year by a margin of 248 to 159. The issue continued to be a source of division, as demonstrated by the number of Unionists' bodies found at Dead Man's Hole,[qv] but in spite of the initial majority opposition to secession, residents of Burnet County contributed both men and supplies to the Confederate war effort. More tension would likely have existed between Unionists and secessionists, except that most of the men who were part of the Confederate Army were in frontier companies formed to protect the county more from outlaws and Indians than from Yankees. Crime was rampant in Burnet County in the 1860s and 1870s. In addition to occasional Indian raids, residents had to contend with counterfeiters and cattle thieves. There were also incidents of white outlaws masquerading as Indians so as to divert blame from themselves. During Reconstruction,[qv] several Burnet County men, who had been active in the pursuit of outlaws and Indian raiders, were arrested by Union forces, taken to Austin, and held for several weeks on charges of impeding Reconstruction. Although the men were later released, the incident caused considerable ill-feeling. In 1869 the county's lopsided election returns for Andrew J. Hamilton over Edmund J. Davis[qqv] indicated that the local government had been returned to Democratic rule.

In presidential politics, Burnet County was staunchly Democratic from the end of Reconstruction until the 1970s, the only exception being a vote of 936 to 467 for Herbert Hoover over Al Smith in 1928. Burnet County voters preferred Republican presidential candidates Richard Nixon in 1972, Ronald Reagan in 1980 and 1984, and George Bush in 1988 and 1992.

Burnet County suffered a severe economic decline immediately after the Civil War[qv] and throughout Reconstruction. Between 1864 and 1866, the county as a whole lost 64 percent of tax revenues. A little more than a quarter of the loss was in slaves; the rest came from declines in total farm acreage, farm value, and livestock value, each of which fell 25 to 50 percent by the time of the 1870 census. Recovery was slow because transportation was poor and the economy was so dependent on agriculture.

After the war some former slaves left the county, but many stayed. A group of them settled on land in the eastern part of Oatmeal. In 1870 the black population of the county had increased to 358, keeping pace with the growth of the total number of residents; the number of blacks had fallen to 248 by 1880, however, and the number of new white residents was such that after 1890, blacks represented less than 3 percent of the total population. Some found work on farms and ranches, but by the turn of the century many had moved into the Marble Falls area to work in town.

The Burnet County economy began to show signs of recovery in the late 1870s and early 1880s. People from other Texas counties and other states had pushed the total population to 6,855 by 1880, and the census reported 951 farms in the county, up from 281 in 1870. Although the number of cattle and hogs on farms had not yet regained prewar levels, the number of sheep had risen from just under 5,800 in 1870 to nearly 25,000 in 1880, when the county produced nearly 90,000 pounds of wool. By 1890 farm values had doubled and livestock production had increased sharply; the county had more than 40,000 cattle, 15,000 pigs, and nearly 59,000 sheep. Also by 1890 the population had risen to 10,747, as the number of people moving in from other states were supplemented by immigrants from England, Scotland, Germany, Sweden, and Mexico. With the exception of a decrease in population in 1920 to 9,500, the number of residents in Burnet County remained fairly stable for the next sixty years.

The Austin and Northwestern finished laying the track between Austin and Burnet in 1882. The track to Granite Mountain [qv] was built in the mid-1880s, and branches to Marble Falls and Llano were completed by 1889 and 1892, respectively. The Houston and Texas Central Railway was completed from Burnet to Lampasas in 1903. Lake Victor and Bertram were established as railroad towns and prospered as shipping points and commercial centers for area farmers and ranchers. Such other communities in the county as Lacy, Naruna, South Gabriel, Sage, Wolf's Crossing, Shady Grove, and Strickling were bypassed by the railroads and faded as their populations were drawn to more promising locations.

One beneficiary of the additional railroad lines was the mining industry. Although the quarry at Granite Mountain had been in operation for several years, shipping became much easier with the arrival of the railroad. Stone from the Granite Mountain quarry was used for the Capitol [qv] in Austin, the Galveston seawall, numerous county courthouses, and several buildings in New York. Graphite proved to be another profitable mining venture. The deposits in the northwestern part of the county, discovered in 1916, were the Western Hemisphere's only fully integrated primary source of graphite. The Southwestern Consolidated Graphite Company began operation in the late teens; the mining stopped because of the Great Depression [qv] of the 1930s, but began again at the request of the War Production Board in 1942. Mining for lead, copper, zinc, iron, and gold was also attempted in Burnet County, but with little success.

Agriculture benefited from the increased accessibility of markets as well. Cotton became an important crop in the 1880s. In 1880 farmers planted just over 7,000 acres, or 12 percent of the county's improved land, and produced about 1,400 bales; cotton acreage had tripled by 1890, when 20,500 acres, or 34 percent of the improved land, produced 8,650 bales. Stock raising, especially sheep and goat ranching, [qqv] was also an important occupation in Burnet County in the late nineteenth and early twentieth centuries. The number of sheep reached 80,800 in 1910, fell sharply to 42,000 by 1920, but then nearly tripled by 1930 to 120,800. The number of goats on farms rose from just over 8,500 in 1920 to nearly 60,000 in 1930; mohair production for the county showed a corresponding increase from 18,000 to 218,000 pounds.

When the depression hit in the 1930s, however, prices for all agricultural products plummeted. Cotton, which averaged sixteen cents a pound in 1929, sold for only five cents in 1931; wheat prices fell as low as forty-five cents a bushel. The value of livestock dropped as well: a ewe and lamb that cost twenty dollars in 1929 sold for two dollars; wool, which sold for forty cents a pound in the late 1920s, fell to seven or eight cents. Lower prices meant lower income for farmers and lower wages for their hired workers. Many farmers had difficulty obtaining enough credit to continue operating. The number of farms in the county fell from 1,548 in 1930 to 810 in 1960.

Unemployed farmers who were unprepared for other kinds of work had to accept help from government relief and public-works projects. Burnet County received more than $387,000 in relief through the Agricultural Adjustment Administration [qv] between 1933 and 1935. The Work Projects Administration [qv] employed men to improve streets and public property and set up sewing rooms and painting classes for women. A company of the Civilian Conservation Corps [qv] was stationed at the newly established Longhorn Cavern State Park [qv] in 1934. In addition, the National Youth Administration [qv] established a camp at Buchanan and Inks dams in 1938 to provide part-time employment for out-of-school youth, ages eighteen to twenty-four. The program was continued for the construction of a national fish hatchery at Inks Dam in 1939.

Another major employer during the depression was the State Highway Department (now the Texas Department of Transportation [qv]). In 1929, construction of the Burnet County section of State Highway 66 (later U.S. Highway 281) began; the project lasted until 1939. State Highway 29, which connected Austin with Burnet and Buchanan Dam was built between 1936 and 1939. These north-south and east-west routes each required a large bridge to cross the Colorado River; one bridge, located at Marble Falls, was completed in 1936, and the second was built across Inks Lake about a mile below Buchanan Dam in 1937.

By far the largest project, however, was the development of the Colorado River as a source of hydroelectric power. Harnessing the power of the river had been a dream of Burnet County residents since the early days of settlement. In 1854, Adam Rankin Johnson [qv] had envisioned a dam that would supply power to factories for the manufacture of cotton and woolen products, as well as help prevent floods. Although several attempts were made to tame the river, none was successful until that of the Lower Colorado River Authority [qv] in the 1930s. Hundreds of people were employed in the construction of Hamilton (later renamed Buchanan) and Roy B. Inks dams (*see* INKS LAKE *and* LAKE BUCHANAN). Many of the jobs were unskilled, but they were steady, and in most cases the income from them enabled people to maintain their standard of living.

Agriculture in Burnet County had for the most part recovered by the early 1940s, but farming as an occupation was less prevalent than it had been before the depression. Land previously under cultivation was now used for grazing; crop raising was relegated primarily to the northeastern part of the county. Larger farms and ranches squeezed out the small farmer and sharecropper. Tenant farming and sharecropping, which had accounted for the operation of nearly 29 percent of the county's farms in 1880, increased steadily in the late nineteenth and early twentieth centuries, peaking at 54 percent in 1930. In 1940 roughly 49 percent of the farms were tenant-run; in 1950 the number had fallen to 23 percent; by the late 1960s fewer than 13 percent of the farms in the county were operated by tenants. The average farm size had increased from 380 acres in 1930 to 695 in 1960.

The LCRA built two more dams on the Colorado in Burnet County in the late 1940s and early 1950s: Alvin J. Wirtz [qv] Dam, which impounded Lake Lyndon B. Johnson, [qv] and Max Starke Dam, on Lake Marble Falls. [qv] Subdivisions on the lake shores were popular sites for retirement and vacation homes. By the 1970s retired couples comprised a significant part of the population; in the early 1980s, Burnet County ranked seventieth of all counties in the United States in percentage of population over age sixty-five. Burnet County had an urban growth of 133 percent between 1970 and 1980, one of the highest in the state. Lake Buchanan, Inks Lake, Lake Lyndon B. Johnson, and Lake Marble Falls were popular recreational sites.

In the early 1980s between 80 and 90 percent of the land in the county was devoted to farming or stock raising. Only about 4 percent of the farmland was under cultivation; hay, oats, and wheat were the primary crops. Most of the farmland was located in the northeastern part of the county. More than 90 percent of the county's agricultural receipts came from livestock, the most important animals being cattle, sheep, angora goats, and hogs. Although agriculture continued to be an important aspect of the economy, farm receipts represented less than 6 percent of the county's annual income in the early 1980s. Roughly three-quarters of the county's farmers and ranchers depended on other work to supplement their income.

Professional and related services, manufacturing, wholesale and retail trade, and construction involved more than 60 percent of the workforce in the 1980s; an additional 17 percent was self-employed, and 24 percent was employed outside the county. Industries with the highest employment included limestone quarrying, agribusiness, general construction, and the manufacture of wood cabinets. In 1980 Burnet County had 17,803 residents, a 56 percent increase over the 1970 population of 11,420; the population increased a further 27 percent in the late 1980s, reaching 22,677 in 1990.

BIBLIOGRAPHY: Malvin George Bowden, History of Burnet County (M.A. thesis, University of Texas, 1940). R. S. Crawford, *Jacob Wolf: Burnet County Pioneer* (Waco: Texian Press, 1969). Darrell Debo, *Burnet County History* (2 vols., Burnet, Texas: Eakin, 1979). Noah Smithwick, *The Evolution of a State, or Recollections of Old Texas Days* (Austin: Gammel, 1900; rpt., Austin: University of Texas Press, 1983).
Vivian Elizabeth Smyrl

BURNET COUNTY (Judicial). Burnet County was established by the Fifth Congress as a judicial county on January 30, 1841. It lay between the Neches and Trinity rivers south of Nacogdoches County and north of Houston County. Fort Houston, the earliest settlement in the area and the temporary seat of justice, had a Sunday school and a temperance society organized in 1840. Peter Fullenwider held Presbyterian services. Magnolia, a projected town on the Trinity River, was intended as a riverport. The *Telegraph and Texas Register*[qv] of September 15, 1841, described the terrain and possibilities of the county and estimated that its population had increased from 250 to 500 between 1839 and 1841. An act of December 6, 1841, provided for a better definition of county boundaries, made Fort Houston the permanent seat of justice, and authorized the county to raise a company of volunteers for protection of the frontier. The county ceased to exist, probably when judicial counties were declared unconstitutional in the case of *Stockton v. Montgomery* in 1842.

BIBLIOGRAPHY: R. L. Batts, "Defunct Counties of Texas," *Quarterly of the Texas State Historical Association* 1 (October 1897). James Wilmer Dallam, *A Digest of the Laws of Texas* (Baltimore: Toy, 1845). Hans Peter Nielsen Gammel, comp., *Laws of Texas, 1822–1897* (10 vols., Austin: Gammel, 1898).
Seymour V. Connor

BURNETT, JOHN H. (1830–1901). John H. Burnett, senator, soldier, and executive, was born in Greene County, Tennessee, on July 8, 1830, the son of Silas E. and Malinda (Howell) Burnett, both of whom were natives of Virginia. He was reared in Summerville, Chattooga County, Georgia. During the Mexican War[qv] he enlisted in Lt. Col. James S. Calhoun's battalion of the Georgia mounted volunteers, a part of Gen. Winfield Scott's army. He was in several engagements, including the storming of the castle of Chapultepec, was twice slightly wounded, and before the end of the campaign was promoted to lieutenant. After the war Burnett was made a colonel in the Georgia militia. He also was elected sheriff of Chattooga County, Georgia, at the early age of twenty-one and served for two years.

In 1854 he moved to Crockett, Texas, where he engaged in farming and merchandising. He was elected to the Texas House of Representatives in 1857. In August 1861 he was elected a member of the Texas Senate from Houston, Anderson, and Trinity counties. He served until February 1862, when he resigned to command the Thirteenth Texas Cavalry. His senatorial colleague, Anderson F. Crawford of Jasper County, became the lieutenant colonel of the regiment, which was soon dismounted and attached to the first brigade of John G. Walker's Texas Division.[qv] In November 1863, after service in Arkansas and Louisiana, Burnett was transferred by medical recommendation to post duty, and he never again commanded his regiment in the field. He resigned his commission in April 1864 because of continuing illness and disability.

He returned to Crockett after the war, then in 1866 moved to Galveston and became a partner with W. B. Wall in the commission business. By 1875 his firm, J. H. Burnett and Company, was doing general contracting and building as well as brokering cotton. The firm was one of the contractors for the third and last Tremont Hotel, completed about 1880. It built the Gulf City Street Railway, added seventy miles to the Gulf, Colorado and Santa Fe Railway, and contracted for $350,000 worth of Galveston streets and sidewalks. For a number of years Burnett was president and director of the Galveston National Bank and a large stockholder in several railroads. In 1899 he moved to Houston, where he had acquired extensive real estate holdings, and became president of the Planters and Merchants Bank. He was thought to be one of the largest taxpayers in South Texas at the time of his death, when his estate was appraised at more than a million dollars. In 1851 Burnett married Catherine Beavers, daughter of Gen. John F. Beavers of Summerville, Georgia. They had three children. Burnett died on June 24, 1901, and was buried in Glenwood Cemetery, Houston.

BIBLIOGRAPHY: Joseph P. Blessington, *Campaigns of Walker's Texas Division* (New York: Lange, Little, 1875; rpt., Austin: Pemberton Press, 1968). John Henry Brown, *Indian Wars and Pioneers of Texas* (Austin: Daniell, 1880; reprod., Easley, South Carolina: Southern Historical Press, 1978). *The War of the Rebellion: A Compilation of the Official Records of the Union and Confederate Armies.*
Anne A. Brindley

BURNETT, MARY COUTS (ca. 1856–1924). Mary Couts Burnett, philanthropist, was born in Parker County around 1856, one of five daughters of James R. Couts, a banker. She was raised in Weatherford, married Claude Barradel, and was widowed. Around 1892 in Weatherford she married Texas rancher and widower Samuel Burk Burnett,[qv] after which the couple settled in Fort Worth. Mary apparently was never comfortable with the frontier life, and tensions also resulted from Burk Burnett's close relationship with his granddaughter, Anne Burnett Tandy,[qv] the daughter of Thomas L. Burnett,[qv] Burk's son from his first marriage. Mary and Burk had one son of their own, Samuel Burk Burnett, Jr., who died in their Fort Worth home in 1917. During the course of their marriage Mary became convinced that her husband was trying to kill her. He attributed these fears to hallucinations, had his wife declared legally insane, and confined her in a private home in Weatherford.

She stayed there until the day of her husband's death in 1922, when she escaped from her confinement, returned to Fort Worth, and quickly succeeded in having her insanity status revoked with the assistance of her physician, Dr. Charles H. Harris. She next challenged her husband's will, in which he had left the bulk of his estate to his granddaughter Anne, and in 1923 was awarded half of his $6 million fortune. She then began organizing her plans for the distribution of her inheritance upon her death. She ultimately decided that Texas Christian University in Fort Worth would receive most of the $3 million. Though she had no immediate ties to the school, her father had been an admirer of Addison Clark,[qv] cofounder and first president of the school, which was then located at Thorp Spring; James Couts had, in fact, contributed money to the school. Moreover, Mary was interested in seeing her money remain in Fort Worth and had expressed, in the deed of trust, an appreciation of TCU's recognition of a broad range of religious faiths, despite its denominational ties to the Christian Church (Mary was Episcopalian). Both Dr. Harris and her lawyer, William J. Slay, approved of her decision, and she probably found no small satisfaction in leaving her money to a university to which her husband had declined to contribute. Her gift to TCU, at that time one of the largest fortunes ever left to an educational institution in Texas, was announced in December 1923, and a board of trustees, which she chaired, was established to administer it. Other trustees were Harris, Slay, Mrs. Ollie Lake Burnett, Mrs. Ella Bardin, and John Sweatt. Although at her death Mary's sisters and their representatives challenged her will by claiming she was insane when she authored it, an out-of-court settlement was reached, with TCU retaining the majority of the initial gift. Included in Mrs. Burnett's decision to leave TCU her estate was the stipulation that part of the bequest be set aside for the construction of a building bearing her name. Work on this building, a new library, began soon after the gift was announced, and she had the satisfaction of seeing the Mary Couts Burnett Library[qv] partially constructed by the time of her death. The library was dedicated in March 1925.

She was described by one historian as a woman of refinement and culture with a strong interest in education. In addition to her gift to TCU, the trust also provided $12,000 for the Dixon Colored Orphanage in Gilmer, for the teaching of domestic science. Because she was believed to have had a heart condition, Mrs. Burnett stipulated that her body be made available for medical researchers at her death. She died in Fort Worth on December 16, 1924, shortly after suffering a stroke. Her funeral was held on December 18 in her Fort Worth home, where those who paid their last respects to her included about 100 female students from TCU. She was ultimately buried with her son and husband at East Oakwood Cemetery, Fort Worth.

bibliography: Betsy Colquitt, *Prologue: The TCU Library to 1983* (Fort Worth: Mary Couts Burnet Library, Texas Christian University, 1983). Fort Worth *Star-Telegram*, December 16, 17, 1924. Colby D. Hall, *History of Texas Christian University* (Fort Worth: Texas Christian University Press, 1947). Jerome A. Moore, *Texas Christian University: A Hundred Years of History* (Fort Worth: Texas Christian University Press, 1974). *Debbie Mauldin Cottrell*

BURNETT, PUMPHREY (1796?–1837). Pumphrey Burnett (Pumphry or Pumpry Burnet), partner of Albert L. Sojourner[qv] as one of Stephen F. Austin's[qv] Old Three Hundred[qv] families, was born around 1796 to Plenander and Elizabeth Burnett. He immigrated from Tennessee to Texas as early as March 1823, when he was listed as a twenty-seven-year-old farmer residing in the Colorado District. In May of that year he enlisted as a private in a scouting company headed by Moses Morrison[qv] that had been raised to control Karankawa Indians around the Colorado and Tres Palacios rivers. With Sojourner, Burnett received title to a sitio[qv] of land now in Matagorda County on July 24, 1824. The census of 1826 listed Burnett as a single man, farmer, and stock raiser. In January 1827 he signed resolutions declaring loyalty to the Mexican government and opposing the Fredonian Rebellion.[qv] By 1830 Burnett owned land near the Tres Palacios, and after his marriage to Elizabeth M. Smalley of Kentucky, the couple lived there. They had no children. Burnett reportedly wanted to found a port, to be called Tidehaven, on the partially navigable Tres Palacios River (*see* tres palacios, texas). With his brother-in-law Abner Smalley, Burnett helped escort Elizabeth and others to the United States during the Runaway Scrape,[qv] but poor health kept him from fighting in the Texas Revolution.[qv] He died on October 31, 1837, and is buried near the Tres Palacios River in Matagorda County.

bibliography: Eugene C. Barker, ed., *The Austin Papers* (3 vols., Washington: GPO, 1924–28). Lester G. Bugbee, "The Old Three Hundred: A List of Settlers in Austin's First Colony," *Quarterly of the Texas State Historical Association* 1 (October 1897). Dan E. Kilgore, *A Ranger Legacy: 150 Years of Service to Texas* (Austin: Madrona, 1973). Matagorda County Historical Commission, *Historic Matagorda County* (3 vols., Houston: Armstrong, 1986). *Rachel Jenkins*

BURNETT, RICHARD WESLEY (1898–1955). Richard Wesley Burnett, oilman and baseball entrepreneur, was born on January 13, 1898, in McLennan County, Texas. When he was two years old the family moved to Gladewater, and the small East Texas town became his lifelong home. After he graduated from high school, Burnett joined the United States Navy and served during World War I.[qv] Afterward he returned to Gladewater, where he pursued several business ventures and jobs. He married Dale Jeter on January 6, 1924, and alternately operated a hardware store, a sawmill, an ice cream plant, and other ventures with only modest success; but when the East Texas oil boom occurred, Burnett found his niche in the business world. He began buying and trading oil leases and in 1932 drilled a well, struck oil, and soon became moderately wealthy. After his successes in East Texas, he became involved in a risky oil-exploration program in Illinois and suffered a ruinous financial setback. Then, in 1944, he discovered the Wesson field in Ouichita County, Arkansas, where he struck oil and gas.

Burnett was an ardent baseball fan. In 1935, shortly after his first success in the East Texas oilfield,[qv] he bought the Shreveport, Louisiana, franchise in the Class C East Texas League and moved it to his hometown. The Gladewater Bears won a pennant in 1936 and whetted Burnett's appetite for further baseball adventures. Between 1935 and 1948, in a addition to the Gladewater team, he owned minor-league franchises in Gainesville and Texarkana, Texas, and Monroe, Louisiana. He enjoyed his association with professional baseball in the low minor leagues, but he had greater ambitions.

In 1948 he drew national attention when he purchased the Texas Rebels of the AA Texas League for $550,000. A few weeks later, Burnett also purchased the Oakcliff ballpark, where the Rebels played their home games, for another $265,000. He promptly renamed the Rebels the Eagles and the park Burnett Field. Burnett intended to make the Eagles a pennant contender in the Texas League,[qv] and he hoped to attract a major-league franchise to Dallas. In 1952 the Eagles won the Texas League pennant for the first time since 1936; they won the league the next year and defeated the Nashville team of the Southern Association in the Dixie Series. Between 1948 and 1953 Burnett turned a lackluster franchise into a powerful force while he pioneered changes in the league. In 1952 he brought David Hoskins to the Eagles and integrated the Texas League five years after the major leagues had ended segregation. He became a noted baseball owner, as he constantly labored to improve his team, his ballpark, and the entertainment value of an evening at Burnett Field.

In 1953 Burnett funded a conference of minor-league owners and operators to discuss the decline of minor-league baseball. Attendance was dwindling in minor-league parks, leagues were collapsing, and the major leagues were uprooting established leagues with their emerging franchise-relocation program and expanded broadcast policies. Burnett, who realized he might negatively affect his chances to acquire a major-league franchise in the future, wanted to reform the business practices in which the interests of minor-league baseball were nearly always considered as secondary to those of the major leagues. But his reform movement failed to make headway against a united and intransigent coterie of major-league owners and executives. Nevertheless, because of his successes as owner of the Eagles and his efforts to improve the conditions of minor league baseball, the *Sporting News* declared him the Minor League Executive of the Year in 1954. On June 1, 1955, Burnett, who was in Shreveport, Louisiana, to see his Eagles play a weekend series against Shreveport, suffered a heart attack and died. He was buried in Hillcrest Cemetery, Dallas.

bibliography: Bill O'Neal, *The Texas League, 1888–1987: A Century of Baseball* (Austin: Eakin Press, 1987). Vertical Files, Barker Texas History Center, University of Texas at Austin. *Larry G. Bowman*

BURNETT, SAMUEL BURK (1849–1922). Burk Burnett, rancher, banker, oilman, son of Jeremiah (Jerry) and Nancy (Turner) Burnett, was born on January 1, 1849, in Bates County, Missouri. In the late 1850s the family moved to Texas and built a home on the banks of Denton Creek in Denton County. Within ten years Jerry Burnett had established a small but successful ranch that enabled Burnett to learn the day-to-day operations of the cattle business. Burk received little formal schooling, but he used his practical education to become eventually one of the wealthiest ranchers in Texas. His first trail drive occurred in 1866. The following year he served as trail boss, driving his father's 1,200 cattle along the Chisholm Trail[qv] to Abilene. In 1868 he became a partner with his father, and in 1871 he acquired his own brand and began building what became one of the largest cattle empires in Texas history—the Four Sixes Ranch.[qv] Burnett weathered the panic of 1873 by holding over the winter the 1,100 cattle he had driven to Kansas. The following year he sold this stock for a profit of $10,000. He was one of the first ranchers in Texas to buy steers and graze them for market. At first his herd consisted of longhorn cattle,[qv] but later he introduced Durhams and then Herefords[qv] into the herd, thus producing what many considered to be among the finest cattle strains in the state.

In 1874 Burnett bought and moved cattle from South Texas to the area of Little Wichita, now Wichita Falls, where he established his ranch headquarters in 1881. The move was partly prompted by the increase in the number of Four Sixes cattle and an agreement drawn up between Burnett and Quanah Parker,[qv] Comanche chief and friend of Burnett. Through Parker's assistance over a period of years Burnett leased 300,000 acres of Kiowa and Comanche land in Indian Territory for 6½ cents an acre. He grazed 10,000 cattle on this land until 1902. After 1898 cattlemen were told to surrender their lease agreements to allow opening of Oklahoma Territory to homesteaders. Burnett once again called on a friend for assistance, this time Theodore Roosevelt. The Texas rancher asked the president for an extension so that the Texas cattle might be removed in an orderly fashion. Roosevelt's agreement to the request enabled Burnett to purchase land to offset the loss of grazing rights in Oklahoma. Between 1900 and 1903 Burnett purchased 107,520 acres in Carson County northeast of Amarillo and bought the Old "8" Ranch, of 141,000 acres, near Guthrie in King County, ninety-three miles east of Lubbock. The two purchases increased the size of the Four Sixes to 206,000 acres. Ultimately, Burnett owned ranches in Oklahoma and Mexico in addition to his holdings in Texas and ran 20,000 cattle under the Four Sixes brand.

In 1905, in return for Roosevelt's assistance, Burnett helped organize a wolf hunt for the president. During the president's visit, Roosevelt influenced the changing of the name of Nesterville, on the Four Sixes spread in Wichita County, to Burkburnett. Five years later Burnett discontinued personal direction of his ranch. He leased the Four Sixes to his eldest son, Tom, so that he could concentrate his attention on his other businesses, banking and oil. After the discovery of oil on land near Burkburnett in 1921, Burnett's wealth increased dramatically. He had already expanded his business interests by buying property in Fort Worth, where he had maintained a residence since 1900. By 1910 the city had become headquarters for his financial enterprises, and he had become the director and principal stockholder of the First National Bank of Fort Worth and president of the Ardmore Oil Milling and Gin Company. He continued his interest in ranching, however, through his association with the Stock-Raisers Association of North-West Texas (*see* texas and southwestern cattle raisers association). He had been a charter member in 1877, and he served as treasurer from 1900 to 1922. Burnett was also president of the National Feeders and Breeders Association and in 1896 of the Fort Worth Fat Stock Show (later the Southwestern Exposition and Livestock Show[qv]).

Burnett married Ruth B. Lloyd in 1869, and they had three children. They were later divorced. Two of their children, Ann and Thomas L. Burnett,[qv] lived to adulthood. Burnett married Mary Couts Barradel (*see* burnett, mary c.) of Weatherford in 1892, and this couple had one son. In the early 1920s Burnett's health failed and he went into semiretirement. On June 27, 1922, he died. At the time of his death his wealth was estimated at $6 million, part of which, through the efforts of his widow, became an endowment for Texas Christian University.

bibliography: Frank W. Johnson, *A History of Texas and Texans* (5 vols., ed. E. C. Barker and E. W. Winkler [Chicago and New York: American Historical Society, 1914; rpt. 1916]). T. J. Powell, *Samuel Burk Burnett* (1916). Jo Stewart Randel, ed., *A Time to Purpose: A Chronicle of Carson County* (4 vols., Hereford, Texas: Pioneer, 1966–72).

David Minor

BURNETT, THOMAS LLOYD (1871–1938). Thomas Lloyd Burnett, rancher, son of Ruth (Lloyd) and Samuel Burk Burnett,[qv] was born in 1871 on the family ranch in Denton County, Texas. When he was four his family moved to Wichita County, where his father established a new ranch headquarters near the future site of Iowa Park and began running his Four Sixes[qv] cattle. Tom received his early education in rural schools near the ranch and later at a private academy in St. Louis, Missouri, prior to attending Virginia Military Institute for three years. His first love was the cattle business, and at age sixteen he was sent as a cowhand to help look after his father's herds in the Big Pasture, the vast acreage in Indian Territory that the Burnetts, Waggoners, and other area ranchers had leased from the Fort Sill Indian Agency. There Tom mastered the Comanche language and developed a lifelong friendship with several in the tribe, including Quanah Parker[qv] and his family. By that time the ranch's base of operations had been moved to the Red River near the future site of Burkburnett. At age twenty-one, Burnett was elevated to wagon boss, and his ability to manage men and cattle quickly won the respect of the ranch employees.

On October 8, 1891, he married Ollie Lake of Fort Worth. They had one child. During the Spanish-American War in 1898 Burnett served as a captain with the Rough Riders (*see* first united states volunteer cavalry). In April 1905 he, his father, Quanah Parker, and John R. Abernathy staged a famous wolf hunt on the Big Pasture for President Theodore Roosevelt. Following the breakup of the pasture shortly thereafter, Burnett moved his family back to the Iowa Park headquarters, which his father had leased to him along with the Wichita County ranch, after developing the Four Sixes Ranch in King County. By then he had accumulated a sizable herd of his own, and in 1912, on the death of his grandfather Martin B. Lloyd, he inherited a fourth of the Wichita County properties and a large sum of money. About that time Burnett adopted Lloyd's Triangle brand as his own. The oil discoveries in the county further enlarged his fortune. In 1918 Burnett and his wife were divorced, a move that offended his father. When Burk Burnett died in 1922, he bequeathed Tom $25,000 a year and left the bulk of his estate in trust for his daughter, with a third of the income to go to her mother.

As an independently wealthy cattleman, Tom Burnett financed and promoted various rodeos at his Iowa Park Ranch and in Wichita Falls. Many of these featured old family friends from Oklahoma, including several of his Comanche friends, whom he invited to hunt antelope and camp on the ranch. He developed a passion for good cow horses and later bred palominos that he featured in fairs, parades, and rodeos. Between 1923 and 1925 he purchased the Pope and McAdams ranches in Foard County and the old Moon Ranch, formerly owned by the W. Q. Richards estate, in Cottle County. In 1929 he added the YL, a 32,000-acre tract that was originally part of the O X Ranch,[qv] near Paducah. In all he owned 449,415 acres, over which he ran from 4,000 to 6,000 head of Hereford stock bearing the Triangle brand during the 1930s. Charlie Hart, longtime Burnett family employee, was hired to oversee this vast enterprise, which had branch headquarters in Iowa Park and Paducah.

On May 3, 1919, Burnett married the famous rodeo queen Lucille Mulhall, but both were strong-willed and separated after a year. He next married Lydia Sheldon of Electra in 1921 and built for her a new house in Iowa Park, but that marriage ended before the house was completed. His fourth wife, Bernice Fassett, was a widow with several daughters from her first marriage and a member of a neighboring ranch family.

During his later years Burnett grew interested in banking and civic developments. He was a major stockholder in the Iowa Park State Bank and maintained an office there. He also became involved in the civic affairs of Wichita Falls and gave generously to various charitable causes. When the Great Depression[qv] hit, he supplied school-lunch funds for needy children and came to the aid of old cowboys who had been hurt economically. In 1938 he made his last purchase by adding the 20,000-acre 7L Ranch, formerly the Dripping Springs pasture of the OX, to his cattle empire. On Christmas Day of that year, when he noticed a group of needy boys on the street at Iowa Park, he took them to a clothing store and had them outfitted entirely. Burnett died of an apparent heart attack on December 26, 1938, and was buried in Highland Cemetery, Iowa Park. He willed all of his estate to his daughter, Anne, who subsequently managed his ranching empire under the name Tom L. Burnett Cattle Company, a major part of the Burnett estates. Mrs. Perry McArthur of Thornton, Washington, filed suit to set aside Burnett's will, claiming to be the daughter of Burnett and Jennie Ho-We-Ah, an Indian woman. Her claim was denied by the Wichita County District Court, and the decision was upheld by the Second Court of Civil Appeals on February 26, 1943. Burnett's home in Iowa Park was given to the city as a library building in 1981 by his granddaughter, Anne Windfohr Sowell.

BIBLIOGRAPHY: Gus L. Ford, ed., *Texas Cattle Brands* (Dallas: Cockrell, 1936). John M. Hendrix, "Tom Burnett," *Cattleman,* May 1939. Dorothy Abbott McCoy, *Texas Ranchmen* (Austin: Eakin Press, 1987). Vertical Files, Barker Texas History Center, University of Texas at Austin. Jesse Wallace Williams, *The Big Ranch Country* (Wichita Falls: Terry, 1954; 2d ed., Wichita Falls: Nortex, 1971).

H. Allen Anderson

BURNETT, THOMAS R. (1842–1916). Thomas R. Burnett, author and newspaper publisher, was probably born in Tennessee; he was taken to Fannin County, Texas, by 1850, and attended Plum Grove Academy nearby. During the Civil War[qv] he served for four years in the Confederate Army in Polignac's Brigade, Texas Calvary. He wrote a collection of short stories and poems during the war called *The Confederate Rhymes.* He later gave every member of his brigade a copy of the book. After the war Burnett became a journalist and established the Bonham *News* and Ladonia *Enterprise.* He was also associated with the Denton *Monitor* and the Paris *Press.* As a master at repartee and sharp retort, he was known as a racy editor. After conversion to the Church of Christ in 1875, Burnett began the *Christian Messenger* in Bonham in 1876. From this date he traveled extensively in North and Central Texas in the interest of his paper, preaching, selling books, and occasionally debating. From September 1876 to September 1888 he kept a journal of numerous trips, during which he averaged three sermons a week. In 1888 he moved to Dallas and continued his paper until 1894, when it was merged with the *Gospel Advocate,* to which Burnett contributed a column called "Burnett's Budget" until 1898, when he began another publication in Dallas called *Burnett's Budget* and published until his death. Only a few issues of the *Budget* and the *Messenger* are extant. In his writings Burnett often combined controversy and good humor. Among his published works were a religious dialog and several volumes of religious poetry, including one collection titled *Doctrinal Poetry.* Burnett was married and had at least five children. He died on June 26, 1916, in Dallas, and was buried in Oak Cliff Cemetery.

BIBLIOGRAPHY: Thomas R. Burnett Papers, Barker Texas History Center, University of Texas at Austin. Dallas *Morning News,* June 27, 1916. *R. L. Roberts*

BURNETTA COLLEGE. Burnetta College, at Venus, operated from 1896 to 1906 under the sponsorship of the Disciples of Christ. The school was named for Burnetta Barnes. Its four-story frame building was built with contributions of $500 by the citizens of Venus and a $5,000 gift from A. D. Leach, who became the school's first president. The college opened with 250 students on September 7, 1896. At its largest Burnetta College had 350 day students, some boarders, and from eight to ten teachers. The building subsequently burned and was rebuilt, but the college was later abandoned, and the building became the property of the Venus public schools.

BIBLIOGRAPHY: Viola Block, *History of Johnson County and Surrounding Areas* (Waco: Texian Press, 1970). Stephen Daniel Eckstein, *History of the Churches of Christ in Texas, 1824–1950* (Austin: Firm Foundation, 1963). Colby D. Hall, *Texas Disciples* (Fort Worth: Texas Christian University Press, 1953). Donald W. Whisenhunt, *The Encyclopedia of Texas Colleges and Universities* (Austin: Eakin, 1986).

David Minor

BURNEY, GEORGE E. (1814–1878). George E. Burney, politician, was born in Robertson County, Tennessee, on August 15, 1814. After moving in 1834 to Independence, Missouri, in 1836 to Fayetteville, Arkansas, for his health, and in 1842 to Carroll County, Arkansas, he settled in Cameron, Texas, in 1847. He married Sara A. Blair in Fayetteville in 1836. He was elected from Carroll County to the Arkansas legislature in 1842. In 1848 Burney was elected to the Third Texas Legislature from the Milam and Williamson district. In 1849 he introduced the bill that established McLennan, Bell, and Falls counties. He also introduced bills granting charters for the Waco Suspension Bridge,[qv] the Waco Tap Railroad, and the Waco Manufacturing Company. He settled at Waco in 1850 and was elected to the Fifth Legislature (1853) from the Waco district. He served in the Texas Senate during the Civil War[qv] years, 1862–66. He was the Senate member of the committee that investigated the burning of Brenham in 1866, conducted much of the investigation personally, and made active efforts to secure redress for the victims. Burney was president of the Waco Manufacturing Company. He was a Methodist. He died at his home near Waco on February 18, 1878.

BIBLIOGRAPHY: John K. Strecker, "Chronicles of George Barnard," Baylor University *Bulletin,* September 1928. Waco *Examiner and Patron,* February 22, 1878.

BURNEY, HANCE MCCAIN (1826–1915). Hance McCain Burney, Kerr County pioneer and county judge, son of Robert H. and Lydia (McCain) Burney, Sr., was born on May 2, 1826, at Guilford Courthouse, North Carolina. His family moved to McNary County, Tennessee, where his father died. Burney first came to Texas in 1853. On December 28 of that year in Washington County he married Mary A. Tatum, who had moved to Texas with her parents from McNary County the same year. After their wedding the couple returned to Tennessee, where they remained until after the birth of their first child in 1854. They returned to Texas, accompanied by Burney's mother and two sisters, and settled in the Guadalupe valley. Burney served as first postmaster of Kerrville from 1858 to 1866. He also served as Kerr county judge in 1864 and 1879–80. As one of Kerrville's early leading citizens, he established a trading business and one of the area's first sawmills, from which he sold to the United States government the building materials for forts and military camps. He owned a ranch on Turtle Creek and served as president of the First National Bank at Center Point. The Burneys had nine sons; one of them, Robert H. Burney,[qv] became a state legislator and district judge. Hance Burney died on April 23, 1915, and Mary died on May 22, 1925.

BIBLIOGRAPHY: Bob Bennett, *Kerr County, Texas, 1856-1956* (San Antonio: Naylor, 1956; bicentennial ed., rev. by Clara Watkins: *Kerr County, Texas, 1856-1976,* Kerrville, Texas: Hill Country Preservation Society, 1975). *Rebecca J. Herring*

BURNEY, ROBERT HANCE (1854–1926). Robert H. Burney, state legislator and district judge, eldest son of Hance McCain and Mary A. (Tatum) Burney, was born in McNary County, Tennessee, on October 22, 1854. His family moved to Texas and settled in the Guadalupe valley while he was still an infant. At the age of twenty he joined the

Texas Rangers[qv] under Capt. Neal Caldwell. He resigned after a year in order to attend Southwestern University at Georgetown. He entered the law department of Vanderbilt University in Nashville, Tennessee, in 1878 and received a bachelor of laws degree in 1879. The same year Southwestern University awarded him the bachelor of arts degree as well. After graduating, he practiced law for a short time in Georgetown in partnership with Judge Thomas P. Hughes.[qv] He returned to Kerr County in 1880 and continued to practice law in Kerrville. He was elected state senator as a Democrat from the Twenty-eighth District in 1886 and reelected in 1890. While a member of the legislature he chaired the Committee on Education, the Committee on State Asylums, and a joint committee established to investigate the state comptroller's office. He also authored a bill establishing the state geological department at the University of Texas. In 1904 he was appointed judge of the Thirty-eighth Judicial District by Governor S. W. T. Lanham.[qv] He held that office until his death and earned a wide reputation for honesty and independence of thought. Burney married Mattie Prather of Palestine, Texas, in September 1879. They had four children. He died on April 2, 1926.

BIBLIOGRAPHY: Bob Bennett, *Kerr County, Texas, 1856-1956* (San Antonio: Naylor, 1956; bicentennial ed., rev. by Clara Watkins: *Kerr County, Texas, 1856-1976*, Kerrville, Texas: Hill Country Preservation Society, 1975). Lewis E. Daniell, *Personnel of the Texas State Government, with Sketches of Representative Men of Texas* (Austin: City Printing, 1887; 3d ed., San Antonio: Maverick, 1892).

Rebecca J. Herring

BURNHAM, TEXAS. Burnham (Burnam) was on the Ascensión Gonsaba land grant six miles southwest of Ennis in southeastern Ellis County. In 1861 the House family received a portion of this grant in exchange for a slave called John. Edeline House had the area surveyed and platted for the town of Burnham and donated the land for the streets, alleys, and a Methodist church. It was a well-planned community with twenty-five blocks covering 6½ acres, arranged around a public square. Mail was routed from the nearby community of Cummin's Creek until Burnham received a post office in 1861, and again after that office was discontinued in 1865. In 1870 a Cumberland Presbyterian church was established at Burnham. At one time the community also had general stores, blacksmith shops, and doctors. When the Houston and Texas Central Railway bypassed Burnham on its way to Ennis in 1872, many of Burnham's businesses were moved to be on the railroad. It had originally been planned that the railroad would go through Burnham, but railroad officials changed the route. Several men from Burnham went to Ennis with guns demanding the railroad for their community. In the ensuing shoot-out one person was killed and several wounded. The community's school, north of the town square, had fifty-eight students in 1894. By 1915 the school was gone, and by the 1930s Burnham was no longer shown on maps. A Texas Historical Commission[qv] marker in Ennis commemorates the Burnham square and cemetery.

BIBLIOGRAPHY: Edna Davis Hawkins et al., *History of Ellis County, Texas* (Waco: Texian, 1972). *Lisa C. Maxwell*

BURNING BUSH COLONY. The Burning Bush Colony was a short-lived Methodist settlement on the Smith-Cherokee county line just south of Bullard, near the site of present Bullard High School. The colony was a project of the Society of the Burning Bush, a splinter group of Free Methodists who broke away from the Methodist Church[qv] in 1900 and organized the Metropolitan Church Association. The movement, commonly known as the Burning Bush, was headquartered in Waukesha, Wisconsin, just outside Milwaukee. Fervently evangelistic, the movement grew quickly during its first decade. The group was heavily subsidized by two wealthy members, Duke M. Farson, a bond broker from Chicago, and Edwin T. Harvey, a millionaire hotel keeper.

After 1900 the group established communal colonies in Virginia, West Virginia, and Louisiana. In 1912 plans were laid for a colony in Texas. The site chosen was a 1,520-acre farm near Bullard. The land had originally been part of the William Pitt Douglas plantation, and the property included a stately two-story antebellum mansion. In 1907 it was purchased by Charles E. Palmer, who planted pecan, peach, plum trees on the land. Duke Farson, acting on behalf of the church, arranged to acquire the land from Palmer in exchange for a tract of land in Idaho, a small plot near Chicago, and a hotel and brickyard in Las Vegas, New Mexico. Representatives from the church arrived in Bullard in 1912 and set up headquarters in the old Douglas house. The next year 375 members of the church arrived on a chartered train. They were temporarily housed in the mansion and the surrounding grounds, while work began on small clapboard residences and a two large dormitories for single male and female colonists. Work was also started on a large wooden tabernacle, which became the focus of colony life.

The colonists gave up all their worldly possessions upon joining the church and lived communally. They had a communal storehouse and ate in a common dining hall. No class distinctions were recognized. Contact with outsiders was kept to a minimum, but visitors were welcomed and treated hospitably. Liquor and tobacco were forbidden. Those who committed transgressions against the colony's strictures were not punished, but were taken to the church and prayed and wailed over.

Most of the colonists' time was occupied with work and worship. Religious services were intense emotional experiences. One local resident later remembered that the "Bushers would even turn back flips in church and roll around on the sawdust floor." Much of the service was devoted to singing, during which the congregation jumped up and down. Because of this practice, the group was sometimes called the "Holy Jumpers."

The colonists supported themselves primarily by farming. Most of the original settlers were from northern states, however, with little knowledge of southern farming practices, and despite the use of tractors and other modern machines, they reaped poor harvests. As a result, most the revenue generated by the colony came from the sale of nuts and fruits of trees that had been planted before their arrival.

From the start financial problems plagued the colony, despite its receipt of large subsidies from the Metropolitan Church Association and Duke Farson. During later years, many community members sought work outside the colony and turned over their wages to the church. Even with this additional revenue, the colony was forced to buy groceries on credit from a local merchant, J. L. Vanderver. In February 1919 Vanderver brought suit against the church for $12,000 in unpaid notes. The county sheriff seized the land and buildings and sold them at auction in Tyler in April 1919. The colonists dispersed, most of them returning to the North, but a small number remained in Texas. The old mansion and other buildings were eventually demolished, and by 1990 only a few foundations and a pecan orchard marked the site.

BIBLIOGRAPHY: T. Lindsay Baker, *Ghost Towns of Texas* (Norman: University of Oklahoma Press, 1986). Edwin Smyrl, "The Burning Bush," *Southwestern Historical Quarterly* 50 (January 1947). Marker Files, Texas Historical Commission, Austin. Tyler *Courier-Times-Telegraph*, September 23, 1962. *Christopher Long*

BURNLEY, ALBERT TRIPLETT (1800–1861). Albert Triplett Burnley, Republic of Texas[qv] loan commissioner, lawyer, and businessman, was born in Hanover County, Virginia, on April 15, 1800. As a businessman, he resided at various times in Kentucky, Louisiana, Mississippi, and Washington, D.C. In 1827 he married Frances Ann Bibb, daughter of Kentucky chief justice George M. Bibb, with whom he studied law and later bought land in Texas. Burnley bought coal mines in Kentucky and subsequently had a commission business in

New Orleans. As an adherent of the Texas cause he accepted a commission from Sam Houston[qv] in April 1837 to negotiate a loan, not to exceed $5,000,000, on the bonds of the republic. Burnley was not successful in securing the loan in the United States, and after withdrawal of the annexation[qv] proposition in October 1838, he attempted similar negotiations in Europe, where he advertised and aroused interest in the republic. He was recommissioned by Mirabeau B. Lamar[qv] in February 1839 but failed again and was finally recalled in January 1840. He spent about six months of each year on his plantations in Mississippi and in Brazoria County, Texas, where he was a nonresident owner. In 1850 he moved to Washington, D. C., where he had established a Whig newspaper, the *Republic*, as an official organ of the Taylor administration sometime earlier. In 1854 he returned to Frankfort, Kentucky, where he died on May 13, 1861.

BIBLIOGRAPHY: Martha A. Burnley, "Albert Triplett Burnley," *Quarterly of the Texas State Historical Association* 14 (October 1910). Herbert Rook Edwards, "Diplomatic Relations between France and the Republic of Texas, 1836–1845," *Southwestern Historical Quarterly* 20 (January 1917). Amelia W. Williams and Eugene C. Barker, eds., *The Writings of Sam Houston, 1813–1863* (8 vols., Austin: University of Texas Press, 1938–43; rpt., Austin and New York: Pemberton Press, 1970).

Seymour V. Connor

BURNS, HUGH (1846–1911). Hugh Burns, identified with much of the railroad construction in Texas, was born in 1846 in County Roscommon, Ireland. He immigrated to the United States about 1850 with his parents and settled first at Nashville, Tennessee, then at Madison, Illinois. Burns, along with his four brothers, attended the Christian Brothers College in St. Louis, but, seeking adventure, he left school when he was sixteen to drive a freight wagon of sugar from Fort Smith, Kansas, to Denver, Colorado. He spent some time mining but lost his stake. His first railroad construction work was on the Fort Scott and Gulf Railroad in Missouri. Burns moved to Texas in the early 1870s and went into partnership with a railroad builder, a Mr. Peters, who was working on the Southern Pacific in West Texas. Later Burns went into the railroad construction business for himself and accepted a contract with the Houston and Texas Central in East Texas. During the early 1880s he formed a partnership with George W. Burkett[qv] and P. Murphy, and they contracted to build the International–Great Northern from Laredo to Palestine. While construction was progressing in Williamson County, Burns bought a 3,000-acre ranch on the San Gabriel River seven miles from Taylor. Several other contracts followed; his last was for construction of a railway for the Jay Gould[qv] interests through the cotton lowlands of the Brazos valley. Burns married Mary Clifford in 1881 in San Antonio. They lived for a while in Taylor after Burns retired, then moved to San Antonio, where he died on March 11, 1911.

BIBLIOGRAPHY: Ellis A. Davis and Edwin H. Grobe, comps., *The New Encyclopedia of Texas* (2 vols., Dallas: Texas Development Bureau, 1925?; 4 vols. 1929?).

Mary Burns Mendel

BURNS, ROLLIE C. (1857–1945). Rollie C. Burns was born in Nodaway County, Missouri, on April 6, 1857. He moved to Texas with his family in 1861 and settled first in Collin County and later in Grayson County. In 1873 he went on the Wegefarth surveying expedition in the Texas Panhandle. His duties included scouting and providing buffalo[qv] meat for the expedition. For the next several years he worked on ranches. He made cattle drives for George Loving in 1874 and 1875 and worked on the 22 Ranch about 1881. In 1883–84 he was manager of the Llano Cattle Company's Curry-Comb Ranch[qv] in Garza County. In November 1884 he married Mary Emma Boles. They had two children. From 1884 to 1888 Burns was manager of the Square and Compass Ranch,[qv] which lay just south of the Curry-Comb. For the next eight years he was range boss on the IOA Ranch[qv] in Lubbock County. In 1891 he helped establish the town of Lubbock. In 1907 he started a business running an automobile stage line from Plainview to Lubbock. He sold his cars in 1909 when the railroad arrived in Lubbock. He died on March 2, 1945.

BIBLIOGRAPHY: William Curry Holden, *Rollie Burns* (Dallas: Southwest, 1932; rpt., College Station: Texas A&M University Press, 1986).

William Curry Holden

BURNS, SAMUEL E. (1810–1836). Samuel E. Burns, Alamo defender, was born in Ireland in 1810 and was a resident of Natchitoches, Louisiana, at the beginning of the Texas Revolution.[qv] He served in the Alamo garrison as a member of Capt. William R. Carey's[qv] artillery company. Burns died in the battle of the Alamo[qv] on March 6, 1836.

BIBLIOGRAPHY: Daughters of the American Revolution, *The Alamo Heroes and Their Revolutionary Ancestors* (San Antonio, 1976). Daughters of the Republic of Texas, *Muster Rolls of the Texas Revolution* (Austin, 1986). Bill Groneman, *Alamo Defenders* (Austin: Eakin, 1990).

Bill Groneman

BURNS, WALLER T. (1858–1917). Waller T. Burns, lawyer and legislator, son of James Randolph and Adelia (Thomas) Burns, was born in Fayette County, Texas, on January 14, 1858. He was admitted to the bar in 1882 and practiced law in Galveston until 1888, when he became attorney for the Houston and Texas Central Railway. In 1882 he married Maggie Evelyn Killough of La Grange; they became the parents of three sons. His second wife was Grace McLemore Willis of Houston, whom he married in 1913. Burns was a delegate to the Republican national conventions in 1884 and in 1892. As senator from the Sixteenth District in the Twenty-fifth and Twenty-sixth Texas legislatures, 1897 to 1901, he was one of the few Republicans ever elected to the Texas Senate from a Democratic district. In 1902 he was appointed United States district judge for the Southern District of Texas. While holding court in Laredo, he became suddenly ill and died, on November 17, 1917. He was buried in La Grange on November 19. Burns was an Episcopalian and a longtime supporter of the Houston Bar Association.

BIBLIOGRAPHY: Benajah Harvey Carroll, Jr., ed., *Standard History of Houston, Texas, from a Study of the Original Sources* (Knoxville, Tennessee: Crew, 1912). Houston *Post*, November 18, 1917. E. H. Loughery, *Texas State Government* (Austin: McLeod and Jackson, 1897). *Proceedings of the Texas Bar Association*, 1918. Ocie Speer, *Texas Jurists* (Austin, 1936).

BURNS CITY, TEXAS. Burns City is on Farm Road 372 fifteen miles southeast of Gainesville in southeastern Cooke County. The community developed in 1881 when mineral water was discovered near the homesite of a man named Burns, who, convinced of the healing properties of the water in the forty-foot well, planned to turn the area into a health resort. He built a sixteen-room hotel in what became the town square. In 1882 a Masonic lodge became the second building on the square, and on June 2, 1884, the residents of the settlement by then known as Burns City voted to incorporate. A post office operated there from 1884 until 1907. Over the next few years the town added a flour mill and a cotton gin. By 1890 the town had an estimated population of 300 and eight businesses, though by the mid-1890s its hotel was no longer in operation. The population of Burns City had dropped below 100 by the 1920s and was twenty-five in 1956 and seventy-five in 1968. In the 1970s Burns City comprised the New Hope Church and a number of scattered dwellings. From the early 1970s through 1990 a population of sixty-one was reported.

BIBLIOGRAPHY: Gainesville *Daily Register*, August 30, 1948. A. Morton Smith, *The First 100 Years in Cooke County* (San Antonio: Naylor, 1955).

David Minor

BURNT BRANCH (Callahan County). Burnt Branch rises five miles west of Cottonwood in southeastern Callahan County (at 32°12′ N, 99°17′ W) and runs southwest for twelve miles to its mouth on Pecan Bayou, a mile south of the Callahan-Coleman county line (at 32°04′ N, 99°20′ W). Most of the creekbed traverses oil and range lands. West Caddo Peak (el. 2,090) lies between the branch's upper forks. Settlers first came to the region in the mid-1870s. A Burnt Branch Cemetery, the only remaining evidence of an early community, is near the stream. Burnt Branch crosses an area of rolling hills, surfaced with clay and sandy loams that support mesquite, scrub brush, cacti, and grasses.

____ (San Saba County). Burnt Branch rises seven miles southeast of San Saba in eastern San Saba County (at 31°09′ N, 98°38′ W) and runs northeast for seven miles to its mouth on the Colorado River (at 31°12′ N, 98°34′ W). It crosses an area of moderately to steeply sloping hills with live oak, Ashe juniper, and grasses growing in clayey and sandy loams.

BURNT HOUSE CREEK. Burnt House Creek rises high in the Glass Mountains thirteen miles north-northeast of Marathon in northeastern Brewster County (at 30°23′ N, 103°10′ W) and extends north-northwest for twenty-four miles to its mouth on Coyanosa Draw in western Pecos County, two miles west of the intersection of U.S. Highway 67 and the Santa Fe Railroad (at 30°39′ N, 103°17′ W). The creek heads in various tributaries in Permian rock more than 5,200 feet above sea level. In its upper reaches it runs through a narrow, steep-sided gorge known as Hess Canyon, with cliffs some 500 to 600 feet high. After 4½ miles this gorge opens out into a wider and shallower canyon called Burnt House Canyon, where Cretaceous formations are encountered. Among residents of the region the name Hess Canyon has largely fallen into disuse, and the two canyons together are known simply as Burnt House Canyon. The Glass Mountains in this area are crossed by numerous northwestward-running faults, and the stream's course may thus be in part fault-controlled. As the stream leaves the mountains, it issues out upon a broad, open plain, crossing Quaternary alluvium derived from erosion of the Glass Mountains. From the mountains to the creek's mouth is semiarid grassland, which is being largely displaced by various encroaching species of Chihuahuan Desert scrub because the grassland has been damaged by overgrazing of cattle. Upstream from the flatlands in its canyons, Burnt House Creek is lined with more riparian vegetation, including southwestern chokecherry trees, willows, and numerous Mexican walnuts. Near the headwaters in the high elevations of the Glass Mountains, piñon and various junipers are also common. The name of the creek comes from a disagreement in the early 1900s between two squatters in this area, one of whom had built a cabin near the creek. This man went to Marathon, and while he was gone the rival squatter burned his cabin. The smoke from the burning house was seen in Marathon, although the owner was unaware of its origin. Reportedly, remnants of the cabin may still be found at the site.

Richard Bruhn

BURR, AARON (1756–1836). Aaron Burr, vice president of the United States from 1801 to 1804, had an important connection with the history of Texas. As early as 1796 he proposed that the United States seize the Spanish colonies in the Southwest and establish a great American empire. After leaving the vice presidency in 1804, he made a tour of the western states and became leader of a conspiracy supposed to have been aimed toward invasion of Texas. In 1805 he announced in Kentucky and New Orleans that his life would be devoted to overthrowing Spanish power in America.

In 1806 he negotiated for the purchase of land in the Baron de Bastrop's[qv] grant near Natchitoches, Louisiana. There he planned to establish a colony that could be used as a rendezvous for his projected invasion of Mexico, basing his plans on the assumption that the United States would go to war with Spain to avenge Spanish depredations along the Louisiana border. He is also suspected of plotting with British authorities and with the Marqués de Casa Yrujo, a Spanish agent. His intrigues with Yrujo gave rise to the idea that he planned to foment a rebellion against the United States and detach the western states from the central government. On Herman Blennerhasset's island in the Ohio, Burr planned for the colonization of his lands.

His plans miscarried because Gen. James Wilkinson,[qv] American military commander in New Orleans Territory, informed President Thomas Jefferson that he had received a coded letter from Burr indicating that Burr meant to seize control of the Mississippi valley. Burr was twice arraigned and tried in Kentucky for instigating an illegal expedition against a friendly nation, but both times he was released for want of sufficient evidence. When his party of colonists set sail from Nashville in December 1808, Jefferson ordered Burr arrested for treason and high misdemeanors.

When Burr arrived at Bayou Pierre, near Natchez, on January 10, he learned that he had been betrayed. On January 17 he surrendered to the governor of Mississippi Territory. After an attempt to escape from the authorities he was tried in Richmond, Virginia. After a prolonged trial Justice John Marshall ruled on October 20, 1807, that Burr was not guilty of treason but was guilty of contemplating an invasion of Spanish territory. He was placed under $3,000 bond.

Burr's exact intentions have never been ascertained, but he probably intended to invade Spanish territory by crossing the Sabine River and marching across Texas. In 1816 he refused the "management" of political affairs of Mexico, but he remained interested in Anglo-American expansion and in Texas colonization and the Texas Revolution,[qv] which occurred near the end of his life.

BIBLIOGRAPHY: Thomas Perkins Abernethy, *The Burr Conspiracy* (New York: Oxford University Press, 1954). Aaron Burr, *Memoirs* (New York: Da Capo Press, 1971). Milton Lomask, *Aaron Burr* (2 vols., New York: Farrar, Strauss and Giroux, 1979, 1982). Walter F. McCaleb, *The Aaron Burr Conspiracy* (New York: Wilson-Ericksson, 1936). Vertical Files, Barker Texas History Center, University of Texas at Austin. Samuel H. Wandell and Meade Minningerode, *Aaron Burr* (2 vols., New York and London: Putnam, 1925, 1927).

Warren French

BURR, TEXAS. Burr, also known as Lawson and Kriegel, on Farm Road 1301 four miles southeast of Wharton in southeastern Wharton County, began when Burr Albert Harrison and a family named Callaway established plantations in the area. Harrison arrived in 1859 and set up sugar, syrup, and grist mills on Caney Creek. The 1860 census recorded eighty-three slaves belonging to Harrison and a total of ninety slaves belonging to four Callaways. The Callaway children were taught by the Harrisons' governess. The community took its first name from Dick Lawson, who built a general store, Lawson's Corner, on the border of the Lawson and Harrison plantations. Harrison died in 1881, and about 1889 his son, Gerard Alexander Harrison, managed the plantation and established a mercantile business that was at one time larger than any general store in Wharton; the brick building remains at Burr. Local plantation owners contributed to a church, which was destroyed by fire soon after the Civil War.[qv] Isam Davenport, a black justice of the peace, was in office during Reconstruction[qv] and also served as county commissioner. According to residents he used his position to get free labor by arresting other black men for drinking or shooting craps and then sentencing them to "ten days hard labor in Isam Davenport's cotton patch." The first of two Baptist churches at Burr was built about 1892, and the other a few years later. The first Lawson school was established sometime after 1889. A second school, which was subsequently moved to a better location, was built after 1893 on land also to be used for a church and cemetery. Because of limited white enrollment in a largely black community, the white Lawson school began with a term that lasted only four months; in 1905 it had twenty-one pupils and one teacher.

When Charles Kriegel, a native of Germany, came to the area in 1896, leased the Lawson Store, and then took it over in 1897, the community and postal station came to be known as Kriegel. Kriegel became a real estate promoter in the area about 1900, when the New York, Texas and Mexican Railway was built from Wharton through Lawson and Van Vleck to Sargent. The switch for loading cane and other products built in front of the school was known as Kriegel Switch. A mile up the road was Dinsmore, and a mile south was Burr. At this time the community comprised a territory of three or four square miles, but in 1902 only five residents were reported. By 1907 the Lawson school had thirty-one white pupils and a teacher, and the Kriegel school, across the street from the store, had 358 black pupils and nine teachers. A post office named Kriegel was established in 1899 and discontinued in 1910, when Kriegel gave up his store and Gerard Harrison moved the post office to his store. Harrison gave the office the new name Burr in honor of his father. In 1915 the community had two stores, a church, and rural school. The post office was discontinued in 1918, and mail was sent to Wharton. A new Lawson school, built in 1919, had five teachers and 100 pupils in 1942 and was made part of the Boling Independent School District in 1947. One store and a population of eighty-three were reported in 1939, but by 1941 many residents had moved. In 1989 only two businesses remained at the townsite, and cemeteries were near the banks of the creek. In 1991 the store built by Gerard Harrison was still standing and was used for storage.

BIBLIOGRAPHY: Annie Lee Williams, *A History of Wharton County* (Austin: Von Boeckmann–Jones, 1964).

Claudia Hazlewood

BURRANTOWN, TEXAS. Burrantown, off Farm Road 1733 twenty miles northeast of Crockett in eastern Houston County, was probably established around 1900. In the mid-1930s the settlement had a store and a number of houses; local children attended school at nearby Glover or in Weches. After World War II[qv] many of the residents moved away, and by the mid-1960s only a few widely scattered houses remained in the area.

Christopher Long

BURRIS PRAIRIE, TEXAS. Burris Prairie was near Bald Hill in south central Angelina County. The area was first settled before the Civil War[qv] by pioneers from the Old South. A post office operated there from 1860 to 1866, but by the 1880s the community was no longer shown on maps.

BIBLIOGRAPHY: Angelina County Historical Survey Committee, *Land of the Little Angel: A History of Angelina County, Texas*, ed. Bob Bowman (Lufkin, Texas: Lufkin Printing, 1976).

Christopher Long

BURR OAK CREEK. Burr Oak Creek, also known as Burnt Oak Creek, rises fifteen miles southwest of Eden in southwestern Concho County (at 31°07′ N, 100°04′ W) and runs 7½ miles northwest to its mouth on Kickapoo Creek, fifteen miles west of Eden (at 31°12′ N, 100°05′ W). It crosses an area of rolling terrain surfaced by clays and loams that support oak, juniper, and mesquite.

BURRO CREEK. Burro Creek rises seven miles southeast of Catarina in southeastern Dimmit County (at 28°16′ N, 99°31′ W) and runs northwest for five miles to its mouth on San Roque Creek, two miles southeast of Catarina (at 28°19′ N, 99°35′ W). It descends from an area of rolling hills to flat terrain with locally shallow depressions, surfaced by sandy and clay loams that support scrub brush, mesquite, cacti, and grasses upstream and water-tolerant hardwoods and grasses downstream. Four miles southeast of Catarina the stream is dammed to form Burro Lake, which has a capacity of 3,500 acre-feet, is owned by R. W. Briggs, Jr., and is used for irrigation.

BURRO MESA. Burro Mesa is a gently westward-sloping mesa standing high above the surrounding desert floor to the northwest of the Chisos Mountains in Big Bend National Park,[qv] southern Brewster County (at 29°15′ N, 103°25′ W). At its highest point the mesa reaches an elevation of 4,431 feet above sea level. Its name derives from the many wild burros that once wandered and grazed there. Burro Mesa is the westward down-thrown fault block of the Burro Mesa fault, which runs along the eastern escarpment of the mesa and extends southward into the Burro Mesa fault group, forming one of the major fault zones in this area of the park. The mesa is composed primarily of interbedded tuffs, ash flows, and lavas. These latter two are generally quite resistant, whereas the tuffs are easily eroded. Such a combination often leads to mesa development as erosion proceeds. The hard, igneous rocks crowning Burro Mesa have weathered so much more slowly than the softer rocks on the opposing side of the fault that they have developed over time into a topographic high. The Burro Mesa rhyolite, the prominent member of the south rim formation, caps the upper elevation of the mesa and derives its name from that feature. Vegetation on Burro Mesa is dominated by Chihuahuan Desert scrub, including various shrubs and such semisucculents as lechuguilla, ocotillo, and creosote bush, as well as cacti. The candelilla wax plant may also be found scattered over the slopes.

BIBLIOGRAPHY: Ross A. Maxwell, *The Big Bend of the Rio Grande* (Bureau of Economic Geology, University of Texas at Austin, 1968). Ross A. Maxwell et al., *Geology of Big Bend National Park* (Austin: Bureau of Economic Geology, University of Texas, 1967). A. Michael Powell, "Vegetation of Trans-Pecos Texas," in *New Mexico Geological Society Guidebook* (Socorro, New Mexico: New Mexico Geological Society, 1980).

BURRO MOUNTAIN. Burro Mountain, or Cerro de las Burras ("Hill of the Jennies"), is six miles northwest of Redford in southeastern Presidio County (at 29°25′ N, 104°07′ W). Its summit, with an elevation of 4,345 feet above sea level, rises 1,855 feet above the nearby Rio Grande floodplain. The mountain stands in an area of the Bofecillos Mountains characterized by Tertiary formations of conglomerate, sandstone, tuff, and basalt. The generally light reddish-brown to brown sands and clay loams in the area support sparse grasses, cacti, and desert shrubs of conifers and oaks.

BURROUGHS, GEORGE H. (?–?). George H. Burroughs, merchant and soldier, was a native of Warren, Massachusetts. In August 1836 he organized a company of cavalry in Zanesville, Ohio, to help the Texans in their ongoing hostilities with Mexico. En route, at Portland, Kentucky, Burroughs's company merged with contingents from Ohio and Pennsylvania. At New Orleans a fourth company, from Norfolk, Virginia, joined the group for the journey to Texas. The contingent arrived at Matagorda in November 1836 and marched to Camp Independence[qv] on the Lavaca River. The ladies of Zanesville, Ohio, had presented a battalion standard to Burroughs. The flag was composed of a field of light blue silk, a border of white silk and fringe, and a dark blue center with a gold five-pointed star superimposed. Above the star the American eagle grasped a streamer bearing the legend "Hero of San Jacinto." Burroughs resigned his commission four months after arriving in Texas and by August 1837 was back in Ohio. In 1838 he received a second-class headright certificate for land in Milam, Upshur, and Wise counties. In 1856 an act of the legislature ordered the General Land Office[qv] to issue Burroughs a certificate for 852 acres of land.

BIBLIOGRAPHY: Austin *Daily Democratic Statesman*, December 18, 1874. Hans Peter Nielsen Gammel, comp., *Laws of Texas, 1822–1897*

(10 vols., Austin: Gammel, 1898). Muster Rolls, Texas General Land Office, Austin. *L. W. Kemp*

BURROUGHS, JAMES M. (1824–?). James M. Burroughs, politician and lawyer, was born in Alabama in 1824. He moved to Texas in 1844 and represented Harris County in the Convention of 1845.[qv] He served in the Texas House from 1846 to 1848 and in the Senate from 1855 to 1858. In the Secession Convention[qv] (1861) he was a member of the foreign relations committee. Afterwards, he served as a scout and as a major in the artillery of the Confederate Army. During his service in the military, Burroughs was recognized for heroism by general orders of the army. In July 1866 he attended a convention at Navasota and was elected to the United States Congress but was not seated because of the radical Reconstruction[qv] policy of the Congress. In 1868 he was a delegate to the Democratic national convention in New York. He subsequently practiced law in Houston and in Galveston, where he was living in the mid-1890s. He served as vice president and later president of the Galveston Wharf Company (*see* GALVESTON WHARVES). One of Burroughs's acquaintances described him as a hard-fighting lawyer and an "unreconstructed rebel."

BIBLIOGRAPHY: Louis Wiltz Kemp Papers, Barker Texas History Center, University of Texas at Austin. Norman Kittrell, *Governors Who Have Been and Other Public Men of Texas* (Houston: Dealy-Adey-Elgin, 1921). William S. Speer and John H. Brown, eds., *Encyclopedia of the New West* (Marshall, Texas: United States Biographical Publishing, 1881; rpt., Easley, South Carolina: Southern Historical Press, 1978). Texas House of Representatives, *Biographical Directory of the Texan Conventions and Congresses, 1832–1845* (Austin: Book Exchange, 1941).

BURROW, TEXAS. Burrow is near State Highway 66 fifteen miles southwest of Greenville in extreme west central Hunt County. The settlement, established in 1886 as a stop on the Missouri, Kansas and Texas line (which began building into the area in 1880), was named for W. T. Burrow, a local landowner. By 1899 a post office had opened there; it served the community until 1923. In 1915 Burrow reported a population of sixty and had a church and a school. By the mid-1920s it reported a population of forty and three businesses. Burrow's population was reported as seventy-five from the mid-1940s through the mid-1960s, after which no population figures were available for the town. *Brian Hart*

BURR'S FERRY. The site of Burr's Ferry, also called Burr Ferry, is on State Highway 63 and the Sabine River in northeast Newton County, about eighty miles northeast of Beaumont. The ferry was located on the middle branch of the Old Beef Trail, which ran from Huntsville, Texas, to Alexandria, Louisiana. It was known as Hickman's Ferry as late as 1840. However, an early Newton County commissioners' court meeting designated the crossing Burr's Ferry, in honor of Dr. Timothy Burr, a second cousin of Aaron Burr.[qv] Dr. Burr was an early settler in the Newton County area who eventually established a plantation on the Texas side of the Sabine River. The town that grew up around the ferry in Louisiana became an important business center for pre–Civil War Newton County. After the fall of Vicksburg in 1863 the United States War Department ordered Gen. Nathaniel P. Banks[qv] to invade Texas. In anticipation of this projected Union thrust, Confederate forces threw up breastworks on the Louisiana side of the Sabine River at Burr's Ferry. They also cleared the adjoining area on the Texas side to give their artillery a better field of fire. A Union map detailing "the best route for Military Operations from Alexandria La. to Huntsville, Texas" listed Burr's Ferry as a good crossing. The bottom on the west side was "good and hard," and a road through rolling open pine woods with ample water and suitable campsites ran to Jasper. The breastworks are still standing. One Union invasion was halted at Sabine Pass, and another projected move against Niblett's Bluff was deemed impossible because of inadequate supplies.

After the war a post office on the Louisiana side served Burr's Ferry during the years 1873–1918, 1922, and 1929–33. The ferry, which eventually included a wire cable and pulley enabling it to serve automobiles, discontinued operations in 1936, when a highway bridge connecting Texas Highway 63 and Louisiana Highway 8 was completed. The town is now a suburb of Leesville, Louisiana.

BIBLIOGRAPHY: Madeleine Martin, "Ghost Towns of the Lower Sabine River," *Texas Gulf Historical and Biographical Record* 2 (1966). Newton County Historical Commission, *Glimpses of Newton County History* (Burnet, Texas: Nortex, 1982). Cooper K. Ragan, ed., "The Diary of Captain George W. O'Brien, 1863," *Southwestern Historical Quarterly* 67 (July, October 1963, January 1964).
Robert Wooster

BURR'S FERRY, BROWNDEL AND CHESTER RAILWAY. John Henry Kirby,[qv] John S. Bonner, and other associates chartered the Burr's Ferry, Browndel and Chester Railway Company on January 2, 1906, to build from Burr's Ferry on the Sabine River west to Peach Tree Village and a junction with the Trinity and Sabine Division of the Missouri, Kansas and Texas Railway Company of Texas. The capital was $80,000, and the business office was located at Browndel. Members of the first board of directors included Nathaniel D. Silsbee of Boston, E. I. Kellie of Jasper, John W. Link[qv] of Orange, William Wiess of Beaumont, James L. Kirby of Kountze, James Irvine of New York, and Bonner, Kirby, and K. H. Cawthon, all of Houston. Both the Kirby Lumber Company and the Aldridge Lumber Company owned extensive timber rights in the area around Aldridge in northwestern Jasper County, and the Aldridge firm also operated a sawmill there. The BFB&C was built as a rail outlet for these rich timber holdings from Rockland on the Texas and New Orleans Railroad in northeastern Tyler County to Aldridge in 1907. The line built further east in 1908, giving the railroad eleven miles of track and linking it to the new turpentine camp at Turpentine in northern Jasper County. The company also graded nearly seventeen miles from Turpentine to Browndel, but never laid track on this extension. The Texas and New Orleans acquired the BFB&C on July 1, 1914, and by 1920 had extended the line another nine miles eastward to the Angelina River. This extension was leased to the P. E. Hamons Company, which operated over the track until August 1922. The new extension was taken up in 1924 and 1925. By 1927, with the timber cut out and expenses ten times greater than income on this spur, the entire line was abandoned. In spite of its name and although its headquarters were in Browndel, the BFB&C did not pass through Burr's Ferry, Browndel, or Chester. *Robert Wooster*

BURT, MARIE ANITA (1899–1975). Sister Marie Anita Burt, O.P., who founded Sacred Heart Dominican College in Houston, daughter of Joseph and Margaret (Hannon) Burt, was born in Olean, New York, on March 25, 1899. She attended Catholic schools in New York and Kansas before her family moved to Brownwood, Texas. She attended boarding school at St. Dominic Villa in Lampasas and after high school studied at the Art Institute in Chicago before joining the Dominican Sisters[qv] in Galveston in 1919. She graduated in 1934 from Rosemont College, Rosemont, Pennsylvania, earned her M.A. in 1946 from Catholic University in Washington, D.C., and received her Ph.D. in 1957 from the University of Texas. Her dissertation was an edition of Jacobus de Cessolis's *Libellus de Moribus*, a medieval moral treatise.

As a member of a large teaching order, Sister Anita focused in her early teaching years on secondary education. In 1937 she was appointed principal in Port Arthur, where she helped organize the city's first Catholic high school. In addition, she taught in other Dominican schools—St. Agnes Academy, Houston; Sacred Heart Academy, Galveston; St. Anthony High School, Beaumont; and St. Mary High School, Taylor. In an effort to realize Mother Pauline (Catherine) Gannon's[qv] dream of a Dominican college, in 1945 Sister Anita founded a junior college in Houston affiliated with the Catholic University of America and intended for the education of Dominican nuns. A few years later, at the suggestion of the Southern Association of Colleges and Schools, the school became a four-year liberal arts college for women, named Sacred Heart Dominican College (later Dominican College). Sister Anita was the academic dean of the college from that time until she retired in 1964, with the exception of three years taken for further study. She was a member of the American Philological Association, the Renaissance Society of America, the Modern Language Association, the National Education Association, and the National Catholic Education Association. Though she received many honors, she maintained that her greatest privilege was being a Dominican sister. After a lengthy illness she died on November 28, 1975, in Houston at St. Dominic Villa, the retired sisters' home.

BIBLIOGRAPHY: *Texas Catholic Herald*, December 5, 1975. *Who's Who of American Women*, 1966–67. *Sister Antoinette Boykin*

BURTON, ISAAC WATTS (1805–1843). Isaac Watts Burton, soldier and legislator, son of William B. Burton, was born in Clarke County, Georgia, in 1805. He was appointed to the United States Military Academy at West Point in 1822 but withdrew in 1823. He traveled to Texas in January 1832 and took part in the battle of Nacogdoches.[qv] On November 29, 1835, he was appointed captain of a ranger company by the General Council[qv] and later served as a private in Henry W. Karnes's[qv] cavalry company at the battle of San Jacinto.[qv] Thomas J. Rusk[qv] commanded Burton and his mounted rangers to watch the Texas coast from Guadalupe to Refugio to keep the Mexicans from landing supplies. On June 2, 1816, Burton and his command, near Copano, captured the boat *Watchman*, loaded with supplies for the Mexican army. After capturing the *Comanche* and the *Fannie Butler*, Burton's command became known as the Horse Marines.[qv] Burton served in the Senate of the Second, Third, and Fourth congresses, September 25, 1837, to February 5, 1840. He was appointed commissioner to treat with the Indians on November 10, 1836, and served on the commission to select a site for a permanent capital of the republic. He practiced law in Nacogdoches for several years and was associated with Charles D. Ferris[qv] in publishing the Nacogdoches *Texas Chronicle*.[qv] In 1841 Burton moved to Crockett, where he died in January 1843.

BIBLIOGRAPHY: Sam Houston Dixon and Louis Wiltz Kemp, *The Heroes of San Jacinto* (Houston: Anson Jones, 1932). Patsy McDonald Spaw, *The Texas Senate*, Vol. 1 (College Station: Texas A&M University Press, 1991). Texas House of Representatives, *Biographical Directory of the Texan Conventions and Congresses, 1832–1845* (Austin: Book Exchange, 1941). Amelia W. Williams and Eugene C. Barker, eds., *The Writings of Sam Houston, 1813–1863* (8 vols., Austin: University of Texas Press, 1938–43; rpt., Austin and New York: Pemberton Press, 1970).

BURTON, WALTER MOSES (1829?–1913). Walter Moses Burton, black state senator, was brought to Texas as a slave from North Carolina in 1850 at the age of twenty-one. He belonged to a planter, Thomas Burke Burton, who owned a plantation and several large farms in Fort Bend County. While a slave, Walter Burton was taught how to read and write by his master, a skill that served him well in later years. Thomas Burton sold Walter several large plots of land for $1,900 dollars. This land made the freedman one of the wealthiest and most influential blacks in Fort Bend County. He became involved in politics as early as 1869, when he was elected sheriff and tax collector of Fort Bend County. Along with these duties, he also served as the president of the Fort Bend County Union League (*see* UNION LEAGUE).

In 1873 Burton campaigned for and won a seat in the Texas Senate, where he served for seven years—from 1874 to 1875 and from 1876 to 1882. In the Senate he championed the education of blacks. Among the many bills that he helped push through was one that called for the establishment of Prairie View Normal School (now Prairie View A&M University). In the Republican party[qv] Burton served as a member of the State Executive Committee at the state convention of 1873, as a vice president of the 1878 and 1880 conventions, and as a member of the Committee on Platform and Resolutions at the 1892 convention. His first term in the Senate was shortened by a contested election, as well as the calling of the Constitutional Convention of 1875.[qv] In January 1874 he was granted a certificate of election from the Thirteenth Senatorial District, but a white Democrat contested the election on the grounds that Burton's name was listed three different ways on the ballot and that, consequently, each name received votes in various counties of the district. The Senate committee on election at first recommended the seating of the Democratic candidate but later reconsidered its decision and based the outcome of the election on the intent of the voters who cast ballots for the different Burtons. The Senate confirmed Burton's election on February 20, 1874. By that time, half of the first session of the Fourteenth Legislature was over, and the second session was abbreviated because of the call for a constitutional convention. Burton ran for and was reelected to the Senate in 1876. He left the Senate in 1882 and upon the request of a white colleague was given an ebony and gold cane for his service in that chamber. He remained active in state and local politics until his death in 1913.

BIBLIOGRAPHY: J. Mason Brewer, *Negro Legislators of Texas and Their Descendants* (Dallas: Mathis, 1935; 2d ed., Austin: Jenkins, 1970). Clarence Wharton, *Wharton's History of Fort Bend County* (San Antonio: Naylor, 1939). *Merline Pitre*

BURTON, TEXAS. Burton, on U.S. Highway 290 in western Washington County, was originally established in 1862 and named for John M. Burton, an early settler in the area. The Burton post office opened in 1870, with A. C. Huberich as first postmaster. In the fall of 1872 the community incorporated, and Nelson Felder served as the first mayor. The town's economy benefited from the extension of the Houston and Texas Central Railway from Brenham to Austin after the Civil War.[qv] During the 1880s Burton had three churches, a bank, a school, and a hotel, and by 1885 it had a population of 150. Its population was reported as 400 in 1896 and nearly 600 in 1910. Burton had a population of 800 and thirty businesses by the mid-1940s. During the 1970s, however, the town declined, and its residents had dwindled to 296 by 1980. The population was an estimated 368 in 1987, and 311 in 1990, when Burton had a post office, an independent school district, a bank, and a number of small businesses. Leander H. McNelly,[qv] one of the most famous Texas Rangers,[qv] was buried near Burton in 1877. In the early 1980s economist Douglas Hutchinson of Burton, Ohio, acquired a Victorian house in Burton and renovated an old cotton gin there as a center for information on cotton ginning.

BIBLIOGRAPHY: W. O. Dietrich, *The Blazing Story of Washington County* (Brenham, Texas: Banner Press, 1950; rev. ed., Wichita Falls: Nortex, 1973). Charles F. Schmidt, *History of Washington County* (San Antonio: Naylor, 1949). Vertical Files, Barker Texas History Center, University of Texas at Austin. *James L. Hailey*

BURTON KNOB. Burton Knob is near Reno in northeastern Parker County (at 32°55′ N, 97°37′ W). It rises 932 feet above sea level.

BUSBY, TEXAS (Falls County). Busby was on Little Deer Creek eleven miles west of Marlin and just east of Carolina in western Falls County. It was one of the earliest settlements in the county west of the Brazos River. A Baptist church, called Little Deer Creek Church, was built there in 1879. In 1881, when the county granted the community's petition for a school, the school was named Busby, in honor of a local family. When the San Antonio and Aransas Pass Railway was built from Waco to Lott in 1889, Busby was bypassed, but its school continued to draw students for a number of years. In 1905 the Busby school had two teachers and 105 students; by the early 1930s, however, its enrollment had fallen to forty-five. The Busby school district was divided between the Chilton and Lott independent school districts in 1949. The Busby church and a few scattered houses marked the community on the 1948 county highway map, but no sign of the community was shown on the 1989 map.

bibliography: Lillian S. St. Romain, *Western Falls County, Texas* (Austin: Texas State Historical Association, 1951).

Vivian Elizabeth Smyrl

BUSBY, TEXAS (Fisher County). Busby, on State Highway 57 ten miles south of Roby in south central Fisher County, had a church, a school, and a community club in 1947. Its population was reported as twelve in 1970, 1980, and 1990.

bibliography: Lora Blount, A Short History of Fisher County (M.A. thesis, Hardin-Simmons University, 1947).

William R. Hunt

BUSBY BRANCH. Busby Branch rises a mile northwest of Byler Point Church in southwestern Fayette County (at 29°54′ N, 97°06′ W) and runs south for about four miles to its mouth on Buckner's Creek (at 29°50′ N, 97°05′ W). The stream traverses terrain that varies from low and moderately rolling to flat and locally dissected. Native vegetation consists of hardwood and pine forests with some mesquite and grasses. The soils are shallow to deep sandy clays. The branch is named for James C. Busby, who served in the Plum Grove Rifles in 1861.

bibliography: Leonie Rummel Weyand and Houston Wade, *An Early History of Fayette County* (La Grange, Texas: La Grange *Journal*, 1936).

BUSH, IRA JEFFERSON (1865–1939). Ira Jefferson Bush, frontier physician, was born in 1865 on his grandfather's plantation in Lawrence, Mississippi, the only son of Rev. Thomas Deloach and Emily (Price) Bush's seven children. He attended public schools and the University of Mississippi, and graduated in 1890 from Louisville Medical College. His first patients were from the cotton plantations of Alto, Louisiana, on the banks of the Boeuf River. After he had swamp fever, on the advice of his doctor to find a better environment for his health, he established a practice at Fort Davis, Jeff Davis County, Texas, in 1891. The army abandoned the post a few months after his arrival, and in 1893 Bush took over the practice of a medical school classmate in Pecos. There he served as surgeon for two railroad companies and was the county health officer. In the summer of 1899 he moved to El Paso. Hobbies of big game hunting and archeological exploration led him to visit Mexico frequently. He served several years as the company doctor for mining and lumber interests in Temósachic, Chihuahua, and elsewhere in Mexico, before returning to El Paso. As a close friend of Francisco (Pancho) Villa,[qv] Bush served as chief surgeon general of the insurrectionist army during the Mexican Revolution.[qv] He was a member of the El Paso County Medical Society, the State Medical Association of Texas, and the American Medical Association. He married Bertha Henderson in 1907. They had no children. Bush died on March 10, 1939, in an El Paso hospital.

bibliography: Ira Jefferson Bush, *Gringo Doctor* (Caldwell, Idaho: Caxton Printers, 1939).

Cheryl Ellis Vaiani

BUSH, WILLIAM HENRY (1849–1931). William Henry Bush, manufacturer, rancher, and businessman, was born in Martinsburg, New York, on October 22, 1849, the son of James and Caroline Lucretia (Hills) Bush. In 1862, after he turned thirteen, he attempted twice to run away and join the Union Army as a drummer boy. As a result his mother apprenticed him to a store owner in Lowville, New York, for an annual salary of $100 plus room and board. In 1866 general merchants Seth Miller and Son of Constableville, New York, hired Bush as a clerk. At age twenty he accepted a job offer from King Brothers and Company, a wholesale hat firm in Chicago. After learning the business, Bush was elevated to a junior partnership in the firm, and by 1877 he had accumulated $28,000. That year he married Elva Glidden, the daughter and only child of barbed wire[qv] manufacturer Joseph F. Glidden. They had no children.

Early in the summer of 1879 Bush arrived in the Panhandle[qv] as an agent for Glidden. His mission was to seek out a suitable ranch site where Glidden's new product could be adequately tested. Bush reported that the fertile land around Tecovas Spring, in southwestern Potter County, was ideal for that purpose and recommended its purchase. Consequently, in 1881, Glidden formed a partnership with Henry B. Sanborn[qv] and established the Frying Pan Ranch.[qv] Bush was made a partner in the endeavor with the understanding that he would make an inspection trip from Chicago on his father-in-law's behalf every two years thereafter.

Meanwhile, he eventually formed his own hat, cap, and glove firm, Bush, Simmons, and Company, in 1885 with his brother-in-law, F. T. Simmons. In 1903 they split, and each formed his own business; Bush became president of the Bush Hat Company. Although Chicago remained his home base, Bush became a leading booster of Amarillo, particularly after the termination of the Glidden-Sanborn partnership in 1894. By then Sanborn's addition had become Amarillo's main business district, and Bush had purchased a block for his sister Harriet and her husband, F. T. Simmons. He also induced H. P. Canode of DeKalb, Illinois, to buy the Amarillo Hotel and turn it into a first-class hostelry. In 1898 Glidden deeded the Frying Pan Ranch properties to his son-in-law for $68,000. Bush was a prime mover in the Chicago, Rock Island and Gulf Railway's purchase of the Choctaw, Oklahoma and Texas line in 1903 and the subsequent extension of that line through Amarillo to Tucumcari, New Mexico. He founded the town of Bushland as a railroad shipping point for the Frying Pan interests and in 1904 induced his sister and brother-in-law to deed their downtown property to Potter County for the establishment of a new courthouse and jail.

After the death of his first wife, Bush married Ruth Russel Gentry, on October 20, 1908, and they became the parents of two daughters. In 1912 the Bushes built a spacious stone house about a mile north of the Amarillo Country Club, where they spent several weeks each summer. The world's largest known helium deposit, from which the government helium plant was supplied, was on their property (*see* helium production). To the end of his life, Bush was one of Amarillo's leading benefactors. He was a member of the Fourth Presbyterian Church in Chicago. He died of influenza on April 9, 1931, and was buried in Chicago. At the time of his death, his estate, half of which was in the Panhandle, was valued at around $5 million. At one time, the Bush properties consisted of 119,000 acres in Potter, Randall, Moore, and Sherman counties. The Bush heirs continued to operate the Frying Pan Ranch; in 1987 they owned about 200 sections in Potter, Randall, Oldham, and Sherman counties.

bibliography: Laura V. Hamner, *Short Grass and Longhorns* (Norman: University of Oklahoma Press, 1943). Della Tyler Key, *In the Cattle Country: History of Potter County, 1887–1966* (Amarillo: Tyler-Berkley, 1961; 2d ed., (Wichita Falls: Nortex, 1972). Mrs. Clyde W. Warwick, comp., *The Randall County Story* (Hereford, Texas: Pioneer, 1969).

H. Allen Anderson

BUSHDALE, TEXAS. Bushdale, near Farm Road 908 three miles northwest of Rockdale in southern Milam County, was supposedly named for the area vegetation. Its early settlers were of German descent. In 1903 Bushdale had a one-teacher school for fifty-seven students. The school, a business, and several scattered houses were reported at Bushdale in the 1940s. Its school was consolidated with the Rockdale Independent School District in 1949. There was no evidence of the community shown on the 1988 county highway map.

BIBLIOGRAPHY: Lelia M. Batte, *History of Milam County, Texas* (San Antonio: Naylor, 1956). Milam County Heritage Preservation Society, *Matchless Milam: History of Milam County* (Dallas: Taylor, 1984).

Vivian Elizabeth Smyrl

BUSH KNOB CREEK. Bush Knob Creek rises two miles west of Masters and six miles south of Throckmorton in south central Throckmorton County (at 33°06′ N, 99°12′ W) and runs northeast fifteen miles to its mouth on Elm Creek, at the Greathouse oilfield just west of the Young county line (at 33°10′ N, 98°59′ W). The stream runs through rolling hills surfaced by clay and sandy loams that support scrub brush, cacti, grasses, live oak, and juniper.

BUSHLAND, TEXAS. Bushland, on Interstate Highway 40 fourteen miles west of Amarillo in southwestern Potter County, was established as a station on the Chicago, Rock Island and Gulf Railway. It was named for William Henry Bush[qv] of Chicago, who gave land that he had bought from the Frying Pan Ranch[qv] for a townsite and a railroad right-of-way. On July 3, 1908, Bush and his associate, S. H. Smiser, dedicated the townsite. A school district was soon established there, with Zulema Clark as its first teacher. Charles B. Bush opened the post office in January 1909. The population grew from twenty in the 1920s to 175 in 1940. By that time Bushland had four businesses, an elementary school, and a Baptist church. By 1984 the town reported three rated businesses, including a grain elevator. Population estimates for the community remained at 130 from 1965 through 1990.

BIBLIOGRAPHY: Della Tyler Key, *In the Cattle Country: History of Potter County, 1887–1966* (Amarillo: Tyler-Berkley, 1961; 2d ed., Wichita Falls: Nortex, 1972). Fred Tarpley, *1001 Texas Place Names* (Austin: University of Texas Press, 1980).

H. Allen Anderson

BUSH MOUNTAIN. Bush Mountain is in Guadalupe Mountains National Park[qv] six miles northwest of U.S. Highway 62/180 in northwestern Culberson County (at 31°56′ N, 104°53′ W). Its summit, with an elevation of 8,631 feet above sea level, rises 3,000 feet above the highway.

BUSING INDUSTRY. Texas inventor and transportation pioneer W. B. Chenoweth inaugurated the era of intercity bus travel in Texas on October 29, 1907, by operating his six-cylinder "motor driven stage coach" from Colorado City to Snyder. He abandoned this line and another operation from Big Spring to Lamesa before leaving the bus business. The first regularly scheduled, successfully maintained, and more or less permanent intercity bus line began operations in Texas between Luling and San Marcos on March 1, 1912. The operator of this bus service was G. J. (Josh) Merritt of Fentress.

The period before, during, and after World War I[qv] saw considerable growth in the Texas busing industry, spurred in part by the passage of the Federal Highway Act in July 1916. Immediately after the war the discovery of oilfields near such Texas towns as Ranger, Breckenridge, Eastland, Mexia, and Desdemona provided new interest in the bus business. Pioneer drivers who were able to develop routes that survived the decline of the oil boom included Ed Abbott, Louis Hardy Creamer, George Wellington (Bill) Hyde, O. C. and W. L. Murphey, Walter E. Nunnelee, and Clarence E. Roberson. The owners and operators soon began to realize the value of organization in order to protect their bus routes from unscrupulous "wildcatters" who might attempt to divert their passengers.

The Fortieth Texas Legislature passed the Motor Bus Law with an effective date of June 15, 1927. The law quickly became known in the industry as the Beck Bus Law of 1927, in honor of its chief architect, Representative Walter H. Beck of Fort Worth. The law gave authority over the state's bus lines to the Railroad Commission[qv] of Texas, which immediately organized a Motor Transportation Division, with Mark Marshall as its first director. The law and subsequent amendments and court interpretations provided Texas bus owners with a definition of the rights and responsibilities of motor carriers and set forth expectations for the industry in terms of punctuality, safety, insurance, and other needs of the traveling public. A principal provision of the law was the authority granted to the Railroad Commission to establish certificates of convenience and necessity, or "franchises," which would guarantee a given company the exclusive right to transport passengers between fixed points. The commission issued certificate number one to Walter E. Nunnelee of Tyler for his operation from Tyler to Marshall.

The Beck Bus Law provided a grandfather clause for those bus owners who could demonstrate continuous service over a given route as of January 11, 1927. Most of the pioneer operators filed their certification papers under this clause. Clarence Roberson stated his original date of operation from Fort Worth to Stephenville as August 8, 1921. O. C. and W. L. Murphey attested that Sun Set Stages had been in continuous operation from Abilene to Ballinger via Winters since August 15, 1923. Walter E. Nunnelee began operations on September 8, 1922.

R. C. Bowen of Fort Worth and Guy J. Shields of Austin soon organized other operators into the Texas Bus Owners Association and incorporated the association under state laws on March 24, 1928. The first meeting of the board of directors of the TBOA was held on April 4, 1928, at the Jefferson Hotel in Dallas; the directors elected Guy J. Shields president, Fred Freeman of Denton vice president, and R. C. Bowen secretary-treasurer. On April 20, 1928, the TBOA appointed Joe C. Carrington, then secretary of the Cuero Chamber of Commerce, its secretary-manager.

Carrington used his organizational and entrepreneurial skills to lead the TBOA through its initial years. He organized support through the chambers of commerce around the state, conducted training sessions for ticket agents, produced a comprehensive set of bus timetables, coordinated safety programs and public-relations events, worked with the Motor Transportation Division to eradicate wildcatters, developed a code of ethics for the bus industry, and began a house publication, Motor Transportation in Texas. By the end of 1928 the Texas intercity bus industry carried 4,744,867 passengers annually over a highway network of 31,000 miles. Total operating revenues for the industry in 1928 amounted to $6,412,483.

Further developments in the industry before World War II[qv] included the founding of the Kerrville Bus Company by Hal and Charlie Peterson in 1929; the sale of three lines by R. C. Bowen to the emerging industry giant, Southland Greyhound Lines, also in 1929; the formation of Airline Motor Coaches in 1930, Central Texas Bus Lines in 1933, Arrow Coach Lines in 1935, and Texas, New Mexico, and Oklahoma Coaches in 1939.

The Texas intercity busing industry suffered some economic reversal during the Great Depression[qv] but rebounded vigorously during World War II, when tire and gasoline rationing encouraged motorists to take the bus. Military installations around the state played a large part in the economic prosperity of the bus lines despite the inability of the owners to acquire sufficient parts, drivers, equipment, and mechanics to keep all of the routes functioning properly. After the end of the war, M. E. Moore founded the Continental Bus System, with corporate headquarters in Dallas, on December 12, 1945. In 1946 all of the franchises of pioneer operator R. C. Bowen were consolidated into Lone Star Coaches and then merged into the new Continental Bus system. On December 9, 1947, all of the Moore and Bowen interests formed the nucleus of the new Transcontinental Bus System (Continental Trailways), with national operations headquartered in Dallas. A symbolic historical transition occurred in the industry on January 1, 1949, when coaches of the Texas Electric Bus Line replaced the interurban rail cars of the Texas Electric Railway between Waco and Dallas.

The postwar optimism of the bus owners did not materialize, and both ridership and revenues entered a period of sustained decline after the war. Most of the small lines ceased operation altogether in the 1950s or sold out to the larger networks of Trailways and Greyhound, which merged in 1987. The Greyhound Corporation sold its bus operations in toto to a group of investors headed by Fred Currey of Dallas in 1986. The entire operation of the Kerrville Bus Company, including Painter Bus Lines, was sold to Fred Kaiser of Kerrville on July 15, 1988. As of 1989 the Texas intercity bus industry was heavily dominated by Greyhound. Other companies still in operation were Arrow Trailways of Texas, Central Texas Trailways, Kerrville Bus Company, Sun Set Stages, and Texas Bus Lines; Texas, New Mexico, and Oklahoma Coaches; and a few smaller operations.

BIBLIOGRAPHY: Jack Rhodes, *Intercity Bus Lines of the Southwest* (College Station: Texas A&M University Press, 1988). San Antonio *Express News*, July 30, 1988. Oscar Schisgall, *Greyhound Story* (Chicago: Ferguson, 1985). Thomas Urbanik II, Intercity Bus Industry in Texas (Ph.D. dissertation, Texas A&M University, 1982). *Jack Rhodes*

BUSTAMANTE, ANASTACIO (1780–1853). Anastacio Bustamante, president of Mexico, son of José Ruiz and Francisca Oseguera Bustamante, was born at Jiquilpan, Michoacán, Mexico, on July 27, 1780. He attended a seminary college in Guadalajara, studied medicine in Mexico City, and practiced medicine in San Luis Potosí. At the time of the Mexican War of Independence,[qv] Bustamante fought for a time as a cavalry officer with the Spanish forces and then changed sides to fight under Agustín de Inturbide,[qv] who appointed him captain general of the Provincias Internas.[qv] In 1822 captain general Bustamante recommended that Stephen F. Austin[qv] be allowed to settle his colony near San Antonio because he foresaw the dangers of allowing American settlers to establish themselves beyond the confines of Mexican rule in Texas. President Guadalupe Victoria reappointed Bustamante captain general of the Provincias Internas. Bustamante was declared vice president of Mexico in January 1829 and was acting president when the Law of April 6, 1830,[qv] was passed. He was again president from April 1837 to March 1839, and from July 1839 to September 1841. He spent the last years of his life in retirement at San Miguel de Allende, where he died on February 6, 1853.

BIBLIOGRAPHY: Vito Alessio Robles, *Coahuila y Texas en la época colonial* (Mexico City: Editorial Cultura, 1938; 2d ed., Mexico City: Editorial Porrúa, 1978). Hubert Howe Bancroft, *History of Mexico* (6 vols., San Francisco: A. L. Bancroft and the History Company, 1883–89). Eugene C. Barker, *The Life of Stephen F. Austin* (Nashville: Cokesbury Press, 1925; rpt., Austin: Texas State Historical Association, 1949; New York: AMS Press, 1970). Manuel Rivera Cambas, *Los Gobernantes de México* (2 vols., Mexico City: Imp. de J. M. Aguilar Ortiz, 1873). *C. A. Hutchinson*

BUSTAMANTE, TEXAS. Bustamante is on State Highway 16 twelve miles northeast of Zapata in central Zapata County. It was named for Pedro José Bustamante, to whom the Las Comitas land grant was made in 1802; the site was settled as the ranch headquarters in the 1870s. A post office was established there in 1913. During the 1930s and 1940s peanuts were grown in the area, and in 1942 family members Francisco Bustamante, Martiniano Garza, and Juan Rodrigues bought a peanut-harvesting machine for $300. In 1945 Bustamante had a population of fifty. Before 1960 several springs near the community furnished sweet water to area residents. The springs have since dried up, and the site is overgrown with vegetation. In the 1990s the Comitas and Aguila oilfields were near the community. The *Texas Almanac*[qv] listed the population of Bustamante as twenty-five in 1990; in 1991 a local source reported that the community comprised only a TransAmerica Compressor Station, the headquarters for Las Comitas Ranch, and three to six houses.

BIBLIOGRAPHY: Jean Y. Fish, *Zapata County Roots Revisited* (Edinburg, Texas: New Santander Press, 1990). Virgil N. Lott and Mercurio Martinez, *The Kingdom of Zapata* (San Antonio: Naylor, 1953). Kathleen E. and Clifton R. St. Clair, eds., *Little Towns of Texas* (Jacksonville, Texas: Jayroe Graphic Arts, 1982). *Dick D. Heller, Jr.*

BUSTAMANTE RANCH. Bustamante Ranch, located on State Highway 16 fifteen miles northeast of Zapata in central Zapata County, was established in 1802 by Pedro Bustamante. Not until January 2, 1848, did he acquire legal ownership to the land. On that date the Mexican government deeded him 22,142 acres as a part of Las Comitas, a land grant. Bustamante was a contemporary of Col. Antonio Zapata,[qv] with whom he often fought against raiding Indians. The primary crop produced on the ranch was peanuts, although Bustamante also raised sheep, goats, and cattle. Bustamante and his wife, Micaela (Villarreal), had ten children, and their son Manuel inherited 22,000 acres in 1856. He and his wife, Anastacia (Salinas), continued the enterprise, raising sheep, goats, cattle, and peanuts. They had eight children, and in 1890 their son Dionicio acquired 1,040 acres. He eventually added 500 more acres. Dionicio married Petra de los Santos, and they had seven children. Among the crops they raised were sugarcane, peanuts, cotton, squash, and watermelons. They also continued raising cattle and added a pond to the ranch; they sold both cattle and crops at market. In 1930 their son Francisco was given 183 acres, and he and his wife, Matiana, continued the tradition of raising cattle and producing peanuts. The great-great-grandson of Dionicio Bustamante, also named Dionicio, acquired the ranch in 1952. In the mid-1980s the ranch consisted of forty-one acres and was dedicated to cattle raising. It was under the management of the Garza brothers, Dionicio's cousins.

BIBLIOGRAPHY: *Guide to Spanish and Mexican Land Grants in South Texas* (Austin: Texas General Land Office, 1988). Virgil N. Lott and Mercurio Martinez, *The Kingdom of Zapata* (San Antonio: Naylor, 1953). *Texas Family Land Heritage Registry*, Vol. 10.

Alicia A. Garza

BUSTER, TEXAS. Buster, on Farm Road 182 five miles south of Turnersville in northern Coryell County, was named for J. V. (Jack) Buster, who had a farm and ranch in the vicinity in 1872 and who gave land for a school in 1883. The school had sixty students and one teacher in 1904; it was consolidated with the Turnersville school in 1929. No evidence of Buster was shown on the 1988 county highway map.

Zelma Scott

BUSTILLO Y CEBALLOS, JUAN ANTONIO (?–?). Juan Antonio Bustillo y Ceballos (Zevallos), soldier and governor of Spanish Texas,[qv] was in Texas for twelve years, seven of them (1724–31) as captain of Nuestra Señora de Loreto Presidio at La Bahía del Espíritu Santo. He assisted in the transfer of the Queretaran missions from East Texas to San Antonio in 1730 and was so successful that he was appointed governor of Texas in 1731. His administration was notable for the settlement of the Canary Islanders[qv] in San Antonio and for a campaign to the San Xavier (San Gabriel) and San Saba rivers against the Apaches in 1732. The expedition, consisting of 160 Spaniards and sixty Indians, tracked the Apaches to their *rancherías* and administered a defeat that was followed by a short period of peace with them. Bustillo resigned the governorship of Texas in 1734 and returned to Mexico. He became *alcalde ordinario* of Mexico City and in 1751 was a member of the Audiencia, the highest judicial and administrative body of New Spain. Although he raised objections against the founding of the San Xavier missions[qv] in 1746, the Audiencia, of which he was then a member, gave its approval in 1751. On December 21, 1754, while he was lieutenant governor and acting governor of Coahuila, Bustillo and Fr. Alonso Giraldo de Terreros[qv] founded San Lorenzo Mission for the Apaches near San Fernando de Austria, Coahuila.

BIBLIOGRAPHY: Herbert Eugene Bolton, *Texas in the Middle Eighteenth Century: Studies in Spanish Colonial History and Administration* (Berkeley: University of California Press, 1915; rpt., Austin: University of Texas Press, 1970). Carlos E. Castañeda, *Our Catholic Heritage in Texas* (7 vols., Austin: Von Boeckmann–Jones, 1936–58; rpt., New York: Arno, 1976). Juan Agustín Morfi, *History of Texas, 1673–1779* (2 vols., Albuquerque: Quivira Society, 1935; rpt., New York: Arno, 1967). Elizabeth Howard West, trans., "Bonilla's Brief Compendium of the History of Texas, 1772," *Quarterly of the Texas State Historical Association* 8 (July 1904). *C. H. Taylor, Jr.*

BUTCHERKNIFE HILL. Butcherknife Hill is forty miles south of Alpine and one mile west of State Highway 118 in west central Brewster County (at 29°50′ N, 103°36′ W). It rises abruptly from the center of a broad, open expanse many miles wide that is surrounded by high mountains and mesas and covered with Chihuahuan Desert scrub. A small body of Tertiary igneous rock makes up the higher portion of the hill, which rises at its peak to an elevation of 4,042 feet above sea level. As a result of this rock's more resistant character, it stands out in bold relief against the surrounding flats. Butcherknife Hill was at one time a stopping place on the stage route between Alpine and Study Butte. One source claims that the name resulted from an incident in which a knife was lost and later found at the spot by passengers of the stagecoach. It is also possible that the name was derived from an incident that occurred in 1860, when Lt. William Echols, leading an army train of camels[qv] through the area, found a butcherknife "not long lost" on the route of a major Indian trail. It is not clear, however, if the event recorded by Echols was indeed at the spot now called Butcherknife Hill.

BUTE, TEXAS. Bute was eight miles south of Athens in southern Henderson County. A post office operated there from 1892 to 1901. In 1896 the reported population was ten. By the mid-1930s the settlement no longer appeared on maps, and in the early 1990s only a few houses remained in the area. *Christopher Long*

BUTLER, ANTHONY (1787?–1849?). Anthony Butler, lawyer, soldier, and politician, was born in South Carolina, probably in 1787 in Clarendon County, and established a sizable plantation in Russellville, Kentucky. At the outbreak of the War of 1812 he was commissioned a lieutenant colonel of the Twenty-eighth United States Infantry, on March 11, 1813. On February 21, 1814, he was promoted to colonel of the Second Rifle Regiment. After discharge he served as a member of the Kentucky legislature for two terms, 1818–19, but failed in a run for governor of that state in 1820. Butler was a resident of Mississippi in 1829 when his friend President Andrew Jackson, appointed him to succeed Joel Poinsett[qv] as United States chargé d'affaires in Mexico City. Historian Justin H. Smith commented that Butler's only qualifications for the post "were an acquaintance with Texas and a strong desire to see the United States obtain it." He had been through bankruptcy more than once, spoke no Spanish, was ignorant of the forms of diplomacy, and "was personally a bully and a swashbuckler." Further, Smith maintained, Butler was "shamefully careless," unprincipled in his methods, and "openly scandalous in his conduct...In brief, he was a national disgrace." Sam Houston wrote of Butler in 1832, "Such men as he is, would destroy a country, but take my word for it, he will never gain one!"

Butler was recalled to Washington early in January 1836 but remained in Mexico on his own authority and continued to report to Jackson on the actions and intentions of the Mexican government toward Texas. He at last returned to the United States in May 1836. He then took residence in Washington County, Texas, and in September 1838 was elected to the House of Representatives of the Third Texas Legislature. At the outbreak of the Mexican War[qv] he offered his services to Gen. Zachary Taylor,[qv] believing that his knowledge of the country would be useful. Butler moved to the North in 1847 or 1848. As a Mason he was grand master of Kentucky in 1812–13 and of Texas in 1840–41. In 1849 or 1850 he died on the Mississippi River attempting to save his fellow passengers from the burning wreck of the steamboat *Anthony Wayne.* His papers are preserved at the Barker Texas History Center,[qv] University of Texas at Austin.

BIBLIOGRAPHY: Eugene C. Barker, "The Private Papers of Anthony Butler," *Nation* 92 (June 15, 1911). Francis B. Heitman, *Historical Register and Dictionary of the United States Army* (2 vols., Washington: GPO, 1903; rpt., Urbana: University of Illinois Press, 1965). John H. Jenkins, ed., *The Papers of the Texas Revolution, 1835–1836* (10 vols., Austin: Presidial Press, 1973). Justin H. Smith, *The War with Mexico* (2 vols., New York: Macmillan, 1919). Texas House of Representatives, *Biographical Directory of the Texan Conventions and Congresses, 1832–1845* (Austin: Book Exchange, 1941). Amelia W. Williams and Eugene C. Barker, eds., *The Writings of Sam Houston, 1813–1863* (8 vols., Austin: University of Texas Press, 1938–43; rpt., Austin and New York: Pemberton Press, 1970). *Thomas W. Cutrer*

BUTLER, GEORGE (?–?). George Butler, early settler, was born in Georgia and came to Texas by 1832, when he was a delegate to the Convention of 1832[qv] from the Tenehaw District (present-day Shelby County). In 1834 he was described on a certificate of character as being "a man of family consisting of five." In 1839 he was elected justice of the peace in Shelby County and associate land commissioner. He was still living in Shelby County in 1841.

BIBLIOGRAPHY: Texas House of Representatives, *Biographical Directory of the Texan Conventions and Congresses, 1832–1845* (Austin: Book Exchange, 1941). *Cecil Harper, Jr.*

BUTLER, GEORGE D. (1813–1836). George D. Butler, Alamo defender, was born in Missouri in 1813 and traveled to Texas by way of New Orleans. During the Texas Revolution[qv] he served in the Alamo garrison. He died in the battle of the Alamo[qv] on March 6, 1836.

BIBLIOGRAPHY: Daughters of the American Revolution, *The Alamo Heroes and Their Revolutionary Ancestors* (San Antonio, 1976). Bill Groneman, *Alamo Defenders* (Austin: Eakin, 1990).

Bill Groneman

BUTLER, WILLIAM G. (1831–1912). William G. Butler, one of the earliest and most active trail drivers of South Texas, was born on June 14, 1831, in Scott County, Mississippi, the son of Burnell and Sarah Ann (Ricks) Butler. In 1852 he moved to Karnes County, Texas, with his parents and twelve siblings. In 1858 he married Adeline Burris, who bore him eight children. During the Civil War[qv] Butler volunteered for Confederate service and was mustered into the Escondido Rifles, a company of mounted riflemen raised in Karnes County in July 1861. Later, as a member of Franklin C. Wilkes's[qv] cavalry, he was transferred to the Trans-Mississippi Department for service in Louisiana, Texas, and Arkansas. After the war, like many other South Texans, Butler started ranching and trail driving "to connect the four-dollar cow with the forty-dollar market." He soon became important in the cattle industry in South Texas. His first string of cattle was driven to Abilene in the spring of 1868. For many years he and Seth Mabry of Austin were partners, and together they sent up the trail an estimated 100,000 cattle. In Karnes County, Butler owned nearly 75,000 acres of land, leased another 25,000, and stocked 10,000 cattle. He also helped secure the passage of the San Antonio and Aransas Pass Railway through the county. He died in Karnes County on June 20, 1912, and was buried in the family cemetery at his home near Kenedy.

BIBLIOGRAPHY: J. Frank Dobie, ed., *A Vaquero of the Brush Country* (Dallas: Southwest, 1929; new ed., Boston: Little, Brown, 1943). Wayne Gard, *The Chisholm Trail; with Drawings by Nick Eggenhofer* (Norman: University of Oklahoma Press, 1954). J. Marvin Hunter, *Trail*

Drivers of Texas (2 vols., San Antonio: Jackson Printing, 1920, 1923; 4th ed., Austin: University of Texas Press, 1985).

Robert H. Thonhoff

BUTLER, TEXAS (Bastrop County). Butler, five miles southeast of Elgin in northern Bastrop County, was established with the coming of the Texas and New Orleans Railroad in 1871. However, the small railroad community never developed enough to establish a post office or, apparently, to have population figures recorded until the 1930s. The estimated population through the 1930s and 1940s stood at 107, then rose to 150 in the late 1940s. It remained at this number till the late 1960s. In the mid-1980s the settlement was still listed as a community. *Paula Mitchell Marks*

BUTLER, TEXAS (Freestone County). Butler is on U.S. Highway 84 fourteen miles southeast of Fairfield in southeast Freestone County. In 1852, at a nearby location known as West Point Hill, John T. Gill built a store and warehouse, which he moved a few miles away from the Trinity River the following year. Several families from Butler County, Alabama, including the Mannings, McDaniels, Mayeses, and Mobleys, settled in the area at the same time. In 1854 a church was organized, and the next year a post office by the name of West Point was established. In 1856 the name of the town was officially changed to Butler. By 1858 the community had a doctor, a general store, several businesses, and a Masonic lodge. The post office was closed in 1867 but reestablished in 1868. Butler Academy was authorized by the Texas legislature in 1870. The major revenue of the town at that time was from cotton, which was shipped through Galveston by steamboat on the Trinity River. In 1872 the International–Great Northern Railroad attempted to build a line through the town, but an agreement with landowners could not be reached. The railroad instead went through Oakwood and Palestine. In 1880 the population of Butler was 300, but by 1892 it had decreased to 150, primarily due to the lack of a railroad and the decline in steamboat traffic.

In 1904 the population was estimated at 115, and by 1914 the community had 100 people, a cotton gin, and a general store. The post office closed in August 1916, and mail was sent through Oakwood. In 1936 Butler had three churches, a cemetery, and a number of scattered dwellings. In 1969 four businesses were in operation there, and the school had been consolidated with the Fairfield schools. From 1943 to 1988 the population of Butler was estimated at between sixty and seventy. In 1990 the population was sixty-seven.

BIBLIOGRAPHY: Phillip Dale Browne, The Early History of Freestone County to 1865 (M.A. thesis, University of Texas, 1925). Freestone County Historical Commission, *History of Freestone County, Texas* (Fairfield, Texas, 1978). *Chris Cravens*

BUTLERBERG, TEXAS. Butlerberg, on State Highway 105 in the eastern part of Montgomery County, was named for an early settler. The settlement was probably founded in the mid-1880s. By the late 1940s it consisted only of a few scattered dwellings along the highway. It has since been incorporated into Conroe. *Becky Borjas*

BUTLER COLLEGE. Butler College, a coeducational school for blacks in Tyler, was established as the Texas Baptist Academy in 1905 by the East Texas Baptist Association. In 1924 the name was changed to Butler College in honor of its president, C. M. Butler, and the institution became a junior college. In 1932 the Texas Baptist Convention agreed to assist in operation of the college. After World War II[qv] the school added such vocational courses as tailoring, photography, and secretarial science, particularly to benefit veterans. In 1949 the plant had a thirty-three-acre campus, eleven buildings, and a 103-acre farm on the Tyler-Kilgore highway. The enrollment in 1948–49 was 361. In 1951 Butler became a senior college and added a program in teacher preparation. The physical plant had fourteen buildings. The college, however, never achieved four-year accreditation. Throughout the 1960s the enrollment declined, and in 1968 only fifty-eight students were enrolled. Although students were bussed to the campus from Kilgore Junior College, Butler closed in the summer of 1972.

BIBLIOGRAPHY:Linda Brown Cross and Robert W. Glover, *History of Tyler Junior College, 1926–1986* (Tyler, Texas: Tyler Junior College, 1985). Robert W. Glover, ed., *Tyler and Smith County, Texas* (n.p.: Walsworth, 1976). Michael R. Heintze, A History of the Black Private Colleges in Texas, 1865–1954 (Ph.D. dissertation, Texas Tech University, 1981; published as *Private Black Colleges in Texas, 1865–1954* [College Station: Texas A&M University Press, 1985]). Donald W. Whisenhunt, *The Encyclopedia of Texas Colleges and Universities* (Austin: Eakin, 1986). *Martin Behnke*

BUTLER CREEK. Butler Creek rises two miles south of Atlanta State Park in northeastern Cass County (at 33°12′ N, 94°14′ W) and flows southeast for five miles to its mouth on Black Bayou, two miles northwest of Atlanta (at 33°08′ N, 94°12′ W). The stream is intermittent in its upper reaches. It traverses gently undulating to hilly land with sandy and loamy soils, heavily wooded with pines and hardwoods.

BUTT, FLORENCE THORNTON (1864–1954). Florence Thornton Butt, whose grocery store was the first link in the H-E-B[qv] chain founded by her son Howard Edward Butt,[qv] was born in Buena Vista, Mississippi, on September 19, 1864, the daughter of John and Mary (Kimbrough) Thornton. She spent her youth in Buena Vista, where she often assisted her two pastor brothers in holding revivals. She later enrolled in Clinton College and, as the only female in her class, graduated with highest honors. Afterward, she taught school. In 1889 she married pharmacist Clarence C. Butt. The couple lived in Mississippi and Tennessee before moving to Texas in 1904 in search of a more suitable climate and better medical facilities to treat Clarence's tuberculosis. After a year in San Antonio, the family, which included their three young sons, moved to Kerrville. With her husband unable to work, Mrs. Butt became an agent for the A&P Tea Company, taking and delivering grocery orders door-to-door. She accumulated a small stock of groceries and invested sixty dollars to open the C. C. Butt Grocery on Main Street in Kerrville. The store was on the ground floor of a two-story building, which Mrs. Butt rented for nine dollars a month. She combined her business and domestic responsibilities by moving her family into the second floor of the building and using her sons as delivery boys. She continued to run the store until 1919, when her son Howard returned from the navy and took over as manager. She then concentrated on religious and civic efforts in Kerrville. She was a devout Baptist and a leader in the Eastern Star. She died at her Kerrville home on March 4, 1954, after suffering a stroke, and was buried in Glen Rest Cemetery. Her survivors included her sons Howard and Eugene. By the end of the twentieth century the H-E-B stores were the largest privately owned food chain in the nation.

BIBLIOGRAPHY: Austin *American*, March 5, 1954. Austin *American-Statesman*, April 9, 1985. San Antonio *Express*, March 5, 1954. Vertical Files, Barker Texas History Center, University of Texas at Austin (Howard Edward Butt, Sr., Howard Edward Butt, Jr., Charles C. Butt). *Debbie Mauldin Cottrell*

BUTT, HOWARD EDWARD (1895–1991). Howard Edward Butt, businessman, was born April 9, 1895, in Memphis, Tennessee, the son of Charles Clarence and Florence (Thornton) Butt.[qv] His father, a pharmacist, suffered from tuberculosis, so the family moved to Kerrville in the Hill Country[qv] of Texas, where the drier climate was believed therapeutic. To support the family, Florence Butt purchased wholesale groceries in 1905 with which she opened a small store in Kerrville later that year. Her cash resources at the time the store opened were sixty dollars. The family of five lived in rented rooms

Florence Butt behind the counter at her grocery store. Kerrville, 1913.

over the store. Howard, the youngest of three boys, helped his mother with the business, delivering groceries first in a child's wagon and later on horseback. He began to manage the store at age sixteen. He graduated as the valedictorian of Tivy High School in 1914. After hitchhiking to California for the summer, he harvested grapes to earn his return train fare and visited the home of his favorite author, Jack London, to whom he introduced himself. Before enlisting in the United States Navy for service in World War I,[qv] Butt chose for himself the middle name Edward. He served from 1917 to 1919, part of that time as aide to the commandant at the Great Lakes Naval Station. In 1919 he returned to Kerrville and joined his mother in managing the small family store. In 1921 he converted the store to cash-and-carry instead of charge and deliver, a move that was considered quite a gamble at the time. He attempted four expansions of the business—a feed store in Kerrville and grocery stores in Center Point, Junction, and Brownwood—all of which failed. Other attempts in such towns as Eagle Pass, Uvalde, and Crystal City also failed.

On December 5, 1924, Butt married Mary Elizabeth Holdsworth of Kerrville (*see* butt, mary e. h.). In 1926 he opened a store in Del Rio that proved successful. In 1928 he borrowed $38,000, moved to the Rio Grande valley, and purchased three small stores. He began calling his stores H. E. Butt Grocery Company in 1935 and changed the name to H-E-B[qv] in 1946. Butt expanded the grocery business in the Rio Grande valley and South and Central Texas, entering Corpus Christi in 1931, Austin in 1938, and San Antonio in 1942. Company headquarters moved to Corpus Christi in 1940. As one of the first to begin developing "one-stop shopping," he added a meat market, delicatessen, and bakery to his stores. By the 1950s H-E-B was the leading food retailer in South and Central Texas. By 1960 the company operated over eighty stores and its own food processing and distribution facilities. Butt's son, Charles C. Butt, succeeded him as president in 1971 and as chairman in 1984.

Butt was a thirty-third-degree Mason and a Baptist deacon. He established the H. E. Butt Foundation in 1933, one of the earliest philanthropic foundations in Texas. He and his wife pioneered programs instrumental in eliminating tuberculosis in South Texas. They provided libraries and recreational facilities—swimming pools and tennis courts—to many South Texas communities, making seed-money gifts and urging municipal governments to implement these projects, particularly in low-income areas. He also began developing the H. E. Butt Foundation Camp in 1954. Under Butt's leadership, H-E-B regularly gave the maximum philanthropic contributions allowable under federal law. He maintained a strong sense of involvement in the communities that his businesses served. He was a member of the board of directors of Texas A&I college and the University of Corpus Christi. On March 30, 1972, the Texas Senate gave Butt a special commendation for his contributions to the state. He died at age ninety-five on March 12, 1991, in Corpus Christi. At the time of his death there were more than 170 H-E-B supermarkets.

bibliography: *Howard E. Butt, Sr., April 9, 1895–March 12, 1991: Special Edition, Fall 1991* (Kerrville, Texas: Laity Lodge, 1991). Vertical Files, Barker Texas History Center, University of Texas at Austin.

Kristy Ozmun

BUTT, MARY ELIZABETH HOLDSWORTH (1903–1993). Mary Elizabeth Holdsworth Butt, social reformer, daughter of Thomas and Rosa (Ross) Holdsworth, was born the fourth of seven children on a ranch near Loma Vista, Texas, on February 4, 1903. Thomas Holdsworth immigrated to Texas as a child in 1880 with his stepmother and father, an English schoolmaster, and settled on a homestead in Zavala County. Mary graduated from Tivy High School in Kerrville, attended the University of Texas in Austin, and taught in the Kerrville public schools during the mid-1920s. On December 5, 1924, she married Howard Edward Butt,[qv] who operated a small grocery store in Kerrville. In 1929 they moved to Brownsville in the Rio Grande valley and later relocated to Harlingen. During this time Mrs. Butt began a series of projects addressing the health and educational needs of South Texas families. Her dining room became the area office for the State Crippled Children's Program, and she served as chairwoman of the Cameron County Child Welfare Board. She worked to expand inadequate library services. She also began an ambitious program of tuberculosis diagnosis and treatment throughout the valley and later bought the first equipment for testing the hearing and vision of the area's elementary school children. While living in the valley she gave birth to three children.

During these years her husband's business, H-E-B,[qv] was expanding. In 1940 the family moved to Corpus Christi, Texas. There the YWCA, the Hearth, the Nueces County home for the aged, the Nueces County Tuberculosis Hospital, and the district American Cancer Society were all organized in the Butt home. Troubled by the lack of day care for African-American children, Mary Butt worked to establish the Mary Bethune Day Nursery, an organization still strong in Corpus Christi in the 1990s. She served on the Community Chest Board and was also the prime mover in establishing a Juvenile Center separate from the jails. Mrs. Butt helped to establish Hilltop, a local tuberculosis hospital for the Corpus Christi area, which opened in 1953. She served for five years as chairman of the Hilltop board. She often testified before state legislative committees regarding the budgetary needs of agencies with which she worked, and in 1934 she and her husband established the H. E. Butt Foundation, one of the earliest philanthropic foundations in Texas, to provide libraries and recreational facilities and fund public school programs. The H. E. Butt Foundation Camp, on the Frio River, yearly provides facilities for over 18,000 campers (many from state mental hospitals) free of charge and is the site of Laity Lodge, a Center for Christian Learning.

In 1953 Mary Butt received an honorary doctor of law degree from Baylor University and in 1955 an honorary doctorate from Paul Quinn College, Waco, Texas. Also in 1955 she was appointed by Governor Allan Shivers[qv] to the governing board of Texas State Hospitals and Special Schools, which was supplanted in 1965 by the Texas Department of Mental Health and Mental Retardation.[qv] For eighteen years she was the only woman member of this board. In 1954 she was selected by citizens of Laredo to receive the annual Mrs. South Texas Award in recognition of her work in the fields of public health, social service, and education and so became the first woman to receive the award. In 1968 Howard and Mary Butt were awarded the Texas Library Association Philanthropic Award of the Year in recognition of their service to the libraries. In 1975 they were presented the Brotherhood Award from the Corpus Christi Chapter of the National Conference of Christians and Jews in appreciation of their humanitarian endeavors on a statewide as well as local basis.

In 1981 Mary Holdsworth Butt was chosen to receive the first Yellow Rose Award by the Parent's Association for the Retarded in Texas. In conjunction with the award, the state Senate and House adopted resolutions commending her life work. On May 13, 1981, Governor William P. Clements designated her a member emeritus of the Texas Department of Mental Health and Mental Retardation.

In September 1986 the Texas Alliance for the Mentally Ill voted to make Mrs. Butt the first recipient of its lifetime award, in honor of her contributions to the field of mental health and her "leadership in improving human services for the people of Texas." On July 12, 1993, the National Council of Juvenile and Family Court Judges' Awards Committee selected her to receive the council's highest award for "Meritorious Service to the Children of America." She died in her home in Corpus Christi on October 6, 1993 and was survived by her three children—Howard E. Butt, Jr., president of H. E. Butt Foundation and founder of Laity Lodge; Margaret Eleanor Butt Crook, a director of Bread for the World, Washington, D.C., whose husband, William H. Crook, served as director of VISTA (Volunteers in Service to America) and later as United States Ambassador to Australia; and Charles C. Butt, president and chairman of H. E. Butt Grocery Company.

BIBLIOGRAPHY: Austin *American-Statesman*, October 7, 1993. Vertical Files, Barker Texas History Center, University of Texas at Austin (H. E. Butt, Sr.). *Kristy Ozmun*

BUTTE, GEORGE CHARLES (1877–1940). George Charles Butte, legal scholar and colonial administrator, the son of Charles Felix and Lena Clara (Stoes) Butte, was born on May 8, 1877, in San Francisco, California. When he was nine years old the family moved to Hunt County, Texas. He was reared on a farm near Commerce and attended the public schools there before taking a B.A. degree at Austin College in 1895 and B.A. and M.A. degrees at the University of Texas in 1903 and 1904. He later moved to Dublin, Texas. He was admitted to the Texas bar in 1903 and to the Oklahoma bar in 1904, and practiced at Muskogee, Oklahoma, until 1911, when he quit to travel and study. He attended the University of Berlin, 1911–12, took a degree in jurisprudence at Heidelberg University in 1913, and studied at the École de Droit in Paris until 1914, when he became professor of law at the University of Texas.

On October 5, 1918, Butte was commissioned a major in the United States Army and appointed chief of the foreign intelligence division of the general staff, a position he held until March 10, 1919. In 1920 Governor William P. Hobby[qv] appointed him to a commission to draft public-utility laws for Texas. In 1921 Butte was granted an honorary doctorate of laws by Austin College. He served as dean of the law school of the University of Texas in 1923–24. In 1924 he was nominated as Republican candidate for governor of Texas. Despite a spirited campaign that drew support of dissident Democrats and members of the Ku Klux Klan[qv] as well as Republicans, he was defeated by Miriam A. (Ma) Ferguson.[qv]

Butte was appointed attorney general of Puerto Rico in 1925 and remained in that office until 1928; he served three times as acting governor of the island. In 1928 he was appointed a special assistant to the attorney general of the United States. He became vice governor of the Philippine Islands on December 31, 1930, and acted as governor general in 1931–32. On July 1, 1932, he resigned to become associate justice of the Supreme Court of the Philippines. In 1936, at the request of the Railroad Commission[qv] of Texas, he was granted a year's leave of absence to organize a division of, and draw up regulations for, oil and gas conservation in Texas.

On August 21, 1898, Butte married Bertha Lattimore at Dublin, Texas; they had five children. Butte was a Baptist, a thirty-third-degree Mason, and a member of the American Society of International Law, the American Law Institute, Alpha Tau Omega, Delta Theta Phi, and a number of clubs. He was an honorary life member of the State Bar of Texas[qv] and in 1928 was honorary president of the Puerto Rican bar association. In 1913 he published two works: *Great Britain and the Panama Canal* and *Amerikanische Prisengerichtsbarkeit.* He was known internationally as an expert on colonial administration and international law. He died in Mexico City on January 18, 1940, and was buried at Dublin, Texas. He was survived by his second wife, Angelina.

BIBLIOGRAPHY: Sam Hanna Acheson, Herbert P. Gambrell, Mary Carter Toomey, and Alex M. Acheson, Jr., *Texian Who's Who,* Vol. 1

(Dallas: Texian, 1937). Austin *Statesman*, January 19, 1940. Dallas *Morning News*, October 22, 1924. *Who Was Who in America*, Vol. 2.

Ernest R. May

BUTTE CREEK. Butte Creek, also known as Buke Creek and Battle Creek, rises two miles south of Clairemont in central Kent County (at 33°08′ N, 100°46′ W) and runs east for seven miles to its mouth on the Salt Fork of the Brazos River (at 33°10′ N, 100°37′ W). Most of the area features moderately steep slopes and locally high relief surfaced by silt loam that supports mesquite and grasses. About a mile west of the creek's mouth the land is flat with local shallow depressions and a surface of sandy and clay loams in which grow hardwoods, conifers, and grasses.

BUTTERCUP, TEXAS. Buttercup (also called Doddville and Dodd's Store) was on Buttercup Creek just south of Cedar Park in southwest Williamson County. Its site now lies under a reservoir beside U.S. Highway 183. The community, situated on the old road from Bagdad to Austin, throve in the 1870s and 1880s. In 1878 Buttercup had a store, a church, a school, a gin, a mill, and two doctors. A post office was located there from 1880 to 1894, except for a two-year interruption (1882–83). The only extant population figure for Buttercup dates from 1892, when the community had forty inhabitants.

BIBLIOGRAPHY: Clara Stearns Scarbrough, *Land of Good Water: A Williamson County History* (Georgetown, Texas: Williamson County Sun Publishers, 1973).

Mark Odintz

BUTTERFIELD, TEXAS. Butterfield was on the old Jim Hogg Highway south of Alto and north of Forest in southern Cherokee County. Around 1900 the area was the site of a Texas Prison System camp, one of several such satellite camps in the region established to provide charcoal for the Texas State Penitentiary foundry at Rusk (*see* RUSK PENITENTIARY). In 1906 a group of investors purchased a large tract of land to develop as a fruit orchard. The operation was known as Butterfield Farm or Butterfield, after a man named Butterfield who served as manager. In 1907 Butterfield hired a number of local farmers to clear the land and plant rows of peach trees with rows of cotton, corn, watermelons, and peas between them. Around 1910 a railroad spur was constructed to connect the orchard with the Texas and Southwestern Railroad three or four miles away, and a flag stop, known as Butterfield, was built. At the site residents built several packing sheds, one of which was said to have been 300 feet long and fifty or sixty feet wide. The orchard operated for six or seven years but was never commercially successful, and the investors eventually sold the operation to a dairy farmer. In 1944 Jeter I. Dean purchased the property and converted it into a cattle ranch. The manager's house constructed by Butterfield was still standing in the early 1990s, but the packing sheds and most of the orchards were no longer extant.

BIBLIOGRAPHY: *Cherokee County History* (Jacksonville, Texas: Cherokee County Historical Commission, 1986).

Christopher Long

BUTTERFIELD OVERLAND MAIL. The Butterfield (or Southern) Overland Mail, which operated from September 15, 1858, until March 1, 1861, was a semiweekly mail and passenger stage service from St. Louis, Missouri, and Memphis, Tennessee, across northern Texas to San Francisco, California. The routes from the two eastern termini united at Fort Smith, Arkansas. From St. Louis to San Francisco the distance was 2,795 miles, probably the longest route of any system using horse-drawn conveyances in the history of the United States. An act of Congress, effective on March 3, 1857, authorized a mail contract calling for the conveying of letter mail twice weekly, in both directions, in four-horse coaches or spring wagons suitable for carrying passengers; it was further specified that each trip should be completed within twenty-five days. Awarded to John Butterfield and associates, the contract provided for a compensation of $600,000 per year, in addition to receipts for passengers and express.

As of 1858 the route extended from San Francisco to Los Angeles, thence by Fort Yuma, California, and Tucson, Arizona, to Franklin, Texas (present El Paso). From Franklin it ran nearly due east to Hueco Tanks, thirty miles; a little north of east to the Pinery, fifty-six miles; twenty-four miles on to Delaware Springs; down Delaware Creek, almost to its junction with the Pecos River, and across the river to Pope's Camp, near the thirty-second parallel, forty miles; down the east side of the Pecos, to Emigrant Crossing, sixty-five miles; and fifty-five miles on to Horsehead Crossing.[qv] Thence the trail ran east-northeast to the headwaters of the Middle Concho River, seventy miles; slightly more northward through the vicinity of Carlsbad, Texas, to a camp or station, about thirty miles; to Grape Creek near the south line of present Coke County, twenty-two miles; to Fort Chadbourne in what is now Coke County. Thence the route ran more to the north across Valley Creek, twelve miles; to Mountain Pass, sixteen miles; passed the route of the Texas and Pacific Railway, a mile west of the site of present Tye, to Fort Phantom Hill, thirty miles; to Smith's station, twelve miles; to Clear Fork station, twenty-six miles; to Franz's station, thirteen miles; and to Fort Belknap, twenty-two miles. From Fort Belknap the line turned eastward to Murphy's station (a site near present Graham), sixteen miles; to Jacksboro, nineteen miles; to Earhart's station, sixteen miles; to Davidson's station, twenty-four miles; to Gainesville, seventeen miles; to Diamond's station (one mile west of the site of present Whitesboro), fifteen miles; to Sherman, fifteen miles; and across the Red River at Colbert's Ferry,[qv] eight miles below Preston. The route was changed slightly from time to time, the most important change being made late in 1858, when, in order to secure a better water supply, the stages between Franklin and the Pecos followed the El Paso–San Antonio road to Camp Stockton (now Fort Stockton) and thence to the Horsehead Crossing.

The mails went through almost without exception in the twenty-five days allowed. The postage rate of ten cents per half ounce resulted in receipts in 1860 of $119,766.77. Early in 1859 Sherman was made a distribution point, through which Texas settlements were given postal service. In addition to mail and express the Concord coaches had room for five or six passengers, and at times more were crowded in. The fare averaged $200 one-way. Passengers, with firearms ready to meet attacks by Indians, generally endured the ordeal of the trip without rest; for if a traveler laid over, he forfeited his seat, and he might be marooned for a month before he could secure another. Stage service on the southern route was terminated in March 1861, when an agreement was made to modify the contract and move the route northward out of Texas.

BIBLIOGRAPHY: Roscoe P. and Margaret B. Conkling, *The Butterfield Overland Mail, 1857–1869* (3 vols., Glendale, California: Clark, 1947). LeRoy R. Hafen, *Overland Mail, 1849–1869* (Cleveland: Clark, 1926). Waterman L. Ormsby, *The Butterfield Overland Mail* (San Marino, California: Huntington Library, 1942; rpt. 1955). Rupert N. Richardson, "Some Details of the Southern Overland Mail," *Southwestern Historical Quarterly* 29 (July 1925). J. W. Williams, "The Butterfield Overland Mail Road across Texas," *Southwestern Historical Quarterly* 61 (July 1957). J. W. Williams, The Marcy and Butterfield Trails across Texas (M.A. thesis, Hardin-Simmons University, 1938).

Rupert N. Richardson

BUTTERFLIES. Because Texas spans so many ecological regions, it has more butterfly species than any other state—at least 400. (The total lepidopteran species—butterflies, moths, and skippers—in Texas number more than 1,600.) This is more than half the butterfly species known from North America north of Mexico. The western limb of the state, bordering New Mexico at Guadalupe Mountains National Park,[qv] holds the southernmost island peaks of the Rocky Mountains, whose pine, juniper, and oak woodlands harbor butterflies typical of the Rockies. In stark contrast, the dense eastern pine forests host butterflies typical of the Gulf Coast through Louisiana, Mississippi, and eastward. At the southern tip of the state, near Brownsville, subtropical species find a home, while the arid west across the Rio Grande from Chihuahua provides dry mountain habitats for endemic desert butterflies. The resulting variety is staggering.

The state's geologic past has further enhanced the diversity of its butterfly fauna. Cold and warm cycles caused by the advance and retreat of continental glaciers have pushed distant species into the region. Many of these have survived, the northern forms occupying niches in cool, shady valleys, and the southern forms colonizing arid hills. In addition to resident butterflies, numerous species stray into the state from the subtropics of Mexico. Most of these cannot survive the cold winters of Central Texas and northward, but many establish temporary colonies for one to several years until freezes annihilate them. Autumn is the best time to look for these visitors.

Although the number of families of North American butterflies has not been settled, all are liberally represented in Texas. The larvae of two families (Hesperiidae and Satyridae) feed upon grasses, and most others eat a wide variety of herbs, shrubs, and trees. One carnivorous species (*Feniseca tarquinius*) feeds on wooly aphids, and two other species (*Calycopis isobeon* and *C. cecrops*) seem able to survive on ground litter and detritus. Most adult butterflies feed on nectar, though some avoid flowers and prefer tree sap. Others visit fermenting or decaying organic matter, including carrion and feces.

The Monarch, *Danaus plexippus,* with which most Texans are familiar, makes its annual migratory flight through Texas en route to its wintering grounds in Mexico. The northward flight in April and May is not as easily recognized as the southward flight in late summer and fall, when the large, soaring butterflies at times fill the air and gather on trees by hundreds or thousands to rest.

Other butterflies are less well known, but at least a few of the nearly twenty species of swallowtails that inhabit the state are familiar to gardeners. A patient nature enthusiast can learn to recognize dozens of other species, and with practice suburbanites in smaller cities such as Austin or San Antonio can find at least sixty species in the backyard.

Although a few of the state's butterflies are threatened by land developments that destroy fragile habitats, human activities have not generally harmed butterfly populations. In fact, because many species prefer open areas, clearing of space for highways, railroads, and recreation spaces and parklands has encouraged the spread of butterflies throughout the state. Only when suburbs become lawn-to-lawn and eliminate vacant lots do butterflies avoid them.

A few of the butterflies of Texas are commercial pests of minor import. The cabbage butterflies and mustard whites (the genera *Artogeia* and *Pontia*) feed on some domestic cabbage-family crops. The alfalfa butterflies (*Colias eurytheme* and relatives) feed on various clovers. And the orange dog, or giant swallowtail (*Heraclides cresphontes*), attacks citrus orchards. None of these is a major threat to crops unless unusual population explosions occur.

In the northern part of the state, where freezes are regular and hard, butterflies are predictably seasonal; they emerge from their pupae at about the same time each year. Farther south, however, butterflies are subject to wet and dry cycles as well as the photoperiod, and seasonal cyclicity is less pronounced. A species that flies in July of one year might not be on the wing at all in July of the following year. In addition, population density varies greatly from year to year, depending upon the same variables. The lepidopterist is hard-pressed to predict the flight of a given species and often is surprised by unexpected periods of scarcity or abundance.

bibliography: Christopher J. Durden, "The Butterfly Fauna of Barton Creek Canyon on the Balcones Fault Zone, Austin, Texas, and a Regional List," *Journal of the Lepidopterists' Society* 36 (1982). William H. Howe, *The Butterflies of North America* (Garden City, New York: Doubleday, 1975). Lee D. Miller and F. Martin Brown, *A Catalog-Checklist of the Butterflies of America North of Mexico* (n.p.: Lepidopterists' Society, 1981). *Samuel A. Johnson*

BUTTERNUT CREEK. Butternut Creek rises a quarter mile north of U.S. Highway 67 and seven miles northeast of Ballinger in east central Runnels County (at 31°46′ N, 99°51′ W) and runs south for nine miles before emptying into Mustang Creek a mile north of the Colorado River and seven miles southeast of Ballinger in southeast Runnels County (at 31°41′ N, 99°51′ W). The vegetation beside the creek comprises juniper, live oak, mesquite, and various grasses. The terrain exhibits steep slopes and benches.

BUTTON PRAIRIE, TEXAS. Button Prairie, seven miles southeast of Milano in eastern Milam County, was supposedly named for the buttonlike acorns produced by oak trees in the region. A church and a few scattered houses appeared on county highway maps of the area in 1941. There was no evidence of the community in 1988.

bibliography: Lelia M. Batte, *History of Milam County, Texas* (San Antonio: Naylor, 1956). *Vivian Elizabeth Smyrl*

BUZZARD MOUNTAIN (Burnet County). Buzzard Mountain is twenty miles northwest of Burnet in the northwestern corner of Burnet County (at 31°00′ N, 98°26′ W). It rises 1,456 feet above sea level, more than 150 feet higher than the surrounding countryside.

——— (Taylor County). Buzzard Mountain is four miles northwest of View in north central Taylor County (at 32°22′ N, 99°58′ W). With an elevation of 2,410 feet above sea level, its summit rises approximately 425 feet above nearby Farm Road 1235.

BUZZARD PEAK. Buzzard Peak is near the intersection of Farm roads 143 and 222 and two miles from the Knox county line in southwest King County (at 33°31′ N, 100°02′ W). Its elevation is 1,881 feet, 155 feet above the surrounding terrain.

BUZZARDWING CREEK. Buzzardwing Creek rises five miles southwest of Ringgold in extreme western Montague County (at 33°45′ N, 97°58′ W) and runs east for five miles to its mouth on Belknap Creek, five miles southeast of Ringgold (at 33°45′ N, 97°55′ W). It crosses flat to rolling terrain surfaced by clay and sandy loams that support water-tolerant hardwood, mesquite, scrub brush, cacti, and various grasses.

BYARS, NOAH TURNER (1808–1888). Noah T. Byars, pioneer Baptist preacher, was born in Spartanburg, South Carolina, on May 17, 1808. He moved to Georgia as a young man and subsequently, in 1835, to Texas, where he established a gunsmith and blacksmith shop at Washington-on-the-Brazos. He was also involved in a real estate business with Peter M. Mercer;[qv] the two were described as "merchants and partners" in the deed records of Washington County in 1835. On January 21, 1838, Byars married Sophia A. Lowden; they had three children.

In 1836 Sam Houston[qv] appointed Byars armorer and blacksmith of the Texas army. He also served as sergeant-at-arms to the Texas Senate from 1837 to 1841 and as armorer and blacksmith to the Indians, a position to which he was appointed by Mirabeau B. Lamar.[qv] Byars was associate judge of Travis County from 1839 to 1841 and was elected for another two-year term but declined to serve because of his ordination in 1841 to the Baptist ministry. When he moved to Burleson County to assume his first pastorate, he was appointed notary public for the county by the president of the Republic of Texas.[qv]

Byars had been one of eight charter members of the first Baptist church in Texas, which Z. N. Morrell[qv] established at Washington-on-the-Brazos. His ordination, on October 16, 1841, was attended by President Lamar and members of his cabinet. In 1848 Byars was appointed the first missionary of the Texas Baptist Convention. His mission field extended from the Brazos River to the Trinity and northwest to Palo Pinto and Young counties. It covered the territory of thirty present-day Texas counties. Byars was instrumental in founding five Baptist associations in Texas: the Trinity River Association in 1848, the West Fork (of the Trinity) Association in 1856, the Brazos River Association in 1858, the Pecan Valley Association in 1876, and the Hamilton County Association in 1877. He also founded more than sixty churches in Texas, including First Baptist, Waco, in 1851, and First Baptist, Brownwood, in 1876.

Though he had little formal education himself, he wanted the church to lead the way in providing education in Texas. Under his leadership, the Brazos River Association founded a school at Golconda (now Palo Pinto). He later founded a school known as Byars Institute in Houston. By 1843 the Texas Baptist Educational Society[qv] was functioning as a separate organization but in connection with the Brazos River Association; it included Byars on its first board of managers. The education society founded Baylor University in Waco and the University of Mary Hardin–Baylor in Belton while Byars served on the board of managers. A year after his death, the Pecan Valley Association established Howard Payne College (now Howard Payne University) in Brownwood.

In his old age Byars served as pastor of First Baptist, Brownwood, for fourteen months in 1881–82. His last full charge was at Clear Creek Baptist in Brown County in 1884. He officiated at the wedding of Katherine Anne Porter's[qv] parents. In 1884–85 he was appointed missionary to the Texas Baptist Convention without definite charge (probably as a means of giving him a livelihood rather than for actual services.) But Byars returned to the pulpit in the last months of his life. In April 1888 he petitioned the conference for permission to preach at least one sermon a month in the Coggin Academy Building across the street from his home in Brownwood. Permission was granted, and he preached there until his death on July 18, 1888. He was survived by his second wife, whom he had married in 1877, and his children from his first marriage. He is buried in Greenleaf Cemetery in Brownwood. In 1936 a special Byars Memorial Thanksgiving Service was held in honor of the Texas Centennial[qv] on the campus of Howard Payne College. A blue marble spire was erected there and later moved to Byars's grave.

BIBLIOGRAPHY: *Baptist Standard*, June 11, 1936. James Milton Carroll, *A History of Texas Baptists* (Dallas: Baptist Standard, 1923). Thomas Robert Havins, Noah T. Byars—A Study in Baptist Missionary Effort on the Frontier (Ph.D. dissertation, University of Texas, 1941).
Charlotte Laughlin

BYARS' INSTITUTE. Byars' Institute, located at Byars' Bluff near Cedar Bayou in Chambers County, was founded by Noah T. Byars,[qv] who led the Baptists of Tryon Baptist Association to provide funds for the opening of the school in 1867. The building, a two-story frame structure, furnished boarding facilities for thirty students. Byars was president of the board of trustees, and A. Goddard was principal. Separate classes for boys and girls were held, although all classes were conducted in the same building. Instruction included elementary and high school subjects. A daily chapel service with compulsory attendance furnished religious instruction. On Sunday, attendance at the services of the local church, of which Byars was pastor, was required. In addition to the principal, who taught all high school subjects, there were two teachers in the elementary department. Tuition was three dollars a month in the elementary school and five dollars in high school. Byars seems to have been the guiding spirit of the school. With his move from Texas to Mississippi in 1868, interest in the institution waned, and its activity ceased in the spring of 1870.

BIBLIOGRAPHY: Thomas Robert Havins, Noah T. Byars—A Study in Baptist Missionary Effort on the Frontier (Ph.D. dissertation, University of Texas, 1941). Carl Bassett Wilson, History of Baptist Educational Efforts in Texas, 1829–1900 (Ph.D. dissertation, University of Texas, 1934).
Thomas Robert Havins

BYBEE, CHARLES L. (1900–1972). Charles L. Bybee, banker and philanthropist, was born in Willis, Texas, on July 7, 1900, the son of Charles T. and Ianthe (Lewis) Bybee. The family moved in 1913 to Houston, where Bybee attended Heights High School and Rice University; he subsequently attended the University of Texas and specialized in engineering and business administration. As a young man Bybee worked as a researcher and clerk for his uncle, Judge John M. Lewis.[qv] He graduated from the American Institute of Banking and began work as a runner for Houston Bank and Trust in the summer of 1917. In 1921 he took a full-time position as a teller, from which he rose through every major post in the firm to become vice president in 1947. He was made president in 1958 and became board chairman in 1964. He was chairman of the Houston Clearing House Association and first chairman of the board of the Westmont National Bank, founded in 1964. Bybee served as vice president and treasurer of the Houston Symphony Society. He was a founder and president in 1953 of the Houston Heart Association, director of the Texas and American Heart associations, treasurer of National Jewish Hospital in Denver, and a trustee of Methodist Hospital of Houston.[qv] In addition, he worked with the United Fund, the Community Chest, Houston Baptist College, and the First Methodist Church. With his wife, Faith (Poorman), whom he married in 1924, Bybee restored Texas homes and buildings at Round Top, Warrenton, Washington-on-the-Brazos, and Frelsburg. He also owned land in Harris, Fort Bend, Galveston, Washington, and Fayette counties. The couple campaigned to preserve Houston's Old Market Square and was active in the Institute of International Education. Bybee and his wife had no children, but raised Faith's nephew, Joseph Newton Westerlage, Jr. Bybee retired in 1971 and died at his summer home at Round Top on April 7, 1972.

BIBLIOGRAPHY: Joseph L. Clark, *Texas Gulf Coast: Its History and Development* (4 vols., New York: Lewis Historical Publishing, 1955). Houston Metropolitan Research Center Files, Houston Public Library. Vertical Files, Barker Texas History Center, University of Texas at Austin.
Diana J. Kleiner

BYBEE, HALBERT PLEASANT (1888–1957). Halbert Pleasant Bybee, geologist and teacher, the son of William Lawson and Martha (Kessler) Bybee, was born on January 7, 1888, on a farm just outside of Rochester, Indiana. He attended Shellbark Grade School and Talma High School and received a B.S. from Rochester College in 1908. He was subsequently principal of Richland Center Township High School for a year before becoming a science instructor at Clinton College in Kentucky. He enrolled in Indiana University in 1911 and was awarded a Ph.D. in 1915. On September 1, 1914, he married Ruth Woolery. They had four children. Bybee became an instructor in geology at the University of Texas that year. In 1916 he was promoted to adjunct professor. The following year he began the university's first summer camp in geology. In 1925 his son, Henry, drowned. Bybee afterward took a job with Dixie Oil Company in West Texas. While in San Angelo he helped organize the West Texas Geological Society and served as president in 1927.

When the Board for Lease of University Lands was formed in June 1929, Bybee assumed the position of geologist in charge. In 1936 he returned to the faculty at the university and for the remainder of his career served in both positions. During World War II[qv] he taught Company D, Texas Defense Guard, at Camp Mabry. Known as "Doc" to his students, Bybee trained and influenced hundreds of geologists. In 1954 he helped establish the Geology Foundation, which administers the Hal P. Bybee Memorial Fund. Bybee belonged to the American Association of Petroleum Geologists, of which he was made a Life

Member in 1952 and an honorary member in 1956, and numerous other geological societies. He was active in the Boy Scouts[qv] and the Kiwanis Club and was a Baptist deacon for forty years. He died in Austin on March 30, 1957.

BIBLIOGRAPHY: L. T. Barrow, "Halbert Pleasant Bybee (1888–1957)," *Bulletin of the American Association of Petroleum Geologists* 41 (October 1957). Fred M. Bullard, "Memorial to Halbert Pleasant Bybee (1888–1957)," *Proceedings Volume of the Geological Society of America Annual Report for 1957*, May 1958. *Kris Ercums*

BYERS, CHESTER ALLEN ARTHUR (1892–1945). Chester (Chet) Byers, rodeo trick roping star, son of Jesse and Eliza J. (Gray) Byers, was born at Knoxville, Illinois, on January 18, 1892. He moved to Mulhall, Oklahoma, in 1895 and soon dreamed of becoming a cowboy. He learned roping and trick and fancy roping, sometimes instructed by the great Will Rogers. Byers's first job was with the Pawnee Bill Wild West Show in 1905. During the next decade he headlined the Miller Brothers' 101 Ranch and Lucky Baldwin Ranch shows, as they toured the United States, Canada, Mexico, South America, and England.

He also began entering contests for trick and fancy roping and calf and steer roping. By 1915 Byers was the world's champion trick and fancy roper and supervisor of the Wild West portion of the Hagenbeck-Wallace Circus. He won the world's championship again at the 1916 Sheepshead Bay Stampede in New York and decided to become a full-time competitor.

After years on the road he established his headquarters at Fort Worth, Texas, and subsequently remained closely identified with that city. He was the undefeated champion of trick and fancy roping at the Madison Square Garden rodeos through 1933, when the event was discontinued. He was also a winner at the Cheyenne Frontier Days and the Houston and San Antonio rodeos and was featured at Fort Worth Southwestern Exposition and Fat Stock Show every year through 1945.

When trick and fancy roping was changed from a contest to a contract act in the mid-1930s, Byers continued to compete in calf and steer roping and became one of the most popular entertainers on the rodeo circuit. His death on November 1, 1945, brought to his wife, Mary (Bosany), and two daughters expressions of sympathy from thousands of rodeo professionals and fans and was front-page news in Fort Worth.

Byers's book, *Roping: Trick and Fancy Rope Spinning* (1928; reprinted in 1966 as *Cowboy Roping and Rope Tricks*), was still the standard work on the subject when he died. He was then the best-known roper in the world, and along with Will Rogers and Vincente Oropeza, one of the greatest of all times. Rogers himself had said, "Chet knows more about roping than any man in the world." A warm and friendly man, Byers was fondly remembered in the rodeo profession and in 1969 was inducted into the Rodeo Hall of Fame at the National Cowboy Hall of Fame in Oklahoma City.

BIBLIOGRAPHY: Fort Worth *Star-Telegram*, November 1, 2, 1945. Willard H. Porter, *Who's Who in Rodeo* (Oklahoma City: Powder River, 1982). *Mary Lou LeCompte*

BYERS, TEXAS. Byers is at the intersection of State Highway 79 and Farm Road 171, two miles south of the conjunction of the Red and Wichita rivers, fourteen miles north of Henrietta, and twenty miles northeast of Wichita Falls in northern Clay County. It was founded by two brothers, Anthony Walter and George Washington Byers, who were partners in a general store in Sherman and acquired over 30,000 acres of land in Clay County. There are several versions of how they acquired the land. One is that Mr. Acers, a large landowner in the area, bought barbed wire[qv] on credit with his land as collateral, and when he was unable to pay off his debt the land was forfeited to the Byers brothers. The other story is that the Byerses traded their mercantile business in Sherman for the land in Clay County.

The real establishment of Byers occurred in 1904, when the Wichita Falls and Oklahoma Railway was completed from Wichita Falls to Byers. The brothers donated $15,000 of the $27,924 raised for the completion of the line. They subdivided their ranch, laid out town lots, and established the Tree Ranch. Because the railroad went three miles west of Benvanue, many of the residents moved their homes and businesses to Byers to have access to the railroad, which was completed through the community in June of 1904. Town lots went on sale on June 10. That year Byers received a post office with A. Harris, the owner of the first store in town, as postmaster. In 1905 Edgar P. Haney established the community's first newspaper, the Byers *Searchlight*, to promote the community, its school, and the "Searchlight Town Band."

By 1906 Byers was a sizable town. Its school had 115 pupils and two teachers, and the town had its first cotton gin. In 1914 the community had a population of 600, the First National Bank, a weekly newspaper named the Byers *Herald*, several cotton gins, cattle breeders and livestock dealers, and cotton buyers. In addition, a variety of stores included furniture dealers, jewelers, grocery and dry goods establishments, and a blacksmith. The population of Byers remained steady throughout the 1920s, but by the 1930s it began to drop. The town was incorporated by 1940. It had a population of 427 and thirty businesses shortly before World War II.[qv] In 1943 the Wichita Falls and Oklahoma Railway was abandoned. By the 1980s twelve businesses remained in Byers. In 1980 and 1990 the population was 510. Byers was one of the five school districts in Clay County; in 1990 its school had 136 students.

BIBLIOGRAPHY: Katherine Christian Douthitt, ed., *Romance and Dim Trails* (Dallas: Tardy, 1938). Kathleen E. and Clifton R. St. Clair, eds., *Little Towns of Texas* (Jacksonville, Texas: Jayroe Graphic Arts, 1982). William Charles Taylor, *A History of Clay County* (Austin: Jenkins, 1972). *Lisa C. Maxwell*

BYFIELD, TEXAS. Byfield, just off Farm Road 1971 sixteen miles southwest of Carthage in southwestern Panola County, was established after the Civil War.[qv] A school began operating there around 1900, and in 1906 it had an enrollment of sixty-two. In the mid-1930s the community had a school, a church, and a number of houses. After World War II[qv] the school was consolidated with the Carthage schools, and by the mid-1960s only a church, a cemetery, and a few scattered houses remained in the area. In the early 1990s Byfield was a dispersed rural community.

BIBLIOGRAPHY: Leila B. LaGrone, ed., *History of Panola County* (Carthage, Texas: Panola County Historical Commission, 1979). *Christopher Long*

BYNUM, TEXAS. Bynum is thirty miles north of Waco and eight miles southeast of Hillsboro on State Highway 171 in east central Hill County. The town was named for a pioneer settler. At the site was an ancient Indian burial ground. In 1882 Judge J. P. Connell built a small establishment with a "stock of goods" and opened a post office that was named Hanover and operated until 1884. Ranches and, to the north, farms surrounded the establishment. Due to a lack of business the store closed by 1884. Henry M. Mucklevane opened a general store about 1890, and a post office called Bynum began operation in 1886 in the same vicinity as the original store. In 1896 the town had a population of 150, a district school, Baptist and Christian churches, a music teacher, a blacksmith, a grocer, the Bynum String Band, a barber, a druggist, a general store, and two doctors.

The town moved a half mile to its present location when the Texas and Brazos Valley Railroad arrived in 1904. The community purchased the farm of W. W. Cabell for its new townsite. In March, town lots were sold. J. C. Barnard's grocery, Dr. Saylor's drugstore, and the privately owned Bank of Bynum were housed in brick buildings. The population was 163. The Baptist, Methodist, and Christian churches were moved from the old townsite. In 1905 the Bynum Independent School District was organized, and residents voted on a bond for the construction of a two-story brick school building for $5,000. Professor T. W. Swofford was hired as the teacher and assisted by older students.

A fire destroyed most of the business district in 1925, but it was rebuilt the same year. By 1926 Bynum had a population of 350, which it maintained until 1964. A tornado destroyed much of the downtown area in 1930. Nevertheless, the town supported twenty businesses in 1931, though half of them closed the following year. The Great Depression and the boll weevil[qqv] plague were mainly responsible for the shrinkage. People along the T&BV railroad called it the "Boll Weevil" route. The railroad was sold to the Burlington–Rock Island in 1930, and in an effort to reduce its losses the B–RI closed the track between Hillsboro and Hubbard in 1935. State Highway 171 connecting Hillsboro and Mexia was built at that time.

Bynum did not recover until 1949, when the number of businesses reached eighteen and the Gilmer-Aikin Laws[qv] forced the consolidation of smaller school districts. Schools in Brandon, Prairie Valley, Davis, Irene, Malone, Watson, and Grove Creek were added to the Bynum system. By 1956 the number of businesses began to decline again. Within thirty years no businesses were reported, and the bank had been moved to Hillsboro. The population of Bynum was 130 in 1972. In 1980 it was 112. In 1988 the town reported a population of 298, and in 1990, 192.

BIBLIOGRAPHY: Ellis Bailey, *A History of Hill County, Texas, 1838–1965* (Waco: Texian Press, 1966). Hill County Historical Commission, *A History of Hill County, Texas, 1853–1980* (Waco: Texian, 1980). Hillsboro *Mirror*, May 26, 1909, June 18, 1930. *Kenneth E. Austin*

BYRD, DAVID HAROLD (1900–1986). D. Harold (Dry Hole) Byrd, oilman, was born in Detroit, Texas, on April 24, 1900, the youngest of five sons and three daughters of Edward and Mary (Easley) Byrd. He grew up in Texas and Oklahoma. His first job in oil was as a roughneck in the Burkburnett oilfield.[qv] In 1917 he went to Trinity University, and from 1919 to 1921 he studied geology at the University of Texas. During the summers he worked on a rig in Santa Anna, where his penchant for wrestling got him into a match with a carnival bear. He lost.

After college Byrd worked for A. E. Humphreys as a geological scout. In 1924 he worked for the Old Dominion Oil Company of San Antonio. In 1925 he decided to become independent and moved to Brownwood, where he worked as a geological consultant and contracted for drilling. During this time he acquired his nickname by drilling fifty-six dry holes. Then, on May 5, 1928, he hit two good wells at once: the Byrd-Daniels produced 1,000 barrels a day, which sold for three dollars a barrel; and one of his wells opened up the Baker gas field in Brown County.

During the East Texas oil boom, Byrd rented office space in the Gregg Hotel in Longview and secretly bought out the Gregg Abstract Company. He then hired seventy-two typists from Dallas and assigned each of them to a volume of the county abstracts. With his control of lease information thus secured, and with an office set up in the courthouse yard, Byrd could force anyone who wanted to verify a lease to consult him; he could also get service to anyone he was dealing with by the end of the day or pay cash for any lease that he wanted to acquire. He comments in his autobiography, "At one time I owned 34,000 acres, but . . . ended up owning 15,000 in partnership with Gulf, Humble, and Atlantic Oil Companies, with whom I drilled about 5,000 wells. . . . Needless to say I became an overnight millionaire."

In 1931 Byrd and Jack Frost founded Byrd-Frost, Incorporated, to operate 492 East Texas wells that were soon producing 4,000 barrels of oil a day. In 1944 Byrd founded Byrd Oil Corporation and B-H Drilling Corporation. Byrd Oil was later bought by Mobil. In 1952 the entrepreneur began to phase out Byrd-Frost and organized the Three States Natural Gas Company, which was purchased by Delhi-Taylor Oil Corporation in 1961. Byrd also invested in Temco Aircraft and, in 1961, helped organize Ling-Temco-Vought, a conglomerate that reflected his continued interest in aviation.

Byrd was a lifelong advocate of aeronautics. He had invested in his cousin Adm. Richard E. Byrd's exploration of the poles, and Admiral Byrd had named a mountain range in Antarctica for him. In 1938 Byrd was appointed by Governor James Allred[qv] to the Texas Civil Aeronautics Commission. In September 1941 Byrd and Gill Robb Wilson formed the Civil Air Patrol. During World War II[qv] Byrd commanded an antisubmarine base for the Civil Air Patrol at Beaumont. In 1968 he received the Alpha Eta Rho annual award for the man outside the aviation education profession to contribute most to aviation. In 1963, in resistance to the activity of the Teamsters' Union among farm workers in Texas, Byrd moved his frozen food business from Crystal City to La Pryor. He regarded the teamsters as "a terrible cancer."

On June 8, 1935, he married Martha Caruth of Dallas. They had two sons. Mrs. Byrd died in 1972, and on February 14, 1974, Byrd married Mavis Barnett Heath, the widow of William W. Heath.[qv] Byrd made two African safaris and was known for his trophy room. He was awarded the University of Texas Ex-Students' Association Distinguished Alumnus award in 1966. He donated the drum Big Bertha to the UT Longhorn Band and gave many scholarships to university students. Byrd was a deacon in the First Presbyterian Church of Dallas, where he contributed the Byrd Fellowship Hall. He died on September 14, 1986, in Dallas.

BIBLIOGRAPHY: David Harold Byrd, *I'm an Endangered Species* (Houston: Pacesetter, 1978). James Anthony Clark and Michael T. Halbouty, *The Last Boom* (New York: Random House, 1972). Dallas *Morning News*, February 21, 1963. Dallas *News*, October 10, 1968.

Jerrell Dean Palmer

BYRD, MICAJAH (?–?). Micajah Byrd, early colonist, was in Texas by January 31, 1824, when he served on a jury to try a theft case. As one of Stephen F. Austin's[qv] Old Three Hundred[qv] colonists, he received title to a sitio[qv] now in Washington County. The census of 1826 classified him as a farmer and stock raiser, aged between twenty-five and forty. He had a wife, Hannah, and one daughter. Byrd was a judge in the alcalde[qv] election in December 1826 and in January 1827 was appointed to a committee to wait upon the political chief to register the protest of Austin's colony against the activities of the Fredonian Rebellion.[qv]

BIBLIOGRAPHY: Eugene C. Barker, ed., *The Austin Papers* (3 vols., Washington: GPO, 1924–28). Lester G. Bugbee, "The Old Three Hundred: A List of Settlers in Austin's First Colony," *Quarterly of the Texas State Historical Association* 1 (October 1897). J. H. Kuykendall, "Reminiscences of Early Texans," *Quarterly of the Texas State Historical Association* 6–7 (January, April, July 1903).

BYRD, ROBERT JAMES, SR. (1934–1990). Robert James Byrd, Sr., black rhythm and blues singer and band leader, was born in Fort Worth in 1934. In 1947 he moved to Los Angeles and began his performing career under the stage name Bobby Day at Johnny Otis's Barrelhouse Club. By 1950 he had formed the group the Hollywood Flames, with whom he made a hit recording, "Buzz Buzz Buzz" (1957). In 1957 Day formed a second musical group, the Satellites, which backed him on his hit "Little Bitty Pretty One," which Day wrote. He was also the first to perform Jimmie Thomas's "Rockin' Robin" (1958), the song by which most pop music lovers recognize

Day. As Bobby Day, Byrd was also the original Bob of the rhythm and blues duo Bob and Earl, when he performed with Earl Nelson from 1957 to 1959. Day and Nelson met in 1957, when the latter joined Day's group, the Hollywood Flames. As the Flames' lead singer, Nelson was spotlighted on Day's "Buzz Buzz Buzz." Byrd's unique baritone voice kept him in demand with a variety of recording labels, including Rendezvous, RCA, and Sureshot. For Jama records he sang lead with the Day Birds. His "doo-wop" style was revived in the works of artists of the 1960s and 1970s. The Jackson 5 and the Dave Clark Five re-recorded, respectively, "Rockin' Robin" and "Over and Over." Byrd established Byrdland Attractions and Quiline Publishing, songwriting enterprises. He died on July 27, 1990, in Los Angeles and was survived by his wife, Jackie, and four children.

BIBLIOGRAPHY: Colin Larkin, ed., *The Guinness Encyclopedia of Popular Music* (Chester, Connecticut: New England Publishing Associates, 1992). Norm N. Nite, *Rock On: The Illustrated Encyclopedia of Rock n' Roll* (New York: Crowell, 1974–). *Peggy Hardman*

BYRD, WILLIAM (1828–1898). William Byrd, lawyer, soldier, and politician, was born at Cottage Farm, Clarke County, Virginia, on September 9, 1828, the son of Richard Evelyn and Anne (Harrison) Byrd. He graduated from Virginia Military Institute on July 4, 1849, and afterward took a degree in law at the University of Virginia. By March 1853 he was practicing law in the Travis County, Texas, community of Webberville, and by 1854 was popular enough to be chosen orator at the annual Fourth of July barbecue. The Austin *Texas State Gazette* (*see* AUSTIN *STATE GAZETTE*) referred to him as "a young lawyer spoken of highly by his friends," and declared his address "to have been quite eloquent and credible to that young gentleman." A clipping from an unidentified newspaper in Byrd's scrapbook, now preserved at the Barker Texas History Center[qv] at the University of Texas at Austin, quotes the 1854 speech in full. Its spread-eagle oratory praises the creed of the Young America movement and attacks the North for "tramping on the constitution" and for "substituting for the wisdom and virtue of their patriotic fathers, the fatuity and villainy of unprincipled fanatics deliberately [inaugurating] a series of legislative acts against slavery."

In August 1854 Byrd moved to Austin, where he formed a partnership with T. Scott Anderson.[qv] He was elected city treasurer and in 1857 ran unsuccessfully for the state legislature. He was a delegate to the Travis County convention that in June 1859 endorsed the nominations of the state convention for governor and lieutenant governor. In Austin on September 12, 1859, Byrd married Jennie Rivers of Colorado, Texas, the daughter of Robert Jones Rivers.[qv] They had nine children. When William Marshall[qv] returned to Mississippi in November 1860 to be with his ailing wife, Byrd became editor of the *Texas State Gazette* and in its pages in December called for a secession[qv] convention in Texas.

He was appointed adjutant general by Governor Edward Clark[qv] on May 11, 1861, and was responsible for putting the Confederate state of Texas on a war footing. In a series of general orders he provided for the recruiting of 11,000 volunteers into infantry companies. As "a well organized citizen soldiery is the strength of a free country," Byrd oversaw the formation of the new companies into battalions, regiments, and brigades at eleven new camps of instruction in various parts of the state. These were commanded by Augustus Buchel, Thomas Green, Hugh McLeod, Joseph L. Hogg, James H. Rogers, W. C. Young, W. H. Parsons, C. C. Herbert,[qqv] M. F. Locke, R. M. Powell, and C. L. Cleveland. Each camp was to accommodate 1,000 recruits for a period of forty days, beginning on July 2, and was to be supplied with food by voluntary subscription from local citizens. This requisition Byrd reckoned at 45,000 pounds of flour, 37,000 pounds of beef, 7,500 pounds of bacon, 2,000 pounds of coffee, 2,400 pounds of sugar, 6 sacks of salt, and 1,600 pounds of soap per camp. "Our citizens will not be less cheerful in contributing to prepare our troops, to uphold our honor and liberties, than our Northern enemies in lavishing their gold, to hire mercenaries to enslave us," he opined.

Byrd served for a time as state ordnance officer during the fall of 1861 before being elected on November 26, 1861, as lieutenant colonel of Col. Edward Clark's[qv] Fourteenth Texas Infantry, a regiment that saw action in the Red River campaign[qv] as a component of Walker's Texas Division.[qv] Byrd, however, was detached from the regiment to command Fort DeRussy on the Red River, some three miles above Marksville, Louisiana. Capt. E. P. Petty described the fort as "a strong work and there are some fine guns there but it is incomplete. . . . When completed no gunboat will be able to pass and they can only be taken by land attack." The fort was garrisoned by some 400 soldiers detached from the regiments of Walker's division. On March 14, 1864, it was surrounded by Union troops and taken by bombardment and assault. Byrd was at first reported killed but was in fact taken prisoner. He was exchanged at Red River Landing, Louisiana, on July 22, 1864, returned to his regiment, and was stationed at Hempstead at the war's end. Thereafter he returned to Winchester, Virginia, to practice law. He died in May 1898. William Byrd was the grandfather of aviator and explorer Richard Byrd, Virginia governor Harry Byrd, and World War I[qv] hero Tom Byrd.

BIBLIOGRAPHY: Norman D. Brown, ed., *Journey to Pleasant Hill: The Civil War Letters of Captain Elijah P. Petty* (San Antonio: University of Texas Institute of Texan Cultures, 1982). Clarksville *Northern Standard*, June 15, 29, 1861. Marilyn M. Sibley, *Lone Stars and State Gazettes: Texas Newspapers before the Civil War* (College Station: Texas A&M University Press, 1983). Marcus J. Wright, comp., and Harold B. Simpson, ed., *Texas in the War, 1861–1865* (Hillsboro, Texas: Hill Junior College Press, 1965). *Thomas W. Cutrer*

BYRD, TEXAS (Ellis County). Byrd was on Farm Road 985 near Clear Creek sixteen miles southeast of Waxahachie and eight miles southwest of Ennis in Ellis County. The original settlers to the Byrd area included H. L. Parker, Dan Faulk, Rube Warren, William I. Champ, and the Gensch family. The settlement, originally called Byron, was on a stage route from Dallas to the Gulf Coast. Rube Warren built a store, which became a replacement point for horses and an overnight stop for travelers. Byron had a post office from 1894 to 1905 in one of several general stores and a blacksmith shop. When the post office was removed from Byron the citizens decided to rename the community Byrd in honor of Charlie Byrd, who donated land for the community's first school. The school was used for social activities and as a union church. In 1897 plans were drafted for an open-sided meetinghouse on a knoll called the Arbor. Later, Byrd had several physicians, one of whom owned a grocery and drug store. The Woodmen of the World Hall was one of the community's most prominent buildings, and all the elections were held in it. The Trinity and Brazos Valley Railway was built through the community in 1907. By 1933 Byrd had an estimated population of fifty and three businesses. The same figures were reported until the 1960s. The school closed in 1957, and the students began attending school in Ennis or other nearby communities. The last grocery store closed in 1968. From 1970 to 1990 the population was estimated at fifteen. *Lisa C. Maxwell*

BYRD, TEXAS (Tom Green County). Byrd was northeast of the site of present Veribest near Farm Road 380 in eastern Tom Green County. George Jefferson Byrd, the founder of Veribest, who came to Tom Green County in 1877, donated the land for the school that was named for him. The Byrd school was consolidated with the Veribest school to form the Veribest-Byrd school in Veribest. In the 1980s a large, well-built storm cellar remained at the Byrd site.

BIBLIOGRAPHY: *Cattleman*, March 1951. *Betty Jane Smith*

BYRDS, TEXAS. Byrds is on a country road at the northern edge of Lake Brownwood in north central Brown County. The site was settled in 1870 and named for Martin H. Byrd, who by 1874 had opened a store there and who also served as postmaster when the community received a post office, called Byrd's Store, in 1877. By 1884 Byrd's Store, which shipped cattle, cotton, and pecans, had a population of seventy-five, a district school, Methodist and Baptist churches, a steam cotton gin, and steam grist and saw mills. By 1896 the post office name had been changed to Byrd's, and the population had fallen to fourteen. In 1914 Byrd's reported only one business, a general store. In 1925 the population was sixty-four. Sometime during the 1930s the Byrd's school was consolidated with the Williams school district, and by 1949 the population had fallen to twenty people, who supported one business. By 1957, when population was still reported at twenty, the post office had closed. *Rachel Jenkins*

BYRDTOWN, TEXAS. Byrdtown is at the head of Brushy Creek, eight miles east of Paris and two miles northeast of Pattonville in eastern Lamar County. The area was inhabited by 1896, when Byrdtown School reported sixty-five students and one teacher. In 1936 the community had a school, a church, and a cluster of dwellings. By 1957 the school had been consolidated into the Blossom Independent School District. Maps for 1964 showed a few scattered dwellings at the site, which still appeared on maps in 1983.

BIBLIOGRAPHY: Thomas S. Justiss, An Administrative Survey of the Schools of Lamar County with a Plan for Their Reorganization (M.A. thesis, University of Texas, 1937). *Vista K. McCroskey*

BYRNE, CHRISTOPHER EDWARD (1867–1950). Christopher Edward Byrne, bishop of the Catholic Diocese of Galveston, was born on April 21, 1867, in Byrnesville, Missouri, the son of Patrick and Rose (Byrne) Byrne. After attending the village school where his father taught, he earned an A.B. degree at the age of nineteen from St. Mary's College, Kansas. After completing his studies at St. Mary's Seminary, Baltimore, on September 23, 1891, he was ordained to the priesthood at St. John's Church in St. Louis. He spent about twenty-eight years in parish work in St. Louis, Columbia, and Edina, Missouri, and built churches and schools in each place. For many years he also did editorial work on the leading church publication in Missouri, *Church Progress.*

On November 27, 1918, he succeeded Bishop Nicholas A. Gallagher[qv] as fourth bishop of Galveston. During his tenure he ordained about 130 priests and received several hundred people into religious communities. In 1922 he sponsored a successful celebration of the diamond jubilee of the Galveston cathedral and diocese (*see* GALVESTON-HOUSTON, CATHOLIC DIOCESE OF). Through his encouragement the church took a lead in planning the 1936 Texas Centennial[qv] program, beginning with the Field Mass at San Jacinto Battleground. Byrne also endorsed and supported the collecting and preserving of documents relative to the church's history by the Knights of Columbus,[qv] an effort that ultimately resulted in the publication of the seven-volume *Our Catholic Heritage in Texas, 1519–1936* by Carlos E. Castañeda,[qv] and the establishment of the Catholic Archives of Texas.[qv] During his administration the Catholic population of the Diocese of Galveston grew from 70,000 to 200,000. The number of schools increased from fifty-one in 1918 to more than 100 in 1950. Bishop Byrne was an avid reader and an eloquent orator and often spoke at religious and civic ceremonies. He died on April 1, 1950, and is buried in Calvary Cemetery, Galveston.

BIBLIOGRAPHY: Catholic Archives of Texas, Files, Austin. Carlos E. Castañeda, *Our Catholic Heritage in Texas* (7 vols., Austin: Von Boeckmann–Jones, 1936–58; rpt., New York: Arno, 1976).
Sister M. Claude Lane, O.P.

BYRNE, JAMES J. (?–1880). James J. Byrne, United States army officer, was born in Ireland and moved to New York at an early age. On July 24, 1862, he was commissioned a first lieutenant and appointed adjutant of the 163d New York Infantry. He left the regiment on December 11, 1862, but on February 24, 1864, was appointed colonel of the Eighteenth New York Cavalry. As a member of Maj. Gen. Nathaniel P. Banks's[qv] Army of the Gulf, he saw extensive action in Louisiana during the Red River campaign[qv] of 1864. Byrne was brevetted to brigadier general for gallantry at the battles of Pleasant Hill[qv] and Campti and to major general for his conduct at the battles of Moore's Plantation (May 5–6, 1864) and Yellow Bayou (May 18, 1864), both brevets being issued on March 13, 1865. According to a report in the Fort Worth *Democrat* (*see* FORT WORTH *STAR-TELEGRAM*), he was the youngest general in the United States Army. He was mustered out of volunteer service on May 13, 1866.

President Andrew Johnson then appointed him United States marshal for the Northern District of Texas, with headquarters in Fort Worth. Byrne was mentioned as a possible conservative candidate for Congress from the Galveston district and was commended by the Dallas *Herald*[qv] for his defense of James W. Throckmorton[qv] in connection with a financial scandal. Although Byrne was popular with the citizens of the district, President Ulysses S. Grant replaced him in office, and the former marshal turned to surveying in the Fort Worth area and was retained as chief engineer of the Texas and Pacific Railway. Early in July 1880 he left Fort Worth for El Paso with a party of fifteen men, guided by the notorious Pat Doolan, to survey railroad lands in the Guadalupe Mountains. On August 2 he was at Ysleta, where he learned that Apache chief Victorio[qv] had once again crossed into the Big Bend region from Mexico and was attacking such targets of opportunity as presented themselves. Perhaps with a sense of foreboding, he penned a letter to his wife, Lilly (Loving), and his last will and testament—"my last goodbye to all I love upon this earth"—at the Texas and Pacific station and, bound by "either honor or self respect," pushed on toward the Guadalupe Mountains. On August 10 Byrne left Fort Quitman for the Pecos on a stagecoach driven by seventeen-year-old Charles D. West. The coach was attacked by Victorio's band about nine miles east of Fort Quitman, and although West managed to turn it around and start for the shelter of the fort, two of the Indians overtook the coach and fired into it, wounding Byrne first in the hip and then in the small of the back. According to newspaper report, Byrne was unarmed, and West's Winchester rifle had only two cartridges. No doctor was nearer than El Paso. Byrne died of gangrene on August 14, 1880. "I never saw a man die braver," said West.

Byrne's estate amounted to an estimated $25,000. His one child died as an infant, and Byrne requested that his own remains, "if they be found," be buried by its side. He was first buried at Fort Quitman but was later removed to Fort Worth, where he was reinterred on November 21. According to the Fort Worth *Democrat* Byrne was "a man of indomitable energy and courage, always ready to discharge any duty fully and freely which came upon him." His final advice to his wife was that she leave Texas "and seek some other home" where she might "find the peace and rest denied you here." A historical marker in Hudspeth County marks the site of Victorio's attack.

BIBLIOGRAPHY: Dallas *Herald*, July 4, 1868, September 6, 1873. Fort Worth *Democrat*, July 11, August 17, November 21, 1880. Miles Hart, "I Never Saw a Man Die Braver," *Panhandle-Plains Historical Review* 43 (1970). Francis B. Heitman, *Historical Register and Dictionary of the United States Army* (2 vols., Washington: GPO, 1903; rpt., Urbana: University of Illinois Press, 1965). Marker Files, Texas Historical Commission, Austin. Vertical Files, Barker Texas History Center, University of Texas at Austin. *Thomas W. Cutrer*

BYRNE, JAMES W. (ca. 1787–1862). James W. Byrne, early Refugio County settler and legislator, was born in County Warwick, Ireland, about 1787. He traveled to Texas from the United States in 1835 or early 1836 and was a private in Ira J. Westover's[qv] company in the Texas army in March 1836. In 1838 Byrne acquired a tract of land on Lookout Peninsula and, in association with George Robert Hall and George Armstrong, founded the town of Lamar. Byrne built wharves and warehouses and established a salt works. He was county clerk of Refugio County from 1839 to 1841. On February 3, 1840, he was appointed commissioner to investigate the Refugio land office. He represented the Refugio district in the Senate of the Fifth, Sixth, and Seventh Congresses of the republic. Before the Civil War[qv] he induced Samuel and James B. Colt, Randolph B. Marcy,[qv] and others to establish a munition works near Lamar, but the war prevented completion of their project. With Pryor Lea[qv] he planned a railroad corporation, hoping to make Lamar a railroad terminus, but the war destroyed those plans also. During the war Byrne served in Edward P. Upton's Lamar Home Guards and was member of a committee to attend to the wants of soldiers' families. A devout Catholic, Byrne gave the funds for the construction of Stella Maris Church at Lamar in 1854. His wife, Harriet (Odin), with whom he had a son, died at Lamar in 1858. Byrne died there on September 10, 1862.

BIBLIOGRAPHY: Texas House of Representatives, *Biographical Directory of the Texan Conventions and Congresses, 1832–1845* (Austin: Book Exchange, 1941).

Hobart Huson

BYROM, JOHN SMITH DAVENPORT (1798–1837). John Byrom, early settler, son of Henry and Catherine Smith (Davenport) Byrom, was born in Hancock, Georgia, on September 24, 1798. In 1806 he moved with his uncle and guardian, John Byrom, to Jasper County, Georgia. There on March 17, 1818, he married Nancy Fitzpatrick; they had three children. Byrom later moved to Heard County, Georgia, and later still to Florida. After his divorce from his first wife, he married Mary Anne Knott; they had a son and a daughter. In 1830 Byrom came to Texas and settled in what is now Brazoria County. He participated in the battle of Velasco[qv] on June 26, 1832. In 1835 he represented Brazoria at the Consultation,[qv] and the General Council[qv] appointed him one of three commissioners to organize the militia in the Municipality of Brazoria. Byrom was one of the four representatives from the municipality to the Convention of 1836[qv] at Washington-on-the-Brazos and there signed the Texas Declaration of Independence.[qv] He died on July 10, 1837.

BIBLIOGRAPHY: Sam Houston Dixon, *Men Who Made Texas Free* (Houston: Texas Historical Publishing, 1924). Louis Wiltz Kemp, *The Signers of the Texas Declaration of Independence* (Salado, Texas: Anson Jones, 1944; rpt. 1959). Worth Stickley Ray, *Austin Colony Pioneers* (Austin: Jenkins, 1949; 2d ed., Austin: Pemberton, 1970). Vertical Files, Barker Texas History Center, University of Texas at Austin.

L. W. Kemp

BYSPOT, TEXAS. Byspot was eighteen miles southeast of Coldspring in southwestern San Jacinto County. The post office, established in 1899, was called Teddy. About 1903, however, J. O. H. Bennett changed the community's name to Byspot, a name derived from spelling his wife Topsy's name backwards and adding a *B*. Bennett also owned and operated a tram railroad at Byspot, an indication that the area was once the site of logging operations. The railroad, which extended to Conroe, was taken over by the Delta Land and Timber Company in 1926. The post office had been discontinued in 1921, and the tram road was abandoned in 1931. The community did not appear on 1985 county highway maps or on United States Geological Survey place name lists.

BIBLIOGRAPHY: Ruth Hansbro, History of San Jacinto County (M.A. thesis, Sam Houston State Teachers College, 1940).

Robert Wooster

BYWATERS, WILLIAMSON GERALD (1906–1989). Jerry Bywaters, artist, son of Porter Ashburn and Hattie (Williamson) Bywaters, was born at Paris, Texas, on May 21, 1906. His emergence on the Dallas art scene began after he graduated from Southern Methodist University in 1926 with a degree in comparative literature. Afterward he traveled for two years in France, Spain, Mexico, and New England and studied at the New York Art Students League. When he returned to Dallas, Bywaters found that his contemporaries had similar interests in expressing their native region in art. He became a central figure and spokesman for a group of young artists including Alexandre Hogue, Otis M. Dozier, William L. Lester,[qqv] Everett Spruce, and others who found inspiration in the Texas landscape.

He was recognized as an artist of national importance in 1933 when *Art Digest* announced that he had "arrived." Bywaters produced a significant body of landscape, still-life and portrait paintings, as well as lithographic prints and public murals. Stylistically and aesthetically, his work paralleled the national movement known as the American Scene. He produced most of his important paintings and murals between 1937 and 1942. His paintings in museum collections include *Self-Portrait* (1935), *Sharecropper* (1937), and *On the Ranch* (1941) at the Dallas Museum of Art;[qv] *Where the Mountain Meets the Plains*, at Southern Methodist University; and *Oil Field Girls* (1940), at the Archer M. Huntington Art Gallery, University of Texas at Austin. Other important paintings include *Texas Subdivision* (1938), *Century Plant, Big Bend* (1939), *Autumn Still Life* (1942), and *Houses in West Texas Big Bend* (1942). His original lithographs include *Gargantua* (1935), which won a prize in the 1935 Allied Arts Exhibition; *Ranch Hand and Pony* (1938), which was exhibited at the 1938 Venice Biennial Exposition; *Texas Courthouse* (1938), purchased by the Dallas Museum of Fine Arts in 1938; and *False Fronts, Colorado* (1939), which received a prize from the Dallas Print Society in 1941. Bywaters was a founding member of Lone Star Printmakers, a group of artists in Texas who produced and published editions of original prints and circulated touring exhibitions of prints from 1938 to 1941.

He and other Dallas artists benefitted from the art programs of the New Deal. During the 1930s and early 1940s, Bywaters successfully competed in federally sponsored mural competitions and completed six projects in Texas, including a series of panels in collaboration with Alexandre Hogue at the Old City Hall in Dallas; a series of panels at the Paris Public Library; one mural each in the post offices of Trinity, Quanah, and Farmersville; and three murals in the Parcel Post Building of Houston. As art critic for the Dallas *Morning News* from 1933 to 1939 Bywaters wrote hundreds of articles on the art and artists of Texas. He served from 1943 to 1964 as director of the Dallas Museum of Fine Arts while teaching art and art history at Southern Methodist University. His university duties included chairmanship of the division of fine arts from 1965 to 1967 and directorship of the Pollock Galleries at the Owens Fine Arts Center. During his twenty-year tenure as director of the Dallas Museum of Fine Arts, Bywaters recognized the educational possibilities of the art museum and produced such ambitious and excellent exhibitions as Religious Art of the Western World (1958) and The Arts of Man (1962). In the mid-1950s he and the museum's board of trustees faced accusations that the museum was exhibiting works by "Reds" or communist artists. City support for the museum was threatened by the accusers, but Bywaters and the trustees of the Dallas Art Association clung to the standard of freedom of expression and professionalism.

Bywaters wrote and produced catalogues for art exhibitions, published an art magazine, and edited books on art. His long association with the *Southwest Review*[qv] included writing articles on the development of regional art, as well as serving as art editor and illustrating articles by other authors. After retirement from Southern Methodist University, he served as regional director of the Texas Project of the Archives of American Art, Smithsonian Institution, and he continued to curate exhibitions including The American Woman as Artist, 1820–1965, and Texas Painting and Sculpture: Twentieth Century for the Pollock Galleries and Seventy-five Years of Art in Dallas for the Dallas Museum of Fine Arts. In 1981, Bywaters presented Southern Methodist University a gift of his papers on the art and artists of the region to form the Jerry Bywaters Collection on Art of the Southwest. In 1972 he was elected a life member of the Dallas Art Association; in 1978 he received the Distinguished Alumni Award from Southern Methodist University; in 1980 the Texas Arts Alliance[qv] recognized him for distinguished service to the arts in the state; in 1987 Southern Methodist University acknowledged his distinctive career with an honorary doctorate. Until his death on March 7, 1989, Bywaters lived in Dallas with his wife of fifty-eight years, Mary McLarry Bywaters.

BIBLIOGRAPHY: Francine Carraro, *Jerry Bywaters: A Life in Art* (Austin: University of Texas Press, 1994). *Francine Carraro*

CJ MOUNTAIN. CJ Mountain, nine miles east of Breckenridge in east central Stephens County (at 32°47′ N, 98°45′ W), has an elevation of 1,390 feet above sea level. It was named for the CJ Ranch. The surrounding rolling hills are surfaced by clay and sandy loams that support scrub brush, mesquite, and grasses.

CAAI INDIANS. The Caai Indians are known from a single 1691 Spanish missionary report. The name occurs on a short list of groups that lived an unspecified distance southwest of the Hasinais. The Caais may be the same as the Caisquetebanas, reported in 1690 as living north of Matagorda Bay and between the Guadalupe and Colorado rivers and also the Caiasbans, named in documents (1687) of the La Salle expedition[qv] as enemies of the Kadohadachos on the Red River. These identifications cannot be demonstrated. If the names all refer to the same group of Indians, a considerable north–south range is indicated. The affiliations of these groups remain unknown.

BIBLIOGRAPHY: Herbert Eugene Bolton, ed., *Spanish Exploration in the Southwest, 1542–1706* (New York: Scribner, 1908; rpt., New York: Barnes and Noble, 1959). Pierre Margry, ed., *Découvertes et établissements des Français dans l'ouest et dans le sud de l'Amérique septentrionale, 1614–1754* (6 vols., Paris: Jouast, 1876–86). John R. Swanton, *Source Material on the History and Ethnology of the Caddo Indians* (Smithsonian Institution, Bureau of American Ethnology Bulletin 132, Washington: GPO, 1942). *Thomas N. Campbell*

CABALLO, JUAN (1812?–1882). Juan Caballo, also known as Juan Coheia, Juan Cavallo, Gopher John, and John Horse, a Black Seminole warrior, diplomat, and civil leader, was a successful farmer and stockman in Florida in the early 1800s. His parents are believed to have been of mixed heritage (African, Spanish, and American Indian). His birth place is believed to be Thonotassassa in East Florida. Caballo, like many of the Black Seminole Indians[qv] (also called maroons), began his life as a slave of the Seminole Indians. In 1843, after he helped a group of Seminoles reach Indian Territory, he was granted his freedom. Throughout his life he served not only the interests of Black Seminoles but also assisted the Seminoles in numerous negotiations with whites. He was fluent in at least four languages. Caballo first achieved prominence during the Second Seminole War as a negotiator and military leader. The conflict had begun in the early 1830s when President Andrew Jackson initiated a policy to move the Five Civilized Tribes of the Southeast to western lands. At first many Seminoles were willing to move west, but their attitude changed once whites began kidnapping their slaves. Seminoles also began to worry about protection of their slaves once they arrived in the West. In 1835 these concerns turned into armed resistance. Once the United States Army promised to allow the Black Seminoles to accompany their Seminole masters, bands of Indians and their slaves began to surrender.

Between 1838 and 1842, Caballo traveled between Florida and Indian Territory helping Indians and other maroons to relocate. During the last two years of the war, he was responsible for convincing at least 535 belligerents to surrender. As in the Seminole homeland, once the groups arrived in Indian Territory, Black Seminoles established autonomous communities adjacent to their Seminole masters. Caballo's band settled on the Little River in Oklahoma at a place he named Wewoka, the "Village of Refuge." Life in the territory was extremely difficult for both Seminoles and Black Seminoles due to the domination of the Creek Indians. Seminoles allowed their slaves to own weapons and to control their own labor. The Creeks put intense pressure on the Seminoles to adopt the more stringent Creek slave codes. By 1849 Caballo, in conjunction with Seminole leader Coacoochee,[qv] organized a group of dissatisfied maroons and Indians to leave the territory and settle in Mexico, where slavery was outlawed. Mexican authorities provided the group with land and supplies in exchange for their promise to patrol the area and subdue renegade Comanche and Apache Indians. For his service to Mexico in fighting Indians, Juan Caballo was given the title of captain in the Mexican army.

By 1870, the internal problems of Mexico forced the Moscogos, as they were called by the Mexicans, to abandon their lands and return to the United States. Many of the Black Seminoles entered the United States Army as scouts, on the army's promise that they and their families would eventually be allowed to move to their own land in Oklahoma. Always skeptical of the white man's promises, Caballo refused to join the Black Seminole scouts,[qv] though he served them as an unofficial interpreter at times. In December 1873, John Kibbetts,[qv] Caballo's longtime second-in-command, beat out the elder leader in a vote for civil chief. Despite the loss, Black Seminoles continued to rely on Caballo's diplomatic skills. Dissatisfied with the delays of the government in giving the Black Seminoles a permanent home, Caballo returned to Mexico in 1876 with a band of followers. Sometime in late 1882, he died while on a mission to Mexico City to secure previously issued government land grants. The exact circumstances of his death are unknown. Some say he was murdered by outlaws; others believe that he died in a Mexico City hospital of pneumonia. During his life, the chief had survived four assassination attempts by various individuals unhappy with his ability to gain positive results for his people. This fact gives some credence to the murder theory. He was married to Susan July and had one son, Joe Coon.

BIBLIOGRAPHY: Kevin Mulroy, *Freedom on the Border: The Seminole Maroons in Florida, the Indian Territory, Coahuila and Texas* (Lubbock: Texas Tech University Press, 1993). Kenneth Wiggins Porter, "Farewell to John Horse," *Phylon* 8 (1947). Kenneth Wiggins Porter, *The Negro on the American Frontier* (New York: Arno Press, 1971). Doug Sivad, *The Black Seminole Indians of Texas* (Boston: American Press, 1984). Dan L. Thrapp, *Encyclopedia of Frontier Biography* (4 vols., Glendale, California: Clark, 1988–94). *E. Douglas Sivad*

CABALLO CREEK. Caballo Creek, sometimes known as Fernando Creek, rises thirteen miles southwest of Tilden in western McMullen County (at 28°20′ N, 98°43′ W) and runs southeast for six miles to its mouth on the Nueces River, fifteen miles southwest of Tilden (at 28°15′ N, 98°39′ W). The stream is dammed in its upper reaches to form Medio de Llano tank. Caballo Creek crosses low-rolling to flat terrain with locally shallow depressions, surfaced by clay and sandy loams that support grasses, mesquite, and chaparral upstream and water-tolerant hardwoods and grasses downstream.

CABAZA, J. (1830–?). J. Cabaza, farmer, one of the 100 wealthiest Texans in 1860, was born in Mexico and lived and worked in Cameron County. By the time he was thirty he owned $100,000 in real property and $2,000 in personal property. In 1860 Cabaza was one of four Spanish-surnamed individuals enumerated in a group of 263 "Wealthy Texans." Other "Wealthy Texans" residing in Cameron County included Juan N. Cabaza, José San Román, John V. Singer, Charles Stillman, and Salome Young.[qqv]

BIBLIOGRAPHY: Ralph A. Wooster, "Wealthy Texans, 1860," *Southwestern Historical Quarterly* 71 (October 1967). *Alicia A. Garza*

CABAZA, JUAN N. (1827–?). Juan N. Cabaza, farmer, one of the 100 wealthiest Texans in 1860, was born around 1827 in Mexico and lived and worked in Cameron County. At age thirty-three he owned real property worth $339,000 and $15,000 in personal property.

BIBLIOGRAPHY: Ralph A. Wooster, "Wealthy Texans, 1860," *Southwestern Historical Quarterly* 71 (October 1967). *Alicia A. Garza*

CABELL, CHARLES PEARRE (1903–1971). Charles Pearre Cabell, air force general and deputy director of the CIA, son of Ben E. and Sadie E. (Pearre) Cabell and grandson of William Lewis Cabell,[qv] was born on October 11, 1903, in Dallas, Texas. He attended Oak Cliff High School, then graduated from the United States Military Academy at West Point in 1925 and the Air Corps Flying School in San Antonio in 1931. He subsequently spent thirty-eight years in the United States Army and Air Force before his retirement as a four-star general in 1963. Cabell was married to Jacklyn Dehymel in 1934; they had two sons and a daughter.

During World War II[qv] Cabell was a member of the advisory council for the United States Army Air Force headquarters in Washington before being made commander of the Forty-fifth Combat Wing of the Eighth Air Force in the European Theater of Operations. He was director of plans for the United States Strategic Air Forces from May until July 1944, when he became director of operations and intelligence for the Mediterranean Allied Air Forces, a post he held until May 1945. Cabell attended the Yalta Conference in 1945 and the London Conference of the United Nations in January and February 1946. He had been promoted to colonel in 1942 and to brigadier general in 1944. After the war he was the United States air representative on the military staff committee of the United Nations in New York. In 1951 he was appointed director of the staff for the Joint Chiefs of Staff, where he worked with Gen. Omar Bradley. From 1953 until his retirement in 1963, General Cabell was deputy director of the Central Intelligence Agency. In 1965 he was appointed a consultant to the National Aeronautics and Space Administration. He was a member of the Philosophical Society of Texas.[qv] He died in Arlington, Virginia, on May 25, 1971, and was buried in Arlington National Cemetery.

BIBLIOGRAPHY: *Proceedings of the Philosophical Society of Texas,* 1970. Vertical Files, Barker Texas History Center, University of Texas at Austin. *Who's Who in America,* 1960–61.

CABELL, WILLIAM LEWIS (1827–1911). William Lewis Cabell, Confederate general and mayor of Dallas, son of Benjamin W. S. and Sarah Epes (Doswell) Cabell, was born on January 1, 1827, in Danville, Virginia. The elder Cabell was a veteran of the War of 1812 and a member of the Virginia General Assembly. William Cabell graduated from the United States Military Academy at West Point in 1850 and entered the United States Army as a brevet second lieutenant with the Seventh Infantry Regiment. In March 1858 he was made a captain in the quartermaster's department. On July 22, 1856, he married Harriet A. Rector in Fort Smith, Arkansas. The couple had seven children.

In March 1861 Cabell resigned his commission in the United States Army and traveled to Montgomery, Alabama, where he was commissioned a major in the Confederate Army. He was assigned to Richmond, Virginia, with the responsibility of organizing the quartermaster, commissary, and ordnance departments. Upon completion of that task, he was made chief quartermaster of the Army of the Potomac. In January 1862 he was transferred to the Trans-Mississippi Department and served on the staff of Gen. Earl Van Dorn.[qv] Later he was promoted to brigadier general. Cabell was wounded during the battles of Corinth and Hatcher's Bridge in the fall of 1862. He was captured near Mine Creek, Kansas, on October 25, 1864, and remained a prisoner of war until August 28, 1865, when he was released at Fort Warren, Massachusetts.

Upon his release Cabell joined his family in Fort Smith, Arkansas, where he studied law and was admitted to the bar in 1868. He and his family moved in 1872 to Dallas, Texas, where he served as agent of the Carolina Life Insurance Company. In 1874 he was elected mayor of the city, a position he held until 1876. He was elected mayor again in 1882. He was a delegate to the Democratic national conventions of 1876, 1884, and 1892. From 1885 to 1889 he was United States marshall for the Northern District of Texas. For four years he served as vice president and general manager of the Texas Trunk Railway.

After the organization of United Confederate Veterans, Cabell devoted increasingly larger amounts of his time to that group. In 1890 he was elected commander of the Trans-Mississippi Department. He remained in that position until he was elected honorary commander in chief shortly before his death. He died in Dallas on February 22, 1911.

BIBLIOGRAPHY: Dallas *Morning News,* February 23, 1911. *Dictionary of American Biography.* Ezra J. Warner, *Generals in Gray* (Baton Rouge: Louisiana State University Press, 1959). *Cecil Harper, Jr.*

CABELL, TEXAS. Cabell, four miles northeast of Richmond in Fort Bend County, was part of the original Oyster Creek settlement. An early landowner in the area was Dr. Matthew A. Moore, who in 1852 established a plantation there. An extension of the Missouri–Pacific line from Sugar Land made Cabell a shipping point for rice, cotton, and other products grown on surrounding farms. By 1936 the entire area had been absorbed by a state prison farm (*see* PRISON SYSTEM). *Stephen L. Hardin*

CABELLO Y ROBLES, DOMINGO (ca. 1725–?). Domingo Cabello y Robles, a career officer in the Spanish Royal Army from León, Spain, served after Juan María de Ripperdá[qv] as governor of Texas from October 29, 1778, to December 3, 1786. He began his military career at an early age when he joined an infantry regiment as a lieutenant in 1741. He first saw action in 1742, on his way to Santiago de Cuba, which was under siege, when the vessel carrying his company was attacked by an English warship. Cabello returned to Spain in 1749 but was quickly promoted to major and sent back to Cuba as commander of four battalions of a fixed regiment constituted to garrison the island and the presidios of Florida. His conduct during the English siege and capture of Havana in 1762 earned him promotion to the governorship of Nicaragua, in which post he served from December 12, 1764, until July 20, 1776.

Cabello must have seemed the ideal replacement for Ripperdá; he had military and administrative experience as well as success in dealing with hostile Indians. His Indian policy first favored the Lipan Apaches over the Comanches, but he later came to view the latter as more worthy of Spanish attention. He successfully achieved peace with the Comanches in Texas and supported their efforts against the Apaches. The high point of Cabello's Indian policy was the peace treaty reached with the Comanches in October 1785, a pact observed until the end of the eighteenth century.

Almost as serious as the Indian question was the protracted livestock controversy in the province. Cattle rustling between vecinos and missions, depletion of cattle through wasteful slaughter and excessive exports, and noncompliance with an ordinance of January 1778 were holdovers from the Ripperdá administration. Enforcing existing regulations and preventing illegal exports became Cabello's major concerns. His bando, or ordinance, of July 10, 1783, imposed strict guidelines for the roundup, branding, and export of unbranded cattle.

A number of important events took place during Cabello's administration. In judicial matters, Texas was transferred from the Audiencia (High Court) of Mexico's jurisdiction to that of Guadalajara. The town of Bucareli,[qv] on the Trinity River, was abandoned in favor of a new site among the Hasinai Indians known as Nacogdoches. A monthly mail service between the province and Provincias Internas[qv] headquarters was established and later made semimonthly. The fort established for the protection of the ranches along Cibolo Creek was abandoned and burned. In 1786 Cabello commissioned Pedro Vial,[qv] whom he had used previously as an intermediary with the Comanches, to seek a direct route between San Antonio and Santa Fe, New Mexico.

Cabello's enforcement of livestock regulations resulted in much animosity from ranchers. Soon after his departure from the province in 1787, the ranchers filed a memorial against Cabello charging him with arbitrary and unjust decrees and misrepresentations that denied them rights to unbranded cattle. Cabello left Texas under suspicion but with a promotion as king's lieutenant for the garrison of Havana and deputy inspector of troops for the island of Cuba. He did not find out about the charges against him, which included misappropriation of funds, until 1790. The case did not adversely affect his career, for by 1797 Cabello had reached the rank of field marshall.

BIBLIOGRAPHY: Herbert Eugene Bolton, *Texas in the Middle Eighteenth Century: Studies in Spanish Colonial History and Administration* (Berkeley: University of California Press, 1915; rpt., Austin: University of Texas Press, 1970). Carlos E. Castañeda, *Our Catholic Heritage in Texas* (7 vols., Austin: Von Boeckmann–Jones, 1936–58; rpt., New York: Arno, 1976). Jack Jackson, *Los Mesteños: Spanish Ranching in Texas, 1721–1821* (College Station: Texas A&M University Press, 1986). Elizabeth A. H. John, *Storms Brewed in Other Men's Worlds: The Confrontation of Indians, Spanish, and French in the Southwest, 1540–1795* (College Station: Texas A&M University Press, 1975).
Jesús F. de la Teja

CABELLOS BLANCOS INDIANS. The Cabellos Blancos (Spanish for "white hairs") Indians are known only from a Spanish document of 1693 that lists the Cabellos Blancos as one of fifty "nations" that lived north of the Rio Grande and "between Texas and New Mexico." This may be interpreted to mean the southern part of western Texas, since the document also mentions that the Apaches were at war with the groups named. Nothing further is known about the Cabellos Blancos.

BIBLIOGRAPHY: Charles W. Hackett, ed., *Historical Documents Relating to New Mexico, Nueva Vizcaya, and Approaches Thereto, to 1773* (3 vols., Washington: Carnegie Institution, 1923–37).
Thomas N. Campbell

CABELLOS COLORADOS. Cabellos Colorados (Red Hair), a Lipan Apache chief, figured prominently in a raid on San Antonio just after the establishment of the villa by the Canary Islanders[qv] in 1731. In 1743 his band seized two citizens in a raid. He stole horses from San Francisco de la Espada Mission and killed Indians from the missions of San Juan Capistrano and Nuestra Señora de la Purísima Concepción de Acuña. After numerous raids in 1736 and 1737, he was captured on December 11, 1737, and imprisoned at Bexar until October 1738, when Apache depredations were renewed, and he was sent as a prisoner to Mexico City.

BIBLIOGRAPHY: Herbert Eugene Bolton, *Texas in the Middle Eighteenth Century* (Berkeley: University of California Press, 1915; rpt., Austin: University of Texas Press, 1970). Carlos E. Castañeda, *Our Catholic Heritage in Texas* (7 vols., Austin: Von Boeckmann–Jones, 1936–58; rpt., New York: Arno, 1976).

CABET, ÉTIENNE (1788–1856). Étienne Cabet, utopian socialist and founder of the Icarian movement, was born in Dijon, France, on January 1, 1788, the son of Claude and Françoise (Bertier) Cabet. He received his law degree in May 1812 and moved to Paris four years later to work for Félix Nicod, a wealthy and influential lawyer with links to the opposition to the restored Bourbon monarchy. Cabet also became closely associated with the opposition and embarked on a career of political and social activism that dominated the rest of his life. As a reward for his participation in the revolution of 1830, he served briefly as attorney general for Corsica and as a representative in the chamber of deputies. He soon became disenchanted with the July Monarchy of Louis Philippe and, in 1833, launched an antigovernment newspaper, *Le Populaire.* The increasingly revolutionary tone of this paper led to his going to England in 1834 to avoid a prison sentence. Cabet married Délphine Lesage, another native of Dijon, while in exile. A daughter, Céline, had been born to the couple earlier. By the time of his return to France in 1839, Cabet, who had been strongly influenced by Robert Owen and by Thomas More's *Utopia* during his exile, had written and produced two books, *Histoire populaire de la Révolution française* (1839) and the more famous novel, *Voyage en Icarie* (1838). The latter book, which outlined Cabet's plan for a perfect utopian community based on the principles of evolutionary communism, captured the imaginations of thousands of French craftsmen. Cabet believed that environment determined human nature and that people, whom he saw as perfectible and rational, would produce a perfect society when placed in a perfect environment.

On February 3, 1848, sixty-nine or seventy of Cabet's adherents left Le Havre to attempt to fabricate such an environment on an expected one million acres of land near the site of present-day Justin, in southern Denton County, Texas. The land had been contracted by Cabet from the Peters Real Estate Company. But upon arriving at the site in late May 1848, the settlers found that only one-tenth of the anticipated land was available and that even that fraction had been allotted in noncontiguous half-section plots. Moreover, they found that they were also required to construct a house on each of their half-sections by July in order to obtain title to the land. Disillusioned and ill with malaria, the surviving settlers returned to New Orleans, their original port of entry in the United States. Cabet, along with another group of Icarians, left France and joined them in that city in December 1848.

Later that same month an advance party traveled north to the town of Nauvoo, Illinois, abandoned two years earlier by the Mormons, and returned to New Orleans to report to Cabet that the vacant town would be an ideal location for another Icarian community. Cabet and 280 followers left New Orleans and arrived in Nauvoo on March 15, 1849. The Nauvoo community had serious problems from the beginning, many of them involving resentment of Cabet's occasionally dictatorial behavior. Cabet also had to return to France in May 1851 to defend himself against charges of fraud in the promotion of his American Icarian projects. After being cleared of wrongdoing, he returned to Nauvoo in 1852 and, in 1854, became a United States citizen. Yet the problems at Nauvoo remained, and in the fall of 1856 the community disintegrated under the combined weight of serious financial difficulties and severe factional strife. After this breakup, Cabet took 180 of his remaining followers to St. Louis to start a new community. He died in that city a week after he arrived, on November 8, 1856. Icarian communities continued to exist in the United States until 1898.

BIBLIOGRAPHY: Odie B. Faulk, "The Icarian Colony in Texas, 1848: A Problem in Historiography," *Texana* 5 (Summer 1967). Christopher

H. Johnson, *Utopian Communism in France: Cabet and the Icarians, 1839–1851* (Ithaca, New York: Cornell University Press, 1974). Jules Jean Prudhommeaux, *Icarie et son fondateur, étienne Cabet* (Paris: Cornély, 1907; rpt., Philadelphia: Porcupine, 1972). Fernand Rude, ed., *Voyage en Icarie: Deux ouvriers viennois aux états-Unis en 1855* (Paris, 1957). Albert Shaw, *Icaria: A Chapter in the History of Communism* (New York: Putnam, 1884; rpt., Philadelphia: Porcupine, 1972). Everett Webber, *Escape to Utopia: The Communal Movement in America* (New York: Hastings House, 1959). *Christopher E. Guthrie*

CABEZA, TEXAS. Cabeza, 5½ miles northwest of Nordheim in western DeWitt County, was named for its location on the headwaters of Cabeza Creek, which in turn was named by the Spaniards. The settlement was founded about 1876 by three sheepmen, P. P. Short, John Riley, and Joshua Butler, at an elevated site. In 1888 Robert E. Magee taught the first session at the new school named for Short, who had donated land for the site. Baptist and Methodist services were held in the school building beginning about 1890. The community had a post office from 1899 to 1907. It also had three stores and a blacksmith. Cabeza was first a sheep-raising center; later, cattle and cotton dominated its economy. A local cotton gin processed about 1,000 bales of cotton annually until boll weevil[qv] devastation ruined the business. In 1948 the community had about 150 pupils in two schools, one for white children, the other for Hispanic. Both schools were discontinued in the 1950s. Cabeza was not shown on the 1965 county highway map.

BIBLIOGRAPHY: Nellie Murphree, *A History of DeWitt County* (Victoria, Texas, 1962). *Craig H. Roell*

CABEZA CREEK. Cabeza Creek rises four miles southwest of Garfield in southwestern DeWitt County (at 28°59′ N, 97°40′ W) and runs southeast for forty miles, across southeastern Karnes County, to its mouth on the San Antonio River, six miles west of Goliad in Goliad County (at 28°38′ N, 97°29′ W). It traverses flat to rolling terrain surfaced by highly permeable calcareous clay that supports scrub brush, cacti, and prairie grasses and, toward the creek's mouth, water-tolerant hardwoods and conifers. The stream has been named Cabeza ("head") since at least 1848.

CABEZA INDIANS. Cabeza (Cavesa, Caveza) is a name (Spanish for "head") that seems to have been applied to several Indian groups in North America. In 1693 a group of Cabezas was reported north of the Rio Grande, presumably in the Trans-Pecos.[qv] It is not known if these were the same as the Cabezas who lived in southern Coahuila during the same period and who were frequently recorded as being closely associated with the Tobosos.

BIBLIOGRAPHY: Herbert E. Bolton, "The Jumano Indians in Texas, 1650–1771," *Quarterly of the Texas State Historical Association* 15 (July 1911). Herbert Eugene Bolton, ed., *Spanish Exploration in the Southwest, 1542–1706* (New York: Scribner, 1908; rpt., New York: Barnes and Noble, 1959). Charles W. Hackett, ed., *Historical Documents Relating to New Mexico, Nueva Vizcaya, and Approaches Thereto, to 1773* (3 vols., Washington: Carnegie Institution, 1923–37).

Thomas N. Campbell

CABEZA DE VACA, ÁLVAR NÚÑEZ (ca. 1490–ca. 1556). Álvar Núñez Cabeza de Vaca, an early Spanish explorer, was born about 1490 in Jerez de la Frontera, an Andalucian town near Cádiz, to Francisco de Vera and Teresa Cabeza de Vaca. Cabeza de Vaca was his preferred surname. It descended from an ancestor who had helped secure victory for Christian forces at the battle of Las Navas de Tolosa (1212) by marking an unguarded pass in the Sierra Moreno with the skull of a cow. In gratitude, King Sancho of Navarra bestowed the surname "Cow's Head" on Cabeza de Vaca's matrilineal progenitors. The Álvar Núñez portion of Cabeza de Vaca's name also came from a prominent ancestor of his mother, who was an accomplished naval officer.

As a young man Cabeza de Vaca gained military experience in Italy, where he campaigned with the Spanish army of Charles V. His service to the crown probably earned him the position of treasurer in the 1527–28 expedition of Pánfilo de Narváez.[qv] Narváez, a minor participant in the conquest of Mexico, had lost an eye and command of his army to Hernán Cortés in 1520. Later, his importunities at the Spanish court resulted in a royal patent to found a colony in Florida, a name applied to the Gulf Coast between the province of Pánuco in Mexico and the Florida peninsula.

Narváez departed from Spain in June 1527, wintered in Cuba, and landed on the west coast of Florida in April 1528. Despite protests from Cabeza de Vaca, Narváez decided to separate 300 men from his support vessels and reconnoiter the land. He was soon permanently separated from his ships and stranded on the Florida coast, which he believed to be only a few leagues from the Pánuco River.

Narváez's expedition then began a march up the interior coast to northwestern Florida, where it remained for approximately three months. Faced with hostile natives and food shortages, Narváez elected to build improvised barges and to leave Florida by sea. His command, which had dwindled to fewer than 250 men, crowded into five craft and set out for Pánuco. The first month at sea went well. Hugging the coast, the small flotilla approached the mouth of the Mississippi River. But on the thirty-first day a storm caught the barges and eventually drove them apart. Several days after passing the mouth of the Great River, two of the battered craft were beached on an island (probably San Luis, now known as Follets Island[qv]) off the Texas coast, in November 1528. Among some eighty survivors were Cabeza de Vaca, Andrés Dorantes de Carranza, his African-born slave Estevanico, and Alonso Castillo Maldonado.[qqv] These men, known as the "four ragged castaways," were among the first non-Indians to set foot on Texas soil, and they were the only survivors of the Narváez expedition. Most of the others succumbed to disease, injuries, drowning, or violence at the hands of hostile coastal tribes.

Shortly after landing on the Texas coast, Cabeza de Vaca became separated from the other survivors. Believing he had died on the mainland, all but two of them proceeded down the coast. Cabeza de Vaca recovered from a near fatal illness and later became the first European merchant in Texas. He ranged inland as well as along the coast, carrying sea shells and mesquite beans to the interior and returning with skins and red ochre. He also enjoyed success as a medicine man; his treatment consisted of blessing the afflicted, breathing on injuries, and praying.

Cabeza de Vaca's reluctance to leave the Galveston area was influenced by a single surviving countryman, Lope de Oviedo, who refused to leave the initial landfall island. In 1532 Cabeza de Vaca convinced the reluctant Spaniard to accompany him along the coast toward Pánuco, as the other survivors had done in the spring of 1529. En route Lope de Oviedo turned back and disappeared from history. Cabeza de Vaca eventually rendezvoused with three astonished colleagues at what they called the "river of nuts," probably the Guadalupe. There the four castaways, who were made slaves of the Mariame Indians, plotted their escape to Mexico. Not until 1534, however, did they start for Pánuco.

Cabeza de Vaca and the other castaways traveled from the environs of Galveston Island to Culiacán, an outpost near the Pacific Coast of Mexico, where they arrived in early 1536. Their path has been the subject of historical controversy for more than a century. Differences over route interpretations continue, for no one can prove with absolute certainty the precise course followed on any part of the journey. It is the Texas portion of the odyssey, however, that has received the most attention.

The *Relación* of Cabeza de Vaca reported the experience, and the joint report, a cooperative account, was written by the three surviving Spaniards. Both accounts were composed shortly after the trek ended in 1536. Biotic, enthnographic, and physiographic information contained in these narratives provides clues as to where the four men spent nearly seven years in Texas and what they saw. Their reports of their experiences provide valuable data on Texas Indians, landforms, flora, and fauna.

The crucial pieces of evidence in the narratives are the dimensions of the island where the initial landing occurred, the distance between and the crossing of four successive streams on the mainland, the description of a series of inlets along the coast toward Pánuco, the mention of a "river of nuts" and extensive stands of prickly pear cactus, the crossing of a large river comparable in width to the Guadalquivir River in Spain, the subsequent appearance of mountains near the coast that ran from the direction of the "North Sea," and the recorded names of Indian tribes. The data, when correlated with the established goal of reaching Pánuco, strongly suggest a southern route along the inner Texas coast and a crossing of the lower Río Grande into Mexico near the site of International Falcon Reservoir.[qv] Ultimately, the castaways' successful flight on foot brought them back to Texas at the junction of the Rio Grande and the Río Conchos near the site of present Presidio, Texas. On that portion of the trek, Cabeza de Vaca removed an arrow from the chest of an Indian. The operation has earned him remembrance as the "patron saint" of the Texas Surgical Society. Cabeza de Vaca also deserves recognition as the first geographer, historian, and ethnologist in Texas. He was the only Spaniard to live among the coastal Indians of Texas and survive to write about them. As a result he, along with Dorantes de Carranza and Castillo Maldonado, may be remembered for producing the first Texas literature.

In the early 1540s Cabeza de Vaca again served the Spanish crown as a governor in what is now Paraguay. He was, however, charged with misrule there, recalled to Spain, tried, and temporarily banished to North Africa. Later he was cleared of charges and permitted to return to Spain, where he died in the mid-1550s.

BIBLIOGRAPHY: Thomas N. Campbell and T. J. Campbell, *Historic Indian Groups of the Choke Canyon Reservoir and Surrounding Area, Southern Texas* (San Antonio: Center for Archaeological Research, University of Texas at San Antonio, 1981). Donald E. Chipman, "In Search of Cabeza de Vaca's Route Across Texas: An Historiographical Survey," *Southwestern Historical Quarterly* 91 (October 1987). Harbert Davenport and Joseph K. Wells, "The First Europeans in Texas, 1528–1536," *Southwestern Historical Quarterly* 22 (October 1918). Martin A. Favata and José B. Fernández, *The Account: Núñez Cabeza de Vaca's Relación* (Houston: Arte Público Press, 1993). Jesse E. Thompson, "Sagittectomy—First Recorded Surgical Procedure in the American Southwest," *New England Journal of Medicine* 289 (December 27, 1973).

Donald E. Chipman

CABIA INDIANS. The Cabia Indians, reported but not located in a document of 1690, have been identified with the Kabaye of the La Salle expedition[qv] records, but the identity has never been demonstrated. J. R. Swanton listed the Cabias among his Coahuiltecan bands. Since only the name is known, the status of the Cabias remains in doubt. It is possible that Cabia is merely a variant of the name Cava.

BIBLIOGRAPHY: Frederick Webb Hodge, ed., *Handbook of American Indians North of Mexico* (2 vols., Washington: GPO, 1907, 1910; rpt., New York: Pageant, 1959). J. R. Swanton, *Linguistic Material from the Tribes of Southern Texas and Northeastern Mexico* (Washington: Smithsonian Institution, 1940).

Thomas N. Campbell

CABILDO. In Spanish Texas[qv] the cabildo was the building that housed meetings of the ayuntamiento,[qv] or town council, though Spanish colonists in America generally used the term to refer to the council itself. Though colonists used the word *ayuntamiento* more frequently in the latter part of the Spanish era, the two terms were interchangeable.

La relacion y comentarios del gouernador Aluar nuñez cabeça de vaca, de lo acaescido en las dos jornadas que hizo a las Indias, *by Álvar Núñez Cabeza de Vaca (Valladolid, 1555). Courtesy CAH; CN 00835a. Cabeza de Vaca's book, also known as* Los Naufragios *or* Shipwrecks, *is the first published eyewitness account of Texas. This title page, a hand-colored woodcut, appeared in the second edition.*

BIBLIOGRAPHY: Marc Simmons, *Spanish Government in New Mexico* (Albuquerque: University of New Mexico Press, 1968).

Geoffrey Pivateau

CACALOTE INDIANS. Cacalote ("crow" or "raven") is a name that was applied by the Spanish to several Indian groups in North America. Two Cacalote groups of northern Mexico can be connected with the Texas area. One of these lived south of the Rio Grande in Nuevo León and Tamaulipas in the seventeenth and eighteenth centuries and may at times have crossed into Texas. This was probably a Coahuiltecan group. The other Cacalote group lived south of the Rio Grande near the site of present Presidio, Texas, in the early eighteenth century but is said to have ranged north of the Rio Grande in the late seventeenth century. These western Cacalotes have been identified as Concho Indians, but this identification is debatable. Both Cacalote groups disappeared in the late eighteenth century.

BIBLIOGRAPHY: Charles W. Hackett, ed., *Historical Documents Relating to New Mexico, Nueva Vizcaya, and Approaches Thereto, to 1773* (3 vols., Washington: Carnegie Institution, 1923–37). J. Charles Kelley, "Factors Involved in the Abandonment of Certain Peripheral Southwestern Settlements," *American Anthropologist* 54 (July–September 1952). J. Charles Kelley, "The Historic Indian Pueblos of La Junta de Los Rios," *New Mexico Historical Review* 27, 28 (October 1952, January 1953). Carl Sauer, *The Distribution of Aboriginal Tribes and Languages in Northwestern Mexico* (Berkeley: University of California Press, 1934).

Thomas N. Campbell

CACAXTLE INDIANS. This was one of the more important early Coahuiltecan bands of southern Texas. Between 1653 and 1663 the Cacaxtle (Casastle, Cataxtle) and their allies repeatedly attacked the Spanish frontier settlements of Coahuila and Nuevo León, and two Spanish military expeditions in 1663 and 1665 finally crossed the Rio Grande to administer punishment. In two decisive battles a total of 200 Cacaxtle were killed and about the same number captured. The captives were sold into slavery for work in the mines of Chihuahua and Zacatecas, a common procedure in northern Mexico during the seventeenth century. The location of the Cacaxtle Indians in southern Texas cannot be precisely determined, but the data available suggest that it was somewhere on the southward bend of the Nueces River in the area of present La Salle and McMullen counties. However, on a map prepared by W. Jiménez Moreno the Cacaxtles are shown as living along the lower Pecos River. It seems likely that the Cacaxtle Indians originally ranged from the Nueces southward across the Rio Grande into what is now northwestern Tamaulipas and northern Nuevo León. This hypothetical range is in accord with reports of repeated raids on Spanish frontier settlements prior to 1663. If Spanish records are accurate, the two battles mentioned above destroyed Cacaxtle power, for little is heard of them afterward. The name of this group appears to be derived from a Coahuiltecan word, "kakaxtle," which refers to a special netted frame used for carrying loads on the back.

BIBLIOGRAPHY: Vito Alessio Robles, *Coahuila y Texas en la época colonial* (Mexico City: Editorial Cultura, 1938; 2d ed., Mexico City: Editorial Porrúa, 1978). Herbert Eugene Bolton, ed., *Spanish Exploration in the Southwest, 1542–1706* (New York: Scribner, 1908; rpt., New York: Barnes and Noble, 1959). Carlos E. Castañeda, *Our Catholic Heritage in Texas* (7 vols., Austin: Von Boeckmann–Jones, 1936–58; rpt., New York: Arno, 1976). David A. Cossio, *Historia de Nuevo León* (6 vols., Monterrey, Nuevo León, Mexico: J. Cantú Leal, 1925). Frederick Ruecking, Jr., "The Economic System of the Coahuiltecan Indians of Southern Texas and Northeastern Mexico," *Texas Journal of Science* 5 (December 1953). J. R. Swanton, *Linguistic Material from the Tribes of Southern Texas and Northeastern Mexico* (Washington: Smithsonian Institution, 1940).

Thomas N. Campbell

CACHAÉ INDIANS. This was a Caddoan tribe of the southwestern or Hasinai division in eastern Texas that is known from a single Spanish document written near the close of the seventeenth century. H. E. Bolton[qv] thought that Cachaé and Cataye were variants of the same name and that they were early names for the people later known as Hainai. It is true that Cachaé and Hainai Indians seem to have occupied the same area. J. R. Swanton followed Bolton's interpretations and also identified the Caxo Indians with the Cachaé. This is all a matter of modern inference and opinion. Cachaé, Caxo, and Cataye are all listed as separate tribes in the same document without any indication that they are names for the same people, and no early Spanish authority ever said that these names were synonyms for Hainai.

BIBLIOGRAPHY: Herbert E. Bolton, "The Native Tribes about the East Texas Missions," *Quarterly of the Texas State Historical Association* 11 (April 1908). John R. Swanton, *Source Material on the History and Ethnology of the Caddo Indians* (Smithsonian Institution, Bureau of American Ethnology Bulletin 132, Washington: GPO, 1942).

Thomas N. Campbell

CACHE CREEK. Cache Creek rises near U.S. Highway 277 and the Burlington Northern line (*see* BURLINGTON RAILROAD SYSTEM) about three miles northeast of Bomarton in southwestern Baylor County (at 33°31′ N, 99°23′ W) and runs east for ten miles to its mouth on the Brazos River, just east of U.S. Highway 183/283 (at 33°31′ N, 99°16′ W). It crosses an area of flat to rolling terrain with sandy soil that supports scattered oak mottes and occasional marsh grasses. Cache Springs was once a major source for the creek; in earlier times the springs maintained a substantial flow, and a small community evolved nearby. By the 1970s, however, both the town and the springs were gone. The creek runs through ranchland north of the Baylor County Regular oilfield.

BIBLIOGRAPHY: Gunnar Brune, *Springs of Texas*, Vol. 1 (Fort Worth: Branch–Smith, 1981).

CACHOPOSTAL INDIANS. The Cachopostals first became known in 1727, when a small remnant of them was reported to be living near the Pampopa Indians on the Nueces River, apparently in the area now embraced by Dimmit and La Salle counties. It is not certain that they were native to this particular locality. After 1727 the Cachopostals are known only from records connected with two Spanish missions. In 1739 an elderly female was recorded twice in the registers of San Antonio de Valero Mission of San Antonio, her ethnic affiliation being given as both Zacpo and Zacpoco, which on phonetic grounds are judged to be variants of the name Cachopostal. Four Cachopostal individuals were recorded in a census taken in 1772 at San Juan Bautista[qv] Mission near the Rio Grande in northeastern Coahuila. According to Spanish missionaries, the Pampopas spoke the Coahuilteco language, and the Cachopostals have usually been classified as Coahuilteco speakers because of their association with Pampopas in 1727. In the early eighteenth century, however, languages other than Coahuilteco were spoken in southern Texas and northeastern Mexico, and remnant Indian groups did not always associate with each other simply because they happened to speak the same language. The identification of the Cachopostal as Coahuilteco-speaking Indians must therefore remain tentative.

BIBLIOGRAPHY: F. D. Almaráz, Jr., *Inventory of the Rio Grande Missions: 1772, San Juan Bautista and San Bernardo* (Archaeology and History of the San Juan Bautista Mission Area, Coahuila and Texas, Report No. 2, Center for Archaeological Research, University of Texas at San Antonio, 1980). Thomas N. Campbell, *Ethnohistoric Notes on Indian Groups Associated with Three Spanish Missions at Guerrero, Coahuila* (Center for Archaeological Research, University of Texas at San Antonio, 1979). San Antonio de Valero Mission, Baptismal and Burial Registers, San Antonio. Robert S. Weddle, *San Juan Bautista: Gateway to Spanish Texas* (Austin: University of Texas Press, 1968).

Thomas N. Campbell

CACTI. More than 100 species of cacti grow in Texas, the widest assortment found in any state in the United States. Many are best known by such nonscientific names as blind pear, cow-tongue cactus, night-blooming cereus, Texas rainbow, tree cactus, early bloomer, and devil's head, so-called because its rigid spines are dangerous to the hoofs of horses and cattle. Numerous other varieties are commonly called strawberry cactus, pincushion, and jumping jack. Cacti are used in Texas for foods, for landscaping, and for commercial and private botanical collections. The tunas, or seed pods, of the prickly pear are used in making salads, wines, and jelly; the pads, or *nopalitos*, with their spines singed off, make a substantial food for cattle and form a minor staple in Tex-Mex food. Other cacti are used to make food colorings, medicines, and candy. The climatic adaptability of cacti and their ease of culture make them useful in gardens and as shrubbery; their unusual forms and multicolored flowers, which vary in shade from green and white to magenta and purple, attract many collectors. The sizes of cacti range from the minute button cactus, smaller than a dime, to the barrel or fishhook cactus, which weighs up to half a ton or more.

The cacti of Texas represent ten genera:

Genus *Echinocereus. Echino-* ("spiny") refers to the very thorny covering of this genus, and *cereus* ("wax candle") comes from the stately appearance of its upright species. *Echinocerei* are oval, conical, or cylindrical cacti, always with ribbed stems. The flowers are usually large and beautiful, though a few have small and inconspicuous greenish flowers. The fruits are always fleshy and thin-skinned and often edible; they are also spiny, but the spines loosen as the fruits mature and may be easily brushed off. The *Echinocerei* grow mostly in exposed places on dry slopes and hills in the full strength of the southwestern sun.

Genus *Wilcoxia.* Five species in this genus are usually recognized, four in Mexico and one in South Texas. The cacti have slender stems of about five-eighths inch or less diameter. The spines are very short, a quarter inch or less long. The flower is large and beautiful, bell-shaped or funnel-shaped, reddish to purplish, and diurnal. The ovary surface is scaly, wooly, and covered with bristly or hairlike spines that remain on the fruits.

Genus *Peniocereus.* The "thread cereus" cacti all have slender stems and an extremely large, fleshy taproot, from which grow stems that are ribbed at first but become round. All have fragrant nocturnal flowers produced from within the spine areole, and all have very short spines on the stems and rigid spines on the fruits.

Genus *Acanthocereus.* There are about a dozen species in the "acanthus candle" genus. These are more or less shrubby plants that grow upright but cannot support their own weight for long and depend on some support, usually other plants. Supported stems may grow to twenty feet tall. All stems are from one to four inches in diameter, and mature stems have from three to seven conspicuous ribs. The flowers are nocturnal, large, and white, and the ovary is usually spiny. These tropical lowland cacti are never found far from a coast and seem to thrive best on semiarid coastal plains. They tolerate much more moisture than most cacti and when water is adequate grow very rapidly. A light frost will kill the tips of the stems, and 32° F will kill all of the plant above the ground, though the roots may sprout again. In the United States the *Acanthocerei* have a precarious existence along the coast in South Texas and Florida.

Genus *Echinocactus.* Most members of this genus, known as the barrel cacti, have strong, rigid, numerous spines. A few have more slender and flexible spines, and the genus includes a some spineless members. The barrels range in size from several hundred pounds to miniature forms only a few inches high. The exterior exhibits from eight to more than twenty vertical or spiraling ribs. Flowers are produced at or near the apex of the plant and have no distinct floral tube; the ovary bears scales and sometimes wool but not spines.

Genus *Lophophora.* The members of this genus, the "crest-bearers," are small, globose, or depressed globose cacti that grow from comparatively large, carrot-shaped taproots. The stem is about three inches in diameter but stands no more than two inches above the ground. Stems may be single or may branch from the base to form large clusters. Surfaces are blue-green and often glaucous. The plants have no spines after the early seedling stage. The ribs are broad and flat. The areoles are small and round with long white to yellowish wool that often persists, and the flowers are small, bell-shaped, and varied in color. In this genus the ovary and fruit are entirely naked, and the fruit remains always fleshy. The stems are ribbed. Monomorphic areoles produce the flowers from the apexes of young tubercles rather than from the axils. Peyote[qv] belongs to this genus.

Genus *Ariocarpus.* This is a small genus with only one species in Texas and the others in Mexico. The body of the plant consists of one or occasionally a cluster of low flattened stems ranging from two inches in diameter to ten inches across. The smaller species may not project above the surface of the ground, whereas the larger ones reach five inches tall. The stem sits on top of a large carrot-like taproot. The surface of the stem is divided into very distinct, usually imbricated but noncoalescent tubercles. There are no spines after first seedling growth. This genus is unusual in that it flowers in the fall. Flowers open widely, are diurnal, and are white, yellowish, or purplish. The ovary and fruit are both naked. The fruit is fleshy at first, becomes dry at maturity, and disintegrates, leaving the seeds in the wool at the center of the plant.

Genus *Epithelantha.* Although a number of species of this genus grow in Mexico, only one grows in the United States. The whole stem is covered with very many, very tiny tubercles, apparently the smallest tubercles of any United States cactus. These are hidden almost entirely from view by many tiny spines. The growing tip of the stem is a distinct depression filled with a great deal of hairlike wool and covered over by the converging, later deciduous, tips of the longer spines; this covering makes it difficult to observe the formation of the tubercles, areoles, and flowers. Also unusual about this cactus is the fact that it produces its flowers not in the axil of the tubercle but at the top of it. This cactus does not produce its flower from within a monomorphic spine areole as previously believed. The blossom is produced after a division of the meristem into a determinate spiny portion and a separate, indeterminate, floral or vegetative meristem.

Genus *Mammillaria.* Members of this genus are small or very small. The stems vary in different species from depressed and almost flat to globular or sometimes columnar and are often referred to as heads. In some species these remain single, but in many others they multiply from the base to become caespitose; one individual sometimes forms a large clump of heads. In a few species branches may occasionally grow from higher up on the stem. Each stem is entirely covered by a system of nipple-like projections called tubercles. These are usually arranged in spiral rows but in a few cases are more loosely organized. The tubercles are usually cylindrical or conical but sometimes have more or less quadrangular bases.

Genus *Opuntia.* This large genus is generally regarded as more primitive than the others. In more than half of the states of the United States opuntias are the only cacti found; it is this genus that allows the claim that cacti grow over almost the entire United States. Characteristics are jointed stems, cylindrical or conical leaves on young stems, the presence of glochidia (barbed hairs or spines), and the production of spreading, rotate flowers with more or less sensitive stamens and with aeroles that often produce glochidia and spines on the ovaries. The fruits have thick rinds.

BIBLIOGRAPHY: Del Weniger, *Cacti of Texas and Neighboring States: A Field Guide* (Austin: University of Texas Press, 1984).

John G. Johnson

CACTUS, TEXAS (Moore County). Cactus is on U.S. Highway 287 near Etter and thirteen miles north of Dumas in northern Moore County. It began as a company town to produce ammunition for World War II.[qv] The Cactus Ordnance Works,[qv] one of the largest plants in the county, was established there as a government project by the Chemical Construction Company in May 1942. About sixteen sections of land were purchased; the cactus and other prickly plants were cleared, and huge dormitories were hastily erected to house construction workers. After its completion in 1943, the plant began production of ammonium nitrate to be used in explosives. Housing was built for the plant employees, who at one time numbered 6,000, and many of whom lived in trailer houses. With the easing of the emergency after several months, officials of the Chemical Construction Company received orders to close the plant. Operations were suspended, and some of the residential structures were sold as surplus before the Shell Union Oil and Gas Corporation assumed control of the plant in early 1944 and began manufacturing aviation gasoline. This arrangement lasted until August 1946, when the Emergency

Export Corporation took over and reconverted the plant to the production of ammonia. This company continued production until August 15, 1948, when Phillips Chemical, a division of Phillips Petroleum Company, assumed management. Phillips had erected another plant near the ordnance works in 1943. The Cactus post office was established in 1948, by which time the local population had decreased to 2,000. In the early 1980s Cactus had a population of 898 and fifteen businesses, including a large beef-packing plant. In 1990 the community's population was 1,529.

BIBLIOGRAPHY: M. D. Minor, The History of Moore County, Stressing Education (M.A. thesis, West Texas State College, 1949). Fred Tarpley, *1001 Texas Place Names* (Austin: University of Texas Press, 1980). *H. Allen Anderson*

CACTUS, TEXAS (Webb County). Cactus is two miles east of Interstate Highway 35 and twenty miles north of Laredo in northern Webb County. The settlement began around 1881 as a shipping point on the International–Great Northern Railroad. A local school enrolled forty-five pupils in 1907, and a post office served area residents from 1884 through 1916. After 1892 the community's reported population never exceeded fifty, and the number of residents had declined to twenty-five by the late 1940s. No population figures were available for Cactus from 1968 through the early 1990s. In the 1980s a combination gas station and grocery, a few scattered dwellings, and a cemetery remained in the vicinity. *Eduardo Pupo*

CACTUS BRANCH. Cactus Branch rises a mile west of Lott in western Falls County (at 31°11′ N, 97°03′ W) and runs south for six miles to its mouth on Pond Creek, five miles northwest of Rosebud (at 31°07′ N, 97°03′ W). It crosses flat to rolling prairie surfaced by dark, calcareous clays that support mesquite, cacti, and grasses.

CACTUS CREEK. Cactus Creek rises four miles northwest of Vivian in northwestern Foard County (at 34°06′ N, 99°57′ W) and runs northeast for ten miles to its mouth on the Pease River, ten miles southwest of Quanah in southwestern Hardeman County (at 34°11′ N, 99°53′ W). One source of the stream is Seven L Springs, which remained active through the 1970s. Cactus Creek crosses terrain that varies from rolling hills to steep slopes, with a surface of shallow sandy and clay loams in which grow juniper, cacti, and sparse grasses. The creek passes through remote rangeland marked with several sinkholes.

BIBLIOGRAPHY: Gunnar Brune, *Springs of Texas*, Vol. 1 (Fort Worth: Branch–Smith, 1981).

CACTUS ORDNANCE WORKS. The Cactus Ordnance Works, on 700 acres in northern Moore County, was begun in the spring of 1942, after the United States government entered into a $5 million contract with the Chemical Construction Company of New York to erect, equip, and staff a plant for the manufacturing of ammonia nitrate, a product of natural gas, to be used in making munitions. Construction was supervised by the United States Army Corps of Engineers, which was given temporary office space at the Moore County Courthouse in Dumas. There the engineers laid out plans for thirty-five staff houses, seven dormitories, seventy-five two-family duplexes, a cafeteria, a canteen, a fire station, and other facilities for an instant industrial town, as well as a railroad spur to the plant. In August 1942 a flag-raising ceremony was held at the COW. By the time of its completion in 1943, recreation clubs had been formed, and a plant newspaper, the *COW Puncher* (later the *Cactuzette*) was being printed. Soon the plant had nearly 3,000 employees, enough to prompt Sunray and Dumas to provide shopping and other services.

On May 5, 1943, with the easing of the wartime emergency, Chemical Construction Company officials received orders from Washington to close the COW down. Operations were suspended, and some of the residential structures, mostly trailer houses, were sold as surplus. Later that summer, however, Shell Union and Gas Corporation of San Francisco assumed control of the plant and in early 1944 began manufacturing aviation gasoline. That arrangement lasted until August 1946, when the Emergency Export Corporation took over and reconverted the plant for the purpose of producing ammonia for fertilizers to help bolster grain production in postwar Europe. About 250 tons was manufactured at the COW each day, and 375 people were employed. Emergency Export continued production there until August 15, 1948, when Phillips Chemical, a division of the Phillips Petroleum Company, which had built another plant near the COW in 1943, assumed management.

During the 1950s the COW was one of the nation's largest producers of chemicals for fertilizers. Despite a few cutbacks, employment was stabilized at around 600. By the end of the decade the aged plant was updated and automated. In 1961 a bitter 105-day strike occurred over a contract dispute between Phillips and the Oil, Chemical, and Atomic Workers of America. Due to increasing competition in fertilizer production, the plant's workforce was reduced to around 200 by the late 1960s. In November 1973 the ammonia section, the facility's largest production unit, was shut down. However, nitric acid and ammonium nitrate were still manufactured at the old COW for some time. By the early 1980s the Cactus Ordnance Works had completely shut down.

BIBLIOGRAPHY: Jay B. Funk and James C. Jarrett, *Moore County: Memories That Count* (Canyon, Texas: Staked Plains, 1986). M. D. Minor, The History of Moore County, Stressing Education (M.A. thesis, West Texas State College, 1949). *H. Allen Anderson*

CADDELL, ANDREW (1795–1869). Andrew Caddell, soldier at San Jacinto and Nacogdoches county official, was born on October 21, 1795, in Person County, North Carolina, the son of John Calvin and Mary (Jay) Caddell. He married Rhoda Doty in 1818 in Tuscaloosa County, Alabama; they had eleven children. The family moved to the Sabine District of Texas in April 1834. Caddell received a grant of a league and a labor of land now in San Augustine and Young counties from the San Augustine board of land commissioners in 1834. He was a member of Capt. William Kimbro's[qv] company at the battle of San Jacinto.[qv] He received a commission as captain and later commanded a company of volunteers from San Augustine County. He served in the army from March 15 to June 15, 1836. Shortly after the Texas Revolution[qv] he moved to Nacogdoches County, where he was tax assessor and collector from 1846 to 1854. He moved to a farm near Belton in 1867. He died in Bell County on October 15, 1869, and was buried there. One of his sons, John C. Caddell, was the first county clerk of Bell County. Another son, William Jay Caddell, also fought in the Texas army.

BIBLIOGRAPHY: Bell County Historical Commission, *Story of Bell County, Texas* (2 vols., Austin: Eakin Press, 1988).

Helen Gomer Schluter

CADDELL, TEXAS. Caddell was on Caddell Creek and a country road twenty-five miles south of San Augustine in far southern San Augustine County. The community received a post office in 1890 and had a population of fifty by 1896. The Caddell school enrolled twenty-eight students in 1904. In 1940 the community had scattered dwellings, a cemetery, and a school. The site was inundated by Sam Rayburn Reservoir[qv] in the 1960s; Caddell Cove, an inlet on the lake, preserves the name of the community. *Mark Odintz*

CADDO CREEK (Harrison County). Caddo Creek rises three miles northwest of Elysian Fields in southeastern Harrison County (at 32°25′ N, 94°12′ W) and runs southwest for fourteen miles to its mouth on the Sabine River, two miles northeast of Grand Bluff in north central Panola County (at 32°18′ N, 94°20′ W). It was probably named for the Caddo Indians, who lived in the area until the mid-1800s. The local terrain is level to rolling and is surfaced by loams and clays that support dense patches of pine and hardwood trees. The land is used predominantly for agriculture.

____ (Henderson County). Caddo Creek rises a mile northwest of Larue in southeastern Henderson County (at 32°08′ N, 95°41′ W) and runs southeast for eighteen miles to its mouth on the Neches River, a mile south of the U.S. Highway 178 bridge in Anderson County (at 32°01′ N, 95°26′ W). It crosses flat to rolling terrain surfaced by sandy and clay loams that support water-tolerant hardwoods, conifers, and grasses.

____ (Stephens County). Caddo Creek, also called Big Caddo Creek, rises in southeastern Stephens County (at 32°34′ N, 98°44′ W) and flows northeast for thirty-two miles to its mouth on Possum Kingdom Lake, in the northwest corner of Palo Pinto County (at 32°49′ N, 98°34′ W). It crosses flat terrain marked with local deep and dense dissection and some rolling hills. The soils are clay and sandy loams, locally shallow and stony. Oak, juniper, mesquite, scrub brush, cacti, and grasses grow in the area.

CADDO FORK OF THE SABINE RIVER. The Caddo Fork of the Sabine River rises a mile north of Quinlan in southwestern Hunt County (at 32°59′ N, 96°09′ W) and flows southeast for 6½ miles, over flat to rolling terrain surfaced with clay and sandy loams that support water-tolerant hardwoods and grasses. The stream is intermittent in its upper reaches. Throughout the history of Hunt County the area has been used as crop and range land. The Caddo Fork empties into the Caddo Inlet of Lake Tawakoni a half mile south of Boles Orphan Home[qv] (at 32°56′ N, 96°06′ W).

BIBLIOGRAPHY: W. Walworth Harrison, *History of Greenville and Hunt County, Texas* (Waco: Texian, 1976). Vertical Files, Barker Texas History Center, University of Texas at Austin (Lake Tawakoni).

CADDO GROVE, TEXAS. Caddo Grove, eight miles northeast of Cleburne in north central Johnson County, was named for nearby Caddo Peak. The settlement apparently developed around a store established by E. M. Heath early in 1869, although J. R. McKinsey, an area pioneer, had operated a school in his home in the area since 1854. After returning from the Civil War,[qv] McKinsey established the Caddo Grove Academy, a private school that, with Heath's store, attracted settlers. McKinsey also owned and operated a sawmill and a flour mill in Caddo Grove. Fifty-three students were enrolled in the local school in 1847. By 1876 two or three families made their homes in Caddo Grove, and a general merchandise store, a blacksmith shop, and three doctors served area residents. By that time Caddo Grove Academy had become a public school. Both the Missouri, Kansas and Texas and the Gulf, Colorado and Santa Fe railroads bypassed Caddo Grove in favor of the nearby settlement of Joshua in 1881. Soon afterward Caddo Grove was abandoned.

BIBLIOGRAPHY: *A Memorial and Biographical History of Johnson and Hill Counties* (Chicago: Lewis, 1892). *Brian Hart*

CADDO INDIANS. Before the middle of the nineteenth century the term *Caddo* denoted only one of at least twenty-five distinct but closely affiliated groups centered around the Red River in Texas, Arkansas, Louisiana, and Oklahoma. The term derives from the French abbreviation of *Kadohadacho,* a word meaning "real chief" or "real Caddo" in the Kadohadacho dialect. European chroniclers referred to the Caddo groups as the Hasinai, Kadohadacho, and Natchitoches confederacies, although the "confederacies" are better interpreted as kin-based affiliated groups or bands of Caddo communities. The Hasinai groups lived in the Neches and Angelina River valleys in East Texas, the Kadohadacho groups on the Red River in the Great Bend area, and the Natchitoches groups on the Red River in the vicinity of the French post of Natchitoches (Fort St. Jean Baptiste aux Natchitos), established in 1714. The first European description of the Caddo peoples came in 1542 from diarists traveling with the De Soto entrada, then led by Luis de Moscoso Alvarado[qv] (Hernando De Soto had died in the spring of 1542). The Spanish described several of the Caddo groups as having dense populations living in scattered settlements and having abundant food reserves of corn. Twentieth-century archeological investigations of many prehistoric Caddoan sites indicate that Caddo communities were widely dispersed throughout the major and minor stream valleys of the Caddoan area by around A.D. 800. The roots of these peoples can be traced to Fourche Maline or Woodland Period culture groups that began to settle down in small communities, to manufacture ceramics for cooking and storage of foodstuffs, and to develop a horticultural way of life based on the raising of tropical cultigens (corn, squash, and later beans) and certain native plants.

The development of prehistoric Caddo culture may have been the result of several factors, including: (a) the rise, elaboration, and maintenance of complex social and political symbols of authority, ritual, and ceremony (centering on the construction, dismantling, remodeling, and use of earthen temple and burial mounds); (b) the development of elite status positions within certain Caddo communities; (c) increased sedentary life; and (d) the expanding reliance on tropical cultigens in the economy, with an intensification in the use of maize agriculture after about A.D. 1200. Regardless of the processes involved, it is clear that after about A.D. 900, the Caddo groups were complex and socially ranked societies with well-planned civic-ceremonial centers, conducted elaborate mortuary rituals and ceremonial practices, and engaged in extensive interregional trade. Caddoan societies shared much with their Mississippian neighbors, particularly the adoption of maize and the development of maize agricultural economies, as well as systems of social authority and ceremony.

In prehistoric times, the Caddos lived in dispersed communities of grass and cane covered houses, with the communities composed of isolated farmsteads, small hamlets, a few larger villages, and the civic-ceremonial centers. These centers had earthen mounds used as platforms for temple structures for civic and religious functions, for burials of the social and political elite, and for ceremonial fire mounds. The largest communities and the most important civic-ceremonial centers were primarily located along the major streams—the Red, Arkansas, Little, Ouachita, and Sabine rivers. The Caddo peoples developed a successful horticultural economy based on the cultivation of maize, beans, and squash, as well as such native cultigens as maygrass, amaranth, chenopods, and sunflowers. By about A.D. 1300 most Caddoan groups were consuming large amounts of maize, and this plant was clearly the most important food source for them after that time. Several varieties of corn were cultivated, an early or "little corn," harvested in July, and the "flour corn," harvested in September at the harvest of the Great Corn. Deer was the most important source of meat to the Caddos, who exploited bison and bear for their furs and meat. After the introduction of the horse in the late seventeenth century, the Caddos began to participate in winter communal bison hunts on the prairies to the west of their settlements.

They developed long-distance trade networks in prehistoric times. Important items of trade were bison hides, salt, and bois d'arc bows, along with copper, stone, turquoise, and marine shell used for gorgets, cups, and dippers, as well as finished objects such as pottery vessels and large ceremonial bifaces. Many of the more important trade items were obtained from great distances (e.g., turquoise from New Mexico, copper from the Great Lakes, and marine shell from the Gulf Coast), and these items were often placed as grave goods in the burials of the social and political elite. The Caddo peoples had a sophisticated technology based on the use of clay, stone, bone, wood, shell, and other media for the manufacture of tools, clothing, ceramic vessels, basketry, ornaments, and other material items. The Caddos are particularly well known for the beautiful artistic and functional ceramic wares they made of many forms and functions, and the ceramics are considered some of the finest aboriginal pottery manufactured in North America. Stone was fashioned into arrowheads, and the Caddos also made ground stone celts and axes for use in removing trees and turning over the soil. They made bone into awls, beamers, digging implements, and hoes, as well as ornaments, beads, and whistles. Hoes and digging tools were also made of freshwater mussel shells, while marine shells obtained through trade were used in the production of shell pendants, gorgets, beads, and cups.

The Caddos traced descent through the maternal line rather than the paternal. Matrilineality was reflected in kinship terms, as the father and father's brothers were called by the same term as the mother and the mother's sisters. The Caddos recognized and ranked clans. Marriage typically occurred between members of different clans. Religious and political authority in historic Caddoan society rested in a hierarchy of key positions within and between the various affiliated communities and groups. The *xinesi* inherited a position of spiritual leadership, the *caddi* the position of principal headman of a community (also a hereditary leadership position), and the *canahas* the position of subordinate headmen or village elders. The Caddo people turned to the *xinesi* for mediation and communication with the supreme god, the *Caddi Ayo,* for religious leadership and decision-making influence between allied villages and in leading certain special rites, including first-fruits, harvest, and naming ceremonies. The *xinesi* imbued everyday life with the supernatural. The *caddi* was primarily responsible for making the important political decisions for the community, sponsoring important ceremonies, leading councils for war expeditions, and conducting the calumet (or peace pipe) ceremony with visitors to the communities. The most influential and politically astute Caddo leaders or *caddices* in historic times were Tinhiouen (from ca. 1760 to 1789) and Dehahuit (from ca. 1800 to 1833) of the Kadohadachos, and Iesh or José María (from about 1842 to 1862) of the Anadarko or Nadaco tribe.

At the time of sustained European (Spanish and French) contact with the Caddo groups in the late seventeenth century, Caddo peoples lived on the Red River and in East Texas. European populations—living in missions, ranches, and trading posts—increased throughout the eighteenth and into the early nineteenth century in the Red River valley and in the vicinity of Natchitoches and Nacogdoches, important fur trading centers, while epidemics between 1691 and 1816 greatly reduced Caddo populations. At the same time, the Caddo peoples participated in the fur trade, traded guns, horses, and other items to Europeans and other Indians, and developed new trade and economic networks. The resulting economic symbiosis between the Caddo groups and Europeans was an important means of acculturation because great quantities of European goods became available to the Caddo. While the Hasinai Caddo groups continued to live through the 1830s in their traditional East Texas homeland in the Neches and Angelina River valleys, the Kadohadacho groups moved off the Red River in the 1790s to get away from Osage depredations and slave-raiding. Their new settlements were between the Sabine River and Caddo Lake,[qv] generally along the boundary between the territory of Louisiana and the province of Texas. Most of the Kadohadachos remained in the Caddo Lake area until about 1842, although with the cession of Caddoan lands in Louisiana in 1835 and increased Texas settlement, other Kadohadacho moved to the Brazos River in north central Texas. By the early 1840s, all Caddo groups had moved to the Brazos River area to remove themselves from Anglo-American repressive measures and colonization efforts. They remained there until they were placed on the Brazos Indian Reservation[qv] in 1855, and then in 1859 the Caddos (about 1,050 people) were removed to the Washita River in Indian Territory (now western Oklahoma) with the help of Robert S. Neighbors,[qv] superintendent of Indian affairs in Texas.

During the Civil War[qv] most of the Caddo groups abandoned the Indian Territory and resettled in southern and eastern Kansas, but they moved back to the Wichita Reservation in 1867. By 1874 the boundaries of the Caddo reservation were defined, and the separate Caddo tribes agreed to unite as the unified Caddo Indian Tribe. Under the terms of the General Allotment Act of 1887, the Caddo reservation was partitioned in 1902 a 160-acre allotment for each enrolled Caddo, and the remaining lands were opened for white settlement. The Caddo peoples continue to live in western Oklahoma, primarily in Caddo County near the Caddo Indian Tribe's Tribal Complex, outside Binger, Oklahoma.

BIBLIOGRAPHY: Hiram F. Gregory, ed., *The Southern Caddo: An Anthology* (New York: Garland, 1986). Thomas R. Hester, *Ethnology of the Texas Indians* (New York: Garland, 1991). Frederick Webb Hodge, ed., *Handbook of American Indians North of Mexico* (2 vols., Washington: GPO, 1907, 1910; rpt., New York: Pageant, 1959). Marvin D. Jeter et al., *Archeology and Bioarcheology of the Lower Mississippi Valley and Trans-Mississippi South in Arkansas and Louisiana* (Research Series No. 37, Fayetteville: Arkansas Archeological Survey, 1989). Michael S. Nassaney and Charles R. Cobb, eds., *Stability, Transformation, and Variation: The Late Woodland Southeast* (New York: Plenum Press, 1991). Vynola B. Newkumet and Howard L. Meredith, *Hasinai: A Traditional History of the Caddo Confederacy* (College Station: Texas A&M University Press, 1988). Timothy K. Perttula, *"The Caddo Nation": Archaeological and Ethnohistoric Perspectives* (Austin: University of Texas Press, 1992). F. Todd Smith, *The Caddo Indians* (College Station: Texas A&M University Press, 1995). F. Todd Smith, "The Red River Caddos: A Historical Overview to 1835," *Bulletin of the Texas Archeological Society* 64 (1994). Dee Ann Story, Cultural History of the Native Americans, in *Archeology and Bioarcheology of the Gulf Coast Plain* (Research Series No. 38, Fayetteville, Arkansas: Arkansas Archeological Survey, 1990). John R. Swanton, *Source Material on the History and Ethnology of the Caddo Indians* (Smithsonian Institution, Bureau of American Ethnology Bulletin 132, Washington: GPO, 1942).

Timothy K. Perttula

CADDO LAKE. Caddo Lake is impounded by Caddo Dam in the Cypress Creek basin in Caddo Parish, Louisiana, and extends into Harrison and Marion counties, Texas; the center of the lake is located twenty-nine miles northeast of Marshall (at 30°42′ N, 97°20′ W). The lake, named for the Caddo Indians, was one of the largest natural lakes in the South prior to the construction of the dam. According to Caddo legend the lake was formed by an earthquake caused by a Caddo chief's failure to obey the Great Spirit. The more prosaic explanation of the lake's origin is that it was formed behind a log jam in the Red River. In 1874 the United States government destroyed the log jam, or Red River Raft, as it was called (*see* RED RIVER).

In 1914 a dam was completed near Mooringsport, Louisiana. Construction was begun on a replacement dam in 1968 and completed in 1971. The dam is owned and operated by the Caddo Lake Levee District. The project was constructed by the United States Army Corps of Engineers for water-supply purposes. Caddo Lake is formed by an earthfill dam some 1,540 feet long and is used for recreation, wildlife preserves, and water conservation. The crest of the spillway is 170.5 feet above mean sea level, the conservation storage capacity is 69,200 acre-feet, and the surface area is 20,700 acres. The drainage area above the dam (including the drainage area of Lake O' the Pines[qv]) comprises 2,700 square miles. The lake is the heart of the 500-acre Caddo State Park, established in 1934; it is noted for its giant cypress trees, plentiful fish, and excellent duck and goose hunting. In 1993, in an attempt to block the construction of a barge canal through the lake, environmentalists secured recognition of Caddo Lake as an international wetlands site, the thirteenth such site in the United States.

Along the shores of Caddo Lake and Cypress Creek are to be found many towns and ghost towns dating back to the days of the Republic of Texas.[qv] Swanson's Landing on Broad Lake was near the place of the burning of the steamer *Mittie Stevens*[qv] in 1869, when some sixty persons were burned to death at night, not realizing that the shore was so close or the water so shallow. Farther up the bayou were Port Caddo, the port of entry for the Republic of Texas in the northeast, and Benton, from which much of the river freight was distributed to other parts of Texas before Jefferson became the head of navigation. A short distance inland from Port Caddo is the site of Macon, called the "Lost Colony" after its settlers moved to Port Caddo. Another point of historical interest is the government ditch that was dredged upstream toward Jefferson so that cotton could be shipped from Texas to New Orleans on the Red River.

BIBLIOGRAPHY: C. L. Dowell and R. G. Petty, *Engineering Data on Dams and Reservoirs in Texas* (Texas Water Development Board Report 126 [3 pts., Austin, 1971–74]). V. H. Hackney, *Historical Hallmarks of Harrison County* (Marshall, Texas: Marshall National Bank, 1964). V. H. Hackney, *Port Caddo—A Vanished Village and Vignettes of Harrison County* (Marshall, Texas: Marshall National Bank, 1966).

Seth D. Breeding and Sallie Starr Lentz

CADDO LAKE STATE PARK. Caddo Lake State Park, on Caddo Lake sixteen miles northeast of Marshall in Harrison County, comprises 478 acres, including an abandoned thirty-acre log pond. The park was first proposed in 1924, but progress was slow until the 1930s. Between 1933 and 1937 various individuals donated land; most notably, Thomas Jefferson Taylor II[qv] gave 385 acres. The park has picnicking, camping, boating, and fishing facilities, as well as nature and hiking trails. It also has a visitor center and museum with interpretive displays of Indian artifacts, pictures and specimens of native fish, wildlife, and birds, and wood samples of prominent trees of the region.

Vernen Liles and Marjorie Seidel

CADDO MILLS, TEXAS. Caddo Mills is at the intersection of State Highway 66 and Farm Road 36, eight miles southwest of Greenville in southwestern Hunt County. Caddo Indians were early inhabitants and camped in the area near the banks of Caddo Creek. The first arrived in the late 1850s. Twenty years later I. T. Johnson and Henry King built a gristmill a mile west of the present townsite. Shortly thereafter, a store opened and a community developed. Residents in the area referred to the community as Caddo Mills, after Johnson and King's gristmill. On June 16, 1879, a post office opened. By the early 1880s the settlement had 100 residents, three churches, a school, and at least a dozen businesses. In 1886 the tracks of the Missouri, Kansas and Texas Railroad reached the area. As a depot of the Katy, Caddo Mills grew rapidly over the next few decades. By 1892 the number of businesses doubled and the population increased to 500. In 1897 the Caddo Mills *Banner* began weekly publication. The State National Bank opened in 1905. The town's population reached 700 on the eve of World War I,[qv] then fell to 600 in the 1920s. By the early 1940s Caddo Mills had incorporated; the population was reported as 390 and the number of businesses as twenty. The population reached 680 by 1964 and 1,302 by 1988. In 1990 it was 1,068.

BIBLIOGRAPHY: W. Walworth Harrison, *History of Greenville and Hunt County, Texas* (Waco: Texian, 1976). *David Minor*

CADDO NATIONAL GRASSLAND. Caddo National Grassland is on Farm Road 100 eleven miles north of Honey Grove in Fannin County. The 17,785-acre preserve was purchased by the United States Department of the Interior during the 1930s under the Bankhead-Jones Farm Tenant Act in an effort to return some of the badly eroded land of the area to its natural state. The preserve, which borders on both Lake Coffeemill and Lake Davy Crockett, is administered by the United States Department of Agriculture Forest Service regional office in Lufkin under a policy of multiple use for range, watershed, recreation, and wildlife. Open grasslands and post oak and blackjack oak savannas provide habitats for a variety of animal life, ranging from deer and opossums to bobwhite quail and mourning doves. Facilities include camping and picnicking areas and boat ramps.

BIBLIOGRAPHY: George Oxford Miller, *Texas Parks and Campgrounds: Central, South, and West Texas* (Austin: Texas Monthly Press, 1984). *Christopher Long*

CADDO PEAK. Caddo Peak is 1½ miles northwest of Joshua in north central Johnson County (at 32°28′ N, 97°24′ W). The brown sandstone hill, located near the Santa Fe Trail,[qv] bears inscriptions chiseled into its face, some dating back to 1836. It rises to a height of 1,065 feet above mean sea level.

BIBLIOGRAPHY: Johnson County History Book Committee, *History of Johnson County, Texas* (Dallas: Curtis Media, 1985).

CADDO PEAK, TEXAS. Caddo Peak was about sixteen miles from Putnam and five miles northwest of Cross Plains in southeastern Callahan County. It was settled in 1870 and received a post office in 1878. This was discontinued in December 1881 but reinstated in November 1882. By 1884 the community had three churches and a district school as well as three general stores, a flour mill, and a physician. From about 1880 through 1900 the community's population remained at about fifty. By 1897 Caddo Peak consisted of a general store, a blacksmith shop, a cotton gin, and a local school with twenty-eight students and one teacher. In March 1907 the post office was discontinued permanently. A 1936 map shows scattered residences and a cemetery in the area; a 1989 map shows only the cemetery.

BIBLIOGRAPHY: Brutus Clay Chrisman, *Early Days in Callahan County* (Abilene, Texas: Abilene Printing and Stationery, 1966).

John G. Johnson

CADDO, TEXAS (Milam County). Caddo (Caddo Springs) was a farming community on Farm Road 2027 two miles northwest of Baileyville in northern Milam County. It was supposedly named for an Indian campground. Area schools were part of the Baileyville system until the early 1970s, when they were consolidated with the Rosebud Independent School District in Falls County.

BIBLIOGRAPHY: Lelia M. Batte, *History of Milam County, Texas* (San Antonio: Naylor, 1956). *Vivian Elizabeth Smyrl*

CADDO, TEXAS (Stephens County). Caddo, at the junction of U.S. Highway 180, Farm Road 717, and Park Road 33 in east central Stephens County, was established in the late 1870s on a Caddo Indian campsite. In 1880 the town had sixty residents, two churches, a school, and a post office. Its reported population was seventy-five in 1890 and 149 in 1900. The Ranger oil boom of 1916–17 increased Caddo's population to 1,000 by 1920. Oil was discovered on the W. L. Carey farm near Caddo in 1916, then on the L. W. Wright property at Caddo. These finds kept interest high and were harbingers of the Breckenridge boom in 1917. Caddo had 600 residents in 1940, but World War II[qv] and the postwar era saw the town decline. In 1980 and 1990 its population was forty, and its post office was still in service.

BIBLIOGRAPHY: Betty E. Hanna, *Doodle Bugs and Cactus Berries: A Historical Sketch of Stephens County* (Quanah, Texas: Nortex, 1975).

William R. Hunt

CADDO, TEXAS (Wilson County). Caddo is on Farm Road 3335 eighteen miles northeast of Floresville in eastern Wilson County. The community was first settled around the time of the Civil War.[qv] A school was in operation there by 1896, when it had an enrollment of sixty-four. In the mid-1930s Caddo had a school, a gin, a church, and a number of houses. After World War II[qv] the school and gin were closed, and in the early 1990s only the church and a few scattered houses remained. *Christopher Long*

CADDOAN MOUNDS STATE HISTORIC SITE. Caddoan Mounds State Historic Site, one of the best known and intensively investigated Indian sites in Texas, is on State Highway 21 about six miles southwest of Alto in southern Cherokee County. It comprises much of what is known to archeologists as the George C. Davis Site, the southwesternmost ceremonial center of the Caddoan peoples who flourished on the western edge of the woodlands of eastern North America between 1000 B.C. and A.D. 1550. Caddoan Mounds consists of three large earthen mounds, as well as a large portion of a prehistoric village.

The large mounds have long been recognized as an ancient Indian settlement. One of the principal routes of the Old San Antonio Road,[qv] which extended diagonally across southern Cherokee County, ran along one edge of the mound site. The earliest mention of the mounds was made by Athanase de Mézières,[qv] a Frenchman in the employ of Spain, who traveled from Louisiana to San Antonio in 1779. Numerous amateur archeologists and other travelers visited the area during the nineteenth century. The first professional archeologist to examine the mounds, James Edwin Pearce,[qv] recorded the site for the Bureau of Ethnology in 1919. An Arizona archeologist, E. B. Sayles, who collected surface artifacts in 1933, concluded that the mounds had been built by the prehistoric Southern Caddos.

The first systematic excavations at the site were conducted by the Work Projects Administration[qv] and the University of Texas archeologist H. Perry Newell from 1939 to 1941. After Newell's death Alex D. Krieger, another UT archeologist, examined Newell's findings and concluded that the site had been a major Caddo community inhabited for several centuries, possibly as early as A.D. 500. Evidence collected in further excavations conducted by a team led by Dee Ann Story in the late 1960s and early 1970s suggested that the mounds had been occupied by the Early Caddos between A.D. 780 and 1260. Additional examination of the excavated material revealed that the site had been occupied by Paleo-Indian (10,000–6,000 B.C.) and Archaic cultures (6,000 B.C.–A.D. 500).

Scholars now believe that Early Caddos, probably from the Red River area to the northeast, founded a permanent settlement at the site sometime between A.D. 850 and 900. The life of these people differed markedly from that of the transient hunters and gathers who had previously used the site. At the same time, the society and material culture of the newcomers reflected a series of cultural developments evident between A.D. 800 and 1000 throughout much of the southeastern United States and central Mississippi valley. Inhabitants of the Davis Site cultivated large quantities of corn, which they supplemented with wild plants and game. They used the bow and arrow and made a decorated pottery that differed from the simpler vessels of earlier people who had camped there. Artifacts suggest that they participated in trade networks that stretched to the Gulf Coast, Central Texas, the Ouachita Mountains of western Arkansas and southeastern Oklahoma, and the Appalachians. Their dwellings were beehive-shaped structures of pole and thatch construction, about twenty-five feet in diameter, possibly occupied by extended families. Archeological evidence indicates a hierarchical social and political organization. Two of the mounds represent communal precincts, where special structures served multiple functions. The third mound served as a burial site for elite members of the community. The mounds developed over time, as burials and destroyed buildings were periodically covered over with earth.

The Davis Site served as a regional center for the middle Neches region for almost 500 years. Then, for reasons unknown, the site was abandoned about A.D. 1300. It was used to some extent by later Caddoan people, but the site never regained its former prominence. When Europeans arrived in the area in the eighteenth century, the Caddoan groups they encountered lived in widely dispersed hamlets and small villages. Their social and political organization had become less hierarchical, and they had ceased to build mounds.

In 1974 the Texas Parks and Wildlife Department[qv] acquired seventy acres at the site and established a historic park. During the late 1970s and early 1980s, the department sponsored a series of excavations by archeologists from the University of Texas at Austin, Texas A&M University, and private contractor Elton R. Prewitt. The digs revealed large concentrations of artifacts and surface features that indicated the village had been significantly larger than previously thought, extending beyond Weeping Mary Road to the north. As a result, the Parks and Wildlife Department acquired an additional twenty-three acres of adjacent land in 1981. The Parks and Wildlife Department subsequently constructed a visitors' center with interpretive exhibits as well as a three-quarter-mile self-guided trail tour that leads visitors through the mounds and village. Also on exhibit is a reconstruction of an Early Caddo dwelling, built using tools and techniques employed by the Caddos.

BIBLIOGRAPHY: Darrell Creel, *Archeological Investigations at the George C. Davis Site, Cherokee County, Texas, Summer, 1978* (College Station: Texas A&M University and Texas Antiquities Committee, 1979). William Bonny Glover, A History of the Caddo Indians (M.A. thesis, University of Texas, 1932). Karen West Scott, An Interpretive Plan for Caddoan Mounds State Historic Site (the George C. Davis Site), Cherokee County, Texas (M.S. thesis, Stephen F. Austin State University, 1984). Dee Ann Story, "Indian Mounds," *Discovery: Research and Scholarship at the University of Texas*, Autumn 1984.

Christopher Long and Mary M. Standifer

CADE LAKES. The Cade Lakes are two man-made reservoirs on upper Davidson Creek three miles west of Caldwell in western Burleson County (at 30°31′ N, 96°42′ W). They were constructed in 1964 and lie 2½ miles below the creek's spring-fed headwaters. The twin, roughly half-mile-long bodies of water are known as East Lake and West Lake and are connected by a narrow channel along the dam near their southern rims. The spillway elevation of the dam is 403 feet. Shiloh and the Shiloh Baptist Church, established in 1869, are situated on the southwest shores of West Lake. The surrounding gently sloping terrain is surfaced by sand that supports post oak, blackjack oak, elm, and hackberry trees on the northern shore of East Lake. The lakes appear to have been named for C. E. Cade, who served as alderman in Caldwell from 1926 to 1936.

BIBLIOGRAPHY: Burleson County Historical Society, *Astride the Old San Antonio Road: A History of Burleson County, Texas* (Dallas: Taylor, 1980).

CADENA CREEK. Cadena Creek rises two miles south of Goliad in central Goliad County (at 28°37′ N, 97°24′ W) and flows east for six miles to its mouth on the San Antonio River, a mile north of Farm Road 239 (at 28°37′ N, 97°19′ W). It traverses flat to rolling terrain surfaced by clay and sandy loam that supports water-tolerant hardwoods and grasses. The name is Spanish for "chain."

CADIZ, TEXAS. Cadiz is on Farm Road 799 near La Para Creek twelve miles west of Beeville in western Bee County. In the early 1870s the community was known as Lapara (perhaps from *la parral*, Spanish for "thicket" or "tangle of vines"). By the late 1870s R. C. Eeds had opened a store, and Amos Barker was minister of the Lapara Baptist Church. Area children attended school at the Turner and McCollom homes. When a post office was established in 1892, the name of the community was changed to Cadiz. In 1914 the population was reported at fifty, but by the early 1930s it had decreased to twenty-five. In the late 1930s the community had two churches, a store, a gin, a three-teacher school, and a service station. The post office was discontinued in 1942, and mail for the community was routed through Beeville. The population of Cadiz was reported at fifteen from the late 1950s through 1990. Community life centered around the Cadiz Baptist Church.

BIBLIOGRAPHY: Grace Bauer, *Bee County Centennial, 1858–1958* (Bee

County Centennial, 1958). Camp Ezell, *Historical Story of Bee County, Texas* (Beeville: Beeville Publishing, 1973).

Rebecca Leigh Kendall

CAESAR, TEXAS. Caesar is on Farm Road 798 eight miles northwest of Pettus in northern Bee County. It was originally called Wolfe's Neighborhood after Peter Wolfe, who settled in the area before 1876. The name was changed to Caesar in the early 1900s, when R. L. Peevy built the first store there and applied for a post office. He sent the postal authorities a list of potential names from his Bible; from this list the authorities chose Caesar. The post office was established in 1903 and was discontinued sometime after 1930. In 1914 the town had a church, a store, and a population of fifteen. Gas and oil were discovered in the area, but old-timers refused to sell any of the land to newcomers. By the late 1980s no residents or businesses were recorded there.

BIBLIOGRAPHY: Grace Bauer, *Bee County Centennial, 1858–1958* (Bee County Centennial, 1958). Camp Ezell, *Historical Story of Bee County, Texas* (Beeville: Beeville Publishing, 1973).

Grace Bauer

CAGAYA INDIANS. This name occurs in a single Spanish missionary report of 1691, which lists eight groups that lived some eighty leagues southwest of the Hasinai Indians of eastern Texas. The Jumano (Chuman) Indians are named on this list. The Cagayas may be the same as the Caynaayas, named in another document of the same year, along with Jumanos and Cíbolas, as having been seen hunting bison near the Guadalupe River east of San Antonio. If the Cagayas and Caynaayas were the same, then the Cagayas can be identified as Indians of Trans-Pecos Texas, the designated home of the Caynaaya, Cibola, and Jumano Indians.

BIBLIOGRAPHY: Herbert E. Bolton, "The Jumano Indians in Texas, 1650–1771," *Quarterly of the Texas State Historical Association* 15 (July 1911). John R. Swanton, *Source Material on the History and Ethnology of the Caddo Indians* (Smithsonian Institution, Bureau of American Ethnology Bulletin 132, Washington: GPO, 1942).

Thomas N. Campbell

CAGUATE INDIANS. The Caguate (Caguase, Caguaze) Indians lived along the Rio Grande valley below El Paso in the late sixteenth century. Some writers regard the Caguates as a Jumano band; others suggest that Caguate was probably an early name for the Sumas, who occupied that area in the seventeenth and eighteenth centuries. The status of the Caguates remains in doubt.

BIBLIOGRAPHY: J. Charles Kelley, "Factors Involved in the Abandonment of Certain Peripheral Southwestern Settlements," *American Anthropologist* 54 (July–September 1952). Diego Pérez de Luxán, *Expedition into New Mexico Made by Antonio de Espejo, 1582–1583,* trans. George Peter Hammond and Agapito Rey (Los Angeles: Quivira Society, 1929). Carl Sauer, *The Distribution of Aboriginal Tribes and Languages in Northwestern Mexico* (Berkeley: University of California Press, 1934).

Thomas N. Campbell

CAIASBAN INDIANS. The Caiasban Indians are known only from the 1687 records of the La Salle expedition,[qv] which merely list these Indians as enemies of the Kadohadachos on the Red River. They may be the same as the Caais, named in a 1691 Spanish missionary report as one of the groups that lived southwest of the Hasinais, and also the Caisquetebanas, who in 1690 lived north of Matagorda Bay between the Guadalupe and Colorado rivers. These identifications cannot be demonstrated. If the names all refer to the same group of Indians, then a considerable north–south range is indicated. The affiliations of the three groups remain unknown.

BIBLIOGRAPHY: Herbert Eugene Bolton, ed., *Spanish Exploration in the Southwest, 1542–1706* (New York: Scribner, 1908; rpt., New York: Barnes and Noble, 1959). Pierre Margry, ed., *Découvertes et établissements des Français dans l'ouest et dans le sud de l'Amérique septentrionale, 1614–1754* (6 vols., Paris: Jouast, 1876–86). John R. Swanton, *Source Material on the History and Ethnology of the Caddo Indians* (Smithsonian Institution, Bureau of American Ethnology Bulletin 132, Washington: GPO, 1942).

Thomas N. Campbell

CAICACHE INDIANS. A few eighteenth century maps show the Caicache (Kaikache) Indians on the Texas coast between the Nueces River and the Rio Grande. The primary sources used by the cartographers have not been identified. Caicache may be a variant of either Aguichacha or Cacaxtle. In the seventeenth century the Aguichachas lived between Monterrey and Cerralvo (Nuevo León) and the Cacaxtles lived farther inland in southern Texas.

BIBLIOGRAPHY: William Bollaert, "Observations on the Indian Tribes in Texas," *Journal of the Ethnological Society of London* 2 (1850). Frederick Webb Hodge, ed., *Handbook of American Indians North of Mexico* (2 vols., Washington: GPO, 1907, 1910; rpt., New York: Pageant, 1959).

Thomas N. Campbell

CAIMAN CREEK. Caiman Creek rises nine miles southwest of Artesia Wells in southwestern La Salle County (at 28°09′ N, 99°21′ W) and runs east for ten miles to its mouth on the Nueces River, eighteen miles southeast of Artesia Wells (at 28°09′ N, 99°02′ W). It crosses low-rolling to flat terrain with locally shallow depressions and a surface of clay and sandy loams that support grasses, mesquite, and chaparral upstream and water-tolerant hardwoods and grasses downstream.

CAIMANE INDIANS. The Caimane Indians are known from a Spanish document of 1683 that does not clearly identify their area, although it seems to have been east of the Pecos River. Their name bears some similarity to Camama, the name of a band, presumable Coahuiltecan, known only from eighteenth-century records pertaining to San José y San Miguel de Aguayo Mission at San Antonio. As yet the two groups cannot otherwise be linked.

BIBLIOGRAPHY: Charles W. Hackett, ed., *Pichardo's Treatise on the Limits of Louisiana and Texas* (4 vols., Austin: University of Texas Press, 1931–46).

Thomas N. Campbell

CAIN, JOHN (1802–1836). John Cain, Alamo defender, was born in Pennsylvania in 1802 and became a resident of Gonzales, Texas. He took part in the siege of Bexar[qv] and was issued a donation certificate for 640 acres of land for his service. After the battle he remained in Bexar as a member of Capt. William R. Carey's[qv] artillery company. He may have left Bexar before the siege of the Alamo began and returned with the relief force from Gonzales on March 1, 1836. He died in the battle of the Alamo[qv] on March 6, 1836.

BIBLIOGRAPHY: Daughters of the American Revolution, *The Alamo Heroes and Their Revolutionary Ancestors* (San Antonio, 1976). Daughters of the Republic of Texas, *Muster Rolls of the Texas Revolution* (Austin, 1986). Bill Groneman, *Alamo Defenders* (Austin: Eakin, 1990). Ethel Zivley Rather, "DeWitt's Colony," *Quarterly of the Texas State Historical Association* 8 (October 1904).

Bill Groneman

CAIN CITY, TEXAS. Cain City, four miles southeast of Fredericksburg in southern Gillespie County, was founded by J. C. Stinson, a Kansas farmer who moved to San Antonio and bought 324 acres in Gillespie County in 1913. He and a surveyor named A. J. Green laid out streets, lots, and parks in anticipation of the arrival of the Fredericksburg and Northern Railway, which was built through Gillespie County in 1913. Cain City was named after San Antonio businessman Charlie Cain, an important fund-raiser for the railroad construction. A depot was built near the railroad tracks, and the town grew into an important shipping center for agricultural products from the surrounding rural area. In 1914 Cain City got a water system, an unpaved road to nearby Luckenbach, and two early businesses, the Farmers' Produce Company warehouse, built by Tom Schmidt, and Alfred Jung's lumberyard. Also in 1914 Stinson petitioned the federal government for a post office, which opened the following year with railroad agent Hugo Pahl as postmaster. In 1915 Mrs. Fletcher Hamilton of Illinois opened the Mountain Home Hotel, which she later sold to Stinson. That year also brought Cain City a telephone exchange, two general stores, owned by Alfred Pahl and by A. M. and Marion Cox and Luther Price, and a schoolhouse, with Katie Striegler as teacher, which had a peak enrollment of thirty students. In 1917 the Cain City Bank was founded with Stinson as president, and in 1919 Gus Bausch opened a cotton gin. In the 1920s, however, Cain City's prosperity began to diminish. In 1922 Stinson sold the hotel and moved back to San Antonio, and the Cain City Bank folded shortly thereafter. Cain City's population reached an estimated high of seventy-five in 1925. In 1927 Edgar Tatsch and Theodore Keller opened a dance hall. Fifteen years later Mrs. Will Bird, who had bought the Mountain Home Hotel from Stinson, razed the hotel. The railroad ceased operation on October 1, 1944. By 1949 the estimated population had sunk to twenty-five, and by the mid-1960s the community was little more than a ghost town. The population was estimated at fifteen in 1964.

BIBLIOGRAPHY: Eileen Schneider, "Cain City—Ghost Town," *Junior Historian*, November 1964. *Martin Donell Kohout*

CAIRO SPRINGS, TEXAS. Cairo Springs, also known as Cairo, is between Farm Road 1004 and the Neches River seven miles northwest of Buna and forty-three miles north of Beaumont in southwestern Jasper County. To serve the heavy river traffic a post office operated at Cairo from 1858 to 1866 and reopened in 1872. The Texas Tram and Lumber Company established a logging camp in 1876 near Yellow Bluff, which overlooked the Neches River. By 1877 Long and Company was leasing the Yellow Bluff Tramway, which extended three miles into Jasper County to Cairo. The following year, about sixty men were employed in the Cairo–Yellow Bluff vicinity, cutting timber near Cairo, shipping it along the tram line to Yellow Bluff, then floating the logs down the Neches River to Beaumont sawmills. Machinery for the Texas Tram and Lumber Company mill at Cairo was sent upriver from Beaumont in 1881. Although headquarters were moved to Magnolia Springs in 1882, the logging camp at Cairo continued until 1894. With the depletion of local timber and the coming of the railroads to Jasper and Tyler counties, the camp was abandoned, and the post office closed in 1895. The Cairo Springs church and Cairo Springs lookout marked the old site in 1990. The Sally Withers and Sally Withers Lake oilfields, first discovered in 1956 and expanded in 1961 and 1977–79, lie just to the southeast of the Cairo Springs site.

BIBLIOGRAPHY: W. T. Block, ed., *Emerald of the Neches: The Chronicles of Beaumont from Reconstruction to Spindletop* (Nederland, Texas: Nederland Publishing, 1980). *Robert Wooster*

CAISQUETEBANA INDIANS. The Caisquetebana Indians are known only from records of Alonso De León's[qv] various expeditions to the Texas coast in search of La Salle's[qv] Fort St. Louis. In 1690 De Leon visited a small settlement of these Indians north of Matagorda Bay and between the Guadalupe and Colorado rivers. The name suggests the possibility of linkage with the Caai Indians, reported in 1691 as living southwest of the Hasinais, and also the Caiasbans, named in the 1687 documents of the La Salle expedition[qv] as enemies of the Kadohadachos on the Red River. These identifications cannot be demonstrated. If the names all refer to the same group of Indians, then a considerable north-south range is indicated. The affiliations of these groups remain unknown.

BIBLIOGRAPHY: Herbert Eugene Bolton, ed., *Spanish Exploration in the Southwest, 1542–1706* (New York: Scribner, 1908; rpt., New York: Barnes and Noble, 1959). Pierre Margry, ed., *Découvertes et établissements des Français dans l'ouest et dans le sud de l'Amérique septentrionale, 1614–1754* (6 vols., Paris: Jouast, 1876–86). John R. Swanton, *Source Material on the History and Ethnology of the Caddo Indians* (Smithsonian Institution, Bureau of American Ethnology Bulletin 132, Washington: GPO, 1942). *Thomas N. Campbell*

CALAHORRA Y SAENZ, JOSÉ FRANCISCO (?–?). Fray José Francisco Calahorra y Saenz was for over twenty years a Franciscan missionary in East Texas. His services demonstrate the superlative use to which the Spanish government put priests as mediators and diplomats. His 1745 report from Nacogdoches to Joaquín de Orobio y Basterra, captain at La Bahía,[qv] concerning Frenchmen wrecked on the Texas coast resulted in Orobio's visit to Los Adaes[qv] to consult Governor Francisco García Larios[qv] on French activities. After the defeat of Diego Ortiz Parrilla[qv] at Spanish Fort in 1759, Calahorra attempted to restore peace with the northern tribes. Tawakonis and Yscanis visited him asking peace and offering to give up Spanish captives and cannons. In September 1760 the governor furnished an escort for the priest to go to the Tawakoni villages on the upper Sabine River to meet a delegation of Taovayas for a peace meeting. He made other trips to the northern Indians in 1762 and 1763 and, as a result of the conference, proposed moving the San Sabá Presidio (*see* SAN LUIS DE LAS AMARILLAS PRESIDIO) to the Tawakoni area or to the country between the Tawakonis and the Taovayas. It was probably as a result of his efforts that the Taovayas took the captive Antonio Treviño to San Antonio in 1765. Though Calahorra may have been at Los Adaes part of the time, he was in Nacogdoches in 1768, when Fray Gaspar José de Solís[qv] inspected the East Texas missions.

BIBLIOGRAPHY: Herbert Eugene Bolton, ed. and trans., *Athanase de Mézières and the Louisiana-Texas Frontier, 1768–1780* (2 vols., Cleveland: Arthur H. Clark, 1914). Carlos E. Castañeda, *Our Catholic Heritage in Texas* (7 vols., Austin: Von Boeckmann–Jones, 1936–58; rpt., New York: Arno, 1976). Gaspar José de Solís, "Diary," trans. Margaret Kenny Kress, *Southwestern Historical Quarterly* 35 (July 1931).

CALALLEN, TEXAS. Calallen, on State Highway 9 in extreme north central Nueces County, was once an independent town but is now part of Corpus Christi. It was named for Calvin Allen, who donated land for the St. Louis, Brownsville and Mexico Railway. A nearby Nueces River dam is named Calallen Dam. The Calallen community received a post office in 1908 with Ira D. Magee as the first postmaster. The post office was discontinued after 1930. In 1914 the town had 150 residents and nine businesses. Its population dwindled to twenty-five by 1925 but reached 100 in 1939; it was 270 by 1965. By 1966 Corpus Christi had annexed Calallen.

BIBLIOGRAPHY: Nueces County Historical Society, *History of Nueces County* (Austin: Jenkins, 1972). *Karen S. Parrish*

CALAMITY CREEK. Calamity Creek rises southeast of Ranger Peak, 6½ miles southwest of Alpine in northwestern Brewster County (at 30°16′ N, 103°43′ W), and flows down a winding course through rugged mountain terrain for a number of miles before issuing out on open desert flatland. Thence it flows south-southeast for sixty-two miles to its intersection with Chalk Draw, about four miles west of Santiago Peak. The stream then continues southeast for thirty-five more miles through Chalk Draw, Nine Point Draw, and Dog Canyon in the north end of Big Bend National Park,[qv] before it finally reaches its mouth on Maravillas Creek, about five miles east of the Persimmon Gap ranger station (at 29°40′ N, 103°10′ W). Calamity Creek is the westernmost tributary of the Maravillas Creek drainage basin, one of the major drainage systems in Brewster County. Its headwaters are on the flank of the now-extinct and deeply eroded Paisano volcano. The rocks there consist primarily of quartz trachyte and rhyolites and are approximately thirty-five million years old. Unlike most streams in the Trans-Pecos, Calamity Creek is perennial in its upper reaches since it is fed by several springs. Over the free-flowing portion of its course the creek is lined with lush vegetation, including thick growths of willow, large cottonwoods, and numerous Mexican walnut and soapberry trees. This vegetation provides cover for numerous small mammals, as well as a large number and variety of small passerine birds, both resident and migratory. The many high cliffs towering over the creek along this mountainous portion of its course also provide habitat for such larger birds as red-tailed hawks and turkey vultures. The outlying area is characterized by high, semiarid grassland. Calamity Creek ceases to be perennial near Elephant Mountain, where it leaves the mountains and grassland habitat and enters lower, flatter, more desert-like terrain. The vegetation in the more southerly reaches of the creek does include grassland, but the area is covered predominantly with invading Chihuahuan Desert scrub. The vegetation along the creek's banks also turns much sparser after the creek becomes intermittent. The name Calamity Creek derives from an incident early in this century. An adobe house built near the creek on the Nevill Ranch about twenty miles south of Alpine was washed away by a particularly destructive flash flood. At least one source claims that several people were drowned in the flood, but the name Calamity appears to be most closely associated with the destruction of the cabin.

BIBLIOGRAPHY: Virginia Madison and Hallie Stillwell, *How Come It's Called That? Place Names in the Big Bend Country* (Albuquerque: University of New Mexico Press, 1958).

CALAVERAS, TEXAS. Calaveras (Spanish for "skulls") is at the junction of U.S. Highway 181 and Farm Road 3444, eight miles northwest of Floresville in northwestern Wilson County. It was originally in Bexar County and was called Wright when it was established in the early 1860s. A boundary change put the site in Wilson County in 1869, and the name was changed when a post office was granted in 1882. The population was twenty in 1885, when B. Johnson was postmaster and mail was brought by horse from San Antonio. The San Antonio and Aransas Pass Railway reached the area in 1886. By 1892 the town had a hotel, three brickyards, a saloon, a barber shop, a bakery, two general stores, a meat market, and a reported 250 residents. A Calaveras school was in operation by 1896, when it had an enrollment of sixty-three. The town reached a peak population of 369 in 1900. In 1925 the post office was closed, and the station was reduced to a flag stop. In 1947 Calaveras had one business and a population of 100. Since that time the population has remained steady, and in 1990 Calaveras still had 100 residents. *Claudia Hazlewood*

CALAVERAS CREEK. Calaveras Creek rises just south of Martinez in eastern Bexar County (at 29°25′ N, 98°21′ W) and runs southeast for fifteen miles to its mouth on the San Antonio River, one mile southwest of Calaveras in eastern Wilson County (at 29°13′ N, 98°16′ W). The creek is dammed just north of Elmendorf to form Calaveras Lake. It traverses rolling terrain surfaced by clay loam that supports mesquite and grasses.

CALDER, ROBERT JAMES (1810–1885). Robert James Calder, soldier and public official, was born in Baltimore, Maryland, on July 17, 1810, the son of James H. and Jane E. (Caldwell) Calder. He was raised by his mother's father after his father's death and moved to Texas from Kentucky in 1832. He joined Stephen F. Austin's[qv] army in 1835, took part as a second lieutenant in the battle of Concepción,[qv] was made third lieutenant of artillery in December, and accompanied James W. Fannin, Jr.,[qv] on a recruiting expedition. In 1836 Calder joined the army at Gonzales and was elected captain of K Company, First Regiment of Texas Volunteers, which he commanded at the battle of San Jacinto.[qv] He was among those who delivered news of the battle to President David G. Burnet[qv] on Galveston Island. Calder received 640 acres of land for his service and was appointed marshal of Texas by Burnet in 1836. In 1837 he was elected sheriff of Brazoria County, a position he held for six years. One source states that "he was Brazoria sheriff during the famous Monroe Edwards[qv] contests with Dart and was swindled by Edwards out of about five thousand dollars, fees and responsibilities undertaken, while in charge of imported Africans." He was elected mayor of Brazoria in 1838 and chief justice of Brazoria County in 1844 and 1846. After moving to Fort Bend County, Calder became mayor of Richmond in 1859 and from 1866 to 1869 served as county chief justice. He later practiced law with the firm of Mitchell, Nolan, and Calder. In 1881 he officially unveiled the monument to the memory of those killed at San Jacinto. Calder married Mary Walker Douglass of Brazoria on January 3, 1837; they had six children. He died at Richmond on August 28, 1885. In 1929 the state of Texas erected a joint monument over the graves of Calder and his wife in the Richmond Masonic Cemetery.

BIBLIOGRAPHY: Sam Houston Dixon and Louis Wiltz Kemp, *The Heroes of San Jacinto* (Houston: Anson Jones, 1932). Vertical Files, Barker Texas History Center, University of Texas at Austin.

Seymour V. Connor

CALDWELL, CLIFTON MOTT (1880–1968). Clifton Mott Caldwell, philanthropist, oilman, and rancher, son of James S. and Janie (Mott) Caldwell, was born in Palo Pinto County, Texas, on May 1, 1880. He spent his early years working on the family farm with his three brothers, and by attending rural and summer normal schools he earned a teaching certificate. In 1896 he moved with his family to Breckenridge, where he met his future wife, Cora Belle Keathley. They were married in 1901 and soon moved to Caddo, where, after teaching for five years, Caldwell became the principal of the Caddo school. In 1908 he moved his wife and three children to Austin, and at the age of twenty-eight, with a total of $400 in savings, he entered the University of Texas law school. After he graduated in 1911 the family returned to Breckenridge, where in 1912 Caldwell was elected county attorney of Stephens County. He served until 1916. In the four years that followed he was appointed county judge and later district judge.

In 1917 Caldwell and his partner, Breck Walker, formed the Walker-Caldwell Oil Company, which was highly successful during the Ranger and Breckenridge oil booms. Caldwell acquired large landholdings in West Texas, and both he and Walker invested much of their time and profits in the future of Breckenridge. They financed the city's first water system and induced three railroads to come to town. In the 1920s and again in the 1950s Caldwell served as director of the Texas and Pacific Railway.

In 1922 the family moved to Abilene, where Caldwell had close ties through his work in the Baptist Church[qv] and his friendship with Jefferson Davis Sandefer,[qv] president of Simmons College (now Hardin-Simmons University). Caldwell served as chairman of the Hardin-Simmons board of trustees for many years, and as a member until his resignation at the age of eighty-five. In 1923 Governor Pat Neff[qv] appointed him a regent of the University of Texas, and he served on both the land and publicity committees. In 1929 Governor Daniel Moody[qv] appointed Caldwell founding director of the Brazos River Authority,[qv] a post he held for the next twenty-five years. Caldwell also donated the land for Hendrick Memorial Hospital (now Hendrick Medical Center[qv]) in Abilene, contributed funds for its operation, and served as a trustee for decades. He was a member of the boards of Citizens National Bank and Abilene Savings Association for over forty years. During both world wars he chaired county war loan drives; during World War II[qv] he raised more than $40 million in bonds and stamps in Taylor County. In 1951 Caldwell was presented the "Top Citizen of the Year" award, the highest civic honor awarded by the Abilene Chamber of Commerce. He died on August 8, 1968, at the age of eighty-eight.

BIBLIOGRAPHY: Abilene *Reporter-News*, October 31, 1965. John L. Beckham, "Clifton Mott Caldwell: Citizen of Texas," West Texas Historical Association *Year Book* 56 (1980). *John Lacy Beckham*

CALDWELL, COLBERT (1822–1892). Colbert Caldwell (Coldwell), lawyer, jurist, and politician, son of Nathaniel Caldwell, was born in Bedford County, Tennessee, on May 16, 1822. After engaging in the Santa Fe trade from 1840 to 1845 he returned to Tennessee, studied law, and was admitted to the bar in Shelbyville in 1846. He began his career as an attorney in St. Francis County, Arkansas, and represented that district in the state legislature before moving to Texas. He settled first in Mansfield in 1859. Before the outbreak of the Civil War[qv] he had moved to Navasota. By the end of the war county tax rolls described Caldwell as the owner of eleven slaves and an estate valued at more than $17,000.

He was named to the bench of the Seventh Judicial District by provisional governor A. J. Hamilton[qv] on August 23, 1865. On October 18, 1867, he was appointed associate justice of the Texas Supreme Court by Gen. Philip H. Sheridan,[qv] commander of the Fifth Military District.[qv] Campaigning for a seat at the Constitutional Convention of 1868–69,[qv] Caldwell, whose outspoken Republican partisanship had earned him a reputation among Democrats as a rabble-rouser, survived an assassination attempt by a white mob during a speech before a mostly black audience in Marshall on December 31, 1867. Although badly frightened by the incident, he resumed his campaign and won the seat. As a delegate Caldwell helped lead the moderate Republican faction and was nominated for the presidency of the convention. He chaired a select committee of that body, which investigated the rampant postbellum lawlessness and violence in the state. The convention also sent Caldwell and Morgan Hamilton[qv] to Washington, D.C., to lobby for their appointment of loyal Republicans to state office and to win authorization for a state militia to quell disorder. However, increasingly perceived by radicals within his party as unsympathetic to freedmen's aspirations and the goals of congressional Reconstruction,[qv] Caldwell was removed from his position on the Supreme Court by the commander of the Military District of Texas on October 31, 1869. In 1876 he was appointed United States collector of customs at El Paso. Upon retirement from that post he and his family left the state for Kansas and later settled in California. Caldwell and his wife, the former Martha Julia Mitchie of Lawrence County, Tennessee, had eight children. Caldwell died in Fresno, California, on April 18, 1892.

BIBLIOGRAPHY: H. L. Bentley and Thomas Pilgrim, *Texas Legal Directory for 1876–77* (Austin: Democratic Statesman Office, 1877). Dallas *Herald*, March 28, June 12, July 11, 1868. Harbert Davenport, *History of the Supreme Court of the State of Texas* (Austin: Southern Law Book Publishers, 1917). Grimes County Historical Commission, *History of Grimes County, Land of Heritage and Progress* (Dallas: Taylor, 1982). Carl H. Moneyhon, *Republicanism in Reconstruction Texas* (Austin: University of Texas Press, 1980). James R. Norvell, "The Reconstruction Courts of Texas, 1867-1873," *Southwestern Historical Quarterly* 62 (1958). Charles W. Ramsdell, *Reconstruction in Texas* (New York: Columbia University Press, 1910; rpt., Austin: Texas State Historical Association, 1970). *Charles Christopher Jackson*

CALDWELL, FRANK (1883–1962). Frank Caldwell, hardware salesman and Texana collector, was born in Austin, Texas, in 1883 and lived his entire life there. He was an employee of Hartwell Brothers Wholesalers, but his true love was book collecting. At the age of seven he purchased for ten cents a copy of *The Life and Adventures of Ben Thompson, the Famous Texan,* published in 1884, forbidden reading for children of that time. After he read it he threw it into the loft of the barn, where rats devoured the evidence. Later he attempted to buy another copy from Gammel's Book Store, but the price kept rising just beyond his willingness to pay. Ten years later he was given a copy of the book by Judge A. E. Wilkinson of Austin. *The Life and Adventures of Ben Thompson* now is part of a collection of 1,000 books and documents, which was given to the University of Texas during the 1950s. Other titles include Arthur Ikin's[qv] *Texas (1841);* Dudley G. Wooten's[qv] *History of Texas* (1898); *Texas—The Home for the Emigrant from Everywhere* (1875), authorized by the Texas legislature; Edmond Bates's *Authentic History of Sam Bass* (1878); and A. J. Jowell's *Life of Big Foot Wallace* (1899). Caldwell also collected stamps, arrowheads, and guns. He was a lifetime member of the Texas State Historical Society,[qv] the Gun Collectors Association, and Stamp Collectors. He and his wife, Winnie, had two children. He died in Austin on January 28, 1962, and was buried in Oakwood Cemetery.

BIBLIOGRAPHY: Austin *American*, January 29, 1962. Dallas *News*, September 6, 1936. Vertical Files, Barker Texas History Center, University of Texas at Austin. *Anne Marie Fikes*

CALDWELL, JAMES PECKHAM (1793–1856). James Peckham Caldwell, Brazoria County planter and soldier, was born in Baltimore, Maryland, on January 6, 1793, and resided for a time in Kentucky. After receiving a land grant from the Mexican government in 1824, he arrived in Texas in 1832 and established one of the first sugar mills on the Brazos River. After Henry William Munson's[qv] death in 1833, Caldwell married the widow, Ann Bynum Pearce Munson, on May 12, 1835, and continued to operate Munson's plantation, Oakland. The couple had two children. In 1852 Oakland produced 200 hogsheads of sugar, and throughout the antebellum period (*see* ANTEBELLUM TEXAS) Caldwell supplied sugar and hired out slaves to nearby plantations. Caldwell was wounded at the battle of Velasco.[qv] In March 1835 he was one of six men who applied to the Louisiana Grand Lodge for a dispensation to form the first Masonic lodge in Texas. Caldwell was to be one of the principal officers of the new lodge. Dispensation for the Holland Lodge was granted, and it opened in December 1835. Caldwell died of yellow fever on November 16, 1856, at Gulf Prairie, Texas, and was buried in Peach Point cemetery.

BIBLIOGRAPHY: James A. Creighton, *A Narrative History of Brazoria County* (Angleton, Texas: Brazoria County Historical Commission, 1975). Abigail Curlee, "History of a Texas Slave Plantation," *Southwestern Historical Quarterly* 26 (October 1922). Joseph W. Hale, "Masonry in the Early Days of Texas," *Southwestern Historical Quarterly* 49 (January 1946). *Diana J. Kleiner*

CALDWELL, JOHN (1802–1870). John Caldwell, attorney and legislator, son of Adam and Phoebe (Gallion) Caldwell, was born on December 10, 1802, in Frankfort, Kentucky. Adam Caldwell had emigrated from Ireland in 1787. After the War of 1812, the Caldwells moved to Nashville, Tennessee, where John studied law and was admitted to the bar in 1823. He opened his law office in Tuscumbia, Alabama, and there married Lucinda Whey Haynie on December 4, 1827. The couple traveled to Texas in 1831 through New Orleans and settled in 1834 in Bastrop County on the Navarro league, which was deeded to Caldwell on April 2, 1833.

Caldwell became commissioner of Bastrop County in 1840. He represented the county as in the House of the Third, Fifth, Sixth, Seventh, and Eighth congresses (*see* CONGRESS OF THE REPUBLIC OF TEXAS) and in the Senate of the Ninth Congress, where he signed the resolution calling for an annexation[qv] convention. He was a member of the Convention of 1845[qv] and a state senator in the Sixth and Seventh legislatures. In 1850 he was one of the organizers of the Colorado Navigation Company, formed to get cotton to market. He opposed secession[qv] but supported the South to the extent of lending the state of Texas, when its treasury was empty in 1861, a quarter of a million dollars in gold, for which he received Confederate bonds that became worthless at the end of the war.

Caldwell built the first two-story house in the area. It came to be called the White House, and his daughter Lucinda put it on canvas. The framed painting in 1988 was in the home of a great-granddaughter. John and Lucinda Caldwell, who had nine children, were Methodists. Caldwell died on October 22, 1870, and was buried in the Caldwell lot in the southeast corner of old Oakwood Cemetery, Austin.

bibliography: John Henry Brown, *Indian Wars and Pioneers of Texas* (Austin: Daniell, 1880; reprod., Easley, South Carolina: Southern Historical Press, 1978). Alice Duggan Gracy, *The Gracy Family of New York and Texas* (Austin, 1986). Loyce Haynie Rossman, comp., *A Haynie Genealogy* (Fredericksburg, Texas, 1963).

Alice Duggan Gracy

CALDWELL, MATHEW (1798–1842). Mathew Caldwell, a signer of the Texas Declaration of Independence[qv] and soldier in the Texas army, was born in Kentucky on March 8, 1798. He moved to Missouri with his family in 1818 and settled in Texas in the DeWitt colony[qv] in 1831. He has been called "the Paul Revere of the Texas Revolution" because he rode from Gonzales to Bastrop to call men to arms before the battle of Gonzales[qv] in October 1835; he was also called "Old Paint" because his whiskers were spotted. Caldwell served as one of the two delegates from Gonzales Municipality at the Convention of 1836[qv] at Washington-on-the-Brazos. On March 2, 1836, after the signing of the Declaration of Independence, the convention dispatched couriers with the news and sent Caldwell with one of the couriers to the Texas army in order to ascertain the condition of the force and the movements of the enemy on the frontier.

On January 15, 1839, President Mirabeau B. Lamar[qv] named Caldwell captain of a company of rangers to be raised for the defense of Goliad. On March 23, 1839, Caldwell became captain of a company in the First Regiment of Infantry. He was wounded at the Council House Fight[qv] in March 1840 but headed a company at the battle of Plum Creek[qv] on August 12. As captain of Company D of the scouting force on the Texan Santa Fe expedition[qv] in 1841, he was captured with the expedition and imprisoned in Mexico. Upon release he hastened to the relief of San Antonio and on September 18, 1842, commanded a force of 200 men who met and defeated Adrián Woll[qv] in the battle of Salado Creek.[qv]

Caldwell was noted as married in the list of DeWitt colony settlers in 1831, but his first wife's name is not known; he married Mrs. Hannah Morrison in Washington County on May 17, 1837, and had at least three children. He died at his home in Gonzales on December 28, 1842, and was buried with military honors. Caldwell County, established in 1848, was named in his honor. In 1930 the state of Texas erected a monument at his grave in the cemetery at Gonzales.

bibliography: Louis Wiltz Kemp, *The Signers of the Texas Declaration of Independence* (Salado, Texas: Anson Jones, 1944; rpt. 1959). George R. Nielsen, "Mathew Caldwell," *Southwestern Historical Quarterly* 64 (April 1961). Texas House of Representatives, *Biographical Directory of the Texan Conventions and Congresses, 1832–1845* (Austin: Book Exchange, 1941).

L. W. Kemp

CALDWELL, PINCKNEY COATSWORTH (1795–1840). Pinckney Caldwell, soldier of the Republic of Texas,[qv] was born in Kentucky in 1795 and came to Texas in December 1830. He was one of the defenders of the famous Gonzales "Come and Take It" cannon.[qv] According to Launcelot Smither[qv] Caldwell sent a communication to Capt. Francisco de Castañeda[qv] on October 1, declaring a truce with the Mexican lancers, but nevertheless the insurrectionists attacked the Mexican camp the following morning. Caldwell was a member of the council of war called by Gen. Stephen F. Austin[qv] on November 2, 1835, which determined that Bexar should be taken by siege rather than storm. Caldwell voted with the majority.

On November 24, 1835, Edward Burleson appointed William A. Pettus[qqv] quartermaster and Caldwell his assistant. Caldwell, with the rank of captain, forwarded supplies from Gonzales to the Texas army besieging Bexar until he was wounded, sometime before December 23, 1835. At the battle of San Jacinto[qv] he served as quartermaster on the staff of Lt. Col. Henry W. Millard,[qv] commander of the Regular Infantry. On August 17, 1836, quartermaster general Almanzon Huston[qv] reprimanded Caldwell and reported him to their superiors for failure to comply with orders to post quarterly returns on government property in his charge. Caldwell was discharged on November 20, 1836, but reentered service as a quartermaster of the Army of the Republic of Texas.[qv] His appointment was confirmed by the Senate on May 22 and again on January 11, 1837. For his service in the Texas Revolution[qv] Caldwell was given a bounty warrant for 960 acres on October 18, 1837. His heirs surveyed and claimed the land in Tarrant County. By May 3, 1839, Caldwell was serving as quartermaster in Houston with the rank of major. William Gordon Cooke[qv] was then quartermaster general. Caldwell, whom pioneer Texas historian John Henry Brown[qv] called "a soldier of repute . . . and a man of talent," was killed in an Indian raid at Victoria on August 6 or 7, 1840 (*see* linnville raid of 1840).

bibliography: Daughters of the Republic of Texas, *Muster Rolls of the Texas Revolution* (Austin, 1986). Sam Houston Dixon and Louis Wiltz Kemp, *The Heroes of San Jacinto* (Houston: Anson Jones, 1932). John H. Jenkins, ed., *The Papers of the Texas Revolution, 1835–1836* (10 vols., Austin: Presidial Press, 1973). William S. Speer and John H. Brown, eds., *Encyclopedia of the New West* (Marshall, Texas: United States Biographical Publishing, 1881; rpt., Easley, South Carolina: Southern Historical Press, 1978).

Thomas W. Cutrer

CALDWELL, TEXAS. Caldwell, the county seat of Burleson County, is at the intersection of State highways 21 and 36, in the center of the county. In 1840, when the Texas Congress annexed to Milam County all of Washington County north of Yegua Creek and west of the Brazos River, Caldwell was designated as the county seat of a new county to be formed. The proposed town, surveyed by George B. Erath and named for Mathew Caldwell,[qqv] was laid out parallel to the Old San Antonio Road[qv] and west of Davidson Creek; the site encompassed a settlement founded by Lewis L. Chiles. Until Burleson County was organized in 1846, Caldwell served as the county seat of Milam County.

By 1856 the population of the town was 300, and the Caldwell House, known as one of the finest hotels in Texas, was the rendezvous of westward-bound travelers on the Old San Antonio Road. Caldwell also had a post office, male and female academies housed in the Masonic building, Baptist and Methodist churches, seven general stores, a saloon, a blacksmith shop, a livery stable, and a fine red-brick courthouse. By 1878 Caldwell had its own newspaper, the Caldwell *Register*, and by 1886 the town owned a fine hearse, "kept for the service of the community" by a local livery stable. It also had a bottling works and an ice house.

In 1880 the Gulf, Colorado and Santa Fe Railway built its main line through Caldwell and located the depot a half mile from the courthouse square. Caldwell soon became an important shipping point for the county. Gins, a cottonseed oil mill, and wholesale groceries were added by 1900, and by 1905 six passenger trains arrived daily. In 1912 the Houston and Texas Central, now the Southern Pacific, built a line from Hearne through Caldwell to Flatonia, where it joined a line to the west coast. Freight and passenger service on this line began in 1913. Although passenger service has been discontinued, Caldwell is still served by these two major railroads and Central Freight Lines. Passenger service, both north and south and east and west, is now provided by Kerrville Bus Lines.

Caldwell was incorporated in 1891 with a mayor-council form of government. The city maintains a library (established in 1976 and a member of the Texas Library System), a municipal airport (dedicated in 1968), five parks, and equipment and housing for a Volunteer Fire Department, organized in 1886. The first school of record was a Male and Female Academy advertised in 1844. In 1852 the Masons opened a Masonic Institute (for males) and in 1855 a Female Academy. By 1872 the Masons had given permission for their building to be used for "free school purposes." The first public school built with tax money was erected in 1882 by the county school district. This school came under the supervision of the city in 1891 and remained there until 1923, when the citizens voted to establish an independent school district. In 1990 the Caldwell ISD, the largest in the county, had four campuses and 1,651 students.

During the Reconstruction qv period, a company of State Police qv was stationed in Caldwell. A company of the Texas National Guard, Company E, was headquartered in Caldwell from 1898 through 1940, when it became part of the Thirty-sixth Infantry Division.qv Caldwell was the smallest town in Texas to have a full infantry company; its soldiers were all volunteers from Caldwell, Somerville, and the rural parts of the county. Many of these men were captured by the Germans at Salerno, Italy, in 1943 and were prisoners of war until the Germans surrendered in 1945.

The population of Caldwell, which was 2,165 in 1940, remained static until the 1970s, when oil was discovered in Burleson County. In 1990 the population was 3,181. At that time the town was a supply point for the agriculture and livestock industries and the oilfields in the county. The Burleson County Industrial Foundation, organized in 1961, and the chamber of commerce have been responsible for locating four manufacturing plants and twelve oil-related industries in the town. The town also had a newspaper, a veterinary clinic, and four financial institutions. The courthouse square, dominated by the fourth courthouse to be built on the site, was the heart of the town. Motels, restaurants, a shopping mall, grocery stores, and service stations lined the two highways. Medical facilities included two clinics, two dentists, a nursing home, and the Burleson Memorial Hospital, operated by a county hospital district. The hospital, opened in 1978, was a successor to Thomas L. Goodnight Memorial Hospital, dedicated in 1956. Recreational facilities included baseball fields, tennis courts, parks, a country club, a swimming pool, and a saddle club arena. The town had twelve churches, two museums, nine civic clubs, and two veterans' organizations. It was also the home of the Burleson County Fair and the Kolache Festival.

BIBLIOGRAPHY: Burleson County Historical Society, *Astride the Old San Antonio Road: A History of Burleson County, Texas* (Dallas: Taylor, 1980).
Catherine G. Alford

CALDWELL COUNTY. Caldwell County (L-17), 120 miles inland from the Gulf of Mexico in south central Texas, is bordered by Bastrop, Fayette, Gonzales, Guadalupe, Hays, and Travis counties. Lockhart, the county seat, is at the intersection of U.S. Highway 183 and Farm Road 20, thirty miles south of Austin and seventy miles northeast of San Antonio. The county's center lies four miles southeast of Lockhart at approximately 29°50′ north latitude and 97°37′ west longitude. The county comprises roughly 546 square miles of flat to rolling terrain with elevations ranging from 375 to 500 feet above sea level. It is bisected from southwest to northeast by the Luling–Darst Creek fault zone. The northwest part of the county is in the blackland prairie region, where the terrain is low-rolling to flat and tall grasses and mesquite flourish in the black, waxy soils. The southeastern half of the county is more hilly, and the sandy soils support a wider variety of vegetation, including hardwoods such as oak and elm as well as mesquite qv and grasses. The county is almost entirely within the Guadalupe River basin; it is drained primarily by Plum Creek and its tributaries, and by the San Marcos River, which forms the boundary with Guadalupe County. Wildlife in the area includes deer, javelinas, coyotes, bobcats, beavers, otters, foxes, raccoons, skunks, turkeys, squirrels, and a variety of small birds, fish, and reptiles. Among the county's mineral resources are clay, industrial sand, gravel, oil, and gas. The climate is subtropical and humid, with an average minimum temperature of 38° F in January and an average high temperature of 96° F in July. The growing season averages 274 days annually, and the rainfall averages thirty-five inches.

Although Caldwell County is on the border between Central Texas and the Coastal Plains, its archeological record is more closely related to that of Central Texas. The region has supported human habitation for several thousand years. Archeological evidence suggests that hunting and gathering peoples established themselves in the area as early as 10,000 years ago. Some of these may have been ancestors of the Tonkawa Indians, who appear to have been native to the region. Other Indian groups included the Karankawas, who sometimes ranged as far inland as Gonzales and Caldwell counties, and the Comanches, who migrated from north and west Texas in the early nineteenth century.

Caldwell County was part of Green DeWitt's qv colony, which was approved by the Mexican government in April 1825. Early settlement in the colony centered around the Gonzales area. The surveying of the Caldwell County area began in the late 1820s. Most of the early grants, made between 1831 and 1835, were located along the San Marcos River and Plum Creek, and most of the early communities, such as Prairie Lea, Plum Creek, and Atlanta, developed along these watercourses in the southwestern and central parts of the county. One exception was the McMahan area on Tinney Creek in eastern Caldwell County, which was settled in the late 1830s. Settlement was disrupted during the Runaway Scrape qv in 1836 but resumed soon after the war ended. The Congress of the Republic of Texas qv made the Caldwell County area part of Gonzales County in 1836. In the early years of the republic residents were threatened by Indian raids, but after the defeat of the Indians in the battle of Plum Creek qv in 1840 only minor skirmishes occurred.

By 1847 the population in the northern part of Gonzales County had increased so much that residents petitioned the Texas legislature to establish a new county, Plum Creek County, with Lockhart Springs as county seat. In March 1848 the legislature approved the formation of the county from Bastrop and Gonzales counties but named it Caldwell instead of Plum Creek; the county seat was called Lockhart. Although the legislature did not say why the name Caldwell was chosen, it was probably in honor of Mathew Caldwell,qv a signer of the Texas Declaration of Independence.qv The county seat was located on a tract of land that had been part of Byrd Lockhart's qv Plum Creek grant.

Caldwell County grew fairly quickly between 1850 and 1860. According to the 1850 census it had 1,055 free residents and 274 slaves; by 1860 the number of free residents had more than doubled to 2,871, and the number of slaves had increased more than 5½ times to 1,610. Among the new communities were Fentress, Martindale, and Lytton Springs. The county's early economy was primarily based on livestock rather than on crops; the number of cattle in the county increased from 3,800 in 1850 to more than 33,000 in 1860, and the number of hogs rose from 3,400 to 11,480 during the same time period. The increase in livestock would probably have been even greater if the region had not had a severe drought from 1857 to 1859.

The earliest schools in Caldwell County were private institutions that met in someone's home or in space donated by Masonic lodges. Although the legislature established a system of public school districts in 1854, the outbreak of the Civil War qv in 1861 delayed improvements in buildings and textbooks. Redistricting in 1875 and in 1884 made districts smaller and more numerous; most districts centered around established communities, allowing children to attend school near their home. It was not until the 1930s and 1940s that improved transportation made large-scale consolidation of schools into independent school districts possible. Until the mid-twentieth century, extensive schooling was for many children in Caldwell County a luxury that took second place to their duties on the family farm, and dropout rates were high. As late as 1940 only 8 percent of the population over twenty-five had completed high school. The percentage of adult residents who had finished school began to rise, however, as the job market expanded; it was nearly 15 percent in 1960 and 58 percent in 1980.

The first church in Caldwell County, the Clear Fork Baptist Church, was organized in 1848. Among the early churches were a Primitive Baptist congregation organized at Prairie Lea in 1851, Christian and Episcopal churches organized at Lockhart in 1852, and a Primitive Baptist church organized at Tinney Creek in 1852. By 1870 the county had eleven churches: five Baptist, two Methodist, two Presbyterian, one Episcopal, and one Christian. Few communities had their own preachers; itinerant ministers went from place to place, sometimes staying two or three months in a town and teaching school to help earn their keep. Camp meetings also played an important role in the county's religious development, especially after 1870, and people came as far as thirty miles to attend them. The first Catholic church in the county was St. Mary's of the Visitation, which was built in Lockhart in the mid-1880s. In 1900 the Southwest Texas Sacred Harp Singing Convention was established in McMahan (*see* SACRED HARP MUSIC). In the early 1980s the county's forty-seven churches had an estimated combined membership of 10,559; Southern Baptist, Catholic, and United Methodist were the largest denominations.

Spencer Ford of Lockhart represented Caldwell County at the Secession Convention[qv] in January 1861 and voted in favor of secession;[qv] Caldwell County voters accepted the ordinance later that year by a margin of 434 to 188. Several hundred men from Caldwell County served in the Confederate Army, in at least six companies that served in the New Mexico and Red River campaigns, in Galveston and Brownsville, and on the frontier. Because most men of military age had enlisted, women, children, old men, and slaves were left to maintain family farms. Many acres lay idle for lack of enough people to work them. The crops and livestock that families did manage to raise were in danger of being confiscated by troops foraging for supplies.

During Reconstruction,[qv] several incidents of racial violence prompted the stationing of federal troops at Lockhart and Prairie Lea, and clashes between federal soldiers and local residents led to considerable ill-feeling, as elsewhere in the South. Because of the loyalty oath required, the first elections after the Civil War attracted few former Confederates as voters, although some residents did turn out to harass blacks who came to the polls. By the election of 1869, however, enough Democrats had regained their eligibility to choose Andrew J. Hamilton[qv] for governor over Edmund J. Davis[qv] by a vote of 413 to 352. In presidential politics Caldwell County was staunchly Democratic from the end of Reconstruction until 1972, when the vote went to Richard Nixon. Ronald Reagan won the county in 1984.

Like most areas in the south, Caldwell County suffered a severe economic decline immediately after the Civil War and throughout the Reconstruction period. Between 1864 and 1866 property-tax receipts declined 70 percent. A little more than half of the loss was in slaves; the rest came from declines in total farm acreage, farm value, and livestock value, each of which fell 33 to 60 percent by the time of the 1870 census. Recovery was slow because transportation was poor and because the economy was so dependent on agriculture.

After the war many former slaves remained in the area. By 1870 the black population in the county had increased to 2,531, 38 percent of the total. With the exception of St. John Colony, which was established by former slaves in the early 1870s, there were no independent black communities in the county. Instead, separate church and school facilities were built in existing communities. The number of black residents increased steadily until 1900, although the number of whites who moved in was such that blacks as a percentage of the total population fell from 34 percent in 1880 to 26 percent in 1900. The black population fell slowly to 4,664 in 1930 and 2,582 in 1960, but remained at a stable 15 percent of the total number of residents. In 1980 the county's 3,867 black residents represented slightly more than 16 percent of the total.

The Caldwell County economy began to show signs of recovery by 1880, thanks in large part to the growth of the cattle industry, improved transportation, and an influx of people from other states and other countries. The Galveston, Harrisburg and San Antonio Railway connected the new community of Luling with Columbus in 1874, thus providing southern Caldwell County with easier access to markets. With the railroads came new towns—Maxwell, Dale, and Reedville; other towns, like Brownsboro, McNeil, Taylorsville, and Elm Grove were bypassed by the railroads and faded as their residents moved away. The county population rose from 6,572 in 1870 to 11,757 in 1880, and the census reported 1,421 farms in 1880, up from 357 ten years earlier. The amount of land in farms rose from 124,690 acres in 1870 to 205,335 acres in 1880, but the average farm size fell from 349 acres to 144 acres. Many of the county's large farms and ranches were divided into smaller units and leased to tenants in the years immediately following the Civil War; other farms were broken up and sold for taxes. New residents were able to take advantage of the availability of land and start new farms of their own.

Although production in 1880 included 190,648 bushels of corn, 11,098 bushels of wheat, and 7,609 bales of cotton, the principal commodity was cattle; the county reported 16,900 head of cattle that year. Large herds passed through the county on trail drives to northern markets. Before the introduction of barbed wire into the region in the 1880s, a shortage of fencing materials made it difficult for farmers to protect their crops. The open prairie lent itself more easily to the grazing of cattle. When barbed wire[qv] did come into use, fence-cutting[qv] was a serious problem until the expansion of railroads eliminated the need for extended trail drives. The Missouri, Kansas and Texas completed its track between Lockhart and San Marcos in 1887, and the San Antonio and Aransas Pass Railway connected Lockhart and Luling to Shiner in 1889. In 1892 the Missouri, Kansas and Texas laid track from Lockhart east to Smithville.

The cattle industry in Caldwell County peaked in the late 1880s and the 1890s, and cotton began to take its place. In 1890 the 38,710 acres planted in cotton represented nearly 30 percent of the county's improved acreage, and the yield of 21,326 bales was nearly three times higher than the 1880 harvest. In 1900 farmers planted more than 90,000 acres in cotton, or nearly 70 percent of the improved land; the yield was 42,660 bales. As marginal land came into use and the soil of good land was depleted, the amount of cotton produced per acre fell. In 1920, 137,197 acres produced only 21,857 bales; in 1930, 124,802 acres produced only 11,878 bales. The low cotton yields, combined with the success of an experimental farm established by the Luling Foundation,[qv] persuaded farmers to diversify their crops and devote more of their resources to livestock.

Immigrants from Mexico began arriving in Caldwell County in large numbers in the late nineteenth and early twentieth centuries. The 1890 census reported 477 native Mexicans, representing 3 percent of the county's population; by 1910 the number totalled 4,113, or 17 percent of the population. Some became tenant farmers or sharecroppers, while others became part of a migratory labor force that helped to sustain the county's cotton-dependent economy. From the 1930s through the 1980s roughly a third of the county's population was of Mexican descent. Other large ancestry groups in the county were German and English, each of which made up 16 percent of the population in the 1980s.

Caldwell County's departure from an almost total dependence on agriculture began after the discovery of oil in 1922. Speculation about the possible presence of oil in Caldwell County had started soon after the discovery of the Spindletop oilfield[qv] in 1901, but it was not until 1914 that various enterprises began to drill test wells around Luling. After Edgar B. Davis[qv] discovered the Luling oilfield[qv] in 1922, the new industry expanded rapidly. By the end of the 1920s significant oil deposits had also been found in the Buchanan, Dale, Larremore, and Salt Flat fields, and production ranged from six to twelve million barrels a year. Although oil prices fell from $1.09 a barrel in 1929 to $0.51 in 1931, they recovered briefly in 1932 and stabilized at $0.95 in 1934. Annual oil production fluctuated between three and five million barrels during the 1930s. The civilian market fell in the early 1940s, but the loss was quickly offset by increased military demand. Production varied between two and four million barrels a year from the 1950s through the 1980s.

Although the economic activity generated by the new oil industry spared Caldwell County some of the hardships of the Great Depression,[qv] the population began a thirty-year decline in the 1930s, falling from 31,397 residents to 17,222 by 1960. Many of the people who left were tenant farmers and sharecroppers. After 1930 the agricultural emphasis of the county shifted from small family farms to larger ranches, and from cotton to pastureland and feed crops. Tenant farming had accounted for nearly half of all the county's farming from 1880 through 1900, and as much as 75 percent, or 2,346 of the 3,149 farms, in 1930; but by 1960 fewer than 20 percent of the county's 819 farms were tenant-run. As the number of farms decreased, the average farm size increased, from eighty-six acres in 1930 to 330 in 1960.

In the early 1980s 83 percent of the land in the county was in farms and ranches, but only 20 percent was under cultivation. Sorghum, hay, cotton, wheat, and corn, the primary crops, accounted for more than 95 percent of the 38,500 acres harvested; other crops were watermelons, peaches, and pecans. More than 80 percent of the county's agricultural receipts came from livestock and livestock products, the most important ones being poultry, eggs, cattle, and hogs. Professional and related services, manufacturing, and wholesale and retail trade involved more than 50 percent of the workforce in the 1980s; 11 percent of workers were self-employed, and 38 percent were employed outside the county. Industries with the highest employment included oil and gas extraction, poultry processing, and the manufacture of clothing, wood products, and engineering and scientific instruments.

Caldwell County's downward population trend seemed to reverse itself in the 1960s; it increased to 21,178 by 1970, 23,637 by 1980, and 26,392 in 1990. The majority of residents lived in three towns: Lockhart (9,205), Luling (4,661) and Martindale (904). Uhland (368) and Niederwald (233) were the next largest, but they are partly in Hays County. Part of San Marcos is also in Caldwell County. Ethnically, the population in the county is white (18,919 or 71.7 percent), Hispanic (9,988 or 37.8 percent), black (2,825 or 10.7 percent), Asian (86 or 0.3 percent), American Indian (65 or 0.2 percent), and other (4,497 or 17 percent).

Recreation available in Caldwell County includes boating and fishing; hunting deer, javelinas, ducks, and geese; a botanic garden in Luling; and Lockhart State Park.[qv] The Chisholm Trail[qv] Roundup and a rodeo are held in Lockhart in June. In May the Luling Watermelon Thump attracts many visitors. The Texas Independence Trail runs through Caldwell County.

BIBLIOGRAPHY: Caldwell County Oral History Collection, Barker Texas History Center, University of Texas at Austin. Mark Withers Trail Drive Museum, *Historical Caldwell County* (Dallas: Taylor, 1984). Carroll L. Mullins, History of the Schools of Caldwell County to 1900 (M.A. thesis, University of Texas, 1929). Maurine M. O'Banion, The History of Caldwell County (M.A. thesis, University of Texas, 1931). *Plum Creek Almanac.*

Vivian Elizabeth Smyrl

CALEDONIA, TEXAS. Caledonia is nine miles east of Mount Enterprise in extreme southeastern Rusk County. Thomas Williams and William Elliott received land grants there in 1828. A post office was established in Caledonia in 1851, with Sam T. Allen as postmaster. It was discontinued in 1866, reestablished in 1870, and discontinued again in 1905. In 1883 the community reported a population of 150, three steam gristmills, a cotton gin, five churches, and a school. Cotton was the principal product of Caledonia. By 1892 the population had declined to fifty, but by 1896 it had risen to 100. In 1944 Caledonia had a population estimated at twenty-five, and in 1990 it was still listed as a community.

BIBLIOGRAPHY: Dorman H. Winfrey, *A History of Rusk County* (Waco: Texian, 1961).

Megan Biesele

CAL FARLEY'S BOYS RANCH. Cal Farley's Boys Ranch was founded in 1939 by Cal Farley,[qv] former professional wrestler and Amarillo businessman, on the site of Old Tascosa in Oldham County. The original 120 acres was given by Julian Bivins, son of Lee Bivins[qv] and himself a prominent Panhandle rancher, who died in a plane crash a year later. The ranch opened in March 1939 with five boys housed in the old county courthouse, which also served as the first headquarters of the institution. Chanslor Weymouth,[qv] Ralph Dykeman, and other leaders from the Maverick Club, the Rotarian boys' club of Amarillo, formed the first board of directors of the ranch. They sought to help Farley provide "the boy nobody wanted" with "a shirttail to hang to," and Farley used his radio program to promote the ranch. As contributions increased, more facilities were added, and full-time staff members were hired; Alton Weeks, a cousin of Cecil (Stuttering Sam) Hunter, was the first superintendent, and Mrs. Maude Thompson was the first cook. Overall, the boys were provided with a "home-ranch" atmosphere. Among their privileges they were allowed to keep pets and maintain a pet cemetery. By 1941 twenty-five young "ranchers" were crowded into the old courthouse.

During World War II[qv] Farley often raised money by having Amarillo school children hold bond drives. The first annual Boys Ranch Rodeo was staged in 1944. That decade the ranch gained national attention through such magazines as the *Saturday Evening Post* and *Reader's Digest.* In 1946 it received its biggest boost when it became the subject of the M-G-M movie *Boys Ranch,* with James Craig and Dorothy Patrick as Cal and Mimi Farley and the young ranchers as extras. Such celebrities as Jack Dempsey, Gene Tunny, J. Edgar Hoover, and Roy Rogers were among the ranch's friends and supporters, along with businessmen like Eugene A. Howe[qv] and Lawrence R. Hagey. By 1949 Boys Ranch had over 100 residents, expanded acreage, and several new buildings moved from military bases after the war, including a gymnasium. By that time Farley had sold his Wun-Stop-Duzzit tire shop to devote full time to the ranch, and that year the ranch began printing its own newsletter, the *Round-up.*

In 1950, after a group of rebellious teenagers had threatened the previous superintendent, Farley averted further problems by hiring a professional wrestler, Dorrance Funk.[qv] Funk and his family became immediate favorites among the youngsters and remained at the ranch for three years, during which time the resident population doubled. In 1955 the new Boys Ranch Independent School facilities were opened. The old courthouse continued to be used as a dormitory until 1963, when it was renovated and opened as the Julian Bivins Museum. By 1966 more than 1,400 acres had been added to the ranch, which cared for 346 formerly homeless boys between the ages of four and eighteen, from thirty-seven states. The boys lived in eleven dormitories, nine of which housed thirty-six boys and two staff families each, and two of which housed the youngest boys. There were sixteen additional buildings for educational, sports, and vocational training and a nonsectarian chapel. In addition to the annual rodeo, football, basketball, and baseball are among popular sports at Boys Ranch, which has its own post office. After the deaths of Cal and Mimi Farley in 1967, the ranch was run by their daughter and son-in-law, Gene and Sherman Harriman.

The ranch is supported solely by contributions. By 1973 2,500 boys from every state and several foreign countries had been educated, trained, and cared for at the ranch without cost to any governmental, church, or civic agency. In April 1987 Girlstown, U.S.A., merged with Cal Farley's Boys Ranch. Afterwards the Boys Ranch general fund financed much of the Girlstown operations. Cal Farley's Family Program oversaw the Girlstown facility at Borger—providing homes for male and female elementary school age children. The Boys Ranch also provided a scholarship and loan fund for eligible applicants at the Girlstown campus at Whiteface. In 1994 the resident population of Boys Ranch was 412, and it was a co-ed facility. In the center of this ranching community stands a memorial to its founder, who dedicated his life to helping "the bottom ten percent of the Nation's youth."

BIBLIOGRAPHY: Beth Feagles Day, *A Shirttail to Hang To: The Story of Cal Farley and His Boys Ranch* (New York: Holt, 1959). Louie Hendricks, *No Rules or Guidelines* (Amarillo: Cal Farley's Boys Ranch, 1971).

H. Allen Anderson

CALF CREEK (Donley County). Calf Creek rises ten miles east of Howardwick in north central Donley County (at 35°04′ N, 100°44′ W) and runs south for three miles to its mouth on Saddlers Creek, thirteen miles northeast of Clarendon (at 35°00′ N, 100°46′ W). The stream flows through an area that was part of the RO range, where the land is flat to rolling with local escarpments. Native vegetation consists primarily of mesquite shrubs and grasses in soil composed of mostly deep, fine sandy loam.

____ (Grayson County). Calf Creek rises three miles northeast of Sherman in east central Grayson County (at 33°41′ N, 96°34′ W) and runs southeast for six miles to its mouth on Choctaw Creek, a mile southwest of Penland (at 33°40′ N, 96°28′ W). The stream is intermittent in its upper and middle reaches. It crosses rolling prairie with locally steep slopes, surfaced by deep to shallow expansive clays and clay loams that support oak, juniper, and various grasses. The area has served as range and crop land.

____ (Grayson County). Calf Creek, also known as Shannon Creek, rises just northeast of Sherman in east central Grayson County (at 33°42′ N, 96°34′ W) and runs southeast for seven miles to its mouth on Choctaw Creek, seven miles east of Sherman (at 33°40′ N, 96°29′ W). It traverses flat to rolling prairie with a dark calcareous clay and clay loam surface that supports oak, juniper, mesquite, cacti, and grasses.

____ (Menard County). Calf Creek rises ten miles northeast of Menard in northeastern Menard County (at 31°00′ N, 99°39′ W) and runs southeast, through the southwestern corner of McCulloch County, to its mouth on the San Saba River, twelve miles west of Katemcy in northwestern Mason County (at 30°55′ N, 99°27′ W). The surrounding flat to rolling prairie is marked by local deep depressions; the soil varies from shallow and stony to deeper clay loams that support oak, juniper, mesquite, and grasses. James Bowie[qv] and ten others fought more than 150 Caddo and Lipan Indians along Calf Creek on November 21, 1831.

CALF CREEK, TEXAS. Calf Creek is on Farm Road 1311 twelve miles southwest of Brady in southwestern McCulloch County. It has had three names and three locations. The first site was two miles south of the present community and was known as Deland, named for a family who moved to the area from Kansas in 1874. The Calf Creek school had one teacher and twenty-three students in 1898. Baptist and Methodist churches were organized in 1903. The Deland post office operated from 1906 to 1909. The focus of the community shifted about a mile to the north, and the new post office, called Tucker in honor of local store owner Lum Tucker, operated from 1909 to 1915. Tucker had a cotton gin, a general store, a blacksmith, and a grocer in 1914. The community moved a mile north to its present location, and the post office changed its name to Calf Creek in 1915. A new school was built in 1921 and at times enrolled as many as 100 students. The community's population gradually declined, however, and the school district was consolidated with the Brady schools in 1949. The post office was discontinued in 1953. Calf Creek had fifty residents and two businesses in 1949; the population was twenty-three in 1990, when only a church and a cemetery appeared on county highway maps.

BIBLIOGRAPHY: T. Lindsay Baker, *Ghost Towns of Texas* (Norman: University of Oklahoma Press, 1986). Jessie Laurie Barfoot, History of McCulloch County, Texas (M.A. thesis, University of Texas, 1937). Wayne Spiller, comp., *Handbook of McCulloch County History* (Vol. 1, Seagraves, Texas: Pioneer, 1976; Vol. 2, Canyon, Texas: Staked Plains Press, 1986). *Vivian Elizabeth Smyrl*

CALHOUN, JAMES HENRY (1849–1919). James Henry Calhoun, judge and state senator, was born in La Grange, Georgia, on January 17, 1849. He graduated in 1870 from Homer College, Louisiana, and moved in August to Waco, Texas, where he was admitted to the bar in August 1873. He engaged in the land business at Eastland from 1873 to 1876, when he became county judge. From 1881 to 1884 he was district attorney for the Twelfth Judicial District. On January 1, 1882, he married Jennie Connor of Eastland; they had three children. In 1885 and 1887 Calhoun was elected to the Texas Senate from the Twenty-ninth District and served as chairman of a committee that investigated the offices of state treasurer and state comptroller. He was subsequently elected judge of the Forty-second District and moved to Cisco in 1903. He died in Cisco on October 1, 1919, and was buried there.

BIBLIOGRAPHY: H. L. Bentley and Thomas Pilgrim, *Texas Legal Directory for 1876–77* (Austin: Democratic Statesman Office, 1877). Carolyne Lavinia Langston, *History of Eastland County* (Dallas: Aldridge 1904). E. H. Loughery, *Personnel of the Texas State Government for 1885* (Austin: Snyder, 1885).

CALHOUN, JOHN WILLIAM (1871–1947). John William Calhoun, comptroller and professor of the University of Texas, was born to George Washington and Maria Frances (Glasgow) Calhoun on October 24, 1871, in Manchester, Tennessee. He attended school at nearby Reddens Chappel for an average three months a year from age five to age nineteen; he then spent a year at a private school in Manchester and fifteen months at Winchester Normal School before teaching in country schools in Tennessee and Texas.

He entered the University of Texas in 1901, took a position as superintendent of schools at Arlington in 1902, returned to the university, and received his B.A. degree in 1905. He worked as a tutor in mathematics from 1905 to 1909 but took the year 1907–08 to earn an M.A. degree from Harvard. He became an instructor at the University of Texas in 1909 and worked his way to full professor by 1923. In 1919 he was transferred from the department of pure mathematics to that of applied mathematics. He also served as comptroller of the university from 1925 until 1937, when he became president ad interim, a post he held for two years. As comptroller he supervised oil production on university lands, investment of funds, and construction of buildings. One of his favorite projects was the planting of live-oak trees on the campus. In 1938 Calhoun received an honorary LL.D. degree from Abilene Christian College. When Homer S. Rainey[qv] was appointed president of the University of Texas in 1939, Calhoun went back to teaching full-time. He was president of the University Cooperative Society for twenty-five years. He was also president of the University Club, a fellow of the Texas Academy of Science,[qv] president of the Texas Alpha chapter of Phi Beta Kappa, and a long-time secretary of the Town and Gown Club of Austin. His publications, primarily official reports and textbooks, included *Unified Mathematics* (1918), *Algebra for Junior and Senior High Schools* (1930), and *The University of Texas: The Position Achieved, The Opportunities Ahead* (1938). Calhoun left in manuscript an account of the trees on the university campus and an autobiography, The Short and Simple Annals of the Poor, which he described as being "an eye-witness account of the lives and manner of living of the POOR WHITES inhabiting the Hill Country of the south-eastern part of Middle Tennessee from 1870 to 1890 A.D."

Calhoun married Evelyn Scott of Fort Worth on August 22, 1910; they had one daughter. He died in Austin on July 7, 1947, and was buried in Memorial Park. Calhoun Hall on the University of Texas campus was named for him when it was completed in 1968.

BIBLIOGRAPHY: John William Calhoun Papers, Barker Texas History Center, University of Texas at Austin. Carl John Eckhardt, *One Hundred Faithful to the University of Texas at Austin* (197-?). Vertical Files, Barker Texas History Center, University of Texas at Austin. *Who's Who in America*, 1948–49. *William James Battle*

CALHOUN, SAMUEL (1788–1875). Samuel Calhoun, plantation owner, a relative of John C. Calhoun, was born in the Abbeyville District of South Carolina in 1788. As a captain in the Indian War of 1812 he was company commander of the Fifth Calvary. He later moved to Georgia, where he operated a plantation and married Elizabeth Finney. They had six children. Elizabeth died in 1836, and Samuel moved to Alabama shortly afterwards. There he married Catherine O'Brien, and they had two children. Calhoun moved his family and slaves to

Texas in 1845. They settled in northern Walker County, where Calhoun amassed a large block of land. Eventually he acquired several thousand acres in Walker, Madison, and Houston counties. His son William built a plantation home called Osceola in Madison County at the junction of Bedias Creek and the Trinity River. The plantation served as a riverport, ferry crossing, and sometimes stage stop. Calhoun died in 1875 and is buried in Walker County.

BIBLIOGRAPHY: Walker County Genealogical Society and Walker County Historical Commission, *Walker County* (Dallas, 1986).

James L. Hailey

CALHOUN, TEXAS (Calhoun County). Calhoun, on Matagorda Island, was projected by the Republic of Texas[qv] in January 1839, when Congress directed the secretary of the treasury to have 640 acres on the north end of the island surveyed as the site for a seaport. Lots in the town went on sale in June 1841. A customhouse was established, and Alexander Somervell[qv] was appointed collector of customs. The town failed to prosper, however, and the customhouse was moved to Port Caballo. Calhoun ceased to exist by 1845.

CALHOUN, TEXAS (Colorado County). Calhoun is on the route of the Atchison, Topeka and Santa Fe Railway five miles south of Eagle Lake near the southeastern boundary of Colorado County. This predominantly black settlement, named for John C. Calhoun, grew around a railroad shipping point. By 1910 it had enough residents to establish two general stores and a railroad express and Wells Fargo office. The post office opened in 1912. Two years later the estimated population reached 105. The land around Calhoun is flat and generally sandy, and small independent farmers and tenant farmers in the area produced good crops of potatoes that were shipped by rail. In 1921 the post office closed, and mail was subsequently delivered daily from Eagle Lake. During the Great Depression[qv] most of the small farmers drifted away and businesses closed. Some of the nearby land was converted to rice and cotton farming. Cotton was replaced during the 1950s by stock grazing, and this remains the predominant use of the land. In addition to ranching and rice growing, there is a certain amount of oil and gas production in the area, and numerous sand and gravel extraction operations are located between Calhoun and the Colorado River.

BIBLIOGRAPHY: *Colorado County Sesquicentennial Commemorative Book* (La Grange, Texas: Hengst Printing, 1986). *Jeff Carroll*

CALHOUN, TEXAS (Dallas County). Calhoun, also known as Fisher, was at the intersection of Fisher Road and the Missouri, Kansas and Texas Railroad, six miles northeast of downtown Dallas in northeastern Dallas County. Northwest Highway is to the north, Mockingbird Road is to the south, and White Rock Lake is one mile to the east. The community was on the original land grants of D. A. Murdock to the northeast and D. Murray to the southwest. The area was first settled in 1844 when Tom Fisher built a home in the area, reportedly one of the first houses in Dallas County. Fisher was a rural agricultural community characterized by a number of small farms and was almost certainly named after this early pioneer.

Sometime in the late 1800s Fisher became known as Calhoun. The change of name may have occurred simultaneously with the construction of the Missouri, Kansas and Texas Railroad through the community in 1886. However, it is most likely that Calhoun was the name of the post office, which was established in Fisher in 1888 and remained until 1906. In 1890 the community was still called Fisher and had two general stores and a population of twenty-five. By 1900 the settlement was called Calhoun and had a population of fifty, a drugstore, a general store, a banker, and a Baptist church. John Body served as postmaster. By the 1930s the site of the community was in the Dallas city limits.

BIBLIOGRAPHY: Ed Ellsworth Bartholomew, *The Encyclopedia of Texas Ghost Towns* (Fort Davis, Texas, 1982). David S. Switzer, *It's Our Dallas County* (Dallas: Switzer, 1954). *Matthew Hayes Nall*

CALHOUN, TEXAS (Gregg County). Calhoun, among the earliest settlements in Gregg County, was probably founded in the 1850s and was located on or near Rabbit Creek in the southern portion of the county, near the site of the present western edge of Kilgore. Maps show a settlement in the area in the mid-1850s, and a post office operated there from 1853 to 1855. After the Civil War[qv] Calhoun disappeared, and no trace remains.

BIBLIOGRAPHY: Eugene W. McWhorter, *Traditions of the Land: The History of Gregg County* (Longview, Texas: Gregg County Historical Foundation, 1989). *Christopher Long*

CALHOUN COLLEGE. Calhoun College, in Kingston, was established and chartered in 1887 as a private, nondenominational, coeducational college. The institution offered instruction until sometime around the turn of the century, likely 1900. Operations began in what had been Kingston High School, a two-story wooden building owned and operated by J. L. Clemmons and J. C. Todd. In 1885 the institution, which enrolled students primarily from Kingston, apparently began offering college-level instruction in addition to primary and secondary courses. Two years later the school was renamed and chartered as Calhoun College. The college's first president, professor T. S. Sligh, was succeeded in 1889 by T. S. Wallis, a member of the original faculty. Wallis remained until the school closed. The college, which had no entrance requirements, offered work leading to the bachelor of arts degree. Courses were offered in six departments: primary, preparatory, teachers', music, elocution, and scientific. Classes in such subjects as mathematics, oratory, ancient and modern languages, grammar, rhetoric, and moral philosophy were offered. Though the building could accommodate up to 400 students, the school's enrollment never seems to have reached that level. Tuition ranged from one dollar to four dollars a month, depending on the level of instruction desired. The institution changed ownership a number of times during its existence. At one time a Professor Booth, who "loved whiskey and drugs," operated Calhoun College and severely lowered its reputation. The school discontinued college-level instruction after 1893. It continued as a private primary and secondary school until sometime around 1900.

BIBLIOGRAPHY: Ethel Cassles, A History of Hunt County (M.A. thesis, University of Texas, 1935). W. Walworth Harrison, *History of Greenville and Hunt County, Texas* (Waco: Texian, 1976). Jackson Massey, A History of College Education in Hunt County, Texas (M.A. thesis, University of Texas, 1928). Donald W. Whisenhunt, *The Encyclopedia of Texas Colleges and Universities* (Austin: Eakin, 1986).

Brian Hart

CALHOUN COUNTY. Calhoun County (G-29) is located on the Gulf Coast between Houston and Corpus Christi. Approximately one-fourth of the county's 540-square-mile area is under water. Calhoun County is bordered by Victoria and Jackson counties on the north, Matagorda Island[qv] and the Gulf on the south, Refugio County on the west, and Matagorda County on the east. The approximate center of the county is at 33°40′ north latitude and 95°06′ west longitude, five miles southwest of Port Lavaca, the county seat. The altitude of this Coastal Prairie county ranges from sea level to fifty feet. The terrain is flat, poorly to moderately well drained, and surfaced with loams underlain by cracking, clayey subsoils, including deep black soils and sandy clay. Matagorda Island, on the southern fringe of the county, is chiefly deep shell sand. The climate is mild, the rainfall averages about forty inches annually, and the growing season lasts 305 days a year. The flora includes tall grasses and live oaks with cordgrasses and sedges along the coast, and the animal life includes quail, deer, doves, cottontail rabbits, jackrabbits, armadillos, skunks, opossums, raccoons, and a few coyotes. Between 21 and 30 percent of the land is considered prime farmland. The county is drained by the Guadalupe River, Chocolate Bayou, and several creeks. Green Lake, a large natural lake, is in Calhoun County. Major incorporated communities include Point Comfort, Port Lavaca, and Seadrift. The county is served by the Southern Pacific, Missouri Pacific, and Point Comfort and Northern railroads, as well as by U.S. Highway 87 and State highways 35 and 185.

Evidence suggests that Calhoun County was inhabited from prehistoric times. A Clovis point is among examples of Paleo-American projectile points found in the area. Shell middens have been located at Mustang Lake, an arm of San Antonio Bay. Karankawa Indians populated the shoreline and roamed the Coastal Plain until the middle of the nineteenth century, when they were notorious among white settlers. Subgroups of the Karankawas occupied Matagorda Bay and Matagorda Peninsula.[qqv] Fletching tools, scrapers, and spear and arrow points have been discovered at Lavaca Bay and Six Mile Creek. Tonkawa shelter sites have been found at Cox's Creek, Keller's Creek, and the mouth of the Guadalupe River, as well as on Green Lake, Chocolate Bayou, and Linn's Bayou in Port Lavaca.

In 1519 Alonso Álvarez de Pineda,[qv] exploring the Gulf Coast for the governor of Jamaica, drafted a map that included Espíritu Santo Bay and named the mainland "Amichal," but it is not clear whether he set foot in the future Calhoun County. René Robert Cavalier, Sieur de La Salle,[qv] is believed to have landed in 1685 near Powderhorn Lake after one of his four ships was wrecked while crossing the bar at Cavallo Pass. A monument placed by the Texas Centennial[qv] Commission in 1936 marks his landing site. The future county was explored by Spaniards, including Alonso De León,[qv] who found the ruins of the French fort in 1689, but no permanent settlement was made until Anglo-American colonization. As early as 1825, empresario[qv] Martín De León of Mexico brought forty-one families to the area and established a ranch near the former site of La Salle's fort. The first Anglo settlement site now in the county was at Linnville, where in 1831 John J. Linn[qv] established a warehouse and wharf three miles north of the future site of Lavaca (later Port Lavaca). Comanche Indians collecting horses sacked and burned the settlement during the Linnville Raid of 1840[qv] before being pursued and defeated. The inhabitants escaped by boat to a bluff about three miles away, where a few men who operated a warehouse welcomed them; this was the beginning of the present town of Port Lavaca. Caught between settlers and the Comanches, the Tonkawas, who numbered 800 in 1836, became loyal to the Texans.

As early as 1836 Mary Austin Holley[qv] reported a population of 200 at Cox's Point. In 1844 Prince Carl of Solms-Braunfels[qv] landed at Indian Point in Calhoun County with a hundred German families. Although few of them remained on the Gulf, their tent village, called Karlshafen, became Indianola, the town that served as Calhoun county seat for many years. In the 1840s other Germans[qv] established a community at Seadrift, and Poles[qv] arrived at Indianola between 1854 and 1856. Many native Tejanos were granted land in Calhoun County, where they developed more of the Spanish ranching culture on the flat, grassy prairie, which was well-suited for rangeland. Plácido Benavides,[qv] one of the Tejanos who fought with the Texans during the Texas Revolution,[qv] owned land in Calhoun County, as did many other prominent Mexican families. The majority of settlers in Calhoun County came from Southern states, including Louisiana, Georgia, Mississippi, Tennessee, and Alabama.

In antebellum Texas,[qv] Calhoun County residents were active in the trade and commerce stimulated by the Federalist wars of Texas and northern Mexico and the French blockade of Mexican ports in 1838 and 1839. Goods and ammunition for South Texas and Northern Mexico went through Lavaca, Cox's Point, Linnville, and Texana for overland distribution by wagon train. Men from Calhoun County participated in the Mier expedition[qv] in 1842. United States Army quartermaster depots were located at Lavaca until 1854, and later Indianola supplied military forts and garrisons.

Newcomers began rounding up cattle during the 1840s and making ranching, traditionally a Hispanic concern, an American occupation. Lavaca, established in 1842 as a port, shipped hides and tallow and transported goods from New Orleans to San Antonio and points west. Its present name, Spanish for "cow port," reflected the importance of cattle to the local economy.

On April 4, 1846, Calhoun County was formed from parts of Victoria, Jackson, and Matagorda counties and named for John C. Calhoun of South Carolina, who had advocated Texas statehood. Lavaca was the first county seat. But, as a result of the development of the Indianola Railroad, the formation of other transportation lines, and a shift of population, Indianola became more important and was made county seat in 1852. The county's earliest newspaper, the Lavaca *Journal*, began publication in 1848; the first county school opened at Lavaca in 1849; and a county courthouse was completed at Indianola in 1857. Both Lavaca and Indianola remained important trade centers until 1861. Exports from Lavaca included cotton, pecans, and lead and copper from Mexico; Indianola exported silver bullion and cattle. The Morgan Lines[qv] moved their headquarters from Lavaca to Indianola in 1849, and in 1852 operated regular service to New York. The San Antonio and Mexican Gulf Railway completed a line from Lavaca to Victoria by 1861, and the Indianola Railroad was completed in the 1870s. Both roads eventually became parts of the Southern Pacific system. Trade development ceased, however, with the beginning of the Civil War.[qv]

Despite cholera epidemics in 1849, 1852, and 1853, the county's population increased between 1850 and 1860 from 867 white and 234 black residents to a total of 2,642, of which 414 were slaves. Plantations operated at Green Lake and Cox's Point, but most blacks were urban dwellers who worked as servants or at seaport trades (*see* SLAVERY, URBAN). Only one free black resided in the county in 1840 and nine in 1850; slave trading peaked at Indianola in 1852. In 1860 Calhoun County, not part of the plantation-based culture that dominated many Texas counties, produced only five bales of cotton, but residents nevertheless voted 276 to 16 the next year for secession.[qv] Calhoun County volunteers, organized in 1859 for the frontier, became part of the Third Texas Infantry of the Confederate Army. Others from the area joined the Indianola Guards or the Lavaca Guards, which became part of Company A of the Sixth Texas Infantry.

Because of the impact on its port facilities, Calhoun County felt the brunt of the war more than many Texas counties. During the war, women and slaves raised cotton, planted vegetables, and subsisted on cattle driven in to feed the families of soldiers. The 1860 census reported among county industries a manufacturer of turtle soup. Fort Esperanza, on Matagorda Island, constructed by Confederate forces using slave labor, covered the approaches to Cavallo Pass,[qv] but in 1863 the fort was captured after the battle of Matagorda Bay.[qv] Wharves, warehouses, railroads, and bridges were destroyed or damaged, and Indianola and Lavaca were taken by federal troops, many of whom were quartered in the county by the end of the war. The only Civil War land battle in Calhoun County was fought on Christmas Eve, 1863, at Norris's Bridge, but Union and Confederate graves remain at the site of Fort Esperanza.

The county recovered during Reconstruction.[qv] The population rose from 2,642 in 1860 to 3,443 by 1870, of which 907 were black; most county residents lived at Lavaca or Indianola, which for a time in the 1870s surpassed Galveston as the leading Texas seaport. Factories increased from fourteen to thirty-three, and sharecropping, which developed in many Texas counties, was not as widespread, probably because the soil facilitated ranching more than farming. In 1870 the wealthiest man in the county, Fletcher S. Stockdale,[qv] a lawyer from Kentucky, had real property valued at $100,000 and personal property at $20,000.

Although Union troops were stationed in Calhoun County, the chief problems of the post–Civil War years were not political. A fire in 1867 destroyed buildings at Indianola, and a yellow fever epidemic reduced the population. In 1875 a Gulf storm brought heavy damage to Indianola, which recovered only briefly before a tidal wave virtually destroyed the community in 1886. By 1880 the county's population had dropped to 1,739. Lavaca, renamed Port Lavaca, became county seat again in 1887, the post office and courthouse were moved there, and Indianola was never rebuilt. In 1878 the Southern Pacific Railroad bought out the property of the Morgan Lines, which had headquartered at Indianola since the 1850s, and in 1887 reopened the war-damaged railroad. This development, along with the growth of other railroads across the state, reduced Port Lavaca from a major seaport to a fishing center. Manufacturing establishments dropped to four by 1880 and disappeared altogether by 1890. The cattle industry peaked in 1890, when 32,629 head were reported, but by then the county population numbered only 815. Among those who registered brands in the county were several African Americans,[qv] including Ann Harred, a "free woman of color" who used the JD brand on her Matagorda Island ranch. Other blacks, who had been cowboys as slaves, continued driving cattle to Texas ports. Of eighty-two farms in operation in 1900, fifty-six were operated by their owners and twenty-six by tenants.

The value of taxable property in Calhoun County grew between 1870 and 1912 from $1.5 million to almost $4 million. At the turn of the century, land companies offering mortgage loans at ordinary interest brought an influx of small farmers, most of whom raised cotton. Oyster shipping began at Port Lavaca, and developers established a new community at Port O'Connor. Swedes[qv] established a Lutheran colony at Olivia in 1892, and by 1900 European immigrants included Irish, Scots,[qqv] Germans, and Bohemians (*see* CZECHS). The population increased gradually, reaching pre-1875 figures again only in 1910, when a total of 3,635 was estimated, and 4,325 by 1920, of which 584 were black. By 1930 roughly one-fourth of the population was described as "Mexican." Hurricanes[qv] in 1914 and 1919 wrought further damage, and to defend itself Port Lavaca built a seawall in 1920.

Transportation improved in 1909 with construction of the St. Louis, Brownsville and Mexico Railway[qv] in the southern part of the county, with its terminus at Port O'Connor. United States participation in World War I[qv] brought significant improvements in the county's economy, but slow growth during the Great Depression[qv] hurt county cattlemen, whose herds were reduced to a total of only 4,007 head by 1930. Livestock was raised on only half the county's acreage in the 1930s, as many farmers raised figs, citrus fruits, and other products. Tenant farming increased in the 1920s and reached a high during the depression. By 1930, of 574 county farms, 372 were operated by tenants. The total number of farms began to decline from 574 in 1930 to 331 in 1950, by which time the average farm size was 731 acres, agribusiness had developed, and more than 200 farms were commercial. Improvements came with the construction in 1931 of a causeway over Lavaca Bay that linked the area to the South Texas highway system, discoveries of natural gas near Port Lavaca in 1934, and oil in 1935. Black schools operated in the Port Lavaca and Long Mott districts. A colony of Christian Scientists was established at Magnolia Beach, which became a major resort. In World War II[qv] an army training camp was built on Matagorda Island, along with a Strategic Air Command base that remained in service until 1975.

The county suffered a tropical storm in 1945 and extensive damage from Hurricane Carla in 1961. From 1940 to 1950 the population increased from 5,911 to 8,971. An Alcoa plant that employed 2,600 workers opened at Point Comfort in 1947, and a Union Carbide and Carbon Chemicals Company plant near Seadrift opened in 1952; in 1980 it provided jobs for 1,400 employees. Other major industry included the Hartzog Shipyards, the U.S. Cold Storage Company, and the fishing and shrimping industry.[qv] By 1958 the county had a total of eleven manufacturers and seventy-seven mineral-related enterprises. In agriculture, a maximum county production of 10,570 bales of cotton and 133,996 pounds of corn were harvested in 1940, when 95,000 acres of land was planted with cotton, corn, sorghum, flax, and rice.

The number of cattle increased steadily after 1940, and by 1969 reached 20,404. National Starch, a manufacturer of vinyl acetate, began operation in 1962, Witco manufactured pitch oil at Point Comfort, and Vistron Corporation was in operation by the 1970s. Other industries produced oilfield products and metal cleaner; there was some marine construction. The population grew steadily after the 1950s, to 17,831 by 1970, of which 957 were black. Of a total of 21,300 in 1982, 34 percent were Hispanic, 18 percent German, and 18 percent of English[qv] descent.

In the 1980s Calhoun County farmers raised cattle, sorghum, rice, corn, pecans, and soybeans. Seventy percent of the land was in farms and ranches, but farmers faced problems of inefficient irrigation, soil compaction, poor drainage, and shoreline erosion. Businesses in 1981 totaled 380. Major industries included oil and gas extraction, fish packaging, heavy construction, and industrial chemical production. In 1982 oil and gas production totaled 849,240 barrels of crude oil, 2,439,971,000 cubic feet of casinghead gas, 43,787,907,000 cubic feet of gas-well gas, and 313,318 barrels of condensate. In 1990 crude production was 1,179,390 barrels. Matagorda Ship Channel traffic in 1981 totaled 4,148,664 short tons, including 3,347,547 tons of imports, 153,501 tons of exports, and 647,616 tons of domestic shipments. Important exports included oil, cotton, seafood, and cattle. Calhoun County's principal natural resources, after discoveries around 1935, remained industrial sand, oil, and gas. Port Lavaca, Port O'Connor, and Magnolia Beach attracted tourists, and hunting, fishing, boating, and bathing offered recreation. In 1988 the Formosa Plastics Corporation of Taiwan, encouraged to locate in Calhoun County to improve employment, established a petrochemical factory at Point Comfort; controversy subsequently developed over the company's environmental practices. Calhoun County school districts consolidated after 1955 and, by the 1980s, a single school district was operating eight elementary schools, three middle schools, and one high school. Many local churches operate schools. Thirty-three percent of high school graduates planned to attend college.

Calhoun County voters have consistently supported Democratic candidates in every presidential election between 1848 and 1992 with six exceptions: Ulysses S. Grant (1872), Dwight D. Eisenhower[qv] (1952, 1956), Ronald Reagan (1980, 1984), and George H. W. Bush (1992).

In 1985 a Texas historical marker was placed at Half Moon Reef Lighthouse. Matagorda Island State Park and Wildlife Management Area,[qv] Calhoun County's principal state park, covered 7,325 acres. Annual special events in the county include the Sea Fest in May, Texas Water Safari in June, Shrimp-Fest in July, Fishing Derby and Youth Rodeo in August, Christmas Parade in December, and Calhoun County Fair in October at Port Lavaca. In 1990 the county's population was 19,053. The largest towns were Port Lavaca, Port O'Connor, and Seadrift.

BIBLIOGRAPHY: Calhoun County Historical Commission, *Shifting Sands of Calhoun County, Texas* (Port Lavaca, Texas, ca. 1980). Isaac Joslin Cox, ed., *The Journeys of René Robert Cavelier, Sieur de La Salle* (2 vols., New York: Barnes, 1905; 2d ed., New York: Allerton, 1922). Paul H. Freier, *A "Looking Back" Scrapbook for Calhoun County and Matagorda Bay, Texas* (Port Lavaca, Texas: Port Lavaca *Wave*, 1979). John B. Hayes, A Survey and Proposed Plan of Reorganization of the Schools of Calhoun County, Texas (M.A. thesis, University of Texas, 1939). Port Lavaca *Wave*, Centennial Edition, May 1940. WPA Texas Historical Records Survey, Inventory of the County Archives of Texas (MS, Barker Texas History Center, University of Texas at Austin).

Diana J. Kleiner

CALIFORNIA COLUMN. The California Column, a force composed of a few more than 1,500 men, chiefly California volunteer troops, was organized in 1862 under Col. James H. Carleton and moved eastward to discourage invasion of California by the Confederates. An advance party under Lt. Col. Edward E. Eyre arrived at Fort Thorne on the Rio Grande on July 4, 1862, and Carleton and the main body arrived in August. Detachments were sent to pursue the

Confederates and reoccupy army posts as far east as Fort Davis, in Jeff Davis County, where the United States flag was raised on August 29, 1862. Carleton replaced Lt. Col. Edward R. S. Canby[qv] as commander of the Department of New Mexico and organized his men for Indian fighting. Most of the members were discharged in August and September 1864. After the war many of the California Column elected to remain in New Mexico and West Texas, and several of them played prominent roles in the history of the region. Charles E. Ellis, killed during the Salt War,[qv] was one member; Albert J. Fountain[qv] and Albert H. French became prominent in El Paso politics of the 1860s. When Texas cattlemen began to settle in the area in the 1870s and 1880s, the men of the California Column lined up with the native Mexicans against the invading Southerners in a number of disturbances.

BIBLIOGRAPHY: Aurora Hunt, *The Army of the Pacific* (Glendale, California: Clark, 1950). Aurora Hunt, *James H. Carlton, 1814–1873: Western Frontier Dragoon* (Glendale, California: Clark, 1958). Darlis A. Miller, *The California Column in New Mexico* (Albuquerque: University of New Mexico Press, 1982). George Henry Pettis, *The California Column* (Santa Fe: New Mexico Printing Company, 1908).

C. L. Sonnichsen

CALIFORNIA CREEK (Fisher County). California Creek, also known as South Paint Creek, rises nine miles east of Rotan in northeastern Fisher County (at 32°51′ N, 100°18′ W) and runs northeast for seventy miles, across northern Jones County and southeastern Haskell County, to its mouth on Paint Creek, near the Haskell-Throckmorton county line (at 33°05′ N, 99°33′ W). The stream is dammed four miles south of Hamlin to form South Lake. It crosses an area of flat to gently rolling to steeply sloping terrain surfaced by moderately deep to shallow silt and clay loam that supports mesquite, grasses, juniper, live oak, and scrub brush.

—— (Val Verde County). California Creek rises four miles west of Feely in south central Val Verde County (at 29°37′ N, 101°02′ W) and runs south for seven miles to its mouth on the northern shore of Amistad Reservoir (at 29°33′ N, 101°01′ W). It dissects cretaceous limestone and ends on an alluvium of gravel, sand, clay, and silt. The surrounding dark, calcareous stony clays and clay loams support oaks, junipers, mesquites, and grasses. The creek was probably named by workmen on the Galveston, Harrisburg and San Antonio Railway, who laid the tracks four miles west of the creek in 1882. The men said the place was as close to California as they ever expected to be.

—— (Young County). California Creek, also known as Paint Creek, rises five miles southwest of Olney in northwestern Young County (at 33°19′ N, 98°50′ W) and flows south for ten miles before joining the Brazos River some six miles west of Newcastle (at 33°12′ N, 98°49′ W). Much of the creek's drainage area is devoted to oil production. The stream flows between the Padgett and Lairmore oilfields across land surfaced by clay and sandy loams that primarily support water-tolerant hardwoods and grasses.

CALIFORNIA HILL. California Hill, sometimes called California Mountain, is halfway between Terlingua and Lajitas in southwestern Brewster County (29°19′ N, 103°41′ W). It rises 3,328 feet above sea level. The hill consists of an erosional high made up of a massive, resistant variety of limestone underlain by a formation of clay and some interbedded flaggy limestone and friable sandstone. The limestone is responsible for the high topography, as it forms a resistant cap over the clay. The mountain is probably a remnant of an eroded mesa. The terrain in this area presents an eroded and rugged desert landscape with sparse Chihuahuan Desert scrub, especially creosote bush, lechuguilla, and ocotillo.

California Hill is the site of the first discovery in 1884 of quicksilver in what was to become the Terlingua Mining District (see MERCURY MINING). A California company took an early interest in the discovery, filed claim to the area, and initiated the first real mining operations in the Big Bend. The site of the operation became known as California Hill when, reportedly, one of the miners inscribed that name on one of the mountain's rock faces. The early endeavors of the Californians proved unsuccessful, although one of the richest mercury deposits in the country lay under the mountain. In 1899 California Hill became the site of the Marfa and Mariposa Mine, the largest quicksilver producer in the area until it closed in 1910. The mine was reopened briefly in 1916 and again during World War II.[qv]

BIBLIOGRAPHY: Kenneth B. Ragsdale, *Quicksilver: Terlingua and the Chisos Mining Company* (College Station: Texas A&M University Press, 1976). Ronnie C. Tyler, *The Big Bend* (Washington: National Park Service, 1975).

CALINA, TEXAS. Calina (Callina) is on Farm Road 936 four miles west of Coolidge in northern Limestone County. It was established in the early 1890s, and by 1897 its population was estimated at fifty. A post office opened at Calina in 1898 with Jesse Q. Rich as postmaster. The community became the focus of a common-school district in 1904. The Calina post office was discontinued in 1906, and mail for the community was sent to Coolidge. Calina had fifty residents and two businesses in the early 1940s, but by 1945 its population was reported as twenty-five. In 1949 the Calina school was consolidated with the Coolidge Independent School District. By the 1980s little remained in the area.

BIBLIOGRAPHY: John J. Germann and Myron Janzen, *Texas Post Offices by County* (1986). Ray A. Walter, *A History of Limestone County* (Austin: Von Boeckmann–Jones, 1959). *Vivian Elizabeth Smyrl*

CALL, TEXAS. Call is at the intersection of Farm roads 1004 and 1013, on the Newton-Jasper county line forty-five miles northeast of Beaumont. The town was founded by George Adams, who named it after a business associate, Dennis Call. The two had joined M. T. Jones in 1890 to form the Cow Creek Tram Company, which established a sawmill at Call in 1895. Two years later Adams bought out his partners and leased the mill to the Industrial Lumber Company, of Beaumont. John Henry Kirby[qv] acquired the Call mill in 1901. In 1906 the Orange and Northwestern Railway was completed, linking Call with Newton, Buna, and Orange. The mill and the Call school were both in Jasper County. The Call post office, established in 1896, burned in 1906 and was reestablished in a new location. Call had a baseball team and hosted Chautauqua performances during the early twentieth century. Fire destroyed the pine mill in 1924, but a hardwood plant was rebuilt to replace the earlier structure. The mill closed during the Great Depression,[qv] forcing an estimated one-third of the community's inhabitants to leave. It subsequently reopened, only to close again in 1953. In 1937 oil was discovered six miles south of Call on land owned by the Peavy-Moore Lumber Company. The Call oilfield had one producing well with an output of 3,600 barrels in 1938. By 1942 the well had been abandoned. The community has survived its economic setbacks, although its estimated population fell from 250 in 1936 to 170 in the early 1970s. It still recorded a population of 170 in 1990.

BIBLIOGRAPHY: Newton County Historical Commission, *Crosscuts: An Anthology of Memoirs of Newton County Folk* (Austin: Eakin, 1984). Newton County Historical Commission, *Glimpses of Newton County History* (Burnet, Texas: Nortex, 1982). *Robert Wooster*

CALL FIELD. Call Field, one of thirty-two United States Army Air Corps training camps established in 1918, was five miles southwest of Wichita Falls in Wichita County. It operated from 1917 until 1919. In 1916 the army announced its intention of establishing a series of camps to train prospective pilots. Frank Kell[qv] of Wichita Falls organized an effort to attract the army to the city. By August 17, 1917, Kell and others successfully raised $35,000 and had a commitment from the Missouri, Kansas and Texas Railroad to extend tracks to the proposed site of the camp. On August 27 construction began. In November, when 85 percent of the work was completed, Maj. J. B. Brooks arrived to inspect the facilities. On November 10 he was named commander. On November 20 the first six army pilots arrived, and the field had 600 pilots by late December. On January 15 the army gave final approval of Call Field. The field was named for Loren H. Call, a native of Washington, D.C., who was killed in a plane crash near Texas City on July 9, 1913.

The training camp had forty-six buildings, which included twelve hangars that housed four to eight planes each, a hospital, and six barracks that held 175 men each. In May four additional hangars and a row of lofts to hold carrier pigeons were built. During its operation 3,000 officers, cadets, and enlisted men were stationed at Call Field, and 500 officers received their wings there. Two squadrons left the training facility for overseas duty. Thirty-four men lost their lives during training exercises, the smallest number of fatalities of any training center. After the war the training center closed. The last military personnel left on October 1, 1919.

In 1919 and 1920 Ernest Hall, a former instructor at Call Field, operated a flying school at the facility. The Wichita Polo Club briefly used a portion of the land for its polo field. In 1937 the Wichita Falls Junior Chamber of Commerce and American Legion erected a small marker near the gates of the old field in memory of the thirty-four men who were killed during training. For a number of years the site was the scene of memorial services by the Call Field Veterans Association. The name is perpetuated by a street named Call Field Road.

BIBLIOGRAPHY: Louise Kelly, *Wichita County Beginnings* (Burnet, Texas: Eakin Press, 1982).

David Minor

CALL JUNCTION, TEXAS. Call Junction is at the intersection of Farm Road 1004 and U.S. Highway 96, forty-five miles north of Beaumont in extreme east central Jasper County. The area around Call Junction and Call, its sister community in Newton County, was developed by lumberman George Adams, who named the site after business associate Dennis Call. Adams and Call joined M. T. Jones in organizing the Cow Creek Tram Company, which built a sawmill at the Call site in 1895, using the newly constructed Gulf, Beaumont and Kansas City Railway to ship its product. With the subsequent completion of the Orange and Northwestern Railway in 1906, the station on the GB&KC line took the name Call Junction. Both Call and Call Junction depended heavily on the sawmill, which was located in the Jasper County section of Call. Nonetheless, Call Junction had a separate post office from 1908 to 1927. It also was organized as a voting precinct in March 1912. The local mill closed in 1953, but Call Junction still reported fifty residents during the early 1970s. The discovery of oil to the south, at the Call, Call Junction, and Sally Withers fields, with new wells dug between the 1930s and the 1970s, gave the community new economic impetus. In 1990 its population was still reported as fifty.

BIBLIOGRAPHY: Newton County Historical Commission, *Glimpses of Newton County History* (Burnet, Texas: Nortex, 1982).

Robert Wooster

CALLAGHAN, BRYAN V., JR. (1852–1912). Bryan V. Callaghan, Jr., political boss, county judge, and mayor of San Antonio, son of Bryan V. and Concepción (Ramón) Callaghan, was born in San Antonio on April 1, 1852. After receiving an elementary education at St. Mary's Institute, he studied at the Lycée de Montpelier in southern France for five years. He then took a position as a guard on a West Texas stagecoach line operated by a family friend, Peter Gallagher.[qv] After a few years he took up the study of law at the University of Virginia, where he received a bachelor of law degree in 1874. Callaghan then returned to San Antonio and set up a private law practice. In 1879 he married Adele Guilbeau; they had six children.

Callaghan was elected alderman in San Antonio in 1879. In 1883 he became city recorder, and in 1885 he won his first term as mayor. He was continuously reelected until 1892, when he resigned to campaign successfully for a seat as a county judge of Bexar County. He returned to the mayor's office in 1897 but lost the post in 1899. He resumed his private law practice, then returned to politics in 1905, once again elected mayor. He continued to hold that office until his death. One of the reasons for his political success was his appeal to the ethnically diverse voters of San Antonio. By birth or by marriage, he had intimate ties to the Irish, Hispanic, and French communities in the city. He was able to deliver political speeches fluently in English, Spanish, French, and German. He was Catholic, like many San Antonio residents. He also entered politics at a time when San Antonio's fiscally conservative leadership was reluctant to provide municipal services that the growing population needed. At the beginning of his career, while he was building his political organization, he favored the expansion of city services, though he later became more conservative in his own views on municipal spending. Nevertheless, he became a civic hero. Throughout his tenure in office he stood as a bulwark against prohibition[qv] agitation and the growing drive for other sumptuary laws.

The Callaghan machine has been accused, with justification, of a variety of sins, including the unethical distribution of patronage, opposition to civil-service reform, lenience toward gambling and vice operations, favoritism in awarding municipal contracts, and widespread vote manipulation. On the other hand, Callaghan accepted advice from and directed resources toward groups of citizens that had been ignored in the past. He worked to expand and modernize the police and fire-fighting forces of the city. He began major road-paving and sewerage projects, and under his guidance the city gained ownership of its waterworks. During his administrations city officials expanded the park system and school facilities and built a new city hospital and city hall. Callaghan may have used irregular methods in the accomplishment of these goals, but he did not benefit personally from the power he wielded; he had built up no personal fortune when he died in his San Antonio home on July 8, 1912.

BIBLIOGRAPHY: Frederick Charles Chabot, *With the Makers of San Antonio* (Yanaguana Society Publications 4, San Antonio, 1937). Mary B. Edelman, Bryan Callaghan II: His Early Political Career, 1885–1899 (M.A. thesis, Trinity University, 1971). Caroline Haley, "Bryan Callaghan, Gilded Age Politician," *Journal of the American Studies Association of Texas* 2 (1971). David R. Johnson et al., eds., *The Politics of San Antonio* (Lincoln: University of Nebraska Press, 1983). Stacy R. Lester, Bryan Callaghan Versus the Reformers, 1905–1912 (M.A. thesis, Trinity University, 1976). *Saturday Evening Post*, April 27, 1912. Vertical Files, Barker Texas History Center, University of Texas at Austin. Randall L. Waller, The Callaghan Machine and San Antonio Politics, 1885–1912 (M.A. thesis, Texas Tech University, 1973).

J. Kaaz Doyle

CALLAGHAN, TEXAS. Callaghan (Callahan) was established in 1881 as a cattle shipping point on the International–Great Northern Railroad in Webb County. The settlement was named for Charles Callaghan of the Callaghan Ranch.[qv] A post office operated there under the name Callahan in 1880–81. The Callaghan Ranch was still operating in the 1980s, but by that time the community was gone.

Karen Gratke

CALLAGHAN RANCH. The Callaghan Ranch, lying athwart the Old San Antonio Road[qv] between Laredo and San Antonio, covered an area of 250,000 acres, with headquarters near Encinal, Texas. The ranch was started after the Civil War[qv] as an eighty-acre homestead south of old Fort Ewell on which Charles Callaghan, a young veteran of the Confederate Army, undertook to raise sheep. Before Callaghan died in 1874, he employed Col. William R. Jones, a former officer under Robert E. Lee[qv] in Virginia, as superintendent. Jones carried on the work for the heirs and built up the ranch by purchase and lease until at its height it ran 100,000 sheep and 6,000 goats and owned 125,000 acres outright, besides 100,000 more under lease. Because of its sheep-raising function, the ranch became the focus of the bitter Sheep Wars[qv] in the 1880s. Two of the Callaghan sheepmen were killed; Jones with a posse trailed and captured the killers, who were imprisoned. The Callaghan Ranch also survived various Indian raids between the period of its founding and the middle 1880s. During the period following the Indian difficulties William Sydney Porter,[qv] later world famous as O. Henry, became acquainted with the Callaghan territory. Fort Ewell was the post office to which he came for his mail, and many of his Western tales deal with the Callaghan terrain. A transition in the function and policy of the ranch came in 1908, when it was purchased by David T. Beals,[qv] and George D. Ford, both of Kansas City, and Thomas Atlee Coleman,[qv] a veteran Texas cattleman. The ranch, incorporated as the Callaghan Land and Pastoral Company, was converted into a cattle operation, and a new and vigorous scheme of expansion was undertaken. In 1946 the ranch comprised 218,500 acres owned outright and 31,500 under lease, in a single block of 250,000 acres, upon which the Swinging Eleven brand was carried by more than 20,000 Hereford cattle.[qv] The Callaghan was one of the best improved ranches in the country, and many of its employees, chiefly Mexican Americans,[qv] were born and lived their entire lives on the ranch. From 1923 to 1947 Joe B. Finley was general manager of the ranch, which was operated in the 1960s by the Finley family. On June 12 of the following year, the Callaghan Ranch was partially liquidated and original stockholders retired from the company. Acreage at that time was reduced to 131,000 acres owned and 46,000 leased.

BIBLIOGRAPHY: Paul H. Carlson, *Texas Woolybacks: The Range Sheep and Goat Industry* (College Station: Texas A&M University Press, 1982). Val W. Lehmann, *Forgotten Legions: Sheep in the Rio Grande Plain of Texas,* Vol. 3 (El Paso: Texas Western Press, 1969). Paul Iselin Wellman, *The Callaghan, Yesterday and Today* (Encinal, Texas: Callaghan Land and Pastoral Company, 1944?).

Paul I. Wellman and Hal R. Taylor

CALLAHAN, JAMES HUGHES (1812–1856). James Hughes Callahan, a soldier of the Texas Revolution[qv] and frontier military leader, was born near Marietta, Georgia, in 1812. He marched to Texas as a sergeant in Capt. J. C. Winn's Third Company of the Georgia Battalion,[qv] which arrived at Velasco just before Christmas of 1835. Callahan served in this unit for more than the next two months but managed to escape the Goliad Massacre,[qv] probably by having been engaged in a labor detail at Victoria during the battles of March 1836. After a postwar visit in the United States, he settled in the southwestern Hill Country.[qv] He helped establish Walnut Springs (now Seguin) in 1838. During the 1840s he moved to Caldwell County, where he operated a 350-acre farm and a store. He also held government land grants in Lavaca and Kimble counties. He married Sarah Melissa Day in 1841; they had four children.

Callahan remained an active citizen and soldier and, like many others who had fought in the revolution, was vigorously anti-Mexican. From 1839 to 1841 he commanded a group of minutemen in Guadalupe County who chased and fought Indians and Mexicans accused of stealing horses. He also volunteered for more formal campaigns between 1840 and 1842. He served as a first lieutenant in Mathew Caldwell's[qv] company in 1840, and became a company commander during the incursion of Rafael Vásquez[qv] in 1841, in which he led a retreat from San Antonio. The next year his sixty-man company helped expel Adrián Woll[qv] from Texas and saw action at the battle of Salado Creek.[qv] Later that year Callahan also served as a lieutenant in the Somervell expedition.[qv]

His military activities then ceased until 1855, when he commanded the punitive expedition into Mexico that bears his name. This campaign originated with Governor E. M. Pease's[qv] authorization to form a ranger company to retaliate against Indian attacks in Bexar and Comal counties. Callahan was also responding to slaveholders' appeals for a military venture that would return runaway slaves from Mexico. Accordingly, his company of about 130 men crossed the Rio Grande at Eagle Pass on September 29, 1855, and fought an inconclusive battle about forty miles south of there on the Río Escondido. Callahan retreated to Piedras Negras, which he first fortified, then looted and burned, before recrossing the Rio Grande under fire.

He failed to gain the support needed for another expedition, but public opinion generally favored his aggressive action. He moved to Blanco in 1854 or early 1855 and was killed there in April 1856 during a feud with Woodson Blassingame. The legislature of 1857–58 named Callahan County in his honor. In 1931 the bodies of Callahan and his wife were removed from the cemetery at Blanco and reinterred in the State Cemetery,[qv] Austin.

BIBLIOGRAPHY: Thomas L. Miller, *Bounty and Donation Land Grants of Texas, 1835–1888* (Austin: University of Texas Press, 1967). Ernest C. Shearer, "The Callahan Expedition, 1855," *Southwestern Historical Quarterly* 54 (October 1951). Ronnie C. Tyler, "The Callahan Expedition of 1855: Indians or Negroes?" *Southwestern Historical Quarterly* 70 (April 1967). *Russell Woodall*

CALLAHAN, TEXAS. Callahan, an early school community five miles east of Yorktown in western DeWitt County, was organized as a school district in 1880. The area was predominantly settled by German immigrants. The school, important in the county's development because of its relatively early establishment as a focus of the surrounding rural area, operated until 1945, when its students were transferred to the Ratcliff School and to Yorktown.

BIBLIOGRAPHY: Nellie Murphree, *A History of DeWitt County* (Victoria, Texas, 1962). *Nellie Murphree*

CALLAHAN CITY, TEXAS. Callahan City was on what is now Farm Road 2228, three miles south of Interstate Highway 20 and four miles southwest of Baird in northwestern Callahan County. The community was founded in 1876 with aspirations of becoming a center of commerce. Its location was chosen at a water hole on the Western Trail[qv] to Dodge City, over which nearly 100,000 cattle passed between 1874 and 1879. The Texas legislature had established the county in 1858, but the region was sparsely settled until the early 1870s. By 1877 Callahan City had several merchants who supplied the traildrivers and who also carried general merchandise for settlers; their goods had to be freighted from Fort Worth and took a month to reach the community. Callahan City never prospered like the cowtowns of Coleman to the south or Albany to the north, and it suffered some early setbacks that led to its swift decline. Although it was the scene of the first Callahan County Commissioners Court session on July 30, 1877, Callahan City lost a disputed county seat election to Belle Plain on December 9 of that year. When the Texas and Pacific Railway bypassed both towns in 1880, their demise was inevitable. In the 1980s only a cemetery remained near the abandoned Callahan City townsite.

BIBLIOGRAPHY: Mrs. L. L. Blackburn, "Early Settlers and Settlements of Callahan County," West Texas Historical Association *Year Book* 23 (1947). Brutus Clay Chrisman, *Early Days in Callahan County* (Abilene, Texas: Abilene Printing and Stationery, 1966). *Frontier Times,* January 1953. S. E. Settle, "Early Days in Callahan County," West Texas Historical Association *Year Book* 12 (1936). Jimmy M. Skaggs, *The Cattle-Trailing Industry: Between Supply and Demand, 1866–1890* (Lawrence: University Press of Kansas, 1973). *Mary Jo Gerngross*

CALLAHAN COUNTY. Callahan County (I–13) is in the Rolling Plains region of Central Texas on Interstate Highway 20 east of Abilene. The county is bounded on the north by Shackelford and Jones counties, on the east by Eastland County, on the south by Coleman and Brown counties, and on the west by Taylor County. The county seat is Baird. The largest town, Clyde, is nine miles east of Abilene and roughly 162 miles west of Fort Worth. The center point of the county is at 32°18′ north latitude and 99°23′ west longitude. In addition to Interstate 20, the county's transportation needs are served by U.S. highways 80 and 283, State highways 6, 36, 206, 279, 351, and the Missouri Pacific Railroad. Callahan County embraces 899 square miles of grassy prairie. The elevation ranges from 1,500 to 1,900 feet. The county is divided by a low range of hills known as the Callahan Divide,[qv] which runs from east to west. The region to the north is in the Brazos River basin, and the area to the south is in the Colorado River basin. Most of the county has light to dark loamy soils with clayey to loamy subsoils. In the southeast the soils are light-colored with loamy to sandy surface layers and clayey subsoils. Between 21 and 30 percent of the land in the county is considered prime farmland. The eastern quarter of the county has vegetation typical of the Cross Timbers[qv] and Prairies regions—a variety of grasses, including mesquite grass, red grama, red love grass, tumble grass, and Texas grama, and small stands of trees, including mesquite, post oak, live oak, and pecan. The southwest corner has tall grasses. The remainder of the county has short to mid-height grasses, with some mesquite, juniper, and cacti (*see* GRASSLANDS). The subtropical and subhumid climate features mild winters and warm summers. Temperatures range in January from an average low of 31° F to an average high of 56°, and in July from 71° to 96°. The average annual rainfall is twenty-five inches. The average annual snowfall is six inches. The growing season averages 230 days a year, with the last freeze in late March and the first in early November. Tornadoes are common in the area. Since its establishment in the last century Callahan County towns have suffered several severe storms, most notably Baird in 1895, Oplin in 1922, and Clyde in 1938 and 1950.

Until the 1870s the county was dominated by Comanche Indians. The area was first explored and described by Dr. Henry C. Connelly[qv] of the Chihuahua expedition[qv] in 1839–40. Callahan County was formed by the Texas legislature in 1858 from Bexar, Bosque, and Travis counties and named for James Hughes Callahan,[qv] a survivor of the Goliad Massacre[qv] and leader of the Callahan expedition.[qv] Because of the threat of Comanche attack, little permanent settlement took place in the area until after the Civil War.[qv] The first white settler to reside in the county was probably James Dulan, a native of Georgia, who built a shelter on Hubbard Creek in 1859 and tended a small herd of cattle. Sometime before November 1863 the Whitten family moved in and established a camp on Deep Creek in the northeastern part of the county. They were followed by the Hittsons and Eubankses, who ranched in both Callahan and Shackelford counties just after the Civil War. The first permanent residence in the county was built by A. A. and Caroline Hart and their four sons, John, Jim, Early, and Jesse, who settled on the South Prong of Pecan Bayou in 1868. They moved to Coleman County shortly thereafter, but returned to Callahan County in 1872 and constructed a double log cabin that for many years was a county landmark.

During the early 1870s a number of other settlers arrived. Most were ranchers, drawn to the area by abundant grazing land. In 1873 John Hittson[qv] established the headquarters of his Three Circle Ranch in Callahan County, and in 1874 Jasper McCoy established a ranch on Pecan Bayou. Other early settlers included the Merchant brothers and Dr. J. D. Windham, a physician, who also started a ranch operated by his sons in the southwestern part of the county. Despite the growing population, the threat of attack from hostile Comanches continued during the early 1870s. In 1874 United States troops under Col. Ranald S. Mackenzie[qv] defeated the Comanches at Palo Duro Canyon, and the same year Company E of the Frontier Battalion[qv] of the Texas Rangers,[qv] under the command of William J. Maltby,[qv] was sent to the area to drive the remaining Indians away. With the danger of Indian attacks over, large numbers of settlers began moving in. By 1875 land promoter Nelson A. Smith established the first town, Belle Plain, near the center of the county. During the mid-1870s Callahan County became a transit area for cattlemen driving their herds to Kansas. On the way to Dodge City the Western Trail[qv] ran up the Pecan Bayou valley, passed near Belle Plain, and extended northward by way of the Bar-be-cue Ranch, just east of the site of present-day Baird. The Jacksboro *Echo* of July 21, 1876, estimated that some 73,000 cattle were driven up the trail in the first part of that year alone, and by 1880 the annual figure surpassed 260,000. The drives ended in the mid-1880s with the coming of the railroads, but they played an important role in drawing settlers to the area (*see* CATTLE TRAILING).

Between 1858 and 1877, Callahan County was attached successively to Bexar County, Travis County, and Eastland County for administrative and judicial purposes. In 1877 the residents, more than 150 strong, signed a petition requesting the organization of Callahan County. At the election of July 3, 1877, Callahan City became the first county seat, a position the town retained only until the election of October 13, 1877, when Belle Plain was voted in as the new county seat. Belle Plain showed signs of rapid growth, and a number of settlers moved there in anticipation of the railroad; by 1878 it had a population of more than 100, and by 1880 the number of residents had grown to nearly 300. In 1880–81 the Texas and Pacific Railway was constructed from Fort Worth to El Paso. Stations for the railroad were located at Putnam, Baird, and Clyde, all of which soon developed into towns, but bypassed Belle Plain six miles to the north. An election on January 16, 1883, made Baird the new county seat. Belle Plain soon declined; the stone jail and many of residences were moved to Baird, and by 1897 only four families remained. The construction of the railroad also opened the way for numerous new settlers. During the 1870s and 1880s several communities formed, including Cottonwood, Atwell, Cross Plains, Caddo Peak, Eagle Cove, and Eula. More settlers continued to arrive during the 1890s, and by the turn of the century there were post offices in Oplin, Tecumseh, Denton, Dressy, Admiral, and Dudley. In 1880 the county population was 3,419; by 1890 it had grown to 5,274.

During the 1880s extensive farming was introduced. Settlers from East Texas began farming in the area around Cottonwood in the mid-1880s, raising cotton, oats, and various varieties of fruit. A severe drought in 1886–87 ruined crops and caused some to wonder if the region was suited to agriculture, but by the late 1880s the farming economy had recovered and was rapidly expanding. Between 1880 and 1890 the number of farms in the county grew from 346 to 518, and by 1900 it had increased to 1,176. During the late nineteenth century corn was the largest crop; by 1900 Callahan County farmers were producing more than 300,000 bushels a year. Wheat and oats were the other main crops; in 1900, 13,450 bushels of wheat and 44,560 bushels oats were harvested. In the early 1890s large-scale cotton production was also introduced, and during the first two decades of the twentieth century cotton became one of the county's leading crops. In 1890, 7,640 bales were ginned; by 1910 that figure had jumped to 52,467, placing Callahan County among the leaders in cotton culture[qv] in the state.

Despite the impressive growth of agriculture, however, ranching continued to form the mainstay of the economy. The total number of cattle in the county during the period from 1890 and 1930 ranged between 25,000 and 35,000. Most were beef cattle, although dairying became more popular after the turn of the century, and for a time the county was a major producer of butter. Some ranchers tried their hands at raising sheep in the 1880s and 1890s—the number of sheep in the county was reported at 6,818 in 1880 and 6,487 in 1890—but by the turn of the century most ranchers had sold their flocks, and in 1910 only fifty-six sheep were recorded. During the first three decades of the twentieth century many farmers raised hogs. After 1900 chickens also were raised in large numbers: 54,246 in 1910 and 73,138 in 1930.

The population grew from 8,768 in 1900 to 12,973 in 1910. After 1910 the pace of growth slowed, and by the mid-teens it had begun to decline. It fell to 11,844 by 1920. Growth in the number of farms was steady at the beginning of the century, as more settlers arrived, lured by the prospect of plentiful land. By 1905 county farms numbered more than 1,600, three times as many as in 1890. Land prices, however, also increased, and many newcomers could not buy land. As a result, the number of tenant farmers grew steadily, until by 1920 nearly half the farmers—823 of 1,649—were tenants. Most were sharecroppers, who farmed the land in exchange for a share of the harvest. In contrast to tenants in many parts of the state, however, virtually all of the Callahan County tenants were white; in 1910 there was only a single black tenant in the county (*see* FARM TENANCY).

Many of the county's farmers, both tenants and owners, were heavily indebted, and with the onset of the Great Depression[qv] in the 1930s a large number experienced hard times. Falling agricultural prices, combined with a boll weevil[qv] outbreak and the unwillingness of most banks to extend additional credit, forced many farmers off the land. By 1940, 1,200 active farmers were left, down more than 600 from the peak in 1910. The downturn in agriculture was partially offset by the discovery of oil in the county in 1923. A number of promising fields were soon located, including the Cross Plains Townsite, Pioneer, Cross Cut, and Blake fields, and by the late 1920s the oil business was in full bloom. Oil and gas revenues helped some landowners to survive the economic slump of the 1930s and made a few large landowners wealthy.

The period after World War II[qv] saw a continuation of the prewar trends. Ranching and farming continued to form the twin pillars of the economy, with the largest proceeds coming from beef and other livestock products. The years after the war saw a trend toward fewer and larger ranches and farms, as well-to-do landowners added to their previous holdings. In 1982, 91 percent of the land in the county was in farms and ranches, with 18 percent of the farmland under cultivation and 4 percent irrigated. That year Callahan County ranked 180th of the 254 Texas counties in agricultural receipts, with 73 percent coming from livestock and livestock products, primarily from cattle. Overgrazing and water problems—erosion, salinity, and a shortage of potable water—had brought about several conservation programs. Principal crops included wheat, oats, hay, sorghums, and peanuts. Other significant agricultural products included watermelons, peaches, and pecans.

Businesses in the county in the early 1980s numbered 174. In 1980, 15 percent of the labor force were self-employed, 18 percent were employed in professional or related services, 13 percent in manufacturing, 21 percent in wholesale and retail trade, and 14 percent in agriculture, forestry, fishing, and mining; 55 percent were employed in other counties; and 1,401 retired workers lived in the county. Nonfarm earnings in 1981 totaled $97,794,000. The industries with the most employment were agribusiness and the manufacture of fabricated metal products. Oil and gas extraction continued to form an important part of the local economy. In the early 1990s oil production averaged a million barrels annually; between 1923 and 1991 crude production totaled 79,523,155 barrels.

The first schools in Callahan County were opened in the 1870s. Among the earliest ones was a private academy in Belle Plain, established in 1877 by Professor and Mrs. W. J. Westmoreland. Belle Plain was also the site of one of the earliest colleges in West Texas, Belle Plain College, which opened in 1881. Another institution of higher learning, Baird College, operated for a brief time around the turn of the century. The first public schools in the county were opened in the mid-1880s. In the early 1990s Callahan County had four school districts with five elementary, one middle, and four high schools. The average daily attendance in 1981–82 was 2,253, with expenditures per pupil of approximately $2,000. Forty-seven percent of the 141 high school graduates planned to attend college. In 1983, 96 percent of the high school graduates were white, 4 percent Hispanic, and 0.1 percent black. Callahan County has generally been staunchly Democratic, although Republicans made advances in the second half of the twentieth century. Of the nine presidential elections between 1952 and 1988, Callahan County voted six times in support of the Democratic candidate and three times for the Republican candidate. In gubernatorial elections since 1952, county voters supported the Democratic candidate in every election except in 1986, when they supported Republican Bill Clements. Of the senatorial elections between 1952 and 1988, Callahan County voted for Democratic candidates in every instance except 1972 and 1984. Democratic officials also continued to maintain control of most county-wide offices. The first organized church in the county was reportedly the Methodist church in Cross Plains, which was established in the 1880s. Other early churches were located in Belle Plain, Clyde, and Baird. In the mid-1980s Callahan County had thirty-one organized churches, with an estimated aggregate membership of 6,505. The largest communions were Southern Baptist, United Methodist, and Church of Christ.

The county's population reached 12,785 in 1960 but fell to 8,205 in 1970. It was 10,992 in 1980 and 11,859 in 1990. That year more than half the residents lived in Baird (1,737), Clyde (3,053), Cross Plains (1,201), and Putnam (131). Whites constituted 96.8 percent of the population, Hispanics 4.1 percent, and American Indians .4 percent. In 1990 only two black people lived in the county. Among the county's attractions are the Callahan County Pioneer Museum and a number of historic houses. Recreational activities include hunting, lake activities, and the old settler reunion, held each July.

BIBLIOGRAPHY: Mrs. L. L. Blackburn, "Early Settlers and Settlements of Callahan County," West Texas Historical Association *Year Book* 23 (1947). Callahan County Historical Commission, *I Remember Callahan: History of Callahan County, Texas* (Dallas: Taylor, 1986). Brutus Clay Chrisman, *Early Days in Callahan County* (Abilene, Texas: Abilene Printing and Stationery, 1966). Fane Downs et al., *Inventory of County Records, Callahan County Courthouse, Baird, Texas* (Denton: Texas County Records Project, North Texas State University, 1977). Thomas Robert Havins, *Belle Plain, Texas: Ghost Town in Callahan* (Brownwood, Texas: Brown Press, 1972). S. E. Settle, "Early Days in Callahan County," West Texas Historical Association *Year Book* 12 (1936). Vertical Files, Callahan County Library and Museum, Baird, Texas. Jimmy West, "Indian Episodes of Callahan County," West Texas Historical Association *Year Book* 23 (1947). *Christopher Long*

CALLAHAN DIVIDE. The Callahan Divide, named for Callahan County, is a range of hills that extend twenty-six miles from west to southeast through Taylor and Callahan counties and that separate the Brazos River from the Colorado River (the center point of the range is 32°18′ N, 99°51′ W). The divide begins near the emergence of Cedar Creek, three miles east of Mountain Pass in central Taylor County, proceeds through Buffalo Gap, and concludes near Lytle Gap at the intersection of Farm roads 1178 and 36, a mile north of Dudley in west central Callahan County. Elevations in the range vary from a low of 1,898 feet above sea level at Buffalo Gap to 2,411 at the western end of the Callahan Divide, two miles south of Round Top Mountain.

CALLAHAN DRAW. Callahan Draw rises from several playas[qv] six miles northwest of Hale Center in west central Hale County (at 34°07′ N, 101°44′ W) and runs mainly southeast through farmlands for twenty-five miles, entering western Floyd County three miles northwest of Barwise before reaching its mouth on the White River, two miles southwest of Sandhill (at 33°59′ N, 101°26′ W). Much of the stream consists of only a dry bed of sandy loam, though numerous wet-weather ponds are located along its course. It traverses gently sloping terrain that supports scrub brush and grasses. The rural community of Callahan is on the draw five miles south of Plainview.

CALLAHAN EXPEDITION. The Callahan Expedition occurred in October 1855, when James Hughes Callahan[qv] led a force of 111 men into Mexico near Piedras Negras, Coahuila. The announced purpose of the unauthorized invasion was to punish Lipan Apache Indians who reportedly had raided along the Texas frontier during the summer and fall of 1855, then returned to Mexico, where they were protected by the authorities. In fact, the expedition likely was an attempt by Texas slaveholders to regain fugitive slaves who had fled to northern Mexico and to prevent Mexican authorities from permitting runaway slaves to settle in their midst. On July 5, 1855, Governor Elisha M. Pease[qv] authorized Callahan to organize a force to punish marauding Indians, who reportedly had increased their raids that summer when 3,000 United States troops were moved from the Texas frontier to Kansas. Callahan mustered his force into service on July 20. As Texas citizens continued to appeal to Pease for defense against the Indian raids, Callahan and his men left Bandera Pass[qv] on September 18 headed for the Rio Grande.

Texas slaveowners, meanwhile, had developed plans to capture fugitive slaves who had taken up refuge in northern Mexico, especially near San Fernando, Coahuila. Newspaper editor John S. (Rip) Ford[qv] estimated that more than 4,000 slaves had run away from Texas by 1855. That summer the slaveowners sent an emissary to talk with Governor Santiago Vidaurri[qv] of Nuevo León y Coahuila, but Vidaurri rebuffed the offer and warned his military commanders on the frontier to be ready for an invasion. The slaveowners apparently contacted Callahan and persuaded him to use his force to chastise the Mexicans as well as Indians, and perhaps to capture fugitive slaves. Callahan, at least, attempted to keep the real goal of his expedition secret, even from his own men. On August 31 he wrote his quartermaster, Edward Burleson, Jr.,[qv] "I am bound to go to the Rio Grand if nothing hapens. . . . I believe some of the boys have found out about the arrangement so I wrote to you as though my intention was to go to the uper country . . . to keep the matter as much of a secret as possible." Callahan crossed the swollen Rio Grande on October 1–3. Marching westward on October 3, the Texans encountered a Mexican detachment at the Río Escondido, about twenty-two miles from Piedras Negras. In the skirmish that followed, the Mexicans under Col. Emilio (Edvard Emil) Langberg[qv] reported a loss of four dead and three wounded, and Callahan reported four killed and seven wounded. The next morning, Callahan retreated to Piedras Negras and took possession of the town. As the Mexican force approached the town on October 5, Callahan ordered his men to set fire to houses to cover their retreat, and on the evening of October 6 Maj. Sidney Burbank, commander of the American forces across the river at Fort Duncan, turned four cannons to cover the Texans as they recrossed the river.

Callahan immediately defended his invasion of Mexico, claiming that he had received permission from the Mexican authorities to cross the river in pursuit of the Lipans. Pease defended Callahan's burning of Piedras Negras, saying that it was justified because the Mexicans had deceived Callahan by leading him into an ambush. Quartermaster Burleson alluded to a different purpose, however, when he wrote on November 11 to editor Ford about a slave who had escaped to Piedras Negras: The "Mexicans took him up and sent him back to this side immediately. We can guess why they did it." Historians have argued for years over the purpose of the expedition, but there was little misunderstanding at the time by those who were there. Even Bvt. Maj. Gen. Persifor F. Smith, who had encouraged Pease to appoint a company of rangers to help defend the frontier, reported to the adjutant general's office that the Texans were organizing a party to retrieve runaway slaves; "I presume," Smith wrote, "that the party of Captain Callahan was the one alluded to." The claims originating with this invasion of Mexico were not officially settled until 1876, when the Claims Commission of 1868 finished its work. The commission awarded approximately 150 Mexican citizens a total of $50,000 in damages.

BIBLIOGRAPHY: Edward Burleson, Jr., Papers, Barker Texas History Center, University of Texas at Austin. Ernest C. Shearer, "The Callahan Expedition, 1855," *Southwestern Historical Quarterly* 54 (October 1951). Ronnie C. Tyler, "The Callahan Expedition of 1855: Indians or Negroes?" *Southwestern Historical Quarterly* 70 (April 1967).

Ron Tyler

CALLAN, CLAUDE CLEMENT (1881–1956). Claude Clement Callan, humorist and newspaper columnist, was born in 1881 in either Menard or Coleman, Texas, the son of James Joseph and Margaret Jane (Sheen) Callan. He worked for his father on the Coleman *Voice* and married Jessie Garrett, with whom he had two children. In 1906 Callan was living in Brady. He started writing a column entitled "Poor Pa" in 1925, and by the 1930s it was syndicated in 101 newspapers. Another of his columns, "Cracks of the Crowd," was also nationally syndicated. Callan moved to San Antonio in 1936. For a time he wrote daily columns for the Fort Worth *Star-Telegram*[qv] and the Kansas City *Star*. He also wrote for the *Ladies Home Journal* and worked as an editor for the Curtis Publishing Company. He died in San Antonio on April 17, 1956, and was buried in Brady.

BIBLIOGRAPHY: Brady *Standard*, April 20, 1956. Menard County Historical Society, *Menard County History—An Anthology* (San Angelo: Anchor, 1982). Vertical Files, Barker Texas History Center, University of Texas at Austin.

Vivian Elizabeth Smyrl

CALLAN, TEXAS. Callan was ten miles northeast of Menard in northeastern Menard County. In 1908 James Callan, a local landowner, gave the Fort Worth and Rio Grande Railroad Company a site for a depot and several miles of right-of-way to cross his land. The track connecting Brady and Menard was completed in July 1911, and the Richey–DeFreest Land Company formed the Callan City Company to build a stopover community on the railroad. The new company bought 542 acres from James Callan and divided them into town lots. At its peak the Callan community had a hotel, a general store, a lumberyard, and a livery stable and wagonyard, in addition to the stockyards that the railroad company had built. Plans were made to open a bank, but the idea was abandoned when a drought threatened the local economy. A post office was in operation at Callan in 1911–12 and from 1915 to 1919. Population estimates for the Callan area in the 1920s ranged from fifty to seventy-five. As cars came into general use and local road conditions improved, travelers were able to cover more distance in a day, and wayside communities like Callan were gradually abandoned. Most of the buildings at Callan were vacant by the 1930s and were sold for scrap in the early 1940s as part of the World War II[qv] effort. The school at Callan closed in 1939. The depot and a few scattered houses marked the community on county highway maps in the late 1940s, but none of these were shown on county maps in the 1980s.

BIBLIOGRAPHY: Menard County Historical Society, *Menard County History—An Anthology* (San Angelo: Anchor, 1982).

Vivian Elizabeth Smyrl

CALLAWAY, FRANCIS OSCAR (1872–1947). Francis Oscar Callaway, congressman, was born in Harmony Hill, Texas, on October 2, 1872, the son of Christopher Columbus (Bud) and Louise Caroline (Atwood) Callaway. Four years later the family moved to Mercers Gap, in Comanche County. Callaway graduated from Comanche High School in 1894, taught school for three years, and entered the University of Texas law school; he received a degree in 1900 and began the practice of law. He was prosecuting attorney of Comanche County from 1900 to 1902.

He was elected to the United States Congress from the Twelfth District of Texas in 1910, 1912, and 1914. Throughout his legislative career Callaway sharply questioned every federal expenditure. In 1912–13 he served on the Committee on Expenditures in the Treasury Department, and in 1914–15 he was on the Committee on Expenditures in the Department of the Interior. Until late 1915, when he was moved up to the Naval Affairs Committee, he had not attracted a great deal of attention except for his vigorous opposition to huge river and harbor appropriations. It was hard for him to see merit in making the Trinity and Brazos rivers navigable. Of these two rivers he once remarked that he had often waded across them, sometimes had spat across them, but never had to swim them. He gained national attention in 1916 by his opposition to the naval appropriation bill. He thought the huge preparedness campaign unnecessary and believed that it favored munition makers and others who would derive excessive profit from it. He also believed that an army of civilians could repel any invasion. So strong were his words against some congressmen that parts of his speech were expunged from the *Congressional Record.* He believed that submarines had made battleships obsolete and that international law would have to be rewritten to cover the situation.

He was defeated for renomination in 1916 by United States attorney James C. Wilson, largely on the issue of preparedness. At the time of his defeat his hometown newspaper, the Comanche *Chief,* editorialized, "One thing marks this man above his fellows and that is his absolute lack of fear of criticism. He has his convictions and lives up to them." In 1917 Callaway returned to Comanche, where he practiced law and engaged in farming and stock raising until his death on January 31, 1947. He was buried in Oakwood Cemetery, Comanche. He was survived by his widow, the former Stella Couch, whom he had married on December 29, 1904. They had no children.

BIBLIOGRAPHY: *Biographical Directory of the American Congress.* Thomas L. Miller, "Oscar Callaway and Preparedness," West Texas Historical Association *Year Book* 43 (1967). *Who's Who in America,* 1930–31.

Thomas Lloyd Miller

CALLAWAY, MORGAN, JR. (1862–1936). Morgan Callaway, Jr., scholar and teacher, the son of Morgan and Eliza Mary (Hinton) Callaway, was born on November 3, 1862, in Cuthbert, Georgia. His father was a professor of English at Emory College, where Callaway obtained his B.A. degree in 1881 and his M.A. in 1883. He was adjunct professor of English at Emory from 1881 to 1883 and moved to Texas as principal of an academy at Chireno for a year. He became professor of English at Southwestern University in 1884 and remained there for two years before going to Johns Hopkins University, where he was made Phi Beta Kappa, was a fellow in English, and took his Ph.D. degree in 1889, after seminar work with the philologist James W. Bright.

Callaway returned to Southwestern in 1889 but in 1890 joined the English staff of the University of Texas, where he rose to the rank of professor. He also served as assistant literary editor of the Library of Southwestern Literature from 1909 to 1923. He was awarded an honorary doctorate by Southern Methodist University in 1924 and was made faculty research lecturer at the University of Texas in 1925. In 1895 he edited a small volume, *Select Poems of Sidney Lanier.* All his other published works grew out of his unceasing research in Old English: *The Absolute Participle in Anglo-Saxon* (1889), *The Appositive Participle in Anglo-Saxon* (1901), *The Infinitive in Anglo-Saxon* (1913), *Studies in the Syntax of the Lindisfarne Gospels* (1918), *The Historic Study of the Mother Tongue* (1925), *The Temporal Subjunctive in Old English* (1931), and *The Consecutive Subjunctive in Old English* (1933). Callaway maintained uncompromising standards in the teaching of English composition and grammar. He married Lora Hanah Smith, a former pupil, on August 3, 1920. He was a Democrat and a member of the Methodist church. Callaway died on April 3, 1936, and was buried in Austin.

BIBLIOGRAPHY: Carl John Eckhardt, *One Hundred Faithful to the University of Texas at Austin* (197-?). Vertical Files, Barker Texas History Center, University of Texas at Austin. *Who Was Who in America,* Vol. 1.

Robert Adger Law

CALLAWAY, SARA ISADORE SUTHERLAND (1863–1916). Sara Callaway [pseud. Pauline Periwinkle], journalist, suffragist, clubwoman, and community activist, was born in Michigan on September 25, 1863, the daughter of a Civil War[qv] soldier and a suffragist. She began writing at age twelve and later worked as a journalist and writer in Michigan and Ohio. She married James Weston Minor (Miner) in 1884 and published two books of children's stories and verse in 1890. After her husband died she moved to Dallas, Texas, to be near her mother and stepfather. She began working at the Dallas *Morning News*[qv] in January 1893 as society editor and editor of the women's page, and for more than twenty years she wrote a popular weekly column under the pen name Pauline Periwinkle. Later she wrote and edited a weekly children's page in the *News.* She was also editor of the *Semi-Weekly Farm News,* published in both Dallas and Galveston. In July 1900 she married William Allen Callaway, an insurance agent and former newspaperman.

As a witty and sometimes acerbic journalist, Mrs. Callaway inaugurated or advocated several successful social and public health crusades. In 1903 and 1904 she wrote several columns urging the establishment of a juvenile court system and a home for juvenile offenders. She initiated a campaign for pure drinking water and a movement for an antiexpectoration ordinance and wrote in favor of a pure-food law. She also promoted women's rights and women's organizations in her columns.

She organized the first woman suffrage[qv] club in Dallas in 1894. She was a founding member of the Texas Women's Press Association in 1893 and helped organize the Woman's Congress, later the State Council of Women of Texas, in 1893. Among the many women who spoke before the council was sculptor Elisabet Ney.[qv] Through the State Council, Isadore Callaway fostered the establishment of the Women's Building at the State Fair of Texas.[qv] She was president of the Oak Cliff Quero Club and an honorary member of the Dallas Pierian Club. She served as seventh president of the Dallas City Federation of Women's Clubs in 1907 and 1908 and was a founding member of the Dallas Woman's Forum in 1906. While president of the Dallas Federation of Women's Clubs, she led the movement for supervised playgrounds for boys and for the employment of a police matron and a woman probation officer. She originated the annual Christmas empty-stocking crusade for poor children and helped organize the Dallas Free Kindergarten Association. She was a charter member of the Dallas Humane Society and the Jane Douglas chapter of the Daughters of the American Revolution,[qv] a director of the Dallas Public Library, and the chairman of the Chamber of Commerce city-beautification committee. As an original member of the Rural Welfare Association, begun in 1913, Mrs. Callaway encouraged the establishment of the Dallas County Rest Room for country women. Child welfare expert Henry S. Curtis ranked her as one of four outstanding American women, along with Jane Addams, Anna Howard Shaw, and Carrie Chapman Catt.

The Callaways lived in Dallas and raised two orphaned nieces. Isadore Callaway died on August 10, 1916, at St. Paul's Sanitarium in Dallas.

BIBLIOGRAPHY: Dallas *Morning News,* August 21, 1916. Martha Lavinia Hunter, *A Quarter of a Century of the Dallas Woman's Forum, 1906–1931* (Dallas: Cockrell, 1932). Jackie McElhaney, "Pauline Periwinkle: Crusading Columnist," *Heritage News,* Summer 1985.

Megan Seaholm

CALLENDER, WILLIAM LARRABEE (1815–1895). William Larrabee Callender, attorney, judge, and prominent Methodist, was born to Nathaniel and Olive Callender in Shippensburg, Pennsylvania, in 1815. Subsequently, the family lived in several locations in New York and on the Ohio frontier. Callender learned the shoemaker's trade from his father and as a youth of thirteen read for college preparation while employed as a printer. He was graduated from Allegheny College in 1839 and, after studying law in Frankfort, Kentucky, under James Harlan, was admitted to the bar in 1848. Callender edited the

Frankfort *Commonwealth* from 1850 to 1856, when he moved to Victoria, Texas. He married Ann Matilda Kellogg in 1842, Lucy W. Roper in 1850, Alice F. Kibbe in 1862, and Sallie R. Sangster in 1869; he had children in each marriage.

Though his views were decidedly pro-Union, Callender was a much respected citizen of Victoria, where he conducted the Victoria Male Academy.[qv] He served as justice of the peace, district clerk, and attorney, while pursuing his avocation of reflecting on current and historical events in poetry and prose, much of which remains among the Callender manuscripts.

The firm of Glass and Callender conducted the bulk of legal business in Victoria County for two decades after the Civil War.[qv] For thirty years Callender led the Methodist movement in the area. At the time of his death on November 4, 1895, he was given generous recognition by the state Supreme Court. The Callender House of Victoria, cited by the United States Department of the Interior and the state of Texas, bears his name. Callender was buried in Evergreen Cemetery, Victoria.

BIBLIOGRAPHY: Callender Papers, Callender House, Victoria, Texas. Victor Marion Rose, *History of Victoria* (Laredo, 1883; rpt., Victoria, Texas: Book Mart, 1961). Robert W. Shook, "A Texas Portrait: William Larrabee Callender," *Texas Bar Journal*, January 22, 1963.

Robert W. Shook

CALLEROS, CLEOFAS (1896–1973). Cleofas Calleros, historian and community leader in El Paso, was born on April 9, 1896, in Río Florido, Chihuahua, Mexico, to Ismael and Refugia (Perales) Calleros. In 1902 the family immigrated to El Paso to farm, and Calleros enrolled in Sacred Heart School, from which he graduated as valedictorian in 1911. He later attended Draughton Business College. Poverty forced him to work throughout his adolescence; one of his first jobs was in a print shop, where he learned how to print and bind books. In October 1917 Calleros lied about his citizenship in order to serve in World War I.[qv] He became a naturalized citizen in June 1918. He later spent forty years organizing free citizenship-preparation classes for thousands of immigrants. Calleros served in the Army of Occupation in Germany in 1919. He was wounded in action and awarded the Purple Heart. He was a member of the United States Army Officers Reserve Corps from 1920 to 1938. In April 1918 he married Benita Blanco, with whom he had one daughter. He worked as a border representative for the Department of Immigration of the United States Catholic Conference for more than twenty years.

Calleros won several awards for his writing, including the Daliet Award and trophies for four years (1925–28) that he spent gathering materials for the Texas Centennial[qv] in 1936. In 1952 he shared first prize and the award of merit of the American Association for State and Local History with the El Paso *Times,* for which he had produced feature articles dealing with the history of West Texas. In 1954 he collaborated with Marjorie F. Graham on *El Paso—Then and Now,* a book based on his series of newspaper articles focusing on El Paso in 1896. He collected the historical data and coauthored with Dr. Ángel Alcázar de Velasco of Madrid, Spain, the book *Historia del Templo de Nuestra Señora de Guadalupe* (1953). It took numerous years to write, illustrate, and hand-print the book on a "workworn Chandler job press." The work includes information on early settlements in Texas. Carlos E. Castañeda[qv] wrote the introduction, and José Cisneros produced twelve illustrations of early Franciscan missionary and expeditionary motifs for it. The unique format of the 200-page limited edition made it a historic "book of the century." Rich printing materials were used, and great care was taken in producing a special copy in vellum for Pope John XXIII. Others were embossed in silk, imitation parchment, and Florentine paper. The borders of each page were of a different design. The entire book was bound in Mexican leather, and a seventeenth-century style of printing was used.

Beginning in the 1920s Calleros became involved in a variety of community activities to clear slums, to improve his old southside neighborhood, and to enrich the arts. He also helped organize the El Paso Boy's Club, the League of United Latin American Citizens[qv] in El Paso, the Chihuahua State Historical Society, and the Western History Association. Calleros was also a founding member of the first Knights of Columbus[qv] chapter in Texas—Council 638—about which he wrote a short history on the occasion of its seventieth anniversary. As a member of the council, he helped establish a boys' center and organized many other councils in the state. His efforts with the Knights of Columbus were honored through his investiture as a Knight Commander of St. Gregory the Great. He was also designated a Knight of the Order of Isabella by the Spanish Government for his work on Spanish history in the Southwest. In addition, Calleros was awarded an honorary master of fine arts degree by New Mexico State University and an honorary doctorate in history by the University of New Mexico. Calleros died on February 22, 1973, and was buried at Fort Bliss National Cemetery with military honors. His daughter later donated his papers to the University of Texas at El Paso Special Collections and Archives.

BIBLIOGRAPHY: El Paso *Times,* November 29, 1953, April 4, 1954, January 24, 1960, April 25, 1968, September 20, 1973, February 23, 1974. Mario T. García, *Desert Immigrants: The Mexicans of El Paso, 1880–1920* (New Haven: Yale University Press, 1981). Kingsville-Bishop *Record-News,* May 24, 1972. Mercedes Lugo, "El Paso's Own Señor Cleofas Calleros," *Junior Historian,* December 1968.

Teresa Palomo Acosta

CALLIHAM, TEXAS. Calliham, originally known as Guffeyola, is on State Highway 72 eleven miles east of Tilden in northwestern McMullen County. The settlement was originally named for Hiram Harvey McGuffey, who owned a store on the site; in 1923 the community was renamed for Joseph Thomas Calliham, a rancher and the owner of the townsite. The community began on the Calliham Ranch during an oil-prospecting boom in 1918. At that time Guffeyola was not much more than a tent city with a general store. But by 1922, when an oil well was drilled on the site, so many people had moved to the area that J. W. Stephenson arranged with Calliham to lay out a formal townsite; according to one account he guaranteed Calliham fifty dollars for every lot sold. In 1923 the community received a post office. During the 1920s the town had four cafes, three two-story hotels, several grocery stores, a bakery, a drugstore, a pool hall, a newspaper office, and a dance pavilion. Temporary classes were held on the nearby Stitz Ranch until 1928, when a brick schoolhouse was built in Calliham. Calliham's development peaked with a population of 400 during the late 1930s. In the late 1940s the community had a reported population of 300, five businesses, a post office, and a school. Its high school closed in 1948, and its elementary school closed in 1963. By 1972 only 121 residents and two businesses were reported in the town, and by 1978 twenty-two families remained at the original site. Calliham by 1988 had been moved three miles south of its original site, which had been inundated by Choke Canyon Reservoir.

BIBLIOGRAPHY: T. Lindsay Baker, *Ghost Towns of Texas* (Norman: University of Oklahoma Press, 1986). Marker Files, Texas Historical Commission, Austin. *McMullen County History* (n.p: McMullen County History Book Committee, 1981).

John Leffler

CALLIHAN, MOSIS A. (?–?). Mosis A. Callihan (Morris Callahan) was a partner of Allen Vince[qv] as one of Stephen F. Austin's[qv] Old Three Hundred[qv] colonists. The pair received title to a league of land now in Harris County on August 3, 1824. Callihan probably died before September 30, 1825, for about that date Humphrey Jackson[qv] wrote Austin that Nicholas Callahan, the brother of Morris Callahan, deceased, was getting a power of attorney from his father to settle the estate.

BIBLIOGRAPHY: Eugene C. Barker, ed., *The Austin Papers* (3 vols., Washington: GPO, 1924–28). Lester G. Bugbee, "The Old Three Hundred: A List of Settlers in Austin's First Colony," *Quarterly of the Texas State Historical Association* 1 (October 1897).

CALLIS, TEXAS. Callis, also known as Oak Grove, was twenty-five miles northeast of McKinney in northeastern Collin County. A post office operated there from 1891 through 1904. By 1900 the community had a population of fifty, two stores, a cotton gin, a church, and a school. Its population stood at twenty-five by the mid-1940s, the last time population statistics were reported.

BIBLIOGRAPHY: Roy Franklin Hall and Helen Gibbard Hall, *Collin County: Pioneering in North Texas* (Quanah, Texas: Nortex, 1975).
Brian Hart

CALLISBURG, TEXAS. Callisburg is eleven miles northeast of Gainesville in eastern Cooke County. The town was near the Butterfield Overland Mail[qv] route and on the Mormon Trail, a route established in 1846 by a group of Mormons led by Lyman Wight,[qv] who were migrating to Texas. The community was named for blacksmith Sam Callis, the first settler there. By 1873 a post office had been established at the community in Billy Rousseau's dry-goods and grocery store, and ten years later Callisburg reported a population of 300, a school, and some twenty businesses, including a steam gristmill–cotton gin. By 1902, however, its population had declined to about 110, and its post office had closed. In 1902 residents thought an electric rail line was to be built between Gainesville and Sherman to the east; Callisburg was to be used as the headquarters for this line, but the project never developed. In 1924 the Big Indian Oil and Development Company Well No. 1 was drilled on B. W. Davis's farm, a mile east of Callisburg. The community's population level fluctuated between 110 and 200 until the early 1970s, when it dropped sharply to around sixty-eight. By 1980, however, Callisburg had become incorporated, and by 1988 its population had reached a new reported high of 329. In 1988 the town had two churches, two stores, a volunteer fire department, a city hall, a community center, and its own independent school district. Its population in 1990 was 344.

BIBLIOGRAPHY: Gainesville *Daily Register*, Centennial Edition, August 30, 1948. C. N. Jones, *Early Days in Cooke County: 1848–1873* (Gainesville, Texas, 1936; rpt., Gainesville: Cooke County Heritage Society, 1977). A. Morton Smith, *The First 100 Years in Cooke County* (San Antonio: Naylor, 1955).
Robert Wayne McDaniel

CALLOWAY, TEXAS. Calloway, one of the earliest settlements in Upshur County, was on Calloway Hill, near Farm Road 49 some ten miles west of Gilmer. The settlement was established around 1853 as a way station on the road from Jefferson. In antebellum Texas[qv] Calloway served as a shipping and trading center for farms and plantations in the western part of the county. A post office opened there in 1855, and by the eve of the Civil War[qv] the town had a cotton gin, a blacksmith shop, and several stores and saloons. After the war, Calloway continued to prosper. In 1885 it had an estimated population of 250, three steam gristmill–cotton gins, three churches, two blacksmith shops, a general store, and a district school. Among the town's prominent citizens was James B. Cranfill,[qv] an influential Baptist leader. By the mid-1890s the population of Calloway reached 300. After 1900, however, the community began to decline. Its post office was closed, and many residents moved away. By the mid-1930s the town was no longer shown on county highway maps.

BIBLIOGRAPHY: G. H. Baird, *A Brief History of Upshur County* (Gilmer, Texas: Gilmer *Mirror*, 1946). Doyal T. Loyd, *History of Upshur County* (Waco: Texian Press, 1987).
Christopher Long

CALOHAN, WILLIAM LAWRENCE (1867–1932). W. Lawrence (Lod) Calohan, cattle inspector, was born in Blanco County, Texas, in 1867, one of five children of William S. and Vibella (McCrocklin) Calohan. He began herding cattle in Southwest Texas and made his first cattle drive to Abilene, Kansas, for the Blocker Ranch. In 1892 he was employed as cattle inspector by the Texas Cattle Raisers Association (later the Texas and Southwestern Cattle Raisers Association[qv]), first at Midland and Fort Worth and after 1909 at Kansas City, Missouri. He was said to have "carried more than 15,000 cattle brands in his head." As brand inspector of the association, he was able to recognize on sight 2,700 brands of members from Texas, New Mexico, Oklahoma, Kansas, Nebraska, Colorado, Montana, and Wyoming. In 1918 he became chief inspector for the cattlemen's association at Kansas City. He married Sarah Alpha Grammer, and they had two children. He died in Kansas City from heat prostration on July 11, 1932.

BIBLIOGRAPHY: *Cattleman*, July 1936, May 1953. *Frontier Times*, July 1936. John Moursund, *Blanco County Families for One Hundred Years* (Austin, 1958). John W. Speer, *A History of Blanco County* (Austin: Pemberton, 1965). Vertical Files, Barker Texas History Center, University of Texas at Austin.
S. G. Reed

CALOSA CREEK. Calosa Creek rises nine miles southwest of Falfurrias in north central Brooks County (at 27°07′ N, 98°15′ W) and runs east for five miles to its mouth, in a pool one mile west of U.S. Highway 281 (at 27°07′ N, 98°10′ W). It crosses flat to gently rolling terrain surfaced by loose sand that supports scrub brush, grasses, and seasonal high-moisture plants.

CALVARY, TEXAS (Trinity County). Calvary, at the junction of Farm roads 233 and 357, fourteen miles northeast of Groveton in northern Trinity County, grew up around a school established in the 1890s. Its school was later consolidated with the school at Apple Springs. In the mid-1930s Calvary had a church, a cemetery, and a few scattered houses. In the early 1990s the church and cemetery were still at the site.

BIBLIOGRAPHY: Patricia B. and Joseph W. Hensley, eds., *Trinity County Beginnings* (Groveton, Texas: Trinity County Book Committee, 1986). Trinity County Historical Commission, *Trinity County Cemeteries* (Burnet, Texas: Nortex, 1980).
Christopher Long

CALVARY, TEXAS (Wood County). Calvary is on Farm Road 779 three miles northeast of Golden in southwestern Wood County. Some reports state that a Calvary community existed as early as 1888. By 1896 a four-teacher school called Bell Founte (also spelled Bellefont and Bell Font) was located in that area and had 120 students; ten years later its enrollment had dropped to eighty-five. In the 1930s the Bell Font school district had fifty-nine students in nine grades. Though the community was not indicated on the 1936 county highway map, newspaper accounts from that time refer to a community named Bellfonte and a "Calvery" Church. By 1959 the community was called Calvary and was the site of Calvary Church and a number of scattered dwellings. In 1988 the settlement had one business.

Rachel Jenkins

CALVERT, TEXAS. Calvert is at the intersection of State Highway 6 and Farm roads 1644 and 979, on the Southern Pacific line nine miles north of Hearne in west central Robertson County. The earliest white settler in the area was Joseph Harlan, whose 1837 land grant lay five miles south of what is now the site of Calvert. In 1850 Robert Calvert, for whom the town was named, established a plantation west of the townsite. Calvert and other area farmers urged the Houston and Texas Central Railway to build through the area; the railroad arrived in 1868. A group of investors purchased land at the townsite and platted the community in January of that year, and by February merchants from nearby communities such as Sterling and Owensville were moving to the new town. A post office also opened at the community in 1868. The first trains arrived there in 1869. Calvert incorporated with an aldermanic form of government in 1870. In 1870, as part of the Reconstruction[qv] political maneuvering in Robertson County, Calvert replaced Owensville as county seat. Early that year the town was briefly occupied by federal troops; that year also the first school was founded in the community. The Republican party[qv] in the county drew much of its strength from black voters on the plantations in the Calvert area, and for a number of years the party was able to elect blacks from Calvert to county and state office. As a rail center and as county seat, Calvert prospered, and in 1871 the town claimed to have the largest cotton gin in the world. In 1873 a severe yellow fever epidemic killed many in the community. A county jail built in 1875 was still a local landmark more than a century later.

In 1878 Calvert was a thriving community with some fifty-two businesses. The next year the town of Morgan became county seat, but Calvert continued to prosper as a commercial center. By 1884 Calvert had an estimated 3,000 inhabitants, with Presbyterian, Methodist, Baptist, Episcopal, and Catholic churches, public schools, two banks, an opera house, and the weekly *Courier*. Around 1900 the community was a major cotton center, with a number of gins, cotton compresses, and cottonseed oil mills (*see* COTTONSEED INDUSTRY). In 1899 the town was damaged by floods, and two years later a fire destroyed much of its business district. Calvert's population was reported as 3,322 in 1900, but thereafter it began to decline. The community had 2,579 residents in 1910, 2,099 in the mid-1920s, 2,366 in 1940, 2,561 in 1950, 2,073 in 1960, and 1,950 in the mid-1960s. In 1968 many former residents of the town visited to help its citizens celebrate Calvert's centennial. The population was 1,714 in 1980 and 1,536 in 1990.

BIBLIOGRAPHY: J. W. Baker, *History of Robertson County, Texas* (Franklin, Texas: Robertson County Historical Survey Committee, 1970).

Mark Odintz

CALVERT CREEK. Calvert Creek rises two miles east of Interstate Highway 30 in southwestern Bowie County (at 33°18′ N, 94°39′ W) and runs southeast for five miles to its mouth on Wright Patman Lake, two miles west of U.S. Highway 67 (at 33°18′ N, 94°37′ W). Before the reservoir was constructed in the mid-1950s, the creek ran into the Sulphur River a mile east of Highway 67 (at 33°16′ N, 94°36′ W). The stream traverses flat to gently rolling terrain surfaced by sandy and clay loams that support grasses and mixed hardwoods and pines.

CALVERT, WACO AND BRAZOS VALLEY RAILROAD. The Calvert, Waco and Brazos Valley Railroad Company was chartered on June 28, 1899. The line was initially projected to extend from the International–Great Northern Railroad at Lewis Switch to Waco. Members of the first board of directors were George J. Gould of Lakewood, New Jersey; Frank J. Gould of Irvington, New York; Leroy Trice, Nathan A. Steadman, George L. Noble, Alfred R. Howard, and William L. Maury, all from Anderson County, Texas; and Leonidas H. Parish and John T. Garrett, both from Robertson County, Texas. The initial capital was $75,000, and the business office was in Calvert in Robertson County. By the end of 1900 the company had completed sixty-six miles between Bryan and Marlin and a branch from Calvert Junction to Calvert. In that year the charter was amended twice, ultimately raising capitalization to $2,830,000 and changing the projected route to run from Spring, just north of Houston, to Fort Worth. On February 12, 1901, the legislature authorized the International and Great Northern to acquire the Calvert, Waco and Brazos Valley. The two lines merged on May 1. The International and Great Northern completed the line between Spring and Fort Worth in 1902.

Chris Cravens

CALVILLO, MARÍA DEL CARMEN (1765–1856). María Calvillo, descendent of early settlers of San Antonio and owner of Rancho de las Cabras in what is now Wilson County (*see* RANCHO DE LAS CABRAS STATE HISTORIC SITE), was born at the Villa of San Fernando de Béxar[qv] (San Antonio) on July 9, 1756, the eldest of six children born to Ygnacio Francisco Xavier Calvillo and Antonia de Arocha. Her father acquired Rancho de las Cabras ("the Goat Ranch"), an outpost of San Francisco de la Espada Mission, after the mission and its lands were secularized. María Calvillo married Juan Gavino de la Trinidad Delgado around 1781. The couple had two sons, Juan Bautista and José Anacleto, and adopted three additional children, Juan José, María Concepción Gortari, and Antonio Durán. During the 1811 and 1814 Gavino played a major role in the overthrow of the Spanish; as a result of his activities he was declared a rebel against the crown. María apparently separated from her husband at this time. On April 15, 1814, Ygnacio Calvillo was murdered at his ranch during a raid; initially the raid was thought to have been perpetrated by Indians, but subsequent investigation revealed that the attackers included Ygnacio's own grandson. At this time María gained control and ownership of the property. On August 28, 1828, she formally petitioned the Mexican government for a new title to her father's ranch; it was granted the next month. Later grants in 1833 placed three leagues of land under her control. Her will passed ownership of the property to two of her adopted children, María Concepción Gortari and Antonio Durán. María Calvillo died on January 15, 1856.

BIBLIOGRAPHY: Frederick Charles Chabot, *With the Makers of San Antonio* (Yanaguana Society Publications 4, San Antonio, 1937). Julia Kathryn Garrett, *Green Flag Over Texas: A Story of the Last Years of Spain in Texas* (Austin: Pemberton Press, 1939).

I. Waynne Cox

CALVIN, TEXAS (Bastrop County). Calvin is between State Highway 95 and Big Sandy Creek five miles north of Bastrop in north central Bastrop County. The town, named after Calvin Silliman, son of Calvin Coal Company founder W. C. Silliman, was established in 1910 on the Missouri, Kansas and Texas Railroad as a planned community to house the local population of predominantly Mexican coal miners. Calvin, like its trackside neighbors to the south, Glenham and Phelan, owed its existence to the lignite industry that began to flourish after 1900 between Sayersville and Bastrop. By 1912 Calvin had a post office run by postmaster Newell L. Trammell, and during the productive 1920s some 100 residents occupied fifty-three neatly arranged buildings there. The miners' children attended school in Bastrop. During the Great Depression[qv] the production of shaft-mined lignite waned, however, relative to increasingly competitive petroleum and more efficient strip-mined coal. Postal service to Calvin was discontinued in the late 1930s, and by 1940 the community had diminished to one store and an agricultural population of about fifty. Mining in Bastrop struggled on into the early 1940s before being abandoned. Calvin, uninhabited after 1950, has been completely razed by the owner of the site, and today little remains to identify the former community.

BIBLIOGRAPHY: Ray D. Kenmotsu, *Cultural Resource Investigations at the Powell Bend Prospect* (Texas Archeological Survey, University of Texas at Austin, 1982). Davis McAuley, "Some Notes on Calvin, Texas," *Sayersville Historical Association Bulletin*, Spring 1983. David G. Robinson, *Additional Cultural Resource Investigations on the Powell Bend Prospect* (Texas Archeological Survey, University of Texas at Austin, 1983).

John J. Buder

CALVIN, TEXAS (Red River County). Calvin, a farming community on a mail route from Clarksville in Red River County, reported one business and a population of seventy-five in 1930. By 1940 its population had dropped to fifty, and by 1984 Calvin no longer existed.

Claudia Hazlewood

CALVIT, ALEXANDER (1784–1836). Alexander Calvit (Calvet), early settler and soldier in the Texas Revolution,[qv] was born in Mississippi on June 17, 1784. In 1814 and 1816 he was a captain in the Mississippi militia. As one of Stephen F. Austin's[qv] Old Three Hundred,[qv] he received title to a league and two labores of land now in Brazoria and Waller counties on August 3, 1824. He was popularly known as Sandy. Calvit lived at Bell's Landing (now East Columbia) at the mouth of the Brazos River, as did his wife's sister, Jane H. W. Long.[qv]

The census of March 1826 listed Calvit as a farmer and stock raiser with a household including his wife, Barbara, three daughters, and thirteen slaves. Despite an early friendship with Austin during which Barbara Calvit and Jane Long made Austin a buckskin suit, Calvit apparently got into difficulties with the empresario qv over land fees and Austin's efforts to prevent speculation in land, for in 1833 Calvit wrote José Antonio Mexía qv that he hoped Austin would continue to be imprisoned in Mexico. At Brazoria on August 9, 1835, Calvit signed resolutions recommending the calling of the Consultation.qv He contracted pneumonia while in charge of a supply camp for the Texas army and died at his home in Brazoria County on January 7, 1836.

BIBLIOGRAPHY: Eugene C. Barker, ed., *The Austin Papers* (3 vols., Washington: GPO, 1924–28). Eugene C. Barker, *The Life of Stephen F. Austin* (Nashville: Cokesbury Press, 1925; rpt., Austin: Texas State Historical Association, 1949; New York: AMS Press, 1970). Eugene C. Barker, ed., "Minutes of the Ayuntamiento of San Felipe de Austin, 1828–1832," 12 parts, *Southwestern Historical Quarterly* 21–24 (January 1918–October 1920). Lester G. Bugbee, "The Old Three Hundred: A List of Settlers in Austin's First Colony," *Quarterly of the Texas State Historical Association* 1 (October 1897). Files, Daughters of the Republic of Texas Museum, Austin. "J. C. Clopper's Journal and Book of Memoranda for 1828," *Southwestern Historical Quarterly* 13 (July 1909). Noah Smithwick, *The Evolution of a State, or Recollections of Old Texas Days* (Austin: Gammel, 1900; rpt., Austin: University of Texas Press, 1983). *Texas State Gazette*, October 9, 1830; November 16, 1850.

CALVIT-HERNDON PLANTATION. The Calvit-Herndon Plantation, on the site of present Clute in southeastern Brazoria County, was a sugar plantation with a frame residence, office, and brick sugar house located on land purchased from the Wharton family. It was called Evergreen by its original owner, Alexander Calvit,qv and known as Herndon Plantation when Calvit's only daughter inherited it and married John Hunter Herndon.qv Herndon raised Arabian horses and had large herds of cattle, which, according to one source, were later purchased by Abel Head (Shanghai) Pierce.qv By 1860 Herndon was one of the wealthiest men in the county; he had a summer house at Velasco, real property valued at $1,605,000, personal property estimated at $106,050, and forty slaves. Little is known about the plantation after the Civil War,qv but it is likely that its operations ceased with the decline of the plantation economy.

BIBLIOGRAPHY: James A. Creighton, *A Narrative History of Brazoria County* (Angleton, Texas: Brazoria County Historical Commission, 1975). Abner J. Strobel, *The Old Plantations and Their Owners of Brazoria County* (Houston, 1926; rev. ed., Houston: Bowman and Ross, 1930; rpt., Austin: Shelby, 1980). Ralph A. Wooster, "Wealthy Texans, 1860," *Southwestern Historical Quarterly* 71 (October 1967).

Diana J. Kleiner

CALZONES COLORADOS (?–?). Calzones Colorados (Red Breeches) was chief of an Akokisa Indian village east of the Trinity River ten or fifteen miles from its mouth. When several Frenchmen under Joseph Blancpain qv were arrested in October 1754, their goods were confiscated, and their huts were given to Calzones Colorados by the Spanish, who had also given him the name. Both the Spanish and French tried to use the chief as a pawn in their diplomatic game for control of Southeast Texas. In 1760 Calzones Colorados reported that Louis Juchereau de St. Denis qv had sent two Bidai Indians to bribe him to come to Natchitoches, Louisiana, to secure ammunition to kill the Spanish at El Orcoquisac qv but that he had refused the bribe. The Spanish contributed to his village two cattle and five fanegas of corn a week to secure the Indians as neophytes of Nuestra Señora de la Luz Mission. In 1764 Calzones was an intermediary in the quarrel between Rafael Martínez Pacheco and Marcos Ruiz qqv over the administration of San Agustín de Ahumada Presidio and was bribed by Pacheco to oppose attempts to remove the Trinity River missions to Los Horconcitos.qv The Spanish finally abandoned the area in 1771 but later named one of the tributaries of the Trinity Arroyo de Calzones in honor of the chief.

BIBLIOGRAPHY: Herbert Eugene Bolton, *Texas in the Middle Eighteenth Century: Studies in Spanish Colonial History and Administration* (Berkeley: University of California Press, 1915; rpt., Austin: University of Texas Press, 1970).

CAMAI INDIANS. In 1740 the name Camai was recorded twice on the same day in the baptismal register of San Antonio de Valero Mission of San Antonio. It is given as the ethnic affiliation of an unnamed woman whose two orphan children were baptized. This woman and her husband, a Tuu (Toho), were said to have previously died "in the woods." Thus, though Herbert E. Bolton qv assumes the presence of Camais at Valero, it is not certain that any Camai individuals were ever actually there. Because the name Camai has not been found in other documents, the original homeland of the Camai Indians remains unknown and their ethnic identity cannot be determined. By 1740 so many Indian groups had been displaced that a record of Camai-Toho intermarriage is no indication that both groups originally lived in the same area or were linguistically and culturally related. J. R. Swanton entered the name Camai on his list of Indian groups who may have spoken the Coahuilteco language. Swanton, who never examined the Valero Mission registers, obtained the name Camai from Bolton's list of Indian groups said to have been represented at Valero. Since Coahuilteco was spoken by many of the Indians at Valero, Swanton evidently thought that the Camais may also have spoken that language. His assumption is not supported by such evidence as is now available.

BIBLIOGRAPHY: Frederick Webb Hodge, ed., *Handbook of American Indians North of Mexico* (2 vols., Washington: GPO, 1907, 1910; rpt., New York: Pageant, 1959). J. R. Swanton, *Linguistic Material from the Tribes of Southern Texas and Northeastern Mexico* (Washington: Smithsonian Institution, 1940).

Thomas N. Campbell

CAMAMA INDIANS. In 1768 Gaspar José de Solís qv listed Camama as the name of one of the eight Indian groups represented at San José y San Miguel de Aguayo Mission of San Antonio. Since no recognizable variant of this name has been found in earlier documents and the registers of Mission San José apparently have not survived, there is not enough information to determine just who the Camamas of Solís actually were. Because most of the Indians at San José came from the coastal plain of southern Texas and northern Tamaulipas, it seems likely that the Camamas were from the same area.

BIBLIOGRAPHY: Thomas N. Campbell, *The Payaya Indians of Southern Texas* (San Antonio: Southern Texas Archeological Association, 1975). Peter P. Forrestal, trans., *The Solís Diary of 1767*, ed. Paul J. Foik (Preliminary Studies of the Texas Catholic Historical Society 1.6 [March 1931]).

Thomas N. Campbell

CAMARGO, DIEGO DE (?–1520?). Although he never visited Texas, Diego de Camargo is often said to have commanded an expedition for Francisco de Garay qv to establish a colony at the mouth of the Rio Grande. The colony was attempted not at the Rio Grande, however, but at the Río Pánuco, in the future Mexican state of Vera Cruz. The expedition commander, according to Bernal Díaz del Castillo, was not Camargo but Alonso Álvarez de Pineda.qv Camargo was an unheralded sailor on Juan de Grijalva's 1518 voyage to the southern Gulf of Mexico and, according to Díaz, a Dominican friar. Early in 1520 he sailed from Jamaica as captain of a ship carrying supplies to the Pánuco settlement already begun by Álvarez de Pineda. Shortly after his arrival, the Huastec Indians rebelled, killing all the Spaniards except those who were able to get aboard Camargo's vessels and escape to Hernán Cortés's settlement of Villa Rica de la Vera Cruz. Álvarez de Pineda was among those slain in the uprising. Wounded, as were most of his men, Camargo died after reaching Villa Rica. Most of those who survived the Huastec attack and the voyage were pressed into Cortés's forces for the final assault on the Aztec capital of Tenochtitlán.

BIBLIOGRAPHY: Bernal Díaz del Castillo, *Historia verdadera de la conquista de la Nueva España* (Madrid, 1632; rpt., Mexico City: Porrúa, 1955). Alonso García Bravo, Probanza de méritos y servicios (MS, Archivo General de Indias, Seville, 1561). Antonio de Herrera y Tordesillas, *Historia general de los hechos de los castellanos en las islas y Tierra-firme de el Mar Océano* (10 vols., Asunción, Paraguay: Guaranía, 1944). *Robert S. Weddle*

CAMARGO, NUEVO SANTANDER. Camargo, Nuevo Santander (now Tamaulipas), was founded on the south side of the San Juan River on March 5, 1749, by José de Escandón,[qv] governor of Nuevo Santander. At this time, Blas María de la Garza Falcón,[qv] a prominent rancher, and forty families from Nuevo León already occupied the general area of the San Juan valley. Camargo was one of five such towns founded by Escandón and local cattle owners between 1749 and 1753 in the Trans-Nueces area. Settlers who went to Camargo in 1749 brought 13,000 sheep to begin ranching; the following year they had increased their stock to 30,000 and their population to 700, thus becoming the largest of Escandón's settlements. In addition to the Spaniards, the town included 241 Indians from the groups of Tareguanos, Pajaritos, Paysanos, Venados, Cueroquemados, and Guajolotes living inside the walls of San Agustín de Laredo Mission, south of the town. Prominent ranchers, including Manuel and Joseph Hinojosa, Nicolás de los Santos Coy, and Garza Falcón, braved two years of drought, as well as floods and malaria, to continue ranching.

In 1751 Camargo remained the largest of the Rio Grande colonies, with ninety-six families numbering 637 persons. Although agriculture afforded the settlers a moderate income, their main subsistence came from cattle and sheep at Camargo. In 1753 Escandón used nineteen families to help found Mier on the Rio Grande. Camargo also remained the largest goat and sheep ranching site of the Rio Grande settlements; in 1757 its seventeen ranches were stocked with 8,000 horses and mules, 2,600 cattle, and 72,000 sheep and goats. By this year constant migration into Camargo began to use up the land for new settlers, and in 1767 a royal commission was appointed to survey the total area of Nuevo Santander. Camargo received 118 *porciones* as a result of this survey, the largest number granted to any of the settlements surveyed. By 1800 Nuevo Santander had a population of 15,000, a large part of which resided in Camargo. After *de facto* Texas independence, Camargo joined the effort in 1839–40 of the northern provinces supported by Americans to separate from Mexico and establish a Republic of the Rio Grande.[qv] During the late 1800s, disputes arose over the *porciones* granted to Camargo, but in a series of rulings between 1889 and 1908 the Supreme Court validated all of the original allocations to Camargo. The present Texas town of Rio Grande City is located on *porciones* eighty and eighty-one of the original jurisdiction of Camargo. In 1967, along with other Mexican border towns, Camargo was badly damaged by the floodwaters of Hurricane Beulah.

BIBLIOGRAPHY: Herbert Eugene Bolton, *Texas in the Middle Eighteenth Century: Studies in Spanish Colonial History and Administration* (Berkeley: University of California Press, 1915; rpt., Austin: University of Texas Press, 1970). Lawrence Francis Hill, *José de Escandón and the Founding of Nuevo Santander* (Columbus: Ohio State University Press, 1926). Florence J. Scott, *Historical Heritage of the Lower Rio Grande* (San Antonio: Naylor, 1937; rev. ed., Waco: Texian, 1966; rpt., Rio Grande City, Texas: La Retama Press, 1970). *Time*, October 6, 1967.

CAMBRIDGE, TEXAS. Cambridge, three miles northeast of Henrietta, was once the principal community and retail center for Clay County. The settlement developed in the early 1870s, and in 1875 it received postal service. A year later the United States Army opened a telegraph office there, and three years later St. Mary's Catholic Church was built. In July 1882 the tracks of the Fort Worth and Denver Railway were extended through Henrietta, which became the county seat. Many Cambridge residents and businesses moved to Henrietta, and the Cambridge post office closed. Soon a second railroad, the Missouri, Kansas and Texas, also bypassed Cambridge for Henrietta, and Cambridge's few remaining residents left. In 1991 only a cemetery remained at the townsite.

BIBLIOGRAPHY: William Charles Taylor, *A History of Clay County* (Austin: Jenkins, 1972). *David Minor*

CAMDEN, TEXAS (Polk County). Camden is at the junction of Farm roads 62 and 942, eighty miles northwest of Beaumont in east central Polk County. The site was developed by the W. T. Carter and Brother Lumber Company in 1898, after its plant at nearby Barnum had burned a year earlier. Local historians credit Mrs. W. T. Carter with naming the town, though postal historians state that surveyor T. H. Woodson named it after his former home, Camden, New Jersey. In any event, the Carter company built a successful lumber plant and company town at Camden. William Thomas and Ernest A. Carter, owners of the company, also constructed the Moscow, Camden and San Augustine Railway, which linked Camden with the Houston, East and West Texas line to the west. The wooden sawmill burned in 1910 but was rebuilt of concrete and steel. Another fire destroyed the planer mill in 1922, but it was also replaced. The Mummert Company, with headquarters in Chicago, Illinois, established another smaller plant there in the early 1930s. The United States Plywood Corporation bought the W. T. Carter mill at Camden in 1968. The tiny Moscow, Camden and San Augustine line continued to be a minor tourist attraction through the early 1970s. The discovery of oil at the Camden field in 1972 also diversified the local economy. The population of Camden, estimated at 500 in 1904, had grown to 1,000 in the mid-1950s; it was reported as 1,200 in 1990.

BIBLIOGRAPHY: *A Pictorial History of Polk County, Texas, 1846–1910* (Livingston, Texas: Polk County Bicentennial Commission, 1976; rev. ed. 1978). *Robert Wooster*

CAMDEN, TEXAS (Gregg County). Camden, also known as Walling's Ferry, was on the south bank of the Sabine River, just north of the site of what is now Easton in the extreme southeastern corner of Gregg County. It was among the earliest settlements in the county. The community grew up around a Sabine ferry crossing operated by John Walling, who moved to the area during the late 1820s or early 1830s. The site was known for many years both as Walling's Ferry and as Camden. Walling's ferry operation, which was on the road between Port Caddo and Henderson County, was licensed by the Mexican government (*see* MEXICAN TEXAS) in the early 1830s, and Camden reportedly served as a stopping point for Sam Houston[qv] on his first trip to Texas in 1832. In 1844 the settlement was formally established as a townsite, and the same year Enoch Hays built a two-story, eight-room log tavern and hotel. A post office under the name Walling's Ferry operated there intermittently from 1847 to 1872; in 1861 its name was briefly changed to Camden. During the 1850s steamboats came up the Sabine as far as Camden. By the Civil War,[qv] however, the settlement had begun to decline. A Confederate colonel who visited the community in 1863 found it unimpressive, and shortly after the war another visitor wrote that the townspeople seemed "notably inert and melancholy." Disease—particularly malaria, which was rampant along low-lying riverbottoms—and the rise of nearby Iron Bridge eventually doomed the town. By the late 1860s most of Camden's remaining residents had moved away, and in the 1870s the town was no longer shown on maps. Camden cemetery was still in use in the 1990s.

BIBLIOGRAPHY: Eugene W. McWhorter, *Traditions of the Land: The History of Gregg County* (Longview, Texas: Gregg County Historical Foundation, 1989). *Christopher Long*

CAMEL DRAW. Camel Draw rises five miles southeast of Dome Peak in east central Hudspeth County (at 31°12′ N, 105°09′ W) and runs southeast for twelve miles before joining Seventeen Draw to form Eagle Flat Draw, five miles southwest of Allamoore (at 31°03′ N, 105°06′ W). It traverses an area of steep to gentle slopes surfaced by variable soil that supports scrub brush and sparse grasses. The name of the draw may come from the camels[qv] imported to Texas by the United States government in the 1850s and later used on an expedition from Camp Verde[qv] to the Big Bend.

CAMELS. In 1836 Maj. George H. Crosman urged the United States War Department to use camels in Indian campaigns in Florida because of the animals' ability to keep on the move with a minimum of food and water. The matter came to the attention of Senator Jefferson Davis,[qv] whom President Franklin Pierce later appointed secretary of war. Davis's first problem was that of coping with Indians and with transportation in Texas, but the enormous expense of the Mexican Cession of 1848 had seriously depleted available army resources. Davis firmly accepted the currently prevalent "Great American Desert" thesis, which held that much of the western United States was virtually uninhabitable. He urged Congress to appropriate money to test the value and efficiency of camels in the Southwest as a partial solution to pressing needs. At the insistence of the War Department, Congress passed, on March 3, 1855, the Shield amendment to the appropriation bill, which made $30,000 available "under the direction of the War Department in the purchase of camels and the importation of dromedaries, to be employed for military purposes."

On May 10, 1855, Maj. H. C. Wayne received the special presidential assignment. The naval storeship *Supply*,[qv] in command of Lt. D. D. Porter, was placed at Wayne's disposal. Wayne traveled ahead to study continental use of camels. After trafficking down the North African coast and spending $12,000 for desirable beasts, he returned with thirty-three camels, three Arabs, and two Turks. Thirty-two of the camels, plus one calf born at sea, arrived at Indianola, Texas, on April 29, 1856, but because of bad weather and shallow water were not unloaded until May 13. On June 4 Wayne started his caravan westward. They stopped near Victoria, where the animals were clipped and Mrs. Mary A. Shirkey spun and knit for the president of the United States a pair of camel-pile socks. The animals were finally located at Camp Verde, where several successful experiments were made to test the camels' utility in the pursuit of Indians and the transportation of burdens. Wayne reported that camels rose and walked with as much as 600 pounds without difficulty, traveled miles without water, and ate almost any kind of plant. One camel trek was made to the unexplored Big Bend.

The first camel importation was followed by a second, consisting of forty-one beasts, which were also quartered at Camp Verde. In the spring of 1857 James Buchanan's secretary of war, John B. Floyd, directed Edward Fitzgerald Beale to use twenty-five of the camels in his survey for a wagon road from Fort Defiance, New Mexico, across the thirty-fifth parallel to the Colorado River. After this survey, the drive continued to Fort Tejon, California, where the camels were used to transport supplies and dispatches across the desert for the army. Eventually some of the animals were turned loose, some were used in salt pack-trains, and others even saw Texas again after Bethel Coopwood,[qv] Confederate spy and Texas lawyer, captured fourteen from Union forces. During the Civil War[qv] eighty camels and two Egyptian drivers passed into Confederate hands. The camels soon were widely scattered; some were turned out on the open range near Camp Verde; some were used to pack cotton bales to Brownsville; and one found its way to the infantry command of Capt. Sterling Price, who used it throughout the war to carry the whole company's baggage. In 1866 the federal government sold the camels at auction; sixty-six of them went to Coopwood. Some of the camels in California were sold at auction in 1863, and others escaped to roam the desert.

The failure of the camel in the United States was not due to its capability; every test showed it to be a superior transport animal. It was instead the nature of the beasts which led to their demise—they smelled horrible, frightened horses, and were detested by handlers accustomed to the more docile mules. Two private importations of camels followed the government experiment. On October 16, 1858, Mrs. M. J. Watson reported to Galveston port authorities that her ship had eighty-nine camels aboard, and claimed that she wanted to test them for purposes of transport. One port official, however, felt that she was using the camels to mask the odor typically associated with a slave ship and refused her petition to unload the cargo. After two months in port, Mrs. Watson sailed for the slave markets in Cuba after dumping the camels ashore in Galveston, where they wandered about the city and died from neglect and slaughter around the coastal sand dunes. A second civilian shipment of a dozen camels arrived at Port Lavaca in 1859, where it met a similar fate.

BIBLIOGRAPHY: Chris Emmett, *Texas Camel Tales* (San Antonio: Naylor, 1932). Odie B. Faulk, *The U.S. Camel Corps: An Army Experiment* (New York: Oxford University Press, 1976).

Chris Emmett and Odie B. Faulk

CAMEL'S HUMP. The Camel's Hump is a pair of knobs two miles east of State Highway 118 on the Terlingua Ranch, sixty-three miles south of Alpine in south central Brewster County (at 29°32′ N, 103°31′ W). They stand isolated on a broad desert flat covered sparsely with Chihuahuan Desert scrub. The knobs at their highest point reach an elevation of 3,662 feet above sea level and stand about 250 feet above the surrounding terrain. The Camel's Hump is a Tertiary-age igneous mass that intrudes into the Upper Cretaceous Boquillas formation, which is a flaggy limestone. The feature's present shape comes from erosion of the comparatively less resistant, thinly bedded limestone away from the more resistant igneous rock. Though the name of the Camel's Hump is very likely a descriptive allusion to its camel-like shape, the knobs also lay on the route through this area of the United States Army camel expedition commanded by Lt. William Echols in 1859 (*see* CAMELS).

BIBLIOGRAPHY: Ronnie C. Tyler, *The Big Bend* (Washington: National Park Service, 1975).

CAMERON, EWEN (1811?–1843). Ewen Cameron, participant in the Mier expedition,[qv] was born in Scotland about 1811. He was named for the Scottish hero Sir Ewen Cameron of Lockhiel, laird of Clan Cameron and a staunch supporter of King Charles II. He traveled to Texas during the Texas Revolution[qv] and served two terms in the Texas army, the first from April 29 through October 21, 1836. On October 20, 1836, he reenlisted as a private in Capt. Clark L. Owen's[qv] Company A of Joseph H. D. Rogers's First Regiment, Permanent Volunteers. He served until the company was mustered out on December 31, 1836. For his service he received bounty warrants for a total of 1,920 acres, which his heirs later claimed in San Patricio County. In the period that followed the revolution he won renown as a leader of the "cowboys" prominent in frontier defense in South Texas. The Telegraph and Texas Register[qv] hailed him on September 14, 1842, as "a bold and chivalrous leader" who promised to become "the Bruce of the West."

On July 7, 1842, Cameron took part in the battle of Lipantitlán[qv] against Gen. Antonio Canales.[qv] Samuel H. Walker[qv] attributed much of the credit for the successful defense of the position to Cameron. At the battle of Mier, "The fearless Cameron, whose company garrisoned the back yard of one of the houses, being charged by an imposing force of the enemy, after emptying his rifles into their lines, beat off the foe until he could reload, with the loose stones in the court." At Pass Suarte, after Fisher and the staff officers had been separated from the command, the Mier prisoners unanimously chose Cameron as their commander. On Saturday, February 19, Cameron and about sixty men were recaptured by Mexicans and subjected with other groups to the Black Bean Episode.[qv] Cameron drew a white bean in the lottery, but was shot for a later attempt at escape. Cameron County is named in his honor.

BIBLIOGRAPHY: Daughters of the Republic of Texas, *Muster Rolls of the Texas Revolution* (Austin, 1986). John Holland Jenkins, *Recollections of Early Texas*, ed. John H. Jenkins III (Austin: University of Texas Press, 1958; rpt. 1973). Marilyn M. Sibley, ed., *Samuel H. Walker's Account of the Mier Expedition* (Austin: Texas State Historical Association, 1978). William P. Stapp, *The Prisoners of Perote: A Journal* (Philadelphia: Zieber, 1845). Vertical Files, Barker Texas History Center, University of Texas at Austin.

Thomas W. Cutrer

CAMERON, JOHN (?–1861). John Cameron, early settler and soldier, was a native of Scotland. On May 21, 1827, the Mexican government granted him an empresario[qv] contract to introduce 100 families on the Colorado River in Texas. On September 12 the congress of Coahuila and Texas[qv] declared him a citizen. The contract was extended in 1832 for an additional three years. In 1828 he received a second contract to introduce 200 families on land along the Red River, an area previously contracted to Reuben Ross.[qv] This agreement was also extended in 1832 for an additional three years. No titles, however, were ever issued in consequence of either contract. Cameron received title to two leagues of land in the Power and Hewetson colony[qv] on October 31, 1834. In 1835 he was a secretary in the executive department of the state government at Monclova, and when Martín Perfecto de Cos[qv] dispersed the legislature, Cameron was taken prisoner with Benjamin R. Milam[qv] and others. They escaped and reached Texas in safety.

Cameron assisted in the siege of Bexar[qv] and was commended for his conduct by Francis W. Johnson.[qv] As interpreter for the Texas army, he signed the capitulation entered into between Cos and Gen. Edward Burleson[qv] on December 11, 1835. Cameron was issued a donation certificate for his part in the capture of Bexar and a bounty certificate for his three months' service in the army. William Fairfax Gray,[qv] who met Cameron at Nacogdoches on February 4, 1836, wrote in his diary that Cameron was a shrewd Scot, particularly well informed and interesting. Cameron became a resident of the Rio Grande valley and was killed in 1861 in one of the fights that took place in the contest between the "Rohos" and "Crinolinos."

BIBLIOGRAPHY: John Henry Brown, *History of Texas from 1685 to 1892* (2 vols., St. Louis: Daniell, 1893). Hans Peter Nielsen Gammel, comp., *Laws of Texas, 1822–1897* (10 vols., Austin: Gammel, 1898). William Fairfax Gray, *From Virginia to Texas, 1835* (Houston: Fletcher Young, 1909, 1965). Mary Virginia Henderson, "Minor Empresario Contracts for the Colonization of Texas, 1825–1834," *Southwestern Historical Quarterly* 31, 32 (April, July 1928). Malcolm D. McLean, comp. and ed., *Papers Concerning Robertson's Colony in Texas* (19 vols., Fort Worth: Texas Christian University Press, 1974–76; Arlington: University of Texas at Arlington Press, 1977–92). Homer S. Thrall, *A Pictorial History of Texas* (St. Louis: Thompson, 1879).

L. W. Kemp

CAMERON, MINNIE BARDENWERPER (1885–1971). Minnie Cameron, librarian, was born in San Antonio on November 21, 1885, the daughter of Max and Eliza (Wefing) Bardenwerper. She was employed by the San Antonio Public Library in 1917. During World War I[qv] she took a leave to serve the United States Censorship Bureau. She spoke English, Spanish, and German. After the Armistice she returned to the San Antonio Public Library, where she served thirty-seven years as reference librarian. During her service, the library's collection of Texana grew from 528 to more than 6,000 volumes. Throughout her professional career she was active in the Texas Library Association[qv] and the American Library Association. She was appointed to many committees to study and implement means of improvement of library services. Her research assistance to historians, journalists, authors, and students led to her involvement in such statewide and national issues as the Tidelands Controversy[qv] and to local projects such as La Villita.[qv] As an expert on San Antonio and Texas history, she contributed to numerous journals, including the *Southwestern Historical Quarterly.* She was praised in 1957 by the San Antonio *Express* (*see* SAN ANTONIO *EXPRESS-NEWS*) for maintaining freedom of speech, information, and press during the 1950s. In 1920 she married Reuben H. Cameron, an executive of A. B. Frank Company of San Antonio. They had a daughter. Mrs. Cameron lived her entire life in San Antonio, although she traveled extensively. She retired from the library in July 1957. She died in San Antonio on September 9, 1971. She was Catholic.

BIBLIOGRAPHY: Frederick Charles Chabot, *With the Makers of San Antonio* (Yanaguana Society Publications 4, San Antonio, 1937). San Antonio *Express*, July 21, 31, 1957, September 10, 1971. Vertical Files, Barker Texas History Center, University of Texas at Austin.

Frederick S. White, Sr.

CAMERON, RALPH H. (1892–1970). Ralph Haywood Cameron, architect, was born in San Antonio, Texas, on November 10, 1892, the son of Antoine Haywood and Nila (Crawford) Cameron. He attended public school and subsequently worked as an architectural draftsman for architect Alfred Giles[qv] and the firm of Adams and Adams. In 1912 he went to Kingsville to supervise construction of the new main house on the King Ranch,[qv] designed by Adams and Adams for Robert J. Kleberg.[qv] While working for the firm, Cameron also designed the Dewitt County Courthouse in Cuero and remodeled the Gonzales County Courthouse.

In August 1914 he opened his own architectural office in the Majestic Building in San Antonio, and between then and the American entry into World War I[qv] he designed numerous houses and small buildings in San Antonio and South Texas. He entered the United States Army in 1917 and attended the first officers' training camp at Camp Funston (now Camp Bullis) and the Army Engineering School at Fort Leavenworth, Kansas. He served as a first lieutenant with the 315th Engineers, Ninetieth Division of the American Expeditionary Force, and saw combat at St. Michel in France. He was gassed on the last day of the war and hospitalized for a time in Paris. While there, he used the opportunity to study architecture briefly at the École des Beaux-Arts.

After the war Cameron returned to San Antonio and in August 1919 reopened his architectural practice. During the 1920s and 1930s he emerged as one of the leading Beaux-Arts-influenced architects in South Texas, along with Atlee B. and Robert M. Ayers[qqv] and his former employer Carleton W. Adams.[qv] Among his best-known works from this period are the Neo-Gothic Medical Arts Building (1925–26), Grace Lutheran Church (1928), the Neo–Spanish Colonial Academic Building at Randolph Field (1929), the Art Deco–influenced Frost Brothers Store Building (1930), and the C. S. Lips residence in Terrell Hills (1940). The Hornaday residence in Monte Vista (1929) is an outstanding San Antonio example of Colonial Revival architecture. Cameron also served as supervising architect for the Scottish Rite Cathedral designed by the Herbert M. Greene Company (1923–24), South Side High School (1930), and the United States Post Office and

Courthouse (1937), for which Paul P. Cret[qv] of Philadelphia served as consulting architect. In addition to his work in San Antonio, Cameron designed numerous buildings in the Rio Grande valley, among them McAllen High School (1928), the Hidalgo County State Bank in Mercedes (1928), and the A. Y. Baker residence in Edinburg (1930).

From 1929 to 1941 he served in the Texas National Guard,[qv] and in October 1941 he was called to active service with the rank of colonel and transferred to the Army Corps of Engineers. He spent forty months in Europe as commander of the 344th Engineer Regiment, which saw action in North Africa, Italy, France, Germany, and Austria. Cameron is credited with building the first bridge over the Rhine near the war's end. After the war he served in the army reserve corps until his retirement in 1952.

He married Mary Fly, the niece of William S. Fly,[qv] on July 22, 1923. The couple had four children. Cameron was a founding member of the Texas Society of Architects and a member of the American Institute of Architects. He served for ten years as the director of the West Texas Chapter of the AIA and in 1932 was responsible for bringing the national convention to San Antonio. Cameron was a Methodist and a member of many fraternal and business organizations, including the Scottish Rite, the Elks, the San Antonio Chamber of Commerce, the Argyle Club, and the Menger Patio Club. He died in San Antonio on May 5, 1970.

BIBLIOGRAPHY: Ralph Cameron Collection (Architectural Drawings Collection, Architecture and Planning Library, University of Texas at Austin). Chris Carson and William B. McDonald, eds., *A Guide to San Antonio Architecture* (San Antonio Chapter, American Institute of Architects, 1986). Ellis A. Davis and Edwin H. Grobe, comps., *The New Encyclopedia of Texas* (2 vols., Dallas: Texas Development Bureau, 1925?). *Christopher Long*

CAMERON, WILLIAM (1834–1899). William Cameron, businessman, was born on a farm near Blairgowrie, Perthshire, Scotland, on January 11, 1834, the son of John and Isabella Cameron. He attended college at Dundee and served three years as an apprentice in a lawyer's office before 1852, when he immigrated to the United States. He subsequently worked in Illinois and Missouri and in 1860 became construction foreman for the Missouri Pacific Railroad. At the outbreak of the Civil War[qv] he organized a militia at Sedalia, Missouri. He was captured in the battle of Springfield on August 10, 1861, sent to St. Louis, and later paroled. In 1864 he married Letitia Stewart of Pleasantown, Missouri, and settled in Sedalia. The couple had two children. About 1865 Cameron contracted with the Missouri, Kansas and Texas Railroad to supply ties and construction timber. He built his first retail lumberyard at Warrensburg, Missouri, in 1867 and continued to establish yards along the railroad line as it advanced to the southwest.

In 1871 he moved to Denison, Texas, and in 1872, in partnership with J. S. Mayfield, established yards at Denison and Dallas. Mrs. Cameron died at Denison in 1873, and on September 1, 1875, Cameron married Flora Ann Berry of Little Rock, Arkansas; they became parents of three children, one of whom, William W. Cameron,[qv] carried on the business after his father's death. On August 1, 1876, Cameron opened a yard at Waco, where he made his home and headquarters after 1878. By 1890 the William Cameron Company had more than sixty retail lumberyards. Cameron entered the sawmill and timber business in 1885 with organization of the Texas Lumber Company to secure virgin timberlands in East Texas and Louisiana. Between 1885 and 1897 he expanded also into the grain and flour mill business. He built mills at Fort Worth and Waco and elevators along the line of the Fort Worth and Denver Railway. Cameron was a director of the First National Bank of Waco, the Hibernia National Bank of New Orleans, and the Southern National Bank of New York. He died at Morgan City, Louisiana, on February 6, 1899.

BIBLIOGRAPHY: R. J. Tolson, *A History of William Cameron and Company* (Waco: Cameron, ca. 1920). Vertical Files, Barker Texas History Center, University of Texas at Austin. *Jeanette H. Flachmeier*

CAMERON, WILLIAM WALDO (1878–1939). William Waldo Cameron, businessman, was born in Waco, Texas, on August 1, 1878, the son of Flora Ann (Berry) and William Cameron.[qv] He attended the Agricultural and Mechanical College of Texas (now Texas A&M University) and St. Albans Military Academy in Virginia. He returned to Waco in 1895 and held a variety of successive positions in the mills, elevators, and lumberyards of the William Cameron Company. In May 1898 he became a partner of his father in the pine and flour mill interests. After his father's death in 1899, the Cameron estate was divided, and on October 10, 1900, Cameron became president of William Cameron and Company, Incorporated. The business then had fourteen retail lumberyards, four yellow-pine mills, forest land, and bank and industrial stock. Between 1900 and 1905 the company added ten lumberyards, two new sawmills, sash and door departments, and wallpaper, paint, and mantel stores. Additional establishments were added up to 1924, when the retail lumberyards totaled seventy-one, the Sash, Door Manufacturing and Wholesale Industry had nine warehouses and branches, and the capital stock of the corporation had increased to $7 million. By 1939 the business included seventy-two yards in Texas, eleven in Oklahoma, and three in New Mexico. In 1910 and 1920 the Cameron family donated land for Cameron Park to the city of Waco. Cameron was married twice: to Faith D. Baird of Buffalo, New York, on January 9, 1901, and to Helen Miller of Waco on June 21, 1922; one daughter was born to each marriage. Cameron died in Waco on October 16, 1939, and was buried in Oakwood Cemetery.

BIBLIOGRAPHY: Dallas *Morning News*, October 17, 1939. R. J. Tolson, *A History of William Cameron and Company* (Waco: Cameron, ca. 1920). Vertical Files, Barker Texas History Center, University of Texas at Austin.

CAMERON, TEXAS (DeWitt County). Cameron was accepted by the DeWitt County Commissioners Court on June 23, 1846, as the first county seat of DeWitt County. It was to be established 3½ miles above Chisholm Ferry (see CLINTON, TEXAS) on land east of the Guadalupe River that Joseph Tumlinson[qv] had donated. The settlement was named for Ewen Cameron,[qv] a Mier expedition[qv] prisoner executed by order of Antonio López de Santa Anna[qv] in 1843. By November 1846, James Norman Smith[qv] had surveyed and platted the new townsite, and though many lots were sold, no houses were ever built. The sole buildings were Smith's county clerk's office and the commissioners' court, both rude log structures. On November 21, 1848, court sessions were moved to nearby Clinton, which claimed to have won the county seat election, but the Texas Supreme Court decided in favor of Cameron. The county government was moved at least four times back and forth across the river from Cameron to Clinton until the latter won the designation of county seat in 1850. The last court session in Cameron was held on August 3, 1850.

BIBLIOGRAPHY: Nellie Murphree, *A History of DeWitt County* (Victoria, Texas, 1962). *Craig H. Roell*

CAMERON, TEXAS (Milam County). Cameron, the county seat of Milam County, is at the intersection of U.S. highways 77 and 190, on the Atchison, Topeka and Santa Fe Railroad fourteen miles north of Rockdale in the north central part of the county. In April 1846 the Texas Legislature authorized a seven-member commission to find a permanent site for the Milam county seat. The commission purchased a sixty-acre tract of Daniel Monroe's headright on the Little River later that year and named the new town Cameron, in honor of Ewen Cameron.[qv]

When the courthouse at Cameron was completed in 1846, the county records were transferred to Cameron from Nashville, which had served as the seat of Milam County during the republic. The new town struggled in its early years because of its isolation, the nearest railroad being more than fifty miles away. In the late 1840s and early 1850s several attempts were made to navigate the Little River in order to give Cameron easier access to trade routes. The most successful of these occurred in 1850 after rains had made the river rise. J. W. McCown, Sr., persuaded Capt. Basil M. Hatfield to bring his steamboat Washington through the upper Brazos and up the Little River. The steamboat and the merchandise it brought caused great excitement among residents, and a two-day celebration was held when the boat tied up 2½ miles east of Cameron. Navigation of the river was impractical on a regular basis, however, and other towns, such as Nashville and later Port Sullivan, prospered in the 1850s and 1860s as the dominant business centers of Milam County. Cameron faced even greater competition in the 1870s, when Rockdale was established on the International–Great Northern Railroad. The arrival of the railroad prompted considerable discussion among Milam County residents as to whether Cameron should remain the county seat, and elections were held in 1874 and 1880 to decide if the county government should be moved to Rockdale.

Cameron survived these challenges, and in 1881 the Gulf, Colorado and Santa Fe Railway arrived; the San Antonio and Aransas Pass came through the town ten years later. The railroads improved the town's economy and increased its prestige. The population grew from an estimated 500 in 1878 to 800 by 1884 and 2,000 by 1892. Cameron had attempted to incorporate in 1856, 1866, and 1873, but each time the charter was allowed to lapse; the town was finally incorporated for good in 1889. Although agriculture, particularly cotton, dominated the town's economy in the nineteenth century, diverse industrial interests came into play in the early twentieth century. The discovery of oil in neighboring Williamson County in 1915 prompted residents in Milam County to look for oil of their own, and the discovery of the Minerva-Rockdale field in 1921 provided new opportunities for investment. Several milk-product companies, including the Kraft-Phenix Cheese Corporation, were in operation at Cameron in the 1920s and 1930s.

Cameron residents received much-needed job opportunities in the 1950s, when the Aluminum Company of America built a plant a few miles southwest of Rockdale. Jobs at the plant, as well as in the lignite industry that supplied the plant's power, revitalized the economy of the entire county. Unfortunately, Cameron suffered setbacks when the Texas and New Orleans discontinued its track from Cameron south to Giddings in 1959, and again in 1977, when the Southern Pacific, which had taken over the Texas and New Orleans, abandoned its track from Cameron north to Rosebud. The population of Cameron rose from 5,227 in 1952 to an estimated 7,500 in 1958; it fell to 5,640 in the early 1960s and, after a brief recovery, to 5,347 in 1978; the town reported 5,817 residents in 1988. The present courthouse, which was constructed in 1890, is listed in the National Register of Historic Places. In 1990 the population was 5,580.

BIBLIOGRAPHY: Ann Arthur, "A New Era for Milam County," *Texas Historian,* March 1972. Lelia M. Batte, *History of Milam County, Texas* (San Antonio: Naylor, 1956). Katherine Bradford Henderson, The Early History of Milam County (M.A. thesis, University of Texas, 1924). Curtis Henley, "Alcoa's Impact on Milam County," *Texas Historian,* September 1974. Margaret Eleanor Lengert, The History of Milam County (M.A. thesis, University of Texas, 1949).

Vivian Elizabeth Smyrl

CAMERON COUNTY. Cameron County (U-17) is 140 miles south of Corpus Christi in the Rio Grande Plains region of South Texas. The county, named for Mier expedition[qv] member Capt. Ewen Cameron,[qv] is bordered on the north by Willacy County, on the west by Hidalgo County, on the east by the Gulf of Mexico, and on the south by Mexico. The county's largest town and county seat is Brownsville, which serves as the terminus of U.S. Highways 77, 83, and 281 and the Missouri Pacific and Southern Pacific railroads. The center point of the county is at 26°10′ north latitude and 97°30′ west longitude. Other large communities include Harlingen, La Feria, Port Isabel, San Benito, and South Padre Island.

Cameron County covers 905 square miles, with an elevation range from sea level to sixty feet. Along the eastern edge of the county the soils are sandy and saline, with some cracking clay. The remainder of the county has brownish to reddish soils, with loamy to clayey surface layers and clayey subsoils. Vegetation along the eastern edge of the county is typical of the Gulf Prairie and Marsh vegetation areas, with marsh grasses, bluestems, and grama grasses predominating. The vegetation of the rest of the county is like that of the South Texas Plains area, with small trees, brush, weeds, and grasses found in abundance. Mesquite, live oak, post oak, and shrubs also grow densely in some areas. Between 41 and 50 percent of the county is considered prime farmland. Natural resources include oil and gas, barite, celestite, chromium, bentonite clay, fluorspar, manganese, and phosphate.

Cameron County's climate is subtropical and subhumid, with hot summers and mild winters. Temperatures range from an average low of 50° F to 69° in January and from an average high of 75° F to 94° in July. Rainfall averages twenty-six inches per year. Snowfall is exceedingly rare. The growing season lasts 320 days, with the first freeze in mid-December and the last in late January.

The area now called Cameron County has long been the site of human habitation. Artifacts dating to the Archaic Period suggest that the first inhabitants arrived more than 10,000 years ago. During historic times as many as seven linguistic groups, including Coahuiltecans and Karankawas, inhabited the lower Rio Grande valley. Seven groups of Coahuiltecans lived there. The Indians hunted a wide variety of animals, fished, and gathered berries, fruits, and roots, as well as mountain laurel and peyote for their narcotic effects. After the arrival of the Spanish in the seventeenth century, much of the native population succumbed to disease; those who survived eventually moved away or intermarried with the Europeans, and by the late eighteenth century they had been largely supplanted by the Lipan Apaches. During the nineteenth century the Comanches occasionally made forays into the area, but by the early twentieth century virtually all trace of the Indians had disappeared.

The first Spanish explorers arrived in the seventeenth century. In August 1638 the governor of León sent a group under Jacinto García de Sepulveda to explore the area; they crossed the Rio Grande near Mier and marched down the north bank of the river as far as the site of present Brownsville. In 1687 Alonso De León,[qv] on his second journey to find the location of Fort St. Louis, crossed the Rio Grande and proceeded north, probably to Baffin Bay. Beginning in January 1747, Miguel de la Garza Falcón[qv] reconnoitered the north bank of the Rio Grande from the site of modern Eagle Pass to the mouth of the river, which he reached on March 3. He listed the numerous Indian groups in the area and described the land as unfit for settlement because of the inadequate fresh water supply. On February 27, 1747, José de Escandón[qv] built a raft to sound the Rio Grande north of present-day Matamoros, Tamaulipas, and crossed into what is now Cameron County. A royal inspection made in 1757 by José Tienda de Cuervo[qv] recommended that titles to the land in the area be given to the colonists. In 1765 the community of San Juan de los Esteros (present-day Matamoros) was established south of the Rio Grande. In 1781 Spanish authorities granted fifty-nine leagues of land lying on the north bank of the river (including all of the site of Brownsville) to José Salvador de la Garza, who established a ranch about sixteen miles northwest of the site. A number of other grants were made in the area before April 18, 1789, when Juan José Ballí was granted the San Salvador del Tule area.

Additional grants were made in Mexican period, but the region was still only sparsely populated at the time of the Texas Revolution.[qv] Before 1836 the area was part of the state of Tamaulipas, but after the signing of the treaties of Velasco[qv] it was claimed as part of Texas and included in San Patricio County. Mexico, however, also claimed the territory, and through the late 1830s and early 1840s Mexican rancheros ranged their herds across the much of the area. By 1840 there were isolated settlements throughout the region, especially along the Rio Grande. The area on the north bank of the river immediately across from Matamoros—the future site of Brownsville—was used by the city as a common pasture, or *ejido.*

In early 1846 United States troops under the command of Gen. Zachary Taylor[qv] marched into the disputed territory between the Nueces River and the Rio Grande and constructed a defensive position across from Matamoros. The temporary fort was originally called Fort Texas but was renamed Fort Brown a short time later, in honor of Maj. Jacob Brown,[qv] who died during a Mexican attack on the stronghold. On April 25, 1846, a skirmish occurred between United States and Mexican troops at Las Rucias (Las Rusias), in southwest Cameron County, which became known as the spot where "American blood was shed on American soil," the verbal spark that ignited the Mexican War.[qv] Two other Mexican War battles were fought in Cameron County, the battle of Palo Alto[qv] (May 8, 1846) and the battle of Resaca de la Palma[qv] (May 9, 1846).

On February 12, 1848, the Texas legislature decreed the existence of Cameron County, and with the signing of the Treaty of Guadalupe Hidalgo[qv] on July 4 the area officially became part of the United States. The new county encompassed 3,308 square miles, including parts of the future Hidalgo, Willacy, Kenedy, and Brooks counties. An election of county officers was held on August 7, but organization was not completed until September 11. Santa Rita, five miles downstream from Fort Brown and believed to be the earliest English-speaking town in the area, was made the county seat. The same year Charles Stillman[qv] established Brownsville just west of Fort Brown. In December another election was held, and after intense effort on Stillman's part Brownsville was chosen county seat.

Much of the economy of the county in its earliest years was based on trade. Merchants on both sides of the border quickly recognized the advantage of shipping goods to Brownsville and then smuggling them across the Rio Grande to avoid paying high Mexican duties. During the Mexican War Richard King, Mifflin Kenedy,[qqv] and Stillman had set up a transport company to haul American troops and supplies up the river. After the war the three men managed to establish a virtual monopoly on river transportation, thus ensuring Anglo dominance of trade in the area and helping to encourage growth. In 1849 and 1850 California-bound gold-seekers came through the area, landing at Port Isabel and taking the military road to the west; some stayed and became settlers. Cholera and yellow fever epidemics struck the area on several occasions, but the population grew rapidly, and by 1850 Cameron County had 8,451 inhabitants.

The early history of the county was marked by a series of ongoing disputes about land titles, especially between the heirs of the original Spanish and Mexican grantees and more recent Anglo-American settlers. In 1852 a board of land commissioners examined the claims to land in the area and confirmed many Spanish and Mexican grants. In 1860 the legislature again authorized Spanish and Mexican grantees to establish their titles by court procedure. But in numerous instances land disputes continued to simmer, and court cases to decide who had legal title dragged on well into the second half of the nineteenth century. The activities of Juan N. Cortina[qv] were partly an expression of this rivalry.

By 1860 Brownsville was a thriving city; the Civil War[qv] made it the principal port for shipment of cotton and supplies to elude the Union blockade, and cotton caravans traversed the county from north to south on their way to Matamoros and Bagdad, Tamaulipas. Other caravans bore salt from El Sal del Rey in nearby Hidalgo County. Federal forces occupied the county in 1864, but it was later recaptured by the Confederates. The last land battle of the Civil War, the battle of Palmito Ranch,[qv] was fought near Brazos Santiago in May 1865.

After the war Fort Brown was rebuilt with brick buildings, and federal troops were once again stationed there. But the lack of a railroad and deepwater port hindered the county's economic recovery. Efforts had been made before the war to build a rail link between Brownsville and the coast. In 1850 and 1853 the Rio Grande Railway and Turn Pike Company and the Brownsville and Rio Grande Railway were planned for the county, but neither was constructed; the first railroad actually built in Cameron County was a military road constructed by Philip H. Sheridan[qv] connecting Brazos Santiago to White Ranch. In 1872 Simón Celaya funded and built a narrow-gauge line, the Rio Grande Valley Railway, between Brownsville and Port Isabel. The railroad served to break the Kenedy-King steamboat monopoly, but the lack of a rail connection to the North proved to be a serious impediment to trade. After 1880 the county's economy stagnated. A new railroad linking San Antonio with Laredo diverted much of the trade away, and the Morgan Lines[qv] quit making regular stops at Brazos Santiago. The population of Cameron County, which had more than doubled between 1860 and 1880 (growing from 6,028 to 14,959), declined slightly over the next decade, to 14,242.

During the latter half of the nineteenth century Cameron County's economy, as in former times, was based largely on ranching. Almost all the land in the county remained in ranches, mostly owned by a few wealthy landholders. Farming showed a marked increase in the period just after the Civil War but dropped off dramatically after 1880, in large part because of a lack of ready access to outside markets. The number of improved acres in the county grew from 4,354 to 116,989 between 1870 and 1880, but declined over the next decade to just over 31,000. During this period corn was the leading crop, with vegetables and other foods accounting for most of the rest of the harvest. Irrigation[qv] was introduced on a small scale during the 1880s, after George Paul Brulay[qv] built the first successful irrigation system in South Texas near Brownsville in 1876; but watered land remained a tiny fraction of the land under cultivation.

The population during the early post–Civil War era was nearly equally split between Anglos and Hispanics. Ethnic relations were generally harmonious: as in the rest of the lower Rio Grande valley, Cameron County leaders consisted of both Anglos and Mexicans, linked socially and economically through marriage and the social-religious custom of *compadrazgo* (compaternity or gossipred, the obligation assumed by godparents). Intermarriage was not practiced exclusively by the elite, but occurred at all levels of society. During the 1880s and 1890s, however, social and ethnic relations in the county began to change. Increasingly, Anglos began taking over the large ranches—usually by purchase or marriage but in some instances also by fraud—and displacing Mexican ranchers. Among the largest landowners were the King and Kenedy families, who owned over 300,000 acres each, and James G. Brown, who held 114,000 acres. By 1890 these large landowners controlled 97 percent of the county.

Political power also came to fall increasingly in the hands of the Anglo elite. James B. Wells,[qv] who arrived in the county during the 1870s, soon established a powerful political machine that extended throughout much of South Texas. Using his connections with the big ranchers of the region, who were able to deliver the votes of most of their Mexican-American employees and neighbors, Wells consolidated the Democratic party[qv] in the area and built up a secure coalition.

Matters began to change dramatically, however, after 1904, when the St. Louis, Brownsville and Mexico Railway was built through the county. The introduction of the much-awaited rail line to the north opened the area for settlement of Midwestern farmers, who began arriving in the lower Valley in large numbers after the turn of the century. During the late teens and 1920s Cameron County underwent a new period of prosperity as the area experienced a prolonged land boom. Enterprising agents went to the Midwest and North hawking the cheap abundant land in and around Brownsville. Special trains were dispatched to bring prospective buyers to the area, and during the height of the boom in the early 1920s as many as 200 land-seekers a day were being brought into the town and its environs. The new settlers cleared the land of brush, built extensive irrigation systems and roads, and introduced large-scale truck farming. In 1904 H. G. Stillwell, Sr., planted the first commercial citrus orchard in the area, opening the way for what was to become one of the Valley's leading industries (*see* CITRUS FRUIT CULTURE).

While the expansion of farming in the area and the railroad connection to the North brought newfound prosperity to the region, it also served to reshape its ethnic and social structure. Before 1900 nearly half of all those born in the area were the products of interracial marriages, and both Anglo and Mexican customs were widely practiced and respected. The county's new residents, however, mostly Protestant and white, were more reluctant to assimilate, and as a result ethnic divisions began to widen. After 1910 social relations came to be increasingly dominated by ethnic separatism. Many of the new arrivals saw their Mexican neighbors as "racial inferiors" ignorant of the American way of life, while Mexican Americans,[qv] the majority of whom worked as common laborers, became increasingly resentful of their situation. The animosities grew even worse during the Mexican Revolution,[qv] when border raids by Mexican bandits wrought havoc.

The decades after the turn of the century also saw a profound shift in the political structure of the county. Although Wells continued to maintain control during the first two decades of the twentieth century, he came under increasing pressure from the new Yankee residents, who resented his power and sought to clean up the political arena. Because of the changing demographics of the county and the rising tide of racial animosity between Anglos and Hispanics, Wells could no longer maintain his position, and his machine collapsed in 1920. In its place a new Anglo elite, made up mostly of recent arrivals, emerged, and a new social order, based on de facto segregation, became the rule. Segregated facilities—including churches, schools, and restaurants—were established for Hispanics and Anglos, and many of the former felt the sharp sting of discrimination. Their leaders, alarmed by the situation, met at the Harlingen Convention[qv] in August 1927 and eventually organized the Latin American Citizens League, a precursor to the League of United Latin American Citizens.[qv] But little changed until the 1960s.

The years from 1910 to 1930 also saw a rapid rise in population. Residents numbered just over 16,000 in 1900, 27,158 in 1910, and 77,540 in 1930. The growth was due not only to the influx of farmers from the Midwest, but also to a growing surge of immigrants from Mexico, who moved to the area in search of jobs and better lives. By 1930 the population was almost equally divided between Anglos and Hispanics; African Americans[qv] composed less than 2 percent of the population.

During the prohibition[qv] years Brownsville became a popular port of entry into Mexico for numerous tourists who wanted to have a few drinks in Matamoros. Smuggling, always an important underground industry, enjoyed a brief heyday as Brownsville became an important port of entry for illegal liquor. The area also saw a steady growth in the volume of legal trade, and after completion of the port of Brownsville in 1936, Brownsville emerged as one of the leading shipping points along the Texas coast.

The farming economy also saw marked growth. Between 1920 and 1930 the number of farms in Cameron County grew from 1,507 to 2,936, and by 1940 the farms numbered 3,243. Similarly, the total number of acres under cultivation rose, from 83,121 in 1920 to 101,376 in 1930 and 120,064 in 1940. The Great Depression[qv] of the 1930s briefly slowed the growth, but the region's economy was much less affected than that of many other areas of the state. The rise of agriculture in the county was fueled in large measure by the introduction of commercial-scale truck farming and the growth of cotton as a cash crop. Farmers discovered that the land and climate were ideally suited to growing vegetables and small fruits, and during the 1920s many abandoned such traditional crops as corn and sorghum to raise carrots, lettuce, onions, strawberries, melons and other such produce. The production of cotton, first grown in the area as early as the Civil War, also increased steadily after 1910, and by the 1920s it was among the area's leading cash crops (*see* AGRICULTURE *and articles cross-referenced there*).

During World War II[qv] Cameron County served as an important food production and shipping center, and in the 1940s the population increased rapidly, rising to 129,170 by 1950. The farming economy also expanded quickly in the early postwar years. Although the number of farms in the county began to decline after 1950 as the result of consolidations, farm output grew tremendously. In 1949 Cameron County farmers grew 214,536 bales of cotton, making the area one of the leading cotton-producing regions in the state. Production of other crops such as grapefruit, oranges, and sugarcane also increased impressively, and by the early 1960s Cameron County had established itself as one of the state's most productive agricultural areas.

In the early 1990s, more than 80 percent of county land was in farms and ranches, with 50 percent of the farmland under cultivation and 90 percent—more than 200,000 acres—irrigated. The county was among the state's largest producers of cotton and sorghum. Other leading crops included corn, sugarcane, hay, soybeans, onions, cabbage, cantaloupes, bell peppers, watermelons, cucumbers, carrots, honeydew melons, tomatoes, grapefruit, oranges, and pecans. Cattle and hogs were also raised in significant numbers.

Much of the county's nonfarm income came from processing fruits and vegetables, fishing, seafood processing, and light manufacturing. The county is also a producer of oil and natural gas. Gas-well gas production in 1982 totaled 2,424,550 thousand cubic feet; in addition, 4,670 thousand cubic feet of casinghead gas and a small amount of crude oil were also produced. Between 1944, when oil was first discovered in the county, and 1990, oil production totaled 434,000 barrels.

The earliest schools in Cameron County were private institutions founded before the Civil War. Among the first of these was the Rio Grande Female Institute, established by Melinda Rankin[qv] in 1852. Other early schools included Villa María, a girls' school founded on March 7, 1853, by the Sisters of the Incarnate Word and Blessed Sacrament,[qv] and St. Joseph's Academy, a boys' school, established by brothers of the Oblates of Mary Immaculate[qv] on November 10, 1862. The first public school system was established in the mid-1850s, and by 1860 Cameron County had six public schools in operation. With the growth of population after the turn of the century the number of schools grew, increasing to fifty-nine by 1904. During the next two decades, however, many of the schools became segregated. Little money was spent on "Mexican schools," and as a result the quality of education offered to Hispanic children was generally inferior. As late as 1960 only 7 percent of the county's population had graduated from high school. The situation subsequently improved, and in the early 1990s the county had eleven school districts with sixty elementary schools, thirteen middle schools, eleven high schools, and three special-education schools. Private schools—predominantly Catholic—enrolled nearly 4,000 students in eleven elementary and five high schools. Texas Southmost College, the University of Texas–Pan American at Brownsville, and Texas State Technical Institute at Harlingen, as well as five vocational schools, offer postsecondary education. Nevertheless, despite efforts to improve the educational system, in the 1990s education levels in Cameron County remained fairly low, and many better-educated young people continued to leave the area.

Before the first American settlers arrived, the populace of the future Cameron County was almost exclusively Catholic. With the arrival of large numbers of English speakers from the Southern states after the Mexican War, several Protestant churches were founded, and by the eve of the Civil War most of the major Protestant denominations were represented. In 1990 Cameron County had 160 churches with an estimated combined membership of more than 150,000. The largest communions were Catholic, Baptist, and Methodist.

Cameron County has generally been staunchly Democratic. Democratic presidential candidates won virtually every race during the nineteenth and twentieth centuries, except for the elections of 1848, 1896, 1952, 1956, 1972, and 1988. Democrats have also dominated local elections, and despite the collapse of the Wells machine in 1920 have continued to maintain a virtual stranglehold on local politics. Republicans, however, made strong gains after the 1970s, particularly in presidential and statewide races. Among the principal reasons for this trend is the influx of retirees from the Midwest.

Between 1960 and 1970 the population of Cameron County fell from 151,089 to 140,368, but it subsequently grew rapidly. In 1980 the residents numbered 209,727, and in 1990, 260,120. In 1990 the largest towns were Brownsville, Harlingen, San Benito, Port Isabel, and La Feria. The growth rate of 22.7 percent during the 1980s was partially attributed to retirees. The county ranked seventh in a 1987 list of the most desirable retirement areas in the United States. Winter Texans, or "snowbirds," often come for a few seasons and then stay permanently.

Cameron County ranks high among United States counties in the size of its Hispanic population. In 1990, 81.9 percent (212,995 of the total population of 260,120) of residents were of Hispanic decent; the actual percentage is probably higher than this census figure, since the census often misses migrant farmworkers, undocumented workers, and refugees. The civil-rights movement[qv] of the 1960s helped to desegregate most of the county, and a growing number of Mexican Americans subsequently attained positions of power. The last vestiges of segregation were removed with the closing of separate schools for migrant farmworkers' children in the 1970s. However, the later influx of refugees from Central and South America again increased tensions in the area. The refugee problem was especially acute in Harlingen, where in 1988 and early 1989 several hundred refugees were living in a condemned hotel building and on the streets. Many poor Hispanics, particularly new arrivals from Mexico and Central America, live in the county's numerous colonias,[qv] or shantytowns, a sizable number of them without electricity or running water.

Despite such problems, Cameron County remains a favored tourist destination. Each winter thousands of visitors arrive from the North, attracted by the mild climate and low cost of living, and during the spring and summer many more come to visit the beaches on Padre Island,[qv] which has seen intense development during the past two decades. Brownsville also serves as a major gateway to and from Mexico for tourists and shoppers. Major attractions in Cameron County include Palo Alto Battlefield National Historic Site, Resaca de la Palma Site State Park, Port Isabel Lighthouse State Historic Structure, Brazos Island State Scenic Park,[qqv] Immaculate Conception Cathedral, the Old Brulay Plantation, and the García Pasture. The county also offers hunting and fishing opportunities throughout the year. Special events include the Tourist Festival and Shuffleboard Tourney, the Winter Olympics, the Cameron County Livestock Show, Golden Gloves Boxing, Charro Days, the Winter Texan Fishing Tourney, the Valley Music Festival, the Tip O'Texas Wildcat Show, Little Bit of Mexico, the All-Valley Winter Texans Golden Tourney, Riofest, the Blessing of the Shrimp Fleet, the Texas International Fishing Tournament, Seafest, Fiesta Internacional, and the Welcome Home Winter Texans Party.

BIBLIOGRAPHY: Evan Anders, *Boss Rule in South Texas: The Progressive Era* (Austin: University of Texas Press, 1982). Polly Pearl Crawford, The Beginnings of Spanish Settlement in the Lower Rio Grande Valley (M.A. thesis, University of Texas, 1925). Walter Wilson Hildebrand, History of Cameron County, Texas (M.A. thesis, North Texas State College, 1950). Frank Cushman Pierce, *Texas' Last Frontier: A Brief History of the Lower Rio Grande Valley* (Menasha, Wisconsin: Banta, 1917; rpt., Brownsville: Rio Grande Valley Historical Society, 1962). Maurice S. Pipkin, An Early History of Cameron County (M.A. thesis, Texas College of Arts and Industries, 1940). Florence Johnson Scott, Spanish Land Grants in the Lower Rio Grande Valley (M.A. thesis, University of Texas, 1939). J. Lee and Lillian J. Stambaugh, *The Lower Rio Grande Valley of Texas* (San Antonio: Naylor, 1954). James Heaven Thompson, A Nineteenth Century History of Cameron County (M.A. thesis, University of Texas, 1965). Virginia Lovelace Thompson, The History of Education in Cameron County (M.A. thesis, University of Texas, 1930). David Martell Vigness, The Lower Rio Grande Valley: 1836–1846 (M.A. thesis, University of Texas, 1948).

Alicia A. Garza and Christopher Long

CAMERON CREEK. Cameron Creek rises six miles west of Jermyn in northeast Young County (at 33°16′ N, 98°30′ W) and flows northeast for eighteen miles to its mouth on the West Fork of the Trinity River, four miles southeast of Antelope in Jack County (at 33°24′ N, 98°18′ W). The stream's name is an alteration of Cambren, the name of a pioneer family from Jack County. The surrounding gently sloping to steep terrain is surfaced by stony loam that supports tall prairie grasses. The area has been used mostly as rangeland and has been the site of mineral production.

BIBLIOGRAPHY: Thomas F. Horton, *History of Jack County* (Jacksboro, Texas: Gazette Print, 193-?).

CAMERON IRON WORKS, HOUSTON. The Cameron Iron Works of Houston began in 1920, when oil wildcatter James Smither Abercrombie[qv] purchased a controlling interest in Harry S. Cameron's shop for use in repairing drilling rigs and for forging high grade steel. The firm incorporated on August 20, 1920, with $25,000 capital, five men, two lathes, a drill press, and hand tools and patented its innovative blowout preventer in April 1922. Until World War II[qv] the firm concentrated on service and manufacture of oilfield equipment and from 1945 to 1950 on research and development. It manufactured army ordnance, particularly depth-charge projectors and arbors for the navy in World War II, along with gun barrels, gun mounts, and rockets, for which it received the Navy "E" award in 1941. The company built its first plant and company headquarters in 1946 on forty acres north of the Katy Highway in Houston, after which the original shop was used as a warehouse. The firm subsequently went public and was listed on the New York Stock Exchange. Between 1950 and 1960 annual sales grew from $10 million to $40 million and employment from 700 to 2,000 workers. During the Korean War Cameron Iron Works supplied armaments and was involved in power generation and manufacture of jet engines and airplane parts. In 1957 it established a guided-missile plant, and the International Association of Machinists went on strike against the company.

At its peak Cameron was involved in atomic and space technology and the military, energy, petrochemical, and aerospace industries, as well as oil and gas exploration. It employed 12,300 workers in thirty-eight countries. A case involving back pay for Cameron workers fired for striking went to the United States Supreme Court in 1961. In 1963 the company built a plant at Livingston, Scotland, near Edinburgh, to construct aircraft engines and power generators to supply the nuclear-power and valve and tool industry. In 1965 Cameron was involved in the military buildup for Vietnam and in 1966 built a new plant at Cypress for high-strength metal production. In 1972, by which year the firm supplied pipelines for Russia and had a plant at Béziers, France, Abercrombie stepped down as company head.

In the 1980s Cameron Iron Works was described as "a Houston-headquartered vertically integrated company that designs, manufactures, and markets a range of oil tools, ball valves, and forged products" through three operating divisions responsible for "sales, supply, and service." Cameron provided its own metals, engineering, forgings, manufacturing and test facilities, and service staff. In 1980 it had sales of over $697 million and net earnings of over $78 million. In 1983 company restructuring allowed Cameron to form a United States holding company with domestic and foreign subsidiaries, but a 46 percent decline in sales in fiscal 1984 caused major inventory reductions, asset sales, and expense controls. By 1985 only 3,200 employees remained, concentrated primarily in the Houston area. In

1989 Cameron Iron Works merged with Cooper Industries, Incorporated, in a stock exchange valued at over $700 million. At the time the firm had 1,800 employees in Houston and 5,500 worldwide.

BIBLIOGRAPHY: Houston Metropolitan Research Center Files, Houston Public Library. Jim Hutton, *Houston: A History of a Giant* (Tulsa, Oklahoma: Continental Heritage, 1976). Marie Phelps McAshan, *A Houston Legacy: On the Corner of Main and Texas* (Houston: Gulf, 1985). Patrick J. Nicholson, *Mr. Jim: The Biography of James Smither Abercrombie* (Houston: Gulf, 1983). Lee and Marsha Tucker, *Houston: A Sesquicentennial Commemorative* (Houston: Pioneer, 1986). Vertical Files, Barker Texas History Center, University of Texas at Austin.

Diana J. Kleiner

CAMEY SPUR, TEXAS. Camey Spur (Camey) was on State Highway 121 sixteen miles southeast of Denton in southeastern Denton County. It was established about 1852 and named for Capt. William McKamy. For a time it served as a spur on the St. Louis–San Francisco Railway. A post office operated in Camey Spur from 1913 through 1925. In 1914 the community had a cotton gin, two general stores, and a population of thirty. It had two businesses and a population of forty-seven during the 1930s and 1940s, after which no population statistics were available.

Brian Hart

CAMILLA, TEXAS. Camilla is at the intersection of Farm roads 222, 3128, and 3278, seventy miles north of Houston in eastern San Jacinto County. The community was named for one of its early settlers, Mrs. Camilla Hardin Davis, shortly after the Civil War.[qv] L. S. McMickin owned the first store at Camilla, and Jim McMurrey opened a second store there, along with a large cotton gin. The agricultural settlement became the site of one of the county's first Farmers' Alliance[qv] groups. Camilla received a post office in 1895, and though this office was subsequently discontinued, the area population, which largely earned its livelihood from locally grown cotton, was estimated to be 100 through the first half of the twentieth century. The community had three rated businesses as late as 1961. By the mid-1960s, however, the number of residents had fallen to about seventy, and the community no longer reported any businesses. The population of Camilla was still reported as seventy in 1990.

BIBLIOGRAPHY: Ruth Hansbro, History of San Jacinto County (M.A. thesis, Sam Houston State Teachers College, 1940).

Robert Wooster

CAMOLE INDIANS. The Camoles, an otherwise unidentified Indian group living on the Texas coast west of the Susolas and Comos, were met by Álvar Núñez Cabeza de Vaca[qv] between 1528 and 1534.

BIBLIOGRAPHY: Frederick Webb Hodge, ed., *Handbook of American Indians North of Mexico* (2 vols., Washington: GPO, 1907, 1910; rpt., New York: Pageant, 1959).

Margery H. Krieger

CAMP, JIM (1877–1964). Jim Camp, pioneer West Texas physician, son of Miles N. and Elizabeth (Gillentine) Camp, was born in White County, Tennessee, on November 7, 1877. As a young man he taught for three years in a rural Tennessee public school. He later attended the University of Tennessee Medical School, where he graduated in the spring of 1900. He soon moved to Pecos, Texas, and set up a medical practice. On October 1, 1901, Camp married Virgie Maude Stroud outside of Dallas, and the couple made their home in Pecos. They had three children. The older son became a physician; in 1929 he and his father built Camp Hospital, the institution that made Pecos a medical center in West Texas. During World War I[qv] Camp served in the medical corps as a first lieutenant. He later led in the formation of the Six County Medical Association in West Texas. In 1950 he was honored as General Practitioner of the Year by the Texas Medical Association.[qv] He served a term as tax assessor in Reeves County and more than twenty years as a member of the county school board. Camp was a York Rite Mason, a Shriner, and a Rotarian. He was an active member of the First Christian Church of Pecos and of the Pecos Chamber of Commerce. He died on January 22, 1964, in Pecos and was buried in Evergreen Cemetery, Reeves County. In 1973, for his civic and humanitarian contributions to West Texas, he was named to the Permian Basin Petroleum Hall of Fame.

BIBLIOGRAPHY: Alton Hughes, *Pecos: A History of the Pioneer West* (Seagraves, Texas: Pioneer, 1978).

Julia Cauble Smith

CAMP, JOHN LAFAYETTE (1828–1891). John Lafayette Camp, soldier and political leader, was born on February 20, 1828, near Birmingham, Alabama, the son of John Lafayette and Elizabeth (Brown) Camp. In 1848 he graduated from the University of Tennessee, and the following year he moved to Gilmer, Upshur County, Texas. There he taught school, became a prosperous cotton planter, and established himself as one of the leading attorneys of East Texas. In 1851 he married Mary Ann Ward, the daughter of William Ward, a well-known physician. The couple eventually had five children.

When the Civil War[qv] began, Camp was first elected captain of a company and then colonel of the Fourteenth Texas Cavalry. The regiment served in Texas and Arkansas in the early months of the war but was later transferred east of the Mississippi River to the Confederate Army of Tennessee. There the regiment was consolidated with the Tenth Texas Cavalry, Dismounted, and assigned to Mathew D. Ector's[qv] brigade. Camp saw action at the battles of Richmond and Cumberland Gap, Kentucky; Murfreesboro (Stone's River), Tennessee; and Chickamauga and Altoona, Georgia. He was twice wounded and twice captured.

In 1866 he was elected to the United States House of Representatives from the First District of Texas but was not permitted to take his seat. He served as a delegate to the Constitutional Convention of 1866,[qv] where he was an advocate of presidential Reconstruction.[qv] In 1872, as a delegate to the national Democratic party[qv] convention, he favored cooperation with the liberal wing of the Republican party.[qv] In 1874 he was elected to the Texas Senate, where he sponsored railroad construction in order to encourage the settlement of West Texas. He was also a firm supporter of constitutional reform and, with two members of the Texas House of Representatives, formed a committee that drafted a proposed new constitution for the state.

In 1878 Governor Richard B. Hubbard[qv] appointed Camp judge of the district comprising Jefferson, Marshall, Palestine, and Tyler, and in 1884, hoping that the change of climate would improve Camp's health, President Grover Cleveland appointed him registrar of the land office in Arizona. His health continued to decline, however, and Camp resigned after two years to return to Texas. He settled in San Antonio, where he died on July 16, 1891. He was the father of John Lafayette Camp, Jr.[qv] Camp County in northeast Texas is named in his honor.

BIBLIOGRAPHY: *Dictionary of American Biography.* Marcus J. Wright, comp., and Harold B. Simpson, ed., *Texas in the War, 1861–1865* (Hillsboro, Texas: Hill Junior College Press, 1965).

Thomas W. Cutrer

CAMP, JOHN LAFAYETTE, JR. (1855–1918). John Lafayette Camp, Jr., judge, was born on September 23, 1855, in Gilmer, Texas, the son of Mary Ann (Ward) and John Lafayette Camp.[qv] After graduating from the Gilmer Academy, Texas Military Institute[qv] (San Antonio), and Trinity University he served in the Texas Senate from 1887 to 1891 and then moved to San Antonio, where he established a legal practice. In 1897 Governor Charles Allen Culberson[qv] appointed Camp judge of the Forty-fifth District Court. He continued to be re-elected for seventeen years, usually without opposition. Among his most notable decisions was that which enabled the preservation of the Alamo chapel. "Care and custody" of the shrine had been granted to the Daughters of the Republic of Texas[qv] by a state law of 1905. In 1912, however, the state legislature, at the prompting of Governor Oscar Branch Colquitt,[qv] appropriated $5,000 to "improve" the Alamo. Colquitt's true intention was to turn the Alamo into a state park. When the DRT filed suit to halt the dismantling of the historic structure, Camp ruled that the 1912 law had not overturned that of 1905 and that the Daughters maintained custody of the property. An appellate court concurred.

In 1913 President Woodrow Wilson appointed Camp United States district attorney for western Texas. In that position he was chiefly responsible for the arrest, on June 27, 1915, of former Mexican president Victoriano Huerta[qv] for the violation of United States neutrality laws. Huerta was released on bond but rearrested on July 3 and confined at Fort Bliss, where he died six months later. In 1916, when Judge Thomas Sheldon Maxey[qv] retired from the bench, the eighteen Texas representatives and two senators endorsed Camp as his successor as federal judge of West Texas, but President Wilson demurred, thinking that no one over the age of sixty should hold such a position. Wilson did, however, appoint Camp to a second term as district attorney.

In 1881 Camp married Lamartine Felder, the daughter of J. L. Felder, a Leesburg physician. Camp died in San Antonio on August 10, 1918. He was survived by his wife, five daughters, and two sons.

BIBLIOGRAPHY: *Dictionary of American Biography.* San Antonio *Express,* August 11, 1918. San Antonio *Light,* August 11, 1918.

Thomas W. Cutrer

CAMP AIR, TEXAS. Camp Air, or simply Air, is at the junction of U.S. Highway 377/Interstate Highway 87 and Ranch Road 1222, two miles southwest of Katemcy in northern Mason County. The area was used for many years as pastureland by Comanche Indians, who periodically burned off the brush to encourage the growth of the prairie grass. In the 1850s soldiers from Fort Mason cut hay there for their animals. Early white settlers began moving into the area around 1862. Many of them had been stationed at the Ranger camp on the San Saba River and moved to the area after their term of enlistment was over. There were originally three separate communities. The school community was named Peter's Prairie after Maj. Sam (or Joshua) Peters, who owned much of the land at one time and used to send his slaves there to cut prairie grass for Fort Mason. The original picket school, where Miss Jane Hurley was an early teacher, was eventually replaced by a rock building. The school was later moved closer to the highway south of town but retained the name Peter's Prairie for many years. The church, built in 1876, and the surrounding community were named by early settler David Hurley after his previous hometown, Bethel, South Carolina. The original building was replaced in the 1930s and is located one-half mile south of the present community.

Camp Air was the name given to the stores that grew up on either side of the Mason-to-Brady highway. John Kyle, who built the first store and filling station, supposedly chose the name as a joke, claiming his stores looked like a camp and he had nothing else but air. Other sources say that the name was chosen because of its brevity when Kyle applied for a post office in 1925. He had wanted to name the community Kyle, but there was already a Texas town by that name. Eventually all three communities became known as Air, and after 1966 as Camp Air, although the post office was never established. The town reached its highest population of seventy-five in the early 1940s. From 1974 through the mid-1980s the population held steady at thirty-one. As of 1980 Camp Air had a store and filling station, the Bethel church and cemetery, and a community center located in the old schoolhouse. In 1990 the population was fifteen.

BIBLIOGRAPHY: Kathryn Burford Eilers, A History of Mason County, Texas (M.A. thesis, University of Texas, 1939). Stella Gipson Polk, *Mason and Mason County: A History* (Austin: Pemberton Press, 1966; rev. ed., Burnet, Texas: Eakin Press, 1980). *Mason County Historical Book* (Mason, Texas: Mason County Historical Commission, 1976).

Alice J. Rhoades

CAMP ALLISON, TEXAS. Camp Allison, on the North Llano River in southeastern Sutton County, was named for George S. Allison, who began grazing cattle on the free range of the area in 1885 and later bought land from which he contributed a free campsite and public park. The one-store supply point was granted a post office in 1927. In 1933 its population was estimated at twenty-five. That number remained steady until 1949, when the *Texas Almanac*[qv] deleted Camp Allison from its list of towns. The community's post office seems to have closed during the 1940s as well.

BIBLIOGRAPHY: Sutton County Historical Society, *Sutton County* (Sonora, Texas, 1979).

CAMP AUSTIN. Camp Austin, on the left bank of the Colorado River in Austin in Travis County, became a military depot on November 20, 1848. The first garrison, commanded by J. H. King, was composed of two companies of the First United States Infantry. Temporary buildings made by sinking cedar posts in the ground were weatherboarded and shingled. They were located on a 236-foot square, enclosed with a plain fence. Supplies were brought first from Indianola and later from San Antonio. While Col. William S. Harney[qv] was in command at the camp, he hoped to make Austin the military center of the state, but there were probably no troops at the post from 1852 until after the Civil War,[qv] when Austin was occupied by the Sixth United States Cavalry.

BIBLIOGRAPHY: Arrie Barrett, Federal Military Outposts in Texas, 1846–1861 (M.A. thesis, University of Texas, 1927). *Texas Almanac,* 1936. Joseph H. and James R. Toulouse, *Pioneer Posts of Texas* (San Antonio: Naylor, 1936).

CAMP BARKELEY. Camp Barkeley was eleven miles southwest of Abilene in Taylor County. It was originally planned as a temporary camp for infantry and supply troops, but during World War II[qv] it became one of the state's largest military installations. The camp was named for David B. Barkley,[qv] a native Texan who was awarded the Medal of Honor in World War I.[qv] A clerical error apparently caused the discrepancy in spelling. Construction of the camp began in December 1940. The government leased 70,229 acres, with the option to purchase a small portion, to accommodate the facility and maneuvering grounds. Although the cost of the camp was originally estimated at $4 million, when it was completed in July 1941 costs totaled $7 million.

The first unit to occupy the camp was the Forty-fifth Infantry Division, consisting of 19,000 men under the command of Maj. Gen. William S. Key. The division occupied the still unfinished camp on February 23, 1941. The *45th Divisional News* was published at Camp Barkeley. One member of the paper's staff, William Mauldin, became a famous war cartoonist during World War II. Other units in addition to the Forty-fifth trained at Camp Barkeley, among them the Ninetieth Infantry Division and the Eleventh and Twelfth Armored divisions. A medical officer candidate school was established at Barkeley in May 1942, and from it 12,500 candidates eventually graduated.

The camp also served as a camp for German prisoners of war.[qv] On February 1, 1944, the 1846th Unit POW Camp was activated under the command of Lt. Col. Harry Slaughter. At its peak in March 1945 the POW camp housed 840 prisoners. Two months after the camp opened, twelve prisoners escaped, but all were recaptured within a week.

On April 30, 1945, Camp Barkeley was deactivated. At its peak it had a total population of 50,000. It was officially closed in September 1945 and dismantled. The War Department estimated the total cost from December 1940 to September 1945, including land and construction, at $27,332,000. At the time it closed, the military reservation encompassed one-ninth of Taylor County—77,436 acres—of which the government owned 18,976. After the camp was abandoned, the leased land reverted to its owners. Camp Barkeley had long-term effects on Abilene. Construction and army payrolls helped the local economy, and the community's demonstrated ability to maintain satisfactory relations with a large military population was a factor in the government's decision in the 1950s to locate Dyess Air Force Base[qv] there.

BIBLIOGRAPHY: John J. Hatcher, "Camp Barkeley: Abilene, Texas," *Texas Military History* 3 (Winter 1963). James M. Myers, World War II as an Instrument of Social Modernization: The Social and Economic Influence of Camp Barkeley on Abilene, Texas (M.A. thesis, Hardin-Simmons University, 1981). *James M. Myers*

CAMP BELKNAP. Camp Belknap, near Fort Belknap in Young County, was established on March 17, 1862, by James M. Norris[qv] as a Texas Ranger station for the Frontier Regiment.[qv] The camp, manned by members of Capt. J. J. (Jack) Cureton's[qv] company, did frontier patrol duty until March 1864, when the Frontier Regiment was consolidated at Fort Belknap.

BIBLIOGRAPHY: William Curry Holden, Frontier Problems and Movements in West Texas, 1846–1900 (Ph.D. dissertation, University of Texas, 1928). Vertical Files, Barker Texas History Center, University of Texas at Austin (Fort Belknap).

CAMPBELL, CHARLES AUGUSTUS ROSENHEIMER (1865–1931). Charles A. R. Campbell, doctor, was born in 1865 in San Antonio. He acquired his early education there, received a medical degree from Tulane University, and returned to San Antonio, where he practiced for many years. He was president of the San Antonio Academy of Medicine at one time. After becoming interested in the extermination of fever-carrying mosquitoes, he discovered that the bat was a foe of the mosquito and constructed large roosts in which bats could feed, sleep, and deposit guano, which attracted mosquitoes. In this manner Campbell attempted to eradicate the insect in large numbers and reduce the incidence of disease. He also benefited financially from the sale of guano. Campbell published his findings in *Bats, Mosquitoes, and Dollars* (1925), which was lauded by such notable naturalists as Theodore Roosevelt, Lord Rothschild, and Ernest Thompson Seton. Later studies, however, have found that only certain species of bats eat mosquitoes in appreciable numbers, and that bats are not as significant a factor in mosquito control as Campbell suggested. Campbell was married to Ida Hoyer, and they had one son. Campbell died on February 22, 1931.

BIBLIOGRAPHY: Vertical Files, Barker Texas History Center, University of Texas at Austin. *S. W. Pease*

CAMPBELL, DONALD (1830–1871). Donald Campbell, lieutenant governor of Texas, was born on March 26, 1830, in Alabama. As a young man he moved to Tennessee and attended Knoxville College, where he graduated with distinction in 1849. He moved to Texas in 1858 and settled in Jefferson, Marion County, where he worked as a druggist, as an insurance agent, and around 1866 as an agent for the United States Internal Revenue Service. By 1865 Campbell was married, had three children, and was a relatively prosperous property owner with 125 acres of improved farmland and five slaves.

Due to his partisan credentials as an old-line Whig and his ardent Unionism, Campbell rose to political prominence during the tumultuous years of Reconstruction.[qv] The wholesale removal of county officials considered by federal authorities to be disloyal to the cause of the Union resulted in Campbell's appointment as chief justice of Marion County in 1868. He was also elected a delegate to the Constitutional Convention of 1868–69,[qv] to fill the unexpired position of another Marion County Unionist, Rev. Aaron Grimsby. Campbell's close cooperation with the military government raised the ire of Marion County Democrats and resulted in his arrest and temporary incarceration by county authorities in 1868 for allegedly falsely swearing to the Union loyalty oath. District Judge Colbert Caldwell[qv] ordered Campbell's release, ruling that he had committed no offense.

Campbell won election to the Texas Senate in 1870. When James Winwright Flanagan[qv] vacated the lieutenant governorship in 1870 for an appointment to the United States Senate, Campbell was elected president pro tem of the Texas Senate and consequently, by constitutional succession, became ex officio lieutenant governor. He once again found himself caught in the maelstrom of Reconstruction politics when, in support of Governor Edmund J. Davis's[qv] legislative agenda, he ordered the arrest of the "Senate bolters," who attempted to break the quorum and prevent the passage of Davis's legislative package. Despite the contentious nature of the political atmosphere, Campbell's Senate colleagues considered him clear, consistent, and honorable as lieutenant governor. He died in Austin on November 8, 1871. The Masonic fraternity performed his funeral rites in the Senate chamber on November 9, 1871. He is buried in the State Cemetery.[qv]

BIBLIOGRAPHY: *Flake's Daily Bulletin*, November 8, 1871. Carl H. Moneyhon, *Republicanism in Reconstruction Texas* (Austin: University of Texas Press, 1980). Texas Legislature, *Senate Journal*, 12th legislative session. *Mark Howard Atkins*

CAMPBELL, ELIZABETH BUNDY (1852–1931). Elizabeth Bundy (Lizzie) Campbell, Panhandle[qv] pioneer, daughter of Williamson and E. Vance (Hamilton) Bundy, was born on October 25, 1852, in Navarro County, Texas. Her mother was the daughter of James Hamilton, a descendent of Alexander Hamilton. Elizabeth married Henry H. Campbell[qv] in Ellis County in 1871. They had a son and a daughter. Their first home was in Ennis.

In 1879 Campbell founded the Matador Ranch.[qv] Lizzie lived in Fort Worth until she decided to join him on their new ranch. In 1880 she rode to Matador, about 300 miles from Fort Worth, with a load of freight for the ranch. When she arrived, she slept in a tent because she refused to sleep in a dugout[qv] as her husband had been doing for the last year. She was one of only two women living in that area at the time, and the other woman was twenty miles away. On March 25, 1880, the Campbells finished building a white, two-room house with supplies shipped from Fort Worth and Fort Griffin by wagon. They enlarged the house after the Texas and Pacific Railway laid track within about twenty miles of the Matador, thus making supplies more accessible.

Lizzie was known for the big Christmas parties she held every year from 1883 until they left the Matador in 1891. The parties lasted for two or three days, and the ranchhands from the surrounding area would come. She took good care of them at all times. Her work as cook, seamstress, doctor, and surgeon, even though she had no medical training, earned her the nickname "Angel of the Matador." She also arranged for preachers to come to the ranch at least once a month for the spiritual wellbeing of the ranchhands. Her son Harry was born in 1881, the first white child born in Motley County.

Lizzie loved ranching as much as her husband. She rode unaccompanied all over the ranch, exploring, analyzing water, and examining the vegetation. She discovered a hill covered with petrified wood; on the old county maps it was labeled "Mrs. Campbell's Petrified Hill." She was the Matador Ranch postmistress from 1883 to 1891. When the county was organized in 1891 Matador became county seat; she was Matador postmistress from 1891 to 1911. Though she lost her eyesight in her latter years, she remained a respected member of the community known for her intelligence and interest in city, state, and national affairs. She died on October 8, 1931.

BIBLIOGRAPHY: Harry H. Campbell, *The Early History of Motley County* (San Antonio: Naylor, 1958; 2d ed., Wichita Falls: Nortex, 1971). James Cox, *Historical and Biographical Record of the Cattle Industry* (2 vols., St. Louis: Woodward and Tiernan Printing, 1894, 1895;

rpt., with an introduction by J. Frank Dobie, New York: Antiquarian, 1959). Marisue Burleson Potts, *Motley County Roundup: Over One Hundred Years of Gathering, a Centennial History*, 2d ed. (Floydada, Texas, 1991). *Amanda Oren*

CAMPBELL, HENRY HARRISON (1840–1911). Henry Harrison (Hank) Campbell, rancher, son of F. and Effie (McLean) Campbell, was born on August 31, 1840, in Cumberland County, North Carolina, where his father was a planter. The family moved to Texas in 1854 and lived successively in Waller, Grimes, and Ellis counties. During the Civil War[qv] Campbell served with the Twentieth Texas Regiment in Texas, Missouri, Arkansas, and Indian Territory; he was wounded three times before he was mustered out in Houston.

He returned to Ellis County, where he contracted to drive his neighbors' cattle to market in California, New Orleans, or Chicago for wages, shares, and later investment. In 1879, as working partner-manager, he secured $50,000 from Alfred M. Britton of Chicago, a Mr. Cato of New York, S. W. Lomax, and John Nichols of Fort Worth to establish the Matador Cattle Company at Ballard Springs on the Pease River. The ranch began operations with a small herd of some 1,300 cattle. Steers sold for seventy-five dollars a head in 1881, and within a few years the Matador under Campbell was branding from 15,000 to 20,000 calves a year. In 1882 the ranch was sold to a group of Scottish investors and became the Matador Land and Cattle Company.[qv] By the time of Campbell's resignation from the post of superintendent in 1890, the ranch had grown to include a million and a half acres in three different ranges and a total herd of some 90,000 head.

Campbell married Elizabeth Bundy of Navarro County in 1871, and they had two children. His first home on the ranch was in an old buffalo hunter's dugout[qv] at Ballard Springs; he later built a frame home there. By the time he left the ranch in early 1891, he had bought a section of land a mile northeast of Ballard Springs. On this he founded the town of Matador. Also in 1891, in order to organize the county formally, he brought in cowboys from the ranch who set up temporary "businesses" so that a patent could be obtained from the land office. Campbell was appointed the first county judge of Motley County and served two one-year terms. He then bought another ranch and operated it for several years before turning it over to his son. He lived in Matador until his death, on May 23, 1911. He was buried there at East Mound Cemetery.

bibliography: Harry H. Campbell, *The Early History of Motley County* (San Antonio: Naylor, 1958; 2d ed., Wichita Falls: Nortex, 1971). Mary Whatley Clarke, *A Century of Cow Business: A History of the Texas and Southwestern Cattle Raisers Association* (Fort Worth: Evans, 1976). James Cox, *Historical and Biographical Record of the Cattle Industry* (2 vols., St. Louis: Woodward and Tiernan Printing, 1894, 1895; rpt., with an introduction by J. Frank Dobie, New York: Antiquarian, 1959). W. M. Pearce, *The Matador Land and Cattle Company* (Norman: University of Oklahoma Press, 1964). Eleanor Traweek, *Of Such as These: A History of Motley County and Its Families* (Quanah, Texas: Nortex, 1973). *H. Allen Anderson*

CAMPBELL, ISAAC (ca. 1813–1843). Isaac Campbell, Republic of Texas[qv] congressman, was born about 1813. He moved to Texas in January 1836 as a single man and settled in San Augustine County, where he married Elizabeth Holman. From December 5, 1838, to January 24, 1839, he represented San Augustine County in the House of Representatives of the Third Congress of the republic and was one of the commissioners who selected the site of the city of Austin. Campbell was a royal arch Mason, a charter member in 1837 of the McFarland Lodge in San Augustine, and a representative in 1838 of the Grand Lodge of the Republic of Texas. He assisted in formation of the Rising Star chapter in 1841. In 1839 early Texas architect and master builder Augustus Phelps built Campbell a two-story Greek-Revival home on Main Street in San Augustine. The home was sold to Matthew Cartwright[qv] in 1847 and was still in excellent condition in 1990. Campbell lived there until his death on September 7, 1843. The probate of his estate was not filed until December 19, 1846.

bibliography: George L. Crocket, *Two Centuries in East Texas* (Dallas: Southwest, 1932; facsimile reprod. 1962). Texas House of Representatives, *Biographical Directory of the Texan Conventions and Congresses, 1832–1845* (Austin: Book Exchange, 1941). *McXie Whitton Martin*

CAMPBELL, ISRAEL S. (1815–1898). Israel S. Campbell, early black Baptist pastor and organizer, was born in Russellville, Kentucky, in 1815. He joined the Baptist Church[qv] in 1836 and began preaching a year later. Campbell ministered at churches in Tennessee, Canada, and Ohio before being ordained in Canada in 1855. He then served as a general missionary to Baptists in Louisiana from his headquarters in Baton Rouge. In 1866 the Baptist convention that met at Nashville, Tennessee, sent Campbell to Texas as a missionary. In August of 1866 he and fellow pastor I. Rhinehart organized the Antioch Baptist Church in Houston. Campbell served that church for a short time, until John Henry Yates[qv] was ordained and chosen as the resident pastor. In 1867 Campbell reorganized the African Baptist Church at Galveston, the first completely independent black Baptist congregation in Texas after emancipation. The church was renamed the First Regular Missionary Baptist Church and grew from forty-seven to 500 members under Campbell's leadership. It is known today as the Avenue L Baptist Church.[qv]

In 1968 Campbell helped organize the Regular Missionary Lincoln Baptist Association with Yates and Peter Diggs, Sr. Campbell, who had served as the moderator of Baptist associations in Michigan and Louisiana and as the president of the Freedmen's Baptist Convention for two years, became the first moderator of the Lincoln Association, the first association of black Baptists in Texas. The association encompassed an area along the coast south of Galveston and north along the Brazos River to McLennan County. It was formed with twenty churches and grew to twenty-seven churches, twenty-four ministers, and almost 2,700 members. Recognizing the need for a formal, statewide organization, Campbell and others formed the Baptist State Missionary Convention in 1872, for which Campbell wrote the constitution. He also worked to establish a vocational school in the tradition of Booker T. Washington. He was forestalled in 1881, however, by the establishment of Bishop College in Marshall, an academic and nonvocational institution supported by the Baptist Church.

Campbell had one child, Mary, who was married in 1873 to James Henry Washington,[qv] a member of the Texas House of Representatives. In 1890 Campbell moved to La Marque with his daughter and son-in-law, where they cultivated a small truck farm and raised chickens. In February 1891 Campbell retired as pastor of the First Regular Missionary Baptist Church. By the time of his retirement he was popularly known as the father of black Baptists in Texas. He died in La Marque on June 13, 1898, and was buried in Lakeview Cemetery, Galveston.

bibliography: Robert A. Baker, *The Blossoming Desert—A Concise History of Texas Baptists* (Waco: Word, 1970). Alwyn Barr, *Black Texans: A History of Negroes in Texas, 1528–1971* (Austin: Jenkins, 1973). *Rosalie Beck*

CAMPBELL, KILLIS (1872–1937). Killis Campbell, writer and professor of literature, the son of Robert Camm and Alice (Hawes) Campbell, was born in Enfield, Virginia, on June 11, 1872. He earned a B.Litt. degree at Peabody College for Teachers in 1892 and a B.A. degree at William and Mary College in 1894. For graduate study in English he went to Johns Hopkins University, where he held a fellowship in 1897–98 and received his Ph.D. in 1898. The summers of 1897, 1902, and 1904 he spent studying in the British Museum and the Bodleian Library.

In 1899 he taught English at Culver Military Academy in Indiana. He then accepted an instructorship in English at the University of Texas, where he was made professor in 1918. He continued to teach until 1937, when he suffered a stroke from which he never fully recovered. Campbell's first scholarly love was the literature of the Middle Ages, and his definitive edition of a version of *The Seven Sages of Rome* (1907) was judged a model of scholarship. In the classroom he was subsequently drawn to the study of American literature, especially to Edgar Allan Poe. As a pioneer in the serious teaching of American literature, he was probably more influential than any other individual in the formation, about 1921, of the American Literature Study Group of the Modern Language Association of America. He was research professor at the University of Texas for 1930–31 and vice president of the MLA in 1934–35. In addition to editing *The Poems of Edgar Allan Poe* (1917) and *Poe's Short Stories* (1927), he collected and revised a number of Poe's essays under the title *The Mind of Poe and Other Studies.* In numerous shorter articles on Walt Whitman and James Russell Lowell as well as Poe, and in similar published works that he inspired his students to undertake and push to completion, Campbell made large contributions to knowledge. He died on August 8, 1937, and was buried in Austin. He was survived by his widow, Mary Hogg (Aitken), whom he had married in 1902, and five children. Campbell was a Democrat and a member of the Christian Church.

bibliography: Carl John Eckhardt, *One Hundred Faithful to the University of Texas at Austin* (197–?). Vertical Files, Barker Texas History Center, University of Texas at Austin. *Who Was Who in America,* 1943.

Robert Adger Law

CAMPBELL, LEE LEWIS (ca. 1865–1927). Lee Lewis Campbell, black Baptist pastor, was born in the mid-1860s in Milam County, Texas. He attended Bishop College in Marshall and then went to the University of Chicago. Sometime afterwards he returned to Texas and in 1887 married Ella Williams. They had three sons and one daughter. Campbell was ordained to the Baptist ministry at Cameron, Milam County. In 1892 he became pastor of Ebenezer Baptist Church in Austin, a position he held for thirty-five years. In Austin he founded St. John's Institute and Orphanage. He was president of the General Baptist State Convention and vice president of the National General Baptist Convention. He was also president of St. John's Encampment Colored Association, in which 10,000 African Americans came to Austin to discuss race relations. Campbell was also moderator of the St. John's Association, which had over 230,000 members across the state. He founded the Austin *Herald* in 1889. It was published every Saturday by the Publication Board of the General Baptist Convention of Texas in Austin. Campbell was ill the last two years of his life and died at Seton Infirmary on August 9, 1927, after surgery. His funeral on August 14 was attended by over 5,000 people. In 1939 L. L. Campbell Elementary School in Austin in his honor.

bibliography: Austin *Herald,* March 10, 1917. Negro Scrapbook, Barker Texas History Center, University of Texas at Austin.

Kharen Monsho

CAMPBELL, MICHAEL (?–?). Michael Campbell, participant in the battle of San Jacinto,[qv] arrived in Texas in January 1836, according to a headright certificate, and joined Capt. Jacob Snively's[qv] company on a two-year enlistment. He later received a land grant for his service from January 1836 to June 1838.

Several other men named Michael Campbell also served in the Texas army from the Texas Revolution[qv] through the years of the Republic of Texas,[qv] but historian Louis W. Kemp[qv] states that none of them fought at San Jacinto. One of these soldiers came to Texas in 1835. He enlisted in Capt. Henry Teal's[qv] company early in 1836 but was transferred to an artillery company under Isaac N. Moreland.[qv] He later served under Capt. Peter B. Dexter[qv] until June 20, 1836. The Texas government issued two bounty certificates in the name Michael Campbell: one for 1,280 acres of land for service from June 1836 to November 1837 and another for 240 acres of land for service from November 1839 to March 1841. Yet another Michael Campbell, born in Ireland in 1813, came to the republic in 1841, participated in the Texan Santa Fe expedition,[qv] and was living in Bastrop County in 1874.

bibliography: DeWitt Clinton Baker, comp., *A Texas Scrap-Book* (New York: Barnes, 1875; rpt. 1887; facsimile rpt., Austin: Steck, 1935). Daughters of the Republic of Texas, *Muster Rolls of the Texas Revolution* (Austin, 1986). Sam Houston Dixon and Louis Wiltz Kemp, *The Heroes of San Jacinto* (Houston: Anson Jones, 1932). Louis Wiltz Kemp Papers, Barker Texas History Center, University of Texas at Austin.

David L. Fisher

CAMPBELL, ROBERT (1810–1836). Robert Campbell, Alamo defender, was born in Tennessee in 1810. He moved to Texas in January 1836 and obtained a commission as lieutenant in the Volunteer Auxillary Corps. He traveled to the Alamo as an officer of Capt. William B. Harrison's[qv] company of volunteers, which included David Crockett.[qv] Campbell died in the battle of the Alamo[qv] on March 6, 1836.

bibliography: Daughters of the American Revolution, *The Alamo Heroes and Their Revolutionary Ancestors* (San Antonio, 1976). Bill Groneman, *Alamo Defenders* (Austin: Eakin, 1990). John H. Jenkins, ed., *The Papers of the Texas Revolution, 1835–1836* (10 vols., Austin: Presidial Press, 1973). Phil Rosenthal and Bill Groneman, *Roll Call at the Alamo* (Fort Collins, Colorado: Old Army, 1985). Amelia W. Williams, A Critical Study of the Siege of the Alamo and of the Personnel of Its Defenders (Ph.D. dissertation, University of Texas, 1931; rpt., *Southwestern Historical Quarterly* 36 (April 1933), 37 (July, October 1933, January, April 1934).

Bill Groneman

CAMPBELL, ROBERT DOUGLAS (1870–1955). Robert D. Campbell, Presbyterian clergyman, was born in Rogersville, Tennessee, in January 1870. His family moved to Texas when he was fifteen and settled in Lancaster. Campbell attended Austin College in Sherman (B.A., 1894), and Union Theological Seminary in Richmond, Virginia (B.D., 1897); he was ordained by the Fort Worth Presbytery in 1898. While in the seminary he met Minnie Gunn, a missionary to Mexico, whom he married in 1899. Through her influence Campbell became interested in a ministry to the Spanish-speaking population of Texas. When a position opened in Laredo the following year, he accepted a call as missionary pastor. With the help of his wife Campbell learned enough Spanish to communicate effectively with his constituents. With Walter S. Scott,[qv] he organized a number of small churches in South Texas. He was a charter member of the Texas-Mexican Presbytery when it was organized in 1908. When Scott left the presbytery to start new work, Campbell assumed leadership in Mexican-American missionary work. As a permanent member of the Home Missions Committee and the treasurer of the Texas Mexican Presbytery, Campbell distributed all the funds authorized by the denomination. Few questioned his decisions regarding the placement of ministers and the locations of new churches. He also functioned as liaison between the Texas Mexican Presbytery and the Synod of Texas and as spokesman for the cause of Mexican-American missions throughout the state. In addition to his pastoral and administrative responsibilities, Campbell served as a part-time instructor in Spanish at Austin Presbyterian Theological Seminary from 1932 until his retirement in 1946. He died in 1955.

bibliography: Robert Douglas Brackenridge and Francisco O. García-Treto, *Iglesia Presbiteriana: A History of Presbyterians and Mexican Americans in the Southwest* (San Antonio: Trinity University Press, 1974; 2d ed. 1987).

R. Douglas Brackenridge

CAMPBELL, THOMAS MITCHELL (1856–1923). Thomas Mitchell Campbell, governor of Texas, was born at Rusk, Texas, on

April 22, 1856, the son of Thomas Duncan and Rachel (Moore) Campbell. He attended common schools at Rusk before entering Trinity University (then located at Tehuacana) to study law in 1873. Lack of finances forced him to withdraw after a year, but he got a job in the Gregg county clerk's office and studied law at night. In 1878 he was admitted to the Texas bar and began his practice in Longview. In the same year, he married Fannie Irene Bruner of Shreveport, Louisiana; they had five children.

Campbell practiced law in Longview until he was appointed a master in chancery for the troubled International–Great Northern Railroad in 1889. Financier Jay Gould[qv] had allowed the ailing railroad to default on its debts in 1888 and then forced it into federal receivership in order to gain eventual control of it. Campbell soon found himself deeply involved in guiding the railroad's recovery. He became its court-appointed receiver in 1891 and moved his family to Palestine. The next year, after lifting the line from bankruptcy, he remained in Palestine as the general manager of the railroad.

However, Gould managed to gain control anyway, and Campbell found his own attitudes clashing with the business practices of his employer. Campbell distrusted monopolistic big business and sympathized with organized labor. He shared many of the reformist political views of his lifelong friend, former governor James Stephen Hogg.[qv] In 1897 Campbell resigned from the railroad, returned to private law practice in Palestine, and became active in Democratic party[qv] politics. He attended several Democratic conventions and subsequently, at Hogg's urging, decided to run for governor. Though Hogg died before the campaign got underway, Campbell used his endorsement and promised to resurrect his friend's antitrust policies. His campaign gained added impetus when Senator Joseph Weldon Bailey[qv] threw his support to the Palestine lawyer, and Campbell was elected governor in 1906.

In his two terms in office, 1907–1911, Campbell initiated a number of reforms involving railroad regulation, antitrust laws, lobbying restrictions, equitable taxation, and pure food and drug laws. Under his administration the Robertson Insurance Law (1907) brought to a halt the insurance companies' practice of realizing large profits in Texas without investing policy reserves in the state. The most significant legislation centered on prison reform, as Campbell's administration ended the contract lease system for inmates and implemented more humane treatment of prisoners. Under Campbell many state agencies also came into being, including the Department of Insurance and Banking (*see* DEPARTMENT OF BANKING), the Bureau of Labor Statistics (*see* TEXAS DEPARTMENT OF LICENSING AND REGULATION), the State Board of Health (*see* TEXAS DEPARTMENT OF HEALTH), and the Texas State Library.[qv]

Upon leaving the governorship Campbell returned to private law practice in Palestine but remained active in Democratic politics. In 1916 he ran unsuccessfully for the United States Senate. In 1917 he served on the exemption board for World War I.[qv] He died in Galveston on April 1, 1923, and was buried in Palestine.

BIBLIOGRAPHY: Thomas Mitchell Campbell Letters and Papers, Texas State Archives, Austin. Thomas Mitchell Campbell Papers, Barker Texas History Center, University of Texas at Austin. Ross Phares, *The Governors of Texas* (Gretna, Louisiana: Pelican, 1976). Janet Schmelzer, "Thomas M. Campbell, Progressive Governor of Texas," *Red River Valley Historical Review* 3 (Fall 1978).

Janet Schmelzer

CAMPBELL, TEXAS (Hunt County). Campbell is a mile north of Interstate Highway 30 and six miles east of Greenville in eastern Hunt County. Settlement began at the site in the fall of 1880, when the long-awaited East Line and Red River Railroad was extended from Black Jack Grove to Greenville. The town was built around the railroad, and a station was constructed. A post office was established in June 1881, and the community was officially named Oliverea. By fall of that year, however, the town was generally referred to as Campbell or sometimes Tom Campbell, perhaps in honor of Thomas M. Campbell,[qv] later governor of Texas, who had played a prominent part in the extension of the railroad. At least one source contends that the Tom Campbell for whom the town was named was not the governor, since the community was established before Governor Campbell became prominent. The name of the post office was officially changed to Campbell in September 1882.

Campbell became a shipping center for area farmers and by 1900 had a population of 508 and twelve businesses, as well as a college, Henry College, founded in 1892. Although the town lost its college in 1906, when Emerson College, the successor of Henry College, was forced to close, Campbell's population remained stable. The town was incorporated in 1912 with an aldermanic form of government. Between 1920, when the population was 583, and 1925, the small farming community experienced a burst of growth. By 1925 Campbell had a telephone exchange, a bank, power and light services, a weekly newspaper, twenty commercial establishments, and an estimated population of 1,000. By 1930 there were only twelve businesses remaining, and the population had fallen to 416. Although the population remained stable thereafter until the early 1960s, the number of businesses continued to decline. By 1936 the bank had closed, and by the early 1950s only seven businesses remained. In 1961 only four were still open. The population reached a low of 204 in 1970. In the mid-1980s, when Campbell had six businesses, the town was reincorporated to take in part of the surrounding rural area; consequently, the population jumped to 549. In 1990 it was 683.

BIBLIOGRAPHY: W. Walworth Harrison, *History of Greenville and Hunt County, Texas* (Waco: Texian, 1976). Fred I. Massengill, *Texas Towns: Origin of Name and Location of Each of the 2,148 Post Offices in Texas* (Terrell, Texas, 1936). Thomas Clarence Richardson, *East Texas: Its History and Its Makers* (4 vols., New York: Lewis Historical Publishing, 1940).

Cecil Harper, Jr.

CAMPBELL, TEXAS (Navarro County). Campbell, on Farm Road 744 near Rush Creek ten miles west of Corsicana in central Navarro County, was probably established before 1900. In the mid-1930s it had a church, a school, and a number of houses. After World War II[qv] its school was consolidated with the Corsicana schools, and in the mid-1960s only a cemetery and a few widely scattered farmhouses remained. In 1990 Campbell was a dispersed rural community.

Christopher Long

CAMPBELL BRANCH (Lavaca County). Campbell Branch rises at the confluence of its east and west branches, on the northwestern outskirts of Hallettsville in north central Lavaca County (at 29°28′ N, 96°57′ W), and runs a mile to its mouth on the Lavaca River, just west of Hallettsville (at 29°27′ N, 96°57′ W). East Campbell Branch rises a mile west of U.S. Highway 77 and four miles north of Hallettsville in north central Lavaca County (at 29°31′ N, 96°56′ W) and flows south for 5½ miles to its confluence with West Campbell Branch, just northwest of Hallettsville. West Campbell Branch rises a mile east of Breslau (at 29°32′ N, 96°58′ W) and runs southeast for 5½ miles, roughly paralleling the route of State Highway 957. The streams are named for James Campbell, a pioneer colonist who arrived in the area before 1830. The loamy and loamy clay soils in the area support range, pasturage, and corn and grain sorghum.

BIBLIOGRAPHY: Paul C. Boethel, *On the Headwaters of the Lavaca and the Navidad* (Austin: Von Boeckmann–Jones, 1967).

____ (Montague County). Campbell Branch rises fifteen miles northeast of Bonita in northeastern Montague County (at 33°52′ N, 97°32′ W) and runs north for four miles to its mouth on the Illinois Bend of the Red River, twenty miles northeast of Bonita (at 33°55′ N, 97°30′ W). The surrounding flat to rolling terrain is surfaced by clay and sandy loams that support hardwoods, conifers, and grasses. For most of the county's history the Campbell Branch area has been used as rangeland.

CAMPBELL CREEK (Armstrong County). Campbell Creek rises south of the JA Ranch[qv] headquarters in southern Armstrong County (at 34°48′ N, 101°12′ W) and runs southwest for 5½ miles through sloping loamy plains of mesquite brush to its mouth, on the Prairie Dog Town Fork of the Red River just across the county line in northern Briscoe County (at 34°44′ N, 101°16′ W). The creek was named for the brothers W. A. (Jud), T. J. (Jeff), and L. M. Campbell, who were outstanding JA employees during the ranch's early years. One of the JA's twelve winter camps was located near the mouth of Campbell Creek.

BIBLIOGRAPHY: Armstrong County Historical Association, *A Collection of Memories: A History of Armstrong County, 1876–1965* (Hereford, Texas: Pioneer, 1965). Harley True Burton, *A History of the JA Ranch* (Austin: Von Boeckmann–Jones, 1928; rpt., New York: Argonaut, 1966).

—— (Franklin County). Campbell Creek rises four miles northeast of Mount Vernon in northeastern Franklin County (at 33°13′ N, 95°10′ W) and runs northwest for 5½ miles to its mouth on White Oak Creek, eight miles northeast of Mount Vernon (at 33°17′ N, 95°11′ W). The creek traverses level to undulating terrain surfaced by loams underlain by clays. Forests of pines and various hardwoods grow in the area.

—— (Guadalupe County). Campbell Creek (Campbell Branch) rises four miles southwest of Seguin in south central Guadalupe County (at 29°31′ N, 98°02′ W) and runs southeast for 4½ miles to its mouth on Elm Creek, five miles south of Seguin (at 29°30′ N, 97°59′ W). The surrounding rolling prairies are surfaced by clay loams that support mesquite and grasses.

CAMPBELL DRAW. Campbell Draw rises ten miles southeast of the Fort McKavett community in southwestern Menard County (at 30°43′ N, 100°02′ W) and runs north for ten miles to its mouth on the San Saba River, five miles west of Fort McKavett (at 30°50′ N, 100°03′ W). The surrounding flat terrain with local shallow depressions is surfaced by clay and sandy loams that support water-tolerant hardwoods, conifers, and grasses.

CAMPBELL LAKE. Campbell Lake (Campbell's Lake) is a natural lake two miles east of the Trinity River in southwestern Anderson County (at 31°46′ N, 95°53′ W). The lake drains into Cedar Lake Slough.

CAMPBELL'S BAYOU, TEXAS. Campbell's Bayou was across Galveston Bay from Galveston on an inlet now in southern Texas City, Galveston County. The site was chosen by the Karankawa Indians as a homesite for their friends, James and Mary (Chirino) Campbell. Campbell (1791–1856), who had served in the United States Navy during the War of 1812, had subsequently been an officer with privateer Jean Laffite[qv] until 1821, when the United States government demanded that Campeche, the privateer's settlement on Galveston Island, be evacuated. Though some sources say that the Campbells settled at Campbell's Bayou in 1821, it is more likely that they did not finally move there until 1837–39.

The land the Indians had shown the Campbells was situated near the smallest of three bayous and was named Campbell's Bayou. The stream has since been renamed Campbell Bayou. Fish, wild horses, wild pigs, and game were plentiful. The Campbells planted gardens and built an underground cistern and a log house with shuttered windows and a shell floor. They signaled passing schooners with a raised white flag and traded fresh meat for goods they could not grow. Other families soon moved to the site because it offered easy access to the protected waters of Galveston Bay. Thus goods made and grown on the mainland could be traded to passing ships or sent to Galveston to be sold. The small settlement was visited by travelers from the inland on their way to Galveston. As the white population increased, the Karankawas left. In 1856 Campbell's fence lines were repeatedly moved by a wealthy Judge Jones, who coveted Campbell's land.

During the Civil War[qv] many men from Campbell's Bayou fought for the Confederacy, and 5,000 Confederate soldiers camped in and around the bayou in preparation for their attack on Union forces at Galveston. The Galveston hurricane of 1900[qv] destroyed the community, however, and many survivors moved inland. The few who remained rebuilt their homes with wood washed ashore during the storm. When the storm of 1915 destroyed the settlement a second time, it was abandoned. A state historical marker placed in the late 1960s commemorates the site, and Laffite's telescope, which he presented to Jim Campbell as a farewell gift, is on display in the Moore Memorial Public Library, Texas City.

BIBLIOGRAPHY: Claude W. Dooley, comp., *Why Stop?* (Odessa: Lone Star Legends, 1978; 2d ed., with Betty Dooley and the Texas Historical Commission, Houston: Lone Star, 1985). Charles Adams Gulick, Jr., Harriet Smither, et al., eds., *The Papers of Mirabeau Buonaparte Lamar* (6 vols., Austin: Texas State Library, 1920–27; rpt., Austin: Pemberton Press, 1968). Vertical Files, Barker Texas History Center, University of Texas at Austin (James Campbell). Vertical File, Moore Memorial Public Library, Texas City, Texas (James Campbell).

Margaret Bearden Hamilton

CAMPBELLS CREEK. Campbells Creek rises five miles south of Wheelock in southeastern Robertson County (at 30°50′ N, 96°25′ W) and flows southwest ten miles to its mouth on the Little Brazos River, three miles west of Benchley (at 30°44′ N, 96°30′ W). The surrounding nearly level terrain is surfaced by sandy loam that supports post oaks and grasses. The stream was named for Roth Campbell, who held an original land grant along its course.

CAMPBELLTON, TEXAS. Campbellton is on U.S. Highway 281A, Farm Road 1099, and the Atascosa River twelve miles east of Christine in southeast Atascosa County. It is named for John F. Campbell, who came to Texas in 1855 from Ireland to establish a ranch. He encouraged other settlers to join him in Atascosa County in the 1860s and was the first postmaster when the town acquired a post office in the 1870s. During that time Campbell opened a general store, founded the first school, and hosted Catholic services in his home. By 1894 the town had a population of twenty-five. Campbellton was strategically located on the highway from San Antonio to the Rio Grande Valley. By 1890 its population had grown to thirty, and the town had three churches (Baptist, Catholic, and Union), a gin, two livestock breeders, and a lumberyard. The communitzy in the mid-1890s had lost population but added a general store and another livestock breeder. In 1904 the local school had thirty students and one teacher. The number of cattle breeders in Campbellton increased to seven by 1914, and the population again rose to thirty. While it remained primarily a ranching community, Campbellton profited from the arrival of the San Antonio, Uvalde and Gulf Railroad in 1912. By 1914 the school had 169 students, and local beekeepers were manufacturing honey for commercial purposes. Campbellton had fifty residents in 1925, 368 in the 1950s, and an average number of ten businesses during that period. Oil was discovered in the area in 1956 but did not eclipse ranching. The school had 240 students and seven teachers in 1938. After 1964 area children beyond elementary school age were sent to Pleasanton to continue their education. The population in Campbellton remained 275 from the 1960s through 1990, when it had three businesses and a post office.

BIBLIOGRAPHY: *Atascosa County Centennial, 1856–1956* (Jourdanton, Texas: Atascosa County Centennial Association, n.d). *Atascosa County History* (Pleasanton, Texas: Atascosa History Committee, 1984). Margaret G. Clover, The Place Names of Atascosa County (M.A. thesis, University of Texas, 1952).

Linda Peterson

CAMP BEN MCCULLOCH. Camp Ben McCulloch, near Driftwood in Hays County, was organized in the summer of 1896 as a reunion camp for Confederate veterans and named for Benjamin McCulloch.[qv] The first commander was Capt. M. L. Reed of Henly. Annual three-day reunions were held at the camp, often with 5,000 to 6,000 persons attending. In 1930 Ben McCulloch was said to be the largest Confederate camp in existence. The last reunion, the Golden Jubilee, was held on August 9, 1946, and included a memorial service for the camp's last two members, who had died the previous year. Subsequently, the camp became the location of the annual meetings of the Sons and Daughters of the Confederacy, with various activities and services spanning a week in early June. The campsite, on a branch of Onion Creek, also remains a popular picnic area for residents of northern Hays County.

BIBLIOGRAPHY: Austin *American*, August 9, 1946. T. F. Harwell, *Eighty Years Under the Stars and Bars* (Kyle, Texas, 1947).

Dorman H. Winfrey

CAMP BLAKE. Camp Blake was established as a temporary federal military installation on the Devils River in southeastern Val Verde County soon after the Mexican War.[qv] The camp was located on the road from San Antonio to El Paso. The camp was named for Lt. Jacob E. Blake,[qv] a topographical engineer who fought in the battle of Palo Alto.[qv]

BIBLIOGRAPHY: Ray Miller, *Ray Miller's Texas Forts* (Houston: Cordovan, 1985).

Julia Cauble Smith

CAMP BOWIE (Brown County). Camp Bowie was established at Brownwood in September 1940 as an infantry and artillery training center for the Thirty-sixth Infantry Division,[qv] Texas National Guard,[qqv] and was named in honor of the Texas patriot James Bowie.[qv] It was the first major defense construction project in Texas in World War II.[qv] The camp was occupied by the end of December 1940 by the 111th Quartermaster Regiment of the Thirty-sixth Division, commanded by Maj. Gen. Claude V. Birkhead.[qv] By October 1942 Camp Bowie had expanded from an original 2,000 acres to a total of 120,000 acres and was occupied, in addition to the Thirty-sixth Division, by the 113th Cavalry of the Iowa National Guard, the Eighth Army Corps with its headquarters, and troops of the Third Army under Gen. Walter Krueger.[qv] The Third Army personnel at Camp Bowie was composed of special troops of the Seventh Headquarters Detachment of the Third Army, medical units ranging from the Second to the Seventeenth, some engineer companies, signal battalions, and chemical companies. The Eighth Corps comprised the 174th and 142nd Field Artillery groups. The Eighteenth Field Artillery Brigade, the Fourth Armored Division, and the Seventh Headquarters Special Troops of the Fourth Army were also stationed at Camp Bowie at various times. A WAC contingent was attached to the Tank Destroyer Group and the Service Command Unit. A rehabilitation center to serve all posts and camps of the Eighth Service Command was set up in January 1942, and in August 1943 a prisoner of war camp with a capacity of 3,000 prisoners was established within the post (*see* GERMAN PRISONERS OF WAR). Camp Bowie was declared surplus by a War Department order, effective August 31, 1946.

CAMP BOWIE (Jackson County). Camp Bowie, the principal encampment of the Army of the Republic of Texas[qv] from April 22 through the middle of June 1837, was located on the east side of the Navidad River at Red Bluff, one mile below Texana. The site is near Red Bluff Cemetery, eight miles southeast of the Jackson County community of Edna. The camp's first commander was Gen. Albert Sidney Johnston,[qv] commanding general of the army. When Johnston left the republic for the United States on May 7, he was succeeded in command by Col. Joseph H. D. Rogers of the First Regiment, Permanent Volunteers, who was in turn replaced by Col. H. R. A. Wiggington, commander of the Second Regiment of Permanent Volunteers, early in June. Camp Bowie was named for Alamo defender James Bowie.[qv] It was the site of the murder, on the night of May 5, 1837, of Col. Henry Teal,[qv] following which President Sam Houston[qv] issued indefinite furloughs to almost all of the men of the dangerously undisciplined and mutinous army. In the latter part of May, Secretary of War William S. Fisher[qv] issued furloughs and travel orders to 1,200 troops, two-thirds of the army. By the third week in June the 200 men remaining at Camp Bowie had been transferred to Camp Crockett, and the post was abandoned.

BIBLIOGRAPHY: Samuel E. Asbury, ed., "Extracts from the Reminiscences of General George W. Morgan," *Southwestern Historical Quarterly* 30 (January 1927). John Henry Brown, *History of Texas from 1685 to 1892* (2 vols., St. Louis: Daniell, 1893). Louis Wiltz Kemp, ed., "The Joseph H. D. Rodgers Letters," *Southwestern Historical Quarterly* 55 (July, October 1951). Gerald S. Pierce, *Texas Under Arms: The Camps, Posts, Forts, and Military Towns of the Republic of Texas* (Austin: Encino, 1969). *Telegraph and Texas Register*, May 30, 1837.

Thomas W. Cutrer

CAMP BOWIE (Tarrant County). Construction of Camp Bowie began on July 18, 1917. The camp, in the Arlington Heights neighborhood about three miles north of downtown Fort Worth, was established by the United States War Department to give training to the Thirty-sixth Infantry Division.[qv] Local officials expected financial gain and urged that the camp be located at Fort Worth. Including the adjacent rifle range and trench system, the site encompassed 2,186 acres. The camp was named for Alamo defender James Bowie.[qv] Cavalrymen of the First Texas Cavalry guarded the camp during its raising. Although classified as a tent camp, it required much construction to accommodate a division of men. Camp Bowie was opened officially on August 24, 1917, with Maj. Gen. Edwin St. John Greble[qv] of the regular army as commandant. During Greble's absence, the camp was commanded by a number of generals, including Brig. Gen. George Blakely.

The Thirty-sixth Division remained at Camp Bowie for ten months. Training dragged, partly because of epidemics and equipment shortages, but morale never flagged, thanks in part to the cooperation of Fort Worth in tending to the social needs of the troops. Relations between town and camp were remarkably good throughout the camp's existence, though the February 18, 1918, issue of *Pass in Review,* the bimonthly newspaper of camps Bowie and Taliaferro (near Saginaw), announced a base-mandated "purity crusade" designed to close down the brothels that thrived near the camp.

Camp Bowie's greatest average monthly strength was recorded in October 1917 as 30,901. On April 11, 1918, the Thirty-sixth went on parade in the city for the first time. The four-hour event drew crowds estimated at 225,000, making it possibly the biggest parade in Fort Worth's history. For about five months after the departure of the Thirty-sixth for France in July 1918, the camp functioned as an infantry replacement and training facility, with monthly population ranging from 4,164 to 10,527. A total of more than 100,000 men trained at the camp. Greble's retirement in September 1918 began a fairly rapid turnover of commandants that did not end until the camp ceased operation.

Shortly after the Armistice on November 11, 1918, Camp Bowie was designated a demobilization center. By May 31, 1919, it had discharged 31,584 men. The heaviest traffic occurred in June, when it processed thousands of combat veterans of the Thirty-sixth and Ninetieth Texas-Oklahoma divisions. The demobilization having been concluded, Camp Bowie was closed on August 15, 1919. After the camp closed it was quickly converted to a residential area, as builders took advantage of utility hookups left by the army.

BIBLIOGRAPHY: Ben-Hur Chastaine, *Story of the 36th: The Experiences of the 36th Division in the World War* (Oklahoma City: Harlow, 1920). Bernice B. M. Maxfield, *Camp Bowie, Fort Worth* (Fort Worth: Maxfield Foundation, 1975). *Order of Battle of the United States Land Forces in the World War* (3 vols., Washington: GPO, 1931–49; facsimile, Washington: United States Army, 1988). Lonnie J. White, "Major General Edwin St. John Greble," *Military History of Texas and the Southwest* 14 (1976). Lonnie J. White, *Panthers to Arrowheads: The 36th Division in World War I* (Austin: Presidial, 1985). Mack H. Williams, comp., *The News-Tribune in Old Fort Worth* (Fort Worth: *News-Tribune*, 1975).

Lonnie J. White

CAMP BRANCH (Erath County). Camp Branch rises several miles east of Duffau in southeastern Erath County (at 32°06′ N, 97°58′ W) and runs seven miles south to its mouth on Duffau Creek, in extreme northwestern Bosque County (at 32°01′ N, 97°57′ W). The surrounding variable terrain is surfaced by shallow, stony clay loams to deep, fine sandy loams that support juniper, oak, grasses, chaparral, cacti, brush, live oak, mesquite, and grasses.

____ (Tyler County). Camp Branch rises five miles east of Woodville in eastern Tyler County (at 30°49′ N, 94°13′ W) and runs northwest for three miles to its mouth on Lake B. A. Steinhagen[qv] (at 30°50′ N, 94°13′ W). Before the impoundment of water at Town Bluff Dam in 1951, Camp Branch flowed into the Neches River. It crosses flat to rolling terrain with local escarpments, surfaced by deep, fine sandy loams that support pine and oak forests and grasses.

CAMP BRECKENRIDGE. Camp Breckenridge was on Gunsolus (now Gonzales) Creek six miles above its confluence with Hubbard Creek, near Crystal Falls in northern Stephens County. The camp was established by Col. James M. Norris[qv] with half of Capt. John Salmon's company of the Frontier Regiment[qv] on March 21, 1862. Salmon's company, which was organized in February 1862 with slightly more than 100 men, maintained Camp Salmon in southwestern Stephens County and Camp Breckenridge as a deterrent against Indian aggression. However, Capt. R. Whiteside, who commanded at Breckenridge in 1863, stated that the only service satisfactorily rendered was to carry the mail, because "the patrol keeps our horses poor and when we find Indians they can outrun us." Beset by inadequate supplies, low morale, and frequent changing of officers, the camp supplied little real service. A report late in 1863 found only twenty-six out of fifty-four men who should have been in camp: one had been killed, four were absent without leave, and the rest were either sick, on patrol, or hunting for lost horses. The entire Frontier Regiment was mustered into regular Confederate service in the last year of the Civil War.[qv] The camp was used briefly during Reconstruction[qv] by area settlers who took refuge there against Indian raids.

BIBLIOGRAPHY: Loy W. Hartsfield, A History of Stephens County (M.A. thesis, University of Texas, 1929). William Curry Holden, "Frontier Defense in Texas during the Civil War," West Texas Historical Association *Year Book* 4 (1928).

Charles G. Davis

CAMP BULLIS. Camp Bullis, a United States Army camp, occupies 12,000 acres on Interstate Highway 10 and Harry Wurzbach Road seventeen miles northwest of San Antonio in Bexar County. Camp Bullis and Camp Stanley make up the Leon Springs Military Reservation.[qv] Camp Bullis was established in 1917 to train troops in preparation for the growing threat of war in Europe. It was named for Brig. Gen. John Lapham Bullis,[qv] who as a lieutenant led the Black Seminole scouts[qv] during the Indian Wars. During World War I[qv] Camp Bullis provided maneuver areas and small arms and rifle ranges for troops from Fort Sam Houston. No units were stationed at the camp. In all, more than 32,000 acres was owned and leased by the government. By 1918, $1,350,000 had been spent on cantonments and improvements in the Leon Springs Military Reservation. After the war Bullis was used as a site for demobilization. Between 1918 and 1940 the army planned and built permanent facilities at the camp. Construction of the cantonment area was begun in 1930. The old arsenal in downtown San Antonio was moved to Camp Stanley in 1931, and the use of that camp for troop training virtually ceased. In 1931 Camp Bullis received a ten-bed infirmary, an officers' mess, vehicle sheds, a landing field, a post exchange, and a swimming pool, in addition to improved firing ranges.

In 1926 two motion pictures were made on the Camp Bullis reservation. For the filming of *The Rough Riders* troops from the Second Division and Fifth Cavalry were used as extras, and Palmtree Hill was made over to simulate the famous charge up San Juan Hill. For *Wings*, the Academy Award–winning film for 1927, extensive trench works and a faux French village were built and manned by Second Division troops in German and American uniforms.

During the 1920s and 1930s Camp Bullis provided facilities for training the Civilian Military Training Corps, the Civilian Conservation Corps,[qv] the Reserve Officer Training Corps, and the Officer Reserve Corps. With World War II[qv] looming, Congress authorized the call-up of the national guard, and in 1940 the Selective Service Act was passed. A reception center was established at Camp Bullis in September 1940 to process and train draftees. By December 7, 1941, expansion of Fort Sam Houston and Camp Bullis was well under way. The camp served for activation and training of infantry divisions, service schools, a reception center, a prisoner of war camp, and a test bed for tactics and organizational units. From January 1942 through November 1943 the Second, Ninety-fifth, and Eighty-eighth Infantry divisions used Camp Bullis. Smaller units continued to use the camp until 1944. After the war 500,000 soldiers were processed out through the separation centers at Fort Sam Houston and Camp Bullis.

The changing medical needs of the army during and after World War II brought major changes to Fort Sam Houston and Camp Bullis. By 1944 a school for enlisted medical technicians and a basic training course for army nurses was added. The greater portion of Fort Sam Houston became hospital wards and a convalescent center, Brooke Army Medical Center.[qv] Camp Bullis provided field training for small arms and a stretcher obstacle course to train combat medics in the handling of wounded on the battlefield. Camp Bullis was largely on stand-by status until the invasion of South Korea by North Korea in June 1950.

At Camp Bullis the Army Food Service School established a field site, the Detroit Arsenal a tire-testing facility, and the Fourth Army a chemical defense school. The growth of San Antonio and commercial aviation increased air traffic over Camp Bullis, making it necessary to restrict the firing of military mortars and artillery. By 1955 Camp Bullis was providing ranges and training areas for medical units of the regular army, reserve component units, ROTC, and United States Army Reserve schools. Trainers conducted field exercises under realistic conditions, including survival techniques, map reading, and escape and evasion. The trainee loads increased significantly when 40,000 medical personnel prepared for Vietnam duty. The Forty-fifth Medical Unit, Self Contained, Transportable, was the first of these units sent overseas. The unit was a modular facility of inflatable shelters developed at Fort Sam Houston and field-tested at Camp Bullis. A mock Vietnam village was constructed at Camp Bullis to help prepare soldiers for service in Vietnam. In 1965 the air force was conducting weapons training for trainees, air police, and the security service at Camp Bullis.

As the war in Vietnam wound down, so did activity at Camp Bullis. The General Services Administration declared 1,140 acres of the reservation excess in 1972. Dwight D. Eisenhower[qv] Park opened on 323 acres transferred to the city of San Antonio in 1988. Another ninety-four acres was transferred to Bexar County in 1977 to allow the widening of Blanco Road, and forty-seven acres was turned over to the county for a park near Borgfield Drive. These reductions had little effect on the mission of the camp.

In 1977 an Air Force Security Police Training Site, known as Victor Base, was constructed to accommodate the Air Force Security Police Academy. The air force was subsequently the largest single user of Camp Bullis until 1987. The army began emergency deployment readiness exercises at Camp Bullis in 1973, when elements of the 101st Airborne Division from Fort Hood were air-dropped at Camp Bullis. Other exercises were conducted by the 101st and the Eighty-second Airborne in 1980 and 1981. In 1985 the 307th Medical Battalion and a French army medical unit were air-dropped on Camp Bullis. A combat assault landing strip was constructed in 1983. The First Marine Amphibious Force conducted landing operations at the strip in 1986 and 1989.

Unit training at Camp Bullis for the garrison and tenant organization of the Department of Defense has been vigorous and sometimes innovative. Commanders have taken their administrative, overhead, and garrison troops to practice "real soldiering" at Camp Bullis. Since the Vietnam War the post has undergone organizational changes. In 1990 the camp was under the operational control of the Directorate of Plans, Training, Mobilization, and Security at Fort Sam Houston.

BIBLIOGRAPHY: *Camp Bullis: A History of the Leon Springs Military Reservation, 1890–1990* (San Antonio: Fort Sam Houston, 1990). Edward S. Wallace, "General John Lapham Bullis, the Thunderbolt of the Texas Frontier," *Southwestern Historical Quarterly* 54, 55 (April, July 1951).

Art Leatherwood

CAMP CABELL. Camp Cabell, a temporary United States military installation during the Spanish-American War, was located at Dallas and named for William Lewis Cabell,[qv] a Confederate general. The camp was occupied for a time by the Second Texas Volunteer Infantry.

BIBLIOGRAPHY: Dallas *Morning News*, July 19, 1925.

CAMP CAZNEAU. Two camps seem to have been named Camp Cazneau. The first may have been on a site on Onion Creek just southeast of Austin and near the site of Bergstrom Air Force Base[qv] in southeast Travis County. It was occupied by the First Infantry Regiment on March 5, 1840, as they moved from Camp Caldwell to San Antonio. The second Camp Cazneau was 2½ miles east of Round Rock on the south bank of Brushy Creek at the old Double File Crossing, below the Missouri, Kansas and Texas Railroad bridge. It was used by George W. Bonnell[qv] when he led the Travis Guards and Rifles[qv] in expeditions against the Comanche Indians in May and June 1840. The camp also served as the final assembly point for the Texan Santa Fe expedition[qv] in June 1841. The school children of Williamson County erected a monument there in 1925. This site was adjacent to Kenney's Fort.[qv] It may have also been the site of the regular-army Camp Caldwell, 1839–40. The camps were probably named for William L. Cazneau,[qv] a merchant, soldier, and commissary general of the Republic of Texas.[qv]

BIBLIOGRAPHY: H. Bailey Carroll, *The Texan Santa Fe Trail* (Canyon, Texas: Panhandle-Plains Historical Society, 1951). Gerald S. Pierce, *Texas Under Arms: The Camps, Posts, Forts, and Military Towns of the Republic of Texas* (Austin: Encino, 1969).

Art Leatherwood

CAMP CHAMBERS (Falls County). Camp Chambers, a regular army post near the site of present Marlin in Falls County, was established in May or June of 1840. The camp was on the east bank of the Brazos River, two miles north of the State Highway 7 crossing. It was first garrisoned by Capt. John Holiday's Company D, First Infantry regiment. Holiday's company joined Col. William Gordon Cooke's[qv] Military Road[qv] expedition in September, however, and was replaced in November by a detachment under Capt. Adam Clendenin. This detachment was moved to Waco in December but returned to Camp Chambers in January 1841; there the men remained until February or March, when they were withdrawn to Austin for discharge.

BIBLIOGRAPHY: Gerald S. Pierce, *Texas Under Arms: The Camps, Posts, Forts, and Military Towns of the Republic of Texas* (Austin: Encino, 1969).

Thomas W. Cutrer

CAMP CHAMBERS (Victoria County). The first Camp Chambers, on the west bank of Arenosa Creek near the Texana-Victoria road crossing, three miles southeast of the site of present Inez in what is now Victoria County, was the last of a series of encampments of the Army of the Republic of Texas[qv] made on the lower Lavaca and Navidad rivers in 1837. The camp was occupied by Capt. Samuel W. Jordan's[qv] company of permanent volunteers and Capt. James Jevons's company of regulars from August through October or early November. It was named for Gen. Thomas Jefferson Chambers[qv] and commanded by Col. Edwin Morehouse.[qv]

BIBLIOGRAPHY: Gerald S. Pierce, *Texas Under Arms: The Camps, Posts, Forts, and Military Towns of the Republic of Texas* (Austin: Encino, 1969).

Thomas W. Cutrer

CAMP CHARLOTTE. Camp Charlotte was a Civil War–era military installation located on the Middle Concho River below its confluence with Kiowa Creek in northwestern Irion County. It was established in April 1858. The site was forty-five miles west of San Angelo at the intersection of the Butterfield Overland[qv] and El Paso mail routes. The purpose of the camp was the usual one for frontier posts—protecting against Indian depredations, especially those against the overland mail. A stockade measuring 115 by 190 feet encompassed some facilities, but the officers' quarters and guardhouse were built outside the compound. A small settlement grew up around the stage station near the fort. By the middle 1870s the post had only infantry troops, who found it difficult to police the area against Indian raids. William Garrison established a post office in the settlement in 1885, when what later became Irion County was still a part of Tom Green County. The office served the area until it was discontinued and moved to San Angelo in 1899. The site of the camp is in an isolated area of northwest Irion County west of State Highway 163. Little of the camp remained there by the 1970s except some foundations and a historical marker.

BIBLIOGRAPHY: Roscoe P. and Margaret B Conkling, *The Butterfield Overland Mail, 1857–1869* (3 vols., Glendale, California: Clark, 1947). J. Evetts Haley, *Fort Concho and the Texas Frontier* (San Angelo *Standard-Times*, 1952).

Charles G. Davis

CAMP CLARK. Camp Clark, on the south side of the San Marcos River seven miles from San Marcos in Guadalupe County, was one of the instruction camps founded by Governor Edward Clark[qv] in 1861. The Fourth Texas Infantry was mobilized there. Several companies were organized at Camp Clark, where the men were trained for several months before going to active duty in the Civil War.[qv] The Fourth Texas became part of Hood's Texas Brigade.[qv] In 1862 Camp Clark served as a training camp for Col. Peter C. Woods's[qv] Thirty-sixth Texas Cavalry, which was composed mostly of Hays County men. Its officers were Woods, Maj. W. O. Hutchinson, and captains James G. Storey, J. L. Holes, R. Blair, L. C. Schrum, J. K. Stevens, John Crook, and Eugene Millet. The regiment, called the Thirty-second Texas Cavalry by its members, served in the Red River campaign[qv] of 1864. In 1966 a large cotton farm was on the site, and no signs of a camp remained.

BIBLIOGRAPHY: Dudley Richard Dobie, *A Brief History of Hays County and San Marcos, Texas* (San Marcos, 1948). Dudley Richard Dobie, The History of Hays County, Texas (M.A. thesis, University of Texas, 1932).

Tula Townsend Wyatt

CAMP COLLIER. Camp Collier, located at Vaughn's Springs on Clear Creek in southwestern Brown County, was one of sixteen military installations established by the Confederacy in Texas after the Union Army evacuated the desolate stretches of the Texas frontier. To staff the camps for protection against Indian depredations, ten companies of Texas Rangers[qv] were supposed to be activated, but only nine could be enlisted. James M. Norris[qv] was appointed colonel of the Frontier Regiment[qv] and, accompanied by Maj. James E. McCord[qv] and Lt. Col. A. T. Obenchain, made an inspection tour in February 1862 from the Wichita River near its confluence with the Red River to the Rio Grande, selecting sites for prospective outposts. On March 23, 1862, Camp Collier was activated, and Capt. Thomas N. Collier took command.

The Frontier Regiment had an aggregate strength of 1,089 men and officers and 1,347 horses. Each camp was manned by about half a company, assigned to patrol the area between the posts and to cover the entire line at least every other day. But troopers found duty at the ranger posts a hardship; they were sheltered poorly in tents, food was frequently in short supply, and they had to supply their own weapons and horses. Because of poor conditions illnesses were rife. Disciplinary problems also occurred.

The original intent of the Texas legislature was that the regiment be a part of the Confederate Army, but Governor Francis R. Lubbock[qv] consented to the transfer only on the condition that the men not be removed from Texas. The regiment was eventually transferred to the Confederate States as the Forth-sixth Texas Cavalry regiment and garrisoned at Fort Belknap until the regiments were consolidated in March 1864. Because there were no permanent structures at Camp Collier the camp was quickly dismantled. No trace remains.

BIBLIOGRAPHY: Thomas Robert Havins, *Something about Brown: A History of Brown County, Texas* (Brownwood, Texas: Banner Printing, 1958). Frances Richard Lubbock, *Six Decades in Texas* (Austin: Ben C. Jones, 1900; rpt., Austin: Pemberton, 1968). Allan Robert Purcell, The History of the Texas Militia (Ph.D. dissertation, University of Texas at Austin, 1981). Robert B. Roberts, *Encyclopedia of Historic Forts: The Military, Pioneer, and Trading Posts of the United States* (New York: Macmillan, 1988). Bill Winsor, *Texas in the Confederacy* (Hillsboro, Texas: Hill Junior College Press, 1978). Dudley Goodall Wooten, ed., *A Comprehensive History of Texas* (2 vols., Dallas: Scarff, 1898; rpt., Austin: Texas State Historical Association, 1986).

Jeanne F. Lively

CAMP COLORADO. In 1855 Camp Colorado was probably temporarily at a site near what is now Ebony, in Mills County. In August 1856, Troops A and F, Second United States Cavalry,[qv] under Maj. Earl Van Dorn[qv] moved the camp to Mukewater Creek about six miles north of the Colorado River, on the route between Fort Belknap and Fort Mason in Coleman County. Because of sickness among the soldiers, the post was moved in July 1857 about twenty-two miles north to Jim Ned Creek. Commanders who succeeded Van Dorn included Edmund Kirby Smith, Lawrence S. (Sul) Ross, John Bell Hood, and Fitzhugh Lee.[qqv] Robert E. Lee[qv] visited the camp at least twice on tours of inspection. From 1857 to 1861 Camp Colorado was the center of Coleman County's settlements. The camp's buildings were of adobe[qv] with shingled roofs and pine-plank floors; the lumber, doors, and windows were hauled by ox team from East Texas. Outside communication was through a post office and a telegraph line along the Wire Road between the camp and army headquarters at San Antonio. People settled at all of the nearby waterholes. In 1857, J. C. Mullins, a graduate of Yale University, settled east of the camp and taught school under an elm tree on the post.

The camp was abandoned on February 26, 1861, by order of Gen. David E. Twiggs.[qv] With the exception of Lt. George B. Cosby, the men stationed at the camp all went into Confederate service. After the departure of United States troops, Capt. W. Pitts and later Capt. James Monroe Holmsley[qv] commanded companies of state troops at the camp until early in 1862. From 1862 to 1864 Capt. J. J. Callan and a company of Texas Rangers[qv] occupied the post. Texas state troops occupied the post until the end of the Civil War. Camp Colorado was not regarrisoned by United States troops after its evacuation by the Confederates. Fourteen years after the Civil War an Englishman, H. H. Sackett, purchased the land in the vicinity of the old post. The headquarters building was dismantled, and the stone was used to build a combination store and residence. Leaving the guardhouse intact, Sackett attached one wall of the residence to it. A stretch of stone corral fence remains, and a quarter of a mile to the east is the post cemetery.

BIBLIOGRAPHY: Beatrice Grady Gay, *Into the Setting Sun: A History of Coleman County* (Coleman?, Texas, 1936?). Thomas R. Havins, "The Texas Mounted Regiment at Camp Colorado," *Texas Military History* 4 (Summer 1964). Joseph Carroll McConnell, *West Texas Frontier* (Vol. 1, Jacksboro, Texas, 1933; Vol. 2, Palo Pinto, Texas, 1939). Robert B. Roberts, *Encyclopedia of Historic Forts: The Military, Pioneer, and Trading Posts of the United States* (New York: Macmillan, 1988).

Beatrice Grady Gay

CAMP COOK. Camp Cook was near the Medina River thirteen miles southwest of San Antonio, probably at the crossing of the San Antonio–Presidio del Rio Grande road. It is believed to have been a rendezvous and headquarters camp for Gen. Alexander Somervell's[qv] Army of the Southwest, which occupied the camp between November 19 and November 23, 1842.

BIBLIOGRAPHY: Gerald S. Pierce, *Texas Under Arms: The Camps, Posts, Forts, and Military Towns of the Republic of Texas* (Austin: Encino, 1969). *Art Leatherwood*

CAMP COOKE. Camp Cooke was on the Colorado River near the mouth of Waller Creek, now in Austin, Travis County. The camp was one of the assembly sites for volunteers of the Texan Santa Fe expedition[qv] in May and June 1841. It was almost certainly named for William Gordon Cooke,[qv] a civilian commissioner on the expedition. The camp was occupied as late as June 11, 1841.

BIBLIOGRAPHY: Gerald S. Pierce, *Texas Under Arms: The Camps, Posts, Forts, and Military Towns of the Republic of Texas* (Austin: Encino, 1969). *Art Leatherwood*

CAMP COOPER. Camp Cooper was on the Clear Fork of the Brazos River seven miles north of the site of present Fort Griffin State Historical Park[qv] in south central Throckmorton County. It was established by the Texas legislature in January 1856 and named for United States Army adjutant general Samuel Cooper. Its mission was to protect the frontier and to monitor the nearby Comanche Indian reservation. The area had been a campsite for three companies of the Fifth Infantry in 1851. The site was subsequently surveyed by Capt. Randolph B. Marcy and Robert S. Neighbors.[qqv] The post was founded by Col. Albert Sidney Johnston[qv] in January 1856 and became headquarters for four companies of the Second United States Cavalry[qv] under the command of Lt. Col. Robert E. Lee.[qv] This was Lee's first command of a fort. He remained in charge for fifteen months, from April 9, 1856, until July 22, 1857. Captains under his command included Earl Van Dorn[qv] and Theodore O'Hara.

Although the camp initially had adequate military stores, it was plagued by severe weather, insects, dust, and irregular supply trains. Rattlesnakes were constant visitors, and Lee kept one as a pet. When he left the camp in 1857 for San Antonio, Maj. George H. Thomas[qv] took over. Thomas commanded the Cimarron expedition into Northwest Texas that same year. Troops from Camp Cooper participated in numerous campaigns and police actions against hostile Indians, including the pursuit of Peta Nocona's[qv] Comanches that resulted in the death of Peta Nocona and the recapture of Cynthia Ann Parker.qv Local unrest declined after 1859, when the Comanche reservation was dissolved and the Indians were removed from the area. During this same time Lt. Joseph F. Minter made a sketch of Cooper showing stone and picket buildings for the officers' quarters, hospital, and commissary. Enlisted men and the regimental band were quartered in barracks with shingle roofs and walls of mud bricks. A post office operated at the camp from March 31 to October 1860, but the coming of the Civil Warqv brought an end to the camp's usefulness. The post was officially abandoned on February 21, 1861, and Capt. S. D. Carpenter surrendered the site to Col. W. C. Dalrympleqv four days later. By March all military activity at Camp Cooper had ceased.

BIBLIOGRAPHY: R. C. Crane, "Robert E. Lee's Expedition in the Upper Brazos and Colorado Country," West Texas Historical Association *Year Book* 13 (1937). M. L. Crimmins, "Camp Cooper and Fort Griffin, Texas," West Texas Historical Association *Year Book* 17 (1941). M. L. Crimmins, "Robert E. Lee in Texas: Letters and Diary," West Texas Historical Association *Year Book* 8 (1932). Tom Crum, "Camp Cooper, A Different Look," West Texas Historical Association *Year Book* 68 (1992). Claude W. Dooley, comp., *Why Stop?* (Odessa: Lone Star Legends, 1978; 2d ed., with Betty Dooley and the Texas Historical Commission, Houston: Lone Star, 1985). Robert W. Frazer, *Forts of the West* (Norman: University of Oklahoma Press, 1965). Carl Coke Rister, *Robert E. Lee in Texas* (Norman: University of Oklahoma Press, 1946).
Charles G. Davis

CAMP CORPUS CHRISTI. Camp Corpus Christi, at Corpus Christi, was established in November 1850, when Lt. Col. J. J. Abercrombie rented quarters there for two companies of the Fifth Infantry. On August 8, 1851, Maj. G. R. Paul moved his troops thirty miles inland from Corpus Christi to a location that was healthful but had bad water and no permanent building material. On November 26, 1851, the camp was manned by two companies of the Seventh Infantry, a total of eighty-five men. Corpus Christi became headquarters under Persifor F. Smithqv in 1852 and remained such until 1855, when headquarters were moved back to San Antonio.

BIBLIOGRAPHY: Arrie Barrett, Federal Military Outposts in Texas, 1845–1861 (M.A. thesis, University of Texas, 1927).

CAMP COUNTY. Camp County (D-21), the third smallest Texas county, comprises 203 square miles of the East Texas timberlands, an area that is heavily forested with a great variety of softwoods and hardwoods, especially pine, cypress, and oak. The terrain ranges from nearly level to hilly; the largest portion of the county is undulating to rolling. The county is located in northeastern Texas, forty miles from the state's eastern boundary and fifty miles from the state's northern boundary. Pittsburg, the county seat and the county's largest town, is located on U.S. Highway 271, sixty miles southwest of Texarkana and ninety miles northeast of Dallas. The county center lies at 32°58′ north latitude and 94°57′ west longitude. Two railroads cross Camp County and intersect in Pittsburg. The St. Louis Southwestern Railway, constructed as the Texas and St. Louis Railway in the late 1870s, crosses the county from north to south, and the Louisiana and Arkansas Railway, constructed in the late 1870s as the East Line and Red River Railway, crosses the county from east to west. The elevation ranges from 250 to 450 feet above mean sea level. The county is drained by Big Cypress Creek, which formed the northern and eastern boundaries of the county when it was organized. There are six major lakes within eighteen miles of Pittsburg that are reputed to be among the best bass-fishing lakes in Texas. By 1983 Lake Bob Sandlin and Lake O' The Pines had subsumed more than half of the creekbed along the boundaries of the county. The soils in Camp County are predominantly light-colored loam with loam and clay subsoils. Between 31 and 40 percent of the land in the county is considered prime farmland. Mineral resources include ceramic clay, industrial sand, oil, gas, and lignite coal. In 1982, 435,159 barrels of oil and 4,322,947,000 cubic feet of gas-well gas were produced. Pine and hardwood production in 1981 totaled 2,168,053 cubic feet. Temperatures range from an average high of 94° F in July to an average low of 30° in January. Rainfall averages forty-four inches a year, and the growing season extends for an average of 240 days.

The area of Camp County has been the site of human habitation for several thousand years, although perhaps not continuously. Artifacts have been recovered from sites to the north in Titus County that date from the Archaic Period (ca. 5000 B.C.–A.D. 500). During historic times, the earliest occupants of the county were the Caddo Indians, an agricultural people with a highly developed culture. During the 1820s and 1830s, American settlements in other parts of Texas caused a number of groups of Indians associated with other tribes such as the Creek, the Choctaw, and the Cherokee to settle in the area. But by the 1840s the Indians had generally been displaced by settlers.

The time of earliest European exploration of the area can not be conclusively determined. If one of the northernmost of the numerous conflicting route interpretations of the Moscoso expeditionqv in 1542 is correct, then that group may have passed through the county. In 1719 the French founded Le Poste des Cadodaquiousqv in what is now Bowie County. Although the French occupied the post for more than fifty years, little is known about their activities. They may have explored as far to the southwest as Camp County.

Anglo settlement began in the late 1830s, with most of the early settlers coming from the southern states of Georgia, Alabama, and Tennessee. The earliest communities in the area were Pittsburg, near the center, and Lilly and Pine, in the southwestern and south central part. There were probably some early settlers along Big Cypress Creek in the northern portion also, but no information is available about their activities. The first post office, established in 1848, was located in the community known now as Pine, and was called Pine Tree. In 1855 a post office was also established at Pittsburg, and by 1860 this town had become the most important supply center for northern Upshur County farmers.

These early, predominantly southern settlers brought with them their southern heritage and institutions. Most of the early settlers were Protestants, especially Baptists and Methodists. A number of the settlers were also slaveholders, who used the fertile soils of the county to grow the two most important southern crops, cotton and corn. Although precise figures are not available, the proportion of the population who were blacks held as slaves probably exceeded the 1860 statewide average of about 30 percent.

Camp County was separated from Upshur County in 1874 and named for John Lafayette Camp,qv who was serving as state senator from Upshur County and presented the petitions that led to the action of the legislature. A county seat election was held, and Pittsburg won with 500 votes. Leesburg, to the west, received 228, and Center Point, in the southeastern part, received sixty-nine. Following the election, a courthouse was constructed of locally manufactured brick on a lot donated by William Pitts. Since the 1874 election the choice of county seat has never been contested.

The 1880 census provided the first population figures for Camp County. In 1880 the county had a population of 5,931, with 3,085 whites and 2,845 blacks. For the next ten years the black population of the county grew at a faster rate than the white, and in 1890 there were 3,328 whites and 3,296 blacks. From that point the white population grew at a faster rate than the black until 1920, when the 4,577 African Americansqv present constituted about 41 percent of the total population of 11,103. Between 1920 until 1960, with the exception of a modest gain between 1930 and 1940, the population of the county declined, with black population declining at a faster rate than the white. By 1960 blacks constituted about 38 percent of a total population of 7,849. From 1960 through 1980 the total population of the county began to rise, but the black population of the county continued to decline. In 1980 the 2,369 blacks constituted approximately 25 percent of the total population of 9,275, and in 1990, 24 percent of the county's 9,904 inhabitants were black.

When voters went to the polls to select the county seat in 1874, they also elected the first county officials. Most of those elected were Republicans. As in most Texas counties controlled by the Republican party[qv] during this Reconstruction[qv] period, the votes for Republican candidates came almost exclusively from black voters, while the candidates themselves were generally white. By 1876 Democrats had regained control of the county. On the local level they were generally successful in maintaining control; in fact, by the 1890s the Republicans no longer fielded a county ticket. But in state and national elections, Republicans waged vigorous campaigns. The vote was generally close through the nineteenth and into the first years of the twentieth century, particularly when third-party efforts divided traditionally Democratic voters. In the 1888 national election, for example, the Democrats won by just thirty-eight votes out of 1,232 votes cast. In 1892, 1896, and 1900, the Republicans carried the county in most state and all national races, as the People's party[qv] waged a generally unsuccessful campaign against the Democratic party for control of the county.

Beginning with the imposition of the poll tax in 1902, the state government implemented a series of procedures that effectively limited black political participation. In Camp County these measures meant that the Democratic hold on the county was strengthened. The measures, coupled with the apparent certainty of a Democratic victory, also acted to keep many whites, particularly poorer ones, away from the polls. In the 1900 general election, 1,596 votes were recorded, while in 1904, although the county population was increasing, only 895 county residents voted.

In the late 1940s the impediments to participation by blacks and poor whites were gradually lifted, beginning with the end of the white primary.[qv] Although the population of the county was declining, voter turnout jumped from 1,488 in 1948 to 2,487 in 1952. Through all these changes, the county has generally remained Democratic. From 1900 to 1992, the Democratic presidential candidate has carried the county in every election except the 1972 and 1984 elections, when Richard Nixon and Ronald Reagan respectively carried the county.

Although Pittsburg had become an important supply center for area farmers by the 1870s, at its beginning, Camp County was largely rural and agricultural. At the time of the 1880 census, most residents lived and worked on the county's 607 farms. For the next sixty years the economic base of the county was agriculture. During that period cotton was the principal cash crop, and for most of this period corn was the principal food crop. From 1880 until 1940 census returns indicated that at least two-thirds of the harvested cropland of the county were planted in these two crops. Although cotton provided the county's major source of income, it did not bring prosperity for most of the farmers. From 1880 until 1930 each census recorded a higher percentage of farmers who did not own the land they farmed. In 1880, 37 percent were tenants. By 1930, 60 percent of farmers fell into that category.

Camp County was hit hard by the Great Depression,[qv] which actually began for most southern farmers in the 1920s. Between 1920 and 1930, although the average size of the county's farms had increased from sixty-one to eighty-six acres, the average value had fallen from $3,253 to $1,722. The programs of the New Deal provided relief that ameliorated the worst effects of the depression for many of the county's residents. In 1933, for example, cotton-reduction payments to county farmers from the Agricultural Adjustment Administration[qv] totaled a little over $56,000. In January 1934, 832 Camp County families were receiving commodities from the local welfare office.

The depression signaled the beginning of the end of a number of long-term Camp County economic and social trends. One of these was population growth. Every census had recorded a larger population from 1880 through 1920. During the decade of the 1920s, though, the population declined for the first time, and, although it rose slightly during the 1930s (from 10,063 to 10,285), it subsequently fell steadily until 1960. The long-term trend in tenant farming was also reversed, beginning in the 1930s. The 1940 census was the first to record a decline in the percentage of farmers in the county who did not own the land they farmed, as the percentage of tenant farmers dropped to just under 50 percent. The initial stages of this process were hard on tenants, as they were forced off the land by governmental policies that paid farmers to remove cotton lands from cultivation. During the 1940s, however, tenants generally continued to desert the land because of other opportunities, offered by the World War II[qv] production boom and afterward by urban jobs produced as the state's industrial base expanded. By 1959 only 15 percent of the county's farmers were tenants.

The agricultural depression and the programs of the New Deal designed to deal with it also signaled the beginning of the end of cotton culture[qv] in Camp County. Between 1930 and 1940 the number of acres farmers planted in cotton declined from a little over 28,600 to a just over 12,700 acres. The decline continued, and by 1969 there were no cotton fields in the county. Cotton was replaced by livestock rather than by other crops. By 1982, 97 percent of the county's income from agriculture was generated by livestock and livestock products. Most of it came from hens, pullets, eggs, and commercial broiler production. Mechanization and the increasing emphasis on livestock also resulted in fewer and larger farms in the county. In 1920 the county had 1,709 farms. By 1959 the number had dropped to 537. In 1982 the 413 farms averaged 169 acres each.

The decline in the number of farmers led to a decline in county population. By 1960 it had fallen from the 1920 high of 11,103 to 7,849. A more dramatic decline was probably prevented by events in Pittsburg, the county seat. As the state began to industrialize, Pittsburg participated in the trend. In 1930, 197 county residents had been employed in manufacturing, and most of the industry was in Pittsburg. By 1947 the number employed in manufacturing had jumped to 507. Many of these jobs may have been in industries related to the war effort that had just ended, however, for by 1958 the number had dropped to 272. Still, the town had established an industrial base that continued to grow. By 1972, 700 county residents were employed in manufacturing. Although the number has continued to grow, census figures have been withheld since 1972 to protect the privacy of Camp County manufacturers. The largest industry in the county in the 1970s and early 1980s was Pilgrim Industries, a poultry-processing company that employed more than 500 people in 1976.

As Pittsburg's manufacturing base expanded, so did its population. In 1890 it was 1,203, or about 18 percent of the county's total population. By 1920 the number had increased to 2,540, a little less than 23 percent of the county's total population. In 1980 the population of the town had grown to 4,245. That figure represented nearly 46 percent of the county's total population. Although Pittsburg continued to serve as a supply and shipping point for area agriculturists, the economy of the town no longer revolved around those functions.

The changing nature of employment opportunities has led to an increasing emphasis on the importance of formal education. In 1897 most of the county's school-aged children attended one-room, ungraded schools. Children generally walked to school, so districts were small. Small districts, and the traditional policy of rigidly segregated schools, meant that the county's limited resources were divided and strained. None of the county's thirty-four common school districts in 1897 contained school libraries, and only one had a graded school. School terms varied from a low of forty-nine days to a high of 140. Most children in the county quit without ever attending high school. By 1937 improvements in transportation had led to consolidation, and the number of school districts in the county had dropped to seventeen. All of the schools were graded, and school terms varied from a low of 110 days to a high of 179 days. More than 600 pupils were attending high school that year. Still, resources were inadequate, and fewer than one-third of the county's teachers had received a bachelor's or higher degree. By 1955 all of the school districts in the county had been consolidated into the Pittsburg Independent School District. In 1980 less than twenty percent of all children between the ages of sixteen and nineteen had dropped out of school before graduating from high school, and for the first time in its history, more than 50 percent of the county's residents over the age of twenty-five had graduated from high school.

BIBLIOGRAPHY: Hollie Max Cummings, An Administrative Survey of the Schools of Camp County, Texas (M.A. thesis, University of Texas, 1937). Artemesia L. B. Spencer, *The Camp County Story* (Fort Worth: Branch-Smith, 1974). *Cecil Harper, Jr.*

CAMP CREEK (Archer County). Camp Creek rises two miles northwest of Mankins in northwest Archer County (at 33°45′ N, 98°50′ W) and runs north for 9½ miles to its mouth on the Wichita River, just north of Kadane in southwestern Wichita County (at 33°52′ N, 98°51′ W). The stream is intermittent in its upper reaches. It traverses flat to rolling terrain surfaced by sandy and clay loams that support hardwoods and grasses. For most of the county's history the Camp Creek area has been used as range and crop land.

____ (Coleman County). Camp Creek rises four miles north of Rockwood in southern Coleman County (at 31°34′ N, 99°25′ W) and runs southeast for twelve miles, through Rockwood and Whon, to its mouth on Home Creek (at 31°30′ N, 99°16′ W), near its junction with the Colorado River. The surrounding level terrain, at 1,450 feet above sea level, is surfaced by deep loam that supports grasses, shrubs, and some hardwoods.

____ (Cooke County). Camp Creek rises five miles northwest of Muenster in north central Cooke County (at 33°43′ N, 97°26′ W) and runs north for eight miles to its mouth on the Red River, two miles northeast of Bulcher (at 33°49′ N, 97°25′ W). It crosses flat to rolling terrain surfaced by deep, fine sandy loam that supports hardwood forests and conifers along the banks of the creek.

____ (Falls County). Camp Creek rises three miles southeast of Belfalls in southwestern Falls County (at 31°09′ N, 97°11′ W) and runs southeast for ten miles, through Falls and Bell counties, to its mouth on Big Elm Creek, near the Milam county line (at 30°58′ N, 97°07′ W). The surrounding nearly level to sloping terrain is surfaced by clay and is used predominantly for agriculture.

____ (Fayette County). Camp Creek rises one mile northeast of Lake Fayette in northeastern Fayette County (at 29°57′ N, 96°43′ W) and runs northeast for four miles, past the Halimecek Cemetery on Farm Road 1291, to its mouth on Clear Creek (at 29°58′ N, 96°40′ W). It crosses gently sloping to rolling terrain surfaced by moderately deep sandy and clay loam. The area is used for agriculture and pasture.

____ (Houston County). Camp Creek rises two miles west of Easley Cemetery in extreme northeastern Houston County (at 31°33′ N, 95°13′ W) and runs southeast for 6½ miles to its mouth on the Neches River, five miles north of Plain (at 31°31′ N, 95°07′ W). The creek is intermittent in its upper reaches. It runs across flat terrain surfaced by clay and sandy loam that supports water-tolerant hardwoods, conifers, and grasses.

____ (Johnson County). Camp Creek rises 3½ miles southwest of Bono in southwestern Johnson County (at 32°19′ N, 97°33′ W) and runs south and then southwest 9½ miles to its mouth on the Brazos River, 1½ miles north of Highland (at 32°11′ N, 97°34′ W). The creek is intermittent in its upper reaches and runs through Cleburne State Park in its middle reaches. Freeland is on its lower banks 1½ miles north of its mouth. The surrounding variable terrain is surfaced by shallow, stony clay loams that support juniper and oak trees, chaparral, cacti, and grasses.

____ (Kent County). Camp Creek rises at the meeting of two forks two miles northeast of Clairemont in central Kent County (at 33°10′ N, 100°39′ W). The South Fork of Camp Creek rises one mile east of Clairemont (at 33°10′ N, 100°44′ W) and runs east until it meets the North Fork. The North Fork rises four miles northeast of Clairemont (at 33°12′ N, 100°42′ W) and runs southeast three miles until it meets the South Fork. Camp Creek then runs east one mile to its mouth on the Salt Fork of the Brazos River (at 33°10′ N, 100°38′ W). The surrounding moderately steep slopes and locally high relief are surfaced by shallow to moderately deep silt loam that supports mesquite and grasses.

____ (Lipscomb County). Camp Creek, fed by Camp Springs, rises five miles east of Higgins in southeastern Lipscomb County (at 36°07′ N, 100°04′ W) and runs north for ten miles to its mouth on Wolf Creek, fifteen miles east of Lipscomb (at 36°15′ N, 100°05′ W). The stream was on Elga Page's ranch and probably was an Indian campsite. The eastern branch of the Jones and Plummer Trail[qv] crossed it, and the headquarters of the Box T Ranch[qv] was established on it in 1885. The terrain varies from flat to rolling, with some local escarpments, and is surfaced by deep, fine sandy loam that supports mesquite and grasses.

BIBLIOGRAPHY: *A History of Lipscomb County, Texas, 1876–1976* (Lipscomb, Texas: Lipscomb County Historical Survey Committee, 1976). Clinton Leon Paine, The History of Lipscomb County (M.A. thesis, West Texas State College, 1941).

____ (McCulloch County). Camp Creek rises three miles northeast of Calf Creek and just south of U.S. Highway 190 in southwestern McCulloch County (at 31°02′ N, 99°27′ W) and runs southeast for 10½ miles to its mouth on the San Saba River, seven miles southwest of Camp San Saba (at 30°58′ N, 99°22′ W). It crosses flat terrain with local deep depressions and rolling prairie, surfaced by shallow, stony soils and clay loams that support oak, juniper, and mesquite.

____ (Robertson County). Camp Creek rises four miles west of Franklin in central Robertson County (at 31°02′ N, 96°25′ W) and runs east for fifteen miles to its mouth on the Navasota River, near the Leon county line (at 31°02′ N, 96°15′ W). The creek is dammed four miles east of its mouth to form Camp Creek Lake, a reservoir for water conservation and flood control. The lake stores approximately 8,400 acre-feet of water and is surrounded by nearly level terrain surfaced by sandy loams that support post oaks and grasses.

____ (Scurry County). Camp Creek rises seven miles east of Snyder in east central Scurry County (at 32°44′ N, 100°48′ W) and runs east and then north for thirteen miles to its mouth on Rough Creek, three miles west of the Fisher county line and two miles northwest of Green Mountain (at 32°50′ N, 100°43′ W). The creek was named either for Judge A. J. Camp, an early settler in the area, or from its use as a campsite by early travelers and settlers. It runs through sparsely settled ranchland characterized by moderately steep slopes with locally high relief and silt loams that support mesquite and grasses.

BIBLIOGRAPHY: Ranch Headquarters Association. Snyder Unit, *Early Ranching and Water Sources in West Texas* (Snyder, Texas, 1972).

____ (Washington County). Camp Creek rises 1½ miles south of Burton in southwest Washington County (at 30°10′ N, 96°37′ W) and runs south for seven miles to its mouth on the West Fork of Mill Creek, three miles southwest of Greenvine (at 30°06′ N, 96°36′ W). It runs through gentle to moderately steep slopes surfaced by clay that supports grass.

____ (Young County). Camp Creek rises one mile west of the Olney Municipal Airport in northwest Young County (at 33°21′ N, 98°50′ W) and runs west for ten miles to its mouth on the Brazos River, just east of the Throckmorton county line (at 33°19′ N, 98°57′ W). It crosses rolling hills surfaced by clay and sandy loams that support water-resistant hardwoods and grasses.

CAMP CREEK LAKE. Camp Creek Lake is on Camp Creek, a tributary of the Navasota River, in the Brazos River basin thirteen miles southeast of Franklin in Robertson County (at 31°04′ N, 96°17′ W). The lake was developed by the Camp Creek Water Company. Construction began in August 1948 and was completed on January 3, 1949. The reservoir has a capacity of 8,550 acre-feet and a surface area of

750 acres at an elevation of 310 feet above mean sea level. It is fed by a drainage area of forty square miles, the site of a retirement community with more than 200 residents. The surrounding nearly level to slightly sloping terrain is surfaced by loam that supports grassland and post oaks.

BIBLIOGRAPHY: Ralph A. Wurbs, *Reservoir Operation in Texas* (College Station: Texas Water Resources Institute, Texas A&M University, 1985).

James L. Hailey

CAMP CROCKETT. Camp Crockett, named for Alamo defender David Crockett,[qv] became the main encampment and headquarters of the Army of the Republic of Texas[qv] following its removal from Camp Bowie[qv] in mid-June 1837. Camp Crockett was somewhere in central Jackson County, probably on the Navidad River near Camp Bowie and just to the south or southwest of the site of present Edna. The camp was commanded by Col. H. R. A. Wiggington, Second Regiment, Permanent Volunteers, from its establishment until it was abandoned in July or August, when the troops were transferred to Camp Chambers.[qv]

BIBLIOGRAPHY: Gerald S. Pierce, *Texas Under Arms: The Camps, Posts, Forts, and Military Towns of the Republic of Texas* (Austin: Encino, 1969).

Thomas W. Cutrer

CAMP CURETON. Camp Cureton was established on March 17, 1862, where the Gainesville–Fort Belknap road crossed the West Fork of the Trinity River southeast of Archer City. It was one of a number of posts set up by the Confederate Army to restrict Indian incursions. The camp was manned by half the men of the Frontier Regiment[qv] company of Capt. J. J. (Jack) Cureton,[qv] for whom it was named. It had long buildings for the rangers and a rock-fence corral for the horses. The camp was closed by March 1864, when the regiment was concentrated at Fort Belknap. All that remained in 1990 was the corner rocks and the base of a chimney. In 1963 a memorial to Camp Cureton was placed on the Archer County Courthouse lawn in Archer City.

BIBLIOGRAPHY: J. Evetts Haley, *Charles Goodnight* (Norman: University of Oklahoma Press, 1949). William Curry Holden, Frontier Problems and Movements in West Texas, 1846–1900 (Ph.D. dissertation, University of Texas, 1928). J. Marvin Hunter, *Trail Drivers of Texas* (2 vols., San Antonio: Jackson Printing, 1920, 1923; 4th ed., Austin: University of Texas Press, 1985). Jack Loftin, *Trails Through Archer* (Burnet, Texas: Nortex, 1979).

CAMP DAVIS. Camp Davis, four miles from the junction of White Oak Creek and the Pedernales River in Gillespie County, was established in March 1862 by James M. Norris[qv] as a ranger station for the Frontier Regiment.[qv] It was one of the sixteen Frontier Regiment posts set up in Central Texas along a generally north-south axis from Camp Cureton on the Trinity River to Rio Grande Station[qv] (formerly Fort Duncan) on the Rio Grande. The camp, manned by members of H. T. Davis's company, sent men on scout duty, probably until the consolidation of the regiment in March 1864.

BIBLIOGRAPHY: William Curry Holden, Frontier Problems and Movements in West Texas, 1846–1900 (Ph.D. dissertation, University of Texas, 1928).

CAMP DIX. Camp Dix, a Confederate outpost established by James M. Norris[qv] on April 4, 1862, was at the crossing of the San Antonio–Eagle Pass road and the Frio River, a spot on the river known as Black Waterhole, seven miles east of Uvalde. The camp was a Frontier Regiment[qv] post under the command of Capt. John J. Dix, Jr.[qv] The road had become a vital commercial route to Mexico for the Confederate cause when the Union forces gained control of the entry points to Mexico along the lower Rio Grande. Camp Dix was one of several encampments established to protect Confederate export wagon trains on their way to Mexico. It was abandoned after the consolidation of the Frontier Regiment in March 1864.

BIBLIOGRAPHY: Marker Files, Texas Historical Commission, Austin.

Ruben E. Ochoa

CAMP DRUM. Camp Drum, a United States military post at Zapata on the Rio Grande, was established in 1852 and abandoned the same year. About the time of its establishment, C. H. Tyler, of the Second United States Dragoons, arrived with orders to establish a camp and call it Camp Bugle. The officer of the Fourth United States Artillery, already on the site, secured an order from another authority to use the name Camp Drum. The abandonment may have been caused by local friction, the reduced fear of border disturbances, or the westward movement of the frontier.

BIBLIOGRAPHY: *Texas Almanac*, 1936. WPA Writers' Program, *Texas: A Guide* (New York: Hastings House, 1940; rev. ed. 1969).

CAMP ELIZABETH. Camp Elizabeth was nine miles northwest of the site of present Sterling City in central Sterling County. It was first established as a camp for Texas Rangers[qv] about 1853. In 1874 it was taken over by Fort Concho and used mainly as an outpost hospital. Fort Concho was activated from 1867 to 1874, when an unusual number of Indian depredations were taking place in West Texas. The camp had officers' quarters, a hospital, a farrier shop, and rock corrals, as remembered by early surveyor W. F. Kellis, who made a diagram of it. The soldiers slept in tents near the officers' quarters. Water was obtained from a nearby spring on the North Concho River. The parade ground between the camp and the river seems to have been used to teach horsemanship. During the time the camp was in operation several black troopers were stationed at the post. Camp Elizabeth was abandoned intact in 1886. Later the buildings were razed by ranchers who objected to the unsavory characters frequenting the place. A commemorative monument was later erected by the state of Texas at the presumed site.

BIBLIOGRAPHY: Beverly Daniels, ed., *Milling around Sterling County* (Canyon, Texas: Staked Plains, 1976). Harold Schoen, comp., *Monuments Erected by the State of Texas to Commemorate the Centenary of Texas Independence* (Austin: Commission of Control for Texas Centennial Celebrations, 1938).

CAMP FANNIN. Camp Fannin, an infantry-replacement training center of World War II,[qv] was located ten miles northeast of Tyler. The reservation was a wooded, hilly site of more than 14,000 acres named for James Walker Fannin, Jr.[qv] Construction was begun on December 1, 1942; Col. John A. Robenson assumed command on March 16, 1943; and the camp headquarters, 361st Service Command Unit, was activated on April 25, 1943. The replacement-training center was activated on May 29, 1943, and the first trainees arrived in June. Formal dedication of the camp was held on September 6, 1943. Colonel Robenson was succeeded as commanding officer by Lt. Col. Charles H. Brammel on August 4, 1943. Maj. Sam H. Burchard commanded the prisoner-of-war camp located at the station. Troop capacity at the height of war operations was 18,680, and the camp had hospital beds for 1,074. All except the cantonment was declared surplus on January 19, 1946. At the end of World War II in 1945, the camp was converted to a separation center for the discharge of soldiers. Two years later, some of the buildings were placed on the new campus of Tyler Junior College. The abandoned base became the East Texas State Tuberculosis Sanatorium the following year.

BIBLIOGRAPHY: Donald W. Whisenhunt, comp., *Chronological History of Smith County* (Tyler, Texas: Smith County Historical Society, 1983). Albert Woldert, *A History of Tyler and Smith County* (San Antonio: Naylor, 1948).

CAMP FELDER. Camp Felder, a Confederate camp for Union prisoners, was located near Chappell Hill in Washington County. It was named for Gabriel Felder,[qv] owner of the Brazos River bottomland where the camp was set up. Previously the site had been a Methodist campground. In September 1864 Union prisoners of war who had been transferred from Camp Groce to a camp in the Bellville vicinity were moved to Camp Felder to avoid a fever epidemic. Col. Clayton C. Gillespie was commander. The camp was on low ground at the foot of the hill; a Confederate cavalry guard and its horses stayed in sheds on the hill above. Apparently prisoners suffered a high mortality rate at Camp Felder and were returned to Camp Groce.

BIBLIOGRAPHY: Mr. and Mrs. Nate Winfield, *All Our Yesterdays: A Brief History of Chappell Hill* (Waco: Texian Press, 1969).

Carole E. Christian

CAMP FORD. In 1862 the Confederacy located a conscript-training camp four miles northeast of Tyler. The installation became known as Camp Ford, in honor of Col. John S. (Rip) Ford.[qv] On July 21, 1863, the Trans-Mississippi Department ordered the establishment of a prison camp at Camp Ford and transferred the prisoners of war then located at Shreveport, Louisiana, to Tyler for confinement. These and other POWs sent to Tyler encamped in the open under guard until November 1863, when reports of a plan to escape caused alarm among the local citizenry and the Confederates in charge. Accordingly, a stockade was built enclosing an area of two to four acres. A large spring ran along the south wall of the stockade and served as a water supply for the prison camp. The prisoners were required to improvise their own shelter, which they fashioned out of logs and other primitive building materials. Until the spring of 1864, morale among the prisoners at Camp Ford was passable, and the ranking federal officers maintained a decent sense of order. Enterprising prisoners made goods for use and sale, including crude furniture, clay dishes, woven baskets, brooms, clothing, and other useful articles. Some of these were traded or sold to local citizens for food and clothes.

Living conditions at Camp Ford became deplorable in April 1864, when the population was suddenly tripled by the addition of about 3,000 prisoners captured at the defeat of the Union army in Arkansas and the battles at Mansfield and Pleasant Hill, Louisiana. The stockade area was doubled in size in an effort to accommodate this influx. The 4,725 inmates were overcrowded and critically short of food, shelter, and clothing. Their plight was desperate for several months, until major exchanges of prisoners in July and October 1864 alleviated somewhat the shocking conditions that had prevailed. For the rest of the war the Confederates encountered great difficulties in supplying adequate rations to both prisoners and guards at Camp Ford. Sometimes the standard daily pint of meal and pound of beef per prisoner was down to a quarter pound of each, depending upon the supply available to the Confederate commissary department. Beginning with the overcrowding in April 1864, the quality of the shelters deteriorated. Nearby timber was less plentiful, and shelters had to be constructed quickly. The prisoners improvised all sorts of crude shelters ranging from brush arbors to blanket tents. Some simply dug holes in the ground for protection from the cold winds. A popular form of shelter was called a "shebang," a burrow into a hillside covered by a crude A-shaped framework made of poles, sticks, and clay to protect the entrance. The majority of the prisoners required the clothes that they were wearing when captured to see them through their captivity. The acute shortage of clothing was due to a lack of manufacturing in the South and to the federal blockade. In response to a letter from the ranking Union officers at Camp Ford, at least two shipments of clothes from the United States government were received by and distributed among the prisoners.

Escapes from Camp Ford were common, but no reliable estimate of the number is available. Postwar accounts of those attempts, some successful, were abundant among the members of the former Camp Ford inmates. After the war the former prisoners leveled charges against the Confederates for mistreatment and failure to provide humane living conditions at Camp Ford. However, the published accounts present many conflicting stories and viewpoints among the former prisoners. Nothing came of the charges. About 6,000 prisoners were confined at Camp Ford over the two years of its existence, making it the largest Confederate prison camp west of the Mississippi River. Of this number, 286 died there. Following the surrender of the Confederate Trans-Mississippi Department, the 1,200 remaining prisoners left Camp Ford, on May 17, 1865, bound for Shreveport. The remains of the prison compound were destroyed in July by a detail of the Tenth Illinois Cavalry.

BIBLIOGRAPHY: A. J. H. Duganne, *Twenty Months in the Department of the Gulf* (New York: J. P. Robens, 1865). B. P. Gallaway, *The Dark Corner of the Confederacy* (Dubuque, Iowa: Brown, 1968). Robert W. Glover, ed., *Tyler and Smith County, Texas* (n.p.: Walsworth, 1976). F. Lee Lawrence and Robert W. Glover, *Camp Ford, C.S.A.: The Story of Union Prisoners in Texas* (Austin: Texas Civil War Centennial Advisory Committee, 1964). Leon Mitchell, Jr., "Camp Ford, Confederate Military Prison," *Southwestern Historical Quarterly* 66 (July 1962). S. A. Swiggett, *The Bright Side of Prison Life* (Baltimore: Fleet, McGinley, 1897). *The War of the Rebellion: A Compilation of the Official Records of the Union and Confederate Armies* (Washington: GPO, 1880–1901).

F. Lee Lawrence

CAMP GRIERSON'S SPRING. Camp Grierson's Spring was between the head of the main Concho River and the Pecos Crossing, thirty miles east of the Pecos River and eight miles southwest of the site of Best in Reagan County. Lt. Mason Maxon of the Tenth United States Cavalry[qv] found the spring, which is at the head of a branch of Live Oak Creek, in the winter of 1877–78. It was named for Col. Benjamin H. Grierson,[qv] who commanded the Tenth Cavalry, Fort Concho, and the district of the Pecos.

The spring was due south of Centralia Station and the overland stage route, on a direct line midway between forts Concho and Stockton. In May and June of 1878 soldiers opened a military wagon road between the two posts, via Grierson's Spring. At about the same time, Camp Grierson's Spring was established as an subpost of Fort Concho, and another road was extended to the Horsehead Crossing of the Pecos. From the spring, detachments of the Sixteenth, Twenty-fourth, and Twenty-fifth Infantry and the Tenth Cavalry explored and scouted the surrounding country and guarded freight trains and travelers. The military telegraph line from San Antonio and Fort Concho also was routed through Camp Grierson's Spring to forts Stockton and Davis. Stone buildings at the camp included a corral and stable, a two-room guardhouse, a two-room officers' quarters, quarters for one company of infantry, a grain storehouse, a kitchen and mess room, and a telegraph office. After the close of the Victorio[qv] campaign in the summer of 1880, the subpost at Grierson's Spring was irregularly garrisoned. It was permanently abandoned at the end of September 1882. Today only rock foundations remain.

BIBLIOGRAPHY: Frank M. Temple, "Grierson's Spring," *Fort Concho Report* 15 (Winter 1983).

Bruce J. Dinges

CAMP GROCE. Camp Groce was on Col. Leonard W. Groce's[qv] Liendo Plantation,[qv] on Clear Creek and the Houston and Texas Central Railway two miles east of Hempstead in Waller County. The camp was the first permanent Confederate military prison west of the Mississippi. It was one of two camps in Texas where northern prisoners were held, probably in 1861–63. It received 110 prisoners from Houston on June 13, 1863. The camp had several long barracks.

BIBLIOGRAPHY: Leon Mitchell, Jr., "Camp Ford, Confederate Military Prison," *Southwestern Historical Quarterly* 66 (July 1962). Frank E. White, History of the Territory that Now Constitutes Waller

County, Texas, from 1821 to 1884 (M.A. thesis, University of Texas, 1936). *Art Leatherwood*

CAMPGROUND, TEXAS. Campground was on State Highway 294 twelve miles southwest of Rusk in southern Cherokee County. It was first settled around the time of the Civil War[qv] and grew up around an early church of the same name. In the mid-1930s the small community had a church and a number of houses. After World War II[qv] many residents left the area, but in the early 1980s a church, a store, a cemetery, and a few scattered houses still remained. *Christopher Long*

CAMPGROUND BAYOU. Campground Bayou rises 2½ miles northeast of Bagwell in central Red River County (at 33°41′ N, 95°07′ W) and runs east for 6½ miles to its mouth on White Oak Bayou, six miles north of Clarksville (at 33°42′ N, 95°02′ W). It crosses flat to rolling terrain surfaced by loams that support pine and oak forests.

CAMPGROUND CREEK. Campground Creek rises four miles north of Bluffton in eastern Llano County (at 30°52′ N, 98°30′ W) and runs southeast for 4½ miles to its mouth on Lake Buchanan, one mile south of Lake Buchanan Village (at 30°50′ N, 98°27′ W). It is in the Llano basin and crosses locally dissected, flat to rolling terrain surfaced by sandy and clay loams that support open stands of live oak and mesquite.

CAMPGROUND TRACE. The Campground Trace was an eighteen-mile-long trail connecting the Middle Coushatta Village (Long King's Village[qv]) with a popular Indian camping area in eastern Polk County, Texas. From Long King's Village this trail crossed Long King Creek north of the site of present Goodrich, extended eastward across what is now central Polk County, crossed Menard Creek, and ended at the junction of Big Sandy Creek and Bear Creek, south of the present Alabama-Coushatta Indian Reservation. On Stephen F. Austin's[qv] Memorandum for a Map of Texas, 1827, this location is shown as the site of an abandoned Alabama village. Also, the surveyor Samuel C. Hirams wrote in the field notes for his survey of land for William Nash that he began the survey at the old Indian campground. This camping site was apparently well known among the Alabama and Coushatta Indian tribes, and members of these two groups frequently used it during their hunting trips in the Big Thicket[qv] of East Texas.

BIBLIOGRAPHY: Howard N. Martin, "Polk County Indians: Alabamas, Coushattas, Pakana Muskogees," *East Texas Historical Journal* 17 (1979). *Howard N. Martin*

CAMP HARNEY. Camp Harney, a temporary military establishment near Bellville, Zapata County (*see* ZAPATA, TEXAS), opened in 1851 and was named for Col. William S. Harney.[qv]

BIBLIOGRAPHY: *Texas Almanac*, 1936.

CAMP HENRY E. MCCULLOCH. Camp Henry E. McCulloch, at Nuner's Mott, four miles north of Victoria, served as a Confederate camp of instruction from September 1861 to May 1862. The post was named in honor of Gen. Henry Eustace McCulloch,[qv] commander of the Department of Texas. Its commanding officer was Col. Robert R. Garland, a native Virginian who entered the United States Army on December 30, 1847, as a second lieutenant in the Seventh Infantry. By 1861 he held the rank of captain. After the fall of Fort Sumter, Garland forfeited his commission while stationed at Fort Fillmore, New Mexico, enrolled in the Confederate Army as a captain, and was assigned to duty as a mustering officer for the Texas cavalry regiments of B. Warren Stone, Jr., and Middleton T. Johnson.[qqv] Later he was authorized to raise and train men for the newly formed Sixth Texas Infantry. Garland was confirmed colonel of the regiment on December 12, 1861, to rank from the preceding September 3.

Ten infantry companies from Calhoun, Victoria, Bell, Matagorda, Bexar, Gonzales, DeWitt, Travis, and Guadalupe counties were assembled at Camp McCulloch. The first one mustered into service there was the Lavaca Guards, from Calhoun County. Included in the ranks of the Sixth Texas Infantry were T. Scott Anderson, Sebron G. Sneed, Jr., George P. Finlay, and John P. White.[qqv] In addition to the infantry companies two cavalry companies, Edward Beaumont's and James C. Borden's, were also stationed at the camp.

The site selected for Camp McCulloch was very disagreeable to some of the soldiers, who complained that the location was insect-infested and unhealthful. In order to provide adequate medical care for the trainees, the Victoria Male Academy[qv] was rented from the Corporation of Victoria and used as the camp's hospital. The troops were issued "butternut"—light brown— uniforms manufactured at the State Penitentiary (*see* TEXAS STATE PENITENTIARY AT HUNTSVILLE). The raw recruits were drilled under the watchful eye of Garland until they became adept at marching with military precision. In December 1861 units of the regiment were ordered to Indianola and Saluria to help defend the region against an anticipated Union attack. When it became apparent that no engagement was forthcoming, the companies returned to Victoria.

Before breaking camp on May 22, 1862, and moving to Arkansas, Garland asked the ladies of Victoria to make a regimental flag. Mrs. Richard (Elizabeth McAnulty) Owens[qv] and her daughters, using materials from the Owens mercantile store, designed and produced a flag. However, the flag was not finished before the regiment left Camp McCulloch and had to be forwarded. Shortly after it was received, it was captured at the battle of Arkansas Post.

BIBLIOGRAPHY: Roy Grimes, ed., *300 Years in Victoria County* (Victoria, Texas: Victoria *Advocate*, 1968; rpt., Austin: Nortex, 1985). James M. McCaffrey, *This Band of Heroes* (Austin: Eakin Press, 1985). George Lee Robertson Papers, Barker Texas History Center, University of Texas at Austin. *Charles D. Spurlin*

CAMP HOLLAND. Camp Holland, twelve miles west of Valentine at Viejo Pass in Presidio County, was constructed in 1918 after the Brite Ranch and Neville Ranch raids[qqv] by Mexican bandits. Viejo Pass was used by Indians in prehistoric times because of its good supply of water and grass. On June 12, 1880, the pass was the scene of the last Apache attack in Presidio County; on that day four Pueblo Indian scouts and Lt. Frank H. Mills of the Twenty-fourth United States Infantry[qv] fought off twenty Apaches. Camp Holland, named for the J. R. Holland Ranch on which it was built, was a base for pack-trains that supplied Col. George T. Langhorne's Eighth United States Cavalry as it patrolled the Mexican border. On September 9, 1919, Troop B of the Second Squadron was assigned to Camp Holland. The buildings of the camp were made of stone and wood and cost over $16,000 to construct. Although soldiers seldom lived there, Camp Holland had two barracks that could house up to 400 men, four officers' houses, a mess hall, and a guardhouse. The soldiers' everyday needs were met by a bakery, a corral, a blacksmith shop, and a quartermaster store. Since the area afforded a good supply of springwater, the camp had a sewer system and a shower house. By 1921 the army began phasing out border patrols in Presidio County. Camp Holland was closed and leased to civilians including Texas Rangers[qv] and customs and immigration border patrols in January 1922. It was eventually sold at auction to C. O. Finley. The deserted buildings were still standing in the late 1960s.

BIBLIOGRAPHY: Cecilia Thompson, *History of Marfa and Presidio County, 1535–1946* (2 vols., Austin: Nortex, 1985). Kim Thornsburg, "Camp Holland," *Junior Historian*, December 1967. *Julia Cauble Smith*

CAMP HOWZE. Camp Howze, northwest of Gainesville in central Cooke County, was established by the United States War Department in 1942 as a United States Army infantry-training camp. It was located on a 59,000-acre tract purchased from local landowners beginning in December 1941 and named for Maj. Robert E. Lee Howze,qv a Medal of Honor winner who had seen action in the Indian campaigns of the late nineteenth century, the Philippine Insurrection, and World War I.qv Col. John P. Wheeler activated the base on August 17, 1942, and Maj. Gen. John H. Hilldring was its first commander. With a troop capacity of 39,963 men, the camp served as the training ground for several hundred thousand men between 1942 and 1946. Among the units prepared for action in World War IIqv were the 84th, 86th, and 103d divisions. The camp provided employment for hundreds of area civilians. In addition, the $20 million spent by the national government on Camp Howze fueled the local economy. In 1946 the camp was declared surplus, disbanded, and leveled.

bibliography: Michael Collins, *Cooke County, Texas: Where the South and West Meet* (Gainesville, Texas: Cooke County Heritage Society, 1981). Gainesville *Daily Register*, August 30, 1948.

Brian Hart

CAMP HUDSON. Camp Hudson, also called Fort Hudson, was located on San Pedro Creek, a tributary of the Devils River, twenty-one miles north of Comstock in central Val Verde County. It was established on June 7, 1857, in what was then Kinney County and named for Lt. Walter W. Hudson, who died in April 1850 of injuries he received in an Indian fight. The camp was one of several posts built between San Antonio and El Paso to protect travelers on the so-called Chihuahua Trail. A local post office was opened in 1857. The post was built along an elevated but isolated section of the creek, and few travelers or settlers came by in the early years. Zenas R. Bliss,qv who was stationed at Camp Hudson for two years, reported seeing only four or five people during that time who were not related to the army. The walls of the buildings at Camp Hudson were constructed of a mixture of gravel and lime. The process was slow, but it made the buildings cool in summer and warm in winter. In 1859 one of the experimental caravans of camelsqv from Camp Verde passed through Camp Hudson. The troops left on March 17, 1861, for service in the Civil War.qv In 1866 the post office closed. In late October 1867 a stage from Camp Hudson to Fort Stockton was ambushed by Indians, and two military escorts were killed. In November, immediately after the stage attack, companies D and G of the Ninth Cavalry were ordered to Camp Hudson. By April 1868 other troops had returned to the area.

In April 1871 Camp Hudson was reorganized with three commissioned officers and sixty enlisted men. In March 1876 Lt. Col. George Pearson Buell came to Camp Hudson from Fort Concho with two companies of cavalry. Under his leadership, the post was to be used as a summer camp to protect newly arrived settlers. The troops at Camp Hudson fought with Indians on several occasions and sometimes followed them into Mexico. In April 1876 Lt. Louis Henry Orleman was sent to Camp Hudson to take command of Company B of the Tenth Cavalry. In January 1877, however, Camp Hudson was permanently closed because the threat of Indian attacks no longer existed. In 1936 the Texas Historical Commissionqv placed a centennial marker at the site of Camp Hudson. By the 1980s no buildings stood on the private property where the camp was once situated.

bibliography: Arrie Barrett, "Western Frontier Forts of Texas, 1845–1861," West Texas Historical Association *Year Book* 7 (1931). Roy L. Swift and Leavitt Corning, Jr., *Three Roads to Chihuahua* (Austin: Eakin Press, 1988). Clayton W. Williams, *Texas' Last Frontier: Fort Stockton and the Trans-Pecos, 1861–1895* (College Station: Texas A&M University Press, 1982). Robert Wooster, *Soldiers, Sutlers and Settlers: Garrison Life of the Texas Frontier* (College Station: Texas A&M University Press, 1987).

Julia Cauble Smith

CAMP HULEN. Camp Hulen, formerly known as Camp Palacios, was on Turtle and Tres Palacios bays just west of Palacios in southwestern Matagorda County. It reached its peak use as a United States Army training center during World War II.qv It was originally established as a summer training camp for the Thirty-sixth Infantry Divisionqv of the Texas National Guardqv after the Palacios Campsite Association donated the land to the state in 1926. The association had in mind the economic benefits a military training center would bring Palacios. Some 6,500 men came to the first training session in the summer of 1926. Beginning in July 1926 Camp Palacios had a newspaper, the Camp Palacios *T-Arrow Daily*, published by the Palacios *Beacon;* its name was derived from the symbols for the two states that largely made up the Thirty-sixth Division: T for Texas and an arrowhead for Oklahoma. In 1930 the camp, where more than $500,000 was spent on housing for the division, was renamed Camp Hulen, after John Augustus Hulen.qv By 1934 some 1,886 concrete tent floors had been laid for the trainees. Because the surrounding bays provided a safe range for target practice, in 1940 the United States War Department began to use the base for antiaircraft training for national guard units from across the country (the Thirty-sixth Division had moved to Camp Bowieqv in Brown County). In January 1941 the first draftees arrived, and the following month saw the first printed issue of the weekly Camp Hulen *Searchlight*, which had begun earlier as a simple mimeographed sheet. The paper ran until 1945; a few 1943 copies are housed at the Barker Texas History Center,qv University of Texas at Austin.

Civil contractors and the Work Projects Administrationqv constructed additions to the camp, which eventually included some 400 semipermanent buildings and 2,825 floored, framed, and screened tents, as well as a tent theater, fire station, bakery, weather station, library, dental clinic, post office, and 500-bed hospital. At its height the installation's troop capacity was 14,560. Associated with Camp Hulen were the Indianola Battalion Camp, the Wells Point rifle range and antiaircraft firing range, the Olivia projectile area, and the Civilian War Housing Project. Camp Hulen proper encompassed some 1,460 acres and adjoined the army air base to the north, which, despite the damage done the area by a September hurricane, saw construction begin in October 1942.

Housing for soldiers' families and other newcomers was limited in nearby Palacios, and the town, a fourth of which did not even have proper sewage facilities, was temporarily overloaded by the sudden rise in population. At one time the Texas Rangersqv were called in to help maintain order. In November 1940 Gen. Harvey C. Allen took command of the camp and the antiaircraft artillery training center. In May 1942 Col. John K. Brown became camp commander, though Allen maintained command of the antiaircraft training center. Several other men commanded the camp before it was deactivated.

In January 1944 Camp Hulen was converted to a prisoner of war camp; the Germans housed there were farmed out to help with agricultural work in the county (*see* german prisoners of war). On May 31, 1946, the War Department declared Camp Hulen surplus and returned it to the Texas National Guard. Rather than use it for summer training, the guard slowly dismantled it for scrap. Though in 1965 the site was sold to developers hoping to construct an industrial park, by 1985 the abandoned camp still remained undeveloped. The army air base became the Palacios Municipal Airport.

bibliography: Matagorda County Historical Commission, *Historic Matagorda County* (3 vols., Houston: Armstrong, 1986). Ruby Penland, *Camp Hulen, Texas* (Palacios, Texas: Palacios Area Historical Association, 1987).

Rachel Jenkins

CAMP INDEPENDENCE. Camp Independence, established in December 1836, was the main camp of the Texas army until March 1837. It was on land belonging to Sylvanus Hatch, east of the Lavaca River and five miles from Texana in Jackson County. On February 4, 1837, Gen. Felix Hustonqv commanded the Texas army at Camp Independence, where he was succeeded in command by Gen. Albert Sidney Johnston,qv an action that precipitated the infamous Huston-Johnston duel. Although seriously wounded in the contest, Johnston kept his headquarters at Camp Independence until the army was transferred to Camp Preston, a move that seems to have occurred during the first week of March 1837. It was reported that on May 5, 1837, Capt. Henry Teal[qv] was assassinated near the camp as he lay asleep in his tent. In 1936 the Texas Centennial[qv] Committee placed a marker at a site, 4½ miles southwest of Edna.

BIBLIOGRAPHY: Gerald S. Pierce, *Texas Under Arms: The Camps, Posts, Forts, and Military Towns of the Republic of Texas* (Austin: Encino, 1969). Harold Schoen, comp., *Monuments Erected by the State of Texas to Commemorate the Centenary of Texas Independence* (Austin: Commission of Control for Texas Centennial Celebrations, 1938). Ira T. Taylor, *The Cavalcade of Jackson County* (San Antonio: Naylor, 1938). *Stephen L. Hardin*

CAMP IRWIN. Camp Irwin, also called Camp Placedo, was a Mexican War[qv] encampment established in October 1846 on Placedo Creek near the Port Lavaca–Victoria road, twelve miles west of Port Lavaca in Victoria County. It was named for James R. Irwin, chief quartermaster of Winfield Scott's army during the Mexico City campaign, and served as a rendezvous for troops assigned to Gen. John E. Wool's[qv] Center Division and as a temporary military supply depot. Military units that used the camp were Col. John J. Hardin's First Regiment, Illinois Volunteers; Col. Humphrey Marshall's regiment of Kentucky Volunteers; Capt. John S. Williams's independent company, Kentucky Volunteers; and Col. Jonas E. Thomas's regiment of Tennessee Volunteers. Accounts describe the site as low, swampy ground where disease was common and conditions were barely tolerable.

BIBLIOGRAPHY: George W. Cullum, *Biographical Register of the Officers and Graduates of the U.S. Military Academy at West Point, New York.* George C. Furber, *The Twelve Months Volunteer* (Cincinnati: James, 1848). Edward D. Mansfield, *The Mexican War* (New York: Barnes, 1848). *Charles D. Spurlin*

CAMP IVES. Camp Ives was a military outpost on Turtle Creek four miles north of Camp Verde in southeastern Kerr County. Second Lt. Wesley Owen, commanding Troop I, Second United States Cavalry,[qv] established the camp on October 2, 1859. Although built in answer to requests from area settlers for government protection against Indians, the camp saw little use. On March 13, 1860, it was evacuated temporarily when soldiers stationed there escorted Lt. Col. Robert E. Lee,[qv] then in temporary command of the Second Cavalry, to the Rio Grande. The camp was reoccupied on October 20, 1860, but remained in operation only until January 28, 1861. On that date its troops abandoned it and moved to Camp Verde in preparation for defense against Confederate occupation as Texas neared secession.[qv]

BIBLIOGRAPHY: James Edward Batson, The Beginnings of Kerr County, Texas (M.A. thesis, University of Texas, 1928). Matilda Maria Real, A History of Kerr County (M.A. thesis, University of Texas, 1942). *Rebecca J. Herring*

CAMP JOHN DICK AVIATION CONCENTRATION CAMP. Camp John Dick Aviation Concentration Camp, also known as Camp Dick, was a personnel holding pool for graduates of ground training schools. It was located on the State Fairgrounds in Dallas from January 1918 until January 1919.

BIBLIOGRAPHY: Robert E. Hays, Jr., Military Aviation Activities in Texas, World Wars I and II (M.A. thesis, University of Texas, 1963). *Art Leatherwood*

CAMP JOHN WISE. Camp John Wise, a balloon training station on 261 acres of leased land four miles north of downtown San Antonio, was established on January 19, 1918. The United States Army Balloon School was transferred there from Fort Omaha, Nebraska. The personnel were quartered at Fort Sam Houston until March, when construction on their barracks was completed. The base reached a maximum strength of thirty-three officers and 1,800 enlisted men and was equipped with four balloons. The camp was named for John Wise of Philadelphia, a pioneer balloonist who constructed a balloon in which he set a world distance record in 1869. The base seems to have closed soon after World War I.[qv]

BIBLIOGRAPHY: Robert E. Hays, Jr., Military Aviation Activities in Texas, World Wars I and II (M.A. thesis, University of Texas, 1963). *Art Leatherwood*

CAMP JOSEPH E. JOHNSTON. Camp Joseph E. Johnston, a temporary federal outpost on the south side of the North Concho River in northwestern Tom Green County, was named for Joseph E. Johnston,[qv] who in 1849 had commanded an army topographic party in surveying the road between San Antonio and El Paso. Five companies of the Eighth United States Infantry,[qv] a total of 284 persons, including families and servants of officers, garrisoned the camp between March 15 and November 18, 1852, under command of General J. Garland.

BIBLIOGRAPHY: Arrie Barrett, Federal Military Outposts in Texas, 1845–1861 (M.A. thesis, University of Texas, 1927). Ray Miller, *Ray Miller's Texas Forts* (Houston: Cordovan, 1985). *Dorman H. Winfrey*

CAMP KENNEY. Camp Kenney, at the head of Gonzales Creek in southern Stephens County, was a temporary patrolling post of the Frontier Battalion.[qv] Following procedures similar to those used by former frontier forces, patrolling squads operated from the camp after October 1874. They went out to scout at irregular intervals, but the Indians quickly learned how to evade the soldiers and sweep in behind them to raid the settlements. Scouting parties had the pack animals with them, making it impossible for those remaining in camp to follow the raiders. The camp probably operated only until September 1875, after which no Indian depredations were reported on that frontier.

BIBLIOGRAPHY: Loy W. Hartsfield, A History of Stephens County (M.A. thesis, University of Texas, 1929).

CAMP KINGSVILLE. Camp Kingsville, at the Kingsville Fairgrounds, was established in September 1915. It was the headquarters of a battalion of the Twenty-sixth Infantry and the operational base for companies K, L, and M, commanded by Lt. Joseph D. Patch, who became a major general in World War II.[qv] The camp operated during the Mexican border troubles and was detailed to defend the Armstrong, Kenedy, and King ranches (*see* ARMSTRONG, JOHN BARCLAY; KENEDY, MIFFLIN; KING RANCH), as well as the rail line between San Antonio and Norias. A Texas historical marker, dedicated to Patch, was placed at Santa Gertrudis Avenue and Texas Highway 141 in Kingsville on February 1, 1971.

BIBLIOGRAPHY: Kleberg County Historical Commission, *Kleberg County, Texas* (Austin: Hart Graphics, 1979). *Art Leatherwood*

CAMP LAKE SLOUGH. Camp Lake Slough rises one-half mile east of U.S. Highway 83 and four miles south of Uvalde in southern Uvalde County (at 29°08′ N, 99°49′ W) and runs southeast for nineteen miles to its mouth on the Leona River, four miles north of Batesville in northeast Zavala County (at 29°01′ N, 99°37′ W). Four impoundments—Ranger, Kenedy, Caliche, and County Line lakes—are located on small tributaries of Camp Lake Slough within a three-mile stretch immediately north of the Uvalde-Zavala county line. The creek rises in flat to rolling terrain with steep margins, surfaced by gravelly loams that support oak, juniper, elm, and grasses. It descends to flat terrain with shallow depressions and low relief, surfaced by expansive clays that support grasses, water-tolerant hardwoods, and conifers, interspersed with pecan and other hardwoods.

CAMP LIENDO. Camp Liendo, also known as Camp Groce, was on Liendo Plantation,[qv] owned by Leonard Waller Groce,[qv] 2½ miles east of Hempstead in Waller County. It was probably established in 1862 to house Union soldiers captured by Confederate forces at the battle of Galveston.[qv] The camp had four rows of barracks and a permanent militia guard of seventy men. Most of the federal prisoners remained at Liendo only temporarily while en route to a larger prisoner of war camp at Camp Ford near Tyler. Camp Liendo also served as a recruiting station for the Confederate Army and a refugee center for women and children fleeing from other Southern states. By the end of the Civil War[qv] Confederate soldiers were using the camp as a rallying point. The Twenty-ninth Texas Cavalry regiment disbanded at Camp Liendo during March and April of 1865. After the war a federal division under the command of Gen. George Armstrong Custer[qv] camped at Liendo, from September to December 1865. Groce lent a rocking chair to Custer's wife, Elizabeth, and also provided milk, vegetables, and other food for the Custer family. When recovering from a brief illness, Elizabeth accepted an invitation from the Groce family to stay in the plantation house until she regained her health.

BIBLIOGRAPHY: John M. Carroll, ed., *Custer in Texas: An Interrupted Narrative* (New York: Sol Lewis/Liveright, 1975). Elizabeth Bacon Custer, *Tenting on the Plains, or General Custer in Kansas and Texas* (New York: Webster, 1887). Waller County Historical Survey Committee, *A History of Waller County, Texas* (Waco: Texian, 1973). Frank E. White, History of the Territory that Now Constitutes Waller County, Texas, from 1821 to 1884 (M.A. thesis, University of Texas, 1936).

Clinton P. Hartmann

CAMP LLANO. Camp Llano, at the junction of Rock Creek and the Llano River in Mason County, was established by James M. Norris[qv] on March 29, 1862, as a ranger station for the Frontier Regiment.[qv] It was manned by members of the ranger company of Capt. H. T. Davis and engaged in scouting duty, probably until the consolidation of the Frontier Regiment in March 1864.

BIBLIOGRAPHY: William Curry Holden, Frontier Problems and Movements in West Texas, 1846–1900 (Ph.D. dissertation, University of Texas, 1928).

CAMP LOGAN. Camp Logan, an emergency training center in World War I,[qv] was earlier a National Guard camp just beyond the western city limits of Houston. Construction of the center began on July 24, 1917. Trouble between local police and black soldiers quartered at the camp resulted in a riot on August 23 and the declaration of martial law in Houston. The camp was used for hospitalization of wounded men in 1918. At the close of the war the site was acquired by William C. Hogg[qv] and his brother, Mike, who turned over to the city of Houston, at cost, more than 1,000 acres. Memorial Park, the city's largest recreational area, is on the site.

BIBLIOGRAPHY: Robert V. Haynes, *A Night of Violence: The Houston Riot of 1917* (Baton Rouge: Louisiana State University Press, 1976). WPA Writers Program, *Houston* (Houston: Anson Jones, 1942).

Claudia Hazlewood

CAMP MABRY. Camp Mabry, in northwestern Austin, was established in the early 1890s as a summer encampment of the Texas Volunteer Guard, a forerunner of the Texas National Guard.[qv] In 1891 a citizens' committee in Austin began looking for a place for the volunteer guard to train. In 1892 they chose an eighty-five-acre site three miles northwest of the Capitol.[qv] The guardsmen chose to name the new camp in honor of Woodford Haywood Mabry,[qv] adjutant general of Texas from January 1891 to May 1898. In 1909 the size of the camp was greatly increased by the addition of 200 acres that the federal government purchased for the state for use in training the national guard. Other gifts brought the size of the encampment to 400 acres by 1911.

Since its establishment Camp Mabry has served in a variety of capacities. It was used as a mobilization area during the Spanish-American War. The state arsenal building was built there in 1915, and all military stores were moved from the state Capitol to the new facility. During World War I[qv] the United States Army used the camp as a training site and built several barracks and administration buildings. The army also used the camp as an engine-rebuilding station during the war. When the Texas National Guard was called into federal service during World War II,[qv] Camp Mabry served as Headquarters for the Texas Defense Guard, the remaining state militia. Camp Mabry served as a training ground for the Texas Department of Public Safety and the Texas Rangers,[qqv] as well as the national guard, until 1953. The state adjutant general's office was moved to Camp Mabry in 1954, and the Texas National Guard State Officer Candidate School was established there in 1959. A historical marker acknowledging the contribution of Camp Mabry was dedicated in December 1972.

In the mid-1980s the size of the Camp Mabry site was just over 375 acres, and the building space was 700,000 square feet. The various offices at Camp Mabry employed 800 people. The Texas National Guard Academy opened at Camp Mabry in June 1984. Also located on the post are the headquarters of the Texas Air National Guard, the Texas State Guard, the United States Property and Fiscal Office, the Texas National Guard Armory Board, the Headquarters Armory of the Forty-ninth Armored Division, a clinic, a parachute packing and storage facility, and numerous supply and warehouse facilities.

Camp Mabry observed its 100th anniversary on Texas Armed Forces Day in May 1992. In addition to battle reenactments and displays, the celebration included an informal opening of the Texas Military Forces Museum, which was completed later that year.

BIBLIOGRAPHY: Ron Dusek, "Mabry Surrounded, Still Sits Pretty," *Third Coast*, April 1985. Marker Files, Texas Historical Commission, Austin.

Vivian Elizabeth Smyrl

CAMP MACARTHUR. Camp MacArthur, a World War I[qv] training camp named for and dedicated by Gen. Arthur MacArthur on July 18, 1917, was on the northwestern side of Waco. Construction began on July 20, 1917, and in September of that year 18,000 troops arrived from Michigan and Wisconsin. The campsite proper covered 1,377 acres, although the entire tract of land reserved for the camp's use encompassed 10,699 acres. Facilities at the camp included a base hospital, administrative offices, and a tent camp, supplemented by 1,284 buildings. Troop capacity was 45,074, although the average strength of the force stationed at MacArthur during any given month did not exceed 28,000 troops. Construction costs were estimated at $5 million. The camp served as an infantry replacement and training camp, an officers' training school, and a demobilization facility. Among the units trained at the facility were the Thirty-second or Red Arrow Division, which saw combat in France in 1918. The camp was ordered salvaged on January 3, 1919, and materials from it were to be used in the construction of United States–Mexican border stations. The camp was officially closed on March 7, 1919, and the grounds became part of the city of Waco. A historical marker was placed at the former site of the camp headquarters in 1966.

BIBLIOGRAPHY: *Order of Battle of the United States Land Forces in the World War* (3 vols., Washington: GPO, 1931-49; facsimile, Washington: United States Army, 1988). Marker Files, Texas Historical Commission, Austin.

Vivian Elizabeth Smyrl

CAMP MCMILLAN. Camp McMillan, at Hall's Spring at the head of Richland Creek in San Saba County, was established by James M. Norris[qv] on March 26, 1862, as a ranger station for the Frontier Regiment.[qv] Under command of Capt. N. D. McMillan, scouts served at the camp until the consolidation of the regiment in March 1864.

BIBLIOGRAPHY: William Curry Holden, Frontier Problems and Movements in West Texas, 1846–1900 (Ph.D. dissertation, University of Texas, 1928).

CAMP MAXEY. Camp Maxey, a World War II[qv] infantry-training camp ten miles north of Paris, Texas, was named in honor of Samuel Bell Maxey.[qv] It was activated on July 15, 1942, under command of Col. C. H. Palmer. The first division to be trained at the camp, the 103rd Infantry Division, was organized and activated on September 15, 1942, under Gen. John B. Anderson. Col. Robert C. Annin succeeded Palmer as commander on March 25, 1943. In addition to the army ground forces trained at Camp Maxey, army service forces and army air forces had a part in the development of camp activities. The varied terrain provided facilities for working out problems of infantry training to meet modern battle conditions. An artillery range, obstacle course, infiltration course, and "German Village" were included in training maneuvers. Troop capacity was 44,931. The camp was put on an inactive status on October 1, 1945. Afterward, the installation served as a training center for the Texas National Guard,[qv] and most of the original buildings were demolished or sold and removed; in 1990 the camp sewage-treatment plant was used by the city of Paris. When Pat Mayse Lake was constructed, parts of the northern edge of the base were inundated.

CAMP MELVIN. Camp Melvin, a little-known temporary outpost, was established in 1868 on the Pecos River two miles west of what is now State Highway 349 in northwestern Crockett County. The site was called by twenty-four different names between 1864 and 1926: San Pantaleon, Connelley's Crossing, Camp Melbourne, Fennelly's Crossing, Pecos Crossing, Camp Melvin, Camp Milvin, Pecos River Station, Mail Station, Mail Station Bridge, Pecos Mail Station, Melvin Station, Melvin Mail Station, Ficklin, Crossing of the Pecos Station, Crossing of the Pecos, Pecos Crossing Bridge, Pecos Bridge, Pecos Stage Station, Pecos Station, Pontoon Bridge Crossing, Pontoon Crossing, Mail Station at Pecos, and Pontoon Bridge. The site was more significant as a river crossing than as a military installation. On May 22, 1684, Juan Domínguez de Mendoza[qv] crossed the river there. His expedition camped at the crossing, and Mendoza called it San Pantaleon. In 1840 Dr. Henry Connelly[qv] returned to Chihuahua after a trading trip to North Texas and crossed at the point. Camp Melvin operated as an outpost of Fort Lancaster from 1868 to 1871 on the Government Road from San Antonio to El Paso. A post office operated at the crossing from 1868 to 1870. From 1868 to 1881 stagecoaches crossed the Pecos at the site, and the stage company maintained a station there. By 1871 the number of soldiers at the camp had been reduced to a few men. The crossing was dangerous since it was subject to Comanche attack. In July 1873 Juan Chabavilla was killed by a raiding party of thirteen Indians that stole the horses and mules of the stage company. Indians attacked the place again on June 2, 1874, wounded the owner of the nearby Torres Ranch, and took his thirty-five horses and mules. In October 1875 only two soldiers were stationed at the former outpost to protect stage-company mules. On June 27, 1878, five Indians fired upon the stage five miles beyond the crossing. A passenger was seriously injured.

In 1882 the crossing was labeled Mail Station on a map. Between 1892 and 1926 the site was called Pontoon Crossing. After 1926 no map designation was given the point. By 1960 the only remnants of Camp Melvin were several crumbling walls of former buildings and a stone corral.

BIBLIOGRAPHY: Grover C. Ramsey, "Camp Melvin, Crockett County, Texas," West Texas Historical Association *Year Book* 37 (1961). Roy L. Swift and Leavitt Corning, Jr., *Three Roads to Chihuahua* (Austin: Eakin Press, 1988).

Julia Cauble Smith

CAMP MERRILL. Camp Merrill, on a site formerly known as Camp Casa Blanca on the south side of the Nueces River in northeastern Jim Wells County, was established in 1852. The camp may have been a subpost of Fort Merrill; both installations were named for Hamilton W. Merrill.[qv] The town of Casa Blanca later developed on the site.

BIBLIOGRAPHY: William Curry Holden, "Frontier Defense in Texas during the Civil War," West Texas Historical Association *Year Book* 4 (1928).

CAMP MONTEL. Camp Montel, at the head of Seco Creek in Bandera County, was established by James M. Norris[qv] in March 1862 as a ranger station for the Frontier Regiment.[qv] The post was manned by rangers under Charles DeMontel[qv] until the consolidation of the Frontier Regiment in March 1864. In 1870 DeMontel, with a large surveying party, located another Camp Montel on the Nueces River in northern Uvalde County. At this site the town of Montell was later established. In 1880 and 1881 Company G of the First Texas Volunteer Cavalry was organized and named the Montell Guards. The company, consisting of thirty-seven men and an ordnance store, was stationed at Montell. A historical marker for Camp Montel is at the Bandera County Courthouse.

BIBLIOGRAPHY: Charles de Montel Papers, Barker Texas History Center, University of Texas at Austin. William Curry Holden, "Frontier Defense in Texas during the Civil War," West Texas Historical Association *Year Book* 4 (1928).

E. C. de Montel

CAMP MYSTIC. Camp Mystic is a summer camp for girls on the South Fork of the Guadalupe River three miles southwest of Hunt in central Kerr County. It was established in 1926 by E. J. (Doc) Stewart, former head football coach at the University of Texas, who had founded Camp Stewart for boys in the same area two years earlier. Camp Mystic, known originally as Stewart's Camp for Girls, provided facilities for outdoor activities and instruction in roping, marksmanship, music, painting, and drama. In 1937 the camp was purchased by Mr. and Mrs. Gilespie Stacy and in 1968 was owned by a group of investors that included Stacy family members. The camp has remained in continuous operation since its founding, except for the years 1943–45, when it was leased by the federal government as a convalescent camp for army air corps veterans of World War II.[qv]

BIBLIOGRAPHY: Frank R. Gilliland, Kerrville, Texas: A Social and Economic History (M.A. thesis, Stephen F. Austin State College, 1951). Kerrville *Daily Times*, February 25, 1968.

Rebecca J. Herring

CAMP NEVILLE SPRINGS. The site of Camp Neville Springs is on Government Spring Road 1½ miles east of the boundary marker and campground in Big Bend National Park.[qv] The camp, on the Comanche Trail,[qv] was established in the 1880s to protect the area from Apaches and bandits from Mexico. It was primarily occupied by a group of Black Seminole scouts[qv] who had enlisted for six months at Fort Clark. They were commanded by a lieutenant of cavalry or infantry from that post. Normally, the small scout command consisted of eighteen to twenty enlisted men and one officer. Two of the scout commanders were Lt. Woodbridge Geary, Nineteenth Infantry, and Lt. J. W. King, Eighth Cavalry. Every sixty days the scouts would return to Fort Clark to be paid and see their families, and the camp would be relieved by eight to ten enlisted soldiers, usually under a sergeant, to guard and protect the permanent structures and equipment. The eponymous spring is in a deep ravine surrounded by cottonwood trees. On top of the ravine and seventy-five feet from the spring is the foundation of a permanent barracks sixty feet long and twenty feet wide. A one-room stone house 600 yards away was probably the officers' quarters; only the north wall and part of the south wall remain. Because this camp was permanent, many of the scouts from Camp Peña Colorado, seventy-five miles to the northeast, stayed overnight or to rest and eat. Camp Neville Springs is presumed to have been permanently closed in January 1883, when Camp Peña

Colorado was abandoned. At that time all military personnel in the surrounding area were called in and transferred to other posts.

BIBLIOGRAPHY: Gunnar Brune, *Springs of Texas*, Vol. 1 (Fort Worth: Branch-Smith, 1981). *Richard A. Thompson*

CAMP NORMOYLE. Camp Normoyle was probably established during World War II[qv] as an engine-replacement depot for Kelly Field. It is located across the railroad at the northeast corner of Kelly Field in western San Antonio. By 1943 it was a quartermaster ordnance depot for Kelly Field, and in 1990 it continued in this function.

BIBLIOGRAPHY: Albert Curtis, *Fabulous San Antonio* (San Antonio: Naylor, 1955). Leah Carter Johnston, *San Antonio: St. Anthony's Town* (San Antonio: Librarians Council, 1947). Green Peyton [Wertenbacker], *San Antonio* (New York: McGraw-Hill, 1946).
Art Leatherwood

CAMP NOWLIN. Camp Nowlin was a temporary military outpost near the Little Wichita River and the site of present Archer City in Archer County. It was established under the direction of Capt. John H. Brown[qv] on August 8, 1859, and served as a post for soldiers whose primary duties included escorting Indians to and from the Brazos Indian Reservation[qv] and Indian Territory. The military outpost only lasted for three weeks, as a series of illnesses forced Brown to close the camp on August 21.

BIBLIOGRAPHY: William Curry Holden, Frontier Problems and Movements in West Texas, 1846–1900 (Ph.D. dissertation, University of Texas, 1928). *David Minor*

CAMP NUECES (La Salle County). Camp Nueces was near the Nueces River and the lower San Antonio–Laredo road in the area of present La Salle County. It served as headquarters for Gen. Alexander Somervell's[qv] Southwestern Army in December 1842.

BIBLIOGRAPHY: Gerald S. Pierce, *Texas Under Arms: The Camps, Posts, Forts, and Military Towns of the Republic of Texas* (Austin: Encino, 1969). *Art Leatherwood*

CAMP NUECES (Nueces County). A Camp Nueces was established in 1842 in the Corpus Christi Bay area near Kenney's Fort[qv] in Nueces County, probably directly on Nueces Bay; the site is now in Corpus Christi. This camp, which was occupied in April and May 1842, may have been a secondary camp for nearby camps Everitt and Williams.

BIBLIOGRAPHY: Gerald S. Pierce, *Texas Under Arms: The Camps, Posts, Forts, and Military Towns of the Republic of Texas* (Austin: Encino, 1969). *Art Leatherwood*

CAMP NUECES (Uvalde County). Camp Nueces, at the San Antonio–Eagle Pass road crossing of the Nueces River in southwestern Uvalde County, was established by James M. Norris[qv] in April 1862, as a ranger station for the Frontier Regiment.[qv] Manned by a company under Capt. John J. Dix, Jr.,[qv] the camp sent out scouts on the frontier, probably until consolidation of the regiment in March 1864.

BIBLIOGRAPHY: William Curry Holden, Frontier Problems and Movements in West Texas, 1846–1900 (Ph.D. dissertation, University of Texas, 1928).

CAMPO, ANDRÉS DO (?–?). Andrés do Campo, a Portuguese soldier and gardener and a member of the Coronado expedition,[qv] accompanied Fray Juan de Padilla[qv] to Quivira[qv] and fled southward after the Franciscan friar was slain by natives in 1542. Campo eventually reached Pánuco and Mexico City. Few facts are verifiable concerning him and his wilderness journey. It is said that he fled the scene of Padilla's martyrdom at the friar's urging that he save the two Indian lay-brothers, for his was the only horse. Yet various accounts indicate that he traveled separately from the Indians.

Campo, from all accounts, might have told a story of wilderness survival to rival that of Álvar Núñez Cabeza de Vaca.[qv] His journey, which finally ended in Mexico City, may have taken several years, perhaps only one. The contemporary chronicler Francisco López de Gómara relates that Campo was seized by natives—seemingly the same ones who slew Padilla—and kept a slave for ten months. In his trek, beginning in the area of Kansas, he crossed extensive plains, spanning what is now Oklahoma and Texas, and traversed the "prickly pear country." He at last came upon the Sierra Madre Oriental in the Mexican state of Nuevo León, crossed the mountains in search of the "North Sea" (Gulf of Mexico), and came to Pánuco. His presence in Mexico was reported in March 1547. A conspiracy of silence, probably stemming from official desire to avoid unauthorized expeditions, seems to have shrouded Campo's journey. It has been alleged that Viceroy Antonio de Mendoza "must have sworn him to silence." Yet the story was known in many different places.

A notation on the so-called "De Soto" map of Alonso de Santa Cruz is believed to derive from Campo; it makes mention of the "great herds of cattle" (buffalo[qv]) found between the Río Solo (Rio Grande) and Quivira. As early as 1547 officials in Mexico City were pondering a new expedition to Quivira over Campo's route, which was much shorter than the one taken by Coronado. In 1560 Viceroy Luis de Velasco, intending to send large droves of horses and cattle to Tristán de Luna y Arellano's[qv] colony in Florida, planned to utilize part of the route "followed by the Portuguese [Campo] through the prickly pear country."

BIBLIOGRAPHY: Herbert Eugene Bolton, *Coronado: Knight of Pueblos and Plains* (New York: Whittlesey; Albuquerque: University of New Mexico Press, 1949). Angelico Chávez, *Coronado's Friars* (Washington: Academy of American Franciscan History, 1968).
Robert S. Weddle

CAMPO ALTO, TEXAS. Campo Alto is a colonia on Farm Road 495 two miles northwest of Alamo in south central Hidalgo County. In 1976 it had a population of 534 and 108 dwellings. *See* COLONIAS.

BIBLIOGRAPHY: *Colonias in the Lower Rio Grande Valley of South Texas: A Summary Report* (Policy Research Project Report No. 18, Lyndon B. Johnson School of Public Affairs, University of Texas at Austin, 1977). *Alicia A. Garza*

CAMP PECAN. Camp Pecan, on Pecan Bayou in Callahan County, was established on March 23, 1862, by James M. Norris[qv] as a ranger post of the Frontier Regiment[qv] on the road from Camp Cooper to Camp Colorado. Under Capt. T. M. Collier the camp probably continued scouting activities until the consolidation of the regiment in March 1864.

BIBLIOGRAPHY: William Curry Holden, "Frontier Defense in Texas during the Civil War," West Texas Historical Association *Year Book* 4 (1928). William Curry Holden, Frontier Problems and Movements in West Texas, 1846–1900 (Ph.D. dissertation, University of Texas, 1928).

CAMP PEÑA COLORADO. Camp Peña Colorado, originally known as Cantonment Peña Colorado, was a post of the United States Army for almost fifteen years in the late 1800s. It was located about four miles southwest of the site of present-day Marathon in north central Brewster County. The post was built on Peña Colorada Creek near a large spring and beneath a high bluff called Peña Colorada (Spanish for "red rock," known also in English as Rainbow Cliffs), after which the creek, spring, and the army post itself were named (though the namers were not fastidious about Spanish grammatical gender).

Indians had apparently occupied the area around Peña Colorada Springs for thousands of years. In historical times the site had been a major stopping place on the Comanche Trail[qv] to Mexico. It was first occupied by United States soldiers in late August 1879, when Companies F and G, Twenty-fifth United States Infantry Regiment, moved there from Fort Stockton. The location lay on the road connecting Fort Clark and Fort Davis, was also on the prospective southern route of the transcontinental railroad, and was within practicable supporting distance of Fort Stockton to the northeast and Fort Davis to the northwest.

The establishment of Camp Peña Colorado was likely part of a larger army strategy to increase pressure on the Apaches living in the Trans-Pecos region, who were still forcefully resisting white settlement. It is probably not coincidence, either, that the outpost was founded the same month that Victorio[qv] and his Warm Springs Apaches escaped confinement on the Mescalero reservation in New Mexico and began their flight across the Southwest and Trans-Pecos.

The primary mission of the garrison at Camp Peña Colorado, as it turned out, was to provide escort through the region, perform scout duty, and pursue bandits, border raiders, horse thieves, and the like. In July 1880 the garrison was relieved by two companies of the Twenty-fourth United States Infantry.[qv] In September Company K, First Infantry, assumed garrison duties. This company, by monthly reports, indicated its chief occupations as road building and escort duty; it remained at the post for four years. During this time the spartan post consisted of several crude huts made of stone and mud and included two long, narrow buildings, one to serve as enlisted men's barracks and the other as a storehouse. Other buildings included two smaller huts for officers' quarters and a stone granary. The coming of the Southern Pacific Railroad in 1882 just to the north, however, brought material refinement in living conditions at the post with the increased availability of commodities from the East.

After July 1884 the garrison was principally composed of units of the Tenth United States Cavalry.[qv] Among the Tenth's famous "buffalo soldiers" who served at Camp Peña Colorado was Lt. Henry O. Flipper,[qv] the army's only black officer at the time. The cavalry was needed for scouting missions and inspection of the Mexican border for Apaches and bandits. The Third Cavalry replaced the Tenth in the summer of 1885, when Geronimo and his band were causing trouble in Arizona and New Mexico. Units of the Third Cavalry made up the garrison until relieved by a temporary detachment of the Eighteenth Infantry.

Camp Peña Colorado was finally abandoned in late January 1893. By that time the settling of the country around the post was well along, and the need for United States Army troops in the Big Bend had shifted closer to the border. The site of the camp is located on Post Ranch, part of the Combs Cattle Company. The company's founder, David St. Clair Combs,[qv] early trail driver and prominent Texas rancher, donated the land around Peña Colorada Springs for a park in 1935. A historical marker was erected the next year on the location of the former outpost. The park is still enjoyed by residents of the area, among whom the spot is commonly known simply as the Post.

bibliography: Clifford B. Casey, *Mirages, Mysteries and Reality: Brewster County, Texas, the Big Bend of the Rio Grande* (Hereford, Texas: Pioneer, 1972). M. L. Crimmins, "Camp Pena Colorado, Texas" (West Texas Historical and Scientific Society Publication 6 [1935]). William H. Leckie, *The Buffalo Soldiers: A Narrative of the Negro Cavalry in the West* (Norman: University of Oklahoma Press, 1967). Clayton W. Williams, *Texas' Last Frontier: Fort Stockton and the Trans-Pecos, 1861–1895* (College Station: Texas A&M University Press, 1982).

Richard A. Thompson

CAMP RABB. Camp Rabb was at the crossing of the road from San Antonio to Eagle Pass and Elm Creek, in Bexar Territory, later northeastern Maverick County. It was established by James M. Norris[qv] on April 7, 1862, as a ranger station for the Frontier Regiment.[qv] Under commander Capt. Thomas Rabb,[qv] the camp guarded the road and the frontier until the consolidation of the regiment at Fort Belknap in March 1864.

bibliography: William Curry Holden, Frontier Problems and Movements in West Texas, 1846–1900 (Ph.D. dissertation, University of Texas, 1928).

William Curry Holden

CAMP RADZIMINSKI. Camp Radziminski was established on September 23, 1858, on the south bank of Otter Creek in Indian Territory by Maj. Earl Van Dorn[qv] as a provision depot on one of his Indian campaigns. It was subsequently moved upstream and maintained as an outpost of Fort Belknap in Young County, Texas. Unlike most other army posts on the frontier, Camp Radziminski was surrounded by a log stockade to protect government animals and supplies. The camp, near the site of Tipton, Tillman County, Oklahoma, was abandoned by the army in the fall of 1859 when its garrison was withdrawn to the newly established Fort Cobb. In 1860 it was reoccupied by Texas Rangers[qv] under Col. Middleton T. Johnson,[qv] who was campaigning against the Comanches. Willis Lang[qv] of Johnson's command wrote in his diary that the camp was "located at the south extremity of a range of Wichita mountains in midst of high piles of rocks. . . . Huge mountains rise on either side." Camp Radziminski was named in honor of Charles Radziminski, a native of Poland, who was living in Louisiana when he was appointed second lieutenant in the Third Dragoons in April 1847. Radziminski served as regimental quartermaster and then regimental adjutant during the Mexican War.[qv] He left the service at the end of the war but was reinstated as a first lieutenant in the Second United States Cavalry[qv] on June 30, 1855. He died of tuberculosis on August 18, 1858. By 1860 very little evidence of the camp remained.

bibliography: Francis B. Heitman, *Historical Register and Dictionary of the United States Army* (2 vols., Washington: GPO, 1903; rpt., Urbana: University of Illinois Press, 1965). Willis Lang, Diary (MS, Barker Texas History Center, University of Texas at Austin). Harold B. Simpson, *Cry Comanche: The Second U.S. Cavalry in Texas* (Hillsboro, Texas: Hill Junior College Press, 1979).

Thomas W. Cutrer

CAMP RESOLUTION. Camp Resolution was the name given to four camps occupied by the main body of the Texan Santa Fe expedition[qv] from August 30 through September 18, 1841. The first camp was near the junction of Quitaque and Los Lingos creeks in northwest Motley County, 5½ miles northwest of the site of present Flomat. This camp was used August 30 through September 3rd. Camp Resolution No. 2, used September 3 through September 5, was on the south side of Quitaque Creek, about where Ranch Road 1065 crosses the creek, in extreme northeast Floyd County. Camp No. 3, used from September 5 through 14, was a half mile above No. 2. No. 4 was three-quarters of a mile above No. 3 and was occupied from September 14 through September 18.

bibliography: "Clayton Erhard's Reminiscences of the Santa Fe Expedition, 1841," *Southwestern Historical Quarterly* 66 (April 1963).

Art Leatherwood

CAMP RUBY, TEXAS. Camp Ruby, also known as Ruby, is on Farm Road 1276 sixty-five miles northwest of Beaumont in south central Polk County. A community was established at the site before the Civil War;[qv] by 1880 residents referred to it as Old Hope. A temporary post office, named Rhoden, was opened in the summer of 1880. Another post office, called Charity, was in operation from 1896 to 1911. The site was renamed Camp Ruby when the W. T. Carter and Brother Lumber Company established a logging camp there in 1926. According to local lore, A. B. Clayton was sent to select a good site; having chosen the heavily wooded area of Old Hope, Clayton renamed it after an acquaintance named Ruby Moore. The location became a major logging camp for the Carter sawmills. A tram line linked

Camp Ruby to Camden, which lay on the Moscow, Camden and San Augustine Railroad. As the timber around Camp Ruby was cut out, the Carter Lumber Company shifted logging operations to other areas. Camp Ruby's population thus dwindled to about twenty-five by the early 1940s. The completion of U.S. Highway 190 led many of the residents to move two miles west to a community called New Camp Ruby on the highway. The Camp Ruby oilfield, discovered in the mid-1960s, has yielded moderate amounts of oil and natural gas, and additional discoveries were made in the early 1980s. Camp Ruby's voting box was restored on May 26, 1969. In 1990 the population was thirty-five.

BIBLIOGRAPHY: *History of Polk County* (2 vols., Livingston, Texas: Keen Printing, 1968). *A Pictorial History of Polk County, Texas, 1846–1910* (Livingston, Texas: Polk County Bicentennial Commission, 1976; rev. ed. 1978). *Robert Wooster*

CAMP RUSK. Camp Rusk, located on the south bank of the North Sulphur River at Treadmill Lake one mile west of Ben Franklin in Delta County, was established in the fall of 1861 as the training site for the Ninth Texas Infantry. The site was chosen by Col. Samuel Bell Maxey[qv] upon his return from Richmond in October with an officer's commission and authorization to raise a regiment of infantry composed of companies from Northeast Texas. Lt. James Patteson, Sr., who remained on Maxey's staff throughout the war, supervised the drill instruction of the Ninth, and his brother, Bernard M. Patteson, headed a commissary department that was called upon to furnish twelve large beef cattle daily and to operate three grain mills continuously in order to supply bread.

In November 1861 Col. William Hugh Young[qv] wrote that he was en route to Colonel Maxey's camp in the southwest corner of Lamar County (now northwest Delta County) to complete the muster of the Ninth Regiment. The ten companies were composed of men from Lamar, Red River, Titus, Grayson, Fannin, Hopkins, and Collin counties. In December an outbreak of measles, along with poor water supplies, caused Maxey to abandon Camp Rusk in favor of a site farther north in Fannin County. The epidemic claimed several men, who were buried in unmarked graves at the Fannin encampment.

On January 5, 1862, Maxey prepared to march off to war by writing his last will and testament, and on the following day, the Ninth left Texas for battles at Shiloh, Corinth, Chickamauga, Atlanta, Missionary Ridge, and Perryville. In the early 1900s a flood-control channel was cut through Treadmill Lake. In 1989 no trace remained of the lake or Camp Rusk. A historical marker was placed at the site in 1967 by the Texas Historical Commission.[qv]

BIBLIOGRAPHY: Cooper *Review*, July 26, 1946. Louise Horton, *Samuel Bell Maxey: A Biography* (Austin: University of Texas Press, 1974). Samuel Bell Maxey Papers, Barker Texas History Center, University of Texas at Austin. A. W. Neville, *The History of Lamar County, Texas* (Paris, Texas: North Texas, 1937; rpt. 1986). Ikie Gray Patteson, *Loose Leaves: A History of Delta County* (Dallas: Mathis, 1935). *The War of the Rebellion: A Compilation of the Official Records of the Union and Confederate Armies.* *Morris E. Smart*

CAMP SABINAL. Camp Sabinal, on the west bank of the Sabinal River one mile west of Sabinal, was established by Capt. Albert G. Brackett on July 12, 1856, to provide protection for commercial traffic and travelers from San Antonio to El Paso. Among the people to settle nearby were John Kenedy, who built a store near the camp, Louis Peter, and Peter Rheiner, future father-in-law of Vice President John Nance Garner.[qv] Remnants of structures built by these settlers were still in evidence when the Texas Centennial[qv] Commission placed a marker at the site in 1936. By the summer of 1856 the Second United States Cavalry,[qv] commanded by Col. Albert S. Johnston[qv] and stationed at Fort Mason, was the lone mounted unit left in Texas. Johnston distributed the six companies under his command to different outposts along the Texas frontier; Company I was assigned to Camp Sabinal. The fort was occupied by United States troops until November 1856, and later served as a Texas Ranger camp. The Second Cavalry and Company I were under the command of Robert E. Lee[qv] for three months in late 1857 and again near the end of 1860.

BIBLIOGRAPHY: *A Proud Heritage: A History of Uvalde County* (Uvalde, Texas: El Progreso Club, 1975). Harold B. Simpson, "The Second U.S. Cavalry in Texas, 1855–1861," *Texas Military History* 8 (1970). *Ruben E. Ochoa*

CAMP SALADO. Camp Salado was the campground occupied by the volunteers under Capt. John Coffee (Jack) Hays[qv] during the battle of Salado Creek[qv] on September 18, 1842. The camp is believed to have been adjacent to the battlefield on Salado Creek, six miles northeast of San Antonio within the bounds of present Fort Sam Houston.

BIBLIOGRAPHY: Gerald S. Pierce, *Texas Under Arms: The Camps, Posts, Forts, and Military Towns of the Republic of Texas* (Austin: Encino, 1969). *Art Leatherwood*

CAMP SALMON. Camp Salmon was on a branch of Hubbard Creek near Sloan's Ranch in northeast Callahan County. It was established in March 1862 by Col. James M. Norris[qv] as a station for the Frontier Regiment.[qv] Norris placed half a company under the command of Capt. John Salmon at or near the site of present Breckinridge in Stephens County and the other half at Camp Salmon, which was named for the company commander. The troops initially lived in the open. Huts were not constructed until the summer of 1862. The principal mission of the soldiers was to protect the Ledbetter Salt Works, located in the southwestern part of Shackelford County, against Indian attacks. Beginning in the early part of 1864 and continuing until the close of the war, the attention of the Frontier Regiment was principally directed to Jayhawkers and deserters. In March 1864 the regiment was consolidated and Camp Salmon was abandoned.

BIBLIOGRAPHY: Brutus Clay Chrisman, *Early Days in Callahan County* (Abilene, Texas: Abilene Printing and Stationery, 1966). William Curry Holden, "Frontier Defense in Texas during the Civil War," West Texas Historical Association *Year Book* 4 (1928). Bill Winsor, *Texas in the Confederacy* (Hillsboro, Texas: Hill Junior College Press, 1978). Dudley Goodall Wooten, ed., *A Comprehensive History of Texas* (2 vols., Dallas: Scarff, 1898; rpt., Austin: Texas State Historical Association, 1986). *Jeanne F. Lively*

CAMP SAN ELIZARIO. Camp San Elizario was on the Rio Grande twenty-one miles below El Paso in El Paso County, at the site of San Elizario Presidio,[qv] which had been established there in 1773. On September 15, 1849, the post was occupied by companies I and K of the Third United States Infantry. In 1862 it was occupied by the California Volunteers, or the California Column,[qv] which had moved eastward to prevent invasion of California by Confederate troops.

BIBLIOGRAPHY: Arrie Barrett, Federal Military Outposts in Texas, 1845–1861 (M.A. thesis, University of Texas, 1927). Charles W. Hackett, ed., *Pichardo's Treatise on the Limits of Louisiana and Texas* (4 vols., Austin: University of Texas Press, 1931–46). Joseph Carroll McConnell, *West Texas Frontier* (Vol. 1, Jacksboro, Texas, 1933; Vol. 2, Palo Pinto, Texas, 1939).

CAMP SAN FELIPE. Camp San Felipe, on San Felipe Creek at the site of present Del Rio, was established in 1857. It was considered an outpost of Fort Clark until 1876, when it was made a permanent post with Company E, Tenth United States Cavalry,[qv] stationed there. Lt. J. M. Kelley was the commanding officer. The installation remained in active use until 1896, when the government ordered it dismantled. All movable and usable parts were sold at auction; the medical and hospital supplies were sent to Fort Clark; and the reservation was returned to the original grantee, the Agricultural, Manufacturing, and Irrigation Company of Del Rio.

BIBLIOGRAPHY: William H. Leckie, *The Buffalo Soldiers: A Narrative of the Negro Cavalry in the West* (Norman: University of Oklahoma Press, 1967). *Axcie Seale*

CAMP SAN SABA. When the Civil War[qv] began, federal troops pulled out of frontier posts, and state companies of mounted volunteers organized to protect settlers from Indian raids. One or more of these companies established a camp on the San Saba River at what was probably the site of an earlier ranger camp. Capt. W. D. McMillan's company, Capt. W. G. O'Brien's regiment, and Lt. Decator Barton's company were among the troops at Camp San Saba. The camp ceased to be active by the end of the Civil War. The community of Camp San Saba grew up near the site and took its name.

BIBLIOGRAPHY: Jessie Laurie Barfoot, History of McCulloch County, Texas (M.A. thesis, University of Texas, 1937). William Curry Holden, Frontier Problems and Movements in West Texas, 1846–1900 (Ph.D. dissertation, University of Texas, 1928). Wayne Spiller, comp., *Handbook of McCulloch County History* (Vol. 1, Seagraves, Texas: Pioneer, 1976; vol. 2, Canyon, Texas: Staked Plains Press, 1986). *Vivian Elizabeth Smyrl*

CAMP SAN SABA, TEXAS. Camp San Saba is on Farm Road 1955 and the San Saba River ten miles southeast of Brady in southeastern McCulloch County. The settlers, who in the early 1860s built the community known as Camp San Saba, were not the first to occupy the region. John O. Meusebach[qv] met with a council of Comanches in 1847 near the present townsite. A group of Texas Rangers[qv] was stationed in the area in the mid-1850s to protect settlers from Indian attacks. The community supposedly took its name from this ranger camp. Confederate troops protected the settlers during the Civil War.[qv] Camp San Saba was the principal settlement in McCulloch County until Brady became the county seat in 1876. A post office opened in Camp San Saba in 1876. In 1884 the community had three churches, a district school, three stores, and a population of 250. Area residents shipped wool and livestock. When the coming of the railroad increased Brady's importance as a shipping point in 1904, Camp San Saba began a steady decline. The post office was discontinued after the 1930s. The population of Camp San Saba was 180 in 1925, fifty in 1939, and thirty-six in 1990.

BIBLIOGRAPHY: Wayne Spiller, comp., *Handbook of McCulloch County History* (Vol. 1, Seagraves, Texas: Pioneer, 1976; Vol. 2, Canyon, Texas: Staked Plains Press, 1986). *Vivian Elizabeth Smyrl*

CAMP SEALE, TEXAS. Camp Seale is east of Farm Road 1276 fifty-five miles northwest of Beaumont in southeastern Polk County. In 1928 the Kirby Lumber Company secured large timber tracts in the area and established Camp Seale as a logging camp. By 1940 the site had a post office and a population of about twenty.

Robert Wooster

CAMP SHAFTER. Camp Shafter was a semipermanent military outpost on Comanche Creek twenty-six miles southeast of Fort Duncan and Eagle Pass in Maverick County. The area later became part of the ranch of Ewing Halsell.[qv] The camp was established on May 28, 1873, by Company M, Fourth United States Cavalry,[qv] commanded by Capt. William O'Connell, and named for Lt. Col. William R. Shafter,[qv] then in command at Fort Duncan. A few days before, six companies of the Fourth Cavalry had returned with Lt. John L. Bullis[qv] of the Twenty-fourth United States Infantry.[qv] Bullis, with his famous Black Seminole scouts,[qv] had just carried out the raid on the Kickapoo Village near Remolino, Coahuila. The troops were under the command of Col. Ranald S. Mackenzie.[qv] Camp Shafter was initially established to guard against potential Indian or Mexican retaliation for the Remolino raid. However, when none occurred, it was used as a base for scouting along the Rio Grande. During May and June 1873 the camp was home for Company M and Company E, Fourth Cavalry. Company E was commanded by First Lt. George Thurston. Various units from forts Clark and Duncan used the camp throughout 1873. The site is now covered by a lake on Comanche Creek.

BIBLIOGRAPHY: Records of the Fourth Regiment of Cavalry, National Archives, Washington. *Richard A. Thompson*

CAMP SPRINGS, TEXAS. Camp Springs is on Farm Road 1614 ten miles east of Snyder in east central Scurry County. Lush grass and springs made the area a popular camping spot, first for Indians and later for travelers and such army men as Gen. Robert E. Lee,[qv] who camped there in 1856 with his troops while on the trail of the Comanches. In 1878 the benefits of the area attracted a sheepherder named W. H. Camp, who settled on Spring Creek. Residents called their town Afra after the postmistress's son when a post office was first established in 1891. They later renamed the town Camp Springs. After reaching a population high of fifty between 1920 and 1940, when it also had a bank, a school, stores, and churches, the town declined. By the early 1950s the post office had closed. In 1990 ten people were still living there. Camp Springs is an important site for archeologists, who have unearthed a number of Indian artifacts and bones.

BIBLIOGRAPHY: Scurry County Historical Survey Committee, *Historical Markers in Scurry County* (Snyder, Texas, 1969). Hooper Shelton, comp., *From Buffalo...to Oil: History of Scurry County, Texas* (Snyder, Texas?: Feather, 1973). *Noel Wiggins*

CAMP STANLEY. Camp Stanley, originally Camp Funston, was a subpost of the San Antonio Arsenal[qv] and operated as an ammunition storage depot. It was named Camp Stanley on October 2, 1917, for Brig. Gen. David Sloane Stanley[qv] and designated at first as an infantry cantonment. It was located at Leon Springs Military Reservation, twenty miles northwest of San Antonio. Chinese refugees brought from Mexico in 1916 by Gen. John J. Pershing[qv] were transferred from Fort Sam Houston to Camp Stanley after World War I.[qv] They were finally registered as legal immigrants in 1922. In 1922 the camp became a subpost of Camp Travis[qv] and was to be used as a temporary garrison at peace strength. In September 1933 Camp Stanley was transferred to the jurisdiction of the Ordnance Department, and new buildings were constructed to eliminate hazards. Magazine and igloo space totaled 232,100 square feet. On July 1, 1947, Camp Stanley was consolidated with the San Antonio General Distribution Depot and on July 1, 1949, was designated the Camp Stanley Area of Red River Arsenal, Texarkana, a class-two installation under the jurisdiction of the chief of ordnance. In 1985 Camp Stanley was a subpost of nearby Camp Bullis.

BIBLIOGRAPHY: Edward Eugene Briscoe, "Pershing's Chinese Refugees in Texas," *Southwestern Historical Quarterly* 62 (April 1959). Leah Carter Johnston, *San Antonio: St. Anthony's Town* (San Antonio: Librarians Council, 1947). Ray Miller, *Ray Miller's Texas Forts* (Houston: Cordovan, 1985). *San Antonio Express Magazine*, May 7, 1950. *Texas Monthly Review*, November 1917.

CAMP SWIFT. Camp Swift is on U.S. Highway 290 twenty-eight miles east of Austin and seven miles north of Bastrop in Bastrop County. It was built in 1942 on 55,906 acres and initially had 2,750 buildings designed to accommodate 44,000 troops. The camp was named after Eben Swift,[qv] a World War I[qv] commander and author. During World War II[qv] it reached a maximum strength of 90,000 troops and included, at different times, the 95th, 97th, and 102nd Infantry divisions, the 10th Mountain Division, the 116th and 120th

Tank Destroyer battalions, and the 5th Headquarters, Special Troops, of the Third Army. Swift was the largest army training and transshipment camp in Texas. It also housed 3,865 German prisoners of war.[qv] After the war much of the site was returned to former owners. The government retained 11,700 acres as a military reservation. That land housed parts of the Texas National Guard,[qv] a medium-security federal prison, and a University of Texas cancer research center. Environmental-impact studies and development plans for the mining of extensive lignite deposits under Camp Swift began in the 1970s. Opposition by environmentalists and former landowners and resulted in decades of litigation.

BIBLIOGRAPHY: Arnold P. Krammer, "When the Afrika Korps Came to Texas," *Southwestern Historical Quarterly* 80 (January 1977). Duford W. Skelton and Martha Doty Freeman, *A Cultural Resource Inventory and Assessment at Camp Swift, Texas* (Texas Archeological Resource Report No. 72, Austin: Texas Archeological Survey, University of Texas at Austin, 1979). *Art Leatherwood*

CAMP SWITCH, TEXAS. Camp Switch, on the Missouri Pacific Railroad between Kilgore and White Oak in central Gregg County, was established before 1880. The small settlement was originally known as Camp or Camps, but the name was changed to Camps Switch for the nearby railroad siding. In 1884 Camps was listed as a station on the Texas and Pacific. In 1949 it had one business and a population of 25. In the mid-1960s the population reached 150, but in 1990 it was 70.

BIBLIOGRAPHY: Eugene W. McWhorter, *Traditions of the Land: The History of Gregg County* (Longview, Texas: Gregg County Historical Foundation, 1989). *Christopher Long*

CAMP TERRETT. Camp Terrett, also known as Fort Terrett, on the banks of the North Llano River in eastern Sutton County, was established on February 2, 1852, by Lt. Col. Henry Bainbridge. It was named for Lt. John Terrett, who was killed in the battle of Monterrey in 1846. The camp was established to protect the settlements along the San Antonio Road from Comanches. It was abandoned by federal troops on February 26, 1854. The state of Texas erected a marker in 1936 at the site, twenty-six miles from Junction off U.S. Highway 290W. The old fort buildings are headquarters of the Noel ranch.

BIBLIOGRAPHY: Arrie Barrett, Federal Military Outposts in Texas, 1845–1861 (M.A. thesis, University of Texas, 1927). Herbert M. Hart, *Tour Guide to Old Western Forts* (Boulder, Colorado: Pruett, 1980). Joseph Carroll McConnell, *West Texas Frontier* (Vol. 1, Jacksboro, Texas, 1933; Vol. 2, Palo Pinto, Texas, 1939). Ray Miller, *Ray Miller's Texas Forts* (Houston: Cordovan, 1985). Harold Schoen, comp., *Monuments Erected by the State of Texas to Commemorate the Centenary of Texas Independence* (Austin: Commission of Control for Texas Centennial Celebrations, 1938).

CAMPTI, TEXAS. Campti is on Farm Road 414 eight miles northeast of Center in northeastern Shelby County. It was founded about 1880 and named for Campti, Louisiana, the hometown of many of the early residents. Its post office was established in 1902 and discontinued in 1908. The town had a store, a church, a cemetery, and several houses in 1946, but by 1988 only the church, the cemetery, and a few widely scattered houses remained. *Cecil Harper, Jr.*

CAMPTOWN, TEXAS. Camptown was on the Sabine and Neches Valley Railway three miles northwest of Deweyville and thirty miles northeast of Beaumont in southern Newton County. The Sabine Tram Company mill was established there after the construction of the Sabine and Neches Valley from Deweyville to Gist in 1922. Although the logging camp was abandoned after the discontinuation of the Sabine and Neches Valley in 1945, the area was found to have oil and gas in 1960. A number of wells, known as the Camptown field, continued to produce as of 1984, although no community was evident.

BIBLIOGRAPHY: Ed Ellsworth Bartholomew, *800 Texas Ghost Towns* (Fort Davis, Texas: Frontier, 1971). *Robert Wooster*

CAMP TRAVIS. Shortly after the United States entered World War I,[qv] the war department ordered the establishment of thirty-two divisional training camps—sixteen tent camps for the National Guard and sixteen camps with wooden buildings for the United States Army. Since the South Texas climate was favorable to uninterrupted training, and since Camp Wilson could easily be prepared to handle a division, San Antonio was chosen as one of the sites. Camp Wilson was five miles northeast of downtown San Antonio on the northeastern adjacent boundary of Fort Sam Houston. In May 1916 it became the mobilization point for the Texas National Guard[qv] during the Mexican border crisis. On July 15, 1917, after its selection as the training site for the Ninetieth (Texas-Oklahoma) Division of the army, it was renamed Camp Travis, in honor of Alamo hero William B. Travis.[qv] The camp was ready for occupancy on August 25, 1917. Additional land was subsequently acquired for vital training facilities, and numerous structures were erected by the soldier welfare agencies. Camp Travis comprised 18,290 acres, of which 5,730 were on the main campsite adjoining Fort Sam Houston.

The Ninetieth Division was organized at Camp Travis in September and October of 1917. The ranking officers, including Maj. Gen. Henry T. Allen,[qv] the division and camp commander, were regular army officers. The junior officers were primarily Texas and Oklahoma graduates of the officer-training camp at Camp Funston. The enlisted personnel consisted of Texas and Oklahoma draftees. Hispanics and Indians were intermixed with Caucasians in the new draft division, but blacks were assigned to the camp depot brigade. By mid-October 1917 the Ninetieth Division numbered more than 31,000 officers and men. Equipment shortages, illness, and transfers to other commands interfered with training, however. At the time the division departed for Europe in June 1918 it was composed in considerable part of recent conscripts, many from states other than Texas and Oklahoma. During General Allen's absence in the late fall and winter of 1917–18 the division and camp were commanded successively by brigadier generals Joseph A. Gaston and William H. Johnston.

During the summer of 1918 Camp Travis served as an induction and replacement center, with an average strength in July of about 34,000 white and black troops. In August and September the Eighteenth Division was formed of old and new units at the post under the command of Brig. Gen. George H. Estes. The Eighteenth was still in training when the war ended on November 11. On December 3 Camp Travis was named as a demobilization center. The facility was also designated a local recruiting station and a regional recruit depot in March 1919. Some 62,500 troops were discharged at Camp Travis in about eight months. The camp then became the home station of the Second Division. Its service as a separate entity was terminated, however, upon its absorption by Fort Sam Houston in 1922.

BIBLIOGRAPHY: E. B. Johns, comp., *Camp Travis and Its Part in the World War* (New York, 1919). George Wythe, *A History of the 90th Division* (New York: 90th Division Association, 1920).

Lonnie J. White

CAMP VAN CAMP. Camp Van Camp, near the site of present Newcastle in central Young County, was a United States military outpost of Fort Belknap. It was established on April 30, 1859, and named in memory of Lt. Cornelius Van Camp, a topographical officer in Earl Van Dorn's[qv] expedition. Van Camp was killed in a battle at Wichita Village, Indian Territory, on October 1, 1858. The camp was abandoned on August 28, 1859. In 1936 the Texas Centennial[qv] Commission placed a marker at the site.

BIBLIOGRAPHY: Robert B. Roberts, *Encyclopedia of Historic Forts: The Military, Pioneer, and Trading Posts of the United States* (New York: Macmillan, 1988). Harold Schoen, comp., *Monuments Erected by the State of Texas to Commemorate the Centenary of Texas Independence* (Austin: Commission of Control for Texas Centennial Celebrations, 1938).

CAMP VERDE. Camp Verde, a United States Army frontier post, was established on July 8, 1855, on the northern bank of Verde Creek three miles outside of Bandera Pass in southern Kerr County. In 1856 the camp was headquarters for forty camels[qv] sent by Secretary of War Jefferson Davis[qv] to be used in a system of overland communications. Albert Sidney Johnston[qv] started from Camp Verde in 1857 on his expedition against the Mormons[qv] in Utah. The post was surrendered to the Confederate government in 1861, reoccupied by United States troops in 1865, and abandoned on April 1, 1869. In 1949 a few ruins of the camel corrals and officers' quarters remained. The Texas Centennial[qv] Commission placed a marker at the site near Camp Verde, Texas, in 1936.

BIBLIOGRAPHY: Arrie Barrett, Federal Military Outposts in Texas, 1845–1861 (M.A. thesis, University of Texas, 1927). Chris Emmett, *Texas Camel Tales* (San Antonio: Naylor, 1932). J. Marvin Hunter, *Old Camp Verde, The Home of the Camels* (Bandera, Texas: *Frontier Times*, 1939). Harold Schoen, comp., *Monuments Erected by the State of Texas to Commemorate the Centenary of Texas Independence* (Austin: Commission of Control for Texas Centennial Celebrations, 1938).

CAMP VERDE. A second Camp Verde, two miles below old Camp Verde in Kerr County, was established on March 31, 1862, by James M. Norris[qv] as a ranger station for the Frontier Regiment.[qv] It was manned by members of Charles S. DeMontel's[qv] company and served as a frontier outpost, probably until the consolidation of the regiment in March 1864.

BIBLIOGRAPHY: William Curry Holden, "Frontier Defense in Texas during the Civil War," West Texas Historical Association *Year Book* 4 (1928).

CAMP VERDE, TEXAS. Camp Verde is on the north bank of Verde Creek six miles southwest of Center Point in southeastern Kerr County. It grew around the Williams community store, established adjacent to Camp Verde[qv] in 1857 in order to serve the needs of soldiers stationed there. It is reported that the primary purpose of the store was to provide liquor to the soldiers because regulations prohibited the sale of intoxicants within the camp. When Williams's health failed in 1858, the store was acquired by Charles Schreiner,[qv] then a young rancher in the nearby Turtle Creek area, who had recently immigrated from Germany. Since the store was open only on army paydays, Schreiner and his brother-in-law, Caspar Real, supplemented the business by contracting with the federal government to supply wood and beef to the military post. A post office and store continued to provide irregular service to area inhabitants after the military camp was abandoned. Camp Verde's first post office was established in 1858, probably operated from Schreiner's store. It discontinued operation in 1866. Charles C. Kelley served as postmaster when the post office was reopened at a different location in 1887. In 1892, however, it too was closed. Walter S. Nowlin reestablished the store and post office in 1899. Both remained in operation in the mid-1980s. In 1974 Camp Verde's population was estimated to be forty-one. That figure was still recorded in 1990.

BIBLIOGRAPHY: T. Lindsay Baker, *Ghost Towns of Texas* (Norman: University of Oklahoma Press, 1986). Bob Bennett, *Kerr County, Texas, 1856–1956* (San Antonio: Naylor, 1956; bicentennial ed., rev. by Clara Watkins: *Kerr County, Texas, 1856–1976*, Kerrville, Texas: Hill Country Preservation Society, 1975). Chris Emmett, *Texas Camel Tales* (San Antonio: Naylor, 1932). J. Evetts Haley, *Charles Schreiner, General Merchandise* (Austin: Texas State Historical Association, 1944; rpt., Kerrville, Texas: Charles Schreiner, 1969). Matilda Maria Real, A History of Kerr County (M.A. thesis, University of Texas, 1942).

Rebecca J. Herring

CAMP WALLACE. Camp Wallace, Galveston County, was designed as a training center for antiaircraft units in World War II.[qv] It was formally opened on February 1, 1941, and named for Col. Elmer J. Wallace of the Fifty-ninth Coast Artillery, who was fatally wounded in the Meuse-Argonne offensive of 1918. For two years Camp Wallace served as an antiaircraft replacement training center. On April 15, 1944, the camp was officially transferred to the United States Navy as a naval training and distribution center and was used as a boot camp. After the war it became the Naval Personnel Separation Center. It was declared surplus in 1946.

BIBLIOGRAPHY: David G. McComb, *Galveston: A History* (Austin: University of Texas Press, 1986). *Texas Almanac*, 1945–46, 1947–48.

CAMP WAUL. Camp Waul, a Confederate training camp, was at Old Gay Hill, seven miles north of Brenham in Washington County. New Year's Creek ran through the camp, which bordered the southern boundary of Glenblythe Plantation.[qv] Camp Waul was named for Thomas Neville Waul.[qv] After Waul's Legion was organized at Brenham on May 13, 1862, it trained at Camp Waul until it was ordered out of state on August 18, 1862. During training a severe measles epidemic resulted in the illness of 600 soldiers, but not many died. Soldiers from Austin, Fayette, and Washington counties trained at Camp Waul. During its brief existence, the camp had plentiful food but shortages of arms and other supplies.

BIBLIOGRAPHY: John Duff Brown, "Reminiscences of Jno. Duff Brown," *Southwestern Historical Quarterly* 12 (April 1909). Robert A. Hasskarl, *Waul's Texas Legion, 1862–1865* (Ada, Oklahoma: Book Bindery, 1976). *Carole E. Christian*

CAMP WICHITA. Camp Wichita was a military post near the site of present Buffalo Springs in southeastern Clay County. It may have been little more than a way station for couriers traveling between Fort Richardson and Red River Station. It was used intermittently by the Sixth United States Cavalry from 1868 to 1873.

BIBLIOGRAPHY: William Charles Taylor, *A History of Clay County* (Austin: Jenkins, 1972). *Brian Hart*

CAMP WOOD. Camp Wood was on the Nueces River near the site of the present-day town of Camp Wood in far southwestern Real County. It was established as a United States military outpost on May 20, 1857, when it was occupied by Lt. E. D. Philips and a company of the First Infantry assigned to protect the San Antonio–El Paso route and the Rio Grande valley from Indian raids. The camp was located near the ruins of San Lorenzo de la Santa Cruz Mission; its water was supplied by the same spring that had earlier served the mission and that later provided water for the town of Camp Wood. The installation was named for Bvt. Maj. George W. F. Wood.

The camp was temporarily abandoned on October 29, 1857. Lt. John Bell Hood,[qv] later commander of Hood's Texas Brigade,[qv] reestablished the post in 1858 with a company of the Second Cavalry and remained until November 1860. The post was abandoned by Union troops in the spring of 1861 and was afterward occupied by Confederate forces. Walter Paye Lane's[qv] rangers arrived on June 14, 1861, and W. W. Heartsill,[qv] a member of this detachment, described its stay in his journals, later published as *Fourteen Hundred and 91 Days in the Confederate Army* (1876). Edward Dixon Westfall,[qv] an early settler of Southwest Texas, also lived at Camp Wood during this period, raising cattle and acting as a guide for the Confederates. After the Civil War[qv] the site was periodically used by United States troops and Texas Rangers,[qv] and the influx of settlers began. Jim Hill, who served as a scout for Gen. John Bullis,[qv] moved to the area with his mother and brothers in 1873. According to local residents, buildings and the camp cemetery, the latter of which continued to be used after the post was abandoned, were still extant at the site in the early twentieth century. The buildings have since disappeared, however, and the headstones from the cemetery were eventually taken up and used to line a flower bed.

BIBLIOGRAPHY: A. B. Bender, "Opening Routes Across West Texas, 1848–1850," *Southwestern Historical Quarterly* 37 (October 1933); cont. as "The Texas Frontier, 1848–1861: Government Explorations in Texas, 1851–1860," ibid. 38 (October 1934). John Bell Hood, *Advance and Retreat: Personal Experiences in the United States and Confederate States Armies* (New Orleans: Beauregard, 1880). Andrew Jackson Sowell, *Early Settlers and Indian Fighters of Southwest Texas* (Austin: Ben C. Jones, 1900; rpt., Austin: State House Press, 1986). Allan A. Stovall, *Breaks of the Balcones: A Regional History* (Barksdale, Texas, 1967). Allan A. Stovall, *Nueces Headwater Country: A Regional History* (San Antonio: Naylor, 1959). University of Texas Department of Anthropology, Data Concerning Texas Forts (MS, Barker Texas History Center, University of Texas at Austin). *John Minton*

CAMP WOOD CREEK. Camp Wood Creek, an intermittent, spring-fed stream, rises just north of Farm Road 337 on the divide separating the Nueces and Frio canyons in southwestern Real County (at 29°45′ N, 99°55′ W) and runs southwest for ten miles to its mouth on the Nueces River, just above Camp Wood (at 29°41′ N, 100°01′ W). It winds down the steep eastern descent into the Nueces canyon over a bed of limestone, gravel, and calcareous soil. The surroundings are typical of the heavily dissected canyonlands of the Balcones Escarpment[qv] on the southern edge of the Edwards Plateau,[qv] forested with open stands of live oak, mesquite, and Ashe juniper.

CAMP WOOD, TEXAS. Camp Wood is on the Nueces River at the intersection of Farm Road 337 and State Highway 55, just below Camp Wood Creek in far southwestern Real County. The settlement was founded in 1920 by workers of the Uvalde Cedar Company for the purpose of exploiting the abundant cedar in the area. The site of the town and the immediate vicinity have, however, been inhabited for several millenia, as revealed by archeological evidence. The town is situated in the Nueces Canyon on the Balcones Escarpment, at the southern edge of the Edwards Plateau,[qv] amid plentiful supplies of water, game, and other natural resources. The excellence of the site for habitation is attested by evidence of successive occupations since the Archaic and Neo-American periods. The modern town's water is supplied by the same spring that earlier served San Lorenzo de la Santa Cruz Mission (1762–71), established by Franciscans[qv] for the Lipan Apaches who inhabited the region during the historic period, and the United States military outpost Camp Wood[qv] (1857–61), from which the town derives its name. After the mission was abandoned, Indians continued to return to the site. White occupation did not cease with the withdrawal of federal troops at the start of the Civil War.[qv] Edward D. Westfall[qv] moved to the site at this time and remained until 1874, raising cattle and serving as a scout for Confederate troops stationed there. Jerusha Sánchez, a midwife in the Nueces Canyon, also reportedly came into the area in the early 1860s, and in 1864 the family of George Schwander was occupying the remains of the old mission when Lipans killed Mrs. Schwander and abducted their son, Albert. In 1873 the widow Elizabeth Hill moved to the canyon with her three sons, John, Ed, and Jim, the last of whom subsequently served as a scout for Gen. John Bullis[qv] and purchased a house from the Sánchez family. The United States military and the Texas Rangers[qv] also briefly reoccupied Camp Wood in the second half of the nineteenth century. In 1917–18 Joe Sweeten ran a store a mile north of the site of present Camp Wood on the Uvalde-Rocksprings road (Highway 55); the store served local ranchers and freighters hauling goods between Rocksprings and Uvalde and was referred to as Real City.

In 1920 Camp Wood became the northern terminus of the Uvalde and Northern Railroad, and the townsite was formally laid out. Cedar workers initially lived in tents, but during the 1920s the settlement rapidly developed into a prosperous community. The post office was established in November 1921, and the town was incorporated in 1936. However, the depression and the depletion of the region's cedar curtailed development. The Uvalde and Northern ceased operation in the early 1940s, and ranching, in particular the raising of Angora goats, replaced cedar as the principal industry, with tourism and hunting assuming increasing importance in the local economy.

In March 1924 Charles A. Lindbergh made an unplanned stop in Camp Wood, three years before his solo flight from New York to Paris. Lindbergh, then waiting to enter Brooks Field at San Antonio as a United States Air Service cadet, was attempting to fly to California with a friend, Leon Klink, and followed the Uvalde and Northern Railroad up the Nueces River, mistaking it for the Southern Pacific along the Rio Grande. When the line ended at the recently established cedar town, Lindbergh, realizing his error, landed in a pasture to the north. Later, having flown to Camp Wood itself and landed on the main street, he attempted to take off, hit a telephone pole with a wing, and crashed into the paint section of Walter Pruett's hardware store. The two fliers remained in Camp Wood for several days, awaiting parts and making repairs, and their visit and the circumstances surrounding it were still vividly recalled and related over half a century later. In 1976 the town of Camp Wood renamed a park and a street after Lindbergh and Klink respectively, and the state placed a historical marker celebrating the event.

Though population estimates for Camp Wood remained at 700 to 800 between 1920 and World War II,[qv] large amounts of local real estate were subsequently purchased by outsiders who are drawn to the area by its natural beauty and who use the land for hunting or vacationing; meanwhile, large numbers of young people have left in search of greater opportunity. In 1990 the population was 595.

BIBLIOGRAPHY: Grace Lorene Lewis, A History of Real County (M.A. thesis, University of Texas, 1956). Allan A. Stovall, *Breaks of the Balcones: A Regional History* (Barksdale, Texas, 1967). Allan A. Stovall, *Nueces Headwater Country: A Regional History* (San Antonio: Naylor, 1959). Curtis D. Tunnell and William W. Newcomb, *A Lipan Apache Mission: San Lorenzo de la Santa Cruz* (Austin: Texas Memorial Museum, 1969). *John Minton*

CAMP WORTH, TEXAS. Camp Worth was on Arenosa Creek and a country road, ten miles northwest of San Augustine in northwestern San Augustine County. It was founded as a timber camp of the Frost Lumber Industries and was named for the lumber mills manager, Worth Whited. A tram line was built to the site in the 1920s or 1930s, and in 1940 the community had a church, scattered dwellings, and a school. By the 1980s no buildings remained on the site, though it was still listed on state highway maps. *Mark Odintz*

CANA, TEXAS. Cana was north of State Highway 243 and eight miles west of Canton in west central Van Zandt County. The 1936 county highway map showed a church, a cemetery, and scattered dwellings at the townsite, but by 1987 the community was no longer shown on maps. *Diana J. Kleiner*

CANAAN SWITCH, TEXAS. Canaan Switch was a flag station on the Houston and Texas Central Railway six miles south of Mexia in Limestone County. Its early residents were former slaves from nearby plantations. In 1888 a post office called Dump was briefly established at Canaan Switch with Zachariah H. Williams as postmaster. After the office was discontinued, mail for the community was sent to

Groesbeck. The community's population was given as ten in 1889. Little remained in the area by the 1940s.

BIBLIOGRAPHY: Walter F. Cotton, *History of Negroes of Limestone County from 1860 to 1939* (Mexia, Texas: Chatman and Merriwether, 1939). John J. Germann and Myron Janzen, *Texas Post Offices by County* (1986). *Vivian Elizabeth Smyrl*

CANABATINU INDIANS. This name is known from a single Spanish missionary report in 1691, which indicates that the Canabatinus were enemies of the Hasinai tribes of eastern Texas and lived an unspecified distance to the west of the Hasinais. J. R. Swanton suggested that the Canabatinus may have been a Wichita group, but he cited no evidence in support of this identification.

BIBLIOGRAPHY: John R. Swanton, *Source Material on the History and Ethnology of the Caddo Indians* (Smithsonian Institution, Bureau of American Ethnology Bulletin 132, Washington: GPO, 1942).
Thomas N. Campbell

CAÑADA VERDE, TEXAS. Cañada Verde is at the junction of Farm roads 1303 and 3444, eight miles northwest of Floresville in western Wilson County. The site was settled around the time of the Civil War.[qv] A school was in operation there by 1896, when it had an enrollment of seventy-one. In the mid-1930s Cañada Verde had a school, a church, three stores, and a number of houses. After World War II[qv] its school was closed, but in the early 1990s a church and several businesses remained at the site. *Christopher Long*

CANADAY, JOHN EDWIN (1907–1985). John Canaday, art critic and author, was born on February 1, 1907, in Fort Scott, Kansas, one of six children of Franklin and Agnes F. (Musson) Canaday. His family moved to Dallas when Canaday was seven and later moved to San Antonio, where he attended Main Avenue High School. Canaday entered the University of Texas in 1924 and earned a B.A. degree in French and English literature in 1929. He subsequently studied painting and art history at Yale University, where he received an M.A. in 1933. He taught at Washburn College (later Washburn University of Topeka) in 1933–34; at Newcomb College, Tulane University, New Orleans (1934–36); Hollins College, Roanoke, Virginia (1936–38); and the University of Virginia, Charlottesville (1938–50). In 1943 he traveled to the Belgian Congo and acted as a French interpreter for the Bureau of Economic Welfare, and the following year he joined the United States Marine Corps. He served as a lieutenant in the South Pacific until the end of World War II,[qv] after which he returned to the University of Virginia. From 1950 to 1952 Canaday headed the art school at Newcomb College in New Orleans. He worked as chief of the educational division at the Philadelphia Museum of Art from 1953 to 1959. During this period he wrote the text for *Metropolitan Seminars in Art,* a widely distributed series of twenty-four portfolios published between 1958 and 1960 by the Metropolitan Museum of Art in New York.

In 1959 Canaday began a seventeen-year career as a critic for the New York *Times.* In his first column on September 6, 1959, he inflamed the art establishment by proclaiming that Abstract Expressionism, the dominant style of the period, allowed "exceptional tolerance for incompetence and deception." Although he acknowledged the talent of the best Abstract Expressionists, he noted that "we have been had" by the "freaks, the charlatans, and the misled who surround this handful of serious and talented artists." Canaday's inaugural column and subsequent articles criticizing this style provoked a much-publicized letter to the *Times* signed by forty-nine of the nation's leading art figures, who denounced Canaday as an agitator. Other artists and critics, however, championed him as an honest and articulate observer of the art scene, which continued to provide ample targets for his barbed wit over the years.

In addition to writing for the *Times,* Canaday published a number of influential books, notably *Mainstreams of Modern Art: David to Picasso* (1959), winner of the Athenaeum Award and a popular art history textbook for many years. His experiences as a critic provided the subject matter of two books, *Embattled Critic: Views on Modern Art* (1962) and *Culture Gulch: Notes on Art and Its Public in the 1960's* (1969). He also wrote *Keys to Art,* with Katherine H. Canaday (1963), *The Lives of the Painters* (1969), *Baroque Painters* (1972), *Late Gothic to Renaissance Painters* (1972), *Neoclassic to Post-Impressionist Painters* (1972), *My Best Girls: 8 Drawings* (1972), *The New York Guide to Dining Out in New York* (1972), *The Artful Avocado* (1973), *Richard Estes: The Urban Landscape* (1979), *What is Art? An Introduction to Painting, Sculpture, and Architecture* (1980), and *Ben Shahn, Voices and Visions* (1981). In the 1940s and 1950s, under the pen name Matthew Head, Canaday wrote seven crime novels with such titles as *The Smell of Money* (1943), *The Congo Venus* (1976), and *Murder at the Flea Club* (1957). Drawing in part on his experiences in the Congo, he set three of his mysteries in Africa, and they were heralded by one critic as subtly foreshadowing a time of change on the African continent.

In 1973 Canaday stepped down from his post as art critic in order to devote more time to writing books, although he continued to write restaurant reviews for the *Times* until his retirement in 1977. Canaday taught several courses as a guest lecturer at the University of Texas in the spring of 1977. He continued to lecture and to write for such publications as *Smithsonian Magazine,* the *New Republic,* and the *New York Times Magazine* until his death. John Canaday married Katherine S. Hoover on September 19, 1935, and they had two sons. He died of pancreatic cancer on July 19, 1985.

BIBLIOGRAPHY: New York *Times,* July 21, 1985. *New Yorker,* January 4, 1964. *Who's Who in America,* 1984–85. *Kendall Curlee*

CANADIAN, TEXAS. Canadian, on U.S. highways 60 and 83 in western Hemphill County, has been the county seat since its founding in 1887. In the spring of that year E. P. Purcell and O. H. Nelson, who headed the Kansas Railway Townsite Company, laid out the 240-acre townsite, which is on the south bank of the Canadian River near its junction with Red Deer Creek. By summer the Southern Kansas Railway had completed a bridge across the river from the settlement of Clear Creek, or Hogtown. As a result, residents of Hogtown moved their homes and businesses to Canadian. Soon the temporary tent city gave way to more permanent structures, as the townsite company's advertisements attracted more prospective settlers and businesses. Nelson Peet established the first hotel, the Log Cabin, and a post office was opened in August. On July 4, 1888, Canadian's reputation as a rodeo (*see* RODEOS) town began when the annual Cowboys' Reunion staged a commercial rodeo, one of the first in Texas. The event has been an annual custom ever since. Baptists, Methodists, Disciples of Christ, and other Christian communions soon established churches in Canadian. By 1900 the incorporated town was a major shipping center with railroad division headquarters and roundhouses, cotton gins, elevators, banks, a public school, and a private academy, as well as various stores and other small businesses. Canadian also had as many as thirteen saloons before the county voted to go dry in 1903. Since then, the Woman's Christian Temperance Union[qv] has had an active chapter in Canadian; the old WCTU building also houses the city library. Canadian has had seven newspapers: the *Free Press* (1887–88), the *Crescent* (1888–93), the *Record* (1893–), the *Enterprise* (1891–1912), the *Advertiser* (which later became the *Hemphill County News,* 1938–71), the *Sand Burr* (1933–49), and the short-lived *Monday Morning News* (1916).

Among the prominent businessmen and civic leaders, some of whose descendants still make Canadian their home, were George and John J. Gerlach, Harvey E. Hoover, Edward H. Brainard, and Nahim Abraham,[qqv] who immigrated from Lebanon. Temple Lea Houston[qv] lived for a time in Canadian, as did the colorful rancher and lawman George W. Arrington.[qv]

In the early 1950s Canadian lost its railroad roundhouses and division headquarters as a result of reorganization by the Santa Fe. Nevertheless, it continued to thrive on ranching and farming, as well as oil and gas production. The population increased from 2,671 in 1950 to 3,491 in 1980. In 1990 it was 2,417. In addition to the annual rodeo, the annual Midsummer Music Festival in August and the Autumn Foliage Tour in October attract visitors. The Pioneer Museum is housed in the old Moody Hotel, which dates from 1906. Lake Marvin and the Gene Howe Wildlife Management area are located east of town.

BIBLIOGRAPHY: F. Stanley [Stanley F. L. Crocchiola], *The Canadian, Texas, Story* (Nazareth, Texas, 1975). F. Stanley [Stanley F. L. Crocchiola], *Rodeo Town (Canadian, Texas)* (Denver: World, 1953).

H. Allen Anderson

CANADIAN ACADEMY. Canadian Academy, a Baptist coeducational institution at Canadian, was established in 1901 and opened in 1903, in a building constructed and equipped in 1900 for the use of the local school system. It opened with a faculty of four and a student body of twenty-seven. The second year the faculty numbered seven and the student enrollment 117. Over the next few years a dining hall and two dormitories were added. The school was divided into departments of literature and composition, music, education, and physical culture. A highlight of the academy's brief history came in the spring of 1907, when the twelve-member science class traveled to dig and examine artifacts on the recently discovered, buried Indian-city site south of Perryton in Ochiltree County. Because it was sustained wholly by contributions, fees, and tuition, Canadian Academy could not compete with tax-supported schools when the latter began to offer more educational opportunities. The academy was closed in 1913. Presidents of the school were J. F. McDonald, O. N. McBride, and R. E. L. Farmer.

BIBLIOGRAPHY: Sallie B. Harris, *Cowmen and Ladies: A History of Hemphill County* (Canyon, Texas: Staked Plains, 1977). F. Stanley [Stanley F. L. Crocchiola], *The Canadian, Texas, Story* (Nazareth, Texas, 1975). F. Stanley [Stanley F. L. Crocchiola], *Rodeo Town (Canadian, Texas)* (Denver: World, 1953). Winifred Morris Stoker, History of Canadian Academy (MS, Canadian Public Library, Canadian, Texas). Winifred Morris Stoker, *A Pictorial History of Early Higher Education in the Texas Panhandle* (Canyon: West Texas State University, 1976).

J. W. Sanders

CANADIAN BREAKS. The Canadian Breaks is a unique valley in Oldham County that dramatically interrupts the Pliocene surface of the High Plains. The breaks were formed where the Canadian River cut through the Caprock[qv] and Triassic sandstone beneath into Permian sandy clay and andydrite.

BIBLIOGRAPHY: Robert A. Sheldon, *Roadside Geology of Texas* (Missoula, Montana: Mountain Press, 1979).

CANADIAN RIVER. The Canadian River, the largest tributary of the Arkansas River, rises in the Sangre de Cristo Mountains in southern Las Animas County, Colorado, near Raton Pass and the boundary line with Colfax County, New Mexico (at 37°01′ N, 105°03′ W), and flows south and southeastward, separating the Llano Estacado[qv] from the northern High Plains. It is roughly 760 miles long; a stretch of about 190 miles is in Texas. The river is dammed to form the Conchas and Ute reservoirs in northeastern New Mexico before it enters Texas at about the midpoint of the western boundary of Oldham County. The Canadian crosses the Panhandle,[qv] flowing eastward and northeastward through Oldham, Potter, Moore, Hutchinson, Roberts, and Hemphill counties. Most of the river's course across the Panhandle passes through a gorge 500 to 800 feet below the plateau. Particularly in its lower reaches in Oklahoma, the riverbed contains great amounts of quicksand; this and the deep gorge make the river difficult to bridge. A tributary, the North Canadian, heads in Union County, New Mexico (at 36°30′ N, 102°09′ W), and flows briefly into the northern Texas Panhandle before continuing on to its confluence with the river in McIntosh County, Oklahoma (at 36°30′ N, 101°55′ W). After crossing the state line back into Oklahoma, the Canadian River flows generally southeastward to its mouth on the Arkansas River, twenty miles east of Canadian in Haskell County, Oklahoma (at 35°27′ N, 95°02′ W).

According to some sources, the river's name came from early explorers who thought that it flowed into Canada. Among the Canadian's principal tributaries in Texas are Big Blue, Tallahone, Red Deer, Pedarosa, Punta Agua, Amarillo, Tascosa, and White Deer creeks. The Texas portion of the Canadian River is noted for archeological sites where extensive remains of Pueblo Indian culture have been found (*see* ANTELOPE CREEK PHASE). Some historians have said that Quivira,[qv] long sought by Francisco Vázquez de Coronado,[qv] was on the Canadian. The Canadian is probably the stream that Juan de Oñate[qv] called the Magdalena in 1601. The area was Comanche country until the latter part of the 1800s, but the stream was well known to the Comancheros,[qv] to Josiah Gregg,[qv] and to others engaged in trade out of St. Louis or Santa Fe. Lt. James William Abert[qv] of the United States Army Corps of Topographical Engineers explored the river in 1845 and made an extensive report of its physical features and of the Indians whom he encountered. With the decimation of the buffalo,[qv] cattlemen replaced Indians in the area, and, except for oil developments, the Canadian valley in Texas remained in 1949 principally a ranching area.

The river is dammed to form Lake Meredith[qv] forty miles northeast of Amarillo near Sanford in Hutchinson County. The Panhandle Water Conservation Authority[qv] as early as 1949 was contemplating construction of Sanford Dam to create a reservoir of some 1,305,000 acre-feet capacity that would furnish a municipal water supply for eleven Panhandle cities and serve the secondary purposes of flood control, soil conservation, recreation, and promotion of wildlife; actual impoundment of water did not begin until 1965. Lake Meredith is named for A. A. Meredith, who was executive secretary of the Canadian River Municipal Water Authority.[qv] An aqueduct to serve Pampa, Amarillo, Lubbock, Lamesa, Borger, Levelland, Littlefield, O'Donnell, Slaton, and Tahoka was estimated to cost $54 million. Cities purchasing the water would repay the major part of the cost of the project over a period of fifty years. The Canadian River Compact[qv] Commissioner, appointed in 1951, negotiates with other states regarding the water of the Canadian. The National Park Service assumed management of recreational facilities at Lake Meredith in 1965.

BIBLIOGRAPHY: *A Summary of the Preliminary Plan for Proposed Water Resources Development in the Canadian River Basin* (Austin: Texas Water Development Board, 1966). Texas Planning Board, *The Canadian River Basin in Texas* (Austin, 1936). U.S. Army Corps of Topographical Engineers, *Guadal P'a: The Journal of Lieutenant J. W. Abert, from Bent's Fort to St. Louis in 1845* (Canyon, Texas: Panhandle-Plains Historical Society, 1941).

Hobart Huson

CANADIAN RIVER COMPACT. Shortly after 1900 interest began to develop in the Panhandle[qv] in large-scale irrigation projects, which require conservation storage of water. In 1918 Eagle Nest Reservoir was constructed on Cimarron Creek, a Canadian River tributary in New Mexico, to impound water for downstream irrigation. In 1925 an organization known as the Canadian River Development Association was formed to foster interstate flood-control and irrigation projects, and to promote such projects a compact apportioning the river's flow among the three riparian states was negotiated in 1926. The Oklahoma legislature ratified the agreement, as did the New Mexico legislature, with modification. The Texas legislature took no action, and the compact did not become effective.

Interest in development of the Canadian continued, however, and in 1938 the United States Army Corps of Engineers was authorized to construct the Conchas Reservoir on the river's main stream in New Mexico, to provide flood protection for all three states and to supply water for a 34,000-acre irrigation project in the headwater state, New Mexico. During the late 1940s, faced with the problems of declining water levels and rising water requirements, a number of pump-dependent Panhandle communities pooled efforts to promote construction of a surface-water reservoir on the river's main stream near Sanford. This was to provide additional flood protection and store water for municipal, industrial, and recreational uses. To expedite the plan, the communities urged negotiation of a second compact to define the rights of each state to use of Canadian River water. On December 6, 1950, a second compact was signed in Santa Fe, New Mexico. The legislatures of the three states ratified the agreement in 1951. Acceptance by Congress followed, and the instrument was signed into law by the president on May 19, 1952. With their equities in the river defined, New Mexico and Texas were able to proceed with development projects—New Mexico at the Clayton and Ute sites and Texas at the Sanford site. Projects in Oklahoma were planned.

The reservoir behind Sanford Dam, completed in 1965 by the United States Bureau of Reclamation, yields about 103,000 acre-feet of water annually for use in eleven Texas communities: Amarillo, Borger, Pampa, Plainview, Lubbock, Slaton, O'Donnell, Tahoka, Levelland, Lamesa, and Brownfield. The aqueduct system includes more than 300 miles of pipeline, pumping stations, and regulating reservoirs, as well as chlorinating facilities. Construction costs were about $103,230,000.

BIBLIOGRAPHY: Canadian River Project Reference File, Southwest Collection, Texas Tech University. *Hudson Davis*

CANADIAN RIVER EXPEDITION. The Canadian River Expedition of 1868 was the westernmost prong of Gen. Philip H. Sheridan's[qv] winter campaign, launched in the late fall of 1868 for the purpose of chasing down Cheyennes and Arapahos who had fled south of the Arkansas River after raiding white settlements in northwestern Kansas. The campaign began after Nathaniel Taylor's peace commission, in a meeting dominated by the military (including Gen. William T. Sherman[qv]), voted to use military strength to force the Indians to move to the reservations set up under the Medicine Lodge Treaty of 1867. The commission also resolved to annul a provision in the treaty that had allowed the Indians to hunt outside the reservation. Many Indians had set up winter camps near the villages of the Comanches and Kiowas in the Canadian and Washita valleys, thus compounding the problem, since those two tribes were not considered hostile in Kansas at the time. Indeed, peaceful Indians were supposed to report to Gen. William B. Hazen[qv] at his base at Fort Cobb, where he was supervising the southern reservations that had been set up under the Medicine Lodge treaty. Sheridan and his immediate superior, Sherman, opted for total war to drive the raiders onto the reserves in Indian Territory.

The main force in the campaign, led by Gen. Alfred Sully and including Lt. Col. George A. Custer's[qv] Seventh Cavalry, moved south from Fort Dodge, Kansas. After establishing Camp Supply on the North Canadian, the troops engaged in several forays, highlighted by Custer's victory in the battle of the Washita, near the site of present Cheyenne, Oklahoma, on November 17. In December Sheridan himself led troops down the Washita to Fort Cobb, which he designated as his temporary headquarters.

Since several hostile groups had fled westward, particularly after the fight on the Washita, Sheridan ordered certain columns of troops to come in from the north and west to act as "beaters-in" for his main forces. The leader of the western contingent was Maj. Andrew Wallace (Beans) Evans, a native of Maryland who had risen through the ranks since his graduation from West Point in 1848. During the Civil War[qv] he had been brevetted twice—for meritorious action at the battle of Valverde[qv] on February 21, 1862, and for his cavalry actions in the Union campaign leading to Lee's surrender at Appomattox in April 1865. One contemporary described him as "the most even tempered man in the Army—always cross," while another recalled him as a "melancholy, philosophically inclined officer, devoted to literature, suffering from an old wound, and having, to all appearance, registered a vow never to smile."

On November 18, 1868, Evans left Fort Bascom, New Mexico, with more than 500 officers and men, including six troops of the Third Cavalry, one company of the Thirty-seventh Infantry, a battery of howitzers, and several civilian scouts and guides. Following the left bank of the Canadian, the column encountered a blizzard two days later, but despite deep snow, sleet, and freezing temperatures the troops trudged their way over the Fort Smith–Santa Fe route across the Panhandle[qv] and eventually established a supply depot between two sand hills at the mouth of Monument Creek, probably in what is now Hemphill County, Texas. From there scouting parties searched the eastern Panhandle for Indians, but none was found. Leaving Capt. Arthur B. Carpenter with twenty men to guard the base, Evans moved down the Canadian on December 15 and struck a fresh Indian trail going southeast a few miles west of the Antelope Hills. After ten days of hard marching, his command came upon a Comanche village of sixty tepees at Soldier Spring, on the North Fork of the Red River in what is now Greer County,[qv] Oklahoma. A sharp battle on Christmas Day drove the surprised Indians from their lodges with several casualties and resulted in the destruction of vast quantities of dried buffalo meat and other provisions on which they depended for winter survival. The troops lost only one killed and two slightly wounded, while the Indians sustained twenty-five fatalities. Evans moved northeast toward the Washita in the still frigid weather and sent a small escort with dispatches for Sheridan at Fort Cobb. On January 3, 1869, he marched his contingent back westward toward his supply base on Monument Creek.

Captain Carpenter, in the meantime, had lent some supplies and forage to the beleaguered northern column from Fort Lyon, Colorado, led by Maj. Eugene A. Carr, whose own base of operations was twenty miles west of Evans's depot. By the time Evans returned on January 13, however, Carr's troops had started back to Fort Lyon without having located any Indians. Evans's own troops were famished and suffering from exposure and had suffered heavy losses in livestock. Nevertheless, as it turned out, the village he and his men had destroyed at Soldier Spring was that of Horseback's Nokoni band, which had committed several depredations in Texas the previous summer and fall. At the height of the engagement the Nokonis had been reinforced by Kiowa braves under Woman's Heart, whose lodges were downstream from Horseback's village, but to no avail. Afterward, several Nokonis and Kiowas surrendered to the authorities at Fort Cobb, while others came in at Fort Bascom in such haste that they arrived even ahead of Evans, who had returned there by February 7.

By the end of December 1868 most of the Kiowa and Comanche bands, except for the isolationist Quahadis, had been consolidated at Fort Cobb. The following spring, after the establishment of Fort Sill as the new headquarters for the Comanche and Kiowa reserve near the Wichita Mountains, Custer made a sortie into the eastern Panhandle and cowed several recalcitrant Cheyenne and Arapaho bands into reporting to Camp Supply for assignment to their new reservation. Although lasting peace was not effected for almost another decade, the raiders of the southern plains realized that the winter season was no longer a guaranteed safeguard against campaigns by white horse-soldiers. Evans, who was brevetted colonel for his action at Soldier

Spring, received a brigadier general's brevet in 1890 for his gallantry in an engagement against Apaches at the Big Dry Wash in Arizona on July 17, 1882.

BIBLIOGRAPHY: Duane F. Guy, "The Canadian River Expedition of 1868," *Panhandle-Plains Historical Review* 48 (1975). Francis B. Heitman, *Historical Register and Dictionary of the United States Army* (2 vols., Washington: GPO, 1903; rpt., Urbana: University of Illinois Press, 1965). William H. Leckie, *The Military Conquest of the Southern Plains* (Norman: University of Oklahoma Press, 1963). Frederick W. Rathjen, *The Texas Panhandle Frontier* (Austin: University of Texas Press, 1973). Robert M. Utley, *Frontier Regulars: The United States Army and the Indian, 1866–1891* (New York: Macmillan, 1973). Robert M. Utley, *The Indian Frontier of the American West, 1846–1890* (Albuquerque: University of New Mexico Press, 1984).

H. Allen Anderson

CANADIAN RIVER MUNICIPAL WATER AUTHORITY. The Canadian River project received federal authorization in December 1950, and in November 1953 the legislature authorized it to organize as a legal entity and independent political subdivision of Texas. Eleven cities formed the authority: Amarillo, Borger, Pampa, Plainview, Lubbock, Slaton, Brownfield, Levelland, Lamesa, Tahoka, and O'Donnell. Under a tri-state compact (Texas, Oklahoma, and New Mexico), Texas was entitled to 100,000 acre-feet of water a year for use by the member cities and 51,000 acre-feet for use by industries. In 1960 a repayment contract between the United States government and the Canadian River Municipal Water Authority was executed for construction of the project. The repayment schedule for the authority provided for the repayment, with interest, over a fifty-year period. Each city negotiated a contract with the Canadian River Municipal Water Authority for that city's estimate of water needs and the city's assumption of a percentage of the construction debt. Sale of water to cities outside of the authority is possible only by a city's willingness to release a portion of its water. The dam, crossing the Canadian River nine miles west of Borger, is 226 feet high and 6,380 feet long. The aqueduct system, with 322 miles of pipeline, ten pumping plants, and three regulating reservoirs, furnishes municipal and industrial water to the cities of the authority.

BIBLIOGRAPHY: Arrell L. Gibson, *The Canadian River Valley* (New York: Teacher's College Press, 1971). *Doris Alexander*

CANA INDIANS. The Cana (Cano) Indians are known only from records pertaining to San José y San Miguel de Aguayo Mission at San Antonio. It is said that they were among the Indians for whom this mission was founded in 1720. This rather clearly indicates that they were Coahuiltecans. It has been assumed by some writers that the Canas were the same as the Sanas, but the Sanas were not Coahuiltecans and did not appear at San Antonio missions until after 1740. In 1691 a group known as Canu was reported as living eighty leagues southwest of the Hasinai Indians of eastern Texas, but it cannot be proved that Canu and Cana were names for the same people. It seems likely that the Canas originally lived in the vicinity of San Antonio, perhaps to the west or southwest.

BIBLIOGRAPHY: Charles W. Hackett, ed., *Pichardo's Treatise on the Limits of Louisiana and Texas* (4 vols., Austin: University of Texas Press, 1931–46). Frederick Webb Hodge, ed., *Handbook of American Indians North of Mexico* (2 vols., Washington: GPO, 1907, 1910; rpt., New York: Pageant, 1959). Gaspar José de Solís, "Diary," trans. Margaret Kenny Kress, *Southwestern Historical Quarterly* 35 (July 1931). John R. Swanton, *Source Material on the History and Ethnology of the Caddo Indians* (Smithsonian Institution, Bureau of American Ethnology Bulletin 132, Washington: GPO, 1942). *Thomas N. Campbell*

CANAL CREEK. Canal Creek rises a mile east of Vivian in northwestern Foard County (at 34°02′ N, 99°53′ W) and runs northeast for six miles to its mouth on the Pease River, at State Highway 6 (at 34°06′ N, 99°47′ W). It crosses an area of steep to moderately sloping hills, surfaced by shallow, stony, sandy and clay loams that support mesquite, oak, and grasses.

CANALES, JOSÉ TOMÁS (1877–1976). José Tomás (J. T.) Canales, lawyer, legislator, landowner, and a founder of the League of United Latin American Citizens,[qv] the son of Andreas and Tomasa (Cavazos) Canales, was born on a ranch in Nueces County, Texas, on March 7, 1877. His mother was a descendant of José Salvador de la Garza, the recipient of the Espíritu Santo grant, an enormous Spanish land grant that occupied most of what is now Cameron County. His mother's family still retained extensive holdings of ranchland in Nueces County at the time of Canales's birth. As a child, Canales lived with his parents and with several relatives and attended a variety of schools in Nueces County and at Tampico, Vera Cruz, and Matamoros and Mier, Tamaulipas. From 1890 to 1892 he attended a secondary school at Austin called Texas Business College. After delivering a shipment of cattle to Oklahoma he befriended a cattle dealer and moved to Kansas City, Kansas, to live with the man's family and complete high school. There Canales left the Catholic Church and became a Presbyterian. In fall 1896 he attended the University of Michigan, where he received a law degree three years later. After practicing law in Corpus Christi and Laredo from 1900 to 1903 he settled in Brownsville, where he worked in the county assessor's office.

Over the next two decades Canales made his mark as both a lawyer and a politician. With the support of the Cameron County Democratic machine under the control of James B. Wells, Jr.,[qv] he served from 1905 to 1910 in the Texas House of Representatives, where he represented the Ninety-fifth District (Cameron, Hidalgo, Starr, and Zapata counties). He worked in irrigation laws, education, and judicial and tax reform. His cooperation with Wells ended when Canales embraced prohibition[qv] in 1909 and campaigned unsuccessfully as an independent candidate for county judge in 1910. Two years later he returned to the Democratic party[qv] and from 1912 to 1914 served as county superintendent of public schools in Cameron County, where he stressed the use of the English language, United States patriotism, and rural education. In 1914 he served as county judge. Canales returned to the Texas House as a representative of the Seventy-seventh District, Cameron and Willacy counties, and served from 1917 to 1920. As chairman of the House Committee on Irrigation, he promoted legislation to organize public irrigation districts. In 1917, during World War I,[qv] he helped to prevent Mexican immigrant workers from fleeing to Mexico to escape the draft and the high cost of living.

During the Mexican border raids of 1915 and 1916 Canales organized a company of Mexican-American scouts to collect intelligence for the United States army. At the same time, he stood out as the only prominent local Democrat to call for an end to Texas Ranger and vigilante oppression of the Hispanic population of the lower Rio Grande valley. His most dramatic maneuver came on January 31, 1918, when he filed nineteen charges against the Texas Rangers[qv] and demanded a legislative investigation and the reorganization of the force. While defending the rights of persons of Mexican descent against the abuses of the rangers, Canales sought white support by embracing such causes as prohibition and woman suffrage.[qv] In 1918 ranger Frank Hamer[qv] threatened the legislator because of his criticism of the force, as did committee chairman William H. Bledsoe[qv] of Lubbock. As a result of the reaction by state legislators against Canales's challenge to the rangers, the Tejano legislator declined to seek reelection in 1920.

After he retired from state office, Canales played an active role in the incipient Mexican-American civil-rights movement. He was in contact with the Order of Sons of America[qv] in San Antonio in 1923 and with the Corpus Christi chapter in 1925. In 1927 at the Harlingen Convention[qv] he played a prominent role in the exclusion of Mexican citizens from the organization formed there, the Latin American Citizens League, for which he served as president. Over the years he was extremely influential in the League of United Latin American Citizens. He addressed its founding meeting in 1929 and later wrote most of its first constitution. He also served on its first board of trustees and was LULAC president in 1932–33. In 1939 he revised the constitution to accommodate the organization's westward expansion as a national organization. Canales was Brownsville city attorney from 1930 to 1940. In 1931 he served as an attorney in *Del Rio ISD v. Salvatierra.*[qv] In 1951 he was temporary chairman of the Texas Council on Human Relations[qv] established by Governor R. Allan Shivers.[qv]

Canales wrote numerous articles, pamphlets, and books, mostly privately published, on religion, law, and history. He wrote for the *LULAC News* in the 1930s and penned *Ethics in the Profession of Law* in 1953. His historical works focused on Mexican-American history; he believed that an understanding of that history could foster better racial relations. He also wrote *Bits of Texas History in the Melting Pot of America,* published in two parts in 1950 and 1957, and two books about his great uncle, Juan N. Cortina,[qv] *Juan N. Cortina: Bandit or Patriot?* and *Juan N. Cortina Presents His Motion for a New Trial,* both published in 1951. Perhaps Canales's best historical works are his "Personal Recollections of J. T. Canales," written in 1945, an account of the economic development of South Texas, and "The Texas Law of Flowing Waters With Special Reference to Irrigation from the Lower Rio Grande," written in collaboration with Harbert Davenport.[qv] In 1958 Canales was chairman of a committee to plan a memorial for Francita Alavez,[qv] as provided for by a legislative resolution.

He was also a wealthy landowner. Around 1900 his family was engaged principally in cattle raising, but by 1930 the emphasis had shifted to raising crops, especially cotton. The family owned 30,000 acres in 1930. Canales was a member of the Fraternal Order of Red Men, the Elks' Lodge, and the Woodmen of the World. He was also a charter member of the Brownsville Historical Society. He married Anne Anderson Wheeler on September 1, 1910, and the couple had one child. Canales died on March 30, 1976, in Brownsville.

José Tomás Canales looking at a portrait of an ancestor, Mexican general Servando Canales. From Houston Chonicle, *April 30, 1950. Reproduced by permission. Photograph courtesy CAH; CN 08485.*

BIBLIOGRAPHY: Evan Anders, *Boss Rule in South Texas: The Progressive Era* (Austin: University of Texas Press, 1982). Brownsville *Herald,* March 31, 1976. Dermont H. Hardy and Ingham S. Roberts, eds., *Historical Review of South-East Texas* (2 vols., Chicago: Lewis, 1910).

Evan Anders

CANALES ROSILLO, ANTONIO (1802–1852?). Antonio Canales Rosillo, military leader and politician, son of Josefa Rosillo Canales and José Antonio Canales Treviño, was born in Monterrey, Nuevo León, in 1802. He studied law, earned his license in 1829, and with his wife, María del Refugio Molano, reared five children. Canales served as a militia officer in fights against Comanche and Lipan raiders. He served a term in the Tamaulipas Chamber of Deputies and in 1834 joined in liberal opposition to Antonio López de Santa Anna's[qv] Centralist move against the Constitution of 1824.[qv] As commander of Federalist forces in Tamaulipas, Canales sent envoys to appraise Anglo-Texan, Tejano, and Indian sentiments. When he discovered that the Texans' intentions were to secede from Mexico, he practiced neutrality while he fostered the idea of an independent border republic. The geographical and ideological boundaries of this republic fluctuated, but Canales easily raised armed forces from both sides of the Rio Grande. In 1839 he visited San Antonio, Austin, and Lipantitlán on the lower Nueces to enlist men. During these visits he offered substantial bounties to those Texans who joined his cause. The Texian Auxiliary Corps, an irregular militia composed of 270 officers and men under separate command of colonels Richard Roman, Reuben Ross, and Samuel W. Jordan,[qqv] allied with Canales and participated in various campaigns.

During this period of revolts and counterrevolts, Canales, Antonio Zapata,[qv] and others met at Guerrero in January 1840 and proclaimed a separate Republic of the Rio Grande,[qv] drafted a constitution, and selected Laredo as their capital. The republic would have included Tamaulipas, Nuevo León, Coahuila, and the sub-Nueces portion of Texas. Jesús Cárdenas was selected president, and Canales was appointed secretary of war and commander in chief of the army. Although Texas did not recognize it politically, the republic existed in the minds of many border people.

As the Centralist state continued to transform Mexico, Canales continued resistance against it, but he was defeated at Monterrey by Centralist forces and retreated to the Rio Grande. At Santa Rita de Morelos, Coahuila, he lost Zapata. Along with several Texan volunteers, Zapata was captured, court-martialed, and executed on March 29, 1840. Canales eventually capitulated to Centralist forces and forsook his Texan allies, a move for which he received a commission as brigadier general in Santa Anna's army. He later led campaigns against Anglo-Texans at Corpus Christi and Lipantitlán and in 1842 was instrumental in stopping a Texan filibuster at Mier. He was dismissed in 1844 for abandonment of his post but was later reinstated.

During the Mexican War[qv] Canales harassed United States troops stationed between Corpus Christi and Matamoros. He fought at Palo Alto and at Resaca de Guerrero. He served under Gen. Pedro de Ampudia[qv] at Cerralvo and under Santa Anna at Buena Vista. Between 1848 and 1851 Canales served Tamaulipas as surveyor general, legislative envoy, and interim governor. On July 22, 1852, he received a gold award for exemplary conduct. His sons Servando and Antonio served several terms as governors of Tamaulipas. Canales apparently died in 1852, after leading government forces that suppressed the Tamaulipas Rebelión de la Loba at El Paso de Azúcar, Camargo.

BIBLIOGRAPHY: Charles Adams Gulick, Jr., Harriet Smither, et al., eds., *The Papers of Mirabeau Buonaparte Lamar* (6 vols., Austin: Texas State Library, 1920–27; rpt., Austin: Pemberton Press, 1968). Hobart Huson, *Refugio: A Comprehensive History of Refugio County from Aboriginal Times to 1953* (2 vols., Woodsboro, Texas: Rooke Foundation, 1953, 1955). Milton Lindheim, *The Republic of the Rio Grande: Texans in Mexico, 1839–40* (Waco: Morrison, 1964). Joseph Milton Nance, *After San Jacinto: The Texas-Mexican Frontier, 1836–1841* (Austin: University of Texas Press, 1963). Juan Fidel Zorrilla and Carlos González Salas, *Diccionario Biográfico de Tamaulipas* (Ciudad Victoria, Tamaulipas: Instituto de Investigaciones Históricas, Universidad Autónoma de Tamaulipas, 1984). *Roberto Mario Salmón*

CANAQ INDIANS. These Indians are known only from a Spanish document of 1693 which lists them as one of fifty "nations" that lived north of the Rio Grande and "between Texas and New Mexico." This may be interpreted to mean the southern part of western Texas, since the document also mentions that the Apaches were at war with the groups named. Nothing further is known about the Canaqs. The name is similar to that of the Cana, who apparently lived in southern Texas, but no connection between the two can be established.

BIBLIOGRAPHY: Charles W. Hackett, ed., *Historical Documents Relating to New Mexico, Nueva Vizcaya, and Approaches Thereto, to 1773* (3 vols., Washington: Carnegie Institution, 1923–37).
Thomas N. Campbell

CANARY, TEXAS. Canary was eighty-five miles north of Houston in west central Polk County. The town, one of a cluster of small communities formed originally by settlers from Louisiana, was part of what nineteenth-century Polk County residents referred to as the Louisiana Settlement.[qv] In 1900 the community's residents secured a post office, which they named Canary and housed at Milliard Hilton's store. Allie Faircloth served as postmistress for the rural office. The Canary post office was discontinued in 1914. The community was not shown on the 1984 county highway map.

BIBLIOGRAPHY: *A Pictorial History of Polk County, Texas, 1846–1910* (Livingston, Texas: Polk County Bicentennial Commission, 1976; rev. ed. 1978). *Robert Wooster*

CANARY ISLANDERS. On February 14, 1729, the Marqués de San Miguel de Aguayo[qv] made a report to the king of Spain proposing that 400 families be transported from the Canary Islands, Galicia, or Havana to populate the province of Texas. His plan was approved, and notice was given the Canary Islanders to furnish 200 families; the Council of the Indies suggested that 400 families should be sent from the Canaries to Texas by way of Havana and Veracruz. By June 1730, twenty-five families had reached Cuba and ten families had been sent on to Veracruz before orders from Spain to stop the movement arrived. Under the leadership of Juan Leal Goraz,[qv] the group marched overland to the presidio of San Antonio de Bexar, where they arrived on March 9, 1731. The party had increased by marriages on the way to fifteen families, a total of fifty-six persons. They joined a military community that had been in existence since 1718. The immigrants formed the nucleus of the villa of San Fernando de Béxar,[qv] the first regularly organized civil government in Texas. Several of the old families of San Antonio trace their descent from the Canary Island colonists. María Rosa Padrón was the first baby born of Canary Islander descent in San Antonio.

BIBLIOGRAPHY: Mattie Alice Austin, "The Municipal Government of San Fernando de Bexar, 1730–1800," *Quarterly of the Texas State Historical Association* 8 (April 1905). Carlos E. Castañeda, *Our Catholic Heritage in Texas* (7 vols., Austin: Von Boeckmann–Jones, 1936–58; rpt., New York: Arno, 1976).

CANA SCHOOL, TEXAS. Cana School is on Farm Road 2225 four miles northwest of Quitman in northwestern Wood County. A school existed at Cana before World War I.[qv] By 1932 the Cana school district offered nine grades of school to seventy-one white students and seven grades to twenty-nine black students. By 1960 the community consisted of a school, a church, and a few scattered dwellings along the road. The 1988 county highway map showed a church and a school at the site. *Rachel Jenkins*

CANBY, EDWARD RICHARD SPRIGG (1817–1873). Edward R. S. Canby, United States Army officer, son of Israel T. and Elizabeth (Piatt) Canby, was born at Piatt's Landing, Kentucky, on November 9, 1817. His father, a country doctor, later moved his family to Indiana. Canby enrolled in Wabash College and was appointed in 1835 to the United States Military Academy; he graduated thirtieth of thirty-one in the class of 1839. He married Louisa Hawkins of Crawfordsville, Indiana, on August 1 of that year. Lieutenant Canby served in the South, notably in the Second Seminole War in Florida (1839–42). During the Mexican War[qv] he earned two brevets in the campaign of Gen. Winfield Scott against Mexico City. Between 1848 and 1855 Major Canby held staff posts on the West Coast and in Washington, D.C. He was ordered to the Tenth Infantry Regiment in the Trans-Mississippi and later took part in the Mormon Expedition (1857–58) under Col. Albert Sidney Johnston.[qv]

Soon after the Civil War[qv] began, Canby was named colonel of the Nineteenth Infantry at Fort Defiance, New Mexico Territory. In a series of battles (Valverde[qv] on February 21, 1862, and Apache Canyon and Glorieta[qv] on March 27 and 28), Canby's troops blunted a Confederate invasion led by Gen. Henry H. Sibley,[qv] who turned back into Texas. Canby's actions prevented Confederate expansion from Texas into the greater Southwest.

After staff duties in Washington, D.C., from January 1863 through May 1864, Canby, as newly promoted major general of volunteers, took command of the Military Division of West Mississippi. He was wounded by guerrillas at White River, Arkansas, on November 6, 1864, but recovered and led the land campaign to capture Mobile, Alabama (March through April 1865), in cooperation with Gen. Gordon Granger[qv] and Adm. David G. Farragut. Canby received the surrender of Confederates under Gen. Richard Taylor on May 4, 1865, and that of the Trans-Mississippi forces of Gen. Edmund Kirby Smith[qv] on May 26.

The army was reorganized in July 1866, and Canby ranked ninth of only ten regular brigadier generals. His command included several states on the Gulf of Mexico, but Gen. Philip H. Sheridan[qv] reduced Canby's department to Louisiana. Sheridan supervised Texas through subordinate officers, Gen. Charles Griffin and Gen. Joseph J. Reynolds.[qqv] All three of these officers were strong Republicans. After devoting Reconstruction[qv] time to Louisiana and the Carolinas, Canby replaced Reynolds in the Fifth Military District,[qv] where he served from November 1868 to March 1869. As an independent in politics, Canby was recognized during Reconstruction as one of the most fair-minded army officers in the South.

His main accomplishment in Texas was supervising the process that led to the ratification of the Constitution of 1869.[qv] New southern state constitutions giving blacks the right to vote were required under the congressional Reconstruction Acts of 1867. Canby saw to it that the convention records were preserved and published. He removed few civilian officials, and his political appointments were judicious. He carefully protected the rights of freedmen without suppressing Democrats.

In March 1869 President U. S. Grant reinstated Reynolds as commander in Texas. Reynolds had been removed by President Andrew Johnson, who thought he was partisan. Grant reassigned him, however, and ordered Canby to the Department of the Columbia, in the Pacific Northwest. There the Modoc Indians, based in an area known as the Lava Beds in California, were attacking settlers in California and Oregon. On April 11, 1873, Canby went unarmed to a parley and was killed when set upon by Modoc negotiators, including their leader, Captain Jack. Canby was the only regular army general killed in the Trans-Mississippi Indian wars.

BIBLIOGRAPHY: Martin Hardwick Hall, *Sibley's New Mexico Campaign* (Austin: University of Texas Press, 1960). Max L. Heyman, Jr., *Prudent Soldier: A Biography of Major General E. R. S. Canby* (Glendale, California: Clark, 1959). William L. Richter, *The Army in Texas during Reconstruction, 1865–1870* (College Station: Texas A&M University Press, 1987). James E. Sefton, *The United States Army and Reconstruction* (Baton Rouge: Louisiana State University Press, 1967).

Joseph G. Dawson III

CANCEPNE INDIANS. The Cancepne (Cancepu, Concepue) Indians are known from a Spanish document of 1748 that lists the names of twenty-five Indian groups of east central and southeastern Texas who had asked for missions in that general area. About half the names on this list, including Cancepne, cannot be identified. The others consist of groups identifiable as Caddoans (including Wichita), Tonkawans, Atakapans, and Karankawans.

BIBLIOGRAPHY: Herbert Eugene Bolton, *Texas in the Middle Eighteenth Century* (Berkeley: University of California Press, 1915; rpt., Austin: University of Texas Press, 1970). Charles W. Hackett, ed., *Pichardo's Treatise on the Limits of Louisiana and Texas* (4 vols., Austin: University of Texas Press, 1931–46). Juan Agustín Morfi, *History of Texas, 1673–1779* (2 vols., Albuquerque: Quivira Society, 1935; rpt., New York: Arno, 1967).

Thomas N. Campbell

CANDELARIA, TEXAS. Candelaria is a ranching community at the end of Farm Road 170, across the Rio Grande from San Antonio El Bravo, Chihuahua, Mexico, and forty-two miles southwest of Marfa in western Presidio County. The Candelaria community was originally known as Gallina. The town lies in an area of rugged mountain terrain in the Chihuahuan Desert, where scrub, sotol, cacti, and sparse grasses grow. The post office at Candelaria was established in 1901. By 1910 the town reported a population of 543, a general merchandise store, a church, and a school. A cotton gin and flour mill were constructed there in 1913, after the introduction of cotton to the area. The United States Army built a cavalry outpost overlooking Candelaria shortly after the mobilization of National Guard troops along the border in May 1916. On August 19, 1919, troopers of the Eighth Cavalry crossed into Chihuahua at Candelaria on the last American punitive expedition into Mexico during the Mexican Revolution.[qv] The army outpost was closed after the cavalry withdrew from the upper Big Bend area in September 1919. After the army camp at Candelaria closed, the community's population began to decline: it fell to 250 in 1925 and to seventy-five by 1940. By 1985 Farm Road 170 to Candelaria had been completed, providing the first paved access to the remote community. In the late 1980s Candelaria comprised a two-room elementary school, a store, a Catholic church, and a cluster of adobe houses. The community had an estimated population of fifty-five in 1990.

BIBLIOGRAPHY: Austin *American-Statesman*, September 19, 1989. Virginia Madison and Hallie Stillwell, *How Come It's Called That? Place Names in the Big Bend Country* (Albuquerque: University of New Mexico Press, 1958).

Glenn Justice

CANDLISH, TEXAS. Candlish was on the Texas and New Orleans Railroad and U.S. Highway 59, eight miles northeast of Beeville in eastern Bee County. It included three pioneer communities: Robinson's, settled by J. W. and J. N. Robinson and later called Medio Hill, where Michael Seeligson became the first postmaster in Bee County in 1857; Cummingsville, later Blanco, where W. D. H. Saunders operated a store at the confluence of Talpacate and Poesta creeks; and Upper Medio, where R. E. Nutt settled in 1857 and R. A. Ezell, a gristmill operator, in 1872. Around 1907, when the railroad was built through the area, William J. Candlish laid out a townsite just north of the rail line. A local post office opened in 1907 but closed in 1930. The town was gone by the 1950s. East of Candlish, on Blanco Creek, one of the nation's richest fossil beds was discovered in 1939.

Grace Bauer

CANE BELT RAILROAD. A group of Eagle Lake businessmen and planters chartered the Cane Belt Railroad on March 10, 1898. Large acreage of sugarcane was grown in the area, and the railroad was needed to move the cane and other agricultural products to market. The charter was signed by William Dunovant, president; William T. Eldridge,[qv] vice president; and Thomas Boulden, secretary-treasurer. Other members of the board were John W. Thatcher, Perry Clark, Osburn Green, and E. P. Newsome, directors; Rudolph Greenbaum, William Jasper McGee, and Frank P. Herbert. The capital was $15,000. The principal place of business was Eagle Lake.

The charter called for a railroad of ten miles from Lakeside on Eagle Lake through the Colorado riverbottom to Bonus, where Dunovant owned a large plantation. Agricultural products, including sugarcane, rice, cattle, and vegetables, were the principal cargo. In 1908, 5,000 cars of sugarcane was shipped to the refinery at Lakeside, which processed more than 70,000 tons of cane that year. Sulfur and oil were other important commodities.

Soon after receiving the charter the Cane Belt purchased a mile of track from Eagle Lake to Lakeside from the Galveston, Harrisburg and San Antonio Railway, and construction of the line to Bonus was completed on November 11, 1898. A charter amendment approved on June 9, 1899, permitted an extension north to Sealy, to connect with the Missouri, Kansas and Texas Railroad for access to northern markets, and south to the Gulf Coast, eventually terminating at Matagorda. On July 18, 1899, shareholders approved issuance of bonds at $12,000 a mile ($1.2 million). Lincoln Trust Company of St. Louis, Missouri, purchased the bonds.

The extension north to Sealy and south to Wharton was completed in 1900. In 1901 the railroad established a major facility in Wharton County at Lane City, named for Jonathan Lane,[qv] president of the Cane Belt. On June 30, 1901, the Cane Belt arrived in Bay City, just in time to collect a $13,000 bonus from the town. The line reached Matagorda in 1903. The choice of Matagorda as a termination point was a fortunate one, as it offered access to the huge sulfur resources discovered at Gulf Hill in 1919. In 1931 the Gulf Hill deposit was exhausted, but another large sulfur discovery near Boling in Wharton County stimulated the construction of a new line of thirty-four miles connecting the old Cane Belt at Lane City with the main line of the Gulf, Colorado and Santa Fe at Thompsons. At its peak the road had 145 miles of track. In 1940 the Eldridge-to-Bonus segment of about five miles was abandoned.

The railroad was profitable from the start. Net earnings for the fiscal year ending on June 30, 1901, were more than $20,000. By 1902, however, an uneven cash flow, construction debt, and friction among the principals contributed to financial problems, and the road was near insolvency. On November 11, 1903, the Cane Belt was sold to the Atchison, Topeka and Santa Fe for $1.6 million. The purchase price included $850,000 for stock and assumption of $750,000 of outstanding bonds. In 1926 the Railroad Commission[qv] established the value of the Cane Belt at $2.5 million. Evidence presented at the hearing indicated an actual value of close to $3.5 million.

The AT&SF operated the Cane Belt as an independent road until the Texas legislature passed an act on April 11, 1905, that allowed it to lease or sell the road to another of its operating companies, the Gulf, Colorado and Santa Fe. The Cane Belt was leased to the GC&SF on July 1, 1905, and operated under lease until December 1948, when it was merged into the GC&SF.

BIBLIOGRAPHY: Charles S. Potts, *Railroad Transportation in Texas* (Austin: University of Texas, 1909). Annie Lee Williams, *A History of Wharton County* (Austin: Von Boeckmann–Jones, 1964).

William J. Reading

CANE CREEK. Cane Creek rises in a pool two miles west of Brookston in western Lamar County (at 33°37′ N, 95°44′ W) and runs south for eleven miles through eastern Roxton to its mouth on the North Sulphur River, just north of the Delta county line and two miles north of Crossroads (at 33°29′ N, 95°42′ W). It is intermittent at its headwaters. The creek crosses flat to rolling terrain surfaced by black clay that forms deep cracks when dry. Local vegetation includes grasses, junipers, and oaks. Low-lying floodplains near the creek's mouth are surfaced by sand and gravel.

CANE ISLAND VILLAGE. The Cane Island Village of the Alabama Indian tribe was between Peach Tree Village[qv] and Fort Terán twenty-two miles northwest of the site of present Woodville, Texas. This site was at the junction of three important trails—the Alabama Trace, the Coushatta Trace, and the Liberty–Nacogdoches Road[qqv]—all of which crossed the Neches River at the site where Fort Terán was constructed later in Tyler County. From Cane Island Village, the Alabama Trace and the Coushatta Trace went westward through Peach Tree Village, and the Liberty–Nacogdoches Road continued south through Fenced-in Village.[qv] Cane Island Village received its name from the dense growths of cane along nearby creeks. Apparently unhealthful conditions prevailed at this location, and the Alabamas referred to this village as "Flea Village." It was abandoned during the years of the Republic of Texas.[qv]

BIBLIOGRAPHY: Howard N. Martin, *Myths and Folktales of the Alabama-Coushatta Indians of Texas* (Austin: Encino Press, 1977).

Howard N. Martin

CANEY, TEXAS (Hopkins County). Caney, off Farm Road 269 in southeastern Hopkins County, was the site of one of eighteen churches that formed the Rehoboth Baptist Association. Services were held for several years before a meetinghouse was built on land owned by G. L. Stacy. A local school was opened before 1898, when it had an enrollment of seventy-one black students. The school was later closed, and in the mid-1930s the community had the church, a cemetery, and a number of scattered dwellings. Around 1944 the Pickton oilfield was in operation near the church. In the late 1980s Caney was the site of a church and cemetery. *J. E. Jennings*

CANEY, TEXAS (Matagorda County). Caney, formerly Caney Crossing, is on Farm Road 457 seven miles east of Bay City in eastern Matagorda County. The site was settled as early as 1838 and received its name from Caney Creek, an old bed of the Colorado River, which flowed through a dense canebrake. Caney had a post office as early as 1838, when Robert H. Williams[qv] was postmaster. This post office closed in 1846, then reopened in 1847 and closed again in 1914. In 1884 Caney reported a population of 130 and a church, a school, a doctor, a general store, a stock breeder, and five cotton gins. By 1896 its reported population had increased to 140, and by 1914 it was 200. In 1936 the town had one business, a cemetery, and about 150 residents. By 1949 the Caney school had been consolidated with the Van Vleck Independent School District, and by 1950 Caney's population had dwindled to about forty. In the late 1960s its population was estimated at 296. It was still reported at that level in 1990, but around that time Caney was shown on the county highway map as only a loose cluster of dwellings.

BIBLIOGRAPHY: Matagorda County Historical Commission, *Historic Matagorda County* (3 vols., Houston: Armstrong, 1986).

Stephen L. Hardin

CANEY CITY, TEXAS. Caney City is on State Highway 198 eleven miles west of Athens in western Henderson County. The largely residential community grew after the construction of Cedar Creek Reservoir in the mid-1960s. During the early 1980s Caney City was incorporated. Its population was 177 in 1980, and in 1991 it had a store and a reported population of 382. *Christopher Long*

CANEY CREEK (Cherokee County). Caney Creek rises just east of New Summerfield in northeastern Cherokee County (at 32°09′ N, 95°06′ W) and runs southwest for five miles to its mouth on Bridge Creek, just north of U.S. Highway 79 (at 32°01′ N, 95°10′ W). The stream is intermittent in its upper reaches. It crosses flat to gently rolling terrain surfaced by clay and sandy loam that supports grasses and mixed hardwoods and pines.

—— (Bowie County). Caney Creek rises within the Red River Army Depot[qv] a mile south of Hooks in central Bowie County (at 33°27′ N, 94°18′ W) and runs south for ten miles to its mouth on Big Creek, three miles east of Maud (at 33°20′ N, 94°17′ W). The upper and middle reaches of the creek have been dammed to form Caney Creek Reservoir just inside the southern boundary of the depot. Along the creek's lower reaches the stream cuts through clay that supports forests.

—— (Cass County). Caney Creek rises 9½ miles northwest of Linden in western Cass County (at 33°05′ N, 94°29′ W) and runs northwest for three miles to its mouth on Kelley Creek, eight miles northeast of Hughes Springs (at 33°05′ N, 94°32′ W). It is intermittent in its upper reaches. The stream crosses gently undulating to rolling terrain surfaced by sandy loam that supports pines and various hardwoods.

—— (Fannin County). Caney Creek rises a half mile north of Whitewright in west central Fannin County (at 33°33′ N, 96°24′ W) and runs northeast for 22½ miles to its mouth on the Red River, a mile west of Mulberry and within a mile of the city limits of Savoy (at 33°43′ N, 96°19′ W). The stream is intermittent in its upper reaches. It traverses flat to rolling terrain surfaced by clays and sandy loams that support oak, juniper, mesquite, and grasses. For most of the county's history the Caney Creek area has been used as crop and range land.

—— (Freestone County). Caney Creek rises less than a mile east of Teague in western Freestone County (at 31°37′ N, 96°14′ W) and runs northwest for fifteen miles to its mouth on Tehuacana Creek, five miles southeast of Streetman (at 31°51′ N, 96°15′ W). It crosses flat to rolling prairies with local shallow depressions, surfaced by clay and sandy loams that support hardwoods, pines, conifers, and grasses. The area is used primarily as dry cropland and forest.

—— (Grimes County). Caney Creek rises three miles southeast of Anderson in south central Grimes County (at 30°27′ N, 95°58′ W) and runs southeast for seventeen miles through mostly open country to its mouth on Lake Creek, in western Montgomery County (at 30°21′ N, 95°45′ W). It crosses gently sloping to nearly level terrain surfaced by sandy and clay loams that support stands of water oak, elm, pecan, loblolly pine, and shortleaf pine. On February 15–16, 1687, the French explorer René Robert Cavelier, Sieur de La Salle,[qv] crossed the creek traveling north toward the Trinity River on one of his many forays into the Texas interior in search of the Mississippi River. Settlement on the prairie near the upper creek began in the mid-1820s when Jesse

Grimes,qv Franklin Greenwood, Margaret McIntire, and her sons William and Robert established Grimes Prairie, one of the first settlements in Grimes County.

BIBLIOGRAPHY: E. L. Blair, *Early History of Grimes County* (Austin, 1930). Robin Navarro Montgomery, *The History of Montgomery County* (Austin: Jenkins, 1975).

—— (Harrison County). Caney Creek rises six miles west of Marshall in northwestern Harrison County (at 32°33′ N, 94°29′ W) and runs northwest for six miles to its mouth on Little Cypress Bayou, five miles southeast of Harleton (at 32°37′ N, 94°31′ W). The surrounding gently undulating to hilly terrain is surfaced by loams and clays that support dense patches of pine and hardwood trees. The land is used predominantly for agriculture.

—— (Harrison County). Caney Creek rises three miles northwest of Elysian Fields in southeastern Harrison County (at 32°25′ N, 94°12′ W) and runs southwest for 6½ miles to its mouth on Caddo Creek, just south of the Harrison county line in Panola County (at 32°21′ N, 94°16′ W). The surrounding level to rolling terrain is surfaced by loams and clays that support dense patches of pine and hardwood trees. The land is used predominantly for agriculture.

—— (Harrison County). Caney Creek rises six miles northwest of Harleton in northwestern Harrison County (at 32°43′ N, 94°40′ W) and runs southwest for 5½ miles to its mouth on Little Cypress Bayou, near the intersection of the Harrison, Gregg, and Upshur county lines (at 32°39′ N, 94°42′ W). The local nearly level to hilly terrain is surfaced by loams and clays that support dense patches of pine and hardwood trees. The land is used predominantly for agriculture.

—— (Henderson County). Caney Creek rises two miles south of Moore Station in eastern Henderson County (at 32°09′ N, 95°35′ W). It formerly ran east for six miles to its mouth on the Neches River. Since the construction of Lake Palestine in the early 1960s, the lower two miles of the creek have been inundated, and the creek now enters the lake just south of Cape Tranquility (at 32°09′ N, 95°30′ W). The surrounding flat to rolling terrain is surfaced by sandy and clay loams that support water-tolerant hardwoods, conifers, and grasses.

—— (Hopkins County). Caney Creek rises a mile north of Pickton in extreme southeastern Hopkins County (at 33°03′ N, 95°22′ W). The stream, which is intermittent in its upper reaches, formerly ran southwest for eighteen miles to its mouth on Lake Fork Creek, three miles west of Quitman in Wood County (at 32°49′ N, 95°33′ W). In the late 1970s its lower streambed was inundated by Lake Fork Reservoir, and since then the creek has flowed into the reservoir two miles east of Yantis in northwestern Wood County. The stream traverses generally flat terrain with local shallow depressions, surfaced by clay and sandy loams that support water-tolerant hardwoods, conifers, and grasses.

—— (Hunt County). Caney Creek rises twelve miles northeast of Lake Tawakoni in east central Hunt County (at 33°09′ N, 95°57′ W) and runs southwest for 5½ miles to its mouth on the Cowleech Fork of the Sabine River, four miles north of Lake Tawakoni (at 33°03′ N, 95°59′ W). It runs through flat to rolling terrain surfaced by clay and sandy loams that support grasses and water-tolerant hardwoods. The area has been used as crop and range land.

—— (Kaufman County). Caney Creek rises two miles northwest of Stubbs in southwestern Kaufman County (at 32°26′ N, 96°19′ W) and runs south for ten miles to its mouth on the Trinity River, two miles south of the Kaufman–Henderson county line (at 32°18′ N, 96°18′ W). It crosses flat to rolling terrain surfaced by sandy and clay loams that support hardwoods and grasses. Throughout most of the county's history the Caney Creek area has been used as range and crop land.

—— (Leon County). Caney Creek rises two miles north of Normangee in southwestern Leon County (at 31°04′ N, 96°08′ W) and runs southeast for thirty-seven miles to its mouth on Bedias Creek, in southern Madison County (at 30°53′ N, 95°48′ W). The surrounding gently sloping to nearly level terrain is surfaced by sandy and clay loams that support pecan, elm, water oak, hackberry, post oak, and black hickory trees. The Old San Antonio Road,qv a thoroughfare for early Spanish and French explorers, crossed the headwaters of the stream. Settlement in the vicinity began during the 1830s when the Pee Dee community was established on the east bank of the creek near its mouth. Madisonville, the seat of Madison County, was founded on the east bank of the lower creek in 1854. Bullard and Center were on the west bank of the lower creek in the late 1800s, and High Prairie was on the west bank of the middle creek.

BIBLIOGRAPHY: Madison County Historical Commission, *A History of Madison County* (Dallas: Taylor, 1984).

—— (Madison County). Caney Creek rises in far northern Madison County (at 31°05′ N, 95°52′ W) and runs northeast for seven miles to its mouth on Boggy Creek in southeastern Leon County (at 31°09′ N, 95°50′ W). It traverses gently sloping to nearly level terrain surfaced by sands and loams that support elm, pecan, water oak, post oak, hackberry, and black hickory along its banks. Settlement in the vicinity began in the mid-1800s. The Spillers Store community is located on the creek's west bank.

—— (Montgomery County). Caney Creek rises west of Farm Road 1791 in extreme northwestern Montgomery County (at 30°36′ N, 95°48′ W) and runs southeast for thirteen miles, traveling parallel to the Walker–Montgomery county line and passing through the Sam Houston National Forestqv before reaching its mouth on Lake Conroe, northeast of Lake Mount Pleasant (at 30°30′ N, 95°40′ W). The stream is intermittent in its upper reaches. It crosses flat terrain with local shallow depressions surfaced by clay and sandy loams that support water-tolerant hardwoods, conifers, and grasses.

—— (Morris County). Caney Creek rises 1½ miles northwest of Naples in northeastern Morris County (at 33°13′ N, 94°42′ W) and runs northeast for six miles to its mouth on Tuck Branch in northwestern Cass County, 1½ miles from the Morris county line (at 33°14′ N, 94°36′ W). The local soils are predominantly loamy, and the area is for the most part used for pasture. Locally the creek has often been called Fleming Creek.

—— (Nacogdoches County). Caney Creek rises just east of Looneyville in northwestern Nacogdoches County (at 31°46′ N, 94°49′ W) and runs south for 6½ miles to its mouth on Little Loco Bayou, two miles southwest of Red Flat (at 31°41′ N, 94°49′ W). The stream is intermittent in its upper reaches. The surrounding flat terrain has local shallow depressions and is surfaced by clay and sandy loams that support water-tolerant hardwoods, conifers, and grasses.

—— (Newton County). Caney Creek rises seven miles north of Newton in western Newton County (at 30°54′ N, 93°47′ W) and runs southeast for 19½ miles to its mouth on the Sabine River, four miles west of Merryville, Louisiana (at 30°44′ N, 93°37′ W). It is intermittent in its upper reaches. The creek was the site of early settlement and several mills. It flows through a flood-prone area of canebrakes.

—— (Polk County). Caney Creek, one of two watercourses by this name that begin in Polk County, rises three miles north of Onalaska in the western part of the county (at 30°51′ N, 95°00′ W) and runs southwest for 2½ miles to its mouth on Lake Livingston, 5½ miles southeast of Carlisle (at 30°49′ N, 95°08′ W). It crosses rolling to steep terrain, some badlands, and some prairies. Clay and sandy loams in the area support pine and hardwood forests, some mesquite, and grasses. Before the completion of Lake Livingston in 1968 Caney Creek ran twice its present length before joining the Trinity River, which now feeds the lake.

—— (Polk County). Caney Creek, one of two Polk County creeks by that name, rises four miles west of Bold Springs in the western part of the county (at 30°48′ N, 95°02′ W) and runs west for 2½ miles to its mouth on Lake Livingston, three miles east of Onalaska (at 30°47′ N, 95°04′ W). It crosses the East Texas timberlands—low rolling hills and prairies surfaced by clay and sandy loams that support pine and hardwood forests, some mesquite, and grasses.

—— (Red River County). Caney Creek rises three miles northeast of Boxelder in southeastern Red River County (at 33°30′ N, 94°50′ W) and runs southeast for 3½ miles to its mouth on Dillard Creek, three miles northwest of Lydia (at 33°27′ N, 94°48′ W). The local soils are mostly clay and sandy loams, best suited for pastureland or grain crops. Surrounding pastures and fields are interspersed with wooded areas where pine trees predominate.

——— (Red River County). Caney Creek rises about a mile southeast of White Rock in northeastern Red River County (at 33°39′ N, 94°55′ W) and runs northeast for 5½ miles to its mouth on Pecan Bayou, about eight miles east of the Bowie county line in northeastern Red River County (at 33°42′ N, 94°54′ W). Local soils are clayey. The creek is intermittent in its upper reaches, where the soils are used mainly as pastureland. As the creek flows toward its mouth, it enters a heavily wooded area where shortleaf pine and post oaks and southern red oaks predominate.

——— (Shelby County). Caney Creek rises five miles northeast of Center in northeastern Shelby County (at 31°49′ N, 94°06′ W) and runs southeast for five miles to its mouth on Tenaha Creek (at 31°48′ N, 94°03′ W). It traverses flat to moderately steep terrain surfaced by soils varying from sandy to clayey and loamy. The local countryside is heavily wooded, with pines and various hardwoods predominating.

——— (Trinity County). Caney Creek rises three miles northeast of Westville in west central Trinity County (at 31°07′ N, 95°11′ W). It formerly ran southwest for fourteen miles to its mouth on the Trinity River, near Sebastopol (at 30°55′ N, 95°16′ W). Since the construction of Livingston Reservoir (later known as Lake Livingston) in the 1960s, the lower portion of the creek has been inundated. The stream runs through flat to rolling terrain surfaced by clay and sandy loams that support conifers, water-tolerant hardwoods, and grasses.

——— (Upshur County). Caney Creek rises two miles northeast of Zion Hill in north central Upshur County (at 32°52′ N, 94°53′ W) and runs southwest for seven miles to its mouth on Little Cypress Creek, two miles west of Friendship (at 32°46′ N, 94°55′ W). The creek traverses flat to rolling terrain surfaced by sandy and clay loam soils that support water-tolerant hardwoods, conifers, and grasses.

——— (Van Zandt County). Caney Creek rises two miles northeast of Lawrence Springs in northeastern Van Zandt County (at 32°39′ N, 95°47′ W) and runs nine miles northeast to its mouth on the Sabine River, three miles northeast of Grand Saline (at 32°44′ N, 95°41′ W). The creek traverses flat terrain with local shallow depressions, surfaced by clay and sandy loam soils that support water-tolerant hardwoods, conifers, and grasses.

——— (Walker County). Caney Creek, a spring-fed perennial stream, rises five miles east of Huntsville in east central Walker County (at 30°42′ N, 95°26′ W) and flows north seventeen miles to its mouth on Harmon Creek, near the southwestern edge of Lake Livingston (at 30°51′ N, 95°26′ W). The upper creek lies within the boundary of Sam Houston National Forest.[qv] The stream traverses gently rolling to nearly level terrain surfaced by sandy and loamy soils. Along the banks of the creek grow pines, including loblolly and shortleaf, and hardwoods, including elm, hickory, oak, and sweet and black gum. Settlement near the upper creek began in the mid-1820s and on the lower creek in the mid-1830s. The Dodge community was established on the upper creek after the Civil War.[qv] In the early 1870s, Riverside was founded as a station on the Houston and Great Northern Railroad near the creek's mouth. For a number of years after World War II,[qv] Sam Houston State Teachers College (later Sam Houston State University) maintained a country campus on the west bank of the middle creek on the site of an abandoned German prisoner-of-war camp (*see* GERMAN PRISONERS OF WAR).

——— (Walker County). Caney Creek, a spring-fed perennial stream, rises two miles northwest of New Waverly in southeastern Walker County (at 30°34′ N, 95°27′ W) and flows southeast for forty-eight miles through eastern Montgomery County to its mouth on the East Fork of the San Jacinto River, just above Lake Houston in northeastern Harris County (at 30°05′ N, 95°09′ W). The upper creek forms part of the southwestern boundary of Sam Houston National Forest.[qv] The stream traverses rolling to nearly level terrain surfaced by sandy and loamy soils. Along its banks grow pines, including loblolly and shortleaf, and hardwoods, including elm, hickory, oak, and sweet and black gum. Settlement in the vicinity began during the mid-1830s. In the late 1860s what is now the community of New Caney was founded on the west bank of the lower creek. Waukegan, on the west bank of the middle creek, served as a station on the Gulf, Colorado and Santa Fe Railway from the late 1800s until the 1930s. During the local oil boom of the early 1930s, Grangerland was established on the west bank of the middle creek. The town of Cut and Shoot was incorporated on the west bank of the middle creek in 1970. Groceville and Black Diamond are on the east bank of the middle creek. Walden Woods, Dogwood Acres, and Dunnam, suburbs of Houston, lie on the west bank of the lower creek near its mouth.

BIBLIOGRAPHY: Montgomery County Genealogical Society, *Montgomery County History* (Winston–Salem, North Carolina: Hunter, 1981).

——— (Washington County). Caney Creek rises six miles west of Chappell Hill in Washington County (at 30°08′ N, 96°21′ W) and runs southeast for sixteen miles to its mouth on the Brazos River, at the juncture of the Washington, Austin, and Waller county lines (at 30°04′ N, 96°09′ W). The creek forms a large part of the Washington–Austin county line. Caney Creek flows through gently to moderately sloping terrain surfaced by clays and fine sandy loam soils that support grasslands. Land near the creek's mouth is cropland.

——— (Wharton County). Caney Creek, originally named Canebrake Creek after the dense cane growth that banked its sides until white settlement of the area, rises one mile south of Matthews in Colorado County, within the maze of irrigation canals, dead-water sloughs, and old stream channels of the flat prairie near the Colorado-Wharton county line in northern Wharton County (at 29°26′ N, 96°18′ W). It runs southeast through rich coastal plains for 155 miles to its mouth on the Gulf Intracoastal Waterway,[qv] in a recreational homesite 5½ miles southeast of Sargent, Matagorda County (at 28°46′ N, 95°39′ W). Several thousand years ago the current Caney Creek channel served as the channel of the Colorado River. The changing course of the Colorado intercepts that of the Caney Creek channel a mile west of Glen Flora (at 29°21′ N, 96°13′ W). They travel together for a mile before separating (at 29°20′ N, 96°12′ W). Since the early 1900s Caney Creek, which has the wide meanders that characterize an old stream, passes several towns and communities as an intermittent streambed until it enters Matagorda County, where it takes on water from several sloughs and drainage areas to become a flowing stream. Most of the area surrounding the stream is used for the production of rice and other grains as well as cotton and improved pasture for cattle. The rich alluvial lands surrounding Caney Creek, described in the field notes of early surveyor and Old Three Hundred[qv] settler Elias R. Wightman[qv] and elsewhere, made it a focal point for settlement in the 1820s (*see* ANGLO-AMERICAN COLONIZATION). Before breaking the land for planting, the colonists would burn off the canebrake, a native bamboo, to enrich the soil. The creek was sometimes navigable for some distance upstream. Sugar production in the area was so successful that stately homes began to line the creek's banks, and part of its course became known as plantation row. In 1825 Robert Harris Williams[qv] established what was reportedly one of the first three cotton gins in colonial Texas on the creek's banks. During the Civil War,[qv] Confederate commander John Bankhead Magruder[qv] had the mouth fortified as part of a strategy to stop the federal advance north along the coast toward Galveston. In January and February 1864, federal gunboats bombarded the area, which was reportedly defended by 4,000 to 6,000 Confederate troops. No ground combat occurred, and by March Magruder had shifted the troops elsewhere. A Texas Historical Commission[qv] marker at the site commemorates the defense. A 1975 archeological survey including the Caney Creek area noted the ruins of a sugar mill and sawmill on the creek's banks, and the sunken remains of a paddle wheeler. The study recommended that the creekside remains of James Boyd Hawkins's nineteenth-century plantation house be considered for renovation. It also noted the presence, dwindling at that time because of ongoing subdivision and development of the preferred creekside land, of a rich cultural complex of descendents of both slaves and plantation owners still living along lower Caney Creek.

BIBLIOGRAPHY: Gayle Jeannine Fritz, *Matagorda Bay Area, Texas* (Research Report 45, Texas Archeological Survey of the University of Texas at Austin, 1975). Matagorda County Historical Commission, *Historic Matagorda County* (3 vols., Houston: Armstrong, 1986). Marker Files, Texas Historical Commission, Austin.

CANFIELD, ALANSON WYLLYS (?–1864). Alanson Wyllys Canfield, editor of the San Augustine *Red-Lander,*[qv] was born in New Milford, Connecticut. In the mid-1830s he married Elizabeth A. Russell in Hamilton, New York, and the couple immigrated with the bride's brother, Robert B. Russell, to Texas in 1836. They settled in Milam. In July 1836 Canfield and Russell enlisted in a company of volunteers from Sabine County. Within two years the trio moved to San Augustine, where Canfield's flair for business soon became evident. As a successful businessman he lived well; his home occupied an entire block and included gardens and a broad avenue that ran to Main Street. In 1840 he purchased the press of W. W. Parker's *Red-Lander* and launched the *Journal and Advertiser.* This venture lasted slightly over a year, after which Canfield revived the *Red-Lander,* by which Canfield publicized his democratic views across the Republic of Texas.[qv] In staunch support of Sam Houston[qv] and tariff reform, Canfield's paper repeatedly proclaimed that "no true friend of Texas" could adhere to the tenets of the Whig party.[qv] In 1842–43 Canfield waged a heated political feud with a rival editor, Charles DeMorse[qv] of the Clarksville *Northern Standard.*[qv] In 1846, after five tumultuous years, Canfield retired from the newspaper business. In 1846 he traveled to Corpus Christi to join the army of Zachary Taylor[qv] as a captain. In the 1850s Canfield was probably a commission merchant in Calhoun County. During the Civil War,[qv] although Northern by birth and marriage, he became an advocate of the Confederacy. He died as Major Canfield of the Confederate Army at the battle of Mansfield on April 8, 1864 (*see* RED RIVER CAMPAIGN).

BIBLIOGRAPHY: George L. Crocket, *Two Centuries in East Texas* (Dallas: Southwest, 1932; facsimile reprod., 1962). Marilyn M. Sibley, *Lone Stars and State Gazettes: Texas Newspapers before the Civil War* (College Station: Texas A&M University Press, 1983).

Randolph Lewis

CANNAHA AND CANNAHIO INDIANS. These Indians are known only from the 1687 documents of the La Salle expedition,[qv] which list them separately as enemies of the Kadohadachos on the Red River. In spite of this separate listing, it has been assumed that the two names refer to the same people, and the Cannaha-Cannahios have been equated with the Kannehouans, who in the same documents were placed far to the south of the Red River near the Gulf Coast. These identifications, which are based on phonetic similarities in names, ignore separate listing in the documents as well as differences in geographic location. Until better evidence is presented, the Cannahas and Cannahios must be considered as different peoples and unrelated to the Kannehouans.

BIBLIOGRAPHY: Frederick Webb Hodge, ed., *Handbook of American Indians North of Mexico* (2 vols., Washington: GPO, 1907, 1910; rpt., New York: Pageant, 1959). Pierre Margry, ed., *Découvertes et établissements des Français dans l'ouest et dans le sud de l'Amérique septentrionale, 1614–1754* (6 vols., Paris: Jouast, 1876–86).

Thomas N. Campbell

CANNAN, WILLIAM JARVIS (1808–1881). William Jarvis Cannan, soldier at the battle of San Jacinto,[qv] was born in Alabama in 1808 and moved to Texas in 1835. He was in the Texas army from March 1 to November 1, 1836, and took part at San Jacinto as a private in Company H, First Regiment of Texas Volunteers, under Robert Stevenson.[qv] For his service Cannan was granted a bounty warrant for 640 acres in Brazoria County. In 1837 he married Matilda Lewis. They had four sons and a daughter. After his wife's death at Brazoria in 1850, Cannan married Parmelia A. Wilcox; they became the parents of three sons and a daughter. Throughout the Civil War and Reconstruction[qqv] era, the Cannan family figured prominently in the Texas cotton trade. Cannan died in September 1881 and was buried in the Oyster Creek Cemetery four miles from Velasco.

BIBLIOGRAPHY: James A. Creighton, *A Narrative History of Brazoria County* (Angleton, Texas: Brazoria County Historical Commission, 1975). Sam Houston Dixon and Louis Wiltz Kemp, *The Heroes of San Jacinto* (Houston: Anson Jones, 1932).

CANNON, TEXAS. Cannon is at the junction of Farm roads 2729 and 121, twelve miles southeast of Sherman in southeastern Grayson County. Settlement of the community occurred in 1852, when Elijah Cannon, a native of Pickens County, South Carolina, built a gristmill and gin. Construction of a school, a church, and several businesses established the community as a center for area farmers in the 1870s. In 1876 John A. and Joseph L. Cobb founded the Centennial Institute,[qv] which burned in 1888. In 1877 a post office opened there. One source indicates that the town may have been called Canaan in its early history. Its population reached its peak in the mid-1880s, with some estimates placing the number of residents at 400. That same decade, however, saw the Houston and Texas Central Railway bypass Cannon. Over the next fifteen years the community's businesses declined and its population decreased. In 1907 the post office closed. Only thirty residents remained in Cannon by 1910. That figure increased slowly over the next few decades, reaching seventy-five by 1989; it remained at that number in 1990.

BIBLIOGRAPHY: Dallas *Morning News,* November 10, 1936. Grayson County Frontier Village, *History of Grayson County, Texas* (2 vols., Winston-Salem, North Carolina: Hunter, 1979, 1981).

David Minor

CANNON GULLY. Cannon Gully rises in the Hufsmith East oilfield in northwestern Harris County (at 30°07′ N, 95°34′ W) and runs southeast for about two miles to its mouth on Willow Creek (at 30°07′ N, 95°32′ W). The local terrain is flat to rolling with local dissection and escarpments. The land surface of shallow to deep sandy and clay loams supports native vegetation including mixed hardwoods and pines. In developed areas native vegetation has been replaced by cultivated row or cover crops.

CANNONSNAP CREEK. Cannonsnap Creek rises a mile northwest of Milano in eastern Milam County (at 30°43′ N, 96°52′ W) and runs north for twelve miles to its mouth on the Little River, seven miles southeast of Cameron (at 30°50′ N, 96°51′ W). It crosses generally flat terrain with local shallow depressions, surfaced by clay and sandy loams that support water-tolerant hardwoods, conifers, and grasses. According to some sources, the creek's name originated when a young sentry, standing guard by the creek in July 1836, thought he heard a Mexican "cannonsnap" and sounded the alarm in his camp.

BIBLIOGRAPHY: John Holland Jenkins, *Recollections of Early Texas,* ed. John H. Jenkins III (Austin: University of Texas Press, 1958; rpt. 1973).

CANNONVILLE, TEXAS. Cannonville, in the hills of central Hays County, was the brainchild of an early county booster, William Cannon. In the mid-1850s Cannon chose and platted the site for a new town about sixteen miles northwest of San Marcos, east of Onion Creek, and on the road to Dripping Springs. After securing a post office in 1857, Cannon led a petition drive to move the county government from San Marcos to his land along Onion Creek, on the grounds that the former town was too far from the center of the county. Cannonville won an election held to decide the issue, but the Civil War[qv] interrupted a lawsuit brought by San Marcos to overturn the election results, and the move was never accomplished. By the end of the war, a change in the southern boundary of the county left Cannonville outside of the accepted central area; the issue was apparently dropped, and San Marcos remained the county seat. Cannonville apparently never attracted many settlers, and by 1862 both its post office and community school had been moved.

BIBLIOGRAPHY: Dudley Richard Dobie, *A Brief History of Hays County and San Marcos, Texas* (San Marcos, 1948).

Daniel P. Greene

CANOE BAYOU. Canoe Bayou rises eight miles southeast of Bay City in the Bay Prairie of east central Matagorda County (at 28°54′ N, 95°51′ W) and runs southeast for 14½ miles, passing through a small lake before reaching its mouth on Live Oak Bayou, two miles east of Lake Austin (at 28°47′ N, 95°44′ W). The creek is intermittent in its upper reaches. It traverses low and rolling to flat terrain surfaced by sandy and clay loams that support grasses and hardwoods.

CANON GRANDE. Canon Grande begins just north of the Kinney-Maverick county line in far southwestern Kinney County (at 29°06′ N, 100°31′ W) and runs southwest for nineteen miles to its mouth on the Rio Grande, three miles south of Quemado in northwestern Maverick County (at 28°57′ N, 100°36′ W). An intermittent stream runs through the canyon. The surrounding variable terrain is surfaced by clay and sandy loams that support scrub brush, some hardwoods, pecans, conifers, and grasses.

CANONIDIBA INDIANS. The Canonidiba Indians are known from a single 1691 Spanish missionary report that lists them as a group that lived to the southeast of the Hasinais of eastern Texas. As no distance was specified, it is impossible to tell whether the Canonidibas were in eastern Texas or western Louisiana. Their affiliations are unknown.

BIBLIOGRAPHY: John R. Swanton, *Source Material on the History and Ethnology of the Caddo Indians* (Smithsonian Institution, Bureau of American Ethnology Bulletin 132, Washington: GPO, 1942).

Thomas N. Campbell

CANONIZOCHITOUI INDIANS. The Canonizochitoui Indians are known from a single 1691 Spanish missionary report, which lists them among the groups that lived southeast of the Hasinais. Since no distance was specified, it is impossible to tell whether these Indians lived in eastern Texas or western Louisiana. The latter part of the name, *-zochitoui,* resembles Souchitiony, an early form of Doustioni, the name of a Caddoan tribe that lived near the site of present Natchitoches, Louisiana, in the eighteenth century. No further evidence in support of this identification has been found.

BIBLIOGRAPHY: John R. Swanton, *Source Material on the History and Ethnology of the Caddo Indians* (Smithsonian Institution, Bureau of American Ethnology Bulletin 132, Washington: GPO, 1942).

Thomas N. Campbell

CANTAGREL, FRANÇOIS JEAN (1810–1887). François Jean Cantagrel, first director of the colony La Réunion,[qv] was born in Amboise, France, on June 27, 1810. He went to Paris as a young man to study engineering and architecture but soon found that socialist theory interested him more. He wrote numerous articles on the subject and, as a result, became the friend and colleague of Victor Considérant,[qv] chief disciple of the socialist theorist Charles Fourier and architect of the plan to found a community on Fourierist principles in Texas. Due to his socialist activities while a member of the National Assembly, Cantagrel ran afoul of government authorities. He demonstrated against Louis Napoleon's illegal force in Italy and joined Considérant and others in seizing the Conservatory of Arts and Crafts. To avoid exile to a penal colony in Algeria, he fled the country in 1849; then, sentenced to exile, he stopped in Belgium and England before settling in the United States in 1854.

Cantagrel arrived in the United States as an employee of the European American Society of Colonization (Considérant's company for the establishment of La Réunion) and served as its main agent in America, with the responsibility of choosing the site in Texas for the future utopian community. He bought land at the site of present-day Dallas and hired Americans to help put up the first buildings and plant the first crops in order to be ready to receive the new colonists. Once this preliminary work had been accomplished, Considérant named Cantagrel as director of the colony and charged him with overseeing its day-to-day operation.

From the very start La Réunion was plagued with problems, including a serious lack of skilled farmers. Cantagrel is claimed to have complained, "I am sent here to direct an agricultural colony and have no agriculturalists to direct." The problems eventually wore out his enthusiasm, and he resigned from the directorship in 1856; he remained with the colony until 1857. Then he went to Belgium and, after being granted amnesty in 1859, to France.

There he became deeply involved in radical politics. He spent many years as vice mayor of Paris and served, at various times, as representative of the Government of National Defense for the department of Loir-et-Cher and municipal counselor in Paris. He also edited the short-lived newspaper *L'Union Démocratique* in 1871 and later played an important role in drawing up labor regulations that helped protect the health and safety of French workers. Cantagrel married and had two children. He died on February 27, 1887, in Paris.

BIBLIOGRAPHY: Victor Prosper Considérant, *Au Texas* (Paris: Librairie Phalanstérienne, 1854; ed., with additions, by Rondel V. Davidson, Philadelphia: Porcupine, 1975). *The French Texans* (San Antonio: University of Texas Institute of Texan Cultures, 1973). William J. and Margaret F. Hammond, *La Réunion: A French Settlement in Texas* (Dallas: Taylor, 1958). George H. Santerre, *White Cliffs of Dallas: The Story of La Reunion* (Dallas: Book Craft, 1955).

Christopher E. Guthrie

CANTAU CREEK. Cantau Creek rises eight miles southeast of Seguin in southeastern Guadalupe County (at 29°28′ N, 97°54′ W) and runs north for six miles to its mouth on the Guadalupe River, five miles southeast of Seguin (at 29°32′ N, 97°53′ W). The creek traverses an area of rolling prairies surfaced by clay loams that support mesquite and grasses. It was probably named for Jesús Cantú, who was granted land in the area by the Mexican government in 1831.

BIBLIOGRAPHY: Willie Mae Weinert, *An Authentic History of Guadalupe County* (Seguin, Texas: Seguin *Enterprise,* 1951; rpt. 1976).

CANTEY INDIANS. This name appears in records of the La Salle expedition,[qv] which indicate that in 1687 these Indians were enemies of the Kadohadachos. The Canteys have been identified as Lipan Apache, but this identification is debatable. A better case can be made for identification of the Canteys with the Chaquanties, who in 1700 lived on the Red River some sixty to seventy-five miles west of the Kadohadachos. This would place them in the area of what is now Lamar and Red River counties. Apparent variants of the name Chaquantie appear on several eighteenth-century maps, some of which show the name on the north side of the Red River, others on the south. Although it has been speculated that the Chaquanties were Caddoans, their affiliations have yet to be documented.

BIBLIOGRAPHY: Frederick Webb Hodge, ed., *Handbook of American Indians North of Mexico* (2 vols., Washington: GPO, 1907, 1910; rpt., New York: Pageant, 1959). Pierre Margry, ed., *Découvertes et établissements des Français dans l'ouest et dans le sud de l'Amérique septentrionale, 1614–1754* (6 vols., Paris: Jouast, 1876–86).

Thomas N. Campbell

CANTON, TEXAS. Canton, the county seat of Van Zandt County, is on State highways 19 and 64 on the Mill Creek tributary of the Sabine River, fourteen miles southeast of Wills Point in the central part of the county. The site, originally in Henderson County, was surveyed as early as 1840 by a company of men under Dr. W. P. King. The community stands on the original survey of Jesse Stockwell, who arrived in the area at that time. No settlement was made until 1850, when the town was laid out and named by settlers moving from Old Canton in Smith County. The first district courthouse at Canton opened in 1850, and a post office, the county's fourth, was established in that year.

When the Texas and Pacific Railway built across the county in 1872, it missed Canton by ten miles, and citizens of Wills Point persuaded the county officials to move the county seat there. In the resulting dispute residents of Canton in 1877 went armed to Wills Point to get the records back, and the county judge wired Governor Richard B. Hubbard[qv] for aid. The Supreme Court of Texas finally decided in favor of Canton. Unwilling to use the railroad at Wills Point, Canton businessmen established Edgewood, ten miles to the northwest of town, and built an extension to the railroad at a siding formerly called Stevenson.

Property for the town's first school, Canton Academy, was acquired in 1853. Sid S. Johnson began publication of the Canton *Weekly Times*, the county's first newspaper, in 1860. A Grange[qv] was founded in 1876. James S. Hogg,[qv] who once served as Canton district attorney, was elected governor in 1880. By 1890 Canton had a population of 421, flour mills, sawmills, cotton gins, and a bank. Brick buildings were under construction by 1892, and a new brick courthouse was completed in 1894. Iron ore and anthracite coal were discovered in 1887 and 1891. By 1896 the town reached a population high of 800 and had several churches, a steam gristmill and gin, two weekly newspapers, three general stores and two hotels. But residents had dropped to 421 by 1904. Notorious bank robbers Bonnie Parker and Clyde Barrow[qqv] once lived briefly at the Dixie Hotel, built in 1915. Canton was incorporated in 1919 and elected a mayor and aldermen. Despite the Great Depression,[qv] development of the Van oilfield[qv] after 1929 brought further expansion, and a Public Works Administration project in the 1930s completed a new courthouse in the community. In 1933 area schools registered 500 white and twenty-eight black students. The population reached 715 in 1940, but residents dwindled again after 1949. In the 1950s, local business included a sweet-potato curing plant, an ice factory, a concrete-tile factory, lumberyards, and a cotton gin. Expansion of the Canton city limits doubled its territory in the 1960s. In 1970 the community had a municipal lake with recreational facilities, seven churches, a school, a bank, a library, a newspaper, and eighty-six businesses. The population doubled between 1960 and 1970 from roughly 1,000 to 2,000, and reached nearly 3,000 by 1990.

Canton is known for its First Monday or Hoss Monday trade day. According to various sources, the tradition began with district court meetings held on the first Monday of each month or with the monthly visit of neighbors in the Confederate times. The custom began with the swapping of surplus stock by barter and grew to include casual bargaining for or swapping of dogs, antiques, junk, and donkeys on a thirty-acre grounds. The Van Zandt County Fair and Rodeo and the Annual Bluegrass Festival take place in the community in August.

BIBLIOGRAPHY: Francis Edward Abernethy, ed., *Some Still Do: Essays on Texas Customs*, Publications of the Texas Folklore Society 39 (Austin: Encino Press, 1975). Carol Barrington, "For Sale or Trade," *Texas Highways*, November 1986. Gayle Essary, "First Monday," *Texas Co-op Power*, October 1964. William Samuel Mills, *History of Van Zandt County* (Canton, Texas, 1950). Jack Raskopf, "Big Bargains in a Little Town," *Texas Parade*, November 1970. Van Zandt County History Book Committee, *History of Van Zandt County* (Dallas, 1984). Fain Williams, "First Monday," *Texas Parade*, June 1967. David Nelson Wren, *Every First Monday: A History of Canton* (Quanah, Texas: Nortex, 1973).

Diana J. Kleiner

CANTONA INDIANS. Although they were reported as numerous and were widely distributed in east central Texas, the Cantona Indians have generally been ignored in studies of Texas Indians. In the late seventeenth and early eighteenth centuries they were known to the Spanish by a variety of names, including Cantanual, Cantujuana, Cantauhaona, Cantuna, Mandone, and Simaomo (Simomo). During this period they ranged the prairies between the Guadalupe and Trinity rivers, particularly east of the sites of present San Antonio, Austin, and Waco. They were most frequently reported along the Colorado and Brazos rivers, where their skill and success in bison hunting were often mentioned. The Cantonas were rarely encountered alone; instead they shared settlements with other Indian groups, and they seem to have been welcome nearly everywhere. At times they encamped with the Jumanos and their associated tribes or with Coahuiltecans (Mescales, Payayas, Xarames) near San Antonio; farther east they sometimes shared villages with the Cava, Emet, Sana, and Tohoho Indians, all considered to be Tonkawans; northeast of Austin they were closely associated with the Yojuanes, also Tonkawan; in eastern Texas they were frequent visitors at the Hasinai Caddo villages; and later in the eighteenth century (1771) they were associated with Wichita groups (Tawakoni, Yscani) east of present Waco. A few Cantonas also entered San Antonio de Valero Mission at San Antonio in the first half of the eighteenth century.

The linguistic and cultural affiliations of the Cantonas are difficult to assess. J. R. Swanton listed them as a Coahuiltecan band, presumably because of their association with Coahuiltecan groups near San Antonio. Others have stressed association with Tonkawan peoples and have argued that the Cantona language must have been Tonkawan. It is clear that linguistic identification on the basis of association leads nowhere in the case of the Cantonas. At one time or another they were associated with nearly every group in or near their area. The same judgment also applies to Cantona cultural affiliations. The Cantonas disappeared in the second half of the eighteenth century. When last mentioned they were living with Wichita groups in the northern part of their range, and it seems likely that most of the Cantona survivors lost their ethnic identity among the southern Wichita groups, particularly the Tawakonis and Yscanis. One question deserves serious consideration: were the Cantonas the same people as the Kanohatinos named in documents of the La Salle expedition?[qv] Both groups occupied the same general area at the same time, and their cultures as known seem to have been similar. This question can be answered only by further archival research. The name Simaomo, clearly stated in one Spanish document to be an alternative name for Cantona, is puzzling. Since another document mentions both Cantonas and Simaomos as being represented in a large congregation of tribes or bands, it is impossible that Simaomo was the name of a Cantona subdivision that was sometimes used as a synonym for Cantona.

BIBLIOGRAPHY: Herbert Eugene Bolton, ed. and trans., *Athanase de Mézières and the Louisiana-Texas Frontier, 1768–1780* (2 vols., Cleveland: Arthur H. Clark, 1914). Herbert E. Bolton, "The Jumano Indians in Texas, 1650–1771," *Quarterly of the Texas State Historical Association* 15 (July 1911). Herbert Eugene Bolton, ed., *Spanish Exploration in the Southwest, 1542–1706* (New York: Scribner, 1908; rpt., New York: Barnes and Noble, 1959). Charles W. Hackett, ed., *Pichardo's Treatise on the Limits of Louisiana and Texas* (4 vols., Austin: University of Texas Press, 1931–46). Frederick Webb Hodge, ed., *Handbook of Amer-*

ican Indians North of Mexico* (2 vols., Washington: GPO, 1907, 1910; rpt., New York: Pageant, 1959). J. R. Swanton, *Linguistic Material from the Tribes of Southern Texas and Northeastern Mexico* (Washington: Smithsonian Institution, 1940). John R. Swanton, *Source Material on the History and Ethnology of the Caddo Indians* (Smithsonian Institution, Bureau of American Ethnology Bulletin 132, Washington: GPO, 1942). *Thomas N. Campbell*

CANTONMENT CREEK. Cantonment Creek rises southwest of Laketon in northeastern Gray County (at 35°32′ N, 100°41′ W) and runs southeast for ten miles to its mouth on the North Fork of the Red River, near Farm Road 1321 (at 35°24′ N, 100°37′ W). It begins in flat to rolling terrain surfaced by deep, fine sandy loams that support hardwood forest, brush, and grasses, and crosses into flat terrain with local shallow depressions, surfaced by clay and sandy loams that support water-tolerant hardwoods, conifers, and grasses.

CANTRELL, CHARLES E. (1859–1919). Charles E. Cantrell, physician, was born on March 15, 1859, at Lead Hill, Arkansas, the son of William and Elizabeth Cantrell. He attended public schools near his home and earned a medical degree from the University of Arkansas in 1893. He practiced in Wolfe City, Texas, until 1899, when he moved to Greenville. Cantrell founded the Physician's and Surgeon's Hospital, later named Cantrell Hospital, after he was joined in practice by his brother Will. Cantrell served as president of the Hunt County Medical Society and president (1908) and member of the board of trustees (1905–13) of the State Medical Association of Texas (later the Texas Medical Association[qv]). He was a member of the Board of Trustees of the American Medical Association (1909–13) and served as chairman of this organization's judicial council (1907). He also served for several years as the Texas delegate to the AMA and the Association of American Medical Colleges. He published several articles involving clinical case reports and philosophical issues in medicine.

During World War I[qv] Cantrell accepted an assignment as chief of the surgical staff of Base Hospital No. 15 in Corpus Christi. He later accepted a commission in the United States Public Health Service and was reassigned as a surgeon to the hospital in Corpus Christi. The United States surgeon general also asked Cantrell to organize the medical services of the War Risk Insurance Bureau. He was active in business groups in Greenville and was a member of the Wesley Methodist Church. He married Perrilda Dosher in 1878, and they had six daughters and four sons. Cantrell died in Greenville on November 20, 1919.

BIBLIOGRAPHY: Greenville *Morning Herald*, November 12, 1919. *Texas State Journal of Medicine*, December 1919. *Chester R. Burns*

CANTÚ, JOSÉ (ca. 1914–1952). José Cantú, radio broadcaster, had a popular weekly evening musical show on KBOR in Brownsville known as the "Programa Popular" that aired from 1946 to 1952. Mexican singers and such local talented Tejanos as Ermilo Montemayor made the show a major success. Cantu's wit and political criticism during intermissions expressed the frustrations of Hispanics along the lower Rio Grande. He lampooned corrupt politicians and unscrupulous businessmen, hired investigators to examine consumer fraud and City Hall graft in numerous towns, and made powerful enemies. Still, Carnation Dairy Products, Royal Crown Hair Dressing, and other well-known companies sponsored the program. In time, Cantú became a major spokesman for local Mexican Americans[qv] in the battle for equality of opportunity and against prejudice. His program became so popular that sometimes he went on for an extra hour before saying on the air to his wife, "Jesusita, keep the pots warm. I will be there soon for supper." Eventually, his enemies asked Minor Wilson, manager of KBOR, to ban him from radio work. Nevertheless, Cantú continued to denounce those "who exploit the community." On June 7, 1952, he crashed into a tree outside Brownsville and was instantly killed; it was rumored that his brakes had been sabotaged. Brownsville was overwhelmed by Cantu's funeral, where honors were bestowed on "a friend of those in poverty."

BIBLIOGRAPHY: Brownsville *Herald*, June 11, 1952.

Carlos M. Larralde

CANTWELL, JAMES WILLIAM (1868–1931). James William Cantwell, educational administrator, son of John T. and Martha Cantwell, was born near Douglass, Texas, on March 6, 1868. He received his B.A. degree at Yale University in 1894 and his M.A. at Baylor University in 1903; Baylor granted him an LL.D in 1917. On May 24, 1895, he married Ada Westmoreland. From 1894 to 1901 Cantwell was president of Southwestern Academy at Magnolia, Arkansas. He was superintendent of schools at Texarkana, Arkansas, in 1901–02; at Corsicana, Texas, from 1902 to 1908; and at Fort Worth from 1908 to 1915. From 1915 to 1921 he was president of Oklahoma Agricultural and Mechanical College. He served as superintendent of the Texas State Juvenile Training School (later Gatesville State School for Boys[qv]) from 1922 to 1923, when he became superintendent of schools and president of Wichita Falls Junior College (*now* MIDWESTERN UNIVERSITY). He was president of the Texas State Teachers Association[qv] and of the state vocational education board. He died on April 2, 1931, at Wichita Falls, where he was buried in Riverside Cemetery.

BIBLIOGRAPHY: *Who Was Who in America*, Vol. 2.

CANU INDIANS. In a Spanish missionary report of 1691 the Canu Indians were mentioned as living about eighty leagues southwest of the Hasinais of eastern Texas. Although there is no proof, the Canus may have been the same as the Canas, one of the Coahuiltecan groups for which San José y San Miguel de Aguayo Mission was founded at San Antonio in 1720. Some writers have assumed that the Canas were the same as the Sanas, but there is little evidence to support this identification.

BIBLIOGRAPHY: Charles W. Hackett, ed., *Pichardo's Treatise on the Limits of Louisiana and Texas* (4 vols., Austin: University of Texas Press, 1931–46). Gaspar José de Solís, "Diary," trans. Margaret Kenny Kress, *Southwestern Historical Quarterly* 35 (July 1931). John R. Swanton, *Source Material on the History and Ethnology of the Caddo Indians* (Smithsonian Institution, Bureau of American Ethnology Bulletin 132, Washington: GPO, 1942). *Thomas N. Campbell*

CANUTILLO, TEXAS. Canutillo is an incorporated community on the east bank of the Rio Grande and on U.S. Highways 80 and 85 about twelve miles northwest of downtown El Paso in northwestern El Paso County. The community also was on the Atchison, Topeka and Santa Fe Railway. The story of the town begins in June 1823, when the Canutillo land grant was assigned to Juan María Ponce De León[qv] and twenty-nine other citizens of El Paso del Norte (what is now Juárez, Chihuahua, Mexico). A small agricultural settlement was established in 1824, but Apache raiders forced residents to abandon it in 1833. The site remained vacant until after the arrival of Anglo-American settlers in the mid-1800s. The Canutillo ranch became a principal source of income for James Wiley Magoffin,[qv] but in 1855 José Sánchez and others established their ownership as descendants of the original grantees. The state of Texas recognized their claim in 1858, and the land grant was surveyed by Anson Mills[qv] two years later. In 1874 a court order divided ownership of the grant among Joseph Magoffin, Josiah F. Crosby, William W. Mills,[qqv] Anson Mills, John S. Watts, and Sánchez. The Canutillo Townsite and Land Company was chartered in 1909, and a post office was established there two years later. In 1914 Canutillo was identified as a rural post office and had four general stores to serve the surrounding population. The community's estimated population was 300 in 1925, some 400 in 1931, and 828 in 1936. By the mid-1940s the number of local residents had declined to 775, but later the town continued to grow. By the mid-1950s its estimated population was 1,326, by the mid-1960s it was 1,425, and by the mid-1970s it was 1,800. That population estimate remained constant until the early 1990s, when it was revised upward to 4,442.

Martin Donell Kohout

CANYON, TEXAS (Lubbock County). Canyon is at the intersection of Farm roads 1729 and 40, six miles east of Lubbock in east central Lubbock County. It was the site of a school built during the 1890s, when the community was a meetingplace for a small congregation of the Church of Christ. At various times the settlement was also known as Canyon School or Wheelock. Canyon became a county rural school district in the 1920s but was consolidated with the similar districts of McClung and Acuff in 1935 to form the Roosevelt Rural School District. The settlement survived in the mid-1980s as a small farming community with no reported businesses. In 1990 Canyon had an estimated population of forty.

BIBLIOGRAPHY: Virginia Hufstedler, A Study of the Activities of the Church of Christ in Lubbock County from 1890 to 1925 (M.A. thesis, Texas Technological College, 1933). Mary Louise McDonald, The History of Lubbock County (M.A. thesis, University of Texas, 1942).

Charles G. Davis

CANYON, TEXAS (Randall County). Canyon is at the junction of U.S. Highway 60 and Interstate Highway 27, near the center of Randall County and southwest of the old T Anchor Ranch qv headquarters. In December 1887 Lincoln Guy Conner qv surveyed and settled at the site. He laid out the town in the spring of 1889, his dugout serving as home, general store, and post office. A. L. Hammond established the second business and a blacksmith shop, and suggested the name Canyon City, after nearby Palo Duro Canyon, when Conner refused to have the settlement named after himself. When Randall County was organized in July 1889 Conner's home was the voting place for that precinct, and Canyon City was chosen as the county seat. Lumber for commercial buildings was hauled from Quanah by mule-drawn freight wagons. A temporary, two-room frame building served as a courthouse, where church services and other community gatherings were held. Conner established the town's first real estate office and built the Victoria Hotel. Beginning in August 1890 several newspapers, the *Echo*, the *Keystone*, the *Headlight*, and the *Battleship*, appeared briefly. In 1896 Mrs. R. W. Morgan began publishing the *Stayer;* George A. Brandon renamed this paper the Canyon City *News* after buying it in 1903. The first telephone line reached Canyon City from Amarillo in 1896.

The arrival of the Pecos and Northern Texas Railway in 1898 made Canyon City a major shipping point for cattle and cotton and a receiving center for such necessities as coal and lumber. Acres of cattle pens were built on land donated by Conner; W. C. Kenyon ran a wagonyard and seven saloons. The population reached 530 by 1904. That year L. T. Lester opened the Stockman's National Bank, later the First National Bank of Canyon. A telephone exchange was installed in 1902, and construction boomed in anticipation of further rail service. By 1910 ten real estate firms, including the Texas Land Company qv and Keiser Brothers and Phillips, were operating in Canyon City. A brick school building and several churches were built, and on September 29, 1906, residents voted to incorporate, with Jasper N. Haney as first mayor. The Commercial Club and other civic and social organizations were begun at that time. In 1907 the completion of the Santa Fe line from Canyon City to Plainview marked the retirement of the mail hack and stage line between the two towns. The following year a volunteer fire department was organized and an electricity and ice plant installed. C. O. Keiser purchased the Canyon City *News* and began calling it the *Randall County News;* R. A. Terrill was editor. In 1909 a waterworks and sewer system were installed, and a brick courthouse replaced the original frame building. Since many of Canyon City's settlers were Confederate veterans, annual reunions of the Stonewall Jackson Camp of United Confederate Veterans were staged there for ten years.

In 1910 the Santa Fe's Llano Estacado line connected Canyon City with Floydada. West Texas State Normal College (now West Texas State University) opened on a forty-acre site donated by Conner, but classes were held in the courthouse until the completion of the college's first building in 1911. That year the town was renamed Canyon. By 1915 the population was 1,500, and industries included two banks, grain elevators, a tannery, and the twenty-five-room Palace Hotel. The Ford Motor Company established Canyon's first automobile dealership in 1919, and in 1920 Clyde W. Warwick, editor of the *Randall County News* since 1910, bought the paper; he later renamed it the Canyon *News.* On December 2, 1921, fire destroyed several buildings on the south side of the town square. Nevertheless, during the 1920s Canyon enjoyed new growth because of above-average rainfall. The first American Legion qv post in the Southwest completed its headquarters at Canyon in 1921. Streets and highways were paved, street lights added, and natural gas piped in from the Panhandle oil and gas field north of Amarillo. The Santa Fe Railroad erected a new depot, new elementary and high school buildings were constructed, and the Methodist, Baptist, and Presbyterian churches built new brick buildings. The Randall County Library opened in 1927.

During the Great Depression qv of the 1930s the city's three banks were consolidated under the ownership of the First National Bank. The Panhandle-Plains Historical Museum qv was established in 1932, new buildings on the university campus were constructed with Work Projects Administration qv funds, and a new post office building was opened in 1937. The population reached 2,622 by 1940 and 4,349 by 1950. After World War II qv the economy continued to depend on the production of wheat, grain sorghums, dairy products, and livestock, as well as on West Texas State University. City projects completed by 1966 included water and sewer improvements and street extensions. Though Canyon's businesses decreased from 163 in 1967 to 137 in 1985, tourism was enhanced by the expanding Panhandle-Plains Museum and the nearby Palo Duro Canyon State Scenic Park, qv with its summer outdoor drama, *Texas.* In 1987 three public schools, two city parks, a hospital and nursing center, a radio station, a new county library and city hall, and new county government facilities attested to Canyon's continuing growth, as did several new housing developments such as Hunsley Hills, just north of town. The population was 5,864 in 1960, 8,333 in 1970, 10,724 in 1980, and 11,365 in 1990.

BIBLIOGRAPHY: C. Boone McClure, A History of Randall County and the T Anchor Ranch (M.A. thesis, University of Texas, 1930). Mrs. Clyde W. Warwick, comp., *The Randall County Story* (Hereford, Texas: Pioneer, 1969).

Claire R. Kuehn and H. Allen Anderson

CANYON CREEK (Clay County). Canyon Creek rises five miles north of Bellevue in eastern Clay County (at 33°45′ N, 98°01′ W) and runs east for seven miles to its mouth on Belknap Creek, four miles north of Stoneburg in Montague County (at 33°44′ N, 97°56′ W). The stream runs through rolling to flat terrain surfaced by sandy and clay loams that support post oak, water-tolerant hardwoods, and conifers. For most of its history the Canyon Creek area has been used as range and crop land.

____ (Jeff Davis County). Canyon Creek rises on Antelope Flat 1½ miles southwest of Red Hills in northeastern Jeff Davis County (at 30°56′ N, 103°57′ W) and runs northeast for twenty-four miles to its mouth on Cherry Creek, four miles northeast of the Saragosa siding of the Pecos Valley Southern Railway in south central Reeves County (at 31°06′ N, 103°41′ W). Its course crosses steep to gentle slopes and flat to rolling terrain of caliche and alluvial sand, gravel, and mud. Soils in the area are brown sands and clay loams that support scrub brush, sparse grasses, creosote bush, and cacti.

____ (Lipscomb County). Canyon Creek rises ten miles northeast of Higgins in southeastern Lipscomb County (at 36°05′ N, 100°10′ W) and runs north for nine miles to its mouth on Wolf Creek, seven miles east of Lipscomb (at 35°15′ N, 100°07′ W). The stream traverses terrain that varies from flat to rolling, with some local escarpments. Native vegetation consists primarily of mesquite and grasses growing in deep, fine sandy loams.

CANYON LAKE. Canyon Lake, formerly known as Canyon Reservoir, is on the Guadalupe River twelve miles northwest of New Braunfels in northern Comal County (at 29°52′ N, 98°12′ W). The project is owned by the United States government and operated by the United States Army Corps of Engineers, Fort Worth District. The local cooperative agency is the Guadalupe-Blanco River Authority,[qv] which, for paying part of the cost, has rights to the conservation storage space and control over the use and release of conservation water. The lake, formed by a rolled earthfill dam 6,830 feet long, is used for flood control, water conservation, and recreation. Construction of the dam was started on June 27, 1958, and impoundment of water began on June 16, 1964. The general contractor was Tecon Corporation of Dallas. The crest of the spillway is 943 feet above mean sea level, and the conservation storage capacity is 382,000 acre-feet with a surface area of 8,240 acres and a sixty-mile shoreline at 909 feet above mean sea level. Stored water is used for municipal, industrial, and irrigation purposes and for the development of hydroelectric power downstream. The drainage area above the dam is 1,432 square miles.

The construction of the dam and subsequent growth of the area surrounding the lake are among the most significant developments in twentieth-century Comal County history. Inundating a portion of the Guadalupe River valley cost the area productive farm and ranch land as well as two rural communities—Cranes Mill and Hancock—but it also stimulated development that transformed the economy and demography of the county. After the lake was filled north central Comal County became one of the largest population centers in Central Texas and the focus of a resort and tourist industry that rivaled manufacturing and agriculture in importance to the county economy. The dam made possible land development along the lake shore and in the area downstream, which for the first time was protected from periodic flooding. Even as the lake was filling, the first residential subdivisions—including Canyon Lake Hills and Canyon Lake Village—began attracting permanent and temporary residents. By 1967 there were forty-six subdivisions on the shores of Canyon Lake and fourteen more in the hills surrounding it. By the mid-1980s more than eighty neighborhoods had been built, and estimates of the permanent population of the lake area ranged from 12,000 to 15,000. Seven lakeside public parks and two public marinas served thousands of weekend visitors. Residents and tourists supported a variety of new businesses and service industries that transformed the former farm and ranch communities of Sattler and Startzville into thriving commercial centers and occasioned the new town of Canyon City. In the late 1980s two schools and thirteen churches served the permanent residents of the lake area. The Canyon Lake community, forty-eight miles from San Antonio and fifty-six from Austin, continued to attract new commuter, retired, and weekend residents.

BIBLIOGRAPHY: C. L. Dowell, *Dams and Reservoirs in Texas: History and Descriptive Information* (Texas Water Commission Bulletin 6408 [Austin, 1964]). *Seth D. Breeding*

CAPELLONE INDIANS. This name, which is known only from the records of San Antonio de Valero Mission of San Antonio, cannot be related to any known group of Indians. It may be a variant of Apion, the name of another group at the same mission. If the two are the same, a former place name near Laredo, La Cañada de los Abiones, suggests residence in Coahuiltecan Indian territory.

BIBLIOGRAPHY: Herbert Eugene Bolton, *Texas in the Middle Eighteenth Century: Studies in Spanish Colonial History and Administration* (Berkeley: University of California Press, 1915; rpt., Austin: University of Texas Press, 1970). *Thomas N. Campbell*

CAPERS, WILLIAM THEODOTUS (1867–1943). William Theodotus Capers, second bishop of the Diocese of West Texas of the Protestant Episcopal Church,[qv] was born in Greenville, South Carolina, on August 9, 1867, the son of Ellison and Charlotte (Palmer) Capers. He was educated at South Carolina College in 1885 and graduated from Furman University in 1887. He received his M.A. from the University of Kentucky and in 1894 graduated from the Virginia Theological Seminary. He held positions in various churches in South Carolina, Mississippi, North Carolina, Kentucky, and Pennsylvania, from 1895 to 1914. Capers was elected bishop coadjutor of the Diocese of West Texas and was consecrated on May 1, 1914. Upon the retirement of Bishop James Steptoe Johnston[qv] in 1914, Capers became bishop of the diocese and served in that capacity until his death. He married Rebecca Holt Bryan and, after her death, Mrs. Louis Cash Myers. He died in San Antonio on March 29, 1943, after being hospitalized for a week at Santa Rosa Hospital. He is buried in Mission Burial Park.

BIBLIOGRAPHY: San Antonio *Express*, March 30, April 1, 1943. Vertical Files, Barker Texas History Center, University of Texas at Austin. *DuBose Murphy*

CAPITALS. Valladolid, the administrative center of Spain before Madrid became capital in 1551, and Madrid and Paris could be considered capitals of Texas under the competing claims of Spain and France. Mexico City could also be considered the first capital of Texas, since at the beginning of Spanish Texas[qv] there was no intermediate provincial capital of the area. Ysleta, said to be the first settlement in Texas, had Santa Fe, New Mexico, as its capital. Monclova, Coahuila, Mexico,[qv] became the first provincial capital of Texas in 1686. In 1721 the Marqués de Aguayo[qv] established headquarters at Los Adaes[qv] (present Robeline, Louisiana), which remained the capital of Texas for half a century. From 1772 until 1824 San Antonio was the seat of government, although Manuel Antonio Cordero y Bustamante[qv] made his headquarters in 1806 in the Old Stone Fort[qv] at Nacogdoches; in 1810 Manuel María de Salcedo[qv] had his headquarters there for three months.

After the Mexican War of Independence,[qv] Texas was united with Coahuila, with Saltillo[qv] as the provincial capital. On March 9, 1833, Monclova was made capital of Coahuila and Texas.[qv] The Department of Texas had become a subdistrict of the province, and San Felipe de Austin was named the capital of the colony of Texas in 1824. Therefore the conventions of 1832 and 1833[qqv] met at San Felipe, as did the Consultation[qv] of 1835, which organized a provisional government[qv] for Texas as a separate Mexican state. Mexico did not recognize the separation. The Convention of 1836,[qv] which declared Texas independent, met at Washington-on-the-Brazos. Harrisburg and Galveston were both occupied by President David G. Burnet[qv] as temporary capitals, and after the battle of San Jacinto,[qv] Burnet and the cabinet met at Sam Houston's[qv] headquarters near the battlefield. The government then returned briefly to Galveston before moving to Velasco, which served as the seat of government through the end of September 1836.

In October 1836 Columbia (now West Columbia) became the first capital of an elected government of the Republic of Texas.[qv] Columbia remained capital for three months. Houston was then selected as a temporary capital, and President Sam Houston ordered the government to move there on December 15, 1836. Houston was capital from April 19, 1837, until 1839. A capital-site commission selected a site near La Grange, Fayette County, in 1838 and Congress passed a bill to build the capital there, but Houston vetoed it. Waterloo, soon renamed Austin, was approved as the capital on January 19, 1839. President Mirabeau B. Lamar[qv] and his cabinet arrived in Austin on October 17, 1839.

Fearing an attack on Austin by the Mexicans, President Houston ordered the government to return to Houston on March 13, 1842. Washington-on-the-Brazos became capital by executive order in September of that year, and the order spawned the Archive War qv when President Houston attempted to move the archives from Austin. The Constitution of 1845 qv provided that Austin be capital until 1850, when a vote was required to choose the premanent capital. Austin received 7,674 votes, a majority. Another election was scheduled for twenty years later and held in 1872. Austin won with 63,297 votes, compared to Houston's 35,188 and Waco's 12,776.

BIBLIOGRAPHY: Robert A. Calvert and Arnoldo De León, *The History of Texas* (Arlington Heights, Illinois: Harlan Davidson, 1990). Dallas *News,* July 24–30, 1960. Lorena Drummond, "Five Texas Capitals," *Texas Monthly,* February 1930. C. W. Raines, "Enduring Laws of the Republic," *Quarterly of the Texas State Historical Association* 1, 2 (October 1897, October 1898). *San Antonio Express Magazine,* October 8, 1950. Dorman H. Winfrey, "The Texan Archive War of 1842," *Southwestern Historical Quarterly* 64 (October 1960). Ernest William Winkler, "The Seat of Government of Texas," *Quarterly of the Texas State Historical Association* 10 (October 1906, January 1907).

John G. Johnson

CAPITOL. The present Capitol building, constructed between 1882 and 1888, is the fourth one in Austin. As a result of the need for a new Capitol, the Constitution of 1876 qv set aside three million acres of land in the Panhandle qv to fund construction. In 1879 the Sixteenth Legislature provided for surveying the Capitol lands in ten counties of the Panhandle, and formed a Capitol Board as well as a building commission consisting of a "superintendent" architect and two building commissioners to oversee the project. After the completion and acceptance of the surveys in late 1880, the building commission announced a design competition for the new statehouse. Eight architects entered a total of eleven different designs in the competition. In May 1881 the Capitol Board approved the design entered by Elijah E. Myers qv of Detroit. The building commission then advertised for a contractor who would build the Capitol in exchange for the three million acres of public land. The state received only two bids: from Mathias Schnell of Rock Island, Illinois, and from Alfred Andrew Burck of Rockdale, Texas. Schnell received the contract but soon assigned three-fourths of it to Taylor, Babcock and Company, a Chicago firm that included Abner Taylor, Amos C. Babcock, Charles B. Farwell, and John V. Farwell.qv A few months later, Schnell signed over the rest of the contract to the same firm. Abner Taylor became the chief contractor but subcontracted the work to Gustav Wilke,qv a young Chicago builder.

The plans and specifications for the Capitol called for its construction of native limestone, but all of the limestone found near Austin contained discoloring iron particles. Abner Taylor proposed using limestone from Bedford, Indiana, but the Capitol Board and Governor John Ireland qv wished to use Texas stone, specifically red granite from Granite Mountain near the site of present-day Marble Falls in Burnet County. The owners of the mountain, George W. Lacy, William H. Westfall, and Nimrod L. Norton, offered to give the state enough granite for the building. Taylor initially refused to use the red granite because he believed the difficulty of working the stone would make it too expensive. In early 1885 subcontractor Wilke informed Taylor that it would cost much less to use donated red granite in a simplified style agreed upon by architect Myers than limestone with the extensive decorative carving originally agreed upon. However, Taylor kept this information a secret, and continued to assure state officials that he could not afford to use red granite because of its additional cost. Finally, on July 25, 1885, he signed a supplementary contract in which he agreed to use red granite for the Capitol if the state would supply it free of charge, share the "extra cost," construct a narrow-gauge railroad from Burnet to Granite Mountain, and furnish convict labor to quarry the stone. Taylor also agreed to pay the state for the use of the convicts and to provide room and board for them.

After labor difficulties arose in 1886, stemming from the use of convict labor to quarry the granite, Wilke imported granite cutters from Scotland, in violation of the Contract Labor Act of 1885 (*see* CAPITOL BOYCOTT). In spite of such difficulties, work began on the Capitol dome in mid-1887 and the Goddess of Liberty was hoisted to the top of it in February 1888. The Capitol first was opened to the public on the evening of April 21, 1888, before its completion. The structure was dedicated during a week-long celebration lasting from May 14 to May 19, 1888, but the Capitol Board refused to accept the structure because its copper roof leaked and because of several other minor problems. After Wilke fixed the roof and corrected several other problems, the Capitol Board received the building on December 6, 1888. In 1882 the three million acres of land in the Capitol reservation was valued at $1.5 million. The total cost of the Capitol was $3,744,630.60, of which the state assumed about $500,000. A hundred years later, the lands exchanged for the Capitol had a tax evaluation of almost $7 billion.

The Texas Capitol is of Renaissance Revival design and was modeled after the national Capitol in Washington. At the time of its completion it contained 392 rooms, 18 vaults, 924 windows, and 404 doors. From the ground to the top of statue on the dome is 311 feet. In February 1983 a fire badly damaged the east wing of the Capitol and provided the impetus for a restoration of the building. A few weeks after the fire, the legislature formed the State Preservation Board. The first project of this board was to replace the figure of Liberty on the dome of the Capitol. In November 1985 the original Goddess of Liberty was removed by helicopter. A new statue, cast of aluminum in molds made from the original zinc statue, was placed on the dome in June 1986. The entire cost of more than $450,000 was raised from private donations. The original statue has been restored and is on exhibition on the Capitol grounds in a special structure built for it in 1995.

The Governor's Public Reception Room, originally the most lavishly decorated space in the building, was restored in 1987. In 1988 work began on a masterplan to restore the Capitol and to build an underground annex north of the building. The legislature approved this plan in 1989, and work began in 1990. The extension was completed by January 1993. The restoration of the 1888 Capitol was finished in early 1995, and the structure was re-dedicated on April 21, 1995. The extension and restoration project cost about $200 million. *See also* CAPITOL FREEHOLD LAND AND INVESTMENT COMPANY and XIT RANCH.

BIBLIOGRAPHY: Robert C. Cotner, *The Texas State Capitol* (Austin: Pemberton Press, 1968). Joubert Lee Greer, The Building of the Texas State Capitol, 1882–1888 (M.A. thesis, University of Texas, 1932). *The Texas Capitol: Selected Essays from the* Southwestern Historical Quarterly (Austin: Texas State Historical Association, 1995).

William Elton Green

CAPITOLA, TEXAS. Capitola was on the old Menard road between State Highway 29 and the Llano River in northwestern Mason County. It was settled in the early 1890s. Its post office was established in 1894, and the postmistress, Sarah E. Jenkins, named the town Capitola, supposedly after a continuing story in a magazine she was reading. The community had a population of twenty-five in 1896. In 1909 its post office was discontinued, and the community was gradually abandoned after the route of the road was changed.

Alice J. Rhoades

CAPITOL BOYCOTT. In 1882 the Texas legislature contracted with Mathias Schnell of Rock Island, Illinois, for construction of a state Capitol,qv promising as compensation more than three million acres of public land. Twelve days later three-quarters interest in the project was transferred to the Illinois firm of Taylor, Babcock, and Company, and five months later Schnell transferred his remaining interest to the

Convict laborers with granite blocks for construction of the state Capitol, ca. 1885. Courtesy Austin History Center, Austin Public Library; photo no. PICA 06359. The use of convict labor on the construction of the Capitol precipitated a boycott of the job by the granite cutters' union.

same company. Principals in the company, which became known as the Capitol Syndicate, were Charles B. Farwell, United States senator from Illinois; his brother, John Villiers Farwell;[qv] Abner Taylor, a United States Representative from Illinois; and Amos Babcock. Initially, the Capitol was to be built of Texas limestone, but when limestone proved unsatisfactory, granite from the Burnet area was substituted. Since a fall in land prices from 1883 to 1885 made it difficult to meet the expenses of the syndicate, Taylor, who acted as chief contractor, asked the legislature to help by furnishing convict labor for quarrying the granite and for building the needed rail line from Burnet to Austin. Taylor agreed to pay sixty-five cents a day to house, feed, and guard the convicts. Owners of the quarries at Marble Falls agreed to furnish the granite free of charge. Shortly after this, construction of the building was subcontracted by Gustav Wilke.[qv]

The use of convict labor in competition with free labor was strongly opposed by all organized labor groups. Moreover, Wilke had already aroused the antagonism of the International Association of Granite Cutters by using nonunion labor on other jobs. He placed an ad in the Journal of the International Association of Granite Cutters for thirty cutters to work "on red granite, steady work, climate good and healthy, union wages." The following month, referring to this ad, the local union in Austin placed a notice that no union men had been hired, there was little work to be done, and workers should not be "gulled" by the description of the climate. Wilke wrote the union headquarters stating he would hire whomever he chose and would not allow the union to dictate to him. The union, by a vote of 500 to 1, declared a boycott against the job and warned all granite cutters to stay away from Austin. Wilke sent a telegram to the union stating that if the union would accept Quincy, Massachusetts, wages, he would guarantee that no convicts would cut granite for the capitol. These wages were $2.75 to $3.00 a day. The custom, however, was that wages on new quarries were set at the level of the nearest competitive quarry, in this case Graniteville, Missouri, where the wages were $3.50 a day. According to the national office of the granite cutters, the official wage for Austin was $4.00 per day, so the offer was refused.

The contractor sent a personal representative, George Berry, to Aberdeen, Scotland, to secure cutters. Berry promised eighteen months' steady work at four to six dollars a day. Eighty-eight Scottish workers came to the United States under contract to work on the building. Transportation expenses were to be deducted from their first two months' wages. At New York they were met by representatives of the union and a United States marshal, who held the bringing in of the workers a clear violation of the Alien Contract Labor Law, passed in February 1885. Twenty-four workers refused to scab, but sixty-four continued on the way to Texas.

As a consequence, charges were filed in the federal district court at Austin against the members of the Capitol Syndicate. All were indicted in March 1886, but the hearing was postponed until August 1887. Aberdeen recruits who left employment with Wilke gave depositions against the syndicate in March 1887, and in July those who remained were asked to sign a statement that they had no contract. Some later admitted signing knowing that the claim was false. Before the case was heard, two years later, members of the syndicate were removed from the suit, leaving only Wilke, who admitted the charges and was fined $1,000 for each Aberdeen man, a total of $64,000. He was given eighteen months to appeal for executive clemency and finally in 1893 paid $8,000 plus costs. The union claimed Wilke pled guilty to shield syndicate members, who then used their influence to reduce the fine. Considering the status of unions in the United States at that time, the fact that the federal prosecutor left town the day of the hearing, leaving prosecution to attorneys hired by the Knights of Labor,[qv] and the fact that two syndicate members were also members of the United States Congress, the claim was probably correct.

Many of the Scottish workers did not remain long in Texas. Anger over the expense of the seven-day train trip from New York and the unpleasant surprise that wages were not as promised left only fifteen working on the Capitol by May 1887. It was estimated that more than one-half had no granite-cutting experience and were unable to earn even a dollar a day. Vouchers from May 1886 through May 1887 indicate that the average wage was twenty-seven cents an hour, although individual wages ranged from four to fifty cents an hour. Wilke had promised to reduce the number of convicts working, but from July to October 1886 the number increased from 300 to 350. From the standpoint of preventing the use of convict labor and use of scabs, the boycott was a failure. In 1890 Wilke and Berry paid a penalty of $500 each and agreed to use union cutters on future jobs. *See also* XIT RANCH.

BIBLIOGRAPHY: Ruth A. Allen, "The Capitol Boycott: A Study in Peaceful Labor Tactics," *Southwestern Historical Quarterly* 42 (April 1939). Marjory Harper, "Emigrant Strikebreakers: Scottish Granite Cutters and the Texas Capitol Boycott," *Southwestern Historical Quarterly* 95 (April 1992). *John G. Johnson*

CAPITOL FREEHOLD LAND AND INVESTMENT COMPANY. The Capitol Freehold Land and Investment Company, Limited, was incorporated in London, England, late in the fall of 1884 with an authorized capital of $15 million. It was organized by John V. Farwell[qv] to raise finances to stock the XIT Ranch[qv] and to meet its tremendous operating expenses. Wealthy English bond buyers like the Earl of Aberdeen and Henry Seton-Karr were shareholders in the investment company but not in the ranch, which was operated by the Capitol Syndicate under John and Charles B. Farwell, Amos C. Babcock, and Abner Taylor. By the late 1890s the British investors had begun clamoring for the redemption of their bonds, and the syndicate began its gradual selling of the XIT properties. The Farwell estate completed the redemption of most of these bonds to the Englishmen's satisfaction in 1909, and the investment company ceased to exist. The final account payment and dissolution of the company came in 1915. The remaining interest went to the Farwell heirs, who set up the Capitol Reservation Lands as a trust, and to shareholders in this country.

BIBLIOGRAPHY: J. Evetts Haley, *The XIT Ranch of Texas and the Early Days of the Llano Estacado* (Chicago: Lakeside, 1929; rpts., Norman: University of Oklahoma Press, 1953, 1967). William D. Mauldin, History of Dallam County, Texas (M.A. thesis, University of Texas, 1938). Lewis Nordyke, *Cattle Empire: The Fabulous Story of the 3,000,000 Acre XIT* (New York: Morrow, 1949. rpt., New York: Arno Press, 1977).

CAPLEN, TEXAS. Caplen, a residential area of Bolivar Peninsula[qv] on State Highway 87 near the Rollover Pass[qv] in eastern Galveston County adjoins the west end of Gilchrist. The Gilchrist post office serves the Caplen area. Caplen has been a resort since the late 1800s and was eventually named for John Caplen, a property owner who surveyed the area in 1909. At one time the local marshlands produced large quantities of muskrats for trappers. Caplen's summer population for a time was between 300 and 500, and two hotels served the visitors. In 1915 Caplen had a population of 200, a post office, a general store, and three hotels. The hurricane of 1915 scared people away until about 1930, when a gradual influx of residents again started. In the 1940s, Caplen was a ranching, tourist, and fishing community that reported two businesses and a population of seventy-five. Its 1990 year-round population was about thirty. In earlier years the site reportedly was a favorite of Indians, who left a burial ground there. Several important archeological finds have led to detailed excavations at the Caplen Site.

BIBLIOGRAPHY: Thomas N. Campbell, "Archeological Investigations at the Caplen Site, Galveston County, Texas," *Texas Journal of Science* 9 (December 1957). A. Pat Daniels, *Bolivar! Gulf Coast Peninsula* (Crystal Beach, Texas: Peninsula, 1985). Houston *Chronicle*, July 21, 1963, May 10, 1982. Vertical Files, Barker Texas History Center, University of Texas at Austin (Bolivar Peninsula). *A. Pat Daniels*

CAP MOUNTAIN. Cap Mountain stands six miles southeast of Llano in eastern Llano County (at 30°43′ N, 98°35′ W). Its summit, at an elevation of 1,376 feet above sea level, rises some 250 feet above the terrain below. The surrounding area is variously flat to rolling to steep, covered by soils ranging from shallow and stony to deep, fine sandy loams. Local vegetation consists primarily of open stands of live oak and mesquite.

CAPOTA CREEK. Capota Creek rises eight miles northwest of Crystal City in southwestern Zavala County (at 28°49′ N, 99°54′ W) and runs south for 9½ miles to its mouth on Turkey Creek, three-quarters of a mile west of Comanche Lake (at 28°41′ N, 99°55′ W). The creek rises in flat to low-rolling terrain with local dissections and descends to flat terrain with shallow depressions. The local soils are clayey and sandy loams. Scrub brush, cacti, and grasses predominate around the creek's upper reaches and water-tolerant hardwoods and grasses near its lower.

CAPOTE, TEXAS. Capote (Capoti) was a rural school community on Farm Road 466 about ten miles southeast of Seguin in southeastern Guadalupe County. Hiram Wilson, a former slave, established a pottery business in Capote in 1869. He also founded the Capote Baptist Church. Wilson died in 1884, but other ex-slaves continued to run the pottery until 1903. Pottery from Capote turned up in many areas of southwestern Texas (*see* WILSON POTTERIES). In 1904 Capote had three one-teacher schools for forty-four white students, and three schools and four teachers for 137 black students. There were a few scattered houses and a cemetery in the area in 1946; by the mid-1980s only a church and a cemetery marked the community on county highway maps. *Vivian Elizabeth Smyrl*

CAPOTE CREEK. Capote Creek rises two miles south of Capote Peak in western Presidio County (at 30°18′ N, 104°35′ W) and runs south and southwest for ten miles, passing over Capote Falls (at 30°13′ N, 104°34′ W) to meet its tributary, Walker Creek. Capote Falls, the highest falls in Texas, drops 175 feet; it is on private property. Capote Creek continues eight miles to its mouth on the Rio Grande, three miles from Candelaria (at 30°10′ N, 104°41′ W). The local terrain is composed primarily of rhyolite and tuff, except where Cretaceous sediments are exposed along the edge of the Sierra Vieja range. The area is surfaced by sand and clay loams, with patches of bare, rough, stony ground. Local vegetation is primarily sparse desert shrubs. The creek was named for Capote Peak, near its origin. Antonio de Espejo's[qv] entrada passed by Capote Creek on its way to the Rio Grande in August 1583. A dam was built across Capote Creek in the winter of 1937 to hold water for irrigation when the Rio Grande was low in the Candelaria area.

BIBLIOGRAPHY: Virginia Madison and Hallie Stillwell, *How Come It's Called That? Place Names in the Big Bend Country* (Albuquerque: University of New Mexico Press, 1958). Cecilia Thompson, *History of Marfa and Presidio County, 1535–1946* (2 vols., Austin: Nortex, 1985).

CAPOTE DRAW. Capote Draw, a shallow valley, rises 2½ miles west of the Cuesta del Burro range in western Presidio County (at 30°05′ N, 104°27′ W) and runs north for twenty-four miles to its mouth on Wild Horse Creek, at the section known as Chispa Creek, ten miles south of the Jeff Davis county line (at 30°18′ N, 104°29′ W). The draw crosses an alluvium of Quaternary sands and gravel washed from the Sierra Vieja range. The land surface of sands and rough stony areas supports desert shrubs. In August 1583 Antonio de Espejo's[qv] entrada camped in Capote Draw.

bibliography: Cecilia Thompson, *History of Marfa and Presidio County, 1535–1946* (2 vols., Austin: Nortex, 1985).

CAPOTE HILLS. The Capote Hills are near the headwaters of O'Neal Creek, twelve miles southeast of Seguin in southeastern Guadalupe County (at 29°29′ N, 97°47′ W). The highest of these hills, Porter Knob, stands at 670 feet above mean sea level, 150 feet above the surrounding landscape. José de la Baume received the first land grant in the area in 1806; he renewed the grant with the Mexican government in 1828. Michael H. Erskine qv bought the Capote Hills Ranch in the early 1840s.

bibliography: Willie Mae Weinert, *An Authentic History of Guadalupe County* (Seguin, Texas: Seguin *Enterprise*, 1951; rpt. 1976).

CAPOTE KNOB. Capote Knob is a small summit just north of the Capote Hills, near the headwaters of O'Neal Creek, and twelve miles southeast of Seguin in Guadalupe County (at 29°30′ N, 97°47′ W). The top of the hill is 726 feet above mean sea level, 150 feet higher than the surrounding landscape.

CAPOTE PEAK. Capote Peak is fourteen miles northwest of Farm Road 2810 in western Presidio County (at 30°17′ N, 104°33′ W). At an elevation of 6,212 feet above sea level, its summit rises 1,882 feet above nearby Capote Creek. The peak stands at the southeastern edge of the Sierra Vieja range. The area is characterized by desert mountains and canyonland of rhyolite and tuff; vegetation includes sparse grasses, cacti, and conifer and oak shrubs. Capote means "cloak" or "cape" and refers to the fog and mist that at times surround the peak. In 1870 William Russell grazed sheep on the southern edge of Capote. Although the shepherds were considered safe from attack because of their distance from Indian trails, Apaches raided the area and allowed only one sheepherder to escape. Lucas Charles Brite II qv brought cattle to Capote Peak in 1885 and built his ranch in its shadow.

bibliography: Virginia Madison and Hallie Stillwell, *How Come It's Called That? Place Names in the Big Bend Country* (Albuquerque: University of New Mexico Press, 1958). Ronnie C. Tyler, *The Big Bend* (Washington: National Park Service, 1975).

CAPOTE SPRINGS. Capote Springs is a group of springs flowing from Quaternary gravel in a remote area eleven miles northeast of Candelaria in western Presidio County (at 30°15′ N, 104°33′ W). The water produces the beautiful Capote Falls, where it drops over a 180-foot-high cliff of Bracks rhyolite in the Vieja Rim. There is a large buildup of travertine at the falls in the shape of a cape; hence the Spanish name, which means "cape" or "shroud." The very rare and acutely endangered Hinckley columbine and the many-stemmed spider flower have been found in Texas only at these springs. Animal life includes the canyon tree frog, the unisexual whiptail lizard, and the mastiff bat. On July 20, 1976, the springs flowed at a rate of two gallons per second. Rockshelters in the vicinity offered protection to prehistoric inhabitants, whose pictographs and bedrock mortar holes were still visible in 1990.

bibliography: Gunnar Brune, *Springs of Texas,* Vol. 1 (Fort Worth: Branch-Smith, 1981).
Gunnar Brune

CAPPS CORNER, TEXAS. Capps Corner is at the intersection of Farm roads 1956 and 677, fifteen miles northeast of Montague in extreme northeastern Montague County. The settlement was established about 1925 and named for E. G. (Cap) Adams. It was still listed as a community in 1990.

bibliography: John Clements, *Flying the Colors: Texas, a Comprehensive Look at Texas Today, County by County* (Dallas: Clements Research, 1984).
Brian Hart

CAPROCK. The cap, or hard layer, underlying the Llano Estacado qv is a major geological feature known to Texans as the Caprock. It is not a rock layer in the usual sense of the term but is more technically a "hard-pan" layer that developed a few feet below the ground as highly mineral subsoil particles cemented themselves together to form a rock-like layer that resists erosion. Although the name Caprock technically applies only to the formation itself, the expression is often loosely used to mean the whole Llano Estacado. The Caprock escarpment was formed by erosion about one million to two million years ago. Prehistoric nomadic hunters, Plains Apaches, and Comanches lived in the region. The Spanish explorer Vásquez de Coronado qv traveled the area in 1541. The Caprock escarpment forms a natural boundary line between the High Plains and the lower rolling plains of West Texas. It stretches from the Panhandle qv into Central Texas and can be seen most prominently in Briscoe, Floyd, Motley, Dickens, Crosby, Garza, and Borden counties, where it reaches its highest elevations, rising abruptly above the plains at 200, 500, or as much as 1,000 feet. The east-facing wall is often cut by rivers, forming canyons such as Palo Duro Canyon.qv
H. Bailey Carroll

CAP ROCK, TEXAS. Cap Rock is at the edge of the Caprock qv on State Highway 207, twenty-seven miles east of Lubbock in Crosby County. It was established in 1925 after ranchlands were broken up for farming use. On March 8, 1929, the Cap Rock school district, originally named Plum Creek School, was established under the jurisdiction of the Robertson school district. Grades one through seven were taught in a one-room building with Estelle Griffin as the first teacher. A grade school remained in operation at Cap Rock until August 23, 1960, when the district was consolidated with Ralls Independent School District. Leading pioneers include C. H. Graham, who donated land for the school; Lawrence Teston, owner of the first store; and John Wheeler, who gave land for the construction of the first gin. Cap Rock was still listed as a community in 1990.

bibliography: Crosby County Pioneer Memorial Museum, *A History of Crosby County, 1876-1977* (Dallas: Taylor, 1978).
Edloe A. Jenkins

CAPROCK CANYONS STATE PARK. Caprock Canyons State Park, in southeastern Briscoe, Floyd, and Hall counties three miles north of Quitaque, was acquired from the estate of Theodore Geisler in May 1975. It comprises 13,960.6 acres and is the third largest park in the Texas state park system; its terrain is the roughest. In addition to Lake Theo (named after Geisler), the park features spectacular landscapes carved by erosion at the edge of the Caprock,qv colorful cliffs and canyons, and abundant wildlife, including mule and white-tailed deer and imported North African aoudad sheep (*see* exotics). One of the park's most interesting features is the Folsom Site near Lake Theo, one of five such sites in the nation. Among the artifacts first excavated there in 1974 were several Folsom points and remains of an extinct Ice Age bison. This bison-kill site gives substantial evidence that Folsom man manufactured and made use of his weapons here about 10,000 years ago. Springs in Holmes Canyon probably contributed to making this area a favorite campsite for pre-Columbian man. Activities available at the park include camping, hiking, horseback riding, fishing, picnicking, swimming, mountain bike riding, rock climbing, and sightseeing.

bibliography: Tommie Pinkard, "Under the Caprock," *Texas Highways,* May 1984.
H. Allen Anderson

CAPS, TEXAS. Caps is near the intersection of U.S. Highway 277 and Farm Road 707 southwest of Abilene in Taylor County. The community began in 1882 when J. Stoddard Johnston of Abilene gave Ira and Anna Rollins Borders a wedding present of an acre of land just north of the current townsite. By 1894 the community had a post office, known as Border's Chapel, that served forty families. This office was replaced by mail delivery from Abilene in 1916. In 1905 residents gathered to select a new name; reportedly, someone threw his cap into the air and said, "Let's call it caps," and the idea was approved. The Caps community had a cotton gin, a telephone office, two churches, two stores, a school, and a blacksmith shop by 1920. Caps and View constructed the Butterfield School halfway between the two communities in 1935. The school, named in honor of the Butterfield Overland Mail[qv] line, had eight grades. It was consolidated with the Wylie Independent School District in 1978. In the mid-1980s it had an average yearly enrollment of seventy-three in kindergarten through the fifth grade. Commercial activity shifted to U.S. 277 after Camp Barkeley opened in 1940 four miles southwest of the community. After the army base was closed in 1945, its site became a commercial feedlot; in the mid-1980s it was still used for that purpose. Dyess Air Force Base was opened in 1953, and aircraft noise forced the two Caps churches to move closer to Abilene on Highway 277. A disagreement over territorial rights between the View-Caps Water Supply Corporation and the city of Abilene began in 1979. The issue, one of Abilene's longest legal battles, lasted through three mayors and two city managers. The population of Caps was reported as twenty in 1936, 125 in 1948, seventy-five in 1965, and 300 in 1985. In 1986 Abilene annexed a portion of Caps, including the churches and fifty View-Caps water customers. In 1990 Caps reported a population of 100.

BIBLIOGRAPHY: Juanita Daniel Zachry, *A History of Rural Taylor County* (Burnet, Texas: Nortex, 1980). *Nita Houlihan Keesee*

CAPUT, TEXAS. Caput was near the site of present Seminole in central Gaines County. Before the county was organized, Caput had the main post office in the area. It opened on December 19, 1904, with William B. Austin as postmaster. However, by 1905 the new town of Seminole had brought an end to its influence, and Caput declined rapidly. The post office moved to Seminole on January 22, 1906.

BIBLIOGRAPHY: Ed Ellsworth Bartholomew, *800 Texas Ghost Towns* (Fort Davis, Texas: Frontier, 1971). Ed Ellsworth Bartholomew, *The Encyclopedia of Texas Ghost Towns* (Fort Davis, Texas, 1982).

Charles G. Davis

CAQUIXADAQUIX INDIANS. The Caquixadaquix Indians are known from a single 1691 Spanish missionary report that lists them among the groups southeast of the Hasinai of eastern Texas. Since no distance was specified, it is impossible to tell whether they lived in eastern Texas or western Louisiana. The first part of the name, "Caquixa-," suggests Catqueza, the name of a tribe that lived southwest of the Hasinai. Since the same report also lists "Caquiza" as living to the southwest of the Hasinai, there seems to be no basis for giving serious consideration to linkage of Caquixadaquix with Catqueza. The affiliations of the Caquixadaquix Indians remain unknown.

BIBLIOGRAPHY: John R. Swanton, *Source Material on the History and Ethnology of the Caddo Indians* (Smithsonian Institution, Bureau of American Ethnology Bulletin 132, Washington: GPO, 1942).

Thomas N. Campbell

CARACOL. *Caracol*, a journal published in San Antonio from September 1974 until October 1977, was a project of the Texas Institute for Educational Development. It began as a monthly, then became bimonthly with the July–August 1977 issue. The last issue was the following one, September–October 1977. The original staff consisted of Cecilio García-Camarillo (editor), Linda García and Mia García-Camarillo (layout), Cesar Augusto Martínez (photography and original woodcuts), Jorge Ramírez (staff), and Jaime Bustos (illustrator). The stated purpose of *Caracol* was to be a forum to raise Chicano[qv] consciousness and to present contemporary politics and the arts from a Hispanic point of view. The title, which means "snail," suggested a spiral of self-expansion and was inspired by Oliver Wendell Holmes's poem "The Chambered Nautilus." Contributors included the poet Alurista (March 1975), the New Mexico novelist Rudolfo Anaya (March 1975), the dramatist Luis Valdez (May 1975), and the short-story writer Tomás Rivera[qv] (August 1977). *Caracol* was issued on newsprint in an 8½ x 11 format, bound with staples, and averaging thirty to forty pages. It printed original stories, poems, and drama and political commentary, women's concerns, reviews of Mexican-American theater and music, and cartoons. After November 1976 *Caracol* devoted entire issues to a single theme. One issue was a children's coloring book, and another issue was entirely short stories.

Russell H. Goodyear

CARACOL CREEK. Caracol Creek rises just west of North San Antonio Hills in western Bexar County (at 29°29′ N, 98°43′ W) and runs southeast for 5½ miles to its mouth on Medio Creek, just east of Loop 1604 (at 29°25′ N, 98°42′ W). It traverses rolling terrain surfaced by clay loam that supports mesquite and grasses. The name is Spanish for "snail."

CARADAN, TEXAS. Caradan is nine miles northeast of Goldthwaite in northeastern Mills County. It was established in the 1880s and named for two pioneer settlers, S. L. Caraway and Dan T. Bush. In 1889 the community of fifteen was granted a post office. Development was slow. In 1930 the community had twenty-nine residents and five businesses. In 1950 Caradan had two businesses and seventy-five residents. In 1970 the population had declined to eighteen, and the community still supported one business. In 1974 the post office was discontinued. The population was twenty in 1990.

BIBLIOGRAPHY: Fred Tarpley, *1001 Texas Place Names* (Austin: University of Texas Press, 1980). *Julius A. Amin*

CARADJA, CATHERINE OLYMPIA (1893–1993). Princess Catherine Caradja (Caragea in Romanian), a celebrated Romanian expatriate who spent much of her later life in the Hill Country[qv] of Texas, daughter of Princess Irene Cantacuzene and Prince Radu Kretzulescu, was born in Bucharest, Romania, on January 28, 1893. A pawn in a financial struggle between her father and her mother's family, the princess was abducted at the age of three by her father and hidden in England. With her identity obscured, she did not return to Romania until 1908. By then her parents had divorced and her mother, subsequently remarried to Prince Nicolae Ghica, had died. After the courts awarded custody of the young princess to the Cantacuzene family, she was reared by her maternal grandmother, the daughter of the last duke of Oltenea, and her maternal grandfather, Prince George Cantacuzene. This prince was a former prime minister of Romania and prominent oilman who developed the major oilfield at Ploesti, as well as the chief of a powerful dynasty that extended back to the Phanariot rulers of imperial Byzantium, when a Cantacuzene had been emperor. The princess was educated in England, France, Romania, and Belgium and conversant in five languages. She married Prince Constantin Caragea, a military officer, in 1914 and thereafter devoted herself to social work, to running wartime hospitals, and to St. Catherine's Crib, a complex of orphanages started by her mother after the princess was abducted. At their height, before the Communist takeover of Romania, the orphanages had a capacity of more than 3,000 children and were considered among the best in that part of Europe. The princess first became known internationally as a result of her opposition to Nazi occupation of Romania during World War II.[qv] When the oilfields at Ploesti were bombed by the Allies in 1943, she personally took custody of surviving Allied crews, saw that they were cared for in her hospitals, and facilitated their escape to Italy. These activities earned her the sobriquet "Angel of Ploesti." Her rank, demeanor, and connections, which had fortified her against most Nazi reprisals, were of little use against the Communists, however. Her orphanages and foundation were nationalized in 1949, and in the winter of 1951–52 the princess was forced to flee.

After eight weeks in the hull of a Danube tanker, Princess Catherine, by then divorced and with only one surviving daughter, emerged in Vienna to a new life as an itinerant public servant and publicist. She directed relief efforts for children in Algiers after the severe 1954 earthquake, and she spoke widely throughout western Europe, Great Britain, and northwestern Africa against Communism. In 1955 she brought her message to North America about the "captive nations" of central and eastern Europe. For the next thirty-five years she traveled the United States and Canada as a public speaker and as a visitor in the homes of the aviators she had saved. She spent part of every year in the Texas Hill Country town of Comfort, which became one of her three places of residence in the United States, the other two having been Baltimore and Kansas City. In 1973 she began an autobiography of her remarkable life. In mid-1991, a year and a half after the overthrow of the Communist government in Romania, she returned to her native country, took up residence in her old orphanage, and inspired much public admiration and media coverage. Nearly two years later, at the age of 100, she died, on May 26, 1993. She was buried in the family tomb in Bucharest, and memorial services were held in the historic Kretzulescu Church in the heart of the city. She was survived by one daughter, in Paris, by a granddaughter who resided in Bucharest and Paris, and by two great-grandsons. Two daughters and her former husband preceded her in death.

BIBLIOGRAPHY: Catherine Caradja, *Princess Catherine* (Comfort, Texas: Gabriel Press, 1991). *Who's Who of American Women*, 17th ed.

Glen E. Lich

CARANCAHUA, TEXAS. Carancahua, in southeastern Jackson County, was originally an informal cluster of log cabins and was apparently named for its position near the banks of Carancahua Bay. By 1880 Carancahua was the site of a mail stop called Freeport, on the route from Texana to Matagorda. There was a post office at Carancahua from 1897 to 1926. In 1908 local boosters offered town lots for sale, but the town's location—conducive to malaria and floods—discouraged prospective investors. In 1915 the community reported a population of fifty. By the 1920s the population hovered around twenty-five, and by 1931 Carancahua no longer reported a population. In the 1960s a community building was at the site. Carancahua was still listed as a community in 1990.

BIBLIOGRAPHY: Ira T. Taylor, *The Cavalcade of Jackson County* (San Antonio: Naylor, 1938).

Stephen L. Hardin

CARANCAHUA BAY. Carancahua Bay, named for the Karankawa Indians, who at one time inhabited its shores, is an inlet of Matagorda Bay in extreme northeastern Calhoun County (at 28°'40 N, 96°'24 W). It is bounded on the north by Jackson County, and the Calhoun-Jackson county line extends through the bay. The Calhoun County community of Port Alto is on the west shore of the bay. Carancahua, a Jackson County community, is on the east shore.

CARANCAHUA BAYOU. Carancahua (Karankawa) Bayou rises south of the Sarah White oilfield and east of the Brazoria county line in southwestern Galveston County (at 29°17′ N, 95°06′ W) and flows 6½ miles southeast, through Carancahua Lake and across the Gulf Intracoastal Waterway,[qv] to its mouth on West Bay, two miles northeast of the Brazoria county line (at 29°14′ N, 95°01′ W). It flows first through low-rolling to flat terrain surfaced by sandy and clay loam that supports hardwoods and pines, then descends to a brackish saltwater marsh where rushes and grasses grow.

CARANCAHUA PASS. Carancahua Pass is a narrow channel joining Carancahua Bay and Matagorda Bay in eastern Calhoun County (at 28°38′ N, 96°22′ W). The waterway is named after the Karankawa Indians. The maximum width of the channel is about a half mile.

CARBAJAL, JOSÉ MARÍA JESÚS (?–1874). José Carbajal, son of José Antonio Carbajal Peña and María Gertrudis Sánchez Soto, was born in San Fernando de Béxar (San Antonio). In 1823 he went to Lexington, Kentucky, and worked two years as a tanner and saddle maker. Later he studied at Bethany, Virginia, under Alexander Campbell, renounced Catholicism, and became an ardent Protestant. Aided by Stephen F. Austin,[qv] he returned to Texas as the official surveyor for Martín De León,[qv] laid out the town of Victoria, and married De León's daughter, María del Refugio De León Garza, around 1830. They had two children. In January 1831 Carbajal accompanied José Francisco Madero[qv] to survey and issue land titles in East Texas, was arrested by John Davis Bradburn,[qv] but was soon released. He acted as ad interim secretary for the ayuntamiento[qv] of Bexar and in February 1835 was elected deputy from Bexar to the legislature of Coahuila and Texas,[qv] where he acted as secretary. In the spring of 1835 the legislature authorized him to publish the laws and decrees of the state in English and Spanish. The laws were published in Texas in 1839. Domingo de Ugartechea[qv] ordered Carbajal arrested for attempting to stir up rebellion, and Carbajal left for New Orleans, where in November 1835 he joined Peter Kerr and Fernando De León[qqv] in chartering the *Hannah Elizabeth* to supply the Texas forces. The vessel was captured by Mexicans, and Carbajal was imprisoned at Brazos Santiago and then at Matamoros. While preparations were underway to transfer him to San Juan de Ulloa, he escaped and returned to Texas, where he or possibly his brother Mariano, who was with James W. Fannin[qv] in 1835, signed the Goliad Declaration of Independence[qv] on December 2, 1835. Carbajal was elected to the Convention of 1836[qv] at Washington-on-the-Brazos but did not attend.

In 1839 Carbajal, in command of a group of American volunteers, defeated a Mexican Centralist army near Mier but was wounded in the engagement and lost the use of his left arm. As an advocate of an independent republic in northern Mexico, he commanded a division of the Mexican army against the United States in 1846. From 1850 to 1853 he led American merchants and filibusters in the border engagements known as the Merchants War.[qv] Although he was arrested twice by United States authorities, he was released both times. He was living in Piedras Negras in 1855, when his house was destroyed by the Callahan expedition.[qv] In 1861 Carbajal was commander in chief of state troops of Tamaulipas and was defeated at Matamoros while supporting the *de jure* government of Jesús de la Serva. In 1862 Carbajal joined the Mexican liberal army to serve against the French. He was governor of the state of Tamaulipas and San Luis Potosí in 1865, when he was commissioned financial agent to negotiate a loan from the United States. Some time later he moved to Hidalgo County, Texas, and from there, in 1872, moved to Soto la Marina, Tamaulipas, where he died in 1874.

BIBLIOGRAPHY: Hubert Howe Bancroft, *History of Mexico* (6 vols., San Francisco: A. L. Bancroft and the History Company, 1883–89). Hubert Howe Bancroft, *History of the North Mexican States and Texas* (2 vols., San Francisco: History Company, 1886, 1889). J. Fred Rippy, "Border Troubles along the Rio Grande, 1848–1860," *Southwestern Historical Quarterly* 23 (October 1919). Ernest C. Shearer, Border Diplomatic Relations between the United States and Mexico, 1848–1860 (Ph.D. dissertation, University of Texas, 1940). Vertical Files, Barker Texas History Center, University of Texas at Austin.

CARBON, TEXAS. Carbon, on State Highway 6 in central Eastland County, derives its name from the mineral deposits in the area. In 1881 N. S. Hayes (or Haynes) bought the first lot on the present townsite and built a store. He became the first postmaster when a post office was granted in 1882. Carbon was considered one of the six principal towns in Eastland County in 1889; it vied to become county seat in 1897 but came in third. By 1904 Carbon had a gin, a lumberyard, a school, a bank, several churches, a Masonic lodge, and 600 residents. The Carbon *Herald,* which carried all important county court news, was called "the local paper for Eastland County." Carbon was among nine towns in Eastland County with independent school districts in 1924 and 1942. Its population fell to 281 by 1980, when the town retained a post office and two businesses. In 1990 the population was 255.

BIBLIOGRAPHY: Edwin T. Cox, *History of Eastland County, Texas* (San Antonio: Naylor, 1950). Ruby Pearl Ghormley, *Eastland County, Texas: A Historical and Biographical Survey* (Austin: Rupegy, 1969).

Noel Wiggins

CARBON BLACK INDUSTRY. Carbon black is produced from "sour" gas—natural gas that contains more than 1½ grains of hydrogen sulfide or more than two grains of sulfur per hundred standard cubic feet. Although J. K. Wright, a Philadelphia ink maker, discovered the process of manufacturing carbon black in 1864, it was little used until improved technology in the twentieth century reduced the high cost of production. After 1915 carbon black became widely used as a reinforcing agent in the production of automobile tires. In early 1923 the first Texas plant for manufacturing carbon black by burning residue gas from gasoline plants was constructed in Stephens County. Two other plants were erected in the same county later that year; together the three plants annually produced 2,633,013 pounds of carbon black valued at $184,306. Carbon black production was limited to Stephens and Eastland counties until March 11, 1926, when the Railroad Commission[qv] permitted the Phillips Petroleum Company to build a plant in the Panhandle[qv] for the casinghead gasoline plants in Carson and Hutchinson counties. This plant, initially run by the Western Carbon Company, was later owned and operated by the Columbian Carbon firm. By 1926 there were seven carbon black plants in Stephens County and two in Eastland County, as well as the one in Hutchinson County; that year Texas produced 20 percent of the nation's output of carbon black. In 1928 the Cabot Carbon Company established the first of several plants near Pampa, and in 1931 a plant was erected at Big Lake. Such corporations as Coltexo, Texas-Elf Carbon, Peerless Carbon, and United Carbon continued to expand and sometimes established their own company towns in more remote areas to house employees and their families. In 1931 thirty-one plants in Texas produced 210,878,000 pounds of carbon black, or 75 percent of the nation's output. In 1937 forty Texas plants, thirty-three of them in the Panhandle, produced 82 percent of the nation's carbon black; the Panhandle plants alone yielded 405,247,000 pounds. Plants were also operating in Winkler and Ward counties during the late 1930s and 1940s. By the close of World War II[qv] there were forty-two carbon black plants in the state, including one at Bunavista, west of Borger, built shortly after the Japanese bombing of Pearl Harbor.

During the 1950s, when eighty-eight billion cubic feet of gas were burned annually to produce carbon black, Texas retained its position as the nation's leading carbon black producer. In 1954 thirty Texas plants with a total daily capacity of three million pounds were located in eighteen counties and produced 65 percent of the nation's total carbon black. Rubber companies absorbed most of the total production; smaller quantities were used as pigments in ink and paint. Production continued to be concentrated in the Panhandle, although some carbon black plants were built along the Gulf Coast. Major locations included five plants (four furnace-type and one channel-type) at Borger, two furnace-type plants at Big Spring, and two plants (one furnace-type and one channel-type) at Seagraves. Other plants were located at Skellytown, Baytown, and Aransas Pass. Of the two methods of production, channel and furnace, the latter was becoming more popular by the 1960s.

In 1964 the industry recovered 1,165,593,000 pounds of carbon black valued at $86,494,000. Thirty-nine plants employed 1,954 persons and had a value added by manufacturing of $29,957,000. The total daily capacity of Texas carbon black plants had increased by that year to 3,945,300 pounds. By 1969 Texas carbon black production was valued at $110,816,000.

The 1970s and 1980s saw a general decline in the number of carbon black plants, due mainly to the decrease in output of natural gas. This was particularly true of the Panhandle, where by the 1980s only a few plants near Pampa and Borger remained in operation. Even so, Texas remained the largest producer of carbon black. In 1973 the state produced 1,511,127,000 pounds of carbon black, valued at $128,144,000. By 1981 only 3,213,899 cubic feet, or about .05 percent of all the natural gas in Texas, went to produce carbon black. In 1984 carbon black was manufactured from 2,456,809 cubic feet, or .04 percent of Texas natural gas.

BIBLIOGRAPHY: R. G. Allen, H. W. Price, and E. V. Reinbold, "The History, Use and Manufacture of Carbon Black," *Panhandle-Plains Historical Review* 12 (1939). Gray County History Book Committee, *Gray County Heritage* (Dallas: Taylor, 1985). Charles Albert Warner, *Texas Oil and Gas Since 1543* (Houston: Gulf, 1939).

H. Allen Anderson

CARBONDALE, TEXAS. Carbondale is on the St. Louis Southwestern Railway ten miles south of Boston in southern Bowie County. It was named for the coal deposits in the area. A post office was established there in 1907 and remained open into the 1950s. In 1925 the reported population was thirty-five. In 1982 the town had thirty residents and no rated businesses. In 1990 the population was still thirty.

BIBLIOGRAPHY: J. J. Scheffelin, *Bowie County Basic Background Book* (n.d.).

Cecil Harper, Jr.

CARDEN, TEXAS. Carden, five miles from Gatesville in eastern Coryell County, was named for Gaines B. Carden, an early settler. By 1949 the school at Carden had been consolidated with the Gatesville schools, but its building continued to be used for church services and community gatherings. There was also a grocery store and filling station at Carden. The community did not appear on county highway maps in the 1980s.

Zelma Scott

CÁRDENAS, ALONSO DE (?–?). Alonso de Cárdenas and Juan Cortinas were sent by the Marqués de Aguayo[qv] in 1720 to select a site for a mission to be placed under the supervision of Father Antonio Margil de Jesús.[qv] The resulting mission was San José y San Miguel de Aguayo in San Antonio. On August 6, 1721, Cárdenas and Cortinas attended the refounding of Nuestra Señora de la Purísima Concepción de los Hainai Mission, which had been abandoned in 1719 and was reestablished in 1721 as Nuestra Señora de la Purísima Concepción de Acuña Mission in San Antonio.

BIBLIOGRAPHY: Eleanor Claire Buckley, "The Aguayo Expedition in Texas and Louisiana, 1719–1722," *Quarterly of the Texas State Historical Association* 15 (July 1911).

Frank Goodwyn

CÁRDENAS, JUSTO (?–?). Justo Cárdenas, journalist, fled from Monterrey, Nuevo León, to Laredo, Texas, after federal authorities proclaimed a state of emergency in Nuevo León. In 1886 he established the Imprenta y Casa Editorial de Justo Cárdenas in Laredo. There he founded two Spanish-language newspapers,[qv] *El Correo de Laredo* (1891–97) and *El Demócrata Fronterizo* (1900–19). Through them he defended the interests of Mexicans in Texas and criticized the abuses of Mexican president Porfirio Díaz. Though it was generally pro-worker, *El Demócrata Fronterizo* strongly criticized Mexican workers in Laredo's Federal Labor Union No. 11,953 when it decided to go on strike against the Mexican National Railway in 1906–07. Cárdenas was named an honorary member of the Primer Congreso

Mexicanista,[qv] held in Laredo, Texas, in September 1911. The Primer Congreso was organized by Nicasio and Clemente Idar,[qqv] editors of *La Crónica*,[qv] in response to several incidents of racial violence against Mexicans in Texas.

BIBLIOGRAPHY: Elliott Young, "Deconstructing *La Raza:* Identifying the *Gente Decente* of Laredo, 1904–1911," *Southwestern Historical Quarterly* 98 (October 1994). Emilio Zamora, *The World of the Mexican Worker in Texas* (College Station: Texas A&M University Press, 1993). *Elliott Young*

CÁRDENAS Y MAGAÑA, MANUEL DE (?–?). Manuel José de Cárdenas y Magaña, a skillful engineer who had built the prison and fort of San Juan de Ulloa in Veracruz, was ordered to accompany Francisco de Llanos on the Llanos-Cárdenas expedition[qv] up the coast from Veracruz in 1690, for the purposes of finding out whether the rivers of the Texas coast were navigable and of locating Fort St. Louis.[qv] They reached Cavallo Pass[qv] on October 24, 1690, and were back in Veracruz on December 9.

BIBLIOGRAPHY: Eugene C. Barker, *Readings in Texas History* (Dallas: Southwest Press, 1929). *Frank Goodwyn*

CARDIS, LOUIS (1825–1877). Louis Cardis, El Paso political figure and first casualty of the Salt War of San Elizario,[qv] was born in the Piedmont region of Italy in 1825. He served as a captain in Giuseppe Garibaldi's army before immigrating to the United States in 1854; he applied for citizenship in New York on March 28, 1864. He moved to El Paso that year and became a citizen on July 19, 1869. In El Paso, Cardis ran a store and became a subcontractor of the San Antonio–El Paso stage line. He spoke fluent Spanish and took an active role in local politics, becoming associated with Father Antonio Borrajos, the priest of San Elizario parish. Their roles as unofficial leaders of local Mexican Americans did not, however, prevent them from joining William Wallace Mills, Albert J. Fountain, Benjamin S. Dowell,[qqv] and others in the 1866 formation of the Salt Ring. This was a group of El Paso businessmen who sought to acquire title to the salt beds at the foot of the Guadalupe Mountains, ninety miles east of the city, and begin charging fees from the Mexican Americans of the valley communities, who had for years collected salt there without charge.

The Salt Ring fell apart in 1868 after a quarrel between Mills and Fountain. The latter thereupon became the leader of the so-called Anti-Salt Ring, but the scheme persisted, as did Cardis's involvement in political affairs. In 1871 an opponent described Cardis as Mills's "right-hand man," and he became closely allied with the Democrat Charles H. Howard,[qv] who opposed Fountain, after Howard's arrival in 1872. In 1874 Cardis helped secure Howard's election as district attorney, while Howard aided Cardis's successful campaign for the state legislature. Within two years the two men had quarreled, most probably over Cardis's attempts to revive the salt scheme, and Howard wrote that Cardis was "a liar, a coward, a mischief maker, a meddler; such a thing as could only spring from the decaying carcass of an effete people." In June 1875 Howard opposed Cardis for delegate to the state constitutional convention at Austin and defeated him at the precinct and district conventions; but Cardis ran as an independent and defeated Howard in the election.

In 1876 Cardis was reelected to the state legislature, which had cleared the way for Howard's appointment as district judge by removing the incumbent. The feud between the two turned even uglier, as Howard twice attacked Cardis physically, once in Austin and once in San Antonio. After Howard filed in the name of his father-in-law on the unlocated portions of the salt lakes, taking over Samuel Maverick's[qv] ten-year-old claim, Cardis fanned the discontent of the Mexican Americans in the Rio Grande valley. In late June 1877 Howard encountered Cardis at the latter's Fort Quitman stage station and beat him again. This time Cardis filed charges against Howard and had him indicted, and in September a mob of angry Mexican Americans held Howard for three days in San Elizario. Eventually Howard agreed to let the courts settle the matter of the salt lakes and to leave the area forever.

On October 7, 1877, however, he returned to El Paso from Mesilla, New Mexico, where he had taken refuge. Three days later he found Cardis dictating letters in the store of Solomon Schutz. Howard killed Cardis, who had attempted to hide behind a desk, with two shotgun blasts. Just over two months later Howard and two associates were executed by a mob in San Elizario.

BIBLIOGRAPHY: J. Morgan Broaddus, *The Legal Heritage of El Paso* (El Paso: Texas Western College Press, 1963). C. L. Sonnichsen, *The El Paso Salt War* (El Paso: Hertzog, 1961). *Martin Donell Kohout*

CARDWELL, JOHN (1837–1893). John Cardwell, newspaperman, was born in Lexington, Georgia, on January 28, 1837. He studied law at the University of Virginia in the mid-1850s and moved to Texas before 1860, having inherited his father's plantation in Wharton County. He married Margaret Dunlap of Brazoria County on January 6, 1860, and they became the parents of one daughter. After the Civil War[qv] Cardwell traveled to Brazil to investigate possible opportunities for the relocation of Texas planters, but returned with a negative report. In July 1871 the Democratic Executive Committee offered Cardwell the position of editor of the Austin *Statesman*, a new Democratic paper (*see* AUSTIN *AMERICAN-STATESMAN*). He accepted and became known for his vigorous attacks against Edmund J. Davis[qv] and other public figures. He resigned from the paper in 1883 and retired to his plantation. Two years later President Grover Cleveland appointed Cardwell United States Consul General to Egypt, a post he held until 1889. Cardwell died at his home on April 17, 1893.

BIBLIOGRAPHY: Vertical Files, Barker Texas History Center, University of Texas at Austin. Vertical Files, Austin History Center. *Marie Giles*

CAREWE, EDWIN (1883–1940). Edwin Carewe, motion picture director and actor, was born to Mr. and Mrs. Frank M. Fox on March 5, 1883, at Gainesville, Texas, and named Jay J. Fox. He became interested in theater in his youth, when he witnessed traveling medicine shows, and by 1900 he had resolved to become an actor. After brief studies at the universities of Texas and Missouri and a period of work with regional theatrical groups, he found himself in New York in 1910 as a member of the Dearborn Stock Company. In 1912 he changed his name to Edwin Carewe, taking the first name from renowned actor Edwin Booth, and Carewe from the name of a character he was portraying at the time. In 1914 he entered the film industry as an actor for the Lubin Company of Philadelphia. Within a year Carewe graduated from actor to director, his debut being *The Final Judgement* (1915), a film of the Rolfe-Metro Company.

Between 1915 and 1934 he directed forty-one feature films, among them *Resurrection* (1927), *Ramona* (1928), *Evangeline* (1929), and *The Spoilers* (1930). During his career Carewe provided early screen exposure to such actors as Gary Cooper, Delores Del Rio, and Francis X. Bushman. Although he directed and produced a number of critically and financially successful pictures during the silent era, he was not fully able to make the transition to sound. After resorting to sound remakes of his earlier successes, and later to low-budget and religious films, he made his last feature in 1934.

Carewe was married to Mary Jane (Mason?) in California in 1908 and to Mary Akin in 1926 and 1929. He was the father of five children, two with his first wife and three with his second. Two brothers followed Carewe into the film industry, Finis Pox, a screenwriter and occasional collaborator with Carewe, and Wallace Fox, a director of westerns. Carewe died of a heart attack at his Hollywood home on

January 22, 1940. Funeral services and burial were in Hollywood two days later.

BIBLIOGRAPHY: Ephraim Katz, *The Film Encyclopedia* (New York: Crowell, 1979). Richard Koszarski, *Hollywood Director, 1914–1940* (New York: Oxford University Press, 1976). James Robert Parish and Michael R. Pitts, *Film Directors: A Guide to Their American Films* (Metuchen, New Jersey: Scarecrow Press, 1974). A. Morton Smith, *The First 100 Years in Cooke County* (San Antonio: Naylor, 1955). *Variety*, January 24, 1940. *John H. Slate*

CAREY, WILLIAM R. (1806–1836). William R. Carey, commander of the Alamo artillery, son of Moses Carey, was born in Virginia in 1806. He was a single man when he arrived at Washington-on-the-Brazos on July 28, 1835, from New Orleans. He joined the volunteer army of Texas at the outbreak of the Texas Revolution[qv] and was among the troops that marched to Gonzales during the fight for the Gonzales "Come and take it" cannon.[qv] He was appointed second lieutenant on October 28, 1835. During the siege of Bexar[qv] Carey received a slight wound to his scalp while manning a cannon. He was promoted to first lieutenant in the field for his actions in the battle. On December 14 he was elected captain of his fifty-six-man artillery company by popular vote of the men. He called his company the Invincibles. The company remained in Bexar as part of the garrison under Lt. Col. James C. Neill.[qv] During the weeks before January 14, when Neill moved his entire force into the Alamo, Carey commanded the Alamo compound while Neill commanded the town of Bexar. Neill utilized Carey's company for tough tasks and even, on one occasion, as military police. During the siege and battle of the Alamo Carey commanded the fort's artillery. He died in the battle of the Alamo[qv] on March 6, 1836. His father traveled to Texas to settle his estate and received $198.65 for Carey's military service.

BIBLIOGRAPHY: Daughters of the American Revolution, *The Alamo Heroes and Their Revolutionary Ancestors* (San Antonio, 1976). Bill Groneman, *Alamo Defenders* (Austin: Eakin, 1990). John H. Jenkins, ed., *The Papers of the Texas Revolution, 1835–1836* (10 vols., Austin: Presidial Press, 1973). Walter Lord, *A Time to Stand* (New York: Harper, 1961; 2d ed., Lincoln: University of Nebraska Press, 1978). Phil Rosenthal and Bill Groneman, *Roll Call at the Alamo* (Fort Collins, Colorado: Old Army, 1985). *Bill Groneman*

CAREY, TEXAS. Carey is on U.S. Highway 287 eight miles northwest of Childress in Childress County. It was originally named Talulah, after Talulah Collier, who taught the first school there in 1888. A post office was established there in 1896. In 1898, however, the Fort Worth and Denver City Railway renamed the town after Dan Carey, building foreman of the road, whose land claim was nearby. In 1940 Carey had a post office, a school, a cotton gin, three churches, and a general store. The population comprised twenty-five families. In 1980 Carey reported a population of fifty-seven, a rural store, and a post office. In the 1960s its school district was merged with that of Childress. In 1990 the population was sixty.

BIBLIOGRAPHY: Paul Ord, ed., *They Followed the Rails: In Retrospect, A History of Childress County* (Childress, Texas: Childress *Reporter*, 1970). Fred Tarpley, *1001 Texas Place Names* (Austin: University of Texas Press, 1980). *H. Allen Anderson*

CARHART, EDWARD ELMER (1863–1946). Edward Elmer Carhart, businessman, the eldest son and third of eight children of Theresa (Mumford) and John Wesley Carhart,[qv] was born on December 15, 1863, in Watertown, New York. The family moved to Racine, Wisconsin, in 1871, and three years later to Oshkosh, where Carhart received the majority of his schooling. In 1876 he and his sister Minnie began publishing a weekly newsletter, the *Early Dawn*, using the basement of their father's church as a printing office. Soon Carhart's journalistic ability attracted the attention of his father's cousin, Lewis H. Carhart,[qv] who had founded Clarendon, Texas, in 1878. Impressed, Lewis invited him to come and edit the settlement's fledgling newspaper, the Clarendon *News*, after sending the proofs of its first edition to Oshkosh to be printed at Ed's shop. With his father's blessing, sixteen-year-old Ed stopped over in Chicago to buy a press, proceeded to Sherman, Texas, then the end of the railroad, and arranged to have the press freighted by wagon to Clarendon. In Sherman he met Mary Estella Brewer, daughter of a Methodist minister, who soon afterward moved with her family to Mobeetie. At Clarendon young Carhart converted the *News* from a monthly to a weekly publication and a year later sold half interest in it to Charles Kimball. On December 23, 1881, Carhart and Mary Brewer became the first white couple to be married in Donley County. They had four children.

After disposing of his paper, Carhart spent about two years riding line on his cousin's Quarter Circle Heart Ranch[qv] and served as county clerk of Donley County. He also worked for a short time as a druggist with Jerome D. Stocking[qv] and later with B. H. White and Company, general merchants and ranch outfitters at Clarendon. In the spring of 1887, shortly before the Santa Fe Railroad reached the town of Panhandle in Carson County, White sent Carhart there with a stock of goods and a portable building to establish a mercantile store, of which Carhart took charge as manager. Later, after White sold the store, Carhart turned it into a thriving drug business with stock he had purchased from Stocking. Among other products he manufactured quality cigars, which he named after his daughters, Nina and Thelma. He also assisted Henry H. Brooks in establishing the Panhandle *Herald.* For eight years, beginning in 1889, Carhart served as postmaster, and in 1896 he succeeded Judge James C. Paul[qv] as treasurer of Carson County. He held that position until 1904, when he ran for county judge. He sold the drugstore in 1906 and for the next twenty-one years worked as cashier of the Panhandle Bank. He retired in 1927 to establish the Carhart Motor Company, the county's first automobile business. In addition, Carhart owned a grain elevator just east of town. Both he and his wife were pillars in the local Methodist church, and their children married and lived in the Panhandle area. Mary Carhart died on November 25, 1938, and Carhart died on February 4, 1946, at Panhandle. Both are buried there.

BIBLIOGRAPHY: Willie Newbury Lewis, *Between Sun and Sod* (Clarendon, Texas: Clarendon Press, 1938; rev. ed., College Station: Texas A&M University Press, 1976). Buckley B. Paddock, ed., *A Twentieth Century History and Biographical Record of North and West Texas* (Chicago: Lewis, 1906). Jo Stewart Randel, ed., *A Time to Purpose: A Chronicle of Carson County* (4 vols., Hereford, Texas: Pioneer, 1966–72). *H. Allen Anderson*

CARHART, JOHN WESLEY (1834–1914). John Wesley Carhart, minister, physician, inventor, and writer, son of Daniel Sutton and Margaret (Martin) Carhart, was born on June 26, 1834, near Couymans, Albany County, New York. As a boy he possessed an inventive nature and once floated his own homemade miniature steam yacht on the Hudson River. He was ordained a Methodist minister at seventeen and received his D.D. degree from Union Seminary in Charlottesville, New York, in 1861. He was pastoring at Richmond, New York, when he met and married Theresa A. Mumford. They became the parents of eight children, one of whom died in infancy. Carhart pastored churches in Vermont, Massachusetts, and New York and published two books of poems, *Sunny Hours* (1859) and *Poets and Poetry of the Hebrews* (1865). In Troy he perfected an oscillating valve for steam engines, which he patented and for which he was paid several thousand dollars. In 1871 he was transferred to a pastorate in Racine, Wisconsin. There he invented a buggy powered by a two-cylinder steam engine called the Spark. Aided by his uncle, former Michigan State University professor H. S. Carhart, and financed by George W. Slausen, a wealthy lumberman, Carhart's Spark proved successful.

However, he was pressured by townspeople to dismantle the machine after it caused the death of a valuable horse that had been frightened by the noise. Nevertheless, Carhart's invention was recognized years later by the American Manufacturers' Association as a forerunner of the automobile.

He subsequently used his plant to supply power for a job printer. After his move to a new pastorate at Oshkosh in 1874, the Carhart children began publishing a weekly newsletter, the *Early Dawn,* from a print shop set up in the church basement. This press printed the first issue of the Clarendon *News* from the proofs sent by Carhart's cousin, Lewis H. Carhart,[qv] who had founded the Clarendon colony in Texas in 1878. The success of that issue prompted Lewis to send for John Wesley's son, Edward Elmer Carhart,[qv] to come and set up the settlement's first local press. In 1880 Carhart resigned from the ministry after some dissensions with members of his conference. Believing his life's work at an end, he published an autobiography, *Four Years on Wheels* (1880). Subsequently, his earlier interest in medicine was renewed, and while pastoring in Pittsfield, Massachusetts, he studied for a semester at Berkshire Medical College. He received an M.D. Degree in 1883 with the first graduating class of the Chicago College of Physicians and practiced for a short time in Oshkosh.

In 1885 Carhart and the rest of his family followed Ed to Texas. They stayed briefly in Clarendon before moving to Lampasas. There Carhart started a weekly newspaper, the Lampasas *Teacher,* and also wrote a serial, "The Sign Rider," for the other Lampasas paper, the *Leader.* He then turned full-time to medicine and established himself in Lampasas and later in La Grange, Austin, and San Antonio as an outstanding skin and nerve specialist. He became a spokesman for better public sanitation practices. In 1893 he served as one of ten assistant secretaries general of the first Pan American Medical Congress in Washington, D.C.

Carhart continued turning out newspaper stories and professional medical articles. His novel *Norma Trist,* published in 1895, was one of the earliest fictional treatments of homosexuality. The book was highly moralistic in tone, but critics as well as the reading public were horrified by such a work, and the author was arrested for "sending obscene literature through the mails." The case against him was later dismissed. In 1899 Carhart published his last work, *Under Palmetto and Pine,* a sensitive treatment of African Americans[qv] in Texas and their struggles against poverty and racial discrimination. He was recognized as the "father of the automobile" by the magazine the *Horseless Age* in 1903. Two years later he went to Paris as a guest of the French government at the International Automobile Exposition. There he received a cash award and certificate of honor for his pioneer invention. Carhart died at San Antonio on December 21, 1914, and was buried in Austin.

bibliography: Violet M. Baird, "John Wesley Carhart," *Texana* 9 (Spring 1971). Willie Newbury Lewis, *Between Sun and Sod* (Clarendon, Texas: Clarendon Press, 1938; rev. ed., College Station: Texas A&M University Press, 1976). Jo Stewart Randel, ed., *A Time to Purpose: A Chronicle of Carson County* (4 vols., Hereford, Texas: Pioneer, 1966–72).

H. Allen Anderson

CARHART, LEWIS HENRY (1833–?). Lewis Henry Carhart, son of Isaac D. and Nancy (Bangs) Carhart, was born in Albany County, New York, in 1833. He graduated from the theological department of Northwestern University and the Garrett Biblical Institute and served in the Union Army during the Civil War.[qv] In 1866 he was assigned on trial to the Arkansas Methodist Conference. By 1877 he was in charge of a pastorate in Sherman, Texas. There he developed an interest in establishing a Christian colony in the Texas Panhandle that would discourage liquor consumption and other "impure" activities. He married Clara Sully, a Canadian whose brother Alfred worked for Austin and Corbett, an influential New York investment firm. The couple had two children.

Carhart launched his advertising campaign from Sherman and attracted prospective colonists from the East and Midwest. Alfred Sully provided the financial backing. In 1878, after traveling via Dodge City and Mobeetie to their colony site in the Panhandle,[qv] the promoters founded their Christian colony and named it Clarendon, in honor of Carhart's wife. In 1879 Carhart established the Panhandle's first newspaper, the Clarendon *News.* Ed Carhart,[qv] son of Lewis's brother John Wesley Carhart[qv] of Wisconsin, acted as the paper's printer and later its editor. Although Clara Sully Carhart lived for a time in Clarendon, she never wanted to live permanently in a frontier environment and throughout the next several years retained family residences at Sherman and Dallas.

In 1880 Carhart was appointed pastor to a large Methodist church in Dallas. He placed his brother-in-law, Benjamin Horton White, and another attorney, J. C. Murdock, in charge of managing the affairs in Clarendon. Carhart went on to a two-year pastorate in Fort Worth, after which he returned to Donley County in 1884 and established his Quarter Circle Heart Ranch.[qv] In 1884 or 1885 he sailed to England on a stock-selling venture and, with Sully's backing, organized the Clarendon Land Investment and Agency Company. He then returned to manage his expanded ranching operations, ably assisted by his foreman, Al S. McKinney. Unfortunately, unwise investments, coupled with the drought and blizzard of 1886–87, resulted in tremendous losses, and when the English stockholders sent Count Cecil Kearney to investigate in June 1887, Carhart resigned his position and moved from Clarendon.

He returned to the Methodist ministry, but, in spite of his affection for people and his powers of persuasion, he never regained the leadership that he had formerly had. He moved to Hot Springs, Arkansas, in 1891 and invested his remaining money in a bathhouse. Afterward, he migrated to Sawtelle, California, where he died in the Union Soldier's Home.

bibliography: Virginia Browder, *Donley County: Land O' Promise* (Wichita Falls, Texas: Nortex, 1975). Willie Newbury Lewis, *Between Sun and Sod* (Clarendon, Texas: Clarendon Press, 1938; rev. ed., College Station: Texas A&M University Press, 1976). Millie Jones Porter, *Memory Cups of Panhandle Pioneers* (Clarendon, Texas: Clarendon Press, 1945). Lonnie J. White, comp., "Dodge City *Times,* 1877–1885," *Panhandle-Plains Historical Review* 40 (1967).

H. Allen Anderson

CARL, TEXAS (Navarro County). Carl was six miles north of Corsicana in northeastern Navarro County. It was probably founded before 1900, and for a time was a stop on the Houston and Texas Central Railway. In the mid-1930s it had a depot, a few stores, and several houses. The town declined after World War II[qv] and by the 1960s no longer appeared on highway maps. In the early 1990s only a few scattered houses remained in the area. *Christopher Long*

CARL, TEXAS (Travis County). Carl is twelve miles south of Austin and two miles north of Creedmoor in southern Travis County. It had an estimated population of thirty in 1886. A post office opened there in 1887 with William T. Hart as postmaster. By the early 1890s the settlement had a steam gristmill and cotton gin, four churches, a school, a hotel, a general store, and 250 residents. By 1900, however, the community began to decline. The post office was discontinued in 1902, and mail was sent to Buda in Hays County. A school, a church, and a few scattered houses marked the site on county highway maps in the 1940s. Carl was still listed as a community in 1990.

bibliography: John J. Germann and Myron Janzen, *Texas Post Offices by County* (1986). *Vivian Elizabeth Smyrl*

CARL B. AND FLORENCE E. KING FOUNDATION. The Carl B. and Florence E. King Foundation, established in 1966, provides support to agencies in the fields of arts and culture, education, community improvement, and health and human services. In 1991 the foundation had assets of over $31 million and income of more than $3 million. Grants were distributed to 156 recipients. Major grants were in the fields of education and arts and culture.

Art Leatherwood

CARLETON, JAMES HENRY (1814–1873). James Henry Carleton, soldier, son of John and Abigail (Phelps) Carleton, was born at Lubec, Maine, on December 27, 1814. He was commissioned a lieutenant in the Maine militia in 1838 and participated in the boundary dispute with Canada known as the Aristook War. He received appointment as a second lieutenant in the First Dragoons on October 18, 1839, and then trained at Carlisle Barracks. In October 1840 he married Henrietta Tracy Loring of Boston. Henrietta accompanied Carleton to his duty assignment at Fort Gibson, Indian Territory, where she died in October 1841. Later in the 1840s Carleton served as assistant commissary of subsistence at Fort Leavenworth, accompanied Maj. Clifton Wharton's expedition to the Pawnee Villages in Nebraska, served as an officer on Col. Stephen Watts Kearny's 1845 expedition to South Pass, and saw action in 1847 in the battle of Buena Vista. In 1848 Carleton married Sophia Garland Wolfe, niece of Gen. John Garland. During the 1850s Carleton served under Garland in New Mexico Territory. In 1859 he was ordered to Salt Lake City to investigate the massacre at Mountain Meadows (1857). Stationed in California at the outbreak of the Civil War, Carleton became brigadier general in the California volunteers and commanded the California Column[qv] on its march to the Rio Grande. In September 1862 he replaced Gen. Edward R. S. Canby[qv] as commander of the Department of New Mexico. One of Carleton's first acts upon assuming command was to reissue Canby's order establishing martial law in New Mexico. He also devised a passport system to distinguish loyal citizens from Confederate spies. Although Carleton never attempted to set himself up as a military governor, he believed he had authority to carry through any policy he deemed essential to the peace and prosperity of the territory. Many of his actions antagonized the citizens.

In addition to securing the territory against Confederate intrigue, Carleton took steps to subdue hostile Indian tribes. He sent Col. Kit (Christopher) Carson[qv] and other subordinates against the Mescalero Apaches with orders to kill all Indian men "whenever and wherever you can find them." By February 1863 the Mescaleros had been relocated on the new Indian reservation of Bosque Redondo on the Pecos River. Carleton then waged war against the Navajos, ordering Carson and other officers to destroy all crops in Navajo country to starve them into submission. Carleton's strategy brought immediate results. Some 8,000 Navajos surrendered and then made the "Long Walk" to Bosque Redondo, where Carleton planned to turn them into Christian farmers. The Bosque Redondo experiment ended in failure, however. The Mescaleros quietly fled the reservation, and the Navajo captives faced death, disease, and a constant shortage of food. The cost of maintaining Bosque Redondo persuaded the government to allow the Navajos to return to their homeland. Carleton's policies became ensnarled in territorial politics. Although his superiors believed him an efficient and capable officer, hostile criticism led to his reassignment early in 1867. He later joined his regiment, the Fourth United States Cavalry,[qv] in Texas. He died in San Antonio on January 7, 1873. Carleton and his second wife, Sophia, had five children; two died in childhood. Carleton published several accounts of his military experiences. His oldest son, Henry Guy Carleton, became a journalist, playwright, and inventor.

BIBLIOGRAPHY: Aurora Hunt, *Major General James H. Carlton, 1814–1873: Western Frontier Dragoon* (Glendale, California: Clark, 1958). Paul Andrew Hutton, ed., *Soldiers West: Biographies from the Military Frontier* (Lincoln: University of Nebraska Press, 1987). William A. Keleher, *Turmoil in New Mexico* (Santa Fe: Rydal Press, 1952). Gerald Thompson, *The Army and the Navajo* (Tucson: University of Arizona Press, 1976).

Darlis A. Miller

CARLETON, WILLIAM (1812–1865). William Carleton, early settler, participant in the Texas Revolution,[qv] and journalist, was born in Taunton, England, on May 7, 1812. After receiving a medical education he married Elizabeth Martha Coxhead, on August 1, 1833. With his wife, an infant, and three servants, he traveled to Texas in January 1835. They remained in the little settlement that centered about Texana during the heated months just before the Texas Revolution. Alarmed by reports of military advances from Mexico, Carleton joined the Matagorda Volunteers in March. At Goliad a unit of the command was sent to attack the Mexican fort at Lipantitlán, and Carleton performed valiant service in the attack. In the few days that the colonists stayed in the vicinity, some of the men slept in a shed filled with damp cotton, and from this Carleton supposedly developed a serious case of inflammatory rheumatism, for which he was invalided back to Texana. Late in 1836 he and his wife went to New Orleans, and twenty years passed before they returned to Texas. Carlton worked for a time on Galveston and Houston newspapers but eventually settled in Austin. For his loyal services at Goliad, the Texas legislature passed a special act that gave him his bounty lands. He sold them, bought presses, and established his own weekly paper, the Austin *Rambler*.[qv] Carleton died in Austin on November 2, 1865, and was buried in Oakwood Cemetery. He was survived by three sons and two daughters.

BIBLIOGRAPHY: Daughters of the Republic of Texas, *Founders and Patriots of the Republic of Texas* (Austin, 1963–). Lorraine Bruce Jeter, *Matagorda: Early History* (Baltimore: Gateway, 1974). Villamae Williams, *Stephen F. Austin's Register of Families* (Nacogdoches, Texas: Ericson, 1984)

Cora Carleton Glassford

CARLISLE, JAMES MCCOY (1851–1922). James McCoy Carlisle, teacher, administrator, and state public education official, was born on May 11, 1851, at Beech Grove, Coffee County, Tennessee, to James M. and Mary (Bird) Carlisle, Sr. Since his father was a farmer, Carlisle attended public schools only when possible. He entered Beech Grove College in Tennessee at the age of sixteen, attended sporadically until 1876, and graduated with an A.B. degree. During this time he also taught school, farmed, and spent a year studying at Cumberland University in Lebanon, Tennessee. Following his graduation from Beech Grove, Carlisle taught school in Tennessee. He received an honorary A.M. degree from Emory College in Oxford, Georgia, in 1879 and later an honorary doctorate from the University of Nashville.

In 1880 he moved to Grayson County, Texas, and established a private school that was soon consolidated with the public schools in the area to form the Whitesboro Normal School. Carlisle served as superintendent of the institution until 1887, when he was named superintendent of the Corsicana public school system. He held this post for two years, during which time he also served for a year as bookkeeper of the City National Bank in Corsicana. In 1890 he was hired as superintendent of the Fort Worth public schools. On August 29, 1891, Governor James S. Hogg[qv] appointed him state superintendent of public instruction. Carlisle was elected three times thereafter and remained in office from September 15, 1891, to January 10, 1899. He did not seek reelection, evidently because of a scandal. It was charged that his teaching certificate was based on an honorary degree; therefore, some claimed that he was unqualified for the job.

After retiring from the position of state superintendent, he resumed teaching and opened a private school in Hillsboro. In 1901 he established the Carlisle Military Academy in Arlington. He remained at the school until 1913, when the judgment in a lawsuit, *J. M. Thompson v. Carlisle Military Academy*, forced him to abandon the school because he was unable to meet his financial obligations. He left Arlington and reestablished Carlisle Military Academy in an old college building at Whitewright, Grayson County. After several years Carlisle moved on and taught in Terrell for a short time before becoming the superintendent at Rock Springs. After a year in that job he retired and returned to Arlington. He suffered a paralytic stroke in 1921 and died on July 14, 1922. State officials ordered the flag to be flown at half-mast over the Capitol.[qv] In addition to his administrative duties within the schools, Carlisle also helped organize and later served as the president of the Texas State Teachers Association.[qv] He was a Mason and a Presbyterian. He was married in January 1878 to Mary E. Anderson, and they had two children. Although some claimed that he was lacking in ability as a financier, many others stated that he was decades ahead of his time in his progressive thinking.

BIBLIOGRAPHY: Lewis E. Daniell, *Personnel of the Texas State Government, with Sketches of Representative Men of Texas* (Austin: City Printing, 1887; 3d ed., San Antonio: Maverick, 1892). Junia Evans Hudspeth, A History of North Texas Agricultural College (M.A. thesis, Southern Methodist University, 1935). *Kristi Strickland*

CARLISLE CREEK. Carlisle Creek rises one mile north of Arneckeville in east central DeWitt County (at 29°01′ N, 97°16′ W) and runs southeast for six miles to its mouth on the Guadalupe River, three miles west of Thomaston (at 29°00′ N, 97°13′ W). It traverses flat terrain with local shallow depressions, surfaced by clay and sandy loams that support water-tolerant hardwoods, conifers, and prairie grasses. Carlisle Creek was named for Henry Carlisle, an early DeWitt County settler, who built his home nearby. In the nineteenth century there was a large spring near the mouth of the creek. This spring, equipped with two buckets, a rope, and a pulley system, provided drinking water for many early settlers of the area. During the 1850s John H. Slaughter operated a water-powered mill on the stream.

CARLISLE, TEXAS (Lubbock County). Carlisle is on State Highway 114 and the Santa Fe Railroad three miles east of Reese Air Force Base[qv] and five miles west of Lubbock in west central Lubbock County. It was named for rancher W. A. Carlisle and grew up around a school in the early twentieth century. A congregation of the Church of Christ met there from 1918 to 1923. By 1927 the Carlisle school was one of twenty-six rural educational districts in the county. Carlisle combined with Hurlwood, Wolfforth, and Foster to form the Frenship Rural School District in 1935. The town had two stores and was known as the site of the largest vineyard in Northwest Texas during the 1940s. In 1983 Carlisle was still listed as a community, but on January 27, 1984, it was annexed to Lubbock.

BIBLIOGRAPHY: Virginia Hufstedler, A Study of the Activities of the Church of Christ in Lubbock County from 1890 to 1925 (M.A. thesis, Texas Technological College, 1933). Mary Louise McDonald, The History of Lubbock County (M.A. thesis, University of Texas, 1942).
Charles G. Davis

CARLISLE, TEXAS (Trinity County). Carlisle is on Farm Road 356 fourteen miles southwest of Groveton in southwestern Trinity County. The area was first settled around the time of the Civil War,[qv] but a settlement did not begin to grow up until the late nineteenth century. The community was named for John Carlisle, who founded mills in the Carlisle and Carmona areas. After 1900 the Beaumont and Great Northern Railway built through the area, and Carlisle became a station. A post office was established there in 1906 and closed in 1955. The population reached 100 in the early 1930s and remained at roughly that level through 1990, when Carlisle was a dispersed farming community with a reported population of ninety-five.

BIBLIOGRAPHY: Patricia B. and Joseph W. Hensley, eds., *Trinity County Beginnings* (Groveton, Texas: Trinity County Book Committee, 1986). Trinity County Historical Commission, *Trinity County Cemeteries* (Burnet, Texas: Nortex, 1980). *Christopher Long*

CARLOS, TEXAS. Carlos, on State Highway 30 and Farm Road 244 in western Grimes County, was founded about 1906. Settlement in the vicinity began as early as the 1830s, but the formation of a community awaited the coming of the railroad. Farm families moved to the newly constructed Houston and Texas Central Railway line from Navasota to Mexia. A post office and a railroad freight depot were established in the settlement by 1907. By 1910 John Lindley was operating a local general merchandise store and a cotton gin, and W. G. Prescott had constructed a sawmill and general store. Carlos was initially a lumbering community and shipping center for cordwood, cattle, cotton, and other products. In 1936 the Missionary Baptist Church was moved to the town from Dry Creek. Electrification arrived in 1947. In 1949 Farm Road 244 reached the community, and ten years later State Highway 30 was extended through town. In the early 1980s the Texas Municipal Power Agency began operating its lignite-powered Gibbons Creek Plant nearby.

In 1910 Carlos had a population of 150. By the late 1920s population losses had resulted in the closing of the post office. In 1936 the community had a school, one business, and an estimated population of sixty. Population figures have been unavailable since 1948, at which time the community had an estimated sixty residents and one rated business.

BIBLIOGRAPHY: Grimes County Historical Commission, *History of Grimes County, Land of Heritage and Progress* (Dallas: Taylor, 1982).
Charles Christopher Jackson

CARLOS BAY. Carlos Bay is a small bay between Mesquite Bay and Aransas Bay in central Aransas County (at 28°'11 N, 96°'53 W). It is separated from the Gulf of Mexico by St. Joseph Island.

CARLOS RANCHO, TEXAS. Carlos Rancho was a Mexican village on the north side of the San Antonio River in what is now Victoria County. It was located at Carlos Crossing, about twelve miles below Goliad on the old road from Victoria to Nuestra Señora del Refugio Mission. The village was established about 1830 and named for Carlos de la Garza,[qv] whose father, Antonio de la Garza, a Mexican soldier stationed at Goliad, settled the area as a ranch. In 1834 Carlos received title to a league of land that included the old ranch, Carlos Crossing, and Carlos Rancho. He had a commissary, barrel house, smithy, and double log cabin at the site and operated a ferry at Carlos Crossing alternately with John White Bower,[qv] another resident. Bower and George B. Amory also had a store there. The settlement had numerous houses and jacals, barns, corrals, and sheds, and a Catholic church where José Antonio Valdez was resident priest. A local school for boys was operating in 1841.

In 1835–36 the population of Carlos Rancho grew substantially as the Mexican residents of Goliad abandoned that town in the wake of its capture and subsequent occupation by George M. Collinsworth, Philip Dimmitt, and especially James W. Fannin, Jr.[qqv] (see GOLIAD CAMPAIGN OF 1835 *and* GOLIAD CAMPAIGN OF 1836). Consequently, Carlos Rancho fell suspect as a nest of spies. Fannin launched at least two attacks on the place and captured several citizens, including Father Valdez, the suspected leader. John Crittenden Duval[qv] wrote of one of these raids in his celebrated *Early Times in Texas* (1892). Carlos de la Garza recruited his Victoriana Guardes, a unit of some eighty horsemen, from among the Goliad refugees and joined Gen. José de Urrea[qv] in defeating Amon B. King and William Ward[qqv] in the battle of Refugio[qv] and in keeping Fannin under surveillance, thus contributing to his defeat in the battle of Coleto.[qv]

After the Texas Revolution,[qv] Carlos Rancho sheltered families from Goliad and Refugio during Indian raids and the 1842 invasions of Rafael Vásquez and Adrián Woll.[qqv] Particularly notorious was the killing of Johnson Gilleland[qv] and his wife and the capture of their two children by Comanches. During the Vásquez and Woll invasions and several Indian raids, Carlos Rancho became the Refugio county seat; it was located in Refugio County until March 1846, when the community became part of Victoria County upon the boundary change from Coleto Creek to the San Antonio River. The settlement also served as headquarters for the Texas army under Albert Sidney Johnston[qv] and as a post for the Texas Rangers.[qv]

Nevertheless, Carlos Rancho steadily declined as its Mexican residents were driven off their lands by incoming whites hostile toward those considered to be sympathizers with Mexico during the revolution. Carlos de la Garza remained, however, fighting Indians and running his commissary, as well as operating the ferry alternately with Bower and others. By the time of his death in 1882, Carlos Rancho had virtually ceased to exist, although records indicate that a post office named Carlos, Texas, existed at the site from April until June 1886.

BIBLIOGRAPHY: Harbert Davenport, "Men of Goliad," *Southwestern Historical Quarterly* 43 (July 1939). Hobart Huson, *Refugio: A Comprehensive History of Refugio County from Aboriginal Times to 1953* (2 vols., Woodsboro, Texas: Rooke Foundation, 1953, 1955). Kathryn Stoner O'Connor, *The Presidio La Bahía del Espíritu Santo de Zúñiga, 1721 to 1846* (Austin: Von Boeckmann–Jones, 1966).

Craig H. Roell

CARLOS VILLALONGÍN DRAMATIC COMPANY. The Carlos Villalongín Dramatic Company (also known as the Compañía Cómico Dramática Carlos Villalongín and the Compañía Lírico-Dramática Villalongín) originated as the Compañía Hernández, founded in Jalisco, Mexico, in 1849 by Encarnación Hernández. Originally the group consisted of five actors, but in 1885 the number increased to six. Upon Hernández's death around 1888, his wife, Antonia Pineda de Hernández, took over the management of the company, which was renamed Compañía Hernández-Villalongín. The Compañía Villalongín was based primarily in Nuevo León, although it toured throughout northern Mexico and the southwestern United States for many years, producing plays then popular in Mexico City. In 1900 the troupe was invited to perform at the new San Antonio Grand Opera House; perhaps prior appearances in the area had warranted a reputation there. The tour also included appearances in Houston, Victoria, and Dallas. By 1904 Carlos Villalongín had married one of the Hernández daughters, Herlinda, and taken over the company after Antonia Hernández retired. The Compañía Villalongín included two prompters, a play copier, a scenic technician, a property master, a costumer, ten to twelve actors, and six to eight actresses. The Villalongín children and those of other troupe families played the children's roles found frequently in the repertory. The company was organized around at least three families, those of Villalongín, Hernández, and Cristóbal Berrones. For the most part, Villalongín and Concepción Hernández were the source of the group's popularity. Their performances included a large repertoire of tragedies, dramas, melodramas, and comedies.

In May 1911 the company arrived in San Antonio, where Villalongín had contracted to perform at the Teatro Aurora for nine months. The theater, a converted saloon, occupied the second floor of a building at 113 South Santa Rosa Avenue. The first performance, on May 22, 1911, featured the first three acts of *Chucho el Roto,* a drama in five acts and an epilogue by the Mexican dramatist Antonio Fuentes. The initial nine-month residency at the Teatro Aurora met with such success that the company continued to work there for a year and a half. The troupe had expected to return to Coahuila, after completing its agreement at the Aurora, but the Mexican Revolution[qv] made Carlos Villalongín, his family, and several other actors decide to remain in San Antonio. Upon his arrival in town or shortly thereafter, Villalongín formed a partnership with Carlos Saldaña. Their venture was called "Compañía Lírico-Dramática Villalongín y Saldaña," and Saldaña had the leading role in performances on May 22 and 23, 1911. By September 30, 1911, however, Saldaña's name no longer appeared on the company's broadsides. In 1911 or 1912 the Compañía Villalongín merged with the Compañía Juan B. Padilla and took a long-term engagement at the new Teatro Zaragoza, which was owned by Sam Lucchese.[qv] The Compañía Villalongín worked with the Compañía Padilla in San Antonio for about five years, but it continued to tour occasionally under its own name.

Villalongín prided himself on establishing the practice in San Antonio of presenting a full-length drama in a single evening, with no incidental entertainment. He wanted to educate and entertain his audiences with performances that were moral, emotionally and intellectually rich, and suitable for entire families. The success of his company produced a demand for high-quality performances in Spanish-language theater not only among Spanish-speaking audiences, but also in Anglo, Italian, and other communities. The troupe gave performances in Brownsville in 1913, in Elmendorf in 1916, and in several other South Texas communities before dispersing in 1924. Villalongín, though he officially retired from professional acting in 1924, continued to direct and produce performances for charity and religious causes until shortly before his death in 1936. *See also* MEXICAN-AMERICAN THEATER.

BIBLIOGRAPHY: John W. Brokaw, "The Repertory of a Mexican-American Theatrical Troupe: 1849–1924," *Latin American Theatre Review* 8 (Fall 1974). Carlos Villalongín Dramatic Company Collection, 1848–1945, Benson Latin American Collection, University of Texas at Austin. Elizabeth C. Ramírez, *Footlights across the Border: A History of Spanish-Language Professional Theatre on the Texas Stage* (New York: Lang, 1990).

Elizabeth C. Ramírez

CARLOW CREEK. Carlow Creek rises two miles south of Douglassville in north central Cass County (at 33°09′ N, 94°21′ W) and runs northwest for four miles to its mouth on Wright Patman Lake, two miles north of Douglassville (at 33°12′ N, 94°22′ W). The creek traverses gently undulating to gently rolling terrain surfaced by sandy and loamy soils. The area was originally heavily wooded, with pines and various hardwoods predominating.

CARLSBAD, TEXAS. Carlsbad, on U.S. Highway 87 in the North Concho valley fifteen miles northwest of San Angelo in northwestern Tom Green County, began in 1907, when T. J. Clegg, Ed Perry, and others organized the Concho Land Company and purchased the 60,000-acre Hughes Ranch. They divided the land into lots, laid out a townsite, built a hotel, named the town Hughes, and advertised free land to anyone who purchased a farm tract. The surrounding area was settled by farmers from Illinois, Indiana, Kentucky, Missouri, and Tennessee. Within two years the land company had attracted a population of 600. Growth was stimulated after the drilling of a deep well revealed medicinal properties in the local water; a bathhouse and efforts to advertise the town as a health resort resulted. The community was required to choose a new name for a post office in 1908. Residents selected Karlsbad, after a spa in Bohemia. The Hughes *Headlight,* first published in 1908, was renamed the Carlsbad *Headlight.* Around 1910 the Panhandle and Santa Fe Railway established a spur to Carlsbad, but a three-year drought decimated the community and most residents moved away. By 1914 the settlement was reduced to 200 residents and a general store. The population declined to 150 by 1925, then rose to 400 by 1932, when the community had eleven businesses. The local school had four teachers in 1931 and an enrollment of eighty-four in 1933. The Great Depression[qv] reduced the population to 150 by 1934, but growth resumed, and by 1944 the population reached a high of 700. State highway maps in 1936 showed three churches, a post office, two stores, and scattered dwellings at the townsite on the Gulf, Colorado, and Santa Fe tracks, near a mining operation. After World War II[qv] the Carlsbad freight station served a local pipe line and cattle shippers; the McKnight State Sanatorium was established in 1950 on acreage to the north donated by the land company. From 1950 to 1972 the population declined to 100, where it remained in 1990. In the 1980s Carlsbad had five churches, a post office, several businesses, and multiple dwellings, but by 1990 only two businesses remained.

BIBLIOGRAPHY: Julia Grace Bitner, The History of Tom Green County, Texas (M.A. thesis, University of Texas, 1931). Clarence George Parsons, Proposed Plan for the Reorganization of the Schools in Tom Green County, Texas (M.A. thesis, University of Texas, 1939). San Angelo *Standard Times*, August 29, 1954. Vertical Files, Barker Texas History Center, University of Texas at Austin.

Alice Gray Upchurch

CARLSON, TEXAS. Carlson is near Farm Road 973 nine miles west of Pflugerville in northeastern Travis County. It was probably named for a local family. As early as 1881 the community had a school, which in 1903 had one teacher and sixty students. Carlson had a store, several residences, and twenty-five residents in the mid-1930s. The Carlson school was consolidated with several neighboring districts in the early 1940s to form the Manda common school district. The population of Carlson was reported at 100 in 1945 and at sixty-one in 1972. Only the name marked the community on county highway maps in the early 1990s. *Vivian Elizabeth Smyrl*

CARLTON, CHARLES (1821–1902). Charles Carlton, minister and school administrator, the son of Charles and Mary (Coveney) Carlton, was born at Eythorne, Kent County, England, on August 25, 1821. At the age of sixteen he left home to see the world. In 1841 he began a three-year tenure as a yard worker in Nova Scotia, Canada. He then traveled to the United States, first to Boston, then to Fredonia, New York, where he was a farmer. There Baptist ministers encouraged him to attend college and enter the ministry. In 1847 he enrolled in Bethany College in West Virginia, where he quickly won the admiration of the school's president, Alexander Campbell, who financed Carlton's education. Carlton completed a three-year course in two years. By the time of his graduation in 1849, he had been converted to the Disciples of Christ, largely through the efforts of Campbell. Carlton left West Virginia for Georgetown, Kentucky, where he taught public school and preached. He then traveled to Kingston, Missouri, and soon thereafter to Van Buren, Arkansas. At Van Buren he met the wife of the governor, whom he convinced to finance a school at Springfield.

In 1861 Carlton's wife, Harriet Ann (Taylor), died. He moved his four children to Dallas, where he taught and organized the local First Christian Church. He taught school at Kentucky town in Grayson County from 1865 to 1867 and in 1867 moved to Bonham. There he established his own school, Carlton College, and organized the town's First Christian Church. He and his new wife, Sallie (Abernathy), and their daughters devoted their entire efforts to the college. The school's president, administrative staff, and teachers were the Carlton family. Their home even served as the dormitory; ten students lived there in 1870. The college, an all-girl's school, quickly established a reputation among county residents. Carlton's emphasis on character and Christianity appealed to families who lived on the frontier and were looking for an appropriate place to send their daughters. Carlton remained at Bonham as president of the college until his death on February 13, 1902. His school was unable to sustain itself without him, however, and closed shortly after his death.

BIBLIOGRAPHY: Kenneth M. Hay, *The Life and Influence of Charles Carlton, 1821–1902* (Fort Worth: Texas Christian University, 1940). Floy Crandall Hodge, *A History of Fannin County* (Hereford, Texas: Pioneer, 1966). *David Minor*

CARLTON, TEXAS. Carlton, at the junction of Farm roads 219, 1744, and 2823, in northwestern Hamilton County, was settled in 1877 by H. H. Armstrong on land belonging to J. M. Evans and Dr. F. M. Carlton. The Honey Creek post office was moved from the Malone gin in 1879 and named after Dr. Carlton. Location on the east–west stage and freight route helped development, and by 1878 a school and churches had been founded. The Stephenville, North and South Texas Railway reached town in 1907. By 1900 Carlton had 161 residents, and businesses included a cotton gin. By 1910 the town had a bank and a population of 750. In 1940 the population was 400; the rail line was abandoned that year. Carlton had two newspapers, the *Courier* (1907–09) and the *Citizen* (1910–36). The school closed in 1969, as the population decline continued. By 1980 the population was only seventy, but Carlton retained its post office and had a renovated community center, a volunteer fire department, and several clubs and associations. In 1990 the population was still seventy.

BIBLIOGRAPHY: Hamilton County Historical Commission, *A History of Hamilton County, Texas* (Dallas: Taylor, 1979).

William R. Hunt

CARLTON COLLEGE. Carlton College began as a school founded by Charles Carlton[qv] in Kentucky Town, Fannin County, in 1866. It was probably the earliest Disciples of Christ school in Texas. It was moved to Bonham in 1867, when a committee acting on behalf of that city expressed interest in Carlton's school as a replacement for the failing Bonham Female Institute. Happy for the opportunity to increase the size of his school and establish a church, Carlton opened the coeducational Bonham Seminary in the institute's former building in September 1867. The school offered a Christian education for primary, preparatory, and collegiate students. Carlton, his second wife Sally, and two of his daughters were the mainstays of the teaching staff throughout the school's tenure in Bonham. Other teachers joined the staff as time and finances allowed. Carlton's son Charles was the school's vice president from 1875 to 1907. Courses were offered in mathematics and surveying, music, astronomy, physics, botany, chemistry, and geology. Latin, French, English, and two courses in Bible were also offered. No deserving student was ever turned away; tuition was paid in goods and labor or even waived as necessity demanded.

In 1881 the school moved into the Christian church for one year while a new building was constructed nearby to house the students. By this time, the name Carlton was deemed so important to the school's identity that its name was changed by charter to Carlton College. The early 1880s saw the school achieve an enrollment of more than 200. Thereafter, the establishment of other Christian schools and the public education system may have contributed to the school's decline. In 1887 the school became a female-only institution. An impressive three-story hall was built in 1895, and the school continued its work despite declining enrollments until Carlton's death in 1902. An arsonist set fire to the college in 1910. In 1914 the institution, under the guidance of C. T. Carlton and his wife, merged with Carr-Burdette College and moved to Sherman for two years. In 1916 the Carltons returned to Bonham, but Carlton College never reopened.

BIBLIOGRAPHY: Kenneth M. Hay, *The Life and Influence of Charles Carlton, 1821–1902* (Fort Worth: Texas Christian University, 1940).

Deborah K. Kilgore

CARMEL, TEXAS. Carmel was on the Medina River near the site of present Losoya in southern Bexar County. It was settled around the time of the Civil War[qv] and by the mid-1880s had a church, a school, and a reported population of 100. A post office, named after the church and school, operated from 1887 to 1889. In the 1890s Carmel was supplanted by nearby Losoya and Cassin and after 1900 no longer appeared on maps. *Christopher Long*

CARMINE, TEXAS. Carmine is on U.S. Highway 290 at the Fayette-Washington county line. Dr. B. J. Thigpen and his family moved to the townsite on Christmas Day, 1885. Thigpen had been promised the position of station agent on the Texas and New Orleans Railroad if he would promote the town. When the post office was established in 1892 the original name, Sylvan, was changed to Carmine in honor of Newton Carmean, the first postmaster. The town grew through active promotion. By 1900 it had four general stores, four saloons, two blacksmith shops, a newspaper named the *New Century*, several churches, and ten other businesses. Both the railroad and the highway provided direct links between Houston and Austin. In 1950 Carmine had twenty-four businesses and a population of 650. Students attended the consolidated school of Carmine–Round Top. During the 1960s, however, cotton gins closed and farmland reverted to pasture. U.S. 290 was straightened between 1958 and 1964 and bypassed the town. The railroad line was closed, and the track was removed between 1980 and 1985. By 1985 the town had twenty-five businesses and a population of 239. In 1990 the population was 192.

BIBLIOGRAPHY: Frank Lotto, *Fayette County: Her History and Her People* (Schulenburg, Texas: Sticker Steam Press, 1902; rpt., Austin: University of Texas Press, 1981). *Jeff Carroll*

CARMONA, TEXAS. Carmona is at the intersection of U.S. Highway 287 and Farm Road 1872, ninety miles northwest of Beaumont in northwestern Polk County. It was named for Juan Carmona, on whose 1833 land grant it was located when it was established as a farming community in the 1850s. With the construction of the Trinity and Sabine Railway through northern Polk County in 1882, new interests came seeking to reap the harvests of the area's rich timber reserves. A sawmill, owned by the William Cameron Lumber Company, was built at Carmona in the latter part of the nineteenth century. In 1894 the Carmona post office was established; by 1897 Carmona was listed as a stop on the railroad, then owned by the Missouri, Kansas and Texas line. The Cameron sawmill burned in 1914, and another logging establishment was set up a mile south of Carmona, at a site known as Ragley or Saner Junction. The newer mill, operated by the Saner-Ragley Lumber Company, was expanded in 1934 but ended operations sometime after 1943. The old mill sites are now farm and ranch land. Population changes reflect the rise and decline of the local lumber industry, falling from an estimated 500 in 1925 to 200 in the late 1940s. Early 1970s estimates set the population at fifty, where it remained in 1990.

BIBLIOGRAPHY: *A Pictorial History of Polk County, Texas, 1846–1910* (Livingston, Texas: Polk County Bicentennial Commission, 1976; rev. ed. 1978). *Robert Wooster*

CARNEGIE LIBRARIES. The public library movement was late in coming to Texas. Before the building program financed by Andrew Carnegie began, the state had only a handful of public libraries; some of the larger were the Galveston Public Library, the Houston Lyceum Library, the El Paso Public Library, and St. Mary's Church Library in San Antonio. Andrew Carnegie believed in giving to those who were willing to help themselves. He defined the public library as one that not only served the public but was supported by public funds. The cities that received his gifts were told they must make themselves responsible for the maintenance of the gifts. He asked that they pledge an amount equal to 10 percent of the grant, to be made available annually for the library, and that the city also provide a suitable site for the building.

Between 1898 and 1917 Carnegie gave thirty-four gifts totaling $645,000 to various Texas communities. These donations were responsible for the construction of thirty-two public library buildings. Pittsburg, a mining town of fewer than 1,500 inhabitants, was the first Texas community to receive a Carnegie building grant. The gift of $5,000 in 1898 helped to finance a building that contained a small library and reading room for the use of local mine workers during their leisure time. In 1899 and 1900 gifts were awarded to the Dallas, Fort Worth, and San Antonio public library associations and the Houston Women's Club. The El Paso Public Library Association received a grant of $37,500 in 1904. Grants to such smaller communities as Clarksville, Waco, Belton, Tyler, Gainesville, and Sherman often resulted from applications from women's clubs, many of which had already started their own subscription libraries.

Typically, the buildings were constructed with two stories and a basement. Club rooms and auditoriums were included in the early buildings to provide rental fees to help defray operating costs. Later the Carnegie Corporation refused to approve plans that included rooms for nonlibrary use. The libraries in smaller communities were located wherever land was made available to them. Usually this property was adjacent to the business section of town, and frequently the development of a park around the library was planned, if one did not already exist.

Construction on the last Texas library built by Carnegie funds began in May 1915 in Vernon. On its completion, the Vernon Library Committee found that it had no money with which to buy books, a problem frequently encountered in small communities. However, two years later the library was able to open with 4,000 volumes provided through the efforts of the city commission and the women's library club.

In many small communities the libraries functioned as the educational institutions they were intended to be. For example, Gainesville expanded service to the entire county, the second Texas library to do so. Sulphur Springs, Tyler, Sherman, and Waco enhanced support of their successful libraries with increases in funding and use. But in some of the smaller communities, interest declined due to the lack of good books and professional guidance. By 1914 fourteen communities were defaulting on the agreements made with the Carnegie Corporation, despite efforts by the Texas State Library and the Texas Historical Commission[qqv] to remedy the situation.

In 1916 Alvin S. Johnson of Columbia University reported to the Carnegie Corporation that Texas libraries were poorly stocked and badly run and suggested that funds might better have been used for both books and buildings, with a provision for competent librarians for the initial period. He recommended that the corporation's attention be directed to education for librarianship. Shortly thereafter, the building grants were discontinued.

Although the libraries were not successful in some small communities because of the lack of financial support, the building program was a worthy experiment. It stimulated interest in the public library movement and supplied the only means by which many library buildings could have been built. The buildings themselves were quite up-to-date. That in Gainesville, for instance, was made of cream-colored brick and steel; wood was used only for doors and windows. In Texas the program resulted in the construction of libraries in five of the largest cities, thus permitting local resources to be spent entirely for staff and book collections. The resulting institutions are among the largest libraries in Texas.

BIBLIOGRAPHY: Alvin S. Johnson, *A Report to the Carnegie Corporation of New York on the Policy of Donations to Free Public Libraries* (n.d). Anne Harwell Teague [Jordan], Carnegie Library Building Grants to Texas Communities (M.L.S. report, University of Texas at Austin, 1967). Texas Library Association, *Handbook of Texas Libraries*, 1–4 (Austin, 1904–35). *Anne H. Jordan*

CARNEY, FRANK (1868–1934). Frank Carney, geologist and teacher, was born in Watkins, New York, on March 15, 1868, the son of Hugh and Esther R. (Beahan) Carney. He graduated from Starkey Seminary in Eddytown, New York, in 1887 and was an instructor in mathematics and history at that institution until 1891, when he entered Cornell University. He received a B.A. degree from Cornell in

1895 and a Ph.D. in 1909. He worked his way through school, serving at various times as principal of Starkey Seminary, instructor at the Keuta Institute, assistant and instructor in the Cornell geology department, and vice principal of Ithaca High School. In 1904 Carney became head of the department of geology and geography at Denison University in Granville, Ohio; he remained there for thirteen years and built a very successful program. He was chief geologist at the National Refining Company at Columbus, Ohio, in 1917 but returned to academics in the fall of 1928. He taught for one year at Texas Christian University before moving to Waco to become head of the geology and geography department at Baylor University. Under his management the department grew to be the largest science department at the university and one of the strongest geography centers in the state. Carney held membership in numerous professional organizations, including the Geological Society of America, the Association of American Geographers, the Ohio Academy of Science, the American Institute of Mining and Metallurgical Engineers, and the Texas Academy of Science.[qv] He published more than forty articles in professional journals and was in great demand as a speaker. He married Mary Ellen Keegan on November 26, 1890, and they became the parents of five children. Carney was a Mason, a Shriner, a member of the Baptist Church, and an independent in politics. He died in Waco on December 13, 1934, and was buried at Wilmer, Texas.

BIBLIOGRAPHY: *Proceedings of the Geological Society of America*, 1934. *Who Was Who in America*, Vol. 2. *Vivian Elizabeth Smyrl*

CARNOHAN, HARRY PEYTON (1904–1969). Harry Carnohan, artist and critic, was born on April 18, 1904, in Milford, Texas, the second of three sons of William George and Maie (Rogers) Carnohan. He grew up in the Oak Cliff area of Dallas after moving there with his family at an early age. He studied art under Vivian Aunspaugh and Frank Reaugh.[qqv] He continued his studies at the Art Institute of Chicago, where in June 1926 he was awarded the Bryan Lathrop Traveling Fellowship for study in Europe. He spent the next 4½ years studying in Paris and other major European art centers. During this period he studied for a year with the influential modernist teacher André L'Hote and exhibited his work at the Salon d'Automne in Paris (1927).

Following his European sojourn Carnohan returned to Dallas, where he became active in the Dallas Nine,[qv] a circle of regionalists. He presented his theories on modern art at meetings of the Dallas Art League and shared information on recent developments in European art with other artists. For the Dallas *Journal* Carnohan wrote articles critiquing a series of exhibitions that influenced the Dallas regionalist group, including the Kress traveling exhibition of early Italian painters (1933), the College Art Association's exhibition of Mexican muralists Diego Rivera and José Clemente Orozco (1934), and an exhibition of contemporary lithographers organized by Lloyd Rollins for the Dallas Museum of Art[qv] (1934). Carnohan was more open to contemporary European styles such as surrealism than Jerry Bywaters[qv] and Alexandre Hogue, the leading exponents of southwestern regionalism.

Carnohan almost certainly came into contact with the Surrealists, who were active in Paris at the time he was there, and whose influence permeates his best-known work, *West Texas Landscape* (1934). He evoked a sense of strangeness in this painting through the precise placement of a bucket, a garden hose, a shed, stones, and other ordinary objects that took on a life of their own in the harsh light of the West Texas sun. The painting was executed in the cool palette favored by the early Italian Renaissance painters, whom Carnohan admired. *West Texas Landscape* won the purchase prize at the Seventh Annual Allied Arts Exhibition at the Dallas Museum of Fine Arts in 1935 and was singled out as one of the two finest paintings exhibited by Texan artists at the Centennial Exposition (1936). Carnohan worked in oil, watercolor, pastel, and tempera and experimented with graphic techniques as a member of the Lone Star Printmakers group. He favored landscapes, figures, and portraits after briefly experimenting with abstraction.

In spite of his limited output, Carnohan won considerable acclaim during his years in Dallas. His work won praise at the 1933 and 1935 Allied Artists annuals in Dallas and the 1936 Texas Centennial[qv] Exposition. He was chosen as one of several artists to represent Texas in a touring exhibition of American art organized by the New York City Museum of Modern Art (1933), and in 1934 he participated in the annual exhibition of contemporary painters sponsored by the Whitney Museum in New York City. He was also represented at the Golden Gate Exposition in San Francisco in 1939.

Carnohan taught at the Dallas Art Institute in the late 1930s and apparently spent some time in Colorado Springs, Colorado, before accepting a position in the art department at Columbia University in 1940. In November 1940 Columbia University mounted a solo exhibition of his work that traced his development over fifteen years, from the early abstractions, to his Texas landscapes with their emphasis on color and space, to his most recent work at that time, gouaches of Vermont scenes characterized by rich patterning.

On December 31, 1942, Carnohan married an artist, Lucille (Michaela) Cimbollek, in New York City; they had two daughters and a son. Uncomfortable with the emerging emphasis on abstract art in New York City, Carnohan left Columbia University in 1953 and subsequently moved with his family to Pacific Beach, California. They later settled in nearby La Jolla, where Carnohan worked as a furniture and antique dealer. The couple were divorced in 1966. Carnohan died in the San Diego area on March 9, 1969. His work is represented in the Dallas Museum of Art.

BIBLIOGRAPHY: Frances Battaile Fisk, *A History of Texas Artists and Sculptors* (Abilene, Texas, 1928; facsimile rpt., Austin: Morrison, 1986). Esse Forrester-O'Brien, *Art and Artists of Texas* (Dallas: Tardy, 1935). Rick Stewart, *Lone Star Regionalism* (Austin: Texas Monthly Press, 1985). *Kendall Curlee*

CARO, TEXAS. Caro is just off State Highway 204 ten miles north of Nacogdoches in north central Nacogdoches County. It was named for José Antonio Caro, who received title to the surrounding land in 1835. The area was settled before the Civil War,[qv] but a community did not grow up until the end of the nineteenth century, when the settlement became the center of intensive logging operations. A post office and a school opened in 1904. Around 1906 the Caro Northern Railway linked the town with Mount Enterprise. Caro flourished in the period just before World War I;[qv] in 1914 the town had two drugstores, a general store, a physician, a grocer, a large sawmill, and a reported population of 1,300. After the war, however, the sawmill closed and the town began to decline. By the mid-1930s the population fell to 150. The population remained steady through the 1970s, but in the intervening years the school, the post office, and all of the businesses closed. By the early 1990s Caro was a dispersed community. The reported population in 1990 was 113.

BIBLIOGRAPHY: Nacogdoches County Genealogical Society, *Nacogdoches County Families* (Dallas: Curtis, 1985). *Christopher Long*

CAROLINA CREEK. Before being unundated in 1969 by Lake Livingston, Carolina Creek was a spring-fed perennial stream that rose at the confluence of two forks, West Carolina and East Carolina creeks, near the northwestern boundary of the Sam Houston National Forest[qv] in far eastern Walker County (at 30°51′ N, 95°20′ W) and flowed north for two miles to its mouth on the Trinity River, near the Walker and San Jacinto county lines (at 30°52′ N, 95°20′ W). East Carolina Creek rises two miles east of Dodge (at 30°45′ N, 95°21′ W) and flows north ten miles through northwestern San Jacinto County along the Walker county line, and West Carolina Creek rises two miles northeast of Dodge (at 30°45′ N, 95°22′ W) and flows north nine miles. Both forks now drain into Lake Livingston. They traverse gently rolling to nearly level terrain surfaced by sandy loam that supports loblolly pine, sweet gum, short-leaf pine, post oak, and black hickory trees near the banks. Settlement in the vicinity began in the mid-1830s. In the late 1830s the original Carolina community was founded in the vicinity of the forks' mouths; a settlement known as Carolina Mill existed farther upstream from 1870 to 1900. The Palmetto Park community is located just west of the west fork, and Staley lies just east of the east fork. The present Carolina community, first known as Gilbert Settlement, was established during the 1850s where the two tributaries meet. The Gospel Hill community has been located on the west bank of the west fork since the early twentieth century.

BIBLIOGRAPHY: D'Anne McAdams Crews, ed., *Huntsville and Walker County, Texas: A Bicentennial History* (Huntsville, Texas: Sam Houston State University, 1976).

CAROLINA, TEXAS. Carolina was just off Farm Road 935 near Deer Creek, three miles southwest of Chilton in western Falls County. It was one of the earliest settlements in Falls County west of the Brazos River. A post office called Deer Creek was established in 1852; the name was soon changed to Carolina by several settlers from North Carolina, who thought that the landscape resembled that of their former home. The first Presbyterian church in Falls County was established there in 1854 when the church at Elm Creek near Cameron in Milam County moved to Carolina. The Carolina post office was discontinued in 1873. When the San Antonio and Aransas Pass Railway bypassed the community in the late 1880s, most of the residents moved. By the 1930s a cemetery was all that remained.

BIBLIOGRAPHY: Walter W. Brawn, The History of Falls County (M.A. thesis, Baylor University, 1938). Lillian S. St. Romain, *Western Falls County, Texas* (Austin: Texas State Historical Association, 1951).

Vivian Elizabeth Smyrl

CARO NORTHERN RAILWAY. The Caro Northern Railway Company was chartered on September 14, 1906, to connect Caro in Nacogdoches County with Mount Enterprise in Rusk County. The railroad originated as a logging road; it was chartered as a common carrier in 1906 with capital stock of $100,000. The principal place of business was Caro. The first board of directors included C. H. Morris and M. W. Jones, both of Winnsboro; Mrs. M. R. Schulter of Dallas; W. T. Whiteman and E. M. Decker, both of Caro; D. W. March of Mount Enterprise; and R. H. Thompson of Henderson. The Caro Northern was recognized by the Railroad Commission[qv] as a common carrier on March 25, 1907. In 1916 the line owned one locomotive and two cars and reported passenger earnings of $1,400 and freight earnings of $15,000. During 1919 the company was operated by a receiver appointed at the direction of the commission due to the failure of the railroad to operate as required by law. According to the Railroad Commission, the company did not operate in 1922 and was abandoned in 1923. However, by 1926 the Caro Northern had resumed service. In that year it was considered a Class III railroad with passenger earnings of $1,300 and freight revenues of $13,000. The railroad was abandoned in 1928. *Nancy Beck Young*

CAROTHERS, ASENATH WALLACE (1859–1933). Asenath (Cenie) W. Carothers, clubwoman and university administrator, daughter of William J. and Susan (Williams) Wallace, was born on the family plantation at New London, Arkansas, on February 6, 1859. She was orphaned by the age of five and was reared by her aunt in Starkville, Mississippi, where she attended Starkville Seminary for Women and graduated with honors. In 1882 she married Neil Carothers of Starkville. The couple had five children, one of whom died in infancy. They lived in Chattanooga, Tennessee, for about five years, where Carothers became an attorney. In 1897 they moved to Arkansas, where Mrs. Carothers became an officer in the Arkansas Federation of Women's Clubs and began writing articles and short stories for newspapers and magazines.

Carothers died in 1901, leaving Cenie with four children. She became head librarian at the University of Arkansas. In 1903 she accepted the position as director of the Woman's Building, a residence hall at the University of Texas, where she remained until her retirement in 1928. She was founder, sponsor, and first regent of the Andrew Carruthers Chapter of the Daughters of the American Revolution, which limited its membership to students, faculty, and ex-students of the University of Texas. She initiated a state DAR scholarship at the university and similar scholarships at other state educational institutions. She also established a scholarship for student teachers. Carothers Dormitory on the University of Texas campus is named for her. A chair in her honor was purchased in Constitution Hall, Philadelphia, by the DAR. Mrs. Carothers was a Presbyterian, a charter member of the Pan-American Round Table in Austin, and a member of the Society of Colonial Dames, the United Daughters of the Confederacy,[qqv] and the University Ladies Club. She died in Grosse Pointe, Michigan, on February 25, 1933, and was buried in Starkville, Mississippi.

BIBLIOGRAPHY: Vertical Files, Barker Texas History Center, University of Texas at Austin. *Margaret C. Berry*

CARPENTER, DAVID (?–?). David Carpenter was a partner of William Harris[qv] as one of Stephen F. Austin's[qv] Old Three Hundred[qv] families. He and Harris received title to a sitio[qv] now in Harris County on August 16, 1824. The census of 1826 classified Carpenter as a blacksmith and a single man aged between twenty-five and forty.

BIBLIOGRAPHY: Lester G. Bugbee, "The Old Three Hundred: A List of Settlers in Austin's First Colony," *Quarterly of the Texas State Historical Association* 1 (October 1897). *Clinton P. Hartmann*

CARPENTER, EUGENE R. (1873–1934). Eugene R. Carpenter, brain surgeon, son of William D. and Emma (Shanks) Carpenter, was born on October 5, 1873, in Knob Noster, Missouri. He attended New Mexico Military Institute and the University of Michigan and graduated from Jefferson Medical College, Philadelphia, in 1898. He served as intern at Kings County Hospital, New York City, and did postgraduate work at Manhattan Eye and Ear Hospital and in London and Vienna. He practiced medicine in El Paso, Texas, and became a member of the county and state medical societies and the American Ophthalmological and Oto-pharyngological Society. On July 20, 1916, he married Lucile Snyder. Carpenter served as a captain in the United States Army Medical Corps in World War I[qv] and in 1921 began practice as a brain surgeon in Dallas. He was also a designer of medical instruments. He became a member of the American Association of Surgeons and was later made a fellow of the American College of Surgeons. He was a Mason. He died on October 9, 1934, in Dallas and was buried at Knob Noster, Missouri.

BIBLIOGRAPHY: Dallas *Morning News*, October 11, 1934. Frank W. Johnson, *A History of Texas and Texans* (5 vols., ed. E. C. Barker and E. W. Winkler [Chicago and New York: American Historical Society, 1914; rpt. 1916]). *Who Was Who in America*, Vol. 2.

Clinton P. Hartmann

CARPENTER, JOHN WILLIAM (1881–1959). John William Carpenter, utility and insurance executive and rancher, was born on August 31, 1881, on a farm near Corsicana, Texas, to Thomas Wirt and Ellen Isaphene (Dickson) Carpenter. He attended a country school as a youth and later took courses at North Texas State Normal College (now the University of North Texas) in Denton, at Draughon's Business College in Fort Worth, and from the International Correspondence School of Scranton, Pennsylvania. In 1900, after a short time with a Corsicana implement-supply firm, Carpenter rose in the Corsicana Gas and Electric Company from day laborer through line man, plant engineer, bookkeeper, collector, and superintendent of distribution to general superintendent. He went to Schenectady, New York, in 1905 to work in the testing department at General Electric and took the company's student apprenticeship course in electrical engineering. For two years he worked in Ohio and Indiana for GE, then returned to Texas in 1907 to become president and general manager of Corsicana Gas and Electric.

In 1918 Carpenter moved to Dallas to become vice president and general manager of Dallas Power and Light Company, and the next year he assumed the same position at Texas Power and Light. In 1927 he become president of TP&L and in 1949 chairman of the board. He resigned this position in 1953 but stayed on as a board member and chairman of the company's executive committee. From 1927 to 1947 he served as president and general manager of Texas Public Utilities Corporation, which ran Texas Electric Service Company as well as TP&L.

In 1930 Carpenter organized Texas Security Life Insurance Company, which through various combinations and mergers became Southland Life Insurance Company and was, at the time of his death, the nation's fifteenth largest publicly owned life insurance company. Carpenter was the founder and first president of Lone Star Steel; this company's contribution to the development of East Texas earned him the East Texas Achievement Award for 1953. He served as president of Dallas Railway and Terminal Company (1927–35) and Texas Refrigeration and Ice Company (1945–49). In all, Carpenter managed or organized nearly twenty-five major companies in the Southwest, including eleven utility companies and the St. Louis and Southwestern Railway Company.

One of his major interests was agriculture and horse and cattle breeding. With his son he owned and operated four ranches and one farm. He introduced the technique of artificial insemination to Texas with a $5,000 grant to Texas A&M.

Carpenter served as president of the Dallas Chamber of Commerce for two terms, chairman of the board of the Southwestern Legal Foundation, vice president of the State Fair of Texas,[qv] a director of the National Safety Council and the Southwest Research Institute,[qv] and chairman of an organizing committee that established the National Conference of Christians and Jews in the Southwest. In an advisory capacity he worked with the United States Chamber of Commerce Southwestern Business Council, the Edison Electric Institute, the Southwestern Regional Committee of the National Association of Manufacturers, and the National Rivers and Harbors Congress.

His concern for agriculture and the Texas landscape placed him on the boards of the Texas Research Foundation and the Texas Forestry Association.[qqv] As a member of the executive committee of the Big Bend National Park[qv] Association, Carpenter was instrumental in obtaining for Texas its first national park. He was an avid supporter of canalizing and developing the Trinity River and served as president of the Trinity Improvement Association for twenty-nine years. He served on the first board of regents of Texas Technological College (now Texas Tech University) and held a bachelor of laws degree from there. He was a fellow in the American Institute of Electrical Engineers and was awarded an honorary doctorate of engineering by Southern Methodist University. His many other activities included memberships in the Dallas Historical Society and the Texas State Historical Association.[qqv] Carpenter Freeway in Dallas is named for him. On June 18, 1913, he married Flossie Belle Gardner of Palestine, Texas; they had three children. Carpenter was a Presbyterian and a Democrat. On June 16, 1959, he died at his home of a heart attack. He was buried in Corsicana.

BIBLIOGRAPHY: Dallas *Morning News*, September 17, 1950, March 11, 1951, February 28, 1953, April 12, June 17, 1959, September 7, 1963, January 24, 1967. *Who Was Who in America*, Vol. 6.

Joan Jenkins Perez

CARPENTER, TEXAS. Carpenter, on Farm Road 1346 eight miles north of Floresville in northern Wilson County, was established in 1893, when the San Antonio and Gulf Railway crossed eastern Wilson County. The settlement, named for a local landowner, had a population of ten in 1900. Joseph Winkler became postmaster when a post office was granted that year and established a cotton gin, a general store, and a saloon in the early 1900s. By 1914 Carpenter had a blacksmith, two general stores, a saloon, a cotton gin, and a reported 100 residents. The post office was discontinued in 1928 and the mail sent to Adkins. In 1947 Carpenter had one store and a population of 100. Subsequently, the population declined, and in the early 1990s only a few scattered houses remained. *Claudia Hazlewood*

CARPENTERS BAYOU. Carpenters Bayou rises at the south end of Sheldon Reservoir in southeastern Harris County (at 29°51′ N, 95°10′ W) and runs southeast for about twelve miles until it joins Buffalo Bayou at the San Jacinto Battleground State Historical Park[qv] (at 29°45′ N, 95°06′ W). The bayou traverses flat to rolling terrain with local escarpments and dissections, surfaced by thin to thick sandy and clay loams that support native vegetation including mixed hardwoods and pines. In developed areas the native vegetation has been replaced by cultivated row or cover crops. The bayou was possibly named for David Carpenter,[qv] who was granted land along its banks in 1824.

CARPENTER'S BLUFF, TEXAS. Carpenter's Bluff is on the Red River and Farm Road 120 twelve miles northeast of Sherman in extreme northeastern Grayson County. The settlement, established about 1860, derived its name from that of an early settler who operated a ferry across the Red River. After 1865 a number of disreputable persons who frequented the local general store and saloon earned the community the nickname Thiefneck. Law-abiding citizens soon drove these men from Carpenter's Bluff, however, and the nickname was forgotten.

By the early twentieth century the Kansas, Oklahoma and Gulf Railway had constructed a bridge across the Red River at Carpenter's Bluff. The Texas and Pacific Railway later owned and operated the bridge. At some time a one-lane shoulder was added to the bridge to allow automobile traffic. The Texas and Pacific relinquished control of the bridge in 1966, turning authority over to officials of Grayson County and Bryan County, Oklahoma. Soon thereafter the bridge was converted to accommodate two lanes of automobile traffic. By 1936 Carpenter's Bluff had a population of seventy-five and four businesses. Ten years later the population had increased to 120, and the town still had four businesses.

BIBLIOGRAPHY: Grayson County Frontier Village, *History of Grayson County, Texas* (2 vols., Winston-Salem, North Carolina: Hunter, 1979, 1981).

Brian Hart

CARPER, WILLIAM M. (ca. 1810–ca. 1859). William M. Carper, soldier and physician of the Republic of Texas,[qv] was born in Virginia and apparently traveled to Texas because he had been promised a commission in the cavalry, but on April 10, 1836, acting secretary of war David Thomas[qv] appointed him a regimental surgeon. Thomas, in a letter to Sam Houston,[qv] described Carper as "a gentleman of fine address." At the battle of San Jacinto[qv] Carper served as surgeon of Lt. Col. Henry Millard's[qv] First Regiment of Regular Infantry. For his military service from March 9, 1836, through June 8, 1837, Carper was issued a bounty warrant for 1,280 acres that he sold to Governor Henry Smith[qv] for $250.

After the war he located his practice in Houston and was apparently appointed chief of surgeons at the city hospital. On May 28, 1839, he married Sarah Ann Minerva Ward of Houston. That same week he was elected president of the Houston Medical and Surgical Society. On September 23 he was elected to the board of the Houston Post Oak Jockey Club; George Washington Hockley[qv] was its president, and Sidney Sherman[qv] was first vice president. Carper finished third in a four-man race for mayor of Houston in 1841. After only two years of marriage his wife died, on May 16, 1841, at the age of nineteen.

In 1850 Carper was living in the Tremont House, Houston, also the residence of his friend Hockley, with a Mrs. Carper, age twenty-four, of Alabama. At the same time he was maintaining a residence in the Rio Grande valley (where he owned $10,000 worth of real estate) with Mary J. D. Carper, age twenty, from Ohio, and a six-month-old orphan named J. W. Crocket.

Carper and Hugh McLeod[qv] were the two Democratic nominees from Galveston for the first House of Representatives of the state of Texas in 1846. On April 8 of that year Carper became a cofounder of the Grand Lodge of the International Order of Odd Fellows in Texas. In 1848 he was elected charter treasurer of the Medical and Surgical Society of Galveston. Pat Ireland Nixon[qv] reported Carper to be in ill health and nearly blind in Brazoria in 1859, so the report of his death in 1847 by Sam Houston Dixon and Lewis W. Kemp[qqv] is in error.

BIBLIOGRAPHY: Clarksville *Northern Standard,* January 7, 1846. Daughters of the Republic of Texas, *Muster Rolls of the Texas Revolution* (Austin, 1986). Sam Houston Dixon and Louis Wiltz Kemp, *The Heroes of San Jacinto* (Houston: Anson Jones, 1932). Houston *Morning Star,* May 31, 1839. John H. Jenkins, ed., *The Papers of the Texas Revolution, 1835–1836* (10 vols., Austin: Presidial Press, 1973). Pat Ireland Nixon, *The Medical Story of Early Texas, 1528–1853* (Lancaster, Pennsylvania: Lupe Memorial Fund, 1946). *Telegraph and Texas Register,* January 6, April 10, May 29, September 25, 1839, May 26, 1841.

Thomas W. Cutrer

CARPER'S CREEK. Carper's Creek rises a half mile east of Big Head Mountain in northern Comal County (at 29°59′ N, 98°19′ W) and runs east for ten miles to its mouth on the Blanco River, five miles southwest of Wimberley in Hays County (at 29°58′ N, 98°11′ W). It crosses an area of the Balcones Escarpment[qv] characterized by steep slopes and limestone benches that give a stairstep appearance to the landscape. Soil in the area is generally dark, calcareous, stony clay and clay loam with rock outcroppings, and vegetation consists primarily of live oak and Ashe juniper woods. The creek was named for William M. Carper,[qv] who was granted ownership of some of the surrounding land in 1847.

CARPETBAGGERS. *Carpetbagger* was the pejorative term applied to Northerners who moved to the South after the Civil War, specifically those who joined state Republican parties formed in 1867 and who were elected as Republicans to public office. Southern Democrats alleged that the newcomers were corrupt and dishonest adventurers, whose property consisted only of what they could carry in their carpetbags (suitcases made of carpeting), who seized political power and plundered the helpless people of the South. This assessment of the carpetbagger became standard in late-nineteenth-century histories and retained its currency among some historians as late as the 1990s. Since the 1950s, however, revisionist historians have challenged the validity of the traditional view and assessed the carpetbaggers more favorably. For Texas, the revised characterization appears to be more appropriate than the traditional one. Carpetbaggers played only a minor role in the state's Reconstruction[qv] history. In part this was because few Northerners who arrived after the Civil War held political offices. In the Constitutional Convention of 1868–69,[qv] seven of the ninety-three delegates were carpetbaggers. In the subsequent administration of Governor Edmund J. Davis,[qv] Northerners held only the positions of state adjutant general and chief justice of the Supreme Court. Eight of sixty district court judges were carpetbaggers. In the Twelfth Legislature just twelve of 142 state legislators were postwar immigrants from the North. At the county level the actual number of carpetbaggers also was small. One scholar has placed their number at no more than 11 percent.

In addition to their numerical insignificance, Texas carpetbaggers generally do not fit the stereotypical pattern. The most important Northern immigrants to hold major political offices in Texas were congressman William T. Clark[qv] from Connecticut, state senator George T. Ruby,[qv] a black man from Maine, state treasurer George W. Honey[qv] from Wisconsin, adjutant general James Davidson[qv] from Scotland, superintendent of public instruction Edwin M. Wheelock[qv] from New Hampshire, and Supreme Court justice Moses B. Walker[qv] from Ohio. Their lives and careers demonstrate the deficiencies with the traditional view of carpetbaggers. Because most of these men arrived in Texas before black enfranchisement under Congressional Reconstruction in 1867, it is not possible that they were political adventurers intending to take advantage of black voters. Clark, a brevet major general, arrived with the army of occupation in 1865, then resigned that year to become the cashier for the First National Bank of Texas at Galveston. Honey, a clergyman and chaplain of the Fourth Wisconsin Cavalry, Ruby, a black newspaperman and teacher, and Wheelock, a Unitarian minister and teacher, all came to Texas in 1865 as employees of the Freedmen's Bureau[qv] school system. Only Walker and Davidson came after 1867, but both were in the United States Army and assigned to units that were already in the state. These men joined the Republican party[qv] for a variety of different reasons. Honey, Ruby, and Wheelock believed that political action was necessary to secure rights for former slaves in the postwar environment. Clark and Walker apparently were Republicans in the North before the war and continued their prewar political ties. Davidson's reasons for supporting local Republicanism are not known. Rather than representing the lowest or the propertyless class of the North, most of these men were of middle-class origin, usually possessing both education and property. Clark, although from a background of poverty, had established a successful law practice in Iowa before the war. Walker was from a prominent Ohio family, attended Yale College and Cincinnati Law School, and by 1860 was a prosperous attorney at Dayton, with more than $70,000 in property. Wheelock was educated at Harvard and was a pastor. Honey, Ruby, and Davidson, while not wealthy, were educated and do not appear to have been fortune hunters.

On the whole, these men were responsible state officials. Wheelock developed the public school idea that became part of the Constitution of 1869.[qv] Walker's career in the state Supreme Court, until his Semicolon ruling in 1874, was considered a conservative one (*see* SEMICOLON COURT). Congressman Clark secured the first major appropriation for the construction of jetties in Galveston harbor. State senator Ruby supported a variety of laws favorable to the people, both black and white, of his district. Only two of these important carpetbagger officials were tied to public corruption. Honey was charged with inappropriate use of funds in the state treasury when he loaned state funds to private individuals. He was removed by the Davis administration, but regained the office by order of the state Supreme Court. The state lost no money in Honey's speculations. In the second instance, Adjutant General Davidson defrauded the state of more than $37,000 by issuing fraudulent warrants, and fled the state in 1872. Few in numbers, never particularly powerful relative to the native white or scalawag element of the Republican party, the carpetbaggers of Texas played a minor role in Texas politics after the Civil War. The traditional idea of carpetbag rule is an unsuitable concept to apply to Texas Reconstruction.

BIBLIOGRAPHY: Randolph B. Campbell, "Grass Roots Reconstruction: The Personnel of County Government in Texas, 1865–1876," *Journal of Southern History* 58 (February 1992). Randolph B. Campbell, "Carpetbagger Rule in Reconstruction Texas: An Enduring Myth," *Southwestern Historical Quarterly* 97 (April 1994). Carl H. Moneyhon, *Republicanism in Reconstruction Texas* (Austin: University of Texas Press, 1980).

Carl H. Moneyhon

CARR, EUGENE ASA (1830–1910). Eugene Asa Carr, army officer, the oldest of four sons born to Clark Merwin and Delia Ann (Torry)

Carr, was born on March 10, 1830, near Hamburg, Erie County, New York. In 1846 he entered the United States Military Academy at West Point, from which he graduated on July 1, 1850. His first tour of duty was at the Carlisle, Pennsylvania, cavalry barracks. He received his commission as a second lieutenant in the Regiment of Mounted Rifles (later the Third Cavalry) at Jefferson Barracks, near St. Louis, Missouri, in 1851. From 1852 to 1854, Carr saw frontier duty at forts Leavenworth and Scott in Kansas, Fort Kearney in Nebraska, and Fort Gibson in Indian Territory. Early in the fall of 1854, in response to Indian troubles along the Rio Grande border in South Texas, Carr's company was transferred to the regimental headquarters at Fort Inge, near the site of present Uvalde. On October 1, Capt. John G. Walker[qv] and about forty troops, including Carr, set out to follow the trail of hostile Lipan Apaches, who had recently stolen livestock in the vicinity. Near the Diablo Mountains on the morning of the third day out, the mounted troopers came upon "about three-hundred" Indians, whom they charged. In the ensuing skirmish, Carr received an arrow wound and was subsequently commended by Gen. Persifor F. Smith[qv] for his "gallantry and coolness."

In the spring of 1855, Carr was promoted to first lieutenant in the newly organized First Cavalry. In that capacity he participated in the Sioux expedition of 1855 and that summer was the hero of the cholera outbreak at Fort Riley, Kansas. During 1856 and 1857, he was involved in the Kansas border troubles and led a company in the so-called Mormon War. After accompanying Col. Edwin V. Sumner's expedition into western Kansas and Nebraska in the summer of 1858, he was promoted to captain and transferred to Fort Washita, in the Indian Territory. By late 1859 he had assumed command of that post. From there, in the summer of 1860, he took part in the campaign against hostile Comanches and Kiowas in Kansas and Nebraska.

When the Civil War[qv] broke out, Lt. Col. William H. Emory[qv] took over command of the fort. Emory escaped from the Confederate forces and marched his command from Fort Washita to Fort Leavenworth, then joined forces with Gen. Nathaniel Lyon in Missouri. Carr was brevetted a lieutenant colonel for his actions in the battle of Wilson's Creek on August 9, 1861, and a week later was made colonel of the Third Illinois Cavalry. He was soon acting brigadier general under Gen. John C. Frémont, and in February 1862 he took command of a division of the Army of the Southwest under Gen. Samuel R. Curtis. In the battle of Pea Ridge, Arkansas, on March 7–8, he was wounded three times and displayed such bravery as eventually (in 1894) to be awarded the Medal of Honor. Shortly afterward, Carr was commissioned a brigadier general of volunteers and during the remainder of 1862 was engaged in Arkansas. In 1863 he commanded a division of the Thirteenth Army Corps in the Vicksburg campaign, where he received a brevet in regular rank to colonel. His division led the assault on Vicksburg on May 18 and was the first to reach the Confederate breastworks four days later. Following brief service at Corinth, Mississippi, he was transferred in December 1863 to the Army of Arkansas, where he participated in numerous small actions, including the capture of Little Rock. He joined Gen. Edward R. S. Canby[qv] for the campaign against Mobile, Alabama, in April 1865. By the cessation of hostilities, Carr had been brevetted twice more, to major general, and had won national renown as "the black-bearded Cossack." It was during the war, while on temporary duty in St. Louis, that he met and fell in love with Mary Patience Magwire. They were married on October 12, 1865. Four sons were born to them, but only the oldest, Clark Magwire, lived to adulthood.

After reverting to permanent rank of major, Carr spent the next two years on Reconstruction[qv] duty in Helena, Arkansas, and Raleigh, North Carolina. Early in 1869 he was involved in the events surrounding the impeachment of President Andrew Johnson and the replacement of Secretary of War Edwin M. Stanton in Washington, D.C. That fall he was transferred to the Fifth Cavalry and returned to the frontier. There he campaigned against recalcitrant Cheyennes and played a leading role in Gen. Philip H. Sheridan's[qv] winter campaign.

On December 2, 1868, Carr led seven troops of the Fifth Cavalry and one company of the Third Infantry out of Fort Lyon, Colorado. His orders were to join Bvt. Brig. Gen. William H. Penrose, who had left Fort Lyon on November 10 with five cavalry troops, and set up a supply base on or near the North Canadian (Beaver) River from which they could scour the area to the southeast. The column, which included 100 pack mules and 130 wagons, fared well for three days but then ran into a severe blizzard. Thus it was not until December 23, after much agony, that Carr finally reached Penrose's beleaguered camp, with its supplies greatly depleted, on Paloduro Creek in present Texas County, Oklahoma. Pushing on south into the Texas Panhandle, Carr sent out scouting parties and on December 28 established a base on the main Canadian, probably in what is now Roberts County, about twenty miles west of the supply camp set up by Maj. Andrew W. Evans's Canadian River expedition.[qv] From there, Carr was able to replenish his stores somewhat, but his search parties were continually dogged by bad weather and were unable to find any Indians. What was more, forty of Carr's teamsters quit and forfeited their pay rather than endure the icy weather any longer. Thus on January 8, 1869, the "Cossack" gave up the attempt and marched back to Fort Lyon, with the loss of 181 animals and two men from exposure. Among the civilian scouts accompanying his "Dandy Fifth" were James Butler (Wild Bill) Hickok and William F. (Buffalo Bill) Cody, whom Carr highly commended after Cody made a ride to Camp Supply in Indian Territory to deliver dispatches and obtain maps; this was the only foray these legendary frontiersmen ever made into Texas as army scouts. One bit of unpleasantness developed when Hickok and Cody reportedly became involved in a brawl with Penrose's Mexican scouts at the Paloduro Creek campsite, where a supply train from Fort Lyon brought back badly needed provisions.

Whatever failures they suffered in the Panhandle[qv] were practically forgotten the following summer after the success of the Republican River campaign, which culminated in the battle of Summit Springs on July 11, 1869, and gave new hero status to both Carr and Cody, who remained lifelong friends. In 1870 Carr was stationed at Fort McPherson, Nebraska, and later assumed command of the garrison. He was promoted to lieutenant colonel in January 1873 and was placed in command of the Black Hills district. He was one of the leaders in the Big Horn and Yellowstone campaign against the Sioux in 1876. In April 1879, Carr was promoted to colonel of the Sixth Cavalry and transferred to Fort Lowell, Arizona, where he became involved in the campaigns against Victorio's[qv] hostile forces. His hero status achieved new heights after his foolhardy stand against Apaches at Cibicu Creek, west of Fort Apache, on August 30, 1881, an episode that caused controversy in army circles. Carr remained in Arizona until 1884, when his regiment was transferred to Fort Wingate, New Mexico, to maintain order on the Navajo reservation. His last Indian campaign occurred in December 1890, when he took part in the sad events leading to the Wounded Knee Massacre in South Dakota. He was in the field helping to restore order in Wyoming in the wake of the Johnson County War when word came of his promotion to brigadier general, effective in July 1892. Carr and his wife moved back east to Washington, D.C., where they maintained a residence after his retirement in February 1893. In addition, he and his son, Clark, owned ranchland in Valencia County, New Mexico. Carr died in Washington on December 2, 1910, and was buried in the cemetery at his alma mater, West Point. Clark M. Carr, who had volunteered for active service in the army during the Spanish-American War and Philippine Insurrection, subsequently became a successful rancher and businessman in New Mexico.

BIBLIOGRAPHY: Francis B. Heitman, *Historical Register and Dictionary of the United States Army* (2 vols., Washington: GPO, 1903; rpt., Urbana: University of Illinois Press, 1965). James T. King, *War Eagle: A Life of General Eugene A. Carr* (Lincoln: University of Nebraska Press, 1963). William H. Leckie, *The Military Conquest of the Southern*

Plains (Norman: University of Oklahoma Press, 1963). Frederick W. Rathjen, *The Texas Panhandle Frontier* (Austin: University of Texas Press, 1973). Don Russell, *The Lives and Legends of Buffalo Bill* (Norman: University of Oklahoma Press, 1960). *H. Allen Anderson*

CARR, ROBERT GAY (1895–1978). Robert Gay Carr, oilman and philanthropist, son of Milford Marshall and Carrie Bright (William) Carr, was born in North Middletown, Kentucky, on November 9, 1895. After attending public schools and Kentucky Wesleyan College, he worked for oil companies in Houston. He married Nona Kathryn Falk of Houston in 1918 and had one daughter. By 1919 he was head of the land, lease, and scouting department of Humble Oil Company (later Exxon Company, U.S.A.[qv]). In 1926 Carr left that position and with P. G. Northrup of San Angelo formed a partnership that became the field representative of Texas and Pacific Land Trust. The two men were also independent oil operators. Their partnership was dissolved in 1950, and Carr continued as an independent oil operator. He was a member of the Midland Petroleum Club, the Texas Mid-Continent Oil and Gas Association, the Texas Independent Producers and Royalty Owners Association, and the Independent Petroleum Association of America.

Carr served in the United States Air Force during both world wars and helped to bring Goodfellow Air Force Base to San Angelo in 1940. In 1943 he helped secure a bombardier-navigator base, commonly known as Mathis Field, for San Angelo. He endowed the Angelo State University Air Force ROTC detachment with over $1 million, thus making it the largest privately endowed ROTC unit in the nation. For his military services Carr received numerous honors.

He donated the Robert Carr Chapel to Texas Christian University and served on various TCU boards, including the board of trustees (for twenty-three years). TCU conferred an honorary doctorate on him in 1954. Carr was also on the Texas Fish and Game Commission. He gave generously to West Texas Boys Ranch at Tankersley, the San Angelo Emergency Corps, the Salvation Army, St. John's Hospital in San Angelo, and the Shriner Orthopedic Hospital in Houston. After having served the Boy Scouts in various capacities for twenty-five years, he was honored with the Silver Beaver Award. And after years of service to the San Angelo Board of City Development, San Angelo College, and the San Angelo Independent School District, he was named Citizen of the year in San Angelo in 1972. He was a member of the First Christian Church in San Angelo.

Carr died on March 17, 1978, in San Angelo. In his will he endowed a scholarship fund at Angelo State University that financed the Robert G. Carr and Nona G. Carr Academic Scholarships for more than 800 students in the late 1980s. After the death of Mrs. Carr in 1987 all of the Carrs' oil and gas holdings became the property of the university, thus doubling the scholarship fund. The education and fine arts buildings and a dormitory at Angelo State are named in honor of the Carrs.

BIBLIOGRAPHY: Vertical Files, Barker Texas History Center, University of Texas at Austin. *Peggy Skaggs*

CARR-BURDETTE COLLEGE. Carr-Burdette College, at Sherman, was a preparatory school and junior college for women that operated from 1894 to 1929. The founders of the school were O. A. and Mattie F. (Myers) Carr. After missionary work in Australia and administrative duties in Kentucky and Missouri, the Carrs moved to Sherman in the early 1890s. The rapid growth of the North Texas area, partly a result of the emerging agribusiness centers Denison and Sherman convinced the Carrs that a preparatory school for young women was needed. Mattie financed the construction of a large brick building by selling 250 lots at $200 each in Sherman. The "Girls' Home," as Carr called it, sat on an eight-acre campus. The Carrs planned to leave the institution to the Christian Church at Sherman. The college opened in 1894, and for the next fourteen years Mrs. Carr directed its development. After her death in 1907 the Christian Church in Sherman took control of the administrative duties. O. A. Carr died in 1913. During the next sixteen years the enrollment and finances of Carr-Burdette College peaked, stabilized, and then began a slow decline. In 1929 the institution closed. In April 1939 the property was sold, and the two brick buildings were razed.

BIBLIOGRAPHY: J. Breckenridge Ellis, ed., *In Memory of Mrs. O. A. Carr* (Barker Texas History Center, University of Texas at Austin). J. Breckenridge Ellis, *The Story of a Life* (Sherman, Texas: Reynolds-Parker, 1910). Graham Landrum and Allen Smith, *Grayson County* (Fort Worth, 1960; 2d ed., Fort Worth: Historical Publishers, 1967). Sherman *Democrat*, September 19, 1948. *David Minor*

CARRELL, WILLIAM BEALL (1883–1944). William Beall Carrell, an orthopedic surgeon known for his humanitarian efforts with crippled children, was born in Lawrenceburg, Tennessee, on December 21, 1883, the only son of six children of Dr. C. A. and Jennie L. (Herrin) Carrell; the elder Carrell practiced medicine in Cedar Hill, Texas. William Carrell attended college at Southwestern University at Georgetown, where he received his bachelor of science degree in 1905. On September 20 of the same year he married Beulah Stewart of Dallas, the daughter of J. H. Stewart, the district clerk of Dallas County. William and Beulah had two sons and one daughter. Carrell received his degree in medicine in 1908 at Southwestern Medical School in Dallas and interned at St. Paul's Sanitarium in Dallas from 1908 to 1910. He remained in the city to practice until the outbreak of World War I.[qv] He joined the United States Army Medical Corp in December 1917 and was assigned successively to Oklahoma City, Houston, New Orleans, Washington, D.C., Liverpool, England, various sites in France, and finally New York City. He left the army in August 1919 with the rank of major.

Upon returning to Dallas after the war he focused his career on orthopedic surgery, especially among children. He was active in getting state legislation passed to secure care for impoverished children suffering from paralysis. Carrell was one of the founding organizers of the Texas Society for Crippled Children, and he also served on the orthopedic board of the National Foundation for Infantile Paralysis. He did his main work at the Carrell-Girard Clinic in Dallas, where he was senior member. He also served as orthopedic surgeon for Baylor, Methodist, and Parkland hospitals. He was the chief surgeon for the Scottish Rite Hospital for Crippled Children and the Dallas Orthopedic Hospital, and he taught at the Baylor School of Medicine as professor of orthopedic surgery. In 1925 Carrell received the Linz Award, a prestigious honor for Dallas citizens, for outstanding service.

He was a member of the American Medical Association, the Southern Medical Association, the Texas, North Texas, and Dallas Medical societies, and the American College of Surgeons. He was also a member of the Phi Delta Theta and the Kappa Psi fraternities. He was a thirty-third-degree Mason and a member of the Scottish Rite and the Hella Temple Shrine. His other memberships included the Dallas Athletic Club, the Dallas Country Club, the Dallas Automobile Country Club, and the Rotary Club. He was a member of Highland Park Methodist Church. He died at his home in Dallas on February 23, 1944.

BIBLIOGRAPHY: Dallas *Morning News*, February 24, 1944. Dallas *Times Herald*, February 23, 1944. Ellis A. Davis and Edwin H. Grobe, comps., *The Encyclopedia of Texas* (2 vol. ed., 1922?). *Texas State Journal of Medicine*, April 1944. *Kelly Pigott*

CARRICITOS, TEXAS. Carricitos is near the junction of U.S. Highway 281 and Farm Road 2520, seven miles southwest of San Benito in southwestern Cameron County. It is on part of the land that made up the Concepción de Carricitos grant from Spain to Bartolomé and Eugenio Fernández in 1789. The town was named before the Civil War[qv] by Mexican ranchers residing in the area. A post office was in operation there from November 1908 until January 1914. In 1914 the town had a population of 300 and six general stores. By

1936 the community had a school, a cemetery, and various dwellings. In 1948 Carricitos consisted of a store, a school, and a population of twenty-five who received mail from San Benito. In 1956 the community had several dwellings and a cemetery. The population of Carricitos remained at twenty-five from 1948 through 1991. During the 1960s a colonia[qv] developed in the area of Carricitos; by 1986 it was known as Carricitos-Landrum and had forty-five dwellings and a population of 203. *Alicia A. Garza*

CARRICITOS CREEK. Carricitos Creek rises twenty-two miles northwest of Callaghan in central Webb County (at 27°56′ N, 99°46′ W) and runs southwest for fourteen miles to its mouth on the Rio Grande, twenty-three miles northwest of Laredo (at 27°47′ N, 99°49′ W). The creek traverses flat terrain with local shallow depressions, surfaced by expansive clays that support water-tolerant hardwoods, conifers, and grasses.

CARRICK, MANTON MARBLE (1879–1932). Manton Marble Carrick, physician and author, the son of White L. and Cammie Rozina (Thompson) Carrick, was born near Keatchie, Louisiana, on August 17, 1879. He spent most of his childhood in Waxahachie, Texas, where his family moved when he was a boy. After graduating from Dallas Academy in 1897 he began his medical career as assistant house surgeon in the Texas and Pacific Railway Company Hospital in Marshall in 1899. The next year he was the house physician at Parkland Hospital in Dallas. While there, he studied medicine at Fort Worth University and graduated in 1901.

Carrick began his twenty-six-year career in public health in 1903 as a medical officer in the Texas National Guard,[qv] a post he held until 1905. The following year he was the state quarantine officer. In 1910 he was assistant superintendent of the State Epileptic Colony in Abilene (*see* ABILENE STATE SCHOOL) and two years later was appointed superintendent of the Texas State Leper Colony. In 1914 Carrick became professor of preventive medicine at Baylor University. Although he enjoyed teaching and was a popular instructor, he left Baylor in 1917 to enlist as a captain in the Medical Corps of the American Expeditionary Forces. He served four years in the army, rose to the rank of major, and received a commission as surgeon in the United States Public Health Service. While in the army, however, he contracted diabetes mellitus, and he received a disability retirement in 1921. The following year Governor Pat M. Neff[qv] appointed Carrick state health officer.

During the 1920s Carrick conducted sanitary surveys of many cities and towns in the United States and, through a series of articles in scholarly journals and popular magazines, publicized methods of health preservation for the general public. Publications in the *Journal of the Southern Medical Association, Pictorial Review,* and *Ladies Home Journal* attracted the interest of public-health officials throughout the country. One result of Carrick's writings was an invitation to study at the Johns Hopkins University School of Hygiene and Public Health. In 1925 and 1926 Carrick also received two scholarships in general medicine and children's diseases from New York Graduate Medical School and Hospital.

In 1927 he was appointed director of public health and welfare for the city of Dallas by Mayor R. E. Burt. While director, Carrick implemented many of the measures he advocated in his publications. For example, by campaigning against the use of common drinking cups he forced the substitution of paper cups in many public places. His efforts did not go unnoticed. One newspaper editor commented that Carrick "did more for the cause of public health in Texas than anyone else ever did." Unfortunately, his work was cut short by diabetes. From 1929 until 1932 Carrick's failing health confined him to bed. He was nursed by his wife, Mai Connor (Gordon), whom he had married in 1926. Shortly before his death the Dallas County Medical Society elected Carrick an honorary member. He was also a member of the State Medical Association of Texas (now the Texas Medical Association[qv]), the American Medical Association, the American Public Health Association, the American Medical Authors Association, and the American Legion.[qv] He was an Episcopalian, a Mason, and a Democrat. He died on September 17, 1932, and was buried in an Episcopalian cemetery in Waxahachie.

BIBLIOGRAPHY: Dallas *Morning News*, September 18, 1932. *Texas State Journal of Medicine*, November 1932. *David Minor*

CARRINGTON, E. J. (1799–?). E. J. Carrington, one of largest slaveholders in Texas in 1860, owned 103 slaves and was living north of Jones Prairie in Polk County, according to the census of that year. He had real property valued at $22,600 and personal property valued at $70,000, owned 500 improved acres, and produced 2,500 bushels of corn and 200 bales of cotton. Carrington, who was born in Virginia, was a member of the Fourth Texas Cavalry, Riley's Regiment, Green's Brigade. He was twice married and had four children; his second wife was Jane Chamber of Liberty County.

BIBLIOGRAPHY: Randolph B. Campbell, *An Empire for Slavery: The Peculiar Institution in Texas, 1821–1865* (Baton Rouge: Louisiana State University Press, 1989). Emma Haynes, The History of Polk County (MS, Sam Houston Regional Library, Liberty, Texas, 1937; rev. ed. 1968). United Confederate Veterans, Ike Turner Camp, Historical Polk County, Texas (Livingston: Polk County Enterprise, 191-?).
Diana J. Kleiner

CARRINGTON, EVELYN MAURINE (1898–1985). Evelyn Maurine Carrington, psychologist, was born in Austin on August 30, 1898, the daughter of William Leonidas and Bertha (Gray) Carrington. She earned three degrees from the University of Texas: a B.A. in 1919, an M.A. in 1920, and a Ph.D. in 1930. She did further work at the Institute for Juvenile Research and the Michael Reese Hospital in Chicago and at Columbia University. From 1930 to 1941 she taught educational psychology at Sam Houston State Teachers College (now Sam Houston State University), and from 1941 to 1952 she was on the faculty at Texas State College for Women (now Texas Woman's University). She served briefly as administrative director for the Children's Development Center in Dallas and as psychologist and director of instruction at the Shady Brook schools before becoming staff psychologist at Children's Medical Center in Dallas in 1955. She remained with the center until 1973. During most of this period she maintained a private practice in child psychology in Dallas, and from 1955 to 1962 she also lectured at Baylor University College of Dentistry.

Carrington's research interests focused on children's learning, especially as related to the process of learning to read, and on the problems of aging. She was a delegate to two White House conferences on aging and a member of the Governor's Commission on Aging and several organizations concerned with the needs of the elderly. She served on the committee that planned and established the Hogg Foundation for Mental Health[qv] and held the offices of vice president of the Texas Society for Mental Health and president of the International Council of Women Psychologists. She was a fellow of both the Texas Psychological Association[qv] and the American Psychological Association. She was the author of *Mental Health for Older People* (1946), *A Psychologist Looks at the Adolescent Girl* (1946), and *The Exceptional Child: His Nature and His Needs* (1951) and the editor of *Women in Early Texas* (1975). She died in Austin on October 4, 1985, and was buried in Oakwood Cemetery.

BIBLIOGRAPHY: *American Men of Science*, 13th ed. Austin *American-Statesman*, October 6, 1985. *Who's Who of American Women*, 1970–71.
Judith N. McArthur

CARRINGTON CREEK. Carrington Creek rises five miles east of Caldwell in central Burleson County (at 30°31′ N, 96°36′ W) and runs east for ten miles through mostly open country to its mouth on the

Old River, two miles northwest of Snook in eastern Burleson County (at 30°31′ N, 96°29′ W). The stream traverses gently sloping to nearly level terrain surfaced with loamy to clayey soils. Post oak, blackjack oak, elm, hackberry, water oak, and pecan woods border the creek along much of its length. Settlement in the vicinity began in the early 1830s. The Providence Baptist Church, for many years one of the Texas frontier's largest Baptist churches, was established near the headwaters of the creek in 1841. In 1866 the Old Bethlehem Missionary Baptist Church was founded on the north bank of the lower creek. In the 1890s, with an influx of immigrants from Sicily into eastern Burleson County, the community of Tunis was founded on the north bank of the lower creek as a trade center for Italians[qv] laboring on plantations in the Brazos bottomlands. Carrington Creek is named for a prominent family of Burleson County settlers, the first of which, E. C. Carrington, served as county commissioner in 1862 and 1868.

BIBLIOGRAPHY: Burleson County Historical Society, *Astride the Old San Antonio Road: A History of Burleson County, Texas* (Dallas: Taylor, 1980).

CARRIZITOS CREEK. Carrizitos Creek rises seven miles southwest of Callaghan in central Webb County (at 27°46′ N, 99°27′ W) and runs northeast for twenty-two miles to its mouth on Venado Creek, thirteen miles northeast of Callaghan in north central Webb County (at 27°58′ N, 99°12′ W). The name is Spanish for "little cane," after the cane plants that once grew along its banks. The creek traverses low-rolling and flat terrain with locally shallow depressions, surfaced by clay and sandy loams. Local vegetation consists of grasses, mesquite, and chaparral in the creek's upper reaches, changing to water-tolerant hardwoods and grasses in its lower reaches.

CARRIZO CREEK (Dallam County). Carrizo Creek (Carrizo Arroyo) rises in Union County, New Mexico (at 36°25′ N, 103°35′ W) and enters Texas at the western boundary of Dallam County (at 36°14′ N, 103°02′ W); it crosses southern Dallam County for thirty miles and empties into Rita Blanca Creek just west of Dalhart in southeastern Dallam County (at 36°04′ N, 102°35′ W). The creek runs through flat to rolling hills surfaced by clay and sandy loams that support hardwoods, brush, and grasses. Much of the creek was part of the Buffalo Springs division of the XIT Ranch.[qv]

—— (Dimmit County). Carrizo Creek rises eight miles southwest of Carrizo Springs in western Dimmit County (at 28°22′ N, 99°57′ W) and runs northeast for fifteen miles to its mouth on Soldier Slough, four miles east of Carrizo Springs (at 28°34′ N, 99°48′ W). The name is Spanish for the cane grass or reed grass that once grew in the area. The creek rises in flat to rolling terrain surfaced by deep, fine, sandy loam that supports brush and grasses, then descends to flat terrain with locally shallow depressions, surfaced by clay and sandy loams that support water-tolerant hardwoods and grasses.

CARRIZO MOUNTAIN. Carrizo Mountain, the tallest peak in the mountain range of the same name, is twenty-four miles southeast of Sierra Blanca in southeastern Hudspeth County (at 31°04′ N, 104°55′ W). It has an elevation of 4,874 feet above sea level. Some of the oldest Precambrian rocks in Texas, about a billion years old, can be found at the surface in the Carrizos. The shallow, stony soils that form the land surface support scrub brush, creosote bush, cacti, grasses, oak, and mesquite. *Carrizo* is Spanish for "reed grass."

CARRIZO SPRINGS. Carrizo Springs is a line of springs through the town of Carrizo Springs in Dimmit County (at 28°31′ N, 99°52′ W), named for the reeds that grow abundantly near Carrizo Creek. In 1689 the Spaniard Alonso De León[qv] probably refreshed himself at the springs while traveling to Fort St. Louis,[qv] usually presumed to have been in what is now Victoria County. Previously, many Coahuiltecan Indian villages were located at the springs. Irrigation wells have greatly lowered the water level in the Carrizo sand. The spring flow of moderately hard water declined radically in the twentieth century.

BIBLIOGRAPHY: Gunnar Brune, *Springs of Texas*, Vol. 1 (Fort Worth: Branch-Smith, 1981).

Gunnar Brune

CARRIZO SPRINGS, TEXAS. Carrizo Springs, the county seat of Dimmit County, is on U.S. Highway 83 eight miles northwest of Asherton. The name of the town comes from the local springs, which were named by the Spanish for the cane grass that once grew around them. Carrizo Springs is the oldest town in Dimmit County; it was founded in 1865 by a group of fifteen families from Atascosa County, led by Levi English,[qv] who had visited the area earlier. A second group of settlers arrived from Goliad about two years later.

The Carrizo Springs settlement was still quite small in 1880, when Dimmit County was organized. Nevertheless, as the largest and oldest community in the county, it was designated the county seat. In 1880 English donated a parcel of land for a townsite, including land designated for schools, churches, and a courthouse. The town began to grow, and the residents constructed their homes of solid, lasting materials. In 1881 a local group of Masons helped to build the first schoolhouse in Carrizo Springs, and two years later construction began on a courthouse. A newspaper, the Carrizo Springs *Javelin*, began operations in 1884. By 1885 Carrizo Springs had two churches, at least one grocery, a livery stable, a harness and boot shop, and a population of 900. By 1892 the town also had two druggists, a steam gristmill and gin, and a nursery.

Until 1900 the local economy relied primarily on sheep and cattle ranching, but when artesian water was discovered to be a cheap source of irrigation, new settlers arrived and land prices rose. By 1904 there were thirty artesian wells in the Carrizo Springs area, with average flows ranging from forty to 300 gallons of water a minute, irrigating over 1,000 acres of new cropland.

In 1910 the San Antonio, Uvalde and Gulf Railroad opened a spur into Carrizo Springs; that same year the town incorporated. By 1915 the community had grown to 1,200 residents, who supported three churches, two banks, two hotels, an ice plant, several grocery stores, two real estate businesses, and a title company. By 1916 Carrizo Springs had electricity. In the early 1920s a period of drought and low agricultural prices depressed most Dimmit County farmers, but between 1925 and 1927 seventeen new businesses opened and fifty-five new homes were built. The old courthouse was remodeled and enlarged, and ten blocks of the town's business district were paved. By 1928 Carrizo Springs had a population of 2,500. In 1936 the town's population was 2,171. By 1943 the town had a population of 2,494 and sixty-two businesses, and in 1952 it had 4,343 residents and 130 businesses. By the 1980s Carrizo Springs was by far the largest town in the county; in 1982 it had a population of 6,886 and 148 businesses. In 1984 Carrizo Springs was home to the county's only newspaper, the Carrizo Springs *Javelin*, and its only radio station. In 1988 the town reported 7,553 residents and 109 businesses. In 1990 the population was 5,745.

BIBLIOGRAPHY: Carrizo Springs *Javelin*, October 28, 1980. Paul S. Taylor, "Historical Note on Dimmit County, Texas," *Southwestern Historical Quarterly* 34 (October 1930). Laura Knowlton Tidwell, *Dimmit County Mesquite Roots* (Austin: Wind River, 1984). Vertical Files, Barker Texas History Center, University of Texas at Austin.

John Leffler

CARROL CREEK. Carrol Creek rises ten miles north of Howardwick in northwestern Donley County (at 35°10′ N, 100°54′ W) and formerly ran south for eleven miles to its mouth on the Salt Fork of the Red River (at 35°01′ N, 100°54′ W). The main headquarters for Lewis Henry Carhart's[qv] Quarter Circle Heart Ranch[qv] was located on Carrol Creek. The mouth of the creek on the Salt Fork was inundated by Greenbelt Reservoir (now Greenbelt Lake). Carrol Creek runs through flat to rolling terrain with local escarpments, surfaced by deep fine sandy loam that supports native mesquite brush and grasses.

BIBLIOGRAPHY: Willie Newbury Lewis, *Between Sun and Sod* (Clarendon, Texas: Clarendon Press, 1938; rev. ed., College Station: Texas A&M University Press, 1976).

CARROLL, BENAJAH HARVEY (1843–1914). Benajah Harvey Carroll, Baptist leader, pastor, teacher, and author, was born near Carrollton, Mississippi, on December 27, 1843, the seventh child of Benajah and Mary Elisa (Mallard) Carroll. His father was a Baptist preacher who supported his family by farming. The family moved to Arkansas in 1850 and to Burleson County, Texas, in 1858. Carroll entered Baylor University, then at Independence, in 1859 with junior standing. He studied philosophy and became a champion debater. In 1861, just before earning his degree, he left to fight for the Confederacy in Benjamin McCulloch's[qv] Texas Rangers.[qv] He later joined the Seventeenth Texas Infantry of the Confederate Army and served until he was wounded in 1864 in Mansfield, Louisiana. Although Carroll left Baylor before graduating, the institution granted him the B.A. degree. Later he received honorary M.A. and D.D. degrees from the University of Tennessee and an honorary LL.D. degree from Keatchie College, Louisiana.

Despite the influence of his parents, Carroll was deeply troubled over his spiritual condition and privately skeptical toward the rudiments of Christianity. After his return from the war he was crippled and in debt and suffered numerous family crises. He was converted in 1865 at a Methodist camp meeting near Caldwell, Texas. The following year he became an ordained Baptist minister. From 1866 to 1869 Carroll preached in rural Baptist churches in Burleson and McLennan counties and participated in revivals throughout Central Texas. He also taught school and farmed to help support his family. In 1871 he became pastor of the First Baptist Church, Waco, where he remained until 1899. During his pastorate this church became a flagship church of Texas Baptists. Carroll's intellectual acumen and oratorical gifts contributed mightily to his prominence, but more than any single factor a doctrinal debate in 1871 and the publicity surrounding it thrust him to the forefront among the state's Baptists. Editor J. B. Link[qv] of the *Texas Baptist Herald* vigorously promoted Carroll as a rising champion of orthodoxy after the young Waco pastor purportedly vanquished a seasoned Methodist polemicist in an acrimonious confrontation. Proclaimed as a "new giant in Israel," Carroll began publishing a steady stream of trenchant editorials, doctrinal discussions, and sermons in the state's Baptist periodicals. Throughout the 1870s he held important positions on boards and committees of the General Association (a regional forerunner of the Baptist General Convention of Texas) and figured prominently in early negotiations and support efforts aimed at centralizing Texas Baptist educational institutions. In the 1880s he took an active role in consolidating regional associations and conventions into a single unified body, the Baptist General Convention of Texas. Carroll also served on several Southern Baptist Convention committees and addressed the convention on various occasions.

Having publicly maintained a firm stand against liquor since the beginning of his Waco ministry, Carroll, a Democrat, was a natural leadership choice in the McLennan County and statewide prohibition[qv] crusades of the late 1880s. In both he matched words and wits with two of the state's most influential politicians, Richard Coke and Roger Q. Mills.[qqv] Before a crowd of 7,000 in Waco he engaged Mills in a heated three-hour debate that almost ended in a brawl. By weathering abuse in the political arena, he developed an imperviousness to criticism that served him well in guiding Texas Baptists through the turbulent 1890s. During the last decade of his ministry at the First Baptist Church, Carroll was involved directly and indirectly in virtually every controversy that touched Baptists in the state.

Carroll left the First Baptist Church to become corresponding secretary for the Educational Commission, an agency dedicated primarily to securing financial stability for Texas Baptist schools. For the remainder of his career he continued to work for the cause of Christian education. He taught Bible and theology at Baylor from 1872 to 1905. He began a fifteen-year term as chairman of the Baylor University Board of Trustees in 1886. He also served as a trustee of the Southern Baptist Theological Seminary in Louisville, Kentucky, in the 1880s. In 1905 he organized Baylor Theological Seminary, which eventuated in the founding of Southwestern Baptist Theological Seminary in 1908. Carroll taught at the new school, which moved to Fort Worth in 1910, and served as its president until his death.

Carroll's publications include addresses, doctrinal works, sermons, and Bible expositions. His magnum opus is *An Interpretation of the English Bible* (1973), a commentary in seventeen volumes. Baptist leader George Truett called Carroll "the greatest preacher our State has ever known." In 1866 Carroll married Ellen Virginia Bell. Nine children were born to this union. In 1899, after Ellen's death, he married Hallie Harrison. To them was born one son. Carroll died in Fort Worth on November 11, 1914, and was buried in Oakwood Cemetery, Waco.

BIBLIOGRAPHY: Benajah Harvey Carroll Collection (Southwestern Baptist Theological Seminary, Fort Worth). Benajah Harvey Carroll Papers, Texas Collection, Baylor University. James Milton Carroll, *A History of Texas Baptists* (Dallas: Baptist Standard, 1923). Alan J. Lefever, The Life and Work of B. H. Carroll (Ph.D. dissertation, Southwestern Baptist Theological Seminary, 1992). Jeff D. Ray, *B. H. Carroll* (Nashville: Southern Baptist Convention, 1927). Vertical Files, Barker Texas History Center, University of Texas at Austin.

J. A. Reynolds

CARROLL, BENAJAH HARVEY, JR. (1874–1922). Benajah Harvey Carroll, Jr., minister, journalist, author, and diplomat, was born at Waco, Texas, on March 3, 1874, the son of Ellen Virginia (Bell) and Benajah Harvey Carroll.[qv] He received his A.B. degree from Baylor University, took an LL.B. degree at the University of Texas in 1894, and received degrees in theology from the Southern Baptist Seminary at Louisville, Kentucky, in 1900 and 1901. His M.A. and Ph.D. degrees were awarded by Friedrich Wilhelm Universität in Berlin in 1904. He was accomplished in Hebrew, Greek, Latin, French, and Spanish.

Carroll was ordained a minister by the First Baptist Church at Waco in 1894 and served various pastorates in Kentucky and Texas before he surrendered his credentials in 1906. For a time he was head of the department of history and political economy at Baylor University. He was captain and field chaplain of the First United States Volunteers, Texas Cavalry, during the Spanish-American War. Governor S. W. T. Lanham[qv] appointed him to his staff as lieutenant colonel and aide-de-camp in the Texas National Guard.[qv] For seven or eight years Carroll was on the editorial staff of the Houston *Chronicle*.[qv] In 1912 and 1913 he owned, published, and edited a weekly magazine, *The Stylus*, at Houston.

In April 1914 he was appointed United States consul to Venice, where he served during World War I.[qv] He had charge of the first Red Cross war work in Venice and was associated with the defense of the city, where his work earned high and unusual honors, including the red handkerchief and the regimental colors of Garibaldi, the Cross of War, membership in the Alpini Brigade, Gonfaloniere of the Lion of St. Mark, and Ufficiale dell' Ordine della Corona d'Italia. He was later consul at Naples and at Cádiz, Spain.

Carroll wrote *The Genesis of American Anti-Missionism* (1902), *Die Annexion von Texas: Ein Beitrag zur Geschichte der Monroe-Doktrin* (1904); and *A Political History of Europe from 1815 to 1848* (1906). He was editor of a *Standard History of Houston* (1912), and he also produced numerous newspaper articles, poems, and short stories.

Carroll married Daisy Crawford on August 6, 1905. He became ill in Cádiz and died at the English Colonial Hospital at Gibraltar on

March 31, 1922. His body was returned to Texas, and he was buried beside his son in Glenwood Cemetery, Houston, on April 21, 1922.

BIBLIOGRAPHY: *Alcalde* (magazine of the Ex-Students' Association of the University of Texas), April 1923. Austin *Statesman*, October 15, 1922. *Who Was Who in America*, 1943–44.

Charles Chauncey Carroll

CARROLL, GEORGE WASHINGTON (1855–1935). George Washington Carroll, lumber and oil businessman, philanthropist, and prohibition[qv] candidate for vice president, the son of Francis Lafayette and Sarah (Long) Carroll, was born in Mansfield, Louisiana, on April 11, 1855. His father took the family to Beaumont from Louisiana in 1868 and, with others, formed the Long Shingle and Saw Mill. George Carroll went to work for his father's company and soon became foreman. On November 20, 1877, he married Underhill Mixson in Beaumont's first church wedding. They had three sons. In 1877 F. L. Carroll, in company with George Carroll, John Gilbert, and others, founded the Beaumont Lumber Company. By 1892 the younger Carroll was its president and general manager. The family sold the Beaumont Lumber Company to the John Henry Kirby[qv] interests in 1900, but George Carroll continued to hold interest in the Nona Mills Company, also founded by his father, and other lumber companies.

In 1892 Carroll was persuaded by fellow First Baptist Church member Pattillo Higgins[qv] to invest a thousand dollars in the Gladys City Oil Company, which was planning to drill for oil on Spindletop Hill, just a few miles south of Beaumont. Carroll, the only investor actually to put up cash instead of land, was elected president of the company. The first efforts to find oil were unsuccessful, but in 1901, on land leased from the Gladys City Oil Company, Anthony Francis Lucas[qv] brought in the Lucas Gusher, the first well of the great Spindletop oilfield.[qv] By 1903 Carroll had become one of Beaumont's wealthiest men, having made one fortune in lumber and another in oil. In spite of the money he made from Spindletop oil, he came to regret Beaumont's sudden prosperity, which he felt had turned the town into a den of iniquity. Consequently, he conducted a constant but largely ineffective war against drinking, gambling, and prostitution in the town. He ran on the prohibition ticket for governor of Texas in 1902 and for vice president of the United States in 1904. Both campaigns were unsuccessful. Carroll did, however, serve two terms as alderman from Ward No. 3 in the city of Beaumont.

Carroll, who was a devout Baptist, made large contributions to the First Baptist Church of Beaumont and was equally generous to other Baptist causes, particularly Baylor University. He was the founder and first president of the Young Men's Christian Association in Beaumont and gave much of the money for the construction of a new YMCA building in the late 1920s. He was also a pioneer ecologist who believed that indiscriminate cutting of young trees was bad for the environment. His effort to educate his fellow lumbermen to this danger met with little success. By the time of his death, Carroll was no longer wealthy, presumably because he had given away most of his money. He died on December 14, 1935, in a small room in the YMCA building that his money had helped to build.

BIBLIOGRAPHY: James Anthony Clark and Michel T. Halbouty, *Spindletop* (New York: Random House, 1952). W. R. Estep, *And God Gave the Increase: The Centennial History of the First Baptist Church of Beaumont, Texas* (Beaumont: First Baptist Church, 1972).

Judith Linsley and Ellen Rienstra

CARROLL, HORACE BAILEY (1903–1966). H. Bailey Carroll, historian, son of J. Speed and Lena (Russell) Carroll, was born in Gatesville, Texas, on April 29, 1903. He successively attended Southern Methodist University, McMurry College, Texas Technological College (now Texas Tech University) (B.A., M.A., 1928), and the University of Texas (Ph.D., 1935). He began teaching history at Texas Technological College in 1928 and subsequently taught at Texas Wesleyan, Lamar State, Hillsboro, West Texas State, Eastern New Mexico, and Arlington State colleges before returning to the University of Texas in 1942 as a member of the history department, director of research in Texas history, and associate director of the Texas State Historical Association.[qv] In 1946 he became professor of history, director of the association, and editor of its *Southwestern Historical Quarterly* and Junior Historian.[qqv]

Under Carroll's direction and coeditorship the two-volume *Handbook of Texas* was published in 1952. His first work was *Gúadal P'a*, published in 1941; the next year he edited *Three New Mexico Chronicles.* He compiled a bibliography of *Texas County Histories* (1943) and wrote *Texan Santa Fe Trail* (1951), which was followed by his indispensable checklist of *Texas History Theses* (1955). These and twenty-six volumes of the *Quarterly* stand as a monument to his editorial skill and scholarly standards. Fourteen of his articles were published in learned journals, and he served six journals in advisory capacities. He held honorary memberships in a number of regional societies, including the Sons of the Republic of Texas,[qv] and was a member of the Mississippi Valley Historical Association (now the Organization of American Historians), the American Association for State and Local History (of which he was vice president), the Texas Folklore Society,[qv] the Bibliographical Society of the United States and Canada, and the Philosophical Society of Texas.[qv] He was a fellow of the Royal Geographic Society of London and of the Society of American Historians. He received a Rockefeller research grant and wide recognition for his pioneer leadership in the Junior Historian movement,[qv] which originated in Texas and spread throughout the country. Largely because of Carroll's efforts, interested citizens established a fund for the benefit of the Texas State Historical Association. In 1948 he initiated a book-publication program that made possible the issuance of eighty books under the association's colophon by 1990.

Carroll was married on June 3, 1935, to Mary Joe Durning, and they had one son. A cerebral stroke in 1961 impaired his health permanently, although he continued his work almost to the day of his death, May 12, 1966. Each year since 1967 the H. Bailey Carroll Award has been presented to honor the best article in the *Southwestern Historical Quarterly* for the past year.

BIBLIOGRAPHY: George P. Isbell, "Dr. H. Bailey Carroll, 1903–1966," *Southwestern Historical Quarterly* 70 (July 1966). *Proceedings of the Philosophical Society of Texas*, 1966. Vertical Files, Barker Texas History Center, University of Texas at Austin. *Herbert Gambrell*

CARROLL, JAMES JUDSON (1876–1938). James J. Carroll, lumber-company executive, ornithologist, and conservationist, son of Francis W. and Sarah (Womble) Carroll, was born on December 27, 1876, in Burleson County, Texas. His father, a Baptist minister, died about 1880, and he was reared by his uncle, James Milton Carroll,[qv] a prominent minister, educator, and historian of Baptist activities in Texas. Carroll became interested in the natural sciences at the age of twelve and eventually became an authority on the identification of birds. He attended public schools. In 1894 he enrolled in the preparatory department at Baylor University and in the following year in the collegiate department. He contributed specimens to the Baylor University Museum for several years before his appointment in 1901 as curator of the museum and university librarian. In 1902 he was relieved of the position of librarian, but he continued to work as curator until September 1903, when he left the museum to enter private business.

His first articles on natural history were published in the *Naturalist* (1894) and the *Oologist* (1897–98). His most important work, published in the October 1900 issue of the *Auk*, consisted of an annotated list of 185 species of birds recorded in Refugio County, Texas.

In 1903 Carroll married Lena Carter, daughter of lumberman W. T. Carter. Three daughters were born to this marriage. Carroll entered business with his father-in-law at Camden, Texas, and eventually became sales manager of the company of W. T. Carter and Brothers, vice president of the Carter Lumber and Building Company, and president of the Carter Lumber Company. After moving to Houston in 1908 he became a director of the Union National Bank, a member of the Houston Club, the Eagle Rod and Gun Club, and the Tejas Club; he was also an organizer of the Houston Open Forum. Carroll was a life member of the American Ornithologists' Union, a member of the National Audubon Society, an accomplished photographer of birds, and, in his later years, an ardent protector of Texas birdlife.

In 1926 he resumed his studies of birds. He published articles on the avifauna of the "bird islands" (1927), the white pelican (1930), the fulvous tree duck (1932), and the nesting of the robin in Houston (1935). Through his hobby of photography, he came to be an acknowledged authority on the birdlife of the islands along the Texas coast. In the mid-1930s he alerted the National Audubon Society to the hazards facing the birds nesting on the bird islands in the Laguna Madre. Through Carroll's efforts wardens were selected to patrol the islands and the Audubon Society secured leases to establish sanctuaries.

In 1933 he suffered a stroke that curtailed his activities. He died at Houston on February 17, 1938, and, in accordance with his wishes, his body was cremated and the ashes scattered over the bird islands. In 1955 the second chain of bird islands, located in the Laguna Madre between Aransas National Wildlife Refuge and Matagorda Island,[qqv] was leased by the National Audubon Society as part of the Robert Allen Porter Sanctuary. The largest of these six small islands was later named Carroll Island and a monument set thereon to commemorate the efforts of James J. Carroll to protect the nesting areas of Texas waterfowl. Carroll Island and the other islands of the second chain are today important nesting sites for great egrets, snowy egrets, reddish egrets, great blue herons, roseate spoonbills, laughing gulls, brown pelicans, and four species of tern.

BIBLIOGRAPHY: Ellis A. Davis and Edwin H. Grobe, comps., *The New Encyclopedia of Texas* (4 vols. 1929?). Houston *Post*, February 18, 1938. Frank W. Johnson, *A History of Texas and Texans* (5 vols., ed. E. C. Barker and E. W. Winkler [Chicago and New York: American Historical Society, 1914; rpt. 1916]). T. S. Palmer, *Biographies of Members of the American Ornithologists' Union* (Washington, 1954).

Stanley D. Casto

J. Ellison Carroll. Courtesy Western History Collections, University of Oklahoma Library.

CARROLL, JAMES MILTON (1852–1931). James Milton Carroll, Baptist leader and historian, was born in Monticello, Arkansas, on January 8, 1852, the son of Benajah and Mary Elizabeth (Mallard) Carroll; Benajah Carroll was a Baptist minister. The family moved to Burleson County, Texas, in 1858. Both of Carroll's parents died before he was seventeen. In spite of a limited educational background, he entered Baylor University at Independence in January 1873 and graduated five years later with awards in oratory and scholarship. He also received an honorary master of arts degree from Baylor in 1884, when he delivered the commencement sermon.

Carroll pastored churches in Anderson, Burleson, Grimes, and Washington counties, as well as in Corpus Christi, Lampasas, Taylor, Waco, and San Antonio. As an administrator and educator, he founded and was the first president of San Marcos Academy. Later he became president of both Oklahoma Baptist University and Howard Payne College (now Howard Payne University). He was the founder and guiding figure of the Education Commission of the Baptist General Convention of Texas during its first decade of existence. Carroll served as solicitor for the *Texas Baptist and Herald*,[qv] agent for the Southern Baptist Foreign Mission Board in Texas, secretary and statistician for the Baptist General Convention of Texas, financial agent for Baylor College (now Mary Hardin-Baylor University) at Belton, and endowment secretary for Baylor University. He is best remembered for his writings. The best known are *Texas Baptist Statistics* (1895); *A History of Texas Baptists* (1923); *The Trail of Blood* (1931), based on a lecture given in many states in the south; and *B. H. Carroll, The Colossus of Baptist History* (1946), a biography of his brother. Carroll, a man of many talents, also enjoyed a reputation as an amateur ornithologist and owned one of the largest collections of bird eggs in Texas. On December 22, 1870, Carroll married Sudie Eliza Wamble of Caldwell, Texas. He died in Fort Worth on January 11, 1931.

BIBLIOGRAPHY: *Encyclopedia of Southern Baptists* (4 vols., Nashville: Broadman, 1958-82).

J. A. Reynolds

CARROLL, JOHN ELLISON (1862–1942). John Ellison Carroll, champion steer roper and rodeo pioneer, son of J. E. and Mary Carroll, was born in San Patricio County, Texas, on September 14, 1862. As a young man he began working as a cowboy and trail driver in the Panhandle.[qv] He later ranched in Oklahoma and in Tarrant and Crockett counties, Texas, before he and Jim Todd established the 07 Ranch in Reagan County. In 1912 Carroll sold his shares in the ranch and moved to Big Lake, where he lived for the remainder of his life. He won his first major professional contest as a steer roper at Canadian, Texas, in 1888 and was soon classed among the best single-steer ropers in the state. He would challenge anybody, any time, primarily in matched contests where earnings from side bets far exceeded contest prizes. His chief opponent in matched roping from 1900 through 1913 was fellow Texan Henry Clay McGonagil,[qv] whom he defeated for the unofficial world's championship in a legendary three-day, ten-steer match in San Antonio. Carroll set a record that still stands by roping and tying a steer in seventeen seconds; he won $2,000. Thereafter, until he retired from competition around 1913, he proclaimed himself the "world's champion steer roper." He issued postcards bearing this title and his picture alongside a "busted" steer. Thanks to his reputation as a roper Carroll also became a Wild West–show star and performed with such notables as Lucille Mulhall, Tom Mix, and Will Rogers between 1900 and 1910.

Carroll married Marie Wiegand Van Wert on October 16, 1916. She died when their son, J. E. Carroll Jr., was born in 1919, and in 1926 Carroll married Frances Wiegand McClour. He was a Methodist and a Democrat. He served as sheriff of Reagan County from 1931 to 1933 and was county commissioner from 1937 until his death. Carroll remained interested in rodeo throughout his life. During the 1930s he judged the Stamford Cowboy Reunion Rodeo and competed in its Oldtimers' Rodeo. He was also president of the Texas Cowboy Reunion[qv] Oldtimers Association in 1941. He died on April 20, 1942, and is buried in Big Lake Cemetery. He was elected to the National Cowboy Hall of Fame Rodeo Division in Oklahoma City in 1976.

BIBLIOGRAPHY: Foghorn Clancy, *My Fifty Years in Rodeo* (San Antonio: Naylor, 1952). Beth Day, *America's First Cowgirl: Lucille Mulhall* (New York: Messner, 1955). Willard H. Porter, *Who's Who in Rodeo* (Oklahoma City: Powder River, 1982). Hooper Shelton, *50 Years of a Living Legend: Texas Cowboy Reunion and Old-Timers Association* (Stamford, Texas: Shelton, 1979). Carl L. Studer, "First Rodeo in Texas," *Southwestern Historical Quarterly* 48 (January 1945). J. L. Werst, Jr., ed., *The Reagan County Story* (Big Lake, Texas: Reagan County Historical Survey Committee, 1974).

Mary Lou LeCompte

CARROLL, MARY JOE DURNING (1914–1995). Mary Joe Carroll, lawyer, was born in Wichita Falls, Texas, on June 25, 1914, to Joseph H. and Mary (Douglas) Durning. When she was two years old her father, as an employee of Texas Power and Light, moved the family to Sherman, where Mary Joe attended public school and graduated second in her class. She attended the University of Texas on a scholarship won in the University Interscholastic League[qv] state debate championship. She graduated from UT with honors in 1934 and received her M.A. on June 3 of the next year, the day she married H. Bailey Carroll,[qv] a history instructor and graduate student at the university. Except for brief periods—the longest being two years when Bailey Carroll accepted a teaching assignment at another university—the couple made Austin their home. They had two sons. During and after college Mary Joe Carroll did research and editing for Texas historian Walter Prescott Webb.[qv] In the late 1930s she worked as an associate editor of the *Handbook of Texas,* of which her husband was managing editor.

Since her days in high school when she read Clarence Darrow's *The Life of Clarence Darrow,* Mrs. Carroll had wanted to be a lawyer. Not until 1944, however, did she begin her studies. Despite her responsibilities at the *Handbook* and with her family, she persevered and, after taking only one or two classes a semester, graduated with honors in 1955. She also made the Law Review during her senior year. She ranked first among those who took the bar exam with her; it is believed that she was the first woman to do so. She subsequently went to work at an Austin firm, Looney, Clark and Moorehead. Her first assignment was as assistant to one of the senior partners, Judge Everett L. Looney, who was the chief litigator for the firm in both appellate and trial matters. One of her first cases involved the Veterans' Land Board Scandal[qv] of the 1950s, in which Looney's firm represented several of the land dealers accused of fraud, including B. R. Sheffield. When Sheffield was convicted, Mary Joe Carroll was given the task of writing up the appeal brief, which was so long in documentation of the original trial's faults that it had to be bound in two thick volumes. Sheffield's conviction was overturned on appeal. In 1961, Mrs. Carroll's law practice was briefly interrupted when she agreed to be parliamentarian to the Texas Senate under the directorship of Lieutenant Governor Ben Ramsey.[qv] She found this experience valuable in subsequent years when she was called on to draft potential legislation for clients. Throughout her career, she represented a variety of clients, including the Licensed Beverage Distributors Association, the Texas Restaurant Association, the Wholesale Beer Distributors of Texas, and the Texas Brewers Institute. She was also advisory counsel to the Texas National Armory Board, the Texas Farm Bureau,[qv] the Texas Press Association,[qv] and the Texas Daily Newspaper Association. For these last two clients she drafted legislation that eventually became the Open Meetings Act (1967) and the Open Records Act (1973). She was also instrumental in drafting an early version of the Texas Education Code. She was made a partner of her firm, renamed Clark, Thomas and Winters, in 1968, after which she spent most of her time working on appellate cases. Her first appearance as a litigator was in the Texas Supreme Court. Her last appearances were in the same court just before and after her eightieth birthday in 1994.

Significant decisions in which Mary Joe Carroll participated included *Myers v. Martinez,* which ended county dominance by holding that there could be a wet city in a dry county; *Texas Alcoholic Beverage Commission v. Major Brands of Texas, Incorporated,* which gave the state the right to control the source of supply of alcoholic beverages; *Oak Cliff Savings and Loan Association v. Gersh,* the so-called county-line case, which gave savings and loan associations the right to ignore county lines in establishing branches; and *Amex Warehouse Company v. Archer,* in which the court held that the state's notice of appeal operates as a supersedeas. Carroll disliked being called a "woman lawyer," and frequently said that she was a woman, who happened to be a lawyer. She often said that she did not consider the practice of law to be a sexual activity. She observed about her life that she "was born before women could vote; held a license to practice law before women could sit on a state jury in Texas, and was a partner in a major law firm before women had any civil rights." She died at her home on March 17, 1995, after a long illness.

BIBLIOGRAPHY: Mary Joe Carroll and Robert W. Stayton, "Proposed Reorganization of the Supreme Court of Texas—Number of Judges," *Texas Law Review* 33 (October 1955). Robert Etnyre, The Texas Open Records Act: A History and an Assessment (M.A. thesis, University of Texas at Austin, 1975). Thomas L. Miller, *The Public Lands of Texas, 1519–1970* (Norman: University of Oklahoma Press, 1972). *Texas Legal Directory,* 1994.

Tracé Etienne-Gray

CARROLL, TEXAS. Carroll is at the intersection of State Highway 110 and Interstate Highway 20, three miles west of Mount Sylvan in northwest Smith County. Rattlesnake Creek flows to the west and Allen Branch to the east. The area was settled by 1890, when the community was granted a post office with Joseph S. Hobbs as the postmaster. In 1892 the community had a population of 125, a teacher, a barber, and a justice of the peace. The only businesses were two general stores, a gristmill, and a cotton gin. The growth of nearby Lindale, on the International–Great Northern Railroad, soon overshadowed Carroll, and in 1901 the post office moved there. In 1903 postmaster John H. Moseley transferred it back to Carroll. That year forty black students attended a one-teacher school at Carroll, and seventy-seven white children were enrolled in a two-teacher facility. The post office moved back to Lindale in 1904. In 1910 Carroll's population was twenty-five. In the 1930s and 1940s Carroll reported ninety-eight inhabitants and never more than three businesses. Maps for 1936 identify the school, a church, three businesses, and approximately fifteen dwellings on bituminous and dirt roads. Carroll school records for that year show 154 white pupils and four teachers. The fifty-one local black children were not in school. In 1940 a school, a church, and two businesses were reported. The population had decreased to sixty in 1950. By 1952 the Carroll schools had been consolidated into the Lindale Independent School District. The community had only one business in 1973, but by 1981 there were two churches and six businesses located along Interstate 20. In 1990 the population remained at sixty.

BIBLIOGRAPHY: Edward Clayton Curry, An Administrative Survey of the Schools of Smith County, Texas (M.Ed. thesis, University of Texas, 1938). "Post Offices and Postmasters of Smith County, Texas: 1847–1929," *Chronicles of Smith County*, Spring 1966. "School Sights," *Chronicles of Smith County*, Fall 1969. Smith County Historical Society, *Historical Atlas of Smith County* (Tyler, Texas: Tyler Print Shop, 1965). Albert Woldert, *A History of Tyler and Smith County* (San Antonio: Naylor, 1948).

Vista K. McCroskey

CARROLL CHAPEL, TEXAS. Carroll Chapel, on State Highway 14 fourteen miles south of Corsicana in southern Navarro County, was established before 1900. By the early 1900s a school was in operation there, and in 1906 it had an enrollment of twenty-five. In the mid-1930s the settlement comprised a church, a cemetery, and a number of houses. After World War II[qv] many of the residents moved away, and by the mid-1960s only the cemetery and a few scattered houses remained. In 1990 Carroll Chapel was a dispersed rural community.

Christopher Long

CARROLL CREEK. Carroll Creek rises six miles south of Jacksboro in south central Jack County (at 33°08′ N, 98°07′ W) and runs northeast for 12½ miles to its mouth on the West Fork of the Trinity River, eight miles northeast of Jacksboro (at 33°15′ N, 98°01′ W). The creek traverses gently sloping to steep terrain with well-drained stony and loamy soils that support tall prairie grasses near its banks. Carroll Creek was named for James A. Carroll, a surveyor for the land near its banks in the mid-1850s. The area has been used as rangeland and for mineral production.

CARROLL SPRINGS, TEXAS. Carroll Springs was just off Farm Road 1615, twelve miles southeast of Athens in far southern Henderson County. It was evidently founded around the time of the Civil War[qv] and was named for a nearby spring. In the mid-1930s the settlement had a church, a school, and a number of houses. After World War II[qv] the school closed. In the early 1990s only a church, a cemetery, and a few houses remained.

Christopher Long

CARROLLTON, TEXAS. Carrollton is on Interstate Highway 35 East fourteen miles north of downtown Dallas in Dallas, Denton, and Collin counties. The site was in the Peters colony[qv] grant. The first settlers in the area were William and Mary Larner, who came in 1842. The A. W. Perry family followed two years later and claimed their headright in the Trinity Mills area. In partnership with Wade H. Witt, Perry established a mill there. Over time he acquired extensive landholdings, which probably included the site of Carrollton. Many early settlers were related by blood or marriage. In the northeastern area of settlement, which extended into Denton County, was the English colony, where many of the large landowners, including the Jackson, Furneaux, Morgan, and Rowe families, were English immigrants. It is most likely that the settlement was named for Carrollton, Illinois, the hometown of many of the early settlers.

In the early days Carrollton was an exclusively agricultural community. In 1846 David Myers, from Illinois, established the first Baptist church in Dallas County near the site of present Carrollton. Around 1856 the Union Baptist Church became the site of the first community school. In 1878 an agent for the unfinished Dallas and Wichita rail line filed an early plat of Carrollton at the Dallas County Courthouse. In the same year the Carrollton post office was established. The unfinished railway was bought and extended to Denton in 1880 by Jay Gould,[qv] who subsequently sold it to the Missouri, Kansas and Texas in 1881. By 1885 Carrollton had cotton gins, flour mills, a school, and two churches serving its population of 150. When the Cotton Belt line crossed the Katy at Carrollton in 1888 the town developed as a shipping center for livestock, grain, cotton, and cottonseed; it eventually surpassed Trinity Mills, an older settlement to the north. In 1913 the city was incorporated, and W. F. Vinson was elected the first mayor. A gravel industry began in 1912 and grew, so that by the late 1940s Carrollton was a "grain and gravel" town that also supported a dairy industry. A brick plant furnished brick for Dallas. During the postwar era the city worked to attract major industries. National Metal Products, a manufacturer of metal utility cabinets and shelving, established itself there in 1946.

With the Sun Belt boom, especially as it affected the Dallas area, Carrollton grew rapidly. The population was 1,610 in 1950, 4,242 in 1960, and 13,855 by 1970. Between 1970 and 1980 it increased 193 percent, to 40,595; almost three-quarters of the year-round housing units in the city were built during that decade. In 1983, when the population was 52,000, the major area industries included auto-parts distribution, food packing, light manufacturing, and manufacturing of computers, semiconductors, and electronic components. Nevertheless, Carrollton retained a remnant of frontier living; in 1983 it still had a working cattle ranch within its city limits. Carrollton is part of the area called Metrocrest, a group of four northwest Dallas County cities (including Addison, Coppell, and Farmers Branch) served by a single chamber of commerce.

Four railroads—the Katy, St. Louis–Southwestern, St. Louis–San Francisco, and Burlington-Northern—provide service to the city, which has access to the airports of the Dallas–Fort Worth metropolitan area. Carrollton is served by the daily Carrollton *Chronicle* and the weekly *Metrocrest News.* The Peters Colony Historical Society researches and records area history and publishes its *Elm Fork Echoes* semiannually. In 1990 the population of Carrollton was 82,169.

BIBLIOGRAPHY: Georgia Myers Ogle, comp., *Elm Fork Settlements: Farmers Branch and Carrollton* (Quanah, Texas?: Nortex, 1977).

Joan Jenkins Perez

CARSON, CHRISTOPHER HOUSTON (1809–1868). Christopher Houston (Kit) Carson, frontiersman, son of Lindsey and Rebecca (Robinson) Carson, was born on December 24, 1809, in Madison County, Kentucky. The family moved in 1811 to Howard County, Missouri, where Kit grew up illiterate. He ran away to Santa Fe in 1826, learned Spanish, and trapped from Taos to California and back in 1829–31. He became a veteran mountain man before he was twenty-one. As a free trapper for many different companies during the next ten years, he led an arduous life and became familiar with a vast area only partly within the United States. In 1842, after eight months as hunter for Bent's Fort in what is now Colorado, he visited relatives in Missouri.

Carson was guide and hunter for John C. Frémont's first three explorations between 1842 and 1846 and became a national hero through Frémont's published reports. Carson's exploits in the Mexican War[qv] and subsequent overland transcontinental journeys with Edward F. Beale and George D. Brewerton caused him to be lionized in Washington, D.C. In 1854 he was appointed Indian agent at Taos, New Mexico, and learned to sign his name, C. Carson. In 1856 he dictated his concise and factual memoirs to his secretary, John Mostin.

Though Carson's knowledge of Indian languages and customs made him an effective agent, he resigned his agency in 1861 and became colonel of the First New Mexico Volunteers. He fought the Confederates at the battle of Valverde[qv] in 1862. In 1863–64, under orders from Gen. James H. Carleton, Carson conducted a successful campaign against the Navajos but was not in charge of the "Long Walk," which transferred them to a reservation at the Bosque Redondo.

Carson was brevetted brigadier general of volunteers and was in command at Fort Garland, Colorado, in 1866–67. He resigned his commission, moved his family to Boggsville, Colorado, and became Indian agent for Colorado Territory in November 1867. Although seriously ill, he conducted a Ute delegation to Washington, D.C., early in 1868. He died at Fort Lyons, Colorado, from an aneurysm of the aorta on May 23, 1868.

From about 1836 to 1840 Carson was married to an Arapaho, Waanibe, by whom he had two daughters. In 1841 he married a Cheyenne, who soon divorced him. In February 1843, after conversion to Catholicism, Carson married Josefa Jaramillo in Taos, and by her he had seven children, of whom four left descendants. The couple also adopted a Navajo orphan. Josefa died after childbirth in April of 1868. Kit and Josefa were first buried in Boggsville in the Colorado Territory. Their remains were moved to Taos in 1869, as Carson's will stipulated.

In Texas history Carson was connected with an international border incident in 1843 (see SNIVELY EXPEDITION). He made a hazardous ride from what is now Kansas to Taos and back in an effort to secure aid for a wagon train, which was ultimately saved by the intervention of United States Dragoons. A second Texas adventure was Carson's fight at the first battle of Adobe Walls[qv] on November 26, 1864, against a large number of Kiowas and Comanches. Aided by two howitzers, Carson made a demonstration of force that may have helped to produce a peace treaty in 1865.

As trapper, explorer, Indian agent, and soldier, Carson fought hostile Indians innumerable times. He also had a variety of peaceable relations with friendly Indians and treated Indians as equals. Myth-makers in his own time made Carson a superhero by exaggerating his Indian fighting. Later myth-makers have tried to make him a supervillain by the same process.

Carson was of short stature and unimpressive demeanor and was extraordinary in his willingness to volunteer for what he believed to be the common good. Although fearless, he had enough caution to survive. He was not a natural leader but acted as difficult circumstances demanded, though he remained modest and unspoiled by adulation. Kit Carson is one of the most deservedly durable of American heroes.

BIBLIOGRAPHY: Harvey Lewis Carter, *"Dear Old Kit": The Historical Christopher Carson with a New Edition of the Carson Memoirs* (Norman: University of Oklahoma Press, 1968). Thelma S. Guild and Harvey L. Carter, *Kit Carson* (Lincoln: University of Nebraska Press, 1984). Lawrence C. Kelly, ed., *Navajo Roundup* (Boulder: Pruett, 1970).

Harvey L. Carter

CARSON, SAMUEL PRICE (1798–1838). Samuel Price Carson, planter and lawmaker, son of John and Mary (Moffitt) Carson, was born at Pleasant Gardens, North Carolina, on January 22, 1798. The elder Carson was a "man of means and an iron will" who represented Burke County in the North Carolina General Assembly for many years. Samuel Carson was educated in the "old Field school" until age nineteen, when his brother, Joseph McDowell Carson, began teaching him grammar and directing a course of reading to prepare him for a political career. As a young man Carson also attended camp meetings with his Methodist mother and was often called upon to lead congregational singing.

In 1822 he was elected to the North Carolina Senate. Two years later he was chosen to the first of his four terms (1825–33) as a member of the United States House of Representatives, where he became a close friend of David Crockett.[qv] Carson was defeated in 1833 because he had supported John C. Calhoun's nullification meeting in spite of his constituents' disapproval. He was reelected to the North Carolina Senate in 1834 and was selected as a delegate to the North Carolina Constitutional Convention in 1835. His failing health prompted him to move to a new home in Mississippi. In a very short time, however, he moved on to Lafayette (now Miller) County, Arkansas, an area then claimed by both Texas and Arkansas. On February 1, 1836, he was elected one of five delegates to represent Pecan Point and its vicinity at the Convention of 1836.[qv] On March 10 he reached Washington-on-the-Brazos and immediately signed the Texas Declaration of Independence.[qv]

With regard to legislative and constitution-drafting experience, Carson was the outstanding member of the convention. On March 17 he was nominated, along with David G. Burnet,[qv] for president ad interim of the Republic of Texas,[qv] but he was defeated by a vote of 29 to 23. Thereupon Carson was elected secretary of state, an office he held only a few months. On April 1, 1836, President Burnet sent him to Washington to help George C. Childress and Robert Hamilton[qqv] secure financial and other aid for the infant republic. In May, Burnet wrote Carson asking him to resign because of his poor health, but Carson evidently did not receive the letter. When Carson read in a June newspaper that two other men were the only authorized agents for Texas, he retired in disgust to his Arkansas home.

On May 10, 1831, he married Catherine Wilson, daughter of James and Rebecca Wilson of Burke County, North Carolina. The couple had a daughter. They also adopted Carson's illegitimate daughter, Emily, whose mother was Emma Trout, a North Carolina neighbor of Carson's. Carson died on November 2, 1838, at Hot Springs and was buried there in the United States government cemetery. Carson County, Texas, is named in his honor.

BIBLIOGRAPHY: Michael R. Hill, The Carson House of Marion, North Carolina (MS, Barker Texas History Center, University of Texas at Austin, 1982). Louis Wiltz Kemp, *The Signers of the Texas Declaration of Independence* (Salado, Texas: Anson Jones, 1944; rpt. 1959). Rupert N. Richardson, "Framing the Constitution of the Republic of Texas," *Southwestern Historical Quarterly* 31 (January 1928). Texas House of Representatives, *Biographical Directory of the Texan Conventions and Congresses, 1832–1845* (Austin: Book Exchange, 1941).

Joe E. Ericson

CARSON, WILLIAM C. (1790–1836). William C. Carson, one of Stephen F. Austin's[qv] Old Three Hundred[qv] colonists, was born in Delaware in 1790 and moved to Texas from Indiana or possibly Louisiana about 1824. He was married to Katherine (Catherine) Patterson, and the couple had five children. Carson received title to a league of land now in Brazoria County on May 15, 1827. He was reportedly in poor health when he arrived in Texas and died before the end of the Texas Revolution[qv] in 1836. His widow and children fled to the Sabine in the Runaway Scrape[qv] that year. His widow married Gail Borden, Sr., in 1842.

BIBLIOGRAPHY: Lester G. Bugbee, "The Old Three Hundred: A List of Settlers in Austin's First Colony," *Quarterly of the Texas State Historical Association* 1 (October 1897). James A. Creighton, *A Narrative History of Brazoria County* (Angleton, Texas: Brazoria County Historical Commission, 1975). Daughters of the Republic of Texas, *Founders and Patriots of the Republic of Texas* (Austin, 1963–).

CARSON, TEXAS. Carson, originally Gum Springs, is on Farm Road 1396 ten miles northeast of Bonham in northeastern Fannin County. In the late nineteenth century the settlement served area farmers as a school and church community. Between 1898 and 1907 Carson had a post office and, at one time, a cotton gin. The population was estimated at twenty-two in 1990.

BIBLIOGRAPHY: *Fannin County Folks and Facts* (Dallas: Taylor, 1977).

David Minor

CARSON COUNTY. Carson County (C-4), in the center of the Panhandle[qv] and on the eastern edge of the Texas High Plains, is bounded on the north by Hutchinson County, on the west by Potter County, on the south by Armstrong County, and on the east by Gray County. Carson County was named for Samuel P. Carson,[qv] the first secretary of state of the Republic of Texas.[qv] The center of the county lies at roughly 35°25′ north latitude and 101°22′ west longitude. The county occupies 900 square miles of level to rolling prairies surfaced by dark clay and loam that make the county almost completely tillable and productive. Native grasses and various crops such as wheat, oats, barley, grain sorghums, and corn flourish. The huge Ogallala Aquifer beneath the surface provides water for people, crops, and livestock. Trees, usually cottonwood, oak, or elm, appear, along with mesquite, in the county's creekbottoms. Antelope and Dixon creeks, both intermittent streams, run northward from central Carson County to their mouths on the Canadian River in Hutchinson County. McClellan Creek, also intermittent, runs eastward across the southeastern corner of the county to join the Red River. Carson County ranges from 3,200 to 3,500 feet in elevation, averages 20.92 inches of rain per year, and varies in temperature from a minimum average of 21° F in January to a maximum average of 93° in July. The growing season averages 191 days a year.

Prehistoric hunters first occupied the area, and then the Plains Apaches arrived. Modern Apaches followed them and were displaced by Comanches, who dominated the region until the 1870s. Spanish exploring parties, including those of Francisco Vázquez de Coronado[qv] in the 1540s and Juan de Oñate[qv] in the early 1600s, crisscrossed the Texas Panhandle, but it is not known if they traversed Carson County. American buffalo[qv] hunters penetrated the Panhandle in the early 1870s as they slaughtered the great southern herd. The ensuing Indian wars, culminated by the Red River War[qv] of 1874, led to the extermination of the buffalo and the removal of the Comanches to Indian Territory. The Panhandle was thus opened to settlement. Carson County was established in 1876, when its territory was marked off from the Bexar District.

Ranchers appeared in Carson County in the early 1880s. The JA Ranch[qv] of Charles Goodnight and John G. Adair[qqv] and the Turkey Track Ranch[qv] both grazed large ranges in Carson County by 1880. In 1882 Charles G. Francklyn purchased 637,440 acres of railroad lands in Gray, Carson, Hutchinson, and Roberts counties, 281,000 of them in Carson County. The newly formed Francklyn Land and Cattle Company,[qv] with B. B. Groom[qv] as manager, attempted to ranch and farm on a large scale, but failed. The lands of the Francklyn Company were sold to the White Deer Lands Trust of British bondholders in 1886 and 1887.

In the later 1880s the railroads reached Carson County. By 1886 the Southern Kansas Railway, a subsidiary of the Atchison, Topeka and Santa Fe, had built from Kiowa, Kansas, to the Texas–Indian Territory border. The Southern Kansas of Texas Railway was formed to extend the line into Texas. Panhandle City, a temporary railhead, was founded in 1887 in anticipation of the railroad line, which finally reached the town in 1888. The town grew, and its occupants hoped that another rail line, the Fort Worth and Denver City, which was building from Fort Worth across the Panhandle to Colorado, would pass through their city. As it happened, the Fort Worth and Denver City missed Panhandle City by fourteen miles to the south, just touching the southwestern corner of the county. In 1889 the two lines were finally linked by a fourteen-mile span between Panhandle City and Washburn, a station on the Fort Worth and Denver City. By 1890 Carson County had a rail network, and its first town, soon known simply as Panhandle; that year, the United States census listed twenty-eight ranches or farms in the area, and 356 people were living in the county, all of them white and twenty-nine of them foreign-born.

The establishment of ranches and railroad construction led to a need for local government. A petition for organization was circulated through the county in 1888, and in November of that year an election was held. Panhandle, the county's only town at that time, was designated the county seat. Despite organization, however, the county remained a ranching area throughout the 1890s, with a small population and only a handful of farmers and stock raisers appearing as the decade wore on. As late as 1900 only 469 people were living in Carson County, and only fifty-six farms and ranches had been established.

Water had to be brought to Panhandle by railroad from the area of Miami in Roberts County, then carried in barrels on wagons to homesteads. This problem hindered development until it was found that abundant underground water could be pumped to the surface by windmills.[qv] That discovery, together with the selling of White Deer lands to small ranchers and farmers in 1902, greatly increased the area's attractiveness. During the next thirty years a modern agricultural economy emerged, based on the production of livestock, wheat, corn, and grain sorghum.

Continued railroad expansion during the first decades of the twentieth century helped to encourage farmers to settle in the area. The Choctaw, Oklahoma and Texas Railroad built from the Texas–Oklahoma Territory border to Yarnall, crossing the southern edge of Carson County on an east–west line. The townsites of Groom, Lark, and Conway appeared at this time along the railroad right-of-way. In 1904 the Chicago, Rock Island and Gulf bought this line. In the early 1900s the Santa Fe Railroad decided to improve its Kansas–Texas–New Mexico line and make it a major transcontinental route. The Santa Fe already had access to the Southern Kansas of Texas line from the Oklahoma Territory border to Panhandle City. In 1908 the Southern Kansas of Texas extended its line from Panhandle City to Amarillo, thus completing the Texas section of the Santa Fe's transcontinental route.

During the early twentieth century both Europeans and Americans built the agricultural economy of the county and added variety to the cultural milieu of the Panhandle. Anglo-American farmers arrived early in the century, settling as early as 1901 and 1902 around the new town of Groom in the southeastern corner of the county. A large number of German Catholics arrived in western Carson County and eastern Potter County between 1909 and the 1920s. They established St. Francis, a community that straddles the Potter-Carson county line. This community retained its ethnic character into the 1990s. Likewise, a large Polish Catholic population developed in the eastern part of the county on lands purchased from White Deer lands by immigrants. They began to arrive in 1909 and centered their community around a new village named White Deer, laid out in the same year. This community has also retained the cultural heritage of the settlers.

Between 1900 and 1930 farming activity in the county markedly increased. By 1910, 284 farms had been established in the county; by 1920, 426; and by 1930, 542. Meanwhile, the United States Census Bureau reported that the number of "improved" acres in the county had jumped from only 4,663 in 1900 to over 241,620 in 1930. Local farmers concentrated on growing corn, oats, sorghum, and particularly wheat; by 1930 wheat culture[qv] occupied more than 182,740 acres. By 1930 242,000 acres, or 42 percent of the entire county, was used for farming. Meanwhile, cattle ranching remained an important component of the economy. Carson County ranchers owned 18,435 cattle in 1900, 22,587 in 1910, 28,370 in 1920, and 16,621 in 1930.

During the 1920s and 1930s the oil and gas industry became another major component of Carson County's economy. Experimental drilling by Gulf Oil Corporation[qv] led to the county's, and the Panhandle's, first oil and gas production in late 1921. Little activity occurred, however, until the discovery of the huge Borger field, thirty miles north, in 1925, when a wave of oil exploration and production swept the Panhandle, including Carson County. By the end of 1926 the county had produced over a million barrels of oil and had also emerged as a large natural gas producer. Oilfield activity led to renewed railroad construction in the county and to the construction of another town. In 1926 the Panhandle and Santa Fe built a thirty-two-mile spur from Panhandle to Borger to tap the oil profits. In 1927 the same railroad built a ten-mile spur from White Deer to Skellytown, a new town built that year by Skelly Oil to serve a recently constructed refinery. Thus, by the 1930s Carson County had a diversified economy based on ranching, farming, petroleum, and transportation.

As the county's economy developed between 1900 and 1930, its population rose. In 1910 the census counted 2,027 residents in Carson County, and by 1930 the population had increased to 7,745. During the Great Depression[qv] of the 1930s, however, agricultural production dropped off, and many local farmers were forced to leave their lands. Cropland harvested in the county dropped from 220,734 acres in 1929 to 180,971 in 1940; the number of farms dropped during the same period from 542 to 493. The population of the county as a whole declined by 15 percent during the years of the depression, falling to 6,624 by 1940.

During and since World War II[qv] defense spending by the federal government has helped the local economy. In September 1942 the Pantex Ordnance Plant (*see* PANTEX, TEXAS) began to manufacture bombs and artillery shells. The plant was on 16,076 acres of southwestern Carson County land, where it operated until August 1945. In 1949 Texas Technological College (now Texas Tech University) acquired the site for use as an agricultural experiment station. During the Korean War, however, the federal government took back more than 10,000 acres of the site for use as a nuclear weapons assembly plant. By the 1980s Pantex had become the only nuclear assembly plant in the country; it employed more than 2,500 people and had been the scene of numerous antinuclear protests.

By the 1920s State Highway 33 (now U.S. Highway 60) ran from Oklahoma through Canadian, Pampa, and Panhandle, then proceeded to Amarillo, where it joined U.S. Highway 66. During the 1930s paved state roads were built from Panhandle north to Borger and south to Conway, on U.S. 66. Farm and ranch roads also appeared during those years. In the 1960s Interstate Highway 40, from Oklahoma City to Amarillo, was built across the southern portion of the county along the route of old U.S. 66, which was originally built in the 1920s.

Though petroleum production in the area has declined, Carson County has remained a substantial, if not spectacular, producer of oil and gas. In 1946 county wells pumped 4,955,000 barrels of petroleum; in 1978, 1,360,000; and in 1990, 747,000. By the end of 1990 more than 172,852,460 barrels of petroleum had been produced from county lands.

Carson County therefore has a balanced and diversified economy based on ranching, farming, oil, transportation, and the Pantex plant. Most of the farmland is located in the eastern part of the county, while the western part remains ranchland. In the 1940s and 1950s many local farmers drilled irrigation wells to tap the Ogallala Aquifer, and by the 1980s about 33 percent of cultivated land in the county was irrigated. The local agricultural economy remained relatively static after the 1940s; by 1982, land under cultivation totaled 281,424 acres. The number of farms and farmers declined, however, as mechanization led to a growth in farm size and corresponding decline in the number of farms.

The population of the county also remained essentially stable after World War II. It rose from 6,624 in 1940 to 6,852 in 1950, and again to 7,781 by 1960. It declined somewhat during the 1960s to 6,358 in 1970, then rose again to 6,672 in 1980. In 1990 the population of the county was 6,576. The bulk of the county's population now lives in its towns, which include White Deer, Skellytown, Groom, and Rocky Mount. Panhandle (1990 population 2,353) is Carson County's largest town and its seat of government.

BIBLIOGRAPHY: Rual Dewey Ford, A Survey History of Carson County, Texas (M.A. thesis, University of Colorado, 1933). Donald E. Green, *Fifty Years of Service to West Texas Agriculture: A History of Texas Tech University's College of Agricultural Sciences, 1925–1975* (Lubbock: Texas Tech University Press, 1977). *Highways of Texas, 1927* (Houston: Gulf Oil and Refining, 1927). Jo Stewart Randel, ed., *A Time to Purpose: A Chronicle of Carson County* (4 vols., Hereford, Texas: Pioneer, 1966–72). Texas Crop and Livestock Reporting Service, *Texas County Statistics* (Austin: Texas Department of Agriculture, 1980).

Donald R. Abbe

CARSON COUNTY SQUARE HOUSE MUSEUM. The Square House Museum in Panhandle, Texas, opened in 1967. The museum complex started with one twenty-four-foot square house, one of the oldest houses in Carson County, and grew by 1986 to eight structures. The buildings and exhibits include the Opal R. Weatherly Purvines Annex with costume and changing art exhibits, the pioneer dugout dwelling, the Santa Fe Railroad Caboose, a bank exhibit and blacksmith shop, Freedom Hall with history exhibits, Moody Hall with wildlife exhibits, and the Finch, Lord, and Nelson farm and ranch exhibits. An Eclipse windmill stands on the grounds. Private and corporate funding has provided for building museum structures and for operation and maintenance of the facility; county support pays for utilities and staff salaries. The museum also holds one major fundraiser annually, at Museum Day in the fall.

More than 10,000 artifacts are housed at the museum, including documents, photographs, historical items, guns, natural history specimens, and archeological artifacts. Bronze sculptures and a large collection of Indian art add to the fine arts collection. Educational tours and outreach programs for local and area schools are an integral part of the educational program. A Summer Youth Arts program involves students from all county towns. Adult organizations tour the museum and attend museum-sponsored lecture series. The museum has an active publication program, which has produced a history of Carson County, a cookbook, a children's book, and historical videos. The museum newsletter is sent quarterly to supporters. The Square House Museum is accredited by the American Association of Museums and has been awarded the American Association for State and Local History National Award of Merit.

BIBLIOGRAPHY: Carson County Square House Museum *Newsletter*, Summer 1986.

Mogie R. McCray

CARSON CREEK. Carson (Kit Carson) Creek rises in northeastern Hutchinson County (at 35°57′ N, 101°16′ W) and runs southeast for eleven miles to its mouth on the Canadian River (at 35°50′ N, 101°12′ W). It crosses flat to rolling plains with sandy and clayey soils that support mesquite and various grasses. The stream was named for Col. Christopher Houston Carson,[qv] who mounted his bold but unsuccessful attack against marauding Comanches and Kiowas at the nearby Adobe Walls site in November 1864. Carson Creek is now part of the Turkey Track Ranch[qv] properties.

BIBLIOGRAPHY: Pauline D. and R. L. Robertson, *Cowman's Country: Fifty Frontier Ranches in the Texas Panhandle, 1876–1887* (Amarillo: Paramount, 1981).

CAR-STABLE CONVENTION. The Texas Democratic gubernatorial nominating convention met in a streetcar stable in Houston on August 16 and 17, 1892. Earlier in the year the state party had apportioned 958 convention votes among the various counties. On Saturdays between May 21 and August 1, county Democratic party[qv] committees conducted conventions or held primary elections to choose candidates. The two gubernatorial candidates, James S. Hogg and George W. Clark,[qqv] met in debates and gave speeches, first in one section of the state and then in another, as the primary and convention battle switched from one county to another. During his first term in office, Governor Hogg had made friends as well as enemies in his push for the establishment of the Railroad Commission,[qv] members of which were appointed by the governor. Clark, a prominent railroad lobbyist, believed that the commission had stifled the Texas economy. Clark wanted Railroad Commission members elected and more open to public influence, but so did populists among farming interests who otherwise were hostile to the railroads.

As convention time approached, votes pledged to Hogg appeared to total more than the two-thirds majority necessary to renominate him. He needed 632 convention votes to be renominated, and estimates appearing in newspapers in Dallas, Austin, and Beeville gave him from 626 to 674. With victory out of the question, the Clark supporters worked to block Hogg's renomination, or, as Hogg supporters put it, "to rule or ruin." If Hogg had failed to get 632 votes, the convention would have been forced to nominate a compromise candidate; former governor James W. Throckmorton,[qv] an avid railroad supporter, was mentioned as a possibility. Clark delegates hoped to gain control of the convention by electing, on a voice vote, a Clark supporter as temporary chairman. By controlling the convention, the Clark supporters could take votes away from Hogg in contested counties such as Bexar and Dallas.

Clark supporters planned to increase the volume of their voices by splitting each of their votes among several persons. The Harris County delegation, for example, planned to use fifty delegates to cast thirteen convention votes. The state executive committee learned of this plan and ruled that a vote could be split between no more than two delegates. The Hogg-controlled committee also decided who would get delegate badges and who would not, and a fence was erected around the car stable to block out all persons without proper badges. Clark delegates said they would not wear the "badge of servitude" but planned to enter the car stable anyway. Newton W. Finley,[qv] the state party chairman and a Hogg supporter, opened the convention with a move to elect a temporary chairman on a roll-call vote. This procedure would ensure the election of T. S. Shepard, Hogg's choice for the position. At the same time, the Clark delegates shouted for the election of their nominee, Jonathan Lane.[qv] Each side declared itself to be the winner of this contest, and Shepard and Lane attempted to preside over the convention simultaneously.

Finally, the Clark delegates bolted down the street to Turner Hall. There they nominated Clark for governor and proclaimed themselves to be the representatives of the true Democratic party. Clark claimed that he had lost out in the main convention because members of a third party, the People's party,[qv] had been allowed to participate in the Democratic conventions and primary elections. He made this accusation despite his earlier support of a decision to allow such participation.

The delegates remaining at the Car-Stable Convention nominated Hogg by a vote of 697 to Clark's 108½ votes; 15½ votes were cast for other candidates. In a compromise with farming interests, Hogg supporters accepted a platform plank calling for staggered, six-year, elected terms for commission members rather than executive appointment. In the general election there were three candidates for governor: two Democrats, Hogg and Clark, and one People's party candidate, Thomas L. Nugent.[qv] Hogg won reelection by a plurality vote over Clark and the Populist candidate. The vote totals were 190,486 for Hogg, 133,395 for Clark, and 108,483 for Nugent. Hogg received 59 percent of the Democratic votes cast for governor.

BIBLIOGRAPHY: Alwyn Barr, *Reconstruction to Reform: Texas Politics, 1876–1906* (Austin: University of Texas Press, 1971). Robert C. Cotner, *James Stephen Hogg: A Biography* (Austin: University of Texas Press, 1959).

John Martin Brockman

CARSWELL, HORACE S., JR. (1916–1944). Horace S. Carswell, Jr., Medal of Honor recipient, was born on July 18, 1916, in Fort Worth, Texas, the son of Horace S. and Bertha Carswell. He attended Texas Christian University in August 1939. He was appointed flying cadet in March 1940 and completed flight training and was appointed second lieutenant in November 1940. By October 1944 Major Carswell was deputy commander of the 308th Bombardment Group in the Pacific Theater. He was flying a B-24 on the night of October 26, 1944, on a single-aircraft night mission against a Japanese convoy in the South China Sea. He elected to make a second low-level run over a thoroughly alerted convoy and scored two direct hits on a large tanker. His copilot was wounded, and his aircraft had two engines knocked out, a third damaged, the hydraulic system damaged, and a fuel tank punctured. He managed to gain enough altitude to reach land, where he ordered the crew to bail out. Finding the bombardier's parachute too badly damaged to use, Carswell stayed with the aircraft and attempted a crash landing. The badly damaged aircraft crashed against a mountain, and both Carswell and the copilot were killed.

Major Carswell was awarded the Medal of Honor in 1946. He was cited for having given "his life...to save all members of his crew" and for "sacrifice far beyond that required of him." He was also posthumously awarded the Distinguished Flying Cross, the Distinguished Service Cross, the Air Medal, and the Purple Heart. The medals were presented to his wife, Virginia, on December 20, 1944, and July 21, 1945. On February 27, 1948, Fort Worth Army Airfield was renamed Carswell Air Force Base[qv] in his honor. Carswell was buried at a Catholic mission in Tungchen, China. He was survived by his wife and one son.

BIBLIOGRAPHY: Dallas *Morning News*, February 12, 1946, February 28, 1948. Committee on Veterans' Affairs, United States Senate, *Medal of Honor Recipients, 1863–1973* (Washington: GPO, 1973). Vertical Files, Barker Texas History Center, University of Texas at Austin.

Art Leatherwood

CARSWELL AIR FORCE BASE. Carswell Air Force Base, at Fort Worth, has been called Tarrant Field (from 1932 to 1943), Fort Worth Army Air Field (until January 1948), Fort Worth Air Force Base (in January 1948), Griffiss Air Force Base (for a few days in January 1948), and Carswell Air Force Base (from 1948). The base is named after Maj. Horace S. Carswell, Jr.[qv] The site of the base was originally selected in 1941 as a Consolidated Vultee factory for the production of B-24 bombers. A separate contract was let for a landing field, Tarrant Field, to be built to support the aircraft factory. The construction of an air force base on the east side of Tarrant Field was authorized after the Japanese attack on Pearl Harbor, and Tarrant Field Airdrome was assigned to the Army Air Forces Flying Training Command in July 1942. The base became one of the first B-24 transition schools to begin operation. After more than 4,000 students were trained in B-24s at the base, its mission was changed to B-34 transition because of the nearness to the Consolidated Vultee[qv] factory. In 1945 the mission was changed from B-34 to B-29 aircraft training. The base was assigned to the newly formed Strategic Air Command in March of 1946. In June 1948 the first B-36 was delivered to the Seventh Bomb Wing at the base. The six-engine, heavy bomber, later augmented by four jet engines, was phased out beginning in August 1957. In February 1949 the B-50, a later-model B-29, took off from Carswell for the first nonstop flight around the world. After mid-air refueling and 23,108 miles in ninety-four hours and one minute, the *Lucky Lady* landed at Carswell. The Seventh Bomb Wing became operational with the all-jet B-52 and KC-135 in January 1959. The unit was deployed to Guam in June 1965, flew more than 1,300 missions over Vietnam, and returned to Carswell in December 1965. In the 1980s the base received several new weapons systems, including modified B-52H aircraft and cruise missiles. By 1984 Carswell was the largest unit of its kind in the Strategic Air Command. The base contributed personnel and recruits to Operation Desert Storm in the Middle East in 1991.

Art Leatherwood

CARTA VALLEY, TEXAS. Carta Valley is on U.S. Highway 377 thirty-two miles southwest of Rocksprings in southwestern Edwards County. The community is named for its location in a valley surrounded by bluffs and for Ed Carta, an early settler. Settlers arrived in the area in 1898, and land was allotted for a cemetery in 1904. W. A. Varga opened a store in the community in 1906 and served as postmaster the following year when the Carta Valley post office was opened. In the early years children from the settlement attended the nearby Double Tank School until a school and church building was erected in Carta Valley sometime before 1913. A separate structure for the Methodist church was built in 1913, and a Baptist church was built in 1923. Carta Valley had an estimated thirty-five inhabitants in 1914. The population of the community was estimated at twenty from the 1920s through the 1950s. In 1948 the community maintained a school, two churches, one business, and a number of scattered dwellings. The settlement had a small boom in the 1960s, when its population briefly shot up to an estimated 150 inhabitants with five businesses, but by

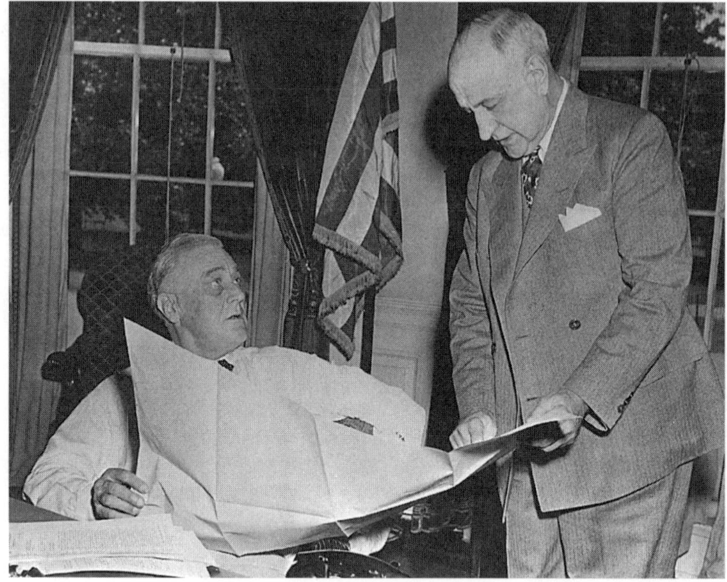

Amon G. Carter, Sr., presenting deed to Big Bend National Park to President Franklin D. Roosevelt, Washington, D.C., 1943. Courtesy Amon Carter Museum Archives, Fort Worth, Texas.

the 1970s the population was once more estimated at twenty. In 1978 Carta Valley had a school, a church, and a few dwellings; it was still marked on highway maps in 1990.

BIBLIOGRAPHY: Rocksprings Woman's Club Historical Committee, *A History of Edwards County* (San Angelo: Anchor, 1984).

Mark Odintz

CARTER, AMON G., SR. (1879–1955). Amon G. Carter, newspaperman and entrepreneur, was born Giles Amon Carter on December 11, 1879, in Crafton, Texas, the son of William Henry and Josephine (Ream) Carter. He changed his name as an adult; he named his son Amon Gary Carter, Jr.,[qv] and was widely known as Amon Carter, Sr. He quit school to help his family when he was eleven years old, did odd jobs in Bowie, and later worked in Oklahoma and California. He moved to Fort Worth in 1905 and became advertising manager of the Fort Worth *Star* the next year. Three years later, with the backing of Col. Paul Waples, he bought the newspaper and merged it with the Fort Worth *Telegram.* He named it the Fort Worth *Star-Telegram;*[qv] Louis J. Wortham[qv] was editor. In 1923 Carter succeeded Wortham as publisher and president, and in 1925 he bought the rival paper, the *Record,* which was published by William Randolph Hearst.

In 1922 Carter established WBAP, Fort Worth's first radio station; it became the first television station in the South and the Southwest in 1948. In 1923 Carter became chairman of the first board of directors of Texas Technological College (now Texas Tech University), where he served until 1927. He was the youngest president of the Fort Worth Chamber of Commerce. When oil was discovered in North Texas in the 1920s he helped persuade oilmen to move to Fort Worth and encouraged construction of such skyscrapers as the Sinclair, W. T. Waggoner,[qv] and Life of America buildings; he later served as director of the American Petroleum Institute.

One of Carter's special interests was transportation. In 1911 he headed a committee that brought the first airplane to the Fort Worth area; by 1928 he was a director and part owner of American Airways, which six years later reorganized as American Airlines, Incorporated (*see* AMR CORPORATION). Before World War II[qv] he helped bring to Fort Worth a huge Convair complex, later to become General Dynamics. In 1952 he persuaded Bell Aircraft Corporation to locate a helicopter plant in nearby Hurst. Amon G. Carter Field, named for him in 1950, was involved in the Fort Worth–Dallas airport controversy (see DALLAS–FORT WORTH INTERNATIONAL AIRPORT).

Carter was noted for his large-scale philanthropy, which was fueled by wealth from the oil business. His first successful well was drilled in New Mexico in 1935, and in 1945 the Amon G. Carter Foundation was established for cultural and educational purposes. Because of his outstanding service to Fort Worth and to Texas, Carter received numerous honors. He was named Range Boss of West Texas in 1939 and Ambassador of Good Will in 1941 by the Texas legislature. He received the Exceptional Service Medal from the United States Air Force and the Frank M. Hawks Memorial Award from American Legion Post 501 of New York City. He was an organizer and director of the Southwest Exposition and Fat Stock Show, president of the Fort Worth Club for thirty-five years, and a contributor to Fort Worth hospitals and civic centers. Many important visitors from business, theater, and public life visited his farm, Shady Oak.

Carter was married to Zetta Thomas, and they had a daughter. He subsequently married Nenetta Burton, and they had a son and a daughter; they were divorced in 1941. Carter subsequently married Minnie Meacham Smith. He died on June 23, 1955, in Fort Worth. Under the terms of his will, the Amon Carter Museum[qv] was established in Fort Worth from his collection of Remingtons and Russells. See also TEXAS FRONTIER CENTENNIAL.

BIBLIOGRAPHY: Seymour V. Connor, ed., *Builders of the Southwest* (Lubbock: Southwest Collection, Texas Technological College, 1959). Fort Worth *Star-Telegram,* June 24, 25, 1955. Vertical Files, Barker Texas History Center, University of Texas at Austin.

Ben H. Procter

CARTER, AMON GARY, JR. (1919–1982). Amon Gary Carter, Jr., publisher, civic leader, and philanthropist, son of Amon G. and Nenetta (Burton) Carter, was born in Fort Worth, Texas, on December 23, 1919. As a youth he sold newspapers on a corner in downtown Fort Worth. During his teens he worked in the summers as a copy boy, staff photographer, and advertising salesman for the Fort Worth *Star-Telegram.*[qv] He graduated from Culver Military Academy in Culver, Indiana, in 1938. He served in the army during World War II[qv] and was captured by German forces in North Africa in 1943. He subsequently spent twenty-seven months as a prisoner of war near Szubin, Poland, where he published a clandestine camp newspaper and established an unofficial pipeline for packages from home.

After the war, Carter attended the University of Texas and graduated in June 1946. He was appointed treasurer of the *Star-Telegram* and in 1952 became president of its parent corporation, Carter Publications, Incorporated. In 1955 he succeeded his father as publisher of the *Star-Telegram,* a position he held until his death. He influenced the move of American Airlines (*see* AMR CORPORATION) from New York City to Fort Worth. As its second largest stockholder, he also brought the Texas Rangers[qv] baseball team to the area. His long list of civic activities included service on the boards of the Texas Sports Hall of Fame[qv] Foundation, the Amon Carter Museum,[qv] the West Texas Chamber of Commerce,[qv] and Texas Christian University.

From 1955 until his death, Carter was the president of the Amon G. Carter Foundation and oversaw the distribution of over $60 million to charitable and cultural organizations. His many honors included the B'nai B'rith Gold Medallion and the Boy Scouts' Silver Beaver Award. He was a renowned collector who built one of the largest coin collections in the country. He also helped found the International Paper Money Society and was appointed to the United States Assay Commission. He was a member of the First United Methodist Church and an independent Democrat who supported political leaders regardless of party. Carter and his wife, George Ann (Brown), had a daughter and two sons. He died in Dallas of a heart attack on July 24, 1982.

BIBLIOGRAPHY: Jerry Flemmons, *Amon: The Life of Amon Carter, Sr., of Texas* (Austin: Jenkins, 1978). Fort Worth *Star-Telegram,* July 25, 26, 27, 1982, August 25, 26, 1983.

Patrick Norris

CARTER, ASA EARL (1925–1979). Asa Earl Carter [pseud. Bedford Forrest Carter], part Indian, segregationist, politician, speech-writer, and novelist, one of five children of Ralph and Hermione (Weatherly) Carter, was born in Anniston, Alabama, on September 4, 1925, and lived near Oxford. He attended schools in Calhoun County, Alabama. He married India Thelma Walker and had four children. Carter served in the United States Navy during World War II[qv] and later returned to the University of Colorado, where he attended naval training school in 1944. By the late 1950s he was in Birmingham, Alabama, where his political activities included hosting a radio show for the American States Rights Association and providing leadership in the Alabama Council movement. Later he founded the North Alabama White Citizens Council in Birmingham. He wrote speeches for Lurleen Wallace when she ran successfully for the governorship of Alabama in 1966 and was one of two writers said to be responsible for the words "segregation today, segregation tomorrow, segregation forever" uttered by Governor George Wallace. Although Carter is associated by the media with George Wallace and publicly claimed that he wrote speeches for Wallace in the 1960s, Wallace denied any association or collaboration. Carter ran unsuccessfully against Wallace in the Democratic primary for governor in 1970.

After his loss to Wallace, Carter gave up politics and left Alabama. He adopted the pseudonym Bedford Forrest Carter and assumed the role of a largely self-taught, part-Cherokee novelist named after Nathan Bedford Forrest, the colorful, uneducated Confederate general. Carter also used a Cherokee Indian name, Gundi Usdi, which he translated as Little Tree. So complete was his break with his old life that it was not widely known until after his death that the novelist and the former politician were the same man. By 1972 Carter was in Sweetwater, Texas, where he used the resources of the City-County Library to work on his first novel, *Gone to Texas* (1973). The highly successful film version starring Clint Eastwood is entitled *The Outlaw Josey Wales* (1976). Carter's residence during the writing of his three other books was St. George's Island, Florida. These books are *The Vengeance Trial of Josey Wales* (1976), a sequel to his first novel; *The Education of Little Tree* (1976, reprint 1986), a purported autobiography of his early years, considered his best book; and *Watch for Me on the Mountain* (1978), a sympathetic portrayal of Geronimo. Carter received various honors, one of which was an appearance at a Wellesley luncheon in Dallas in 1978 with J. Lon Tinkle,[qv] Barbara Tuchman, and Elizabeth Forsythe Hailey. Carter was a masterful storyteller whose prose style is characterized by sparsely phrased, often fragmentary sentences and fast-paced plot. The influence of the Civil War[qv] and his Cherokee heritage are evident, and from these he drew his themes of courage, honor, kinship, and blood-feud. He spent his last years traveling to promote his books, attempting to arrange for films of the last three of them, writing the screenplay for one himself, and composing *The Wanderings of Little Tree,* an unfinished sequel to his third book. In addition, Bruce Marshall, an artist from Austin, prepared illustrations for a volume of Carter's poetry. All of these efforts collapsed with Carter's untimely death. In Abilene, Texas, on June 7, 1979, he choked on food and clotted blood after a fist fight, and died; he is buried near Anniston, Alabama.

BIBLIOGRAPHY: Birmingham (Alabama) *News,* April 20, 1970, July 4, 1979. Lawrence Clayton, "The Enigma of Forrest Carter," *Texas Books in Review* 5 (1983). Lawrence Clayton and Randall Parks, "Forrest Carter's Use of History," *Heritage of the Great Plains* 15 (1982).

Lawrence Clayton

CARTER, GEORGE WASHINGTON (ca. 1826–1901). George Washington Carter, minister and educator, Confederate colonel, legislator, and diplomat, was born in Virginia about 1826. He became a minister in the Methodist Church when he was twenty-one years old. He served congregations in the Richmond, Petersburg, and Fredericksburg, Virginia, districts and in 1858 received an appointment to the University of Mississippi as professor of ethics. In January 1860 the Texas Methodist Conference invited him to become president of Soule University at Chappell Hill, Texas. After participating in the Secession Convention[qv] in 1861, Carter resigned his position and returned to Virginia, where the Confederate secretary of war authorized him to recruit a regiment for the army. He returned to Texas, raised three regiments instead of one, and planned to arm his recruits with lances. The regiments—his own Twenty-first Texas Cavalry, Franklin C. Wilkes's[qv] Twenty-fourth Texas Cavalry, and Clayton C. Gillespie's Twenty-fifth Texas Cavalry—became known as Carter's Lancers. When the force arrived in Arkansas in the autumn of 1862 the Twenty-fourth and Twenty-fifth Texas withdrew from Carter's command, leaving him with only the Twenty-first Texas; this regiment joined a brigade under Col. William Henry Parsons.[qv] Throughout the war Carter claimed that he should have had command of Parsons's brigade because his commission as colonel came from the secretary of war and predated that of Parsons. This dispute was not settled until the Twenty-first Texas left Parsons's brigade early in 1865. At times during the war Carter did command portions of the brigade, and when it was under him it was known as Carter's brigade. He led this force with Brig. Gen. John S. Marmaduke into Missouri in 1863. Although both he and Colonel Parsons participated in the Red River campaign[qv] in 1864, the brigade was placed under Brig. Gen. William Steele.[qv]

After the war Carter moved to Louisiana, where he was a controversial figure in Reconstruction[qv] politics. He served in the legislature as speaker in 1871–72. He was minister resident to Venezuela from June 30, 1881, to May 16, 1882, and in his later life was a lecturer. Carter was married and divorced three times. He died at the Maryland Line Confederate Soldiers' Home in Pikesville, Maryland, on May 11, 1901, and is buried at Loudon Park Cemetery in Baltimore.

BIBLIOGRAPHY: Anne J. Bailey, *Between the Enemy and Texas: Parsons's Texas Cavalry in the Civil War* (Fort Worth: Texas Christian University Press, 1989). Macum Phelan, *History of Early Methodism in Texas, 1817–1866* (Nashville: Cokesbury, 1924); *A History of the Expansion of Methodism in Texas, 1867–1902* (Dallas: Mathis, Van Nort, 1937).

Anne J. Bailey

CARTER, JAMES W. (1845–1916). James W. Carter, the first permanent white resident of Castro County, was born on February 13, 1845, and spent much of his youth in Stephenville, where he grew up in the cattle business. In 1874 he became one of the first settlers to locate on Jim Ned Creek near Buffalo Gap in Taylor County. Two years later A. J. Breeding, a native of West Virginia, took his family from Minnesota to Cedar Gap, four miles from Buffalo Gap; in 1878 Carter married Breeding's daughter Ellen. In 1879 he and his half-brothers John and Lish took some 300 cattle to the vicinity of present Pecos, Texas. The following year they gathered the remainder of the herd, about 3,000 head, and established a headquarters about eight miles below the future townsite. To this ranch the Carters freighted supplies and brought their wives; Lish Carter married Ellen's sister Jennie in 1881. They resided in half-dugout huts of native materials (*see* DUGOUT).

After the Texas and Pacific Railway came through in 1882 the Carters sold their Pecos ranch to Colonel Gottard of St. Louis and returned briefly to Taylor County. In 1883 J. W. Carter purchased seventy-two sections in Castro County at seventy-nine cents an acre. He, his wife, and three small children made their way in wagons from Taylor County to their new homestead, bringing with them carpenters, lumber, all necessary supplies and tools to build and equip a four-room house, and a year's supply of groceries. Carter established headquarters on the north side of Running Water Draw about fourteen miles southwest of the site of present Dimmitt. He fenced in eighteen sections for a horse pasture and erected a two-story, four-room dugout on top of the slope overlooking the draw. On his 53,000-acre range, he grazed 3,000 head of cattle that bore his Seven-Up brand. Elizabeth Carter, born in 1886, was the first white child born in the county; the Carters eventually had two sons and three daughters. The family obtained supplies at Colorado City and after 1887 at Amarillo. In 1887 Carter added to his herd 15,000 two-year-old steers from Taylor County.

From 1884 to 1890 the Carters were the only settlers in Castro County. Their nearest neighbors were at the Springlake and Escarbada divisions of the XIT Ranch [qv] and C. C. Slaughter's [qv] Circle Cross, then managed by Ellen's brother, Bill Breeding. Lish and Jennie Breeding Carter settled on Tierra Blanca Creek, in Deaf Smith County, in 1886. As the family grew, J. W. and Ellen Carter added to their house and later began hosting Saturday night dances. Mrs. Carter also won a reputation among area cowboys and nesters as a nurse and midwife. In 1888 the Carters hired Elizabeth (Lizzie) Bayne of Amarillo as a governess and tutor for their children since there was no school for them to attend. After Dimmitt was founded and Castro County was organized in 1891, Miss Bayne became the county's first schoolteacher. To help make up the list of 150 residents required for county organization, Carter is said to have given fictitious surnames to his horses.

In 1891 he went into a business partnership with two store owners in Amarillo. Unfortunately that move proved unwise, for by 1895 the Seven-Up Ranch was encumbered with a $52,000 debt. Hoping to save at least part of this land and cattle, Carter bought into the store, only to learn that there was a $100,000 note against it. Thus he was compelled to sell the land at public auction in May 1895 to pay his numerous creditors. The highest bidder was the Scottish American Mortgage Company.

The Carters moved to Dimmitt, where they established the thirty-room Castro Hotel, one of the first Panhandle [qv] lodgings to have piped hot and cold water. They managed this business until Carter's death on June 25, 1916. The following year Ellen sold it with the provision that it would be her home for as long as she lived. She died on May 16, 1942, and the hotel was subsequently sold to J. E. Hyatt and moved to Plainview. J. W. and Ellen Carter are buried in the Castro Memorial Gardens in Dimmitt.

BIBLIOGRAPHY: Lana Payne Barnett and Elizabeth Brooks Buhrkuhl, eds., *Presenting the Texas Panhandle* (Canyon, Texas: Lan-Bea, 1979). Castro County Historical Commission, *Castro County, 1891–1981* (Dallas: Taylor, 1981).

H. Allen Anderson

CARTER, JOHN (1929–1991). John Carter, jazz composer and clarinetist, was born in Fort Worth, Texas, in 1929. He was influenced by the music at his Baptist church and records his parents owned by jazz greats, such as Duke Ellington, Count Basie, and Cab Calloway. Carter began playing clarinet at the age of twelve; he also played flute and saxophone. He played with Ornette Coleman in Fort Worth. He received his B.A. in music in 1949 at Lincoln University in Jefferson, Missouri, and his M.A. at the University of Colorado in 1956. He taught music in the Fort Worth public schools from 1949 to 1961, when he secured a position as a traveling elementary-school music teacher in Los Angeles, California. There he and Bobby Bradford, also from Texas, collaborated to form the New Art Jazz Ensemble. Some of their music was released as "West Coast Hot" in 1969. In Los Angeles Carter opened a jazz establishment, Rudolph's, where progressive musicians met. He was critics' choice for best jazz clarinetist for most of the 1980s.

Between 1985 and 1990 Carter composed and recorded "Roots and Folklore: Episodes in the Development of American Folk Music," in five albums focused on African-Americans [qv]—*Dauwhe* (1985), *Castles of Ghana* (1985), *Dance of the Love Ghosts* (1986), *Fields* (1988), and *Shadows on a Wall* (1989). The complete set was acclaimed by jazz critics as containing some of the best releases of the 1980s. In February 1990 Carter had a nonmalignant tumor that resulted in the removal of his left lung. He made an appearance in Los Angeles in September of that year, in which he stated that he expected a full recovery. He died on March 31, 1991, in Los Angeles from complications due to lung cancer. He was survived by his wife, Gloria, three sons, and a daughter.

BIBLIOGRAPHY: Austin *Chronicle*, April 12, 1991. Barry Kernfeld, ed., *The New Grove Dictionary of Jazz* (London: Macmillan, 1988). Los Angeles *Times*, September 5, 1990, April 14, 1991. New York *Times*, February 5, 1988.

Kristi Strickland

CARTER, KATHERINE POLLARD (1900–1989). Katherine Pollard Carter, religious writer, was born on January 20, 1900, in Wichita Falls, Texas, the eldest of William T. and Addie (Ford) Pollard's three living children. She grew up in various Texas communities where her father worked as a school administrator, including Wichita Falls, Alpine, Orange, Dallas, Austin, Cameron, Pearsall, Gonzales, and Houston. She completed high school in Del Rio. She studied journalism at the University of Texas, where she graduated in 1922. She then took graduate journalism courses at Columbia University in New York before returning to Texas by 1924. She settled in Houston and began a career in public relations and advertising. In June 1938 Katherine Pollard married Kenneth I. Carter, a Bay City farmer. She taught school for several years, then worked in the curriculum department of the Houston Independent School District. In 1946 she wrote a set of graded books, the "Carter Sono-Speller Work Book and Spelling Tablets," distributed mostly in Texas. In 1951 she received a master's degree from the University of Houston. She subsequently returned to writing, primarily radio copy and newspaper articles. She took assignments at the *Daily Tribune* and the weekly *Matagorda County Tribune*, both published in Bay City. For a few years she was editor of another local weekly.

During the 1960s Mrs. Carter's spiritual interests prompted her to resign the editorial post to write inspirational books. In 1972 she produced *Hand on the Helm: Phantoms, Visions, Voices and Dreams That Have Changed the Course of History.* Three years later she followed with *Heard in Heaven: Miraculous Answers to Prayer That Have Affected the Fate of Nations.* Portions of these home-published books were combined with another of her manuscripts in a paperback edition titled *Hand on the Helm*, which Whitaker House published in 1977. That year Carter died, and Katherine Carter moved to Weslaco in 1978. She devoted most of her last years to writing scripts based on her books. Her hope was to interest producers in adapting them for a television series, but she was unsuccessful in this. She died on September 8, 1989, in Weslaco and was buried in Bay City.

BIBLIOGRAPHY: *Alcalde* (magazine of the Ex-Students' Association of the University of Texas), January 1947. Vertical Files, Barker Texas History Center, University of Texas at Austin.

Sherilyn Brandenstein

CARTER, RICHARD (ca. 1790–1863). Richard Carter, early settler, the son of Joseph and Nancy (Menefee) Carter of Virginia, was born about 1790. He may have been a constituent of the "Alabama Settlement," which migrated from Virginia to Tennessee, Alabama, and finally East Texas, by the first quarter of the nineteenth century. Carter married Elizabeth Lones in 1811 in Knoxville, Tennessee, and later moved to Morgan County, Alabama. They had several children. Carter may have served in the War of 1812. On April 30, 1831, he received a grant for a league of land in Stephen F. Austin's [qv] colony, now in Brazos County. The family settled at Sabine Creek (subsequently renamed Carter Creek). Carter was reported to be the first white settler in the area of present College Station. In describing their early life in Texas his daughter, Evaline Burton, states that the only women she saw from the arrival of their family in 1831 until the following July were those in her own family and friendly Indians and that during this time their family lived exclusively on wild meats and honey. Another early Brazos County settler, Harvey Mitchell, described the Carter Creek bottom as "an unbroken canebrake, infested with bear, panthers, wild cats, and other enemies of hogs and cattle, as well as of men."

After 1835 Carter moved his family to Tinninville, north of the Old San Antonio Road[qv] at the Navasota River in the area that became Robertson County. He is listed in 1838 as paying taxes on 1,476 acres originally granted to Jeremiah Tinnan in 1835. According to Mitchell, he boarded with the Carters at Tinninville during 1839 and 1840. He later visited their home, again on Carter Creek in Brazos County, during Christmas of 1840. At that time the Carters were living in a one-room log cabin, and stock raising was widespread locally. Carter's property was close to Boonville, which was made the county seat in 1841. The first area school was conducted in his home, and Carter, John H. Jones, and Hiram Hanover served as the first board of commissioners in 1841 to survey the town and auction off the lots. Hanover bought the first lot and built a log cabin home that served as the first post office in Boonville, with Hanover as postmaster. Carter's son Wiley served at the first meeting of the grand jury in Boonville. In 1848 Carter served again as a commissioner.

By 1845 he had real and personal property worth $5,800. In the 1850 census he was listed as a farmer who owned 350 cattle, five horses, and five slaves. In the 1850s Carter was prosecuted for allowing a slave to carry a gun off his property without proper supervision. The case went all the way to the Texas Supreme Court. By 1860 he had a herd of 1,000 cattle and was among the top cotton and corn producers in the county. The 1860 census listed his real estate at a value of $4,000 and his personal property at $26,150. From 1846 to 1860 Carter's estate increased in value from $5,800 to $30,000. This was in part due to an increase in the value of land and cattle. Also, increased production of corn and cotton was possible through an expanded number of improved acres. However, the most significant factor accounting for his prosperity was the value of slaves. Half of Carter's taxable property was based upon slave ownership—each slave averaging $800 in 1860.

Carter died on May 12, 1863. Popular legend held that a substantial amount of Confederate money was buried with him, but the story was never substantiated. Apparently he had no desire for emancipation to be proclaimed within the lifetime of his family, for his will stated that upon the death of his wife, Elizabeth, who died in 1876, his property, including his two slave families, should be divided among his children and grandchildren. Through the war years Carter's estate climbed to an unprecedented $44,000. But after the 1865 taxes were assessed, the value of the estate had plummeted to $9,800, which still left the Carters in the upper economic bracket of Brazos County. In spite of the loss of three-fourths of their accumulated wealth, Elizabeth Carter was the second largest cattle owner in the county in 1865 and remained among the richest 2 percent of county residents. During Reconstruction[qv] her finances were relatively grim compared to the prewar years. Between 1865 and her death her property dwindled in value to $3,400.

In 1986 the Richard Carter homesite was dedicated as Richard Carter Park, on Brazoswood Drive, College Station, at a Texas historical marker ceremony conducted by the Brazos County Historical Commission. In the early 1990s the remains of the Carters and probably several slaves were moved to a new site in the park.

BIBLIOGRAPHY: Glenna Fourman Brundidge, *Brazos County History: Rich Past—Bright Future* (Bryan, Texas: Family History Foundation, 1986). Virginia H. Taylor, *Index to Spanish and Mexican Land Grants* (Austin: General Land Office, 1976). Vertical Files, Barker Texas History Center, University of Texas at Austin.

Eleanor Hanover Nance

CARTER, ROBERT GOLDTHWAITE (1845–1936). Robert Goldthwaite Carter, soldier and writer, was born at Bridgton, Maine, on October 29, 1845. The family moved in 1847 to Portland, where young Carter was educated, and in 1857 to Massachusetts, where he was about to enter Phillips (Andover) Academy when the Civil War[qv] broke out. Carter enlisted as a private in Company H, Twenty-second Massachusetts Infantry, and served from August 5, 1862, to October 4, 1864. He entered the United States Military Academy in 1865, graduated on June 15, 1870, and was assigned to Troop E, Fourth United States Cavalry.[qv] He married on September 4, 1870, and started with his bride, Mary, to San Antonio, Texas, on September 12, 1870. Carter was promoted to first lieutenant on February 21, 1875, and retired from the army on June 28, 1876, because of disability contracted in the line of duty. He was brevetted captain on February 27, 1890, for gallant service in action against the Kickapoo and Apache Indians at Remolino, Mexico, in May 1873. On January 23, 1900, he was awarded the Medal of Honor for his action in the Brazos River campaign in October 1871.

The Carters had three children, two of whom were born at Fort Richardson. Mrs. Carter died in November 1923. After his retirement from the army, Carter wrote several books concerning his military career and that of early members of his family: *The Boy Soldier at Gettysburg* (1887), *Four Brothers in Blue* (1913), and *The Old Sergeant's Story* (1926). An autobiographical work, *Record of the Military Service of First Lieutenant and Brevet Captain Robert Goldthwaite Carter, U. S. Army 1862–1876*, was published in 1904. Carter also wrote several pamphlets on his Texas experiences; these were reprinted as part of his book *On the Border with Mackenzie* in 1935. Carter died in Washington on January 4, 1936, and was buried in Arlington National Cemetery.

BIBLIOGRAPHY: Francis B. Heitman, *Historical Register and Dictionary of the United States Army* (2 vols., Washington: GPO, 1903; rpt., Urbana: University of Illinois Press, 1965).

CARTER, SAMUEL C. (ca. 1790–1825). Samuel C. Carter, one of Stephen F. Austin's[qv] Old Three Hundred,[qv] was born about 1790 in Georgia. He was a merchant in business with Benjamin Fowler at San Felipe de Austin as early as February 1824. He apparently had a trading vessel with which he brought supplies from New Orleans. Carter participated in colonial elections in April and took his oath of loyalty to the Mexican government in May. He received title to a league of land on the east bank of the Brazos River three miles south of Manor Lake in what is now Brazoria County on July 8, 1824. On September 4, 1825, Joshua Marsh wrote Austin from New Orleans that Carter had died at his house of yellow fever and that his sloop had been delivered to the probate court for sale.

BIBLIOGRAPHY: Eugene C. Barker, ed., *The Austin Papers* (3 vols., Washington: GPO, 1924–28). Lester G. Bugbee, "The Old Three Hundred: A List of Settlers in Austin's First Colony," *Quarterly of the Texas State Historical Association* 1 (October 1897). Daughters of the Republic of Texas, *Founders and Patriots of the Republic of Texas* (Austin, 1963–).

CARTER, SAMUEL FAIN (1857–1928). Samuel Fain Carter, lumberman and businessman, son of John Quincy Adams and Mildred Ann (Richards) Carter, was born near Huntsville, Alabama, on September 14, 1857. In 1858 the family moved to Sherman, Texas, where in 1870 Samuel began work on the Sherman *Courier* as printer's devil, compositor, and typesetter. From 1876 to 1881 he worked on the Galveston *News*.[qv] He married Carrie E. Banks of Galveston on June 23, 1882. Carter entered the lumber business in 1881 as bookkeeper for the Texas Train and Lumber Company in Beaumont; he became so familiar with the industry that he was soon managing the sawmill plant at Village Mills. Subsequently, he returned to Beaumont, where he was made manager of the business and bought a stock interest in 1883. He moved in 1892 to Houston, where he and M. T. Jones organized the Emporia Lumber Company, which Carter managed until the sale of his lumber interests in 1906. In 1907 he organized the Lumberman's National Bank (later the Second National Bank) of Houston, of which he was president until January 1, 1927, when he became chairman of the board. He was president of the Houston Building Company and director of the American Maid Flour Mills, the First Texas Joint Stock Land Bank, and the Houston and Texas Central Railway. Carter died in Houston on March 1, 1928, and was buried in Glenwood Cemetery.

BIBLIOGRAPHY: Hugh Nugent Fitzgerald, ed., *Texans and Their State: A Newspaper Reference Work* (2 vols., Houston: Texas Biographical Association, 1918). Houston *Post-Dispatch*, March 2, 1928. Clarence R. Wharton, ed., *Texas under Many Flags* (5 vols., Chicago: American Historical Society, 1930). *Jeanette H. Flachmeier*

CARTER, WILLIAM SAMUEL (1859–1923). William Samuel Carter, government railroad official, the son of Samuel Miles and Margaret Francis (Oliphant) Carter, was born on August 11, 1859, in Austin, Texas. He attended school in Williamson County and the Agricultural and Mechanical College of Texas (now Texas A&M University). In 1879 he became connected with railroading and was in charge of hauling lumber on a wooden tramway. That year he became a fireman on the Gulf, Colorado and Santa Fe Railway. He worked on various railroads until 1894, when he became editor of the *Brotherhood of Locomotive Firemen and Enginemen's Magazine*. He retained this position until January 1, 1904, when he became general secretary and treasurer of the brotherhood. Five years later he became its president. In February 1918 he was appointed director of the division of labor of the United States Railway Administration. Carter was married twice: on December 26, 1880, to Evelyn Gorsuch of Austin, who died on June 22, 1892, and on November 27, 1902, to Julia I. Cross. He died in Baltimore on March 15, 1923.

BIBLIOGRAPHY: *Dictionary of American Biography*.

CARTER, WILLIAM SPENCER (1869–1944). William S. Carter, medical college teacher and administrator, was born in Still Valley, Warren County, New Jersey, on April 11, 1869, the son of William and Ann (Stewart) Carter. After studies at Easton (Pennsylvania) High School and the University of Pennsylvania School of Medicine, he received an M.D. degree in 1890. He then interned in two Philadelphia hospitals. After working in several teaching positions, including those of assistant demonstrator of pathology (1891–94) and assistant professor of physiology (1894–97), and serving as attending physician at his alma mater, Carter was appointed professor of physiology and hygiene at the University of Texas Medical Branch, Galveston, in 1897. He established one of the earliest research and teaching laboratories in physiology in the South, taught hygiene and public health for several years, and encouraged his assistant, Oscar Plant, to offer the first course in pharmacology at UTMB.

In 1903 Carter became UTMB's fourth dean. During nineteen years in that position, he nurtured the growth and development of the institution. He founded the department of pharmacology and equipped physiology and pharmacology labs. He encouraged educational campaigns for the promotion of public hygiene and control of tuberculosis. He was instrumental in building an isolation hospital behind the Main Building at UTMB and also helped establish a Children's Hospital in Galveston, which was donated by the Texas Public Health Association and operated by a staff from the medical college. In 1913 UTMB became a member of the Association of American Medical Colleges, then a national organization of medical school deans. Fellow deans elected Carter vice president in 1916 and president in 1917.

He left UTMB in 1922 to become a staff member of the Division of Medical Sciences of the Rockefeller Foundation, and in 1923 he was named associate director. For the next twelve years he skillfully orchestrated the development of medical schools in the Philippines, Australia, South Africa, Java, New Zealand, China, and India. In China he was acting director of Peking Union Medical College in 1925, and he helped organize the School of Tropical Medicine in Calcutta the next year. Carter retired in 1934. Urged by alumni and faculty, he returned to UTMB in 1935 as dean. He resigned in 1938.

His memberships included the National Board of Medical Examiners, the American Physiological Society, the American Medical Association, the Texas State Medical Association (now the Texas Medical Association[qv]), and the Texas Academy of Sciences.[qv] He was the author of *Notes on Pathology and Bacteriology* (with David Riesman, 1895) and *Laboratory Exercises in Physiology* (1916). For his medical essays he received the Boylston Prize in 1892 and the Alvarenga Prize in 1903. On October 18, 1894, Carter married Lillian V. McCleavy. They had two daughters. He died on May 12, 1944, in Auburndale, Massachusetts.

BIBLIOGRAPHY: Sam Hanna Acheson, Herbert P. Gambrell, Mary Carter Toomey, and Alex M. Acheson, Jr., *Texian Who's Who*, Vol. 1 (Dallas: Texian, 1937). William Keuller, "William Spencer Carter, M.D.," *Alcalde*, June 1922. Chauncey D. Leake et al., "William Spencer Carter, 1869–1944," *Science* 100 (July 21, 1944). *The University of Texas Medical Branch at Galveston: A Seventy-five Year History* (Austin: University of Texas Press, 1967). *Who's Who in America*, 1944–45.

Chester R. Burns

CARTER, TEXAS (Parker County). Carter was ten miles north of Weatherford in north central Parker County. It was established by Judge W. F. Carter and two partners, T. Parkinson, and H. C. Vardy, in 1866–67. The three men built a flour mill near the banks of Clear Fork Creek and added a cotton gin within a year. A general store, a blacksmith shop, a common school, and a church soon were erected. The community, originally called Cartersville or Carterville, established a statewide reputation for its flour, which was judged the best in Texas at the State Fair of Texas[qv] in Houston in 1873. In 1888 the seventy-five residents of the community received a post office branch and adopted the town's present name. Postal service to the community was discontinued in 1907. The population gradually declined, and by the 1920s the town was a memory.

BIBLIOGRAPHY: Gustavus Adolphus Holland, *History of Parker County and the Double Log Cabin* (Weatherford, Texas: Herald, 1931; rpt. 1937). H. Bryant Prather, *Texas Pioneer Days* (Dallas: Egan, 1965). Henry Smythe, *Historical Sketch of Parker County and Weatherford* (St. Louis: Lavat, 1877; rpt., Waco: Morrison, 1973).

David Minor

CARTER, TEXAS (Stephens County). Carter was on Farm Road 717 in southeastern Stephens County. It was served by the Wichita Falls and Southern Railway. Highway maps of 1948 indicate widely scattered residences and a school called Bullock two miles south of Carter. By the 1990s Carter was a ghost town and no longer appeared on county maps; all that was left of the community was an abandoned railway station. *Julius A. Amin*

CARTER BEND. Carter Bend, a bend in the Brazos River, was inundated by Possum Kingdom Lake in Young and Palo Pinto counties. There is now a Carter Island in the vicinity of the former bend (at 32°58′ N, 98°25′ W).

CARTER CREEK. Carter Creek (Prewetts Creek) rises four miles south of North Zulch in southwestern Madison County (at 30°51′ N, 96°06′ W) and flows west six miles to its mouth on the Navasota River, near the Brazos county line in far northwestern Grimes County (at 30°49′ N, 96°10′ W). The stream traverses gently sloping to nearly level terrain surfaced by loamy and clayey soils that support post oak, blackjack oak, elm, hackberry, water oak, and pecan woods along its banks. Settlement in the vicinity began during the mid-1830s. In 1881 the Pleasant Grove Baptist Church was constructed near the headwaters of the creek. The Oak Grove community was established on the north bank of the middle creek in the late nineteenth century.

bibliography: Madison County Historical Commission, *A History of Madison County* (Dallas: Taylor, 1984).

CARTERS CREEK. Carters Creek (Saline Creek) rises three-quarters of a mile northwest of U.S. Highway 190 and 1½ miles north of Bryan in southeastern Brazos County (at 30°34′ N, 96°21′ W) and runs southeast nearly eighteen miles to its mouth on the Navasota River, at the Brazos-Grimes county line (at 30°34′ N, 96°10′ W). The creek traverses flat to moderately rolling terrain with local shallow depressions, surfaced by clayey or sandy loams that support oak, mesquite, juniper, and native and introduced grasses. The creek was probably named for Richard Carter,[qv] who received an original land grant south of the site of present College Station from Stephen F. Austin[qv] on April 30, 1831.

bibliography: W. Broadus Smith, *Pioneers of Brazos County, Texas, 1800–1850* (Bryan, Texas, 1962).

CARTER'S MILL, TEXAS. Carter's Mill was six miles west of Longview near the site of present White Oak in central Gregg County. It was probably established after the Civil War.[qv] A post office operated there from 1877 until 1881. At its height in the early 1880s, the small settlement had a general store, a mill, and a number of houses. By 1900 the community no longer appeared on maps.

Christopher Long

CARTERVILLE, TEXAS. Carterville is on Farm Road 130 seven miles northwest of Linden in western Cass County. It was probably named for the Carter family, early settlers in the area, and was apparently settled in the 1860s. It reached its largest point in the 1960s with a population of seventy-five. In 1983 the community had one small business, a town hall, and a church, and in 1990 the population was twenty-five. *Cecil Harper, Jr.*

CARTHAGE, TEXAS. Carthage is at the intersection of U.S. highways 59 and 79, forty-two miles west of Shreveport, Louisiana, near the center of Panola County. Carthage is Panola County's second county seat. When an act of the Texas legislature delineated the county in 1846, the temporary county seat was Pulaski, a settlement on the east bank of the Sabine River. In 1848 the county commissioners selected a site at the county's geographic center as the permanent county seat. Jonathan Anderson,[qv] who owned the proposed site, agreed to donate 100 acres for the town. Spearman Holland[qv] is credited with naming the community in honor of Carthage, Mississippi. A post office was established in 1849. The first courthouse, made of peeled pine logs and financed by the sale of town lots, was completed in August of the same year. The log courthouse was used until 1853, when a brick structure was built. In 1860 Carthage had a school, a church, and the Panola Male and Female Academy, founded by L. C. Libby. The courthouse soon became overcrowded, and a third courthouse, built in Gothic style, was completed in 1885. By that time a local newspaper, the Panola *Watchman,* was being published by T. E. Boren, and a second weekly, the Panola *Banner,* published by G. D. Guest and H. M. Knight, was in operation by 1890. In 1888 the Texas, Sabine Valley and Northwestern Railway was extended to Carthage. This line later became part of the Gulf, Colorado and Santa Fe and in 1965 was conveyed to the Atchison, Topeka and Santa Fe.

Carthage was incorporated in 1874, but it soon reverted to management by the county court. In 1902 the community was incorporated under the council form, but it later dissolved again. In 1913 the town adopted the commission form of government, still in place today, which consists of a mayor, a city manager, and city commissioners. In 1953 a brick courthouse was dedicated on Sycamore Street, two blocks west of the old site on Carthage Square. The old courthouse was auctioned off and the square cleared for a public park, named for Jonathan Anderson, in 1956. In 1920 Carthage had a population of 1,366. The community expanded steadily afterward, spurred by the growth of the oil and gas industry and general commerce in the area. In 1940 the population had risen to 2,178, and by 1980 it had reached 6,477. The town had a shopping mall and a renovated downtown, as well as a cup company and a chicken-processing plant. In 1990 the population was 6,496.

bibliography: Leila B. LaGrone, ed., *History of Panola County* (Carthage, Texas: Panola County Historical Commission, 1979).

Leila B. LaGrone

CART WAR. The so called "Cart War" erupted in 1857 and had national and international repercussions. The underlying causes of the event, historians believe, were ethnic and racial hostilities of Texans toward Mexican Texans, exacerbated by the ethnocentrism of the Know-Nothing party[qv] and the white anger over Mexican sympathy with black slaves. By the mid-1850s, Mexicans and *Tejanos* had built a successful business of hauling food and merchandise from the port of Indianola to San Antonio and other towns in the interior of Texas. Using oxcarts, Mexicans moved freight more rapidly and cheaply than their Anglo competitors. Some Anglos retaliated by destroying the Mexicans' oxcarts, stealing their freight, and reportedly killing and wounding a number of Mexican carters. An attack on Mexican carters occurred in 1855 near Seguin, but sustained violence did not begin until July 1857. Local authorities made no serious effort to apprehend the criminals, and violence increased so much that some feared that a "campaign of death" against Mexicans was under way.

Public opinion in some counties between San Antonio and the coast ran heavily against the carters, who were regarded as an "intolerable nuisance." Some newspapers, however, spoke out against the violence. The Austin *Southern Intelligencer* and the San Antonio *Herald*[qqv] expressed concern that the "war" would raise prices. The *Intelligencer* also worried that if attacks on a "weak race" were permitted, the next victims would be the German Texans, and that finally "a war between the poor and the rich" might occur. Some humanitarians also expressed concern for the Mexicans, notwithstanding "the fact of their being low in the scale of intelligence," as the *Nueces Valley Weekly* of Corpus Christi stated.

News of the violence in Texas soon reached the Mexican minister in Washington, Manuel Robles y Pezuela, who on October 14 protested the affair to Secretary of State Lewis Cass. Cass urged Texas governor Elisha M. Pease[qv] to end the hostilities. In a message to the state legislature of November 30, 1857, Pease declared: "It is now very evident that there is no security for the lives of citizens of Mexican origin engaged in the business of transportation, along the road from San Antonio to the Gulf." Pease asked for a special appropriation for the militia, and the legislators approved the expenditure with little opposition. Though some citizens of Karnes County, who wanted the "peon Mexican teamsters" out of business, were angry at the arrival of armed escorts for *Tejano*[qv] carters, the "war" subsided in December of 1857.

bibliography: Arnoldo De León, *They Called Them Greasers: Anglo Attitudes Toward Mexicans in Texas, 1821–1900* (Austin: University of Texas Press, 1983). John J. Linn, *Reminiscences of Fifty Years in Texas* (New York: Sadlier, 1883; 2d ed., Austin: Steck, 1935; rpt., Austin: State House, 1986). Sister Paul of the Cross McGrath, *Political Nativism in Texas, 1825–1860* (Washington: Catholic University of America, 1930). *Reports of the Committee of Investigations, sent in 1873 by the Mexican Government to the Frontier of Texas* (New York: Baker and Godwin, 1875). J. Fred Rippy, "Border Troubles along the Rio Grande, 1848–1860," *Southwestern Historical Quarterly* 23 (October 1919).

David J. Weber

CARTWRIGHT, JESSE H. (ca. 1787–1848). Jesse H. Cartwright, public official, early settler, and one of Stephen F. Austin's[qv] Old Three Hundred,[qv] was born about 1787 in Nashville, Tennessee. He moved to Texas from Woodville, Mississippi, in 1825. The census of March

1826 listed him as a farmer and stock raiser aged between twenty-five and forty. His household included his wife, Nancy (Gray), a son, a daughter, two servants, and eight slaves. Cartwright's title to a league and a labor of land now in Fort Bend and Lavaca counties was granted on March 31, 1828. In 1830 he built his home on the Samuel Isaacks[qv] league at the head of Oyster Creek. Cartwright presided over the August 1830 election of electors for choosing the state governor and vice governor; as second regidor[qv] at San Felipe de Austin in December 1830 he was on a committee to examine the validity of land titles in Austin's first colony. Cartwright, along with Randolph Foster[qv] and William Walker, apparently served on a procurement committee during the early stages of the Texas Revolution,[qv] for on October 11, 1835, Richard Royster Royall[qv] requested that the trio bring lead and powder to San Felipe for the use of the Texas army. In June 1836 Cartwright blossomed as a realtor and advertised lots in Fayetteville, to be located on Round Lake, on the east side of the Brazos River. This town he tried, unsuccessfully, to make the county seat of Fort Bend County in 1838. In October 1836 Cartwright represented Harrisburg County in the House of the First Congress. About 1841 he sold most of his Fort Bend County holdings and moved west to the Guadalupe River. Apparently Cartwright divorced Nancy; he married Martha Adcock on May 31, 1843, in Harris County. Nancy died in Fort Bend before May 4, 1847, and Jesse was administrator of her estate. He died on March 11, 1848, in Guadalupe County.

BIBLIOGRAPHY: Eugene C. Barker, ed., *The Austin Papers* (3 vols., Washington: GPO, 1924–28). Eugene C. Barker, ed., "Minutes of the Ayuntamiento of San Felipe de Austin, 1828–1832," 12 parts, *Southwestern Historical Quarterly* 21–24 (January 1918–October 1920). Lester G. Bugbee, "The Old Three Hundred: A List of Settlers in Austin's First Colony," *Quarterly of the Texas State Historical Association* 1 (October 1897). John H. Jenkins, ed., *The Papers of the Texas Revolution, 1835–1836* (10 vols., Austin: Presidial Press, 1973). Louis Wiltz Kemp Papers, Barker Texas History Center, University of Texas at Austin. Texas House of Representatives, *Biographical Directory of the Texan Conventions and Congresses, 1832–1845* (Austin: Book Exchange, 1941). Leonie L. Weyand, Early History of Fayette County, 1822–1865 (M.A. thesis, University of Texas, 1932).

CARTWRIGHT, JOHN (1787–1841). John Cartwright, pioneer, son of Matthew and Polly (Grimmer) Cartwright, was born on March 10, 1787, in Pitt County, North Carolina. At a young age he moved to Tennessee with his parents and five sisters. There he grew to manhood, married, and lived near Lebanon until he left for Texas. He is said to have moved to Texas as early as 1819 and staked his claim in the Ayish Bayou District near the site of present San Augustine. Stephen F. Austin[qv] wrote to him in Ayish Bayou inquiring about travel conditions through East Texas before he came to Texas with his colony. As late as 1958 the letter was preserved at the Texas Memorial Museum[qv] in Austin but has since disappeared.

Cartwright brought his eldest son, Matthew Cartwright,[qv] and a few servants to clear the land and in 1825 brought the rest of the family, which consisted of his wife Polly, five sons, and two daughters, to settle permanently. However, possibly due to the unrest in East Texas, in 1830 he visited S. F. Austin in San Felipe and requested permission to join his colony. He did not move, however, but remained at his home place on the Palo Gaucho five miles northeast of San Augustine to the end of his life.

In 1826 Cartwright was listed one of the free males in the Ayish Bayou District and a member of the local militia. In 1834 he was elected one of the four primary judges of San Augustine Municipality and was one of the original trustees of the University of San Augustine, incorporated by the First Congress, June 5, 1837. Cartwright was an expert ironsmith and carpenter and is said to have built the first cotton gin in Texas. His cotton gin and mill was in operation by 1825, and he and his sons merchandised, ginned, and hauled cotton to Natchitoches, New Orleans, and later to Sabine Town, where he and his son-in-law William Garrett owned a warehouse for storage and shipment of goods down the Sabine River. Texas had no banks at the time, so Cartwright lent money at interest and kept deposits for his customers. He and Matthew helped supply the Texas army during the Texas Revolution.[qv]

Cartwright was noted for his size—so large he had a reinforced carriage in which he alone occupied the wide seat. He invested in the proposed town of San Augustine as early as 1830 by buying seventeen lots from developer Thomas S. McFarland.[qv] The town was finally laid out in 1833. Shortly afterward Cartwright moved his mercantile store there and ran it in partnership with his son Matthew. He also continued his ironworks, ginning, and hauling and some merchandising at his home place east of town. He died on July 18, 1841.

BIBLIOGRAPHY: Cartwright Collection, Barker Texas History Center, University of Texas at Austin. George L. Crocket, *Two Centuries in East Texas* (Dallas: Southwest, 1932; facsimile reprod., 1962). John S. Ford, *Rip Ford's Texas*, ed. Stephen B. Oates (Austin: University of Texas Press, 1963). Frank W. Johnson, *A History of Texas and Texans* (5 vols., ed. E. C. Barker and E. W. Winkler [Chicago and New York: American Historical Society, 1914; rpt. 1916]). William Seale, *San Augustine in the Texas Republic* (Austin: Encino, 1969).

Sandra Kardell Calpakis

CARTWRIGHT, MATTHEW (1807–1870). Matthew Cartwright, early merchant and landowner, the son of John and Polly (Cruchfield) Cartwright, was born in Wilson County, Tennessee, on November 11, 1807, and moved with his family to the Ayish Bayou District of Texas when he was fourteen. He went into partnership with his father at an early age, and by the late 1820s he and his father and brothers had a cotton gin and mill and hauled cotton to Natchitoches, Louisiana, and down the Sabine River. They also provided merchandise and extended credit on returns from New Orleans. They operated from their settlement on the Palo Gaucho until San Augustine was founded, at which time they started a store there. Cartwright bought out his father eventually and went into partnership with his sons after they returned from the Civil War.[qv] The store continued until after his death.

In 1826 Cartwright was a member of the local Ayish Bayou District Militia. From 1829 to 1832 he went back occasionally to Portershill Academy in Smith County, Tennessee, to further his education. In 1832 he was on the committee to find a location for the town of San Augustine. After the death of his father in 1840, he became a member of the board of trustees of the University of San Augustine. In 1848 he was on the board of trustees of the University of Eastern Texas.

Between 1847 and 1860 Cartwright dealt extensively in Texas lands. At the time of his death in 1870 he owned a million acres of land in Texas. It is said that he traveled a total of 20,000 miles on one favorite horse looking after his property. Although he was wealthy, he owned few slaves, just enough for the household. After the war he was required to apply for amnesty because of his large holdings but managed to survive and prosper, unlike many in similar circumstances. In 1849 he bought the house of his sister-in-law, Mrs. Isaac Campbell, which was built in 1839 by New England architect Augustus Phelps. This home was still in the Cartwright family in 1991.

Cartwright married Amanda Holman, the daughter of Isaac Holman, on October 18, 1836. They were the parents of two daughters and four sons, three of whom fought in the Civil War. Amanda's brother James S. Holman[qv] joined Austin's colony and later became the first mayor of Houston. On April 2, 1870, Cartwright died; he was buried in San Augustine. His wife survived him by twenty-four years. After her death their remains were transferred from San Augustine to Terrell by his youngest son, Matthew Cartwright, who was residing there.

BIBLIOGRAPHY: John Henry Brown, *Indian Wars and Pioneers of Texas* (Austin: Daniell, 1880; reprod., Easley, South Carolina: Southern Historical Press, 1978). Matthew Cartwright Papers, Barker Texas History Center, University of Texas at Austin. George L. Crocket, *Two Centuries in East Texas* (Dallas: Southwest, 1932; facsimile reprod., 1962). Hans Peter Nielsen Gammel, comp., *Laws of Texas, 1822–1897* (10 vols., Austin: Gammel, 1898). Frank W. Johnson, *A History of Texas and Texans* (5 vols., ed. E. C. Barker and E. W. Winkler [Chicago and New York: American Historical Society, 1914; rpt. 1916]). William Seale, *San Augustine in the Texas Republic* (Austin: Encino, 1969). Ralph A. Wooster, "Wealthy Texans, 1860," *Southwestern Historical Quarterly* 71 (October 1967). *Sandra Kardell Calpakis*

CARTWRIGHT, THOMAS NOTLEY (ca. 1798–1846). Thomas Notley Cartwright, soldier in the War of 1812 and one of Stephen F. Austin's[qv] Old Three Hundred,[qv] was born about 1798 in Georgia, the second son of Thomas Notley and Martha Cartwright and a cousin of John Cartwright[qv] of San Augustine County, Texas. His father moved the family to Wilson County, Tennessee, by 1812, where his three brothers had settled. Young Cartwright served at the battle of New Orleans with the Tennessee militia and received bounty land. He settled in Natchitoches Parish, Louisiana, where he married Ann Davis in 1823.

The same year he moved to Ayish Bayou in Texas after buying the improvements of Daniel McLean. He moved the following year to Austin's grant, where he received a league on the Colorado River and a labor just below San Felipe on August 10, 1824. He voted in the alcalde[qv] election at San Felipe on December 22, 1824. Early in 1825 he sold his land and returned to Ayish Bayou, where he farmed and worked at his cousin's cotton gin over the next decade. He applied for and received a headright in the area that became Polk County from special commissioner Charles S. Taylor[qv] in 1835. At this time he had five children and one slave. Cartwright served in the Texas army from July to September 1836 and located his bounty land in San Augustine County, where he lived until about 1845. He then moved his family to Houston County. There he died in October 1846. His widow and sons still lived there as late as 1860.

bibliography: Eugene C. Barker, ed., *The Austin Papers* (3 vols., Washington: GPO, 1924–28). Mary Smith Fay, *War of 1812 Veterans in Texas* (New Orleans: Polyanthos, 1979). Thomas L. Miller, *Bounty and Donation Land Grants of Texas, 1835–1888* (Austin: University of Texas Press, 1967). Marion Day Mullins, *First Census of Texas, 1829–1836, and Other Early Records of the Republic of Texas* (Washington: National Genealogical Society, 1959). Virginia H. Taylor, *Index to Spanish and Mexican Land Grants* (Austin: General Land Office, 1976).

Margaret Swett Henson

CARTWRIGHT, TEXAS. Cartwright is on Farm Road 1643 seven miles northeast of Quitman in north central Wood County. The Cartwright area, which probably had settlers as early as 1851, was first called the Barrens because of its isolation and the danger from wolves. Around 1874 a log school was constructed at the community. Cartwright was probably named for Matthew Cartwright,[qv] whose family in 1882 donated land for a school. By 1894 Cartwright had its first store and a post office. Around that time a Baptist church was organized. In 1895 the Cartwright school burned and was replaced with a two-room building; the next year the community's public school reported ninety-two white students. That same year Cartwright had at least eight businesses, including two carpenters, two music teachers, a barber, and a gin and mill. In 1905 the community's three-teacher school served 149 students. In 1907 the post office closed. In the 1930s Cartwright had a population of 100, two schools, a seasonal industry, and a number of dwellings. By 1945 the population had fallen to seventy-five, where it remained until the mid-1960s. Sometime after 1960 Cartwright lost its school. The population fell to sixty-one in 1968 and was still reported at that level in 1990. In 1988 highway maps showed two businesses, a church, and a community hall.

bibliography: *Wood County, 1850–1900* (Quitman, Texas: Wood County Historical Society, 1976). *Rachel Jenkins*

CARUTH, TEXAS. Caruth (Carruth) was on the Jacobs survey in southwestern Caldwell County. It was centered around a cotton gin and store. A post office operated there from 1902 until 1908. Children in the area attended the Unity School, which had one teacher and thirty-seven students in 1905. In 1912 Sarah Elizabeth Spencer purchased the community site and built her home there. Most of the early buildings were destroyed by a tornado in 1940.

bibliography: Mark Withers Trail Drive Museum, *Historical Caldwell County* (Dallas: Taylor, 1984). *Vivian Elizabeth Smyrl*

CARUTHERS, TEXAS. Caruthers was near Clawson in west central Angelina County. Around 1900 a logging camp was established at the site and named for an official with the logging company. At one time the Peavy family operated a small sawmill nearby. A post office opened in June 1908 but was suspended in August of the same year. In the early 1990s only a few scattered houses remained in the area.

bibliography: Angelina County Historical Survey Committee, *Land of the Little Angel: A History of Angelina County, Texas*, ed. Bob Bowman (Lufkin, Texas: Lufkin Printing, 1976).

Christopher Long

CARVAJAL CROSSING. Carvajal Crossing, a natural rock-bottomed ford across Cibolo Creek in north central Karnes County, was the best-known ford along the old cart road that went from the Texas coast to San Antonio. Situated halfway between Goliad and San Antonio, the crossing was in close proximity to the old Fuerte del Santa Cruz[qv] and the ranch headquarters of Andrés Hernández,[qv] who may have had the first ranch in Texas. Old maps and journals designated the crossing at various times as Tawakoni Crossing, the Crossing of the Tehuacanas, or Cibolo Crossing. About 1830 José Luis Carvajal, scion of Canary Islanders[qv] from San Antonio, acquired the ranch property adjoining the crossing, and since that time the ford has been called the Carvajal Crossing.

bibliography: Robert H. Thonhoff, "The First Ranch of Texas," West Texas Historical Association *Year Book* 40 (1964).

Robert H. Thonhoff

CARVAJAL Y DE LA CUEVA, LUIS DE (ca. 1540–1590). Luis de Carvajal y de la Cueva, governor, adventurer, slave trader, and the first Spanish subject to enter Texas, was born in Mogodorio, Portugal, about 1540, the son of Gaspar de Carvajal and Francisca De León, Jewish converts to the Christian faith. As a young man he spent three years at Cape Verde as the king's accountant and treasurer in the black slave trade. Then he emigrated to Spain, traded in grain and wines at Seville, and about 1565 married Guiomar de Ribera, daughter of a Portuguese royal slave factor and a native of Lisbon. Two years later, driven by financial losses and marital discord, Carvajal sailed for New Spain with his own ship as admiral (second in command) of the Spanish Indies fleet. Upon arrival he was accorded the viceroy's appointment as alcalde ordinario of Tampico.

In that capacity, in the fall of 1568, Carvajal rounded up seventy-seven defenseless Englishmen marooned on the Tamaulipas shore by master John Hawkins, who had lost some of his ships in a shootout with the Spanish fleet at Veracruz. Impressed by this deed, which seems to have grown with each telling, Viceroy Martín Enríquez de Almanza commissioned Carvajal a captain and sent him to open a road between Pánuco province and the Mazapil mines, then to chastise hostile Indian bands at the mouth of the Río Bravo (Rio Grande). In carrying out the latter assignment, Carvajal claimed to have punished the natives responsible for the massacre of 400 castaways from three ships wrecked on the coast while en route to Spain—doubtless the Padre Island Spanish shipwrecks of 1554.qv During the campaign, he crossed the lower Rio Grande into what is now Texas, thus becoming the first Spanish subject to do so.

In 1578 Carvajal was summoned to Mexico City to answer charges that such exploits were but a thin disguise of his traffic in Indian slaves. Witnesses at the hearing generally upheld his probity, but the affront hastened the plan that may have been in his mind from the beginning. He soon embarked for Spain, where in March 1579 he presented to the Council of the Indies one of the most sweeping proposals it had ever seen. He sought authority to develop all the ports from the Río Pánuco to Santa Elena on the Atlantic coast; to settle the area between Tampico and the mines of Mazapil and Zacatecas; and to extend exploration and settlement across Mexico "from sea to sea."

So fervently did the council recommend the plan that the king approved it, in substance, without consulting the viceroy. For his life and that of his heir, Carvajal was granted the title of governor and captain-general with authority to "discover, pacify, and settle" a new province to be called the Nuevo Reyno de León. The jurisdiction was defined as extending west from the port of Tampico to the borders of Nueva Galicia and Nueva Vizcaya and northward into undiscovered lands. Within five years Carvajal was to reconnoiter the interior, convert the Indians, and settle all the ports from Tampico to St. Joseph Bay, which bordered the Florida jurisdiction of Pedro Menéndez de Avilés. North of Nueva Galicia and Nueva Vizcaya, he might "discover" from sea to sea, but no farther than 200 leagues of latitude and the same of longitude, without infringing on prior rights. Implicit in such a description was the crown's profound ignorance of the territory it claimed; the distance from Tampico to St. Joseph Bay was far greater than 200 leagues.

After buying a ship and recruiting 100 families—many of them his wife's kin or his own—Carvajal again sailed for New Spain in June 1580, in the same fleet that carried a new viceroy, Conde de la Coruña. A bit heady over his success, the governor found Coruña an irritant. In a grave strategic blunder, he complained to the king.

Although no details are found, Carvajal claimed to have reconnoitered his grant, the northern limits of which extended almost to the site of Austin, Texas. Sixty leagues northwest of Tampico, by his estimate, he discovered silver mines and founded, at the site of present Cerralvo, Nuevo León, a village pretentiously called Ciudad de León. His claims consistently exceeded his accomplishments. He established a village called San Luis at the site of present Monterrey and another called Almadén at that of Monclova. But litigation in the next century discredits many of his purported achievements, establishing that virtually all the places he occupied had been settled previously under authority of the governor of Nueva Vizcaya.

Indeed, charges of usurpation were brought against Carvajal in his own time. To these were added allegations that the governor made a habit of slave raiding on the Río de las Palmas (present Soto la Marina) and the Río Bravo and was selling Indian captives into slavery by the hundreds. In January 1587 he was brought again before the royal audiencia in Mexico City to face an inquiry. His renewed complaint to the crown brought an order for his recall to Spain. Carvajal, however, had already disappeared into his wilderness jurisdiction to resume his slave raiding.

The viceroy's agent sent to arrest him found in the New Kingdom of León only two meager settlements of four or five huts each, distant from each other by fifteen to twenty days' march. Carvajal finally was overtaken at Almadén, which he had established with "renegades who acknowledged neither God nor king," to carry on his slaving operation among peaceful Indians. Arrested and taken to Mexico, Carvajal left Gaspar Castaño de Sosa qv in charge of the Almadén settlement.

While in prison awaiting disposition of the viceroy's charges, Carvajal was accused by the Inquisition of heresy. He remained Catholic, but members of his extended family had reverted to Judaism; notably, his niece, Isabel Rodríguez. It became apparent that the governor had known of Isabel's leanings and had failed in his obligation to denounce her. As a result, he was sentenced on February 23, 1590, to a six-year exile from New Spain. Before the year was out, while still awaiting execution of the sentence, Carvajal died in the Mexico prison.

In the years that followed, the Inquisition indicted other members of the family. In 1596 charges were brought against Luis de Carvajal the younger, the governor's nephew and heir. Luis broke under torture and implicated up to 120 other practicing Judaists among the Carvajal colonists, including his own mother, brothers, and sisters. Many of them were subjected to the rack and burned on Mexico City's main plaza on December 8, 1596.

bibliography: Archivo General de Indias, *Archivo General de Indias de Sevilla* (Madrid, 1958). Carl L. Duaine, *Caverns of Oblivion* (Manchaca, Texas: Packrat, 1971). Alfonso Toro, *La familia Carvajal: Estudio histórico sobre los judíos y la Inquisición de la Nueva España en el siglo XVI* (2 vols., Mexico City: Patria, 1944). Robert S. Weddle, *Spanish Sea: The Gulf of Mexico in North American Discovery, 1500–1685* (College Station: Texas A&M University Press, 1985).

Robert S. Weddle

CARVER, CHARLES (1915–1982). Charles Carver, writer and teacher, was born on June 19, 1915, in Ardmore, Pennsylvania, the son of Alexander Henry and Gertrude (Nason) Carver. After graduating from St. Albans School in Washington, D.C., he attended Yale University, where he received his B.A. degree in 1938. He married Elizabeth Preston in April 1836, and they had a daughter. At Yale, Carver served as editor of the *Yale Literary Magazine*; he altered the format of the publication to include photographs, student drawings, and feature columns. In 1939, after a year's apprenticeship with the Reynal and Hitchcock publishing company, he became assistant editor of the *Journal of Accounting*, a professional magazine for certified public accountants. He served in the navy in World War II qv and rose in rank from ensign to lieutenant in command of a mine sweeper. He was stationed off Sicily and Salerno before the Allied invasions of those islands. He subsequently taught navigation and seamanship for nine months before receiving a transfer to another command in Okinawa. The ship transporting Carver to Okinawa capsized during a typhoon a short distance from its destination, and Carver and the other survivors were in the water for four hours before being rescued.

After his discharge from the navy Carver and his wife moved to Texas, first to Weatherford and then to Waco. He ran an ad agency and, as a freelance writer, published short stories in *Esquire*, *Collier's*, *American*, and other magazines. He taught play writing part-time at Baylor University from 1947 to 1950. He was a member of the Episcopal Church and served as president of the Waco Civic Theater. In Waco he also wrote a book about William Cowper Brann,qv *Brann and the Iconoclast*, published by the University of Texas Press qv in 1957. Carver moved to New York that year and joined the staff of an ad agency in Manhattan. He retired in 1966 and spent his summers in Blue Hill, Maine, and his winters in Pound Ridge, New York. He died in Blue Hill on July 27, 1982.

bibliography: Vertical Files, Barker Texas History Center, University of Texas at Austin.

Vivian Elizabeth Smyrl

CARY, EDWARD HENRY (1872–1953). Edward Henry Cary, physician, medical educator, and civic leader, son of Joseph Milton and Lucy Janette (Powell) Cary, was born in Union Springs, Alabama, on February 28, 1872. He was a descendent of one of the first families of Virginia. He originally worked in Dallas for his older brother, but went to New York in 1895 to be trained as a physician at Bellevue Hospital Medical College. He graduated in 1898 and returned to Dallas in 1901 to set up a practice in ophthalmology that spanned a half century.

Cary was the father of both the present-day Baylor University Medical Center and the University of Texas Southwestern Medical Center,qqv both in Dallas. The former was founded in 1903 after Cary gained control of the financially troubled University of Dallas Medical Department and persuaded Baylor University to make this proprietary institution the nucleus of a school of medicine. As dean between 1903 and 1920 and dean emeritus until 1943, Cary helped the school to become one of the leading medical institutions in the Southwest. He also served it for decades (1903–43) as professor of ophthalmology and otolaryngology. During World War I[qv] he organized the Baylor Medical and Surgical Unit, which saw duty in France. In 1939 he founded and directed the Southwestern Medical Foundation, primarily Dallas businessmen who were interested in promoting medical education and research in Dallas. This group founded Southwestern Medical College in 1943, after Baylor Medical School moved to Houston. In 1949, at Cary's instigation, the school became associated with the University of Texas.

Cary headed the Cary-Schneider Investment Company and in 1921 built the Medical Arts Building, the first Dallas skyscraper with offices primarily for physicians. He was one of the founders of the Dallas Historical Society[qv] (1922–) and played a major role in its development. In the years both before and after World War II,[qv] he was an outspoken opponent of national health insurance. In 1943 he helped to found and lead the National Physicians Committee that successfully fought it. He became one of the principal proponents of group hospitalization as an alternative.

Cary maintained a highly successful practice and served as a consultant in ophthalmology at Baylor University Hospital, Parkland Hospital, and Medical Arts Hospital. He published over sixty papers on ophthalmology and otolaryngology. He was elected to the presidencies of the Texas Society of Ophthalmology and Otolaryngology, the Dallas County Medical Society (1912), the Texas State Medical Association (1917–18), the Southern Medical Association (1919–20), and the American Medical Association (1932–33). In 1916 Baylor University conferred an honorary LL.D. degree on him. In 1945 he was presented the Linz Award as the outstanding citizen of Dallas. On his seventy-fifth birthday, in 1947, a scholarship fund was established in his name at Southwestern Medical School. In 1959 a junior high school in Dallas was named for him. The first permanent building at Southwestern Medical School, dedicated in 1960, was named Edward H. Cary Science Hall. On April 19, 1911, Cary married Georgie Fonda Schneider. They had five children. Cary died in Dallas on December 11, 1953.

bibliography: John S. Chapman, *The University of Texas Southwestern Medical School: Medical Education in Dallas, 1900–1975* (Dallas: Southern Methodist University Press, 1976). Morris Fishbein, *A History of the American Medical Association, 1847 to 1947* (Philadelphia and London: Saunders, 1947). Lana Henderson, *Baylor University Medical Center* (Waco: Baylor University Press, 1978). Booth Mooney, *More Than Armies: The Story of Edward H. Cary, M.D* (Dallas: Mathis, Van Nort, 1948).

James O. Breeden

CASA BLANCA, TEXAS. Casa Blanca was two miles southwest of Sandia and twenty miles northeast of Alice in extreme northeastern Jim Wells County. The Casa Blanca or White House was part of a settlement established at the site around 1754 by Tomás Sánchez de la Barrera y Gallardo,[qv] captain of Laredo, who was ordered to find a suitable site for a new settlement. After surveying the country Sánchez selected a site on the banks of Peñitas Creek. A settlement was established there, and the White House was constructed of caliche blocks known as *ciares.* The house was built in the shape of a square with a courtyard in the center; the well in the courtyard also served as a the end of a tunnel out of the building. Toward the end of the eighteenth century the house was used as a mission.

The Spanish crown granted the land to Juan José de la Garza Montemayor[qv] and his sons Agustín, Perfecto, and Manuel on April 2, 1807. They used the Casa Blanca as a ranchhouse. According to records the land was occupied by their heirs until 1852. However, local legend has it that the Montemayor family was driven away by a band of outlaws, who in turn were driven out by hostile Indians. Subsequently various families occupied the house and the surrounding area, and a post office operated at the site from 1860 to 1866. The area continued to be inhabited by several families, and in 1893 the post office was reactivated. In 1896 the land was purchased by John L. Wade. Because Casa Blanca was already established as a stopping point Wade established Wade City adjacent to it, platting streets and setting aside land for stores and churches. In 1896 Casa Blanca–Wade City had a combined estimated population of 150, a Methodist church, a general store, a gin, and a lumberyard. Wade City did not prosper, however, and by 1914 its population had decreased to thirty-five. The post office ceased operation in 1922.

Around 1936 Wade's heirs petitioned for the site of Wade City to revert to them, arguing that the town never developed and showed no promise of doing so and that the land would be more valuable as ranchland. The petition was granted, and Wade City reverted to pastureland; Casa Blanca continued to be an independent community, but by 1945 only ruins remained.

bibliography: Neva Virginia Pollard, The History of Jim Wells County (M.A. thesis, Texas A&I University, 1945).

Alicia A. Garza

CASA BLANCA CREEK. Casa Blanca Creek rises in eastern Victoria County (at 28°53′ N, 96°55′ W) and runs southeast for eleven miles to its mouth on Placedo Creek (at 28°52′ N, 96°47′ W). It traverses flat to rolling prairie surfaced by permeable loam that supports mesquite and various prairie grasses.

CASA BLANCA LAKE. Casa Blanca Lake is on Chacon Creek, a tributary of the Rio Grande, just east of Laredo International Airport in southern Webb County (at 27° 32' N, 99° 27' W). It is owned and operated by Webb County for recreational purposes. The first dam, built in 1946, with top elevation at 455 above mean sea level, was damaged by the first floodwaters impounded by piping underneath the earth embankment. Construction of the second dam began in 1947 and was completed in 1951. The lake has a capacity of 20,000 acre-feet and a surface area of 1,656 acres at elevation 446.5 feet above mean sea level. Among its recreational uses, the lake supplies water to a golf course owned by the county. The drainage area above the dam is 117 square miles. The surrounding flat to rolling terrain is surfaced by clay and sandy loam that supports mesquite, cacti, and grasses.

Seth D. Breeding

CASA CALVO, MARQUÉS DE (1751–?). Sebastián Nicolás de Bari Calvo de la Puerta, Marqués de Casa Calvo, Spanish military officer, was born in Havana on August 11, 1751, the son of Pedro Calvo de la Puerta and Catalina de O'Farril. He joined the Company of Nobles as a cadet on April 1, 1763. On July 3, 1769, he was named interim captain of cavalry volunteers and on September 14 was given full captain's rank. He was transferred to the regular army with the rank of captain in 1776 and advanced to colonel by 1802. Casa Calvo participated in the reconquest of Louisiana by Spain in 1769. He fought in the campaign at Mobile in 1780, but a hurricane prevented him from fighting at Pensacola. When Manuel Gayoso de Lemos[qv] died in 1799, Casa Calvo was sent by the captain general of Cuba to take military command of Louisiana, which he did on September 18. The following June he was succeeded by Juan Manuel de Salcedo. Together with Salcedo, Casa Calvo delivered Louisiana to the French on April 10, 1803, but he remained in New Orleans after the American flag was raised. In 1805–06 he led an expedition with Nicolas de Finiels[qv] into western Louisiana and Texas. His analysis of mission and presidial records at Nacogdoches and survey of the jurisdiction of Los Adaes[qv] convinced him of the just claims of Spain to territory as far east as Arroyo Hondo, which formed the boundary between Louisiana and Texas. Upon his return to New Orleans in 1806, he was expelled from Louisiana by

Governor W. C. C. Claiborne. He was almost shipwrecked off Pass Christian, but he survived the storm to arrive at Pensacola in March 1806, where he asked permission to lead a military expedition against Louisiana. He regarded this as the only hope of saving Spanish North America from the rapacious conquest by Anglo-Americans. He was a Knight of the Order of Santiago.

BIBLIOGRAPHY: Charles Gayarré, *History of Louisiana* (4 vols., New York: Widdleton, 1866). Jack D. L. Holmes, *Documentos inéditos para la historia de la Luisiana, 1782–1810* (Madrid: Porrúa Turanzas, 1963). Jack D. L. Holmes, "The Marqués de Casa-Calvo, Nicolás de Finiels, and the 1805 Spanish Expedition through East Texas and Louisiana," *Southwestern Historical Quarterly* 69 (January 1966). Micheline Walsh, *Spanish Knights of Irish Origin* (Dublin: Stationery Office for the Irish Manuscripts Commission, 1960). *Jack D. L. Homes*

CASA EDITORIAL LOZANO. The Casa Editorial Lozano was founded between 1915 and 1920 in San Antonio as an offshoot of the Spanish-language newspaper *La Prensa.*[qv] Ignacio E. Lozano,[qv] a Mexican national who immigrated to the United States just before the outbreak of the Mexican Revolution[qv] in 1910, founded *La Prensa* in 1913. He intended the newspaper to report primarily current events in Mexico, but also to provide coverage of United States and worldwide events of interest to Mexicans and Mexican Americans in Texas, so as to help them maintain national identity until the immigrants could return to their homeland.

In accord with this purpose, Lozano opened a bookstore adjacent to the newspaper's facilities. He subsequently became aware of the availability in San Antonio of unpublished Spanish-language manuscripts, some of which had been written by his staff writers. It was natural for the bookstore to begin a publishing operation, which became La Casa Editorial Lozano. Though La Casa Lozano published some patriotic biographies and romantic novels, its most important publications were a series of seven Novels of the Mexican Revolution, published between 1920 and 1928. These novels are particularly significant because the multiple editions of four of them published by 1929, suggest that the Novels of the Mexican Revolution, as a literary genre, enjoyed widespread popularity in the United States before their public acclaim in Mexico, which occurred after 1931. Mexican exiles, aware of the chaos taking place in the fatherland, were evidently avidly interested in novels portraying the Revolution. Ironically, the reverse was probably true in Mexico. A distinguished Mexican literary historian contends that the Novels of the Revolution received belated popularity in Mexico because Mexicans in the 1920s looked to the novel primarily as a means of escape from the harsh reality of daily life. Only after peace had been firmly reestablished by the 1930s was the Mexican populace able to look to the revolution as a suitable literary topic. During the first two decades of publication, the intended readership of both *La Prensa* and the Casa Lozano was an educated and refined elite. This is evident in the elevated style, replete with allusions to classical literature and art, characteristic not only of the Casa Lozano novels, but also of the literary selections published regularly in *La Prensa.*

BIBLIOGRAPHY: Richard Garcia, "Class Consciousness and Identity: The Mexican Community of San Antonio, Texas, 1930–1940," *Aztlán* 9 (Spring 1979). Dennis Parle, "The Novels of the Mexican Revolution Published by the Casa Editorial Lozano," *Americas Review* 17 (Fall–Winter 1989). *Dennis J. Parle*

CASA GRANDE. Casa Grande is a prominent mountain on the east side of the basin of the Chisos Mountains of Big Bend National Park[qv] in Brewster County (at 29°16′ N, 103°17′ W). The name Casa Grande (Spanish for "Big House") probably refers to the massive profile the mountain presents. Casa Grande rises in wooded slopes to a tremendous square-topped monolith of bare rock with sheer, towering cliffs overlooking the National Park Service ranger station in the basin some 2,000 feet below. At its highest point Casa Grande reaches an elevation of 7,325 feet above sea level. Casa Grande is a lava-capped erosional remnant with constituent stones that are 30 to 33 million years old. The vegetation on its lower slopes is dominated by an association of juniper, oak, and piñon that is found at higher elevations in many of the mountainous areas of the Trans-Pecos[qv] region. Some Douglas firs also grow on the upper slopes of the northeast side of the mountain.

BIBLIOGRAPHY: Ross A. Maxwell, *The Big Bend of the Rio Grande* (Bureau of Economic Geology, University of Texas at Austin, 1968).

CASA PIEDRA, TEXAS. Casa Piedra is on Alamito Creek and the Atchison, Topeka and Santa Fe Railway in southeastern Presidio County. A winding, unpaved road leads there from Plata, ten miles to the north. Casa Piedra began in 1883 when Domenicio Mata settled at the site on preemption land. In the late 1890s he built a rock house, which gave the settlement its Spanish name. By 1900 more than fifty farm families lived at Casa Piedra. The community was close-knit because many of the residents were related. Among them were the Russell and the Vásquez families. The families of Casa Piedra observed holidays with music, dancing, feasting, and horse racing. They raised large crops of cotton, corn, beans, and hay and enjoyed prosperity throughout the first three decades of the twentieth century. In 1906, through the encouragement of Lucia Hernández Russell, the community opened a one-room school. When the growing number of students warranted a larger school, a two-room building was completed. A post office was established in 1912. In 1930 the Santa Fe brought its tracks to the community, and Conrado Vásquez served as the first depot agent. The 1930s also brought an end to Casa Piedra's prosperity when drought and economic depression hit most of the nation. By 1933 the community's population had declined to ten. As late as 1939 a public school continued in the community, and the Ted Harper Ranch shipped livestock from the Casa Piedra station in the 1940s. But the post office was closed by 1953, and the Vásquez family shut down its mercantile store, the community's only business, in 1957. The community reported a population of twenty-one in 1968 and by 1988 was a ghost town.

BIBLIOGRAPHY: Ed Ellsworth Bartholomew, *The Encyclopedia of Texas Ghost Towns* (Fort Davis, Texas, 1982). Cecilia Thompson, *History of Marfa and Presidio County, 1535–1946* (2 vols., Austin: Nortex, 1985). *Julia Cauble Smith*

CASAÑAS DE JESÚS MARÍA, FRANCISCO (1656?–1696). Fray Francisco Casañas de Jesús María was born of noble parents about 1656 in Barcelona, Spain. He joined the Franciscans[qv] and in 1682 was selected as one of the first members of the College of Santa Cruz de Querétaro.[qv] He did mission work in Mexico City, Veracruz, San Juan de Ulloa, Campeche, and Mérida. After returning to Querétaro for a short time, he resumed his missionary activities in 1689, this time among the Indians of the Nuevo León frontier. His work met with so little success that he returned to Querétaro and accompanied Alonso De León[qv] on his fifth expedition to Texas, in 1690. Casañas aided in the establishment of the first missions in East Texas and was left at San Francisco de los Tejas Mission by Fray Damián Massanet.[qv] In the fall of 1691 Casañas founded Santísimo Nombre de María Mission. Early in 1692 he returned to Mexico with Domingo Terán de los Ríos[qv] in hope of securing additional aid for the Texas mission field. He went first to his college then to Mexico City to plead his cause but was informed that conditions in Texas did not warrant the undertaking of additional work, and the matter was apparently dropped. With the discontinuation of his Texas work in 1693, Fray Casañas began mission work among the Xemes Indians of New Mexico. He was killed in 1696 by Apaches.

BIBLIOGRAPHY: Carlos E. Castañeda, *Our Catholic Heritage in Texas* (7 vols., Austin: Von Boeckmann–Jones, 1936–58; rpt., New York:

Arno, 1976). Mattie Austin Hatcher, "Description of the Tejas or Asinai Indians," *Southwestern Historical Quarterly* 30 (January 1937). Vertical Files, Barker Texas History Center, University of Texas at Austin.

CASAS AMARILLAS. The name Casas Amarillas, Spanish for "yellow houses," was given by early explorers to a geological formation near Levelland in Hockley County that at a distance looked like yellow houses. Spanish missionaries visited Indians at the site in the seventeenth century. The formation, long considered a landmark on the South Plains, became the location of a trading post for buffalo hunters, freighters, and cattlemen. It was acquired by the XIT Ranch[qv] syndicate in 1882 and by George Washington Littlefield[qv] in 1901. A marker was placed at the site of Casas Amarillas by the Texas Centennial[qv] Commission in 1936.

BIBLIOGRAPHY: Harold Schoen, comp., *Monuments Erected by the State of Texas to Commemorate the Centenary of Texas Independence* (Austin: Commission of Control for Texas Centennial Celebrations, 1938).

CASAS BLANCAS, TEXAS. Casas Blancas, begun in 1776 as an outgrowth of the colonizing activities of José de Escandón,[qv] is a ghost town seven miles west of Roma in southwestern Starr County. The land was originally granted to Antonio García by the Spanish government in 1767. The García family occupied the site as late as 1852 and owned it until about 1880. Through marriage and purchase the González family acquired the entire grant and eventually occupied the fifteen rock houses erected by the Garcías. The whole family left suddenly in 1894. According to a local story a feud divided them into two factions and resulted in one man's murder. Reportedly, the rest of the family secretly buried the victim in the family cemetery and left their homes. Another story says that a ghostly apparition of the murdered man caused the evacuation. In 1899 a school at Casa Blancas had twenty-five students and one teacher. Years later locals asserted that a curse was on the site. The old rock houses gradually deteriorated, and by 1949 all that remained of the community was a few stones, the rest having been used to build new houses a few miles away.

BIBLIOGRAPHY: *Guide to Spanish and Mexican Land Grants in South Texas* (Austin: Texas General Land Office, 1988). Randy McMillon, "Vanished Towns of the Rio Grande Valley," *Junior Historian*, May 1955. Vertical Files, Barker Texas History Center, University of Texas at Austin. *Dick D. Heller, Jr., and Alicia A. Garza*

CASAS BLANCAS CREEK. Casas Blancas Creek, also known as Arroyo La Minita, rises in western Starr County (at 26°37′ N, 99°03′ W) and runs southwest for fifteen miles to its mouth on the Rio Grande, four miles south of Salineno (at 26°28′ N, 99°06′ W). It traverses flat to rolling terrain with steep margins, surfaced by shallow to deep sandy loams that support pecan, willow, and grasses.

Dick D. Heller, Jr.

CASAS CHIQUITAS INDIANS. These Indians, whose name is Spanish for "small houses," lived somewhere along the Rio Grande below Laredo during the second half of the eighteenth century. They are among the various small Coahuiltecan bands of that area which the Spaniards referred to as Carrizo.

BIBLIOGRAPHY: Frederick Webb Hodge, ed., *Handbook of American Indians North of Mexico* (2 vols., Washington: GPO, 1907, 1910; rpt., New York: Pageant, 1959). *Thomas N. Campbell*

CASAS MORADAS INDIANS. The Casas Moradas (Spanish for "purple [or mulberry-colored] houses") are known only from a Spanish document of 1693 that lists them as one of fifty "nations" that lived north of the Rio Grande and "between Texas and New Mexico." This may be interpreted to mean the southern part of western Texas, since the document also mentions that the Apaches were at war with the groups named. The document further states that the Casas Moradas consisted of "four nations of the same name." Nothing further is known about them.

BIBLIOGRAPHY: Charles W. Hackett, ed., *Historical Documents Relating to New Mexico, Nueva Vizcaya, and Approaches Thereto, to 1773* (3 vols., Washington: Carnegie Institution, 1923–37).

Thomas N. Campbell

CASAS REVOLT. The Casas Revolt of 1811 was one of the many challenges to imperial authority that convulsed New Spain after Miguel Hidalgo y Costilla's[qv] initial action to achieve Mexican independence from Spain in September 1810. The royalist governor of Texas, Manuel María de Salcedo,[qv] found that Mexican revolutionaries seeking to overthrow Spanish rule hoped to get aid from the United States via Texas. In late 1810 Salcedo discovered two revolutionary agents from Nuevo Santander, militia lieutenants Francisco Ignacio Escamilla and Antonio Saenz, working among his troops. After ordering their imprisonment in San Antonio de Valero Mission, Salcedo decided to take preemptive action. Aware that the viceregal authorities could not spare forces to protect Texas, he tried in January to muster his men to crush the rebellion on the Rio Grande. Members of the garrison were unhappy at the prospect of leaving their families unprotected against Indians and other dangers. Equally disconcerted were the alcaldes (*see* ALCALDE), led by Francisco Travieso, who would be faced with mounting a citizen guard during the militia's absence. Along with a militia representative, Travieso called upon Capt. Juan Bautista de las Casas to assume command of the San Antonio troops. Casas, a native of San Fernando, Nuevo Santander, and a retired captain of the Villa de Croix frontier defenses in his home province, was living in San Antonio de Béxar at the time. The next morning, January 22, 1811, Casas, leading the rebellious militia, arrested Governor Salcedo and the garrison commandant and ordered the release of Saenz and Escamilla.

Casas and his supporters declared themselves against government by European-born Spaniards, *gachupines*, in accordance with Hidalgo's declaration. Casas ordered the arrest of all *gachupines* in the province and the confiscation of their property. The revolutionary leadership in Coahuila, upon word of Casas's success, appointed him ad interim governor of Texas. Meanwhile, Casas sent Saenz and alcalde Gavino Delgado, at the head of eighty troops, to establish the revolutionary government in Nacogdoches, where they arrived on February 1. There they arrested *gachupines*, confiscated property, and erected a provisional government before returning to San Antonio with prisoners in tow.

When the successful Nacogdoches expedition returned, Casas had Saenz arrested for pocketing some of the confiscated wealth. The charges were dropped, but neither Saenz nor Delgado received recognition for the mission. The slighted revolutionaries made common cause with the remaining royalists. The two groups found a leader in Lt. Col. Juan Manuel Zambrano,[qv] a scandalous churchman and Bexar native who had long been out of favor with local authorities. Delgado persuaded leading townsmen to support Zambrano's efforts at undermining Casas, while Saenz agitated among the militia.

Events soon came to a head. Ignacio Aldama, Hidalgo's ambassador to the United States, arrived at Bexar with a retinue and a substantial sum of money and silver to solicit arms and troops. After determining that Aldama would not remove Casas from the governorship, Zambrano and his fellow conspirators spread the rumor that Aldama was actually a Napoleonic agent. Fear of the French cemented the support of the populace for the counterrevolutionaries. In a predawn movement on March 2, Zambrano's forces captured and arrested Casas and Aldama. Casas was sent as a prisoner to Monclova for court-martial as a traitor. On August 3, 1811, he was demoted, shot in the back, and beheaded. The body was buried at Monclova, and the head was sent to San Antonio to be publicly displayed. With the troops loyal to the new junta, royal authority was soon reestablished throughout the province of Texas. Salcedo was restored to the governorship.

BIBLIOGRAPHY: Carlos E. Castañeda, *Our Catholic Heritage in Texas* (7 vols., Austin: Von Boeckmann–Jones, 1936–58; rpt., New York: Arno, 1976). Frederick Charles Chabot, ed., *Texas in 1811: The Las Casas and Sambrano Revolutions* (San Antonio: Yanaguana Society, 1941).
Laura Caldwell

CASCADE CAVERNS. Cascade Caverns, five miles south of Boerne in Kendall County, was first commercially operated from 1933 to about 1941; it was reopened about 1950. The cave, originally known as Hester's Cave, became famous as a result of Frank Nicholson's publication of cave explorations. In it a commercial tour passes through a half mile of flowstone-decorated passages and rooms. See also CAVES AND CAVE STUDIES.

BIBLIOGRAPHY: Victor S. Craun, "Commercial Caves of Texas," in *The Caves of Texas* (National Speleological Society Bulletin 10, April 1948). Frank E. Nicholson, "A Celebrated Cave Exploration," in *The Caves of Texas* (National Speleological Society Bulletin 10 [April 1948]).
A. Richard Smith

CASE, JOEL TITUS (1802–1868). Joel Titus Case, teacher, editor, and pastor, was born on June 30, 1802, in Austinburg, Ashtabula County, Ohio. He attended Burton Academy in Ohio, then taught there from 1821 to 1826, studied theology in Cincinnati, and graduated from Yale in 1828 with an A.B. degree and in 1854 with an M.A. degree. In 1834–35 he was editor of a paper in Mobile, Alabama. In October 1835 he acted as secretary at a meeting held to raise money and volunteers for Texas. In 1838 he traveled to Texas, where he lived for a time in Houston, helped organize the University of Galveston, edited the Galveston *Daily Courier*,[qv] and at one time was a Refugio district surveyor. As a member of the Texan Santa Fe expedition,[qv] he was captured and imprisoned by the Mexicans. Upon his release he returned to Mobile, where he edited the Mobile *Advertiser* from 1842 to 1847. Case was first married while in Ohio to the niece of a Bishop McIlvane. This marriage ended in divorce. After his move to Texas he married a widow, Mrs. Raymond (Cook) Gaylord, who died in October 1853. They had a daughter.

Case was licensed to preach in 1849 in Alabama. He was ordained and became pastor of a Presbyterian church at Victoria, Texas, on December 29, 1850. There he married, in 1862, his third wife, Mrs. Viola H. Shive, whose first husband had founded Victoria Female Academy.[qv] The Cases continued the operation of the academy as Case School until 1862, when they moved to Clinton, where they continued the school and Case became pastor. From 1854 to 1861 he was agent for Aranama College at Goliad; he was also the stated clerk for the Western Texas Presbytery for fourteen years. In 1866 the Cases returned to Victoria, where Case died on June 10, 1868.

BIBLIOGRAPHY: Frances Terry Ingmire, *Victoria County, Texas, Marriage Records, 1838–1890* (St. Louis, 1981). Claude Elliott, "Alabama and the Texas Revolution," *Southwestern Historical Quarterly* 50 (January 1947). *Ministerial Directory of the Presbyterian Church, U.S.* (Presbyterian Church in the United States, 1942). William Stuart Red, *A History of the Presbyterian Church in Texas* (Austin: Steck, 1936). Victor Marion Rose, *History of Victoria* (Laredo, 1883; rpt., Victoria, Texas: Book Mart, 1961).
Clinton P. Hartmann

CASE CREEK. Case Creek rises 4½ miles northeast of Ethel in southwestern Grayson County (at 33°36′ N, 96°48′ W) and runs southwest for seven miles to its mouth on Range Creek, 1½ miles southeast of Ethel (at 33°31′ N, 96°49′ W). The surrounding flat to rolling prairie with local shallow depressions is surfaced by soils ranging from dark, commonly calcareous clays to clay and sandy loams that support mesquite, water-tolerant hardwoods, conifers, cacti, and various grasses.

CASE'S MILLS, TEXAS. Case's Mills (Case's) was six miles east of Austin and two miles north of the Colorado River in east central Travis County. A post office called Case's was in operation from 1852 to 1853, and one called Case's Mills operated from 1855 to 1859. The community was named in honor of Sherman Case, postmaster and mill owner.

BIBLIOGRAPHY: John J. Germann and Myron Janzen, *Texas Post Offices by County* (1986).
Vivian Elizabeth Smyrl

CASEYVILLE, TEXAS. Caseyville, on the Brazos River in southern Young County, was settled about 1880, when John C. Casey and George Aynesworth purchased the site, upon which Casey later built a cotton gin and mill. Although the exact location of Caseyville is uncertain, it was near the Palo Pinto county line. The settlement grew up around a ferry marked "K Z" and operated by Casey. It was one of the first ferries on the Brazos and was the only means of crossing when the river was up. Several families built homes 300 yards or more from the river bank, and Casey started a general store, a gin, and a blacksmith shop. Although Casey sold his ferry to a Mr. Bellamy, its "K Z" label was not changed. L. W. Aynesworth bought the store, and other settlers moved in to develop the river country. Sketchy school records put Caseyville in county district ten and show a school from 1881 to 1884.

BIBLIOGRAPHY: Carrie J. Crouch, *Young County: History and Biography* (Dallas: Dealey and Love, 1937; rev. ed., *A History of Young County, Texas*, Austin: Texas State Historical Association, 1956). Young County Federation of Women's Clubs, *Scrapbook of Young County* (Graham, Texas?, 194–?).
Jeanne F. Lively

CASH, CHRISTINE BENTON (1889–1988). Christine Benton Cash, teacher, administrator, and civil-rights activist, was born on August 9, 1889, in the New Zion Baptist Church community, eight miles southwest of Jefferson in Marion County, Texas, the second child of James and Kizzia (Dotson) Benton. She attended Central Elementary School in Jefferson from 1898 to 1902 and Bishop College Academy in Marshall from 1902 to 1906; she was the first honor graduate of both the normal school and the scientific college preparatory department of the academy. Upon completion of county and state examinations, she began her professional career with a contract to teach in a one-room school in Marion County. For five years she taught in rural schools, during which time she successfully lobbied to lengthen the school year for black children from five to eight months.

In 1909 she married Larry Brown Cash of Pittsburg, Texas, with whom she had two sons. At the time of their marriage Larry Cash was principal of the Center Point school, ten miles east of Pittsburg. He was the state treasurer of the National Association for the Advancement of Colored People and later left the teaching profession for the ministry. In 1911, when he resigned as principal of the Center Point school, Christine took his place. The following year planning began for a community high school. In 1916 a building was erected that had five classrooms and an industrial lab. Financing came from a bond issue and local subscription. The school comprised eleven grades in 1918, and in 1928 it became a state-accredited school with twelve grades. Mrs. Cash continued as principal of the school until 1949. By 1937 the Center Point Training School had an enrollment of 289 students, representing seven counties in Northeast Texas. Monthly tuition was paid in specie or in kind, and students could defray part of their expenses by working at the school. The school had ten teachers, a fourteen-acre campus, and six buildings, all but one of them built by the students. Facilities included a library, which was open to the public, a cannery, a farm shop, and a home economics building. The school raised crops on its own acreage and on other land that it rented. During Cash's tenure the value of the physical plant increased from

$100 to $100,000. She was responsible for the installation of rural electrification; health, sanitation, and home-improvement projects; and cultural enrichment programs. She encouraged the intermediate-grade teachers to institute extracurricular reading programs for students. Those who read thirty books during the year received reading certificates. When the books on the state-approved list did not interest the students, she asked for and received permission to include books about African Americans.[qv] As a result more students entered the program and received reading certificates.

Christine Cash attended the summer session at Hampton Institute in Virginia in 1919, 1922, and 1923. She attended Bishop College in 1925–26, and received her B.A. She earned an M.A. degree from Atlanta University in 1943 and a Ph.D. from the University of Wisconsin in 1947, thus becoming one of the first Texas-born black women to earn a doctorate. In 1948 she was a member of the statewide legislative committee that initiated public school reforms (*see* GILMER-AIKEN LAWS). From 1951 to 1955 she participated in the Southwestern Cooperative Project in Education Administration. From 1948 to 1958 she taught education and sociology at Bishop College, where she served as secretary of the graduate division of education. From 1958 to 1965 she taught at Jarvis Christian College; she was chairman of the division of social sciences from 1958 to 1960 and chairman of the division of teacher education and certification from 1962 to 1965. A serious automobile accident in 1966 forced her to retire from her professional duties at Jarvis. She spent her last years in Marshall, writing her autobiography, "Confrontation, Conflict, Conquest."

Christine Cash was a member of Pi Lambda Theta (an honor society for women in education), Delta Sigma Theta, the National Education Association, the American Teachers Association, the Teachers State Association of Texas,[qv] the National Council of Teachers of Social Studies, the National Society for the Study of Education, the Association of Social Science Teachers, the American Association of University Women,[qv] and the American Association of University Professors. She served as a trustee of Bishop College, as recording secretary for the Northeast Texas Baptist Women's Convention, and as statistical secretary for the Baptist Women's Missionary and Educational Convention of Texas. In 1942 she listed her political affiliation as Republican.

She was awarded the title of Piper Professor in 1960 by the Minnie Stevens Piper Foundation. In 1962 she received a plaque from the Teachers State Association of Texas recognizing her distinguished career and contributions in the field of education. In 1966 she and her husband were honored at a testimonial dinner. She was named educator of the year by Upsilon Zeta chapter of Zeta Phi Beta in 1968 and outstanding educator by the Alpha Zeta Chapter of Delta Sigma Theta in 1969. In 1969 she also received the Distinguished Service Award from Bishop College. The Longview branch of the NAACP gave her a plaque recognizing her many decades of service. Christine Cash died in Harris County on December 12, 1988.

BIBLIOGRAPHY: Effie Kaye Adams, *Tall Black Texans: Men of Courage* (Dubuque, Iowa: Kendall-Hunt, 1972). Dallas *Morning News*, June 13, 1937. *Who's Who in American Education*, 23d ed. *Who's Who in Colored America*, 6th ed. *Kharen Monsho*

CASH, TEXAS. Cash is on State Highway 34 five miles south of Greenville in south central Hunt County. It was one of several communities established in the mid-1890s by the president of the Texas Midland Railroad, Edward H. R. Green,[qv] and was originally named Sylvia, in honor of Green's sister. Sylvia quickly became a church and school community for area farmers. Residents, however, wanted to rename the settlement Money, for John A. Money, who owned a store there. When this name was submitted to postal authorities, though, it was rejected and the name Cash substituted. A post office branch opened in 1895 with John A. Money as postmaster. Since its founding Cash has served as a community center for farmers in south central Hunt County, but the town never reported more than 150 residents until 1949, when it claimed 250 residents. Cash's population decreased to fifty-six by 1968 and remained at that figure through 1990.

BIBLIOGRAPHY: W. Walworth Harrison, *History of Greenville and Hunt County, Texas* (Waco: Texian, 1976). *David Minor*

CASHS CREEK. Cashs (Cash) Creek rises two miles north of Blessing in western Matagorda County (at 28°53′ N, 96°13′ W) and runs southeast for 11½ miles to its mouth on Tres Palacios Bay, three miles northeast of Palacios (at 28°45′ N, 96°11′ W). The surrounding terrain is flat with some low rolling hills and local dissection and is surfaced by sandy and clay loam that supports hardwoods and grasses. The creek was called Post Oak Creek by the area's first white settlers and was renamed Cash around 1842 after a family by that name settled near its mouth.

CASIBA INDIANS. The name is known from a single 1691 Spanish missionary report which indicates that the Casiba Indians were neighbors of the Hasinai tribes of eastern Texas. It is said that they lived an unspecified distance southeast of the Hasinais. This location suggests that the Casibas were probably not the same as the Cassias, reported in 1687 documents of the La Salle expedition[qv] as allies of the Kadohadachos on the Red River. The affiliations of both groups remain unknown.

BIBLIOGRAPHY: Pierre Margry, ed., *Découvertes et établissements des Français dans l'ouest et dans le sud de l'Amérique septentrionale, 1614–1754* (6 vols., Paris: Jouast, 1876–86). John R. Swanton, *Source Material on the History and Ethnology of the Caddo Indians* (Smithsonian Institution, Bureau of American Ethnology Bulletin 132, Washington: GPO, 1942). *Thomas N. Campbell*

CASINO CLUB. The Casino Club, San Antonio's first social club and theater, originated from meetings of twenty Germans[qv] who gathered for conversation and sociability in 1854. The club was chartered in 1857, with a membership of 106 men—all German Texans. The club's building on Market Street, formally opened in 1858, had on its west side a bar with skat tables and reading room, in the center a ballroom that could be converted into a theater with a stage and balcony, and on the east side a salon and lounge. Commissioned army officers stationed in San Antonio were honorary guests. The names of generals Robert E. Lee[qv] and Ulysses S. Grant appear on the guest list. The club was open daily to its members; a monthly entertainment (usually a concert or an amateur play followed by a dance or hop) was provided for the families. The New Year's Ball was a formal affair with supper and champagne. The children had their Kinderball and Maskenball. Revenue was collected from the rental of the theater. Many leading actors, stock companies, entertainers, and lecturers engaged it. The Casino Club had existed sixty-nine years when its building was sold in 1923. Its reputation as a social center was famous, with its old German flavor and European traditions. Fathers reserved memberships for their sons and formally introduced their daughters. In 1946 the organization was exclusively a man's club. There were Casino Clubs listed in the San Antonio telephone directory into the early 1960s.

BIBLIOGRAPHY: San Antonio *Express*, February 24, 1924. Adolf Paul Weber, *Deutsche Pioniere: zur Geschichte des Deutschthums in Texas* (San Antonio, 1894). *Minnie B. Cameron*

CASIS, LILIA MARY (1869–1947). Lilia Mary Casis, teacher, dean, and language scholar, was born in Kingston, Jamaica, on May 12, 1869, the daughter of José Marie Salomé and Coelestine Auguste Marie (Sack) de Casís. Her father, a wealthy lawyer, was of Spanish and French descent; her mother was a German related to the Kleberg family in Texas. Lilia received most of her early education, which included extensive training in classical and modern languages, from her father at home. She hoped to study medicine but when her father died, Lilia, at age nineteen, began private tutoring to supplement her family's income. In 1890 she, her mother, and her younger sister Josephine moved to Texas. Their mother died soon after their arrival, and the Casis sisters supported themselves in various teaching jobs in rural areas.

In 1894 Lilia Casis entered the University of Texas in Austin; by placing out of many classes through examinations, she completed her bachelor's degree in one year. In 1896, while holding the first student assistantship offered in the modern language department, she completed her master's degree in Romance languages, and in that same year the university named her a tutor in that subject. She was affiliated with the University of Texas for the rest of her life, as she became an instructor (1897), adjunct professor (1899), and associate professor (1908). She was appointed a full professor in 1916 and served as dean of women from 1919 to 1921. Casis additionally studied at the University of Chicago in summers and for a year in France and Spain. Her teaching specialties included elementary language courses as well as advanced linguistics and classical Spanish literature. She also wrote several articles and textbooks.

She was raised Catholic but later became a Methodist. She was a member of the Delta Kappa Gamma Society,[qv] an honorary organization for women teachers, and also was active in the YMCA, YWCA, University Ladies Club, and American Association of University Women.[qv] In 1945 she was named an honorary life member of the Texas State Historical Association.[qv] When she retired to part-time service in 1939, her friends and colleagues established a scholarship in her name. Shortly before her death Casis made the university the beneficiary of her life insurance policy and stipulated that this money was to be used for an annual scholarship for graduate study in Spanish. In addition, both Casis sisters left large sums of money to the university and the Austin school district.

Lilia Casis died in Austin on October 19, 1947, a few months after the death of her sister. She was buried in Oakwood Cemetery, Austin. In 1951 the Austin Independent School District dedicated Casis Elementary School, named for Lilia and Josephine, who was a longtime teacher in the Austin schools. The school was opened as a cooperative effort between the Austin Independent School District and the University of Texas; in addition to serving the children in its West Austin neighborhood, it included special facilities for physically handicapped students from across the city. For many years the school served as a demonstration center for the university and was noted for its trilingual classes (English, French, and Spanish) and for offering the only public kindergarten and only summer school for Austin elementary students.

BIBLIOGRAPHY: *Alcalde* (magazine of the Ex-Students' Association of the University of Texas), January 1920, June 1939, December 1947. Austin *American*, October 20, 21, 1947. *Daily Texan*, October 21, 1947, April 6, 1951. Mabelle and Stuart Purcell et al., *This Is Texas* (Austin: Futura, 1977). Vertical Files, Barker Texas History Center, University of Texas at Austin.

Debbie Mauldin Cottrell

CASKET MOUNTAIN. Casket Mountain is six miles northwest of Fort Davis in central Jeff Davis County (at 30°39′ N, 103°55′ W). It rises to an elevation of 6,183 feet above sea level, some 900 feet higher than the radio tower a mile southwest. On the mountain shallow, stony soils support Douglas fir, aspen, Arizona cypress, maple, ponderosa pine, and madrone.

CASO INDIANS. The Caso Indians are known from a Spanish document of 1748 that lists the names of twenty-five Indian groups of east central and southeastern Texas who had asked for missions in the general area. Although it cannot be demonstrated, it seems likely that the Casos were the same as the Caxos, who were reported in a Spanish missionary report from eastern Texas in 1691. The Caxos are generally considered to have been Caddoans of the southwestern or Hasinai division.

BIBLIOGRAPHY: Herbert Eugene Bolton, *Texas in the Middle Eighteenth Century* (Berkeley: University of California Press, 1915; rpt., Austin: University of Texas Press, 1970). Charles W. Hackett, ed., *Pichardo's Treatise on the Limits of Louisiana and Texas* (4 vols., Austin: University of Texas Press, 1931–46). Juan Agustín Morfi, *History of Texas, 1673–1779* (2 vols., Albuquerque: Quivira Society, 1935; rpt., New York: Arno, 1967). John R. Swanton, *Source Material on the History and Ethnology of the Caddo Indians* (Smithsonian Institution, Bureau of American Ethnology Bulletin 132, Washington: GPO, 1942).

Thomas N. Campbell

CASON, TEXAS. Cason is on State Highway 11 and the Louisiana and Arkansas Railway, five miles west of Daingerfield in southwestern Morris County. The town grew up around a station on the East Line and Red River Railroad, which was constructed through western Morris County in the late 1870s. Many of the early businesses were transferred from Snow Hill, three miles north. When the post office, which had been in Snow Hill, was moved in 1878, the postmaster, William M. Cason, named the new town Cason in honor of his father, J. W. By 1884 the settlement had an estimated population of 200, a church, a district school, and businesses that included sawmills and gristmills and two cotton gins. By 1892 the population had grown to 250, and a bedspring factory was in operation. The town reached its peak in the late 1920s, when the population was estimated at 500. The population declined between World War II[qv] and 1972, when a population of 160 and five rated businesses were reported. In 1986 the population was estimated at 165, and Cason had four rated businesses. In 1990 the population was 173.

BIBLIOGRAPHY: Jean Connor, *A Short History of Morris County* (Daingerfield, Texas: Daingerfield Bicentennial Commission, 1975).

Cecil Harper, Jr.

CASON TOWN, TEXAS. Cason Town was ten miles southwest of Emory in extreme southwestern Rains County. It was probably first settled after the Civil War[qv] and was named for a early resident. In the mid-1930s the settlement had a school and a number of scattered houses. With the construction of Lake Tawakoni in the late 1950s and early 1960s the entire area was inundated. *Christopher Long*

CASS, TEXAS. Cass is on the Kansas City Southern Railway and Farm Road 251, eight miles northeast of Atlanta in northeastern Cass County. It was settled in the early 1890s, when the Texarkana and Fort Smith Railway was built through the county. The first post office was established in March 1894 and named Sheffield, but the name was changed to Cass in 1896. At that time the settlement was little more than a country post office and a general store. By 1914 it had two stores, two gins, and a population of 100. In 1925 Cass had a population of twenty, and the post office closed in 1928. In 1964 the population was reported at forty, and the town had no rated businesses. In 1983 Cass had a town hall, a church, two businesses, and a population estimated at fifty. The population was still fifty in 1990.

BIBLIOGRAPHY: Wright Patman, *History of Post Offices—First Congressional District of Texas* (Texarkana, Texas, 1946?).

Cecil Harper, Jr.

CASS COUNTY. Cass County (C-22), bordered by Arkansas and Louisiana on the east, is located in northeastern Texas on the state's eastern boundary; it is one county removed from the northern boundary. Linden, the county seat, is in the south central portion of the county fourteen miles southwest of Atlanta, the county's largest town. The county's center lies at approximately 33°05′ north latitude and 94°21′ west longitude. U.S. Highway 59 connects Linden, Atlanta, and Queen City with Jefferson to the south and Texarkana to the north. The county's transportation needs are also served by State highways 8, 11, 77, and 155, and by two rail lines, the Missouri Pacific and the Louisiana and Arkansas. Cass County comprises 937 square miles of the East Texas timberlands, an area that is heavily forested with a great variety of softwoods and hardwoods, especially pine, cypress, and oak. The terrain ranges from nearly level to hilly, with an elevation ranging from 200 to 632 feet above sea level. Several stony hills in the western part of the county rise to a height of more than 200 feet and have been protected from erosion by the ironstone material that caps them. The largest of these hills are the Cusseta Mountains, five miles east of Marietta. Northern Cass County is drained by the Sulphur River, and the remainder is drained by Cypress Creek. The soil is light-colored and predominantly sandy and loamy. Between 21 and 30 percent of the land in Cass County is considered prime farmland. Mineral resources include ceramic clay, granite, industrial sand, oil, gas, iron, and lignite coal. Pine and hardwood production in 1981 totaled 16,920,041 cubic feet. Temperatures range from an average high of 92° F in July to an average low of 31° F in January. Rainfall averages almost forty-seven inches a year, and the growing season extends for an average of 237 days.

The Caddo Indians, an agricultural people with a highly developed culture, had occupied the area for centuries before the arrival of Europeans, but disease and threats from other Indians forced them to abandon the region in the final years of the eighteenth century. During the 1820s bands of Shawnee, Delaware, and Kickapoo Indians inhabited the area for a few years, but they abandoned their settlements in the mid-1830s.

It seems probable that the first European entry into what would become Cass County occurred between 1687, when Henri Joutel[qv] traveled north in search of Henri de Tonti,[qv] and 1690, when Tonti returned to Texas in search of survivors of the LaSalle expedition.[qv] Prolonged European activity in the area began in 1719, when Le Poste des Cadodaquious[qv] was founded by Bénard de La Harpe.[qv]

Anglo settlement in the area that became Cass County began in the 1830s. Among the earliest settlers was Reece Hughes,[qv] who built a cabin near three mineral springs which later became known as Hughes Springs. The county was formed from Bowie County in 1846. Jefferson was chosen as the first county seat, but, after several fiercely contested elections, in 1852 Linden became county seat. The county's boundaries were reduced in 1860 with the formation of Marion County, but, with the exception of small adjustments, have remained unchanged since that time. The county was originally named Cass County in honor of Lewis Cass, a United States Senator from Michigan who had favored the annexation[qv] of Texas. During the secession[qv] crisis Cass, who had formerly been known as a Northern man with Southern principles, resigned his post as secretary of state when President James Buchanan declined to defend the federal forts in Charleston, South Carolina. When word of his actions reached Texas, the name of the county was changed to Davis in honor of Jefferson Davis.[qv] The republican-controlled state legislature of 1871 changed the name back to Cass.

As settlers began to pour in, the lands to the west were being settled, so that Cass County was never really a frontier community in the sense of being on the western edge of settlement. Neither was it isolated from access to larger markets, except for a very brief period during its earliest years. Jefferson, a major riverport in antebellum Texas,[qv] served as a supply point and shipping center for produce. Those who settled Cass County were for the most part southerners, and many of them were slaveholders. The white population built a way of life similar to the one they had known in the older Southern states and an agricultural economy based on cotton as the cash crop and corn and hogs as primary food crops. During the antebellum years agricultural production in the county expanded steadily; the amount of cotton produced grew from 1,573 bales in 1849 to 9,968 bales in 1859. Corn production expanded also, from 167,250 bushels in 1849 to 289,979 bushels in 1859. The number of hogs in the county expanded only slightly, from 16,732 in 1849 to 17,432 in 1859. The labor force in this agricultural economy was composed almost entirely of black slaves (*see* SLAVERY). As agricultural production expanded, the slave population grew faster than the free. In 1847 the 943 slaves in the county constituted roughly 31 percent of the total population of 2,949. The 3,475 slaves in 1860 constituted 41 percent of the 8,411 people counted. In 1847 one free black lived in the county, and the census of 1860 reported none.

Cass County's white population overwhelmingly supported the secession[qv] movement during the winter of 1860–61. When the secession ordinance was voted on in February 1861 Cass County voters approved it by a vote of 423 to 32. They also wholeheartedly supported the war effort of the Confederacy, but no estimates of the number of men from the county who served in the Confederate armed forces are available. Because Cass County was never invaded it escaped the physical destruction that devastated other parts of the South. Nonetheless, the war years were trying times for the county's citizens. They were forced to deal with disruptions to the local economy caused by an unstable Confederate currency and the lack of a market for their cotton, as well as concern for those on the battlefield. The end of the war brought wrenching changes in the county's economic foundation. While the end of slavery meant freedom for the black, it meant a serious loss of capital for the white slaveholder. In 1859 Cass County slaveholders had paid taxes on 4,697 slaves valued at $2,387,500. This represented 60 percent of all taxable property in the county. The loss brought about by emancipation, together with the widespread belief that free blacks would not work and the uncertain status of the South in the nation, led to a loss of confidence that caused property values to plummet in 1865.

Throughout 1867 and 1868 there were repeated reports from agents of the Freedmen's Bureau[qv] in Marshall that freedmen were being cheated and physically abused in Cass County, but neither federal troops nor an agent of the bureau was ever stationed in the county. Thus the county never experienced military occupation by a conquering army. Still, the county's citizens felt the effects of Reconstruction[qv] because troops stationed at various times in Marion, Bowie, and Harrison counties occasionally passed through Cass County while chasing fugitives or traveling to their posts. Military commanders also removed Cass County officeholders as "impediments to reconstruction." Reconstruction, however, was of short duration in the county, as the county was returned to white Democratic control at the election that determined the contents of the Constitution of 1869[qv] (*see also* CONSTITUTIONAL CONVENTION OF 1868–69).

Since Reconstruction, with the exception of a brief period in the 1890s when the Populists (*see* PEOPLE'S PARTY) controlled the county, Cass County has generally voted Democratic in local and state elections. In presidential elections, the county has been more changeable. Democrats have carried the county in most elections through 1992, but in 1892 the Populist candidate received a majority, and in 1968 George Wallace was the choice of county voters. Republican candidates have carried the county in most presidential elections starting with 1956.

For more than sixty years after Reconstruction, the economic base of Cass County was agricultural, as it had been since the county's beginnings. Cotton remained the principal cash crop, and corn remained the principal food crop. Hogs remained the other principal food product until, beginning in the 1920s, changes in diet led to declining swine production. As late as 1940, 57 percent of the county's labor force worked in agriculture, and three-quarters of the county's cropland was devoted to cotton and corn. Although cotton provided the major source of income, however, it did not provide prosperity for many of the county's residents. From 1880, when the statistics were first compiled, through 1930, each census recorded a higher percentage of farmers who did not own the land they farmed. In 1880, 24 percent of the farmers in the county were listed as tenants. In 1930, 61 percent of all farmers in the county fell into that category.

Though agriculture was the foundation of the county's economic base, the county was never exclusively agricultural. Manufacturing provided jobs for a small portion of the county's population beginning in 1850, when twenty-four persons were employed to produce goods valued at $13,860. With the exception of a modest decline in the early 1900s, the number of those involved in manufacturing expanded steadily. In 1940, 842 individuals manufactured products valued at $1,340,999. Although the number had grown, those employed in manufacturing in 1940 constituted less than 8 percent of the county's labor force.

One other important industry in Cass County was the lumber industry.[qv] The abundant forests in the county initially provided wood for houses and fences for the county's residents, but production gradually expanded to include the production of lumber and lumber products for export. By the 1940s Cass County lumbermills were producing 75 million board feet of lumber annually. Most of this wood was softwood from the shortleaf pines prominent in the county's forests. Though the timber industry was important, it employed about the same number of individuals as manufacturing and thus provided jobs for less than 10 percent of the county's labor force.

In many areas there seemed to be little change in the county between the end of Reconstruction and 1940. Cotton and corn remained the principal crops, and most people in the county worked in agriculture. The county was still overwhelmingly rural. In 1890, 14 percent of the population lived in the county's four largest towns. In 1940 the percentage had not changed. Still there had been changes, some of which were dramatically altering the lives of Cass County residents. First, there were dramatic changes in the county's transportation system. During the antebellum period, the primary major market and supply center had been the riverport and supply center, Jefferson. In 1873 the Texas and Pacific Railway was constructed through eastern Cass County, and the towns of Atlanta and Queen City grew up along that line. In 1876 the East Line and Red River was constructed through the southwestern corner of the county; its principal Cass County station was Hughes Springs. The two railroads gave residents more reliable transportation for their crops and enabled Hughes Springs and Atlanta to develop as supply centers. Within the county the predominant means of transportation remained horses and mules[qv] into the 1930s. By 1940, however, the automobile had become predominant. In 1922 only 775 automobiles were registered in the county. By 1940 there were 5,504. By 1940 the major highways that crossed the county in the 1990s had been constructed.

The 1930s saw the birth of a new industry in the county, as the oil reserves beneath the surface were tapped, beginning with the exploration of the Rodessa oilfield[qv] south of Atlanta. By 1936 over 100 wells had been drilled. Although this activity brought a new town, McLeod, and prosperity to some landowners in the area of the oilfields, its impact on the economic base of the county is hard to measure. Although exploration and production continued, Cass County never really became a major oil-producing county. In 1937, following the initial boom, the wells in the county produced 11,511,838 barrels of oil. But over the next several years production declined sharply, and in 1948 the county's wells produced only 880,575 barrels of oil.

Profound changes also occurred in the size and structure of the county's farms. Although the county's population had increased from 30,030 in 1930 to 33,496 in 1940, the number of farms in the county had dropped from 5,841 to 4,404. The size of the average county farm had increased from sixty-eight to ninety-two acres. For the first time since 1910 a majority of the farmers in Cass County owned all or at least part of the land they farmed, with farm tenancy dropping from its 1930 high of 61 percent to 48 percent in 1940. These changes were largely the result of the Great Depression[qv] of the 1920s and 1930s and federal programs implemented to deal with the crisis.

The depression, which began for farmers in the mid-1920s, had hit Cass County farmers hard. Between 1920 and 1930 the value of the average farm in the county plummeted from $2,504 to $1,554. The farmers' initial response to falling crop prices had been to plant more cotton. The 1929 cotton crop was the largest ever reported to census takers, both in output (37,508 bales) and in acreage (123,753 acres planted). In fact, 60 percent of the county's total cropland had been planted in cotton, the largest proportion ever recorded. During the 1930s, under the programs of the New Deal, county landowners began to restrict the acreage planted in return for payments from the federal government. Apparently, many Cass County farmers, like others throughout the South, took the land that was to lie fallow away from tenants and sharecroppers. Though the number of farms cultivated by owners in Cass County fell by only twenty-six between 1930 and 1940, the number of farms cultivated by tenants and sharecroppers fell by 1,411. The exodus from the farms was forced on landless farmers by landlords during the hard years of the depression. Later, during the 1940s and 1950s, farmers voluntarily left the land as other sectors of the economy and parts of the country provided greater opportunities. By 1959 only 13 percent of Cass County farmers were tenants. The trend continued until 1969, when the figure had fallen to 7 percent.

The trend towards larger and fewer farms begun in the 1930s has also continued. By 1982 only 894 farms were in operation in Cass County, and their average size had grown to 277 acres. The trend away from cotton continued and expanded to include all harvested crops. In 1930 the county's farmers reported that they had harvested crops from over 206,000 acres of cropland in 1929. In 1982 the total cropland harvested was only 25,000 acres. Replaced by a wide variety of crops, the former mainstays of cotton and corn had been totally abandoned. The county's farmers had turned to livestock, particularly beef and poultry, as their major source of income. In 1982, 80 percent of the county's total agricultural income came from livestock.

As the changes in agriculture that had begun in the 1930s continued in the 1940s and 1950s, the county began to change in other ways. The percentage of the county's residents who lived in the four largest towns doubled between 1940 and 1950, as many of those who were leaving the farms moved into town. These four towns continued to grow, until, by 1970, 43 percent of the county's population lived in them. In 1980 the 12,661 people who lived in the four largest towns were also 43 percent of the county's total population of 29,430.

The county's manufacturing base continued to expand in the 1940s, and by 1947, 1,008 people were employed in Cass County's forty-one manufacturing establishments. But afterward, the continued growth of Lone Star Steel in neighboring Morris County made that county the industrial center of the region, and manufacturing in Cass County declined precipitously. In 1958 the number of Cass County manufactories had fallen from forty-one to twenty-one, and those twenty-one employed just 174 people. Afterward, manufacturing in the county expanded slowly until in 1982 it employed 700 people.

The decline in manufacturing in the late 1940s and 1950s, coupled with the changes in agriculture, led to a fall in the county's population as people left to take advantage of opportunities elsewhere. The shrinkage continued until 1960, when Cass County's population was recorded as 23,496. After that, the county grew slowly in the 1960s to a population of 24,133 in 1970, then more rapidly in the 1970s to a population of 29,430 in 1980. During the period of decline, the county's black population fell more rapidly than the white population; it continued to decline through the 1960s. In 1970 the 6,395 blacks constituted just 26 percent of the county's total population. The black population grew only marginally during the 1970s; the 6,460 blacks present in 1980 constituted only 22 percent of the county's population.

In 1982 many county residents worked at jobs beyond the county line, predominantly at Lone Star Steel in Morris County and Red River Arsenal and Lone Star Army Ammunition Plant[qv] in Bowie County. Of those who worked in Cass County, the largest numbers worked in manufacturing, trade, and local government. Income figures for 1981 indicated that Cass County was poorer than most Texas counties. With a per-capita income of $7,457 annually, it ranked 218th among the state's 254 counties. By way of contrast, Bowie and Morris counties ranked 139th and 29th, with per-capita incomes of $9,065 and $11,602, respectively. In 1990 Cass County had 29,982 inhabitants.

BIBLIOGRAPHY: Carl H. Moneyhon, *Republicanism in Reconstruction Texas* (Austin: University of Texas Press, 1980). Thomas Clarence Richardson, *East Texas: Its History and Its Makers* (4 vols., New York: Lewis Historical Publishing, 1940). *Cecil Harper, Jr.*

CASSATA, JOHN JOSEPH (1908–1989). John Joseph Cassata, the first bishop of the Catholic Diocese of Fort Worth,[qv] was born in Galveston, Texas, on November 8, 1908, the son of Vincent and Anna (Pizzitola) Cassata, natives of Sicily. He attended St. Mary's Cathedral[qv] School in Galveston and St. Mary's boarding school in La Porte and began his studies for the priesthood at St. Mary's Seminary in La Porte, the first seminarian of Italian parentage to enter that seminary. Upon completion of his studies in La Porte, Cassata was sent to the North American College in Rome, where he was ordained on December 8, 1932. He was the second native Texan of Italian parentage to be ordained a priest for the state of Texas and the first for the Catholic Diocese of Galveston-Houston.[qv]

Shortly after his ordination he was assigned to Holy Name parish in Houston as assistant pastor. He became pastor in 1945 and served in this capacity until 1968. In 1956 he was elevated to domestic prelate. In addition to his pastoral duties Cassata was appointed vicar general of the Galveston-Houston diocese and served as the diocesan procurator at Vatican II. He was diocesan synodal judge of the matrimonial court and a member of the diocesan board of examiners, the Catholic Youth Organization board, and the diocesan board of education. He was also diocesan moderator for the Confraternity of Christian Doctrine; director of diocesan radio and TV programing; chairman of the diocesan building commission, development fund, and War on Poverty; and a lieutenant colonel in the Texas State Guard,[qv] Eighth District.

On March 20, 1968, Pope Paul VI appointed Cassata titular bishop of Bida and auxiliary bishop of the Diocese of Dallas–Fort Worth. Following his consecration on June 5, 1968, he served as vicar general of the diocese, episcopal vicar for Fort Worth, vice chancellor of the University of Dallas, and pastor of St. Patrick Co-Cathedral in Fort Worth. On August 22, 1969, he was appointed bishop of the newly formed diocese of Fort Worth. He retired on September 16, 1980, due to ill health.

During Cassata's years of leadership in Fort Worth twelve new parishes were formed, and the Catholic population grew from 67,690 to 93,500. He was a strong advocate of more lay involvement in the church and encouraged strong parish councils. He established the lay assembly as a liaison between parish councils and the diocesan pastoral council. Under his direction permanent deacons were ordained, and the marriage tribunal was established. Seminarians were encouraged to learn Spanish and study Mexican-American culture to serve the people of the diocese better. In order to assure stability and quality in the Catholic schools of the diocese, Cassata established an elected diocesan board of education and elected local school boards, unified under a diocesan Catholic school system. Cassata Learning Center, an alternative school in Fort Worth, was named for him.

He was grand prior of the Southern Lieutenancy of the Equestrian Order of the Holy Sepulchre of Jerusalem from October 1968 until November 1984. Bishop Cassata died on September 8, 1989, in Houston and was buried in the family plot at Garden of Gethsemane in Forest Park Cemetery, Houston.

BIBLIOGRAPHY: Austin *American-Statesman*, September 17, 1989. *Texas Catholic*, June 29, 1968, August 30, 1969, September 14, 1989. *Texas Catholic Herald*, September 22, 1989. *Kathryn Fialho*

CASSELLS BOYKIN STATE RECREATION AREA. Cassells Boykin State Recreation Area is on the western shore of Sam Rayburn Reservoir just off State Highway 147, nine miles east of Zavalla in Angelina County. The 265-acre park was built by the United States Army Corps of Engineers in the mid-1960s and was leased to the state in 1982, when the corps developed financial problems. The heavily wooded site, in Angelina National Forest,[qv] attracts numerous migratory birds and waterfowl. Archeological surveys have revealed extensive Caddoan settlements in the area; Cherokees occupied the site from about 1828 to 1839. Facilities include a boat ramp, toilets, picnic tables, campsites, a well, and a dump station.

BIBLIOGRAPHY: Ray Miller, *Texas Parks* (Houston: Cordovan, 1984).
Christopher Long

CASSIA INDIANS. In the 1687 documents of the La Salle expedition[qv] the Cassia Indians were reported as allies of the Kadohadachos on the Red River. Apparently the Cassias were not the same as the Casibas, reported in a Spanish document of 1691 as living southeast of the Hasinais. The affiliations of both groups remain unknown.

BIBLIOGRAPHY: Pierre Margry, ed., *Découvertes et établissements des Français dans l'ouest et dans le sud de l'Amérique septentrionale, 1614–1754* (6 vols., Paris: Jouast, 1876–86). John R. Swanton, *Source Material on the History and Ethnology of the Caddo Indians* (Smithsonian Institution, Bureau of American Ethnology Bulletin 132, Washington: GPO, 1942). *Thomas N. Campbell*

CASSIANO, JOSÉ (1791–1862). José Cassiano, patriot, merchant, and landowner, was born Giuseppe Cassini in San Remo, Italy, the son of Geronimo and Catalina Cassini. As a young man he became an experienced seaman. He arrived in New Orleans on November 20, 1816, with a British passport, as a resident of Gibraltar. In New Orleans he became a successful merchant and property owner. In connection with his business he made frequent trips to Texas and sometime in the 1820s moved to San Antonio, where he opened a store. He acquired extensive property in San Antonio and landholdings throughout South Texas.

During the siege of Bexar[qv] in December 1835 his home and store with its supplies were turned over to the revolutionary army.[qv] In 1835–36 he served as a scout along the Rio Grande. Just before the attack on the Alamo he sent messages to William B. Travis[qv] on the movements of Antonio López de Santa Anna.[qv] He made substantial contributions to finance the revolution. His aid to the cause of independence was recognized when Thomas J. Rusk,[qv] secretary of war, issued instructions on June 21, 1836, that Cassiano be permitted to travel freely between Texas and the United States.

Cassiano served as alderman in San Antonio in 1839–40, 1841–42, and 1845–46. He contributed generously to San Fernando de Béxar Cathedral.[qv] He was married successively to Josefa Menchaca; Gertrudis Pérez (Peres) de Cordero, widow of Governor Manuel Antonio Cordero y Bustamante;[qv] Margarita Valdez in 1833; and Trinidad Soto in 1842. He had three children. The first Cassiano homestead in San Antonio was the old Juan Ignacio Pérez[qv] property on Dolorosa Street between Main and Military plazas. Both there and at their ranch, Calaveras, the Cassianos extended hospitality to newly arriving Americans in the early days of the Republic of Texas.[qv] Among them were Samuel A. Maverick[qv] and his family, who spent their first few months in San Antonio as guests of the Cassianos. Cassiano died on January 1, 1862, and is buried in San Fernando Cemetery in San Antonio.

BIBLIOGRAPHY: Frederick Charles Chabot, *With the Makers of San Antonio* (Yanaguana Society Publications 4, San Antonio, 1937). Rena Maverick Green, ed., *Memoirs of Mary A. Maverick* (San Antonio: Alamo Printing, 1921; rpt., Lincoln: University of Nebraska Press, 1989). John H. Jenkins, ed., *The Papers of the Texas Revolution, 1835–1836* (10 vols., Austin: Presidial Press, 1973). Walter Lord, *A Time to*

Stand (New York: Harper, 1961; 2d ed., Lincoln: University of Nebraska Press, 1978). San Antonio *Express*, August 30, 1936. August Santleben, *A Texas Pioneer* (New York and Washington: Neale, 1910).

Bernice Strong

CASSIANO, MARÍA GERTRUDIS PÉREZ (1790–1832). María Gertrudis Pérez Cassiano, a descendant of the Canary Islanders,[qv] daughter of Juan Ignacio Pérez[qv] and Clemencia Hernández, was born on January 2, 1790, in the Pérez homestead in Villa de San Fernando, Royal Presidio of San Antonio de Béxar. Her father, a lieutenant colonel in the Spanish army, was later interim governor of Texas. In 1804 the family paid 800 pesos for the Spanish Governor's Palace[qv] and made it their home; it was in the family's possession for over a hundred years. The palace, a center of "military and social activity" during María's youth, later became run-down. In the late 1920s, under the leadership of Adina de Zavala,[qv] it was acquired by the city of San Antonio and restored as a museum. In 1813, Col. Manuel Antonio Cordero y Bustamante[qv] requested permission from the viceroy to marry María and was granted the favor on January 1, 1814. With her marriage to Cordero, María became known as La Brigaviella ("the Brigadier-General") and was permitted to carry out her husband's duties, including reviewing the troops, in his absence. Her apparent ease in handling his duties may have come from the fact that she was considered an equal to men in some business dealings, such as the inheritance, administration, buying, and selling of property. Upon her father's death, María inherited the Pérez homestead. After Cordero's death in 1823, she married a wealthy Italian, José Cassiano,[qv] on April 12, 1826. With him she had a son. María died of dropsy and was buried in San Fernando de Béxar on September 29, 1832. In her will she refused to leave any money for "pious works," allegedly to ensure that her assets would not fall into the hands of the Mexican government. Nonetheless, her husband donated a small amount of money shortly after her death to public charities and school funds. In his correspondence transmitting these funds, Cassiano noted that it would have been his late wife's desire to see that some of her wealth be used in the public interest.

Carlos Castañeda, ca. 1941–1948. Eleuterio Escobar Papers, Benson Latin American Collection, University of Texas at Austin.

BIBLIOGRAPHY: Nettie Lee Benson, "Texas Failure to Send a Deputy to the Spanish Cortes, 1810–1812," *Southwestern Historical Quarterly* 64 (July 1960). Evelyn M. Carrington, ed., *Women in Early Texas* (Austin: Pemberton Press, 1975).

Teresa Palomo Acosta

CASSIN, TEXAS. Cassin is off U.S. Highway 281 just south of Mitchell Lake, twelve miles south of downtown San Antonio in southern Bexar County. It was settled before 1900 and was named for local landowner William Cassin. After the construction of the San Antonio, Uvalde and Gulf Railroad in 1913 Cassin served as a flag stop. In the mid-1930s the settlement was the site of the Asa Mitchell[qv] school, a church, and a store. The population in 1946 was 175. By 1990 the population had fallen to a reported fifty.

Minnie B. Cameron

CASSIN LAKE. Cassin Lake is in the San Antonio River basin on Minita Creek two miles west of Southton in southeastern Bexar County (at 29°18′ N, 98°27′ W). The artificial lake was built in 1907 for irrigation purposes and was evidently named for William Cassin, an early landowner for whom the town of Cassin was also named. In the early 1990s the lake, which has a maximum capacity of 580 acre-feet, was owned and operated by Medina Properties Limited. The surrounding terrain is flat to gently rolling and is surfaced by clay loam that supports mesquite, cacti, and grasses.

CASTAÑEDA, CARLOS EDUARDO (1896–1958). Carlos Eduardo Castañeda, historian and professor, was born on November 11, 1896, in Ciudad Camargo, Tamaulipas, Mexico, the seventh child of Timoteo and Elisa (Leroux) Castañeda. He moved to the United States in 1906 and graduated as valedictorian from Brownsville High School in 1916; a year later he moved to Austin and embarked on a long and distinguished academic career. He received his A.B. in 1921 (with induction in Phi Beta Kappa), his M.A. in 1923, and Ph.D. in 1932, all from the University of Texas. During this period he worked as a teacher of Spanish in high schools in Beaumont and San Antonio and from 1923 to 1927 as associate professor at the College of William and Mary in Virginia. In 1927 Castañeda became librarian of the Genaro García Collection (*see* NETTIE LEE BENSON LATIN AMERICAN COLLECTION) at the University of Texas. While retaining his position as librarian, he also served as associate professor of history from 1939 to 1946. During World War II[qv] Castañeda took a leave of absence to serve as regional director of the President's Committee on Fair Employment Practice. In 1946 he became professor of Latin-American history, a position he held until his death.

Castañeda's scholarly interests centered in the history of the Catholic Church[qv] in the Spanish Borderlands. His principal work was the seven-volume *Our Catholic Heritage in Texas, 1519–1936*, with *Supplement* that brought the story to 1950. He translated Juan Agustín Morfi's[qv] *History of Texas, 1673–1779* (1935) and (with Jack A. Dabbs) compiled the *Guide to the Latin American Manuscripts in the University of Texas Library* (1939). He also published numerous scholarly articles on history.

Castañeda was awarded many honors, among them the presidency of the American Catholic Historical Association (1939), knighthood in the Equestrian Order of the Holy Sepulchre of Jerusalem (1941), and Knight Commander of the Order of Isabel the Catholic from the Spanish Government (1950). He also received honorary doctorates from St. Edward's University in Austin (1941) and the Catholic University of America in Washington (1951), as well as the Junípero Serra Award of the Americas from the Academy of American Franciscan History in Washington (1951). On December 27, 1921, at San Fernando de Bexar Cathedral[qv] in San Antonio, Castañeda married Elisa Ríos; they had three daughters. Castañeda died on April 3, 1958, and was buried at Mount Calvary Cemetery in Austin. The Perry-Castañeda Library at the University of Texas at Austin, which opened in 1977, was named for him and Ervin S. Perry.[qv]

BIBLIOGRAPHY: Félix D. Almaráz, Jr., "Carlos Eduardo Castañeda, Mexican-American Historian: The Formative Years, 1896–1927," *Pacific Historical Review* 42 (August 1973). Félix D. Almaráz, Jr., "Carlos E. Castañeda and *Our Catholic Heritage*: The Initial Volumes," *Social Science Journal*, April 1976. Félix D. Almaráz, Jr., "Carlos E. Castañeda's Rendezvous with a Library: The Latin American Collection, 1920–1927—The First Phase," *Journal of Library History* 16 (Spring 1981). Félix D. Almaráz, Jr., "The Making of a Boltonian: Carlos E. Castañeda of Texas—The Early Years," *Red River Valley Historical Review* 1 (Winter 1974). Vertical Files, Barker Texas History Center, University of Texas at Austin. John R. Wunder, *Historians of the American Frontier* (New York: Greenwood Press, 1988).

Félix D. Almaráz, Jr.

CASTAÑEDA, FRANCISCO DE (?–?) Francisco de Castañeda (Castonado), lieutenant in the Mexican army and commander of the Mexican contingent at the battle of Gonzales,[qv] was attached to the Presidial Company of Alamo de Parras (*see* SECOND FLYING COMPANY OF SAN CARLOS), billeted in the old San Antonio de Valero Mission in the fall of 1835. He saw action against hostile Indians. On September 27, 1835, Castañeda was sent by Domingo de Ugartechea[qv] with a force of 100 cavalrymen to retrieve a cannon lent to the citizens of Gonzales in 1831 for Indian defense. The citizens refused to relinquish the Gonzales "come and take it" cannon,[qv] and the battle of Gonzales resulted.

BIBLIOGRAPHY: Bexar Archives, Barker Texas History Center, University of Texas at Austin. Hubert Howe Bancroft, *History of the North Mexican States and Texas* (2 vols., San Francisco: History Company, 1886, 1889). Miles S. Bennet, "The Battle of Gonzales: The 'Lexington' of the Texas Revolution," *Quarterly of the Texas State Historical Association* 2 (April 1899). Henry Stuart Foote, *Texas and the Texans* (2 vols., Philadelphia: Cowperthwait, 1841; rpt., Austin: Steck, 1935). Edward Albert Lukes, *De Witt Colony of Texas* (Austin: Jenkins, 1976). Malcolm D. McLean, comp. and ed., *Papers Concerning Robertson's Colony in Texas* (19 vols., Fort Worth: Texas Christian University Press, 1974–76; Arlington: University of Texas at Arlington Press, 1977–92). Ethel Zivley Rather, "DeWitt's Colony," *Quarterly of the Texas State Historical Association* 8 (October 1904). Harold Schoen, comp., *Monuments Erected by the State of Texas to Commemorate the Centenary of Texas Independence* (Austin: Commission of Control for Texas Centennial Celebrations, 1938). Dudley Goodall Wooten, ed., *A Comprehensive History of Texas* (2 vols., Dallas: Scarff, 1898; rpt., Austin: Texas State Historical Association, 1986).

Stephen L. Hardin

CASTAÑEDA, PEDRO DE (?–?). Pedro de Castañeda, a member and chronicler of the Coronado expedition,[qv] was a native of Nájera, a town in the state of Vizcaya in northern Spain. At the time of the organization of the Coronado expedition, Castañeda was at a Spanish outpost at Culiacán, in northwestern Mexico. He was married and had at least eight children. Castañeda's original account, *Relación de la jornada de Cíbola compuesta por Pedro de Castañeda de Nácera donde se trata de todas aquellos poblados y ritos, y costumbres, la cual fué el año de 1540*, has been lost, but a copy made in 1596 is in the Lenox Library in New York City. The narrative appears most recently in both Spanish and English, edited by George Parker Winship.

BIBLIOGRAPHY: George Parker Winship, trans. and ed., *The Coronado Expedition, 1540–1542* (Extract from the Fourteenth Annual Report of the Bureau of Ethnology, Washington: GPO, 1896; rpt., New York: AMS Press, 1973).

CASTAÑO DE SOSA, GASPAR (?–?). Gaspar Castaño de Sosa was born in Portugal, probably around the middle of the sixteenth century. By the late 1580s, he was a longtime associate of Luis de Carvajal y de la Cueva[qv] on the northeastern frontier of New Spain. Carvajal named Castaño as *alcalde mayor* of Villa San Luis (later Monterrey), and with the arrest of Carvajal on orders of the Holy Office of the Inquisition, Don Gaspar assumed leadership at Villa de Almadén (now Monclova). On July 27, 1590, Castaño, who had become disillusioned with the unproductive mines of Almadén, packed up most of the colony and set out on an arduous march to northern New Mexico. Under the guidance of a young Indian named Miguel, the expedition comprised 170 persons, as well as heavily laden carts, yokes of oxen, tools, and provisions. Castaño marched north to the Rio Grande, and thence along the course of the Pecos River to Pecos Pueblo. He later established his headquarters at Santo Domingo, north of the site of present-day Albuquerque. Meanwhile, Carvajal, as a suspected Jewish apostate, had been brought to trial in New Spain. The case disclosed many Judaists in Carvajal's extended family, and it also cast suspicion on the orthodoxy of his colonists at Almadén—especially Castaño, who become the victim of guilt by association. Upon discovering that Castaño was not present at Almadén, Capt. Juan Morlete, a viceregal agent, received authorization to pursue him into New Mexico with a force of twenty men. Charged with leading an unauthorized entrada into New Mexico, Castaño was returned in chains to New Spain. There he was tried, convicted, and exiled to the Philippines. His sentence was appealed to the Council of the Indies, where it was eventually reversed, but the reversal benefited only the man's reputation. The unfortunate Castaño had already been slain aboard a ship in the South China Sea—the victim of a slave insurrection.

BIBLIOGRAPHY: Vito Alessio Robles, *Coahuila y Texas en la época colonial* (Mexico City: Editorial Cultura, 1938; 2d ed., Mexico City: Editorial Porrúa, 1978). Donald E. Chipman, *Spanish Texas, 1519–1821* (Austin: University of Texas Press, 1992). Robert S. Weddle, *Spanish Sea: The Gulf of Mexico in North American Discovery, 1500–1685* (College Station: Texas A&M University Press, 1985).

Donald E. Chipman

CASTELL, TEXAS. Castell is at the intersection of Farm roads 2768 and 152, on the south bank of the Llano River in extreme western Llano County. Castell was established in 1847 on the north side of the Llano River by German immigrants under the auspices of the Adelsverein.[qv] They were led from Fredericksburg by Count Emil von Kriewitz to a site selected by John O. Meusebach[qv] to comply with the terms of the Fisher-Miller land grant,[qv] which the organization had acquired. The town was named for Count Carl Frederick Castell-Castell,[qv] business manager of the Adelsverein. Other Adelsverein settlements—Leiningen, Bettina, and Schoenburg—were established at the same time but did not survive. In 1872 a post office was established on the south side of the Llano River, where the community has since been centered. The site held the first church services in the region, conducted by Rev. Charles A. Grote in 1852. Castell has remained a center of religious activity. The local Methodist and Lutheran churches date their founding from that year. By 1972 the ranching and recreational community had declined to a population of seventy-two, mainly descendants of the original German settlers. A population of seventy-two was still reported in 1990, when the community was the oldest surviving settlement in the county.

BIBLIOGRAPHY: Tillie Badu Moss Fry, A History of Llano County (M.A. thesis, University of Texas, 1943). Irene M. King, *John O. Meusebach, German Colonizer in Texas* (Austin: University of Texas Press, 1967). Wilburn Oatman, *Llano, Gem of the Hill Country: A History of Llano County* (Hereford, Texas: Pioneer, 1970).

James B. Heckert-Greene

CASTELL-CASTELL, CARL FREDERICK CHRISTIAN, COUNT OF (1801–1850). Count Carl of Castell-Castell, initiator, vice president, and business manager of the Adelsverein,[qv] the son of Count Albrecht Frederick Carl zu Castell Remlingen and Sophie Amalie Charlotte (née Countess of Löwenstein-Wertheim), was born at Castell, Lower Franconia, near Würzburg, Germany, on December 8, 1801. He was descended from a long line of Franconian knights and nobles dating back to the thirteenth century. After receiving his basic education at the private school of Castell and military training in the royal Bavarian cadet corps, Castell entered military service in 1819 with the rank of cornet in a royal Hanoverian hussar regiment. In 1833, after having attained the rank of major, he left Hanoverian service. The same year he entered the Austrian army, and for the next several years he served in Moravia, Hungary, Dalmatia, and Vienna. In 1841 he was appointed to the post of governmental adjutant, with the rank of captain, at the Austrian garrison in Mainz. Inspired by books that he had read about Texas and by the Texans' struggle for independence, in 1842 he organized a society in Mainz for the purpose of directing German emigration to Texas. On April 20, 1842, when twenty-one noblemen met at Biebrich-on-the-Rhein, near Mainz, to form the association later called the Adelsverein, Count Carl of Castell was elected vice president and business manager of the organization. Under his management the society was reorganized in March 1844 into a stock company, and eight months later the society's first shipload of immigrants disembarked at Port Lavaca, Texas. Castell served the society as business manager and vice president until 1847, when the conduct of the society's business was placed in the hands of a committee. In 1848 he returned to his post as business manager but remained only until the society was reorganized that same year under new leadership. Count Carl of Castell led the society through its formative years as well as during the financial difficulties in the mid-1840s of settling immigrants on the Fisher-Miller Land Grant.[qv] He had an intense personal interest in the success of the colonization venture but little business acumen. The failure of the society was due in part to Castell's own blunders and omissions. In the latter years of his administration, in desperate attempts to save the reputation of the society and the investments of its stockholders, he even practiced deception and intrigue.

In 1846 Count Carl of Castell succeeded Count Ludwig Joseph von Boos-Waldeck[qv] as aide-de-camp to Duke Adolf of Nassau, the protector of the society, and early in 1850 he was promoted by the duke to the rank of colonel and appointed chief director of the war department in the Nassau Ministry of State. A few weeks later, however, on March 2, 1850, Castell succumbed to a fatal liver disorder. Among the several settlements founded in the 1840s by the Adelsverein, one was named Castell in honor of the count. The community was originally on the north bank of the Llano River but now is on the south bank in the western part of Llano County near the Mason county line.

BIBLIOGRAPHY: Rudolph L. Biesele, *The History of the German Settlements in Texas, 1831–1861* (Austin: Von Boeckmann–Jones, 1930; rpt. 1964). Irene M. King, *John O. Meusebach, German Colonizer in Texas* (Austin: University of Texas Press, 1967). Solms-Braunfels Archives (transcripts, Sophienburg Museum, New Braunfels, Texas; Barker Texas History Center, University of Texas at Austin). Prince Carl of Solms-Braunfels, *Texas, 1844–1845* (Houston: Anson Jones Press, 1936).

Louis E. Brister

CASTELLANOS, MANUEL (16??–17??). Manuel Castellanos was a Franciscan priest assigned to the College of Santa Cruz de Querétaro.[qv] Father Castellanos, along with Francisco Hidalgo[qv] and three other missionaries, left the college on January 21, 1716, for Saltillo. There they joined the expedition of Domingo Ramón,[qv] charged with reestablishing the Spanish presence in East Texas. On April 16 the contingent of priests reached San Juan Bautista,[qv] where they were reunited with three additional brethren of the college. On April 27, 1716, Castellanos left the gateway mission as a member of the Ramón expedition. En route to East Texas, he narrowly escaped drowning while fording the rain-swollen Colorado River near the site of present Austin. Ramón and his followers reached the land of the Tejas Indians in late June, and on July 3 Mission San Francisco was reestablished under the name of Nuestro Padre San Francisco de los Tejas. Joining Francisco Hidalgo, who served as minister of the new mission, was Manuel Castellanos. The latter was also given responsibility for the spiritual care of the soldiers at nearby Nuestra Señora de los Dolores de los Tejas Presidio. In late 1716 Father Castellanos fell ill while ministering to soldiers of the garrison. He evidently recovered from an illness believed to have been malaria, and he apparently remained in East Texas until the Spanish withdrew to San Antonio during the course of the Chicken War.[qv]

BIBLIOGRAPHY: Carlos E. Castañeda, *Our Catholic Heritage in Texas* (7 vols., Austin: Von Boeckmann–Jones, 1936–58; rpt., New York: Arno, 1976). Isidro Félix de Espinosa, *Chrónica apostólica y seráphica de todos los colegios de propaganda fide de esta Nueva España, parte primera* (Mexico, 1746; new ed., *Crónica de los colegios de propaganda fide de la Nueva España*, ed. Lino G. Caneda, Washington: Academy of American Franciscan History, 1964). Robert S. Weddle, *San Juan Bautista: Gateway to Spanish Texas* (Austin: University of Texas Press, 1968).

Donald E. Chipman

CASTILLO, DIEGO DEL (?–?). Captain Diego del Castillo led an expedition with Capt. Hernán Martín[qv] from Santa Fe in 1650 to explore north central Texas by order of Gen. Hernando de Ugarte y la Concha, governor of New Mexico. Their expedition penetrated as far as the territory of the Tejas Indians, and their report of pearls on the Nueces River (the present Concho) led to the expedition of Diego de Guadalajara.[qv]

BIBLIOGRAPHY: Hubert Howe Bancroft, *History of Arizona and New Mexico, 1530–1888* (San Francisco: History Company, 1889; facsimile ed., Albuquerque: Horn and Wallace, 1962). Herbert Eugene Bolton, ed., *Spanish Exploration in the Southwest, 1542–1706* (New York: Scribner, 1908; rpt., New York: Barnes and Noble, 1959). Charles W. Hackett, ed., *Pichardo's Treatise on the Limits of Louisiana and Texas* (4 vols., Austin: University of Texas Press, 1931–46).

CASTILLO MALDONADO, ALONSO (?–?). Alonso Castillo Maldonado, early Spanish explorer and Indian captive, a native of the Spanish university town of Salamanca, was the son of a physician and Aldonza Maldonado; both his parents were members of the Spanish nobility. As a well-bred but impoverished hidalgo, Castillo sought fame and fortune in the New World. He volunteered in 1527 as a captain in the expedition of Pánfilo de Narváez[qv] to Florida. After the expedition abandoned its attempt to go from the area of present-day Tampa, Florida, to Tampico, Mexico, by land, Castillo and Andrés Dorantes de Carranza[qv] were placed in joint command of a boat. In early November the makeshift vessel bearing Castillo and some forty men, including Cabeza de Vaca,[qv] was wrecked on or near the western extremity of Galveston Island. In the spring of 1529 a party of twelve, led by Dorantes and Castillo, started south along the coast;

the survivors eventually arrived in Matagorda Bay. Castillo is credited with introducing faith healing among the coastal Indians. His ritual consisted of prayers and a gentle blowing of breath on the bodies of afflicted natives. Dorantes and Cabeza de Vaca were among his pupils, and Castillo's quiet demeanor and piety are credited with transforming Cabeza de Vaca's mechanical religiosity to genuine devoutness.

After nearly seven years of precarious existence among hostile Indians, Castillo, Dorantes, Estevanico,[qv] and Cabeza de Vaca escaped inland. They were the first Europeans to traverse Texas. Traveling a circuitous and now disputed west-by-northwest route, they may have passed near the sites of San Antonio, New Braunfels, Austin, Big Spring, and Pecos. After a brief trek through the south part of what became New Mexico, they reentered and left Texas at El Paso in late 1535. Walking southward through Sonora and Sinaloa, Castillo and his companions were reunited with their Spanish countrymen north of Culiacán in 1536. From there they traveled to Mexico City for an audience with Viceroy Antonio de Mendoza.

Castillo chose to continue his career in the New World. After a brief visit in Spain he served as a treasury official in Guatemala (1545), and as an encomendero he later enjoyed one-fourth of the revenues of Tehuacán in New Spain. Castillo appeared as a witness in a lawsuit in 1547, and he is believed to have died in the late 1540s.

BIBLIOGRAPHY: Stephen Clissold, *The Seven Cities of Cíbola* (London: Eyre and Spottiswood, 1961). Cyclone Covey, trans. and ed., *Cabeza de Vaca's Adventures in the Unknown Interior of America* (New York: Collier, 1961; rpt., Albuquerque: University of New Mexico Press, 1983). Harbert Davenport, and Joseph K. Wells, "The First Europeans in Texas, 1528–1536," *Southwestern Historical Quarterly* 22 (October 1918). *Donald E. Chipman*

CASTLEBERRY, TEXAS. Castleberry was in an area that became the west side of Fort Worth in Tarrant County. It was a separate community from 1940 to 1947. Residents decided to incorporate in response to the dramatic population growth brought about by the construction of nearby Carswell Air Force Base and the Fort Worth Quartermaster Depot,[qqv] both activated in 1942. By the end of World War II[qv] Castleberry's population exceeded 5,000. In 1947 the community was annexed by Fort Worth.

BIBLIOGRAPHY: Janet L. Schmelzer, *Where the West Begins: Fort Worth and Tarrant County* (Northridge, California: Windsor, 1985). *David Minor*

CASTLE CANYON. Castle Canyon, a valley that runs along the last two miles of Evans Creek, begins a mile west of U.S. Highway 90 in southern Val Verde County (at 29°32′ N, 101°06′ W) and runs southeast to its mouth on the north shore of Amistad Reservoir, one-half mile east of the Southern Pacific Railroad tracks (at 29°32′ N, 101°04′ W). The path of the arroyo sharply dissects massive limestone to form vertical cliffs. Wash deposits of gravel, sand, clay, and silt cover the floor. The area's flat to rolling prairies are surfaced by generally dark, calcarecus stony clays and clay loams that support oaks, junipers, grasses, and mesquites. The canyon was named for the castle-shaped cones carved from its limestone walls by water erosion. In the 1880s a railroad station was located on Castle Canyon.

CASTLE GAP. Castle Gap is a pass through the Castle Mountains, whose rimrock suggests the parapets of a castle, between Crane and McCamey at the edge of the Edwards Plateau[qv] in extreme western Upton County (at 31°18′ N, 102°17′ W). The gap is a mile long and only yards wide at its narrowest point. It lies 421 feet below the summits of Castle Mountain to the north and King Mountain to the south, each of which rises to an elevation of 3,141 feet. The pass opens westward to the arid lowlands of the Pecos valley and toward Horsehead Crossing, twelve miles west-southwest.

Geologically, Castle Gap originated 135 million years ago as marine limestone deposits that eventually resulted in a great mesa subsequently split by erosion. In prehistoric times the gap was a natural gateway to and from crossings on the Pecos River for Indian nomads seeking buffalo[qv] on the Edwards Plateau or salt at Juan Cordona Lake, fifteen miles westward. Springs at the gap later prompted Comanches to name it Weick Pah, "Gap-Water."

Álvar Núñez Cabeza de Vaca[qv] describes a river flowing north to south with thirty leagues of plain on the west and an eastern ridge, identical to the topography of the Pecos River adjacent to Castle Gap. This fact suggests he may have passed through the break in 1535, when he traveled from the Texas coast to settlements in Mexico. In the fall of 1760 forty-one Spaniards dispatched by Capt. Felipe Rábago y Terán[qv] likely passed through Castle Gap in scouting a route from the presidio at the site of present-day Menard to Santa Fe. With the advent of the Comanche War Trail by 1800, Comanches, Kiowas, Rocky Mountain Utahs, and Plains Apaches used Castle Gap as a route to and from their raiding grounds in Mexico. Dr. Henry Connelly[qv] became one of the first English-speaking men to pass through the gap when he and a guard of fifty dragoons freighted seven wagons of bullion from Chihuahua City, Chihuahua, to an army post in what is now Oklahoma in 1839. By the late 1840s California-bound prospectors had established a wagon route from the confluence of the branches of the Concho in what is now Tom Green County up the Middle Concho to its head and across sixty-two miles of desert to Castle Gap.

The necessity of surveying the region brought several parties to Castle Gap in 1849 and 1850, including those of John S. (Rip) Ford and Maj. Robert S. Neighbors[qqv] in April 1849, Bvt. 1st Lt. Francis T. Bryan[qv] in July 1849, and John Russell Bartlett[qv] in October 1850. From 1858 to 1861 Butterfield Overland Mail[qv] stages passed through the gap twice a week on their 2,795-mile, twenty-five-day trips between Tipton, Missouri, and San Francisco. The first stage traversed the pass on the night of September 25, 1858, en route to fresh mules at Horsehead Crossing. Butterfield soon constructed a two-story stage station of native rock at the gap's west end, where a spring supplied the needs of attendants and stage teams. In an 1869 sketch, Col. Thomas B. Hunt pictured the station as two structures lying immediately south of the road.

In 1864 William A. Peril drove the first cattle herd of any size through Castle Gap en route from the Hill Country[qv] to Chihuahua. The most noteworthy drive occurred in the spring of 1866, when Charles Goodnight, Oliver Loving,[qqv] and eighteen men trailed 2,000 longhorn steers and breeding cows to Fort Sumner, New Mexico, from the Brazos in North Texas by way of the Middle Concho and Castle Gap. The drive opened up the Goodnight-Loving Trail[qv] for hundreds of succeeding drovers, who used the route as a springboard to push cattle as far north as Montana.

In the 1860s and 1870s Castle Gap was the frequent site of raids on cattle herds by Indians, who used the cattle as barter with Comancheros[qv] in New Mexico. Because of this, alternate routes were employed as early as 1859. The railroad subsequently bypassed the gap to the south, and erosion destroyed the wagon road. Castle Gap was closed as a practical route between 1910 and 1920.

Treasure hunters still frequent the gap in search of any of eight treasures supposedly lost in the vicinity. They include gold said to have been cached by Francisco Vásquez de Coronado[qv] in 1540, the Catholic Cross Cache of 1780, a horseshoe keg full of gold lost by a returning California Forty-niner, a Butterfield stage treasure hidden in 1860, gold cached by Old Bill Castle and Little Bill Castle in the 1860s, $40,000 stashed by outlaws who preyed on passing wagoners, gold and rifles from a United States Army wagon train of the late 1860s, and the treasure of Mexican emperor Maximilian, stashed in 1867.

BIBLIOGRAPHY: John Russell Bartlett, *Personal Narrative of Explorations . . . Connected with the United States and Mexican Boundary Commission* (New York: Appleton, 1854; rpt., Chicago: Rio Grande

Press, 1965). Patrick Dearen, *Castle Gap and the Pecos Frontier* (Fort Worth: Texas Christian University Press, 1988). John S. Ford, *Rip Ford's Texas*, ed. Stephen B. Oates (Austin: University of Texas Press, 1963). Clayton W. Williams, *Never Again, Texas* (3 vols., San Antonio: Naylor, 1969).

Patrick Dearen

CASTLE HILLS, TEXAS. Castle Hills is on Interstate Loop 410 nine miles north of downtown San Antonio in northern Bexar County. It was developed in the late 1940s and had a population of 2,622 in 1960 and 5,311 in 1970. In 1990 the population was 4,198.

Christopher Long

CASTLEMAN, SYLVANUS (?–1832). Sylvanus Castleman, one of Stephen F. Austin's[qv] Old Three Hundred,[qv] moved to Texas from Missouri, probably in 1821 or 1822, for in March 1822 Austin took a lot in Ste. Genevieve, Missouri, as payment for surveying Castleman's land in Texas. Seth Ingram[qv] surveyed the Castleman land on the west side of the Colorado River above La Grange in 1823. Indians raided the Castleman farm and stole cattle from him just before Austin and the Baron de Bastrop[qv] lodged with him in August of the same year. In December Castleman was appointed judge for the alcalde[qv] election and, being himself elected alcalde, took his oath of office on January 10, 1824. In April 1824 his daughter Nancy married John Crownover.[qv] On July 7, 1824, Castleman received title to two sitios of land in what is now Wharton County, one-half sitio now in Fayette County, and two labores now in Austin County. The census of March 1826 listed him as a farmer and stock raiser aged between forty and fifty. His household included his wife, four sons, two daughters, one servant, and one slave. Castleman died before March 10, 1832, when it was announced that all movable property of Sylvanus Castleman, deceased, would be sold at his house. Elizabeth Castleman, administratrix, gave notice in the *Telegraph and Texas Register*[qv] of July 8, 1840, that she would present her account for final settlement of the estate at the next term of Austin county court, and the July 1841 term of the Fayette county court divided Castleman's Fayette County land among his wife and children.

BIBLIOGRAPHY: Eugene C. Barker, ed., *The Austin Papers* (3 vols., Washington: GPO, 1924–28). Lester G. Bugbee, "The Old Three Hundred: A List of Settlers in Austin's First Colony," *Quarterly of the Texas State Historical Association* 1 (October 1897). J. H. Kuykendall, "Reminiscences of Early Texans," *Quarterly of the Texas State Historical Association* 6–7 (January, April, July 1903). La Grange High School, *Fayette County: Past and Present* (La Grange, Texas, 1976). Worth Stickley Ray, *Austin Colony Pioneers* (Austin: Jenkins, 1949; 2d ed., Austin: Pemberton, 1970). *Texas Gazette*, February 20, 1832. Leonie Rummel Weyand and Houston Wade, *An Early History of Fayette County* (La Grange, Texas: La Grange *Journal*, 1936).

CASTLEMAN CREEK (McLennan County). Castleman Creek rises two miles west of Hewitt in south central McLennan County (at 31°28′ N, 97°14′ W) and runs southeast for seventeen miles to its mouth on the Brazos River, a mile north of the Falls county line (at 31°25′ N, 97°01′ W). The surrounding flat to rolling prairie with locally steep slopes is surfaced by expansive clays and clay loams that support juniper, oak, mesquite, and grasses in the upper and middle reaches of the creek and water-tolerant hardwoods and conifers in the lower reaches.

CASTLE MOUNTAIN (Bell County). Castle Mountain is inside Fort Hood[qv] one mile north of Killeen in southwestern Bell County (at 31°09′ N, 97°43′ W). At an elevation of 1,015 feet above sea level, its summit rises 100 feet above the surrounding terrain.

—— (Crane-Upton County). Castle Mountain, on the Crane-Upton county line six miles south of Crane (at 31°18′ N, 102°17′ W), reaches an elevation of 3,151 feet at its summit. The mountain received its name from early Spanish explorers who thought it resembled a castle. It is composed of limestone and calcareous clay mud substrate with shallow, dark clay soil. Juniper, oak, grasses, chaparral, and cacti grow on it. Castle Gap[qv] divides Castle Mountain and is a landmark and spring-fed watering place that has been used by travelers for centuries. In 1968 a 100-acre park at Castle Gap was given to Upton County by the family of Caton Jacobs, owner of the property since the 1930s.

BIBLIOGRAPHY: Claude W. Dooley, comp., *Why Stop?* (Odessa: Lone Star Legends, 1978; 2d ed., with Betty Dooley and the Texas Historical Commission, Houston: Lone Star, 1985). Clayton W. Williams, *Never Again, Texas* (3 vols., San Antonio: Naylor, 1969).

CASTLE PEAK (Lampasas County). Castle Peak is two miles southeast of Moline in northern Lampasas County (at 31°21′ N, 98°18′ W). At an elevation of 1,531 feet above sea level, its summit rises 200 feet above nearby Ranch Road 1047. The peak stands in an area of the Grand Prairies, where steep to moderately sloping hills are surfaced by shallow, stony, sandy and clay loams that support grasses, live oak, mesquite, and juniper.

—— (Taylor County). Castle Peak is eight miles south of Merkel in southwest Taylor County (at 32°22′ N, 100°00′ W). It was originally named Abercrombie Peak for Lt. Col. J. J. Abercrombie, who commanded the first troops at Fort Phantom, from which the peak and the adjoining mountain range were visible. As the only prominent landmark in the flat West Texas landscape, the 2,400-foot peak was used as a beacon by the Butterfield Overland Mail.[qv] Waterman L. Ormsby of the New York *Herald*, the first through passenger on the Butterfield Overland Mail, said Castle Peak resembled a fortress that could be seen from thirty miles away. Castle Peak's soils are typical of the Tarrant Rock outcrop. Mesquite, cedar, brush, and grasses grow at the peak. A historical marker commemorating the use of the Castle Peak as a landmark on the Butterfield route was erected and dedicated in 1968 on Farm Road 1235, 2½ miles northeast of Castle Peak.

BIBLIOGRAPHY: Abilene *Reporter-News*, September 8, 1958. Marker Files, Texas Historical Commission, Austin.

Sherry L. McCormick

CASTOLON, TEXAS. Castolon, also known as Santa Helena, was on the Rio Grande in Big Bend National Park,[qv] twenty-three miles southwest of Panther Junction in southwestern Brewster County. The first known resident was Cipriano Hernández, a native of Camargo, Chihuahua, who in 1903 bought three sections of land on the American side of the Rio Grande five or six miles downstream from the mouth of Santa Elena Canyon. Hernández, who called the place Santa Helena, irrigated the fertile bottomland and grew wheat, corn, oats, and other grains, which he sold. He also opened the first store in the area.

Hernández's success inspired others to move to the region, and Castolon soon became a center of agricultural activity. Patricio Márquez opened a second store; Agapito Carrasco settled six Mexican families about a mile downstream from Hernández and called his community El Ojito; and Ruperto Chavarria led a larger group of immigrants to the west bank of Alamo Creek, two miles upriver from Castolon, and named the settlement La Coyota. Eventually Castolon and the nearby communities of El Ojito, La Coyota, Terlingua Abaja, and Buenos Aires, five miles downriver, had some 200 or 300 residents, most of whom engaged in subsistence farming. In 1910, at the outbreak of the Mexican Revolution,[qv] the inhabitants requested protection from the United States Army. By 1911 a cavalry troop was stationed at Castolon. It was later supplemented by infantry units from Camp Marfa.[qv]

In 1914 Hernández sold out to Clyde Buttrill, a prominent rancher in the Rosillos Mountains, and moved to Terlingua Abaja, where he and his son Guadalupe opened a large mercantile business. Buttrill hired James L. Sublett of Sweetwater to grow alfalfa. Sublett may have been the first man to use mechanized farming techniques in the Big Bend region. He installed the area's first pump irrigation system and brought the first wheat-threshing machine into the valley. By February 1916 he had become Buttrill's partner.

In 1918, however, Buttrill sold out and established a new farm two miles upriver from Castolon in partnership with a German-born architect from Detroit named Albert W. Dorgan. They bought a piece of property from brothers Tom and Charlie Metcalf. This spread was known as the Steele Ranch, after prospector L. V. Steele, who inherited it through his marriage to the daughter of a prominent Mexican rancher. Sublett built himself a house atop a small hill, and Dorgan moved about a half mile upriver. They developed an extensive irrigation system along the floodplain, and Sublett converted the old Metcalf house into a store, managed by his son-in-law, Fred Spann.

In 1919 the federal government leased four acres near Castolon, intending to construct permanent quarters for a cavalry troop. Camp Santa Helena, as the installation was called, was completed in 1920 but never used. Also in 1919 Wayne Cartledge, whose father was a prominent Austin lawyer and partner of Terlingua mining baron Howard E. Perry,[qv] bought the old Sublett-Buttrill place. Cartledge, who had been manager of the Chisos Mining Company store in Terlingua, was as ambitious as Sublett. He set up a partnership called La Harmonía with Perry, opened a new, larger trading post, and in 1921 began commercial cotton farming in the area. At first La Harmonía shipped its cotton to Houston for ginning, but in the spring of 1923 Cartledge bought a cotton gin that became operational in October of that year.

In 1924 he brought in a former shipbuilder named Richard W. Derrick to get the gin working more efficiently. Derrick trained Alvino Ybarra, a Mexican immigrant, to keep the gin running and in 1926 became the first Castolon postmaster. The establishment of the post office also marked the change of the community's name to Castolon, derived from the nearby Cerro Castellan; there was already another post office in Texas called Santa Helena. Cartledge's gin produced 150 to 200 bales of cotton each season, marketed in El Paso and Houston, and between 1923 and 1942 ginned more than 2,000 bales. Though the cotton operation never became a major financial success, it was a steady source of local employment for decades.

Cartledge also introduced fruit trees, hogs, turkeys, and bees to Castolon's agricultural repertoire. He served as middleman for Mexican trappers who supplied him with fox, beaver, wolf, and bobcat fur, and as a wholesale distributor for local producers of candelilla wax. In 1921 the army allowed Cartledge to move his store into the abandoned barracks at Camp Santa Helena. He and his employees lived in the other buildings. In January 1925 the War Department offered for sale all its abandoned military installations along the Rio Grande, including Camp Santa Helena. Cartledge and Perry bought the nine buildings for $1,280 in April 1926. Cartledge moved the headquarters of La Harmonía into the abandoned military camp.

Unfortunately, after 1927 the Castolon cotton industry began to decline. In that year the United States Immigration Service began strictly enforcing immigration laws, a move that interfered with the ready supply of cheap labor from across the Rio Grande. Many Mexican families left Castolon to avoid deportation. Within ten years Perry began to accuse Cartledge of mismanagement, and in 1940 Cartledge dissolved the partnership. In 1942 La Harmonía ceased cotton farming, and Cartledge turned over the management of the Castolon store to his son.

After the establishment of Big Bend National Park in 1944, Castolon's days were numbered. The estimated population declined from twenty-five in the late 1930s to just three by the early 1960s. The post office closed in 1954, and three years later Cartledge finally signed the deed transferring his holdings at Castolon to the National Park Service, though he retained the right to operate the store for three more years. By the mid-1980s the only residents of Castolon were National Park Service employees, although the Castolon store was still open under NPS management and remained a tourist attraction.

BIBLIOGRAPHY: T. Lindsay Baker, *Ghost Towns of Texas* (Norman: University of Oklahoma Press, 1986). Clifford B. Casey, *Mirages, Mysteries and Reality: Brewster County, Texas, the Big Bend of the Rio Grande* (Hereford, Texas: Pioneer, 1972). Arthur R. Gomez, *A Most Singular Country: A History of Occupation in the Big Bend* (Santa Fe: National Park Service; Salt Lake City: Charles Redd Center for Western Studies, Brigham Young University, 1990).

Martin Donell Kohout

CASTRO, CUELGAS DE (?–1842). Cuelgas de Castro, a Lipan Apache chief in Texas during the first half of the nineteenth century, was probably born in the 1790s; he was a leading Apache chief at the time Mexico won independence from Spain (1821). He inherited his rank from his father, Josef Castro, and, by several wives, fathered several children, including Juan Castro, who succeeded him. As a friend of the white settlers in Texas, Castro allied his people with the Austin colonists and the Republic of Texas[qv] in an effort to defend the Lipans from the Comanches. In 1812 he and other Lipans and members of other groups joined Samuel Kemper[qv] in attacking San Antonio during the Gutiérrez-Magee expedition.[qv] Kemper had succeeded the deceased Augustus William Magee[qv] as commander of pro-Hidalgo forces (*see* HIDALGO Y COSTILLA, MIGUEL) organized by José Bernardo Gutiérrez de Lara[qv] to establish an independent Texas republic; he encouraged Indian enlistments. Castro and his people returned home after the successful battle and took no part in Gen. Joaquín de Arredondo's[qv] subsequent defeat of the republican forces on the Medina River. The Apaches continued to support filibustering expeditions into Texas during the remaining years of Spanish rule. After the establishment of an independent Mexico, Castro and other Lipans visited Mexico City and signed a treaty of peace with the Mexican government. In this agreement the Lipans promised to keep the peace in Texas—a promise they did not honor. Mexican authorities promised trade in return but also failed to make good on their word. As a result the Lipans had no guns for fighting the Comanches. The arrival of settlers led by Stephen F. Austin,[qv] however, provided the Lipans with new trading partners and military allies.

During the Republic of Texas Castro enlisted in the Texas Rangers[qv] as a scout. In his first expedition he led a force under John H. Moore[qv] to attack a Comanche village. The white men ignored Castro's advice to run off the horses of the Comanches, who were therefore able to escape. In disgust, Castro and his men deserted Moore's force. From that time, Castro fought only with the ranger companies commanded by John Coffee Hays.[qv] In 1838 he signed a treaty of friendship and mutual aid between his people and the Republic of Texas. The Lipans supported the Somervell expedition[qv] against Mexico in 1842 and eagerly accepted the gifts the Texans provided them. Castro died in 1842, and his son Juan became chief. Juan Castro served as a leading spokesman for the Indians on the Brazos Indian Reservation[qv] in the 1850s. Rather than accept removal to Indian Territory in 1859, the Lipans fled to Mexico and joined the Kickapoos.

BIBLIOGRAPHY: Roy D. Holt, *Heap Many Texas Chiefs* (San Antonio: Naylor, 1966). Adele B. Looscan, "Capt. Joseph Daniels," *Quarterly of the Texas State Historical Association* 5 (July 1901). Amelia W. Williams and Eugene C. Barker, eds., *The Writings of Sam Houston, 1813–1863* (8 vols., Austin: University of Texas Press, 1938–43; rpt., Austin and New York: Pemberton Press, 1970). Dorman H. Winfrey and James M. Day, eds., *Texas Indian Papers* (4 vols., Austin: Texas State Library, 1959–61; rpt., 5 vols., Austin: Pemberton Press, 1966).

Thomas F. Schilz

CASTRO, HENRI (1786–1865). Henri Castro, empresario[qv] and founder of Castro's colony,[qv] was born in the department of Landes, France, in July 1786. His family, descended from Portuguese Jews who had fled to France after the inception of the Spanish Inquisition, occupied a position of wealth and status in southwestern France. At nineteen Castro was appointed by the governor of Landes to a committee to welcome Napoleon during a visit to the province, and in 1806 he served as a member of Napoleon's guard of honor when the emperor installed his brother Joseph as king of Spain. In 1813 Castro married a wealthy widow, Amelia Mathias, who brought him a dowry of 50,000 francs. After the fall of Napoleon, he immigrated to the United States and in 1827 became a naturalized citizen. He returned to France in 1838 and became a partner in the banking house of Lafitte and Company. While with that firm he was active in trying to negotiate a loan for the Republic of Texas[qv] and thus became interested in the young republic. Out of gratitude for his influence and kindness to Texas, President Sam Houston[qv] appointed him consul general for Texas at Paris. In 1842 Castro entered into a contract with the Texas government to settle a colony in Southwest Texas on the Medina River. After great expense, labor, and vexing delays, between 1843 and 1847 he succeeded in chartering twenty-seven ships, in which he brought to Texas 485 families and 457 single men. His task was made difficult because at this same time the French government was trying to colonize Algeria and because the Mexican War[qv] made Texas ports often unsafe harbors for the landing of immigrants. Castro was able, however, to settle his first shipload of families at Castroville in September 1844; in 1845 he established the village of Quihi; in 1846, the town of Vandenburg; the last village, D'Hanis, was founded in 1847. Castro was a learned, wise, humane man. In the management of his colony he is more comparable to Stephen F. Austin than is any other Texas empresario. He expended his own money freely—more than $200,000—for the welfare of his colonists, furnishing them cows, farm implements, seeds for planting, medicines, and whatever they really needed that he was able to procure for them. He had unbounded faith in the capacity of intelligent men for self-government. Among his duties Castro found the time to publish his memoirs. He made many maps of his colonial grant and of the area bordering on it and circulated them throughout the Rhine districts of France to induce colonists to join his settlements. These maps did much to advertise Texas in Europe. Despite his scholarship, his exceedingly great energy, and his rare aptitude for work, he was exceptionally modest and retiring. While on his way to France in 1865, he became severely ill at Monterrey, Nuevo León, and died there on November 31, 1865. He was buried in Monterrey at the foot of the Sierra Madre. His many interests were carried on by his son, Lorenzo. Castro County, in the Panhandle,[qv] was named in his honor.

BIBLIOGRAPHY: Rudolph L. Biesele, *The History of the German Settlements in Texas, 1831–1861* (Austin: Von Boeckmann–Jones, 1930; rpt. 1964). Henri Castro Papers, Barker Texas History Center, University of Texas at Austin. Cornelia E. Crook, *Henry Castro* (San Antonio: St. Mary's University Press, 1988). Audrey G. Goldthorp, Castro's Colony (M.A. thesis, University of Texas, 1928). Julia Nott Waugh, *Castro-Ville and Henry Castro, Empresario* (San Antonio: Standard, 1934). Bobby D. Weaver, *Castro's Colony: Empresario Development in Texas, 1842–1865* (College Station: Texas A&M University Press, 1985).

Amelia W. Williams

CASTRO COUNTY. Castro County (D-8) is located in the western Panhandle[qv] on the Texas High Plains, bordered on the west by Parmer County, on the north by Deaf Smith and Randall counties, on the east by Swisher County, and on the south by Lamb and Hall counties. The county was named for Henri Castro,[qv] the empresario[qv] who was consul general to Paris for the Republic of Texas.[qv] The center of the county lies at approximately 34°32′ north latitude and 102°20′ west longitude. Dimmitt, the county seat, is near the center of the county, approximately fifty miles southwest of Amarillo. Castro County comprises 900.33 square miles of level plains. Its sandy loam and black soils once supported native grasses but now produce abundant corn, wheat, sorghum, cotton, sugarbeets, and soybeans. Seasonally waterless draws or arroyos drain the county; Frio Draw runs southeasterly into Swisher County, and Running Water Draw, which begins about twenty-five miles northwest of Clovis, New Mexico, meanders southeasterly across Castro County into Lamb and then Hale counties. More than 500 playas dot the surface of the county. Elevation ranges from 3,500 to 4,000 feet above sea level, and annual precipitation averages 17.72 inches. The average minimum temperature of 22° F occurs in January, and the average maximum of 93° in July. The growing season averages 193 days a year.

The area now known as Castro County was once occupied by Apaches, who were forced out of the region by Comanches around 1720. The Comanches ruled the Panhandle-Plains area until they were defeated by the United States Army in the Red River War[qv] of 1874. The Indians were confined to reservations in Indian Territory during 1875 and 1876. Buffalo hunters arrived in the region in 1876 and by the early 1880s had eliminated the last remnants of the formerly huge herds. The Texas legislature established Castro County in 1876.

Ranchers began to arrive in the county in the early and middle 1880s. James W. Carter[qv] brought his family in 1884 and established a medium-sized ranch of seventy-two sections, the 7-UP Ranch, in the southwestern part of the county on Running Water Draw. Other ranches, headquartered in surrounding counties, controlled Castro County lands. The XIT Ranch[qv] held some land in the southern and western parts of the county, while the T Anchor Ranch[qv] controlled some of the land in the north. The Cross L had lands in southeastern Castro County, and the Circle Cross controlled ranges in the eastern part of the county. In 1888 Lysius Gough[qv] filed on land south of the site of present-day Dimmitt, and in 1889 James L. Beach and his six sons from Grayson County each filed on sections of land in the same general area and dug dugouts (*see* DUGOUT), confident that a county seat would be soon be established nearby. In 1890 only nine people lived in Castro County; most of them were members of the Carter family.

Between 1890 and 1900 Castro County slowly developed but remained a sparsely populated stock-farming and ranching region. Some settlers arrived in the nineties to claim land for agricultural or commercial uses. On March 4, 1890, the Bedford Town and Land Development Company was formed in Grayson County with H. G. Bedford as president. On May 27, the company, eager to establish a county seat for Castro County, bought a section of land near the center of the county, dug a well, built a water tower, and platted a town. The new town was called Dimmitt because of the close bond between H. G. Bedford and the Rev. W. C. Dimmitt, a partner in the venture. In 1890 and 1891 a number of settlers, including Ira Aten,[qv] Thornton and Will Jones, Mrs. M. B. Fowle, the Tates, the Turnbows, and the J. E. Turners, moved into the county and established themselves near Dimmitt.

By 1891 Castro County's new settlers felt a need for local government. A petition for organization was circulated in August 1891. Meanwhile, developers of different townsites were competing for the location of the county seat, though only one of the proposed sites, Castro City, posed a real threat to the Bedford group. After much struggle to obtain the 150 names necessary for organization, the petition was presented to the Oldham County Commissioners Court on December 9, 1891. Castro County was formally organized by an election on December 21, and Dimmitt was designated the county seat. By 1900, seventy-six farms and ranches in the county encompassed 191,362 acres of land (including 12,131 acres classified as "improved"), and the county's population had risen to 400.

Soon after 1900 the XIT and other Panhandle ranches began to sell lands to arriving settlers, and the advent of German farmers in the eastern part of the county between 1902 and 1906 helped to stimulate farming on a large scale. The German immigrants came to Castro County as a result of the colonization efforts of a Catholic priest, Father Joseph Reisdorff.[qv] Reisdorff, founder of other German colonies at Rhineland, Windthorst, and Slaton, began his Castro County promotions in league with an Irish Catholic, Tom McCormick, who had lived in the eastern part of the county since 1892. McCormick's attempt to establish an Irish Catholic colony named Wind on his property in 1892 had failed, so he was amenable to Reisdorff's plans. Reisdorff established a town, Nazareth, in 1902 to serve as the center of his new colony.

The Germans and other newcomers took up both farming and stock raising, and farming gradually grew in importance over the years. Meanwhile, a rapid rise in agricultural mechanization, coupled with a rising demand for agricultural products in the 1920s, helped to stimulate the county's farm economy. The number of farms in the area consequently grew steadily between 1900 and 1930. By 1910, 327 had been established in Castro County, 365 by 1920, 521 by 1925, and 751 by 1930. Corn, sorghum, and, especially, wheat, were the principal crops grown by these new farmers; by 1930 crops were harvested on more than 220,000 acres of land in the county, including 132,665 acres devoted to wheat production. The number of cattle also grew during this period. In 1900 about 9,500 head were counted in Castro County; by 1930 the census counted almost 31,460. As the agricultural economy developed, county population grew: Castro County had 1,850 residents in 1910 and 1,948 in 1920; in 1930 the census enumerated 4,720.

The hard years of the Great Depression[qv] marked an end to this first period of development; during the 1930s crop production dropped and some farmers were forced to give up their lands. In 1939 farmers harvested only about 212,000 acres in the county, and the number of farms had dropped to 703; the population declined during the depression to 4,631.

After World War II,[qv] however, the county's economy began to expand again as underground irrigation[qv] water began to play an important role in the local farming economy and farming acreage increased. By the 1980s more than 400,000 acres of Castro County (over 70 percent of county lands) was under cultivation, with over 300,000 acres irrigated by underground water. As the farming economy grew, the county prospered. Population rose in 1950 to 5,417, to 8,923 in 1960, to 10,394 in 1970, and to 10,556 in 1980. During the 1980s, however, it shrank; by 1992, only 9,070 people lived in Castro County.

The transportation system of Castro County has developed along with the area's economy and population. Crude wagon roads of the 1890s evolved into dirt auto roads by the World War I[qv] era. Most of these wound across the county along section lines and fence lines. By the mid-1920s a graded dirt road linked Dimmitt to Tulia via Nazareth and Bovina. Ungraded dirt roads also ran from Dimmitt to Hereford and from Dimmitt to Plainview. In the 1930s Work Projects Administration[qv] projects in Castro County included the construction of caliche auto roads in and around Dimmitt. After 1934 the Texas State Highway Department began to build and maintain intercounty dirt roads, which were paved after World War II. The county's first paved highway, State Highway 86, from Dimmitt to Tulia, was not completed until 1941. Castro County was thus the last Texas county to acquire a paved road. In the years between the 1940s and the 1960s, a network of paved farm-to-market roads evolved to link the rural parts of the county to main routes (*see* HIGHWAY DEVELOPMENT).

Railroads came into the area relatively late. The county's only rail line is a branch of the Fort Worth and Denver Railway built from Plainview to Dimmitt in 1928. The Pecos and Northern Texas Railway, an Atchison, Topeka and Santa Fe subsidiary, built across the far northwestern corner of the county in 1898 but made no real contribution to the local economy.

By the 1980s Castro County ranked as one of the state's most productive agricultural counties. Its yearly average crop, valued at over $195 million, consists principally of corn, wheat, sorghum, cotton, soybeans, sugarbeets, and vegetables. The county maintains several large vegetable-processing plants. The cattle feedlot industry developed on a large scale after the 1950s and reached a capacity of over 200,000 head. In 1972 a large sheep feedlot went into production with a capacity of 20,000 head. Since then two or three large-scale hog operations have been started. The county also has a fertilizer industry and a number of cotton gins. Most people in Castro County live in the towns and communities, including Nazareth (1980 population 299), Hart (1,008), Summerfield (60), Easter (91), Flagg (50), and Sunnyside (106). Dimmitt, the county's largest town and seat of government, had an estimated population in 1992 of 4,408, and hosts Castro County's yearly harvest festival.

Henri Castro. Albumin print. Henri Castro Papers, CAH; CN 00930.

BIBLIOGRAPHY: Castro County Historical Commission, *Castro County, 1891–1981* (Dallas: Taylor, 1981). Charles P. Flanagin, The Origins of Nazareth, Texas (M.A. thesis, West Texas State College, 1948). *Highways of Texas, 1927* (Houston: Gulf Oil and Refining, 1927).

Donald R. Abbe

CASTRO'S COLONY. On February 15, 1842, Henri Castro,[qv] an empresario[qv] of the Republic of Texas,[qv] received contracts for two grants of land on which he was to establish 600 families. One grant lay west of San Antonio; the other was along the Rio Grande between Camargo and La Sal del Rey.[qv] Castro recruited his colonists in France, particularly in Alsace. On September 1, 1844, he left San Antonio for his land grant beyond the Medina River with his first thirty-five colonists. On September 3 the group reached its destination and began building homes. On September 12 an election was held for two justices of the peace and a constable, and the name Castroville was adopted for the settlement. During the colony's first year 558 headrights were issued, and 485 families and 457 single men were introduced, for a total of 2,134 settlers. The colony suffered from Indian depredations, cholera, and the drought of 1848, but population increased sufficiently for the formation of Medina County in 1848. The present towns of Castroville, D'Hanis, Quihi, and Vandenburg were founded by the colonists.

BIBLIOGRAPHY: Cornelia E. Crook, *Henry Castro* (San Antonio: St. Mary's University Press, 1988). Audrey G. Goldthorp, Castro's Colony

(M.A. thesis, University of Texas, 1928). Julia Nott Waugh, *Castro-Ville and Henry Castro, Empresario* (San Antonio: Standard, 1934). Bobby D. Weaver, *Castro's Colony: Empresario Development in Texas, 1842–1865* (College Station: Texas A&M University Press, 1985).

Curtis Bishop

CASTROVILLE, TEXAS. Castroville, the "little Alsace" of Texas, is located on the Medina River and U.S. Highway 90 twenty-five miles west of San Antonio in eastern Medina County. The town was named for its founder, Henri Castro,[qv] with whom the Republic of Texas[qv] negotiated an empresario[qv] contract on January 15, 1842. Castro's grant began four miles west of the Medina River and comprised frontier lands in Comanche territory. Wanting to locate his first settlement on the Medina River, Castro purchased the sixteen leagues between his grant and the river from John McMullen[qv] of San Antonio.

He arranged transport for mostly Catholic Alsatian farmers to the Texas coast, from where the colonists were escorted overland to San Antonio. On September 2, 1844, Castro set out from San Antonio with his colonists, accompanied by Texas Ranger John C. Hays[qv] and five of his rangers, to decide upon a site for settlement. The company chose a level, park-like area near a sharp bend of the Medina River covered with pecan trees. Castro recounts in his memoirs that after crossing the river members of his party killed two deer, three bears, and one alligator and caught numerous fish. Subsequently, the colonists endured raids by Comanches and Mexicans, droughts in 1848 and 1849, an invasion of locusts, and a cholera epidemic in 1849.

Castro patterned his town after European villages in which small town lots were surrounded by individual farming plots. The town was surveyed by John James; its streets were named in honor of Castro's relatives and friends and the capitals of Europe. In 1844 citizens of Castroville built St. Louis Catholic Church, the first church in Medina County. Zion Lutheran Church was built in 1853; the first public school classes taught in Medina County were held in this church in 1854. By 1856 Castroville supported three large stores, a brewery, and a water-powered gristmill. The community raised corn, cattle, horses, hogs, and poultry, and sold produce to the military posts in the area.

Castroville architecture and style were distinctly European. A cross was erected on Mount Gentilz (*see* GENTILZ, J. L. T.). A visitor in the 1850s described Castroville as quite "un-Texan," with its "steep thatched roofs and narrow lanes" and the inn whose interior suggested "Europe rather than the frontier." The houses were not arranged along parallel lines but were spread out over many acres. Stores and residences were constructed without the broad front porches common to the South. The house builders used rough-cut stone or stone and timber combinations and smoothed over the exterior with lime plaster. The European method of building ground floors of stone and second floors with vertically placed timbers was characteristic of two-story construction. Many of the structures erected in Castroville's earliest days continued to house people and businesses 150 years later. Local builders made use of large cypress trees growing along the Medina River to produce shingles for home use or for market. (*See also* GERMAN VERNACULAR ARCHITECTURE.)

The first post office in Medina County opened in Castroville in 1847 with M. Laroch as postmaster. In 1848 the Texas legislature established Medina County and designated Castroville its county seat. In 1853 Castro donated two lots for the site of the new courthouse, which when completed in 1855 served as a school. A rock dam, still intact in 1945, was built in 1854 to furnish power for a gristmill.

During the Civil War[qv] wagon trains loaded with freight stopped overnight at Castroville on their way to Mexico, and the town thrived. By the mid-1860s Castroville was the twelfth largest city in Texas. In 1884 the town had a population of 1,000, a weekly newspaper called the *Brackett Weekly News*, a steam gristmill and cotton gin, a brewery, Catholic and Lutheran churches, a convent, and a public school. The principal marketable goods produced at this time were cotton, hides, and grain. By 1890 pecans were being marketed, the Castroville *Anvil* was being published, and a telephone system had been installed. A bank opened by 1896, when the population was 750.

In 1880 the Southern Pacific Railroad, extending its line to the west, passed south of Castroville because the town refused to grant the railroad a bonus. Hondo became the county seat in 1892. Castroville citizens voted that year to disincorporate their town, and it remained unincorporated until 1948. In 1908 the Castroville school had 172 white students, twelve black students, and four teachers. In 1915 the old courthouse was converted into a school with three large classrooms.

In 1914 Castroville had a population of 700 and a new weekly newspaper called the Castroville *Quill*. The population dropped to 500 during Prohibition.[qv] By 1931 the town had a population of 325 and nineteen businesses. In 1936 the population was 787; 65 percent were German, 15 percent were Mexican American, and 20 percent were French or American. Most farmers in the community lived in town and farmed their small tracts in the surrounding territory. The population in 1940 was 865. By 1953 Castroville had a population of 992 and thirty businesses. In 1962 it had 1,508 residents and forty businesses. The following year the Castroville Public Library, the first public library in Medina County, opened. In 1979 Castroville had a population estimated at 2,146 and thirty-five businesses.

In 1984 the major agricultural products grown in the area were corn, maize, oats, wheat, vegetables, and hay. Agribusinesses in Castroville included a firm that processed whole-grain corn for local tortilla and corn-chip manufacturers, feed mills, and irrigation, tractor, and farm-implement dealers. Castroville is also a center for applied research in genetics and artificial breeding of livestock. By 1989 Castroville had a population of 2,037 and thirty-three businesses. In 1990 the population was 2,159.

Castroville has been recognized as a national and a Texas historic district. Many of the ninety-seven Historical American buildings in Castroville can be seen on a walking tour; they include the Landmark Inn State Historic Site, the St. Louis Catholic and the Zion Lutheran churches, the Moye Formation Center, the Tarde Hotel, and Henri Castro's original homestead. Castroville celebrates St. Louis Day on August 22 each year.

BIBLIOGRAPHY: Castro Colonies Heritage Association, *The History of Medina County, Texas* (Dallas: National Share Graphics, 1983). Houston B. Eggen, History of Public Education in Medina County, Texas, 1848–1928 (M.A. thesis, University of Texas, 1950). John J. Germann and Myron Janzen, *Texas Post Offices by County* (1986). Vertical Files, Barker Texas History Center, University of Texas at Austin. Bobby D. Weaver, *Castro's Colony: Empresario Development in Texas, 1842–1865* (College Station: Texas A&M University Press, 1985).

Ruben E. Ochoa

CATALINE, TEXAS. Cataline, at the mouth of Gageby Creek on the Washita River in southeastern Hemphill County, was established in 1890 on the Houston and Great Northern Railroad survey. The town, located on the Alexander Ranch, was allegedly named by Lucy Alexander for the ancient Roman politician Catiline, about whom she had read and whose name she misspelled. One historian, however, states that a Kansas land promoter named Cataline named the community after himself. Although it had a post office and a combination school and church building, the town failed when the railroad changed plans. Cataline was too remote to prosper. The post office remained in operation until 1912. In 1990 only the community cemetery remained.

BIBLIOGRAPHY: Sallie B. Harris, *Cowmen and Ladies: A History of Hemphill County* (Canyon, Texas: Staked Plains, 1977). Glyndon M. Riley, The History of Hemphill County (M.A. thesis, West Texas State

College, 1939). F. Stanley [Stanley F. L. Crocchiola], *Story of the Texas Panhandle Railroads* (Borger, Texas: Hess, 1976).

H. Allen Anderson

CATARINA, TEXAS. Catarina is on U.S. Highway 83 ten miles southeast of Asherton in southern Dimmit County. The name has been associated with the area since at least 1778; legend holds that it is the name of a Mexican woman killed by Indians on or near the site. The town was established after Asher Richardson, a rancher, decided to build a railway link from Artesia Wells to his planned town of Asherton. In return for an easement through the nearby Taft-Catarina Ranch (*see* COLEMAN-FULTON PASTURE COMPANY), Richardson agreed to allow the ranch to establish a railroad depot, with cattle-shipping pens, on his railroad. By 1910, when the Asherton and Gulf Railway began operations, these cattle pens had become the nucleus of a small community built by Joseph F. Green,[qv] the manager of the ranch. Green moved the ranch headquarters to the depot and added a bunkhouse, a commissary, a hotel, a post office, and a small schoolhouse. By 1915 the little town had twenty-five residents and had become famous in the area for the Taft House, an expensive mansion that Charles Taft, the owner of the ranch, supposedly built with oversized bathtubs to accommodate his brother, President William Howard Taft. Catarina Farms, a development project, built roads, sidewalks, a waterworks, and an impressive new hotel and installed electric power and a telephone exchange. Agent Charles Ladd imported entire orchards of fruit-laden citrus trees to impress prospective investors with the area's agricultural possibilities. By 1929 Catarina had between 1,000 and 2,500 residents, a bank, at least two groceries, a lumber company, and a bakery. Short supplies of water, marketing problems, and the Great Depression[qv] hurt the town. By 1931 the population had dropped to 592, and many of its businesses had been forced to close. In 1943 Catarina had 403 residents and seven businesses; in 1956 it had 380 residents and three businesses. By 1969 some of the town's most picturesque old buildings had been abandoned, and the population was 160. In 1990 the population was forty-five.

BIBLIOGRAPHY: Laura Knowlton Tidwell, *Dimmit County Mesquite Roots* (Austin: Wind River, 1984). Frank X. Tolbert, "Tolbert's Texas" Scrapbook, Barker Texas History Center, University of Texas at Austin. Vertical Files, Barker Texas History Center, University of Texas at Austin.

John Leffler

CATARINA CREEK. Catarina Creek rises eleven miles southwest of Catarina in south central Dimmit County (at 28°18′N, 99°49′W) and runs southeast for nine miles before emptying into San Roque Creek 7½ miles southwest of Catarina (at 28°15′ N, 99°42′ W). The stream rises in rolling hills and ends in flat terrain with shallow depressions. The surrounding clay and sandy loams support scrub brush, mesquite, grasses, and cacti in the upper reaches and water-tolerant hardwoods and grasses in the lower.

CATAYE INDIANS. The Cataye Indians, a Caddoan tribe of the southwestern or Hasinai division in eastern Texas, are known from a single Spanish document that was written near the end of the seventeenth century. H. E. Bolton[qv] assumed that Cataye was a variant of the name Cachaé, but these similar names both occur in the same document without any indication that they are variants of the same name. Bolton also argued that Cachaé was an early name for the Hainai Indians (they seem to have occupied the same territory). J. R. Swanton accepted Bolton's interpretations and also linked Caxo with Cachaé. This is all largely a matter of modern inference and opinion. As no early Spanish authority ever stated that Cataye, Cachaé, Caxo, and Hainai were names that referred to the same people, the case is still open.

BIBLIOGRAPHY: Herbert E. Bolton, "The Native Tribes about the East Texas Missions," *Quarterly of the Texas State Historical Association* 11 (April 1908). John R. Swanton, *Source Material on the History and Ethnology of the Caddo Indians* (Smithsonian Institution, Bureau of American Ethnology Bulletin 132, Washington: GPO, 1942).

Thomas N. Campbell

CAT CLAW CREEK. Cat Claw Creek rises a half mile east of Farm Road 89 and five miles northeast of Buffalo Gap in north central Taylor County (at 32°22′ N, 99°47′ W) and runs northeast for thirteen miles to its mouth on Elm Creek, a quarter mile north of U.S. Highway 20 in north Abilene (at 32°30′ N, 99°45′ W). Mesquite, catclaw, and various grasses grow beside the stream, which flows through flat to gently sloping terrain.

CAT CREEK (Lipscomb County). Cat Creek rises five miles northeast of Lipscomb in central Lipscomb County (at 36°14′ N, 100°15′ W) and runs south for four miles to its mouth on Wolf Creek, two miles east of Lipscomb (at 36°14′ N, 100°14′ W). It crosses flat to rolling terrain with some local escarpments, surfaced by deep, fine sandy loams that support mesquite and grasses.

____ (Newton County). Cat Creek rises four miles southeast of Weeks Settlement in northwest Newton County (at 31°03′ N, 93°48′ W) and runs southeast for 10½ miles to its mouth on Yellow Bayou, three miles southwest of Burkeville (at 30°58′ N, 93°41′ W). It flows through the heavily forested areas typical of Newton County.

CATFISH, TEXAS. Catfish was twelve miles southeast of Athens in southeastern Henderson County. A post office operated there from 1888 to 1910. At its height around 1900 the settlement had a flour mill, a gin, and a grocer. By the mid-1930s Catfish no longer appeared on maps, and in the early 1990s only a few houses remained in the area.

Christopher Long

CATFISH CREEK (Cottle County). Catfish Creek rises at the confluence of two of its three tributaries, the East and West prongs, eighteen miles northeast of Paducah in east central Cottle County (at 34°11′ N, 100°05′ W) and runs four miles northeast to its mouth on the Pease River, twenty miles northeast of Paducah and one mile east of Farm Road 104 (at 34°13′ N, 100°04′ W). The East Prong rises a mile north of U.S. Highway 70 and two miles west of the Foard county line (at 34°06′ N, 100°05′ W), and the West Prong rises two miles southeast of Swearingen (at 34°07′ N, 100°07′ W). The third tributary, the Middle Prong, rises two miles north of U.S. Highway 70 and three miles west of the Foard county line (at 34°07′ N, 100°06′ W) and runs north to its mouth on the West Prong, one mile upstream from its confluence with the East Prong (at 34°10′ N, 100°05′ W). Each of the tributaries flows six miles northeast. The system traverses locally faulted rolling to steep terrain surfaced by shallow clay and sandy loams that support juniper, cacti, and sparse grasses.

____ (Henderson County). Catfish Creek, also known as Catfish Bayou, rises just south of the Steele lakes in southwestern Henderson County (at 32°08′ N, 95°43′ W) and runs southwest for thirty-seven miles through southwestern Henderson County and western Anderson County to its mouth on the Trinity River, by the Coffield State Department of Corrections facility (at 31°46′ N, 95°56′ W). The banks of the stream are heavily wooded in places with mixed pine and hardwood trees, and the gently sloping to moderately steep terrain is surfaced by sand, clay, and loam. The area is used as woodland and for agriculture. The major tributaries of Catfish Creek include Beaver Creek and Coon Creek. Catfish Creek has been dammed at two points in Henderson County to form Rainbo Lake and Catfish Creek Ranch Lake.

CATFISH DRAW. Catfish Draw begins near the state line in Curry County, New Mexico (at 34°38′ N, 103°11′ W), and runs southeast into Parmer County, Texas, for twelve miles to its mouth on Runningwater Draw, east of Bovina (at 34°31′ N, 102°51′ W). The draw is cut through loose sand that covers flat to gently sloping terrain; the vegetation is mainly scrub brush and grasses. Several playas, including Mustang Lake, are on its course. The area was once part of the XIT Ranch's[qv] Spring Lake and Bovina divisions.

CATHEDRAL MOUNTAIN. Cathedral Mountain is ten miles northwest of Marathon in northern Brewster County (at 30°19′ N, 103°21′ W). With an elevation of 6,220 feet above sea level, it rises some 1,800 feet above U.S. Highway 90, four miles southwest. Cathedral Mountain is a ridge of tilted limestone roughly 250 million years old. It is the southern tip of the Glass Mountains.[qv] Its shallow, stony soils support live oak, piñon, juniper, and grasses.

A second Cathedral Mountain is twelve miles south of Alpine in northwestern Brewster County (at 30°11′ N, 103°40′ W). With an elevation of 6,868 feet above sea level, it rises 1,900 feet above State Highway 118, four miles east. Cathedral Mountain is an intrusive mass of igneous rock that has been exposed by erosion. Its shallow, stony soils support Douglas fir, aspen, Arizona cypress, maple, ponderosa pine, and madrone.

CATHEDRAL PEAK. Cathedral Peak is just southeast of Pinto Canyon in west central Presidio County (at 30°00′ N, 104°30′ W). With an elevation of over 4,400 feet above sea level, the peak stands encircled by canyons and higher summits in all directions. Cathedral Peak is composed of intrusive igneous rock from which grow sparse grasses, cacti, and desert shrubs of conifers and oaks.

CATHOLIC ARCHIVES OF TEXAS. The Catholic Archives of Texas, in Austin, serves as a central depository for records and documents pertaining to the activities of the Catholic Church[qv] in the state. The holdings of the collection range from earliest sixteenth-century Spanish explorations to present-day events. The depository had its beginning with the formal organization of the state Knights of Columbus[qv] Historical Commission in 1924, when the group, with the endorsement of the Texas bishops, resolved to publish a history of the church in Texas. Soon after launching their project, the commission named as chairman Paul J. Foik,[qv] librarian at St. Edward's University, Austin, who had established the Catholic Archives of America at Notre Dame University, where he was librarian for twelve years. Carlos E. Castañeda,[qv] professor of history at the University of Texas, was selected as historiographer.

Castañeda spent years researching and collecting source materials from depositories in Mexico City and other seats of government such as Saltillo, Matamoros, and Monterrey. His work culminated in the seven-volume *Our Catholic Heritage in Texas, 1519–1936*, published between 1936 and 1958. Castañeda gave care of the collection to Bishop Lawrence FitzSimon[qv] in 1948, and it became the core of the Catholic Archives of Texas. FitzSimon transferred the materials to Amarillo and during several trips to Europe added materials. These documents include correspondence of early French missionaries, biographical information on early priests, and information on Catholic newspapers, of which the *Southern Messenger*[qv] collection is the most valuable.

After FitzSimon died in 1958, the collection was again transferred to Austin, where it was housed in the chancery of the Catholic Diocese of Austin.[qv] With the establishment of the Texas Catholic Conference in 1963, the bishops of Texas placed the care of the archives under its direction. Holdings include records of the Texas Catholic Conference, the Texas Knights of Columbus Historical Commission, the Texas Catholic Historical Society,[qv] and religious associations, societies, and Catholic clubs in Texas; papers of Paul J. Foik, William H. Oberste, Sam Houston, Charles S. Taylor, Francis Bouchu,[qqv] and Fred Bomar; diocese and parish collections; copies of governmental and religious documents in other archives; personal papers and biographical files of the bishops and clergy of Texas; documents dealing with the various religious orders formed or stationed in the state; and newspapers, pamphlets, books, maps, photographs, artifacts, and periodicals relating to the history of the Catholic Church in Texas. The depository, owned and supported by the Catholic hierarchy of Texas, solicits records from institutions and organizations in all parts of the state and is open to researchers.

BIBLIOGRAPHY: Sister M. Claude Lane, O.P., Catholic Archives of Texas: History and Preliminary Inventory (M.A. thesis, University of Texas, 1961). Karl M. Schmitt, "The History of the Texas Catholic Historical Society," *U.S. Catholic Historian* 3 (1983).

Sister Dolores Kasner, O.P.

CATHOLIC CHURCH. The Catholic Church has been a part of Texas history ever since Europeans first set foot on the land in 1528. In fact for the three centuries up to 1821—that is, during the Spanish Texas[qv] period—Hispanic Catholicism had a rarely challenged religious and civil monopoly among the European-origin settlers in what is now Texas. This in turn gave Hispanic Catholics complete control over Christianization efforts among the Indians. However, events after Mexican independence in 1821 soon left Catholics in a minority status in the land. But even then they always remained one of the largest single religious bodies in Texas, and Hispanics continued to be one of the largest ethnic groups among Texas Catholics. For more than a century, beginning with the odyssey of Álvar Núñez Cabeza de Vaca[qv] and his three companions (1528–35), transient expeditions of Catholic Hispanics (usually including Catholic clergy as well as such non-Spaniards as Estevanico[qv] "the Moor," of African origin) were the first Christians encountered by various indigenous peoples in what is now Texas. In the eyes of both the explorers and the natives, these sporadic religiocultural as well as military-political encounters ranged from wondrous to atrocious. In the 1680s and 1690s the first European foundations were attempted on various edges of the territory that was eventually incorporated in Texas. Tigua and Piro refugees from the Pueblo Revolt in northern New Mexico established the Franciscan-directed mission villages of Corpus Christi de la Isleta and Nuestra Señora de la Limpia Concepción del Socorro in the El Paso area in 1682. These proved to be the first permanent European-directed settlements in the future Texas. Nonpermanent, on the other hand, were the first mission efforts at La Junta de los Ríos[qv] (modern-day Presidio) in 1683–84; the French Catholic post established by La Salle along the Texas Gulf Coast in 1685–89, and the Spanish mission effort from 1690 to 1693 on the East Texas border in defensive response to French plans.

Missions at La Junta were re-established in 1715, and continued thereafter with occasional interruptions of several years at a time. La Junta's instability left the missionary-led Indian settlement at San Antonio de Valero Mission and the soldier-settler town of San Antonio de Béxar Presidio, both established in 1718, as the beginnings of the second permanent Hispanic Catholic foundation in Texas. Throughout the rest of that century, a total of twenty-six Spanish missions existed for greater or lesser periods of time in what is now East, Southeast, Central, South, and West Texas. To this number should be added those missionary centers established immediately across the Rio Grande whose sphere of influence also extended to the Texas side of the river, such as those at Camargo, Nuevo Santandes[qv] (across from the site of present Rio Grande City), San Juan Bautista (at Guerrero, Coahuila, below the site of present Eagle Pass), and in the La Junta and El Paso districts. Some missions, such as that of Santa Cruz de San Sabá at the locale of present-day Menard, proved to be disasters. Most were unsuccessful in terms of converting any significant number of Indians. But those in the El Paso district, San Antonio, La Bahía (Goliad), and Camargo were relatively successful for several decades or longer not only in economic terms, but also in terms of assimilating natives into Hispanic Catholic society. Franciscans[qv] founded and supervised all the mission efforts in Texas during the Spanish colonial period. They were sent by several of their missionary organizations: the Holy Gospel Province, the San Francisco de Zacatecas Province, the College of Santa Cruz de Querétaro,[qv] the College of Nuestra Señora de Guadalupe de Zacatecas,[qv] and the College of San Fernando de Mexico.

Even more important than the missions in the development and permanence of Hispanic Catholicism in Texas, however, were the communities of Hispanic Catholics themselves who planted their religious institutions in Texas during and after the colonial period. In towns and in the countryside they gathered for worship and celebrations, instructed their children in the faith, and built their own churches and chapels. Even the mission establishments were eventually meant to be "secularized"—that is, merged into the Catholic diocesan church. The diocesan church, the church under a bishop's direct jurisdiction, had already been developing in Texas decades before any mission secularizations occurred. From the beginning, the huge Diocese of Guadalajara supervised church work east of the Pecos River, while the equally immense Diocese of Durango gradually made good its claim to jurisdiction over the Trans-Pecos[qv] region in the eighteenth century. In 1779 the new Diocese of Linares or Nuevo León, soon headquartered in Monterrey, took over supervision of the east-of-the-Pecos lands from the Guadalajara diocese. While the Franciscans initially cared for the Hispanic Catholics as well as the missionized natives throughout Texas, gradually diocesan clergy arrived to take over this role in one place after another, beginning with the secular priest who became the first pastor of San Fernando de Béxar parish in San Antonio in 1731. By 1808 at least thirteen Franciscans and twelve secular priests were serving eighteen different Hispanic Catholic population centers within or on the edge of the territory of today's Texas, and native Hispanics were joining the ranks of the clergy.

In the 1810 to 1846 period—that is, during the last decade of the Spanish regime and the first decades of Mexican Texas[qv]—a volatile combination of insurgencies, invasions, new economic systems, massive foreign and particularly Anglo-Protestant immigration, sociopolitical discord, and changes of sovereignty resulted in serious trials and new challenges for the Mexican Catholic Church in the old province of Texas east of the Medina River and above the Nueces River. Almost all the Catholic population centers remained staffed by priests up until the Texas Revolution,[qv] but the increasing numbers of foreign and mostly non-Catholic immigrants east of the Guadalupe River rarely saw a Catholic clergyman—a situation that pleased most of them. The revolution wreaked havoc on the Mexican Catholic communities above the Nueces, totally displacing some, damaging and in some cases expropriating their church buildings, and reducing the clergy presence to San Antonio alone. Wherever Mexicans remained, however, their Catholic faith communities endured, thanks to continuing lay initiative as well as the ministry of whatever priests were available. Along the Rio Grande the changes were real but much less drastic, and Mexican priests managed to continue to provide pastoral care to all the communities.

In response to the radical changes in the newly independent Republic of Texas,[qv] Catholic Church authorities made the fledgling nation a separate jurisdiction from the Mexican church in 1840. Jean Marie Odin,[qv] a Vincentian priest, was sent to supervise the transition. He became the first vicar apostolic of Texas in 1842. After annexation[qv] to the United States, the vicariate was raised to the status of a diocese (1847). Odin thus became the first bishop of the Diocese of Galveston, which embraced all of Texas above the Nueces. As a result of the Mexican War,[qv] which ended that same year, the diocese's boundaries were declared to reach all the way to the Rio Grande. In practice, however, the westernmost settlements, that is, the El Paso and La Junta districts, continued to be pastored by Mexican priests of the Diocese of Durango until 1872 and 1892 respectively. By 1850, the year that the present Texas boundaries were determined for the most part, Mexicans and indeed Catholics in general had become a clearly subordinated minority in Texas above the Nueces River. Irish and other European Catholic immigrants were numerous enough, however, in combination with Mexican Catholics, to become the target of Anglo-Protestant nativist campaigns in the 1850s. Along the Rio Grande mainly Mexican but also a few European-origin Catholics exercised enough numerical and political power to oblige newcomers from the dominant United States society to adopt a generally more accommodating approach.

In keeping with the general population growth in Texas, the estimated number of Catholics swelled from fewer than 40,000 in 1850 to 150,000 in 1880. To attend to this mixed population of Mexican, European, and Anglo-American Catholics, Bishop Odin and his successor, Claude Marie Dubuis,[qv] recruited heavily from Europe to obtain Catholic congregations of men, Catholic congregations of women,[qqv] and secular clergy. The religious congregations contributed greatly to the development of institutions of Catholic education[qv] in Texas. The women religious established the first centers of Catholic health care[qv] and other Catholic social services such as St. Mary's Hospital and St. Mary's Orphanage[qqv] in Galveston. To tend better to the rapid growth of post–Civil War Texas, several new church jurisdictions were established. In 1872 the Vicariate Apostolic of Tucson in Arizona took over the El Paso district from the Mexican church. The Diocese of San Antonio (elevated to an archdiocese in 1926) and the Vicariate Apostolic of Brownsville were established in 1874. Holy Rosary Church and its accompanying school, the first church and school expressly for black Catholics[qv] in the state, began in 1887.

Railroads and major irrigation works in the late 1800s and early 1900s prompted major new immigration into North, West, and South Texas, and the Mexican Revolution[qv] (1910–) pushed thousands more into the state from Mexico. One response to the ever-increasing Catholic population was the inauguration of Catholic journalism[qv] in the 1890s. Another was the further division of church jurisdictions: the Catholic Diocese of Dallas was begun in 1890, the Vicariate of Brownsville was upgraded and renamed the Diocese of Corpus Christi[qv] in 1912, the Diocese of El Paso[qv] (extending into southern New Mexico) was established in 1914, and the Diocese of Amarillo[qv] was formed in 1926. The greater population base also helped to make possible the first permanent Catholic schools of ministry (seminaries) in Texas, St. Mary's University at La Porte and the San Antonio Philosophical and Theological Seminary (now the Oblate School of Theology), both founded at the beginning of the century.

By 1930 there were some 750,000 Catholics in Texas, a fivefold increase in half a century. They were served by their own lay leaders as well as around 630 priests, plus religious sisters and brothers. Secular priests were the great majority in the northern and eastern parts of the state, while religious priests were the majority in the Mexican-border dioceses. The new influx of Anglo and Mexican immigration during this period heightened racial and ethnic tensions, which were only exacerbated by the Great Depression[qv] of the 1930s. These tensions were addressed in the following decades by the social-action policies advocated by certain church leaders sympathetic to the New Deal such as Robert E. Lucey,[qv] archbishop of San Antonio, and Carmelo Tranchese,[qv] S.J. Among the notable results of such efforts was the development of the Bishops' Committee for Hispanic Affairs[qv] on the national level.

Renewed population growth in Texas after World War II[qv] led to the near doubling of the number of dioceses in the next two decades: the Diocese of Austin[qv] in 1947, the Diocese of San Angelo[qv] in 1961, the Diocese of Brownsville[qv] in 1965, the Diocese of Beaumont[qv] in 1966, and the Diocese of Fort Worth[qv] in 1969. A more publicly confident Catholicism emerged from the Catholic integration into the national war efforts. Texas Catholics numbered 1,800,000 by 1960; they were served by 1,570 priests, 4,950 women religious, and 330 religious brothers. The appearance of Catholic presidential candidate John F.

Kennedy before the Ministerial Association of Protestant leaders in Houston in 1960 marked a threshold in Catholic respectability within the country. But the Kennedy assassination[qv] in Dallas three years later signaled the beginning of the loss of postwar American self-assurance. The confusing and divisive times of the next two decades in both the nation and the Catholic Church—sorting out civil rights, the Vietnam War, and the church's Vatican Council II—were reflected in the numerical leveling off or even decline among the church's traditional ministerial personnel. The number of sisters did not increase in the 1960s and actually began a steady decline after 1968; there were only 3,270 in the state in 1993. The number of brothers, which had grown to 440 in 1967, plummeted to 240 in 1972 and has remained stable since. The number of priests has remained at 1,900 to 2,100 since reaching that level in the mid-1960s. And yet the Catholic population more than doubled between 1960 and 1993. In the latter year there were 3,975,000 Catholics in Texas, 23 percent of the state's total population. Catholic educational institutions, which relied heavily upon the contributed services of sisters, brothers, and priests, were especially affected by these changes. The number of Catholic schools decreased, with those remaining being staffed mostly by laity. The percentage of Catholic youth who received formal religious instruction declined. As the aging ranks of priests, sisters, and brothers are replaced by relatively few new recruits in the 1990s, there will be an even more significant decline in the number of these church personnel.

In response to these major sociocultural and ministerial shifts, however, new avenues of church life and outreach began developing. Among the more important of these have been such lay movements as the Cursillo (which entered the United States through the Texas church), Charismatic Renewal, and Marriage Encounter. The Texas Catholic Conference was established by the Texas bishops in 1964 to coordinate Texas Catholic activities and serve as a clearinghouse for information on federal and state legislation. PADRES,[qv] a Mexican-American priests' advocacy association, together with its female counterpart, Las Hermanas,[qv] worked hard in the 1970s for the advancement of Hispanics in both church and civil life. The efforts of these groups and others contributed to the appointment of such Hispanic bishops as Patricio F. Flores, the first Mexican-American Catholic bishop in the nation, and to the establishment of a national pastoral center, the Mexican American Cultural Center,[qv] in San Antonio. Church-based community organizing projects, beginning with Communities Organized for Public Service (COPS) in San Antonio, politically empowered neglected populations.

By the 1980s the ministry of deacons was being redeveloped in the Catholic Church and, even more importantly, serious training of lay ministers began. There were 450 deacons in Texas in 1980, and 1,030 deacons by 1994. Full-time and part-time lay ministers with various levels of training were much more numerous. Hispanics figure prominently in the growing Catholic population of Texas today, and Asians have brought a significant new presence.

New dioceses have been established to serve the continually increasing number of Catholics in the state. The Diocese of Victoria[qv] was founded in 1982, the Diocese of Lubbock[qv] in 1983, and the Diocese of Tyler[qv] in 1987. Another new diocese is being planned for the Laredo area. Today four million Texas Catholics continue to face the challenges of ethnic, racial, and religious pluralism, economic and social inequality, and renewed ministerial structures, in the hope of a better society for all peoples in Texas and beyond. *See also* SPANISH MISSIONS, CATHOLIC DIOCESAN CHURCH OF SPANISH AND MEXICAN TEXAS, BOUNDARIES.

BIBLIOGRAPHY: T. Lindsay Baker, "Holy Rosary School and Church, 1887–1914: A Pioneer Catholic Effort among African American Texans," *Journal of Texas Catholic History and Culture* 6 (1996). Carlos E. Castañeda, *Our Catholic Heritage in Texas* (7 vols., Austin: Von Boeckmann–Jones, 1936–58; rpt., New York: Arno, 1976). Jay P. Dolan and Gilberto M. Hinojosa, eds., *Mexican Americans and the Catholic Church, 1900–1965* (Notre Dame: University of Notre Dame Press, 1994). Gilberto M. Hinojosa, "The Enduring Hispanic Faith Communities: Spanish and Texas Church Historiography," *Journal of Texas Catholic History and Culture* 1 (1990). James Talmadge Moore, *Through Fire and Flood: The Catholic Church in Frontier Texas, 1836–1900* (College Station: Texas A&M University Press, 1992). Charles E. Nolan, "Modest and Humble Crosses: A History of Catholic Parishes in the South Central Region (1850–1984)," in *The American Catholic Parish: A History from 1850 to the Present,* Vol. 1, ed. Jay P. Dolan (New York: Paulist, 1987). *The Official Catholic Directory.*

Robert E. Wright, O.M.I.

CATHOLIC CONGREGATIONS OF MEN. From the initial foundations of Christianity within the present borders of Texas in 1682 until the present time, Catholic societies referred to as "religious congregations" or, in certain cases, "religious orders," have been present to provide important services to Catholics and others. The members of a religious congregation vow life-long commitment to God and to each other for the sake of their shared calling or "charism," through a lifestyle patterned after the evangelical counsels of celibacy, simplicity of lifestyle, and spiritual obedience. Each congregation has a certain degree of autonomy within the Catholic Church,[qv] places its resources in common, and determines the places and ways its members will minister. Due to the way they are constituted as corporate bodies sharing a specific calling, religious congregations can promptly respond to pastoral situations that demand a considerable commitment of personnel and organizational resources. These same characteristics can help provide continuity in a certain ministry. On the other hand, the relative autonomy of religious congregations in relation to diocesan authorities can also allow those congregations to withdraw from a location or ministry, leaving diocesan authorities to look for replacements. Whereas discontinuity was more prevalent among the religious congregations of men in Texas in the nineteenth century, continuity has been more the norm in the twentieth century.

Franciscan (O.F.M.) men from Spain and Mexico were the first and only religious congregation of either men or women to labor within what is now Texas during the entire century and a half of Spanish and then independent Mexican direction from the 1680s up through the 1830s. After establishing missions for Indians (*see* SPANISH MISSIONS) as well as providing pastoral care for the Hispanics, the friars were gradually aided or even replaced by secular priests, who were directly under episcopal authority. By the time of the Texas Revolution[qv] in 1835–36 the only Franciscans[qv] left in Texas were in the Rio Grande settlements of far west Texas (*see* CATHOLIC DIOCESAN CHURCH OF SPANISH AND MEXICAN TEXAS). The Catholic hierarchy responsible for the church's direction in post revolutionary Texas sought out, among others, religious congregations whose communal resources, ethnic backgrounds, or special ministerial emphases made them particularly suitable for various urgent needs among Texas Catholics. Among the most pressing needs were the pastoral care of vast geographical districts and various linguistic or ethnic (or multiethnic) populations, and the establishment of educational institutions.

The Vincentian Fathers[qv] (C.M.) accepted responsibility for the Catholic Church in Texas above the Nueces River during the crucial decade of the 1840s. Led by Jean Marie Odin,[qv] who was soon named the first bishop of Texas, they and a handful of immigrant diocesan priests did an admirable job in spite of their insufficient numbers in attending to both the Mexican and new immigrant Catholics scattered throughout the country. But Bishop Odin's Vincentian colleagues were all withdrawn by the end of 1852, leaving him the task to find helpers elsewhere. While the bishop actively recruited secular clergy for his diocese, he and his successors also importuned religious congregations of various nationalities—German, Irish, Polish, Italian, and especially French—to come to their aid. The first to do so (after the Vincentians) were the Oblates in 1849 and the Marianists in 1852. Both have remained ever since. The Oblates of Mary Immaculate[qv] (O.M.I.) rapidly expanded from their nineteenth-century base in Mexican South Texas into almost every area of the state during the twentieth century. They have worked in parishes, renewal ministry, foreign missions, ministry formation, shrines, institutional chaplaincies, and communications media. The Marianists[qv] (S.M.) have maintained a strong educational presence in San Antonio along with some parish ministry, and in this century directed schools in Victoria and Fort Worth. The 1870s brought two other groups that remained in Texas. The Holy Cross Fathers and Brothers[qv] (C.S.C.) established a strong educational and pastoral presence in Austin and the surrounding area, and entered San Antonio's Westside in 1957. One group of Jesuits[qv] (S.J.) temporarily ministered in the San Antonio area from 1874 to 1884, and a separate group worked in Galveston from 1884 to 1924. A third group that arrived in far west Texas in 1881 made the first permanent Jesuit foundation in the state. After 1930 Jesuits gradually developed new pastoral and educational establishments in the principal Texas cities.

Three religious congregations that remained in Texas only a decade or two provided crucial leadership to their immigrant minority groups during trying times. The Conventual Franciscans (O.F.M.Conv.) worked among their fellow German and Polish-speakers in the San Antonio area during the nativist 1850s. The Benedictines (O.S.B.) replaced the Conventuals among the German-speaking during the tense Civil War[qv] years. The Polish Resurrectionists (C.R.) gave strong leadership to their people during the Reconstruction[qv] period. When the railroad opened West Texas to settlement in the 1880s, Carmelite Fathers (O.Carm.) pioneered the parishes from Colorado City to the Davis Mountains and even reached out to the vast Big Bend area before they withdrew in 1901. Benedictines returned to the state in 1893 to serve rural German communities in North Texas, added Italian ministry in Bryan in 1922, and entered the Corpus Christi area in the 1950s. The twelve religious congregations of men who worked in Texas from 1847 to 1897 provided anywhere from 30 to 54 percent of the Catholic priests in Texas during those years. They provided much-needed ministry to speakers of various languages and developed the first Catholic institutions of higher learning for young men in Texas. In 1897 there were forty-six religious priests and sixty-three religious brothers in the state.

Texas entered its modern era around the turn of the century as the result of an expanding railroad network, massive irrigation projects, oil production, and a concomitant strong immigration from the midwestern United States and Mexico. Many new religious congregations of men joined the five pioneer groups still remaining to help respond to the changing needs. Eight congregations that arrived in Texas during the pre–World War I years (1899–1913) are still active in the state today. The Josephite Fathers[qv] (S.S.J.) dedicated themselves to ministry to African Americans[qv] throughout the state. The Basilian Fathers[qv] (C.S.B.), Marist Brothers (F.M.S.), and Paulist Fathers (C.S.P.) came primarily as teachers in urban settings. The Basilians later developed extensive Spanish-speaking ministry to the west of Houston. The Claretians (C.M.F.) and Redemptorists (C.Ss.R.) worked with the Spanish-speaking in the San Antonio vicinity. The Claretians later entered North Texas and El Paso. The Redemptorists also preached missions (revivals) and later engaged in multiethnic ministry in Houston and other cities. The Vincentians returned to Texas after a fifty-year absence to engage in educational and parish ministry in the northeast part of the state. They gradually took on parish work in other sections, and for a few decades directed the major diocesan seminaries in San Antonio and Houston. The Dominicans (O.P.) engaged in parish work and college chaplaincies in Houston, South Texas, and later in other areas of the state.

From 1914 to 1930 the Catholic Church in Texas experienced not only the nationwide effects of World War I,[qv] but also the impact of the ongoing civil strife and serious church-state conflict in neighboring Mexico. Thousands of Mexican refugees and immigrants crossed the border. Among them were Spanish and Mexican exiles belonging to male religious congregations who temporarily or permanently began working among Hispanics in Texas. Most were from religious congregations already represented in the state, such as the Franciscans, who had just returned in 1924 and who were soon working in various areas of Texas. On the other hand, the exiled Discalced Carmelites (O.C.D.) who moved to Dallas and San Antonio were the first of their congregation to establish themselves in the state. Other congregations whose first members arrived in Texas at this time to help in Spanish-speaking ministry were the Spanish Third Order Franciscans (T.O.R.) in central and north central Texas, the Spanish Augustinians (O.S.A.) originally in the San Angelo and Beaumont areas and eventually also in North and South Texas, and the Holy Family Missionaries (M.S.F.) in South Texas. At least four more congregations arrived during these same years in response to varying needs. The Passionists (C.P.) served parishes in South Texas from 1914 to 1928 before withdrawing; two decades later they returned to work in renewal ministry in Houston and San Antonio. The Atonement Friars (S.A.) accepted parishes in the Panhandle,[qv] and later moved to the South Plains. The La Salette Fathers (M.S.) ministered in East Texas and later in Houston. The Brothers of the Christian Schools[qv] (F.S.C.), who had attempted foundations in Texas in the 1860s, returned to direct schools at opposite corners of the state from each other, at El Paso, Galveston, and Amarillo.

In 1930 there were around 270 religious priests in Texas, forming 43 percent of the total number of Catholic clergy in the state. In the next four decades, mostly after World War II,[qv] at least twenty-two more religious congregations of men entered the Texas field. In 1970 there were 886 religious priests, forming 48 percent of the total number of Catholic priests, and 258 religious brothers. The number of religious brothers in the state reached an all-time high of around 440 in the mid-1960s, only to experience a sharp drop soon thereafter. The number of religious priests reached a plateau of around 900 to 1,000 during the same period. Almost all of the new congregations came to help pastor the growing number of local Catholic churches or parishes, which doubled during these years. Specializing in Spanish-speaking ministry were the Spanish Capuchins (O.F.M.Cap.) in Dallas–Fort Worth, South Texas, and Houston; the Trinitarians (O.SS.T.) in the Victoria area; the Mexican Servites (O.S.M.) and Augustinian Recollect Fathers (O.A.R.) in El Paso; and the Missionhurst (C.I.C.M.) and Sacred Heart Fathers (SS.CC.) in South Texas. The Sacred Heart Priests (S.C.J.) and Holy Ghost Fathers (C.S.Sp.) served in Southeast and South Texas. The Sacred Heart Missionaries (M.S.C.) scattered their members thinly across the state. The Pallottines (S.A.C.) covered much of Northwest Texas, while the Glenmary Home Missioners (Glmy.) served in the Northeast. The Divine Word Fathers (S.V.D.) came to Central Texas and Houston. The Carmelites returned to Texas to work in both educational and parish ministry in the Houston area. Refugee Hungarian members of another monastic order, the Cistercian Fathers[qv] (O.Cist.), helped refound the University of Dallas.

Between 1970 and 1993 at least eighteen more religious congregations of men entered Texas, several of recent foundation. However, none of them had more than a few members in the entire state, and thus they had a very limited impact, even if they were quite helpful in the localities where they served. Most engaged in parish ministry. Those having at least a half dozen members in Texas were the Precious Blood Fathers (C.PP.S.) in the Abilene–San Angelo area; the Blessed Sacrament Fathers (S.S.S.) in San Antonio and Houston; the Conventual Franciscans (who returned to Texas after more than a century's absence) in San Antonio, Austin, and El Paso; the Nigerian Missionaries of St. Paul (M.S.P.) in Southeast Texas; the Vietnamese Congregation of the Mother Coredemptrix (C.M.C.) in Southeast Texas, the Panhandle, and around Fort Worth; the Marianist Fathers (S.M.) scattered in South, Central, and West Texas; the Society of Our Lady of the Most Holy Trinity (S.O.L.T.) in Robstown (dedicated to international missionary work among the poor); and the Blessed Sacrament Missionaries (M.S.S.) in Corpus Christi, who concentrated upon preaching devotional missions.

Almost all of the religious congregations of men who came to Texas at one time or another in its history, even those who left for a certain period, were active in the state in 1993. In that year members of sixty-nine different religious congregations of men—946 priests and 256 brothers—worked in parishes (in general or special ethnic ministry), schools, ministerial formation, renewal ministry, hospital and prison chaplaincies, and other specialized ministries. They still contributed 45 percent of the total number of Catholic priests working in Texas. The members of those congregations, however, which have traditionally provided the great majority of the religious priests and brothers in Texas are all aging, while their congregations have insufficient new recruits to prevent a rapid decline in numbers for at least a decade or two. Consequently many are refocusing and reducing their commitments in the state. But they will continue to respond to the needs of Catholics and others as their numbers permit in keeping with their special calling.

BIBLIOGRAPHY: Carlos E. Castañeda, *Our Catholic Heritage in Texas* (7 vols., Austin: Von Boeckmann–Jones, 1936–58; rpt., New York: Arno, 1976). Robert E. Wright, O.M.I., "Pioneer Religious Congregations of Men in Texas before 1900," *Journal of Texas Catholic History and Culture* 5 (1994). *Robert E. Wright, O.M.I.*

CATHOLIC CONGREGATIONS OF WOMEN. The first religious order to enter Texas was the Ursuline Sisters,[qv] who came from New Orleans to establish the Ursuline Academy in Galveston in January 1847. Other orders followed, coming from all classes of society and trained in particular areas of teaching and nursing, to teach the Gospel as Franciscans[qv] had done in Spanish Texas.[qv] After long and arduous travels, they often found empty buildings awaiting them and had to gather furniture, equipment, and supplies for convent, school, or hospital. Like other pioneer women and men they had to endure yellow fever epidemics, hurricanes,[qv] Indian raids, and other hardships of the frontier. Schools operated by orders of nuns added quality and variety to Texas culture. The Ursuline Academy in Galveston, for example, offered courses in reading, grammar, composition, rhetoric, poetry, English literature, French literature, sacred and profane history, chronology, mythology, ancient and modern geography, the principles of natural philosophy, arithmetic, chemistry, astronomy, music, drawing, and plain and ornamental needlework. Other schools run by nuns offered geometry, algebra, ethics, logic, and, somewhat later, various commercial subjects. They attempted to combine practical and cultural fields.

In addition to the Ursulines, orders that came before 1900 and established headquarters in the state were the Sisters of the Incarnate Word and Blessed Sacrament (1853), Sisters of Divine Providence (1866), Sisters of Charity of the Incarnate Word (1866), Sisters of St. Mary of Namur (1860s), Holy Cross Sisters (1874), Sisters of Mercy (1875), Dominican Sisters (1882), and Sisters of the Holy Ghost and Mary Immaculate (1893).[qqv]

BIBLIOGRAPHY: Catholic Archives of Texas, Files, Austin. James Talmadge Moore, *Through Fire and Flood: The Catholic Church in Frontier Texas, 1836–1900* (College Station: Texas A&M University Press, 1992). *Sister M. Claude Lane, O.P.*

CATHOLIC DIOCESAN CHURCH OF SPANISH AND MEXICAN TEXAS. In addition to the Franciscan missions in Texas under New Spain and Mexico (*see* FRANCISCANS and SPANISH MISSIONS), significant development within the same area was conducted by the Hispanic Catholic diocesan church. By "diocesan church" is meant the Catholic communities of a certain territory under the supervision of a bishop. The ordained ministers who are directly bound to a diocese are called diocesan or secular clergy, in distinction to those who belong to religious congregations and are called religious clergy, or, in previous times, regular clergy, from the fact that they live under a *regula,* or rule. The latter's work usually extends across many dioceses and even nations, and their members are subject, in the first place, to their own congregational leadership.

The history of the church in Texas before 1850 is complicated by the fact that the various sections of its vast current territory belonged to different civil divisions of New Spain and Mexico. Church organization more or less mirrored these divisions, with a great variety of Franciscan provinces and missionary colleges responsible for the different areas of today's Texas. In turn, these areas all eventually came under the supervision of two major diocesan organizations; one of these dioceses later transferred its northern territory to a new frontier diocese. Far West Texas, the stretch of the Rio Grande from the Big Bend up through the El Paso valley, was claimed by the northwestern diocese of Durango soon after the first foundations in the area in the later 1600s. But that claim was generally successfully contested up into the early 1800s by the Franciscans of the Holy Gospel Province. In contrast, the jurisdiction of the huge Guadalajara diocese was recognized almost immediately by all the Franciscan-staffed settlements permanently established in the early 1700s between San Juan Bautista[qv] on the Rio Grande (near the site of present-day Eagle Pass) and the Louisiana border. The lower Rio Grande towns were part of major new colonization along the Gulf of Mexico around 1750. The new colony raised the question of establishing a separate diocese for the whole northeastern frontier, including the province of Texas and San Juan Bautista. Apparently none of the lower Rio Grande settlements except Laredo, the only town at that time staffed by a diocesan priest rather than a Franciscan, recognized any diocesan jurisdiction until just before the new diocese of Linares or Nuevo León was finally instituted in 1779. This new diocese was headquartered in Monterrey by the early 1780s.

From the first years of Hispanic foundations, the diocesan church began to develop not only through the missionary work specifically designed to incorporate the indigenous nations into the church, but also through the implantation and growth of local Hispanic Catholic communities. Where the Franciscans were the only clergy in a certain area, they served both the indigenous nations and the Hispanic military and civilians. But in Texas, decades before any other region of the Southwest (even the much older New Mexico province), the Franciscans were also joined by diocesan pastors in a slow but progressive fashion, to a much greater extent than has heretofore been recognized. Between 1731 and 1776 San Antonio, Laredo, San Juan Bautista, and La Bahía received secular pastors or chaplains.

The people of San Juan Bautista[qv] and the other settlements on what is now the Mexican side of the Rio Grande, from Matamoros all the way up to the original El Paso (now Ciudad Juárez, Chihuahua), spread to the Texas side decades before it became a part of Texas. The original settlements, including those downriver from El Paso that ended up on the Texas side due to changes in the river's course, all eventually received diocesan priests while still under the jurisdiction of the church of New Spain or Mexico. In the first decade of the 1800s the American acquisition of Louisiana led to a military and civilian buildup by New Spain in East Texas, with a concomitant increase in clergy for the new settlements and military chaplaincies. By 1808 there were at least seven Franciscan and five diocesan priests in Texas above the Nueces, and more than six Franciscan and seven diocesan clergy along the Rio Grande.

It is to these local parishes and their substantially Hispanic populations, whether staffed by diocesan clergy or Franciscans, that the strong Hispanic Catholic heritage in Texas must be credited. The people's faith was expressed in mandated public worship and sacramental participation, solemn public processions, special confraternities, home devotions, religious art, songs, gestures, and prayers. The growing maturity of several of these local Hispanic church communities by the last decades of the 1700s was further indicated by the fact that they began to produce native Hispanic clergy, who were serving on the northern frontier of New Spain by 1800. San Antonio, Reynosa, and Revilla (the latter two towns situated on the lower Rio Grande) each saw several native sons ordained before 1810. In fact, for all but four years between 1804 and 1840 San Antonio had one or another native son as pastor.

This flourishing diocesan church was dealt a heavy blow by a period of internal strife and border wars that began with the 1810 insurgencies (*see* MEXICAN WAR OF INDEPENDENCE) and was especially destructive along the lower Rio Grande and in Texas above the Nueces. Above that river, church buildings were damaged, local economies were devastated, and even entire towns were temporarily abandoned. Everywhere, certain clergy and their parishioners paid dearly for their sympathy with the insurgent cause or their loyalty to the Mexican nation between 1836 and 1846. During these troubled times, a greater incidence of moral weakening began to manifest itself among some of the diocesan clergy, but there were at least as many others who gave good personal witness and even performed heroically. The only brief respite enjoyed by most of the settlements was in the 1820s. El Paso, on the other hand, which had become the most populous and prosperous settlement in New Mexico and benefited further by the opening of trade with St. Louis under independent Mexico, avoided these conflicts until 1846.

The northern frontier dioceses, aided by the Franciscans, managed to maintain almost continuous ministry in all the principally Catholic settlements throughout the wide expanse of what is now Texas. But the Texas Revolution[qv] in 1835–36 shattered the fragile organization that the Mexico diocesan church had struggled to maintain in Texas above the Nueces. All of the mainly Catholic towns west of the Colorado River except San Antonio were evacuated. Their churches were damaged in the battles and then pillaged and vandalized. The clergy was decimated: one died a natural death, another violently, a third was led off as a prisoner of war, and two others were forced into exile.

Above the Nueces in Texas, that left only the pastor of San Antonio, which was the only mainly Catholic settlement still functioning in the new Republic of Texas[qv] during its initial years. Eventually the captive pastor of the desolate Goliad found his way to the San Antonio vicinity but apparently refrained from active pastoral work. In 1840 representatives of the United States–related Catholic Church established jurisdiction for the Republic of Texas (*see* CATHOLIC CHURCH); the two old priests were accused of scandalous conduct by their political enemies in the pro-Anglo party and were summarily dismissed.

However, the settlements along what became the Texas side of the Rio Grande after its conquest by United States troops in 1846 continued to receive almost continuous pastoral care from the Mexican church, both before and after the United States occupation, until the United States church gradually took over the border areas. This takeover occurred anywhere from a few years to several decades after the conquest. It occurred as late as 1892 in the Presidio area of far west Texas.

BIBLIOGRAPHY: Eleanor B. Adams, ed., *Bishop Tamarón's Visitation of New Mexico, 1760* (Albuquerque: Historical Society of New Mexico, 1954). Hubert Howe Bancroft, *History of the North Mexican States and Texas* (2 vols., San Francisco: History Company, 1886, 1889). Herbert Eugene Bolton, *Texas in the Middle Eighteenth Century: Studies in Spanish Colonial History and Administration* (Berkeley: University of California Press, 1915; rpt., Austin: University of Texas Press, 1970). Carlos E. Castañeda, *Our Catholic Heritage in Texas* (7 vols., Austin: Von Boeckmann–Jones, 1936–1958; rpt., New York: Arno, 1976). "Diocese," *Catholic Encyclopedia*, Vol. 5 (New York: Appleton, 1967). Mary Angela Fitzmorris, Four Decades of Catholicism in Texas, 1820–1860 (Ph.D. dissertation, Catholic University of America, 1926). Peter Gerhard, *North Frontier of New Spain* (Princeton University Press, 1982). Myra Ellen Jenkins, "History and Administration of the Tigua Indians of Ysleta del Sur during the Spanish Colonial Period," in *Apache Indians*, Vol. 3, by Rex E. Gerald et al. (New York: Garland, 1974). P. Otto Maas, ed., *Viajes de Misioneros Franciscanos a la conquista del Nuevo México* (Seville: Imprenta de San Antonio, 1915). Aureliano Tapia Méndez, "La creación del primitivo Obispado de Linares," *Humanitas* 20 (1979). William Stuart Red, *The Texas Colonists and Religion, 1821–1836* (Austin: Shettles, 1924). David J. Weber, *The Mexican Frontier, 1821–1846* (Albuquerque: University of New Mexico Press, 1982).

Robert E. Wright, O.M.I.

CATHOLIC EDUCATION. The Catholic Church,[qv] always concerned with the education and training of youth, brought its educational system to Texas in 1682 when Franciscans[qv] established the first Texas mission at Corpus Christi de la Isleta (Ysleta) near El Paso. In mission schools the Indians were taught not only religion by a special Indian catechism, but reading and writing in the Spanish language; they were given instruction in vocational training, agriculture, and caring for the sick, along with cultural training in crafts, painting, sculpture, and music. More than 100 years later, with the secularization of the missions beginning in 1794 and finally ending in 1830, this work was abandoned. When Jean Marie Odin[qv] arrived in Texas in 1840, he was distressed at what appeared to be a spiritual neglect of the people, and he recommended to his superior a need for Catholic schools in Galveston and San Antonio. He organized a school in Galveston in 1842 with twenty-two pupils, one-third of whom were non-Catholics. After purchasing the Love estate in Galveston in 1845, he invited the Ursuline Sisters[qv] from New Orleans to open a school for young ladies. Ursuline Academy,[qv] in Galveston, opened on February 8, 1847. Two other schools operating in 1847 were St. Mary's School at Brown's Settlement in Lavaca County and a school for boys at Brazoria. A fourth school was listed in Houston in 1848, taught by the pastor of St. Vincent's Church there, and in 1849 schools in Castroville and Cummings Creek were reported.

With help from the Ursuline convent in New Orleans the Galveston Ursuline Sisters opened a girls' school in San Antonio in 1851. The Marianists[qv] arrived in San Antonio from France in 1851 and opened St. Mary's School for boys in 1852 (*see* ST. MARY'S UNIVERSITY). Bishop Odin established the Sisters of the Incarnate Word and Blessed Sacrament[qv] from Lyons, France, in Brownsville, where they opened Villa Maria Academy for girls in 1853, after arriving in Galveston in June 1852. By 1856 schools for boys were reported in Brownsville and Laredo.

For training a native clergy, Bishop Odin persuaded a young missionary society in France, the Oblates of Mary Immaculate,[qv] to come to Texas in 1852. They opened Immaculate Conception College and Seminary in Galveston in November 1854, which was chartered in 1856 as St. Mary's University of Galveston and continued as such until 1924. In 1926 the original charter was amended to read "at La Porte."

In 1866 Bishop Claude-Marie Dubuis[qv] brought two groups from France. Two Sisters of Divine Providence[qv] arrived in Austin in October 1866 and opened the first Catholic school there in December; in 1868 they opened schools in Corpus Christi and Castroville. In 1895 they established Our Lady of the Lake Academy in San Antonio, a school that was expanded into a four-year college in 1913. The second group, three *Soeurs Hôpitalières,* who at Bishop Dubuis's request were trained for work in Texas by the Sisters of the Incarnate Word and Blessed Sacrament in Lyons, opened St. Mary's Infirmary, Galveston, in 1866, and Santa Rosa Infirmary, San Antonio, in 1869 (*see* CATHOLIC HEALTH CARE). These nuns, later known as Sisters of Charity of the Incarnate Word,[qv] opened a parochial school in connection with St. Joseph's Orphanage in 1875 and in 1893 established Incarnate Word Academy, to which a college program was added in 1909.

After the Civil War the Incarnate Word sisters of Brownsville started academies at Victoria (1866), Corpus Christi (1871), and Houston (1873). The Ursulines formed separate communities and academies at Laredo (1868), Dallas (1874), Puebla, Mexico (1892), and at Bryan after the Galveston hurricane of 1900.qv The Sisters of St. Mary of Namurqv moved to Waco in 1873 and established Sacred Heart Academy. In 1885 they established Saint Ignatius Academy in Fort Worth, which became their headquarters and Our Lady of Victory College (now merged with the University of Dallas). The Sisters of Mercyqv of New Orleans arrived in Indianola in January 1875 and opened a school in September, but within a month that building, along with most of the town, was destroyed by a hurricane; they moved to Refugio, where they opened their first permanent school. A second group of Mercy sisters, from San Francisco, established a school in the German community of Mariensfeld (Mariensfield, later changed to Stanton), which operated from 1894 until 1938, when it was moved to Slaton. In 1874 Holy Crossqv priests, brothers, and sisters from Indiana arrived in Austin. The priests assumed charge of St. Mary's parish, and the brothers prepared buildings for a Catholic boys' school, which was formally opened in 1881 as St. Edward's School for Boys and chartered as St. Edward's College in 1885. The sisters established St. Mary's Academyqv in Austin in 1874 and in 1880 opened a parish school in Marshall, also called St. Mary's Academy. Five Sisters of Lorettoqv from New Mexico opened St. Joseph's School in San Elizario in 1879 and moved it to El Paso in 1892, where they also sponsored the new Sacred Heart School. Dominican Sistersqv of Somerset, Ohio, moved their new foundation to Galveston in 1882 and opened a select day and boarding school for girls, Sacred Heart Academy (later Dominican High School). Holy Rosary School for Negroes, begun by the Dominican sisters in Galveston in 1887, grew so rapidly that a new and larger building was constructed the following year. The order also staffed the following schools: St. Mary's Cathedral, Galvestonqv (1893); St. Mary's, Taylor (1896); and Sacred Heart, Houston (1897). With the opening of schools in Galveston and Houston in 1887, interest in education for African Americansqv began to increase. In 1893 Margaret Mary Healy-Murphyqv founded a congregation in San Antonio, the Sister-Servants of the Holy Ghost and Mary Immaculate (later the Sisters of the Holy Spirit and Mary Immaculateqv). Beginning at St. Peter Claver's parish school, they expanded to Dallas, Fort Worth, Houston, and Beaumont. Sisters of the Holy Family, a community of black nuns founded in 1842 in New Orleans, took charge of Holy Rosary School in Galveston in 1897, reorganizing it into a grammar and industrial training school. Their work was extended to Houston, San Antonio, Ames, and Marshall. A third group dedicated to work among blacks, the Sisters of the Blessed Sacrament for Indians and Colored People, founded in 1891 in Philadelphia, established a school in Beaumont in 1916 and later founded schools in Port Arthur, Houston, and Orange. Parochial schools assumed a major role in Catholic education with immigration in the nineteenth century. Schools for German, Polish, Czech, Mexican, and Anglo children often were established along with new churches. After 1900 parochial schools increased steadily in number and quality, although many of the earlier ones closed or were consolidated with public schools.

Higher education also was a Catholic concern. Although St. Mary's University in Galveston (1854–1924) and the University of Dallas (1907–27) closed, St. Mary's University in San Antonio and St. Edward's University in Austin continued to operate with increased enrollment, as did two Catholic women's colleges in San Antonio, Our Lady of the Lake University (coed 1969) and Incarnate Word College (coed 1971). Subsequently established colleges were Dominican College in Houston (1945; closed 1975); the University of St. Thomas in Houston (1946), established by the Basilian Fathers,qv who entered Texas in 1899; and the University of Dallas, reestablished in 1956. A trend toward junior colleges developed in the early 1960s with the opening of Our Lady of Perpetual Help College in Houston and Christopher College of Corpus Christi (closed in 1968) by the Sisters of the Incarnate Word and Blessed Sacrament. In a move toward coeducational universities, Maryhill College for Women was founded at St. Edwards University (Austin) in 1966, administered by the Sisters of the Immaculate Heart of Mary. By 1971 Maryhill College had become a part of St. Edwards University, the sisters remaining as part of the faculty and staff.

Despite the demise of numerous Catholic schools over the years, and partly as a result of controversy over the quality of public schools as well as increasing crime and drug use in them, Catholic education was thriving in the early 1990s. In 1992 statistics on Catholic education in Texas showed 579 sisters, 68 brothers, 148 priests, 2 scholastics (post-novitiate teaching assistants), and 4,673 lay teachers, a total of 5,470 teachers in 16 seminaries, 7 colleges and universities, 23 diocesan and 24 private high schools, 207 parochial and 21 private elementary schools, and 7 protective institutions. Enrollment comprised 301 seminarians, 17,688 collegians, 15,141 high school students, 58,838 elementary pupils, 461 students in protective schools, and 69,725 high school students and 238,967 elementary students in Confraternity of Christian Doctrine classes (parish-run religion classes); this brought the total number receiving Catholic instruction to 400,660.

BIBLIOGRAPHY: Max Berger, "Education in Texas during the Spanish and Mexican Periods," *Southwestern Historical Quarterly* 51 (July 1947). Carlos E. Castañeda, *Our Catholic Heritage in Texas* (7 vols., Austin: Von Boeckmann–Jones, 1936–58; rpt., New York: Arno, 1976). *The Official Catholic Directory.* *Sister M. Claude Lane, O.P.*

CATHOLIC HEALTH CARE. The Texas Conference of Catholic Health Facilities is a state-wide organization of Catholic hospitals, systems, and long-term-care facilities, and their sponsoring religious congregations. It exercises the ministry of healing within the Catholic Churchqv and the broader society through programs of education, facilitation, and advocacy. The extant health-care facilities named in this article belong to the TCCHF.

In 1971, in order to adapt to changes in health-care delivery and to improve coordination of its sponsored health-care facilities, the Sisters of Charity of the Incarnate Wordqv in Houston established the Sisters of Charity of the Incarnate Word Health Care System of Houston. The SCH System, one of the largest Catholic health care systems in the United States, operates eleven acute-care and four long-term-care centers. Six of these centers are in Texas. In 1867 St. Mary's Hospital,qv Galveston, the first Catholic hospital in Texas, was established by Bishop Claude M. Dubuisqv and by the recently founded Sisters of Charity of the Incarnate Word, who were trained in France and came to Texas specifically to start a hospital. The original thirty-bed hospital developed by 1994 into an acute-care facility with 322 licensed beds. The sisters so impressed the citizens of Galveston with their dedication and service during a yellow fever epidemic that the city council recommended turning over the city hospital to them in 1868. In 1887 St. Joseph Hospital, Houston, was opened by sisters from St. Mary's in Galveston. For over a century St. Joseph's has provided health care and health education to the citizens of Houston. In 1994 St. Joseph Hospital, licensed for 840 beds, was a full-service, acute-care facility. In 1962 St. Elizabeth Hospital, Beaumont, became the third hospital operated in Beaumont by the Sisters of Charity of the Incarnate Word, having been preceded by the Hotel Dieu (founded in 1897) and St. Therese Hospital (1934). By 1994 St. Elizabeth's had grown from the initial 200 licensed beds to 497, and was widely recognized for medical and surgical services. It is a major referral center for a large area of Southeast Texas and neighboring Louisiana. St. Mary Hospital, Port Arthur, began as a 150-bed acute-care facility in 1928. In 1994 it had 278 licensed beds and offered a full spectrum of medical and surgical services. The Bishop Byrne Wellness Center, Port Arthur, opened in 1985 and is a central facility for outpatient services. St. John Hospital, Nassau Bay, formerly a United States public health facility, became a member of the SCH System in 1981. It is an acute-care facility, licensed for 141 beds. The SCH System acquired the Regis and St. Elizabeth centers, Waco, from the Catholic Diocese of Austin[qv] in 1985. The Regis offers living units for 196 independent retired persons. St. Elizabeth provides 179 beds for long-term care.

In 1981 the Sisters of Charity of the Incarnate Word, San Antonio, established Incarnate Word Health Services as a multi-hospital system charged with providing leadership and services to its members. The Texas members of IWHS are Santa Rosa Health Care, San Antonio; Spohn Health System, Corpus Christi; St. Anthony's Hospital, Amarillo; and St. Joseph's Hospital and Health Service, Paris. Santa Rosa Health Care, a 1,098-bed complex, includes Santa Rosa Hospital, which developed from the original 1869 facility. In 1924, Santa Rosa Hospital won a four-year battle against the city of San Antonio when the Texas Supreme Court ruled that this and all Catholic-run hospitals were tax-exempt, nonprofit organizations. Santa Rosa offers a full range of services. Its component units include Santa Rosa Long Term Hospital, which houses patients requiring extended hospitalization; Santa Rosa Children's Hospital; Santa Rosa Northwest Hospital and Santa Rosa Rehabilitation Hospital, both located in the South Texas Medical Center; and Villa Rosa Hospital, San Antonio's first and largest free-standing, private psychiatric hospital. Included also is Yoakum Community Hospital, a forty-six-bed facility in Yoakum. Spohn Health System, Corpus Christi, comprises Spohn Hospital[qv] (founded in 1905), licensed for 560 beds, the leading general acute-care hospital south of San Antonio; Spohn Kleberg Hospital, Kingsville, a 100-bed hospital serving Kleberg County and surrounding areas; and Spohn Hospital South, a full-service, 120-bed, acute-care facility. In 1901 St. Anthony's Hospital, Amarillo, became the first Catholic hospital in the Panhandle.[qv] With 336 licensed beds, it is the Panhandle's premier tertiary-care center and is a major referral hospital. St. Joseph's Hospital and Health Center, Paris, was originally established in 1906 by the Sisters of Mercy[qv] and known as St. Patrick's Infirmary. The hospital passed to the San Antonio Sisters of Charity of the Incarnate Word in 1911. In 1994, with 212 licensed beds, St. Joseph's offered comprehensive health service to Paris.

In addition to the health-care facilities sponsored by the Incarnate Word Sisters, the Daughters of Charity National Health System, West Central Region, administers several major health-care institutions (*see* daughters of charity of st. vincent de paul). St. Paul Medical Center, founded in 1896, the oldest, private, nonprofit hospital in Dallas, is a 600-bed, full-service, acute-care facility. St. Paul's opened its first free clinic in 1908 and another in 1920 in a Hispanic neighborhood. In 1923 another branch, the Marillac Clinic, opened its doors. It is also a teaching hospital, providing education for sixty resident physicians in four specialties. St. Joseph Hospital,[qv] Fort Worth, was founded in 1883 as a hospital for railroad workers. From 1885 until 1991 it was sponsored by the Sisters of Charity of the Incarnate Word, San Antonio. The Daughters of Charity assumed sponsorship on October 5, 1991. St. Joseph, with 475 licensed beds, is the oldest hospital in Fort Worth and the only Catholic one. Waco's first hospital, now Providence Health Center, opened in 1903, amid a barrage of anti-Catholic sentiment. Because the hospital had few private patients to cover the costs of treating the indigent, the sisters contracted with the Missouri, Kansas and Texas Railroad to treat sick railroad employees. Through the care of more than 3,000 such patients over seven years, the hospital's reputation flourished. In 1994 its four divisions included the medical-surgical area, DePaul Psychiatric Center, Providence Home Care, and St. Catherine Center (a center for the elderly that includes an Alzheimer's unit). The health center campus features a 136-bed acute-care hospital and an ambulatory-services building for outpatients. The Daughters of Charity Services of Austin includes Seton Medical Center (founded in 1902), Seton Northwest Hospital, and Seton East Community Center. Seton Medical Center, with 503 licensed beds, is the largest medical and surgical acute-care center in Austin. Seton Northwest Hospital, with eighty-two beds, provides acute-care services in northwest Austin. Seton East Community Center offers primary health care at reduced rates, social services, and health education for residents of east and south Austin.

Other Catholic orders and institutions have served health care in Texas. Holy Cross Hospital, Austin, was established in 1940 by Father F. R. Weber, pastor of Holy Cross Church, and the Missionary Sisters of the Immaculate Conception. Its mission was to offer care to African Americans[qv] who had difficulty getting quality service at other hospitals. The sisters originally had twelve beds, six bassinets, and one second-hand operating table, located in an old two-story school building. Supplies and equipment were so limited that the staff had to use pressure cookers and kitchen pots to sterilize instruments. Under the direction of Sister Celine Heitzman, M.D., who became the resident physician in 1942, the hospital improved. During the 1940s, Sister Celine instituted a racially mixed staff. Through intensive fund-raising a new facility was built in 1951 with a fifty-bed capacity. The hospital was closed in 1989. Bethania Regional Health Care Center, Wichita Falls, was opened by the Sisters of the Holy Family of Nazareth as a thirty-five-bed hospital in 1935. In 1994 it had 258 licensed beds and managed an additional sixty-five beds at three regional hospitals. Mother Francis Regional Health Care Center, Tyler, which opened in 1937 as a municipal hospital operated by the Sisters of the Holy Family of Nazareth, was purchased by the sisters in 1947. In 1994 it was a 358-bed acute-care facility that offered a full spectrum of services. Since 1937 it has been committed to caring in a special way for the family, in cooperation with the Tyler Health District. St. Joseph Hospital and Health Center, in Bryan, originated as Bryan Hospital in 1912. The Sisters of St. Francis from Sylvania, Ohio, purchased the hospital in 1935 and reopened it in 1936 under its present name. The original twenty-five-bed hospital, now a regional medical center with 196 licensed beds, is the largest hospital in Bryan–College Station. Trinity Community Medical Center of Brenham was founded on March 1, 1989, by the consolidation of St. Jude and Bohne Memorial hospitals. This seventy-three-bed acute-care hospital is also sponsored by the Sisters of St. Francis. The organization operates at the St. Jude and Bohne Memorial locations under a single board of trustees and a single administrative team. Mercy Regional Medical Center, Laredo, sponsored by the Institute of the Sisters of Mercy of the Americas (St. Louis Province) originated when three Sisters of Mercy opened a twelve-bed hospital. Within five years, a twenty-bed hospital was in operation. In 1955 ground was broken for a new hospital at the present location. Through the 1970s and 1980s, facilities and services continued to be added or expanded. In 1994 the 420-bed acute-care center celebrated "a hundred years of community health and the wellness of generations to come." St. Mary of the Plains Hospital, Lubbock, sponsored by the Sisters of St. Joseph of Orange, California, originated as the Plains Hospital and Clinic of Lubbock, built by a group of physicians. It was acquired by the Sisters of St. Joseph of Orange in 1939 and renamed St. Mary of the Plains Hospital. In 1994 this full-service acute-care hospital had a bed capacity of 434.

bibliography: Carlos E. Castañeda, *Our Catholic Heritage in Texas* (7 vols., Austin: Von Boeckmann–Jones, 1936–58; rpt., New York: Arno, 1976). Catholic Archives of Texas, Files, Austin. Sister Mary Loyola Hegarty, C.C.V.I., *Serving with Gladness: The Origin and History of the Congregation of the Sisters of Charity of the Incarnate Word, Houston, Texas* (Milwaukee: Bruce, 1967).

Sister M. Loyola Hegarty, C.C.V.I.

CATHOLIC JOURNALISM. For many years journalism has played an important role in the ministry of teaching in the Catholic Church;[qv] the decree on communications, the first of the sixteen documents issued by the Second Vatican Council in the early 1960s, has given impetus to the Catholic press. Catholic journalism had its beginning in Texas long before that, however. In the nineteenth century the dioceses of Dallas and Galveston briefly attempted to produce papers. Individual Catholic ethnic groups produced papers. Parishes sometimes produced newsletters, though usually for the purpose of raising funds.

The most important Catholic newspaper in Texas, the *Southern Messenger*,[qv] started as a parish-sponsored paper in San Antonio and was taken over by the Menger family. It went through a series of titles: *Saint Mary's Review* (January 15–May 15, 1891), *Saint Mary's Weekly Review* (June 6, 1891–January 30, 1892), and *Southern Messenger* (March 8, 1894–August 8, 1957). The *Southern Messenger* was consolidated with the *Alamo Register* (June 5, 1942–August 9, 1957) to form the *Alamo Messenger*, published August 18, 1957, to July 21, 1972.

Each of the fourteen dioceses of Texas has its own journalistic history. The Diocese of Amarillo[qv] was the first to publish its own newspaper, which has changed names several times. It has been known as the *Texas Panhandle Register* (1936–47), the *Amarillo Register* (1948–56), the *West Texas Register* (1956–84), and the *West Texas Catholic* (1985–).

The Diocese of Austin[qv] published its paper under the names *Lone Star Catholic* (1957–61), *Lone Star Register* (1961–68), and *Texas Catholic Herald—Austin Edition* (1968–80) before suspending publication. It was revived as the *Catholic Journal* (1982–83) and subsequently renamed the *Catholic Spirit* (January 1983–).

The Diocese of Beaumont[qv] has published a paper since its beginning, first under the name *Texas Catholic Herald* (1966–82) and then under the title *East Texas Catholic* (1982–).

The Diocese of Brownsville[qv] briefly published a paper titled *Valley Catholic Witness* (1967–72).

In the Diocese of Corpus Christi[qv] a privately owned and published Catholic paper titled *Corpus Christi Post* was published from 1954 to 1966. The official diocesan newspaper started with the *Texas Gulf Coast Register* (1966–70), which became the *Texas Gulf Coast Catholic* (1970–79) and afterward the *South Texas Catholic* (1980–). The staff of the diocesan paper published a thirty-two-page supplement on the life of Bishop Thomas Drury that was placed in each copy of the *South Texas Catholic* and the secular daily Corpus Christi *Caller-Times*.[qv]

The Diocese of Dallas[qv] sponsored a paper in the nineteenth century titled the *Texas Catholic* (1891–92). In Jefferson the local pastor privately published a paper, the *Jeffersonian* (1948–53), for the Catholics of the east end of the diocese. The diocese began a paper on September 24, 1952, under the title *Texas Catholic*. Father James Tucek, an editor of the *Texas Catholic*, was promoted to the Vatican Office of Communications and was in charge of the English-speaking world during the Second Vatican Council. He also wrote four books.

The Diocese of El Paso[qv] has had three different papers. The original one, *Revista Católica*, was owned by the Society of Jesus (Jesuits[qv]). The diocese's own first paper, the *South West Catholic Register*, was published from 1922 to February 24, 1967. A new one was begun on May 1, 1991, and titled the *Rio Grande Catholic*.

The Diocese of Fort Worth[qv] has published a paper since its beginning in 1969. It has had two titles, *Texas Catholic, Fort Worth Edition* (1969–84), and *North Texas Catholic* (1985–). An independent Catholic paper was published in 1924 called the *Fort Worth Catholic Review*.

The Diocese of Galveston (*see* GALVESTON-HOUSTON, CATHOLIC DIOCESE OF) had a paper briefly in the nineteenth century, the *Texas Catholic Herald*. It began publishing again on May 14, 1964, under the same name. For a while it published an edition for the dioceses of Beaumont (1966–82) and Austin (1968–80).

The Diocese of Lubbock[qv] began publication of the *South Plains Catholic* on July 14, 1985.

The Diocese of San Angelo[qv] published the *Texas Concho Register* (1964–80) and changed the name to the *West Texas Angeles* in 1980.

The Archdiocese of San Antonio[qv] began publication of its own paper with the *Alamo Register* (June 5, 1942–August 9, 1957). The paper was renamed *Alamo Messenger* on August 15, 1957, when it merged with the *Southern Messenger*, and continued publication under this title until July 21, 1972, when it changed its name to *Today's Catholic*. Also published in San Antonio were three Spanish-language papers: *Ecos de la Catedral* (February to June 1918), *La Fe Católica* (March 27, 1897–August 4, 1900) and *La Voz* (October 11, 1937–January 14, 1951), and one German paper, *Katholische Rundschau* (December 2, 1897–August 14, 1918).

The Diocese of Tyler[qv] has published *Catholic East Texas* since 1987.

The Diocese of Victoria[qv] has published the *Catholic Lighthouse* since May 29, 1986.

BIBLIOGRAPHY: Elizabeth Anne Delaney, Diocesan Newspaper Reading and Church Activity: How Reading *The Catholic Spirit* is Related to Church Participation in the Diocese of Austin (M.A. thesis, University of Texas at Austin, 1989). James Hasdorff, The *Southern Messenger* and the Mexican Church-State Controversy, 1917–1941 (M.A. thesis, St. Mary's University, 1968). Sister M. Alpheus Murphy, The Efforts of Louis William Menger to Combat the A.P.A. through the *Southern Messenger*, 1892–1898 (Ph.D. dissertation, Catholic University of America, 1964). Eugene P. Willging and Herta Hatzfeld, *Catholic Serials of the Nineteenth Century in the United States*, Second Series, Part 13 (Washington: Catholic University of America Press, 1966).

James F. Vanderholt

CATLETT CREEK. Catlett (Callett, Catlertt) Creek rises five miles north of Decatur in north central Wise County (at 33°19′ N, 97°36′ W) and runs southeast for twelve miles to its mouth on Sweetwater Creek, five miles north of Bluett (at 33°14′ N, 97°26′ W). The stream is dammed in its upper reaches. It traverses flat terrain surfaced by clay and sandy loams that support water-tolerant hardwood trees, conifers, brushes, and grasses.

CATLIN, GEORGE (1796–1872). George Catlin, painter and chronicler of American Indians, son of Putnam and Polly (Sutton) Catlin, was born in Wilkes-Barre, Pennsylvania, on July 26, 1796. He grew up on farms in the Susquehanna valley of New York and Pennsylvania, where he hunted, fished, and absorbed local stories about Indians, including an account of the Wyoming (Pennsylvania) massacre of 1778, during which Indians briefly detained his mother and grandmother. At his father's behest, Catlin entered the prestigious law school of Tapping Reeve and James Gould at Litchfield, Connecticut, in 1817 and passed the bars for Connecticut and Pennsylvania the following year. In 1821 he abandoned his legal practice and moved to Philadelphia to pursue a career as an artist. He exhibited as a miniaturist from 1821 to 1823 at the Pennsylvania Academy of Fine Arts, which elected him a member the next year. His miniature of Sam Houston[qv] from this period is unparalleled. Catlin turned to portraiture, exhibited for two more years in Philadelphia before moving to New York City, and produced a fine portrait of Stephen F. Austin.[qv] While in Albany to execute his first major commission, a full-length portrait of Governor De Witt Clinton, Catlin met Clara B. Gregory, whom he married on May 10, 1828. In the summer of 1828 Catlin received the inspiration that guided him for the rest of his life when he witnessed the visit to Philadelphia by a delegation of "noble and dignified-looking Indians, from the wilds of the 'Far West.'" He promptly decided to devote his life to painting Indians to lend "a hand to a dying nation, who have no historian or biographer of their own," thereby "snatching from a hasty oblivion what could be saved for the benefit of posterity." He spent 1829–30 painting portraits of the delegates to the Virginia Constitutional Convention while awaiting an opportunity to pursue the consuming passion to paint all of the Indian tribes in the United States.

From 1830 to 1836 Catlin traveled and painted Indians of the West much of each spring, summer, and fall. After spending part of two years painting subjects immediately accessible from St. Louis, he boarded the steamer *Yellow Stone*[qv] in 1832 for its maiden voyage to Fort Union, which stood at the confluence of the Yellowstone and upper Missouri rivers. Catlin painted furiously during the five months up river. He outlined about 170 paintings, including the only eyewitness accounts of the exotic Okeepa ceremony of the Mandans, which he completed during the winters spent with Clara. He accompanied a contingent of dragoons from Fort Gibson, Arkansas Territory, in 1834 on their expedition to consult with the elusive Comanche and Pawnee tribes. The expedition, on which more than 200 men died from disease, was the source for several paintings depicting "Texas" as well as the basis for Catlin's later claims of prolonged experience traversing Texas. But Catlin never crossed the international boundary between Indian Territory and Texas, the Red River. His final major expedition took him in 1836 to the sacred Indian pipestone quarry in the southwest corner of what is now Minnesota. He saw himself as the first white man to record that "classic ground." From his "mission" as historian of the Indians, Catlin collected the "North American Indian Gallery," which eventually contained more than 600 paintings and thousands of costumes and cultural artifacts. The portraits, landscapes, and cultural events he painted continue to be invaluable historical and anthropological documents, as well as intriguing artistic accomplishments.

Catlin exhibited his Indian Gallery in major cities along the Ohio River and the East Coast from 1837 to 1839. To reap larger returns from exhibiting and enhance the value of the gallery and his own prestige and thus improve the chances for purchase by the federal government, an almost constant aim for him for the next dozen years, Catlin sailed for England, where for five years he circulated his gallery. In London he published his great work, the two-volume *Letters and Notes on the Manners, Customs, and Condition of the North American Indian* (1841), which not only championed the Indian but indicted frontier "civilization." Faced with declining interest in his gallery, which now included Indian performers, he moved to the continent, where he again found royal audiences, this time in Paris and Brussels, and diminishing general interest. During the three years on the continent, Catlin suffered the sudden deaths of Clara and their only son, George, Jr. In the wake of the 1848 revolution, which deposed his presumed patron, Louis Philippe, Catlin and his three daughters returned to London. Insolvent, despondent, virtually ignored by the British, yet obsessed with keeping his gallery intact after eighteen years and devoted to making and promoting regardless of the substantial emotional and financial price, Catlin turned to itinerant lecturing to support his family and resuscitate interest. Displaying a few paintings and artifacts, he utilized a new hook for his old subject: his knowledge of that amorphous Eden, the American West, for the thousands of potential British emigrants. Soon, his paintings became mere travel posters, and he became a spokesman for British companies representing large Texas land speculators, principally James B. Reily. His unremunerated task was to encourage organized emigration activity and to direct it to Reily's lands. To supplement his emigration lectures, he published in November 1848 a persuasive pamphlet, *Notes for the Emigrant to America,* which concluded, "I fearlessly and unhesitatingly pronounce the new State of Texas the finest and fairest field for [emigrants'] consideration." Catlin's efforts on behalf of Texas landowners persuaded one Midlands emigration group in 1849 to engage Edward Smith and John Barrow to "examine the Country pointed out by Mr. Catlin," and report their findings. Catlin's employers, holders of the large tracts of James Reily, took in the Midlands group shortly after the return, and glowing report, of Smith and Barrow. The speculation group changed names twice in a year, finally settling on the United States Land Company in early 1850.

Newspapers from Galveston to Austin cited Catlin in connection with impending settlement in Central Texas, not just as organizer abroad but as leader of the party as well. In June 1850 the Universal Emigration and Colonization Company, with a house newspaper, the *Universal Emigration and Colonization Messenger,* and agreements with the Black Star Line for transporting emigrants, absorbed the United States Land Company. For his investment in time, money, and energy, Catlin became the "local superintendent in Texas" for the newly consolidated company. The August issue of the *Messenger* included an article on the proposed "New Colony of Milam County, Texas"—on 60,000 acres of Reily's tract now in Coryell County—that discussed the "class of persons who are now accompanying Mr. Catlin to his first settlement in Texas." The report of Catlin's departure for Texas was premature, however, and in fact a few days later he severed relations with the company in a disagreement concerning compensation. He received no money for his two years' recruiting nor for his investment.

Catlin's efforts as Texas colonization expert proved disastrous for himself and the colonists. He mortgaged his gallery to invest in the Texas scheme and to meet expenses during two years spent promoting it and continued to borrow against it to mollify initial creditors and support his family. In 1852 creditors seized the gallery and sold it to industrialist Joseph Harrison, who immediately shipped it to a warehouse in Philadelphia. A sometime benefactor wrote Catlin years later that "I remember I constantly warned you of the imprudent manner in which you were acting, wasting your money upon Texas gamblings." The colonists received dangerously inaccurate and misleading information concerning the intended destination, Central Texas, that reflected Catlin's ignorance of the area, his financial desperation, the interests of the land speculators, and the complete incompetence of the colonization company. Though the British colonists founded the Colony of Kent[qv] in what is now Bosque County, their ordeal in Catlin's Eden ended shortly afterward, with high casualty rates.

Catlin saw "the second starting point of my life" in an expedition to South America in 1852 and within five years claimed to have traversed the Western Hemisphere from Kamchatka to Tierra del Fuego, including a trip down the entire Rio Grande. He produced hundreds of paintings depicting North and South American Indian life, which he called the Catlin Cartoon Collection. His return to the United States in 1871 reunited him with his daughters, whom Clara's brother had taken during the days of the gallery seizure. He died on December 23, 1872, and was buried in Greenwood Cemetery, Long Island, New York. Mrs. Joseph Harrison donated the gallery, which Catlin had not seen since 1852, to the Smithsonian Institution in 1879, where it remains today. Catlin's published works include, in addition to those mentioned, *Catlin's North American Indian Portfolio: Hunting, Rocky Mountains, and Prairies of America* (1845); *Catlin's Notes on Eight Years' Travels and Residence in Europe* (2 vols., 1848); *Life Among the Indians* (1867); and *Last Rambles amongst the Indians of the Rocky Mountains and the Andes* (1867).

BIBLIOGRAPHY: George Catlin Collection, Thomas Gilcrease Institute of American History and Art, Tulsa, Oklahoma. Brian W. Dippie, *Catlin and His Contemporaries: The Politics of Patronage* (Lincoln: University of Nebraska Press, 1990). Richard H. Ribb, George Catlin's Crash: "Texas Gamblings" and the Loss of His Indian Gallery (M.A. thesis, University of Texas at Austin, 1992). Marjorie Catlin Roehm, *The Letters of George Catlin and His Family: A Chronicle of the American West* (Berkeley and Los Angeles: University of California Press, 1966). William H. Truettner, *The Natural Man Observed: A Study of Catlin's Indian Gallery* (Washington: Smithsonian Institution Press, 1979).

Richard H. Ribb

CATON, TEXAS. Caton is four miles southwest of Bagwell in southern Red River County. Although settlement in the area began much earlier, apparently a community did not emerge until the mid-1880s. In 1888 a post office was opened for a few months, and the settlement was called Catonville. When the post office was reestablished in 1892 the name was shortened to Caton. In 1896 the community had two churches, a doctor, and a music teacher. The post office was closed in 1905, and by 1984 only a few widely scattered houses and Catonville Cemetery remained.

Cecil Harper, Jr.

CATOR, JAMES HAMILTON (1852–1927). James Hamilton Cator, buffalo hunter, Panhandle[qv] pioneer, and rancher, one of five children of Capt. John Bertie Cator, administrator of the Port of Hull, England, was born on September 2, 1852, near Fintra, Ireland, where his father was on duty at the time. As a British naval officer, Captain Bertie had already distinguished himself in the Chinese Opium Wars and in his attempts to find the polar expedition of Sir John Franklin. However, he determined that his two oldest sons, James and Arthur J. L. (Bob), would seek less hazardous careers and had them trained in engineering and draftsmanship. After a fruitless effort to find suitable employment for his sons in the British Empire, the captain wrote the American consul in London inquiring of opportunities for young men in the less settled parts of the United States. In 1871, after hearing glowing reports of the Kansas Land and Immigration Company, he sent James and Bob over to strike it rich by farming in Kansas.

The brothers, however, found farming to be different from what it was in England and were scorned by most Kansas frontiersmen. Soon they became enthusiastic over the buffalo-hide trade. Having had previous experience in hunting game, the Cators joined in this profitable business and killed 300 buffalo soon after purchasing new Sharps buffalo rifles.[qv] With their earnings they bought a wagon, mules, horses, and food. Between July 1 and September 1, 1873, the Cators killed nearly 7,000 buffalo and had in their employ seven skinners. When the Panic of 1873 caused the price of hides to drop momentarily, the Cators took up "wolfing" and killed over 600 gray wolves and coyotes for bounty. However, soon they were hunting buffalo again, and late in the fall they followed Josiah Wright and John Wesley Mooar[qqv] from Clay Center, Kansas, to the Texas Panhandle, where the animals were still abundant. A severe snowstorm on Christmas Day 1873 caught the Cators' hunting party in a break along North Palo Duro Creek (in what is now Hansford County) huddling against an earthen wall. There they constructed a crude dugout[qv] of cottonwood pickets and buffalo hides and waited out the winter. The success that the Cators and Mooars enjoyed led to the establishment of the trading center at Adobe Walls the following spring; the Cators, in fact, entered the post from their camp on Aroja Bonita Creek, in Potter County twelve miles away, the day after the Indian attack that took place on June 27, 1874 (see adobe walls, second battle of). Subsequently the brothers and their companions filed claims for property burned or stolen by the Indians, but not until 1892 was their case heard by a federal court, in Wichita, Kansas. After Adobe Walls was abandoned, the Cators settled down to quiet lives at their Palo Duro Creek shelter. Never bothered by Indians in the course of the Red River War,[qv] they continued hunting buffalo until 1877, when decimation of the herds prompted them to seek another occupation.

With the arrival of free-range cattle outfits, the Cators decided to try ranching on a small scale. From the LX Ranch[qv] in 1878 they bought forty two-year-olds, eleven cows, and ten heifers and drove them back to their dugout to range along North Palo Duro Creek. As this herd expanded, James Cator used a Diamond C brand, while Bob used a VP. In that same year, 1878, the Cators erected a three-room picket house and started a store they called Zulu Stockade because they considered their territory "as wild as the Zululand region of Africa." Bob hauled supplies on a freight line he established to Dodge City, bringing in additional orders for other settlers moving into the region. Buffalo hunters, soldiers, and ranchers traveling over the military road between forts Dodge and Bascom stopped at Zulu for supplies, and the first Hansford County post office was opened there in December 1880 with Bob Cator as postmaster.

Letters from the Cator brothers to their family back in England prompted their sister Clara and younger brother Bert O. to join them at Zulu Stockade in 1879. Traveling with them was Jennie Ludlow, who married Bob in 1882. Clara and Jennie were the first white women to settle in the Panhandle north of the Canadian River. They helped tend the store and added such refinements as gunnysack carpets and wall whitewash made from creekbed gyp and crushed rocks.

James Cator returned to England in the fall of 1879 to recover from the ague. There he met Edith Land, daughter of a Hull physician, and promised to return and marry her later. That promise, however, was delayed by the "Big Die-up"[qv] of January 1886, in which blizzards nearly wiped out the Cator herd. Disheartened, Bob and Jennie Cator sold their share of the business and cattle and moved to Oregon. As a result, James sent for his fiancée in the spring of 1887 to meet him at Dodge City, where their wedding was held. Arriving with Edith was her brother, Arthur Land. For his bride Cator had built a multiroom house from native stone, and there they raised a son and two daughters.

Business at the Cator Ranch picked up after the town of Hansford was platted in 1887. Clara and her husband Clayton McCrea, who taught the first school at Tascosa, took charge of the stockade. Another brother, Leslie Stewart Cator, immigrated from England, brought over his bride, Bessie Donelson, and stayed to put down roots in the Panhandle. After Hansford County was organized in 1889, James Cator was elected the first county judge and Arthur Land the first county treasurer; fewer than thirty ballots were cast. Bert Cator, who operated a lumber and grain firm in Hansford, served as a county commissioner. Later, from 1898 to 1900, Leslie Cator served as county judge.

After retiring from the bench in 1894, James Cator devoted himself to improving his cattle herds with selective breeding. He also became involved in the move to promote agriculture in the northern Panhandle and with Clate McCrea introduced alfalfa into the county. In 1907 Cator organized the county's first bank, which was moved from Hansford to Spearman with the building of the North Texas and Santa Fe Railway in 1917. Zulu Stockade was abandoned in 1912, and after World War I[qv] the McCreas moved to California. James H. Cator lived in the rock house until his death on October 4, 1927. He was buried in the family cemetery near the ghost town of Hansford. His widow continued to reside in the house until her death in 1950. Although the original Diamond C and VP brands were no longer used, in the late 1980s Cator's heirs still operated the ranch on Palo Duro Creek. His "Big 50" Sharps rifle, with which he killed 16,000 buffalo in three years, is on display at the Panhandle-Plains Historical Museum[qv] in Canyon.

See also buffalo, buffalo hunting.

bibliography: Ernest Cabe, Jr., "A Sketch of the Life of James Hamilton Cator," *Panhandle-Plains Historical Review* 6 (1933). Angie Debo, "An English View of the Wild West," *Panhandle-Plains Historical Review* 6 (1933). Laura V. Hamner, *Short Grass and Longhorns* (Norman: University of Oklahoma Press, 1943). Hansford County Historical Commission, *Hansford County, Texas* (2 vols., Dallas: Taylor, 1980?). *H. Allen Anderson*

CATQUEZA INDIANS. The Catqueza (Caquiza, Casqueza, Catcueza) Indians are known only from a brief period near the close of the seventeenth century. At this time they ranged an area east and northeast of San Antonio, principally in the Guadalupe valley between the sites of present San Marcos and Gonzales. Certain Spanish documents indicate that the Catquezas were not Coahuiltecans. Some writers have suggested that they spoke Tonkawan, apparently because they lived in an area where other Tonkawans also lived. It is possible that the Catquezas were seventeenth-century migrants from western Texas or northern Mexico. They were sometimes associated with the Jumanos and Cíbolas, and a Spanish document of 1691 mentions a Catqueza chief who was "reared in Parras, Saltillo, and Parral. Later he went to New Mexico and returned again to his people."

bibliography: Herbert E. Bolton, "The Jumano Indians in Texas, 1650–1771," *Quarterly of the Texas State Historical Association* 15 (July 1911). Charles W. Hackett, ed., *Pichardo's Treatise on the Limits of Louisiana and Texas* (4 vols., Austin: University of Texas Press, 1931–46). Frederick Webb Hodge, ed., *Handbook of American Indians North of Mexico* (2 vols., Washington: GPO, 1907, 1910; rpt., New York: Pageant, 1959). John R. Swanton, *Source Material on the History and Ethnology of the Caddo Indians* (Smithsonian Institution, Bureau of American Ethnology Bulletin 132, Washington: GPO, 1942).

Thomas N. Campbell

CAT SPRING. Cat Spring is in Cat Spring, Texas, in Austin County (at 29°51′ N, 96°20′ W). The area was settled in 1835 by Franz Ferdinand Albrecht von Roeder[qv] and his brothers. Before European-Americans moved into the area wildcats were numerous in the woods around the spring. The first night the Roeders camped at the spring a wildcat came to drink, and some sources indicate that the cat was shot and killed by one of the Roeder boys. Thus arose the name Katzenquelle, later known as Wildcat Spring, and finally shortened to Cat Spring. The springwaters rise from Willis sand. In 1978 the rate of flow was 0.72 liters per second.

BIBLIOGRAPHY: Gunnar Brune, *Springs of Texas*, Vol. 1 (Fort Worth: Branch-Smith, 1981).

Gunnar Brune

CAT SPRING, TEXAS. Cat Spring, at the intersection of Farm roads 2187 and 949, on the Missouri, Kansas and Texas Railroad and the west bank of Bernard Creek in western Austin County, was first settled in 1834 by a group of German immigrants from the duchies of Oldenburg and Westphalia led by Ludwig Anton Siegmund von Roeder and Robert Kleberg.[qv] Many of these immigrants had been attracted to Texas by the letters of an earlier Oldenburg migrant, Friedrich Ernst,[qv] who had taken up land nearby in the valley of Mill Creek in 1831. The community received its name when a son of Leopold von Roeder killed a puma at one of the springs of the San Bernard River near the family farm. A German Protestant congregation was organized at Cat Spring by Rev. Louis C. Ervendberg[qv] between 1840 and 1844. The earliest agricultural society in Texas was formed in the town immediately after the Civil War.[qv] A post office was established by 1878. By the early 1890s the Missouri, Kansas and Texas Railroad linked Cat Spring with New Ulm to the west and Sealy to the east. In 1836 Cat Spring had a population estimated at 350, and fifteen businesses. However, decline set in after World War II,[qv] and by 1950 it had an estimated 200 people and nine businesses. In 1990 Cat Spring had a population of seventy-six and two accredited businesses.

BIBLIOGRAPHY: Rudolph L. Biesele, *The History of the German Settlements in Texas, 1831–1861* (Austin: Von Boeckmann-Jones, 1930; rpt. 1964). C. W. Schmidt, *Footprints of Five Generations* (New Ulm, Texas: New Ulm *Enterprise*, 1930).

Charles Christopher Jackson

CATTAIL CREEK. Cattail Creek rises six miles southeast of Cuero in southeastern DeWitt County (at 29°01′ N, 97°16′ W) and runs northeast for 4½ miles to its mouth on the Guadalupe River, four miles north of Arneckeville (at 29°03′ N, 97°14′ W). It runs through flat to rolling terrain surfaced by clay loam that supports scrub brush, grasses, and cattail bushes.

CATTLE BRANDS. Cattle brands still play an important role in identifying an animal's owner in Texas cattle ranching. The practice of branding is ancient. Some Egyptian tomb paintings at least 4,000 years old depict scenes of roundups and cattle branding, and biblical evidence suggests that Jacob the herdsman branded his stock. Burning an identifying mark into the hide of an animal was, until the invention of the tattoo, the only method of marking that lasted the life of the animal. The practice of branding came to the New World with the Spaniards, who brought the first cattle to New Spain. When Hernán Cortés experimented with cattle breeding during the late sixteenth century in the valley of Mexicalzimgo, south of modern Toluca, Mexico, he branded his cattle. His brand, three Latin crosses, may have been the first brand used in the Western Hemisphere. As cattle raising grew, in 1537 the crown ordered the establishment of a stockmen's organization called Mesta throughout New Spain. Each cattle owner had to have a different brand, and each brand had to be registered in what undoubtedly was the first brand book in the Western Hemisphere, kept at Mexico City. Soon after the Spaniards moved north into Texas and cattle raising developed on a large scale during the middle eighteenth century, the crown ordered the branding of all cattle. The early Spanish brands in Texas were more generally pictographs than letters. The Spaniards chose their brands to represent beautiful sentiments in beautiful ways. Most of the early Spanish brands found in the Bexar and Nacogdoches archives[qqv] are pictographs made with curlicues and pendants. A cattle raiser would compose his own brand. When his first son acquired cattle, a curlicue or pendant was added to the father's brand, and as other sons acquired their own cattle, additional curlicues or pendants were added to what became the family brand. Only a few Spanish brands found in the Bexar and Nacogdoches archives are made of letters.

Many early Anglo-American Texas ranchers were unable to interpret the brands used under the Spanish and Mexican regimes. Texans often referred to them as "dog irons" or "quién sabes" (*quién sabe?* = "who knows?") since they could not be read. Most of the early brands of Texans, by contrast, were made of initials and could be read with ease. Richard H. Chisholm owned perhaps the first recorded brand, registered in Gonzales County in 1832. During the years of the Republic of Texas,[qv] the recording of brands was provided for but not rigidly enforced. The oldest brand records under state government are those found along the Texas coast. Harris County began keeping records in 1836. Stephen F. Austin[qv] recorded his initial brand in Brazoria County in 1838, about four years after he began using it. Galveston County records began in 1839, the year Gail Borden, Jr.,[qv] first recorded his brand, the first one entered in the Galveston County brand book. When Nueces County was organized in 1847, brands were recorded, but the cattle industry in the county was not dignified by having a separate brand-registration book. During the first seven years brand registrations in Nueces County were sandwiched between marriage licenses, sales of slaves, declarations of citizenship, oaths of office, bonds for administration of estates, wills, and construction contracts. Beginning in 1848, Texas provided for recording brands with the county clerk, with the stipulation that an unrecorded brand did not constitute legal evidence of ownership. This provision was modified in 1913 after thefts went unpunished where unrecorded brands were involved. A considerable body of Texas law deals with brands. At one time the office of hide and cattle inspector was an elective county office.

Many western counties did not begin brand registration until the 1870s or 1880s. By then letters, numerals, and even names were popular brands in Texas. Though such brands were easily read, others have to be seen. Among them are the "Hogeye," "Fishtail," "Milliron," "Buzzard on a rail," "Coon on a rail," "Saddle Pockets" or "Swinging blocks," "Quién sabe," "Grab-all," and countless others with intriguing names. Representations of such common subjects as an anvil, truck handle, hash knife, door key, bridle bit, spur, pitchfork, old woman, doll baby, broadax, boot, shoe, hat, rocking chair, frying pan, and so on were commonplace.

In branding terminology, a leaning letter or character is "tumbling." In the horizontal position it is "lazy." Short curved strokes or wings added at the top make a "Flying T." The addition of short bars at the bottom of a symbol makes it "walking." Changing angular lines into curves makes a brand "running." Half-circles, quarter-circles, and triangles were frequently used in late-nineteenth-century brands. An open triangle was a "rafter." If a letter rested in a quarter-circle it was "rocking." There were "bars," "stripes," "rails," and "slashes" that differed only in length and angle. When a straight line connected characters, a "chain" was made. A picture of a fish marked the cattle owned by Mrs. Fish of Houston. A. Coffin of Port Lavaca used a representation of a coffin with a large A on it. Bud Christmas of Seminole had his XMAS brand, and S. A. Hightower of Breckenridge placed "HI" beside a mushroom-like object.

C. C. Slaughter,[qv] who was instrumental in organizing the Texas Cattle Raisers' Association, established his cattle business on the Trinity River in Freestone County during the 1850s. He became dissatisfied with his location and moved twice, finally locating the Long S Ranch at the headwaters of the Colorado River in 1877. His brand, however, was not recorded until September 1879, when it was subsequently run in Howard, Martin, Dawson, Borden, Cochran, and Hockley counties. Many old-time Texas cattlemen believed that during the latter half of the nineteenth century more cattle were sold in the open markets with Slaughter's brand than with any other brand in the world. The famous XIT brand of the Capitol Freehold Land and Investment Company,[qv] once registered in nine counties, was designed by Ab (Abner P.) Blocker,[qv] a well-known traildriver.

No law dictated the exact spot on a cow's hide for the branding, yet through the years the left side of the animal, especially the hip, became the customary spot. Nowhere in old documents or recollections does anyone say why the left side was chosen, but the recollections of some old-time cowboys suggest that cattle have a peculiar habit of milling more to the left than to the right; hence brands on their left sides would be more visible to cowboys inside the roundup herds. Still other cowboys recalled that cattle were branded on their left hips "because persons read from left to right" and thus read "from the head toward the tail." As one cowboy added, "A right-handed roper would ride slightly to the left of the animal and could see the brand better if it were on that side." Regardless of the reason for the position of a brand on an animal, the position was recorded in brand books.

Marks besides brands were used. Some ranchers marked their cattle with a wattle, a mark of ownership made on the neck or the jaw of an animal by pinching up a quantity of skin and cutting it. The skin, however, is not cut entirely off, and when the cut is healed, a hanging flap is left. Wattles, however, were not as common as earmarks, which were used by nearly every cattleman during the open-range days and were recorded along with brands. As the name suggests, an earmark was a design cut into one or both ears of an animal. Sometimes a portion of the ear might be removed. A semicircular nick was an "underbit" or "overbit." A square clip at the tip of roughly half of the ear was a "crop," while cutting the ear close to the head was a "grub." A V-shaped cut in the tip of the ear was a "swallow-fork." The same mark on both ears became known as a "flickerbob." A "double over-bit" was the mark made by cutting two triangular pieces in the upper part of the animal's ear. One of the better-known earmarks in Texas was the "jinglebob," a deep slit that left the lower half of the ear flapping down. Many cattlemen considered it one of the most hideous earmarks ever devised. It was the mark of John S. Chisum,[qv] whose great ranch lay in West Texas and southeastern New Mexico.

By the 1940s numerous brands that were no longer in use had been registered in county records. On April 14, 1943, the Texas legislature passed a bill designed to deregister many of the unused brands. The bill included a grace period until October 1, 1945, giving cattlemen the opportunity to reregister their brands. Among the oldest continual brands is the Running W of the King Ranch,[qv] which was originated by Richard King[qv] in 1869 and reregistered in 1943. *See also* RANCHING, RANCHING IN SPANISH TEXAS.

BIBLIOGRAPHY: Oren Arnold and John P. Hale, *Hot Irons, Heraldry of the Range* (New York: Macmillan, 1940). David Dary, *Cowboy Culture: A Saga of Five Centuries* (New York: Knopf, 1981). Gus L. Ford, ed., *Texas Cattle Brands* (Dallas: Cockrell, 1936). Wayne Gard, *Cattle Brands of Texas* (Dallas: First National Bank, 1956). J. Evetts Haley, *The Heraldry of the Range: Some Southwestern Brands* (Canyon, Texas: Panhandle-Plains Historical Society, 1949). J. Evetts Haley, *The XIT Ranch of Texas and the Early Days of the Llano Estacado* (Chicago: Lakeside, 1929; rpts., Norman: University of Oklahoma Press, 1953, 1967). Hortense Warner Ward, *Cattle Brands and Cow Hides* (Dallas: Story Book Press, 1953). Manfred R. Wolfenstine, *The Manual of Brands and Marks* (Norman: University of Oklahoma Press, 1970).

David Dary

CATTLE EGRET. The cattle egret (*Bubulcus ibis*) is a member of the Ardeidae (heron family) included in the order Ciconiiformes (stork-like birds). It is gregarious and usually associates with cattle and other grazing animals. Adults are about seventeen inches (43.2 cm) in length, have a wingspan of about thirty-seven inches (94.0 cm), and weigh between 0.6 and 1.0 pound (0.3–0.5 kg). Their plumage is white, but during the breeding season orange-buff plumes appear on the head, neck, and back. Cattle egrets are native to Africa and Asia. The nature and success of their almost worldwide range expansion is dynamic and complex, but well-documented. Although the mechanisms and details of original range expansion are not known, cattle egrets spread from the west coast of Africa in the late 1800s across the Atlantic Ocean to the coastal area of northeastern South America, then northward into North America and the West Indies in the early 1940s and 1950s. Cattle egrets originally entered Texas in 1954, migrating south and west along the Gulf Coast states from initial heronries in Florida. They increased from about ten pairs in the state in 1959 to about 300,000 pairs by 1990. By 1995 they occupied 266 heronries in Texas, mostly along the coast and east of the Balcones Escarpment, but between 1987 and 1995, a few small scattered colonies nested in the South Plains, Trans-Pecos, and Panhandle.

Cattle egrets nest in woodlands and swamps and on inland and coastal islands. There is no correlation between distribution or density of grazing cattle and the breeding range of cattle egrets. In inland heronries, they associate primarily with the little blue heron (*Egretta caerulea*) and snowy egret (*E. thula*). In coastal heronries, they primarily associate with the snowy egret and tricolored heron (*E. tricolor*). They are generally beneficial because of their insect-eating habits. However, in nesting colonies, the deposition of cattle egret guano changes soil chemistry. Some plant species, such as hackberry, cedar elm, and chinaberry, can survive the changes, but others, such as oak, pecan, and winged elm, are killed. Cattle egrets nest about three weeks later than native herons and egrets; their breeding season is seven to nine weeks longer, and they are less selective of nest sites. Their nests consist of twigs and are bowl-shaped. The average clutch size is 3.4; egg-laying intervals are about two days, and the incubation period is about twenty-four days. Cattle egrets lose about 14 percent of their eggs, but hatching failure of remaining eggs is low (7 percent). Chick mortality is about 4 percent. Thus, 2.5 young are fledged per brood.

Mixed clutches of cattle egrets and native ardeids are occasionally found. But since cattle egrets nest later than native herons and egrets, they are mostly noncompetitive with the natives, and interspecific aggression is relatively low. Cattle egrets reuse abandoned nests or take them apart for materials for their own nests, a behavior which is also common among native herons and egrets. From 1959 to 1972 the cattle egret population increased at an average rate of 180 percent a year. Between 1972 and 1990 the rate of increase dropped to an average of 120 percent per year. This decrease may indicate that the bird is reaching its maximum population in Texas.

Annual mortality rates among age groups are: juveniles (56 percent), yearlings (30 percent), and adults (28 percent). Few birds (about 4 percent) live longer than 7–8 years. Maximum life span is unknown, but may reach 20 years. Mortality factors are natural causes such as predation, diseases, injuries, and accidents and human causes such as shooting, trapping, being struck by farm machinery, and entanglement in fishing line. The major cause of mortality is shooting, most of which occurs when migrating birds disperse into Mexico during the winter. Agricultural pesticide residues have been found in eggs and bird tissues in Texas and Mexico; however, there is no indication of adverse effects to cattle egret populations.

Most cattle egrets hatched in Texas winter in Mexico—in the Gulf states of Tamaulipas and Vera Cruz and in the Pacific states of Sinaloa, Michoacán, Jalisco, and Najarit. Band recoveries and sight records of colored leg tags indicate that few cattle egret adults return to natal Texas colonies, but most disperse to other heronries, some at considerable distances from the natal heronry (in Mexico and Central America, for instance). Similar records indicate that they move as far as extreme southern and southwestern Mexico, Guatemala, El Salvador, and Cocos Island (Costa Rica). A few have also been noted in Arkansas, California, Florida, and Louisiana. Compared to the large breeding population in Texas, the winter population of cattle egrets in the state is extremely small with most of them in coastline counties, increasing southward. Sightings away from coastal areas are inconsistent and numbers are small; occasionally, single birds are seen far inland during mild winters.

Cattle egrets obtain 95 percent of their food in association with grazing animals. Major prey items are grasshoppers and cattle-associated flies. Rare prey items include ticks, earthworms, crayfish, fish, and small birds. Frogs and toads are apparently important food items for chicks. After the breeding season, cattle egrets often feed in cotton and grain fields and follow farm equipment. Lack of food may limit their winter distribution in Texas. Consumption of grasshoppers and cattle-associated flies may be of great economic benefit to cattlemen. Cattle egrets reduce the number of tabanids and, thereby, the incidence of bovine anaplasmosis. Laboratory tests have shown that cattle egrets are not carriers of brucellosis, as was once suspected. Heronries near human habitation cause noise, odor, and fear of diseases such as ornithosis and histoplasmosis. There is no evidence, however, that cattle egrets have introduced diseases or parasites detrimental to humans or native herons and egrets.

bibliography: R. C. Telfair II, "Additional Inland Nesting Records in Texas of Four Species of Colonial Waterbirds," *Bulletin of the Texas Ornithological Society* 13 (1980). R. C. Telfair II, The African Cattle Egret in Texas and Its Relation to the Little Blue Heron, Snowy Egret, and Louisiana Heron (Ph.D. dissertation, Texas A&M University, 1979). R. C. Telfair II, *Cattle Egret (Bubulcus ibis) Population Trends and Dynamics in Texas (1954–1990)* (Austin: Texas Parks and Wildlife Department, 1993). R. C. Telfair II, "The Cattle Egret in Texas: Range Expansion and Interrelations with Other Colonial Waterbirds," *Bulletin of the Texas Ornithological Society* 13 (1980). R. C. Telfair II, *The Cattle Egret: A Texas Focus and World View* (College Station: Texas A&M University Press, 1983). R. C. Telfair II, "Cattle Egrets, Inland Heronries, and the Availability of Crayfish," *Southwestern Naturalist* 26 (1981). R. C. Telfair II and L. E. Marcy, "Cattle Egrets . . . in Texas," *Texas Journal of Science* 35 (1984). R. C. Telfair II, and B. C. Thompson, *Nuisance Heronries in Texas: Characteristics and Management* (Austin: Texas Parks and Wildlife Department, 1986).

Raymond C. Telfair II

CATTLE FEEDING. Texas has long been considered the Number 1 cattle state in the nation. In fact, during its early years Texas had more cattle on its ranges than people. By the mid-1980s Texas had also become the Number 1 cattle feeding state. The cattle-feeding industry annually contributes $12 billion dollars to the state's economy. In this industry, cattle are confined in feedyards to add weight and improve quality. A typical yearling, weighing 500 to 700 pounds off grass, will double its weight during its 150-to-200 day stay in a feedyard. Its quality will improve from "unpredictable" to Choice or Select grade—the quality that consumers prefer. Besides adding weight and improving quality, cattle feeding in its early years also helped to dispose of unwanted by-products. Apparently there were some feedlots in operation in New England during colonial times, but the first widespread early cattle feedyards in the nation were built by cottonseed oil–mill operators in the 1850s. The arrangement spread, and by 1895 Texas had eighty-four yards. Initially, the owners viewed mill by-products—meal and hulls—as a burden and dumped them into nearby ravines or swamps. When the owners discovered that cattle would eat cottonseed meal and hulls, the mill owners started feedyards though the yards were still located near draws, ravines, or creeks for drainage. For example, the 6,000-head yard in Lubbock drained into the Yellow House Fork. In time, owners became concerned about polluting the environment and avoided building yards on streams and lakes.

Texas cattlemen early believed that cattle feeding would become a major industry in the state. At the Cattle Raisers Association of Texas meeting in Fort Worth in 1895, Greenlief W. Simpson predicted that by 1900 the state would lead the world in cattle feeding (Texas attained this distinction in the 1990s). A problem arose in the early 1900s when cattle numbers dropped rapidly from 50.8 million to 35.8 million by 1914. A few cattle raisers suggested that feeding young animals would be more efficient than waiting until they were two or older. J. E. Boog-Scott, a major rancher-feeder at Coleman, promoted the idea and believed the best way to gain acceptance was by influencing future ranchers. In 1912 he organized the first Boys Baby Beef Club, a forerunner of the Four-H Clubs. In the 1890s the Brownwood Cotton Oil Company, in Brownwood, was one of the first Texas oil mills to operate a sizable feedyard—500 to 1,000 head capacity. From 1900 to 1927 the Planters Oil Company ran a feeding operation in the Brazos River bottoms near Hearne. By the late 1920s, the Simmons Cotton Oil Mills had processing units—most with feedyards—at Lubbock, Rotan, Sweetwater, Quanah, and Childress. Tom B. Simmons, Jr. of Lubbock, son of one of the founders, entered the business in 1930 and fed cattle yearly until 1992. His first exposure to the industry was as the manager of the pens at Quanah. These pens were made of wire and could handle 7,000 head, but they offered scant restraint against stampedes during lightning storms. Oil-mill feedyards became an expanding industry. During the 1920s and 1930s these yards numbered in the scores. Swift and Company,[qv] for example, bought cattle in Fort Worth, and fed them in as many as twenty yards at a time. But there were lean years when fewer than 50,000 head were fed statewide (some individual yards could finish this many in the 1990s). During the depression era, large feedyards flourished on the South Plains. Two were at Brownfield—the D. H. Snyder pens and the Baricora Development Company feedyard. The latter, owned by newspaper millionaire William Randolph Hearst, had 10,000 head on feed in 1937. H. W. Stanton built a large yard along Yellow House Canyon, which later was engulfed by a growing Lubbock. To provide clean running water Stanton equipped his pens with what Ripley's "Believe It or Not" billed as the world's longest water trough—2,230 feet running the length of the pens. A pump on one well daily fed the trough until it went dry in 1946 and the yard was closed.

The Sudan Livestock and Feeding Company, in Sudan, was one of the first feedyards to operate year-round. Ben H. Davidson and Anton Rieder opened the lot in the fall of 1940 with a capacity of 2,000 head. Eventually, the size expanded to handle 25,000 head and the ownership changed, but it still retained its original name in 1993. During the 1950s and 1960s several sizable feedyards opened and closed in East and Central Texas. Cattle were available locally, but grain was in short supply and the mud problem was unmanageable. In the early 1950s, Durward W. Lewter, a county agent at Big Spring, learned how to feed grain sorghum to Four-H Club steers and won blue ribbons across the nation. To test the commercial market, he secured the financial backing of oilman Clint Murchison, Sr.,[qv] of Dallas and in 1955 built the largest commercial feedyard in West Texas. Lewter quickly illustrated the profit potential of large-scale cattle feeding. He fed mainly company-owned cattle to High Choice and Low Prime grades and expanded the yard until by 1960 he had more than 30,000 head of cattle on feed. During the market drop in the early 1960s, Lewter experienced hard times and became entangled in a legal dispute with Murchison. In 1962 the giant feedyard was sold by the court. E. C. Crofoot and his son, Jay, of Kansas, bought the operation and renamed it Lubbock Feed Lots. In the late 1950s an El Paso feedyard became involved in a boundary dispute with Mexico. When the United States entered World War I,[qv] Joe Peyton, an El Paso butcher, obtained a contract to supply beef to the army at Fort Bliss. As the demand escalated, Peyton built a packing plant on the Rio Grande with a 3,000-head feedyard. Through the years the yard grew to a capacity of 17,000 head. But a hitch developed for Peyton Packing Company and Peyton Feedyard. Since the Treaty of Guadalupe Hidalgo[qv] (1848) the Rio Grande had shifted, and for a century Mexico claimed 630 acres (the

Chamizal Strip) in south El Paso. In 1962 President John F. Kennedy met with President Adolfo López-Mateos and discussed the disputed tract, a meeting that led to the signing of the Chamizal Treaty in 1963 (*see* CHAMIZAL DISPUTE). Peyton was compensated, and he moved his packing plant to the eastern edge of El Paso and placed his feedyard forty-eight miles downriver at Tornillo.

During the years following World War II,[qv] the increased use of technology changed the landscape and economy of the High Plains of West Texas. Two major breakthroughs spurred this changed—the discovery of hybrid grain sorghum and the development of irrigation.[qv] Yields doubled and quadrupled—up to 7,000 and 8,000 pounds per acre—but the huge surpluses depressed prices. In 1955 farmers organized the Grain Sorghum Producers Association in an effort to find new markets with cattle feeders at home and abroad. In 1959, GSPA joined with the West Texas Chamber of Commerce[qv] and announced the first of three tours to study feeding practices in the Midwest and the Far West. West Texas farmers, cattlemen, bankers, and agribusiness leaders traveled by train and bus to Iowa, Illinois, Arizona, and California. After the 1962 tour to Arizona and California, where commercial feedyards were booming, a concerted effort was begun in West Texas to expand the feedyard operations there. A group that included Wenzel L. Stangel, former dean of agriculture at Texas Tech and chairman of the WTCC Agriculture Committee; Sam Thomas, manager of agricultural development, Southwestern Public Service Company; and D. G. (Bill) Nelson, executive vice president of the Grain Sorghum Producers Association, launched a campaign to attract entrepreneurs from other states. Cattle feeding in West Texas boomed. The number of fed cattle increased from 300,000 head marketed in 1958 to nearly two million in 1968 and 4.8 million in 1973—a 1,600 percent increase in fifteen years. During the 1980s, the number stabilized at around 4.8 million per year, or about 22 percent of the United States total. In a 1973 speech Charles E. Ball, executive vice president of the Texas Cattle Feeders Association, attributed the boom to available feeder cattle, bountiful grain supply, good climate, reasonable financing, and entrepreneurship.

Cattle feeders believed that an association of cattle feeders was needed. In 1961 the Texas and Southwestern Cattle Raisers Association,[qv] headquartered in Fort Worth, formed a Cattle Feeders Committee. TSCRA president Dolph Briscoe[qv] (later Texas governor) appointed Norman Moser, a rancher-feeder at DeKalb, as chairman. The committee hired Lloyd Bergsma, extension livestock marketing specialist at Texas A&M University, to be executive director. The committee was made a division of TSCRA. As most of the new feedyards were built in the Panhandle—300 miles from Fort Worth—a majority of the owners soon desired more autonomy, a closer head office, and separation from the rancher-controlled TSCRA. On May 18, 1967, ten cattle feeders met in Amarillo to discuss the matter. Attending were Jack Carrothers of Friona, Robert Allen of Tulia, J. O. Parker of Happy, Richard Jagels of Hereford, R. M. (Bob) Carter of Plainview, H. D. King of Muleshoe, Grady Shepard of Hale Center, Walter Lasley of Stratford, Rex McAnelly of Pampa, and Gene Newman of San Angelo. A questionnaire mailed to all known feedyards in the state showed that sixty-three of eighty-one respondents wanted a new organization. At the May 18 meeting the feedyard owners formed the Texas Cattle Feeders Association. The first officers were Jack Carrothers, president; R. M. (Bob) Carter, vice president; and Robert Allen, treasurer. They hired Lloyd Bergsma as the executive director and James W. Witherspoon of Hereford as TCFA attorney. By the fall of 1967, TCFA had seventy-two regular members and forty-eight associate members. Its five standing committees included Research and University, Membership and Finance, Insurance, Water and Air Pollution, and Technical. TCFA grew rapidly in services, membership, and finances.

To speed market information, the organization installed a telephone-computer network to permit TCFA market analysts to communicate with feedyard members, hired lobbyists to represent the organization in Austin and Washington, established a liaison with the fifteen state and national agencies that regulated feedyards, promoted beef promotion, sponsored research at universities, offered group insurance, initiated safety programs, published a weekly newsletter and the *Cattle Feeders Annual* magazine, and funded educational seminars. Membership grew from 390 in 1968 to a peak of 7,128 in 1984, then leveled off at 6,500. In the 1980s feedyard members numbered around 160, including most of the 150 commercial feedyards in Texas as well as yards in New Mexico and Oklahoma. "Custom feedyards" were developed. In them, operators handle from 2,000 to 50,000 head that they feed on a custom basis (cost of feed plus a service charge). Very few feedyards own the cattle they feed, because of the investment, credit requirements, and risk. In the 1990s a 20,000-head feedyard could cost more than $2 million for equipment and facilities, plus as much as $16 million for cattle. As TCFA grew it reflected the changing nature and needs of the industry. The annual budget increased from $40,675 in 1968 to nearly $3 million in 1993. The staff increased from three in 1968 to nineteen in the 1980s. At its twenty-fifth anniversary convention in November 1992 in Amarillo, TCFA honored the eighteen presidents and three executive vice presidents who had served the organization.

Since the boom years that began in the 1960s, the Texas feedyard industry has faced both economic and political challenges. In late 1972 and early 1973, for example, there was a flurry of consumer boycotts of beef and public protests against rising beef prices. On March 29, 1973, President Richard Nixon imposed a price freeze. As feeders delayed the marketing of cattle, this caused a buildup in supply and a price drop when the freeze was lifted in the fall of 1973. Cattle raisers suffered losses that ran $100 to $200 per head, and many declared bankruptcy. A number of feedyards closed. The episode became known as "the Wreck." Meanwhile, TCFA had called on its members to contribute a dollar a head for an emergency fund—to tell the cattlemen's story in Washington. In three weeks the organization raised $519,350. This ultimately led to the national dollar-per-head checkoff, authorized in the Agricultural Act of 1985 for beef promotion and research. In the 1970s, when packers were delaying payment for cattle for seven to eighteen days, TCFA took the lead and secured federal legislation requiring payment by the close of the next business day after delivery. During these years as consumers became concerned about dietary goals, leaner beef, food safety, animal welfare, and the environment, Texas cattle feeders addressed these issues in their programs and operations.

By 1984 Texas was the Number 1 cattle feeding state. The economic impact of this relatively new industry had mushroomed within less than thirty years. Economists estimated that the 4.8 million head marketed in 1990 contributed $11.5 billion to the Texas economy. The state comptroller's office reported that year that feedyards spent more than $1.1 billion in purchasing Texas-grown feeder cattle, bought $355 million worth of feeds, and paid $105 million for trucking. The industry had 5,000 regular employees and several hundred contract workers. An estimated 40,000 jobs in the state depended on cattle feeding.

BIBLIOGRAPHY: Charles E. Ball, *The Finishing Touch* (Amarillo: Texas Cattle Feeders Association, 1992). James Cox, *Historical and Biographical Record of the Cattle Industry* (2 vols., St. Louis: Woodward and Tiernan Printing, 1894, 1895; rpt., with an introduction by J. Frank Dobie, New York: Antiquarian, 1959). Henry C. Dethloff and Irvin M. May, Jr., eds., *Southwestern Agriculture: Pre-Columbian to Modern* (College Station: Texas A&M University Press, 1982). Robert L. Haney, *Milestones: Marking Ten Decades of Research* (College Station: Texas Agricultural Experiment Station, 1989). John H. McCoy, *Livestock and Meat Marketing* (Westport: AVI, 1979). J'Nell Pate, *Livestock Legacy: The Fort Worth Stockyards, 1887–1987* (College Station: Texas A&M University Press, 1988). Jimmy M. Skaggs, *Prime Cut: Livestock Raising and Meatpacking in the United States, 1607–1983* (College Station: Texas A&M University Press, 1986).

Charles E. Ball

CATTLEMAN. The *Cattleman,* the official publication of the Texas and Southwestern Cattle Raisers Association,[qv] is a widely read beef-cattle journal. In June 1914 the twenty-four-page premier issue of this monthly magazine was published in Fort Worth, Texas. In its first year the *Cattleman* reached 2,905 subscribers; in 1994 the magazine was almost nine times its original size, with 200-page monthly issues and an average total paid circulation of 20,500. About two-thirds of the subscribers are members of TSCRA. Readers live in every state and more than forty foreign countries and include commercial cattlemen, producers of purebred seed-stock, cattle feeders, and horsemen. As a whole, they owned or managed a total of 9.8 million cattle on 93.7 million acres of land in 1985. The magazine is nonpartisan and deals with issues of importance to the livestock industry, such as commercial ranch operations, cattle breeding and feeding, range and pasture management, and profit tips. Issues of the *Cattleman* frequently, but not always, focus on a particular breed of cattle. In those instances, there is usually a photo of the featured breed on the front cover, a principal article on the breed, and an advertising section especially for breeders of the featured breed. In December, the *Cattleman* publishes an issue devoted to the cattle industry in Mexico. Articles are written in both Spanish and English.

BIBLIOGRAPHY: Mary Whatley Clarke, *A Century of Cow Business: A History of the Texas and Southwestern Cattle Raisers Association* (Fort Worth: Evans, 1976). *Kipp Shackelford*

CATTLE RUSTLING. Cattle theft by Indians was a common hazard of early settlers in Texas. Though the Indians more often stole horses, when their food supply was short, they drove off and butchered beeves, dairy cows, and oxen. Sometimes they stole beyond their needs to avenge wrongs or to drive white settlers from their hunting grounds. Occasionally they started stampedes and killed cattle they could not drive off. In the Civil War and Reconstruction[qqv] periods, Mexican rustlers gave much trouble along the border. In claims made against the Mexican government, it was asserted that from 1859 through 1872 Mexican bandits stole 145,298 cattle from various South Texas ranches. The depredations of Indian and Mexican rustlers, however, fell far short of those perpetrated by white renegades. In fact, ranchmen in Mexico often were victimized by Texas thieves who swam large herds of "wet stock" across the Rio Grande by night and trailed them to Kansas markets. Other rustlers stampeded herds on the northward trails and drove off as many cattle as they could, using six-shooters to defend themselves if pursued. Many preyed on herds that grazed on the western ranges, especially where canyons or high brush afforded hiding places.

Most rustlers of the open-range era were cowboys who had drifted into dubious practices. They knew the cattle country and were adept at roping, branding, and trailing. One needed only to buy a few cows, register a brand, and begin branding strays. Many cowboys' herds increased so rapidly that some ranchmen refused to hire any hand who had stock of his own. The altering of brands was a frequent practice among rustlers. Instead of the stamp iron used by most cattlemen, the rustler used a running iron—a straight rod with a curve at the heated end. When this was outlawed, he sometimes used a piece of heavy wire that he could bend into any shape and carry in his pocket.

More common was the theft of large unbranded calves. When a ranchman neglected to brand some of his calves before they were weaned, it was easy for the rustler to cut a pasture fence, drive the calves to his corral, and stamp his own brand upon them. Often he was not content with this but would return to take also the smaller calves, not yet weaned. This was more ticklish procedure, since Longhorn cows and calves had a strong instinct for returning to each other, even when separated by miles. Such reunions had to be prevented, for if a ranchman found a calf with a rustler's brand nursing from one of his cows, there likely would be trouble. Before branding unweaned calves, often the rustler kept them penned until they quit bawling and learned to eat grass. Other measures used to keep them from getting back to their mothers and to hasten weaning were to cut the muscles supporting the calf's eyelids and thus make it temporarily blind, to apply a hot iron between the toes to make the calf's feet too sore for walking, or, in uncommon cases, to split the calf's tongue to prevent suckling. The rustler might also kill the mother to make the calf a genuine orphan.

With county seats far apart, grand juries disinclined to indict, and trial juries reluctant to convict, early cattlemen often had to take law enforcement into their own hands in dealing with rustlers. Following the transition from the open range to fenced ranches, rustling gradually was lessened by efforts of local officers, the Texas Rangers,[qv] and inspectors of cattlemen's associations, who checked brands as cattle were sold at livestock markets. Rustling was not entirely stamped out, however, and in the 1930s it broke out in a new form. Thieves equipped with fast trucks stole cattle at night, butchered them in nearby thickets, and sold the meat the next day in markets perhaps several hundred miles away. The extent of this rustling and the fact that the thieves often crossed state lines led Congress in 1941 to pass the McCarran Act, which provided a maximum penalty of a $5,000 fine and five years in prison for transporting across state lines stolen cattle or meat from such cattle. This measure, however, did not prevent the sale of stolen meat in black markets during World War II.[qv]

In the late 1970s, a new type of thief emerged known as the "Suburban rustler." This individual usually attacked unattended ranchettes, stole four or five head, and took the cattle immediately to auction. Techniques of theft in the later twentieth century included anesthetizing cattle with hypodermic darts, using trained bulldogs to bring the animals down, and herding the booty with helicopters. As the price of beef escalated, so did the ingenuity of the rustlers. Since the early twentieth century, the Texas and Southwestern Cattle Raisers Association[qv] has employed field inspectors to police cattle rustling. These agents, deputized by the Texas Department of Public Safety[qv] as Special Texas Rangers, helped to recover 4,000 cattle in 1993.

BIBLIOGRAPHY: Dallas *Morning News,* May 31, 1988. J. Evetts Haley, *The XIT Ranch of Texas and the Early Days of the Llano Estacado* (Chicago: Lakeside, 1929; rpts., Norman: University of Oklahoma Press, 1953, 1967). Philip Ashton Rollins, *The Cowboy: His Characteristics, His Equipment, and His Part in the Development of the West* (New York: Scribner, 1922). Doug Perkins, *Brave Men and Cold Steel: A History of Range Detectives and Their Peacemakers* (Fort Worth: Texas and Southwestern Cattle Raisers Foundation, 1984). Vertical Files, Barker Texas History Center, University of Texas at Austin.

Wayne Gard

CATTLE TRAILING. Cattle trailing was the principal method of getting cattle to market in the late nineteenth century. It provided Texans with a practical, economical means of marketing surplus livestock. It also achieved mythological stature as an aspect of the American frontier. Although their heyday was from 1866 to 1890, organized livestock drives to market in the United States date to the seventeenth century, especially in the Carolinas, Massachusetts, New York, and Pennsylvania. Easterners, however, often afoot and aided by shepherd dogs, herded relatively tame animals, whereas Texas drives during the nineteenth century usually featured mounted riders tending decidedly wilder beasts, at first mostly longhorn cattle[qv] and usually mavericks.[qv] As early as the 1830s, opportunists drove surplus Texas cattle from Stephen F. Austin's[qv] colony eastward through treacherous swamp country to New Orleans, where animals fetched twice their Texas market value. After statehood, during the 1840s and 1850s, some cattlemen drove Texas cattle northward over the Shawnee Trail[qv] to Illinois, Indiana, Iowa, Missouri, and Ohio, where they were sold mostly to farmers who fattened them for local slaughter markets. The first recorded large cattle drive occurred in 1846, when

Edward Piper herded 1,000 head from Texas to Ohio. Outbreaks of "Texas fever"[qv] during the mid-1850s caused both Missouri and Kansas legislatures to quarantine their states against "southern cattle." The gold rush to California created substantial demand for slaughter beeves, and during the early to mid-1850s some adventurous Texans herded steers westward through rugged mountains and deserts to West Coast mining camps, where animals worth fourteen dollars in Texas marketed for $100 or more. During the Civil War[qv] some Texans drove cattle to New Orleans, where they were sold, but, mostly, animals were left untended at home, where they multiplied.

At the war's end, Texas possessed between three million and six million head of cattle, many of them wild unbranded mavericks worth locally as little as two dollars each. However, the same beasts were potentially far more valuable elsewhere, especially in the North, which had been largely denuded of its livestock by wartime demand and where longhorns commanded forty dollars or more a head. As early as 1865 a few Texans reportedly tested export markets by trailing cattle to Mexico and Louisiana, but most cattlemen waited until the spring of 1866 to mount large trail drives, especially to the North. That year Texans drove more than 260,000 cattle to assorted markets. Some went eastward to Louisiana, where many animals were shipped by boat to Cairo, Illinois, and St. Louis, Missouri. In search of possible sales among Rocky Mountain miners, veteran cattleman Oliver Loving and his young partner Charles Goodnight[qqv] that year drove a herd of cattle westward through dangerous Indian country to New Mexico and sold them profitably at Fort Sumner, New Mexico, and at Denver, thereby inaugurating the famed Goodnight-Loving Trail.[qv] Yet the vast majority of Texans who drove cattle to market in 1866 apparently followed the familiar and safer Shawnee Trail through Indian Territory either to Kansas City or to Sedalia, Missouri, both of which possessed railroad facilities for transshipment eastward, especially to meatpackers at Chicago. While many drovers found profitable markets and sold cattle for as much as sixty dollars a head, others encountered armed, hostile farmers, especially in Missouri, where new outbreaks of Texas fever engendered much anger. Therefore, many cattlemen reportedly resolved not to drive cattle northward again. A number of states, including Colorado, Nebraska, Kansas, Missouri, Illinois, and Kentucky, either barred or severely restricted the trailing of Texas cattle across their borders. The restrictions included fines up to $1,000, and in some areas herds were either impounded or killed.

Postwar cattle trailing might have ended had not Illinois cattle buyer Joseph G. McCoy established a marketplace away from settled areas. Selecting Abilene, Kansas, near the center of the mostly uninhabited Great Plains—then a veritable sea of grass—McCoy enticed Kansas Pacific Railroad executives to provide sidings and other facilities and even to pay him a commission on each carload of cattle it shipped from Abilene. He also persuaded Kansas officials not to enforce the state's quarantine law at Abilene in order to attract trail herds; he later successfully lobbied the Illinois legislature to revise its restrictions to allow entry of Texas cattle that had been "wintered" in Kansas, documentation of which soon accompanied every shipment eastward. McCoy advertised his facilities with handbills and by word of mouth, attracting drovers and an estimated 35,000 head of cattle in 1867. Thereafter, until closed to southern cattle by renewed quarantine in 1873, Abilene, Kansas, was the principal railhead-market for Texas cattle. The most important cow path from Texas to Abilene was the Chisholm Trail.[qv] Between the Civil War and 1873 more than 1.5 million Texas cattle were driven over it to Abilene, as well as to Wichita and Ellsworth, rival Kansas cattle towns along the trail.

This enormous traffic gave rise to contract drovers, who, for a fee (usually $1 to $1.50 per head) walked Texas animals to market for their owners, large and small cattle raisers alike who mostly remained at home, tending their breeding stock. Railroad connections with northern and eastern markets, available in Texas after 1873, did not immediately diminish trail traffic because freight rates were two to three times more expensive than drovers' fees. Numerous Texans, mostly young former Confederates, became contract drovers. The most active of these was probably John T. Lytle,[qv] who, in association with at least three partners between 1871 and 1886, delivered about a half million head of cattle to Kansas markets. Also important were John R. and William B. Blocker, George W. Littlefield, Ike (Isaac Thomas) Pryor,[qqv] Moses Coggin, Eugene B. Millett, Charles Goodnight, William H. Jennings, and numerous others, most of whom also became substantial ranchers. In addition to contract deliveries, they often included their own livestock on drives, as well as animals they bought cheaply in Texas and drove to market for speculation. However, most of their profits derived from volume and efficient use of manpower. All told, contract drovers accounted for as much as 90 percent of total trail traffic between 1866 and 1890, the rest being moved by those who had actually raised the animals.

A herd delivered by contract drovers typically consisted of as many as 3,000 head and employed about eleven persons. An estimated two-thirds of these individuals were whites—"cowboys" mostly, youths aged twelve to eighteen who were readily available for seasonal work as "waddies," as trail hands then were often called. Trail bosses and ramrods—also usually whites—were somewhat older, often in their twenties. The rest were members of minorities—blacks, Hispanics, or Indians—mature men usually, who often served as cooks and as horse wranglers. A few adventurous young women rode the trail, frequently disguised as boys. Wages ranged from $25 to $40 a month for waddies, $50 for wranglers, and $75 for cooks and ramrods, to $100 or more for trail bosses, who often also shared the profits. With chuck and equipment wagons leading the way toward suitable campsites, followed closely by horse wranglers and remudas (spare horses), drives were herded by a couple of waddies on "point," two or more on "flank," and two or more on "drag," that dusty rear position often reserved for greenhorns or meted out as punishment to enforce discipline. Little of the work was glamorous. Most days were uneventful; a plodding, leisurely pace of ten to fifteen miles a day allowed cattle to graze their way to market in about six weeks. Drudgery was occasionally punctuated with violent weather, stampedes, dangerous river crossings, and, rarely, hostile Indians. Even so, few trail bosses allowed youthful waddies to carry pistols, which were prone to discharge and stampede cattle. The gun-totin' image of cowboys owes more to Hollywood than to history.

About 1876 most northern cattle drives shifted westward from the Texas Road (or Chisholm Trail) to the Western (Dodge City or Ogallala) Trail.[qv] By then much of the eastern trail in Texas traversed settled country, and farmers strenuously objected to cattle being driven through their fields. Civilized tribes in Indian Territory increasingly demanded grazing fees from the drovers who crossed their reservations. And, after 1873, Texas herds capable of carrying Texas fever were quarantined from Abilene, Ellsworth, and Wichita, forcing drovers who continued to use the Chisholm Trail westward to Hays. Looking for an alternate route and market, in 1874 contract drover John Lytle blazed the Western Trail to Dodge City, but few of his contemporaries immediately followed his path. Most of them waited until Comanche and Kiowas Indians had been disarmed and forced onto reservations after the Red River War[qv] (1871–76). Thereafter, until Kansas and other northern states and territories totally quarantined themselves against Texas fever in 1885, the trail to Dodge was the principal thoroughfare over which between 2.7 million and 6 million Texas cattle were moved to market. To forestall the end of trailing, contract drovers and South Texas cattlemen sought to circumvent quarantines by asking Congress to establish a National Trail, a federal highway for cattle that would have departed the Western Trail south of the Kansas border, run westward through the Oklahoma Panhandle, and then turned northward to pass through Colorado, Nebraska, Wyoming, and Montana, ending at the international boundary. But the bill died in the House of Representatives. By then the Western Trail had been blocked in innumerable places with barbed wire[qv] fences, legally erected and not, both in Texas and north of the Red River. With the movement of cattle thus greatly impeded by quarantines and barbed wire, Texas cattlemen increasingly shifted to railroads to transport their animals to market.

bibliography: Edward Everett Dale, *The Range Cattle Industry* (Norman: University of Oklahoma Press, 1930). Wayne Gard, *The Chisholm Trail; with Drawings by Nick Eggenhofer* (Norman: University of Oklahoma Press, 1954). J. Evetts Haley, "Texas Fever and the Winchester Quarantine," *Panhandle-Plains Historical Review* 8 (1935). J. Marvin Hunter, *Trail Drivers of Texas* (2 vols., San Antonio: Jackson Printing, 1920, 1923; 4th ed., Austin: University of Texas Press, 1985). Terry G. Jordan, *Trails to Texas: Southern Roots of Western Cattle Ranching* (Lincoln: University of Nebraska Press, 1981). Joseph G. McCoy, *Historic Sketches of the Cattle Trade of the West and Southwest* (Kansas City, Missouri: Ramsey, Millett, and Hudson, 1874; rpt., Philadelphia: Porcupine, 1974). Joseph Nimmo, Jr., *Report in Regard to the Range and Cattle Business of the United States* (Washington: GPO, 1885; rpt., New York: Arno Press, 1972). Jimmy M. Skaggs, *The Cattle-Trailing Industry: Between Supply and Demand, 1866–1890* (Lawrence: University Press of Kansas, 1973). Jimmy M. Skaggs, *Prime Cut: Livestock Raising and Meatpacking in the United States, 1607–1983* (College Station: Texas A&M University Press, 1986). Jack Weston, *The Real American Cowboy* (New York: Schocken Books, 1985).

Jimmy M. Skaggs

CATUJANO INDIANS. In the late seventeenth century the Catujano (Catajane, Catuxane) Indians, apparently a Coahuiltecan-speaking people, ranged from northeastern Coahuila across the Rio Grande into the southwestern part of the Edwards Plateau[qv] in Texas. They do not seem to have survived into the eighteenth century.

bibliography: Herbert Eugene Bolton, ed., *Spanish Exploration in the Southwest, 1542–1706* (New York: Scribner, 1908; rpt., New York: Barnes and Noble, 1959). Frederick Webb Hodge, ed., *Handbook of American Indians North of Mexico* (2 vols., Washington: GPO, 1907, 1910; rpt., New York: Pageant, 1959).

Thomas N. Campbell

CAUBLE, PETER (1786–1870). Peter Cauble, early Texas settler, was born in Guilford County, North Carolina, in 1786. He received a good education and taught school for many years. About 1811 he moved to Tennessee, where he met and married Mary Ann Rotan of South Carolina. They had nine children. Cauble may have moved to Texas from Alabama before 1830 and lived for a short time in Nacogdoches County. In 1831 he brought his family to Texas and settled at Peach Tree Village in old Liberty (now Tyler) County. Like hundreds of settlers living in old Liberty County before and during the Texas Revolution,[qv] he failed to secure a land title from the Mexican government. Although he was living and farming at Peach Tree Village from 1831, the area was included in a five-league tract granted on March 17, 1834, to Gavino Aranjo, a Mexican company commander at Fort Terán. Aranjo, however, never took possession, and without regard to the land's legal ownership Cauble built a large hewn-log house in 1835, which became a landmark. It was used to describe the boundary of the newly established Polk County in 1846. The Cauble house was also the dividing point for the roads in Tyler County—that is, overseers were appointed for either direction away from the house.

Cauble served in the volunteer army during the Texas struggle for independence. When the General Land Office[qv] awarded headrights in 1838, he received Certificate No. 56 for 640 acres. An early deed by Frost Thorn[qv] conveyed land at Peach Tree Village to Peter Cauble on April 2, 1844. By 1860, with the Aranjo land available, Cauble built the 5,000-acre Peach Tree Plantation and began operating one of the county's first cotton gins. He was road commissioner and justice of Tyler County for several years. In August 1861 he enlisted as a private in the Mount Hope Home Guards, an organization to protect Tyler County. Cauble acquired substantial holdings through the use of "borrowed" land and slave labor. He stubbornly stood his ground in the conflicts that arose, which included lawsuits and fistfights. He died on March 9, 1870, at his home and was buried in the Cauble-Burch Cemetery, a few hundred yards from his log plantation house.

bibliography: Hans Peter Nielsen Gammel, comp., *Laws of Texas, 1822–1897* (10 vols., Austin: Gammel, 1898). *It's Dogwood Time in Tyler County*, 1967. Thomas L. Miller, *The Public Lands of Texas, 1519–1970* (Norman: University of Oklahoma Press, 1972). Lou Ella Moseley, *Pioneer Days of Tyler County* (Fort Worth: Miran, 1975). Buckley B. Paddock, *History of Central and Western Texas* (2 vols., Chicago: Lewis, 1911). James E. and Josiah Wheat et al., *Sketches of Tyler County History* (Woodville, Texas: Tyler County Sesquicentennial Committee, 1986).

Julia Cauble Smith

CAUDILL, WILLIAM WAYNE (1914–1983). William Wayne Caudill, architect and teacher, was born on May 25, 1914, in Hobart, Oklahoma, the son of Walter H. and Josephine (Moores) Caudill. He attended Oklahoma State University (B.S. Arch., 1937) and the Massachusetts Institute of Technology (M. Arch., 1939). He was a teacher, a proponent of architectural research and publication, and an innovator in the organization of professional architectural practice.

From 1939 until 1942 and again from 1946 until 1949 Caudill taught architecture at Texas A&M. From 1946 until 1949 he also was research architect at the Texas Engineering Experiment Station, where he coordinated work on optimizing natural ventilation and daylighting in school buildings. The results of this research were incorporated into buildings designed by the architectural firm that Caudill and John Miles Rowlett (1914–78) organized in Austin in 1946, moved to College Station in 1947, and reorganized as Caudill, Rowlett, and Scott in 1948, upon the admission of Wallie E. Scott, Jr. (1921–89) to partnership. Beginning in 1949 Caudill Rowlett Scott, as the firm was commonly called, produced a series of acclaimed school buildings that propelled it by the end of the 1950s to nationwide practice. In 1958 the firm moved its office from Bryan to Houston, where during the 1960s it developed an additional specialized practice in hospital design. Caudill Rowlett Scott's buildings received numerous state and national design awards. By 1969 Caudill had developed an international reputation as an authority on school design and had received commissions for schools, colleges, and universities from twenty-six states and eight foreign countries.

He served as director of the School of Architecture at Rice University from 1961 until 1969; from 1969 until 1971 he was William Ward Watkin[qv] professor of architecture at Rice. There he assembled a young and enthusiastic faculty and skillfully publicized the school by developing a visiting critic program, a student intern program, and a publication series, *Architecture at Rice.*

Caudill was the author or coauthor of twelve books, the most influential of which were *Space for Teaching* (1941) and *Architecture by Team* (1971). The latter is an exposition of his idea that comprehensive architectural services for complex building programs were more effectively provided by interdisciplinary teams than by single designers. This notion was reflected in the organization of Caudill Rowlett Scott and guided its development during the 1970s, when its range of professional services, numbers of employees, and volume of work increased until it became one of the largest architectural and engineering firms in the United States. In recognition of this professional entrepreneurship, the American Institute of Architects conferred its Architecture Firm Award on the partners in 1972.

Caudill was a member of the Advisory Committee on New Educational Media of the Department of Health, Education, and Welfare (1966–68), a member of the Advisory Panel on Architectural Services of the General Services Administration (1966–69), architectural consultant to the Department of State on foreign buildings (1974–77), and a member of the United States Energy Research and Development Ad-Hoc Commission. He was a member of the board of directors of Herman Miller, Incorporated, and of the American Institute of Architects. Caudill joined the AIA in 1946, was elected to fellowship in 1962, and became the first Texas architect to receive the Gold Medal of the AIA, which was awarded to him posthumously in 1985. During World War II[qv] he served in the United States Army Corps of Engineers (1942–44) and the United States Navy (1944–46). He married Edith Roselle Woodman in 1940, and they had two children. After Edith died, Caudill married Aleen Plumer Harrison, in 1974. He died in Houston on June 25, 1983.

BIBLIOGRAPHY: *American Architects Directory. Contemporary Architects* (New York: St. Martin's Press, 1980; 2d ed., Chicago: St. James Press, 1987). Nancy Acker Elisei, *The TIBs of Bill Caudill* (Houston: CRS Sirrine, 1984). *Texas Architect*, July–August 1983. *Who's Who in America*, 1982–83.

Stephen Fox

CAUDLE, JOHN H. (ca. 1835–?). John H. Caudle, pioneer and Confederate soldier, was born in Alabama about 1835. He moved to Texas, settled in Red River County as a merchant in the 1850s, and was married by 1860. In 1861 he was a member of the local Red River County Rangers and in 1862 raised a company that joined Col. Almerine M. Alexander's[qv] Thirty-fourth Texas Cavalry. The regiment served in Indian Territory and, as part of what became Polignac's Brigade,[qv] fought at Shirley's Ford and Newtonia, Missouri, and Prairie Grove, Arkansas, in 1862. In the spring of 1863 the unit was reorganized with Caudle in command, first as lieutenant colonel and later as colonel. He led the regiment in action at Vidalia and Harrisonburg and in the Red River campaign[qv] in Louisiana during 1864. He subsequently continued as commander until the regiment was disbanded in Texas in the spring of 1865. After the war Caudle returned to Red River County, which he represented in Democratic congressional district conventions of 1871 and 1872.

BIBLIOGRAPHY: Alwyn Barr, *Polignac's Texas Brigade*, Texas Gulf Coast Historical Association Publication Series 8.1 (November 1964). Dallas *Herald*, July 8, 1871, August 24, 1872.

Alwyn Barr

CAUFIELD MOUNTAIN, TEXAS. Caufield (Caulfield, Cawlfield) Mountain is three miles northeast of Gatesville in eastern Coryell County. It was named for Tom Caufield, who came to Coryell County in the early 1850s. A school and a Baptist church provided the main focus for the community. Mountain School had fifty-one students and one teacher in 1904. In the 1920s thirty to forty families lived in the Caufield Mountain vicinity. With the completion of U.S. Highway 84 in the late 1930s, Caufield Mountain became more accessible, and gradually more people moved into the area. Several residential subdivisions had been established by the late 1970s, when the Sunday school at the Mountain Baptist Church had an enrollment of 190.

BIBLIOGRAPHY: Coryell County Genealogical Society, *Coryell County, Texas, Families, 1854–1985* (Dallas: Taylor, 1986). Frank E. Simmons, *History of Coryell County* (Gatesville, Texas: *Coryell County News*, 1936).

Vivian Elizabeth Smyrl

CAULA INDIANS. The Caula Indians were one of twenty Indian groups that joined Juan Domínguez de Mendoza[qv] on his journey from El Paso to the vicinity of present San Angelo in 1683–1684. Since Mendoza did not indicate at what point the Caulas joined his party, it is impossible to determine their range or affiliations. However, the Indians between the Pecos River and the San Angelo area were being hard pressed by Apache Indians at that time, and it seems likely that the Caulas ranged between these two localities.

BIBLIOGRAPHY: Herbert Eugene Bolton, ed., *Spanish Exploration in the Southwest, 1542–1706* (New York: Scribner, 1908; rpt., New York: Barnes and Noble, 1959).

Thomas N. Campbell

CAUSEY, R. L. (?–1937). R. L. (Bob) Causey, brother of John V. and Thomas L. Causey,[qv] learned the blacksmith trade from his father, G. W. Causey, in Missouri, then became the first blacksmith on the Llano Estacado[qv] after moving to Thomas's ranch in New Mexico in the 1880s. Shortly thereafter he moved to Odessa, Texas, where he also served as town constable. Among horsemen with a taste for splendor he achieved great fame with his "gal-leg" spurs and bridle bits; the shanks of the spurs and side bars of the bits were forged and filed into the shape of a woman's legs and decorated with Mexican silver coins. In 1895 Causey moved to Eddy, New Mexico, where he later married Agnes Bogle. In 1905 he moved to Stafford, Arizona, where he operated a blacksmith shop until his death in 1937.

BIBLIOGRAPHY: Vivian H. Whitlock, *Cowboy Life on the Llano Estacado* (Norman: University of Oklahoma Press, 1970).

William R. Hunt

CAUSEY, THOMAS L. (1850–1903). Thomas L. (George) Causey, buffalo hunter and West Texas pioneer rancher, son of G. W. Causey and brother of R. L. Causey,[qv] was born in Alton, Illinois, in 1850. In the late 1860s he hauled supplies to army outposts and traders in western Kansas by mule team. When railroad competition diminished the hauling business, he took up buffalo hunting,[qv] using Hays City and later Fort Dodge as marketing points. In 1874 he crossed the Arkansas River and moved south to hunt the more plentiful herds on the Texas plains. Within a few years the Causey outfit was one of the largest ever organized for hunting buffalo commercially. Initially Causey hauled his skins to Dodge City, Kansas, then, after a trading post was established, to Adobe Walls, Texas. Indians were a constant threat until army campaigns cleared them from the region. Causey was among those who relieved other hunters and traders at the second battle of Adobe Walls[qv] in 1874. Although they repulsed the Indians, the hunters abandoned Adobe Walls and again used Dodge City as their marketing base. As the buffalo grew scarce, Causey prepared to join the gold rush to the Black Hills of South Dakota, but was deterred by news of the Sioux Indian uprising. His disappointment was relieved at reports of huge buffalo herds roaming the Llano Estacado[qv] of West Texas, and of Col. Ranald S. Mackenzie's[qv] removal of the Comanches and Kiowas from their former hunting grounds. Causey seized the opportunity and hunted along the Canadian and Washita rivers, trading at Camp Supply and then at Fort Elliott, where the town of Mobeetie developed.

As the buffalo herds moved, the hunters and traders followed across the Red River and the Pease River in increasing numbers, thus setting the stage for the last great hunts. Soon Fort Griffin, on the Clear Fork of the Brazos River, became the trading center for hunters as well as for cattle drivers bringing cattle north to markets. Causey moved south to the Salt Fork and Double Mountain Fork of the Brazos and found splendid hunting. It was said, perhaps with some exaggeration, that a single hunt yielded a bounty of 4,000 hides. Fort Griffin was Causey's usual market, but occasionally he hauled hides all the way to Fort Worth, where prices were slightly higher than the Fort Griffin price of two dollars for bulls and one dollar for cows. In early 1877 Causey changed his location once again to establish a permanent camp in Yellow House Canyon, where he built the first house in Hockley County. Sources differ on whether his house was sod or adobe.[qv] As time passed the herds grew smaller, and the returns to hunters were reduced. Causey found a supplementary income from the sale of salted and dried buffalo meat, particularly the hump, tenderloin, and tongue. His market was Las Vegas, New Mexico, where Santa Fe Railroad construction camps were located. Railroad construction also benefited his business when the Texas and Pacific Railway established service within reach of his hunting ground. Causey hauled buffalo bones to the rail point of Colorado City by bull team (*see* BONE BUSINESS) and served the growing numbers of pioneer settlers by hauling supplies to them on his return trips.

After six years at Yellow House Canyon, during which Causey's home had become something of a cultural center for military visitors and pioneer ranchers like Charles Goodnight and George W. Littlefield,[qqv] he observed a considerable change in the country. The day of the Indian and the buffalo had passed, and with it the day of the hunter. Increasing settlement offered hazards as well as amenities. On one occasion vigilantes in pursuit of rustlers visited Causey's camp on the Cedar Fork of the Brazos and almost lynched him because he had received the rustlers hospitably. Hunter Jim White, an old friend, interceded just in time to prevent the hanging. In 1882 Causey killed the last herd of wild buffalo on the Llano Estacado at Cedar Lake, near Seminole, Gaines County. After hauling the hides to Midland, he closed down an operation of thirteen years' duration that had been comparable in success to that of John W. and J. Wright Mooar.[qqv] His total estimated kill was some 40,000 animals, with records of 7,500 skins in 1876–77 and 7,800 skins in 1878. Such skillful associates as Sam Carr and Bob Parrack could kill and skin as many as thirty animals a day, and earned twenty to twenty-five cents for each hide. George Causey himself, sensitive to the belated outcry at the buffalo's virtual extermination, did not make any estimates.

Statewide events affected Causey's next moves. He had taken up horse and cattle raising in 1882 at Yellow House Canyon, where he mated mustangs[qv] with stallions brought from East Texas. Because his holdings were threatened by the establishment of the XIT Ranch,[qv] which encompassed his range, he sold his stock and buildings and moved to Lea County, New Mexico. He then sold his water rights and improvements to the Littlefield Cattle Company and moved thirty-five miles south to the future site of Knowles, New Mexico. Midland, Texas, was the supply center for his cattle ranch.

In 1902 Causey received a spinal injury when his horse threw him during a mustang roundup. Seeking help beyond the little relief available locally, he visited hospitals in Saint Louis and Kirksville, Missouri, exhausting most of his life's savings in the process. In Missouri he married his German-born nurse, Johanna Feuson. The couple returned to New Mexico and soon moved to Kenna, where they built a smaller home. Causey continued to suffer "severe head pains," however, and, on May 19, 1903, committed suicide. He was buried in Roswell, New Mexico. Two Texas hills bear his name: one in the eastern part of Lubbock and another in western Cochran County near the Texas–New Mexico line. A third place perhaps named for him is the hamlet of Causey, platted in 1908 twenty-five miles southeast of Portales, just inside New Mexico.

BIBLIOGRAPHY: Lillian Brasher, *Hockley County* (2 vols., Canyon, Texas: Staked Plains, 1976). Wayne Gard, *The Great Buffalo Hunt* (New York: Knopf, 1959). Lawrence L. Graves, ed., *A History of Lubbock* (Lubbock: West Texas Museum Association, 1962). Orville R. Watkins, "Hockley County: From Cattle Ranches to Farms," West Texas Historical Association *Year Book* 17 (1941). Vivian H. Whitlock, *Cowboy Life on the Llano Estacado* (Norman: University of Oklahoma Press, 1970).

James I. Fenton

CAUTHORN DRAW. Cauthorn Draw begins 1½ miles east of the junction of State Highway 55 and U.S. Highway 277 in south central Sutton County (at 30°17′ N, 100°37′ W) and runs northwest for 14½ miles until it meets the Dry Devil's River two miles west of U.S. 277 (at 30°25′ N, 100°44′ W). The hollow is surrounded by the gently rolling limestone terrain of the western Edwards Plateau and surfaced by loam, occasionally broken by rock outcrops, that supports grasses with scattered small stands of oak, juniper, and mesquite.

CAUX INDIANS. These are the Indians who held François Simars de Bellisle[qv] captive for several months in 1719–20. Their location has now been established as the vicinity of Galveston Bay in southeastern Texas. They have been tentatively identified as Coco Indians, but their location and De Bellisle's description of their culture strongly indicate that they were the Akokisas, well known to the Spanish through missionary activity in this area later in the eighteenth century. The Akokisas were Atakapan-speaking Indians who dominated the coastal strip that lies between present Houston and Beaumont.

BIBLIOGRAPHY: Henri Folmer, "De Bellisle on the Texas Coast," *Southwestern Historical Quarterly* 44 (October 1940). Pierre Margry, ed., *Découvertes et établissements des Français dans l'ouest et dans le sud de l'Amérique septentrionale, 1614–1754* (6 vols., Paris: Jouast, 1876–86). M. de Villiers du Terrage and P. Rivet, "Les Indiens du Texas et les expéditions françaises de 1720 et 1721 a la Baie Saint-Bernard," *Journal de la Société des Américanistes de Paris* 11 (1919).

Thomas N. Campbell

CAVA INDIANS. The Cava (Caba, Cagua, Caouache, Lava) Indians lived on the coastal plain north of Matagorda Bay and between the Guadalupe and Colorado rivers in the late seventeenth century and during the first half of the eighteenth century. When encountered by Europeans they were usually occupying settlements jointly with other groups, especially Cantona, Emet, Sana, Toho, and Tohaha Indians. Between 1740 and 1750 some of the Cavas entered San Antonio de Valero Mission at San Antonio. The linguistic and cultural affiliations of the Cava Indians are still debatable. Most writers have said that the Cavas were probably Tonkawan; however, others have suggested either a Karankawan or a Coahuiltecan affiliation. Attempts to link the Cava Indians with various groups encountered by the La Salle party, such as Kabaye and Kouyam Indians, are not very convincing.

BIBLIOGRAPHY: Herbert Eugene Bolton, ed., *Spanish Exploration in the Southwest, 1542–1706* (New York: Scribner, 1908; rpt., New York: Barnes and Noble, 1959). Frederick Webb Hodge, ed., *Handbook of American Indians North of Mexico* (2 vols., Washington: GPO, 1907, 1910; rpt., New York: Pageant, 1959). William W. Newcomb, *The Indians of Texas* (Austin: University of Texas Press, 1961). A. F. Sjoberg, "The Culture of the Tonkawa, A Texas Indian," *Texas Journal of Science* 5 (September 1953). John R. Swanton, *The Indian Tribes of North America* (Gross Pointe, Michigan: Scholarly Press, 1968).

Thomas N. Campbell

CAVALLO PASS. Cavallo Pass (Pass Cavallo) connects Matagorda Bay with the Gulf of Mexico between Matagorda Island and the Matagorda Peninsula in southeastern Calhoun County (at 28°23′ N, 96°24′ W). In the nineteenth century it was a major point of entry to the Texas interior. Cotton, cattle, molasses, lumber, potatoes, and corn were shipped through the pass. A reported 10,000 to 12,000 bales of cotton was shipped from Lavaca and Indianola in 1852. A lighthouse was constructed on Matagorda Island in 1852 to mark the entrance to the pass. Federal forces captured Cavallo Pass and Matagorda Island, along with other Texas coastal areas, in 1863. Most of the troops in the vicinity were withdrawn in March 1864 to participate in Gen. Nathaniel P. Banks's[qv] Red River campaign.[qv]

BIBLIOGRAPHY: Brownson Malsch, *Indianola—the Mother Of Western Texas* (Austin: Shoal Creek, 1977).

CAVASSO CREEK. Cavasso Creek rises a mile south of Zapata Lake in southeastern Refugio County (at 28°17′ N, 97°04′ W) and runs southeast fourteen miles across Aransas County to its mouth on St. Charles Bay (at 28°12′ N, 96°59′ W). The surrounding flat to rolling prairie is surfaced by calcareous expansive clay that supports hardwoods, pines, and numerous prairie grasses.

CAVAZOS, TEXAS. Cavazos was at the junction of U.S. Highway 281 and Farm Road 1732, six miles southeast of San Benito in south central Cameron County. The community was first settled by Mexican ranchers in the late 1890s. The introduction of irrigation to the area in 1910 facilitated intensive diversified agriculture. In 1936 there were two cemeteries, various dwellings and farms, and a school in the area of Cavazos. By 1955 the community comprised only dwellings and the two cemeteries. In 1976 all that remained at the site was a colonia known as Villa Cavazos or Cavazos. At that time it had forty-four dwellings and an estimated population of 231. By 1983 the number of dwellings had increased to seventy-one, and there was a cemetery at the site. In 1986 the colonia had a population of 225 and encompassed thirty-eight acres; at that time it received its water from the Military Water Supply Corporation.

BIBLIOGRAPHY: *Colonias in the Lower Rio Grande Valley of South Texas: A Summary Report* (Policy Research Project Report No. 18, Lyndon B. Johnson School of Public Affairs, University of Texas at Austin, 1977). *Alicia A. Garza*

CAVE, EBER WORTHINGTON (1831–1904). Eber Worthington Cave, editor, Texas secretary of state, and promoter of the Houston Ship Channel,[qv] was born on July 14, 1831, in Philadelphia, Pennsylvania. He received his early education in Philadelphia and learned the printing trade in New Jersey before he moved to Nacogdoches in January 1853. He became foreman on the Nacogdoches *Chronicle* and purchased the newspaper in early 1854. He soon became one of the most influential editors in Texas and was the first Texas editor to mention James Buchanan as a Democratic presidential candidate in 1856.

Cave opposed internal improvements by the state but also opposed the reopening of the African slave trade. He supported Sam Houston[qv] as candidate for governor in 1857 with an extra, the *Campaign Chronicle*, printed every Saturday during the campaign. When Houston ran for governor again in 1859, Cave revived the *Campaign Chronicle* and Houston was elected. Cave served as Texas secretary of state during the Houston administration. He resigned his office when Houston was deposed in 1861 and initially refused to support Texas efforts to join the Confederate States of America. Cave moved his family to Houston and when war came supported the Confederacy by organizing and preparing military companies for service in the defense of Texas.

After the war he formed a partnership with Edward Hopkins Cushing,[qv] editor of the Houston *Telegraph* (*see* TELEGRAPH AND TEXAS REGISTER), to engage in the book and stationery business in Houston. Cave sold his interest in the book business after a few years and from 1869 until 1874 was manager of the Houston Navigation Company, owned by Charles Morgan[qv] of New York. Cave made an intensive study of the possibility of a ship channel from Galveston to Houston. He was responsible for collecting information that would enable Houston to become a port, and he compiled additional information that led to the successful completion of the channel in later years. He was appointed treasurer of the Houston and Texas Central Railway, also owned by Morgan, in 1874; he remained associated with that company for twenty-five years. In 1877 he was made a director.

On April 15, 1857, Cave married Laura Sterne, daughter of Nacogdoches pioneer Adolphus Sterne.[qv] They had two daughters. Mrs. Cave died on August 26, 1872. Cave died on March 28, 1904, after falling from a streetcar several days before. He was buried in Glenwood Cemetery, Houston.

BIBLIOGRAPHY: Biographical Files, Special Collections, Steen Library, Stephen F. Austin State University. William DeRyee and R. E. Moore, *The Texas Album of the Eighth Legislature, 1860* (Austin: Miner, Lambert, and Perry, 1860). Douglas Ann Johnson, Press-stone to Politics: The Career of Eber Worthington Cave, Nineteenth-Century Texas Editor (M.Journ. thesis, University of Texas, 1956). Amelia W. Williams and Eugene C. Barker, eds., *The Writings of Sam Houston, 1813–1863* (8 vols., Austin: University of Texas Press, 1938–43; rpt., Austin and New York: Pemberton Press, 1970). *Linda Sybert Hudson*

CAVE CREEK (Coryell County). Cave Creek rises seven miles north of Gatesville in northern Coryell County (at 31°34′ N, 97°43′ W) and runs northeast for nine miles to its mouth on Middle Bosque Creek, a mile west of the Bosque county line (at 31°35′ N, 97°37′ W). The surrounding terrain is generally flat to rolling, with local deep dissections, and is surfaced by shallow, stony clay loams that support juniper, oak, mesquite, and grasses. The creek was named by early settlers who found numerous caves along its banks.

____ (Edwards County). Cave Creek rises one mile south of Goode Triangulation Station in south central Edwards County (at 29°45′ N, 100°18′ W) and runs southwest fifteen miles to its mouth on the West Nueces River, one mile north of DeLong Ranch in north central Kinney County (at 29°38′ N, 100°22′ W). It crosses flat terrain with local deep and dense dissection, surfaced by shallow, stony soils that support oak, juniper, and mesquite.

____ (Gillespie County). Cave Creek rises a quarter mile west of Farm Road 1631 in east central Gillespie County (at 30°19′ N, 98°43′ W) and runs southeast for eight miles to its mouth on the Pedernales River west of Stonewall (at 30°14′ N, 98°42′ W). The creek rises in the hills of the eastern edge of the Edwards Plateau and crosses generally flat terrain broken by sections of steep slopes and limestone benches, which give a stairstep appearance to the landscape. The area is surfaced by clays and loams that support open stands of live oak and Ashe juniper and grasses.

CAVE CREEK, TEXAS. Cave Creek was a small rural community ten miles north of Gatesville in northern Coryell County. It was nicknamed Peruna or Perunie after a patented medicine, high in alcohol content, which was sold at the general store. On paper the Cave Creek community had a post office called Peruna from July until October 1899, but the office was never in operation. The Cave Creek school had twenty-nine students and one teacher in 1904; it was consolidated with the White Hall school in 1929. The community was not shown on county highway maps in the 1980s.

BIBLIOGRAPHY: Coryell County Genealogical Society, *Coryell County, Texas, Families, 1854–1985* (Dallas: Taylor, 1986). *Vivian Elizabeth Smyrl*

CAVES. At least 3,000 caves and sinkholes are known in Texas, distributed in karst areas covering about 20 percent of the state. Karst is terrain formed by the dissolution of bedrock, and generally is characterized by sinkholes and caves that channel water underground. Texas caves and karst aquifers are important economic, scientific, and recreational resources. Karst requires soluble rocks. The majority of Texas caves occur in the Cretaceous limestones of the Edwards Group, Glen Rose, and Austin Chalk, distributed in the Balcones Fault Zone, the Edwards Plateau,[qv] the Stockton Plateau, and the Cibolo Creek and Guadalupe River basins. In the Llano region the Ellenburger Group carbonates (Ordovician age) are intensely cavernous. Permian reef limestones in West Texas contain important caves. Two gypsum karst areas (Permian age) occur north of Van Horn, Culberson County, and in fourteen counties in Northwest Texas. Some unusual caves occur in granite (Enchanted Rock Cave, Llano County), volcanic tuff and conglomerate (Big Bend), sandstone, travertine, selenite, shale, caliche, and other materials. Many caves are being degraded, filled, or quarried before their contents can be adequately studied. Honey Creek Cave is the state's longest at thirty-two kilometers (twenty miles) and is still being explored. The cave, a tributary to the Guadalupe River, extends under Comal and Kendall counties. Powell's Cave System, a complex of three caves in Menard County, is at least twenty-one kilometers (13 miles) long and "growing" as cavers continue to map it. There are at least 100 caves longer than 1,000 feet, and there are at least thirteen caves deeper than ninety-one meters (300 feet). Sorcerer's Cave (Terrell County) is the deepest at 170 meters (558 feet). The largest cave in terms of volume may be Fern Cave (Val Verde County), estimated at about 300,000 cubic meters (ten million cubic feet).

The scientific resources of Texas caves are many. Hundreds of ancient species, specially adapted to an energy-efficient life in permanent darkness, are scattered through the karst of Central Texas. Cave-adapted salamanders, catfishes, shrimps, isopods, amphipods, snails, spiders, harvestmen, pseudoscorpions, beetles, millipedes, centipedes, and other life forms have been described. Most of these eyeless troglodytes occur in the Balcones Fault Zone, where geologic isolation in faulted, river-dissected karst blocks has resulted in an evolutionary history like that of an archipelago. Some of these species are endangered by land development, overuse of groundwater, pollution, and such pests as the imported fire ant. About two dozen Texas caverns harbor about 100 million Mexican free-tailed bats from April to November every year. These migratory bats consume 6,000 to 18,000 metric tons of insects annually in Texas. The largest known mammal colony in the world is the colony of twenty million or more Mexican freetails in Bracken Bat Cave, Comal County. Bats are recognized as important but are feared by many nevertheless. A 1917 state law protecting them was rescinded during a rabies scare in 1957. Several other insectivorous bat species inhabit hundreds of Texas caves, but have been killed or driven out of some caves by vandals. Bat Conservation International moved its headquarters to Austin in 1986 and has been educating the public on the ecological importance of bats.

About twenty-five Texas caves have yielded important fossils of vertebrate animals. Extinct species, such as the scimitar cat, dire wolf, Columbian mammoth, ground sloth, glyptodon, spectacled bear, and flat-headed peccary, denned in, fell in, or were eaten in Texas caves. Radiocarbon dates up to 23,000 years before the present have been recorded. Bats have utilized Texas caves for many millenia. The remains of small mammals found in cave soil and flowstone strata have chronicled the climatic shifts in Texas since the ice ages ended about 11,000 years ago. Central Texas was a cool, moist environment until about 3,000 years ago. Such burrowing mammals as moles and gophers were common. With the increasing aridity there was a massive loss of soil. A second episode of soil loss was caused by fire and overgrazing by domestic animals that continues to this day. Paleo Indians utilized Texas cliffs and rockshelters for "animal kills." As long ago as 12,400 years, Bonfire Shelter[qv] near the Rio Grande received animals driven off a cliff. People processed the carcasses in the shelter. Kills of mammoth, bison, and horse occurred several times. In the Archaic Period (9,000–1,000 years ago) many shelters in the lower Pecos River and Devils River area were inhabited by hunter-gatherers. Fine pictographs may still be seen in Fate Bell Shelter at Seminole Canyon State Historical Park[qqv] near Comstock. Pit burials, where the dead were dropped into deep sinkholes, also have been documented. Important archeological materials no doubt remain to be found in caves and are protected by law.

Early scientific work in Texas caves began in 1896 with the description of the Texas blind salamander, *Typhlomolge rathbuni,* from an artesian well at San Marcos. Important bat guano caves were documented in 1901; the caves had been sources of nitrates for gunpowder but became fertilizer mines for citrus and vegetable farms. Serious speleology in Texas began with the 1948 publication of *The Caves of Texas* by the National Speleological Society. Caving groups (grottos) formed in the 1950s and systematic documentation of the state's caves began, first by the grottos and the Texas Cave Survey, then by the Texas Speleological Survey, founded in 1961. NSS conventions were held in Texas in 1964, 1978, and 1994. In 1994 the Texas Speleological Association included eleven grottos in major cities. Caves are conserved and managed by the Texas Cave Management Association, the Nature Conservancy, the Texas Parks and Wildlife Department,[qv] Bat Conservation International, and many private landowners. The State Caverns Protection Act protects caves from vandalism and destruction. Another statute protects landowners from liability for injuries to cave visitors, unless they have paid for access to the cave.

The Edwards Aquifer, which extends from Del Rio to north of Austin along the margin of the Edwards Plateau, is a karst aquifer that supplies drinking water to 1.5 million people in the San Antonio area. As pumping began to exceed natural recharge and water levels declined, several rare species and the human economy were threatened. The Comal and San Marcos rivers, which originate from large karst springs, are important in maintaining the Guadalupe River ecosystem all the way to the San Antonio Bay estuary on the Texas coast.

Texas caves abound with natural delights. Eight show caves are open to the public: Cascade Caverns and Cave Without A Name (both at Boerne), Caverns of Sonora (Sonora), Inner Space Cavern (Georgetown), Longhorn Cavern (Burnet), Natural Bridge Caverns (New Braunfels), Wonder Cave (San Marcos),[qqv] and West Cave (a botanical preserve and travertine cave near Austin). The Caverns of Sonora is considered by many to be the most beautiful cave in the world. The other caves offer an amazing variety of beautiful speleothems (rock formations), fossils, and history. Wild caving tours are now offered at Colorado Bend State Park and Kickapoo Caverns State Natural Area.

BIBLIOGRAPHY: *The Caves of Texas* (National Speleological Society Bulletin 10, Washington, 1948). W. R. Elliott, "Texas' Caves," *Texas Almanac,* 1994–95. W. R. Elliott and G. Veni, eds., *The Caves and Karst of Texas* (Huntsville, Alabama: National Speleological Society, 1994). James R. Reddell, "A Checklist of the Cave Fauna of Texas," *Texas Journal of Science* 17–19 (June 1965, May 1966, August 1967).

William R. Elliott

CAVE SPRINGS, TEXAS. Cave Springs was near the intersection of State Highway 43 and Farm Road 2625 some nine miles southwest of Marshall near the site of what is now Darco in southwestern Harrison County. The community was founded sometime before 1897, when the Cave Springs school had fifteen white pupils. In 1904 the community had two schools, one with thirty white pupils and another with seventy-seven black pupils. The Cave Springs schools were still operating in the 1930s and 1940s, and the community around this time also had three churches, one business, and a number of scattered dwellings. In 1983 a church, a cemetery, and a few dwellings were still at the site, but Cave Springs was no longer named on government survey or county highway maps.

BIBLIOGRAPHY: Ennis B. Carrington, An Administrative Survey and Proposed Plan of Reorganization for the Public Schools of Harrison County, Texas (M.A. thesis, University of Texas, 1940).

Mark Odintz

CAVE WITHOUT A NAME. Cave Without a Name is four miles off Farm Road 474 and ten miles northeast of Boerne in southeast central Kendall County (at 29°53′ N, 98°37′ W). It was discovered in 1927, when a goat fell through a hole into the cavern. In the mid-1930s some exploration was conducted. The property was originally owned by a rancher named Short and then purchased by James L. Horne. The Horne Ranch, Incorporated, developed the cavern, which was opened to the public in 1939. Horne held a contest to name the cave. While visiting it a young boy commented that it was too pretty to have a name. He won the contest with his suggestion, Cave Without A Name. Over the years, however, the cave has been known by various other names, such as Century Caverns and Short Ranch Cave. Estimates of the cave's age vary from 100 million up to 400 million years, when the land was covered by a shallow sea that carved out large underground cavities. The temperature in the cavern is a constant 66° F, and the cavern floor is approximately 100 feet below the surface. Cave Without A Name is at least 80 percent active and consists of a large corridor that is subdivided into several rooms. The cavern contains many large formations that vary in color from white to amber, brown, and red, due to mineral content. Also present are some of the largest calcite formations called bacon strips in the United States, as well as deposits resembling white grapes and other shapes. Striking features include the formation called "Mary and Christ" and a series of travertine-dammed pools. Gravel walkways wind through each room. The tour ends at an underground river that spelunkers have explored and mapped up to 3½ miles upstream. In the 1990s the cave was owned by Eugene and Jolene Ebell and open to tourists Wednesday through Monday. Though heralded as one of the state's more scenic caves, it was not largely advertised. No other recreational or camping facilities were on the property.

BIBLIOGRAPHY: San Antonio *Express News,* February 3, 1990. Jerry and Dorothy Sinise, *Texas Show Caves* (Austin: Eakin Press, 1983). *Texas Parade,* May 1940.

Laurie E. Jasinski

CAVELIER, COLIN (ca. 1674–?). Colin Cavelier was born about 1674, probably in Rouen, France. He was a nephew of René Robert Cavelier, Sieur de La Salle,[qv] evidently the son of La Salle's brother Nicolas, a lawyer who died quite young. Colin is said to have been about ten years old when he embarked with his uncle for the Gulf of Mexico in 1684 to establish a colony on the lower Mississippi River but landed instead at Matagorda Bay in Texas. When La Salle left Fort St. Louis the last time to seek his post on the Illinois river, Colin was among the group of seventeen who accompanied him, as were La Salle's brother, Abbé Jean Cavelier,[qv] and another nephew, Crevel de Moranger.[qv] After the murder of La Salle, Crevel de Moranger, and several others, Colin continued the journey to the Illinois and thence to Canada and to France with his uncle, the abbé.

BIBLIOGRAPHY: Paul Chesnel, *History of Cavelier de La Salle, 1643–1687*, trans. Andrée Chesnel Meany (New York: Putnam, 1932). Robert S. Weddle et al., eds., *La Salle, the Mississippi, and the Gulf: Three Primary Documents* (College Station: Texas A&M University Press, 1987).

Robert S. Weddle

CAVELIER, JEAN (?–?). Jean Cavelier, priest and adventurer, was born in Rouen, France, in St. Herbland parish. He was the older brother of René Robert Cavelier, Sieur de La Salle,[qv] and accompanied him on the French expedition that landed at Matagorda Bay, Texas, in February 1685. The parents had one other son, Nicolas, and a daughter who married Nicolas Crevel. The father, also named Jean, and his brother, Henri, were wealthy merchants at Rouen, "living more like nobles than burghers."

The younger Jean Cavelier became a Sulpician priest. He migrated to Canada in 1665 and served as curate at Montreal. A year later he influenced his younger brother Robert to join him there, thus opening the door to La Salle's career as an explorer. Abbé Cavelier handled some of La Salle's business affairs and advanced him capital to engage in the fur trade. In 1679 the abbé went to court to collect what his brother owed him, which amounted to more than the value of all the peltries La Salle had shipped to Montreal. Cavelier also resorted to intercepting La Salle's mail. "In his double character of priest and elder brother," says Francis Parkman, "he seems to have constituted himself the counselor, monitor, and guide of a man who, though many years his junior, was in all respects incomparably superior to him."

Despite the bitterness thus engendered, Cavelier joined the La Salle expedition[qv] to the Gulf of Mexico and shared in its hardships. He wrote a journal of that undertaking, but ended it more than a month before La Salle was murdered in eastern Texas. The accuracy of the document has often been questioned.

In the fall and winter of 1685–86 Abbé Cavelier accompanied his brother on a mysterious trek west of Matagorda Bay, the journal account of which is both confusing and at odds with La Salle's equally obfuscatory version. He was also among the seventeen who accompanied La Salle on a journey intended to reach Fort Saint Louis of the Illinois in January 1687. After the murder of La Salle and their nephew Crevel de Moranget,[qv] in March 1687, the abbé feared for his own life. He and his nephew, Colin Cavelier,[qv] were visited following La Salle's death by the murderer, (Pierre) Duhaut, who "told them that they could withdraw and go wherever they wished, for he would not be able from then on to see them without pain."

Cavelier, his nephew, and five others at last resumed the march for the Illinois post, to proceed thence to Canada and France. In the spring of 1688, Henri de Tonti,[qv] having searched for La Salle at the mouth of the Mississippi, returned to Fort Saint Louis of the Illinois to find Cavelier and his associates. To obtain a loan from La Salle's funds for the voyage to France, the abbé concealed from Tonti his brother's death, assuring him that La Salle was in good health in his Gulf Coast colony. Not until a year later did Tonti learn the truth. In the meantime, all possibility of rescuing the more than twenty colonists who had remained at Fort St. Louis of Texas was removed by the Karankawa Indians, who destroyed the settlement late in 1688.

On reaching Montreal in July 1688 Cavelier and his nephew remained for a time, while the others went on to Quebec to be lodged in the Recollect monastery. They sailed together for France on August 21, 1688. Their ship docked at La Rochelle on October 9.

A few years later, as a clamor arose for renewal of La Salle's Mississippi valley enterprise, Cavelier added his voice, warning that if the English seized control of the Mississippi River, they also would gain the Illinois and Ottawa Indians, and "all the nations with whom the French of New France carry on trade." He nevertheless declined to join the expedition of Pierre Le Moyne, Sieur de Iberville, which left France for Louisiana on October 24, 1698.

Sometime after Iberville's second voyage to Louisiana, he received an inquiry from Abbé Cavelier—perhaps seeking to salve his conscience for having sent no aid to the Texas colony since his return to France—concerning the possibility that survivors of La Salle's settlement might remain alive among the natives. Iberville, replying on May 3, 1704, enclosed an extract of the Talon children's[qv] answers to interrogations, assuring the cleric that every effort had been made to find any remaining Frenchmen without success. Cavelier died not long afterward.

BIBLIOGRAPHY: Paul Chesnel, *History of Cavelier de La Salle, 1643–1687*, trans. Andrée Chesnel Meany (New York: Putnam, 1932). Jean Delanglez, trans. and ed., *The Journal of Jean Cavelier* (Chicago: Institute of Jesuit History, 1938). Francis Parkman, *The Discovery of the Great West* (London: Murray, 1869; *La Salle and the Discovery of the Great West*, new ed., New York: New American Library, 1963). Robert S. Weddle et al., eds., *La Salle, the Mississippi, and the Gulf: Three Primary Documents* (College Station: Texas A&M University Press, 1987).

Robert S. Weddle

CAVEN, WILLIAM JOHN (1833–1907). William John Caven, soldier, businessman, and politician, was born in Augusta, Georgia, on October 27, 1833, the son of David and Eliza (Scott) Caven. His family moved to Harrison County, Texas, before the Civil War,[qv] and he settled near Caddo Lake as a planter about 1859. When Col. Elkanah Greer's[qv] Third Texas Cavalry was organized in 1861, Caven joined Company A, a unit primarily recruited from wealthy planters in eastern Harrison County, under Capt. Thomas W. Winston. Caven served in the regiment for four years, rose to the rank of lieutenant, and was wounded twice. After the war he returned to Marshall, where he was one of the leading cotton growers in East Texas. He married Virginia Driscoll of Tyler in 1867; they had six children. Beginning in 1872 Caven anticipated that the railroad would lead to an economic boom in the Dallas area and made a fortune by investing heavily in Dallas real estate. He continued to live in Marshall and represented the Fourteenth District in the Seventeenth, Eighteenth, and Nineteenth legislatures. In 1886 he moved to Dallas to take over his real estate business and became president of the Central National Bank of Dallas. Caven was not affiliated with any church but believed in the "universal brotherhood of man." He died in Dallas on July 25, 1907, and was buried in Greenwood Cemetery.

BIBLIOGRAPHY: Samuel Barron, *The Lone Star Defenders: A Chronicle of the Third Texas Cavalry, Ross' Brigade* (New York: Neale, 1908; rpt., Waco: Morrison, 1964). Dallas *Morning News*, July 26, 1907. Sidney S. Johnson, *Texans Who Wore the Gray* (Tyler, Texas, 1907). *Memorial and Biographical History of Dallas County* (Chicago: Lewis, 1892; rpt., Dallas: Walsworth, 1976).

CAVERNS OF SONORA. The Caverns of Sonora are ten miles southwest of Sonora in Sutton County (at 30°33′ N, 100°49′ W). Their formation began during the Cretaceous Period, several million years ago, while the area was submerged. Limestone pockets were dissolved by acidic groundwater, and when the sea receded, empty chambers were left underground. Millions of years of dripping water subsequently deposited a variety of colorful formations. The cave entrance was discovered on Stanley Mayfield's ranch in 1900, but extensive exploration did not begin until 1955. A 1,800-foot section of the cave was opened to the public in 1960, and an additional 1,700 feet was made accessible in 1961; by mid-1979 the cave's public tour was 1½ miles long. Although small in size—the 7½-mile cave has no huge rooms or giant formations—the Caverns of Sonora have been ranked as one of the most spectacular cave complexes in the world. It has been said that the caverns' beauty "cannot be exaggerated, even by Texans." Unlike most caves, the caverns have hundreds of helictites, ranging in shape from soda straws to fish fins. The most famous attraction is a pair of symmetrical fishtail helictites that form a butterfly shape.

The people who prepared the cave for public viewing took care to preserve the cave's natural humidity levels, and the temperature inside is a constant 71° F. Ninety-five percent of the cave is "alive," with formations still growing. The Caverns of Sonora were named a National Natural Landmark in 1966. In addition to the underground tours, the caverns offer aboveground facilities for camping and picnicking. In the 1990s visitors averaged 40,000 annually.

BIBLIOGRAPHY: George Macias, "Cave of the Butterfly," *Texas Co-op Power,* April 1991. Laurence Parent, "Caverns of Sonora," *Texas Highways,* March 1987. Jerry and Dorothy Sinise, *Texas Show Caves* (Austin: Eakin Press, 1983). *Vivian Elizabeth Smyrl*

CAVINESS, TEXAS. Caviness is on Farm Road 1499 eight miles from Paris in north central Lamar County. A post office operated there from 1895 until sometime after 1930. The post office was originally to be named Sidney, after early settler Sidney Caviness, but to avoid duplicating another office's name, Caviness was substituted. In 1896 the settlement's population was recorded as fifteen. By 1914 the number of residents had risen to forty, and the community had a cotton gin and two general stores. In the 1930s the town had a population of fifty, a school, a church, a cemetery, a factory, at least one other business, and scattered dwellings on a graded and drained metal surface road. In 1990 Caviness had a population of eighty and a town hall. *Sarah E. Calcote*

CAVITT, TEXAS. Cavitt is at the intersection of Farm roads 1996 and 107, four miles south of Oglesby in eastern Coryell County. The Cavitt switch was established two miles west of the community on the Texas and Saint Louis Railway, which built through the area in 1882. Both the switch and the community were named after Andrew Cavitt, who owned a land headright in the area in the 1830s. The Cavitt school had twenty-nine students and one teacher in 1904; it was consolidated with the Oglesby Independent School District by the early 1950s.

BIBLIOGRAPHY: Coryell County Genealogical Society, *Coryell County, Texas, Families, 1854–1985* (Dallas: Taylor, 1986).
Vivian Elizabeth Smyrl

CAWTHON, TEXAS. Cawthon is a small rural community on Farm Road 159 four miles south of Millican and seventeen miles south of Bryan in southern Brazos County. The site was within the lands of Stephen F. Austin's[qv] colony and was settled before the Civil War.[qv] A townsite did not develop, however, until after the International–Great Northern Railroad was built from Navasota to Hearne in the early 1900s. The town was named for early settler Will Cawthon. A post office operated at the community from 1912 to 1956. In 1925 the town had a population of twenty-five, two general stores, a railroad express and telegraph agent, a physician, a butcher, and a blacksmith. The community had a store and a population of ten in 1940. The 1948 county highway map indicated a church, a school, two businesses, and several scattered dwellings at Cawthon. By 1964 the community reported a population of seventy-five and no businesses. Cawthon in 1990 had scattered farm buildings, the old International–Great Northern Depot, and an estimated seventy-five residents.

BIBLIOGRAPHY: Glenna Fourman Brundidge, *Brazos County History: Rich Past—Bright Future* (Bryan, Texas: Family History Foundation, 1986). *Christina L. Gray*

CAWTHON, PETER WILLIS (1898–1962). Peter Willis (Pete) Cawthon, football coach, was born on March 24, 1898, in Houston, the tenth of thirteen children and the oldest surviving son of Peter W. and Frances Pauline (Harrison) Cawthon. After graduating from Houston Central High School in 1917 he entered Southwestern University, Georgetown. There he lettered in football, basketball, and baseball his freshman year and coached the baseball team after the coach left to fight in World War I.[qv] Cawthon earned four letters his sophomore year and was selected as an All-State halfback. At Southwestern he met and married Virginia Smith of Mexia; they had two sons.

In 1919 Cawthon took his first coaching job, at Beaumont High School. The following year he became varsity baseball and basketball coach at Rice Institute (now Rice University) and also directed freshman sports. He took charge of athletics at Terrell Prep School in Dallas in 1921 and carried its football team through two victorious seasons. When Cawthon went to Austin College at Sherman in 1923 to become head coach there, seven of the gridders who had played under him at Terrell followed him. Already he had begun to establish a reputation as a hard-nosed but big-hearted disciplinarian. When Notre Dame coach Knute Rockne (*see* ROCKNE, TEXAS) came to conduct a coaching school at Austin in 1925, Cawthon met him; thereafter he utilized many of Rockne's methods. Cawthon also established the annual Cawthon Trophy, awarded to an outstanding individual on the basis of athletic participation, leadership, and sportsmanship, at Austin College. In 1927 he resigned his position because of poor health resulting from overwork and went to the Ozark Mountains in Arkansas for a rest. After a few months of recuperation, he returned to Texas, where he spent the next two years working as an official for the Southwest Conference.[qv]

In February 1930 Cawthon was hired as head football coach and athletic director at Texas Technological College (now Texas Tech University) in Lubbock, with Russell T. (Dutch) Smith and John O'Dell (Dell) Morgan as assistants. By 1932 his Matadors had become the highest-scoring team in the nation. Elmer Tarbox[qv] and Ed Irons were among "Pete's Boys" at Tech. In Lubbock Cawthon taught the men's Downtown Bible Class and helped begin the city's first Jewish synagogue. During his tenure the Tech athletic programs and facilities were expanded and improved. In the fall of 1934 he outfitted his team in red satin uniforms and set out to build their reputation by scheduling games across the nation. As a result sports writers began referring to the Matadors as the "Red Raiders." In 1937 they became the nation's first college football team to fly to a road game when Cawthon, backed by the Tech athletic council, chartered a DC-3 to fly from Meecham Field in Fort Worth to Michigan to play the University of Detroit. In all, Cawthon led the Raiders through seventy-nine wins, twenty-seven losses, and six ties, including an appearance in the Sun Bowl in 1938. In 1939 he led the Tech team through its first undefeated season to an appearance in the Cotton Bowl.[qv] Controversy developed over his use of an ineligible player, however, and Tech was expelled for two years from the Border Conference. Even so, Cawthon coached for two more seasons. His traveling schedules increasingly conflicted with attempts by the athletic council, headed by W. L. Stangel,[qv] to gain Tech's admission into the Southwest Conference. Cawthon resigned in January 1941, after presenting a schedule without a single Texas team on it.

He and his family retreated briefly to Daytona Beach, Florida. When the United States entered World War II,[qv] Cawthon helped recruit coaches for the navy's preflight athletic program at Annapolis, Maryland, before taking a job as line coach at the University of Alabama in the fall of 1942. In 1943 he launched his professional football career as head coach of the Brooklyn Dodgers. He stayed in Brooklyn for two seasons and then served three years as associate coach and head scout for the Detroit Lions. He returned to college football in 1952, when he became athletic director for the University of Alabama, a position he held for two seasons, both of which brought the Crimson Tide to postseason bowl games. After 1953 Cawthon devoted full time to his summer youth camp in the Blue Ridge Mountains near Lexington, Virginia.

He and his wife maintained homes in both Sherman and Tuscaloosa during his last years. Among the honors bestowed upon Cawthon was the Meritorious Service Award from Austin College in 1957. He was enrolled in the Sports Hall of Fame in Dallas, inducted into the Texas Tech Athletic Hall of Honor, and recognized at a testimonial dinner in Houston, all in 1961. Late in December 1962 he was stricken with infectious hepatitis, and although he recovered from that, he subsequently suffered two heart attacks. He died at the Wilson and Jones Hospital in Sherman on December 31, 1962, and was interred in the Mexia Cemetery.

BIBLIOGRAPHY: Lubbock *Avalanche-Journal*, January 1, 2, 1963. Etta Lynch, *Tender Tyrant: The Legend of Pete Cawthon* (Canyon, Texas: Staked Plains Press, 1976). Jane Gilmore Rushing and Kline A. Knall, *Evolution of a University: Texas Tech's First Fifty Years* (Austin: Madrona, 1975).

H. Allen Anderson

CAXO INDIANS. The Caxo Indians, a tribe of the southwestern or Hasinai division of Caddo Indians, are known from a single 1691 Spanish missionary report. J. R. Swanton identified the Caxos with the Cachaés and followed H. E. Bolton[qv] in equating the Cachaés with the Hainais. This is strictly a matter of modern inference and opinion. Caxo and Cachaé both occur as names of tribes in the same document without any indication that they refer to the same people. Bolton argued that Cachaé was an early name for the Hainai (both names are associated with the same area) and that Cataye was a synonym for Cachaé. No early Spanish authority ever stated that Caxo, Cachaé, Cataye, and Hainai were different names for the same people.

BIBLIOGRAPHY: Herbert E. Bolton, "The Native Tribes about the East Texas Missions," *Quarterly of the Texas State Historical Association* 11 (April 1908). John R. Swanton, *Source Material on the History and Ethnology of the Caddo Indians* (Smithsonian Institution, Bureau of American Ethnology Bulletin 132, Washington: GPO, 1942).

Thomas N. Campbell

CAYCE, HENRY PETTY (1819–1875). Henry Petty Cayce, a Texas soldier through five wars and thirty years, was born at Franklin, Williamson County, Tennessee, on September 5, 1819, to Thomas Dodson and Hannah (Stanley) Cayce. The family came to Texas in December 1829, and Thomas Cayce received a league of land on the Colorado River, just below the present Wharton-Matagorda county line. Where the road from Columbia to Goliad crossed the river he built a ferry that became known as Cayce's Ferry. In the fall of 1835, just a few days after his sixteenth birthday, Henry Cayce, under the command of Captain Goodwin and Philip Dimmitt,[qv] rode to Goliad to capture La Bahía[qv] from the Mexicans. Early in November 1835 Dimmitt sent Cayce on special duty, under Capt. Bailey Hardeman,[qv] to move an eighteen-pound cannon from Dimitt's Landing,[qv] at the mouth of the Lavaca River, to San Antonio for use in the siege of Bexar.[qv] Twenty men from the Bay Prairie area started on the trip. They were joined along the way by others, including twenty members of the Mobile Grays,[qv] until they numbered seventy-five. They pushed and pulled the cannon for almost 200 miles and made it to San Antonio two days after the Mexicans surrendered. Some say they surrendered because Gen. Martín Perfecto de Cos[qv] knew the cannon was coming. Cayce went back to Goliad and was discharged on January 14, 1836, when Dimmitt and the Bay Prairie men were sent home. He received a bounty grant of 320 acres for this service.

Cayce returned to Goliad with some of the men that were marching to join James W. Fannin, Jr.[qv] He was still at Goliad when Fannin started the retreat to Victoria and was sent a few miles ahead of the main body of troops to guard some wagons. When Fannin and his men were surrounded, Cayce and the others with the wagons eluded the enemy and escaped. Cayce made his way to the Colorado River and found Sam Houston[qv] and the Texas army. Houston believed the sixteen-year-old-boy was too young to fight another battle, and he sent him to guard the women and children in the Runaway Scrape.[qv] This caused him to miss the battle of San Jacinto,[qv] and he always regretted it.

After the war Cayce's father sent him back to Tennessee to finish his education. He studied law and returned to Texas four years later. He came home just in time to learn of the death of his brother, George Washington Cayce, who was killed by Comanches at the Council House Fight[qv] in San Antonio. In March of 1842 he joined Albert Clinton Horton[qv] after the invasion of Rafael Vásquez.[qv] In September he joined Colonel Horton again when Gen. Adrián Woll[qv] and a thousand Mexican troops captured San Antonio.

Cayce married Mary Francis Slade on November 29, 1842, in Matagorda County, and subsequently started buying land in Wharton County. He became a prosperous farmer with extensive holdings. He owned many slaves but was a kindhearted man and never sold any of them.

In 1846 he served with Gen. Zachary Taylor[qv] in the Mexican War[qv] and fought at Matamoros. He was elected county commissioner of Wharton County in 1848 and served until 1852. In 1861 he joined the Confederate Army and was commissioned a lieutenant in Col. Joseph Bates's[qv] Fourth Texas Volunteer regiment. On October 22, 1861, Cayce placed an advertisement in the Columbia *Democrat and Planter* asking for volunteers to join the "Flying Artillery." One of the first to answer the call was his sixteen-year-old son, Henry P. Cayce, Jr. Father and son rode off to fight this war together. Henry Cayce spent four years using the big guns of his artillery battery to keep the Yankees from invading the Texas coast. By 1865 he was a lieutenant colonel and was sent to Louisiana to stop the Union forces from overrunning Texas from the east.

After the war he returned again to Wharton County. His slaves were gone, the land was overgrown, and he had no money. He practiced law in Wharton for a few years, but the problems of Reconstruction[qv] were too much, and he decided to move on and start over again. In the winter of 1873 he set out for Coryell County with his wife, most of their nine children, and many members of both of their families. Many illnesses and some deaths occurred on the long, cold trip. The caravan stopped in Milam County to rest and to let Cayce practice law for a while because they needed the money. But without recovering from the cold and exposure of the trip he died, on November 26, 1875, and was buried at Davilla in Milam County.

BIBLIOGRAPHY: Matagorda County Historical Commission, *Historic Matagorda County* (3 vols., Houston: Armstrong, 1986). Malcolm D. McLean, comp. and ed., *Papers Concerning Robertson's Colony in Texas* (19 vols., Fort Worth: Texas Christian University Press, 1974–76; Arlington: University of Texas at Arlington Press, 1977–92). Thomas L. Miller, *Bounty and Donation Land Grants of Texas, 1835–1888* (Austin: University of Texas Press, 1967).

Barbara L. Young

CAYLOR, HARVEY WALLACE (1867–1932). Harvey Wallace Caylor, frontier painter, son of Henry I. and Nancy Ann (Rambo) Caylor, was born at Noblesville, Indiana, on February 20, 1867. He achieved a degree of prominence as a self-taught artist, particularly among ranch families. He had little formal education, academically or artistically. He left home at the age of twelve or fourteen and, when he ran out of money in Kansas, became a cowboy. He worked his way as a cowhand to California and back to Indiana, all the while sketching scenes and characters. He had studied briefly as a child under Frank Finch, a local artist; he was later taught by Jacob Cox of Indianapolis, who had instructed the portraitist William Chase. While staying with an aunt in Parsons, Kansas, Caylor did black-and-white portraits. On July 1, 1889, he married one of his subjects, Florence

Nephler, "a frowzy-headed girl from New Orleans." Though they had no children, she was his perfect complement, his traveling companion on the range and in rugged mountains, and the driving force of his art.

In 1890, after a few years as an itinerant artist, Caylor and his wife settled in the frontier railroad town of Big Spring, Texas, where his sister lived. Probably because of his frail health, they spent a year in the open country on the Fore Ranch in northern Sterling County, living in a rigid-topped hack with roll-down canvas sides, while Caylor sketched feverishly. He began painting in oils seriously in 1894, and during the next decade he exhibited his paintings where he could. He won prizes at San Antonio and Dallas. He also did commissioned works for such ranchers as C. C. Slaughter and George T. Reynolds.[qqv] Ranch families still own most of his paintings, though the Heritage Museum in Big Spring has a substantial collection.

Caylor's favorite subjects included stampedes and trail herds. He depicted the latter in *Coming Up the Trail,* which hangs in the Kansas City stockyard headquarters. *His Prayer for Rain* (privately owned), depicting a rancher with bowed head beside his horse, reflects something of Caylor's faith, although he rarely attended his (Presbyterian) church. Caylor caught West Texas at the moment of transition from open range to barbed wire[qv] fences and painted it realistically and without extravagance. He was variously illustrator, landscapist, portrait painter, and even sculptor. Although he acknowledged that Caylor was not comparable to Charles Russell or Frederic Remington, J. Frank Dobie[qv] stated that Caylor's "deep appeal to men who drove up the trail, faced blizzards, loved horses and regarded longhorns as a symbol for Texas itself . . . marks him as important, significant and genuine." Edward G. Eisenlohr,[qv] widely known Dallas artist in the 1920s, thought that Caylor ranked among the great artists of the West.

Caylor started acquiring land in 1898 and by around 1906 had a showplace on his four-section ranch sixteen miles south of Big Spring. But ranching cut into his painting and his health. He devoted his talent only to painting after 1916 and moved into town in 1918. With a severe drought, the demand for his paintings declined. He died of nephritis, heavily in debt, at his cottage in Big Spring on Christmas Eve, 1932. His tombstone bears the inscription, "Harvey Wallace Caylor, 'The Artist.'"

BIBLIOGRAPHY: Dallas *News,* December 15, 1932. Dallas *Morning News,* March 11, 1940. Fort Worth *Star-Telegram,* October 1, 1972. Joe Pickle, comp., *H. W. Caylor, Frontier Artist* (College Station: Texas A&M University Press, 1981).

Joe Pickle

CAYNAAYA INDIANS. The Caynaaya (Caynaagua) Indians are known mainly from a document of 1691 which reported them encamped with Cíbola and Jumano Indians on the Guadalupe River east of San Antonio, where they were hunting bison. In this document it is stated that these three groups lived far to the west on the Rio Grande and that their country was adjacent to that of the Salineros, who lived along the lower stretches of the Pecos River. This seems to place the Caynaaya in Trans-Pecos Texas. As their name does not occur on contemporary lists of Indians living in western Texas, it is possible that the Caynaayas were also known by some alternate name. They were probably the same as the Cagaya, who are named in a Spanish missionary report of 1691 from eastern Texas. This report placed them about eighty leagues southwest of the Hasinai and lists them along with the Jumano (Chuman) Indians.

BIBLIOGRAPHY: Herbert E. Bolton, "The Jumano Indians in Texas, 1650–1771," *Quarterly of the Texas State Historical Association* 15 (July 1911). John R. Swanton, *Source Material on the History and Ethnology of the Caddo Indians* (Smithsonian Institution, Bureau of American Ethnology Bulletin 132, Washington: GPO, 1942).

Thomas N. Campbell

CAYOTE, TEXAS. Cayote is on Farm Road 56 by Childress Creek seven miles north of Valley Mills and twenty-three miles northwest of Waco in southeastern Bosque County. The community was founded in 1866–67 when John Cox built a grocery store two miles southwest of the future townsite. Cox sold his store in 1870, and the new owners moved the store to the town's present location to be close to a good source of water. Shortly thereafter, the town was designated Coyote because of the number of these animals in the area, but a spelling error changed the name to Cayote. The store acquired a post office in 1879. In the mid-1880s Cayote had the store, a gristmill and cotton gin, and a population estimated at fifty. Its population rose to 100 during the 1890s; by the end of 1909, however, the local post office had closed. Cayote's estimated population was twenty-five in 1933; its population estimate remained constant at seventy-five from 1943 to 1990.

BIBLIOGRAPHY: Bosque County History Book Committee, *Bosque County, Land and People* (Dallas: Curtis Media, 1985). William C. Pool, *Bosque Territory* (Kyle, Texas: Chaparral, 1964).

Karen Yancy

CAYUGA. The small river steamer *Cayuga,* the first commercially successful steamboat in Texas, played an important role during the Texas Revolution.[qv] She carried supplies for the revolutionary army,[qv] transported government officials and refugees, and was the floating capitol of Texas in April 1836. The *Cayuga,* an eighty-eight-ton sidewheeler, was built in 1832 in Pittsburg, Pennsylvania. She was 96′11″ long, 17′4″ wide, and 5′4″ deep. The *Cayuga* had one deck, two boilers, a high-compression engine, a cabin on deck, a plain head, and a pointed stern.

The steamer's first owners were Pennsylvanians who sold her to Mississippi interests; they in turn sold to J. F. Aisles of New Orleans. William P. Harris and Robert Wilson,[qqv] Texas entrepreneurs and partners, bought the vessel in 1834 from Aisles. Having been in the Mississippi steamboat trade, Harris and Wilson knew the virtues of river transportation, and in order to finance their purchase they secured pledges from Texas investors for 5,000 acres of land and $800. The *Cayuga* cleared New Orleans for Galveston Bay on August 1, 1834, under Capt. John E. Ross.[qv]

The *Cayuga* was the only steamer in Texas at this time. She operated on the Brazos River during the fall of 1834 under the command of Capt. William P. Harris and ascended the river as high as Washington. The necessity of waiting for three different rises of the river in running upstream and three in going downstream gave Harris the opportunity to clear and plant corn on 300 acres of the pledged land. On January 8, 1835, a ball was given in San Felipe, the capital of Stephen F. Austin's[qv] colony, in honor of the arrival of the *Cayuga.* The steamer left San Felipe on January 15 and ran aground downstream. Throughout 1835 she continued to ply the Brazos River, Galveston Bay, and Buffalo Bayou, where Harris and Wilson maintained a store, warehouse, and sawmill at Harrisburg.

In April 1836 David G. Burnet,[qv] ad interim president of the new Republic of Texas,[qv] impressed the *Cayuga* for public service. The ship began transporting provisions to the Texas army and rescuing officials and citizens fleeing the advancing Mexican armies. On April 15 Captain Harris, in command of the steamer, evacuated Harrisburg just ahead of Gen. Antonio López de Santa Anna[qv] and his troops. The refugees included President Burnet, his cabinet, and all the inhabitants of the town. After stopping at Lynch's Ferry and New Washington the *Cayuga* preceded to Anahuac and Galveston, where the passengers disembarked. The cabinet members remained aboard and on April 19 were rejoined by Burnet, who had left the steamer at Lynch's Ferry to get his family and had narrowly escaped being captured by the Mexicans at New Washington. The business of the republic was conducted through April 26 on the *Cayuga,* the temporary capitol. During this time the republic bought the steamer for $5,000 from Harris.

The Republic of Texas[qv] spent $300 for repairs on the *Cayuga* and by the end of the year authorized the secretary of the navy to sell it. The steamer was sold at auction on December 15, 1836, at Lynch's Ferry. The new owners refitted the vessel and renamed her the *Branch T. Archer;* she was thus one of two Texas ships named after Branch Tanner Archer.[qv] The *Archer* remained in the Houston-Galveston trade during 1837 and 1838. In June 1838 the ship was reported to have ascended the Trinity River as far as the Coushatta Indian Village. John E. Ross was captain of the vessel during these years.

The last mention of the little steamer was a Liberty County sheriff's sale on September 4, 1839, advertising all the right, title, and interest of John Huffman in the steamboat *Pioneer,* the late *Branch T. Archer,* together with the tackle and furniture. The vessel lay near the residence of Robert Wiseman in the Old River. The sale was to settle claims of John E. Ross and Robert Adkinson.

BIBLIOGRAPHY: William Fairfax Gray, *From Virginia to Texas, 1835* (Houston: Fletcher Young, 1909, 1965). *Telegraph and Texas Register,* November 26, 1836, June 9, 1838, September 4, 1839. John H. Jenkins, ed., *The Papers of the Texas Revolution, 1835–1836* (10 vols., Austin: Presidial Press, 1973). Pamela A. Puryear and Nath Winfield, Jr., *Sandbars and Sternwheelers: Steam Navigation on the Brazos* (College Station: Texas A&M University Press, 1976). *Jean L. Epperson*

CAYUGA, TEXAS. Cayuga is at the intersection of U.S. Highway 287 and Farm Road 59, five miles west of the Trinity River in northwestern Anderson County. The area was first settled in the late 1840s. The forerunner of Cayuga was a settlement called Wild Cat Bluff, located a short distance away on the Trinity River, which served as a shipping point for area farmers. Wild Cat Bluff flourished briefly during the heyday of river traffic on the Trinity but began to decline in the early 1870s, when the river became unnavigable. By the 1880s a new settlement began to grow up nearby. A post office was opened in 1894; W. A. Davenport, a native of Cayuga, New York, was the first postmaster. He operated a steam barge on the Trinity River for several years, shipping cotton, cross ties, and staves to Galveston. The earliest church in the area, the Judson Baptist Church, was organized in 1854. The Joppa Holiness Church worshiped in the town from 1899 to 1907; the Freeman Baptist Church was organized in 1910 and held regular services until 1934. The first school in the area was taught by G. W. Tuggle, chief justice of Anderson County. Tuggle and his wife Elizabeth gave a half acre of land near Tuggle Springs for the school on May 7, 1860; the school remained there until the 1880s, when it was moved to the Cayuga-Blackfoot road. In 1922, after a bitter fight, the school was moved to a location just off Farm Road 59.

Cayuga remained a small farming community until 1934, when the Tidewater Oil Company brought in the discovery well of a new field, the J. N. Edens No. 1. Cayuga became a oil boomtown almost overnight, and by 1936 it reported a population of 1,000 and fifteen business. After World War II[qv] the oil business began to decline, and the number of residents dropped to 200 by 1952. By 1974 the population was only fifty-six, and the town only had two businesses. The school was closed and moved to Bethel. With the opening of the Richland–Chambers Creek Reservoir in nearby Freestone and Navarro counties and the establishment of four state prison units in the area, the town grew some. In the mid-1970s large lignite reserves were discovered in the area. In 1988 approximately 700 people lived around Cayuga, and the town had several businesses, including the regional offices of two major petroleum companies. The reported population in 1990 was fifty-six.

BIBLIOGRAPHY: Michael J. Vaughn, *The History of Cayuga and Cross Roads* (Waco: Texian Press, 1967). *Michael J. Vaughn*

CAZNEAU, JANE MARIA ELIZA MCMANUS (1807–1878). Jane Cazneau [pseuds.: Montgomery, Cora Montgomery, Corrine Montgomery], journalist, author, promoter, and unofficial diplomat, daughter of William Telemachus and Catharina (Coons) McManus, was born in or near Troy, New York, on April 6, 1807. Her father served in the United States Congress from 1825 to 1827. She had three brothers, including Robert O. W. She was apparently raised Lutheran but seems to have become Catholic as a young woman. She married William F. (or Allen B.) Storms in 1825 and had a son but was divorced in 1831. Three years later she was named as Aaron Burr's[qv] mistress in a divorce suit brought against the former United States vice president. Jane McManus Storms (she used both surnames at different times after her divorce) first became active in Texas in 1832, when, to offset declining family fortunes, she investigated opportunities both to resettle her parents and to contract to bring immigrants to Stephen F. Austin's[qv] colonies, in what was then the Mexican state of Coahuila and Texas.[qv] With her brother Robert she traveled to Texas on the first of nine trips that she made there between 1832 and 1849. She applied to Austin for a headright and a league of coastal land in 1834 and 1835, respectively. An acquaintance recollected that the Mexican government granted her eleven leagues of land for her project but that she lacked the financial means to move her settlers, a group of Germans, from the Texas coast to the designated colony. According to this account, the enterprise broke up at Matagorda, where Jane resided for several months. She may not have lived on her land long enough to get final title and may have forfeited her claim. In a letter posted from New York in 1835, she alluded to owning 1,000 acres in Austin's colony, over and above a league she claimed as a settler. She speculated actively in Texas land from 1834 to 1851. Meanwhile, apparently in 1833, her brother Robert and her parents moved to Matagorda, Texas, although her father returned north before his death in 1835.

Land interests and the presence of family gave Jane McManus a vested interest in the future of Texas. When the Texas Revolution[qv] erupted, she announced an intent to contribute money and arms to the cause of Texas independence. In the mid-1840s her columns in the New York *Sun* helped swing United States public opinion in favor of the annexation[qv] of the Republic of Texas.[qv] She contributed "The Presidents of Texas" to the March 1845 issue of the *Democratic Review.* That same year her *Texas and Her Presidents, With a Glance at Her Climate and Agricultural Capabilities* was published in New York. In December 1849 she married Texas entrepreneur and politician William Leslie Cazneau.[qv] From 1840 to 1852 she and her new husband lived at Eagle Pass, where he founded a town, opened a trade depot, and investigated mining opportunities. Jane recounted her experiences there in *Eagle Pass; or Life on the Border* (1852). In this book, in letters to United States Senator William H. Seward, and in columns for the New York *Tribune,* she charged that Mexicans had been kidnapping Texas residents into peonage in Mexico. Her complaints induced the United States Department of State to broach the issue with the government of Mexico. *Eagle Pass* also inspired Frederick Law Olmsted[qv] to investigate the matter. Olmsted reported in *A Journey Through Texas* that he found no evidence to corroborate Mrs. Cazneau's accusations. Throughout the antebellum period, she maintained close ties to Mirabeau B. Lamar,[qv] second president of the Republic of Texas. Lamar dedicated a volume of poetry to her (*Verse Memorials,* 1857). Her will, drafted in 1877, lists 1,000 acres at Eagle Pass and other Texas properties among her assets.

Jane Cazneau participated in United States diplomacy almost a century before the first woman was appointed to the United States Foreign Service. During the Mexican War[qv] she played an important, if unofficial, part in the unsuccessful secret peace mission of *Sun* editor Moses Yale Beach to Mexico City, from November 1846 to April 1847, an assignment authorized by President James K. Polk. During that mission she became the only female war correspondent and the only American journalist to issue reports from behind enemy lines. Upon returning to the states she championed the "All Mexico" movement. Between 1847 and her death she also promoted United

States annexation of Cuba, United States commercial penetration of the Dominican Republic, American Filibuster William Walker's conquest of Nicaragua, United States control of transit routes across the Mexican and Nicaraguan isthmuses, and other variants of "Manifest Destiny." She resided for much of the 1850s in the Dominican Republic, where her husband was serving as United States secret agent and commissioner, diplomatic missions which she helped initiate. It is difficult to separate ideology from self-interest when it comes to her expansionist advocacy; she and her husband made substantial investments that promised profit if the United States government implemented her policies. To promote these causes as well as her opinions on domestic political issues, she wrote letters to presidents and demanded and received presidential audiences. She socialized with and sent letters to politicians and journalists, including James K. Polk, James Buchanan, Jefferson Davis, Horace Greeley, Thurlow Weed, and William H. Seward. She contributed pieces to city newspapers on the East Coast, including the New York *Sun*, the Philadelphia *Public Ledger*, the Washington *States*, and the New York *Tribune*, as well as magazines such as *Hunt's Commercial Magazine* and the *Democratic Review*. She bought into the New York *Morning Star*, so that she could use its press to publish her own expansionist journal, the short-lived *Our Times*. Between 1848 and 1853 her column "The Truth," regularly published in the Spanish-and-English-language newspaper *La Verdad*, advocated the annexation of Cuba to the United States. Her books, particularly *The Queen of Islands* (1850) and *Our Winter Eden: Pen Pictures of the Tropics* (1878), conveyed her expansionist message.

The Cazneaus purchased Esmeralda, an estate in the Dominican Republic, in 1855. Though the Abraham Lincoln administration terminated Cazneau's diplomatic appointment to that country in 1861, around the time that Spain was reannexing the Dominican Republic, he and his wife remained at their estate. When Spanish troops destroyed Esmeralda in October 1863, they fled to Keith Hall in Jamaica, another of their properties. After Spanish evacuation of the Dominican Republic in 1865, they returned and became involved in both the project of President Andrew Johnson to acquire a United States coaling station at Samaná Bay and President U. S. Grant's attempt to annex the Dominican Republic to the United States. William Cazneau died in 1876. Jane Cazneau died in the sinking of the steamship *Emily B. Souder*, bound from New York to Santo Domingo, on December 10, 1878. Her will left her property to Ann S. Stephens, a prolific New York writer.

BIBLIOGRAPHY: Jane Cazneau Papers, Barker Texas History Center, University of Texas at Austin. Jane Cazneau Papers, New York Historical Society, New York City; Barker Texas History Center, University of Texas at Austin. Edward P. Crapol, ed., *Women and American Foreign Policy: Lobbyists, Critics, and Insiders* (New York: Greenwood, 1987). Marker Files, Texas Historical Commission, Austin. Anna Kasten Nelson, "Jane Storms Cazneau: Disciple of Manifest Destiny," *Prologue* 18 (Spring 1986). Tom Reilly, "Jane McManus Storms: Letters from the Mexican War, 1846–1848," *Southwestern Historical Quarterly* 85 (July 1981).

Robert E. May

CAZNEAU, WILLIAM LESLIE (1807–1876). William Leslie Cazneau, soldier and politician, was born on October 5, 1807, in Boston, Massachusetts, and arrived in Matagorda, Texas, in 1830 to establish a general store. He served on the staff of Gen. Thomas J. Chambers qv in 1835 and was a member of the guard that escorted Antonio López de Santa Anna qv and his staff as prisoners to Galveston Island after the battle of San Jacinto. qv At the direction of Col. Juan N. Seguín qv he collected the remains of the Texan soldiers at the Alamo and saw to their burial with full military honors. In 1839 Cazneau moved to Austin and was appointed commissary general by Mirabeau B. Lamar. qv His association with Lamar was personal as well as professional, and Lamar later dedicated a volume of his poetry to Cazneau and his wife. As a representative from Travis County, Cazneau served in the Seventh, Eighth, and Ninth congresses. He opposed moving the government archives from the frontier community of Austin and was considered a frequent opponent of other plans of Sam Houston qv as well (*see* ARCHIVE WAR). Cazneau served in the Convention of 1845 qv and the First Legislature. His military career included service in the Mexican War qv until August 1847, when he entered into a partnership with Henry L. Kinney qv that involved land speculation along the Nueces River valley. Also at this time he married Jane McManus Storms (*see* CAZNEAU, JANE), and together they were instrumental in establishing the town of Eagle Pass. Under the administrations of President Franklin Pierce and his successor, James Buchanan, Cazneau was twice appointed special agent to the Dominican Republic (1853 and 1859). He supported annexation of that nation to the United States but was defeated in this project by a combination of changing conditions there and a temporary loss of enthusiasm for imperial adventures on the part of the administration in Washington. Various schemes and development projects kept him occupied in the Caribbean region for the remainder of his life. He died on January 7, 1876, at Keith Hall, his estate in Jamaica. His wife perished in a shipwreck two years later. They had no children.

BIBLIOGRAPHY: Vertical Files, Barker Texas History Center, University of Texas at Austin.

Frank Wagner

CAZORLA, LUIS (?–1788). Luis Cazorla served as captain of Nuestra Señora de Loreto Presidio from 1772 to 1778 and again from 1784 to 1788. He was first appointed by Viceroy Antonio María Bucareli y Ursúa qv on April 28, 1772, and succeeded Francisco de Tovar, qv who had resigned. Cazorla was captain of the presidio when the New Regulations for Presidios qv (1772) were adopted, and it was his task to implement them. His administration is best remembered for his explorations along the Texas coast to watch for English intrusions and for the murder at La Bahía qv of El Mocho, qv a Tonkawa chieftain, and three companions. During his travels he became the first European to reach the mouths of the San Jacinto and Brazos rivers by land. Previous maps, including those of Diego Ortiz Parrilla (1767) and Bernardo de Miranda qqv (1757) showed the San Jacinto flowing directly into the Gulf instead of into Galveston Bay.

In 1776 Cazorla investigated the wreck on Matagorda Island of an English frigate whose crew had been murdered by Karankawas. Afterward, he deplored in a letter to the viceroy "the pitiful misfortunes of the countless ships lost on the coast. The poor sailors fortunate enough to escape the shipwreck fall into the hands of the heathen Indians . . . the Karankawas, Copano, and other small nations, and are victims of their cruelty and ferocity." As a remedy, Cazorla proposed placing on one of the barrier islands a fort with thirty or forty men equipped with a shallow-draft vessel with which to reconnoiter the coast constantly, after first clearing "the heathen nations" from the swamps and sending them to exile in Mexico. Cazorla's recommendations ran afoul of an age-old Spanish dread: that the opening of ports would give rise to contraband trade that would deprive the crown of revenue. Probably as a result of the influence of Hugo Oconór, qv the plan was not acted upon.

In 1778 Teodoro de Croix, qv commandant general of the presidios along the northern frontier of New Spain, chose Cazorla to be the inspector of presidios in Texas and Coahuila. On October 28, 1784, he was transferred back to La Bahía, where he continued as captain until his death there on October 3, 1788.

BIBLIOGRAPHY: Bexar Archives, Barker Texas History Center, University of Texas at Austin. Jack Jackson, *Los Mesteños: Spanish Ranching in Texas, 1721–1821* (College Station: Texas A&M University Press, 1986). Kathryn Stoner O'Connor, *The Presidio La Bahía del Espíritu Santo de Zúñiga, 1721 to 1846* (Austin: Von Boeckmann–Jones, 1966). Robert S. Weddle and Robert H. Thonhoff, *Drama and Conflict: The Texas Saga of 1776* (Austin: Madrona, 1976).

Robert H. Thonhoff